INTERLINEAR
FOR THE REST OF US

Also by William D. Mounce

Basics of Biblical Greek Grammar
Basics of Biblical Greek Workbook
Morphology of Biblical Greek
The Analytical Lexicon to the Greek New Testament
A Graded Reader of Biblical Greek
Greek for the Rest of Us

WILLIAM D. MOUNCE

INTERLINEAR
FOR THE REST OF US

THE REVERSE INTERLINEAR FOR
NEW TESTAMENT WORD STUDIES

ZONDERVAN™

GRAND RAPIDS, MICHIGAN 49530 USA

ZONDERVAN.COM/
AUTHORTRACKER

ZONDERVAN™

Interlinear for the Rest of Us
Copyright © 2006 by William D. Mounce

Requests for information should be addressed to:
Zondervan, *Grand Rapids, Michigan 49530*

Library of Congress Cataloging-in-Publication Data

Bible. N.T. Greek 2005
    Interlinear for the rest of us : the reverse interlinear for New Testament word studies / edited by William D. Mounce.
      p. cm.
    Includes bibliographical references.
    ISBN-10: 0-310-26303-4
    ISBN-13: 978-0-310-26303-6
    1. Bible. N.T.—Interlinear translations, English. I. Mounce, William D. II. Bible. N.T. English. New International. 2005.
  BS1965.5 2005
  225.4'8—dc22

2005022807

This edition printed on acid-free paper.

The website addresses recommended throughout this book are offered as a resource to you. These websites are not intended in any way to be or imply an endorsement on the part of Zondervan, nor do we vouch for their content for the life of this book.

Interior design by William D. Mounce

Printed in China

06 07 08 09 10 11 • • 18 17 16 15 14 13 12 11 10 9 8 7 6 5 4 3 2

to Billy Graham

a model of Christian integrity and single-minded focus

and all others who preach the Word of God

who have always wanted to study the Greek New Testament

Table of Contents

Preface

The New Testament is the revelation of God's will. Unfortunately for many, it was given in a language they cannot understand. Either they never learned Greek, or what Greek they did learn in college or seminary has drifted off into the fog of strange paradigms and hard-to-remember vocabulary cards.

I will never forget when my four-year-old daughter asked our pastor, five minutes before the Sunday morning service started, if he knew the Greek alphabet. Talk about timing! He admitted, much to his chagrin, that he no longer did, and Kiersten proceeded to sing it to him. (I did *not* initiate the discussion, and I did *not* require my children to learn Greek; they asked me to teach them.) I have also reflected on my own feeling of uncertainty when I preach from the Old Testament. While I have not forgotten the Hebrew alphabet, my ability in Hebrew is below that of my Greek, and as a result I often am not sure what the Hebrew text "really" says. What is discouraging is that most pastors feel this way every Sunday, no matter whether they are preaching from the Old or New Testament. So what can I do to help?

Some would say, "Leave it. If the pastor or layperson is not able to learn Greek, stay immersed in it, and develop a facility and 'feel' for the language and the biblical text, then they should not even dabble." There is much to be said for this position. The abuse that exegetical dilettantes have wreaked on the text is almost beyond comprehension, and the thought of producing a tool that could aid such people in their abuse of the text has kept me from this project for years.

My favorite story along these lines is of a well-known Christian speaker who based her entire message on the "fact" that a certain Greek word is in the "genital" case. (It's "genitive.") If she cannot even get the name of the case right, I doubt she knows how to exegete it.

Another time a visitor came to my Sunday School class. When he noticed that the women's heads were not covered, he decided I was a sinner and needed to be confronted, challenged, and attacked. (It seems this was his mission in life, going from church to church.) He took a sheet of paper out of his pocket with the same verse written on it ten times, in ten different colors of ink, thrust it into my face, and exclaimed that if I "really" knew Greek, I would know that he was right. When the class broke out in laughter, the matter was diffused.

I am sure that many of you can add your own stories of how a little bit of Greek knowledge is a dangerous thing, and perhaps caution would suggest that this book should never be published. But I have come to the conclusion that *it is not a little bit of Greek that can be dangerous; it is a little bit of pride.* I am convinced that if a person will recognize the limitations of this approach, if this text can be approached with humility and integrity, then *The Interlinear for the Rest of Us (IRU)* can be used properly. I was not comfortable abandoning the vast majority of pastors and laypeople, saying it is just "too bad" if they don't know Greek. There had to be something that I could do to help.

Once I had made this commitment to help, the question became how I could guard against misuse. Of course, there is nothing I can do about arrogance and pride; I will leave that to the Holy Spirit. But I could do something about ignorance and lack of training. So I wrote another text, *Greek for the Rest of Us*, which will help you learn enough about Greek so that you can use *IRU* properly. It is my prayer that by using these two texts, a good word-study book, and an excellent set of commentaries, you will be able to study your New Testament in ways you could not previously even imagine.

IRU is not a traditional interlinear. From my experience of watching pastors use, or perhaps I should say misuse, interlinears, I came to the conclusion that the interlinear format suffers from two basic flaws. *IRU* corrects those flaws.

- *IRU* assumes that the user's primary language is English, not Greek. This is why the top line is English. It is also why I maintain the English word order and alter the Greek word order. The Greek is given along the bottom of each page in Greek order for the purists among us.

- You can study from *IRU* and not just reference it. Because interlinears alter the English word order, they are difficult to read. Most people study with an English Bible and then check the interlinear here and there. But since the English order has not been changed, you can make *IRU* your study Bible for the New Testament.

One of my fears is that the format of this text may imply that there is a word-for-word equivalence between languages, that if you see ὁ under "the," you may think ὁ is the exact Greek equivalent to the English "the." Let me say clearly up front that this perception is false. There is rarely, if ever, an exact equivalence between words in different languages, and language conveys meaning more in groups of words, in phrases, than it does in individual words.

Please do not draw the wrong implications from the format of this text. This issue is discussed in detail in my *Greek for the Rest of Us* and the "Detailed Guidelines" in Appendix A.

The parsings are the same as I used in my *The Analytical Lexicon to the Greek New Testament*. The methodology I adopted is listed in the back of that text. The parsings are a combination of computer generated parsings plus hundreds of hours of manual checking. Sometimes it was difficult to make a decision between two possibilities, such as whether a present or perfect form is middle or passive, since the forms are identical. I thought about including alternate forms but decided the book was long enough as is. It was also difficult at times to decide what Greek text the NIV translators were following because of their dynamic view of translating (see Appendix A).

I have tried my best to tag the Greek to the English on the basis of what I felt the NIV translators had done. This does not mean that I agree with them at every point. So much for disclaimers.

The Greek text along the bottom of the page was supplied by John R. Kohlenberger III, which he constructed from the NIV; where it is different from the modern critical text I have indicated with variants.

The Greek dictionary in the back is a revised edition of the Greek dictionary in my *The Analytical Lexicon to the Greek New Testament*.

There are a few people I wish to thank, but none more so than Miles Van Pelt. Miles is the type of student every teacher dreams of teaching. He has helped me on many projects, but none so much as this one. The first stage of writing *IRU* was to "tag" the NIV text, connecting the English word to the Greek word in a database. I wrote a computer program to make it as easy as possible, and Miles did the initial tagging. The computer program then creates a file with all the raw data, it runs through a conversion program, and out comes *IRU*, all typeset. I proofed the work, and then Verlyn Verbrugge, my editor at Zondervan, and Robert Mounce, my father, proofed the book again. Finally, I proofed it one more time. The second edition was created with the help of Gabriel Schmidt, Clarissa Keinath, W. H. Tinkler, Rex Koivisto, and my friends at Oaksoft. As careful as I have been, I am sure there are mistakes and inconsistencies, and these are my sole responsibility. I can be contacted through email (support@teknia.com) and through regular mail at Zondervan. I will not be able to respond, but I do appreciate the feedback. You can also visit my website at www.teknia.com. I should also thank Stan Gundry and Ed van der Maas at Zondervan for believing in the project and publishing it, Verlyn and Dad for all their editing work, Matt Smith for helping me finish the project, and my wife, Robin, and my children, Tyler, Kiersten, and Hayden, for all their encouragement and patience.

My prayer is that you find this book a valuable resource in your study of the New Testament. My prayer is also that you will not think you actually know Greek just because *IRU* parses the words. Learning a language is an art, one that takes a substantial commitment of time if it is to be done properly. But for those who are not able to spend the time, this text can help you to better understand the Word of God.

Bill Mounce
August, 2005

General Guidelines

Because *IRU* is unique in its layout, it is important that you spend time reading through these guidelines. They will help you understand the principles that guided my work and will in turn help you use it more efficiently and correctly. The detailed guidelines are listed in Appendix A. If you have never had a class in Greek, you may want to get my *Greek for the Rest of Us* to fully understand these guidelines.

1. **Each "staff" has four "lines." The first is the English translation, then the Greek, then the parsing, and finally the G/K number.**

	This	is	the	message		we have	heard	from	him
Καὶ	αὕτη	ἔστιν	ἡ	ἀγγελία	ἣν	→ →	ἀκηκόαμεν	ἀπ'	αὐτοῦ
cj	r.nsf	v.pai.3s	d.nsf	n.nsf	r.asf		v.rai.1p	p.g	r.gsm.3
2779	4047	1639	3836	32	4005		201	608	899

In Appendix B (*The Greek-English Dictionary*) you will find the Strong's numbers listed at the end of each dictionary entry.*

2. **I maintain English order, and the Greek word is listed under the English word it translates, if possible.**

For this reason I often refer to *IRU* as a "reverse interlinear." A traditional interlinear follows Greek order and lists the English under the Greek. For example:

οὕτως	γὰρ	ἠγάπησεν	ὁ	θεὸς	τὸν	κόσμον,	ὥστε	τὸν	υἱὸν
so	for	he loved	the	God	the	world	so that	the	son

3. **If two or more English words translate a single Greek word, an arrow is placed under the English word(s) pointing to the Greek word.**

"That which" is the translation of the single Ὅ.

That which	was	from	the	beginning,	which		we have heard,
→ Ὅ	ἦν	ἀπ'		ἀρχῆς	ὃ	→ →	ἀκηκόαμεν
r.nsn	v.iai.3s	p.g		n.gsf	r.asn		v.rai.1p
4005	1639	608		794	4005		201

"Atoning sacrifice" is the translation of the single ἱλασμός.

	He	is	the	**atoning**	**sacrifice**	for	our	sins,
καὶ	αὐτὸς	ἔστιν		ἱλασμός	←	περὶ	ἡμῶν	⌐τῶν ἁμαρτιῶν⌐
cj	r.nsm	v.pai.3s		n.nsm		p.g	r.gp.1	d.gpf n.gpf
2779	899	1639		2662		4309	7005	3836 281

I try to place the Greek word under the English word that conveys most of the meaning of that Greek word.

Therefore,	**just**	**as**	sin		entered		the	world
⌐Διὰ τούτο⌐	ὥσπερ	←	⌐ἡ	ἁμαρτία⌐	εἰσῆλθεν	εἰς	τὸν	κόσμον
p.a r.asn	cj		d.nsf	n.nsf	v.aai.3s	p.a	d.asm	n.asm
1328 4047	6061		3836	281	1656	1650	3836	3180

When there are two or more arrows in a row, all English words are derived from the same Greek word (i.e., the first is not derived from the second). In this example, "we" is not derived from "have"; both are derived from the Greek word under "seen."

	The	life	appeared;		**we have**	**seen**	it	and	testify
καὶ	ἡ	ζωὴ	ἐφανερώθη	καὶ	→	→	ἑωράκαμεν	καὶ	μαρτυροῦμεν
cj	d.nsf	n.nsf	v.api.3s	cj			v.rai.1p	cj	v.pai.1p
2779	3836	2437	5746	2779			3972	2779	3455

* The "G/K" numbers were developed by Edward W. Goodrick and John R. Kohlenberger III and are used throughout Zondervan's publications. They addressed certain problems with Strong's numbering system that come out of the differences between the Received Text (used by the KJV and the NKJV) and the Critical Text (used by most modern translations, including the NIV).

There are many reasons why it often takes more than one English word to translate a Greek word. Sometimes it is the nature of the Greek grammatical construction. (μένειν as an infinitive means "to live.")

Whoever	claims	**to**	**live**	in	him				must
ὁ	λέγων →		μένειν	ἐν	αὐτῷ	καὶ	αὐτὸς	οὕτως	ὀφείλει
d.nsm	pt.pa.nsm		f.pa	p.d	r.dsm.3	adv	r.nsm	adv	v.pai.3s
3836	3306		3531	1877	899	2779	899	4048	4053

Other times the actual meaning of the Greek word requires multiple English words.

	Jesus	stepped	into	a	boat,	**crossed**	**over**	and	came
Καὶ		ἐμβὰς	εἰς		πλοῖον	διεπέρασεν	←	καὶ	ἦλθεν
cj		pt.aa.nsm	p.a		n.asn	v.aai.3s		cj	v.aai.3sa
2779		1832	1650		4450	1385		2779	2262

If you do not know Greek at all, be careful with using these arrows. It might be better to stick to those English words that have Greek words directly under them and ignore the arrows.

4. **If a word comes between the two English words translating a single Greek word, a corner arrow is used. The number of the main Greek word is listed under the other word.**

"Do" and "love" both come from the Greek word ἀγαπᾶτε, word #26.

Do	not	**love**	the	world	or	anything	in	the	world.
↱	Μὴ	ἀγαπᾶτε	τὸν	κόσμον	μηδὲ	τὰ	ἐν	τῷ	κόσμῳ
	pl	v.pam.2p	d.asm	n.asm	cj	d.apn	p.d	d.dsm	n.dsm
26	3590	26	3836	3180	3593	3836	1877	3836	3180

5. **When two Greek words are translated by a single English word, the two Greek words have corner brackets.**

"Pregnant" is a translation of the two Greek words ⌊ἐν γαστρί⌋.

	She	was	**pregnant**		and	cried	out
καὶ	→	ἔχουσα	⌊ἐν	γαστρὶ⌋	καὶ	κράζει	←
cj		pt.pa.nsf	p.d	n.dsf	cj	v.pai.3s	
2779		2400	1877	1143	2779	3189	

When this happens with nouns, the first word is often the definite article.

If	we	confess	our	**sins**,		he	is	faithful	and	just
ἐὰν	→	ὁμολογῶμεν	ἡμῶν	⌊τὰς	ἁμαρτίας⌋	→	ἐστιν	πιστός	καὶ	δίκαιος
cj		v.pas.1p	r.gp.1	d.apf	n.apf		v.pai.3s	a.nsm	cj	a.nsm
1569		3933	7005	3836	281		1639	4412	2779	1465

6. **When the subject of a sentence is assumed in the verb and the translation supplies a personal pronoun, I place an arrow under the subject pointing toward the verb.**

They	went	out	from	us,	but	they	did	not	really	belong
→	ἐξῆλθαν	ἐξ	←	ἡμῶν	ἀλλ᾽	↱	↱	οὐκ		ἦσαν
	v.aai.3p	p.g		r.gp.1	cj			pl		v.iai.3p
	2002	1666		7005	247	1639	1639	4024		1639

This includes the expressions "this / there is / was."

Dear	children,	**this**	**is**	the	last	hour;
→	Παιδία	→	ἐστίν		ἐσχάτη	ὥρα
	n.vpn		v.pai.3s		a.nsf	n.nsf
	4086		1639		2274	6052

	There	**was**	a	violent	earthquake,	for	an	angel
ἰδοὺ	→	ἐγένετο		μέγας	σεισμὸς	γὰρ		ἄγγελος
j		v.ami.3s		a.nsm	n.nsm	cj		n.nsm
2627		1181		3489	4939	1142		34

If the translation supplies a specific noun instead of a personal pronoun, I usually do not include an arrow under it. However, it is usually clear that the noun is derived from both the verb and the context.

Jesus	replied,			"Moses	permitted	you	to	divorce
	λέγει	αὐτοῖς	ὅτι	Μωϋσῆς	ἐπέτρεψεν	ὑμῖν	→	ἀπολῦσαι
	v.pai.3s	r.dpm.3	cj	n.nsm	v.aai.3s	r.dp.2		f.aa
	3306	899	4022	3707	2205	7007		668

And	the	**dragon**	stood	on	the	shore	of	the	sea.
Καὶ			ἐστάθη	ἐπὶ	τὴν	ἄμμον	→	τῆς	θαλάσσης
cj			v.api.3s	p.a	d.asf	n.asf		d.gsf	n.gsf
2779			2705	2093	3836	302		3836	2498

But if the supplied word is general, such as "person" but not "man" (see Detailed Guidelines), I include the arrow.

People	went		out	to	him	from	Jerusalem
Τότε	→		ἐξεπορεύετο	←	πρὸς	αὐτὸν	Ἱεροσόλυμα
adv			v.imi.3s		p.a	r.asm.3	n.npn
5538			1744		4639	899	2642

If	there	is	no	interpreter,	**the speaker**	should	keep	quiet
ἐὰν	→	ᾖ	μὴ	διερμηνευτής	→ →	→	→	σιγάτω
cj		v.pas.3s	pl	n.nsm				v.pam.3s
1569		1639	3590	1449				4967

7. **English often requires helping words to translate a Greek verb ("is, can, will, have, do, may," etc.). There are arrows under these words pointing to the verb.**

In	this	way,	love		**is**	made	complete	among	us
Ἐν	τούτῳ	←	ἡ	ἀγάπη	→ →		τετελείωται	μεθ᾽	ἡμῶν
p.d	r.dsn		d.nsf	n.nsf			v.rpi.3s	p.g	r.gp.1
1877	4047		3836	27			5457	3552	7005

This		is	how	you	**can**	recognize	the		Spirit	of	God:
ἐν	τούτῳ	←	←	→	→	γινώσκετε	τὸ		πνεῦμα	→	τοῦ θεοῦ
p.d	r.dsn					v.pai.2p	d.asn		n.asn		d.gsm n.gsm
1877	4047					1182	3836		4460		3836 2536

And	we	**have**	seen	and	testify	that	the	Father
καὶ	ἡμεῖς	→	τεθεάμεθα	καὶ	μαρτυροῦμεν	ὅτι	ὁ	πατὴρ
cj	r.np.1		v.rmi.1p	cj	v.pai.1p	cj	d.nsm	n.nsm
2779	7005		2517	2779	3455	4022	3836	4252

Brothers,	I	**do**	not	consider	myself	yet	to	have	taken	hold		of it.
ἀδελφοί	ἐγὼ	↱	οὐ	λογίζομαι	ἐμαυτὸν	→	→	→		κατειληφέναι	←
n.vpm	r.ns.1		pl	v.pmi.1s	r.asm.1					f.ra
81	1609	3357	4024	3357	1831					2898

He	who	has		ears,	**let**	him	hear.
ὁ	←	ἔχων	ὦτα		ἀκουέτω		
d.nsm		pt.pa.nsm	n.apn		v.pam.3s		
3836		2400	4044		201		

so	that	your	faith		**might**	not	rest	on	men's	wisdom,
ἵνα	←	ὑμῶν	ἡ	πίστις	↱	μὴ	ᾖ	ἐν	ἀνθρώπων	σοφίᾳ
cj		r.gp.2	d.nsf	n.nsf		pl	v.pas.3s	p.d	n.gpm	n.dsf
2671		7007	3836	4411	1639	3590	1639	1877	476	5053

8. **Greek frequently omits a verb's direct object (as well as other words), and English translations usually must insert it.**

Though	you	have	not	seen	him,	you	love	**him;**
↱	↱	↱	οὐκ	ἰδόντες	ὃν	→	ἀγαπᾶτε	
			pl	pt.aa.npm	r.asm		v.pai.2p	
1625	1625	1625	4024	1625	4005		26	

English does the same type of thing. For example, in certain cases indirect objects in English are omitted but they are included in Greek. English tends to say, "Jesus said" while Greek says, "Jesus said to him" (αὐτῷ).

"Be	quiet!"	said	Jesus			sternly.		"Come	out
→	φιμώθητι	λέγων	ὁ	Ἰησοῦς‚	αὐτῷ	ἐπετίμησεν	καὶ	ἔξελθε	←
	v.apm.2s	pt.pa.nsm	d.nsm	n.nsm	r.dsm.3	v.aai.3s	cj	v.aam.2s	
	5821	3306	3836	2652	899	2203	2779	2002	

9. **Greek substantives may require a helping word in translation (e.g., "of, to, for"). This word is often connected with the Greek case. An arrow is placed under these words pointing to the substantive.**

"The	kingdom	of	heaven		is	like	treasure	hidden
ἡ	βασιλεία	→	‚τῶν	οὐρανῶν‚	ἐστιν	Ὁμοία	θησαυρῷ	κεκρυμμένῳ
d.nsf	n.nsf		d.gpm	n.gpm	v.pai.3s	a.nsf	n.dsm	pt.rp.dsm
3836	993		3836	4041	1639	3927	2565	3221

I	write	these	things	**to**	you	who	believe	in	the	name
→	ἔγραψα	Ταῦτα	←	→	ὑμῖν	τοῖς	πιστεύουσιν	εἰς	τὸ	ὄνομα
	v.aai.1s	r.apn			r.dp.2	d.dpm	pt.pa.dpm	p.a	d.asn	n.asn
	1211	4047			7007	3836	4409	1650	3836	3950

"Do	not	store	up	**for**	yourselves	treasures	on	earth,
→	Μὴ	θησαυρίζετε	←	→	ὑμῖν	θησαυροὺς	ἐπὶ	‚τῆς	γῆς‚
	pl	v.pam.2p			r.dp.2	n.apm	p.g	d.gsf	n.gsf
	2564	3590	2564		7007	2565	2093	3836	1178

In	Damascus	the	governor	**under**	King		Aretas
ἐν	Δαμασκῷ	ὁ	ἐθνάρχης	→	‚τοῦ	βασιλέως‚	Ἀρέτα
p.d	n.dsf	d.nsm	n.nsm	745	d.gsm	n.gsm	n.gsm
1877	1242	3836	1617		3836	995	745

because	our	testimony	**about**	Christ		was	confirmed
καθὼς	τὸ	μαρτύριον	→	‚τοῦ	Χριστοῦ‚	→	ἐβεβαιώθη
cj	d.nsn	n.nsn		d.gsm	n.gsm		v.api.3s
2777	3836	3457		3836	5986		1011

making	peace		through	his	blood,		**shed**	**on**	the	cross.
→	εἰρηνοποιήσας	διὰ	αὐτοῦ	‚τοῦ	αἵματος‚		→		τοῦ	σταυροῦ
	pt.aa.nsm	p.g	r.gsm.3	d.gsn	n.gsn				d.gsm	n.gsm
	1647	1328	899	3836	135				3836	5089

For	the	grace	of	God		**that**	**brings**	salvation
γὰρ	ἡ	χάρις	→	‚τοῦ	θεοῦ‚	→	→	σωτήριος
cj	d.nsf	n.nsf		d.gsm	n.gsm			a.nsf
1142	3836	5921		3836	2536			5402

10. **Troublesome constructions (including idioms). When there is simply no way to place a Greek word under an English word, I put the English words in italics. This means that the English word cannot be derived from the Greek word underneath it and you should not attempt a word study unless you know some Greek and can see what is happening. Often this situation is due to a Greek idiom.**

A	*few*	*days*	*later*,	when	Jesus	again	entered		Capernaum,
δι᾽	ἡμερῶν		→			πάλιν	εἰσελθὼν	εἰς	Καφαρναοὺμ
p.g	n.gpf					adv	pt.aa.nsm	p.a	n.asf
1328	2465		1656			4099	1656	1650	3019

to	whom	be	glory		*for*	*ever*		*and*	*ever*.		Amen.
→	ᾧ	‚ἡ	δόξα‚	εἰς	‚τοὺς	αἰῶνας‚		‚τῶν	αἰώνων‚		ἀμήν
	r.dsm	d.nsf	n.nsf	p.a	d.apm	n.apm		d.gpm	n.gpm		pl
	4005	3836	1518	1650	3836	172		3836	172		297

11. **I use the NIV's paragraphing and section names. Sections start a new paragraph and the heading is given. Paragraphs are marked with the paragraph symbol (¶) to save space.**

John,	¶	To	the	seven	churches
Ἰωάννης	→		ταῖς	ἑπτὰ	ἐκκλησίαις
n.nsm			d.dpf	a.dpf	n.dpf
2722			3836	2231	1711

If the translation starts a new paragraph because of a change in speaker, the new paragraph may not be marked.

12. **The major parsing codes are as follows.**

   a. Most parsing codes first list the type of word following by a period.

n. Noun	r. Pronoun	v. Verb	f. Infinitive
a. Adjective	d. Definite article	pt. Participle	

   b. Substantives are parsed as case–number–gender. "n.asm" means "noun . accusative singular masculine"

n	Nominative	s	Singular	m	Masculine
g	Genitive	p	Plural	f	Feminine
d	Dative			n	Neuter
a	Accusative				
v	Vocative				

   Adjectives can be followed by ".c" ("Comparative") or ".s" ("superlative"). "a.gpn.c" means "adjective . genitive plural neuter . comparative."

   Personal pronouns are parsed "case–number–gender . person–number." "r.apf.3p" means "pronoun . accusative plural feminine . third person plural."

   c. Verbs are parsed "tense–voice–mood . person–number." "v.pai.1s" means "verb . present active indicative . first person singular."

p	Present	a	Active	i	Indicative	1	First
i	Imperfect	m	Middle	s	Subjunctive	2	Second
f	Future	p	Passive	o	Optative	3	Third
a	Aorist			m	Imperative		
r	Perfect					s	Singular
l	Pluperfect					p	Plural

   Participles are parsed "tense–voice . case–number–gender." "pt.pa.nsm" means "participle . present active . nominative singular masculine."

   Infinitives are parsed "tense–voice." "f.ra" means "infinitive . perfect active."

   d. The following codes are used by themselves for other parsing tags.

adv	Adverb	cj	Conjunction
adv.c	Comparative adverb	j	Interjection
adv.s	Superlative adverb	pl	Particle
p.g	Preposition with the genitive		
p.d	Preposition with the dative		
p.a	Preposition with the accusative		

Matthew

The Genealogy of Jesus

1:1 A record of the genealogy of Jesus Christ the son of David, the son of Abraham: ¶ **2** Abraham was the
Βίβλος → γενέσεως → Ἰησοῦ Χριστοῦ υἱοῦ → Δαυὶδ υἱοῦ → Ἀβραάμ. Ἀβραὰμ →
n.nsf n.gsf n.gsm n.gsm n.gsm n.gsm n.nsm
1047 1161 2652 5986 5626 1253 5626 11 11

father of Isaac, Isaac the father of Jacob, Jacob the father of Judah and his
ἐγέννησεν ⸂τὸν Ἰσαάκ,⸃ δὲ Ἰσαὰκ ἐγέννησεν ⸂τὸν Ἰακώβ,⸃ δὲ Ἰακὼβ ἐγέννησεν ⸂τὸν Ἰούδαν⸃ καὶ αὐτοῦ,
v.aai.3s d.asm n.asm cj n.nsm v.aai.3s d.asm n.asm cj n.nsm v.aai.3s d.asm n.asm cj r.gsm
1164 3836 2693 1254 2693 1164 3836 2609 1254 2609 1164 3836 2683 2779 899

brothers, **3** Judah the father of Perez and Zerah, whose mother was Tamar, Perez the
⸂τοὺς ἀδελφοὺς⸃ δὲ Ἰούδας ἐγέννησεν ⸂τὸν Φάρες⸃ καὶ ⸂τὸν Ζάρα⸃ ἐκ ⸂τῆς Θαμάρ⸃ δὲ Φάρες
d.apm n.apm cj n.nsm v.aai.3s d.asm n.asm cj d.asm n.asm p.g d.gsf n.gsf cj n.nsm
3836 81 1254 2683 1164 3836 5756 2779 3836 2406 1666 3836 2500 1254 5756

father of Hezron, Hezron the father of Ram, **4** Ram the father of Amminadab, Amminadab
ἐγέννησεν ⸂τὸν Ἑσρώμ⸃ δὲ Ἑσρὼμ ἐγέννησεν ⸂τὸν Ἀράμ⸃ δὲ Ἀρὰμ ἐγέννησεν ⸂τὸν Ἀμιναδάβ⸃ δὲ Ἀμιναδὰβ
v.aai.3s d.asm n.asm cj n.nsm v.aai.3s d.asm n.asm cj n.nsm v.aai.3s d.asm n.asm cj n.nsm
1164 3836 2272 1254 2272 1164 3836 730 1254 730 1164 3836 300 1254 300

the father of Nahshon, Nahshon the father of Salmon, **5** Salmon the father of Boaz, whose
ἐγέννησεν ⸂τὸν Ναασσών⸃ δὲ Ναασσὼν ἐγέννησεν ⸂τὸν Σαλμών⸃ δὲ Σαλμὼν ἐγέννησεν ⸂τὸν Βόες⸃
v.aai.3s d.asm n.asm cj n.nsm v.aai.3s d.asm n.asm cj n.nsm v.aai.3s d.asm n.asm
1164 3836 3709 1254 3709 1164 3836 4891 1254 4891 1164 3836 1067

mother was Rahab, Boaz the father of Obed, whose mother was Ruth, Obed the father
ἐκ ⸂τῆς Ῥαχάβ⸃ δὲ Βόες ἐγέννησεν ⸂τὸν Ἰωβὴδ⸃ ἐκ ⸂τῆς Ῥούθ⸃ δὲ Ἰωβὴδ ἐγέννησεν
p.g d.gsf n.gsf cj n.nsm v.aai.3s d.asm n.asm p.g d.gsf n.gsf cj n.nsm v.aai.3s
1666 3836 4829 1254 1067 1164 3836 2725 1666 3836 4858 1254 2725 1164

of Jesse, **6** and Jesse the father of King David. ¶ David was the father of Solomon,
⸂τὸν Ἰεσσαί⸃ δὲ Ἰεσσαὶ ἐγέννησεν ⸂τὸν βασιλέα⸃ ⸂τὸν Δαυίδ⸃ δὲ Δαυὶδ → ἐγέννησεν ⸂τὸν Σολομῶνα⸃
d.asm n.asm cj n.nsm v.aai.3s d.asm n.asm d.asm n.asm cj n.nsm v.aai.3s d.asm n.asm
3836 2649 1254 2649 1164 3836 995 3836 1253 1254 1253 1164 3836 5048

whose mother had been Uriah's wife, **7** Solomon the father of Rehoboam, Rehoboam the father
ἐκ τῆς ⸂τοῦ Οὐρίου⸃ ↩ δὲ Σολομὼν ἐγέννησεν ⸂τὸν Ῥοβοάμ⸃ δὲ Ῥοβοὰμ ἐγέννησεν
p.g d.gsf d.gsm n.gsm cj n.nsm v.aai.3s d.asm n.asm cj n.nsm v.aai.3s
1666 3836 3836 4043 3836 1254 5048 1164 3836 4850 1254 4850 1164

of Abijah, Abijah the father of Asa, **8** Asa the father of Jehoshaphat, Jehoshaphat the father
⸂τὸν Ἀβιά⸃ δὲ Ἀβιὰ ἐγέννησεν ⸂τὸν Ἀσάφ⸃ δὲ Ἀσὰ ἐγέννησεν ⸂τὸν Ἰωσαφάτ⸃ δὲ Ἰωσαφὰτ ἐγέννησεν
d.asm n.asm cj n.nsm v.aai.3s d.asm n.asm cj n.nsm v.aai.3s d.asm n.asm cj n.nsm v.aai.3s
3836 7 1254 7 1164 3836 811 1254 811 1164 3836 2734 1254 2734 1164

of Jehoram, Jehoram the father of Uzziah, **9** Uzziah the father of Jotham, Jotham the father
⸂τὸν Ἰωράμ⸃ δὲ Ἰωρὰμ ἐγέννησεν ⸂τὸν Ὀζίαν⸃ δὲ Ὀζίας ἐγέννησεν ⸂τὸν Ἰωαθάμ⸃ δὲ Ἰωαθὰμ ἐγέννησεν
d.asm n.asm cj n.nsm v.aai.3s d.asm n.asm cj n.nsm v.aai.3s d.asm n.asm cj n.nsm v.aai.3s
3836 2732 1254 2732 1164 3836 3852 1254 3852 1164 3836 2718 1254 2718 1164

of Ahaz, Ahaz the father of Hezekiah, **10** Hezekiah the father of Manasseh, Manasseh the
⸂τὸν Ἀχάζ⸃ δὲ Ἀχὰζ ἐγέννησεν ⸂τὸν Ἑζεκίαν⸃ δὲ Ἑζεκίας ἐγέννησεν ⸂τὸν Μανασσῆ⸃ δὲ Μανασσῆς
d.asm n.asm cj n.nsm v.aai.3s d.asm n.asm cj n.nsm v.aai.3s d.asm n.asm cj n.nsm
3836 937 1254 937 1164 3836 1614 1254 1614 1164 3836 3442 1254 3442

father of Amon, Amon the father of Josiah, **11** and Josiah the father of Jeconiah and his
ἐγέννησεν ⸂τὸν Ἀμώς⸃ δὲ Ἀμὼς ἐγέννησεν ⸂τὸν Ἰωσίαν⸃ δὲ Ἰωσίας ἐγέννησεν ⸂τὸν Ἰεχονίαν⸃ καὶ αὐτοῦ
v.aai.3s d.asm n.asm cj n.nsm v.aai.3s d.asm n.asm cj n.nsm v.aai.3s d.asm n.asm cj r.gsm
1164 3836 322 1254 322 1164 3836 2739 1254 2739 1164 3836 2651 2779 899

brothers at the time of the exile to Babylon. ¶ **12** After the exile to Babylon: Jeconiah was
⸂τοὺς ἀδελφοὺς⸃ ἐπὶ ↩ ← τῆς μετοικεσίας → Βαβυλῶνος δὲ Μετὰ τὴν μετοικεσίαν → Βαβυλῶνος Ἰεχονίας →
d.apm n.apm p.g d.gsf n.gsf n.gsf cj p.a d.asf n.asf n.gsf n.nsm
3836 81 2093 3836 3578 956 1254 3552 3836 3578 956 2651

1:1 Βίβλος γενέσεως Ἰησοῦ Χριστοῦ υἱοῦ Δαυὶδ υἱοῦ Ἀβραάμ. ¶ **2** Ἀβραὰμ ἐγέννησεν τὸν Ἰσαάκ, Ἰσαὰκ δὲ ἐγέννησεν τὸν Ἰακώβ, Ἰακὼβ δὲ ἐγέννησεν τὸν Ἰούδαν καὶ τοὺς ἀδελφοὺς αὐτοῦ, **3** Ἰούδας δὲ ἐγέννησεν τὸν Φάρες καὶ τὸν Ζάρα ἐκ τῆς Θαμάρ, Φάρες δὲ ἐγέννησεν τὸν Ἑσρώμ, Ἑσρὼμ δὲ ἐγέννησεν τὸν Ἀράμ, **4** Ἀρὰμ δὲ ἐγέννησεν τὸν Ἀμιναδάβ, Ἀμιναδὰβ δὲ ἐγέννησεν τὸν Ναασσών, Ναασσὼν δὲ ἐγέννησεν τὸν Σαλμών, **5** Σαλμὼν δὲ ἐγέννησεν τὸν Βόες ἐκ τῆς Ῥαχάβ, Βόες δὲ ἐγέννησεν τὸν Ἰωβὴδ ἐκ τῆς Ῥούθ, Ἰωβὴδ δὲ ἐγέννησεν τὸν Ἰεσσαί, **6** Ἰεσσαὶ δὲ ἐγέννησεν τὸν Δαυὶδ τὸν βασιλέα. ¶ Δαυὶδ δὲ ἐγέννησεν τὸν Σολομῶνα ἐκ τῆς τοῦ Οὐρίου, **7** Σολομὼν δὲ ἐγέννησεν τὸν Ῥοβοάμ, Ῥοβοὰμ δὲ ἐγέννησεν τὸν Ἀβιά, Ἀβιὰ δὲ ἐγέννησεν τὸν Ἀσά, «Ἀσάφ,» **8** Ἀσὰ «Ἀσάφ» δὲ ἐγέννησεν τὸν Ἰωσαφάτ, Ἰωσαφὰτ δὲ ἐγέννησεν τὸν Ἰωράμ, Ἰωρὰμ δὲ ἐγέννησεν τὸν Ὀζίαν, **9** Ὀζίας δὲ ἐγέννησεν τὸν Ἰωαθάμ, Ἰωαθὰμ δὲ ἐγέννησεν τὸν Ἀχάζ, Ἀχὰζ δὲ ἐγέννησεν τὸν Ἑζεκίαν, **10** Ἑζεκίας δὲ ἐγέννησεν τὸν Μανασσῆ, Μανασσῆς δὲ ἐγέννησεν τὸν Ἀμών, «Ἀμώς,» Ἀμὼν «Ἀμώς» δὲ ἐγέννησεν τὸν Ἰωσίαν, **11** Ἰωσίας δὲ ἐγέννησεν τὸν Ἰεχονίαν καὶ τοὺς ἀδελφοὺς αὐτοῦ ἐπὶ τῆς μετοικεσίας Βαβυλῶνος. ¶ **12** Μετὰ δὲ τὴν μετοικεσίαν Βαβυλῶνος

the father of Shealtiel, Shealtiel the father of Zerubbabel, **13** Zerubbabel the father of Abiud,
ἐγέννησεν ⌐τὸν Σαλαθιήλ⌐ δὲ Σαλαθιὴλ ἐγέννησεν ⌐τὸν Ζοροβαβέλ⌐ δὲ Ζοροβαβὲλ ἐγέννησεν ⌐τὸν Ἀβιούδ⌐
v.aai.3s d.asm n.asm cj n.nsm v.aai.3s d.asm n.asm cj n.nsm v.aai.3s d.asm n.asm
1164 3836 4886 1254 4886 1164 3836 2431 1254 2431 1164 3836 10

Abiud the father of Eliakim, Eliakim the father of Azor, **14** Azor the father of Zadok,
δὲ Ἀβιοὺδ ἐγέννησεν ⌐τὸν Ἐλιακίμ⌐ δὲ Ἐλιακὶμ ἐγέννησεν ⌐τὸν Ἀζώρ⌐ δὲ Ἀζὼρ ἐγέννησεν ⌐τὸν Σαδώκ⌐ δὲ
cj n.nsm v.aai.3s d.asm n.asm cj n.nsm v.aai.3s d.asm n.asm cj n.nsm v.aai.3s d.asm n.asm cj
1254 10 1164 3836 1806 1254 1806 1164 3836 110 1254 110 1164 3836 4882 1254

Zadok the father of Akim, Akim the father of Eliud, **15** Eliud the father of Eleazar,
Σαδὼκ ἐγέννησεν ⌐τὸν Ἀχίμ⌐ δὲ Ἀχὶμ ἐγέννησεν ⌐τὸν Ἐλιούδ⌐ δὲ Ἐλιοὺδ ἐγέννησεν ⌐τὸν Ἐλεάζαρ⌐ δὲ
n.nsm v.aai.3s d.asm n.asm cj n.nsm v.aai.3s d.asm n.asm cj n.nsm v.aai.3s d.asm n.asm cj
4882 1164 3836 943 1254 943 1164 3836 1809 1254 1809 1164 3836 1789 1254

Eleazar the father of Matthan, Matthan the father of Jacob, **16** and Jacob the father of Joseph, the
Ἐλεάζαρ ἐγέννησεν ⌐τὸν Ματθάν⌐ δὲ Ματθὰν ἐγέννησεν ⌐τὸν Ἰακώβ⌐ δὲ Ἰακὼβ ἐγέννησεν ⌐τὸν Ἰωσὴφ⌐ τὸν
n.nsm v.aai.3s d.asm n.asm cj n.nsm v.aai.3s d.asm n.asm cj n.nsm v.aai.3s d.asm n.asm d.asm
1789 1164 3836 3474 1254 3474 1164 3836 2609 1254 2609 1164 3836 2737 3836

husband of Mary, of whom was born Jesus, who is called Christ. ¶ **17** Thus there were fourteen
ἄνδρα → Μαρίας ἐξ ἧς → ἐγεννήθη Ἰησοῦς ὁ → λεγόμενος χριστός οὖν δεκατέσσαρες
n.asm n.gsf p.g r.gsf v.api.3s n.nsm d.nsm pt.pp.nsm n.nsm a.npf
467 3451 1666 4005 1164 2652 3836 3306 5986 4036 1280

generations in all from Abraham to David, fourteen from David to the exile to
γενεαὶ Πᾶσαι αἱ γενεαὶ ἀπὸ Ἀβραὰμ ἕως Δαυὶδ καὶ γενεαὶ δεκατέσσαρες ἀπὸ Δαυὶδ ἕως τῆς μετοικεσίας →
n.npf a.npf d.npf n.npf p.g n.gsm p.g n.gsm cj n.npf a.npf p.g n.gsm p.g d.gsf n.gsf
1155 4246 3836 1155 608 11 2401 1253 2779 1155 1280 608 1253 2401 3836 3578

Babylon, and fourteen from the exile to the Christ.
Βαβυλῶνος καὶ γενεαὶ δεκατέσσαρες ἀπὸ τῆς μετοικεσίας Βαβυλῶνος ἕως τοῦ Χριστοῦ
n.gsf cj n.npf a.npf p.g d.gsf n.gsf n.gsf p.g d.gsm n.gsm
956 2779 1155 1280 608 3836 3578 956 2401 3836 5986

The Birth of Jesus Christ

1:18 This is how the birth of Jesus Christ came about: His mother Mary was pledged to be
δὲ → → οὕτως ἡ γένεσις → ⌐Τοῦ Ἰησοῦ⌐ Χριστοῦ ἦν ← αὐτοῦ ⌐τῆς μητρὸς⌐ Μαρίας → μνηστευθείσης ← ←
cj adv d.nsf n.nsf d.gsm n.gsm n.gsm v.iai.3s r.gsm d.gsf n.gsf n.gsf pt.ap.gsf
1254 4048 3836 1161 3836 2652 5986 1639 899 3836 3613 3451 3650

married to Joseph, but before they came together, she was found *to be* *with child* through the Holy
← → ⌐τῷ Ἰωσήφ⌐ ⌐πρὶν ἢ⌐ αὐτοὺς συνελθεῖν ← → εὑρέθη ἔχουσα ἐν γαστρὶ ἐκ ἁγίου
d.dsm n.dsm cj pl r.apm f.aa v.api.3s pt.pa.nsf p.d n.dsf p.g a.gsn
3836 2737 4570 2445 899 5302 2351 2400 1877 1143 1666 41

Spirit. **19** Because Joseph her husband was a righteous man and did not want to expose her to public
πνεύματος δὲ Ἰωσὴφ αὐτῆς ὁ ἀνήρ, ὢν δίκαιος ← καὶ μὴ θέλων → δειγματίσαι αὐτὴν ←
n.gsn cj n.nsm r.gsf d.nsm n.nsm pt.pa.nsm a.nsm cj pl pt.pa.nsm f.aa r.asf
4460 1254 1639 2737 899 3836 467 1639 1465 2779 2527 3590 2527 1258 899 1258 1258

disgrace, he had in mind to divorce her quietly. ¶ **20** But after he had considered this, an angel of
← → → ἐβουλήθη ἀπολῦσαι αὐτὴν λάθρα δὲ → αὐτοῦ ἐνθυμηθέντος ταῦτα ἰδοὺ ἄγγελος →
v.api.3s f.aa r.asf adv cj r.gsm pt.ap.gsm r.apn j n.nsm
1258 1089 668 899 3277 1254 1926 899 1926 4047 2627 34

the Lord appeared to him in a dream and said, "Joseph son of David, do not be afraid to take Mary
κυρίου ἐφάνη → αὐτῷ κατ' ὄναρ λέγων Ἰωσὴφ υἱὸς Δαυὶδ μὴ → φοβηθῇς → παραλαβεῖν Μαρίαν
n.gsm v.api.3s r.dsm p.a n.asn pt.pa.nsm n.vsm n.nsm n.gsm pl v.aps.2s f.aa n.asf
3261 5743 899 2848 3941 3306 2737 5626 1253 5828 3590 5828 4161 3451

home as your wife, because what is conceived in her is from the Holy Spirit. **21** She will give birth to
σου ⌐τὴν γυναῖκα⌐ γὰρ τὸ → γεννηθὲν ἐν αὐτῇ ἐστιν ἐκ ἁγίου πνεύματος δὲ → → → τέξεται ←
r.gs.2 d.asf n.asf cj d.nsn pt.ap.nsn p.d r.dsf v.pai.3s p.g a.gsn n.gsn cj v.fmi.3s
5148 3836 1222 1142 3836 1164 1877 899 1639 1666 41 4460 1254 5503

a son, and you are to give him the name Jesus, because he will save his people from their sins." ¶
υἱόν καὶ → καλέσεις αὐτοῦ τὸ ὄνομα Ἰησοῦν γὰρ αὐτὸς → σώσει αὐτοῦ ⌐τὸν λαὸν⌐ ἀπὸ αὐτῶν ⌐τῶν ἁμαρτιῶν⌐
n.asm cj v.fai.2s r.gsm d.asn n.asn n.asm cj r.nsm v.fai.3s r.gsm.3 d.asm n.asm p.g r.gpm.3 d.gpf n.gpf
5626 2779 2813 899 3836 3950 2652 1142 899 5392 899 3836 3295 608 899 3836 281

Ἰεχονίας ἐγέννησεν τὸν Σαλαθιήλ, Σαλαθιὴλ δὲ ἐγέννησεν τὸν Ζοροβαβέλ, **13** Ζοροβαβὲλ δὲ ἐγέννησεν τὸν Ἀβιούδ, Ἀβιοὺδ δὲ ἐγέννησεν τὸν Ἐλιακίμ, Ἐλιακὶμ δὲ ἐγέννησεν τὸν Ἀζώρ, **14** Ἀζὼρ δὲ ἐγέννησεν τὸν Σαδώκ, Σαδὼκ δὲ ἐγέννησεν τὸν Ἀχίμ, Ἀχὶμ δὲ ἐγέννησεν τὸν Ἐλιούδ, **15** Ἐλιοὺδ δὲ ἐγέννησεν τὸν Ἐλεάζαρ, Ἐλεάζαρ δὲ ἐγέννησεν τὸν Ματθάν, Ματθὰν δὲ ἐγέννησεν τὸν Ἰακώβ, **16** Ἰακὼβ δὲ ἐγέννησεν τὸν Ἰωσὴφ τὸν ἄνδρα Μαρίας, ἐξ ἧς ἐγεννήθη Ἰησοῦς ὁ λεγόμενος Χριστός. ¶ **17** Πᾶσαι οὖν αἱ γενεαὶ ἀπὸ Ἀβραὰμ ἕως Δαυὶδ γενεαὶ δεκατέσσαρες, καὶ ἀπὸ Δαυὶδ ἕως τῆς μετοικεσίας Βαβυλῶνος γενεαὶ δεκατέσσαρες, καὶ ἀπὸ τῆς μετοικεσίας Βαβυλῶνος ἕως τοῦ Χριστοῦ γενεαὶ δεκατέσσαρες.

1:18 Τοῦ δὲ Ἰησοῦ Χριστοῦ ἡ γένεσις οὕτως ἦν. μνηστευθείσης τῆς μητρὸς αὐτοῦ Μαρίας τῷ Ἰωσήφ, πρὶν ἢ συνελθεῖν αὐτοὺς εὑρέθη ἐν γαστρὶ ἔχουσα ἐκ πνεύματος ἁγίου. **19** Ἰωσὴφ δὲ ὁ ἀνὴρ αὐτῆς, δίκαιος ὢν καὶ μὴ θέλων αὐτὴν δειγματίσαι, ἐβουλήθη λάθρᾳ ἀπολῦσαι αὐτήν. ¶ **20** ταῦτα δὲ αὐτοῦ ἐνθυμηθέντος ἰδοὺ ἄγγελος κυρίου κατ' ὄναρ ἐφάνη αὐτῷ λέγων, Ἰωσὴφ υἱὸς Δαυίδ, μὴ φοβηθῇς παραλαβεῖν Μαριὰν τὴν γυναῖκά σου· τὸ γὰρ ἐν αὐτῇ γεννηθὲν ἐκ πνεύματός ἐστιν ἁγίου. **21** τέξεται δὲ υἱόν, καὶ καλέσεις τὸ ὄνομα αὐτοῦ Ἰησοῦν· αὐτὸς γὰρ σώσει τὸν λαὸν αὐτοῦ ἀπὸ τῶν ἁμαρτιῶν αὐτῶν.

22 All this took place to fulfill what the Lord had said through the prophet: **23** "The
δὲ ὅλον τοῦτο γέγονεν ← ἵνα πληρωθῇ τὸ ὑπὸ κυρίου → ῥηθὲν διὰ τοῦ προφήτου λέγοντος ἰδοὺ ἡ
cj a.nsn r.nsn v.rai.3s cj v.aps.3s d.nsn p.g n.gsm pt.ap.nsn p.g d.gsm n.gsm pt.pa.gsm j d.nsf
1254 3910 4047 1181 2671 4444 3836 5679 3261 3306 1328 3836 4737 3306 2627 3836

virgin *will be with child* and will give birth to a son, and they will call him Immanuel" –
παρθένος → ἕξει ἐν γαστρὶ καὶ → → τέξεται υἱόν καὶ → → καλέσουσιν ⌐τὸ ὄνομα αὐτοῦ⌐ Ἐμμανουήλ
n.nsf v.fai.3s p.d n.dsf cj v.fmi.3s n.asm cj v.fai.3p d.asn n.asn r.gsm.3 n.asm
4221 2400 1877 1143 2779 5503 5626 2779 2813 3836 3950 899 1842

which means, "God with us." ¶ **24** When Joseph woke up, he did
ὅ ἐστιν μεθερμηνευόμενον ⌐ὁ θεός μεθ' ἡμῶν⌐ δὲ → ὁ Ἰωσὴφ ἐγερθεὶς ἀπὸ τοῦ ὕπνου ἐποίησεν
r.nsn v.pai.3s pt.pp.nsn d.nsm n.nsm p.g r.gp.1 cj d.nsm n.nsm pt.ap.nsm p.g d.gsm n.gsm v.aai.3s
4005 1639 3493 3836 2536 3552 7005 1254 1586 3836 2737 1586 608 3836 5678 1586 4472

what the angel of the Lord had commanded him and took Mary home as his wife. **25** But he had no
ὡς ὁ ἄγγελος → κυρίου → προσέταξεν αὐτῷ καὶ παρέλαβεν αὐτοῦ ⌐τὴν γυναῖκα⌐ καὶ → → οὐκ
cj d.nsm n.nsm n.gsm v.aai.3s r.dsm.3 cj v.aai.3s r.gsm.3 d.asf n.asf cj adv
6055 3836 34 3261 4705 899 2779 4161 899 3836 1222 2779 1182 1182 4024

union with her until she gave birth to a son. And he gave him the name Jesus.
ἐγίνωσκεν ← αὐτὴν ⌐ἕως οὗ⌐ → ἔτεκεν υἱόν καὶ → ἐκάλεσεν αὐτοῦ τὸ ὄνομα Ἰησοῦν
v.iai.3s r.asf.3 p.g r.gsm v.aai.3s n.asm cj v.aai.3s r.gsm.3 d.asn n.asn n.asm
1182 899 2401 4005 5503 5626 2779 2813 899 3836 3950 2652

The Visit of the Magi

2:1 After Jesus was born in Bethlehem in Judea, during the time of King Herod,
δὲ → ⌐Τοῦ Ἰησοῦ⌐ → γεννηθέντος ἐν Βηθλέεμ → ⌐τῆς Ἰουδαίας⌐ ἐν ἡμέραις → ⌐τοῦ βασιλέως⌐ Ἡρῴδου
cj d.gsm n.gsm pt.ap.gsm p.d n.dsf d.gsf n.gsf p.d n.dpf d.gsm n.gsm n.gsm
1254 1164 3836 2652 1164 1877 1033 3836 2677 1877 2465 3836 995 2476

Magi from the east came to Jerusalem **2** and asked, "Where is the one who has been born king
ἰδοὺ μάγοι ἀπὸ ἀνατολῶν παρεγένοντο εἰς Ἰεροσόλυμα λέγοντες ποῦ ἐστιν ὁ ← ← → τεχθεὶς βασιλεὺς
j n.npm p.g n.gpf v.ami.3p p.a n.apn pt.pa.npm adv v.pai.3s d.nsm pt.ap.nsm n.nsm
2627 3407 608 424 4134 1650 2642 3306 4544 1639 3836 5503 995

of the Jews? We saw his star in the east and have come to worship him." ¶ **3**
→ τῶν Ἰουδαίων γὰρ → εἴδομεν αὐτοῦ ⌐τὸν ἀστέρα⌐ ἐν τῇ ἀνατολῇ καὶ → ἤλθομεν → προσκυνῆσαι αὐτῷ δὲ
d.gpm a.gpm cj v.aai.1p r.gsm.3 d.asm n.asm p.d d.dsf n.dsf cj v.aai.1p f.aa r.dsm.3 cj
3836 2681 1142 1625 899 3836 843 1877 3836 424 2779 2262 4686 899 1254

When King Herod heard this he was disturbed, and all Jerusalem with him. **4** When he had called
→ ὁ βασιλεὺς Ἡρῴδης ἀκούσας → → ἐταράχθη καὶ πᾶσα Ἰεροσόλυμα μετ' αὐτοῦ καὶ → → συναγαγὼν
d.nsm n.nsm n.nsm pt.aa.nsm v.api.3s cj a.nsf n.nsf p.g r.gsm.3 cj pt.aa.nsm
201 3836 995 2476 201 5429 2779 4246 2642 3552 899 2779 5251

together all the people's chief priests and teachers of the law, he asked them where the Christ was
πάντας τοὺς ⌐τοῦ λαοῦ⌐ ἀρχιερεῖς καὶ γραμματεῖς → → ἐπυνθάνετο παρ' αὐτῶν ποῦ ὁ χριστὸς →
a.apm d.apm d.gsm n.gsm n.apm cj n.apm v.imi.3s p.g r.gpm.3 adv d.nsm n.nsm
4246 3836 3836 3295 797 2779 1208 4785 4123 899 4544 3836 5986

to be born. **5** "In Bethlehem in Judea," they replied, "for *this is what* the prophet has written:
→ γεννᾶται δὲ ἐν Βηθλέεμ → ⌐τῆς Ἰουδαίας⌐ οἱ εἶπαν αὐτῷ γὰρ οὕτως διὰ τοῦ προφήτου → γέγραπται
v.ppi.3s cj p.d n.dsf d.gsf n.gsf d.npm v.aai.3p r.dsm.3 cj adv p.g d.gsm n.gsm v.rpi.3s
1164 1254 1877 1033 3836 2677 3836 3306 899 1142 4048 1328 3836 4737 1211

6 "'But you, Bethlehem, in the land of Judah, are *by no means* least among the rulers of Judah; for out of you
καὶ σὺ Βηθλέεμ γῆ → Ἰούδα εἶ οὐδαμῶς ἐλαχίστη ἐν τοῖς ἡγεμόσιν → Ἰούδα γὰρ ἐκ ← σοῦ
cj r.ns.2 n.vsf n.vsf n.gsm v.pai.2s adv a.nsf.s p.d d.dpm n.dpm n.gsm cj p.g r.gs.2
2779 5148 1033 1178 2683 1639 4027 1788 1877 3836 2450 2683 1142 1666 5148

will come a ruler who will be the shepherd of my people Israel.'" ¶ **7** Then Herod called the
→ ἐξελεύσεται ἡγούμενος ὅστις → → ποιμανεῖ μου ⌐τὸν λαόν⌐ ⌐τὸν Ἰσραήλ⌐ Τότε Ἡρῴδης καλέσας τοὺς
v.fmi.3s pt.pm.nsm r.nsm v.fai.3s r.gs.1 d.asm n.asm d.asm n.asm adv n.nsm pt.aa.nsm d.apm
2002 2451 4015 4477 1609 3836 3295 3836 2702 5538 2476 2813 3836

Magi secretly and found out from them the exact time the star had appeared. **8** He sent them to
μάγους λάθρᾳ ἠκρίβωσεν ← παρ' αὐτῶν τὸν χρόνον ἀστέρος ⌐τοῦ φαινομένου⌐ καὶ → πέμψας αὐτοὺς εἰς
n.apm adv v.aai.3s p.g r.gpm.3 d.asm n.asm n.gsm d.gsm pt.pm.gsm cj pt.aa.nsm r.apm.3 p.a
3407 3277 208 4123 899 3836 5989 843 3836 5743 2779 4287 899 1650

---

²² Τοῦτο δὲ ὅλον γέγονεν ἵνα πληρωθῇ τὸ ῥηθὲν ὑπὸ κυρίου διὰ τοῦ προφήτου λέγοντος, ²³ Ἰδοὺ ἡ παρθένος ἐν γαστρὶ ἕξει καὶ τέξεται υἱόν, καὶ καλέσουσιν τὸ ὄνομα αὐτοῦ Ἐμμανουήλ, ὅ ἐστιν μεθερμηνευόμενον Μεθ' ἡμῶν ὁ θεός. ¶ ²⁴ ἐγερθεὶς δὲ ὁ Ἰωσὴφ ἀπὸ τοῦ ὕπνου ἐποίησεν ὡς προσέταξεν αὐτῷ ὁ ἄγγελος κυρίου καὶ παρέλαβεν τὴν γυναῖκα αὐτοῦ, ²⁵ καὶ οὐκ ἐγίνωσκεν αὐτὴν ἕως οὗ ἔτεκεν υἱόν· καὶ ἐκάλεσεν τὸ ὄνομα αὐτοῦ Ἰησοῦν.

²:¹ Τοῦ δὲ Ἰησοῦ γεννηθέντος ἐν Βηθλέεμ τῆς Ἰουδαίας ἐν ἡμέραις Ἡρῴδου τοῦ βασιλέως, ἰδοὺ μάγοι ἀπὸ ἀνατολῶν παρεγένοντο εἰς Ἰεροσόλυμα ² λέγοντες, Ποῦ ἐστιν ὁ τεχθεὶς βασιλεὺς τῶν Ἰουδαίων; εἴδομεν γὰρ αὐτοῦ τὸν ἀστέρα ἐν τῇ ἀνατολῇ καὶ ἤλθομεν προσκυνῆσαι αὐτῷ. ¶ ³ ἀκούσας δὲ ὁ βασιλεὺς Ἡρῴδης ἐταράχθη καὶ πᾶσα Ἰεροσόλυμα μετ' αὐτοῦ, ⁴ καὶ συναγαγὼν πάντας τοὺς ἀρχιερεῖς καὶ γραμματεῖς τοῦ λαοῦ ἐπυνθάνετο παρ' αὐτῶν ποῦ ὁ Χριστὸς γεννᾶται. ⁵ οἱ δὲ εἶπαν αὐτῷ, Ἐν Βηθλέεμ τῆς Ἰουδαίας· οὕτως γὰρ γέγραπται διὰ τοῦ προφήτου· ⁶ Καὶ σὺ Βηθλέεμ, γῆ Ἰούδα, οὐδαμῶς ἐλαχίστη εἶ ἐν τοῖς ἡγεμόσιν Ἰούδα· ἐκ σοῦ γὰρ ἐξελεύσεται ἡγούμενος, ὅστις ποιμανεῖ τὸν λαόν μου τὸν Ἰσραήλ. ¶ ⁷ Τότε Ἡρῴδης λάθρᾳ καλέσας τοὺς μάγους ἠκρίβωσεν παρ' αὐτῶν τὸν χρόνον τοῦ φαινομένου ἀστέρος, ⁸ καὶ πέμψας αὐτοὺς εἰς Βηθλέεμ

Bethlehem and said, "Go and make a careful search for the child. *As soon as* you find him,
Βηθλέεμ εἶπεν πορευθέντες → ἀκριβῶς ἐξετάσατε περὶ τοῦ παιδίου δὲ ἐπὰν → εὕρητε
n.asf v.aai.3s pt.ap.npm adv v.aam.2p p.g d.gsn n.gsn cj cj v.aas.2p
1033 3306 4513 2004 209 2004 4309 4086 1254 2054 2351

report to me, so that I too may go and worship him." ¶ **9** After they had heard the
ἀπαγγείλατέ → μοι ὅπως ← κἀγὼ ← → ἐλθὼν προσκυνήσω αὐτῷ δὲ → οἱ → ἀκούσαντες τοῦ
v.aam.2p r.ds.1 cj crasis pt.aa.nsm v.aas.1s r.dsm.3 cj d.npm pt.aa.npm d.gsn
550 1609 3968 2743 4686 2262 4686 899 1254 201 3836 201 3836

king, they went on their way, and the star they had seen in the east went ahead of them
βασιλέως → ἐπορεύθησαν ← καὶ ἰδοὺ ὁ ἀστὴρ ὃν → εἶδον ἐν τῇ ἀνατολῇ προῆγεν ← ← αὐτούς
n.gsm v.api.3p cj j d.nsm n.nsm r.asm v.aai.3p p.d d.dsf n.dsf v.iai.3s r.apm.3
995 4513 2779 2627 3836 843 4005 1625 1877 3836 424 4575 899

until it stopped over the place where the child was. **10** When they saw the star, they were
ἕως → ἐλθὼν ἐστάθη ἐπάνω οὗ τὸ παιδίον ἦν δὲ → → ἰδόντες τὸν ἀστέρα →
cj pt.aa.nsm v.api.3s adv adv d.nsn n.nsn v.iai.3s cj pt.aa.npm d.asm n.asm
2401 2705 2262 2705 2062 4023 3836 4086 1639 1254 1625 3836 843

overjoyed. **11** On coming to the house, they saw the child with his mother Mary, and
ἐχάρησαν χαρὰν μεγάλην σφόδρα καὶ ἐλθόντες εἰς τὴν οἰκίαν → εἶδον τὸ παιδίον μετὰ αὐτοῦ τῆς μητρὸς Μαρίας καὶ
v.api.3p n.asf a.asf adv cj pt.aa.npm p.a d.asf n.asf v.aai.3p d.asn n.asn p.g r.gsm.3 d.gsf n.gsf n.gsf cj
5897 5915 3489 5379 2779 2262 1650 3836 3864 1625 3836 4086 3552 899 3836 3613 3451 2779

they bowed down and worshiped him. Then they opened their treasures and presented him with gifts of
→ πεσόντες ← προσεκύνησαν αὐτῷ καὶ → ἀνοίξαντες αὐτῶν τοὺς θησαυροὺς προσήνεγκαν αὐτῷ ↰ δῶρα
pt.aa.npm v.aai.3p r.dsm.3 cj pt.aa.npm r.gpm.3 d.apm n.apm v.aai.3p r.dsm.3 n.apn
4406 4686 899 2779 487 3836 2565 4712 899 4712 1565

gold and of incense and of myrrh. **12** And having been warned in a dream not to go back to Herod,
χρυσὸν καὶ λίβανον καὶ σμύρναν καὶ → → χρηματισθέντες κατ᾽ ὄναρ μὴ ἀνακάμψαι ← πρὸς Ἡρῴδην
n.asm cj n.asm cj n.asf cj pt.ap.npm p.a n.asn pl f.aa p.a n.asm
5996 2779 3337 2779 5043 2779 5976 2848 3941 3590 366 4639 2476

they returned to their country by another route.
→ ἀνεχώρησαν εἰς αὐτῶν τὴν χώραν δι᾽ ἄλλης ὁδοῦ
v.aai.3p p.a r.gpm.3 d.asf n.asf p.g r.gsf n.gsf
432 1650 899 3836 6001 1328 257 3847

The Escape to Egypt

2:13 When they had gone, an angel of the Lord appeared to Joseph in a dream. "Get
δὲ → αὐτῶν → Ἀναχωρησάντων ἰδοὺ ἄγγελος → κυρίου φαίνεται → τῷ Ἰωσὴφ κατ᾽ ὄναρ ἐγερθεὶς
cj r.gpm.3 pt.aa.gpm j n.nsm n.gsm v.pmi.3s d.dsm n.dsm p.a n.asn pt.ap.nsm
1254 432 899 432 2627 34 3261 5743 3836 2737 2848 3941 1586

up," he said, "take the child and his mother and escape to Egypt. Stay there until I tell you, for
← → λέγων παράλαβε τὸ παιδίον καὶ αὐτοῦ τὴν μητέρα καὶ φεῦγε εἰς Αἴγυπτον καὶ ἴσθι ἐκεῖ ἕως ἂν → εἴπω σοι γὰρ
pt.pa.nsm v.aam.2s d.asn n.asn cj r.gsm.3 d.asf n.asf cj v.pam.2s p.a n.asf cj v.pam.2s adv adv pl v.aas.1s r.ds.2 cj
3306 4161 3836 4086 2779 899 3836 3613 2779 5771 1650 131 2779 1639 1695 2401 323 3306 5148 1142

Herod is going to search for the child to kill him." ¶ **14** So he got up, took the child and
Ἡρῴδης → μέλλει → ζητεῖν ← τὸ παιδίον τοῦ ἀπολέσαι αὐτό δὲ ὁ ἐγερθεὶς ← παρέλαβεν τὸ παιδίον καὶ
n.nsm v.pai.3s f.pa d.asn n.asn d.gsn f.aa r.asn.3 cj d.nsm pt.ap.nsm v.aai.3s d.asn n.asn cj
2476 3516 2426 3836 4086 3836 660 899 1254 3836 1586 4161 3836 4086 2779

his mother during the night and left for Egypt, **15** where he stayed until the death of Herod. And so
αὐτοῦ τὴν μητέρα → νυκτὸς καὶ ἀνεχώρησεν εἰς Αἴγυπτον καὶ ἐκεῖ → ἔως τῆς τελευτῆς → Ἡρῴδου ἵνα
r.gsm.3 d.asf n.asf n.gsf cj v.aai.3s p.a n.asf cj adv p.g d.gsf n.gsf n.gsm cj
899 3836 3613 3816 2779 432 1650 131 2779 1695 1639 2401 3836 5463 2476 2671

was fulfilled what the Lord had said through the prophet: "Out of Egypt I called my son." ¶
→ πληρωθῇ τὸ ὑπὸ κυρίου ῥηθὲν διὰ τοῦ προφήτου λέγοντος ἐξ ← Αἰγύπτου → ἐκάλεσα μου τὸν υἱόν
v.aps.3s d.nsn p.g n.gsm pt.ap.nsn p.g d.gsn n.gsm pt.pa.gsm p.g n.gsf v.aai.1s r.gs.1 d.asm n.asm
4444 3836 5679 3261 3306 1328 3836 4737 3306 1666 131 2813 1609 3836 5626

16 When Herod realized that he had been outwitted by the Magi, he was furious, and he gave orders to
Τότε Ἡρῴδης ἰδὼν ὅτι → → ἐνεπαίχθη ὑπὸ τῶν μάγων → ἐθυμώθη λίαν καὶ → → ἀποστείλας
adv n.nsm pt.aa.nsm cj v.api.3s p.g d.gpm n.gpm v.api.3s adv cj pt.aa.nsm
5538 2476 1625 4022 1850 5679 3836 3407 2597 3336 2779 690

εἶπεν, Πορευθέντες ἐξετάσατε ἀκριβῶς περὶ τοῦ παιδίου· ἐπὰν δὲ εὕρητε, ἀπαγγείλατέ μοι, ὅπως κἀγὼ ἐλθὼν προσκυνήσω αὐτῷ. ¶ 9 οἱ δὲ ἀκούσαντες τοῦ βασιλέως ἐπορεύθησαν καὶ ἰδοὺ ὁ ἀστήρ, ὃν εἶδον ἐν τῇ ἀνατολῇ, προῆγεν αὐτούς, ἕως ἐλθὼν ἐστάθη ἐπάνω οὗ ἦν τὸ παιδίον. 10 ἰδόντες δὲ τὸν ἀστέρα ἐχάρησαν χαρὰν μεγάλην σφόδρα. 11 καὶ ἐλθόντες εἰς τὴν οἰκίαν εἶδον τὸ παιδίον μετὰ Μαρίας τῆς μητρὸς αὐτοῦ, καὶ πεσόντες προσεκύνησαν αὐτῷ καὶ ἀνοίξαντες τοὺς θησαυροὺς αὐτῶν προσήνεγκαν αὐτῷ δῶρα, χρυσὸν καὶ λίβανον καὶ σμύρναν. 12 καὶ χρηματισθέντες κατ᾽ ὄναρ μὴ ἀνακάμψαι πρὸς Ἡρῴδην, δι᾽ ἄλλης ὁδοῦ ἀνεχώρησαν εἰς τὴν χώραν αὐτῶν.
2:13 Ἀναχωρησάντων δὲ αὐτῶν ἰδοὺ ἄγγελος κυρίου φαίνεται κατ᾽ ὄναρ τῷ Ἰωσὴφ λέγων, Ἐγερθεὶς παράλαβε τὸ παιδίον καὶ τὴν μητέρα αὐτοῦ καὶ φεῦγε εἰς Αἴγυπτον καὶ ἴσθι ἐκεῖ ἕως ἂν εἴπω σοι· μέλλει γὰρ Ἡρῴδης ζητεῖν τὸ παιδίον τοῦ ἀπολέσαι αὐτό. ¶ 14 ὁ δὲ ἐγερθεὶς παρέλαβεν τὸ παιδίον καὶ τὴν μητέρα αὐτοῦ νυκτὸς καὶ ἀνεχώρησεν εἰς Αἴγυπτον, 15 καὶ ἦν ἐκεῖ ἕως τῆς τελευτῆς Ἡρῴδου· ἵνα πληρωθῇ τὸ ῥηθὲν ὑπὸ κυρίου διὰ τοῦ προφήτου λέγοντος, Ἐξ Αἰγύπτου ἐκάλεσα τὸν υἱόν μου. ¶ 16 Τότε Ἡρῴδης ἰδὼν ὅτι ἐνεπαίχθη ὑπὸ τῶν μάγων ἐθυμώθη λίαν, καὶ ἀποστείλας ἀνεῖλεν πάντας τοὺς παῖδας τοὺς ἐν Βηθλέεμ

kill	all	the	boys	in	Bethlehem	and		its	vicinity		who were		two	years old and
ἀνεῖλεν	πάντας	τοὺς	παῖδας	τοὺς ἐν	Βηθλέεμ	καὶ	ἐν πᾶσι αὐτῆς	τοῖς ὁρίοις			ἀπὸ διετοῦς ← ←			καὶ
v.aai.3s	a.apm	d.apm	n.apm	d.apm p.d	n.dsf	cj	p.d a.dpn n.gsf.3	d.dpn n.dpn			p.g a.gsm			cj
359	4246	3836	4090	3836 1877	1033	2779	1877 4246 899	3836 3990			608 1453			2779

under,	in accordance with the time				he had learned	from	the	Magi.	**17** Then	what	was	said	through	the prophet
κατωτέρω → →		κατὰ	τὸν	χρόνον ὃν	ἠκρίβωσεν	παρὰ	τῶν	μάγων	τότε	τὸ	→	ῥηθὲν	διὰ	τοῦ προφήτου
adv.c		p.a	d.asm	n.asm r.asm	v.aai.3s	p.g	d.gpm	n.gpm	adv	d.nsn		pt.ap.nsn	p.g	d.gsm n.gsm
3006		2848	3836	5989 4005	208	4123	3836	3407	5538	3836		3306	1328	3836 4737

Jeremiah	was fulfilled:		**18** "A voice	is heard	in	Ramah,	weeping	and	great	mourning,	Rachel	weeping	for her
Ἰερεμίου	→ ἐπληρώθη	λέγοντος	φωνὴ	→ ἠκούσθη	ἐν	Ῥαμὰ	κλαυθμὸς	καὶ	πολὺς	ὀδυρμὸς	Ῥαχὴλ	κλαίουσα ←	αὐτῆς
n.gsm	v.api.3s	pt.pa.gsm	n.nsf	v.api.3s	p.d	n.dsf	n.nsm	cj	a.nsm	n.nsm	n.nsf	pt.pa.nsf	r.gsf.3
2635	4444	3306	5889	201	1877	4821	3088	2779	4498	3851	4830	3081	899

children	and	refusing		to be comforted,	because	they are	no more."
τὰ τέκνα	καὶ	οὐκ ἤθελεν	→ →	παρακληθῆναι	ὅτι	→ εἰσίν	οὐκ ←
d.apn n.apn	cj	adv v.iai.3s		f.ap	cj	v.pai.3p	adv
3836 5451	2779	4024 2527		4151	4022	1639	4024

The Return to Nazareth

2:19	After	Herod		died,		an	angel	of the	Lord	appeared	in	a dream	to Joseph	in
	δὲ →	τοῦ Ἡρῴδου	Τελευτήσαντος	ἰδοὺ		ἄγγελος	→	κυρίου		φαίνεται	κατ'	ὄναρ	τῷ Ἰωσὴφ	ἐν
	cj	d.gsm n.gsm	pt.aa.gsm	j		n.nsm		n.gsm		v.pmi.3s	p.a	n.asn	d.dsm n.dsm	p.d
	1254 5462	3836 2476	5462	2627		34		3261		5743	2848	3941	3836 2737	1877

Egypt	**20** and said,	"Get	up,	take		the	child	and	his	mother	and	go	to	the	land	of Israel,	for	those
Αἰγύπτῳ	λέγων ἐγερθεὶς ←			παράλαβε	τὸ		παιδίον	καὶ	αὐτοῦ	τὴν μητέρα	καὶ	πορεύου	εἰς		γῆν →	Ἰσραὴλ	γὰρ	οἱ
n.dsf	pt.pa.nsm pt.ap.nsm			v.aam.2s	d.asn		n.asn	cj	r.gsm.3	d.asf n.asf	cj	v.pmm.2s	p.a		n.asf	n.gsm	cj	d.npm
131	3306 1586			4161	3836		4086	2779	899	3836 3613	2779	4513	1650		1178	2702	1142	3836

who were trying to take				the	child's	life		are dead."	¶	**21** So	he	got	up,	took		the	child	and
← ← → →	ζητοῦντες	τὴν	τοῦ παιδίου		ψυχὴν	→	τεθνήκασιν			δὲ	ὁ	ἐγερθεὶς ←		παρέλαβεν	τὸ		παιδίον	καὶ
	pt.pa.npm	d.asf	d.gsm n.gsm		n.asf		v.rai.3p			cj	d.nsm	pt.ap.nsm		v.aai.3s	d.asn		n.asn	cj
	2426	3836	3836 4086		6034		2569			1254	3836	1586		4161	3836		4086	2779

his	mother	and	went	to	the	land	of Israel.	**22** But	when	he heard		that	Archelaus	was	reigning in
αὐτοῦ	τὴν μητέρα	καὶ	εἰσῆλθεν	εἰς		γῆν →	Ἰσραήλ	δὲ	→	Ἀκούσας	ὅτι		Ἀρχέλαος	→	βασιλεύει →
r.gsm.3	d.asf n.asf	cj	v.aai.3s	p.a		n.asf	n.gsm	cj		pt.aa.nsm	cj		n.nsm		v.pai.3s
899	3836 3613	2779	1656	1650		1178	2702	1254		201	4022		793		996

Judea		in	place of his		father		Herod,	he was afraid	to go		there.		Having been warned	in
τῆς Ἰουδαίας	ἀντὶ ←		← αὐτοῦ	τοῦ πατρὸς		Ἡρῴδου	→	ἐφοβήθη	ἀπελθεῖν	ἐκεῖ	δὲ		χρηματισθεὶς	καὶ
d.gsf n.gsf	p.g		r.gsm.3	d.gsm n.gsm		n.gsm		v.api.3s	f.aa	adv	cj		pt.ap.nsm	p.a
3836 2677	505		899	3836 4252		2476		5828	599	1695	1254		5976	2848

a dream,	he	withdrew	to	the	district	of Galilee,		**23** and	he went	and	lived	in	a town	called	Nazareth.	So
ὄναρ	→	ἀνεχώρησεν	εἰς	τὰ	μέρη	τῆς Γαλιλαίας		καὶ	→ ἐλθὼν		κατῴκησεν	εἰς	πόλιν	λεγομένην	Ναζαρέτ	ὅπως
n.asn		v.aai.3s	p.a	d.apn	n.apn	d.gsf n.gsf		cj	pt.aa.nsm		v.aai.3s	p.a	n.asf	pt.pp.asf	n.asf	cj
3941		432	1650	3836	3538	3836 1133		2779	2262		2997	1650	4484	3306	3715	3968

was fulfilled	what	was	said	through	the prophets:		"He will be	called	a Nazarene."
→ πληρωθῇ	τὸ	→	ῥηθὲν	διὰ	τῶν προφητῶν	ὅτι →	→ →	κληθήσεται	Ναζωραῖος
v.aps.3s	d.nsn		pt.ap.nsn	p.g	d.gpm n.gpm	cj		v.fpi.3s	n.nsm
4444	3836		3306	1328	3836 4737	4022		2813	3717

John the Baptist Prepares the Way

3:1	In	those	days		John	the	Baptist	came,		preaching	in	the	Desert	of Judea		**2** and
	δὲ	Ἐν ἐκείναις	ταῖς ἡμέραις		Ἰωάννης	ὁ	βαπτιστὴς	παραγίνεται		κηρύσσων	ἐν	τῇ	ἐρήμῳ →	τῆς Ἰουδαίας		καὶ
	cj	p.d r.dpf	d.dpf n.dpf		n.nsm	d.nsm	n.nsm	v.pmi.3s		pt.pa.nsm	p.d	d.dsf	a.dsf	d.gsf n.gsf		cj
	1254	1877 1697	3836 2465		2722	3836	969	4134		3062	1877	3836	2245	3836 2677		2779

saying,	"Repent,	for	the	kingdom	of heaven		is near."	**3**	This	is	he	who	was	spoken of	through	the
λέγων	μετανοεῖτε	γὰρ	ἡ	βασιλεία	τῶν οὐρανῶν	→	ἤγγικεν	γὰρ	οὗτός	ἐστιν	ὁ	→	→	ῥηθεὶς	← διὰ	τοῦ
pt.pa.nsm	v.pam.2p	cj	d.nsf	n.nsf	d.gpm n.gpm		v.rai.3s	cj	r.nsm	v.pai.3s	d.nsm			pt.ap.nsm	p.g	d.gsm
3306	3566	1142	3836	993	3836 4041		1581	1142	4047	1639	3836			3306	1328	3836

καὶ ἐν πᾶσι τοῖς ὁρίοις αὐτῆς ἀπὸ διετοῦς καὶ κατωτέρω, κατὰ τὸν χρόνον ὃν ἠκρίβωσεν παρὰ τῶν μάγων. [17] τότε ἐπληρώθη τὸ ῥηθὲν διὰ Ἰερεμίου τοῦ προφήτου λέγοντος, [18] Φωνὴ ἐν Ῥαμὰ ἠκούσθη, κλαυθμὸς καὶ ὀδυρμὸς πολύς· Ῥαχὴλ κλαίουσα τὰ τέκνα αὐτῆς, καὶ οὐκ ἤθελεν παρακληθῆναι, ὅτι οὐκ εἰσίν.

[2:19] Τελευτήσαντος δὲ τοῦ Ἡρῴδου ἰδοὺ ἄγγελος κυρίου φαίνεται κατ' ὄναρ τῷ Ἰωσὴφ ἐν Αἰγύπτῳ [20] λέγων, Ἐγερθεὶς παράλαβε τὸ παιδίον καὶ τὴν μητέρα αὐτοῦ καὶ πορεύου εἰς γῆν Ἰσραήλ· τεθνήκασιν γὰρ οἱ ζητοῦντες τὴν ψυχὴν τοῦ παιδίου. ¶ [21] ὁ δὲ ἐγερθεὶς παρέλαβεν τὸ παιδίον καὶ τὴν μητέρα αὐτοῦ καὶ εἰσῆλθεν εἰς γῆν Ἰσραήλ. [22] ἀκούσας δὲ ὅτι Ἀρχέλαος βασιλεύει τῆς Ἰουδαίας ἀντὶ τοῦ πατρὸς αὐτοῦ Ἡρῴδου ἐφοβήθη ἐκεῖ ἀπελθεῖν· χρηματισθεὶς δὲ κατ' ὄναρ ἀνεχώρησεν εἰς τὰ μέρη τῆς Γαλιλαίας, [23] καὶ ἐλθὼν κατῴκησεν εἰς πόλιν λεγομένην Ναζαρέτ· ὅπως πληρωθῇ τὸ ῥηθὲν διὰ τῶν προφητῶν ὅτι Ναζωραῖος κληθήσεται.

[3:1] Ἐν δὲ ταῖς ἡμέραις ἐκείναις παραγίνεται Ἰωάννης ὁ βαπτιστὴς κηρύσσων ἐν τῇ ἐρήμῳ τῆς Ἰουδαίας [2] [καὶ] λέγων, Μετανοεῖτε· ἤγγικεν γὰρ ἡ βασιλεία τῶν οὐρανῶν. [3] οὗτος γάρ ἐστιν ὁ ῥηθεὶς διὰ Ἠσαΐου τοῦ προφήτου λέγοντος, Φωνὴ

prophet Isaiah: "A voice of one calling in the desert, 'Prepare the way for the Lord, make straight
προφήτου Ἠσαΐου λέγοντος φωνὴ → → βοῶντος ἐν τῇ ἐρήμῳ ἑτοιμάσατε τὴν ὁδὸν → κυρίου ποιεῖτε εὐθείας
n.gsm n.gsm pt.pa.gsm n.nsf pt.pa.gsm p.d d.dsf a.dsf v.aam.2p d.asf n.asf n.gsm v.pam.2p a.apf
4737 2480 3306 5889 1066 1877 3836 2245 2286 3836 3847 3261 4472 2318

paths for him.'" ¶ 4 John's clothes were made of camel's hair, and he had a
τὰς τρίβους, → αὐτοῦ δὲ ὁ Ἰωάννης, αὐτὸς τὸ ἔνδυμα αὐτοῦ ἀπὸ καμήλου τριχῶν καὶ → εἶχεν
d.apf n.apf r.gsm.3 cj d.nsm n.nsm r.nsm d.asn n.asn r.gsm.3 p.g n.gsf n.gpf cj v.iai.3s
3836 5561 899 1254 3836 2722 899 3836 1903 899 608 2823 2582 2779 2400

leather belt around his waist. His food was locusts and wild honey. ¶ 5 People
δερματίνην ζώνην περὶ αὐτοῦ τὴν ὀσφὺν δὲ αὐτοῦ ἡ τροφὴ, ἦν ἀκρίδες καὶ ἄγριον μέλι Τότε →
a.asf n.asf p.a r.gsm.3 d.asf n.asf cj r.gsm.3 d.nsf n.nsf v.iai.3s n.npf cj a.nsn n.nsn adv
1294 2438 4309 899 3836 4019 1254 899 3836 5575 1639 210 2779 67 3510 5538

went out to him from Jerusalem and all Judea and the whole region of the Jordan. 6
ἐξεπορεύετο → πρὸς αὐτὸν Ἰεροσόλυμα καὶ πᾶσα ἡ Ἰουδαία καὶ ἡ πᾶσα περίχωρος → τοῦ Ἰορδάνου καὶ
v.imi.3s p.a r.asm.3 n.npn cj a.nsf d.nsf n.nsf cj d.nsf a.nsf n.nsf d.gsm n.gsm cj
1744 4639 899 2642 2779 4246 3836 2677 2779 3836 4246 4369 3836 2674 2779

Confessing their sins, they were baptized by him in the Jordan River. ¶ 7 But when he saw
ἐξομολογούμενοι αὐτῶν τὰς ἁμαρτίας, → → ἐβαπτίζοντο ὑπ᾽ αὐτοῦ ἐν τῷ Ἰορδάνῃ ποταμῷ δὲ → → ἰδὼν
pt.pm.npm r.gpm.3 d.apf n.apf v.ipi.3p p.g r.gsm.3 p.d d.dsm n.dsm n.dsm cj pt.aa.nsm
2018 899 3836 281 5679 1877 899 1877 3836 2674 4532 1254 1625

many of the Pharisees and Sadducees coming to where he was baptizing, he said to them: "You brood
πολλοὺς τῶν Φαρισαίων καὶ Σαδδουκαίων ἐρχομένους ἐπὶ ← αὐτοῦ τὸ βάπτισμα, → εἶπεν → αὐτοῖς → γεννήματα
a.apm d.gpm n.gpm cj n.gpm pt.pm.apm p.a r.gsm.3 d.asn n.asn v.aai.3s r.dpm.3 n.vpn
4498 3836 5757 2779 4881 2262 2093 899 3836 967 3306 899 1165

of vipers! Who warned you to flee from the coming wrath? 8 Produce fruit in keeping with repentance.
→ ἐχιδνῶν τίς ὑπέδειξεν ὑμῖν φυγεῖν ἀπὸ τῆς μελλούσης ὀργῆς οὖν ποιήσατε καρπὸν → ἄξιον ← τῆς μετανοίας,
n.gpf r.nsm v.aai.3s r.dp.2 f.aa p.g d.gsf pt.pa.gsf n.gsf cj v.aam.2p n.asm a.asm d.gsf n.gsf
2399 5515 5683 7007 5771 608 3836 3516 3973 4036 4472 2843 545 3836 3567

9 And do not think you can say to yourselves, 'We have Abraham as our father.' I tell you that out of
καὶ → μὴ δόξητε → → λέγειν ἐν ἑαυτοῖς → ἔχομεν τὸν Ἀβραάμ, πατέρα γὰρ → λέγω ὑμῖν ὅτι ἐκ ←
cj pl v.aas.2p f.pa p.d r.dpm.2 v.pai.1p d.asm n.asm n.asm cj v.pai.1s r.dp.2 cj p.g
2779 1506 3590 1506 3306 1877 1571 2400 3836 11 4252 1142 3306 7007 4022 1666

these stones God can raise up children for Abraham. 10 The ax is already at the root of the
τούτων τῶν λίθων, ὁ θεὸς, δύναται ἐγεῖραι ← τέκνα → τῷ Ἀβραάμ, δὲ ἡ ἀξίνη κεῖται ἤδη πρὸς τὴν ῥίζαν → τῶν
r.gpm d.gpm n.gpm d.nsm n.nsm v.pmi.3s f.aa n.apn d.dsm n.dsm cj d.nsf n.nsf v.pmi.3s adv p.a d.asf n.asf d.gpn
4047 3836 3345 3836 2536 1538 1586 5451 3836 11 1254 3836 544 3023 2453 4639 3836 4844 3836

trees, and every tree that does not produce good fruit will be cut down and thrown into the fire. ¶
δένδρων οὖν πᾶν δένδρον → μὴ ποιοῦν καλὸν καρπὸν → → ἐκκόπτεται καὶ βάλλεται εἰς πῦρ
n.gpn cj a.nsn n.nsn pl pt.pa.nsn a.asm n.asm v.ppi.3s cj v.ppi.3s p.a n.asn
1285 4036 4246 1285 4472 3590 4472 2819 2843 1716 2779 965 1650 4786

11 "I baptize you with water for repentance. But after me will come one who is more powerful than
μὲν Ἐγὼ βαπτίζω ὑμᾶς ἐν ὕδατι εἰς μετάνοιαν δὲ ὀπίσω μου ὁ → ἐρχόμενος → ἐστιν ἰσχυρότερος →
pl r.ns.1 v.pai.1s r.ap.2 p.d n.dsn p.a n.asf cj p.g r.gs.1 d.nsm pt.pm.nsm v.pai.3s a.nsm.c
3525 1609 966 7007 1877 5623 1650 3567 1254 3958 1609 3836 2262 1639 2708

I, whose sandals I am not fit to carry. He will baptize you with the Holy Spirit and with fire.
μού οὗ τὰ ὑποδήματα → εἰμὶ οὐκ ἱκανὸς → βαστάσαι αὐτὸς → βαπτίσει ὑμᾶς ἐν ἁγίῳ πνεύματι καὶ → πυρί
r.gs.1 r.gsm d.apn n.apn v.pai.1s adv a.nsm f.aa r.nsm v.fai.3s r.ap.2 p.d a.dsn n.dsn cj n.dsn
1609 4005 3836 5687 1639 4024 2653 1002 899 966 7007 1877 41 4460 2779 4786

12 His winnowing fork is in his hand, and he will clear his threshing floor, gathering his
οὗ → τὸ πτύον, ἐν αὐτοῦ τῇ χειρί, καὶ → → διακαθαριεῖ αὐτοῦ → τὴν ἅλωνα, καὶ συνάξει αὐτοῦ
r.gsm d.nsn n.nsn p.d r.gsm.3 d.dsf n.dsf cj v.fai.3s r.gsm.3 d.asf n.asf cj v.fai.3s r.gsm.3
4005 3836 4768 1877 899 3836 5931 2779 1351 899 3836 272 2779 5251 899

wheat into the barn and burning up the chaff with unquenchable fire."
τὸν σῖτον, εἰς τὴν ἀποθήκην δὲ κατακαύσει ← τὸ ἄχυρον → ἀσβέστῳ πυρί
d.asm n.asm p.a d.asf n.asf cj v.fai.3s d.asn n.asn a.dsn n.dsn
3836 4992 1650 3836 630 1254 2876 3836 949 812 4786

βοῶντος ἐν τῇ ἐρήμῳ· Ἑτοιμάσατε τὴν ὁδὸν κυρίου, εὐθείας ποιεῖτε τὰς τρίβους αὐτοῦ. ¶ 4 Αὐτὸς δὲ ὁ Ἰωάννης εἶχεν τὸ ἔνδυμα αὐτοῦ ἀπὸ τριχῶν καμήλου καὶ ζώνην δερματίνην περὶ τὴν ὀσφὺν αὐτοῦ, ἡ δὲ τροφὴ ἦν αὐτοῦ ἀκρίδες καὶ μέλι ἄγριον. ¶ 5 τότε ἐξεπορεύετο πρὸς αὐτὸν Ἰεροσόλυμα καὶ πᾶσα ἡ Ἰουδαία καὶ πᾶσα ἡ περίχωρος τοῦ Ἰορδάνου, 6 καὶ ἐβαπτίζοντο ἐν τῷ Ἰορδάνῃ ποταμῷ ὑπ᾽ αὐτοῦ ἐξομολογούμενοι τὰς ἁμαρτίας αὐτῶν. ¶ 7 Ἰδὼν δὲ πολλοὺς τῶν Φαρισαίων καὶ Σαδδουκαίων ἐρχομένους ἐπὶ τὸ βάπτισμα αὐτοῦ εἶπεν αὐτοῖς, Γεννήματα ἐχιδνῶν, τίς ὑπέδειξεν ὑμῖν φυγεῖν ἀπὸ τῆς μελλούσης ὀργῆς; 8 ποιήσατε οὖν καρπὸν ἄξιον τῆς μετανοίας 9 καὶ μὴ δόξητε λέγειν ἐν ἑαυτοῖς, Πατέρα ἔχομεν τὸν Ἀβραάμ. λέγω γὰρ ὑμῖν ὅτι δύναται ὁ θεὸς ἐκ τῶν λίθων τούτων ἐγεῖραι τέκνα τῷ Ἀβραάμ. 10 ἤδη δὲ ἡ ἀξίνη πρὸς τὴν ῥίζαν τῶν δένδρων κεῖται· πᾶν οὖν δένδρον μὴ ποιοῦν καρπὸν καλὸν ἐκκόπτεται καὶ εἰς πῦρ βάλλεται. ¶ 11 ἐγὼ μὲν ὑμᾶς βαπτίζω ἐν ὕδατι εἰς μετάνοιαν, ὁ δὲ ὀπίσω μου ἐρχόμενος ἰσχυρότερός μού ἐστιν, οὗ οὐκ εἰμὶ ἱκανὸς τὰ ὑποδήματα βαστάσαι· αὐτὸς ὑμᾶς βαπτίσει ἐν πνεύματι ἁγίῳ καὶ πυρί· 12 οὗ τὸ πτύον ἐν τῇ χειρὶ αὐτοῦ καὶ διακαθαριεῖ τὴν ἅλωνα αὐτοῦ καὶ συνάξει τὸν σῖτον αὐτοῦ εἰς τὴν ἀποθήκην, τὸ δὲ ἄχυρον κατακαύσει πυρὶ ἀσβέστῳ.

The Baptism of Jesus

3:13 Then Jesus came from Galilee to the Jordan to be baptized by
Τότε ὁ Ἰησοῦς παραγίνεται ἀπὸ τῆς Γαλιλαίας ἐπὶ τὸν Ἰορδάνην πρὸς τὸν Ἰωάννην → → τοῦ βαπτισθῆναι ὑπ᾽
adv d.nsm n.nsm v.pmi.3s p.g d.gsf n.gsf p.a d.asm n.asm p.a d.asm n.asm d.gsn f.ap p.g
5538 3836 2652 4134 608 3836 1133 2093 3836 2674 4639 3836 2722 3836 966 5679

John. **14** But John tried to deter him, saying, "I need to be baptized by you, and do you come
αὐτοῦ δὲ ὁ Ἰωάννης → → διεκώλυεν αὐτὸν λέγων ἐγὼ χρείαν ἔχω → → βαπτισθῆναι ὑπὸ σοῦ καὶ ↱ σὺ ἔρχῃ
r.gsm.3 cj d.nsm n.nsm v.iai.3s r.asm.3 pt.pa.nsm r.ns.1 n.asf v.pai.1s f.ap p.g r.gs.2 cj r.ns.2 v.pmi.2s
899 1254 3836 2722 1361 899 3306 1609 5970 2400 966 5679 5148 2779 2262 5148 2262

to me?" **15** Jesus replied, "Let it be so now; it is proper for us to do this to
πρός με δὲ ὁ Ἰησοῦς ἀποκριθεὶς εἶπεν πρὸς αὐτόν ἄφες ← ← ἄρτι γὰρ οὕτως ἐστὶν πρέπον ἡμῖν → →
p.a r.as.1 cj d.nsm n.nsm pt.ap.nsm v.aai.3s p.a r.asm.3 v.aam.2s adv cj adv v.pai.3s pt.pa.nsn r.dp.1
4639 1609 1254 3836 2652 646 3306 4639 899 918 785 1142 4048 1639 4560 7005

fulfill all righteousness." Then John consented. ¶ **16** As soon as Jesus was baptized, he went up
πληρῶσαι πᾶσαν δικαιοσύνην τότε αὐτόν ἀφίησιν δὲ → εὐθὺς ← ὁ Ἰησοῦς → βαπτισθεὶς → ἀνέβη ←
f.aa a.asf n.asf adv r.asm.3 v.pai.3s cj adv d.nsm n.nsm pt.ap.nsm v.aai.3s
4444 4246 1466 5538 899 918 1254 2318 3836 2652 966 326

out of the water. At that moment heaven was opened, and he saw the Spirit of God
ἀπὸ τοῦ ὕδατος καὶ → → ἰδοὺ οἱ οὐρανοί → ἠνεῴχθησαν [αὐτῷ] καὶ → εἶδεν τὸ πνεῦμα τοῦ θεοῦ
p.g d.gsn n.gsn cj j d.npm n.npm v.api.3p r.dsm.3 cj v.aai.3s d.asn n.asn d.gsm n.gsm
608 3836 5623 2779 2627 3836 4041 487 899 2779 1625 3836 4460 3836 2536

descending like a dove and lighting on him. **17** And a voice from heaven said, "This is my Son,
καταβαῖνον ὡσεὶ περιστερὰν καὶ ἐρχόμενον ἐπ᾽ αὐτόν καὶ ἰδοὺ φωνὴ ἐκ τῶν οὐρανῶν λέγουσα οὗτος ἐστιν μου ὁ υἱός
pt.pa.asn pl n.asf cj pt.pm.asn p.a r.asm.3 cj j n.nsf p.g d.gpm n.gpm pt.pa.nsf r.nsm v.pai.3s r.gs.1 d.nsm n.nsm
2849 6059 4361 2779 2262 2093 899 2779 2627 5889 1666 3836 4041 3306 4047 1639 1609 3836 5626

whom I love; with him I am well pleased."
ὁ ἀγαπητός ἐν ᾧ → → εὐδόκησα
d.nsm a.nsm p.d r.dsm v.aai.1s
3836 28 1877 4005 2305

The Temptation of Jesus

4:1 Then Jesus was led by the Spirit into the desert to be tempted by the devil. **2** After
Τότε ὁ Ἰησοῦς → ἀνήχθη ὑπὸ τοῦ πνεύματος εἰς τὴν ἔρημον → → πειρασθῆναι ὑπὸ τοῦ διαβόλου καὶ →
adv d.nsm n.nsm v.api.3s p.g d.gsn n.gsn p.a d.asf n.asf f.ap p.g d.gsm n.gsm cj
5538 3836 2652 343 5679 3836 4460 1650 3836 2245 4279 5679 3836 1333 2779

fasting forty days and forty nights, he was hungry. **3** The tempter came to him and
νηστεύσας τεσσεράκοντα ἡμέρας καὶ τεσσεράκοντα νύκτας ὕστερον → ἐπείνασεν καὶ ὁ πειράζων προσελθὼν ← αὐτῷ
pt.aa.nsm a.apf n.apf cj a.apf n.apf adv.c v.aai.3s cj d.nsm pt.pa.nsm pt.aa.nsm r.dsm.3
3764 5477 2465 2779 5477 3816 5731 4277 2779 3836 4279 4665 899

said, "If you are the Son of God, tell these stones to become bread." **4** Jesus answered, "It is
εἶπεν εἰ → εἶ υἱός τοῦ θεοῦ εἰπὲ ἵνα οὗτοι οἱ λίθοι → γένωνται ἄρτοι δὲ ὁ ἀποκριθεὶς εἶπεν → →
v.aai.3s cj v.pai.2s n.nsm d.gsm n.gsm v.aam.2s cj r.npm d.npm n.npm v.ams.3p n.npm cj d.nsm pt.ap.nsm v.aai.3s
3306 1623 1639 5626 3836 2536 3306 2671 4047 3836 3345 1181 788 1254 3836 646 3306

written: 'Man does not live on bread alone, but on every word that comes from the mouth of
γέγραπται ὁ ἄνθρωπος ↱ οὐκ ζήσεται ἐπ᾽ ἄρτῳ μόνῳ ἀλλ᾽ ἐπὶ παντὶ ῥήματι → ἐκπορευομένῳ διὰ στόματος →
v.rpi.3s d.nsm n.nsm adv v.fmi.3s p.d n.dsm a.dsm cj p.d a.dsn n.dsn pt.pm.dsn p.g n.gsn
1211 3836 476 2409 4024 2409 2093 788 3668 247 2093 4246 4839 1744 1328 5125

God.'" ¶ **5** Then the devil took him to the holy city and had him stand on the highest point
θεοῦ Τότε ὁ διάβολος παραλαμβάνει αὐτὸν εἰς τὴν ἁγίαν πόλιν καὶ → αὐτὸν ἔστησεν ἐπὶ τὸ πτερύγιον ←
n.gsm adv d.nsm n.nsm v.pai.3s r.asm.3 p.a d.asf a.asf n.asf cj r.asm.3 v.aai.3s p.a d.asn n.asn
2536 5538 3836 1333 4161 899 1650 3836 41 4484 2779 2705 899 2705 2093 3836 4762

of the temple. **6** "If you are the Son of God," he said, "throw yourself down. For it is written: "'He
→ τοῦ ἱεροῦ καὶ εἰ → εἶ υἱός τοῦ θεοῦ λέγει αὐτῷ βάλε σεαυτὸν κάτω γὰρ → → γέγραπται ὅτι
d.gsn n.gsn cj cj v.pai.2s n.nsm d.gsm n.gsm v.pai.3s r.dsm.3 v.aam.2s r.asm.2 adv cj v.rpi.3s cj
3836 2639 2779 1623 1639 5626 3836 2536 3306 899 965 4932 3004 1142 1211 4022

---

³¹³ Τότε παραγίνεται ὁ Ἰησοῦς ἀπὸ τῆς Γαλιλαίας ἐπὶ τὸν Ἰορδάνην πρὸς τὸν Ἰωάννην τοῦ βαπτισθῆναι ὑπ᾽ αὐτοῦ. ¹⁴ ὁ
δὲ Ἰωάννης διεκώλυεν αὐτὸν λέγων, Ἐγὼ χρείαν ἔχω ὑπὸ σοῦ βαπτισθῆναι, καὶ σὺ ἔρχῃ πρός με; ¹⁵ ἀποκριθεὶς δὲ ὁ Ἰησοῦς
εἶπεν πρὸς αὐτόν, Ἄφες ἄρτι, οὕτως γὰρ πρέπον ἐστὶν ἡμῖν πληρῶσαι πᾶσαν δικαιοσύνην. τότε ἀφίησιν αὐτόν. ¶ ¹⁶ βαπτισθεὶς
δὲ ὁ Ἰησοῦς εὐθὺς ἀνέβη ἀπὸ τοῦ ὕδατος· καὶ ἰδοὺ ἠνεῴχθησαν [αὐτῷ] οἱ οὐρανοί, καὶ εἶδεν [τὸ] πνεῦμα [τοῦ] θεοῦ καταβαῖνον
ὡσεὶ περιστερὰν [καὶ] ἐρχόμενον ἐπ᾽ αὐτόν· ¹⁷ καὶ ἰδοὺ φωνὴ ἐκ τῶν οὐρανῶν λέγουσα, Οὗτός ἐστιν ὁ υἱός μου ὁ ἀγαπητός,
ἐν ᾧ εὐδόκησα.

⁴·¹ Τότε ὁ Ἰησοῦς ἀνήχθη εἰς τὴν ἔρημον ὑπὸ τοῦ πνεύματος πειρασθῆναι ὑπὸ τοῦ διαβόλου. ² καὶ νηστεύσας ἡμέρας
τεσσεράκοντα καὶ νύκτας τεσσεράκοντα, ὕστερον ἐπείνασεν. ³ Καὶ προσελθὼν ὁ πειράζων εἶπεν αὐτῷ, Εἰ υἱὸς εἶ τοῦ θεοῦ,
εἰπὲ ἵνα οἱ λίθοι οὗτοι ἄρτοι γένωνται. ⁴ ὁ δὲ ἀποκριθεὶς εἶπεν, Γέγραπται, Οὐκ ἐπ᾽ ἄρτῳ μόνῳ ζήσεται ὁ ἄνθρωπος, ἀλλ᾽ ἐπὶ
παντὶ ῥήματι ἐκπορευομένῳ διὰ στόματος θεοῦ. ¶ ⁵ Τότε παραλαμβάνει αὐτὸν ὁ διάβολος εἰς τὴν ἁγίαν πόλιν καὶ ἔστησεν
αὐτὸν ἐπὶ τὸ πτερύγιον τοῦ ἱεροῦ ⁶ καὶ λέγει αὐτῷ, Εἰ υἱὸς εἶ τοῦ θεοῦ, βάλε σεαυτὸν κάτω· γέγραπται γὰρ ὅτι Τοῖς ἀγγέλοις

will command his angles | concerning you, | and they will lift | you up in their hands, so that you will
→ ἐντελεῖται αὐτοῦ ⸀τοῖς ἀγγέλοις⸀ περὶ σοῦ καὶ → ἀροῦσίν σε ← ἐπὶ χειρῶν, → → →
v.fmi.3s r.gsm.3 d.dpm n.dpm p.g r.gs.2 cj v.fai.3p r.as.2 p.g n.gpf
1948 899 3836 34 4309 5148 2779 149 5148 149 2093 5931 3607 3607 4684 4684

not strike your foot | against a stone."' ⁷ Jesus | answered him, "It is | also | written: 'Do not put the
μήποτε προσκόψῃς σου ⸀τὸν πόδα⸀ πρὸς λίθον ὁ Ἰησοῦς⸀ ἔφη αὐτῷ → → πάλιν γέγραπται → οὐκ →
cj v.aas.2s r.gs.2 d.asm n.asm p.a n.asm d.nsm n.nsm v.iai.3s r.dsm.3 adv v.rpi.3s adv
3607 4684 5148 3836 4546 4639 3345 3836 2652 5774 899 1211 1211 4099 1211 1733 4024 1733

Lord your God | to the test."' ¶ ⁸ Again, the devil | took | him to a very high mountain and
κύριον σου ⸀τὸν θεόν⸀ → → ἐκπειράσεις Πάλιν ὁ διάβολος παραλαμβάνει αὐτὸν εἰς λίαν ὑψηλὸν ὄρος καὶ
n.asm r.gs.2 d.asm n.asm v.fai.2s adv d.nsm n.nsm v.pai.3s r.asm.3 p.a adv a.asn n.asn cj
3261 5148 3836 2536 1733 4099 3836 1333 4161 899 1650 3336 5734 4001 2779

showed him all the kingdoms of the world and their splendor. ⁹ "All this I will give you," he said, "if
δείκνυσιν αὐτῷ πάσας τὰς βασιλείας → τοῦ κόσμου καὶ αὐτῶν ⸀τὴν δόξαν⸀ καὶ πάντα ταῦτα → → δώσω σοι → εἶπεν αὐτῷ ἐὰν
v.pai.3s r.dsm.3 a.apf d.apf n.apf d.gsm n.gsm cj r.gpf3 d.asf n.asf cj a.apn r.apn v.fai.1s r.ds.2 v.aai.3s r.dsm.3 cj
1259 899 4246 3836 993 3836 3180 2779 1518 3836 1518 2779 4246 4047 1443 5148 3306 899 1569

you will bow down and worship me." ¹⁰ Jesus said to him, "Away from me, Satan! For it is written:
→ → πεσὼν ← προσκυνήσῃς μοι τότε ὁ Ἰησοῦς⸀ λέγει αὐτῷ ὕπαγε ← ← σατανᾶ γάρ → → γέγραπται
pt.aa.nsm v.aas.2s r.ds.1 adv d.nsm n.nsm v.pai.3s r.dsm.3 v.pam.2s n.vsm cj v.rpi.3s
4406 4686 1609 5538 3836 2652 3306 899 5632 4928 1142 1211

'Worship the Lord your God, and serve him only.'" ¶ ¹¹ Then the devil left him, and
προσκυνήσεις κύριον σου ⸀τὸν θεόν⸀ καὶ λατρεύσεις αὐτῷ μόνῳ Τότε ὁ διάβολος ἀφίησιν αὐτὸν καὶ ἰδοὺ
v.fai.2s n.asm r.gs.2 d.asm n.asm cj v.fai.2s r.dsm.3 a.dsm adv d.nsm n.nsm v.pai.3s r.asm.3 cj j
4686 3261 5148 3836 2536 2779 3302 899 3668 5538 3836 1333 918 899 2779 2627

angels came and attended him.
ἄγγελοι προσῆλθον καὶ διηκόνουν αὐτῷ
n.npm v.aai.3p cj v.iai.3p r.dsm.3
34 4665 2779 1354 899

Jesus Begins to Preach

4:12 When Jesus heard that John had been put in prison, he returned to Galilee. ¹³ Leaving
δὲ → Ἀκούσας ὅτι Ἰωάννης → → παρεδόθη → ἀνεχώρησεν εἰς ⸀τὴν Γαλιλαίαν⸀ καὶ καταλιπὼν
cj pt.aa.nsm cj n.nsm v.api.3s v.aai.3s p.a d.asf n.asf cj pt.aa.nsm
1254 201 4022 2722 4140 432 1650 3836 1133 2779 2901

Nazareth, he went and lived in Capernaum, which was by the lake in the area of Zebulun and
⸀τὴν Ναζαρὰ⸀ → ἐλθὼν κατῴκησεν εἰς Καφαρναοὺμ → τὴν παραθαλασσίαν ἐν ὁρίοις → Ζαβουλὼν καὶ
d.asf n.asf pt.aa.nsm v.aai.3s p.a n.asf d.asf a.asf p.d n.dpn n.gsm cj
3836 3836 2262 2997 1650 3019 3836 4144 1877 3990 2404 2779

Naphtali – ¹⁴ to fulfill what was said through the prophet Isaiah: ¹⁵ "Land of Zebulun and land of Naphtali,
Νεφθαλίμ ἵνα πληρωθῇ τὸ → ῥηθὲν διὰ τοῦ προφήτου Ἠσαΐου λέγοντος γῆ → Ζαβουλὼν καὶ γῆ → Νεφθαλίμ
n.gsm cj v.aps.3s d.nsn pt.ap.nsn p.g d.gsm n.gsm n.gsm pt.pa.gsm n.nsf n.nsf cj n.nsf n.gsm
3750 2671 4444 3836 3306 1328 3836 4737 2480 3306 1178 2404 2779 1178 3750

the way to the sea, along the Jordan, Galilee of the Gentiles – ¹⁶ the people living in darkness have
ὁδὸν → θαλάσσης πέραν τοῦ Ἰορδάνου Γαλιλαία → τῶν ἐθνῶν ὁ λαὸς ὁ καθήμενος⸀ ἐν σκότει →
n.asf n.gsf p.g d.gsm n.gsm n.nsf d.gpn n.gpn d.nsm n.nsm d.nsm pt.pm.nsm p.d n.dsn
3847 2498 4305 3836 2674 1133 3836 1620 3836 3295 3836 2764 1877 5030

seen a great light; on those living in the land of the shadow of death a light has dawned." ¶
εἶδεν μέγα φῶς καὶ → τοῖς καθημένοις ἐν χώρᾳ καὶ → σκιᾷ → θανάτου φῶς → ἀνέτειλεν αὐτοῖς
v.aai.3s a.asn n.asn cj d.dpm pt.pm.dpm p.d n.dsf cj n.dsf n.gsm n.nsn v.aai.3s r.dpm.3
1625 3489 5890 2779 3836 2764 1877 6001 2779 5014 2505 5890 422 899

¹⁷ From that time on Jesus began to preach, "Repent, for the kingdom of heaven is near."
Ἀπὸ → τότε ← ὁ Ἰησοῦς⸀ ἤρξατο → κηρύσσειν καὶ λέγειν μετανοεῖτε γάρ ἡ βασιλεία → ⸀τῶν οὐρανῶν⸀ → ἤγγικεν
p.g adv d.nsm n.nsm v.ami.3s f.pa cj f.pa v.pam.2p cj d.nsf n.nsf d.gpm n.gpm v.rai.3s
608 5538 3836 2652 806 3062 2779 3306 3566 1142 3836 993 3836 4041 1581

The Calling of the First Disciples

4:18 As Jesus was walking beside the Sea of Galilee, he saw two brothers, Simon called
δὲ → → Περιπατῶν παρὰ τὴν θάλασσαν → ⸀τῆς Γαλιλαίας⸀ → εἶδεν δύο ἀδελφούς Σίμωνα ⸀τὸν λεγόμενον⸀
cj pt.pa.nsm p.a d.asf n.asf d.gsf n.gsf v.aai.3s a.apm n.apm n.asm d.asm pt.pp.asm
1254 4344 4123 3836 2498 3836 1133 1625 1545 81 4981 3836 3306

αὐτοῦ ἐντελεῖται περὶ σοῦ καὶ ἐπὶ χειρῶν ἀροῦσίν σε, μήποτε προσκόψῃς πρὸς λίθον τὸν πόδα σου. ⁷ ἔφη αὐτῷ ὁ Ἰησοῦς, Πάλιν γέγραπται, Οὐκ ἐκπειράσεις κύριον τὸν θεόν σου. ¶ ⁸ Πάλιν παραλαμβάνει αὐτὸν ὁ διάβολος εἰς ὄρος ὑψηλὸν λίαν καὶ δείκνυσιν αὐτῷ πάσας τὰς βασιλείας τοῦ κόσμου καὶ τὴν δόξαν αὐτῶν ⁹ καὶ εἶπεν αὐτῷ, Ταῦτά σοι πάντα δώσω, ἐὰν πεσὼν προσκυνήσῃς μοι. ¹⁰ τότε λέγει αὐτῷ ὁ Ἰησοῦς, Ὕπαγε, ὀπίσω μου Σατανᾶ· γέγραπται γάρ, Κύριον τὸν θεόν σου προσκυνήσεις καὶ αὐτῷ μόνῳ λατρεύσεις. ¶ ¹¹ Τότε ἀφίησιν αὐτὸν ὁ διάβολος, καὶ ἰδοὺ ἄγγελοι προσῆλθον καὶ διηκόνουν αὐτῷ.

⁴:¹² Ἀκούσας δὲ ὅτι Ἰωάννης παρεδόθη ἀνεχώρησεν εἰς τὴν Γαλιλαίαν. ¹³ καὶ καταλιπὼν τὴν Ναζαρὰ ἐλθὼν κατῴκησεν εἰς Καφαρναοὺμ τὴν παραθαλασσίαν ἐν ὁρίοις Ζαβουλὼν καὶ Νεφθαλίμ· ¹⁴ ἵνα πληρωθῇ τὸ ῥηθὲν διὰ Ἠσαΐου τοῦ προφήτου λέγοντος, ¹⁵ Γῆ Ζαβουλὼν καὶ γῆ Νεφθαλίμ, ὁδὸν θαλάσσης, πέραν τοῦ Ἰορδάνου, Γαλιλαία τῶν ἐθνῶν, ¹⁶ ὁ λαὸς ὁ καθήμενος ἐν σκότει φῶς εἶδεν μέγα, καὶ τοῖς καθημένοις ἐν χώρᾳ καὶ σκιᾷ θανάτου φῶς ἀνέτειλεν αὐτοῖς. ¶ ¹⁷ Ἀπὸ τότε ἤρξατο ὁ Ἰησοῦς κηρύσσειν καὶ λέγειν, Μετανοεῖτε· ἤγγικεν γὰρ ἡ βασιλεία τῶν οὐρανῶν.

⁴:¹⁸ Περιπατῶν δὲ παρὰ τὴν θάλασσαν τῆς Γαλιλαίας εἶδεν δύο ἀδελφούς, Σίμωνα τὸν λεγόμενον Πέτρον καὶ Ἀνδρέαν τὸν

Peter	and	his	brother	Andrew.	They	were	casting	a net		into the	lake,	for	they	were	fishermen.
Πέτρον	καὶ	αὐτοῦ	τὸν ἀδελφὸν	Ἀνδρέαν	→	→	βάλλοντας	ἀμφίβληστρον	εἰς	τὴν	θάλασσαν	γὰρ	→	ἦσαν	ἁλιεῖς
n.asm	cj	r.gsm.3	d.asm n.asm	n.asm			pt.pa.apm	n.asn	p.a	d.asf	n.asf	cj		v.iai.3p	n.npm
4377	2779	899	3836 81	436			965	312	1650	3836	2498	1142		1639	243

19 "Come, follow me," Jesus said, "and I will make you fishers of men." **20** At once they left their

καὶ	δεῦτε	ὀπίσω	μου	λέγει	αὐτοῖς	καὶ	→	→	ποιήσω	ὑμᾶς	ἁλιεῖς	→	ἀνθρώπων	δὲ	→	εὐθέως	οἱ	ἀφέντες	τὰ
cj	adv	p.g	r.gs.1	v.pai.3s	r.dpm.3	cj			v.fai.1s	r.ap.2	n.apm		n.gpm	cj		adv	d.npm	pt.aa.npm	d.apn
2779	1307	3958	1609	3306	899	2779			4472	7007	243		476	1254		2311	3836	918	3836

nets and followed him. ¶ **21** Going on from there, he saw two other brothers, James son of

δίκτυα	ἠκολούθησαν	αὐτῷ		καὶ	προβὰς	←	→	ἐκεῖθεν	→	εἶδεν	δύο	ἄλλους	ἀδελφούς	Ἰάκωβον	τὸν
n.apn	v.aai.3p	r.dsm.3		cj	pt.aa.nsm			adv		v.aai.3s	a.apm	a.apm	n.apm	n.asm	d.asm
1473	199	899		2779	4581			1696		1625	1545	257	81	2610	3836

Zebedee and his brother John. They were in a boat with their father Zebedee, preparing

τοῦ Ζεβεδαίου	καὶ	αὐτοῦ	τὸν ἀδελφὸν	Ἰωάννην		ἐν	τῷ πλοίῳ	μετὰ	αὐτῶν	τοῦ πατρὸς	Ζεβεδαίου	καταρτίζοντας
d.gsm n.gsm	cj	r.gsm.3	d.asm n.asm	n.asm		p.d	d.dsn n.dsn	p.g	r.gpm.3	d.gsm n.gsm	n.gsm	pt.pa.apm
3836 2411	2779	899	3836 81	2722		1877	3836 4450	3552	899	3836 4252	2411	2936

their nets. Jesus called them, **22** and immediately they left the boat and their father and followed

αὐτῶν	τὰ δίκτυα	καὶ	ἐκάλεσεν	αὐτούς	δὲ	εὐθέως	οἱ	ἀφέντες	τὸ	πλοῖον	καὶ	αὐτῶν	τὸν πατέρα	ἠκολούθησαν
r.gpm.3	d.apn n.apn	cj	v.aai.3s	r.apm.3	cj	adv	d.npm	pt.aa.npm	d.asn	n.asn	cj	r.gpm.3	d.asm n.asm	v.aai.3p
899	3836 1473	2779	2813	899	1254	2311	3836	918	3836	4450	2779	899	3836 4252	199

him.

αὐτῷ
r.dsm.3
899

Jesus Heals the Sick

4:23 Jesus went throughout Galilee, teaching in their synagogues, preaching the good

Καὶ		περιῆγεν	ἐν ὅλῃ	τῇ Γαλιλαίᾳ	διδάσκων	ἐν	αὐτῶν	ταῖς συναγωγαῖς	καὶ	κηρύσσων	τὸ	→
cj		v.iai.3s	p.d a.dsf	d.dsf n.dsf	pt.pa.nsm	p.d	r.gpm.3	d.dpf n.dpf	cj	pt.pa.nsm	d.asn	
2779		4310	1877 3910	3836 1133	1438	1877	899	3836 5252	2779	3062	3836	

news of the kingdom, and healing every disease and sickness among the people. **24** News about

εὐαγγέλιον	→	τῆς	βασιλείας	καὶ	θεραπεύων	πᾶσαν	νόσον	καὶ	πᾶσαν	μαλακίαν	ἐν	τῷ	λαῷ	Καὶ	ἡ	ἀκοὴ	→
n.asn		d.gsf	n.gsf	cj	pt.pa.nsm	a.asf	n.asf	cj	a.asf	n.asf	p.d	d.dsm	n.dsm	cj	d.nsf	n.nsf	
2295		3836	993	2779	2543	4246	3798	2779	4246	3433	1877	3836	3295	2779	3836	198	

him spread all over Syria, and people brought to him all who were ill with various diseases,

αὐτοῦ	ἀπῆλθεν	εἰς	→	ὅλην	τὴν Συρίαν	καὶ	→	προσήνεγκαν	αὐτῷ	πάντας	τοὺς	ἔχοντας	κακῶς	→	ποικίλαις	νόσοις
r.gsm.3	v.aai.3s	p.a		a.asf	d.asf n.asf	cj		v.aai.3p	r.dsm.3	a.apm	d.apm	pt.pa.apm	adv		a.dpf	n.dpf
899	618	1650		3910	3836 5353	2779		4712	899	4246	2400	2400	2809		4476	3798

those suffering severe pain, the demon-possessed, those having seizures, and the

καὶ	→	συνεχομένους	→	βασάνοις	[καὶ]	δαιμονιζομένους	καὶ	→	σεληνιαζομένους	καὶ
cj		pt.pp.apm		n.dpf	cj	pt.pp.apm	cj		pt.pp.apm	cj
2779		5309		992	2779	1227	2779		4944	2779

paralyzed, and he healed them. **25** Large crowds from Galilee, the Decapolis, Jerusalem,

παραλυτικούς	καὶ	→	ἐθεράπευσεν	αὐτούς	καὶ	πολλοὶ	ὄχλοι	ἀπὸ	τῆς Γαλιλαίας	καὶ	Δεκαπόλεως	καὶ	Ἰεροσολύμων	καὶ
a.apm	cj		v.aai.3s	r.apm.3	cj	a.npm	n.npm	p.g	d.gsf n.gsf	cj	n.gsf	cj	n.gpn	cj
4166	2779		2543	899	2779	4498	4063	608	3836 1133	2779	1279	2779	2642	2779

Judea and the region across the Jordan followed him.

Ἰουδαίας	καὶ		πέραν	τοῦ	Ἰορδάνου	ἠκολούθησαν	αὐτῷ
n.gsf	cj		p.g	d.gsm	n.gsm	v.aai.3p	r.dsm.3
2677	2779		4305	3836	2674	199	899

The Beatitudes

5:1 Now when he saw the crowds, he went up on a mountainside and sat down. His disciples

δὲ	when	→	ἰδὼν	τοὺς ὄχλους	he	ἀνέβη	←	εἰς	τὸ ὄρος	καὶ	αὐτοῦ	καθίσαντος	←	αὐτοῦ	οἱ	μαθηταὶ
cj			pt.aa.nsm	d.apm n.apm		v.aai.3s		p.a	d.asn n.asn	cj	r.gsm.3	pt.aa.gsm		r.gsm.3	d.npm	n.npm
1254			1625	3836 4063		326		1650	3836 4001	2779	899	2767		899	3836	3412

ἀδελφὸν αὐτοῦ, βάλλοντας ἀμφίβληστρον εἰς τὴν θάλασσαν· ἦσαν γὰρ ἁλιεῖς. **19** καὶ λέγει αὐτοῖς, Δεῦτε ὀπίσω μου, καὶ ποιήσω ὑμᾶς ἁλιεῖς ἀνθρώπων. **20** οἱ δὲ εὐθέως ἀφέντες τὰ δίκτυα ἠκολούθησαν αὐτῷ. ¶ **21** Καὶ προβὰς ἐκεῖθεν εἶδεν ἄλλους δύο ἀδελφούς, Ἰάκωβον τὸν τοῦ Ζεβεδαίου καὶ Ἰωάννην τὸν ἀδελφὸν αὐτοῦ, ἐν τῷ πλοίῳ μετὰ Ζεβεδαίου τοῦ πατρὸς αὐτῶν καταρτίζοντας τὰ δίκτυα αὐτῶν, καὶ ἐκάλεσεν αὐτούς. **22** οἱ δὲ εὐθέως ἀφέντες τὸ πλοῖον καὶ τὸν πατέρα αὐτῶν ἠκολούθησαν αὐτῷ.

4:23 Καὶ περιῆγεν ἐν ὅλῃ τῇ Γαλιλαίᾳ διδάσκων ἐν ταῖς συναγωγαῖς αὐτῶν καὶ κηρύσσων τὸ εὐαγγέλιον τῆς βασιλείας καὶ θεραπεύων πᾶσαν νόσον καὶ πᾶσαν μαλακίαν ἐν τῷ λαῷ. **24** καὶ ἀπῆλθεν ἡ ἀκοὴ αὐτοῦ εἰς ὅλην τὴν Συρίαν· καὶ προσήνεγκαν αὐτῷ πάντας τοὺς κακῶς ἔχοντας ποικίλαις νόσοις καὶ βασάνοις συνεχομένους [καὶ] δαιμονιζομένους καὶ σεληνιαζομένους καὶ παραλυτικούς, καὶ ἐθεράπευσεν αὐτούς. **25** καὶ ἠκολούθησαν αὐτῷ ὄχλοι πολλοὶ ἀπὸ τῆς Γαλιλαίας καὶ Δεκαπόλεως καὶ Ἰεροσολύμων καὶ Ἰουδαίας καὶ πέραν τοῦ Ἰορδάνου.

5:1 Ἰδὼν δὲ τοὺς ὄχλους ἀνέβη εἰς τὸ ὄρος, καὶ καθίσαντος αὐτοῦ προσῆλθαν αὐτῷ οἱ μαθηταὶ αὐτοῦ· **2** καὶ ἀνοίξας τὸ

came | to him, | **2** and | | | | | he began to teach | | them, saying: | **3** "Blessed | are | the | poor | in
προσῆλθαν ← | αὐτῷ | καὶ | ἀνοίξας | τὸ | στόμα | αὐτοῦ | | ἐδίδασκεν | αὐτοὺς | λέγων | Μακάριοι | οἱ | πτωχοὶ →
v.aai.3p | r.dsm.3 | cj | pt.aa.nsm | d.asn | n.asn | r.gsm.3 | | v.iai.3s | r.apm.3 | pt.pa.nsm | a.npm | | d.npm | a.npm
4665 | 899 | 2779 | 487 | 3836 | 5125 | 899 | | 1438 | 899 | 3306 | 3421 | | 3836 | 4777

spirit, | | for theirs is | | the | kingdom | of heaven. | | **4** Blessed | are those who | | mourn, | for | they | will be
⸂τῷ πνεύματι⸃ | ὅτι | αὐτῶν ἐστιν | ἡ | | βασιλεία → | ⸂τῶν οὐρανῶν⸃ | μακάριοι | οἱ | ← | πενθοῦντες | ὅτι | αὐτοὶ → | will be
d.dsn n.dsn | cj | r.gpm.3 v.pai.3s | d.nsf | | n.nsf | d.gpm n.gpm | a.npm | d.npm | | pt.pa.npm | cj | r.npm |
3836 4460 | 4022 | 899 1639 | 3836 | | 993 | 3836 4041 | 3421 | 3836 | | 4291 | 4022 | 899 |

comforted. | **5** Blessed | are | the | meek, | for | they | will inherit | | the | earth. | **6** Blessed | are those who | | hunger | and
παρακληθήσονται | μακάριοι | | οἱ | πραεῖς | ὅτι | αὐτοὶ → | κληρονομήσουσιν | | τὴν | γῆν | μακάριοι | οἱ | ← | πεινῶντες | καὶ
v.fpi.3p | a.npm | | d.npm | a.npm | cj | r.npm | v.fai.3p | | d.asf | n.asf | a.npm | d.npm | | pt.pa.npm | cj
4151 | 3421 | | 3836 | 4558 | 4022 | 899 | 3099 | | 3836 | 1178 | 3421 | 3836 | | 4277 | 2779

thirst | for righteousness, | | for | they | | will be filled. | **7** Blessed | are | the | merciful, | for | they | | will be | shown
διψῶντες → | ⸂τὴν δικαιοσύνην⸃ | | ὅτι | αὐτοὶ → | → | χορτασθήσονται | μακάριοι | | οἱ | ἐλεήμονες | ὅτι | αὐτοὶ → | → |
pt.pa.npm | d.asf n.asf | | cj | r.npm | | v.fpi.3p | a.npm | | d.npm | a.npm | cj | r.npm | |
1498 | 3836 1466 | | 4022 | 899 | | 5963 | 3421 | | 3836 | 1798 | 4022 | 899 | |

mercy. | **8** Blessed | are | the | pure | in heart, | | for | they | | will see | God. | **9** Blessed | are | the | peacemakers, | for
ἐλεηθήσονται | μακάριοι | | οἱ | καθαροὶ → | ⸂τῇ καρδίᾳ⸃ | | ὅτι | αὐτοὶ → | → | ὄψονται | ⸂τὸν θεὸν⸃ | μακάριοι | | οἱ | εἰρηνοποιοί | ὅτι
v.fpi.3p | a.npm | | d.npm | a.npm | d.dsf n.dsf | | cj | r.npm | | v.fmi.3p | d.asm n.asm | a.npm | | d.npm | n.npm | cj
1796 | 3421 | | 3836 | 2754 | 3836 2840 | | 4022 | 899 | | 3972 | 3836 2536 | 3421 | | 3836 | 1648 | 4022

they | will be called | | sons | of God. | **10** Blessed | are those who | | are persecuted | because | of | righteousness, | for | theirs | is
αὐτοὶ → | → | κληθήσονται | υἱοὶ → | θεοῦ | μακάριοι | οἱ | ← | → | δεδιωγμένοι | ἕνεκεν | ← | δικαιοσύνης | ὅτι | αὐτῶν → | ἐστιν
r.npm | | v.fpi.3p | n.npm | n.gsm | a.npm | d.npm | | | pt.rp.npm | p.g | | n.gsf | cj | r.gpm.3 | v.pai.3s
899 | | 2813 | 5626 | 2536 | 3421 | 3836 | | | 1503 | 1914 | | 1466 | 4022 | 899 | 1639

the | kingdom | of heaven. | **11** "Blessed | are | you | when | people | insult | | you, | | persecute you | and | falsely | | | say
ἡ | βασιλεία → | ⸂τῶν οὐρανῶν⸃ | μακάριοί | ἐστε | ← | ὅταν | → | ὀνειδίσωσιν | ὑμᾶς | καὶ | διώξωσιν | | | καὶ | ψευδόμενοι | εἴπωσιν
d.nsf | n.nsf | d.gpm n.gpm | a.npm | v.pai.2p | | cj | | v.aas.3p | r.ap.2 | cj | v.aas.3p | | | cj | pt.pm.npm | v.aas.3p
3836 | 993 | 3836 4041 | 3421 | 1639 | | 4020 | | 3943 | 7007 | 2779 | 1503 | | | 2779 | 6017 | 3306

all | kinds of | evil | against | you | because | of me. | **12** Rejoice | and | be glad, | | because | great | is | your | reward | | in
πᾶν ← | ← | πονηρὸν | καθ᾽ | ὑμῶν | ἕνεκεν | ← | ἐμοῦ | χαίρετε | καὶ | → | ἀγαλλιᾶσθε | ὅτι | | πολὺς | ὑμῶν | ⸤ὁ | μισθὸς⸥ | ἐν
a.asn | | a.asn | p.g | r.gp.2 | p.g | | r.gs.1 | v.pam.2p | cj | | v.pmm.2p | cj | | a.nsm | r.gp.2 | d.nsm | n.nsm | p.d
4246 | | 4505 | 2848 | 7007 | 1914 | | 1609 | 5897 | 2779 | | 22 | 4022 | | 4498 | 7007 | 3836 | 3635 | 1877

heaven, | | for | in the same way | | they | persecuted | the | prophets | who | were before | you.
⸤τοῖς οὐρανοῖς⸥ | γὰρ → | → | οὕτως → | → | ἐδίωξαν | τοὺς | προφήτας | τοὺς | πρὸ | ὑμῶν
d.dpm | cj | | adv | | v.aai.3p | d.apm | n.apm | d.apm | p.g | r.gp.2
3836 | 1142 | | 4048 | | 1503 | 3836 | 4737 | 3836 | 4574 | 7007

Salt and Light

5:13 "You | are | the | salt | of the earth. | But | if | the | salt | loses | | its saltiness, | how | | can it be made salty
ὑμεῖς | ἐστε | τὸ | ἅλας → | τῆς γῆς | δὲ | ἐὰν | τὸ | ἅλας | μωρανθῇ | ← | ← | | ἐν | τίνι → | | ἁλισθήσεται
r.np.2 | v.pai.2p | d.nsn | n.nsn | d.gsf n.gsf | cj | cj | d.nsn | n.nsn | v.aps.3s | | | | p.d | r.dsn | | v.fpi.3s
7007 | 1639 | 3836 | 229 | 3836 1178 | 1254 | 1569 | 3836 | 229 | 3701 | | | | 1877 | 5515 | | 245

again? | It | is | no longer | good | for | anything, | except | to be | thrown | out | and | trampled | | by | men. | ¶
→ | → | → | ἔτι | ἰσχύει | εἰς | οὐδὲν | ⸂εἰ | μὴ⸃ | → | βληθὲν | ἔξω | καταπατεῖσθαι | ὑπὸ | ⸤τῶν ἀνθρώπων⸥ |
| | | adv | v.pai.3s | p.a | a.asn | cj | pl | | pt.ap.asn | adv | f.pp | p.g | d.gpm n.gpm |
2710 2710 4029 | 2285 | 2710 | 1650 | 4029 | 1623 | 3590 | | 965 | 2032 | 2922 | 5679 | 3836 476 |

14 "You | are | the | light | of the world. | A city | | on | a hill | cannot | | be hidden. | **15** Neither | do | people | light | a
ὑμεῖς | ἐστε | τὸ | φῶς → | τοῦ κόσμου | πόλις | κειμένη | ἐπάνω | ὄρους | ⸤οὐ | δύναται⸥ | → | κρυβῆναι | οὐδὲ | → | → | καίουσιν
r.np.2 | v.pai.2p | d.nsn | n.nsn | d.gsm n.gsm | n.nsf | pt.pm.nsf | p.g | n.gsn | adv | v.pmi.3s | | f.ap | cj | | | v.pai.3p
7007 | 1639 | 3836 | 5890 | 3836 3180 | 4484 | 3023 | 2062 | 4001 | 4024 | 1538 | | 3221 | 4028 | | | 2794

lamp | and | put | it | under | a bowl. | Instead | | they put | it on | its | stand, | and | it | gives | light | to | everyone | | in
λύχνον | καὶ | τιθέασιν | αὐτὸν | ὑπὸ | τὸν μόδιον | ἀλλ᾽ | | → | ἐπὶ | τὴν | λυχνίαν | καὶ | → | → | λάμπει → | πᾶσιν | τοῖς | ἐν
n.asm | cj | v.pai.3p | r.asm.3 | p.a | d.asm n.asm | cj | | | p.a | d.asf | n.asf | cj | | | v.pai.3s | a.dpm | d.dpm | p.d
3394 | 2779 | 5502 | 899 | 5679 | 3836 3654 | 247 | | | 2093 | 3836 | 3393 | 2779 | | | 3290 | 4246 | 3836 | 1877

the | house. | **16** In the same way, | let | your | light | | shine | before | men, | | that | they | may see | your | good
τῇ | οἰκίᾳ | οὕτως ← | → | ⸤ὑμῶν | ⸤τὸ | φῶς⸥ | λαμψάτω | ἔμπροσθεν | ⸤τῶν ἀνθρώπων⸥ | ὅπως → | → | ἴδωσιν | ὑμῶν | καλὰ
d.dsf | n.dsf | adv | | r.gp.2 | d.nsn | n.nsn | v.aam.3s | p.g | d.gpm n.gpm | cj | | v.aas.3p | r.gp.2 | a.apn
3836 | 3864 | 4048 | | 3290 7007 | 3836 | 5890 | 3290 | 1869 | 3836 476 | 3968 | | 1625 | 7007 | 2819

στόμα αὐτοῦ ἐδίδασκεν αὐτοὺς λέγων, **3** Μακάριοι οἱ πτωχοὶ τῷ πνεύματι, ὅτι αὐτῶν ἐστιν ἡ βασιλεία τῶν οὐρανῶν. **4** μακάριοι οἱ πενθοῦντες, ὅτι αὐτοὶ παρακληθήσονται. **5** μακάριοι οἱ πραεῖς, ὅτι αὐτοὶ κληρονομήσουσιν τὴν γῆν. **6** μακάριοι οἱ πεινῶντες καὶ διψῶντες τὴν δικαιοσύνην, ὅτι αὐτοὶ χορτασθήσονται. **7** μακάριοι οἱ ἐλεήμονες, ὅτι αὐτοὶ ἐλεηθήσονται. **8** μακάριοι οἱ καθαροὶ τῇ καρδίᾳ, ὅτι αὐτοὶ τὸν θεὸν ὄψονται. **9** μακάριοι οἱ εἰρηνοποιοί, ὅτι αὐτοὶ υἱοὶ θεοῦ κληθήσονται. **10** μακάριοι οἱ δεδιωγμένοι ἕνεκεν δικαιοσύνης, ὅτι αὐτῶν ἐστιν ἡ βασιλεία τῶν οὐρανῶν. **11** μακάριοί ἐστε ὅταν ὀνειδίσωσιν ὑμᾶς καὶ διώξωσιν καὶ εἴπωσιν πᾶν πονηρὸν καθ᾽ ὑμῶν [ψευδόμενοι] ἕνεκεν ἐμοῦ. **12** χαίρετε καὶ ἀγαλλιᾶσθε, ὅτι ὁ μισθὸς ὑμῶν πολὺς ἐν τοῖς οὐρανοῖς· οὕτως γὰρ ἐδίωξαν τοὺς προφήτας τοὺς πρὸ ὑμῶν.

5:13 Ὑμεῖς ἐστε τὸ ἅλας τῆς γῆς· ἐὰν δὲ τὸ ἅλας μωρανθῇ, ἐν τίνι ἁλισθήσεται; εἰς οὐδὲν ἰσχύει ἔτι εἰ μὴ βληθὲν ἔξω καταπατεῖσθαι ὑπὸ τῶν ἀνθρώπων. ¶ **14** Ὑμεῖς ἐστε τὸ φῶς τοῦ κόσμου. οὐ δύναται πόλις κρυβῆναι ἐπάνω ὄρους κειμένη· **15** οὐδὲ καίουσιν λύχνον καὶ τιθέασιν αὐτὸν ὑπὸ τὸν μόδιον ἀλλ᾽ ἐπὶ τὴν λυχνίαν, καὶ λάμπει πᾶσιν τοῖς ἐν τῇ οἰκίᾳ. **16** οὕτως

deeds	and	praise	your	Father		in	heaven.
⸂τὰ ἔργα	καὶ	δοξάσωσιν	ὑμῶν	⸃τὸν πατέρα	τὸν	ἐν	⸂τοῖς οὐρανοῖς⸃
d.apn n.apn	cj	v.aas.3p	r.gp.2	d.asm n.asm	d.asm	p.d	d.dpm n.dpm
3836 2240	2779	1519	7007	3836 4252	3836	1877	3836 4041

The Fulfillment of the Law

5:17"Do	not	think	that	I	have	come	to abolish	the	Law	or	the	Prophets;	I	have	not	come	to abolish
⸂	Μὴ	νομίσητε	ὅτι	⸂	⸂	ἦλθον	καταλῦσαι	τὸν	νόμον	ἢ	τοὺς	προφήτας·	⸂	⸂	οὐκ	ἦλθον	καταλῦσαι
	pl	v.aas.2p	cj			v.aai.1s	f.aa	d.asm	n.asm	cj	d.apm	n.apm			adv	v.aai.1s	f.aa
	3787	3590	3787	4022		2262	2907	3836	3795	2445	3836	4737		2262	2262	4024	2262	2907

them	but	to fulfill	them.	18	I	tell	you	the truth,	until		heaven		and	earth	disappear,	not	the	smallest
ἀλλὰ	⸂	πληρῶσαι			γὰρ	⸂	λέγω ὑμῖν		ἀμὴν	ἕως	ἂν		ὁ οὐρανὸς	καὶ	ἡ γῆ	παρέλθῃ	⸂	ἓν
cj		f.aa			cj		v.pai.1s	r.dp.2	pl	cj	pl		d.nsm n.nsm	cj	d.nsf n.nsf	v.aas.3s		a.nsn
247		4444			1142		3306	7007	297	2401	323		3836 4041	2779	3836 1178	4216		4024	1651

letter,		not	the least	stroke of a pen,	will	*by any means*	disappear	from	the	Law	until		everything	is
ἰῶτα	ἢ	⸂	μία	κεραία	⸂		⸂οὐ μὴ	παρέλθῃ	ἀπὸ	τοῦ	νόμου	ἕως	ἂν	πάντα	⸂
n.nsn	cj		a.nsf	n.nsf			adv pl	v.aas.3s	p.g	d.gsm	n.gsm	cj	pl	a.npn	
2740	2445	4024	1651	3037		4216	4024 3590	4216	608	3836	3795	2401	323	4246	

accomplished.	19	Anyone	who	breaks	one	of	the	least		of these	commandments	and	teaches	others		to
γένηται		οὖν	ὃς ἐάν	⸂	λύσῃ	μίαν	⸂	τῶν ἐλαχίστων	τούτων	⸂τῶν ἐντολῶν⸃	καὶ	διδάξῃ	⸂τοὺς ἀνθρώπους⸃		
v.ams.3s		cj	r.nsm pl		v.aas.3s	a.asf		d.gpf a.gpf.s	r.gpf	d.gpf n.gpf	cj	v.aas.3s	d.apm n.apm		
1181		4036	4005 1569		3395	1651		3836 1788	4047	3836 1953	2779	1438	3836 476		

do	the	same	will	be	called	least		in	the	kingdom	of heaven,		but	whoever	practices	and	teaches	these
⸂	⸂	οὕτως	⸂	⸂	κληθήσεται	ἐλάχιστος	ἐν	τῇ	βασιλείᾳ	⸂	⸂τῶν οὐρανῶν⸃	δ᾽	ὃς ἂν	ποιήσῃ	καὶ	διδάξῃ	
		adv			v.fpi.3s	a.nsm.s		p.d	d.dsf	n.dsf		d.gpm n.gpm	cj	r.nsm pl	v.aas.3s	cj	v.aas.3s	
		4048			2813	1788		1877	3836	993		3836 4041	1254	4005 323	4472	2779	1438	

commands		will	be	called	great	in	the	kingdom	of heaven.	20	For	I	tell	you	that	unless		your
οὗτος	⸂	⸂	κληθήσεται	μέγας	ἐν	τῇ	βασιλείᾳ	⸂	⸂τῶν οὐρανῶν⸃		γὰρ	⸂	Λέγω	ὑμῖν ὅτι	⸂ἐὰν μὴ	ὑμῶν	
r.nsm			v.fpi.3s	a.nsm	p.d	d.dsf	n.dsf		d.gpm n.gpm		cj		v.pai.1s	r.dp.2 cj	cj pl	r.gp.2	
4047			2813	3489	1877	3836	993		3836 4041		1142		3306	7007 4022	1569 3590	7007	

righteousness	surpasses		that of	the	Pharisees	and	the	teachers	of the law,	you	will	certainly	not		enter
⸂ἡ δικαιοσύνη⸃	⸂περισσεύσῃ	πλεῖον⸃			Φαρισαίων	καὶ	τῶν γραμματέων				⸂	⸂	⸂	⸂οὐ μὴ	εἰσέλθητε
d.nsf n.nsf	v.aas.3s	adv.c			n.gpm	cj	d.gpm n.gpm							adv pl	v.aas.2p
3836 1466	4355	4498			5757	2779	3836 1208				1656	1656		4024 3590	1656

the	kingdom	of heaven.		
εἰς	τὴν βασιλείαν	⸂	⸂τῶν οὐρανῶν⸃	
p.a	d.asf n.asf		d.gpm n.gpm	
1650	3836 993		3836 4041	

Murder

5:21"You	have	heard	that	it was	said	to	the	people	long	ago,	'Do	not	murder,	and	anyone	who	murders
⸂	⸂	Ἠκούσατε	ὅτι	⸂	ἐρρέθη	τοῖς	⸂		ἀρχαίοις	⸂		οὐ	φονεύσεις	δ᾽	⸂ὃς ἂν	⸂	φονεύσῃ
		v.aai.2p	cj		v.api.3s	d.dpm			a.dpm			adv	v.fai.2s	cj	r.nsm pl		v.aas.3s
		201	4022		3306	3836			792		5839	4024	5839	1254	4005 323		5839

will	be	subject	to judgment.'	22	But	I	tell	you	that	anyone	who	is	angry		with	his	brother		will	be
⸂	ἔσται	ἔνοχος	⸂τῇ κρίσει⸃		δὲ	ἐγὼ	λέγω	ὑμῖν ὅτι		πᾶς	ὁ	⸂	ὀργιζόμενος			αὐτοῦ	⸂τῷ ἀδελφῷ⸃	⸂	ἔσται
	v.fmi.3s	a.nsm	d.dsf n.dsf		cj	r.ns.1	v.pai.1s	r.dp.2 cj		a.nsm	d.nsm		pt.pp.nsm			r.gsm.3	d.dsm n.dsm		v.fmi.3s
	1639	1944	3836 3213		1254	1609	3306	7007 4022		4246	3836		3974			81	899 3836 81		1639

subject	to judgment.	Again,	anyone	who	says	to	his	brother,	'Raca,'	is		answerable	to	the	Sanhedrin.	But
ἔνοχος	⸂τῇ κρίσει⸃	δ᾽	ὃς ἂν	⸂	εἴπῃ	⸂	αὐτοῦ	⸂τῷ ἀδελφῷ⸃	ῥακά	ἔσται	ἔνοχος	⸂	τῷ	συνεδρίῳ		δ᾽
a.nsm	d.dsf n.dsf	cj	r.nsm pl		v.aas.3s		r.gsm.3	d.dsm n.dsm	n.vsn	v.fmi.3s	a.nsm		d.dsn n.dsn			cj
1944	3836 3213	1254	4005 323		3306		81 899	3836 81	4819	1639	1944		3836 5284			1254

anyone	who	says,	'You fool!'	will	be	in	danger	of	the	fire	of hell.	¶	23 "Therefore,	if	you	are
⸂ὃς ἂν	⸂	εἴπῃ	μωρέ	⸂	ἔσται	⸂	ἔνοχος	⸂	τοῦ	πυρός	εἰς	⸂τὴν γέενναν⸃	οὖν	ἐὰν	⸂	⸂
r.nsm pl		v.aas.3s	a.vsm		v.fmi.3s		a.nsm		d.gsn	n.gsn	p.a	d.asf n.asf	cj	cj		
4005 323		3306	3704		1639		1944		3836	4786	1650	3836 1147	4036	1569		

λαμψάτω τὸ φῶς ὑμῶν ἔμπροσθεν τῶν ἀνθρώπων, ὅπως ἴδωσιν ὑμῶν τὰ καλὰ ἔργα καὶ δοξάσωσιν τὸν πατέρα ὑμῶν τὸν ἐν τοῖς οὐρανοῖς.

5:17 Μὴ νομίσητε ὅτι ἦλθον καταλῦσαι τὸν νόμον ἢ τοὺς προφήτας· οὐκ ἦλθον καταλῦσαι ἀλλὰ πληρῶσαι. 18 ἀμὴν γὰρ λέγω ὑμῖν· ἕως ἂν παρέλθῃ ὁ οὐρανὸς καὶ ἡ γῆ, ἰῶτα ἓν ἢ μία κεραία οὐ μὴ παρέλθῃ ἀπὸ τοῦ νόμου, ἕως ἂν πάντα γένηται. 19 ὃς ἐὰν οὖν λύσῃ μίαν τῶν ἐντολῶν τούτων τῶν ἐλαχίστων καὶ διδάξῃ οὕτως τοὺς ἀνθρώπους, ἐλάχιστος κληθήσεται ἐν τῇ βασιλείᾳ τῶν οὐρανῶν· ὃς δ᾽ ἂν ποιήσῃ καὶ διδάξῃ, οὗτος μέγας κληθήσεται ἐν τῇ βασιλείᾳ τῶν οὐρανῶν. 20 λέγω γὰρ ὑμῖν ὅτι ἐὰν μὴ περισσεύσῃ ὑμῶν ἡ δικαιοσύνη πλεῖον τῶν γραμματέων καὶ Φαρισαίων, οὐ μὴ εἰσέλθητε εἰς τὴν βασιλείαν τῶν οὐρανῶν. 21 Ἠκούσατε ὅτι ἐρρέθη τοῖς ἀρχαίοις, Οὐ φονεύσεις· ὃς δ᾽ ἂν φονεύσῃ, ἔνοχος ἔσται τῇ κρίσει. 22 ἐγὼ δὲ λέγω ὑμῖν ὅτι πᾶς ὁ ὀργιζόμενος τῷ ἀδελφῷ αὐτοῦ ἔνοχος ἔσται τῇ κρίσει· ὃς δ᾽ ἂν εἴπῃ τῷ ἀδελφῷ αὐτοῦ, Ῥακά, ἔνοχος ἔσται τῷ συνεδρίῳ· ὃς δ᾽ ἂν εἴπῃ, Μωρέ, ἔνοχος ἔσται εἰς τὴν γέενναν τοῦ πυρός. ¶ 23 ἐὰν οὖν προσφέρῃς τὸ δῶρόν σου ἐπὶ τὸ θυσιαστήριον κἀκεῖ

offering	your	gift	at	the	altar	and there	remember	that	your	brother	has	something	against	you,
προσφέρῃς	σου	ˌτὸ δῶρονˌ	ἐπὶ	τὸ	θυσιαστήριον	κἀκεῖ ←	μνησθῇς	ὅτι	σου	ὁ ἀδελφός	ἔχει	τι	κατὰ	σοῦ
v.pas.2s	r.gs.2	d.asn n.asn	p.a	d.asn	n.asn	crasis	v.aps.2s	cj	r.gs.2	d.nsm n.nsm	v.pai.3s	r.asn	p.g	r.gs.2
4712	5148	3836 1565	2093	3836	2603	2795	3630	4022	5148	3836 81	2400	5516	2848	5148

24 leave your gift there in front of the altar. First go and be reconciled to your brother;

ἄφες	σου	ˌτὸ δῶρονˌ	ἐκεῖ	→	ἔμπροσθεν ←	τοῦ θυσιαστηρίου	καὶ	πρῶτον	ὕπαγε	→	διαλλάγηθι	↱	σου	ˌτῷ ἀδελφῷˌ	καὶ
v.aam.2s	r.gs.2	d.asn n.asn	adv		p.g	d.gsn n.gsn	cj	adv	v.pam.2s		v.apm.2s		r.gs.2	d.dsm n.dsm	cj
918	5148	3836 1565	1695		1869	3836 2603	2779	4754	5632		1367		81	3836 81	2779

then come and offer your gift. ¶ **25** "Settle matters quickly with your adversary who is taking you to

τότε	ἐλθὼν	πρόσφερε	σου	ˌτὸ δῶρονˌ		ἴσθι	εὐνοῶν	ταχύ	↱	σου	ˌτῷ ἀντιδίκῳˌ	
adv	pt.aa.nsm	v.pam.2s	r.gs.2	d.asn n.asn		v.pam.2s	pt.pa.nsm	adv		r.gs.2	d.dsm n.dsm	
5538	2262	4712	5148	3836 1565		1639	2333	5444		5148	3836 508	

court. Do it while you are still with him on the way, or he may hand you over to the judge,

	ˌἕως ὅτουˌ	→	εἶ	←	μετ'	αὐτοῦ	ἐν	τῇ	ὁδῷ	μήποτε	ὁ ἀντίδικος	→	παραδῷ	σε	←	→	τῷ κριτῇ
	p.g r.gsn		v.pai.2s		p.g	r.gsm.3	p.d	d.dsf	n.dsf	cj	d.nsm n.nsm		v.aas.3s	r.as.2			d.dsm n.dsm
	2401 4015		1639	4015	3552	899	1877	3836	3847	3607	3836 508		4140	5148	4140		3836 3216

and the judge may hand you over to the officer, and you may be thrown into prison. **26** I tell you the truth, you will

καὶ	ὁ	κριτῆς	→	→	→	τῷ ὑπηρέτῃ	καὶ	→	→	βληθήσῃ	εἰς	φυλακὴν	→	λέγω	σοι	ἀμὴν	↱	↱
cj	d.nsm	n.nsm				d.dsm n.dsm	cj			v.fpi.2s	p.a	n.asf		v.pai.1s	r.ds.2	pl		
2779	3836	3216				3836 5677	2779			965	1650	5871		3306	5148	297	2002	2002

not get out until you have paid the last penny.

ˌοὐ μὴˌ	ἐξέλθῃς	←	ἐκεῖθεν	ἕως ἄνˌ	→	→	ἀποδῷς	τὸν	ἔσχατον	κοδράντην
adv	pl	v.aas.2s	adv	cj pl			v.aas.2s	d.asn	a.asm	n.asm
4024	3590	2002	1696	2401 323			625	3836	2274	3119

Adultery

5:27 "You have heard that it was said, 'Do not commit adultery.' **28** But I tell you that anyone who looks at a

→	→	Ἠκούσατε ὅτι	→	ἐρρέθη	↱	οὐ	→	μοιχεύσεις	δὲ	ἐγὼ	λέγω	ὑμῖν	ὅτι	πᾶς	ὁ	βλέπων ←
		v.aai.2p cj		v.api.3s		adv		v.fai.2s	cj	r.ns.1	v.pai.1s	r.dp.2	cj	a.nsm	d.nsm	pt.pa.nsm
201		4022		3306	3658	4024		3658	1254	1609	3306	7007	4022	4246	3836	1063

woman lustfully has already committed adultery with her in his heart. **29** If your

γυναῖκα	ˌπρὸς τὸ ἐπιθυμῆσαιˌ	αὐτὴν	ἤδη	→	ἐμοίχευσεν	→	αὐτὴν	ἐν	αὐτοῦ	ˌτῇ καρδίᾳˌ	δὲ	εἰ	σου
n.asf	p.a d.asn f.aa	r.asf.3	adv		v.aai.3s		r.asf.3	p.d	r.gsm.3	d.dsf n.dsf	cj	cj	r.gs.2
1222	4639 3836 2121	899	3658		3658		899	1877	899	3836 2840	1254	1623	5148

right eye causes you to sin, gouge it out and throw it away. It is better for you to

ˌὁ δεξιὸςˌ	ˌὁ ὀφθαλμόςˌ	→	σε	→ σκανδαλίζει	ἔξελε	αὐτὸν	←	καὶ	βάλε	ˌἀπὸ σοῦˌ	γάρ	→	συμφέρει	→	σοι	ἵνα
d.nsm a.nsm	d.nsm n.nsm		r.as.2	v.pai.3s	v.aam.2s	r.asm.3		cj	v.aam.2s	p.g r.gs.2	cj		v.pai.3s		r.ds.2	cj
3836 1288	3836 4057	4997	5148	4997	1975	899	1975	2779	965	608 5148	1142		5237		5148	2671

lose one part of your body than for your whole body to be thrown into hell. **30** And if your right

ἀπόληται	ἓν	ˌτῶν μελῶνˌ	σου	ˌκαὶ μὴˌ	σου	ὅλον	ˌτὸ σῶμαˌ	→	βληθῇ	εἰς	γέενναν	καὶ	εἰ	σου	δεξιά
v.ams.3s	a.nsn	d.gpn n.gpn	r.gs.2	cj pl	r.gs.2	a.nsn	d.nsn n.nsn		v.aps.3s	p.a	n.asf	cj	cj	r.gs.2	a.nsf
660	1651	3836 3517	5148	2779 3590	5148	3910	3836 5393		965	1650	1147	2779	1623	5148	1288

hand causes you to sin, cut it off and throw it away. It is better for you to lose one

ˌἡ χεὶρˌ	→	σε	→ σκανδαλίζει	ἔκκοψον	αὐτὴν	←	καὶ	βάλε	ˌἀπὸ σοῦˌ	γάρ	→	συμφέρει	→	σοι	ἵνα	ἀπόληται	ἓν
d.nsf n.nsf		r.as.2	v.pai.3s	v.aam.2s	r.asf.3		cj	v.aam.2s	p.g r.gs.2	cj		v.pai.3s		r.ds.2	cj	v.ams.3s	a.nsn
3836 5931	4997	5148	4997	1716	899	1716	2779	965	608 5148	1142		5237		5148	2671	660	1651

part of your body than for your whole body to go into hell.

ˌτῶν μελῶνˌ	→	σου	ˌκαὶ μὴˌ	σου	ὅλον	ˌτὸ σῶμαˌ	→	ἀπέλθῃ	εἰς	γέενναν
d.gpn n.gpn		r.gs.2	cj pl	r.gs.2	a.nsn	d.nsn n.nsn		v.aas.3s	p.a	n.asf
3836 3517		5148	2779 3590	5148	3910	3836 5393		599	1650	1147

Divorce

5:31 "It has been said, 'Anyone who divorces his wife must give her a certificate of divorce.' **32** But

δὲ	→	→	Ἐρρέθη	ˌὃς ἄνˌ	→	ἀπολύσῃ	αὐτοῦ	ˌτὴν γυναῖκαˌ	→	δότω	αὐτῇ	ἀποστάσιον	←	←	δὲ
cj			v.api.3s	r.nsm pl		v.aas.3s	r.gsm.3	d.asf n.asf		v.aam.3s	r.dsf.3	n.asn			cj
1254			3306	4005 323		668	899	3836 1222		1443	899	687			1254

μνησθῇς ὅτι ὁ ἀδελφός σου ἔχει τι κατὰ σοῦ, ²⁴ ἄφες ἐκεῖ τὸ δῶρόν σου ἔμπροσθεν τοῦ θυσιαστηρίου καὶ ὕπαγε πρῶτον διαλλάγηθι τῷ ἀδελφῷ σου, καὶ τότε ἐλθὼν πρόσφερε τὸ δῶρόν σου. ¶ ²⁵ ἴσθι εὐνοῶν τῷ ἀντιδίκῳ σου ταχύ, ἕως ὅτου εἶ μετ' αὐτοῦ ἐν τῇ ὁδῷ, μήποτέ σε παραδῷ ὁ ἀντίδικος τῷ κριτῇ καὶ ὁ κριτὴς τῷ ὑπηρέτῃ καὶ εἰς φυλακὴν βληθήσῃ· ²⁶ ἀμὴν λέγω σοι, οὐ μὴ ἐξέλθῃς ἐκεῖθεν, ἕως ἂν ἀποδῷς τὸν ἔσχατον κοδράντην.

⁵·²⁷ Ἠκούσατε ὅτι ἐρρέθη, Οὐ μοιχεύσεις. ²⁸ ἐγὼ δὲ λέγω ὑμῖν ὅτι πᾶς ὁ βλέπων γυναῖκα πρὸς τὸ ἐπιθυμῆσαι αὐτὴν ἤδη ἐμοίχευσεν αὐτὴν ἐν τῇ καρδίᾳ αὐτοῦ. ²⁹ εἰ δὲ ὁ ὀφθαλμός σου ὁ δεξιὸς σκανδαλίζει σε, ἔξελε αὐτὸν καὶ βάλε ἀπὸ σοῦ· συμφέρει γάρ σοι ἵνα ἀπόληται ἓν τῶν μελῶν σου καὶ μὴ ὅλον τὸ σῶμά σου βληθῇ εἰς γέενναν. ³⁰ καὶ εἰ ἡ δεξιά σου χεὶρ σκανδαλίζει σε, ἔκκοψον αὐτὴν καὶ βάλε ἀπὸ σοῦ· συμφέρει γάρ σοι ἵνα ἀπόληται ἓν τῶν μελῶν σου καὶ μὴ ὅλον τὸ σῶμά σου εἰς γέενναν ἀπέλθῃ.

⁵·³¹ Ἐρρέθη δέ, Ὃς ἂν ἀπολύσῃ τὴν γυναῖκα αὐτοῦ, δότω αὐτῇ ἀποστάσιον. ³² ἐγὼ δὲ λέγω ὑμῖν ὅτι πᾶς ὁ ἀπολύων τὴν

I	tell	you	that	anyone	who	divorces	his	wife,		except	for		marital	unfaithfulness,	causes	her	to
ἐγὼ	λέγω	ὑμῖν	ὅτι	πᾶς	ὁ	ἀπολύων	αὐτοῦ	τὴν γυναῖκα		παρεκτὸς	←	λόγου →		πορνείας	ποιεῖ	αὐτὴν	
r.ns.1	v.pai.1s	r.dp.2	cj	a.nsm	d.nsm	pt.pa.nsm	r.gsm.3	d.asf n.asf		p.g		n.gsm		n.gsf	v.pai.3s	r.asf.3	
1609	3306	7007	4022	4246	3836	668	899	3836 1222		4211		3364		4518	4472	899	

become	an adulteress,	and	anyone	who	marries	the	divorced	woman	commits	adultery.
→	μοιχευθῆναι	καὶ	ὃς	ἐὰν ←	γαμήσῃ		ἀπολελυμένην ←	→	μοιχᾶται
	f.ap	cj	r.nsm	pl	v.aas.3s		pt.rp.asf		v.ppi.3s
	3658	2779	4005	1569	1138		668		3656

Oaths

5:33 "Again, you have heard that it was said to the people long ago, 'Do not break your oath, but

Πάλιν	→	→	ἠκούσατε	ὅτι	→	→	ἐρρέθη	→	τοῖς		ἀρχαίοις	←		οὐκ	ἐπιορκήσεις	←	←	δὲ
adv			v.aai.2p	cj			v.api.3s		d.dpm		a.dpm			adv	v.fai.2s			cj
4099			201	4022			3306		3836		792			2155	4024	2155		1254

keep		the	oaths	you	have	made	to	the	Lord.'	34 But	I	tell	you,	Do	not	swear	at all:	either	by	heaven,		for it
ἀποδώσεις		τοὺς	ὅρκους	σου		→	τῷ	κυρίῳ		δὲ	ἐγὼ	λέγω	ὑμῖν	→	μὴ	ὀμόσαι	→ ὅλως	μήτε	ἐν	τῷ οὐρανῷ	ὅτι →	
v.fai.2s		d.apm	n.apm	r.gs.2			d.dsm	n.dsm		cj	r.ns.1	v.pai.1s	r.dp.2		pl	f.aa	adv	cj	p.d	d.dsm n.dsm	cj	
625		3836	3992	5148			3836	3261		1254	1609	3306	7007		3923	3590	3923	3914	3612	1877 3836 4041	4022	

is	God's		throne;	35 or	by	the	earth,	for it is		his	footstool;			or	by	Jerusalem,	for it is		the	city
ἐστιν	τοῦ θεοῦ	θρόνος		μήτε	ἐν	τῇ	γῇ	ὅτι →	ἐστιν	αὐτοῦ	ὑποπόδιον	τῶν	ποδῶν	μήτε	εἰς	Ἰεροσόλυμα	ὅτι →	ἐστιν		πόλις
v.pai.3s	d.gsm n.gsm	n.nsm		cj	p.d	d.dsf	n.dsf	cj	v.pai.3s	r.gsm.3	n.nsn	d.gpm	n.gpm	cj	p.a	n.apn	cj	v.pai.3s		n.nsf
1639	3836 2536	2585		3612	1877	3836	1178	4022	1639	899	5711	3836	4546	3612	1650	2642	4022	1639		4484

of the	Great	King.	36 And	do	not	swear	by	your	head,		for	you	cannot		make	even	one	hair	white	or
τοῦ	μεγάλου	βασιλέως		μήτε	ὀμόσῃς	ἐν	σου	τῇ κεφαλῇ		ὅτι →		οὐ	δύνασαι	ποιῆσαι		μίαν	τρίχα	λευκὴν	ἢ
d.gsm	a.gsm	n.gsm		cj	v.aas.2s	p.d	r.gs.2	d.dsf n.dsf		cj		adv	v.ppi.2s	f.aa		a.asf	n.asf	a.asf	a.asf
3836	3489	995		3612	3923	3612	5148	3836 3051		4022		4024	1538	4472		1651	2582	3328	2445

black.	37 Simply	let		your	'Yes'	be	'Yes,'	and	your	'No,'	'No';		anything	beyond	this	comes	from	the
μέλαιναν	δὲ	ἔστω	ὁ	λόγος	ὑμῶν	ναὶ	ναὶ			οὐ	οὔ	δὲ	τὸ	περισσὸν	τούτων	ἐστιν	ἐκ	τοῦ
a.asf	cj	v.pam.3s	d.nsm	n.nsm	r.gp.2	pl	pl			pl	pl	cj	d.nsn	a.nsn	r.gpn	v.pai.3s	p.g	d.gsm
3506	1254	1639	3836	3364	7007	3721	3721			4024	4024	1254	3836	4356	4047	1639	1666	3836

evil	one.
πονηροῦ	←
a.gsm	
4505	

An Eye for an Eye

5:38 "You have heard that it was said, 'Eye for eye, and tooth for tooth.' 39 But I tell you, Do not

	→	Ἠκούσατε	ὅτι	→	→	ἐρρέθη	ὀφθαλμὸν	ἀντὶ	ὀφθαλμοῦ	καὶ	ὀδόντα	ἀντὶ	ὀδόντος	δὲ	ἐγὼ	λέγω	ὑμῖν	→	μὴ
		v.aai.2p	cj			v.api.3s	n.asm	p.g	n.gsm	cj	n.asm	p.g	n.gsm	cj	r.ns.1	v.pai.1s	r.dp.2		pl
		201	4022			3306	4057	505	4057	2779	3848	505	3848	1254	1609	3306	7007	468	3590

resist	an evil		person.	If	someone	strikes	you	on	the	right	cheek,		turn	to	him	the	other
ἀντιστῆναι	τῷ πονηρῷ	←	ἀλλ'	ὅστις		ῥαπίζει	σε	εἰς	τὴν	δεξιὰν	σιαγόνα	[σου]	στρέψον	→	αὐτῷ	τὴν	ἄλλην
f.aa	d.dsm a.dsm		cj	r.nsm		v.pai.3s	r.as.2	p.a	d.asf	a.asf	n.asf	r.gs.2	v.aam.2s		r.dsm.3	d.asf	r.asf
468	3836 4505		247	4015		4824	5148	1650	3836	1288	4965	5148	5138		899	3836	257

also.	40 And	if	someone	wants	to sue	you	and	take	your	tunic,		let him	have	your	cloak	as	well.	41		If
καὶ	καὶ	τῷ	θέλοντι		κριθῆναι	σοι	καὶ	λαβεῖν	σου	τὸν χιτῶνα	→	αὐτῷ	ἄφες	τὸ	ἱμάτιον	καὶ				καὶ
adv	cj	d.dsm	pt.pa.dsm		f.ap	r.ds.2	cj	f.aa	r.gs.2	d.asm n.asm		r.dsm.3	v.aam.2s	d.asn	n.asn	adv				cj
2779	2779	3836	2527		3212	5148	2779	3284	5148	3836 5945		918	899	918	3836	2668	2779			2779

someone	forces	you	to go	one	mile,	go	with	him	two miles.	42	Give	to	the one	who	asks	you,	and	do	not
ὅστις	ἀγγαρεύσει	σε	ὕπαγε	ἓν	μίλιον		μετ'	αὐτοῦ	δύο		δός	→	τῷ	←	αἰτοῦντι	σε	καὶ	→	μὴ
r.nsm	v.fai.3s	r.as.2	v.pam.2s	a.asn	n.asn		p.g	r.gsm.3	a.apn		v.aam.2s		d.dsm		pt.pa.dsm	r.as.2	cj		pl
4015	30	5148	5632	1651	3627		3552	899	1545		1443		3836		160	5148	2779	695	3590

turn	away	from	the one	who	wants	to	borrow	from	you.
ἀποστραφῇς	←	←	τὸν	←	θέλοντα	→	δανίσασθαι	ἀπὸ	σου
v.aps.2s			d.asm		pt.pa.asm		f.am	p.g	r.gs.2
695			3836		2527		1244	608	5148

γυναῖκα αὐτοῦ παρεκτὸς λόγου πορνείας ποιεῖ αὐτὴν μοιχευθῆναι, καὶ ὃς ἐὰν ἀπολελυμένην γαμήσῃ, μοιχᾶται. **5:33** Πάλιν ἠκούσατε ὅτι ἐρρέθη τοῖς ἀρχαίοις, Οὐκ ἐπιορκήσεις, ἀποδώσεις δὲ τῷ κυρίῳ τοὺς ὅρκους σου. 34 ἐγὼ δὲ λέγω ὑμῖν μὴ ὀμόσαι ὅλως· μήτε ἐν τῷ οὐρανῷ, ὅτι θρόνος ἐστιν τοῦ θεοῦ, 35 μήτε ἐν τῇ γῇ, ὅτι ὑποπόδιόν ἐστιν τῶν ποδῶν αὐτοῦ, μήτε εἰς Ἰεροσόλυμα, ὅτι πόλις ἐστιν τοῦ μεγάλου βασιλέως, 36 μήτε ἐν τῇ κεφαλῇ σου ὀμόσῃς, ὅτι οὐ δύνασαι μίαν τρίχα λευκὴν ποιῆσαι ἢ μέλαιναν. 37 ἔστω δὲ ὁ λόγος ὑμῶν ναὶ ναί, οὒ οὔ· τὸ δὲ περισσὸν τούτων ἐκ τοῦ πονηροῦ ἐστιν. **5:38** Ἠκούσατε ὅτι ἐρρέθη, Ὀφθαλμὸν ἀντὶ ὀφθαλμοῦ καὶ ὀδόντα ἀντὶ ὀδόντος. 39 ἐγὼ δὲ λέγω ὑμῖν μὴ ἀντιστῆναι τῷ πονηρῷ· ἀλλ' ὅστις σε ῥαπίζει εἰς τὴν δεξιὰν σιαγόνα [σου], στρέψον αὐτῷ καὶ τὴν ἄλλην· 40 καὶ τῷ θέλοντί σοι κριθῆναι καὶ τὸν χιτῶνά σου λαβεῖν, ἄφες αὐτῷ καὶ τὸ ἱμάτιον· 41 καὶ ὅστις σε ἀγγαρεύσει μίλιον ἕν, ὕπαγε μετ' αὐτοῦ δύο. 42 τῷ αἰτοῦντί σε δός, καὶ τὸν θέλοντα ἀπὸ σοῦ δανίσασθαι μὴ ἀποστραφῇς.

Love for Enemies

5:43 "You have heard　that it was said, 'Love　your neighbor　and hate　your enemy.' **44** But I　tell you:
Ἠκούσατε ὅτι　ἐρρέθη ἀγαπήσεις σου τὸν πλησίον καὶ μισήσεις σου τὸν ἐχθρόν δὲ ἐγὼ λέγω ὑμῖν
v.aai.2p cj　v.api.3s v.fai.2s r.gs.2 d.asm adv cj v.fai.2s r.gs.2 d.asm a.asm cj r.ns.1 v.pai.1s r.dp.2
201 4022　3306 26 5148 3836 4446 2779 3631 5148 3836 2398 1254 1609 3306 7007

Love　your enemies　and pray　for those who persecute you, **45** that you may be　sons of your
ἀγαπᾶτε ὑμῶν τοὺς ἐχθρούς καὶ προσεύχεσθε ὑπὲρ τῶν διωκόντων ὑμᾶς ὅπως γένησθε υἱοὶ ὑμῶν
v.pam.2p r.gp.2 d.apm a.apm cj v.pmm.2p p.g d.gpm pt.pa.gpm r.ap.2 cj v.ams.2p n.npm r.gp.2
26 7007 3836 2398 2779 4667 5642 3836 1503 7007 3968 1181 5626 4252 7007

Father　in heaven. He causes his　sun　to rise　on the evil　and the good, and sends
τοῦ πατρὸς τοῦ ἐν οὐρανοῖς ὅτι αὐτοῦ τὸν ἥλιον ἀνατέλλει ἐπὶ πονηροὺς καὶ ἀγαθοὺς καὶ
d.gsm n.gsm d.gsm p.d n.dpm cj r.gsm.3 d.asm n.asm v.pai.3s p.a a.apm cj a.apm cj
3836 4252 3836 1877 4041 4022 899 3836 2463 422 2093 4505 2779 19 2779

rain　on the righteous and the unrighteous. **46**　If you love　those who love　you, what reward will you
βρέχει ἐπὶ δικαίους καὶ ἀδίκους γὰρ ἐὰν ἀγαπήσητε τοὺς ἀγαπῶντας ὑμᾶς τίνα μισθὸν
v.pai.3s p.a a.apm cj a.apm cj cj v.aas.2p d.apm pt.pa.apm r.ap.2 r.asm n.asm
1101 2093 1465 2779 96 1142 1569 26 3836 26 7007 5515 3635

get? Are not even the tax　collectors doing　that? **47** And if　you greet　only your brothers,　what are
ἔχετε οὐχὶ καὶ οἱ τελῶναι ποιοῦσιν τὸ αὐτό καὶ ἐὰν ἀσπάσησθε μόνον ὑμῶν τοὺς ἀδελφούς τί
v.pai.2p adv cj d.npm n.npm v.pai.3p d.asn r.asn cj cj v.ams.2p adv r.gp.2 d.apm n.apm r.asn
2400 4472 4049 2779 3836 5467 4472 3836 899 2779 1569 832 3667 7007 3836 81 5515

you doing more　than others? Do not　even pagans　do　that? **48**　Be　perfect, therefore, as your
ποιεῖτε περισσόν οὐχὶ καὶ οἱ ἐθνικοὶ ποιοῦσιν τὸ αὐτό ὑμεῖς ἔσεσθε τέλειοι οὖν ὡς ὑμῶν
v.pai.2p a.asn pl cj d.npm a.npm v.pai.3p d.asn r.asn r.np.2 v.fmi.2p a.npm cj cj r.gp.2
4472 4356 4472 4049 2779 3836 1618 4472 3836 899 7007 1639 5455 4036 6055 7007

heavenly　Father　is　perfect.
ὁ οὐράνιος ὁ πατὴρ ἐστιν τέλειος
d.nsm a.nsm d.nsm n.nsm v.pai.3s a.nsm
3836 4039 3836 4252 1639 5455

Giving to the Needy

6:1　"Be careful　not to do　your 'acts of righteousness' before　men,　to　be seen　by
[δὲ] Προσέχετε μὴ ποιεῖν ὑμῶν τὴν δικαιοσύνην ἔμπροσθεν τῶν ἀνθρώπων πρὸς τὸ θεαθῆναι
cj v.pam.2p pl f.pa r.gp.2 d.asf n.asf p.g d.gpm n.gpm p.a d.asn f.ap
1254 4668 3590 4472 7007 3836 1466 1869 3836 476 4639 3836 2517

them. If you do,　you will have no reward from your Father　in heaven. ¶ **2** "So when you
αὐτοῖς δὲ εἰ μὴ γε ἔχετε οὐκ μισθὸν παρὰ ὑμῶν τῷ πατρὶ τῷ ἐν τοῖς οὐρανοῖς οὖν Ὅταν
r.dpm.3 cj cj pl pl v.pai.2p adv n.asm p.d r.gp.2 d.dsm n.dsm d.dsm p.d d.dpm n.dpm cj cj
899 1254 1623 3590 1145 2400 4024 3635 4123 7007 3836 4252 3836 1877 3836 4041 4036 4020

give to the needy,　do not announce it with trumpets,　as　the hypocrites do　in the
ποιῇς ἐλεημοσύνην μὴ σαλπίσῃς ἔμπροσθεν σου ὥσπερ οἱ ὑποκριταὶ ποιοῦσιν ἐν ταῖς
v.pas.2s n.asf pl v.aas.2s p.g r.gs.2 cj d.npm n.npm v.pai.3p p.d d.dpf
4472 1797 4895 3590 4895 1869 5148 6061 3836 5695 4472 1877 3836

synagogues and on the streets, to　be honored　by men.　I tell you the truth, they have received their
συναγωγαῖς καὶ ἐν ταῖς ῥύμαις ὅπως δοξασθῶσιν ὑπὸ τῶν ἀνθρώπων λέγω ὑμῖν ἀμὴν ἀπέχουσιν αὐτῶν
n.dpf cj p.d d.dpf n.dpf cj v.aps.3p p.g d.gpm n.gpm v.pai.1s r.dp.2 pl v.pai.3p r.gpm.3
5252 2779 1877 3836 4860 3968 1519 5679 3836 476 3306 7007 297 600 899

reward　in full. **3** But when you give　to the needy,　do not let your left　hand know what your
τὸν μισθὸν δὲ σοῦ ποιοῦντος ἐλεημοσύνην μὴ σου ἡ ἀριστερά γνώτω τί σου
d.asm n.asm cj r.gs.2 pt.pa.gsm n.asf pl r.gs.2 d.nsf n.nsf v.aam.3s r.asn r.gs.2
3836 3635 600 600 5148 4472 1797 3590 5148 3836 754 1182 5515 5148

right　hand is doing, **4** so　that your giving　may be　in secret. Then your Father,　who sees　what
ἡ δεξιά ποιεῖ ὅπως σου ἡ ἐλεημοσύνη ᾖ ἐν τῷ κρυπτῷ καὶ σου ὁ πατὴρ ὁ βλέπων
d.nsf a.nsf v.pai.3s cj r.gs.2 d.nsf n.nsf v.pas.3s p.d d.dsn a.dsn cj r.gs.2 d.nsm n.nsm d.nsm pt.pa.nsm
3836 1288 4472 3968 5148 3836 1797 1639 1877 3836 3220 2779 5148 3836 4252 3836 1063

is done in secret,　will reward you.
ἐν τῷ κρυπτῷ ἀποδώσει σοι
p.d d.dsn a.dsn v.fai.3s r.ds.2
1877 3836 3220 625 5148

5:43 Ἠκούσατε ὅτι ἐρρέθη, Ἀγαπήσεις τὸν πλησίον σου καὶ μισήσεις τὸν ἐχθρόν σου. **44** ἐγὼ δὲ λέγω ὑμῖν, ἀγαπᾶτε τοὺς ἐχθροὺς ὑμῶν καὶ προσεύχεσθε ὑπὲρ τῶν διωκόντων ὑμᾶς, **45** ὅπως γένησθε υἱοὶ τοῦ πατρὸς ὑμῶν τοῦ ἐν οὐρανοῖς, ὅτι τὸν ἥλιον αὐτοῦ ἀνατέλλει ἐπὶ πονηροὺς καὶ ἀγαθοὺς καὶ βρέχει ἐπὶ δικαίους καὶ ἀδίκους. **46** ἐὰν γὰρ ἀγαπήσητε τοὺς ἀγαπῶντας ὑμᾶς, τίνα μισθὸν ἔχετε; οὐχὶ καὶ οἱ τελῶναι τὸ αὐτὸ ποιοῦσιν; **47** καὶ ἐὰν ἀσπάσησθε τοὺς ἀδελφοὺς ὑμῶν μόνον, τί περισσὸν ποιεῖτε; οὐχὶ καὶ οἱ ἐθνικοὶ τὸ αὐτὸ ποιοῦσιν; **48** Ἔσεσθε οὖν ὑμεῖς τέλειοι ὡς ὁ πατὴρ ὑμῶν ὁ οὐράνιος τέλειός ἐστιν.

6:1 Προσέχετε [δὲ] τὴν δικαιοσύνην ὑμῶν μὴ ποιεῖν ἔμπροσθεν τῶν ἀνθρώπων πρὸς τὸ θεαθῆναι αὐτοῖς· εἰ δὲ μή γε, μισθὸν οὐκ ἔχετε παρὰ τῷ πατρὶ ὑμῶν τῷ ἐν τοῖς οὐρανοῖς. ¶ **2** Ὅταν οὖν ποιῇς ἐλεημοσύνην, μὴ σαλπίσῃς ἔμπροσθέν σου, ὥσπερ οἱ ὑποκριταὶ ποιοῦσιν ἐν ταῖς συναγωγαῖς καὶ ἐν ταῖς ῥύμαις, ὅπως δοξασθῶσιν ὑπὸ τῶν ἀνθρώπων· ἀμὴν λέγω ὑμῖν, ἀπέχουσιν τὸν μισθὸν αὐτῶν. **3** σοῦ δὲ ποιοῦντος ἐλεημοσύνην μὴ γνώτω ἡ ἀριστερά σου τί ποιεῖ ἡ δεξιά σου, **4** ὅπως ᾖ σου ἡ ἐλεημοσύνη ἐν τῷ κρυπτῷ· καὶ ὁ πατήρ σου ὁ βλέπων ἐν τῷ κρυπτῷ ἀποδώσει σοι.

Prayer

6:5 "And when you pray, do not be like the hypocrites, for they love to pray standing in the
Καὶ ὅταν → προσεύχησθε → οὐκ ἔσεσθε ὡς οἱ ὑποκριταί ὅτι → φιλοῦσιν → προσεύχεσθαι ἑστῶτες ἐν ταῖς
cj cj v.pms.2p adv v.fmi.2p cj d.npm n.npm cj v.pai.3p f.pm pt.ra.npm p.d d.dpf
2779 4020 4667 1639 4024 1639 6055 3836 5695 4022 5797 4667 2705 1877 3836

synagogues and on the street corners to be seen by men. I tell you the truth, they have
συναγωγαῖς καὶ ἐν ταῖς τῶν πλατειῶν γωνίαις ὅπως → φανῶσιν → τοῖς ἀνθρώποις· → λέγω ὑμῖν ἀμὴν → →
n.dpf cj p.d d.dpf d.gpf n.gpf n.dpf cj v.aps.3p d.dpm n.dpm v.pai.1s r.dp.2 pl
5252 2779 1877 3836 3836 4426 1224 3968 5743 3836 476 3306 7007 297

received their reward in full. **6** But when you pray, go into your room, close the door and
ἀπέχουσιν αὐτῶν ⸢τὸν μισθὸν⸣ ← ← δὲ ὅταν σὺ προσεύχῃ εἴσελθε εἰς σου ⸢τὸ ταμεῖον⸣ καὶ κλείσας τὴν θύραν σου
v.pai.3p r.gpm.3 d.asm n.asm cj cj r.ns.2 v.pms.2s v.aam.2s p.a r.gs.2 d.asn n.asn cj pt.aa.nsm d.asf n.asf r.gs.2
600 899 3836 3635 600 600 1254 4020 5148 4667 1656 1650 5148 3836 5421 2779 3091 3836 2598 5148

pray to your Father, who is unseen. Then your Father, who sees what is done in secret, will
πρόσευξαι → σου ⸢τῷ πατρί⸣ τῷ ⸢ἐν τῷ κρυπτῷ⸣ καὶ σου ὁ πατήρ ὁ βλέπων ⸢ἐν τῷ κρυπτῷ⸣ →
v.amm.2s r.gs.2 d.dsm n.dsm d.dsm p.d d.dsn a.dsn cj r.gs.2 d.nsm n.nsm d.nsm pt.pa.nsm p.d d.dsn a.dsn
4667 4252 5148 3836 4252 3836 1877 3836 3220 2779 5148 3836 4252 3836 1063 1877 3836 3220

reward you. **7** And when you pray, do not keep on babbling like pagans, for they think they
ἀποδώσει σοι δὲ → → Προσευχόμενοι μὴ → βατταλογήσητε ὥσπερ οἱ ἐθνικοί γὰρ → δοκοῦσιν ὅτι →
v.fai.3s r.ds.2 cj pt.pm.npm pl v.aas.2p cj d.npm a.npm cj v.pai.3p cj
625 5148 1254 4667 1006 3590 1006 6061 3836 1618 1142 1506 4022

will be heard because of their many words. **8** Do not be like them, for your Father knows
→ → εἰσακουσθήσονται ἐν → ← αὐτῶν ⸢τῇ πολυλογίᾳ⸣ οὖν → μὴ ὁμοιωθῆτε αὐτοῖς γὰρ ὑμῶν ὁ πατὴρ οἶδεν
v.fpi.3p p.d r.gpm.3 d.dsf n.dsf cj pl v.aps.2p r.dpm.3 cj r.gp.2 d.nsm n.nsm v.rai.3s
1653 1877 899 3836 4494 4036 3929 3590 3929 899 1142 7007 3836 4252 3857

what you need before you ask him. ¶ **9** "This, then, is how you should pray: "'Our
ὧν → ⸢χρείαν ἔχετε⸣ πρὸ ὑμᾶς ⸢τοῦ αἰτῆσαι⸣ αὐτόν οὕτως οὖν ← ← ὑμεῖς → προσεύχεσθε ἡμῶν
r.gpn n.asf v.pai.2p p.a r.ap.2 d.gsn f.aa r.asm.3 adv cj r.np.2 v.pmm.2p r.gp.1
4005 5970 2400 4574 7007 3836 160 899 4048 4036 4048 4048 7007 4667 7005

Father in heaven, hallowed be your name, **10** your kingdom come, your will be done on
Πάτερ ὁ ἐν ⸢τοῖς οὐρανοῖς⸣ ἁγιασθήτω → σου ⸢τὸ ὄνομα⸣ σου ἡ βασιλεία ἐλθέτω σου ⸢τὸ θέλημα⸣ → γενηθήτω καὶ ἐπὶ
n.vsm d.vsm p.d d.dpm n.dpm v.apm.3s r.gs.2 d.nsn n.nsn r.gs.2 d.nsf n.nsf v.aam.3s r.gs.2 d.nsn n.nsn v.apm.3s adv p.g
4252 3836 1877 3836 4041 39 5148 3836 3950 5148 3836 993 2262 5148 3836 2525 1181 2779 2093

earth as it is in heaven. **11** Give us today our daily bread. **12** Forgive us our debts, as we
γῆς ὡς ἐν οὐρανῷ δὸς ἡμῖν σήμερον ἡμῶν ⸢τὸν ἐπιούσιον⸣ ⸢τὸν ἄρτον⸣ καὶ ἄφες ἡμῖν ἡμῶν ⸢τὰ ὀφειλήματα⸣ ὡς ἡμεῖς
n.gsf cj p.d n.dsm v.aam.2s r.dp.1 adv r.gp.1 d.asm a.asm d.asm n.asm cj v.aam.2s r.dp.1 r.gp.1 d.apn n.apn cj r.np.1
11/8 6055 1877 4041 1443 7005 4958 7005 3836 2157 3836 788 2779 918 7005 7005 3836 4052 6055 7005

also have forgiven our debtors. **13** And lead us not into temptation, but deliver us from the evil
καὶ → ἀφήκαμεν ἡμῶν ⸢τοῖς ὀφειλέταις⸣ καὶ εἰσενέγκῃς ἡμᾶς μὴ εἰς πειρασμόν ἀλλὰ ῥῦσαι ἡμᾶς ἀπὸ τοῦ πονηροῦ
adv v.aai.1p r.gp.1 d.dpm n.dpm cj v.aas.2s r.ap.1 pl p.a n.asm cj v.amm.2s r.ap.1 p.g d.gsn a.gsn
2779 918 7005 3836 4050 2779 1662 7005 3590 1650 4280 247 4861 7005 608 3836 4505

one.' **14** For if you forgive men when they sin against you, your heavenly Father will
← γὰρ Ἐὰν → ἀφῆτε ⸢τοῖς ἀνθρώποις⸣ αὐτῶν ⸢τὰ παραπτώματα⸣ ὑμῶν ὁ οὐράνιος ὁ πατὴρ →
cj cj v.aas.2p d.dpm n.dpm r.gp.3 d.apn n.apn r.gp.2 d.nsm a.nsm d.nsm n.nsm
1142 1569 918 3836 476 899 3836 4183 7007 3836 4039 3836 4252 918

also forgive you. **15** But if you do not forgive men their sins, your Father will not forgive your
καὶ ἀφήσει ὑμῖν δὲ ἐὰν → μὴ ἀφῆτε ⸢τοῖς ἀνθρώποις⸣ ὑμῶν ὁ πατὴρ → οὐδὲ ἀφήσει ὑμῶν
adv v.fai.3s r.dp.2 cj cj pl v.aas.2p d.dpm n.dpm r.gp.2 d.nsm n.nsm cj v.fai.3s r.gp.2
2779 918 7007 1254 1569 918 918 3590 918 3836 476 7007 3836 4252 4028 918 7007

sins.
⸢τὰ παραπτώματα⸣
d.apn n.apn
3836 4183

6:5 Καὶ ὅταν προσεύχησθε, οὐκ ἔσεσθε ὡς οἱ ὑποκριταί, ὅτι φιλοῦσιν ἐν ταῖς συναγωγαῖς καὶ ἐν ταῖς γωνίαις τῶν πλατειῶν ἑστῶτες προσεύχεσθαι, ὅπως φανῶσιν τοῖς ἀνθρώποις· ἀμὴν λέγω ὑμῖν, ἀπέχουσιν τὸν μισθὸν αὐτῶν. **6** σὺ δὲ ὅταν προσεύχῃ, εἴσελθε εἰς τὸ ταμεῖόν σου καὶ κλείσας τὴν θύραν σου πρόσευξαι τῷ πατρί σου τῷ ἐν τῷ κρυπτῷ· καὶ ὁ πατήρ σου ὁ βλέπων ἐν τῷ κρυπτῷ ἀποδώσει σοι. **7** Προσευχόμενοι δὲ μὴ βατταλογήσητε ὥσπερ οἱ ἐθνικοί, δοκοῦσιν γὰρ ὅτι ἐν τῇ πολυλογίᾳ αὐτῶν εἰσακουσθήσονται. **8** μὴ οὖν ὁμοιωθῆτε αὐτοῖς· οἶδεν γὰρ ὁ πατὴρ ὑμῶν ὧν χρείαν ἔχετε πρὸ τοῦ ὑμᾶς αἰτῆσαι αὐτόν. ¶ **9** Οὕτως οὖν προσεύχεσθε ὑμεῖς· Πάτερ ἡμῶν ὁ ἐν τοῖς οὐρανοῖς· ἁγιασθήτω τὸ ὄνομά σου· **10** ἐλθέτω ἡ βασιλεία σου· γενηθήτω τὸ θέλημά σου, ὡς ἐν οὐρανῷ καὶ ἐπὶ γῆς· **11** Τὸν ἄρτον ἡμῶν τὸν ἐπιούσιον δὸς ἡμῖν σήμερον· **12** καὶ ἄφες ἡμῖν τὰ ὀφειλήματα ἡμῶν, ὡς καὶ ἡμεῖς ἀφήκαμεν τοῖς ὀφειλέταις ἡμῶν· **13** καὶ μὴ εἰσενέγκῃς ἡμᾶς εἰς πειρασμόν, ἀλλὰ ῥῦσαι ἡμᾶς ἀπὸ τοῦ πονηροῦ. **14** Ἐὰν γὰρ ἀφῆτε τοῖς ἀνθρώποις τὰ παραπτώματα αὐτῶν, ἀφήσει καὶ ὑμῖν ὁ πατὴρ ὑμῶν ὁ οὐράνιος· **15** ἐὰν δὲ μὴ ἀφῆτε τοῖς ἀνθρώποις, τὰ παραπτώματα αὐτῶν οὐδὲ ὁ πατὴρ ὑμῶν ἀφήσει τὰ παραπτώματα ὑμῶν.

Fasting

6:16 "When you fast, do not look somber as the hypocrites do, for they disfigure their faces
δὲ Ὅταν → νηστεύητε μὴ γίνεσθε σκυθρωποί ὡς οἱ ὑποκριταὶ γὰρ → ἀφανίζουσιν αὐτῶν τὰ πρόσωπα
cj cj v.pas.2p pl v.pmm.2p a.npm conj d.npm n.npm cj v.pai.3p r.gpm.3 d.apn n.apn
1254 4020 3764 3590 1181 5034 6055 3836 5695 1142 906 899 3836 4725

to show men they are fasting. I tell you the truth, they have received their reward in full.
ὅπως φανῶσιν τοῖς ἀνθρώποις νηστεύοντες λέγω ὑμῖν ἀμὴν ἀπέχουσιν αὐτῶν τὸν μισθὸν
cj v.aps.3p d.dpm n.dpm pt.pa.npm v.pai.1s r.dp.2 pl v.pai.3p r.gpm.3 d.asm n.asm
3968 5743 3836 476 3764 3306 7007 297 600 899 3836 3635 600 600

17 But when you fast, put oil on your head and wash your face, **18** so that it will not be obvious
δὲ σὺ νηστεύων ἄλειψαι σου τὴν κεφαλὴν καὶ νίψαι σου τὸ πρόσωπον ὅπως μὴ φανῇς
cj r.ns.2 pt.pa.nsm v.amm.2s r.gs.2 d.asf n.asf cj v.amm.2s r.gs.2 d.asn n.asn cj pl v.aps.2s
1254 3764 5148 3764 230 5148 3836 3051 2779 3782 5148 3836 4725 3968 5743 5743 3590 5743

to men that you are fasting, but only to your Father, who is unseen; and your Father, who
τοῖς ἀνθρώποις νηστεύων ἀλλὰ σου τῷ πατρί τῷ ἐν τῷ κρυφαίῳ καὶ σου ὁ πατήρ ὁ
d.dpm n.dpm pt.pa.nsm cj r.gs.2 d.dsm n.dsm d.dsm p.d d.dsn n.dsn cj r.gs.2 d.nsm n.nsm d.nsm
3836 476 3764 247 4252 5148 3836 4252 3836 1877 3836 3224 2779 5148 3836 4252 3836

sees what is done in secret, will reward you.
βλέπων ἐν τῷ κρυφαίῳ → ἀποδώσει σοι
pt.pa.nsm p.d d.dsn a.dsn v.fai.3s r.ds.2
1063 1877 3836 3224 625 5148

Treasures in Heaven

6:19 "Do not store up for yourselves treasures on earth, where moth and rust destroy, and where thieves
Μὴ θησαυρίζετε ὑμῖν θησαυροὺς ἐπὶ τῆς γῆς ὅπου σὴς καὶ βρῶσις ἀφανίζει καὶ ὅπου κλέπται
pl v.pam.2p r.dp.2 n.apm p.g d.gsf n.gsf pl n.nsm cj n.nsf v.pai.3s cj pl n.npm
2564 3590 2564 7007 2565 2093 3836 1178 3963 4962 2779 1111 906 2779 3963 3095

break in and steal. **20** But store up for yourselves treasures in heaven, where moth and rust do
διορύσσουσιν καὶ κλέπτουσιν δὲ θησαυρίζετε ὑμῖν θησαυροὺς ἐν οὐρανῷ ὅπου οὔτε σὴς οὔτε βρῶσις
v.pai.3p cj v.pai.3p cj v.pam.2p r.dp.2 n.apm p.d n.dsm pl cj n.nsm cj n.nsf
1482 2779 3096 1254 2564 7007 2565 1877 4041 3963 4046 4962 4046 1111 906

not destroy, and where thieves do not break in and steal. **21** For where your treasure is, there your
ἀφανίζει καὶ ὅπου κλέπται οὐ διορύσσουσιν οὐδὲ κλέπτουσιν γὰρ ὅπου σου ὁ θησαυρός, ἐστιν ἐκεῖ σου
v.pai.3s cj pl n.npm adv v.pai.3p cj v.pai.3p cj pl r.gs.2 d.nsm n.nsm v.pai.3s adv r.gs.2
4046 906 2779 3963 3095 1482 4024 1482 4028 3096 1142 3963 5148 3836 2565 1639 1695 5148

heart will be also. ¶ **22** "The eye is the lamp of the body. If your eyes are good,
ἡ καρδία → ἔσται καὶ ὁ ὀφθαλμός ἐστιν Ὁ λύχνος τοῦ σώματος οὖν ἐὰν σου ὁ ὀφθαλμός ᾖ ἁπλοῦς
d.nsf n.nsf v.fmi.3s adv d.nsm n.nsm v.pai.3s d.nsm n.nsm d.gsn n.gsn cj cj r.gs.2 d.nsm n.nsm v.pas.3s a.nsm
3836 2840 1639 2779 3836 4057 1639 3836 3394 3836 5393 4036 1569 5148 3836 4057 1639 606

your whole body will be full of light. **23** But if your eyes are bad, your whole body will be
σου ὅλον τὸ σῶμα → ἔσται φωτεινόν δὲ ἐὰν σου ὁ ὀφθαλμός, ᾖ πονηρός σου ὅλον τὸ σῶμα → ἔσται
r.gs.2 a.nsn d.nsn n.nsn v.fmi.3s a.nsn cj cj r.gs.2 d.nsm n.nsm v.pas.3s a.nsm r.gs.2 a.nsn d.nsn n.nsn v.fmi.3s
5148 3910 3836 5393 1639 5893 1254 1569 5148 3836 4057 1639 4505 5148 3910 3836 5393 1639

full of darkness. If then the light within you is darkness, how great is that darkness! ¶ **24** "No one
σκοτεινόν εἰ οὖν τὸ φῶς τὸ ἐν σοὶ ἐστίν σκότος πόσον τὸ σκότος Οὐδεὶς
a.nsn cj cj d.nsn n.nsn d.nsn p.d r.ds.2 v.pai.3s n.nsn r.nsn d.nsn n.nsn a.nsm
5027 1623 4036 3836 5890 3836 1877 5148 1639 5030 4531 3836 5030 4029

can serve two masters. Either he will hate the one and love the other, or he will be devoted to the
δύναται δουλεύειν δυσὶ κυρίοις γὰρ ἢ μισήσει τὸν ἕνα καὶ ἀγαπήσει τὸν ἕτερον ἢ → ἀνθέξεται
v.ppi.3s f.pa a.dpm n.dpm cj cj v.fai.3s d.asm a.asm cj v.fai.3s d.asm r.asm cj v.fmi.3s
1538 1526 1545 3261 1142 2445 3631 3836 1651 2779 26 3836 2283 2445 504

one and despise the other. You cannot serve both God and Money.
ἑνὸς καὶ καταφρονήσει τοῦ ἑτέρου οὐ δύνασθε δουλεύειν θεῷ καὶ μαμωνᾷ
a.gsm cj v.fai.3s d.gsm r.gsm adv v.ppi.2p f.pa n.dsm cj n.dsm
1651 2779 2969 3836 2283 4024 1538 1526 2536 2779 3440

6:16 Ὅταν δὲ νηστεύητε, μὴ γίνεσθε ὡς οἱ ὑποκριταὶ σκυθρωποί, ἀφανίζουσιν γὰρ τὰ πρόσωπα αὐτῶν ὅπως φανῶσιν τοῖς ἀνθρώποις νηστεύοντες· ἀμὴν λέγω ὑμῖν, ἀπέχουσιν τὸν μισθὸν αὐτῶν. 17 σὺ δὲ νηστεύων ἄλειψαί σου τὴν κεφαλὴν καὶ τὸ πρόσωπόν σου νίψαι, 18 ὅπως μὴ φανῇς τοῖς ἀνθρώποις νηστεύων ἀλλὰ τῷ πατρί σου τῷ ἐν τῷ κρυφαίῳ· καὶ ὁ πατήρ σου ὁ βλέπων ἐν τῷ κρυφαίῳ ἀποδώσει σοι.

6:19 Μὴ θησαυρίζετε ὑμῖν θησαυροὺς ἐπὶ τῆς γῆς, ὅπου σὴς καὶ βρῶσις ἀφανίζει καὶ ὅπου κλέπται διορύσσουσιν καὶ κλέπτουσιν· 20 θησαυρίζετε δὲ ὑμῖν θησαυροὺς ἐν οὐρανῷ, ὅπου οὔτε σὴς οὔτε βρῶσις ἀφανίζει καὶ ὅπου κλέπται οὐ διορύσσουσιν οὐδὲ κλέπτουσιν· 21 ὅπου γάρ ἐστιν ὁ θησαυρός σου, ἐκεῖ ἔσται καὶ ἡ καρδία σου. ¶ 22 Ὁ λύχνος τοῦ σώματός ἐστιν ὁ ὀφθαλμός. ἐὰν οὖν ᾖ ὁ ὀφθαλμός σου ἁπλοῦς, ὅλον τὸ σῶμά σου φωτεινὸν ἔσται· 23 ἐὰν δὲ ὁ ὀφθαλμός σου πονηρὸς ᾖ, ὅλον τὸ σῶμά σου σκοτεινὸν ἔσται. εἰ οὖν τὸ φῶς τὸ ἐν σοὶ σκότος ἐστίν, τὸ σκότος πόσον. ¶ 24 Οὐδεὶς δύναται δυσὶ κυρίοις δουλεύειν· ἢ γὰρ τὸν ἕνα μισήσει καὶ τὸν ἕτερον ἀγαπήσει, ἢ ἑνὸς ἀνθέξεται καὶ τοῦ ἑτέρου καταφρονήσει. οὐ δύνασθε θεῷ δουλεύειν καὶ μαμωνᾷ.

Do Not Worry

6:25 "Therefore I tell you, do not worry about your life, what you will eat or drink; or about
Διὰ τοῦτο → λέγω ὑμῖν, → μὴ μεριμνᾶτε → ὑμῶν τῇ ψυχῇ τί → → φάγητε ἢ τί πίητε μηδὲ
p.a r.asn v.pai.1s r.dp.2 pl v.pam.2p r.gp.2 d.dsf n.dsf r.asn v.aas.2p cj r.asn v.aas.2p cj
1328 4047 3306 7007 3534 3590 3534 6034 7007 3836 6034 5515 2266 2445 5515 4403 3593 5393

your body, what you will wear. Is not life more important than food, and the body more
ὑμῶν τῷ σώματι τί → → ἐνδύσησθε ἐστιν οὐχὶ ἡ ψυχὴ πλεῖόν ← τῆς τροφῆς καὶ τὸ σῶμα
r.gp.2 d.dsn n.dsn r.asn v.ams.2p v.pai.3s d.nsf d.nsf n.nsf a.nsn.c d.gsf n.gsf cj d.nsn n.nsn
7007 3836 5393 5515 1907 1639 4049 3836 6034 4498 3836 5575 2779 3836 5393

important than clothes? **26** Look at the birds of the air; they do not sow or reap or
→ τοῦ ἐνδύματος ἐμβλέψατε εἰς τὰ πετεινὰ τοῦ οὐρανοῦ ὅτι → οὐ σπείρουσιν οὐδὲ θερίζουσιν οὐδὲ
d.gsn n.gsn v.aam.2p p.a d.apn n.apn d.gsm n.gsm cj adv v.pai.3p cj v.pai.3p cj
3836 1903 1838 1650 3836 4041 3836 4041 4022 5062 5062 4024 5062 4028 2545 4028

store away in barns, and yet your heavenly Father feeds them. Are you not much more valuable
συνάγουσιν ← εἰς ἀποθήκας καὶ ὑμῶν ὁ οὐράνιος ὁ πατὴρ τρέφει αὐτά → ὑμεῖς οὐχ → μᾶλλον διαφέρετε
v.pai.3p p.a n.apf cj r.gp.2 d.nsm a.nsm d.nsm n.nsm v.pai.3s r.apn.3 r.np.2 adv adv.c v.pai.2p
5251 1650 630 2779 7007 3836 4039 3836 4252 5555 899 1422 7007 4024 3437 1422

than they? **27** Who of you by worrying can add a single hour to his life? ¶ **28** "And why do
αὐτῶν δὲ τίς ἐξ ὑμῶν μεριμνῶν δύναται προσθεῖναι ἕνα πῆχυν ἐπὶ αὐτοῦ τὴν ἡλικίαν καὶ τί →
r.gpn.3 cj r.nsm p.g r.gp.2 pt.pa.nsm v.ppi.3s f.aa a.asm n.asm p.a r.gsm.3 d.asf n.asf cj r.asn
899 1254 5515 1666 7007 3534 1538 4707 1651 4388 2093 899 3836 2461 2779 5515

you worry about clothes? See how the lilies of the field grow. They do not labor or spin. **29** Yet I
→ μεριμνᾶτε περὶ ἐνδύματος καταμάθετε πῶς τὰ κρίνα → τοῦ ἀγροῦ αὐξάνουσιν → οὐ κοπιῶσιν οὐδὲ νήθουσιν δὲ →
v.pai.2p p.g n.gsn v.aam.2p pl d.apn n.apn d.gsm n.gsm v.pai.3p adv v.pai.3p cj v.pai.3p cj
3534 4309 1903 2908 4802 3836 3211 3836 69 889 3159 3159 4024 3159 4028 3756 1254

tell you that not even Solomon in all his splendor was dressed like one of these. **30** If that is how
λέγω ὑμῖν ὅτι οὐδὲ ← Σολομὼν ἐν πάσῃ τῇ δόξῃ → περιεβάλετο ὡς ἓν → τούτων δὲ εἰ οὕτως
v.pai.1s r.dp.2 cj adv n.d a.dsf r.gsf.3 d.dsf n.dsf v.ami.3s conj a.nsn r.gpn cj cj adv
3306 7007 4022 4028 5048 1877 4246 899 3836 1518 4314 6055 1651 4047 1254 1623 4048

God clothes the grass of the field, which is here today and tomorrow is thrown into the fire, will
ὁ θεὸς ἀμφιέννυσιν τὸν χόρτον τοῦ ἀγροῦ ὄντα ← σήμερον καὶ αὔριον → βαλλόμενον εἰς κλίβανον
d.nsm n.nsm v.pai.3s d.asm n.asm d.gsm n.gsm pt.pa.asm adv cj adv pt.pp.asm p.a n.asm
3836 2536 314 3836 5965 3836 69 1639 4958 2779 892 965 1650 3106

he not much more clothe you, O you of little faith? **31** So do not worry, saying, 'What shall we eat?' or
οὐ πολλῷ μᾶλλον ὑμᾶς → → ὀλιγόπιστοι οὖν → μὴ μεριμνήσητε λέγοντες τί → φάγωμεν ἢ
pl a.dsn adv.c r.ap.2 a.vpm cj pl v.aas.2p pt.pa.npm r.asn v.aas.1p cj
4024 4498 3437 7007 3899 4036 3534 3590 3534 3306 5515 2266 2445

'What shall we drink?' or 'What shall we wear?' **32** For the pagans run after all these things, and your
τί → → πίωμεν ἢ τί → περιβαλώμεθα γὰρ τὰ ἔθνη ἐπιζητοῦσιν πάντα ταῦτα ← γὰρ ὑμῶν
r.asn v.aas.1p cj r.asn v.ams.1p cj d.npn n.npn v.pai.3p a.apn r.apn cj r.gp.2
5515 4403 2445 5515 4314 1142 3836 1620 2118 4246 4047 1142 7007

heavenly Father knows that you need them. **33** But seek first his kingdom and his
ὁ οὐράνιος ὁ πατὴρ οἶδεν ὅτι → χρῄζετε τούτων ἁπάντων δὲ ζητεῖτε πρῶτον τὴν βασιλείαν [τοῦ θεοῦ] καὶ αὐτοῦ
d.nsm a.nsm d.nsm n.nsm v.rai.3s cj v.pai.2p r.gpn a.gpn cj v.pam.2p adv d.asf n.asf d.gsm n.gsm cj r.gsm.3
3836 4039 3836 4252 3857 4022 5974 4047 570 1254 2426 4754 3836 993 3836 2536 2779 899

righteousness, and all these things will be given to you as well. **34** Therefore do not worry about
τὴν δικαιοσύνην καὶ πάντα ταῦτα → προστεθήσεται ὑμῖν οὖν → μὴ μεριμνήσητε εἰς
d.asf n.asf cj a.npn r.npn v.fpi.3s r.dp.2 cj pl v.aas.2p p.a
3836 1466 2779 4246 4047 4707 7007 4707 4707 4036 3534 3590 3534 1650

tomorrow, for tomorrow will worry about itself. Each day has enough trouble of its own.
τὴν αὔριον γὰρ ἡ αὔριον → μεριμνήσει → ἑαυτῆς τῇ ἡμέρᾳ ἀρκετὸν ἡ κακία → αὐτῆς ←
d.asf adv cj d.nsf adv v.fai.3s r.gsf.3 d.dsf n.dsf a.nsn d.nsf n.nsf r.gsf.3
3836 892 1142 3836 892 3534 1571 899 3836 2465 757 3836 2798 899

6:25 Διὰ τοῦτο λέγω ὑμῖν, μὴ μεριμνᾶτε τῇ ψυχῇ ὑμῶν τί φάγητε [ἢ τί πίητε], μηδὲ τῷ σώματι ὑμῶν τί ἐνδύσησθε. οὐχὶ ἡ ψυχὴ πλεῖόν ἐστιν τῆς τροφῆς καὶ τὸ σῶμα τοῦ ἐνδύματος; **26** ἐμβλέψατε εἰς τὰ πετεινὰ τοῦ οὐρανοῦ ὅτι οὐ σπείρουσιν οὐδὲ θερίζουσιν οὐδὲ συνάγουσιν εἰς ἀποθήκας, καὶ ὁ πατὴρ ὑμῶν ὁ οὐράνιος τρέφει αὐτά· οὐχ ὑμεῖς μᾶλλον διαφέρετε αὐτῶν; **27** τίς δὲ ἐξ ὑμῶν μεριμνῶν δύναται προσθεῖναι ἐπὶ τὴν ἡλικίαν αὐτοῦ πῆχυν ἕνα; ¶ **28** καὶ περὶ ἐνδύματος τί μεριμνᾶτε; καταμάθετε τὰ κρίνα τοῦ ἀγροῦ πῶς αὐξάνουσιν· οὐ κοπιῶσιν οὐδὲ νήθουσιν· **29** λέγω δὲ ὑμῖν ὅτι οὐδὲ Σολομὼν ἐν πάσῃ τῇ δόξῃ αὐτοῦ περιεβάλετο ὡς ἓν τούτων. **30** εἰ δὲ τὸν χόρτον τοῦ ἀγροῦ σήμερον ὄντα καὶ αὔριον εἰς κλίβανον βαλλόμενον ὁ θεὸς οὕτως ἀμφιέννυσιν, οὐ πολλῷ μᾶλλον ὑμᾶς, ὀλιγόπιστοι; **31** μὴ οὖν μεριμνήσητε λέγοντες, Τί φάγωμεν; ἤ, Τί πίωμεν; ἤ, Τί περιβαλώμεθα; **32** πάντα γὰρ ταῦτα τὰ ἔθνη ἐπιζητοῦσιν· οἶδεν γὰρ ὁ πατὴρ ὑμῶν ὁ οὐράνιος ὅτι χρῄζετε τούτων ἁπάντων. **33** ζητεῖτε δὲ πρῶτον τὴν βασιλείαν [τοῦ θεοῦ] καὶ τὴν δικαιοσύνην αὐτοῦ, καὶ ταῦτα πάντα προστεθήσεται ὑμῖν. **34** μὴ οὖν μεριμνήσητε εἰς τὴν αὔριον, ἡ γὰρ αὔριον μεριμνήσει ἑαυτῆς· ἀρκετὸν τῇ ἡμέρᾳ ἡ κακία αὐτῆς.

Judging Others

7:1 "Do not judge, or you too will be judged. **2** For in the same way you judge others, you will

Μὴ κρίνετε ἵνα μὴ | κριθῆτε γὰρ ἐν ᾧ | κρίματι κρίνετε
pl v.pam.2p cj pl — v.aps.2p cj p.d r.dsn — n.dsn v.pai.2p
3212 3590 3212 2671 3590 — 3212 1142 1877 4005 — 3210 3212

be judged, and with the measure you use, it will be measured to you. ¶ **3** "Why do you look at the

κριθήσεσθε καὶ ἐν ᾧ μέτρῳ μετρεῖτε μετρηθήσεται ὑμῖν δὲ τί βλέπεις τὸ
v.fpi.2p cj p.d r.dsn n.dsn v.pai.2p v.fpi.3s r.dp.2 cj r.asn v.pai.2s d.asn
3212 2779 1877 4005 3586 3582 3582 7007 1254 5515 1063 3836

speck of sawdust in your brother's eye and pay no attention to the plank in your own eye? **4**

κάρφος τὸ ἐν σου τοῦ ἀδελφοῦ τῷ ὀφθαλμῷ δὲ οὐ κατανοεῖς τὴν δοκὸν ἐν σῷ τῷ ὀφθαλμῷ ἢ
n.asn d.asn p.d r.gs.2 d.gsm n.gsm d.dsm n.dsm cj adv v.pai.2s d.asf n.asf p.d r.dsm.2 d.dsm n.dsm cj
2847 3836 1877 5148 3836 81 3836 4057 1254 2917 4024 2917 3836 1512 1877 5050 3836 4057 2445

How can you say to your brother, 'Let me take the speck out of your eye,' when all the time

πῶς ἐρεῖς σου τῷ ἀδελφῷ ἄφες ἐκβάλω τὸ κάρφος ἐκ σου τοῦ ὀφθαλμοῦ καὶ ἰδοὺ
pl v.fai.2s r.gs.2 d.dsm n.dsm v.aam.2s v.aas.1s d.asn n.asn p.g r.gs.2 d.gsm n.gsm cj j
4802 3306 81 5148 3836 81 918 1675 3836 2847 1666 5148 3836 4057 2779 2627

there is a plank in your own eye? **5** You hypocrite, first take the plank out of your own eye, and then

ἡ δοκὸς ἐν σοῦ τῷ ὀφθαλμῷ ὑποκριτά πρῶτον ἔκβαλε τὴν δοκὸν ἐκ σοῦ τοῦ ὀφθαλμοῦ καὶ τότε
d.nsf n.nsf p.d r.gs.2 d.dsm n.dsm n.vsm adv v.aam.2s d.asf n.asf p.g r.gs.2 d.gsm n.gsm cj adv
3836 1512 1877 5148 3836 4057 5695 4754 1675 3836 1512 1666 5148 3836 4057 2779 5538

you will see clearly to remove the speck from your brother's eye. ¶ **6** "Do not give dogs

διαβλέψεις ἐκβαλεῖν τὸ κάρφος ἐκ σου τοῦ ἀδελφοῦ τοῦ ὀφθαλμοῦ Μὴ δῶτε τοῖς κυσὶν
v.fai.2s f.aa d.asn n.asn p.g r.gs.2 d.gsm n.gsm d.gsm n.gsm pl v.aas.2p d.dpm n.dpm
1332 1675 3836 2847 1666 5148 3836 81 3836 4057 3590 1443 3836 3264

what is sacred; do not throw your pearls to pigs. If you do, they may trample them

τὸ ἅγιον μηδὲ βάλητε ὑμῶν τοὺς μαργαρίτας ἔμπροσθεν τῶν χοίρων μήποτε καταπατήσουσιν αὐτοὺς
d.asn a.asn cj v.aas.2p r.gp.2 d.apm n.apm p.g d.gpm n.gpm cj v.fai.3p r.apm.3
3836 41 3593 965 7007 3836 3449 1869 3836 5956 3607 2922 899

under their feet, and then turn and tear you to pieces.

ἐν αὐτῶν τοῖς ποσὶν καὶ στραφέντες ῥήξωσιν ὑμᾶς
p.d r.gpm.3 d.dpm n.dpm cj pt.ap.npm v.aas.3p r.ap.2
1877 899 3836 4546 2779 5138 4838 7007 4838 4838

Ask, Seek, Knock

7:7 "Ask and it will be given to you; seek and you will find; knock and the door will be opened to you.

Αἰτεῖτε καὶ δοθήσεται ὑμῖν ζητεῖτε καὶ εὑρήσετε κρούετε καὶ ἀνοιγήσεται ὑμῖν
v.pam.2p cj v.fpi.3s r.dp.2 v.pam.2p cj v.fai.2p v.pam.2p cj v.fpi.3s r.dp.2
160 2779 1443 7007 2426 2779 2351 3218 2779 487 7007

8 For everyone who asks receives; he who seeks finds; and to him who knocks, the door will be opened. ¶

γὰρ πᾶς ὁ αἰτῶν λαμβάνει καὶ ὁ ζητῶν εὑρίσκει καὶ τῷ κρούοντι ἀνοιγήσεται
cj a.nsm d.nsm pt.pa.nsm v.pai.3s cj d.nsm pt.pa.nsm v.pai.3s cj d.dsm pt.pa.dsm v.fpi.3s
1142 4246 3836 160 3284 2779 3836 2426 2351 2779 3836 3218 487

9 "Which of you, if his son asks for bread, will give him a stone? **10** Or if he

ἢ τίς ἐξ ὑμῶν ἐστιν ἄνθρωπος ὃν αὐτοῦ ὁ υἱὸς αἰτήσει ἄρτον μὴ ἐπιδώσει αὐτῷ λίθον ἢ καὶ
cj r.nsm p.g r.gp.2 v.pai.3s n.nsm r.asm r.gsm.3 d.nsm n.nsm v.fai.3s n.asm pl v.fai.3s r.dsm.3 n.asm cj adv
2445 5515 1666 7007 1639 476 4005 899 3836 5626 160 788 3590 2113 899 3345 2445 2779

asks for a fish, will give him a snake? **11** If you, then, though you are evil, know how to give good

αἰτήσει ἰχθὺν μὴ ἐπιδώσει αὐτῷ ὄφιν εἰ ὑμεῖς οὖν ὄντες πονηροὶ οἴδατε διδόναι ἀγαθὰ
v.fai.3s n.asm pl v.fai.3s r.dsm.3 n.asm cj r.np.2 cj pt.pa.npm a.npm v.rai.2p f.pa a.apn
160 2716 3590 2113 899 4058 1623 7007 4036 1639 4505 3857 1443 19

gifts to your children, how much more will your Father in heaven give good gifts to those who

δόματα ὑμῶν τοῖς τέκνοις πόσῳ μᾶλλον ὑμῶν ὁ πατὴρ ὁ ἐν τοῖς οὐρανοῖς δώσει ἀγαθὰ τοῖς
n.apn r.gp.2 d.dpn n.dpn r.dsn adv.c r.gp.2 d.nsm n.nsm d.nsm p.d d.dpm n.dpm v.fai.3s a.apn d.dpm
1517 5451 7007 3836 5451 4531 3437 1443 7007 3836 4252 3836 1877 3836 4041 1443 19 3836

7:1 Μὴ κρίνετε, ἵνα μὴ κριθῆτε· **2** ἐν ᾧ γὰρ κρίματι κρίνετε κριθήσεσθε, καὶ ἐν ᾧ μέτρῳ μετρεῖτε μετρηθήσεται ὑμῖν. ¶ **3** τί δὲ βλέπεις τὸ κάρφος τὸ ἐν τῷ ὀφθαλμῷ τοῦ ἀδελφοῦ σου, τὴν δὲ ἐν τῷ σῷ ὀφθαλμῷ δοκὸν οὐ κατανοεῖς; **4** ἢ πῶς ἐρεῖς τῷ ἀδελφῷ σου, Ἄφες ἐκβάλω τὸ κάρφος ἐκ τοῦ ὀφθαλμοῦ σου, καὶ ἰδοὺ ἡ δοκὸς ἐν τῷ ὀφθαλμῷ σοῦ; **5** ὑποκριτά, ἔκβαλε πρῶτον ἐκ τοῦ ὀφθαλμοῦ σοῦ τὴν δοκόν, καὶ τότε διαβλέψεις ἐκβαλεῖν τὸ κάρφος ἐκ τοῦ ὀφθαλμοῦ τοῦ ἀδελφοῦ σου. ¶ **6** Μὴ δῶτε τὸ ἅγιον τοῖς κυσὶν μηδὲ βάλητε τοὺς μαργαρίτας ὑμῶν ἔμπροσθεν τῶν χοίρων, μήποτε καταπατήσουσιν αὐτοὺς ἐν τοῖς ποσὶν αὐτῶν καὶ στραφέντες ῥήξωσιν ὑμᾶς.

7:7 Αἰτεῖτε καὶ δοθήσεται ὑμῖν, ζητεῖτε καὶ εὑρήσετε, κρούετε καὶ ἀνοιγήσεται ὑμῖν· **8** πᾶς γὰρ ὁ αἰτῶν λαμβάνει καὶ ὁ ζητῶν εὑρίσκει καὶ τῷ κρούοντι ἀνοιγήσεται. ¶ **9** ἢ τίς ἐστιν ἐξ ὑμῶν ἄνθρωπος, ὃν ἐὰν αἰτήσῃ «αἰτήσει» ὁ υἱὸς αὐτοῦ ἄρτον, μὴ λίθον ἐπιδώσει αὐτῷ; **10** ἢ καὶ ἰχθὺν αἰτήσει, μὴ ὄφιν ἐπιδώσει αὐτῷ; **11** εἰ οὖν ὑμεῖς πονηροὶ ὄντες οἴδατε δόματα ἀγαθὰ διδόναι τοῖς τέκνοις ὑμῶν, πόσῳ μᾶλλον ὁ πατὴρ ὑμῶν ὁ ἐν τοῖς οὐρανοῖς δώσει ἀγαθὰ τοῖς αἰτοῦσιν αὐτόν. **12** Πάντα οὖν ὅσα ἐὰν

ask	him!	**12** So	in everything,		do	to others	what	you would		have	them		do	to
αἰτοῦσιν	αὐτόν	οὖν Πάντα		οὕτως καὶ	ὑμεῖς ποιεῖτε →	αὐτοῖς	ὅσα ἐὰν →	θέλητε	ἵνα →		οἱ ἄνθρωποι		ποιῶσιν →	
pt.pa.dpm	r.asm.3	cj a.apn		adv adv	r.np.2 v.pam.2p	r.dpm.3	r.apn pl	v.pas.2p	cj		d.npm n.npm		v.pas.3p	
160	899	4036 4246		4048 2779	7007 4472	899	4012 1569	2527	2671		3836 4/6		4472	

you,	for	this	sums up	the Law	and	the Prophets.
ὑμῖν	γὰρ	οὗτος	ἐστιν ←	ὁ νόμος	καὶ	οἱ προφῆται
r.dp.2	cj	r.nsm	v.pai.3s	d.nsm n.nsm	cj	d.npm n.npm
7007	1142	4047	1639	3836 3795	2779	3836 4737

The Narrow and Wide Gates

7:13 "Enter	through	the narrow	gate.	For wide		is the	gate	and	broad		is the	road	that	leads		to
Εἰσέλθατε	διὰ	τῆς στενῆς	πύλης	ὅτι πλατεῖα		ἡ	πύλη	καὶ	εὐρύχωρος		ἡ	ὁδὸς	ἡ	ἀπάγουσα		εἰς
v.aam.2p	p.g	d.gsf a.gsf	n.gsf	ὅτι a.nsf		d.nsf	n.nsf	cj	a.nsf		d.nsf	n.nsf	d.nsf	pt.pa.nsf		p.a
1656	1328	3836 5101	4783	4022 4426		3836	4783	2779	2353		3836	3847	3836	552		1650

destruction,	and	many	enter		through it.		**14** But small	is the	gate	and	narrow	the	road	that	leads
⌞τὴν ἀπώλειαν⌟	καὶ	πολλοί	⌞εἰσιν οἱ εἰσερχόμενοι⌟		δι' αὐτῆς		στενὴ	ἡ	πύλη	καὶ	τεθλιμμένη	ἡ	ὁδὸς	ἡ	ἀπάγουσα
d.asf n.asf	cj	a.npm	v.pai.3p d.npm pt.pm.npm		p.g r.gsf.3		a.nsf	d.nsf	n.nsf	cj	pt.rp.nsf	d.nsf	n.nsf	d.nsf	pt.pa.nsf
3836 724	2779	4498	1639 3836 1656		1328 899		5101	3836	4783	2779	2567	3836	3847	3836	552

to life,		and	only a few	find		it.
εἰς	⌞τὴν ζωὴν⌟	καὶ	ὀλίγοι	⌞εἰσιν οἱ εὑρίσκοντες⌟		αὐτήν
p.a	d.asf n.asf	cj	a.npm	v.pai.3p d.npm pt.pa.npm		r.asf.3
1650	3836 2437	2779	3900	1639 3836 2351		899

A Tree and Its Fruit

7:15 "Watch	out	for	false prophets.		They	come	to	you	in	sheep's	clothing,	but	inwardly	they	are
Προσέχετε ←	ἀπὸ →		⌞τῶν ψευδοπροφητῶν⌟		οἵτινες	ἔρχονται	πρὸς	ὑμᾶς	ἐν	προβάτων	ἐνδύμασιν	δὲ	ἔσωθεν →		εἰσιν
v.pam.2p	p.g		d.gpm n.gpm		r.npm	v.pmi.3p	p.a	r.ap.2	p.d	n.gpn	n.dpn	cj	adv		v.pai.3p
4668	608		3836 6021		4015	2262	4639	7007	1877	4585	1903	1254	2277		1639

ferocious	wolves.	**16** By their	fruit		you will recognize	them.	Do	people	pick		grapes	from	thornbushes,
ἅρπαγες	λύκοι	ἀπὸ αὐτῶν	⌞τῶν καρπῶν⌟ →	→	ἐπιγνώσεσθε	αὐτούς	μήτι →		συλλέγουσιν		σταφυλὰς	ἀπὸ	ἀκανθῶν
a.npm	n.npm	p.g r.gpm.3	d.gpm n.gpm		v.fmi.2p	r.apm.3	pl		v.pai.3p		n.apf	p.g	n.gpf
774	3380	608 899	3836 2843		2105	899	3614		5198		5091	608	180

or	figs	from	thistles?	**17** Likewise	every	good	tree	bears	good	fruit,	but	a bad	tree		bears	bad
ἢ	σῦκα	ἀπὸ	τριβόλων	οὕτως	πᾶν	ἀγαθὸν	δένδρον	ποιεῖ	καλοὺς	καρπούς	δὲ	σαπρὸν	⌞τὸ δένδρον⌟		ποιεῖ	πονηροὺς
cj	n.apn	p.g	n.gpm	adv	a.nsn	a.nsn	n.nsn	v.pai.3s	a.apm	n.apm	cj	a.nsn	d.nsn n.nsn		v.pai.3s	a.apm
2445	5192	608	5560	4048	4246	19	1285	4472	2819	2843	1254	4911	3836 1285		4472	4505

fruit.	**18** A good	tree	cannot		bear	bad	fruit,	and	a bad	tree	cannot	bear	good	fruit.	**19** Every
καρπούς	ἀγαθὸν	δένδρον	⌞οὐ δύναται⌟		ποιεῖν	πονηροὺς	καρπούς	οὐδὲ	σαπρὸν	δένδρον		ποιεῖν	καλοὺς	καρπούς	πᾶν
n.apm	a.nsn	n.nsn	adv v.ppi.3s		f.pa	a.apm	n.apm	cj	a.nsn	n.nsn		t.pa	a.apm	n.apm	a.nsn
2843	19	1285	4024 1538		4472	4505	2843	4028	4911	1285		4472	2819	2843	4246

tree	that does not	bear	good	fruit	is cut		down	and	thrown	into	the	fire.	**20** Thus,	by	their	fruit	you
δένδρον	μὴ	ποιοῦν	καλὸν	καρπὸν	ἐκκόπτεται			καὶ	βάλλεται	εἰς		πῦρ	⌞ἄρα γε⌟	ἀπὸ	⌞τῶν καρπῶν⌟	→	
n.nsn	pl	pt.pa.nsn	a.asm	n.asm	v.ppi.3s			cj	v.ppi.3s	p.a		n.asn	cj pl	p.g	d.gpm n.gpm		
1285	4472 3590	4472	2819	2843	1716			2779	965	1650		4786	726 1145	608	899 3836 2843		

will recognize	them.	¶	**21** "Not	everyone	who	says	to me,	'Lord,	Lord,'		will	enter		the	kingdom	of
→ ἐπιγνώσεσθε	αὐτούς		Οὐ	πᾶς	ὁ	λέγων →	μοι	κύριε	κύριε	→		εἰσελεύσεται	εἰς	τὴν	βασιλείαν	→
v.fmi.2p	r.apm.3		adv	a.nsm	d.nsm	pt.pa.nsm	r.ds.1	n.vsm	n.vsm			v.fmi.3s	p.a	d.asf	n.asf	
2105	899		4024	4246	3836	3306	1609	3261	3261			1656	1650	3836	993	

heaven,	but	only he	who	does	the	will	of	my	Father	who	is	in	heaven.	**22** Many	will say		to	me
⌞τῶν οὐρανῶν⌟	ἀλλ'	ὁ	←	ποιῶν	τὸ	θέλημα	⌞μου	τοῦ πατρός⌟		τοῦ		ἐν	⌞τοῖς οὐρανοῖς⌟	πολλοί	→ ἐροῦσιν		μοι	
d.gpm n.gpm	cj	d.nsm		pt.pa.nsm	d.asn	n.asn	r.gs.1	d.gsm n.gsm		d.gsm		p.d	d.dpm n.dpm	a.npm	v.fai.3p		r.ds.1	
3836 4041	247	3836		4472	3836	2525	4252	1609 4252		3836		1877	3836 4041	4498	3306		1609	

on	that	day,	'Lord,	Lord,	did	we	not	prophesy		in	your	name,	and	in	your	name	drive	out
ἐν	ἐκείνῃ	⌞τῇ ἡμέρᾳ⌟	κύριε	κύριε			οὐ	ἐπροφητεύσαμεν →			σῷ	⌞τῷ ὀνόματι⌟	καὶ →		σῷ	⌞τῷ ὀνόματι⌟	ἐξεβάλομεν	→
p.d	r.dsf	d.dsf n.dsf	n.vsm	n.vsm	pl		v.aai.1p				r.dsn.2	d.dsn n.dsn	cj		r.dsn.2	d.dsn n.dsn	v.aai.1p	
1877	1697	3836 2465	3261	3261	4736	4736	4024	4736			3950	5050 3836 3950	2779		3950	5050 3836 3950	1675	

θέλητε ἵνα ποιῶσιν ὑμῖν οἱ ἄνθρωποι, οὕτως καὶ ὑμεῖς ποιεῖτε αὐτοῖς· οὗτος γάρ ἐστιν ὁ νόμος καὶ οἱ προφῆται.

7:13 Εἰσέλθατε διὰ τῆς στενῆς πύλης· ὅτι πλατεῖα ἡ πύλη καὶ εὐρύχωρος ἡ ὁδὸς ἡ ἀπάγουσα εἰς τὴν ἀπώλειαν καὶ πολλοί εἰσιν οἱ εἰσερχόμενοι δι' αὐτῆς· **14** ὅτι δὲ «τί» στενὴ ἡ πύλη καὶ τεθλιμμένη ἡ ὁδὸς ἡ ἀπάγουσα εἰς τὴν ζωὴν καὶ ὀλίγοι εἰσιν οἱ εὑρίσκοντες αὐτήν.

7:15 Προσέχετε ἀπὸ τῶν ψευδοπροφητῶν, οἵτινες ἔρχονται πρὸς ὑμᾶς ἐν ἐνδύμασιν προβάτων, ἔσωθεν δέ εἰσιν λύκοι ἅρπαγες. **16** ἀπὸ τῶν καρπῶν αὐτῶν ἐπιγνώσεσθε αὐτούς. μήτι συλλέγουσιν ἀπὸ ἀκανθῶν σταφυλὰς ἢ ἀπὸ τριβόλων σῦκα; **17** οὕτως πᾶν δένδρον ἀγαθὸν καρποὺς καλοὺς ποιεῖ, τὸ δὲ σαπρὸν δένδρον καρποὺς πονηροὺς ποιεῖ. **18** οὐ δύναται δένδρον ἀγαθὸν καρποὺς πονηροὺς ποιεῖν οὐδὲ δένδρον σαπρὸν καρποὺς καλοὺς ποιεῖν. **19** πᾶν δένδρον μὴ ποιοῦν καρπὸν καλὸν ἐκκόπτεται καὶ εἰς πῦρ βάλλεται. **20** ἄρα γε ἀπὸ τῶν καρπῶν αὐτῶν ἐπιγνώσεσθε αὐτούς. ¶ **21** Οὐ πᾶς ὁ λέγων μοι, Κύριε κύριε, εἰσελεύσεται εἰς τὴν βασιλείαν τῶν οὐρανῶν, ἀλλ' ὁ ποιῶν τὸ θέλημα τοῦ πατρός μου τοῦ ἐν τοῖς οὐρανοῖς. **22** πολλοὶ ἐροῦσίν μοι ἐν ἐκείνῃ τῇ ἡμέρᾳ, Κύριε κύριε, οὐ τῷ σῷ ὀνόματι ἐπροφητεύσαμεν, καὶ τῷ σῷ ὀνόματι δαιμόνια ἐξεβάλομεν, καὶ τῷ σῷ

demons and | | | perform many miracles?' **23** Then I will tell | them plainly, | 'I | never knew
δαιμόνια καὶ τῷ σῷ ὀνόματι ἐποιήσαμεν πολλὰς δυνάμεις | καὶ τότε → ὁμολογήσω αὐτοῖς | ὅτι → οὐδέποτε ἔγνων
n.apn / cj / d.dsn / r.dsn.2 / n.dsn / v.aai.1p / a.apf / n.apf / cj / adv / v.fai.1s / r.dpm.3 / cj / adv / v.aai.1s
1228 / 2779 / 3836 / 5050 / 3950 / 4472 / 4498 / 1539 / 2779 / 5538 / 3933 / 899 / 3933 / 4022 / 1182 / 4030 / 1182

you. Away | from me, you evildoers!'
ὑμᾶς ἀποχωρεῖτε ἀπ' ἐμοῦ οἱ ἐργαζόμενοι τὴν ἀνομίαν
r.ap.2 / v.pam.2p / p.g / r.gs.1 / r.vpm / d.vpm / pt.pm.vpm / d.asf / n.asf
7007 / 713 / 608 / 1609 / 3836 / 2237 / 3836 / 490

The Wise and Foolish Builders

7:24 "Therefore everyone who hears these words | of mine and puts them into practice is like | a
οὖν Πᾶς ὅστις ἀκούει τούτους τοὺς λόγους μου καὶ ποιεῖ αὐτοὺς ← → ὁμοιωθήσεται
cj / a.nsm / r.nsm / r.pai.3s / r.apm / d.apm / n.apm / r.gs.1 / cj / v.pai.3s / r.apm.3 / v.fpi.3s
4036 / 4246 / 4015 / 201 / 4047 / 3836 / 3364 / 1609 / 2779 / 4472 / 899 / 4472 / 4472 / 3929

wise man who built his house on the rock. **25** The rain came down, the streams rose, and the
φρονίμῳ ἀνδρὶ ὅστις ᾠκοδόμησεν αὐτοῦ τὴν οἰκίαν ἐπὶ τὴν πέτραν καὶ ἡ βροχὴ κατέβη ← καὶ οἱ ποταμοὶ ἦλθον καὶ οἱ
a.dsm / n.dsm / r.nsm / v.aai.3s / r.gsm.3 / d.asf / n.asf / p.a / d.asf / n.asf / cj / d.nsf / n.nsf / v.aai.3s / cj / d.npm / n.npm / v.aai.3p / cj / d.npm
5861 / 467 / 4015 / 3868 / 899 / 3836 / 3864 / 2093 / 3836 / 4376 / 2779 / 3836 / 1104 / 2849 / 2779 / 3836 / 4532 / 2262 / 2779 / 3836

winds blew and beat against that house; yet it did not fall, because it had its foundation on the rock.
ἄνεμοι ἔπνευσαν καὶ προσέπεσαν ἐκείνῃ τῇ οἰκίᾳ καὶ οὐκ ἔπεσεν γὰρ τεθεμελίωτο ἐπὶ τὴν πέτραν
n.npm / v.aai.3p / cj / v.aai.3p / r.dsf / d.dsf / n.dsf / cj / adv / v.aai.3s / cj / v.lpi.3s / p.a / d.asf / n.asf
449 / 4463 / 2779 / 4700 / 3864 / 1697 / 3836 / 3864 / 2779 / 4406 / 4406 / 4024 / 4406 / 1142 / 2530 / 2093 / 3836 / 4376

26 But everyone who hears these words | of mine and does not put them into practice is like | a foolish
καὶ πᾶς ὁ ἀκούων τούτους τοὺς λόγους μου καὶ μὴ ποιῶν αὐτοὺς ← → ὁμοιωθήσεται μωρῷ
cj / a.nsm / d.nsm / pt.pa.nsm / r.apm / d.apm / n.apm / r.gs.1 / cj / pl / pt.pa.nsm / r.apm.3 / v.fpi.3s / a.dsm
2779 / 4246 / 3836 / 201 / 4047 / 3836 / 3364 / 1609 / 2779 / 3590 / 4472 / 899 / 4472 / 4472 / 3929 / 3704

man who built his house on sand. **27** The rain came down, the streams rose, and the winds
ἀνδρὶ ὅστις ᾠκοδόμησεν αὐτοῦ τὴν οἰκίαν ἐπὶ τὴν ἄμμον καὶ ἡ βροχὴ κατέβη ← καὶ οἱ ποταμοὶ ἦλθον καὶ οἱ ἄνεμοι
n.dsm / r.nsm / v.aai.3s / r.gsm.3 / d.asf / n.asf / p.a / d.asf / n.asf / cj / d.nsf / n.nsf / v.aai.3s / cj / d.npm / n.npm / v.aai.3p / cj / d.npm / n.npm
467 / 4015 / 3868 / 899 / 3836 / 3864 / 2093 / 3836 / 302 / 2779 / 3836 / 1104 / 2849 / 2779 / 3836 / 4532 / 2262 / 2779 / 3836 / 449

blew and beat against that house, and it fell with a great crash." ¶ **28**
ἔπνευσαν καὶ προσέκοψαν ἐκείνῃ τῇ οἰκίᾳ καὶ → ἔπεσεν καὶ ἦν μεγάλη ἡ πτῶσις αὐτῆς Καὶ ἐγένετο
v.aai.3p / cj / v.aai.3p / r.dsf / d.dsf / n.dsf / cj / v.aai.3s / cj / v.iai.3s / a.nsf / d.nsf / n.nsf / r.gsf.3 / cj / v.ami.3s
4463 / 2779 / 4684 / 3864 / 1697 / 3836 / 3864 / 2779 / 4406 / 2779 / 1639 / 3489 / 3836 / 4774 / 899 / 2779 / 1181

When Jesus had finished saying these things, the crowds were amazed at his teaching, **29** because
ὅτε ὁ Ἰησοῦς → ἐτέλεσεν τούτους τοὺς λόγους οἱ ὄχλοι → ἐξεπλήσσοντο ἐπὶ αὐτοῦ τῇ διδαχῇ γὰρ
cj / d.nsm / n.nsm / v.aai.3s / r.apm / d.apm / n.apm / d.npm / n.npm / v.ipi.3p / p.d / r.gsm.3 / d.dsf / n.dsf / cj
4021 / 3836 / 2652 / 5464 / 4047 / 3836 / 3364 / 3836 / 4063 / 1742 / 2093 / 899 / 3836 / 1439 / 1142

he taught as one who had authority, and not as their teachers of the law.
→ ἦν διδάσκων αὐτοὺς ὡς → ἔχων ἐξουσίαν καὶ οὐχ ὡς αὐτῶν οἱ γραμματεῖς
v.iai.3s / pt.pa.nsm / r.apm.3 / conj / pt.pa.nsm / n.asf / cj / adv / conj / r.gpm.3 / d.npm / n.npm
1639 / 1438 / 899 / 6055 / 2400 / 2026 / 2779 / 4024 / 6055 / 899 / 3836 / 1208

The Man With Leprosy

8:1 When he came down from the mountainside, large crowds followed him. **2** A man with
δὲ αὐτοῦ Καταβάντος ← ἀπὸ τοῦ ὄρους πολλοί ὄχλοι ἠκολούθησαν αὐτῷ καὶ ἰδοὺ →
cj / r.gsm.3 / pt.aa.gsm / p.g / d.gsn / n.gsn / a.npm / n.npm / v.aai.3p / r.dsm.3 / cj / j
1254 / 2849 / 899 / 2849 / 608 / 3836 / 4001 / 4498 / 4063 / 199 / 899 / 2779 / 2627

leprosy came and knelt before him and said, "Lord, if you are willing, you can make me clean." ¶
λεπρὸς προσελθὼν προσεκύνει ← αὐτῷ λέγων κύριε ἐὰν → θέλῃς → δύνασαι → με καθαρίσαι
a.nsm / pt.aa.nsm / v.iai.3s / r.dsm.3 / pt.pa.nsm / n.vsm / cj / v.pas.2s / v.ppi.2s / r.as.1 / f.aa
3320 / 4665 / 4686 / 899 / 3306 / 3261 / 1569 / 2527 / 1538 / 2751 / 1609 / 2751

3 Jesus reached out his hand and touched the man. "I am willing," he said. "Be clean!" Immediately he
καὶ ἐκτείνας ← τὴν χεῖρα ἥψατο αὐτοῦ θέλω λέγων καθαρίσθητι καὶ εὐθέως
cj / pt.aa.nsm / d.asf / n.asf / v.ami.3s / r.gsm.3 / v.pai.1s / pt.pa.nsm / v.apm.2s / cj / adv
2779 / 1753 / 3836 / 5931 / 721 / 899 / 2527 / 3306 / 2751 / 2779 / 2311

ὀνόματι δυνάμεις πολλὰς ἐποιήσαμεν; ²³ καὶ τότε ὁμολογήσω αὐτοῖς ὅτι Οὐδέποτε ἔγνων ὑμᾶς· ἀποχωρεῖτε ἀπ' ἐμοῦ οἱ ἐργαζόμενοι τὴν ἀνομίαν.

⁷:²⁴ Πᾶς οὖν ὅστις ἀκούει μου τοὺς λόγους τούτους καὶ ποιεῖ αὐτούς, ὁμοιωθήσεται ἀνδρὶ φρονίμῳ, ὅστις ᾠκοδόμησεν αὐτοῦ τὴν οἰκίαν ἐπὶ τὴν πέτραν· ²⁵ καὶ κατέβη ἡ βροχὴ καὶ ἦλθον οἱ ποταμοὶ καὶ ἔπνευσαν οἱ ἄνεμοι καὶ προσέπεσαν τῇ οἰκίᾳ ἐκείνῃ, καὶ οὐκ ἔπεσεν, τεθεμελίωτο γὰρ ἐπὶ τὴν πέτραν. ²⁶ καὶ πᾶς ὁ ἀκούων μου τοὺς λόγους τούτους καὶ μὴ ποιῶν αὐτοὺς ὁμοιωθήσεται ἀνδρὶ μωρῷ, ὅστις ᾠκοδόμησεν αὐτοῦ τὴν οἰκίαν ἐπὶ τὴν ἄμμον· ²⁷ καὶ κατέβη ἡ βροχὴ καὶ ἦλθον οἱ ποταμοὶ καὶ ἔπνευσαν οἱ ἄνεμοι καὶ προσέκοψαν τῇ οἰκίᾳ ἐκείνῃ, καὶ ἔπεσεν καὶ ἦν ἡ πτῶσις αὐτῆς μεγάλη. ¶ ²⁸ Καὶ ἐγένετο ὅτε ἐτέλεσεν ὁ Ἰησοῦς τοὺς λόγους τούτους, ἐξεπλήσσοντο οἱ ὄχλοι ἐπὶ τῇ διδαχῇ αὐτοῦ· ²⁹ ἦν γὰρ διδάσκων αὐτοὺς ὡς ἐξουσίαν ἔχων καὶ οὐχ ὡς οἱ γραμματεῖς αὐτῶν.

⁸:¹ Καταβάντος δὲ αὐτοῦ ἀπὸ τοῦ ὄρους ἠκολούθησαν αὐτῷ ὄχλοι πολλοί. ² καὶ ἰδοὺ λεπρὸς προσελθὼν προσεκύνει αὐτῷ λέγων, Κύριε, ἐὰν θέλῃς δύνασαί με καθαρίσαι. ¶ ³ καὶ ἐκτείνας τὴν χεῖρα ἥψατο αὐτοῦ λέγων, Θέλω, καθαρίσθητι· καὶ εὐθέως ἐκαθαρίσθη αὐτοῦ ἡ λέπρα. ⁴ καὶ λέγει αὐτῷ ὁ Ἰησοῦς, Ὅρα μηδενὶ εἴπῃς, ἀλλὰ ὕπαγε σεαυτὸν δεῖξον τῷ ἱερεῖ καὶ προσένεγκον

was cured   of his   leprosy.   **4** Then Jesus   said to him, "See that you don't tell anyone. But go, show
→ ἐκαθαρίσθη ← αὐτοῦ ἡ λέπρα καὶ ὁ Ἰησοῦς λέγει αὐτῷ ὅρα   → μηδενὶ εἴπῃς ← ἀλλὰ ὕπαγε δεῖξον
v.api.3s   r.gsm.3 d.nsf n.nsf cj   d.nsm n.nsm v.pai.3s r.dsm.3 v.pam.2s   a.dsm v.aas.2s   247 v.pam.2s v.aam.2s
2751   899   3836 3319 2779 3836 2652 3306   899   3972   3594 3306 3594   247 5632   1259

yourself to the priest and offer   the gift   Moses commanded, as a testimony to them."
σεαυτὸν → τῷ ἱερεῖ καὶ προσένεγκον τὸ δῶρον ὃ Μωϋσῆς προσέταξεν εἰς μαρτύριον → αὐτοῖς
r.asm.2   d.dsm n.dsm cj v.aam.2s   d.asn n.asn r.asn n.nsm v.aai.3s p.a n.asn   r.dpm.3
4932   3836 2636 2779 4712   3836 1565 4005 3707 4705   1650 3457   899

The Faith of the Centurion

8:5 When Jesus had entered   Capernaum, a centurion   came   to him, asking   for help.   **6**
δὲ → αὐτοῦ → Εἰσελθόντος εἰς Καφαρναοὺμ ἑκατόνταρχος προσῆλθεν ← αὐτῷ παρακαλῶν ← ← αὐτὸν καὶ
1254 1656 r.gsm.3   pt.aa.gsm   p.a n.asf   n.nsm   v.aai.3s   r.dsm.3 pt.pa.nsm   r.asm.3
     1656 899   1656   1650 3019   1672   4665   899   4151   899   2779

"Lord," he said, "my servant lies   at home   paralyzed and in terrible suffering." **7** Jesus said to him,
κύριε → λέγων μου ὁ παῖς βέβληται ἐν τῇ οἰκίᾳ παραλυτικός   δεινῶς βασανιζόμενος καὶ   λέγει → αὐτῷ
n.vsm   pt.pa.nsm r.gs.1 d.nsm n.nsm v.rpi.3s p.d d.dsf n.dsf a.nsm   adv   pt.pp.nsm   cj   v.pai.3s r.dsm.3
3261   3306 1609 3836 4090 965   1877 3836 3864 4166   1267   989   2779 3306   899

"I will go   and heal   him."   ¶ **8** The centurion   replied,   "Lord, I do not deserve to have
ἐγὼ → ἐλθὼν θεραπεύσω αὐτόν   καὶ ὁ ἑκατόνταρχος ἀποκριθεὶς ἔφη   κύριε → εἰμι οὐκ ἱκανὸς ἵνα →
r.ns.1   pt.aa.nsm v.fai.1s r.asm.3 cj d.nsm n.nsm   pt.ap.nsm v.iai.3s n.vsm   v.pai.1s adv a.nsm   cj
1609   2262   2543   899   2779 3836 1672   646   5774 3261   1639 4024 2653   2671

you come   under my roof. But just   say the word, and my servant   will be healed. **9** For I myself am
→ εἰσέλθῃς ὑπὸ μου τὴν στέγην ἀλλὰ μόνον εἰπὲ   λόγῳ καὶ μου ὁ παῖς → → ἰαθήσεται γὰρ καὶ ἐγὼ εἰμι
v.aas.2s   p.a r.gs.1 d.asf n.asf cj adv   v.aam.2s n.dsm cj r.gs.1 d.nsm n.nsm v.fpi.3s cj adv r.ns.1 v.pai.1s
1656   5679 1609 3836 5094 247 3667   3306   3364 2779 1609 3836 4090   2615   1142 2779 1639 1609 1639

a man   under authority, with soldiers   under me.   I tell this one, 'Go,'   and he goes;   and that
ἄνθρωπος ὑπὸ ἐξουσίαν, ἔχων στρατιώτας ὑπ' ἐμαυτὸν καὶ λέγω τούτῳ ←   πορεύθητι καὶ → πορεύεται καὶ ἄλλῳ
n.nsm   p.a n.asf   pt.pa.nsm n.apm p.a r.asm.1 cj v.pai.1s r.dsm   v.apm.2s cj   v.pmi.3s cj r.dsm
476   5679 2026   2400   5132   5679 1831   2779 3306 4047   4513   2779 4513   2779 257

one, 'Come,' and he comes. I say to my servant, 'Do this,' and he does it." ¶ **10** When Jesus
← ἔρχου καὶ → ἔρχεται καὶ   → μου τῷ δούλῳ ποίησον τοῦτο καὶ → ποιεῖ   δὲ → ὁ Ἰησοῦς
v.pmm.2s cj v.pmi.3s cj   r.gs.1 d.dsm n.dsm v.aam.2s r.asn cj v.pai.3s   1254 201 d.nsm n.nsm
2262   2779 2262   2779   1529 1609 3836 1529 4472   4047 2779 4472   1254 201 3836 2652

heard this, he was astonished and said to those following   him, "I tell you the truth, I have not found
ἀκούσας → ἐθαύμασεν καὶ εἶπεν → τοῖς ἀκολουθοῦσιν   → λέγω ὑμῖν ἀμὴν →   οὐδενὶ εὗρον παρ'
pt.aa.nsm   v.aai.3s cj v.aai.3s d.dpm pt.pa.dpm   v.pai.1s r.dp.2 pl   a.dsm v.aai.1s p.d
201   2513   2779 3306   3836 199   3306 7007 297   2351 2351   4029 2351   4123

anyone in Israel   with such great   faith. **11** I say to you that many will come from the east   and the
← ἐν τῷ Ἰσραὴλ   τοσαύτην πίστιν δὲ → λέγω ὑμῖν ὅτι πολλοὶ → ἥξουσιν ἀπὸ ἀνατολῶν καὶ
    p.d d.dsm n.dsm   r.asf   n.asf cj v.pai.1s r.dp.2 cj a.npm v.fai.3p p.g n.gpf   cj
4029 1877 3836 2702   5537   4411 1254 3306 7007 4022 4498 2457   608 424   2779

west, and will take   their places at the feast with Abraham, Isaac and Jacob in the kingdom of
δυσμῶν καὶ → ἀνακλιθήσονται ←   μετὰ Ἀβραὰμ καὶ Ἰσαὰκ καὶ Ἰακὼβ ἐν τῇ βασιλείᾳ
n.gpf cj   v.fpi.3p   p.g n.gsm   cj n.gsm cj n.gsm p.d d.dsf n.dsf
1553   2779 369   3552 11   2779 2693 2779 2609 1877 3836 993

heaven. **12** But the subjects of the kingdom will be thrown   outside,   into the darkness, where there will
τῶν οὐρανῶν, δὲ οἱ υἱοὶ → τῆς βασιλείας → ἐκβληθήσονται τὸ ἐξώτερον εἰς τὸ σκότος ἐκεῖ → →
d.gpm n.gpm cj d.npm n.npm d.gsf n.gsf   v.fpi.3p   d.asn a.asn.c p.a d.asn n.asn adv
3836 4041   1254 3836 5626 3836 993   1675   3836 2035   1650 3836 5030 1695

be weeping   and gnashing of teeth." ¶ **13** Then Jesus   said to the centurion, "Go! It will be
ἔσται ὁ κλαυθμὸς καὶ ὁ βρυγμὸς → τῶν ὀδόντων   καὶ ὁ Ἰησοῦς εἶπεν τῷ ἑκατοντάρχῃ ὕπαγε → →
v.fmi.3s d.nsm n.nsm cj d.nsm n.nsm d.gpm n.gpm   cj d.nsm n.nsm v.aai.3s d.dsm n.dsm v.pam.2s
1639 3836 3088 2779 3836 1106   3836 3848   2779 3836 2652 3306   3836 1672   5632

done   just as you believed it would." And his servant was healed at that very hour.
γενηθήτω σοι → ὡς → ἐπίστευσας   καὶ αὐτοῦ ὁ παῖς → ἰάθη ἐν ἐκείνῃ τῇ ὥρᾳ
v.apm.3s r.ds.2 cj v.aai.2s   cj r.gsm.3 d.nsm n.nsm v.api.3s p.d r.dsf d.dsf n.dsf
1181   5148 6055 4409   2779 899 3836 4090   2615   1877 1697 3836 6052

τὸ δῶρον ὃ προσέταξεν Μωϋσῆς, εἰς μαρτύριον αὐτοῖς.

8:5 Εἰσελθόντος δὲ αὐτοῦ εἰς Καφαρναοὺμ προσῆλθεν αὐτῷ ἑκατόνταρχος παρακαλῶν αὐτὸν **6** καὶ λέγων, Κύριε, ὁ παῖς μου βέβληται ἐν τῇ οἰκίᾳ παραλυτικός, δεινῶς βασανιζόμενος. **7** καὶ λέγει αὐτῷ, Ἐγὼ ἐλθὼν θεραπεύσω αὐτόν. ¶ **8** καὶ ἀποκριθεὶς ὁ ἑκατόνταρχος ἔφη, Κύριε, οὐκ εἰμι ἱκανὸς ἵνα μου ὑπὸ τὴν στέγην εἰσέλθῃς, ἀλλὰ μόνον εἰπὲ λόγῳ, καὶ ἰαθήσεται ὁ παῖς μου. **9** καὶ γὰρ ἐγὼ ἄνθρωπός εἰμι ὑπὸ ἐξουσίαν, ἔχων ὑπ' ἐμαυτὸν στρατιώτας, καὶ λέγω τούτῳ, Πορεύθητι, καὶ πορεύεται, καὶ ἄλλῳ, Ἔρχου, καὶ ἔρχεται, καὶ τῷ δούλῳ μου, Ποίησον τοῦτο, καὶ ποιεῖ. ¶ **10** ἀκούσας δὲ ὁ Ἰησοῦς ἐθαύμασεν καὶ εἶπεν τοῖς ἀκολουθοῦσιν, Ἀμὴν λέγω ὑμῖν, παρ' οὐδενὶ τοσαύτην πίστιν ἐν τῷ Ἰσραὴλ εὗρον. **11** λέγω δὲ ὑμῖν ὅτι πολλοὶ ἀπὸ ἀνατολῶν καὶ δυσμῶν ἥξουσιν καὶ ἀνακλιθήσονται μετὰ Ἀβραὰμ καὶ Ἰσαὰκ καὶ Ἰακὼβ ἐν τῇ βασιλείᾳ τῶν οὐρανῶν, **12** οἱ δὲ υἱοὶ τῆς βασιλείας ἐκβληθήσονται εἰς τὸ σκότος τὸ ἐξώτερον· ἐκεῖ ἔσται ὁ κλαυθμὸς καὶ ὁ βρυγμὸς τῶν ὀδόντων. ¶ **13** καὶ εἶπεν ὁ Ἰησοῦς τῷ ἑκατοντάρχῃ, Ὕπαγε, ὡς ἐπίστευσας γενηθήτω σοι. καὶ ἰάθη ὁ παῖς [αὐτοῦ] ἐν τῇ ὥρᾳ ἐκείνῃ.

8:14 Καὶ ἐλθὼν ὁ Ἰησοῦς εἰς τὴν οἰκίαν Πέτρου εἶδεν τὴν πενθερὰν αὐτοῦ βεβλημένην καὶ πυρέσσουσαν· **15** καὶ ἥψατο τῆς

Jesus Heals Many

8:14

When Jesus came into Peter's house, he saw Peter's mother-in-law lying in bed with a
Καὶ → ὁ Ἰησοῦς, ἐλθὼν εἰς Πέτρου ⌐τὴν οἰκίαν⌐ → εἶδεν αὐτοῦ ⌐τὴν πενθερὰν⌐ βεβλημένην ← καὶ →
cj d.nsm n.nsm pt.aa.nsm p.a n.gsm d.asf n.asf v.aai.3s r.gsm.3 d.asf n.asf pt.rp.asf cj
2779 2262 3836 2652 2262 1650 4377 3836 3864 1625 899 3836 4289 965 2779

fever. **15** He touched her hand and the fever left her, and she got up and began to wait on
πυρέσσουσαν καὶ → ἥψατο αὐτῆς ⌐τῆς χειρός⌐ καὶ ὁ πυρετός ἀφῆκεν αὐτὴν καὶ → ἠγέρθη ← καὶ → → διηκόνει →
pt.pa.asf cj v.ami.3s r.gsf.3 d.gsf n.gsf cj d.nsm n.nsm v.aai.3s r.asf.3 cj v.api.3s cj v.iai.3s
4789 2779 721 899 3836 5931 2779 3836 4790 918 899 2779 1586 2779 1354

him. ¶ **16** When evening came, many who were demon-possessed were brought to him, and he drove
αὐτῷ δὲ → Ὀψίας γενομένης πολλούς → → δαιμονιζομένους → προσήνεγκαν → αὐτῷ καὶ → ἐξέβαλεν
r.dsm.3 cj n.gsf pt.am.gsf a.apm pt.pp.apm v.aai.3p r.dsm.3 cj v.aai.3s
899 1254 1181 4068 1181 4498 1227 4712 899 2779 1675

out the spirits with a word and healed all the sick. **17** This was to fulfill what was spoken through
← τὰ πνεύματα → λόγῳ καὶ ἐθεράπευσεν πάντας τοὺς ⌐κακῶς ἔχοντας⌐ ὅπως πληρωθῇ τὸ → ῥηθὲν διὰ
d.apn n.apn n.dsm cj v.aai.3s a.apm d.apm adv pt.pa.apm cj v.aps.3s d.nsn pt.ap.nsn p.g
3836 4460 3364 2779 2543 4246 3836 2809 2400 3968 4444 3836 3306 1328

the prophet Isaiah: "He took up our infirmities and carried our diseases."
τοῦ προφήτου Ἠσαΐου λέγοντος αὐτὸς ἔλαβεν ← ἡμῶν ⌐τὰς ἀσθενείας⌐ καὶ ἐβάστασεν τὰς νόσους
d.gsm n.gsm n.gsm pt.pa.gsm r.nsm v.aai.3s r.gp.1 d.apf n.apf cj v.aai.3s d.apf n.apf
3836 4737 2480 3306 899 3284 7005 3836 819 2779 1002 3836 3798

The Cost of Following Jesus

8:18

When Jesus saw the crowd around him, he gave orders to cross to the other side of the lake.
δὲ → ὁ Ἰησοῦς, ἰδὼν ὄχλον περὶ αὐτὸν ἐκέλευσεν → ἀπελθεῖν εἰς τὸ πέραν
cj d.nsm n.nsm pt.aa.nsm n.asm p.a r.asm.3 v.aai.3s f.aa p.a d.asn adv
1254 1625 3836 2652 1625 4063 4309 899 3027 599 1650 3836 4305

19 Then a teacher of the law came to him and said, "Teacher, I will follow you wherever you go." **20**
καὶ εἷς γραμματεὺς ← ← προσελθὼν αὐτῷ εἶπεν διδάσκαλε → ἀκολουθήσω σοι ⌐ὅπου ἐὰν⌐ → ἀπέρχῃ καὶ
cj a.nsm n.nsm pt.aa.nsm r.ds.3 v.aai.3s n.vsm v.fai.1s r.ds.2 pl v.pms.2s cj
2779 1651 1208 4665 899 3306 1437 199 5148 3963 1569 599 2779

Jesus replied, "Foxes have holes and birds of the air have nests, but the Son of
ὁ Ἰησοῦς, λέγει αὐτῷ ⌐αἱ ἀλώπεκες⌐ ἔχουσιν φωλεοὺς καὶ ⌐τὰ πετεινὰ⌐ → τοῦ οὐρανοῦ → κατασκηνώσεις δὲ ὁ υἱὸς →
d.nsm n.nsm v.pai.3s r.dsm.3 d.npf n.npf v.pai.3p n.apm cj d.npn n.npn d.gsm n.gsm n.apf cj d.nsm n.nsm
3836 2652 3306 899 3836 273 2400 5887 2779 3836 4374 3836 4041 2943 1254 3836 5626

Man has no place to lay his head." ¶ **21** Another disciple said to him, "Lord, first
⌐τοῦ ἀνθρώπου⌐ ἔχει οὐκ ποῦ → κλίνῃ τὴν κεφαλὴν δὲ ἕτερος ⌐τῶν μαθητῶν⌐ [αὐτοῦ] εἶπεν → αὐτῷ κύριε πρῶτον
d.gsm n.gsm v.pai.3s adv adv v.pas.3s d.asf n.asf cj r.nsm d.gpm n.gpm r.gsm.3 v.aai.3s r.dsm.3 n.vsm adv
3836 476 2400 4024 4543 3111 3836 3051 1254 2283 3836 3412 899 3306 899 3261 4754

let me go and bury my father." **22** But Jesus told him, "Follow me, and let the dead bury
ἐπίτρεψόν μοι ἀπελθεῖν καὶ θάψαι μου ⌐τὸν πατέρα⌐ δὲ ὁ Ἰησοῦς, λέγει αὐτῷ ἀκολούθει μοι καὶ ἄφες τοὺς νεκροὺς θάψαι
v.aam.2s r.ds.1 f.aa cj f.aa r.gs.1 d.asm n.asm cj d.nsm n.nsm v.pai.3s r.dsm.3 v.pam.2s r.ds.1 cj v.aam.2s d.apm a.apm f.aa
2205 1609 599 2779 2507 1609 3836 4252 1254 3836 2652 3306 899 199 1609 2779 918 3836 3738 2507

their own dead."
τοὺς ἑαυτῶν νεκρούς
d.apm r.gpm.3 a.apm
3836 1571 3738

Jesus Calms the Storm

8:23 Then he got into the boat and his disciples followed him. **24** *Without warning,* a furious storm
Καὶ αὐτῷ ἐμβάντι εἰς τὸ πλοῖον αὐτοῦ ⌐οἱ μαθηταὶ⌐ ἠκολούθησαν αὐτῷ καὶ ἰδοὺ μέγας σεισμός
cj r.dsm.3 pt.aa.dsm p.a d.asn n.asn r.gsm.3 d.npm n.npm v.aai.3p r.dsm.3 cj j a.nsm n.nsm
2779 899 1832 1650 3836 4450 899 3836 3412 199 899 2779 2627 3489 4939

came up on the lake, so that the waves swept over the boat. But Jesus was sleeping. **25** The
ἐγένετο ← ἐν τῇ θαλάσσῃ ὥστε → ὑπὸ τῶν κυμάτων καλύπτεσθαι ← τὸ πλοῖον δὲ αὐτὸς → ἐκάθευδεν καὶ
v.ami.3s p.d d.dsf n.dsf cj p.g d.gpn n.gpn f.pp d.asn n.asn cj r.nsm v.iai.3s cj
1181 1877 3836 2498 6063 5679 3836 3246 2821 3836 4450 1254 899 2761 2779

χειρὸς αὐτῆς, καὶ ἀφῆκεν αὐτὴν ὁ πυρετός, καὶ ἠγέρθη καὶ διηκόνει αὐτῷ. ¶ **16** Ὀψίας δὲ γενομένης προσήνεγκαν αὐτῷ δαιμονιζομένους πολλούς· καὶ ἐξέβαλεν τὰ πνεύματα λόγῳ καὶ πάντας τοὺς κακῶς ἔχοντας ἐθεράπευσεν, **17** ὅπως πληρωθῇ τὸ ῥηθὲν διὰ Ἠσαΐου τοῦ προφήτου λέγοντος, Αὐτὸς τὰς ἀσθενείας ἡμῶν ἔλαβεν καὶ τὰς νόσους ἐβάστασεν. **8:18** Ἰδὼν δὲ ὁ Ἰησοῦς ὄχλον περὶ αὐτὸν ἐκέλευσεν ἀπελθεῖν εἰς τὸ πέραν. **19** καὶ προσελθὼν εἷς γραμματεὺς εἶπεν αὐτῷ, Διδάσκαλε, ἀκολουθήσω σοι ὅπου ἐὰν ἀπέρχῃ **20** καὶ λέγει αὐτῷ ὁ Ἰησοῦς, Αἱ ἀλώπεκες φωλεοὺς ἔχουσιν καὶ τὰ πετεινὰ τοῦ οὐρανοῦ κατασκηνώσεις, ὁ δὲ υἱὸς τοῦ ἀνθρώπου οὐκ ἔχει ποῦ τὴν κεφαλὴν κλίνῃ. ¶ **21** ἕτερος δὲ τῶν μαθητῶν [αὐτοῦ] εἶπεν αὐτῷ, Κύριε, ἐπίτρεψόν μοι πρῶτον ἀπελθεῖν καὶ θάψαι τὸν πατέρα μου. **22** ὁ δὲ Ἰησοῦς λέγει αὐτῷ, Ἀκολούθει μοι καὶ ἄφες τοὺς νεκροὺς θάψαι τοὺς ἑαυτῶν νεκρούς. **8:23** Καὶ ἐμβάντι αὐτῷ εἰς τὸ πλοῖον ἠκολούθησαν αὐτῷ οἱ μαθηταὶ αὐτοῦ. **24** καὶ ἰδοὺ σεισμὸς μέγας ἐγένετο ἐν τῇ θαλάσσῃ, ὥστε τὸ πλοῖον καλύπτεσθαι ὑπὸ τῶν κυμάτων, αὐτὸς δὲ ἐκάθευδεν. **25** καὶ προσελθόντες ἤγειραν αὐτὸν λέγοντες, Κύριε, σῶσον,

disciples went   and woke   him, saying, "Lord, save us! We're going to drown!"   ¶   26   He replied,
→   προσελθόντες   ἤγειραν   αὐτὸν λέγοντες κύριε   σῶσον   →   →   ἀπολλύμεθα   καὶ → λέγει
   pt.aa.npm   v.aai.3p   r.asm.3 pt.pa.npm n.vsm   v.aam.2s   v.pmi.1p   cj   v.pai.3s
   4665   1586   899   3306   3261   5392   660   2779   3306

"You of little faith,   why are you so afraid?" Then he got   up and rebuked the winds and the
αὐτοῖς →   →   →   ὀλιγόπιστοι τί   ἐστε   ←   δειλοί   τότε   →   ἐγερθεὶς ←   ἐπετίμησεν τοῖς ἀνέμοις καὶ τῇ
r.dpm.3   a.vpm   τί   ἐστε   δειλοί   adv   pt.ap.nsm   v.aai.3s   d.dpm n.dpm cj d.dsf
899   3899   5515   1639   1264   5538   1586   2203   3836 449   2779 3836

waves, and it was   completely calm.   27   The men   were amazed and asked, "What kind of man is   this?
θαλάσσῃ καὶ → ἐγένετο μεγάλη   γαλήνη   δὲ οἱ   ἄνθρωποι →   ἐθαύμασαν   λέγοντες ποταπός ←   ←   ἐστιν οὗτος
n.dsf   cj   v.ami.3s   a.nsf   n.nsf   cj d.npm n.npm   v.aai.3p   pt.pa.npm r.nsm   v.pai.3s r.nsm
2498   2779   1181   3489   1132   1254 3836 476   2513   3306 4534   1639 4047

Even the winds and the waves   obey   him!"
ὅτι καὶ   οἱ ἄνεμοι καὶ ἡ   θάλασσα ὑπακούουσιν αὐτῷ
cj   adv   d.npm n.npm cj d.nsf n.nsf   v.pai.3p   r.dsm.3
4022 2779   3836 449   2779 3836 2498   5634   899

The Healing of Two Demon-possessed Men

8:28   When he   arrived at the other side in the region of the Gadarenes, two demon-possessed men
Καὶ →   αὐτοῦ ἐλθόντος εἰς τὸ   πέραν ←   εἰς τὴν χώραν → τῶν Γαδαρηνῶν δύο δαιμονιζόμενοι ←
   cj   r.gsm.3 pt.aa.gsm p.a d.asn adv   p.a d.asf n.asf   d.gpm a.gpm   a.npm pt.pp.npm
2779 2262   899   2262   1650 3836 4305   1650 3836 6001   3836 1123   1545 1227

coming from the tombs met   him. They were so   violent that no one could pass   that way.
ἐξερχόμενοι ἐκ   τῶν μνημείων ὑπήντησαν αὐτῷ   λίαν χαλεποί ὥστε μὴ   τινὰ ἰσχύειν παρελθεῖν διὰ ἐκείνης ⌐τῆς ὁδοῦ⌐
pt.pm.npm p.g   d.gpn n.gpn   v.aai.3p   r.dsm.3   adv a.npm   cj pl   r.asm f.pa   f.aa   p.g ε.gsf d.gsf n.gsf
2002   1666   3836 3646   5636   899   3336 5901   6063 3590   5516 2710   4216   1328 1697 3836 3847

29 "What do   you want with us, Son of God?"   they shouted.   "Have you come here to torture
τί   καὶ σοί   ἡμῖν υἱὲ → ⌐τοῦ θεοῦ⌐ καὶ ἰδοὺ →   ἔκραξαν λέγοντες →   →   ἦλθες ὧδε → βασανίσαι
r.nsn   cj r.ds.2   r.dp.1 n.vsm   d.gsm n.gsm cj j   v.aai.3p pt.pa.npm   v.aai.2s adv   f.aa
5515   2779 5148   7005 5626   3836 2536   2779 2627   3189   3306   2262 6045   989

us before the appointed time?"   ¶   30   Some distance from them a large herd of pigs was feeding.
ἡμᾶς πρὸ   καιροῦ   δὲ ἦν   μακρὰν ἀπ' αὐτῶν πολλῶν ἀγέλη → χοίρων → βοσκομένη
r.ap.1 p.g   n.gsm   cj v.iai.3s   adv   p.g r.gpm.3 a.gpm n.nsf   n.gpm   pt.pp.nsf
7005 4574   2789   1254 1639   3426   608 899   4498 36   5956   1081

31   The demons begged   Jesus,   "If you drive   us   out, send   us   into the herd of pigs."
δὲ οἱ   δαίμονες παρεκάλουν αὐτὸν λέγοντες εἰ →   ἐκβάλλεις ἡμᾶς   ἀπόστειλον ἡμᾶς εἰς τὴν ἀγέλην → ⌐τῶν χοίρων⌐
cj d.npm   n.npm   v.iai.3p   r.asm.3 pt.pa.npm cj   v.pai.2s r.ap.1   v.aam.2s r.ap.1 p.a d.asf n.asf   d.gpm n.gpm
1254 3836   1230   4151   899   3306   1623   1675 1675   690   7005 1650 3836 36   3836 5956

32   He said to them, "Go!" So they came   out and went   into the pigs, and   the whole herd   rushed
καὶ → εἶπεν → αὐτοῖς ὑπάγετε δὲ οἱ ἐξελθόντες ←   ἀπῆλθον εἰς τοὺς χοίρους καὶ ἰδοὺ   πᾶσα ἡ ἀγέλη ὥρμησεν
cj → v.aai.3s   r.dpm.3 v.pam.2p δὲ οἱ   pt.aa.npm ←   v.aai.3p p.a d.apm n.npm cj j   a.nsf d.nsf n.nsf v.aai.3s
2779   3306   899   5632   1254 3836 2002   599   1650 3836 5956 2779 2627   4246 3836 36   3994

down the steep bank into the lake   and died   in the water. 33   Those tending the pigs ran   off,
κατὰ τοῦ → κρημνοῦ εἰς τὴν θάλασσαν καὶ ἀπέθανον ἐν τοῖς ὕδασιν   δὲ οἱ   βόσκοντες   ἔφυγον ←   καὶ
p.g d.gsm → n.gsm εἰς d.asf n.asf   cj v.aai.3p p.d d.dpn n.dpn   cj d.npm   pt.pa.npm   v.aai.3p   cj
2848 3836   3204   1650 3836 2498   2779 633   1877 3836 5623   1254 3836   1081   5771   2779

went   into the town and reported all   this, including what had happened to the demon-possessed men.
ἀπελθόντες εἰς τὴν πόλιν ἀπήγγειλαν πάντα   καὶ   τὰ   ←   →   τῶν δαιμονιζομένων
pt.aa.npm p.a d.asf n.asf   v.aai.3p   a.apn   cj   d.apn   d.gpm pt.pp.gpm
599   1650 3836 4484   550   4246   2779   3836   3836

34 Then   the whole town   went out to meet   Jesus.   And when they saw   him, they pleaded   with
καὶ ἰδοὺ   πᾶσα ἡ πόλις ἐξῆλθεν ←   εἰς ὑπάντησιν ⌐τῷ Ἰησοῦ⌐ καὶ →   ἰδόντες αὐτὸν → παρεκάλεσαν
cj j   a.nsf d.nsf n.nsf v.aai.3s   p.a n.asf   d.dsm n.dsm cj   pt.aa.npm r.asm.3   v.aai.3p
2779 2627   4246 3836 4484   2002   1650 5637   3836 2652   2779   1625 899   4151

him to   leave   their region.
ὅπως μεταβῇ ἀπὸ αὐτῶν ⌐τῶν ὁρίων⌐
cj   v.aas.3s p.g r.gpm.3 d.gpn n.gpn
3968   3553   608 899   3836 3990

ἡμᾶς ἀπολλύμεθα. ¶ 26 καὶ λέγει αὐτοῖς, Τί δειλοί ἐστε, ὀλιγόπιστοι; τότε ἐγερθεὶς ἐπετίμησεν τοῖς ἀνέμοις καὶ τῇ θαλάσσῃ, καὶ ἐγένετο γαλήνη μεγάλη. 27 οἱ δὲ ἄνθρωποι ἐθαύμασαν λέγοντες, Ποταπός ἐστιν οὗτος ὅτι καὶ οἱ ἄνεμοι καὶ ἡ θάλασσα αὐτῷ ὑπακούουσιν;

8:28 Καὶ ἐλθόντος αὐτοῦ εἰς τὸ πέραν εἰς τὴν χώραν τῶν Γαδαρηνῶν ὑπήντησαν αὐτῷ δύο δαιμονιζόμενοι ἐκ τῶν μνημείων ἐξερχόμενοι, χαλεποὶ λίαν, ὥστε μὴ ἰσχύειν τινὰ παρελθεῖν διὰ τῆς ὁδοῦ ἐκείνης. 29 καὶ ἰδοὺ ἔκραξαν λέγοντες, Τί ἡμῖν καὶ σοί, υἱὲ τοῦ θεοῦ; ἦλθες ὧδε πρὸ καιροῦ βασανίσαι ἡμᾶς; ¶ 30 ἦν δὲ μακρὰν ἀπ' αὐτῶν ἀγέλη χοίρων πολλῶν βοσκομένη. 31 οἱ δὲ δαίμονες παρεκάλουν αὐτὸν λέγοντες, Εἰ ἐκβάλλεις ἡμᾶς, ἀπόστειλον ἡμᾶς εἰς τὴν ἀγέλην τῶν χοίρων. 32 καὶ εἶπεν αὐτοῖς, Ὑπάγετε. οἱ δὲ ἐξελθόντες ἀπῆλθον εἰς τοὺς χοίρους· καὶ ἰδοὺ ὥρμησεν πᾶσα ἡ ἀγέλη κατὰ τοῦ κρημνοῦ εἰς τὴν θάλασσαν καὶ ἀπέθανον ἐν τοῖς ὕδασιν. 33 οἱ δὲ βόσκοντες ἔφυγον, καὶ ἀπελθόντες εἰς τὴν πόλιν ἀπήγγειλαν πάντα καὶ τὰ τῶν δαιμονιζομένων. 34 καὶ ἰδοὺ πᾶσα ἡ πόλις ἐξῆλθεν εἰς ὑπάντησιν τῷ Ἰησοῦ καὶ ἰδόντες αὐτὸν παρεκάλεσαν ὅπως μεταβῇ ἀπὸ τῶν ὁρίων αὐτῶν.

Jesus Heals a Paralytic

9:1

Jesus stepped	into	a boat,	crossed	over	and	came	to	his own	town.	**2**		Some men	brought	to
Καὶ ἐμβὰς	εἰς	πλοῖον	διεπέρασεν ←		καὶ	ἦλθεν	εἰς	τὴν ἰδίαν	πόλιν		καὶ ἰδοὺ		προσέφερον →	
cj pt.aa.nsm	p.a	n.asn	v.aai.3s		cj	v.aai.3s	p.a	d.asf a.asf	n.asf		cj j		v.iai.3p	
2779 1832	1650	4450	1385		2779	2262	1650	3836 2625	4484		2779 2627		4712	

him	a paralytic,	lying	on	a mat.	When	Jesus	saw	their	faith,	he said	to the	paralytic,	"Take
αὐτῷ	παραλυτικὸν	βεβλημένον	ἐπὶ	κλίνης	καὶ →	ὁ Ἰησοῦς	ἰδὼν	αὐτῶν	τὴν πίστιν	εἶπεν →	τῷ	παραλυτικῷ →	
r.dsm.3	a.asm	pt.rp.asm	p.g	n.gsf	cj	d.nsm n.nsm	pt.aa.nsm	r.gpm.3	d.asf n.asf	v.aai.3s	d.dsm	a.dsm	
899	4166	965	2093	3109	2779 1625	3836 2652	1625	899	3836 4411	3306	3836	4166	

heart,	son;	your	sins	are forgiven."	**3**	*At this*,	some	of the	teachers	of the law	said	to themselves,	"This
θάρσει	τέκνον	σου	αἱ ἁμαρτίαι →	ἀφίενται		καὶ ἰδού	τινες	τῶν	γραμματέων ←	←	εἶπαν	ἐν ἑαυτοῖς	οὗτος
v.pam.2s	n.vsn	r.gs.2	d.npf n.npf	v.ppi.3p		cj j	r.npm	d.gpm	n.gpm		v.aai.3p	p.d r.dpm.3	r.nsm
2510	5451	5148	3836 281	918		2779 2627	5516	3836	1208		3306	1877 1571	4047

fellow	is blaspheming!"	¶	**4**	Knowing	their	thoughts,	Jesus	said,	"Why	do you	entertain	evil
←	→ βλασφημεῖ			καὶ ἰδὼν	αὐτῶν	τὰς ἐνθυμήσεις	ὁ Ἰησοῦς	εἶπεν	ἱνατί	→ →	ἐνθυμεῖσθε	πονηρὰ
	v.pai.3s			cj pt.aa.nsm	r.gpm.3	d.apf n.apf	d.nsm n.nsm	v.aai.3s	cj		v.pmi.2p	a.apf
	1059			2779 1625	899	3836 1927	3836 2652	3306	2672		1926	4505

thoughts	in	your	hearts?	**5**	Which	is	easier:	to say,	'Your	sins	are forgiven,'	or	to say,
ἐν	ὑμῶν	ταῖς	καρδίαις		γάρ	τί	ἐστιν	εὐκοπώτερον →	εἰπεῖν	σου	αἱ ἁμαρτίαι →	ἀφίενται	ἢ →	εἰπεῖν
p.d	r.gp.2	d.dpf	n.dpf		cj	r.nsn	v.pai.3s	a.nsn.c	f.aa	r.gs.2	d.npf n.npf	v.ppi.3p	cj	f.aa
1877	7007	3836	2840		1142	5515	1639	2324	3306	5148	3836 281	918	2445	3306

'Get up	and	walk'?	**6**	But	so	that	you	may	know	that	the	Son	of Man	has	authority	on	earth	to	forgive
ἔγειρε ←	καὶ	περίπάτει	δὲ	ἵνα ←		→		→	εἰδῆτε	ὅτι	ὁ	υἱὸς	τοῦ ἀνθρώπου	ἔχει	ἐξουσίαν	ἐπὶ	τῆς γῆς	→	ἀφιέναι
v.pam.2s	cj	v.pam.2s	cj	cj					v.ras.2p	cj	d.nsm	n.nsm	d.gsm n.gsm	v.pai.3s	n.asf	p.g	d.gsf n.gsf		f.pa
1586	2779	4344	1254	2671					3857	4022	3836	5626	3836 476	2400	2026	2093	3836 1178		918

sins	...."	Then	he said	to the	paralytic,	"Get	up,	take	your	mat	and	go	home."	**7**	And	the
ἁμαρτίας	τότε	→	λέγει	τῷ	παραλυτικῷ	ἐγερθεὶς	→	ἆρον	σου	τὴν κλίνην	καὶ	ὕπαγε	εἰς τὸν οἶκον		καὶ	→
n.apf	adv		v.pai.3s	d.dsm	n.dsm	pt.ap.nsm		v.aam.2s	r.gs.2	d.asf n.asf	cj	v.pam.2s	p.a d.asm n.asm		cj	
281	5538		3306	3836	4166	1586		149	5148	3836 3109	2779	5632	1650 3836 3875		5148	2779

man	got	up	and went	home.	**8**	When	the	crowd	saw	this,	they	were	filled	with	awe;	and
→	ἐγερθεὶς ←		ἀπῆλθεν εἰς	τὸν οἶκον	αὐτοῦ	δὲ	→	οἱ ὄχλοι	ἰδόντες						ἐφοβήθησαν	καὶ
	pt.ap.nsm		v.aai.3s p.a	d.asm n.asm	r.gsm.3	cj		d.npm n.npm	pt.aa.npm						v.api.3p	cj
	1586		599 1650	3836 3875	899	1254 1625		3836 4063	1625						5828	2779

they	praised	God,	who	had	given	such	authority	to	men.
→	ἐδόξασαν	τὸν θεὸν	τὸν	→	δόντα	τοιαύτην	ἐξουσίαν	τοῖς	ἀνθρώποις
	v.aai.3p	d.asm n.asm	d.asm		pt.aa.asm	r.asf	n.asf	d.dpm	n.dpm
	1519	3836 2536	3836		1443	5525	2026	3836	476

The Calling of Matthew

9:9

As	Jesus	went	on	from there,	he saw	a man	named	Matthew	sitting	at	the	tax
Καὶ →	ὁ Ἰησοῦς	παράγων ←	→	ἐκεῖθεν	εἶδεν	ἄνθρωπον	λεγόμενον	Μαθθαῖον	καθήμενον	ἐπὶ	τὸ	
cj	d.nsm n.nsm	pt.pa.nsm	adv	adv	v.aai.3s	n.asm	pt.pp.asm	n.asm	pt.pm.asm	p.a	d.asn	
2779	4135 3836 2652	4135		1696	1625	476	3306	3414	2764	2093	3836	

collector's	booth.	"Follow	me,"	he told	him,	and	Matthew	got	up	and	followed	him.	¶	**10**
τελώνιον	καὶ	ἀκολούθει	μοι	→ λέγει	αὐτῷ	καὶ		ἀναστὰς ←			ἠκολούθησεν	αὐτῷ		καὶ ἐγένετο
n.asn	cj	v.pam.2s	r.ds.1	v.pai.3s	r.dsm.3	cj		pt.aa.nsm			v.aai.3s	r.dsm.3		cj v.ami.3s
5468	2779	199	1609	3306	899	2779		482			199	899		2779 1181

While	Jesus	was	having	dinner	at	Matthew's	house,		many	tax	collectors	and	"sinners"	came	and
→	αὐτοῦ	→	→	ἀνακειμένου	ἐν		τῇ οἰκίᾳ	καὶ ἰδοὺ	πολλοὶ	→	τελῶναι	καὶ	ἁμαρτωλοὶ	ἐλθόντες	
	r.gsm.3			pt.pm.gsm	p.d		d.dsf n.dsf	cj j	a.npm		n.npm	cj	a.npm	pt.aa.npm	
	367			367	1877		3836 3864	2779 2627	4498		5467	2779	283	2262	

ate	with	him	and	his	disciples.	**11**	When	the	Pharisees	saw	this,	they	asked	his
συνανέκειντο ←	τῷ	Ἰησοῦ	καὶ	αὐτοῦ	τοῖς μαθηταῖς		καὶ →	οἱ	Φαρισαῖοι	ἰδόντες		they	ἔλεγον	αὐτοῦ
v.imi.3p	d.dsm	n.dsm	cj	r.gsm.3	d.dpm n.dpm		cj	d.npm	n.npm	pt.aa.npm			v.iai.3p	r.gsm.3
5263	3836	2652	2779	899	3836 3412		2779 1625	3836	5757	1625			3306	899

9:1 Καὶ ἐμβὰς ὁ Ἰησοῦς εἰς πλοῖον διεπέρασεν καὶ ἦλθεν εἰς τὴν ἰδίαν πόλιν. ² καὶ ἰδοὺ προσέφερον αὐτῷ παραλυτικὸν ἐπὶ κλίνης βεβλημένον. καὶ ἰδὼν ὁ Ἰησοῦς τὴν πίστιν αὐτῶν εἶπεν τῷ παραλυτικῷ, Θάρσει, τέκνον, ἀφίενταί σου αἱ ἁμαρτίαι. ³ καὶ ἰδού τινες τῶν γραμματέων εἶπαν ἐν ἑαυτοῖς, Οὗτος βλασφημεῖ. ¶ ⁴ καὶ εἰδὼς «ἰδὼν» ὁ Ἰησοῦς τὰς ἐνθυμήσεις αὐτῶν εἶπεν, Ἱνατί ἐνθυμεῖσθε πονηρὰ ἐν ταῖς καρδίαις ὑμῶν; ⁵ τί γάρ ἐστιν εὐκοπώτερον, εἰπεῖν, Ἀφίενταί σου αἱ ἁμαρτίαι, ἢ εἰπεῖν, Ἔγειρε καὶ περιπάτει; ⁶ ἵνα δὲ εἰδῆτε ὅτι ἐξουσίαν ἔχει ὁ υἱὸς τοῦ ἀνθρώπου ἐπὶ τῆς γῆς ἀφιέναι ἁμαρτίας τότε λέγει τῷ παραλυτικῷ, Ἐγερθεὶς ἆρόν σου τὴν κλίνην καὶ ὕπαγε εἰς τὸν οἶκόν σου. ⁷ καὶ ἐγερθεὶς ἀπῆλθεν εἰς τὸν οἶκον αὐτοῦ. ⁸ ἰδόντες δὲ οἱ ὄχλοι ἐφοβήθησαν καὶ ἐδόξασαν τὸν θεὸν τὸν δόντα ἐξουσίαν τοιαύτην τοῖς ἀνθρώποις.

9:9 Καὶ παράγων ὁ Ἰησοῦς ἐκεῖθεν εἶδεν ἄνθρωπον καθήμενον ἐπὶ τὸ τελώνιον, Μαθθαῖον λεγόμενον, καὶ λέγει αὐτῷ, Ἀκολούθει μοι. καὶ ἀναστὰς ἠκολούθησεν αὐτῷ. ¶ ¹⁰ Καὶ ἐγένετο αὐτοῦ ἀνακειμένου ἐν τῇ οἰκίᾳ, καὶ ἰδοὺ πολλοὶ τελῶναι καὶ ἁμαρτωλοὶ ἐλθόντες συνανέκειντο τῷ Ἰησοῦ καὶ τοῖς μαθηταῖς αὐτοῦ. ¹¹ καὶ ἰδόντες οἱ Φαρισαῖοι ἔλεγον τοῖς μαθηταῖς

disciples,	"Why	does your	teacher		eat	with	tax collectors	and 'sinners'?"	¶	**12**	On hearing
τοῖς μαθηταῖς	διὰ τί	→ ὑμῶν ὁ	διδάσκαλος		ἐσθίει μετὰ →		τῶν τελωνῶν	καὶ ἁμαρτωλῶν		δὲ →	ἀκούσας
d.dpm n.dpm	p.a r.asn	r.gp.2 d.nsm n.nsm			v.pai.3s p.g		d.gpm n.gpm	cj a.gpm		cj	pt.aa.nsm
3836 3412	1328 5515	2266 7007 3836 1437			2266 3552		3836 5467	2779 283		1254	201

this, Jesus said,	"It is not the	healthy	who need		a doctor,	but	the sick.	**13** But	go		and learn
ὁ εἶπεν	οὐ οἱ	ἰσχύοντες	χρείαν ἔχουσιν		ἰατροῦ	ἀλλ᾽ οἱ	κακῶς ἔχοντες	δὲ	πορευθέντες		μάθετε
d.nsm v.aai.3s	adv d.npm	pt.pa.npm	n.asf v.pai.3p		n.gsm	cj d.npm	adv pt.pa.npm	cj	pt.ap.npm		v.aam.2p
3836 3306	4024 3836	2710	5970 2400		2620	247 3836	2809 2400	1254	4513		3443

what this means:	'I desire	mercy,		not sacrifice.'	For I		have not	come	to call	the righteous,	but	sinners."
τί → ἐστιν	θέλω	ἔλεος	καὶ	οὐ θυσίαν	γὰρ		οὐ	ἦλθον	καλέσαι	δικαίους	ἀλλὰ	ἁμαρτωλούς
r.nsn v.pai.3s	v.pai.1s	n.asn	cj	adv n.asf	cj		adv	v.aai.1s	f.aa	a.apm	cj	a.apm
5515 1639	2527	1799	2779	4024 2602	1142	2262 2262	4024	2262	2813	1465	247	283

Jesus Questioned About Fasting

9:14 Then	John's	disciples	came		and asked	him,	"How	is it that	we	and the	Pharisees
Τότε	Ἰωάννου	οἱ μαθηταὶ	προσέρχονται	αὐτῷ	λέγοντες	↰	διὰ τί	↰	ἡμεῖς	καὶ οἱ	Φαρισαῖοι
adv	n.gsm	d.npm n.npm	v.pmi.3p	r.dsm.3	pt.pa.npm		p.a r.asn		r.np.1	cj d.npm	n.npm
5538	2722	3836 3412	4665	899	3306		1328 5515		7005	2779 3836	5757

fast,	but your	disciples	do not fast?"	**15**	Jesus		answered,		"How can	the
νηστεύομεν [πολλά]	δὲ σου οἱ μαθηταὶ		οὐ νηστεύουσιν	καὶ ὁ Ἰησοῦς	εἶπεν		αὐτοῖς μὴ		δύνανται	οἱ
v.pai.1p a.apn	cj r.gs.2 d.npm n.npm		adv v.pai.3p	cj d.nsm n.nsm	v.aai.3s		r.dpm.3 pl		v.ppi.3p	d.npm
3764 4498	1254 5148 3836 3412		3764 4024 3764	2779 3836 2652	3306		899 3590		1538	3836

guests	of the	bridegroom	mourn	while	he		is	with them?	The time	will come	when	the
υἱοὶ	→ τοῦ	νυμφῶνος	πενθεῖν	ἐφ᾽ ὅσον	ὁ	νυμφίος	ἐστιν	μετ᾽ αὐτῶν	δὲ ἡμέραι →	ἐλεύσονται	ὅταν	ὁ
n.npm	d.gsm	n.gsm	f.pa	p.a r.asm	d.nsm	n.nsm	v.pai.3s	p.g r.gpm.3	cj n.npf	v.fmi.3p	pl	d.nsm
5626	3836	3813	4291	2093 4012	3836	3812	1639	3552 899	1254 2465	2262	4020	3836

bridegroom	will be taken	from them;		then	they will fast.	¶	**16**	"No one	sews	a patch	of
νυμφίος	→ → ἀπαρθῇ ἀπ᾽	αὐτῶν	καὶ	τότε →	νηστεύσουσιν		δὲ →	οὐδεὶς	ἐπιβάλλει	ἐπίβλημα →	
n.nsm	v.aps.3s p.g	r.gpm.3	cj	adv	v.fai.3p		cj	a.nsm	v.pai.3s	n.asn	
3812	554 608	899	2779	5538	3764		1254	4029	2095	2099	

unshrunk	cloth	on an	old	garment,	for the	patch		will pull	away	from	the	garment,		making	the
ἀγνάφου	ῥάκους	ἐπὶ	παλαιῷ	ἱματίῳ	γὰρ τὸ	πλήρωμα	αὐτοῦ →	αἴρει		ἀπὸ	τοῦ	ἱματίου	καὶ	γίνεται	
a.gsn	n.gsn	p.d	a.dsn	n.dsn	cj d.asn	n.asn	r.gsn.3	v.pai.3s		p.g	d.gsn	n.gsn	cj	v.pmi.3s	
47	4820	2093	4094	2668	1142 3836	4445	899	149		608	3836	2668	2779	1181	

tear	worse.	**17** Neither	do men	pour		new	wine	into	old		wineskins.	If	they do,	the skins	will burst,
σχίσμα	χεῖρον	οὐδὲ	→	βάλλουσιν	νέον	οἶνον	εἰς	παλαιούς	ἀσκούς		δὲ εἰ		οἱ	ἀσκοὶ →	ῥήγνυνται	καὶ
n.nsn	a.nsn.c	cj		v.pai.3p	a.asm	n.asm	p.a	a.apm	n.apm		cj cj		d.npm n.npm		v.ppi.3p	cj
5388	5937	4028		965	3742	3885	1650	4094	829		1254 1623		3836 829		660	2779

the wine	will run	out	and the	wineskins	will be ruined.	No,	they pour		new	wine	into	new	wineskins,
ὁ οἶνος →	ἐκχεῖται	↰	καὶ οἱ	ἀσκοὶ	→ ἀπόλλυνται	ἀλλὰ	→ βάλλουσιν		νέον	οἶνον	εἰς	καινούς	ἀσκούς
d.nsm n.nsm	v.ppi.3s		cj d.npm	n.npm	v.ppi.3p	cj	v.pai.3p		a.asm	n.asm	p.a	a.apm	n.apm
3836 3885	1772		2779 3836	829	660	247	965		3742	3885	1650	2785	829

and both		are preserved."
καὶ ἀμφότεροι	→	συντηροῦνται
cj a.npm		v.ppi.3p
2779 317		5337

A Dead Girl and a Sick Woman

9:18 While	he	was saying	this,		a	ruler	came	and knelt	before	him	and said,		"My
↰	αὐτοῦ	→ λαλοῦντος	Ταῦτα	αὐτοῖς	ἰδοὺ	εἷς ἄρχων	ἐλθὼν		προσεκύνει ↰	αὐτῷ	λέγων ὅτι	μου	
	r.gsm.3	pt.pa.gsm	r.apn	r.dpm.3	pt.aa.nsm	n.nsm n.nsm	pt.aa.nsm		v.iai.3s	r.dsm.3	pt.pa.nsm	r.gs.1	
3281	899	3281	4047	899	2627	1651 807	2262		4686	899	3306 4022	1609	

daughter	has	just	died.	But	come	and	put	your	hand	on her,	and	she will live."	**19**	Jesus
ἡ θυγάτηρ	→	ἄρτι	ἐτελεύτησεν	ἀλλὰ	ἐλθὼν	→	ἐπίθες	σου	τὴν χεῖρα	ἐπ᾽ αὐτὴν	καὶ	→ ζήσεται		καὶ ὁ Ἰησοῦς
d.nsf n.nsf		adv	v.aai.3s	cj	pt.aa.nsm		v.aam.2s	r.gs.2	d.asf n.asf	p.a r.asf.3	cj	v.fmi.3s		cj d.nsm n.nsm
3836 2588		5462 785	5462	247	2262		2202	5148	3836 5931	2093 899	2779	2409		2779 3836 2652

αὐτοῦ, Διὰ τί μετὰ τῶν τελωνῶν καὶ ἁμαρτωλῶν ἐσθίει ὁ διδάσκαλος ὑμῶν; ¶ **12** ὁ δὲ ἀκούσας εἶπεν, Οὐ χρείαν ἔχουσιν οἱ ἰσχύοντες ἰατροῦ ἀλλ᾽ οἱ κακῶς ἔχοντες. **13** πορευθέντες δὲ μάθετε τί ἐστιν, Ἔλεος θέλω καὶ οὐ θυσίαν· οὐ γὰρ ἦλθον καλέσαι δικαίους ἀλλὰ ἁμαρτωλούς.

9:14 Τότε προσέρχονται αὐτῷ οἱ μαθηταὶ Ἰωάννου λέγοντες, Διὰ τί ἡμεῖς καὶ οἱ Φαρισαῖοι νηστεύομεν [πολλά], οἱ δὲ μαθηταί σου οὐ νηστεύουσιν; **15** καὶ εἶπεν αὐτοῖς ὁ Ἰησοῦς, Μὴ δύνανται οἱ υἱοὶ τοῦ νυμφῶνος πενθεῖν ἐφ᾽ ὅσον μετ᾽ αὐτῶν ἐστιν ὁ νυμφίος; ἐλεύσονται δὲ ἡμέραι ὅταν ἀπαρθῇ ἀπ᾽ αὐτῶν ὁ νυμφίος, καὶ τότε νηστεύσουσιν. ¶ **16** οὐδεὶς δὲ ἐπιβάλλει ἐπίβλημα ῥάκους ἀγνάφου ἐπὶ ἱματίῳ παλαιῷ· αἴρει γὰρ τὸ πλήρωμα αὐτοῦ ἀπὸ τοῦ ἱματίου καὶ χεῖρον σχίσμα γίνεται. **17** οὐδὲ βάλλουσιν οἶνον νέον εἰς ἀσκοὺς παλαιούς· εἰ δὲ μή γε, ῥήγνυνται οἱ ἀσκοὶ καὶ ὁ οἶνος ἐκχεῖται καὶ οἱ ἀσκοὶ ἀπόλλυνται· ἀλλὰ βάλλουσιν οἶνον νέον εἰς ἀσκοὺς καινούς, καὶ ἀμφότεροι συντηροῦνται.

9:18 Ταῦτα αὐτοῦ λαλοῦντος αὐτοῖς ἰδοὺ ἄρχων εἷς ἐλθὼν προσεκύνει αὐτῷ λέγων ὅτι Ἡ θυγάτηρ μου ἄρτι ἐτελεύτησεν· ἀλλὰ ἐλθὼν ἐπίθες τὴν χεῖρά σου ἐπ᾽ αὐτήν, καὶ ζήσεται. **19** καὶ ἐγερθεὶς ὁ Ἰησοῦς ἠκολούθησεν αὐτῷ καὶ οἱ μαθηταὶ αὐτοῦ.¶

got | up and went | with him, and so did his | disciples. | ¶ | **20** *Just then* a woman who had been subject
ἐγερθεὶς ← | ἠκολούθησεν → | αὐτῷ καὶ | αὐτοῦ ‚οἱ μαθηταὶ‚ | | Καὶ ἰδοὺ γυνὴ
pt.ap.nsm | v.aai.3s | r.dsm.3 cj | r.gsm.3 d.npm n.npm | | cj cj n.nsf
1586 | 199 | 899 2779 | 899 3836 3412 | | 2779 2627 1222

to bleeding | for twelve years came | up behind him and touched the edge | of his | cloak. | **21** She
→ αἱμορροοῦσα | → δώδεκα ἔτη προσελθοῦσα ← | ὄπισθεν ἥψατο τοῦ κρασπέδου → | αὐτοῦ ‚τοῦ ἱματίου‚ | | γὰρ →
pt.pa.nsf | a.apn n.apn pt.aa.nsf | adv v.ami.3s d.gsn n.gsn | r.gsm.3 d.gsn n.gsn | | cj
137 | 1557 2291 4665 | 3957 721 3836 3192 | 2668 899 3836 2668 | | 1142

said to herself, "If I | only touch his | cloak, | I will be healed." | **22** Jesus | turned and saw her.
ἔλεγεν ἐν ἑαυτῇ ἐὰν → | μόνον ἅψωμαι αὐτοῦ | ‚τοῦ ἱματίου‚ | → → σωθήσομαι | δὲ ‚ὁ Ἰησοῦς‚ | στραφεὶς καὶ ἰδὼν αὐτὴν
v.iai.3s p.d r.dsf.3 cj → | adv v.ams.1s r.gsm.3 | d.gsn n.gsn | v.fpi.1s | cj d.nsm n.nsm | pt.ap.nsm cj pt.aa.nsm r.asf.3
3306 1877 1571 1569 | 721 3667 721 | 899 | 5392 | 1254 3836 2652 | 5138 2779 1625 899

"Take heart, daughter," he said, "your faith | has healed you." And the woman was healed from that | moment.
→ θάρσει θύγατερ → εἶπεν σου ‚ἡ πίστις‚ | σέσωκέν σε. καὶ ἡ γυνὴ → ἐσώθη ἀπὸ ἐκείνης ‚τῆς ὥρας‚
v.pam.2s n.vsf → v.aai.3s r.gs.2 d.nsf n.nsf | v.rai.3s r.as.2 cj d.nsf n.nsf v.api.3s p.g r.gsf d.gsf n.gsf
2510 2588 3306 5148 3836 4411 | 5392 5148 2779 3836 1222 5392 608 1697 3836 6052

¶ **23** When Jesus | entered | the ruler's | house and saw | the flute players and the noisy
Καὶ → ‚ὁ Ἰησοῦς‚ ἐλθὼν | εἰς τὴν ‚τοῦ ἄρχοντος‚ | οἰκίαν καὶ ἰδὼν | τοὺς | αὐλητὰς καὶ τὸν θορυβούμενον
cj d.nsm n.nsm pt.aa.nsm | p.a d.asf d.gsm n.gsm | n.asf cj pt.aa.nsm | d.apm | n.apm cj d.asm pt.pp.asm
2779 2262 3836 2652 2262 | 1650 3836 3836 807 | 3864 2779 1625 | 3836 | 886 2779 3836 2572

crowd, **24** he said, "Go | away. | The girl | is not dead | but asleep." But they laughed at him. | **25** After
ὄχλον | → ἔλεγεν ἀναχωρεῖτε ← | γὰρ τὸ | κοράσιον | οὐ ἀπέθανεν ἀλλὰ καθεύδει καὶ → | κατεγέλων ← αὐτοῦ | δὲ ὅτε
n.asm | v.iai.3s v.pam.2p | cj d.nsn n.nsn | οὐ v.aai.3s cj v.pai.3s cj | v.iai.3p r.gsm.3 | cj cj
4063 | 3306 432 | 1142 3836 3166 | 633 4024 633 247 2761 2779 | 2860 899 | 1254 4021

the crowd had been put | outside, he went | in and took | the girl by the hand, | and she | got
ὁ ὄχλος → | ἐξεβλήθη ← | εἰσελθὼν ← | ἐκράτησεν | τῆς χειρὸς αὐτῆς καὶ ‚τὸ κοράσιον‚ | ἠγέρθη
d.nsm n.nsm | v.api.3s | pt.aa.nsm | v.aai.3s | d.gsf n.gsf r.gsf.3 cj d.nsn n.nsn | v.api.3s
3836 4063 | 1675 | 1656 | 3195 | 3836 5931 899 2779 3836 3166 | 1586

up. **26** News | of this spread through all that | region.
← καὶ ‚ἡ φήμη‚ | αὕτη ἐξῆλθεν εἰς | ὅλην ἐκείνην ‚τὴν γῆν‚
cj d.nsf n.nsf | r.nsf v.aai.3s p.a | a.asf r.asf d.asf n.asf
2779 3836 5773 | 4047 2002 1650 | 3910 1697 3836 1178

Jesus Heals the Blind and Mute

9:27 As Jesus | went | on from there, two blind men followed | him, calling out, | "Have
Καὶ → ‚τῷ Ἰησοῦ‚ παράγοντι | ἐκεῖθεν ← | δύο τυφλοὶ | ἠκολούθησαν αὐτῷ κράζοντες ← | καὶ λέγοντες →
cj d.dsm n.dsm pt.pa.dsm | adv | a.npm a.npm | v.aai.3p r.dsm.3 pt.pa.npm | cj pt.pa.npm
2779 4135 3836 2652 4135 | 1696 | 1545 5603 | 199 899 3189 | 2779 3306

mercy on us, Son of David!" | ¶ **28** When he had gone indoors, | the blind men came | to him, and
ἐλέησον ἡμᾶς υἱὸς Δαυίδ | δὲ → | ἐλθόντι εἰς τὴν οἰκίαν | οἱ τυφλοὶ ← | προσῆλθον ← αὐτῷ καὶ
v.aam.2s r.ap.1 n.nsm n.gsm | cj → | pt.aa.dsm p.a d.asf n.asf | d.npm a.npm | v.aai.3p r.dsm.3 cj
1796 7005 5626 1253 | 1254 | 2262 1650 3836 3864 | 3836 5603 | 4665 899 2779

he | asked them, "Do you believe that I am able | to do | this?" "Yes, Lord," they replied. | **29** Then
‚ὁ Ἰησοῦς‚ λέγει αὐτοῖς → | → πιστεύετε ὅτι → | δύναμαι → ποιῆσαι τοῦτο ναὶ | κύριε → λέγουσιν αὐτῷ | τότε
d.nsm n.nsm v.pai.3s r.dpm.3 | v.pai.2p cj | v.ppi.1s f.aa r.asn pl | n.vsm v.pai.3p r.dsm.3 | adv
3836 2652 3306 899 | 4409 4022 | 1538 4472 4047 3721 | 3261 3306 899 | 5538

he touched their eyes | and said, "According to your faith | will it be done | to you"; **30** and their
→ ἥψατο αὐτῶν ‚τῶν ὀφθαλμῶν‚ | λέγων κατὰ | ὑμῶν ‚τὴν πίστιν‚ | → γενηθήτω ὑμῖν | καὶ αὐτῶν
v.ami.3s r.gpm.3 d.gpm n.gpm | pt.pa.nsm p.a | r.gp.2 d.asf n.asf | v.apm.3s r.dp.2 | cj r.gpm.3
721 899 3836 4057 | 3306 2848 | 7007 3836 4411 | 1181 7007 | 2779 899

sight | was restored. Jesus | warned them sternly, | "See that no one | knows | about this."
‚οἱ ὀφθαλμοί‚ → | ἠνεῴχθησαν καὶ ‚ὁ Ἰησοῦς‚ | ἐνεβριμήθη αὐτοῖς | λέγων ὁρᾶτε | μηδεὶς γινωσκέτω
d.npm n.npm | v.api.3p cj d.nsm n.nsm | v.api.3s r.dpm.3 | pt.pa.nsm v.pam.2p | a.nsm v.pam.3s
3836 4057 | 487 2779 3836 2652 | 1839 899 | 3306 3972 | 3594 1182

31 But they went | out and spread | the news about him *all* *over* that region. | ¶ **32** While they were
δὲ οἱ ἐξελθόντες ← | διεφήμισαν | αὐτὸν ἐν ὅλῃ ἐκείνῃ ‚τῇ γῇ‚ | δὲ → Αὐτῶν →
cj d.npm pt.aa.npm | v.aai.3p | r.asm.3 p.d a.dsf r.dsf d.dsf n.dsf | cj r.gpm.3
1254 3836 2002 | 1424 | 899 1877 3910 1697 3836 1178 | 1254 2002 899

20 Καὶ ἰδοὺ γυνὴ αἱμορροοῦσα δώδεκα ἔτη προσελθοῦσα ὄπισθεν ἥψατο τοῦ κρασπέδου τοῦ ἱματίου αὐτοῦ· 21 ἔλεγεν γὰρ ἐν ἑαυτῇ, Ἐὰν μόνον ἅψωμαι τοῦ ἱματίου αὐτοῦ σωθήσομαι. 22 ὁ δὲ Ἰησοῦς στραφεὶς καὶ ἰδὼν αὐτὴν εἶπεν, Θάρσει, θύγατερ· ἡ πίστις σου σέσωκέν σε. καὶ ἐσώθη ἡ γυνὴ ἀπὸ τῆς ὥρας ἐκείνης. ¶ 23 Καὶ ἐλθὼν ὁ Ἰησοῦς εἰς τὴν οἰκίαν τοῦ ἄρχοντος καὶ ἰδὼν τοὺς αὐλητὰς καὶ τὸν ὄχλον θορυβούμενον 24 ἔλεγεν, Ἀναχωρεῖτε, οὐ γὰρ ἀπέθανεν τὸ κοράσιον ἀλλὰ καθεύδει. καὶ κατεγέλων αὐτοῦ. 25 ὅτε δὲ ἐξεβλήθη ὁ ὄχλος εἰσελθὼν ἐκράτησεν τῆς χειρὸς αὐτῆς, καὶ ἠγέρθη τὸ κοράσιον. 26 καὶ ἐξῆλθεν ἡ φήμη αὕτη εἰς ὅλην τὴν γῆν ἐκείνην. ¶

9:27 Καὶ παράγοντι ἐκεῖθεν τῷ Ἰησοῦ ἠκολούθησαν [αὐτῷ] δύο τυφλοὶ κράζοντες καὶ λέγοντες, Ἐλέησον ἡμᾶς, υἱὸς Δαυίδ. ¶ 28 ἐλθόντι δὲ εἰς τὴν οἰκίαν προσῆλθον αὐτῷ οἱ τυφλοί, καὶ λέγει αὐτοῖς ὁ Ἰησοῦς, Πιστεύετε ὅτι δύναμαι τοῦτο ποιῆσαι; λέγουσιν αὐτῷ, Ναὶ κύριε. 29 τότε ἥψατο τῶν ὀφθαλμῶν αὐτῶν λέγων, Κατὰ τὴν πίστιν ὑμῶν γενηθήτω ὑμῖν. 30 καὶ ἠνεῴχθησαν αὐτῶν οἱ ὀφθαλμοί. καὶ ἐνεβριμήθη αὐτοῖς ὁ Ἰησοῦς λέγων, Ὁρᾶτε μηδεὶς γινωσκέτω. 31 οἱ δὲ ἐξελθόντες διεφήμισαν αὐτὸν ἐν ὅλῃ τῇ γῇ ἐκείνῃ. ¶ 32 Αὐτῶν δὲ ἐξερχομένων ἰδοὺ προσήνεγκαν αὐτῷ ἄνθρωπον κωφὸν δαιμονιζόμενον. 33 καὶ ἐκβληθέντος τοῦ

going   out,   a man   who was demon-possessed and could not talk   was brought   to Jesus. [33] And when
ἐξερχομένων ←   ἰδοὺ   ἄνθρωπον →   →   δαιμονιζόμενον   →   κωφὸν   προσήνεγκαν → αὐτῷ   καὶ ↱
pt.pm.gpm   j   n.asm   pt.pp.asm   a.asm   v.aai.3p   r.dsm.3   cj
2002   2627   476   1227   3273   4712   899   2779   1675

the demon   was driven   out, the man who had been mute spoke.   The crowd was amazed   and said,
τοῦ δαιμονίου →   ἐκβληθέντος ←   ὁ   κωφός ἐλάλησεν καὶ οἱ   ὄχλοι   →   ἐθαύμασαν   λέγοντες
d.gsn n.gsn   pt.ap.gsn   d.nsm   a.nsm v.aai.3s   cj   d.npm n.npm   v.aai.3p   pt.pa.npm
3836 1228   1675   3836   3273 3281   2779 3836 4063   2513   3306

"Nothing like this has ever been seen in Israel."   [34] But the Pharisees said, "It is by the prince of demons
οὐδέποτε οὕτως ←   ἐφάνη ἐν ⸤τῷ Ἰσραήλ⸥   δὲ   οἱ   Φαρισαῖοι ἔλεγον   ἐν   τῷ   ἄρχοντι ⸤τῶν δαιμονίων⸥
adv   adv   v.api.3s   p.d   d.dsm n.dsm   cj   d.npm   n.npm   v.iai.3p   p.d   d.dsm   n.dsm   d.gpn n.gpn
4030   4048   5743   1877   3836 2702   1254   3836   5757   3306   1877   3836   807   3836 1228

that he drives   out demons."
→   ἐκβάλλει ←   ⸤τὰ δαιμόνια⸥
v.pai.3s   d.apn n.apn
1675   3836 1228

The Workers Are Few

9:35   Jesus   went   through all   the towns and villages,   teaching in   their synagogues,
Καὶ ὁ   Ἰησοῦς,   περιῆγεν ←   πάσας τὰς πόλεις καὶ ⸤τὰς κώμας⸥ διδάσκων ἐν   αὐτῶν ⸤ταῖς συναγωγαῖς⸥ καὶ
cj   d.nsm n.nsm   v.iai.3s   a.apf d.apf n.apf cj   d.apf n.apf   pt.pa.nsm   p.d   r.gpm.3   d.dpf n.dpf   cj
2779   3836 2652   4310   4246 3836 4484   2779   3836 3267   1438   1877   899   3836 5252   2779

preaching the good news   of the kingdom and healing   every disease and   sickness. [36]   When he saw   the
κηρύσσων τὸ   →   εὐαγγέλιον →   τῆς βασιλείας καὶ θεραπεύων πᾶσαν νόσον   καὶ πᾶσαν μαλακίαν   δὲ →   →   ἰδὼν   τοὺς
pt.pa.nsm   d.asn   n.asn   d.gsf n.gsf   cj   pt.pa.nsm   a.asf n.asf   cj   a.asf   n.asf   cj   pt.aa.nsm d.apm
3062   3836   2295   3836 993   2779 2543   4246 3798   2779 4246   3433   1254   1625   3836

crowds, he had compassion on them, because they were harassed and helpless, like sheep   without   a shepherd.
ὄχλους →   →   ἐσπλαγχνίσθη περὶ αὐτῶν ὅτι   →   ἦσαν ἐσκυλμένοι καὶ ἐρριμμένοι ὡσεὶ πρόβατα ⸤μὴ ἔχοντα⸥   ποιμένα
n.apm   v.api.3s   p.g   r.gpm.3 cj   v.iai.3p pt.rp.npm   cj   pt.rp.npm   pl   n.npn   pl   pt.pa.npn   n.asm
4063   5072   4309   899   4022   1639   5035   2779   4849   6059 4585   3590 2400   4478

[37] Then he said to his   disciples,   "The harvest is plentiful but the workers are few. [38] Ask   the Lord of the
τότε   →   λέγει →   αὐτοῦ ⸤τοῖς μαθηταῖς⸥ μὲν ὁ   θερισμὸς   πολύς   δὲ   οἱ   ἐργάται   ὀλίγοι   δεήθητε τοῦ κυρίου →   τοῦ
adv   v.pai.3s   r.gsm.3   d.dpm n.dpm   pl   d.nsm   n.nsm   a.nsm   cj   d.npm n.npm   a.npm   v.apm.2p d.gsm n.gsm   d.gsm
5538   3306   3412 899   3836 3412   3525 3836   2546   4498   1254 3836 2239   3900   1289   3836 3261   3836

harvest, therefore, to   send   out workers into his   harvest   field."
θερισμοῦ οὖν   ὅπως ἐκβάλῃ ←   ἐργάτας εἰς   αὐτοῦ ⸤τὸν θερισμὸν⸥ ←
n.gsm   cj   cj   v.aas.3s   n.apm   p.a   r.gsm.3 d.asm n.asm
2546   4036   3968   1675   2239   1650   899   3836 2546

Jesus Sends Out the Twelve

10:1   He called   his   twelve disciples   to him and gave   them authority to   drive   out
Καὶ →   προσκαλεσάμενος αὐτοῦ δώδεκα ⸤τοὺς μαθητὰς⸥   ←   ἔδωκεν αὐτοῖς ἐξουσίαν ὥστε ἐκβάλλειν ←   αὐτὰ
cj   pt.am.nsm   r.gsm.3   a.apm   d.apm n.apm   v.aai.3s   r.dpm.3 n.asf   cj   f.pa   r.apn.3
2779   4673   899   1557   3836 3412   4673 4673   1443   899   2026   6063 1675   899

evil   spirits   and to heal   every disease and   sickness. ¶   [2]   These are   the names of the
ἀκαθάρτων πνευμάτων καὶ   →   θεραπεύειν πᾶσαν νόσον   καὶ   πᾶσαν μαλακίαν   δὲ   ταῦτα ἐστιν τὰ   ὀνόματα →   Τῶν
a.gpn   n.gpn   cj   f.pa   a.asf   n.asf   cj   a.asf   n.asf   cj   r.npn   v.pai.3s d.npn n.npn   d.gpm
176   4460   2779   2543   4246   3798   2779   4246   3433   1254 4047   1639   3836 3950   3836

twelve apostles: first,   Simon (who is called   Peter) and his   brother   Andrew;   James   son of
δώδεκα ἀποστόλων πρῶτος Σίμων ὁ   → λεγόμενος Πέτρος καὶ αὐτοῦ ὁ   ἀδελφὸς,   Ἀνδρέας   καὶ Ἰάκωβος ὁ   →
a.gpm   n.gpm   a.nsm   n.nsm d.nsm   pt.pp.nsm   n.nsm   cj   r.gsm.3 d.nsm n.nsm   n.nsm   cj   n.nsm   d.nsm
1557   693   4755   4981   3836   3306   4377   2779 899   3836 81   436   2779 2610   3836

Zebedee,   and his   brother   John;   [3] Philip   and Bartholomew; Thomas and Matthew the tax collector;
⸤τοῦ Ζεβεδαίου⸥ καὶ αὐτοῦ ὁ   ἀδελφὸς,   Ἰωάννης   Φίλιππος καὶ Βαρθολομαῖος Θωμᾶς   καὶ Μαθθαῖος ὁ   →   τελώνης
d.gsm n.gsm   cj   r.gsm.3 d.nsm n.nsm   n.nsm   n.nsm   cj   n.nsm   n.nsm   cj   n.nsm   d.nsm   n.nsm
3836 2411   2779 899   3836 81   2722   5805   2779 978   2605   2779 3414   3836   5467

δαιμονίου ἐλάλησεν ὁ κωφός. καὶ ἐθαύμασαν οἱ ὄχλοι λέγοντες, Οὐδέποτε ἐφάνη οὕτως ἐν τῷ Ἰσραήλ.   [34] οἱ δὲ Φαρισαῖοι ἔλεγον, Ἐν τῷ ἄρχοντι τῶν δαιμονίων ἐκβάλλει τὰ δαιμόνια.

  [9:35] Καὶ περιῆγεν ὁ Ἰησοῦς τὰς πόλεις πάσας καὶ τὰς κώμας διδάσκων ἐν ταῖς συναγωγαῖς αὐτῶν καὶ κηρύσσων τὸ εὐαγγέλιον τῆς βασιλείας καὶ θεραπεύων πᾶσαν νόσον καὶ πᾶσαν μαλακίαν.   [36] Ἰδὼν δὲ τοὺς ὄχλους ἐσπλαγχνίσθη περὶ αὐτῶν, ὅτι ἦσαν ἐσκυλμένοι καὶ ἐρριμμένοι ὡσεὶ πρόβατα μὴ ἔχοντα ποιμένα.   [37] τότε λέγει τοῖς μαθηταῖς αὐτοῦ, Ὁ μὲν θερισμὸς πολύς, οἱ δὲ ἐργάται ὀλίγοι·   [38] δεήθητε οὖν τοῦ κυρίου τοῦ θερισμοῦ ὅπως ἐκβάλῃ ἐργάτας εἰς τὸν θερισμὸν αὐτοῦ.

  [10:1] Καὶ προσκαλεσάμενος τοὺς δώδεκα μαθητὰς αὐτοῦ ἔδωκεν αὐτοῖς ἐξουσίαν πνευμάτων ἀκαθάρτων ὥστε ἐκβάλλειν αὐτὰ καὶ θεραπεύειν πᾶσαν νόσον καὶ πᾶσαν μαλακίαν. ¶   [2] Τῶν δὲ δώδεκα ἀποστόλων τὰ ὀνόματά ἐστιν ταῦτα· πρῶτος Σίμων ὁ λεγόμενος Πέτρος καὶ Ἀνδρέας ὁ ἀδελφὸς αὐτοῦ, καὶ Ἰάκωβος ὁ τοῦ Ζεβεδαίου καὶ Ἰωάννης ὁ ἀδελφὸς αὐτοῦ,   [3] Φίλιππος καὶ Βαρθολομαῖος, Θωμᾶς καὶ Μαθθαῖος ὁ τελώνης, Ἰάκωβος ὁ τοῦ Ἀλφαίου καὶ Θαδδαῖος,   [4] Σίμων ὁ Καναναῖος

James　　son of Alphaeus,　and Thaddaeus;　⁴Simon the Zealot　and Judas Iscariot,　who　betrayed
Ἰάκωβος ὁ → ‚τοῦ⸥ Ἀλφαίου‚ καὶ Θαδδαῖος Σίμων ὁ Καναναῖος καὶ Ἰούδας ‚ὁ⸥ ‚Ἰσκαριώτης⸥ ‚ὁ⸥ καὶ παραδοὺς
n.nsm d.nsm　d.gsm n.gsm cj n.nsm n.nsm d.nsm n.nsm cj n.nsm d.nsm n.nsm d.nsm adv pt.aa.nsm
2610 3836　3836 271 2779 2497 4981 3836 2831 2779 2683 3836 2697 3836 2779 4140

him.　¶　⁵These twelve　Jesus　sent　out with the following instructions:　　"Do not
αὐτόν　Τούτους ‚τοὺς δώδεκα⸥ ‚ὁ⸥ Ἰησοῦς ἀπέστειλεν ←　παραγγείλας αὐτοῖς λέγων → μὴ
r.asm.3　r.apm d.apm a.apm d.nsm n.nsm v.aai.3s　pt.aa.nsm r.dpm.3 pt.pa.nsm pl
899　4047 3836 1557 3836 2652 690　4133 899 3306 599 3590

go　among　the Gentiles or　enter　any town of the Samaritans.　⁶Go　rather to　the lost
ἀπέλθητε εἰς ὁδὸν‚ ἐθνῶν καὶ μὴ εἰσέλθητε εἰς πόλιν → Σαμαριτῶν δὲ πορεύεσθε μᾶλλον πρὸς τὰ ἀπολωλότα
v.aas.2p p.a n.asf n.gpn cj pl v.aas.2p p.a n.asf n.gpm cj v.pmm.2p adv.c p.a d.apn pt.ra.apn
599 1650 3847 1620 2779 3590 1656 1650 4484 4901 1254 4513 3437 4639 3836 660

sheep　of　Israel.　⁷As you go,　preach this message:　'The kingdom of heaven　is
‚τὰ πρόβατα⸥ → οἴκου‚ Ἰσραήλ δὲ → → πορευόμενοι κηρύσσετε λέγοντες ὅτι ἡ βασιλεία → ‚τῶν οὐρανῶν⸥ →
d.apn n.apn n.gsm n.gsm cj pt.pm.npm v.pam.2p pt.pa.npm cj d.nsf n.nsf d.gpm n.gpm
3836 4585 3875 2702 1254 4513 3062 3306 4022 3836 993 3836 4041

near.'　⁸Heal　the sick,　raise　the dead,　cleanse　those who have leprosy,　drive　out demons. Freely you
ἤγγικεν θεραπεύετε ἀσθενοῦντας ἐγείρετε νεκροὺς καθαρίζετε → → → λεπροὺς ἐκβάλλετε ← δαιμόνια δωρεὰν
v.rai.3s v.pam.2p pt.pa.apm v.pam.2p a.apm v.pam.2p a.apm v.pam.2p n.apn adv
1581 2543 820 1586 3738 2751 3320 1675 1228 1562

have received, freely give.　⁹Do not take　along any gold　or silver　or copper in your belts;　¹⁰take no
→ ἐλάβετε δωρεὰν δότε Μὴ κτήσησθε ← χρυσὸν μηδὲ ἄργυρον μηδὲ χαλκὸν εἰς ὑμῶν ‚τὰς ζώνας⸥ μὴ
v.aai.2p adv v.aam.2p pl v.ams.2p n.asm cj n.asm cj n.asm p.a r.gp.2 d.apf n.apf pl
3284 1562 1443 3227 3590 3227 5996 3593 738 3593 5910 1650 7007 3836 2438 3590

bag　for the journey, or　extra tunic,　or　sandals　or a staff; for the worker is worth his　keep.　¶
πήραν εἰς ὁδὸν μηδὲ δύο χιτῶνας μηδὲ ὑποδήματα μηδὲ ῥάβδον γὰρ ὁ ἐργάτης ἄξιος αὐτοῦ ‚τῆς τροφῆς⸥
n.asf p.a n.asf cj a.apm n.apm cj n.apn cj n.asf cj d.nsm n.nsm a.nsm r.gsm.3 d.gsf n.gsf
4385 1650 3847 3593 1545 5945 3593 5687 3593 4811 1142 3836 2239 545 899 3836 5575

¹¹　"Whatever town or village you enter,　search　for some　worthy person there　and stay　at his
δ' εἰς ἣν ἂν πόλιν ἢ κώμην → εἰσέλθητε ἐξετάσατε ← τίς ἐστιν ἄξιος ‚ἐν αὐτῇ⸥ κἀκεῖ μείνατε ←
cj p.a r.asf pl n.asf cj n.asf v.aas.2p v.aam.2p r.nsm v.pai.3s a.nsm p.d r.dsf.3 crasis v.aam.2p
1254 1650 4005 323 4484 2445 3267 1656 2004 5515 1639 545 1877 899 2795 3531 2795 2795

house until　you leave.　¹²As you enter　the home, give it　your greeting.　¹³If the home is
← ‚ἕως ἂν⸥ → ἐξέλθητε δὲ → → εἰσερχόμενοι εἰς τὴν οἰκίαν αὐτήν ἀσπάσασθε καὶ μὲν ἐὰν ἡ οἰκία ἢ
cj pl v.aas.2p cj pt.pm.npm p.a d.asf n.asf r.asf.3 v.amm.2p cj pl cj d.nsf n.nsf v.pas.3s
2795 2401 323 2002 1254 1656 1650 3836 3864 832 832 2779 3525 1569 3836 3864 1639

deserving, let your peace　rest　on it;　if it is　not,　let your peace　return　to you.　¹⁴If
ἀξία → ὑμῶν ἡ εἰρήνη ἐλθάτω ἐπ' αὐτὴν δὲ ἐὰν → μὴ ἀξία → ὑμῶν ἡ εἰρήνη ἐπιστραφήτω πρὸς ὑμᾶς καὶ
a.nsf r.gp.2 d.nsf n.nsf v.aam.3s p.a r.asf.3 cj cj v.pas.3s pl a.nsf r.gp.2 d.nsf n.nsf v.apm.3s p.a r.ap.2 cj
545 2262 7007 3836 1645 2262 2093 899 1254 1569 1639 3590 545 2188 7007 3836 1645 2188 4639 7007 2779

anyone will not welcome you or　listen to your words,　shake　the dust　off your feet　when you
‚ὃς ἂν⸥ → μὴ δέξηται ὑμᾶς μηδὲ ἀκούσῃ ὑμῶν ‚τοὺς λόγους⸥ ἐκτινάξατε τὸν κονιορτὸν ὑμῶν ‚τῶν ποδῶν⸥ →
r.nsm pl pl v.ams.3s r.ap.2 cj v.aas.3s r.gp.2 d.apm n.apm v.aam.2p d.asm n.asm r.gp.2 d.gpm n.gpm
4005 323 1312 3590 1312 7007 3593 201 7007 3836 3364 1759 3836 3155 1759 7007 3836 4546

leave　that home　or town.　¹⁵I tell you the truth, it will be　more bearable for　Sodom and
ἐξερχόμενοι ἔξω ἐκείνης ‚τῆς οἰκίας⸥ ἢ ‚τῆς πόλεως⸥ → λέγω ὑμῖν ἀμὴν → ἔσται ἀνεκτότερον γῇ Σοδόμων καὶ
pt.pm.npm p.g r.gsf d.gsf n.gsf cj d.gsf n.gsf v.pai.1s r.dp.2 pl v.fmi.3s a.nsn.c n.dsf n.gpn cj
2002 2032 1697 3836 3864 2445 3836 4484 3306 7007 297 1639 445 1178 5047 2779

Gomorrah on the day　of judgment than for that town.　¹⁶I am sending you out like sheep　among
Γομόρρων ἐν ἡμέρᾳ κρίσεως ἢ → ἐκείνῃ τῇ πόλει Ἰδοὺ ἐγώ ἀποστέλλω ὑμᾶς ← ὡς πρόβατα ἐν μέσῳ
n.gpn p.d n.dsf n.gsf cj r.dsf d.dsf n.dsf j r.ns.1 v.pai.1s r.ap.2 conj n.apn p.d n.dsn
1202 1877 2465 3213 2445 4484 1697 3836 4484 2627 1609 690 7007 690 6055 4585 1877 3545

wolves. Therefore be　as shrewd as snakes　and as innocent as doves.　¶　¹⁷"Be on your guard
λύκων οὖν γίνεσθε φρόνιμοι ὡς ‚οἱ ὄφεις⸥ καὶ ἀκέραιοι ὡς ‚αἱ περιστεραί⸥ δὲ → → Προσέχετε
n.gpm cj v.pmm.2p a.npm conj d.npm n.npm cj a.npm conj d.npf n.npf cj v.pam.2p
3380 4036 1181 5861 6055 3836 4058 2779 193 6055 3836 4361 1254 4668

καὶ Ἰούδας ὁ Ἰσκαριώτης ὁ καὶ παραδοὺς αὐτόν. ¶ ⁵ Τούτους τοὺς δώδεκα ἀπέστειλεν ὁ Ἰησοῦς παραγγείλας αὐτοῖς λέγων, Εἰς ὁδὸν ἐθνῶν μὴ ἀπέλθητε καὶ εἰς πόλιν Σαμαριτῶν μὴ εἰσέλθητε· ⁶ πορεύεσθε δὲ μᾶλλον πρὸς τὰ πρόβατα τὰ ἀπολωλότα οἴκου Ἰσραήλ. ⁷ πορευόμενοι δὲ κηρύσσετε λέγοντες ὅτι Ἤγγικεν ἡ βασιλεία τῶν οὐρανῶν. ⁸ ἀσθενοῦντας θεραπεύετε, νεκροὺς ἐγείρετε, λεπροὺς καθαρίζετε, δαιμόνια ἐκβάλλετε· δωρεὰν ἐλάβετε, δωρεὰν δότε. ⁹ Μὴ κτήσησθε χρυσὸν μηδὲ ἄργυρον μηδὲ χαλκὸν εἰς τὰς ζώνας ὑμῶν, ¹⁰ μὴ πήραν εἰς ὁδὸν μηδὲ δύο χιτῶνας μηδὲ ὑποδήματα μηδὲ ῥάβδον· ἄξιος γὰρ ὁ ἐργάτης τῆς τροφῆς αὐτοῦ. ¶ ¹¹ εἰς ἣν δ' ἂν πόλιν ἢ κώμην εἰσέλθητε, ἐξετάσατε τίς ἐν αὐτῇ ἄξιός ἐστιν· κἀκεῖ μείνατε ἕως ἂν ἐξέλθητε. ¹² εἰσερχόμενοι δὲ εἰς τὴν οἰκίαν ἀσπάσασθε αὐτήν· ¹³ καὶ ἐὰν μὲν ᾖ ἡ οἰκία ἀξία, ἐλθάτω ἡ εἰρήνη ὑμῶν ἐπ' αὐτήν, ἐὰν δὲ μὴ ᾖ ἀξία, ἡ εἰρήνη ὑμῶν πρὸς ὑμᾶς ἐπιστραφήτω. ¹⁴ καὶ ὃς ἂν μὴ δέξηται ὑμᾶς μηδὲ ἀκούσῃ τοὺς λόγους ὑμῶν, ἐξερχόμενοι ἔξω τῆς οἰκίας ἢ τῆς πόλεως ἐκείνης ἐκτινάξατε τὸν κονιορτὸν τῶν ποδῶν ὑμῶν. ¹⁵ ἀμὴν λέγω ὑμῖν, ἀνεκτότερον ἔσται γῇ Σοδόμων καὶ Γομόρρων ἐν ἡμέρᾳ κρίσεως ἢ τῇ πόλει ἐκείνῃ. ¹⁶ Ἰδοὺ ἐγὼ ἀποστέλλω ὑμᾶς ὡς πρόβατα ἐν μέσῳ λύκων· γίνεσθε οὖν φρόνιμοι ὡς οἱ ὄφεις καὶ ἀκέραιοι ὡς αἱ περιστεραί. ¶ ¹⁷ προσέχετε δὲ ἀπὸ τῶν ἀνθρώπων· παραδώσουσιν γὰρ ὑμᾶς εἰς συνέδρια καὶ ἐν

against men;   they will hand   you over to the local councils and flog   you in their
ἀπὸ τῶν ἀνθρώπων γὰρ   →   παραδώσουσιν ὑμᾶς εἰς   συνέδρια καὶ μαστιγώσουσιν ὑμᾶς ἐν αὐτῶν
p.g   d.gpm n.gpm   cj   v.fai.3p   r.ap.2 p.a   n.apn   cj   v.fai.3p   r.ap.2 p.d r.gpm.3
608   3836 476   1142   4140   7007 4140 1650   5284   2779 3463   7007 1877 899

synagogues.   **18**   On my account you will be brought before governors and kings   as witnesses to them
ταῖς συναγωγαῖς δὲ καὶ   ἐμοῦ ἕνεκεν   →   →   →   ἀχθήσεσθε ἐπὶ ἡγεμόνας καὶ βασιλεῖς εἰς μαρτύριον → αὐτοῖς
d.dpf n.dpf   cj cj   r.gs.1 p.g   v.fpi.2p p.a   n.apm   adv   n.apm   p.a n.asn   r.dpm.3
3836 5252   1254 2779   1914 1914   72   2093   2450   2779 995   1650 3457   899

and to the Gentiles. **19** But when they arrest   you, do not worry   about what to say or how to say   it.   At
καὶ τοῖς ἔθνεσιν   δὲ ὅταν → παραδῶσιν ὑμᾶς μὴ μεριμνήσητε   πῶς   ἢ τί → λαλήσητε   γὰρ ἐν
cj   d.dpn n.dpn   cj   cj   v.aas.3p r.ap.2 pl   v.aas.2p   adv   cj r.asn   v.aas.2p   cj p.d
2779 3836 1620   1254 4020   4140   7007 3534 3534   4802   2445 5515 3281   1142 1877

that time   you will be given   what to say,   **20** for it will not be you speaking,   but the Spirit of your
ἐκείνη τῇ ὥρᾳ ὑμῖν → δοθήσεται τί → λαλήσητε γὰρ   →   οὐ ἐστε ὑμεῖς οἱ λαλοῦντες ἀλλὰ τὸ πνεῦμα → ὑμῶν
r.dsf d.dsf n.dsf r.dp.2   v.fpi.3s r.asn   v.aas.2p   cj   adv v.pai.2p r.np.2 d.npm pt.pa.npm   cj   d.nsn n.nsn   r.gp.2
1697 3836 6052   7007   1443   5515   3281   1142   1639 1639 4024 1639 7007 3836 3281   247 3836 4460   4252 7007

Father   speaking   through you. ¶ **21** "Brother will betray   brother to death, and a father his child;
τοῦ πατρὸς τὸ λαλοῦν ἐν   ὑμῖν   δὲ ἀδελφὸς   Παραδώσει ἀδελφὸν εἰς θάνατον καὶ πατὴρ   τέκνον καὶ
d.gsm n.gsm d.nsn pt.pa.nsn p.d   r.dp.2   cj   n.nsm   v.fai.3s   n.asm   p.a n.asn   cj   n.nsm   n.asn   cj
3836 4252   3836 3281   1877 7007   1254 81   4140   81   1650 2505   2779 4252   5451   2779

children will rebel   against their parents and have them put to death.   **22**   All   men will
τέκνα   → ἐπαναστήσονται ἐπὶ   γονεῖς καὶ   αὐτοὺς → → θανατώσουσιν καὶ ὑπὸ πάντων   ἔσεσθε
n.npn   v.fmi.3p   p.a   n.apm   cj   r.apm.3   v.fai.3p   cj   p.g a.gpm   v.fmi.2p
5451   2060   2093   1204   2779   899   2506   2779 5679 4246   1639

hate   you because of me,   but he who stands   firm to the end   will be saved. **23**   When you
μισούμενοι διὰ   τὸ ὄνομα μου δὲ ὁ   ὑπομείνας εἰς τέλος οὗτος → → σωθήσεται δὲ Ὅταν ὑμᾶς
pt.pp.npm   p.a   d.asn n.asn r.gs.1 cj d.nsm   pt.aa.nsm   p.a   n.asn r.nsm   v.fpi.3s   cj   cj   r.ap.2
3631   1639   3836 3950 1609 1254 3836   5702   1650 5465 4047   5392   1254 4020 7007

are persecuted in one place,   flee to another.   I tell you the truth, you will not finish going
→ διώκωσιν ἐν ταύτῃ τῇ πόλει φεύγετε εἰς τὴν ἑτέραν γὰρ →ʼ λέγω ὑμῖν ἀμὴν   οὐ μὴ τελέσητε
v.pas.3p   p.d   r.dsf d.dsf n.dsf   v.pam.2p p.a d.asf r.asf   cj   v.pai.1s r.dp.2   pl   adv pl   v.aas.2p
1503   1877 4047 3836 4484 5771   1650 3836 2283   1142   3306 7007   297   4024 3590 5464

through the cities of Israel   before the Son of Man   comes. ¶ **24** "A student is   not above his
τὰς πόλεις → τοῦ Ἰσραὴλ ἕως ἂν ὁ υἱὸς → τοῦ ἀνθρώπου ἔλθῃ   μαθητὴς ἔστιν Οὐκ ὑπὲρ τὸν
d.apf n.apf   d.gsm n.gsm   cj pl d.nsm n.nsm   d.gsm n.gsm   v.aas.3s   n.nsm   v.pai.3s adv p.a   d.asm
3836 4484   3836 2702   2401 323 3836 5626   3836 476   2262   3412   1639 4024 5642   3836

teacher, nor a servant above his   master. **25** It is enough for the student to be   like his   teacher, and
διδάσκαλον οὐδὲ δοῦλος ὑπὲρ αὐτοῦ τὸν κύριον → ἀρκετὸν → τῷ μαθητῇ ἵνα γένηται ὡς αὐτοῦ ὁ διδάσκαλος καὶ
n.asm   cj   n.nsm   p.a r.gsm.3 d.asm n.asm   a.nsn   d.dsm n.dsm cj v.ams.3s pl r.gsm.3 d.nsm n.nsm   cj
1437   4028 1529   5642 899   3836 3261   757   3836 3412 2671 1181   6055 899   3836 1437   2779

the servant like his   master. If the head   of the house has been called   Beelzebub, how much more
ὁ δοῦλος ὡς αὐτοῦ ὁ κύριος εἰ τὸν οἰκοδεσπότην ← ←   ←   ἐπεκάλεσαν Βεελζεβοὺλ πόσῳ ← μᾶλλον
d.nsm n.nsm pl r.gsm.3 d.nsm n.nsm cj d.asm n.asm   v.aai.3p   n.nsm   r.dsn   adv
3836 1529   6055 899   3836 3261 1623 3836 3867   2126   1015   4531   3437

the members of his   household! ¶ **26** "So do not be afraid of them. There is   nothing concealed that
τοὺς οἰκιακοὺς → αὐτοῦ ←   οὖν ⸆ Μὴ → φοβηθῆτε αὐτοὺς γὰρ → ἐστιν οὐδὲν κεκαλυμμένον ὃ
d.apm n.apm   r.gsm.3   cj   pl   pl   v.aps.2p   r.apm.3 cj   v.pai.3s a.nsn pt.rp.nsn   r.nsn
3836 3865   899   3865   4036 5828 3590   5828   899   1142   1639 4029 5828   4005

will not be disclosed,   or hidden that will not be made known. **27** What I tell you in the dark, speak in the
→ οὐκ → ἀποκαλυφθήσεται καὶ κρυπτὸν ὃ → οὐ → γνωσθήσεται   ὃ   → λέγω ὑμῖν ἐν τῇ σκοτίᾳ εἴπατε ἐν τῷ
adv   v.fpi.3s   cj a.nsn   r.nsn   adv   v.fpi.3s   r.asn   v.pai.1s r.dp.2 p.d d.dsf n.dsf v.aam.2p p.d d.dsn
636   4024 636 4005   2779 3220   4005   1182 4024 1182   4005   3306 7007 1877 3836 5028 3306   1877 3836

daylight;   what is whispered in your ear, proclaim from the roofs. **28**   Do not be afraid of those who
φωτί   καὶ ὃ   → ἀκούετε εἰς τὸ οὖς κηρύξατε ἐπὶ τῶν δωμάτων καὶ μὴ → φοβεῖσθε ἀπὸ τῶν ←
n.dsn   cj r.asn v.pai.2p p.a d.asn n.asn v.aam.2p p.g d.gpn n.gpn   cj   pl   v.ppm.2p   p.g d.gpm
5890   2779 4005   201   1650 3836 4044 3062   2093 3836 1560   2779 5828 3590 5828   608 3836

ταῖς συναγωγαῖς αὐτῶν μαστιγώσουσιν ὑμᾶς· 18 καὶ ἐπὶ ἡγεμόνας δὲ καὶ βασιλεῖς ἀχθήσεσθε ἕνεκεν ἐμοῦ εἰς μαρτύριον αὐτοῖς καὶ τοῖς ἔθνεσιν. 19 ὅταν δὲ παραδῶσιν ὑμᾶς, μὴ μεριμνήσητε πῶς ἢ τί λαλήσητε· δοθήσεται γὰρ ὑμῖν ἐν ἐκείνῃ τῇ ὥρᾳ τί λαλήσητε· 20 οὐ γὰρ ὑμεῖς ἐστε οἱ λαλοῦντες ἀλλὰ τὸ πνεῦμα τοῦ πατρὸς ὑμῶν τὸ λαλοῦν ἐν ὑμῖν. ¶ 21 παραδώσει δὲ ἀδελφὸς ἀδελφὸν εἰς θάνατον καὶ πατὴρ τέκνον, καὶ ἐπαναστήσονται τέκνα ἐπὶ γονεῖς καὶ θανατώσουσιν αὐτούς. 22 καὶ ἔσεσθε μισούμενοι ὑπὸ πάντων διὰ τὸ ὄνομά μου· ὁ δὲ ὑπομείνας εἰς τέλος οὗτος σωθήσεται. 23 ὅταν δὲ διώκωσιν ὑμᾶς ἐν τῇ πόλει ταύτῃ, φεύγετε εἰς τὴν ἑτέραν· ἀμὴν γὰρ λέγω ὑμῖν, οὐ μὴ τελέσητε τὰς πόλεις τοῦ Ἰσραὴλ ἕως ἂν ἔλθῃ ὁ υἱὸς τοῦ ἀνθρώπου. ¶ 10:24 Οὐκ ἔστιν μαθητὴς ὑπὲρ τὸν διδάσκαλον οὐδὲ δοῦλος ὑπὲρ τὸν κύριον αὐτοῦ. 25 ἀρκετὸν τῷ μαθητῇ ἵνα γένηται ὡς ὁ διδάσκαλος αὐτοῦ καὶ ὁ δοῦλος ὡς ὁ κύριος αὐτοῦ. εἰ τὸν οἰκοδεσπότην Βεελζεβοὺλ ἐπεκάλεσαν, πόσῳ μᾶλλον τοὺς οἰκιακοὺς αὐτοῦ. ¶ 26 Μὴ οὖν φοβηθῆτε αὐτούς· οὐδὲν γάρ ἐστιν κεκαλυμμένον ὃ οὐκ ἀποκαλυφθήσεται καὶ κρυπτὸν ὃ οὐ γνωσθήσεται. 27 ὃ λέγω ὑμῖν ἐν τῇ σκοτίᾳ εἴπατε ἐν τῷ φωτί, καὶ ὃ εἰς τὸ οὖς ἀκούετε κηρύξατε ἐπὶ τῶν δωμάτων. 28 καὶ μὴ φοβεῖσθε ἀπὸ

kill		the	body	but		cannot		kill		the	soul.		Rather,	be afraid		of the	One who can		destroy
ἀποκτεννόντων		τὸ	σῶμα	δὲ	μὴ	δυναμένων		ἀποκτεῖναι		τὴν	ψυχὴν	δὲ	μᾶλλον	→ φοβεῖσθε ←		τὸν		δυνάμενον	ἀπολέσαι
pt.pa.gpm		d.asn	n.asn	cj	pl	pt.pp.gpm		v.aa		d.asf	n.asf	cj	adv.c	v.ppm.2p		d.asm		pt.pp.asm	f.aa
650		3836	5393	1254	3590	1538		650		3836	6034	1254	3437	5828		3836		1538	660

both	soul	and	body	in	hell.	**29** Are not	two	sparrows	sold		for a penny?	Yet	not	one	of	them	will	fall		to	the
καὶ	ψυχὴν	καὶ	σῶμα	ἐν	γεέννῃ	→ οὐχὶ	δύο	στρουθία	πωλεῖται	→	ἀσσαρίου	καὶ	οὐ	ἓν	ἐξ	αὐτῶν	→	πεσεῖται	ἐπὶ	τὴν
cj	n.asf	cj	n.asn	p.d	n.dsf	pl	a.npn	n.npn	v.ppi.3s		n.gsn	cj	adv	a.nsn	p.g	r.gpn.3		v.fmi.3s	p.a	d.asf
2779	6034	2779	5393	1877	1147	4797	4049	1545	5141		837	2779	4024	1651	1666	899		4406	2093	3836

ground	apart	from	the	will	of your	Father.	**30** And	even	the	very	hairs	of	your	head		are	all	numbered.
γῆν	ἄνευ ←				ὑμῶν	⌐τοῦ πατρὸς⌐	δὲ	καὶ	αἱ		τρίχες	→	ὑμῶν	⌐τῆς κεφαλῆς⌐		εἰσίν	πᾶσαι	ἠριθμημέναι
n.asf	p.g				r.gp.2	d.gsm n.gsm	cj	adv	d.npf		n.npf		r.gp.2	d.gsf n.gsf		v.pai.3p	a.npf	pt.rp.npf
1178	459				7007	3836 4252	1254	2779	3836		2582		3051	7007	3836 3051		1639	4246	749

31 So	don't	be afraid;	you	are worth		more	than	many	sparrows.	¶	**32**	"Whoever	acknowledges	me
οὖν μὴ	→	φοβεῖσθε	ὑμεῖς	→ διαφέρετε ←	→		πολλῶν	στρουθίων				οὖν ⌐Πᾶς⌐ ὅστις	ὁμολογήσει	⌐ἐν ἐμοὶ⌐
cj	pl	v.ppm.2p	r.np.2	v.pai.2p			a.gpn	n.gpn				cj a.nsm r.nsm	v.fai.3s	p.d r.ds.1
4036	3590	5828	7007	1422			4498	5141				4036 4246 4015	3933	1877 1609

before	men,	I	will also	acknowledge	him		before	my	Father		in	heaven.	**33** But
ἔμπροσθεν	⌐τῶν ἀνθρώπων⌐		καγὼ ὁμολογήσω		⌐ἐν αὐτῷ⌐	ἔμπροσθεν	μου	⌐τοῦ πατρός⌐	τοῦ	ἐν	⌐τοῖς οὐρανοῖς⌐	δ'
p.g	d.gpm n.gpm		crasis v.fai.1s		p.d r.dsm.3	p.g	r.gs.1	d.gsm n.gsm	d.gsm	p.d	d.dpm n.dpm	cj
1869	3836 476		2743 3933	2743	3933	1877 899	1869	1609 3836 4252	3836	1877	3836 4041	1254

whoever	disowns	me	before	men,		I	will	disown	him	before	my	Father		in	heaven.
⌐ὅστις	ἂν	ἀρνήσηται	με	ἔμπροσθεν	⌐τῶν ἀνθρώπων⌐	καγὼ	→	ἀρνήσομαι	αὐτὸν	ἔμπροσθεν	μου	⌐τοῦ πατρός⌐	τοῦ	ἐν	⌐τοῖς οὐρανοῖς⌐
r.nsm	pl	v.ams.3s	r.as.1	p.g	d.gpm n.gpm	crasis		v.fmi.1s	r.asm.3	p.g	r.gs.1	d.gsm n.gsm	d.gsm	p.d	d.dpm n.dpm
4015	323	766	1609	1869	3836 476	2743		766	899	1869	1609	3836 4252	3836	1877	3836 4041

¶	**34** "Do	not	suppose	that	I	have	come	to	bring	peace	to	the	earth.	I	did	not	come	to	bring	peace,	but	a
→	Μὴ	νομίσητε	ὅτι	→	→		ἦλθον	→	βαλεῖν	εἰρήνην	ἐπὶ	τὴν	γῆν		→	οὐκ	ἦλθον	→	βαλεῖν	εἰρήνην	ἀλλὰ
	pl	v.aas.2p	cj				v.aai.1s		f.aa	n.asf	p.a	d.asf	n.asf			adv	v.aai.1s		f.aa	n.asf	cj
3787	3590	3787	4022				2262		965	1645	2093	3836	1178		2262	2262	4024	2262	965	1645	247

sword.	**35** For	I	have	come	to	turn	'a	man		against	his	father,		a	daughter	against	her	mother,		a
μάχαιραν	γὰρ	→	→	ἦλθον	→	διχάσαι		ἄνθρωπον	κατὰ		αὐτοῦ	⌐τοῦ πατρός⌐	καὶ		θυγατέρα	κατὰ	αὐτῆς	⌐τῆς μητρὸς⌐	καὶ
n.asf	cj			v.aai.1s		f.aa		n.asm	p.g		r.gsm.3	d.gsm n.gsm	cj		n.asf	p.g	r.gsf.3	d.gsf n.gsf	cj
3479	1142			2262		1495		476	2848		899	3836 4252	2779		2588	2848	899	3836 3613	2779

daughter-in-law	against	her	mother-in-law –	**36**	a	man's		enemies	will be	the	members of his		own
νύμφην	κατὰ	αὐτῆς	⌐τῆς πενθερᾶς⌐	καὶ		⌐τοῦ ἀνθρώπου⌐	ἐχθροὶ		οἱ	οἰκιακοὶ	→	αὐτοῦ
n.asf	p.g	r.gsf.3	d.gsf n.gsf	cj		d.gsm n.gsm	a.npm		d.npm	n.npm		r.gsm.3
3811	2848	899	3836 4289	2779		3836 476	2398		3836	3865		899

household.'	¶	**37** "Anyone	who	loves	his	father	or	mother	more	than	me	is	not	worthy	of me;		anyone	who
←		Ὁ	←	φιλῶν		πατέρα	ἢ	μητέρα	ὑπὲρ		ἐμὲ	ἔστιν	οὐκ	ἄξιος	→	μου	καὶ	ὁ
		d.nsm		pt.pa.nsm		n.asm	cj	n.asf	p.a		r.as.1	v.pai.3s	adv	a.nsm		r.gs.1	cj	d.nsm
3865		3836		5797		4252	2445	3613	5642		1609	1639	4024	545		1609	2779	3836

loves	his	son	or	daughter	more	than	me	is	not	worthy	of me;	**38** and	anyone	who	does	not	take		his	cross
φιλῶν		υἱὸν	ἢ	θυγατέρα	ὑπὲρ		ἐμὲ	ἔστιν	οὐκ	ἄξιος	→ μου	καὶ		ὃς	→	οὐ	λαμβάνει	αὐτοῦ	⌐τὸν σταυρὸν⌐
pt.pa.nsm		n.asm	cj	n.asf	p.a		r.as.1	v.pai.3s	adv	a.nsm	r.gs.1	cj		r.nsm		adv	v.pai.3s	r.gsm.3	d.asm n.asm
5797		5626	2445	2588	5642		1609	1639	4024	545	1609	2779		4005		3284	4024	3284	899	3836 5089

and	follow	me	is	not	worthy	of me.	**39** Whoever	finds	his	life		will	lose	it,		and	whoever
καὶ	ἀκολουθεῖ	ὀπίσω	μου	ἔστιν	οὐκ	ἄξιος	→ μου	ὁ	εὑρὼν	αὐτοῦ	⌐τὴν ψυχὴν⌐	→	ἀπολέσει	αὐτὴν	καὶ	ὁ
cj	v.pai.3s	p.g	r.gs.1	v.pai.3s	adv	a.nsm	r.gs.1	d.nsm	pt.aa.nsm	r.gsm.3	d.asf n.asf		v.fai.3s	r.asf.3	cj	d.nsm
2779	199	3958	1609	1639	4024	545	1609	3836	2351	899	3836 6034		660	899	2779	3836

loses	his	life	for	my	sake	will	find	it.	¶	**40** "He	who	receives	you	receives	me, and	he	who
ἀπολέσας	αὐτοῦ	⌐τὴν ψυχὴν⌐	→	ἐμοῦ	ἕνεκεν	→	εὑρήσει	αὐτήν	¶	Ὁ		δεχόμενος	ὑμᾶς	δέχεται	ἐμὲ	καὶ ὁ	
pt.aa.nsm	r.gsm.3	d.asf n.asf		r.gs.1	p.g		v.fai.3s	r.asf.3		d.nsm		pt.pm.nsm	r.ap.2	v.pmi.3s	r.as.1	cj d.nsm	
660	899	3836 6034		1914	1609	1914	2351	899		3836		1312	7007	1312	1609	2779 3836	

receives	me	receives	the	one who sent		me.	**41** Anyone	who	receives	a	prophet	because	he is	a prophet	will
δεχόμενος	ἐμὲ	δέχεται	τὸν	←	ἀποστείλαντα	με	ὁ	←	δεχόμενος	προφήτην	εἰς ὄνομα	←		προφήτου	→
pt.pm.nsm	r.as.1	v.pmi.3s	d.asm		pt.aa.asm	r.as.1	d.nsm		pt.pm.nsm	n.asm	p.a n.asn			n.gsm	
1312	1609	1312	3836		690	1609	3836		1312	4737	1650 3950			4737	

τῶν ἀποκτεννόντων τὸ σῶμα, τὴν δὲ ψυχὴν μὴ δυναμένων ἀποκτεῖναι· φοβεῖσθε δὲ μᾶλλον τὸν δυνάμενον καὶ ψυχὴν καὶ σῶμα ἀπολέσαι ἐν γεέννῃ. ²⁹ οὐχὶ δύο στρουθία ἀσσαρίου πωλεῖται; καὶ ἓν ἐξ αὐτῶν οὐ πεσεῖται ἐπὶ τὴν γῆν ἄνευ τοῦ πατρὸς ὑμῶν. ³⁰ ὑμῶν δὲ καὶ αἱ τρίχες τῆς κεφαλῆς πᾶσαι ἠριθμημέναι εἰσίν. ³¹ μὴ οὖν φοβεῖσθε· πολλῶν στρουθίων διαφέρετε ὑμεῖς. ¶ ³² Πᾶς οὖν ὅστις ὁμολογήσει ἐν ἐμοὶ ἔμπροσθεν τῶν ἀνθρώπων, ὁμολογήσω καγὼ ἐν αὐτῷ ἔμπροσθεν τοῦ πατρός μου τοῦ ἐν [τοῖς] οὐρανοῖς· ³³ ὅστις δ' ἂν ἀρνήσηται με ἔμπροσθεν τῶν ἀνθρώπων, ἀρνήσομαι καγὼ αὐτὸν ἔμπροσθεν τοῦ πατρός μου τοῦ ἐν [τοῖς] οὐρανοῖς. ¶ ³⁴ Μὴ νομίσητε ὅτι ἦλθον βαλεῖν εἰρήνην ἐπὶ τὴν γῆν· οὐκ ἦλθον βαλεῖν εἰρήνην ἀλλὰ μάχαιραν. ³⁵ ἦλθον γὰρ διχάσαι ἄνθρωπον κατὰ τοῦ πατρὸς αὐτοῦ καὶ θυγατέρα κατὰ τῆς μητρὸς αὐτῆς καὶ νύμφην κατὰ τῆς πενθερᾶς αὐτῆς, ³⁶ καὶ ἐχθροὶ τοῦ ἀνθρώπου οἱ οἰκιακοὶ αὐτοῦ. ¶ ³⁷ Ὁ φιλῶν πατέρα ἢ μητέρα ὑπὲρ ἐμὲ οὐκ ἔστιν μου ἄξιος, καὶ ὁ φιλῶν υἱὸν ἢ θυγατέρα ὑπὲρ ἐμὲ οὐκ ἔστιν μου ἄξιος· ³⁸ καὶ ὃς οὐ λαμβάνει τὸν σταυρὸν αὐτοῦ καὶ ἀκολουθεῖ ὀπίσω μου, οὐκ ἔστιν μου ἄξιος. ³⁹ ὁ εὑρὼν τὴν ψυχὴν αὐτοῦ ἀπολέσει αὐτήν, καὶ ὁ ἀπολέσας τὴν ψυχὴν αὐτοῦ ἕνεκεν ἐμοῦ εὑρήσει αὐτήν. ¶ ⁴⁰ Ὁ δεχόμενος ὑμᾶς ἐμὲ δέχεται, καὶ ὁ ἐμὲ δεχόμενος δέχεται τὸν ἀποστείλαντά με. ⁴¹ ὁ δεχόμενος προφήτην εἰς ὄνομα προφήτου μισθὸν

receive	a prophet's	reward,	and		anyone	who	receives	a righteous man	because		he is	a righteous man	will	receive
λήμψεται	προφήτου	μισθὸν	καὶ	ὁ		←	δεχόμενος	δίκαιον	εἰς ὄνομα	←	←	δικαίου	→	λήμψεται
v.fmi.3s	n.gsm	n.asm	cj	d.nsm			pt.pm.nsm	a.asm	p.a n.asn			a.gsm		v.fmi.3s
3284	4737	3635	2779	3836			1312	1465	1650 3950			1465		3284

a righteous man's	reward.	[42] And	if	anyone	gives	even	a cup	of cold	water	to	one	of these	little		ones
δικαίου	μισθὸν	καὶ	→	ὅς ἄν	ποτίσῃ	μόνον	ποτήριον	→	ψυχροῦ	←	ἕνα	τούτων	τῶν μικρῶν	←	
a.gsm	n.asm	cj		r.nsm pl	v.aas.3s	adv	n.asn		n.gsn		a.asm	r.gpm	d.gpm a.gpm		
1465	3635	2779		4005 323	4540	3667	4539		6037		1651	4047	3836 3625		

because	he is	my disciple,	I	tell	you	the truth,	he will	certainly	not	lose	his	reward."
εἰς ὄνομα	←	μαθητοῦ	→	λέγω	ὑμῖν	ἀμὴν	→	→	οὐ μὴ	ἀπολέσῃ	αὐτοῦ	τὸν μισθὸν
p.a n.asn		n.gsm		v.pai.1s	r.dp.2	pl			adv pl	v.aas.3s	r.gsm.3	d.asm n.asm
1650 3950		3412		3306	7007	297	660	660	4024 3590	660	899	3836 3635

Jesus and John the Baptist

11:1

After	Jesus		had finished	instructing	his	twelve	disciples,		he went on	from	there	to
Καὶ ἐγένετο ὅτε	ὁ	Ἰησοῦς,	→ ἐτέλεσεν	διατάσσων	αὐτοῦ	δώδεκα	τοῖς μαθηταῖς,	→	μετέβη	ἐκεῖθεν ←		→
cj v.ami.3s cj	d.nsm	n.nsm	v.aai.3s	pt.pa.nsm	r.gsm.3	a.dpm	d.dpm n.dpm		v.aai.3s	adv		
2779 1181 4021	3836	2652	5464	1411	899	1557	3836 3412		3553	1696		

teach	and	preach	in	the	towns	of	Galilee.	¶	[2]	When	John		heard	in	prison
τοῦ διδάσκειν	καὶ	κηρύσσειν	ἐν	ταῖς	πόλεσιν	→	αὐτῶν			δὲ →	Ὁ Ἰωάννης		ἀκούσας	ἐν	τῷ δεσμωτηρίῳ
d.gsn f.pa	cj	f.pa	p.d	d.dpf	n.dpf		r.gpm.3			cj	d.nsm n.nsm		pt.aa.nsm	p.d	d.dsn n.dsn
3836 1438	2779	3062	1877	3836	4484		899			1254 201	3836 2722		201	1877	3836 1303

what	Christ		was doing,	he sent		his	disciples	[3]	to ask	him,	"Are	you	the one	who was to		come,
τὰ ἔργα	τοῦ Χριστοῦ		πέμψας	διὰ	αὐτοῦ	τῶν μαθητῶν		εἶπεν	αὐτῷ	εἶ	σὺ	ὁ	→	→	ἐρχόμενος
d.apn n.apn	d.gsm n.gsm		pt.aa.nsm	p.g	r.gsm.3	d.gpm n.gpm		v.aai.3s	r.dsm.3	v.pai.2s	r.ns.2	d.nsm			pt.pm.nsm
3836 2240	3836 5986		4287	1328	899	3836 3412		3306	899	1639	5148	3836			2262

or		should we expect	someone else?"	[4]		Jesus		replied,		"Go		back	and report		to
ἤ	→	→ προσδοκῶμεν	ἕτερον	←	καὶ	ὁ	Ἰησοῦς,	ἀποκριθεὶς	εἶπεν αὐτοῖς	πορευθέντες ←					ἀπαγγείλατε →
cj		v.pai.1p	r.asn		cj	d.nsm	n.nsm	pt.ap.nsm	v.aai.3s r.dpm.3	pt.ap.npm					v.aam.2p
2445		4659	2283		2779	3836	2652	646	3306 899	4513					550

John	what	you hear		and	see:	[5]	The blind	receive sight,		the lame	walk,		those who have	leprosy
Ἰωάννῃ	ἃ	ἀκούετε	καὶ	βλέπετε			τυφλοὶ	→ ἀναβλέπουσιν	καὶ	χωλοὶ	περιπατοῦσιν	→	→	λεπροὶ
n.dsm	r.apn	v.pai.2p	cj	v.pai.2p			a.npm	v.pai.3p	cj	a.npm	v.pai.3p			a.npm
2722	4005	201	2779	1063			5603	329	2779	6000	4344			3320

are cured,		the deaf	hear,		the dead	are raised,		and	the good news	is preached		to the poor.
→ καθαρίζονται	καὶ	κωφοὶ	ἀκούουσιν	καὶ	νεκροὶ	→ ἐγείρονται	καὶ			→ εὐαγγελίζονται	→	πτωχοὶ
v.ppi.3p	cj	a.npm	v.pai.3p	cj	a.npm	v.ppi.3p	cj			v.ppi.3p		a.npm
2751	2779	3273	201	2779	3738	1586	2779			2294		4777

[6]	Blessed	is	the	man	who	does	not	fall	away	on account of me."	¶	[7]	As	John's	disciples
καὶ	μακάριος	ἐστιν		ὅς	ἐὰν	μὴ		σκανδαλισθῇ	←	ἐν ← ἐμοί		δὲ → →			Τούτων
cj	a.nsm	v.pai.3s		r.nsm	pl	pl		v.aps.3s		p.d r.ds.1		cj			r.gpm
2779	3421	1639		4005	1569	4997		3590	4997	1877 1609		1254 4513			4047

were leaving,		Jesus		began	to speak	to the	crowd	about	John:	"What	did you	go		out	into	the	desert
→ πορευομένων	ὁ	Ἰησοῦς,	ἤρξατο	→	λέγειν	τοῖς	ὄχλοις	περὶ	Ἰωάννου	τί	→	ἐξήλθατε	←	εἰς	τὴν		ἔρημον
pt.pm.gpm	d.nsm	n.nsm	v.ami.3s		f.pa	d.dpm	n.dpm	p.g	n.gsm	r.asn		v.aai.2p		p.a	d.asf		n.asf
4513	3836	2652	806		3306	3836	4063	4309	2722	5515		2002		1650	3836		2245

to see?	A reed	swayed	by	the wind?	[8]	If	not,	what	did you	go		out	to see?	A man	dressed		in
→ θεάσασθαι	κάλαμον	σαλευόμενον	ὑπὸ	ἀνέμου	ἀλλὰ		τί		→	ἐξήλθατε	←	→	ἰδεῖν	ἄνθρωπον	ἠμφιεσμένον	ἐν
f.am	n.asm	pt.pp.asm	p.g	n.gsm	cj		r.asn			v.aai.2p			f.aa	n.asm	pt.rp.asm	p.d
2517	2812	4888	5679	449	247		5515			2002			1625	476	314	1877

fine clothes?	No,	those	who	wear		fine	clothes	are	in	kings'		palaces.	[9]	Then	what	did	you	go
μαλακοῖς	ἰδοὺ	οἱ	←	φοροῦντες		τὰ	μαλακὰ	εἰσίν	ἐν	τῶν βασιλέων		τοῖς οἴκοις		ἀλλὰ	τί		→	ἐξήλθατε
a.dpn	j	d.npm		pt.pa.npm		d.apn	a.apn	v.pai.3p	p.d	d.gpm n.gpm		d.dpm n.dpm		cj	r.asn			v.aai.2p
3434	2627	3836		5841		3836	3434	1639	1877	3836 995		3836 3875		247	5515			2002

out to see?	A prophet?	Yes,	I	tell	you,	and	more		than a prophet.	[10]	This	is		the one	about	whom	it is
← → ἰδεῖν	προφήτην	ναί	→	λέγω	ὑμῖν	καὶ	περισσότερον	←	προφήτου		οὗτος	ἐστιν			περὶ	οὗ	→ →
f.aa	n.asm	pl		v.pai.1s	r.dp.2	cj	adv.c		n.gsm		r.nsm	v.pai.3s			p.g	r.gsm	
1625	4737	3721		3306	7007	2779	4358		4737		4047	1639			4309	4005	

προφήτου λήμψεται, καὶ ὁ δεχόμενος δίκαιον εἰς ὄνομα δικαίου μισθὸν δικαίου λήμψεται. **42** καὶ ὃς ἂν ποτίσῃ ἕνα τῶν μικρῶν τούτων ποτήριον ψυχροῦ μόνον εἰς ὄνομα μαθητοῦ, ἀμὴν λέγω ὑμῖν, οὐ μὴ ἀπολέσῃ τὸν μισθὸν αὐτοῦ.

11:1 Καὶ ἐγένετο ὅτε ἐτέλεσεν ὁ Ἰησοῦς διατάσσων τοῖς δώδεκα μαθηταῖς αὐτοῦ, μετέβη ἐκεῖθεν τοῦ διδάσκειν καὶ κηρύσσειν ἐν ταῖς πόλεσιν αὐτῶν. ¶ **2** Ὁ δὲ Ἰωάννης ἀκούσας ἐν τῷ δεσμωτηρίῳ τὰ ἔργα τοῦ Χριστοῦ πέμψας διὰ τῶν μαθητῶν αὐτοῦ **3** εἶπεν αὐτῷ, Σὺ εἶ ὁ ἐρχόμενος ἢ ἕτερον προσδοκῶμεν; **4** καὶ ἀποκριθεὶς ὁ Ἰησοῦς εἶπεν αὐτοῖς, Πορευθέντες ἀπαγγείλατε Ἰωάννῃ ἃ ἀκούετε καὶ βλέπετε· **5** τυφλοὶ ἀναβλέπουσιν καὶ χωλοὶ περιπατοῦσιν, λεπροὶ καθαρίζονται καὶ κωφοὶ ἀκούουσιν, καὶ νεκροὶ ἐγείρονται καὶ πτωχοὶ εὐαγγελίζονται· **6** καὶ μακάριός ἐστιν ὃς ἐὰν μὴ σκανδαλισθῇ ἐν ἐμοί. ¶ **7** Τούτων δὲ πορευομένων ἤρξατο ὁ Ἰησοῦς λέγειν τοῖς ὄχλοις περὶ Ἰωάννου, Τί ἐξήλθατε εἰς τὴν ἔρημον θεάσασθαι; κάλαμον ὑπὸ ἀνέμου σαλευόμενον; **8** ἀλλὰ τί ἐξήλθατε ἰδεῖν; ἄνθρωπον ἐν μαλακοῖς ἠμφιεσμένον; ἰδοὺ οἱ τὰ μαλακὰ φοροῦντες ἐν τοῖς οἴκοις τῶν βασιλέων εἰσίν. **9** ἀλλὰ τί ἐξήλθατε ἰδεῖν; προφήτην; ναὶ λέγω ὑμῖν, καὶ περισσότερον προφήτου. **10** οὗτός ἐστιν περὶ οὗ

written:　　　"'I　will　send　　　my　messenger　ahead of you,　　　who will prepare　　your way　　before
γέγραπται　ἰδοὺ　ἐγὼ　→　ἀποστέλλω μου　⸤τὸν ἄγγελον⸥　πρὸ　←　⸤προσώπου σου⸥　ὃς　→　κατασκευάσει σου　⸤τὴν ὁδόν⸥　ἔμπροσθεν
v.rpi.3s　j　r.ns.1　　v.pai.1s r.gs.1　d.asm n.asm　p.g　　n.gsn r.gs.2　r.nsm　　v.fai.3s r.gs.2　d.asf n.asf　p.g
1211　　2627　1609　　690　　　1609　3836 34　　4574　　　4725　　5148　4005　　2941　　5148　3836 3847　1869

you.'　11 I　tell　you the truth:　Among those born　　of women　there has not risen　　anyone greater than John　the
σου　→ λέγω ὑμῖν　Ἀμὴν　ἐν　→　γεννητοῖς　→ γυναικῶν ↗　↗　οὐκ ἐγήγερται　　μείζων　←　Ἰωάννου τοῦ
r.gs.2　　v.pai.1s r.dp.2　pl　p.d　　n.dpm　　　n.gpf　　　　adv v.rpi.3s　　a.nsm.c　　n.gsm d.gsm
5148　　3306 7007　297　1877　　1168　　　1222　　1586 1586 4024 1586　　3489　　　2722 3836

Baptist; yet he who is least　　in the kingdom of heaven　　is　greater than he.　12　From the days of
βαπτιστοῦ δὲ ὁ　←　μικρότερος ἐν τῇ βασιλείᾳ　→ ⸤τῶν οὐρανῶν⸥ ἐστιν μείζων　→　αὐτοῦ　δὲ ἀπὸ　τῶν ἡμερῶν →
n.gsm　cj d.nsm　a.nsm.c　p.d d.dsf n.dsf　　d.gpm n.gpm　v.pai.3s a.nsm.c　　r.gsm.3　cj p.g　d.gpf n.gpf
969　　1254 3836　3625　　1877 3836 993　　3836 4041　1639 3489　　899　　1254 608　3836 2465

John　　the Baptist　until now, the kingdom of heaven　　has been forcefully advancing, and forceful men
Ἰωάννου τοῦ βαπτιστοῦ ἕως ἄρτι ἡ βασιλεία ⸤τῶν οὐρανῶν⸥ →　→　βιάζεται　　　　and βιασταὶ ←
n.gsm　d.gsm n.gsm　p.g adv d.nsf n.nsf　d.gpm n.gpm　　v.ppi.3s　　　　cj n.npm
2722　3836 969　　2401 785 3836 993　3836 4041　　1041　　　　2779 1043

lay　　hold of it.　13 For all　　the Prophets and the Law prophesied until John.　14 And if　you are willing to
ἁρπάζουσιν ←　← αὐτήν γὰρ πάντες οἱ προφῆται καὶ ὁ νόμος ἐπροφήτευσαν ἕως Ἰωάννου καὶ εἰ →　→　θέλετε →
v.pai.3p　　　r.asf.3　cj a.npm d.npm n.npm　cj d.nsm n.nsm v.aai.3p　　p.g n.gsm　cj cj　　　v.pai.2p
773　　　　899　1142 4246 3836 4737　2779 3836 3795 4736　　2401 2722　2779 1623　　2527

accept it, he　is　the Elijah who was　to come.　15 He who has　ears, let him hear.　¶　16　"To what can
δέξασθαι αὐτός ἐστιν Ἠλίας ὁ μέλλων → ἔρχεσθαι ὁ ← ἔχων ὦτα　→ ἀκουέτω　δὲ → Τίνι →
f.am　r.nsm v.pai.3s n.nsm d.nsm pt.pa.nsm　f.pm　d.nsm pt.pa.nsm n.apn　v.pam.3s　cj　r.dsn
1312　899 1639　2460 3836 3516　　2262　3836　2400 4044　201　　1254　5515

I compare this　generation? They are like children sitting　　in the marketplaces　　and calling　　out to
→ ὁμοιώσω ταύτην ⸤τὴν γενεάν⸥ → ἐστιν ὁμοία παιδίοις καθημένοις ἐν ταῖς ἀγοραῖς　ἃ　προσφωνοῦντα →
v.fai.1s　r.asf　d.asf n.asf　　v.pai.3s a.nsf n.dpn pt.pp.dpn　p.d d.dpf n.dpf　r.npn　pt.pa.npn
3929　4047　3836 1155　　1639 3927 4086　2764　1877 3836 59　4005　4715

others:　　17 "We played　the flute for you, and you did not dance;　we sang　　a dirge, and you did
⸤τοῖς ἑτέροις⸥ λέγουσιν　ηὐλήσαμεν ←　→ ὑμῖν καὶ ↗　οὐκ ὠρχήσασθε　ἐθρηνήσαμεν　　καὶ ↗
d.dpn r.dpn　v.pai.3p　　v.aai.1p　　　r.dp.2 cj　adv v.ami.2p　v.aai.1p　　　cj
3836 2283　3306　　884　　　7007 2779 4004 4004 4024 4004　2577　　　2779 3164 3164

not mourn.'　18 For John　came neither eating nor drinking, and they say,　'He has a demon.'　19 The Son of
οὐκ ἐκόψασθε γὰρ Ἰωάννης ἦλθεν μήτε ἐσθίων μήτε πίνων καὶ → λέγουσιν → ἔχει δαιμόνιον ὁ υἱὸς →
adv v.ami.2p cj n.nsm　v.aai.3s cj　pt.pa.nsm cj pt.pa.nsm cj　v.pai.3p　v.pai.3s n.asn　d.nsm n.nsm
4024 3164　1142 2722　2262 3612 2266 3612 4403 2779　3306　2400 1228　3836 5626

Man　came eating and drinking, and they say,　'Here is a glutton　　and a drunkard, a friend of tax
⸤τοῦ ἀνθρώπου⸥ ἦλθεν ἐσθίων καὶ πίνων καὶ → λέγουσιν ἰδοὺ ← ⸤ἄνθρωπος φάγος⸥ καὶ οἰνοπότης φίλος → →
d.gsm n.gsm　v.aai.3s pt.pa.nsm cj pt.pa.nsm cj　v.pai.3p j　　n.nsm　　cj n.nsm　a.nsm
3836 476　2262 2266 2779 4403 2779　3306 2627　476　5741　2779 3884　5813

collectors and "sinners." 'But wisdom　is proved right　by her　actions."
τελωνῶν καὶ ἁμαρτωλῶν καὶ ⸤ἡ σοφία⸥ → → ἐδικαιώθη ἀπὸ αὐτῆς ⸤τῶν ἔργων⸥
n.gpm　cj a.gpm　cj d.nsf n.nsf　　v.api.3s p.g r.gsf.3 d.gpn n.gpn
5467　2779 283　2779 3836 5053　　1467　608 899 3836 2240

Woe on Unrepentant Cities

11:20 Then Jesus began to denounce the cities in which most　　of his　miracles had been performed,
Τότε　ἤρξατο → ὀνειδίζειν τὰς πόλεις ἐν αἷς　⸤αἱ πλεῖσται⸥ αὐτοῦ δυνάμεις → ἐγένοντο
adv　v.ami.3s　f.pa　　d.apf n.apf p.d d.dpf　d.npf a.npf.s　r.gsm.3 n.npf　　v.ami.3p
5538　806　3943　　3836 4484 1877 4005　3836 4498　899 1539　　1181

because they did not repent.　21 "Woe to you, Korazin! Woe to you, Bethsaida!　If the miracles that were
ὅτι　↗ → οὐ μετενόησαν οὐαί → σοι Χοραζίν οὐαί → σοι Βηθσαϊδά ὅτι εἰ αἱ δυνάμεις αἱ →
cj　　adv v.aai.3p　j → r.ds.2 n.vsf　j → r.ds.2 n.vsf　cj cj d.npf n.npf　d.npf
4022　3566 3566 4024 3566　4026　5148 5960　4026　5148 1034　4022 1623 3836 1539　3836

performed in you had been performed in Tyre and Sidon, they would have repented long ago in sackcloth and
γενόμεναι ἐν ὑμῖν → → ἐγένοντο ἐν Τύρῳ καὶ Σιδῶνι ↗ ἂν → μετενόησαν πάλαι ← ἐν σάκκῳ καὶ
pt.am.npf p.d r.dp.2　　v.ami.3p p.d n.dsf cj n.dsf　pl　v.aai.3p　adv　p.d n.dsm cj
1181　1877 7007　　1181　1877 5602 2779 4972　3566　3566　4093　1877 4884 2779

γέγραπται, Ἰδοὺ ἐγὼ ἀποστέλλω τὸν ἄγγελόν μου πρὸ προσώπου σου, ὃς κατασκευάσει τὴν ὁδόν σου ἔμπροσθέν σου. 11 ἀμὴν λέγω ὑμῖν· οὐκ ἐγήγερται ἐν γεννητοῖς γυναικῶν μείζων Ἰωάννου τοῦ βαπτιστοῦ· ὁ δὲ μικρότερος ἐν τῇ βασιλείᾳ τῶν οὐρανῶν μείζων αὐτοῦ ἐστιν. 12 ἀπὸ δὲ τῶν ἡμερῶν Ἰωάννου τοῦ βαπτιστοῦ ἕως ἄρτι ἡ βασιλεία τῶν οὐρανῶν βιάζεται καὶ βιασταὶ ἁρπάζουσιν αὐτήν. 13 πάντες γὰρ οἱ προφῆται καὶ ὁ νόμος ἕως Ἰωάννου ἐπροφήτευσαν· 14 καὶ εἰ θέλετε δέξασθαι, αὐτός ἐστιν Ἠλίας ὁ μέλλων ἔρχεσθαι. 15 ὁ ἔχων ὦτα ἀκουέτω. ¶ 16 Τίνι δὲ ὁμοιώσω τὴν γενεὰν ταύτην; ὁμοία ἐστὶν παιδίοις καθημένοις ἐν ταῖς ἀγοραῖς ἃ προσφωνοῦντα τοῖς ἑτέροις 17 λέγουσιν, Ηὐλήσαμεν ὑμῖν καὶ οὐκ ὠρχήσασθε, ἐθρηνήσαμεν καὶ οὐκ ἐκόψασθε. 18 ἦλθεν γὰρ Ἰωάννης μήτε ἐσθίων μήτε πίνων, καὶ λέγουσιν, Δαιμόνιον ἔχει. 19 ἦλθεν ὁ υἱὸς τοῦ ἀνθρώπου ἐσθίων καὶ πίνων, καὶ λέγουσιν, Ἰδοὺ ἄνθρωπος φάγος καὶ οἰνοπότης, τελωνῶν φίλος καὶ ἁμαρτωλῶν. καὶ ἐδικαιώθη ἡ σοφία ἀπὸ τῶν ἔργων αὐτῆς. 11:20 Τότε ἤρξατο ὁ Ἰησοῦς ὀνειδίζειν τὰς πόλεις ἐν αἷς ἐγένοντο αἱ πλεῖσται δυνάμεις αὐτοῦ, ὅτι οὐ μετενόησαν· 21 Οὐαί σοι, Χοραζίν, οὐαί σοι, Βηθσαϊδά· ὅτι εἰ ἐν Τύρῳ καὶ Σιδῶνι ἐγένοντο αἱ δυνάμεις αἱ γενόμεναι ἐν ὑμῖν, πάλαι ἂν ἐν σάκκῳ

ashes. **22** But I tell you, it will be more bearable for Tyre and Sidon on the day of judgment than for you.
σποδῷ πλὴν λέγω ὑμῖν → ἔσται → ἀνεκτότερον → Τύρῳ καὶ Σιδῶνι ἐν ἡμέρᾳ κρίσεως ἢ → ὑμῖν
n.dsf cj v.pai.1s r.dp.2 v.fmi.3s a.nsn.c n.dsf cj n.dsf p.d n.dsf n.gsf pl r.dp.2
5075 4440 3306 7007 1639 445 5602 2779 4972 1877 2465 3213 2445 7007

23 And you, Capernaum, will you be lifted up to the skies? No, you will go down to the depths. If the
καὶ σύ Καφαρναούμ → → ὑψωθήσῃ ← ἕως οὐρανοῦ μὴ → → καταβήσῃ ← ἕως ᾅδου ὅτι εἰ αἱ
cj r.ns.2 n.vsf v.fpi.2s p.g n.gsm pl v.fmi.2s p.g n.gsm cj cj d.npf
2779 5148 3019 5738 2401 4041 3590 2849 2401 87 4022 1623 3836

miracles that were performed in you had been performed in Sodom, it would have remained to this day.
δυνάμεις αἱ → γενόμεναι ἐν σοί → → ἐγενήθησαν ἐν Σοδόμοις → ἂν → → ἔμεινεν μέχρι τῆς σήμερον
n.npf d.npf pt.am.npf p.d r.ds.2 v.api.3p p.d n.dpn pl v.aai.3s p.g d.gsf adv
1539 3836 1181 1877 5148 1181 1877 5047 3531 323 3531 3588 3836 4958

24 But I tell you that it will be more bearable for Sodom on the day of judgment than for you."
πλὴν λέγω ὑμῖν ὅτι → → ἔσται → ἀνεκτότερον → γῇ Σοδόμων ἐν ἡμέρᾳ κρίσεως ἢ → σοί
cj v.pai.1s r.dp.2 cj v.fmi.3s a.nsn.c n.dsf n.gpn p.d n.dsf n.gsf pl r.ds.2
4440 3306 7007 4022 1639 445 1178 5047 1877 2465 3213 2445 5148

Rest for the Weary

11:25 At that time Jesus said, "I praise you, Father, Lord of heaven and earth,
Ἐν ἐκείνῳ τῷ καιρῷ ὁ Ἰησοῦς ἀποκριθεὶς εἶπεν Ἐξομολογοῦμαι σοι πάτερ κύριε τοῦ οὐρανοῦ καὶ τῆς γῆς
p.d r.dsm d.dsm n.dsm d.nsm n.nsm pt.ap.nsm v.aai.3s v.pmi.1s r.ds.2 n.vsm n.vsm d.gsm n.gsm cj d.gsf n.gsf
1877 1697 3836 2789 3836 2652 646 3306 2018 5148 4252 3261 3836 4041 2779 3836 1178

because you have hidden these things from the wise and learned, and revealed them to little children. **26** Yes,
ὅτι → → ἔκρυψας ταῦτα ← ἀπὸ σοφῶν καὶ συνετῶν καὶ ἀπεκάλυψας αὐτὰ → νηπίοις ναὶ
cj v.aai.2s r.apn p.g a.gpm cj a.gpm cj v.aai.2s r.apn.3 a.dpm pl
4022 3221 4047 608 5055 2779 5305 2779 636 899 3758 3721

Father, for this was your good pleasure. ¶ **27** "All things have been committed to me by my
ὁ πατήρ ὅτι οὕτως ἐγένετο ἔμπροσθεν σου → εὐδοκία Πάντα ← → παρεδόθη μοι ὑπὸ μου
d.vsm n.vsm cj adv v.ami.3s p.g r.gs.2 n.nsf a.npn v.api.3s r.ds.1 p.g r.gs.1
3836 4252 4022 4048 1181 1869 5148 2306 4246 4140 1609 5679 1609

Father. No one knows the Son except the Father, and no one knows the Father except the Son
τοῦ πατρός καὶ → οὐδεὶς ἐπιγινώσκει τὸν υἱὸν εἰ μὴ ὁ πατήρ → οὐδὲ τις ἐπιγινώσκει τὸν πατέρα εἰ μὴ ὁ υἱός
d.gsm n.gsm cj a.nsm v.pai.3s d.asm n.asm cj pl d.nsm n.nsm cj r.nsm v.pai.3s d.asm n.asm cj pl d.nsm n.nsm
3836 4252 2779 4029 2105 3836 5626 1623 3590 3836 4252 4028 5516 2105 3836 4252 1623 3590 3836 5626

and those to whom the Son chooses to reveal him. ¶ **28** "Come to me, all you who are weary
καὶ → ᾧ ἐὰν ὁ υἱὸς βούληται → ἀποκαλύψαι Δεῦτε πρός με πάντες οἱ → κοπιῶντες
cj r.dsm pl d.nsm n.nsm v.pms.3s f.aa adv p.a r.as.1 a.vpm d.vpm pt.pa.vpm
2779 4005 1569 3836 5626 636 1307 4639 1609 4246 3836 3159

and burdened, and I will give you rest. **29** Take my yoke upon you and learn from me, for I am gentle
καὶ πεφορτισμένοι καγὼ ὑμᾶς ἀναπαύσω ἄρατε μου τὸν ζυγόν ἐφ ὑμᾶς καὶ μάθετε ἀπ ἐμοῦ ὅτι εἰμι πραΰς
cj pt.rp.vpm crasis r.ap.2 v.fai.1s v.aam.2p r.gs.1 d.asm n.asm p.a r.ap.2 cj v.aam.2p p.g r.gs.1 cj v.pai.1s a.nsm
2779 5844 2743 399 399 7007 399 149 1609 3836 2433 2093 7007 2779 3443 608 1609 4022 1639 4558

and humble in heart, and you will find rest for your souls. **30** For my yoke is easy and my
καὶ ταπεινὸς τῇ καρδίᾳ καὶ → εὑρήσετε ἀνάπαυσιν ὑμῶν ταῖς ψυχαῖς γὰρ μου ὁ ζυγός χρηστὸς καὶ μου
cj a.nsm d.dsf n.dsf cj v.fai.2p n.asf r.gp.2 d.dpf n.dpf cj r.gs.1 d.nsm n.nsm a.nsm cj r.gs.1
2779 5424 3836 2840 2779 2351 398 6034 7007 3836 6034 1142 1609 3836 2433 5982 2779 1609

burden is light."
τὸ φορτίον ἐστιν ἐλαφρόν
d.nsn n.nsn v.pai.3s a.nsn
3836 5845 1639 1787

Lord of the Sabbath

12:1 At that time Jesus went through the grainfields on the Sabbath. His disciples were
Ἐν ἐκείνῳ τῷ καιρῷ ὁ Ἰησοῦς ἐπορεύθη διὰ τῶν σπορίμων → τοῖς σάββασιν δὲ αὐτοῦ οἱ μαθηταὶ →
p.d r.dsm d.dsm n.dsm d.nsm n.nsm v.api.3s p.g d.gpn n.gpn d.dpn n.dpn cj r.gsm.3 d.npm n.npm
1877 1697 3836 2789 3836 2652 4513 1328 3836 5077 3836 4879 1254 899 3836 3412

καὶ σποδῷ μετενόησαν. **22** πλὴν λέγω ὑμῖν, Τύρῳ καὶ Σιδῶνι ἀνεκτότερον ἔσται ἐν ἡμέρᾳ κρίσεως ἢ ὑμῖν. **23** καὶ σύ, Καφαρναούμ, μὴ ἕως οὐρανοῦ ὑψωθήσῃ; ἕως ᾅδου καταβήσῃ· ὅτι εἰ ἐν Σοδόμοις ἐγενήθησαν αἱ δυνάμεις αἱ γενόμεναι ἐν σοί, ἔμεινεν ἂν μέχρι τῆς σήμερον. **24** πλὴν λέγω ὑμῖν ὅτι γῇ Σοδόμων ἀνεκτότερον ἔσται ἐν ἡμέρᾳ κρίσεως ἢ σοί.

11:25 Ἐν ἐκείνῳ τῷ καιρῷ ἀποκριθεὶς ὁ Ἰησοῦς εἶπεν, Ἐξομολογοῦμαί σοι, πάτερ, κύριε τοῦ οὐρανοῦ καὶ τῆς γῆς, ὅτι ἔκρυψας ταῦτα ἀπὸ σοφῶν καὶ συνετῶν καὶ ἀπεκάλυψας αὐτὰ νηπίοις· **26** ναὶ ὁ πατήρ, ὅτι οὕτως εὐδοκία ἐγένετο ἔμπροσθέν σου. ¶ **27** Πάντα μοι παρεδόθη ὑπὸ τοῦ πατρός μου, καὶ οὐδεὶς ἐπιγινώσκει τὸν υἱὸν εἰ μὴ ὁ πατήρ, οὐδὲ τὸν πατέρα τις ἐπιγινώσκει εἰ μὴ ὁ υἱὸς καὶ ᾧ ἐὰν βούληται ὁ υἱὸς ἀποκαλύψαι. ¶ **28** Δεῦτε πρός με πάντες οἱ κοπιῶντες καὶ πεφορτισμένοι, κἀγὼ ἀναπαύσω ὑμᾶς. **29** ἄρατε τὸν ζυγόν μου ἐφ ὑμᾶς καὶ μάθετε ἀπ ἐμοῦ, ὅτι πραΰς εἰμι καὶ ταπεινὸς τῇ καρδίᾳ, καὶ εὑρήσετε ἀνάπαυσιν ταῖς ψυχαῖς ὑμῶν· **30** ὁ γὰρ ζυγός μου χρηστὸς καὶ τὸ φορτίον μου ἐλαφρόν ἐστιν.

12:1 Ἐν ἐκείνῳ τῷ καιρῷ ἐπορεύθη ὁ Ἰησοῦς τοῖς σάββασιν διὰ τῶν σπορίμων· οἱ δὲ μαθηταὶ αὐτοῦ ἐπείνασαν καὶ ἤρξαντο

hungry | and | began | to | pick | some | heads | of | grain | and | eat | | them. | **2** | When | the | Pharisees | saw | this, | they | said
ἐπείνασαν | καὶ | ἤρξαντο | → | τίλλειν | → | → | στάχυας | καὶ | ἐσθίειν | | | δὲ | → | οἱ | Φαρισαῖοι | ἰδόντες | | | εἶπαν
v.aai.3p | cj | v.ami.3p | | f.pa | | | n.apm | cj | f.pa | | | cj | | d.npm | n.npm | pt.aa.npm | | | v.aai.3p
4277 | 2779 | 806 | | 5504 | | | 5092 | 2779 | 2266 | | | 1254 | 1625 | 3836 | 5757 | 1625 | | | 3306

to him, | "Look! | Your | disciples | | are doing | what | is | unlawful | | on | the Sabbath." | ¶ | **3** | He | answered,
→ | αὐτῷ | ἰδοὺ | σου | οἱ | μαθηταί, | → | ποιοῦσιν | ὃ | → | ｢οὐκ | ἔξεστιν｣ | ποιεῖν | ἐν | σαββάτῳ | | | δὲ | ὁ | εἶπεν
| r.dsm.3 | j | r.gs.2 | d.npm | n.npm | | v.pai.3p | r.asn | | adv | v.pai.3s | f.pa | p.d | n.dsn | | | cj | d.nsm | v.aai.3s
| 899 | 2627 | 5148 | 3836 | 3412 | | 4472 | 4005 | | 4024 | 1997 | 4472 | 1877 | 4879 | | | 1254 | 3836 | 3306

"Haven't | you | read | | what | David | did | when | he and | his | companions | were hungry? | **4** | He | entered | into
αὐτοῖς | οὐκ | → | ἀνέγνωτε | τί | Δαυὶδ | ἐποίησεν | ὅτε | → καὶ | αὐτοῦ | οἱ | μετ᾽ | → | ἐπείνασεν | πῶς | → | εἰσῆλθεν | εἰς
r.dpm.3 | pl | | v.aai.2p | r.asn | n.nsm | v.aai.3s | cj | cj | r.gsm.3 | d.npm | p.g | | v.aai.3s | cj | | v.aai.3s | p.a
899 | 4024 | | 336 | 5515 | 1253 | 4472 | 4021 | 4277 2779 | 899 | 3836 | 3552 | | 4277 | 4802 | | 1656 | 1650

the house | of | God, | | and | he and | his | companions | ate | | the consecrated | bread – | which | was | not | lawful | for | them
τὸν | οἶκον | ┌τοῦ θεοῦ┐ | καὶ | → | οὐδὲ | αὐτοῦ | ┌τοῖς μετ᾽┐ | ἔφαγον | τοὺς | ┌τῆς προθέσεως┐ | ἄρτους | ὃ | ἦν | οὐκ | ἐξὸν | → | αὐτῷ
d.asm | n.asm | d.gsm n.gsm | cj | | r.gsm.3 | | d.dpm p.g | v.aai.3p | d.apm | d.gsf n.gsf | n.apm | r.asn | v.iai.3s | adv | pt.pa.nsn | | r.dsm.3
3836 | 3875 | 3836 2536 | 2779 | | 4028 899 | | 3836 3552 | 2266 | 788 | 4606 4005 | | 1639 | 4024 | 1997 | | 899

to | do, | but | only | for | the priests. | **5** | Or | haven't | you | read | | in | the | Law | that | on | the Sabbath | the | priests | in | the
→ | φαγεῖν | ┌εἰ μὴ┐ | μόνοις | → | τοῖς ἱερεῦσιν | | ἢ | οὐκ | → | ἀνέγνωτε | ἐν | τῷ | νόμῳ | ὅτι | → | τοῖς | σάββασιν | οἱ | ἱερεῖς | ἐν | τῷ
| f.aa | cj pl | a.dpm | | d.dpm n.dpm | | cj | pl | | v.aai.2p | p.d | d.dsm | n.dsm | cj | | d.dpn | n.dpn | d.npm | n.npm | p.d | d.dsn
| 2266 | 1623 3590 | 3668 | | 3836 2636 | | 2445 | 4024 | | 336 | 1877 | 3836 | 3795 | 4022 | | 3836 | 4879 | 3836 | 2636 | 1877 | 3836

temple | desecrate | the | day | | and yet | are | innocent? | **6** | I | tell | you | that | one greater | than | the | temple | is | here. | **7**
ἱερῷ | βεβηλοῦσιν | τὸ | σάββατον | καὶ | → | εἰσιν | ἀναίτιοι | | δὲ | → λέγω | ὑμῖν | ὅτι | → | μεῖζον | → | τοῦ | ἱεροῦ | ἐστιν | ὧδε | δὲ
n.dsn | v.pai.3p | d.asn | n.asn | cj | | v.pai.3p | a.npm | | cj | v.pai.1s | r.dp.2 | cj | | a.nsn.c | | d.gsn | n.gsn | v.pai.3s | adv | cj
2639 | 1014 | 3836 | 4879 | 2779 | | 1639 | 360 | | 1254 | 3306 | 7007 | 4022 | | 3489 | | 3836 | 2639 | 1639 | 6045 | 1254

If | you | had | known | what | these words | mean, | 'I | desire | mercy, | | not | sacrifice,' | you | would | not | have | condemned | the
εἰ | → | → | ἐγνώκειτε | τί | → | ἐστιν | θέλω | ἔλεος | καὶ | οὐ | θυσίαν | → | ἂν | οὐκ | → | κατεδικάσατε | τοὺς
cj | | | v.lai.2p | r.nsn | | v.pai.3s | v.pai.1s | n.asn | cj | adv | n.asf | | pl | adv | | v.aai.2p | d.apm
1623 | | | 1182 | 5515 | | 1639 | 2527 | 1799 | 2779 | 4024 | 2602 | | 2868 | 4024 | | 2868 | 3836

innocent. | **8** | For | the | Son | of Man | | is | Lord | of the | Sabbath." | ¶ | **9** | Going | on | from | that place, | he
ἀναιτίους | | γὰρ | ὁ | υἱὸς | ┌τοῦ ἀνθρώπου┐ | ἐστιν | κύριος | τοῦ | σαββάτου | | | Καὶ | μεταβὰς | ἐκεῖθεν
a.apm | | cj | d.nsm | n.nsm | d.gsm n.gsm | v.pai.3s | n.nsm | d.gsn | n.gsn | | | cj | pt.aa.nsm | adv
360 | | 1142 | 3836 | 5626 | 3836 476 | 1639 | 3261 | 3836 | 4879 | | | 2779 | 3553 | 1696

went | into | their | synagogue, | **10** | and | | a man | with a | shriveled | hand | was there. | Looking | for | a reason | to
ἦλθεν | εἰς | αὐτῶν | ┌τὴν συναγωγήν┐ | | καὶ | ἰδοὺ | ἄνθρωπος | ἔχων | ξηρὰν | χεῖρα | | | | | ἵνα
v.aai.3s | p.a | r.gpm.3 | d.asf n.asf | | cj | j | n.nsm | pt.pa.nsm | a.asf | n.asf | | | | | cj
2262 | 1650 | 899 | 5252 | | 2779 | 2627 | 476 | 2400 | 3831 | 5931 | | | | | 2671

accuse | | Jesus, | they | asked | him, | | "Is it | lawful | to | heal | | on | the Sabbath?" | **11** | He | said | to
κατηγορήσωσιν | αὐτοῦ | καὶ | → | ἐπηρώτησαν | αὐτὸν | λέγοντες | εἰ | → | ἔξεστιν | → | θεραπεῦσαι | → | τοῖς | σάββασιν | | δὲ | ὁ | εἶπεν | →
v.aas.3p | r.gsm.3 | cj | | v.aai.3p | r.asm.3 | pt.pa.npm | cj | | v.pai.3s | | f.aa | | d.dpn | n.dpn | | cj | d.nsm | v.aai.3s
2989 | 899 | 2779 | | 2089 | 899 | 3306 | 1623 | | 1997 | | 2543 | | 3836 | 4879 | | 1254 | 3836 | 3306

them, | "If | any | | of you | has | a | sheep | and | it | falls | into a | pit | | on | the Sabbath, | will you
αὐτοῖς | → | ἔσται | ┌τίς ἄνθρωπος┐ | ἐξ | ὑμῶν | ὃς | ἕξει | ἓν | πρόβατον | καὶ | ἐὰν | τοῦτο | ἐμπέσῃ | εἰς | βόθυνον | → | τοῖς | σάββασιν
r.dpm.3 | | v.fmi.3s | r.nsm n.nsm | p.g | r.gp.2 | r.nsm | v.fai.3s | a.asn | n.asn | cj | cj | r.nsn | v.aas.3s | p.a | n.asm | | d.dpn | n.dpn
899 | | 5515 | 1639 5515 476 | 1666 | 7007 | 4005 | 2400 | 1651 | 4585 | 2779 | 1569 | 4047 | 1860 | 1650 | 1073 | | 3836 | 4879 | 3195 3195

not | take | hold | of it | and | lift | it out? | **12** | How | much | more | valuable | is a | man | than | a sheep! | Therefore | it is
οὐχὶ | → | κρατήσει | αὐτὸ καὶ | ἐγερεῖ | | | οὖν | πόσῳ | → | διαφέρει | ἄνθρωπος | → | προβάτου | ὥστε | → | →
pl | | v.fai.3s | r.asn.3 cj | v.fai.3s | | | cj | a.dsn | | v.pai.3s | n.nsm | | n.gsn | cj | |
4049 | | 3195 | 899 2779 | 1586 | | | 4036 | 4531 | | 1422 | 476 | | 4585 | 6063

lawful | to do | good | on | the Sabbath." | **13** | Then | he | said | to | the man, | "Stretch | out | your | hand." | So | he | stretched | it
ἔξεστιν | → ποιεῖν | καλῶς | → | τοῖς σάββασιν | | τότε | → | λέγει | τῷ | ἀνθρώπῳ | ἔκτεινον | → | σου | ┌τὴν χεῖρα┐ | καὶ | → | ἐξέτεινεν
v.pai.3s | f.pa | adv | d.dpn | n.dpn | | adv | | v.pai.3s | d.dsm | n.dsm | v.aam.2s | | r.gs.2 | d.asf n.asf | cj | | v.aai.3s
1997 | 4472 | 2822 | 3836 | 4879 | | 5538 | | 3306 | 3836 | 476 | 1753 | | 5148 | 3836 5931 | 2779 | | 1753

out and | it | was | completely | restored, | | just as | sound | as | the | other. | **14** | But | the | Pharisees | went | | out and
καὶ | → | → | → | ἀπεκατεστάθη | ὑγιὴς | ὡς | ἡ | ἄλλη | | δὲ | οἱ | Φαρισαῖοι | ἐξελθόντες
cj | | | | v.api.3s | a.nsf | pl | d.nsf | r.nsf | | cj | d.npm | n.npm | pt.aa.npm
2779 | | | | 635 | 5618 | 6055 | 3836 | 257 | | 1254 | 3836 | 5757 | 2002

τίλλειν στάχυας καὶ ἐσθίειν. ² οἱ δὲ Φαρισαῖοι ἰδόντες εἶπαν αὐτῷ, Ἰδοὺ οἱ μαθηταί σου ποιοῦσιν ὃ οὐκ ἔξεστιν ποιεῖν ἐν σαββάτῳ. ¶ ³ ὁ δὲ εἶπεν αὐτοῖς, Οὐκ ἀνέγνωτε τί ἐποίησεν Δαυὶδ ὅτε ἐπείνασεν καὶ οἱ μετ᾽ αὐτοῦ, ⁴ πῶς εἰσῆλθεν εἰς τὸν οἶκον τοῦ θεοῦ καὶ τοὺς ἄρτους τῆς προθέσεως ἔφαγον, ὃ οὐκ ἐξὸν ἦν αὐτῷ φαγεῖν οὐδὲ τοῖς μετ᾽ αὐτοῦ εἰ μὴ τοῖς ἱερεῦσιν μόνοις; ⁵ ἢ οὐκ ἀνέγνωτε ἐν τῷ νόμῳ ὅτι τοῖς σάββασιν οἱ ἱερεῖς ἐν τῷ ἱερῷ τὸ σάββατον βεβηλοῦσιν καὶ ἀναίτιοί εἰσιν; ⁶ λέγω δὲ ὑμῖν ὅτι τοῦ ἱεροῦ μεῖζόν ἐστιν ὧδε. ⁷ εἰ δὲ ἐγνώκειτε τί ἐστιν, Ἔλεος θέλω καὶ οὐ θυσίαν, οὐκ ἂν κατεδικάσατε τοὺς ἀναιτίους. ¶ ⁸ κύριος γάρ ἐστιν τοῦ σαββάτου ὁ υἱὸς τοῦ ἀνθρώπου. ¶ ⁹ Καὶ μεταβὰς ἐκεῖθεν ἦλθεν εἰς τὴν συναγωγὴν αὐτῶν· ¹⁰ καὶ ἰδοὺ ἄνθρωπος χεῖρα ἔχων ξηράν. καὶ ἐπηρώτησαν αὐτὸν λέγοντες, Εἰ ἔξεστιν τοῖς σάββασιν θεραπεῦσαι; ἵνα κατηγορήσωσιν αὐτοῦ. ¹¹ ὁ δὲ εἶπεν αὐτοῖς, Τίς ἔσται ἐξ ὑμῶν ἄνθρωπος ὃς ἕξει πρόβατον ἓν καὶ ἐὰν ἐμπέσῃ τοῦτο τοῖς σάββασιν εἰς βόθυνον, οὐχὶ κρατήσει αὐτὸ καὶ ἐγερεῖ; ¹² πόσῳ οὖν διαφέρει ἄνθρωπος προβάτου. ὥστε ἔξεστιν τοῖς σάββασιν καλῶς ποιεῖν. ¹³ τότε λέγει τῷ ἀνθρώπῳ, Ἔκτεινόν σου τὴν χεῖρα. καὶ ἐξέτεινεν καὶ ἀπεκατεστάθη ὑγιὴς ὡς ἡ ἄλλη. ¹⁴ ἐξελθόντες δὲ οἱ Φαρισαῖοι συμβούλιον ἔλαβον

plotted		how they might kill			Jesus.	
⌐συμβούλιον	ἔλαβον⌐	κατ'	αὐτοῦ	ὅπως →	→ ἀπολέσωσιν	αὐτόν
n.asn	v.aai.3p	p.g	r.gsm.3	cj	v.aas.3p	r.asm.3
5206	3284	2848	899	3968	660	899

God's Chosen Servant

12:15

Aware of this,		Jesus		withdrew	from	that place.		Many				followed	him,	and he
δὲ	γνοὺς	⌐Ὁ	Ἰησοῦς⌐	ἀνεχώρησεν	ἐκεῖθεν ←	←		καὶ	πολλοί	[ὄχλοι]		ἠκολούθησαν	αὐτῷ	καὶ →
cj	pt.aa.nsm	d.nsm	n.nsm	v.aai.3s	adv			cj	a.npm	n.npm		v.aai.3p	r.dsm.3	cj
1254	1182	3836	2652	432	1696			2779	4498	4063		199	899	2779

healed	all	their	sick,	**16** warning	them	not to		tell		who he was.	**17**This was	to	fulfill	what
ἐθεράπευσεν	πάντας	αὐτοὺς	καὶ	ἐπετίμησεν	αὐτοῖς	μὴ	ἵνα	⌐ποιήσωσιν	φανερὸν⌐	αὐτὸν	ἵνα	πληρωθῇ	τὸ	
v.aai.3s	a.apm	r.apm.3	cj	v.aai.3s	r.dpm.3	pl	cj	v.aas.3p	a.asm	r.asm.3	cj	v.aps.3s	d.nsn	
2543	4246	899	2779	2203	899	3590	2671	4472	5745	899	2671	4444	3836	

was	spoken	through	the	prophet	Isaiah:		**18** "Here is		my	servant		whom	I have	chosen,	the one	I	love,
→	ῥηθὲν	διὰ	τοῦ	προφήτου	Ἠσαΐου	λέγοντος	ἰδοὺ		μου	⌐ὁ	παῖς⌐	ὃν	→	→ ἡρέτισα	ὁ ←	μου	ἀγαπητός
	pt.ap.nsn	p.g	d.gsm	n.gsm	n.gsm	pt.pa.gsm	j		r.gs.1	d.nsm	n.nsm	r.asm		v.aai.1s	d.nsm	r.gs.1	a.nsm
	3306	1328	3836	4737	2480	3306	2627		1609	3836	4090	4005		147	3836	1609	28

in	whom	I		delight;	I will	put	my	Spirit		on	him,	and		he will	proclaim	justice	to the	nations.	**19** He
εἰς	ὃν	⌐ἡ	ψυχή	μου⌐	εὐδόκησεν	→	θήσω	μου	⌐τὸ	πνεῦμα⌐	ἐπ'	αὐτὸν	καὶ	→	ἀπαγγελεῖ	κρίσιν	→ τοῖς	ἔθνεσιν	→
p.a	r.asm	d.nsf	n.nsf	r.gs.1	v.aai.3s		v.fai.1s	r.gs.1	d.asn	n.asn	p.a	r.asm.3	cj		v.fai.3s	n.asf	d.dpn	n.dpn	
1650	4005	3836	6034	1609	2305		5502	1609	3836	4460	2093	899	2779		550	3213	3836 1620	2248	

will not	quarrel	or	cry	out;	no	one	will	hear	his	voice	in	the	streets.	**20** A bruised		reed	he
→ οὐκ	ἐρίσει	οὐδὲ	κραυγάσει ←	οὐδὲ	τις	→	ἀκούσει	αὐτοῦ	⌐τὴν φωνὴν⌐	ἐν	ταῖς	πλατείαις	συντετριμμένον	κάλαμον	→	
adv	v.fai.3s	cj	v.fai.3s	cj	r.nsm		v.fai.3s	r.gsm.3	d.asf n.asf	p.d	d.dpf	n.dpf	pt.rp.asm	n.asm		
2248	4024	2248	4028 3198	4028	5516		201	899	3836 5889	1877	3836	4426	5341	2812	2862	

will not	break,	and	a	smoldering	wick	he	will	not	snuff	out,	till		he	leads	justice	to	victory.	**21**	In	his
→ οὐ	κατεάξει	καὶ		τυφόμενον	λίνον	→	οὐ	σβέσει ←			⌐ἕως	ἄν⌐	→	ἐκβάλῃ	⌐τὴν κρίσιν⌐	εἰς	νῖκος		καὶ →	αὐτοῦ
adv	v.fai.3s	cj		pt.pp.asn	n.asn		adv	v.fai.3s			cj	pl		v.aas.3s	d.asf n.asf	p.a	n.asn		cj	r.gsm.3
2862	2862	2779		5606	3351	4931	4931	4024 4931			2401	323		1675	3836 3213	1650	3777		2779 3950	899

name		the nations	will	put	their	hope."	
⌐τῷ	ὀνόματι⌐	ἔθνη	→	→		ἐλπιοῦσιν	
d.dsn	n.dsn	n.npn				v.fai.3p	
3836	3950	1620				1827	

Jesus and Beelzebub

12:22

Then	they brought	him	a	demon-possessed	man	who was	blind	and	mute,	and	Jesus	healed	him,	so
Τότε	→ προσηνέχθη	αὐτῷ		δαιμονιζόμενος	←		τυφλὸς	καὶ	κωφός	καὶ		ἐθεράπευσεν	αὐτόν	ὥστε
adv	v.api.3s	r.dsm.3		pt.pm.nsm			a.nsm	cj	a.nsm	cj		v.aai.3s	r.asm.3	cj
5538	4712	899		1227			5603	2779	3273	2779		2543	899	6063

that he		could both	talk	and	see.	**23**	All		the	people		were astonished	and	said,	"Could	this	be	the
←	⌐τὸν κωφὸν⌐	→	λαλεῖν	καὶ	βλέπειν		καὶ	πάντες	οἱ	ὄχλοι	→	ἐξίσταντο	καὶ	ἔλεγον	μήτι	οὗτός	ἐστιν	ὁ
d.asm	a.asm		f.pa	cj	f.pa		cj	a.npm	d.npm	n.npm		v.imi.3p	cj	v.iai.3p	pl	r.nsm	v.pai.3s	d.nsm
3836	3273		3281	2779	1063		2779	4246	3836	4063		2014	2779	3306	3614	4047	1639	3836

Son	of David?"	¶	**24** But	when	the	Pharisees	heard	this,	they	said,	"It is	only		by	Beelzebub,		the prince
υἱὸς	→ Δαυίδ		δὲ	→	οἱ	Φαρισαῖοι	ἀκούσαντες	→		εἶπον	⌐εἰ	μὴ⌐	ἐν	⌐τῷ	Βεελζεβοὺλ⌐		ἄρχοντι
n.nsm	n.gsm		cj		d.npm	n.npm	pt.aa.npm			v.aai.3p		cj pl	p.d	d.dsm	n.dsm		n.dsm
5626	1253		1254		3836	5757	201			3306	1623 3590		1877	3836	1015		807

of demons,		that	this	fellow		drives	out	demons."	¶	**25**	Jesus	knew	their	thoughts		and	said
→	⌐τῶν δαιμονίων⌐	οὗτος ←			οὐκ	ἐκβάλλει ←		⌐τὰ δαιμόνια⌐		δὲ		εἰδὼς	αὐτῶν	⌐τὰς ἐνθυμήσεις⌐			εἶπεν
d.gpn	n.gpn	r.nsm			adv	v.pai.3s		d.apn n.apn		cj		pt.ra.nsm	r.gpm.3	d.apf n.apf			v.aai.3s
3836	1228	4047			4024	1675		3836 1228		1254		3857	899	3836 1927			3306

to them,	"Every	kingdom	divided	against	itself	will	be	ruined,	and	every	city	or	household	divided	against
αὐτοῖς	πᾶσα	βασιλεία	μερισθεῖσα	καθ'	ἑαυτῆς	→		ἐρημοῦται	καὶ	πᾶσα	πόλις	ἢ	οἰκία	μερισθεῖσα	καθ'
r.dpm.3	a.nsf	n.nsf	pt.ap.nsf	p.g	r.gsf.3			v.ppi.3s	cj	a.nsf	n.nsf	cj	n.nsf	pt.ap.nsf	p.g
899	4246	993	3532	2848	1571			2246	2779	4246	4484	2445	3864	3532	2848

κατ' αὐτοῦ ὅπως αὐτὸν ἀπολέσωσιν.
12:15 Ὁ δὲ Ἰησοῦς γνοὺς ἀνεχώρησεν ἐκεῖθεν. καὶ ἠκολούθησαν αὐτῷ [ὄχλοι] πολλοί, καὶ ἐθεράπευσεν αὐτοὺς πάντας
16 καὶ ἐπετίμησεν αὐτοῖς ἵνα μὴ φανερὸν αὐτὸν ποιήσωσιν, **17** ἵνα πληρωθῇ τὸ ῥηθὲν διὰ Ἠσαΐου τοῦ προφήτου λέγοντος,
18 Ἰδοὺ ὁ παῖς μου ὃν ἡρέτισα, ὁ ἀγαπητός μου εἰς ὃν εὐδόκησεν ἡ ψυχή μου· θήσω τὸ πνεῦμά μου ἐπ' αὐτόν, καὶ κρίσιν τοῖς
ἔθνεσιν ἀπαγγελεῖ. **19** οὐκ ἐρίσει οὐδὲ κραυγάσει, οὐδὲ ἀκούσει τις ἐν ταῖς πλατείαις τὴν φωνὴν αὐτοῦ. **20** κάλαμον
συντετριμμένον οὐ κατεάξει καὶ λίνον τυφόμενον οὐ σβέσει, ἕως ἂν ἐκβάλῃ εἰς νῖκος τὴν κρίσιν. **21** καὶ τῷ ὀνόματι αὐτοῦ ἔθνη
ἐλπιοῦσιν.
12:22 Τότε προσήνεγκαν «προσηνέχθη» αὐτῷ δαιμονιζόμενον «δαιμονιζόμενος» τυφλὸν «τυφλός» καὶ κωφόν, «κωφός,» καὶ
ἐθεράπευσεν αὐτόν, ὥστε τὸν κωφὸν λαλεῖν καὶ βλέπειν. **23** καὶ ἐξίσταντο πάντες οἱ ὄχλοι καὶ ἔλεγον, Μήτι οὗτός ἐστιν ὁ υἱὸς
Δαυίδ; ¶ **24** οἱ δὲ Φαρισαῖοι ἀκούσαντες εἶπον, Οὗτος οὐκ ἐκβάλλει τὰ δαιμόνια εἰ μὴ ἐν τῷ Βεελζεβοὺλ ἄρχοντι τῶν
δαιμονίων. ¶ **25** εἰδὼς δὲ τὰς ἐνθυμήσεις αὐτῶν εἶπεν αὐτοῖς, Πᾶσα βασιλεία μερισθεῖσα καθ' ἑαυτῆς ἐρημοῦται καὶ πᾶσα

itself will not stand. **26** If Satan drives out Satan, he is divided against himself. How then can
ἑαυτῆς ↱ οὐ σταθήσεται καὶ εἰ ὁ σατανᾶς ἐκβάλλει ← ⸤τὸν σατανᾶν⸥ → → ἐμερίσθη ἐφ᾽ ἑαυτὸν πῶς οὖν
r.gsf.3   adv v.fpi.3s cj cj d.nsm n.nsm v.pai.3s d.asm n.asm v.api.3s p.a r.asm.3 cj cj
1571   2705 4024 2705 2779 1623 3836 4928 1675 3836 4928 3532 2093 1571 4802 4036

his kingdom stand? **27** And if I drive out demons by Beelzebub, by whom do your people
αὐτοῦ ἡ βασιλεία σταθήσεται καὶ εἰ ἐγὼ ἐκβάλλω ← ⸤τὰ δαιμόνια⸥ ἐν Βεελζεβοὺλ ἐν τίνι → ὑμῶν οἱ υἱοὶ
r.gsm.3 d.nsf n.nsf v.fpi.3s cj cj r.ns.1 v.pai.1s d.apn n.apn p.d n.dsm p.d r.dsm r.gp.2 d.npm n.npm
899 3836 993 2705 2779 1623 1609 1675 3836 1228 1877 1015 1877 5515 1675 7007 3836 5626

drive them out? *So then,* they will be your judges. **28** But if I drive out demons by the Spirit of
ἐκβάλλουσιν ← διὰ τοῦτο αὐτοὶ ἔσονται ὑμῶν κριταί δὲ εἰ ἐγὼ ἐκβάλλω ← ⸤τὰ δαιμόνια⸥ ἐν πνεύματι →
v.pai.3p p.a r.asn r.npm v.fmi.3p r.gp.2 n.npm cj cj r.ns.1 v.pai.1s d.apn n.apn p.d n.dsn
1675 1328 4047 1639 7007 3216 1254 1623 1609 1675 3836 1228 1877 4460

God, then the kingdom of God has come upon you. ¶ **29** "Or again, how can anyone enter a
θεοῦ ἄρα ἡ βασιλεία → ⸤τοῦ θεοῦ⸥ → ἔφθασεν ἐφ᾽ ὑμᾶς ἢ πῶς δύναταί τις εἰσελθεῖν εἰς
n.gsm cj d.nsf n.nsf d.gsm n.gsm v.aai.3s p.a r.ap.2 cj cj v.ppi.3s r.nsm f.aa p.a
2536 726 3836 993 3836 2536 5777 2093 7007 2445 4802 1538 5516 1656 1650

strong man's house and carry off his possessions unless he first ties up the strong man? Then
⸤τοῦ ἰσχυροῦ⸥ ⸤τὴν οἰκίαν⸥ καὶ ἁρπάσαι ← αὐτοῦ ⸤τὰ σκεύη⸥ ἐὰν μὴ → πρῶτον δήσῃ ← τὸν ἰσχυρόν ← καὶ τότε
d.gsm a.gsm d.asf n.asf cj f.aa r.gsm.3 d.apn n.apn cj pl adv v.aas.3s d.asm a.asm cj adv
3836 2708 3836 3864 2779 773 899 3836 5007 1569 3590 1313 4754 1313 3836 2708 2779 5538

he can rob his house. ¶ **30** "He who is not with me is against me, and he who does not
→ → διαρπάσει αὐτοῦ ⸤τὴν οἰκίαν⸥ ὁ ← ὢν μὴ μετ᾽ ἐμοῦ ἐστιν κατ᾽ ἐμοῦ καὶ ὁ ← ↱ μὴ
v.fai.3s r.gsm.3 d.asf n.asf d.nsm pt.pa.nsm pl p.g r.gs.1 v.pai.3s p.g r.gs.1 cj d.nsm pl
1395 899 3836 3864 3836 1639 3590 3552 1609 1639 2848 1609 2779 3836 5251 3590

gather with me scatters. **31** And so I tell you, every sin and blasphemy will be forgiven men,
συνάγων μετ᾽ ἐμοῦ σκορπίζει ⸤Διὰ τοῦτο⸥ → λέγω ὑμῖν πᾶσα ἁμαρτία καὶ βλασφημία → → ἀφεθήσεται ⸤τοῖς ἀνθρώποις⸥
pt.pa.nsm p.g r.gs.1 v.pai.3s p.a r.asn v.pai.1s r.dp.2 a.nsf n.nsf cj n.nsf v.fpi.3s d.dpm n.dpm
5251 3552 1609 5025 1328 4047 3306 7007 4246 281 2779 1060 918 3836 476

but the blasphemy against the Spirit will not be forgiven. **32** Anyone who speaks a word against the Son of
δὲ ἡ βλασφημία → τοῦ πνεύματος ↱ οὐκ → ἀφεθήσεται καὶ ↱ ὃς ἐὰν εἴπῃ λόγον κατὰ τοῦ υἱοῦ →
cj d.nsf n.nsf d.gsn n.gsn adv v.fpi.3s cj r.nsm cj v.aas.3s n.asm p.g d.gsm n.gsm
1254 3836 1060 3836 4460 4024 918 2779 1569 4005 1569 3306 3364 2848 3836 5626

Man will be forgiven, but anyone who speaks against the Holy Spirit will not be forgiven,
⸤τοῦ ἀνθρώπου⸥ → → ἀφεθήσεται αὐτῷ δ᾽ ὃς ἂν εἴπῃ κατὰ τοῦ ἁγίου ⸤τοῦ πνεύματος⸥ ↱ οὐκ → ἀφεθήσεται
d.gsm n.gsm v.fpi.3s r.dsm.3 cj r.nsm pl v.aas.3s p.g d.gsn a.gsn d.gsn n.gsn adv v.fpi.3s
3836 476 918 899 1254 323 4005 323 3306 2848 3836 41 3836 4460 918 4024 918

either in this age or in the age to come. ¶ **33** "Make a tree good and its fruit
αὐτῷ οὔτε ἐν τούτῳ ⸤τῷ αἰῶνι⸥ οὔτε ἐν τῷ → μέλλοντι Ἢ ποιήσατε ⸤τὸ δένδρον⸥ καλὸν καὶ αὐτοῦ ⸤τὸν καρπὸν⸥
r.dsm.3 cj p.d r.dsm d.dsm n.dsm cj p.d d.dsm pt.pa.dsm cj v.aam.2p d.asn n.asn a.asn cj r.gsn.3 d.asm n.asm
899 4046 1877 4047 3836 172 4046 1877 3836 3516 2445 4472 3836 1285 2819 2779 899 3836 2843

will be good, or make a tree bad and its fruit will be bad, for a tree is recognized by
καλόν ἢ ποιήσατε ⸤τὸ δένδρον⸥ σαπρὸν καὶ αὐτοῦ ⸤τὸν καρπὸν⸥ σαπρόν γὰρ ⸤τὸ δένδρον⸥ → γινώσκεται ἐκ
a.asm cj v.aam.2p d.asn n.asn a.asn cj r.gsn.3 d.asm n.asm a.asn cj d.nsn n.nsn v.ppi.3s p.g
2819 2445 4472 3836 1285 4911 2779 899 3836 2843 4911 1142 3836 1285 1182 1666

its fruit. **34** You brood of vipers, how can you who are evil say anything good? For out of the
τοῦ καρποῦ γεννήματα ἐχιδνῶν πῶς δύνασθε ← → ὄντες πονηροὶ λαλεῖν → ἀγαθὰ γὰρ ἐκ ← τοῦ
d.gsm n.gsm n.vpn n.gpf cj v.ppi.2p pt.pa.npm a.npm f.pa a.apn cj p.g d.gsn
3836 2843 1165 2399 4802 1538 1639 4505 3281 19 1142 1666 3836

overflow of the heart the mouth speaks. **35** The good man brings good things out of the good stored
περισσεύματος τῆς καρδίας τὸ στόμα λαλεῖ ὁ ἀγαθὸς ἄνθρωπος ἐκβάλλει ἀγαθὰ ← ἐκ ← τοῦ ἀγαθοῦ θησαυροῦ
n.gsn d.gsf n.gsf d.nsn n.nsn v.pai.3s d.nsm a.nsm n.nsm v.pai.3s a.apn p.g d.gsm a.gsm n.gsm
4354 3836 2840 3836 5125 3281 3836 19 476 1675 19 1666 3836 19 2565

up in him, and the evil man brings evil things out of the evil stored up in him. **36** But I tell you that
← καὶ ὁ πονηρὸς ἄνθρωπος ἐκβάλλει πονηρά ἐκ ← τοῦ πονηροῦ θησαυροῦ ← δὲ → λέγω ὑμῖν ὅτι
cj d.nsm a.nsm n.nsm v.pai.3s a.apn p.g d.gsm a.gsm n.gsm cj v.pai.1s r.dp.2 cj
2779 3836 4505 476 1675 4505 1666 3836 4505 2565 1254 3306 7007 4022

πόλις ἢ οἰκία μερισθεῖσα καθ᾽ ἑαυτῆς οὐ σταθήσεται. ²⁶ καὶ εἰ ὁ Σατανᾶς τὸν Σατανᾶν ἐκβάλλει, ἐφ᾽ ἑαυτὸν ἐμερίσθη· πῶς οὖν σταθήσεται ἡ βασιλεία αὐτοῦ; ²⁷ καὶ εἰ ἐγὼ ἐν Βεελζεβοὺλ ἐκβάλλω τὰ δαιμόνια, οἱ υἱοὶ ὑμῶν ἐν τίνι ἐκβάλλουσιν; διὰ τοῦτο αὐτοὶ κριταὶ ἔσονται ὑμῶν. ²⁸ εἰ δὲ ἐν πνεύματι θεοῦ ἐγὼ ἐκβάλλω τὰ δαιμόνια, ἄρα ἔφθασεν ἐφ᾽ ὑμᾶς ἡ βασιλεία τοῦ θεοῦ. ¶ ²⁹ ἢ πῶς δύναταί τις εἰσελθεῖν εἰς τὴν οἰκίαν τοῦ ἰσχυροῦ καὶ τὰ σκεύη αὐτοῦ ἁρπάσαι, ἐὰν μὴ πρῶτον δήσῃ τὸν ἰσχυρόν; καὶ τότε τὴν οἰκίαν αὐτοῦ διαρπάσῃ. «διαρπάσει.» ¶ ³⁰ ὁ μὴ ὢν μετ᾽ ἐμοῦ κατ᾽ ἐμοῦ ἐστιν, καὶ ὁ μὴ συνάγων μετ᾽ ἐμοῦ σκορπίζει. ³¹ Διὰ τοῦτο λέγω ὑμῖν, πᾶσα ἁμαρτία καὶ βλασφημία ἀφεθήσεται τοῖς ἀνθρώποις, ἡ δὲ τοῦ πνεύματος βλασφημία οὐκ ἀφεθήσεται. ³² καὶ ὃς ἐὰν εἴπῃ λόγον κατὰ τοῦ υἱοῦ τοῦ ἀνθρώπου, ἀφεθήσεται αὐτῷ· ὃς δ᾽ ἂν εἴπῃ κατὰ τοῦ πνεύματος τοῦ ἁγίου, οὐκ ἀφεθήσεται αὐτῷ οὔτε ἐν τούτῳ τῷ αἰῶνι οὔτε ἐν τῷ μέλλοντι. ¶ ³³ Ἢ ποιήσατε τὸ δένδρον καλὸν καὶ τὸν καρπὸν αὐτοῦ καλόν, ἢ ποιήσατε τὸ δένδρον σαπρὸν καὶ τὸν καρπὸν αὐτοῦ σαπρόν· ἐκ γὰρ τοῦ καρποῦ τὸ δένδρον γινώσκεται. ³⁴ γεννήματα ἐχιδνῶν, πῶς δύνασθε ἀγαθὰ λαλεῖν πονηροὶ ὄντες; ἐκ γὰρ τοῦ περισσεύματος τῆς καρδίας τὸ στόμα λαλεῖ. ³⁵ ὁ ἀγαθὸς ἄνθρωπος ἐκ τοῦ ἀγαθοῦ θησαυροῦ ἐκβάλλει ἀγαθά, καὶ ὁ πονηρὸς ἄνθρωπος ἐκ τοῦ πονηροῦ θησαυροῦ ἐκβάλλει πονηρά. ³⁶ λέγω δὲ ὑμῖν ὅτι

men		will have	to give		account	on	the day	of judgment	for	every	careless	word		they
οἱ ἄνθρωποι	→	→	ἀποδώσουσιν	περὶ	αὐτοῦ	λόγον	ἐν	ἡμέρᾳ	→ κρίσεως		πᾶν	ἀργὸν	ῥῆμα	ὃ
d.npm n.npm			v.fai.3p	p.g	r.gsn.3	n.asm	p.d	n.dsf	n.gsf		a.asn	a.asn	n.asn	r.asn
3836 476			625	4309	899	3364	1877	2465	3213		4246	734	4839	4005

have spoken.	**37** For	by	your	words	you will be	acquitted,	and	by	your	words	you will be	condemned."
→ λαλήσουσιν	γὰρ	ἐκ	σου	⌐τῶν λόγων⌐	→ →	δικαιωθήσῃ	καὶ	ἐκ	σου	⌐τῶν λόγων⌐	→ →	καταδικασθήσῃ
v.fai.3p	cj	p.g	r.gs.2	d.gpm n.gpm		v.fpi.2s	cj	p.g	r.gs.2	d.gpm n.gpm		v.fpi.2s
3281	1142	1666	5148	3836 3364		1467	2779	1666	5148	3836 3364		2868

The Sign of Jonah

12:38 Then	some	of	the	Pharisees	and	teachers	of the law	said		to him,		"Teacher,	we want	to
Τότε	τινες	→	τῶν	Φαρισαίων	καὶ	γραμματέων	← ←	ἀπεκρίθησαν	→	αὐτῷ	λέγοντες	διδάσκαλε	θέλομεν	→
adv	r.npm		d.gpm	n.gpm	cj	n.gpm		v.api.3p		r.dsm.3	pt.pa.npm	n.vsm	v.pai.1p
5538	5516		3836	5757	2779	1208		646		899	3306	1437	2527

see	a miraculous	sign	from you."	**39**	He answered,		"A	wicked	and	adulterous	generation	asks	for a
ἰδεῖν	σημεῖον	ἀπὸ	σοῦ	δὲ	ὁ ἀποκριθεὶς	αὐτοῖς	εἶπεν	πονηρὰ	καὶ	μοιχαλὶς	γενεὰ	ἐπιζητεῖ ←
f.aa	n.asn	p.g	r.gs.2	cj	d.nsm pt.ap.nsm	r.dpm.3	v.aai.3s	a.nsf	cj	a.nsf	n.nsf	v.pai.3s
1625	4956	608	5148	1254	3836 646	899	3306	4505	2779	3655	1155	2118

miraculous	sign!	But	none		will be	given	it	except	the	sign	of	the	prophet	Jonah.	**40** For	as	Jonah
→	σημεῖον	καὶ	οὐ	σημεῖον	→ →	δοθήσεται	αὐτῇ	εἰ μὴ	τὸ	σημεῖον	→	τοῦ	προφήτου	Ἰωνᾶ	γὰρ	ὥσπερ	Ἰωνᾶς
n.asn	cj	adv	n.nsn		v.fpi.3s	r.dsf.3	cj pl	d.nsn	n.nsn		d.gsm	n.gsm	n.gsm	cj		n.nsm
4956	2779	4024	4956		1443	899	1623 3590	3836	4956		3836	4737	2731	1142	6061	2731

was	three	days	and	three	nights	in	the	belly	of a huge fish,		so	the	Son	of Man		will be	three
ἦν	τρεῖς	ἡμέρας	καὶ	τρεῖς	νύκτας	ἐν	τῇ	κοιλίᾳ	⌐τοῦ κήτους⌐	→	οὕτως ὁ	υἱὸς	→	⌐τοῦ ἀνθρώπου⌐	→	ἔσται	τρεῖς
v.iai.3s	a.apf	n.apf	cj	a.apf	n.apf	p.d	d.dsf	n.dsf	d.gsn n.gsn		adv d.nsm	n.nsm		d.gsm n.gsm		v.fmi.3s	a.apf
1639	5552	2465	2779	5552	3816	1877	3836	3120	3836 3063		4048 3836	5626		3836 476		1639	5552

days | and | three | nights | in | the | heart | of the earth. | **41** The | men | of | Nineveh | will stand | | up | at | the | judgment | with
--- | --- | --- | --- | --- | --- | --- | --- | --- | --- | --- | --- | --- | --- | --- | --- | --- | ---
ἡμέρας | καὶ | τρεῖς | νύκτας | ἐν | τῇ | καρδίᾳ | → τῆς γῆς | | ἄνδρες | → | Νινευῖται | → ἀναστήσονται | ← | | ἐν | τῇ | κρίσει | μετὰ
n.apf | cj | a.apf | n.apf | p.d | d.dsf | n.dsf | d.gsf n.gsf | | n.npm | | n.npm | v.fmi.3p | | | p.d | d.dsf | n.dsf | p.g
2465 | 2779 | 5552 | 3816 | 1877 | 3836 | 2840 | 3836 1178 | | 467 | | 3780 | 482 | | | 1877 | 3836 | 3213 | 3552

this	generation	and	condemn	it;	for	they	repented	at	the	preaching	of Jonah,	and	now	one	greater	than
ταύτης	⌐τῆς γενεᾶς⌐	καὶ	κατακρινοῦσιν	αὐτὴν	ὅτι		μετενόησαν	εἰς	τὸ	κήρυγμα	→ Ἰωνᾶ	καὶ	ἰδοὺ	→	πλεῖον
r.gsf	d.gsf n.gsf	cj	v.fai.3p	r.asf.3	cj		v.aai.3p	p.a	d.asn	n.asn	n.gsm	cj	j		a.nsn.c
4047	3836 1155	2779	2891	899	4022		3566	1650	3836	3060	2731	2779	2627		4498

Jonah	is here.	**42** The	Queen	of	the South	will rise		at	the	judgment	with	this	generation	and	condemn it;
Ἰωνᾶ	ὧδε		βασίλισσα	→	νότου	→	ἐγερθήσεται	ἐν	τῇ	κρίσει	μετὰ	ταύτης	⌐τῆς γενεᾶς⌐	καὶ	κατακρινεῖ	αὐτὴν
n.gsm	adv		n.nsf		n.gsm		v.fpi.3s	p.d	d.dsf	n.dsf	p.g	r.gsf	d.gsf n.gsf	cj	v.fai.3s	r.asf.3
2731	6045		999		3803		1586	1877	3836	3213	3552	4047	3836 1155	2779	2891	899

for | she | came | from | the | ends | of | the | earth | to listen | to Solomon's | wisdom, | | and | now | one | greater | than | Solomon | is
--- | --- | --- | --- | --- | --- | --- | --- | --- | --- | --- | --- | --- | --- | --- | --- | --- | ---
ὅτι | → | ἦλθεν | ἐκ | τῶν | περάτων | → | τῆς | γῆς | → ἀκοῦσαι | Σολομῶνος | ⌐τὴν σοφίαν⌐ | | καὶ | ἰδοὺ | → | πλεῖον | → | Σολομῶνος
cj | | v.aai.3s | p.g | d.gpn | n.gpn | | d.gsf | n.gsf | t.aa | n.gsm | d.asf n.asf | | cj | j | | a.nsn.c | | n.gsm
4022 | | 2262 | 1666 | 3836 | 4306 | | 3836 | 1178 | 201 | 5048 | 3836 5053 | | 2779 | 2627 | | 4498 | | 5048

here. ¶	**43**	"When	an	evil	spirit	comes out	of	a man,		it goes	through	arid	places
ὧδε	δὲ	Ὅταν	ἀκάθαρτον	τὸ	πνεῦμα	ἐξέλθῃ ←	ἀπὸ	⌐τοῦ ἀνθρώπου⌐	→	διέρχεται	δι'	ἀνύδρων	τόπων
adv	cj	cj	a.nsn	d.nsn	n.nsn	v.aas.3s	p.g	d.gsm n.gsm		v.pmi.3s	p.g	a.gpm	n.gpm
6045	1254	4020	176	3836	4460	2002	608	3836 476		1451	1328	536	5536

seeking	rest	and	does not	find	it.	**44** Then	it says,	'I will return	to	the	house	I	left.'		When	it
ζητοῦν	ἀνάπαυσιν	καὶ	⌐→ οὐχ	εὑρίσκει		τότε	→ λέγει	ἐπιστρέψω εἰς	τὸν	οἶκον	μου	ὅθεν	ἐξῆλθον	καὶ	→	→
pt.pa.nsn	n.asf	cj	adv	v.pai.3s		adv	v.pai.3s	v.fai.1s	d.asm	n.asm	r.gs.1	cj	v.aai.1s	cj
2426	398	2779	2351 4024	2351		5538	3306	2188 1650	3836	3875	1609	3854	2002	2779

arrives, | it finds | the | house | unoccupied, | swept | | clean | and | put | in order. | **45** Then | it goes | | and
--- | --- | --- | --- | --- | --- | --- | --- | --- | --- | --- | --- | --- | ---
ἐλθὸν | → εὑρίσκει | | σχολάζοντα | σεσαρωμένον | → | καὶ | κεκοσμημένον ← | | τότε | → πορεύεται | καὶ
pt.aa.nsn | v.pai.3s | | pt.pa.asm | pt.rp.asm | | cj | pt.rp.asm | | adv | v.pmi.3s | cj
2262 | 2351 | | 5390 | 4924 | | 2779 | 3175 | | 5538 | 4513 | 2779

takes | | with | it | seven | other | spirits | more | wicked | than | itself, | and | they | go | | in | and | live | there. | And
--- | --- | --- | --- | --- | --- | --- | --- | --- | --- | --- | --- | --- | --- | --- | --- | --- | ---
παραλαμβάνει | μεθ' | ἑαυτοῦ | ἑπτὰ | ἕτερα | πνεύματα | → | πονηρότερα | → | ἑαυτοῦ καὶ | ⌐→ | εἰσελθόντα ← | | κατοικεῖ | ἐκεῖ | καὶ
v.pai.3s | p.g | r.gsn.3 | a.apn | r.apn | n.apn | | a.apn.c | | r.gsn.3 cj | | pt.aa.npn | | v.pai.3s | adv | cj
4161 | 3552 | 1571 | 2231 | 2283 | 4460 | | 4505 | | 1571 2779 | | 1656 | | 2997 | 1695 | 2779

πᾶν ῥῆμα ἀργὸν ὃ λαλήσουσιν οἱ ἄνθρωποι ἀποδώσουσιν περὶ αὐτοῦ λόγον ἐν ἡμέρᾳ κρίσεως· **37** ἐκ γὰρ τῶν λόγων σου δικαιωθήσῃ, καὶ ἐκ τῶν λόγων σου καταδικασθήσῃ.

12:38 Τότε ἀπεκρίθησαν αὐτῷ τινες τῶν γραμματέων καὶ Φαρισαίων λέγοντες, Διδάσκαλε, θέλομεν ἀπὸ σοῦ σημεῖον ἰδεῖν. **39** ὁ δὲ ἀποκριθεὶς εἶπεν αὐτοῖς, Γενεὰ πονηρὰ καὶ μοιχαλὶς σημεῖον ἐπιζητεῖ, καὶ σημεῖον οὐ δοθήσεται αὐτῇ εἰ μὴ τὸ σημεῖον Ἰωνᾶ τοῦ προφήτου. **40** ὥσπερ γὰρ ἦν Ἰωνᾶς ἐν τῇ κοιλίᾳ τοῦ κήτους τρεῖς ἡμέρας καὶ τρεῖς νύκτας, οὕτως ἔσται ὁ υἱὸς τοῦ ἀνθρώπου ἐν τῇ καρδίᾳ τῆς γῆς τρεῖς ἡμέρας καὶ τρεῖς νύκτας. **41** ἄνδρες Νινευῖται ἀναστήσονται ἐν τῇ κρίσει μετὰ τῆς γενεᾶς ταύτης καὶ κατακρινοῦσιν αὐτήν, ὅτι μετενόησαν εἰς τὸ κήρυγμα Ἰωνᾶ, καὶ ἰδοὺ πλεῖον Ἰωνᾶ ὧδε. **42** βασίλισσα νότου ἐγερθήσεται ἐν τῇ κρίσει μετὰ τῆς γενεᾶς ταύτης καὶ κατακρινεῖ αὐτήν, ὅτι ἦλθεν ἐκ τῶν περάτων τῆς γῆς ἀκοῦσαι τὴν σοφίαν Σολομῶνος, καὶ ἰδοὺ πλεῖον Σολομῶνος ὧδε. ¶ **43** Ὅταν δὲ τὸ ἀκάθαρτον πνεῦμα ἐξέλθῃ ἀπὸ τοῦ ἀνθρώπου, διέρχεται δι' ἀνύδρων τόπων ζητοῦν ἀνάπαυσιν καὶ οὐχ εὑρίσκει. **44** τότε λέγει, Εἰς τὸν οἶκόν μου ἐπιστρέψω ὅθεν ἐξῆλθον· καὶ ἐλθὸν εὑρίσκει τὸν οἶκον σχολάζοντα σεσαρωμένον καὶ κεκοσμημένον. **45** τότε πορεύεται καὶ παραλαμβάνει μεθ' ἑαυτοῦ ἑπτὰ ἕτερα

the final	condition	of that		man		is	worse	than the first.		That is how	it will be		with	this
τὰ ἔσχατα		ἐκείνου	τοῦ ἀνθρώπου		γίνεται	χείρονα	→	τῶν πρώτων καὶ	→	→ οὕτως →	ἔσται καὶ	→	ταύτῃ
d.npn a.npn		r.gsm	d.gsm n.gsm		v.pmi.3s	a.npn.c		d.gpn a.gpn cj		adv	v.fmi.3s cj		r.dsf
3836 2274		476	1697	3836 476	1181	5937		3836 4755 2779		4048	1639 2779		4047

wicked	generation."
τῇ πονηρᾷ	τῇ γενεᾷ
d.dsf a.dsf	d.dsf n.dsf
3836 4505	3836 1155

Jesus' Mother and Brothers

12:46

While	Jesus	was still	talking	to the crowd,		his	mother	and	brothers		stood	outside,
→	αὐτοῦ →	Ἔτι	λαλοῦντος →	τοῖς ὄχλοις	ἰδοὺ	αὐτοῦ	ἡ μήτηρ	καὶ	οἱ ἀδελφοὶ	αὐτοῦ	εἱστήκεισαν	ἔξω
	r.gsm.3	adv	pt.pa.gsm	d.dpm n.dpm	j	r.gsm.3	d.nsf n.nsf	cj	d.npm n.npm	r.gsm.3	v.lai.3p	adv
3281	899 3281	2285	3281	3836 4063	2627	899	3836 3613	2779	3836 81	899	2705	2032

wanting	to speak	to him.	**47**	Someone	told	him,	"Your	mother	and	brothers		are standing	outside,
ζητοῦντες →	λαλῆσαι →	αὐτῷ	δέ τις		εἶπεν αὐτῷ	ἰδοὺ	σου	ἡ μήτηρ	καὶ	οἱ ἀδελφοὶ	σου →	ἑστήκασιν	ἔξω
pt.pa.npm	f.aa	r.dsm.3	cj r.nsm		v.aai.3s r.dsm.3	j	r.gs.2	d.nsf n.nsf	cj	d.npm n.npm	r.gs.2	v.rai.3p	adv
2426	3281	899	1254 5516		3306 899	2627	5148	3836 3613	2779	3836 81	5148	2705	2032

wanting	to speak	to you."	**48**	He replied			to him,	"Who is		my	mother,	and	who are		my
ζητοῦντες →	λαλῆσαι →	σοι	δὲ	ὁ ἀποκριθεὶς	εἶπεν τῷ	λέγοντι	→ αὐτῷ	τίς	ἐστίν	μου	ἡ μήτηρ	καὶ	τίνες εἰσίν	μου
pt.pa.npm	f.aa	r.ds.2	cj	d.nsm pt.ap.nsm	v.aai.3s d.dsm	pt.pa.dsm	r.dsm.3	r.nsf	v.pai.3s	r.gs.1	d.nsf n.nsf	cj	r.npm v.pai.3p	r.gs.1
2426	3281	5148	1254	3836 646	3306 3836	3306	899	5515	1639	1609	3836 3613	2779	5515 1639	1609

brothers?"	**49**	Pointing		to his	disciples,		he said,	"Here	are my	mother	and	my	brothers.
οἱ ἀδελφοί	καὶ	ἐκτείνας	τὴν χεῖρα αὐτοῦ	ἐπὶ αὐτοῦ	τοὺς μαθητὰς		εἶπεν ἰδοὺ		μου	ἡ μήτηρ	καὶ	μου	οἱ ἀδελφοί
d.npm n.npm	cj	pt.aa.nsm	d.asf n.asf r.gsm.3	p.a r.gsm.3	d.apm n.apm		v.aai.3s j		r.gs.1	d.nsf n.nsf	cj	r.gs.1	d.npm n.npm
3836 81	2779	1753	3836 5931 899	2093 899	3836 3412		3306 2627		1609	3836 3613	2779	1609	3836 81

50	For	whoever	does	the	will	of my	Father	in	heaven		is	my	brother	and	sister	and	mother."
	γὰρ	ὅστις ἂν	ποιήσῃ	τὸ	θέλημα	→ μου	τοῦ πατρός	τοῦ ἐν	οὐρανοῖς	αὐτός	ἐστίν μου	ἀδελφὸς	καὶ	ἀδελφὴ	καὶ	μήτηρ	
	cj	r.nsm pl	v.aas.3s	d.asn	n.asn	r.gs.1	d.gsm n.gsm	d.gsm p.d	n.dpm	r.nsm	v.pai.3s r.gs.1	n.nsm	cj	n.nsf	cj	n.nsf	
	1142	4015 323	4472	3836	2525	4252 1609	3836 4252	3836 1877	4041	899	1639 1609	81	2779	80	2779	3613	

The Parable of the Sower

13:1

That	same	day		Jesus	went	out of the	house	and sat		by	the	lake.	**2**	Such	large
Ἐν ἐκείνῃ		τῇ ἡμέρᾳ	ὁ Ἰησοῦς	ἐξελθὼν	←	τῆς οἰκίας		ἐκάθητο	παρὰ	τὴν	θάλασσαν	καὶ	→	πολλοί
p.d r.dsf		d.dsf n.dsf	d.nsm n.nsm	pt.aa.nsm		d.gsf n.gsf		v.imi.3s	p.a	d.asf	n.asf	cj		a.npm
1877 1697		3836 2465	3836 2652	2002		3836 3864		2764	4123	3836	2498	2779		6063 4498

crowds	gathered	around	him	that	he	got	into a	boat	and sat		in it,	while	all	the	people	stood	on	the
ὄχλοι	συνήχθησαν	πρὸς	αὐτὸν	ὥστε	αὐτὸν	ἐμβάντα	εἰς	πλοῖον	καθῆσθαι		καὶ	πᾶς	ὁ	ὄχλος	εἱστήκει	ἐπὶ	τὸν
n.npm	v.api.3p	p.a	r.asm.3	cj	r.asm.3	pt.aa.asm	p.a	n.asn	f.pm		cj	a.nsm	d.nsm	n.nsm	v.lai.3s	p.a	d.asm
4063	5251	4639	899	6063	899	1832	1650	4450	2764		2779	4246	3836	4063	2705	2093	3836

shore.	**3**	Then	he	told	them	many	things	in	parables,	saying:	"A	farmer	went	out	to sow		his seed.
αἰγιαλὸν	Καὶ			ἐλάλησεν	αὐτοῖς	πολλὰ	←	ἐν	παραβολαῖς	λέγων	ἰδοὺ ὁ	σπείρων	ἐξῆλθεν	←	τοῦ σπείρειν		
n.asn	cj			v.aai.3s	r.dpm.3	a.apn		p.d	n.dpf	pt.pa.nsm	j d.nsm	pt.pa.nsm	v.aai.3s		d.gsn f.pa		
129	2779			3281	899	4498		1877	4130	3306	2627 3836	5062	2002		3836 5062		

4	As he	was scattering	the seed,		some	fell	along	the	path,	and	the	birds	came	and ate		it	up.
	καὶ ἐν αὐτὸν →	τῷ σπείρειν		μὲν ἃ	ἔπεσεν	παρὰ	τὴν	ὁδόν	καὶ	τὰ	πετεινὰ	ἐλθόντα		κατέφαγεν	αὐτά	←
	cj p.d r.asm.3	d.dsn f.pa		pl r.npn	v.aai.3s	p.a	d.asf	n.asf	cj	d.npn	n.npn	pt.aa.npn		v.aai.3s	r.apn.3	
	2779 1877 899	3836 5062		3525 4005	4406	4123	3836	3847	2779	3836	4374	2262		2983	899 2983	

5	Some	fell	on	rocky	places,	where	it	did not	have	much	soil.		It sprang	up	quickly,	because	the soil
	δὲ ἄλλα	ἔπεσεν	ἐπὶ	τὰ πετρώδη		ὅπου	→	οὐκ	εἶχεν	πολλὴν γῆν	καὶ	→	ἐξανέτειλεν ←	εὐθέως		διὰ	γῆς
	pl r.npn	v.aai.3s	p.a	d.apn n.apn		cj		adv	v.iai.3s	a.asf n.asf	cj		v.aai.3s	adv		p.a	n.gsf
	1254 257	4406	2093	3836 4378		3963	2400 2400	4024	2400	4498 1178	2779		1984	2311		1328	1178

was shallow.	**6**	But	when	the	sun	came		up,	the plants were	scorched,		and they withered	because
τὸ μὴ ἔχειν βάθος	δὲ				ἡλίου	ἀνατείλαντος	←		ἐκαυματίσθη	καὶ	→	ἐξηράνθη	διὰ
d.asn pl f.pa n.asn	cj				n.gsm	pt.aa.gsm			v.api.3s	cj		v.api.3s	p.a
3836 3590 2400 958	1254				2463	422			3009	2779		3830	1328

πνεύματα πονηρότερα ἑαυτοῦ καὶ εἰσελθόντα κατοικεῖ ἐκεῖ· καὶ γίνεται τὰ ἔσχατα τοῦ ἀνθρώπου ἐκείνου χείρονα τῶν πρώτων. οὕτως ἔσται καὶ τῇ γενεᾷ ταύτῃ τῇ πονηρᾷ.

¹²:⁴⁶ Ἔτι αὐτοῦ λαλοῦντος τοῖς ὄχλοις ἰδοὺ ἡ μήτηρ καὶ οἱ ἀδελφοὶ αὐτοῦ εἱστήκεισαν ἔξω ζητοῦντες αὐτῷ λαλῆσαι. ⁴⁷ [εἶπεν δέ τις αὐτῷ, Ἰδοὺ ἡ μήτηρ σου καὶ οἱ ἀδελφοί σου ἔξω ἑστήκασιν ζητοῦντές σοι λαλῆσαι.] ⁴⁸ ὁ δὲ ἀποκριθεὶς εἶπεν τῷ λέγοντι αὐτῷ, Τίς ἐστιν ἡ μήτηρ μου καὶ τίνες εἰσὶν οἱ ἀδελφοί μου; ⁴⁹ καὶ ἐκτείνας τὴν χεῖρα αὐτοῦ ἐπὶ τοὺς μαθητὰς αὐτοῦ εἶπεν, Ἰδοὺ ἡ μήτηρ μου καὶ οἱ ἀδελφοί μου. ⁵⁰ ὅστις γὰρ ἂν ποιήσῃ τὸ θέλημα τοῦ πατρός μου τοῦ ἐν οὐρανοῖς αὐτός μου ἀδελφὸς καὶ ἀδελφὴ καὶ μήτηρ ἐστίν.

¹³:¹ Ἐν τῇ ἡμέρᾳ ἐκείνῃ ἐξελθὼν ὁ Ἰησοῦς τῆς οἰκίας ἐκάθητο παρὰ τὴν θάλασσαν· ² καὶ συνήχθησαν πρὸς αὐτὸν ὄχλοι πολλοί, ὥστε αὐτὸν εἰς πλοῖον ἐμβάντα καθῆσθαι, καὶ πᾶς ὁ ὄχλος ἐπὶ τὸν αἰγιαλὸν εἱστήκει. ³ καὶ ἐλάλησεν αὐτοῖς πολλὰ ἐν παραβολαῖς λέγων, Ἰδοὺ ἐξῆλθεν ὁ σπείρων τοῦ σπείρειν. ⁴ καὶ ἐν τῷ σπείρειν αὐτὸν ἃ μὲν ἔπεσεν παρὰ τὴν ὁδόν, καὶ ἐλθόντα τὰ πετεινὰ κατέφαγεν αὐτά. ⁵ ἄλλα δὲ ἔπεσεν ἐπὶ τὰ πετρώδη ὅπου οὐκ εἶχεν γῆν πολλήν, καὶ εὐθέως ἐξανέτειλεν διὰ τὸ μὴ ἔχειν βάθος γῆς· ⁶ ἡλίου δὲ ἀνατείλαντος ἐκαυματίσθη καὶ διὰ τὸ μὴ ἔχειν ῥίζαν ἐξηράνθη. ⁷ ἄλλα δὲ ἔπεσεν ἐπὶ τὰς ἀκάνθας,

they had   no root. [7]   Other seed fell   among thorns,   which   grew   up and choked the plants.
ιτὸ ἔχειν, μὴ ῥίζαν δὲ ἄλλα   ἔπεσεν ἐπὶ ιτὰς ἀκάνθας, καὶ ιαἱ ἄκανθαι, ἀνέβησαν ←   καὶ ἔπνιξαν αὐτά
d.asn f.pa pl n.asf pl r.npn   v.aai.3s p.a d.apf n.apf cj d.npf n.npf v.aai.3p   cj v.aai.3p r.apn.3
3836 2400 3590 4844 1254 257   4406 2093 3836 180 2779 3836 180 326   2779 4464 899

[8] Still other seed fell   on good   soil,   where it produced a crop   –   a hundred,   sixty   or
δὲ ἄλλα   ἔπεσεν ἐπὶ ιτὴν καλήν, ιτὴν γῆν, καὶ →ἐδίδου καρπόν μὲν ὃ ἑκατόν δὲ ὃ ἑξήκοντα δὲ ὃ
pl r.npn   v.aai.3s p.a d.asf d.asf d.asf n.asf cj v.iai.3s n.asm pl r.nsn a.apm pl r.nsn a.apm pl r.nsn
1254 257   4406 2093 3836 2819 3836 1178 2779 1443 2843 3525 4005 1669 1254 4005 2008 1254 4005

thirty   times what was sown. [9] He who has   ears, let him hear." ¶   [10]   The disciples came   to him and
τριάκοντα   ὁ ← ἔχων ὦτα → ἀκουέτω   Καὶ οἱ μαθηταὶ προσελθόντες ←
a.apm   d.nsm pt.pa.nsm n.apn v.pam.3s   cj d.npm n.npm pt.aa.npm
5558   3836 2400 4044 201   2779 3836 3412 4665

asked,   "Why   do you speak to the people in   parables?" [11]   He replied,   "The knowledge of
εἶπαν αὐτῷ ιδιὰ τί, → → λαλεῖς → αὐτοῖς ἐν παραβολαῖς δὲ ὁ ἀποκριθεὶς εἶπεν αὐτοῖς ὅτι   γνῶναι
v.aai.3p r.dsm.3 p.a r.asn v.pai.2s r.dpm.3 p.d n.dpf cj d.nsm pt.ap.nsm v.aai.3s r.dpm.3 cj f.aa
3306 899 1328 5515 3281 899 1877 4130 1254 3836 646 3306 899 4022 1182

the secrets   of the kingdom of heaven   has been given to you, but not   to them. [12]   Whoever has will
τὰ μυστήρια → τῆς βασιλείας ιτῶν οὐρανῶν, → δέδοται ὑμῖν δὲ οὐ δέδοται → ἐκείνοις γὰρ ὅστις   ἔχει →
d.apn n.apn d.gsf n.gsf d.gpm n.gpm v.rpi.3s r.dp.2 cj adv v.rpi.3s r.dpm cj r.nsm v.pai.3s
3836 3696 3836 993 3836 4041 1443 7007 1254 4024 1443 1697 1142 4015 2400

be given   more,   and he will have an abundance.   Whoever does not have, even what he has will be
→ δοθήσεται αὐτῷ καὶ → → → περισσευθήσεται δὲ ὅστις → οὐκ ἔχει καὶ ὃ → ἔχει →
v.fpi.3s r.dsm.3 cj v.fpi.3s cj r.nsm adv v.pai.3s adv r.asn v.pai.3s
1443 899 2779 4355 1254 4015 2400 4024 2400 2779 4005 2400

taken   from him. [13] This   is why I speak to them in   parables: "Though seeing,   they do not see;
ἀρθήσεται ἀπ' αὐτοῦ ιδιὰ τοῦτο, ← ← → λαλῶ → αὐτοῖς ἐν παραβολαῖς ὅτι →   βλέποντες ↱ → οὐ βλέπουσιν καὶ
v.fpi.3s p.g r.gsm.3 p.a r.asn v.pai.1s r.dpm.3 p.d n.dpf cj pt.pa.npm adv v.pai.3p cj
149 608 899 1328 4047 3281 899 1877 4130 4022 1063 1063 1063 4024 1063 2779

though hearing,   they do not hear   or   understand. [14]   In them is fulfilled   the prophecy of Isaiah:
→ ἀκούοντες ↱ → οὐκ ἀκούουσιν οὐδὲ συνίουσιν   καὶ → αὐτοῖς → ἀναπληροῦται ἡ προφητεία → Ἡσαΐου ἡ
pt.pa.npm adv v.pai.3p cj v.pai.3p cj r.dpm.3 v.ppi.3s d.nsf n.nsf n.gsm d.nsf
201 201 201 4024 201 4028 5317 2779 899 405 3836 4735 2480 3836

"'You will be ever hearing   but never   understanding;   you will be ever seeing   but
λέγουσα → → → ιἀκοῇ ἀκούσετε, καὶ ιοὐ μὴ, συνῆτε   καὶ → → ιβλέποντες βλέψετε, καὶ
pt.pa.nsf n.dsf v.fai.2p cj adv v.aas.2p cj pt.pa.npm v.fai.2p cj
3306 198 201 2779 4024 3590 5317 2779 1063 1063 2779

never   perceiving. [15] For this   people's   heart   has become calloused;   they hardly hear   with their ears, and
ιοὐ μὴ, ἴδητε   γὰρ τούτου ιτοῦ λαοῦ, ιἡ καρδία, → → ἐπαχύνθη καὶ ↱ βαρέως ἤκουσαν → τοῖς ὠσὶν καὶ
adv pl v.aas.2p cj r.gsm d.gsm n.gsm d.nsf n.nsf v.api.3s cj adv v.aai.3p d.dpn n.dpn cj
4024 3590 1625 1142 4047 3836 3295 3836 2840 4266 2779 201 977 201 3836 4044 2779

they have closed   their eyes.   Otherwise they might see   with their eyes,   hear   with their
→ → ἐκάμμυσαν αὐτῶν ιτοὺς ὀφθαλμούς, μήποτε → → ἴδωσιν → τοῖς ὀφθαλμοῖς καὶ ἀκούσωσιν → τοῖς
v.aai.3p r.gpm.3 d.apm n.apm cj v.aas.3p d.dpm n.dpm cj v.aas.3p d.dpn
2826 899 3836 4057 3607 1625 3836 4057 2779 201 3836

ears,   understand with their hearts and turn,   and I would heal   them.' [16] But blessed are your eyes
ὠσὶν καὶ συνῶσιν → τῇ καρδίᾳ καὶ ἐπιστρέψωσιν καὶ → → ἰάσομαι αὐτούς δὲ μακάριοι ὑμῶν οἱ ὀφθαλμοὶ
n.dpn cj v.aas.3p d.dsf n.dsf cj v.aas.3p cj v.fmi.1s r.apm.3 cj a.npm r.gp.2 d.npm n.npm
4044 2779 5317 3836 2840 2779 2188 2779 2615 899 1254 3421 7007 3836 4057

because they see,   and your ears   because they hear. [17] For I tell   you the truth,   many prophets and
ὅτι → βλέπουσιν καὶ ὑμῶν ιτὰ ὦτα, ὅτι → ἀκούουσιν γὰρ → λέγω ὑμῖν ἀμὴν ὅτι πολλοὶ προφῆται καὶ
cj v.pai.3p cj r.gp.2 d.npn n.npn cj v.pai.3p cj v.pai.1s r.dp.2 pl cj a.npm n.npm cj
4022 1063 2779 7007 3836 4044 4022 201 1142 3306 7007 297 4022 4498 4737 2779

righteous men longed   to see   what you see   but did not see   it, and to hear   what you hear   but did not
δίκαιοι ἐπεθύμησαν → ἰδεῖν ἃ → βλέπετε καὶ ↱ οὐκ εἶδαν καὶ → ἀκοῦσαι ἃ → ἀκούετε καὶ ↱ οὐκ
a.npm v.aai.3p f.aa r.apn v.pai.2p cj adv v.aai.3p cj f.aa r.apn v.pai.2p cj adv
1465 2121 1625 4005 1063 2779 1625 1625 2779 201 4005 201 2779 201 4024

καὶ ἀνέβησαν αἱ ἄκανθαι καὶ ἔπνιξαν αὐτά. [8] ἄλλα δὲ ἔπεσεν ἐπὶ τὴν γῆν τὴν καλὴν καὶ ἐδίδου καρπόν, ὃ μὲν ἑκατόν, ὃ δὲ ἑξήκοντα, ὃ δὲ τριάκοντα. [9] ὁ ἔχων ὦτα ἀκουέτω. ¶ [10] Καὶ προσελθόντες οἱ μαθηταὶ εἶπαν αὐτῷ, Διὰ τί ἐν παραβολαῖς λαλεῖς αὐτοῖς; [11] ὁ δὲ ἀποκριθεὶς εἶπεν αὐτοῖς, ὅτι «Ὅτι» Ὑμῖν «ὑμῖν» δέδοται γνῶναι τὰ μυστήρια τῆς βασιλείας τῶν οὐρανῶν, ἐκείνοις δὲ οὐ δέδοται. [12] ὅστις γὰρ ἔχει, δοθήσεται αὐτῷ καὶ περισσευθήσεται· ὅστις δὲ οὐκ ἔχει, καὶ ὃ ἔχει ἀρθήσεται ἀπ' αὐτοῦ. [13] διὰ τοῦτο ἐν παραβολαῖς αὐτοῖς λαλῶ, ὅτι βλέποντες οὐ βλέπουσιν καὶ ἀκούοντες οὐκ ἀκούουσιν οὐδὲ συνίουσιν, [14] καὶ ἀναπληροῦται αὐτοῖς ἡ προφητεία Ἡσαΐου ἡ λέγουσα, Ἀκοῇ ἀκούσετε καὶ οὐ μὴ συνῆτε, καὶ βλέποντες βλέψετε καὶ οὐ μὴ ἴδητε. [15] ἐπαχύνθη γὰρ ἡ καρδία τοῦ λαοῦ τούτου, καὶ τοῖς ὠσὶν βαρέως ἤκουσαν καὶ τοὺς ὀφθαλμοὺς αὐτῶν ἐκάμμυσαν, μήποτε ἴδωσιν τοῖς ὀφθαλμοῖς καὶ τοῖς ὠσὶν ἀκούσωσιν καὶ τῇ καρδίᾳ συνῶσιν καὶ ἐπιστρέψωσιν καὶ ἰάσομαι αὐτούς. [16] ὑμῶν δὲ μακάριοι οἱ ὀφθαλμοὶ ὅτι βλέπουσιν καὶ τὰ ὦτα ὑμῶν ὅτι ἀκούουσιν. [17] ἀμὴν γὰρ λέγω ὑμῖν ὅτι πολλοὶ προφῆται καὶ δίκαιοι ἐπεθύμησαν ἰδεῖν ἃ βλέπετε καὶ οὐκ εἶδαν, καὶ ἀκοῦσαι ἃ ἀκούετε καὶ οὐκ ἤκουσαν. ¶ [18] Ὑμεῖς οὖν ἀκούσατε τὴν

hear it. ¶ **18** "Listen then to what the parable of the sower means: **19** When anyone hears the
ἤκουσαν   ὑμεῖς ἀκούσατε οὖν   τὴν παραβολὴν → τοῦ σπείραντος   παντὸς ἀκούοντος τὸν
v.aai.3p   r.np.2 v.aam.2p cj   d.asf n.asf   d.gsm pt.aa.gsm   a.gsm pt.pa.gsm d.asm
201   7007 201 4036   3836 4130   3836 5062   201 4246 201 3836

message about the kingdom and does not understand it, the evil   one comes and snatches away what was
λόγον → τῆς βασιλείας καὶ ↑ μὴ συνιέντος   ὁ πονηρὸς   ← ἔρχεται καὶ ἁρπάζει   ← τὸ →
n.asm   d.gsf n.gsf cj   pl pt.pa.gsn   d.nsm a.nsm   v.pmi.3s cj v.pai.3s   d.asn
3364   3836 993 2779   3590 5317   3836 4505   2262 2779 773   3836

sown in his heart. This is the seed sown along the path. **20** The one who received the seed that
ἐσπαρμένον ἐν αὐτοῦ ⌊τῇ καρδίᾳ⌋ οὗτός ἐστιν ὁ   σπαρείς παρὰ τὴν ὁδόν δὲ ὁ   ←   → σπαρείς
pt.rp.asn p.d r.gsm.3 d.dsf n.dsf r.nsm v.pai.3s d.nsm   pt.ap.nsm p.a d.asf n.asf cj d.nsm   pt.ap.nsm
5062 1877 899 3836 2840 4047 1639 3836   5062 4123 3836 3847 1254 3836   5062

fell on rocky places is the man who hears the word and at once receives it with joy. **21** But since
ἐπὶ ⌊τὰ πετρώδη⌋ ← οὗτός ἐστιν ὁ   ← ἀκούων τὸν λόγον καὶ → εὐθὺς λαμβάνων αὐτὸν μετὰ χαρᾶς δὲ
p.a d.apn n.apn   r.nsm v.pai.3s d.nsm   pt.pa.nsm d.asm n.asm cj   adv pt.pa.nsm r.asm.3 p.g n.gsf cj
2093 3836 4378   4047 1639 3836   201 3836 3364 2779   2318 3284 899 3552 5915 1254

he has no root, *he lasts only a short time.* When trouble or persecution comes because
→ ἔχει οὐκ ῥίζαν ἐν ἑαυτῷ ἀλλὰ ἐστιν πρόσκαιρος δὲ → θλίψεως ἢ διωγμοῦ γενομένης διὰ
v.pai.3s adv n.asf p.d r.dsm.3 cj v.pai.3s a.nsm cj   n.gsf cj n.gsm pt.am.gsf p.a
2400 4024 4844 1877 1571 247 1639 4672 1254   2568 2445 1501 1181 1328

of the word, he quickly falls away. **22** The one who received the seed that fell among the thorns
← τὸν λόγον εὐθὺς σκανδαλίζεται ← δὲ ὁ ← ← → σπαρείς εἰς τὰς ἀκάνθας οὗτος
d.asm n.asm adv v.ppi.3s   cj d.nsm   pt.ap.nsm p.a d.apf n.apf r.nsm
3836 3364 4997 2318 4997   1254 3836   5062 1650 3836 180 4047

is the man who hears the word, but the worries of this life and the deceitfulness of wealth choke
ἐστιν ὁ ← ἀκούων τὸν λόγον καὶ ἡ μέριμνα → τοῦ αἰῶνος καὶ ἡ ἀπάτη → ⌊τοῦ πλούτου⌋ συμπνίγει
v.pai.3s d.nsm   pt.pa.nsm d.asm n.asm cj d.nsf n.nsf   d.gsm n.gsm cj d.nsf n.nsf   d.gsm n.gsm v.pai.3s
1639 3836   201 3836 3364 2779 3836 3533   3836 172 2779 3836 573   3836 4458 5231

it, making it unfruitful. **23** But the one who received the seed that fell on good soil is the
⌊τὸν λόγον⌋ καὶ γίνεται ← ἄκαρπος δὲ ὁ ← → σπαρείς ἐπὶ ⌊τὴν καλὴν⌋ γῆν οὗτός ἐστιν ὁ
d.asm n.asm cj v.pmi.3s a.nsm cj d.nsm   pt.ap.nsm p.a d.asf a.asf n.asf r.nsm v.pai.3s d.nsm
3836 3364 2779 1181 182 1254 3836   5062 2093 3836 2819 1178 4047 1639 3836

man who hears the word and understands it. He produces a crop, yielding a hundred,
← ἀκούων τὸν λόγον καὶ συνιείς δὴ ὃς καρποφορεῖ ← καὶ ποιεῖ μὲν ὁ ἑκατόν δὲ ὁ
pt.pa.nsm d.asm n.asm cj pt.pa.nsm pl r.nsm v.pai.3s   cj v.pai.3s pl r.nsn a.apn pl r.nsn
201 3836 3364 2779 5317 1314 4005 2844   2779 4472 3525 4005 1669 1254 4005

sixty or thirty times what was sown."
ἑξήκοντα δὲ ὁ τριάκοντα
a.apn pl r.nsn a.apn
2008 1254 4005 5558

The Parable of the Weeds

13:24 Jesus told them another parable: "The kingdom of heaven is like a man who
παρέθηκεν αὐτοῖς Ἄλλην παραβολὴν λέγων ἡ βασιλεία → ⌊τῶν οὐρανῶν⌋ → ὡμοιώθη ἀνθρώπῳ →
v.aai.3s r.dpm.3 r.asf n.asf pt.pa.nsm d.nsf n.nsf   d.gpm n.gpm   v.api.3s n.dsm
4192 899 257 4130 3306 3836 993   3836 4041   3929 476

sowed good seed in his field. **25** But while everyone was sleeping, his enemy came and
σπείραντι καλὸν σπέρμα ἐν αὐτοῦ ⌊τῷ ἀγρῷ⌋ δὲ ἐν ⌊τοὺς ἀνθρώπους⌋ → ⌊τῷ καθεύδειν⌋ αὐτοῦ ὁ ἐχθρὸς ἦλθεν καὶ
pt.aa.dsm a.asn n.asn p.d r.gsm.3 d.dsm n.dsm cj p.d d.apm n.apm   d.dsn f.pa r.gsm.3 d.nsm n.nsm v.aai.3s cj
5062 2819 5065 1877 899 3836 69 1254 1877 3836 476   3836 2761 899 3836 2398 2262 2779

sowed weeds among the wheat, and went away. **26** When the wheat sprouted and formed heads, then the
ἐπέσπειρεν ζιζάνια ἀνὰ μέσον τοῦ σίτου καὶ ἀπῆλθεν δὲ ὅτε ὁ χόρτος ἐβλάστησεν καὶ ἐποίησεν καρπὸν τότε τὰ
v.aai.3s n.apn p.a n.asn d.gsm n.gsm cj v.aai.3s cj cj d.nsm n.nsm v.aai.3s cj v.aai.3s n.asm adv d.npn
2178 2429 324 3545 3836 4992 2779 599 1254 4021 3836 5965 1056 2779 4472 2843 5538 3836

weeds also appeared. ¶ **27** "The owner's servants came to him and said, 'Sir, didn't you
ζιζάνια καὶ ἐφάνη δὲ οἱ ⌊τοῦ οἰκοδεσπότου⌋ δοῦλοι προσελθόντες ← εἶπον αὐτῷ κύριε οὐχὶ →
n.npn adv v.api.3s cj d.npm d.gsm n.gsm n.npm pt.aa.npm   v.aai.3p r.dsm.3 n.vsm pl
2429 2779 5743 1254 3836 3836 3867 1529 4665   3306 899 3261 4049

παραβολὴν τοῦ σπείραντος. ¹⁹ παντὸς ἀκούοντος τὸν λόγον τῆς βασιλείας καὶ μὴ συνιέντος ἔρχεται ὁ πονηρὸς καὶ ἁρπάζει τὸ ἐσπαρμένον ἐν τῇ καρδίᾳ αὐτοῦ, οὗτός ἐστιν ὁ παρὰ τὴν ὁδὸν σπαρείς. ²⁰ ὁ δὲ ἐπὶ τὰ πετρώδη σπαρείς, οὗτός ἐστιν ὁ τὸν λόγον ἀκούων καὶ εὐθὺς μετὰ χαρᾶς λαμβάνων αὐτόν, ²¹ οὐκ ἔχει δὲ ῥίζαν ἐν ἑαυτῷ ἀλλὰ πρόσκαιρός ἐστιν, γενομένης δὲ θλίψεως ἢ διωγμοῦ διὰ τὸν λόγον εὐθὺς σκανδαλίζεται. ²² ὁ δὲ εἰς τὰς ἀκάνθας σπαρείς, οὗτός ἐστιν ὁ τὸν λόγον ἀκούων, καὶ ἡ μέριμνα τοῦ αἰῶνος καὶ ἡ ἀπάτη τοῦ πλούτου συμπνίγει τὸν λόγον καὶ ἄκαρπος γίνεται. ²³ ὁ δὲ ἐπὶ τὴν καλὴν γῆν σπαρείς, οὗτός ἐστιν ὁ τὸν λόγον ἀκούων καὶ συνιείς, ὃς δὴ καρποφορεῖ καὶ ποιεῖ ὃ μὲν ἑκατόν, ὃ δὲ ἑξήκοντα, ὃ δὲ τριάκοντα.

¹³:²⁴ Ἄλλην παραβολὴν παρέθηκεν αὐτοῖς λέγων, Ὡμοιώθη ἡ βασιλεία τῶν οὐρανῶν ἀνθρώπῳ σπείραντι καλὸν σπέρμα ἐν τῷ ἀγρῷ αὐτοῦ. ²⁵ ἐν δὲ τῷ καθεύδειν τοὺς ἀνθρώπους ἦλθεν αὐτοῦ ὁ ἐχθρὸς καὶ ἐπέσπειρεν ζιζάνια ἀνὰ μέσον τοῦ σίτου καὶ ἀπῆλθεν. ²⁶ ὅτε δὲ ἐβλάστησεν ὁ χόρτος καὶ καρπὸν ἐποίησεν, τότε ἐφάνη καὶ τὰ ζιζάνια. ¶ ²⁷ προσελθόντες δὲ οἱ δοῦλοι τοῦ

sow   good seed   in   your field?   Where then did the weeds come from?' **28**   "'An enemy   did
ἔσπειρας καλὸν σπέρμα ἐν σῷ ⌐τῷ ἀγρῷ⌐ πόθεν οὖν →   ζιζάνια ἔχει ←   δὲ   ⌐ἐχθρὸς ἄνθρωπος ἐποίησεν
v.aai.2s a.asn n.asn p.d r.dsm.2 d.dsm n.dsm cj   cj   n.apn v.pai.3s   cj   a.nsm n.nsm   v.aai.3s
5062   2819 5065 1877 5050 3836 69   4470 4036 2400 2429 2400   4470 1254   2398 476   4472

this,' he replied.   ¶   "The servants asked   him, 'Do you want us to go   and pull
τοῦτο ὁ   ἔφη   αὐτοῖς   δὲ οἱ   δοῦλοι λέγουσιν αὐτῷ οὖν →   →   θέλεις → ἀπελθόντες συλλέξωμεν
r.asn d.nsm v.iai.3s r.dpm.3   cj d.npm n.npm   v.pai.3p r.dsm.3 cj   v.pai.2s   pt.aa.npm   v.aas.1p
4047 3836 5774   899   1254 3836 1529   3306   899   4036   2527   599   5198

them up?' **29**   "'No,' he answered, 'because while you are pulling   the weeds, you may root   up the wheat
αὐτά ←   δὲ οὖ ὁ   φησιν μήποτε →   →   →   συλλέγοντες τὰ ζιζάνια →   ἐκριζώσητε ←   τὸν σῖτον
r.apn.3   cj pl d.nsm v.pai.3s cj   pt.pa.npm   d.apn n.apn   v.aas.2p   d.asm n.asm
899   5198 4024 3836 5774 3607   5198   3836 2429   1748   3836 4992

with them. **30** Let both   grow   together until the harvest.   At that   time I will tell the harvesters:
ἅμα αὐτοῖς ἄφετε ἀμφότερα συναυξάνεσθαι ←   ἕως τοῦ θερισμοῦ καὶ ἐν ⌐τοῦ θερισμοῦ⌐ καιρῷ → ἐρῶ τοῖς θερισταῖς
p.d r.dpn.3 v.aam.2p a.apn f.pp   p.g d.gsm n.gsm cj p.d d.gsm n.gsm   n.dsm   v.fai.1s d.dpm n.dpm
275 899   918   317   5277   2401 3836 2546 2779 1877 3836 2546   2789   3306 3836 2547

First collect the weeds and tie   them in bundles to be burned;   then gather   the wheat and
πρῶτον συλλέξατε τὰ ζιζάνια καὶ δήσατε αὐτὰ εἰς δέσμας πρὸς → ⌐τὸ κατακαῦσαι αὐτὰ δὲ συναγάγετε τὸν σῖτον
adv   v.aam.2p d.apn n.apn cj v.aam.2p r.apn.3 p.a n.apf p.a   d.asn f.aa   r.apn.3 cj v.aam.2p d.asm n.asm
4754   5198   3836 2429 2779 1313   899 1650 1299 4639   3836 2876   899 1254 5251   3836 4992

bring it into my barn.'"
εἰς μου ⌐τὴν ἀποθήκην⌐
p.a r.gs.1 d.asf n.asf
1650 1609 3836 630

The Parables of the Mustard Seed and the Yeast

13:31 He told   them another parable: "The kingdom of heaven   is   like a mustard seed, which
→   παρέθηκεν αὐτοῖς Ἄλλην παραβολὴν λέγων ἡ   βασιλεία → ⌐τῶν οὐρανῶν⌐ ἐστὶν ὁμοία σινάπεως κόκκῳ ὃν
v.aai.3s   r.dpm.3 r.asf n.asf   pt.pa.nsm n.nsf   d.gpm n.gpm   v.pai.3s a.nsf n.gsn   n.dsm r.asm
4192   899   257   4130   3306   3836 993   3836 4041   1639   3927 4983   3133 4005

a man   took and planted in his field. **32** Though it is   the smallest of all   your seeds,   yet when it
ἄνθρωπος λαβὼν ἔσπειρεν ἐν αὐτοῦ ⌐τῷ ἀγρῷ⌐   μὲν   ὃ ἐστιν μικρότερον → πάντων τῶν σπερμάτων δὲ ὅταν
n.nsm   pt.aa.nsm v.aai.3s p.d r.gsm.3 d.dsm n.dsm   pl   r.nsn v.pai.3s a.nsn.c   a.gpn d.gpn n.gpn   rj cj
476   3284   5062   1877 899 3036 69   4005   1639   3625   4246 3836 5065   1254 4020

grows, it is   the largest of garden plants   and becomes a tree,   so   that the birds of the air   come and
αὐξηθῇ → ἐστὶν μεῖζον →   ⌐τῶν λαχάνων⌐ καὶ γίνεται δένδρον ὥστε   → τὰ πετεινὰ → τοῦ οὐρανοῦ ἐλθεῖν καὶ
v.aps.3s v.pai.3s a.nsn.c   d.gpn n.gpn   cj v.pmi.3s n.nsn cj   d.apn n.apn d.gsm n.gsm   f.aa   cj
889   1639   3489   3836 3303   2779 1181   1285   6063   3836 4374   3836 4041   2262   2779

perch   in its branches."   ¶   **33** He told   them still another parable: "The kingdom of heaven
κατασκηνοῦν ἐν αὐτοῦ ⌐τοῖς κλάδοις⌐   →   ἐλάλησεν αὐτοῖς Ἄλλην παραβολὴ ἡ   βασιλεία → ⌐τῶν οὐρανῶν⌐
f.pa   p.d r.gsn.3 d.dpm n.dpm   v.aai.3s   r.dpm.3 r.asf n.asf   d.nsf n.nsf   d.gpm n.gpm
2942   1877 899   3836 3080   3281   899   257   4130   3836 993   3836 4041

is   like yeast that a woman took   and mixed into a *large amount* of flour until it worked all   through
ἐστὶν ὁμοία ζύμη ἣν γυνὴ λαβοῦσα ἐνέκρυψεν εἰς τρία σάτα → ἀλεύρου ἕως οὗ ἐζυμώθη ὅλον
v.pai.3s a.nsf n.dsf r.asf n.nsf pt.aa.nsf v.aai.3s p.a a.apn n.apn   n.gsn   p.g r.gsm v.api.3s a.nsn
1639   3927 2434 4005 1222 3284   1606   1650 5552 4929   236   2401 4005 2435   3910

the dough." ¶   **34** Jesus   spoke   all   these things to the crowd in parables; he did not say   anything
⌐ὁ Ἰησοῦς⌐ ἐλάλησεν πάντα ταῦτα ←   →   τοῖς ὄχλοις ἐν παραβολαῖς καὶ → → οὐδὲν ἐλάλει ←
d.nsm n.nsm   v.aai.3s a.apn r.apn   d.dpm n.dpm p.d n.dpf   cj   a.asn v.iai.3s
3836 2652   3281   4246 4047   3836 4063   1877 4130   2779 3281 3281 4029 3281   4029

to them without using a parable. **35** So   was fulfilled what was spoken through the prophet: "I will open my
→ αὐτοῖς χωρὶς   παραβολῆς ὅπως → πληρωθῇ τὸ →   ῥηθὲν   διὰ τοῦ προφήτου λέγοντος →   ἀνοίξω μου
   r.dpm.3 p.g   n.gsf   cj   v.aps.3s d.nsn   pt.ap.nsn p.g d.gsm n.gsm   pt.pa.gsm   v.fai.1s r.gs.1
   899   6006   4130   3968   4444   3836   3306   1328 3836 4737   3306   487   1609

οἰκοδεσπότου εἶπον αὐτῷ, Κύριε, οὐχὶ καλὸν σπέρμα ἔσπειρας ἐν τῷ σῷ ἀγρῷ; πόθεν οὖν ἔχει ζιζάνια; **28** ὁ δὲ ἔφη αὐτοῖς, Ἐχθρὸς ἄνθρωπος τοῦτο ἐποίησεν. ¶ οἱ δὲ δοῦλοι λέγουσιν αὐτῷ, Θέλεις οὖν ἀπελθόντες συλλέξωμεν αὐτά; **29** ὁ δέ φησιν, Οὔ, μήποτε συλλέγοντες τὰ ζιζάνια ἐκριζώσητε ἅμα αὐτοῖς τὸν σῖτον. **30** ἄφετε συναυξάνεσθαι ἀμφότερα ἕως τοῦ θερισμοῦ, καὶ ἐν καιρῷ τοῦ θερισμοῦ ἐρῶ τοῖς θερισταῖς, Συλλέξατε πρῶτον τὰ ζιζάνια καὶ δήσατε αὐτὰ εἰς δέσμας πρὸς τὸ κατακαῦσαι αὐτά, τὸν δὲ σῖτον συναγάγετε εἰς τὴν ἀποθήκην μου.
13:31 Ἄλλην παραβολὴν παρέθηκεν αὐτοῖς λέγων, Ὁμοία ἐστὶν ἡ βασιλεία τῶν οὐρανῶν κόκκῳ σινάπεως, ὃν λαβὼν ἄνθρωπος ἔσπειρεν ἐν τῷ ἀγρῷ αὐτοῦ· **32** ὃ μικρότερον μέν ἐστιν πάντων τῶν σπερμάτων, ὅταν δὲ αὐξηθῇ μεῖζον τῶν λαχάνων ἐστὶν καὶ γίνεται δένδρον, ὥστε ἐλθεῖν τὰ πετεινὰ τοῦ οὐρανοῦ καὶ κατασκηνοῦν ἐν τοῖς κλάδοις αὐτοῦ. ¶ **33** Ἄλλην παραβολὴν ἐλάλησεν αὐτοῖς· Ὁμοία ἐστὶν ἡ βασιλεία τῶν οὐρανῶν ζύμη, ἣν λαβοῦσα γυνὴ ἐνέκρυψεν εἰς ἀλεύρου σάτα τρία ἕως οὗ ἐζυμώθη ὅλον. ¶ **34** Ταῦτα πάντα ἐλάλησεν ὁ Ἰησοῦς ἐν παραβολαῖς τοῖς ὄχλοις καὶ χωρὶς παραβολῆς οὐδὲν ἐλάλει αὐτοῖς, **35** ὅπως πληρωθῇ τὸ ῥηθὲν διὰ τοῦ προφήτου λέγοντος, Ἀνοίξω ἐν παραβολαῖς τὸ στόμα μου, ἐρεύξομαι κεκρυμμένα ἀπὸ καταβολῆς [κόσμου].

mouth | in | parables, | I will utter | | things hidden | since | the creation | | of the world."
╷τὸ στόμα╵ | ἐν | παραβολαῖς | → → | ἐρεύξομαι | → | κεκρυμμένα ἀπὸ | | καταβολῆς | → | κόσμου
d.asn n.asn | p.d | n.dpf | | v.fmi.1s | | pt.rp.apn p.g | | n.gsf | | n.gsm
3836 5125 | 1877 | 4130 | | 2243 | | 3221 608 | | 2856 | | 3180

The Parable of the Weeds Explained

13:36 Then | he left | the crowd | and | went | into | the house. | His | disciples | came | to him | and said,
Τότε | → ἀφεὶς | τοὺς ὄχλους | | ἦλθεν εἰς | | τὴν οἰκίαν | καὶ αὐτοῦ | οἱ μαθηταὶ | προσῆλθον ← | αὐτῷ | λέγοντες
adv | pt.aa.nsm | d.apm n.apm | | v.aai.3s p.a | | d.asf n.asf | cj r.gsm.3 | d.npm n.npm | v.aai.3p | r.dsm.3 | pt.pa.npm
5538 | 918 3836 | 4063 | | 2262 1650 | | 3836 3864 | 2779 899 | 3836 3412 | 4665 | 899 | 3306

"Explain | to us | the | parable | of the weeds | in the field." | ¶ | **37** | He answered, | "The one who sowed
διασάφησον | → ἡμῖν | τὴν | παραβολὴν | → τῶν ζιζανίων | → τοῦ ἀγροῦ | | | δὲ ὁ ἀποκριθεὶς εἶπεν ὁ | σπείρων
v.aam.2s | r.dp.1 | d.asf | n.asf | d.gpn n.gpn | d.gsm n.gsm | | | cj d.nsm pt.ap.nsm v.aai.3s d.nsm | pt.pa.nsm
1397 | 7005 | 3836 | 4130 | 3836 2429 | 3836 69 | | | 1254 3836 646 3306 3836 | 5062

the | good | seed | is | the | Son | of Man. | | **38** | The | field | is | the | world, | and | the | good | seed | stands for | the
τὸ | καλὸν | σπέρμα | ἐστὶν | ὁ | υἱὸς | ╷τοῦ ἀνθρώπου╵ | | | δὲ ὁ | ἀγρός | ἐστιν ὁ | κόσμος | δὲ | τὸ | καλὸν | σπέρμα | οὗτοι | εἰσιν | οἱ
d.asn | a.asn | n.asn | v.pai.3s | d.nsm | n.nsm | d.gsm n.gsm | | | cj d.nsm | n.nsm | v.pai.3s d.nsm | n.nsm | cj | d.nsn | a.nsn | n.nsn | r.npm | v.pai.3p | d.npm
3836 | 2819 | 5065 | 1639 | 3836 | 5626 | 3836 476 | | | 1254 3836 | 69 | 1639 3836 | 3180 | 1254 | 3836 | 2819 | 5065 | 4047 | 1639 | 3836

sons | of the kingdom. | | The | weeds | are | the | sons | of the evil | one, | **39** | and | the | enemy | who | sows | them | is | the
υἱοὶ | → τῆς βασιλείας | | δὲ | τὰ | ζιζάνιά | εἰσιν | οἱ | υἱοὶ | → τοῦ πονηροῦ ← | | | δὲ | ὁ | ἐχθρὸς | ὁ | σπείρας | αὐτά | ἐστιν | ὁ
n.npm | d.gsf n.gsf | | cj | d.npn | n.npn | v.pai.3p | d.npm | n.npm | d.gsm a.gsm | | | cj | d.nsm | n.nsm | d.nsm | pt.aa.nsm | r.apn.3 | v.pai.3s | d.nsm
5626 | 3836 993 | | 1254 | 3836 | 2429 | 1639 | 3836 | 5626 | 3836 4505 | | | 1254 | 3836 | 2398 | 3836 | 5062 | 899 | 1639 | 3836

devil. | | The | harvest | is | the | end | of the age, | | and | the | harvesters | are | angels. | ¶ | **40** | "As | the | weeds
διάβολος | | δὲ | ὁ | θερισμὸς | ἐστιν | | συντέλεια | → αἰῶνος | δὲ | οἱ | θερισταὶ | εἰσιν | ἄγγελοι | | | οὖν | ὥσπερ | τὰ | ζιζάνια
n.nsm | | cj | d.nsm | n.nsm | v.pai.3s | | n.nsf | n.gsm | cj | d.npm | n.npm | v.pai.3p | n.npm | | | cj | cj | d.npn | n.npn
1333 | | 1254 | 3836 | 2546 | 1639 | | 5333 | 172 | 1254 | 3836 | 2547 | 1639 | 34 | | | 4036 | 6061 | 3836 | 2429

are | pulled | up | and | burned | | in | the fire, | so | | it will be | at | the | end | | of the age. | **41** | The | Son | of Man
→ | συλλέγεται ← | | καὶ | κατακαίεται | → | | πυρὶ | οὕτως | → | → ἔσται ἐν | | τῇ | συντελείᾳ | → | τοῦ αἰῶνος | | ὁ | υἱὸς | ╷τοῦ ἀνθρώπου╵
| v.ppi.3s | | cj | v.ppi.3s | | | n.dsn | adv | | v.fmi.3s p.d | | d.dsf | n.dsf | | d.gsm n.gsm | | d.nsm | n.nsm | d.gsm n.gsm
| 5198 | | 2779 | 2876 | | | 4786 | 4048 | | 1639 1877 | | 3836 | 5333 | | 3836 172 | | 3836 | 5626 | 3836 476

will send | out | his | angels, | | and | they will weed | out of | his | kingdom | everything | that | causes | sin
→ ἀποστελεῖ ← | | αὐτοῦ | ╷τοὺς ἀγγέλους╵ | καὶ | → | → συλλέξουσιν ἐκ | ← | αὐτοῦ | ╷τῆς βασιλείας╵ | πάντα | τὰ | σκάνδαλα
v.fai.3s | | r.gsm.3 | d.apm n.apm | cj | | v.fai.3p | p.g | r.gsm.3 | d.gsf n.gsf | a.apn | d.apn | n.apn
690 | | 899 | 3836 34 | 2779 | | 5198 | 1666 | 899 | 3836 993 | 4246 | 3836 | 4998

and | all | who | do | evil. | **42** | They will throw | them | into | the | fiery | furnace, | where | there will be
καὶ | τοὺς | ποιοῦντας | ╷τὴν ἀνομίαν╵ | | | καὶ → | → βαλοῦσιν | αὐτοὺς εἰς | τὴν | ╷τοῦ πυρός╵ | κάμινον | ἐκεῖ | → → ἔσται
cj | d.apm | pt.pa.apm | d.asf n.asf | | | cj | v.fai.3p | r.apm.3 p.a | d.asf | d.gsn n.gsn | n.asf | adv | v.fmi.3s
2779 | 3836 | 4472 | 3836 490 | | | 2779 | 965 | 899 1650 | 3836 | 2825 | 2825 | 1695 | 1639

weeping | and | gnashing | of teeth. | **43** | Then | the | righteous | will shine | like | the | sun | in | the | kingdom of
╷ὁ κλαυθμὸς╵ | καὶ | ὁ | βρυγμὸς | ╷τῶν ὀδόντων╵ | | τότε | οἱ | δίκαιοι | → ἐκλάμψουσιν | ὡς | ὁ | ἥλιος | ἐν | τῇ | βασιλείᾳ | →
d.nsm n.nsm | cj | d.nsm | n.nsm | d.gpn n.gpn | | adv | d.npm | a.npm | v.fai.3p | pl | d.nsm | n.nsm | p.d | d.dsf | n.dsf
3836 3088 | 2779 | 3836 | 1106 | 3836 3848 | | 5538 | 3836 | 1465 | 1719 | 6055 | 3836 | 2463 | 1877 | 3836 | 993 | 4252

their | Father. | He | who | has | ears, | let him hear.
αὐτῶν | ╷τοῦ πατρός╵ | ὁ | ← | ἔχων | ὦτα | → ἀκουέτω
r.gpm.3 | d.gsm n.gsm | d.nsm | | pt.pa.nsm | n.apn | v.pam.3s
899 | 3836 4252 | 3836 | | 2400 | 4044 | 201

The Parables of the Hidden Treasure and the Pearl

13:44 "The | kingdom | of heaven | is | like | treasure | hidden | in a field. | When | a | man | found it, | he
ἡ | βασιλεία | ╷τῶν οὐρανῶν╵ | ἐστιν | Ὁμοία | θησαυρῷ | κεκρυμμένῳ ἐν | ╷τῷ ἀγρῷ╵ | → | | ἄνθρωπος | εὑρὼν ὃν | →
d.nsf | n.nsf | d.gpm n.gpm | v.pai.3s | a.nsf | n.dsm | pt.rp.dsm p.d | d.dsm n.dsm | | | n.nsm | pt.aa.nsm r.asm
3836 | 993 | 3836 4041 | 1639 | 3927 | 2565 | 3221 1877 | 3836 69 | | | 476 | 2351 4005

hid | it again, | and | then | in | his | joy | went | and | sold | all | he had | and | bought | that | field. | ¶
ἔκρυψεν | καὶ | | ἀπὸ | αὐτοῦ | ╷τῆς χαρᾶς╵ | ὑπάγει | καὶ | πωλεῖ | ╷πάντα ὅσα╵ | → | ἔχει | καὶ | ἀγοράζει | ἐκεῖνον | ╷τὸν ἀγρὸν╵
v.aai.3s | cj | | p.g | r.gsm.3 | d.gsf n.gsf | v.pai.3s | cj | v.pai.3s | a.apn r.apn | | v.pai.3s | cj | v.pai.3s | r.asm | d.asm n.asm
3221 | 2779 | | 608 | 899 | 3836 5915 | 5632 | 2779 | 4797 | 4246 4012 | | 2400 | 2779 | 60 | 1697 | 3836 69

45 "Again, | the | kingdom | of heaven | is | like | a merchant | looking for | fine | pearls. | **46** | When he found
Πάλιν | ἡ | βασιλεία | ╷τῶν οὐρανῶν╵ | ἐστιν ὁμοία | | ╷ἀνθρώπῳ ἐμπόρῳ╵ | ζητοῦντι ← | καλοὺς | μαργαρίτας | δὲ | → → εὑρὼν
adv | d.nsf | n.nsf | d.gpm n.gpm | v.pai.3s a.nsf | | n.dsm n.dsm | pt.pa.dsm | a.apm | n.apm | cj | pt.aa.nsm
4099 | 3836 | 993 | 3836 4041 | 1639 3927 | | 476 1867 | 2426 | 2819 | 3449 | 1254 | 2351

13:36 Τότε ἀφεὶς τοὺς ὄχλους ἦλθεν εἰς τὴν οἰκίαν. καὶ προσῆλθον αὐτῷ οἱ μαθηταὶ αὐτοῦ λέγοντες, Διασάφησον ἡμῖν τὴν παραβολὴν τῶν ζιζανίων τοῦ ἀγροῦ. ¶ **37** ὁ δὲ ἀποκριθεὶς εἶπεν, Ὁ σπείρων τὸ καλὸν σπέρμα ἐστὶν ὁ υἱὸς τοῦ ἀνθρώπου, **38** ὁ δὲ ἀγρός ἐστιν ὁ κόσμος, τὸ δὲ καλὸν σπέρμα οὗτοί εἰσιν οἱ υἱοὶ τῆς βασιλείας· τὰ δὲ ζιζάνια εἰσιν οἱ υἱοὶ τοῦ πονηροῦ, **39** ὁ δὲ ἐχθρὸς ὁ σπείρας αὐτά ἐστιν ὁ διάβολος, ὁ δὲ θερισμὸς συντέλεια αἰῶνός ἐστιν, οἱ δὲ θερισταὶ ἄγγελοί εἰσιν. ¶ **40** ὥσπερ οὖν συλλέγεται τὰ ζιζάνια καὶ πυρὶ [κατα]καίεται, οὕτως ἔσται ἐν τῇ συντελείᾳ τοῦ αἰῶνος· **41** ἀποστελεῖ ὁ υἱὸς τοῦ ἀνθρώπου τοὺς ἀγγέλους αὐτοῦ, καὶ συλλέξουσιν ἐκ τῆς βασιλείας αὐτοῦ πάντα τὰ σκάνδαλα καὶ τοὺς ποιοῦντας τὴν ἀνομίαν **42** καὶ βαλοῦσιν αὐτοὺς εἰς τὴν κάμινον τοῦ πυρός· ἐκεῖ ἔσται ὁ κλαυθμὸς καὶ ὁ βρυγμὸς τῶν ὀδόντων. **43** Τότε οἱ δίκαιοι ἐκλάμψουσιν ὡς ὁ ἥλιος ἐν τῇ βασιλείᾳ τοῦ πατρὸς αὐτῶν. ὁ ἔχων ὦτα ἀκουέτω.

13:44 Ὁμοία ἐστὶν ἡ βασιλεία τῶν οὐρανῶν θησαυρῷ κεκρυμμένῳ ἐν τῷ ἀγρῷ, ὃν εὑρὼν ἄνθρωπος ἔκρυψεν, καὶ ἀπὸ τῆς χαρᾶς αὐτοῦ ὑπάγει καὶ πωλεῖ πάντα ὅσα ἔχει καὶ ἀγοράζει τὸν ἀγρὸν ἐκεῖνον. ¶ **45** Πάλιν ὁμοία ἐστὶν ἡ βασιλεία τῶν οὐρανῶν ἀνθρώπῳ ἐμπόρῳ ζητοῦντι καλοὺς μαργαρίτας· **46** εὑρὼν δὲ ἕνα πολύτιμον μαργαρίτην ἀπελθὼν πέπρακεν πάντα ὅσα εἶχεν καὶ

one of great value,			he went	away and sold		everything he had		and bought	it.
ἕνα → →	πολύτιμον μαργαρίτην →		ἀπελθὼν ←	πέπρακεν	πάντα ὅσα →	εἶχεν καὶ		ἠγόρασεν	αὐτόν
a.asm	a.asm n.asm		pt.aa.nsm	v.rai.3s	a.apn r.apn	v.iai.3s cj		v.aai.3s	r.asm.3
1651	4501 3449		599	4405	4246 4012	2400 2779		60	899

The Parable of the Net

13:47 "Once again, the kingdom of heaven is like a net that was let down into the lake and

Πάλιν	ἡ	βασιλεία →	˻τῶν οὐρανῶν˼	ἐστὶν	ὁμοία	σαγήνη →	→	βληθείσῃ ←	εἰς	τὴν θάλασσαν	καὶ
adv	d.nsf	n.nsf	d.gpm n.gpm	v.pai.3s	a.nsf	n.nsf		pt.ap.dsf	p.a	d.asf n.asf	cj
4099	3836	993	3836 4041	1639	3927	4880		965	1650	3836 2498	2779

caught all kinds of fish. **48** When it was full, the fishermen pulled it up on the shore. Then

συναγαγούσῃ	˻ἐκ παντὸς˼ ←	← γένους	ὅτε	ἦν	ἐπληρώθη		ἀναβιβάσαντες	←	ἐπὶ τὸν αἰγιαλὸν	καὶ
pt.aa.dsf	p.g a.gsn	n.gsn	cj	v.iai.3s	v.api.3s		pt.aa.npm		p.a d.asm n.asm	cj
5251	1666 4246	1169	4021	4005	4444		328		2093 3836 129	2779

they sat down and collected the good fish in baskets, but threw the bad away. **49** This is how it will be at

→	καθίσαντες ←		συνέλεξαν	τὰ καλὰ	εἰς ἄγγη	δὲ	ἔβαλον	τὰ σαπρὰ ἔξω		→	οὕτως →		ἔσται	ἐν
	pt.aa.npm		v.aai.3p	d.apn a.apn	p.a n.apn	cj	v.aai.3p	d.apn a.apn adv			adv		v.fmi.3s	p.d
	2767		5198	3836 2819	1650 35	1254	965	3836 4911 2032			4048		1639	1877

the end of the age. The angels will come and separate the wicked from the righteous **50** and throw

τῇ	συντελείᾳ →	τοῦ αἰῶνος	οἱ	ἄγγελοι	ἐξελεύσονται καὶ	ἀφοριοῦσιν	τοὺς πονηροὺς	˻ἐκ μέσου˼	τῶν δικαίων	καὶ	βαλοῦσιν
d.dsf	n.dsf	d.gsm n.gsm	d.npm	n.npm	v.fmi.3p cj	v.fai.3p	d.apm a.apm	p.g n.gsn	d.gpm a.gpm	cj	v.fai.3p
3836	5333	3836 172	3836	34	2002 2779	928	3836 4505	1666 3545	3836 1465	2779	965

them into the fiery furnace, where there will be weeping and gnashing of teeth. ¶

αὐτοὺς	εἰς	τὴν	˻τοῦ πυρός˼	κάμινον	ἐκεῖ →	→	ἔσται	ὁ κλαυθμὸς	καὶ	ὁ βρυγμὸς	→	˻τῶν ὀδόντων˼
r.apm.3	p.a	d.asf	d.gsn n.gsn	n.asf	adv		v.fmi.3s	d.nsm n.nsm	cj	d.nsm n.nsm		d.gpm n.gpm
899	1650	3836	3836 4786	2825	1695		1639	3836 3088	2779	3836 1106		3836 3848

51 "Have you understood all these things?" Jesus asked. "Yes," they replied. **52** He said to them, "Therefore

→	→	Συνήκατε	πάντα ταῦτα ←		ναί	→	λέγουσιν αὐτῷ	δὲ	ὁ	εἶπεν →	αὐτοῖς	˻διὰ τοῦτο˼
		v.aai.2p	a.apn r.apn		pl		v.pai.3p r.dsm.3	cj	d.nsm	v.aai.3s	r.dpm.3	p.a r.asn
		5317	4246 4047		3721		3306 899	1254	3836	3306	899	1328 4047

every teacher of the law who has been instructed about the kingdom of heaven is like the

πᾶς	γραμματεὺς ← ← ←	μαθητευθεὶς →	τῇ	βασιλείᾳ →	˻τῶν οὐρανῶν˼	ἐστὶν	ὅμοιος
a.nsm	n.nsm	pt.ap.nsm	d.dsf	n.dsf	d.gpm n.gpm	v.pai.3s	a.nsm
4246	1208	3411	3836	993	3836 4041	1639	3927

owner of a house who brings out of his storeroom new treasures as well as old."

˻ἀνθρώπῳ	οἰκοδεσπότῃ˼ ← ← ←	ὅστις	ἐκβάλλει	ἐκ	αὐτοῦ	˻τοῦ θησαυροῦ˼	καινὰ		καὶ ←	← παλαιά
n.dsm	n.dsm	r.nsm	v.pai.3s	p.g	r.gsm.3	d.gsm n.gsm	a.apn		cj	a.apn
476	3867	4015	1675	1666	899	3836 2565	2785		2779	4094

A Prophet Without Honor

13:53 When Jesus had finished these parables, he moved on from there. **54** Coming to

Καὶ	ἐγένετο ὅτε	ὁ	Ἰησοῦς →	ἐτέλεσεν	ταύτας	˻τὰς παραβολὰς˼	→	μετῆρεν ←	ἐκεῖθεν		καὶ	ἐλθὼν	εἰς
cj	v.ami.3s cj	d.nsm	n.nsm	v.aai.3s	r.apf	d.apf n.apf		v.aai.3s	adv		cj	pt.aa.nsm	p.a
2779	1181 4021	3836	2652	5464	4047	3836 4130		3558	1696		2779	2262	1650

his hometown, he began teaching the people in their synagogue, and they were amazed. "Where did this

αὐτοῦ	˻τὴν πατρίδα˼	→	ἐδίδασκεν	αὐτοὺς	ἐν αὐτῶν	˻τῇ συναγωγῇ˼	ὥστε αὐτοὺς	→	ἐκπλήσσεσθαι	πόθεν		τούτῳ
r.gsm.3	d.asf n.asf		v.iai.3s	r.apm.3	p.d r.gpm.3	d.dsf n.dsf	cj r.apm.3		f.pp	cj		r.dsm
899	3836 4258		1438	899	1877 899	3836 5252	6063 899		1742	4470		4047

man get this wisdom and these miraculous powers?" they asked. **55** "Isn't this the carpenter's son? Isn't his

←	αὕτη	ἡ σοφία	καὶ αἱ	→	δυνάμεις	καὶ →	λέγειν	˻οὐχ ἐστιν˼	οὗτος ὁ	˻τοῦ τέκτονος˼	υἱός	οὐχ	αὐτοῦ
	r.nsf	d.nsf n.nsf	cj d.npf		n.npf	cj	f.pa	pl v.pai.3s	r.nsm d.nsm	d.gsm n.gsm	n.nsm	pl	r.gsm.3
	4047	3836 5053	2779 3836		1539	2779	3306	4024 1639	4047 3836	3836 5454	5626	4024	899

mother's name Mary, and aren't his brothers James, Joseph, Simon and Judas? **56** Aren't all

ἡ	μήτηρ	λέγεται	Μαριὰμ	καὶ	αὐτοῦ	˻οἱ ἀδελφοὶ˼	Ἰάκωβος	καὶ	Ἰωσὴφ	καὶ	Σίμων	καὶ	Ἰούδας	καὶ	˻οὐχὶ εἰσιν˼	πᾶσαι
d.nsf	n.nsf	v.ppi.3s	n.nsf	cj	r.gsm.3	d.npm n.npm	n.nsm	cj	n.nsm	cj	n.nsm	cj	n.nsm	cj	pl v.pai.3p	a.npf
3836	3613	3306	3452	2779	899	3836 81	2610	2779	2737	2779	4981	2779	2683	2779	4049 1639	4246

ἠγόρασεν αὐτόν.
    13:47 Πάλιν ὁμοία ἐστὶν ἡ βασιλεία τῶν οὐρανῶν σαγήνῃ βληθείσῃ εἰς τὴν θάλασσαν καὶ ἐκ παντὸς γένους συναγαγούσῃ **48** ἣν ὅτε ἐπληρώθη ἀναβιβάσαντες ἐπὶ τὸν αἰγιαλὸν καὶ καθίσαντες συνέλεξαν τὰ καλὰ εἰς ἄγγη, τὰ δὲ σαπρὰ ἔξω ἔβαλον. **49** οὕτως ἔσται ἐν τῇ συντελείᾳ τοῦ αἰῶνος· ἐξελεύσονται οἱ ἄγγελοι καὶ ἀφοριοῦσιν τοὺς πονηροὺς ἐκ μέσου τῶν δικαίων **50** καὶ βαλοῦσιν αὐτοὺς εἰς τὴν κάμινον τοῦ πυρός· ἐκεῖ ἔσται ὁ κλαυθμὸς καὶ ὁ βρυγμὸς τῶν ὀδόντων. ¶ **51** Λέγει αὐτοῖς ὁ Ἰησοῦς, Συνήκατε ταῦτα πάντα; λέγουσιν αὐτῷ, Ναί. **52** ὁ δὲ εἶπεν αὐτοῖς, Διὰ τοῦτο πᾶς γραμματεὺς μαθητευθεὶς τῇ βασιλείᾳ τῶν οὐρανῶν ὅμοιός ἐστιν ἀνθρώπῳ οἰκοδεσπότῃ, ὅστις ἐκβάλλει ἐκ τοῦ θησαυροῦ αὐτοῦ καινὰ καὶ παλαιά.
    13:53 Καὶ ἐγένετο ὅτε ἐτέλεσεν ὁ Ἰησοῦς τὰς παραβολὰς ταύτας, μετῆρεν ἐκεῖθεν. **54** καὶ ἐλθὼν εἰς τὴν πατρίδα αὐτοῦ ἐδίδασκεν αὐτοὺς ἐν τῇ συναγωγῇ αὐτῶν, ὥστε ἐκπλήσσεσθαι αὐτοὺς καὶ λέγειν, Πόθεν τούτῳ ἡ σοφία αὕτη καὶ αἱ δυνάμεις; **55** οὐχ οὗτός ἐστιν ὁ τοῦ τέκτονος υἱός; οὐχ ἡ μήτηρ αὐτοῦ λέγεται Μαριὰμ καὶ οἱ ἀδελφοὶ αὐτοῦ Ἰάκωβος καὶ Ἰωσὴφ καὶ Σίμων καὶ Ἰούδας; **56** καὶ αἱ ἀδελφαὶ αὐτοῦ οὐχὶ πᾶσαι πρὸς ἡμᾶς εἰσιν; πόθεν οὖν τούτῳ ταῦτα πάντα; **57** καὶ ἐσκανδαλίζοντο

his   sisters   with us?   Where then did this man get all   these things?" **57** And they took offense   at   him.
αὐτοῦ   αἱ ἀδελφαὶ πρὸς ἡμᾶς πόθεν οὖν   τούτῳ ←   πάντα ταῦτα ←   καὶ →   →   ἐσκανδαλίζοντο ἐν αὐτῷ
r.gsm.3   d.npf n.npf r.ap.1   r.ap.1   r.dsm   a.npn r.npn   cj   v.ipi.3p   p.d r.dsm.3
899   3836 80   4639 7005   4470 4036   4047   4246 4047   2779   4997   1877 899

But Jesus   said   to them, "Only in his hometown and in his   own house   is   a prophet without honor."
δὲ ὁ Ἰησοῦς,   εἶπεν → αὐτοῖς εἰ μὴ ἐν τῇ πατρίδι καὶ ἐν αὐτοῦ τῇ οἰκίᾳ οὐκ ἔστιν προφήτης → ἄτιμος
cj d.nsm n.nsm v.aai.3s r.dpm.3 cj pl p.d d.dsf n.dsf cj   p.d r.gsm.3 d.dsf n.dsf adv v.pai.3s n.nsm   a.nsm
1254 3836 2652   3306   899   1623 3590 1877 3836 4258 2779 1877 899 3836 3864 4024 1639 4737   872

¶   **58** And he did not do   many miracles there because of their lack of faith.
καὶ →   οὐκ ἐποίησεν πολλὰς δυνάμεις ἐκεῖ διὰ ← αὐτῶν → → ⸢τὴν ἀπιστίαν⸣
cj   adv v.aai.3s a.apf n.apf adv   p.a   r.gpm.3   d.asf n.asf
2779 4472 4472 4024 4472 4498 1539 1695 1328   899   3836 602

John the Baptist Beheaded

14:1 At that time   Herod the tetrarch heard the reports about Jesus, **2** and he said to his attendants,
Ἐν ἐκείνῳ ⸢τῷ καιρῷ⸣ Ἡρῴδης ὁ τετραάρχης ἤκουσεν τὴν ἀκοὴν →   Ἰησοῦ καὶ → εἶπεν αὐτοῦ ⸢τοῖς παισὶν⸣
p.d r.dsm d.dsm n.dsm n.nsm d.nsm n.nsm v.aai.3s d.asf n.asf   n.gsm cj   v.aai.3s r.gsm.3 d.dpm n.dpm
1877 1697 3836 2789   2476   3836 5490 201   3836 198   2652   2779   3306   4090 3836 4090

"This is John   the Baptist; he has risen from the dead!   That is why   miraculous powers   are at
οὗτος ἐστιν Ἰωάννης ὁ βαπτιστής αὐτος → ἠγέρθη ἀπὸ τῶν νεκρῶν καὶ → ⸢διὰ τοῦτο⸣   ⸢αἱ δυνάμεις⸣ →
r.nsm v.pai.3s n.nsm d.nsm n.nsm r.nsm   v.api.3s p.g d.gpm a.gpm cj   p.a r.asn   d.npf n.npf
4047 1639 2722 3836 969   899   1586 608 3836 3738 2779   1328 4047   3836 1539

work in him." ¶ **3** Now Herod   had arrested John   and bound him and put   him in prison
ἐνεργοῦσιν ἐν αὐτῷ   γὰρ ὁ Ἡρῴδης → κρατήσας ⸢τὸν Ἰωάννην⸣ ἔδησεν αὐτὸν καὶ ἀπέθετο ἐν φυλακῇ
v.pai.3p p.d r.dsm.3   cj d.nsm n.nsm pt.aa.nsm d.asm n.asm   v.aai.3s r.asm.3 cj v.ami.3s p.d n.dsf
1919   1877 899   1142 3836 2476   3195   3836 2722   1313   899   2779 700   1877 5871

because of Herodias, his brother   Philip's wife,   **4** for John   had been saying to him: "It is not
διὰ ← Ἡρῳδιάδα αὐτοῦ ⸢τοῦ ἀδελφοῦ⸣ Φιλίππου τὴν γυναῖκα γὰρ ὁ Ἰωάννης → → ἔλεγεν αὐτῷ → → οὐκ
p.a   n.asf   r.gsm.3 d.gsm n.gsm n.gsm d.asf n.asf cj d.nsm n.nsm   v.iai.3s r.dsm.3   adv
1328   2478   899   3836 81   5805   3836 1222 1142 3836 2722   3306   899 1997 1997 4024

lawful for you to have her." **5**   Herod wanted to kill   John, but he was afraid of the people, because they
ἔξεστιν → σοι → ἔχειν αὐτήν καὶ   θέλων → ἀποκτεῖναι αὐτὸν   →   ἐφοβήθη ← τὸν ὄχλον ὅτι   →
v.pai.3s   r.ds.2 f.pa r.asf.3 cj   pt.pa.nsm f.aa   r.asm.3   v.api.3s   d.asm n.asm cj
1997   5148   2400   899   2779   2527   650   899   5828   3836 4063 4022

considered him   a prophet. ¶ **6** On   Herod's   birthday the daughter of Herodias   danced for
εἶχον   αὐτὸν ὡς προφήτην δὲ γενομένοις ⸢τοῦ Ἡρῴδου⸣ Γενεσίοις ἡ θυγάτηρ ⸢τῆς Ἡρῳδιάδος⸣ ὠρχήσατο ἐν
v.iai.3p r.asm.3 pl n.asm   cj pt.am.dpn d.gsm n.gsm n.dpn   d.nsf n.nsf d.gsf n.gsf   v.ami.3s p.d
2400   899   6055 4737   1254 1181   3836 2476 1160   3836 2588 3836 2478   4004   1877

them and pleased Herod   so much **7** that he promised with an oath to give her whatever she asked. **8**
⸢τῷ μέσῳ⸣ καὶ ἤρεσεν ⸢τῷ Ἡρῴδῃ⸣   ὅθεν → ὡμολόγησεν μεθ' ὅρκου → δοῦναι αὐτῇ ὃ ἐάν →   αἰτήσηται δὲ
d.dsn n.dsn cj v.aai.3s d.dsm n.dsm   cj   v.aai.3s   p.g   n.gsm   f.aa r.dsf.3 r.asn pl v.ams.3s cj
3836 3545   2779 743   3836 2476   3854 3933   3552   3992   1443 899 4005 1569   160   1254

Prompted   by her mother,   she said, "Give me here on a platter the head of John   the Baptist." **9**   The
προβιβασθεῖσα ὑπὸ αὐτῆς ⸢τῆς μητρός⸣ ἡ φησίν δός μοι ὧδε ἐπὶ πίνακι τὴν κεφαλὴν → Ἰωάννου τοῦ βαπτιστοῦ καὶ ὁ
pt.ap.nsf p.g r.gsf.3 d.gsf n.gsf d.nsf v.pai.3s v.aam.2s r.ds.1 adv p.d n.dsm d.asf n.asf   n.gsm d.gsm n.gsm cj d.nsm
4586   5679 899   3836 3613 3836 5774 1443 1609 6045 2093 4402 3836 3051   2722 3836 969   2779 3836

king   was distressed, but because of his oaths and his dinner guests,   he ordered that her request be
βασιλεὺς → λυπηθεὶς διὰ ← τοὺς ὅρκους καὶ τοὺς συνανακειμένους → ἐκέλευσεν →
n.nsm   pt.ap.nsm p.a   d.apm n.apm cj d.apm pt.pm.apm   v.aai.3s
995   3382   1328   3836 3992 2779 3836 5263   3027

granted **10** and   had John   beheaded in the prison. **11** His head   was brought in on a platter and
δοθῆναι καὶ πέμψας ⸢τὸν Ἰωάννην⸣ ἀπεκεφάλισεν ἐν τῇ φυλακῇ καὶ αὐτοῦ ἡ κεφαλὴ → ἠνέχθη ← ἐπὶ πίνακι καὶ
f.ap   cj pt.aa.nsm d.asm n.asm v.aai.3s p.d d.dsf n.dsf cj r.gsm.3 d.nsf n.nsf v.api.3s p.d n.dsm cj
1443   2779 4287   3836 2722   642   1877 3836 5871 2779 899 3836 3051   5770 2093 4402 2779

given to the girl,   who carried it to her mother. **12** John's disciples   came   and took his body and
ἐδόθη → τῷ κορασίῳ καὶ → ἤνεγκεν → αὐτῆς τῇ μητρί, καὶ αὐτοῦ ⸢οἱ μαθηταὶ⸣ προσελθόντες ἦραν τὸ πτῶμα καὶ
v.api.3s d.dsn n.dsn cj   v.aai.3s   r.gsf.3 d.dsf n.dsf cj r.gsm.3 d.npm n.npm pt.aa.npm   v.aai.3p d.asn n.asn cj
1443   3836 3166   2779   5770   3613 899 3836 3613 2779 899 3836 3412 4665   149   3836 4773 2779

ἐν αὐτῷ. ὁ δὲ Ἰησοῦς εἶπεν αὐτοῖς, Οὐκ ἔστιν προφήτης ἄτιμος εἰ μὴ ἐν τῇ πατρίδι καὶ ἐν τῇ οἰκίᾳ αὐτοῦ. ¶ **58** καὶ οὐκ ἐποίησεν
ἐκεῖ δυνάμεις πολλὰς διὰ τὴν ἀπιστίαν αὐτῶν.

14:1 Ἐν ἐκείνῳ τῷ καιρῷ ἤκουσεν Ἡρῴδης ὁ τετραάρχης τὴν ἀκοὴν Ἰησοῦ, **2** καὶ εἶπεν τοῖς παισὶν αὐτοῦ, Οὗτός ἐστιν
Ἰωάννης ὁ βαπτιστής· αὐτὸς ἠγέρθη ἀπὸ τῶν νεκρῶν καὶ διὰ τοῦτο αἱ δυνάμεις ἐνεργοῦσιν ἐν αὐτῷ. ¶ **3** Ὁ γὰρ Ἡρῴδης κρατήσας
τὸν Ἰωάννην ἔδησεν [αὐτὸν] καὶ ἐν φυλακῇ ἀπέθετο διὰ Ἡρῳδιάδα τὴν γυναῖκα Φιλίππου τοῦ ἀδελφοῦ αὐτοῦ· **4** ἔλεγεν γὰρ ὁ
Ἰωάννης αὐτῷ, Οὐκ ἔξεστίν σοι ἔχειν αὐτήν. **5** καὶ θέλων αὐτὸν ἀποκτεῖναι ἐφοβήθη τὸν ὄχλον, ὅτι ὡς προφήτην αὐτὸν εἶχον. ¶
6 γενεσίοις δὲ γενομένοις τοῦ Ἡρῴδου ὠρχήσατο ἡ θυγάτηρ τῆς Ἡρῳδιάδος ἐν τῷ μέσῳ καὶ ἤρεσεν τῷ Ἡρῴδῃ, **7** ὅθεν μεθ' ὅρκου
ὡμολόγησεν αὐτῇ δοῦναι ὃ ἐὰν αἰτήσηται. **8** ἡ δὲ προβιβασθεῖσα ὑπὸ τῆς μητρὸς αὐτῆς, Δός μοι, φησίν, ὧδε ἐπὶ πίνακι τὴν κεφαλὴν
Ἰωάννου τοῦ βαπτιστοῦ. **9** καὶ λυπηθεὶς ὁ βασιλεὺς διὰ τοὺς ὅρκους καὶ τοὺς συνανακειμένους ἐκέλευσεν δοθῆναι, **10** καὶ πέμψας
ἀπεκεφάλισεν [τὸν] Ἰωάννην ἐν τῇ φυλακῇ. **11** καὶ ἠνέχθη ἡ κεφαλὴ αὐτοῦ ἐπὶ πίνακι καὶ ἐδόθη τῷ κορασίῳ, καὶ ἤνεγκεν τῇ
μητρὶ αὐτῆς. **12** καὶ προσελθόντες οἱ μαθηταὶ αὐτοῦ ἦραν τὸ πτῶμα καὶ ἔθαψαν αὐτὸ «αὐτό[ν],» καὶ ἐλθόντες ἀπήγγειλαν τῷ
Ἰησοῦ.

buried it.   Then they went   and told   Jesus.
ἔθαψαν αὐτὸν καὶ   →   ἐλθόντες ἀπήγγειλαν ‚τῷ Ἰησοῦ‚
v.aai.3p r.asm.3 cj   pt.aa.npm   v.aai.3p   d.dsm n.dsm
2507   899   2779   2262   550   3836 2652

Jesus Feeds the Five Thousand

14:13 When Jesus   heard   what had happened, he withdrew   by boat privately   to a solitary
δὲ →   ‚ὁ Ἰησοῦς‚ Ἀκούσας   → ἀνεχώρησεν ἐκεῖθεν ἐν πλοίῳ ‚κατ᾽ ἰδίαν‚ εἰς ἔρημον
cj →   d.nsm n.nsm pt.aa.nsm   v.aai.3s   adv   p.d n.dsn p.a a.asf p.a a.asm
1254 201   3836 2652 201   432   1696   1877 4450 2848 2625 1650 2245

place.   Hearing   of this, the crowds followed   him on foot from the towns.   **14** When Jesus landed and saw a
τόπον καὶ ἀκούσαντες ← ← οἱ ὄχλοι ἠκολούθησαν αὐτῷ → πεζῇ ἀπὸ τῶν πόλεων   Καὶ →   ἐξελθὼν   εἶδεν
n.asm cj pt.aa.npm   d.npm n.npm v.aai.3p   r.dsm.3 adv p.g d.gpf n.gpf   cj →   pt.aa.nsm   v.aai.3s
5536 2779 201   3836 4063 199   899   4270 608 3836 4484   2779   2002   1625

large crowd,   he had compassion on them and healed   their sick.   ¶   **15** As evening
πολὺν ὄχλον καὶ → → ἐσπλαγχνίσθη ἐπ᾽ αὐτοῖς καὶ ἐθεράπευσεν αὐτῶν ‚τοὺς ἀρρώστους‚   δὲ → Ὀψίας
a.asm n.asm cj   v.api.3s p.d r.dpm.3 cj v.aai.3s r.gpm.3 d.apm a.apm   cj   n.gsf
4498 4063 2779   5072 2093 899 2779 2543 899 3836 779   1254 1181 4068

approached, the disciples came   to him and said,   "This is   a remote place,   and it's already *getting*
γενομένης οἱ μαθηταὶ προσῆλθον ← αὐτῷ λέγοντες → ἐστιν ἔρημος ‚ὁ τόπος‚ καὶ ᾽ ἤδη παρῆλθεν
pt.am.gsf d.npm n.npm v.aai.3p   r.dsm.3 pt.pa.npm   v.pai.3s a.nsm d.nsm n.nsm cj   adv v.aai.3s
1181 3836 3412 4665   899 3306   1639 2245 3836 5536 2779 4216 2453 4216

late.   Send   the crowds away, so they can go   to the villages and buy   themselves some food."
ἡ ὥρα ἀπόλυσον τοὺς ὄχλους ← → ἵνα → ἀπελθόντες εἰς τὰς κώμας ἀγοράσωσιν ἑαυτοῖς   βρώματα
d.nsf n.nsf v.aam.2s d.apm n.apm   cj → pt.aa.npm p.a d.apf n.apf v.aas.3p r.dpm.3   n.apn
3836 6052 668 3836 4063 668   2671   599   1650 3836 3267 60   1571   1109

¶   **16** Jesus   replied,   "They do not need   to go   away. You give them something to eat."
δὲ ‚ὁ Ἰησοῦς‚ εἶπεν αὐτοῖς → ᾽ οὐ ‚χρείαν ἔχουσιν‚ ἀπελθεῖν ← ὑμεῖς δότε αὐτοῖς → φαγεῖν
cj d.nsm n.nsm v.aai.3s r.dpm.3   adv n.asf v.pai.3p f.aa   r.np.2 v.aam.2p r.dpm.3   f.aa
1254 3836 2652 3306 899   2400 4024 5970 2400 599   7007 1443 899   2266

17 "We have here only   five loaves of bread and two fish,"   they answered.   ¶   **18** "Bring them
οὐκ → ἔχομεν ὧδε εἰ μὴ πέντε → ἄρτους καὶ δύο ἰχθύας δὲ οἱ λέγουσιν αὐτῷ   δὲ φέρετε αὐτούς
adv → v.pai.1p adv εἰ μὴ pl a.apm   a.apm cj a.apm a.apm cj d.npm v.pai.3p r.dsm.3   cj v.pam.2p r.apm.3
4024 2400 6045 1623 3590 4297   788 2779 1545 2716 1254 3836 3306 899   1254 5770 899

here to me," he said. **19** And he directed the people to sit   down on the grass. Taking the five loaves and
ὧδε → μοι ὁ εἶπεν καὶ → κελεύσας τοὺς ὄχλους ἀνακλιθῆναι ← ἐπὶ τοῦ χόρτου λαβὼν τοὺς πέντε ἄρτους καὶ
adv → r.ds.1 d.nsm v.aai.3s cj → pt.aa.nsm d.apm n.apm f.ap   p.g d.gsm n.gsm pt.aa.nsm d.apm a.apm n.apm cj
6045 1609 3836 3306 2779   3027 3836 4063 369   2093 3836 5965 3284 3836 4297 788 2779

the two fish   and looking   up to heaven,   he gave thanks   and broke the loaves. Then he gave
τοὺς δύο ἰχθύας ἀναβλέψας ← εἰς ‚τὸν οὐρανόν‚ → → εὐλόγησεν καὶ κλάσας   → ἔδωκεν
d.apm a.apm n.apm pt.aa.nsm   p.a d.asm n.asm   v.aai.3s cj pt.aa.nsm   v.aai.3s
3836 1545 2716 329   1650 3836 4041   2328 2779 3089   1443

them   to the disciples, and the disciples gave them to the people. **20** They all   ate   and were satisfied,
‚τοὺς ἄρτους‚ → τοῖς μαθηταῖς δὲ οἱ μαθηταὶ → τοῖς ὄχλοις καὶ ᾽ πάντες ἔφαγον καὶ → ἐχορτάσθησαν
d.apm n.apm   d.dpm n.dpm cj d.npm n.npm → d.dpm n.dpm cj a.npm v.aai.3p cj → v.api.3p
3836 788   3836 3412 1254 3836 3412   3836 4063 2779 2266 4246 2266 2779 5963

and the disciples picked up twelve basketfuls   of broken pieces   that were left   over. **21** The
καὶ   ἦραν ← δώδεκα ‚κοφίνους πλήρεις‚ → → ‚τῶν κλασμάτων‚ τὸ → περισσεῦον ←   δὲ
cj   v.aai.3p a.apm n.apm a.apm   d.gpn n.gpn d.asn → pt.pa.asn   cj
2779   149 1557 3186 4441   3836 3083 3836 4355   1254

number of those who ate   was about five   thousand men, besides women and children.
οἱ   ἐσθίοντες ἦσαν ὡσεὶ πεντακισχίλιοι ← ἄνδρες χωρὶς γυναικῶν καὶ παιδίων
d.npm   pt.pa.npm v.iai.3p pl a.npm   n.npm p.g n.gpf cj n.gpn
3836   2266 1639 6059 4295   467 6006 1222 2779 4086

14:13 Ἀκούσας δὲ ὁ Ἰησοῦς ἀνεχώρησεν ἐκεῖθεν ἐν πλοίῳ εἰς ἔρημον τόπον κατ᾽ ἰδίαν· καὶ ἀκούσαντες οἱ ὄχλοι ἠκολούθησαν αὐτῷ πεζῇ ἀπὸ τῶν πόλεων. **14** καὶ ἐξελθὼν εἶδεν πολὺν ὄχλον καὶ ἐσπλαγχνίσθη ἐπ᾽ αὐτοῖς καὶ ἐθεράπευσεν τοὺς ἀρρώστους αὐτῶν. ¶ **15** ὀψίας δὲ γενομένης προσῆλθον αὐτῷ οἱ μαθηταὶ λέγοντες, Ἔρημός ἐστιν ὁ τόπος καὶ ἡ ὥρα ἤδη παρῆλθεν· ἀπόλυσον τοὺς ὄχλους, ἵνα ἀπελθόντες εἰς τὰς κώμας ἀγοράσωσιν ἑαυτοῖς βρώματα. ¶ **16** ὁ δὲ [Ἰησοῦς] εἶπεν αὐτοῖς, Οὐ χρείαν ἔχουσιν ἀπελθεῖν, δότε αὐτοῖς ὑμεῖς φαγεῖν. **17** οἱ δὲ λέγουσιν αὐτῷ, Οὐκ ἔχομεν ὧδε εἰ μὴ πέντε ἄρτους καὶ δύο ἰχθύας. ¶ **18** ὁ δὲ εἶπεν, Φέρετέ μοι ὧδε αὐτούς. **19** καὶ κελεύσας τοὺς ὄχλους ἀνακλιθῆναι ἐπὶ τοῦ χόρτου, λαβὼν τοὺς πέντε ἄρτους καὶ τοὺς δύο ἰχθύας, ἀναβλέψας εἰς τὸν οὐρανὸν εὐλόγησεν καὶ κλάσας ἔδωκεν τοῖς μαθηταῖς τοὺς ἄρτους, οἱ δὲ μαθηταὶ τοῖς ὄχλοις. **20** καὶ ἔφαγον πάντες καὶ ἐχορτάσθησαν, καὶ ἦραν τὸ περισσεῦον τῶν κλασμάτων δώδεκα κοφίνους πλήρεις. **21** οἱ δὲ ἐσθίοντες ἦσαν ἄνδρες ὡσεὶ πεντακισχίλιοι χωρὶς γυναικῶν καὶ παιδίων.

14:22 Καὶ εὐθέως ἠνάγκασεν τοὺς μαθητὰς ἐμβῆναι εἰς τὸ πλοῖον καὶ προάγειν αὐτὸν εἰς τὸ πέραν, ἕως οὗ ἀπολύσῃ τοὺς ὄχλους. **23** καὶ ἀπολύσας τοὺς ὄχλους ἀνέβη εἰς τὸ ὄρος κατ᾽ ἰδίαν προσεύξασθαι. ὀψίας δὲ γενομένης μόνος ἦν ἐκεῖ. **24** τὸ δὲ

Jesus Walks on the Water

14:22

Immediately		Jesus	made		the	disciples	get		into	the	boat	and	go		on ahead of	him	to	the
Καὶ	εὐθέως		ἠνάγκασεν		τοὺς	μαθητὰς	ἐμβῆναι	εἰς		τὸ	πλοῖον	καὶ	προάγειν	←		αὐτὸν	εἰς	τὸ
cj	adv		v.aai.3s		d.apm	n.apm	f.aa	p.a		d.asn	n.asn	cj	f.pa			r.asm.3	p.a	d.asn
2779	2311		337		3836	3412	1832	1650		3836	4450	2779	4575			899	1650	3836

other side,	while		he dismissed	the	crowd.	**23**	After he had	dismissed	them,		he went up	on	a	mountainside
πέραν	←	ἕως οὗ	→	ἀπολύσῃ	τοὺς	ὄχλους	καὶ	→	→	ἀπολύσας	τοὺς ὄχλους	ἀνέβη	←	εἰς	τὸ ὄρος
adv		p.g r.gsm		v.aas.3s	d.apm	n.apm	cj			pt.aa.nsm	d.apm n.apm	v.aai.3s		p.a	d.asn n.asn
4305		2401 4005		668	3836	4063	2779			668	3836 4063	326		1650	3836 4001

by	himself	to pray.		When	evening	came,		he was	there	alone,	**24** but	the	boat	was	already	a
κατ'	ἰδίαν	→ προσεύξασθαι	δὲ		ὀψίας	γενομένης		ἦν	ἐκεῖ	μόνος	δὲ	τὸ	πλοῖον	ἀπεῖχεν	ἤδη	
p.a	a.asf	f.am	cj		n.gsf	pt.am.gsf		v.iai.3s	adv	a.nsm	cj	d.nsn	n.nsn	v.iai.3s	adv	
2848	2625	4667	1254		4068	1181		1639	1695	3668	1254	3836	4450	600	2453	

considerable	distance	from	land,		buffeted		by	the	waves	because	the	wind	was	against	it.	¶	**25**		During
πολλοὺς	σταδίους	ἀπὸ	τῆς γῆς	βασανιζόμενον		ὑπὸ	τῶν	κυμάτων	γὰρ		ὁ	ἄνεμος	ἦν	ἐναντίος				δὲ	→
a.apm	n.apm	p.g	d.gsf n.gsf	pt.pp.nsn		p.g	d.gpn	n.gpn	cj		d.nsm	n.nsm	v.iai.3s	a.nsm				cj	
4498	5084	608	3836 1178	989		5679	3836	3246	1142		3836	449	1639	1885				1254	

the	fourth	watch	of	the	night	Jesus	went out	to		them,	walking	on	the	lake.	**26**		When the	disciples	saw
τετάρτῃ	φυλακῇ		τῆς	νυκτὸς		ἦλθεν		πρὸς	αὐτοὺς	περιπατῶν	ἐπὶ	τὴν	θάλασσαν		δὲ		οἱ	μαθηταὶ	ἰδόντες
a.dsf	n.dsf		d.gsf	n.gsf		v.aai.3s		p.a	r.apm.3	pt.pa.nsm	p.a	d.asf	n.asf		cj		d.npm	n.npm	pt.aa.npm
5480	5871		3836	3816		2262		4639	899	4344	2093	3836	2498		1254		1625	3836 3412	1625

him	walking	on	the	lake,		they were	terrified.			"It's a	ghost,"		they said,	and	cried	out	in
αὐτὸν	περιπατοῦντα	ἐπὶ	τῆς	θαλάσσης	→	→	ἐταράχθησαν	ὅτι	ἐστιν	φάντασμα		→	λέγοντες	καὶ	ἔκραξαν	←	ἀπὸ
r.asm.3	pt.pa.asm	p.g	d.gsf	n.gsf			v.api.3p	cj	v.pai.3s	n.nsn			pt.pa.npm	cj	v.aai.3p		p.g
899	4344	2093	3836	2498			5429	4022	1639	5753			3306	2779	3189		608

fear.	**27** But	Jesus		immediately	said		to them:		"Take	courage!	It is	I.	Don't	be afraid."	¶
τοῦ φόβου	δὲ	ὁ Ἰησοῦς	εὐθὺς		ἐλάλησεν	→	αὐτοῖς	λέγων	→	θαρσεῖτε	→	εἰμι	ἐγώ	μὴ	→	φοβεῖσθε
d.gsm n.gsm	cj	d.nsm n.nsm	adv		v.aai.3s		r.dpm.3	v.pap		v.pam.2p		v.pai.1s	r.ns.1	pl		v.ppm.2p
3836 5832	1254	3836 2652	2318		3281		899	3306		2510		1639	1609	3590		

28	"Lord,	if	it's	you,"	Peter		replied,		"tell	me	to come	to	you	on	the	water."	**29** "Come,"	
δὲ	κύριε	εἰ	εἶ	σὺ	ὁ Πέτρος	ἀποκριθεὶς	αὐτῷ εἶπεν		κέλευσον	με	→ ἐλθεῖν	πρός	σε	ἐπὶ	τὰ	ὕδατα	ἐλθέ	δὲ
cj	n.vsm	cj	v.pai.2s	r.ns.2	d.nsm n.nsm	pt.ap.nsm	r.dsm.3 v.aai.3s		v.aam.2s	r.as.1	f.aa	p.a	r.as.2	p.a	d.apn	n.apn	v.aam.2s	cj
1254	3261	1623	1639	5148	3836 4377	646	899 3306		3027	1609	2262	4639	5148	2093	3836	5623	2262	1254

he said.	¶	Then	Peter		got	down	out of	the	boat,	walked		on	the	water	and	came	toward
ὁ εἶπεν		καὶ	ὁ Πέτρος	καταβὰς	←	ἀπὸ	τοῦ	πλοίου	περιεπάτησεν	ἐπὶ	τὰ	ὕδατα	καὶ	ἦλθεν	πρὸς
d.nsm v.aai.3s		cj	d.nsm n.nsm	pt.aa.nsm		p.g	d.gsn	n.gsn	v.aai.3s	p.a	d.apn	n.apn	cj	v.aai.3s	p.a
3836 3306		2779	3836 4377	2849		608	3836	4450	4344	2093	3836	5623	2779	2262	4639

Jesus.	**30** But	when	he saw	the	wind,		he was	afraid	and,	beginning	to sink,		cried	out,
τὸν Ἰησοῦν	δὲ		βλέπων	τὸν	ἄνεμον	[ἰσχυρὸν]	→	→	ἐφοβήθη	καὶ	ἀρξάμενος	→	καταποντίζεσθαι	ἔκραξεν	←
d.asn n.asm	cj		pt.pa.nsm	d.asn	n.asm	a.asm			v.api.3s	cj	pt.am.nsm		f.pp	v.aai.3s
3836 2652	1254		1063	3836	449	2708			5828	2779	806		2931	3189

"Lord,	save	me!"	¶	**31**	Immediately	Jesus		reached	out his	hand	and	caught	him.	"You of	little
λέγων	κύριε	σῶσον	με		δὲ	εὐθέως	ὁ Ἰησοῦς	ἐκτείνας	←	τὴν χεῖρα		ἐπελάβετο αὐτοῦ	→	→
pt.pa.nsm	n.vsm	v.aam.2s	r.as.1		cj	adv	d.nsm n.nsm	pt.aa.nsm		d.asf n.asf		v.ami.3s r.gsm.3		
3306	3261	5392	1609		1254	2311	3836 2652	1753		3836 5931		2138 899		

faith,"		he said,		"why	did you doubt?"	¶	**32** And when	they	climbed	into	the	boat,	the	wind
ὀλιγόπιστε	καὶ	λέγει αὐτῷ	εἰς τί	→	→	ἐδίστασας		καὶ	αὐτῶν ἀναβάντων	εἰς	τὸ	πλοῖον	ὁ	ἄνεμος
a.vsm	cj	v.pai.3s r.dsm.3	p.a r.asn			v.aai.2s		cj	r.gpm.3 pt.aa.gpm	p.a	d.asn	n.asn	d.nsm	n.nsm
3899	2779	3306 899	1650 5515			1491		2779	899 326	1650	3836	4450	3836	449

died	down.	**33** Then	those who	were	in	the	boat	worshiped	him,	saying,	"Truly	you are	the	Son	of God."	¶
ἐκόπασεν	←	δὲ	οἱ		ἐν	τῷ	πλοίῳ	προσεκύνησαν	αὐτῷ	λέγοντες	ἀληθῶς	→	εἶ	υἱὸς	→ θεοῦ	
v.aai.3s		cj	d.npm		p.d	d.dsn	n.dsn	v.aai.3p	r.dsm.3	pt.pa.npm	adv		v.pai.2s	n.nsm	n.gsm	
3156		1254	3836		1877	3836	4450	4686	899	3306	242		1639	5626	2536	

34	When they had	crossed		over,	they	landed		at	Gennesaret.	**35** And	when	the	men	of	that
Καὶ	→	διαπεράσαντες	←	→	ἦλθον		ἐπὶ	τὴν γῆν	εἰς	Γεννησαρέτ	καὶ	→	οἱ	ἄνδρες	→	ἐκείνου
cj		pt.aa.npm			v.aai.3p		p.a	d.asf n.asf	p.a	n.asf	cj		d.npm	n.npm		r.gsm
2779		1385			2262		2093	3836 1178	1650	1166	2779		3836	467		1697

πλοῖον ἤδη σταδίους πολλοὺς ἀπὸ τῆς γῆς ἀπεῖχεν βασανιζόμενον ὑπὸ τῶν κυμάτων, ἦν γὰρ ἐναντίος ὁ ἄνεμος. ¶ ²⁵ τετάρτῃ δὲ φυλακῇ τῆς νυκτὸς ἀπῆλθεν «ἦλθεν» πρὸς αὐτοὺς περιπατῶν ἐπὶ τὴν θάλασσαν. ²⁶ οἱ δὲ μαθηταὶ ἰδόντες αὐτὸν ἐπὶ τῆς θαλάσσης περιπατοῦντα ἐταράχθησαν λέγοντες ὅτι Φάντασμά ἐστιν, καὶ ἀπὸ τοῦ φόβου ἔκραξαν. ²⁷ εὐθὺς δὲ ἐλάλησεν [ὁ Ἰησοῦς] αὐτοῖς λέγων, Θαρσεῖτε, ἐγώ εἰμι· μὴ φοβεῖσθε. ¶ ²⁸ ἀποκριθεὶς δὲ αὐτῷ ὁ Πέτρος εἶπεν, Κύριε, εἰ σὺ εἶ, κέλευσόν με ἐλθεῖν πρὸς σὲ ἐπὶ τὰ ὕδατα. ²⁹ ὁ δὲ εἶπεν, Ἐλθέ. ¶ καὶ καταβὰς ἀπὸ τοῦ πλοίου [ὁ] Πέτρος περιεπάτησεν ἐπὶ τὰ ὕδατα καὶ ἦλθεν πρὸς τὸν Ἰησοῦν. ³⁰ βλέπων δὲ τὸν ἄνεμον [ἰσχυρὸν] ἐφοβήθη, καὶ ἀρξάμενος καταποντίζεσθαι ἔκραξεν λέγων, Κύριε, σῶσόν με. ¶ ³¹ εὐθέως δὲ ὁ Ἰησοῦς ἐκτείνας τὴν χεῖρα ἐπελάβετο αὐτοῦ καὶ λέγει αὐτῷ, Ὀλιγόπιστε, εἰς τί ἐδίστασας; ¶ ³² καὶ ἀναβάντων αὐτῶν εἰς τὸ πλοῖον ἐκόπασεν ὁ ἄνεμος. ³³ οἱ δὲ ἐν τῷ πλοίῳ προσεκύνησαν αὐτῷ λέγοντες, Ἀληθῶς θεοῦ υἱὸς εἶ. ¶ ³⁴ Καὶ διαπεράσαντες ἦλθον ἐπὶ τὴν γῆν εἰς Γεννησαρέτ. ³⁵ καὶ ἐπιγνόντες αὐτὸν οἱ ἄνδρες τοῦ τόπου ἐκείνου ἀπέστειλαν εἰς ὅλην τὴν

place　　　recognized　Jesus,　they sent　　　　word to　all　the surrounding country.　　　　　People brought
ͺτοῦ τόπουͺ ἐπιγνόντες　αὐτὸν →　ἀπέστειλαν ←　εἰς ὅλην τὴν →　　περίχωρον ἐκείνην καὶ →　　προσήνεγκαν
d.gsm n.gsm　pt.aa.npm　r.asm.3　v.aai.3p　　p.a a.asf d.asf　　a.asf　r.asf　cj　　v.aai.3p
3836 5536　2105　　899　　690　　　　1650 3910 3836　　4369　1697　2779　　4712

all　their sick　　　　to him ³⁶ and begged　　him to let the sick just touch the edge　of his
πάντας τοὺς ͺκακῶς ἔχονταςͺ →　αὐτῷ καὶ παρεκάλουν αὐτὸν ἵνα ↱　　μόνον ἅψωνται τοῦ κρασπέδου　αὐτοῦ
a.apm d.apm adv pt.pa.apm　r.dsm.3 cj v.iai.3p　r.asm.3 cj　　adv v.ams.3p d.gsn n.gsn　r.gsm.3
4246 3836 2809 2400　　899 2779 4151　899 2671 721　　3667 721 3836 3192　　899

cloak,　and all who touched him were healed.
ͺτοῦ ἱματίουͺ καὶ ὅσοι ←　ἥψαντο →　διεσώθησαν
d.gsn n.gsn cj r.npm v.ami.3p　v.api.3p
3836 2668 2779 4012 721　　1407

Clean and Unclean

¹⁵:¹Then some Pharisees and teachers of the law came　　to Jesus　from Jerusalem and asked, ² "Why
Τότε　Φαρισαῖοι καὶ γραμματεῖς ← ← ←　προσέρχονται ← τῷ Ἰησοῦ ἀπὸ Ἰεροσολύμων λέγοντες ͺδιὰ τί
adv　n.npm cj n.npm　v.pmi.3p　d.dsm n.dsm p.g n.gpn　pt.pa.npm p.a r.asn
5538　5757 2779 1208　4665　3836 2652 608 2642　3306　1328 5515

do your disciples break　the tradition of the elders?　They don't wash their hands before
↱ σου οἱ μαθηταί παραβαίνουσιν τὴν παράδοσιν → τῶν πρεσβυτέρων γὰρ ↱ οὐ νίπτονται αὐτῶν ͺτὰς χεῖραςͺ ὅταν
r.gs.2 d.npm n.npm v.pai.3p d.asf n.asf d.gpm a.gpm cj adv v.pmi.3p r.gpm.3 d.apf n.apf cj
4124 5148 3836 3412 4124 3836 4142 3836 4565 1142 3782 4024 3782 899 3836 5931 4020

they eat!"　³ Jesus replied,　　"And why do you break the command of God for
ἐσθίωσιν ἄρτον δὲ ὁ ἀποκριθεὶς εἶπεν αὐτοῖς καὶ ͺδιὰ τί ↱ ὑμεῖς παραβαίνετε τὴν ἐντολὴν → ͺτοῦ θεοῦ διὰ
v.pas.3p n.asm cj d.nsm pt.ap.nsm v.aai.3s r.dpm.3 adv p.a r.asn r.np.2 v.pai.2p d.asf n.asf d.gsm n.gsm p.a
2266 788 1254 3836 646 3306 899 2779 1328 5515 4124 7007 4124 3836 1953 3836 2536 1328

the sake of your tradition? ⁴ For God　said, 'Honor your father and mother' and 'Anyone who curses his
← ← ← ὑμῶν ͺτὴν παράδοσινͺ γὰρ ὁ θεός εἶπεν τίμα τὸν πατέρα καὶ ͺτὴν μητέρα καὶ ὁ ← κακολογῶν
r.gp.2 d.asf n.asf cj d.nsm n.nsm v.aai.3s v.pam.2s d.asm n.asm cj d.asf n.asf cj d.nsm pt.pa.nsm
7007 3836 4142 1142 3836 2536 3306 5506 3836 4252 2779 3836 3613 2779 3836 2800

father or mother must be put　　to death.' ⁵ But you say that if a man says to his father or mother,
πατέρα ἢ μητέρα → → τελευτάτω θανάτῳ δὲ ὑμεῖς λέγετε ͺὃς ἂν εἴπῃ → τῷ πατρὶ ἢ ͺτῇ μητρί
n.asm cj n.asf v.pam.3s n.dsm cj r.np.2 v.pai.2p r.nsm pl v.aas.3s d.dsm n.dsm cj d.dsf n.dsf
4252 2445 3613 5462 2505 1254 7007 3306 4005 323 3306 3836 4252 2445 3836 3613

'Whatever help you might otherwise have received from me is a gift devoted to God,' ⁶ he is not to 'honor
ͺὃ ἐάνͺ → → → ὠφεληθῇς ἐξ ἐμοῦ δῶρον ↱ ͺοὐ μὴͺ τιμήσει
r.asn pl v.aps.2s p.g r.gs.1 n.nsn adv pl v.fai.3s
4005 1569 6067 1666 1609 1565 5506 5506 4024 3590 5506

his father' with it. Thus you nullify the word of God for the sake of your tradition. ⁷ You hypocrites!
αὐτοῦ ͺτὸν πατέραͺ καὶ → ἠκυρώσατε τὸν λόγον → ͺτοῦ θεοῦ διὰ ← ← ὑμῶν ͺτὴν παράδοσινͺ ὑποκριταί
r.gsm.3 d.asm n.asm cj v.aai.2p d.asm n.asm d.gsm n.gsm p.a r.gp.2 d.asf n.asf n.vpm
899 3836 4252 2779 218 3836 3364 3836 2536 1328 7007 3836 4142 5695

Isaiah was right when he prophesied about you: ⁸ "'These people honor me with their lips, but their
Ἠσαΐας καλῶς → ἐπροφήτευσεν περὶ ὑμῶν λέγων οὗτος ὁ λαὸς τιμᾷ με → τοῖς χείλεσιν δὲ αὐτῶν
n.nsm adv v.aai.3s p.g r.gp.2 pt.pa.nsm r.nsm d.nsm n.nsm v.pai.3s r.as.1 d.dpn n.dpn cj r.gpm.3
2480 2822 4736 4309 7007 3306 4047 3836 3295 5506 1609 3836 5927 1254 899

hearts are far from me. ⁹ They worship me in vain; their teachings are but rules taught by
ἡ καρδία ἀπέχει πόρρω ἀπ᾽ ἐμοῦ δὲ → σέβονταί με → μάτην διδασκαλίας ἐντάλματα διδάσκοντες →
d.nsf n.nsf v.pai.3s adv p.g r.gs.1 cj v.pmi.3p r.as.1 adv n.apf n.apn pt.pa.npm
3836 2840 600 4522 608 1609 1254 4936 1609 3472 1436 1945 1438

men.'" ¹⁰ Jesus called the crowd to him and said, "Listen and understand. ¹¹ What goes into a
ἀνθρώπων καὶ προσκαλεσάμενος τὸν ὄχλον ← εἶπεν αὐτοῖς ἀκούετε καὶ συνίετε τὸ εἰσερχόμενον εἰς
n.gpm cj pt.am.nsm d.asm n.asm v.aai.3s r.dpm.3 v.pam.2p cj v.pam.2p d.nsn pt.pm.nsn p.a
476 2779 4673 3836 4063 3306 899 201 2779 5317 3836 1656 1650

man's mouth does not make him 'unclean,' but what comes out of his mouth, that is what makes
ͺτὸ στόμαͺ οὐ ↱ ͺτὸν ἄνθρωπονͺ κοινοῖ ἀλλὰ τὸ ἐκπορευόμενον ἐκ ← τοῦ στόματος τοῦτο ↱
d.asn n.asn adv d.asm n.asm v.pai.3s cj d.nsn pt.pm.nsn p.g d.gsn n.gsn r.nsn
3836 5125 4024 3124 3836 476 3124 247 3836 1744 1666 3836 5125 4047 3124

περίχωρον ἐκείνην καὶ προσήνεγκαν αὐτῷ πάντας τοὺς κακῶς ἔχοντας, ³⁶ καὶ παρεκάλουν αὐτὸν ἵνα μόνον ἅψωνται τοῦ κρασπέδου τοῦ ἱματίου αὐτοῦ· καὶ ὅσοι ἥψαντο διεσώθησαν.

¹⁵:¹ Τότε προσέρχονται τῷ Ἰησοῦ ἀπὸ Ἰεροσολύμων Φαρισαῖοι καὶ γραμματεῖς λέγοντες, ² Διὰ τί οἱ μαθηταί σου παραβαίνουσιν τὴν παράδοσιν τῶν πρεσβυτέρων; οὐ γὰρ νίπτονται τὰς χεῖρας [αὐτῶν] ὅταν ἄρτον ἐσθίωσιν. ³ ὁ δὲ ἀποκριθεὶς εἶπεν αὐτοῖς, Διὰ τί καὶ ὑμεῖς παραβαίνετε τὴν ἐντολὴν τοῦ θεοῦ διὰ τὴν παράδοσιν ὑμῶν; ⁴ ὁ γὰρ θεὸς εἶπεν, Τίμα τὸν πατέρα καὶ τὴν μητέρα, καί, Ὁ κακολογῶν πατέρα ἢ μητέρα θανάτῳ τελευτάτω. ⁵ ὑμεῖς δὲ λέγετε, Ὃς ἂν εἴπῃ τῷ πατρὶ ἢ τῇ μητρί, Δῶρον ὃ ἐὰν ἐξ ἐμοῦ ὠφεληθῇς, ⁶ οὐ μὴ τιμήσει τὸν πατέρα αὐτοῦ· καὶ ἠκυρώσατε τὸν λόγον τοῦ θεοῦ διὰ τὴν παράδοσιν ὑμῶν. ⁷ ὑποκριταί, καλῶς ἐπροφήτευσεν περὶ ὑμῶν Ἠσαΐας λέγων, ⁸ Ὁ λαὸς οὗτος τοῖς χείλεσίν με τιμᾷ, ἡ δὲ καρδία αὐτῶν πόρρω ἀπέχει ἀπ᾽ ἐμοῦ· ⁹ μάτην δὲ σέβονταί με διδάσκοντες διδασκαλίας ἐντάλματα ἀνθρώπων. ¹⁰ Καὶ προσκαλεσάμενος τὸν ὄχλον εἶπεν αὐτοῖς, Ἀκούετε καὶ συνίετε· ¹¹ οὐ τὸ εἰσερχόμενον εἰς τὸ στόμα κοινοῖ τὸν ἄνθρωπον, ἀλλὰ τὸ ἐκπορευόμενον

him 'unclean.'" **12** Then the disciples came to him and asked, "Do you know that the Pharisees
ˌτὸν ἄνθρωπον˳ κοινοῖ   Τότε οἱ μαθηταὶ προσελθόντες ← λέγουσιν αὐτῷ → → οἶδας ὅτι οἱ Φαρισαῖοι
d.asm n.asm v.pai.3s   adv d.npm n.npm pt.aa.npm   v.pai.3p r.dsm.3   v.rai.2s cj d.npm n.npm
3836 476 3124   5538 3836 3412   3306 899   3857 4022 3836 5757

were offended when they heard this?" **13** He replied, "Every plant that my heavenly
→ ἐσκανδαλίσθησαν → → ἀκούσαντες ˌτὸν λόγον˳ δὲ ὁ ἀποκριθεὶς εἶπεν πᾶσα φυτεία ἣν μου ὁ οὐράνιος˳
v.api.3p   pt.aa.npm d.asm n.asm cj d.nsm pt.ap.nsm v.aai.3s a.nsf n.nsf r.asf r.gs.1 d.nsm a.nsm
4997   201 3836 3364 1254 3836 646 3306 4246 5884 4005 1609 3836 4039

Father has not planted will be pulled up by the roots. **14** Leave them; they are blind guides.
ˌὁ πατήρ˳ → οὐκ ἐφύτευσεν → ἐκριζωθήσεται ←   ἄφετε αὐτούς εἰσιν τυφλοὶ ὁδηγοί [τυφλῶν] δὲ
d.nsm n.nsm adv v.aai.3s v.fpi.3s   v.aam.2p r.apm.3 v.pai.3p a.npm n.npm a.gpm cj
3836 4252 5885 4024 5885 1748   918 899 1639 5603 3843 5603 1254

If a blind man leads a blind man, both will fall into a pit." **15** Peter said, "Explain
ἐὰν τυφλὸς ὁδηγῇ τυφλὸν ἀμφότεροι → πεσοῦνται εἰς βόθυνον δὲ ὁ Πέτρος Ἀποκριθεὶς εἶπεν αὐτῷ φράσον
cj a.nsm v.pas.3s a.asm a.npm v.fmi.3p p.a n.asm cj d.nsm n.nsm pt.ap.nsm v.aai.3s r.dsm.3 v.aam.2s
1569 5603 3842 5603 317 4406 1650 1073 1254 3836 4377 646 3306 899 5851

the parable to us." **16** "Are you still so dull?" Jesus asked them. **17** "Don't you see that whatever
τὴν παραβολὴν [ταύτην] → ἡμῖν δὲ ἐστε ὑμεῖς ἀκμὴν καὶ ἀσύνετοι ὁ εἶπεν οὐ → νοεῖτε ὅτι πᾶν
d.asf n.asf r.asf r.dp.1 cj v.pai.2p r.np.2 adv adv a.npm d.nsm v.aai.3s pl v.pai.2p cj a.nsn
3836 4130 4047 7005 1254 7007 197 2779 852 3836 3306 4024 3783 4022 4246

enters the mouth goes into the stomach and then out of the body? **18** But the things
ˌτὸ εἰσπορευόμενον˳ εἰς τὸ στόμα χωρεῖ εἰς τὴν κοιλίαν καὶ ˌεἰς ἀφεδρῶνα ἐκβάλλεται˳ ← ← δὲ τὰ ←
d.nsn pt.pm.nsn p.a d.asn n.asn v.pai.3s p.a d.asf n.asf cj p.a n.asm v.ppi.3s cj d.npn
3836 1660 1650 3836 5125 6003 1650 3836 3120 2779 1650 909 1675 1254 3836

that come out of the mouth come from the heart, and these make a man 'unclean.' **19** For out of
← ἐκπορευόμενα ἐκ τοῦ στόματος ἐξέρχεται ἐκ τῆς καρδίας κακεῖνα ← → ˌτὸν ἄνθρωπον˳ κοινοῖ γὰρ ἐκ
pt.pm.npn p.g d.gsn n.gsn v.pmi.3s p.g d.gsf n.gsf r.apn d.asm n.asm v.pai.3s cj p.g
1744 1666 3836 5125 2002 1666 3836 2840 2797 3124 3836 476 3124 1142 1666

the heart come evil thoughts, murder, adultery, sexual immorality, theft, false testimony, slander.
τῆς καρδίας ἐξέρχονται πονηροὶ διαλογισμοί φόνοι μοιχεῖαι → πορνεῖαι κλοπαί → ψευδομαρτυρίαι βλασφημίαι
d.gsf n.gsf v.pmi.3p a.npm n.npm n.npm n.npf n.npf n.npf n.npf n.npf
3836 2840 2002 4505 1369 5840 3657 4518 3113 6019 1060

20 These are what make a man 'unclean'; but eating with unwashed hands does not make him
ταῦτα ἐστιν τὰ → ˌτὸν ἄνθρωπον˳ κοινοῦντα δὲ ˌτὸ φαγεῖν˳ → ἀνίπτοις χερσὶν οὐ → ˌτὸν ἄνθρωπον˳
r.npn v.pai.3s d.npn d.asm n.asm pt.pa.npn cj d.nsn f.aa a.dpf n.dpf adv d.asm n.asm
4047 1639 3836 3124 3836 476 3124 1254 3836 2266 481 5931 4024 3124 3836 476

'unclean.'"
κοινοῖ
v.pai.3s
3124

The Faith of the Canaanite Woman

15:21 Leaving that place, Jesus withdrew to the region of Tyre and Sidon. **22** A Canaanite
Καὶ ἐξελθὼν ἐκεῖθεν ← ὁ Ἰησοῦς ἀνεχώρησεν εἰς τὰ μέρη → Τύρου καὶ Σιδῶνος καὶ ἰδοὺ Χαναναία
cj pt.aa.nsm adv d.nsm n.nsm v.aai.3s p.a d.apn n.apn n.gsf cj n.gsf cj j a.nsf
2779 2002 1696 3836 2652 432 1650 3836 3538 5602 2779 4972 2779 2627 5914

woman from that vicinity came to him, crying out, "Lord, Son of David, have mercy on me! My
γυνὴ ἀπὸ ἐκείνων ˌτῶν ὁρίων˳ ἐξελθοῦσα ἔκραζεν ← λέγουσα κύριε υἱὸς → Δαυίδ → ἐλέησον ← με μου
n.nsf p.g r.gpn d.gpn n.gpn pt.aa.nsf v.iai.3s pt.pa.nsf n.vsm n.nsm n.gsm v.aam.2s r.as.1 r.gs.1
1222 608 1697 3836 3990 2002 3189 3306 3261 5626 1253 1796 1609 1609

daughter is suffering terribly from demon-possession." **23** Jesus did not answer a word. So his disciples
ˌἡ θυγάτηρ˳ → → κακῶς → δαιμονίζεται δὲ ὁ οὐκ ἀπεκρίθη αὐτῇ λόγον καὶ αὐτοῦ ˌοἱ μαθηταὶ˳
d.nsf n.nsf adv v.ppi.3s cj d.nsm adv v.api.3s r.dsf.3 n.asm cj r.gsm.3 d.npm n.npm
3836 2588 1227 1227 2809 1227 1254 3836 646 4024 646 899 3364 2779 899 3836 3412

came to him and urged him, "Send her away, for she keeps crying out after us." **24** He
προσελθόντες ← ἠρώτουν αὐτὸν λέγοντες ἀπόλυσον αὐτὴν ← ὅτι → → κράζει ← ὄπισθεν ἡμῶν δὲ ὁ
pt.aa.npm v.iai.3p r.asm.3 pt.pa.npm v.aam.2s r.asf.3 cj v.pai.3s p.g r.gp.1 cj d.nsm
4665 2263 899 3306 668 899 668 4022 3189 3957 7005 1254 3836

ἐκ τοῦ στόματος τοῦτο κοινοῖ τὸν ἄνθρωπον. **12** Τότε προσελθόντες οἱ μαθηταὶ λέγουσιν αὐτῷ, Οἶδας ὅτι οἱ Φαρισαῖοι ἀκούσαντες τὸν λόγον ἐσκανδαλίσθησαν; **13** ὁ δὲ ἀποκριθεὶς εἶπεν, Πᾶσα φυτεία ἣν οὐκ ἐφύτευσεν ὁ πατήρ μου ὁ οὐράνιος ἐκριζωθήσεται. **14** ἄφετε αὐτούς· τυφλοί εἰσιν ὁδηγοί· «ὁδηγοί» [τυφλῶν]· τυφλὸς δὲ τυφλὸν ἐὰν ὁδηγῇ, ἀμφότεροι εἰς βόθυνον πεσοῦνται. **15** Ἀποκριθεὶς δὲ ὁ Πέτρος εἶπεν αὐτῷ, Φράσον ἡμῖν τὴν παραβολὴν [ταύτην]. **16** ὁ δὲ εἶπεν, Ἀκμὴν καὶ ὑμεῖς ἀσύνετοί ἐστε; **17** οὐ νοεῖτε ὅτι πᾶν τὸ εἰσπορευόμενον εἰς τὸ στόμα εἰς τὴν κοιλίαν χωρεῖ καὶ εἰς ἀφεδρῶνα ἐκβάλλεται; **18** τὰ δὲ ἐκπορευόμενα ἐκ τοῦ στόματος ἐκ τῆς καρδίας ἐξέρχεται, κἀκεῖνα κοινοῖ τὸν ἄνθρωπον. **19** ἐκ γὰρ τῆς καρδίας ἐξέρχονται διαλογισμοὶ πονηροί, φόνοι, μοιχεῖαι, πορνεῖαι, κλοπαί, ψευδομαρτυρίαι, βλασφημίαι. **20** ταῦτά ἐστιν τὰ κοινοῦντα τὸν ἄνθρωπον, τὸ δὲ ἀνίπτοις χερσὶν φαγεῖν οὐ κοινοῖ τὸν ἄνθρωπον.

15:21 Καὶ ἐξελθὼν ἐκεῖθεν ὁ Ἰησοῦς ἀνεχώρησεν εἰς τὰ μέρη Τύρου καὶ Σιδῶνος. **22** καὶ ἰδοὺ γυνὴ Χαναναία ἀπὸ τῶν ὁρίων ἐκείνων ἐξελθοῦσα ἔκραζεν λέγουσα, Ἐλέησόν με, κύριε υἱὸς Δαυίδ· ἡ θυγάτηρ μου κακῶς δαιμονίζεται. **23** ὁ δὲ οὐκ ἀπεκρίθη αὐτῇ λόγον. καὶ προσελθόντες οἱ μαθηταὶ αὐτοῦ ἠρώτουν αὐτὸν λέγοντες, Ἀπόλυσον αὐτήν, ὅτι κράζει ὄπισθεν ἡμῶν. **24** ὁ δὲ

answered, "I was sent only to the lost sheep of Israel." **25** The woman came and
ἀποκριθεὶς εἶπεν → → ἀπεστάλην οὐκ εἰ μὴ εἰς τὰ ⌐τὰ ἀπολωλότα⌐ πρόβατα → οἴκου Ἰσραήλ δὲ ἡ ← ἐλθοῦσα
pt.ap.nsm v.aai.3s v.api.1s adv cj pl p.a d.apn d.apn pt.ra.apn n.apn n.gsm n.gsm cj d.nsf pt.aa.nsf
646 3306 690 4024 1623 3590 1650 3836 3836 660 4585 3875 2702 1254 3836 2262

knelt before him. "Lord, help me!" she said. **26** He replied, "It is not right to take the children's
προσεκύνει← αὐτῷ κύριε βοήθει μοι → λέγουσα δὲ ὁ ἀποκριθεὶς εἶπεν → ἔστιν οὐκ καλόν → λαβεῖν τὸν ⌐τῶν τέκνων⌐
v.iai.3s r.dsm.3 n.vsm v.pam.2s r.ds.1 pt.pa.nsf cj d.nsm pt.ap.nsm v.aai.3s v.pai.3s adv a.nsn f.aa d.asm d.gpn n.gpn
4686 899 3261 1070 1609 3306 1254 3836 646 3306 1639 4024 2819 3284 3836 3836 5451

bread and toss it to their dogs." **27** "Yes, Lord," she said, "but even the dogs eat the crumbs that
ἄρτον καὶ βαλεῖν → τοῖς κυναρίοις δὲ ναὶ κύριε ἡ εἶπεν γὰρ καὶ τὰ κυνάρια ἐσθίει ἀπὸ τῶν ψιχίων τῶν
n.asm cj f.aa d.dpn n.dpn cj pl n.vsm d.nsf v.aai.3s cj adv d.npn n.npn v.pai.3s p.g d.gpn n.gpn d.gpn
788 2779 965 3836 3249 1254 3721 3261 3836 3306 1142 2779 3836 3249 2266 608 3836 6033 3836

fall from their masters' table." **28** Then Jesus answered, "Woman, you have great
πιπτόντων ἀπὸ αὐτῶν ⌐τῶν κυρίων⌐ ⌐τῆς τραπέζης⌐ τότε ὁ Ἰησοῦς ἀποκριθεὶς εἶπεν αὐτῇ ὦ γύναι σου μεγάλη
pt.pa.gpn p.g r.gpm.3 d.gpm n.gpm d.gsf n.gsf adv d.nsm n.nsm pt.ap.nsm v.aai.3s r.dsf.3 j n.vsf r.gs.2 a.nsf
4406 608 899 3836 3261 3836 5544 5538 3836 2652 646 3306 899 6043 1222 5148 3489

faith! Your request is granted." And her daughter was healed from that very hour.
⌐ἡ πίστις⌐ ὡς σοι θέλεις → γενηθήτω καὶ αὐτῆς ἡ θυγάτηρ → ἰάθη ἀπὸ ἐκείνης τῆς ὥρας
d.nsf n.nsf cj r.ds.2 v.pai.2s v.apm.3s cj r.gsf.3 d.nsf n.nsf v.api.3s p.g r.gsf d.gsf n.gsf
3836 4411 6055 5148 2527 1181 2779 899 3836 2588 2615 608 1697 3836 6052

Jesus Feeds the Four Thousand

15:29 Jesus left there and went along the Sea of Galilee. Then he went up on a
Καὶ ⌐ὁ Ἰησοῦς⌐ μεταβὰς ἐκεῖθεν ἦλθεν παρὰ τὴν θάλασσαν ⌐τῆς Γαλιλαίας⌐ καὶ → ἀναβὰς ← εἰς
cj d.nsm n.nsm pt.aa.nsm adv v.aai.3s p.a d.asf n.asf d.gsf n.gsf cj pt.aa.nsm p.a
2779 3836 2652 3553 1696 2262 4123 3836 2498 3836 1133 2779 326 1650

mountainside and sat down. **30** Great crowds came to him, bringing the lame, the blind, the
⌐τὸ ὄρος⌐ ἐκάθητο← ἐκεῖ καὶ πολλοὶ ὄχλοι προσῆλθον← αὐτῷ ἔχοντες μεθ᾽ ἑαυτῶν χωλοὺς τυφλοὺς
d.asn n.asn v.imi.3s adv cj a.npm n.npm v.aai.3p r.dsm.3 pt.pa.npm p.g r.gpm.3 a.apm a.apm
3836 4001 2764 1695 2779 4498 4063 4665 899 2400 3552 1571 6000 5603

crippled, the mute and many others, and laid them at his feet; and he healed them. **31** The
κυλλούς κωφούς καὶ πολλοὺς ἑτέρους καὶ ἔρριψαν αὐτοὺς παρὰ αὐτοῦ ⌐τοὺς πόδας⌐ καὶ → ἐθεράπευσεν αὐτούς ὥστε τὸν
a.apm a.apm cj a.apm a.apm cj v.aai.3p r.apm.3 p.a r.gsm.3 d.apm n.apm cj v.aai.3s r.apm.3 cj d.asm
3245 3273 2779 4498 2283 2779 4849 899 4123 899 3836 4546 2779 2543 899 6063 3836

people were amazed when they saw the mute speaking, the crippled made well, the lame walking
ὄχλον → θαυμάσαι → → βλέποντας κωφοὺς λαλοῦντας κυλλοὺς ὑγιεῖς καὶ χωλοὺς περιπατοῦντας
n.asm f.aa pt.pa.apm a.apm pt.pa.apm a.apm a.apm cj a.apm pt.pa.apm
4063 2513 1063 3273 3281 3245 5618 2779 6000 4344

and the blind seeing. And they praised the God of Israel. **32** Jesus called his disciples to
καὶ τυφλοὺς βλέποντας καὶ ἐδόξασαν τὸν θεὸν → Ἰσραήλ δὲ ⌐Ὁ Ἰησοῦς⌐ προσκαλεσάμενος αὐτοῦ ⌐τοὺς μαθητὰς⌐ ←
cj a.apm pt.pa.apm cj v.aai.3p d.asm n.asm n.gsm cj d.nsm n.nsm pt.am.nsm r.gsm.3 d.apm n.apm
2779 5603 1063 2779 1519 3836 2536 2702 1254 3836 2652 4673 899 3836 3412 4673

him and said, "I have compassion for these people; they have already been with me three days and
← εἶπεν σπλαγχνίζομαι ἐπὶ τὸν ὄχλον ὅτι → ἤδη προσμένουσιν ← μοι τρεῖς ἡμέραι καὶ
v.aai.3s v.ppi.1s p.a d.asm n.asm cj adv v.pai.3p r.ds.1 a.npf n.npf cj
4673 3306 5072 2093 3836 4063 4022 4693 4693 2453 4693 1609 5552 2465 2779

have nothing to eat. I do not want to send them away hungry, or they may collapse on the
ἔχουσιν ⌐οὐκ τί⌐ → φάγωσιν καὶ → → οὐ θέλω → ἀπολῦσαι αὐτοὺς ← νήστεις μήποτε → ἐκλυθῶσιν ἐν τῇ
v.pai.3p adv r.asn v.aas.3p cj adv v.pai.1s f.aa r.apm.3 a.apm cj v.aps.3p p.d d.dsf
2400 4024 5515 2266 2779 2527 2527 4024 2527 668 899 668 3765 3607 1725 1877 3836

way." **33** His disciples answered, "Where could we get enough bread in this remote place to feed
ὁδῷ καὶ οἱ μαθηταί λέγουσιν αὐτῷ πόθεν ἡμῖν τοσοῦτοι ἄρτοι ἐν ἐρημίᾳ ← ὥστε χορτάσαι
n.dsf cj d.npm n.npm v.pai.3p r.dsm.3 r.npm r.dp.1 r.npm n.npm p.d n.dsf cj f.aa
3847 2779 3836 3412 3306 899 4470 7005 5537 788 1877 2244 6063 5963

ἀποκριθεὶς εἶπεν, Οὐκ ἀπεστάλην εἰ μὴ εἰς τὰ πρόβατα τὰ ἀπολωλότα οἴκου Ἰσραήλ. **25** ἡ δὲ ἐλθοῦσα προσεκύνει αὐτῷ λέγουσα, Κύριε, βοήθει μοι. **26** ὁ δὲ ἀποκριθεὶς εἶπεν, Οὐκ ἔστιν καλὸν λαβεῖν τὸν ἄρτον τῶν τέκνων καὶ βαλεῖν τοῖς κυναρίοις. **27** ἡ δὲ εἶπεν, Ναὶ κύριε, καὶ γὰρ τὰ κυνάρια ἐσθίει ἀπὸ τῶν ψιχίων τῶν πιπτόντων ἀπὸ τῆς τραπέζης τῶν κυρίων αὐτῶν. **28** τότε ἀποκριθεὶς ὁ Ἰησοῦς εἶπεν αὐτῇ, Ὦ γύναι, μεγάλη σου ἡ πίστις· γενηθήτω σοι ὡς θέλεις. καὶ ἰάθη ἡ θυγάτηρ αὐτῆς ἀπὸ τῆς ὥρας ἐκείνης.

15:29 Καὶ μεταβὰς ἐκεῖθεν ὁ Ἰησοῦς ἦλθεν παρὰ τὴν θάλασσαν τῆς Γαλιλαίας, καὶ ἀναβὰς εἰς τὸ ὄρος ἐκάθητο ἐκεῖ. **30** καὶ προσῆλθον αὐτῷ ὄχλοι πολλοὶ ἔχοντες μεθ᾽ ἑαυτῶν χωλούς, τυφλούς, κυλλούς, κωφούς, καὶ ἑτέρους πολλοὺς καὶ ἔρριψαν αὐτοὺς παρὰ τοὺς πόδας αὐτοῦ, καὶ ἐθεράπευσεν αὐτούς· **31** ὥστε τὸν ὄχλον θαυμάσαι βλέποντας κωφοὺς λαλοῦντας, κυλλοὺς ὑγιεῖς καὶ χωλοὺς περιπατοῦντας καὶ τυφλοὺς βλέποντας· καὶ ἐδόξασαν τὸν θεὸν Ἰσραήλ. **32** Ὁ δὲ Ἰησοῦς προσκαλεσάμενος τοὺς μαθητὰς αὐτοῦ εἶπεν, Σπλαγχνίζομαι ἐπὶ τὸν ὄχλον, ὅτι ἤδη ἡμέραι τρεῖς προσμένουσίν μοι καὶ οὐκ ἔχουσιν τί φάγωσιν· καὶ ἀπολῦσαι αὐτοὺς νήστεις οὐ θέλω, μήποτε ἐκλυθῶσιν ἐν τῇ ὁδῷ. **33** καὶ λέγουσιν αὐτῷ οἱ μαθηταί, Πόθεν ἡμῖν ἐν ἐρημίᾳ

such   a crowd?" **34** "How many loaves do you have?"   Jesus   asked.   "Seven," they replied, "and a
τοσοῦτον ὄχλον   πόσους ←   ἄρτους →   ἔχετε   καὶ ὁ Ἰησοῦς λέγει   αὐτοῖς δὲ ἑπτὰ   οἱ εἶπαν   καὶ
r.asm   n.asm   r.apm   n.apm   v.pai.2p   cj d.nsm n.nsm v.pai.3s   r.dpm.3 cj a.apm   d.npm v.aai.3p cj
5537   4063   4531   788   2400   2779 3836 2652 3306   899 1254 2231   3836 3306 2779

few small fish." **35**   He told   the crowd to sit   down on the ground. **36** Then he took the seven loaves
ὀλίγα →   ἰχθύδια   καὶ →   παραγγείλας τῷ ὄχλῳ → ἀναπεσεῖν ←   ἐπὶ τὴν γῆν   ἔλαβεν τοὺς ἑπτὰ ἄρτους
a.apn   n.apn   cj   pt.aa.nsm   d.dsm n.dsm f.aa   p.a d.asf n.asf   v.aai.3s d.apm a.apm n.apm
3900   2715   2779   4133   3836 4063 404   2093 3836 1178   3284 3836 2231 788

and the fish, and when he had given thanks,   he broke them and gave them to the disciples, and
καὶ τοὺς ἰχθύας καὶ →   εὐχαριστήσας → ἔκλασεν   καὶ ἐδίδου   → τοῖς μαθηταῖς δὲ
cj d.apm n.apm cj   pt.aa.nsm → v.aai.3s   cj v.iai.3s   d.dpm n.dpm cj
2779 3836 2716 2779   2373   3089   2779 1443   3836 3412 1254

they   in turn to the people. **37** They all ate and were satisfied. Afterward the disciples picked up
οἱ μαθηταὶ   → τοῖς ὄχλοις   καὶ ↱   πάντες ἔφαγον καὶ   → ἐχορτάσθησαν καὶ   ἦραν ←
d.npm n.npm   d.dpm n.dpm   cj   a.npm v.aai.3p cj   v.api.3p   cj   v.aai.3p
3836 3412   3836 4063   2779 2266 4246 2266 2779   5963   2779   149

seven basketfuls   of broken pieces that were left over. **38**   The number of those who ate   was
ἑπτὰ σπυρίδας πλήρεις. →   τῶν κλασμάτων τὸ → περισσεῦον   δὲ   οἱ ← ἐσθίοντες ἦσαν
a.apf n.apf a.apf   d.gpn n.gpn d.asn pt.pa.asn   cj   d.npm pt.pa.npm v.iai.3p
2231 5083 4441   3836 3083 3836 4355   1254   3836 2266 1639

four   thousand,   besides women and children. **39** After Jesus had sent the crowd away, he got
τετρακισχίλιοι ←   ἄνδρες χωρὶς γυναικῶν καὶ παιδίων   Καὶ →   → ἀπολύσας τοὺς ὄχλους ←   → ἐνέβη
a.npm   n.npm p.g n.gpf cj n.gpn   cj   pt.aa.nsm d.apm n.apm   v.aai.3s
5483   467 6006 1222 2779 4086   2779   668   3836 4063 668   1832

into the boat and went to the vicinity of Magadan.
εἰς τὸ πλοῖον καὶ ἦλθεν εἰς τὰ ὅρια → Μαγαδάν
p.a d.asn n.asn cj v.aai.3s p.a d.apn n.apn n.gsf
1650 3836 4450 2779 2262 1650 3836 3990 3400

The Demand for a Sign

16:1 The Pharisees and Sadducees came   to Jesus and tested   him by asking   him to show
Καὶ οἱ   Φαρισαῖοι καὶ Σαδδουκαῖοι προσελθόντες ←   πειράζοντες   ἐπηρώτησαν αὐτὸν → ἐπιδεῖξαι
cj d.npm n.npm   cj   n.npm   pt.aa.npm   pt.pa.npm   v.aai.3p   r.asm.3 f.aa
2779 3836 5757   2779 4881   4665   4279   2089   899   2109

them a sign from heaven. **2**   He replied,   "When evening comes, you say, 'It will be fair
αὐτοῖς σημεῖον ἐκ τοῦ οὐρανοῦ   δὲ ὁ ἀποκριθεὶς εἶπεν αὐτοῖς ↱   ὀψίας γενομένης → λέγετε   εὐδία
r.dpm.3 n.asn p.g d.gsm n.gsm   cj d.nsm pt.ap.nsm v.aai.3s r.dpm.3   n.gsf pt.am.gsf v.pai.2p   n.nsf
899   4956   1666 3836 4041   1254 3836 646   3306 899 1181   4068 1181   3306   2304

weather, for the sky   is red,' **3** and in the morning, 'Today it will be stormy, for the sky   is red   and
γὰρ ὁ οὐρανός → πυρράζει   καὶ →   πρωῒ   σήμερον   χειμών γὰρ ὁ οὐρανός → πυρράζει
cj d.nsm n.nsm v.pai.3s   cj   adv   adv   n.nsm cj d.nsm n.nsm v.pai.3s
1142 3836 4041 4793   2779   4745   4958   5930 1142 3836 4041 4793

overcast.' You know how to interpret the appearance of the sky, but you cannot   interpret the signs
στυγνάζων μὲν → γινώσκετε   → διακρίνειν τὸ πρόσωπον   → τοῦ οὐρανοῦ δὲ →   οὐ δύνασθε   τὰ σημεῖα
pt.pa.nsm pl v.pai.2p   f.pa   d.asn n.asn   d.gsm n.gsm cj   adv v.ppi.2p   d.apn n.apn
5145   3525 1182   1359   3836 4725   3836 4041 1254   4024 1538   3836 4956

of the times. **4** A wicked and adulterous generation looks for a miraculous sign, but   none will be given
→ τῶν καιρῶν   πονηρὰ καὶ μοιχαλὶς   γενεὰ   ἐπιζητεῖ →   σημεῖον καὶ σημεῖον οὐ →   → δοθήσεται
d.gpm n.gpm   a.nsf cj a.nsf   n.nsf   v.pai.3s   n.asn cj n.nsn adv   v.fpi.3s
3836 2789   4505 2779 3655   1155   2118   4956 2779 4956 4024   1443

it except the sign of Jonah." Jesus then left   them and went away.
αὐτῇ εἰ μὴ τὸ σημεῖον → Ἰωνᾶ   καὶ καταλιπὼν αὐτοὺς   ἀπῆλθεν ←
r.dsf.3 cj pl d.nsn n.nsn n.gsm   cj pt.aa.nsm r.apm.3   v.aai.3s
899 1623 3590 3836 4956 2731   2779 2901   899   599

The Yeast of the Pharisees and Sadducees

16:5 When they went across   the lake, the disciples forgot   to take bread. **6** "Be careful,"
Καὶ →   → ἐλθόντες εἰς τὸ πέραν   οἱ μαθηταὶ ἐπελάθοντο → λαβεῖν ἄρτους   → ὁρᾶτε   δὲ
cj   pt.aa.npm εἰς τὸ adv   d.npm n.npm v.ami.3p   f.aa   n.apm   v.pam.2p cj
2779   2262   1650 3836 4305   3836 3412 2140   3284 788   3972   1254

ἄρτοι τοσοῦτοι ὥστε χορτάσαι ὄχλον τοσοῦτον; ³⁴ καὶ λέγει αὐτοῖς ὁ Ἰησοῦς, Πόσους ἄρτους ἔχετε; οἱ δὲ εἶπαν, Ἑπτὰ καὶ ὀλίγα ἰχθύδια. ³⁵ καὶ παραγγείλας τῷ ὄχλῳ ἀναπεσεῖν ἐπὶ τὴν γῆν ³⁶ ἔλαβεν τοὺς ἑπτὰ ἄρτους καὶ τοὺς ἰχθύας καὶ εὐχαριστήσας ἔκλασεν καὶ ἐδίδου τοῖς μαθηταῖς, οἱ δὲ μαθηταὶ τοῖς ὄχλοις. ³⁷ καὶ ἔφαγον πάντες καὶ ἐχορτάσθησαν. καὶ τὸ περισσεῦον τῶν κλασμάτων ἦραν ἑπτὰ σπυρίδας πλήρεις. ³⁸ οἱ δὲ ἐσθίοντες ἦσαν τετρακισχίλιοι ἄνδρες χωρὶς γυναικῶν καὶ παιδίων. ³⁹ Καὶ ἀπολύσας τοὺς ὄχλους ἐνέβη εἰς τὸ πλοῖον καὶ ἦλθεν εἰς τὰ ὅρια Μαγαδάν.

^{16:1} Καὶ προσελθόντες οἱ Φαρισαῖοι καὶ Σαδδουκαῖοι πειράζοντες ἐπηρώτησαν αὐτὸν σημεῖον ἐκ τοῦ οὐρανοῦ ἐπιδεῖξαι αὐτοῖς. ² ὁ δὲ ἀποκριθεὶς εἶπεν αὐτοῖς, [Ὀψίας γενομένης λέγετε, Εὐδία, πυρράζει γὰρ ὁ οὐρανός· ³ καὶ πρωΐ, Σήμερον χειμών, πυρράζει γὰρ στυγνάζων ὁ οὐρανός. τὸ μὲν πρόσωπον τοῦ οὐρανοῦ γινώσκετε διακρίνειν, τὰ δὲ σημεῖα τῶν καιρῶν οὐ δύνασθε;] ⁴ Γενεὰ πονηρὰ καὶ μοιχαλὶς σημεῖον ἐπιζητεῖ, καὶ σημεῖον οὐ δοθήσεται αὐτῇ εἰ μὴ τὸ σημεῖον Ἰωνᾶ. καὶ καταλιπὼν αὐτοὺς ἀπῆλθεν.

^{16:5} Καὶ ἐλθόντες οἱ μαθηταὶ εἰς τὸ πέραν ἐπελάθοντο ἄρτους λαβεῖν. ⁶ ὁ δὲ Ἰησοῦς εἶπεν αὐτοῖς, Ὁρᾶτε καὶ προσέχετε ἀπὸ

Jesus   said to them.   "Be on your guard   against the yeast of the Pharisees and Sadducees." 7   They
ὁ Ἰησοῦς, εἶπεν αὐτοῖς καὶ → → προσέχετε ἀπὸ τῆς ζύμης → τῶν Φαρισαίων καὶ Σαδδουκαίων δὲ οἱ
d.nsm n.nsm v.aai.3s r.dpm.3 cj   v.pam.2p p.g d.gsf n.gsf d.gpm n.gpm cj n.gpm cj d.npm
3836 2652 3306 899 2779   4668 608 3836 2434 3836 5757 2779 4881 1254 3836

discussed   this among themselves and said,   "It is because we didn't bring   any bread."   8   Aware of their
διελογίζοντο ἐν ἑαυτοῖς λέγοντες ὅτι → οὐκ ἐλάβομεν ἄρτους δὲ γνοὺς
v.imi.3p p.d r.dpm.3 pt.pa.npm cj adv v.aai.1p n.apm cj pt.aa.nsm
1368 1877 1571 3306 4022 4024 3284 788 1254 1182

discussion, Jesus   asked, "You of little faith,   why are you talking   among yourselves about having no
ὁ Ἰησοῦς εἶπεν ὀλιγόπιστοι τί → → διαλογίζεσθε ἐν ἑαυτοῖς ὅτι ἔχετε οὐκ
d.nsm n.nsm v.aai.3s a.vpm r.asn v.pmi.2p p.d r.dpm.2 cj v.pai.2p adv
3836 2652 3306 3899 5515 1368 1877 1571 4022 2400 4024

bread? 9 Do you still not understand? Don't you remember the five loaves for the five   thousand, and how
ἄρτους → → οὔπω νοεῖτε οὐδὲ → μνημονεύετε τοὺς πέντε ἄρτους → τῶν πεντακισχιλίων ← καὶ →
n.apm adv v.pai.2p cj v.pai.2p d.apm a.apm n.apm d.gpm a.gpm cj
788 3783 3783 4037 3783 4028 3648 3836 4297 788 3836 4295 2779

many basketfuls you gathered? 10 Or the seven loaves for the four   thousand, and how many basketfuls you
πόσους κοφίνους → ἐλάβετε οὐδὲ τοὺς ἑπτὰ ἄρτους → τῶν τετρακισχιλίων καὶ → πόσας σπυρίδας →
r.apm n.apm v.aai.2p cj d.apm a.apm n.apm d.gpm a.gpm cj r.apf n.apf
4531 3186 3284 4028 3836 2231 788 3836 5483 2779 4531 5083

gathered? 11 How is it you don't understand that I   was not talking to you about bread? But be on your guard
ἐλάβετε πῶς ← ← οὐ νοεῖτε ὅτι → → οὐ εἶπον → ὑμῖν περὶ ἄρτων δὲ → → προσέχετε
v.aai.2p cj adv v.pai.2p cj adv v.aai.1s r.dp.2 p.g n.gpm cj v.pam.2p
3284 4802 3783 4024 3783 4022 3306 3306 4024 3306 7007 4309 788 1254 4668

against the yeast of the Pharisees and Sadducees." 12 Then they understood that he was not telling them to guard
ἀπὸ τῆς ζύμης → τῶν Φαρισαίων καὶ Σαδδουκαίων τότε → συνῆκαν ὅτι → → οὐκ εἶπεν → προσέχειν
p.g d.gsf n.gsf d.gpm n.gpm cj n.gpm adv v.aai.3p cj adv v.aai.3s f.pa
608 3836 2434 3836 5757 2779 4881 5538 5317 4022 3306 3306 4024 3306 4668

against the yeast used in bread,   but against the teaching of the Pharisees and Sadducees.
ἀπὸ τῆς ζύμης → τῶν ἄρτων ἀλλὰ ἀπὸ τῆς διδαχῆς → τῶν Φαρισαίων καὶ Σαδδουκαίων
p.g d.gsf n.gsf d.gpm n.gpm cj p.g d.gsf n.gsf d.gpm n.gpm cj n.gpm
608 3836 2434 3836 788 247 608 3836 1439 3836 5757 2779 4881

Peter's Confession of Christ

16:13 When Jesus   came to the region of Caesarea Philippi,   he asked his   disciples,
δὲ → ὁ Ἰησοῦς Ἐλθὼν εἰς τὰ μέρη → Καισαρείας τῆς Φιλίππου → ἠρώτα αὐτοῦ τοὺς μαθητὰς λέγων
cj d.nsm n.nsm pt.aa.nsm p.a d.apn a.apn n.gsf d.gsf n.gsn v.iai.3s r.gsm.3 d.apm n.apm pt.pa.nsm
1254 2262 3836 2652 2262 1650 3836 3538 2791 3836 5805 2263 899 3836 3412 3306

"Who do people   say   the Son of Man   is?"   14   They replied, "Some say John   the Baptist;
τίνα οἱ ἄνθρωποι λέγουσιν τὸν υἱὸν → τοῦ ἀνθρώπου εἶναι δὲ οἱ εἶπαν μὲν οἱ Ἰωάννην τὸν βαπτιστὴν
r.asm d.npm n.npm v.pai.3p d.asm n.asm d.gsm n.gsm f.pa cj d.npm v.aai.3p pl oi n.asm d.asm n.asm
5515 3836 476 3306 3836 5626 3836 476 1639 1254 3836 3306 3525 3836 2722 3836 969

others say Elijah; and still others, Jeremiah or one of the prophets." 15 "But what about you?" he asked.
δὲ ἄλλοι Ἠλίαν δὲ ἕτεροι Ἰερεμίαν ἢ ἕνα → τῶν προφητῶν ὑμεῖς → λέγει αὐτοῖς δὲ
pl r.npm n.asm pl r.npm n.asm cj a.asm d.gpm n.gpm r.np.2 v.pai.3s r.dpm.3 cj
1254 257 2460 1254 2283 2635 2445 1651 3836 4737 7007 3306 899 1254

"Who do you say   I am?" 16   Simon Peter answered,   "You are the Christ, the Son of the living
τίνα → λέγετε με εἶναι δὲ Σίμων Πέτρος ἀποκριθεὶς εἶπεν σὺ εἶ ὁ χριστὸς ὁ υἱὸς → τοῦ τοῦ ζῶντος
r.asm v.pai.2p r.as.1 f.pa cj n.nsm n.nsm pt.ap.nsm v.aai.3s r.ns.2 v.pai.2s d.nsm n.nsm d.nsm n.nsm d.gsm d.gsm a.gsm
5515 3306 1609 1639 1254 4981 4377 646 3306 5148 1639 3836 5986 3836 5626 3836 3836 2409

God." 17   Jesus   replied,   "Blessed are you, Simon son of Jonah,   for this was not revealed   to you
θεοῦ δὲ ὁ Ἰησοῦς ἀποκριθεὶς εἶπεν αὐτῷ μακάριος εἶ ← Σίμων → Βαριωνᾶ ὅτι οὐκ ἀπεκάλυψεν → σοι
n.gsm cj d.nsm n.nsm pt.ap.nsm v.aai.3s r.dsm.3 a.nsm v.pai.2s n.vsm n.vsm cj adv v.aai.3s r.ds.2
2536 1254 3836 2652 646 3306 899 3421 1639 4981 980 4022 4024 636 5148

by man,   but by my Father   in heaven.   18   And I   tell you that you are Peter, and on
σὰρξ καὶ αἷμα ἀλλ' μου ὁ πατήρ ὁ ἐν τοῖς οὐρανοῖς δὲ → κἀγὼ λέγω σοι ὅτι σὺ εἶ Πέτρος καὶ ἐπὶ
n.nsf cj n.nsn cj r.gs.1 d.nsm n.nsm d.nsm p.d d.dpm n.dpm cj crasis v.pai.1s r.ds.2 cj r.ns.2 v.pai.2s n.nsm cj p.d
4922 2779 135 247 1609 3836 4252 3836 1877 3836 4041 1254 2743 3306 5148 4022 5148 1639 4377 2779 2093

τῆς ζύμης τῶν Φαρισαίων καὶ Σαδδουκαίων. 7 οἱ δὲ διελογίζοντο ἐν ἑαυτοῖς λέγοντες ὅτι Ἄρτους οὐκ ἐλάβομεν. 8 γνοὺς δὲ ὁ Ἰησοῦς εἶπεν, Τί διαλογίζεσθε ἐν ἑαυτοῖς, ὀλιγόπιστοι, ὅτι ἄρτους οὐκ ἔχετε; 9 οὔπω νοεῖτε, οὐδὲ μνημονεύετε τοὺς πέντε ἄρτους τῶν πεντακισχιλίων καὶ πόσους κοφίνους ἐλάβετε; 10 οὐδὲ τοὺς ἑπτὰ ἄρτους τῶν τετρακισχιλίων καὶ πόσας σπυρίδας ἐλάβετε; 11 πῶς οὐ νοεῖτε ὅτι οὐ περὶ ἄρτων εἶπον ὑμῖν; προσέχετε δὲ ἀπὸ τῆς ζύμης τῶν Φαρισαίων καὶ Σαδδουκαίων. 12 τότε συνῆκαν ὅτι οὐκ εἶπεν προσέχειν ἀπὸ τῆς ζύμης τῶν ἄρτων ἀλλὰ ἀπὸ τῆς διδαχῆς τῶν Φαρισαίων καὶ Σαδδουκαίων.

16:13 Ἐλθὼν δὲ ὁ Ἰησοῦς εἰς τὰ μέρη Καισαρείας τῆς Φιλίππου ἠρώτα τοὺς μαθητὰς αὐτοῦ λέγων, Τίνα λέγουσιν οἱ ἄνθρωποι εἶναι τὸν υἱὸν τοῦ ἀνθρώπου; 14 οἱ δὲ εἶπαν, Οἱ μὲν Ἰωάννην τὸν βαπτιστήν, ἄλλοι δὲ Ἠλίαν, ἕτεροι δὲ Ἰερεμίαν ἢ ἕνα τῶν προφητῶν. 15 λέγει αὐτοῖς, Ὑμεῖς δὲ τίνα με λέγετε εἶναι; 16 ἀποκριθεὶς δὲ Σίμων Πέτρος εἶπεν, Σὺ εἶ ὁ Χριστὸς ὁ υἱὸς τοῦ θεοῦ τοῦ ζῶντος. 17 ἀποκριθεὶς δὲ ὁ Ἰησοῦς εἶπεν αὐτῷ, Μακάριος εἶ, Σίμων Βαριωνᾶ, ὅτι σὰρξ καὶ αἷμα οὐκ ἀπεκάλυψέν σοι ἀλλ' ὁ πατήρ μου ὁ ἐν τοῖς οὐρανοῖς. 18 κἀγὼ δέ σοι λέγω ὅτι σὺ εἶ Πέτρος, καὶ ἐπὶ ταύτῃ τῇ πέτρᾳ οἰκοδομήσω

| this | rock | I will build | | my church, | and | the gates | of Hades | will not | overcome | | it. | ¹⁹ I | will give | you |

ταύτῃ τῇ πέτρᾳ → οἰκοδομήσω μου τὴν ἐκκλησίαν, καὶ πύλαι → ᾅδου → οὐ κατισχύσουσιν αὐτῆς → δώσω σοι
r.dsf d.dsf n.dsf | v.fai.1s r.gs.1 d.asf n.asf | cj n.npf | n.gsm | adv v.fai.3p | r.gsf.3 | v.fai.1s r.ds.2
4047 3836 4376 | 3868 | 1609 3836 1711 | 2779 4783 | 87 | 2996 4024 2996 | 899 | 1443 5148

| the keys | of the kingdom | of heaven; | | whatever | you bind | on | earth | | will be | bound | in | heaven, |

τὰς κλεῖδας → τῆς βασιλείας → τῶν οὐρανῶν, καὶ ὃ ἐὰν → δήσῃς ἐπὶ τῆς γῆς → ἔσται δεδεμένον ἐν τοῖς οὐρανοῖς,
d.apf n.apf | d.gsf n.gsf | d.gpm n.gpm | cj r.asn pl | v.aas.2s p.g d.gsf n.gsf | v.fmi.3s pt.rp.nsn p.d d.dpm n.dpm
3836 3090 | 3836 993 | 3836 4041 | 2779 4005 1569 | 1313 2093 3836 1178 | 1639 1313 | 1877 3836 4041

| and | whatever | you loose | on | earth | | will be | loosed | in | heaven." | ²⁰ Then | he warned | his disciples | | not to |

καὶ ὃ ἐὰν → λύσῃς ἐπὶ τῆς γῆς → ἔσται λελυμένον ἐν τοῖς οὐρανοῖς, τότε → διεστείλατο τοῖς μαθηταῖς ἵνα →
cj r.asn pl | v.aas.2s p.g d.gsf n.gsf | v.fmi.3s pt.rp.nsn p.d d.dpm n.dpm | adv | v.ami.3s d.dpm n.dpm cj
2779 4005 1569 | 3395 2093 3836 1178 | 1639 3395 | 1877 3836 4041 | 5538 | 1403 3836 3412 2671 3594

| tell | anyone | that | he | was | the Christ. |

εἴπωσιν μηδενὶ ὅτι αὐτός ἐστιν ὁ χριστός
v.aas.3p a.dsm cj r.nsm v.pai.3s d.nsm n.nsm
3306 3594 4022 899 1639 3836 5986

Jesus Predicts His Death

^{16:21} From that time on | Jesus | | began | to explain | to | his | disciples | that | he | must | go | to

Ἀπὸ τότε ← ὁ Ἰησοῦς, ἤρξατο → δεικνύειν αὐτοῦ τοῖς μαθηταῖς, ὅτι αὐτὸν δεῖ ἀπελθεῖν εἰς
p.g adv | d.nsm n.nsm | v.ami.3s f.pa | r.gsm.3 d.dpm n.dpm | cj r.asm.3 v.pai.3s f.aa p.a
608 5538 | 3836 2652 | 806 1260 | 899 3836 3412 | 4022 899 1256 599 1650

Jerusalem | and | suffer | many things | at | the hands of | the elders, | | chief priests | and | teachers | of the law, and

Ἰεροσόλυμα καὶ παθεῖν πολλὰ ← ἀπὸ ← → τῶν πρεσβυτέρων καὶ ἀρχιερέων καὶ γραμματέων ← ← καὶ
n.apn cj f.aa a.apn p.g | d.gpm a.gpm cj n.gpm cj n.gpm | cj
2642 2779 4248 4498 608 | 3836 4565 2779 797 2779 1208 | 2779

| that | he must | be killed | | and | on | the third | day | be raised | to life. | ²² | Peter | | took | | him | aside and

→ ἀποκτανθῆναι καὶ → τῇ τρίτῃ ἡμέρᾳ ἐγερθῆναι καὶ ὁ Πέτρος, προσλαβόμενος αὐτὸν ←
f.ap cj d.dsf a.dsf n.dsf f.ap | cj d.nsm n.nsm pt.am.nsm r.asm.3
650 2779 3836 5569 2465 1586 | 2779 3836 4377 4689 899 4689

| began | to rebuke | him. | "Never, | Lord!" | he said. | "This | shall | never | happen | to you!" | ²³ | | Jesus | turned | and | said to

ἤρξατο → ἐπιτιμᾶν αὐτῷ ἵλεώς σοι, κύριε → λέγων τοῦτο οὐ μὴ ἔσται → σοι δὲ ὁ στραφεὶς εἶπεν →
v.ami.3s f.pa r.dsm.3 a.nsm r.ds.2 n.vsm pt.pa.nsm r.nsn adv pl v.fmi.3s r.ds.2 | cj d.nsm pt.ap.nsm v.aai.3s
806 2203 899 2664 5148 3261 3306 4047 1639 4024 3590 1639 5148 | 1254 3836 5138 3306

Peter, | "Get | behind | me, | Satan! | You | are | a stumbling block | | to me; | | you do | not | have | in mind | the things

τῷ Πέτρῳ, ὕπαγε ὀπίσω μου σατανᾶ → εἶ σκάνδαλον ἐμοῦ ὅτι → → οὐ → φρονεῖς τὰ ←
d.dsm n.dsm v.pam.2s p.g r.gs.1 n.vsm v.pai.2s n.nsn r.gs.1 cj adv v.pai.2s d.apn
3836 4377 5632 3958 1609 4928 1639 4998 1609 4022 5858 5858 4024 5858 3836

| of God, | | but | the things | of men." | ²⁴ Then | Jesus | | said | to | his | disciples, | "If | anyone | would | come

→ τοῦ θεοῦ, ἀλλὰ τὰ ← τῶν ἀνθρώπων. Τότε ὁ Ἰησοῦς, εἶπεν αὐτοῦ τοῖς μαθηταῖς, εἴ τις θέλει ἐλθεῖν
d.gsm n.gsm cj d.apn d.gpm n.gpm | adv d.nsm n.nsm v.aai.3s r.gsm.3 d.dpm n.dpm | cj r.nsm v.pai.3s f.aa
3836 2536 247 3836 3836 476 | 5538 3836 2652 3306 899 3836 3412 | 1623 5516 2527 2262

after | me, | he must | deny | | himself | and | take | up | his | cross | | and | follow | me. | ²⁵ For | whoever | wants to

ὀπίσω μου → → ἀπαρνησάσθω ἑαυτὸν καὶ ἀράτω αὐτοῦ τὸν σταυρὸν καὶ ἀκολουθείτω μοι γὰρ ὃς ἐὰν θέλῃ →
p.g r.gs.1 v.amm.3s r.asm.3 cj v.aam.3s r.gsm.3 d.asm n.asm cj v.pam.3s r.ds.1 | cj r.nsm pl v.pas.3s
3958 1609 565 1571 2779 149 899 3836 5089 2779 199 1609 | 1142 4005 1569 2527

save | his | life | | will lose | it, | but | whoever | loses | his | life | | for | me | will find | it. | ²⁶ | What

σῶσαι αὐτοῦ τὴν ψυχὴν → ἀπολέσει αὐτήν δ' ὃς ἂν ἀπολέσῃ αὐτοῦ τὴν ψυχὴν, ἕνεκεν ἐμοῦ → εὑρήσει αὐτήν γὰρ τί
f.aa r.gsm.3 d.asf n.asf v.fai.3s r.asf.3 cj r.nsm pl v.aas.3s r.gsm.3 d.asf n.asf p.g r.gs.1 v.fai.3s r.asf.3 cj r.asn
5392 899 3836 6034 660 899 1254 4005 323 660 899 3836 6034 1914 1609 2351 899 1142 5515

good | will it be | for a man | | if | he gains | the whole | world, | yet | forfeits | his | soul? | Or | what | can | a

ὠφεληθήσεται ← ← → ἄνθρωπος ἐὰν κερδήσῃ τὸν ὅλον κόσμον δὲ ζημιωθῇ αὐτοῦ τὴν ψυχὴν, ἢ τί →
v.fpi.3s n.nsm cj v.aas.3s d.asm a.asm n.asm cj v.aps.3s r.gsm.3 d.asf n.asf cj r.asn
6067 476 1569 3045 3836 3910 3180 1254 2423 899 3836 6034 2445 5515 1443

man | give | in exchange | for | his | soul? | ²⁷ For | the | Son | of Man | | is going | to come | in | his | Father's

ἄνθρωπος δώσει → ἀντάλλαγμα → αὐτοῦ τῆς ψυχῆς, γὰρ ὁ υἱὸς → τοῦ ἀνθρώπου, → μέλλει → ἔρχεσθαι ἐν αὐτοῦ τοῦ πατρὸς,
n.nsm v.fai.3s n.asn r.gsm.3 d.gsf n.gsf | cj d.nsm n.nsm d.gsm n.gsm | v.pai.3s f.pm p.d r.gsm.3 d.gsm n.gsm
476 1443 498 6034 899 3836 6034 | 1142 3836 5626 3836 476 | 3516 2262 1877 899 3836 4252

μου τὴν ἐκκλησίαν καὶ πύλαι ᾅδου οὐ κατισχύσουσιν αὐτῆς. ¹⁹ δώσω σοι τὰς κλεῖδας τῆς βασιλείας τῶν οὐρανῶν, καὶ ὃ ἐὰν δήσῃς ἐπὶ τῆς γῆς ἔσται δεδεμένον ἐν τοῖς οὐρανοῖς, καὶ ὃ ἐὰν λύσῃς ἐπὶ τῆς γῆς ἔσται λελυμένον ἐν τοῖς οὐρανοῖς. ²⁰ τότε ἐπετίμησεν «διεστείλατο» τοῖς μαθηταῖς ἵνα μηδενὶ εἴπωσιν ὅτι αὐτός ἐστιν ὁ Χριστός.

^{16:21} Ἀπὸ τότε ἤρξατο ὁ Ἰησοῦς δεικνύειν τοῖς μαθηταῖς αὐτοῦ ὅτι δεῖ αὐτὸν εἰς Ἰεροσόλυμα ἀπελθεῖν καὶ πολλὰ παθεῖν ἀπὸ τῶν πρεσβυτέρων καὶ ἀρχιερέων καὶ γραμματέων καὶ ἀποκτανθῆναι καὶ τῇ τρίτῃ ἡμέρᾳ ἐγερθῆναι. ²² καὶ προσλαβόμενος αὐτὸν ὁ Πέτρος ἤρξατο ἐπιτιμᾶν αὐτῷ λέγων, Ἵλεώς σοι, κύριε· οὐ μὴ ἔσται σοι τοῦτο. ²³ ὁ δὲ στραφεὶς εἶπεν τῷ Πέτρῳ, Ὕπαγε ὀπίσω μου, Σατανᾶ· σκάνδαλον εἶ ἐμοῦ, ὅτι οὐ φρονεῖς τὰ τοῦ θεοῦ ἀλλὰ τὰ τῶν ἀνθρώπων. ²⁴ Τότε ὁ Ἰησοῦς εἶπεν τοῖς μαθηταῖς αὐτοῦ, Εἴ τις θέλει ὀπίσω μου ἐλθεῖν, ἀπαρνησάσθω ἑαυτὸν καὶ ἀράτω τὸν σταυρὸν αὐτοῦ καὶ ἀκολουθείτω μοι. ²⁵ ὃς γὰρ ἐὰν θέλῃ τὴν ψυχὴν αὐτοῦ σῶσαι ἀπολέσει αὐτήν· ὃς δ' ἂν ἀπολέσῃ τὴν ψυχὴν αὐτοῦ ἕνεκεν ἐμοῦ εὑρήσει αὐτήν. ²⁶ τί γὰρ ὠφεληθήσεται ἄνθρωπος ἐὰν τὸν κόσμον ὅλον κερδήσῃ τὴν δὲ ψυχὴν αὐτοῦ ζημιωθῇ; ἢ τί δώσει ἄνθρωπος ἀντάλλαγμα τῆς ψυχῆς αὐτοῦ; ²⁷ μέλλει γὰρ ὁ υἱὸς τοῦ ἀνθρώπου ἔρχεσθαι ἐν τῇ δόξῃ τοῦ πατρὸς αὐτοῦ μετὰ τῶν ἀγγέλων αὐτοῦ, καὶ τότε ἀποδώσει

glory	with	his	angels,		and then	he will reward	each		person according	to	what	he	has done.	**28** I tell	you
˪τῇ δόξῃ	μετὰ	αὐτοῦ	˪τῶν ἀγγέλων˩	καὶ	τότε →	→ ἀποδώσει	ἑκάστῳ ←		κατὰ	←	τὴν	αὐτοῦ	πρᾶξιν →	→ λέγω	ὑμῖν
d.dsf n.dsf	p.g	r.gsm.3	r.gpm n.gpm	cj	adv	v.fai.3s	r.dsm		p.a		d.asf	r.gsm.3	n.asf	v.pai.1s	r.dp.2
3836 1518	3552	899	3836 34	2779	5538	625	1667		2848		3836	899	4552	3306	7007

the truth,		some who are	standing	here		will not	taste	death	before	they see	the Son of
ἀμὴν	ὅτι	εἰσίν τινες →	→ ˪τῶν ἑστώτων˩	ὧδε	οἵτινες	→ ˪οὐ μὴ˩	γεύσωνται	θανάτου	ἕως ἂν →	→ ἴδωσιν	τὸν υἱὸν →
pl	cj	v.pai.3p r.npm	d.gpm pt.ra.gpm	adv	r.npm	adv pl	v.ams.3p	n.gsm	cj pl	v.aas.3p	d.asm n.asm
297	4022	1639 5516	3836 2705	6045	4015	1174 4024	3590	2505	2401 323	1625	3836 5626

Man		coming	in	his	kingdom.”
˪τοῦ ἀνθρώπου˩	ἐρχόμενον	ἐν	αὐτοῦ	˪τῇ βασιλείᾳ˩
d.gsm n.gsm	pt.pm.asm	p.d	r.gsm.3	d.dsf n.dsf
3836 476	2262	1877	899	3836 993

The Transfiguration

17:1

After six days		Jesus	took	with him Peter,		James	and John	the brother of
Καὶ μεθ᾽ ἓξ ἡμέρας	ὁ	Ἰησοῦς	παραλαμβάνει ←	˪τὸν Πέτρον	καὶ Ἰάκωβον	καὶ	Ἰωάννην	τὸν ἀδελφὸν →
cj p.a a.apf n.apf	d.nsm	n.nsm	v.pai.3s	d.asm n.asm	cj n.asm	cj	n.asm	d.asm n.asm
2779 3552 1971 2465	3836	2652	4161	3836 4377	2779 2610	2779	2722	3836 81

James,	and led	them	up a high	mountain by	themselves.	**2**	There he was	transfigured	before	them.
αὐτοῦ	καὶ ἀναφέρει	αὐτοὺς εἰς	ὑψηλὸν ὄρος	κατ᾽ ἰδίαν		καὶ	→ →	μετεμορφώθη	ἔμπροσθεν	αὐτῶν καὶ
r.gsm.3	cj v.pai.3s	r.apm.3 p.a	a.asn n.asn	p.a a.asf		cj		v.api.3s	p.g	r.gpm.3 cj
899	2779 429	899 1650	5734 4001	2848 2625		2779		3565	1869	899 2779

His	face	shone	like	the	sun,	and his	clothes	became	as white	as	the light.	**3** *Just then*	there appeared
αὐτοῦ	˪τὸ πρόσωπον˩	ἔλαμψεν	ὡς	ὁ	ἥλιος	δὲ αὐτοῦ	˪τὰ ἱμάτια˩	ἐγένετο	λευκὰ ὡς	τὸ	φῶς	καὶ ἰδοὺ →	→ ὤφθη
r.gsm.3	d.nsn n.nsn	v.aai.3s	pl	d.nsm	n.nsm	cj r.gsm.3	d.npn n.npn	v.ami.3s	a.npn pl	d.nsn	n.nsn	cj	v.api.3s
899	3836 4725	3290	6055	3836	2463	1254 899	3836 2668	1181	3328 6055	3836	5890	2779 2627	3972

before them	Moses	and	Elijah,	talking		with Jesus.	**4**	Peter	said		to Jesus,	“Lord,	it is
→	αὐτοῖς Μωϋσῆς	καὶ	Ἠλίας	συλλαλοῦντες	μετ᾽	αὐτοῦ	δὲ	ὁ Πέτρος	ἀποκριθεὶς	εἶπεν →	˪τῷ Ἰησοῦ˩	κύριε	→ ἐστιν
	r.dpm.3 n.nsm	cj	n.nsm	pt.pa.npm	p.g	r.gsm.3	cj	d.nsm n.nsm	pt.ap.nsm	v.aai.3s	d.dsm n.dsm	n.vsm	v.pai.3s
	899 3707	2779	2460	5196	3552	899	1254	3836 4377	646	3306	2652 3261	3261	1639

good	for us	to be	here.	If	you wish,	I will put	up	three	shelters –	one for you,		one for Moses and
καλόν	ἡμᾶς	εἶναι	ὧδε	εἰ →	→ θέλεις →	→ ποιήσω	ὧδε	τρεῖς	σκηνάς	μίαν →	→ σοὶ	καὶ μίαν → → Μωϋσεῖ καὶ
a.nsn	r.ap.1	f.pa	adv	cj	v.pai.2s	v.fai.1s	adv	a.apf	n.apf	a.asf	r.ds.2	cj a.asf n.dsm cj
2819	7005	1639	6045	1623	2527	4477	6045	5552	5008	1651	5148	2779 1651 3707 2779

one for Elijah.”	**5** While he		was still	speaking,		a bright	cloud	enveloped	them, and		a voice	from	the cloud
μίαν →	Ἠλίᾳ		˪αὐτοῦ˩ →	ἔτι	λαλοῦντος	ἰδοὺ	φωτεινὴ	νεφέλη	ἐπεσκίασεν	αὐτούς καὶ	ἰδοὺ	φωνὴ	ἐκ	τῆς νεφέλης
a.asf	n.dsm		r.gsm.3	adv	pt.pa.gsm	j	a.nsf	n.nsf	v.aai.3s	r.apm.3 cj	j	n.nsf	p.g	d.gsf n.gsf
1651	2460		3281	2285	3281	2627	5893	3749	2173	899 2779	2627	5889	1666	3836 3749

said,	“This is	my	Son,	whom I love;		with	him	I am well pleased.	Listen to him!”	**6**	When the
λέγουσα	οὗτος	ἐστιν μου	ὁ υἱός	ὁ	ἀγαπητός →	ἐν	ᾧ	εὐδόκησα	ἀκούετε ← αὐτοῦ	καὶ →	οἱ
pt.pa.nsf	r.nsm	v.pai.3s r.gs.1	d.nsm n.nsm	d.nsm	a.nsm	p.d	r.dsm	v.aai.1s	v.pam.2p r.gsm.3	cj	d.npm
3306	4047	1639 1609	3836 5626	3836	28	1877	4005	2305	201 899	2779 201	3836

disciples	heard	this,	they fell	facedown		to the ground,		terrified.	**7** But	Jesus		came
μαθηταὶ	ἀκούσαντες	→	ἔπεσαν	ἐπὶ πρόσωπον	αὐτῶν˩		καὶ	˪ἐφοβήθησαν σφόδρα˩	καὶ ὁ	Ἰησοῦς	προσῆλθεν
n.npm	pt.aa.npm		v.aai.3p	p.a n.asn	r.gpm.3		cj	v.api.3p adv	cj d.nsm	n.nsm	v.aai.3s
3412	201		4406	2093 4725	899		2779	5828 5379	2779 3836	2652	4665

and	touched	them.	“Get	up,”	he said.	“Don’t	be afraid.”	**8**	When they looked			up,
καὶ	ἁψάμενος	αὐτῶν	ἐγέρθητε ←	→	εἶπεν καὶ	μὴ	→ φοβεῖσθε	δὲ	→ ἐπάραντες	τοὺς ὀφθαλμοὺς	αὐτῶν˩ →
cj	pt.am.nsm	r.gpm.3	v.apm.2p		v.aai.3s cj	pl	v.ppm.2p	cj	pt.aa.npm	d.apm n.apm	r.gpm.3
2779	721	899	1586		3306 2779	3590	5828	1254	2048	3836 4057	899

they saw	no one	except	Jesus.	**9**	As they	were coming		down	the mountain,	Jesus
→ εἶδον →	οὐδένα	εἰ μὴ	αὐτὸν Ἰησοῦν μόνον	Καὶ	→ αὐτῶν →	καταβαινόντων		ἐκ	τοῦ ὄρους	ὁ Ἰησοῦς
v.aai.3p	a.asm	cj pl	r.asm n.asm adv	cj	r.gpm.3	pt.pa.gpm		p.g	d.gsn n.gsn	d.nsm n.nsm
1625	4029	1623 3590	899 2652 3668	2779	2849 899	2849		1666	3836 4001	3836 2652

instructed	them,	“Don’t	tell	anyone	what	you have	seen,	until	the Son of Man		has been	raised
ἐνετείλατο	αὐτοῖς	λέγων	μηδενὶ	εἴπητε ←	τὸ		ὅραμα	ἕως οὗ	ὁ υἱὸς →	˪τοῦ ἀνθρώπου˩ →		ἐγέρθη
v.ami.3s	r.dpm.3	pt.pa.nsm	a.dsm	v.aas.2p	d.asn		n.asn	p.g r.gsm	d.nsm n.nsm	d.gsm n.gsm		v.aps.3s
1948	899	3306	3594	3306	3836		3969	2401 4005	3836 5626	3836 476		1586

ἑκάστῳ κατὰ τὴν πρᾶξιν αὐτοῦ. **28** ἀμὴν λέγω ὑμῖν ὅτι εἰσίν τινες τῶν ὧδε ἑστώτων οἵτινες οὐ μὴ γεύσωνται θανάτου ἕως ἂν ἴδωσιν τὸν υἱὸν τοῦ ἀνθρώπου ἐρχόμενον ἐν τῇ βασιλείᾳ αὐτοῦ.

17:1 Καὶ μεθ᾽ ἡμέρας ἓξ παραλαμβάνει ὁ Ἰησοῦς τὸν Πέτρον καὶ Ἰάκωβον καὶ Ἰωάννην τὸν ἀδελφὸν αὐτοῦ καὶ ἀναφέρει αὐτοὺς εἰς ὄρος ὑψηλὸν κατ᾽ ἰδίαν. **2** καὶ μετεμορφώθη ἔμπροσθεν αὐτῶν, καὶ ἔλαμψεν τὸ πρόσωπον αὐτοῦ ὡς ὁ ἥλιος, τὰ δὲ ἱμάτια αὐτοῦ ἐγένετο λευκὰ ὡς τὸ φῶς. **3** καὶ ἰδοὺ ὤφθη αὐτοῖς Μωϋσῆς καὶ Ἠλίας συλλαλοῦντες μετ᾽ αὐτοῦ. **4** ἀποκριθεὶς δὲ ὁ Πέτρος εἶπεν τῷ Ἰησοῦ, Κύριε, καλόν ἐστιν ἡμᾶς ὧδε εἶναι· εἰ θέλεις, ποιήσω ὧδε τρεῖς σκηνάς, σοὶ μίαν καὶ Μωϋσεῖ μίαν καὶ Ἠλίᾳ μίαν. **5** ἔτι αὐτοῦ λαλοῦντος ἰδοὺ νεφέλη φωτεινὴ ἐπεσκίασεν αὐτούς, καὶ ἰδοὺ φωνὴ ἐκ τῆς νεφέλης λέγουσα, Οὗτός ἐστιν ὁ υἱός μου ὁ ἀγαπητός, ἐν ᾧ εὐδόκησα· ἀκούετε αὐτοῦ. **6** καὶ ἀκούσαντες οἱ μαθηταὶ ἔπεσαν ἐπὶ πρόσωπον αὐτῶν καὶ ἐφοβήθησαν σφόδρα. **7** καὶ προσῆλθεν ὁ Ἰησοῦς καὶ ἁψάμενος αὐτῶν εἶπεν, Ἐγέρθητε καὶ μὴ φοβεῖσθε. **8** ἐπάραντες δὲ τοὺς ὀφθαλμοὺς αὐτῶν οὐδένα εἶδον εἰ μὴ αὐτὸν Ἰησοῦν μόνον. **9** Καὶ καταβαινόντων αὐτῶν ἐκ τοῦ ὄρους ἐνετείλατο αὐτοῖς ὁ Ἰησοῦς λέγων, Μηδενὶ εἴπητε τὸ ὅραμα ἕως οὗ ὁ υἱὸς τοῦ ἀνθρώπου ἐκ νεκρῶν ἐγερθῇ. **10** καὶ ἐπηρώτησαν αὐτὸν οἱ μαθηταὶ

from the dead." **10**   The disciples asked   him,   "Why then do the teachers   of the law say   that
ἐκ   νεκρῶν   Καὶ οἱ   μαθηταὶ   ἐπηρώτησαν αὐτὸν λέγοντες τί   οὖν → οἱ γραμματεῖς ← ← ←   λέγουσιν ὅτι
p.g   a.gpm   cj d.npm n.npm   v.aai.3p   r.asm.3 pt.pa.npm r.asn cj   d.npm n.npm   v.pai.3p cj
1666   3738   2779 3836 3412   2089   899   3306   5515   4036   3306 1208   3306   4022

Elijah must come first?" **11**   Jesus replied,   "To be sure, Elijah comes and will restore   all   things. **12**But I
Ἠλίαν δεῖ ἐλθεῖν πρῶτον δὲ ὁ   ἀποκριθεὶς εἶπεν →   → μὲν Ἠλίας ἔρχεται καὶ → ἀποκαταστήσει πάντα ←   δὲ →
n.asm v.pai.3s f.aa adv   cj d.nsm pt.ap.nsm v.aai.3s   pl   n.nsm v.pmi.3s cj   v.fai.3s   a.apn   cj
2460 1256   4754 2262   1254 3836 646   3306   3525 2460 2262   2779   635   4246   1254

tell you,   Elijah has already come, and they did not recognize him, but have done   to him everything they
λέγω ὑμῖν ὅτι Ἠλίας → ἤδη   ἦλθεν καὶ   → οὐκ ἐπέγνωσαν αὐτὸν ἀλλὰ → ἐποίησαν ἐν αὐτῷ ὅσα   →
v.pai.1s r.dp.2 cj n.nsm   adv   v.aai.3s cj   adv v.aai.3p   r.asm.3 cj   v.aai.3p p.d r.dsm.3 r.apn
3306 7007 4022 2460   2453 2262 2779   4024 2105   899   247   4472   1877 899   4012

wished. In the same way   the Son of Man   is going to suffer at their hands." **13** Then the disciples
ἠθέλησαν → → οὕτως ←   καὶ ὁ υἱὸς τοῦ ἀνθρώπου   μέλλει → πάσχειν ὑπ' αὐτῶν   τότε οἱ μαθηταὶ
v.aai.3p   adv   adv d.nsm n.nsm d.gsm n.gsm   v.pai.3s   f.pa   p.g r.gpm.3   adv d.npm n.npm
2527   4048   2779 3836 5626 3836 476   3516   4248   5679 899   5538 3836 3412

understood that he was talking to them about John   the Baptist.
συνῆκαν ὅτι → εἶπεν → αὐτοῖς περὶ Ἰωάννου τοῦ βαπτιστοῦ
v.aai.3p cj   v.aai.3s r.dpm.3 p.g n.gsm   d.gsm n.gsm
5317   4022   3306   899   4309 2722   3836 969

The Healing of a Boy With a Demon

17:14 When they came to   the crowd, a man   approached Jesus and knelt   before him. **15** "Lord,
Καὶ →   → ἐλθόντων πρὸς τὸν ὄχλον ἄνθρωπος προσῆλθεν αὐτῷ   γονυπετῶν ←   αὐτὸν καὶ κύριε
cj   pt.aa.gpm p.a d.asm n.asm n.nsm   v.aai.3s   r.dsm.3 pt.pa.nsm   r.asm.3 cj n.vsm
2779   2262   4639 3836 4063   476   4665   899   1206   899   2779 3261

have mercy on my son,"   he said. "He has seizures   and is suffering greatly. He often   falls into the
→ ἐλέησον ← μου τὸν υἱόν   → λέγων ὅτι → σεληνιάζεται καὶ πάσχει κακῶς γὰρ → πολλάκις πίπτει εἰς τὸ
v.aam.2s r.gs.1 d.asm n.asm pt.pa.nsm cj   v.ppi.3s   cj v.pai.3s adv cj   adv   v.pai.3s p.a d.asn
1796   1609 3836 5626   3306 4022   4944   2779 4248 2809 1142   4406   4406   1650 3836

fire or   into the water. **16** I brought him to   your disciples, but they could   not heal   him."
πῦρ καὶ πολλάκις εἰς τὸ ὕδωρ καὶ → προσήνεγκα αὐτὸν τοῖς σου μαθηταῖς καὶ → ἠδυνήθησαν οὐκ θεραπεῦσαι αὐτὸν
n.asn cj adv   p.a d.asn n.asn cj   v.aai.1s   r.asm.3 d.dpm r.gs.2 n.dpm   cj   v.api.3p   adv f.aa   r.asm.3
4786 2779 4490   1650 3836 5623 2779   4712   899   3836 5148 3412   2779   1538   4024 2543   899

17 "O unbelieving and perverse   generation," Jesus   replied,   "how long shall I stay with you? How
δὲ ὦ ἄπιστος καὶ διεστραμμένη γενεὰ   ὁ Ἰησοῦς ἀποκριθεὶς εἶπεν ἕως πότε →   ἔσομαι μεθ' ὑμῶν ἕως
cj j a.vsf   cj pt.rp.vsf   n.vsf   d.nsm n.nsm pt.ap.nsm v.aai.3s p.g adv   v.fmi.1s p.g r.gp.2 p.g
1254 6043 603   2779 1406   1155   3836 2652 646   3306   2401 4537   1639   3552 7007 2401

long shall I put   up with you? Bring the boy here to me." **18** Jesus   rebuked the demon, and
πότε → ἀνέξομαι ← ὑμῶν φέρετε αὐτὸν ὧδε → μοι   καὶ ὁ Ἰησοῦς ἐπετίμησεν αὐτῷ καὶ
adv   v.fmi.1s   r.gp.2 v.pam.2p r.asm.3 adv r.ds.1   cj d.nsm n.nsm v.aai.3s   r.dsm.3 cj
4537   462   7007 5770   899   6045 1609   2779 3836 2652 2203   899   2779

it   came out of the boy, and he   was healed from that moment. **19** Then the disciples
τὸ δαιμόνιον ἐξῆλθεν ← ἀπ' αὐτοῦ καὶ ὁ παῖς → ἐθεραπεύθη ἀπὸ ἐκείνης τῆς ὥρας   Τότε οἱ μαθηταὶ
d.nsn n.nsn   v.aai.3s   p.g r.gsm.3 cj d.nsm n.nsm   v.api.3s p.g r.gsf   d.gsf n.gsf adv d.npm n.npm
3836 1228   2002   608 899   2779 3836 4090   2543   608 1697   3836 6052   5538 3836 3412

came   to Jesus   in private and asked, "Why couldn't   we drive   it out?" **20** He replied,
προσελθόντες ← τῷ Ἰησοῦ κατ' ἰδίαν   εἶπον διὰ τί οὐκ ἠδυνήθημεν ἡμεῖς ἐκβαλεῖν αὐτό ←   δὲ ὁ λέγει
pt.aa.npm   d.dsm n.dsm p.a r.asn   v.aai.3p p.a r.asn adv v.api.1p   r.np.1 f.aa   r.asn.3   cj d.nsm v.pai.3s
4665   3836 2652 2848 2625   3306 1328 5515 4024 1538   7005 1675 899   1254 3836 3306

"Because you have so little faith.   I tell you the truth, if you have faith as small as a
αὐτοῖς διὰ ὑμῶν → τὴν ὀλιγοπιστίαν γὰρ → λέγω ὑμῖν ἀμὴν ἐὰν → ἔχητε πίστιν ὡς
r.dpm.3 p.a r.gp.2   d.asf n.asf   cj   v.pai.1s r.dp.2 pl cj   v.pas.2p n.asf pl
899   1328 7007   3836 3898   1142 3306 7007 297 1569   2400   4411 6055

mustard seed, you can say to this mountain, 'Move from here to there' and it will move.   Nothing will be
σινάπεως κόκκον → ἐρεῖτε τούτῳ τῷ ὄρει μετάβα → ἔνθεν → ἐκεῖ καὶ → μεταβήσεται καὶ οὐδὲν →
n.gsn   n.asn   v.fai.2p r.dsn d.dsn n.dsn v.aam.2s   adv   adv cj   v.fmi.3s   cj a.nsn
4983   3133   3306   4001 4047 3836 4001 3553   1925   1695 2779   3553   2779 4029

λέγοντες, Τί οὖν οἱ γραμματεῖς λέγουσιν ὅτι Ἠλίαν δεῖ ἐλθεῖν πρῶτον; **11** ὁ δὲ ἀποκριθεὶς εἶπεν, Ἠλίας μὲν ἔρχεται καὶ
ἀποκαταστήσει πάντα· **12** λέγω δὲ ὑμῖν ὅτι Ἠλίας ἤδη ἦλθεν, καὶ οὐκ ἐπέγνωσαν αὐτὸν ἀλλὰ ἐποίησαν ἐν αὐτῷ ὅσα ἠθέλησαν·
οὕτως καὶ ὁ υἱὸς τοῦ ἀνθρώπου μέλλει πάσχειν ὑπ' αὐτῶν. **13** τότε συνῆκαν οἱ μαθηταὶ ὅτι περὶ Ἰωάννου τοῦ βαπτιστοῦ εἶπεν
αὐτοῖς.
  17:14 Καὶ ἐλθόντων πρὸς τὸν ὄχλον προσῆλθεν αὐτῷ ἄνθρωπος γονυπετῶν αὐτὸν **15** καὶ λέγων, Κύριε, ἐλέησόν μου τὸν υἱόν,
ὅτι σεληνιάζεται καὶ κακῶς πάσχει· πολλάκις γὰρ πίπτει εἰς τὸ πῦρ καὶ πολλάκις εἰς τὸ ὕδωρ. **16** καὶ προσήνεγκα αὐτὸν τοῖς
μαθηταῖς σου, καὶ οὐκ ἠδυνήθησαν αὐτὸν θεραπεῦσαι. **17** ἀποκριθεὶς δὲ ὁ Ἰησοῦς εἶπεν, Ὦ γενεὰ ἄπιστος καὶ διεστραμμένη,
ἕως πότε μεθ' ὑμῶν ἔσομαι; ἕως πότε ἀνέξομαι ὑμῶν; φέρετέ μοι αὐτὸν ὧδε. **18** καὶ ἐπετίμησεν αὐτῷ ὁ Ἰησοῦς καὶ ἐξῆλθεν ἀπ'
αὐτοῦ τὸ δαιμόνιον καὶ ἐθεραπεύθη ὁ παῖς ἀπὸ τῆς ὥρας ἐκείνης. **19** Τότε προσελθόντες οἱ μαθηταὶ τῷ Ἰησοῦ κατ' ἰδίαν εἶπον,
Διὰ τί ἡμεῖς οὐκ ἠδυνήθημεν ἐκβαλεῖν αὐτό; **20** ὁ δὲ λέγει αὐτοῖς, Διὰ τὴν ὀλιγοπιστίαν ὑμῶν· ἀμὴν γὰρ λέγω ὑμῖν, ἐὰν ἔχητε
πίστιν ὡς κόκκον σινάπεως, ἐρεῖτε τῷ ὄρει τούτῳ, Μετάβα ἔνθεν ἐκεῖ, καὶ μεταβήσεται· καὶ οὐδὲν ἀδυνατήσει ὑμῖν.

impossible for you." **22** When they came   together in Galilee,   he   said to them, "The Son of
ἀδυνατήσει → ὑμῖν   δὲ ⌐→ αὐτῶν Συστρεφομένων ←   ἐν ⌐τῇ Γαλιλαίᾳ ὁ Ἰησοῦς, εἶπεν → αὐτοῖς ὁ   υἱὸς
v.fai.3s   r.dp.2   cj   r.gpm.3   pt.pp.gpm   p.d d.dsf n.dsf   d.nsm n.nsm   v.aai.3s   r.dpm.3 d.nsm n.nsm
104   7007   1254 5370   899   5370   1877 3836 1133   3836 2652   3306   899 3836 5626

Man   is going to be betrayed   into the hands of men.   **23** They will kill   him, and on the third
⌐τοῦ ἀνθρώπου, → μέλλει → → παραδίδοσθαι εἰς   χεῖρας → ἀνθρώπων   καὶ →   → ἀποκτενοῦσιν αὐτόν καὶ →   τῇ   τρίτῃ
⌐d.gsm n.gsm   v.pai.3s   f.pp   p.a   n.apf → n.gpm   cj   v.fai.3p   r.asm.3 cj   d.dsf d.dsf
3836 476   3516   4140   1650   5931   476   2779   650   899   2779   3836 5569

day he will be raised   to life." And the disciples were filled with grief.
ἡμέρᾳ → → → ἐγερθήσεται   καὶ →   →   → ἐλυπήθησαν σφόδρα,
n.dsf   v.fpi.3s   cj   v.api.3p   adv
7465   1586   2779   3382   5379

The Temple Tax

17:24 After Jesus and his disciples arrived   in Capernaum, the collectors   of the two-drachma tax came   to
      δὲ   αὐτῶν ←   ←   ←   Ἐλθόντων εἰς Καφαρναοὺμ οἱ λαμβάνοντες τὰ δίδραχμα   προσῆλθον ←
      cj   r.gpm.3   pt.aa.gpm p.a n.asf   d.npm pt.pa.npm   d.apn n.apn   v.aai.3p
      1254 2262   899   2262   1650 3019   3836 3284   3836 1440   4665

Peter   and asked, "Doesn't your teacher   pay the *temple tax?*"   **25** "Yes, he does," he replied.   When
⌐τῷ Πέτρῳ, καὶ εἶπαν   οὐ   ὑμῶν ὁ διδάσκαλος, τελεῖ τὰ   δίδραχμα   ναί   → λέγει   καὶ →
d.dsm n.dsm   cj   v.aai.3p   pl   r.gp.2 d.nsm n.nsm   v.pai.3s d.apn   n.apn   pl   v.pai.3s   cj
3836 4377   2779 4024   7007   3836 1437   5464 3836   1440   3721   3306   2779

Peter came   into the house, Jesus   was the first to speak.   "What do you think, Simon?" he asked.
ἐλθόντα εἰς   τὴν οἰκίαν ὁ Ἰησοῦς, → → → προέφθασεν αὐτὸν τί   ⌐→ σοι δοκεῖ Σίμων   λέγων
pt.aa.asm p.a   d.asf n.asf d.nsm n.nsm   v.aai.3s   r.asm.3 r.nsn   r.ds.2 v.pai.3s n.vsm   pt.pa.nsm
2262   1650   3836 3864 3836 2652   4740   899   5515   1506 5148 1506 4981   3306

"From whom do the kings   of the earth collect   duty and taxes – from their own sons or from others?"
ἀπὸ   τίνων   ⌐→ οἱ βασιλεῖς → τῆς γῆς   λαμβάνουσιν τέλη ἢ   κῆνσον ἀπὸ   αὐτῶν τῶν υἱῶν ἢ   ἀπὸ   ⌐τῶν ἀλλοτρίων,
p.g   r.gpm   d.npm n.npm   d.gsf n.gsf   v.pai.3p   n.apn cj   n.asm   p.g   r.gpm.3 d.gpm n.gpm cj   p.g   d.gpm a.gpm
608   5515   3284 3836   995   3836 1178   3284   5465 2445   3056   608   899   3836 5626 2445 608   3836 259

26 "From others,"   Peter answered. "Then   the sons are   exempt," Jesus   said to him.   **27** "But so that we
δὲ   ἀπὸ   ⌐τῶν ἀλλοτρίων, εἰπόντος   ⌐ἄρα γε   οἱ υἱοί   εἰσιν ἐλεύθεροι ὁ   Ἰησοῦς, ἔφη →   αὐτῷ   δὲ   ἵνα
cj   p.g   d.gpm n.gpm   pt.aa.gsm   cj   pl   d.npm n.npm v.pai.3p a.npm   d.nsm n.nsm   v.iai.3s   r.dsm.3   cj   cj
1254 608   3836 259   3306   726 1145   3836 5626 1639 1801   3836 2652   5774   899   1254 2671   4997

may not offend   them, go   to the lake   and throw out your line.   Take   the first   fish you
⌐→ μὴ σκανδαλίσωμεν αὐτούς, πορευθεὶς εἰς   θάλασσαν   βάλε   ἄγκιστρον καὶ ἀναβάντα τὸν πρῶτον ἰχθὺν →
pl   v.aas.1p   r.apm.3 pt.ap.nsm p.a   n.asf   v.aam.2s   n.asn   cj   pt.aa.asm d.asm a.asm n.asm
4997 3590 4997   899   4513   1650   2498   965   45   2779 326   3836 4755 2716

catch;   open its   mouth   and you will find   a four-drachma coin. Take it   and give it to them for
ἆρον   καὶ ἀνοίξας αὐτοῦ ⌐τὸ στόμα, → → εὑρήσεις →   στατῆρα λαβὼν ἐκεῖνον   δὸς →   αὐτοῖς ἀντὶ
v.aam.2s   cj   pt.aa.nsm r.gsm.3 d.asn n.asn   v.fai.2s   n.asm pt.aa.nsm r.asm   v.aam.2s   r.dpm.3 p.g
149   2779 487   899   3836 5125   2351   5088   3284   1697   1443   899   505

my tax and yours."
ἐμοῦ   καὶ   σοῦ,
r.gs.1   cj   r.gs.2
1609   2779 5148

The Greatest in the Kingdom of Heaven

18:1 At that time   the disciples came   to Jesus   and asked,   "Who is   the greatest in   the
Ἐν ἐκείνῃ ⌐τῇ ὥρᾳ, οἱ μαθηταὶ προσῆλθον ← τῷ Ἰησοῦ, λέγοντες ἄρα τίς   ἐστιν μείζων ἐν τῇ
p.d r.dsf   d.dsf n.dsf d.npm n.npm   v.aai.3p   d.dsm n.dsm   pt.pa.npm cj   r.nsm   v.pai.3s a.nsm.c   p.d d.dsf
1877 1697   3836 6052 3836 3412   4665   3836 2652   3306   726 5515   1639   3489   1877 3836

kingdom of heaven?"   **2** He called   a little child   and had him stand   among   them.   **3** And he said: "I
βασιλεία → ⌐τῶν οὐρανῶν, καὶ   προσκαλεσάμενος → παιδίον   αὐτὸ ἔστησεν ἐν μέσῳ αὐτῶν   καὶ   εἶπεν
n.dsf   d.gpm n.gpm   cj   pt.am.nsm   n.asn   r.asn.3 v.aai.3s p.d n.dsn r.gpm.3   cj   v.aai.3s
993   3836 4041   2779   4673   4086   2705 899   2705 1877 3545 899   2779   3306

tell you the truth, unless   you change and become like little children,   you will never   enter   the kingdom
λέγω ὑμῖν   ἀμὴν ⌐ἐὰν μὴ, → στραφῆτε καὶ γένησθε ὡς → ⌐τὰ παιδία,   ⌐→ οὐ μὴ, εἰσέλθητε εἰς τὴν βασιλείαν
v.pai.1s r.dp.2   pl   cj   pl   v.aps.2p   cj   v.ams.2p   pl   d.npn n.npn   adv pl   v.aas.2p   p.a d.asf n.asf
3306 7007   297   1569 3590   5138   2779 1181   6055   3836 4086   4024 3590 1656   1650 3836 993

---

22 Συστρεφομένων δὲ αὐτῶν ἐν τῇ Γαλιλαίᾳ εἶπεν αὐτοῖς ὁ Ἰησοῦς, Μέλλει ὁ υἱὸς τοῦ ἀνθρώπου παραδίδοσθαι εἰς χεῖρας ἀνθρώπων, 23 καὶ ἀποκτενοῦσιν αὐτόν, καὶ τῇ τρίτῃ ἡμέρᾳ ἐγερθήσεται. καὶ ἐλυπήθησαν σφόδρα.

17:24 Ἐλθόντων δὲ αὐτῶν εἰς Καφαρναοὺμ προσῆλθον οἱ τὰ δίδραχμα λαμβάνοντες τῷ Πέτρῳ καὶ εἶπαν, Ὁ διδάσκαλος ὑμῶν οὐ τελεῖ [τὰ] δίδραχμα; 25 λέγει, Ναί. καὶ ἐλθόντα εἰς τὴν οἰκίαν προέφθασεν αὐτὸν ὁ Ἰησοῦς λέγων, Τί σοι δοκεῖ, Σίμων; οἱ βασιλεῖς τῆς γῆς ἀπὸ τίνων λαμβάνουσιν τέλη ἢ κῆνσον; ἀπὸ τῶν υἱῶν αὐτῶν ἢ ἀπὸ τῶν ἀλλοτρίων; 26 εἰπόντος δέ, Ἀπὸ τῶν ἀλλοτρίων, ἔφη αὐτῷ ὁ Ἰησοῦς, Ἄρα γε ἐλεύθεροί εἰσιν οἱ υἱοί. 27 ἵνα δὲ μὴ σκανδαλίσωμεν αὐτούς, πορευθεὶς εἰς τὴν θάλασσαν βάλε ἄγκιστρον καὶ τὸν ἀναβάντα πρῶτον ἰχθὺν ἆρον, καὶ ἀνοίξας τὸ στόμα αὐτοῦ εὑρήσεις στατῆρα· ἐκεῖνον λαβὼν δὸς αὐτοῖς ἀντὶ ἐμοῦ καὶ σοῦ.

18:1 Ἐν ἐκείνῃ τῇ ὥρᾳ προσῆλθον οἱ μαθηταὶ τῷ Ἰησοῦ λέγοντες, Τίς ἄρα μείζων ἐστὶν ἐν τῇ βασιλείᾳ τῶν οὐρανῶν; 2 καὶ προσκαλεσάμενος παιδίον ἔστησεν αὐτὸ ἐν μέσῳ αὐτῶν 3 καὶ εἶπεν, Ἀμὴν λέγω ὑμῖν, ἐὰν μὴ στραφῆτε καὶ γένησθε ὡς τὰ

of heaven. **4** Therefore, whoever humbles himself like this child is the greatest in the kingdom of
→ ⌐τῶν οὐρανῶν┐ οὖν ὅστις ταπεινώσει ἑαυτὸν ὡς τοῦτο ⌐τὸ παιδίον┐ οὗτος ἐστιν ὁ μείζων ἐν τῇ βασιλείᾳ →
d.gpm n.gpm cj r.nsm v.fai.3s r.asm.3 pl r.nsn d.nsn n.nsn r.nsm v.pai.3s d.nsm a.nsm.c p.d d.dsf n.dsf
3836 4041 4036 4015 5427 1571 6055 4047 3836 4086 4047 1639 3836 3489 1877 3836 993

heaven. **5** "And whoever welcomes a little child like this in my name welcomes me. **6** But if anyone
⌐τῶν οὐρανῶν┐ καὶ ὃς ἐὰν δέξηται ἓν → παιδίον → τοιοῦτο ἐπὶ μου ⌐τῷ ὀνόματι┐ δέχεται ἐμὲ δ᾽ ⌐Ὃς ἂν┐
d.gpm n.gpm cj r.nsm pl v.ams.3s a.asn n.asn r.asn p.d r.gs.1 d.dsn n.dsn v.pmi.3s r.as.1 cj r.nsm an
3836 4041 2779 4005 1569 1312 1651 4086 5525 2093 1609 3836 3950 1312 1609 1254 4005 323

causes one of these little ones who believe in me to sin, it would be better for him to have a
ἕνα → τούτων ⌐τῶν μικρῶν┐ τῶν πιστευόντων εἰς ἐμὲ σκανδαλίσῃ → → συμφέρει αὐτῷ ἵνα →
a.asm r.gpm d.gpm a.gpm d.gpm pt.pa.gpm p.a r.as.1 v.aas.3s v.pai.3s r.dsm.3 cj
4997 1651 3625 4047 3836 3625 3836 4409 1650 1609 4997 5237 899 2671 3203

large millstone hung around his neck and to be drowned in the depths of the sea. **7** "Woe to the
ὀνικὸς μύλος κρεμασθῇ περὶ αὐτοῦ ⌐τὸν τράχηλον┐ καὶ → καταποντισθῇ ἐν τῷ πελάγει → τῆς θαλάσσης Οὐαὶ → τῷ
a.nsm n.nsm v.aps.3s p.a r.gsm.3 d.asm n.asm cj v.aps.3s p.d d.dsn n.dsn d.gsf n.gsf j d.dsm
3948 3685 3203 4309 899 3836 5549 2779 2931 1877 3836 4283 3836 2498 4026 3836

world because of the things that cause people to sin! Such things must come, but woe to the
κόσμῳ ἀπὸ ← τῶν ← → σκανδάλων γὰρ ⌐τὰ σκάνδαλα┐ ἀνάγκη ἐλθεῖν πλὴν οὐαὶ → τῷ
n.dsm p.g d.gpn n.gpn cj d.apn n.apn n.nsf f.aa cj j d.dsm
3180 608 3836 4998 1142 3836 4998 340 2262 4440 4026 3836

man through whom they come! **8** If your hand or your foot causes you to sin cut
ἀνθρώπῳ δι᾽ οὗ ⌐τὸ σκάνδαλον┐ ἔρχεται δὲ Εἰ σου ⌐ἡ χείρ┐ ἢ σου ⌐ὁ πούς┐ → σε → σκανδαλίζει ἔκκοψον
n.dsm p.g r.gsm d.nsn n.nsn v.pmi.3s cj cj r.gs.2 d.nsf n.nsf cj r.gs.2 d.nsm n.nsm r.as.2 v.pai.3s v.aam.2s
476 1328 4005 3836 4998 2262 1254 1623 5148 3836 5931 2445 5148 3836 4546 4997 5148 4997 1716

it off and throw it away. It is better for you to enter life maimed or crippled than to have two
αὐτὸν ← καὶ βάλε ⌐ἀπὸ σοῦ┐ ἐστιν καλόν → σοί → εἰσελθεῖν εἰς ⌐τὴν ζωήν┐ κυλλὸν ἢ χωλὸν ἢ → ἔχοντα δύο
r.asm.3 cj v.aam.2s p.g r.gs.2 v.pai.3s a.nsn r.ds.2 f.aa p.a d.asf n.asf a.asm cj a.asm pl pt.pa.asm a.apf
899 1716 2779 965 608 5148 1639 2819 5148 1656 1650 3836 2437 3245 2445 6000 2445 2400 1545

hands or two feet and be thrown into eternal fire. **9** And if your eye causes you to sin,
χεῖρας ἢ δύο πόδας → βληθῆναι εἰς ⌐τὸ αἰώνιον┐ ⌐τὸ πῦρ┐ καὶ εἰ σου ⌐ὁ ὀφθαλμός┐ σε → σκανδαλίζει
n.apf cj a.apm n.apm f.ap p.a d.asn a.asn d.asn n.asn cj cj r.gs.2 d.nsm n.nsm r.as.2 v.pai.3s
5931 2445 1545 4546 965 1650 3836 173 3836 4786 2779 1623 5148 3836 4057 4997 5148 4997

gouge it out and throw it away. It is better for you to enter life with one eye than to
ἔξελε αὐτὸν καὶ βάλε ⌐ἀπὸ σοῦ┐ ἐστιν καλόν → σοί → εἰσελθεῖν εἰς ⌐τὴν ζωήν┐ → μονόφθαλμον ἢ →
v.aam.2s r.asm.3 cj v.aam.2s p.g r.gs.2 v.pai.3s a.nsn r.ds.2 f.aa p.a d.asf n.asf a.asn pl
1975 899 1975 2779 965 608 5148 1639 2819 5148 1656 1650 3836 2437 3669 2445

have two eyes and be thrown into the fire of hell.
ἔχοντα δύο ὀφθαλμοὺς → βληθῆναι εἰς τοῦ πυρὸς ⌐τὴν γέενναν┐
pt.pa.asm a.apm n.apm f.ap p.a d.gsn n.gsn d.asf n.asf
2400 1545 4057 965 1650 3836 4786 3836 1147

The Parable of the Lost Sheep

18:10 "See that you do not look down on one of these little ones. For I tell you that their
Ὁρᾶτε → μὴ καταφρονήσητε ← ← ἑνὸς → τούτων ⌐τῶν μικρῶν┐ γὰρ → λέγω ὑμῖν ὅτι αὐτῶν
v.pam.2p cj v.aas.2p a.gsm r.gpm d.gpm a.gpm cj v.pai.1s r.dp.2 cj r.gpm.3
3972 2969 2969 2969 1651 3625 4047 3836 3625 1142 3306 7007 4022 899

angels in heaven always see the face of my Father in heaven. **12** "What do you think? If
⌐οἱ ἄγγελοι┐ ἐν οὐρανοῖς ⌐διὰ παντὸς┐ βλέπουσι τὸ πρόσωπον → μου ⌐τοῦ πατρός┐ τοῦ ἐν οὐρανοῖς Τί → ὑμῖν δοκεῖ ἐὰν
d.npm n.npm p.d n.dpm p.g a.gsm v.pai.3p d.asn n.asn r.gs.1 d.gsm n.gsm d.gsm p.d n.dpm r.nsn r.dp.2 v.pai.3s cj
3836 34 1877 4041 1328 4246 1063 3836 4725 1609 3836 4252 3836 1877 4041 5515 7007 1506 1569

a man owns a hundred sheep, and one of them wanders away, will he not leave the ninety-nine on
τινι ἀνθρώπῳ γένηται ἑκατὸν πρόβατα καὶ ἓν ἐξ αὐτῶν πλανηθῇ ← → οὐχὶ ἀφήσει τὰ ⌐ἐνενήκοντα ἐννέα┐ ἐπὶ
r.dsm n.dsm v.ams.3s a.npn n.npn cj a.nsn p.g r.gpn.3 v.aps.3s pl v.fai.3s d.apn a.apn a.apn p.a
5516 476 1181 1669 4585 2779 1651 1666 899 4414 918 918 4049 918 3836 1916 1933 2093

the hills and go to look for the one that wandered off? **13** And if he finds it, I tell you the truth,
τὰ ὄρη καὶ πορευθεὶς → ζητεῖ τὸ ← ← πλανώμενον καὶ ἐὰν γένηται εὑρεῖν αὐτό → λέγω ὑμῖν ἀμὴν ὅτι
d.apn n.apn cj pt.ap.nsm v.pai.3s d.asn pt.pp.asn cj cj v.ams.3s f.aa r.asn.3 v.pai.1s r.dp.2 j cj
3836 4001 2779 4513 2426 3836 4414 2779 1569 1181 2351 899 3306 7007 297 4022

παιδία, οὐ μὴ εἰσέλθητε εἰς τὴν βασιλείαν τῶν οὐρανῶν. **4** ὅστις οὖν ταπεινώσει ἑαυτὸν ὡς τὸ παιδίον τοῦτο, οὗτός ἐστιν ὁ μείζων ἐν τῇ βασιλείᾳ τῶν οὐρανῶν. **5** καὶ ὃς ἐὰν δέξηται ἓν παιδίον τοιοῦτο ἐπὶ τῷ ὀνόματί μου, ἐμὲ δέχεται. **6** Ὃς δ᾽ ἂν σκανδαλίσῃ ἕνα τῶν μικρῶν τούτων τῶν πιστευόντων εἰς ἐμέ, συμφέρει αὐτῷ ἵνα κρεμασθῇ μύλος ὀνικὸς περὶ τὸν τράχηλον αὐτοῦ καὶ καταποντισθῇ ἐν τῷ πελάγει τῆς θαλάσσης. **7** οὐαὶ τῷ κόσμῳ ἀπὸ τῶν σκανδάλων· ἀνάγκη γὰρ ἐλθεῖν τὰ σκάνδαλα, πλὴν οὐαὶ τῷ ἀνθρώπῳ δι᾽ οὗ τὸ σκάνδαλον ἔρχεται. **8** Εἰ δὲ ἡ χείρ σου ἢ ὁ πούς σου σκανδαλίζει σε, ἔκκοψον αὐτὸν καὶ βάλε ἀπὸ σοῦ· καλόν σοί ἐστιν εἰσελθεῖν εἰς τὴν ζωὴν κυλλὸν ἢ χωλὸν ἢ δύο χεῖρας ἢ δύο πόδας ἔχοντα βληθῆναι εἰς τὸ πῦρ τὸ αἰώνιον. **9** καὶ εἰ ὁ ὀφθαλμός σου σκανδαλίζει σε, ἔξελε αὐτὸν καὶ βάλε ἀπὸ σοῦ· καλόν σοί ἐστιν μονόφθαλμον εἰς τὴν ζωὴν εἰσελθεῖν ἢ δύο ὀφθαλμοὺς ἔχοντα βληθῆναι εἰς τὴν γέενναν τοῦ πυρός.

18:10 Ὁρᾶτε μὴ καταφρονήσητε ἑνὸς τῶν μικρῶν τούτων· λέγω γὰρ ὑμῖν ὅτι οἱ ἄγγελοι αὐτῶν ἐν οὐρανοῖς διὰ παντὸς βλέπουσι τὸ πρόσωπον τοῦ πατρός μου τοῦ ἐν οὐρανοῖς. **12** Τί ὑμῖν δοκεῖ; ἐὰν γένηταί τινι ἀνθρώπῳ ἑκατὸν πρόβατα καὶ πλανηθῇ ἓν ἐξ αὐτῶν, οὐχὶ ἀφήσει τὰ ἐνενήκοντα ἐννέα ἐπὶ τὰ ὄρη καὶ πορευθεὶς ζητεῖ τὸ πλανώμενον; **13** καὶ ἐὰν γένηται εὑρεῖν αὐτό, ἀμὴν

he is happier	about	that	one sheep	than	about	the	ninety-nine	that	did not	wander	off.	14 In the same
→ → χαίρει	ἐπ᾽	αὐτῷ	∟μᾶλλον ἢ	ἐπὶ	τοῖς	ἐνενήκοντα ἐννέα	τοῖς	→ μὴ	πεπλανημένοις ←	→ → →	οὕτως
v.pai.3s	p.d	r.dsn.3	adv.c pl	p.d	d.dpn	a.dpn	d.dpn	pl	pt.rp.dpn		adv
5897	2093	899	3437 2445	2093	3836	1916	3836	4414	3590 4414		4048

way		your Father		in heaven	is	not	willing that	any of	these	little	ones should be lost.
←	ἔμπροσθεν	ὑμῶν ∟τοῦ πατρὸς	τοῦ	ἐν οὐρανοῖς	ἔστιν οὐκ		θέλημα ἵνα	→	τούτων	∟τῶν μικρῶν	→ → ἀπόληται
	p.g	r.gp.2 d.gsm n.gsm	d.gsm	p.d n.dpm	v.pai.3s adv		n.nsn cj	a.nsn	r.gpn	d.gpn a.gpn	v.ams.3s
	1869	7007 3836 4252	3836	1877 4041	1639 4024		2525 2671	1651	3625	4047 3836 3625	660

A Brother Who Sins Against You

18:15
"If	your brother	sins	against you,	go	and show	him	his fault,	just	between the	two of
δὲ ∟Ἐὰν	σοι ὁ ἀδελφός	ἁμαρτήσῃ	εἰς	σὲ ὕπαγε	ἔλεγξον	αὐτὸν ←		μόνου	μεταξὺ
cj cj	r.gs.2 d.nsm n.nsm	v.aas.3s	p.a	p.a v.pam.2s	v.aam.2s	r.asm.3		a.gsm	p.g
1254 1569	5148 3836 81	279	1650	5148 5632	1794	899 1794 1794		3668	3568

you.		If	he listens to you,	you have won	your brother	over.	16 But if	he	will not	listen,	take
∟σοῦ	καὶ αὐτοῦ ∟ἐὰν	→ ἀκούσῃ	← σου	→ → ἐκέρδησας σου	∟τὸν ἀδελφόν ←		δὲ ἐὰν	→ →	μὴ	ἀκούσῃ	παράλαβε
r.gs.2	cj r.gsm.3 cj	v.aas.3s	r.gs.2	v.aai.2s r.gs.2	d.asm n.asm		cj cj		pl	v.aas.3s	v.aam.2s
5148	2779 899 1569	3045	5148	3045 5148	3836 81	3045	1254 1569	201 201	3590	201	4161

one or	two	others	along,	so that	'every	matter	may be	established	by	the testimony of	two	or	three witnesses.'
ἕνα ἢ	δύο	ἔτι	∟μετὰ σοῦ	∟ἵνα ←	πᾶν	ῥῆμα	→	σταθῇ	ἐπὶ	στόματος	→ δύο	ἢ	τριῶν μαρτύρων
a.asm cj	a.apm	adv	p.g r.gs.2	cj	a.nsn	n.nsn		v.aps.3s	p.g	n.gsn	a.gpm	cj	a.gpm n.gpm
1651 2445	1545	2285	3552 5148	2671	4246	4839		2705	2093	5125	1545	2445	5552 3459

17
If	he	refuses to listen		to them,	tell	it to the	church;	and if	he	refuses to listen	even	to the	church,
δὲ ἐὰν	→ →	→ παρακούσῃ	←	αὐτῶν	εἰπὲ	→ τῇ	ἐκκλησίᾳ	δὲ ἐὰν	→ →	→ παρακούσῃ	καὶ	← τῆς	ἐκκλησίας
cj cj		v.aas.3s		r.gpm.3	v.aam.2s	d.dsf	n.dsf	cj cj		v.aas.3s	adv	d.gsf	n.gsf
1254 1569		4159		899	3306	3836	1711	1254 1569		4159	2779	4159 3836	1711

treat	him as	you would a	pagan	or a	tax collector.	18 "I	tell	you the truth,	whatever	you bind	on	earth
ἔστω ←	ὥσπερ σοι		ὁ ἐθνικὸς	καὶ →	ὁ τελώνης	→ λέγω	ὑμῖν	Ἀμήν	∟ὅσα ἐὰν	→ δήσητε	ἐπὶ	∟τῆς γῆς
v.pam.3s	pl r.ds.2		d.nsm n.nsm	cj	d.nsm n.nsm	v.pai.1s	r.dp.2	pl	r.apn cj	v.aas.2p	p.g	d.gsf n.gsf
1639	6061 5148		3836 1618	2779	3836 5467	3306	7007	297	4012 1569	1313	2093	3836 1178

will be bound	in	heaven,	and	whatever	you loose	on	earth	will be loosed	in	heaven.	19 "Again, I	tell	you
ἔσται → δεδεμένα	ἐν	οὐρανῷ	καὶ	∟ὅσα ἐὰν	→ λύσητε	ἐπὶ	∟τῆς γῆς	ἔσται → λελυμένα	ἐν	οὐρανῷ	Πάλιν	→ λέγω	ὑμῖν
v.fmi.3s pt.rp.npn	p.d	n.dsm	cj	r.apn pl	v.aas.2p	p.g	d.gsf n.gsf	v.fmi.3s pt.rp.npn	p.d	n.dsm	adv	v.pai.1s	r.dp.2
1639 1313	1877	4041	2779	4012 1569	3395	2093	3836 1178	1639 3395	1877	4041	4099	3306	7007

	that if	two of	you	on	earth	agree	about	anything		you ask	for, it will be
[ἀμὴν]	ὅτι ἐὰν	δύο ἐξ	ὑμῶν	ἐπὶ	∟τῆς γῆς	συμφωνήσωσιν	περὶ	∟παντὸς πράγματος	οὗ ἐὰν	αἰτήσωνται ←	→ → →
pl	cj cj	a.npm p.g	r.gp.2	p.g	d.gsf n.gsf	v.aas.3p	p.g	a.gsn n.gsn	r.gsn pl	v.ams.3p	
297	4022 1569	1545 1666	7007	2093	3836 1178	5244	4309	4246 4547	4005 1569	160	

done	for you	by	my Father		in heaven.	20 For	where	two	or	three	come	together	in	my
γενήσεται	→ αὐτοῖς	παρὰ	μου ∟τοῦ πατρός	τοῦ	ἐν οὐρανοῖς	γὰρ	οὗ	δύο	ἢ	τρεῖς	∟εἰσιν	συνηγμένοι	εἰς	ἐμὸν
v.fmi.3s	r.dpm.3	p.g	r.gs.1 d.gsm n.gsm	d.gsm	p.d n.dpm	cj	adv	a.npm	cj	a.npm	v.pai.3p	pt.rp.npm	p.a	r.asn.1
1181	899	4123	1609 3836 4252	3836	1877 4041	1142	4023	1545	2445	5552	1639	5251	1650	1847

name,	there	am	I	with	them."
∟τὸ ὄνομα	ἐκεῖ	εἰμι	←	ἐν μέσῳ	αὐτῶν
d.asn n.asn	adv	v.pai.1s		p.d n.dsn	r.gpm.3
3836 3950	1695	1639		1877 3545	899

The Parable of the Unmerciful Servant

18:21
Then	Peter	came	to	Jesus and asked,	"Lord,	how	many times shall I	forgive		my
Τότε	∟ὁ Πέτρος	προσελθὼν ←		εἶπεν αὐτῷ	κύριε	ποσάκις ←	← →	ἀφήσω	αὐτῷ	μου
adv	d.nsm n.nsm	pt.aa.nsm		v.aai.3s r.dsm.3	n.vsm	adv		v.fai.1s	r.dsm.3	r.gs.1
5538	3836 4377	4665		3306 899	3261	4529		918	899	1609

brother	when	he sins	against	me?	Up to	seven	times?"	22 Jesus		answered,	"I	tell	you,	not		seven
ὁ ἀδελφός	καὶ	→ ἁμαρτήσει	εἰς	ἐμὲ	ἕως ←	ἑπτάκις ←		∟ὁ Ἰησοῦς	λέγει		αὐτῷ	→ λέγω	σοι	οὐ	ἕως	ἑπτάκις
d.nsm n.nsm	cj	v.fai.3s	p.a	r.as.1	p.g	adv		d.nsm n.nsm	v.pai.3s		r.dsm.3	v.pai.1s	r.ds.2	adv	p.g	adv
3836 81	2779	279	1650	1609	2401	2232		3836 2652	3306		899	3306	5148	4024	2401	2232

λέγω ὑμῖν ὅτι χαίρει ἐπ᾽ αὐτῷ μᾶλλον ἢ ἐπὶ τοῖς ἐνενήκοντα ἐννέα τοῖς μὴ πεπλανημένοις. 14 οὕτως οὐκ ἔστιν θέλημα ἔμπροσθεν τοῦ πατρὸς ὑμῶν τοῦ ἐν οὐρανοῖς ἵνα ἀπόληται ἓν τῶν μικρῶν τούτων.

18:15 Ἐὰν δὲ ἁμαρτήσῃ [εἰς σὲ] ὁ ἀδελφός σου, ὕπαγε ἔλεγξον αὐτὸν μεταξὺ σοῦ καὶ αὐτοῦ μόνου. ἐάν σου ἀκούσῃ, ἐκέρδησας τὸν ἀδελφόν σου· 16 ἐὰν δὲ μὴ ἀκούσῃ, παράλαβε μετὰ σοῦ ἔτι ἕνα ἢ δύο, ἵνα ἐπὶ στόματος δύο μαρτύρων ἢ τριῶν σταθῇ πᾶν ῥῆμα· 17 ἐὰν δὲ παρακούσῃ αὐτῶν, εἰπὲ τῇ ἐκκλησίᾳ· ἐὰν δὲ καὶ τῆς ἐκκλησίας παρακούσῃ, ἔστω σοι ὥσπερ ὁ ἐθνικὸς καὶ ὁ τελώνης. 18 Ἀμὴν λέγω ὑμῖν· ὅσα ἐὰν δήσητε ἐπὶ τῆς γῆς ἔσται δεδεμένα ἐν οὐρανῷ, καὶ ὅσα ἐὰν λύσητε ἐπὶ τῆς γῆς ἔσται λελυμένα ἐν οὐρανῷ. 19 Πάλιν [ἀμὴν] λέγω ὑμῖν ὅτι ἐὰν δύο συμφωνήσωσιν ἐξ ὑμῶν ἐπὶ τῆς γῆς περὶ παντὸς πράγματος οὗ ἐὰν αἰτήσωνται, γενήσεται αὐτοῖς παρὰ τοῦ πατρός μου τοῦ ἐν οὐρανοῖς. 20 οὗ γάρ εἰσιν δύο ἢ τρεῖς συνηγμένοι εἰς τὸ ἐμὸν ὄνομα, ἐκεῖ εἰμι ἐν μέσῳ αὐτῶν.

18:21 Τότε προσελθὼν ὁ Πέτρος εἶπεν αὐτῷ, Κύριε, ποσάκις ἁμαρτήσει εἰς ἐμὲ ὁ ἀδελφός μου καὶ ἀφήσω αὐτῷ; ἕως ἑπτάκις; 22 λέγει αὐτῷ ὁ Ἰησοῦς, Οὐ λέγω σοι ἕως ἑπτάκις ἀλλὰ ἕως ἑβδομηκοντάκις ἑπτά. 23 Διὰ τοῦτο ὡμοιώθη ἡ βασιλεία τῶν

times, but   seventy-seven   times. 23 "Therefore,   the kingdom of heaven   is like a   king who
← ἀλλὰ ἕως ⌐ἑβδομηκοντάκις ἑπτά⌐ ← ⌐Διὰ τοῦτο⌐ ἡ βασιλεία → ⌐τῶν οὐρανῶν⌐ → ὡμοιώθη ἀνθρώπῳ βασιλεῖ ὃς
   cj   p.g   adv   a.apn   p.a   r.asn   d.nsf n.nsf   d.gpm n.gpm   v.api.3s   n.dsm   n.dsm   r.nsm
   247   2401 1574   2231   1328 4047   3836 993   3836 4041   3929   476   995   4005

wanted to settle accounts with his servants. 24 As he began the settlement, a man who owed   him ten
ἠθέλησεν → συνᾶραι λόγον μετὰ αὐτοῦ ⌐τῶν δούλων⌐ δὲ → αὐτοῦ ἀρξαμένου συναίρειν εἰς ὀφειλέτης
v.aai.3s   f.aa   n.asm   p.g   r.gsm.3 d.gpm n.gpm   cj   r.gsm.3 pt.am.gsm   f.pa   a.nsm   n.nsm
2527   5256   3364   3552 899   3836 1529   1254 806   899   806   5256   1651   4050

thousand talents was brought to him. 25 Since he was not able to pay, the master ordered that he
μυρίων ταλάντων → προσηνέχθη → αὐτῷ δὲ → αὐτοῦ → μὴ ἔχοντος ἀποδοῦναι ὁ κύριος ἐκέλευσεν αὐτὸν
a.gpn   n.gpn   v.api.3s   r.dsm.3 cj   r.gsm.3   pl   pt.pa.gsm f.aa   d.nsm n.nsm v.aai.3s   r.asm.3
3692   5419   4712   899   1254 2400 899   2400 3590 2400   625   3836 3261 3027   899

and his wife   and his children and all   that he had be sold   to repay   the debt. 26 "The servant
καὶ τὴν γυναῖκα καὶ τὰ τέκνα καὶ πάντα ὅσα → ἔχει → πραθῆναι καὶ → ἀποδοθῆναι οὖν ὁ δοῦλος
cj   d.asf n.asf   cj d.apn n.apn cj   a.apn r.apn   v.pai.3s   f.ap   cj   f.ap   cj   d.nsm n.nsm
2779 3836 1222   2779 3836 5451 2779 4246 4012   2400   4405   2779   625   4036 3836 1529

fell on his knees   before him. 'Be patient   with me,' he begged, 'and I will pay back everything.'
πεσὼν → προσεκύνει → αὐτῷ → μακροθύμησον ἐπ' ἐμοί → λέγων καὶ → ἀποδώσω ← πάντα
pt.aa.nsm   v.iai.3s   r.dsm.3   v.aam.2s   p.d r.ds.1 pt.pa.nsm cj   v.fai.1s   a.apn
4406   4686   899   3428   2093 1609 3306   2779   625   4246

27 The servant's master took pity   on him, canceled   the debt and let   him go. 28 "But
σοι δὲ ὁ ⌐τοῦ δούλου⌐ κύριος → σπλαγχνισθεὶς ← ἐκείνου ἀφῆκεν αὐτῷ τὸ δάνειον καὶ ἀπέλυσεν αὐτὸν ↵ δὲ
r.ds.2 cj d.nsm d.gsm n.gsm   n.nsm   pt.ap.nsm   r.gsm   v.aai.3s r.dsm.3 d.asn n.asn cj   v.aai.3s r.asm.3   cj
5148 1254 3836 3836 1529   3261   5072   1697   918   899   3836 1245 2779 668   899   668   1254

when that servant   went out, he found one of his   fellow servants   who owed him a hundred denarii.
→ ἐκεῖνος ὁ ⌐δοῦλος⌐ ἐξελθὼν ← εὗρεν ἕνα → αὐτοῦ ⌐τῶν συνδούλων⌐ ὃς ὤφειλεν αὐτῷ ἑκατὸν δηνάρια
   r.nsm   d.nsm n.nsm   pt.aa.nsm   v.aai.3s a.asm   r.gsm.3   d.gpm n.gpm   r.nsm v.iai.3s r.dsm.3 a.apn   n.apn
2002   1697 3836 1529   2002   2351   1651 5281 899   3836 5281   4005 4053   899   1669   1324

He grabbed him and began to choke him. 'Pay back   what you owe me!' he demanded. 29 "His fellow
καὶ → κρατήσας αὐτὸν → → ἔπνιγεν ἀπόδος ← εἴ τι → ὀφείλεις → λέγων οὖν αὐτοῦ →
cj   pt.aa.nsm r.asm.3   v.iai.3s v.aam.2s   cj r.asn   v.pai.2s   pt.pa.nsm   cj   r.gsm.3
2779   3195   899   4464   625   1623 5516   4053   3306   4036 899

servant   fell   to his knees and begged him,   'Be patient   with me, and I will pay you back.'
ὁ σύνδουλος πεσὼν → παρεκάλει αὐτὸν λέγων → μακροθύμησον ἐπ' ἐμοί καὶ → → ἀποδώσω σοι ↵
d.nsm n.nsm   pt.aa.nsm   v.iai.3s r.asm.3 pt.pa.nsm   v.aam.2s   p.d r.ds.1 cj   v.fai.1s r.ds.2
3836 5281   4406   4151   899   3306   3428   2093 1609 2779   625   5148 625

30 "But he refused.   Instead, he went off and had the man thrown into prison until he could pay the
δὲ ὁ ⌐οὐκ ἤθελεν⌐ ἀλλὰ → ἀπελθὼν ← → αὐτὸν ἔβαλεν εἰς φυλακὴν ἕως → → ἀποδῷ τὸ
cj d.nsm adv v.iai.3s cj   pt.aa.nsm   r.asm.3 v.aai.3s p.a n.asf   cj   v.aas.3s d.asn
1254 3836 4024 2527   247   599   965   899   965   1650 5871   2401   625   3836

debt. 31 When the other servants   saw what had happened, they were greatly distressed and went
ὀφειλόμενον οὖν → οἱ → σύνδουλοι αὐτοῦ ἰδόντες τὰ → γενόμενα → → σφόδρα ἐλυπήθησαν καὶ ἐλθόντες
pt.pp.asn   cj   d.npm   n.npm   r.gsm.3 pt.aa.npm d.apn   pt.am.apn   adv   v.api.3p   cj   pt.aa.npm
4053   4036 1625   3836   5281   899   1625   3836   1181   3382 3382 5379   3382   2779 2262

and told   their master everything that had happened. 32 "Then the master   called   the servant in.
διεσάφησαν ἑαυτῶν ⌐τῷ κυρίῳ⌐ πάντα τὰ → γενόμενα τότε ὁ κύριος αὐτοῦ προσκαλεσάμενος αὐτὸν ↵
v.aai.3p   r.gpm.3 d.dsm n.dsm a.apn d.apn   pt.am.apn   adv d.nsm n.nsm r.gsm.3 pt.am.nsm   r.asm.3
1397   1571   3836 3261 4246 3836   1181   5538 3836 3261 899   4673   899   4673

'You wicked servant,' he said,   'I canceled all   that debt   of yours because you begged me to.
→ πονηρέ δοῦλε → λέγει αὐτῷ → ἀφῆκα πᾶσαν ἐκείνην ⌐τὴν ὀφειλὴν⌐ σοι ἐπεὶ → παρεκάλεσας με
  a.vsm   n.vsm   v.pai.3s r.dsm.3 v.aai.1s a.asf   r.asf   d.asf n.asf   r.ds.2 cj   v.aai.2s   r.as.1
4505   1529   3306 899   918   4246   1697   3836 4051   5148 2075   4151   1609

33 Shouldn't   you   have had mercy on your fellow servant   just as I had   on you?' 34 In anger his
⌐οὐκ ἔδει⌐ σὲ καὶ → ἐλεῆσαι ← σου → ⌐τὸν σύνδουλον⌐ ὡς κἀγὼ ἠλέησα ← σὲ καὶ → ὀργισθεὶς αὐτοῦ
pl   v.iai.3s r.as.2 adv   f.aa   r.gs.2   d.asm n.asm   ὡς crasis v.aai.1s r.as.2 cj   pt.ap.nsm r.gsm.3
4024 1256   5148 2779   1796   5148   3836 5281   2743 6055 2743 1796   5148 2779 3974   899

οὐρανῶν ἀνθρώπῳ βασιλεῖ, ὃς ἠθέλησεν συνᾶραι λόγον μετὰ τῶν δούλων αὐτοῦ. 24 ἀρξαμένου δὲ αὐτοῦ συναίρειν προσηνέχθη αὐτῷ εἷς ὀφειλέτης μυρίων ταλάντων. 25 μὴ ἔχοντος δὲ αὐτοῦ ἀποδοῦναι ἐκέλευσεν αὐτὸν ὁ κύριος πραθῆναι καὶ τὴν γυναῖκα καὶ τὰ τέκνα καὶ πάντα ὅσα ἔχει, καὶ ἀποδοθῆναι. 26 πεσὼν οὖν ὁ δοῦλος προσεκύνει αὐτῷ λέγων, Μακροθύμησον ἐπ' ἐμοί, καὶ πάντα ἀποδώσω σοι. 27 σπλαγχνισθεὶς δὲ ὁ κύριος τοῦ δούλου ἐκείνου ἀπέλυσεν αὐτὸν καὶ τὸ δάνειον ἀφῆκεν αὐτῷ. 28 ἐξελθὼν δὲ ὁ δοῦλος ἐκεῖνος εὗρεν ἕνα τῶν συνδούλων αὐτοῦ, ὃς ὤφειλεν αὐτῷ ἑκατὸν δηνάρια, καὶ κρατήσας αὐτὸν ἔπνιγεν λέγων, Ἀπόδος εἴ τι ὀφείλεις. 29 πεσὼν οὖν ὁ σύνδουλος αὐτοῦ παρεκάλει αὐτὸν λέγων, Μακροθύμησον ἐπ' ἐμοί, καὶ ἀποδώσω σοι. 30 ὁ δὲ οὐκ ἤθελεν ἀλλὰ ἀπελθὼν ἔβαλεν αὐτὸν εἰς φυλακὴν ἕως ἀποδῷ τὸ ὀφειλόμενον. 31 ἰδόντες οὖν οἱ σύνδουλοι αὐτοῦ τὰ γενόμενα ἐλυπήθησαν σφόδρα καὶ ἐλθόντες διεσάφησαν τῷ κυρίῳ ἑαυτῶν πάντα τὰ γενόμενα. 32 τότε προσκαλεσάμενος αὐτὸν ὁ κύριος αὐτοῦ λέγει αὐτῷ, Δοῦλε πονηρέ, πᾶσαν τὴν ὀφειλὴν ἐκείνην ἀφῆκά σοι, ἐπεὶ παρεκάλεσάς με· 33 οὐκ ἔδει καὶ σὲ ἐλεῆσαι τὸν σύνδουλόν σου, ὡς κἀγὼ σὲ ἠλέησα; 34 καὶ ὀργισθεὶς ὁ κύριος αὐτοῦ παρέδωκεν αὐτὸν τοῖς βασανισταῖς ἕως οὗ

master turned him over to the jailers to be tortured, until he should pay back all he
ὁ κύριος παρέδωκεν αὐτὸν ← → τοῖς βασανισταῖς ← ← ← ἕως οὗ → → ἀποδῷ ← πᾶν
d.nsm n.nsm v.aai.3s r.asm.3 d.dpm n.dpm p.g r.gsn v.aas.3s a.asn
3836 3261 4140 899 4140 3836 991 2401 4005 625 4246

owed. **35** "This is how my heavenly Father will treat each of you unless you forgive your
ιτὸ ὀφειλόμενον, οὕτως ← ← καὶ μου ὁ οὐράνιος, ὁ πατήρ → ποιήσει ἕκαστος → ὑμῖν ἐὰν μὴ → ἀφῆτε αὐτοῦ
d.asn pt.pp.asn adv adv r.gs.1 d.nsm a.nsm d.nsm n.nsm v.fai.3s r.nsm r.dp.2 cj pl v.aas.2p r.gsm.3
3836 4053 4048 2779 1609 3836 4039 3836 4252 4472 1667 7007 1569 3590 918 899

brother from your heart."
ιτῷ ἀδελφῷ, ἀπὸ ὑμῶν ιτῶν καρδιῶν,
d.dsm n.dsm p.g r.gp.2 d.gpf n.gpf
3836 81 608 7007 3836 2840

Divorce

19:1 When Jesus had finished saying these things, he left Galilee and went
Καὶ ἐγένετο ὅτε ὁ Ἰησοῦς → ἐτέλεσεν ιτοὺς λόγους, τούτους ← → μετῆρεν ἀπὸ ιτῆς Γαλιλαίας, καὶ ἦλθεν
cj v.ami.3s cj d.nsm n.nsm v.aai.3s d.apm n.apm r.apm v.aai.3s p.g d.gsf n.gsf cj v.aai.3s
2779 1181 4021 3836 2652 5464 3836 3364 4047 3558 608 3836 1133 2779 2262

into the region of Judea to the other side of the Jordan. **2** Large crowds followed him, and he healed
εἰς τὰ ὅρια → ιτῆς Ἰουδαίας, → πέραν ← τοῦ Ἰορδάνου καὶ πολλοί ὄχλοι ἠκολούθησαν αὐτῷ καὶ → ἐθεράπευσεν
p.a d.apn n.apn d.gsf n.gsf p.g d.gsm n.gsm cj a.npm n.npm v.aai.3p r.dsm.3 cj v.aai.3s
1650 3836 3990 3836 2677 4305 3836 2674 2779 4498 4063 199 899 2779 2543

them there. ¶ **3** Some Pharisees came to him to test him. They asked, "Is it lawful for a
αὐτοὺς ἐκεῖ Καὶ Φαρισαῖοι προσῆλθον ← αὐτῷ → πειράζοντες αὐτὸν καὶ → λέγοντες εἰ → ἔξεστιν →
r.apm.3 adv cj n.npm v.aai.3p r.dsm.3 pt.pa.npm r.asm.3 cj pt.pa.npm cj v.pai.3s
899 1695 2779 5757 4665 899 4279 899 2779 3306 1623 1997

man to divorce his wife for any and every reason?" **4** "Haven't you read," he replied, "that
ἀνθρώπῳ → ἀπολῦσαι αὐτοῦ ιτὴν γυναῖκα, κατὰ → πᾶσαν αἰτίαν δὲ οὐκ → ἀνέγνωτε ὁ ἀποκριθεὶς εἶπεν ὅτι
n.dsm f.aa r.gsm.3 d.asf n.asf p.a a.asf n.asf cj pl v.aai.2p d.nsm pt.ap.nsm v.aai.3s cj
476 668 899 3836 1222 2848 4246 162 1254 4024 336 3836 646 3306 4022

at the beginning the Creator 'made them male and female,' **5** and said, 'For this reason a man will leave
ἀπ' ἀρχῆς ὁ κτίσας ἐποίησεν αὐτοὺς ἄρσεν καὶ θῆλυ καὶ εἶπεν ἕνεκα τούτου ἄνθρωπος → καταλείψει
p.g n.gsf d.nsm pt.aa.nsm v.aai.3s r.apm.3 a.asn cj a.asn cj v.aai.3s p.g r.gsn n.nsm v.fai.3s
608 794 3836 3231 4472 899 781 2779 2559 2779 3306 1914 4047 476 2901

his father and mother and be united to his wife, and the two will become one flesh'? **6** So they
τὸν πατέρα καὶ ιτὴν μητέρα, καὶ → κολληθήσεται → αὐτοῦ ιτῇ γυναικὶ, καὶ οἱ δύο → ἔσονται εἰς μίαν σάρκα ὥστε →
d.asm n.asm cj d.asf n.asf cj v.fpi.3s r.gsm.3 d.dsf n.dsf cj d.npm a.npm v.fmi.3p p.a a.asf n.asf cj
3836 4252 2779 3836 3613 2779 3140 1222 3836 1222 2779 3836 1545 1639 1650 1651 4922 6063

are no longer two, but one. Therefore what God has joined together, let man not separate." ¶
εἰσὶν οὐκέτι ← δύο ἀλλὰ μία σὰρξ οὖν ὃ ιὁ θεὸς, → συνέζευξεν → ἄνθρωπος μὴ χωριζέτω
v.pai.3p adv a.npm cj a.nsf n.nsf cj r.asn d.nsm n.nsm v.aai.3s n.nsm pl v.pam.3s
1639 4033 1545 247 1651 4922 4036 4005 3836 2536 5183 6004 476 3590 6004

7 "Why then," they asked, "did Moses command that a man give his wife a certificate of divorce and
τί οὖν → λέγουσιν αὐτῷ Μωϋσῆς ἐνετείλατο δοῦναι βιβλίον → ἀποστασίου καὶ
r.asn cj v.pai.3p r.dsm.3 n.nsm v.ami.3s f.aa n.asn n.gsn cj
5515 4036 3306 899 1948 3707 1948 1443 1046 687 2779

send her away?" **8** Jesus replied, "Moses permitted you to divorce your wives because your
ἀπολῦσαι αὐτήν, ← λέγει αὐτοῖς ὅτι Μωϋσῆς ἐπέτρεψεν ὑμῖν → ἀπολῦσαι ὑμῶν ιτὰς γυναῖκας, πρὸς ὑμῶν
f.aa r.asf.3 v.pai.3s r.dpm.3 cj n.nsm v.aai.3s r.dp.2 f.aa r.gp.2 d.apf n.apf p.a r.gp.2
668 899 668 3306 899 4022 3707 2205 7007 668 7007 3836 1222 4639 7007

hearts were hard. But it was not this way from the beginning. **9** I tell you that anyone who
→ → ιτὴν σκληροκαρδίαν, δὲ → γέγονεν οὐ → οὕτως ἀπ' ἀρχῆς δὲ → λέγω ὑμῖν ὅτι ιὃς ἂν, ←
d.asf n.asf cj v.rai.3s adv adv p.g n.gsf cj v.pai.1s r.dp.2 cj r.nsm pl
3836 5016 1254 1181 4024 4048 608 794 1254 3306 7007 4022 4005 323

divorces his wife, except for marital unfaithfulness, and marries another woman commits adultery." ¶
ἀπολύσῃ αὐτοῦ ιτὴν γυναῖκα, μὴ ἐπὶ → πορνείᾳ καὶ γαμήσῃ ἄλλην ← → μοιχᾶται
v.aas.3s r.gsm.3 d.asf n.asf pl p.d n.dsf cj v.aas.3s r.asf v.ppi.3s
668 899 3836 1222 3590 2093 4518 2779 1138 257 3656

ἀποδῷ πᾶν τὸ ὀφειλόμενον. **35** Οὕτως καὶ ὁ πατήρ μου ὁ οὐράνιος ποιήσει ὑμῖν, ἐὰν μὴ ἀφῆτε ἕκαστος τῷ ἀδελφῷ αὐτοῦ ἀπὸ τῶν καρδιῶν ὑμῶν.

19:1 Καὶ ἐγένετο ὅτε ἐτέλεσεν ὁ Ἰησοῦς τοὺς λόγους τούτους, μετῆρεν ἀπὸ τῆς Γαλιλαίας καὶ ἦλθεν εἰς τὰ ὅρια τῆς Ἰουδαίας πέραν τοῦ Ἰορδάνου. **2** καὶ ἠκολούθησαν αὐτῷ ὄχλοι πολλοί, καὶ ἐθεράπευσεν αὐτοὺς ἐκεῖ. ¶ **3** Καὶ προσῆλθον αὐτῷ Φαρισαῖοι πειράζοντες αὐτὸν καὶ λέγοντες, Εἰ ἔξεστιν ἀνθρώπῳ ἀπολῦσαι τὴν γυναῖκα αὐτοῦ κατὰ πᾶσαν αἰτίαν; **4** ὁ δὲ ἀποκριθεὶς εἶπεν, Οὐκ ἀνέγνωτε ὅτι ὁ κτίσας ἀπ' ἀρχῆς ἄρσεν καὶ θῆλυ ἐποίησεν αὐτούς; **5** καὶ εἶπεν, Ἕνεκα τούτου καταλείψει ἄνθρωπος τὸν πατέρα καὶ τὴν μητέρα καὶ κολληθήσεται τῇ γυναικὶ αὐτοῦ, καὶ ἔσονται οἱ δύο εἰς σάρκα μίαν. **6** ὥστε οὐκέτι εἰσὶν δύο ἀλλὰ σὰρξ μία. ὃ οὖν ὁ θεὸς συνέζευξεν ἄνθρωπος μὴ χωριζέτω. ¶ **7** λέγουσιν αὐτῷ, Τί οὖν Μωϋσῆς ἐνετείλατο δοῦναι βιβλίον ἀποστασίου καὶ ἀπολῦσαι [αὐτήν]; **8** λέγει αὐτοῖς ὅτι Μωϋσῆς πρὸς τὴν σκληροκαρδίαν ὑμῶν ἐπέτρεψεν ὑμῖν ἀπολῦσαι τὰς γυναῖκας ὑμῶν, ἀπ' ἀρχῆς δὲ οὐ γέγονεν οὕτως. **9** λέγω δὲ ὑμῖν ὅτι ὃς ἂν ἀπολύσῃ τὴν γυναῖκα αὐτοῦ μὴ ἐπὶ πορνείᾳ καὶ γαμήσῃ ἄλλην μοιχᾶται. ¶ **10** λέγουσιν αὐτῷ οἱ μαθηταί, «μαθηταὶ» [αὐτοῦ], Εἰ οὕτως ἐστὶν ἡ αἰτία

10 The disciples said to him, "If this is the situation between a husband and wife, it is
οἱ μαθηταὶ [αὐτοῦ] Λέγουσιν → αὐτῷ εἰ οὕτως ἐστὶν ἡ αἰτία → τοῦ ἀνθρώπου μετὰ ⸢τῆς γυναικός⸣ → →
d.npm n.npm r.gsm.3 v.pai.3p r.dsm.3 cj adv v.pai.3s d.nsf n.nsf d.gsn n.gsm p.g d.gsf n.gsf
3836 3412 899 3306 899 1623 4048 1639 3836 162 3836 476 3552 3836 1222

better not to marry." **11** Jesus replied, "Not everyone can accept this word, but only those to whom
συμφέρει οὐ → γαμῆσαι δὲ → εἶπεν αὐτοῖς οὐ πάντες → χωροῦσιν τοῦτον ⸢τὸν λόγον⸣ ἀλλ' → οἷς
v.pai.3s adv f.aa cj d.nsm v.aai.3s r.dpm.3 adv a.npm v.pai.3p r.asm d.asm n.asm cj r.dpm
5237 4024 1138 1254 3836 3306 899 4024 4246 6003 4047 3836 3364 247 4005

it has been given. **12** For some are eunuchs because they were born that way; others
→ → → δέδοται γὰρ οἵτινες εἰσὶν εὐνοῦχοι → → ἐκ κοιλίας μητρὸς ἐγεννήθησαν → οὕτως καὶ οἵτινες εἰσὶν
v.rpi.3s cj r.npm v.pai.3p n.npm p.g n.gsf n.gsf v.api.3p adv cj r.npm v.pai.3p
1443 1142 4015 1639 2336 1164 1164 1666 3120 3613 1164 4048 2779 4015 1639

were made that way by men; and others have renounced marriage because of
εὐνοῦχοι → εὐνουχίσθησαν ← ← ὑπὸ ⸢τῶν ἀνθρώπων⸣ καὶ οἵτινες εἰσὶν εὐνοῦχοι → εὐνούχισαν ἑαυτοὺς διὰ ←
n.npm v.api.3p p.g d.gpm n.gpm cj r.npm v.pai.3p n.npm v.aai.3p r.apm.3 p.a
2336 2335 5679 3836 476 2779 4015 1639 2336 2335 1571 1328

the kingdom of heaven. The one who can accept this should accept it."
τὴν βασιλείαν → ⸢τῶν οὐρανῶν⸣ ὁ → δυνάμενος χωρεῖν → χωρείτω
d.asf n.asf d.gpm n.gpm d.nsm pt.pp.nsm f.pa v.pam.3s
3836 993 3836 4041 3836 1538 6003 6003

The Little Children and Jesus

19:13 Then little children were brought to Jesus for him to place his hands on them and pray for them.
Τότε → παιδία → προσηνέχθησαν → αὐτῷ ἵνα → → ἐπιθῇ τὰς χεῖρας → αὐτοῖς καὶ προσεύξηται
adv n.npn v.api.3p r.dsm.3 cj v.aas.3s d.apf n.apf r.dpm.3 cj v.ams.3s
5538 4086 4712 899 2671 2202 3836 5931 899 2779 4667

But the disciples rebuked those who brought them. **14** Jesus said, "Let the little children come to me, and
δὲ οἱ μαθηταὶ ἐπετίμησαν αὐτοῖς δὲ ὁ Ἰησοῦς εἶπεν Ἄφετε τὰ → παιδία ἐλθεῖν πρός με καὶ
cj d.npm n.npm v.aai.3p r.dpm.3 cj d.nsm n.nsm v.aai.3s v.aam.2p d.apn n.apn f.aa p.a r.as.1 cj
1254 3836 3412 2203 899 1254 3836 2652 3306 918 3836 4086 2262 4639 1609 2779

do not hinder them, for the kingdom of heaven belongs to such as these." **15** When he had placed his
→ μὴ κωλύετε αὐτὰ γὰρ ἡ βασιλεία → ⸢τῶν οὐρανῶν⸣ ἐστιν → ⸢τῶν τοιούτων⸣ ← καὶ → → ἐπιθεὶς τὰς
pl v.pam.2p r.apn.3 cj d.nsf n.nsf d.gpm n.gpm v.pai.3s d.gpm r.gpm cj pt.aa.nsm d.apf
3266 3590 3266 899 1142 3836 993 3836 4041 1639 3836 5525 2779 2202 3836

hands on them, he went on from there.
χεῖρας → αὐτοῖς → ἐπορεύθη ἐκεῖθεν ←
n.apf r.dpm.3 v.api.3s adv
5931 899 4513 1696

The Rich Young Man

19:16 Now a man came up to Jesus and asked, "Teacher, what good thing must I do to get eternal
Καὶ ἰδοὺ εἷς προσελθὼν ← ← αὐτῷ εἶπεν διδάσκαλε τί ἀγαθὸν ← → ποιήσω ἵνα σχῶ αἰώνιον
cj j a.nsm pt.aa.nsm r.dsm.3 v.aai.3s n.vsm r.asn a.asn v.aas.1s cj v.aas.1s a.asf
2779 2627 1651 4665 899 3306 1437 5515 19 4472 2671 2400 173

life?" **17** "Why do you ask me about what is good?" Jesus replied. "There is only One who is good.
ζωὴν δὲ τί → → ἐρωτᾷς με περὶ τοῦ ἀγαθοῦ ὁ εἶπεν αὐτῷ → ἐστιν εἷς ὁ ἀγαθός δὲ
n.asf cj r.asn v.pai.2s r.as.1 p.g d.gsn a.gsn d.nsm v.aai.3s r.dsm.3 v.pai.3s a.nsm d.nsm a.nsm cj
2437 1254 5515 2263 1609 4309 3836 19 3836 3306 899 1639 1651 3836 19 1254

If you want to enter life, obey the commandments." ¶ **18** "Which ones?" the man inquired.
εἰ → θέλεις → εἰσελθεῖν εἰς ⸢τὴν ζωὴν⸣ τήρησον τὰς ἐντολάς ποίας ← λέγει αὐτῷ
cj v.pai.2s f.aa p.a d.asf n.asf v.aam.2s d.apf n.apf r.apf v.pai.3s r.dsm.3
1623 2527 1656 1650 3836 2437 5498 3836 1953 4481 3306 899

Jesus replied, "'Do not murder, do not commit adultery, do not steal, do not give false
δὲ ὁ ⸢Ἰησοῦς⸣ εἶπεν τὸ Οὐ φονεύσεις → Οὐ μοιχεύσεις → Οὐ κλέψεις Οὐ →
cj d.nsm n.nsm v.aai.3s d.asn adv v.fai.2s adv v.fai.2s adv v.fai.2s adv
1254 3836 2652 3306 3836 5839 4024 5839 3658 4024 3096 4024 3096 6018 4024

testimony, **19** honor your father and mother,' and 'love your neighbor as yourself.'" ¶ **20** "All these I
ψευδομαρτυρήσεις τίμα τὸν πατέρα καὶ ⸢τὴν μητέρα⸣ καὶ ἀγαπήσεις σου ⸢τὸν πλησίον⸣ ὡς σεαυτόν πάντα ταῦτα →
v.fai.2s v.pam.2s d.asm n.asm cj d.asf n.asf cj v.fai.2s r.gs.2 d.asm adv cj r.asm.2 a.apn r.apn
6018 5506 3836 4252 2779 3836 3613 2779 26 5148 3836 4446 6055 4932 4246 4047

τοῦ ἀνθρώπου μετὰ τῆς γυναικός, οὐ συμφέρει γαμῆσαι. **11** ὁ δὲ εἶπεν αὐτοῖς, Οὐ πάντες χωροῦσιν τὸν λόγον [τοῦτον] ἀλλ' οἷς δέδοται. **12** εἰσὶν γὰρ εὐνοῦχοι οἵτινες ἐκ κοιλίας μητρὸς ἐγεννήθησαν οὕτως, καὶ εἰσὶν εὐνοῦχοι οἵτινες εὐνουχίσθησαν ὑπὸ τῶν ἀνθρώπων, καὶ εἰσὶν εὐνοῦχοι οἵτινες εὐνούχισαν ἑαυτοὺς διὰ τὴν βασιλείαν τῶν οὐρανῶν. ὁ δυνάμενος χωρεῖν χωρείτω.

19:13 Τότε προσηνέχθησαν αὐτῷ παιδία ἵνα τὰς χεῖρας ἐπιθῇ αὐτοῖς καὶ προσεύξηται· οἱ δὲ μαθηταὶ ἐπετίμησαν αὐτοῖς. **14** ὁ δὲ Ἰησοῦς εἶπεν, Ἄφετε τὰ παιδία καὶ μὴ κωλύετε αὐτὰ ἐλθεῖν πρός με, τῶν γὰρ τοιούτων ἐστὶν ἡ βασιλεία τῶν οὐρανῶν. **15** καὶ ἐπιθεὶς τὰς χεῖρας αὐτοῖς ἐπορεύθη ἐκεῖθεν.

19:16 Καὶ ἰδοὺ εἷς προσελθὼν αὐτῷ εἶπεν, Διδάσκαλε, τί ἀγαθὸν ποιήσω ἵνα σχῶ ζωὴν αἰώνιον; **17** ὁ δὲ εἶπεν αὐτῷ, Τί με ἐρωτᾷς περὶ τοῦ ἀγαθοῦ; εἷς ἐστιν ὁ ἀγαθός· εἰ δὲ θέλεις εἰς τὴν ζωὴν εἰσελθεῖν, τήρησον τὰς ἐντολάς. ¶ **18** λέγει αὐτῷ, Ποίας; ὁ δὲ Ἰησοῦς εἶπεν, Τὸ Οὐ φονεύσεις, Οὐ μοιχεύσεις, Οὐ κλέψεις, Οὐ ψευδομαρτυρήσεις, **19** Τίμα τὸν πατέρα καὶ τὴν μητέρα, καί, Ἀγαπήσεις τὸν πλησίον σου ὡς σεαυτόν. ¶ **20** λέγει αὐτῷ ὁ νεανίσκος, Πάντα ταῦτα ἐφύλαξα· τί ἔτι ὑστερῶ; **21** ἔφη αὐτῷ ὁ

have kept," the young man said.   "What do I still lack?" [21] Jesus answered,   "If you want to be
ἐφύλαξα ὁ νεανίσκος ← λέγει αὐτῷ τί ⌐ ┌ ἔτι ὑστερῶ ὁ Ἰησοῦς ἔφη αὐτῷ εἰ → θέλεις → εἶναι
v.aai.1s d.nsm n.nsm   v.pai.3s r.dsm.3 r.asn   adv v.pai.1s d.nsm n.nsm v.iai.3s r.dsm.3 cj v.pai.2s f.pa
5875 3836 3734   3306 899 5515   5728 5728 2285 5728 3836 2652 5774 899 1623 2527 1639

perfect, go, sell your possessions and give to the poor, and you will have treasure in heaven. Then come,
τέλειος ὕπαγε πώλησον σου τὰ ὑπάρχοντα καὶ δὸς → τοῖς πτωχοῖς καὶ → → ἕξεις θησαυρὸν ἐν οὐρανοῖς καὶ δεῦρο
a.nsm v.pam.2s v.aam.2s r.gs.2 d.apn pt.pa.apn cj v.aam.2s d.dpm a.dpm cj   v.fai.2s n.asm p.d n.dpm cj adv
5455 5632 4797 5148 3836 5639 2779 1443 3836 4777 2779   2400 2565 1877 4041 2779 1306

follow me." [22]   When the young man heard this, he went away sad, because he had great
ἀκολούθει μοι δὲ ┌ ὁ νεανίσκος ← ἀκούσας τὸν λόγον ἀπῆλθεν ← λυπούμενος γὰρ → ἦν ἔχων πολλά
v.pam.2s r.ds.1 cj d.nsm n.nsm pt.aa.nsm d.asm n.asm v.aai.3s pt.pp.nsm cj   v.iai.3s pt.pa.nsm a.apn
199 1609 1254 201 3836 3734 201 3836 3364 599 3382 1142   1639 2400 4498

wealth. ¶ [23] Then Jesus said to his disciples, "I tell you the truth, it is hard for a rich
κτήματα δὲ Ὁ Ἰησοῦς εἶπεν ┌ αὐτοῦ τοῖς μαθηταῖς → λέγω ὑμῖν ἀμὴν ὅτι δυσκόλως πλούσιος
n.apn cj d.nsm n.nsm v.aai.3s r.gsm.3 d.dpm n.dpm v.pai.1s r.dp.2 pl cj adv a.nsm
3228 1254 3836 2652 3306 3412 899 3836 3412 3306 7007 297 4022 1552 4454

man to enter the kingdom of heaven. [24] Again I tell you, it is easier for a camel to go
→ εἰσελεύσεται εἰς τὴν βασιλείαν → τῶν οὐρανῶν δὲ πάλιν λέγω ὑμῖν → ἐστιν εὐκοπώτερον κάμηλον → διελθεῖν
v.fmi.3s p.a d.asf n.asf d.gpm n.gpm cj adv v.pai.1s r.dp.2 v.pai.3s a.nsn.c n.asf f.aa
1656 1650 3836 993 3836 4041 1254 4099 3306 7007 1639 2324 2823 1451

through the eye of a needle than for a rich man to enter the kingdom of God." ¶ [25] When
διὰ τρυπήματος → ῥαφίδος ἢ πλούσιον → εἰσελθεῖν εἰς τὴν βασιλείαν → τοῦ θεοῦ δὲ ┌
p.g n.gsn n.gsf pl a.asm f.aa p.a d.asf n.asf d.gsm n.gsm cj
1328 5585 4827 2445 4454 1656 1650 3836 993 3836 2536 1254 201

the disciples heard this, they were greatly astonished and asked, "Who then can be saved?" [26] Jesus
οἱ μαθηταὶ ἀκούσαντες ┌ ┌ σφόδρα ἐξεπλήσσοντο λέγοντες τίς ἄρα δύναται → σωθῆναι δὲ ὁ Ἰησοῦς
d.npm n.npm pt.aa.npm   adv v.ipi.3s pt.pa.npm r.nsm cj v.ppi.3s f.ap cj d.nsm n.nsm
3836 3412 201   1742 1742 5379 1742 3306 5515 726 1538 5392 1254 3836 2652

looked at them and said, "With man this is impossible, but with God all things are possible." ¶
ἐμβλέψας ← αὐτοῖς εἶπεν παρὰ ἀνθρώποις τοῦτο ἐστιν ἀδύνατον δὲ παρὰ θεῷ πάντα ← δυνατά
pt.aa.nsm r.dpm.3 v.aai.3s p.d n.dpm r.nsn v.pai.3s a.nsn cj p.d n.dsm a.npn a.npn
1838 899 3306 4123 476 4047 1639 105 1254 4123 2536 4246 1543

[27] Peter answered him, "We have left everything to follow you! What then will there
Τότε ὁ Πέτρος ἀποκριθεὶς εἶπεν αὐτῷ ἰδοὺ ἡμεῖς → ἀφήκαμεν πάντα καὶ ἠκολουθήσαμεν σοι τί ἄρα → →
adv d.nsm n.nsm pt.ap.nsm v.aai.3s r.dsm.3 pl r.np.1 v.aai.1p a.apn cj v.aai.1p r.ds.2 r.nsn cj
5538 3836 4377 646 3306 899 2627 7005 918 4246 2779 199 5148 5515 726

be for us?" [28] Jesus said to them, "I tell you the truth, at the renewal of all things, when the Son
ἔσται → ἡμῖν δὲ ὁ Ἰησοῦς εἶπεν αὐτοῖς → λέγω ὑμῖν ἀμὴν ὅτι ἐν τῇ παλιγγενεσίᾳ ὅταν ὁ υἱὸς
v.fmi.3s r.dp.1 cj d.nsm n.nsm v.aai.3s r.dpm.3 v.pai.1s r.dp.2 pl cj p.d d.dsf n.dsf cj d.nsm n.nsm
1639 7005 1254 3836 2652 3306 899 3306 7007 297 4022 1877 3836 4098 4020 3836 5626

of Man sits on his glorious throne, you who have followed me will also sit on twelve
→ τοῦ ἀνθρώπου καθίσῃ ἐπὶ αὐτοῦ δόξης θρόνου ὑμεῖς οἱ → ἀκολουθήσαντες μοι ὑμεῖς ┌ καὶ καθήσεσθε ἐπὶ δώδεκα
d.gsm n.gsm v.ams.3s p.g r.gsm.3 n.gsf n.gsm r.np.2 d.npm pt.aa.npm r.ds.1 r.np.2 adv v.fmi.2p p.a a.apm
3836 476 2767 2093 899 1518 2585 7007 3836 199 1609 7007 2764 2779 2764 2093 1557

thrones, judging the twelve tribes of Israel. [29] And everyone who has left houses or brothers or sisters or
θρόνους κρίνοντες τὰς δώδεκα φυλὰς → τοῦ Ἰσραήλ καὶ πᾶς ὅστις → ἀφῆκεν οἰκίας ἢ ἀδελφοὺς ἢ ἀδελφὰς ἢ
n.apm pt.pa.npm d.apf a.apf n.apf d.gsm n.gsm cj a.nsm r.nsm v.aai.3s n.apf cj n.apm cj n.apf cj
2585 3212 3836 1557 5876 3836 2702 2779 4246 4015 918 3864 2445 81 2445 80 2445

father or mother or children or fields for my sake will receive a hundred times as much
πατέρα ἢ μητέρα ἢ τέκνα ἢ ἀγροὺς ἕνεκεν τοῦ ὀνόματος μου ┌ → λήμψεται ἑκατονταπλασίονα ←
n.asm cj n.asf cj n.apn cj n.apm p.g d.gsn n.gsn r.gs.1 v.fmi.3s a.apn
4252 2445 3613 2445 5451 2445 69 1914 3836 3950 1609 3950 3284 1671

and will inherit eternal life. [30] But many who are first will be last, and many who are last will be first.
καὶ → κληρονομήσει αἰώνιον ζωὴν δὲ πολλοὶ πρῶτοι → ἔσονται ἔσχατοι καὶ ἔσχατοι πρῶτοι
cj v.fai.3s a.asf n.asf cj a.npm a.npm v.fmi.3p a.npm cj a.npm a.npm
2779 3099 173 2437 1254 4498 4755 1639 2274 2779 2274 4755

Ἰησοῦς, Εἰ θέλεις τέλειος εἶναι, ὕπαγε πώλησόν σου τὰ ὑπάρχοντα καὶ δὸς [τοῖς] πτωχοῖς, καὶ ἕξεις θησαυρὸν ἐν οὐρανοῖς, καὶ δεῦρο ἀκολούθει μοι. [22] ἀκούσας δὲ ὁ νεανίσκος τὸν λόγον ἀπῆλθεν λυπούμενος· ἦν γὰρ ἔχων κτήματα πολλά. ¶ [23] Ὁ δὲ Ἰησοῦς εἶπεν τοῖς μαθηταῖς αὐτοῦ, Ἀμὴν λέγω ὑμῖν ὅτι πλούσιος δυσκόλως εἰσελεύσεται εἰς τὴν βασιλείαν τῶν οὐρανῶν. [24] πάλιν δὲ λέγω ὑμῖν, εὐκοπώτερόν ἐστιν κάμηλον διὰ τρυπήματος ῥαφίδος διελθεῖν ἢ πλούσιον εἰσελθεῖν εἰς τὴν βασιλείαν τοῦ θεοῦ. ¶ [25] ἀκούσαντες δὲ οἱ μαθηταὶ ἐξεπλήσσοντο σφόδρα λέγοντες, Τίς ἄρα δύναται σωθῆναι; [26] ἐμβλέψας δὲ ὁ Ἰησοῦς εἶπεν αὐτοῖς, Παρὰ ἀνθρώποις τοῦτο ἀδύνατόν ἐστιν, παρὰ δὲ θεῷ πάντα δυνατά. ¶ [27] Τότε ἀποκριθεὶς ὁ Πέτρος εἶπεν αὐτῷ, Ἰδοὺ ἡμεῖς ἀφήκαμεν πάντα καὶ ἠκολουθήσαμέν σοι· τί ἄρα ἔσται ἡμῖν; [28] ὁ δὲ Ἰησοῦς εἶπεν αὐτοῖς, Ἀμὴν λέγω ὑμῖν ὅτι ὑμεῖς οἱ ἀκολουθήσαντές μοι ἐν τῇ παλιγγενεσίᾳ, ὅταν καθίσῃ ὁ υἱὸς τοῦ ἀνθρώπου ἐπὶ θρόνου δόξης αὐτοῦ, καθήσεσθε καὶ ὑμεῖς ἐπὶ δώδεκα θρόνους κρίνοντες τὰς δώδεκα φυλὰς τοῦ Ἰσραήλ. [29] καὶ πᾶς ὅστις ἀφῆκεν οἰκίας ἢ ἀδελφοὺς ἢ ἀδελφὰς ἢ πατέρα ἢ μητέρα ἢ τέκνα ἢ ἀγροὺς ἕνεκεν τοῦ ὀνόματός μου, ἑκατονταπλασίονα λήμψεται καὶ ζωὴν αἰώνιον κληρονομήσει. [30] Πολλοὶ δὲ ἔσονται πρῶτοι ἔσχατοι καὶ ἔσχατοι πρῶτοι.

The Parable of the Workers in the Vineyard

20:1 "For the kingdom of heaven   is   like   a landowner   who went out early   in the morning
γὰρ   ἡ   βασιλεία → ⸂τῶν οὐρανῶν⸃ ἐστιν Ὁμοία ⸆ἀνθρώπῳ οἰκοδεσπότῃ, ὅστις ἐξῆλθεν → ⸂ἅμα πρωῒ⸃ ←   ←
cj   d.nsf n.nsf   d.gpm n.gpm   v.pai.3s a.nsf   n.dsm   n.dsm   r.nsm   v.aai.3s   p.d adv
1142 3836 993   3836   4041   1639   3927   476   3867   4015   2002   275 4745

to hire   men to work   in   his   vineyard.   **2**   He agreed   to pay them a denarius for
μισθώσασθαι →   ἐργάτας εἰς αὐτοῦ ⸂τὸν ἀμπελῶνα⸃, δὲ → συμφωνήσας μετὰ τῶν ἐργατῶν ἐκ   δηναρίου →
f.am   n.apm   p.a r.gsm.3 d.asm n.asm   cj   pt.aa.nsm p.g d.gpm n.gpm p.g   n.gsn
3636   2239   1650 899   3836 308   1254   5244   3552 3836   2239   1666   1324

the day   and sent   them into his   vineyard. ¶   **3**   "About the third hour he went   out and saw
τὴν ἡμέραν ἀπέστειλεν αὐτοὺς εἰς αὐτοῦ ⸂τὸν ἀμπελῶνα⸃ καὶ περὶ   τρίτην ὥραν → ἐξελθὼν ←   εἶδεν
d.asf n.asf v.aai.3s r.apm.3 p.a r.gsm.3 d.asm n.asm   cj   p.a   a.asf n.asf   pt.aa.nsm   v.aai.3s
3836 2465   690   899   1650 899   3836 308   2779 4309   5569   6052   2002   1625

others standing in   the marketplace doing nothing. **4**   He told them, 'You also go   and work in my vineyard,
ἄλλους ἑστῶτας ἐν τῇ ἀγορᾷ   ἀργούς   καὶ → εἶπεν ἐκείνοις ὑμεῖς καὶ ὑπάγετε   εἰς τὸν ἀμπελῶνα
r.apm pt.ra.apm p.d d.dsf n.dsf   a.apm   cj   v.aai.3s r.dpm   r.np.2 cj   v.pam.2p   p.a d.asm n.asm
257   2705   1877 3836 59   734   2779   3306   1697   7007   2779 5632   1650 3836 308

and I will pay you whatever is   right.' **5** So they went. ¶   "He went out again about the sixth
καὶ → → δώσω ὑμῖν ⸂ὃ ἐὰν⸃ ᾖ δίκαιον δὲ οἱ ἀπῆλθον.   [δὲ] → ἐξελθὼν ← πάλιν περὶ ἕκτην
cj   v.fai.1s r.dp.2 r.nsn pl v.pas.3s a.nsn cj d.npm v.aai.3p   cj   pt.aa.nsm adv p.a   a.asf
2779   1443   7007   4005 1569 1639   1465 1254 3836 599   1254   2002   4099 4309 1761

hour and the ninth hour and did   the same   thing. **6** About the eleventh hour he went   out and found still
καὶ   ἐνάτην ὥραν ἐποίησεν ὡσαύτως ←   δὲ περὶ τὴν ἑνδεκάτην → ἐξελθὼν ← εὗρεν
cj   a.asf   n.asf v.aai.3s adv   cj p.a   d.asf a.asf   pt.aa.nsm   v.aai.3s
2779 1888   6052   4472   6058   1254 4309 3836 1895   2002   2351

others standing around.   He asked them, 'Why have you been standing here all day   long doing nothing?'
ἄλλους ἑστῶτας   καὶ λέγει αὐτοῖς τί ἑστήκατε ὧδε ὅλην ⸂τὴν ἡμέραν⸃ ←   ἀργοί
r.apm pt.ra.apm   cj   v.pai.3s r.dpm.3 r.asn v.rai.2p adv a.asf d.asf n.asf   a.npm
257   2705   2779 3306   899   5515   2705   6045 3910 3836 2465   734

7 "'Because no one has hired   us,' they answered.   "He said to them, 'You also go   and work in my
ὅτι   → οὐδεὶς → ἐμισθώσατο ἡμᾶς → λέγουσιν αὐτῷ → λέγει → αὐτοῖς ὑμεῖς καὶ ὑπάγετε   εἰς τὸν
cj   a.nsm   v.ami.3s   r.ap.1   v.pai.3p r.dsm.3   v.pai.3s   r.dpm.3 r.np.2 cj   v.pam.2p   p.a d.asm
4022   4029   3636   7005   3306   899   3306   899   7007   2779 5632   1650 3836

vineyard.' **8** "When evening came,   the owner of the vineyard said to his   foreman, 'Call   the workers
ἀμπελῶνα δὲ → ὀψίας γενομένης ὁ κύριος → τοῦ ἀμπελῶνος λέγει → αὐτοῦ ⸂τῷ ἐπιτρόπῳ⸃ κάλεσον τοὺς ἐργάτας
n.asm   cj   n.gsf pt.am.gsf d.nsm n.nsm   d.gsm n.gsm   v.pai.3s r.gsm.3 d.dsm n.dsm   v.aam.2s d.apm n.apm
308   1254   4068   1181   3836 3261   3836 308   3306   899   3836 2207   2813   3836 2239

and pay   them their wages, beginning with the last   ones hired and going on to   the first.' ¶ **9** "The
καὶ ἀπόδος αὐτοῖς τὸν μισθόν ἀρξάμενος ἀπὸ τῶν ἐσχάτων   → → ἕως τῶν πρώτων   καὶ οἱ
cj   v.aam.2s r.dpm.3 d.asm n.asm pt.am.nsm p.g d.gpm a.gpm   p.g d.gpm a.gpm   cj   d.npm
2779 625   899   3836 3635 806   608 3836 2274   2401 3836 4755   2779 3836

workers who were hired about the eleventh hour came   and each received a denarius. **10** So when those came   who
περὶ   τὴν ἑνδεκάτην ὥραν ἐλθόντες ἀνὰ ἔλαβον δηνάριον   καὶ → → ἐλθόντες οἱ
p.a   d.asf a.asf   n.asf pt.aa.npm p.a v.aai.3p n.asn   cj   pt.aa.npm d.npm
4309   3836 1895   6052 2262   324 3284   1324   2779   2262   3836

were hired first, they expected   to receive more. But each one of them also received a denarius. **11** When
πρῶτοι → ἐνόμισαν ὅτι → λήμψονται πλεῖον καὶ ἀνὰ   αὐτοί καὶ ἔλαβον ⸂τὸ δηνάριον⸃ δὲ →
a.npm   v.aai.3p   cj   v.fmi.3p a.asn.c cj   p.a   r.npm adv v.aai.3p d.asn n.asn   cj
4755   3787   4022   3284   4498   2779 324   899   2779 3284   3836 1324   1254

they received it, they began to grumble against the landowner. **12** 'These men who were hired last   worked only one
→ λαβόντες → → → ἐγόγγυζον κατὰ τοῦ οἰκοδεσπότου οὗτοι ← οἱ   ἔσχατοι ἐποίησαν μίαν
pt.aa.npm   v.iai.3p p.g   d.gsm n.gsm   r.npm   d.npm   a.npm   v.aai.3p a.asf
3284   1197   2848 3836 3867   4047   3836   2274   4472   1651

hour,' they said, 'and you have made   them equal to us who have borne   the burden of the work and the
ὥραν → λέγοντες καὶ → ἐποίησας αὐτοὺς ἴσους → ἡμῖν τοῖς βαστάσασι τὸ βάρος   καὶ τὸν
n.asf   pt.pa.npm cj   v.aai.2s r.apm.3 a.apm   r.dp.1 d.dpm pt.aa.dpm d.asn n.asn   cj   d.asm
6052   3306   2779   4472   899   2698   7005 3836   1002   3836 983   2779 3836

20:1 Ὁμοία γὰρ ἐστιν ἡ βασιλεία τῶν οὐρανῶν ἀνθρώπῳ οἰκοδεσπότῃ, ὅστις ἐξῆλθεν ἅμα πρωῒ μισθώσασθαι ἐργάτας εἰς τὸν ἀμπελῶνα αὐτοῦ. **2** συμφωνήσας δὲ μετὰ τῶν ἐργατῶν ἐκ δηναρίου τὴν ἡμέραν ἀπέστειλεν αὐτοὺς εἰς τὸν ἀμπελῶνα αὐτοῦ. ¶ **3** καὶ ἐξελθὼν περὶ τρίτην ὥραν εἶδεν ἄλλους ἑστῶτας ἐν τῇ ἀγορᾷ ἀργοὺς **4** καὶ ἐκείνοις εἶπεν, Ὑπάγετε καὶ ὑμεῖς εἰς τὸν ἀμπελῶνα, καὶ ὃ ἐὰν ᾖ δίκαιον δώσω ὑμῖν. **5** οἱ δὲ ἀπῆλθον. ¶ πάλιν [δὲ] ἐξελθὼν περὶ ἕκτην καὶ ἐνάτην ὥραν ἐποίησεν ὡσαύτως. **6** περὶ δὲ τὴν ἑνδεκάτην ἐξελθὼν εὗρεν ἄλλους ἑστῶτας καὶ λέγει αὐτοῖς, Τί ὧδε ἑστήκατε ὅλην τὴν ἡμέραν ἀργοί; **7** λέγουσιν αὐτῷ, Ὅτι οὐδεὶς ἡμᾶς ἐμισθώσατο. λέγει αὐτοῖς, Ὑπάγετε καὶ ὑμεῖς εἰς τὸν ἀμπελῶνα. **8** ὀψίας δὲ γενομένης λέγει ὁ κύριος τοῦ ἀμπελῶνος τῷ ἐπιτρόπῳ αὐτοῦ, Κάλεσον τοὺς ἐργάτας καὶ ἀπόδος αὐτοῖς τὸν μισθὸν ἀρξάμενος ἀπὸ τῶν ἐσχάτων ἕως τῶν πρώτων. ¶ **9** καὶ ἐλθόντες οἱ περὶ τὴν ἑνδεκάτην ὥραν ἔλαβον ἀνὰ δηνάριον. **10** καὶ ἐλθόντες οἱ πρῶτοι ἐνόμισαν ὅτι πλεῖον λήμψονται· καὶ ἔλαβον [τὸ] ἀνὰ δηνάριον καὶ αὐτοί. **11** λαβόντες δὲ ἐγόγγυζον κατὰ τοῦ οἰκοδεσπότου **12** λέγοντες, Οὗτοι οἱ ἔσχατοι μίαν ὥραν ἐποίησαν, καὶ ἴσους ἡμῖν αὐτοὺς ἐποίησας τοῖς βαστάσασι τὸ βάρος τῆς ἡμέρας καὶ τὸν καύσωνα. ¶ **13** ὁ δὲ

heat   of the day.'   ¶ **13** "But he   answered one of them,   'Friend, I am not being unfair to you. Didn't
καύσωνα → τῆς ἡμέρας   δὲ   ὁ   ἀποκριθεὶς ἑνὶ → αὐτῶν εἶπεν ἑταῖρε   οὐκ → ἀδικῶ σε   οὐχὶ
n.asm   d.gsf n.gsf   cj   d.nsm pt.ap.nsm a.dsm   r.gpm.3 v.aai.3s n.vsm   adv   v.pai.1s r.as.2 pl
3014   3836 2465   1254 3836 646   1651   899   3306 2279   92 92 4024   92   5148 4049

you agree   to work for a denarius? **14** Take *your*   *pay* and go.   I want to give   the man who was
→   συνεφώνησας μοι →   δηναρίου   ἆρον ⸂τὸ σὸν⸃ καὶ ὕπαγε δὲ → θέλω → δοῦναι τούτῳ τῷ
    v.aai.2s   r.ds.1   n.gsn   v.aam.2s d.asn r.as.2 cj v.pam.2s cj v.pai.1s → f.aa r.dsm d.dsm
    5244   1609   1324   149   3836 5050 2779 5632 1254 2527   1443 4047   3836

hired last   the same as   I gave you. **15**   Don't I have the right to do   what I want with *my own*
ἐσχάτῳ   ὡς καὶ   σοί   [ἢ] οὐκ   μοι →   →   ἔξεστιν ποιῆσαι ὃ → θέλω ἐν τοῖς ἐμοῖς
a.dsm   cj cj   r.ds.2   pl   r.ds.1   v.pai.3s f.aa r.asn v.pai.1s d.p d.dpn r.dpn.1
2274   6055 2779 5148   2445   4024 1609   1997   4472   4005   2527 1877 3836 1847

money? Or are you envious   because I am generous?' ¶ **16** "So the last   will be   first, and
ἢ ἐστιν σου ὁ ὀφθαλμός πονηρός⸃ ὅτι   ἐγὼ εἰμι ἀγαθός   οὕτως οἱ ἔσχατοι → ἔσονται πρῶτοι καὶ
cj v.pai.3s r.gs.2 d.nsm n.nsm a.nsm   cj   r.ns.1 v.pai.1s a.nsm   adv   d.npm a.npm   v.fmi.3p a.npm cj
2445 1639 5148 3836 4057 4505   4022 1609 1639 19   4048 3836 2274   1639   4755 2779

the first   will be last."
οἱ πρῶτοι ἔσχατοι
d.npm a.npm a.npm
3836 4755   2274

Jesus Again Predicts His Death

20:17 Now as Jesus   was going   up to Jerusalem, he took   the twelve disciples aside   and
Καὶ → ὁ Ἰησοῦς⸃ → ἀναβαίνων ← εἰς Ἱεροσόλυμα → παρέλαβεν τοὺς δώδεκα μαθητὰς ⸤κατʼ ἰδίαν⸥ καὶ ἐν τῇ
cj   d.nsm n.nsm pt.pa.nsm   p.a n.apn   v.aai.3s d.apm a.apm n.apm   p.a a.asf cj p.d d.dsf
2779 326 3836 2652 326   1650 2642   4161   3836 1557 3412   2848 2625 2779 1877 3836

said to them, **18**   "We are going   up to Jerusalem, and the Son of Man   will be betrayed   to
ὁδῷ εἶπεν αὐτοῖς ἰδοὺ → → ἀναβαίνομεν ← εἰς Ἱεροσόλυμα καὶ ὁ υἱὸς ⸤τοῦ ἀνθρώπου⸥ → παραδοθήσεται →
n.dsf v.aai.3s r.dpm.3 j   v.pai.1p   p.a n.apn   cj d.nsm n.nsm d.gsm n.gsn   v.fpi.3s
3847 3306 899   2627   326   1650 2642   2779 3836 5626 3836 476   4140

the chief priests   and the teachers   of the law.   They will condemn   him to death **19** and will turn
τοῖς   ἀρχιερεῦσιν καὶ   γραμματεῦσιν ←   καὶ   κατακρινοῦσιν αὐτὸν → θανάτῳ καὶ → παραδώσουσιν
d.dpm   n.dpm cj   n.dpm   cj   v.fai.3p   r.asm.3 n.dsm   cj   v.fai.3μ
3836   797 2779   1208   2779   2891   899   2505   2779   4140

him over to the Gentiles to be mocked   and flogged   and crucified.   On the third day   he will be
αὐτὸν ← → τοῖς ἔθνεσιν εἰς → ⸤τὸ ἐμπαῖξαι⸥ καὶ μαστιγῶσαι καὶ σταυρῶσαι καὶ → τῇ τρίτῃ ἡμέρᾳ → →
r.asm.3   d.dpn n.dpn p.a d.asn f.aa cj f.aa   cj f.aa   cj   d.dsf a.dsf n.dsf
899 4140   3836 1620 1650   3836 1850 2779 3463   2779 5090   2779 3836 5569 2465

raised   to life!"
ἐγερθήσεται
v.fpi.3s
1586

A Mother's Request

20:20 Then the mother of Zebedee's sons   came   to Jesus with her   sons   and, kneeling   down,
Τότε ἡ μήτηρ → Ζεβεδαίου ⸤τῶν υἱῶν⸥ προσῆλθεν ← αὐτῷ μετὰ αὐτῆς ⸤τῶν υἱῶν⸥   προσκυνοῦσα ←   καὶ
adv d.nsf n.nsf   n.gsm   d.gpm n.gpm v.aai.3s   r.dsm.3 p.g r.gsf.3 d.gpm n.gpm pt.pa.nsf   cj
5538 3836 3613   5626 2411 3836 5626 4665   899   3552 899   3836 5626   4686   2779

asked a favor of him. **21** "What is it you want?"   he asked. ¶ She said,   "Grant that one of these
αἰτοῦσα τι ἀπʼ αὐτοῦ τί →   → θέλεις δὲ ὁ εἶπεν αὐτῇ   → λέγει αὐτῷ εἰπὲ ἵνα εἷς οὗτοι
pt.pa.nsf r.asn p.g r.gsm.3 r.asn   v.pai.2s cj d.nsm v.aai.3s r.dsf.3 v.pai.3s r.dsm.3 v.aam.2s cj a.nsm r.npm
160   5516 608 899 5515   2527 1254 3836 3306 899   3306 899 3306 2671 1651 4047

two sons   of mine may sit   at your right and the other at your left   in your kingdom." **22** "You
δύο οἱ υἱοί → μου → καθίσωσιν ἐκ σου δεξιῶν καὶ εἷς ἐξ σου εὐωνύμων ἐν σου ⸤τῇ βασιλείᾳ⸥ δὲ →
a.npm d.npm n.npm r.gs.1   v.aas.3p p.g r.gs.2 a.gpf cj a.nsm p.g r.gs.2 a.gpf p.d r.gs.2 d.dsf n.dsf cj
1545 3836 5626 1609   2767   1666 5148 1288 2779 1651 1666 5148 2381   1877 5148 3836 993   1254 3857

don't know what you are asking," Jesus   said   to them. "Can you drink the cup   I am going
οὐκ οἴδατε τί → αἰτεῖσθε ὁ Ἰησοῦς⸃ ἀποκριθεὶς εἶπεν   δύνασθε ← πιεῖν τὸ ποτήριον ὃ ἐγὼ μέλλω
adv v.rai.2p r.asn v.pmi.2p d.nsm n.nsm pt.ap.nsm v.aai.3s   v.ppi.2p f.aa d.asn n.asn r.asn r.ns.1 v.pai.1s
4024 3857 5515   160   3836 2652 646   3306   1538   4403 3836 4539 4005 1609 3516

ἀποκριθεὶς ἑνὶ αὐτῶν εἶπεν, Ἑταῖρε, οὐκ ἀδικῶ σε· οὐχὶ δηναρίου συνεφώνησάς μοι; **14** ἆρον τὸ σὸν καὶ ὕπαγε. θέλω δὲ τούτῳ τῷ ἐσχάτῳ δοῦναι ὡς καὶ σοί· **15** [ἢ] οὐκ ἔξεστίν μοι ὃ θέλω ποιῆσαι ἐν τοῖς ἐμοῖς; ἢ ὁ ὀφθαλμός σου πονηρός ἐστιν ὅτι ἐγὼ ἀγαθός εἰμι; ¶ **16** Οὕτως ἔσονται οἱ ἔσχατοι πρῶτοι καὶ οἱ πρῶτοι ἔσχατοι.

20:17 Καὶ ἀναβαίνων ὁ Ἰησοῦς εἰς Ἱεροσόλυμα παρέλαβεν τοὺς δώδεκα [μαθητὰς] κατʼ ἰδίαν καὶ ἐν τῇ ὁδῷ εἶπεν αὐτοῖς, **18** Ἰδοὺ ἀναβαίνομεν εἰς Ἱεροσόλυμα, καὶ ὁ υἱὸς τοῦ ἀνθρώπου παραδοθήσεται τοῖς ἀρχιερεῦσιν καὶ γραμματεῦσιν, καὶ κατακρινοῦσιν αὐτὸν θανάτῳ **19** καὶ παραδώσουσιν αὐτὸν τοῖς ἔθνεσιν εἰς τὸ ἐμπαῖξαι καὶ μαστιγῶσαι καὶ σταυρῶσαι, καὶ τῇ τρίτῃ ἡμέρᾳ ἐγερθήσεται.

20:20 Τότε προσῆλθεν αὐτῷ ἡ μήτηρ τῶν υἱῶν Ζεβεδαίου μετὰ τῶν υἱῶν αὐτῆς προσκυνοῦσα καὶ αἰτοῦσά τι ἀπʼ αὐτοῦ. **21** ὁ δὲ εἶπεν αὐτῇ, Τί θέλεις; ¶ λέγει αὐτῷ, Εἰπὲ ἵνα καθίσωσιν οὗτοι οἱ δύο υἱοί μου εἷς ἐκ δεξιῶν σου καὶ εἷς ἐξ εὐωνύμων σου ἐν τῇ βασιλείᾳ σου. **22** ἀποκριθεὶς δὲ ὁ Ἰησοῦς εἶπεν, Οὐκ οἴδατε τί αἰτεῖσθε. δύνασθε πιεῖν τὸ ποτήριον ὃ ἐγὼ μέλλω

to drink?" ¶ "We can," they answered. 23 Jesus said to them, "You will indeed drink from my
→ πίνειν → δυνάμεθα → λέγουσιν αὐτῷ λέγει → αὐτοῖς μὲν πίεσθε μου
f.pa v.ppi.1p v.pai.3p r.dsm.3 v.pai.3s r.dpm.3 pl v.fmi.2p r.gs.1
4403 1538 3306 899 3306 899 3525 4403 1609

cup, but to sit at my right or left is not for me to grant. These places
ιτὸ ποτήριον, δὲ → ιτὸ καθίσαι ἐκ μου δεξιῶν καὶ ἐξ εὐωνύμων ἔστιν οὐκ → ἐμὸν δοῦναι [τοῦτο] ἀλλ'
d.asn n.asn cj d.nsn f.aa p.g r.gs.1 a.gpf cj p.g a.gpf v.pai.3s adv r.nsn.1 f.aa r.nsn cj
3836 4539 1254 3836 2767 1666 1609 1288 2779 1666 2381 1639 4024 1847 1443 4047 247

belong to those for whom they have been prepared by my Father." ¶ 24 When the ten heard about
→ οἷς → → → ἡτοίμασται ὑπὸ μου ιτοῦ πατρός, Καὶ → οἱ δέκα ἀκούσαντες
r.dpm v.rpi.3s p.g r.gs.1 d.gsm n.gsm cj d.npm a.npm pt.aa.npm
4005 2286 5679 1609 3836 4252 2779 201 3836 1274 201

this, they were indignant with the two brothers. 25 Jesus called them together and said, "You know
→ → ἠγανάκτησαν περὶ τῶν δύο ἀδελφῶν δὲ ὁ Ἰησοῦς, προσκαλεσάμενος αὐτοὺς ← εἶπεν → οἴδατε
v.aai.3p p.g d.gpm a.gpm n.gpm cj d.nsm n.nsm pt.am.nsm r.apm.3 v.aai.3s v.rai.2p
24 4309 3836 1545 81 1254 3836 2652 4673 899 3306 3857

that the rulers of the Gentiles lord it over them, and their high officials exercise authority over
ὅτι οἱ ἄρχοντες → τῶν ἐθνῶν κατακυριεύουσιν ← αὐτῶν καὶ οἱ μεγάλοι κατεξουσιάζουσιν
cj d.npm n.npm d.gpn n.gpn v.pai.3p r.gpm.3 cj d.npm a.npm v.pai.3p
4022 3836 807 3836 1620 2894 899 2779 3836 3489 2980

them. 26 Not so with you. Instead, whoever wants to become great among you must be your servant, 27 and
αὐτῶν οὐχ οὕτως ἔσται ἐν ὑμῖν ἀλλ' ιὃς ἐὰν, θέλῃ → γενέσθαι μέγας ἐν ὑμῖν ἔσται ὑμῶν διάκονος καὶ
r.gpm.3 adv adv v.fmi.3s p.d r.dp.2 cj r.nsm pl v.pas.3s f.am a.nsm p.d r.dp.2 v.fmi.3s r.gp.2 n.nsm cj
899 4024 4048 1639 1877 7007 247 4005 1569 2527 1181 3489 1877 7007 1639 7007 1356 2779

whoever wants to be first must be your slave – 28 just as the Son of Man did not come to be
ιὃς ἂν, θέλῃ → εἶναι πρῶτος ἐν ὑμῖν ἔσται ὑμῶν δοῦλος ὥσπερ ὁ υἱὸς ιτοῦ ἀνθρώπου, → οὐκ ἦλθεν →
r.nsm pl v.pas.3s f.pa a.nsm p.d r.dp.2 v.fmi.3s r.gp.2 n.nsm cj d.nsm n.nsm d.gsm n.gsm adv v.aai.3s
4005 323 2527 1639 4755 1877 7007 1639 7007 1529 6061 3836 5626 3836 476 2262 4024 2262

served, but to serve, and to give his life as a ransom for many."
διακονηθῆναι ἀλλὰ → διακονῆσαι καὶ → δοῦναι αὐτοῦ ιτὴν ψυχὴν, λύτρον ἀντὶ πολλῶν
f.ap cj f.aa cj f.aa r.gsm.3 d.asf n.asf n.asn p.g a.gpm
1354 247 1354 2779 1443 899 3836 6034 3389 505 4498

Two Blind Men Receive Sight

20:29 As Jesus and his disciples were leaving Jericho, a large crowd followed him. 30 Two
Καὶ → αὐτῶν ← → ← → ἐκπορευομένων ἀπὸ Ἰεριχὼ πολὺς ὄχλος ἠκολούθησεν αὐτῷ καὶ ἰδοὺ δύο
cj r.gpm.3 pt.pm.gpm p.g n.gsf a.nsm n.nsm v.aai.3s r.dsm.3 cj cj a.npm
2779 1744 899 1744 608 2637 4498 4063 199 899 2779 2627 1545

blind men were sitting by the roadside, and when they heard that Jesus was going by, they shouted,
τυφλοὶ ← → καθήμενοι παρὰ τὴν ὁδόν → → → ἀκούσαντες ὅτι Ἰησοῦς → παράγει ← ἔκραξαν
a.npm pt.pm.npm p.a d.asf n.asf pt.aa.npm cj n.nsm v.pai.3s v.aai.3p
5603 2764 4123 3836 3847 201 4022 2652 4135 3189

"Lord, Son of David, have mercy on us!" ¶ 31 The crowd rebuked them and told them to be
λέγοντες κύριε υἱὸς → Δαυίδ → ἐλέησον → ἡμᾶς δὲ ὁ ὄχλος ἐπετίμησεν αὐτοῖς ἵνα →
pt.pa.npm n.vsm n.nsm n.gsm v.aam.2s r.ap.1 cj d.nsm n.nsm v.aai.3s r.dpm.3 cj
3306 3261 5626 1253 1796 7005 1254 3836 4063 2203 899 2671

quiet, but they shouted all the louder, "Lord, Son of David, have mercy on us!" ¶ 32 Jesus
σιωπήσωσιν δὲ οἱ ἔκραξαν → μεῖζον λέγοντες κύριε υἱὸς → Δαυίδ → ἐλέησον ← ἡμᾶς καὶ ὁ Ἰησοῦς,
v.aas.3p cj d.npm v.aai.3p adv.c pt.pa.npm n.vsm n.nsm n.gsm v.aam.2s r.ap.1 cj d.nsm n.nsm
4995 1254 3836 3189 3489 3306 3261 5626 1253 1796 7005 2779 3836 2652

stopped and called them. "What do you want me to do for you?" he asked. 33 "Lord," they answered,
στὰς ἐφώνησεν αὐτοὺς καὶ τί → → θέλετε → ποιήσω → ὑμῖν εἶπεν κύριε → λέγουσιν αὐτῷ
pt.aa.nsm v.aai.3s r.apm.3 cj r.asn v.pai.2p v.aas.1s r.dp.2 v.aai.3s n.vsm v.pai.3p r.dsm.3
2705 5888 899 2779 5515 2527 4472 7007 3306 3261 3306 899

"we want our sight." ¶ 34 Jesus had compassion on them and touched their eyes.
ἵνα ἀνοιγῶσιν ἡμῶν ιοἱ ὀφθαλμοί, δὲ ιὁ Ἰησοῦς, → σπλαγχνισθεὶς ἥψατο αὐτῶν ιτῶν ὀμμάτων,
cj v.aps.3p r.gp.1 d.npm n.npm cj d.nsm n.nsm pt.ap.nsm v.ami.3s r.gpm.3 d.gpn n.gpn
2671 487 7005 3836 4057 1254 3836 2652 5072 721 899 3836 3921

πίνειν; ¶λέγουσιν αὐτῷ, Δυνάμεθα. 23 λέγει αὐτοῖς, Τὸ μὲν ποτήριόν μου πίεσθε, τὸ δὲ καθίσαι ἐκ δεξιῶν μου καὶ ἐξ εὐωνύμων οὐκ ἔστιν ἐμὸν [τοῦτο] δοῦναι, ἀλλ' οἷς ἡτοίμασται ὑπὸ τοῦ πατρός μου. ¶ 24 Καὶ ἀκούσαντες οἱ δέκα ἠγανάκτησαν περὶ τῶν δύο ἀδελφῶν. 25 ὁ δὲ Ἰησοῦς προσκαλεσάμενος αὐτοὺς εἶπεν, Οἴδατε ὅτι οἱ ἄρχοντες τῶν ἐθνῶν κατακυριεύουσιν αὐτῶν καὶ οἱ μεγάλοι κατεξουσιάζουσιν αὐτῶν. 26 οὐχ οὕτως ἔσται ἐν ὑμῖν, ἀλλ' ὃς ἐὰν θέλῃ ἐν ὑμῖν μέγας γενέσθαι ἔσται ὑμῶν διάκονος, 27 καὶ ὃς ἂν θέλῃ ἐν ὑμῖν εἶναι πρῶτος ἔσται ὑμῶν δοῦλος· 28 ὥσπερ ὁ υἱὸς τοῦ ἀνθρώπου οὐκ ἦλθεν διακονηθῆναι ἀλλὰ διακονῆσαι καὶ δοῦναι τὴν ψυχὴν αὐτοῦ λύτρον ἀντὶ πολλῶν.

20:29 Καὶ ἐκπορευομένων αὐτῶν ἀπὸ Ἰεριχὼ ἠκολούθησεν αὐτῷ ὄχλος πολύς. 30 καὶ ἰδοὺ δύο τυφλοὶ καθήμενοι παρὰ τὴν ὁδόν ἀκούσαντες ὅτι Ἰησοῦς παράγει, ἔκραξαν λέγοντες, Ἐλέησον ἡμᾶς, [κύριε,] υἱὸς Δαυίδ. ¶ 31 ὁ δὲ ὄχλος ἐπετίμησεν αὐτοῖς ἵνα σιωπήσωσιν· οἱ δὲ μεῖζον ἔκραξαν λέγοντες, Κύριε, «κύριε,» ἐλέησον «Ἐλέησον» ἡμᾶς, υἱὲ «υἱὸς» Δαυίδ. ¶ 32 καὶ στὰς ὁ Ἰησοῦς ἐφώνησεν αὐτοὺς καὶ εἶπεν, Τί θέλετε ποιήσω ὑμῖν; 33 λέγουσιν αὐτῷ, Κύριε, ἵνα ἀνοιγῶσιν οἱ ὀφθαλμοὶ ἡμῶν. ¶ 34 σπλαγχνισθεὶς δὲ ὁ Ἰησοῦς ἥψατο τῶν ὀμμάτων αὐτῶν, καὶ εὐθέως ἀνέβλεψαν καὶ ἠκολούθησαν αὐτῷ.

Immediately they received their sight   and followed   him.
καὶ εὐθέως   →   →   →   ἀνέβλεψαν καὶ ἠκολούθησαν αὐτῷ
cj   adv   v.aai.3p   cj   v.aai.3p   r.dsm.3
2779 2311   329   2779 199   899

The Triumphal Entry

21:1 As they approached   Jerusalem and came to Bethphage on the Mount of Olives,   Jesus sent
Καὶ ὅτε →   ἤγγισαν   εἰς Ἰεροσόλυμα καὶ ἦλθον εἰς Βηθφαγὴ εἰς τὸ ὄρος τῶν ἐλαιῶν τότε Ἰησοῦς ἀπέστειλεν
cj   cj   v.aai.3p   p.a n.apn   cj   v.aai.3p p.a n.asf   p.a d.asn n.asn d.gpf n.gpf   adv   n.nsm   v.aai.3s
2779 4021   1581   1650 2642   2779 2262   1650 1036   1650 3836 4001 3836 1777   5538 2652   690

two disciples, **2** saying to them, "Go   to the village   ahead   of you, and at once you will find   a donkey
δύο μαθητάς   λέγων › αὐτοῖς πορεύεσθε εἰς τὴν κώμην τὴν κατέναντι → ὑμῶν καὶ → εὐθέως → → εὑρήσετε ὄνον
a.apm n.apm   pt.pa.nsm r.dpm.3 v.pmm.2p p.a d.asf n.asf d.asf p.g   r.gp.2 cj   adv   v.fai.2p n.asf
1545 3412   3306   899   4513   1650 3836 3267   3836 2978   7007 2779   2311   2351   3952

tied there, with her colt by her. Untie them and bring them to me. **3** If anyone says anything to
δεδεμένην   καὶ   πῶλον μετ᾽ αὐτῆς λύσαντες   ἀγάγετε   → μοι καὶ ἐάν τις   εἴπῃ τι   →
pt.rp.asf   cj   n.asm p.g r.gsf.3 pt.aa.npm   v.aam.2p   r.ds.1 cj cj   r.nsm   v.aas.3s r.asn
1313   2779   4798 3552 899   3395   72   1609 2779 1569 5516   3306   5516

you, tell him that the Lord needs   them, and he will send   them right away." ¶   **4** This took
ὑμῖν ἐρεῖτε   ὅτι ὁ κύριος χρείαν ἔχει αὐτῶν δὲ → ἀποστελεῖ αὐτούς εὐθὺς ←   δὲ τοῦτο γέγονεν
r.dp.2 v.fai.2p   cj   d.nsm n.nsm n.asf   v.pai.3s r.gpm.3 cj   v.fai.3s r.apm.3 adv   cj   r.nsn v.rai.3s
7007 3306   4022 3836 3261   5970   2400   899   1254   690   899   2318   1254 4047   1181

place to fulfill what was spoken through the prophet: **5** "Say to the Daughter of Zion, 'See, your
← ἵνα πληρωθῇ τὸ → ῥηθὲν διὰ τοῦ προφήτου λέγοντος εἴπατε → τῇ θυγατρὶ Σιών ἰδοὺ σου
cj   v.aps.3s d.nsn   pt.ap.nsn p.g d.gsm n.gsm   pt.pa.gsm v.aam.2p   d.dsf n.dsf   n.gsf j   r.gs.2
2671 4444   3836   3306   1328 3836 4737   3306   3306   3836 2588   4994 2627   5148

king   comes to you, gentle and riding   on a donkey,   on a colt, the foal of a donkey.'" ¶   **6**
ὁ βασιλεύς ἔρχεται → σοι πραΰς καὶ ἐπιβεβηκὼς ἐπὶ ὄνον   καὶ ἐπὶ πῶλον υἱὸν → ὑποζυγίου   δὲ
d.nsm n.nsm v.pmi.3s   r.ds.2 a.nsm cj   pt.ra.nsm p.a n.asm   cj   p.a n.asm n.asm   n.gsn   cj
3836 995   2262   5148 4558   2779 2094   2093 3952   2779 2093 4798   5626   5689   1254

The disciples went   and did   as   Jesus   had instructed them. **7** They brought the donkey and the
οἱ μαθηταὶ πορευθέντες καὶ ποιήσαντες καθὼς ὁ Ἰησοῦς → συνέταξεν αὐτοῖς   ἤγαγον τὴν ὄνον καὶ τὸν
d.npm n.npm pt.ap.npm cj   pt.aa.npm cj   d.nsm n.nsm   v.aai.3s r.dpm.3   v.aai.3p d.asf n.asf cj   d.asm
3836 3412   4513   2779 4472   2777   3836 2652   5332   899   72   3836 3952 2779 3836

colt,   placed their cloaks on them, and Jesus sat   on   them. **8** A very large   crowd spread their
πῶλον καὶ ἐπέθηκαν τὰ ἱμάτια ἐπ᾽ αὐτῶν καὶ ἐπεκάθισεν ἐπάνω αὐτῶν δὲ ὁ → πλεῖστος ὄχλος ἔστρωσαν ἑαυτῶν
n.asm cj   v.aai.3p d.apn n.apn   p.g r.gpm.3 cj   v.aai.3s   p.g r.gpm.3 cj   d.nsm   a.nsm.s   n.nsm   v.aai.3p r.gpm.3
4798 2779 2202   3836 2668   2093 899   2779 2125   2062 899   1254 3836   4498   4063   5143   1571

cloaks   on the road, while others cut   branches from the trees   and spread   them on the road. **9** The
τὰ ἱμάτια ἐν τῇ ὁδῷ δὲ ἄλλοι ἔκοπτον κλάδους ἀπὸ τῶν δένδρων καὶ ἐστρώννυον   ἐν τῇ ὁδῷ δὲ οἱ
d.apn n.apn p.d d.dsf n.dsf cj   r.npm v.iai.3p n.apm   p.g d.gpn n.gpn   cj   v.iai.3p   p.d d.dsf n.dsf cj   d.npm
3836 2668   1877 3836 3847 1254 257   3164   3080   608 3836 1285   2779 5143   1877 3836 3847 1254 3836

crowds that went   ahead of him and those that followed   shouted,   "Hosanna to the Son of David!"
ὄχλοι οἱ προάγοντες ← ← αὐτὸν καὶ οἱ ← ἀκολουθοῦντες ἔκραζον λέγοντες ὡσαννὰ → τῷ υἱῷ → Δαυίδ
n.npm d.npm pt.pa.npm   r.asm.3 cj   d.npm   pt.pa.npm   v.iai.3p pt.pa.npm j   d.dsm n.dsm   n.gsm
4063   3836 4575   899   2779 3836   199   3189   3306   6057   3836 5626   1253

"Blessed is he who comes   in the name of the Lord!" "Hosanna in the highest!" ¶   **10** When Jesus
εὐλογημένος ὁ ← ἐρχόμενος ἐν ὀνόματι → κυρίου ὡσαννὰ ἐν τοῖς ὑψίστοις   Καὶ → αὐτοῦ
pt.rp.nsm   d.nsm   pt.pm.nsm p.d n.dsn   n.gsm   j   p.d d.dpn a.dpn.s   cj   r.gsm.3
2328   3836   2262   1877 3950   3261   6057   1877 3836 5736   2779   899

entered   Jerusalem, the whole city was stirred and asked, "Who is   this?" **11** The crowds answered, "This
εἰσελθόντος εἰς Ἰεροσόλυμα ἡ πᾶσα πόλις → ἐσείσθη λέγουσα τίς ἐστιν οὗτος δὲ οἱ ὄχλοι ἔλεγον οὗτος
pt.aa.gsm   p.a n.apn   d.nsf a.nsf n.nsf   v.api.3s pt.pa.nsf r.nsm v.pai.3s r.nsm cj   d.npm n.npm v.iai.3p r.nsm
1656   1650 2642   3836 4246   4484   4940   3306   5515 1639   4047   1254 3836 4063   3306   4047

is Jesus, the prophet   from Nazareth in Galilee."
ἐστιν Ἰησοῦς ὁ προφήτης ὁ ἀπὸ Ναζαρὲθ τῆς Γαλιλαίας
v.pai.3s n.nsm d.nsm n.nsm   d.nsm p.g n.gsf   d.gsf n.gsf
1639   2652   3836 4737   3836 608 3714   3836 1133

21:1 Καὶ ὅτε ἤγγισαν εἰς Ἰεροσόλυμα καὶ ἦλθον εἰς Βηθφαγὴ εἰς τὸ Ὄρος τῶν Ἐλαιῶν, τότε Ἰησοῦς ἀπέστειλεν δύο μαθητὰς **2** λέγων αὐτοῖς, Πορεύεσθε εἰς τὴν κώμην τὴν κατέναντι ὑμῶν, καὶ εὐθέως εὑρήσετε ὄνον δεδεμένην καὶ πῶλον μετ᾽ αὐτῆς· λύσαντες ἀγάγετέ μοι. **3** καὶ ἐάν τις ὑμῖν εἴπῃ τι, ἐρεῖτε ὅτι Ὁ κύριος αὐτῶν χρείαν ἔχει· εὐθὺς δὲ ἀποστελεῖ αὐτούς. ¶ **4** Τοῦτο δὲ γέγονεν ἵνα πληρωθῇ τὸ ῥηθὲν διὰ τοῦ προφήτου λέγοντος, **5** Εἴπατε τῇ θυγατρὶ Σιών, Ἰδοὺ ὁ βασιλεύς σου ἔρχεταί σοι πραΰς καὶ ἐπιβεβηκὼς ἐπὶ ὄνον καὶ ἐπὶ πῶλον υἱὸν ὑποζυγίου. ¶ **6** πορευθέντες δὲ οἱ μαθηταὶ καὶ ποιήσαντες καθὼς συνέταξεν αὐτοῖς ὁ Ἰησοῦς **7** ἤγαγον τὴν ὄνον καὶ τὸν πῶλον καὶ ἐπέθηκαν ἐπ᾽ αὐτῶν τὰ ἱμάτια, καὶ ἐπεκάθισεν ἐπάνω αὐτῶν. **8** ὁ δὲ πλεῖστος ὄχλος ἔστρωσαν ἑαυτῶν τὰ ἱμάτια ἐν τῇ ὁδῷ, ἄλλοι δὲ ἔκοπτον κλάδους ἀπὸ τῶν δένδρων καὶ ἐστρώννυον ἐν τῇ ὁδῷ. **9** οἱ δὲ ὄχλοι οἱ προάγοντες αὐτὸν καὶ οἱ ἀκολουθοῦντες ἔκραζον λέγοντες, Ὡσαννὰ τῷ υἱῷ Δαυίδ· Εὐλογημένος ὁ ἐρχόμενος ἐν ὀνόματι κυρίου· Ὡσαννὰ ἐν τοῖς ὑψίστοις. ¶ **10** καὶ εἰσελθόντος αὐτοῦ εἰς Ἰεροσόλυμα ἐσείσθη πᾶσα ἡ πόλις λέγουσα, Τίς ἐστιν οὗτος; **11** οἱ δὲ ὄχλοι ἔλεγον, Οὗτός ἐστιν ὁ προφήτης Ἰησοῦς ὁ ἀπὸ Ναζαρὲθ τῆς Γαλιλαίας.

Jesus at the Temple

21:12

Jesus	entered		the	temple area	and	drove out	all		who were	buying	and	selling
Καὶ	Ἰησοῦς	εἰσῆλθεν	εἰς	τὸ	ἱερὸν	←	καὶ	ἐξέβαλεν ←	πάντας	τοὺς →	πωλοῦντας	καὶ	ἀγοράζοντας
cj	n.nsm	v.aai.3s	p.a	d.asn	n.asn		cj	v.aai.3s	a.apm	d.apm	pt.pa.apm	cj	pt.pa.apm
2779	2652	1656	1650	3836	2639		2779	1675	4246	3836	4797	2779	60

there.		He overturned	the	tables		of the		money changers	and	the	benches	of those	selling
ἐν τῷ ἱερῷ	καὶ	κατέστρεψεν	τὰς	τραπέζας	→	τῶν	→	κολλυβιστῶν	καὶ	τὰς	καθέδρας	τῶν	πωλούντων
p.d d.dsn n.dsn	cj	v.aai.3s	d.apf	n.apf		d.gpm		n.gpm	cj	d.apf	n.apf	d.gpm	pt.pa.gpm
1877 3836 2639	2779	2951	3836	5544		3836		3142	2779	3836	2756	3836	4797

doves.	**13** "It is written,"			he said	to them,	"'My		house		will be called	a house	of prayer,'	but	you
τὰς περιστεράς.		→	γέγραπται	καὶ	→	λέγει	αὐτοῖς	μου	ὁ	οἶκος,	→	κληθήσεται	οἶκος	→	προσευχῆς	δὲ	ὑμεῖς
d.apf n.apf			v.rpi.3s	cj		v.pai.3s	r.dpm.3	r.gs.1	d.nsm	n.nsm		v.fpi.3s	n.nsm		n.gsf	cj	r.np.2
3836 4361			1211	2779		3306	899	1609	3836	3875		2813	3875		4666	1254	7007

are	making	it	a 'den	of robbers.'"	¶	**14**		The	blind	and	the	lame	came		to him	at	the	temple,	and
→	ποιεῖτε	αὐτὸν	σπήλαιον	λῃστῶν			καὶ		τυφλοὶ	καὶ		χωλοὶ	προσῆλθον ←		αὐτῷ	ἐν	τῷ	ἱερῷ	καὶ
	v.pai.2p	r.asm.3	n.asn	n.gpm			cj		a.npm	cj		a.npm	v.aai.3p		r.dsm.3	p.d	d.dsn	n.dsn	cj
	4472	899	5068	3334			2779		5603	2779		6000	4665		899	1877	3836	2639	2779

he healed	them.	**15** But	when	the	chief priests		and	the	teachers	of the law	saw			the	wonderful things		he
→	ἐθεράπευσεν	αὐτούς	δὲ	οἱ	ἀρχιερεῖς	καὶ	οἱ	γραμματεῖς ←	←	←	ἰδόντες	τὰ	θαυμάσια	←	ἃ
	v.aai.3s	r.apm.3	cj	d.npm	n.npm	cj	d.npm	n.npm			pt.aa.npm	d.apn	n.apn		r.apn
	2543	899	1254	1625	3836	797	2779	3836	1208		1625	3836	2514		4005

did	and	the	children	shouting		in	the	temple area,		"Hosanna	to the	Son	of David,"		they
ἐποίησεν	καὶ	τοὺς	παῖδας	τοὺς κράζοντας	ἐν	τῷ	ἱερῷ	←	καὶ	λέγοντας	ὡσαννὰ	→	τῷ	υἱῷ	→	Δαυίδ	καὶ
v.aai.3s	cj	d.apm	n.apm	d.apm pt.pa.apm	p.d	d.dsn	n.dsn		cj	pt.pa.apm	j		d.dsm	n.dsm		n.gsm	cj
4472	2779	3836	4090	3836 3189	1877	3836	2639		2779	3306	6057		3836	5626		1253	2779

were	indignant.	¶	**16** "Do you hear	what	these	children	are saying?"	they asked	him.	"Yes,"	replied
→	ἠγανάκτησαν			ἀκούεις	τί	οὗτοι	→	λέγουσιν	εἶπαν	αὐτῷ	δὲ	ναί	λέγει
	v.aai.3p			v.pai.2s	r.asn	r.npm		v.pai.3p	v.aai.3p	r.dsm.3	cj	pl	v.pai.3s
	24			201	5515	4047		3306	3306	899	1254	3721	3306

Jesus,		"have you	never	read,	"'From	the	lips	of children	and	infants	you have	ordained
ὁ	Ἰησοῦς,	αὐτοῖς		οὐδέποτε	ἀνέγνωτε	ὅτι	ἐκ	στόματος	→	νηπίων	καὶ	θηλαζόντων	→	→	κατηρτίσω
d.nsm	n.nsm	r.dpm.3		adv	v.aai.2p	cj	p.g	n.gsn		a.gpm	cj	pt.pa.gpm			v.ami.2s
3836	2652	899	336	336	4030	336	4022	1666		5125	3758	2779	2558		2936

praise'?"	¶	**17** And	he left		them	and	went	out	of the	city	to	Bethany,		where	he spent	the night.
αἶνον		καὶ	→	καταλιπὼν	αὐτούς	ἐξῆλθεν	ἔξω		τῆς	πόλεως	εἰς	Βηθανίαν	καὶ	ἐκεῖ	→	ηὐλίσθη ←	←
n.asm		cj		pt.aa.nsm	r.apm.3	v.aai.3s	p.g		d.gsf	n.gsf	p.a	n.asf	cj	adv		v.api.3s
142		2779		2901	899	2002	2032		3836	4484	1650	1029	2779	1695		887

The Fig Tree Withers

21:18

Early	in the	morning,	as he was	on his way		back	to	the	city,	he was hungry.	**19**	Seeing	a	fig
δὲ	Πρωὶ	←	←	→	→	ἐπανάγων	←	εἰς	τὴν	πόλιν	→	ἐπείνασεν	καὶ	ἰδὼν	μίαν	→
cj	adv					pt.pa.nsm		p.a	d.asf	n.asf		v.aai.3s	cj	pt.aa.nsm	a.asf
1254	4745					2056		1650	3836	4484		4277	2779	1625	1651

tree	by	the	road,	he went	up to	it	but	found	nothing	on	it	except	leaves.		Then	he said	to it,	"May
συκῆν	ἐπὶ	τῆς	ὁδοῦ	→	ἦλθεν	ἐπ᾽	αὐτὴν	καὶ	εὗρεν	οὐδὲν	ἐν	αὐτῇ	εἰ	μὴ	φύλλα	μόνον	καὶ	→	λέγει	→	αὐτῇ
n.asf	p.g	d.gsf	n.gsf		v.aai.3s	p.a	r.asf.3	cj	v.aai.3s	a.asn	p.d	r.dsf.3	cj	pl	n.apn	adv	cj		v.pai.3s		r.dsf.3
5190	2093	3836	3847		2262	2093	899	2779	2351	4029	1877	899	1623	3590	5877	3667	2779		3306		899	1181

you	never	bear	fruit	again!"		Immediately	the	tree	withered.	¶	**20**	When	the	disciples	saw
ἐκ	σοῦ	μηκέτι	γένηται	καρπὸς	εἰς	τὸν	αἰῶνα	καὶ	παραχρῆμα	ἡ	συκῆ	ἐξηράνθη		Καὶ	→	οἱ	μαθηταὶ	ἰδόντες
p.g	r.gs.2	adv	v.ams.3s	n.nsm	p.a	d.asm	n.asm	cj	adv	d.nsf	n.nsf	v.api.3s		cj		d.npm	n.npm	pt.aa.npm
1666	5148	3600	1181	2843	1650	3836	172	2779	4202	3836	5190	3830		2779		3836	3412	1625

this,	they were	amazed.	"How	did	the fig tree	wither	so quickly?"	they asked.	**21**	Jesus	replied,
→	ἐθαύμασαν	πῶς	ἡ	συκῆ	ἐξηράνθη	παραχρῆμα	→	λέγοντες	δὲ	ὁ	Ἰησοῦς	ἀποκριθεὶς	εἶπεν
	v.aai.3p	pl	d.nsf	n.nsf	v.api.3s	adv		pt.pa.npm	cj	d.nsm	n.nsm	pt.ap.nsm	v.aai.3s
	2513	4802	3830	3836	5190	3830	4202		3306	1254	3836	2652	646	3306

"I tell	you	the truth,	if	you have	faith	and	do	not	doubt,		not	only	can	you	do		what was	done	to
αὐτοῖς	→	λέγω	ὑμῖν	ἀμὴν	ἐὰν	→	ἔχητε	πίστιν	καὶ	→	μὴ	διακριθῆτε	οὐ	μόνον	→	ποιήσετε	τὸ	←	←
r.dpm.3		v.pai.1s	r.dp.2	pl	cj		v.pas.2p	n.asf	cj		pl	v.aps.2p	pl	adv		v.fai.2p	d.asn
899		3306	7007	297	1569		2400	4411	2779		3590	1359	4024	3667		4472	3836

²¹:¹² Καὶ εἰσῆλθεν Ἰησοῦς εἰς τὸ ἱερὸν καὶ ἐξέβαλεν πάντας τοὺς πωλοῦντας καὶ ἀγοράζοντας ἐν τῷ ἱερῷ, καὶ τὰς τραπέζας τῶν κολλυβιστῶν κατέστρεψεν καὶ τὰς καθέδρας τῶν πωλούντων τὰς περιστεράς, ¹³ καὶ λέγει αὐτοῖς, Γέγραπται, Ὁ οἶκός μου οἶκος προσευχῆς κληθήσεται, ὑμεῖς δὲ αὐτὸν ποιεῖτε σπήλαιον λῃστῶν. ¶ ¹⁴ Καὶ προσῆλθον αὐτῷ τυφλοὶ καὶ χωλοὶ ἐν τῷ ἱερῷ, καὶ ἐθεράπευσεν αὐτούς. ¹⁵ ἰδόντες δὲ οἱ ἀρχιερεῖς καὶ οἱ γραμματεῖς τὰ θαυμάσια ἃ ἐποίησεν καὶ τοὺς παῖδας τοὺς κράζοντας ἐν τῷ ἱερῷ καὶ λέγοντας, Ὡσαννὰ τῷ υἱῷ Δαυίδ, ἠγανάκτησαν ¶ ¹⁶ καὶ εἶπαν αὐτῷ, Ἀκούεις τί οὗτοι λέγουσιν; ὁ δὲ Ἰησοῦς λέγει αὐτοῖς, Ναί. οὐδέποτε ἀνέγνωτε ὅτι Ἐκ στόματος νηπίων καὶ θηλαζόντων κατηρτίσω αἶνον; ¶ ¹⁷ Καὶ καταλιπὼν αὐτοὺς ἐξῆλθεν ἔξω τῆς πόλεως εἰς Βηθανίαν καὶ ηὐλίσθη ἐκεῖ.

²¹:¹⁸ Πρωὶ δὲ ἐπανάγων εἰς τὴν πόλιν ἐπείνασεν. ¹⁹ καὶ ἰδὼν συκῆν μίαν ἐπὶ τῆς ὁδοῦ ἦλθεν ἐπ᾽ αὐτὴν καὶ οὐδὲν εὗρεν ἐν αὐτῇ εἰ μὴ φύλλα μόνον, καὶ λέγει αὐτῇ, Μηκέτι ἐκ σοῦ καρπὸς γένηται εἰς τὸν αἰῶνα. καὶ ἐξηράνθη παραχρῆμα ἡ συκῆ. ¶ ²⁰ καὶ ἰδόντες οἱ μαθηταὶ ἐθαύμασαν λέγοντες, Πῶς παραχρῆμα ἐξηράνθη ἡ συκῆ; ²¹ ἀποκριθεὶς δὲ ὁ Ἰησοῦς εἶπεν αὐτοῖς, Ἀμὴν

the fig tree,	but	also	you can	say	to	this	mountain,	'Go,		throw	yourself	into	the	sea,'		and it will be
τῆς → συκῆς	ἀλλὰ	κἂν →	→	εἴπητε τῷ	τούτῳ	ὄρει		ἄρθητι	καὶ	βλήθητι ←		εἰς	τὴν	θάλασσαν	→ →	
d.gsf n.gsf	cj	crasis		v.aas.2p d.dsn	r.dsn	n.dsn		v.apm.2s	cj	v.apm.2s		p.a	d.asf	n.asf		
3836 5190	247	2829		3306 3836	4047	4001		149	2779	965		1650	3836	2498		

done.	**22**	If you believe,		you will	receive	whatever			you ask		for	in	prayer."
γενήσεται	καὶ →	→ πιστεύοντες	→	→	λήμψεσθε	πάντα ὅσα	ἂν	→	αἰτήσητε ←		ἐν	τῇ	προσευχῇ
v.fmi.3s	cj	pt.pa.npm			v.fmi.2p	a.apn r.apn	r.apn		v.aas.2p		p.d	d.dsf	n.dsf
1181	2779	4409			3284	4246 4012	323		160		1877	3836	4666

The Authority of Jesus Questioned

21:23

	Jesus	entered		the	temple courts,	and,	while he was	teaching,	the	chief	priests	and	the	elders	of
Καὶ	αὐτοῦ	ἐλθόντος	εἰς	τὸ	ἱερὸν	→ →	→ →	διδάσκοντι	οἱ		ἀρχιερεῖς	καὶ	οἱ	πρεσβύτεροι	
cj	r.gsm.3	pt.aa.gsm	p.a	d.asn	n.asn			pt.pa.dsm	d.npm		n.npm	cj	d.npm	a.npm	
2779	899	2262	1650	3836	2639			1438	3836		797	2779	3836	4565	

the	people	came		to him.	"By	what	authority	are you	doing	these	things?"	they asked.	"And	who	gave	you
τοῦ	λαοῦ	προσῆλθον ←		αὐτῷ	ἐν	ποίᾳ	ἐξουσίᾳ	→ →	ποιεῖς	ταῦτα ←		→ λέγοντες	καὶ	τίς	ἔδωκέν	σοι
d.gsm	n.gsm	v.aai.3p		r.dsm.3	p.d	r.dsf	n.dsf		v.pai.2s	r.apn		pt.pa.npm	cj	r.nsm	v.aai.3s	r.ds.2
3836	3295	4665		899	1877	4481	2026		4472	4047		3306	2779	5515	1443	5148

this	authority?"	¶	**24**	Jesus		replied,		"I	will also	ask	you	one	question.	If	you
ταύτην ⌐τὴν ἐξουσίαν⌐				δὲ ὁ	Ἰησοῦς⌐	⌐ἀποκριθεὶς	εἶπεν	αὐτοῖς	κἀγὼ →		ἐρωτήσω ὑμᾶς	ἕνα	λόγον	ὃν	ἐὰν →
r.asf d.asf n.asf				cj d.nsm	n.nsm	pt.ap.nsm	v.aai.3s	r.dpm.3	adv		v.fai.1s r.ap.2	a.asm	n.asm	r.asm	cj
4047 3836 2026				1254 3836	2652	646	3306	899	2743 2263	2743	2263 7007	1651	3364	4005	1569

answer	me,	I	will	tell	you	by	what	authority	I am	doing	these	things.	**25**	John's		baptism	— where	did it
εἴπητε	μοι	κἀγὼ →		ἐρῶ	ὑμῖν	ἐν	ποίᾳ	ἐξουσίᾳ	→	ποιῶ	ταῦτα ←			⌐τὸ Ἰωάννου⌐		⌐τὸ βάπτισμα⌐	πόθεν	→ →
v.aas.2p	r.ds.1	crasis		v.fai.1s	r.dp.2	p.d	r.dsf	n.dsf		v.pai.1s	r.apn			d.nsn n.gsm		d.nsn n.nsn	cj	
3306	1609	2743		3306	7007	1877	4481	2026		4472	4047			3836 2722		3836 967	4470	

come	from?	Was it		from	heaven,	or	from	men?"	¶		They	discussed	it	among	themselves	and	said,	"If
ἦν	↰			ἐξ	οὐρανοῦ	ἢ	ἐξ	ἀνθρώπων		δὲ	οἱ	διελογίζοντο	ἐν	ἑαυτοῖς		λέγοντες		ἐὰν
v.iai.3s				p.g	n.gsm	cj	p.g	n.gpm		cj	d.npm	v.imi.3p	p.d	r.dpm.3		pt.pa.npm		cj
1639	4470			1666	4041	2445	1666	476		1254	3836	1368	1877	1571		3306		1569

we say,	'From	heaven,'		he will ask,		'Then	why		didn't	you believe	him?'	**26**	But if		we say,	'From
→ εἴπωμεν	ἐξ	οὐρανοῦ	→	→	ἐρεῖ	ἡμῖν	οὖν	⌐διὰ τί⌐	οὐκ	→ ἐπιστεύσατε	αὐτῷ		δὲ	ἐὰν →	εἴπωμεν	ἐξ
v.aas.1p	p.g	n.gsm			v.fai.3s	r.dp.1	cj	p.a r.asn	pl	v.aai.2p	r.dsm.3		cj	cj	v.aas.1p	p.g
3306	1666	4041			3306	7005	4036	1328 5515	4024	4409	899		1254	1569	3306	1666

men'	— we	are afraid		of	the	people,	for	they	all	hold	that	John		was	a prophet."	**27**	So	they
ἀνθρώπων	→	φοβούμεθα ←		τὸν	ὄχλον	γὰρ ↰		πάντες	ἔχουσιν		⌐τὸν Ἰωάννην⌐	ὡς		προφήτην		καὶ		
n.gpm		v.ppi.1p		d.asm	n.asm	cj		a.npm	v.pai.3p		d.asm n.asm	pl		n.asm		cj		
476		5828		3836	4063	1142 2400		4246	2400		3836 2722	6055		4737		2779		

answered	Jesus,	"We	don't know."	¶		Then	he	said,		"Neither	will	I	tell	you	by	what
⌐ἀποκριθέντες	εἶπαν	⌐τῷ Ἰησοῦ⌐	→ οὐκ οἴδαμεν		καὶ	αὐτὸς	ἔφη	αὐτοῖς	οὐδὲ			ἐγὼ	λέγω	ὑμῖν	ἐν	ποίᾳ
pt.ap.npm	v.aai.3p	d.dsm n.dsm	pl v.rai.1p		adv	r.nsm	v.iai.3s	r.dpm.3	cj			r.ns.1	v.pai.1s	r.dp.2	p.d	r.dsf
646	3306	3836 2652	3857 4024 3857		2779	899	5774	899	4028			3306 1609	3306	7007	1877	4481

authority	I am	doing	these	things.
ἐξουσίᾳ	→	ποιῶ	ταῦτα ←	
n.dsf		v.pai.1s	r.apn	
2026		4472	4047	

The Parable of the Two Sons

21:28

	"What	do	you	think?	There was	a	man		who had	two	sons.		He	went		to	the	first	and	said,
δὲ	Τί	↰	ὑμῖν	δοκεῖ			ἄνθρωπος		εἶχεν	δύο	τέκνα	καὶ	→	προσελθὼν ←		τῷ		πρώτῳ		εἶπεν
cj	r.nsn		r.dp.2	v.pai.3s			n.nsm		v.iai.3s	a.apn	n.apn	cj		pt.aa.nsm		d.dsn		a.dsn		v.aai.3s
1254	5515		7007	1506			476		2400	1545	5451	2779		4665		3836		4755		3306

'Son,	go	and	work	today	in	the	vineyard.'	**29**		"'I	will not,'	he	answered,		but	later	he	changed	his
τέκνον	ὕπαγε		ἐργάζου	σήμερον	ἐν	τῷ	ἀμπελῶνι	δὲ	→	θέλω	οὐ	ὁ	⌐ἀποκριθεὶς	εἶπεν⌐	δὲ	ὕστερον	→	μεταμεληθεὶς ←	
n.vsn	v.pam.2s		v.pmm.2s	adv	p.d	d.dsm	n.dsm	cj		v.pai.1s	pl	d.nsm	pt.ap.nsm	v.aai.3s	cj	adv.c		pt.ap.nsm	
5451	5632		2237	4958	1877	3836	308	1254		2527	4024	646		3306	1254	5731		3564	

mind	and went.	**30**	"Then	the	father	went		to	the	other	son	and	said	the	same		thing.		He	answered,	'I
←	ἀπῆλθεν	δὲ				προσελθὼν ←		τῷ		ἑτέρῳ			εἶπεν		ὡσαύτως			δὲ	ὁ	⌐ἀποκριθεὶς	εἶπεν⌐ ⌐ἐγὼ⌐
	v.aai.3s	cj				pt.aa.nsm		d.dsm		r.dsm			v.aai.3s		adv			cj	d.nsm	pt.ap.nsm	v.aai.3s r.ns.1
	599	1254				4665		3836		2283			3306		6058			1254	3836	646	3306 1609

λέγω ὑμῖν, ἐὰν ἔχητε πίστιν καὶ μὴ διακριθῆτε, οὐ μόνον τὸ τῆς συκῆς ποιήσετε, ἀλλὰ κἂν τῷ ὄρει τούτῳ εἴπητε, Ἄρθητι καὶ βλήθητι εἰς τὴν θάλασσαν, γενήσεται· ²² καὶ πάντα ὅσα ἂν αἰτήσητε ἐν τῇ προσευχῇ πιστεύοντες λήμψεσθε.

²¹·²³ Καὶ ἐλθόντος αὐτοῦ εἰς τὸ ἱερὸν προσῆλθον αὐτῷ διδάσκοντι οἱ ἀρχιερεῖς καὶ οἱ πρεσβύτεροι τοῦ λαοῦ λέγοντες, Ἐν ποίᾳ ἐξουσίᾳ ταῦτα ποιεῖς; καὶ τίς σοι ἔδωκεν τὴν ἐξουσίαν ταύτην; ¶ ²⁴ ἀποκριθεὶς δὲ ὁ Ἰησοῦς εἶπεν αὐτοῖς, Ἐρωτήσω ὑμᾶς κἀγὼ λόγον ἕνα, ὃν ἐὰν εἴπητέ μοι κἀγὼ ὑμῖν ἐρῶ ἐν ποίᾳ ἐξουσίᾳ ταῦτα ποιῶ· ²⁵ τὸ βάπτισμα τὸ Ἰωάννου πόθεν ἦν; ἐξ οὐρανοῦ ἢ ἐξ ἀνθρώπων; ¶ οἱ δὲ διελογίζοντο ἐν ἑαυτοῖς λέγοντες, Ἐὰν εἴπωμεν, Ἐξ οὐρανοῦ, ἐρεῖ ἡμῖν, Διὰ τί οὖν οὐκ ἐπιστεύσατε αὐτῷ; ²⁶ ἐὰν δὲ εἴπωμεν, Ἐξ ἀνθρώπων, φοβούμεθα τὸν ὄχλον, πάντες γὰρ ὡς προφήτην ἔχουσιν τὸν Ἰωάννην. ²⁷ καὶ ἀποκριθέντες τῷ Ἰησοῦ εἶπαν, Οὐκ οἴδαμεν. ¶ ἔφη αὐτοῖς καὶ αὐτός, Οὐδὲ ἐγὼ λέγω ὑμῖν ἐν ποίᾳ ἐξουσίᾳ ταῦτα ποιῶ.

²¹·²⁸ Τί δὲ ὑμῖν δοκεῖ; ἄνθρωπος εἶχεν τέκνα δύο. καὶ προσελθὼν τῷ πρώτῳ εἶπεν, Τέκνον, ὕπαγε σήμερον ἐργάζου ἐν τῷ ἀμπελῶνι. ²⁹ ὁ δὲ ἀποκριθεὶς εἶπεν, Οὐ θέλω, ὕστερον δὲ μεταμεληθεὶς ἀπῆλθεν. ³⁰ προσελθὼν δὲ τῷ ἑτέρῳ εἶπεν ὡσαύτως. ὁ

will, sir,' but he did not go. ¶ **31** "Which of the two did what his father wanted?" "The first," they
κύριε καί → ↱ οὐκ ἀπῆλθεν τίς ἐκ τῶν δύο ἐποίησεν τὸ τοῦ πατρὸς θέλημα ὁ πρῶτος →
n.vsm cj pl v.aai.3s r.nsm p.g d.gpm a.gpm v.aai.3s d.asn d.gsm n.gsm n.asn d.nsm a.nsm
3261 2779 599 599 4024 599 5515 1666 3836 1545 4472 3836 3836 4252 2525 3836 4755

answered. Jesus said to them, "I tell you the truth, the tax collectors and the prostitutes are entering
λέγουσιν ὁ Ἰησοῦς, λέγει → αὐτοῖς → λέγω ὑμῖν ἀμὴν ὅτι οἱ → τελῶναι καὶ αἱ πόρναι → προάγουσιν εἰς
v.pai.3p d.nsm n.nsm v.pai.3s r.dpm.3 v.pai.1s r.dp.2 pl cj d.npm n.npm cj d.npf n.npf v.pai.3p p.a
3306 3836 2652 3306 899 3306 7007 297 4022 3836 5467 2779 3836 4520 4575 1650

the kingdom of God ahead of you. **32** For John came to you to show you the way of righteousness, and you
τὴν βασιλείαν τοῦ θεοῦ → ↤ ὑμᾶς γὰρ Ἰωάννης ἦλθεν πρὸς ὑμᾶς ἐν ὁδῷ → δικαιοσύνης καὶ →
d.asf n.asf d.gsm n.gsm r.ap.2 cj n.nsm v.aai.3s p.a r.ap.2 p.d n.dsf n.gsf cj
3836 993 3836 2536 4575 4575 7007 1142 2722 2262 4639 7007 1877 3847 1466 2779 4409

did not believe him, but the tax collectors and the prostitutes did. And even after you saw this,
↱ οὐκ ἐπιστεύσατε αὐτῷ δὲ οἱ → τελῶναι καὶ αἱ πόρναι ἐπίστευσαν αὐτῷ δὲ ὕστερον → ἰδόντες
pl v.aai.2p r.dsm.3 cj d.npm n.npm cj d.npf n.npf v.aai.3p r.dsm.3 cj adv.c pt.aa.npm
4409 4024 4409 899 1254 3836 5467 2779 3836 4520 4409 899 1254 5731 1625

you did not repent and believe him.
ὑμεῖς → οὐδὲ μετεμελήθητε τοῦ πιστεῦσαι αὐτῷ
r.np.2 adv v.api.2p d.gsn n.faa r.dsm.3
7007 3564 4028 3564 3836 4409 899

The Parable of the Tenants

21:33 "Listen to another parable: There was a landowner who planted a vineyard. He put a
ἀκούσατε ← Ἄλλην παραβολὴν → ἦν ἄνθρωπος οἰκοδεσπότης ὅστις ἐφύτευσεν ἀμπελῶνα καὶ → περιέθηκεν
v.aam.2p r.asf n.asf v.iai.3s n.nsm n.nsm r.nsm v.aai.3s n.asm cj v.aai.3s
201 257 4130 1639 476 3867 4015 5885 308 2779 4363

wall around it, dug a winepress in it and built a watchtower. Then he rented the vineyard to
φραγμὸν ← αὐτῷ καὶ ὤρυξεν ληνὸν ἐν αὐτῷ καὶ ᾠκοδόμησεν πύργον καὶ → ἐξέδετο αὐτὸν →
n.asm r.dsm.3 cj v.aai.3s n.asn p.d r.dsm.3 cj v.aai.3s n.asm cj v.ami.3s r.asm.3
5850 4363 899 2779 4002 3332 1877 899 2779 3868 4788 2779 1686 899

some farmers and went away on a journey. **34** When the harvest time approached, he sent his
γεωργοῖς καὶ ἀπεδήμησεν ← δὲ ὅτε τῶν καρπῶν ὁ καιρὸς ἤγγισεν → ἀπέστειλεν αὐτοῦ
n.dpm cj v.aai.3s cj cj d.gpm n.gpm d.nsm n.nsm v.aai.3s v.aai.3s r.gsm.3
1177 2779 623 1254 4021 3836 2843 3836 2789 1581 690 899

servants to the tenants to collect his fruit. ¶ **35** "The tenants seized his servants;
τοὺς δούλους πρὸς τοὺς γεωργοὺς λαβεῖν αὐτοῦ τοὺς καρπούς καὶ οἱ γεωργοὶ λαβόντες αὐτοῦ τοὺς δούλους μὲν
d.apm n.apm p.a d.apm n.apm f.aa r.gsm.3 d.apm n.apm cj d.npm n.npm pt.aa.npm r.gsm.3 d.apm n.apm pl
3836 1529 4639 3836 1177 3284 899 3836 2843 2779 3836 1177 3284 899 3836 1529 3525

they beat one, killed another, and stoned a third. **36** Then he sent other servants to them, more
→ ἔδειραν ὃν δὲ ἀπέκτειναν ὃν δὲ ἐλιθοβόλησαν ὃν πάλιν → ἀπέστειλεν ἄλλους δούλους πλείονας
v.aai.3p r.asm cj v.aai.3p r.asm cj v.aai.3p r.asm adv v.aai.3s r.apm n.apm a.apm.c
1296 4005 1254 650 4005 1254 3344 4005 4099 690 257 1529 4498

than the first time, and the tenants treated them the same way. **37** Last of all, he sent his son
→ τῶν πρώτων καὶ ἐποίησαν αὐτοῖς ὡσαύτως ← δὲ ὕστερον ← ἀπέστειλεν αὐτοῦ τὸν υἱὸν
d.gpm a.gpm cj v.aai.3p r.dpm.3 adv cj adv.c v.aai.3s r.gsm.3 d.asm n.asm
3836 4755 2779 4472 899 6058 1254 5731 690 899 3836 5626

to them. 'They will respect my son,' he said. ¶ **38** "But when the tenants saw the son, they said to
πρὸς αὐτοὺς → → ἐντραπήσονται μου τὸν υἱόν → λέγων δὲ ↱ οἱ γεωργοὶ ἰδόντες τὸν υἱὸν εἶπον ἐν
p.a r.apm.3 v.fpi.3p r.gs.1 d.asm n.asm pt.pa.nsm cj d.npm n.npm pt.aa.npm d.asm n.asm v.aai.3p p.d
4639 899 1956 1609 3836 5626 3306 1254 1625 3836 1177 1625 3836 5626 3306 1877

each other, 'This is the heir. Come, let's kill him and take his inheritance.' **39** So they took
ἑαυτοῖς ← οὗτος ἐστιν ὁ κληρονόμος δεῦτε ἀποκτείνωμεν αὐτὸν καὶ σχῶμεν αὐτοῦ τὴν κληρονομίαν καὶ → λαβόντες
r.dpm.3 r.nsm v.pai.3s d.nsm n.nsm adv v.aas.1p r.asm.3 cj v.aas.1p r.gsm.3 d.asf n.asf cj pt.aa.npm
1571 4047 1639 3836 3101 1307 650 899 2779 2400 899 3836 3100 2779 3284

him and threw him out of the vineyard and killed him. ¶ **40** "Therefore, when the owner of the vineyard
αὐτὸν ἐξέβαλον ἔξω → τοῦ ἀμπελῶνος καὶ ἀπέκτειναν οὖν ὅταν ὁ κύριος → τοῦ ἀμπελῶνος
r.asm.3 v.aai.3p p.g d.gsm n.gsm cj v.aai.3p cj cj d.nsm n.nsm d.gsm n.gsm
899 1675 2032 3836 308 2779 650 4036 4020 3836 3261 3836 308

δὲ ἀποκριθεὶς εἶπεν, Ἐγώ, κύριε, καὶ οὐκ ἀπῆλθεν. ¶ **31** τίς ἐκ τῶν δύο ἐποίησεν τὸ θέλημα τοῦ πατρός; λέγουσιν, Ὁ πρῶτος. λέγει αὐτοῖς ὁ Ἰησοῦς, Ἀμὴν λέγω ὑμῖν ὅτι οἱ τελῶναι καὶ αἱ πόρναι προάγουσιν ὑμᾶς εἰς τὴν βασιλείαν τοῦ θεοῦ. **32** ἦλθεν γὰρ Ἰωάννης πρὸς ὑμᾶς ἐν ὁδῷ δικαιοσύνης, καὶ οὐκ ἐπιστεύσατε αὐτῷ, οἱ δὲ τελῶναι καὶ αἱ πόρναι ἐπίστευσαν αὐτῷ· ὑμεῖς δὲ ἰδόντες οὐδὲ μετεμελήθητε ὕστερον τοῦ πιστεῦσαι αὐτῷ.

21:33 Ἄλλην παραβολὴν ἀκούσατε. Ἄνθρωπος ἦν οἰκοδεσπότης ὅστις ἐφύτευσεν ἀμπελῶνα καὶ φραγμὸν αὐτῷ περιέθηκεν καὶ ὤρυξεν ἐν αὐτῷ ληνὸν καὶ ᾠκοδόμησεν πύργον καὶ ἐξέδετο αὐτὸν γεωργοῖς καὶ ἀπεδήμησεν. **34** ὅτε δὲ ἤγγισεν ὁ καιρὸς τῶν καρπῶν, ἀπέστειλεν τοὺς δούλους αὐτοῦ πρὸς τοὺς γεωργοὺς λαβεῖν τοὺς καρποὺς αὐτοῦ. ¶ **35** καὶ λαβόντες οἱ γεωργοὶ τοὺς δούλους αὐτοῦ ὃν μὲν ἔδειραν, ὃν δὲ ἀπέκτειναν, ὃν δὲ ἐλιθοβόλησαν. **36** πάλιν ἀπέστειλεν ἄλλους δούλους πλείονας τῶν πρώτων, καὶ ἐποίησαν αὐτοῖς ὡσαύτως. **37** ὕστερον δὲ ἀπέστειλεν πρὸς αὐτοὺς τὸν υἱὸν αὐτοῦ λέγων, Ἐντραπήσονται τὸν υἱόν μου. **38** οἱ δὲ γεωργοὶ ἰδόντες τὸν υἱὸν εἶπον ἐν ἑαυτοῖς, Οὗτός ἐστιν ὁ κληρονόμος· δεῦτε ἀποκτείνωμεν αὐτὸν καὶ σχῶμεν τὴν κληρονομίαν αὐτοῦ, **39** καὶ λαβόντες αὐτὸν ἐξέβαλον ἔξω τοῦ ἀμπελῶνος καὶ ἀπέκτειναν. ¶ **40** ὅταν οὖν ἔλθῃ ὁ κύριος τοῦ

comes, what will he do to those tenants?" ¶ [41] "He will bring those wretches to a wretched end," they
ἔλθη τί → → ποιήσει τοῖς ἐκείνοις γεωργοῖς   αὐτοὺς κακοὺς → κακῶς ἀπολέσει →
v.aas.3s r.asn   v.fai.3s d.dpm r.dpm n.dpm   r.apm.3 a.apm adv v.fai.3s
2262 5515   4472 3836 1697 1177   660 660 660 899 2805 660 660 2809 660

replied, "and he will rent the vineyard to other tenants, who will give him his share of the
λέγουσιν αὐτῷ καὶ → → ἐκδώσεται τὸν ἀμπελῶνα → ἄλλοις γεωργοῖς οἵτινες → ἀποδώσουσιν αὐτῷ → τοὺς
v.pai.3p r.dsm.3 cj   v.fmi.3s d.asm n.asm   r.dpm n.dpm r.npm   v.fai.3p r.dsm.3   d.apm
3306 899 2779   1686 3836 308   257 1177 4015   625 899   3836

crop at harvest time." ¶ [42] Jesus said to them, "Have you never read in the Scriptures:
καρποὺς ἐν → τοῖς καιροῖς αὐτῶν   ὁ Ἰησοῦς Λέγει → αὐτοῖς   οὐδέποτε ἀνέγνωτε ἐν ταῖς γραφαῖς
n.apm p.d   d.dpm n.dpm r.gpm.3   d.nsm n.nsm v.pai.3s r.dpm.3   adv v.aai.2p p.d d.dpf n.dpf
2843 1877   3836 2789 899   3836 2652 3306 899 336 336 4030 336 1877 3836 1210

"'The stone the builders rejected has become the capstone; the Lord has done this,
λίθον ὃν οἱ οἰκοδομοῦντες ἀπεδοκίμασαν οὗτος → ἐγενήθη εἰς κεφαλὴν γωνίας παρὰ κυρίου → ἐγένετο αὕτη
n.asm r.asm d.npm pt.pa.npm v.aai.3p r.nsm   v.api.3s p.a n.asf n.gsf p.g n.gsm   v.ami.3s r.nsf
3345 4005 3836 3868 627 4047   1181 1650 3051 1224 4123 3261   1181 4047

and it is marvelous in our eyes'? ¶ [43] "Therefore I tell you that the kingdom of God will be taken
καὶ → ἔστιν θαυμαστὴ ἐν ἡμῶν ὀφθαλμοῖς   διὰ τοῦτο → λέγω ὑμῖν ὅτι ἡ βασιλεία τοῦ θεοῦ → ἀρθήσεται
cj   v.pai.3s a.nsf p.d r.gp.1 n.dpm   p.a r.asn   v.pai.1s r.dp.2 cj d.nsf n.nsf d.gsm n.gsm   v.fpi.3s
2779   1639 2515 1877 7005 4057   1328 4047   3306 7007 4022 3836 993 3836 2536   149

away from you and given to a people who will produce its fruit. [44] He who falls on this stone
→ ἀφ' ὑμῶν καὶ δοθήσεται → ἔθνει → ποιοῦντι αὐτῆς τοὺς καρποὺς καὶ ὁ ← πεσὼν ἐπὶ τοῦτον τὸν λίθον
  p.g r.gp.2 cj v.fpi.3s   n.dsn   pt.pa.dsn r.gsf.3 d.apm n.apm cj d.nsm   pt.aa.nsm p.a r.asm d.asm n.asm
608 7007 2779 1443   1620   4472 899 3836 2843 2779 3836   4406 2093 4047 3836 3345

will be broken to pieces, but he on whom it falls will be crushed." [45] When the chief priests and the
→ → συνθλασθήσεται ← δ' αὐτὸν ἐφ' ὃν ἂν → πέσῃ → λικμήσει Καὶ → οἱ ἀρχιερεῖς ← καὶ οἱ
    v.fpi.3s   cj r.asm.3 p.a r.asm pl v.aas.3s   v.fai.3s cj   d.npm n.npm   cj d.npm
    5314   1254 899 2093 4005 323 4406   3347 2779 201   3836 797   2779 3836

Pharisees heard Jesus' parables, they knew he was talking about them. [46] They looked for a way to
Φαρισαῖοι ἀκούσαντες αὐτοῦ τὰς παραβολὰς → ἔγνωσαν ὅτι → λέγει περὶ αὐτῶν καὶ → ζητοῦντες
n.npm pt.aa.npm r.gsm.3 d.apf n.apf   v.aai.3p cj   v.pai.3s p.g r.gpm.3 cj   pt.pa.npm
5757 201 899 3836 4130   1182 4022   3306 4309 899 2779   2426

arrest him, but they were afraid of the crowd because the people held that he was a prophet.
κρατῆσαι αὐτὸν → → ἐφοβήθησαν τοὺς ὄχλους ἐπεὶ εἶχον αὐτὸν εἰς προφήτην
f.aa r.asm.3   v.api.3p d.apm n.apm cj v.iai.3p r.asm.3 p.a n.asm
3195 899   5828 3836 4063 2075 2400 899 1650 4737

The Parable of the Wedding Banquet

[22:1] Jesus spoke to them again in parables, saying: [2] "The kingdom of heaven is like a
Καὶ ὁ Ἰησοῦς ἀποκριθεὶς εἶπεν → αὐτοῖς πάλιν ἐν παραβολαῖς λέγων ἡ βασιλεία → τῶν οὐρανῶν → ὡμοιώθη
cj d.nsm n.nsm pt.ap.nsm v.aai.3s   r.dpm.3 adv p.d n.dpf pt.pa.nsm d.nsf n.nsf   d.gpm n.gpm   v.api.3s
2779 3836 2652 646 3306   899 4099 1877 4130 3306 3836 993   3836 4041   3929

king who prepared a wedding banquet for his son. [3] He sent his servants to those
ἀνθρώπῳ βασιλεῖ ὅστις ἐποίησεν γάμους ← → αὐτοῦ τῷ υἱῷ καὶ → ἀπέστειλεν αὐτοῦ τοὺς δούλους τοὺς
n.dsm n.dsm r.nsm v.aai.3s n.apm   r.gsm.3 d.dsm n.dsm cj   v.aai.3s r.gsm.3 d.apm n.apm d.apm
476 995 4015 4472 1141   5626 899 3836 5626 2779   690 899 3836 1529 3836

who had been invited to the banquet to tell them to come, but they refused to come. [4] "Then he
← κεκλημένους εἰς τοὺς γάμους → καλέσαι καὶ → οὐκ ἤθελον ἐλθεῖν πάλιν →
  pt.rp.apm p.a d.apm n.apm   f.aa cj   pl v.iai.3p f.aa adv
  2813 1650 3836 1141   2813 2779   4024 2527 2262 4099

sent some more servants and said, 'Tell those who have been invited that I have prepared my
ἀπέστειλεν ἄλλους δούλους λέγων εἴπατε τοῖς ← → κεκλημένοις ἰδοὺ → ἡτοίμακα μου
v.aai.3s r.apm n.apm pt.pa.nsm v.aam.2p d.dpm   pt.rp.dpm j   v.rai.1s r.gs.1
690 257 1529 3306 3306 3836   2813 2627   2286 1609

dinner: My oxen and fattened cattle have been butchered, and everything is ready. Come to the
τὸ ἄριστον μου οἱ ταῦροι καὶ τὰ σιτιστὰ ← → τεθυμένα καὶ πάντα ἕτοιμα δεῦτε εἰς τοὺς
d.asn n.asn r.gs.1 d.npm n.npm cj d.npn a.npn   pt.rp.npn cj a.npn a.npn adv p.a d.apm
3836 756 1609 3836 5436 2779 3836 4990   2604 2779 4246 2289 1307 1650 3836

ἀμπελῶνος, τί ποιήσει τοῖς γεωργοῖς ἐκείνοις; ¶ [41] λέγουσιν αὐτῷ, Κακοὺς κακῶς ἀπολέσει αὐτοὺς καὶ τὸν ἀμπελῶνα ἐκδώσεται ἄλλοις γεωργοῖς, οἵτινες ἀποδώσουσιν αὐτῷ τοὺς καρποὺς ἐν τοῖς καιροῖς αὐτῶν. ¶ [42] λέγει αὐτοῖς ὁ Ἰησοῦς, Οὐδέποτε ἀνέγνωτε ἐν ταῖς γραφαῖς, Λίθον ὃν ἀπεδοκίμασαν οἱ οἰκοδομοῦντες, οὗτος ἐγενήθη εἰς κεφαλὴν γωνίας· παρὰ κυρίου ἐγένετο αὕτη καὶ ἔστιν θαυμαστὴ ἐν ὀφθαλμοῖς ἡμῶν; ¶ [43] διὰ τοῦτο λέγω ὑμῖν ὅτι ἀρθήσεται ἀφ' ὑμῶν ἡ βασιλεία τοῦ θεοῦ καὶ δοθήσεται ἔθνει ποιοῦντι τοὺς καρποὺς αὐτῆς. [44] [Καὶ ὁ πεσὼν ἐπὶ τὸν λίθον τοῦτον συνθλασθήσεται· ἐφ' ὃν δ' ἂν πέσῃ λικμήσει αὐτόν.] [45] Καὶ ἀκούσαντες οἱ ἀρχιερεῖς καὶ οἱ Φαρισαῖοι τὰς παραβολὰς αὐτοῦ ἔγνωσαν ὅτι περὶ αὐτῶν λέγει· [46] καὶ ζητοῦντες αὐτὸν κρατῆσαι ἐφοβήθησαν τοὺς ὄχλους, ἐπεὶ εἰς προφήτην αὐτὸν εἶχον.

[22:1] Καὶ ἀποκριθεὶς ὁ Ἰησοῦς πάλιν εἶπεν ἐν παραβολαῖς αὐτοῖς λέγων, [2] Ὡμοιώθη ἡ βασιλεία τῶν οὐρανῶν ἀνθρώπῳ βασιλεῖ, ὅστις ἐποίησεν γάμους τῷ υἱῷ αὐτοῦ. [3] καὶ ἀπέστειλεν τοὺς δούλους αὐτοῦ καλέσαι τοὺς κεκλημένους εἰς τοὺς γάμους, καὶ οὐκ ἤθελον ἐλθεῖν. [4] πάλιν ἀπέστειλεν ἄλλους δούλους λέγων, Εἴπατε τοῖς κεκλημένοις, Ἰδοὺ τὸ ἄριστόν μου ἡτοίμακα, οἱ ταῦροί μου καὶ τὰ σιτιστὰ τεθυμένα καὶ πάντα ἕτοιμα· δεῦτε εἰς τοὺς γάμους. [5] οἱ δὲ ἀμελήσαντες ἀπῆλθον, ὃς

wedding banquet.' **5** "But they paid no attention and went off — one to his field, another to his
γάμους ← δὲ οἱ → → ἀμελήσαντες ἀπῆλθον ← μὲν ὃς εἰς ἴδιον τὸν ἀγρόν δὲ ὃς ἐπὶ αὐτοῦ
n.apm cj d.npm pt.aa.npm v.aai.3p pl r.nsm p.a a.asm d.asm n.asm pl r.nsm p.a r.gsm.3
1141 1254 3836 288 599 3525 4005 1650 2625 3836 69 1254 4005 2093 899

business. **6** The rest seized his servants, mistreated them and killed them. **7** The king was
τὴν ἐμπορίαν δὲ οἱ λοιποὶ κρατήσαντες αὐτοῦ τοὺς δούλους ὕβρισαν καὶ ἀπέκτειναν δὲ ὁ βασιλεὺς →
d.asf n.asf pl d.npm a.npm pt.aa.npm r.gsm.3 d.apm n.apm v.aai.3p cj v.aai.3p cj d.nsm n.nsm
3836 1865 1254 3836 3370 3195 899 3836 1529 5614 2779 650 1254 3836 995

enraged. He sent his army and destroyed those murderers and burned their city. **8** "Then
ὠργίσθη καὶ → πέμψας αὐτοῦ τὰ στρατεύματα ἀπώλεσεν ἐκείνους τοὺς φονεῖς καὶ ἐνέπρησεν αὐτῶν τὴν πόλιν τότε
v.api.3s cj pt.aa.nsm r.gsm.3 d.apn n.apn v.aai.3s r.apm d.apm n.apm cj v.aai.3s r.gpm.3 d.asf n.asf adv
3974 2779 4287 899 3836 5128 660 1697 3836 5838 2779 1856 899 3836 4484 5538

he said to his servants, 'The wedding banquet is ready, but those I invited did not deserve to come.
→ λέγει → αὐτοῦ τοῖς δούλοις μὲν ὁ γάμος ← ἐστιν ἕτοιμος δὲ οἱ → κεκλημένοι ἦσαν οὐκ ἄξιοι
v.pai.3s r.gsm.3 d.dpm n.dpm pl d.nsm n.nsm v.pai.3s a.nsm cj d.npm pt.rp.npm v.iai.3p pl a.npm
3306 1529 899 3836 1529 3525 3836 1141 1639 2289 1254 3836 2813 1639 4024 545

9 Go to the street corners and invite to the banquet anyone you find.' **10** So the servants
οὖν πορεύεσθε ἐπὶ τῶν ὁδῶν τὰς διεξόδους καὶ καλέσατε εἰς τοὺς γάμους ὅσους ἐὰν → εὕρητε καὶ οἱ δοῦλοι ἐκεῖνοι
cj v.pmm.2p p.a d.gpf n.gpf d.apf n.apf cj v.aam.2p p.a d.apm n.apm r.apm pl v.aas.2p cj d.npm n.npm r.npm
4036 4513 2093 3836 3847 3836 1447 2779 2813 1650 3836 1141 4012 1569 2351 2779 3836 1529 1697

went out into the streets and gathered all the people they could find, both good and bad, and the
ἐξελθόντες ← εἰς τὰς ὁδοὺς συνήγαγον πάντας οὓς → → εὗρον τε ἀγαθούς καὶ πονηροὺς καὶ ὁ
pt.aa.npm p.a d.apf n.apf v.aai.3p a.apm r.apm v.aai.3p cj a.apm cj a.apm cj d.nsm
2002 1650 3836 3847 5251 4246 4005 2351 5445 19 2779 4505 2779 3836

wedding hall was filled with guests. **11** "But when the king came in to see the guests, he noticed
γάμος → ἐπλήσθη → ἀνακειμένων δὲ ὁ βασιλεὺς εἰσελθὼν → θεάσασθαι τοὺς ἀνακειμένους → εἶδεν
n.nsm v.api.3s pt.pm.gpm cj d.nsm n.nsm pt.aa.nsm f.am d.apm pt.pm.apm v.aai.3s
1141 4398 367 1254 1656 3836 995 1656 2517 3836 367 1625

a man there who was not wearing wedding clothes. **12** 'Friend,' he asked, 'how did you get in here
ἄνθρωπον ἐκεῖ → → οὐκ ἐνδεδυμένον γάμου ἔνδυμα ἑταῖρε καὶ → λέγει αὐτῷ πῶς → → εἰσῆλθες ← ὧδε
n.asm adv pl pt.rm.asm n.gsm n.asn n.vsm cj v.pai.3s r.dsm.3 cj v.aai.2s adv
476 1695 1907 1907 4024 1907 1141 1903 2279 2779 3306 899 4802 1656 6045

without wedding clothes?' The man was speechless. **13** "Then the king told the attendants, 'Tie him
μὴ ἔχων γάμου ἔνδυμα δὲ ὁ ← → ἐφιμώθη τότε ὁ βασιλεὺς εἶπεν τοῖς διακόνοις δήσαντες αὐτοῦ
pl pt.pa.nsm n.gsm n.asn cj d.nsm v.api.3s adv d.nsm n.nsm v.aai.3s d.dpm n.dpm pt.aa.npm r.gsm.3
3590 2400 1141 1903 1254 3836 5821 5538 3836 995 3306 3836 1356 1313 899

hand and foot, and throw him outside, into the darkness, where there will be weeping and gnashing
χεῖρας καὶ πόδας ἐκβάλετε αὐτὸν τὸ ἐξώτερον εἰς τὸ σκότος ἐκεῖ → → ἔσται ὁ κλαυθμὸς καὶ ὁ βρυγμὸς
n.apf cj n.apm v.aam.2p r.asm.3 d.asn a.asn.c p.a d.asn n.asn adv v.fmi.3s d.nsm n.nsm cj d.nsm n.nsm
5931 2779 4546 1675 899 3836 2035 1650 3836 5030 1695 1639 3836 3088 2779 3836 1106

of teeth.' **14** "For many are invited, but few are chosen."
→ τῶν ὀδόντων γάρ πολλοί εἰσιν κλητοί δὲ ὀλίγοι ἐκλεκτοί
d.gpm n.gpm cj a.npm v.pai.3p a.npm cj a.npm a.npm
3836 3848 1142 4498 1639 3105 1254 3900 1723

Paying Taxes to Caesar

22:15 Then the Pharisees went out and laid plans to trap him in his words. **16** They
Τότε οἱ Φαρισαῖοι πορευθέντες → συμβούλιον ἔλαβον ὅπως παγιδεύσωσιν αὐτὸν ἐν λόγῳ καὶ →
adv d.npm n.npm pt.ap.npm n.asn v.aai.3p cj v.aas.3p r.asm.3 p.d n.dsm cj
5538 3836 5757 4513 5206 3284 3968 4074 899 1877 3364 2779

sent their disciples to him along with the Herodians. "Teacher," they said, "we know you are
ἀποστέλλουσιν αὐτῶν τοὺς μαθητὰς → αὐτῷ → μετὰ τῶν Ἡρῳδιανῶν διδάσκαλε → λέγοντες οἴδαμεν ὅτι → εἶ
v.pai.3p r.gpm.3 d.apm n.apm r.dsm.3 p.g d.gpm n.gpm n.vsm pt.pa.npm v.rai.1p cj v.pai.2s
690 899 3836 3412 899 3552 3836 2477 1437 3306 3857 4022 1639

a man of integrity and that you teach the way of God in accordance with the truth. *You aren't swayed*
→ → ἀληθής καὶ διδάσκεις τὴν ὁδὸν τοῦ θεοῦ ἐν ← ← ἀληθείᾳ καὶ σοι οὐ μέλει
a.nsm cj v.pai.2s d.asf n.asf d.gsm n.gsm p.d n.dsf cj r.ds.2 pl v.pai.3s
239 2779 1438 3836 3847 3836 2536 1877 237 2779 5148 4024 3508

μὲν εἰς τὸν ἴδιον ἀγρόν, ὃς δὲ ἐπὶ τὴν ἐμπορίαν αὐτοῦ· **6** οἱ δὲ λοιποὶ κρατήσαντες τοὺς δούλους αὐτοῦ ὕβρισαν καὶ ἀπέκτειναν. **7** ὁ δὲ βασιλεὺς ὠργίσθη καὶ πέμψας τὰ στρατεύματα αὐτοῦ ἀπώλεσεν τοὺς φονεῖς ἐκείνους καὶ τὴν πόλιν αὐτῶν ἐνέπρησεν. **8** τότε λέγει τοῖς δούλοις αὐτοῦ, Ὁ μὲν γάμος ἕτοιμός ἐστιν, οἱ δὲ κεκλημένοι οὐκ ἦσαν ἄξιοι· **9** πορεύεσθε οὖν ἐπὶ τὰς διεξόδους τῶν ὁδῶν καὶ ὅσους ἐὰν εὕρητε καλέσατε εἰς τοὺς γάμους. **10** καὶ ἐξελθόντες οἱ δοῦλοι ἐκεῖνοι εἰς τὰς ὁδοὺς συνήγαγον πάντας οὓς εὗρον, πονηρούς τε καὶ ἀγαθούς· καὶ ἐπλήσθη ὁ γάμος ἀνακειμένων. **11** εἰσελθὼν δὲ ὁ βασιλεὺς θεάσασθαι τοὺς ἀνακειμένους εἶδεν ἐκεῖ ἄνθρωπον οὐκ ἐνδεδυμένον ἔνδυμα γάμου, **12** καὶ λέγει αὐτῷ, Ἑταῖρε, πῶς εἰσῆλθες ὧδε μὴ ἔχων ἔνδυμα γάμου; ὁ δὲ ἐφιμώθη. **13** τότε ὁ βασιλεὺς εἶπεν τοῖς διακόνοις, Δήσαντες αὐτοῦ πόδας καὶ χεῖρας ἐκβάλετε αὐτὸν εἰς τὸ σκότος τὸ ἐξώτερον· ἐκεῖ ἔσται ὁ κλαυθμὸς καὶ ὁ βρυγμὸς τῶν ὀδόντων. **14** πολλοὶ γάρ εἰσιν κλητοί, ὀλίγοι δὲ ἐκλεκτοί.

22:15 Τότε πορευθέντες οἱ Φαρισαῖοι συμβούλιον ἔλαβον ὅπως αὐτὸν παγιδεύσωσιν ἐν λόγῳ. **16** καὶ ἀποστέλλουσιν αὐτῷ τοὺς μαθητὰς αὐτῶν μετὰ τῶν Ἡρῳδιανῶν λέγοντες, Διδάσκαλε, οἴδαμεν ὅτι ἀληθὴς εἶ καὶ τὴν ὁδὸν τοῦ θεοῦ ἐν ἀληθείᾳ

by men, because *you pay no attention to*   *who they are.* [17] Tell us then, what is your opinion?
περὶ οὐδενός γὰρ → → οὐ βλέπεις εἰς πρόσωπον ἀνθρώπων εἰπὲ ἡμῖν οὖν τί → σοι δοκεῖ
p.g a.gsm cj   pl v.pai.2s p.a n.asn n.gpm v.aam.2s r.dp.1 cj r.nsn r.ds.2 v.pai.3s
4309 4029 1142 1063 1063 4024 1063 1650 4725 476 3306 7005 4036 5515 1506 5148 1506

Is it right to pay taxes to Caesar or not?" [18] But Jesus, knowing their evil intent, said, "You
→ → ἔξεστιν → δοῦναι κῆνσον Καίσαρι ἢ οὔ δὲ ὁ Ἰησοῦς γνοὺς αὐτῶν τὴν πονηρίαν ← εἶπεν
  v.pai.3s f.aa n.asm n.dsm ptcl pl cj d.nsm n.nsm pt.aa.nsm r.gpm.3 d.asf n.asf v.aai.3s
  1997 1443 3056 2790 2445 4024 1254 3836 2652 1182 899 3836 4504 3306

hypocrites, why are you trying to trap me? [19] Show me the coin used for paying the tax." They
ὑποκριταί τί → → πειράζετε με ἐπιδείξατε μοι τὸ νόμισμα τοῦ κήνσου δὲ οἱ
n.vpm r.asn   v.pai.2p r.as.1 v.aam.2p r.ds.1 d.asn n.asn d.gsm n.gsm cj d.npm
5695 5515   4279 1609 2109 1609 3836 3790 3836 3056 1254 3836

brought him a denarius, [20] and he asked them, "Whose portrait is this? And whose inscription?" [21] "Caesar's," they
προσήνεγκαν αὐτῷ δηνάριον καὶ → λέγει αὐτοῖς τίνος ἡ εἰκὼν αὕτη καὶ ἡ ἐπιγραφή Καίσαρος →
v.aai.3p r.dsm.3 n.asn cj v.pai.3s r.dpm.3 r.gsm d.nsf n.nsf r.nsf cj d.nsf n.nsf n.gsm
4712 899 1324 2779 3306 899 5515 3836 1635 4047 2779 3836 2107 2790

replied. Then he said to them, "Give to Caesar what is Caesar's, and to God what is God's." [22]
λέγουσιν αὐτῷ τότε → λέγει → αὐτοῖς οὖν ἀπόδοτε → Καίσαρι τὰ Καίσαρος καὶ → τῷ θεῷ τὰ τοῦ θεοῦ καὶ
v.pai.3p r.dsm.3 adv v.pai.3s r.dpm.3 cj v.aam.2p n.dsm d.apn n.gsm cj d.dsm n.dsm d.apn d.gsm n.gsm cj
3306 899 5538 3306 899 4036 625 2790 3836 2790 2779 3836 2536 3836 3836 2536 2779

When they heard this, they were amazed. So they left him and went away.
→ → ἀκούσαντες → ἐθαύμασαν καὶ → ἀφέντες αὐτὸν ἀπῆλθαν →
  pt.aa.npm v.aai.3p cj pt.aa.npm r.asm.3 v.aai.3p
  201 2513 2779 918 899 599

Marriage at the Resurrection

22:23 That same day the Sadducees, who say there is no resurrection, came to him with a
Ἐν ἐκείνῃ τῇ ἡμέρᾳ Σαδδουκαῖοι → λέγοντες → εἶναι μὴ ἀνάστασιν προσῆλθον αὐτῷ καὶ
p.d r.dsf d.dsf n.dsf n.npm pt.pa.npm f.pa pl n.asf v.aai.3p r.dsm.3 cj
1877 1697 3836 2465 4881 3306 1639 3590 414 4665 899 2779

question. [24] "Teacher," they said, "Moses told us that if a man dies without having children, his
ἐπηρώτησαν αὐτόν διδάσκαλε → λέγοντες Μωϋσῆς εἶπεν ἐάν τις ἀποθάνῃ μὴ ἔχων τέκνα αὐτοῦ
v.aai.3p r.asm.3 n.vsm pt.pa.npm n.nsm v.aai.3s cj r.nsm v.aas.3s pl pt.pa.nsm n.apn r.gsm.3
2089 899 1437 3306 3707 3306 1569 5516 633 3590 2400 5451 899

brother must marry the widow and have children for him. [25] Now there were seven
ὁ ἀδελφός → ἐπιγαμβρεύσει τὴν γυναῖκα αὐτοῦ καὶ ἀναστήσει σπέρμα τῷ ἀδελφῷ αὐτοῦ δὲ → ἦσαν ἑπτά
d.nsm n.nsm v.fai.3s d.asf n.asf r.gsm.3 cj v.fai.3s n.asn d.dsm n.dsm r.gsm.3 cj v.iai.3p a.npm
3836 81 2102 3836 1222 899 2779 482 5065 3836 81 899 1254 1639 2231

brothers among us. The first one married and died, and since he had no children, he left his
ἀδελφοί παρ' ἡμῖν καὶ ὁ πρῶτος ← γήμας ἐτελεύτησεν καὶ → → ἔχων μὴ σπέρμα → ἀφῆκεν αὐτοῦ
n.npm p.d r.dp.1 cj d.nsm a.nsm pt.aa.nsm v.aai.3s cj pt.pa.nsm pl n.asn v.aai.3s r.gsm.3
81 4123 7005 2779 3836 4755 1138 5462 2779 2400 3590 5065 918 899

wife to his brother. [26] The same thing happened to the second and third brother, right on down
τὴν γυναῖκα → αὐτοῦ τῷ ἀδελφῷ ὁμοίως ← καὶ ὁ δεύτερος καὶ ὁ τρίτος right on down
d.asf n.asf r.gsm.3 d.dsm n.dsm adv adv d.nsm a.nsm cj d.nsm a.nsm
3836 1222 81 899 3836 81 3931 2779 3836 1311 2779 3836 5569

to the seventh. [27] Finally, the woman died. [28] Now then, at the resurrection, whose wife will she be of
ἕως τῶν ἑπτά δὲ ὕστερον πάντων ἡ γυνὴ ἀπέθανεν → οὖν ἐν τῇ ἀναστάσει τίνος γυνή → ἔσται →
p.g d.gpm a.gpm cj adv.c a.gpn d.nsf n.nsf v.aai.3s cj p.d d.dsf n.dsf r.gsm n.nsf v.fmi.3s
2401 3836 2231 1254 5731 4246 3836 1222 633 4036 1877 3836 414 5515 1222 1639

the seven, since all of them were married to her?" [29] Jesus replied, "You are in error
τῶν ἑπτά γὰρ πάντες → ἔσχον ← αὐτήν δὲ ὁ Ἰησοῦς ἀποκριθεὶς εἶπεν αὐτοῖς → πλανᾶσθε
d.gpm a.gpm cj a.npm v.aai.3p r.asf.3 cj d.nsm n.nsm pt.ap.nsm v.aai.3s r.dpm.3 v.ppi.2p
3836 2231 1142 4246 2400 899 1254 3836 2652 646 3306 899 4414

because you do not know the Scriptures or the power of God. [30] At the resurrection people will neither
→ → μὴ εἰδότες τὰς γραφὰς μηδὲ τὴν δύναμιν → τοῦ θεοῦ γὰρ ἐν τῇ ἀναστάσει → → οὔτε
  pl pt.ra.npm d.apf n.apf cj d.asf n.asf d.gsm n.gsm cj p.d d.dsf n.dsf cj
3857 3857 3857 3590 3857 3836 1210 3593 3836 1539 3836 2536 1142 1877 3836 414 1138 1138 4046

διδάσκεις καὶ οὐ μέλει σοι περὶ οὐδενός· οὐ γὰρ βλέπεις εἰς πρόσωπον ἀνθρώπων. [17] εἰπὲ οὖν ἡμῖν τί σοι δοκεῖ· ἔξεστιν δοῦναι κῆνσον Καίσαρι ἢ οὔ; [18] γνοὺς δὲ ὁ Ἰησοῦς τὴν πονηρίαν αὐτῶν εἶπεν, Τί με πειράζετε, ὑποκριταί; [19] ἐπιδείξατέ μοι τὸ νόμισμα τοῦ κήνσου. οἱ δὲ προσήνεγκαν αὐτῷ δηνάριον. [20] καὶ λέγει αὐτοῖς, Τίνος ἡ εἰκὼν αὕτη καὶ ἡ ἐπιγραφή; [21] λέγουσιν αὐτῷ, Καίσαρος. τότε λέγει αὐτοῖς, Ἀπόδοτε οὖν τὰ Καίσαρος Καίσαρι καὶ τὰ τοῦ θεοῦ τῷ θεῷ. [22] καὶ ἀκούσαντες ἐθαύμασαν, καὶ ἀφέντες αὐτὸν ἀπῆλθαν.

[22:23] Ἐν ἐκείνῃ τῇ ἡμέρᾳ προσῆλθον αὐτῷ Σαδδουκαῖοι, λέγοντες μὴ εἶναι ἀνάστασιν, καὶ ἐπηρώτησαν αὐτὸν [24] λέγοντες, Διδάσκαλε, Μωϋσῆς εἶπεν, Ἐάν τις ἀποθάνῃ μὴ ἔχων τέκνα, ἐπιγαμβρεύσει ὁ ἀδελφὸς αὐτοῦ τὴν γυναῖκα αὐτοῦ καὶ ἀναστήσει σπέρμα τῷ ἀδελφῷ αὐτοῦ. [25] ἦσαν δὲ παρ' ἡμῖν ἑπτὰ ἀδελφοί· καὶ ὁ πρῶτος γήμας ἐτελεύτησεν, καὶ μὴ ἔχων σπέρμα ἀφῆκεν τὴν γυναῖκα αὐτοῦ τῷ ἀδελφῷ αὐτοῦ. [26] ὁμοίως καὶ ὁ δεύτερος καὶ ὁ τρίτος ἕως τῶν ἑπτά. [27] ὕστερον δὲ πάντων ἀπέθανεν ἡ γυνή. [28] ἐν τῇ ἀναστάσει οὖν τίνος τῶν ἑπτὰ ἔσται γυνή; πάντες γὰρ ἔσχον αὐτήν· [29] ἀποκριθεὶς δὲ ὁ Ἰησοῦς εἶπεν αὐτοῖς, Πλανᾶσθε μὴ εἰδότες τὰς γραφὰς μηδὲ τὴν δύναμιν τοῦ θεοῦ· [30] ἐν γὰρ τῇ ἀναστάσει οὔτε γαμοῦσιν οὔτε γαμίζονται, ἀλλ' ὡς

marry	nor		be given in marriage;			they will be	like	the angels	in	the	heaven.	**31** But	about	the	resurrection of
γαμοῦσιν	οὔτε →	→	→ γαμίζονται	ἀλλ᾽	→	→ εἰσιν	ὡς	ἄγγελοι	ἐν	⌐τῷ	οὐρανῷ	δὲ	περὶ	τῆς	ἀναστάσεως →
v.pai.3p	cj		v.ppi.3p	cj		v.pai.3p	cj	n.npm	p.d	d.dsm	n.dsm	cj	p.g	d.gsf	n.gsf
1138	4046		1139	247		1639	6055	34	1877	3836	4041	1254	4309	3836	414

the dead	– have	you not read		what	God	said	to you,	**32** 'I	am	the	God	of Abraham,	the
τῶν νεκρῶν	⌐	⌐	οὐκ ἀνέγνωτε ⌐	ὑπὸ	⌐τοῦ θεοῦ	τὸ ῥηθὲν	ὑμῖν λέγοντος	ἐγώ	εἰμι	ὁ	θεὸς →	Ἀβραὰμ	καὶ ὁ
d.gpm a.gpm			pl v.aai.2p	p.g	d.asn	d.asn pt.ap.asn	r.dp.2 pt.pa.gsm	r.ns.1	v.pai.1s	d.nsm	n.nsm	n.gsm	cj d.nsm
3836 3738	336	336	4024 336	5679	3836 2536	3836 3306	7007 3306	1609	1639	3836	2536	11	2779 3836

God	of Isaac,	and	the	God	of Jacob'?	He is	not	the	God	of the dead	but	of the living."	**33**	When	the crowds
θεὸς →	Ἰσαὰκ	καὶ	ὁ	θεὸς →	Ἰακώβ	ἔστιν	οὐκ	ὁ	θεὸς →	νεκρῶν	ἀλλὰ →	ζώντων	καὶ		οἱ ὄχλοι
n.nsm	n.gsm	cj	d.nsm	n.nsm	n.gsm	v.pai.3s	pl	d.nsm	n.nsm	a.gpm	cj	pt.pa.gpm	cj		d.npm n.npm
2536	2693	2779	3836	2536	2609	1639	4024	3836	2536	3738	247	2409	2779		3836 4063

heard		this, they were	astonished	at	his	teaching.
ἀκούσαντες	→	→ ἐξεπλήσσοντο	ἐπὶ	αὐτοῦ	⌐τῇ	διδαχῇ⌐
pt.aa.npm		v.ipi.3p	p.d	r.gsm.3	d.dsf	n.dsf
201		1742	2093	899	3836	1439

The Greatest Commandment

22:34	Hearing	that	Jesus had		silenced	the	Sadducees,	the Pharisees	got	together.	**35**	One of
δὲ	ἀκούσαντες	ὅτι	→	ἐφίμωσεν	τοὺς	Σαδδουκαίους	Οἱ Φαρισαῖοι	συνήχθησαν	⌐ἐπὶ τὸ αὐτό⌐	καὶ εἷς	ἐξ
cj	pt.aa.npm	cj		v.aai.3s	d.apm	n.apm	d.npm n.npm	v.api.3p	p.a d.asn r.asn	cj a.nsm	p.g
1254	201	4022		5821	3836	4881	3836 5757	5251	2093 3836 899	2779 1651	1666

them,	an	expert	in the law,	tested	him	with this question:	**36** "Teacher,	which	is	the	greatest	commandment	in	the
αὐτῶν	νομικὸς ←	←	← πειράζων	αὐτόν		ἐπηρώτησεν	διδάσκαλε	ποία			μεγάλη	ἐντολὴ	ἐν	τῷ
r.gpm.3	n.nsm		pt.pa.nsm	r.asm.3		v.aai.3s	n.vsm	r.nsf			a.nsf	n.nsf	p.d	d.dsm
899	3788		4279	899		2089	1437	4481			3489	1953	1877	3836

Law?"	**37**	Jesus	replied:	"'Love	the	Lord	your	God	with	all	your	heart	and	with	all	your	soul
νόμῳ	δὲ	ὁ	ἔφη	αὐτῷ	ἀγαπήσεις	κύριον	σου	⌐τὸν θεόν⌐	ἐν	ὅλῃ	σου	⌐τῇ καρδίᾳ⌐	καὶ	ἐν	ὅλῃ	σου	⌐τῇ ψυχῇ⌐
n.dsm	cj	d.nsm	v.iai.3s	r.dsm.3	v.fai.2s	n.asm	r.gs.2	d.asm n.asm	p.d	a.dsf	r.gs.2	d.dsf n.dsf	cj	p.d	a.dsf	r.gs.2	d.dsf n.dsf
3795	1254	3836	5774	899	26	3261	5148	3836 2536	1877	3910	5148	3836 2840	2779	1877	3910	5148	3836 6034

and	with	all	your	mind.'	**38** This is		the	first	and	greatest	commandment.	**39** And	the second	is like	it:	'Love
καὶ	ἐν	ὅλῃ	σου	⌐τῇ διανοίᾳ⌐	αὕτη ἐστὶν	ἡ		πρώτη	καὶ	μεγάλη	ἐντολή	δὲ	δευτέρα	ὁμοία	αὕτη	ἀγαπήσεις
cj	p.d	a.dsf	r.gs.2	d.dsf n.dsf	r.nsf v.pai.3s	d.nsf		a.nsf	cj	a.nsf	n.nsf	cj	a.nsf	a.nsf	r.dsf.3	v.fai.2s
2779	1877	3910	5148	3836 1379	4047 1639	3836		4755	2779	3489	1953	1254	1311	3927	899	26

your	neighbor	as	yourself.'	**40** All	the	Law	and	the	Prophets	hang	on	these	two	commandments."
σου	⌐τὸν πλησίον⌐	ὡς	σεαυτόν	ὅλος	ὁ	νόμος	καὶ	οἱ	προφῆται	κρέμαται	ἐν	ταύταις	δυσὶν	⌐ταῖς ἐντολαῖς⌐
r.gs.2	d.asm adv	cj	r.asm.2	a.nsm	d.nsm	n.nsm	cj	d.npm	n.npm	v.ppi.3s	p.d	r.dpf	a.dpf	d.dpf n.dpf
5148	3836 4446	6055	4932	3910	3836	3795	2779	3836	4737	3203	1877	4047	1545	3836 1953

Whose Son is the Christ?

22:41	While	the Pharisees	were	gathered	together,	Jesus	asked	them,	**42** "What	do you	think
δὲ	⌐	τῶν Φαρισαίων →		Συνηγμένων ←		⌐ὁ Ἰησοῦς⌐	ἐπηρώτησεν	αὐτοὺς λέγων	τί	→	ὑμῖν δοκεῖ
cj		d.gpm n.gpm		pt.rp.gpm		d.nsm n.nsm	v.aai.3s	r.apm.3 pt.pa.nsm	r.nsn		r.dp.2 v.pai.3s
1254	5251	3836 5757		2652		3836 2652	2089	899 3306	5515		7007 1506

about	the Christ?	Whose	son	is	he?"	"The	son	of David,"		they replied.	**43** He said	to them,	"How	is it	then
περὶ	τοῦ χριστοῦ	τίνος	υἱός	ἐστιν		⌐τοῦ Δαυίδ⌐			λέγουσιν αὐτῷ	→	λέγει →	αὐτοῖς	πῶς	→	οὖν
p.g	d.gsm n.gsm	r.gsn	n.nsm	v.pai.3s		d.gsm n.gsm			v.pai.3p r.dsm.3		v.pai.3s	r.dpm.3	cj		cj
4309	3836 5986	5515	5626	1639		3836 1253			3306 899		3306	899	4802		4036

that	David,	speaking	by	the	Spirit,	calls	him	'Lord'?	For he	says,	**44** "'The	Lord	said	to	my	Lord:	"Sit	at	my
Δαυὶδ		ἐν	πνεύματι	καλεῖ	αὐτὸν	κύριον	→	λέγων		κύριος	εἶπεν ⌐	μου	⌐τῷ κυρίῳ⌐	κάθου	ἐκ	μου
n.nsm		p.d	n.dsn	v.pai.3s	r.asm.3	n.asm		pt.pa.nsm		n.nsm	v.aai.3s	r.gs.1	d.dsm n.dsm	v.pmm.2s	p.g	r.gs.1
1253		1877	4460	2813	899	3261		3306		3261	3306	1609	3836 3261	2764	1666	1609

right	hand	until	I	put	your	enemies	under	your	feet."'	**45** If	then	David	calls	him	'Lord,'	how	can he
δεξιῶν ←		⌐ἕως ἄν⌐		θῶ	σου	τοὺς ἐχθρούς	ὑποκάτω	σου	⌐τῶν ποδῶν⌐	εἰ	οὖν	Δαυὶδ	καλεῖ	αὐτὸν	κύριον	πῶς →	→
a.gpf		cj pl		v.aas.1s	r.gs.2	d.apm a.apm	p.g	r.gs.2	d.gpm n.gpm	cj	cj	n.nsm	v.pai.3s	r.asm.3	n.asm	cj
1288		2401 323		5502	5148	3836 2398	5691	5148	3836 4546	1623	4036	1253	2813	899	3261	4802

ἄγγελοι ἐν τῷ οὐρανῷ εἰσιν. ³¹ περὶ δὲ τῆς ἀναστάσεως τῶν νεκρῶν οὐκ ἀνέγνωτε τὸ ῥηθὲν ὑμῖν ὑπὸ τοῦ θεοῦ λέγοντος, ³² Ἐγώ εἰμι ὁ θεὸς Ἀβραὰμ καὶ ὁ θεὸς Ἰσαὰκ καὶ ὁ θεὸς Ἰακώβ; οὐκ ἔστιν [ὁ] θεὸς νεκρῶν ἀλλὰ ζώντων. ³³ καὶ ἀκούσαντες οἱ ὄχλοι ἐξεπλήσσοντο ἐπὶ τῇ διδαχῇ αὐτοῦ.

²²:³⁴ Οἱ δὲ Φαρισαῖοι ἀκούσαντες ὅτι ἐφίμωσεν τοὺς Σαδδουκαίους συνήχθησαν ἐπὶ τὸ αὐτό, ³⁵ καὶ ἐπηρώτησεν εἷς ἐξ αὐτῶν [νομικὸς] πειράζων αὐτόν, ³⁶ Διδάσκαλε, ποία ἐντολὴ μεγάλη ἐν τῷ νόμῳ; ³⁷ ὁ δὲ ἔφη αὐτῷ, Ἀγαπήσεις κύριον τὸν θεόν σου ἐν ὅλῃ τῇ καρδίᾳ σου καὶ ἐν ὅλῃ τῇ ψυχῇ σου καὶ ἐν ὅλῃ τῇ διανοίᾳ σου· ³⁸ αὕτη ἐστὶν ἡ μεγάλη καὶ πρώτη ἐντολή. ³⁹ δευτέρα δὲ ὁμοία αὐτῇ, Ἀγαπήσεις τὸν πλησίον σου ὡς σεαυτόν. ⁴⁰ ἐν ταύταις ταῖς δυσὶν ἐντολαῖς ὅλος ὁ νόμος κρέμαται καὶ οἱ προφῆται.

²²:⁴¹ Συνηγμένων δὲ τῶν Φαρισαίων ἐπηρώτησεν αὐτοὺς ὁ Ἰησοῦς ⁴² λέγων, Τί ὑμῖν δοκεῖ περὶ τοῦ Χριστοῦ; τίνος υἱός ἐστιν; λέγουσιν αὐτῷ, Τοῦ Δαυίδ. ⁴³ λέγει αὐτοῖς, Πῶς οὖν Δαυὶδ ἐν πνεύματι καλεῖ αὐτὸν κύριον λέγων, ⁴⁴ Εἶπεν κύριος τῷ κυρίῳ μου, Κάθου ἐκ δεξιῶν μου, ἕως ἂν θῶ τοὺς ἐχθρούς σου ὑποκάτω τῶν ποδῶν σου; ⁴⁵ εἰ οὖν Δαυὶδ καλεῖ αὐτὸν κύριον,

be his son?" **46** No one could say a word in reply, and from that day on no one dared
ἐστιν αὐτοῦ υἱός καὶ → οὐδεὶς ἐδύνατο → λόγον → ἀποκριθῆναι αὐτῷ οὐδὲ ἀπ᾽ ἐκείνης ⌐τῆς ἡμέρας⌐ → τις ἐτόλμησεν
v.pai.3s r.gsm.3 n.nsm cj a.nsm v.ipi.3s n.asm f.ap r.dsm.3 cj p.g r.gsf d.gsf n.gsf r.nsm v.aai.3s
1639 899 5626 2779 4029 1538 646 3364 646 899 4028 608 1697 3836 2465 5516 5528

to ask him any more questions.
→ ἐπερωτῆσαι αὐτὸν οὐκέτι ← ↰
f.aa r.asm.3 adv
2089 899 4033 2089

Seven Woes

23:1 Then Jesus said to the crowds and to his disciples: **2** "The teachers of the law and the
Τότε ὁ Ἰησοῦς ἐλάλησεν → τοῖς ὄχλοις καὶ → αὐτοῦ ⌐τοῖς μαθηταῖς⌐ λέγων οἱ γραμματεῖς ← ← καὶ οἱ
adv d.nsm n.nsm v.aai.3s d.dpm n.dpm cj r.gsm.3 d.dpm n.dpm pt.pa.nsm d.npm n.npm cj d.npm
5538 3836 2652 3281 3836 4063 2779 3412 899 3836 3412 3306 3836 1208 2779 3836

Pharisees sit in Moses' seat. **3** So you must obey them and do everything they tell you.
Φαρισαῖοι ἐκάθισαν ἐπὶ τῆς Μωϋσέως καθέδρας οὖν → → τηρεῖτε καὶ ποιήσατε ⌐πάντα ὅσα⌐ ἐὰν → εἴπωσιν ὑμῖν
n.npm v.aai.3p p.g d.gsf n.gsm n.gsf cj v.pam.2p cj v.aam.2p a.apn r.apn pl v.aas.3p r.dp.2
5757 2767 2093 3836 3707 2756 4036 5498 2779 4472 4246 4012 1569 3306 7007

But do not do what they do, for they do not practice what they preach. **4** They tie up heavy
δὲ → μὴ ποιεῖτε κατὰ αὐτῶν ⌐τὰ ἔργα⌐ γὰρ → → οὐ καὶ ποιοῦσιν → λέγουσιν δὲ → δεσμεύουσιν ← βαρέα
cj pl v.pam.2p p.a r.gpm.3 d.apn n.apn cj pl cj v.pai.3p v.pai.3p cj v.pai.3p a.apn
1254 4472 3590 4472 2848 899 3836 2240 1142 4472 4472 4024 2779 4472 3306 1254 1297 987

loads and put them on men's shoulders, but they themselves are not willing to
φορτία [καὶ δυσβάστακτα] καὶ ἐπιτιθέασιν ἐπὶ τῶν ἀνθρώπων ⌐τοὺς ὤμους⌐ δὲ → αὐτοὶ → οὐ θέλουσιν
n.apn cj a.apn cj v.pai.3p p.a d.gpm n.gpm d.apm n.apm cj r.npm pl v.pai.3p
5845 2779 1546 2779 2202 2093 3836 476 3836 6049 1254 2527 899 2527 4024 2527

lift a finger to move them. **5** "Everything they do is done for men to see:
⌐τῷ δακτύλῳ⌐ αὐτῶν → κινῆσαι αὐτά δὲ πάντα αὐτῶν ⌐τὰ ἔργα⌐ → ποιοῦσιν πρὸς ⌐τοῖς ἀνθρώποις⌐ → ⌐τὸ θεαθῆναι⌐
d.dsm n.dsm r.gpm.3 f.aa r.apn.3 cj a.apn r.gpm.3 d.apn n.apn v.pai.3p p.a d.dpm n.dpm d.asn f.ap
3836 1235 899 3075 899 1254 4246 899 3836 2240 4472 4639 3836 476 3836 2517

They make their phylacteries wide and the tassels on their garments long; **6** they love the
γὰρ → → αὐτῶν ⌐τὰ φυλακτήρια⌐ πλατύνουσιν καὶ τὰ κράσπεδα ← → → μεγαλύνουσιν δὲ → φιλοῦσιν τὴν
cj r.gpm.3 d.apn n.apn v.pai.3p cj d.apn n.apn v.pai.3p cj v.pai.3p d.asf
1142 4425 4425 899 3836 5873 4425 2779 3836 3197 3486 1254 5797 3836

place of honor at banquets and the most important seats in the synagogues; **7** they love to be
→ → πρωτοκλισίαν ἐν ⌐τοῖς δείπνοις⌐ καὶ τὰς → → πρωτοκαθεδρίας ἐν ταῖς συναγωγαῖς καὶ
n.asf p.d d.dpn n.dpn cj d.apf n.apf p.d d.dpf n.dpf cj
4752 1877 3836 1270 2779 3836 4751 1877 3836 5252 2779

greeted in the marketplaces and to have men call them 'Rabbi.' **8** "But you are not to be
⌐τοὺς ἀσπασμοὺς⌐ ἐν ταῖς ἀγοραῖς καὶ ὑπὸ ⌐τῶν ἀνθρώπων⌐ καλεῖσθαι ῥαββί δὲ ὑμεῖς → μὴ → →
d.apm n.apm p.d d.dpf n.dpf cj p.g d.gpm n.gpm f.pp n.nsm cj r.np.2 pl
3836 833 1877 3836 59 2779 5679 3836 476 2813 4806 1254 7007 2813 3590

called 'Rabbi,' for you have only one Master and you are all brothers. **9** And do not call anyone on
κληθῆτε ῥαββί γὰρ ὑμῶν ἐστιν εἷς ⌐ὁ διδάσκαλος⌐ δὲ ὑμεῖς ἐστε πάντες ἀδελφοί καὶ → μὴ καλέσητε ἐπὶ
v.aps.2p n.nsm cj r.gp.2 v.pai.3s a.nsm d.nsm n.nsm cj r.np.2 v.pai.2p a.npm n.npm cj pl v.aas.2p p.g
2813 4806 1142 7007 1639 1651 3836 1437 1254 7007 1639 4246 81 2779 3590 2813 2093

earth 'father,' for you have one Father, and he is in heaven. **10** Nor are you to be called 'teacher,' for
⌐τῆς γῆς⌐ πατέρα ὑμῶν γὰρ ὑμῶν ἐστιν εἷς ⌐ὁ πατήρ⌐ → → → ⌐ὁ οὐράνιος⌐ μηδὲ → → κληθῆτε καθηγηταί ὅτι
d.gsf n.gsf n.asm r.gp.2 cj r.gp.2 v.pai.3s a.nsm d.nsm n.nsm d.nsm n.nsm cj v.aps.2p n.npm cj
3836 1178 4252 7007 1142 7007 1639 1651 3836 4252 3836 4039 3593 2813 2762 4022

you have one Teacher, the Christ. **11** The greatest among you will be your servant. **12** For whoever exalts himself
ὑμῶν ἐστιν εἷς καθηγητής ὁ Χριστός δὲ ὁ μείζων → ὑμῶν → ἔσται ὑμῶν διάκονος δὲ ὅστις ὑψώσει ἑαυτὸν
r.gp.2 v.pai.3s a.nsm n.nsm d.nsm n.nsm cj d.nsm n.nsm r.gp.2 v.fmi.3s r.gp.2 n.nsm cj r.nsm v.fai.3s r.asm.3
7007 1639 1651 2762 3836 5986 1254 3836 3489 7007 1639 1356 7007 1254 4015 5738 1571

πῶς υἱὸς αὐτοῦ ἐστιν; ⁴⁶ καὶ οὐδεὶς ἐδύνατο ἀποκριθῆναι αὐτῷ λόγον οὐδὲ ἐτόλμησέν τις ἀπ᾽ ἐκείνης τῆς ἡμέρας ἐπερωτῆσαι αὐτὸν οὐκέτι.

²³¹ Τότε ὁ Ἰησοῦς ἐλάλησεν τοῖς ὄχλοις καὶ τοῖς μαθηταῖς αὐτοῦ ² λέγων, Ἐπὶ τῆς Μωϋσέως καθέδρας ἐκάθισαν οἱ γραμματεῖς καὶ οἱ Φαρισαῖοι. ³ πάντα οὖν ὅσα ἐὰν εἴπωσιν ὑμῖν ποιήσατε καὶ τηρεῖτε, κατὰ δὲ τὰ ἔργα αὐτῶν μὴ ποιεῖτε· λέγουσιν γὰρ καὶ οὐ ποιοῦσιν. ⁴ δεσμεύουσιν δὲ φορτία βαρέα [καὶ δυσβάστακτα] καὶ ἐπιτιθέασιν ἐπὶ τοὺς ὤμους τῶν ἀνθρώπων, αὐτοὶ δὲ τῷ δακτύλῳ αὐτῶν οὐ θέλουσιν κινῆσαι αὐτά. ⁵ πάντα δὲ τὰ ἔργα αὐτῶν ποιοῦσιν πρὸς τὸ θεαθῆναι τοῖς ἀνθρώποις· πλατύνουσιν γὰρ τὰ φυλακτήρια αὐτῶν καὶ μεγαλύνουσιν τὰ κράσπεδα «κράσπεδα,» τῶν ἱματίων αὐτῶν, ⁶ φιλοῦσιν δὲ τὴν πρωτοκλισίαν ἐν τοῖς δείπνοις καὶ τὰς πρωτοκαθεδρίας ἐν ταῖς συναγωγαῖς ⁷ καὶ τοὺς ἀσπασμοὺς ἐν ταῖς ἀγοραῖς καὶ καλεῖσθαι ὑπὸ τῶν ἀνθρώπων, Ῥαββί. ⁸ ὑμεῖς δὲ μὴ κληθῆτε, Ῥαββί· εἷς γάρ ἐστιν ὑμῶν ὁ διδάσκαλος, πάντες δὲ ὑμεῖς ἀδελφοί ἐστε. ⁹ καὶ πατέρα μὴ καλέσητε ὑμῶν ἐπὶ τῆς γῆς, εἷς γάρ ἐστιν ὑμῶν ὁ πατὴρ ὁ οὐράνιος. ¹⁰ μηδὲ κληθῆτε καθηγηταί, ὅτι καθηγητὴς ὑμῶν ἐστιν εἷς ὁ Χριστός. ¹¹ ὁ δὲ μείζων ὑμῶν ἔσται ὑμῶν διάκονος. ¹² ὅστις δὲ ὑψώσει ἑαυτὸν

will be humbled, and whoever humbles himself will be exalted. ¹³ "Woe to you, teachers of the law and
→ → ταπεινωθήσεται καὶ ὅστις ταπεινώσει ἑαυτὸν → → ὑψωθήσεται δὲ Οὐαὶ → ὑμῖν γραμματεῖς ← ← καὶ
v.fpi.3s cj r.nsm v.fai.3s r.asm.3 v.fpi.3s cj j r.dp.2 n.vpm cj
5427 2779 4015 5427 1571 5738 1254 4026 7007 1208 2779

Pharisees, you hypocrites! You shut the kingdom of heaven in men's faces. You
Φαρισαῖοι → ὑποκριταί ὅτι → κλείετε τὴν βασιλείαν → ⌐τῶν οὐρανῶν⌐ ἔμπροσθεν ⌐τῶν ἀνθρώπων⌐ ↤ γὰρ →
n.vpm n.vpm cj v.pai.2p d.asf n.asf d.gpm n.gpm d.gpm n.gpm cj
5757 5695 4022 3091 3836 993 3836 4041 1869 3836 476 1869 1142 1656

yourselves do not enter, nor will you let those enter who are trying to. ¹⁵ "Woe to you, teachers
ὑμεῖς ↦ οὐκ εἰσέρχεσθε οὐδὲ → ἀφίετε εἰσελθεῖν τοὺς → → εἰσερχομένους Οὐαὶ → ὑμῖν γραμματεῖς
r.np.2 pl v.pmi.2p cj v.pai.2p f.aa d.apm pt.pm.apm j r.dp.2 n.vpm
7007 1656 4024 1656 4028 918 1656 3836 1656 4026 7007 1208

of the law and Pharisees, you hypocrites! You travel over land and sea to win a single
← ← ← καὶ Φαρισαῖοι → ὑποκριταί ὅτι → περιάγετε ← ⌐τὴν ξηρὰν⌐ καὶ ⌐τὴν θάλασσαν⌐ → ποιῆσαι ἕνα
cj n.vpm n.vpm cj v.pai.2p d.asf a.asf cj d.asf n.asf f.aa a.asm
2779 5757 5695 4022 4310 3836 3831 2779 3836 2498 4472 1651

convert, and when he becomes one, you make him twice as much a son of hell as you are. ¹⁶ "Woe to you,
προσήλυτον καὶ ὅταν → γένηται → ποιεῖτε αὐτὸν διπλότερον ← υἱὸν → γεέννης → ὑμῶν Οὐαὶ → ὑμῖν
n.asm cj cj v.ams.3s v.pai.2p r.asm.3 adv.c n.asm n.gsf r.gp.2 j r.dp.2
4670 2779 4020 1181 4472 899 1487 5626 1147 7007 4026 7007

blind guides! You say, 'If anyone swears by the temple, it means nothing; but if anyone swears by the gold of
τυφλοὶ ὁδηγοὶ οἱ λέγοντες → ⌐ὃς ἂν ὀμόσῃ ἐν τῷ ναῷ → ἐστιν οὐδέν δ᾽ → ⌐ὃς ἂν ὀμόσῃ ἐν τῷ χρυσῷ →
a.vpm n.vpm d.vpm pt.pa.vpm r.nsm pl v.aas.3s p.d d.dsm n.dsm v.pai.3s a.nsn cj r.nsm pl v.aas.3s p.d d.dsm n.dsm
5603 3843 3836 3306 4005 323 3923 1877 3836 3724 1639 4029 1254 4005 323 3923 1877 3836 5996

the temple, he is bound by his oath.' ¹⁷ You blind fools! Which is greater: the gold, or the temple that
τοῦ ναοῦ → → ὀφείλει → τυφλοὶ καὶ μωροὶ γὰρ τίς ἐστίν μείζων ὁ χρυσὸς ἢ ὁ ναὸς ὁ
d.gsm n.gsm v.pai.3s a.vpm cj a.vpm cj r.nsm v.pai.3s a.nsm.c d.nsm n.nsm cj d.nsm n.nsm d.nsm
3836 3724 4053 5603 2779 3704 1142 5515 1639 3505 3836 5996 2445 3836 3724 3836

makes the gold sacred? ¹⁸ You also say, 'If anyone swears by the altar, it means nothing; but if anyone swears
→ τὸν χρυσόν ἁγιάσας καὶ → ὃς ἂν ὀμόσῃ ἐν τῷ θυσιαστηρίῳ → ἐστιν οὐδέν δ᾽ → ⌐ὃς ἂν ὀμόσῃ
d.asm n.asm pt.aa.nsm cj r.nsm pl v.aas.3s p.d d.dsn n.dsn v.pai.3s a.nsn cj r.nsm pl v.aas.3s
39 3836 5996 39 2779 4005 323 3923 1877 3836 2603 1639 4029 1254 4005 323 3923

by the gift on it, he is bound by his oath.' ¹⁹ You blind men! Which is greater: the gift, or the
ἐν τῷ δώρῳ ⌐τῷ ἐπάνω⌐ αὐτοῦ → → ὀφείλει → τυφλοί ← γὰρ τί μεῖζον τὸ δῶρον ἢ τὸ
p.d d.dsn n.dsn d.dsn p.g r.gsn v.pai.3s a.vpm cj r.nsn a.nsn.c d.nsn n.nsn cj d.nsn
1877 3836 1565 3836 2062 899 4053 5603 1142 5515 3489 3836 1565 2445 3836

altar that makes the gift sacred? ²⁰ Therefore, he who swears by the altar swears by it and by
θυσιαστήριον τὸ → τὸ δῶρον ἁγιάζον οὖν → ὁ ← ὀμόσας ἐν τῷ θυσιαστηρίῳ ὀμνύει ἐν αὐτῷ καὶ ἐν
n.nsn d.nsn d.asn n.asn pt.pa.nsn cj d.nsm pt.aa.nsm p.d d.dsn n.dsn v.pai.3s p.d r.dsn.3 cj p.d
2603 3836 39 3836 1565 39 4036 3836 3923 1877 3836 2603 3923 1877 899 2779 1877

everything on it. ²¹ And he who swears by the temple swears by it and by the one who dwells in
πᾶσι ⌐τοῖς ἐπάνω⌐ αὐτοῦ καὶ ὁ ← ὀμόσας ἐν τῷ ναῷ ὀμνύει ἐν αὐτῷ καὶ ἐν τῷ ← ← κατοικοῦντι
a.dpn d.dpn p.g r.gsn.3 cj d.nsm pt.aa.nsm p.d d.dsm n.dsm v.pai.3s p.d r.dsn.3 cj p.d d.dsm pt.pa.dsm
4246 3836 2062 899 2779 3836 3923 1877 3836 3724 3923 1877 899 2779 1877 3836 2997

it. ²² And he who swears by heaven swears by God's throne and by the one who sits on it.
αὐτόν καὶ ὁ ← ὀμόσας ἐν ⌐τῷ οὐρανῷ⌐ ὀμνύει ἐν ⌐τοῦ θεοῦ⌐ ⌐τῷ θρόνῳ⌐ καὶ ἐν τῷ ← καθημένῳ ἐπάνω αὐτοῦ
r.asm.3 cj d.nsm pt.aa.nsm p.d d.dsm n.dsm v.pai.3s p.d d.gsm n.gsm d.dsm n.dsm cj p.d d.dsm pt.pm.dsm p.g r.gsn.3
899 2779 3836 3923 1877 3836 4041 3923 1877 3836 2536 3836 2585 2779 1877 3836 2764 2062 899

²³ "Woe to you, teachers of the law and Pharisees, you hypocrites! You give a tenth of your spices –
Οὐαὶ → ὑμῖν γραμματεῖς ← ← καὶ Φαρισαῖοι → ὑποκριταί ὅτι → ἀποδεκατοῦτε
j r.dp.2 n.vpm cj n.vpm n.vpm cj v.pai.2p
4026 7007 1208 2779 5757 5695 4022 620

mint, dill and cummin. But you have neglected the more important matters of the law –
⌐τὸ ἡδύοσμον⌐ καὶ ⌐τὸ ἄνηθον⌐ καὶ ⌐τὸ κύμινον⌐ καὶ → ἀφήκατε τὰ → βαρύτερα ← → τοῦ νόμου
d.asn n.asn cj d.asn n.asn cj d.asn n.asn cj v.aai.2p d.apn a.apn.c d.gsm n.gsm
3836 2455 2779 3836 464 2779 3836 3248 2779 918 3836 987 3836 3795

ταπεινωθήσεται καὶ ὅστις ταπεινώσει ἑαυτὸν ὑψωθήσεται. ¹³ Οὐαὶ δὲ ὑμῖν, γραμματεῖς καὶ Φαρισαῖοι ὑποκριταί, ὅτι κλείετε τὴν βασιλείαν τῶν οὐρανῶν ἔμπροσθεν τῶν ἀνθρώπων· ὑμεῖς γὰρ οὐκ εἰσέρχεσθε οὐδὲ τοὺς εἰσερχομένους ἀφίετε εἰσελθεῖν. ¹⁵ Οὐαὶ ὑμῖν, γραμματεῖς καὶ Φαρισαῖοι ὑποκριταί, ὅτι περιάγετε τὴν θάλασσαν καὶ τὴν ξηρὰν ποιῆσαι ἕνα προσήλυτον, καὶ ὅταν γένηται ποιεῖτε αὐτὸν υἱὸν γεέννης διπλότερον ὑμῶν. ¹⁶ Οὐαὶ ὑμῖν, ὁδηγοὶ τυφλοὶ οἱ λέγοντες, Ὃς ἂν ὀμόσῃ ἐν τῷ ναῷ, οὐδέν ἐστιν· ὃς δ᾽ ἂν ὀμόσῃ ἐν τῷ χρυσῷ τοῦ ναοῦ, ὀφείλει. ¹⁷ μωροὶ καὶ τυφλοί, τίς γὰρ μείζων ἐστίν, ὁ χρυσὸς ἢ ὁ ναὸς ὁ ἁγιάσας τὸν χρυσόν; ¹⁸ καί, Ὃς ἂν ὀμόσῃ ἐν τῷ θυσιαστηρίῳ, οὐδέν ἐστιν· ὃς δ᾽ ἂν ὀμόσῃ ἐν τῷ δώρῳ τῷ ἐπάνω αὐτοῦ, ὀφείλει. ¹⁹ τυφλοί, τί γὰρ μεῖζον, τὸ δῶρον ἢ τὸ θυσιαστήριον τὸ ἁγιάζον τὸ δῶρον; ²⁰ ὁ οὖν ὀμόσας ἐν τῷ θυσιαστηρίῳ ὀμνύει ἐν αὐτῷ καὶ ἐν πᾶσι τοῖς ἐπάνω αὐτοῦ· ²¹ καὶ ὁ ὀμόσας ἐν τῷ ναῷ ὀμνύει ἐν αὐτῷ καὶ ἐν τῷ κατοικοῦντι αὐτόν, ²² καὶ ὁ ὀμόσας ἐν τῷ οὐρανῷ ὀμνύει ἐν τῷ θρόνῳ τοῦ θεοῦ καὶ ἐν τῷ καθημένῳ ἐπάνω αὐτοῦ. ²³ Οὐαὶ ὑμῖν, γραμματεῖς καὶ Φαρισαῖοι ὑποκριταί, ὅτι ἀποδεκατοῦτε τὸ ἡδύοσμον καὶ τὸ ἄνηθον καὶ τὸ κύμινον καὶ ἀφήκατε τὰ βαρύτερα τοῦ νόμου, τὴν κρίσιν καὶ τὸ ἔλεος καὶ

justice,   mercy   and faithfulness.   You should have practiced the latter, without neglecting the former.
⌐τὴν κρίσιν⌐ καὶ ⌐τὸ ἔλεος⌐ καὶ ⌐τὴν πίστιν⌐   [δὲ]   →   ἔδει   →   ποιῆσαι   ταῦτα   μὴ   ἀφιέναι   κἀκεῖνα
d.asf n.asf   cj   d.asn n.asn   cj   d.asf n.asf   cj   v.iai.3s   f.aa   r.apn   pl   f.pa   adv
3836 3213   2779   3836 1799   2779   3836 4411   1254   1256   4472   4047   3590   918   2797

24 You blind guides! You strain   out a gnat   but swallow   a camel.   **25** "Woe to you, teachers   of the law
→   τυφλοὶ ὁδηγοὶ   οἱ διϋλίζοντες ←   ⌐τὸν κώνωπα⌐   δὲ   καταπίνοντες   ⌐τὴν κάμηλον⌐   Οὐαὶ   →   ὑμῖν   γραμματεῖς ← ← ←
   a.vpm d.vpm   d.vpm pt.pa.vpm   d.asm n.asm   cj   pt.pa.vpm   d.asf n.asf   j   r.dp.2   n.vpm
   5603 3843   3836 1494   3836 3270   1254   2927   3836 2823   4026   7007   1208

and Pharisees, you hypocrites!   You clean   the outside of the cup   and dish,   but inside they are   →
καὶ Φαρισαῖοι   →   ὑποκριταί   ὅτι   →   καθαρίζετε τὸ   ἔξωθεν   →   τοῦ ποτηρίου καὶ   ⌐τῆς παροψίδος⌐   δὲ   ἔσωθεν   →
cj   n.vpm   n.vpm   cj   v.pai.2p   d.asn   a.g   d.gsn n.gsn   cj   d.gsf n.gsf   cj   adv
2779 5757   5695   4022   2751   3836 2033   3836 4539   2779   3836 4243   1254   2277

full   of greed   and self-indulgence.   **26** Blind Pharisee!   First clean   the inside of the cup   and dish, and then
γέμουσιν ἐξ   ἁρπαγῆς καὶ   ἀκρασίας   τυφλέ   Φαρισαῖε   πρῶτον καθάρισον τὸ   ἐντὸς   →   τοῦ ποτηρίου   →   ἵνα
v.pai.3p   p.g   n.gsf   cj   n.gsf   a.vsm   n.vsm   a.asn   v.aam.2s   d.asn   p.g   d.gsn n.gsn   cj
1154   1666   771   2779   202   5603   5757   4754   2751   3836   1955   3836 4539   2671

the outside   also will be   clean.   **27** "Woe to you, teachers   of the law and Pharisees, you hypocrites!   You
τὸ   ἐκτὸς   αὐτοῦ καὶ   →   γένηται καθαρόν   Οὐαὶ   →   ὑμῖν   γραμματεῖς ← ←   καὶ   Φαρισαῖοι   →   ὑποκριταί   ὅτι   →
d.nsn   adv   r.gsn.3   adv   v.ams.3s   a.nsn   j   r.dp.2   n.vpm   cj   n.vpm   n.vpm   cj
3836   1760   899   2779   1181   2754   4026   7007   1208   2779   5757   5695   4022

are like   whitewashed tombs, which   look   beautiful on the outside but on the inside are full   of
→   παρομοιάζετε κεκονιαμένοις τάφοις   οἵτινες   μὲν   φαίνονται   ὡραῖοι   →   →   ἔξωθεν   δὲ   →   →   ἔσωθεν   γέμουσιν ←
   v.pai.2p   pt.rp.dpm   n.dpm   r.npm   pl   v.ppi.3p   a.npm   adv   cj   adv   v.pai.3p
   4234   3154   5439   4015   3525 5743   6053   2033   1254   2277   1154

dead   men's bones and everything unclean.   **28** In the same way,   on the outside you   appear to people
νεκρῶν   ὀστέων   καὶ   πάσης   ἀκαθαρσίας   →   οὕτως ←   μὲν   →   ἔξωθεν   ὑμεῖς καὶ   φαίνεσθε   →   ⌐τοῖς ἀνθρώποις⌐
a.gpm   n.gpn   cj   a.gsf   n.gsf   adv   pl   adv   r.np.2   adv   v.ppi.2p   d.dpm n.dpm
3738   4014   2779   4246   174   4048   3525   2033   7007   2779   5743   3836 476

as righteous but on the inside you   are   full   of hypocrisy and wickedness.   **29** "Woe to you, teachers   of the law and
δίκαιοι   δὲ   →   →   ἔσωθεν   ἐστε   μεστοὶ   ὑποκρίσεως καὶ   ἀνομίας   Οὐαὶ   →   ὑμῖν   γραμματεῖς ← ←   καὶ
a.npm   cj   adv   v.pai.2p a.npm   n.gsf   cj   n.gsf   j   r.dp.2   n.vpm   cj
1465   1254   2277   1639   3550   5694   2779   490   4026   7007   1208   2779

Pharisees, you hypocrites!   You build   tombs   for the prophets and decorate the graves of the righteous.
Φαρισαῖοι   →   ὑποκριταί   ὅτι   →   οἰκοδομεῖτε ⌐τοὺς τάφους⌐   →   τῶν προφητῶν   καὶ   κοσμεῖτε   τὰ   μνημεῖα   →   τῶν δικαίων
n.vpm   n.vpm   cj   v.pai.2p   d.apm n.apm   d.gpm n.gpm   cj   v.pai.2p   d.apn n.apn   d.gpm a.gpm
5757   5695   4022   3868   3836 5439   3836 4737   2779   3175   3836 3646   3836 1465

30 And you say, 'If we had lived in the days   of our forefathers, we would not have taken part   with them in
καὶ   →   λέγετε εἰ   →   ἤμεθα ἐν   ταῖς ἡμέραις   ⌐ ἡμῶν ⌐τῶν πατέρων⌐   →   ἂν   οὐκ   →   ἤμεθα κοινωνοὶ   →   αὐτῶν ἐν
cj   v.pai.2p cj   v.imi.1p   p.d   d.dpf   n.dpf   r.gp.1   d.gpm n.gpm   pl   pl   v.imi.1p   n.npm   r.gpm.3   p.d
2779   3306   1623   1639   1877   3836   2465   4252   7005   3836 4252   1639   323   4024   1639   3128   899   1877

shedding the blood of the prophets.'   **31** So   you testify   against yourselves that you   are   the descendants of those
τῷ   αἵματι   →   τῶν προφητῶν   ὥστε   →   μαρτυρεῖτε   ἑαυτοῖς   ὅτι   →   ἐστε   υἱοί   →   τῶν
d.dsn   n.dsn   d.gpm n.gpm   cj   v.pai.2p   r.dpm.2   cj   v.pai.2p   n.npm   d.gpm
3836   135   3836 4737   6063   3455   1571   4022   1639   5626   3836

who murdered   the prophets.   **32**   Fill   up, then, the measure of the sin of your forefathers!   **33** "You snakes!
←   φονευσάντων τοὺς προφήτας   καὶ ὑμεῖς πληρώσατε ←   τὸ   μέτρον   ὑμῶν ⌐τῶν πατέρων⌐   ὄφεις
   pt.aa.gpm   d.apm n.apm   cj   r.np.2   v.aam.2p   d.asn   n.asn   r.gp.2   d.gpm n.gpm   n.vpm
   5839   3836 4737   2779 7007   4444   3836   3586   4252 7007   3836 4252   4058

You brood   of vipers! How will you escape   being condemned to hell?   **34** Therefore   I   am sending
→   γεννήματα   →   ἐχιδνῶν πῶς   →   φύγητε ἀπὸ   ⌐τῆς κρίσεως⌐   →   ⌐τῆς γεέννης⌐   ⌐Διὰ τοῦτο⌐   ἰδοὺ ἐγὼ   →   ἀποστέλλω
   n.vpn   n.gpf   cj   v.aas.2p   p.g   d.gsf n.gsf   d.gsf n.gsf   p.a   r.asn   j   r.ns.1   v.pai.1s
   1165   2399   4802   5771   608   3836 3213   3836 1147   1328   4047   2627   1609   690

you prophets and wise   men and teachers. Some of them you will kill   and crucify;   others   you
πρὸς ὑμᾶς προφήτας καὶ   σοφοὺς ←   καὶ   γραμματεῖς   →   ἐξ   αὐτῶν   →   ἀποκτενεῖτε καὶ   σταυρώσετε καὶ   ἐξ   αὐτῶν   →
p.a   r.ap.2   n.apm   cj   a.apm   cj   n.apm   p.g   r.gpm.3   v.fai.2p   cj   v.fai.2p   cj   p.g   r.gpm.3
4639   7007   4737   2779   5055   2779   1208   1666   899   650   2779   5090   2779   1666 899

τὴν πίστιν· ταῦτα [δὲ] ἔδει ποιῆσαι κἀκεῖνα μὴ ἀφιέναι. **24** ὁδηγοὶ τυφλοί, οἱ διϋλίζοντες τὸν κώνωπα, τὴν δὲ κάμηλον καταπίνοντες. **25** Οὐαὶ ὑμῖν, γραμματεῖς καὶ Φαρισαῖοι ὑποκριταί, ὅτι καθαρίζετε τὸ ἔξωθεν τοῦ ποτηρίου καὶ τῆς παροψίδος, ἔσωθεν δὲ γέμουσιν ἐξ ἁρπαγῆς καὶ ἀκρασίας. **26** Φαρισαῖε τυφλέ, καθάρισον πρῶτον τὸ ἐντὸς τοῦ ποτηρίου «ποτηρίου,» καὶ τῆς παροψίδος, ἵνα γένηται καὶ τὸ ἐκτὸς αὐτοῦ καθαρόν. **27** Οὐαὶ ὑμῖν, γραμματεῖς καὶ Φαρισαῖοι ὑποκριταί, ὅτι παρομοιάζετε τάφοις κεκονιαμένοις, οἵτινες ἔξωθεν μὲν φαίνονται ὡραῖοι, ἔσωθεν δὲ γέμουσιν ὀστέων νεκρῶν καὶ πάσης ἀκαθαρσίας. **28** οὕτως καὶ ὑμεῖς ἔξωθεν μὲν φαίνεσθε τοῖς ἀνθρώποις δίκαιοι, ἔσωθεν δέ ἐστε μεστοὶ ὑποκρίσεως καὶ ἀνομίας. **29** Οὐαὶ ὑμῖν, γραμματεῖς καὶ Φαρισαῖοι ὑποκριταί, ὅτι οἰκοδομεῖτε τοὺς τάφους τῶν προφητῶν καὶ κοσμεῖτε τὰ μνημεῖα τῶν δικαίων, **30** καὶ λέγετε, Εἰ ἤμεθα ἐν ταῖς ἡμέραις τῶν πατέρων ἡμῶν, οὐκ ἂν ἤμεθα αὐτῶν κοινωνοὶ ἐν τῷ αἵματι τῶν προφητῶν. **31** ὥστε μαρτυρεῖτε ἑαυτοῖς ὅτι υἱοί ἐστε τῶν φονευσάντων τοὺς προφήτας. **32** καὶ ὑμεῖς πληρώσατε τὸ μέτρον τῶν πατέρων ὑμῶν. **33** ὄφεις, γεννήματα ἐχιδνῶν, πῶς φύγητε ἀπὸ τῆς κρίσεως τῆς γεέννης; **34** διὰ τοῦτο ἰδοὺ ἐγὼ ἀποστέλλω πρὸς ὑμᾶς προφήτας καὶ σοφοὺς

will flog		in	your	synagogues		and	pursue	from	town	to	town.	[35] And so		upon	you		will come	all	the
→ μαστιγώσετε		ἐν	ὑμῶν	˪ταῖς	συναγωγαῖς˩	καὶ	διώξετε	ἀπὸ	πόλεως	εἰς	πόλιν	ὅπως	ἐφ'	ὑμᾶς		→	ἔλθῃ	πᾶν
v.fai.2p		p.d	r.gp.2	d.dpf	n.dpf	cj	v.fai.2p	p.g	n.gsf	p.a	n.asf	cj	p.a	r.ap.2		v.aas.3s	a.nsn
3463		1877	7007	3836	5252	2779	1503	608	4484	1650	4484	3968	2093	7007		2262	4246

righteous	blood	that	has	been	shed		on	earth,	from	the	blood	of	righteous	Abel	to	the	blood	of
δίκαιον	αἷμα	→	→	→	ἐκχυννόμενον	ἐπὶ	τῆς	γῆς,	ἀπὸ	τοῦ	αἵματος	˪τοῦ	δικαίου˩	Ἄβελ	ἕως	τοῦ	αἵματος	→
a.nsn	n.nsn				pt.pp.nsn	p.g	d.gsf	n.gsf	p.g	d.gsn	n.gsn	d.gsm	a.gsm	n.gsm	p.g	d.gsn	n.gsn	
1465	135				1773	2093	3836	1178	608	3836	135	6	3836	6	2401	3836	135	

Zechariah	son	of Berekiah,	whom	you	murdered	between	the	temple	and	the	altar.	[36] I	tell	you	the truth,
Ζαχαρίου	υἱοῦ	Βαραχίου	ὃν	→	ἐφονεύσατε	μεταξὺ	τοῦ	ναοῦ	καὶ	τοῦ	θυσιαστηρίου	→ λέγω	ὑμῖν	ἀμὴν
n.gsm	n.gsm	n.gsm	r.asm		v.aai.2p	p.g	d.gsn	n.gsn	cj	d.gsn	n.gsn	v.pai.1s	r.dp.2	pl
2408	5626	974	4005		5839	3568	3836	3724	2779	3836	2603	3306	7007	297

all	this	will	come	upon	this	generation.	[37] "O Jerusalem,	Jerusalem,	you	who	kill		the	prophets	and
πάντα	ταῦτα	→	ἥξει	ἐπὶ	ταύτην	˪τὴν γενεὰν˩	→ Ἰερουσαλὴμ	Ἰερουσαλὴμ	ἡ	←	ἀποκτείνουσα		τοὺς	προφήτας	καὶ
a.npn	r.npn		v.fai.3s	p.a	r.asf	d.asf n.asf	n.vsf	n.vsf	d.vsf		pt.pa.vsf		d.apm	n.apm	cj
4246	4047		2457	2093	4047	3836 1155	2647	2647	3836		650		3836	4737	2779

stone	those	sent	to	you,	how	often	I	have	longed	to gather		your	children	together,	
λιθοβολοῦσα	τοὺς	ἀπεσταλμένους	πρὸς	αὐτήν	ποσάκις	←	→	→	ἠθέλησα	→ ἐπισυναγαγεῖν		σου	˪τὰ τέκνα˩	←	ὃν
pt.pa.vsf	d.apm	pt.rp.apm	p.a	r.asf.3	adv				v.aai.1s	f.aa		r.gs.2	d.apn n.apn		r.asm
3344	3836	690	4639	899	4529				2527	2190		5148	3836 5451	2190	4005

as	a	hen	gathers	her	chicks	under	her	wings,	but	you	were	not	willing.	[38] Look,	your	house		is left
τρόπον	ὄρνις		ἐπισυνάγει	αὐτῆς	˪τὰ νοσσία˩	ὑπὸ	τὰς	πτέρυγας	καὶ	→	→	οὐκ	ἠθελήσατε	ἰδοὺ	ὑμῶν	ὁ	οἶκος˩	ἀφίεται
n.asm	n.nsf		v.pai.3s	r.gsf.3	d.apn n.apn	p.a	d.apf	n.apf	cj			pl	v.aai.2p	j	r.gp.2	d.nsm	n.nsm	v.ppi.3s
5573	3998		2190	899	3836 3800	5679	3836	4763	2779			4024	2527	2627	7007	3836	3875	918

to you	desolate.	[39] For	I	tell	you,	you	will	not		see	me	again	until		you	say,	'Blessed	is he	who comes
→ ὑμῖν	ἔρημος˩	γὰρ	→	λέγω	ὑμῖν	→	→	˪οὐ μή˩	ἴδητέ	με	˪ἀπ'	ἄρτι˩	˪ἕως	ἄν˩	εἴπητε	εὐλογημένος	ὁ	←	ἐρχόμενος
r.dp.2	a.nsm	cj		v.pai.1s	r.dp.2			pl pl	v.aas.2p	r.as.1	p.g	adv	cj	pl	v.aas.2p	pt.rp.nsm	d.nsm		pt.pm.nsm
7007	2245	1142		3306	7007			4024 3590	1625	1609	608	785	2401	323	3306	2328	3836		2262

in	the	name	of the Lord.'"
ἐν		ὀνόματι	→ κυρίου
p.d		n.dsn	n.gsm
1877		3950	3261

Signs of the End of the Age

24:1 | Jesus | | left | | the | temple | and was | walking | away | when | his | disciples | | came | up to him to |
|---|---|---|---|---|---|---|---|---|---|---|---|---|---|---|
| Καὶ | ὁ | Ἰησοῦς, | ἐξελθὼν | ἀπὸ | τοῦ | ἱεροῦ | → | ἐπορεύετο | ← | καὶ | αὐτοῦ | οἱ | μαθηταὶ | προσῆλθον ← ← |
| cj | d.nsm | n.nsm | pt.aa.nsm | p.g | d.gsn | n.gsn | | v.imi.3s | | cj | r.gsm.3 | d.npm | n.npm | v.aai.3p |
| 2779 | 3836 | 2652 | 2002 | 608 | 3836 | 2639 | | 4513 | | 2779 | 899 | 3836 | 3412 | 4665 |

call	his	attention	to its		buildings.	[2]	"Do you	see	all	these things?"			he	asked.
ἐπιδεῖξαι	αὐτῷ		←	˪τοῦ ἱεροῦ˩	˪τὰς οἰκοδομὰς˩	οὐ	→	βλέπετε	πάντα	ταῦτα	←	δὲ	ὁ	ἀποκριθεὶς	εἶπεν
f.aa	r.dsm.3			d.gsn n.gsn	d.apf n.apf	pl		v.pai.2p	a.apn	r.apn		cj	d.nsm	pt.ap.nsm	v.aai.3s
2109	899	2109		3836 2639	3836 3869	4024		1063	4246	4047		1254	3836	646	3306

	"I	tell	you	the truth,	not		one	stone	here	will	be	left	on	another;	every	one		will	be	thrown
αὐτοῖς	→	λέγω	ὑμῖν	ἀμὴν	˪οὐ μή˩		λίθος	ὧδε	→	→	ἀφεθῇ	ἐπὶ	λίθον		ὃς	οὐ	→	→	καταλυθήσεται
r.dpm.3		v.pai.1s	r.dp.2	pl	pl pl		n.nsm	adv			v.aps.3s	p.a	n.asm		r.nsm	pl			v.fpi.3s
899		3306	7007	297	4024 3590		3345	6045			918	2093	3345		4005	4024			2907

down."	¶	[3]	As	Jesus	was	sitting		on	the	Mount	of Olives,		the	disciples	came		to	him	privately.
←			δὲ	→ αὐτοῦ	→	Καθημένου	ἐπὶ	τοῦ	ὄρους	˪τῶν ἐλαιῶν˩	οἱ	μαθηταὶ	προσῆλθον	αὐτῷ	˪κατ'	ἰδίαν˩
			cj	1254 2764	r.gsm.3	pt.pm.gsm	p.g	d.gsn	n.gsn	d.gpf n.gpf	d.npm	n.npm	v.aai.3p	r.dsm.3	p.a	a.asf
			1254 2764	899	2764	2093	3836	4001	3836 1777	3836	3412	4665	899	2848	2625

"Tell us,"	they	said,	"when	will	this	happen,	and	what	will be	the	sign	of	your	coming		and	of the
εἰπὲ	ἡμῖν	λέγοντες	πότε	→	ταῦτα	ἔσται	καὶ	τί	→	τὸ	σημεῖον	→	σῆς	˪τῆς παρουσίας˩	καὶ	→
v.aam.2s	r.dp.1	pt.pa.npm	cj		r.npn	v.fmi.3s	cj	r.nsn		d.nsn	n.nsn		r.gsf.2	d.gsf n.gsf	cj	
3306	7005	3306	4537		4047	1639	2779	5515		3836	4956		5050	3836 4242	2779	

end		of the age?"	¶	[4]	Jesus		answered:		"Watch	out	that	no	one	deceives	you.	[5] For
συντελείας	→	τοῦ αἰῶνος			Καὶ	ὁ	Ἰησοῦς,	ἀποκριθεὶς	εἶπεν	αὐτοῖς	βλέπετε	←	→	μή	τις	πλανήσῃ	ὑμᾶς	γὰρ
n.gsf		d.gsm n.gsm			cj	d.nsm	n.nsm	pt.ap.nsm	v.aai.3s	r.dpm.3	v.pam.2p			cj	r.nsm	v.aas.3s	r.ap.2	cj
5333		3836 172			2779	3836	2652	646	3306	899	1063			3590	5516	4414	7007	1142

καὶ γραμματεῖς· ἐξ αὐτῶν ἀποκτενεῖτε καὶ σταυρώσετε καὶ ἐξ αὐτῶν μαστιγώσετε ἐν ταῖς συναγωγαῖς ὑμῶν καὶ διώξετε ἀπὸ πόλεως εἰς πόλιν· [35] ὅπως ἔλθῃ ἐφ' ὑμᾶς πᾶν αἷμα δίκαιον ἐκχυννόμενον ἐπὶ τῆς γῆς ἀπὸ τοῦ αἵματος Ἄβελ τοῦ δικαίου ἕως τοῦ αἵματος Ζαχαρίου υἱοῦ Βαραχίου, ὃν ἐφονεύσατε μεταξὺ τοῦ ναοῦ καὶ τοῦ θυσιαστηρίου. [36] ἀμὴν λέγω ὑμῖν, ἥξει ταῦτα πάντα ἐπὶ τὴν γενεὰν ταύτην. [37] Ἰερουσαλὴμ Ἰερουσαλήμ, ἡ ἀποκτείνουσα τοὺς προφήτας καὶ λιθοβολοῦσα τοὺς ἀπεσταλμένους πρὸς αὐτήν, ποσάκις ἠθέλησα ἐπισυναγαγεῖν τὰ τέκνα σου, ὃν τρόπον ὄρνις ἐπισυνάγει τὰ νοσσία αὐτῆς ὑπὸ τὰς πτέρυγας, καὶ οὐκ ἠθελήσατε. [38] ἰδοὺ ἀφίεται ὑμῖν ὁ οἶκος ὑμῶν ἔρημος. [39] λέγω γὰρ ὑμῖν, οὐ μή με ἴδητε ἀπ' ἄρτι ἕως ἂν εἴπητε, Εὐλογημένος ὁ ἐρχόμενος ἐν ὀνόματι κυρίου.

[24:1] Καὶ ἐξελθὼν ὁ Ἰησοῦς ἀπὸ τοῦ ἱεροῦ ἐπορεύετο, καὶ προσῆλθον οἱ μαθηταὶ αὐτοῦ ἐπιδεῖξαι αὐτῷ τὰς οἰκοδομὰς τοῦ ἱεροῦ. [2] ὁ δὲ ἀποκριθεὶς εἶπεν αὐτοῖς, Οὐ βλέπετε ταῦτα πάντα; ἀμὴν λέγω ὑμῖν, οὐ μὴ ἀφεθῇ ὧδε λίθος ἐπὶ λίθον ὃς οὐ καταλυθήσεται. ¶ [3] Καθημένου δὲ αὐτοῦ ἐπὶ τοῦ Ὄρους τῶν Ἐλαιῶν προσῆλθον αὐτῷ οἱ μαθηταὶ κατ' ἰδίαν λέγοντες, Εἰπὲ ἡμῖν πότε ταῦτα ἔσται καὶ τί τὸ σημεῖον τῆς σῆς παρουσίας καὶ συντελείας τοῦ αἰῶνος; ¶ [4] καὶ ἀποκριθεὶς ὁ Ἰησοῦς εἶπεν

many will come | in | my name, | claiming, | 'I | am | the | Christ,' | and | will deceive | many. | **6** | You will
πολλοὶ → ἐλεύσονται ἐπὶ μου ⌐τῷ ὀνόματι⌐ λέγοντες Ἐγώ εἰμι ὁ χριστός καὶ → πλανήσουσιν πολλούς δὲ → μελλήσετε
a.npm / v.fmi.3p / p.d / r.gs.1 / d.dsn n.dsn / pt.pa.npm / r.ns.1 / v.pai.1s / d.nsm / n.nsm / cj / v.fai.3p / a.apm / cj / v.fai.2p
4498 / 2262 / 2093 / 1609 / 3836 3950 / 3306 / 1609 / 1639 / 3836 / 5986 / 2779 / 4414 / 4498 / 1254 / 3516

hear | of wars | and | rumors | of wars, | but see | | | to it that | you are not | alarmed. | | Such things must happen, | but
ἀκούειν πολέμους καὶ ἀκοὰς → πολέμων ὁρᾶτε ← ← → → μὴ θροεῖσθε γὰρ δεῖ γενέσθαι ἀλλʼ
f.pa / n.apm / cj / n.apf / n.gpm / v.pam.2p / / / / v.pam.2p / cj / v.pai.3s / f.am / cj
201 / 4483 / 2779 / 198 / 4483 / 3972 / 2583 / 2583 / 3590 / 2583 / 1142 / 1256 / 1181 / 247

the end | is | still | to come. | **7** | | Nation | will rise | against | nation, | and | kingdom | against | kingdom. | | There will
τὸ τέλος ἐστίν οὔπω ← γὰρ ἔθνος → ἐγερθήσεται ἐπὶ ἔθνος καὶ βασιλεία ἐπὶ βασιλείαν καὶ
d.nsn n.nsn / v.pai.3s / adv / cj / n.nsn / v.fpi.3s / p.a / n.asn / cj / n.nsf / p.a / n.asf / cj
3836 5465 / 1639 / 4037 / 1142 / 1620 / 1586 / 2093 / 1620 / 2779 / 993 / 2093 / 993 / 2779

be | famines | and | earthquakes | in | various | places. | **8** | All | these are | the beginning | of | birth pains. | ¶
ἔσονται λιμοὶ καὶ σεισμοὶ κατὰ ← τόπους δὲ πάντα ταῦτα ἀρχὴ → → ὠδίνων
v.fmi.3p / n.npf / cj / n.npm / p.a / n.apm / cj / a.npn r.npn / n.nsf / n.gpf
1639 / 3350 / 2779 / 4939 / 2848 / 5536 / 1254 / 4246 4047 / 794 / 6047

9 "Then | you | will be handed | over to | be persecuted | and | | put to death, | | and you will be | | | hated | by
Τότε ὑμᾶς → παραδώσουσιν ← εἰς θλῖψιν καὶ ὑμᾶς → → ἀποκτενοῦσιν καὶ → → ἔσεσθε μισούμενοι ὑπὸ
adv / r.ap.2 / v.fai.3p / p.a / n.asf / cj / r.ap.2 / v.fai.3p / cj / v.fmi.2p / pt.pp.npm / p.g
5538 / 7007 / 4140 / 1650 / 2568 / 2779 / 7007 / 650 / 2779 / 1639 / 3631 / 5679

all | nations | because of | me. | **10** | At that time | many | will turn | | away from the faith | and will
πάντων ⌐τῶν ἐθνῶν⌐ διὰ ← ⌐τὸ ὄνομα μου⌐ καὶ τότε πολλοὶ σκανδαλισθήσονται ← καὶ →
a.gpn / d.gpn n.gpn / p.a / d.asn n.asn r.gs.1 / cj adv / a.npm / v.fpi.3p / cj
4246 / 3836 1620 / 1328 / 3836 3950 1609 / 2779 5538 / 4498 / 4997 / 2779

betray | | and hate | each | other, | **11** | and many | false prophets | | will appear | and | deceive
παραδώσουσιν ἀλλήλους καὶ μισήσουσιν ἀλλήλους ← καὶ πολλοὶ → ψευδοπροφῆται → ἐγερθήσονται καὶ πλανήσουσιν
v.fai.3p / r.apm / cj / v.fai.3p / r.apm / cj / a.npm / n.npm / v.fpi.3p / cj / v.fai.3p
4140 / 253 / 2779 / 3631 / 253 / 2779 / 4498 / 6021 / 1586 / 2779 / 4414

many | people. | **12** | Because of | the increase | of wickedness, | the love | of most | | will grow cold, | **13** but | he
πολλούς ← καὶ διὰ ← → ⌐τὸ πληθυνθῆναι⌐ ⌐τὴν ἀνομίαν⌐ ἡ ἀγάπη ⌐τῶν πολλῶν⌐ → ψυγήσεται δὲ ὁ
a.apm / cj / p.a / d.asn f.ap / d.asf n.asf / d.nsf n.nsf / d.gpm a.gpm / v.fpi.3s / cj / d.nsm
4498 / 2779 / 1328 / 3836 4437 / 3836 490 / 3836 27 / 3836 4498 / 6038 / 1254 / 3836

who | stands | firm | to | the end | | will be saved. | **14** And | this | gospel | | of the | kingdom | will be preached | in
← ὑπομείνας ← εἰς τέλος οὗτος → → σωθήσεται καὶ τοῦτο ⌐τὸ εὐαγγέλιον⌐ → τῆς βασιλείας → → κηρυχθήσεται ἐν
pt.aa.nsm / p.a / n.asn r.nsm / v.fpi.3s / cj / r.nsn / d.nsn n.nsn / d.gsf n.gsf / v.fpi.3s / p.d
5702 / 1650 / 5465 4047 / 5392 / 2779 / 4047 / 3836 2295 / 3836 993 / 3062 / 1877

the | whole | world | as | a testimony | to | all | nations, | and | then | the | end | will come. | ¶ | **15** "So | when | you | see
τῇ ὅλῃ οἰκουμένῃ εἰς μαρτύριον ⌐ πᾶσιν τοῖς ἔθνεσιν, καὶ τότε τὸ τέλος → ἥξει οὖν Ὅταν → ἴδητε
d.dsf a.dsf n.dsf / p.a / n.asn / a.dpn / d.dpn n.dpn / cj / adv / d.nsn n.nsn / v.fai.3s / cj / cj / v.aas.2p
3836 3910 3876 / 1650 / 3457 / 1620 4246 / 3836 1620 / 2779 / 5538 / 3836 5465 / 2457 / 4036 / 4020 / 1625

standing | in | the holy | place | 'the | abomination | that | causes | desolation,' | spoken | of | through | the | prophet | Daniel – let
ἑστὸς ἐν ἁγίῳ τόπῳ τὸ βδέλυγμα → → ⌐τῆς ἐρημώσεως⌐ ⌐τὸ ῥηθὲν⌐ ← διὰ τοῦ προφήτου Δανιὴλ →
pt.ra.asn / p.d / a.dsm / n.dsm / d.asn n.asn / d.gsf n.gsf / d.asn pt.ap.asn / p.g / d.gsm n.gsm / n.gsm
2705 / 1877 / 41 / 5536 / 3836 1007 / 3836 2247 / 3836 3306 / 1328 / 3836 4737 / 1248 / 3783

the | reader | understand – | **16** then | let | those who are | in | Judea | | flee | to | the mountains. | **17** Let | no one on | the
ὁ ἀναγινώσκων νοείτω τότε οἱ ἐν τῇ Ἰουδαίᾳ φευγέτωσαν εἰς τὰ ὄρη → μὴ ὁ ἐπὶ τοῦ
d.nsm / pt.pa.nsm / v.pam.3s / adv / d.npm / p.d / d.dsf n.dsf / v.pam.3p / p.a d.apn / n.apn / pl / d.nsm / p.g / d.gsm
3836 / 336 / 3783 / 5538 / 3836 / 1877 / 3836 2677 / 5771 / 1650 3836 / 4001 / 2849 / 3590 / 3836 / 2093 / 3836

roof | of his | house | go | down | to | take | anything | out of | the house. | **18** | Let no one | in | the | field | go
δώματος ← ← καταβάτω → ἆραι τὰ ἐκ τῆς οἰκίας αὐτοῦ καὶ μὴ ὁ ἐν τῷ ἀγρῷ ἐπιστρεψάτω
n.gsn / v.aam.3s / f.aa / d.apn / p.g / d.gsf n.gsf / r.gsm.3 / cj / pl / d.nsm / p.d / d.dsm n.dsm / v.aam.3s
1560 / 2849 / 149 / 3836 / 1666 / 3836 3864 / 899 / 2779 / 3590 / 3836 / 1877 / 3836 69 / 2188

back | to get | his | cloak. | **19** | How | dreadful it will be | in | those | days | | for pregnant
ὀπίσω → ἆραι αὐτοῦ ⌐τὸ ἱμάτιον⌐ δὲ → οὐαὶ ἐν ἐκείναις ⌐ταῖς ἡμέραις⌐ → ⌐ταῖς ἐν γαστρὶ ἐχούσαις⌐
adv / f.aa / r.gsm.3 / d.asn n.asn / cj / j / p.d / r.dpf / d.dpf n.dpf / d.dpf p.d n.dsf pt.pa.dpf
3958 / 149 / 899 / 3836 2668 / 1254 / 4026 / 1877 / 1697 / 3836 2465 / 3836 1877 1143 2400

αὐτοῖς, Βλέπετε μή τις ὑμᾶς πλανήσῃ· ⁵ πολλοὶ γὰρ ἐλεύσονται ἐπὶ τῷ ὀνόματί μου λέγοντες, Ἐγώ εἰμι ὁ Χριστός, καὶ πολλοὺς πλανήσουσιν. ⁶ μελλήσετε δὲ ἀκούειν πολέμους καὶ ἀκοὰς πολέμων· ὁρᾶτε μὴ θροεῖσθε· δεῖ γὰρ γενέσθαι, ἀλλʼ οὔπω ἐστὶν τὸ τέλος. ⁷ ἐγερθήσεται γὰρ ἔθνος ἐπὶ ἔθνος καὶ βασιλεία ἐπὶ βασιλείαν καὶ ἔσονται λιμοὶ καὶ σεισμοὶ κατὰ τόπους· ⁸ πάντα δὲ ταῦτα ἀρχὴ ὠδίνων. ¶ ⁹ τότε παραδώσουσιν ὑμᾶς εἰς θλῖψιν καὶ ἀποκτενοῦσιν ὑμᾶς, καὶ ἔσεσθε μισούμενοι ὑπὸ πάντων τῶν ἐθνῶν διὰ τὸ ὄνομά μου. ¹⁰ καὶ τότε σκανδαλισθήσονται πολλοὶ καὶ ἀλλήλους παραδώσουσιν καὶ μισήσουσιν ἀλλήλους· ¹¹ καὶ πολλοὶ ψευδοπροφῆται ἐγερθήσονται καὶ πλανήσουσιν πολλούς· ¹² καὶ διὰ τὸ πληθυνθῆναι τὴν ἀνομίαν ψυγήσεται ἡ ἀγάπη τῶν πολλῶν. ¹³ ὁ δὲ ὑπομείνας εἰς τέλος οὗτος σωθήσεται. ¹⁴ καὶ κηρυχθήσεται τοῦτο τὸ εὐαγγέλιον τῆς βασιλείας ἐν ὅλῃ τῇ οἰκουμένῃ εἰς μαρτύριον πᾶσιν τοῖς ἔθνεσιν, καὶ τότε ἥξει τὸ τέλος. ¶ ¹⁵ Ὅταν οὖν ἴδητε τὸ βδέλυγμα τῆς ἐρημώσεως τὸ ῥηθὲν διὰ Δανιὴλ τοῦ προφήτου ἑστὸς ἐν τόπῳ ἁγίῳ, ὁ ἀναγινώσκων νοείτω, ¹⁶ τότε οἱ ἐν τῇ Ἰουδαίᾳ φευγέτωσαν εἰς τὰ ὄρη, ¹⁷ ὁ ἐπὶ τοῦ δώματος μὴ καταβάτω ἆραι τὰ ἐκ τῆς οἰκίας αὐτοῦ, ¹⁸ καὶ ὁ ἐν τῷ ἀγρῷ μὴ ἐπιστρεψάτω ὀπίσω ἆραι τὸ ἱμάτιον αὐτοῦ. ¹⁹ οὐαὶ δὲ ταῖς ἐν γαστρὶ ἐχούσαις καὶ ταῖς θηλαζούσαις ἐν ἐκείναις ταῖς ἡμέραις. ²⁰ προσεύχεσθε δὲ ἵνα μὴ

women and nursing   mothers! 20   Pray   that your flight   will not take   place in winter   or   on the
←   καὶ   ταῖς θηλαζούσαις   δὲ   προσεύχεσθε ἵνα   ὑμῶν ἡ φυγὴ   →   μὴ γένηται   ←   →   χειμῶνος μηδὲ   →
         cj   d.dpf   pt.pa.dpf   cj   v.pmm.2p   cj   r.gp.2 d.nsf n.nsf   pl   v.ams.3s   n.gsm   cj
         2779   3836   2558   1254   4667   2671   7007   3836 5870   1181   3590   1181   5930   3593

Sabbath. 21 For then there will be   great distress, unequaled   from the beginning of the world until now   –
σαββάτῳ   γὰρ   τότε →   →   ἔσται μεγάλη θλῖψις   οἵα οὐ γέγονεν ἀπ'   ἀρχῆς   →   κόσμου ἕως τοῦ νῦν
n.dsn   cj   adv   v.fmi.3s a.nsf n.nsf   r.nsf p.g v.rai.3s p.g   n.gsf   n.gsm   p.g   d.gsn adv
4879   1142   5538   1639   3489 2568   3888 4024 1181 608   794   3180   2401   3836 3814

and never   to be   equaled again. 22   If those days   had not been cut   short, no one   would
οὐδ'   οὐ μὴ   →   γένηται   καὶ εἰ ἐκεῖναι αἱ ἡμέραι   →   μὴ   →   ἐκολοβώθησαν   ←   οὐκ πᾶσα σὰρξ   ἂν
cj   pl pl   pl   v.ams.3s   cj cj r.npf d.npf n.npf   →   pl   →   v.api.3p   pl a.nsf n.nsf   pl
4028   4024 3590   1181   2779 1623 1697 3836 2465   3143 3590   3143   4024 4246 4922   323

survive, but for the sake of the elect   those days   will be shortened.   23 At that time if anyone says to you,
ἐσώθη   δὲ   διὰ ←   ←   τοὺς ἐκλεκτοὺς ἐκεῖναι αἱ ἡμέραι   →   κολοβωθήσονται   →   →   Τότε ἐάν τις   εἴπῃ   → ὑμῖν
v.api.3s   cj   p.a   d.apm a.apm   r.npf d.npf n.npf   →   v.fpi.3p   adv ἐάν r.nsm   v.aas.3s   r.dp.2
5392   1254   1328   3836 1723   1697 3836 2465   3143   5538 1569 5516   3306   7007

'Look, here is the Christ!' or, 'There he is!' do not believe it. 24 For false Christs   and false prophets   will
ἰδοὺ   ὧδε   ὁ χριστός ἢ   ὧδε   →   μὴ πιστεύσητε   γὰρ   ψευδόχριστοι καὶ   ψευδοπροφῆται   →
j   adv   d.nsm n.nsm cj   adv   pl v.aas.2p   cj   n.npm   cj   n.npm
2627   6045   3836 5986 2445 6045   4409 3590 4409   1142   6023   2779   6021

appear   and perform great   signs and miracles to deceive even the elect   – if that were possible. 25 See, I
ἐγερθήσονται καὶ   δώσουσιν μεγάλα σημεῖα καὶ   τέρατα   ὥστε πλανῆσαι καὶ   τοὺς ἐκλεκτούς εἰ   →   →   δυνατόν   ἰδοὺ   →
v.fpi.3p   cj   v.fai.3p a.apn   n.apn cj   n.apn   cj f.aa   adv   d.apm a.apm   cj   a.nsn   j
1586   2779   1443 3489   4956 2779   5469   6063 4414   2779   3836 1623   1623   1543   2627

have told   you ahead of time. ¶ 26 "So if   anyone tells   you, 'There he is,   out in the desert,' do not
→   προείρηκα ὑμῖν   ←   ←   →   οὖν ἐὰν   →   εἴπωσιν ὑμῖν ἰδοὺ   →   ἐστίν   ἐν τῇ ἐρήμῳ   μὴ
→   v.rai.1s   r.dp.2   cj ἐὰν   →   v.aas.3p r.dp.2   j   →   v.pai.3s   p.d d.dsf n.dsf   pl
4597   7007 4597   4597 4597   4036 1569   3306 7007 2627   1639   1877 3836 2245   2002 3590

go   out; or, 'Here he is, in the inner rooms,' do not believe it. 27 For as   lightning   that comes   from the
ἐξέλθητε ←   ἰδοὺ   ἐν τοῖς   →   ταμείοις   μὴ πιστεύσητε   γὰρ ὥσπερ ἡ ἀστραπὴ   ἐξέρχεται ἀπὸ
v.aas.2p   j   p.d d.dpn   →   n.dpn   pl v.aas.2p   cj cj   d.nsf n.nsf   v.pmi.3s   p.g
2002   2627   1877 3836   5421   4409 3590 4409   1142 6061   3836 847   2002   608

east   is visible even in the west, so   will be the coming of the Son of Man.   28 Wherever   there
ἀνατολῶν καὶ   φαίνεται ἕως   →   δυσμῶν οὕτως   →   ἔσται ἡ παρουσία τοῦ υἱοῦ   τοῦ ἀνθρώπου   ὅπου ἐὰν   →
n.gpf   cj   v.ppi.3s p.g   →   n.gpf adv   →   v.fmi.3s d.nsf n.nsf   d.gsm n.gsm   d.gsm n.gsm   cj ἐὰν
424   2779   5743 2401   4048 4048   1639 3836 4242   3836 5626   3836 476   3963 1569

is a carcass, there the vultures will gather.   ¶   29   "Immediately after the distress of those
ἦ   τὸ πτῶμα   ἐκεῖ οἱ ἀετοί   →   συναχθήσονται   δὲ   Εὐθέως   μετὰ τὴν θλῖψιν   ἐκείνων
v.pas.3s   d.nsn n.nsn   adv d.npm n.npm   v.fpi.3p   cj   adv   p.a d.asf n.asf   r.gpf
1639   3836 4773   1695 3836 108   5251   1254   2311   3552 3836 2568   1697

days   "'the sun will be darkened,   and the moon will not give its   light;   the stars   will fall
τῶν ἡμερῶν ὁ   ἥλιος   →   →   σκοτισθήσεται καὶ ἡ   σελήνη   οὐ   δώσει αὐτῆς το φέγγος   καὶ οἱ   ἀστέρες   →   πεσοῦνται
d.gpf n.gpf d.nsm   n.nsm   v.fpi.3s cj d.nsf   n.nsf   pl   v.fai.3s r.gsf.3 d.asn n.asn   cj d.npm n.npm   v.fmi.3p
3836 2465 3836   2463   5029 2779 3836   4943   4024   899 3836 5766   2779 3836 843   4406

from the sky,   and the heavenly   bodies   will be shaken.'   ¶   30   "At that time the sign   of the Son
ἀπὸ   τοῦ οὐρανοῦ καὶ αἱ τῶν οὐρανῶν   δυνάμεις   →   σαλευθήσονται   καὶ   →   τότε τὸ σημεῖον   τοῦ υἱοῦ
p.g   d.gsm n.gsm   cj d.npf d.gpm n.gpm   n.npf   →   v.fpi.3p   cj   →   adv d.nsn n.nsn   d.gsm n.gsm
608   3836 4041   2779 3836 3836 4041   1539   4888   2779   5538 3836 4956   3836 5626

of Man   will appear in the sky,   and   all the nations of the earth will mourn.   They will see
τοῦ ἀνθρώπου   →   φανήσεται ἐν   οὐρανῷ καὶ   τότε πᾶσαι αἱ φυλαὶ   τῆς γῆς   →   κόψονται καὶ   →   ὄψονται
d.gsm n.gsm   →   v.fpi.3s ἐν   n.dsm cj   adv a.npf d.npf n.npf   d.gsf n.gsf   →   v.fmi.3p cj   v.fmi.3p
3836 476   5743   1877   4041 2779   5538 4246 3836 5876   3836 1178   3164 2779   3972

the Son of Man   coming   on the clouds of the sky,   with power   and great glory. 31 And he will send
τὸν υἱὸν   τοῦ ἀνθρώπου   ἐρχόμενον ἐπὶ τῶν νεφελῶν   τοῦ οὐρανοῦ μετὰ   δυνάμεως καὶ πολλῆς δόξης   καὶ   →   ἀποστελεῖ
d.asm n.asm   d.gsm n.gsm   pt.pm.asm p.g d.gpf n.gpf   d.gsm n.gsm p.a   n.gsf cj a.gsf   n.gsf   cj   v.fai.3s
3836 5626   3836 476   2262 2093 3836 3749   3836 4041 3552   1539 2779 4498   1518   2779   690

γένηται ἡ φυγὴ ὑμῶν χειμῶνος μηδὲ σαββάτου. 21 ἔσται γὰρ τότε θλῖψις μεγάλη οἵα οὐ γέγονεν ἀπ' ἀρχῆς κόσμου ἕως τοῦ νῦν οὐδ' οὐ μὴ γένηται. 22 καὶ εἰ μὴ ἐκολοβώθησαν αἱ ἡμέραι ἐκεῖναι, οὐκ ἂν ἐσώθη πᾶσα σάρξ· διὰ δὲ τοὺς ἐκλεκτοὺς κολοβωθήσονται αἱ ἡμέραι ἐκεῖναι. 23 τότε ἐάν τις ὑμῖν εἴπῃ, Ἰδοὺ ὧδε ὁ Χριστός, ἤ, Ὧδε, μὴ πιστεύσητε· 24 ἐγερθήσονται γὰρ ψευδόχριστοι καὶ ψευδοπροφῆται καὶ δώσουσιν σημεῖα μεγάλα καὶ τέρατα ὥστε πλανῆσαι, εἰ δυνατόν, καὶ τοὺς ἐκλεκτούς. 25 ἰδοὺ προείρηκα ὑμῖν. ¶ 26 ἐὰν οὖν εἴπωσιν ὑμῖν, Ἰδοὺ ἐν τῇ ἐρήμῳ ἐστίν, μὴ ἐξέλθητε· Ἰδοὺ ἐν τοῖς ταμείοις, μὴ πιστεύσητε· 27 ὥσπερ γὰρ ἡ ἀστραπὴ ἐξέρχεται ἀπὸ ἀνατολῶν καὶ φαίνεται ἕως δυσμῶν, οὕτως ἔσται ἡ παρουσία τοῦ υἱοῦ τοῦ ἀνθρώπου· 28 ὅπου ἐὰν ᾖ τὸ πτῶμα, ἐκεῖ συναχθήσονται οἱ ἀετοί. ¶ 29 Εὐθέως δὲ μετὰ τὴν θλῖψιν τῶν ἡμερῶν ἐκείνων ὁ ἥλιος σκοτισθήσεται, καὶ ἡ σελήνη οὐ δώσει τὸ φέγγος αὐτῆς, καὶ οἱ ἀστέρες πεσοῦνται ἀπὸ τοῦ οὐρανοῦ, καὶ αἱ δυνάμεις τῶν οὐρανῶν σαλευθήσονται. ¶ 30 καὶ τότε φανήσεται τὸ σημεῖον τοῦ υἱοῦ τοῦ ἀνθρώπου ἐν οὐρανῷ, καὶ τότε κόψονται πᾶσαι αἱ φυλαὶ τῆς γῆς καὶ ὄψονται τὸν υἱὸν τοῦ ἀνθρώπου ἐρχόμενον ἐπὶ τῶν νεφελῶν τοῦ οὐρανοῦ μετὰ δυνάμεως καὶ δόξης πολλῆς· 31 καὶ ἀποστελεῖ τοὺς ἀγγέλους

his angels | with a loud | trumpet call, | and | they will | gather | his | elect | from | the | four
αὐτοῦ ⸤τοὺς ἀγγέλους⸥ | μετὰ μεγάλης | σάλπιγγος | καὶ | → | ἐπισυνάξουσιν | αὐτοῦ | ⸤τοὺς ἐκλεκτοὺς⸥ | ἐκ | τῶν | τεσσάρων
r.gsm.3 d.apm n.apm | p.g a.gsf | n.gsf | cj | | v.fai.3p | r.gsm.3 | d.apm a.apm | p.g | d.gpm | a.gpm
899 3836 34 | 3552 3489 | 4894 | 2779 | | 2190 | 899 | 3836 1723 | 1666 | 3836 | 5475

winds, from | one end | | of the heavens | to | the other. | ¶ | 32 "Now | learn | this | lesson | from | the fig tree:
ἀνέμων ἀπ᾽ | ἄκρων → | | οὐρανῶν | ἕως | τῶν ἄκρων αὐτῶν. | | δὲ | μάθετε | τὴν | παραβολήν | Ἀπὸ | τῆς → συκῆς·
n.gpm p.g | n.gpn | | n.gpm | p.g | d.gpn n.gpn r.gpn.3 | | cj | v.aam.2p | d.asf | n.asf | p.g | d.gsf n.gsf
449 608 | 216 | | 4041 | 2401 | 3836 216 899 | | 1254 | 3443 | 3836 | 4130 | 608 | 3836 5190

As | soon as | its | twigs | get | tender | and | its | leaves | come out, | you know | that | summer | is | near.
⸤ὅταν | ἤδη ← | ← αὐτῆς | ὁ κλάδος, | γένηται | ἁπαλὸς | καὶ | τὰ | φύλλα | ἐκφύῃ ← | → γινώσκετε | ὅτι | ⸤τὸ θέρος· | | ἐγγὺς
cj | adv | r.gsf.3 | d.nsm n.nsm | v.ams.3s | a.nsm | cj | d.apn | n.apn | v.pas.3s | v.pai.2p | cj | d.nsn n.nsn | | adv
4020 | 2453 | 899 | 3836 3080 | 1181 | 559 | 2779 | 3836 | 5877 | 1770 | 1182 | 4022 | 3836 2550 | | 1584

33 Even so, | when | you | see | all | these things, | you | know | that | it is | near, | right at | the | door. | 34 I | tell | you | the
καὶ οὕτως | ὅταν | → | ἴδητε | πάντα | ταῦτα ← | ὑμεῖς | γινώσκετε | ὅτι | → ἐστὶν | ἐγγύς | ἐπὶ | | θύραις | → | λέγω | ὑμῖν |
adv adv | cj | | v.aas.2p | a.apn | r.apn | r.np.2 | v.pai.2p | cj | v.pai.3s | adv | p.d | | n.dpf | | v.pai.1s | r.dp.2 |
2779 4048 | 4020 | | 1625 | 4246 | 4047 | 7007 | 1182 | 4022 | 1639 | 1584 | 2093 | | 2598 | | 3306 | 7007 |

truth, | this | generation | will | certainly not | pass | away | until | all | these things | have happened. | 35 Heaven | and
ἀμὴν | ὅτι αὕτη | ⸤ἡ γενεά⸥ | → | οὐ μὴ | παρέλθῃ | | ἕως ἂν | πάντα | ταῦτα ← | → γένηται | 35 ⸤ὁ οὐρανὸς | καὶ
pl | cj r.nsf | d.nsf n.nsf | | pl pl | v.aas.3s | | cj pl | a.npn | r.npn | v.ams.3s | d.nsm n.nsm | cj
297 | 4022 4047 | 3836 1155 | | 4024 3590 | 4216 | | 2401 323 | 4246 | 4047 | 1181 | 3836 4041 | 2779

earth | will pass | away, | but | my | words | will never | pass away.
⸤ἡ γῆ⸥ | → παρελεύσεται ← | | δὲ | μου | οἱ λόγοι | → οὐ μὴ → | παρέλθωσιν
d.nsf n.nsf | v.fmi.3s | | cj | r.gs.1 | d.npm n.npm | pl pl | v.aas.3p
3836 1178 | 4216 | | 1254 | 1609 | 3836 3364 | 4216 4024 3590 | 4216

The Day and Hour Unknown

24:36 | "No one | knows | about | that | day | or | hour, | not even | the | angels | in heaven, | nor | the | Son,
| δὲ → | οὐδεὶς οἶδεν | Περὶ | ἐκείνης | ⸤τῆς ἡμέρας⸥ | καὶ | ὥρας | οὐδὲ ← | οἱ | ἄγγελοι | → ⸤τῶν οὐρανῶν⸥ | οὐδὲ | ὁ | υἱός,
| cj | a.nsm v.rai.3s | p.g | r.gsf | d.gsf n.gsf | cj | n.gsf | adv | d.npm | n.npm | d.gpm n.gpm | adv | d.nsm | n.nsm
| 1254 | 4029 3857 | 4309 | 1697 | 3836 2465 | 2779 | 6052 | 4028 | 3836 | 34 | 3836 4041 | 4028 | 3836 | 5626

but | only | the Father. | 37 As | it was | in | the days | of Noah, | so | it will be | at | the | coming | of | the | Son of
εἰ μὴ | μόνος | ὁ πατήρ. | γὰρ Ὥσπερ | | | αἱ ἡμέραι | ⸤τοῦ Νῶε⸥ | οὕτως | → ἔσται | | ἡ | παρουσία | → | τοῦ | υἱοῦ
cj pl | a.nsm | d.nsm n.nsm | cj cj | | | d.npf n.npf | d.gsm n.gsm | adv | v.fmi.3s | | d.nsf | n.nsf | | d.gsm | n.gsm
1623 3590 | 3668 | 3836 4252 | 1142 6061 | | | 3836 2465 | 3836 3820 | 4048 | 1639 | | 3836 | 4242 | | 3836 | 5626

Man. | 38 For | | in | the days | | before | the flood, | people were | eating | and | drinking,
⸤τοῦ ἀνθρώπου· | γὰρ | ὡς | ἦσαν ἐν | ταῖς ἡμέραις | [ἐκείναις] | ταῖς πρὸ | τοῦ κατακλυσμοῦ → | → | τρώγοντες | καὶ | πίνοντες
d.gsm n.gsm | cj | cj | v.iai.3p p.d | d.dpf n.dpf | r.dpf | d.dpf p.g | d.gsm n.gsm | | pt.pa.npm | cj | pt.pa.npm
3836 476 | 1142 | 6055 | 1639 1877 | 3836 2465 | 1697 | 3836 4574 | 3836 2886 | | 5592 | 2779 | 4403

marrying | and | giving in marriage, | up | to the day | Noah | entered | | the | ark; | 39 and | they | knew | nothing about
γαμοῦντες | καὶ | → → γαμίζοντες | ⸤ἄχρι | ἧς ← | ἡμέρας | Νῶε | εἰσῆλθεν | εἰς | τὴν | κιβωτόν· | καὶ | → | ἔγνωσαν | οὐκ
pt.pa.npm | cj | pt.pa.npm | p.g | r.gsf | n.gsf | n.gsm | v.aai.3s | p.a | d.asf | n.asf | cj | | v.aai.3p | pl
1138 | 2779 | 1139 | 948 | 4005 | 2465 | 3820 | 1656 | 1650 | 3836 | 3066 | 2779 | | 1182 | 4024

what would happen | until | the | flood | came | and | took | them | all | away. | That is how | it will be | | at the
| ἕως | ὁ | κατακλυσμὸς | ἦλθεν | καὶ | ἦρεν | → | ἅπαντας | → | → οὕτως | → ἔσται | [καὶ] | ἡ
| cj | d.nsm | n.nsm | v.aai.3s | cj | v.aai.3s | | a.apm | | adv | v.fmi.3s | adv | d.nsf
| 2401 | 3836 | 2886 | 2262 | 2779 | 149 | | 570 | 149 | 4048 | 1639 | 2779 | 3836

coming | of | the | Son of Man. | 40 | Two | men | will be | in | the field; | one | will be | taken | | and | the other
παρουσία | → | τοῦ | υἱοῦ | ⸤τοῦ ἀνθρώπου⸥ | τότε δύο | ← | → | ἔσονται ἐν | τῷ ἀγρῷ | εἷς | → | παραλαμβάνεται | | καὶ | εἷς
n.nsf | | d.gsm | n.gsm | d.gsm n.gsm | adv a.npm | | | v.fmi.3p p.d | d.dsm n.dsm | a.nsm | | v.ppi.3s | | cj | a.nsm
4242 | | 3836 | 5626 | 3836 476 | 5538 1545 | | | 1639 1877 | 3836 69 | 1651 | | 4161 | | 2779 | 1651

left. | 41 Two | women | will be | grinding | with | a hand mill; | one | will be | taken | | and | the other | left. | ¶
ἀφίεται | δύο | → | → | ἀλήθουσαι ἐν | | ⸤τῷ μύλῳ· | μία | → | παραλαμβάνεται | | καὶ | μία | ἀφίεται |
v.ppi.3s | a.npf | | | pt.pa.npf p.d | | d.dsm n.dsm | a.nsf | | v.ppi.3s | | cj | a.nsf | v.ppi.3s |
918 | 1545 | | | 241 1877 | | 3836 3685 | 1651 | | 4161 | | 2779 | 1651 | 918 |

αὐτοῦ μετὰ σάλπιγγος μεγάλης, καὶ ἐπισυνάξουσιν τοὺς ἐκλεκτοὺς αὐτοῦ ἐκ τῶν τεσσάρων ἀνέμων ἀπ᾽ ἄκρων οὐρανῶν ἕως [τῶν] ἄκρων αὐτῶν. ¶ 32 Ἀπὸ δὲ τῆς συκῆς μάθετε τὴν παραβολήν· ὅταν ἤδη ὁ κλάδος αὐτῆς γένηται ἁπαλὸς καὶ τὰ φύλλα ἐκφύῃ, γινώσκετε ὅτι ἐγγὺς τὸ θέρος· 33 οὕτως καὶ ὑμεῖς, ὅταν ἴδητε πάντα ταῦτα γινώσκετε ὅτι ἐγγύς ἐστιν ἐπὶ θύραις. 34 ἀμὴν λέγω ὑμῖν ὅτι οὐ μὴ παρέλθῃ ἡ γενεὰ αὕτη ἕως ἂν πάντα ταῦτα γένηται. 35 ὁ οὐρανὸς καὶ ἡ γῆ παρελεύσεται, οἱ δὲ λόγοι μου οὐ μὴ παρέλθωσιν.

24:36 Περὶ δὲ τῆς ἡμέρας ἐκείνης καὶ ὥρας οὐδεὶς οἶδεν, οὐδὲ οἱ ἄγγελοι τῶν οὐρανῶν οὐδὲ ὁ υἱός, εἰ μὴ ὁ πατὴρ μόνος. 37 ὥσπερ γὰρ αἱ ἡμέραι τοῦ Νῶε, οὕτως ἔσται ἡ παρουσία τοῦ υἱοῦ τοῦ ἀνθρώπου. 38 ὡς γὰρ ἦσαν ἐν ταῖς ἡμέραις [ἐκείναις] ταῖς πρὸ τοῦ κατακλυσμοῦ τρώγοντες καὶ πίνοντες, γαμοῦντες καὶ γαμίζοντες, ἄχρι ἧς ἡμέρας εἰσῆλθεν Νῶε εἰς τὴν κιβωτόν, 39 καὶ οὐκ ἔγνωσαν ἕως ἦλθεν ὁ κατακλυσμὸς καὶ ἦρεν ἅπαντας, οὕτως ἔσται [καὶ] ἡ παρουσία τοῦ υἱοῦ τοῦ ἀνθρώπου. 40 τότε δύο ἔσονται ἐν τῷ ἀγρῷ, εἷς παραλαμβάνεται καὶ εἷς ἀφίεται· 41 δύο ἀλήθουσαι ἐν τῷ μύλῳ, μία παραλαμβάνεται καὶ

[42] "Therefore keep watch, because you do not know on what day your Lord will come. [43] But understand
οὖν Γρηγορεῖτε ← ὅτι → οὐκ οἴδατε → ποίᾳ ἡμέρᾳ ὑμῶν ὁ κύριος → ἔρχεται δὲ γινώσκετε
cj v.pam.2p cj pl v.rai.2p r.dsf n.dsf r.gp.2 d.nsm n.nsm v.pmi.3s cj v.pam.2p
4036 1213 4022 3857 3857 4024 3857 4481 2465 7007 3836 3261 2262 1254 1182

this: If the owner of the house had known at what time of night the thief was coming, he would
Ἐκεῖνο ὅτι εἰ ὁ οἰκοδεσπότης ← ← → ᾔδει → ποίᾳ φυλακῇ ← ← ὁ κλέπτης → ἔρχεται → ἂν
r.asn cj cj d.nsm n.nsm v.lai.3s r.dsf n.dsf d.nsm n.nsm v.pmi.3s pl
1697 4022 1623 3836 3867 3857 4481 5871 3836 3095 2262 1213 323

have kept watch and would not have let his house be broken into. [44] So you also must be
→ ἐγρηγόρησεν ← καὶ ἂν οὐκ → εἴασεν αὐτοῦ ⌞τὴν οἰκίαν⌟ → διορυχθῆναι ← ⌞διὰ τοῦτο⌟ ὑμεῖς καὶ → γίνεσθε
v.aai.3s cj pl pl v.aai.3s r.gsm.3 d.asf n.asf f.ap p.a r.asn r.np.2 adv v.pmm.2p
1213 2779 323 4024 1572 899 3836 3864 1482 1328 4047 7007 2779 1181

ready, because the Son of Man will come at an hour when you do not expect him. ¶ [45] "Who then
ἕτοιμοι ὅτι ὁ υἱὸς → ⌞τοῦ ἀνθρώπου⌟ → ἔρχεται → ὥρᾳ ᾗ → → οὐ δοκεῖτε Τίς ἄρα
a.npm cj d.nsm n.nsm d.gsm n.gsm v.pmi.3s n.dsf r.dsf pl v.pai.2p r.nsm cj
2289 4022 3836 5626 3836 476 2262 6052 4005 1506 1506 4024 1506 5515 726

is the faithful and wise servant, whom the master has put in charge of the servants in his household
ἐστιν ὁ πιστὸς καὶ φρόνιμος δοῦλος ὃν ὁ κύριος κατέστησεν ← ἐπὶ αὐτοῦ ⌞τῆς οἰκετείας⌟
v.pai.3s d.nsm a.nsm cj a.nsm n.nsm r.asm d.nsm n.nsm v.aai.3s p.g r.gsm.3 d.gsf n.gsf
1639 3836 4412 2779 5861 1529 4005 3836 3261 2770 2093 899 3836 3859

to give them their food at the proper time? [46] It will be good for that servant whose master finds
→ ⌞τοῦ δοῦναι⌟ αὐτοῖς τὴν τροφὴν ἐν → καιρῷ μακάριος ἐκεῖνος ὁ δοῦλος⌟ αὐτοῦ ὁ κύριος⌟ εὑρήσει
d.gsn f.aa r.dpm.3 d.asf n.asf p.d n.dsm a.nsm r.nsm d.nsm n.nsm r.gsm.3 d.nsm n.nsm v.fai.3s
3836 1443 899 3836 5575 1877 2789 3421 1697 3836 1529 899 3836 3261 2351

him doing so when he returns. [47] I tell you the truth, he will put him in charge of all his
ὃν ποιοῦντα οὕτως → → ἐλθὼν → λέγω ὑμῖν ἀμὴν ὅτι → → καταστήσει αὐτὸν ← ἐπὶ πᾶσιν αὐτοῦ
r.asm pt.pa.asm adv pt.aa.nsm v.pai.1s r.dp.2 pl cj v.fai.3s r.asm.3 p.d a.dpn r.gsm.3
4005 4472 4048 2262 3306 7007 297 4022 2770 899 2770 2770 2093 4246 899

possessions. [48] But suppose that servant is wicked and says to himself, 'My master is staying
⌞τοῖς ὑπάρχουσιν⌟ δὲ ἐὰν ἐκεῖνος ⌞ὁ δοῦλος⌟ κακὸς εἴπῃ ἐν τῇ καρδίᾳ αὐτοῦ⌟ μου ⌞ὁ κύριος⌟ χρονίζει
d.dpn pt.pa.dpn cj cj r.nsm d.nsm n.nsm a.nsm v.aas.3s p.d d.dsf n.dsf r.gsm.3 r.gs.1 d.nsm n.nsm v.pai.3s
3836 5639 1254 1569 1697 3836 1529 2805 3306 1877 3836 2840 899 1609 3836 3261 5988

away a long time,' [49] and he then begins to beat his fellow servants and to eat and drink with
← ← ← καὶ ἄρξηται → τύπτειν αὐτοῦ ⌞τοὺς συνδούλους⌟ δὲ ἐσθίῃ καὶ πίνῃ μετὰ
cj v.ams.3s f.pa r.gsm.3 d.apm n.apm cj v.pas.3s cj v.pas.3s p.g
2779 806 5597 899 3836 5281 1254 2266 2779 4403 3552

drunkards. [50] The master of that servant will come on a day when he does not expect him and at an
⌞τῶν μεθυόντων⌟ ὁ κύριος → ἐκείνου ⌞τοῦ δούλου⌟ → ἥξει ἐν ἡμέρᾳ ᾗ → → οὐ προσδοκᾷ καὶ ἐν
d.gpm pt.pa.gpm d.nsm n.nsm r.gsm d.gsm n.gsm v.fai.3s p.d n.dsf r.dsf pl v.pai.3s cj p.d
3836 3501 3836 3261 1529 3836 1529 2457 1877 2465 4005 4659 4659 4024 4659 2779 1877

hour he is not aware of. [51] He will cut him to pieces and assign him a place with the
ὥρᾳ ᾗ → → οὐ γινώσκει καὶ → → διχοτομήσει αὐτὸν ← ← καὶ θήσει αὐτοῦ ⌞τὸ μέρος⌟ μετὰ τῶν
n.dsf r.dsf pl v.pai.3s cj v.fai.3s r.asm.3 cj v.fai.3s r.gsm.3 d.asn n.asn p.g d.gpm
6052 4005 1182 1182 4024 1182 2779 1497 1497 1497 2779 5502 899 3836 3538 3552 3836

hypocrites, where there will be weeping and gnashing of teeth.
ὑποκριτῶν ἐκεῖ → ἔσται κλαυθμὸς καὶ βρυγμὸς ⌞τῶν ὀδόντων⌟
n.gpm adv v.fmi.3s d.nsm n.nsm cj d.nsm n.nsm d.gpm n.gpm
5695 1695 1639 3836 3088 2779 3836 1106 3836 3848

The Parable of the Ten Virgins

[25:1] "At that time the kingdom of heaven will be like ten virgins who took their
Τότε ἡ βασιλεία → ⌞τῶν οὐρανῶν⌟ → → ὁμοιωθήσεται δέκα παρθένοις αἵτινες λαβοῦσαι ἑαυτῶν
adv d.nsf n.nsf d.gpm n.gpm v.fpi.3s a.dpf n.dpf r.npf pt.aa.npf r.gpf.3
5538 3836 993 3836 4041 3929 1274 4221 4015 3284 1571

lamps and went out to meet the bridegroom. [2] Five of them were foolish and five were wise.
⌞τὰς λαμπάδας⌟ ἐξῆλθον ← εἰς ὑπάντησιν τοῦ νυμφίου δὲ πέντε ἐξ αὐτῶν ἦσαν μωραὶ καὶ πέντε φρόνιμοι
d.apf n.apf v.aai.3p p.a n.asf d.gsm n.gsm cj a.npf p.g r.gpf.3 v.iai.3p a.npf cj a.npf a.npf
3836 3286 2002 1650 5637 3836 3812 1254 4297 1666 899 1639 3704 2779 4297 5861

μία ἀφίεται. ¶ [42] γρηγορεῖτε οὖν, ὅτι οὐκ οἴδατε ποίᾳ ἡμέρᾳ ὁ κύριος ὑμῶν ἔρχεται. [43] ἐκεῖνο δὲ γινώσκετε ὅτι εἰ ᾔδει ὁ οἰκοδεσπότης ποίᾳ φυλακῇ ὁ κλέπτης ἔρχεται, ἐγρηγόρησεν ἂν καὶ οὐκ ἂν εἴασεν διορυχθῆναι τὴν οἰκίαν αὐτοῦ. [44] διὰ τοῦτο καὶ ὑμεῖς γίνεσθε ἕτοιμοι, ὅτι ᾗ οὐ δοκεῖτε ὥρᾳ ὁ υἱὸς τοῦ ἀνθρώπου ἔρχεται. ¶ [45] Τίς ἄρα ἐστὶν ὁ πιστὸς δοῦλος καὶ φρόνιμος ὃν κατέστησεν ὁ κύριος ἐπὶ τῆς οἰκετείας αὐτοῦ τοῦ δοῦναι αὐτοῖς τὴν τροφὴν ἐν καιρῷ; [46] μακάριος ὁ δοῦλος ἐκεῖνος ὃν ἐλθὼν ὁ κύριος αὐτοῦ εὑρήσει οὕτως ποιοῦντα· [47] ἀμὴν λέγω ὑμῖν ὅτι ἐπὶ πᾶσιν τοῖς ὑπάρχουσιν αὐτοῦ καταστήσει αὐτόν. [48] ἐὰν δὲ εἴπῃ ὁ κακὸς δοῦλος ἐκεῖνος ἐν τῇ καρδίᾳ αὐτοῦ, Χρονίζει μου ὁ κύριος, [49] καὶ ἄρξηται τύπτειν τοὺς συνδούλους αὐτοῦ, ἐσθίῃ δὲ καὶ πίνῃ μετὰ τῶν μεθυόντων, [50] ἥξει ὁ κύριος τοῦ δούλου ἐκείνου ἐν ἡμέρᾳ ᾗ οὐ προσδοκᾷ καὶ ἐν ὥρᾳ ᾗ οὐ γινώσκει, [51] καὶ διχοτομήσει αὐτὸν καὶ τὸ μέρος αὐτοῦ μετὰ τῶν ὑποκριτῶν θήσει· ἐκεῖ ἔσται ὁ κλαυθμὸς καὶ ὁ βρυγμὸς τῶν ὀδόντων.

[25:1] Τότε ὁμοιωθήσεται ἡ βασιλεία τῶν οὐρανῶν δέκα παρθένοις, αἵτινες λαβοῦσαι τὰς λαμπάδας ἑαυτῶν ἐξῆλθον εἰς ὑπάντησιν τοῦ νυμφίου. [2] πέντε δὲ ἐξ αὐτῶν ἦσαν μωραὶ καὶ πέντε φρόνιμοι. [3] αἱ γὰρ μωραὶ λαβοῦσαι τὰς λαμπάδας αὐτῶν

3 The foolish ones took · their lamps · but did not take · any oil · with them. **4** The wise, however,
γὰρ αἱ μωραὶ ← λαβοῦσαι αὐτῶν ⸤τὰς λαμπάδας⸥ ↗ οὐκ ἔλαβον ἔλαβον μεθ' ἑαυτῶν αἱ φρόνιμοι δὲ
cj d.npf a.npf / pt.aa.npf r.gpf.3 d.apf n.apf / pl v.aai.3p / n.asn / r.gpf.3 / d.npf a.npf cj
1142 3836 3704 · 3284 899 3836 3286 · 3284 4024 3284 · 1778 · 3552 1571 · 3836 5861 1254

took oil in jars · along with their lamps. **5** The bridegroom was a long time in coming,
ἔλαβον ἔλαιον ἐν ⸤τοῖς ἀγγείοις⸥ → μετὰ ἑαυτῶν ⸤τῶν λαμπάδων⸥ δὲ τοῦ νυμφίου → → χρονίζοντος ← ← ←
v.aai.3p n.asn p.d d.dpn n.dpn / p.g r.gpf.3 d.gpf n.gpf / cj d.gsm n.gsm / pt.pa.gsm
3284 1778 1877 3836 31 · 3552 1571 3836 3286 · 1254 3836 3812 · 5988

and they all became drowsy and fell asleep. ¶ **6** "At midnight the cry rang out: 'Here's the
↗ πᾶσαι → ἐνύσταξαν καὶ → ἐκάθευδον δὲ → ⸤μέσης νυκτὸς⸥ κραυγὴ γέγονεν ← ἰδοὺ ὁ
a.npf / v.aai.3p cj v.iai.3p / cj a.gsf n.gsf n.nsf v.rai.3s j d.nsm
3818 4246 · 3818 2779 2761 · 1254 3545 3816 3199 1181 2627 3836

bridegroom! Come out to meet him!' ¶ **7** "Then all the virgins woke up and trimmed
νυμφίος ἐξέρχεσθε ← εἰς ἀπάντησιν αὐτοῦ τότε πᾶσαι αἱ παρθένοι ἐκεῖναι ἠγέρθησαν ← καὶ ἐκόσμησαν
n.nsm v.pmm.2p p.a n.asf r.gsm.3 / adv a.npf d.npf n.npf r.npf v.api.3p cj v.aai.3p
3812 2002 1650 561 899 · 5538 4246 3836 4221 1697 1586 2779 3175

their lamps. **8** The foolish ones said to the wise, 'Give us some of your oil; our
ἑαυτῶν ⸤τὰς λαμπάδας⸥ δὲ αἱ μωραὶ εἶπαν ταῖς φρονίμοις δότε ἡμῖν ἐκ ὑμῶν ⸤τοῦ ἐλαίου⸥ ὅτι ἡμῶν
r.gpf.3 d.apf n.apf / cj d.npf a.npf v.aai.3p d.dpf a.dpf v.aam.2p r.dp.1 p.g r.gp.2 d.gsn n.gsn cj r.gp.1
1571 3836 3286 · 1254 3836 3704 3306 3836 5861 1443 7005 1666 7007 3836 1778 4022 7005

lamps are going out.' ¶ **9** "'No,' they replied, 'there may not be enough for
⸤αἱ λαμπάδες⸥ → → σβέννυνται δὲ μήποτε ⸤αἱ φρόνιμοι⸥ ἀπεκρίθησαν λέγουσαι ⸤οὐ μὴ⸥ → ἀρκέσῃ →
d.npf n.npf / v.ppi.3p / cj cj d.npf a.npf v.api.3p pt.pa.npf pl pl v.aas.3s
3836 3286 · 4931 · 1254 3607 3836 5861 646 3306 758 758 4024 3590 758

both us and you. Instead, go to those who sell oil and buy some for yourselves.' ¶ **10** "But
ἡμῖν καὶ ὑμῖν μᾶλλον πορεύεσθε πρὸς τοὺς ← πωλοῦντας καὶ ἀγοράσατε → ἑαυταῖς δὲ
r.dp.1 cj r.dp.2 adv.c v.pmm.2p p.a d.apm pt.pa.apm cj v.aam.2p r.dpf.2 cj
7005 2779 7007 3437 4513 4639 3836 4797 2779 60 1571 1254

while they were on their way to buy the oil, the bridegroom arrived. The virgins who were ready
↗ αὐτῶν → → ἀπερχομένων ἀγοράσαι ὁ νυμφίος ἦλθεν καὶ αἱ ἕτοιμοι
r.gpf.3 / pt.pm.gpf f.aa / d.nsm n.nsm v.aai.3s cj d.npf / a.npf
599 899 · 599 60 · 3836 3812 2262 2779 3836 · 2289

went in with him to the wedding banquet. And the door was shut. ¶ **11** "Later the others also
εἰσῆλθον ← μετ' αὐτοῦ εἰς τοὺς γάμους καὶ ἡ θύρα → ἐκλείσθη δὲ ὕστερον αἱ λοιπαὶ παρθένοι καὶ
v.aai.3p p.g r.gsm.3 p.a d.apm n.apm / cj d.nsf n.nsf v.api.3s / cj adv.c d.npf a.npf n.npf cj
1656 3552 899 1650 3836 1141 · 2779 3836 2598 3091 · 1254 5731 3836 3370 4221 2779

came. 'Sir! Sir!' they said. 'Open the door for us!' ¶ **12** "But he replied, 'I tell you the truth, I
ἔρχονται κύριε κύριε λέγουσαι ἄνοιξον → ἡμῖν δὲ ὁ ἀποκριθεὶς εἶπεν → λέγω ὑμῖν ἀμὴν ↗
v.pmi.3p n.vsm n.vsm pt.pa.npf v.aam.2s / r.dp.1 cj d.nsm pt.ap.nsm v.aai.3s v.pai.1s r.dp.2 pl
2262 3261 3261 3306 487 · 7005 1254 3836 646 3306 3306 7007 297 7007

don't know you.' ¶ **13** "Therefore keep watch, because you do not know the day or the hour.
οὐκ οἶδα ὑμᾶς οὖν → γρηγορεῖτε ὅτι → οὐκ οἴδατε τὴν ἡμέραν οὐδὲ τὴν ὥραν
pl v.rai.1s r.ap.2 cj / v.pam.2p cj / pl v.rai.2p d.asf n.asf cj d.asf n.asf
4024 3857 7007 4036 · 1213 4022 · 3857 3857 4024 3857 3836 2465 4028 3836 6052

The Parable of the Talents

25:14 "Again, it will be like a man going on a journey, who called his servants and entrusted his
γὰρ Ὥσπερ ἄνθρωπος → → ἀποδημῶν → ἐκάλεσεν ἰδίους ⸤τοὺς δούλους⸥ καὶ παρέδωκεν αὐτοῦ
cj cj n.nsm pt.pa.nsm v.aai.3s a.apm d.apm n.apm cj v.aai.3s r.gsm.3
1142 6061 476 623 2813 2625 3836 1529 2779 4140 899

property to them. **15** To one he gave five talents of money, to another two talents, and to another
⸤τὰ ὑπάρχοντα⸥ αὐτοῖς καὶ μὲν → ᾧ → ἔδωκεν πέντε τάλαντα δὲ → ᾧ δύο δὲ → ᾧ
d.apn pt.pa.apn r.dpm.3 cj pl r.dsm v.aai.3s a.apn n.apn cj r.dsm a.apn cj r.dsm
3836 5639 899 2779 3525 4005 1443 4297 5419 1254 4005 1545 1254 4005

one talent, each according to his ability. Then he went on his journey. **16** The man who had received the five
ἓν ἑκάστῳ κατὰ ← ἰδίαν ⸤τὴν δύναμιν⸥ καὶ → → ἀπεδήμησεν ὁ → λαβὼν τὰ πέντε
a.asn r.dsm p.a a.asf d.asf n.asf cj v.aai.3s d.nsm pt.aa.nsm d.apn a.apn
1651 1667 2848 2625 3836 1539 2779 623 3836 3284 3836 4297

οὐκ ἔλαβον μεθ᾽ ἑαυτῶν ἔλαιον. ⁴ αἱ δὲ φρόνιμοι ἔλαβον ἔλαιον ἐν τοῖς ἀγγείοις μετὰ τῶν λαμπάδων ἑαυτῶν. ⁵ χρονίζοντος
δὲ τοῦ νυμφίου ἐνύσταξαν πᾶσαι καὶ ἐκάθευδον. ¶ ⁶ μέσης δὲ νυκτὸς κραυγὴ γέγονεν, Ἰδοὺ ὁ νυμφίος, ἐξέρχεσθε εἰς ἀπάντησιν
[αὐτοῦ]. ¶ ⁷ τότε ἠγέρθησαν πᾶσαι αἱ παρθένοι ἐκεῖναι καὶ ἐκόσμησαν τὰς λαμπάδας ἑαυτῶν. ⁸ αἱ δὲ μωραὶ ταῖς φρονίμοις
εἶπαν, Δότε ἡμῖν ἐκ τοῦ ἐλαίου ὑμῶν, ὅτι αἱ λαμπάδες ἡμῶν σβέννυνται. ¶ ⁹ ἀπεκρίθησαν δὲ αἱ φρόνιμοι λέγουσαι, Μήποτε
οὐ μὴ ἀρκέσῃ ἡμῖν καὶ ὑμῖν· πορεύεσθε μᾶλλον πρὸς τοὺς πωλοῦντας καὶ ἀγοράσατε ἑαυταῖς. ¶ ¹⁰ ἀπερχομένων δὲ αὐτῶν
ἀγοράσαι ἦλθεν ὁ νυμφίος, καὶ αἱ ἕτοιμοι εἰσῆλθον μετ᾽ αὐτοῦ εἰς τοὺς γάμους καὶ ἐκλείσθη ἡ θύρα. ¶ ¹¹ ὕστερον δὲ ἔρχονται
καὶ αἱ λοιπαὶ παρθένοι λέγουσαι, Κύριε κύριε, ἄνοιξον ἡμῖν. ¶ ¹² ὁ δὲ ἀποκριθεὶς εἶπεν, Ἀμὴν λέγω ὑμῖν, οὐκ οἶδα ὑμᾶς. ¶
¹³ Γρηγορεῖτε οὖν, ὅτι οὐκ οἴδατε τὴν ἡμέραν οὐδὲ τὴν ὥραν.

25:14 Ὥσπερ γὰρ ἄνθρωπος ἀποδημῶν ἐκάλεσεν τοὺς ἰδίους δούλους καὶ παρέδωκεν αὐτοῖς τὰ ὑπάρχοντα αὐτοῦ, ¹⁵ καὶ
ᾧ μὲν ἔδωκεν πέντε τάλαντα, ᾧ δὲ δύο, ᾧ δὲ ἕν, ἑκάστῳ κατὰ τὴν ἰδίαν δύναμιν, καὶ ἀπεδήμησεν. εὐθέως ¹⁶ πορευθεὶς ὁ τὰ

talents went | at once | and put his money to work | and gained | five more. **17** So | also, the one with
τάλαντα πορευθεὶς | εὐθέως | ἠργάσατο ἐν αὐτοῖς καὶ | ἐκέρδησεν | πέντε ἄλλα | ὡσαύτως ὁ
n.apn pt.ap.nsm | adv | v.ami.3s p.d r.dpn.3 cj | v.aai.3s | a.apn r.apn | adv d.nsm
5419 4513 | 2311 | 2237 1877 899 2779 | 3045 | 4297 257 | 6058 3836

the two talents gained | two more. **18** But the man who had received | the one talent | went | off, dug | a hole in the
τὰ δύο ἐκέρδησεν δύο ἄλλα | δὲ ὁ | λαβὼν τὸ ἓν | ἀπελθὼν | ὤρυξεν
d.apn a.apn v.aai.3s a.apn r.apn | cj d.nsm | pt.aa.nsm d.asn a.asn | pt.aa.nsm | v.aai.3s
3836 1545 3045 1545 257 | 1254 3836 | 3284 3836 1651 | 599 | 4002

ground and hid his master's money. ¶ **19** "After a long time the master of those servants
γῆν καὶ ἔκρυψεν αὐτοῦ ⌐τοῦ κυρίου⌐ ⌐τὸ ἀργύριον⌐ | δὲ μετὰ πολὺν χρόνον ὁ κύριος ἐκείνων ⌐τῶν δούλων⌐
n.asf cj v.aai.3s r.gsm.3 d.gsm n.gsm d.asn n.asn | cj p.a a.asm n.asm d.nsm n.nsm r.gpm d.gpm n.gpm
1178 2779 3221 899 3836 3261 3836 736 | 1254 3552 4498 5989 3836 3261 1529 1697 3836 1529

returned and settled accounts with them. **20** The man who had received the five talents brought the
ἔρχεται καὶ συναίρει λόγον μετ᾽ αὐτῶν καὶ ὁ | λαβὼν τὰ πέντε τάλαντα προσελθὼν προσήνεγκεν
v.pmi.3s cj v.pai.3s n.asm p.g r.gpm.3 cj d.nsm | pt.aa.nsm d.apn a.apn n.apn pt.aa.nsm v.aai.3s
2262 2779 5256 3364 3552 899 2779 3836 | 3284 3836 4297 5419 4665 4712

other five. 'Master,' he said, 'you entrusted me with five talents. See, I have gained five more.' ¶
ἄλλα πέντε τάλαντα κύριε | λέγων | παρέδωκας μοι | πέντε τάλαντα ἴδε | ἐκέρδησα πέντε ἄλλα τάλαντα
r.apn a.apn n.apn n.vsm | pt.pa.nsm | v.aai.2s r.ds.1 | a.apn n.apn pl | v.aai.1s a.apn r.apn n.apn
257 4297 5419 3261 | 3306 | 4140 1609 | 4297 5419 2623 | 3045 4297 257 5419

21 "His master replied, 'Well done, good and faithful servant! You have been faithful with a few things; I
αὐτοῦ ὁ κύριος, ἔφη αὐτῷ εὖ ἀγαθὲ καὶ πιστέ δοῦλε ἧς πιστός ἐπὶ ὀλίγα
r.gsm.3 d.nsm n.nsm v.iai.3s r.dsm.3 adv a.vsm cj a.vsm n.vsm v.iai.2s a.nsm p.a a.apn
899 3836 3261 5774 899 2292 19 2779 4412 1529 1639 4412 2093 3900

will put you in charge of many things. Come and share your master's happiness!' ¶ **22** "The
καταστήσω σε ἐπὶ πολλῶν εἴσελθε εἰς σου ⌐τοῦ κυρίου⌐ ⌐τὴν χαρὰν⌐ [δὲ] ὁ
v.fai.1s r.as.2 p.g a.gpn v.aam.2s p.a r.gs.2 d.gsm n.gsm d.asf n.asf cj d.nsm
2770 5148 2093 4498 1656 1650 5148 3836 3261 3836 5915 1254 3836

man with the two talents also came. 'Master,' he said, 'you entrusted me with two talents; see, I have gained
τὰ δύο τάλαντα καὶ προσελθὼν κύριε εἶπεν παρέδωκας μοι δύο τάλαντα ἴδε ἐκέρδησα
d.apn a.apn n.apn adv pt.aa.nsm n.vsm v.aai.3s v.aai.2s r.ds.1 a.apn n.apn pl v.aai.1s
3836 1545 5419 2779 4665 3261 3306 4140 1609 1545 5419 2623 3045

two more.' ¶ **23** "His master replied, 'Well done, good and faithful servant! You have been
δύο ἄλλα τάλαντα αὐτοῦ ⌐ὁ κύριος⌐ ἔφη αὐτῷ εὖ ἀγαθὲ καὶ πιστέ δοῦλε ἧς
a.apn r.apn n.apn r.gsm.3 d.nsm n.nsm v.iai.3s r.dsm.3 adv a.vsm cj a.vsm n.vsm v.iai.2s
1545 257 5419 899 3836 3261 5774 899 2292 19 2779 4412 1529 1639

faithful with a few things; I will put you in charge of many things. Come and share your master's
πιστός ἐπὶ ὀλίγα καταστήσω σε ἐπὶ πολλῶν εἴσελθε εἰς σου ⌐τοῦ κυρίου⌐
a.nsm p.a a.apn v.fai.1s r.as.2 p.g a.gpn v.aam.2s p.a r.gs.2 d.gsm n.gsm
4412 2093 3900 2770 5148 2093 4498 1656 1650 5148 3836 3261

happiness!' ¶ **24** "Then the man who had received the one talent came. 'Master,' he said, 'I knew
⌐τὴν χαρὰν⌐ καὶ δὲ ὁ εἰληφὼς τὸ ἓν τάλαντον προσελθὼν κύριε εἶπεν ἔγνων σε
d.asf n.asf adv cj d.nsm pt.ra.nsm d.asn a.asn n.asn pt.aa.nsm n.vsm v.aai.3s v.aai.1s r.as.2
3836 5915 2779 1254 3836 3284 3836 1651 5419 4665 3261 3306 1182 5148

that you are a hard man, harvesting where you have not sown and gathering where you have not
ὅτι εἶ σκληρὸς ἄνθρωπος θερίζων ὅπου οὐκ ἔσπειρας καὶ συνάγων ὅθεν οὐ
cj v.pai.2s a.nsm n.nsm pt.pa.nsm cj pl v.aai.2s cj pt.pa.nsm cj pl
4022 1639 5017 476 2545 3963 5062 5062 4024 5062 2779 5251 3854 1399 1399 4024

scattered seed. **25** So I was afraid and went out and hid your talent in the ground. See, here is what
διεσκόρπισας καὶ φοβηθεὶς ἀπελθὼν ἔκρυψα σου ⌐τὸ τάλαντον⌐ ἐν τῇ γῇ ἴδε
v.aai.2s cj pt.ap.nsm pt.aa.nsm v.aai.1s r.gs.2 d.asn n.asn p.d d.dsf n.dsf pl
1399 2779 5828 599 3221 5148 3836 5419 1877 3836 1178 2623

belongs to you.' ¶ **26** "His master replied, 'You wicked, lazy servant! So you knew
ἔχεις ⌐τὸ σόν⌐ δὲ αὐτοῦ ὁ κύριος, ἀποκριθεὶς εἶπεν αὐτῷ πονηρὲ καὶ ὀκνηρὲ δοῦλε ᾔδεις
v.pai.2s d.asn r.asn.2 cj r.gsm.3 d.nsm n.nsm pt.ap.nsm v.aai.3s r.dsm.3 a.vsm cj a.vsm n.vsm v.lai.2s
2400 3836 5050 1254 899 3836 3261 646 3306 899 4505 2779 3891 1529 3857

that I harvest where I have not sown and gather where I have not scattered seed? **27** Well then, you should
ὅτι θερίζω ὅπου οὐκ ἔσπειρα καὶ συνάγω ὅθεν οὐ διεσκόρπισα οὖν σε ἔδει
cj v.pai.1s cj pl v.aai.1s cj v.pai.1s cj pl v.aai.1s cj r.as.2 v.lai.3s
4022 2545 3963 5062 5062 4024 5062 2779 5251 3854 1399 1399 4024 1399 4036 5148 1256

πέντε τάλαντα λαβὼν ἠργάσατο ἐν αὐτοῖς καὶ ἐκέρδησεν ἄλλα πέντε· **17** ὡσαύτως ὁ τὰ δύο ἐκέρδησεν ἄλλα δύο. **18** ὁ δὲ τὸ ἓν λαβὼν ἀπελθὼν ὤρυξεν γῆν καὶ ἔκρυψεν τὸ ἀργύριον τοῦ κυρίου αὐτοῦ. **19** μετὰ δὲ πολὺν χρόνον ἔρχεται ὁ κύριος τῶν δούλων ἐκείνων καὶ συναίρει λόγον μετ᾽ αὐτῶν. **20** καὶ προσελθὼν ὁ τὰ πέντε τάλαντα λαβὼν προσήνεγκεν ἄλλα πέντε τάλαντα λέγων, Κύριε, πέντε τάλαντά μοι παρέδωκας· ἴδε ἄλλα πέντε τάλαντα ἐκέρδησα. ¶ **21** ἔφη αὐτῷ ὁ κύριος αὐτοῦ, Εὖ, δοῦλε ἀγαθὲ καὶ πιστέ, ἐπὶ ὀλίγα ἧς πιστός, ἐπὶ πολλῶν σε καταστήσω· εἴσελθε εἰς τὴν χαρὰν τοῦ κυρίου σου. ¶ **22** προσελθὼν [δὲ] καὶ ὁ τὰ δύο τάλαντα εἶπεν, Κύριε, δύο τάλαντά μοι παρέδωκας· ἴδε ἄλλα δύο τάλαντα ἐκέρδησα. ¶ **23** ἔφη αὐτῷ ὁ κύριος αὐτοῦ, Εὖ, δοῦλε ἀγαθὲ καὶ πιστέ, ἐπὶ ὀλίγα ἧς πιστός, ἐπὶ πολλῶν σε καταστήσω· εἴσελθε εἰς τὴν χαρὰν τοῦ κυρίου σου. ¶ **24** προσελθὼν δὲ καὶ ὁ τὸ ἓν τάλαντον εἰληφὼς εἶπεν, Κύριε, ἔγνων σε ὅτι σκληρὸς εἶ ἄνθρωπος, θερίζων ὅπου οὐκ ἔσπειρας καὶ συνάγων ὅθεν οὐ διεσκόρπισας, **25** καὶ φοβηθεὶς ἀπελθὼν ἔκρυψα τὸ τάλαντόν σου ἐν τῇ γῇ· ἴδε ἔχεις τὸ σόν. ¶ **26** ἀποκριθεὶς δὲ ὁ κύριος αὐτοῦ εἶπεν αὐτῷ, Πονηρὲ δοῦλε καὶ ὀκνηρέ, ᾔδεις ὅτι θερίζω ὅπου οὐκ ἔσπειρα καὶ συνάγω ὅθεν οὐ διεσκόρπισα; **27** ἔδει σε οὖν βαλεῖν

have put   my money   on deposit with the bankers,   so that when I returned I   would have received
→ βαλεῖν μου ⌐τὰ ἀργύρια⌐   → τοῖς τραπεζίταις καὶ   → ἐλθὼν ἐγὼ ἂν   → ἐκομισάμην
f.aa r.gs.1 d.apn n.apn   d.dpm n.dpm   cj   pt.aa.nsm r.ns.1 pl   v.ami.1s
965 1609 3836 736   3836 5545   2779   2262 1609 323   3152

it   back with interest. ¶   **28** "'Take the talent   from him and give it to the one who has   the ten
⌐τὸ ἐμὸν⌐ ↰ σὺν τόκῳ   οὖν ἄρατε τὸ τάλαντον ἀπ᾿ αὐτοῦ καὶ δότε → τῷ ← ← ἔχοντι τὰ δέκα
d.asn r.asn.1   p.d n.dsm   cj v.aam.2p d.asn n.asn p.g r.gsm.3 cj v.aam.2p d.dsm   pt.pa.dsm d.apn a.apn
3836 1847 3152 5250 5527   4036 5419   3836 5419   608 899   2779 1443 3836   2400 3836 1274

talents. **29** For everyone who has   will be given   more, and he will have an abundance.   Whoever does not
τάλαντα γὰρ παντὶ τῷ ἔχοντι → → δοθήσεται καὶ → → → περισσευθήσεται δὲ τοῦ   μὴ
n.apn cj a.dsm d.dsm pt.pa.dsm   v.fpi.3s   cj   v.fpi.3s   cj d.gsm   pl
5419 1147 4246 3836 2400   1443   2779   4355   1254 3836   2400   3590

have, even what he has   will be taken   from him. **30** And throw   that worthless servant outside,   into the
ἔχοντος καὶ ὃ → ἔχει → ἀρθήσεται ἀπ᾿ αὐτοῦ καὶ ἐκβάλετε τὸν ἀχρεῖον δοῦλον ⌐τὸ ἐξώτερον⌐ εἰς τὸ
pt.pa.gsm adv r.asn   v.pai.3s   v.fpi.3s   p.g r.gsm.3 cj v.aam.2p d.asm a.asm n.asm d.asn a.asn.c p.a d.asn
2400 2779 4005   2400   149   608 899 2779 1675 3836 945 1529 3836 2035 1650 3836

darkness, where there will be   weeping   and gnashing   of teeth.'
σκότος ἐκεῖ → → ἔσται ὁ κλαυθμὸς καὶ ὁ βρυγμὸς → ⌐τῶν ὀδόντων⌐
n.asn adv   v.fmi.3s d.nsm n.nsm cj d.nsm n.nsm   d.gpm n.gpm
5030 1695   1639 3836 3088 2779 3836 1106   3836 3848

The Sheep and the Goats

25:31 "When the Son of Man   comes in his   glory, and all   the angels with him,   he will
δὲ Ὅταν ὁ υἱὸς → ⌐τοῦ ἀνθρώπου⌐ ἔλθῃ ἐν αὐτοῦ ⌐τῇ δόξῃ⌐ καὶ πάντες οἱ ἄγγελοι μετ᾿ αὐτοῦ τότε → →
cj cj d.nsm n.nsm   d.gsm n.gsm   v.aas.3s p.d r.gsm.3 d.dsf n.dsf cj a.npm d.npm n.npm p.g r.gsm.3 adv
1254 4020 3836 5626   3836 476   2262 1877 899 3836 1518 2779 4246 3836 34 3552 899 5538

sit   on his   throne in heavenly glory. **32**   All   the nations will be gathered   before   him, and he will
καθίσει ἐπὶ αὐτοῦ θρόνου →   δόξης καὶ πάντα τὰ ἔθνη → συναχθήσονται ἔμπροσθεν αὐτοῦ καὶ
v.fai.3s p.g r.gsm.3 n.gsm   n.gsf cj a.npn d.npn n.npn   v.fpi.3s   p.g r.gsm.3 cj
2767 2093 899 2585   1518 2779 4246 3836 1620   5251   1869 899 2779

separate the people one from another as   a   shepherd separates the sheep   from the goats. **33**   He will put
ἀφορίσει αὐτοὺς ἀπ᾿ ἀλλήλων ὥσπερ ὁ ποιμὴν ἀφορίζει τὰ πρόβατα ἀπὸ τῶν ἐρίφων καὶ → στήσει μὲν
v.fai.3s r.apm.3 p.g r.gpm   d.nsm n.nsm v.pai.3s d.apn n.apn p.g d.gpn n.gpn cj   v.fai.3s pl
928 899 253 608 253   6061 3836 4478 928   3836 4585 608 3836 2253 2779   2705 3525

the sheep   on his   right   and the goats on his left.   ¶   **34** "Then the King   will say to those on his
τὰ πρόβατα ἐκ αὐτοῦ δεξιῶν δὲ τὰ ἐρίφια ἐξ εὐωνύμων   τότε ὁ βασιλεὺς → ἐρεῖ → τοῖς ἐκ αὐτοῦ
d.apn n.apn p.g r.gsm.3 a.gpf cj d.apn n.apn p.g a.gpf   adv d.nsm n.nsm   v.fai.3s   d.dpm p.g r.gsm.3
3836 4585 1666 899 1288 1254 3836 2252 1666 2381   5538 3836 995   3306   3836 1666 899

right, 'Come, you who are blessed   by my Father;   take your inheritance, the kingdom prepared   for you
δεξιῶν δεῦτε → οἱ εὐλογημένοι μου ⌐τοῦ πατρός⌐ → κληρονομήσατε τὴν βασιλείαν ἡτοιμασμένην → ὑμῖν
a.gpf adv   d.vpm pt.rp.vpm r.gs.1 d.gsm n.gsm   v.aam.2p d.asf n.asf pt.rp.asf   r.dp.2
1288 1307   3836 2328 4252 1609 3836 4252   3099 3836 993 2286   7007

since the creation   of the world. **35** For I was hungry and you gave   me something to eat,   I was thirsty and you
ἀπὸ καταβολῆς → κόσμου γὰρ → ἐπείνασα καὶ → ἐδώκατέ μοι → φαγεῖν → ἐδίψησα καὶ →
p.g n.gsf   n.gsm cj   v.aai.1s cj   v.aai.2p r.ds.1   f.aa   v.aai.1s cj
608 2856   3180 1142   4277 2779   1443 1609   2266   1498 2779 4540

gave me something to drink, I was a stranger and you invited   me in, **36** I needed clothes and you clothed   me, I
→ με → ἐποτίσατε → ἤμην ξένος καὶ → συνηγάγετέ με ← → γυμνὸς ← καὶ → περιεβάλετέ με →
r.as.1   v.aai.2p → v.imi.1s n.nsm cj   v.aai.2p r.as.1   a.nsm   cj   v.aai.2p r.as.1
4540 1609   4540   1639 3828 2779   5251 1609   5251 1218   2779   4314 1609

was sick   and you looked   after me, I was in   prison and you came to   visit me.'   ¶ **37** "Then the
→ ἠσθένησα καὶ → ἐπεσκέψασθε ← με → ἤμην ἐν φυλακῇ καὶ → ἤλθατε πρός με   τότε οἱ
v.aai.1s cj   v.ami.2p   r.as.1   v.iai.1s p.d n.dsf cj   v.aai.2p p.a r.as.1   adv d.npm
820 2779   2170   1609 1639 1877 5871 2779   2262 4639 1609   5538 3836

righteous will answer   him,   'Lord, when did we see   you hungry and feed   you, or thirsty and
δίκαιοι → ἀποκριθήσονται αὐτῷ λέγοντες κύριε πότε → → εἴδομεν σε πεινῶντα καὶ ἐθρέψαμεν ἢ διψῶντα καὶ
a.npm   v.fpi.3p r.dsm.3 pt.pa.npm n.vsm cj   v.aai.1p r.as.2 pt.pa.asm cj v.aai.1p cj pt.pa.asm cj
1465   646 899 3306 3261 4537   1625 5148 4277 2779 5555   2445 1498 2779

τὰ ἀργύριά μου τοῖς τραπεζίταις, καὶ ἐλθὼν ἐγὼ ἐκομισάμην ἂν τὸ ἐμὸν σὺν τόκῳ. ¶ ²⁸ ἄρατε οὖν ἀπ᾿ αὐτοῦ τὸ τάλαντον καὶ δότε τῷ ἔχοντι τὰ δέκα τάλαντα· ²⁹ τῷ γὰρ ἔχοντι παντὶ δοθήσεται καὶ περισσευθήσεται, τοῦ δὲ μὴ ἔχοντος καὶ ὃ ἔχει ἀρθήσεται ἀπ᾿ αὐτοῦ. ³⁰ καὶ τὸν ἀχρεῖον δοῦλον ἐκβάλετε εἰς τὸ σκότος τὸ ἐξώτερον· ἐκεῖ ἔσται ὁ κλαυθμὸς καὶ ὁ βρυγμὸς τῶν ὀδόντων.
²⁵:³¹ Ὅταν δὲ ἔλθῃ ὁ υἱὸς τοῦ ἀνθρώπου ἐν τῇ δόξῃ αὐτοῦ καὶ πάντες οἱ ἄγγελοι μετ᾿ αὐτοῦ, τότε καθίσει ἐπὶ θρόνου δόξης αὐτοῦ· ³² καὶ συναχθήσονται ἔμπροσθεν αὐτοῦ πάντα τὰ ἔθνη, καὶ ἀφορίσει αὐτοὺς ἀπ᾿ ἀλλήλων, ὥσπερ ὁ ποιμὴν ἀφορίζει τὰ πρόβατα ἀπὸ τῶν ἐρίφων, ³³ καὶ στήσει τὰ μὲν πρόβατα ἐκ δεξιῶν αὐτοῦ, τὰ δὲ ἐρίφια ἐξ εὐωνύμων. ¶ ³⁴ τότε ἐρεῖ ὁ βασιλεὺς τοῖς ἐκ δεξιῶν αὐτοῦ, Δεῦτε οἱ εὐλογημένοι τοῦ πατρός μου, κληρονομήσατε τὴν ἡτοιμασμένην ὑμῖν βασιλείαν ἀπὸ καταβολῆς κόσμου. ³⁵ ἐπείνασα γὰρ καὶ ἐδώκατέ μοι φαγεῖν, ἐδίψησα καὶ ἐποτίσατέ με, ξένος ἤμην καὶ συνηγάγετέ με, ³⁶ γυμνὸς καὶ περιεβάλετέ με, ἠσθένησα καὶ ἐπεσκέψασθέ με, ἐν φυλακῇ ἤμην καὶ ἤλθατε πρός με. ¶ ³⁷ τότε ἀποκριθήσονται

give you something to drink? **38** When did we see   you a stranger and invite   you in, or needing clothes
→   ἐποτίσαμεν   δέ πότε   did we εἴδομεν σε   ξένον   καὶ συνηγάγομεν   ← ἢ γυμνὸν
                 v.aai.1p   cj cj   v.aai.1p r.as.2 n.asm   cj v.aai.1p   ἢ a.asm
                 4540   1254 4537   1625 5148 3828   2779 5251   2445 1218

and clothe   you? **39** When did we see you   sick   or in prison and go   to visit you?’ ¶   **40**
καὶ περιεβάλομεν   δέ πότε   → → σε εἴδομεν ἀσθενοῦντα ἢ ἐν φυλακῇ καὶ ἤλθομεν πρός σε   καὶ
cj v.aai.1p   cj cj   r.as.2 v.aai.1p pt.pa.asm cj p.d n.dsf cj v.aai.1p p.a r.as.2   cj
2779 4314   1254 4537   5148 1625 820   1877 1877 5871 2779 2262 4639 5148   2779

“The King   will reply,   ‘I tell you the truth, whatever you did   for one of the least   of these
ὁ   βασιλεὺς → ἀποκριθεὶς ἐρεῖ αὐτοῖς   λέγω ὑμῖν   ἀμὴν ἐφ’ ὅσον → ἐποιήσατε → ἑνὶ τῶν ἐλαχίστων τούτων
d.nsm n.nsm   pt.ap.nsm v.fai.3s r.dpm.3 v.pai.1s r.dp.2 pl p.a r.asn   v.aai.2p   a.dsm d.gpm a.gpm.s r.gpm
3836 995   646 3306 899   3306 7007   297 2093 4012   4472   1651 3836 1788   81 4047

brothers   of mine, you did   for me.’ ¶ **41** “Then he will say to those on his left,   ‘Depart from me,
τῶν ἀδελφῶν μου → ἐποιήσατε   ἐμοὶ   καὶ τότε   →   ἐρεῖ → τοῖς ἐξ εὐωνύμων πορεύεσθε ἀπ’ ἐμοῦ
d.gpm n.gpm r.gs.1   v.aai.2p   r.ds.1   adv adv   v.fai.3s d.dpm p.g a.gpf v.pmm.2p p.g r.gs.1
3836 81   1609   4472   1609   2779 5538   3306 3836 1666 2381   4513 608   1609

you who are cursed,   into the eternal   fire prepared   for the devil   and his   angels.   **42** For I was
οἱ   → → κατηραμένοι εἰς τὸ τὸ αἰώνιον πῦρ τὸ ἡτοιμασμένον → τῷ διαβόλῳ καὶ αὐτοῦ τοῖς ἀγγέλοις   γὰρ →
d.vpm   pt.rp.vpm   p.a d.asn d.asn a.asn n.asn d.asn pt.rp.asn   d.dsm n.dsm cj r.gsm.3 d.dpm n.dpm   cj
3836   2933   1650 3836 3836 173   4786 3836 2286   2779 1333   899 34   1142

hungry and you gave   me nothing to eat,   I was thirsty and you gave me nothing to drink, **43** I was a stranger
ἐπείνασα καὶ → ἐδώκατέ μοι οὐκ → φαγεῖν → ἐδίψησα καὶ → → με οὐκ → ἐποτίσατε   ἤμην ξένος
v.aai.1s cj   v.aai.2p r.ds.1 pl f.aa   v.aai.1s cj   r.as.1 pl   v.aai.2p   v.imi.1s n.nsm
4277 2779   1443 1609 4024   2266   1498 2779   1609 4024   4540   1639 3828

and you did not invite   me in, I needed clothes and you did not clothe   me, I was sick   and in prison and
καὶ → οὐ συνηγάγετε με → γυμνὸς ← καὶ → → οὐ περιεβάλετέ με   ἀσθενὴς καὶ ἐν φυλακῇ καὶ
cj   pl v.aai.2p r.as.1 a.nsm   cj   pl v.aai.2p r.as.1   a.nsm cj p.d n.dsf cj
2779 5251 5251 1609   1218   2779 2779 4314 4024 4314 1609   822   2779 1877 5871 2779

you did not look   after me.’ ¶ **44** “They also will answer,   ‘Lord, when did we see   you
→ → οὐκ ἐπεσκέψασθε ← με   τότε αὐτοὶ καὶ → ἀποκριθήσονται λέγοντες κύριε πότε → → εἴδομεν σε
pl v.ami.2p r.as.1   adv r.npm adv   v.fpi.3p   pt.pa.npm n.vsm cj   v.aai.1p r.as.2
2170 2170 4024 2170 1609   5538 899 2779   646   3306 3261 4537   1625 5148

hungry or thirsty or a stranger or needing clothes or sick   or in prison, and did not help   you?’ ¶
πεινῶντα ἢ διψῶντα ἢ ξένον ἢ γυμνὸν ← ἢ ἀσθενῆ ἢ ἐν φυλακῇ καὶ → οὐ διηκονήσαμεν σοι
pt.pa.asm cj pt.pa.asm cj n.asm cj a.asm   cj a.asn cj p.d n.dsf cj pl v.aai.1p   r.ds.2
4277 2445 1498 2445 3828 2445 1218   2445 822 2445 1877 5871 2779 1354 4024 1354 5148

45 “He will reply,   ‘I tell you the truth, whatever you did not do   for one of the least   of
τότε → → ἀποκριθήσεται αὐτοῖς λέγων → λέγω ὑμῖν   ἀμὴν ἐφ’ ὅσον   → οὐκ ἐποιήσατε → ἑνὶ τῶν ἐλαχίστων →
adv   v.fpi.3s   r.dpm.3 pt.pa.nsm v.pai.1s r.dp.2 pl p.a r.asn   pl v.aai.2p   a.dsm d.gpm a.gpm.s
5538   646   899 3306   3306 7007   297 2093 4012   4472 4472 4024 4472   1651 3836 1788

these, you did not do   for me.’ ¶ **46** “Then they will go   away to eternal punishment, but the
τούτων → → οὐδὲ ἐποιήσατε → ἐμοὶ   καὶ οὗτοι → ἀπελεύσονται ← εἰς αἰώνιον κόλασιν δὲ οἱ
r.gpm   cj   v.aai.2p   r.ds.1   cj r.npm   v.fmi.3p   p.a a.asf n.asf   cj d.npm
4047 4472 4472 4028 4472   1609   2779 4047   599   1650 173 3136   1254 3836

righteous to eternal life.”
δίκαιοι εἰς αἰώνιον ζωήν
a.npm   p.a a.asf n.asf
1465   1650 173   2437

The Plot Against Jesus

26:1   When Jesus   had finished saying all   these things,   he said to his   disciples,
Καὶ ἐγένετο ὅτε ὁ Ἰησοῦς → ἐτέλεσεν   πάντας τούτους τοὺς λόγους → εἶπεν → αὐτοῦ τοῖς μαθηταῖς
cj v.ami.3s cj d.nsm n.nsm   v.aai.3s   a.apm r.apm d.apm n.apm   v.aai.3s   r.gsm.3 d.dpm n.dpm
2779 1181 4021 3836 2652   5464   4246 4047 3836 3364   3306 3412   899 3836 3412

2 “As you know,   the Passover is   two days away – and the Son of Man   will be handed   over to
→ οἴδατε ὅτι τὸ πάσχα γίνεται δύο ἡμέρας μετὰ καὶ ὁ υἱὸς τοῦ ἀνθρώπου   → παραδίδοται ← εἰς
v.rai.2p cj d.nsn n.nsn v.ppi.3s a.apf n.apf p.a cj d.nsm n.nsm d.gsm n.gsm v.ppi.3s   p.a
3857 4022 3836 4247 1181 1545 2465 3552 2779 3836 5626 3836 476   4140   1650

αὐτῷ οἱ δίκαιοι λέγοντες, Κύριε, πότε σε εἴδομεν πεινῶντα καὶ ἐθρέψαμεν, ἢ διψῶντα καὶ ἐποτίσαμεν; ³⁸ πότε δέ σε εἴδομεν ξένον
καὶ συνηγάγομεν; ἢ γυμνὸν καὶ περιεβάλομεν; ³⁹ πότε δέ σε εἴδομεν ἀσθενοῦντα ἢ ἐν φυλακῇ καὶ ἤλθομεν πρός σε; ¶ ⁴⁰ καὶ
ἀποκριθεὶς ὁ βασιλεὺς ἐρεῖ αὐτοῖς, Ἀμὴν λέγω ὑμῖν, ἐφ’ ὅσον ἐποιήσατε ἑνὶ τούτων τῶν ἀδελφῶν μου τῶν ἐλαχίστων, ἐμοὶ
ἐποιήσατε. ¶ ⁴¹ Τότε ἐρεῖ καὶ τοῖς ἐξ εὐωνύμων, Πορεύεσθε ἀπ’ ἐμοῦ [οἱ] κατηραμένοι εἰς τὸ πῦρ τὸ αἰώνιον τὸ ἡτοιμασμένον
τῷ διαβόλῳ καὶ τοῖς ἀγγέλοις αὐτοῦ. ⁴² ἐπείνασα γὰρ καὶ οὐκ ἐδώκατέ μοι φαγεῖν, ἐδίψησα καὶ οὐκ ἐποτίσατέ με, ⁴³ ξένος
ἤμην καὶ οὐ συνηγάγετέ με, γυμνὸς καὶ οὐ περιεβάλετέ με, ἀσθενὴς καὶ ἐν φυλακῇ καὶ οὐκ ἐπεσκέψασθέ με. ¶ ⁴⁴ τότε
ἀποκριθήσονται καὶ αὐτοὶ λέγοντες, Κύριε, πότε σε εἴδομεν πεινῶντα ἢ διψῶντα ἢ ξένον ἢ γυμνὸν ἢ ἀσθενῆ ἢ ἐν φυλακῇ καὶ οὐ
διηκονήσαμέν σοι; ¶ ⁴⁵ τότε ἀποκριθήσεται αὐτοῖς λέγων, Ἀμὴν λέγω ὑμῖν, ἐφ’ ὅσον οὐκ ἐποιήσατε ἑνὶ τούτων τῶν ἐλαχίστων,
οὐδὲ ἐμοὶ ἐποιήσατε. ¶ ⁴⁶ καὶ ἀπελεύσονται οὗτοι εἰς κόλασιν αἰώνιον, οἱ δὲ δίκαιοι εἰς ζωὴν αἰώνιον.
²⁶:¹ Καὶ ἐγένετο ὅτε ἐτέλεσεν ὁ Ἰησοῦς πάντας τοὺς λόγους τούτους, εἶπεν τοῖς μαθηταῖς αὐτοῦ, ² Οἴδατε ὅτι μετὰ δύο ἡμέρας

be crucified." ¶ **3** Then the chief priests and the elders of the people assembled in the palace of the
→ ⌐τὸ σταυρωθῆναι⌐ Τότε οἱ → ἀρχιερεῖς καὶ οἱ πρεσβύτεροι → τοῦ λαοῦ συνήχθησαν εἰς τὴν αὐλὴν → τοῦ
d.asn f.ap adv d.npm n.npm cj d.npm a.npm d.gsm n.gsm v.api.3p p.a d.asf n.asf d.gsm
3836 5090 5538 3836 797 2779 3836 4565 3836 3295 5251 1650 3836 885 3836

high priest, whose name was Caiaphas, **4** and they plotted to arrest Jesus in some sly way and
→ ἀρχιερέως τοῦ λεγομένου ← Καϊάφα καὶ → συνεβουλεύσαντο ἵνα κρατήσωσιν ⌐τὸν Ἰησοῦν⌐ → δόλῳ ← καὶ
n.gsm d.gsm pt.pp.gsm n.gsm cj v.ami.3p cj v.aas.3p d.asm n.asm n.dsm cj
797 3836 3306 2780 2779 5205 2671 3195 3836 2652 1515 2779

kill him. **5** "But not during the Feast," they said, "or there may be a riot among the people."
ἀποκτείνωσιν μὴ ἐν τῇ ἑορτῇ δέ → ἔλεγον ἵνα μὴ → → γένηται θόρυβος ἐν τῷ λαῷ
v.aas.3p pl p.d d.dsf n.dsf cj v.iai.3p cj pl v.ams.3s n.nsm p.d d.dsm n.dsm
650 3590 1877 3836 2038 1254 3306 2671 3590 1181 2573 1877 3836 3295

Jesus Anointed at Bethany

26:6 While Jesus was in Bethany in the home of a man known as Simon the Leper, **7** a woman
δὲ → ⌐Τοῦ Ἰησοῦ⌐ γενομένου ἐν Βηθανίᾳ ἐν οἰκίᾳ → Σίμωνος τοῦ λεπροῦ γυνὴ
cj d.gsm n.gsm pt.am.gsm p.d n.dsf p.d n.dsf n.gsm d.gsm a.gsm n.nsf
1254 1181 3836 2652 1181 1877 1029 1877 3864 4981 3836 3320 1222

came to him with an alabaster jar of very expensive perfume, which she poured on his head as he
προσῆλθεν αὐτῷ ἔχουσα ἀλάβαστρον ← → → βαρυτίμου μύρου καὶ → κατέχεεν ἐπὶ αὐτοῦ ⌐τῆς κεφαλῆς⌐ → →
v.aai.3s r.dsm.3 pt.pa.nsf n.asn a.gsn n.gsn cj v.aai.3s p.g r.gsm.3 d.gsf n.gsf
4665 899 2400 223 3693 988 3693 2779 2972 2093 899 3836 3051

was reclining at the table. ¶ **8** When the disciples saw this, they were indignant. "Why this
→ ἀνακειμένου ← ← δὲ ⌐ οἱ μαθηταὶ ἰδόντες → → ἠγανάκτησαν ⌐εἰς τί⌐ αὕτη
pt.pm.gsm cj ⌐ d.npm n.npm pt.aa.npm v.aai.3p p.a r.asn r.nsf
367 1254 1625 3836 3412 1625 24 1650 5515 4047

waste?" they asked. **9** "This perfume could have been sold at a high price and the money given to
⌐ἡ ἀπώλεια⌐ → λέγοντες γὰρ τοῦτο ἐδύνατο → → πραθῆναι → πολλοῦ καὶ → δοθῆναι →
d.nsf n.nsf pt.pa.npm cj r.asn v.ipi.3s f.ap a.gsn cj f.ap
3836 724 3306 1142 4047 1538 4405 4498 2779 1443

the poor." ¶ **10** Aware of this, Jesus said to them, "Why are you bothering this woman? She
πτωχοῖς δὲ γνοὺς ὁ Ἰησοῦς⌐ εἶπεν → αὐτοῖς τί → ⌐κόπους παρέχετε⌐ τῇ γυναικί γὰρ →
a.dpm cj pt.aa.nsm d.nsm n.nsm v.aai.3s r.dpm.3 r.asn n.apm v.pai.2p d.dsf n.dsf cj
4777 1254 1182 3836 2652 3306 899 5515 3160 4218 3836 1222 1142

has done a beautiful thing to me. **11** The poor you will always have with you, but you will not always have
→ ἠργάσατο καλὸν ἔργον εἰς ἐμέ γὰρ τοὺς πτωχοὺς → → πάντοτε ἔχετε μεθ' ἑαυτῶν δὲ → → οὐ πάντοτε ἔχετε
v.ami.3s a.asn n.asn p.a r.as.1 cj d.apm a.apm adv v.pai.2p p.g r.gpm.2 cj pl adv v.pai.2p
2237 2819 2240 1650 1609 1142 3836 4777 2400 2400 4121 2400 3552 1571 1254 2400 2400 4024 4121 2400

me. **12** When she poured this perfume on my body, she did it to prepare me for burial. **13** I tell
ἐμέ γὰρ → αὕτη βαλοῦσα τοῦτο ⌐τὸ μύρον⌐ ἐπὶ μου ⌐τοῦ σώματος⌐ → ἐποίησεν πρὸς ⌐τὸ ἐνταφιάσαι⌐ με ← ← → λέγω
r.as.1 cj r.nsf pt.aa.nsf r.asn d.asn n.asn p.g r.gs.1 d.gsn n.gsn v.aai.3s p.a d.asn f.aa r.as.1 v.pai.1s
1609 1142 965 4047 965 4047 3836 3693 2093 1609 3836 5393 4472 4639 3836 1946 1609 1946 1946 3306

you the truth, wherever this gospel is preached throughout the world, what she has done will also be
ὑμῖν ἀμὴν ⌐ὅπου ἐάν⌐ τοῦτο ⌐τὸ εὐαγγέλιον⌐ → κηρυχθῇ ἐν ὅλῳ τῷ κόσμῳ ὃ αὕτη → ἐποίησεν ← καὶ →
r.dp.2 pl cj pl r.nsn d.nsn n.nsn v.aps.3s p.d a.dsm d.dsm n.dsm r.asn r.nsf v.aai.3s cj
7007 297 3963 1569 4047 3836 2295 3062 1877 3910 3836 3180 4005 4047 4472 3281 2779

told, in memory of her."
λαληθήσεται εἰς μνημόσυνον αὐτῆς
v.fpi.3s p.a n.asn r.gsf.3
3281 1650 3649 899

Judas Agrees to Betray Jesus

26:14 Then one of the Twelve – the one called Judas Iscariot – went to the chief priests **15** and asked,
Τότε εἷς → τῶν δώδεκα ὁ → λεγόμενος Ἰούδας Ἰσκαριώτης πορευθεὶς πρὸς τοὺς → ἀρχιερεῖς εἶπεν
adv a.nsm d.gpm a.gpm d.nsm pt.pp.nsm n.nsm n.nsm pt.ap.nsm p.a d.apm n.apm v.aai.3s
5538 1651 3836 1557 3836 3306 2683 2697 4513 4639 3836 797 3306

τὸ πάσχα γίνεται, καὶ ὁ υἱὸς τοῦ ἀνθρώπου παραδίδοται εἰς τὸ σταυρωθῆναι. ¶ **3** Τότε συνήχθησαν οἱ ἀρχιερεῖς καὶ οἱ πρεσβύτεροι τοῦ λαοῦ εἰς τὴν αὐλὴν τοῦ ἀρχιερέως τοῦ λεγομένου Καϊάφα **4** καὶ συνεβουλεύσαντο ἵνα τὸν Ἰησοῦν δόλῳ κρατήσωσιν καὶ ἀποκτείνωσιν· **5** ἔλεγον δέ, Μὴ ἐν τῇ ἑορτῇ, ἵνα μὴ θόρυβος γένηται ἐν τῷ λαῷ.
26:6 Τοῦ δὲ Ἰησοῦ γενομένου ἐν Βηθανίᾳ ἐν οἰκίᾳ Σίμωνος τοῦ λεπροῦ, **7** προσῆλθεν αὐτῷ γυνὴ ἔχουσα ἀλάβαστρον μύρου βαρυτίμου καὶ κατέχεεν ἐπὶ τῆς κεφαλῆς αὐτοῦ ἀνακειμένου. ¶ **8** ἰδόντες δὲ οἱ μαθηταὶ ἠγανάκτησαν λέγοντες, Εἰς τί ἡ ἀπώλεια αὕτη; **9** ἐδύνατο γὰρ τοῦτο τὸ μύρον πραθῆναι πολλοῦ καὶ δοθῆναι πτωχοῖς. ¶ **10** γνοὺς δὲ ὁ Ἰησοῦς εἶπεν αὐτοῖς, Τί κόπους παρέχετε τῇ γυναικί; ἔργον γὰρ καλὸν ἠργάσατο εἰς ἐμέ· **11** πάντοτε γὰρ τοὺς πτωχοὺς ἔχετε μεθ' ἑαυτῶν, ἐμὲ δὲ οὐ πάντοτε ἔχετε· **12** βαλοῦσα γὰρ αὕτη τὸ μύρον τοῦτο ἐπὶ τοῦ σώματός μου πρὸς τὸ ἐνταφιάσαι με ἐποίησεν. **13** ἀμὴν λέγω ὑμῖν, ὅπου ἐὰν κηρυχθῇ τὸ εὐαγγέλιον τοῦτο ἐν ὅλῳ τῷ κόσμῳ, λαληθήσεται καὶ ὃ ἐποίησεν αὕτη εἰς μνημόσυνον αὐτῆς.

"What are you willing to give me if I hand him over to you?" So they counted out for him thirty
τί → → θέλετε → δοῦναι μοι → κἀγὼ παραδώσω αὐτόν ← → ὑμῖν δὲ οἱ ἔστησαν → → αὐτῷ τριάκοντα
r.asn   θέλετε f.aa r.ds.1 crasis v.fai.1s r.asm.3   r.dp.2 cj d.npm v.aai.3p   r.dsm.3 a.apn
5515   2527 1443 1609 2743 4140 899 4140 7007 1254 3836 2705   899 5558

silver coins. **16** From then on Judas watched for an opportunity to hand him over.
ἀργύρια ← καὶ ἀπὸ τότε ← ἐζήτει ← εὐκαιρίαν ἵνα παραδῷ αὐτὸν ←
n.apn cj p.g adv   v.iai.3s   n.asf cj v.aas.3s r.asm.3
736 2779 608 5538   2426   2321 2671 4140 899 4140

The Lord's Supper

26:17 On the first day of the Feast of Unleavened Bread, the disciples came to Jesus and asked,
δὲ → Τῇ πρώτῃ → τῶν → → ἀζύμων ← οἱ μαθηταὶ προσῆλθον ← τῷ Ἰησοῦ, λέγοντες
cj → d.dsf a.dsf d.gpn   n.gpn   d.npm n.npm v.aai.3p   d.dsm n.dsm pt.pa.npm
1254 3836 4755 3836   109   3836 3412 4665   3836 2652 3306

"Where do you want us to make preparations for you to eat the Passover?" ¶ **18** He replied, "Go into
ποῦ → → θέλεις → → ἑτοιμάσωμεν → σοι → φαγεῖν τὸ πάσχα   δὲ ὁ εἶπεν ὑπάγετε εἰς
adv   v.pai.2s   v.aas.1p → r.ds.2 f.aa d.asn n.asn   cj d.nsm v.aai.3s v.pam.2p p.a
4543   2527 2286   5148 2266 3836 4247   1254 3836 3306 5632 1650

the city to a certain man and tell him, 'The Teacher says: My appointed time is near. I am going
τὴν πόλιν πρὸς τὸν δεῖνα ← καὶ εἴπατε αὐτῷ ὁ διδάσκαλος λέγει μου → ὁ καιρός, ἐστιν ἐγγύς → → ποιῶ
d.asf n.asf p.g d.asm n.asm   cj v.aam.2p r.dsm.3 d.nsm n.nsm v.pai.3s r.gs.1   d.nsm n.nsm v.pai.3s adv   v.pai.1s
3836 4484 4639 3836 1265   2779 3306 899 3836 1437 3306 1609   3836 2789 1639 1584   4472

to celebrate the Passover with my disciples at your house.'" **19** So the disciples did as Jesus had
← → τὸ πάσχα μετὰ μου τῶν μαθητῶν, πρὸς σὲ καὶ οἱ μαθηταὶ ἐποίησαν ὡς ὁ Ἰησοῦς, →
d.asn n.asn p.g r.gs.1 d.gpm n.gpm p.g r.as.2 cj d.npm n.npm v.aai.3p cj d.nsm n.nsm
3836 4247 3552 1609 3836 3412 4639 5148 2779 3836 3412 4472 6055 3836 2652

directed them and prepared the Passover. ¶ **20** When evening came, Jesus was reclining at the table with
συνέταξεν αὐτοῖς καὶ ἡτοίμασαν τὸ πάσχα   δὲ → Ὀψίας γενομένης → ἀνέκειτο ← ← ← μετὰ
v.aai.3s r.dpm.3 cj v.aai.3p d.asn n.asn   cj   n.gsf pt.am.gsf   v.imi.3s   p.g
5332 899 2779 2286 3836 4247   1254 1181 4068 1181   367   3552

the Twelve. **21** And while they were eating, he said, "I tell you the truth, one of you will betray me." ¶
τῶν δώδεκα καὶ → αὐτῶν → ἐσθιόντων → εἶπεν → λέγω ὑμῖν ἀμὴν ὅτι εἷς ἐξ ὑμῶν παραδώσει με
d.gpm a.gpm cj → r.gpm.3   pt.pa.gpm   v.aai.3s   v.pai.1s r.dp.2 pl cj a.nsm p.g r.gp.2 v.fai.3s r.as.1
3836 1557 2779 2266 899   2266   3306   3306 7007 297 4022 1651 1666 7007 4140 1609

22 They were very sad and began to say to him one after the other, "Surely not I, Lord?" ¶
καὶ → → σφόδρα λυπούμενοι ἤρξαντο → λέγειν αὐτῷ εἷς ἕκαστος → μήτι ἐγώ εἰμι κύριε
cj   adv pt.pp.npm v.ami.3p   f.pa r.dsm.3 a.nsm r.nsm   pl r.ns.1 v.pai.1s n.vsm
2779 3382 3382 5379 3382 806   3306 899 1651 1667   3614 1609 1639 3261

23 Jesus replied, "The one who has dipped his hand into the bowl with me will betray me. **24**
δὲ ὁ ἀποκριθεὶς εἶπεν ὁ ← → → ἐμβάψας τὴν χεῖρα ἐν τῷ τρυβλίῳ μετ' ἐμοῦ οὗτος → παραδώσει με μὲν
cj d.nsm pt.ap.nsm v.aai.3s d.nsm   pt.aa.nsm d.asf n.asf p.d d.dsn n.dsn p.g r.gs.1 r.nsm   v.fai.3s r.as.1 pl
1254 3836 646 3306 3836   1835 3836 5931 1877 3836 5581 3552 1609 4047   4140 1609 3525

The Son of Man will go just as it is written about him. But woe to that man who
ὁ υἱὸς τοῦ ἀνθρώπου, → ὑπάγει καθὼς ← → γέγραπται περὶ αὐτοῦ δὲ οὐαὶ → ἐκείνῳ τῷ ἀνθρώπῳ δι' οὗ
d.nsm n.nsm d.gsm n.gsm   v.pai.3s cj   v.rpi.3s p.g r.gsm.3 cj j   r.dsm d.dsm n.dsm p.g r.gsm
3836 5626 3836 476   5632 2777   1211 4309 899 1254 4026 476 1697 3836 476 1328 4005

betrays the Son of Man! It would be better for him if he had not been born." ¶
παραδίδοται ὁ υἱὸς → τοῦ ἀνθρώπου, → → ἦν καλὸν → αὐτῷ εἰ ὁ ἄνθρωπος ἐκεῖνος, οὐκ → ἐγεννήθη
v.ppi.3s d.nsm n.nsm d.gsm n.gsm   v.iai.3s a.nsn   r.dsm.3 cj d.nsm n.nsm r.nsm pl   v.api.3s
4140 3836 5626 3836 476   1639 2819   899 1623 3836 476 1697 1164   1164

25 Then Judas, the one who would betray him, said, "Surely not I, Rabbi?" ¶ Jesus
δὲ Ἰούδας ὁ ← ← → παραδιδοὺς αὐτὸν ἀποκριθεὶς εἶπεν μήτι ἐγώ εἰμι ῥαββί
cj n.nsm d.nsm   pt.pa.nsm r.asm.3 pt.ap.nsm v.aai.3s pl r.ns.1 v.pai.1s n.vsm
1254 2683 3836   4140 899 646 3306 3614 1609 1639 4806

answered, "Yes, it is you." ¶ **26** While they were eating, Jesus took bread, gave
λέγει αὐτῷ σὺ εἶπας   δὲ → αὐτῶν → Ἐσθιόντων ὁ Ἰησοῦς, λαβὼν ἄρτον καὶ →
v.pai.3s r.dsm.3 r.ns.2 v.aai.2s   cj   r.gpm.3   pt.pa.gpm d.nsm n.nsm pt.aa.nsm n.asm cj
3306 899 5148 3306   1254 2266 899   2266 3836 2652 3284 788 2779

²⁶:¹⁴ Τότε πορευθεὶς εἷς τῶν δώδεκα, ὁ λεγόμενος Ἰούδας Ἰσκαριώτης, πρὸς τοὺς ἀρχιερεῖς ¹⁵ εἶπεν, Τί θέλετέ μοι δοῦναι, κἀγὼ ὑμῖν παραδώσω αὐτόν; οἱ δὲ ἔστησαν αὐτῷ τριάκοντα ἀργύρια. ¹⁶ καὶ ἀπὸ τότε ἐζήτει εὐκαιρίαν ἵνα αὐτὸν παραδῷ.

²⁶:¹⁷ Τῇ δὲ πρώτῃ τῶν ἀζύμων προσῆλθον οἱ μαθηταὶ τῷ Ἰησοῦ λέγοντες, Ποῦ θέλεις ἑτοιμάσωμέν σοι φαγεῖν τὸ πάσχα; ¹⁸ ὁ δὲ εἶπεν, Ὑπάγετε εἰς τὴν πόλιν πρὸς τὸν δεῖνα καὶ εἴπατε αὐτῷ, Ὁ διδάσκαλος λέγει, Ὁ καιρός μου ἐγγύς ἐστιν, πρὸς σὲ ποιῶ τὸ πάσχα μετὰ τῶν μαθητῶν μου. ¹⁹ καὶ ἐποίησαν οἱ μαθηταὶ ὡς συνέταξεν αὐτοῖς ὁ Ἰησοῦς καὶ ἡτοίμασαν τὸ πάσχα. ¶ ²⁰ Ὀψίας δὲ γενομένης ἀνέκειτο μετὰ τῶν δώδεκα. ²¹ καὶ ἐσθιόντων αὐτῶν εἶπεν, Ἀμὴν λέγω ὑμῖν ὅτι εἷς ἐξ ὑμῶν παραδώσει με. ¶ ²² καὶ λυπούμενοι σφόδρα ἤρξαντο λέγειν αὐτῷ εἷς ἕκαστος, Μήτι ἐγώ εἰμι, κύριε; ¶ ²³ ὁ δὲ ἀποκριθεὶς εἶπεν, Ὁ ἐμβάψας μετ' ἐμοῦ τὴν χεῖρα ἐν τῷ τρυβλίῳ οὗτός με παραδώσει. ²⁴ ὁ μὲν υἱὸς τοῦ ἀνθρώπου ὑπάγει καθὼς γέγραπται περὶ αὐτοῦ, οὐαὶ δὲ τῷ ἀνθρώπῳ ἐκείνῳ δι' οὗ ὁ υἱὸς τοῦ ἀνθρώπου παραδίδοται· καλὸν ἦν αὐτῷ εἰ οὐκ ἐγεννήθη ὁ ἄνθρωπος ἐκεῖνος. ¶

thanks and broke it, and gave it to his disciples, saying, "Take and eat; this is my body." ¶
εὐλογήσας ἔκλασεν καὶ δοὺς → τοῖς μαθηταῖς εἶπεν λάβετε φάγετε τοῦτο ἐστιν μου ⌜τὸ σῶμα⌟
pt.aa.nsm v.aai.3s cj pt.aa.nsm d.dpm n.dpm v.aai.3s v.aam.2p v.aam.2p r.nsn v.pai.3s r.gs.1 d.nsn n.nsn
2328 3089 2779 1443 3836 3412 3306 3284 2266 4047 1639 1609 3836 5393

27 Then he took the cup, gave thanks and offered it to them, saying, "Drink from it, all of you.
καὶ → λαβὼν ποτήριον καὶ → εὐχαριστήσας ἔδωκεν → αὐτοῖς λέγων πίετε ἐξ αὐτοῦ πάντες ← ←
cj pt.aa.nsm n.asn cj pt.aa.nsm v.aai.3s r.dpm.3 pt.pa.nsm v.aam.2p p.g r.gsn.3 a.vpm
2779 3284 4539 2779 2373 1443 899 3306 4403 1666 899 4246

28 This is my blood of the covenant, which is poured out for many for the forgiveness of sins. **29** I
γάρ τοῦτο ἐστιν μου ⌜τὸ αἷμα⌟ → τῆς διαθήκης τὸ → ἐκχυννόμενον ← περὶ πολλῶν εἰς ἄφεσιν → ἁμαρτιῶν δὲ →
cj r.nsn v.pai.3s r.gs.1 d.nsn n.nsn d.gsf n.gsf d.nsn pt.pp.nsn p.g a.gpm p.a n.asf n.gpf cj
1142 4047 1639 1609 3836 135 3836 1347 3836 1773 4309 4498 1650 912 281 1254

tell you, I will not drink of this fruit of the vine from now on until that day when I
λέγω ὑμῖν ↗ ↗ ⌜οὐ μὴ⌟ πίω ἐκ τούτου ⌜τοῦ γενήματος⌟ → τῆς ἀμπέλου ἀπ᾽ ἄρτι ← ἕως ἐκείνης ⌜τῆς ἡμέρας⌟ ὅταν →
v.pai.1s r.dp.2 pl pl v.aas.1s p.g r.gsn d.gsn n.gsn d.gsf n.gsf p.g adv p.g r.gsf d.gsf n.gsf cj
3306 7007 4403 4403 4024 3590 4403 1666 4047 3836 1163 3836 306 608 785 2401 1697 3836 2465 4020

drink it anew with you in my Father's kingdom." ¶ **30** When they had sung a hymn, they
πίνω αὐτὸ καινὸν μεθ᾽ ὑμῶν ἐν μου ⌜τοῦ πατρός⌟ ⌜τῇ βασιλείᾳ⌟ Καὶ → → → ὑμνήσαντες ← ← →
v.pas.1s r.asn.3 a.asn p.g r.gp.2 p.d r.gs.1 d.gsm n.gsm d.dsf n.dsf cj pt.aa.npm
4403 899 2785 3552 7007 1877 1609 3836 4252 3836 993 2779 5630

went out to the Mount of Olives.
ἐξῆλθον ← εἰς τὸ ὄρος → ⌜τῶν ἐλαιῶν⌟
v.aai.3p p.a d.asn n.asn d.gpf n.gpf
2002 1650 3836 4001 3836 1777

Jesus Predicts Peter's Denial

26:31 Then Jesus told them, "This very night you will all fall away on account of me,
Τότε ⌜ὁ Ἰησοῦς⌟ λέγει αὐτοῖς ἐν ταύτῃ τῇ νυκτὶ ὑμεῖς ↗ πάντες σκανδαλισθήσεσθε ← ἐν ← ← ἐμοὶ
adv d.nsm n.nsm v.pai.3s r.dpm.3 p.d r.dsf d.dsf n.dsf r.np.2 a.npm v.fpi.2p p.d r.ds.1
5538 3836 2652 3306 899 1877 4047 3836 3816 7007 4997 4246 4997 1877 1609

for it is written: "'I will strike the shepherd, and the sheep of the flock will be scattered.' But after I
γάρ → γέγραπται → → πατάξω τὸν ποιμένα καὶ τὰ πρόβατα → τῆς ποίμνης → διασκορπισθήσονται δὲ μετὰ με
cj v.rpi.3s v.fai.1s d.asm n.asm cj d.npn n.npn d.gsf n.gsf v.fpi.3p cj p.a r.as.1
1142 1211 4250 3836 4478 2779 3836 4585 3836 4479 1399 1254 3552 1609

have risen, I will go ahead of you into Galilee." ¶ **33** Peter replied, "Even
→ ⌜τὸ ἐγερθῆναι⌟ → προάξω ← ← ὑμᾶς εἰς ⌜τὴν Γαλιλαίαν⌟ δὲ ὁ Πέτρος⌟ ἀποκριθεὶς εἶπεν αὐτῷ
d.asn f.ap v.fai.1s r.ap.2 p.a d.asf n.asf cj d.nsm n.nsm pt.ap.nsm v.aai.3s r.dsm.3
3836 1586 4575 7007 1650 3836 1133 1254 3836 4377 646 3306 899

if all fall away on account of you, I never will." ¶ **34** "I tell you the truth,"
εἰ πάντες σκανδαλισθήσονται ← ἐν ← σοί ἐγὼ οὐδέποτε σκανδαλισθήσομαι → λέγω σοι ἀμὴν
cj a.npm v.fpi.3p p.d r.ds.2 r.ns.1 adv v.fpi.1s v.pai.1s r.ds.2 pl
1623 4246 4997 1877 5148 1609 4030 4997 3306 5148 297

Jesus answered, "this very night, before the rooster crows, you will disown me three times." ¶
⌜ὁ Ἰησοῦς⌟ ἔφη αὐτῷ ὅτι ἐν ταύτῃ τῇ νυκτὶ πρὶν ἀλέκτορα φωνῆσαι → → ἀπαρνήσῃ με τρὶς
d.nsm n.nsm v.iai.3s r.dsm.3 cj p.d r.dsf d.dsf n.dsf cj n.asm f.aa v.fmi.2s r.as.1 adv
3836 2652 5774 899 4022 1877 4047 3836 3816 4570 232 5888 565 1609 5565

35 But Peter declared, "Even if I have to die with you, I will never disown you." And all
⌜ὁ Πέτρος⌟ λέγει αὐτῷ κἂν → με δέῃ → ἀποθανεῖν σὺν σοὶ ↗ ↗ ⌜οὐ μή⌟ ἀπαρνήσομαι σε καὶ πάντες
d.nsm n.nsm v.pai.3s r.dsm.3 crasis r.as.1 v.pas.3s f.aa p.d r.ds.2 pl pl v.fmi.1s r.as.2 adv a.npm
3836 4377 3306 899 2829 1609 1256 633 5250 5148 565 565 4024 3590 565 5148 2779 4246

the other disciples said the same.
οἱ μαθηταὶ εἶπαν ὁμοίως
d.npm n.npm v.aai.3p adv
3836 3412 3306 3931

²⁵ ἀποκριθεὶς δὲ Ἰούδας ὁ παραδιδοὺς αὐτὸν εἶπεν, Μήτι ἐγώ εἰμι, ῥαββί; ¶ λέγει αὐτῷ, Σὺ εἶπας. ¶ ²⁶ Ἐσθιόντων δὲ αὐτῶν λαβὼν ὁ Ἰησοῦς ἄρτον καὶ εὐλογήσας ἔκλασεν καὶ δοὺς τοῖς μαθηταῖς εἶπεν, Λάβετε φάγετε, τοῦτό ἐστιν τὸ σῶμά μου. ¶ ²⁷ καὶ λαβὼν ποτήριον καὶ εὐχαριστήσας ἔδωκεν αὐτοῖς λέγων, Πίετε ἐξ αὐτοῦ πάντες, ²⁸ τοῦτο γάρ ἐστιν τὸ αἷμά μου τῆς διαθήκης τὸ περὶ πολλῶν ἐκχυννόμενον εἰς ἄφεσιν ἁμαρτιῶν. ²⁹ λέγω δὲ ὑμῖν, οὐ μὴ πίω ἀπ᾽ ἄρτι ἐκ τούτου τοῦ γενήματος τῆς ἀμπέλου ἕως τῆς ἡμέρας ἐκείνης ὅταν αὐτὸ πίνω μεθ᾽ ὑμῶν καινὸν ἐν τῇ βασιλείᾳ τοῦ πατρός μου. ¶ ³⁰ Καὶ ὑμνήσαντες ἐξῆλθον εἰς τὸ Ὄρος τῶν Ἐλαιῶν.

²⁶:³¹ Τότε λέγει αὐτοῖς ὁ Ἰησοῦς, Πάντες ὑμεῖς σκανδαλισθήσεσθε ἐν ἐμοὶ ἐν τῇ νυκτὶ ταύτῃ, γέγραπται γάρ, Πατάξω τὸν ποιμένα, καὶ διασκορπισθήσονται τὰ πρόβατα τῆς ποίμνης. ³² μετὰ δὲ τὸ ἐγερθῆναί με προάξω ὑμᾶς εἰς τὴν Γαλιλαίαν. ¶ ³³ ἀποκριθεὶς δὲ ὁ Πέτρος εἶπεν αὐτῷ, Εἰ πάντες σκανδαλισθήσονται ἐν σοί, ἐγὼ οὐδέποτε σκανδαλισθήσομαι. ¶ ³⁴ ἔφη αὐτῷ ὁ Ἰησοῦς, Ἀμὴν λέγω σοι ὅτι ἐν ταύτῃ τῇ νυκτὶ πρὶν ἀλέκτορα φωνῆσαι τρὶς ἀπαρνήσῃ με. ³⁵ λέγει αὐτῷ ὁ Πέτρος, Κἂν δέῃ με σὺν σοὶ ἀποθανεῖν, οὐ μή σε ἀπαρνήσομαι. ὁμοίως καὶ πάντες οἱ μαθηταὶ εἶπαν.

Gethsemane

26:36 Then Jesus went with his disciples to a place called Gethsemane, and he said to them,
Τότε ὁ Ἰησοῦς ἔρχεται μετ' αὐτῶν εἰς χωρίον λεγόμενον Γεθσημανὶ καὶ → λέγει → τοῖς μαθηταῖς,
adv d.nsm n.nsm v.pmi.3s p.g r.gpm.3 p.a n.asn pt.pp.asn n.asn cj v.pai.3s d.dpm n.dpm
5538 3836 2652 2262 3552 899 1650 6005 3306 1149 2779 3306 3836 3412

"Sit here while I go over there and pray." **37** He took Peter and the two sons of
καθίσατε αὐτοῦ ἕως οὗ → ἀπελθὼν → ἐκεῖ προσεύξωμαι καὶ → παραλαβὼν τὸν Πέτρον καὶ τοὺς δύο υἱοὺς →
v.aam.2p adv r.gsm → pt.aa.nsm adv v.ams.1s cj pt.aa.nsm d.asm n.asm cj d.apm a.apm n.apm
2767 7008 2401 4005 599 1695 4667 2779 4161 3836 4377 2779 3836 1545 5626

Zebedee along with him, and he began to be sorrowful and troubled. **38** Then he said to them, "My soul is
Ζεβεδαίου ← → ἤρξατο → λυπεῖσθαι καὶ ἀδημονεῖν τότε → λέγει αὐτοῖς μου ἡ ψυχή ἐστιν
n.gsm v.ami.3s f.pp cj f.pa adv v.pai.3s r.dpm.3 r.gs.1 d.nsf n.nsf v.pai.3s
2411 4161 806 3382 2779 86 5538 3306 899 1609 3836 6034 1639

overwhelmed with sorrow to the point of death. Stay here and keep watch with me." ¶ **39** Going a
→ → περίλυπος ἕως ← ← θανάτου μείνατε ὧδε καὶ → γρηγορεῖτε μετ' ἐμοῦ καὶ προελθὼν
a.nsf p.g n.gsm v.aam.2p adv cj v.pam.2p p.g r.gs.1 cj pt.aa.nsm
4337 2401 2505 3531 6045 2779 1213 3552 1609 2779 4601

little farther, he fell with his face to the ground and prayed, "My Father, if it is possible,
μικρὸν ← → ἔπεσεν ἐπὶ αὐτοῦ πρόσωπον προσευχόμενος λέγων καὶ μου πάτερ εἰ → ἐστιν δυνατόν
a.asn v.aai.3s p.a r.gsm.3 n.asn pt.pm.nsm pt.pa.nsm cj r.gs.1 n.vsm cj v.pai.3s a.nsn
3625 4406 2093 899 4725 4667 3306 2779 1609 4252 1623 1639 1543

may this cup be taken from me. Yet not as I will, but as you will." ¶ **40** Then he returned to
→ τοῦτο τὸ ποτήριον → παρελθάτω ἀπ' ἐμοῦ πλὴν οὐχ ὡς ἐγὼ θέλω ἀλλ' ὡς σύ καὶ → ἔρχεται πρὸς
r.nsn d.nsn n.nsn v.aam.3s p.g r.gs.1 cj pl cj r.ns.1 v.pai.1s cj cj r.ns.2 cj v.pmi.3s p.a
4216 4047 3836 4539 4216 608 1609 4440 4024 6055 1609 2527 247 6055 5148 2779 2262 4639

his disciples and found them sleeping. "Could you men not keep watch with me for one hour?"
τοὺς μαθητὰς καὶ εὑρίσκει αὐτοὺς καθεύδοντας οὕτως καὶ ἰσχύσατε ← οὐκ γρηγορῆσαι μετ' ἐμοῦ → μίαν ὥραν
d.apm n.apm cj v.pai.3s r.apm.3 pt.pa.apm adv cj v.aai.2p pl f.aa p.g r.gs.1 a.asf n.asf
3836 3412 2779 2351 899 2761 4048 2779 2710 4024 1213 3552 1609 1651 6052

he asked Peter. **41** "Watch and pray so that you will not fall into temptation. The spirit is willing,
→ λέγει τῷ Πέτρῳ γρηγορεῖτε καὶ προσεύχεσθε ἵνα ← → μὴ εἰσέλθητε εἰς πειρασμόν μὲν τὸ πνεῦμα πρόθυμον
v.pai.3s d.dsm n.dsm v.pam.2p cj v.pmm.2p cj pl v.aas.2p p.a n.asm pl d.nsn n.nsn a.nsn
3306 3836 4377 1213 2779 4667 2671 1656 1656 3590 1656 1650 4280 3525 3836 4460 4609

but the body is weak." ¶ **42** He went away a second time and prayed, "My Father, if it is
δὲ ἡ σὰρξ ἀσθενής πάλιν → ἀπελθὼν ἐκ δευτέρου προσηύξατο λέγων μου πάτερ εἰ → →
cj d.nsf n.nsf a.nsf adv pt.aa.nsm p.g a.gsn v.ami.3s pt.pa.nsm r.gs.1 n.vsm cj
1254 3836 4922 822 4099 599 1666 1311 4667 3306 1609 4252 1623 1538 1538

not possible for this cup to be taken away unless I drink it, may your will be done." ¶ **43**
οὐ δύναται τοῦτο → παρελθεῖν ← ἐὰν μὴ → πίω ← σου τὸ θέλημα → γενηθήτω καὶ
pl v.ppi.3s r.asn f.aa cj pl v.aas.1s r.asn.3 r.gs.2 d.nsn n.nsn v.aps.3s cj
4024 1538 4047 4216 1569 3590 4403 899 1181 5148 3836 2525 1181 2779

When he came back, he again found them sleeping, because their eyes were heavy. **44** So he left
→ → ἐλθὼν → πάλιν εὗρεν αὐτοὺς καθεύδοντας γὰρ αὐτῶν οἱ ὀφθαλμοὶ ἦσαν βεβαρημένοι καὶ → ἀφεὶς
pt.aa.nsm adv v.aai.3s r.apm.3 pt.pa.apm cj r.gpm.3 d.npm n.npm v.iai.3p pt.rp.npm cj pt.aa.nsm
2262 4099 2351 899 2761 1142 899 3836 4057 1639 976 2779 918

them and went away once more and prayed the third time, saying the same thing. ¶ **45** Then he
αὐτοὺς ἀπελθὼν ← πάλιν προσηύξατο ἐκ τρίτου εἰπὼν τὸν αὐτὸν λόγον πάλιν τότε →
r.apm.3 pt.aa.nsm adv v.ami.3s p.g a.gsn pt.aa.nsm d.asm r.asm n.asm adv adv
899 599 4099 4667 1666 5569 3306 3836 899 3364 4099 5538

returned to the disciples and said to them, "Are you still sleeping and resting? Look, the hour is near,
ἔρχεται πρὸς τοὺς μαθητὰς καὶ λέγει αὐτοῖς τὸ λοιπὸν καθεύδετε καὶ ἀναπαύεσθε ἰδοὺ ἡ ὥρα → ἤγγικεν
v.pmi.3s p.a d.apm n.apm cj v.pai.3s r.dpm.3 d.asn adv v.pai.2p cj v.pmm.2p j d.nsf n.nsf v.rai.3s
2262 4639 3836 3412 2779 3306 899 2761 3370 2761 2779 399 2627 3836 6052 1581

and the Son of Man is betrayed into the hands of sinners. **46** Rise, let us go! Here comes my
καὶ ὁ υἱὸς τοῦ ἀνθρώπου → παραδίδοται εἰς χεῖρας ἁμαρτωλῶν ἐγείρεσθε → ἄγωμεν ἰδοὺ → ἤγγικεν με
cj d.nsm n.nsm d.gsm n.gsm v.ppi.3s p.a n.apf a.gpm v.ppm.2p v.pas.1p j v.rai.3s r.as.1
2779 3836 5626 3836 476 4140 1650 5931 283 1586 72 2627 1581 1609

26:36 Τότε ἔρχεται μετ' αὐτῶν ὁ Ἰησοῦς εἰς χωρίον λεγόμενον Γεθσημανὶ καὶ λέγει τοῖς μαθηταῖς, Καθίσατε αὐτοῦ ἕως [οὗ] ἀπελθὼν ἐκεῖ προσεύξωμαι. 37 καὶ παραλαβὼν τὸν Πέτρον καὶ τοὺς δύο υἱοὺς Ζεβεδαίου ἤρξατο λυπεῖσθαι καὶ ἀδημονεῖν. 38 τότε λέγει αὐτοῖς, Περίλυπός ἐστιν ἡ ψυχή μου ἕως θανάτου· μείνατε ὧδε καὶ γρηγορεῖτε μετ' ἐμοῦ. ¶ 39 καὶ προελθὼν μικρὸν ἔπεσεν ἐπὶ πρόσωπον αὐτοῦ προσευχόμενος καὶ λέγων, Πάτερ μου, εἰ δυνατόν ἐστιν, παρελθάτω ἀπ' ἐμοῦ τὸ ποτήριον τοῦτο· πλὴν οὐχ ὡς ἐγὼ θέλω ἀλλ' ὡς σύ. ¶ 40 καὶ ἔρχεται πρὸς τοὺς μαθητὰς καὶ εὑρίσκει αὐτοὺς καθεύδοντας, καὶ λέγει τῷ Πέτρῳ, Οὕτως οὐκ ἰσχύσατε μίαν ὥραν γρηγορῆσαι μετ' ἐμοῦ; 41 γρηγορεῖτε καὶ προσεύχεσθε, ἵνα μὴ εἰσέλθητε εἰς πειρασμόν· τὸ μὲν πνεῦμα πρόθυμον ἡ δὲ σὰρξ ἀσθενής. ¶ 42 πάλιν ἐκ δευτέρου ἀπελθὼν προσηύξατο λέγων, Πάτερ μου, εἰ οὐ δύναται τοῦτο παρελθεῖν ἐὰν μὴ αὐτὸ πίω, γενηθήτω τὸ θέλημά σου. ¶ 43 καὶ ἐλθὼν πάλιν εὗρεν αὐτοὺς καθεύδοντας, ἦσαν γὰρ αὐτῶν οἱ ὀφθαλμοὶ βεβαρημένοι. 44 καὶ ἀφεὶς αὐτοὺς πάλιν ἀπελθὼν προσηύξατο ἐκ τρίτου τὸν αὐτὸν λόγον εἰπὼν πάλιν. ¶ 45 τότε ἔρχεται πρὸς τοὺς μαθητὰς καὶ λέγει αὐτοῖς, Καθεύδετε [τὸ] λοιπὸν καὶ ἀναπαύεσθε· ἰδοὺ ἤγγικεν ἡ ὥρα καὶ ὁ υἱὸς τοῦ ἀνθρώπου παραδίδοται εἰς χεῖρας ἁμαρτωλῶν. 46 ἐγείρεσθε ἄγωμεν· ἰδοὺ ἤγγικεν ὁ παραδιδούς με.

betrayer!"
ὁ   παραδιδούς⌋
d.nsm pt.pa.nsm
3836   4140

Jesus Arrested

26:47
While	he	was	still	speaking,		Judas,	one	of the	Twelve,	arrived.		With	him	was	a	large	crowd
Καὶ	↱	αὐτοῦ	↱	ἔτι	λαλοῦντος	ἰδοὺ	Ἰούδας	εἷς	→	τῶν δώδεκα	ἦλθεν	καὶ	μετ᾽	αὐτοῦ		πολὺς	ὄχλος
cj		r.gsm.3		adv	pt.pa.gsm	j	n.nsm	a.nsm		d.gpm a.gpm	v.aai.3s	cj	p.g	r.gsm.3		a.nsm	n.nsm
2779	3281	899	3281	2285	3281	2627	2683	1651		3836 1557	2262	2779	3552	899		4498	4063

armed with	swords	and	clubs,	sent	from	the	chief priests	and	the	elders		of the	people.	[48]	Now	the	betrayer
μετὰ	μαχαιρῶν	καὶ	ξύλων		ἀπὸ	τῶν	ἀρχιερέων	καὶ		πρεσβυτέρων	→	τοῦ	λαοῦ		δὲ	ὁ	παραδιδοὺς
p.g	n.gpf	cj	n.gpn		p.g	d.gpm	n.gpm	cj		a.gpm		d.gsm	n.gsm		cj	d.nsm	pt.pa.nsm
3552	3479	2779	3833		608	3836	797	2779		4565		3836	3295		1254	3836	4140

	had arranged	a	signal	with them:		"The	one		I	kiss	is		the man;	arrest	him."	[49]		Going	at
αὐτὸν	→	ἔδωκεν	σημεῖον	→	αὐτοῖς λέγων		Ὃν	ἂν	→	φιλήσω	ἐστιν		αὐτός	κρατήσατε	αὐτόν		καὶ	προσελθὼν	→
r.asm.3		v.aai.3s	n.asn		r.dpm.3 pt.pa.nsm		r.asm	pl		v.aas.1s	v.pai.3s		r.nsm	v.aam.2p	r.asm.3		cj	pt.aa.nsm	
899		1443	4956		899 3306		4005	323		5797	1639		899	3195	899		2779	4665	

once	to	Jesus,		Judas said,	"Greetings,	Rabbi!"	and	kissed	him.	¶	[50]		Jesus		replied,
εὐθέως	↰	⌊τῷ Ἰησοῦ⌋		εἶπεν χαῖρε		ῥαββί	καὶ	κατεφίλησεν	αὐτόν		δὲ	ὁ	Ἰησοῦς	εἶπεν	αὐτῷ
adv		d.dsm n.dsm		v.aai.3s v.pam.2s		n.vsm	cj	v.aai.3s	r.asm.3		cj	d.nsm	n.nsm	v.aai.3s	r.dsm.3
2311	4665	3836 2652		3306 5897		4806	2779	2968	899		1254	3836	2652	3306	899

"Friend,	do		what	you came for."	¶		Then	the men	stepped	forward,	seized			Jesus
ἑταῖρε	ἐφ᾽	ὃ	→	πάρει			τότε		προσελθόντες	←	ἐπέβαλον	τὰς χεῖρας	ἐπὶ	⌊τὸν Ἰησοῦν⌋
n.vsm	p.a	r.asn		v.pai.2s			adv		pt.aa.npm		v.aai.3p	d.apf n.apf	p.a	d.asm n.asm
2279	2093	4005	4205				5538		4665		2095	3836 5931	2093	3836 2652

and	arrested	him.	[51]	*With that,*	one of		Jesus'	companions	reached	for his	sword,	drew	it			out	and
καὶ	ἐκράτησαν	αὐτόν		Καὶ	ἰδοὺ	εἷς	↱	⌊τῶν μετὰ⌋	Ἰησοῦ	ἐκτείνας	←	τὴν χεῖρα	ἀπέσπασεν	⌊τὴν μάχαιραν⌋	αὐτοῦ	↰	καὶ
cj	v.aai.3p	r.asm.3		cj	j	a.nsm		d.gpm p.g	n.gsm	pt.aa.nsm		d.asf n.asf	v.aai.3s	d.asf n.asf	r.gsm.3		cj
2779	3195	899		2779	2627	1651		3836 3552	2652	1753		3836 5931	685	3836 3479	899		2779

struck	the	servant	of the	high priest,	cutting off	his		ear.	¶	[52]	"Put		your	sword		back	in
πατάξας	τὸν	δοῦλον	→	τοῦ	ἀρχιερέως	ἀφεῖλεν	←	αὐτοῦ	⌊τὸ ὠτίον⌋			ἀπόστρεψον	σου	⌊τὴν μάχαιραν⌋			εἰς
pt.aa.nsm	d.asm	n.asm		d.gsm	n.gsm	v.aai.3s		r.gsm.3	d.asn n.asn			v.aam.2s	r.gs.?	d.asf n.asf			p.a
4250	3836	1529		3836	797	904		899	3836 6065			695	5148	3836 3479		695	1650

its	place,"		Jesus		said to him,	"for	all		who	draw	the	sword		will die		by the	sword.	[53]
αὐτῆς	⌊τὸν τόπον⌋	τότε	ὁ	Ἰησοῦς	λέγει	αὐτῷ	γὰρ	πάντες	οἱ	λαβόντες		μάχαιραν	→	ἀπολοῦνται	ἐν		μαχαίρῃ	ἢ
r.gsf.3	d.asm n.asm	adv	d.nsm	n.nsm	v.pai.3s	r.dsm.3	cj	a.npm	d.npm	pt.aa.npm		n.asf		v.fmi.3p	p.d		n.dsf	cj
899	3836 5536	5538	3836	2652	3306	899	1142	4246	3836	3284		3479		660	1877		3479	2445

Do	you think		I	cannot		call		on my	Father,		and	he	will at		once	put		at my	disposal	more
→	→	δοκεῖς	ὅτι	→	οὐ	δύναμαι	παρακαλέσαι	←	μου	⌊τὸν πατέρα⌋	καὶ	↱	↱		ἄρτι	παραστήσει	→	μοι		πλείω
		v.pai.2s	cj		pl	v.ppi.1s	f.aa		r.gs.1	d.asm n.asm	cj				adv	v.fai.3s		r.ds.1		adv.c
1506		4022	4024	1538			4151		1609	3836 4252	2779	4225	4225		785	4225		1609		4498

than	twelve	legions	of angels?	[54]	But	how	then	would	the	Scriptures	be	fulfilled		that	say	it must	happen	in	this
←	δώδεκα	λεγιῶνας	→ ἀγγέλων		πῶς	οὖν			αἱ	γραφαὶ	→	πληρωθῶσιν	ὅτι		→	δεῖ	γενέσθαι		
	a.apf	n.apf	n.gpm		cj	cj			d.npf	n.npf		v.aps.3p	cj			v.pai.3s	f.am		
1557	3305	34			4802	4036			3836	1210		4444	4022			1256	1181		

way?"	¶	[55]	At that	time		Jesus		said	to the	crowd,	"Am I	leading	a	rebellion,		that	you have	come
οὕτως			Ἐν ἐκείνῃ	⌊τῇ ὥρᾳ⌋	ὁ	Ἰησοῦς		εἶπεν	→	τοῖς ὄχλοις		⌊ὡς ἐπὶ λῃστὴν⌋			→	→		ἐξήλθατε
adv			p.d r.dsf	d.dsf n.dsf	d.nsm	n.nsm		v.aai.3s		d.dpm n.dpm		pl p.a n.asm						v.aai.2p
4048			1877 1697	3836 6052	3836	2652		3306		3836 4063		6055 2093 3334						2002

out	with	swords	and	clubs	to	capture	me?	Every	day		I	sat		in	the	temple courts	teaching,	and	you did
←	μετὰ	μαχαιρῶν	καὶ	ξύλων		συλλαβεῖν	με	καθ᾽	ἡμέραν	→	ἐκαθεζόμην		ἐν	τῷ	ἱερῷ		διδάσκων	καὶ	↱
	p.g	n.gpf	cj	n.gpn		f.aa	r.as.1	p.a	n.asf		v.imi.1s		p.d	d.dsn	n.dsn		pt.pa.nsm	cj	
3552	3479	2779	3833		5197	1609		2848	2465		2757		1877	3836	2639		1438	2779	3195 3195

26:47 Καὶ ἔτι αὐτοῦ λαλοῦντος ἰδοὺ Ἰούδας εἷς τῶν δώδεκα ἦλθεν καὶ μετ᾽ αὐτοῦ ὄχλος πολὺς μετὰ μαχαιρῶν καὶ ξύλων ἀπὸ τῶν ἀρχιερέων καὶ πρεσβυτέρων τοῦ λαοῦ. [48] ὁ δὲ παραδιδοὺς αὐτὸν ἔδωκεν αὐτοῖς σημεῖον λέγων, Ὃν ἂν φιλήσω αὐτός ἐστιν, κρατήσατε αὐτόν. [49] καὶ εὐθέως προσελθὼν τῷ Ἰησοῦ εἶπεν, Χαῖρε, ῥαββί, καὶ κατεφίλησεν αὐτόν. ¶ [50] ὁ δὲ Ἰησοῦς εἶπεν αὐτῷ, Ἑταῖρε, ἐφ᾽ ὃ πάρει. ¶ τότε προσελθόντες ἐπέβαλον τὰς χεῖρας ἐπὶ τὸν Ἰησοῦν καὶ ἐκράτησαν αὐτόν. [51] καὶ ἰδοὺ εἷς τῶν μετὰ Ἰησοῦ ἐκτείνας τὴν χεῖρα ἀπέσπασεν τὴν μάχαιραν αὐτοῦ καὶ πατάξας τὸν δοῦλον τοῦ ἀρχιερέως ἀφεῖλεν αὐτοῦ τὸ ὠτίον. ¶ [52] τότε λέγει αὐτῷ ὁ Ἰησοῦς, Ἀπόστρεψον τὴν μάχαιράν σου εἰς τὸν τόπον αὐτῆς· πάντες γὰρ οἱ λαβόντες μάχαιραν ἐν μαχαίρῃ ἀπολοῦνται. [53] ἢ δοκεῖς ὅτι οὐ δύναμαι παρακαλέσαι τὸν πατέρα μου, καὶ παραστήσει μοι ἄρτι πλείω δώδεκα λεγιῶνας ἀγγέλων; [54] πῶς οὖν πληρωθῶσιν αἱ γραφαὶ ὅτι οὕτως δεῖ γενέσθαι; ¶ [55] Ἐν ἐκείνῃ τῇ ὥρᾳ εἶπεν ὁ Ἰησοῦς τοῖς ὄχλοις, Ὡς ἐπὶ λῃστὴν ἐξήλθατε μετὰ μαχαιρῶν καὶ ξύλων συλλαβεῖν με; καθ᾽ ἡμέραν ἐν τῷ ἱερῷ ἐκαθεζόμην διδάσκων καὶ

not arrest me. **56** But this has all taken place that the writings of the prophets might be fulfilled." Then all
οὐκ ἐκρατήσατε με δὲ τοῦτο → ὅλον γέγονεν ← ἵνα αἱ γραφαὶ → τῶν προφητῶν → → πληρωθῶσιν Τότε πάντες
pl v.aai.2p r.as.1 cj r.nsn a.nsn v.rai.3s cj d.npf n.npf d.gpm n.gpm v.aps.3p adv a.npm
4024 3195 1609 1254 4047 1181 3910 1181 2671 3836 1210 3836 4737 4444 5538 4246

the disciples deserted him and fled.
οἱ μαθηταὶ ἀφέντες αὐτὸν ἔφυγον
d.npm n.npm pt.aa.npm r.asm.3 v.aai.3p
3836 3412 918 899 5771

Before the Sanhedrin

26:57 Those who had arrested Jesus took him to Caiaphas, the high priest, where the teachers
δὲ Οἱ ← → κρατήσαντες τὸν Ἰησοῦν ἀπήγαγον πρὸς Καϊάφαν τὸν → ἀρχιερέα ὅπου οἱ γραμματεῖς
cj d.npm pt.aa.npm d.asm n.asm v.aai.3p p.a n.asm d.asm n.asm cj d.npm n.npm
1254 3836 3195 3836 2652 552 4639 2780 3836 797 3963 3836 1208

of the law and the elders had assembled. **58** But Peter followed him at a distance, right up to the courtyard
← ← ← καὶ οἱ πρεσβύτεροι συνήχθησαν δὲ ὁ Πέτρος ἠκολούθει αὐτῷ ἀπὸ μακρόθεν → ἕως τῆς αὐλῆς
cj d.npm a.npm v.api.3p cj d.nsm n.nsm v.iai.3s r.dsm.3 p.g adv p.g d.gsf n.gsf
2779 3836 4565 5251 1254 3836 4377 199 899 608 3427 2401 3836 885

of the high priest. He entered and sat down with the guards to see the outcome. ¶ **59** The
→ τοῦ ἀρχιερέως καὶ → εἰσελθὼν ἔσω ἐκάθητο μετὰ τῶν ὑπηρετῶν → ἰδεῖν τὸ τέλος δὲ Οἱ
d.gsm n.gsm cj pt.aa.nsm adv v.imi.3s p.g d.gpm n.gpm f.aa d.asn n.asn cj d.npm
3836 797 2779 1656 2276 2764 3552 3836 5677 1625 3836 5465 1254 3836

chief priests and the whole Sanhedrin were looking for false evidence against Jesus so that they could
ἀρχιερεῖς καὶ τὸ ὅλον συνέδριον ἐζήτουν ← ψευδομαρτυρίαν κατὰ τοῦ Ἰησοῦ ὅπως ←
n.npm cj d.nsn a.nsn n.nsn v.iai.3p n.asf p.g d.gsm n.gsm cj
797 2779 3836 3910 5284 2426 6019 2848 3836 2652 3968 2506 2506

put him to death. **60** But they did not find any, though many false witnesses came forward. ¶
→ αὐτὸν → θανατώσωσιν καὶ → ← οὐχ εὗρον → πολλῶν → ψευδομαρτύρων προσελθόντων ←
r.asm.3 v.aas.3p cj pl v.aai.3p a.gpm n.gpm pt.aa.gpm
2506 899 2506 2779 2351 2351 4024 2351 4665 4498 6020 4665

Finally two came forward **61** and declared, "This fellow said, 'I am able to destroy the temple of God
δὲ ὕστερον δύο προσελθόντες ← εἶπαν οὗτος ← ἔφη δύναμαι καταλῦσαι τὸν ναὸν → τοῦ θεοῦ
cj adv.c a.npm pt.aa.npm v.aai.3p r.nsm v.iai.3s v.ppi.1s f.aa d.asm n.asm d.gsm n.gsm
1254 5731 1545 4665 3306 4047 5774 1538 2907 3836 3724 3836 2536

and rebuild it in three days.'" ¶ **62** Then the high priest stood up and said to Jesus, "Are you not
καὶ οἰκοδομῆσαι διὰ τριῶν ἡμερῶν καὶ ὁ → ἀρχιερεὺς ἀναστὰς ← εἶπεν αὐτῷ → → οὐδὲν
cj f.aa p.g a.gpf n.gpf cj d.nsm n.nsm pt.aa.nsm v.aai.3s r.dsm.3 a.asn
2779 3868 1328 5552 2465 2779 3836 797 482 3306 899 646 646 4029

going to answer? What is this testimony that these men are bringing against you?" **63** But Jesus remained
→ → ἀποκρίνῃ τί ← οὗτοι καταμαρτυροῦσιν σου δὲ ὁ Ἰησοῦς
v.pmi.2s r.asn r.npm v.pai.3p r.gs.2 cj d.nsm n.nsm
646 5515 4047 2909 5148 1254 3836 2652

silent. ¶ The high priest said to him, "I charge you under oath by the living God: Tell us
ἐσιώπα καὶ ὁ → ἀρχιερεὺς εἶπεν → αὐτῷ ἐξορκίζω σε ← → κατὰ τοῦ ζῶντος τοῦ θεοῦ ἵνα εἴπῃς ἡμῖν
v.iai.3s cj d.nsm n.nsm v.aai.3s r.dsm.3 v.pai.1s r.as.2 p.g d.gsm pt.pa.gsm d.gsm n.gsm cj v.aas.2s r.dp.1
4995 2779 3836 797 3306 899 2019 5148 2019 2019 2848 3836 2409 3836 2536 2671 3306 7005

if you are the Christ, the Son of God." ¶ **64** "Yes, it is as you say," Jesus replied. "But I say to
εἰ σὺ εἶ ὁ χριστὸς ὁ υἱὸς τοῦ θεοῦ σὺ εἶπας ὁ Ἰησοῦς λέγει αὐτῷ πλὴν λέγω →
cj r.ns.2 v.pai.2s d.nsm n.nsm d.nsm n.nsm d.gsm n.gsm r.ns.2 v.aai.2s d.nsm n.nsm v.pai.3s r.dsm.3 cj v.pai.1s
1623 5148 1639 3836 5986 3836 5626 3836 2536 5148 3306 3836 2652 3306 899 4440 3306

all of you: *In the future* you will see the Son of Man sitting at the right hand of the Mighty One
ὑμῖν ἀπ' ἄρτι → ὄψεσθε τὸν υἱὸν τοῦ ἀνθρώπου καθήμενον ἐκ δεξιῶν ← → τῆς δυνάμεως
r.dp.2 p.g adv v.fmi.2p d.asm n.asm d.gsm n.gsm pt.pm.asm p.g a.gpf d.gsf n.gsf
7007 608 785 3972 3836 5626 3836 476 2764 1666 1288 3836 1539

and coming on the clouds of heaven." ¶ **65** Then the high priest tore his clothes and said, "He
καὶ ἐρχόμενον ἐπὶ τῶν νεφελῶν τοῦ οὐρανοῦ τότε ὁ → ἀρχιερεὺς διέρρηξεν αὐτοῦ τὰ ἱμάτια λέγων →
cj pt.pm.asm p.g d.gpf n.gpf d.gsm n.gsm adv d.nsm n.nsm v.aai.3s r.gsm.3 d.apn n.apn pt.pa.nsm
2779 2262 2093 3836 3749 3836 4041 5538 3836 797 1396 899 3836 2668 3306

οὐκ ἐκρατήσατέ με. ⁵⁶ τοῦτο δὲ ὅλον γέγονεν ἵνα πληρωθῶσιν αἱ γραφαὶ τῶν προφητῶν. Τότε οἱ μαθηταὶ πάντες ἀφέντες αὐτὸν ἔφυγον.

²⁶:⁵⁷ Οἱ δὲ κρατήσαντες τὸν Ἰησοῦν ἀπήγαγον πρὸς Καϊάφαν τὸν ἀρχιερέα, ὅπου οἱ γραμματεῖς καὶ οἱ πρεσβύτεροι συνήχθησαν. ⁵⁸ ὁ δὲ Πέτρος ἠκολούθει αὐτῷ ἀπὸ μακρόθεν ἕως τῆς αὐλῆς τοῦ ἀρχιερέως καὶ εἰσελθὼν ἔσω ἐκάθητο μετὰ τῶν ὑπηρετῶν ἰδεῖν τὸ τέλος. ¶ ⁵⁹ οἱ δὲ ἀρχιερεῖς καὶ τὸ συνέδριον ὅλον ἐζήτουν ψευδομαρτυρίαν κατὰ τοῦ Ἰησοῦ ὅπως αὐτὸν θανατώσωσιν, ⁶⁰ καὶ οὐχ εὗρον πολλῶν προσελθόντων ψευδομαρτύρων. ¶ ὕστερον δὲ προσελθόντες δύο ⁶¹ εἶπαν, Οὗτος ἔφη, Δύναμαι καταλῦσαι τὸν ναὸν τοῦ θεοῦ καὶ διὰ τριῶν ἡμερῶν οἰκοδομῆσαι. ¶ ⁶² καὶ ἀναστὰς ὁ ἀρχιερεὺς εἶπεν αὐτῷ, Οὐδὲν ἀποκρίνῃ τί οὗτοί σου καταμαρτυροῦσιν; ⁶³ ὁ δὲ Ἰησοῦς ἐσιώπα. ¶ καὶ ὁ ἀρχιερεὺς εἶπεν αὐτῷ, Ἐξορκίζω σε κατὰ τοῦ θεοῦ τοῦ ζῶντος ἵνα ἡμῖν εἴπῃς εἰ σὺ εἶ ὁ Χριστὸς ὁ υἱὸς τοῦ θεοῦ. ¶ ⁶⁴ λέγει αὐτῷ ὁ Ἰησοῦς, Σὺ εἶπας· πλὴν λέγω ὑμῖν, ἀπ' ἄρτι ὄψεσθε τὸν υἱὸν τοῦ ἀνθρώπου καθήμενον ἐκ δεξιῶν τῆς δυνάμεως καὶ ἐρχόμενον ἐπὶ τῶν νεφελῶν τοῦ οὐρανοῦ. ⁶⁵ τότε ὁ

has spoken blasphemy! Why do we need   any more witnesses? Look, now you have heard   the blasphemy.
→   →   ἐβλασφήμησεν τί →   →   χρείαν ἔχομεν ἔτι ←   μαρτύρων ἴδε νῦν →   ἠκούσατε τὴν βλασφημίαν
                v.aai.3s   r.asn   n.asf v.pai.1p adv   n.gpm   pl   adv   v.aai.2p d.asf n.asf
                1059   5515   5970   2400   2285   3459   2623 3814   201   3836   1060

66 What do you think?”   ¶   “He is   worthy of death,” they answered.   ¶   **67** Then they spit in
τί →   ὑμῖν δοκεῖ   δὲ → ἐστίν ἔνοχος → θανάτου οἱ ἀποκριθέντες εἶπαν   Τότε → ἐνέπτυσαν εἰς
r.nsn   r.dp.2 v.pai.3s   cj   v.pai.3s a.nsm   n.gsm d.npm v.ap.npm v.aai.3p   adv   v.aai.3p   p.a
5515   1506 7007 1506   1254   1639 1944   2505   3836 646   3306   5538   1870   1650

his face   and struck   him with their fists. Others slapped him **68** and said,   “Prophesy to us, Christ.
αὐτοῦ ⸂τὸ πρόσωπον⸃ καὶ ἐκολάφισαν αὐτόν ← →   δὲ οἱ ἐράπισαν   λέγοντες προφήτευσον → ἡμῖν χριστέ
r.gsm.3 d.asn n.asn   cj   v.aai.3p   r.asm.3   cj d.npm v.aai.3p   pt.pa.npm v.aam.2s   r.dp.1 n.vsm
899   3836 4125   2779   3139   899   3139 3139 1254 3836 4824   3306   4736   7005 5986

Who   hit   you?”
τίς ἐστιν ὁ παίσας σε
r.nsm v.pai.3s d.nsm pt.aa.nsm r.as.2
5515 1639   3836 4091   5148

Peter Disowns Jesus

26:69 Now Peter   was sitting out in the courtyard, and a servant girl came   to him. “You also were
δὲ Ὁ Πέτρος⸃ → ἐκάθητο ἔξω ἐν τῇ αὐλῇ   καὶ μία παιδίσκη ← προσῆλθεν αὐτῷ σὺ καὶ ἦσθα
cj d.nsm n.nsm   v.imi.3s adv p.d d.dsf n.dsf   cj a.nsf n.nsf   v.aai.3s r.dsm.3 r.ns.2 adv v.iai.2s
1254 3836 4377   2764   2032 1877 3836 885   2779 1651 4087   4665   899 5148 2779 1639

with Jesus of Galilee,”   she said.   ¶   **70** But he denied it before   them all.   “I don’t know what you’re
μετὰ Ἰησοῦ → ⸂τοῦ Γαλιλαίου⸃ → λέγουσα   δὲ ὁ ἠρνήσατο ἔμπροσθεν →   πάντων ⸂οὐκ οἶδα τί →
p.g n.gsm   d.gsm a.gsm   pt.pa.nsf   cj d.nsm v.ami.3s p.g   a.gpm   pl v.rai.1s r.asn
3552 2652   3836 1134   3306   1254 3836 766   1869   4246   3857 4024 3857 5515

talking about,” he said.   ¶   **71** Then he went   out to the gateway, where another girl saw him and said to
λέγεις   → λέγων   δὲ → ἐξελθόντα ← εἰς τὸν πυλῶνα   ἄλλη ← εἶδεν αὐτὸν καὶ λέγει →
v.pai.2s   pt.pa.nsm   cj   pt.aa.asm   p.a d.asm n.asm   r.nsf   v.aai.3s r.asm.3 cj v.pai.3s
3306   3306   1254   2002   1650 3836 4784   257   1625   899   2779 3306

the people there, “This fellow was with Jesus of Nazareth.”   ¶   **72**   He denied it again, with an oath:
τοῖς ← ἐκεῖ οὗτος ἦν μετὰ Ἰησοῦ → ⸂τοῦ Ναζωραίου⸃   καὶ → ἠρνήσατο πάλιν μετὰ ὅρκου ὅτι
d.dpm   adv r.nsm   v.iai.3s p.g n.gsm   d.gsm n.gsm   cj   v.ami.3s adv   p.g n.gsm cj
3836   1695 4047   1639 3552 2652   3836 3717   2779   766   4099 3552 3992 4022

“I don’t know the man!”   ¶ **73**   After a little while, those standing there went   up to Peter   and
⸂οὐκ οἶδα τὸν ἄνθρωπον δὲ μετὰ μικρὸν ← οἱ ἑστῶτες   προσελθόντες ← ← ⸂τῷ Πέτρῳ⸃
3857 4024 3857 3836 476   cj p.g   a.asn   d.npm pt.ra.npm   pt.aa.npm   d.dsm n.dsm
                           1254 3552 3625   3836 2705   4665   3836 4377

said, “Surely you   are one of them, for   your accent gives you away.”   ¶ **74** Then he began to call
εἶπον ἀληθῶς σὺ καὶ εἶ ἐξ αὐτῶν γὰρ καὶ σου ⸂ἡ λαλιά⸃ ποιεῖ σε δῆλον   τότε → ἤρξατο
v.aai.3p adv   r.ns.2 adv v.pai.2s p.g r.gpm.3 cj cj r.gs.2 d.nsf n.nsf v.pai.3s r.as.2 a.asm   adv   v.ami.3s
3306 242   5148 2779 1639 1666 899   1142 2779 5148 3836 3282 4472 5148 1316   5538   806

down curses   on himself and he swore to them,   “I don’t know the man!”   ¶   Immediately a
→   καταθεματίζειν   καὶ → ὀμνύειν   ὅτι → οὐκ οἶδα τὸν ἄνθρωπον   καὶ εὐθέως
    f.pa   cj   f.pa   cj pl v.rai.1s d.asm n.asm   cj adv
    2874   2779   3923   4022 3857 4024 3857 3836 476   2779 2311

rooster crowed. **75** Then Peter   remembered the word Jesus had spoken: “Before the rooster crows, you
ἀλέκτωρ ἐφώνησεν καὶ ὁ Πέτρος⸃ ἐμνήσθη   τοῦ ῥήματος Ἰησοῦ → εἰρηκότος ὅτι πρὶν   ἀλέκτορα φωνῆσαι →
n.nsm v.aai.3s   cj d.nsm n.nsm v.api.3s   d.gsn n.gsn   n.gsm   pt.ra.gsm cj adv   n.asm   f.aa
232   5888   2779 3836 4377 3630   3836 4839   2652   3306   4022 4570   232   5888

will disown me three times.” And he went outside and wept   bitterly.
→   ἀπαρνήσῃ με τρὶς ←   καὶ → ἐξελθὼν ἔξω ἔκλαυσεν πικρῶς
    v.fmi.2s r.as.1 adv   cj   pt.aa.nsm adv v.aai.3s adv
    565   1609 5565   2779   2002 2032 3081   4396

Judas Hangs Himself

27:1   Early in the morning, all the chief priests and the elders   of the people came to the
δὲ γενομένης Πρωΐας ← ← → πάντες οἱ → ἀρχιερεῖς καὶ οἱ πρεσβύτεροι → τοῦ λαοῦ ἔλαβον ←
cj pt.am.gsf n.gsf   a.npm d.npm   n.npm   cj d.npm a.npm   d.gsm n.gsm v.aai.3p
1254 1181   4746   4246 3836   797   2779 3836 4565   3836 3295 3284

ἀρχιερεὺς διέρρηξεν τὰ ἱμάτια αὐτοῦ λέγων, Ἐβλασφήμησεν· τί ἔτι χρείαν ἔχομεν μαρτύρων; ἴδε νῦν ἠκούσατε τὴν βλασφημίαν·
⁶⁶ τί ὑμῖν δοκεῖ; ¶ οἱ δὲ ἀποκριθέντες εἶπαν, Ἔνοχος θανάτου ἐστίν. ¶ ⁶⁷ Τότε ἐνέπτυσαν εἰς τὸ πρόσωπον αὐτοῦ καὶ
ἐκολάφισαν αὐτόν, οἱ δὲ ἐράπισαν ⁶⁸ λέγοντες, Προφήτευσον ἡμῖν, Χριστέ, τίς ἐστιν ὁ παίσας σε;
²⁶:⁶⁹ Ὁ δὲ Πέτρος ἐκάθητο ἔξω ἐν τῇ αὐλῇ· καὶ προσῆλθεν αὐτῷ μία παιδίσκη λέγουσα, Καὶ σὺ ἦσθα μετὰ Ἰησοῦ τοῦ
Γαλιλαίου. ¶ ⁷⁰ ὁ δὲ ἠρνήσατο ἔμπροσθεν πάντων λέγων, Οὐκ οἶδα τί λέγεις. ¶ ⁷¹ ἐξελθόντα δὲ εἰς τὸν πυλῶνα εἶδεν αὐτὸν
ἄλλη καὶ λέγει τοῖς ἐκεῖ, Οὗτος ἦν μετὰ Ἰησοῦ τοῦ Ναζωραίου. ¶ ⁷² καὶ πάλιν ἠρνήσατο μετὰ ὅρκου ὅτι Οὐκ οἶδα τὸν
ἄνθρωπον. ⁷³ μετὰ μικρὸν δὲ προσελθόντες οἱ ἑστῶτες εἶπον τῷ Πέτρῳ, Ἀληθῶς καὶ σὺ ἐξ αὐτῶν εἶ, καὶ γὰρ ἡ λαλιά σου
δῆλόν σε ποιεῖ. ¶ ⁷⁴ τότε ἤρξατο καταθεματίζειν καὶ ὀμνύειν ὅτι Οὐκ οἶδα τὸν ἄνθρωπον. ¶ καὶ εὐθέως ἀλέκτωρ ἐφώνησεν.
⁷⁵ καὶ ἐμνήσθη ὁ Πέτρος τοῦ ῥήματος Ἰησοῦ εἰρηκότος ὅτι Πρὶν ἀλέκτορα φωνῆσαι τρὶς ἀπαρνήσῃ με· καὶ ἐξελθὼν ἔξω ἔκλαυσεν
πικρῶς.
²⁷:¹ Πρωΐας δὲ γενομένης συμβούλιον ἔλαβον πάντες οἱ ἀρχιερεῖς καὶ οἱ πρεσβύτεροι τοῦ λαοῦ κατὰ τοῦ Ἰησοῦ ὥστε

decision | to | put Jesus to death. | **2** | They bound | him, | led | him away | and | handed | him
συμβούλιον | κατὰ | τοῦ Ἰησοῦ | ὥστε | → | αὐτὸν | θανατῶσαι | καὶ | → | δήσαντες | αὐτὸν | ἀπήγαγον | ← | καὶ | παρέδωκαν
n.asn | p.g | d.gsm n.gsm | cj | | r.asm.3 | f.aa | cj | | pt.aa.npm | r.asm.3 | v.aai.3p | | cj | v.aai.3p
5206 | 2848 | 3836 2652 | 6063 | 2506 | 899 | 2779 | | 1313 | 899 | 552 | | 2779 | 4140

over to Pilate, the governor. | ¶ | **3** When Judas, | who | had betrayed | him, | saw | that Jesus was condemned, | he
→ → Πιλάτῳ τῷ ἡγεμόνι | | Τότε Ἰούδας ὁ | → | παραδιδοὺς | αὐτὸν ἰδὼν | ὅτι | → | κατεκρίθη
| n.dsm d.dsm n.dsm | | adv n.nsm d.nsm | | pt.pa.nsm | r.asm.3 pt.aa.nsm | cj | | v.api.3s
4397 3836 2450 | | 5538 2683 3836 | | 4140 | 899 1625 | 4022 | | 2891

was seized with remorse | and returned | the thirty | silver | coins | to the | chief priests | and the elders. | **4** "I
→ → μεταμεληθεὶς | ἔστρεψεν | τὰ τριάκοντα | ἀργύρια | ← | τοῖς | ἀρχιερεῦσιν | καὶ πρεσβυτέροις | →
pt.ap.nsm | v.aai.3s | d.apn a.apn | n.apn | | d.dpm | n.dpm | cj a.dpm
3564 | 5138 | 3836 5558 | 736 | | 3836 | 797 | 2779 4565

have sinned," he said, "for I have betrayed | innocent | blood." | ¶ | "What | is that to | us?" | they | replied.
→ ἥμαρτον → λέγων → → παραδοὺς | ἀθῷον | αἷμα | | δὲ τί | πρὸς | ἡμᾶς | οἱ | εἶπαν
v.aai.1s pt.pa.nsm pt.aa.nsm | a.asn | n.asn | | cj r.nsn | p.a | r.ap.1 | d.nsm | v.aai.3p
279 3306 4140 | 127 | 135 | | 1254 5515 | 4639 | 7005 | 3836 | 3306

"That's your responsibility." | ¶ | **5** So Judas threw | the money | into | the temple | and left. | Then he went
σὺ ὄψῃ | | καὶ ῥίψας | τὰ ἀργύρια | εἰς | τὸν ναὸν | ἀνεχώρησεν καὶ | → ἀπελθὼν
r.ns.2 v.fmi.2s | | cj pt.aa.nsm | d.apn n.apn | p.a | d.asm n.asm | v.aai.3s cj | pt.aa.nsm
5148 3972 | | 2779 4849 | 3836 736 | 1650 | 3836 3724 | 432 2779 | 599

away and hanged himself. | ¶ | **6** | The | chief priests | picked up | the coins | and said, "It is | against the law
← ἀπήγξατο ← | | δὲ Οἱ | → | ἀρχιερεῖς | λαβόντες ← | τὰ ἀργύρια | εἶπαν → → | οὐκ ἔξεστιν
v.ami.3s | | cj d.npm | | n.npm | pt.aa.npm | d.apn n.apn | v.aai.3p | pl v.pai.3s
551 | | 1254 3836 | | 797 | 3284 | 3836 736 | 3306 1997 | 1997 4024 1997

to put | this | into the treasury, | since it is | blood | money." | **7** So | they | decided | to use the money to
→ βαλεῖν | αὐτὰ εἰς | τὸν κορβανᾶν | ἐπεὶ → ἐστιν | αἵματος | τιμή | δὲ ἐξ | αὐτῶν | συμβούλιον λαβόντες | →
f.aa | r.apn.3 p.a | d.asm n.asm | cj v.pai.3s | n.gsn | n.nsf | cj p.g | r.gpn.3 | n.asn pt.aa.npm
965 | 899 1650 | 3836 3168 | 2075 1639 | 135 | 5507 | 1254 1666 | 899 | 5206 3284

buy | the potter's | field | as a burial place | for foreigners. | **8** That is why it | has been called the
ἠγόρασαν | τὸν τοῦ κεραμέως | ἀγρὸν | εἰς ταφὴν ← | → τοῖς ξένοις | διὸ ← | ὁ ἀγρὸς ἐκεῖνος → → | ἐκλήθη
v.aai.3p | d.asm d.gsm n.gsm | n.asm | p.a n.asf | d.dpm n.dpm | cj | d.nsm n.nsm r.nsm | v.api.3s
60 | 3836 3836 3038 | 69 | 1650 5438 | 3836 3828 | 1475 | 3836 69 1697 | 2813

Field of Blood to this day. | **9** Then what was spoken | by Jeremiah | the prophet | was fulfilled: | "They
ἀγρὸς → αἵματος ἕως τῆς σήμερον | τότε τὸ → ῥηθὲν | διὰ Ἰερεμίου | τοῦ προφήτου | → ἐπληρώθη | λέγοντος καὶ →
n.nsm n.gsn p.g d.gsf | adv d.nsn pt.ap.nsn | p.g n.gsm | d.gsm n.gsm | v.api.3s | pt.pa.gsn cj
69 135 2401 3836 4958 | 5538 3836 3306 | 1328 2635 | 3836 4737 | 4444 | 3306 2779

took | the thirty | silver | coins, the | price | set | on him | by | the people | of Israel, | **10** and they used
ἔλαβον | τὰ τριάκοντα | ἀργύρια | ← τὴν | τιμὴν | τοῦ τετιμημένου | ὃν ἐτιμήσαντο | ἀπὸ | υἱῶν → | Ἰσραήλ | καὶ → ἔδωκαν
v.aai.3p | d.apn a.apn | n.apn | d.asf | n.asf | d.gsm pt.rp.gsm | r.asm v.ami.3p | p.g | n.gpm | n.gsm | cj v.aai.3p
3284 | 3836 5558 | 736 | 3836 | 5507 | 3836 5506 | 4005 5506 | 608 | 5626 | 2702 | 2779 1443

them | to buy the potter's | field, as | the Lord | commanded me."
αὐτὰ | εἰς τὸν τοῦ κεραμέως | ἀγρὸν καθὰ | κύριος | συνέταξεν | μοι
r.apn.3 | p.a d.asm d.gsm n.gsm | n.asm cj | n.nsm | v.aai.3s | r.ds.1
899 | 1650 3836 3836 3038 | 69 2745 | 3261 | 5332 | 1609

Jesus Before Pilate

27:11 Meanwhile Jesus | stood before | the governor, and the governor | asked | him, | "Are you the
δὲ ὁ Ἰησοῦς | ἐστάθη ἔμπροσθεν | τοῦ ἡγεμόνος | καὶ ὁ ἡγεμὼν | ἐπηρώτησεν | αὐτὸν λέγων | εἶ σὺ ὁ
cj d.nsm n.nsm | v.api.3s p.g | d.gsm n.gsm | cj d.nsm n.nsm | v.aai.3s | r.asm.3 pt.pa.nsm | v.pai.2s r.ns.2 d.nsm
1254 3836 2652 | 2705 1869 | 3836 2450 | 2779 3836 2450 | 2089 | 899 3306 | 1639 5148 3836

king | of the Jews?" | ¶ | "Yes, it is as you say," | Jesus | replied. | ¶ | **12** | When he | was
βασιλεὺς | → τῶν Ἰουδαίων | | δὲ | σὺ λέγεις ὁ | Ἰησοῦς | ἔφη | | | καὶ ἐν | αὐτὸν
n.nsm | d.gpm a.gpm | | cj | r.ns.2 v.pai.2s d.nsm | n.nsm | v.iai.3s | | | cj p.d | r.asm.3
995 | 3836 2681 | | 1254 | 5148 3306 3836 | 2652 | 5774 | | | 2779 1877 | 899

accused | by the chief | priests | and the elders, | he gave no | answer. | **13** Then | Pilate | asked him,
τῷ κατηγορεῖσθαι | ὑπὸ τῶν → | ἀρχιερέων | καὶ πρεσβυτέρων → → | οὐδὲν | ἀπεκρίνατο | τότε | ὁ Πιλάτος | λέγει αὐτῷ
d.dsn f.pp | p.g d.gpm | n.gpm | cj a.gpm | a.asn | v.ami.3s | adv | d.nsm n.nsm | v.pai.3s r.dsm.3
3836 2989 | 5679 3836 | 797 | 2779 4565 | 646 646 | 4029 646 | 5538 | 3836 4397 | 3306 899

θανατῶσαι αὐτόν· ² καὶ δήσαντες αὐτὸν ἀπήγαγον καὶ παρέδωκαν Πιλάτῳ τῷ ἡγεμόνι. ¶ ³ Τότε ἰδὼν Ἰούδας ὁ παραδιδοὺς αὐτὸν ὅτι κατεκρίθη, μεταμεληθεὶς ἔστρεψεν τὰ τριάκοντα ἀργύρια τοῖς ἀρχιερεῦσιν καὶ πρεσβυτέροις ⁴ λέγων, Ἥμαρτον παραδοὺς αἷμα ἀθῷον. ¶ οἱ δὲ εἶπαν, Τί πρὸς ἡμᾶς; σὺ ὄψῃ. ¶ ⁵ καὶ ῥίψας τὰ ἀργύρια εἰς τὸν ναὸν ἀνεχώρησεν, καὶ ἀπελθὼν ἀπήγξατο. ¶ ⁶ οἱ δὲ ἀρχιερεῖς λαβόντες τὰ ἀργύρια εἶπαν, Οὐκ ἔξεστιν βαλεῖν αὐτὰ εἰς τὸν κορβανᾶν, ἐπεὶ τιμὴ αἵματός ἐστιν. ⁷ συμβούλιον δὲ λαβόντες ἠγόρασαν ἐξ αὐτῶν τὸν Ἀγρὸν τοῦ Κεραμέως εἰς ταφὴν τοῖς ξένοις. ⁸ διὸ ἐκλήθη ὁ ἀγρὸς ἐκεῖνος Ἀγρὸς Αἵματος ἕως τῆς σήμερον. ⁹ τότε ἐπληρώθη τὸ ῥηθὲν διὰ Ἰερεμίου τοῦ προφήτου λέγοντος, Καὶ ἔλαβον τὰ τριάκοντα ἀργύρια, τὴν τιμὴν τοῦ τετιμημένου ὃν ἐτιμήσαντο ἀπὸ υἱῶν Ἰσραήλ, ¹⁰ καὶ ἔδωκαν αὐτὰ εἰς τὸν ἀγρὸν τοῦ κεραμέως, καθὰ συνέταξέν μοι κύριος.

27:11 Ὁ δὲ Ἰησοῦς ἐστάθη ἔμπροσθεν τοῦ ἡγεμόνος· καὶ ἐπηρώτησεν αὐτὸν ὁ ἡγεμὼν λέγων, Σὺ εἶ ὁ βασιλεὺς τῶν Ἰουδαίων; ¶ ὁ δὲ Ἰησοῦς ἔφη, Σὺ λέγεις. ¶ ¹² καὶ ἐν τῷ κατηγορεῖσθαι αὐτὸν ὑπὸ τῶν ἀρχιερέων καὶ πρεσβυτέρων οὐδὲν ἀπεκρίνατο.

"Don't you hear   the testimony   they are bringing against you?" **14** But Jesus made no reply,   not
οὐκ → ἀκούεις πόσα καταμαρτυροῦσιν ← σου καὶ → οὐκ ἀπεκρίθη αὐτῷ οὐδὲ
pl v.pai.2s r.apn v.pai.3p r.gs.2 cj pl v.api.3s r.dsm.3 adv
4024 201 4531 2909 5148 2779 646 4024 646 899 4028

even to a single charge – to   the great amazement of the governor. ¶ **15** Now it was the governor's custom
← πρὸς ἓν ῥῆμα ὥστε λίαν θαυμάζειν τὸν ἡγεμόνα δὲ → → ὁ ἡγεμὼν εἰώθει
p.a a.asn n.asn cj adv f.pa d.asm n.asm cj d.nsm n.nsm v.lai.3s
4639 1651 4839 6063 3336 2513 3836 2450 1254 1665 1665 3836 2450 1665

at   the Feast to release a prisoner chosen by the crowd. **16**   At that time they had a notorious prisoner,
Κατὰ ἑορτὴν → ἀπολύειν ἕνα δέσμιον ὃν ἤθελον τῷ ὄχλῳ δὲ → τότε εἶχον ἐπίσημον δέσμιον
p.a n.asf f.pa a.asm n.asm r.asm v.iai.3p d.dsm n.dsm cj adv v.iai.3p a.asm n.asm
2848 2038 668 1651 1300 4005 2527 3836 4063 1254 5538 2400 2168 1300

called   Barabbas. **17** So when the crowd had gathered, Pilate   asked them, "Which one do you want
λεγόμενον [Ἰησοῦν] Βαραββᾶν οὖν → αὐτῶν → συνηγμένων ὁ Πιλᾶτος εἶπεν αὐτοῖς τίνα → → θέλετε
pt.pp.asm n.asm n.asm cj r.gpm.3 pt.rp.gpm d.nsm n.nsm v.aai.3s r.dpm.3 r.asm v.pai.2p
3306 2652 972 4036 5251 899 5251 3836 4397 3306 899 5515 2527

me to release to you: Barabbas, or Jesus who is called Christ?" **18** For he knew it was out of
→ → ἀπολύσω ὑμῖν [Ἰησοῦν] ιτὸν Βαραββᾶν ἢ Ἰησοῦν τὸν → λεγόμενον χριστόν γὰρ → ᾔδει ὅτι διὰ ←
v.aas.1s r.dp.2 n.asm d.asm n.asm cj n.asm d.asm pt.pp.asm n.asm cj v.lai.3s cj p.a
668 7007 2652 3836 972 2445 2652 3836 3306 5986 1142 3857 4022 1328

envy that they had handed Jesus over to him. ¶ **19** While Pilate was sitting   on the judge's seat,   his
φθόνον → → παρέδωκαν αὐτόν δὲ αὐτοῦ → Καθημένου ἐπὶ τοῦ βήματος αὐτοῦ
n.asm v.aai.3p r.asm.3 cj r.gsm.3 pt.pm.gsm p.g d.gsn n.gsn r.gsm.3
5784 4140 4140 1254 2764 899 2764 2093 3836 1037 899

wife   sent   him this message: "Don't   have anything to do with that   innocent   man, for I have
ιἡ γυνὴ ἀπέστειλεν πρὸς αὐτὸν λέγουσα μηδὲν σοὶ καὶ ἐκείνῳ ιτῷ δικαίῳ ← γὰρ →
d.nsf n.nsf v.aai.3s p.a r.asm.3 pt.pa.nsf a.nsn r.ds.2 cj r.dsm d.dsm a.dsm cj
3836 1222 690 4639 899 3306 3594 5148 2779 1465 1697 3836 1465 1142

suffered a great deal today in a dream because of him." ¶ **20** But the chief priests   and the elders
ἔπαθον πολλὰ ← σήμερον κατ' ὄναρ δι' ← αὐτόν δὲ Οἱ ἀρχιερεῖς καὶ οἱ πρεσβύτεροι
v.aai.1s a.apn adv p.a n.asn p.a r.asm.3 cj d.npm n.npm cj d.npm a.npm
4248 4498 4958 2848 3941 1328 899 1254 3836 797 2779 3836 4565

persuaded the crowd to ask   for Barabbas   and to have Jesus   executed. ¶ **21** "Which of the two
ἔπεισαν τοὺς ὄχλους ἵνα αἰτήσωνται ← ιτὸν Βαραββᾶν δὲ → → ιτὸν Ἰησοῦν ἀπολέσωσιν τίνα ἀπὸ τῶν δύο
v.aai.3p d.apm n.apm cj v.ams.3p d.asm n.asm cj d.asm n.asm v.aas.3p r.asn p.g d.gpm a.gpm
4275 3836 4063 2671 160 3836 972 1254 660 660 3836 2652 660 5515 608 3836 1545

do you want me to release to you?"   asked the governor.   ¶   "Barabbas," they answered.   ¶
→ θέλετε → ἀπολύσω ὑμῖν δὲ ἀποκριθεὶς ὁ ἡγεμών δὲ ιτὸν Βαραββᾶν οἱ εἶπαν
v.pai.2p v.aas.1s r.dp.2 cj pt.ap.nsm d.nsm n.nsm cj d.asm n.asm d.npm v.aai.3p
2527 668 7007 1254 646 3836 2450 1254 3836 972 3836 3306

22 "What shall I do,   then, with Jesus who is called Christ?" Pilate   asked.   ¶   They all
τί → → ποιήσω οὖν Ἰησοῦν τὸν → λεγόμενον χριστόν ὁ Πιλᾶτος λέγει αὐτοῖς πάντες
r.asn v.aas.1s cj n.asm d.asm pt.pp.asm n.asm d.nsm n.nsm v.pai.3s r.dpm.3 a.npm
5515 4472 4036 2652 3836 3306 5986 3836 4397 3306 899 3306 4246

answered, "Crucify him!"   ¶ **23** "Why? What crime has he committed?"   asked Pilate. ¶   But they
λέγουσιν σταυρωθήτω γὰρ τί κακὸν → ἐποίησεν δὲ ἔφη ὁ δὲ οἱ
v.pai.3p v.apm.3s cj r.asn a.asn v.iai.3s cj v.iai.3s d.nsm cj d.npm
3306 5090 1142 5515 2805 4472 1254 5774 3836 1254 3836

shouted all the louder,   "Crucify him!" ¶ **24** When Pilate   saw   that he was getting nowhere,
ἔκραζον → → περισσῶς λέγοντες σταυρωθήτω ← δὲ ὁ Πιλᾶτος ἰδὼν ὅτι → → ὠφελεῖ οὐδὲν
v.iai.3p adv pt.pa.npm v.apm.3s cj d.nsm n.nsm pt.aa.nsm cj v.pai.3s a.asn
3189 4360 3306 5090 1254 1625 3836 4397 1625 4022 6067 4029

but that instead an uproar was starting, he took water and washed his hands in front   of the crowd. "I am
ἀλλὰ μᾶλλον θόρυβος → γίνεται → λαβὼν ὕδωρ ἀπενίψατο τὰς χεῖρας → ἀπέναντι ← τοῦ ὄχλου → εἰμι
cj adv.c n.nsm v.pmi.3s pt.aa.nsm n.asn v.ami.3s d.apf n.apf p.g d.gsm n.gsm v.pai.1s
247 3437 2573 1181 3284 5623 672 3836 5931 595 3836 4063 1639

¹³ τότε λέγει αὐτῷ ὁ Πιλᾶτος, Οὐκ ἀκούεις πόσα σου καταμαρτυροῦσιν; ¹⁴ καὶ οὐκ ἀπεκρίθη αὐτῷ πρὸς οὐδὲ ἓν ῥῆμα, ὥστε θαυμάζειν τὸν ἡγεμόνα λίαν. ¶ ¹⁵ Κατὰ δὲ ἑορτὴν εἰώθει ὁ ἡγεμὼν ἀπολύειν ἕνα τῷ ὄχλῳ δέσμιον ὃν ἤθελον. ¹⁶ εἶχον δὲ τότε δέσμιον ἐπίσημον λεγόμενον [Ἰησοῦν] Βαραββᾶν. ¹⁷ συνηγμένων οὖν αὐτῶν εἶπεν αὐτοῖς ὁ Πιλᾶτος, Τίνα θέλετε ἀπολύσω ὑμῖν, [Ἰησοῦν τὸν] Βαραββᾶν ἢ Ἰησοῦν τὸν λεγόμενον Χριστόν; ¹⁸ ᾔδει γὰρ ὅτι διὰ φθόνον παρέδωκαν αὐτόν. ¶ ¹⁹ Καθημένου δὲ αὐτοῦ ἐπὶ τοῦ βήματος ἀπέστειλεν πρὸς αὐτὸν ἡ γυνὴ αὐτοῦ λέγουσα, Μηδὲν σοὶ καὶ τῷ δικαίῳ ἐκείνῳ· πολλὰ γὰρ ἔπαθον σήμερον κατ' ὄναρ δι' αὐτόν. ¶ ²⁰ Οἱ δὲ ἀρχιερεῖς καὶ οἱ πρεσβύτεροι ἔπεισαν τοὺς ὄχλους ἵνα αἰτήσωνται τὸν Βαραββᾶν, τὸν δὲ Ἰησοῦν ἀπολέσωσιν. ¶ ²¹ ἀποκριθεὶς δὲ ὁ ἡγεμὼν εἶπεν αὐτοῖς, Τίνα θέλετε ἀπὸ τῶν δύο ἀπολύσω ὑμῖν; ¶ οἱ δὲ εἶπαν, Τὸν Βαραββᾶν. ¶ ²² λέγει αὐτοῖς ὁ Πιλᾶτος, Τί οὖν ποιήσω Ἰησοῦν τὸν λεγόμενον Χριστόν; ¶ λέγουσιν πάντες, Σταυρωθήτω. ²³ ὁ δὲ ἔφη, Τί γὰρ κακὸν ἐποίησεν; ¶ οἱ δὲ περισσῶς ἔκραζον λέγοντες, Σταυρωθήτω. ¶ ²⁴ ἰδὼν δὲ ὁ Πιλᾶτος ὅτι οὐδὲν ὠφελεῖ ἀλλὰ μᾶλλον θόρυβος γίνεται, λαβὼν ὕδωρ ἀπενίψατο τὰς χεῖρας ἀπέναντι τοῦ ὄχλου λέγων, Ἀθῷός εἰμι ἀπὸ τοῦ

innocent of this man's blood," he said. *"It is your responsibility!"* ¶ **25** All the people answered,
ἀθῷος ἀπὸ τούτου ← ⌞τοῦ αἵματος⌟ → λέγων → → ὑμεῖς ὄψεσθε καὶ πᾶς ὁ λαὸς ἀποκριθεὶς εἶπεν
a.nsm a.pg r.gsm d.gsn n.gsn pt.pa.nsm r.np.2 v.fmi.2p cj a.nsm d.nsm n.nsm pt.ap.nsm v.aai.3s
127 608 4047 3836 135 3306 3972 3972 7007 3972 2779 4246 3836 3295 646 3306

"Let his blood be on us and on our children!" ¶ **26** Then he released Barabbas to them. But he had
αὐτοῦ ⌞τὸ αἷμα⌟ ἐφ᾽ ἡμᾶς καὶ ἐπὶ ἡμῶν ⌞τὰ τέκνα⌟ τότε → ἀπέλυσεν ⌞τὸν Βαραββᾶν⌟ αὐτοῖς δὲ ↱ ↱
r.gsm.3 d.nsn n.nsn p.a r.ap.1 cj p.a r.gp.1 d.apn n.apn adv v.aai.3s d.asm n.asm r.dpm.3 cj
899 3836 135 2093 7005 2779 2093 7005 3836 5451 5538 668 3836 972 899 1254 5849 5849

Jesus flogged, and handed him over to be crucified.
⌞τὸν Ἰησοῦν⌟ φραγελλώσας παρέδωκεν ← ἵνα → σταυρωθῇ
d.asm n.asm pt.aa.nsm v.aai.3s cj v.aps.3s
3836 2652 5849 4140 2671 5090

The Soldiers Mock Jesus

27:27 Then the governor's soldiers took Jesus into the Praetorium and gathered the whole
Τότε οἱ ⌞τοῦ ἡγεμόνος⌟ στρατιῶται παραλαβόντες ⌞τὸν Ἰησοῦν⌟ εἰς τὸ πραιτώριον συνήγαγον τὴν ὅλην
adv d.npm d.gsm n.gsm n.npm pt.aa.npm d.asm n.asm p.a d.asn n.asn v.aai.3p d.asf a.asf
5538 3836 3836 2450 5132 4161 3836 2652 1650 3836 4550 5251 3836 3910

company of soldiers around him. **28** They stripped him and put a scarlet robe on him, **29** and then
σπεῖραν ← ← ἐπ᾽ αὐτόν καὶ → ἐκδύσαντες αὐτὸν περιέθηκαν κοκκίνην χλαμύδα ↰ αὐτῷ καὶ
n.asf p.a r.asm.3 cj pt.aa.npm r.asm.3 v.aai.3p a.asf n.asf r.dsm.3 cj
5061 2093 899 2779 1694 899 4363 3132 5948 4363 899 2779

twisted together a crown of thorns and set it on his head. They put a staff in his right
πλέξαντες ← στέφανον ἐξ ἀκανθῶν ἐπέθηκαν ἐπὶ αὐτοῦ ⌞τῆς κεφαλῆς⌟ καὶ κάλαμον ἐν αὐτοῦ ⌞τῇ δεξιᾷ⌟
pt.aa.npm n.asm p.g n.gpf v.aai.3p p.g r.gsm.3 d.gsf n.gsf cj n.asm p.d r.gsm.3 d.dsf a.dsf
4428 5109 1666 180 2202 2093 899 3836 3051 2779 2812 1877 899 3836 1288

hand and knelt in front of him and mocked him. "Hail, king of the Jews!" they said. **30** They
← καὶ γονυπετήσαντες → ἔμπροσθεν ← αὐτοῦ ἐνέπαιξαν αὐτῷ χαῖρε βασιλεῦ τῶν Ἰουδαίων → λέγοντες καὶ →
cj pt.aa.npm p.g r.gsm.3 v.aai.3p r.dsm.3 v.pam.2s n.vsm d.gpm a.gpm pt.pa.npm cj
2779 1206 1869 899 1850 899 5897 995 3836 2681 3306 2779

spit on him, and took the staff and struck him on the head again and again. **31** After they had
ἐμπτύσαντες εἰς αὐτὸν ἔλαβον τὸν κάλαμον καὶ ἔτυπτον εἰς τὴν κεφαλὴν αὐτοῦ καὶ ὅτε →
pt.aa.npm p.a r.asm.3 v.aai.3p d.asm n.asm cj v.iai.3p p.a d.asf n.asf r.gsm.3 cj cj
1870 1650 899 3284 3836 2812 2779 5597 1650 3836 3051 899 5597 5597 5597 2779 4021

mocked him, they took off the robe and put his own clothes on him. Then they led him
ἐνέπαιξαν αὐτῷ ἐξέδυσαν ← αὐτὸν τὴν χλαμύδα καὶ ἐνέδυσαν αὐτοῦ τὰ ἱμάτια αὐτὸν καὶ → ἀπήγαγον αὐτὸν
v.aai.3p r.dsm.3 v.aai.3p r.asm.3 d.asf n.asf cj v.aai.3p r.gsm.3 d.apn n.apn r.asm.3 cj v.aai.3p r.asm.3
1850 899 1694 899 3836 5948 2779 1907 899 3836 2668 899 2779 552 899

away to crucify him.
↰ εἰς ⌞τὸ σταυρῶσαι⌟
p.a d.asn f.aa
552 1650 3836 5090

The Crucifixion

27:32 As they were going out, they met a man from Cyrene, named Simon, and they forced
δὲ → → Ἐξερχόμενοι ← → εὗρον ἄνθρωπον → Κυρηναῖον ὀνόματι Σίμωνα → ἠγγάρευσαν
cj pt.pm.npm v.aai.3p n.asm n.asm n.dsn n.asm v.aai.3p
1254 2002 2351 476 3254 3950 4981 30

him to carry the cross. **33** They came to a place called Golgotha (which means The Place of
τοῦτον ἵνα ἄρῃ τὸν σταυρὸν αὐτοῦ Καὶ → ἐλθόντες εἰς τόπον λεγόμενον Γολγοθᾶ ὃ ⌞ἐστιν λεγόμενος⌟ Τόπος →
r.asm cj v.aas.3s d.asm n.asm r.gsm.3 cj pt.aa.npm p.a n.asm pt.pp.asm n.asf r.nsn v.pai.3s pt.pp.nsm n.nsm
4047 2671 149 3836 5089 899 2779 2262 1650 5536 3306 1201 4005 1639 3306 5536

the Skull). **34** There they offered Jesus wine to drink, mixed with gall; but after tasting it, he refused to
Κρανίου → ἔδωκαν αὐτῷ οἶνον → πιεῖν μεμιγμένον μετὰ χολῆς καὶ → γευσάμενος → ⌞οὐκ ἠθέλησεν⌟ →
n.gsn v.aai.3p r.dsm.3 n.asm f.aa pt.rp.asm p.g n.gsf cj pt.am.nsm pl v.aai.3s
3191 1443 899 3885 4403 3624 3552 5958 2779 1174 4024 2527

drink it. **35** When they had crucified him, they divided up his clothes by casting lots. **36** And sitting
πιεῖν δὲ → → Σταυρώσαντες αὐτὸν → διεμερίσαντο ← αὐτοῦ ⌞τὰ ἱμάτια⌟ → βάλλοντες κλῆρον καὶ καθήμενοι
f.aa cj pt.aa.npm r.asm.3 v.ami.3p r.gsm.3 d.apn n.apn pt.pa.npm n.asm cj pt.pm.npm
4403 1254 5090 899 1374 899 3836 2668 965 3102 2779 2764

αἵματος τούτου· ὑμεῖς ὄψεσθε. ¶ 25 καὶ ἀποκριθεὶς πᾶς ὁ λαὸς εἶπεν, Τὸ αἷμα αὐτοῦ ἐφ᾽ ἡμᾶς καὶ ἐπὶ τὰ τέκνα ἡμῶν. ¶ 26 τότε ἀπέλυσεν αὐτοῖς τὸν Βαραββᾶν, τὸν δὲ Ἰησοῦν φραγελλώσας παρέδωκεν ἵνα σταυρωθῇ.

27:27 Τότε οἱ στρατιῶται τοῦ ἡγεμόνος παραλαβόντες τὸν Ἰησοῦν εἰς τὸ πραιτώριον συνήγαγον ἐπ᾽ αὐτὸν ὅλην τὴν σπεῖραν. 28 καὶ ἐκδύσαντες αὐτὸν χλαμύδα κοκκίνην περιέθηκαν αὐτῷ, 29 καὶ πλέξαντες στέφανον ἐξ ἀκανθῶν ἐπέθηκαν ἐπὶ τῆς κεφαλῆς αὐτοῦ καὶ κάλαμον ἐν τῇ δεξιᾷ αὐτοῦ, καὶ γονυπετήσαντες ἔμπροσθεν αὐτοῦ ἐνέπαιξαν αὐτῷ λέγοντες, Χαῖρε, βασιλεῦ τῶν Ἰουδαίων, 30 καὶ ἐμπτύσαντες εἰς αὐτὸν ἔλαβον τὸν κάλαμον καὶ ἔτυπτον εἰς τὴν κεφαλὴν αὐτοῦ. 31 καὶ ὅτε ἐνέπαιξαν αὐτῷ, ἐξέδυσαν αὐτὸν τὴν χλαμύδα καὶ ἐνέδυσαν αὐτὸν τὰ ἱμάτια αὐτοῦ καὶ ἀπήγαγον αὐτὸν εἰς τὸ σταυρῶσαι.

27:32 Ἐξερχόμενοι δὲ εὗρον ἄνθρωπον Κυρηναῖον ὀνόματι Σίμωνα, τοῦτον ἠγγάρευσαν ἵνα ἄρῃ τὸν σταυρὸν αὐτοῦ. 33 Καὶ ἐλθόντες εἰς τόπον λεγόμενον Γολγοθᾶ, ὅ ἐστιν Κρανίου Τόπος λεγόμενος, 34 ἔδωκαν αὐτῷ πιεῖν οἶνον μετὰ χολῆς μεμιγμένον· καὶ γευσάμενος οὐκ ἠθέλησεν πιεῖν. 35 σταυρώσαντες δὲ αὐτὸν διεμερίσαντο τὰ ἱμάτια αὐτοῦ βάλλοντες κλῆρον, 36 καὶ

down, they kept watch over him there. **37** Above his head they placed the written charge against
→   →   ἐτήρουν ←   αὐτὸν ἐκεῖ Καὶ ἐπάνω αὐτοῦ ⌐τῆς κεφαλῆς⌐ → ἐπέθηκαν τὴν γεγραμμένην αἰτίαν
             v.iai.3p   r.asm.3 adv cj p.g   r.gsm.3 d.gsf n.gsf   v.aai.3p d.asf pt.rp.asf n.asf
             5498   1695   2779 2062 899   3836 3051   2202   3836 1211   162

him: THIS IS JESUS, THE KING OF THE JEWS. **38** Two robbers were crucified with him, one on his
αὐτοῦ οὗτος ἐστιν Ἰησοῦς ὁ βασιλεὺς → τῶν Ἰουδαίων Τότε δύο λῃσταί → σταυροῦνται σὺν αὐτῷ εἷς ἐκ
r.gsm.3 r.nsm v.pai.3s n.nsm d.nsm n.nsm d.gpm a.gpm adv a.npm n.npm v.ppi.3p p.d r.dsm.3 a.nsm p.g
899   4047 1639 2652 3836 995   3836 2681 5538 1545 3334 5090 5250 899 1651 1666

right and one on his left. **39** Those who passed by hurled insults at him, shaking their
δεξιῶν καὶ εἷς ἐξ εὐωνύμων δὲ Οἱ ← παραπορευόμενοι ← ἐβλασφήμουν ← αὐτὸν κινοῦντες αὐτῶν
a.gpf cj a.nsm p.g a.gpf cj d.npm pt.pm.npm v.iai.3p r.asm.3 pt.pa.npm r.gpm.3
1288 2779 1651 1666 2381 1254 3836 4182 1059 899 3075 899

heads **40** and saying, "You who are going to destroy the temple and build it in three days, save yourself!
⌐τὰς κεφαλὰς⌐ καὶ λέγοντες ὁ ← → → καταλύων τὸν ναὸν καὶ οἰκοδομῶν ἐν τρισὶν ἡμέραις σῶσον σεαυτὸν
d.apf n.apf cj pt.pa.npm d.vsm pt.pa.vsm d.asm n.asm cj pt.pa.vsm p.d a.dpf n.dpf v.aam.2s r.asm.2
3836 3051 2779 3306 3836 2907 3836 3724 2779 3868 1877 5552 2465 5392 4932

Come down from the cross, if you are the Son of God!" ¶ **41** In the same way the chief
[καὶ] κατάβηθι ἀπὸ τοῦ σταυροῦ εἰ → εἰ υἱὸς ⌐τοῦθεοῦ⌐ → ὁμοίως ← καὶ οἱ
cj v.aam.2s p.g d.gsm n.gsm cj v.pai.2s n.nsm d.gsmn.gsm adv adv d.npm
2779 2849 608 3836 5089 1623 1639 5626 3836 2536 3931 2779 3836

priests, the teachers of the law and the elders mocked him. **42** "He saved others," they said, "but he
ἀρχιερεῖς μετὰ τῶν γραμματέων ← ← καὶ πρεσβυτέρων ἐμπαίζοντες → ἔσωσεν ἄλλους → ἔλεγον →
n.npm p.g d.gpm n.gpm cj a.gpm pt.pa.npm v.aai.3s r.apm v.iai.3p
797 3552 3836 1208 2779 4565 1850 5392 257 3306

can't save himself! He's the King of Israel! Let him come down now from the cross, and we will
⌐οὐ δύναται⌐ σῶσαι ἑαυτὸν ἐστιν βασιλεὺς → Ἰσραήλ → → καταβάτω ← νῦν ἀπὸ τοῦ σταυροῦ καὶ →
pl v.ppi.3s f.aa r.asm.3 v.pai.3s n.nsm n.nsm v.aam.3s adv p.g d.gsm n.gsm cj
4024 1538 5392 1571 1639 995 2702 2849 3814 608 3836 5089 2779

believe in him. **43** He trusts in God. Let God rescue him now if he wants him, for he said, 'I am the
πιστεύσωμεν ἐπ᾽ αὐτόν → πέποιθεν ἐπὶ ⌐τὸν θεόν⌐ → ῥυσάσθω νῦν εἰ → θέλει αὐτόν γὰρ → εἶπεν ὅτι εἰμι
v.fai.1p p.a r.asm.3 v.rai.3s p.a r.asm.n.asm v.amm.3s adv cj v.pai.3s r.asm.3 cj v.aai.3s cj v.pai.1s
4409 2093 899 4275 2093 3836 2536 4861 3814 1623 2527 899 1142 3306 4022 1639

Son of God.'" **44** In the same way the robbers who were crucified with him also heaped insults on him.
υἱός → θεοῦ δ᾽ Τὸ αὐτὸ οἱ λῃσταὶ οἱ → συσταυρωθέντες σὺν αὐτῷ καὶ → ὠνείδιζον αὐτόν
n.nsm n.gsm cj d.asn r.asn d.npm n.npm d.npm pt.ap.npm p.d r.dsm.3 adv v.iai.3p r.asm.3
5626 2536 1254 3836 899 3836 3334 3836 5365 5250 899 2779 3943 899

The Death of Jesus

27:45 From the sixth hour until the ninth hour darkness came over all the land. **46** About the ninth hour
δὲ Ἀπὸ ἕκτης ὥρας ἕως ἐνάτης ὥρας σκότος ἐγένετο ἐπὶ πᾶσαν τὴν γῆν δὲ περὶ τὴν ἐνάτην ὥραν
cj p.g a.gsf n.gsf p.g a.gsf n.gsf n.nsn v.ami.3s p.a a.asf d.asf n.asf cj p.a d.asf a.asf n.asf
1254 608 1761 6052 2401 1888 6052 5030 1181 2093 4246 3836 1178 1254 4309 3836 1888 6052

Jesus cried out in a loud voice, "Eloi, Eloi, lama sabachthani?" —which means, "My God, my God,
ὁ Ἰησοῦς ἀνεβόησεν ← → μεγάλῃ φωνῇ λέγων ηλι ηλι λεμα σαβαχθανι τοῦτ᾽ ἔστιν μου Θεέ μου θεέ
d.nsm n.nsm v.aai.3s a.dsf n.dsf pt.pa.nsm j j j j r.nsn v.pai.3s r.gs.1 n.vsm r.gs.1 n.vsm
3836 2652 331 3489 5889 3306 2458 2458 3316 4876 4047 1639 1609 2536 1609 2536

why have you forsaken me?" ¶ **47** When some of those standing there heard this, they said, "He's
ἱνατί → ἐγκατέλιπες με δὲ → τινες → τῶν ἑστηκότων ἐκεῖ ἀκούσαντες → ἔλεγον ὅτι οὗτος
v.aai.2s r.as.1 cj r.npm d.gpm pt.ra.gpm adv pt.aa.npm v.iai.3p cj r.nsm
2672 1593 1609 1254 2705 5516 3836 2705 1695 201 3306 4022 4047

calling Elijah." ¶ **48** Immediately one of them ran and got a sponge. He filled it with wine vinegar,
φωνεῖ Ἠλίαν καὶ εὐθέως εἷς ἐξ αὐτῶν δραμὼν καὶ λαβὼν σπόγγον τε → πλήσας → ὄξους
v.pai.3s n.asm cj adv a.nsm p.g r.gpm.3 pt.aa.nsm cj pt.aa.nsm n.asm cj pt.aa.nsm n.gsn
5888 2460 2779 2311 1651 1666 899 5556 2779 3284 5074 5445 4398 3954

put it on a stick, and offered it to Jesus to drink. **49** The rest said, "Now leave him alone. Let's see
καὶ περιθεὶς → καλάμῳ ἐπότιζεν αὐτόν ← δὲ οἱ λοιποὶ ἔλεγον ἄφες → → ἴδωμεν
cj pt.aa.nsm n.dsm v.iai.3s r.asm.3 cj d.npm a.npm v.iai.3p v.aam.2s v.aas.1p
2779 4363 2812 4540 899 4540 4540 1254 3836 3370 3306 918 1625

καθήμενοι ἐτήρουν αὐτὸν ἐκεῖ. **37** καὶ ἐπέθηκαν ἐπάνω τῆς κεφαλῆς αὐτοῦ τὴν αἰτίαν αὐτοῦ γεγραμμένην· Οὗτός ἐστιν Ἰησοῦς
ὁ βασιλεὺς τῶν Ἰουδαίων. **38** Τότε σταυροῦνται σὺν αὐτῷ δύο λῃσταί, εἷς ἐκ δεξιῶν καὶ εἷς ἐξ εὐωνύμων. **39** Οἱ δὲ
παραπορευόμενοι ἐβλασφήμουν αὐτὸν κινοῦντες τὰς κεφαλὰς αὐτῶν **40** καὶ λέγοντες, Ὁ καταλύων τὸν ναὸν καὶ ἐν τρισὶν
ἡμέραις οἰκοδομῶν, σῶσον σεαυτόν, εἰ υἱὸς εἶ τοῦ θεοῦ, [καὶ] κατάβηθι ἀπὸ τοῦ σταυροῦ. ¶ **41** ὁμοίως καὶ οἱ ἀρχιερεῖς
ἐμπαίζοντες μετὰ τῶν γραμματέων καὶ πρεσβυτέρων ἔλεγον, **42** Ἄλλους ἔσωσεν, ἑαυτὸν οὐ δύναται σῶσαι· βασιλεὺς Ἰσραήλ
ἐστιν, καταβάτω νῦν ἀπὸ τοῦ σταυροῦ καὶ πιστεύσωμεν ἐπ᾽ αὐτόν. **43** πέποιθεν ἐπὶ τὸν θεόν, ῥυσάσθω νῦν εἰ θέλει αὐτόν·
εἶπεν γὰρ ὅτι Θεοῦ εἰμι υἱός. **44** τὸ δ᾽ αὐτὸ καὶ οἱ λῃσταὶ οἱ συσταυρωθέντες σὺν αὐτῷ ὠνείδιζον αὐτόν.
27:45 Ἀπὸ δὲ ἕκτης ὥρας σκότος ἐγένετο ἐπὶ πᾶσαν τὴν γῆν ἕως ὥρας ἐνάτης. **46** περὶ δὲ τὴν ἐνάτην ὥραν ἀνεβόησεν ὁ
Ἰησοῦς φωνῇ μεγάλῃ λέγων, Ελωι «Ηλι» ελωι «ηλι» λεμα σαβαχθανι; τοῦτ᾽ ἔστιν, Θεέ μου θεέ μου, ἱνατί με ἐγκατέλιπες; ¶
47 τινὲς δὲ τῶν ἐκεῖ ἑστηκότων ἀκούσαντες ἔλεγον ὅτι Ἠλίαν φωνεῖ οὗτος. ¶ **48** καὶ εὐθέως δραμὼν εἷς ἐξ αὐτῶν καὶ λαβὼν
σπόγγον πλήσας τε ὄξους καὶ περιθεὶς καλάμῳ ἐπότιζεν αὐτόν. **49** οἱ δὲ λοιποὶ ἔλεγον, Ἄφες ἴδωμεν εἰ ἔρχεται Ἠλίας σώσων

if　Elijah　comes　to　save　him."　¶　⁵⁰ And　when　Jesus　　　had　cried　out　again　in a　loud　voice,　he　gave　up
εἰ　Ἠλίας　ἔρχεται　→　σώσων　αὐτόν　　　δὲ　↱　ὁ Ἰησοῦς　→　κράξας　←　πάλιν　→　μεγάλῃ　φωνῇ　→　ἀφῆκεν　←
cj　n.nsm　v.pmi.3s　　pt.fa.nsm　r.asm.3　　　cj　　d.nsm n.nsm　　pt.aa.nsm　　adv　　a.dsf　n.dsf　　v.aai.3s
1623　2460　2262　　　5392　899　　　　1254　3189　　3836　2652　　3189　　4099　　3489　5889　　918

his　spirit.　¶　⁵¹ At　that　moment　the　curtain　　of the　temple　was　torn　　in　two　from　top　　to　bottom.
τὸ　πνεῦμα　　Καὶ　ἰδοὺ　τὸ　καταπέτασμα　→　τοῦ　ναοῦ　→　ἐσχίσθη　εἰς　δύο　ἀπ'　ἄνωθεν　ἕως　κάτω　καὶ
d.asn n.asn　　cj　j　　d.nsn　n.nsn　　d.gsn n.gsn　　v.api.3s　p.a　a.apn　p.g　adv　　adv　　cj
3836　4460　　2779　2627　3836　2925　　3836　3724　　5387　1650　1545　608　540　　2401　3004　2779

The　earth　shook　and　the　rocks　split.　　⁵²　The　tombs　broke　　open　and　the　bodies　of many　holy　　people
ἡ　γῆ　ἐσείσθη　καὶ　αἱ　πέτραι　ἐσχίσθησαν　καὶ　τὰ　μνημεῖα　ἀνεῴχθησαν　←　καὶ　σώματα　πολλὰ　⌐τῶν ἁγίων⌐
d.nsf n.nsf v.api.3s cj d.npf n.npf v.api.3p　　cj d.npn n.npn v.api.3p　　　cj　n.npn　a.npn　d.gpm a.gpm
3836 1178 4940 2779 3836 4376 5387　　2779 3836 3646 487　　　2779 5393 4498 3836 41

who　had　died　　were　raised　to life.　⁵³ They　came　out of　the　tombs,　and　after　Jesus'　resurrection　they
→　→　κεκοιμημένων　→　ἠγέρθησαν　　καὶ　ἐξελθόντες　←　ἐκ　τῶν μνημείων　μετὰ　αὐτοῦ　⌐τὴν ἔγερσιν⌐　→
　　pt.rp.gpm　　　v.api.3p　　　cj　pt.aa.npm　　p.g　d.gpn n.gpn　　p.a　r.gsm.3　d.asf n.asf
　　3121　　　　1586　　　2779　2002　　1666 3836 3646　3552 899　3836 1587

went　into the　holy　city　and　appeared　　to　many　people.　¶　⁵⁴　When　the　centurion　and　those　with
εἰσῆλθον　εἰς　τὴν ἁγίαν　πόλιν　καὶ　ἐνεφανίσθησαν　→　πολλοῖς　←　　δὲ　↱　Ὁ　ἑκατόνταρχος　καὶ　οἱ　μετ'
v.aai.3p p.a d.asf a.asf n.asf cj v.api.3p　　a.dpm　　　cj　　d.nsm n.nsm　cj d.npm p.g
1656 1650 3836 41 4484 2779 1872　　4498　　　1254　　3836 1672　　2779 3836 3552

him　who　were　guarding　Jesus　　saw　the　earthquake　and　all that　had　happened,　they　were　terrified,
αὐτοῦ　→　→　τηροῦντες　⌐τὸν Ἰησοῦν⌐　ἰδόντες　τὸν　σεισμὸν　καὶ　τὰ　→　γενόμενα　→　→　⌐ἐφοβήθησαν σφόδρα⌐
r.gsm.3　　　　pt.pa.npm　d.asm n.asm　pt.aa.npm d.asm n.asm　cj　d.apn　pt.am.apn　　　v.api.3p　adv
899　　　　5498　3836 2652　1625 3836 4939　2779 3836　1181　　　5828　5379

and　exclaimed,　"Surely　he　　was the　Son　of God!"　¶　⁵⁵　Many　women　were　there,　watching　from a
λέγοντες　ἀληθῶς　οὗτος　ἦν　υἱὸς　→　θεοῦ　　δὲ　πολλαὶ　γυναῖκες　Ἦσαν　ἐκεῖ　θεωροῦσαι　ἀπὸ
pt.pa.npm　adv　　r.nsm v.iai.3s　n.nsm　　n.gsm　　cj　a.npf　n.npf　v.iai.3p adv　pt.pa.npf　p.g
3306　242　　4047 1639　5626　　2536　　1254 4498 1222　1639 1695 2555　608

distance.　They　had　followed　Jesus　from　Galilee　　to　care　for his　needs.　⁵⁶ Among　them　were　Mary
μακρόθεν　αἵτινες　→　ἠκολούθησαν　⌐τῷ Ἰησοῦ⌐　ἀπὸ　⌐τῆς Γαλιλαίας⌐　→　διακονοῦσαι　←　αὐτῷ　ἐν　αἷς　ἦν　Μαρία
adv　　r.npf　　v.aai.3p　d.dsm n.dsm　p.g　d.gsf n.gsf　　pt.pa.npf　　r.dsm.3　p.d r.dpf v.iai.3s n.nsf
3427　4015　　199　3836 2652　608 3836 1133　　1354　　　899　1877 4005 1639 3451

Magdalene,　　Mary　the　mother　of James　　and　Joses, and　the　mother　of　Zebedee's　sons.
⌐ἡ　Μαγδαληνή⌐　καὶ　Μαρία　ἡ　μήτηρ　→　⌐τοῦ Ἰακώβου⌐　καὶ　Ἰωσὴφ　καὶ　ἡ　μήτηρ　↱　Ζεβεδαίου　⌐τῶν υἱῶν⌐
d.nsf n.nsf　　cj　n.nsf　d.nsf n.nsf　　d.gsm n.gsm　cj　n.gsm　cj　d.nsf n.nsf　　n.gsm　d.gpm n.gpm
3836 3402　　2779 3451 3836 3613　　3836 2610　2779 2737　2779 3836 3613　　5626 2411　3836 5626

The Burial of Jesus

27:57　As　evening　approached,　there　came　a　rich　　man　　from　Arimathea,　named　Joseph,　who　　had
δὲ　↱　Ὀψίας　γενομένης　　ἦλθεν　πλούσιος　ἄνθρωπος　ἀπὸ　Ἀριμαθαίας　τοὔνομα　Ἰωσήφ　ὃς　καὶ　↱
cj　　n.gsf　pt.am.gsf　　v.aai.3s　a.nsm　　n.nsm　　p.g　n.gsf　　crasis　n.nsm　r.nsm adv
1254　1181 4068　1181　　2262　4454　　476　　608 751　　5540　2737　4047 2779 3411

himself　become　a　disciple　of Jesus.　⁵⁸ Going　　to Pilate,　　he　asked　for Jesus'　　body,　and
αὐτὸς　→　→　ἐμαθητεύθη　→　⌐τῷ Ἰησοῦ⌐　προσελθὼν　←　⌐τῷ Πιλάτῳ⌐　οὗτος　ᾐτήσατο　←　⌐τοῦ Ἰησοῦ⌐　⌐τὸ σῶμα⌐　τότε
r.nsm　　　v.api.3s　　d.dsm n.dsm　pt.aa.nsm　d.dsm n.dsm　r.nsm v.ami.3s　d.gsm n.gsm　d.asn n.asn　adv
899　　　3411　　3836 2652　4665　　3836 4397　4047 2652　　3836 2652　3836 5393　5538

Pilate　　ordered　that　it be　given　　to him.　⁵⁹　Joseph　took　the　body,　wrapped it　in a　clean　linen
⌐ὁ　Πιλάτος⌐　ἐκέλευσεν　→　→　ἀποδοθῆναι　→　　καὶ　ὁ　Ἰωσὴφ　λαβὼν　τὸ　σῶμα　ἐνετύλιξεν αὐτὸ ἐν　καθαρᾷ　σινδόνι
d.nsm n.nsm　v.aai.3s　　　f.ap　　　　cj d.nsm n.nsm pt.aa.nsm d.asn n.asn v.aai.3s r.asn.3 p.d a.dsf　n.dsf
3836 4397　3027　　　625　　　2779 3836 2737 3284 3836 5393 1962 899 1877 2754　4984

cloth,　⁶⁰ and　placed　it　in　his　own　new　tomb　that　he　had　cut　　out of the　rock.　He　rolled　　a　big
←　　καὶ　ἔθηκεν　αὐτὸ ἐν　αὐτοῦ τῷ　καινῷ　μνημείῳ　ὃ　→　　ἐλατόμησεν　ἐν τῇ πέτρᾳ καὶ　προσκυλίσας　μέγαν
　　cj　v.aai.3s　r.asn.3 p.d r.gsm.3 d.dsn a.dsn n.dsn　r.asn　　v.aai.3s　p.d d.dsf n.dsf cj　pt.aa.nsm　a.asm
　　2779 5502　899 1877 899 3836 2785 3646　4005　　3300　　1877 3836 4376 2779 4685　3489

stone　in　front　of the　entrance　to　the　tomb　　and　went　　away.　⁶¹　Mary　　Magdalene　and　the　other　Mary　were
λίθον　→　→　τῇ　θύρᾳ　→　τοῦ　μνημείου　ἀπῆλθεν　　δὲ　Μαριὰμ　ἡ　Μαγδαληνή　καὶ　ἡ　ἄλλη　Μαρία　Ἦν
n.asn　　　d.dsf n.dsf　　d.gsn n.gsn　v.aai.3s　　cj　n.nsf　d.nsf n.nsf　cj d.nsf r.nsf n.nsf v.iai.3s
3345　　　3836 2598　　3836 3646　599　　1254 3452 3836 3402　2779 3836 257 3451 1639

αὐτόν. ¶ ⁵⁰ ὁ δὲ Ἰησοῦς πάλιν κράξας φωνῇ μεγάλῃ ἀφῆκεν τὸ πνεῦμα. ¶ ⁵¹ Καὶ ἰδοὺ τὸ καταπέτασμα τοῦ ναοῦ ἐσχίσθη ἀπ'
ἄνωθεν ἕως κάτω εἰς δύο καὶ ἡ γῆ ἐσείσθη καὶ αἱ πέτραι ἐσχίσθησαν, ⁵² καὶ τὰ μνημεῖα ἀνεῴχθησαν καὶ πολλὰ σώματα τῶν
κεκοιμημένων ἁγίων ἠγέρθησαν, ⁵³ καὶ ἐξελθόντες ἐκ τῶν μνημείων μετὰ τὴν ἔγερσιν αὐτοῦ εἰσῆλθον εἰς τὴν ἁγίαν πόλιν καὶ
ἐνεφανίσθησαν πολλοῖς. ¶ ⁵⁴ Ὁ δὲ ἑκατόνταρχος καὶ οἱ μετ' αὐτοῦ τηροῦντες τὸν Ἰησοῦν ἰδόντες τὸν σεισμὸν καὶ τὰ γενόμενα
ἐφοβήθησαν σφόδρα, λέγοντες, Ἀληθῶς θεοῦ υἱὸς ἦν οὗτος. ¶ ⁵⁵ Ἦσαν δὲ ἐκεῖ γυναῖκες πολλαὶ ἀπὸ μακρόθεν θεωροῦσαι, αἵτινες
ἠκολούθησαν τῷ Ἰησοῦ ἀπὸ τῆς Γαλιλαίας διακονοῦσαι αὐτῷ· ⁵⁶ ἐν αἷς ἦν Μαρία ἡ Μαγδαληνὴ καὶ Μαρία ἡ τοῦ Ἰακώβου
καὶ Ἰωσῆ «Ἰωσὴφ» μήτηρ καὶ ἡ μήτηρ τῶν υἱῶν Ζεβεδαίου.
²⁷:⁵⁷ Ὀψίας δὲ γενομένης ἦλθεν ἄνθρωπος πλούσιος ἀπὸ Ἀριμαθαίας, τοὔνομα Ἰωσήφ, ὃς καὶ αὐτὸς ἐμαθητεύθη τῷ Ἰησοῦ·
⁵⁸ οὗτος προσελθὼν τῷ Πιλάτῳ ᾐτήσατο τὸ σῶμα τοῦ Ἰησοῦ. τότε ὁ Πιλάτος ἐκέλευσεν ἀποδοθῆναι. ⁵⁹ καὶ λαβὼν τὸ σῶμα ὁ
Ἰωσὴφ ἐνετύλιξεν αὐτὸ [ἐν] σινδόνι καθαρᾷ ⁶⁰ καὶ ἔθηκεν αὐτὸ ἐν τῷ καινῷ αὐτοῦ μνημείῳ ὃ ἐλατόμησεν ἐν τῇ πέτρᾳ καὶ
προσκυλίσας λίθον μέγαν τῇ θύρᾳ τοῦ μνημείου ἀπῆλθεν. ⁶¹ ἦν δὲ ἐκεῖ Μαριὰμ ἡ Μαγδαληνὴ καὶ ἡ ἄλλη Μαρία καθήμεναι

sitting   there opposite the tomb.
καθήμεναι ἐκεῖ ἀπέναντι τοῦ τάφου
pt.pm.npf   adv   p.g   d.gsm n.gsm
2764   1695   595   3836   5439

The Guard at the Tomb

27:62 The next   day, the one   after Preparation Day, the chief priests and the Pharisees went
δὲ Τῇ ἐπαύριον ←   ἥτις ἐστὶν μετὰ τὴν παρασκευήν ←   οἱ →   ἀρχιερεῖς καὶ οἱ Φαρισαῖοι συνήχθησαν
cj d.dsf adv   r.nsf v.pai.3s mta d.asf n.asf   d.npm   n.npm   cj d.npm n.npm   v.api.3p
1254 3836 2069   4015 1639   3552 3836 4187   3836   797   2779 3836 5757   5251

to Pilate. **63** "Sir," they said,   "we remember that while he was still alive that deceiver said, 'After three
πρὸς Πιλᾶτον κύριε   λέγοντες →   ἐμνήσθημεν ὅτι →   ἔτι ζῶν ἐκεῖνος ὁ πλάνος, εἶπεν μετὰ τρεῖς
p.a   n.asm   n.vsm   pt.pa.npm   v.api.1p   cj   adv pt.pa.nsm r.nsm d.nsm n.nsm v.aai.3s p.a a.apf
4639 4397   3261   3306   3630   4022 2409 2409 2409 2285 2409 1697 3836 4418 3306 3552 5552

days I will rise   again.' **64** So give the order   for the tomb to be made secure   until the third day.
ἡμέρας → →   ἐγείρομαι   οὖν →   → κέλευσον →   τὸν τάφον →   → ἀσφαλισθῆναι ἕως τῆς τρίτης ἡμέρας
n.apf   v.ppi.1s   cj   v.aam.2s   d.asm n.asm   f.ap   p.g d.gsf a.gsf n.gsf
2465   1586   4036   3027   3836 5439   856   2401 3836 5569 2465

Otherwise, his   disciples   may come   and steal   the body and tell   the people that he has been raised from
μήποτε   αὐτοῦ οἱ μαθηταὶ, →   ἐλθόντες κλέψωσιν αὐτὸν καὶ εἴπωσιν τῷ λαῷ →   → →   ἠγέρθη ἀπὸ
cj   r.gsm.3 d.npm n.npm   pt.aa.npm v.aas.3p r.asm.3 cj v.aas.3p d.dsm n.dsm   v.api.3s p.g
3607   899   3836 3412   2262   3096   899   2779 3306   3836 3295   1586   608

the dead.   This last   deception will be   worse than the first." ¶ **65** "Take a guard," Pilate
τῶν νεκρῶν καὶ ἡ   ἐσχάτη πλάνη   →   ἔσται χείρων →   τῆς πρώτης   ἔχετε   κουστωδίαν ὁ Πιλᾶτος,
d.gpm a.gpm cj d.nsf a.nsf n.nsf   v.fmi.3s a.nsf.c   d.gsf a.gsf   v.pai.2p   n.asf   d.nsm n.nsm
3836 3738 2779 3836 2274 4415   1639 5937   3836 4755   2400   3184   3836 4397

answered.   "Go,   make the tomb as secure   as you know how." **66** So they went   and made the tomb
ἔφη   αὐτοῖς ὑπάγετε →   ἀσφαλίσασθε ὡς → οἴδατε   δὲ οἱ πορευθέντες →   → τὸν τάφον
v.iai.3s r.dpm.3 v.pam.2p   v.amm.2p   cj   v.rai.2p   cj d.npm pt.ap.npm   d.asm n.asm
5774   899   5632   856   6055   3857   1254 3836 4513   856   3836 5439

secure   by putting a seal   on the stone and posting the guard.
ἠσφαλίσαντο →   → σφραγίσαντες ←   τὸν λίθον   μετὰ τῆς κουστωδίας
v.ami.3p   pt.aa.npm   d.asm n.asm   p.g d.gsf n.gsf
856   5381   3836 3345   3552 3836 3184

The Resurrection

28:1 After the Sabbath, at dawn   on the first day of the week,   Mary   Magdalene   and the other
δὲ Ὀψὲ σαββάτων → τῇ ἐπιφωσκούσῃ εἰς μίαν ← →   σαββάτων Μαριὰμ ἡ Μαγδαληνὴ καὶ ἡ ἄλλη
cj p.g n.gpn   d.dsf pt.pa.dsf   p.a a.asf   n.gpn   n.nsf d.nsf n.nsf   cj d.nsf r.nsf
1254 4067 4879   3836 2216   1650 1651   4879   3452 3836 3402   2779 3836 257

Mary went to look   at the tomb. ¶ **2** There was   a violent earthquake, for an angel   of the Lord
Μαρία ἦλθεν → θεωρῆσαι ← τὸν τάφον   καὶ ἰδοὺ   ἐγένετο μέγας σεισμός γὰρ ἄγγελος →   κυρίου
n.nsf v.aai.3s f.aa   d.asm n.asm   cj j   v.ami.3s a.nsm n.nsm   cj n.nsm   n.gsm
3451 2262   2555   3836 5439   2779 2627   1181   3489 4939   1142 34   3261

came down from heaven and, going   to the tomb, rolled   back the stone and sat   on it. **3** His
καταβὰς ←   ἐξ οὐρανοῦ καὶ προσελθὼν ←   ἀπεκύλισεν ← τὸν λίθον καὶ ἐκάθητο ἐπάνω αὐτοῦ δὲ αὐτοῦ
pt.aa.nsm   p.g n.gsm   cj pt.aa.nsm   v.aai.3s   d.asm n.asm cj v.imi.3s p.g r.gsm.3 cj r.gsm.3
2849   1666 4041 2779 4665   653   3836 3345 2779 2064   2062 899 1254 899

appearance was like lightning, and his   clothes   were white as snow. **4** The guards were so   afraid of
ἡ εἰδέα,   ἦν ὡς ἀστραπὴ καὶ αὐτοῦ τὸ ἔνδυμα, λευκὸν ὡς χιών δὲ οἱ τηροῦντες   ἀπὸ τοῦ φόβου, →
d.nsf n.nsf v.iai.3s conj n.nsf   cj r.gsm.3 d.nsn n.nsn   a.nsn conj n.nsf cj d.npm pt.pa.npm   p.g d.gsm n.gsm
3836 1624 1639 6055 847   2779 899 3836 1903   3328 6055 5946 1254 3836 5498   608 3836 5832

him that they shook   and became   like dead men. ¶ **5** The angel   said   to the women,
αὐτοῦ →   ἐσείσθησαν καὶ ἐγενήθησαν ὡς νεκροί, →   δὲ ὁ ἄγγελος ἀποκριθεὶς εἶπεν → ταῖς γυναιξίν ὑμεῖς
r.gsm.3   v.api.3p   cj v.api.3p   conj a.npm   cj d.nsm n.nsm pt.ap.nsm v.aai.3s d.dpf n.dpf r.np.2
899   4940   2779 1181   6055 3738   1254 3836 34   646   3306 3836 1222 7007

ἀπέναντι τοῦ τάφου.
²⁷:⁶² Τῇ δὲ ἐπαύριον, ἥτις ἐστὶν μετὰ τὴν παρασκευήν, συνήχθησαν οἱ ἀρχιερεῖς καὶ οἱ Φαρισαῖοι πρὸς Πιλᾶτον ⁶³ λέγοντες, Κύριε, ἐμνήσθημεν ὅτι ἐκεῖνος ὁ πλάνος εἶπεν ἔτι ζῶν, Μετὰ τρεῖς ἡμέρας ἐγείρομαι. ⁶⁴ κέλευσον οὖν ἀσφαλισθῆναι τὸν τάφον ἕως τῆς τρίτης ἡμέρας, μήποτε ἐλθόντες οἱ μαθηταὶ αὐτοῦ κλέψωσιν αὐτὸν καὶ εἴπωσιν τῷ λαῷ, Ἠγέρθη ἀπὸ τῶν νεκρῶν, καὶ ἔσται ἡ ἐσχάτη πλάνη χείρων τῆς πρώτης. ¶ ⁶⁵ ἔφη αὐτοῖς ὁ Πιλᾶτος, Ἔχετε κουστωδίαν· ὑπάγετε ἀσφαλίσασθε ὡς οἴδατε. ⁶⁶ οἱ δὲ πορευθέντες ἠσφαλίσαντο τὸν τάφον σφραγίσαντες τὸν λίθον μετὰ τῆς κουστωδίας.

²⁸:¹ Ὀψὲ δὲ σαββάτων, τῇ ἐπιφωσκούσῃ εἰς μίαν σαββάτων ἦλθεν Μαριὰμ ἡ Μαγδαληνὴ καὶ ἡ ἄλλη Μαρία θεωρῆσαι τὸν τάφον. ¶ ² καὶ ἰδοὺ σεισμὸς ἐγένετο μέγας· ἄγγελος γὰρ κυρίου καταβὰς ἐξ οὐρανοῦ καὶ προσελθὼν ἀπεκύλισεν τὸν λίθον καὶ ἐκάθητο ἐπάνω αὐτοῦ. ³ ἦν δὲ ἡ εἰδέα αὐτοῦ ὡς ἀστραπὴ καὶ τὸ ἔνδυμα αὐτοῦ λευκὸν ὡς χιών. ⁴ ἀπὸ δὲ τοῦ φόβου αὐτοῦ ἐσείσθησαν οἱ τηροῦντες καὶ ἐγενήθησαν ὡς νεκροί. ¶ ⁵ ἀποκριθεὶς δὲ ὁ ἄγγελος εἶπεν ταῖς γυναιξίν, Μὴ φοβεῖσθε

"Do not be afraid, for I know that you are looking for Jesus, who was crucified. **6** He is not here; he has
μὴ φοβεῖσθε γὰρ οἶδα ὅτι ζητεῖτε Ἰησοῦν τὸν ἐσταυρωμένον ἔστιν οὐκ ὧδε γὰρ
pl v.ppm.2p cj v.rai.1s cj v.pai.2p n.asm d.asm pt.rp.asm v.pai.3s adv adv cj
5828 3590 5828 1142 3857 4022 2426 2652 3836 5090 1639 4024 6045 1142

risen, just as he said. Come and see the place where he lay. **7** Then go quickly and tell his
ἠγέρθη καθὼς εἶπεν δεῦτε ἴδετε τὸν τόπον ὅπου ἔκειτο καὶ πορευθεῖσαι ταχὺ εἴπατε αὐτοῦ
v.api.3s adv v.aai.3s adv v.aam.2p d.asm n.asm pl v.imi.3s cj pt.ap.npf adv v.aam.2p r.gsm.3
1586 2777 3306 1307 1625 3836 5536 3963 3023 2779 4513 5444 3306 899

disciples: 'He has risen from the dead and is going ahead of you into Galilee. There you will
τοῖς μαθηταῖς ὅτι ἠγέρθη ἀπὸ τῶν νεκρῶν καὶ ἰδοὺ προάγει ὑμᾶς εἰς τὴν Γαλιλαίαν ἐκεῖ
d.dpm n.dpm cj v.api.3s p.g d.gpm a.gpm cj j v.pai.3s r.ap.2 p.a d.asf n.asf adv
3836 3412 4022 1586 608 3836 3738 2779 2627 4575 7007 1650 3836 1133 1695

see him.' Now I have told you." ¶ **8** So the women hurried away from the tomb, afraid yet
ὄψεσθε αὐτὸν ἰδοὺ εἶπον ὑμῖν Καὶ ταχὺ ἀπελθοῦσαι ἀπὸ τοῦ μνημείου μετὰ φόβου καὶ
v.fmi.2p r.asm.3 j v.aai.1s r.dp.2 cj adv pt.aa.npf p.g d.gsn n.gsn p.g n.gsm cj
3972 899 2627 3306 7007 2779 599 5444 608 3836 3646 3552 5832 2779

filled with joy, and ran to tell his disciples. **9** Suddenly Jesus met them. "Greetings," he
μεγάλης χαρᾶς ἔδραμον ἀπαγγεῖλαι αὐτοῦ τοῖς μαθηταῖς καὶ ἰδοὺ Ἰησοῦς ὑπήντησεν αὐταῖς χαίρετε
a.gsf n.gsf v.aai.3p f.aa r.gsm.3 d.dpm n.dpm cj j n.nsm v.aai.3s r.dpf.3 v.pam.2p
3489 5915 5556 550 899 3836 3412 2779 2627 2652 5636 899 5897

said. They came to him, clasped his feet and worshiped him. **10** Then Jesus said to them,
λέγων δὲ αἱ προσελθοῦσαι ἐκράτησαν αὐτοῦ τοὺς πόδας καὶ προσεκύνησαν αὐτῷ τότε ὁ Ἰησοῦς λέγει αὐταῖς
pt.pa.nsm cj d.npf pt.aa.npf v.aai.3p r.gsm.3 d.apm n.apm cj v.aai.3p r.dsm.3 adv d.nsm n.nsm v.pai.3s r.dpf.3
3306 1254 3836 4665 3195 899 3836 4546 2779 4686 899 5538 3836 2652 3306 899

"Do not be afraid. Go and tell my brothers to go to Galilee; there they will see
μὴ φοβεῖσθε ὑπάγετε ἀπαγγείλατε μου τοῖς ἀδελφοῖς ἵνα ἀπέλθωσιν εἰς τὴν Γαλιλαίαν κἀκεῖ ὄψονται
pl v.ppm.2p v.pam.2p v.aam.2p r.gs.1 d.dpm n.dpm cj v.aas.3p p.a d.asf n.asf crasis v.fmi.3p
5828 3590 5828 5632 550 1609 3836 81 2671 599 1650 3836 1133 2795 3972

me."
με
r.as.1
1609

The Guard's Report

28:11 While the women were on their way, some of the guards went into the city and
δὲ αὐτῶν Πορευομένων ἰδού τινες τῆς κουστωδίας ἐλθόντες εἰς τὴν πόλιν
cj r.gpf.3 pt.pm.gpf j r.npm d.gsf n.gsf pt.aa.npm p.a d.asf n.asf
1254 4513 4513 2627 5516 3836 3184 2262 1650 3836 4484

reported to the chief priests everything that had happened. **12** When the chief priests had met with the
ἀπήγγειλαν τοῖς ἀρχιερεῦσιν ἅπαντα τὰ γενόμενα καὶ συναχθέντες μετὰ τῶν
v.aai.3p d.dpm n.dpm a.apn d.apn pt.am.apn cj pt.ap.npm p.g d.gpm
550 3836 797 570 3836 1181 2779 5251 3552 3836

elders and devised a plan, they gave the soldiers a large sum of money, **13** telling them, "You are to
πρεσβυτέρων τε λαβόντες συμβούλιον ἔδωκαν τοῖς στρατιώταις ἱκανὰ ἀργύρια λέγοντες
a.gpm cj pt.aa.npm n.asn v.aai.3p d.dpm n.dpm a.apn n.apn pt.pa.npm
4565 5445 3284 5206 1443 3836 5132 2653 736 3306

say, 'His disciples came during the night and stole him away while we were asleep.' **14** If this
εἴπατε ὅτι αὐτοῦ οἱ μαθηταὶ ἐλθόντες νυκτὸς ἔκλεψαν αὐτὸν ἡμῶν κοιμωμένων καὶ ἐὰν τοῦτο
v.aam.2p cj r.gsm.3 d.npm n.npm pt.aa.npm n.gsf v.aai.3p r.asm.3 r.gp.1 pt.pp.gpm cj cj r.asn
3306 4022 899 3836 3412 2262 3816 3096 899 7005 3121 2779 1569 4047

report gets to the governor, we will satisfy him and keep you out of trouble." **15** So the soldiers took the
ἀκουσθῇ ἐπὶ τοῦ ἡγεμόνος ἡμεῖς πείσομεν αὐτὸν καὶ ποιήσομεν ὑμᾶς ἀμερίμνους δὲ οἱ λαβόντες τὰ
v.aps.3s p.g d.gsm n.gsm r.np.1 v.fai.1p r.asm.3 cj v.fai.1p r.ap.2 a.apm cj d.npm pt.aa.npm d.apn
201 2093 3836 2450 7005 4275 899 2779 4472 7007 291 1254 3836 3284 3836

money and did as they were instructed. And this story has been widely circulated among the Jews
ἀργύρια ἐποίησαν ὡς ἐδιδάχθησαν καὶ οὗτος ὁ λόγος διεφημίσθη παρὰ Ἰουδαίοις
n.apn v.aai.3p cj v.api.3p cj r.nsm d.nsm n.nsm v.api.3s p.d a.dpm
736 4472 6055 1438 2779 4047 3836 3364 1424 4123 2681

ὑμεῖς, οἶδα γὰρ ὅτι Ἰησοῦν τὸν ἐσταυρωμένον ζητεῖτε· **6** οὐκ ἔστιν ὧδε, ἠγέρθη γὰρ καθὼς εἶπεν· δεῦτε ἴδετε τὸν τόπον ὅπου ἔκειτο. **7** καὶ ταχὺ πορευθεῖσαι εἴπατε τοῖς μαθηταῖς αὐτοῦ ὅτι Ἠγέρθη ἀπὸ τῶν νεκρῶν, καὶ ἰδοὺ προάγει ὑμᾶς εἰς τὴν Γαλιλαίαν, ἐκεῖ αὐτὸν ὄψεσθε· ἰδοὺ εἶπον ὑμῖν. ¶ **8** καὶ ἀπελθοῦσαι ταχὺ ἀπὸ τοῦ μνημείου μετὰ φόβου καὶ χαρᾶς μεγάλης ἔδραμον ἀπαγγεῖλαι τοῖς μαθηταῖς αὐτοῦ. **9** καὶ ἰδοὺ Ἰησοῦς ὑπήντησεν αὐταῖς λέγων, Χαίρετε. αἱ δὲ προσελθοῦσαι ἐκράτησαν αὐτοῦ τοὺς πόδας καὶ προσεκύνησαν αὐτῷ. **10** τότε λέγει αὐταῖς ὁ Ἰησοῦς, Μὴ φοβεῖσθε· ὑπάγετε ἀπαγγείλατε τοῖς ἀδελφοῖς μου ἵνα ἀπέλθωσιν εἰς τὴν Γαλιλαίαν, κἀκεῖ με ὄψονται.

28:11 Πορευομένων δὲ αὐτῶν ἰδού τινες τῆς κουστωδίας ἐλθόντες εἰς τὴν πόλιν ἀπήγγειλαν τοῖς ἀρχιερεῦσιν ἅπαντα τὰ γενόμενα. **12** καὶ συναχθέντες μετὰ τῶν πρεσβυτέρων συμβούλιόν τε λαβόντες ἀργύρια ἱκανὰ ἔδωκαν τοῖς στρατιώταις **13** λέγοντες, Εἴπατε ὅτι Οἱ μαθηταὶ αὐτοῦ νυκτὸς ἐλθόντες ἔκλεψαν αὐτὸν ἡμῶν κοιμωμένων. **14** καὶ ἐὰν ἀκουσθῇ τοῦτο ἐπὶ τοῦ ἡγεμόνος, ἡμεῖς πείσομεν [αὐτὸν] καὶ ὑμᾶς ἀμερίμνους ποιήσομεν. **15** οἱ δὲ λαβόντες τὰ ἀργύρια ἐποίησαν ὡς ἐδιδάχθησαν. Καὶ

to	this	very	day.
μέχρι →	τῆς	σήμερον	[ἡμέρας]
p.g	d.gsf	adv	n.gsf
3588	3836	4958	2465

The Great Commission

28:16 Then the eleven disciples went to Galilee, to the mountain where Jesus had told them

δὲ	Οἱ	ἔνδεκα	μαθηταὶ	ἐπορεύθησαν	εἰς	₍τὴν Γαλιλαίαν₎	εἰς	τὸ	ὄρος	οὗ	₍ὁ Ἰησοῦς₎ →	ἐτάξατο	αὐτοῖς
cj	d.npm	a.npm	n.npm	v.api.3p	p.a	d.asf n.asf	p.a	d.asn	n.asn	adv	d.nsm n.nsm	v.ami.3s	r.dpm.3
1254	3836	1894	3412	4513	1650	3836 1133	1650	3836	4001	4023	3836 2652	5435	899

to go. **17** When they saw him, they worshiped him; but some doubted. **18** Then Jesus came to them and

καὶ →	→	ἰδόντες	αὐτὸν →	προσεκύνησαν	δὲ	οἱ	ἐδίστασαν	καὶ	₍ὁ Ἰησοῦς₎	προσελθὼν ←	αὐτοῖς
cj		pt.aa.npm	r.asm.3	v.aai.3p	pl	d.npm	v.aai.3p	cj	d.nsm n.nsm	pt.aa.nsm	r.dpm.3
2779		1625	899	4686	1254	3836	1491	2779	3836 2652	4665	899

said, "All authority in heaven and on earth has been given to me. **19** Therefore go and make

ἐλάλησεν	λέγων	πᾶσα	ἐξουσία	ἐν	οὐρανῷ	καὶ	ἐπὶ	₍τῆς γῆς₎ →	→	ἐδόθη →	μοι	οὖν	πορευθέντες →
v.aai.3s	pt.pa.nsm	a.nsf	n.nsf	p.d	n.dsm	cj	p.g	d.gsf n.gsf		v.api.3s	r.ds.1	cj	pt.ap.npm
3281	3306	4246	2026	1877	4041	2779	2093	3836 1178		1443	1609	4036	4513

disciples of all nations, baptizing them in the name of the Father and of the Son and of the Holy Spirit,

μαθητεύσατε	πάντα	₍τὰ ἔθνη₎	βαπτίζοντες	αὐτοὺς	εἰς	τὸ	ὄνομα →	τοῦ	πατρὸς	καὶ →	τοῦ	υἱοῦ	καὶ →	τοῦ	ἁγίου	πνεύματος
v.aam.2p	a.apn	d.apn n.apn	pt.pa.npm	r.apm.3	p.a	d.asn	n.asn	d.gsm	n.gsm	cj	d.gsm	n.gsm	cj	d.gsn	a.gsn	n.gsn
3411	4246	3836 1620	966	899	1650	3836	3950	3836	4252	2779	3836	5626	2779	3836	41	4460

20 and teaching them to obey everything I have commanded you. And surely I am with you always,

διδάσκοντες	αὐτοὺς →	τηρεῖν	₍πάντα ὅσα₎	→ →	ἐνετειλάμην	ὑμῖν	καὶ	ἰδοὺ	ἐγὼ	εἰμι	μεθ᾽	ὑμῶν	₍πάσας τὰς ἡμέρας₎
pt.pa.npm	r.apm.3	f.pa	a.apn r.apn		v.ami.1s	r.dp.2	cj	j	r.ns.1	v.pai.1s	p.g	r.gp.2	a.apf d.apf n.apf
1438	899	5498	4246 4012		1948	7007	2779	2627	1609	1639	3552	7007	4246 3836 2465

to the very end of the age."

to	the	very	end	of	the	age."
ἕως	τῆς	συντελείας →	τοῦ	αἰῶνος
p.g	d.gsf	n.gsf	d.gsm	n.gsm
2401	3836	5333	3836	172

διεφημίσθη ὁ λόγος οὗτος παρὰ Ἰουδαίοις μέχρι τῆς σήμερον [ἡμέρας].

28:16 Οἱ δὲ ἕνδεκα μαθηταὶ ἐπορεύθησαν εἰς τὴν Γαλιλαίαν εἰς τὸ ὄρος οὗ ἐτάξατο αὐτοῖς ὁ Ἰησοῦς, **17** καὶ ἰδόντες αὐτὸν προσεκύνησαν, οἱ δὲ ἐδίστασαν. **18** καὶ προσελθὼν ὁ Ἰησοῦς ἐλάλησεν αὐτοῖς λέγων, Ἐδόθη μοι πᾶσα ἐξουσία ἐν οὐρανῷ καὶ ἐπὶ [τῆς] γῆς. **19** πορευθέντες οὖν μαθητεύσατε πάντα τὰ ἔθνη, βαπτίζοντες αὐτοὺς εἰς τὸ ὄνομα τοῦ πατρὸς καὶ τοῦ υἱοῦ καὶ τοῦ ἁγίου πνεύματος, **20** διδάσκοντες αὐτοὺς τηρεῖν πάντα ὅσα ἐνετειλάμην ὑμῖν· καὶ ἰδοὺ ἐγὼ μεθ᾽ ὑμῶν εἰμι πάσας τὰς ἡμέρας ἕως τῆς συντελείας τοῦ αἰῶνος.

Mark

John the Baptist Prepares the Way

1:1 The beginning of the gospel about Jesus Christ, the Son of God. ¶ **2** It is written in
Ἀρχὴ → τοῦ εὐαγγελίου → Ἰησοῦ Χριστοῦ υἱοῦ → θεοῦ Καθὼς → γέγραπται ἐν
n.nsf d.gsn n.gsn n.gsm n.gsm n.gsm n.gsm cj v.rpi.3s p.d
794 3836 2295 2652 5986 5626 2536 2777 1211 1877

Isaiah the prophet: ¶ "I will send my messenger ahead of you, who will prepare
ⸯτῷ Ἡσαΐᾳⸯ τῷ προφήτῃ ἰδοὺ → ἀποστέλλω μου ⸯτὸν ἄγγελονⸯ ⸯπρὸ προσώπουⸯ ← σου ὃς → κατασκευάσει
d.dsm n.dsm d.dsm n.dsm j v.pai.1s r.gs.1 d.asm n.asm p.g n.gsn r.gs.2 r.nsm v.fai.3s
3836 2480 3836 4737 2627 690 1609 3836 34 4574 4725 5148 4005 2941

your way" – **3** "a voice of one calling in the desert, 'Prepare the way for the Lord, make straight paths for
σου ⸯτὴν ὁδόνⸯ φωνὴ → → βοῶντος ἐν τῇ ἐρήμῳ ἑτοιμάσατε τὴν ὁδὸν → κυρίου ποιεῖτε εὐθείας ⸯτὰς τρίβουςⸯ
r.gs.2 d.asf n.asf n.nsf pt.pa.gsm p.d d.dsf n.dsf v.aam.2p d.asf n.asf n.gsm v.pam.2p a.apf d.apf n.apf
5148 3836 3847 5889 1066 1877 3836 2245 2286 3836 3847 3261 4472 2318 3836 5561

him.'" ¶ **4** And so John came, baptizing in the desert region and preaching a baptism of repentance for
αὐτοῦ Ἰωάννης ἐγένετο ὁ βαπτίζων ἐν τῇ ἐρήμῳ ← καὶ κηρύσσων βάπτισμα → μετανοίας εἰς
r.gsm.3 n.nsm v.ami.3s d.nsm pt.pa.nsm p.d d.dsf n.dsf cj pt.pa.nsm n.asn n.gsf p.a
899 2722 1181 3836 966 1877 3836 2245 2779 3062 967 3567 1650

the forgiveness of sins. **5** The whole Judean countryside and all the people of Jerusalem went out
ἄφεσιν → ἁμαρτιῶν καὶ ἡ πᾶσα Ἰουδαία χώρα καὶ πάντες οἱ → → Ἱεροσολυμῖται ἐξεπορεύετο ←
n.asf n.gpf cj d.nsf a.nsf a.nsf n.nsf cj a.npm d.npm n.npm v.imi.3s
912 281 2779 3836 4246 2677 6001 2779 4246 3836 2643 1744

to him. Confessing their sins, they were baptized by him in the Jordan River. **6** John
πρὸς αὐτὸν καὶ ἐξομολογούμενοι αὐτῶν ⸯτὰς ἁμαρτίαςⸯ → → ἐβαπτίζοντο ὑπ᾽ αὐτοῦ ἐν τῷ Ἰορδάνῃ ποταμῷ καὶ ὁ Ἰωάννης
p.a r.asm.3 cj pt.pm.npm r.gpm.3 d.apf n.apf v.ipi.3p p.g r.gsm.3 p.d d.dsm n.dsm n.dsm cj d.nsm n.nsm
4639 899 2779 2018 899 3836 281 966 5679 899 1877 3836 2674 4532 2779 3836 2722

wore clothing made of camel's hair, with a leather belt around his waist, and he ate locusts
ⸯἦν ἐνδεδυμένοςⸯ ← → → καμήλου τρίχας καὶ δερματίνην ζώνην περὶ αὐτοῦ ⸯτὴν ὀσφὺνⸯ καὶ → ἐσθίων ἀκρίδας
v.iai.3s pt.rp.nsm n.gsf n.apf cj a.asf n.asf p.a r.gsm.3 d.asf n.asf cj pt.pa.nsm n.apf
1639 1907 2823 2502 2779 1294 2438 4309 899 3836 4019 2779 2266 210

and wild honey. **7** And this was his message: "After me will come one more powerful than I, the thongs of
καὶ ἄγριον μέλι Καὶ → ἐκήρυσσεν λέγων ὀπίσω μου → ἔρχεται ὁ → ἰσχυρότερός → μου τὸν ἱμάντα ⸯ
cj a.asn n.asn cj v.iai.3s pt.pa.nsm p.g r.gs.1 v.pmi.3s d.nsm a.nsm.c r.gs.1 d.asm n.asm
2779 67 3510 2779 3062 3306 3958 1609 2262 3836 2708 1609 3836 2666 5687

whose sandals I am not worthy to stoop down and untie. **8** I baptize you with water, but he will
αὐτοῦ ⸯτῶν ὑποδημάτωνⸯ οὗ → εἰμὶ οὐκ ἱκανὸς κύψας ← λῦσαι ἐγὼ ἐβάπτισα ὑμᾶς → ὕδατι δὲ αὐτὸς →
r.gsm.3 d.gpn n.gpn r.gsm v.pai.1s pl a.nsm pt.aa.nsm f.aa r.ns.1 v.aai.1s r.ap.2 n.dsn cj r.nsm
899 3836 5687 4005 1639 4024 2653 3252 3395 1609 966 7007 5623 1254 899

baptize you with the Holy Spirit."
βαπτίσει ὑμᾶς ἐν ἁγίῳ πνεύματι
v.fai.3s r.ap.2 p.d a.dsn n.dsn
966 7007 1877 41 4460

The Baptism and Temptation of Jesus

1:9 At that time Jesus came from Nazareth in Galilee and was baptized by John
Καὶ ἐγένετο ἐν ἐκείναις ⸯταῖς ἡμέραιςⸯ Ἰησοῦς ἦλθεν ἀπὸ Ναζαρὲτ → ⸯτῆς Γαλιλαίαςⸯ καὶ → ἐβαπτίσθη ὑπὸ Ἰωάννου
cj v.ami.3s p.d r.dpf d.dpf n.dpf n.nsm v.aai.3s p.g n.gsf d.gsf n.gsf cj v.api.3s p.g n.gsm
2779 1181 1877 1697 3836 2465 2652 2262 608 3715 3836 1133 2779 966 5679 2722

in the Jordan. **10** As Jesus was coming up out of the water, he saw heaven being torn open
εἰς τὸν Ἰορδάνην καὶ εὐθὺς → ἀναβαίνων ἐκ ← τοῦ ὕδατος → εἶδεν ⸯτοὺς οὐρανοὺςⸯ → σχιζομένους ←
p.a d.asm n.asm cj adv pt.pa.nsm p.g d.gsn n.gsn v.aai.3s d.apm n.apm pt.pp.apm
1650 3836 2674 2779 2318 326 1666 3836 5623 1625 3836 4041 5387

1:1 Ἀρχὴ τοῦ εὐαγγελίου Ἰησοῦ Χριστοῦ [υἱοῦ θεοῦ]. ¶ **2** Καθὼς γέγραπται ἐν τῷ Ἡσαΐᾳ τῷ προφήτῃ, ¶ Ἰδοὺ ἀποστέλλω τὸν ἄγγελόν μου πρὸ προσώπου σου, ὃς κατασκευάσει τὴν ὁδόν σου· **3** φωνὴ βοῶντος ἐν τῇ ἐρήμῳ, Ἑτοιμάσατε τὴν ὁδὸν κυρίου, εὐθείας ποιεῖτε τὰς τρίβους αὐτοῦ, ¶ **4** ἐγένετο Ἰωάννης [ὁ] βαπτίζων ἐν τῇ ἐρήμῳ καὶ κηρύσσων βάπτισμα μετανοίας εἰς ἄφεσιν ἁμαρτιῶν. **5** καὶ ἐξεπορεύετο πρὸς αὐτὸν πᾶσα ἡ Ἰουδαία χώρα καὶ οἱ Ἱεροσολυμῖται πάντες, καὶ ἐβαπτίζοντο ὑπ᾽ αὐτοῦ ἐν τῷ Ἰορδάνῃ ποταμῷ ἐξομολογούμενοι τὰς ἁμαρτίας αὐτῶν. **6** καὶ ἦν ὁ Ἰωάννης ἐνδεδυμένος τρίχας καμήλου καὶ ζώνην δερματίνην περὶ τὴν ὀσφὺν αὐτοῦ καὶ ἐσθίων ἀκρίδας καὶ μέλι ἄγριον. **7** καὶ ἐκήρυσσεν λέγων, Ἔρχεται ὁ ἰσχυρότερός μου ὀπίσω μου, οὗ οὐκ εἰμὶ ἱκανὸς κύψας λῦσαι τὸν ἱμάντα τῶν ὑποδημάτων αὐτοῦ. **8** ἐγὼ ἐβάπτισα ὑμᾶς ὕδατι, αὐτὸς δὲ βαπτίσει ὑμᾶς ἐν πνεύματι ἁγίῳ.

1:9 Καὶ ἐγένετο ἐν ἐκείναις ταῖς ἡμέραις ἦλθεν Ἰησοῦς ἀπὸ Ναζαρὲτ τῆς Γαλιλαίας καὶ ἐβαπτίσθη εἰς τὸν Ἰορδάνην ὑπὸ Ἰωάννου. **10** καὶ εὐθὺς ἀναβαίνων ἐκ τοῦ ὕδατος εἶδεν σχιζομένους τοὺς οὐρανοὺς καὶ τὸ πνεῦμα ὡς περιστερὰν καταβαῖνον

and the Spirit descending on him like a dove. 　**11** And a voice came from heaven: "You are my Son,
καὶ τὸ πνεῦμα καταβαῖνον εἰς αὐτόν ὡς περιστερὰν 　καὶ φωνὴ ἐγένετο ἐκ ⌐τῶν οὐρανῶν⌐ σὺ εἶ μου ὁ υἱός,
cj d.asn n.asn pt.pa.asn p.a r.asm.3 pl n.asf 　cj n.nsf v.ami.3s p.g d.gpm n.gpm r.ns.2 v.pai.2s r.gs.1 d.nsm n.nsm
2779 3836 4460 2849 1650 899 6055 4361 　2779 5889 1181 1666 3836 4041 5148 1639 1609 3836 5626

whom I love; 　with you I am well pleased." ¶ 　**12** 　At once the Spirit sent him out into the desert,
ὁ → ἀγαπητός ἐν σοὶ → → → εὐδόκησα 　Καὶ → εὐθὺς τὸ πνεῦμα ἐκβάλλει αὐτὸν ← εἰς τὴν ἔρημον
d.nsm a.nsm p.d r.ds.2 v.aai.1s 　adv d.asn n.asn v.pai.3s r.asm.3 p.a d.asf n.asf
3836 28 1877 5148 2305 　2779 2318 3836 4460 1675 899 1675 1650 3836 2245

13 and he was in the desert forty days, being tempted by Satan. 　He was with the wild animals, and
καὶ → ἦν ἐν τῇ ἐρήμῳ τεσσεράκοντα ἡμέρας → πειραζόμενος ὑπὸ ⌐τοῦ σατανᾶ⌐ καὶ → ἦν μετὰ τῶν → θηρίων καὶ
cj v.iai.3s p.d d.dsf n.dsf a.apf n.apf pt.pp.nsm p.g d.gsm n.gsm cj v.iai.3s p.g d.gpn n.gpn cj
2779 1639 1877 3836 2245 5477 2465 4279 5679 3836 4928 2779 1639 3552 3836 2563 2779

angels attended him.
⌐οἱ ἄγγελοι⌐ διηκόνουν αὐτῷ.
d.npm n.npm v.iai.3p r.dsm.3
3836 34 1354 899

The Calling of the First Disciples

1:14 　After John was put in prison, Jesus went into Galilee, proclaiming the
δὲ Μετὰ τὸν Ἰωάννην → ⌐τὸ παραδοθῆναι⌐ ← ← ὁ Ἰησοῦς ἦλθεν εἰς ⌐τὴν Γαλιλαίαν⌐ κηρύσσων τὸ
cj p.g d.asn n.asm d.asn f.ap d.nsm n.nsm v.aai.3s p.a d.asf n.asf pt.pa.nsm d.asn
1254 3552 3836 2722 3836 4140 3836 2652 2262 1650 3836 1133 3062 3836

good news of God. 　**15** "The time has come," he said. "The kingdom of God is near.
εὐαγγέλιον ← → ⌐τοῦ θεοῦ⌐ καὶ ὅτι ὁ καιρὸς → πεπλήρωται → λέγων καὶ ἡ βασιλεία ⌐τοῦ θεοῦ⌐ ἤγγικεν
n.asn d.gsm n.gsm cj cj d.nsm n.nsm v.rpi.3s pt.pa.nsm cj d.nsf n.nsf d.gsm n.gsm v.rai.3s
2295 3836 2536 2779 4022 3836 2789 4444 3306 2779 3836 993 3836 2536 1581

Repent and believe the good news!" ¶ 　**16** 　As Jesus walked beside the Sea of Galilee, he
μετανοεῖτε καὶ πιστεύετε ἐν τῷ εὐαγγελίῳ ← 　Καὶ → παράγων παρὰ τὴν θάλασσαν → ⌐τῆς Γαλιλαίας⌐ →
v.pam.2p cj v.pam.2p p.d d.dsn n.dsn 　cj pt.pa.nsm p.a d.asf n.asf d.gsf n.gsf
3566 2779 4409 1877 3836 2295 　2779 4135 4123 3836 2498 3836 1133

saw Simon and his brother Andrew casting a net into the lake, for they were fishermen. 　**17**
εἶδεν Σίμωνα καὶ Σίμωνος ⌐τὸν ἀδελφὸν⌐ Ἀνδρέαν ἀμφιβάλλοντας ← ἐν τῇ θαλάσσῃ γὰρ → ἦσαν ἁλιεῖς καὶ
v.aai.3s n.asm cj n.gsm d.asm n.asm n.asm pt.pa.apm p.d d.dsf n.dsf cj v.iai.3p n.npm cj
1625 4981 2779 4981 3836 81 436 311 1877 3836 2498 1142 1639 243 2779

"Come, follow me," Jesus said, "and I will make you fishers of men." 　**18** At once they
δεῦτε ὀπίσω μου ⌐ὁ Ἰησοῦς⌐ εἶπεν αὐτοῖς καὶ → → ποιήσω ὑμᾶς γενέσθαι ἁλιεῖς → ἀνθρώπων καὶ → εὐθὺς
adv p.g r.gs.1 d.nsm n.nsm v.aai.3s r.dpm.3 cj v.fai.1s r.ap.2 f.am n.apm n.gpm cj adv
1307 3958 1609 3836 2652 3306 899 2779 4472 7007 1181 243 476 2779 2318

left their nets and followed him. ¶ 　**19** When he had gone a little farther, he saw James son of
ἀφέντες τὰ δίκτυα ἠκολούθησαν αὐτῷ 　Καὶ → → προβὰς ὀλίγον ← → εἶδεν Ἰάκωβον τὸν
pt.aa.npm d.apn n.apn v.aai.3p r.dsm.3 　cj pt.aa.nsm adv v.aai.3s n.asm d.asm
918 3836 1473 199 899 　2779 4581 3900 1625 2610 3836

Zebedee and his brother John in a boat, preparing their nets. **20** Without delay he
⌐τοῦ Ζεβεδαίου⌐ καὶ αὐτοῦ ⌐τὸν ἀδελφὸν⌐ Ἰωάννην καὶ αὐτοὺς ἐν ⌐τῷ πλοίῳ⌐ καταρτίζοντας τὰ δίκτυα καὶ → εὐθὺς →
d.gsm n.gsm cj r.gsm.3 d.asm n.asm n.asm cj r.apm.3 p.d d.dsn n.dsn pt.pa.apm d.apn n.apn cj adv
3836 2411 2779 899 3836 81 2722 2779 899 1877 3836 4450 2936 3836 1473 2779 2318

called them, and they left their father Zebedee in the boat with the hired men and followed him
ἐκάλεσεν αὐτούς καὶ → ἀφέντες αὐτῶν ⌐τὸν πατέρα⌐ Ζεβεδαῖον ἐν τῷ πλοίῳ μετὰ τῶν μισθωτῶν ← ἀπῆλθον ὀπίσω αὐτου
v.aai.3s r.apm.3 cj pt.aa.npm r.gpm.3 d.asm n.asm n.asm p.d d.dsn n.dsn p.g d.gpm n.gpm v.aai.3p p.g r.gsm.3
2813 899 2779 918 899 3836 4252 2411 1877 3836 4450 3552 3836 3638 599 3958 899

Jesus Drives Out an Evil Spirit

1:21 　They went to Capernaum, and when the Sabbath came, Jesus went into the synagogue
Καὶ → εἰσπορεύονται εἰς Καφαρναούμ καὶ εὐθὺς → τοῖς σάββασιν ← εἰσελθὼν εἰς τὴν συναγωγὴν
cj v.pmi.3p p.a n.asf cj adv d.dpn n.dpn pt.aa.nsm p.a d.asf n.asf
2779 1660 1650 3019 2779 2318 3836 4879 1656 1650 3836 5252

εἰς αὐτόν· **11** καὶ φωνὴ ἐγένετο ἐκ τῶν οὐρανῶν, Σὺ εἶ ὁ υἱός μου ὁ ἀγαπητός, ἐν σοὶ εὐδόκησα. ¶ **12** Καὶ εὐθὺς τὸ πνεῦμα αὐτὸν ἐκβάλλει εἰς τὴν ἔρημον. **13** καὶ ἦν ἐν τῇ ἐρήμῳ τεσσεράκοντα ἡμέρας πειραζόμενος ὑπὸ τοῦ Σατανᾶ, καὶ ἦν μετὰ τῶν θηρίων, καὶ οἱ ἄγγελοι διηκόνουν αὐτῷ.

1:14 Μετὰ δὲ τὸ παραδοθῆναι τὸν Ἰωάννην ἦλθεν ὁ Ἰησοῦς εἰς τὴν Γαλιλαίαν κηρύσσων τὸ εὐαγγέλιον τοῦ θεοῦ **15** καὶ λέγων ὅτι Πεπλήρωται ὁ καιρὸς καὶ ἤγγικεν ἡ βασιλεία τοῦ θεοῦ· μετανοεῖτε καὶ πιστεύετε ἐν τῷ εὐαγγελίῳ. ¶ **16** Καὶ παράγων παρὰ τὴν θάλασσαν τῆς Γαλιλαίας εἶδεν Σίμωνα καὶ Ἀνδρέαν τὸν ἀδελφὸν Σίμωνος ἀμφιβάλλοντας ἐν τῇ θαλάσσῃ· ἦσαν γὰρ ἁλιεῖς. **17** καὶ εἶπεν αὐτοῖς ὁ Ἰησοῦς, Δεῦτε ὀπίσω μου, καὶ ποιήσω ὑμᾶς γενέσθαι ἁλιεῖς ἀνθρώπων. **18** καὶ εὐθὺς ἀφέντες τὰ δίκτυα ἠκολούθησαν αὐτῷ. ¶ **19** Καὶ προβὰς ὀλίγον εἶδεν Ἰάκωβον τὸν τοῦ Ζεβεδαίου καὶ Ἰωάννην τὸν ἀδελφὸν αὐτοῦ καὶ αὐτοὺς ἐν τῷ πλοίῳ καταρτίζοντας τὰ δίκτυα, **20** καὶ εὐθὺς ἐκάλεσεν αὐτούς. καὶ ἀφέντες τὸν πατέρα αὐτῶν Ζεβεδαῖον ἐν τῷ πλοίῳ μετὰ τῶν μισθωτῶν ἀπῆλθον ὀπίσω αὐτοῦ.

1:21 Καὶ εἰσπορεύονται εἰς Καφαρναούμ· καὶ εὐθὺς τοῖς σάββασιν εἰσελθὼν εἰς τὴν συναγωγὴν ἐδίδασκεν. **22** καὶ

and began to teach. **22** The people were amazed at his teaching, because he taught them as one
→ → ἐδίδασκεν καί → ἐξεπλήσσοντο ἐπὶ αὐτοῦ ˌτῇ διδαχῇ˩ γάρ → ˌἦν διδάσκων αὐτοὺς ὡς →
v.iai.3s cj v.ipi.3p p.d r.gsm.3 d.dsf n.dsf cj v.iai.3s pt.pa.nsm r.apm.3 pl
1438 2779 1742 2093 899 3836 1439 1142 1639 1438 899 6055

who had authority, not as the teachers of the law. **23** Just then a man in their synagogue who
→ ἔχων ἐξουσίαν καὶ οὐχ ὡς οἱ γραμματεῖς ← ← Καὶ εὐθὺς ← ἄνθρωπος ἦν ἐν αὐτῶν ˌτῇ συναγωγῇ˩
pt.pa.nsm n.asf cj pl pl d.npm n.npm cj adv n.nsm v.iai.1s p.d r.gpm.3 d.dsf n.dsf
2400 2026 2779 4024 6055 3836 1208 2779 2318 476 1639 1877 899 3836 5252

was possessed by an evil spirit cried out, **24** "What do you want with us, Jesus of Nazareth?
→ ἐν ἀκαθάρτῳ πνεύματι καὶ ἀνέκραξεν ← λέγων τί σοί καὶ → ἡμῖν Ἰησοῦ → Ναζαρηνέ·
p.d a.dsn n.dsn cj v.aai.3s pt.pa.nsm r.nsn r.ds.2 cj r.dp.1 n.vsm a.vsm
1877 176 4460 2779 371 3306 5515 5148 2779 7005 2652 3716

Have you come to destroy us? I know who you are – the Holy One of God!" ¶ **25** "Be quiet!" said
→ ἦλθες ἀπολέσαι ἡμᾶς → οἶδα σε τίς → εἶ ὁ ἅγιος ← ˌτοῦ θεοῦ˩ καὶ → φιμώθητι λέγων
v.aai.2s f.aa r.ap.1 v.rai.1s r.as.2 r.nsm v.pai.2s d.nsm a.nsm d.gsm n.gsm cj v.apm.2s pt.pa.nsm
2262 660 7005 3857 5148 5515 1639 3836 41 3836 2536 2779 5821 3306

Jesus sternly. "Come out of him!" **26** The evil spirit shook the man violently and
ˌὁ Ἰησοῦς˩ αὐτῷ ἐπετίμησεν καὶ ἔξελθε ← ἐξ αὐτοῦ καὶ τὸ ˌτὸ ἀκάθαρτον˩ πνεῦμα σπαράξαν αὐτὸν καὶ
d.nsm n.nsm r.dsm.3 v.aai.3s cj v.aam.2s p.g r.gsm.3 cj d.nsn d.nsn a.nsn n.nsn pt.aa.nsn r.asm.3 cj
3836 2652 899 2203 2779 2002 1666 899 2779 3836 3836 176 4460 5057 899 5057 2779

came out of him with a shriek. ¶ **27** The people were all so amazed that they asked
ἐξῆλθεν ἐξ ← αὐτοῦ → ˌφωνῆσαν φωνῇ μεγάλῃ˩ καὶ → → ἅπαντες ἐθαμβήθησαν ὥστε → συζητεῖν
v.aai.3s p.g r.gsm.3 pt.aa.nsn n.dsf a.dsf cj a.npm v.api.3p cj f.pa
2002 1666 899 5888 5889 3489 2779 2501 2501 570 2501 6063 5184

each other, "What is this? A new teaching – and with authority! He even gives orders to
πρὸς ἑαυτοὺς ← λέγοντας τί ἐστιν τοῦτο καινὴ διδαχὴ κατ᾽ ἐξουσίαν → καὶ ἐπιτάσσει ← →
p.a r.apm.3 pt.pa.apm r.nsn v.pai.3s r.nsn a.nsf n.nsf p.a n.asf cj v.pai.3s
4639 1571 3306 5515 1639 4047 2785 1439 2848 2026 2199 2779 2199 4460

evil spirits and they obey him." **28** News about him spread quickly over the
ˌτοῖς ἀκαθάρτοις˩ ˌτοῖς πνεύμασι˩ καὶ → ὑπακούουσιν αὐτῷ καὶ ἡ ἀκοὴ αὐτοῦ ἐξῆλθεν εὐθὺς πανταχοῦ εἰς τὴν
d.dpn a.dpn d.dpn n.dpn cj v.pai.3p r.dsm.3 cj d.nsf n.nsf r.gsm.3 v.aai.3s adv adv p.a d.asf
3836 176 3836 4460 2779 5634 899 2779 3836 198 899 2002 2318 4116 1650 3836

whole region of Galilee.
ὅλην περίχωρον → ˌτῆς Γαλιλαίας˩
a.asf a.asf d.gsf n.gsf
3910 4369 3836 1133

Jesus Heals Many

1:29 As soon as they left the synagogue, they went with James and John to the home of
Καὶ εὐθὺς ← ← ← ἐξελθόντες ἐκ τῆς συναγωγῆς → ἦλθον μετὰ Ἰακώβου καὶ Ἰωάννου εἰς τὴν οἰκίαν
cj adv pt.aa.npm p.g d.gsf n.gsf v.aai.3p p.g n.gsm cj n.gsm p.a d.asf n.asf
2779 2318 2002 1666 3836 5252 2262 3552 2610 2779 2722 1650 3836 3864

Simon and Andrew. **30** Simon's mother-in-law was in bed with a fever, and they told Jesus about
Σίμωνος καὶ Ἀνδρέου δὲ Σίμωνος ἡ πενθερὰ → → κατέκειτο → πυρέσσουσα καὶ εὐθὺς → λέγουσιν αὐτῷ περὶ
n.gsm cj n.gsm cj n.gsm d.nsf n.nsf v.imi.3s pt.pa.nsf cj adv v.pai.3p r.dsm.3 p.g
4981 2779 436 1254 4981 3836 4289 2879 4789 2779 2318 3306 899 4309

her. **31** So he went to her, took her hand and helped her up. The fever left her and she began to
αὐτῆς καὶ → προσελθὼν ← κρατήσας τῆς χειρός· ἤγειρεν αὐτὴν καὶ ὁ πυρετός ἀφῆκεν αὐτὴν καὶ → → →
r.gsf.3 cj pt.aa.nsm pt.aa.nsm d.gsf n.gsf v.aai.3s r.asf.3 cj d.nsm n.nsm v.aai.3s r.asf.3 cj
899 2779 4665 3195 3836 5931 1586 899 1586 2779 3836 4790 918 899 2779

wait on them. ¶ **32** That evening after sunset the people brought to Jesus all the
διηκόνει ← αὐτοῖς δὲ γενομένης Ὀψίας ὅτε ἔδυ ὁ ἥλιος˩ ἔφερον πρὸς αὐτὸν πάντας τοὺς
v.iai.3s r.dpm.3 cj pt.am.gsf n.gsf cj v.aai.3s d.nsm n.nsm v.iai.3p p.a r.asm.3 a.apm d.apm
1354 899 1254 1181 4068 4021 1544 3836 2463 5770 4639 899 4246 3836

sick and demon-possessed. **33** The whole town gathered at the door, **34** and Jesus healed
ˌκακῶς ἔχοντας˩ καὶ ˌτοὺς δαιμονιζομένους˩ καὶ ἡ ὅλη πόλις ˌἦν ἐπισυνηγμένη˩ πρὸς τὴν θύραν καὶ ἐθεράπευσεν
adv pt.pa.apm cj d.apm pt.pp.apm cj d.nsf a.nsf n.nsf v.iai.3s pt.rp.nsf p.a d.asf n.asf cj v.aai.3s
2809 2400 2779 3836 1227 2779 3836 3910 4484 1639 2190 4639 3836 2598 2779 2543

ἐξεπλήσσοντο ἐπὶ τῇ διδαχῇ αὐτοῦ· ἦν γὰρ διδάσκων αὐτοὺς ὡς ἐξουσίαν ἔχων καὶ οὐχ ὡς οἱ γραμματεῖς. **23** καὶ εὐθὺς ἦν ἐν τῇ συναγωγῇ αὐτῶν ἄνθρωπος ἐν πνεύματι ἀκαθάρτῳ καὶ ἀνέκραξεν **24** λέγων, Τί ἡμῖν καὶ σοί, Ἰησοῦ Ναζαρηνέ; ἦλθες ἀπολέσαι ἡμᾶς; οἶδά σε τίς εἶ, ὁ ἅγιος τοῦ θεοῦ. ¶ **25** καὶ ἐπετίμησεν αὐτῷ ὁ Ἰησοῦς λέγων, Φιμώθητι καὶ ἔξελθε ἐξ αὐτοῦ. **26** καὶ σπαράξαν αὐτὸν τὸ πνεῦμα τὸ ἀκάθαρτον καὶ φωνῆσαν φωνῇ μεγάλῃ ἐξῆλθεν ἐξ αὐτοῦ. ¶ **27** καὶ ἐθαμβήθησαν ἅπαντες ὥστε συζητεῖν πρὸς ἑαυτοὺς λέγοντας, Τί ἐστιν τοῦτο; διδαχὴ καινὴ κατ᾽ ἐξουσίαν· καὶ τοῖς πνεύμασι τοῖς ἀκαθάρτοις ἐπιτάσσει, καὶ ὑπακούουσιν αὐτῷ. **28** καὶ ἐξῆλθεν ἡ ἀκοὴ αὐτοῦ εὐθὺς πανταχοῦ εἰς ὅλην τὴν περίχωρον τῆς Γαλιλαίας.

1:29 Καὶ εὐθὺς ἐκ τῆς συναγωγῆς ἐξελθόντες ἦλθον εἰς τὴν οἰκίαν Σίμωνος καὶ Ἀνδρέου μετὰ Ἰακώβου καὶ Ἰωάννου. **30** ἡ δὲ πενθερὰ Σίμωνος κατέκειτο πυρέσσουσα, καὶ εὐθὺς λέγουσιν αὐτῷ περὶ αὐτῆς. **31** καὶ προσελθὼν ἤγειρεν αὐτὴν κρατήσας τῆς χειρός· καὶ ἀφῆκεν αὐτὴν ὁ πυρετός, καὶ διηκόνει αὐτοῖς. ¶ **32** Ὀψίας δὲ γενομένης, ὅτε ἔδυ ὁ ἥλιος, ἔφερον πρὸς αὐτὸν πάντας τοὺς κακῶς ἔχοντας καὶ τοὺς δαιμονιζομένους· **33** καὶ ἦν ὅλη ἡ πόλις ἐπισυνηγμένη πρὸς τὴν θύραν. **34** καὶ ἐθεράπευσεν

many	who had		various	diseases.	He	also	drove	out	many	demons,	but	he	would	not	let	the	demons
πολλοὺς →	ἔχοντας	κακῶς	ποικίλαις	νόσοις		καὶ	ἐξέβαλεν ←		πολλὰ	δαιμόνια	καὶ →			οὐκ	ἤφιεν	τὰ	δαιμόνια
a.apm	pt.pa.apm	adv	a.dpf	n.dpf		cj	v.aai.3s		a.apn	n.apn	cj			pl	v.iai.3s	d.apn	n.apn
4498	2400	2809	4476	3798	1675	2779	1675		4498	1228	2779	918	918	4024	918	3836	1228

speak	because	they	knew	who	he	was.
λαλεῖν	ὅτι	→	ᾔδεισαν		αὐτόν	
f.pa	cj		v.lai.3p		r.asm.3	
3281	4022	3857		899		

Jesus Prays in a Solitary Place

1:35

Very	early	in the morning,	while it was still	dark,	Jesus got up,		left	the house	and	went	off	to
Καὶ	λίαν	πρωῒ ← ←		ἔννυχα	→ ἀναστὰς	ἐξῆλθεν			καὶ	ἀπῆλθεν ←		εἰς
cj	adv	adv		adv	pt.aa.nsm	v.aai.3s			cj	v.aai.3s		p.a
2779	3336	4745		1939	482	2002			2779	599		1650

a solitary	place,	where	he prayed.	**36**		Simon	and	his	companions	went to look		for him,	**37**	and	when they
ἔρημον	τόπον	κἀκεῖ	προσηύχετο	καὶ	Σίμων	καὶ	αὐτοῦ	οἱ μετ᾽	→	κατεδίωξεν		αὐτὸν	καὶ	→
a.asm	n.asm	crasis	v.imi.3s	cj	n.nsm	cj	r.gsm.3	d.npm p.g		v.aai.3s		r.asm.3	cj	
2245	5536	2779	4667	2779	4981	2779	899	3836 3552		2870		899	2779

found him,		they	exclaimed:	"Everyone	is looking	for you!"	¶	**38**		Jesus replied,		"Let us
εὗρον	αὐτὸν καὶ	→	λέγουσιν	αὐτῷ ὅτι πάντες	→ ζητοῦσίν ←	σε			καὶ	λέγει	αὐτοῖς →	
v.aai.3p	r.asm.3 cj		v.pai.3p	r.dsm.3 cj a.npm	v.pai.3s	r.as.2			cj	v.pai.3s	r.dpm.3	
2351	899 2779	3306		899 4022 4246	2426	5148			2779	3306	899	

go	somewhere	else	– to	the	nearby	villages	– so	I can	preach	there	also.	That		is why I have come."
ἄγωμεν	ἀλλαχοῦ		εἰς	τὰς	ἐχομένας	κωμοπόλεις	ἵνα →		κηρύξω	ἐκεῖ	καὶ	γὰρ	εἰς τοῦτο	← ←	ἐξῆλθον
v.pas.1p	adv		p.a	d.apf	pt.pm.apf	n.apf	cj		v.aas.1s	adv	adv	cj	p.a r.asn		v.aai.1s
72	250		1650	3836	2400	3268	2671		3062	1695	2779	1142	1650 4047		2002

39 So	he	traveled	throughout	Galilee,		preaching	in	their	synagogues		and	driving	out	demons.
Καὶ	→	ἦλθεν	εἰς ὅλην	τὴν Γαλιλαίαν		κηρύσσων	εἰς	αὐτῶν	τὰς συναγωγὰς		καὶ	ἐκβάλλων		τὰ δαιμόνια
cj		v.aai.3s	p.a a.asf	d.asf n.asf		pt.pa.nsm	p.a	r.gpm.3	d.apf n.apf		cj	pt.pa.nsm		d.apn n.apn
2779	2262		1650 3910	3836 1133		3062	1650	899	3836 5252		2779	1675		3836 1228

A Man With Leprosy

1:40

A man	with	leprosy	came	to	him	and	begged	him		on his knees,			"If you	
Καὶ	→	λεπρὸς	ἔρχεται	πρὸς	αὐτὸν	καὶ →	παρακαλῶν	αὐτὸν	καὶ →	γονυπετῶν	καὶ	λέγων αὐτῷ ὅτι ἐὰν		→
cj		a.nsm	v.pmi.3s	p.a	r.asm.3		pt.pa.nsm	r.asm.3	cj	pt.pa.nsm		pt.pa.nsm r.dsm.3 cj		
2779	3320		2262	4639	899	4151		899	2779	1206	2779	3306 899 4022 1569		

are willing,	you can		make	me	clean."	¶	**41**		Filled with	compassion,	Jesus	reached out	his	hand	and
→ θέλῃς	→ δύνασαι		με	καθαρίσαι				καὶ	→	σπλαγχνισθεὶς		ἐκτείνας	αὐτοῦ	τὴν χεῖρα	
v.pas.2s	v.ppi.2s		r.as.1	f.aa				cj		pt.ap.nsm		pt.aa.nsm	r.gsm.3	d.asf n.asf	
2527	1538	2751	1609	2751				2779		5072	1753		899	3836 5931	

touched	the man.	"I am willing,"	he said.	"Be clean!"	**42**		Immediately	the	leprosy	left		him	and
ἥψατο	καὶ →	θέλω	→ λέγει αὐτῷ	→ καθαρίσθητι	καὶ	εὐθὺς	ἡ	λέπρα	ἀπῆλθεν	ἀπ᾽	αὐτοῦ καὶ	
v.ami.3s	cj	v.pai.1s	v.pai.3s r.dsm.3	v.apm.2s	cj	adv	d.nsf	n.nsf	v.aai.3s	p.g	r.gsm.3 cj	
721	2779	2527	3306 899	2751	2779	2318	3836	3319	599	608	899 2779	

he was cured.	¶	**43**		Jesus sent	him	away	at once	with a strong	warning:				**44**	"See
→ → ἐκαθαρίσθη			καὶ	ἐξέβαλεν	αὐτὸν	→	εὐθὺς	ἐμβριμησάμενος	αὐτῷ	καὶ	λέγει αὐτῷ			ὅρα
v.api.3s			cj	v.aai.3s	r.asm.3		adv	pt.am.nsm	r.dsm.3	cj	v.pai.3s r.dsm.3			v.pam.2s
2751			2779	1675	899	1675	2318	1839	899	2779	3306 899			3972

that you	don't	tell	this	to anyone.	But	go,	show	yourself	to the	priest	and	offer		the	sacrifices	that	Moses
→ μηδὲν	εἴπῃς	→ μηδενὶ		ἀλλὰ	ὕπαγε	δεῖξον	σεαυτὸν	→	τῷ	ἱερεῖ	καὶ	προσένεγκε ← ←		ἃ			Μωϋσῆς
r.asn	v.aas.2s	a.dsn		cj	v.pam.2s	v.aam.2s	r.asm.2		d.dsm	n.dsm	cj	v.aam.2s		r.apn			n.nsm
3306	3594	3306 3594		247	5632	1259	4932		3836	2636	2779	4712		4005			3707

commanded	for	your	cleansing,	as	a	testimony	to them."	**45**	Instead	he	went	out	and	began	to	talk		freely,
προσέταξεν	περὶ	σου	τοῦ καθαρισμοῦ	εἰς		μαρτύριον	αὐτοῖς	δὲ	ὁ	ἐξελθὼν			→	ἤρξατο →		κηρύσσειν		πολλὰ
v.aai.3s	p.g	r.gs.2	d.gsm n.gsm	p.a		n.asn	r.dpm.3		d.nsm	pt.aa.nsm				v.ami.3s		f.pa		a.apn
4705	4309	5148	3836 2752	1650		3457	899	1254	3836	2002			806		3062		4498

spreading	the news.	As	a result,	Jesus	could	no	longer	enter		a town	openly	but	stayed	outside	in
καὶ	διαφημίζειν	τὸν λόγον	ὥστε ←		αὐτὸν	δύνασθαι	μηκέτι ←		εἰσελθεῖν εἰς		πόλιν	φανερῶς	ἀλλ᾽	ἦν	ἔξω	ἐπ᾽
cj	f.pa	d.asm n.asm	cj		r.asm.3	f.pp	adv		f.aa	p.a	n.asf	adv	cj	v.iai.3s	adv	p.d
2779	1424	3836 3364	6063		899	1538	3600		1656	1650	4484	5747	247	1639	2032	2093

πολλοὺς κακῶς ἔχοντας ποικίλαις νόσοις καὶ δαιμόνια πολλὰ ἐξέβαλεν καὶ οὐκ ἤφιεν λαλεῖν τὰ δαιμόνια, ὅτι ᾔδεισαν αὐτόν.

¹:³⁵ Καὶ πρωῒ ἔννυχα λίαν ἀναστὰς ἐξῆλθεν καὶ ἀπῆλθεν εἰς ἔρημον τόπον κἀκεῖ προσηύχετο. ³⁶ καὶ κατεδίωξεν αὐτὸν Σίμων καὶ οἱ μετ᾽ αὐτοῦ. ³⁷ καὶ εὗρον αὐτὸν καὶ λέγουσιν αὐτῷ ὅτι Πάντες ζητοῦσίν σε. ¶ ³⁸ καὶ λέγει αὐτοῖς, Ἄγωμεν ἀλλαχοῦ εἰς τὰς ἐχομένας κωμοπόλεις, ἵνα καὶ ἐκεῖ κηρύξω· εἰς τοῦτο γὰρ ἐξῆλθον. ³⁹ καὶ ἦλθεν κηρύσσων εἰς τὰς συναγωγὰς αὐτῶν εἰς ὅλην τὴν Γαλιλαίαν καὶ τὰ δαιμόνια ἐκβάλλων.

¹:⁴⁰ Καὶ ἔρχεται πρὸς αὐτὸν λεπρὸς παρακαλῶν αὐτὸν [καὶ γονυπετῶν] καὶ λέγων αὐτῷ ὅτι Ἐὰν θέλῃς δύνασαί με καθαρίσαι ¶ ⁴¹ καὶ σπλαγχνισθεὶς ἐκτείνας τὴν χεῖρα αὐτοῦ ἥψατο καὶ λέγει αὐτῷ, Θέλω, καθαρίσθητι· ⁴² καὶ εὐθὺς ἀπῆλθεν ἀπ᾽ αὐτοῦ ἡ λέπρα, καὶ ἐκαθαρίσθη. ¶ ⁴³ καὶ ἐμβριμησάμενος αὐτῷ εὐθὺς ἐξέβαλεν αὐτὸν ⁴⁴ καὶ λέγει αὐτῷ, Ὅρα μηδενὶ μηδὲν εἴπῃς, ἀλλὰ ὕπαγε σεαυτὸν δεῖξον τῷ ἱερεῖ καὶ προσένεγκε περὶ τοῦ καθαρισμοῦ σου ἃ προσέταξεν Μωϋσῆς, εἰς μαρτύριον αὐτοῖς. ⁴⁵ ὁ δὲ ἐξελθὼν ἤρξατο κηρύσσειν πολλὰ καὶ διαφημίζειν τὸν λόγον, ὥστε μηκέτι αὐτὸν δύνασθαι φανερῶς εἰς πόλιν εἰσελθεῖν,

lonely places. Yet the people still came to him from everywhere.
ἐρήμοις τόποις καὶ → ἤρχοντο πρὸς αὐτὸν → πάντοθεν
a.dpm n.dpm cj v.imi.3p p.a r.asm.3 adv
2245 5536 2779 2262 4639 899 4119

Jesus Heals a Paralytic

2:1 *A few days later,* when Jesus again entered Capernaum, the people heard that he had come
Καὶ δι᾽ ἡμερῶν → πάλιν εἰσελθὼν εἰς Καφαρναοὺμ ἠκούσθη ὅτι → → ἐστίν
cj p.g n.gpf adv pt.aa.nsm p.a n.asf v.api.3s cj v.pai.3s
2779 1328 2465 1656 4099 1656 1650 3019 201 4022 1639

home. **2** So many gathered that there was no room left, not even outside the door, and he preached the
ἐν οἴκῳ καὶ πολλοὶ συνήχθησαν ὥστε → → μηκέτι χωρεῖν μηδὲ τὰ πρὸς τὴν θύραν καὶ → ἐλάλει τὸν
p.d n.dsm cj a.npm v.api.3p cj adv f.pa adv d.apn p.a d.asf n.asf cj v.iai.3s d.asm
1877 3875 2779 4498 5251 6063 6003 6003 3600 6003 3593 3836 4639 3836 2598 2779 3281 3836

word to them. **3** Some men came, bringing to him a paralytic, carried by four of them. **4** Since they
λόγον → αὐτοῖς καὶ → ἔρχονται φέροντες πρὸς αὐτὸν παραλυτικὸν αἰρόμενον ὑπὸ τεσσάρων καὶ →
n.asm r.dpm.3 cj v.pmi.3p pt.pa.npm p.a r.asm.3 a.asm pt.pp.asm p.g a.gpm cj
3364 899 2779 2262 5770 4639 899 4166 149 5679 5475 2779

could not get him to Jesus because of the crowd, they made an opening in the roof above Jesus
δυνάμενοι μὴ προσενέγκαι → αὐτῷ διὰ ← τὸν ὄχλον → ἀπεστέγασαν ← τὴν στέγην ὅπου ἦν
pt.pp.npm pl f.aa r.dsm.3 p.a d.asm n.asm v.aai.3p d.asf n.asf cj v.iai.3s
1538 3590 4712 899 1328 3836 4063 689 3836 5094 3963 1639

and, after digging through it, lowered the mat the paralyzed man was lying on. **5** When
καὶ ἐξορύξαντες ← χαλῶσι τὸν κράβαττον ὅπου ὁ παραλυτικὸς ← → κατέκειτο ← καὶ
cj pt.aa.npm v.pai.3p d.asm n.asm cj d.nsm a.nsm v.imi.3s cj
2779 2021 5899 3836 3187 3963 3836 4166 2879 2779 1625

Jesus saw their faith, he said to the paralytic, "Son, your sins are forgiven." ¶ **6** Now some
ὁ Ἰησοῦς ἰδὼν αὐτῶν τὴν πίστιν → λέγει τῷ παραλυτικῷ τέκνον σου αἱ ἁμαρτίαι → ἀφίενται δὲ τινες
d.nsm n.nsm pt.aa.nsm r.gpm.3 d.asf n.asf v.pai.3s d.dsm a.dsm n.vsn r.gs.2 d.npf n.npf v.ppi.3p cj r.npm
3836 2652 1625 899 3836 4411 3306 3836 4166 5451 5148 3836 281 918 1254 5516

teachers of the law were sitting there, thinking to themselves, **7** "Why does this fellow talk
τῶν γραμματέων ← ← ἦσαν καθήμενοι ἐκεῖ καὶ διαλογιζόμενοι ἐν ταῖς καρδίαις αὐτῶν τί οὗτος ← λαλεῖ
d.gpm n.gpm v.iai.3p pt.pm.npm adv cj pt.pm.npm p.d d.dpf n.dpf r.gpm.3 r.asn r.nsm v.pai.3s
3836 1208 1639 2764 1695 2779 1368 1877 3836 2840 899 5515 3281 4047 3281

like that? He's blaspheming! Who can forgive sins but God alone?" ¶ **8** Immediately
οὕτως ← → βλασφημεῖ τίς δύναται ἀφιέναι ἁμαρτίας εἰ μὴ ὁ θεός εἷς καὶ εὐθὺς
adv v.pai.3s r.nsm v.ppi.3s f.pa n.apf cj pl d.nsm n.nsm a.nsm cj adv
4048 1059 5515 1538 918 281 1623 3590 3836 2536 1651 2779 2318

Jesus knew in his spirit that this was what they were thinking in their hearts, and he said to
ὁ Ἰησοῦς ἐπιγνοὺς → αὐτοῦ τῷ πνεύματι ὅτι οὕτως ← → διαλογίζονται ἐν ἑαυτοῖς → λέγει
d.nsm n.nsm pt.aa.nsm r.gsm.3 d.dsn n.dsn cj adv v.pmi.3p p.d r.dpm.3 v.pai.3s
3836 2652 2105 4460 899 3836 4460 4022 4048 1368 1877 1571 3306

them, "Why are you thinking these things? **9** Which is easier: to say to the paralytic,
αὐτοῖς τί → → διαλογίζεσθε ταῦτα ἐν ταῖς καρδίαις ὑμῶν τί ἐστιν εὐκοπώτερον → εἰπεῖν τῷ παραλυτικῷ
r.dpm.3 r.asn v.pmi.2p r.apn p.d d.dpf n.dpf r.gp.2 r.nsn v.pai.3s a.nsn f.aa d.dsm a.dsm
899 5515 1368 4047 1877 3836 2840 7007 5515 1639 2324 3306 3836 4166

'Your sins are forgiven,' or to say, 'Get up, take your mat and walk'? **10** But that you may
σου αἱ ἁμαρτίαι → ἀφίενται ἢ → εἰπεῖν ἔγειρε καὶ ἆρον σου τὸν κράβαττον καὶ περιπάτει δὲ ἵνα →
r.gs.2 d.npf n.npf v.ppi.3p cj f.aa v.pam.2s cj v.aam.2s r.gs.2 d.asm n.asm cj v.pam.2s cj cj
5148 3836 281 918 2445 3306 1586 2779 149 5148 3836 3187 2779 4344 1254 2671

know that the Son of Man has authority on earth to forgive sins . . . ." He said to the paralytic,
εἰδῆτε ὅτι ὁ υἱὸς τοῦ ἀνθρώπου ἔχει ἐξουσίαν ἐπὶ τῆς γῆς → ἀφιέναι ἁμαρτίας → λέγει → τῷ παραλυτικῷ
v.ras.2p cj d.nsm n.nsm d.gsm n.gsm v.pai.3s n.asf p.g d.gsf n.gsf f.pa n.apf v.pai.3s d.dsm a.dsm
3857 4022 3836 5626 3836 476 2400 2026 2093 3836 1178 918 281 3306 3836 4166

11 "I tell you, get up, take your mat and go home." **12** He got up, took his
→ λέγω σοί ἔγειρε ← ἆρον σου τὸν κράβαττον καὶ ὕπαγε εἰς τὸν οἶκον σου καὶ → ἠγέρθη ← καὶ εὐθὺς ἄρας τὸν
v.pai.1s r.ds.2 v.aam.2s v.aam.2s r.gs.2 d.asm n.asm cj v.pam.2s p.a d.asm n.asm r.gs.2 cj v.api.3s cj adv pt.aa.nsm d.asm
3306 5148 1586 149 5148 3836 3187 2779 5632 1650 3836 3875 5148 2779 1586 2779 2318 149 3836

ἀλλ᾽ ἔξω ἐπ᾽ ἐρήμοις τόποις ἦν· καὶ ἤρχοντο πρὸς αὐτὸν πάντοθεν.
2:1 Καὶ εἰσελθὼν πάλιν εἰς Καφαρναοὺμ δι᾽ ἡμερῶν ἠκούσθη ὅτι ἐν οἴκῳ ἐστίν. 2 καὶ συνήχθησαν πολλοὶ ὥστε μηκέτι
χωρεῖν μηδὲ τὰ πρὸς τὴν θύραν, καὶ ἐλάλει αὐτοῖς τὸν λόγον. 3 καὶ ἔρχονται φέροντες πρὸς αὐτὸν παραλυτικὸν αἰρόμενον ὑπὸ
τεσσάρων. 4 καὶ μὴ δυνάμενοι προσενέγκαι αὐτῷ διὰ τὸν ὄχλον ἀπεστέγασαν τὴν στέγην ὅπου ἦν, καὶ ἐξορύξαντες χαλῶσι
τὸν κράβαττον ὅπου ὁ παραλυτικὸς κατέκειτο. 5 καὶ ἰδὼν ὁ Ἰησοῦς τὴν πίστιν αὐτῶν λέγει τῷ παραλυτικῷ, Τέκνον, ἀφίενταί
σου αἱ ἁμαρτίαι. ¶ 6 ἦσαν δέ τινες τῶν γραμματέων ἐκεῖ καθήμενοι καὶ διαλογιζόμενοι ἐν ταῖς καρδίαις αὐτῶν, 7 Τί οὗτος
οὕτως λαλεῖ; βλασφημεῖ· τίς δύναται ἀφιέναι ἁμαρτίας εἰ μὴ εἷς ὁ θεός; ¶ 8 καὶ εὐθὺς ἐπιγνοὺς ὁ Ἰησοῦς τῷ πνεύματι αὐτοῦ
ὅτι οὕτως διαλογίζονται ἐν ἑαυτοῖς λέγει αὐτοῖς, Τί ταῦτα διαλογίζεσθε ἐν ταῖς καρδίαις ὑμῶν; 9 τί ἐστιν εὐκοπώτερον, εἰπεῖν
τῷ παραλυτικῷ, Ἀφίενταί σου αἱ ἁμαρτίαι, ἢ εἰπεῖν, Ἔγειρε καὶ ἆρον τὸν κράβαττόν σου καὶ περιπάτει; 10 ἵνα δὲ εἰδῆτε ὅτι
ἐξουσίαν ἔχει ὁ υἱὸς τοῦ ἀνθρώπου ἀφιέναι ἁμαρτίας ἐπὶ τῆς γῆς— λέγει τῷ παραλυτικῷ, 11 Σοὶ λέγω, ἔγειρε ἆρον τὸν
κράβαττόν σου καὶ ὕπαγε εἰς τὸν οἶκόν σου. 12 καὶ ἠγέρθη καὶ εὐθὺς ἄρας τὸν κράβαττον ἐξῆλθεν ἔμπροσθεν πάντων, ὥστε

mat | and | walked out in full view | | of them all. | This | amazed | everyone | and | they praised | God, | saying,
κράβαττον | ἐξῆλθεν ← → | ἔμπροσθεν ← → | | πάντων | ὥστε | ἐξίστασθαι | πάντας | καὶ | δοξάζειν | ⸤τὸν θεὸν | λέγοντας
n.asm | v.aai.3s | p.g | | a.gpm | cj | f.pm | a.apm | cj | f.pa | d.asm n.asm | pt.pa.apm
3187 | 2002 | 1869 | | 4246 | 6063 | 2014 | 4246 | 2779 | 1519 | 3836 2536 | 3306

"We | have | never | seen | anything | like | this!"
ὅτι ⸢ | ⸢ | οὐδέποτε | εἴδομεν | | | οὕτως
cj | | adv | v.aai.1p | | | adv
4022 1625 | 1625 | 4030 | 1625 | | | 4048

The Calling of Levi

2:13 Once | again | Jesus | went | out | beside | the | lake. | A | large | crowd | came to | him, | and | he began | to
Καὶ | πάλιν | | ἐξῆλθεν ← | παρὰ | τὴν | θάλασσαν | καὶ | πᾶς | ὁ | ὄχλος | ἤρχετο | πρὸς αὐτόν | καὶ → | →
cj | adv | | v.aai.3s | p.a | d.asf | n.asf | cj | a.nsm | d.nsm | n.nsm | v.imi.3s | p.a r.asm.3 | cj
2779 | 4099 | | 2002 | 4123 | 3836 | 2498 | 2779 | 4246 | 3836 | 4063 | 2262 | 4639 899 | 2779

teach | them. | **14** | As | he walked | along, he | saw | Levi | son of Alphaeus | sitting | at | the | tax collector's
ἐδίδασκεν | αὐτούς | Καὶ → | → | παράγων ← | → | εἶδεν | Λευὶν | τὸν → ⸤τοῦ Ἀλφαίου | καθήμενον | ἐπὶ | τὸ →
v.iai.3s | r.apm.3 | Καὶ | | pt.pa.nsm | | v.aai.3s | n.asm | d.asm n.gsm | pt.pm.asm | p.a | d.asn
1438 | 899 | 2779 | | 4135 | | 1625 | 3322 | 3836 271 | 2764 | 2093 | 3836

booth. | "Follow | me," | Jesus told | him, | and | Levi | got | up and | followed | him. | ¶ | **15** | | While | Jesus
τελώνιον | καὶ ἀκολούθει | μοι | λέγει | αὐτῷ | καὶ | | ἀναστὰς ← | | ἠκολούθησεν | αὐτῷ | | | | Καὶ | γίνεται ⸢ | αὐτὸν
n.asn | cj v.pam.2s | r.ds.1 | v.pai.3s | r.dsm.3 | cj | | pt.aa.nsm | | v.aai.3s | r.dsm.3 | | | | cj | v.pmi.3s | r.asm.3
5468 | 2779 199 | 1609 | 3306 | 899 | 2779 | | 482 | | 199 | 899 | | | | 2779 | 1181 2879 | 899

was | having | dinner | at | Levi's | house, | | many | tax | collectors and | "sinners" | were | eating | | with him
→ | → | κατακεῖσθαι | ἐν | αὐτοῦ | ⸤τῇ οἰκίᾳ | καὶ | πολλοὶ | τελῶναι ← | καὶ | ἁμαρτωλοὶ → | | συνανέκειντο ← | | ⸤τῷ Ἰησοῦ
| | f.pm | p.d | r.gsm.3 | d.dsf n.dsf | cj | a.npm | n.npm | cj | a.npm | | v.imi.3p | | d.dsm n.dsm
| | 2879 | 1877 | 899 | 3836 3864 | 2779 | 4498 | 5467 | 2779 | 283 | | 5263 | | 3836 2652

and | his | disciples, | for | there | were | many | | who | followed | him. | **16** | When | the | teachers | of the law | who were
καὶ | ⸤αὐτοῦ | ⸤τοῖς μαθηταῖς⸥ | γὰρ → | | ἦσαν | πολλοὶ | καὶ | | ἠκολούθουν | αὐτῷ | καὶ ⸢ | | οἱ | γραμματεῖς ← | ← | τῶν
cj | r.gsm.3 | d.dpm n.dpm | cj | | v.iai.3p | a.npm | cj | | v.iai.3p | r.dsm.3 | cj | | d.npm | n.npm | | d.gpm
2779 | 899 | 3836 3412 | 1142 | | 1639 | 4498 | 2779 | | 199 | 899 | 2779 1625 | | 3836 | 1208 | | 3836

Pharisees | saw | | him | eating | with the | "sinners" | and | tax | collectors, | they | asked | his | disciples: | | "Why
Φαρισαίων | ἰδόντες | ὅτι → | | ἐσθίει | μετὰ | τῶν ἁμαρτωλῶν | καὶ | | τελωνῶν | | ἔλεγον | αὐτοῦ | ⸤τοῖς μαθηταῖς⸥ | ὅτι
n.gpm | pt.aa.npm | cj | | v.pai.3s | p.g | d.gpm a.gpm | cj | | n.gpm | | v.iai.3p | r.gsm.3 | d.dpm n.dpm | cj
5757 | 1625 | 4022 | | 2266 | 3552 | 3836 283 | 2779 | | 5467 | | 3306 | 899 | 3836 3412 | 4022

does he | eat | with | tax | collectors and | 'sinners'?" | ¶ | **17** | On | hearing | this, | Jesus | | said | to them,
→ | → | ἐσθίει | μετὰ | ⸤τῶν τελωνῶν⸥ ← | καὶ | ἁμαρτωλῶν | | | καὶ | ἀκούσας | ὁ | Ἰησοῦς | λέγει → | αὐτοῖς
| | v.pai.3s | p.g | d.gpm n.gpm | cj | n.gpm | | | cj | pt.aa.nsm | d.nsm | n.nsm | v.pai.3s | r.dpm.3
| | 2266 | 3552 | 3836 5467 | 2779 | 283 | | | 2779 | 201 | 3836 | 2652 | 3306 | 899

"It is | not | the | healthy | who | need | a | doctor, | but | the | sick. | | I | have | not | come | to | call | | the
[ὅτι] | ⸢ ⸢ | οὐ | οἱ | ἰσχύοντες | ⸤χρείαν | ἔχουσιν⸥ | ἰατροῦ | ἀλλ᾽ | οἱ | ⸤κακῶς | ἔχοντες⸥ | | → | οὐκ | ἦλθον | → | καλέσαι | |
cj | | pl | d.npm | pt.pa.npm | n.asf | v.pai.3p | n.gsm | cj | d.npm | adv | pt.pa.npm | | | pl | v.aai.1s | | f.aa
4022 | 2400 2400 | 4024 | 3836 | 2710 | 5970 | 2400 | 2620 | 247 | 3836 | 2809 | 2400 | | 2262 2262 | 4024 | 2262 | | 2813

righteous, | but | sinners."
δικαίους | ἀλλὰ | ἁμαρτωλούς
a.apm | cj | a.apm
1465 | 247 | 283

Jesus Questioned About Fasting

2:18 Now | John's | disciples | and | the | Pharisees | were | fasting. | | Some people | came | and | asked | Jesus,
Καὶ | Ἰωάννου | οἱ μαθηταὶ | καὶ | οἱ | Φαρισαῖοι | ἦσαν | νηστεύοντες | καὶ | → | ἔρχονται | καὶ | λέγουσιν | αὐτῷ
cj | n.gsm | d.npm n.npm | cj | d.npm | n.npm | v.iai.3p | pt.pa.npm | cj | | v.pmi.3p | cj | v.pai.3p | r.dsm.3
2779 | 2722 | 3836 3412 | 2779 | 3836 | 5757 | 1639 | 3764 | 2779 | | 2262 | 2779 | 3306 | 899

"How | is it that | John's | disciples | and | the | disciples | of the | Pharisees | are | fasting, | but | yours
⸤διὰ | τί⸥ ← ← | Ἰωάννου | ⸤οἱ μαθηταὶ | καὶ | οἱ | μαθηταὶ → | τῶν | Φαρισαίων | → | νηστεύουσιν | δὲ | ⸤οἱ σοὶ | μαθηταὶ
p.a | r.asn | n.gsm | d.npm n.npm | cj | d.npm | n.npm | d.gpm | n.gpm | | v.pai.3p | cj | d.npm r.npm.2 | n.npm
1328 | 5515 | 2722 | 3836 3412 | 2779 | 3836 | 3412 | 3836 | 5757 | | 3764 | 1254 | 3836 5050 | 3412

are | not?" | **19** | Jesus | | answered, | | "How | can | the | guests | of the | bridegroom | fast | while
νηστεύουσιν | οὐ | καὶ | ⸤ὁ Ἰησοῦς | εἶπεν | αὐτοῖς | μὴ | δύνανται | οἱ | υἱοὶ | → | τοῦ | νυμφῶνος | νηστεύειν | ⸤ἐν ᾧ
v.pai.3p | pl | cj | d.nsm n.nsm | v.aai.3s | r.dpm.3 | pl | v.ppi.3p | d.npm | n.npm | | d.gsm | n.gsm | f.pa | p.d r.dsm
3764 | 4024 | 2779 | 3836 2652 | 3306 | 899 | 3590 | 1538 | 3836 | 5626 | | 3836 | 3813 | 3764 | 1877 4005

ἐξίστασθαι πάντας καὶ δοξάζειν τὸν θεὸν λέγοντας ὅτι Οὕτως οὐδέποτε εἴδομεν. 2:13 Καὶ ἐξῆλθεν πάλιν παρὰ τὴν θάλασσαν· καὶ πᾶς ὁ ὄχλος ἤρχετο πρὸς αὐτόν, καὶ ἐδίδασκεν αὐτούς. 14 καὶ παράγων εἶδεν Λευὶν τὸν τοῦ Ἀλφαίου καθήμενον ἐπὶ τὸ τελώνιον, καὶ λέγει αὐτῷ, Ἀκολούθει μοι. καὶ ἀναστὰς ἠκολούθησεν αὐτῷ. ¶ 15 Καὶ γίνεται κατακεῖσθαι αὐτὸν ἐν τῇ οἰκίᾳ αὐτοῦ, καὶ πολλοὶ τελῶναι καὶ ἁμαρτωλοὶ συνανέκειντο τῷ Ἰησοῦ καὶ τοῖς μαθηταῖς αὐτοῦ· ἦσαν γὰρ πολλοὶ καὶ ἠκολούθουν αὐτῷ. 16 καὶ οἱ γραμματεῖς τῶν Φαρισαίων ἰδόντες ὅτι ἐσθίει μετὰ τῶν ἁμαρτωλῶν καὶ τελωνῶν ἔλεγον τοῖς μαθηταῖς αὐτοῦ, Ὅτι μετὰ τῶν τελωνῶν καὶ ἁμαρτωλῶν ἐσθίει; ¶ 17 καὶ ἀκούσας ὁ Ἰησοῦς λέγει αὐτοῖς [ὅτι] Οὐ χρείαν ἔχουσιν οἱ ἰσχύοντες ἰατροῦ ἀλλ᾽ οἱ κακῶς ἔχοντες· οὐκ ἦλθον καλέσαι δικαίους ἀλλὰ ἁμαρτωλούς.

2:18 Καὶ ἦσαν οἱ μαθηταὶ Ἰωάννου καὶ οἱ Φαρισαῖοι νηστεύοντες. καὶ ἔρχονται καὶ λέγουσιν αὐτῷ, Διὰ τί οἱ μαθηταὶ Ἰωάννου καὶ οἱ μαθηταὶ τῶν Φαρισαίων νηστεύουσιν, οἱ δὲ σοὶ μαθηταὶ οὐ νηστεύουσιν; 19 καὶ εἶπεν αὐτοῖς ὁ Ἰησοῦς, Μὴ δύνανται οἱ υἱοὶ τοῦ νυμφῶνος ἐν ᾧ ὁ νυμφίος μετ᾽ αὐτῶν ἐστιν νηστεύειν; ὅσον χρόνον ἔχουσιν τὸν νυμφίον μετ᾽ αὐτῶν οὐ

he   is   with   them? They cannot,   so   long as they have   him   with   them.
ὁ   νυμφίος   ἐστιν   μετ᾽   αὐτῶν → οὐ δύνανται νηστεύειν ὅσον χρόνον ← ← ἔχουσιν τὸν νυμφίον μετ᾽ αὐτῶν
d.nsm   n.nsm   v.pai.3s   p.g   r.gpm.3   pl   v.ppi.3p   f.pa   r.asm   n.asm   v.pai.3p   d.asm   n.asm   p.g   r.gpm.3
3836   3812   1639   3552   899   1538   4024   1538   3764   4012   5989   2400   3836   3812   3552   899

20 But the time   will come   when the bridegroom will be taken from them, and   on that day   they will
δὲ   ἡμέραι → ἐλεύσονται ὅταν ὁ   νυμφίος → → ἀπαρθῇ ἀπ᾽ αὐτῶν καὶ τότε ἐν ἐκείνῃ τῇ ἡμέρᾳ → →
cj   n.npf → v.fmi.3p   cj   d.nsm   n.nsm   v.aps.3s   p.g   r.gpm.3   cj   adv   p.d   r.dsf   d.dsf   n.dsf
1254   2465   2262   4020   3836   3812   554   608   899   2779   5538   1877   1697   3836   2465

fast. ¶ **21** "No   one sews   a patch   of unshrunk cloth on an old   garment. If *he does*, the
νηστεύσουσιν   Οὐδεὶς ← ἐπιράπτει ἐπίβλημα → ἀγνάφου ῥάκους ἐπὶ παλαιὸν ἱμάτιον δὲ εἰ   μὴ   τὸ
v.fai.3p   a.nsm   v.pai.3s   n.asn   a.gsn   n.gsn   p.a   a.asn   n.asn   cj   cj   pl   d.asn
3764   4029   2165   2099   47   4820   2093   4094   2668   1254   1623   3590   3836

new   piece will pull away from   the old,   making the tear   worse. **22** And no   one pours new
τὸ καινὸν πλήρωμα   αἴρει ← ἀπ᾽ αὐτοῦ τοῦ παλαιοῦ καὶ γίνεται σχίσμα χεῖρον   καὶ οὐδεὶς ← βάλλει νέον
d.nsn   a.nsn   n.nsn   v.pai.3s   p.g   r.gsn.3   d.gsn   a.gsn   cj   v.pmi.3s   n.nsn   a.nsn.c   cj   a.nsm   v.pai.3s   a.asm
3836   2785   4445   149   608   899   3836   4094   2779   1181   5388   5937   2779   4029   965   3742

wine into old   wineskins. If *he does*, the wine will burst the skins, and both the wine and the wineskins
οἶνον εἰς παλαιούς ἀσκοὺς   δὲ εἰ   μὴ   ὁ   οἶνος → ῥήξει τοὺς ἀσκοὺς καὶ   ὁ   οἶνος καὶ οἱ   ἀσκοὶ
n.asm   p.a   a.apm   n.apm   cj   cj   pl   d.nsm   n.nsm   v.fai.3s   d.apm   n.apm   cj   d.nsm   n.nsm   cj   d.npm   n.npm
3885   1650   4094   829   1254   1623   3590   3836   3885   4838   3836   829   2779   3836   3885   2779   3836   829

will be ruined. No,   he pours new wine into new   wineskins."
→ → ἀπόλλυται ἀλλὰ   νέον οἶνον εἰς καινοὺς ἀσκούς
v.pmi.3s   cj   a.asm   n.asm   p.a   a.apm   n.apm
660   247   3742   3885   1650   2785   829

Lord of the Sabbath

2:23   One   Sabbath   Jesus was going   through the grainfields, and as his   disciples
Καὶ ἐγένετο   ἐν τοῖς σάββασιν αὐτὸν   παραπορεύεσθαι διὰ   τῶν σπορίμων   καὶ   αὐτοῦ οἱ μαθηταὶ
cj   v.ami.3s   p.d   d.dpn   n.dpn   r.asm.3   f.pm   p.g   d.gpn   n.gpn   cj   r.gsm.3   d.npm   n.npm
2779   1181   1877   3836   4879   899   4182   1328   3836   5077   2779   899   3836   3412

walked along, they began   to   pick   some heads of grain. **24** The Pharisees said   to him, "Look,
→ ἤρξαντο ὁδὸν ποιεῖν τίλλοντες → τοὺς στάχυας   καὶ οἱ   Φαρισαῖοι ἔλεγον → αὐτῷ ἴδε
v.ami.3p   n.asf   f.pa   pt.pa.npm   d.apm   n.apm   cj   d.npm   n.npm   v.iai.3p   r.dsm.3   pl
806   3847   4472   5504   3836   5092   2779   3836   5757   3306   899   2623

why are they doing   what is unlawful   on the Sabbath?" ¶ **25** He answered,   "Have you never
τί → → ποιοῦσιν ὃ → οὐκ ἔξεστιν → τοῖς σάββασιν   καὶ → λέγει   αὐτοῖς → → οὐδέποτε
r.asn   v.pai.3p   r.nsn   pl   v.pai.3s   d.dpn   n.dpn   cj   v.pai.3s   r.dpm.3   adv
5515   4472   4005   4024   1997   3836   4879   2779   3306   899   336   336   4030

read   what David did   when he   and his   companions were hungry and in need? **26** In the days of
ἀνέγνωτε τί   Δαυὶδ ἐποίησεν ὅτε   αὐτὸς καὶ   αὐτοῦ οἱ μετ᾽   ἐπείνασεν → χρείαν ἔσχεν → → → ἐπὶ
v.aai.2p   r.asn   n.nsm   v.aai.3s   cj   r.nsm   cj   r.gsm.3   d.npm   p.g   v.aai.3s   n.asf   v.aai.3s   p.g
336   5515   1253   4472   4021   899   2779   899   3836   3552   4277   5970   2400   2093

Abiathar the high   priest,   he entered   the house of God   and ate   the consecrated bread, which
Ἀβιαθὰρ   ἀρχιερέως ← πῶς → εἰσῆλθεν εἰς τὸν οἶκον   τοῦ θεοῦ καὶ ἔφαγεν τοὺς τῆς προθέσεως ἄρτους οὓς   οὐκ
n.gsm   n.gsm   cj   v.aai.3s   p.a   d.asm   n.asm   d.gsm   n.gsm   cj   v.aai.3s   d.apm   d.gsf   n.gsf   n.apm   r.apm   pl
8   797   4802   1656   1650   3836   3875   3836   2536   2779   2266   3836   3836   4606   788   4005   4024

is lawful only   for priests   to eat.   And he also gave   some to his companions." ¶ **27** Then he said
→ ἔξεστιν εἰ μὴ   τοὺς ἱερεῖς   φαγεῖν καὶ → καὶ ἔδωκεν → τοῖς σὺν αὐτῷ οὖσιν   καὶ → ἔλεγεν
v.pai.3s   cj   pl   d.apm   n.apm   f.aa   cj   cj   v.aai.3s   d.dpm   p.d   r.dsm.3   pt.pa.dpm   cj   v.iai.3s
1997   1623   3590   3836   2636   2266   2779   1443   2779   1443   899   3836   5250   1639   2779   3306

to them, "The Sabbath was made for man,   not man   for the Sabbath. **28** So   the Son of
αὐτοῖς τὸ   σάββατον → ἐγένετο διὰ τὸν ἄνθρωπον καὶ οὐχ ὁ   ἄνθρωπος διὰ τὸ   σάββατον   ὥστε ὁ   υἱὸς
r.dpm.3   d.nsn   n.nsn   v.ami.3s   p.a   d.asm   n.asm   cj   pl   d.nsm   n.nsm   p.a   d.asn   n.asn   cj   d.nsm   n.nsm
899   3836   4879   1181   1328   3836   476   2779   4024   3836   476   1328   3836   4879   6063   3836   5626

Man   is   Lord even of the Sabbath." ¶ **3:1** Another time he went   into the synagogue, and a
τοῦ ἀνθρώπου   ἐστιν κύριος καὶ → τοῦ σαββάτου   Καὶ πάλιν ← → εἰσῆλθεν εἰς τὴν συναγωγὴν καὶ
d.gsm   n.gsm   v.pai.3s   n.nsm   adv   d.gsn   n.gsn   cj   adv   v.aai.3s   p.a   d.asf   n.asf   cj
3836   476   1639   3261   2779   3836   4879   2779   4099   1656   1650   3836   5252   2779

δύνανται νηστεύειν. 20 ἐλεύσονται δὲ ἡμέραι ὅταν ἀπαρθῇ ἀπ᾽ αὐτῶν ὁ νυμφίος, καὶ τότε νηστεύσουσιν ἐν ἐκείνῃ τῇ ἡμέρᾳ ¶ 21 οὐδεὶς ἐπίβλημα ῥάκους ἀγνάφου ἐπιράπτει ἐπὶ ἱμάτιον παλαιόν· εἰ δὲ μή, αἴρει τὸ πλήρωμα ἀπ᾽ αὐτοῦ τὸ καινὸν τοῦ παλαιοῦ καὶ χεῖρον σχίσμα γίνεται. 22 καὶ οὐδεὶς βάλλει οἶνον νέον εἰς ἀσκοὺς παλαιούς· εἰ δὲ μή, ῥήξει ὁ οἶνος τοὺς ἀσκοὺς καὶ ὁ οἶνος ἀπόλλυται καὶ οἱ ἀσκοί· ἀλλὰ οἶνον νέον εἰς ἀσκοὺς καινούς.

2:23 Καὶ ἐγένετο αὐτὸν ἐν τοῖς σάββασιν παραπορεύεσθαι διὰ τῶν σπορίμων, καὶ οἱ μαθηταὶ αὐτοῦ ἤρξαντο ὁδὸν ποιεῖν τίλλοντες τοὺς στάχυας. 24 καὶ οἱ Φαρισαῖοι ἔλεγον αὐτῷ, Ἴδε τί ποιοῦσιν τοῖς σάββασιν ὃ οὐκ ἔξεστιν; ¶ 25 καὶ λέγει αὐτοῖς, Οὐδέποτε ἀνέγνωτε τί ἐποίησεν Δαυὶδ ὅτε χρείαν ἔσχεν καὶ ἐπείνασεν αὐτὸς καὶ οἱ μετ᾽ αὐτοῦ, 26 —πῶς εἰσῆλθεν εἰς τὸν οἶκον τοῦ θεοῦ ἐπὶ Ἀβιαθὰρ ἀρχιερέως καὶ τοὺς ἄρτους τῆς προθέσεως ἔφαγεν, οὓς οὐκ ἔξεστιν φαγεῖν εἰ μὴ τοὺς ἱερεῖς, καὶ ἔδωκεν καὶ τοῖς σὺν αὐτῷ οὖσιν; ¶ 27 καὶ ἔλεγεν αὐτοῖς, Τὸ σάββατον διὰ τὸν ἄνθρωπον ἐγένετο καὶ οὐχ ὁ ἄνθρωπος διὰ τὸ σάββατον· 28 ὥστε κύριός ἐστιν ὁ υἱὸς τοῦ ἀνθρώπου καὶ τοῦ σαββάτου. 3:1 Καὶ εἰσῆλθεν πάλιν εἰς τὴν συναγωγήν. καὶ ἦν ἐκεῖ ἄνθρωπος ἐξηραμμένην ἔχων τὴν χεῖρα. 2 καὶ παρετήρουν αὐτὸν εἰ τοῖς σάββασιν θεραπεύσει αὐτόν, ἵνα κατηγορήσωσιν αὐτοῦ. 3 καὶ

man   with   a shriveled   hand   was there. **2** Some of them were looking for a reason to accuse   Jesus, so
ἄνθρωπος   ἔχων   ἐξηραμμένην ⸢τὴν χεῖρα⸣ ἦν   ἐκεῖ   →   → ἵνα   → κατηγορήσωσιν αὐτοῦ καὶ
n.nsm   pt.pa.nsm   pt.rp.asf   d.asf n.asf   v.iai.3s adv   cj   v.aas.3p   r.gsm.3 cj
476   2400   3830   3836 5931   1639 1695   2671   2989   899   2779

they watched   him   closely to see if he would   heal   him   on the Sabbath. **3**   Jesus said to the man
→   παρετήρουν αὐτὸν ⸤   εἰ →   θεραπεύσει αὐτὸν → τοῖς σάββασιν καὶ   λέγει → τῷ ἀνθρώπῳ
     v.iai.3p   r.asm.3   cj →   v.fai.3s   r.asm.3   d.dpn n.dpn   cj   v.pai.3s   d.dsm n.dsm
     4190   899   4190   1623   2543   899   3836 4879   2779   3306   3836 476

with   the shriveled hand, "Stand up in front   of everyone." ¶   **4** Then Jesus asked them, "Which is   →
⸤τῷ ἐχοντι⸥ τὴν ξηρὰν   χεῖρα   ἔγειρε εἰς τὸ μέσον⸥ ←   καὶ   λέγει αὐτοῖς
d.dsm pt.pa.dsm d.asf a.asf n.asf v.pam.2s   p.a d.asn n.asn   cj   v.pai.3s r.dpm.3
3836 2400   3836 3831   5931   1586   1650 3836 3545   2779   3306   899

lawful on the Sabbath: to do   good   or to do evil,   to save life   or to kill?"   But they remained
ἔξεστιν → τοῖς σάββασιν → ποιῆσαι ἀγαθὸν ἢ → → κακοποιῆσαι → σῶσαι ψυχὴν ἢ → ἀποκτεῖναι δὲ   οἱ   →
v.pai.3s   d.dpn n.dpn   f.aa   a.asn   cj   f.aa   f.aa n.asf   cj   f.aa   cj   d.npm
1997   3836 4879   4472   19   2445   2803   5392 6034   2445 650   1254 3836

silent. ¶   **5** He looked   around   at them in anger and, deeply distressed   at their stubborn
ἐσιώπων   καὶ → περιβλεψάμενος ←   αὐτοὺς μετ' ὀργῆς   συλλυπούμενος ἐπὶ αὐτῶν ⸤τῇ πωρώσει⸥
v.iai.3p cj   pt.am.nsm   r.apm.3 p.g n.gsf   pt.pp.nsm   p.d r.gpm.3 d.dsf n.dsf
4995   2779   4315   899   3552 3973   5200   2093 899   3836 4801

hearts,   said to the man,   "Stretch out your hand."   He stretched it out, and his   hand   was completely
⸤τῆς καρδίας⸥ λέγει → τῷ ἀνθρώπῳ ἔκτεινον ←   τὴν χεῖρα καὶ → ἐξέτεινεν   ←   καὶ αὐτοῦ ⸤ἡ χεὶρ →
d.gsf n.gsf   v.pai.3s d.dsm n.dsm v.aam.2s   d.asf n.asf cj   v.aai.3s   cj   r.gsm.3 d.nsf n.nsf
3836 2840   3306   3836 476   1753   3836 5931   2779   1753   2779 899   3836 5931

restored.   **6** Then the Pharisees   went   out and began to plot   with the Herodians
ἀπεκατεστάθη καὶ οἱ Φαρισαῖοι εὐθὺς ἐξελθόντες ←   → ⸤συμβούλιον ἐδίδουν⸥ κατ' αὐτοῦ μετὰ τῶν Ἡρῳδιανῶν
v.api.3s   cj   d.npm n.npm   adv   pt.aa.npm   n.asn   v.iai.3p p.g r.gsm.3 p.g   d.gpm n.gpm
635   2779 3836 5757   2318   2002   5206   1443   2848 899   3552 3836 2477

how they might kill   Jesus.
ὅπως → → ἀπολέσωσιν αὐτὸν
cj   v.aas.3p   r.asm.3
3968   660   899

Crowds Follow Jesus

3:7   Jesus   withdrew with his   disciples   to the lake,   and a large crowd   from Galilee
Καὶ ὁ Ἰησοῦς ἀνεχώρησεν μετὰ αὐτοῦ ⸤τῶν μαθητῶν⸥ πρὸς τὴν θάλασσαν καὶ πολὺ πλῆθος καὶ ἀπὸ ⸤τῆς Γαλιλαίας⸥
cj   d.nsm n.nsm v.aai.3s   p.g   r.gsm.3 d.gpm n.gpm p.a d.asf n.asf   cj   a.nsn n.nsn   cj   p.g d.gsf n.gsf
2779 3836 2652   432   3552 899   3836 3412   4639 3836 2498   2779 4498 4436   2779 608 3836 1133

followed. **8** When they heard   all   he was doing, many people came to him   from Judea,
ἠκολούθησεν →   → ἀκούοντες ὅσα → ἐποίει πολὺ πλῆθος ἦλθον πρὸς αὐτόν καὶ ἀπὸ ⸤τῆς Ἰουδαίας⸥ καὶ ἀπὸ
v.aai.3s   pt.pa.npm r.apn   v.iai.3s a.nsn n.nsn   v.aai.3p p.a r.asm.3 cj   p.g d.gsf n.gsf   cj   p.g
199   201   4012   4472   4498 4436   2262   4639 899   2779 608 3836 2677   2779 608

Jerusalem,   Idumea,   and the regions across the Jordan   and around Tyre and Sidon. **9**   Because of
Ἱεροσολύμων καὶ ἀπὸ ⸤τῆς Ἰδουμαίας⸥ καὶ   πέραν τοῦ Ἰορδάνου καὶ περὶ Τύρον καὶ Σιδῶνα καὶ διὰ ←
n.gpn   cj   p.g d.gsf n.gsf   cj   p.g   d.gsm n.gsm   cj   p.a   n.asf cj   n.asf   cj   p.a
2642   2779 608 3836 2628   2779   4305   3836 2674   2779 4309 5602   2779 4972   2779 1328

the crowd he told his   disciples   to have a small boat   ready   for him, *to keep* the people from
τὸν ὄχλον → εἶπεν αὐτοῦ ⸤τοῖς μαθηταῖς⸥ ἵνα → →   → πλοιάριον προσκαρτερῇ αὐτῷ ἵνα μὴ   →
d.asm n.asm   v.aai.3s r.gsm.3 d.dpm n.dpm   cj   n.nsn   v.pas.3s   r.dsm.3 cj   pl
3836 4063   3306   899   3836 3412   2671 4674 4674   4449   4674   899   2671 3590

crowding him. **10** For he had healed   many,   so   that those with diseases were pushing forward   to touch
θλίβωσιν αὐτόν καὶ → ἐθεράπευσεν πολλοὺς ὥστε ← ὅσοι   εἶχον μάστιγας → ἐπιπίπτειν ←   αὐτῷ ἵνα ἄψωνται
v.pas.3p r.asm.3 cj   v.aai.3s   a.apm   cj   r.npm   v.iai.3p n.apf   f.pa   r.dsm.3 cj   v.ams.3p
2567   899   2779   2543   4498   6063   4012   2400   3465   2158   899   2671 721

him. **11** Whenever the evil   spirits   saw   him, they fell   down before him and cried   out,
αὐτοῦ καὶ ὅταν   τὰ ⸤τὰ ἀκάθαρτα⸥ πνεύματα ἐθεώρουν αὐτόν → προσέπιπτον ←   ←   αὐτῷ καὶ ἔκραζον ←
r.gsm.3 cj   cj   d.npn d.npn a.npn   n.npn   v.iai.3p r.asm.3   v.iai.3p   r.dsm.3 cj   v.iai.3p
899   2779 4020   3836 3836 176   4460   2555   899   4700   899   2779 3189

λέγει τῷ ἀνθρώπῳ τῷ τὴν ξηρὰν χεῖρα ἔχοντι, Ἔγειρε εἰς τὸ μέσον. ¶ **4** καὶ λέγει αὐτοῖς, Ἔξεστιν τοῖς σάββασιν ἀγαθὸν ποιῆσαι ἢ κακοποιῆσαι, ψυχὴν σῶσαι ἢ ἀποκτεῖναι; οἱ δὲ ἐσιώπων. **5** καὶ περιβλεψάμενος αὐτοὺς μετ' ὀργῆς, συλλυπούμενος ἐπὶ τῇ πωρώσει τῆς καρδίας αὐτῶν λέγει τῷ ἀνθρώπῳ, Ἔκτεινον τὴν χεῖρα. καὶ ἐξέτεινεν καὶ ἀπεκατεστάθη ἡ χεὶρ αὐτοῦ. **6** καὶ ἐξελθόντες οἱ Φαρισαῖοι εὐθὺς μετὰ τῶν Ἡρῳδιανῶν συμβούλιον ἐδίδουν κατ' αὐτοῦ ὅπως αὐτὸν ἀπολέσωσιν.

3:7 Καὶ ὁ Ἰησοῦς μετὰ τῶν μαθητῶν αὐτοῦ ἀνεχώρησεν πρὸς τὴν θάλασσαν, καὶ πολὺ πλῆθος ἀπὸ τῆς Γαλιλαίας [ἠκολούθησεν], καὶ ἀπὸ τῆς Ἰουδαίας **8** καὶ ἀπὸ Ἱεροσολύμων καὶ ἀπὸ τῆς Ἰδουμαίας καὶ οἱ πέραν τοῦ Ἰορδάνου καὶ περὶ Τύρον καὶ Σιδῶνα, πλῆθος πολὺ ἀκούοντες ὅσα ἐποίει ἦλθον πρὸς αὐτόν. **9** καὶ εἶπεν τοῖς μαθηταῖς αὐτοῦ ἵνα πλοιάριον προσκαρτερῇ αὐτῷ διὰ τὸν ὄχλον ἵνα μὴ θλίβωσιν αὐτόν· **10** πολλοὺς γὰρ ἐθεράπευσεν, ὥστε ἐπιπίπτειν αὐτῷ ἵνα αὐτοῦ ἅψωνται ὅσοι εἶχον μάστιγας. **11** καὶ τὰ πνεύματα τὰ ἀκάθαρτα, ὅταν αὐτὸν ἐθεώρουν, προσέπιπτον αὐτῷ καὶ ἔκραζον λέγοντες ὅτι Σὺ

"You are the Son of God." **12** But he gave them strict orders not to tell who he was.

λέγοντες ὅτι σὺ εἶ ὁ υἱός → ⌐τοῦ θεοῦ⌐ καὶ → → αὐτοῖς πολλὰ ἐπετίμα ἵνα μὴ → ⌐φανερὸν ποιήσωσιν⌐ αὐτὸν
pt.pa.npm cj r.ns.2 v.pai.2s d.nsm n.nsm d.gsm n.gsm cj r.dpm.3 a.apn v.iai.3s cj pl a.asm v.aas.3p r.asm.3
3306 4022 5148 1639 3836 5626 3836 2536 2779 2203 2203 899 4498 2203 2671 3590 5745 4472 899

The Appointing of the Twelve Apostles

3:13 Jesus went up on a mountainside and called to him those he wanted, and they came to

Καὶ ἀναβαίνει ‹ εἰς ⌐τὸ ὄρος⌐ καὶ προσκαλεῖται ← ← οὓς αὐτός ἤθελεν καὶ → ἀπῆλθον πρὸς
cj v.pai.3s p.a d.asn n.asn cj v.pmi.3s r.apm r.nsm v.iai.3s cj v.aai.3p p.a
2779 326 1650 3836 4001 2779 4673 4005 899 2527 2779 599 4639

him. **14** He appointed twelve – designating them apostles – that they might be with him and that he might

αὐτόν καὶ → ἐποίησεν δώδεκα ὠνόμασεν οὓς καὶ ἀποστόλους ἵνα → → ὦσιν μετ᾽ αὐτοῦ καὶ ἵνα → →
r.asm.3 cj v.aai.3s a.apm v.aai.3s r.apm adv n.apm cj v.pas.3p p.g r.gsm.3 cj cj
899 2779 4472 1557 3951 4005 2779 693 2671 1639 3552 899 2779 2671

send them out to preach **15** and to have authority to drive out demons. **16** These are the twelve he

ἀποστέλλη αὐτοὺς ← → κηρύσσειν καὶ → ἔχειν ἐξουσίαν → ἐκβάλλειν ← ⌐τὰ δαιμόνια⌐ καὶ τοὺς δώδεκα →
v.pas.3s r.apm.3 f.pa cj f.pa n.asf f.pa d.apn n.apn cj d.apm a.apm
690 899 690 3062 2779 2400 2026 1675 3836 1228 2779 3836 1557

appointed: Simon (to whom he gave the name Peter); **17** James son of Zebedee and

ἐποίησεν καὶ ⌐τῷ Σίμωνι⌐ → ἐπέθηκεν ὄνομα Πέτρον καὶ Ἰάκωβον τὸν → ⌐τοῦ Ζεβεδαίου⌐ καὶ
v.aai.3s cj d.dsm n.dsm v.aai.3s n.asn n.asm cj n.asm d.asm d.gsm n.gsm cj
4472 2779 3836 4981 2202 3950 4377 2779 2610 3836 3836 2411 2779

his brother John (to them he gave the name Boanerges, which means Sons of Thunder);

⌐τοῦ Ἰακώβου⌐ ⌐τὸν ἀδελφὸν⌐ Ἰωάννην καὶ → αὐτοῖς → ἐπέθηκεν ὀνόματα βοανηργές ὅ ἐστιν υἱοὶ → βροντῆς
d.gsm n.gsm d.asm n.asm n.asm cj r.dpm.3 v.aai.3s n.apn n.apn r.nsn v.pai.3s n.npm n.gsf
3836 2610 3836 81 2722 2779 899 2202 3950 1065 4005 1639 5626 1103

18 Andrew, Philip, Bartholomew, Matthew, Thomas, James son of Alphaeus and

καὶ Ἀνδρέαν καὶ Φίλιππον καὶ Βαρθολομαῖον καὶ Μαθθαῖον καὶ Θωμᾶν καὶ Ἰάκωβον τὸν → ⌐τοῦ Ἁλφαίου⌐ καὶ
cj n.asm cj n.asm cj n.asm cj n.asm cj n.asm cj n.asm d.asm d.gsm n.gsm cj
2779 436 2779 5805 2779 978 2779 3414 2779 2605 2779 2610 3836 3836 271 2779

Thaddaeus, Simon the Zealot **19** and Judas Iscariot, who betrayed him.

Θαδδαῖον καὶ Σίμωνα τὸν Καναναῖον καὶ Ἰούδαν Ἰσκαριώθ ὃς καὶ παρέδωκεν αὐτόν
n.asm cj n.asm d.asm n.asm cj n.asm n.asm r.nsm cj v.aai.3s r.asm.3
2497 2779 4981 3836 2831 2779 2683 2696 4005 2779 4140 899

Jesus and Beelzebub

3:20 Then Jesus entered a house, and again a crowd gathered, so that he and his disciples were not

Καὶ ἔρχεται εἰς οἶκον καὶ πάλιν ὁ ὄχλος συνέρχεται ὥστε ← αὐτοὺς ← ← → μὴ
cj v.pmi.3s p.a n.asm cj adv d.nsm n.nsm v.pmi.3s cj r.apm.3 pl
2779 2262 1650 3875 2779 4099 3836 4063 5302 6063 899 1538 3590

even able to eat. **21** When his family heard about this, they went to take charge of him, for

μηδὲ δύνασθαι → φαγεῖν ἄρτον καὶ αὐτοῦ οἱ παρ᾽ ἀκούσαντες → ἐξῆλθον → → κρατῆσαι ← αὐτόν γὰρ
adv f.pp f.aa n.asm cj r.gsm.3 d.npm p.g pt.aa.npm v.aai.3p f.aa r.asm.3 cj
3593 1538 2266 788 2779 899 3836 4123 201 2002 3195 899 1142

they said, "He is out of his mind." ¶ **22** And the teachers of the law who came down from Jerusalem

→ ἔλεγον ὅτι → → → → ἐξέστη Καὶ οἱ γραμματεῖς ← ← οἱ καταβάντες ← ἀπὸ Ἱεροσολύμων
v.iai.3p cj v.aai.3s cj d.npm n.npm d.npm pt.aa.npm p.g n.gpn
3306 4022 2014 2779 3836 1208 3836 2849 608 2642

said, "He is possessed by Beelzebub! By the prince of demons he is driving out demons." ¶

ἔλεγον ὅτι → → ἔχει ← Βεελζεβοὺλ καὶ ὅτι ἐν τῷ ἄρχοντι → ⌐τῶν δαιμονίων⌐ → ἐκβάλλει ← ⌐τὰ δαιμόνια⌐
v.iai.3p cj v.pai.3s n.asm cj cj p.d d.dsm n.dsm d.gpn n.gpn v.pai.3s d.apn n.apn
3306 4022 2400 1015 2779 4022 1877 3836 807 3836 1228 1675 3836 1228

εἶ ὁ υἱὸς τοῦ θεοῦ. **12** καὶ πολλὰ ἐπετίμα αὐτοῖς ἵνα μὴ αὐτὸν φανερὸν ποιήσωσιν.

3:13 Καὶ ἀναβαίνει εἰς τὸ ὄρος καὶ προσκαλεῖται οὓς ἤθελεν αὐτός, καὶ ἀπῆλθον πρὸς αὐτόν. **14** καὶ ἐποίησεν δώδεκα [οὓς καὶ ἀποστόλους ὠνόμασεν] ἵνα ὦσιν μετ᾽ αὐτοῦ καὶ ἵνα ἀποστέλλῃ αὐτοὺς κηρύσσειν **15** καὶ ἔχειν ἐξουσίαν ἐκβάλλειν τὰ δαιμόνια· **16** [καὶ ἐποίησεν τοὺς δώδεκα,] καὶ ἐπέθηκεν ὄνομα τῷ Σίμωνι Πέτρον, **17** καὶ Ἰάκωβον τὸν τοῦ Ζεβεδαίου καὶ Ἰωάννην τὸν ἀδελφὸν τοῦ Ἰακώβου καὶ ἐπέθηκεν αὐτοῖς ὀνόμα[τα] Βοανηργές, ὅ ἐστιν Υἱοὶ Βροντῆς· **18** καὶ Ἀνδρέαν καὶ Φίλιππον καὶ Βαρθολομαῖον καὶ Μαθθαῖον καὶ Θωμᾶν καὶ Ἰάκωβον τὸν τοῦ Ἁλφαίου καὶ Θαδδαῖον καὶ Σίμωνα τὸν Καναναῖον **19** καὶ Ἰούδαν Ἰσκαριώθ, ὃς καὶ παρέδωκεν αὐτόν.

3:20 Καὶ ἔρχεται εἰς οἶκον· καὶ συνέρχεται πάλιν [ὁ] ὄχλος, ὥστε μὴ δύνασθαι αὐτοὺς μηδὲ ἄρτον φαγεῖν. **21** καὶ ἀκούσαντες οἱ παρ᾽ αὐτοῦ ἐξῆλθον κρατῆσαι αὐτόν· ἔλεγον γὰρ ὅτι ἐξέστη. ¶ **22** καὶ οἱ γραμματεῖς οἱ ἀπὸ Ἱεροσολύμων καταβάντες ἔλεγον ὅτι Βεελζεβοὺλ ἔχει καὶ ὅτι ἐν τῷ ἄρχοντι τῶν δαιμονίων ἐκβάλλει τὰ δαιμόνια. ¶ **23** καὶ προσκαλεσάμενος αὐτοὺς ἐν

23 So Jesus called them and spoke to them in parables: "How can Satan drive out Satan? **24** If
Καὶ προσκαλεσάμενος αὐτοὺς ἔλεγεν → αὐτοῖς ἐν παραβολαῖς πῶς δύναται σατανᾶς ἐκβάλλειν ← σαταναν καὶ ἐὰν
cj pt.am.nsm r.apm.3 v.iai.3s r.dpm.3 p.d n.dpf cj v.ppi.3s n.nsm f.pa n.asm cj cj
2779 4673 899 3306 899 1877 4130 4802 1538 4928 1675 4928 2779 1569

a kingdom is divided against itself, that kingdom cannot stand. **25** If a house is divided against itself,
βασιλεία → μερισθῇ ἐφ᾽ ἑαυτὴν ἐκείνη ἡ βασιλεία οὐ δύναται σταθῆναι καὶ ἐὰν οἰκία → μερισθῇ ἐφ᾽ ἑαυτὴν
n.nsf v.aps.3s p.a r.asf.3 r.nsf r.nsf n.nsf pl v.ppi.3s f.ap cj cj n.nsf v.aps.3s p.a r.asf.3
993 3532 2093 1571 1697 3836 993 4024 1538 2705 2779 1569 3864 3532 2093 1571

that house cannot stand. **26** And if Satan opposes himself and is divided, he cannot stand;
ἐκείνη ἡ οἰκία οὐ δυνήσεται σταθῆναι καὶ εἰ ὁ σατανᾶς ἀνέστη ἐφ᾽ ἑαυτὸν καὶ → ἐμερίσθη → οὐ δύναται στῆναι
r.nsf d.nsf n.nsf pl v.fpi.3s f.ap cj cj d.nsm n.nsm v.aai.3s p.a r.asm.3 cj v.api.3s pl v.ppi.3s f.aa
1697 3836 3864 4024 1538 2705 2779 1623 3836 4928 482 2093 1571 2779 3532 1538 4024 1538 2705

his end has come. **27** In fact, no one can enter a strong man's house and carry off
ἀλλὰ τέλος ἔχει ἀλλ᾽ ← οὐδεὶς οὐ δύναται εἰσελθὼν εἰς τοῦ ἰσχυροῦ τὴν οἰκίαν διαρπάσαι ←
cj n.asn v.pai.3s cj a.nsm pl v.ppi.3s pt.aa.nsm p.a d.gsm a.gsm d.asf n.asf f.aa
247 5465 2400 247 4029 4024 1538 1656 1650 3836 2708 3836 3864 1395

his possessions unless he first ties up the strong man. Then he can rob his house. **28** I tell you
αὐτοῦ τὰ σκεύη ἐὰν μὴ → πρῶτον δήσῃ ← τὸν ἰσχυρὸν καὶ τότε διαρπάσει αὐτοῦ τὴν οἰκίαν → λέγω ὑμῖν
r.gsm.3 d.apn n.apn cj pl adv v.aas.3s d.asm a.asm cj adv v.fai.3s r.gsm.3 d.asf n.asf v.pai.1s r.dp.2
899 3836 5007 1569 3590 1313 4754 1313 3836 2708 2779 5538 1395 899 3836 3864 3306 7007

the truth, all the sins and blasphemies of men will be forgiven
Ἀμὴν ὅτι πάντα τὰ ἁμαρτήματα καὶ αἱ βλασφημίαι ὅσα ἐὰν βλασφημήσωσιν → → → ἀφεθήσεται
pl cj a.npn d.npn n.npn cj d.npf n.npf r.apn pl v.aas.3p v.fpi.3s
297 4022 4246 3836 280 2779 3836 1060 4012 1569 1059 476 918

them. **29** But whoever blasphemes against the Holy Spirit will never be forgiven;
τοῖς υἱοῖς τῶν ἀνθρώπων, δ᾽ ὃς ἂν βλασφημήσῃ εἰς τὸ ἅγιον πνεῦμα οὐκ εἰς τὸν αἰῶνα ἔχει ἄφεσιν
d.dpm n.dpm d.gpm n.gpm cj r.nsm pl v.aas.3s p.a d.asn d.asn a.asn n.asn pl p.a d.asm n.asm v.pai.3s n.asf
3836 5626 3836 476 1254 4005 323 1059 1650 3836 3836 41 4460 2400 4024 1650 3836 172 2400 912

he is guilty of an eternal sin." ¶ **30** He said this because they were saying, "He has an evil spirit."
ἀλλὰ → ἐστιν ἔνοχος → αἰωνίου ἁμαρτήματος ὅτι → → ἔλεγον → ἔχει ἀκάθαρτον πνεῦμα
cj v.pai.3s a.nsm a.gsn n.gsn cj v.iai.3p v.pai.3s a.asn n.asn
247 1639 1944 173 280 4022 3306 2400 176 4460

Jesus' Mother and Brothers

3:31 Then Jesus' mother and brothers arrived. Standing outside, they sent someone in
Καὶ αὐτοῦ ἡ μήτηρ καὶ οἱ ἀδελφοὶ αὐτοῦ ἔρχεται καὶ στήκοντες ἔξω → ἀπέστειλαν πρὸς
cj r.gsm.3 d.nsf n.nsf cj d.npm n.npm r.gsm.3 v.pmi.3s cj pt.pa.npm adv v.aai.3p p.a
2779 899 3836 3613 2779 3836 81 899 2262 2779 5112 2032 690 4639

to call him. **32** A crowd was sitting around him, and they told him, "Your mother and
αὐτὸν → καλοῦντες αὐτόν καὶ ὄχλος → ἐκάθητο περὶ αὐτὸν καὶ λέγουσιν αὐτῷ ἰδοὺ σου ἡ μήτηρ καὶ
r.asm.3 pt.pa.npm r.asm.3 cj n.nsm v.imi.3s p.a r.asm.3 cj v.pai.3p r.dsm.3 j r.gs.2 d.nsf n.nsf cj
899 2813 899 2779 4063 2764 4309 899 2779 3306 899 2627 5148 3836 3613 2779

brothers are outside looking for you." ¶ **33** "Who are my mother and my
οἱ ἀδελφοί σου [καὶ αἱ ἀδελφαί σου] → ἔξω ζητοῦσιν ← σε καὶ τίς ἐστιν μου ἡ μήτηρ καὶ μου
d.npm n.npm r.gs.2 cj d.npf n.npf r.gs.2 adv v.pai.3p r.as.2 cj r.nsm v.pai.3s r.gs.1 d.nsf n.nsf cj r.gs.1
3836 81 5148 2779 3836 80 5148 2032 2426 5148 2779 5515 1639 1609 3836 3613 2779 1609

brothers?" he asked. ¶ **34** Then he looked at those seated in a circle around him and
οἱ ἀδελφοί → ἀποκριθεὶς αὐτοῖς λέγει καὶ → περιβλεψάμενος ← τοὺς καθημένους → κύκλῳ περὶ αὐτὸν
d.npm n.npm pt.ap.nsm r.dpm.3 v.pai.3s cj pt.am.nsm d.apm pt.pm.apm adv p.a r.asm.3
3836 81 646 899 3306 2779 4315 3836 2764 3241 4309 899

said, "Here are my mother and my brothers! **35** Whoever does God's will is my brother
λέγει ἴδε μου ἡ μήτηρ καὶ μου οἱ ἀδελφοί [γὰρ] ὃς ἂν ποιήσῃ τοῦ θεοῦ τὸ θέλημα οὗτος ἐστίν μου ἀδελφός
v.pai.3s pl r.gs.1 d.nsf n.nsf cj r.gs.1 d.npm n.npm cj r.nsm pl v.aas.3s d.gsm n.gsm d.asn n.asn r.nsm v.pai.3s r.gs.1 n.nsm
3306 2623 1609 3836 3613 2779 1609 3836 81 1142 4005 323 4472 3836 2536 3836 2525 4047 1639 1609 81

and sister and mother."
καὶ ἀδελφὴ καὶ μήτηρ
cj n.nsf cj n.nsf
2779 80 2779 3613

παραβολαῖς ἔλεγεν αὐτοῖς, Πῶς δύναται Σατανᾶς Σατανᾶν ἐκβάλλειν; ²⁴ καὶ ἐὰν βασιλεία ἐφ᾽ ἑαυτὴν μερισθῇ, οὐ δύναται σταθῆναι ἡ βασιλεία ἐκείνη· ²⁵ καὶ ἐὰν οἰκία ἐφ᾽ ἑαυτὴν μερισθῇ, οὐ δυνήσεται ἡ οἰκία ἐκείνη σταθῆναι. ²⁶ καὶ εἰ ὁ Σατανᾶς ἀνέστη ἐφ᾽ ἑαυτὸν καὶ ἐμερίσθη, οὐ δύναται στῆναι ἀλλὰ τέλος ἔχει. ²⁷ ἀλλ᾽ οὐ δύναται οὐδεὶς εἰς τὴν οἰκίαν τοῦ ἰσχυροῦ εἰσελθὼν τὰ σκεύη αὐτοῦ διαρπάσαι, ἐὰν μὴ πρῶτον τὸν ἰσχυρὸν δήσῃ, καὶ τότε τὴν οἰκίαν αὐτοῦ διαρπάσει. ²⁸ Ἀμὴν λέγω ὑμῖν ὅτι πάντα ἀφεθήσεται τοῖς υἱοῖς τῶν ἀνθρώπων τὰ ἁμαρτήματα καὶ αἱ βλασφημίαι ὅσα ἐὰν βλασφημήσωσιν· ²⁹ ὃς δ᾽ ἂν βλασφημήσῃ εἰς τὸ πνεῦμα τὸ ἅγιον, οὐκ ἔχει ἄφεσιν εἰς τὸν αἰῶνα, ἀλλὰ ἔνοχός ἐστιν αἰωνίου ἁμαρτήματος. ¶ ³⁰ ὅτι ἔλεγον, Πνεῦμα ἀκάθαρτον ἔχει.

³:³¹ Καὶ ἔρχεται ἡ μήτηρ αὐτοῦ καὶ οἱ ἀδελφοὶ αὐτοῦ καὶ ἔξω στήκοντες ἀπέστειλαν πρὸς αὐτὸν καλοῦντες αὐτόν. ³² καὶ ἐκάθητο περὶ αὐτὸν ὄχλος, καὶ λέγουσιν αὐτῷ, Ἰδοὺ ἡ μήτηρ σου καὶ οἱ ἀδελφοί σου [καὶ αἱ ἀδελφαί σου] ἔξω ζητοῦσίν σε ¶ ³³ καὶ ἀποκριθεὶς αὐτοῖς λέγει, Τίς ἐστιν ἡ μήτηρ μου καὶ οἱ ἀδελφοί [μου]; ¶ ³⁴ καὶ περιβλεψάμενος τοὺς περὶ αὐτὸν κύκλῳ καθημένους λέγει, Ἴδε ἡ μήτηρ μου καὶ οἱ ἀδελφοί μου. ³⁵ ὃς [γὰρ] ἂν ποιήσῃ τὸ θέλημα τοῦ θεοῦ, οὗτος ἀδελφός μου καὶ ἀδελφὴ καὶ μήτηρ ἐστίν.

The Parable of the Sower

4:1 Again Jesus began to teach by the lake. The crowd that gathered around him was so large
Καὶ πάλιν ἤρξατο → διδάσκειν παρὰ τὴν θάλασσαν καὶ ὄχλος συνάγεται πρὸς αὐτὸν πλεῖστος
cj adv v.ami.3s f.pa p.a d.asf n.asf cj n.nsm v.ppi.3s p.a r.asm.3 a.nsm.s
2779 4099 806 1438 4123 3836 2498 2779 4063 5251 4639 899 4498

that he got into a boat and sat in it out on the lake, while all the people were along the shore at
ὥστε αὐτὸν ἐμβάντα εἰς πλοῖον καθῆσθαι → ἐν τῇ θαλάσσῃ καὶ πᾶς ὁ ὄχλος ἦσαν ἐπὶ τῆς γῆς πρὸς
cj r.asm.3 pt.aa.asm p.a n.asn f.pm p.d d.dsf n.dsf cj a.nsm d.nsm n.nsm v.iai.3p p.g d.gsf n.gsf p.a
6063 899 1832 1650 4450 2764 1877 3836 2498 2779 4246 3836 4063 1639 2093 3836 1178 4639

the water's edge. **2** He taught them many things by parables, and in his teaching said: **3** "Listen!
τὴν θάλασσαν ← καὶ → ἐδίδασκεν αὐτοὺς πολλὰ ἐν παραβολαῖς καὶ ἐν αὐτοῦ ἐτῇ διδαχῇ ἔλεγεν αὐτοῖς Ἀκούετε
d.asf n.asf cj v.iai.3s r.apm.3 a.apn p.d n.dpf cj p.d r.gsm.3 d.dsf n.dsf v.iai.3s r.dpm.3 v.pam.2p
3836 2498 2779 1438 899 4498 1877 4130 2779 1877 899 3836 1439 3306 899 201

A farmer went out to sow his seed. **4** As he was scattering the seed, some fell along the
ἰδοὺ ὁ σπείρων ἐξῆλθεν ← → σπεῖραι καὶ ἐγένετο ἐν → → ἐτῷ σπείρειν μὲν ὃ ἔπεσεν παρὰ τὴν
j d.nsm pt.pa.nsm v.aai.3s f.aa cj v.ami.3s p.d d.dsn f.pa pl r.nsn v.aai.3s p.a d.asf
2627 3836 5062 2002 5062 2779 1181 1877 3836 5062 3525 4005 4406 4123 3836

path, and the birds came and ate it up. **5** Some fell on rocky places, where it did not have
ὁδόν καὶ τὰ πετεινὰ ἦλθεν καὶ κατέφαγεν αὐτό ← καὶ ἄλλο ἔπεσεν ἐπὶ ἐτὸ πετρῶδες ← ὅπου → → οὐκ εἶχεν
n.asf cj d.npn n.npn v.aai.3s cj v.aai.3s r.asn.3 cj r.nsn v.aai.3s p.a d.asn n.asn cj pl v.iai.3s
3847 2779 3836 4374 2262 2779 2983 899 2983 2779 257 4406 2093 3836 4378 3963 2400 2400 4024 2400

much soil. It sprang up quickly, because the soil was shallow. **6** But when the sun came up, the
πολλήν γῆν καὶ → ἐξανέτειλεν ← εὐθὺς διὰ γῆς → ἐτὸ μὴ ἔχειν βάθος καὶ ὅτε ὁ ἥλιος ἀνέτειλεν ←
a.asf n.asf cj v.aai.3s adv p.a n.gsf d.asn pl f.pa n.asn cj cj d.nsm n.nsm v.aai.3s
4498 1178 2779 1984 2318 1328 1178 3836 3590 2400 958 2779 4021 3836 2463 422

plants were scorched, and they withered because they had no root. **7** Other seed fell among thorns,
→ ἐκαυματίσθη καὶ → ἐξηράνθη διὰ → ἐτὸ ἔχειν μὴ ῥίζαν καὶ ἄλλο ἔπεσεν εἰς ἐτὰς ἀκάνθας
v.api.3s cj v.api.3s p.a d.asn f.pa pl n.asf cj r.nsn v.aai.3s p.a d.apf n.apf
3009 2779 3830 1328 3836 2400 3590 4844 2779 257 4406 1650 3836 180

which grew up and choked the plants, so that they did not bear grain. **8** Still other seed fell on
καὶ ἐαἱ ἄκανθαι ἀνέβησαν ← καὶ συνέπνιξαν αὐτό καὶ → → οὐκ ἔδωκεν καρπὸν καὶ ἄλλα ἔπεσεν εἰς
cj d.npf n.npf v.aai.3p cj v.aai.3p r.asn.3 cj pl v.aai.3s n.asm cj r.npn v.aai.3s p.a
2779 3836 180 326 2779 5231 899 2779 1443 4024 1443 2843 2779 257 4406 1650

good soil. It came up, grew and produced a crop, multiplying thirty,
ἐτὴν καλὴν ἐτὴν γῆν καὶ → ἀναβαίνοντα ← καὶ αὐξανόμενα καὶ ἐδίδου καρπὸν ἔφερεν ἐν τριάκοντα καὶ
d.asf a.asf d.asf n.asf cj pt.pa.npn cj pt.pp.npn cj v.iai.3s n.asm v.iai.3s a.nsn a.apn cj
3836 2819 3836 1178 2779 326 2779 889 2779 1443 2843 5770 1651 5558 2779

sixty, or even a hundred times." ¶ **9** Then Jesus said, "He who has ears to hear, let him hear." ¶
ἐν ἑξήκοντα καὶ ← ἐν ἑκατόν καὶ ἔλεγεν → ὃς ἔχει ὦτα → ἀκούειν → ἀκουέτω
a.nsn a.apn cj a.nsn a.apn cj v.iai.3s r.nsm v.pai.3s n.apn f.pa v.pam.3s
1651 2008 2779 1651 1669 2779 3306 4005 2400 4044 201 201

10 When he was alone, the Twelve and the others around him asked him about the parables. **11**
Καὶ ὅτε → ἐγένετο ἐκατὰ μόνας σὺν τοῖς δώδεκα οἱ ← περὶ αὐτὸν ἠρώτων αὐτὸν ← τὰς παραβολάς καὶ
cj cj v.ami.3s p.a a.apf p.d d.dpm a.dpm d.npm p.a r.asm.3 v.iai.3p r.asm.3 d.apf n.apf cj
2779 4021 1181 2848 3668 5250 3836 1557 3836 4309 899 2263 899 2263 3836 4130 2779

He told them, "The secret of the kingdom of God has been given to you. But to those on the outside
→ ἔλεγεν αὐτοῖς τὸ μυστήριον → τῆς βασιλείας → τοῦ θεοῦ → δέδοται → ὑμῖν δὲ → ἐκείνοις → τοῖς ἔξω
v.iai.3s r.dpm.3 d.nsn n.nsn d.gsf n.gsf d.gsm n.gsm v.rpi.3s r.dp.2 cj r.dpm adv d.dpm adv
3306 899 3836 3696 3836 993 3836 2536 1443 7007 1254 1697 3836 2032

everything is said in parables **12** so that, "'they may be ever seeing but never perceiving, and ever
ἐτὰ πάντα γίνεται ← ἐν παραβολαῖς ἵνα ἐβλέποντες βλέπωσιν καὶ μὴ ἴδωσιν καὶ
d.npn a.npn v.pmi.3s p.d n.dpf cj pt.pa.npm v.pas.3p cj pl v.aas.3p cj
3836 4246 1181 1877 4130 2671 1063 1063 2779 3590 1625 2779

hearing but never understanding; otherwise they might turn and be forgiven!'" ¶
ἐἀκούοντες ἀκούωσιν καὶ μὴ συνιῶσιν μήποτε → ἐπιστρέψωσιν καὶ → ἀφεθῇ αὐτοῖς
pt.pa.npm v.pas.3p cj pl v.pas.3p cj v.aas.3p cj v.aps.3s r.dpm.3
201 201 2779 3590 5317 3607 2188 2779 918 899

4:1 Καὶ πάλιν ἤρξατο διδάσκειν παρὰ τὴν θάλασσαν· καὶ συνάγεται πρὸς αὐτὸν ὄχλος πλεῖστος, ὥστε αὐτὸν εἰς πλοῖον ἐμβάντα καθῆσθαι ἐν τῇ θαλάσσῃ, καὶ πᾶς ὁ ὄχλος πρὸς τὴν θάλασσαν ἐπὶ τῆς γῆς ἦσαν. **2** καὶ ἐδίδασκεν αὐτοὺς ἐν παραβολαῖς πολλά καὶ ἔλεγεν αὐτοῖς ἐν τῇ διδαχῇ αὐτοῦ, **3** Ἀκούετε. ἰδοὺ ἐξῆλθεν ὁ σπείρων σπεῖραι. **4** καὶ ἐγένετο ἐν τῷ σπείρειν ὃ μὲν ἔπεσεν παρὰ τὴν ὁδόν, καὶ ἦλθεν τὰ πετεινὰ καὶ κατέφαγεν αὐτό. **5** καὶ ἄλλο ἔπεσεν ἐπὶ τὸ πετρῶδες ὅπου οὐκ εἶχεν γῆν πολλήν, καὶ εὐθὺς ἐξανέτειλεν διὰ τὸ μὴ ἔχειν βάθος γῆς· **6** καὶ ὅτε ἀνέτειλεν ὁ ἥλιος ἐκαυματίσθησαν «ἐκαυματίσθη» καὶ διὰ τὸ μὴ ἔχειν ῥίζαν ἐξηράνθη. **7** καὶ ἄλλο ἔπεσεν εἰς τὰς ἀκάνθας, καὶ ἀνέβησαν αἱ ἄκανθαι καὶ συνέπνιξαν αὐτό, καὶ καρπὸν οὐκ ἔδωκεν. **8** καὶ ἄλλα ἔπεσεν εἰς τὴν γῆν τὴν καλὴν καὶ ἐδίδου καρπὸν ἀναβαίνοντα καὶ αὐξανόμενα καὶ ἔφερεν ἐν τριάκοντα καὶ ἐν ἑξήκοντα καὶ ἐν ἑκατόν. ¶ **9** καὶ ἔλεγεν, Ὃς ἔχει ὦτα ἀκούειν ἀκουέτω. ¶ **10** Καὶ ὅτε ἐγένετο κατὰ μόνας, ἠρώτων αὐτὸν οἱ περὶ αὐτὸν σὺν τοῖς δώδεκα τὰς παραβολάς. **11** καὶ ἔλεγεν αὐτοῖς, Ὑμῖν τὸ μυστήριον δέδοται τῆς βασιλείας τοῦ θεοῦ· ἐκείνοις δὲ τοῖς ἔξω ἐν παραβολαῖς τὰ πάντα γίνεται, **12** ἵνα βλέποντες βλέπωσιν καὶ μὴ ἴδωσιν, καὶ ἀκούοντες ἀκούωσιν καὶ μὴ συνιῶσιν, μήποτε ἐπιστρέψωσιν καὶ ἀφεθῇ αὐτοῖς. ¶ **13** Καὶ λέγει αὐτοῖς, Οὐκ οἴδατε τὴν παραβολὴν ταύτην.

13 Then Jesus said to them, "Don't you understand this   parable?   How then will you understand any
Καὶ   λέγει → αὐτοῖς οὐκ → οἴδατε   ταύτην ⌐τὴν παραβολήν⌐ πῶς καὶ → γνώσεσθε πάσας
cj   v.pai.3s r.dpm.3 pl   v.rai.2p r.asf d.asf n.asf   cj cj   v.fmi.2p a.apf
2779   3306   899   4024   3857   4047   3836 4130   4802 2779   1182   4246

parable?   **14** The farmer sows   the word. **15**   Some people are   like seed along the path, where the word is
⌐τὰς παραβολὰς⌐ ὁ   σπείρων σπείρει τὸν λόγον   δὲ οὗτοι ←   εἰσιν   οἱ παρὰ τὴν ὁδόν ὅπου ὁ   λόγος →
d.apf n.apf   d.nsm pt.pa.nsm v.pai.3s d.asm n.asm δὲ r.npm   v.pai.3p d.npm p.a d.asf n.asf cj   d.nsm n.nsm
3836 4130   3836 5062   5062   3836 3364   1254 4047   1639   3836 4123 3836 3847 3963 3836 3364

sown.   As soon as they hear   it,   Satan   comes and takes away the word that was sown   in
σπείρεται καὶ ὅταν ←   ←   ἀκούσωσιν εὐθὺς ὁ   σατανᾶς ἔρχεται καὶ αἴρει →   τὸν λόγον τὸν → ἐσπαρμένον εἰς
v.ppi.3s cj   cj   v.aas.3p   adv   d.nsm n.nsm   v.pmi.3s cj v.pai.3s   d.asm n.asm d.asm   pt.rp.asm p.a
5062   2779 4020   201   2318 3836 4928   2262   2779 149   3836 3364 3836   5062   1650

them. **16**   Others,   like seed sown   on rocky   places,   hear   the word and at once receive
αὐτούς καὶ οὗτοι εἰσιν   οἱ σπειρόμενοι ἐπὶ ⌐τὰ πετρώδη⌐ ←   οἳ   ὅταν ἀκούσωσιν τὸν λόγον → εὐθὺς λαμβάνουσιν
r.apm.3 cj   r.npm v.pai.3p d.npm pt.pp.npm p.a d.apn n.apn   r.npm 4020 v.aas.3p   d.asm n.asm   adv   v.pai.3p
899   2779 4047 1639   3836 5062   2093 3836 4378   4005 4020 v.aas.3p   3836 3364   2318 3284

it   with joy. **17** But since they have   no root,   they last only a short   time. When trouble or
αὐτὸν μετὰ χαρᾶς καὶ   →   ἔχουσιν οὐκ ῥίζαν ἐν ἑαυτοῖς ἀλλὰ →   εἰσιν   πρόσκαιροι ←   εἶτα θλίψεως ἢ
r.asm.3 p.g n.gsf cj   v.pai.3p pl   n.asf p.d r.dpm.3 cj   v.pai.3p a.npm   adv n.gsf   cj
899   3552 5915 2779   2400   4024 1877 4844 1571 247   1639   4672   1663 2568   2445

persecution comes   because of the word, they quickly fall   away. **18** Still others,   like seed sown
διωγμοῦ   γενομένης διὰ ←   τὸν λόγον → εὐθὺς σκανδαλίζονται καὶ ἄλλοι εἰσιν   οἱ σπειρόμενοι
n.gsm   pt.am.gsf p.a   d.asm n.asm   adv v.ppi.3p   cj   r.npm v.pai.3p d.npm pt.pp.npm
1501   1181   1328   3836 3364   2318 4997   2779 257   1639   3836 5062

among thorns,   hear   the word; **19** but the worries of this life,   the deceitfulness of
εἰς ⌐τὰς ἀκάνθας⌐ οὗτοι εἰσιν ⌐οἱ ἀκούσαντες⌐ τὸν λόγον καὶ αἱ μέριμναι → τοῦ αἰῶνος καὶ ἡ   ἀπάτη   →
p.a d.apf n.apf   r.npm v.pai.3p d.npm pt.aa.npm d.asm n.asm cj d.npf n.npf   d.gsm n.gsm cj d.nsf n.nsf
1650 3836 180   4047 1639 3836 201   3836 3364   2779 3836 3533   3836 172   2779 3836 573

wealth   and the desires for other   things come   in and choke   the word,   making it unfruitful.
⌐τοῦ πλούτου⌐ καὶ αἱ ἐπιθυμίαι περὶ ⌐τὰ λοιπὰ⌐ ←   εἰσπορευόμεναι ←   συμπνίγουσιν τὸν λόγον καὶ γίνεται ← ἄκαρπος
d.gsm n.gsm   cj d.npf n.npf   p.a d.apn a.apn   pt.pm.npf   v.pai.3p   d.asm n.asm cj v.pmi.3s   a.nsm
3836 4458   2779 3836 2123   4309 3836 3370   1660   5231   3836 3364   2779 1181   182

20   Others, like seed sown   on good   soil,   hear   the word,   accept   it, and produce   a
καὶ εἰσιν   οἱ σπαρέντες ἐπὶ ⌐τὴν καλὴν⌐ ⌐τὴν γῆν⌐ οἵτινες ἀκούουσιν τὸν λόγον καὶ παραδέχονται καὶ καρποφοροῦσιν
cj v.pai.3p d.npm pt.ap.npm p.a d.asf a.asf   d.asf n.asf r.npm v.pai.3p   d.asm n.asm cj v.pmi.3p   cj v.pai.3p
2779 1639   3836 5062   2093 3836 2819   3836 1178 4015 201   3836 3364   2779 4138   2779 2844

crop –   thirty,   sixty   or even a   hundred times what was sown."
ἐν τριάκοντα καὶ ἐν ἑξήκοντα καὶ   ἐν ἑκατόν
a.nsn a.apn   cj a.nsn a.apn   cj   a.nsn a.apn
1651 5558   2779 1651 2008   2779   1651 1669

A Lamp on a Stand
4:21   He said to them,   "Do you bring in a lamp   to put it under a bowl   or   a bed?
Καὶ →   ἔλεγεν → αὐτοῖς μήτι →   ἔρχεται ←   ὁ   λύχνος ἵνα τεθῇ   ὑπὸ ⌐τὸν μόδιον⌐ ἢ   ὑπὸ ⌐τὴν κλίνην⌐
cj   v.iai.3s r.dpm.3 pl   v.pmi.3s   d.nsm n.nsm cj v.aps.3s p.a d.asm n.asm cj p.a d.asf n.asf
2779   3306   899   3614   2262   3836 3394 2671 5502   5679 3836 3654   2445 5679 3836 3109

Instead, don't   you put it on its stand? **22** For   whatever is   hidden   is *meant*   to be disclosed, and
οὐχ ἵνα   τεθῇ   ἐπὶ τὴν λυχνίαν γὰρ οὐ →   ἐστιν κρυπτὸν ἐὰν μὴ   ἵνα → φανερωθῇ οὐδὲ
pl cj   v.aps.3s p.a d.asf n.asf cj pl   v.pai.3s a.nsn cj pl   cj   v.aps.3s cj
4024 2671 5502   2093 3836 3393   1142 4024   1639 3220   1569 3590 2671 5746   4028

whatever is   concealed *is meant* to be brought out into the open. **23** If anyone has ears to hear,   let him
→   ἐγένετο ἀπόκρυφον ἀλλ' ἵνα   →   ἔλθῃ ←   εἰς φανερόν   εἴ τις   ἔχει ὦτα → ἀκούειν
     v.ami.3s a.nsn   cj   cj   v.aas.3s p.a a.asn   cj r.nsm v.pai.3s n.apn f.pa
     1181   649   247 2671   2262   1650 5745   1623 5516 2400 4044   201

hear." ¶   **24**   "Consider carefully what you hear," he continued.   "With the measure you use,   it will
ἀκουέτω   Καὶ βλέπετε   ←   τί → ἀκούετε → ἔλεγεν   αὐτοῖς ἐν ᾧ   μέτρῳ →   μετρεῖτε → →
v.pam.3s   cj v.pam.2p   r.asn v.pai.2p   v.iai.3s r.dpm.3 p.d r.dsn n.dsn   v.pai.2p
201   2779 1063   5515 201   3306   899   1877 4005 3586   3582

καὶ πῶς πάσας τὰς παραβολὰς γνώσεσθε; **14** ὁ σπείρων τὸν λόγον σπείρει. **15** οὗτοι δέ εἰσιν οἱ παρὰ τὴν ὁδόν· ὅπου σπείρεται ὁ λόγος καὶ ὅταν ἀκούσωσιν, εὐθὺς ἔρχεται ὁ Σατανᾶς καὶ αἴρει τὸν λόγον τὸν ἐσπαρμένον εἰς αὐτούς. **16** καὶ οὗτοί εἰσιν ὁμοίως οἱ ἐπὶ τὰ πετρώδη σπειρόμενοι, οἳ ὅταν ἀκούσωσιν τὸν λόγον εὐθὺς μετὰ χαρᾶς λαμβάνουσιν αὐτόν, **17** καὶ οὐκ ἔχουσιν ῥίζαν ἐν ἑαυτοῖς ἀλλὰ πρόσκαιροί εἰσιν, εἶτα γενομένης θλίψεως ἢ διωγμοῦ διὰ τὸν λόγον εὐθὺς σκανδαλίζονται. **18** καὶ ἄλλοι εἰσὶν οἱ εἰς τὰς ἀκάνθας σπειρόμενοι· οὗτοί εἰσιν οἱ τὸν λόγον ἀκούσαντες, **19** καὶ αἱ μέριμναι τοῦ βίου «αἰῶνος» καὶ ἡ ἀπάτη τοῦ πλούτου καὶ αἱ περὶ τὰ λοιπὰ ἐπιθυμίαι εἰσπορευόμεναι συμπνίγουσιν τὸν λόγον καὶ ἄκαρπος γίνεται. **20** καὶ ἐκεῖνοί εἰσιν οἱ ἐπὶ τὴν γῆν τὴν καλὴν σπαρέντες, οἵτινες ἀκούουσιν τὸν λόγον καὶ παραδέχονται καὶ καρποφοροῦσιν ἐν τριάκοντα καὶ ἐν ἑξήκοντα καὶ ἐν ἑκατόν.

4:21 Καὶ ἔλεγεν αὐτοῖς, Μήτι ἔρχεται ὁ λύχνος ἵνα ὑπὸ τὸν μόδιον τεθῇ ἢ ὑπὸ τὴν κλίνην; οὐχ ἵνα ἐπὶ τὴν λυχνίαν τεθῇ; **22** οὐ γάρ ἐστιν κρυπτὸν ἐὰν μὴ ἵνα φανερωθῇ, οὐδὲ ἐγένετο ἀπόκρυφον ἀλλ' ἵνα ἔλθῃ εἰς φανερόν. **23** εἴ τις ἔχει ὦτα ἀκούειν ἀκουέτω. ¶ **24** Καὶ ἔλεγεν αὐτοῖς, Βλέπετε τί ἀκούετε. ἐν ᾧ μέτρῳ μετρεῖτε μετρηθήσεται ὑμῖν καὶ προστεθήσεται ὑμῖν. **25** ὃς

be measured   to you – and *even more.*   **25**   Whoever has will be given   more;   whoever does
→ μετρηθήσεται → ὑμῖν καὶ   προστεθήσεται ὑμῖν   γὰρ ὃς   ἔχει → → δοθήσεται   αὐτῷ καὶ ὃς
v.fpi.3s   r.dp.2 cj   v.fpi.3s   r.dp.2 cj   r.nsm v.pai.3s   v.fpi.3s   r.dsm.3 cj   r.nsm
3582   7007   2779   4707   7007   1142 4005 2400   1443   899   2779 4005   2400

not have, even what he has will be taken   from him.”
οὐκ ἔχει καὶ   ὃ   → ἔχει → → ἀρθήσεται ἀπ' αὐτοῦ
pl   v.pai.3s adv r.asn   v.pai.3s   v.fpi.3s   p.g   r.gsm.3
4024 2400   2779 4005   2400   149   608   899

The Parable of the Growing Seed

4:26 He also said, "This is   what the kingdom of God   is like. A man   scatters seed   on the ground.
       Καὶ ἔλεγεν οὕτως ἐστιν   ἡ   βασιλεία → τοῦ θεοῦ ὡς   ἄνθρωπος βάλῃ   τὸν σπόρον ἐπὶ τῆς γῆς
       cj   v.iai.3s adv   v.pai.3s d.nsf n.nsf   d.gsm n.gsm cj   n.nsm   v.aas.3s d.asm n.asm p.g d.gsf n.gsf
       3306 2779   3306 4048   1639 993   3836 2536 6055 476   965   3836 5078   2093 3836 1178

27 Night and day,   whether he sleeps or gets   up,   the seed sprouts and grows,   though he   does not know
νύκτα καὶ ἡμέραν καὶ   → καθεύδῃ καὶ ἐγείρηται ←   καὶ ὁ σπόρος βλαστᾷ καὶ μηκύνηται ὡς   αὐτός →   οὐκ οἶδεν
n.asf cj   n.asf cj   v.pas.3s cj   v.pps.3s   cj d.nsm n.nsm v.pas.3s cj   v.pps.3s cj   r.nsm   pl   v.rai.3s
3816   2779 2465 2779   2761   2779 1586   2779 3836 5078 5078   2779 3602   6055 899   3857 4024 3857

how. **28** All   by itself the soil produces grain – first   the stalk, then the head, then the full   kernel in the head.
←   αὐτομάτη ←   ἡ γῆ καρποφορεῖ   πρῶτον   χόρτον εἶτα στάχυν εἶτα   πλήρης σῖτον ἐν τῷ στάχυϊ
       a.nsf   d.nsf n.nsf v.pai.3s   adv   n.asm   adv   n.asm   adv   a.asm n.asm p.d d.dsm n.dsm
       897   3836 1178 2844   4754   5965   1663 5092   1663   4441   4992   1877 3836 5092

29 As soon as the grain is ripe,   he puts   the sickle   to it, because the harvest has come.”
δὲ ὅταν ←   ←   ὁ   καρπός → παραδοῖ εὐθὺς → ἀποστέλλει τὸ δρέπανον ←   ὅτι   ὁ   θερισμός → παρέστηκεν
cj   cj   d.nsm n.nsm   v.aas.3s adv   v.pai.3s   d.asn n.asn   cj   d.nsm n.nsm   v.rai.3s
1254 4020   3836 2843   4140   2318   690   3836 1535   4022 3836 2546   4225

The Parable of the Mustard Seed

4:30 Again he said, "What shall we say the kingdom of God   is like,   or   what parable shall we use to
Καὶ → ἔλεγεν πῶς → → → τὴν βασιλείαν → τοῦ θεοῦ → ὁμοιώσωμεν ἢ   ἐν τίνι παραβολῇ → → →
cj   v.iai.3s cj   d.asf n.asf   d.gsm n.gsm   v.aas.1p   cj   p.d r.dsf n.dsf
2779   3306   4802 3929 3929 3929 3836 993   3836 2536   3929   2445 1877 5515 4130

describe it? **31** It is like a mustard seed, which is   the smallest   seed   you
θῶμεν αὐτῇ   ὡς σινάπεως κόκκῳ   ὃν   μικρότερον πάντων τῶν σπερμάτων τῶν ἐπὶ τῆς γῆς ὃς   ὅταν
v.aas.1p r.asf.3   pl   n.gsn   n.dsn   pt.pa.nsn a.nsn.c   a.gpn   d.gpn n.gpn   d.gpn p.g d.gsf n.gsf r.nsm cj
5502   899   6055 4983   3133   1639   3625   4246   3836 5065   3836 2093 3836 1178 4005   4020

plant in the ground. **32** Yet when planted, it grows   and becomes the largest of all   garden plants,
σπαρῇ ἐπὶ τῆς γῆς   καὶ ὅταν σπαρῇ → ἀναβαίνει καὶ γίνεται   μεῖζον → πάντων → τῶν λαχάνων καὶ ποιεῖ
v.aps.3s p.g d.gsf n.gsf   cj   cj   v.aps.3s   v.pai.3s   cj   v.pmi.3s   a.nsn.c   a.gpn   d.gpn n.gpn   cj   v.pai.3s
5062   2093 3836 1178   2779 4020 5062   326   2779 1181   3489   4246   3836 3303   2779 4472

with such big   branches that the birds of the air   can   perch   in its shade."   ¶   **33** With
μεγάλους κλάδους ὥστε τὰ πετεινὰ → τοῦ οὐρανοῦ δύνασθαι κατασκηνοῦν ὑπὸ αὐτοῦ τὴν σκιὰν   Καὶ →
a.apm   n.apm   cj   d.apn n.apn   d.gsn n.gsn   f.pp   f.pa   p.a r.gsn.3 d.asf n.asf   cj
3489   3080   6063 3836 4374   3836 4041   1538   2947   5679 899   3836 5014   2779

many similar parables Jesus spoke the word to them, as   much as they could   understand. **34** He did not
πολλαῖς τοιαύταις παραβολαῖς   ἐλάλει τὸν λόγον αὐτοῖς καθὼς ←   ←   ἠδύναντο ἀκούειν   δὲ → → οὐκ
a.dpf   r.dpf   n.dpf   v.iai.3s d.asm n.asm r.dpm.3 cj   v.ipi.3p f.pa   cj   pl
4498   5525   4130   3281   3836 3364   899   2777   1538   201   1254 3281 3281 4024

say anything to them without using a parable. But when he was alone   with his own   disciples, he
ἐλάλει → αὐτοῖς χωρὶς   παραβολῆς δὲ → → → κατ' ἰδίαν → τοῖς ἰδίοις μαθηταῖς →
v.iai.3s   r.dpm.3 p.g   n.gsf   cj   p.a a.asf   d.dpm a.dpm n.dpm
3281   899   6006   4130   1254   2848 2625   3412 3836 2625 3412

explained everything.
ἐπέλυεν πάντα
v.iai.3s a.apn
2147   4246

γὰρ ἔχει, δοθήσεται αὐτῷ· καὶ ὃς οὐκ ἔχει, καὶ ὃ ἔχει ἀρθήσεται ἀπ' αὐτοῦ. **4:26** Καὶ ἔλεγεν, Οὕτως ἐστὶν ἡ βασιλεία τοῦ θεοῦ ὡς ἄνθρωπος βάλῃ τὸν σπόρον ἐπὶ τῆς γῆς **27** καὶ καθεύδῃ καὶ ἐγείρηται νύκτα καὶ ἡμέραν, καὶ ὁ σπόρος βλαστᾷ καὶ μηκύνηται ὡς οὐκ οἶδεν αὐτός. **28** αὐτομάτη ἡ γῆ καρποφορεῖ, πρῶτον χόρτον εἶτα στάχυν εἶτα πλήρη[ς] σῖτον ἐν τῷ στάχυϊ. **29** ὅταν δὲ παραδοῖ ὁ καρπός, εὐθὺς ἀποστέλλει τὸ δρέπανον, ὅτι παρέστηκεν ὁ θερισμός. **4:30** Καὶ ἔλεγεν, Πῶς ὁμοιώσωμεν τὴν βασιλείαν τοῦ θεοῦ ἢ ἐν τίνι αὐτὴν παραβολῇ θῶμεν; **31** ὡς κόκκῳ σινάπεως, ὃς ὅταν σπαρῇ ἐπὶ τῆς γῆς, μικρότερον ὂν πάντων τῶν σπερμάτων τῶν ἐπὶ τῆς γῆς, **32** καὶ ὅταν σπαρῇ, ἀναβαίνει καὶ γίνεται μεῖζον πάντων τῶν λαχάνων καὶ ποιεῖ κλάδους μεγάλους, ὥστε δύνασθαι ὑπὸ τὴν σκιὰν αὐτοῦ τὰ πετεινὰ τοῦ οὐρανοῦ κατασκηνοῦν. ¶ **33** Καὶ τοιαύταις παραβολαῖς πολλαῖς ἐλάλει αὐτοῖς τὸν λόγον καθὼς ἠδύναντο ἀκούειν· **34** χωρὶς δὲ παραβολῆς οὐκ ἐλάλει αὐτοῖς, κατ' ἰδίαν δὲ τοῖς ἰδίοις μαθηταῖς ἐπέλυεν πάντα.

Jesus Calms the Storm

4:35

That day		when	evening came,		he said	to his disciples,	"Let us go	over to	the other
Καὶ ἐν ἐκείνῃ τῇ ἡμέρᾳ		→	ὀψίας γενομένης	→	λέγει →	αὐτοῖς	διέλθωμεν	εἰς τὸ	
cj p.d r.dsf d.dsf n.dsf			n.gsf pt.am.gsf		v.pai.3s	r.dpm.3	v.aas.1p	p.a d.asn	
2779 1877 1697 3836 2465	1181		4068 1181		3306	899	1451	1650 3836	

side." **36**	Leaving	the crowd	behind,	they took		him	along,	just as	he was,	in	the boat.		There were
πέραν	καὶ ἀφέντες	τὸν ὄχλον	←	παραλαμβάνουσιν		αὐτὸν	→	ὡς →	ἦν	ἐν	τῷ πλοίῳ	ἄλλα →	ἦν
adv	cj pt.aa.npm	d.asm n.asm		v.pai.3p		r.asm.3		cj	v.iai.3s	p.d	d.dsn n.dsn	r.npn	v.iai.3s
4305	2779 918	3836 4063	918	4161		899	4161	6055	1639	1877	3836 4450	257	1639

also other boats	with	him.	**37**	A	furious	squall		came up,	and the	waves	broke	over	the	boat,	so that
καὶ	πλοῖα μετ'	αὐτοῦ	καὶ	μεγάλη	λαῖλαψ	ἀνέμου	γίνεται	→	καὶ τὰ	κύματα	ἐπέβαλλεν	εἰς	τὸ	πλοῖον	ὥστε ←
cj	n.npn p.g	r.gsm.3	cj	a.nsf	n.nsf	n.gsm	v.pmi.3s		cj d.npn	n.npn	v.iai.3s	p.a	d.asn	n.asn	cj
2779	4450 3552	899	2779	3489	3278	449	1181		2779 3836	3246	2095	1650	3836	4450	6063

it	was	nearly	swamped.	**38**	Jesus	was	in	the stern,	sleeping	on	a cushion.		The disciples
τὸ πλοῖον	→	ἤδη	γεμίζεσθαι	καὶ	αὐτὸς	ἦν	ἐν	τῇ πρύμνῃ	καθεύδων	ἐπὶ	τὸ προσκεφάλαιον	καὶ	
d.asn n.asn		adv	f.pp	cj	r.nsm	v.iai.3s	p.d	d.dsf n.dsf	pt.pa.nsm	p.a	d.asn n.asn	cj	
3836 4450	1153	2453	1153	2779	899	1639	1877	3836 4744	2761	2093	3836 4676	2779	

woke	him	and said	to him,	"Teacher,	don't you care	if	we drown?"	¶	**39**	He got	up,	rebuked
ἐγείρουσιν	αὐτὸν	καὶ λέγουσιν	αὐτῷ	διδάσκαλε	οὐ σοι μέλει	ὅτι	ἀπολλύμεθα			καὶ →	διεγερθεὶς ←	ἐπετίμησεν
v.pai.3p	r.asm.3	cj v.pai.3p	r.dsm.3	n.vsm	pl r.ds.2 v.pai.3s	cj	v.pmi.1p			cj	pt.ap.nsm	v.aai.3s
1586	899	2779 3306	899	1437	4024 5148 3508	4022	660			2779	1444	2203

the wind	and said	to the waves,	"Quiet!	Be still!"	Then	the wind	died	down	and it was		completely	calm.
τῷ ἀνέμῳ	καὶ εἶπεν	τῇ θαλάσσῃ	σιώπα	πεφίμωσο	καὶ	ὁ ἄνεμος	ἐκόπασεν ←		καὶ	ἐγένετο	μεγάλη	γαλήνη
d.dsm n.dsm	cj v.aai.3s	d.dsf n.dsf	v.pam.2s	v.rpm.2s	cj	d.nsm n.nsm	v.aai.3s		cj	v.ami.3s	a.nsf	n.nsf
3836 449	2779 3306	3836 2498	4995	5821	2779	3836 449	3156		2779	1181	3489	1132

¶ **40**	He said	to his disciples,	"Why	are you	so afraid?	Do you still	have	no faith?"	¶	**41**	They were
καὶ →	εἶπεν →	αὐτοῖς	τί	ἐστε ←	δειλοί →	→	οὔπω ἔχετε ←	πίστιν			καὶ →
cj	v.aai.3s	r.dpm.3	r.asn	v.pai.2p	a.npm		adv v.pai.2p	n.asf			cj
2779	3306	899	5515	1639	1264	2400 2400	4037 2400	4037 4411			2779

terrified		and asked	each other,		"Who	is	this?	Even	the wind	and the waves
ἐφοβήθησαν	φόβον μέγαν	καὶ ἔλεγον	πρὸς →	ἀλλήλους	ἄρα τίς	ἐστιν	οὗτος	ὅτι	καὶ ὁ ἄνεμος	καὶ ἡ θάλασσα
v.api.3p	n.asm a.asm	cj v.iai.3p	p.a	r.apm	r.nsm	v.pai.3s	r.nsm	cj	adv d.nsm n.nsm	cj d.nsf n.nsf
5828	5832 3489	2779 3306	4639	253	726 5515	1639	4047	4022	2779 3836 449	2779 3836 2498

obey	him!"
ὑπακούει	αὐτῷ
v.pai.3s	r.dsm.3
5634	899

The Healing of a Demon-possessed Man

5:1

They	went	across	the lake		to	the region	of the	Gerasenes.	**2**	When	Jesus	got	out of	the
Καὶ →	ἦλθον	εἰς τὸ πέραν	τῆς θαλάσσης		εἰς	τὴν χώραν	→ τῶν	Γερασηνῶν	καὶ	→	αὐτοῦ	ἐξελθόντος	ἐκ	τοῦ
cj	v.aai.3p	p.a d.asn n.asn	d.gsf n.gsf		p.a	d.asf n.asf	d.gpm	n.gpm	cj		r.gsm.3	pt.aa.gsm	p.g	d.gsn
2779	2262	1650 3836 4305	3836 2498		1650	3836 6001	3836	1170	2779	2002	899	2002	1666	3836

boat,	a man	with	an evil	spirit	came from	the	tombs	to meet	him.	**3** This man
πλοίου	εὐθὺς ἄνθρωπος	ἐν	ἀκαθάρτῳ	πνεύματι	→ ἐκ	τῶν	μνημείων	ὑπήντησεν	αὐτῷ	ὃς
n.gsn	adv n.nsm	p.d	a.dsn	n.dsn	p.g	d.gpn	n.gpn	v.aai.3s	r.dsm.3	r.nsm
4450	2318 476	1877	176	4460	5636 1666	3836	3646	5636	899	4005

lived		in	the tombs,	and	no one	could	bind	him	any more,	not even	with	a chain.	**4** For	he
τὴν κατοίκησιν	εἶχεν	ἐν	τοῖς μνήμασιν	καὶ	οὐδεὶς	ἐδύνατο	δῆσαι	αὐτὸν	οὐκέτι ←	οὐδὲ ←	→	→ ἁλύσει	διὰ	αὐτὸν
d.asf n.asf	v.iai.3s	p.d	d.dpn n.dpn	cj	a.nsm	v.ipi.3s	f.aa	r.asm.3	adv	adv		n.dsf	p.a	r.asm.3
3836 2998	2400	1877	3836 3645	2779	4029	1538	1313	899	4033	4028		268	1328	899

had often	been	chained	hand	and foot,	but he	tore	the chains	apart	and	broke	the irons
πολλάκις	→	τὸ δεδέσθαι	ἁλύσεσιν	καὶ πέδαις	καὶ ὑπ' αὐτοῦ	διεσπάσθαι	τὰς ἁλύσεις ←		καὶ	συντετρῖφθαι	
adv		d.asn f.rp	n.dpf	cj n.dpf	cj p.g r.gsm.3	f.rp	d.apf n.apf		cj	f.rp	
1313 4490		3836 1313	268	2779 4267	2779 5679 899	1400	3836 268	1400	2779	5341	

on his feet.	No	one was	strong enough	to subdue	him.	**5**		Night	and	day	among	the tombs
τὰς πέδας	καὶ οὐδεὶς	←	ἴσχυεν ←	→ δαμάσαι	αὐτὸν	καὶ διὰ παντὸς	νυκτὸς	καὶ	ἡμέρας	ἐν	τοῖς	μνήμασιν
d.apf n.apf	cj a.nsm		v.iai.3s	f.aa	r.asm.3	cj p.g a.gsm	n.gsf	cj	n.gsf	p.d	d.dpn	n.dpn
3836 4267	2779 4029		2710	1238	899	2779 1328 4246	3816	2779	2465	1877	3836	3645

4:35 Καὶ λέγει αὐτοῖς ἐν ἐκείνῃ τῇ ἡμέρᾳ ὀψίας γενομένης, Διέλθωμεν εἰς τὸ πέραν. **36** καὶ ἀφέντες τὸν ὄχλον παραλαμβάνουσιν αὐτὸν ὡς ἦν ἐν τῷ πλοίῳ, καὶ ἄλλα πλοῖα ἦν μετ' αὐτοῦ. **37** καὶ γίνεται λαῖλαψ μεγάλη ἀνέμου καὶ τὰ κύματα ἐπέβαλλεν εἰς τὸ πλοῖον, ὥστε ἤδη γεμίζεσθαι τὸ πλοῖον. **38** καὶ αὐτὸς ἦν ἐν τῇ πρύμνῃ ἐπὶ τὸ προσκεφάλαιον καθεύδων. καὶ ἐγείρουσιν αὐτὸν καὶ λέγουσιν αὐτῷ, Διδάσκαλε, οὐ μέλει σοι ὅτι ἀπολλύμεθα; ¶ **39** καὶ διεγερθεὶς ἐπετίμησεν τῷ ἀνέμῳ καὶ εἶπεν τῇ θαλάσσῃ, Σιώπα, πεφίμωσο. καὶ ἐκόπασεν ὁ ἄνεμος καὶ ἐγένετο γαλήνη μεγάλη. ¶ **40** καὶ εἶπεν αὐτοῖς, Τί δειλοί ἐστε; οὔπω ἔχετε πίστιν; ¶ **41** καὶ ἐφοβήθησαν φόβον μέγαν καὶ ἔλεγον πρὸς ἀλλήλους, Τίς ἄρα οὗτός ἐστιν ὅτι καὶ ὁ ἄνεμος καὶ ἡ θάλασσα ὑπακούει αὐτῷ;

5:1 Καὶ ἦλθον εἰς τὸ πέραν τῆς θαλάσσης εἰς τὴν χώραν τῶν Γερασηνῶν. **2** καὶ ἐξελθόντος αὐτοῦ ἐκ τοῦ πλοίου εὐθὺς ὑπήντησεν αὐτῷ ἐκ τῶν μνημείων ἄνθρωπος ἐν πνεύματι ἀκαθάρτῳ, **3** ὃς τὴν κατοίκησιν εἶχεν ἐν τοῖς μνήμασιν, καὶ οὐδὲ ἁλύσει οὐκέτι οὐδεὶς ἐδύνατο αὐτὸν δῆσαι **4** διὰ τὸ αὐτὸν πολλάκις πέδαις καὶ ἁλύσεσιν δεδέσθαι καὶ διεσπάσθαι ὑπ' αὐτοῦ τὰς ἁλύσεις καὶ τὰς πέδας συντετρῖφθαι, καὶ οὐδεὶς ἴσχυεν αὐτὸν δαμάσαι· **5** καὶ διὰ παντὸς νυκτὸς καὶ ἡμέρας ἐν τοῖς μνήμασιν καὶ ἐν τοῖς

and in the hills he would cry out and cut himself with stones. ¶ **6** When he saw Jesus
καὶ ἐν τοῖς ὄρεσιν → ἦν κράζων ← καὶ κατακόπτων ἑαυτὸν → λίθοις καὶ → ἰδὼν ⸂τὸν Ἰησοῦν⸃
cj p.d d.dpn n.dpn v.iai.3s pt.pa.nsm cj pt.pa.nsm r.asm.3 n.dpm cj pt.aa.nsm d.asm n.asm
2779 1877 3836 4001 1639 3189 2779 2888 1571 3345 2779 1625 3836 2652

from a distance, he ran and fell on his knees in front of him. **7** He shouted at the top of his voice,
ἀπὸ μακρόθεν → ἔδραμεν καὶ προσεκύνησεν ← → → → αὐτῷ καὶ κράξας → → μεγάλῃ ← φωνῇ
p.g adv v.aai.3s cj v.aai.3s r.dsm.3 cj pt.aa.nsm a.dsf n.dsf
608 3427 5556 2779 4686 899 2779 3189 3489 5889

"What do you want with me, Jesus, Son of the Most High God? Swear to God that you
λέγει τί σοί καὶ → ἐμοὶ Ἰησοῦ υἱὲ → τοῦ ⸂τοῦ ὑψίστου⸃ θεοῦ ὁρκίζω σε → ⸂τὸν θεόν⸃ ↱ ↱
v.pai.3s r.nsn r.ds.2 cj r.ds.1 n.vsm n.vsm d.gsm d.gsm a.gsm.s n.gsm v.pai.1s r.as.2 d.asm n.asm
3306 5515 5148 2779 1609 2652 5626 3836 3836 5736 2536 3991 5148 3836 2536 3590 989

won't torture me!" **8** For Jesus had said to him, "Come out of this man, you evil spirit!" ¶
μὴ βασανίσῃς με γάρ → ἔλεγεν αὐτῷ ἔξελθε ἐκ ← τοῦ ἀνθρώπου → ⸂τὸ ἀκάθαρτον⸃ ⸂τὸ πνεῦμα⸃
pl v.aas.2s r.as.1 cj v.iai.3s r.dsm.3 v.aam.2s p.g d.gsm n.gsm d.vsn a.vsn d.vsn n.vsn
3590 989 1609 1142 3306 899 2002 1666 3836 476 3836 176 3836 4460

9 Then Jesus asked him, "What is your name?" ¶ "My name is Legion," he replied, "for we are
καὶ ἐπηρώτα αὐτόν τί σοι ὄνομα καὶ μοι ὄνομα λεγιών → λέγει αὐτῷ ὅτι → ἐσμεν
cj v.iai.3s r.asm.3 r.nsn r.ds.2 n.nsn cj r.ds.1 n.nsn n.nsf v.pai.3s r.dsm.3 cj v.pai.1p
2779 2089 899 5515 5148 3950 2779 1609 3950 3305 3306 899 4022 1639

many." **10** And he begged Jesus again and again not to send them out of the area. ¶ **11** A large herd
πολλοί καὶ → παρεκάλει αὐτὸν πολλὰ ← ἵνα μὴ → ἀποστείλῃ αὐτὰ ἔξω ← τῆς χώρας δὲ μεγάλη ἀγέλη
a.npm cj v.iai.3s r.asm.3 a.apn cj pl v.aas.3s r.apn.3 p.g d.gsf n.gsf cj a.nsf n.nsf
4498 2779 4151 899 4498 2671 3590 690 899 2032 3836 6001 1254 3489 36

of pigs was feeding on the nearby hillside. **12** The demons begged Jesus, "Send us among the
→ χοίρων ἦν βοσκομένη πρὸς τῷ ἐκεῖ ὄρει καὶ παρεκάλεσαν αὐτὸν λέγοντες πέμψον ἡμᾶς εἰς τοὺς
n.gpm v.iai.3s pt.pp.nsf p.d d.dsn adv n.dsn cj v.aai.3p r.asm.3 pt.pa.npm v.aam.2s r.ap.1 p.a d.apm
5956 1639 1081 4639 3836 1695 4001 2779 4151 899 3306 4287 7005 1650 3836

pigs; allow us to go into them." **13** He gave them permission, and the evil spirits came out
χοίρους ἵνα → → εἰσέλθωμεν εἰς αὐτούς καὶ αὐτοῖς ἐπέτρεψεν καὶ τὰ ⸂τὰ ἀκάθαρτα⸃ πνεύματα ἐξελθόντα ←
n.apm cj v.aas.1p p.a r.apm.3 cj r.dpn.3 v.aai.3s cj d.npn d.npn a.npn n.npn pt.aa.npn
5956 2671 1656 1650 899 2779 2205 2205 899 2205 2779 3836 3836 176 4460 2002

and went into the pigs. The herd, about two thousand in number, rushed down the steep bank into
εἰσῆλθον εἰς τοὺς χοίρους καὶ ἡ ἀγέλη ὡς δισχίλιοι ← ὥρμησεν κατὰ τοῦ κρημνοῦ εἰς
v.aai.3p p.a d.apm n.apm cj d.nsf n.nsf cj a.npm v.aai.3s p.g d.gsm n.gsm p.a
1656 1650 3836 5956 2779 3836 36 6055 1493 3994 2848 3836 3204 1650

the lake and were drowned. ¶ **14** Those tending the pigs ran off and reported this
τὴν θάλασσαν καὶ → ἐπνίγοντο ἐν τῇ θαλάσσῃ Καὶ οἱ βόσκοντες αὐτοὺς ἔφυγον ← καὶ ἀπήγγειλαν
d.asf n.asf cj v.ipi.3p p.d d.dsf n.dsf cj d.npm pt.pa.npm r.apm.3 v.aai.3p cj v.aai.3p
3836 2498 2779 4464 1877 3836 2498 2779 3836 1081 899 5771 2779 550

in the town and countryside, and the people went out to see what had happened. **15** When they came to
εἰς τὴν πόλιν καὶ εἰς ⸂τοὺς ἀγρούς⸃ καὶ → ἦλθον ← ἰδεῖν τί ἐστιν ⸂τὸ γεγονὸς⸃ καὶ → ἔρχονται πρὸς
p.a d.asf n.asf cj p.a d.apm n.apm cj v.aai.3p f.aa r.nsn v.pai.3s d.nsn pt.ra.nsn cj v.pmi.3p p.a
1650 3836 4484 2779 1650 3836 69 2779 2262 1625 5515 1639 3836 1181 2779 2262 4639

Jesus, they saw the man who had been possessed by the legion of demons, sitting
⸂τὸν Ἰησοῦν⸃ καὶ → θεωροῦσιν τὸν ← ← δαιμονιζόμενον τὸν ἐσχηκότα τὸν λεγιῶνα καθήμενον
d.asm n.asm cj v.pai.3p d.asm pt.pp.asm d.asm pt.ra.asm d.asm n.asm pt.pp.asm
3836 2652 2779 2555 3836 1227 3836 2400 3836 3305 2764

there, dressed and in his right mind; and they were afraid. **16** Those who had seen it told the
ἱματισμένον καὶ → → σωφρονοῦντα καὶ → → ἐφοβήθησαν καὶ οἱ ← → ἰδόντες διηγήσαντο
pt.rp.asm cj pt.pa.asm cj v.api.3p cj d.npm pt.aa.npm v.ami.3p
2667 2779 5404 2779 5828 2779 3836 1625 1455

people what had happened to the demon-possessed man – and told about the pigs as well. **17** Then the people
αὐτοῖς πῶς → ἐγένετο → τῷ δαιμονιζομένῳ ← καὶ περὶ τῶν χοίρων καὶ →
r.dpm.3 cj v.ami.3s d.dsm pt.pp.dsm cj p.g d.gpm n.gpm cj
899 4802 1181 3836 1227 2779 4309 3836 5956 2779

ὄρεσιν ἦν κράζων καὶ κατακόπτων ἑαυτὸν λίθοις. ¶ **6** καὶ ἰδὼν τὸν Ἰησοῦν ἀπὸ μακρόθεν ἔδραμεν καὶ προσεκύνησεν αὐτῷ **7** καὶ κράξας φωνῇ μεγάλῃ λέγει, Τί ἐμοὶ καὶ σοί, Ἰησοῦ υἱὲ τοῦ θεοῦ τοῦ ὑψίστου; ὁρκίζω σε τὸν θεόν, μή με βασανίσῃς. **8** ἔλεγεν γὰρ αὐτῷ, Ἔξελθε τὸ πνεῦμα τὸ ἀκάθαρτον ἐκ τοῦ ἀνθρώπου. ¶ **9** καὶ ἐπηρώτα αὐτόν, Τί ὄνομά σοι ¶ καὶ λέγει αὐτῷ, Λεγιὼν ὄνομά μοι, ὅτι πολλοί ἐσμεν. **10** καὶ παρεκάλει αὐτὸν πολλὰ ἵνα μὴ αὐτὰ ἀποστείλῃ ἔξω τῆς χώρας ¶ **11** Ἦν δὲ ἐκεῖ πρὸς τῷ ὄρει ἀγέλη χοίρων μεγάλη βοσκομένη· **12** καὶ παρεκάλεσαν αὐτὸν λέγοντες, Πέμψον ἡμᾶς εἰς τοὺς χοίρους, ἵνα εἰς αὐτοὺς εἰσέλθωμεν. **13** καὶ ἐπέτρεψεν αὐτοῖς. καὶ ἐξελθόντα τὰ πνεύματα τὰ ἀκάθαρτα εἰσῆλθον εἰς τοὺς χοίρους, καὶ ὥρμησεν ἡ ἀγέλη κατὰ τοῦ κρημνοῦ εἰς τὴν θάλασσαν, ὡς δισχίλιοι, καὶ ἐπνίγοντο ἐν τῇ θαλάσσῃ. ¶ **14** καὶ οἱ βόσκοντες αὐτοὺς ἔφυγον καὶ ἀπήγγειλαν εἰς τὴν πόλιν καὶ εἰς τοὺς ἀγρούς· καὶ ἦλθον ἰδεῖν τί ἐστιν τὸ γεγονὸς **15** καὶ ἔρχονται πρὸς τὸν Ἰησοῦν καὶ θεωροῦσιν τὸν δαιμονιζόμενον καθήμενον ἱματισμένον καὶ σωφρονοῦντα, τὸν ἐσχηκότα τὸν λεγιῶνα, καὶ ἐφοβήθησαν. **16** καὶ διηγήσαντο αὐτοῖς οἱ ἰδόντες πῶς ἐγένετο τῷ δαιμονιζομένῳ καὶ περὶ τῶν χοίρων. **17** καὶ ἤρξαντο

began to plead   with Jesus to leave   their region. ¶   **18** As Jesus was getting   into the boat,
ἤρξαντο → παρακαλεῖν ←   αὐτὸν → ἀπελθεῖν ἀπὸ αὐτῶν ⌞τῶν ὁρίων⌟   Καὶ αὐτοῦ → ἐμβαίνοντος εἰς τὸ πλοῖον
v.ami.3p   f.pa   r.asm.3 f.aa   p.g r.gpm.3 d.gpn n.gpn   cj r.gsm.3   pt.pa.gsm   p.a d.asn n.asn
806   4151   899   599   608 899 3836 3990   2779 1832 899   1832   1650 3836 4450

the man who had been demon-possessed begged   to go with him. **19** Jesus did not let   him, but said,
ὁ ← ← → δαιμονισθεὶς   παρεκάλει αὐτὸν ἵνα ᾖ μετ᾽ αὐτοῦ καὶ   → οὐκ ἀφῆκεν αὐτόν ἀλλὰ λέγει
d.nsm   pt.ap.nsm   v.iai.3s r.asm.3 cj v.pas.3s p.g r.gsm.3 cj   pl   918 v.aai.3s r.asm.3 cj v.pai.3s
3836   1227   4151 899 2671 1639 3552 899 2779   918 4024 918 899 247 3306

"Go home   to your family and tell   them how much the Lord has done   for you, and how he
αὐτῷ εἰς ⌞τὸν οἶκον σου⌟ πρὸς σοὺς τοὺς καὶ ἀπάγγειλον αὐτοῖς ὅσα ← ὁ κύριος → πεποίηκεν → σοι καὶ →
r.dsm.3 p.a d.asm n.asm r.gs.2 p.a r.apm.2 d.apm cj v.aam.2s r.dpm.3 r.apn   d.nsm n.nsm   v.rai.3s   r.ds.2 cj
899 1650 3836 3875 5148 4639 5050 3836 2779 550 899 4012   3836 3261   4472   5148 2779

has had mercy on you." **20** So the man went   away and began to tell   in the Decapolis how much Jesus
→ → ἠλέησεν → σε καὶ   ἀπῆλθεν   καὶ ἤρξατο → κηρύσσειν ἐν τῇ Δεκαπόλει ὅσα ← ⌞ὁ Ἰησοῦς⌟
   v.aai.3s   r.as.2 cj   v.aai.3s   cj v.ami.3s   f.pa   p.d d.dsf n.dsf   r.apn   d.nsm n.nsm
   1796   5148 2779   599   2779 806   3062   1877 3836 1279   4012   3836 2652

had done   for him. And all   the people were amazed.
→ ἐποίησεν → αὐτῷ καὶ πάντες ← ← ἐθαύμαζον
   v.aai.3s   r.dsm.3 cj a.npm   v.iai.3p
   4472   899 2779 4246   2513

A Dead Girl and a Sick Woman

5:21 When Jesus   had again crossed   over by boat   to the other side of the lake, a large crowd
⌞τοῦ Ἰησοῦ⌟ → πάλιν διαπεράσαντος ← ἐν ⌞τῷ πλοίῳ⌟ εἰς τὸ πέραν ←   πολὺς ὄχλος
d.gsn n.gsm   adv pt.aa.gsm   p.d d.dsn n.dsn p.a d.asn adv   a.nsm n.nsm
1385 3836 2652 1385 4099 1385   1877 3836 4450 1650 3836 4305   4498 4063

gathered around him while he was by   the lake. **22** Then one of the synagogue rulers,   named Jairus,
συνήχθη ἐπ᾽ αὐτὸν καὶ → ἦν παρὰ τὴν θάλασσαν Καὶ εἷς → τῶν   ἀρχισυναγώγων ὀνόματι Ἰάϊρος
v.api.3s p.a r.asm.3 cj   v.iai.3s p.a d.asf n.asf cj a.nsm d.gpm   n.gpm   n.dsn n.nsm
5251 2093 899 2779   1639 4123 3836 2498 2779 1651 3836   801   3950 2608

came there.   Seeing Jesus, he fell at   his feet   **23** and pleaded earnestly with him,   "My little
ἔρχεται   καὶ ἰδὼν αὐτὸν → πίπτει πρὸς αὐτοῦ ⌞τοὺς πόδας⌟   καὶ παρακαλεῖ πολλὰ ← αὐτὸν λέγων ὅτι μου →
v.pmi.3s   cj pt.aa.nsm r.asm.3   v.pai.3s p.a r.gsm.3 d.apm n.apm   cj v.pai.3s a.apn   r.asm.3 pt.pa.nsm r.gs.1
2262   2779 1625 899   4406 4639 899 3836 4546   2779 4151 4498   899 3306 4022 1609

daughter is dying.   Please come and put   your hands on her   so that she will be healed and live." **24** So
⌞τὸ θυγάτριον⌟ ἔχει ἐσχάτως ἵνα ἐλθὼν   ἐπιθῇς τὰς χεῖρας → αὐτῇ ἵνα ← → → σωθῇ καὶ ζήσῃ καὶ
d.nsn n.nsn v.pai.3s adv cj pt.aa.nsm   v.aas.2s d.apf n.apf   r.dsf.3 cj   v.aps.3s cj v.aas.3s cj
3836 2589 2400 2275 2262   2202 3836 5931   899 2671   5392 2779 2409 2779

Jesus went with him. ¶   A large crowd followed   and pressed   around him. **25** And a woman was
ἀπῆλθεν μετ᾽ αὐτοῦ   καὶ πολὺς ὄχλος ἠκολούθει αὐτῷ καὶ συνέθλιβον ← αὐτόν Καὶ γυνὴ
v.aai.3s p.a r.gsm.3   cj a.nsm n.nsm v.iai.3s r.dsm.3 cj v.iai.3p   r.asm.3 cj n.nsf
599 3552 899   2779 4498 4063 199 899 2779 5315   899 2779 1222

there who had been subject to bleeding for twelve years. **26** She had suffered a great deal under the care of
→ → → οὖσα ἐν ῥύσει αἵματος → δώδεκα ἔτη καὶ → παθοῦσα πολλὰ ὑπὸ
    pt.pa.nsf p.d n.dsf n.gsn   a.apn n.apn cj   pt.aa.nsf a.apn p.g
    1639 1877 4864 135   1557 2291 2779   4248 4498 5679

many doctors and had spent   all she   had, yet instead of getting better   she grew
πολλῶν ἰατρῶν καὶ → δαπανήσασα ⌞τὰ πάντα⌟ ⌞παρ᾽ αὐτῆς⌟ ← καὶ μηδὲν ← ὠφεληθεῖσα ἀλλὰ μᾶλλον → ἐλθοῦσα
a.gpm n.gpm cj   pt.aa.nsf d.apn a.apn p.g r.gsf.3   cj a.asn   pt.ap.nsf cj adv.c   pt.aa.nsf
4498 2620 2779   1251 3836 4246 4123 899   2779 3594   6067 247 3437   2262

worse. **27** When she heard   about Jesus,   she came up behind him in the crowd and touched his
εἰς ⌞τὸ χεῖρον⌟ → ἀκούσασα περὶ ⌞τοῦ Ἰησοῦ⌟ → ἐλθοῦσα ὄπισθεν ἐν τῷ ὄχλῳ ἥψατο αὐτοῦ
p.a d.asn a.asn.c   pt.aa.nsf p.g d.gsm n.gsm   pt.aa.nsf adv   p.d d.dsm n.dsm v.ami.3s r.gsm.3
1650 3836 5937   201 4309 3836 2652   2262 3957   1877 3836 4063 721 899

cloak, **28** because she thought,   "If I just touch his clothes,   I will be healed." **29** Immediately her
⌞τοῦ ἱματίου⌟ γὰρ → ἔλεγεν ὅτι ἐὰν → κἂν ἅψωμαι αὐτοῦ ⌞τῶν ἱματίων⌟ → → σωθήσομαι καὶ εὐθὺς αὐτῆς
d.gsn n.gsn cj   v.iai.3s cj cj → v.ams.1s r.gsm.3 d.gpn n.gpn   v.fpi.1s cj adv r.gsf.3
3836 2668 1142   3306 4022 1569 721 2829 721 899 3836 2668   5392 2779 2318 899

παρακαλεῖν αὐτὸν ἀπελθεῖν ἀπὸ τῶν ὁρίων αὐτῶν. ¶ **18** καὶ ἐμβαίνοντος αὐτοῦ εἰς τὸ πλοῖον παρεκάλει αὐτὸν ὁ δαιμονισθεὶς ἵνα μετ᾽ αὐτοῦ ᾖ. **19** καὶ οὐκ ἀφῆκεν αὐτόν, ἀλλὰ λέγει αὐτῷ, Ὕπαγε εἰς τὸν οἶκόν σου πρὸς τοὺς σοὺς καὶ ἀπάγγειλον αὐτοῖς ὅσα ὁ κύριός σοι πεποίηκεν καὶ ἠλέησέν σε. **20** καὶ ἀπῆλθεν καὶ ἤρξατο κηρύσσειν ἐν τῇ Δεκαπόλει ὅσα ἐποίησεν αὐτῷ ὁ Ἰησοῦς, καὶ πάντες ἐθαύμαζον.
5:21 Καὶ διαπεράσαντος τοῦ Ἰησοῦ [ἐν τῷ πλοίῳ] πάλιν εἰς τὸ πέραν συνήχθη ὄχλος πολὺς ἐπ᾽ αὐτόν, καὶ ἦν παρὰ τὴν θάλασσαν. **22** καὶ ἔρχεται εἷς τῶν ἀρχισυναγώγων, ὀνόματι Ἰάϊρος, καὶ ἰδὼν αὐτὸν πίπτει πρὸς τοὺς πόδας αὐτοῦ **23** καὶ παρακαλεῖ αὐτὸν πολλὰ λέγων ὅτι Τὸ θυγάτριόν μου ἐσχάτως ἔχει, ἵνα ἐλθὼν ἐπιθῇς τὰς χεῖρας αὐτῇ ἵνα σωθῇ καὶ ζήσῃ. **24** καὶ ἀπῆλθεν μετ᾽ αὐτοῦ. ¶ Καὶ ἠκολούθει αὐτῷ ὄχλος πολὺς καὶ συνέθλιβον αὐτόν. **25** καὶ γυνὴ οὖσα ἐν ῥύσει αἵματος δώδεκα ἔτη **26** καὶ πολλὰ παθοῦσα ὑπὸ πολλῶν ἰατρῶν καὶ δαπανήσασα τὰ παρ᾽ αὐτῆς πάντα καὶ μηδὲν ὠφεληθεῖσα ἀλλὰ μᾶλλον εἰς τὸ χεῖρον ἐλθοῦσα, **27** ἀκούσασα περὶ τοῦ Ἰησοῦ, ἐλθοῦσα ἐν τῷ ὄχλῳ ὄπισθεν ἥψατο τοῦ ἱματίου αὐτοῦ· **28** ἔλεγεν γὰρ ὅτι Ἐὰν ἅψωμαι κἂν τῶν ἱματίων αὐτοῦ σωθήσομαι. **29** καὶ εὐθὺς ἐξηράνθη ἡ πηγὴ τοῦ αἵματος αὐτῆς καὶ ἔγνω τῷ σώματι ὅτι

bleeding | stopped | and | she felt | in her | body | that | she was freed | from | her suffering. | ¶ **30** | At once
ἡ πηγὴ τοῦ αἵματος | ἐξηράνθη | καὶ → | ἔγνω | τῷ | σώματι | ὅτι | ἴαται | ἀπὸ | τῆς μάστιγος | | καὶ εὐθὺς ←
d.nsf n.nsf d.gsn n.gsn | v.api.3s | cj | v.aai.3s | d.dsn | n.dsn | cj | v.rpi.3s | p.g | d.gsf n.gsf | | cj adv
3836 4380 3836 135 | 3830 | 2779 | 1182 | 3836 | 5393 | 4022 | 2615 | 608 | 3836 3465 | | 2779 2318

Jesus | realized | that power | had gone | out | from | him. | He turned | around | in | the crowd and
ὁ Ἰησοῦς | ἐπιγνοὺς ἐν ἑαυτῷ | τὴν δύναμιν → | ἐξελθοῦσαν ← | ἐξ | αὐτοῦ → | ἐπιστραφεὶς ← | ἐν | τῷ ὄχλῳ
d.nsm n.nsm | pt.aa.nsm p.d r.dsm.3 | d.asf n.asf | pt.aa.asf | p.g | r.gsm.3 | pt.ap.nsm | p.d | d.dsm n.dsm
3836 2652 | 2105 1877 1571 | 3836 1539 | 2002 | 1666 | 899 | 2188 | 1877 | 3836 4063

asked, "Who | touched | my clothes?" | ¶ **31** | "You | see | the people | crowding | against you," | his | disciples
ἔλεγεν τίς | ἥψατο | μου τῶν ἱματίων | καὶ → | βλέπεις | τὸν ὄχλον | συνθλίβοντα → | σε | αὐτοῦ | οἱ μαθηταὶ
v.iai.3s r.nsm | v.ami.3s | r.gs.1 d.gpn n.gpn | cj | v.pai.2s | d.asm n.asm | pt.pa.asm | r.as.2 | r.gsm.3 | d.npm n.npm
3306 5515 | 721 | 1609 3836 2668 | 2779 | 1063 | 3836 4063 | 5315 | 5148 | 899 | 3836 3412

answered, | "and yet you can ask, | 'Who | touched | me?'" | ¶ | **32** But Jesus kept | looking | around to see | who
ἔλεγον αὐτῷ καὶ ← → | λέγεις τίς | ἥψατο | μου | καὶ → | περιεβλέπετο ← | → ἰδεῖν | τὴν
v.iai.3p r.dsm.3 cj | v.pai.2s r.nsm | v.ami.3s | r.gs.1 | cj | v.imi.3s | f.aa | d.asf
3306 899 2779 | 3306 5515 | 721 | 1609 | 2779 | 4315 | 1625 | 3836

had done | it. | **33** Then | the woman, | knowing | what | had happened | to her, | came and | fell | at | his feet and,
ποιήσασαν τοῦτο | δὲ | ἡ γυνὴ | εἰδυῖα | ὃ → | γέγονεν | αὐτῇ | ἦλθεν καὶ | προσέπεσεν → | αὐτῷ ← | καὶ
pt.aa.asf r.asn | cj | d.nsf n.nsf | pt.ra.nsf | r.nsn | v.rai.3s | r.dsf.3 | v.aai.3s | v.aai.3s | r.dsm.3 | cj
4472 4047 | 1254 | 3836 1222 | 3857 | 4005 | 1181 | 899 | 2262 2779 | 4700 | 899 | 2779

trembling | with fear, | told | him | the whole | truth. | **34** | He | said | to her, | "Daughter, | your | faith | has | healed
τρέμουσα → | φοβηθεῖσα καὶ | εἶπεν αὐτῷ | τὴν πᾶσαν | ἀλήθειαν | δὲ ὁ | εἶπεν | αὐτῇ | θυγάτηρ | σου | ἡ πίστις | → | σέσωκεν
pt.pa.nsf | pt.ap.nsf cj | v.aai.3s r.dsm.3 | d.asf a.asf | n.asf | cj d.nsm | v.aai.3s | r.dsf.3 | n.vsf | r.gs.2 | d.nsf n.nsf | | v.rai.3s
5554 | 5828 2779 | 3306 899 | 3836 4246 | 237 | 1254 3836 | 3306 | 899 | 2588 | 5148 | 3836 4411 | | 5392

you. | Go | in | peace | and | be | freed | from | your | suffering." | ¶ | **35** While | Jesus | was still | speaking, | some men
σε | ὕπαγε | εἰς | εἰρήνην | καὶ | ἴσθι | ὑγιὴς | ἀπὸ | σου | τῆς μάστιγος | | → αὐτοῦ → | Ἔτι λαλοῦντος
r.as.2 | v.pam.2s | p.a | n.asf | cj | v.pam.2s | a.nsf | p.g | r.gs.2 | d.gsf n.gsf | | r.gsm.3 | adv pt.pa.gsm
5148 | 5632 | 1650 | 1645 | 2779 | 1639 | 5618 | 608 | 5148 | 3836 3465 | | 3281 899 3281 | 2285 3281

came | from | the house | of Jairus, the synagogue | ruler. | "Your | daughter | is dead," | they said. | "Why
ἔρχονται ἀπὸ | τοῦ | ἀρχισυναγώγου | ὅτι σου | ἡ θυγάτηρ | ἀπέθανεν → | λέγοντες | τί
v.pmi.3p p.g | d.gsm | n.gsm | cj r.gs.2 | d.nsf n.nsf | v.aai.3s | pt.pa.npm | r.asn
2262 608 | 3836 | 801 | 4022 5148 | 3836 2588 | 633 | 3306 | 5515

bother | the | teacher | any more?" | ¶ | **36** | Ignoring | what | they said, | Jesus | told | the synagogue
σκύλλεις | τὸν | διδάσκαλον | ἔτι | | δὲ | παρακούσας | τὸν λόγον | λαλούμενον | ὁ Ἰησοῦς | λέγει | τῷ →
v.pai.2s | d.asm | n.asm | adv | | cj | pt.aa.nsm | d.asm n.asm | pt.pp.asm | d.nsm n.nsm | v.pai.3s | d.dsm
5035 | 3836 | 1437 | 2285 | | 1254 | 4159 | 3836 3364 | 3281 | 3836 2652 | 3306 | 3836

ruler, | "Don't be afraid; | just | believe." | ¶ | **37** | He did not let | anyone | follow | him | except
ἀρχισυναγώγῳ μὴ → | φοβοῦ | μόνον | πίστευε | | καὶ → | οὐκ ἀφῆκεν | οὐδένα | συνακολουθῆσαι | μετ' αὐτοῦ | εἰ μὴ
n.dsm pl | v.ppm.2s | adv | v.pam.2s | | cj | pl v.aai.3s | a.asm | f.aa | p.g r.gsm.3 | cj pl
801 3590 | 5828 | 3667 | 4409 | | 2779 918 918 | 4024 918 | 4029 | 5258 | 3552 899 | 1623 3590

Peter, | James | and | John | the brother | of James. | **38** | When they came | to | the home | of the synagogue
τὸν Πέτρον | καὶ Ἰάκωβον | καὶ | Ἰωάννην | τὸν ἀδελφὸν → | Ἰακώβου | καὶ | ἔρχονται | εἰς | τὸν οἶκον → | τοῦ
d.asm n.asm | cj n.asm | cj | n.asm | d.asm n.asm | n.gsm | cj | v.pmi.3p | p.a | d.asm n.asm | d.gsm
3836 4377 | 2779 2610 | 2779 | 2722 | 3836 81 | 2610 | 2779 | 2262 | 1650 | 3836 3875 | 3836

ruler, | Jesus | saw | a commotion, | with | people | crying | and | wailing | loudly. | **39** | He went | in and | said
ἀρχισυναγώγου καὶ | θεωρεῖ | θόρυβον | καὶ → | κλαίοντας | καὶ | ἀλαλάζοντας | πολλὰ | καὶ → | εἰσελθὼν ← | λέγει
n.gsm cj | v.pai.3s | n.asm | cj | pt.pa.apm | cj | pt.pa.apm | a.apm | cj | pt.aa.nsm | v.pai.3s
801 2779 | 2555 | 2573 | 2779 | 3081 | 2779 | 226 | 4498 | 2779 | 1656 | 3306

to them, | "Why | all this | commotion | and | wailing? | The child | is not | dead | but | asleep." | **40** But | they | laughed | at him.
αὐτοῖς τί | θορυβεῖσθε | καὶ | κλαίετε | τὸ | παιδίον | οὐκ ἀπέθανεν | ἀλλὰ | καθεύδει | καὶ → | κατεγέλων ← | αὐτοῦ
r.dpm.3 r.asn | v.ppi.2p | cj | v.pai.2p | d.nsn | n.nsn | pl v.aai.3s | cj | v.pai.3s | cj | v.iai.3p | r.gsm.3
899 5515 | 2572 | 2779 | 3081 | 3836 | 4086 | 633 4024 633 | 247 | 2761 | 2779 | 2860 | 899

¶ | After he put | them | all | out, | he | took | the child's | father | and | mother | and the | disciples
δὲ → | ἐκβαλὼν | πάντας | αὐτὸς | παραλαμβάνει | τὸν τοῦ παιδίου | πατέρα καὶ | τὴν μητέρα | καὶ τοὺς
cj | pt.aa.nsm | a.apm | r.nsm | v.pai.3s | d.asm d.gsn n.gsn | n.asm cj | d.asf n.asf | cj d.apm
1254 | 1675 | 4246 | 899 | 4161 | 3836 3836 4086 | 4252 2779 | 3836 3613 | 2779 3836

ἴαται ἀπὸ τῆς μάστιγος. ¶ 30 καὶ εὐθὺς ὁ Ἰησοῦς ἐπιγνοὺς ἐν ἑαυτῷ τὴν ἐξ αὐτοῦ δύναμιν ἐξελθοῦσαν ἐπιστραφεὶς ἐν τῷ ὄχλῳ ἔλεγεν, Τίς μου ἥψατο τῶν ἱματίων; ¶ 31 καὶ ἔλεγον αὐτῷ οἱ μαθηταὶ αὐτοῦ, Βλέπεις τὸν ὄχλον συνθλίβοντά σε καὶ λέγεις, Τίς μου ἥψατο; ¶ 32 καὶ περιεβλέπετο ἰδεῖν τὴν τοῦτο ποιήσασαν. 33 ἡ δὲ γυνὴ φοβηθεῖσα καὶ τρέμουσα, εἰδυῖα ὃ γέγονεν αὐτῇ, ἦλθεν καὶ προσέπεσεν αὐτῷ καὶ εἶπεν αὐτῷ πᾶσαν τὴν ἀλήθειαν. 34 ὁ δὲ εἶπεν αὐτῇ, Θυγάτηρ, ἡ πίστις σου σέσωκέν σε· ὕπαγε εἰς εἰρήνην καὶ ἴσθι ὑγιὴς ἀπὸ τῆς μάστιγός σου. ¶ 35 Ἔτι αὐτοῦ λαλοῦντος ἔρχονται ἀπὸ τοῦ ἀρχισυναγώγου λέγοντες ὅτι Ἡ θυγάτηρ σου ἀπέθανεν· τί ἔτι σκύλλεις τὸν διδάσκαλον; ¶ 36 ὁ δὲ Ἰησοῦς παρακούσας τὸν λόγον λαλούμενον λέγει τῷ ἀρχισυναγώγῳ, Μὴ φοβοῦ, μόνον πίστευε. ¶ 37 καὶ οὐκ ἀφῆκεν οὐδένα μετ' αὐτοῦ συνακολουθῆσαι εἰ μὴ τὸν Πέτρον καὶ Ἰάκωβον καὶ Ἰωάννην τὸν ἀδελφὸν Ἰακώβου. 38 καὶ ἔρχονται εἰς τὸν οἶκον τοῦ ἀρχισυναγώγου, καὶ θεωρεῖ θόρυβον καὶ κλαίοντας καὶ ἀλαλάζοντας πολλά, 39 καὶ εἰσελθὼν λέγει αὐτοῖς, Τί θορυβεῖσθε καὶ κλαίετε; τὸ παιδίον οὐκ ἀπέθανεν ἀλλὰ καθεύδει. 40 καὶ κατεγέλων αὐτοῦ. ¶ αὐτὸς δὲ ἐκβαλὼν πάντας παραλαμβάνει τὸν πατέρα τοῦ παιδίου καὶ τὴν μητέρα καὶ

who were	with	him,	and	went		in where	the	child	was.		He took		her		by the	hand	and said to
	μετ᾿	αὐτοῦ	καὶ	εἰσπορεύεται ←		ὅπου	τὸ	παιδίον	ἦν	καὶ →	κρατήσας	⌐τοῦ παιδίου⌐		τῆς	χειρὸς	λέγει →
	p.g	r.gsm.3	cj	v.pmi.3s		cj	d.nsn	n.nsn	v.iai.3s	cj	pt.aa.nsm	d.gsn n.gsn		d.gsf	n.gsf	v.pai.3s
3552	899	2779	1660		3963	3836	4086	1639	2779	3195	3836 4086		3195	5931	3306

41

her,	"Talitha	koum!"	(which	means,		"Little girl,		I say	to you,	get	up!").		Immediately
αὐτῇ	ταλιθα	κουμ	ὅ	ἐστιν	μεθερμηνευόμενον⌐ →	⌐τὸ κοράσιον⌐	→	λέγω	σοὶ	ἔγειρε⌐		καὶ	εὐθὺς
r.dsf.3	j	j	r.nsn	v.pai.3s	pt.pp.nsn	d.vsn n.vsn		v.pai.1s	r.ds.2	v.pam.2s		cj	adv
899	5420	3182	4005	1639	3493	3836 3166		3306	5148	1586		2779	2318

42

the	girl	stood up	and	walked	around		(she was	twelve	years	old).	*At this*	they were	completely
τὸ	κοράσιον	ἀνέστη ←	καὶ	περιεπάτει ←		γὰρ →	ἦν	δώδεκα	ἐτῶν		καὶ	εὐθὺς		μεγάλη
d.nsn	n.nsn	v.aai.3s	cj	v.iai.3s		cj	v.iai.3s	a.gpn	n.gpn		cj	adv		a.dsf
3836	3166	482	2779	4344		1142	1639	1557	2291		2779	2318	2014 2014	3489

astonished.		He gave	strict	orders		not to let	anyone	know	about this,	and	told	them to
⌐ἐξέστησαν ἐκστάσει⌐	καὶ ↱	→	πολλὰ	διεστείλατο	αὐτοῖς	ἵνα ↱	→ ↱	μηδεὶς	γνοῖ ←	τοῦτο	καὶ	εἶπεν →
v.aai.3p	n.dsf	cj	a.apn	v.ami.3s	r.dpm.3	cj		a.nsm	v.aas.3s	r.asn	cj	v.aai.3s
2014	1749	2779	1403 1403	4498	4483	899	2671	3594	1182 1182	3594	1182	4047	2779	3306

43

give	her	something	to eat.
δοθῆναι	αὐτῇ	→	φαγεῖν
f.ap	r.dsf.3		f.aa
1443	899		2266

A Prophet Without Honor

6:1

Jesus	left	there	and	went	to	his	hometown,	accompanied	by his		disciples.		When
Καὶ	ἐξῆλθεν	ἐκεῖθεν	καὶ	ἔρχεται	εἰς	αὐτοῦ	⌐τὴν πατρίδα⌐	καὶ	ἀκολουθοῦσιν	αὐτῷ	αὐτοῦ οἱ μαθηταὶ	καὶ →	
cj	v.aai.3s	adv	cj	v.pmi.3s	p.a	r.gsm.3	d.asf n.asf	cj	v.pai.3p	r.dsm.3	r.gsm.3 d.npm n.npm	cj	
2779	2002	1696	2779	2262	1650	899	3836 4258	2779	199	899	899 3836 3412	2779	1181

the	Sabbath	came,	he began	to teach	in	the	synagogue,	and	many	who	heard	him	were amazed.	¶
σαββάτου	γενομένου →	ἤρξατο →	διδάσκειν	ἐν	τῇ	συναγωγῇ	καὶ	πολλοὶ →	ἀκούοντες	→	ἐξεπλήσσοντο			
n.gsn	pt.am.gsn	v.ami.3s	f.pa	p.d	d.dsf	n.dsf	cj	a.npm	pt.pa.npm		v.ipi.3p			
4879	1181	806	1438	1877	3836	5252	2779	4498	201		1742			

"Where	did this	man	get	these things?"	they	asked.		"What's	this	wisdom	that	has been	given	him,	that
πόθεν	τούτῳ ←		ταῦτα ←		λέγοντες	καὶ	τίς	ἡ	σοφία	ἡ	→ →	δοθεῖσα	τούτῳ καὶ		
cj	r.dsm		r.npn		pt.pa.npm	cj	r.nsf	d.nsf	n.nsf	d.nsf		pt.ap.nsf	r.dsm	adv	
4470	4047		4047		3306	2779	5515	3836	5053	3836		1443	4047	2779	

he			even	does	miracles!		**3** Isn't		this	the	carpenter?	Isn't this	Mary's		son
⌐διὰ	τῶν χειρῶν	αὐτοῦ⌐		γινόμεναι	⌐αἱ δυνάμεις τοιαῦται⌐		⌐οὐχ	ἐστιν	οὗτος	ὁ	τέκτων⌐		⌐τῆς Μαρίας⌐	ὁ	υἱὸς⌐
p.g	d.gpf	r.gsm.3		pt.pm.npf	d.npf n.npf		pl	v.pai.3s	r.nsm	d.nsm	n.nsm		d.gsf n.gsf	d.nsm	n.nsm
1328	3836	5931		1181	3836 1539		r.npf	4024	4047	3836	5454		3836 3451	3836	5626
															5525

and	the	brother	of James,		Joseph,		Judas	and	Simon?		Aren't	his	sisters		here	with	us?"	And
καὶ		ἀδελφὸς →	Ἰακώβου	καὶ	Ἰωσῆτος	καὶ	Ἰούδα	καὶ	Σίμωνος	καὶ	⌐οὐκ εἰσὶν⌐	αὐτοῦ	⌐αἱ ἀδελφαὶ⌐	ὧδε	πρὸς	ἡμᾶς	καὶ
cj		n.nsm	n.gsm	cj	n.gsm	cj	n.gsm	cj	n.gsm	cj	pl v.pai.3p	r.gsm.3	d.npf n.npf	adv	p.a	r.ap.1	cj
2779	81	2610	2779	2736	2779	2683	2779	4981	2779	4024 1639	899	3836 80	6045	4639	7005	2779

they	took		offense	at him.	¶	**4**	Jesus		said	to them,	"Only	in	his	hometown,		among
→	ἐσκανδαλίζοντο		ἐν	αὐτῷ		καὶ	⌐ὁ	Ἰησοῦς⌐	ἔλεγεν	αὐτοῖς	ὅτι	⌐εἰ	μὴ⌐	ἐν	αὐτοῦ	⌐τῇ πατρίδι⌐	καὶ	ἐν
v.ipi.3p		p.d	r.dsm.3		cj	d.nsm	n.nsm	v.iai.3s	r.dpm.3	cj	pl	pl	p.d	r.gsm.3	d.dsf n.dsf	cj	p.d
4997		1877	899		2779	3836	2652	3306	899	4022	1623	3590	1877	899	3836 4258	2779	1877

his	relatives	and in	his	own	house	is	a	prophet	without	honor."		He could	not do		any
αὐτοῦ	⌐τοῖς συγγενεῦσιν⌐	καὶ	αὐτοῦ ⌐τῇ		οἰκίᾳ⌐	⌐οὐκ ἐστιν⌐		προφήτης →		ἄτιμος	καὶ →	ἐδύνατο	οὐκ ποιῆσαι		οὐδεμίαν
r.gsm.3	d.dpm n.dpm	cj	r.gsm.3 d.dsf		n.dsf	pl v.pai.3s		n.nsm		a.nsm	cj	v.ipi.3s	pl f.aa		a.asf
899	3836 5150	2779	1877 899	3836	3864	4024 1639		4737		872	2779	1538	4024 4472		4029

5

miracles	there,	except	lay	his	hands	on a	few		sick	people	and	heal		them.	And he	was	amazed	at
δύναμιν	ἐκεῖ	⌐εἰ μὴ⌐	ἐπιθεὶς	τὰς	χεῖρας ←		ὀλίγοις	ἀρρώστοις ←				ἐθεράπευσεν			καὶ →	→	ἐθαύμαζεν	διὰ
n.asf	adv	cj pl	pt.aa.nsm	d.apf	n.apf		a.dpm	a.dpm				v.aai.3s			cj		v.iai.3s	p.a
1539	1695	1623 3590	2202	3836	5931	2202	3900	779				2543			2779		2513	1328

6

their	lack of faith.
αὐτῶν →	→ ⌐τὴν ἀπιστίαν⌐
r.gpm.3	d.asf n.asf
899	3836 602

τοὺς μετ᾿ αὐτοῦ καὶ εἰσπορεύεται ὅπου ἦν τὸ παιδίον. **41** καὶ κρατήσας τῆς χειρὸς τοῦ παιδίου λέγει αὐτῇ, Ταλιθα κουμ, ὅ ἐστιν μεθερμηνευόμενον Τὸ κοράσιον, σοὶ λέγω, ἔγειρε. **42** καὶ εὐθὺς ἀνέστη τὸ κοράσιον καὶ περιεπάτει· ἦν γὰρ ἐτῶν δώδεκα. καὶ ἐξέστησαν [εὐθὺς] ἐκστάσει μεγάλῃ. **43** καὶ διεστείλατο αὐτοῖς πολλὰ ἵνα μηδεὶς γνοῖ τοῦτο, καὶ εἶπεν δοθῆναι αὐτῇ φαγεῖν.

6:1 Καὶ ἐξῆλθεν ἐκεῖθεν καὶ ἔρχεται εἰς τὴν πατρίδα αὐτοῦ, καὶ ἀκολουθοῦσιν αὐτῷ οἱ μαθηταὶ αὐτοῦ. **2** καὶ γενομένου σαββάτου ἤρξατο διδάσκειν ἐν τῇ συναγωγῇ, καὶ πολλοὶ ἀκούοντες ἐξεπλήσσοντο λέγοντες, ¶ Πόθεν τούτῳ ταῦτα, καὶ τίς ἡ σοφία ἡ δοθεῖσα τούτῳ, καὶ αἱ δυνάμεις τοιαῦται διὰ τῶν χειρῶν αὐτοῦ γινόμεναι; **3** οὐχ οὗτός ἐστιν ὁ τέκτων, ὁ υἱὸς τῆς Μαρίας καὶ ἀδελφὸς Ἰακώβου καὶ Ἰωσῆτος καὶ Ἰούδα καὶ Σίμωνος; καὶ οὐκ εἰσὶν αἱ ἀδελφαὶ αὐτοῦ ὧδε πρὸς ἡμᾶς; καὶ ἐσκανδαλίζοντο ἐν αὐτῷ. ¶ **4** καὶ ἔλεγεν αὐτοῖς ὁ Ἰησοῦς ὅτι Οὐκ ἔστιν προφήτης ἄτιμος εἰ μὴ ἐν τῇ πατρίδι αὐτοῦ καὶ ἐν τοῖς συγγενεῦσιν αὐτοῦ καὶ ἐν τῇ οἰκίᾳ αὐτοῦ. **5** καὶ οὐκ ἐδύνατο ἐκεῖ ποιῆσαι οὐδεμίαν δύναμιν, εἰ μὴ ὀλίγοις ἀρρώστοις ἐπιθεὶς τὰς χεῖρας ἐθεράπευσεν.

Jesus Sends Out the Twelve

6:6 Then Jesus went around teaching *from village to village.* **7** Calling the Twelve to him, he
Καὶ   περιῆγεν ←   διδάσκων ⌊τὰς κώμας⌋ κύκλῳ   Καὶ προσκαλεῖται τοὺς δώδεκα ←   καὶ →
cj   v.iai.3s   pt.pa.nsm   d.apf n.apf   adv   v.pmi.3s   d.apm a.apm   cj
2779   4310   1438   3836 3267   3241   2779 4673   3836 1557   4673 4673 2779

sent them out two by two and gave them authority over evil spirits. ¶ **8**
ἤρξατο ἀποστέλλειν αὐτούς ↰ δύο   δύο καὶ ἐδίδου αὐτοῖς ἐξουσίαν → ⌊τῶν ἀκαθάρτων⌋ ⌊τῶν πνευμάτων⌋   καὶ
v.ami.3s f.pa   r.apm.3   a.apm   a.apm cj v.iai.3s r.dpm.3 n.asf   d.gpn a.gpn   d.gpn n.gpn   cj
806   690   899   1545   1545 2779 1443   899   2026   3836 176   3836 4460   2779

These were his instructions: "Take nothing for the journey except a staff – no bread, no bag, no
→ παρήγγειλεν   αὐτοῖς ἵνα αἴρωσιν μηδὲν εἰς ὁδὸν ⌊εἰ μὴ⌋ ῥάβδον μόνον   μὴ ἄρτον μὴ πήραν μὴ
v.aai.3s   r.dpm.3 cj v.pas.3p a.asn p.a n.asf ⌊pl⌋ n.asf adv   pl n.asm pl n.asf pl
4133   899   2671 149   3594 1650 3847 1623 3590 4811 3667   3590 788 3590 4385 3590

money in your belts. **9** Wear sandals but not an extra tunic. **10** Whenever you →
χαλκόν εἰς τὴν ζώνην ἀλλὰ ὑποδεδεμένους σανδάλια καὶ μὴ ἐνδύσησθε δύο χιτῶνας   καὶ ἔλεγεν αὐτοῖς ⌊ὅπου ἐὰν⌋ →
n.asm p.a d.asf n.asf cj pt.rm.apm n.apn cj pl v.ams.2p a.apm n.apm   cj v.iai.3s r.dpm.3 cj pl
5910 1650 3836 2438 247 5686 4908 2779 3590 1907 1545 5945   2779 3306 899 3963 1569

enter a house, stay there until you leave that town. **11** And if any place will not welcome you or
εἰσέλθητε εἰς οἰκίαν μένετε ἐκεῖ ⌊ἕως ἂν⌋ → ἐξέλθητε ἐκεῖθεν   καὶ → ⌊ὃς ἂν⌋ τόπος ↱ μὴ δέξηται ὑμᾶς μηδὲ
v.aas.2p p.a n.asf v.pam.2p adv cj pl v.aas.2p adv   cj r.nsm n.nsm pl v.ams.3s r.ap.2 pl
1656 1650 3864 3531 1695 2401 323 2002 1696   2779 4005 323 5536 3590 1312 7007 3593

listen to you, shake the dust off your feet when you leave, as a testimony
ἀκούσωσιν ← ὑμῶν ἐκτινάξατε τὸν χοῦν τὸν ὑποκάτω ὑμῶν ⌊τῶν ποδῶν⌋ → ἐκπορευόμενοι ἐκεῖθεν εἰς μαρτύριον
v.aas.3p r.gp.2 v.aam.2p d.asm n.asm d.asm p.g r.gp.2 d.gpn n.gpn → pt.pm.npm adv p.a n.asn
201 7007 1759 3836 5967 1759 3836 5691 7007 3836 4546 1744 1696 1650 3457

against them." ¶ **12** They went out and preached that people should repent. **13** They drove out
→ αὐτοῖς   Καὶ → ἐξελθόντες ← ἐκήρυξαν ἵνα → μετανοῶσιν καὶ → ἐξέβαλλον
r.dpm.3   cj pt.aa.npm v.aai.3p cj v.pas.3p cj v.iai.3p
899   2779 2002 3062 2671 3566 2779 1675

many demons and anointed many sick people with oil and healed them.
πολλὰ δαιμόνια καὶ ἤλειφον πολλοὺς ἀρρώστους ← → ἐλαίῳ καὶ ἐθεράπευον
a.apn n.apn cj v.iai.3p a.apm a.apm n.dsn cj v.iai.3p
4498 1228 2779 230 4498 779 1778 2779 2543

John the Baptist Beheaded

6:14 King Herod heard about this, for Jesus' name had become well known. Some were
Καὶ ὁ βασιλεὺς Ἡρῴδης ἤκουσεν γὰρ αὐτοῦ ⌊τὸ ὄνομα⌋ → ἐγένετο φανερὸν καὶ
cj d.nsm n.nsm n.nsm v.aai.3s cj r.gsm.3 d.nsn n.nsn v.ami.3s a.nsn cj
2779 3836 995 2476 201 1142 899 3836 3950 1181 5745 2779

saying, "John the Baptist has been raised from the dead, and *that is why* miraculous powers are
ἔλεγον ὅτι Ἰωάννης ὁ βαπτίζων → → ἐγήγερται ἐκ νεκρῶν καὶ ⌊διὰ τοῦτο⌋ ⌊αἱ δυνάμεις⌋ →
v.iai.3p cj n.nsm d.nsm pt.pa.nsm v.rpi.3s p.g a.gpm cj p.a r.asn d.npf n.npf
3306 4022 2722 3836 966 1586 1666 3738 2779 1328 4047 3836 1539

at work in him." ¶ **15** Others said, "He is Elijah." And still others claimed, "He is a prophet,
→ ἐνεργοῦσιν ἐν αὐτῷ δὲ ἄλλοι ἔλεγον ὅτι ἐστίν Ἠλίας δὲ ἄλλοι ἔλεγον ὅτι προφήτης
v.pai.3p p.d r.dsm.3 cj r.npm v.iai.3p cj v.pai.3s n.nsm cj r.npm v.iai.3p cj n.nsm
1919 1877 899 1254 257 3306 4022 1639 2460 1254 257 3306 4022 4737

like one of the prophets of long ago." ¶ **16** But when Herod heard this, he said, "John, the man I
ὡς εἰς → τῶν προφητῶν δὲ ↱ ὁ Ἡρῴδης ἀκούσας → ἔλεγεν Ἰωάννην ὃν ← ἐγὼ
pl a.nsm d.gpm n.gpm cj d.nsm n.nsm pt.aa.nsm v.iai.3s n.asm r.asm r.ns.1
6055 1651 3836 4737 1254 201 3836 2476 201 3306 2722 4005 1609

beheaded, has been raised from the dead!" ¶ **17** For Herod himself had given orders to have
ἀπεκεφάλισα οὗτος → → ἠγέρθη γὰρ ὁ Ἡρῴδης Αὐτὸς → ἀποστείλας ←
v.aai.1s r.nsm v.api.3s cj d.nsm n.nsm r.nsm pt.aa.nsm
642 4047 1586 1142 3836 2476 899 690 3195 3195

6:6 καὶ ἐθαύμαζεν διὰ τὴν ἀπιστίαν αὐτῶν. Καὶ περιῆγεν τὰς κώμας κύκλῳ διδάσκων. 7 καὶ προσκαλεῖται τοὺς δώδεκα καὶ ἤρξατο αὐτοὺς ἀποστέλλειν δύο δύο καὶ ἐδίδου αὐτοῖς ἐξουσίαν τῶν πνευμάτων τῶν ἀκαθάρτων, ¶ 8 καὶ παρήγγειλεν αὐτοῖς ἵνα μηδὲν αἴρωσιν εἰς ὁδὸν εἰ μὴ ῥάβδον μόνον, μὴ ἄρτον, μὴ πήραν, μὴ εἰς τὴν ζώνην χαλκόν, 9 ἀλλὰ ὑποδεδεμένους σανδάλια, καὶ μὴ ἐνδύσησθε δύο χιτῶνας. 10 καὶ ἔλεγεν αὐτοῖς, Ὅπου ἐὰν εἰσέλθητε εἰς οἰκίαν, ἐκεῖ μένετε ἕως ἂν ἐξέλθητε ἐκεῖθεν. 11 καὶ ὃς ἂν τόπος μὴ δέξηται ὑμᾶς μηδὲ ἀκούσωσιν ὑμῶν, ἐκπορευόμενοι ἐκεῖθεν ἐκτινάξατε τὸν χοῦν τὸν ὑποκάτω τῶν ποδῶν ὑμῶν εἰς μαρτύριον αὐτοῖς. ¶ 12 Καὶ ἐξελθόντες ἐκήρυξαν ἵνα μετανοῶσιν, 13 καὶ δαιμόνια πολλὰ ἐξέβαλλον, καὶ ἤλειφον ἐλαίῳ πολλοὺς ἀρρώστους καὶ ἐθεράπευον.

6:14 Καὶ ἤκουσεν ὁ βασιλεὺς Ἡρῴδης, φανερὸν γὰρ ἐγένετο τὸ ὄνομα αὐτοῦ, καὶ ἔλεγον ὅτι Ἰωάννης ὁ βαπτίζων ἐγήγερται ἐκ νεκρῶν καὶ διὰ τοῦτο ἐνεργοῦσιν αἱ δυνάμεις ἐν αὐτῷ. ¶ 15 ἄλλοι δὲ ἔλεγον ὅτι Ἠλίας ἐστίν· ἄλλοι δὲ ἔλεγον ὅτι προφήτης ὡς εἷς τῶν προφητῶν. ¶ 16 ἀκούσας δὲ ὁ Ἡρῴδης ἔλεγεν, Ὃν ἐγὼ ἀπεκεφάλισα Ἰωάννην, οὗτος ἐκ νεκρῶν ἠγέρθη. ¶ 17 Αὐτὸς

John   arrested, and he had him bound and put in   prison. He did this because of Herodias, his
ⸯτὸν Ἰωάννηνⸯ ἐκράτησεν καὶ → → αὐτὸν ἔδησεν   ἐν φυλακῇ   διὰ ← Ἡρῳδιάδα αὐτοῦ
d.asm n.asm   v.aai.3s cj   r.asm.3 v.aai.3s   p.d n.dsf   p.a   n.asf r.gsm.3
3836 2722   3195 2779 1313 1313 899 1313   1877 5871   1328   2478 899

brother   Philip's   wife,   whom he had married. **18** For John   had been saying to Herod,   "It
ⸯτοῦ ἀδελφοῦⸯ Φιλίππου ⸯτὴν γυναῖκαⸯ ὅτι αὐτὴν → → ἐγάμησεν γὰρ ὁ Ἰωάννηςⸯ → → ἔλεγεν → ⸯτῷ Ἡρῴδῃ ὅτι
d.gsm n.gsm n.gsm d.asf n.asf cj r.asf.3 v.aai.3s v.pai.3s d.nsm n.nsm v.iai.3s d.dsm n.dsm cj
3836 81 5805 3836 1222 4022 899 1138 1142 3836 2722 3306 3836 2476 4022 1997

is not lawful for you to have your brother's   wife."   **19** So Herodias   nursed a grudge against John and
→ οὐκ ἔξεστιν → σοι → ἔχειν σου ⸯτοῦ ἀδελφοῦⸯ ⸯτὴν γυναῖκαⸯ δὲ ἡ Ἡρῳδιὰςⸯ ἐνεῖχεν ← αὐτῷ καὶ
pl v.pai.3s r.ds.2 f.pa r.gs.2 d.gsm n.gsm d.asf n.asf cj d.nsf n.nsf v.iai.3s r.dsm.3 cj
1997 4024 1997 5148 2400 5148 3836 81 3836 1222 1254 3836 2478 1923 899 2779

wanted to kill   him. But she was not able   to, **20** because Herod   feared John   and protected him,
ἤθελεν → ἀποκτεῖναι αὐτὸν καὶ → οὐκ ἠδύνατο ← γὰρ ὁ Ἡρῴδης ἐφοβεῖτο τὸν Ἰωάννηνⸯ καὶ συνετήρει αὐτὸν
v.iai.3s f.aa r.asm.3 cj pl v.ipi.3s cj d.nsm n.nsm v.ipi.3s d.asm n.asm cj v.iai.3s r.asm.3
2527 650 899 2779 1538 1538 4024 1538 1142 3836 2476 5828 3836 2722 2779 5337 899

knowing him to be a righteous and holy man.   When Herod heard   John, he was greatly puzzled; yet he liked
εἰδὼς αὐτὸν → → δίκαιον καὶ ἅγιον ἄνδρα καὶ → ἀκούσας αὐτοῦ → → πολλὰ ἠπόρει καὶ → ἡδέως
pt.ra.nsm r.asm.3 a.asm cj a.asm n.asm cj pt.aa.nsm r.gsm.3 a.apn v.iai.3s cj adv
3857 899 1465 2779 41 467 2779 201 899 679 679 4498 679 2779 201 2452

to listen to him. ¶   **21**   Finally the opportune time   came.   On his birthday   Herod gave   a
→ ἤκουεν ← αὐτοῦ   Καὶ εὐκαίρου ἡμέρας γενομένης ὅτε → αὐτοῦ ⸯτοῖς γενεσίοιςⸯ Ἡρῴδης ἐποίησεν
v.iai.3s r.gsm.3 cj a.gsf n.gsf pt.am.gsf cj r.gsm.3 d.dpn n.dpn n.nsm v.aai.3s
201 899 2779 2322 2465 1181 4021 1160 899 3836 1160 2476 4472

banquet for his   high officials   and military commanders   and the leading men of Galilee.   **22**   When
δεῖπνον → αὐτοῦ → ⸯτοῖς μεγιστᾶσινⸯ καὶ → ⸯτοῖς χιλιάρχοιςⸯ καὶ τοῖς πρώτοις → ⸯτῆς Γαλιλαίαςⸯ καὶ
n.asn r.gsm.3 d.dpm n.dpm cj d.dpm n.dpm cj d.dpm a.dpm d.gsf n.gsf cj
1270 3491 899 3836 3491 2779 3836 5941 2779 3836 4755 3836 1133 2779 1656

the daughter   of Herodias came   in and danced,   she pleased Herod   and his dinner guests.
τῆς θυγατρὸς αὐτοῦ → Ἡρῳδιάδος εἰσελθούσης ← καὶ ὀρχησαμένης → ἤρεσεν ⸯτῷ Ἡρῴδῃⸯ καὶ τοῖς → συνανακειμένοις
d.gsf n.gsf r.gsm.3 n.gsf pt.aa.gsf cj pt.am.gsf v.aai.3s d.dsm n.dsm cj d.dpm pt.pm.dpm
3836 2588 899 2478 1656 2779 4004 743 3836 2476 2779 3836 5263

¶   The king   said to the girl,   "Ask   me for anything you want, and I'll give it to you." **23** And he promised
ὁ βασιλεὺς εἶπεν → τῷ κορασίῳ αἴτησόν με ← ⸯὃ ἐὰνⸯ → θέλῃς καὶ → δώσω → σοι   καὶ → ὤμοσεν
d.nsm n.nsm v.aai.3s d.dsn n.dsn v.aam.2s r.as.1 r.asn pl v.pas.2s cj v.fai.1s r.ds.2 cj v.aai.3s
3836 995 3306 3836 3166 160 1609 160 1569 2527 2779 1443 5148 2779 3923

her with an oath,   "Whatever you ask   I will give you, up to half   my kingdom." ¶
αὐτῇ ← →   [πολλὰ] ὅ τι ἐάνⸯ αἰτήσῃς με → → δώσω σοι ἕως ἡμίσους μου ⸯτῆς βασιλείαςⸯ
r.dsf.3 a.apn r.asn r.asn pl v.aas.2s r.as.1 v.fai.1s r.ds.2 p.g a.gsn r.gs.1 d.gsf n.gsf
899 3923 3923 3923 4498 4005 5516 1569 160 1609 1443 5148 2401 2468 1609 3836 993

24   She went   out and said to   her   mother, "What shall I ask   for?" ¶   "The head   of John
καὶ → ἐξελθοῦσα ← εἶπεν αὐτῆς ⸯτῇ μητρὶ τί → → αἰτήσωμαι ← δὲ τὴν κεφαλὴν → Ἰωάννου
cj pt.aa.nsf v.aai.3s r.gsf.3 d.dsf n.dsf r.asn v.ams.1s cj d.asf n.asf n.gsm
2779 2002 3306 3613 899 3836 3613 5515 160 1254 3836 3051 2722

the Baptist," she answered. ¶   **25**   At once the girl hurried   in to   the king   with the
τοῦ βαπτίζοντος ἡ εἶπεν   καὶ εὐθὺς → ⸯεἰσελθοῦσα μετὰ σπουδῆςⸯ → πρὸς τὸν βασιλέα
d.gsm pt.pa.gsm d.nsf v.aai.3s cj adv pt.aa.nsf p.g n.gsf p.a d.asm n.asm
3836 966 3836 3306 2779 2318 1656 3552 5082 4639 3836 995

request: "I want you to   give me right now   the head   of John   the Baptist on a platter." **26**   The
ἠτήσατο λέγουσα → θέλω   ἵνα δῷς μοι → ἐξαυτῆς τὴν κεφαλὴν → Ἰωάννου τοῦ βαπτιστοῦ ἐπὶ πίνακι καὶ ὁ
v.ami.3s pt.pa.nsf v.pai.1s cj v.aas.2s r.ds.1 adv d.asf n.asf n.gsm d.gsm n.gsm p.d n.dsm cj d.nsm
160 3306 2527 1443 2671 1443 1609 1994 3836 3051 2722 3836 969 2093 4402 2779 3836

king was greatly distressed, but because of his oaths and his dinner guests,   he did not want   to
βασιλεὺς γενόμενος → περίλυπος διὰ ← τοὺς ὅρκους καὶ τοὺς → ἀνακειμένους → οὐκ ἠθέλησεν →
n.nsm pt.am.nsm a.nsm p.a d.apm n.apm cj d.apm pt.pm.apm pl v.aai.3s
995 1181 4337 1328 3836 3992 2779 3836 367 2527 2527 4024 2527

γὰρ ὁ Ἡρῴδης ἀποστείλας ἐκράτησεν τὸν Ἰωάννην καὶ ἔδησεν αὐτὸν ἐν φυλακῇ διὰ Ἡρῳδιάδα τὴν γυναῖκα Φιλίππου τοῦ ἀδελφοῦ αὐτοῦ, ὅτι αὐτὴν ἐγάμησεν· **18** ἔλεγεν γὰρ ὁ Ἰωάννης τῷ Ἡρῴδῃ ὅτι Οὐκ ἔξεστίν σοι ἔχειν τὴν γυναῖκα τοῦ ἀδελφοῦ σου. **19** ἡ δὲ Ἡρῳδιὰς ἐνεῖχεν αὐτῷ καὶ ἤθελεν αὐτὸν ἀποκτεῖναι, καὶ οὐκ ἠδύνατο· **20** ὁ γὰρ Ἡρῴδης ἐφοβεῖτο τὸν Ἰωάννην, εἰδὼς αὐτὸν ἄνδρα δίκαιον καὶ ἅγιον, καὶ συνετήρει αὐτόν, καὶ ἀκούσας αὐτοῦ πολλὰ ἠπόρει, καὶ ἡδέως αὐτοῦ ἤκουεν. ¶ **21** Καὶ γενομένης ἡμέρας εὐκαίρου ὅτε Ἡρῴδης τοῖς γενεσίοις αὐτοῦ δεῖπνον ἐποίησεν τοῖς μεγιστᾶσιν αὐτοῦ καὶ τοῖς χιλιάρχοις καὶ τοῖς πρώτοις τῆς Γαλιλαίας, **22** καὶ εἰσελθούσης τῆς θυγατρὸς αὐτοῦ Ἡρῳδιάδος καὶ ὀρχησαμένης ἤρεσεν τῷ Ἡρῴδῃ καὶ τοῖς συνανακειμένοις. ¶ εἶπεν ὁ βασιλεὺς τῷ κορασίῳ, Αἴτησόν με ὃ ἐὰν θέλῃς, καὶ δώσω σοι· **23** καὶ ὤμοσεν αὐτῇ, «αὐτῇ» [πολλά], Ὅ τι ἐάν με αἰτήσῃς δώσω σοι ἕως ἡμίσους τῆς βασιλείας μου. ¶ **24** καὶ ἐξελθοῦσα εἶπεν τῇ μητρὶ αὐτῆς, Τί αἰτήσωμαι ¶ ἡ δὲ εἶπεν, Τὴν κεφαλὴν Ἰωάννου τοῦ βαπτίζοντος. ¶ **25** καὶ εἰσελθοῦσα εὐθὺς μετὰ σπουδῆς πρὸς τὸν βασιλέα ἠτήσατο λέγουσα, Θέλω ἵνα ἐξαυτῆς δῷς μοι ἐπὶ πίνακι τὴν κεφαλὴν Ἰωάννου τοῦ βαπτιστοῦ. **26** καὶ περίλυπος γενόμενος ὁ βασιλεὺς διὰ τοὺς

refuse her. **27** So he   immediately sent   an executioner with orders to bring John's head.
ἀθετῆσαι αὐτήν   καὶ ὁ βασιλεὺς εὐθὺς ἀποστείλας σπεκουλάτορα → ἐπέταξεν → ἐνέγκαι αὐτοῦ τὴν κεφαλὴν καὶ
f.aa r.asf.3 cj d.nsm n.nsm adv pt.aa.nsm n.asm v.aai.3s f.aa r.gsm.3 d.asf n.asf cj
119 899 2779 3836 995 2318 690 5063 2199 5770 899 3836 3051 2779

The man went,   beheaded   John in the prison, **28** and brought back his   head   on a platter.   He presented
→ → ἀπελθὼν ἀπεκεφάλισεν αὐτὸν ἐν τῇ φυλακῇ καὶ ἤνεγκεν ← αὐτοῦ τὴν κεφαλὴν ἐπὶ πίνακι καὶ → ἔδωκεν
pt.aa.nsm v.aai.3s r.asm.3 p.d d.dsf n.dsf cj v.aai.3s r.gsm.3 d.asf n.asf p.d n.dsm cj v.aai.3s
599 642 899 1877 3836 5871 2779 5770 899 3836 3051 2093 4402 2779 1443

it to the girl,   and she   gave it to her mother. **29** On hearing of this, John's disciples
αὐτὴν → τῷ κορασίῳ καὶ τὸ κοράσιον ἔδωκεν αὐτὴν αὐτῆς τῇ μητρί καὶ → ἀκούσαντες αὐτοῦ οἱ μαθηταὶ
r.asf.3 d.dsn n.dsn cj d.nsn n.nsn v.aai.3s r.asf.3 r.gsf.3 d.dsf n.dsf cj pt.aa.npm r.gsm.3 d.npm n.npm
899 3836 3166 2779 3836 3166 1443 899 3613 899 3836 3613 2779 201 899 3836 3412

came and took his   body   and laid it in a tomb.
ἦλθον καὶ ἦραν αὐτοῦ τὸ πτῶμα καὶ ἔθηκαν αὐτὸ ἐν μνημείῳ
v.aai.3p cj v.aai.3p r.gsm.3 d.asn n.asn cj v.aai.3p r.asn.3 p.d n.dsn
2262 2779 149 899 3836 4773 2779 5502 899 1877 3646

Jesus Feeds the Five Thousand

6:30 The apostles gathered around Jesus   and reported to him all   they had done   and
Καὶ οἱ ἀπόστολοι συνάγονται πρὸς τὸν Ἰησοῦν καὶ ἀπήγγειλαν → αὐτῷ πάντα ὅσα → → ἐποίησαν καὶ ὅσα
cj d.npm n.npm v.ppi.3p p.a d.asm n.asm cj v.aai.3p r.dsm.3 a.apn r.apn v.aai.3p cj r.apn
2779 3836 693 5251 4639 3836 2652 2779 550 899 4246 4012 4472 2779 4012

taught. **31** Then, because so many people were coming   and going   that they did not even have   a
ἐδίδαξαν καὶ γὰρ πολλοί ← ἦσαν οἱ ἐρχόμενοι καὶ οἱ ὑπάγοντες καὶ → → οὐδὲ ← εὐκαίρουν ←
v.aai.3p cj cj a.npm v.iai.3p d.npm pt.pm.npm cj d.npm pt.pa.npm cj adv v.iai.3p
1438 2779 1142 4498 1639 3836 2262 2779 3836 5632 2779 2320 2320 4028 2320

chance to eat, he said to them,   "Come with me by yourselves to a quiet place and get some
→ φαγεῖν → λέγει → αὐτοῖς ὑμεῖς αὐτοὶ δεῦτε κατ' ἰδίαν εἰς ἔρημον τόπον καὶ → ὀλίγον
f.aa v.pai.3s r.dpm.3 r.np.2 r.npm adv p.a a.asf p.a a.asm n.asm cj adv
2266 3306 899 7007 899 1307 2848 2625 1650 2245 5536 2779 399 3900

rest." ¶ **32** So they went   away by themselves in a boat   to a solitary place. **33** But many who saw
ἀναπαύσασθε Καὶ → ἀπῆλθον ← κατ' ἰδίαν ἐν τῷ πλοίῳ εἰς ἔρημον τόπον καὶ πολλοὶ εἶδον
v.amm.2p cj v.aai.3p p.a a.asf p.d d.dsn n.dsn p.a a.asm n.asm cj a.npm v.aai.3p
399 2779 599 2848 2625 1877 3836 4450 1650 2245 5536 2779 4498 1625

them leaving   recognized them and ran   on foot from all   the towns and got   there ahead of them.
αὐτοὺς ὑπάγοντας καὶ ἐπέγνωσαν καὶ συνέδραμον → πεζῇ ἀπὸ πασῶν τῶν πόλεων καὶ προῆλθον ἐκεῖ ← ← αὐτούς
r.apm.3 pt.pa.apm cj v.aai.3p cj v.aai.3p adv p.g a.gpf d.gpf n.gpf cj v.aai.3p adv r.apm.3
899 5632 2779 2105 2779 5340 4270 608 4246 3836 4484 2779 4601 1695 4601 899

34 When Jesus landed and saw a large crowd,   he had compassion on them, because they were like sheep
Καὶ → ἐξελθὼν εἶδεν πολὺν ὄχλον καὶ ἐσπλαγχνίσθη ἐπ' αὐτούς ὅτι → ἦσαν ὡς πρόβατα
cj pt.aa.nsm v.aai.3s a.asm n.asm cj v.api.3s p.a r.apm.3 cj v.iai.3p pl n.npn
2779 2002 1625 4498 4063 2779 5072 2093 899 4022 1639 6055 4585

without a shepherd. So he began teaching them many things. ¶ **35** By this time it was   late
μὴ ἔχοντα ποιμένα καὶ ἤρξατο διδάσκειν αὐτοὺς πολλά ← Καὶ → ἤδη ← γενομένης ὥρας πολλῆς
pl pt.pa.npn n.asm cj v.ami.3s f.pa r.apm.3 a.apn cj adv pt.am.gsf n.gsf a.gsf
3590 2400 4478 2779 806 1438 899 4498 2779 2453 1181 6052 4498

in the day, so his   disciples came   to him.   "This is a remote place,"   they said, "and it's already
αὐτῷ οἱ μαθηταὶ προσελθόντες ← αὐτῷ ὅτι ἐστιν ἔρημος ὁ τόπος → ἔλεγον καὶ ἤδη
r.gsm.3 d.npm n.npm pt.aa.npm r.dsm.3 cj v.pai.3s a.nsm d.nsm n.nsm v.iai.3p cj adv
899 3836 3412 4665 899 4022 1639 2245 3836 5536 3306 2779 2453

very late. **36** Send   the people away so they can go   to the surrounding countryside and villages and
πολλή ὥρα ἀπόλυσον αὐτούς ἵνα → ἀπελθόντες εἰς τοὺς κύκλῳ ἀγροὺς καὶ κώμας
a.nsf n.nsf v.aam.2s r.apm.3 cj pt.aa.npm p.a d.apm adv n.apm cj n.apf
4498 6052 668 899 668 2671 599 1650 3836 3241 69 2779 3267

buy   themselves something to eat." ¶ **37** But he answered,   "You give them something to
ἀγοράσωσιν ἑαυτοῖς τί → φάγωσιν δὲ ὁ ἀποκριθεὶς εἶπεν αὐτοῖς ὑμεῖς δότε αὐτοῖς →
v.aas.3p r.dpm.3 r.asn v.aas.3p cj d.nsm pt.ap.nsm v.aai.3s r.dpm.3 r.np.2 v.aam.2p r.dpm.3
60 1571 5515 2266 1254 3836 646 3306 899 7007 1443 899

ὅρκους καὶ τοὺς ἀνακειμένους οὐκ ἠθέλησεν ἀθετῆσαι αὐτήν· ²⁷ καὶ εὐθὺς ἀποστείλας ὁ βασιλεὺς σπεκουλάτορα ἐπέταξεν ἐνέγκαι τὴν κεφαλὴν αὐτοῦ. καὶ ἀπελθὼν ἀπεκεφάλισεν αὐτὸν ἐν τῇ φυλακῇ ²⁸ καὶ ἤνεγκεν τὴν κεφαλὴν αὐτοῦ ἐπὶ πίνακι καὶ ἔδωκεν αὐτὴν τῷ κορασίῳ, καὶ τὸ κοράσιον ἔδωκεν αὐτὴν τῇ μητρὶ αὐτῆς. ²⁹ καὶ ἀκούσαντες οἱ μαθηταὶ αὐτοῦ ἦλθον καὶ ἦραν τὸ πτῶμα αὐτοῦ καὶ ἔθηκαν αὐτὸ ἐν μνημείῳ.

⁶:³⁰ Καὶ συνάγονται οἱ ἀπόστολοι πρὸς τὸν Ἰησοῦν καὶ ἀπήγγειλαν αὐτῷ πάντα ὅσα ἐποίησαν καὶ ὅσα ἐδίδαξαν. ³¹ καὶ λέγει αὐτοῖς, Δεῦτε ὑμεῖς αὐτοὶ κατ' ἰδίαν εἰς ἔρημον τόπον καὶ ἀναπαύσασθε ὀλίγον. ἦσαν γὰρ οἱ ἐρχόμενοι καὶ οἱ ὑπάγοντες πολλοί, καὶ οὐδὲ φαγεῖν εὐκαίρουν. ¶ ³² καὶ ἀπῆλθον ἐν τῷ πλοίῳ εἰς ἔρημον τόπον κατ' ἰδίαν. ³³ καὶ εἶδον αὐτοὺς ὑπάγοντας καὶ ἐπέγνωσαν πολλοὶ καὶ πεζῇ ἀπὸ πασῶν τῶν πόλεων συνέδραμον ἐκεῖ καὶ προῆλθον αὐτούς. ³⁴ καὶ ἐξελθὼν εἶδεν πολὺν ὄχλον καὶ ἐσπλαγχνίσθη ἐπ' αὐτούς, ὅτι ἦσαν ὡς πρόβατα μὴ ἔχοντα ποιμένα, καὶ ἤρξατο διδάσκειν αὐτοὺς πολλά. ¶ ³⁵ Καὶ ἤδη ὥρας πολλῆς γενομένης προσελθόντες αὐτῷ οἱ μαθηταὶ αὐτοῦ ἔλεγον ὅτι Ἔρημός ἐστιν ὁ τόπος καὶ ἤδη ὥρα πολλή· ³⁶ ἀπόλυσον αὐτούς, ἵνα ἀπελθόντες εἰς τοὺς κύκλῳ ἀγροὺς καὶ κώμας ἀγοράσωσιν ἑαυτοῖς τί φάγωσιν. ¶ ³⁷ ὁ δὲ ἀποκριθεὶς

eat." ¶   They said   to him, "That would take *eight months of a man's wages!*   Are we to
φαγεῖν   καὶ   λέγουσιν → αὐτῷ   δηναρίων διακοσίων → → →
f.aa   cj   v.pai.3p   r.dsm.3   n.gpn   a.gpn
2266   2779   3306   899   1324   1357

go   and spend   that much on bread and give   it to them to eat?" ¶   **38** "How many loaves do
ἀπελθόντες ἀγοράσωμεν   ἄρτους καὶ δώσομεν → αὐτοῖς → φαγεῖν   δὲ   πόσους ← ἄρτους →
pt.aa.npm   v.aas.1p   n.apm   cj   v.fai.1p   r.dpm.3   f.aa   cj   a.apm   n.apm
599   60   788   2779 1443   899   2266   1254 4531   788

you have?" he asked.   "Go   and see." ¶   When they found out, they said,   "Five – and two
→ ἔχετε ὁ   λέγει αὐτοῖς ὑπάγετε ἴδετε   καὶ →   γνόντες ←   λέγουσιν πέντε καὶ δύο
v.pai.2p d.nsm v.pai.3s r.dpm.3 v.pam.2p v.aam.2p cj   pt.aa.npm   v.pai.3p a.apm cj   a.apm
2400   3836 3306   899   5632   1625   2779   1182   3306   4297 2779 1545

fish." ¶ **39** Then Jesus directed them to have all   the people sit   down in groups   on the
ἰχθύας   καὶ   ἐπέταξεν αὐτοῖς → → πάντας ←   ←   ἀνακλῖναι ←   → συμπόσια συμπόσια ἐπὶ τῷ
n.apm   cj   v.aai.3s r.dpm.3   a.apm   f.aa   n.apn   n.apn   p.d d.dsm
2716   2779   2199   899   369 369 4246   369   5235   5235   2093 3836

green grass. **40** So they sat   down in groups   of hundreds and   fifties.   **41** Taking the five loaves
χλωρῷ χόρτῳ   καὶ → ἀνέπεσαν ←   → πρασιαὶ πρασιαὶ κατὰ ἑκατὸν καὶ κατὰ πεντήκοντα καὶ λαβὼν τοὺς πέντε ἄρτους
a.dsm n.dsm   cj   v.aai.3p   n.npf   n.npf   p.a a.apm   cj   p.a a.apm   cj   pt.aa.nsm d.apm a.apm n.apm
5952 5965   2779   404   4555   4555   2848 1669   2779 2848 4299   2779 3284   3836 4297 788

and the two fish and looking   up to heaven,   he gave thanks and broke   the loaves. Then he gave
καὶ τοὺς δύο ἰχθύας ἀναβλέψας ←   εἰς τὸν οὐρανόν, → εὐλόγησεν ←   καὶ κατέκλασεν τοὺς ἄρτους καὶ → ἐδίδου
cj   d.apm a.apm n.apm pt.aa.nsm   p.a d.asm n.asm   v.aai.3s   cj   v.aai.3s   d.apm n.apm cj   v.iai.3s
2779 3836 1545 2716   329   1650 3836 4041   2328   2779 2880   3836 788   2779   1443

them to his disciples   to set   before the people. He also divided the two fish   among them all.
→ αὐτοῦ τοῖς μαθηταῖς ἵνα παρατιθῶσιν ←   αὐτοῖς καὶ ἐμέρισεν τοὺς δύο ἰχθύας →   → πᾶσιν
r.gsm.3 d.dpm n.dpm   cj v.pas.3p   r.dpm.3 cj   v.aai.3s d.apm a.apm n.apm   a.dpm
3412 899 3836 3412   2671 4192   899   3532 3532   3836 1545 2716   4246

42 They all ate   and were satisfied, **43** and the disciples picked up twelve basketfuls   of broken pieces
καὶ → πάντες ἔφαγον καὶ → ἐχορτάσθησαν καὶ   ἦραν ← δώδεκα κοφίνων πληρώματα κλάσματα ←
cj   a.npm v.aai.3p cj   v.api.3p   cj   v.aai.3p a.gpm n.gpm   n.apn   n.apn
2779   4246   2266   2779   5963   2779   149   1557   3186   4445   3083

of bread and   fish.   **44** The number of the men   who had eaten   was five
καὶ ἀπὸ τῶν ἰχθύων, καὶ   οἱ ἄνδρες →   → φαγόντες [τοὺς ἄρτους] ἦσαν πεντακισχίλιοι
cj   p.g d.gpm n.gpm   cj   d.npm n.npm   pt.aa.npm d.apm n.apm   v.iai.3p a.npm
2779 608 3836 2716   2779   3836 467   2266   3836 788   1639   4295

thousand.
←

Jesus Walks on the Water

6:45 Immediately Jesus made   his   disciples   get   into the boat and go   on ahead of him
Καὶ εὐθὺς   ἠνάγκασεν αὐτοῦ τοὺς μαθητὰς ἐμβῆναι εἰς τὸ πλοῖον καὶ προάγειν ← ←   εἰς
cj   adv   v.aai.3s r.gsm.3 d.apm n.apm f.aa   p.a d.asn n.asn cj   f.pa   p.a
2779 2318   337   899 3836 3412   1832   1650 3836 4450   2779 4575   1650

to   Bethsaida, while he dismissed the crowd. **46** After leaving   them, he went   up on a
τὸ πέραν πρὸς Βηθσαϊδάν, ἕως αὐτὸς ἀπολύει τὸν ὄχλον   καὶ   ἀποταξάμενος αὐτοῖς → ἀπῆλθεν ← εἰς
d.asn adv p.a n.asf   cj   r.nsm v.pai.3s d.asm n.asm   cj   pt.am.nsm   r.dpm.3   v.aai.3s   p.a
3836 4305 4639 1034   2401 899 668   3836 4063   2779   698   899   599   1650

mountainside to pray.   ¶ **47** When evening came,   the boat was in the middle of the lake, and
τὸ ὄρος   → προσεύξασθαι καὶ →   ὀψίας γενομένης τὸ πλοῖον ἦν ἐν μέσῳ → τῆς θαλάσσης καὶ
d.asn n.asn   f.am   cj   n.gsf pt.am.gsf d.nsn n.nsn v.iai.3s p.d n.dsn d.gsf n.gsf   cj
3836 4001   4667   2779   1181   4068   1181   3836 4450 1639 1877 3545 3836 2498   2779

he was alone on land. **48** He saw the disciples straining   at the oars,   because the wind was
αὐτὸς μόνος ἐπὶ τῆς γῆς, καὶ → ἰδὼν   αὐτοὺς βασανιζομένους ἐν → τῷ ἐλαύνειν γὰρ ὁ   ἄνεμος ἦν
r.nsm a.nsm p.g d.gsf n.gsf cj   pt.aa.nsm r.apm.3 pt.pp.apm   p.d   d.dsn f.pa   cj   d.nsm n.nsm v.iai.3s
899   3668 2093 3836 1178 2779   1625   899   989   1877   3836 1785   1142 3836 449   1639

εἶπεν αὐτοῖς, Δότε αὐτοῖς ὑμεῖς φαγεῖν. ¶ καὶ λέγουσιν αὐτῷ, Ἀπελθόντες ἀγοράσωμεν δηναρίων διακοσίων ἄρτους καὶ δώσομεν
αὐτοῖς φαγεῖν; ¶ **38** ὁ δὲ λέγει αὐτοῖς, Πόσους ἄρτους ἔχετε; ὑπάγετε ἴδετε. ¶ καὶ γνόντες λέγουσιν, Πέντε, καὶ δύο ἰχθύας. ¶
39 καὶ ἐπέταξεν αὐτοῖς ἀνακλῖναι πάντας συμπόσια συμπόσια ἐπὶ τῷ χλωρῷ χόρτῳ. **40** καὶ ἀνέπεσαν πρασιαὶ πρασιαὶ κατὰ
ἑκατὸν καὶ κατὰ πεντήκοντα. **41** καὶ λαβὼν τοὺς πέντε ἄρτους καὶ τοὺς δύο ἰχθύας ἀναβλέψας εἰς τὸν οὐρανὸν εὐλόγησεν καὶ
κατέκλασεν τοὺς ἄρτους καὶ ἐδίδου τοῖς μαθηταῖς [αὐτοῦ] ἵνα παρατιθῶσιν αὐτοῖς, καὶ τοὺς δύο ἰχθύας ἐμέρισεν πᾶσιν. **42** καὶ
ἔφαγον πάντες καὶ ἐχορτάσθησαν, **43** καὶ ἦραν κλάσματα δώδεκα κοφίνων πληρώματα καὶ ἀπὸ τῶν ἰχθύων. **44** καὶ ἦσαν οἱ
φαγόντες [τοὺς ἄρτους] πεντακισχίλιοι ἄνδρες.
    6:45 Καὶ εὐθὺς ἠνάγκασεν τοὺς μαθητὰς αὐτοῦ ἐμβῆναι εἰς τὸ πλοῖον καὶ προάγειν εἰς τὸ πέραν πρὸς Βηθσαϊδάν, ἕως αὐτὸς
ἀπολύει τὸν ὄχλον. **46** καὶ ἀποταξάμενος αὐτοῖς ἀπῆλθεν εἰς τὸ ὄρος προσεύξασθαι. ¶ **47** καὶ ὀψίας γενομένης ἦν τὸ πλοῖον ἐν
μέσῳ τῆς θαλάσσης, καὶ αὐτὸς μόνος ἐπὶ τῆς γῆς. **48** καὶ ἰδὼν αὐτοὺς βασανιζομένους ἐν τῷ ἐλαύνειν, ἦν γὰρ ὁ ἄνεμος ἐναντίος

against them. About the fourth watch of the night he went out to them, walking on the lake.   He was
ἐναντίος αὐτοῖς περὶ τετάρτην φυλακὴν → τῆς νυκτὸς ἔρχεται ← πρὸς αὐτοὺς περιπατῶν ἐπὶ τῆς θαλάσσης καὶ →
a.nsm r.dpm.3 p.a a.asf n.asf d.gsf n.gsf v.pmi.3s p.a r.apm.3 pt.pa.nsm p.g d.gsf n.gsf cj
1885 899 4309 5480 5871 3836 3816 2262 4639 899 4344 2093 3836 2498 2779

about to pass by them, [49] but when they saw him walking on the lake, they thought he was a
ἤθελεν → παρελθεῖν ← αὐτούς δὲ → ἰδόντες αὐτὸν περιπατοῦντα ἐπὶ τῆς θαλάσσης οἱ ἔδοξαν ὅτι → ἐστιν
v.iai.3s f.aa r.apm.3 cj pt.aa.npm r.asm.3 pt.pa.asm p.g d.gsf n.gsf d.npm v.aai.3p cj v.pai.3s
2527 4216 899 1254 1625 899 4344 2093 3836 2498 3836 1506 4022 1639

ghost. They cried out, [50] because they all saw him and were terrified. ¶ Immediately he
φάντασμα καὶ ἀνέκραξαν ← γὰρ ↱ πάντες εἶδον αὐτὸν καὶ → ἐταράχθησαν δὲ εὐθὺς ὁ
n.nsn cj v.aai.3p cj a.npm v.aai.3p r.asm.3 cj v.api.3p cj adv d.nsm
5753 2779 371 1142 1625 4246 1625 899 2779 5429 1254 2318 3836

spoke to them and said, "Take courage! It is I. Don't be afraid." [51] Then he climbed into the boat with
ἐλάλησεν μετ' αὐτῶν καὶ λέγει αὐτοῖς → θαρσεῖτε → εἰμι ἐγὼ μὴ → φοβεῖσθε καὶ → ἀνέβη εἰς τὸ πλοῖον πρὸς
v.aai.3s p.g r.gpm.3 cj v.pai.3s r.dpm.3 v.pam.2p v.pai.1s r.ns.1 pl v.ppm.2p cj v.aai.3s p.a d.asn n.asn p.a
3281 3552 899 2779 3306 899 2510 1639 1609 3590 5828 2779 326 1650 3836 4450 4639

them, and the wind died down. They were completely amazed, [52] for they had not
αὐτοὺς καὶ ὁ ἄνεμος ἐκόπασεν καὶ → λίαν ἐκ περισσοῦ ἐν ἑαυτοῖς ἐξίσταντο γὰρ ↱ ↱ οὐ
r.apm.3 cj d.nsm n.nsm v.aai.3s cj adv p.g a.gsn p.d r.dpm.3 v.imi.3p cj pl
899 2779 3836 449 3156 2779 2014 2014 3336 1666 4356 1877 1571 2014 1142 5317 5317 4024

understood about the loaves; their hearts were hardened. ¶ [53] When they had crossed over,
συνῆκαν ἐπὶ τοῖς ἄρτοις ἀλλ' αὐτῶν ἡ καρδία ἦν πεπωρωμένη Καὶ → → διαπεράσαντες ←
v.aai.3p p.d d.dpm n.dpm cj r.gpm.3 d.nsf n.nsf v.iai.3s pt.rp.nsf cj pt.aa.npm
5317 2093 3836 788 247 899 3836 2840 1639 4800 2779 1385

they landed at Gennesaret and anchored there. [54] As soon as they got out of the boat,
ἐπὶ τὴν γῆν → ἦλθον εἰς Γεννησαρὲτ καὶ προσωρμίσθησαν καὶ εὐθὺς ← ← αὐτῶν ἐξελθόντων ἐκ → τοῦ πλοίου
p.a d.asf n.asf v.aai.3p p.a n.asf cj v.api.3p cj adv r.gpm.3 pt.aa.gpm p.g d.gsn n.gsn
2093 3836 1178 2262 1650 1166 2779 4694 2779 2318 899 2002 1666 3836 4450

people recognized Jesus. [55] They ran throughout that whole region and carried the sick
→ ἐπιγνόντες αὐτὸν → περιέδραμον ἐκείνην ὅλην τὴν χώραν καὶ ἤρξαντο περιφέρειν τοὺς κακῶς ἔχοντας
pt.aa.npm r.asm.3 v.aai.3p r.asf a.asf d.asf n.asf cj v.ami.3p f.pa d.apm adv pt.pa.apm
2105 899 4366 1697 3910 3836 6001 2779 806 4367 3836 2809 2400

on mats to wherever they heard he was. [56] And wherever he went – into villages, towns or
ἐπὶ τοῖς κραβάττοις ὅπου → ἤκουον ὅτι ἐστίν καὶ ὅπου ἂν → εἰσεπορεύετο εἰς κώμας ἢ εἰς πόλεις ἢ
p.d d.dpm n.dpm cj v.iai.3p cj v.pai.3s cj cj pl v.imi.3s p.a n.apf cj p.a n.apf cj
2093 3836 3187 3963 201 4022 1639 2779 3963 323 1660 1650 3267 2445 1650 4484 2445

countryside – they placed the sick in the marketplaces. They begged him to let them touch
εἰς ἀγρούς → ἐτίθεσαν τοὺς ἀσθενοῦντας ἐν ταῖς ἀγοραῖς καὶ → παρεκάλουν αὐτὸν ἵνα → ἅψωνται
p.a n.apm v.iai.3p d.apm pt.pa.apm p.d d.dpf n.dpf cj v.iai.3p r.asm.3 cj v.ams.3p
1650 69 5502 3836 820 1877 3836 59 2779 4151 899 2671 721

even the edge of his cloak, and all who touched him were healed.
κἂν τοῦ κρασπέδου αὐτοῦ τοῦ ἱματίου καὶ ὅσοι ἂν ← ἥψαντο αὐτοῦ → ἐσῴζοντο
crasis d.gsn n.gsn r.gsm.3 d.gsn n.gsn cj r.npm pl v.ami.3p r.gsm.3 v.ipi.3p
2829 3836 3192 2668 899 3836 2668 2779 4012 323 4012 721 899 5392

Clean and Unclean

[7:1] The Pharisees and some of the teachers of the law who had come from Jerusalem gathered around
Καὶ οἱ Φαρισαῖοι καὶ τινες → τῶν γραμματέων ← ← → ← ἐλθόντες ἀπὸ Ἱεροσολύμων συνάγονται πρὸς
cj d.npm n.npm cj r.npm d.gpm n.gpm pt.aa.npm p.g n.gpn v.ppi.3p p.a
2779 3836 5757 2779 5516 3836 1208 2262 608 2642 5251 4639

Jesus [2] and saw some of his disciples eating food with hands that were "unclean," that is,
αὐτὸν καὶ ἰδόντες τινὰς → αὐτοῦ τῶν μαθητῶν ἐσθίουσιν τοὺς ἄρτους ὅτι → χερσίν κοιναῖς τοῦτ' ἐστιν
r.asm.3 cj pt.aa.npm r.apm r.gsm.3 d.gpm n.gpm v.pai.3p d.apm n.apm cj n.dpf a.dpf r.nsn v.pai.3s
899 2779 1625 5516 3412 899 3836 3412 2266 3836 788 4022 5931 3123 4047 1639

unwashed. [3] (The Pharisees and all the Jews do not eat unless they give their hands a ceremonial
ἀνίπτοις γὰρ οἱ Φαρισαῖοι καὶ πάντες οἱ Ἰουδαῖοι → οὐκ ἐσθίουσιν ἐὰν μὴ → τὰς χεῖρας πυγμῇ
a.dpf cj d.npm n.npm cj a.npm d.npm a.npm pl v.pai.3p pl v.pai.3s d.apf n.apf n.dsf
481 1142 3836 5757 2779 4246 3836 2681 2266 4024 2266 1569 3590 3782 3782 3836 5931 4778

αὐτοῖς, περὶ τετάρτην φυλακὴν τῆς νυκτὸς ἔρχεται πρὸς αὐτοὺς περιπατῶν ἐπὶ τῆς θαλάσσης καὶ ἤθελεν παρελθεῖν αὐτούς. [49] οἱ δὲ ἰδόντες αὐτὸν ἐπὶ τῆς θαλάσσης περιπατοῦντα ἔδοξαν ὅτι φάντασμά ἐστιν, καὶ ἀνέκραξαν· [50] πάντες γὰρ αὐτὸν εἶδον καὶ ἐταράχθησαν. ¶ ὁ δὲ εὐθὺς ἐλάλησεν μετ' αὐτῶν, καὶ λέγει αὐτοῖς, Θαρσεῖτε, ἐγώ εἰμι· μὴ φοβεῖσθε. [51] καὶ ἀνέβη πρὸς αὐτοὺς εἰς τὸ πλοῖον καὶ ἐκόπασεν ὁ ἄνεμος, καὶ λίαν [ἐκ περισσοῦ] ἐν ἑαυτοῖς ἐξίσταντο· [52] οὐ γὰρ συνῆκαν ἐπὶ τοῖς ἄρτοις, ἀλλ' ἦν αὐτῶν ἡ καρδία πεπωρωμένη. ¶ [53] Καὶ διαπεράσαντες ἐπὶ τὴν γῆν ἦλθον εἰς Γεννησαρὲτ καὶ προσωρμίσθησαν. [54] καὶ ἐξελθόντων αὐτῶν ἐκ τοῦ πλοίου εὐθὺς ἐπιγνόντες αὐτὸν [55] περιέδραμον ὅλην τὴν χώραν ἐκείνην καὶ ἤρξαντο ἐπὶ τοῖς κραβάττοις τοὺς κακῶς ἔχοντας περιφέρειν ὅπου ἤκουον ὅτι ἐστίν. [56] καὶ ὅπου ἂν εἰσεπορεύετο εἰς κώμας ἢ εἰς πόλεις ἢ εἰς ἀγρούς, ἐν ταῖς ἀγοραῖς ἐτίθεσαν τοὺς ἀσθενοῦντας καὶ παρεκάλουν αὐτὸν ἵνα κἂν τοῦ κρασπέδου τοῦ ἱματίου αὐτοῦ ἅψωνται· καὶ ὅσοι ἂν ἥψαντο αὐτοῦ ἐσῴζοντο.

[7:1] Καὶ συνάγονται πρὸς αὐτὸν οἱ Φαρισαῖοι καί τινες τῶν γραμματέων ἐλθόντες ἀπὸ Ἱεροσολύμων. [2] καὶ ἰδόντες τινὰς τῶν μαθητῶν αὐτοῦ ὅτι κοιναῖς χερσίν, τοῦτ' ἔστιν ἀνίπτοις, ἐσθίουσιν τοὺς ἄρτους [3] —οἱ γὰρ Φαρισαῖοι καὶ πάντες οἱ

washing, holding   to the tradition of the elders.   **4** When they come from the marketplace they do not eat
νίψωνται κρατοῦντες ← τὴν παράδοσιν → τῶν πρεσβυτέρων καὶ   ἀπ'   ἀγορᾶς   →   → οὐκ ἐσθίουσιν
v.ams.3p pt.pa.npm   d.asf n.asf   d.gpm a.gpm   cj   p.g   n.gsf   pl v.pai.3p
3782   3195   3836 4142   3836 4565   2779   608   59   2266 2266 4024 2266

unless   they wash.   And they observe   many other traditions,   such as the washing   of cups,
ἐὰν μὴ → βαπτίσωνται καὶ → ἐστιν κρατεῖν πολλὰ ἄλλα ἃ παρέλαβον   βαπτισμοὺς → ποτηρίων καὶ
cj pl   v.ams.3p   cj   v.pai.3s f.pa a.npn a.npn r.apn v.aai.3p   n.apm   n.gpn   cj
1569 3590 966   2779   1639 3195 4498 257 4005 4161   968   4539   2779

pitchers and kettles.)   ¶   **5** So the Pharisees and teachers   of the law asked   Jesus, "Why
ξεστῶν καὶ χαλκίων [καὶ κλινῶν]   καὶ οἱ Φαρισαῖοι καὶ οἱ γραμματεῖς ←   ἐπερωτῶσιν αὐτὸν διὰ τί
n.gpm   cj n.gpn   cj n.gpf   cj d.npm n.npm   cj d.npm n.npm   v.pai.3p   r.asm.3 p.a r.asn
3829   2779 5908   2779 3109   2779 3836 5757   2779 3836 1208   2089   899   1328 5515

don't your disciples   live   according to the tradition of the elders   instead of eating   their food with
οὐ   σου οἱ μαθηταὶ περιπατοῦσιν κατὰ   ← τὴν παράδοσιν → τῶν πρεσβυτέρων ἀλλὰ ← ἐσθίουσιν τὸν ἄρτον →
pl   r.gs.2 d.npm n.npm v.pai.3p p.a   d.asf n.asf   d.gpm a.gpm   cj   v.pai.3p   d.asm n.asm
4024 5148 3836 3412 4344   2848   3836 4142   3836 4565   247   2266   3836 788

'unclean' hands?"   ¶   **6** He replied,   "Isaiah was right when he prophesied about you hypocrites;   as
κοιναῖς χερσὶν   δὲ Ὁ εἶπεν   αὐτοῖς Ἡσαΐας καλῶς   → ἐπροφήτευσεν περὶ ὑμῶν τῶν ὑποκριτῶν ὡς
a.dpf   n.dpf   cj d.nsm v.aai.3s r.dpm.3 n.nsm adv   v.aai.3s   p.g r.gp.2 d.gpm n.gpm adv
3123   5931   1254 3836 3306 899   2480   2822   4736   4309 7007 3836 5695   6055

it is written: "'These people   honor me with their lips,   but their hearts   are far   from me.   **7**
→ → γέγραπται [ὅτι] οὗτος ὁ λαὸς τιμᾷ με → τοῖς χείλεσιν δὲ αὐτῶν ἡ καρδία ἀπέχει πόρρω ἀπ' ἐμοῦ δὲ
v.rpi.3s   r.nsm d.nsm n.nsm v.pai.3s r.as.1   d.dpn n.dpn cj r.gpm.3 d.nsf n.nsf v.pai.3s adv p.g r.gs.1 cj
1211   4022   4047   3836 3295 5506 1609   3836 5927   1254 899   3836 2840 600   4522 608 1609 1254

They worship me in vain; their teachings   are but rules   taught   by men.'   ¶ **8** You have let   go of
→ σέβονται με μάτην διδασκαλίας   ἐντάλματα διδάσκοντες ἀνθρώπων   → ἀφέντες ← ←
v.pmi.3p r.as.1 adv n.apf   n.apn   pt.pa.npm   n.gpm   pt.aa.npm
4936   1609   3472 1436   1945   1438   476   918

the commands of God   and are holding on to the traditions of men."   ¶   **9** And he said   to them:
τὴν ἐντολὴν → τοῦ θεοῦ → κρατεῖτε ← τὴν παράδοσιν → τῶν ἀνθρώπων   καὶ → ἔλεγεν → αὐτοῖς
d.asf n.asf   d.gsm n.gsm   v.pai.2p   d.asf n.asf   d.gpm n.gpm   cj   v.iai.3s   r.dpm.3
3836 1953   3836 2536   3195   3836 4142   3836 476   2779   3306   899

"You have a fine way of setting aside the commands of God in order to observe your own traditions! **10** For
→ → καλῶς   ἀθετεῖτε → τὴν ἐντολὴν → τοῦ θεοῦ ἵνα   ← στήσητε ὑμῶν τὴν παράδοσιν   γὰρ
adv   v.pai.2p   d.asf n.asf   d.gsm n.gsm cj   v.aas.2p r.gp.2 d.asf n.asf   cj
119 119 2822   3455   3836 1953   3836 2536 2671   4123   7007 3836 4142   1142

Moses said, 'Honor your father   and your mother,' and, 'Anyone who curses   his father or mother must be
Μωϋσῆς εἶπεν τίμα σου τὸν πατέρα καὶ σου τὴν μητέρα καὶ ὁ   κακολογῶν πατέρα ἢ μητέρα →
n.nsm v.aai.3s v.pam.2s r.gs.2 d.asm n.asm cj r.gs.2 d.asf n.asf cj d.nsm   pt.pa.nsm n.asm cj n.asf
3707   3306   5506 5148 3836 4252   2779 5148 3836 3613 2779 3836   2800   4252 2445 3613

put   to death.' **11** But you say   that if a man   says to his father or mother: 'Whatever help   you might
τελευτάτω → θανάτῳ δὲ ὑμεῖς λέγετε   ἐὰν ἄνθρωπος εἴπῃ → τῷ πατρὶ ἢ τῇ μητρί, ὃ ἐὰν   ὠφεληθῇς ←
v.pam.3s   n.dsm   cj r.np.2 v.pai.2p cj   n.nsm   v.aas.3s d.dsm n.dsm cj d.dsf n.dsf r.asn pl v.aps.2s
5462   2505   1254 7007 3306   1569 476   3306   3836 4252 2445 3836 3613 4005 1569 6067

otherwise have received from me is Corban' (that is, a gift devoted to God), **12** then you no longer let   him
←   ← ἐξ ἐμοῦ κορβᾶν ὃ ἐστιν δῶρον   →   οὐκέτι ←   ἀφίετε αὐτὸν
         p.g r.gs.1 n.nsn r.nsn v.pai.3s n.nsn   adv   v.pai.2p r.asm.3
         1666 1609 3167   4005 1639 1565   4033   918   899

do   anything for his father or mother. **13** Thus you nullify   the word of God   by your tradition that you
ποιῆσαι οὐδὲν → τῷ πατρὶ ἢ τῇ μητρί.   ἀκυροῦντες τὸν λόγον → τοῦ θεοῦ → ὑμῶν τῇ παραδόσει ᾗ →
f.aa   a.asn   d.dsm n.dsm cj d.dsf n.dsf   pt.pa.npm d.asm n.asm d.gsm n.gsm r.gp.2 d.dsf n.dsf r.dsf
4472   4029   3836 4252 2445 3836 3613   218   3836 3364   3836 2536 7007 3836 4142   4005

have handed   down. And you do   many things like   that."   ¶   **14** Again Jesus called   the crowd
→ παρεδώκατε ←   καὶ → ποιεῖτε πολλὰ τοιαῦτα παρόμοια ←   Καὶ πάλιν προσκαλεσάμενος τὸν ὄχλον
v.aai.2p   cj   v.pai.2p a.apn r.apn a.apn   cj adv   pt.am.nsm   d.asm n.asm
4140   2779   4472   4498 5525   4235   2779 4099   4673   3836 4063

Ἰουδαῖοι ἐὰν μὴ πυγμῇ νίψωνται τὰς χεῖρας οὐκ ἐσθίουσιν, κρατοῦντες τὴν παράδοσιν τῶν πρεσβυτέρων, **4** καὶ ἀπ' ἀγορᾶς ὅταν ἔλθωσιν ἐὰν μὴ βαπτίσωνται οὐκ ἐσθίουσιν, καὶ ἄλλα πολλά ἐστιν ἃ παρέλαβον κρατεῖν, βαπτισμοὺς ποτηρίων καὶ ξεστῶν καὶ χαλκίων— «χαλκίων» [καὶ κλινῶν] ¶ **5** καὶ ἐπερωτῶσιν αὐτὸν οἱ Φαρισαῖοι καὶ οἱ γραμματεῖς, Διὰ τί οὐ περιπατοῦσιν οἱ μαθηταί σου κατὰ τὴν παράδοσιν τῶν πρεσβυτέρων, ἀλλὰ κοιναῖς χερσὶν ἐσθίουσιν τὸν ἄρτον; ¶ **6** ὁ δὲ εἶπεν αὐτοῖς, Καλῶς ἐπροφήτευσεν Ἡσαΐας περὶ ὑμῶν τῶν ὑποκριτῶν, ὡς γέγραπται [ὅτι] Οὗτος ὁ λαὸς τοῖς χείλεσίν με τιμᾷ, ἡ δὲ καρδία αὐτῶν πόρρω ἀπέχει ἀπ' ἐμοῦ· **7** μάτην δὲ σέβονταί με διδάσκοντες διδασκαλίας ἐντάλματα ἀνθρώπων. ¶ **8** ἀφέντες τὴν ἐντολὴν τοῦ θεοῦ κρατεῖτε τὴν παράδοσιν τῶν ἀνθρώπων. ¶ **9** Καὶ ἔλεγεν αὐτοῖς, Καλῶς ἀθετεῖτε τὴν ἐντολὴν τοῦ θεοῦ, ἵνα τὴν παράδοσιν ὑμῶν τηρήσητε. «στήσητε.» **10** Μωϋσῆς γὰρ εἶπεν, Τίμα τὸν πατέρα σου καὶ τὴν μητέρα σου, καί, Ὁ κακολογῶν πατέρα ἢ μητέρα θανάτῳ τελευτάτω. **11** ὑμεῖς δὲ λέγετε, Ἐὰν εἴπῃ ἄνθρωπος τῷ πατρὶ ἢ τῇ μητρί, Κορβᾶν, ὅ ἐστιν, Δῶρον, ὃ ἐὰν ἐξ ἐμοῦ ὠφεληθῇς, **12** οὐκέτι ἀφίετε αὐτὸν οὐδὲν ποιῆσαι τῷ πατρὶ ἢ τῇ μητρί, **13** ἀκυροῦντες τὸν λόγον τοῦ θεοῦ τῇ παραδόσει ὑμῶν ᾗ παρεδώκατε· καὶ παρόμοια τοιαῦτα πολλὰ ποιεῖτε. ¶ **14** Καὶ προσκαλεσάμενος πάλιν τὸν ὄχλον ἔλεγεν αὐτοῖς, Ἀκούσατέ μου

to him and said, "Listen to me, everyone, and understand this. **15** Nothing outside a man
ἔλεγεν αὐτοῖς ἀκούσατε ← μου πάντες καὶ σύνετε οὐδέν ἐστιν ἔξωθεν ⌐τοῦ ἀνθρώπου⌐ ὃ
v.iai.3s r.dpm.3 v.aam.2p r.gs.1 a.npm cj v.aam.2p a.nsn v.pai.3s p.g d.gsm n.gsm r.nsn
4673 4673 3306 899 201 1609 4246 2779 5317 4029 1639 2033 3836 476 4005

can make him 'unclean' by going into him. Rather, it is what comes out of a man that
δύναται ↱ αὐτὸν κοινῶσαι → εἰσπορευόμενον εἰς αὐτὸν ἀλλὰ → ἐστιν τὰ ἐκπορευόμενα ἐκ ← ⌐τοῦ ἀνθρώπου⌐
v.ppi.3s r.asm.3 f.aa pt.pm.nsn p.a r.asm.3 cj v.pai.3s d.npn pt.pm.npn p.g d.gsm n.gsm
1538 3124 899 3124 1660 1650 899 247 1639 3836 1744 1666 3836 476

makes him 'unclean.'" ¶ **17** After he had left the crowd and entered the house, his
⌐τὸν ἄνθρωπον⌐ ⌐τὰ κοινοῦντα⌐ Καὶ ὅτε ↱ ἀπὸ τοῦ ὄχλου εἰσῆλθεν εἰς οἶκον αὐτοῦ
d.asm n.asm d.npn pt.pa.npn cj cj p.g d.gsm n.gsm v.aai.3s p.a n.asm r.gsm.3
3124 3836 476 3836 3124 2779 4021 1656 1656 608 3836 4063 1656 1650 3875 899

disciples asked him about this parable. **18** "Are you so dull?" he asked. "Don't you see
⌐οἱ μαθηταὶ⌐ ἐπηρώτων αὐτὸν τὴν παραβολήν καὶ ἐστε ὑμεῖς ⌐οὕτως καὶ⌐ ἀσύνετοι → λέγει αὐτοῖς οὐ → νοεῖτε
d.npm n.npm v.iai.3p r.asm.3 d.asf n.asf cj v.pai.2p r.np.2 adv cj a.npm v.pai.3s r.dpm.3 pl v.pai.2p
3836 3412 2089 899 3836 4130 2779 1639 7007 4048 2779 852 3306 899 4024 3783

that nothing that enters a man from the outside can make him 'unclean'? **19** For it doesn't
ὅτι πᾶν → εἰσπορευόμενον εἰς ⌐τὸν ἄνθρωπον⌐ → τὸ ἔξωθεν οὐ δύναται ↱ αὐτὸν κοινῶσαι ὅτι ↱ οὐκ
cj a.nsn pt.pm.nsn p.a d.asm n.asm d.nsn adv pl v.ppi.3s r.asm.3 f.aa cj pl
4022 4246 1660 1650 3836 476 3836 2033 4024 1538 3124 899 3124 4022 1660 4024

go into his heart but into his stomach, and then out *of his body.*" (In saying this, Jesus
εἰσπορεύεται εἰς αὐτοῦ ⌐τὴν καρδίαν⌐ ἀλλ' εἰς τὴν κοιλίαν καὶ ἐκπορεύεται εἰς τὸν ἀφεδρῶνα
v.pmi.3s p.a r.gsm.3 d.asf n.asf cj p.a d.asf n.asf cj v.pmi.3s p.a d.asm n.asm
1660 1650 899 3836 2840 247 1650 3836 3120 2779 1744 1650 3836 909

declared all foods "clean.") ¶ **20** He went on: "What comes out of a man is
↱ πάντα ⌐τὰ βρώματα⌐ καθαρίζων δὲ → ἔλεγεν ← ὅτι τὸ ἐκπορευόμενον ἐκ ← ⌐τοῦ ἀνθρώπου⌐ ἐκεῖνο
a.apn d.apn n.apn pt.pa.nsm cj v.iai.3s cj d.nsn pt.pm.nsn p.g d.gsm n.gsm r.nsn
2751 4246 3836 1109 2751 1254 3306 4022 3836 1744 1666 3836 476 1697

what makes him 'unclean.' **21** For from within, out of men's hearts, come evil
↱ ⌐τὸν ἄνθρωπον⌐ κοινοῖ γὰρ → ἔσωθεν ἐκ ← ⌐τῶν ἀνθρώπων⌐ ⌐τῆς καρδίας⌐ ἐκπορεύονται ⌐οἱ κακοὶ⌐
d.asm n.asm v.pai.3s cj adv p.g d.gpm n.gpm d.gsf n.gsf v.pmi.3p d.npm a.npm
3124 3836 476 3124 1142 2277 1666 3836 476 3836 2840 1744 3836 2805

thoughts, sexual immorality, theft, murder, adultery, **22** greed, malice, deceit, lewdness, envy,
⌐οἱ διαλογισμοὶ⌐ πορνεῖαι κλοπαὶ φόνοι μοιχεῖαι πλεονεξίαι πονηρίαι δόλος ἀσέλγεια ⌐ὀφθαλμὸς πονηρός⌐
d.npm n.npm n.npf n.npf n.npm n.npf n.npf n.npf n.nsm n.nsf n.nsm a.nsm
3836 1369 4518 3113 5840 3657 4432 4504 1515 816 4057 4505

slander, arrogance and folly. **23** All these evils come from inside and make a man 'unclean.'"
βλασφημία ὑπερηφανία ἀφροσύνη πάντα ταῦτα ⌐τὰ πονηρὰ⌐ ἐκπορεύεται → ἔσωθεν καὶ ↱ ⌐τὸν ἄνθρωπον⌐ κοινοῖ
n.nsf n.nsf n.nsf n.npn r.apn d.npn a.npn v.pmi.3s adv cj d.asm n.asm v.pai.3s
1060 5661 932 4246 4047 3836 4505 1744 2277 2779 3124 3836 476 3124

The Faith of a Syrophoenician Woman

7:24 Jesus left that place and went to the vicinity of Tyre. He entered a house and did not
δὲ ἀναστὰς Ἐκεῖθεν ← ἀπῆλθεν εἰς τὰ ὅρια → Τύρου Καὶ εἰσελθὼν εἰς οἰκίαν
cj pt.aa.nsm adv v.aai.3s p.a d.apn n.apn n.gsf cj pt.aa.nsm p.a n.asf
1254 482 1696 599 1650 3836 3990 5602 2779 1656 1650 3864 2527 4029

want anyone to know it; yet he could not keep his presence secret. **25** In fact, as soon as she heard about
ἤθελεν οὐδένα → γνῶναι καὶ → ἠδυνήθη οὐκ → → → λαθεῖν ἀλλ' ← εὐθὺς ← ← ἀκούσασα περὶ
v.iai.3s a.asm f.aa cj v.api.3s pl f.aa cj adv pt.aa.nsf p.g
2527 4029 1182 2779 1538 4024 3291 247 2318 201 4309

him, a woman whose little daughter was possessed by an evil spirit came and fell at his
αὐτοῦ γυνὴ ἧς ⌐τὸ θυγάτριον⌐ αὐτῆς εἶχεν ἀκάθαρτον πνεῦμα ἐλθοῦσα προσέπεσεν πρὸς αὐτοῦ
r.gsm.3 n.nsf r.gsf d.nsn n.nsn r.gsf.3 v.iai.3s a.asn n.asn pt.aa.nsf v.aai.3s p.a r.gsm.3
899 1222 4005 3836 2589 899 2400 176 4460 2262 4700 4639 899

feet. **26** The woman was a Greek, born in Syrian Phoenicia. She begged Jesus to drive the
⌐τοὺς πόδας⌐ δὲ ἡ γυνὴ ἦν Ἑλληνίς ⌐τῷ γένει⌐ Συροφοινίκισσα καὶ → ἠρώτα αὐτὸν ἵνα ἐκβάλῃ τὸ
d.apm n.apm cj d.nsf n.nsf v.iai.3s n.nsf d.dsn n.dsn n.nsf cj v.iai.3s r.asm.3 cj v.aas.3s d.asn
3836 4546 1254 3836 1222 1639 1820 3836 1169 5355 2779 2263 899 2671 1675 3836

πάντες καὶ σύνετε. ¹⁵ οὐδέν ἐστιν ἔξωθεν τοῦ ἀνθρώπου εἰσπορευόμενον εἰς αὐτὸν ὃ δύναται κοινῶσαι αὐτόν, ἀλλὰ τὰ ἐκ τοῦ ἀνθρώπου ἐκπορευόμενά ἐστιν τὰ κοινοῦντα τὸν ἄνθρωπον. ¶ ¹⁷ Καὶ ὅτε εἰσῆλθεν εἰς τὸν οἶκον ἀπὸ τοῦ ὄχλου, ἐπηρώτων αὐτὸν οἱ μαθηταὶ αὐτοῦ τὴν παραβολήν. ¹⁸ καὶ λέγει αὐτοῖς, Οὕτως καὶ ὑμεῖς ἀσύνετοί ἐστε; οὐ νοεῖτε ὅτι πᾶν τὸ ἔξωθεν εἰσπορευόμενον εἰς τὸν ἄνθρωπον οὐ δύναται αὐτὸν κοινῶσαι ¹⁹ ὅτι οὐκ εἰσπορεύεται αὐτοῦ εἰς τὴν καρδίαν ἀλλ' εἰς τὴν κοιλίαν, καὶ εἰς τὸν ἀφεδρῶνα ἐκπορεύεται; «ἐκπορεύεται,» καθαρίζων πάντα τὰ βρώματα. «βρώματα;» ¶ ²⁰ ἔλεγεν δὲ ὅτι Τὸ ἐκ τοῦ ἀνθρώπου ἐκπορευόμενον, ἐκεῖνο κοινοῖ τὸν ἄνθρωπον. ²¹ ἔσωθεν γὰρ ἐκ τῆς καρδίας τῶν ἀνθρώπων οἱ διαλογισμοὶ οἱ κακοὶ ἐκπορεύονται, πορνεῖαι, κλοπαί, φόνοι, ²² μοιχεῖαι, πλεονεξίαι, πονηρίαι, δόλος, ἀσέλγεια, ὀφθαλμὸς πονηρός, βλασφημία, ὑπερηφανία, ἀφροσύνη· ²³ πάντα ταῦτα τὰ πονηρὰ ἔσωθεν ἐκπορεύεται καὶ κοινοῖ τὸν ἄνθρωπον.

⁷·²⁴ Ἐκεῖθεν δὲ ἀναστὰς ἀπῆλθεν εἰς τὰ ὅρια Τύρου. καὶ εἰσελθὼν εἰς οἰκίαν οὐδένα ἤθελεν γνῶναι, καὶ οὐκ ἠδυνήθη λαθεῖν· ²⁵ ἀλλ' εὐθὺς ἀκούσασα γυνὴ περὶ αὐτοῦ, ἧς εἶχεν τὸ θυγάτριον αὐτῆς πνεῦμα ἀκάθαρτον, ἐλθοῦσα προσέπεσεν πρὸς τοὺς πόδας αὐτοῦ· ²⁶ ἡ δὲ γυνὴ ἦν Ἑλληνίς, Συροφοινίκισσα τῷ γένει· καὶ ἠρώτα αὐτὸν ἵνα τὸ δαιμόνιον ἐκβάλῃ ἐκ τῆς

demon out of her daughter. ¶ **27** "First let the children eat all they want," he told her, "for
δαιμόνιον ἐκ ← αὐτῆς ⌞τῆς θυγατρὸς⌟ καὶ πρῶτον ἄφες τὰ τέκνα χορτασθῆναι ← ← ← ἔλεγεν αὐτῇ γάρ
n.asn p.g r.gsf.3 d.gsf n.gsf cj a.asn v.aam.2s d.apn n.apn f.ap v.iai.3s r.dsf.3 cj
1228 1666 899 899 2588 2779 4754 918 3836 5451 5963 3306 899 1142

it is not right to take the children's bread and toss it to their dogs." ¶ **28** "Yes, Lord," she replied,
→ ἐστιν οὐ καλὸν → λαβεῖν τὸν ⌞τῶν τέκνων⌟ ἄρτον καὶ βαλεῖν → τοῖς κυναρίοις δὲ κύριε ἡ ἀπεκρίθη
v.pai.3s ou a.nsn f.aa d.asm d.gpn n.asm cj f.aa d.dpn n.dpn cj n.vsm d.nsf v.api.3s
1639 4024 2819 3284 3836 3836 3836 788 2779 965 3836 3249 1254 3261 3836 646

"but even the dogs under the table eat the children's crumbs." ¶ **29** Then he told
καὶ λέγει αὐτῷ καὶ ← τὰ κυνάρια ὑποκάτω τῆς τραπέζης ἐσθίουσιν ἀπὸ τῶν ⌞τῶν παιδίων⌟ ψιχίων καὶ → εἶπεν
cj v.pai.3s r.dsm.3 adv d.npn n.npn p.g d.gsf n.gsf v.pai.3p p.g d.gpn d.gpn n.gpn n.gpn cj v.aai.3s
2779 3306 899 2779 3836 3249 5691 3836 5544 2266 608 3836 3836 4086 6033 2779 3306

her, "For such a reply, you may go; the demon has left your daughter." ¶ **30** She went
αὐτῇ διὰ τοῦτον ⌞τὸν λόγον⌟ → → ὕπαγε τὸ δαιμόνιον → ἐξελήλυθεν ἐκ σου ⌞τῆς θυγατρὸς⌟ καὶ → ἀπελθοῦσα
r.dsf.3 p.a r.asm d.asm n.asm v.pam.2s d.nsn n.nsn v.rai.3s p.g r.gs.2 d.gsf n.gsf cj pt.aa.nsf
899 1328 4047 3836 3364 5632 3836 1228 2002 1666 5148 3836 2588 2779 599

home and found her child lying on the bed, and the demon gone.
εἰς ⌞τὸν οἶκον αὐτῆς⌟ εὗρεν τὸ παιδίον βεβλημένον ἐπὶ τὴν κλίνην καὶ τὸ δαιμόνιον ἐξεληλυθός
p.a d.asm n.asm r.gsf.3 v.aai.3s d.asn n.asn pt.rp.asn p.a d.asf n.asf cj d.asn n.asn pt.ra.asn
1650 3836 3875 899 2351 3836 4086 965 2093 3836 3109 2779 3836 1228 2002

The Healing of a Deaf and Mute Man

7:31 Then Jesus left the vicinity of Tyre and went through Sidon, down to the Sea of
⌞Καὶ πάλιν⌟ ἐξελθὼν ἐκ τῶν ὁρίων → Τύρου ἦλθεν διὰ Σιδῶνος εἰς τὴν θάλασσαν τῆς
cj adv pt.aa.nsm p.g d.gpn n.gpn n.gsf v.aai.3s p.g n.gsf p.a d.asf n.asf d.gsf
2779 4099 2002 1666 3836 3990 5602 2262 1328 4972 1650 3836 2498 3836

Galilee and into the region of the Decapolis. **32** There some people brought to him a man who was deaf
Γαλιλαίας ⌞ἀνὰ μέσον⌟ τῶν ὁρίων → Δεκαπόλεως Καὶ → φέρουσιν → αὐτῷ → → → κωφὸν
n.gsf p.a n.asn d.gpn n.gpn n.gsf cj v.pai.3p r.dsm.3 a.asm
1133 324 3545 3836 3990 1279 2779 5770 899 3273

and could hardly talk, and they begged him to place his hand on the man. ¶ **33** After he
καὶ → μογιλάλον καὶ → παρακαλοῦσιν αὐτὸν ἵνα ἐπιθῇ τὴν χεῖρα → αὐτῷ καὶ →
cj a.asm cj v.pai.3p r.asm.3 cj v.aas.3s d.asf n.asf r.dsm.3 cj
2779 3652 2779 4151 899 2671 2202 3836 5931 899 2779

took him aside, away from the crowd, Jesus put his fingers into the man's ears. Then he
ἀπολαβόμενος αὐτὸν ← ⌞κατ᾽ ἰδίαν⌟ ἀπὸ τοῦ ὄχλου ἔβαλεν αὐτοῦ ⌞τοὺς δακτύλους⌟ εἰς τὰ αὐτοῦ ὦτα καὶ →
pt.am.nsm r.asm.3 p.g a.asf p.g d.gsm n.gsm v.aai.3s r.gsm.3 d.apm n.apm p.a d.apn r.gsm.3 n.apn cj
655 899 655 2848 2625 608 3836 4063 965 899 3836 1235 1650 3836 899 4044 2779

spit and touched the man's tongue. **34** He looked up to heaven and with a deep sigh said to
πτύσας ἥψατο τῆς αὐτοῦ γλώσσης καὶ → ἀναβλέψας ← εἰς ⌞τὸν οὐρανὸν⌟ → ἐστέναξεν καὶ λέγει
pt.aa.nsm v.ami.3s d.gsf r.gsm.3 n.gsf cj pt.aa.nsm p.a d.asm n.asm v.aai.3s cj v.pai.3s
4772 721 3836 899 1185 2779 329 1650 3836 4041 5100 2779 3306

him, "Ephphatha!" (which means, "Be opened!"). **35** At this, the man's ears were opened, his
αὐτῷ Ἐφφαθα ὅ ἐστιν → διανοίχθητι καὶ εὐθέως αἱ αὐτοῦ ἀκοαί → ἠνοίγησαν καὶ ὁ δεσμὸς αὐτοῦ
r.dsm.3 j r.nsn v.pai.3s v.apm.2s cj adv d.npf r.gsm.3 n.npf v.api.3p cj d.nsm n.nsm r.gsm.3
899 2395 4005 1639 1380 2779 2311 3836 899 198 487 2779 3836 1301 899

tongue was loosened and he began to speak plainly. ¶ **36** Jesus commanded them not to tell
⌞τῆς γλώσσης⌟ ἐλύθη καὶ → → ἐλάλει ὀρθῶς καὶ διεστείλατο αὐτοῖς → ἵνα λέγωσιν
d.gsf n.gsf v.api.3s cj v.iai.3s adv cj v.ami.3s r.dpm.3 cj v.pas.3p
3836 1185 3395 2779 3281 3987 2779 1403 899 3594 2671 3306

anyone. But the more he did so, the more they kept talking about it. **37** People were
μηδενὶ δὲ ὅσον διεστέλλετο ← αὐτοῖς ⌞μᾶλλον περισσότερον⌟ αὐτοὶ → ἐκήρυσσον καὶ
a.dsm cj r.asn v.imi.3s r.dpm.3 adv.c adv.c r.npm v.iai.3p cj
3594 1254 4012 1403 899 3437 4358 899 3062 2779

overwhelmed with amazement. "He has done everything well," they said. "He even makes the deaf hear
ἐξεπλήσσοντο → ὑπερπερισσῶς → → πεποίηκεν πάντα καλῶς → λέγοντες ⌞ καὶ ποιεῖ τοὺς κωφοὺς ἀκούειν
v.ipi.3p adv v.rai.3s a.apn adv pt.pa.npm cj v.pai.3s d.apm a.apm f.pa
1742 5669 4472 4246 2822 3306 2779 4472 3836 3273 201

θυγατρὸς αὐτῆς. ¶ **27** καὶ ἔλεγεν αὐτῇ, Ἄφες πρῶτον χορτασθῆναι τὰ τέκνα, οὐ γάρ ἐστιν καλὸν λαβεῖν τὸν ἄρτον τῶν τέκνων καὶ τοῖς κυναρίοις βαλεῖν. ¶ **28** ἡ δὲ ἀπεκρίθη καὶ λέγει αὐτῷ, ναί, Κύριε· καὶ γὰρ τὰ κυνάρια ὑποκάτω τῆς τραπέζης ἐσθίουσιν ἀπὸ τῶν ψιχίων τῶν παιδίων. ¶ **29** καὶ εἶπεν αὐτῇ, Διὰ τοῦτον τὸν λόγον ὕπαγε, ἐξελήλυθεν ἐκ τῆς θυγατρός σου τὸ δαιμόνιον. ¶ **30** καὶ ἀπελθοῦσα εἰς τὸν οἶκον αὐτῆς εὗρεν τὸ παιδίον βεβλημένον ἐπὶ τὴν κλίνην καὶ τὸ δαιμόνιον ἐξεληλυθός.

7:31 Καὶ πάλιν ἐξελθὼν ἐκ τῶν ὁρίων Τύρου ἦλθεν διὰ Σιδῶνος εἰς τὴν θάλασσαν τῆς Γαλιλαίας ἀνὰ μέσον τῶν ὁρίων Δεκαπόλεως. **32** καὶ φέρουσιν αὐτῷ κωφὸν καὶ μογιλάλον καὶ παρακαλοῦσιν αὐτὸν ἵνα ἐπιθῇ αὐτῷ τὴν χεῖρα. ¶ **33** καὶ ἀπολαβόμενος αὐτὸν ἀπὸ τοῦ ὄχλου κατ᾽ ἰδίαν ἔβαλεν τοὺς δακτύλους αὐτοῦ εἰς τὰ ὦτα αὐτοῦ καὶ πτύσας ἥψατο τῆς γλώσσης αὐτοῦ, **34** καὶ ἀναβλέψας εἰς τὸν οὐρανὸν ἐστέναξεν καὶ λέγει αὐτῷ, Εφφαθα, ὅ ἐστιν, Διανοίχθητι. **35** καὶ [εὐθέως] ἠνοίγησαν αὐτοῦ αἱ ἀκοαί, καὶ ἐλύθη ὁ δεσμὸς τῆς γλώσσης αὐτοῦ καὶ ἐλάλει ὀρθῶς. ¶ **36** καὶ διεστείλατο αὐτοῖς ἵνα μηδενὶ λέγωσιν· ὅσον δὲ αὐτοῖς διεστέλλετο, αὐτοὶ μᾶλλον περισσότερον ἐκήρυσσον. **37** καὶ ὑπερπερισσῶς ἐξεπλήσσοντο λέγοντες, Καλῶς πάντα

and   the   mute   speak.”
καὶ   [τοὺς]   ἀλάλους   λαλεῖν
cj   d.apm   a.apm   f.pa
2779   3836   228   3281

Jesus Feeds the Four Thousand

8:1 During   those   days   another   large   crowd   gathered.   Since they had   nothing to eat,   Jesus
Ἐν   ἐκείναις   ⌞ταῖς ἡμέραις⌟   πάλιν   πολλοῦ   ὄχλου   ὄντος   καὶ →   →   ἐχόντων   μὴ τί   →   φάγωσιν
p.d   r.dpf   d.dpf   n.dpf   adv   a.gsm   n.gsm   pt.pa.gsm   cj   pt.pa.gpm   pl   r.asn   v.aas.3p
1877   1697   3836   2465   4099   4498   4063   1639   2779   2400   3590   5515   2266

called   his   disciples to him and said,   **2** “I have compassion   for these people;   they have already
προσκαλεσάμενος   τοὺς μαθητὰς   ←   ←   λέγει αὐτοῖς   →   →   σπλαγχνίζομαι   ἐπὶ τὸν   ὄχλον   ὅτι →   →   ἤδη
pt.am.nsm   d.apm   n.apm   v.pai.3s   r.dpm.3   v.ppi.1s   p.a   d.asm   n.asm   cj   adv
4673   3836   3412   4673 4673   3306   899   5072   2093 3836   4063   4022 4693   4693   2453

been   with me three days   and have   nothing to eat.   **3**   If I send   them home   hungry, they
προσμένουσιν   ←   μοι τρεῖς   ἡμέραι   καὶ   ἔχουσιν   οὐκ τί   →   φάγωσιν   καὶ ἐὰν   ἀπολύσω αὐτοὺς   εἰς οἶκον αὐτῶν   νήστεις   →
v.pai.3p   r.ds.1   a.npf   n.npf   cj   v.pai.3p   pl   r.asn   v.aas.3p   cj   cj   v.aas.1s   r.apm.3   p.a   n.asm   r.gpm.3   a.apm
4693   1609   5552   2465   2779   2400   4024   5515   2266   2779 1569   668   899   1650 3875   899   3765

will collapse   on the way, because some of them have   come a long distance.”   ¶   **4**   His   disciples
→   ἐκλυθήσονται   ἐν τῇ   ὁδῷ   καὶ   τινες   →   αὐτῶν   →   ἥκασιν   →   ⌞ἀπὸ μακρόθεν⌟   καὶ αὐτοῦ ⌞οἱ μαθηταί⌟
v.fpi.3p   p.d   d.dsf   n.dsf   cj   r.npm   r.gpm.3   v.rai.3p   p.g   adv   cj   r.gsm.3   d.npm n.npm
1725   1877   3836   3847   2779   5516   899   2457   608   3427   2779   899   3836 3412

answered,   “But where in this remote place   can   anyone get enough bread to feed   them?”   ¶
ἀπεκρίθησαν   αὐτῷ ὅτι   “Πόθεν   ἐπ’   ἐρημίας   ←   ὧδε δυνήσεταί τις   ἄρτων   →   χορτάσαι τούτους
v.api.3p   r.dsm.3 cj   cj   p.g   n.gsf   adv   v.fpi.3s   r.nsm   n.gpm   f.aa   r.apm
646   899   4022   4470   2093   2244   6045   1538   5516   788   5963   4047

5   “How many loaves do you have?”   Jesus asked.   “Seven,” they replied.   ¶   **6**   He told   the
καὶ πόσους   ←   ἄρτους   →   →   ἔχετε   ἠρώτα αὐτούς   δὲ ἑπτά   οἱ εἶπαν   καὶ →   παραγγέλλει τῷ
cj   r.apm   n.apm   v.pai.2p   v.iai.3s   r.apm.3   cj   a.apm   d.npm v.aai.3p   cj   v.pai.3s   d.dsm
2779   4531   788   2400   2263   899   1254   2231   3836 3306   2779   4133   3836

crowd to sit   down on the ground.   When he had taken the seven loaves and given thanks,   he broke
ὄχλῳ   →   ἀναπεσεῖν   ἐπὶ τῆς γῆς   καὶ →   →   λαβὼν   τοὺς ἑπτὰ   ἄρτους   →   εὐχαριστήσας   →   ἔκλασεν
n.dsm   f.aa   p.g   d.gsf   n.gsf   cj   pt.aa.nsm   d.apm   a.apm   n.apm   pt.aa.nsm   v.aai.3s
4063   404   2093 3836   1178   2779   3284   3836   2231   788   2373   3089

them and gave   them to his   disciples to set   before the people, and they did   so.   **7** They had a few
καὶ ἐδίδου   τοῖς αὐτοῦ   μαθηταῖς   ἵνα παρατιθῶσιν   ←   τῷ ὄχλῳ   καὶ →   παρέθηκαν   εἶχον ὀλίγα
cj   v.iai.3s   d.dpm r.gsm.3   n.dpm   cj   v.pas.3p   d.dsm n.dsm   cj   v.aai.3p   v.iai.3p   a.apn
2779   1443   3836   899   3412   2671   4192   3836   4063   2779   4192   2400   3900

small fish   as well; he gave thanks   for them also and told the disciples to distribute   them.   **8**   The people
→   ἰχθύδια   καὶ   ←   εὐλογήσας   ←   αὐτὰ   καὶ εἶπεν   →   παρατιθέναι ταῦτα   καὶ   →
n.apn   cj   pt.aa.nsm   r.apn.3   adv   v.aai.3s   f.pa   r.apn   cj
2715   2779   2328   899   2779   3306   4192   4047   2779

ate   and were satisfied.   Afterward the disciples picked up seven basketfuls of broken   pieces that were
ἔφαγον   καὶ →   ἐχορτάσθησαν   καὶ   ἦραν   →   ἑπτὰ   σπυρίδας   →   κλασμάτων   ←
v.aai.3p   cj   v.api.3p   cj   v.aai.3p   a.apf   n.apf   n.gpn
2266   2779   5963   2779   149   2231   5083   3083

left   over.   **9**   About four   thousand men were present. And having sent   them away,   **10**   he
περισσεύματα   ←   δὲ ὡς   τετρακισχίλιοι   ←   ←   ἦσαν   ←   καὶ →   ἀπέλυσεν αὐτούς   Καὶ εὐθὺς   →
n.apn   cj   adv   a.npm   v.iai.3p   cj   v.aai.3s   r.apm.3   cj   adv
4354   1254 6055   5483   1639   2779   668   899   668   2779 2318

got   into the boat   with his   disciples   and went to the region of Dalmanutha.   ¶   **11**   The Pharisees
ἐμβὰς   εἰς   τὸ   πλοῖον   μετὰ αὐτοῦ   ⌞τῶν μαθητῶν⌟   ἦλθεν εἰς τὰ   μέρη   →   Δαλμανουθά   Καὶ οἱ   Φαρισαῖοι
pt.aa.nsm   p.a   d.asn   n.asn   p.g   r.gsm.3   d.gpm n.gpm   v.aai.3s   p.a   d.apn n.apn   n.gsf   cj   d.npm n.npm
1832   1650   3836   4450   3552   899   3836   3412   2262   1650   3836   3538   1236   2779   3836   5757

came   and began to question Jesus. To test   him, they asked   him for a sign   from heaven.   **12**
ἐξῆλθον   καὶ   ἤρξαντο →   συζητεῖν   αὐτῷ   →   πειράζοντες αὐτόν   →   ζητοῦντες παρ’ αὐτοῦ   ↩   σημεῖον ἀπὸ   ⌞τοῦ οὐρανοῦ⌟   καὶ
v.aai.3p   cj   v.ami.3p   f.pa   r.dsm.3   pt.pa.npm   r.asm.3   pt.pa.npm   p.g   r.gsm.3   n.asn   p.g   d.gsm n.gsm   cj
2002   2779   806   5184   899   4279   899   2426   4123   899   2426   4956   608   3836 4041   2779

πεποίηκεν, καὶ τοὺς κωφοὺς ποιεῖ ἀκούειν καὶ [τοὺς] ἀλάλους λαλεῖν.

    8:1 Ἐν ἐκείναις ταῖς ἡμέραις πάλιν πολλοῦ ὄχλου ὄντος καὶ μὴ ἐχόντων τί φάγωσιν, προσκαλεσάμενος τοὺς μαθητὰς λέγει αὐτοῖς, **2** Σπλαγχνίζομαι ἐπὶ τὸν ὄχλον, ὅτι ἤδη ἡμέραι τρεῖς προσμένουσίν μοι καὶ οὐκ ἔχουσιν τί φάγωσιν· **3** καὶ ἐὰν ἀπολύσω αὐτοὺς νήστεις εἰς οἶκον αὐτῶν, ἐκλυθήσονται ἐν τῇ ὁδῷ· καί τινες αὐτῶν ἀπὸ μακρόθεν ἥκασιν. ¶ **4** καὶ ἀπεκρίθησαν αὐτῷ οἱ μαθηταὶ αὐτοῦ ὅτι Πόθεν τούτους δυνήσεταί τις ὧδε χορτάσαι ἄρτων ἐπ’ ἐρημίας; ¶ **5** καὶ ἠρώτα αὐτούς, Πόσους ἔχετε ἄρτους; οἱ δὲ εἶπαν, Ἑπτά. ¶ **6** καὶ παραγγέλλει τῷ ὄχλῳ ἀναπεσεῖν ἐπὶ τῆς γῆς· καὶ λαβὼν τοὺς ἑπτὰ ἄρτους εὐχαριστήσας ἔκλασεν καὶ ἐδίδου τοῖς μαθηταῖς αὐτοῦ ἵνα παρατιθῶσιν, καὶ παρέθηκαν τῷ ὄχλῳ. **7** καὶ εἶχον ἰχθύδια ὀλίγα· καὶ εὐλογήσας αὐτὰ εἶπεν καὶ ταῦτα παρατιθέναι. **8** καὶ ἔφαγον καὶ ἐχορτάσθησαν, καὶ ἦραν περισσεύματα κλασμάτων ἑπτὰ σπυρίδας. **9** ἦσαν δὲ ὡς τετρακισχίλιοι. καὶ ἀπέλυσεν αὐτούς. **10** Καὶ εὐθὺς ἐμβὰς εἰς τὸ πλοῖον μετὰ τῶν μαθητῶν αὐτοῦ ἦλθεν εἰς τὰ μέρη Δαλμανουθά. ¶ **11** Καὶ ἐξῆλθον οἱ Φαρισαῖοι καὶ ἤρξαντο συζητεῖν αὐτῷ, ζητοῦντες παρ’ αὐτοῦ σημεῖον ἀπὸ τοῦ οὐρανοῦ, πειράζοντες αὐτόν. **12** καὶ ἀναστενάξας τῷ πνεύματι αὐτοῦ λέγει, Τί ἡ γενεὰ αὕτη ζητεῖ σημεῖον; ἀμὴν λέγω ὑμῖν, εἰ δοθήσεται

He sighed   deeply   and said, "Why does this generation ask for a miraculous sign? I tell you the
→ ἀναστενάξας ⌐τῷ πνεύματι αὐτοῦ⌐ λέγει τί   αὕτη ἡ γενεᾷ ζητεῖ ←   σημεῖον → λέγω ὑμῖν
pt.aa.nsm   d.dsn n.dsn   r.gsm.3   v.pai.3s r.asn   r.nsf d.nsf n.nsf   v.pai.3s   n.nsn   v.pai.1s r.dp.2
417   3836 4460   899   3306 5515   2426   4047 3836 1155   2426   4956   3306 7007

truth, no sign   will be given   to it."   [13] Then he left   them, got   back into the boat and crossed to
ἀμὴν εἰ σημεῖον →   δοθήσεται → ⌐τῇ γενεᾷ ταύτῃ⌐ καὶ → ἀφεὶς αὐτοὺς ἐμβὰς πάλιν   ἀπῆλθεν εἰς
pl   cj n.nsn   v.fpi.3s   d.dsf n.dsf r.dsf   cj   pt.aa.nsm r.apm.3 pt.aa.nsm adv   v.aai.3s   p.a
297   1623 4956   1443   3836 1155 4047   2779   918   899   1832   4099   599   1650

the other side.
τὸ πέραν ←
d.asn adv
3836 4305

The Yeast of the Pharisees and Herod

8:14   The disciples had forgotten to bring bread,   except for one loaf   they had with them in the
Καὶ   → ἐπελάθοντο → λαβεῖν ἄρτους καὶ ⌐εἰ μὴ⌐   ἕνα ἄρτον οὐκ →   εἶχον μεθ᾽ ἑαυτῶν ἐν τῷ
cj   v.ami.3p   f.aa   n.apm   cj   cj pl   a.asm n.asm pl   v.iai.3p p.g   r.gpm.3 p.d d.dsn
2779   2140   3284   788   2779 1623 3590   1651 788 4024   2400   3552   1571   1877 3836

boat. **15**   "Be careful," Jesus warned   them.   "Watch out for the yeast of the Pharisees and that   of
πλοίῳ καὶ → ὁρᾶτε   διεστέλλετο αὐτοῖς λέγων βλέπετε ← ἀπὸ τῆς ζύμης → τῶν Φαρισαίων καὶ ⌐τῆς ζύμης⌐ →
n.dsn   cj   v.pam.2p   v.imi.3s   r.dpm.3 pt.pa.nsm v.pam.2p   p.g d.gsf n.gsf   d.gsm n.gpm   cj   d.gsf n.gsf
4450   2779   3972   1403   899   3306   1063   608 3836 2434   3836 5757   2779 3836 2434

Herod." ¶   **16**   They discussed this with one   another and said, "It is because we have   no bread." ¶
Ἡρῴδου   καὶ → διελογίζοντο πρὸς ἀλλήλους ←   ὅτι → ἔχουσιν οὐκ ἄρτους
n.gsm   cj   v.imi.3p   p.a r.apm   cj   v.pai.3p pl   n.apm
2476   2779   1368   4639 253   4022   2400   4024 788

17   Aware of their discussion, Jesus asked them: "Why are you talking   about having no bread? Do you still not
καὶ γνοὺς   λέγει αὐτοῖς τί →   διαλογίζεσθε ὅτι   ἔχετε οὐκ ἄρτους ↱   ↱   οὔπω ←
cj pt.aa.nsm   v.pai.3s r.dpm.3 r.asn →   v.pmi.2p   cj   v.pai.2p pl   n.apm   adv
2779 1182   3306   899   5515   1368   4022   2400   4024 788   3783 3783   4037

see   or understand? Are your hearts   hardened?   **18** Do you have   eyes   but fail to see,   and
νοεῖτε οὐδὲ συνίετε   ↱ ὑμῶν ⌐τὴν καρδίαν⌐ ⌐πεπωρωμένην ἔχετε⌐   →   ἔχοντες ὀφθαλμοὺς   οὐ → βλέπετε καὶ ἔχοντες
v.pai.2p cj   v.pai.2p   r.gp.2 d.asf n.asf   pt.rp.asf v.pai.2p   pt.pa.npm n.apm   pl   v.pai.2p cj   pt.pa.npm
3783   4028 5317   2400 7007 3836 2840   4800   2400   2400   4057   4024   1063   2779 2400

ears but fail to hear? And don't you remember? **19** When I broke the five loaves for the five   thousand,
ὦτα   οὐκ   ἀκούετε καὶ οὐ → μνημονεύετε ὅτε → ἔκλασα τοὺς πέντε ἄρτους εἰς τοὺς πεντακισχιλίους ←
n.apn   pl   v.pai.2p cj   pl →   v.pai.2p   cj → v.aai.1s d.apm a.apm n.apm p.a d.apm a.apm
4044   4024   201   2779 4024   3648   4021   3089   3836 4297 788   1650 3836 4295

how many basketfuls   of pieces   did you pick up?" ¶   "Twelve," they replied.   **20** "And when I
πόσους ← ⌐κοφίνους πλήρεις⌐ → κλασμάτων →   ἤρατε ←   δώδεκα   → λέγουσιν αὐτῷ   ὅτε
r.apm   n.apm   a.apm   n.gpn   v.aai.2p   a.apm   v.pai.3p r.dsm.3   cj
4531   3186   4441   3083   149   1557   3306   899   4021

broke the seven loaves for the four   thousand, how many basketfuls   of pieces   did you pick
τοὺς ἑπτὰ   εἰς τοὺς τετρακισχιλίους ←   πόσων ← ⌐σπυρίδων πληρώματα⌐ → κλασμάτων →   → ἤρατε
d.apm a.apm   p.a d.apm a.apm   r.gpf   r.gpf n.apn   n.gpn   v.aai.2p
3836 2231   1650 3836 5483   4531   5083 4445   3083   149

up?" ¶   They answered,   "Seven." ¶   **21** He said   to them, "Do you still not understand?"
←   καὶ → λέγουσιν [αὐτῷ] ἑπτά   καὶ → ἔλεγεν αὐτοῖς ↱   ↱   οὔπω ← συνίετε
     cj → v.pai.3p r.dsm.3   a.gpf   cj   v.iai.3s r.dpm.3   adv   v.pai.2p
     2779   3306   899   2231   2779   3306   899   5317   5317   4037   5317

The Healing of a Blind Man at Bethsaida

8:22   They came   to Bethsaida, and some people brought   a blind man and begged   Jesus to touch
Καὶ → ἔρχονται εἰς Βηθσαϊδάν Καὶ   φέρουσιν αὐτῷ   τυφλὸν ←   καὶ παρακαλοῦσιν αὐτὸν ἵνα ἅψηται
cj → v.pmi.3p   p.a n.asf   cj   v.pai.3p r.dsm.3   a.asm   cj   v.pai.3p   r.asm.3 cj   v.ams.3s
2779   2262   1650 1034   2779   5770   899   5603   2779 4151   899   2671 721

him. **23**   He took   the blind man by the hand and led   him outside the village.   When he had spit
αὐτοῦ καὶ → ἐπιλαβόμενος τοῦ τυφλοῦ ← → τῆς χειρὸς ἐξήνεγκεν αὐτὸν ἔξω   τῆς κώμης καὶ →   → πτύσας
r.gsm.3   cj   pt.am.nsm   d.gsm a.gsm   d.gsf n.gsf   v.aai.3s   r.asm.3 p.g   d.gsf n.gsf   cj   pt.aa.nsm
899   2779   2138   3836 5603   3836 5931   1766   899   2032   3836 3267   2779   4772

τῇ γενεᾷ ταύτῃ σημεῖον. [13] καὶ ἀφεὶς αὐτοὺς ἐμβὰς πάλιν εἰς τὸ πλοῖον ἀπῆλθεν εἰς τὸ πέραν.

    8:14 Καὶ ἐπελάθοντο λαβεῖν ἄρτους καὶ εἰ μὴ ἕνα ἄρτον οὐκ εἶχον μεθ᾽ ἑαυτῶν ἐν τῷ πλοίῳ. [15] καὶ διεστέλλετο αὐτοῖς λέγων, Ὁρᾶτε, βλέπετε ἀπὸ τῆς ζύμης τῶν Φαρισαίων καὶ τῆς ζύμης Ἡρῴδου. ¶ [16] καὶ διελογίζοντο πρὸς ἀλλήλους λέγοντες ὅτι Ἄρτους «ἄρτους» οὐκ ἔχομεν. «ἔχουσιν.» ¶ [17] καὶ γνοὺς ὁ Ἰησοῦς λέγει αὐτοῖς, Τί διαλογίζεσθε ὅτι ἄρτους οὐκ ἔχετε; οὔπω νοεῖτε οὐδὲ συνίετε; πεπωρωμένην ἔχετε τὴν καρδίαν ὑμῶν; [18] ὀφθαλμοὺς ἔχοντες οὐ βλέπετε καὶ ὦτα ἔχοντες οὐκ ἀκούετε; καὶ οὐ μνημονεύετε, [19] ὅτε τοὺς πέντε ἄρτους ἔκλασα εἰς τοὺς πεντακισχιλίους, πόσους κοφίνους κλασμάτων πλήρεις ἤρατε; ¶ λέγουσιν αὐτῷ, Δώδεκα. [20] Ὅτε καὶ τοὺς ἑπτὰ εἰς τοὺς τετρακισχιλίους, πόσων σπυρίδων πληρώματα κλασμάτων ἤρατε; καὶ ¶ λέγουσιν [αὐτῷ], Ἑπτά. ¶ [21] καὶ ἔλεγεν αὐτοῖς, Οὔπω συνίετε;

    8:22 Καὶ ἔρχονται εἰς Βηθσαϊδάν. καὶ φέρουσιν αὐτῷ τυφλὸν καὶ παρακαλοῦσιν αὐτὸν ἵνα αὐτοῦ ἅψηται. [23] καὶ ἐπιλαβόμενος τῆς χειρὸς τοῦ τυφλοῦ ἐξήνεγκεν αὐτὸν ἔξω τῆς κώμης καὶ πτύσας εἰς τὰ ὄμματα αὐτοῦ, ἐπιθεὶς τὰς χεῖρας αὐτῷ

on the man's eyes   and put   his hands on him, Jesus asked,   "Do you see   anything?"   ¶   **24**   He
εἰς τὰ αὐτοῦ ὄμματα   ἐπιθεὶς τὰς χεῖρας → αὐτῷ   ἐπηρώτα αὐτόν εἰ → βλέπεις τι   καὶ →
p.a d.apn n.gsm.3 n.apn   pt.aa.nsm d.apf n.apf   r.dsm.3   v.iai.3s r.asm.3 cj   v.pai.2s r.asn   cj
1650 3836 899 3921   2202 3836 5931   899   2089 899 1623   1063 5516   2779

looked   up and said, "I see   people;   they look like trees   walking   around."   ¶   **25** Once more
ἀναβλέψας ←   ἔλεγεν → βλέπω ⌐τοὺς ἀνθρώπους⌐ ὅτι → ὁρῶ ὡς δένδρα περιπατοῦντας ←   εἶτα πάλιν
pt.aa.nsm   v.pai.3s   v.pai.1s d.apm n.apm   cj   v.pai.1s rc n.apn pt.pa.apm   adv   adv
329   3306   1063 3836 476   4022 3972 6055 1285 4344   1663 4099

Jesus put   his hands on the man's eyes.   Then his eyes were opened,   his sight was restored,   and he
ἐπέθηκεν τὰς χεῖρας ἐπὶ τοὺς αὐτοῦ ὀφθαλμοὺς καὶ →   διέβλεψεν καὶ →   ἀπεκατέστη καὶ
v.aai.3s d.apf n.apf p.a d.apm r.gsm.3 n.apm   cj   v.aai.3s cj   v.aai.3s cj
2202 3836 5931 2093 3836 899   4057   2779   1332 2779   635   2779

saw   everything clearly.   **26**   Jesus sent   him home,   saying, "Don't go   into the village."
ἐνέβλεπεν ἅπαντα τηλαυγῶς   καὶ   ἀπέστειλεν αὐτὸν εἰς οἶκον αὐτοῦ, λέγων   μηδὲ εἰσέλθῃς εἰς τὴν κώμην
v.iai.3s a.apn adv   cj   v.aai.3s r.asm.3 p.a n.asm r.gsm.3 pt.pa.nsm adv v.aas.2s p.a d.asf n.asf
1838 570   5495   2779   690   899 1650 3875 899   3306   3593 1656 1650 3836 3267

Peter's Confession of Christ

8:27 Jesus   and his   disciples   went   on to the villages around Caesarea   Philippi.   On the
καὶ ⌐ὁ Ἰησοῦς⌐ καὶ αὐτοῦ ⌐οἱ μαθηταὶ⌐ ἐξῆλθεν → εἰς τὰς κώμας →   Καισαρείας ⌐τῆς Φιλίππου⌐ καὶ ἐν τῇ
cj   d.nsm n.nsm cj r.gsm.3 d.npm n.npm v.aai.3s p.a d.apf n.apf   n.gsf   d.gsf n.gsm   cj p.d d.dsf
2779 3836 2652 2779 899   3836 3412   2002   1650 3836 3267   2791   3836 5805   2779 1877 3836

way he asked   them, "Who do people   say   I am?"   ¶   **28**   They replied,
ὁδῷ → ἐπηρώτα ⌐τοὺς μαθητὰς⌐ αὐτοῦ λέγων αὐτοῖς τίνα → οἱ ἄνθρωποι λέγουσιν με εἶναι   Καὶ οἱ εἶπαν
n.dsf v.iai.3s d.apm n.apm   r.gsm.3 pt.pa.nsm r.dpm.3 r.asn d.npm n.npm v.pai.3p r.as.1 f.pa   cj d.npm v.aai.3p
3847   2089 3836 3412   899   3306 899   5515 3306 3836 476 3306 1609 1639   2779 3836 3306

         "Some say John   the Baptist;   others say Elijah; and still others,   one of the prophets."
αὐτῷ λέγοντες [ὅτι]   Ἰωάννην τὸν βαπτιστὴν καὶ ἄλλοι Ἠλίαν δὲ ἄλλοι ὅτι εἷς → τῶν προφητῶν
r.dsm.3 pt.pa.npm cj   n.asm d.asm n.asm   cj r.npm n.asm cj r.npm cj a.nsm d.gpm n.gpm
899 3306   4022   2722   3836 969   2779 257   2460   1254 257   4022 1651 3836 4737

¶ **29** "But what about you?" he   asked.   "Who do you say I   am?"   ¶   Peter   answered,
καὶ   ὑμεῖς αὐτὸς ἐπηρώτα αὐτούς δὲ τίνα → λέγετε με εἶναι   ⌐ὁ Πέτρος⌐ ἀποκριθεὶς λέγει
cj   r.np.2 r.nsm v.iai.3s r.apm.3 cj r.asn v.pai.2p r.as.1 f.pa   d.nsm n.nsm pt.ap.nsm v.pai.3s
2779   7007 899   2089 899   1254 5515   3306 1609 1639   3836 4377 646   3306

"You are the Christ."   ¶   **30**   Jesus warned them   not to tell   anyone about him.
αὐτῷ σὺ εἶ ὁ χριστός   καὶ   ἐπετίμησεν αὐτοῖς ἵνα → → λέγωσιν μηδενὶ περὶ αὐτοῦ
r.dsm.3 r.ns.2 v.pai.2s d.nsm n.nsm   cj   v.aai.3s r.dpm.3 cj   v.pas.3p a.dsm p.g r.gsm.3
899 5148 1639 3836 5986   2779   2203 899   2671 3594   3306 3594 4309 899

Jesus Predicts His Death

8:31 He then began to teach   them that the Son of Man   must suffer many things and be
→ Καὶ ἤρξατο → διδάσκειν αὐτοὺς ὅτι τὸν υἱὸν ⌐τοῦ ἀνθρώπου⌐ δεῖ παθεῖν πολλὰ   καὶ
   cj   v.ami.3s   f.pa   r.apm.3 cj r.asm n.asm d.gsm n.gsm   v.pai.3s f.aa a.apn   cj
806 2779 806   1438   899   4022 3836 5676 3836 476   1256 4248 4498   2779

rejected   by the elders,   chief   priests and teachers   of the law, and that he must be
ἀποδοκιμασθῆναι ὑπὸ τῶν πρεσβυτέρων καὶ ⌐τῶν ἀρχιερέων⌐   καὶ ⌐τῶν γραμματέων⌐ ←   καὶ →   →
f.ap   p.g d.gpm a.gpm   cj d.gpm n.gpm   cj d.gpm n.gpm   cj
627   5679 3836 4565   2779 3836 797   2779 3836 1208   2779

killed   and after three days   rise   again.   **32** He spoke plainly   about this,   and Peter
ἀποκτανθῆναι καὶ μετὰ τρεῖς ἡμέρας ἀναστῆναι   καὶ → ἐλάλει παρρησίᾳ ⌐τὸν λόγον⌐ καὶ ⌐ὁ Πέτρος⌐
f.ap   cj p.a a.apf n.apf f.aa   cj   v.iai.3s n.dsf d.asm n.asm cj d.nsm n.nsm
650   2779 3552 5552 2465 482   2779 3281 4244   3836 3364 2779 3836 4377

took   him   aside and began to rebuke him.   ¶   **33** But when Jesus turned   and looked at his
προσλαβόμενος αὐτὸν ←   ἤρξατο → ἐπιτιμᾶν αὐτῷ   δὲ →   ἐπιστραφεὶς καὶ ἰδὼν ← αὐτοῦ
pt.am.nsm r.asm.3   v.ami.3s f.pa r.dsm.3   cj   pt.ap.nsm cj pt.aa.nsm r.gsm.3
4689   899   806   2203 899   1254   2188   2779 1625   899

ἐπηρώτα αὐτόν, Εἴ τι βλέπεις; ¶ 24 καὶ ἀναβλέψας ἔλεγεν, Βλέπω τοὺς ἀνθρώπους ὅτι ὡς δένδρα ὁρῶ περιπατοῦντας. ¶ 25 εἶτα
πάλιν ἐπέθηκεν τὰς χεῖρας ἐπὶ τοὺς ὀφθαλμοὺς αὐτοῦ, καὶ διέβλεψεν καὶ ἀπεκατέστη καὶ ἐνέβλεπεν τηλαυγῶς ἅπαντα. 26 καὶ
ἀπέστειλεν αὐτὸν εἰς οἶκον αὐτοῦ λέγων, Μηδὲ εἰς τὴν κώμην εἰσέλθῃς.

8:27 Καὶ ἐξῆλθεν ὁ Ἰησοῦς καὶ οἱ μαθηταὶ αὐτοῦ εἰς τὰς κώμας Καισαρείας τῆς Φιλίππου· καὶ ἐν τῇ ὁδῷ ἐπηρώτα τοὺς
μαθητὰς αὐτοῦ λέγων αὐτοῖς, Τίνα με λέγουσιν οἱ ἄνθρωποι εἶναι; ¶ 28 οἱ δὲ εἶπαν αὐτῷ λέγοντες [ὅτι] Ἰωάννην τὸν βαπτιστήν,
καὶ ἄλλοι, Ἠλίαν, ἄλλοι δὲ ὅτι εἷς τῶν προφητῶν. ¶ 29 καὶ αὐτὸς ἐπηρώτα αὐτούς, Ὑμεῖς δὲ τίνα με λέγετε εἶναι; ¶ ἀποκριθεὶς
ὁ Πέτρος λέγει αὐτῷ, Σὺ εἶ ὁ Χριστός. ¶ 30 καὶ ἐπετίμησεν αὐτοῖς ἵνα μηδενὶ λέγωσιν περὶ αὐτοῦ.

8:31 Καὶ ἤρξατο διδάσκειν αὐτοὺς ὅτι δεῖ τὸν υἱὸν τοῦ ἀνθρώπου πολλὰ παθεῖν καὶ ἀποδοκιμασθῆναι ὑπὸ τῶν πρεσβυτέρων
καὶ τῶν ἀρχιερέων καὶ τῶν γραμματέων καὶ ἀποκτανθῆναι καὶ μετὰ τρεῖς ἡμέρας ἀναστῆναι· 32 καὶ παρρησίᾳ τὸν λόγον
ἐλάλει. καὶ προσλαβόμενος ὁ Πέτρος αὐτὸν ἤρξατο ἐπιτιμᾶν αὐτῷ. ¶ 33 ὁ δὲ ἐπιστραφεὶς καὶ ἰδὼν τοὺς μαθητὰς αὐτοῦ

disciples,   he rebuked Peter.   "Get behind me, Satan!" he said.   "You do not have   in mind the things
ⸯτοὺς μαθητάς⸴ ὁ ἐπετίμησεν Πέτρῳ καὶ ὕπαγε ὀπίσω μου σατανᾶ → λέγει ὅτι → → οὐ φρονεῖς ← → τὰ ←
d.apm n.apm d.nsm v.aai.3s n.dsm cj v.pam.2s p.g r.gs.1 n.vsm v.pai.3s cj pl v.pai.2s d.apn
3836 3412 3836 2203 4377 2779 5632 3958 1609 4928 3306 4022 5858 5858 4024 5858 3836

of God,   but the things of men."   ¶   34 Then he called   the crowd to him along with his
→ ⸯτοῦ θεοῦ⸴ ἀλλὰ τὰ ← ⸯτῶν ἀνθρώπων⸴   Καὶ προσκαλεσάμενος τὸν ὄχλον ← ← → σὺν αὐτοῦ
→ d.gsm n.gsm cj d.apn d.gsm n.gpm   cj pt.am.nsm d.asm n.asm p.d r.gsm.3
3836 2536 247 3836 3836 476   2779 4673 3836 4063 4673 4673 5250 899

disciples   and said: "If anyone would come   after me, he must deny   himself and take up his
ⸯτοῖς μαθηταῖς⸴ εἶπεν αὐτοῖς εἴ τις θέλει ἀκολουθεῖν ὀπίσω μου → → ἀπαρνησάσθω ἑαυτὸν καὶ ἀράτω αὐτοῦ
d.dpm n.dpm v.aai.3s r.dpm.3 cj r.nsm v.pai.3s f.pa p.g r.gs.1 v.amm.3s r.asm.3 cj v.aam.3s r.gsm.3
3836 3412 3306 899 1623 5516 2527 199 3958 1609 565 1571 2779 149 899

cross   and follow me.   35 For whoever wants to save his life   will lose it,   but whoever loses
ⸯτὸν σταυρὸν⸴ καὶ ἀκολουθείτω μοι γὰρ ὃς ἐὰν θέλῃ → σῶσαι αὐτοῦ ⸯτὴν ψυχήν⸴ → ἀπολέσει αὐτήν δ᾽ ὃς ἂν ἀπολέσει
d.asm n.asm cj v.pam.3s r.ds.1 cj r.nsm pl v.pas.3s f.aa r.gsm.3 d.asf n.asf v.fai.3s r.asf.3 cj r.nsm pl v.fai.3s
3836 5089 2779 199 1609 1142 4005 1569 2527 5392 899 3836 6034 660 899 1254 4005 323 660

his life   for me and for the gospel will save it.   36 What good is it for a man   to gain the
αὐτοῦ ⸯτὴν ψυχήν⸴ ἕνεκεν ἐμοῦ καὶ τοῦ εὐαγγελίου → σώσει αὐτήν γὰρ τί ὠφελεῖ ← ἄνθρωπον → κερδῆσαι τὸν
r.gsm.3 d.asf n.asf p.g r.gs.1 cj d.gsn n.gsn v.fai.3s r.asf.3 cj r.asn v.pai.3s n.asm f.aa d.asm
899 3836 6034 1914 1609 2779 3836 2295 5392 899 1142 5515 6067 476 3045 3836

whole world, yet forfeit his soul?   37 Or what can a man   give in exchange for his soul?   38 If
ὅλον κόσμον καὶ ζημιωθῆναι αὐτοῦ ⸯτὴν ψυχήν⸴ γὰρ τί ἄνθρωπος δοῖ → ἀντάλλαγμα ← αὐτοῦ ⸯτῆς ψυχῆς⸴ γὰρ
a.asm n.asm cj f.ap r.gsm.3 d.asf n.asf cj r.asn n.nsm v.aas.3s n.asn r.gsm.3 d.gsf n.gsf cj
3910 3180 2779 2423 899 3836 6034 1142 5515 476 1443 498 899 3836 6034 1142

anyone is ashamed of me and my words   in this adulterous   and sinful generation,   the Son of
ⸯὃς ἐὰν⸴ → ἐπαισχυνθῇ ← με καὶ ἐμοὺς ⸯτοὺς λόγους⸴ ἐν ταύτῃ ⸯτῇ μοιχαλίδι⸴ καὶ ἁμαρτωλῷ ⸯτῇ γενεᾷ⸴ καὶ ὁ υἱὸς →
r.nsm cj v.aps.3s r.as.1 cj r.apm.1 d.apm n.apm p.d r.dsf d.dsf n.dsf cj a.dsf d.dsf n.dsf adv d.nsm n.nsm
4005 1569 2049 1609 2779 1847 3836 3364 1877 4047 3836 3655 2779 283 3836 1155 2779 3836 5626

Man   will be ashamed   of him when he comes in his Father's glory   with the holy angels."
ⸯτοῦ ἀνθρώπου⸴ → → ἐπαισχυνθήσεται ← αὐτόν ὅταν → ἔλθῃ ἐν αὐτοῦ ⸯτοῦ πατρὸς⸴ ⸯτῇ δόξῃ⸴ μετὰ τῶν ἁγίων ⸯτῶν ἀγγέλων⸴
d.gsm n.gsm v.fpi.3s r.asm.3 cj v.aas.3s p.d r.gsm.3 d.gsm n.gsm d.dsf n.dsf p.g d.gpm a.gpm d.gpm n.gpm
3836 476 2049 899 4020 2262 1877 899 3836 4252 3836 1518 3552 3836 41 3836 34

¶   9:1 And he said to them, "I tell you the truth,   some who are standing   here will not   taste
Καὶ → ἔλεγεν → αὐτοῖς → λέγω ὑμῖν ἀμὴν ὅτι τινες οἵτινες εἰσίν ⸯτῶν ἑστηκότων⸴ ὧδε → οὐ μὴ γεύσωνται
cj v.iai.3s r.dpm.3 v.pai.1s r.dp.2 pl cj r.npm r.npm v.pai.3p d.gpm pt.ra.gpm adv pl pl v.ams.3p
2779 3306 899 3306 7007 297 4022 5516 4015 1639 3836 2705 6045 1174 4024 3590 1174

death before they see the kingdom of God come with power."
θανάτου ἕως ἂν → ἴδωσιν τὴν βασιλείαν → τοῦ θεοῦ ἐληλυθυῖαν ἐν δυνάμει
n.gsm cj pl v.aas.3p d.asf n.asf d.gsm n.gsm pt.ra.asf p.d n.dsf
2505 2401 323 1625 3836 993 3836 2536 2262 1877 1539

The Transfiguration

9:2   After six days Jesus   took   Peter,   James   and John   with him and
Καὶ μετὰ ἓξ ἡμέρας ὁ Ἰησοῦς παραλαμβάνει ⸯτὸν Πέτρον⸴ καὶ ⸯτὸν Ἰάκωβον⸴ καὶ ⸯτὸν Ἰωάννην⸴ ← καὶ
cj p.a a.apf n.apf d.nsm n.nsm v.pai.3s d.asm n.asm cj d.asm n.asm cj d.asm n.asm cj
2779 3552 1971 2465 3836 2652 4161 3836 4377 2779 3836 2610 2779 3836 2722 4161 4161 2779

led   them up a high   mountain, where they were all alone.   There he was transfigured before
ἀναφέρει αὐτοὺς εἰς ὑψηλὸν ὄρος → ⸯκατ᾽ ἰδίαν μόνους⸴ καὶ → μετεμορφώθη ἔμπροσθεν
v.pai.3s r.apm.3 p.a a.asn n.asn p.a a.asf a.apm cj v.api.3s p.g
429 899 1650 5734 4001 2848 2625 3668 2779 3565 1869

them.   3 His clothes   became dazzling   white, whiter than anyone in the world could   bleach
αὐτῶν καὶ αὐτοῦ τὰ ἱμάτια ἐγένετο ⸯστίλβοντα λίαν λευκὰ οἷα γναφεὺς ἐπὶ τῆς γῆς οὐ δύναται οὕτως λευκᾶναι
r.gpm.3 cj r.gsm.3 d.npn n.npn v.ami.3s pt.pa.npn adv a.npn r.apn n.nsm p.g d.gsf n.gsf pl v.ppi.3s adv f.aa
899 2779 899 3836 2668 1181 5118 3336 3328 3888 1187 2093 3836 1178 4024 1538 4048 3326

them.   4 And there appeared before them Elijah and Moses,   who were talking   with Jesus.   ¶   5
καὶ → ὤφθη → αὐτοῖς Ἠλίας σὺν Μωϋσεῖ καὶ → ἦσαν συλλαλοῦντες ← ⸯτῷ Ἰησοῦ⸴ καὶ
cj v.api.3s r.dpm.3 n.nsm p.d n.dsm cj v.iai.3p pt.pa.npm d.dsm n.dsm cj
2779 3972 899 2460 5250 3707 2779 1639 5196 3836 2652 2779

ἐπετίμησεν Πέτρῳ καὶ λέγει, Ὕπαγε ὀπίσω μου, Σατανᾶ, ὅτι οὐ φρονεῖς τὰ τοῦ θεοῦ ἀλλὰ τὰ τῶν ἀνθρώπων. ¶ 34 Καὶ προσκαλεσάμενος τὸν ὄχλον σὺν τοῖς μαθηταῖς αὐτοῦ εἶπεν αὐτοῖς, Εἴ τις θέλει ὀπίσω μου ἀκολουθεῖν, ἀπαρνησάσθω ἑαυτὸν καὶ ἀράτω τὸν σταυρὸν αὐτοῦ καὶ ἀκολουθείτω μοι. 35 ὃς γὰρ ἐὰν θέλῃ τὴν ψυχὴν αὐτοῦ σῶσαι ἀπολέσει αὐτήν· ὃς δ᾽ ἂν ἀπολέσει τὴν ψυχὴν αὐτοῦ ἕνεκεν ἐμοῦ καὶ τοῦ εὐαγγελίου σώσει αὐτήν. 36 τί γὰρ ὠφελεῖ ἄνθρωπον κερδῆσαι τὸν κόσμον ὅλον καὶ ζημιωθῆναι τὴν ψυχὴν αὐτοῦ; 37 τί γὰρ δοῖ ἄνθρωπος ἀντάλλαγμα τῆς ψυχῆς αὐτοῦ; 38 ὃς γὰρ ἐὰν ἐπαισχυνθῇ με καὶ τοὺς ἐμοὺς λόγους ἐν τῇ γενεᾷ ταύτῃ τῇ μοιχαλίδι καὶ ἁμαρτωλῷ, καὶ ὁ υἱὸς τοῦ ἀνθρώπου ἐπαισχυνθήσεται αὐτόν, ὅταν ἔλθῃ ἐν τῇ δόξῃ τοῦ πατρὸς αὐτοῦ μετὰ τῶν ἀγγέλων τῶν ἁγίων. ¶ 1 Καὶ ἔλεγεν αὐτοῖς, Ἀμὴν λέγω ὑμῖν ὅτι εἰσίν τινες ὧδε τῶν ἑστηκότων οἵτινες οὐ μὴ γεύσωνται θανάτου ἕως ἂν ἴδωσιν τὴν βασιλείαν τοῦ θεοῦ ἐληλυθυῖαν ἐν δυνάμει.

9:2 Καὶ μετὰ ἡμέρας ἓξ παραλαμβάνει ὁ Ἰησοῦς τὸν Πέτρον καὶ τὸν Ἰάκωβον καὶ τὸν Ἰωάννην καὶ ἀναφέρει αὐτοὺς εἰς ὄρος ὑψηλὸν κατ᾽ ἰδίαν μόνους. καὶ μετεμορφώθη ἔμπροσθεν αὐτῶν, 3 καὶ τὰ ἱμάτια αὐτοῦ ἐγένετο στίλβοντα λευκὰ λίαν, οἷα γναφεὺς ἐπὶ τῆς γῆς οὐ δύναται οὕτως λευκᾶναι. 4 καὶ ὤφθη αὐτοῖς Ἠλίας σὺν Μωϋσεῖ καὶ ἦσαν συλλαλοῦντες τῷ Ἰησοῦ ¶ 5 καὶ

Peter		said	to Jesus,	"Rabbi,		it is	good	for	us		to be	here.		Let us put		up	three
˻ὁ	Πέτρος˼	ἀποκριθεὶς	λέγει →	˻τῷ	Ἰησοῦ˼	ῥαββί	→ ἐστιν	καλὸν	ἡμᾶς	→	εἶναι	ὧδε	καὶ	→	ποιήσωμεν ←		τρεῖς
d.nsm	n.nsm	pt.ap.nsm	v.pai.3s	d.dsm	n.dsm	n.vsm	v.pai.3s	a.nsn	r.ap.1		f.pa	adv	cj		v.aas.1p		a.apf
3836	4377	646	3306	3836	2652	4806	1639	2819	7005		1639	6045	2779		4472		5552

shelters –	one	for you,		one	for Moses	and	one	for Elijah."	**6**		(He did	not	know	what	to say,		they
σκηνάς,	μίαν →	σοὶ	καὶ	μίαν →	Μωϋσεῖ	καὶ	μίαν →	Ἠλίᾳ	γὰρ →		→	οὐ	ᾔδει	τί	→ ἀποκριθῇ	γὰρ →	
n.apf	a.asf	r.ds.2	cj	a.asf	n.dsm	cj	a.asf	n.dsm	cj			pl	v.lai.3s	r.asn	v.aps.3s	cj	
5008	1651	5148	2779	1651	3707	2779	1651	2460	1142		3857	3857	4024	5515	646	1142	

were	so frightened.)	¶	**7**	Then	a cloud	appeared	and	enveloped	them,	and	a voice	came	from	the cloud:
ἐγένοντο	ἔκφοβοι			καὶ	νεφέλη	ἐγένετο		ἐπισκιάζουσα	αὐτοῖς	καὶ	φωνὴ	ἐγένετο	ἐκ	τῆς νεφέλης
v.ami.3p	a.npm			cj	n.nsf	v.ami.3s		pt.pa.nsf	r.dpm.3	cj	n.nsf	v.ami.3s	p.g	d.gsf n.gsf
1181	1769			2779	3749	1181		2173	899	2779	5889	1181	1666	3836 3749

"This	is	my	Son,		whom	I love.	Listen	to him!"	¶	**8**	Suddenly,	when they	looked		around,
οὗτος	ἐστιν	μου	ὁ	υἱός	ὁ	ἀγαπητός	ἀκούετε →	αὐτοῦ		καὶ	ἐξάπινα	→	→ περιβλεψάμενοι ←		
r.nsm	v.pai.3s	r.gs.1	d.nsm	n.nsm	d.nsm	a.nsm	v.pam.2p	r.gsm.3		cj	adv		pt.am.npm		
4047	1639	1609	3836	5626	3836	28	201	899		2779	1988		4315		

they	no	longer	saw	anyone	with	them	except		Jesus.	¶	**9**	As	they	were	coming		down	
→	οὐκέτι ←		εἶδον	οὐδένα	μεθ'	ἑαυτῶν	˻ἀλλὰ	μόνον˼	˻τὸν Ἰησοῦν˼		Καὶ →		αὐτῶν →		καταβαινόντων		ἐκ
	adv		v.aai.3p	a.asm	p.g	r.gpm.3	cj	adv	d.asm n.asm		cj		r.gpm.3		pt.pa.gpm		p.g
1625	4033		1625	4029	3552	1571	247	3668	3836 2652		2779		2849 899		2849		1666

the	mountain,	Jesus	gave	them	orders		not	to tell		anyone	what	they	had	seen	until		the	Son of
τοῦ	ὄρους	Ἰησοῦς	αὐτοῖς	διεστείλατο →		ἵνα	διηγήσωνται	μηδενὶ	ἃ	→		→	εἶδον	εἰ μὴ ὅταν˼	ὁ	υἱὸς
d.gsn	n.gsn		r.dpm.3	v.ami.3s		cj	v.ams.3p	a.dsm	r.apn				v.aai.3p	cj pl cj	d.nsm	n.nsm
3836	4001		1403	899	1403		3594	2671	1455	3594	4005		1625	1623 3590 4020	3836	5626

Man		had risen	from	the dead.	**10**		They	kept		the	matter	to	themselves,	discussing	what		"rising
˻τοῦ ἀνθρώπου˼	→	ἀναστῇ	ἐκ	νεκρῶν	καὶ		ἐκράτησαν	τὸν	λόγον	πρὸς	ἑαυτοὺς	συζητοῦντες	τί		˻τὸ ἀναστῆναι˼
d.gsm n.gsm		v.aas.3s	p.g	a.gpm	cj		v.aai.3p	d.asm	n.asm	p.a	r.apm.3	pt.pa.npm	r.nsn		d.nsn f.aa
3836 476		482	1666	3738	2779		3195	3836	3364	4639	1571	5184	5515		3836 482

from	the dead"	meant.	¶	**11**	And	they	asked	him,		"Why	do	the	teachers	of the law	say		that
ἐκ	νεκρῶν	ἐστιν		Καὶ		ἐπηρώτων	αὐτὸν	λέγοντες	ὅτι			οἱ	γραμματεῖς ←	←	λέγουσιν	ὅτι
p.g	a.gpm	v.pai.3s		cj		v.iai.3p	r.asm.3	pt.pa.npm	cj			d.npm	n.npm		v.pai.3p	cj
1666	3738	1639		2779		2089	899	3306	4022		3306	3836	1208		3306	4022

Elijah	must	come	first?"	¶	**12**		Jesus	replied,		"To be sure,	Elijah	does	come	first,		and	restores
Ἠλίαν	δεῖ	ἐλθεῖν	πρῶτον		δὲ	ὁ		ἔφη	αὐτοῖς	μὲν ←		Ἠλίας →		ἐλθὼν	πρῶτον		ἀποκαθιστάνει
n.asm	v.pai.3s	f.aa	a.asn		cj	d.nsm		v.iai.3s	r.dpm.3	pl		n.nsm		pt.aa.nsm	a.asn		v.pai.3s
2460	1256	2262	4754		1254	3836		5774	899	3525		2460		2262	4754		635

all	things.	Why	then	is it	written	that		the	Son	of Man		must suffer	much	and	be rejected?	**13**	But	I
πάντα		καὶ	πῶς	→	γέγραπται	ἵνα	ἐπὶ	τὸν	υἱὸν	τοῦ ἀνθρώπου		πάθῃ	πολλὰ	καὶ	→ ἐξουδενηθῇ		ἀλλὰ →	
a.apn		cj	cj		v.rpi.3s	cj	p.a	d.asm	n.asm	d.gsm n.gsm		v.aas.3s	a.apn	cj	v.aps.3s		cj	
4246		2779	4802		1211	2671	2093	3836	5626	3836 476		4248	4498	2779	2022		247	

tell	you,		Elijah	has	come,	and	they	have	done		to	him	everything	they	wished,	just		as it is	written
λέγω	ὑμῖν	ὅτι	καὶ	Ἠλίας	→	ἐλήλυθεν	καὶ	→	→	ἐποίησαν	→	αὐτῷ	ὅσα	˻	ἤθελον	καθὼς	←	→	γέγραπται
v.pai.1s	r.dp.2	cj	adv	n.nsm		v.rai.3s	cj			v.aai.3p		r.dsm.3	r.apn		v.iai.3p	cj			v.rpi.3s
3306	7007	4022	2779	2460		2262	2779			4472		899	4012		2527	2777			1211

about	him."
ἐπ'	αὐτόν
p.a	r.asm.3
2093	899

The Healing of a Boy With an Evil Spirit

9:14		When	they	came	to	the	other	disciples,	they	saw	a	large	crowd	around	them	and	the	teachers	of
Καὶ →			→	ἐλθόντες	πρὸς	τοὺς		μαθητὰς	→	εἶδον		πολὺν	ὄχλον	περὶ	αὐτοὺς	καὶ		γραμματεῖς	
cj				pt.aa.npm	p.a	d.apm		n.apm		v.aai.3p		a.asm	n.asm	p.a	r.apm.3	cj		n.npm	
2779				2262	4639	3836		3412		1625		4498	4063	4309	899	2779		1208	

the law	arguing		with them.	**15**		As	soon as	all	the	people	saw	Jesus,	they	were	overwhelmed	with wonder
←	συζητοῦντας	πρὸς	αὐτούς	καὶ	εὐθὺς		→	πᾶς	ὁ	ὄχλος	ἰδόντες	αὐτὸν	→	→	ἐξεθαμβήθησαν	
	pt.pa.apm	p.a	r.apm	cj	adv			a.nsm	d.nsm	n.nsm	pt.aa.npm	r.asm.3			v.api.3p	
5184		4639	899	2779	2318			4246	3836	4063	1625	899			1701	

ἀποκριθεὶς ὁ Πέτρος λέγει τῷ Ἰησοῦ, Ῥαββί, καλόν ἐστιν ἡμᾶς ὧδε εἶναι, καὶ ποιήσωμεν τρεῖς σκηνάς, σοὶ μίαν καὶ Μωϋσεῖ μίαν καὶ Ἠλίᾳ μίαν. [6] οὐ γὰρ ᾔδει τί ἀποκριθῇ, ἔκφοβοι γὰρ ἐγένοντο. ¶ [7] καὶ ἐγένετο νεφέλη ἐπισκιάζουσα αὐτοῖς, καὶ ἐγένετο φωνὴ ἐκ τῆς νεφέλης, Οὗτός ἐστιν ὁ υἱός μου ὁ ἀγαπητός, ἀκούετε αὐτοῦ. ¶ [8] καὶ ἐξάπινα περιβλεψάμενοι οὐκέτι οὐδένα εἶδον ἀλλὰ τὸν Ἰησοῦν μόνον μεθ' ἑαυτῶν. ¶ [9] Καὶ καταβαινόντων αὐτῶν ἐκ τοῦ ὄρους διεστείλατο αὐτοῖς ἵνα μηδενὶ ἃ εἶδον διηγήσωνται, εἰ μὴ ὅταν ὁ υἱὸς τοῦ ἀνθρώπου ἐκ νεκρῶν ἀναστῇ. [10] καὶ τὸν λόγον ἐκράτησαν πρὸς ἑαυτοὺς συζητοῦντες τί ἐστιν τὸ ἐκ νεκρῶν ἀναστῆναι. ¶ [11] καὶ ἐπηρώτων αὐτὸν λέγοντες, Ὅτι λέγουσιν οἱ γραμματεῖς ὅτι Ἠλίαν δεῖ ἐλθεῖν πρῶτον; ¶ [12] ὁ δὲ ἔφη αὐτοῖς, Ἠλίας μὲν ἐλθὼν πρῶτον ἀποκαθιστάνει πάντα· καὶ πῶς γέγραπται ἐπὶ τὸν υἱὸν τοῦ ἀνθρώπου ἵνα πολλὰ πάθῃ καὶ ἐξουδενηθῇ; [13] ἀλλὰ λέγω ὑμῖν ὅτι καὶ Ἠλίας ἐλήλυθεν, καὶ ἐποίησαν αὐτῷ ὅσα ἤθελον, καθὼς γέγραπται ἐπ' αὐτόν.

[9:14] Καὶ ἐλθόντες πρὸς τοὺς μαθητὰς εἶδον ὄχλον πολὺν περὶ αὐτοὺς καὶ γραμματεῖς συζητοῦντας πρὸς αὐτούς. [15] καὶ

and ran   to greet   him.   ¶ **16** "What are you arguing with them about?" he asked.   ¶
καὶ προστρέχοντες → ἠσπάζοντο αὐτόν   καὶ τί →   → συζητεῖτε πρὸς αὐτούς ←   → ἐπηρώτησεν αὐτούς
cj   pt.pa.npm   v.imi.3p   r.asm.3   cj   r.asn   v.pai.2p p.a r.apm.3   v.aai.3s   r.apm.3
2779 4708   832   899   2779 5515   5184   4639 899   5184   2089   899

17 A man in the crowd answered,   "Teacher, I brought   you my son,   who is possessed by a spirit
καὶ εἷς ἐκ τοῦ ὄχλου ἀπεκρίθη αὐτῷ διδάσκαλε → ἤνεγκα πρὸς σέ μου τὸν υἱόν, → ἔχοντα   ← πνεῦμα
cj   a.nsm p.g d.gsm n.gsm v.api.3s r.dsm.3 n.vsm v.aai.1s p.a r.as.2 r.gs.1 d.asm n.asm pt.pa.asm   n.asn
2779 1651 1666 3836 4063 646   899   1437   5770   4639 5148 1609 3836 5626   2400   4460

that has robbed him of speech. **18** Whenever it seizes him, it throws him to the ground.   He foams at the
→   →   →   →   ἄλαλον   καὶ ὅπου ἐάν → καταλάβη αὐτόν → ῥήσσει αὐτόν ← ←   καὶ → ἀφρίζει ←
               a.asn   cj   cj pl   v.aas.3s r.asm.3 v.pai.3s r.asm.3   cj   v.pai.3s
               228   2779 3963 1569   2898   899   4841   899   4841 4841 4841 2779 930

mouth, gnashes his teeth   and becomes rigid.   I asked your disciples   to drive   out the spirit,
←   καὶ τρίζει τοὺς ὀδόντας καὶ →   ξηραίνεται καὶ → εἶπα σου τοῖς μαθηταῖς ἵνα ἐκβάλωσιν ←   αὐτό
     cj v.pai.3s d.apm n.apm cj   v.pai.3s   cj   v.aai.1s r.gs.2 d.dpm n.dpm cj v.aas.3p   r.asn.3
     2779 5563   3836 3848   2779   3830   2779 3306 5148 3836 3412 2671 1675   899

but they could not." ¶ **19** "O unbelieving generation," Jesus replied,   "how long shall I stay
καὶ → ἴσχυσαν οὐκ   δὲ ὧ ἄπιστος γενεά   ὁ   ἀποκριθεὶς αὐτοῖς λέγει ἕως πότε → → ἔσομαι
cj   v.aai.3p pl   cj j a.vsf   n.vsf   d.nsm pt.ap.nsm r.dpm.3 v.pai.3s p.g adv   v.fmi.1s
2779   2710   4024   1254 6043 603   1155   3836 646   899   3306 2401 4537   1639

with you? How long shall I put   up with you? Bring the boy to me." ¶ **20** So they brought him.
πρὸς ὑμᾶς ἕως πότε → → ἀνέξομαι ← ← ὑμῶν φέρετε αὐτὸν πρός με   καὶ → ἤνεγκαν αὐτὸν πρὸς
p.a r.ap.2 p.g adv   v.fmi.1s   r.gp.2 v.pam.2p r.asm.3 p.a r.as.1   cj   v.aai.3p r.asm.3 p.a
4639 7007 2401 4537   462   5770   5770   899   4639 1609   2779 5770   899   4639

When the spirit saw Jesus, it immediately threw the boy into a convulsion. He fell   to the
αὐτόν καὶ τὸ πνεῦμα ἰδὸν αὐτὸν → εὐθὺς   →   αὐτόν → συνεσπάραξεν καὶ → πεσὼν ἐπὶ τῆς
r.asm.3 cj d.nsn n.nsn pt.aa.nsm r.asm.3 adv   r.asm.3 v.aai.3s   cj   pt.aa.nsm p.g d.gsf
899   2779 3836 4460 1625   899   5360 2318   899   5360   2779 4406   2093 3836

ground and rolled around, foaming at the mouth.   ¶   **21** Jesus asked   the boy's father, "How long has
γῆς   ἐκυλίετο ←   ἀφρίζων ← ← ←   καὶ   ἐπηρώτησεν τὸν αὐτοῦ πατέρα πόσος χρόνος ἐστὶν
n.gsf   v.imi.3s   pt.pa.nsm   cj   v.aai.3s   d.asm r.gsm.3 n.asm r.nsm n.nsm v.pai.3s
1178   3244   930   2779   2089   3836 899   4252 4531   5989   1639

he been like this?" ¶   "From childhood," he answered. **22** "It has often thrown him   into fire
αὐτῷ γέγονεν ὡς τοῦτο   δὲ ἐκ παιδιόθεν ὁ   εἶπεν   καὶ → → πολλάκις ἔβαλεν αὐτὸν καὶ εἰς πῦρ
r.dsm.3 v.rai.3s ὡς r.asn cj p.g adv   d.nsm v.aai.3s cj   adv   v.aai.3s r.asm.3 cj p.a n.asn
899   1181   6055 4047   1254 1666 4085   3836 3306   2779 965 965 4490   4490   899   2779 1650 4786

or   water to kill him. But if you can do anything, take pity   on us and help   us." ¶
καὶ εἰς ὕδατα ἵνα ἀπολέση αὐτόν ἀλλ᾽ εἰ → → δύνη τι   σπλαγχνισθεὶς ἐφ᾽ ἡμᾶς βοήθησον ἡμῖν
cj p.a n.apn cj v.aas.3s r.asm.3 cj cj   v.ppi.2s r.asn   pt.ap.nsm   p.a r.ap.1 v.aam.2s r.dp.1
2779 1650 5623 2671 660   899   660 247   1623 1538 5516 5072   2093 7005 1070   7005

23 "'If you can'?" said Jesus.   "Everything is possible for him who believes." **24** Immediately the
δὲ τὸ εἰ → δύνη   εἶπεν ὁ Ἰησοῦς αὐτῷ πάντα → δυνατὰ → τῷ   πιστεύοντι εὐθὺς   ὁ
cj d.asn cj v.ppi.2s v.aai.3s d.nsm n.nsm r.dsm.3 a.npn a.npn   d.dsm pt.pa.dsm   adv   d.nsm
1254 3836 1623 1538 3306 2652 899 4246   1543   3836 4409   2318   3836

boy's   father exclaimed, "I do believe; help me overcome my unbelief!"   ¶ **25** When Jesus
τοῦ παιδίου πατὴρ κράξας ἔλεγεν → πιστεύω βοήθει →   μου τῇ ἀπιστία,   δὲ   ὁ Ἰησοῦς
d.gsn n.gsn n.nsm pt.aa.nsm v.iai.3s v.pai.1s v.pam.2s   r.gs.1 d.dsf n.dsf   cj   d.nsm n.nsm
3836 4086   4252 3189   3306   4409   1070   1609 3836 602   1254   1625 3836 2652

saw that a crowd was running   to the scene, he rebuked the evil   spirit. "You deaf and mute
ἰδὼν ὅτι ὄχλος → ἐπισυντρέχει ← ←   → ἐπετίμησεν τῷ τῷ ἀκαθάρτῳ πνεύματι κωφὸν καὶ ἄλαλον
pt.aa.nsm cj n.nsm v.pai.3s   v.aai.3s   d.dsn d.dsn a.dsn n.dsn   a.vsn cj a.vsn
1625 4022 4063 2192   2203   3836 3836 176   4460   3273   2779 228

spirit," he said, "I command you, come out of him and never enter him again." ¶ **26** The
τὸ πνεῦμα λέγων αὐτῷ ἐγὼ ἐπιτάσσω σοι ἔξελθε ἐξ → αὐτοῦ καὶ μηκέτι εἰσέλθης εἰς αὐτόν ←   καὶ
d.vsn n.vsn pt.pa.nsm r.dsn.3 r.ns.1 v.pai.1s r.ds.2 v.aam.2s p.g r.gsm.3 cj adv v.aas.2s p.a r.asm.3   cj
3836 4460 3306   899 1609 2199   5148 2002   1666 899   2779 3600 1656   1650 899 3600   2779

εὐθὺς πᾶς ὁ ὄχλος ἰδόντες αὐτὸν ἐξεθαμβήθησαν καὶ προστρέχοντες ἠσπάζοντο αὐτόν. ¶ **16** καὶ ἐπηρώτησεν αὐτούς, Τί συζητεῖτε πρὸς αὐτούς; ¶ **17** καὶ ἀπεκρίθη αὐτῷ εἷς ἐκ τοῦ ὄχλου, Διδάσκαλε, ἤνεγκα τὸν υἱόν μου πρὸς σέ, ἔχοντα πνεῦμα ἄλαλον· **18** καὶ ὅπου ἐὰν αὐτὸν καταλάβη ῥήσσει αὐτόν, καὶ ἀφρίζει καὶ τρίζει τοὺς ὀδόντας καὶ ξηραίνεται· καὶ εἶπα τοῖς μαθηταῖς σου ἵνα αὐτὸ ἐκβάλωσιν, καὶ οὐκ ἴσχυσαν. ¶ **19** ὁ δὲ ἀποκριθεὶς αὐτοῖς λέγει, Ὦ γενεὰ ἄπιστος, ἕως πότε πρὸς ὑμᾶς ἔσομαι; ἕως πότε ἀνέξομαι ὑμῶν; φέρετε αὐτὸν πρός με. ¶ **20** καὶ ἤνεγκαν αὐτὸν πρὸς αὐτόν. καὶ ἰδὼν αὐτὸν τὸ πνεῦμα εὐθὺς συνεσπάραξεν αὐτόν, καὶ πεσὼν ἐπὶ τῆς γῆς ἐκυλίετο ἀφρίζων. ¶ **21** καὶ ἐπηρώτησεν τὸν πατέρα αὐτοῦ, Πόσος χρόνος ἐστὶν ὡς τοῦτο γέγονεν αὐτῷ; ¶ ὁ δὲ εἶπεν, Ἐκ παιδιόθεν· **22** καὶ πολλάκις καὶ εἰς πῦρ αὐτὸν ἔβαλεν καὶ εἰς ὕδατα ἵνα ἀπολέση αὐτόν· ἀλλ᾽ εἴ τι δύνη, βοήθησον ἡμῖν σπλαγχνισθεὶς ἐφ᾽ ἡμᾶς. ¶ **23** ὁ δὲ Ἰησοῦς εἶπεν αὐτῷ, Τὸ Εἰ δύνη, πάντα δυνατὰ τῷ πιστεύοντι. **24** εὐθὺς κράξας ὁ πατὴρ τοῦ παιδίου ἔλεγεν, Πιστεύω· βοήθει μου τῇ ἀπιστία. ¶ **25** ἰδὼν δὲ ὁ Ἰησοῦς ὅτι ἐπισυντρέχει ὄχλος, ἐπετίμησεν τῷ πνεύματι τῷ ἀκαθάρτῳ λέγων αὐτῷ, Τὸ ἄλαλον καὶ κωφὸν πνεῦμα, ἐγὼ ἐπιτάσσω σοι, ἔξελθε ἐξ αὐτοῦ καὶ μηκέτι εἰσέλθης

spirit shrieked,   convulsed him violently and came out.   The boy looked so much like a corpse that
κράξας   καὶ σπαράξας   πολλὰ   ἐξῆλθεν ←   καὶ   ἐγένετο → →   ὡσεὶ νεκρὸς ὥστε
pt.aa.nsm   cj   pt.aa.nsm   a.apn   v.aai.3s   cj   v.ami.3s   pl   a.nsm   cj
3189   2779 5057   4498   2002   2779   1181   6059   3738   6063

many   said,   "He's dead."   ¶   27 But Jesus   took   him by the hand and lifted him to his
⸢τοὺς πολλοὺς⸥ λέγειν ὅτι →   ἀπέθανεν   δὲ ⸤ὁ Ἰησοῦς⸥ κρατήσας αὐτοῦ → τῆς χειρὸς ἤγειρεν αὐτόν
d.apm   a.apm f.pa cj   v.aai.3s   cj d.nsm n.nsm pt.aa.nsm r.gsm.3   d.gsf n.gsf v.aai.3s r.asm.3
3836   4498 3306 4022   633   1254 3836 2652 3195 899   3836 5931 1586 899

feet, and he stood up.   ¶   28   After Jesus had gone   indoors, his disciples asked him privately,
καὶ → ἀνέστη ←   Καὶ   αὐτοῦ   εἰσελθόντος εἰς οἶκον αὐτοῦ οἱ μαθηταὶ ἐπηρώτων αὐτόν ⸢κατ᾽ ἰδίαν⸥
cj   v.aai.3s   cj   r.gsm.3   pt.aa.gsm p.a n.asm r.gsm.3 d.npm n.npm v.iai.3p r.asm.3 p.a a.asf
2779   482   2779 1656 899   1656 1650 3875 899 3836 3412 2089 899 2848 2625

"Why couldn't   we   drive it out?"   ¶   29   He replied,   "This kind   can
ὅτι   ⸢οὐκ ἠδυνήθημεν⸥ ἡμεῖς ἐκβαλεῖν αὐτό   καὶ → εἶπεν αὐτοῖς τοῦτο ⸢τὸ γένος⸥ ἐν οὐδενὶ δύναται
cj   pl v.api.1p r.np.1 f.aa r.asn.3   cj v.aai.3s r.dpm.3 r.asn d.asn n.asn p.d a.dsn v.ppi.3s
4022   4024 1538 7005 1675 899 1675   2779 3306 899 4047 3836 1169 1877 4029 1538

come out only   by prayer."   ¶   30 They left   that   place and passed   through Galilee.
ἐξελθεῖν ←   εἰ μὴ ἐν προσευχῇ   → ἐξελθόντες Κἀκεῖθεν ←   παρεπορεύοντο διὰ ⸢τῆς Γαλιλαίας⸥ καὶ
f.aa   cj pl p.d n.dsf   pt.aa.npm crasis   v.imi.3p p.g d.gsf n.gsf cj
2002   1623 3590 1877 4666   2002 2796   4182 1328 3836 1133 2779

Jesus did not want   anyone to know where they were,   31 because he was teaching his   disciples.   He said
→ οὐκ ἤθελεν ἵνα τις → γνοῖ   γὰρ → → ἐδίδασκεν αὐτοῦ ⸢τοὺς μαθητὰς⸥ καὶ → ἔλεγεν
  pl v.iai.3s cj r.nsm   v.aas.3s   cj   v.iai.3s r.gsm.3 d.apm n.apm cj v.iai.3s
  2527 4024 2527 2671 5516   1182   1142   1438 899 3836 3412 2779 3306

to them,   "The Son of Man   is going to be betrayed   into the hands of men.   They will
→ αὐτοῖς ὅτι ὁ   υἱὸς → ⸤τοῦ ἀνθρώπου⸥ →   → παραδίδοται εἰς   χεῖρας   ἀνθρώπων καὶ → →
  r.dpm.3 cj d.nsm   n.nsm d.gsm n.gsm   v.ppi.3s p.a   n.apf   n.gpm cj
  899 4022 3836   5626 3836 476   4140 1650   5931   476 2779

kill   him, and   after three days he will rise."   32 But they did not understand what he meant
ἀποκτενοῦσιν αὐτόν καὶ   ἀποκτανθεὶς μετὰ τρεῖς ἡμέρας → → ἀναστήσεται   δὲ οἱ → → ἠγνόουν τὸ → ῥῆμα
v.fai.3p r.asm.3 cj   pt.ap.nsm p.a a.apf n.apf   v.fmi.3s   cj d.npm v.iai.3p d.asn n.asn
650   899 2779   650 3552 5552 2465   482   1254 3836 51 3836 4839

and were afraid   to ask   him about it.
καὶ → ἐφοβοῦντο → ἐπερωτῆσαι αὐτόν
cj   v.ipi.3p   f.aa r.asm.3
2779   5828   2089 899

Who Is the Greatest?

9:33   They came to Capernaum.   When he was   in the house, he asked   them, "What were you
Καὶ → ἦλθον εἰς Καφαρναούμ Καὶ → → γενόμενος ἐν τῇ οἰκίᾳ → ἐπηρώτα αὐτούς τί
cj   v.aai.3p p.a n.asf cj   pt.am.nsm p.d d.dsf n.dsf v.iai.3s r.apm.3 r.asn
2779   2262 1650 3019 2779   1181 1877 3836 3864 2089 899 5515

arguing   about on the road?"   34 But they kept quiet   because on the way they had argued   about
διελογίζεσθε ←   ἐν τῇ ὁδῷ   δὲ οἱ → ἐσιώπων γὰρ   ἐν τῇ ὁδῷ → διελέχθησαν ←   πρὸς ἀλλήλους
v.imi.2p   p.d d.dsf n.dsf   cj d.npm v.iai.3p cj   p.d d.dsf n.dsf v.api.3p   p.a r.apm
1368   1877 3836 3847   1254 3836 4995 1142   1877 3836 3847 1363   4639 253

who was the greatest.   ¶   35   Sitting down, Jesus called   the Twelve and said,   "If anyone wants to be
τίς   μείζων   καὶ καθίσας ←   ἐφώνησεν τοὺς δώδεκα καὶ λέγει αὐτοῖς εἴ τις   θέλει → εἶναι
r.nsm   a.nsm.c   cj pt.aa.nsm   v.aai.3s d.apm a.apm cj v.pai.3s r.dpm.3 cj r.nsm   v.pai.3s f.pa
5515   3489   2779 2767   5888 3836 1557 2779 3306 899 1623 5516   2527 1639

first, he must be   the very last,   and the servant of all."   ¶   36   He took a little child and had him
πρῶτος → → ἔσται   πάντων ἔσχατος καὶ   διάκονος → πάντων   καὶ → λαβὼν   παιδίον   αὐτὸ
a.nsm   v.fmi.3s   a.gpm a.nsm cj   n.nsm a.gpm   cj pt.aa.nsm   n.asn   r.asn.3
4755   1639   4246 2274 2779   1356 4246   2779 3284   4086   2705 899

stand among them.   Taking   him in his arms, he said to them,   37 "Whoever   welcomes one of these little
ἔστησεν ⸤ἐν μέσῳ⸥ αὐτῶν καὶ ἐναγκαλισάμενος αὐτὸ ← ← → εἶπεν → αὐτοῖς ⸢ὃς ἂν⸥ δέξηται ἓν → τοιούτων →
v.aai.3s p.d n.dsn r.gpm.3 cj pt.am.nsm r.asn.3   v.aai.3s r.dpm.3 r.nsm pl v.ams.3s a.asn r.gpn
2705   1877 3545 899 2779 1878 899 1878 1878 1878   3306 899 4005 323 1312 1651 5525

εἰς αὐτόν. ¶ 26 καὶ κράξας καὶ πολλὰ σπαράξας ἐξῆλθεν· καὶ ἐγένετο ὡσεὶ νεκρός, ὥστε τοὺς πολλοὺς λέγειν ὅτι ἀπέθανεν ¶
27 ὁ δὲ Ἰησοῦς κρατήσας τῆς χειρὸς αὐτοῦ ἤγειρεν αὐτόν, καὶ ἀνέστη. ¶ 28 καὶ εἰσελθόντος αὐτοῦ εἰς οἶκον οἱ μαθηταὶ αὐτοῦ
κατ᾽ ἰδίαν ἐπηρώτων αὐτόν, Ὅτι ἡμεῖς οὐκ ἠδυνήθημεν ἐκβαλεῖν αὐτό; ¶ 29 καὶ εἶπεν αὐτοῖς, Τοῦτο τὸ γένος ἐν οὐδενὶ δύναται
ἐξελθεῖν εἰ μὴ ἐν προσευχῇ. ¶ 30 Κἀκεῖθεν ἐξελθόντες παρεπορεύοντο διὰ τῆς Γαλιλαίας, καὶ οὐκ ἤθελεν ἵνα τις γνοῖ·
31 ἐδίδασκεν γὰρ τοὺς μαθητὰς αὐτοῦ καὶ ἔλεγεν αὐτοῖς ὅτι Ὁ υἱὸς τοῦ ἀνθρώπου παραδίδοται εἰς χεῖρας ἀνθρώπων, καὶ
ἀποκτενοῦσιν αὐτόν, καὶ ἀποκτανθεὶς μετὰ τρεῖς ἡμέρας ἀναστήσεται. 32 οἱ δὲ ἠγνόουν τὸ ῥῆμα, καὶ ἐφοβοῦντο αὐτὸν
ἐπερωτῆσαι.
   9:33 Καὶ ἦλθον εἰς Καφαρναούμ. καὶ ἐν τῇ οἰκίᾳ γενόμενος ἐπηρώτα αὐτούς, Τί ἐν τῇ ὁδῷ διελογίζεσθε; 34 οἱ δὲ ἐσιώπων·
πρὸς ἀλλήλους γὰρ διελέχθησαν ἐν τῇ ὁδῷ τίς μείζων. ¶ 35 καὶ καθίσας ἐφώνησεν τοὺς δώδεκα καὶ λέγει αὐτοῖς, Εἴ τις θέλει
πρῶτος εἶναι, ἔσται πάντων ἔσχατος καὶ πάντων διάκονος. ¶ 36 καὶ λαβὼν παιδίον ἔστησεν αὐτὸ ἐν μέσῳ αὐτῶν καὶ
ἐναγκαλισάμενος αὐτὸ εἶπεν αὐτοῖς, 37 Ὃς ἂν ἓν τῶν τοιούτων παιδίων δέξηται ἐπὶ τῷ ὀνόματί μου, ἐμὲ δέχεται· καὶ ὃς ἂν

children	in	my	name	welcomes	me; and	whoever	welcomes	me	does	not	welcome	me	but	the one who
⌐τῶν παιδίων⌐	ἐπὶ	μου	⌐τῷ ὀνόματι⌐	δέχεται	ἐμὲ καὶ	⌐ὃς ἂν⌐	δέχηται	ἐμὲ →		οὐκ	δέχεται	ἐμὲ	ἀλλὰ	τὸν
d.gpn n.gpn	p.d	r.gs.1	d.dsn n.dsn	v.pmi.3s	r.as.1 cj	r.nsm pl	v.pms.3s	r.as.1	1312	pl	v.pmi.3s	r.as.1	247	d.asm
3836 4086	2093	1609	3836 3950	1312	1609 2779	4005 323	1312	1609		4024	1312	1609		3836

sent	me."
ἀποστείλαντα	με
pt.aa.asm	r.as.1
690	1609

Whoever Is Not Against Us Is for Us

9:38	"Teacher,"	said	John,	"we saw	a man	driving	out demons	in	your	name	and we told
	διδάσκαλε	Ἔφη αὐτῷ	ὁ Ἰωάννης, →	εἴδομεν	τινα	ἐκβάλλοντα ←	δαιμόνια	ἐν	σου	⌐τῷ ὀνόματι⌐	καὶ → →
	n.vsm	v.iai.3s r.dsm.3	d.nsm n.nsm	v.aai.1p	r.asm	pt.pa.asm	n.apn	p.d	r.gs.2	d.dsn n.dsn	cj
	1437	5774 899	3836 2722	1625	5516	1675	1228	1877	5148	3836 3950	2779 3266 3266

him	to stop,	because	he was	not one of us."	¶	39	"Do not	stop	him,"	Jesus	said.	"No
αὐτόν →	ἐκωλύομεν ὅτι	→	ἠκολούθει οὐκ	→ ἡμῖν		δὲ	μὴ	κωλύετε	αὐτόν	ὁ Ἰησοῦς,	εἶπεν γὰρ	οὐδεὶς
r.asm.3	v.iai.1p cj		v.iai.3s pl	r.dp.1		1254	pl	v.pam.2p	r.asm.3	d.nsm n.nsm	v.aai.3s cj	a.nsm
899	3266 4022		199 4024	7005		3266	3590	3266	899	3836 2652	3306 1142	4029

one	who	does	a miracle	in	my	name		can	in	the next moment	say		anything bad about
←	ἐστιν ὃς	ποιήσει	δύναμιν	ἐπὶ	μου	⌐τῷ ὀνόματι⌐	καὶ	δυνήσεται	ταχὺ ←		←	κακολογῆσαι	
v.pai.3s	r.nsm	v.fai.3s	n.asf	p.d	r.gs.1	d.dsn n.dsn	cj	v.fmi.3s	adv			f.aa	
1639	4005	4472	1539	2093	1609	3836 3950	2779	1538	5444			2800	

me,	40	for	whoever	is	not against	us	is	for us.	41	I tell	you the truth,	anyone	who	gives	you	a cup	of
με		γὰρ	ὃς	ἔστιν	οὐκ καθ'	ἡμῶν,	ἔστιν	ὑπὲρ ἡμῶν.		γὰρ → λέγω	ὑμῖν	ἀμὴν	⌐Ὃς ἂν⌐ ←		ποτίσῃ	ὑμᾶς	ποτήριον
r.as.1		cj	r.nsm	v.pai.3s	pl p.g	r.gp.1	v.pai.3s	p.g r.gp.1		cj v.pai.1s	r.dp.2	pl	r.nsm cj		v.aas.3s	r.ap.2	n.asn
1609		1142	4005	1639	4024 2848	7005	1639	5642 7005		1142 3306	7007	297	4005 323		4540	7007	4539

water	in	my	name	because	you belong	to Christ	will certainly	not	lose	his	reward.
ὕδατος	ἐν		ὀνόματι	ὅτι	→ ἐστε	→ Χριστοῦ	ὅτι → →	οὐ μὴ	ἀπολέσῃ	αὐτοῦ	⌐τὸν μισθὸν⌐
n.gsn	p.d		n.dsn	cj	v.pai.2p	n.gsm	cj	pl pl	v.aas.3s	r.gsm.3	d.asm n.asm
5623	1877		3950	4022	1639	5986	4022 660	4024 3590	660	899	3836 3635

Causing to Sin

9:42	"And	if	anyone	causes	one	of	these	little		ones	who	believe	in	me to sin,		it would be		better
	Καὶ	→ ⌐ὃς ἂν⌐			ἕνα	→	τούτων	⌐τῶν μικρῶν⌐	←	τῶν	πιστευόντων	εἰς	ἐμέ	→ σκανδαλίσῃ	→ →		ἐστιν	καλόν
	cj	r.nsm pl			a.asm		r.gpm	d.gpm a.gpm		d.gpm	pt.pa.gpm	p.a	r.as.1	v.aas.3s			v.pai.3s	a.nsn
	2779	4005 323		4997	1651	3625	4047	3836 3625		3836	4409	1650	1609	4997			1639	2819

for	him			to be thrown	into	the	sea	with	a large	millstone	tied	around	his	neck.
→	αὐτῷ	μᾶλλον	εἰ καὶ →	βέβληται	εἰς	τὴν	θάλασσαν	ὀνικὸς	μύλος		περίκειται	περὶ	αὐτοῦ	⌐τὸν τράχηλον⌐
	r.dsm.3	adv.c	cj cj	v.rpi.3s	p.a	d.asf	n.asf	a.nsm	n.nsm		v.pmi.3s	p.a	r.gsm.3	d.asm n.asm
	899	3437	1623 2779	965	1650	3836	2498	3948	3685		4329	4309	899	3836 5549

43	If	your	hand	causes	you	to sin,		cut	it	off.	It is		better	for	you	to enter		life
	Καὶ	ἐὰν	σου	⌐ἡ χείρ,⌐	→	σε	→	σκανδαλίζῃ	ἀπόκοψον	αὐτήν ←	→	ἐστίν	καλόν		σε	→ εἰσελθεῖν	εἰς	⌐τὴν ζωὴν⌐
	cj	cj	r.gs.2	d.nsf n.nsf		r.as.2		v.pas.3s	v.aam.2s	r.asf.3		v.pai.3s	a.nsn		r.as.2	f.aa	p.a	d.asf n.asf
	2779	1569	5148	3836 5931		4997		5148	644	899		1639	2819		5148	1656	1650	3836 2437

maimed	than	with	two	hands	to go		into	hell,		where	the	fire	never		goes out.	45	And	if	your
κυλλὸν	ἢ	ἔχοντα	δύο	⌐τὰς χεῖρας⌐	→ ἀπελθεῖν	εἰς		⌐τὴν γέενναν,⌐	→	εἰς	τὸ	πῦρ	⌐τὸ ἄσβεστον⌐	←	←		Καὶ	ἐὰν	σου
a.asm	pl	pt.pa.asm	a.apf	d.apf n.apf	f.aa	p.a		d.asf n.asf		p.a	d.asn	n.asn	d.asn a.asn				cj	cj	r.gs.2
3245	2445	2400	1545	3836 5931	599	1650		3836 1147		1650	3836	4786	3836 812				2779	1569	5148

foot	causes	you	to sin,		cut	it	off.	It is		better	for	you	to enter		life	crippled	than	to
⌐ὁ πούς,⌐	→	σε	→	σκανδαλίζῃ	ἀπόκοψον	αὐτόν	←	→	ἐστίν	καλόν		σε	→ εἰσελθεῖν	εἰς	⌐τὴν ζωὴν⌐	χωλὸν	ἢ	→
d.nsm n.nsm		r.as.2		v.pas.3s	v.aam.2s	r.asm.3			v.pai.3s	a.nsn		r.as.2	f.aa	p.a	d.asf n.asf	a.asm	pl	
3836 4546		4997		5148	644	899			1639	2819		5148	1656	1650	3836 2437	6000	2445	

have	two	feet	and	be thrown	into	hell.	47	And	if	your	eye		causes	you	to sin,		pluck
ἔχοντα	δύο	⌐τοὺς πόδας⌐	→	βληθῆναι	εἰς	⌐τὴν γέενναν,⌐		καὶ	ἐὰν	σου	⌐ὁ ὀφθαλμός,⌐	→	→	σε	→	σκανδαλίζῃ	ἔκβαλε
pt.pa.asm	a.apm	d.apm n.apm		f.ap	p.a	d.asf n.asf		cj	cj	r.gs.2	d.nsm n.nsm			r.as.2		v.pas.3s	v.aam.2s
2400	1545	3836 4546		965	1650	3836 1147		2779	1569	5148	3836 4057		4997	5148		4997	1675

it out.	It is		better	for	you	to enter		the	kingdom	of God		with one eye		than	to have	two
αὐτόν ←	→	ἐστιν	καλόν		σέ	→ εἰσελθεῖν	εἰς	τὴν	βασιλείαν	→ ⌐τοῦ θεοῦ,⌐	→	μονόφθαλμον	ἢ	→	ἔχοντα	δύο
r.asm.3		v.pai.3s	a.nsn		r.as.2	f.aa	p.a	d.asf	n.asf	d.gsm n.gsm		a.asm	pl		pt.pa.asm	a.apm
899		1675	1639	2819	5148	1656	1650	3836	993	3836 2536		3669	2445		2400	1545

ἐμὲ δέχηται, οὐκ ἐμὲ δέχεται ἀλλὰ τὸν ἀποστείλαντά με.

9:38 Ἔφη αὐτῷ ὁ Ἰωάννης, Διδάσκαλε, εἴδομέν τινα ἐν τῷ ὀνόματί σου ἐκβάλλοντα δαιμόνια καὶ ἐκωλύομεν αὐτόν, ὅτι οὐκ ἠκολούθει ἡμῖν. ¶ 39 ὁ δὲ Ἰησοῦς εἶπεν, Μὴ κωλύετε αὐτόν. οὐδεὶς γάρ ἐστιν ὃς ποιήσει δύναμιν ἐπὶ τῷ ὀνόματί μου καὶ δυνήσεται ταχὺ κακολογῆσαί με· 40 ὃς γὰρ οὐκ ἔστιν καθ᾽ ἡμῶν, ὑπὲρ ἡμῶν ἐστιν. 41 Ὃς γὰρ ἂν ποτίσῃ ὑμᾶς ποτήριον ὕδατος ἐν ὀνόματι ὅτι Χριστοῦ ἐστε, ἀμὴν λέγω ὑμῖν ὅτι οὐ μὴ ἀπολέσῃ τὸν μισθὸν αὐτοῦ.

9:42 Καὶ ὃς ἂν σκανδαλίσῃ ἕνα τῶν μικρῶν τούτων τῶν πιστευόντων [εἰς ἐμέ], καλόν ἐστιν αὐτῷ μᾶλλον εἰ περίκειται μύλος ὀνικὸς περὶ τὸν τράχηλον αὐτοῦ καὶ βέβληται εἰς τὴν θάλασσαν. 43 Καὶ ἐὰν σκανδαλίζῃ σε ἡ χείρ σου, ἀπόκοψον αὐτήν· καλόν ἐστίν σε κυλλὸν εἰσελθεῖν εἰς τὴν ζωὴν ἢ τὰς δύο χεῖρας ἔχοντα ἀπελθεῖν εἰς τὴν γέενναν, εἰς τὸ πῦρ τὸ ἄσβεστον. 45 καὶ ἐὰν ὁ πούς σου σκανδαλίζῃ σε, ἀπόκοψον αὐτόν· καλόν ἐστίν σε εἰσελθεῖν εἰς τὴν ζωὴν χωλὸν ἢ τοὺς δύο πόδας ἔχοντα βληθῆναι εἰς τὴν γέενναν. 47 καὶ ἐὰν ὁ ὀφθαλμός σου σκανδαλίζῃ σε, ἔκβαλε αὐτόν· καλόν σέ ἐστιν μονόφθαλμον εἰσελθεῖν εἰς τὴν

eyes   and be thrown   into   hell,   **48** where "'their worm   does not die,   and the fire is   not quenched.'
ὀφθαλμοὺς   →   βληθῆναι   εἰς ⌐τὴν γέενναν⌐   ὅπου αὐτῶν ὁ σκώληξ ⟶ οὐ τελευτᾷ καὶ τὸ πῦρ → οὐ σβέννυται
n.apm   f.ap   p.a d.asf n.asf   cj   r.gpm.3 d.nsm n.nsm   pl v.pai.3s cj d.nsn n.nsn   pl v.ppi.3s
4057   965   1650 3836 1147   3963 899   3836 5038   4024 5462   2779 3836 4786   4931 4024 4931

¶ **49** Everyone will be salted   with fire. ¶ **50** "Salt   is good, but if it   *loses its saltiness,* how
γὰρ Πᾶς   →   →   ἀλισθήσεται → πυρὶ   ⌐τὸ ἅλας⌐ → καλὸν δὲ ἐὰν ⌐τὸ ἅλας⌐ γένηται ἄναλον ἐν τίνι
cj a.nsm   v.fpi.3s   n.dsn   d.nsn n.nsn   a.nsn cj cj d.nsn n.nsn v.ams.3s a.nsn p.d r.dsn
1142 4246   245   4786   3836 229   2819 1254 1569 3836 229   1181   383   1877 5515

can you make it   salty   again? Have salt in yourselves, and be at peace   with each   other."
⟶ ⟶   ⟶ αὐτὸ ἀρτύσετε   ἔχετε ἅλα ἐν ἑαυτοῖς   καὶ → εἰρηνεύετε ἐν ἀλλήλοις ⟵
           r.asn.3 v.fai.2p   v.pam.2p n.asn p.d r.dpm.2   cj   v.pam.2p   p.d r.dpm
789 789 789 899   789   2400   229 1877 1571   2779   1644   1877 253

Divorce

10:1 Jesus then left   that   place and went into the region of Judea   and across the Jordan.   Again
Καὶ ἀναστὰς ἐκεῖθεν ⟵   ἔρχεται εἰς τὰ ὅρια → ⌐τῆς Ἰουδαίας⌐ καὶ πέραν τοῦ Ἰορδάνου καὶ πάλιν
cj pt.aa.nsm adv   v.pmi.3s p.a d.apn n.apn   d.gsf n.gsf   cj p.g   d.gsm n.gsm   cj adv
2779 482   1696   2262   1650 3836 3990   3836 2677   2779 4305 3836 2674   2779 4099

crowds of people came   to   him, and as was his custom,   he taught them. ¶ **2** Some
ὄχλοι   συμπορεύονται πρὸς αὐτόν καὶ ὡς →   εἰώθει   πάλιν ⟶ ἐδίδασκεν αὐτούς   Καὶ
n.npm   v.pmi.3p   p.a r.asm.3 cj cj   v.lai.3s   adv   v.iai.3s r.apm   cj
4063   5233   4639 899   2779 6055   1665   4099 1438   899   2779

Pharisees came   and tested   him by asking,   "Is it lawful for a man to divorce his wife?" ¶
Φαρισαῖοι προσελθόντες   πειράζοντες αὐτόν ἐπηρώτων αὐτὸν εἰ → ἔξεστιν ἀνδρὶ → ἀπολῦσαι γυναῖκα
n.npm   pt.aa.npm   pt.pa.npm   r.asm.3 v.iai.3p r.asm.3 cj   v.pai.3s n.dsm   f.aa   n.asf
5757   4665   4279   899   2089   899   1623 1997   467   668   1222

3 "What did Moses command you?" he replied.   ¶ **4** They said, "Moses permitted a man to
δὲ τί ⟶ Μωϋσῆς ἐνετείλατο ὑμῖν ὁ   ἀποκριθεὶς εἰπεν αὐτοῖς   δὲ οἱ   εἶπαν Μωϋσῆς ἐπέτρεψεν →
cj r.asn   n.nsm v.ami.3s   r.dp.2 d.nsm pt.ap.nsm v.aai.3s r.dpm.3   cj d.npm v.aai.3p n.nsm v.aai.3s
1254 5515   1948 1948   7007 3836 646   3306   3306   1254 3836 3306 3707 2205

write a certificate of divorce   and send   her away." ¶ **5** "It was because your hearts   were
γράψαι βιβλίον   → ἀποστασίου καὶ ἀπολῦσαι   δὲ   πρὸς ὑμῶν ⌐τὴν σκληροκαρδίαν⌐ ⟵
f.aa   n.asn   n.gsn   cj f.aa   cj   p.a rgp.2 d.asf n.asf
1711   1046   687   2779 668   1254   4639 7007 3836 5016

hard that Moses wrote you this law,"   Jesus   replied.   **6** "But at the beginning of creation God
⟵   ἔγραψεν ὑμῖν ταύτην ⌐τὴν ἐντολὴν⌐ ὁ Ἰησοῦς εἶπεν αὐτοῖς δὲ ἀπὸ ἀρχῆς → κτίσεως
         v.aai.3s r.dp.2 r.asf d.asf n.asf   d.nsm n.nsm v.aai.3s r.dpm.3 cj p.g n.gsf   n.gsf
         1211   7007 4047   3836 1953   3836 2652   3306   899   1254 608 794   3232

'made them male and female.' **7** 'For this reason a man   will leave his father   and mother   and be
ἐποίησεν αὐτοὺς ἄρσεν καὶ θῆλυ   ἕνεκεν τούτου ⟵   ἄνθρωπος καταλείψει αὐτοῦ ⌐τὸν πατέρα⌐ καὶ ⌐τὴν μητέρα⌐ καὶ ⟶
v.aai.3s r.apm.3 a.asn cj a.asn   p.g   r.gsn   n.nsm   v.fai.3s   r.gsm.3 d.asm n.asm cj d.asf n.asf   cj
4472   899   781   2779 2559   1914   4047   476   2901   899   3836 4252   2779 3836 3613   2779

united   to   his wife,   **8** and the two will become   one flesh.' So   they are no   longer two, but
προσκολληθήσεται πρὸς αὐτοῦ ⌐τὴν γυναῖκα⌐ καὶ οἱ δύο → ἔσονται εἰς μίαν σάρκα ὥστε → εἰσὶν οὐκέτι   δύο ἀλλὰ
v.fpi.3s   p.a r.gsm.3 d.asf n.asf   cj d.npm a.npm v.fmi.3p p.a a.asf n.asf cj   v.pai.3p adv   a.npm cj
4681   4639 899   3836 1222   2779 3836 1545 1639   1650 1651 4922 6063   1639 4033   1545 247

one.   **9** Therefore what God   has joined   together, let man   not separate." ¶ **10** When they were in
μία σάρξ οὖν   ὃ ὁ θεὸς⌐ συνέζευξεν ⟵   → ἄνθρωπος μὴ χωριζέτω   Καὶ   εἰς
a.nsf n.nsf cj   r.asn d.nsm n.nsm v.aai.3s   n.nsm pl v.pam.3s   cj   p.a
1651 4922 4036   4005 3836 2536   5183   6004 476 3590 6004   2779   1650

the house again, the disciples asked   Jesus about this. **11** He answered,   "Anyone who divorces his
τὴν οἰκίαν πάλιν οἱ μαθηταὶ ἐπηρώτων αὐτὸν περὶ τούτου καὶ → λέγει αὐτοῖς ἂν   ὃς ἀπολύσῃ αὐτοῦ
d.asf n.asf adv d.npm n.npm v.iai.3p r.asm.3 p.g r.gsn   cj v.pai.3s r.dpm.3 pl   r.nsm v.aas.3s r.gsm.3
3836 3864 4099 3836 3412 2089   899   4309 4047   2779 3306   899   323   4005 668   899

wife   and marries another woman commits adultery against her. **12** And if she divorces her husband and
⌐τὴν γυναῖκα⌐ καὶ γαμήσῃ ἄλλην ⟵ → μοιχᾶται ἐπ' αὐτήν   καὶ ἐὰν αὐτὴ ἀπολύσασα αὐτῆς ⌐τὸν ἄνδρα⌐
d.asf n.asf   cj v.aas.3s r.asf   v.ppi.3s p.a r.asf.3   cj cj r.nsf pt.aa.nsf r.gsf.3 d.asm n.asm
3836 1222   2779 1138   257   3656   2093 899   2779 1569 899   668   899   3836 467

βασιλείαν τοῦ θεοῦ ἢ δύο ὀφθαλμοὺς ἔχοντα βληθῆναι εἰς τὴν γέενναν, ⁴⁸ ὅπου ὁ σκώληξ αὐτῶν οὐ τελευτᾷ καὶ τὸ πῦρ οὐ σβέννυται. ¶ ⁴⁹ πᾶς γὰρ πυρὶ ἁλισθήσεται. ¶ ⁵⁰ Καλὸν τὸ ἅλας· ἐὰν δὲ τὸ ἅλας ἄναλον γένηται, ἐν τίνι αὐτὸ ἀρτύσετε; ἔχετε ἐν ἑαυτοῖς ἅλα καὶ εἰρηνεύετε ἐν ἀλλήλοις.

¹⁰:¹ Καὶ ἐκεῖθεν ἀναστὰς ἔρχεται εἰς τὰ ὅρια τῆς Ἰουδαίας [καὶ] πέραν τοῦ Ἰορδάνου, καὶ συμπορεύονται πάλιν ὄχλοι πρὸς αὐτόν, καὶ ὡς εἰώθει πάλιν ἐδίδασκεν αὐτούς. ¶ ² καὶ προσελθόντες Φαρισαῖοι ἐπηρώτων αὐτὸν εἰ ἔξεστιν ἀνδρὶ γυναῖκα ἀπολῦσαι, πειράζοντες αὐτόν. ¶ ³ ὁ δὲ ἀποκριθεὶς εἶπεν αὐτοῖς, Τί ὑμῖν ἐνετείλατο Μωϋσῆς; ¶ ⁴ οἱ δὲ εἶπαν, Ἐπέτρεψεν Μωϋσῆς βιβλίον ἀποστασίου γράψαι καὶ ἀπολῦσαι. ¶ ⁵ ὁ δὲ Ἰησοῦς εἶπεν αὐτοῖς, Πρὸς τὴν σκληροκαρδίαν ὑμῶν ἔγραψεν ὑμῖν τὴν ἐντολὴν ταύτην. ⁶ ἀπὸ δὲ ἀρχῆς κτίσεως ἄρσεν καὶ θῆλυ ἐποίησεν αὐτούς· ⁷ ἕνεκεν τούτου καταλείψει ἄνθρωπος τὸν πατέρα αὐτοῦ καὶ τὴν μητέρα [καὶ προσκολληθήσεται πρὸς τὴν γυναῖκα αὐτοῦ], ⁸ καὶ ἔσονται οἱ δύο εἰς σάρκα μίαν· ὥστε οὐκέτι εἰσὶν δύο ἀλλὰ μία σάρξ. ⁹ ὃ οὖν ὁ θεὸς συνέζευξεν ἄνθρωπος μὴ χωριζέτω. ¶ ¹⁰ Καὶ εἰς τὴν οἰκίαν πάλιν οἱ μαθηταὶ περὶ τούτου ἐπηρώτων αὐτόν. ¹¹ καὶ λέγει αὐτοῖς, Ὃς ἂν ἀπολύσῃ τὴν γυναῖκα αὐτοῦ καὶ γαμήσῃ ἄλλην μοιχᾶται ἐπ' αὐτήν· ¹² καὶ ἐὰν αὐτὴ ἀπολύσασα τὸν ἄνδρα αὐτῆς γαμήσῃ ἄλλον μοιχᾶται.

marries another man, she commits adultery."
γαμήσῃ ἄλλον ←　　　μοιχᾶται
v.aas.3s r.asm　　　　　v.ppi.3s
1138 257　　　　　　　3656

The Little Children and Jesus

10:13 People were bringing little children to Jesus to have him touch them, but the disciples rebuked
Καὶ →　→ προσέφερον → παιδία → αὐτῷ ἵνα →　→ ἅψηται αὐτῶν δὲ οἱ μαθηταὶ ἐπετίμησαν
cj　　　　v.iai.3p　n.apn　r.dsm.3 cj　　　　v.ams.3s r.gpn.3 cj d.npm n.npm v.aai.3p
2779　　　　4712　　4086　　899 2671　　　　721　　899　1254 3836 3412　2203

them. **14** When Jesus saw this, he was indignant. He said to them, "Let the little children come to
αὐτοῖς δὲ →　ὁ Ἰησοῦς, ἰδὼν →　ἠγανάκτησεν καὶ → εἶπεν αὐτοῖς ἄφετε τὰ παιδία ἔρχεσθαι πρός
r.dpm.3 cj　d.nsm n.nsm pt.aa.nsm　　v.aai.3s cj　v.aai.3s r.dpm.3 v.aam.2p d.apn n.apn f.pm p.a
899 1254 1625 3836 2652 1625　　24　　2779　3306 899 918 3836 4086 2262 4639

me, and do not hinder them, for the kingdom of God belongs to such as these. **15** I tell you the truth,
με →　μὴ κωλύετε αὐτά γὰρ ἡ βασιλεία → ⸂τοῦ θεοῦ⸃ ἐστιν → → ⸂τῶν τοιούτων⸃ → λέγω ὑμῖν ἀμὴν
r.as.1　pl v.pam.2p r.apn.3 cj d.nsf n.nsf　　d.gsm n.gsm v.pai.3s　　　d.gpn r.gpn　　v.pai.1s r.dp.2 pl
1609　　3266 3590 3266 899 1142 3836 993　　3836 2536 1639　　　　3836 5525　　3306 7007 297

anyone who will not receive the kingdom of God like a little child will never enter it." **16** And he
ἂν ὃς →　μὴ δέξηται τὴν βασιλείαν → ⸂τοῦ θεοῦ⸃ ὡς →　παιδίον → οὐ μὴ εἰσέλθῃ εἰς αὐτήν καὶ →
pl r.nsm　pl v.ams.3s d.asf n.asf　　d.gsm n.gsm p.a　　　n.nsn　　pl pl v.aas.3s p.a r.asf.3 cj
323 4005 1312 3590 1312 3836 993　3836 2536 6055　　4086　　1656 4024 3590 1656 1650 899 2779

took the children in his arms, put his hands on them and blessed them.
ἐναγκαλισάμενος αὐτὰ ←　←　τιθεὶς τὰς χεῖρας ἐπ' αὐτὰ κατευλόγει
pt.am.nsm　　　r.apn.3　　　　pt.pa.nsm d.apf n.apf p.a r.apn.3 v.iai.3s
1878　　　　　899　1878 1878 1878 5502 3836 5931 2093 899 2986

The Rich Young Man

10:17 As Jesus started on his way, a man ran up to him and fell on his knees before him.
Καὶ ⸂ αὐτοῦ ἐκπορευομένου εἰς ὁδὸν εἰς προσδραμὼν ←　καὶ γονυπετήσας ←　←　←　αὐτὸν
cj ⸂ r.gsm.3 pt.pm.gsm p.a n.asf a.nsm pt.aa.nsm　　cj pt.aa.nsm　　　　r.asm.3
2779 1744 899 1744 1650 3847 1651 4708　　2779 1206　　　　899

"Good teacher," he asked, "what must I do to inherit eternal life?" ¶ **18** "Why do you call
ἀγαθέ διδάσκαλε → ἐπηρώτα αὐτὸν τί →　→ ποιήσω ἵνα κληρονομήσω αἰώνιον ζωὴν δὲ τί →　λέγεις
a.vsm n.vsm　　v.iai.3s r.asm.3 r.asn　　v.aas.1s cj v.aas.1s a.asf n.asf cj r.asn　v.pai.2s
19 1437　　2089 899 5515　　4472 2671 3099 173 2437 1254 5515　3306

me good?" Jesus answered. "No one is good – except God alone. **19** You know the commandments:
με ἀγαθόν ὁ Ἰησοῦς, εἶπεν αὐτῷ οὐδεὶς ←　ἀγαθὸς ⸂εἰ μὴ⸃ ὁ θεός εἷς → οἶδας τὰς ἐντολάς
r.as.1 a.asm d.nsm n.nsm v.aai.3s r.dsm.3 a.nsm　　a.nsm cj pl d.nsm n.nsm a.nsm　v.rai.2s d.apf n.apf
1609 19 3836 2652 3306 899 4029　　19　1623 3590 3836 2536 1651　3857 3836 1953

'Do not murder, do not commit adultery, do not steal, do not give false testimony, do not defraud, honor
→ μὴ φονεύσῃς → μὴ →　μοιχεύσῃς → μὴ κλέψῃς → μὴ →　ψευδομαρτυρήσῃς → μὴ ἀποστερήσῃς τίμα
→ pl v.aas.2s → pl　　v.aas.2s → pl v.aas.2s → pl　　v.aas.2s　　→ pl v.aas.2s v.pam.2s
5839 3590 5839 3658 3590　3658　3096 3590 3096 6018 3590　6018　691 3590 691 5506

your father and mother.'" ¶ **20** "Teacher," he declared, "all these I have kept since I was
σου ⸂τὸν πατέρα⸃ καὶ ⸂τὴν μητέρα⸃ δὲ διδάσκαλε ὁ ἔφη αὐτῷ πάντα ταῦτα →　→ ἐφυλαξάμην ἐκ μου
r.gs.2 d.asm n.asm cj d.asf n.asf cj n.vsm d.nsm v.iai.3s r.dsm.3 a.apn r.apn　　v.ami.1s p.g r.gs.1
5148 3836 4252 2779 3836 3613 1254 1437 3836 5774 899 4246 4047　　5875 1666 1609

a boy." ¶ **21** Jesus looked at him and loved him. "One thing you lack," he said. "Go,
νεότητος δὲ ⸂ὁ Ἰησοῦς, ἐμβλέψας → αὐτῷ ἠγάπησεν αὐτὸν καὶ ἕν →　σε ὑστερεῖ → εἶπεν αὐτῷ ὕπαγε
n.gsf cj d.nsm n.nsm pt.aa.nsm　r.dsm.3 v.aai.3s r.asm.3 cj a.nsn　r.as.2 v.pai.3s　v.aai.3s r.dsm.3 v.pam.2s
3744 1254 3836 2652 1063　899 26 899 2779 1651　5148 5728　3306 899 5632

sell everything you have and give to the poor, and you will have treasure in heaven. Then come, follow
πώλησον ὅσα →　ἔχεις καὶ δὸς → τοῖς πτωχοῖς καὶ →　ἕξεις θησαυρὸν ἐν οὐρανῷ καὶ δεῦρο ἀκολούθει
v.aam.2s r.apn　v.pai.2s cj v.aam.2s d.dpm a.dpm cj　v.fai.2s n.asm p.d n.dsm cj j v.pam.2s
4797 4012　2400 2779 1443 3836 4777 2779　2400 2565 1877 4041 2779 1306 199

me." ¶ **22** At this the man's face fell. He went away sad, because he had great
μοι δὲ ἐπὶ ⸂τῷ λόγῳ⸃ στυγνάσας ὁ ἀπῆλθεν λυπούμενος γὰρ →　ἦν ἔχων πολλά
r.ds.1 cj p.d d.dsm n.dsm pt.aa.nsm d.nsm v.aai.3s pt.pp.nsm cj　v.iai.3s pt.pa.nsm a.apn
1609 1254 2093 3836 3364 5145 3836 599 3382 1142　1639 2400 4498

10:13 Καὶ προσέφερον αὐτῷ παιδία ἵνα αὐτῶν ἅψηται· οἱ δὲ μαθηταὶ ἐπετίμησαν αὐτοῖς. **14** ἰδὼν δὲ ὁ Ἰησοῦς ἠγανάκτησεν καὶ εἶπεν αὐτοῖς, Ἄφετε τὰ παιδία ἔρχεσθαι πρός με, μὴ κωλύετε αὐτά, τῶν γὰρ τοιούτων ἐστὶν ἡ βασιλεία τοῦ θεοῦ. **15** ἀμὴν λέγω ὑμῖν, ὃς ἂν μὴ δέξηται τὴν βασιλείαν τοῦ θεοῦ ὡς παιδίον, οὐ μὴ εἰσέλθῃ εἰς αὐτήν. **16** καὶ ἐναγκαλισάμενος αὐτὰ κατευλόγει τιθεὶς τὰς χεῖρας ἐπ' αὐτά. **17** Καὶ ἐκπορευομένου αὐτοῦ εἰς ὁδὸν προσδραμὼν εἷς καὶ γονυπετήσας αὐτὸν ἐπηρώτα αὐτόν, Διδάσκαλε ἀγαθέ, τί ποιήσω ἵνα ζωὴν αἰώνιον κληρονομήσω; ¶ **18** ὁ δὲ Ἰησοῦς εἶπεν αὐτῷ, Τί με λέγεις ἀγαθόν; οὐδεὶς ἀγαθὸς εἰ μὴ εἷς ὁ θεός. **19** τὰς ἐντολὰς οἶδας· Μὴ φονεύσῃς, Μὴ μοιχεύσῃς, Μὴ κλέψῃς, Μὴ ψευδομαρτυρήσῃς, Μὴ ἀποστερήσῃς, Τίμα τὸν πατέρα σου καὶ τὴν μητέρα. ¶ **20** ὁ δὲ ἔφη αὐτῷ, Διδάσκαλε, ταῦτα πάντα ἐφυλαξάμην ἐκ νεότητός μου. ¶ **21** ὁ δὲ Ἰησοῦς ἐμβλέψας αὐτῷ ἠγάπησεν αὐτὸν καὶ εἶπεν αὐτῷ, Ἕν σε ὑστερεῖ· ὕπαγε, ὅσα ἔχεις πώλησον καὶ δὸς [τοῖς] πτωχοῖς, καὶ ἕξεις θησαυρὸν ἐν οὐρανῷ, καὶ δεῦρο ἀκολούθει μοι. ¶ **22** ὁ δὲ στυγνάσας ἐπὶ τῷ λόγῳ ἀπῆλθεν λυπούμενος· ἦν γὰρ ἔχων κτήματα

wealth. ¶ **23** Jesus looked around and said to his disciples, "How hard it is for the
κτήματα　Καὶ ὁ Ἰησοῦς περιβλεψάμενος ← λέγει → αὐτοῦ τοῖς μαθηταῖς πῶς δυσκόλως οἱ
n.apn　d.nsm n.nsm pt.am.nsm　v.pai.3s r.gsm.3 d.dpm n.dpm pl adv d.npm
3228　2779 3836 2652 4315　3306 3412 899 3836 3412 4802 1552 3836

rich to enter the kingdom of God!" ¶ **24** The disciples were amazed at his
τὰ χρήματα ἔχοντες → εἰσελεύσονται εἰς τὴν βασιλείαν → τοῦ θεοῦ δὲ οἱ μαθηταὶ → ἐθαμβοῦντο ἐπὶ αὐτοῦ
d.apn n.apn pt.pa.npm　v.fmi.3p p.a d.asf n.asf d.gsm n.gsm cj d.npm n.dpm v.ipi.3p p.d r.gsm.3
3836 5975 2400　1656 1650 3836 993 3836 2536 1254 3836 3412 2501 2093 899

words. But Jesus said again, "Children, how hard it is to enter the kingdom
τοῖς λόγοις δὲ ὁ Ἰησοῦς ἀποκριθεὶς λέγει πάλιν αὐτοῖς τέκνα πῶς δύσκολόν → ἐστιν → εἰσελθεῖν εἰς τὴν βασιλείαν
d.dpm n.dpm cj d.nsm n.nsm pt.ap.nsm v.pai.3s adv r.dpm.3 n.vpn pl a.nsn v.pai.3s f.aa p.a d.asf n.asf
3836 3364 1254 3836 2652 646 3306 4099 899 5451 4802 1551 1639 1656 1650 3836 993

of God! **25** It is easier for a camel to go through the eye of a needle than for a rich man to
→ τοῦ θεοῦ → ἐστιν εὐκοπώτερον κάμηλον → διελθεῖν διὰ τῆς τρυμαλιᾶς → ῥαφίδος ἢ πλούσιον →
d.gsm n.gsm v.pai.3s a.nsn.c n.asf f.aa p.g d.gsf n.gsf n.gsf pl n.asm
3836 2536 1639 2324 2823 1451 1328 3836 5584 4827 2445 4454

enter the kingdom of God." ¶ **26** The disciples were even more amazed, and said to each
εἰσελθεῖν εἰς τὴν βασιλείαν → τοῦ θεοῦ δὲ οἱ ↗ → περισσῶς ἐξεπλήσσοντο λέγοντες πρὸς ἑαυτούς
f.aa p.a d.asf n.asf d.gsm n.gsm cj d.npm adv v.ipi.3p pt.pa.npm p.a r.apm.3
1656 1650 3836 993 3836 2536 1254 3836 4360 1742 3306 4639 1571

other, "Who then can be saved?" ¶ **27** Jesus looked at them and said, "With man this is impossible,
← τίς καὶ δύναται → σωθῆναι ὁ Ἰησοῦς ἐμβλέψας → αὐτοῖς λέγει παρὰ ἀνθρώποις ἀδύνατον
r.nsm cj v.ppi.3s f.ap d.nsm n.nsm pt.aa.nsm r.dpm.3 v.pai.3s p.d n.dpm a.nsn
5515 2779 1538 5392 3836 2652 1838 899 3306 4123 476 105

but not with God; all things are possible with God." ¶ **28** Peter said to him, "We have
ἀλλ' οὐ παρὰ θεῷ γὰρ πάντα ← δυνατὰ παρὰ τῷ θεῷ ὁ Πέτρος Ἤρξατο λέγειν αὐτῷ ἰδοὺ ἡμεῖς →
cj pl p.d n.dsm cj a.npn a.npn p.d d.dsm n.dsm d.nsm n.nsm v.ami.3s f.pa r.dsm.3 j r.np.1
247 4024 4123 2536 1142 4246 1543 4123 3836 2536 3836 4377 806 3306 899 2627 7005

left everything to follow you!" ¶ **29** "I tell you the truth," Jesus replied, "no one who
ἀφήκαμεν πάντα καὶ → ἠκολουθήκαμεν σοι λέγω ὑμῖν ἀμὴν ὁ Ἰησοῦς ἔφη οὐδείς ← ἐστιν ὃς
v.aai.1p a.apn cj v.rai.1p r.ds.2 v.pai.1s r.dp.2 pl d.nsm n.nsm v.iai.3s a.nsm v.pai.3s r.nsm
918 4246 2779 199 5148 3306 7007 297 3836 2652 5774 4029 1639 4005

has left home or brothers or sisters or mother or father or children or fields for me and the
→ ἀφῆκεν οἰκίαν ἢ ἀδελφοὺς ἢ ἀδελφὰς ἢ μητέρα ἢ πατέρα ἢ τέκνα ἢ ἀγροὺς ἕνεκεν ἐμοῦ καὶ ἕνεκεν τοῦ
v.aai.3s n.asf cj n.apm cj n.apf cj n.asf cj n.asm cj n.apn cj n.apm p.g r.gs.1 cj p.g d.gsn
918 3864 2445 81 2445 80 2445 3613 2445 4252 2445 5451 2445 69 1914 1609 2779 1914 3836

gospel **30** *will fail* to receive a hundred times as much in this present age (homes, brothers,
εὐαγγελίου ἐὰν μὴ λάβῃ ἑκατονταπλασίονα ← ἐν τούτῳ νῦν τῷ καιρῷ οἰκίας καὶ ἀδελφοὺς καὶ
n.gsn cj pl v.aas.3s a.apn p.d r.dsm adv d.dsm n.dsm n.apf cj n.apm cj
2295 1569 3590 3284 1671 1877 4047 3814 3836 2789 3864 2779 81 2779

sisters, mothers, children and fields – and with them, persecutions) and in the age to come, eternal
ἀδελφὰς καὶ μητέρας καὶ τέκνα καὶ ἀγροὺς μετὰ διωγμῶν καὶ ἐν τῷ αἰῶνι → τῷ ἐρχομένῳ αἰώνιον
n.apf cj n.apf cj n.apn cj n.apm p.g n.gpm cj p.d d.dsm n.dsm d.dsm pt.pm.dsm a.asf
80 2779 3613 2779 5451 2779 69 3552 1501 2779 1877 3836 172 3836 2262 173

life. **31** But many who are first will be last, and the last first."
ζωὴν δὲ πολλοὶ πρῶτοι → ἔσονται ἔσχατοι καὶ οἱ ἔσχατοι πρῶτοι
n.asf cj a.npm a.npm v.fmi.3p a.npm cj d.npm a.npm a.npm
2437 1254 4498 4755 1639 2274 2779 3836 2274 4755

Jesus Again Predicts His Death

10:32 They were on their way up to Jerusalem, with Jesus leading the way, and the
δὲ → Ἦσαν ἐν τῇ ὁδῷ ἀναβαίνοντες εἰς Ἱεροσόλυμα καὶ ὁ Ἰησοῦς ἦν προάγων αὐτοὺς ← καὶ
cj v.iai.3p p.d d.dsf n.dsf pt.pa.npm p.a n.apn cj d.nsm n.nsm v.iai.3s pt.pa.nsm r.apm.3 cj
1254 1639 1877 3836 3847 326 1650 2642 2779 3836 2652 1639 4575 899 4575 4575 2779

disciples were astonished, while those who followed were afraid. Again he took the Twelve aside and
→ ἐθαμβοῦντο δὲ οἱ ← ἀκολουθοῦντες → ἐφοβοῦντο καὶ πάλιν → παραλαβὼν τοὺς δώδεκα ←
v.ipi.3p cj d.npm pt.pa.npm v.ipi.3p cj adv pt.aa.nsm d.apm a.apm
2501 1254 3836 199 5828 2779 4099 4161 3836 1557 4161

πολλά. ¶ 23 Καὶ περιβλεψάμενος ὁ Ἰησοῦς λέγει τοῖς μαθηταῖς αὐτοῦ, Πῶς δυσκόλως οἱ τὰ χρήματα ἔχοντες εἰς τὴν βασιλείαν τοῦ θεοῦ εἰσελεύσονται. ¶ 24 οἱ δὲ μαθηταὶ ἐθαμβοῦντο ἐπὶ τοῖς λόγοις αὐτοῦ. ὁ δὲ Ἰησοῦς πάλιν ἀποκριθεὶς λέγει αὐτοῖς, Τέκνα, πῶς δύσκολόν ἐστιν εἰς τὴν βασιλείαν τοῦ θεοῦ εἰσελθεῖν· 25 εὐκοπώτερόν ἐστιν κάμηλον διὰ [τῆς] τρυμαλιᾶς [τῆς] ῥαφίδος διελθεῖν ἢ πλούσιον εἰς τὴν βασιλείαν τοῦ θεοῦ εἰσελθεῖν. ¶ 26 οἱ δὲ περισσῶς ἐξεπλήσσοντο λέγοντες πρὸς ἑαυτούς, Καὶ τίς δύναται σωθῆναι; ¶ 27 ἐμβλέψας αὐτοῖς ὁ Ἰησοῦς λέγει, Παρὰ ἀνθρώποις ἀδύνατον, ἀλλ' οὐ παρὰ θεῷ· πάντα γὰρ δυνατὰ παρὰ τῷ θεῷ. ¶ 28 Ἤρξατο λέγειν ὁ Πέτρος αὐτῷ, Ἰδοὺ ἡμεῖς ἀφήκαμεν πάντα καὶ ἠκολουθήκαμέν σοι ¶ 29 ἔφη ὁ Ἰησοῦς, Ἀμὴν λέγω ὑμῖν, οὐδείς ἐστιν ὃς ἀφῆκεν οἰκίαν ἢ ἀδελφοὺς ἢ ἀδελφὰς ἢ μητέρα ἢ πατέρα ἢ τέκνα ἢ ἀγροὺς ἕνεκεν ἐμοῦ καὶ ἕνεκεν τοῦ εὐαγγελίου, 30 ἐὰν μὴ λάβῃ ἑκατονταπλασίονα νῦν ἐν τῷ καιρῷ τούτῳ οἰκίας καὶ ἀδελφοὺς καὶ ἀδελφὰς καὶ μητέρας καὶ τέκνα καὶ ἀγροὺς μετὰ διωγμῶν, καὶ ἐν τῷ αἰῶνι τῷ ἐρχομένῳ ζωὴν αἰώνιον. 31 πολλοὶ δὲ ἔσονται πρῶτοι ἔσχατοι καὶ [οἱ] ἔσχατοι πρῶτοι.

10:32 5Ἦσαν δὲ ἐν τῇ ὁδῷ ἀναβαίνοντες εἰς Ἱεροσόλυμα, καὶ ἦν προάγων αὐτοὺς ὁ Ἰησοῦς, καὶ ἐθαμβοῦντο, οἱ δὲ

told them what was going to happen to him. [33] "We are going up to Jerusalem," he said,
ἤρξατο λέγειν αὐτοῖς τὰ → μέλλοντα → συμβαίνειν → αὐτῷ ὅτι ἰδοὺ → ἀναβαίνομεν ← εἰς Ἰεροσόλυμα
v.ami.3s f.pa r.dpm.3 d.apn pt.pa.apn f.pa r.dsm.3 cj j v.pai.1p p.a n.apn
806 3306 899 3836 3516 5201 899 4022 2627 326 1650 2642

"and the Son of Man will be betrayed to the chief priests and teachers of the law.
καὶ ὁ υἱὸς → ⌐τοῦ ἀνθρώπου⌐ → → παραδοθήσεται → τοῖς ἀρχιερεῦσιν ← καὶ ⌐τοῖς γραμματεῦσιν⌐ ← ← ← καὶ
cj d.nsm n.nsm d.gsm n.gsm v.fpi.3s d.dpm n.dpm cj d.dpm n.dpm cj
2779 3836 5626 3836 476 4140 3836 797 2779 3836 1208 2779

They will condemn him to death and will hand him over to the Gentiles, [34] who will mock him
→ κατακρινοῦσιν αὐτὸν → θανάτῳ καὶ → παραδώσουσιν αὐτὸν ↶ → τοῖς ἔθνεσιν καὶ → → ἐμπαίξουσιν αὐτῷ
v.fai.3p r.asm.3 n.dsm cj v.fai.3p r.asm.3 d.dpm n.dpn cj v.fai.3p r.dsm.3
2891 899 2505 2779 4140 899 4140 3836 1620 2779 1850 899

and spit on him, flog him and kill him. Three days later he will rise."
καὶ ἐμπτύσουσιν αὐτῷ καὶ μαστιγώσουσιν αὐτὸν καὶ ἀποκτενοῦσιν καὶ μετὰ τρεῖς ἡμέρας ↶ → ἀναστήσεται
cj v.fai.3p r.dsm.3 cj v.fai.3p r.asm.3 cj v.fai.3p cj p.a a.apf n.apf v.fmi.3s
2779 1870 899 2779 3463 899 2779 650 2779 3552 5552 2465 3552 482

The Request of James and John

[10:35] Then James and John, the sons of Zebedee, came to him. "Teacher," they said, "we
Καὶ Ἰάκωβος καὶ Ἰωάννης οἱ υἱοὶ → Ζεβεδαίου προσπορεύονται → αὐτῷ διδάσκαλε → λέγοντες αὐτῷ →
cj n.nsm cj n.nsm d.npm n.npm n.gsm v.pmi.3p r.dsm.3 n.vsm pt.pa.npm r.dsm.3
2779 2610 2779 2722 3836 5626 2411 4702 899 1437 3306 899

want you to do for us whatever we ask." ¶ [36] "What do you want me to do for you?"
θέλομεν ἵνα → → ποιήσῃς → ἡμῖν ὃ ἐὰν → αἰτήσωμεν σε δὲ τί → → θέλετέ με → ποιήσω ὑμῖν
v.pai.1p cj v.aas.2s r.dp.1 r.asn pl v.aas.1p r.as.2 cj r.asn v.pai.2p r.as.1 v.aas.1s r.dp.2
2527 2671 4472 7005 4005 1569 160 5148 1254 5515 2527 1609 4472 7007

he asked. ¶ [37] They replied, "Let one of us sit at your right and the other at your
ὁ εἶπεν αὐτοῖς δὲ οἱ εἶπαν αὐτῷ δὸς εἷς ἡμῖν ἵνα καθίσωμεν ἐκ σου δεξιῶν καὶ εἷς ἐξ
d.nsm v.aai.3s r.dpm.3 cj d.npm v.aai.3p r.dsm.3 v.aam.2s a.nsm r.dp.1 cj v.aas.1p p.g r.gs.2 a.gpf cj a.nsm p.g
3836 3306 899 1254 3836 3306 899 1443 1651 7005 2671 2767 1666 5148 1288 2779 1651 1666

left in your glory." ¶ [38] "You don't know what you are asking," Jesus said. "Can you
ἀριστερῶν ἐν σου τῇ δόξῃ δὲ → οὐκ οἴδατε τί → → αἰτεῖσθε ὁ Ἰησοῦς εἶπεν αὐτοῖς δύνασθε ←
a.gpf p.d r.gs.2 d.dsf n.dsf cj pl v.rai.2p r.asn v.pmi.2p d.nsm n.nsm v.aai.3s r.dpm.3 v.ppi.2p
754 1877 5148 3836 1518 1254 3857 4024 3857 5515 160 3836 2652 3306 899 1538

drink the cup I drink or be baptized with the baptism I am baptized with?" ¶ [39] "We
πιεῖν τὸ ποτήριον ὃ ἐγὼ πίνω ἢ → βαπτισθῆναι τὸ βάπτισμα ὃ ἐγὼ → βαπτίζομαι δὲ →
f.aa d.asn n.asn r.asn r.ns.1 v.pai.1s cj f.ap d.asn n.asn r.asn r.ns.1 v.ppi.1s cj
4403 3836 4539 4005 1609 4403 2445 966 3836 967 4005 1609 966 1254

can," they answered. Jesus said to them, "You will drink the cup I drink and be
δυνάμεθα οἱ εἶπαν αὐτῷ δὲ ὁ Ἰησοῦς εἶπεν αὐτοῖς → πίεσθε τὸ ποτήριον ὃ ἐγὼ πίνω καὶ →
v.ppi.1p d.npm v.aai.3p r.dsm.3 cj d.nsm n.nsm v.aai.3s r.dpm.3 v.fmi.2p d.asn n.asn r.asn r.ns.1 v.pai.1s cj
1538 3836 3306 899 1254 3836 2652 3306 899 4403 3836 4539 4005 1609 4403 2779

baptized with the baptism I am baptized with, [40] but to sit at my right or left is not for
βαπτισθήσεσθε τὸ βάπτισμα ὃ ἐγὼ → βαπτίζομαι δὲ → ⌐τὸ καθίσαι⌐ ἐκ μου δεξιῶν ἢ ἐξ εὐωνύμων ἔστιν οὐκ
v.fpi.2p d.asn n.asn r.asn r.ns.1 v.ppi.1s cj d.nsn f.aa p.g r.gs.1 a.gpf cj p.g a.gpf v.pai.3s pl
966 3836 967 4005 1609 966 1254 3836 2767 1666 1609 1288 2445 1666 2381 1639 4024

me to grant. These places belong to those for whom they have been prepared." ¶ [41] When the ten
ἐμὸν → δοῦναι ἀλλ' → → οἷς → → ἡτοίμασται Καὶ → οἱ δέκα
r.nsn.1 f.aa cj r.dpm v.rpi.3s cj d.npm a.npm
1847 1443 247 4005 2286 2779 201 3836 1274

heard about this, they became indignant with James and John. [42] Jesus called them together
ἀκούσαντες → ἤρξαντο ἀγανακτεῖν περὶ Ἰακώβου καὶ Ἰωάννου καὶ ὁ Ἰησοῦς προσκαλεσάμενος αὐτοὺς →
pt.aa.npm v.ami.3p f.pa p.g n.gsm cj n.gsm cj d.nsm n.nsm pt.am.nsm r.apm.3
201 806 24 4309 2610 2779 2722 2779 3836 2652 4673 899 4673

and said, "You know that those who are regarded as rulers of the Gentiles lord it over them, and
λέγει αὐτοῖς → οἴδατε ὅτι οἱ ← → δοκοῦντες → ἄρχειν → τῶν ἐθνῶν κατακυριεύουσιν ← αὐτῶν καὶ
v.pai.3s r.dpm.3 v.rai.2p cj d.npm pt.pa.npm f.pa d.gpn n.gpn v.pai.3p r.gpn.3 cj
3306 899 3857 4022 3836 1506 806 3836 1620 2894 899 2779

ἀκολουθοῦντες ἐφοβοῦντο. καὶ παραλαβὼν πάλιν τοὺς δώδεκα ἤρξατο αὐτοῖς λέγειν τὰ μέλλοντα αὐτῷ συμβαίνειν [33] ὅτι Ἰδοὺ ἀναβαίνομεν εἰς Ἱεροσόλυμα, καὶ ὁ υἱὸς τοῦ ἀνθρώπου παραδοθήσεται τοῖς ἀρχιερεῦσιν καὶ τοῖς γραμματεῦσιν, καὶ κατακρινοῦσιν αὐτὸν θανάτῳ καὶ παραδώσουσιν αὐτὸν τοῖς ἔθνεσιν [34] καὶ ἐμπαίξουσιν αὐτῷ καὶ ἐμπτύσουσιν αὐτῷ καὶ μαστιγώσουσιν αὐτὸν καὶ ἀποκτενοῦσιν, καὶ μετὰ τρεῖς ἡμέρας ἀναστήσεται.

[10:35] Καὶ προσπορεύονται αὐτῷ Ἰάκωβος καὶ Ἰωάννης οἱ υἱοὶ Ζεβεδαίου λέγοντες αὐτῷ, Διδάσκαλε, θέλομεν ἵνα ὃ ἐὰν αἰτήσωμέν σε ποιήσῃς ἡμῖν. ¶ [36] ὁ δὲ εἶπεν αὐτοῖς, Τί θέλετέ [με] ποιήσω ὑμῖν; ¶ [37] οἱ δὲ εἶπαν αὐτῷ, Δὸς ἡμῖν ἵνα εἷς σου ἐκ δεξιῶν καὶ εἷς ἐξ ἀριστερῶν καθίσωμεν ἐν τῇ δόξῃ σου. ¶ [38] ὁ δὲ Ἰησοῦς εἶπεν αὐτοῖς, Οὐκ οἴδατε τί αἰτεῖσθε. δύνασθε πιεῖν τὸ ποτήριον ὃ ἐγὼ πίνω ἢ τὸ βάπτισμα ὃ ἐγὼ βαπτίζομαι βαπτισθῆναι; ¶ [39] οἱ δὲ εἶπαν αὐτῷ, Δυνάμεθα. ὁ δὲ Ἰησοῦς εἶπεν αὐτοῖς, Τὸ ποτήριον ὃ ἐγὼ πίνω πίεσθε καὶ τὸ βάπτισμα ὃ ἐγὼ βαπτίζομαι βαπτισθήσεσθε, [40] τὸ δὲ καθίσαι ἐκ δεξιῶν μου ἢ ἐξ εὐωνύμων οὐκ ἔστιν ἐμὸν δοῦναι, ἀλλ' οἷς ἡτοίμασται. ¶ [41] Καὶ ἀκούσαντες οἱ δέκα ἤρξαντο ἀγανακτεῖν περὶ Ἰακώβου καὶ Ἰωάννου. [42] καὶ προσκαλεσάμενος αὐτοὺς ὁ Ἰησοῦς λέγει αὐτοῖς, Οἴδατε ὅτι οἱ δοκοῦντες ἄρχειν τῶν ἐθνῶν κατακυριεύουσιν

their high   officials exercise   authority over them. **43** Not so   with you. Instead, whoever wants to
αὐτῶν ‹οἱ μεγάλοι› ← κατεξουσιάζουσιν ←   ← αὐτῶν δὲ οὐχ οὕτως ἐστιν ἐν ὑμῖν ἀλλ᾽ ‹ὃς ἂν θέλῃ →
r.gpn.3 d.npm a.npm   v.pai.3p   r.gpn.3 cj pl adv v.pai.3s p.d r.dp.2 cj r.nsm pl v.pas.3s
899 3836 3489   2980   899 1254 4024 4048 1639 1877 7007 247 4005 323 2527

become great among you must be   your servant, **44** and whoever wants to be first   must be slave of
γενέσθαι μέγας ἐν ὑμῖν → ἔσται ὑμῶν διάκονος καὶ ‹ὃς ἂν› θέλῃ → εἶναι πρῶτος ἐν ὑμῖν → ἔσται δοῦλος →
f.am a.nsm p.d r.dp.2   v.fmi.3s r.gp.2 n.nsm cj r.nsm pl v.pas.3s f.pa a.nsm p.d r.dp.2 v.fmi.3s n.nsm
1181 3489 1877 7007   1639 7007 1356 2779 4005 323 2527 1639 4755 1877 7007 1639 1529

all. **45** For even the Son of Man   did not come to be served,   but to serve,   and to give his
πάντων γὰρ καὶ ὁ υἱὸς → ‹τοῦ ἀνθρώπου› → οὐκ ἦλθεν → → διακονηθῆναι ἀλλὰ → διακονῆσαι καὶ → δοῦναι αὐτοῦ
a.gpm cj adv d.nsm n.nsm d.gsm n.gsm pl v.aai.3s f.ap cj f.aa cj f.aa r.gsm.3
4246 1142 2779 3836 5626 3836 476   2262 4024 2262   1354 247 1354 2779 1443 899

life   as a ransom for many."
‹τὴν ψυχὴν› λύτρον ἀντὶ πολλῶν
d.asf n.asf n.asn p.g a.gpm
3836 6034 3389 505 4498

Blind Bartimaeus Receives His Sight

10:46 Then they came   to Jericho.   As Jesus and his   disciples,   together with a large   crowd, were
Καὶ → ἔρχονται εἰς Ἰεριχώ Καὶ → αὐτοῦ καὶ αὐτοῦ ‹τῶν μαθητῶν› καὶ ← ἱκανοῦ ὄχλου →
cj v.pmi.3p p.a n.asf cj r.gsm.3 cj r.gsm.3 d.gpm n.gpm cj a.gsm n.gsm
2779 2262 1650 2637 2779 1744 899 2779 899 3836 3412 2779 2653 4063

leaving   the city, a blind man, Bartimaeus (that is, the Son of Timaeus),   was sitting by the roadside
ἐκπορευομένου ἀπὸ Ἰεριχώ τυφλὸς ← Βαρτιμαῖος ὁ υἱὸς → Τιμαίου → ἐκάθητο παρὰ τὴν ὁδόν
pt.pm.gsm p.g n.dsf a.nsm n.nsm d.nsm n.nsm n.gsm v.imi.3s p.a d.asf n.asf
1744 608 2637 5603 985 3836 5626 5505 2764 4123 3836 3847

begging. **47** When he heard   that it was Jesus of Nazareth,   he began to shout,   "Jesus, Son of
προσαίτης καὶ → → ἀκούσας ὅτι → ἐστιν Ἰησοῦς → ὁ Ναζαρηνός → ἤρξατο → κράζειν καὶ λέγειν Ἰησοῦ υἱὲ →
n.nsm cj pt.aa.nsm cj v.pai.3s n.nsm d.nsm n.nsm v.ami.3s f.pa cj f.pa n.vsm n.vsm
4645 2779 201 4022 1639 2652 3836 3716 806 3189 2779 3306 2652 5626

David, have mercy on me!" ¶ **48** Many rebuked him   and told him to be quiet,   but he shouted all
Δαυίδ → ἐλέησον ← με καὶ πολλοὶ ἐπετίμων αὐτῷ ἵνα → → σιωπήσῃ δὲ ὁ ἔκραζεν πολλῷ
n.gsm v.aam.2s r.as.1 cj a.npm v.iai.3p r.dsm.3 cj v.aas.3s cj d.nsm v.iai.3s a.dsn
1253 1796 1609 2779 4498 2203 899 2671 4995 1254 3836 3189 4498

the more, "Son of David, have mercy on me!" ¶ **49** Jesus   stopped and said, "Call him." ¶ So
μᾶλλον υἱὲ → Δαυίδ → ἐλέησον ← με καὶ ὁ Ἰησοῦς στὰς εἶπεν φωνήσατε αὐτόν καὶ
adv.c n.vsm n.gsm v.aam.2s r.as.1 cj d.nsm n.nsm pt.aa.nsm v.aai.3s v.aam.2p r.asm.3 cj
3437 5626 1253 1796 1609 2779 3836 2652 2705 3306 5888 899 2779

they called to the blind man,   "Cheer up! On your feet! He's calling you." ¶ **50** Throwing
→ φωνοῦσιν ← τὸν τυφλὸν λέγοντες αὐτῷ θάρσει → ἔγειρε ← φωνεῖ σε δὲ ἀποβαλὼν
v.pai.3p d.asm a.asm pt.pa.npm r.dsm.3 v.pam.2s v.pam.2s v.pai.3s r.as.2 cj pt.aa.nsm
5888 3836 5603 3306 899 2510 1586 5888 5148 1254 610

his cloak   aside, he jumped to his feet and came to Jesus. ¶ **51** "What do you want me to
αὐτοῦ ‹τὸ ἱμάτιον› ὁ ἀναπηδήσας ← ← ἦλθεν πρὸς τὸν Ἰησοῦν καὶ τί → → θέλεις →
r.gsm.3 d.asn n.asn d.nsm pt.aa.nsm v.aai.3s p.a d.asm n.asm cj r.asn v.pai.2s
899 3836 2668 610 3836 403 2262 4639 3836 2652 2779 5515 2527

do for you?" Jesus   asked him. The blind man said, "Rabbi, I want to see." ¶
ποιήσω → σοι ὁ Ἰησοῦς ἀποκριθεὶς αὐτῷ εἶπεν δὲ ὁ τυφλὸς ← εἶπεν αὐτῷ ῥαββουνί ἵνα → → ἀναβλέψω
v.aas.1s r.ds.2 d.nsm n.nsm pt.ap.nsm r.dsm.3 v.aai.3s cj d.nsm a.nsm v.aai.3s r.dsm.3 n.nsm cj v.aas.1s
4472 5148 3836 2652 646 899 3306 1254 3836 5603 3306 899 4808 2671 329

52 "Go," said Jesus,   "your faith   has healed you." Immediately he received his sight and followed
καὶ ὕπαγε εἶπεν ὁ Ἰησοῦς αὐτῷ σου ‹ἡ πίστις› → σέσωκεν σε καὶ εὐθὺς → ἀνέβλεψεν καὶ ἠκολούθει
cj v.pam.2s v.aai.3s d.nsm n.nsm r.dsm.3 r.gs.2 d.nsf n.nsf v.rai.3s r.as.2 cj adv v.aai.3s cj v.iai.3s
2779 5632 3306 3836 2652 899 5148 3836 4411 5392 5148 2779 2318 329 2779 199

Jesus along the road.
αὐτῷ ἐν τῇ ὁδῷ
r.dsm.3 p.d d.dsf n.dsf
899 1877 3836 3847

αὐτῶν καὶ οἱ μεγάλοι αὐτῶν κατεξουσιάζουσιν αὐτῶν. **43** οὐχ οὕτως δέ ἐστιν ἐν ὑμῖν, ἀλλ᾽ ὃς ἂν θέλῃ μέγας γενέσθαι ἐν ὑμῖν ἔσται ὑμῶν διάκονος, **44** καὶ ὃς ἂν θέλῃ ἐν ὑμῖν εἶναι πρῶτος ἔσται πάντων δοῦλος· **45** καὶ γὰρ ὁ υἱὸς τοῦ ἀνθρώπου οὐκ ἦλθεν διακονηθῆναι ἀλλὰ διακονῆσαι καὶ δοῦναι τὴν ψυχὴν αὐτοῦ λύτρον ἀντὶ πολλῶν.

10:46 Καὶ ἔρχονται εἰς Ἰεριχώ. καὶ ἐκπορευομένου αὐτοῦ ἀπὸ Ἰεριχὼ καὶ τῶν μαθητῶν αὐτοῦ καὶ ὄχλου ἱκανοῦ ὁ υἱὸς Τιμαίου Βαρτιμαῖος, τυφλὸς ἐκάθητο παρὰ τὴν ὁδὸν «ὁδόν.» προσαιτῶν. «προσαίτης,» **47** καὶ ἀκούσας ὅτι Ἰησοῦς ὁ Ναζαρηνός ἐστιν ἤρξατο κράζειν καὶ λέγειν, Υἱὲ Δαυὶδ Ἰησοῦ, ἐλέησόν με. ¶ **48** καὶ ἐπετίμων αὐτῷ πολλοὶ ἵνα σιωπήσῃ· ὁ δὲ πολλῷ μᾶλλον ἔκραζεν, Υἱὲ Δαυίδ, ἐλέησόν με. ¶ **49** καὶ στὰς ὁ Ἰησοῦς εἶπεν, Φωνήσατε αὐτόν. ¶ καὶ φωνοῦσιν τὸν τυφλὸν λέγοντες αὐτῷ, Θάρσει, ἔγειρε, φωνεῖ σε. ¶ **50** ὁ δὲ ἀποβαλὼν τὸ ἱμάτιον αὐτοῦ ἀναπηδήσας ἦλθεν πρὸς τὸν Ἰησοῦν. ¶ **51** καὶ ἀποκριθεὶς αὐτῷ ὁ Ἰησοῦς εἶπεν, Τί σοι θέλεις ποιήσω; ὁ δὲ τυφλὸς εἶπεν αὐτῷ, Ραββουνι, ἵνα ἀναβλέψω. ¶ **52** καὶ ὁ Ἰησοῦς εἶπεν αὐτῷ, Ὕπαγε, ἡ πίστις σου σέσωκέν σε. καὶ εὐθὺς ἀνέβλεψεν καὶ ἠκολούθει αὐτῷ ἐν τῇ ὁδῷ.

The Triumphal Entry

11:1 As they approached Jerusalem and came to Bethphage and Bethany at the Mount of Olives,
Καὶ ὅτε → ἐγγίζουσιν εἰς Ἱεροσόλυμα εἰς Βηθφαγὴ καὶ Βηθανίαν πρὸς τὸ ὄρος → ⸆τῶν ἐλαιῶν⸆
cj cj v.pai.3p p.a n.apn p.a n.asf cj n.asf p.a d.asn n.asn d.gpf n.gpf
2779 4021 1581 1650 2642 1650 1036 2779 1029 4639 3836 4001 3836 1777

Jesus sent two of his disciples, **2** saying to them, "Go to the village ahead of you, and just as
ἀποστέλλει δύο → αὐτοῦ ⸆τῶν μαθητῶν⸆ καὶ λέγει → αὐτοῖς Ὑπάγετε εἰς τὴν κώμην τὴν κατέναντι ← ὑμῶν καὶ εὐθὺς →
v.pai.3s a.apm r.gsm.3 d.gpm n.gpm cj v.pai.3s r.dpm.3 v.pam.2p p.a d.asf n.asf d.asf p.g r.gp.2 cj adv
690 1545 3412 3836 3412 2779 3306 899 5632 1650 3836 3267 3836 2978 7007 2779 2318

you enter it, you will find a colt tied there, which no one has ever ridden. Untie
→ εἰσπορευόμενοι εἰς αὐτὴν → → εὑρήσετε πῶλον δεδεμένον ἐφ' ὃν οὐδεὶς ἀνθρώπων ⸆ οὔπω ἐκάθισεν λύσατε
pt.pm.npm p.a r.asf.3 v.fai.2p n.asm pt.rp.asm p.a r.asm a.nsm n.gpm adv v.aai.3s v.aam.2p
1660 1650 899 2351 4798 1313 2093 4005 4029 476 2767 4037 2767 3395

it and bring it here. **3** If anyone asks you, 'Why are you doing this?' tell him, 'The Lord needs it
αὐτὸν καὶ φέρετε καὶ ἐάν τις εἴπῃ ὑμῖν τί → → ποιεῖτε τοῦτο εἴπατε ὁ κύριος ⸆χρείαν ἔχει αὐτοῦ
r.asm.3 cj v.pam.2p cj cj r.nsm v.aas.3s r.dp.2 r.asn v.pai.2p r.asn v.aam.2p d.nsm n.nsm n.asf v.pai.3s r.gsm.3
899 2779 5770 2779 1569 5516 3306 7007 5515 4472 4047 3306 3836 3261 5970 2400 899

and will send it back here shortly.'" ¶ **4** They went and found a colt outside in the street,
καὶ → ἀποστέλλει αὐτὸν πάλιν ὧδε εὐθὺς καὶ → ἀπῆλθον καὶ εὗρον πῶλον ἔξω ἐπὶ τοῦ ἀμφόδου
cj v.pai.3s r.asm.3 adv adv adv cj v.aai.3p cj v.aai.3p n.asm adv p.g d.gsn n.gsn
2779 690 899 4099 6045 2318 2779 599 2779 2351 4798 2032 2093 3836 316

tied at a doorway. As they untied it, **5** some people standing there asked, "What are you
δεδεμένον πρὸς θύραν καὶ → λύουσιν αὐτὸν καί τινες ← ⸆τῶν ἑστηκότων⸆ ἐκεῖ ἔλεγον αὐτοῖς τί →
pt.rp.asm p.a n.asf cj v.pai.3p r.asm.3 cj r.npm d.gpm pt.ra.gpm adv v.iai.3p r.dpm.3 r.asn
1313 4639 2598 2779 3395 899 2779 5516 3836 2705 1695 3306 899 5515

doing, untying that colt?" **6** They answered as Jesus had told them to, and the people let them
ποιεῖτε λύοντες τὸν πῶλον δὲ οἱ εἶπαν αὐτοῖς καθὼς ὁ Ἰησοῦς → εἶπεν καὶ → ἀφῆκαν αὐτούς
v.pai.2p pt.pa.npm d.asm n.asm cj d.npm v.aai.3p r.dpm.3 cj d.nsm n.nsm v.aai.3s cj v.aai.3p r.apm.3
4472 3395 3836 4798 1254 3836 3306 899 2777 3836 2652 3306 2779 918 899

go. **7** When they brought the colt to Jesus and threw their cloaks over it, he sat on it.
← καὶ → φέρουσιν τὸν πῶλον πρὸς ⸆τὸν Ἰησοῦν⸆ καὶ ἐπιβάλλουσιν αὐτῷ ⸆τὰ ἱμάτια⸆ → αὐτῷ καὶ → ἐκάθισεν ἐπ' αὐτόν
cj v.pai.3p d.asm n.asm p.a d.asm n.asm cj v.pai.3p r.gpm.3 d.apn n.apn r.dsm.3 cj v.aai.3s p.a r.asm.3
918 2779 5770 3836 4798 4639 3836 2652 2779 2095 899 3836 2668 2095 899 2779 2767 2093 899

8 Many people spread their cloaks on the road, while others spread branches they had cut in the
καὶ πολλοὶ ← ἔστρωσαν αὐτῶν ⸆τὰ ἱμάτια⸆ εἰς τὴν ὁδόν δὲ ἄλλοι στιβάδας → → κόψαντες ἐκ τῶν
cj a.npm v.aai.3p r.gpm.3 d.apn n.apn p.a d.asf n.asf pl r.npm n.apf pt.aa.npm p.g d.gpm
2779 4498 5143 899 3836 2668 1650 3836 3847 1254 257 5115 3164 1666 3836

fields. **9** Those who went ahead and those who followed shouted, "Hosanna!" "Blessed is he who
ἀγρῶν καὶ οἱ προάγοντες καὶ οἱ ἀκολουθοῦντες ἔκραζον ὡσαννά εὐλογημένος ὁ
n.gpm cj d.npm pt.pa.npm cj d.npm pt.pa.npm v.iai.3p j pt.rp.nsm d.nsm
69 2779 3836 4575 2779 3836 199 3189 6057 2328 3836

comes in the name of the Lord!" **10** "Blessed is the coming kingdom of our father David!" ¶ "Hosanna
ἐρχόμενος ἐν ὀνόματι → κυρίου εὐλογημένη ἡ ἐρχομένη βασιλεία → ἡμῶν πατρὸς ⸆τοῦ πατρὸς⸆ ὡσαννά
pt.pm.nsm p.d n.dsn n.gsn pt.rp.nsf d.nsf pt.pm.nsf n.nsf r.gp.1 n.gsn d.gsm n.gsm j
2262 1877 3950 3261 2328 3836 2262 993 4252 7005 4252 3836 4252 6057

in the highest!" **11** Jesus entered Jerusalem and went to the temple. He looked around at
ἐν τοῖς ὑψίστοις Καὶ εἰσῆλθεν εἰς Ἱεροσόλυμα εἰς τὸ ἱερὸν καὶ → περιβλεψάμενος
p.d d.dpn a.dpn.s cj v.aai.3s p.a n.apn p.a d.asn n.asn cj pt.am.nsm
1877 3836 5736 2779 1656 1650 2642 1650 3836 2639 2779 4315

everything, but since it was already late, he went out to Bethany with the Twelve.
πάντα → → οὔσης ἤδη ⸆ὀψίας τῆς ὥρας⸆ → ἐξῆλθεν ← εἰς Βηθανίαν μετὰ τῶν δώδεκα
a.apn pt.pa.gsf adv n.gsf d.gsf n.gsf v.aai.3s p.a n.asf p.g d.gpm a.gpm
4246 1639 2453 4068 3836 6052 2002 1650 1029 3552 3836 1557

Jesus Clears the Temple

11:12 The next day as they were leaving Bethany, Jesus was hungry. **13** Seeing in the distance
Καὶ τῇ → ἐπαύριον αὐτῶν ⸆ἐξελθόντων ἀπὸ Βηθανίας → ἐπείνασεν καὶ ἰδὼν ἀπὸ μακρόθεν
cj d.dsf adv r.gpm.3 pt.aa.gpm p.g n.gsf v.aai.3s cj pt.aa.nsm p.g adv
2779 3836 2069 2002 2002 608 1029 4277 2779 1625 608 3427

11:1 Καὶ ὅτε ἐγγίζουσιν εἰς Ἱεροσόλυμα εἰς Βηθφαγὴ καὶ Βηθανίαν πρὸς τὸ Ὄρος τῶν Ἐλαιῶν, ἀποστέλλει δύο τῶν μαθητῶν αὐτοῦ ² καὶ λέγει αὐτοῖς, Ὑπάγετε εἰς τὴν κώμην τὴν κατέναντι ὑμῶν, καὶ εὐθὺς εἰσπορευόμενοι εἰς αὐτὴν εὑρήσετε πῶλον δεδεμένον ἐφ' ὃν οὐδεὶς οὔπω ἀνθρώπων ἐκάθισεν· λύσατε αὐτὸν καὶ φέρετε. ³ καὶ ἐάν τις ὑμῖν εἴπῃ, Τί ποιεῖτε τοῦτο; εἴπατε, Ὁ κύριος αὐτοῦ χρείαν ἔχει, καὶ εὐθὺς αὐτὸν ἀποστέλλει πάλιν ὧδε. ¶ ⁴ καὶ ἀπῆλθον καὶ εὗρον πῶλον δεδεμένον πρὸς θύραν ἔξω ἐπὶ τοῦ ἀμφόδου καὶ λύουσιν αὐτόν. ⁵ καί τινες τῶν ἐκεῖ ἑστηκότων ἔλεγον αὐτοῖς, Τί ποιεῖτε λύοντες τὸν πῶλον; ⁶ οἱ δὲ εἶπαν αὐτοῖς καθὼς εἶπεν ὁ Ἰησοῦς, καὶ ἀφῆκαν αὐτούς. ⁷ καὶ φέρουσιν τὸν πῶλον πρὸς τὸν Ἰησοῦν καὶ ἐπιβάλλουσιν αὐτῷ τὰ ἱμάτια αὐτῶν, καὶ ἐκάθισεν ἐπ' αὐτόν. ⁸ καὶ πολλοὶ τὰ ἱμάτια αὐτῶν ἔστρωσαν εἰς τὴν ὁδόν, ἄλλοι δὲ στιβάδας κόψαντες ἐκ τῶν ἀγρῶν. ⁹ καὶ οἱ προάγοντες καὶ οἱ ἀκολουθοῦντες ἔκραζον, Ὡσαννά· Εὐλογημένος ὁ ἐρχόμενος ἐν ὀνόματι κυρίου· ¹⁰ Εὐλογημένη ἡ ἐρχομένη βασιλεία τοῦ πατρὸς ἡμῶν Δαυίδ· ¶ Ὡσαννὰ ἐν τοῖς ὑψίστοις. ¹¹ Καὶ εἰσῆλθεν εἰς Ἱεροσόλυμα εἰς τὸ ἱερὸν καὶ περιβλεψάμενος πάντα, ὀψίας ἤδη οὔσης τῆς ὥρας, ἐξῆλθεν εἰς Βηθανίαν μετὰ τῶν δώδεκα.

¹¹:¹² Καὶ τῇ ἐπαύριον ἐξελθόντων αὐτῶν ἀπὸ Βηθανίας ἐπείνασεν. ¹³ καὶ ἰδὼν συκῆν ἀπὸ μακρόθεν ἔχουσαν φύλλα ἦλθεν,

a fig tree in leaf, he went to find out if it had any fruit. When he reached it, he found
→ συκῆν ἔχουσαν φύλλα → ἦλθεν εὑρήσει ← εἰ ἄρα ἐν αὐτῇ τι καὶ → ἐλθὼν ἐπ' αὐτὴν εὗρεν
n.asf pt.pa.asf n.apn v.aai.3s v.fai.3s cj cj p.d r.dsf.3 r.asn cj pt.aa.nsm p.a r.asf.3 v.aai.3s
5190 2400 5877 2262 2351 1623 726 1877 899 5516 2779 2262 2093 899 2351

nothing but leaves, because it was not the season for figs. **14** Then he said to the tree, "May no one
οὐδὲν εἰ μὴ φύλλα γὰρ → ἦν οὐκ ὁ καιρὸς → σύκων καὶ ἀποκριθεὶς → εἶπεν → αὐτῇ → μηδεὶς ←
a.asn cj pl n.apn cj v.iai.3s pl d.nsm n.nsm n.npm cj pt.ap.nsm v.aai.3s r.dsf.3 a.nsm
4029 1623 3590 5877 1142 1639 4024 3836 2789 5192 2779 646 3306 899 3594

ever eat fruit from you again." And his disciples heard him say it. ¶ **15** On reaching
εἰς τὸν αἰῶνα φάγοι καρπὸν ἐκ σοῦ μηκέτι καὶ αὐτοῦ οἱ μαθηταὶ ἤκουον Καὶ → ἔρχονται εἰς
p.a d.asm n.asm v.aao.3s n.asm p.g r.gs.2 adv cj r.gsm.3 d.npm n.npm v.iai.3p cj v.pmi.3p p.a
1650 3836 172 2266 2843 1666 5148 3600 2779 899 3836 3412 201 2779 2262 1650

Jerusalem, Jesus entered the temple area and began driving out those who were buying and
Ἱεροσόλυμα Καὶ εἰσελθὼν εἰς τὸ ἱερὸν ← ἤρξατο ἐκβάλλειν ← τοὺς ← → πωλοῦντας καὶ
n.apn cj pt.aa.nsm p.a d.asn n.asn v.ami.3s f.pa d.apm pt.pa.apm cj
2642 2779 1656 1650 3836 2639 806 1675 3836 4797 2779

selling there. He overturned the tables of the money changers and the benches of those
τοὺς ἀγοράζοντας ἐν τῷ ἱερῷ καὶ → κατέστρεψεν τὰς τραπέζας → τῶν κολλυβιστῶν καὶ τὰς καθέδρας → τῶν
d.apm pt.pa.apm p.d d.dsn n.dsn cj v.aai.3s d.apf n.apf d.gpm n.gpm cj d.apf n.apf d.gpm
3836 60 1877 3836 2639 2779 2951 3836 5544 3836 3142 2779 3836 2756 3836

selling doves, **16** and would not allow anyone to carry merchandise through the temple courts. **17** And as
πωλούντων τὰς περιστερὰς καὶ → οὐκ ἤφιεν ἵνα τις → διενέγκῃ σκεῦος διὰ τοῦ ἱεροῦ ← καὶ
pt.pa.gpm d.apf n.apf cj pl v.iai.3s cj r.nsm v.aas.3s n.asn p.g d.gsn n.gsn cj
4797 3836 4361 2779 918 4024 918 2671 5516 1422 5007 1328 3836 2639 2779

he taught them, he said, "Is it not written: "'My house will be called a house of prayer for
→ ἐδίδασκεν αὐτοῖς καὶ → ἔλεγεν → → οὐ γέγραπται ὅτι Ὁ οἶκός μου ὁ οἶκος → → κληθήσεται οἶκος → προσευχῆς →
v.iai.3s r.dpm.3 cj v.iai.3s pl v.rpi.3s cj r.gs.1 d.nsm n.nsm v.fpi.3s n.nsm n.gsf
1438 899 2779 3306 1211 1211 4024 1211 4022 1609 3836 3875 2813 3875 4666

all nations'? ¶ But you have made it 'a den of robbers.'" ¶ **18** The chief priests
πᾶσιν τοῖς ἔθνεσιν δὲ ὑμεῖς → πεποιήκατε αὐτὸν σπήλαιον λῃστῶν Καὶ οἱ ἀρχιερεῖς
a.dpn d.dpn n.dpn cj r.np.2 v.rai.2p r.asm.3 n.asn n.gpm cj d.npm n.npm
4246 3836 1620 1254 7007 4472 899 5068 3334 2779 3836 797

and the teachers of the law heard this and began looking for a way to kill him, for they feared him,
καὶ οἱ γραμματεῖς ← ← ἤκουσαν καὶ → ἐζήτουν πῶς ← → ἀπολέσωσιν αὐτὸν γὰρ → ἐφοβοῦντο αὐτὸν
cj d.npm n.npm v.aai.3p cj v.iai.3s cj v.aas.3p r.asm.3 cj v.ipi.3p r.asm.3
2779 3836 1208 201 2779 2426 4802 660 899 1142 5828 899

because the whole crowd was amazed at his teaching. ¶ **19** When evening came, they went out of
γὰρ ὁ πᾶς ὄχλος → ἐξεπλήσσετο ἐπὶ αὐτοῦ τῇ διδαχῇ Καὶ ὅταν ὀψὲ ἐγένετο ἐξεπορεύοντο ἔξω ←
cj d.nsm a.nsm n.nsm v.ipi.3s p.d r.gsm.3 d.dsf n.dsf cj cj adv v.ami.3s v.imi.3p p.g
1142 3836 4246 4063 1742 2093 899 3836 1439 2779 4020 4067 1181 1744 2032

the city.
τῆς πόλεως
d.gsf n.gsf
3836 4484

The Withered Fig Tree

11:20 In the morning, as they went along, they saw the fig tree withered from the roots.
Καὶ → πρωῒ → παραπορευόμενοι ← → εἶδον τὴν → συκῆν ἐξηραμμένην ἐκ ῥιζῶν καὶ
cj adv pt.pm.npm v.aai.3p d.asf n.asf pt.rp.asf p.g n.gpf cj
2779 4745 4182 1625 3836 5190 3830 1666 4844 2779

21 Peter remembered and said to Jesus, "Rabbi, look! The fig tree you cursed has withered!" ¶ **22** and
ὁ Πέτρος ἀναμνησθεὶς λέγει αὐτῷ ῥαββί ἴδε ἡ συκῆ ἣν κατηράσω → ἐξήρανται καὶ
d.nsm n.nsm pt.ap.nsm v.pai.3s r.dsm.3 n.vsm pl d.nsf n.nsf r.asf v.ami.2s v.rpi.3s cj
3836 4377 389 3306 899 4806 2623 3836 5190 4005 2933 3830 2779

"Have faith in God," Jesus answered. **23** "I tell you the truth, if anyone says to this mountain,
ἔχετε πίστιν θεοῦ ὁ Ἰησοῦς ἀποκριθεὶς λέγει αὐτοῖς → λέγω ὑμῖν ἀμὴν ὅτι ὃς ἂν εἴπῃ → τούτῳ τῷ ὄρει
v.pam.2p n.asf n.gsm d.nsm n.nsm pt.ap.nsm v.pai.3s r.dpm.3 v.pai.1s r.dp.2 pl cj r.nsm pl v.aas.3s r.dsn d.dsn n.dsn
2400 4411 2536 3836 2652 646 3306 899 3306 7007 297 4022 4005 323 3306 4047 3836 4001

εἰ ἄρα τι εὑρήσει ἐν αὐτῇ, καὶ ἐλθὼν ἐπ' αὐτὴν οὐδὲν εὗρεν εἰ μὴ φύλλα· ὁ γὰρ καιρὸς οὐκ ἦν σύκων. **14** καὶ ἀποκριθεὶς εἶπεν αὐτῇ, Μηκέτι εἰς τὸν αἰῶνα ἐκ σοῦ μηδεὶς καρπὸν φάγοι. καὶ ἤκουον οἱ μαθηταὶ αὐτοῦ. ¶ **15** Καὶ ἔρχονται εἰς Ἱεροσόλυμα. καὶ εἰσελθὼν εἰς τὸ ἱερὸν ἤρξατο ἐκβάλλειν τοὺς πωλοῦντας καὶ τοὺς ἀγοράζοντας ἐν τῷ ἱερῷ, καὶ τὰς τραπέζας τῶν κολλυβιστῶν καὶ τὰς καθέδρας τῶν πωλούντων τὰς περιστερὰς κατέστρεψεν, **16** καὶ οὐκ ἤφιεν ἵνα τις διενέγκῃ σκεῦος διὰ τοῦ ἱεροῦ. **17** καὶ ἐδίδασκεν καὶ ἔλεγεν αὐτοῖς, Οὐ γέγραπται ὅτι Ὁ οἶκός μου οἶκος προσευχῆς κληθήσεται πᾶσιν τοῖς ἔθνεσιν; ¶ ὑμεῖς δὲ πεποιήκατε αὐτὸν σπήλαιον λῃστῶν. ¶ **18** καὶ ἤκουσαν οἱ ἀρχιερεῖς καὶ οἱ γραμματεῖς καὶ ἐζήτουν πῶς αὐτὸν ἀπολέσωσιν· ἐφοβοῦντο γὰρ αὐτόν, πᾶς γὰρ ὁ ὄχλος ἐξεπλήσσετο ἐπὶ τῇ διδαχῇ αὐτοῦ. ¶ **19** Καὶ ὅταν ὀψὲ ἐγένετο, ἐξεπορεύοντο ἔξω τῆς πόλεως.

11:20 Καὶ παραπορευόμενοι πρωῒ εἶδον τὴν συκῆν ἐξηραμμένην ἐκ ῥιζῶν. **21** καὶ ἀναμνησθεὶς ὁ Πέτρος λέγει αὐτῷ, Ῥαββί, ἴδε ἡ συκῆ ἣν κατηράσω ἐξήρανται. ¶ **22** καὶ ἀποκριθεὶς ὁ Ἰησοῦς λέγει αὐτοῖς, Ἔχετε πίστιν θεοῦ. **23** ἀμὴν λέγω ὑμῖν ὅτι

'Go,   throw yourself into the sea,'   and does not doubt   in his heart   but believes that what he
ἄρθητι καὶ βλήθητι ←   εἰς τὴν θάλασσαν καὶ →   μὴ διακριθῇ ἐν αὐτοῦ ⌜τῇ καρδίᾳ⌝   ἀλλὰ πιστεύῃ ὅτι ὃ
v.apm.2s cj v.apm.2s   p.a d.asf n.asf cj   pl v.aps.3s p.d r.gsm.3 d.dsf n.dsf   cj v.pas.3s cj r.asn
149 2779 965   1650 3836 2498 2779   1359 3590 1359 1877 899 3836 2840   247 4409 4022 4005

says will happen, it will be   done for him. **24** Therefore   I tell you, whatever   you ask   for   in prayer,
λαλεῖ → γίνεται → ἔσται   → αὐτῷ ⌜διὰ τοῦτο⌝   → λέγω ὑμῖν ⌜πάντα ὅσα⌝   → αἰτεῖσθε ←   καὶ   προσεύχεσθε
v.pai.3s v.pmi.3s v.fmi.3s   r.dsm.3 p.a r.asn   v.pai.1s r.dp.2 r.apn r.apn   v.pmi.2p   cj   v.pmi.2p
3281 1181 1639   899 1328 4047   3306 7007 4246 4012   160   2779   4667

believe that you have received it, and it will be   yours. **25** And when you stand praying,   if   you hold anything
πιστεύετε ὅτι → → ἐλάβετε καὶ → → ἔσται ὑμῖν   Καὶ ὅταν → στήκετε προσευχόμενοι εἴ   → ἔχετε τι
v.pam.2p cj v.aai.2p cj v.fmi.3s r.dp.2   cj cj v.pai.2p pt.pm.npm cj   v.pai.2p r.asn
4409 4022 3284 2779 1639 7007   2779 4020 5112 4667 1623   2400 5516

against anyone, forgive him, so that   your Father   in heaven   may forgive you your sins."
κατά τινος ἀφίετε   ἵνα ←   καὶ ὑμῶν ὁ πατὴρ ὁ ἐν ⌜τοῖς οὐρανοῖς⌝   → ἀφῇ ὑμῖν ὑμῶν ⌜τὰ παραπτώματα⌝
p.g r.gsm v.pam.2p   cj adv r.gp.2 d.nsm n.nsm d.nsm d.nsm p.d d.dpm n.dpm   v.aas.3s r.dp.2 r.gp.2 d.apn n.apn
2848 5516 918   2671 2779 7007 3836 4252 3836 1877 3836 4041   918 7007 7007 3836 4183

The Authority of Jesus Questioned

11:27 They arrived again in Jerusalem, and while Jesus was walking   in the temple courts, the chief
Καὶ → ἔρχονται πάλιν εἰς Ἱεροσόλυμα καὶ → αὐτοῦ → περιπατοῦντος ἐν τῷ ἱερῷ ←   οἱ ἀρχιερεῖς
cj v.pmi.3p adv p.a n.apn cj r.gsm.3 pt.pa.gsm p.d d.dsn n.dsn   d.npm n.npm
2779 2262 4099 1650 2642 2779 4344 899 4344 1877 3836 2639   3836 797

priests,   the teachers of the law and the elders   came   to him. **28** "By what authority are you doing
←   καὶ οἱ γραμματεῖς ←   καὶ οἱ πρεσβύτεροι ἔρχονται πρὸς αὐτόν   καὶ ἐν ποίᾳ ἐξουσίᾳ → → ποιεῖς
cj d.npm n.npm   cj d.npm a.npm v.pmi.3p p.a r.asm.3   cj p.d r.dsf n.dsf v.pai.2s
2779 3836 1208   2779 3836 4565 2262 4639 899   2779 1877 4481 2026 4472

these things?" they asked.   "And who gave you authority   to do this?" ¶   **29** Jesus
ταῦτα ←   → ἔλεγον αὐτῷ ἢ τίς ἔδωκεν σοι ⌜τὴν ἐξουσίαν ταύτην⌝ ἵνα ποιῇς ταῦτα   δὲ ὁ Ἰησοῦς
r.apn   v.iai.3p r.dsm.3 cj r.nsm v.aai.3s r.ds.2 d.asf n.asf r.asf cj v.pas.2s r.apn   cj d.nsm n.nsm
4047   3306 899 2445 5515 1443 5148 3836 2026 4047 2671 4472 4047   1254 3836 2652

replied,   "I will ask   you one question.   Answer me, and I will tell you by what authority I am
εἶπεν αὐτοῖς → → ἐπερωτήσω ὑμᾶς ἕνα λόγον   καὶ ἀποκρίθητε μοι καὶ → → ἐρῶ ὑμῖν ἐν ποίᾳ ἐξουσίᾳ → →
v.aai.3s r.dpm.3 v.fai.1s r.ap.2 a.asm n.asm   cj v.apm.2p r.ds.1 cj v.fai.1s r.dp.2 p.d r.dsf n.dsf
3306 899 2089 7007 1651 3364   2779 646 1609 2779 3306 7007 1877 4481 2026

doing these things. **30** John's   baptism   – was it from heaven, or from men?   Tell   me!" ¶ **31** They
ποιῶ ταῦτα ←   ⌜τὸ Ἰωάννου⌝ ⌜τὸ βάπτισμα⌝ ἦν ← ἐξ οὐρανοῦ ἢ ἐξ ἀνθρώπων ἀποκρίθητε μοι   καὶ →
v.pai.1s r.apn   d.nsn n.gsm d.nsn n.nsn v.iai.3s p.g n.gsn cj p.g n.gpm v.apm.2p r.ds.1   cj
4472 4047   3836 2722 3836 967 1639 1666 4041 2445 1666 476 646 1609   2779

discussed it among themselves and said,   "If we say,   'From heaven,' he will ask, 'Then why   didn't you
διελογίζοντο πρὸς ἑαυτοὺς   λέγοντες ἐὰν   εἴπωμεν ἐξ οὐρανοῦ   ἐρεῖ οὖν ⌜διὰ τί⌝ οὐκ
v.imi.3p p.a r.apm.3   pt.pa.npm cj   v.aas.1p p.g n.gsm   v.fai.3s cj p.a r.asn pl
1368 4639 1571   3306 1569   3306 1666 4041   3306 4036 1328 5515 4024

believe him?' **32** But if we say,   'From men' . . . ." (They feared   the people, for everyone held that
ἐπιστεύσατε αὐτῷ   ἀλλὰ → εἴπωμεν ἐξ ἀνθρώπων   ἐφοβοῦντο τὸν ὄχλον γὰρ ἅπαντες εἶχον ὅτι
v.aai.2p r.dsm.3   cj v.aas.1p p.g n.gpm   v.ipi.3p d.asm n.asm cj a.npm v.iai.3p cj
4409 899   247 3306 1666 476   5828 3836 4063 1142 570 2400 4022

John   really was a prophet.) ¶   **33** So they answered Jesus,   "We don't know." ¶
⌜τὸν Ἰωάννην⌝ ὄντως ἦν προφήτης   καὶ → ἀποκριθέντες ⌜τῷ Ἰησοῦ⌝ λέγουσιν → οὐκ οἴδαμεν   καὶ
d.asm n.asm adv v.iai.3s n.nsm   cj pt.ap.npm d.dsm n.dsm v.pai.3p pl v.rai.1p   cj
3836 2722 3953 1639 4737   2779 646 3836 2652 3306 3857 4024 3857   2779

Jesus   said,   "Neither will I tell you by what authority I am doing these things."
ὁ Ἰησοῦς⌝ λέγει αὐτοῖς οὐδὲ → ἐγὼ λέγω ὑμῖν ἐν ποίᾳ ἐξουσίᾳ → → ποιῶ ταῦτα ←
d.nsm n.nsm v.pai.3s r.dpm.3 cj r.ns.1 v.pai.1s r.dp.2 p.d r.dsf n.dsf v.pai.1s r.apn
3836 2652 3306 899 4028 3306 1609 3306 7007 1877 4481 2026 4472 4047

ὃς ἂν εἴπῃ τῷ ὄρει τούτῳ, Ἄρθητι καὶ βλήθητι εἰς τὴν θάλασσαν, καὶ μὴ διακριθῇ ἐν τῇ καρδίᾳ αὐτοῦ ἀλλὰ πιστεύῃ ὅτι ὃ λαλεῖ γίνεται, ἔσται αὐτῷ. ²⁴ διὰ τοῦτο λέγω ὑμῖν, πάντα ὅσα προσεύχεσθε καὶ αἰτεῖσθε, πιστεύετε ὅτι ἐλάβετε, καὶ ἔσται ὑμῖν. ²⁵ καὶ ὅταν στήκετε προσευχόμενοι, ἀφίετε εἴ τι ἔχετε κατά τινος, ἵνα καὶ ὁ πατὴρ ὑμῶν ὁ ἐν τοῖς οὐρανοῖς ἀφῇ ὑμῖν τὰ παραπτώματα ὑμῶν.

11:27 Καὶ ἔρχονται πάλιν εἰς Ἱεροσόλυμα. καὶ ἐν τῷ ἱερῷ περιπατοῦντος αὐτοῦ ἔρχονται πρὸς αὐτὸν οἱ ἀρχιερεῖς καὶ οἱ γραμματεῖς καὶ οἱ πρεσβύτεροι ²⁸ καὶ ἔλεγον αὐτῷ, Ἐν ποίᾳ ἐξουσίᾳ ταῦτα ποιεῖς; ἢ τίς σοι ἔδωκεν τὴν ἐξουσίαν ταύτην ἵνα ταῦτα ποιῇς; ¶ ²⁹ ὁ δὲ Ἰησοῦς εἶπεν αὐτοῖς, Ἐπερωτήσω ὑμᾶς ἕνα λόγον, καὶ ἀποκρίθητέ μοι καὶ ἐρῶ ὑμῖν ἐν ποίᾳ ἐξουσίᾳ ταῦτα ποιῶ· ³⁰ τὸ βάπτισμα τὸ Ἰωάννου ἐξ οὐρανοῦ ἦν ἢ ἐξ ἀνθρώπων; ἀποκρίθητέ μοι. ¶ ³¹ καὶ διελογίζοντο πρὸς ἑαυτοὺς λέγοντες, Ἐὰν εἴπωμεν, Ἐξ οὐρανοῦ, ἐρεῖ, Διὰ τί [οὖν] οὐκ ἐπιστεύσατε αὐτῷ; ³² ἀλλὰ εἴπωμεν, Ἐξ ἀνθρώπων;-- ἐφοβοῦντο τὸν ὄχλον· ἅπαντες γὰρ εἶχον τὸν Ἰωάννην ὄντως ὅτι προφήτης ἦν. ¶ ³³ καὶ ἀποκριθέντες τῷ Ἰησοῦ λέγουσιν, Οὐκ οἴδαμεν ¶ καὶ ὁ Ἰησοῦς λέγει αὐτοῖς, Οὐδὲ ἐγὼ λέγω ὑμῖν ἐν ποίᾳ ἐξουσίᾳ ταῦτα ποιῶ.

The Parable of the Tenants

12:1 He then began to speak to them in parables: "A man planted a vineyard. He put a wall
　　　　Καὶ ἤρξατο　→ λαλεῖν　→ αὐτοῖς ἐν παραβολαῖς　ἄνθρωπος ἐφύτευσεν ἀμπελῶνα καὶ → περιέθηκεν φραγμὸν
　　　　cj v.ami.3s f.pa r.dpm.3 p.d n.dpf n.nsm v.aai.3s n.asm cj v.aai.3s n.asm
　　　806 2779 806 3281 899 1877 4130 476 5885 308 2779 4363 5850

around it, dug a pit for the winepress and built a watchtower. Then he rented the vineyard to some
←　　καὶ ὤρυξεν ὑπολήνιον ←　←　καὶ ᾠκοδόμησεν πύργον καὶ → ἐξέδετο αὐτὸν →
4363 καὶ v.aai.3s n.asn cj v.aai.3s n.asm cj v.ami.3s r.asm.3
　　2779 4002 5700 2779 3868 4788 2779 1686 899

farmers and went away on a journey. **2** At harvest time he sent a servant to the tenants to
γεωργοῖς καὶ ἀπεδήμησεν ←　　καὶ →　τῷ καιρῷ → ἀπέστειλεν δοῦλον πρὸς τοὺς γεωργοὺς ἵνα
n.dpm cj v.aai.3s cj d.dsm n.dsm v.aai.3s n.asm p.a d.apm n.apm cj
1177 2779 623 2779 3836 2789 690 1529 4639 3836 1177 2671

collect from them some of the fruit of the vineyard. **3** But they seized him, beat him and sent him
λάβῃ παρὰ τῶν γεωργῶν ἀπὸ → τῶν καρπῶν → τοῦ ἀμπελῶνος καὶ → λαβόντες αὐτὸν ἔδειραν καὶ ἀπέστειλαν
v.aas.3s p.g d.gpm n.gpm p.g d.gpm n.gpm d.gsm n.gsm cj pt.aa.npm r.asm.3 v.aai.3p cj v.aai.3p
3284 4123 3836 1177 608 3836 2843 3836 308 2779 3284 899 1296 2779 690

away empty-handed. **4** Then he sent another servant to them; they struck this man on the head
←　κενόν καὶ πάλιν → ἀπέστειλεν ἄλλον δοῦλον πρὸς αὐτοὺς → ἐκεφαλίωσαν κἀκεῖνον ←　←　←
a.asm cj adv v.aai.3s r.asm n.asm p.a r.apm.3 v.aai.3p cj
3031 2779 4099 690 257 1529 4639 899 3052 2797 3052 3052 3052

and treated him shamefully. **5** He sent still another, and that one they killed. He sent many
καὶ → ἠτίμασαν καὶ → ἀπέστειλεν ἄλλον κἀκεῖνον ←　→ ἀπέκτειναν καὶ πολλοὺς
cj v.aai.3p cj v.aai.3s r.asm cj v.aai.3p cj a.apm
2779 869 2779 690 257 2797 650 2779 4498

others; some of them they beat, others they killed. ¶ **6** "He had one left to send, a son, whom
ἄλλους μὲν οὓς → δέροντες δὲ οὓς → ἀποκτέννοντες → εἶχεν ἕνα ἔτι υἱὸν →
r.apm pl r.apm pt.pa.npm cj r.apm pt.pa.npm v.iai.3s a.asm adv n.asm
257 3525 4005 1296 1254 4005 650 2400 1651 2285 5626

he loved. He sent him last of all, saying, 'They will respect my son.'
ἀγαπητόν → ἀπέστειλεν αὐτὸν ἔσχατον πρὸς αὐτοὺς λέγων ὅτι ἐντραπήσονται μου τὸν υἱόν
a.asm v.aai.3s r.asm.3 a.asm p.a r.apm.3 pt.pa.nsm cj v.fpi.3s r.gs.1 d.asm n.asm
28 690 899 2274 4639 899 3306 4022 1956 1609 3836 5626

7 "But the tenants said to one another, 'This is the heir. Come, let's kill him, and the
δὲ ἐκεῖνοι οἱ γεωργοὶ εἶπαν πρὸς ἑαυτοὺς ←　ὅτι οὗτος ἐστιν ὁ κληρονόμος δεῦτε → ἀποκτείνωμεν αὐτὸν καὶ ἡ
cj r.npm d.npm n.npm v.aai.3p p.a r.apm.3 cj r.nsm v.pai.3s d.nsm n.nsm adv v.aas.1p r.asm.3 cj d.nsf
1254 1697 3836 1177 3306 4639 1571 4022 4047 1639 3836 3101 1307 650 899 2779 3836

inheritance will be ours.' **8** So they took him and killed him, and threw him out of the vineyard. ¶
κληρονομία → ἔσται ἡμῶν καὶ λαβόντες ἀπέκτειναν αὐτὸν καὶ ἐξέβαλον αὐτὸν ἔξω ←　τοῦ ἀμπελῶνος
n.nsf v.fmi.3s r.gp.1 cj pt.aa.npm v.aai.3p r.asm.3 cj v.aai.3p r.asm.3 p.g d.gsm n.gsm
3100 1639 7005 2779 3284 650 899 2779 1675 899 2032 3836 308

9 "What then will the owner of the vineyard do? He will come and kill those tenants and give the vineyard
τί οὖν → ὁ κύριος → τοῦ ἀμπελῶνος ποιήσει → ἐλεύσεται καὶ ἀπολέσει τοὺς γεωργοὺς καὶ δώσει τὸν ἀμπελῶνα
r.asn cj d.nsm n.nsm d.gsm n.gsm v.fai.3s v.fmi.3s cj v.fai.3s d.apm n.apm cj v.fai.3s d.asm n.asm
5515 4036 4472 3836 3261 3836 308 4472 2262 2779 660 3836 1177 2779 1443 3836 308

to others. **10** Haven't you read this scripture: "'The stone the builders rejected has become
→ ἄλλοις οὐδὲ → ἀνέγνωτε ταύτην τὴν γραφὴν λίθον ὃν οἱ οἰκοδομοῦντες ἀπεδοκίμασαν οὗτος → ἐγενήθη εἰς
r.dpm adv v.aai.2p r.asf d.asf n.asf n.asm r.asm d.npm pt.pa.npm v.aai.3p r.nsm v.api.3s p.a
257 4028 336 4047 3836 1210 3345 4005 3836 3868 627 4047 1181 1650

the capstone; **11** the Lord has done this, and it is marvelous in our eyes'?" ¶ **12** Then they
κεφαλὴν γωνίας παρὰ κυρίου → ἐγένετο αὕτη καὶ → ἔστιν θαυμαστὴ ἐν ἡμῶν ὀφθαλμοῖς Καὶ
n.asf n.gsf p.g n.gsm v.ami.3s r.nsf cj v.pai.3s a.nsf p.d r.gp.1 n.dpm cj
3051 1224 4123 3261 1181 4047 2779 1639 2515 1877 7005 4057 2779

looked for a way to arrest him because they knew he had spoken the parable against them. But they were
ἐζήτουν ←　→ κρατῆσαι αὐτὸν γὰρ → ἔγνωσαν ὅτι → εἶπεν τὴν παραβολὴν πρὸς αὐτοὺς καὶ → →
v.iai.3p f.aa r.asm.3 cj v.aai.3p cj v.aai.3s d.asf n.asf p.a r.apm.3 cj
2426 3195 899 1142 1182 4022 3306 3836 4130 4639 899 2779

12:1 Καὶ ἤρξατο αὐτοῖς ἐν παραβολαῖς λαλεῖν, Ἀμπελῶνα ἄνθρωπος ἐφύτευσεν καὶ περιέθηκεν φραγμὸν καὶ ὤρυξεν ὑπολήνιον καὶ ᾠκοδόμησεν πύργον καὶ ἐξέδετο αὐτὸν γεωργοῖς καὶ ἀπεδήμησεν. **2** καὶ ἀπέστειλεν πρὸς τοὺς γεωργοὺς τῷ καιρῷ δοῦλον ἵνα παρὰ τῶν γεωργῶν λάβῃ ἀπὸ τῶν καρπῶν τοῦ ἀμπελῶνος· **3** καὶ λαβόντες αὐτὸν ἔδειραν καὶ ἀπέστειλαν κενόν. **4** καὶ πάλιν ἀπέστειλεν πρὸς αὐτοὺς ἄλλον δοῦλον· κἀκεῖνον ἐκεφαλίωσαν καὶ ἠτίμασαν. **5** καὶ ἄλλον ἀπέστειλεν· κἀκεῖνον ἀπέκτειναν, καὶ πολλοὺς ἄλλους, οὓς μὲν δέροντες, οὓς δὲ ἀποκτέννοντες. ¶ **6** ἔτι ἕνα εἶχεν υἱὸν ἀγαπητόν· ἀπέστειλεν αὐτὸν ἔσχατον πρὸς αὐτοὺς λέγων ὅτι Ἐντραπήσονται τὸν υἱόν μου. **7** ἐκεῖνοι δὲ οἱ γεωργοὶ πρὸς ἑαυτοὺς εἶπαν ὅτι Οὗτός ἐστιν ὁ κληρονόμος· δεῦτε ἀποκτείνωμεν αὐτόν, καὶ ἡμῶν ἔσται ἡ κληρονομία. **8** καὶ λαβόντες ἀπέκτειναν αὐτὸν καὶ ἐξέβαλον αὐτὸν ἔξω τοῦ ἀμπελῶνος. ¶ **9** τί [οὖν] ποιήσει ὁ κύριος τοῦ ἀμπελῶνος; ἐλεύσεται καὶ ἀπολέσει τοὺς γεωργοὺς καὶ δώσει τὸν ἀμπελῶνα ἄλλοις. **10** οὐδὲ τὴν γραφὴν ταύτην ἀνέγνωτε, Λίθον ὃν ἀπεδοκίμασαν οἱ οἰκοδομοῦντες, οὗτος ἐγενήθη εἰς κεφαλὴν γωνίας· **11** παρὰ κυρίου ἐγένετο αὕτη καὶ ἔστιν θαυμαστὴ ἐν ὀφθαλμοῖς ἡμῶν; ¶ **12** Καὶ ἐζήτουν αὐτὸν κρατῆσαι, καὶ ἐφοβήθησαν τὸν ὄχλον, ἔγνωσαν γὰρ ὅτι πρὸς αὐτοὺς τὴν παραβολὴν εἶπεν. καὶ ἀφέντες αὐτὸν ἀπῆλθον.

afraid　of the crowd;　so　they left　him　and went　away.
ἐφοβήθησαν ← τὸν ὄχλον καὶ → ἀφέντες αὐτὸν ἀπῆλθον ←
v.api.3p　d.asm n.asm　cj　pt.aa.npm r.asm.3　v.aai.3p
5828　3836 4063　2779　918　899　599

Paying Taxes to Caesar

12:13 Later they sent　some of the Pharisees and Herodians　to　Jesus to catch　him in his
Καὶ → ἀποστέλλουσιν τινας → τῶν Φαρισαίων καὶ τῶν Ἡρῳδιανῶν πρὸς αὐτὸν ἵνα ἀγρεύσωσιν αὐτὸν →
cj　v.pai.3p　r.apm　d.gpm n.gpm　cj　d.gpm n.gpm　p.a　r.asm.3 cj　v.aas.3p　r.asm.3
2779　690　5516　3836 5757　2779 3836 2477　4639 899　2671 65　899

words. **14** They came　to him and said,　"Teacher, we know　you are a man of integrity.　You aren't
λόγῳ καὶ → ἐλθόντες → αὐτῷ → λέγουσιν διδάσκαλε → οἴδαμεν ὅτι → εἶ → → ἀληθὴς καὶ → σοι οὐ
n.dsm cj　pt.aa.npm r.dsm.3　v.pai.3p n.vsm　v.rai.1p cj　v.pai.2s　a.nsm　cj r.ds.2 pl
3364 2779　2262 899　3306 1437　3857 4022　1639　239　2779 5148 4024

swayed by men,　because *you pay*　*no attention to who*　*they are;* but you teach　the way of
μέλει περὶ οὐδενός γὰρ → βλέπεις οὐ　εἰς πρόσωπον ἀνθρώπων　ἀλλ' → διδάσκεις τὴν ὁδὸν →
v.pai.3s p.g a.gsm cj　v.pai.2s pl　p.a n.asn n.gpm　cj　v.pai.2s d.asf n.asf
3508 4309 4029 1142　1063 4024 1063　1650 4725 476　247　1438 3836 3847

God　in accordance with the truth.　Is it right　to pay　taxes to Caesar or not? **15** Should we pay　or
τοῦ θεοῦ ἐπ' ← ← ἀληθείας → ἔξεστιν δοῦναι κῆνσον → Καίσαρι ἢ οὔ → → δῶμεν ἢ
d.gsm n.gsm p.a　n.gsf　v.pai.3s f.aa n.asm　n.dsm cj pl　v.aas.1p cj
3836 2536 2093　237　1997 1443 3056　2790 2445 4024　1443 2445

shouldn't we?" ¶　But Jesus knew their hypocrisy.　"Why are you trying to trap　me?" he asked.
μὴ δῶμεν δὲ ὁ εἰδὼς αὐτῶν τὴν ὑπόκρισιν τί → → → → πειράζετε με → εἶπεν αὐτοῖς
pl v.aas.1p cj d.nsm pt.ra.nsm r.gpm.3 d.asf n.asf r.asn　v.pai.2p r.as.1 v.aai.3s r.dpm.3
3590 1443　1254 3836 3857 899 3836 5694 5515　4279 1609 3306 899

"Bring me a denarius and let me look at it." **16**　They brought the coin,　and he asked them, "Whose portrait is
φέρετε μοι δηνάριον ἵνα → → ἴδω δὲ οἱ ἤνεγκαν καὶ → λέγει αὐτοῖς τίνος ἡ εἰκὼν
v.pam.2p r.ds.1 n.asn cj　v.aas.1s　cj d.npm v.aai.3p　cj　v.pai.3s r.dpm.3 r.gsm d.nsf n.nsf
5770 1609 1324 2671　1625　1254 3836 5770　2779　3306 899 5515 3836 1635

this? And whose inscription?" ¶　"Caesar's," they replied. ¶ **17** Then Jesus　said to them,
αὕτη καὶ ἡ ἐπιγραφή δὲ Καίσαρος οἱ εἶπαν αὐτῷ δὲ ὁ Ἰησοῦς εἶπεν → αὐτοῖς
r.nsf cj d.nsf n.nsf cj n.gsm d.npm v.aai.3p r.dsm.3 cj d.nsm n.nsm v.aai.3s r.dpm.3
4047 2779 3836 2107　1254 2790 3836 3306 899　1254 3836 2652 3306 899

"Give to Caesar what is Caesar's and to God　what is God's."　And they were amazed　at him.
ἀπόδοτε ← Καίσαρι τὰ Καίσαρος καὶ → τῷ θεῷ τὰ τοῦ θεοῦ καὶ → → ἐξεθαύμαζον ἐπ' αὐτῷ
v.aam.2p n.dsm d.apn n.gsm cj d.dsm n.dsm d.apn d.gsm n.gsm cj　v.iai.3p p.d r.dsm.3
625 2790 3836 2790 2779 3836 2536 3836 3836 2536 2779　1703 2093 899

Marriage at the Resurrection

12:18 Then the Sadducees, who　say　there is　no resurrection, came　to　him with a question.
Καὶ → Σαδδουκαῖοι οἵτινες λέγουσιν → εἶναι μὴ ἀνάστασιν ἔρχονται πρὸς αὐτὸν καὶ ἐπηρώτων αὐτὸν
cj　n.npm　r.npm v.pai.3p　f.pa pl n.asf　v.pmi.3p p.a r.asm.3 cj v.iai.3p r.asm.3
2779　4881　4015 3306　1639 3590 414　2262 4639 899 2779 2089 899

19 "Teacher," they said,　"Moses wrote for us that if a man's brother dies　and leaves a wife but no
διδάσκαλε → λέγοντες Μωϋσῆς ἔγραψεν → ἡμῖν ὅτι ἐὰν τινος ἀδελφὸς ἀποθάνῃ καὶ καταλίπῃ γυναῖκα καὶ μὴ ἀφῇ
n.vsm　pt.pa.npm n.nsm v.aai.3s　r.dp.1 cj cj r.gsm n.nsm v.aas.3s cj v.aas.3s n.asf cj pl v.aas.3s
1437　3306 3707 1211　7005 4022 1569 5516 81 633　2779 2901 1222 2779 3590 918

children, the man　must marry the widow and have　children for his　brother. **20** Now there were
τέκνον ὁ ἀδελφὸς αὐτοῦ ἵνα λάβῃ τὴν γυναῖκα καὶ ἐξαναστήσῃ σπέρμα → αὐτοῦ τῷ ἀδελφῷ → ἦσαν
n.asn d.nsm n.nsm r.gsm.3 cj v.aas.3s d.asf n.asf cj v.aas.3s n.asn　r.gsm.3 d.dsm n.dsm　v.iai.3p
5451 3836 81 899 2671 3284 3836 1222 2779 1985 5065　81 899 3836 81　1639

seven brothers.　The first　one married　and died　without leaving any children. **21** The second one
ἑπτὰ ἀδελφοὶ καὶ ὁ πρῶτος ← ἔλαβεν γυναῖκα καὶ ἀποθνήσκων οὐκ ἀφῆκεν σπέρμα καὶ ὁ δεύτερος ←
a.npm n.npm cj d.nsm a.nsm　v.aai.3s n.asf cj pt.pa.nsm pl v.aai.3s n.asn cj d.nsm a.nsm
2231 81 2779 3836 4755　3284 1222 2779 633 4024 918 5065 2779 3836 1311

married the widow, but he also died,　leaving　no child.　It was the same　with the third. **22** *In fact*, none of
ἔλαβεν αὐτὴν καὶ → ἀπέθανεν καταλιπὼν μὴ σπέρμα καὶ → → ὡσαύτως ← ὁ τρίτος καὶ οὐκ
v.aai.3s r.asf.3 cj　v.aai.3s pt.aa.nsm pl n.asn cj　adv　d.nsm a.nsm cj pl
3284 899 2779　633 2901 3590 5065 2779　6058　3836 5569 2779 4024

12:13 Καὶ ἀποστέλλουσιν πρὸς αὐτόν τινας τῶν Φαρισαίων καὶ τῶν Ἡρῳδιανῶν ἵνα αὐτὸν ἀγρεύσωσιν λόγῳ. **14** καὶ ἐλθόντες λέγουσιν αὐτῷ, Διδάσκαλε, οἴδαμεν ὅτι ἀληθὴς εἶ καὶ οὐ μέλει σοι περὶ οὐδενός· οὐ γὰρ βλέπεις εἰς πρόσωπον ἀνθρώπων, ἀλλ' ἐπ' ἀληθείας τὴν ὁδὸν τοῦ θεοῦ διδάσκεις· ἔξεστιν δοῦναι κῆνσον Καίσαρι ἢ οὔ; δῶμεν ἢ μὴ δῶμεν ¶ **15** ὁ δὲ εἰδὼς αὐτῶν τὴν ὑπόκρισιν εἶπεν αὐτοῖς, Τί με πειράζετε; φέρετέ μοι δηνάριον ἵνα ἴδω. **16** οἱ δὲ ἤνεγκαν. καὶ λέγει αὐτοῖς, Τίνος ἡ εἰκὼν αὕτη καὶ ἡ ἐπιγραφή; ¶ οἱ δὲ εἶπαν αὐτῷ, Καίσαρος. ¶ **17** ὁ δὲ Ἰησοῦς εἶπεν αὐτοῖς, Τὰ Καίσαρος ἀπόδοτε Καίσαρι καὶ τὰ τοῦ θεοῦ τῷ θεῷ. καὶ ἐξεθαύμαζον ἐπ' αὐτῷ.

12:18 Καὶ ἔρχονται Σαδδουκαῖοι πρὸς αὐτόν, οἵτινες λέγουσιν ἀνάστασιν μὴ εἶναι, καὶ ἐπηρώτων αὐτὸν λέγοντες, **19** Διδάσκαλε, Μωϋσῆς ἔγραψεν ἡμῖν ὅτι ἐάν τινος ἀδελφὸς ἀποθάνῃ καὶ καταλίπῃ γυναῖκα καὶ μὴ ἀφῇ τέκνον, ἵνα λάβῃ ὁ ἀδελφὸς αὐτοῦ τὴν γυναῖκα καὶ ἐξαναστήσῃ σπέρμα τῷ ἀδελφῷ αὐτοῦ. **20** ἑπτὰ ἀδελφοὶ ἦσαν· καὶ ὁ πρῶτος ἔλαβεν γυναῖκα καὶ ἀποθνήσκων οὐκ ἀφῆκεν σπέρμα· **21** καὶ ὁ δεύτερος ἔλαβεν αὐτὴν καὶ ἀπέθανεν μὴ καταλιπὼν σπέρμα· καὶ ὁ τρίτος ὡσαύτως·

the	seven	left	any	children.	Last	of all,	the	woman	died	too.	[23] At	the	resurrection		
οἱ	ἑπτὰ	ἀφῆκαν	σπέρμα		ἔσχατον	→	πάντων	ἡ γυνὴ	ἀπέθανεν	καὶ	ἐν	τῇ	ἀναστάσει	[ὅταν	ἀναστῶσιν]
d.npm	a.npm	v.aai.3p	n.asn		adv		a.gpn	d.nsf n.nsf	v.aai.3s	adv	p.d	d.dsf	n.dsf	cj	v.aas.3p
3836	2231	918	5065		2274		4246	3836 1222	633	2779	1877	3836	414	4020	482

whose		wife	will she be,	since	the	seven	were married	to her?"	¶	[24] Jesus		replied,	"Are	you	not
⌜τίνος	αὐτῶν⌝	γυνή	→ → ἔσται	γὰρ	οἱ	ἑπτὰ	ἔσχον	γυναῖκα αὐτήν		ὁ	Ἰησοῦς	ἔφη	αὐτοῖς →	→	οὐ
r.gsm	r.gpm.3	n.nsf	v.fmi.3s	cj	d.npm	a.npm	v.aai.3p	n.asf r.asf.3		d.nsm	n.nsm	v.iai.3s	r.dpm.3		pl
5515	899	1222	1639	1142	3836	2231	2400	1222 899		3836	2652	5774	899	4414 4414	4024

in error	because	you do	not know	the	Scriptures	or	the	power	of God?	[25]	When	the	dead	rise,
→ πλανᾶσθε	⌜διὰ τοῦτο⌝	→	μὴ εἰδότες	τὰς	γραφὰς	μηδὲ	τὴν	δύναμιν	⌜τοῦ θεοῦ⌝	γὰρ	ὅταν	ἐκ	νεκρῶν	ἀναστῶσιν
v.ppi.2p	p.a r.asn		pl pt.ra.npm	d.apf	n.apf	cj	d.asf	n.asf	d.gsm n.gsm	cj	cj	p.g	a.gpm	v.aas.3p
4414	1328 4047	3857	3857 3590	3836	1210	3593	3836	1539	3836 2536	1142	4020	1666	3738	482

		they will neither	marry	nor	be given in marriage;		they will be	like	the angels	in	heaven.		[26] Now	about
→	→ οὔτε	γαμοῦσιν	οὔτε →	→ → γαμίζονται	ἀλλ'	→	→ εἰσὶν	ὡς	ἄγγελοι	ἐν	⌜τοῖς οὐρανοῖς⌝	δὲ	περὶ
	cj	v.pai.3p	cj	v.ppi.3p	cj		v.pai.3p	cj	n.npm	p.d	d.dpm n.dpm	cj	p.g
1138	1138 4046	1138	4046	1139	247		1639	6055	34	1877	3836 4041	1254	4309

the dead		rising	– have	you not read	in	the	book	of Moses,	in the account of the bush,	how	God		
τῶν νεκρῶν	ὅτι	ἐγείρονται	→	→ οὐκ ἀνέγνωτε	ἐν	τῇ	βίβλῳ	→ Μωϋσέως	ἐπὶ ← ← ← τοῦ βάτου	πῶς	ὁ	θεὸς	
d.gpm a.gpm	cj	v.ppi.3p		pl v.aai.2p	p.d	d.dsf	n.dsf	n.gsm	p.g d.gsm n.gsm	cj	d.nsm	n.nsm	
3836 3738	4022	1586	336	336 4024 336	1877	3836	1047	3707	2093 3836 1004	4802	3836	2536	

said to him,		'I	am	the God	of Abraham,		the God	of Isaac,	and the God	of Jacob'?	[27] He	is	not	the God
εἶπεν →	αὐτῷ λέγων	Ἐγὼ		ὁ θεὸς	→ Ἀβραὰμ	καὶ ὁ	θεὸς	→ Ἰσαὰκ	καὶ ὁ θεὸς	→ Ἰακώβ	→	ἔστιν	οὐκ	θεὸς
v.aai.3s	r.dsm.3 pt.pa.nsm	r.ns.1		d.nsm n.nsm	n.gsm	cj d.nsm	n.nsm	n.gsm	cj d.nsm n.nsm	n.gsm		v.pai.3s	pl	n.nsm
3306	899 3306	1609		3836 2536	11	2779 3836	2536	2693	2779 3836 2536	2609		1639	4024	2536

of the dead,	but	of the living.	You are	badly	mistaken!"									
→ νεκρῶν	ἀλλὰ	→ ζώντων	→	πολὺ	πλανᾶσθε									
a.gpm	cj	pt.pa.gpm		adv	v.ppi.2p									
3738	247	2409	4414	4414 4498	4414									

The Greatest Commandment

12:28	One	of	the teachers	of the law	came		and heard	them	debating.	Noticing	that	Jesus had	given
Καὶ	εἷς	→	⌜τῶν γραμματέων⌝ ← ← ←		προσελθὼν		ἀκούσας	αὐτῶν	συζητούντων	ἰδὼν	ὅτι		
cj	a.nsm		d.gpm n.gpm		pt.aa.nsm		pt.aa.nsm	r.gpm.3	pt.pa.gpm	pt.aa.nsm	cj		
2779	1651	3836	1208		4665		201	899	5184	1625	4022	646	646

them	a good	answer,	he asked		him,	"Of all		the commandments,	which	is	the most important?"	¶
αὐτοῖς	καλῶς	ἀπεκρίθη	→ ἐπηρώτησεν	αὐτόν		→ πάντων		ἐντολὴ	ποία	ἐστιν	→ πρώτη	
r.dpm.3	adv	v.api.3s	v.aai.3s	r.asm.3		a.gpn		n.nsf	r.nsf	v.pai.3s	a.nsf	
899	2822	646	2089	899		4246		1953	4481	1639	4755	

[29]	"The most	important one,"	answered	Jesus,	"is	this:	'Hear,	O Israel,	the Lord	our	God,	the Lord
ὅτι	→	πρώτη	← ἀπεκρίθη	ὁ Ἰησοῦς	ἐστιν	→	ἄκουε	Ἰσραήλ	κύριος	ἡμῶν	ὁ θεὸς	κύριος
cj		a.nsf	v.api.3s	d.nsm n.nsm	v.pai.3s		v.pam.2s	n.vsm	n.nsm	r.gp.1	d.nsm n.nsm	n.nsm
4022	4755		646	3836 2652	1639	201		2702	3261	7005	3836 2536	3261

is	one.	[30]	Love	the Lord	your	God	with	all	your	heart	and with	all	your	soul	and with
ἐστιν	εἷς		καὶ ἀγαπήσεις	κύριον	σου	⌜τὸν θεόν⌝	ἐξ	ὅλης	σου	⌜τῆς καρδίας⌝	καὶ ἐξ	ὅλης	σου	⌜τῆς ψυχῆς⌝	καὶ ἐξ
v.pai.3s	a.nsm		cj v.fai.2s	n.asm	r.gs.2	d.asm n.asm	p.g	a.gsf	r.gs.2	d.gsf n.gsf	cj p.g	a.gsf	r.gs.2	d.gsf n.gsf	cj p.g
1639	1651		2779 26	3261	5148	3836 2536	1666	3910	5148	3836 2840	2779 1666	3910	5148	3836 6034	2779 1666

all	your	mind	and with	all	your	strength.'	[31] The	second	is this:	'Love	your	neighbor	as	yourself.'
ὅλης	σου	⌜τῆς διανοίας⌝	καὶ ἐξ	ὅλης	σου	⌜τῆς ἰσχύος⌝	δευτέρα	→	αὕτη	ἀγαπήσεις	σου	⌜τὸν πλησίον⌝	ὡς	σεαυτόν
a.gsf	r.gs.2	d.gsf n.gsf	cj p.g	a.gsf	r.gs.2	d.gsf n.gsf	a.nsf		r.nsf	v.fai.2s	r.gs.2	d.asm adv	cj	r.asm.2
3910	5148	3836 1379	2779 1666	3910	5148	3836 2709	1311		4047	26	5148	3836 4446	6055	4932

There is		no	commandment	greater	than	these."	¶	[32]	"Well	said,	teacher,"	the	man	replied.
→	ἔστιν	οὐκ ἄλλη	ἐντολὴ	μείζων	→	τούτων			καὶ	καλῶς	διδάσκαλε	ὁ	γραμματεύς	εἶπεν	αὐτῷ
v.pai.3s		pl r.nsf	n.nsf	a.nsf.c		r.gpf			cj	adv	n.vsm	d.nsm	n.nsm	v.aai.3s	r.dsm.3
1639	4024	257	1953	3489		4047			2779	2822	1437	3836	1208	3306	899

"You are		right	in saying	that	God	is	one	and there	is	no	other	but	him.	¶	[33]	To	love
→	→ ἐπ'	ἀληθείας	εἶπες	ὅτι	→	ἐστιν	εἷς	καὶ →	ἔστιν	οὐκ	ἄλλος	πλὴν	αὐτοῦ			καὶ →	⌜τὸ ἀγαπᾶν⌝
	p.g	n.gsf	v.aai.2s	cj		v.pai.3s	a.nsm	cj	v.pai.3s	pl	r.nsm	p.g	r.gsm.3			cj	d.nsn f.pa
3306	3306	2093 237	3306	4022		1639 1651		2779	1639	4024	257	4440	899			2779	3836 26

---

22 καὶ οἱ ἑπτὰ οὐκ ἀφῆκαν σπέρμα. ἔσχατον πάντων καὶ ἡ γυνὴ ἀπέθανεν. 23 ἐν τῇ ἀναστάσει [ὅταν ἀναστῶσιν] τίνος αὐτῶν ἔσται γυνή; οἱ γὰρ ἑπτὰ ἔσχον αὐτὴν γυναῖκα. ¶ 24 ἔφη αὐτοῖς ὁ Ἰησοῦς, Οὐ διὰ τοῦτο πλανᾶσθε μὴ εἰδότες τὰς γραφὰς μηδὲ τὴν δύναμιν τοῦ θεοῦ; 25 ὅταν γὰρ ἐκ νεκρῶν ἀναστῶσιν οὔτε γαμοῦσιν οὔτε γαμίζονται, ἀλλ' εἰσὶν ὡς ἄγγελοι ἐν τοῖς οὐρανοῖς. 26 περὶ δὲ τῶν νεκρῶν ὅτι ἐγείρονται οὐκ ἀνέγνωτε ἐν τῇ βίβλῳ Μωϋσέως ἐπὶ τοῦ βάτου πῶς εἶπεν αὐτῷ ὁ θεὸς λέγων, Ἐγὼ ὁ θεὸς Ἀβραὰμ καὶ [ὁ] θεὸς Ἰσαὰκ καὶ [ὁ] θεὸς Ἰακώβ; 27 οὐκ ἔστιν ὁ θεὸς νεκρῶν ἀλλὰ ζώντων· πολὺ πλανᾶσθε.

12:28 Καὶ προσελθὼν εἷς τῶν γραμματέων ἀκούσας αὐτῶν συζητούντων, ἰδὼν ὅτι καλῶς ἀπεκρίθη αὐτοῖς ἐπηρώτησεν αὐτόν, Ποία ἐστὶν ἐντολὴ πρώτη πάντων; ¶ 29 ἀπεκρίθη ὁ Ἰησοῦς ὅτι Πρώτη ἐστίν, Ἄκουε, Ἰσραήλ, κύριος ὁ θεὸς ἡμῶν κύριος εἷς ἐστιν, 30 καὶ ἀγαπήσεις κύριον τὸν θεόν σου ἐξ ὅλης τῆς καρδίας σου καὶ ἐξ ὅλης τῆς ψυχῆς σου καὶ ἐξ ὅλης τῆς διανοίας σου καὶ ἐξ ὅλης τῆς ἰσχύος σου. 31 δευτέρα αὕτη, Ἀγαπήσεις τὸν πλησίον σου ὡς σεαυτόν. μείζων τούτων ἄλλη ἐντολὴ οὐκ ἔστιν. ¶ 32 καὶ εἶπεν αὐτῷ ὁ γραμματεύς, Καλῶς, διδάσκαλε, ἐπ' ἀληθείας εἶπες ὅτι εἷς ἐστιν καὶ οὐκ ἔστιν ἄλλος πλὴν αὐτοῦ ¶ 33 καὶ τὸ ἀγαπᾶν αὐτὸν ἐξ ὅλης τῆς καρδίας καὶ ἐξ ὅλης τῆς συνέσεως καὶ ἐξ ὅλης τῆς ἰσχύος καὶ τὸ ἀγαπᾶν τὸν

him with all your heart,   with all your understanding and with all your strength, and to love   your
αὐτοῦ ἐξ ὅλης τῆς καρδίας καὶ ἐξ ὅλης τῆς συνέσεως καὶ ἐξ ὅλης τῆς ἰσχύος καὶ → τὸ ἀγαπᾶν τὸν
r.asm.3 p.g a.gsf d.gsf n.gsf cj p.g a.gsf d.gsf n.gsf cj p.g a.gsf d.gsf n.gsf cj d.nsn f.pa d.asm
899 1666 3910 3836 2840 2779 1666 3910 3836 5304 2779 1666 3910 3836 2709 2779 3836 26 3836

neighbor as yourself is more   important than all   burnt offerings and sacrifices.” ¶ 34
πλησίον ὡς ἑαυτὸν ἐστιν περισσότερον ← → πάντων τῶν ὁλοκαυτωμάτων καὶ θυσιῶν   καὶ
adv cj r.asm.3 v.pai.3s a.nsn.c a.gpn d.gpn n.gpn cj n.gpf cj
4446 6055 1571 1639 4358 4246 3836 3906 2779 2602 2779

When Jesus saw   that he had answered wisely, he said to him, “You are not far   from the
→ ὁ Ἰησοῦς ἰδὼν [αὐτὸν] ὅτι → → ἀπεκρίθη νουνεχῶς → εἶπεν → αὐτῷ εἶ οὐ μακρὰν ἀπὸ τῆς
→ d.nsm n.nsm pt.aa.nsm r.asm.3 cj v.api.3s adv v.aai.3s r.dsm.3 v.pai.2s pl adv p.g d.gsf
1625 3836 2652 1625 899 4022 646 3807 3306 899 1639 4024 3426 608 3836

kingdom of God.” And from then on no   one dared ask   him any more questions.
βασιλείας → τοῦ θεοῦ καὶ   οὐδεὶς ← ἐτόλμα ἐπερωτῆσαι αὐτὸν οὐκέτι ←   ←
n.gsf d.gsn n.gsm cj a.nsm v.iai.3s f.aa r.asm.3 adv
993 3836 2536 2779 4029 5528 2089 899 4033 2089

Whose Son Is the Christ?

12:35   While Jesus   was teaching in the temple courts, he asked, “How is it that the teachers
Καὶ ἀποκριθεὶς → ὁ Ἰησοῦς → διδάσκων ἐν τῷ ἱερῷ → ἔλεγεν πῶς ← ← οἱ γραμματεῖς
cj pt.ap.nsm d.nsm n.nsm pt.pa.nsm p.d d.dsn n.dsn v.iai.3s cj d.npm n.npm
2779 646 1438 3836 2652 1438 1877 3836 2639 3306 4802 3836 1208

of the law say   that the Christ is   the son of David? 36 David himself, speaking by the Holy   Spirit, declared:
← ← ← λέγουσιν ὅτι ὁ χριστὸς ἐστιν υἱὸς → Δαυὶδ Δαυὶδ αὐτὸς   ἐν τῷ τῷ ἁγίῳ πνεύματι εἶπεν
v.pai.3p cj d.nsm n.nsm v.pai.3s n.nsm n.gsm n.nsm r.nsm p.d d.dsn d.dsn a.dsn n.dsn v.aai.3s
3306 4022 3836 5986 1639 5626 1253 1253 899 1877 3836 3836 41 4460 3306

“‘The Lord said to my Lord: “Sit at my right hand until   I put your enemies   under your feet.”’
κύριος εἶπεν → μου τῷ κυρίῳ, κάθου ἐκ μου δεξιῶν → ἕως ἂν → θῶ σου τοὺς ἐχθρούς, ὑποκάτω σου τῶν ποδῶν,
n.nsm v.aai.3s r.gs.1 d.dsm n.dsm v.pmm.2s p.g r.gs.1 a.gpf cj pl v.aas.1s r.gs.2 d.apm a.apm p.g r.gs.2 d.gpm n.gpm
3261 3306 3261 1609 3836 3261 2764 1666 1609 1288 2401 323 5502 5148 3836 2398 5691 5148 3836 4546

37 David himself calls him ‘Lord.’ How then can he be   his son?” ¶   The large crowd listened to him
Δαυὶδ αὐτὸς λέγει αὐτὸν κύριον πόθεν καὶ →   ἐστιν αὐτοῦ υἱὸς   Καὶ ὁ πολὺς ὄχλος ἤκουεν ← αὐτοῦ
n.nsm r.nsm v.pai.3s r.asm.3 n.asm cj cj v.pai.3s r.gsm.3 n.nsm cj d.nsm a.nsm n.nsm v.iai.3s r.gsm.3
1253 899 3306 899 3261 4470 2779 1639 899 5626 2779 3836 4498 4063 201 899

with delight. ¶ 38   As he   taught, Jesus said, “Watch out for the teachers   of the law. They like   to
→ ἡδέως   Καὶ ἐν αὐτοῦ τῇ διδαχῇ,   ἔλεγεν βλέπετε ← ἀπὸ τῶν γραμματέων ← ← τῶν θελόντων →
adv cj p.d r.gsm.3 d.dsf n.dsf v.iai.3s v.pam.2p p.g d.gpm n.gpm d.gpm pt.pa.gpm
2452 2779 1877 899 3836 1439 3306 1063 608 3836 1208 3836 2527

walk   around in flowing robes and be greeted in the marketplaces, 39 and have the most important
περιπατεῖν ← ἐν   στολαῖς καὶ ἀσπασμοὺς ἐν ταῖς ἀγοραῖς καὶ → → →
f.pa p.d n.dpf cj n.apm p.d d.dpf n.dpf cj
4344 1877 5124 2779 833 1877 3836 59 2779

seats   in the synagogues and the places of honor   at banquets. 40 They devour   widows’
πρωτοκαθεδρίας ἐν ταῖς συναγωγαῖς καὶ → → πρωτοκλισίας ἐν τοῖς δείπνοις, οἱ κατεσθίοντες τῶν χηρῶν,
n.apf p.d d.dpf n.dpf cj n.apf p.d d.dpn n.dpn d.npm pt.pa.npm d.gpf n.gpf
4751 1877 3836 5252 2779 4752 1877 3836 1270 3836 2983 3836 5939

houses   and for a show   make lengthy prayers.   Such men will be   punished most severely.”
τὰς οἰκίας, καὶ → προφάσει   μακρὰ προσευχόμενοι οὗτοι   → λήμψονται κρίμα → περισσότερον
d.apf n.apf cj n.dsf adv pt.pm.npm r.npm v.fmi.3p n.asn a.asn.c
3836 3864 2779 4733 3431 4667 4047 3284 3210 4358

The Widow’s Offering

12:41   Jesus sat   down opposite the place   where the offerings were put and watched   the crowd
Καὶ   καθίσας ← κατέναντι τοῦ γαζοφυλακίου → ← ← → ἐθεώρει πῶς ὁ ὄχλος
cj pt.aa.nsm p.g d.gsn n.gsn v.iai.3s cj d.nsm n.nsm
2779 2767 2978 3836 1126 2555 4802 3836 4063

putting their money into the temple treasury.   Many rich   people threw in large amounts. 42 But a   poor
βάλλει   χαλκὸν εἰς τὸ → γαζοφυλάκιον καὶ πολλοὶ πλούσιοι → ἔβαλλον πολλὰ ←   καὶ μία πτωχὴ
v.pai.3s n.asm p.a d.asn n.asn cj a.npm a.npm v.iai.3p a.apn cj a.nsf a.nsf
965 5910 1650 3836 1126 2779 4498 4454 965 4498 2779 1651 4777

πλησίον ὡς ἑαυτὸν περισσότερόν ἐστιν πάντων τῶν ὁλοκαυτωμάτων καὶ θυσιῶν. ³⁴ καὶ ὁ Ἰησοῦς ἰδὼν [αὐτὸν] ὅτι νουνεχῶς ἀπεκρίθη εἶπεν αὐτῷ, Οὐ μακρὰν εἶ ἀπὸ τῆς βασιλείας τοῦ θεοῦ. καὶ οὐδεὶς οὐκέτι ἐτόλμα αὐτὸν ἐπερωτῆσαι.

¹²:³⁵ Καὶ ἀποκριθεὶς ὁ Ἰησοῦς ἔλεγεν διδάσκων ἐν τῷ ἱερῷ, Πῶς λέγουσιν οἱ γραμματεῖς ὅτι ὁ Χριστὸς υἱὸς Δαυὶδ ἐστιν; ³⁶ αὐτὸς Δαυὶδ εἶπεν ἐν τῷ πνεύματι τῷ ἁγίῳ, Εἶπεν κύριος τῷ κυρίῳ μου, Κάθου ἐκ δεξιῶν μου, ἕως ἂν θῶ τοὺς ἐχθρούς σου ὑποκάτω τῶν ποδῶν σου. ³⁷ αὐτὸς Δαυὶδ λέγει αὐτὸν κύριον, καὶ πόθεν αὐτοῦ ἐστιν υἱός; ¶ καὶ [ὁ] πολὺς ὄχλος ἤκουεν αὐτοῦ ἡδέως. ¶ ³⁸ Καὶ ἐν τῇ διδαχῇ αὐτοῦ ἔλεγεν, Βλέπετε ἀπὸ τῶν γραμματέων τῶν θελόντων ἐν στολαῖς περιπατεῖν καὶ ἀσπασμοὺς ἐν ταῖς ἀγοραῖς ³⁹ καὶ πρωτοκαθεδρίας ἐν ταῖς συναγωγαῖς καὶ πρωτοκλισίας ἐν τοῖς δείπνοις, ⁴⁰ οἱ κατεσθίοντες τὰς οἰκίας τῶν χηρῶν καὶ προφάσει μακρὰ προσευχόμενοι· οὗτοι λήμψονται περισσότερον κρίμα.

¹²:⁴¹ Καὶ καθίσας κατέναντι τοῦ γαζοφυλακίου ἐθεώρει πῶς ὁ ὄχλος βάλλει χαλκὸν εἰς τὸ γαζοφυλάκιον. καὶ πολλοὶ πλούσιοι ἔβαλλον πολλά· ⁴² καὶ ἐλθοῦσα μία χήρα πτωχὴ ἔβαλεν λεπτὰ δύο, ὅ ἐστιν κοδράντης. ¶ ⁴³ καὶ προσκαλεσάμενος τοὺς μαθητὰς

widow came and put in two very small copper coins, worth only a fraction of a penny. ¶ **43**
χήρα ἐλθοῦσα ἔβαλεν ← δύο → λεπτὰ ὅ ἐστιν → → → → κοδράντης καί
n.nsf pt.aa.nsf v.aai.3s a.apn n.apn r.nsn v.pai.3s n.nsm cj
5939 2262 965 1545 3321 4005 1639 3119 2779

Calling his disciples to him, Jesus said, "I tell you the truth, this poor widow has
προσκαλεσάμενος αὐτοῦ ⸢τοὺς μαθητὰς⸥ εἶπεν αὐτοῖς λέγω ὑμῖν ἀμὴν ὅτι αὕτη ἡ πτωχὴ ἡ χήρα →
pt.am.nsm r.gsm.3 d.apm n.apm v.aai.3s r.dpm.3 v.pai.1s r.dp.2 pl cj r.nsf d.nsf a.nsf d.nsf n.nsf
4673 899 3836 3412 3306 899 3306 7007 297 4022 4047 3836 4777 3836 5939

put more into the treasury than all the others. **44** They all gave out of their wealth; but
ἔβαλεν πλεῖον εἰς τὸ γαζοφυλάκιον → πάντων τῶν βαλλόντων γὰρ → πάντες ἔβαλον ἐκ ← αὐτοῖς ⸢τοῦ περισσεύοντος⸥ δὲ
v.aai.3s a.asn.c p.a d.asn n.asn a.gpm d.gpm pt.pa.gpm cj a.npm v.aai.3p p.g r.dpm.3 d.gsn pt.pa.gsn cj
965 4498 1650 3836 1126 4246 3836 965 1142 4246 965 1666 899 3836 4355 1254

she, out of her poverty, put in everything – all she had to live on."
αὕτη ἐκ ← αὐτῆς ⸢τῆς ὑστερήσεως⸥ ἔβαλεν ← πάντα ὅσα εἶχεν ὅλον αὐτῆς → → ⸢τὸν βίον⸥ ←
r.nsf p.g r.gsf.3 d.gsf n.gsf v.aai.3s a.apn r.apn v.iai.3s a.asm r.gsf.3 d.asm n.asm
4047 1666 899 3836 5730 965 4246 4012 2400 3910 899 3836 1050

Signs of the End of the Age

13:1 As he was leaving the temple, one of his disciples said to him, "Look, Teacher! What
Καὶ → αὐτοῦ → ἐκπορευομένου ἐκ τοῦ ἱεροῦ εἷς → αὐτοῦ ⸢τῶν μαθητῶν⸥ λέγει αὐτῷ ἴδε διδάσκαλε ποταποὶ
cj r.gsm.3 pt.pm.gsm p.g d.gsn n.gsn a.nsm r.gsm.3 d.gpm n.gpm v.pai.3s r.dsm.3 pl n.vsm r.npm
2779 1744 899 1744 1666 3836 2639 1651 3412 899 3836 3412 3306 899 2623 1437 4534

massive stones! What magnificent buildings!" ¶ **2** "Do you see all these great buildings?"
← λίθοι καὶ ποταπαὶ οἰκοδομαί καὶ → βλέπεις ταύτας μεγάλας ⸢τὰς οἰκοδομάς⸥
n.npm cj r.npf n.npf cj v.pai.2s r.apf a.apf d.apf n.apf
3345 2779 4534 3869 2779 1063 4047 3489 3836 3869

replied Jesus. "Not one stone here will be left on another; every one will be thrown down."
εἶπεν ⸤ὁ Ἰησοῦς⸥ αὐτῷ ⸢οὐ μὴ⸥ λίθος ὧδε → → ἀφεθῇ ἐπὶ λίθον ὃς ← → → ⸢οὐ μὴ⸥ καταλυθῇ ←
v.aai.3s d.nsm n.nsm r.dsm.3 pl pl n.nsm adv v.aps.3s p.a n.asm r.nsm pl pl v.aps.3s
3306 3836 2652 899 4024 3590 3345 6045 918 2093 3345 4005 4024 3590 2907

¶ **3** As Jesus was sitting on the Mount of Olives opposite the temple, Peter, James, John and
Καὶ → αὐτοῦ → καθημένου εἰς τὸ ὄρος → ⸢τῶν ἐλαιῶν⸥ κατέναντι τοῦ ἱεροῦ Πέτρος καὶ Ἰάκωβος καὶ Ἰωάννης καὶ
cj r.gsm.3 pt.pm.gsm p.a d.asn n.asn d.gpf n.gpf p.g d.gsn n.gsn n.nsm cj n.nsm cj n.nsm cj
2779 2761 899 2764 1650 3836 4001 3836 1777 2978 3836 2639 4377 2779 2610 2779 2722 2779

Andrew asked him privately, **4** "Tell us, when will these things happen? And what will be the sign that they
Ἀνδρέας ἐπηρώτα αὐτὸν ⸢κατ᾽ ἰδίαν⸥ εἰπὸν ἡμῖν πότε → ταῦτα ← ἔσται καὶ τί τὸ σημεῖον ὅταν ταῦτα
n.nsm v.iai.3s r.asm.3 p.a a.asf v.aam.2s r.dp.1 adv r.npn v.fmi.3s cj r.nsn d.nsn n.nsn cj r.npn
436 2089 899 2848 2625 3306 7005 4537 1639 4047 2770 2779 5515 3836 4956 4020 4047

are all about to be fulfilled?" ¶ **5** Jesus said to them: "Watch out that no one deceives you.
→ πάντα μέλλῃ → συντελεῖσθαι δὲ ὁ Ἰησοῦς ἤρξατο λέγειν → αὐτοῖς βλέπετε μή τις πλανήσῃ ὑμᾶς
a.npn v.pas.3s f.pp cj d.nsm n.nsm v.ami.3s f.pa r.dpm.3 v.pam.2p cj r.nsm v.aas.3s r.ap.2
3516 4246 3516 5334 1254 3836 2652 806 3306 899 1063 3590 5516 4414 7007

6 Many will come in my name, claiming, 'I am he,' and will deceive many. **7** When you hear
πολλοὶ → ἐλεύσονται ἐπὶ μου ⸢τῷ ὀνόματι⸥ λέγοντες ὅτι ἐγώ εἰμι καὶ → πλανήσουσιν πολλούς δὲ ὅταν → ἀκούσητε
a.npm v.fmi.3p p.d r.gs.1 d.dsn n.dsn pt.pa.npm cj r.ns.1 v.pai.1s cj v.fai.3p a.apm cj cj v.aas.2p
4498 2262 2093 1609 3836 3950 3306 4022 1609 1639 2779 4414 4498 1254 4020 201

of wars and rumors of wars, do not be alarmed. Such things must happen, but the end is still to come. **8**
← πολέμους καὶ ἀκοὰς → πολέμων → μὴ → θροεῖσθε → δεῖ γενέσθαι ἀλλ᾽ τὸ τέλος οὔπω γὰρ
n.apm cj n.apf n.gpm pl v.pam.2p v.pai.3s f.am cj d.nsn n.nsn adv cj
4483 2779 198 4483 3590 2583 1256 1181 247 3836 5465 4037 1142

Nation will rise against nation, and kingdom against kingdom. There will be earthquakes in various
ἔθνος → ἐγερθήσεται ἐπ᾽ ἔθνος καὶ βασιλεία ἐπὶ βασιλείαν → → ἔσονται σεισμοὶ κατὰ ←
n.nsn v.fpi.3s p.a n.asn cj n.nsf p.a n.asf v.fmi.3p n.npm p.a
1620 1586 2093 1620 2779 993 2093 993 1639 4939 2848

places, and famines. These are the beginning of birth pains. ¶ **9** "You must be on your guard.
τόπους ἔσονται λιμοί ταῦτα ἀρχὴ → → ὠδίνων δὲ ὑμεῖς → → → ἑαυτοὺς βλέπετε
n.apm v.fmi.3p n.npf r.npn n.nsf n.gpf cj r.np.2 r.apm.2 v.pam.2p
5536 1639 3350 4047 794 6047 1254 7007 1063 1063 1063 1571 1063

αὐτοῦ εἶπεν αὐτοῖς, Ἀμὴν λέγω ὑμῖν ὅτι ἡ χήρα αὕτη ἡ πτωχὴ πλεῖον πάντων ἔβαλεν τῶν βαλλόντων εἰς τὸ γαζοφυλάκιον· ⁴⁴ πάντες γὰρ ἐκ τοῦ περισσεύοντος αὐτοῖς ἔβαλον, αὕτη δὲ ἐκ τῆς ὑστερήσεως αὐτῆς πάντα ὅσα εἶχεν ἔβαλεν ὅλον τὸν βίον αὐτῆς.

13:1 Καὶ ἐκπορευομένου αὐτοῦ ἐκ τοῦ ἱεροῦ λέγει αὐτῷ εἷς τῶν μαθητῶν αὐτοῦ, Διδάσκαλε, ἴδε ποταποὶ λίθοι καὶ ποταποὶ οἰκοδομαί. ¶ ² καὶ ὁ Ἰησοῦς εἶπεν αὐτῷ, Βλέπεις ταύτας τὰς μεγάλας οἰκοδομάς; οὐ μὴ ἀφεθῇ ὧδε λίθος ἐπὶ λίθον ὃς οὐ μὴ καταλυθῇ. ¶ ³ Καὶ καθημένου αὐτοῦ εἰς τὸ Ὄρος τῶν Ἐλαιῶν κατέναντι τοῦ ἱεροῦ ἐπηρώτα αὐτὸν κατ᾽ ἰδίαν Πέτρος καὶ Ἰάκωβος καὶ Ἰωάννης καὶ Ἀνδρέας, ⁴ Εἰπὸν ἡμῖν, πότε ταῦτα ἔσται καὶ τί τὸ σημεῖον ὅταν μέλλῃ ταῦτα συντελεῖσθαι πάντα ¶ ⁵ ὁ δὲ Ἰησοῦς ἤρξατο λέγειν αὐτοῖς, Βλέπετε μή τις ὑμᾶς πλανήσῃ· ⁶ πολλοὶ ἐλεύσονται ἐπὶ τῷ ὀνόματί μου λέγοντες ὅτι Ἐγώ εἰμι, καὶ πολλοὺς πλανήσουσιν. ⁷ ὅταν δὲ ἀκούσητε πολέμους καὶ ἀκοὰς πολέμων, μὴ θροεῖσθε· δεῖ γενέσθαι, ἀλλ᾽ οὔπω τὸ τέλος. ⁸ ἐγερθήσεται γὰρ ἔθνος ἐπ᾽ ἔθνος καὶ βασιλεία ἐπὶ βασιλείαν, ἔσονται σεισμοὶ κατὰ τόπους, ἔσονται λιμοί· ἀρχὴ ὠδίνων ταῦτα. ¶ ⁹ βλέπετε δὲ ὑμεῖς ἑαυτούς· παραδώσουσιν ὑμᾶς εἰς συνέδρια καὶ εἰς συναγωγὰς δαρήσεσθε καὶ ἐπὶ ἡγεμόνων καὶ

You will be handed | over to the local councils and flogged | in the synagogues. | On | account of me you
ὑμᾶς → → παραδώσουσιν ← εἰς → συνέδρια καὶ δαρήσεσθε εἰς συναγωγὰς καὶ ἕνεκεν ← ← ἐμοῦ →
r.ap.2 v.fai.3p p.a n.apn cj v.fpi.2p p.a n.apf cj p.g r.gs.1
7007 4140 1650 5284 2779 1296 1650 5252 2779 1914 1609

will stand | before governors and kings | as witnesses to them. 10 And the gospel | must first | be preached to
→ σταθήσεσθε ἐπὶ ἡγεμόνων καὶ βασιλέων εἰς μαρτύριον → αὐτοῖς καὶ τὸ εὐαγγέλιον δεῖ πρῶτον κηρυχθῆναι εἰς
v.fpi.2p p.g n.gpm cj n.gpm p.a n.apn r.dpm.3 cj d.asn n.asn v.pai.3s adv f.ap p.a
2705 2093 2450 2779 995 1650 3457 899 2779 3836 2295 1256 4754 3062 1650

all nations. 11 Whenever you are arrested and brought | to trial, do not worry | beforehand about what to
πάντα τὰ ἔθνη καὶ ὅταν ὑμᾶς → ἄγωσιν παραδιδόντες ← μὴ προμεριμνᾶτε ← τί →
a.apn d.apn n.apn cj cj r.ap.2 v.pas.3p pt.pa.npm pl v.pam.2p r.asn
4246 3836 1620 2779 4020 7007 72 4140 4628 3590 4628 5515

say. Just say | whatever is given you at the time, for it is not you speaking, but the
λαλήσητε ἀλλ' λαλεῖτε τοῦτο ὃ ἐὰν → δοθῇ ὑμῖν ἐν ἐκείνῃ τῇ ὥρᾳ γάρ ἐστε οὐ ὑμεῖς οἱ λαλοῦντες ἀλλὰ τὸ
v.aas.2p cj v.pam.2p r.asn r.nsn pl v.aps.3s r.d.p p.d r.dsf d.dsf n.dsf cj v.pai.2p pl r.np.2 d.nsn pt.pa.npm cj d.nsn
3281 247 3281 4047 4005 1569 1443 7007 1877 1697 3836 6052 1142 1639 4024 7007 3836 3281 247 3836

Holy Spirit. ¶ 12 "Brother will betray brother to death, and a father his child. Children will
τὸ ἅγιον πνεῦμα καὶ ἀδελφὸς → παραδώσει ἀδελφὸν εἰς θάνατον καὶ πατὴρ τέκνον καὶ τέκνα →
d.nsn a.nsn n.nsn cj n.nsm v.fai.3s n.asm p.a n.asm cj n.nsm n.asn cj n.npn
3836 41 4460 2779 81 4140 81 1650 2505 2779 4252 5451 2779 5451

rebel | against their parents and have them put to death. 13 All men will hate you
ἐπαναστήσονται ἐπὶ γονεῖς καὶ → αὐτούς → → θανατώσουσιν καὶ ὑπὸ πάντων ἔσεσθε μισούμενοι ←
v.fmi.3p p.a n.apm cj r.apm.3 v.fai.3p cj p.g a.gpm v.fmi.2p pt.pp.npm
2060 2093 1204 2779 2506 899 2506 2779 5679 4246 1639 3631 1639

because of me, | but he who stands firm to the end | will be saved. ¶ 14 "When you see
διὰ ← τὸ ὄνομα μου δὲ ὁ → ὑπομείνας ← εἰς τέλος οὗτος → σωθήσεται δὲ Ὅταν → ἴδητε
p.a d.asn n.asn r.gs.1 cj d.nsm pt.aa.nsm p.a n.asn r.nsm v.fpi.3s cj cj v.aas.2p
1328 3836 3950 1609 1254 3836 5702 1650 5465 4047 5392 1254 4020 1625

'the abomination that causes desolation' | standing where it does not belong – let the reader | understand –
τὸ βδέλυγμα → τῆς ἐρημώσεως, ἑστηκότα ὅπου → → οὐ δεῖ → ὁ ἀναγινώσκων νοείτω
d.asn n.asn d.gsf n.gsf pt.ra.asn cj pl v.pai.3s d.nsm pt.pa.nsm v.pam.3s
3836 1007 3836 2247 2705 3963 1256 4024 1256 3783 3836 336 3783

then let those who are in Judea | flee | to the mountains. 15 Let no one on the roof | of his
τότε → οἱ ← ἐν τῇ Ἰουδαίᾳ φευγέτωσαν εἰς τὰ ὄρη [δὲ] → μὴ ὁ ἐπὶ τοῦ δώματος ἐκ αὐτοῦ
adv d.npm p.d d.dsf n.dsf v.pam.3p p.a d.apn n.apn cj pl d.nsm p.a d.gsn n.gsn p.g r.gsm.3
5538 5771 3836 1877 3836 2677 5771 1650 3836 4001 1254 2849 3590 3836 2093 3836 1560 1666 899

house | go down or enter the house to take anything out. 16 Let no one in the field go
τῆς οἰκίας, καταβάτω ← μηδὲ εἰσελθάτω → ἆραί τι ← καὶ → μὴ ὁ εἰς τὸν ἀγρὸν ἐπιστρεψάτω
d.gsf n.gsf v.aam.3s cj v.aam.3s f.aa r.asn cj pl d.nsm p.a d.asm n.asm v.aam.3s
3836 3864 2849 3593 1656 149 5516 149 2779 2188 3590 3836 1650 3836 69 2188

back | to get his cloak. 17 How dreadful it will be | in those days | for
εἰς τὰ ὀπίσω → ἆραι αὐτοῦ τὸ ἱμάτιον, δὲ οὐαὶ ← ← ἐν ἐκείναις ταῖς ἡμέραις, →
p.a d.apn adv f.aa r.gsm.3 d.asn n.asn cj cj p.d r.dpf d.dpf n.dpf
1650 3836 3958 149 899 3836 2668 1254 4026 1877 1697 3836 2465

pregnant | women and nursing | mothers! 18 Pray | that this will not take | place in
ταῖς ἐν γαστρὶ ἐχούσαις, καὶ ταῖς θηλαζούσαις, ← δὲ προσεύχεσθε ἵνα → μὴ γένηται ←
d.dpf p.d n.dsf pt.pa.dpf cj d.dpf pt.pa.dpf cj v.pmm.2p cj pl v.ams.3s
3836 1877 1143 2400 2779 3836 2558 1254 4667 2671 1181 1181 3590 1181

winter, 19 because those will be | days | of distress unequaled | from the beginning, | when
χειμῶνος γὰρ ἐκεῖναι → ἔσονται αἱ ἡμέραι, θλῖψις οἵα οὐ γέγονεν τοιαύτη ἀπ' ἀρχῆς κτίσεως ἣν
n.gsm cj r.npf v.fmi.3p d.npf n.npf n.nsf r.nsf pl v.rai.3s r.nsf p.g n.gsf n.gsf r.asf
5930 1142 1697 1639 3836 2465 2568 3888 4024 1181 5525 608 794 3232 4005

God created the world, until now – and never to be equaled again. 20 If the Lord had not cut
ὁ θεὸς ἔκτισεν ἕως τοῦ νῦν, καὶ οὐ μὴ → γένηται καὶ εἰ κύριος → μὴ ἐκολόβωσεν
d.nsm n.nsm v.aai.3s p.g d.gsn adv cj pl pl v.ams.3s cj cj n.nsm pl v.aai.3s
3836 2536 3231 2401 3836 3814 2779 4024 3590 1181 2779 1623 3261 3590 3143

βασιλέων σταθήσεσθε ἕνεκεν ἐμοῦ εἰς μαρτύριον αὐτοῖς. 10 καὶ εἰς πάντα τὰ ἔθνη πρῶτον δεῖ κηρυχθῆναι τὸ εὐαγγέλιον. 11 καὶ ὅταν ἄγωσιν ὑμᾶς παραδιδόντες, μὴ προμεριμνᾶτε τί λαλήσητε, ἀλλ' ὃ ἐὰν δοθῇ ὑμῖν ἐν ἐκείνῃ τῇ ὥρᾳ τοῦτο λαλεῖτε· οὐ γάρ ἐστε ὑμεῖς οἱ λαλοῦντες ἀλλὰ τὸ πνεῦμα τὸ ἅγιον. ¶ 12 καὶ παραδώσει ἀδελφὸς ἀδελφὸν εἰς θάνατον καὶ πατὴρ τέκνον, καὶ ἐπαναστήσονται τέκνα ἐπὶ γονεῖς καὶ θανατώσουσιν αὐτούς· 13 καὶ ἔσεσθε μισούμενοι ὑπὸ πάντων διὰ τὸ ὄνομά μου. ὁ δὲ ὑπομείνας εἰς τέλος οὗτος σωθήσεται. ¶ 14 Ὅταν δὲ ἴδητε τὸ βδέλυγμα τῆς ἐρημώσεως ἑστηκότα ὅπου οὐ δεῖ, ὁ ἀναγινώσκων νοείτω, τότε οἱ ἐν τῇ Ἰουδαίᾳ φευγέτωσαν εἰς τὰ ὄρη, 15 ὁ [δὲ] ἐπὶ τοῦ δώματος μὴ καταβάτω μηδὲ εἰσελθάτω ἆραί τι ἐκ τῆς οἰκίας αὐτοῦ, 16 καὶ ὁ εἰς τὸν ἀγρὸν μὴ ἐπιστρεψάτω εἰς τὰ ὀπίσω ἆραι τὸ ἱμάτιον αὐτοῦ. 17 οὐαὶ δὲ ταῖς ἐν γαστρὶ ἐχούσαις καὶ ταῖς θηλαζούσαις ἐν ἐκείναις ταῖς ἡμέραις. 18 προσεύχεσθε δὲ ἵνα μὴ γένηται χειμῶνος· 19 ἔσονται γὰρ αἱ ἡμέραι ἐκεῖναι θλῖψις οἵα οὐ γέγονεν τοιαύτη ἀπ' ἀρχῆς κτίσεως ἣν ἔκτισεν ὁ θεὸς ἕως τοῦ νῦν καὶ οὐ μὴ γένηται. 20 καὶ εἰ μὴ ἐκολόβωσεν

short those days,   no one   would survive. But for the sake of the   elect,   whom he has chosen, he has
←   τὰς   ἡμέρας οὐκ πᾶσα σάρξ ἂν   ἐσώθη   ἀλλὰ διὰ ←   ←   τοὺς ἐκλεκτοὺς οὓς   →   → ἐξελέξατο →
     d.apf n.apf pl a.nsf n.nsf pl v.api.3s cj   p.a   d.apm a.apm   r.apm   v.ami.3s
     3836 2465   4024 4246 4922   323 5392   247 1328   3836 1723   4005   1721

shortened them.   21   At that time if   anyone says to you, 'Look, here is the Christ!' or, 'Look, there he is!' do
ἐκολόβωσεν τὰς ἡμέρας. Καὶ τότε ←   ←   ἐάν τις   εἴπῃ → ὑμῖν ἴδε ὧδε ὁ   χριστός. ἴδε   ἐκεῖ
v.aai.3s   d.apf n.apf   cj adv   cj r.nsm v.aas.3s r.dp.2 pl adv d.nsm n.nsm   pl   adv
3143   3836 2465   2779 5538   1569 5516 3306   7007 2623 6045 3836 5986   2623 1695   4409

not believe it. 22 For false Christs   and false prophets   will appear and perform signs and miracles to
μὴ πιστεύετε   γὰρ → ψευδόχριστοι καὶ → ψευδοπροφῆται → ἐγερθήσονται καὶ δώσουσιν σημεῖα καὶ τέρατα πρὸς
pl v.pam.2p   cj   n.npm   cj   n.npm   v.fpi.3p   cj v.fai.3p n.apn cj n.apn p.a
3590 4409   1142   6023   2779   6021   1586   2779 1443   4956 2779 5469 4639

deceive   the elect   – if that were possible. 23 So be on your guard; I have told   you everything ahead of
.τὸ ἀποπλανᾶν. τοὺς ἐκλεκτούς εἰ → → δυνατόν δὲ ↱ ↱ ὑμεῖς βλέπετε → → προείρηκα ὑμῖν πάντα ←   ←
d.asn f.pa   d.apm a.apm   cj   a.nsn   cj   r.np.2 v.pam.2p   v.rai.1s r.dp.2 a.apn
3836 675   3836 1723   1623   1543   1254 1063 1063 7007 1063   4597   7007 4246   4597 4597

time. ¶   24 "But in those   days,   following that distress, "'the sun will be darkened,   and the moon
←   Ἀλλὰ ἐν ἐκείναις .ταῖς ἡμέραις. μετὰ   ἐκείνην .τὴν θλῖψιν. ὁ   ἥλιος →   → σκοτισθήσεται καὶ ἡ σελήνη
          cj   p.d r.dpf   d.dpf n.dpf   p.a   r.asf   d.asf n.asf d.nsm n.nsm   v.fpi.3s   cj d.nsf n.nsf
4597   247 1877 1697   3836 2465   3552   1697   3836 2568   3836 2463   5029   2779 3836 4943

will not give its light;   25   the stars will fall   from the sky, and   the heavenly bodies
↱ οὐ δώσει αὐτῆς .τὸ φέγγος. καὶ οἱ ἀστέρες ἔσονται πίπτοντες ἐκ τοῦ οὐρανοῦ καὶ αἱ ἐν τοῖς οὐρανοῖς .αἱ δυνάμεις.
pl v.fai.3s r.gsf.3 d.asn n.asn cj d.npm n.npm v.fmi.3p pt.pa.npm p.g d.gsm n.gsm cj d.npf p.d d.dpm n.dpm d.npf n.npf
1443 4024 1443   3836 5766   2779 3836 843   1639   4406   1666 3836 4041 2779 3836 1877 3836 4041 3836 1539

will be shaken.'   ¶   26   "At that time men will see   the Son of Man   coming in clouds with
→ → σαλευθήσονται   καὶ τότε ← ←   → ὄψονται τὸν υἱὸν .τοῦ ἀνθρώπου. ἐρχόμενον ἐν νεφέλαις μετὰ
   v.fpi.3p   cj adv   v.fmi.3p d.asn n.asn d.gsm n.gsm pt.pm.asm p.d n.dpf p.g
4888   2779 5538   3972   3836 5626 3836 476   2262   1877 3749 3552

great power and glory. 27 And   he will send his angels and gather his elect   from the four
πολλῆς δυνάμεως καὶ δόξης. καὶ τότε → ἀποστελεῖ τοὺς ἀγγέλους καὶ ἐπισυνάξει αὐτοῦ τοὺς ἐκλεκτούς. ἐκ τῶν τεσσάρων
a.gsf n.gsf   cj n.gsf cj adv   v.fai.3s d.apm n.apm   cj v.fai.3s r.gsm.3 d.apm a.apm   p.g d.gpm a.gpm
4498 1539   2779 1518 2779 5538   690   3836 34   2779 2190   899 3836 1723   1666 3836 5475

winds, from the ends of the earth to the ends of the heavens. ¶ 28 "Now learn this lesson   from the fig
ἀνέμων ἀπ'   ἄκρου → γῆς ἕως ἄκρου → οὐρανοῦ   δὲ μάθετε τὴν παραβολήν Ἀπὸ τῆς →
n.gpm p.g   n.gsn   n.gsf p.g n.gsn   n.gsm   cj v.aam.2p d.asf n.asf   p.g d.gsf
449 608   216   1178 2401 216   4041   1254 3443 3836 4130   608 3836

tree: As   soon as its   twigs   get   tender and its leaves come out, you know   that summer is
συκῆς ὅταν ἤδη ← ← αὐτῆς ὁ κλάδος. γένηται ἁπαλὸς καὶ τὰ φύλλα ἐκφύῃ → γινώσκετε ὅτι .τὸ θέρος. ἐστίν
n.gsf adv adv   r.gsf.3 d.nsm n.nsm v.ams.3s a.nsm cj d.apn n.apn v.pas.3s v.pai.2p ὅτι d.nsn n.nsn v.pai.3s
5190 4020 2453   899   3836 3080   1181   559   2779 3836 5877 1770   1182   4022 3836 2550 1639

near. 29 Even so,   when you see these things happening, you know   that it is   near, right at the door. 30 I tell
ἐγγὶς καὶ οὕτως ὅταν ὑμεῖς ἴδητε ταῦτα → γινόμενα γινώσκετε ὅτι › ἐστιν ἐγγύς → ἐπὶ θύραις → λέγω
adv   adv adv cj   r.np.2 v.aas.2p rapn   pt.pm.apn v.pam.2p cj   v.pai.3s adv   p.d n.dpf   v.pai.1s
1584 2779 4048 4020 7007 1625   4047   1181   4022   1639 1639 1584   2093 2598   3306

you the truth,   this generation will certainly not   pass   away until   all   these things have happened.
ὑμῖν Ἀμὴν ὅτι αὕτη .ἡ γενεὰ. → οὐ μὴ παρέλθῃ → μέχρις οὗ πάντα ταῦτα → γένηται
r.dp.2 pl ὅτι r.nsf d.nsf n.nsf   pl pl v.aas.3s   r.gsm   a.npn r.npn   v.ams.3s
7007 297 4022 4047 3836 1155   4024 3590 4216   3588 4005 4246 4047   1181

31 Heaven   and earth will pass   away, but my words   will never pass   away.
.ὁ οὐρανὸς. καὶ .ἡ γῆ. → παρελεύσονται ← δὲ μου .οἱ λόγοι. → οὐ μὴ παρελεύσονται ←
d.nsm n.nsm cj d.nsf n.nsf v.fmi.3p   cj r.gs.1 d.npm n.npm pl pl v.fmi.3p
3836 4041   2779 3836 1178   4216   1254 1609 3836 3364   4216 4024 3590 4216

The Day and Hour Unknown

13:32   "No one knows about that day   or hour, not even the angels in heaven, nor the Son,
δὲ οὐδεὶς ← οἶδεν Περὶ ἐκείνης .τῆς ἡμέρας. ἢ .τῆς ὥρας. οὐδὲ ←   οἱ ἄγγελοι ἐν οὐρανῷ οὐδὲ ὁ υἱός
cj a.nsm   v.rai.3s p.g r.gsf d.gsf n.gsf ἢ d.gsf n.gsf adv   d.npm n.npm p.d n.dsm cj d.nsm n.nsm
1254 4029   3857 4309 1697 3836 2465   2445 3836 6052 4028   3836 34   1877 4041 4028 3836 5626

κύριος τὰς ἡμέρας, οὐκ ἂν ἐσώθη πᾶσα σάρξ· ἀλλὰ διὰ τοὺς ἐκλεκτοὺς οὓς ἐξελέξατο ἐκολόβωσεν τὰς ἡμέρας. 21 καὶ τότε ἐὰν τις ὑμῖν εἴπῃ, Ἴδε ὧδε ὁ Χριστός, Ἴδε ἐκεῖ, μὴ πιστεύετε· 22 ἐγερθήσονται γὰρ ψευδόχριστοι καὶ ψευδοπροφῆται καὶ δώσουσιν σημεῖα καὶ τέρατα πρὸς τὸ ἀποπλανᾶν, εἰ δυνατόν, τοὺς ἐκλεκτούς. 23 ὑμεῖς δὲ βλέπετε· προείρηκα ὑμῖν πάντα ¶ 24 Ἀλλὰ ἐν ἐκείναις ταῖς ἡμέραις μετὰ τὴν θλῖψιν ἐκείνην ὁ ἥλιος σκοτισθήσεται, καὶ ἡ σελήνη οὐ δώσει τὸ φέγγος αὐτῆς, 25 καὶ οἱ ἀστέρες ἔσονται ἐκ τοῦ οὐρανοῦ πίπτοντες, καὶ αἱ δυνάμεις αἱ ἐν τοῖς οὐρανοῖς σαλευθήσονται. ¶ 26 καὶ τότε ὄψονται τὸν υἱὸν τοῦ ἀνθρώπου ἐρχόμενον ἐν νεφέλαις μετὰ δυνάμεως πολλῆς καὶ δόξης. 27 καὶ τότε ἀποστελεῖ τοὺς ἀγγέλους καὶ ἐπισυνάξει τοὺς ἐκλεκτοὺς [αὐτοῦ] ἐκ τῶν τεσσάρων ἀνέμων ἀπ' ἄκρου γῆς ἕως ἄκρου οὐρανοῦ. ¶ 28 Ἀπὸ δὲ τῆς συκῆς μάθετε τὴν παραβολήν· ὅταν ἤδη ὁ κλάδος αὐτῆς ἁπαλὸς γένηται καὶ ἐκφύῃ τὰ φύλλα, γινώσκετε ὅτι ἐγγὺς τὸ θέρος ἐστίν· 29 οὕτως καὶ ὑμεῖς, ὅταν ἴδητε ταῦτα γινόμενα, γινώσκετε ὅτι ἐγγύς ἐστιν ἐπὶ θύραις. 30 ἀμὴν λέγω ὑμῖν ὅτι οὐ μὴ παρέλθῃ ἡ γενεὰ αὕτη μέχρις οὗ ταῦτα πάντα γένηται. 31 ὁ οὐρανὸς καὶ ἡ γῆ παρελεύσονται, οἱ δὲ λόγοι μου οὐ μὴ παρελεύσονται.
13:32 Περὶ δὲ τῆς ἡμέρας ἐκείνης ἢ τῆς ὥρας οὐδεὶς οἶδεν, οὐδὲ οἱ ἄγγελοι ἐν οὐρανῷ οὐδὲ ὁ υἱός, εἰ μὴ ὁ πατήρ. 33 βλέπετε,

but   only the Father. **33** Be on guard! Be alert!   You do not know when that time will come. **34** It's like a
ɩεἰ μὴ ← ὁ πατήρ → → Βλέπετε → ἀγρυπνεῖτε γάρ → οὐκ οἴδατε πότε ὁ καιρός ἐστιν ← Ὡς
cj   pl   d.nsm n.nsm   v.pam.2p   v.pam.2p   cj   pl v.rai.2p cj   d.nsm n.nsm v.pai.3s   cj
1623 3590   3836 4252   1063   70   1142   4024 3857   3857   3836 2789 1639   6055

man   going away: He leaves his   house   and puts his   servants   in charge,   each with his
ἄνθρωπος ἀπόδημος → ἀφείς αὐτοῦ τὴν οἰκίαν καὶ δοὺς αὐτοῦ ɩτοῖς δούλοις, → ɩτὴν ἐξουσίαν, ἑκάστῳ αὐτοῦ
n.nsm   a.nsm   pt.aa.nsm r.gsm.3 d.asf n.asf cj pt.aa.nsm r.gsm.3 d.dpm n.dpm   d.asf n.asf   r.dsm   r.gsm.3
476   624   918   899   3836 3864 2779 1443 899   3836 1529   3836 2026   1667   899

assigned task,   and tells   the one at the door   to keep watch.   ¶   **35** "Therefore keep watch   because
ɩτὸ ἔργον, καὶ ἐνετείλατο τῷ ← → θυρωρῷ ἵνα → γρηγορῇ   οὖν   → γρηγορεῖτε γάρ
d.asn n.asn cj   v.ami.3s d.dsm   n.dsm cj v.pas.3s   cj   v.pam.2p   cj
3836 2240 2779 1948   3836   2601 2671   1213   4036   1213   1142

you do not know when the owner of the house will come back – whether in the evening, or at midnight, or when
ɩ→ → οὐκ οἴδατε πότε ὁ κύριος → τῆς οἰκίας ἔρχεται   ἤ   → ὀψὲ ἤ → μεσονύκτιον ἤ →
pl v.rai.2p πότε d.nsm n.nsm d.gsf n.gsf v.pmi.3s   cj   adv cj   n.asn   cj
3857 3857 4024 3857 4537 3836 3261 3836 3864 2262   2445   4067 2445 3543   2445

the rooster   crows, or at dawn. **36** If he comes suddenly, do not let him find you sleeping. **37** What I say to
ἀλεκτοροφωνίας → ἤ → πρωΐ   ἐλθὼν ἐξαίφνης μὴ → εὕρῃ ὑμᾶς καθεύδοντας δὲ ὃ → λέγω
n.gsf   cj adv   pt.aa.nsm adv   cj   v.aas.3s r.ap.2 pt.pa.apm cj r.asn v.pai.1s
231   2445 4745   2262   1978   2351 3590 2351 7007 2761   1254 4005 3306

you, I say to everyone: 'Watch!'"
ὑμῖν → λέγω → πᾶσιν γρηγορεῖτε
r.dp.2   v.pai.1s a.dpm v.pam.2p
7007   3306   4246   1213

Jesus Anointed at Bethany

14:1 Now the Passover and the Feast of Unleavened Bread were only two days away, and the chief priests and
δὲ τὸ πάσχα καὶ τὰ ἄζυμα ←   Ἦν   δύο ἡμέρας μετὰ καὶ οἱ → ἀρχιερεῖς καὶ
cj d.nsn n.nsn cj d.npn n.npn   v.iai.3s a.apf n.apf p.a cj d.npm   n.npm   cj
1254 3836 4247 2779 3836 109   1639 1545 2465 3552 2779 3836   797   2779

the teachers of the law were looking for some sly   way to arrest   Jesus and kill   him. **2** "But not
οἱ γραμματεῖς ← ← ← ἐζήτουν → πῶς ἐν δόλῳ → κρατήσαντες ἀποκτείνωσιν αὐτόν γάρ μὴ
d.npm n.npm   v.iai.3p   cj p.d n.dsm   pt.aa.npm   v.pas.3p   r.asm.3 cj   pl
3836 1208   2426   4802 1877 1515   3195   650   899   1142 3590

during the Feast," they said, "or   the people may riot." ¶ **3**   While he   was in Bethany,
ἐν τῇ ἑορτῇ → ἔλεγον μήποτε τοῦ λαοῦ ἔσται θόρυβος   Καὶ → αὐτοῦ ὄντος ἐν Βηθανίᾳ αὐτοῦ
p.d d.dsf n.dsf   v.iai.3p cj   d.gsm n.gsm v.fmi.3s n.nsm   cj   r.gsm.3 pt.pa.gsm p.d n.dsf   r.gsm.3
1877 3836 2038   3306 3607 3836 2973 1639 2573   2779   1639   899   3836 1877 1029   899

reclining at the table in the home of a man known as Simon the Leper, a woman came with an alabaster jar
κατακειμένου ← ← ἐν τῇ οἰκίᾳ → → → Σίμωνος τοῦ λεπροῦ, γυνὴ ἦλθεν ἔχουσα ἀλάβαστρον →
pt.pm.gsm   p.d d.dsf n.dsf   n.gsm d.gsm a.gsm   n.nsf v.aai.3s pt.pa.nsf n.asf
2879   1877 3836 3864   4981 3836 3320   1222 2262 2400   223

of very expensive perfume, made of pure nard. She broke   the jar   and poured the perfume on his
→ → πολυτελοῦς μύρου, → πιστικῆς νάρδου → συντρίψασα τὴν ἀλάβαστρον κατέχεεν → αὐτοῦ
n.gsf   n.gsn   a.gsf n.gsf   pt.aa.nsf d.asf n.asf   v.aai.3s   r.gsm.3
4500   3693   4410 3726   5341 3836 223   2972   3051 899

head. ¶ **4** Some of those present were saying   indignantly to one another, "Why   this
ɩτῆς κεφαλῆς. δέ τινες ἦσαν ἀγανακτοῦντες ← προς ἑαυτούς ← ɩεἰς τί γέγονεν αὕτη
d.gsf n.gsf   cj n.npm v.iai.3p pt.pa.npm   p.a r.apm.3   p.a r.asn v.rai.3s r.nsf
3836 3051   1254 5516 1639   24   4639 1571   1650 5515 1181   4047

waste   of perfume? **5**   It   could have been sold   for more than a year's wages
ɩἡ ἀπώλεια → ɩτοῦ μύρου, γάρ ɩτοῦτο τὸ μύρον ἠδύνατο → → πραθῆναι → ἐπάνω → → δηναρίων τριακοσίων
d.nsf n.nsf   d.gsn n.gsn cj r.nsn d.nsn n.nsn v.ipi.3s   f.ap   p.g   n.gpn   a.gpn
3836 724   3836 3693   1142 4047 3836 3693 1538   4405   2062   1324   5559

and the money given to the poor." And they rebuked her harshly. ¶ **6** "Leave her alone," said
καὶ δοθῆναι → τοῖς πτωχοῖς καὶ → ἐνεβριμῶντο αὐτῇ   δὲ ἄφετε αὐτήν ← εἶπεν
cj   f.ap   d.dpm a.dpm cj   v.imi.3p   r.dsf.3   cj v.aam.2p r.asf.3   v.aai.3s
2779 1443   3836 4777   2779   1839   1839   1254 918 899   918   3306

ἀγρυπνεῖτε· οὐκ οἴδατε γὰρ πότε ὁ καιρός ἐστιν. ³⁴ ὡς ἄνθρωπος ἀπόδημος ἀφεὶς τὴν οἰκίαν αὐτοῦ καὶ δοὺς τοῖς δούλοις αὐτοῦ τὴν ἐξουσίαν ἑκάστῳ τὸ ἔργον αὐτοῦ καὶ τῷ θυρωρῷ ἐνετείλατο ἵνα γρηγορῇ. ¶ ³⁵ γρηγορεῖτε οὖν· οὐκ οἴδατε γὰρ πότε ὁ κύριος τῆς οἰκίας ἔρχεται, ἢ ὀψὲ ἢ μεσονύκτιον ἢ ἀλεκτοροφωνίας ἢ πρωΐ, ³⁶ μὴ ἐλθὼν ἐξαίφνης εὕρῃ ὑμᾶς καθεύδοντας. ³⁷ ὃ δὲ ὑμῖν λέγω πᾶσιν λέγω, γρηγορεῖτε.

14:1 ⁵Ἦν δὲ τὸ πάσχα καὶ τὰ ἄζυμα μετὰ δύο ἡμέρας. καὶ ἐζήτουν οἱ ἀρχιερεῖς καὶ οἱ γραμματεῖς πῶς αὐτὸν ἐν δόλῳ κρατήσαντες ἀποκτείνωσιν· ² ἔλεγον γάρ, Μὴ ἐν τῇ ἑορτῇ, μήποτε ἔσται θόρυβος τοῦ λαοῦ. ¶ ³ Καὶ ὄντος αὐτοῦ ἐν Βηθανίᾳ ἐν τῇ οἰκίᾳ Σίμωνος τοῦ λεπροῦ, κατακειμένου αὐτοῦ ἦλθεν γυνὴ ἔχουσα ἀλάβαστρον μύρου νάρδου πιστικῆς πολυτελοῦς, συντρίψασα τὴν ἀλάβαστρον κατέχεεν αὐτοῦ τῆς κεφαλῆς. ¶ ⁴ ἦσαν δέ τινες ἀγανακτοῦντες πρὸς ἑαυτούς, Εἰς τί ἡ ἀπώλεια αὕτη τοῦ μύρου γέγονεν; ⁵ ἠδύνατο γὰρ τοῦτο τὸ μύρον πραθῆναι ἐπάνω δηναρίων τριακοσίων καὶ δοθῆναι τοῖς πτωχοῖς· καὶ ἐνεβριμῶντο αὐτῇ. ¶ ⁶ ὁ δὲ Ἰησοῦς εἶπεν, Ἄφετε αὐτήν· τί αὐτῇ κόπους παρέχετε; καλὸν ἔργον ἠργάσατο ἐν ἐμοί. ⁷ πάντοτε

Jesus.   "Why are you bothering   her? She has done   a beautiful thing to me. **7** The poor   you will
ὁ Ἰησοῦς τί   ⸤παρέχετε κόπους⸥ αὐτῇ →   ἠργάσατο καλὸν ἔργον ἐν ἐμοί γὰρ τοὺς πτωχοὺς ↱ ↱
d.nsm n.nsm r.asn   v.pai.2p n.apm   r.dsf.3   v.ami.3s a.asn n.asn p.d r.ds.1 cj d.apm a.apm
3836 2652 5515   4218   3160   899   2237   2240   2819 1877 1609 1142 3836 4777   2400 2400

always have with you,   and you can   help   them any time you want. But you will not always have me.
πάντοτε ἔχετε μεθ ἑαυτῶν καὶ →   δύνασθε εὖ ποιῆσαι⸥ αὐτοῖς ὅταν ←   → θέλητε δὲ ↱ ↱ οὐ πάντοτε ἔχετε ἐμέ
adv v.pai.2p p.g r.gpm.2 cj   v.ppi.2p adv f.aa   r.dpm.3 cj   v.pas.2p cj   pl adv v.pai.2p r.as.1
4121 2400 3552 1571 2779   1538   2292 4472   899   4020   2527   1254 2400 2400 4024 4121 2400 1609

8 She did   what she could. She poured   perfume on my body   beforehand to prepare   for my burial.
ἐποίησεν ὃ →   ἔσχεν προέλαβεν μυρίσαι ← μου ⸤τὸ σῶμα⸥   →   εἰς ⸤τὸν ἐνταφιασμόν⸥ ← ←
v.aai.3s r.asn   v.aai.3s v.aai.3s f.aa r.gs.1 d.asn n.asn   p.a d.asm n.asm
4472 4005   2400   4624   3690   4624 1609 3836 5393   4624   1650 3836 1947

9 I tell you the truth, wherever the gospel   is preached throughout the world, what she has done   will also
δὲ → λέγω ὑμῖν   ἀμὴν ὅπου ἐὰν τὸ εὐαγγέλιον → κηρυχθῇ εἰς ὅλον τὸν κόσμον ὃ αὕτη ἐποίησεν → καὶ
cj v.pai.1s r.dp.2   pl cj pl d.nsn n.nsn   v.aps.3s p.a a.asm d.asm n.asm r.asn r.nsf v.aai.3s adv
1254 3306 7007   297 3963 1569 3836 2295   3062 1650 3910 3836 3180 4005 4047 4472   2779

be told,   in memory of her." ¶ **10** Then Judas Iscariot,   one of the Twelve, went   to the chief
→ λαληθήσεται εἰς μνημόσυνον → αὐτῆς Καὶ Ἰούδας Ἰσκαριὼθ ὁ εἷς → τῶν δώδεκα ἀπῆλθεν πρὸς τοὺς
v.fpi.3s p.a n.asn r.gsf.3 cj n.nsm n.nsm d.nsm a.nsm d.gpm a.gpm v.aai.3s p.a d.apm
3281 1650 3649 899 2779 2683 2696 3836 1651 3836 1557 599 4639 3836

priests to betray Jesus to them. **11** They were delighted to hear   this and promised   to give him money.
ἀρχιερεῖς ἵνα παραδοῖ αὐτὸν → αὐτοῖς δὲ οἱ   ἐχάρησαν ἀκούσαντες καὶ ἐπηγγείλαντο → δοῦναι αὐτῷ ἀργύριον
n.apm cj v.aas.3s r.asm.3 r.dpm.3 cj d.npm   v.api.3p pt.aa.npm cj v.ami.3p f.aa r.dsm.3 n.asn
797 2671 4140 899 899 1254 3836   5897 201 2779 2040 1443 899 736

So he watched for an opportunity to hand him over.
καὶ → ἐζήτει πῶς εὐκαίρως → παραδοῖ αὐτὸν ←
cj v.iai.3s cj adv v.aas.3s r.asm.3
2779 2426 4802 2323 4140 899 4140

The Lord's Supper

14:12 On the first day of the Feast of Unleavened Bread, when it was customary to sacrifice the Passover
Καὶ → τῇ πρώτῃ ἡμέρᾳ → τῶν ἀζύμων ←   ὅτε   →   ἔθυον τὸ πάσχα
cj d.dsf a.dsf n.dsf d.gpn n.gpn   cj   v.iai.3p d.asn n.asn
2779 3836 4755 2465 3836 109   4021   2604 3836 4247

lamb, Jesus' disciples   asked him, "Where do you want us to go   and make preparations for you to eat
← αὐτοῦ οἱ μαθηταὶ λέγουσιν αὐτῷ ποῦ →   θέλεις → ἀπελθόντες → ἑτοιμάσωμεν ἵνα → → φάγῃς
r.gsm.3 d.npm n.npm v.pai.3p r.dsm.3 adv v.pai.2s pt.aa.npm v.aas.1p cj v.aas.2s
899 3836 3412 3306 899 4543 2527 599 2286 2671 2266

the Passover?" ¶ **13** So he sent   two of his disciples,   telling them, "Go   into the city, and a
τὸ πάσχα καὶ → ἀποστέλλει δύο → αὐτοῦ ⸤τῶν μαθητῶν⸥ καὶ λέγει αὐτοῖς ὑπάγετε εἰς τὴν πόλιν καὶ
d.asn n.asn cj v.pai.3s a.apm r.gsm.3 d.gpm n.gpm cj v.pai.3s r.dpm.3 v.pam.2p p.a d.asf n.asf cj
3836 4247 2779 690 1545 899 3836 3412 2779 3306 899 5632 1650 3836 4484 2779

man carrying a jar   of water will meet   you. Follow   him. **14** Say to the owner   of the house
ἄνθρωπος βαστάζων κεράμιον → ὕδατος → ἀπαντήσει ὑμῖν ἀκολουθήσατε αὐτῷ καὶ εἴπατε → τῷ οἰκοδεσπότῃ ← ←
n.nsm pt.pa.nsm n.asn n.gsn v.fai.3s r.dp.2 v.aam.2p r.dsm.3 cj v.aam.2p d.dsm n.dsm
476 1002 3040 5623 560 7007 199 899 2779 3306 3836 3867

he enters, 'The Teacher asks: Where is   my guest room,   where I may eat the Passover with
ὅπου ἐὰν → εἰσέλθῃ ὅτι ὁ διδάσκαλος λέγει ποῦ ἐστιν μου → ⸤τὸ κατάλυμα⸥ ὅπου → φάγω τὸ πάσχα μετὰ
cj pl v.aas.3s cj d.nsm n.nsm v.pai.3s adv v.pai.3s r.gs.1 d.nsn n.nsn cj v.aas.1s d.asn n.asn p.g
3963 1569 1656 4022 3836 1437 3306 4543 1639 1609 3836 2906 3963 2266 3836 4247 3552

my disciples?' **15** He will show you a large upper room, furnished and ready.   Make preparations for us
μου ⸤τῶν μαθητῶν⸥ καὶ αὐτὸς → δείξει ὑμῖν μέγα → ἀνάγαιον ἐστρωμένον ἕτοιμον καὶ → ἑτοιμάσατε → ἡμῖν
r.gs.1 d.gpm n.gpm cj r.nsm v.fai.3s r.dp.2 a.asn n.asn pt.rp.asn a.asn cj v.aam.2p r.dp.1
1609 3836 3412 2779 899 1259 7007 3489 333 5143 2289 2779 2286 7005

there." ¶ **16** The disciples left,   went into the city and found things just   as Jesus had told them. So
ἐκεῖ καὶ οἱ μαθηταὶ ἐξῆλθον καὶ ἦλθον εἰς τὴν πόλιν καὶ εὗρον   καθὼς ←   εἶπεν αὐτοῖς καὶ
adv cj d.npm n.npm v.aai.3p cj v.aai.3p p.a d.asf n.asf cj v.aai.3p cj   v.aai.3s r.dpm.3 cj
1695 2779 3836 3412 2002 2779 2262 1650 3836 4484 2779 2351 2777   3306 899 2779

γὰρ τοὺς πτωχοὺς ἔχετε μεθ᾽ ἑαυτῶν καὶ ὅταν θέλητε δύνασθε αὐτοῖς εὖ ποιῆσαι, ἐμὲ δὲ οὐ πάντοτε ἔχετε. **8** ὃ ἔσχεν ἐποίησεν· προέλαβεν μυρίσαι τὸ σῶμά μου εἰς τὸν ἐνταφιασμόν. **9** ἀμὴν δὲ λέγω ὑμῖν, ὅπου ἐὰν κηρυχθῇ τὸ εὐαγγέλιον εἰς ὅλον τὸν κόσμον, καὶ ὃ ἐποίησεν αὕτη λαληθήσεται εἰς μνημόσυνον αὐτῆς. ¶ **10** Καὶ Ἰούδας Ἰσκαριὼθ ὁ εἷς τῶν δώδεκα ἀπῆλθεν πρὸς τοὺς ἀρχιερεῖς ἵνα αὐτὸν παραδοῖ αὐτοῖς. **11** οἱ δὲ ἀκούσαντες ἐχάρησαν καὶ ἐπηγγείλαντο αὐτῷ ἀργύριον δοῦναι. καὶ ἐζήτει πῶς αὐτὸν εὐκαίρως παραδοῖ.

14:12 Καὶ τῇ πρώτῃ ἡμέρᾳ τῶν ἀζύμων, ὅτε τὸ πάσχα ἔθυον, λέγουσιν αὐτῷ οἱ μαθηταὶ αὐτοῦ, Ποῦ θέλεις ἀπελθόντες ἑτοιμάσωμεν ἵνα φάγῃς τὸ πάσχα; ¶ **13** καὶ ἀποστέλλει δύο τῶν μαθητῶν αὐτοῦ καὶ λέγει αὐτοῖς, Ὑπάγετε εἰς τὴν πόλιν, καὶ ἀπαντήσει ὑμῖν ἄνθρωπος κεράμιον ὕδατος βαστάζων· ἀκολουθήσατε αὐτῷ **14** καὶ ὅπου ἐὰν εἰσέλθῃ εἴπατε τῷ οἰκοδεσπότῃ ὅτι Ὁ διδάσκαλος λέγει, Ποῦ ἐστιν τὸ κατάλυμά μου ὅπου τὸ πάσχα μετὰ τῶν μαθητῶν μου φάγω; **15** καὶ αὐτὸς ὑμῖν δείξει ἀνάγαιον μέγα ἐστρωμένον ἕτοιμον· καὶ ἐκεῖ ἑτοιμάσατε ἡμῖν. ¶ **16** καὶ ἐξῆλθον οἱ μαθηταὶ καὶ ἦλθον εἰς τὴν πόλιν καὶ εὗρον

they prepared the Passover. ¶ **17** When evening came, Jesus arrived with the Twelve. **18** While they were
→ ἡτοίμασαν τὸ πάσχα   Καὶ → ὀψίας γενομένης   ἔρχεται μετὰ τῶν δώδεκα   καὶ → αὐτῶν →
v.aai.3p d.asn n.asn   cj   n.gsf pt.am.gsf   v.pmi.3s p.g d.gpm a.gpm   cj   r.gpm.3
2286 3836 4247   2779 1181   4068 1181   2262 3552 3836 1557   2779 367   899

reclining at the table eating, he said, "I tell you the truth, one of you will betray me – one
ἀνακειμένων ← ← ← καὶ ἐσθιόντων ὁ Ἰησοῦς, εἶπεν → λέγω ὑμῖν ἀμὴν ὅτι εἰς ἐξ ὑμῶν → παραδώσει με ὁ
pt.pm.gpm   cj pt.pa.gpm d.nsm n.nsm v.aai.3s v.pai.1s r.dp.2 pl ὅτι r.nsm p.g r.gp.2 v.fai.3s r.as.1 d.nsm
367   2779 2266 3836 2652 3306 3306 7007 297 4022 1651 1666 7007   4140 1609 3836

who is eating with me." ¶ **19** They were saddened, and one by one they said to him, "Surely not I?"
← → ἐσθίων μετ' ἐμοῦ   ἤρξαντο → λυπεῖσθαι καὶ εἰς κατὰ εἰς λέγειν → αὐτῷ μήτι ἐγώ
pt.pa.nsm p.g r.gs.1   v.ami.3p   f.pp cj a.nsm p.a a.nsm f.pa r.dsm.3 pl r.ns.1
2266 3552 1609   806   3382 2779 1651 2848 1651 3306 899 3614 1609

¶ **20** "It is one of the Twelve," he replied, "one who dips bread into the bowl with me. **21**
δὲ εἰς → τῶν δώδεκα ὁ εἶπεν αὐτοῖς ὁ ← ἐμβαπτόμενος εἰς τὸ τρύβλιον μετ' ἐμοῦ ὅτι μὲν
cj a.nsm d.gpm a.gpm d.nsm v.aai.3s r.dpm.3 d.nsm pt.pm.nsm p.a d.asn n.asn p.g r.gs.1 cj pl
1254 1651 3836 1557 3836 3306 899 3836 1835 1650 3836 5581 3552 1609 4022 3525

The Son of Man will go just as it is written about him. But woe to that man who
ὁ υἱὸς → τοῦ ἀνθρώπου → ὑπάγει καθὼς ← → γέγραπται περὶ αὐτοῦ δὲ οὐαὶ ᾿ ἐκείνῳ τῷ ἀνθρώπῳ δι' οὗ
d.nsm n.nsm d.gsm n.gsm v.pai.3s cj v.rpi.3s p.g r.gsm.3 cj j r.dsm d.dsm n.dsm p.g r.gsm
3836 5626 3836 476 5632 2777 1211 4309 899 1254 4026 476 1697 3836 476 1328 4005

betrays the Son of Man! It would be better for him if he had not been born." ¶
παραδίδοται ὁ υἱὸς → τοῦ ἀνθρώπου καλὸν → αὐτῷ εἰ ὁ ἄνθρωπος ἐκεῖνος ᾿ οὐκ ἐγεννήθη
v.ppi.3s d.nsm n.nsm d.gsm n.gsm a.nsn r.dsm.3 cj d.nsm n.nsm r.nsm pl v.api.3s
4140 3836 5626 3836 476 2819 899 1623 3836 476 1697 4024 1164

22 While they were eating, Jesus took bread, gave thanks and broke it, and gave it to his disciples,
Καὶ ᾿ αὐτῶν ἐσθιόντων λαβὼν ἄρτον → εὐλογήσας ἔκλασεν καὶ ἔδωκεν → αὐτοῖς καὶ
cj r.gpm.3 pt.pa.gpm pt.aa.nsm n.asm pt.aa.nsm v.aai.3s cj v.aai.3s r.dpm.3 cj
2779 2266 899 2266 3284 788 2328 3089 2779 1443 899 2779

saying, "Take it; this is my body." ¶ **23** Then he took the cup, gave thanks and offered it to them,
εἶπεν λάβετε τοῦτο ἐστιν μου τὸ σῶμα καὶ → λαβὼν ποτήριον εὐχαριστήσας ἔδωκεν → αὐτοῖς
v.aai.3s v.aam.2p r.nsn v.pai.3s r.gs.1 d.nsn n.nsn cj pt.aa.nsm n.asn pt.aa.nsm v.aai.3s r.dpm.3
3306 3284 4047 1639 1609 3836 5393 2779 3284 4539 2373 1443 899

and they all drank from it. ¶ **24** "This is my blood of the covenant, which is poured out for
καὶ ᾿ πάντες ἔπιον ἐξ αὐτοῦ καὶ τοῦτο ἐστιν μου τὸ αἷμα → τῆς διαθήκης τὸ → ἐκχυννόμενον ← ὑπὲρ
cj a.npm v.aai.3p p.g r.gsn.3 cj r.nsn v.pai.3s r.gs.1 d.nsn n.nsn d.gsf n.gsf d.nsn pt.pp.nsn p.g
2779 4246 4246 1666 899 2779 4047 1639 1609 3836 135 3836 1347 3836 1773 5642

many," he said to them. **25** "I tell you the truth, I will not drink again of the fruit of the vine until
πολλῶν → εἶπεν → αὐτοῖς → λέγω ὑμῖν ἀμὴν ὅτι → οὐ μὴ πίω οὐκέτι ἐκ τοῦ γενήματος → τῆς ἀμπέλου ἕως
a.gpm v.aai.3s r.dpm.3 v.pai.1s r.dp.2 pl cj pl pl v.aas.1s adv p.g d.gsn n.gsn d.gsf n.gsf p.g
4498 3306 899 3306 7007 297 4022 4403 4403 4024 3590 4403 4033 1666 3836 1163 3836 306 2401

that day when I drink it anew in the kingdom of God." ¶ **26** When they had sung a
ἐκείνης τῆς ἡμέρας ὅταν → πίνω αὐτὸ καινὸν ἐν τῇ βασιλείᾳ → τοῦ θεοῦ Καὶ → → → ὑμνήσαντες ←
r.gsf d.gsf n.gsf cj v.pas.1s r.asn.3 a.asn p.d d.dsf n.dsf d.gsm n.gsm cj pt.aa.npm
1697 3836 2465 4020 4403 899 2785 1877 3836 993 3836 2536 2779 5630

hymn, they went out to the Mount of Olives.
← → ἐξῆλθον ← εἰς τὸ ὄρος → τῶν ἐλαιῶν
v.aai.3p p.a d.asn n.asn d.gpf n.gpf
2002 1650 3836 4001 3836 1777

Jesus Predicts Peter's Denial

14:27 "You will all fall away," Jesus told them, "for it is written: "'I will strike the
καὶ ὅτι πάντες σκανδαλισθήσεσθε ὁ Ἰησοῦς, λέγει αὐτοῖς ὅτι → γέγραπται → Πατάξω τὸν
cj cj a.npm v.fpi.2p d.nsm n.nsm v.pai.3s r.dpm.3 cj v.rpi.3s v.fai.1s d.asm
2779 4022 4997 4997 4246 4997 3836 2652 3306 899 4022 1211 4250 3836

shepherd, and the sheep will be scattered.' **28** But after I have risen, I will go ahead of you into
ποιμένα καὶ τὰ πρόβατα → → διασκορπισθήσονται ἀλλὰ μετὰ με → τὸ ἐγερθῆναι → προάξω ← ← ὑμᾶς εἰς
n.asm cj d.npn n.npn v.fpi.3p cj p.a r.as.1 d.asn f.ap v.fai.1s r.ap.2 p.a
4478 2779 3836 4585 1399 247 3552 1609 3836 1586 4575 7007 1650

κάθως εἶπεν αὐτοῖς καὶ ἡτοίμασαν τὸ πάσχα. ¶ **17** Καὶ ὀψίας γενομένης ἔρχεται μετὰ τῶν δώδεκα. **18** καὶ ἀνακειμένων αὐτῶν καὶ ἐσθιόντων ὁ Ἰησοῦς εἶπεν, Ἀμὴν λέγω ὑμῖν ὅτι εἷς ἐξ ὑμῶν παραδώσει με ὁ ἐσθίων μετ' ἐμοῦ. ¶ **19** ἤρξαντο λυπεῖσθαι καὶ λέγειν αὐτῷ εἷς κατὰ εἷς, Μήτι ἐγώ; **20** ὁ δὲ εἶπεν αὐτοῖς, Εἷς τῶν δώδεκα, ὁ ἐμβαπτόμενος μετ' ἐμοῦ εἰς τὸ τρύβλιον. **21** ὅτι ὁ μὲν υἱὸς τοῦ ἀνθρώπου ὑπάγει καθὼς γέγραπται περὶ αὐτοῦ, οὐαὶ δὲ τῷ ἀνθρώπῳ ἐκείνῳ δι' οὗ ὁ υἱὸς τοῦ ἀνθρώπου παραδίδοται· καλὸν αὐτῷ εἰ οὐκ ἐγεννήθη ὁ ἄνθρωπος ἐκεῖνος. ¶ **22** Καὶ ἐσθιόντων αὐτῶν λαβὼν ὁ Ἰησοῦς ἄρτον εὐλογήσας ἔκλασεν καὶ ἔδωκεν αὐτοῖς καὶ εἶπεν, Λάβετε, τοῦτό ἐστιν τὸ σῶμά μου. ¶ **23** καὶ λαβὼν ποτήριον εὐχαριστήσας ἔδωκεν αὐτοῖς, καὶ ἔπιον ἐξ αὐτοῦ πάντες. ¶ **24** καὶ εἶπεν αὐτοῖς, Τοῦτό ἐστιν τὸ αἷμά μου τῆς διαθήκης τὸ ἐκχυννόμενον ὑπὲρ πολλῶν. **25** ἀμὴν λέγω ὑμῖν ὅτι οὐκέτι οὐ μὴ πίω ἐκ τοῦ γενήματος τῆς ἀμπέλου ἕως τῆς ἡμέρας ἐκείνης ὅταν αὐτὸ πίνω καινὸν ἐν τῇ βασιλείᾳ τοῦ θεοῦ. ¶ **26** Καὶ ὑμνήσαντες ἐξῆλθον εἰς τὸ Ὄρος τῶν Ἐλαιῶν.

14:27 Καὶ λέγει αὐτοῖς ὁ Ἰησοῦς ὅτι Πάντες σκανδαλισθήσεσθε, ὅτι γέγραπται, Πατάξω τὸν ποιμένα, καὶ τὰ πρόβατα διασκορπισθήσονται. **28** ἀλλὰ μετὰ τὸ ἐγερθῆναί με προάξω ὑμᾶς εἰς τὴν Γαλιλαίαν. ¶ **29** ὁ δὲ Πέτρος ἔφη αὐτῷ, Εἰ καὶ πάντες

Galilee." ¶ **29** Peter declared, "Even if all fall away, I will not." ¶
τὴν Γαλιλαίαν δὲ ὁ Πέτρος ἔφη αὐτῷ καὶ εἰ πάντες σκανδαλισθήσονται ← ἀλλ᾽ ἐγὼ οὐκ
d.asf n.asf   cj d.nsm n.nsm v.iai.3s r.dsm.3 adv cj a.npm v.fpi.3p   cj r.ns.1 pl
3836 1133   1254 3836 5774 5774 899 2779 1623 4246 4997   247 1609 4024

30 "I tell you the truth," Jesus answered, "today – yes, tonight – before the rooster
καὶ → λέγω σοι ἀμὴν ὁ Ἰησοῦς λέγει αὐτῷ ὅτι σήμερον ταύτῃ τῇ νυκτὶ πρὶν ἢ ἀλέκτορα
cj v.pai.1s r.ds.2 pl d.nsm n.nsm v.pai.3s r.dsm.3 cj adv r.dsf d.dsf n.dsf pl pl n.asm
2779 3306 5148 297 3836 2652 3306 899 4022 4958 4047 3836 3816 4570 2445 232

crows twice you yourself will disown me three times." ¶ **31** But Peter insisted emphatically, "Even if I have
φωνῆσαι δὶς σὺ ← → ἀπαρνήσῃ με τρίς ← δὲ ὁ ἐλάλει ἐκπερισσῶς ἐὰν με δέῃ
f.aa adv r.ns.2   v.fmi.2s r.as.1 adv   cj d.nsm v.iai.3s adv cj r.as.1 v.pas.3s
5888 1489 5148   565 1609 5565   1254 3836 3281 1735 1569 1609 1256

to die with you, I will never disown you." And all the others said the same.
→ συναποθανεῖν → σοι → οὐ μὴ ἀπαρνήσομαι σε δὲ καὶ πάντες ἔλεγον → ὡσαύτως
f.aa r.ds.2 pl pl v.fmi.1s r.as.2 cj adv a.npm v.iai.3p adv
5271 5148 565 565 4024 3590 565 5148 1254 2779 4246 3306 6058

Gethsemane

14:32 They went to a place called Gethsemane, and Jesus said to his disciples, "Sit here
Καὶ → ἔρχονται εἰς χωρίον οὗ τὸ ὄνομα Γεθσημανί καὶ λέγει αὐτοῦ τοῖς μαθηταῖς καθίσατε ὧδε
cj v.pmi.3p p.a n.asn r.gsn d.nsn n.nsn n.nsn cj v.pai.3s r.gsm.3 d.dpm n.dpm v.aam.2p adv
2779 2262 1650 6005 4005 3836 3950 1149 2779 3306 899 3836 3412 2767 6045

while I pray." **33** He took Peter, James and John along with him, and he began
ἕως → προσεύξωμαι καὶ → παραλαμβάνει τὸν Πέτρον καὶ τὸν Ἰάκωβον καὶ τὸν Ἰωάννην ← μετ᾽ αὐτοῦ καὶ → ἤρξατο
cj v.ams.1s cj v.pai.3s d.asm n.asm cj d.asm n.asm cj d.asm n.asm p.g r.gsm.3 cj v.ami.3s
2401 4667 2779 4161 3836 4377 2779 3836 2610 2779 3836 2722 4161 3552 899 2779 806

to be deeply distressed and troubled. **34** "My soul is overwhelmed with sorrow to the point of death," he
→ ἐκθαμβεῖσθαι καὶ ἀδημονεῖν καὶ μου ἡ ψυχή ἐστιν περίλυπος ← ← ἕως ← ← θανάτου →
f.pp cj f.pa cj r.gs.1 d.nsf n.nsf v.pai.3s a.nsf p.g n.gsm
1701 2779 86 2779 1609 3836 6034 1639 4337 2401 2505

said to them. "Stay here and keep watch." ¶ **35** Going a little farther, he fell to the ground and
λέγει → αὐτοῖς μείνατε ὧδε καὶ → γρηγορεῖτε καὶ προελθὼν μικρὸν ← → ἔπιπτεν ἐπὶ τῆς γῆς καὶ
v.pai.3s r.dpm.3 v.aam.2p adv cj v.pam.2p cj pt.aa.nsm a.asn v.iai.3s p.g d.gsf n.gsf cj
3306 899 3531 6045 2779 1213 2779 4601 3625 4406 2093 3836 1178 2779

prayed that if possible the hour might pass from him. **36** "Abba, Father," he said, "everything is
προσηύχετο ἵνα εἰ ἔστιν δυνατόν ἡ ὥρα → παρέλθῃ ἀπ᾽ αὐτοῦ καὶ ἀββα ὁ πατήρ → ἔλεγεν πάντα
v.imi.3s cj cj v.pai.3s a.nsn d.nsf n.nsf v.aas.3s p.g r.gsm.3 cj n.vsm d.nsm n.nsm v.iai.3s a.npn
4667 2671 1623 1639 1543 3836 6052 4216 608 899 2779 5 3836 4252 3306 4246

possible for you. Take this cup from me. Yet not what I will, but what you will." ¶ **37** Then he
δυνατά → σοι παρένεγκε τοῦτο τὸ ποτήριον ἀπ᾽ ἐμοῦ ἀλλ᾽ οὐ τί ἐγὼ θέλω ἀλλὰ τί σύ καὶ
a.npn r.ds.2 v.aam.2s r.asn d.asn n.asn p.g r.gs.1 pl r.asn r.ns.1 v.pai.1s cj r.asn r.ns.2 cj
1543 5148 4195 4047 3836 4539 608 1609 247 4024 5515 1609 2527 247 5515 5148 2779

returned to his disciples and found them sleeping. "Simon," he said to Peter, "are you asleep? Could
ἔρχεται καὶ εὑρίσκει αὐτοὺς καθεύδοντας καὶ Σίμων → λέγει τῷ Πέτρῳ → → καθεύδεις ἴσχυσας
v.pmi.3s cj v.pai.3s r.apm.3 pt.pa.apm cj n.vsm v.pai.3s d.dsm n.dsm v.pai.2s v.aai.2s
2262 2779 2351 899 2761 2779 4981 3306 3836 4377 2761 2710

you not keep watch for one hour? **38** Watch and pray so that you will not fall into temptation. The
← οὐκ γρηγορῆσαι → μίαν ὥραν γρηγορεῖτε καὶ προσεύχεσθε ἵνα μὴ ἔλθητε εἰς πειρασμόν μὲν τὸ
pl f.aa a.asf n.asf v.pam.2p cj v.pmm.2p cj pl v.aas.2p p.a n.asm pl d.nsn
4024 1213 1651 6052 1213 2779 4667 2671 2262 2262 3590 2262 1650 4280 3525 3836

spirit is willing, but the body is weak." ¶ **39** Once more he went away and prayed the same thing.
πνεῦμα πρόθυμον δὲ ἡ σὰρξ ἀσθενής καὶ πάλιν → ἀπελθὼν ← εἰπὼν προσηύξατο τὸν αὐτὸν λόγον
n.nsn a.nsn cj d.nsf n.nsf a.nsf cj adv pt.aa.nsm pt.aa.nsm v.ami.3s d.asm r.asm n.asm
4460 4609 1254 3836 4922 822 2779 4099 599 3306 4667 3836 899 3364

40 When he came back, he again found them sleeping, because their eyes were heavy. They
καὶ → ἐλθὼν → πάλιν εὗρεν αὐτοὺς καθεύδοντας γὰρ αὐτῶν οἱ ὀφθαλμοὶ ἦσαν καταβαρυνόμενοι καὶ →
cj pt.aa.nsm adv v.aai.3s r.apm.3 pt.pa.apm cj r.gpm.3 d.npm n.npm v.iai.3p pt.pm.npm cj
2779 2262 2351 4099 2351 899 2761 1142 899 3836 4057 1639 2852 2779 3857

σκανδαλισθήσονται, ἀλλ᾽ οὐκ ἐγώ. ¶ **30** καὶ λέγει αὐτῷ ὁ Ἰησοῦς, Ἀμὴν λέγω σοι ὅτι σὺ σήμερον ταύτῃ τῇ νυκτὶ πρὶν ἢ δὶς ἀλέκτορα φωνῆσαι τρίς με ἀπαρνήσῃ. ¶ **31** ὁ δὲ ἐκπερισσῶς ἐλάλει, Ἐὰν δέῃ με συναποθανεῖν σοι, οὐ μή σε ἀπαρνήσομαι. ὡσαύτως δὲ καὶ πάντες ἔλεγον.
14:32 Καὶ ἔρχονται εἰς χωρίον οὗ τὸ ὄνομα Γεθσημανί καὶ λέγει τοῖς μαθηταῖς αὐτοῦ, Καθίσατε ὧδε ἕως προσεύξωμαι. **33** καὶ παραλαμβάνει τὸν Πέτρον καὶ [τὸν] Ἰάκωβον καὶ [τὸν] Ἰωάννην μετ᾽ αὐτοῦ καὶ ἤρξατο ἐκθαμβεῖσθαι καὶ ἀδημονεῖν **34** καὶ λέγει αὐτοῖς, Περίλυπός ἐστιν ἡ ψυχή μου ἕως θανάτου· μείνατε ὧδε καὶ γρηγορεῖτε. ¶ **35** καὶ προελθὼν μικρὸν ἔπιπτεν ἐπὶ τῆς γῆς καὶ προσηύχετο ἵνα εἰ δυνατόν ἐστιν παρέλθῃ ἀπ᾽ αὐτοῦ ἡ ὥρα, **36** καὶ ἔλεγεν, Αββα ὁ πατήρ, πάντα δυνατά σοι· παρένεγκε τὸ ποτήριον τοῦτο ἀπ᾽ ἐμοῦ· ἀλλ᾽ οὐ τί ἐγὼ θέλω ἀλλὰ τί σύ. ¶ **37** καὶ ἔρχεται καὶ εὑρίσκει αὐτοὺς καθεύδοντας, καὶ λέγει τῷ Πέτρῳ, Σίμων, καθεύδεις; οὐκ ἴσχυσας μίαν ὥραν γρηγορῆσαι; **38** γρηγορεῖτε καὶ προσεύχεσθε, ἵνα μὴ ἔλθητε εἰς πειρασμόν· τὸ μὲν πνεῦμα πρόθυμον ἡ δὲ σὰρξ ἀσθενής. ¶ **39** καὶ πάλιν ἀπελθὼν προσηύξατο τὸν αὐτὸν λόγον εἰπών. **40** καὶ πάλιν ἐλθὼν εὗρεν αὐτοὺς καθεύδοντας, ἦσαν γὰρ αὐτῶν οἱ ὀφθαλμοὶ καταβαρυνόμενοι, καὶ οὐκ ᾔδεισαν τί ἀποκριθῶσιν

did not know | what to say | to him. | ¶ | 41 | Returning the third time, | he said to them, "Are you
→ οὐκ ἤδεισαν | τί → ἀποκριθῶσιν | αὐτῷ | | | καὶ ἔρχεται τὸ τρίτον ← | καὶ → λέγει αὐτοῖς ↱
pl v.lai.3p | r.asn v.aas.3p | r.dsm.3 | | | cj v.pmi.3s d.asn a.asn | cj v.pai.3s r.dpm.3
3857 4024 3857 | 5515 646 | 899 | | | 2779 2262 3836 5568 | 2779 3306 899 2761 2761

still | sleeping and resting? | Enough! | The | hour has come. | Look, | the Son of Man | is betrayed | into
ιτὸ λοιπόν, | Καθεύδετε καὶ ἀναπαύεσθε | ἀπέχει | ἡ | ὥρα, → ἦλθεν | ἰδοὺ | ὁ | υἱὸς → ιτοῦ ἀνθρώπου, | → παραδίδοται | εἰς
d.asn adv | v.pai.2p cj v.pmi.2p | v.pai.3s | d.nsf | n.nsf v.aai.3s | j | d.nsm n.nsm | d.gsm n.gsm | v.ppi.3s | p.a
3836 3370 | 2761 2779 399 | 600 | 3836 | 6052 2262 | 2627 | 3836 5626 | 3836 476 | 4140 | 1650

the hands of sinners. | 42 Rise! | Let us go! | Here comes my betrayer!"
τὰς χεῖρας → ιτῶν ἁμαρτωλῶν, | ἐγείρεσθε → | ἄγωμεν | ἰδοὺ ἤγγικεν με ιὁ παραδιδούς,
d.apf n.apf → d.gpm a.gpm | v.ppm.2p | v.pas.1p | j v.rai.3s r.as.1 d.nsm pt.pa.nsm
3836 5931 3836 283 | 1586 | 72 | 2627 1581 1609 3836 4140

Jesus Arrested

14:43 | Just | as he | was speaking, Judas, | one | of the Twelve, | appeared. | With him | was a crowd
Καὶ | ιεὐθὺς ἔτι ← | αὐτοῦ → | λαλοῦντος Ἰούδας | εἷς → | τῶν δώδεκα | παραγίνεται | καὶ μετ᾿ | αὐτοῦ | ὄχλος
cj | adv adv | r.gsm.3 | pt.pa.gsm n.nsm | a.nsm | d.gpm a.gpm | v.pmi.3s | cj p.g | r.gsm.3 | n.nsm
2779 | 2318 2285 | 899 | 3281 2683 | 1651 | 3836 1557 | 4134 | 2779 3552 | 899 | 4063

armed with swords and clubs, | sent from the chief priests, | the teachers | of the law, | and the elders. | ¶
μετὰ μαχαιρῶν καὶ ξύλων | παρὰ τῶν → ἀρχιερέων καὶ τῶν | γραμματέων ← | | καὶ τῶν πρεσβυτέρων
p.g n.gpf cj n.gpn | p.g d.gpm n.gpm cj d.gpm | n.gpm | | cj d.gpm a.gpm
3552 3479 2779 3833 | 4123 3836 797 2779 3836 | 1208 | | 2779 3836 4565

44 Now the betrayer | had arranged a signal | with them: | "The one I kiss | is | the man; arrest | him
δὲ ὁ παραδιδοὺς αὐτὸν → | δεδώκει | σύσσημον → | αὐτοῖς λέγων ιὃν ἄν, | → φιλήσω ἐστιν | αὐτός κρατήσατε αὐτὸν
cj d.nsm pt.pa.nsm r.asm.3 | v.lai.3s | n.asn | r.dpm.3 pt.pa.nsm r.asm pl | v.aas.1s v.pai.3s | r.nsm v.aam.2p r.asm.3
1254 3836 4140 899 | 1443 | 5361 | 899 3306 4005 323 | 5797 1639 | 899 3195 899

and lead | him away under guard." | 45 | Going | at | once to Jesus, Judas said, | "Rabbi!" and kissed
καὶ ἀπάγετε ← | ← → ἀσφαλῶς | | καὶ ἐλθὼν προσελθὼν εὐθὺς ← | ↱ | αὐτῷ | λέγει ῥαββί | καὶ κατεφίλησεν
cj v.pam.2p | adv | | cj pt.aa.nsm pt.aa.nsm adv | | r.dsm.3 | v.pai.3s n.vsm | cj v.aai.3s
2779 552 | 857 | | 2779 2262 4665 2318 | 4665 | 899 | 3306 4806 | 2779 2968

him. | 46 | The men seized | Jesus and arrested him. | 47 Then one | of those standing | near
αὐτόν | δὲ οἱ | ἐπέβαλον τὰς χεῖρας | αὐτῷ καὶ ἐκράτησαν αὐτόν | δὲ εἷς [τις] → | τῶν παρεστηκότων ←
r.asm.3 | cj d.npm | v.aai.3p d.apf n.apf | r.dsm.3 cj v.aai.3p r.asm.3 | cj a.nsm r.nsm | d.gpm pt.ra.gpm
899 | 1254 3836 | 2095 3836 5931 | 899 2779 3195 899 | 1254 1651 5516 | 3836 4225

drew | his sword | and struck the servant | of the | high priest, | cutting off his | ear. | ¶ | 48
σπασάμενος τὴν μάχαιραν | ἔπαισεν τὸν δοῦλον → | τοῦ → | ἀρχιερέως καὶ ἀφεῖλεν ← | αὐτοῦ ιτὸ ὠτάριον, | | Καὶ
pt.am.nsm d.asf n.asf | v.aai.3s d.asm n.asm | d.gsm | n.gsm cj v.aai.3s | r.gsm.3 d.asn n.asn | | cj
5060 3836 3479 | 4091 3836 1529 | 3836 | 797 2779 904 | 899 3836 6064 | | 2779

"Am I leading a rebellion," | said | Jesus, | "that you have come | out with swords | and clubs
ιὡς ἐπὶ λῃστὴν, ἀποκριθεὶς | εἶπεν αὐτοῖς ὁ | Ἰησοῦς, | → | ἐξήλθατε | μετὰ μαχαιρῶν | καὶ ξύλων
pl p.a n.asm pt.ap.nsm | v.aai.3s r.dpm.3 d.nsm | n.nsm | | v.aai.2p | p.g n.gpf | cj n.gpn
6055 2093 3334 646 | 3306 899 3836 | 2652 | | 2002 | 3552 3479 | 2779 3833

to capture me? | 49 Every day | I was with you, teaching in | the temple courts, and you did not arrest | me. But
→ συλλαβεῖν με | καθ᾿ ἡμέραν → | ἤμην πρὸς ὑμᾶς διδάσκων ἐν | τῷ ἱερῷ καὶ ↱ → οὐκ ἐκρατήσατέ με | ἀλλ᾿ ἵνα
f.aa r.as.1 | p.a n.asf | v.imi.1s p.a r.ap.2 pt.pa.nsm p.d | d.dsn n.dsn cj v.pai.2p r.as.1 | cj cj
5197 1609 | 2848 2465 | 1639 4639 7007 1438 1877 | 2639 2779 3195 3195 4024 3195 1609 | 247 2671

the Scriptures must be fulfilled." | 50 Then everyone deserted him and fled. | ¶ | 51 | A | young | man,
αἱ γραφαί ← → πληρωθῶσιν | Καὶ πάντες ἀφέντες αὐτὸν ἔφυγον | | καὶ τις νεανίσκος ←
d.npf n.npf v.aps.3p | cj a.npm pt.aa.npm r.asm.3 v.aai.3p | | cj r.nsm n.nsm
3836 1210 2671 4444 | 2779 4246 918 899 5771 | | 2779 5516 3734

wearing | nothing | but a linen | garment, | was following | Jesus. When they seized | him, | 52 | he | fled | naked,
περιβεβλημένος ιἐπὶ γυμνοῦ, | → σινδόνα → | συνηκολούθει αὐτῷ | καὶ → | κρατοῦσιν αὐτόν | δὲ ὁ | ἔφυγεν γυμνὸς
pt.rp.nsm p.g a.gsn | n.asf | v.iai.3s r.dsm.3 | cj | v.pai.3p r.asm.3 | cj d.nsm | v.aai.3s a.nsm
4314 2093 1218 | 4984 | 5258 899 | 2779 | 3195 899 | 1254 3836 | 5771 1218

leaving | his garment behind.
καταλιπὼν τὴν σινδόνα ↰
pt.aa.nsm d.asf n.asf
2901 3836 4984 2901

αὐτῷ ¶ 41 καὶ ἔρχεται τὸ τρίτον καὶ λέγει αὐτοῖς, Καθεύδετε τὸ λοιπὸν καὶ ἀναπαύεσθε; «ἀναπαύεσθε·» ἀπέχει· ἦλθεν ἡ ὥρα, ἰδοὺ παραδίδοται ὁ υἱὸς τοῦ ἀνθρώπου εἰς τὰς χεῖρας τῶν ἁμαρτωλῶν. 42 ἐγείρεσθε ἄγωμεν· ἰδοὺ ὁ παραδιδούς με ἤγγικεν.

14:43 Καὶ εὐθὺς ἔτι αὐτοῦ λαλοῦντος παραγίνεται Ἰούδας εἷς τῶν δώδεκα καὶ μετ᾿ αὐτοῦ ὄχλος μετὰ μαχαιρῶν καὶ ξύλων παρὰ τῶν ἀρχιερέων καὶ τῶν γραμματέων καὶ τῶν πρεσβυτέρων. ¶ 44 δεδώκει δὲ ὁ παραδιδοὺς αὐτὸν σύσσημον αὐτοῖς λέγων, Ὃν ἂν φιλήσω αὐτός ἐστιν, κρατήσατε αὐτὸν καὶ ἀπάγετε ἀσφαλῶς. 45 καὶ ἐλθὼν εὐθὺς προσελθὼν αὐτῷ λέγει, Ῥαββί, καὶ κατεφίλησεν αὐτόν· 46 οἱ δὲ ἐπέβαλον τὰς χεῖρας αὐτῷ καὶ ἐκράτησαν αὐτόν. 47 εἷς δέ [τις] τῶν παρεστηκότων σπασάμενος τὴν μάχαιραν ἔπαισεν τὸν δοῦλον τοῦ ἀρχιερέως καὶ ἀφεῖλεν αὐτοῦ τὸ ὠτάριον. ¶ 48 καὶ ἀποκριθεὶς ὁ Ἰησοῦς εἶπεν αὐτοῖς, Ὡς ἐπὶ λῃστὴν ἐξήλθατε μετὰ μαχαιρῶν καὶ ξύλων συλλαβεῖν με; 49 καθ᾿ ἡμέραν ἤμην πρὸς ὑμᾶς ἐν τῷ ἱερῷ διδάσκων καὶ οὐκ ἐκρατήσατέ με· ἀλλ᾿ ἵνα πληρωθῶσιν αἱ γραφαί. 50 καὶ ἀφέντες αὐτὸν ἔφυγον πάντες. ¶ 51 Καὶ νεανίσκος τις συνηκολούθει αὐτῷ περιβεβλημένος σινδόνα ἐπὶ γυμνοῦ, καὶ κρατοῦσιν αὐτόν· 52 ὁ δὲ καταλιπὼν τὴν σινδόνα γυμνὸς ἔφυγεν.

Before the Sanhedrin

14:53 They took Jesus to the high priest, and all the chief priests, elders and
Καὶ → ἀπήγαγον ⸤τὸν Ἰησοῦν⸥ πρὸς τὸν → ἀρχιερέα καὶ πάντες οἱ ἀρχιερεῖς καὶ ⸤οἱ πρεσβύτεροι⸥ καὶ
cj   v.aai.3p   d.asm n.asm   p.a d.asm   n.asm cj a.npm d.npm   n.npm cj d.npm a.npm   cj
2779 552   3836 2652   4639 3836   797 2779 4246 3836   797 2779 3836 4565   2779

teachers of the law came together. **54** Peter followed him at a distance, right into the
⸤οἱ γραμματεῖς⸥ ← ← συνέρχονται καὶ ὁ Πέτρος ἠκολούθησεν αὐτῷ ἀπὸ μακρόθεν ἕως ἔσω εἰς τὴν
d.nsm n.nsm   v.pmi.3p   cj d.nsm n.nsm   v.aai.3s   r.dsm.3 p.g adv   p.g adv p.a d.asf
3836 1208   5302   2779 3836 4377   199 899 608   3427 2401 2276 1650 3836

courtyard of the high priest. There he sat with the guards and warmed himself at the
αὐλὴν → τοῦ → ἀρχιερέως καὶ → ἦν συγκαθήμενος, μετὰ τῶν ὑπηρετῶν καὶ θερμαινόμενος ← πρὸς τὸ
n.asf d.gsm n.gsm cj v.iai.3s pt.pm.nsm p.g d.gpm n.gpm cj pt.pm.nsm p.a d.asn
885 3836 797 2779 1639 5153 3552 3836 5677 2779 2548 4639 3836

fire. ¶ **55** The chief priests and the whole Sanhedrin were looking for evidence against Jesus so that
φῶς, δὲ Οἱ → ἀρχιερεῖς καὶ τὸ ὅλον συνέδριον → ἐζήτουν ← μαρτυρίαν κατὰ ⸤τοῦ Ἰησοῦ⸥ εἰς ←
n.asn cj d.npm n.npm cj d.nsn a.nsn n.nsn v.iai.3p n.asf p.g d.gsm n.gsm p.a
5890 1254 3836 797 2779 3836 3910 5284 2426 3456 2848 3836 2652 1650

they could put him to death, but they did not find any. **56** Many testified falsely against him,
→ → αὐτόν ⸤τὸ θανατῶσαι⸥ καὶ → οὐχ ηὕρισκον γὰρ πολλοὶ ἐψευδομαρτύρουν ← κατ' αὐτοῦ
r.asm.3 d.asn f.aai cj pl v.iai.3p cj a.npm v.iai.3p p.g r.gsm.3
2506 2506 2506 899 3836 2506 2779 2351 2351 4024 2351 1142 4498 6018 2848 899

but their statements did not agree. ¶ **57** Then some stood up and gave this false testimony against him:
καὶ αἱ μαρτυρίαι ἦσαν οὐκ ἴσαι καὶ τινες ἀναστάντες ← ἐψευδομαρτύρουν κατ' αὐτοῦ
cj d.npf n.npf v.iai.3p pl a.npf cj r.npm pt.aa.npm v.iai.3p p.g r.gsm.3
2779 3836 3456 1639 4024 2698 2779 5516 482 6018 2848 899

58 "We heard him say, 'I will destroy this man-made temple and in three days will
λέγοντες ὅτι ἡμεῖς ἠκούσαμεν αὐτοῦ λέγοντος ὅτι ἐγὼ → καταλύσω τοῦτον ⸤τὸν χειροποίητον⸥ ⸤τὸν ναὸν⸥ καὶ διὰ τριῶν ἡμερῶν →
pt.pa.npm cj r.np.1 v.aai.1p r.gsm.3 pt.pa.gsm cj r.ns.1 v.fai.1s r.asm d.asm a.asm d.asm n.asm cj p.g a.gpf n.gpf
3306 4022 7005 201 899 3306 4022 1609 2907 4047 3836 5935 3836 3724 2779 1328 5552 2465

build another, not made by man.'" **59** Yet even then their testimony did not agree. ¶
οἰκοδομήσω ἄλλον → ἀχειροποίητον ← καὶ ⸤οὐδὲ οὕτως⸥ ← αὐτῶν ἡ μαρτυρία ἦν ← ἴση
v.fai.1s r.asm a.asm cj adv adv r.gpm.3 d.nsf n.nsf v.iai.3s a.nsf
3868 257 942 2779 4028 4048 899 3836 3456 1639 4028 7698

60 Then the high priest stood up before them and asked Jesus, "Are you not going to answer?
καὶ ὁ → ἀρχιερεὺς ἀναστὰς ⸤εἰς μέσον⸥ ← ἐπηρώτησεν ⸤τὸν Ἰησοῦν⸥ λέγων → → οὐκ → ἀποκρίνη
cj d.nsm n.nsm pt.aa.nsm p.a n.asn v.aai.3s d.asm n.asm pt.pa.nsm pl v.pmi.2s
2779 3836 797 482 1650 3545 2089 3836 2652 3306 646 646 4024 646

What is this testimony that these men are bringing against you?" **61** But Jesus remained silent and gave no
οὐδὲν τί → καταμαρτυροῦσιν οὗτοι ← ← σου δὲ ὁ → ἐσιώπα καὶ → οὐκ
a.asn r.asn v.pai.3p r.npm r.gs.2 cj d.nsm v.iai.3s cj pl
4029 5515 2909 4047 2909 2909 2909 5148 1254 3836 4995 2779 646 4024

answer. ¶ Again the high priest asked him, "Are you the Christ, the Son of the
ἀπεκρίνατο οὐδέν πάλιν ὁ → ἀρχιερεὺς ἐπηρώτα αὐτὸν καὶ λέγει αὐτῷ εἰ σὺ ὁ χριστὸς ὁ υἱὸς → τοῦ
v.ami.3s a.asn adv d.nsm n.nsm v.iai.3s r.asm.3 cj v.pai.3s r.dsm.3 v.pai.2s r.ns.2 d.nsm n.nsm d.nsm n.nsm d.gsm
646 4029 4099 3836 797 2089 899 2779 3306 899 1639 5148 3836 5986 3836 5626 3836

Blessed One?" ¶ **62** "I am," said Jesus. "And you will see the Son of Man sitting at the
εὐλογητοῦ ← δὲ ἐγώ εἰμι εἶπεν ὁ Ἰησοῦς, καὶ → ὄψεσθε τὸν υἱὸν ⸤τοῦ ἀνθρώπου⸥ καθήμενον ἐκ
a.gsm cj r.ns.1 v.pai.1s v.aai.3s d.nsm n.nsm cj v.fmi.2p d.asm n.asm d.gsm n.gsm pt.pm.asm p.g
2329 1254 1609 1639 3306 3836 2652 2779 3972 3836 5626 3836 476 2764 1666

right hand of the Mighty One and coming on the clouds of heaven." ¶ **63** The high priest tore
δεξιῶν ← τῆς δυνάμεως καὶ ἐρχόμενον μετὰ τῶν νεφελῶν ⸤τοῦ οὐρανοῦ⸥ δὲ ὁ → ἀρχιερεὺς διαρρήξας
a.gpf d.gsf n.gsf cj pt.pm.asm p.g d.gpf n.gpf d.gsm n.gsm cj d.nsm n.nsm pt.aa.nsm
1288 3836 1539 2779 2262 3552 3836 3749 3836 4041 1254 3836 797 1396

his clothes. "Why do we need any more witnesses?" he asked. **64** "You have heard the blasphemy.
αὐτοῦ ⸤τοὺς χιτῶνας⸥ τί → ⸤χρείαν ἔχομεν⸥ ἔτι ← μαρτύρων → λέγει → → ἠκούσατε τῆς βλασφημίας
r.gsm.3 d.apm n.apm r.asn n.asf v.pai.1p adv n.gpm v.pai.3s v.aai.2p d.gsf n.gsf
899 3836 5945 5515 5970 2400 2285 3459 3306 201 3836 1060

14:53 Καὶ ἀπήγαγον τὸν Ἰησοῦν πρὸς τὸν ἀρχιερέα, καὶ συνέρχονται πάντες οἱ ἀρχιερεῖς καὶ οἱ πρεσβύτεροι καὶ οἱ γραμματεῖς. **54** καὶ ὁ Πέτρος ἀπὸ μακρόθεν ἠκολούθησεν αὐτῷ ἕως ἔσω εἰς τὴν αὐλὴν τοῦ ἀρχιερέως καὶ ἦν συγκαθήμενος μετὰ τῶν ὑπηρετῶν καὶ θερμαινόμενος πρὸς τὸ φῶς. ¶ **55** οἱ δὲ ἀρχιερεῖς καὶ ὅλον τὸ συνέδριον ἐζήτουν κατὰ τοῦ Ἰησοῦ μαρτυρίαν εἰς τὸ θανατῶσαι αὐτόν, καὶ οὐχ ηὕρισκον· **56** πολλοὶ γὰρ ἐψευδομαρτύρουν κατ' αὐτοῦ, καὶ ἴσαι αἱ μαρτυρίαι οὐκ ἦσαν. ¶ **57** καὶ τινες ἀναστάντες ἐψευδομαρτύρουν κατ' αὐτοῦ λέγοντες **58** ὅτι Ἡμεῖς ἠκούσαμεν αὐτοῦ λέγοντος ὅτι Ἐγὼ καταλύσω τὸν ναὸν τοῦτον τὸν χειροποίητον καὶ διὰ τριῶν ἡμερῶν ἄλλον ἀχειροποίητον οἰκοδομήσω **59** καὶ οὐδὲ οὕτως ἴση ἦν ἡ μαρτυρία αὐτῶν. ¶ **60** καὶ ἀναστὰς ὁ ἀρχιερεὺς εἰς μέσον ἐπηρώτησεν τὸν Ἰησοῦν λέγων, Οὐκ ἀποκρίνη οὐδέν; «οὐδὲν» τί οὗτοί σου καταμαρτυροῦσιν; **61** ὁ δὲ ἐσιώπα καὶ οὐκ ἀπεκρίνατο οὐδέν. ¶ πάλιν ὁ ἀρχιερεὺς ἐπηρώτα αὐτὸν καὶ λέγει αὐτῷ, Σὺ εἶ ὁ Χριστὸς ὁ υἱὸς τοῦ εὐλογητοῦ; ¶ **62** ὁ δὲ Ἰησοῦς εἶπεν, Ἐγώ εἰμι, καὶ ὄψεσθε τὸν υἱὸν τοῦ ἀνθρώπου ἐκ δεξιῶν καθήμενον τῆς δυνάμεως καὶ ἐρχόμενον μετὰ τῶν νεφελῶν τοῦ οὐρανοῦ. ¶ **63** ὁ δὲ ἀρχιερεὺς διαρρήξας τοὺς χιτῶνας αὐτοῦ λέγει, Τί ἔτι χρείαν ἔχομεν μαρτύρων; **64** ἠκούσατε τῆς βλασφημίας· τί ὑμῖν φαίνεται; ¶ οἱ δὲ πάντες κατέκριναν αὐτὸν ἔνοχον

What do you think?" ¶ They all condemned him as worthy of death. **65** Then some began to spit
τί → ὑμῖν φαίνεται δὲ οἱ πάντες κατέκριναν αὐτὸν εἶναι ἔνοχον → θανάτου Καὶ τινες ἤρξαντο → ἐμπτύειν
r.nsn r.dp2 v.ppi.3s cj d.npm a.npm v.aai.3p r.asm f.pa a.asm n.gsm cj r.npm v.ami.3p f.pa
5515 5743 7007 5743 1254 3836 4246 2891 899 1639 1944 2505 2779 5516 806 1870

at him; they blindfolded him, struck him with their fists, and said, "Prophesy!" And
→ αὐτῷ καὶ → περικαλύπτειν αὐτοῦ τὸ πρόσωπον, καὶ κολαφίζειν αὐτὸν ← ← ← καὶ λέγειν αὐτῷ προφήτευσον καὶ
r.dsm.3 cj f.pa r.gsm.3 d.asn n.asn cj f.pa r.asm.3 cj f.pa r.dsm.3 v.aam.2s cj
899 2779 4328 899 3836 4725 2779 3139 899 3139 3139 3139 2779 3306 899 4736 2779

the guards took him and beat him.
οἱ ὑπηρέται ἔλαβον αὐτὸν ῥαπίσμασιν
d.npm n.npm v.aai.3p r.asm.3 n.dpn
3836 5677 3284 899 4825

Peter Disowns Jesus

14:66 While Peter was below in the courtyard, one of the servant girls of the high priest came
Καὶ → ὄντος τοῦ Πέτρου, ὄντος κάτω ἐν τῇ αὐλῇ μία → τῶν → παιδισκῶν → τοῦ → ἀρχιερέως ἔρχεται
cj d.gsm n.gsm pt.pa.gsm adv p.d d.dsf n.dsf a.nsf d.gpf n.gpf d.gsm n.gsm v.pmi.3s
2779 1639 3836 4377 1639 3004 1877 3836 885 1651 3836 4087 3836 797 2262

by. **67** When she saw Peter warming himself, she looked closely at him. ¶ "You also were with
← καὶ → → ἰδοῦσα τὸν Πέτρον θερμαινόμενον ← → ἐμβλέψασα → αὐτῷ σὺ καὶ ἦσθα μετὰ
cj pt.aa.nsf d.asm n.asm pt.pm.asm pt.aa.nsf r.dsm.3 r.ns.2 adv v.iai.2s p.g
2779 1625 3836 4377 2548 1838 899 5148 2779 1639 3552

that Nazarene, Jesus," she said. ¶ **68** But he denied it. "I don't know or understand what you're talking
τοῦ Ναζαρηνοῦ ιτοῦ Ἰησοῦ, → λέγει δὲ ὁ ἠρνήσατο → οὔτε οἶδα οὔτε ἐπίσταμαι τί σὺ λέγεις
d.gsm a.gsm d.gsm n.gsm v.pai.3s cj d.nsm v.ami.3s cj v.rai.1s cj v.ppi.1s r.asn r.ns.2 v.pai.2s
3836 3716 3836 2652 3306 1254 3836 766 3857 4046 3857 4046 2179 5515 5148 3306

about," he said, and went out into the entryway. ¶ **69** When the servant girl
→ λέγων καὶ ἐξῆλθεν ἔξω εἰς τὸ προαύλιον [καὶ ἀλέκτωρ ἐφώνησεν] καὶ → ἡ → παιδίσκη
pt.pa.nsm cj v.aai.3s adv p.a d.asn n.asn cj n.nsm v.aai.3s cj d.nsf n.nsf
3306 2779 2002 2032 1650 3836 4580 2779 232 5888 2779 1625 3836 4087

saw him there, she said again to those standing around, "This fellow is one of them." **70** Again
ἰδοῦσα αὐτὸν → ἤρξατο λέγειν πάλιν → τοῖς παρεστῶσιν ὅτι οὗτος → ἐστιν → ἐξ αὐτῶν δὲ πάλιν
pt.aa.nsf r.asm.3 v.ami.3s f.pa adv d.dpm pt.ra.dpm cj r.nsm v.pai.3s p.g r.gpm.3 cj adv
1625 899 806 3306 4099 3836 4225 4022 4047 1639 1666 899 1254 4099

he denied it. ¶ After a little while, those standing near said to Peter, "Surely you are one
ὁ ἠρνεῖτο καὶ πάλιν μετὰ μικρὸν οἱ παρεστῶτες ἔλεγον → ιτῷ Πέτρῳ ἀληθῶς → εἶ →
d.nsm v.imi.3s cj adv p.a a.asn d.npm pt.ra.npm v.iai.3p d.dsm n.dsm adv v.pai.2s
3836 766 2779 4099 3552 3625 3836 4225 3306 3836 4377 242 1639

of them, for you are a Galilean." ¶ **71** He began to call down curses on himself, and he swore
ἐξ αὐτῶν γὰρ → καὶ εἶ Γαλιλαῖος δὲ ὁ ἤρξατο ἀναθεματίζειν ← ← καὶ → ὀμνύναι
p.g r.gpm.3 cj adv v.pai.2s a.nsm cj d.nsm v.ami.3s f.pa cj f.pa
1666 899 1142 1639 2779 1639 1134 1254 3836 806 354 2779 3923

to them, "I don't know this man you're talking about." ¶ **72** Immediately the rooster
ὅτι → οὐκ οἶδα τοῦτον ιτὸν ἄνθρωπον, ὃν → λέγετε ← καὶ εὐθὺς ἀλέκτωρ
cj pl v.rai.1s r.asn d.asm n.asm r.asm v.pai.2p cj adv n.nsm
4022 3857 4024 3857 4047 3836 476 4005 3306 2779 2318 232

crowed the second time. Then Peter remembered the word Jesus had spoken to him: "Before
ἐφώνησεν ἐκ δευτέρου ← καὶ ὁ Πέτρος, ἀνεμνήσθη τὸ ῥῆμα ὡς ιὁ Ἰησοῦς, → εἶπεν αὐτῷ ὅτι πρὶν
v.aai.3s p.g a.gsn cj d.nsm n.nsm v.api.3s d.asn n.asn cj d.nsm n.nsm v.aai.3s r.dsm.3 cj cj
5888 1666 1311 2779 3836 4377 389 3836 4839 6055 3836 2652 3306 899 4022 4570

the rooster crows twice you will disown me three times." And he broke down and wept.
ἀλέκτορα φωνῆσαι δὶς → → ἀπαρνήσῃ με τρίς → καὶ → ἐπιβαλὼν ἔκλαιεν
n.asm f.aa adv v.fmi.2s r.as.1 adv cj pt.aa.nsm v.iai.3s
232 5888 1489 565 1609 5565 2779 2095 3081

Jesus Before Pilate

15:1 Very early in the morning, the chief priests, with the elders, the teachers of the law and
Καὶ εὐθὺς → πρωΐ ← ← → οἱ ἀρχιερεῖς μετὰ τῶν πρεσβυτέρων καὶ γραμματέων ← ← καὶ
cj adv adv d.npm n.npm p.g d.gpm a.gpm cj n.gpm cj
2779 2318 4745 3836 797 3552 3836 4565 2779 1208 2779

εἶναι θανάτου. ⁶⁵ Καὶ ἤρξαντό τινες ἐμπτύειν αὐτῷ καὶ περικαλύπτειν αὐτοῦ τὸ πρόσωπον καὶ κολαφίζειν αὐτὸν καὶ λέγειν αὐτῷ, Προφήτευσον, καὶ οἱ ὑπηρέται ῥαπίσμασιν αὐτὸν ἔλαβον.

¹⁴⁶⁶ Καὶ ὄντος τοῦ Πέτρου κάτω ἐν τῇ αὐλῇ ἔρχεται μία τῶν παιδισκῶν τοῦ ἀρχιερέως ⁶⁷ καὶ ἰδοῦσα τὸν Πέτρον θερμαινόμενον ἐμβλέψασα ¶ αὐτῷ λέγει, Καὶ σὺ μετὰ τοῦ Ναζαρηνοῦ ἦσθα τοῦ Ἰησοῦ. ¶ ⁶⁸ ὁ δὲ ἠρνήσατο λέγων, Οὔτε οἶδα οὔτε ἐπίσταμαι σὺ τί λέγεις. καὶ ἐξῆλθεν ἔξω εἰς τὸ προαύλιον. «προαύλιον» [καὶ ἀλέκτωρ ἐφώνησεν]. ¶ ⁶⁹ καὶ ἡ παιδίσκη ἰδοῦσα αὐτὸν ἤρξατο πάλιν λέγειν τοῖς παρεστῶσιν ὅτι Οὗτος ἐξ αὐτῶν ἐστιν. ⁷⁰ ὁ δὲ πάλιν ἠρνεῖτο. ¶ καὶ μετὰ μικρὸν πάλιν οἱ παρεστῶτες ἔλεγον τῷ Πέτρῳ, Ἀληθῶς ἐξ αὐτῶν εἶ, καὶ γὰρ Γαλιλαῖος εἶ. ¶ ⁷¹ ὁ δὲ ἤρξατο ἀναθεματίζειν καὶ ὀμνύναι ὅτι Οὐκ οἶδα τὸν ἄνθρωπον τοῦτον ὃν λέγετε. ¶ ⁷² καὶ εὐθὺς ἐκ δευτέρου ἀλέκτωρ ἐφώνησεν. καὶ ἀνεμνήσθη ὁ Πέτρος τὸ ῥῆμα ὡς εἶπεν αὐτῷ ὁ Ἰησοῦς ὅτι Πρὶν ἀλέκτορα φωνῆσαι δὶς τρίς με ἀπαρνήσῃ· καὶ ἐπιβαλὼν ἔκλαιεν.

¹⁵¹ Καὶ εὐθὺς πρωῒ συμβούλιον ποιήσαντες οἱ ἀρχιερεῖς μετὰ τῶν πρεσβυτέρων καὶ γραμματέων καὶ ὅλον τὸ συνέδριον,

the whole Sanhedrin, reached a decision. They bound Jesus, led him away and handed him over to
τὸ ὅλον συνέδριον ποιήσαντες συμβούλιον → δήσαντες ⌐τὸν Ἰησοῦν⌐ ἀπήνεγκαν καὶ παρέδωκαν ←
d.nsn a.nsn n.nsn pt.aa.npm n.asn   pt.aa.npm d.asm n.asm v.aai.3p   cj v.aai.3p
3836 3910 5284 4472 5206   1313 3836 2652 708   2779 4140

Pilate. ¶ 2 "Are you the king of the Jews?" asked Pilate. ¶ "Yes, it is as you
Πιλάτῳ Καὶ εἶ σὺ ὁ βασιλεὺς → τῶν Ἰουδαίων ἐπηρώτησεν αὐτὸν ὁ Πιλᾶτος⌐ δὲ σὺ
n.dsm cj v.pai.2s r.ns.2 d.nsm n.nsm d.gpm a.gpm v.aai.3s r.asm.3 d.nsm n.nsm cj r.ns.2
4397 2779 1639 5148 3836 995 3836 2681 2089 899 3836 4397 1254 5148

say," Jesus replied. ¶ 3 The chief priests accused him of many things. 4 So again Pilate
λέγεις ὁ ἀποκριθεὶς αὐτῷ λέγει καὶ οἱ ἀρχιερεῖς κατηγόρουν αὐτοῦ πολλὰ ← δὲ πάλιν ὁ Πιλᾶτος⌐
v.pai.2s d.nsm pt.ap.nsm r.dsm.3 v.pai.3s cj d.npm n.npm v.iai.3p r.gsm.3 a.apn cj adv d.nsm n.nsm
3306 3836 646 899 3306 2779 3836 797 2989 899 4498 1254 4099 3836 4397

asked him, "Aren't you going to answer? See how many things they are accusing you of." ¶
ἐπηρώτα αὐτὸν λέγων οὐκ → → → ἀποκρίνῃ οὐδὲν ἴδε πόσα ← ← → → κατηγοροῦσιν σου
v.iai.3s r.asm.3 pt.pa.nsm pl v.ppi.2s a.asn pl r.apn v.pai.3p r.gs.2
2089 899 3306 4024 646 4029 2623 4531 2989 5148

5 But Jesus still made no reply, and Pilate was amazed. ¶ 6 Now it was the custom at the
δὲ Ἰησοῦς οὐκέτι →ʳ οὐδὲν ἀπεκρίθη ὥστε ⌐τὸν Πιλᾶτον⌐ → θαυμάζειν δὲ →ʳ →ʳ →ʳ Κατὰ
cj d.nsm n.nsm adv a.asn v.api.3s cj d.asm n.asm f.pa cj p.a
1254 3836 2652 4033 646 4029 646 6063 3836 4397 2513 1254 668 668 668 668 2848

Feast to release a prisoner whom the people requested. 7 A man called Barabbas was in prison with
ἑορτὴν → ἀπέλυεν αὐτοῖς ἕνα δέσμιον ὃν → παρητοῦντο δὲ ὁ λεγόμενος Βαραββᾶς ἦν → δεδεμένος μετὰ
n.asf v.iai.3s r.dpm.3 a.asm n.asm r.asm v.imi.3p cj d.nsm pt.pp.nsm n.nsm v.iai.3s pt.rp.nsm p.g
2038 668 899 1651 1300 4005 4148 1254 3836 3306 972 1639 1313 3552

the insurrectionists who had committed murder in the uprising. 8 The crowd came up and asked
τῶν στασιαστῶν οἵτινες → πεποιήκεισαν φόνον ἐν τῇ στάσει καὶ ὁ ὄχλος ἀναβὰς ← ἤρξατο αἰτεῖσθαι
d.gpm n.gpm r.npm v.lai.3p n.asm p.d d.dsf n.dsf cj d.nsm n.nsm pt.aa.nsm v.ami.3s f.pm
3836 5086 4015 4472 5840 1877 3836 5087 2779 3836 4063 326 806 160

Pilate to do for them what he usually did. ¶ 9 "Do you want me to release to you the king of the
→ ἐποίει → αὐτοῖς καθὼς ← ← δὲ → θέλετε → ἀπολύσω ὑμῖν τὸν βασιλέα → τῶν
v.iai.3s r.dpm.3 r.dpm.3 cj v.pai.2p v.aas.1s r.dp.2 d.asm n.asm d.gpm
4472 899 2777 1254 2527 668 7007 3836 995 3836

Jews?" asked Pilate, 10 knowing it was out of envy that the chief priests had
Ἰουδαίων ἀπεκρίθη αὐτοῖς λέγων ὁ Πιλᾶτος⌐ γὰρ ἐγίνωσκεν ὅτι διὰ ← φθόνον οἱ → ἀρχιερεῖς →
a.gpm v.api.3s r.dpm.3 pt.pa.nsm d.nsm n.nsm cj v.iai.3s cj p.a n.asm d.npm n.npm
2681 646 899 3306 3836 4397 1142 1182 4022 1328 5784 3836 797

handed Jesus over to him. 11 But the chief priests stirred up the crowd to have Pilate release
παραδεδώκεισαν αὐτὸν ← δὲ οἱ ἀρχιερεῖς ἀνέσεισαν ← τὸν ὄχλον ἵνα → ἀπολύσῃ αὐτοῖς
v.lai.3p r.asm.3 cj d.npm n.npm v.aai.3p d.asm n.asm cj v.aas.3s r.dpm.3
4140 899 4140 1254 3836 797 411 3836 4063 2671 668 899

Barabbas instead. ¶ 12 "What shall I do, then, with the one you call the king of the
⌐τὸν Βαραββᾶν⌐ μᾶλλον δὲ τί →ʳ [θέλετε] → ποιήσω οὖν ὃν → λέγετε τὸν βασιλέα → τῶν
d.asm n.asm adv.c cj r.asn v.pai.2p v.aas.1s cj r.asm v.pai.2p d.asm n.asm d.gpm
3836 972 3437 1254 5515 4472 2527 4472 4036 4005 3306 3836 995 3836

Jews?" Pilate asked them. ¶ 13 "Crucify him!" they shouted. ¶ 14 "Why?
Ἰουδαίων ὁ Πιλᾶτος⌐ πάλιν ἀποκριθεὶς ἔλεγεν αὐτοῖς δὲ σταύρωσον αὐτὸν οἱ πάλιν ἔκραξαν δὲ γὰρ
a.gpm d.nsm n.nsm adv pt.ap.nsm v.iai.3s r.dpm.3 cj v.aam.2s r.asm.3 d.npm adv v.aai.3p cj cj
2681 3836 4397 4099 3306 3306 899 1254 5090 899 3836 4099 3189 1254 1142

What crime has he committed?" asked Pilate. ¶ But they shouted all the louder, "Crucify him!"
τί κακόν → → ἐποίησεν ἔλεγεν ὁ Πιλᾶτος⌐ αὐτοῖς δὲ οἱ ἔκραξαν ← → περισσῶς σταύρωσον αὐτὸν
r.asn a.asn v.aai.3s v.iai.3s d.nsm n.nsm r.dpm.3 cj d.npm v.aai.3p adv v.aam.2s r.asm.3
5515 2805 4472 3306 3836 4397 899 1254 3836 3189 4360 5090 899

15 Wanting to satisfy the crowd, Pilate released Barabbas to them. He had Jesus
δὲ βουλόμενος → ⌐τὸ ἱκανὸν ποιῆσαι τῷ ὄχλῳ Ὁ Πιλᾶτος⌐ ἀπέλυσεν τὸν Βαραββᾶν → αὐτοῖς καὶ →ʳ ⌐τὸν Ἰησοῦν⌐
cj pt.pm.nsm d.asn a.asn f.aa d.dsm n.dsm d.nsm n.nsm v.aai.3s d.asm n.asm r.dpm.3 cj d.asm n.asm
1254 1089 3836 2653 4472 3836 4063 3836 4397 668 3836 972 899 2779 5849 5849 3836 2652

δήσαντες τὸν Ἰησοῦν ἀπήνεγκαν καὶ παρέδωκαν Πιλάτῳ. ¶ 2 καὶ ἐπηρώτησεν αὐτὸν ὁ Πιλᾶτος, Σὺ εἶ ὁ βασιλεὺς τῶν
Ἰουδαίων; ¶ ὁ δὲ ἀποκριθεὶς αὐτῷ λέγει, Σὺ λέγεις. ¶ 3 καὶ κατηγόρουν αὐτοῦ οἱ ἀρχιερεῖς πολλά. 4 ὁ δὲ Πιλᾶτος πάλιν
ἐπηρώτα αὐτὸν λέγων, Οὐκ ἀποκρίνῃ οὐδέν; ἴδε πόσα σου κατηγοροῦσιν. ¶ 5 ὁ δὲ Ἰησοῦς οὐκέτι οὐδὲν ἀπεκρίθη, ὥστε
θαυμάζειν τὸν Πιλᾶτον. ¶ 6 Κατὰ δὲ ἑορτὴν ἀπέλυεν αὐτοῖς ἕνα δέσμιον ὃν παρῃτοῦντο. 7 ἦν δὲ ὁ λεγόμενος Βαραββᾶς μετὰ
τῶν στασιαστῶν δεδεμένος οἵτινες ἐν τῇ στάσει φόνον πεποιήκεισαν. 8 καὶ ἀναβὰς ὁ ὄχλος ἤρξατο αἰτεῖσθαι καθὼς ἐποίει
αὐτοῖς. ¶ 9 ὁ δὲ Πιλᾶτος ἀπεκρίθη αὐτοῖς λέγων, Θέλετε ἀπολύσω ὑμῖν τὸν βασιλέα τῶν Ἰουδαίων; 10 ἐγίνωσκεν γὰρ ὅτι
διὰ φθόνον παραδεδώκεισαν αὐτὸν οἱ ἀρχιερεῖς. 11 οἱ δὲ ἀρχιερεῖς ἀνέσεισαν τὸν ὄχλον ἵνα μᾶλλον τὸν Βαραββᾶν ἀπολύσῃ
αὐτοῖς. ¶ 12 ὁ δὲ Πιλᾶτος πάλιν ἀποκριθεὶς ἔλεγεν αὐτοῖς, Τί οὖν [θέλετε] ποιήσω [ὃν λέγετε] τὸν βασιλέα τῶν Ἰουδαίων; ¶
13 οἱ δὲ πάλιν ἔκραξαν, Σταύρωσον αὐτόν. ¶ 14 ὁ δὲ Πιλᾶτος ἔλεγεν αὐτοῖς, Τί γὰρ ἐποίησεν κακόν; ¶ οἱ δὲ περισσῶς ἔκραξαν,
Σταύρωσον αὐτόν. 15 ὁ δὲ Πιλᾶτος βουλόμενος τῷ ὄχλῳ τὸ ἱκανὸν ποιῆσαι ἀπέλυσεν αὐτοῖς τὸν Βαραββᾶν, καὶ παρέδωκεν

flogged, and handed him over to be crucified.
φραγελλώσας παρέδωκεν ἵνα → σταυρωθῇ
pt.aa.nsm v.aai.3s cj v.aps.3s
5849 4140 2671 5090

The Soldiers Mock Jesus

15:16 The soldiers led Jesus away into the palace (that is, the Praetorium) and called together the
δὲ Οἱ στρατιῶται ἀπήγαγον αὐτὸν ↩ ἔσω τῆς αὐλῆς ὃ ἐστιν πραιτώριον καὶ συγκαλοῦσιν ← τὴν
cj d.npm n.npm v.aai.3p r.asm.3 p.g d.gsf n.gsf r.nsn v.pai.3s n.nsn cj v.pai.3p d.asf
1254 3836 5132 552 899 552 2276 3836 885 4005 1639 4550 2779 5157 3836

whole company of soldiers. **17** They put a purple robe on him, then twisted together a crown of
ὅλην σπεῖραν ← καὶ → ἐνδιδύσκουσιν πορφύραν ↩ αὐτὸν καὶ πλέξαντες ← στέφανον
a.asf n.asf cj v.pai.3p n.asf r.asm.3 cj pt.aa.npm n.asm
3910 5061 2779 1898 4525 1898 899 2779 4428 5109

thorns and set it on him. **18** And they began to call out to him, "Hail, king of the Jews!" **19**
ἀκάνθινον περιτιθέασιν ← αὐτῷ καὶ → ἤρξαντο ἀσπάζεσθαι ← ← αὐτόν χαῖρε βασιλεῦ → τῶν Ἰουδαίων καὶ
a.asm v.pai.3p r.dsm.3 cj v.ami.3p f.pm r.asm.3 v.pam.2s n.vsm d.gpm a.gpm cj
181 4363 899 2779 806 832 899 5897 995 3836 2681 2779

Again and again they struck him on the head with a staff and spit on him. Falling on their knees, they
→ → → ἔτυπτον αὐτοῦ → τὴν κεφαλὴν → καλάμῳ καὶ ἐνέπτυον → αὐτῷ καὶ τιθέντες ← τὰ γόνατα →
v.iai.3p r.gsm.3 d.asf n.asf n.dsm cj v.iai.3p r.dsm.3 cj pt.pa.npm d.apn n.apn
5597 899 3836 3051 2812 2779 1870 899 2779 5502 3836 1205

paid homage to him. **20** And when they had mocked him, they took off the purple robe and put his
→ προσεκύνουν → αὐτῷ καὶ ὅτε → → ἐνέπαιξαν αὐτῷ → ἐξέδυσαν αὐτὸν τὴν πορφύραν καὶ ἐνέδυσαν αὐτοῦ
v.iai.3p r.dsm.3 cj cj v.aai.3p r.dsm.3 v.aai.3p r.asm.3 d.asf n.asf cj v.aai.3p r.gsm.3
4686 899 2779 4021 1850 899 1694 1694 899 3836 4525 2779 1907 899

own clothes on him. Then they led him out to crucify him.
τὰ ἱμάτια ↩ αὐτὸν Καὶ → ἐξάγουσιν αὐτὸν ↩ ἵνα σταυρώσωσιν αὐτόν
d.apn n.apn r.asm.3 cj v.pai.3p r.asm.3 cj v.aas.3p r.asm.3
3836 2668 1907 899 2779 1974 899 1974 2671 5090 899

The Crucifixion

15:21 A certain man from Cyrene, Simon, the father of Alexander and Rufus, was passing by on his way
τινα ← → Κυρηναῖον Σίμωνα τὸν πατέρα → Ἀλεξάνδρου καὶ Ῥούφου → παράγοντα ← → ἐρχόμενον
r.asm n.asm n.asm d.asm n.asm n.gsm cj n.gsm pt.pa.asm pt.pm.asm
5516 3254 4981 3836 4252 235 2779 4859 4135 2262

in from the country, and they forced him to carry the cross. **22** They brought Jesus to the place
← ἀπ' ἀγροῦ καὶ → ἀγγαρεύουσιν ἵνα ἄρῃ τὸν σταυρὸν αὐτοῦ Καὶ → φέρουσιν αὐτὸν ἐπὶ τὸν τόπον
p.g n.gsm cj v.pai.3p cj v.aas.3s d.asm n.asm r.gsm.3 cj v.pai.3p r.asm.3 p.a d.asm n.asm
608 69 2779 30 2671 149 3836 5089 899 2779 5770 899 2093 3836 5536

called Golgotha (which means The Place of the Skull). **23** Then they offered him wine mixed
Γολγοθᾶν ὃ ἐστιν μεθερμηνευόμενον Τόπος → Κρανίου καὶ → ἐδίδουν αὐτῷ οἶνον ἐσμυρνισμένον
n.asf r.nsn v.pai.3s pt.pp.nsn n.nsm n.gsn cj v.iai.3p r.dsm.3 n.asm pt.rp.asm
1201 4005 1639 3493 5536 3191 2779 1443 899 3885 5046

with myrrh, but he did not take it. **24** And they crucified him. Dividing up his clothes, they cast
← δὲ ὃς → οὐκ ἔλαβεν Καὶ → σταυροῦσιν αὐτὸν καὶ διαμερίζονται ← αὐτοῦ ⌐τὰ ἱμάτια⌐ βάλλοντες
cj r.nsm pl v.aai.3s cj v.pai.3p r.asm.3 cj v.pmi.3p r.gsm.3 d.apn n.apn pt.pa.npm
1254 4005 3284 4024 3284 2779 5090 899 2779 1374 899 3836 2668 965

lots to see what each would get. **25** It was the third hour when they crucified him. **26** The
κλῆρον ἐπ' αὐτὰ τί τίς → ἄρῃ δὲ ἦν τρίτη ὥρα καὶ → ἐσταύρωσαν αὐτόν καὶ ἡ
n.asm p.a r.apn.3 r.asn r.nsm v.aas.3s cj v.iai.3s a.nsf n.nsf cj v.aai.3p r.asm.3 cj d.nsf
3102 2093 899 5515 5515 149 1254 1639 5569 6052 2779 5090 899 2779 3836

written notice of the charge against him read: THE KING OF THE JEWS. **27** They crucified two
ἐπιγεγραμμένη ἐπιγραφὴ → τῆς αἰτίας → αὐτοῦ ἦν ὁ βασιλεὺς → τῶν Ἰουδαίων Καὶ → σταυροῦσιν δύο
pt.rp.nsf n.nsf d.gsf n.gsf r.gsm.3 v.iai.3s d.nsm n.nsm d.gpm a.gpm cj v.pai.3p a.apm
2108 2107 3836 162 899 1639 3836 995 3836 2681 2779 5090 1545

robbers with him, one on his right and one on his left. **29** Those who passed by hurled insults
λῃστάς σὺν αὐτῷ ἕνα ἐκ δεξιῶν καὶ ἕνα ἐξ αὐτοῦ εὐωνύμων Καὶ οἱ ← παραπορευόμενοι ← → ἐβλασφήμουν
n.apm p.d r.dsm.3 a.asm p.g a.gpf cj a.asm p.g r.gsm.3 a.gpf cj d.npm pt.pm.npm v.iai.3p
3334 5250 899 1651 1666 1288 2779 1651 1666 899 2381 2779 3836 4182 1059

τὸν Ἰησοῦν φραγελλώσας ἵνα σταυρωθῇ.

15:16 Οἱ δὲ στρατιῶται ἀπήγαγον αὐτὸν ἔσω τῆς αὐλῆς, ὅ ἐστιν πραιτώριον, καὶ συγκαλοῦσιν ὅλην τὴν σπεῖραν. **17** καὶ ἐνδιδύσκουσιν αὐτὸν πορφύραν καὶ περιτιθέασιν αὐτῷ πλέξαντες ἀκάνθινον στέφανον· **18** καὶ ἤρξαντο ἀσπάζεσθαι αὐτόν, Χαῖρε, βασιλεῦ τῶν Ἰουδαίων· **19** καὶ ἔτυπτον αὐτοῦ τὴν κεφαλὴν καλάμῳ καὶ ἐνέπτυον αὐτῷ καὶ τιθέντες τὰ γόνατα προσεκύνουν αὐτῷ. **20** καὶ ὅτε ἐνέπαιξαν αὐτῷ, ἐξέδυσαν αὐτὸν τὴν πορφύραν καὶ ἐνέδυσαν αὐτὸν τὰ ἱμάτια αὐτοῦ. καὶ ἐξάγουσιν αὐτὸν ἵνα σταυρώσωσιν αὐτόν.

15:21 Καὶ ἀγγαρεύουσιν παράγοντά τινα Σίμωνα Κυρηναῖον ἐρχόμενον ἀπ' ἀγροῦ, τὸν πατέρα Ἀλεξάνδρου καὶ Ῥούφου, ἵνα ἄρῃ τὸν σταυρὸν αὐτοῦ. **22** καὶ φέρουσιν αὐτὸν ἐπὶ τὸν Γολγοθᾶν τόπον, ὅ ἐστιν μεθερμηνευόμενον Κρανίου Τόπος. **23** καὶ ἐδίδουν αὐτῷ ἐσμυρνισμένον οἶνον· ὃς δὲ οὐκ ἔλαβεν. **24** καὶ σταυροῦσιν αὐτὸν καὶ διαμερίζονται τὰ ἱμάτια αὐτοῦ, βάλλοντες κλῆρον ἐπ' αὐτὰ τίς τί ἄρῃ. **25** ἦν δὲ ὥρα τρίτη καὶ ἐσταύρωσαν αὐτόν. **26** καὶ ἦν ἡ ἐπιγραφὴ τῆς αἰτίας αὐτοῦ ἐπιγεγραμμένη, Ὁ βασιλεὺς τῶν Ἰουδαίων. **27** Καὶ σὺν αὐτῷ σταυροῦσιν δύο λῃστάς, ἕνα ἐκ δεξιῶν καὶ ἕνα ἐξ εὐωνύμων αὐτοῦ. **29** Καὶ οἱ

at him,　shaking　their　heads　　and saying,　"So!　You who are going to destroy　the temple　and build　　it in
← αὐτὸν κινοῦντες αὐτῶν ⌐τὰς κεφαλὰς⌐ καὶ λέγοντες Οὐὰ ὁ　　　　　　　→ καταλύων τὸν ναὸν καὶ οἰκοδομῶν ἐν
r.asm.3 pt.pa.npm r.gpm.3 d.apf n.apf cj pt.pa.npm j d.vsm　　　　　pt.pa.vsm d.asm n.asm cj pt.pa.vsm p.d
899 3075 899 3836 3051 2779 3306 4025 3836　　　　　2907 3836 3724 2779 3868 1877

three days,　 30 come　down from the cross　and save　yourself!" ¶　31 In the same way　the chief priests
τρισὶν ἡμέραις καταβὰς ← ἀπὸ τοῦ σταυροῦ σῶσον σεαυτὸν　　→ → ὁμοίως ← καὶ οἱ → ἀρχιερεῖς
a.dpf n.dpf pt.aa.nsm p.g d.gsm n.gsm v.aam.2s r.asm.2　　adv adv d.npm d.nsm n.npm
5552 2465 2849 608 3836 5089 5392 4932　　3931 2779 3836 797

and the teachers　of the law mocked　him among themselves. "He saved others," they said, "but he can't
μετὰ τῶν γραμματέων ἐμπαίζοντες πρὸς ἀλλήλους ἔσωσεν ἄλλους ἔλεγον →　ⴒού δύναται⌐
p.g d.gpm n.gpm pt.pa.npm p.a r.apm v.aai.3s r.apm v.iai.3p pl v.ppi.3s
3552 3836 1208 1850 4639 253 5392 257 3306 1538 4024 1538

save himself! 32 Let this Christ, this King　of Israel, come　down now from the cross,　that we may see　and
σῶσαι ἑαυτὸν ⌐→ ὁ χριστὸς ὁ βασιλεὺς → Ἰσραὴλ καταβάτω ← νῦν ἀπὸ τοῦ σταυροῦ ἵνα → → ἴδωμεν καὶ
f.aa r.asm.3 d.nsm d.nsm n.nsm n.nsm n.gsm v.aam.3s adv p.g d.gsm n.gsm cj v.aas.1p cj
5392 1571 2849 3836 5986 3836 995 2702 2849 3814 608 3836 5089 2671 1625 2779

believe."　　Those crucified　with him also heaped insults　on him.
πιστεύσωμεν καὶ οἱ συνεσταυρωμένοι σὺν αὐτῷ → ὠνείδιζον αὐτόν
v.aas.1p cj d.npm pt.rp.npm p.d r.dsm.3 v.iai.3p r.asm.3
4409 2779 3836 5365 5250 899 3943 899

The Death of Jesus
15:33　　　　At the sixth hour darkness came　over the whole land until the ninth hour.　34 And at the ninth
Καὶ γενομένης → ἕκτης ὥρας σκότος ἐγένετο ἐφ᾽ τὴν ὅλην γῆν ἕως ἐνάτης ὥρας καὶ → τῇ ἐνάτῃ
cj pt.am.gsf a.gsf n.gsf n.nsn v.ami.3s p.a d.asf a.asf n.asf p.g a.gsf n.gsf cj d.dsf a.dsf
2779 1181 1761 6052 5030 1181 2093 3836 3910 1178 2401 1888 6052 2779 3836 1888

hour Jesus　cried out in a loud　voice, "Eloi, Eloi, lama sabachthani?" –which means,　　　"My
ὥρᾳ ὁ Ἰησοῦς ἐβόησεν ← μεγάλῃ φωνῇ ἐλωι ἐλωι λεμα σαβαχθανι ὅ ἐστιν μεθερμηνευόμενον μου
n.dsf d.nsm n.nsm v.aai.3s a.dsf n.dsf j j j j r.nsn v.pai.3s pt.pp.nsn r.gs.1
6052 3836 2652 1066 3489 5889 1830 1830 3316 4876 4005 1639 3493 1609

God, my God,　why　have you forsaken me?" ¶　35 When some of those standing　near heard
ὁ θεός μου ὁ θεός εἰς τί → ἐγκατέλιπες με καὶ τινες τῶν παρεστηκότων ← ἀκούσαντες
d.vsm n.vsm r.gs.1 d.vsm n.vsm p.a r.asn v.aai.2s r.as.1 cj r.npm d.gpm pt.ra.gpm pt.aa.npm
3836 2536 1609 3836 2536 1650 5515 1593 1609 2779 201 5516 3836 4225 201

this, they said, "Listen, he's calling Elijah." ¶　36 One man ran,　　filled　a sponge with wine
→ ἔλεγον ἴδε → φωνεῖ Ἠλίαν δέ τις δραμὼν [καὶ] γεμίσας σπόγγον → ὄξους
v.iai.3p pl v.pai.3s n.asm cj r.nsm pt.aa.nsm cj pt.aa.nsm n.asm n.gsn
3306 2623 5888 2460 1254 5516 5556 2779 1153 5074 3954

vinegar, put　it on a stick,　and offered it to Jesus to drink. "Now leave him alone. Let's see　if Elijah comes
← περιθεὶς → καλάμῳ ἐπότιζεν → αὐτόν ← ἄφετε ← → ἴδωμεν εἰ Ἠλίας ἔρχεται
pt.aa.nsm n.dsm v.iai.3s r.asm.3 v.aam.2p v.aas.1p cj n.nsm v.pmi.3s
4363 2812 4540 899 4540 4540 918 1625 1623 2460 2262

to take　him down," he said. ¶　37 With a loud　cry, Jesus　breathed his last. ¶　38
→ καθελεῖν αὐτόν ← → λέγων δέ ἀφεὶς μεγάλην φωνὴν ὁ Ἰησοῦς ἐξέπνευσεν ← Καὶ
f.aa r.asm.3 pt.pa.nsm cj pt.aa.nsm a.asf n.asf d.nsm n.nsm v.aai.3s cj
2747 899 2747 3306 1254 918 3489 5889 3836 2652 1743 2779

The curtain　of the temple was torn　in two from top　to bottom. 39 And when the centurion, who stood
τὸ καταπέτασμα → τοῦ ναοῦ → ἐσχίσθη εἰς δύο ἀπ᾽ ἄνωθεν ἕως κάτω δέ → ὁ κεντυρίων ὁ παρεστηκὼς
d.nsn n.nsn d.gsm n.gsm v.api.3s p.a a.apn p.g adv p.g adv cj d.nsm n.nsm d.nsm pt.ra.nsm
3836 2925 3836 3724 5387 1650 1545 608 540 2401 3004 1254 1625 3836 3035 3836 4225

there in front　of Jesus, heard his cry and saw　how he died,　he said, "Surely this man　was the
ἐξ ἐναντίας → αὐτοῦ ἰδὼν ὅτι οὕτως → ἐξέπνευσεν → εἶπεν ἀληθῶς οὗτος ὁ ἄνθρωπος ἦν
p.g a.gsf r.gsm.3 pt.aa.nsm cj adv v.aai.3s v.aai.3s adv r.nsm d.nsm n.nsm v.iai.3s
1666 1885 899 1625 4022 4048 1743 3306 242 4047 3836 476 1639

Son of God!" ¶　40　　Some women were watching from a distance. Among them　were Mary
υἱὸς → θεοῦ δὲ καὶ γυναῖκες Ἦσαν θεωροῦσαι ἀπὸ μακρόθεν ἐν αἷς καὶ Μαρία
n.nsm n.gsm cj adv n.npf v.iai.3p pt.pa.npf p.g adv p.d r.dpf adv n.nsf
5626 2536 1254 2779 1222 1639 2555 608 3427 1877 4005 2779 3451

παραπορευόμενοι ἐβλασφήμουν αὐτὸν κινοῦντες τὰς κεφαλὰς αὐτῶν καὶ λέγοντες, Οὐὰ ὁ καταλύων τὸν ναὸν καὶ οἰκοδομῶν ἐν τρισὶν ἡμέραις, 30 σῶσον σεαυτὸν καταβὰς ἀπὸ τοῦ σταυροῦ. ¶ 31 ὁμοίως καὶ οἱ ἀρχιερεῖς ἐμπαίζοντες πρὸς ἀλλήλους μετὰ τῶν γραμματέων ἔλεγον, Ἄλλους ἔσωσεν, ἑαυτὸν οὐ δύναται σῶσαι· 32 ὁ Χριστὸς ὁ βασιλεὺς Ἰσραὴλ καταβάτω νῦν ἀπὸ τοῦ σταυροῦ, ἵνα ἴδωμεν καὶ πιστεύσωμεν. καὶ οἱ συνεσταυρωμένοι σὺν αὐτῷ ὠνείδιζον αὐτόν.

15:33 Καὶ γενομένης ὥρας ἕκτης σκότος ἐγένετο ἐφ᾽ ὅλην τὴν γῆν ἕως ὥρας ἐνάτης. 34 καὶ τῇ ἐνάτῃ ὥρᾳ ἐβόησεν ὁ Ἰησοῦς φωνῇ μεγάλῃ, Ελωι ελωι λεμα σαβαχθανι; ὅ ἐστιν μεθερμηνευόμενον Ὁ θεός μου ὁ θεός μου, εἰς τί ἐγκατέλιπές με; ¶ 35 καὶ τινες τῶν παρεστηκότων ἀκούσαντες ἔλεγον, Ἴδε Ἠλίαν φωνεῖ. ¶ 36 δραμὼν δέ τις [καὶ] γεμίσας σπόγγον ὄξους περιθεὶς καλάμῳ ἐπότιζεν αὐτὸν λέγων, Ἄφετε ἴδωμεν εἰ ἔρχεται Ἠλίας καθελεῖν αὐτόν. ¶ 37 ὁ δὲ Ἰησοῦς ἀφεὶς φωνὴν μεγάλην ἐξέπνευσεν. ¶ 38 Καὶ τὸ καταπέτασμα τοῦ ναοῦ ἐσχίσθη εἰς δύο ἀπ᾽ ἄνωθεν ἕως κάτω. 39 Ἰδὼν δὲ ὁ κεντυρίων ὁ παρεστηκὼς ἐξ ἐναντίας αὐτοῦ ὅτι οὕτως κράξας ἐξέπνευσεν εἶπεν, Ἀληθῶς οὗτος ὁ ἄνθρωπος υἱὸς θεοῦ ἦν. ¶ 40 Ἦσαν δὲ καὶ γυναῖκες

Magdalene,	Mary	the	mother	of	James	the	younger	and	of	Joses,	and	Salome. [41]		In	Galilee
ἡ Μαγδαληνὴ	καὶ Μαρία	ἡ	μήτηρ	→	Ἰακώβου	τοῦ	μικροῦ	καὶ	→	Ἰωσῆτος	καὶ	Σαλώμη	ὅτε ἦν	ἐν ‿τῇ	Γαλιλαίᾳ‿
d.nsf n.nsf	cj n.nsf	d.nsf	n.nsf		n.gsm	d.gsm	a.gsm	cj		n.gsm	cj	n.nsf	cj v.iai.3s	p.d	d.dsf n.dsf
3836 3402	2779 3451	3836	3613		2610	3836	3625	2779		2736	2779	4897	4021 1639	1877	3836 1133

these	women	had	followed	him	and	cared	for	his	needs.		Many	other	women	who	had	come		up	with
αἱ	←	→	ἠκολούθουν	αὐτῷ	καὶ	→	→	αὐτῷ	διηκόνουν	καὶ	πολλαὶ	ἄλλαι	←		αἱ	→	συναναβᾶσαι	←	→
r.npf			v.iai.3p	r.dsm.3	cj			r.dsm.3	v.iai.3p	cj	a.npf	r.npf			d.npf		pt.aa.npf		
4005			199	899	2779			899	1354	2779	4498	257			3836		5262		

him	to	Jerusalem	were	also	there.
αὐτῷ	εἰς	Ἰεροσόλυμα
r.dsm.3	p.a	n.apn
899	1650	2642

The Burial of Jesus

15:42	It	was	Preparation	Day	(that	is,	the	day	before	the	Sabbath).	So	as	evening	approached,
	Καὶ ἐπεὶ	→ ἦν	παρασκευὴ	←	ὅ	ἐστιν	→	→	→	→	προσάββατον	‿	ἤδη	ὀψίας	γενομένης
	cj cj	v.iai.3s	n.nsf		r.nsn	v.pai.3s					a.nsn		adv	n.gsf	pt.am.gsf
	2779 2075	1639	4187		4005	1639					4640		2075 2453	4068	1181

[43]	Joseph		of	Arimathea,	a	prominent	member	of	the	Council,	who		was	himself	waiting		for	the
	ἐλθὼν Ἰωσὴφ	[ὁ]	ἀπὸ	Ἁριμαθαίας	→		εὐσχήμων	→	→	βουλευτής	ὃς	καὶ	ἦν	αὐτὸς	προσδεχόμενος	←	τὴν
	pt.aa.nsm n.nsm	d.nsm	p.g	n.gsf			a.nsm			n.nsm	r.nsm	adv	v.iai.3s	r.nsm	pt.pm.nsm		d.asf
	2262 2737	3836	608	751			2363			1085	4005	2779	1639	899	4657		3836

kingdom	of	God,	went	boldly	to	Pilate	and	asked	for	Jesus'	body.	[44]	Pilate		was
βασιλείαν	→	‿τοῦ θεοῦ‿	εἰσῆλθεν	τολμήσας	πρὸς	‿τὸν Πιλᾶτον‿	καὶ	ἠτήσατο	←	‿τοῦ Ἰησοῦ‿	‿τὸ σῶμα‿	δὲ	ὁ	Πιλᾶτος‿	→
n.asf		d.gsm n.gsm	v.aai.3s	pt.aa.nsm	p.a	d.asm n.asm	cj	v.ami.3s		d.gsm n.gsm	d.asn n.asn	cj	d.nsm	n.nsm	
993		3836 2536	1656	5528	4639	3836 4397	2779	160		3836 2652	3836 5393	1254	3836	4397	

surprised	to	hear	that	he	was	already	dead.		Summoning	the	centurion,	he	asked		him	if	Jesus	had
ἐθαύμασεν	εἰ	‿→	ἤδη	τέθνηκεν	καὶ	προσκαλεσάμενος	τὸν	κεντυρίωνα	→	ἐπηρώτησεν	αὐτὸν	εἰ	→
v.aai.3s	cj		adv	v.rai.3s	cj	pt.am.nsm	d.asm	n.asm		v.aai.3s	r.asm.3	cj	
2513	1623	2569 2569	2453	2569	2779	4673	3836	3035		2089	899	1623	633

already	died.	[45]	When	he	learned	from	the	centurion	that	it	was	so,	he	gave		the	body	to	Joseph.	[46]	So
πάλαι	ἀπέθανεν	καὶ	→	→	γνοὺς	ἀπὸ	τοῦ	κεντυρίωνος					→	ἐδωρήσατο	τὸ	πτῶμα	→	‿τῷ Ἰωσήφ‿	καὶ
adv	v.aai.3s	cj			pt.aa.nsm	p.g	d.gsm	n.gsm						v.ami.3s	d.asn	n.asn		d.dsm n.nsm	cj
4093	633	2779			1182	608	3836	3035						1563	3836	4773		3836 2737	2779

Joseph	bought	some	linen	cloth,	took		down	the	body,	wrapped	it	in	the	linen,	and	placed	it		in	a	tomb
	ἀγοράσας		σινδόνα		καθελὼν	←			αὐτὸν	ἐνείλησεν	→	τῇ	σινδόνι	καὶ	ἔθηκεν	αὐτὸν	ἐν	μνημείῳ
	pt.aa.nsm		n.asf		pt.aa.nsm				r.asm.3	v.aai.3s		d.dsf	n.dsf	cj	v.aai.3s	r.asm.3	p.d	n.dsn
	60		4984		2747				899	1912		3836	4984	2779	5502	899	1877	3646

	cut		out	of	rock.	Then	he	rolled		a	stone	against	the	entrance	of	the	tomb.	[47]		Mary
ὃ	ἦν	λελατομημένον	ἐκ	→	πέτρας	καὶ	→	προσεκύλισεν	λίθον	ἐπὶ	τὴν	θύραν	→	τοῦ	μνημείου	δὲ	ἡ	Μαρία‿
r.nsn	v.iai.3s	pt.rp.nsn	p.g		n.gsf	cj		v.aai.3s	n.asm	p.a	d.asf	n.asf		d.gsn	n.gsn	cj	d.nsf	n.nsf
4005	1639	3300	1666		4376	2779		4685	3345	2093	3836	2598		3836	3646	1254	3836	3451

Magdalene		and	Mary	the	mother	of	Joses	saw		where	he	was	laid.
‿ἡ Μαγδαληνὴ‿		καὶ	Μαρία	ἡ		→	Ἰωσῆτος	ἐθεώρουν	ποῦ	→	→	τέθειται
d.nsf n.nsf		cj	n.nsf	d.nsf			n.gsm	v.iai.3p	adv			v.rpi.3s
3836 3402		2779	3451	3836			2736	2555	4543			5502

The Resurrection

16:1	When	the	Sabbath	was	over,		Mary	Magdalene,		Mary	the	mother	of	James,		and
	Καὶ	→	τοῦ σαββάτου	→	διαγενομένου	Μαρία	ἡ	Μαγδαληνὴ	καὶ	Μαρία	ἡ		→	‿τοῦ Ἰακώβου‿	καὶ
	cj		d.gsn n.gsn		pt.am.gsn	n.nsf	d.nsf	n.nsf	cj	n.nsf	d.nsf			d.gsn n.gsn	cj
	2779 1335		3836 4879		1335	3451	3836 3402		2779	3451	3836			3836 2610	2779

Salome	bought	spices	so	that	they	might	go		to	anoint	Jesus'	body.	[2]		Very	early	on	the	first	day	of	the
Σαλώμη	ἠγόρασαν	ἀρώματα	ἵνα				→		→	ἐλθοῦσαι	ἀλείψωσιν	αὐτόν		καὶ	λίαν	πρωῒ	→	τῇ	μιᾷ		→	τῶν
n.nsf	v.aai.3p	n.apn	cj							pt.aa.npf	v.aas.3p	r.asm.3		cj	adv	adv		d.dsf	a.dsf			d.gpn
4897	60	808	2671							2262	230	899		2779	3336	4745		3836	1651			3836

week,	just	after	sunrise,		they	were		on	their	way	to	the	tomb	[3]	and	they	asked		each	other,
σαββάτων	→	→	‿ἀνατείλαντος	τοῦ	ἡλίου‿	ἔρχονται	←	←	ἐπὶ	τὸ	μνημεῖον	καὶ	→	ἔλεγον	πρὸς	ἑαυτάς	←
n.gpn			pt.aa.gsm	d.gsm	n.gsm	v.pmi.3p			p.a	d.asn	n.asn	cj		v.iai.3p	p.a	r.apf.3	
4879			422	3836	2463	2262			2093	3836	3646	2779		3306	4639	1571	

ἀπὸ μακρόθεν θεωροῦσαι, ἐν αἷς καὶ Μαρία ἡ Μαγδαληνὴ καὶ Μαρία ἡ Ἰακώβου τοῦ μικροῦ καὶ Ἰωσῆτος μήτηρ καὶ Σαλώμη, [41] αἳ ὅτε ἦν ἐν τῇ Γαλιλαίᾳ ἠκολούθουν αὐτῷ καὶ διηκόνουν αὐτῷ, καὶ ἄλλαι πολλαὶ αἱ συναναβᾶσαι αὐτῷ εἰς Ἰεροσόλυμα.

[15:42] Καὶ ἤδη ὀψίας γενομένης, ἐπεὶ ἦν παρασκευὴ ὅ ἐστιν προσάββατον, [43] ἐλθὼν Ἰωσὴφ [ὁ] ἀπὸ Ἁριμαθαίας εὐσχήμων βουλευτής, ὃς καὶ αὐτὸς ἦν προσδεχόμενος τὴν βασιλείαν τοῦ θεοῦ, τολμήσας εἰσῆλθεν πρὸς τὸν Πιλᾶτον καὶ ἠτήσατο τὸ σῶμα τοῦ Ἰησοῦ. [44] ὁ δὲ Πιλᾶτος ἐθαύμασεν εἰ ἤδη τέθνηκεν καὶ προσκαλεσάμενος τὸν κεντυρίωνα ἐπηρώτησεν αὐτὸν εἰ πάλαι ἀπέθανεν· [45] καὶ γνοὺς ἀπὸ τοῦ κεντυρίωνος ἐδωρήσατο τὸ πτῶμα τῷ Ἰωσήφ. [46] καὶ ἀγοράσας σινδόνα καθελὼν αὐτὸν ἐνείλησεν τῇ σινδόνι καὶ ἔθηκεν αὐτὸν ἐν μνημείῳ ὃ ἦν λελατομημένον ἐκ πέτρας καὶ προσεκύλισεν λίθον ἐπὶ τὴν θύραν τοῦ μνημείου. [47] ἡ δὲ Μαρία ἡ Μαγδαληνὴ καὶ Μαρία ἡ Ἰωσῆτος ἐθεώρουν ποῦ τέθειται.

[16:1] Καὶ διαγενομένου τοῦ σαββάτου Μαρία ἡ Μαγδαληνὴ καὶ Μαρία ἡ [τοῦ] Ἰακώβου καὶ Σαλώμη ἠγόρασαν ἀρώματα ἵνα ἐλθοῦσαι ἀλείψωσιν αὐτόν. [2] καὶ λίαν πρωῒ τῇ μιᾷ τῶν σαββάτων ἔρχονται ἐπὶ τὸ μνημεῖον ἀνατείλαντος τοῦ ἡλίου. [3] καὶ

"Who will roll   the stone away   from the entrance of the tomb?"   ¶   **4** But when they looked   up,
τίς   →   ἀποκυλίσει τὸν λίθον ←   ἡμῖν ἐκ   τῆς θύρας   →   τοῦ μνημείου   καὶ   →   →   ἀναβλέψασαι ←
r.nsm   v.fai.3s   d.asm n.asm   r.dp.1 p.g   d.gsf n.gsf   d.gsn n.gsn   cj   pt.aa.npf
5515   653   3836 3345   653   7005 1666   3836 2598   3836 3646   2779   329

they saw   that the stone,   which was very   large, had been rolled   away.   **5**   As they entered   the
→   θεωροῦσιν ὅτι   ὁ   λίθος γὰρ   ἦν   σφόδρα μέγας   →   →   ἀποκεκύλισται ←   Καὶ   →   εἰσελθοῦσαι εἰς   τὸ
→   v.pai.3p   cj   d.nsm n.nsm   cj   v.iai.3s adv   a.nsm   →   →   v.rpi.3s   cj   pt.aa.npf   p.a d.asn
2555   4022   3836 3345   1142   1639 5379   3489   653   2779   1656   1650 3836

tomb,   they saw   a young man   dressed   in a white robe   sitting   on the right   side, and they were
μνημεῖον   →   εἶδον   →   νεανίσκον περιβεβλημένον ←   λευκήν στολὴν καθήμενον ἐν   τοῖς δεξιοῖς ←   καὶ   →   →
n.asn   v.aai.3p   n.asm   pt.rm.asm   a.asf n.asf   pt.pm.asm   p.d   d.dpn a.dpn   cj
3646   1625   3734   4314   3328 5124   2764   1877   3836 1288   2779

alarmed.   ¶   **6**   "Don't be alarmed," he said.   "You are looking for Jesus the Nazarene, who was
ἐξεθαμβήθησαν   δὲ   μὴ   →   ἐκθαμβεῖσθε ὁ   λέγει αὐταῖς   →   →   ζητεῖτε ←   Ἰησοῦν τὸν Ναζαρηνὸν τὸν   →
v.api.3p   cj   pl   v.ppm.2p   d.nsm v.pai.3s r.dpf.3   v.pai.2p   n.asm   d.asm a.asm   d.asm
1701   1254 3590   1701   3836 3306 899   2426   2652   3836 3716   3836

crucified.   He has risen! He is   not here. See the place where they laid   him.   **7** But go,   tell   his
ἐσταυρωμένον   →   ἠγέρθη   ἔστιν οὐκ ὧδε ἴδε ὁ   τόπος ὅπου   →   ἔθηκαν αὐτόν   ἀλλὰ ὑπάγετε εἴπατε αὐτοῦ
pt.rp.asm   →   v.api.3s   v.pai.3s pl adv   pl   d.nsm n.nsm   cj   v.aai.3p r.asm.3   cj   v.pam.2p   v.aam.2p r.gsm.3
5090   1586   1639 4024 6045 2623 3836 5536 3963   5502 899   247   5632   3306 899

disciples   and Peter,   'He is going   ahead of you into Galilee.   There you will see   him, just   as
⸢τοῖς μαθηταῖς⸣ καὶ   ⸢τῷ Πέτρῳ⸣ ὅτι   →   προάγει   ←   ὑμᾶς εἰς   ⸢τὴν Γαλιλαίαν⸣ ἐκεῖ   →   →   ὄψεσθε αὐτὸν καθὼς ←
d.dpm n.dpm   cj   d.dsm n.dsm   cj   v.pai.3s   r.ap.2 p.a   d.asf n.asf   adv   v.fmi.2p r.asm.3 cj
3836 3412   2779   3836 4377   4022   4575   7007 1650   3836 1133   1695   3972 899 2777

he told you.'"   ¶   **8**   Trembling and bewildered, the women went   out and fled   from the
→   εἶπεν ὑμῖν   καὶ γὰρ εἶχεν αὐτὰς τρόμος   καὶ   ἔκστασις   ἐξελθοῦσαι ←   ἔφυγον ἀπὸ   τοῦ
v.aai.3s r.dp.2   cj   cj   v.iai.3s r.apf.3 n.nsm   cj   n.nsf   pt.aa.npf   v.aai.3p p.g   d.gsn
3306 7007   2779 1142 2400 899   5571   2779   1749   2002   5771   608   3836

tomb.   They said nothing to anyone, because they were afraid.
μνημείου καὶ   εἶπαν οὐδὲν   →   οὐδενὶ γὰρ   →   →   ἐφοβοῦντο
n.gsn   cj   v.aai.3p a.asn   a.dsm   cj   v.imi.3p
3646   2779   3306 4029   4029   1142   5828

The Longer Ending of Mark

16:9   When Jesus rose   early on the first   day of the week,   he appeared first   to Mary Magdalene,
⟦δὲ   →   Ἀναστὰς πρωῒ   →   →   πρώτῃ   →   σαββάτου   →   ἐφάνη   πρῶτον   →   Μαρίᾳ ⸢τῇ Μαγδαληνῇ⸣
cj   pt.aa.nsm   adv   a.dsf   n.gsn   v.api.3s   adv   n.dsf   d.dsf n.dsf
1254   482   4745   4755   4879   5743   4754   3451   3836 3402

out of whom he had driven   seven demons. **10** She went   and told   those who had been   with him and
παρ' ἧς   →   ἐκβεβλήκει ἑπτὰ   δαιμόνια   ἐκείνη πορευθεῖσα   ἀπήγγειλεν τοῖς ←   γενομένοις μετ' αὐτοῦ
p.g   r.gsf   v.lai.3s   a.apn   n.apn   r.nsf   pt.ap.nsf   v.aai.3s   d.dpm   pt.am.dpm   p.g   r.gsm.3
4123   4005   1675   2231   1228   1697   4513   550   3836   1181   3552 899

who were mourning and weeping. **11** When they heard   that Jesus was alive and that   she had seen him,
→   πενθοῦσι   καὶ   κλαίουσιν   ἀκούσαντες ὅτι   →   ζῇ   καὶ   ὑπ' αὐτῆς   →   ἐθεάθη ←
pt.pa.dpm   cj   pt.pa.dpm   pt.aa.npm   cj   v.pai.3s cj   p.g   r.gsf.3   v.api.3s
4291   2779   3081   201   4022   2409   2779   5679 899   2517

they   did not believe it.   ¶   **12**   Afterward   Jesus appeared in a different form to two   of them while they
κἀκεῖνοι →   →   ἠπίστησαν   δὲ   ⸢Μετὰ ταῦτα⸣   ἐφανερώθη ἐν   ἑτέρᾳ   μορφῇ   δυσὶν ἐξ   αὐτῶν   →
cj   v.aai.3p   cj   r.apn   v.api.3s   p.d   r.dsf   n.dsf   a.dpm   p.g   r.gpm.3
2797   601   1254 3552   4047   5746   1877   2283   3671   1545   1666   899

were walking   in the country. **13** These   returned   and reported   it to the rest;   but they   did not
→   περιπατοῦσιν πορευομένοις εἰς   ἀγρόν   κἀκεῖνοι ἀπελθόντες   ἀπήγγειλαν   →   τοῖς λοιποῖς οὐδὲ ἐκείνοις ⌐ →
pt.pa.dpm   pt.pm.dpm   p.a   n.asm   cj   pt.aa.npm   v.aai.3p   d.dpm a.dpm   cj   r.dpm
4344   4513   1650   69   2797   599   550   3836 3370   4028   1697   4409   4028

ἔλεγον πρὸς ἑαυτάς, Τίς ἀποκυλίσει ἡμῖν τὸν λίθον ἐκ τῆς θύρας τοῦ μνημείου; ¶ **4** καὶ ἀναβλέψασαι θεωροῦσιν ὅτι ἀποκεκύλισται ὁ λίθος· ἦν γὰρ μέγας σφόδρα. **5** καὶ εἰσελθοῦσαι εἰς τὸ μνημεῖον εἶδον νεανίσκον καθήμενον ἐν τοῖς δεξιοῖς περιβεβλημένον στολὴν λευκήν, καὶ ἐξεθαμβήθησαν. ¶ **6** ὁ δὲ λέγει αὐταῖς, Μὴ ἐκθαμβεῖσθε· Ἰησοῦν ζητεῖτε τὸν Ναζαρηνὸν τὸν ἐσταυρωμένον· ἠγέρθη, οὐκ ἔστιν ὧδε· ἴδε ὁ τόπος ὅπου ἔθηκαν αὐτόν. **7** ἀλλὰ ὑπάγετε εἴπατε τοῖς μαθηταῖς αὐτοῦ καὶ τῷ Πέτρῳ ὅτι Προάγει ὑμᾶς εἰς τὴν Γαλιλαίαν· ἐκεῖ αὐτὸν ὄψεσθε, καθὼς εἶπεν ὑμῖν. ¶ **8** καὶ ἐξελθοῦσαι ἔφυγον ἀπὸ τοῦ μνημείου, εἶχεν γὰρ αὐτὰς τρόμος καὶ ἔκστασις· καὶ οὐδενὶ οὐδὲν εἶπαν· ἐφοβοῦντο γάρ.

16:9 ⟦Ἀναστὰς δὲ πρωῒ πρώτῃ σαββάτου ἐφάνη πρῶτον Μαρίᾳ τῇ Μαγδαληνῇ, παρ' ἧς ἐκβεβλήκει ἑπτὰ δαιμόνια. **10** ἐκείνη πορευθεῖσα ἀπήγγειλεν τοῖς μετ' αὐτοῦ γενομένοις πενθοῦσι καὶ κλαίουσιν· **11** κἀκεῖνοι ἀκούσαντες ὅτι ζῇ καὶ ἐθεάθη ὑπ' αὐτῆς ἠπίστησαν. ¶ **12** Μετὰ δὲ ταῦτα δυσὶν ἐξ αὐτῶν περιπατοῦσιν ἐφανερώθη ἐν ἑτέρᾳ μορφῇ πορευομένοις εἰς ἀγρόν· **13** κἀκεῖνοι ἀπελθόντες ἀπήγγειλαν τοῖς λοιποῖς· οὐδὲ ἐκείνοις ἐπίστευσαν. ¶ **14** Ὕστερον [δὲ] ἀνακειμένοις αὐτοῖς τοῖς ἕνδεκα

believe them either. ¶ **14**   Later Jesus appeared to the Eleven as they were eating;   he rebuked
ἐπίστευσαν   [δὲ] Ὕστερον ἐφανερώθη → τοῖς ἕνδεκα → αὐτοῖς → ἀνακειμένοις καὶ → ὠνείδισεν
v.aai.3p   cj   adv.c   v.api.3s   d.dpm a.dpm   r.dpm   pt.pm.dpm   cj   v.aai.3s
4409   1254   5731   5746   3836 1894   367 899   367   2779   3943

them for their lack of faith   and their stubborn   refusal to believe those who had seen   him after he
αὐτῶν τὴν → → ἀπιστίαν καὶ → σκληροκαρδίαν ὅτι οὐκ → ἐπίστευσαν τοῖς ← → θεασαμένοις αὐτὸν → →
r.gpm.3 d.asf   n.asf cj   n.asf   cj pl   v.aai.3p d.dpm   pt.am.dpm r.asm.3
899 3836   602 2779   5016   4022 4024   4409 3836   2517 899

had risen. ¶ **15**   He said to them, "Go   into all the world and preach the good news to
→ ἐγηγερμένον καὶ → εἶπεν αὐτοῖς πορευθέντες εἰς ἅπαντα τὸν κόσμον κηρύξατε τὸ εὐαγγέλιον ←
pt.rp.asm   cj   v.aai.3s r.dpm.3 pt.ap.npm p.a a.asm d.asm n.asm   v.aam.2p d.asn n.asn
1586   2779   3306 899   4513 1650 570 3836 3180   3062 3836 2295   3232

all creation. **16** Whoever believes and is baptized will be saved, but whoever does not believe will be
πάσῃ ⌐τῇ κτίσει⌐ ὁ → πιστεύσας καὶ → βαπτισθεὶς → → σωθήσεται δὲ ὁ → → → ἀπιστήσας
a.dsf d.dsf n.dsf   d.nsm   pt.aa.nsm cj   pt.ap.nsm   v.fpi.3s cj d.nsm   pt.aa.nsm
4246 3836 3232   3836   4409 2779   966   5392 1254 3836   601

condemned. **17** And these signs will accompany those who believe: In my name   they will drive out
κατακριθήσεται δὲ ταῦτα σημεῖα → παρακολουθήσει τοῖς ← πιστεύσασιν ἐν μου ⌐τῷ ὀνόματι⌐ → → ἐκβαλοῦσιν
v.fpi.3s   cj r.npn n.npn   v.fai.3s   d.dpm   pt.aa.dpm p.d r.gs.1 d.dsn n.dsn   v.fai.3p
2891   1254 4047 4956   4158   3836   4409 1877 1609 3836 3950   1675

demons; they will speak in new tongues; **18**   they will pick up snakes with their hands; and when they
δαιμόνια → → λαλήσουσιν → καιναῖς γλώσσαις καὶ → → ἀροῦσιν ← ὄφεις ἐν ταῖς χερσὶν κἂν
n.apn → v.fai.3p → a.dpf n.dpf   cj → v.fai.3p   n.apm p.d d.dpf n.dpf   crasis
1228 3281   2785 1185   2779   149   4058 1877 3836 5931   2829

drink deadly poison, it will not hurt them at all; they will place their hands on sick people,
πίωσιν τι θανάσιμον ← → ⌐οὐ μὴ⌐ βλάψῃ αὐτοὺς ← → ἐπιθήσουσιν χεῖρας ἐπὶ ἀρρώστους ←
v.aas.3p r.asn r.asn   pl pl v.aas.3s r.apm.3   v.fai.3p   n.apf p.a a.apm
4403 5516 2503   1055 1055 4024 3590 1055 3590 899 4024 4024   2202   5931 2093 779

and they will get well." ¶ **19**   After the Lord Jesus had spoken to them, he was taken up into
καὶ → → ἕξουσιν καλῶς οὖν μὲν μετὰ Ὁ κύριος Ἰησοῦς → ⌐τὸ λαλῆσαι⌐ → αὐτοῖς → ἀνελήμφθη εἰς
cj → v.fai.3p adv cj pl p.a d.nsm n.nsm n.nsm   d.asn f.aa   r.dpm.3   v.api.3s p.a
2779 2400 2822 4036 3525 3552 3836 3261 2652   3836 3281   899   377 1650

heaven and he sat at the right hand of God. **20** Then the disciples went out and preached
⌐τὸν οὐρανὸν⌐ καὶ → ἐκάθισεν ἐκ δεξιῶν → ⌐τοῦ θεοῦ⌐ δὲ ἐκεῖνοι ἐξελθόντες ← ἐκήρυξαν
d.asm n.asm cj → v.aai.3s p.g a.gpf   d.gsm n.gsm cj r.npm   pt.aa.npm   v.aai.3p
3836 4041 2779 2767 1666 1288   3836 2536 1254 1697   2002   3062

everywhere, and the Lord worked with them and confirmed his word by the signs that accompanied it.
πανταχοῦ τοῦ κυρίου συνεργοῦντος ← ← καὶ βεβαιοῦντος τὸν λόγον διὰ τῶν σημείων → ἐπακολουθούντων ⟧
adv d.gsm n.gsm pt.pa.gsm   cj pt.pa.gsn d.asm n.asm p.g d.gpn n.gpn   pt.pa.gpn
4116 3836 3261 5300   2779 1011 3836 3364 1328 3836 4956   2051

ἐφανερώθη καὶ ὠνείδισεν τὴν ἀπιστίαν αὐτῶν καὶ σκληροκαρδίαν ὅτι τοῖς θεασαμένοις αὐτὸν ἐγηγερμένον οὐκ ἐπίστευσαν. ¶
15 καὶ εἶπεν αὐτοῖς, Πορευθέντες εἰς τὸν κόσμον ἅπαντα κηρύξατε τὸ εὐαγγέλιον πάσῃ τῇ κτίσει. 16 ὁ πιστεύσας καὶ βαπτισθεὶς
σωθήσεται, ὁ δὲ ἀπιστήσας κατακριθήσεται. 17 σημεῖα δὲ τοῖς πιστεύσασιν ταῦτα παρακολουθήσει· ἐν τῷ ὀνόματί μου δαιμόνια
ἐκβαλοῦσιν, γλώσσαις λαλήσουσιν καιναῖς, 18 [καὶ ἐν ταῖς χερσὶν] ὄφεις ἀροῦσιν κἂν θανάσιμόν τι πίωσιν οὐ μὴ αὐτοὺς βλάψῃ
, ἐπὶ ἀρρώστους χεῖρας ἐπιθήσουσιν καὶ καλῶς ἕξουσιν. ¶ 19 Ὁ μὲν οὖν κύριος Ἰησοῦς μετὰ τὸ λαλῆσαι αὐτοῖς ἀνελήμφθη εἰς
τὸν οὐρανὸν καὶ ἐκάθισεν ἐκ δεξιῶν τοῦ θεοῦ. 20 ἐκεῖνοι δὲ ἐξελθόντες ἐκήρυξαν πανταχοῦ, τοῦ κυρίου συνεργοῦντος καὶ τὸν
λόγον βεβαιοῦντος διὰ τῶν ἐπακολουθούντων σημείων.⟧

Luke

Introduction

1:1 Many have undertaken to draw up an account of the things that have been
ἐπειδήπερ πολλοὶ ἐπεχείρησαν ἀνατάξασθαι διήγησιν περὶ τῶν πραγμάτων
cj a.npm v.aai.3p f.am n.asf p.g d.gpn n.gpn
2077 4498 2217 421 1456 4309 3836 4547

fulfilled among us, **2** just as they were handed down to us by those who from the first were
πεπληροφορημένων ἐν ἡμῖν καθὼς παρέδοσαν ἡμῖν οἱ ἀπ' ἀρχῆς γενόμενοι
pt.rp.gpn p.d r.dp.1 cj v.aai.3p r.dp.1 d.npm p.g n.gsf pt.am.npm
4442 1877 7005 2777 4140 7005 3836 608 794 1181

eyewitnesses and servants of the word. **3** Therefore, since I myself have carefully investigated everything from the
αὐτόπται καὶ ὑπηρέται τοῦ λόγου ἀκριβῶς παρηκολουθηκότι πᾶσιν
n.npm cj n.npm d.gsm n.gsm adv pt.ra.dsm a.dpn
898 2779 5677 3836 3364 2077 4158 4158 4158 209 4158 4246

beginning, it seemed good also to me to write an orderly account for you, most excellent Theophilus, **4** so that you
ἄνωθεν ἔδοξε καμοὶ γράψαι καθεξῆς σοι κράτιστε Θεόφιλε ἵνα
adv v.aai.3s crasis f.aa adv r.ds.2 a.vsm.s n.vsm cj
540 1506 2743 1211 2759 5148 3196 2541 2671

may know the certainty of the things you have been taught.
ἐπιγνῷς τὴν ἀσφάλειαν περὶ λόγων ὧν κατηχήθης
v.aas.2s d.asf n.asf p.g n.gpm r.gpm v.api.2s
2105 3836 854 4309 3364 4005 2994

The Birth of John the Baptist Foretold

1:5 In the time of Herod king of Judea there was a priest named Zechariah, who belonged to
ἐν ταῖς ἡμέραις Ἡρῴδου βασιλέως τῆς Ἰουδαίας Ἐγένετο τις ἱερεύς ὀνόματι Ζαχαρίας ἐξ
p.d d.dpf n.dpf n.gsm n.gsm d.gsf n.gsf v.ami.3s r.nsm n.nsm n.dsn n.nsm
1877 3836 2465 2476 995 3836 2677 1181 5516 2636 3950 2408 1666

the priestly division of Abijah; his wife Elizabeth was also a descendant of Aaron. **6**
ἐφημερίας Ἀβιὰ καὶ αὐτῷ γυνὴ τὸ ὄνομα αὐτῆς Ἐλισάβετ καὶ ἐκ τῶν θυγατέρων Ἀαρὼν δὲ
n.gsf n.gsm cj r.dsm.3 n.nsf d.nsn n.nsn r.gsf.3 n.nsf cj p.g d.gpf n.gpf n.gsm cj
2389 7 2779 899 1222 3836 3950 899 1810 2779 1666 3836 2588 2 1254

Both of them were upright in the sight of God, observing all the Lord's commandments and
ἀμφότεροι ἦσαν δίκαιοι ἐναντίον τοῦ θεοῦ πορευόμενοι ἐν πάσαις ταῖς τοῦ κυρίου ἐντολαῖς καὶ
a.npm v.iai.3p a.npm p.g d.gsm n.gsm pt.pm.npm p.d a.dpf d.dpf d.gsm n.gsm n.dpf cj
317 1639 1465 1883 3836 2536 4513 1877 4246 3836 3836 3261 1953 2779

regulations blamelessly. **7** But they had no children, because Elizabeth was barren; and they were both well
δικαιώμασιν ἄμεμπτοι καὶ αὐτοῖς ἦν οὐκ τέκνον καθότι ἡ Ἐλισάβετ ἦν στεῖρα καὶ ἦσαν ἀμφότεροι
n.dpn a.npm cj r.dpm.3 v.iai.3s pl n.nsn cj d.nsf n.nsf v.iai.3s a.nsf cj v.iai.3p a.npm
1468 289 2779 899 1639 4024 5451 2776 3836 1810 1639 5096 2779 1639 317

along in years. ¶ **8** Once when Zechariah's division was on duty and
προβεβηκότες ἐν ταῖς ἡμέραις αὐτῶν δὲ Ἐγένετο ἐν αὐτὸν ἐν τῇ τάξει τῷ ἱερατεύειν
pt.ra.npm p.d d.dpf n.dpf r.gpm.3 cj v.ami.3s p.d r.asm.3 p.d d.dsf n.dsf d.dsn f.pa
4581 1877 3836 1254 1181 1877 3836 5423 3836 2634

he was serving as priest before God, **9** he was chosen by lot, according to the custom of the priesthood, to
αὐτοῦ τῆς ἐφημερίας ἔναντι τοῦ θεοῦ ἔλαχε κατὰ τὸ ἔθος τῆς ἱερατείας
r.gsm.3 d.gsf n.gsf p.g d.gsm n.gsm v.aai.3s p.a d.asn n.asn d.gsf n.gsf
899 3836 2389 1882 3836 2536 3275 2848 3836 1621 3836 2632

go into the temple of the Lord and burn incense. **10** And when the time for the burning of incense
εἰσελθὼν εἰς τὸν ναὸν τοῦ κυρίου τοῦ θυμιᾶσαι καὶ τῇ ὥρᾳ τοῦ θυμιάματος
pt.aa.nsm p.a d.asm n.asm d.gsm n.gsm d.gsn f.aa cj d.dsf n.dsf d.gsn n.gsn
1656 1650 3836 3724 3836 3261 3836 2594 2779 3836 6052 3836 2592

came, all the *assembled* *worshipers* were praying outside. ¶ **11** Then an angel of the Lord appeared to
πᾶν τὸ πλῆθος τοῦ λαοῦ ἦν προσευχόμενον ἔξω δὲ ἄγγελος κυρίου ὤφθη
a.nsn d.nsn n.nsn d.gsm n.gsm v.iai.3s pt.pm.nsn adv cj n.nsm n.gsm v.api.3s
4246 3836 4436 3836 3295 1639 4667 2032 1254 34 3261 3972

1:1 Ἐπειδήπερ πολλοὶ ἐπεχείρησαν ἀνατάξασθαι διήγησιν περὶ τῶν πεπληροφορημένων ἐν ἡμῖν πραγμάτων, **2** καθὼς παρέδοσαν ἡμῖν οἱ ἀπ' ἀρχῆς αὐτόπται καὶ ὑπηρέται γενόμενοι τοῦ λόγου, **3** ἔδοξε καμοὶ παρηκολουθηκότι ἄνωθεν πᾶσιν ἀκριβῶς καθεξῆς σοι γράψαι, κράτιστε Θεόφιλε, **4** ἵνα ἐπιγνῷς περὶ ὧν κατηχήθης λόγων τὴν ἀσφάλειαν.

1:5 Ἐγένετο ἐν ταῖς ἡμέραις Ἡρῴδου βασιλέως τῆς Ἰουδαίας ἱερεύς τις ὀνόματι Ζαχαρίας ἐξ ἐφημερίας Ἀβιά, καὶ γυνὴ αὐτῷ ἐκ τῶν θυγατέρων Ἀαρὼν καὶ τὸ ὄνομα αὐτῆς Ἐλισάβετ. **6** ἦσαν δὲ δίκαιοι ἀμφότεροι ἐναντίον τοῦ θεοῦ, πορευόμενοι ἐν πάσαις ταῖς ἐντολαῖς καὶ δικαιώμασιν τοῦ κυρίου ἄμεμπτοι. **7** καὶ οὐκ ἦν αὐτοῖς τέκνον, καθότι ἦν ἡ Ἐλισάβετ στεῖρα, καὶ ἀμφότεροι προβεβηκότες ἐν ταῖς ἡμέραις αὐτῶν ἦσαν. ¶ **8** Ἐγένετο δὲ ἐν τῷ ἱερατεύειν αὐτὸν ἐν τῇ τάξει τῆς ἐφημερίας αὐτοῦ ἔναντι τοῦ θεοῦ, **9** κατὰ τὸ ἔθος τῆς ἱερατείας ἔλαχε τοῦ θυμιᾶσαι εἰσελθὼν εἰς τὸν ναὸν τοῦ κυρίου, **10** καὶ πᾶν τὸ πλῆθος ἦν τοῦ λαοῦ προσευχόμενον ἔξω τῇ ὥρᾳ τοῦ θυμιάματος. ¶ **11** ὤφθη δὲ αὐτῷ ἄγγελος κυρίου ἑστὼς ἐκ δεξιῶν τοῦ

him, standing at the right side of the altar of incense. **12** When Zechariah saw him, he was startled
αὐτῷ ἑστὼς ἐκ δεξιῶν ← → τοῦ θυσιαστηρίου → ⌊τοῦ θυμιάματος⌋ καὶ → Ζαχαρίας ἰδὼν → → ἐταράχθη
r.dsm.3 pt.ra.nsm p.g a.gpf d.gsn n.gsn d.gsn n.gsn cj n.nsm pt.aa.nsm v.api.3s
899 2705 1666 1288 3836 2603 3836 2592 2779 1625 2408 1625 5429

and was gripped with fear. **13** But the angel said to him: "Do not be afraid, Zechariah; your
καὶ → ἐπέπεσεν ← φόβος ἐπ᾽ αὐτόν δὲ ὁ ἄγγελος εἶπεν πρὸς αὐτόν → μὴ φοβοῦ Ζαχαρία διότι σου
cj v.aai.3s n.nsm p.a r.asm.3 cj d.nsm n.nsm v.aai.3s p.a r.asm.3 pl v.ppm.2s n.vsm cj r.gs.2
2779 2158 5832 2093 899 1254 3836 34 3306 4639 899 3590 5828 2408 1484 5148

prayer has been heard. Your wife Elizabeth will bear you a son, and you are to give him the
⌊ἡ δέησις⌋ → → εἰσηκούσθη καὶ σου ⌊ἡ γυνὴ⌋ Ἐλισάβετ → γεννήσει σοι υἱόν καὶ → → καλέσεις αὐτοῦ τὸ
d.nsf n.nsf v.api.3s cj r.gs.2 d.nsf n.nsf n.nsf v.fai.3s r.ds.2 n.asm cj v.fai.2s r.gsm.3 d.asn
3836 1255 1653 2779 5148 3836 1222 1810 1164 5148 5626 2779 2813 899 3836

name John. **14** He will be a joy and delight to you, and many will rejoice because of his birth,
ὄνομα Ἰωάννην καὶ → → ἔσται χαρά καὶ ἀγαλλίασις → σοι καὶ πολλοὶ → χαρήσονται ἐπὶ ← αὐτοῦ ⌊τῇ γενέσει⌋
n.asn n.asm cj v.fmi.3s n.nsf cj n.nsf r.ds.2 cj a.npm v.fpi.3p p.d r.gsm.3 d.dsf n.dsf
3950 2722 2779 1639 5915 2779 21 5148 2779 4498 5897 2093 899 3836 1161

15 for he will be great in the sight of the Lord. He is never to take wine or other fermented drink, and he
γὰρ → ἔσται μέγας → ἐνώπιον ← τοῦ κυρίου καὶ → ⌊οὐ μὴ⌋ → πίῃ οἶνον καὶ σίκερα καὶ →
cj v.fmi.3s a.nsm p.g d.gsm n.gsm cj pl pl v.aas.3s n.asm cj n.asn cj
1142 1639 3489 1967 3836 3261 2779 4403 4403 4024 3590 4403 3885 2779 4975 2779

will be filled with the Holy Spirit even from birth. **16** Many of the people of Israel will he
→ → πλησθήσεται → ἁγίου πνεύματος ἔτι ἐκ ⌊κοιλίας μητρὸς⌋ αὐτοῦ καὶ πολλοὺς → τῶν υἱῶν → Ἰσραὴλ →
v.fpi.3s a.gsn n.gsn adv p.g n.gsf n.gsf r.gsm.3 cj a.apm d.gpm n.gpm n.gsm
4398 41 4460 2285 1666 3120 3613 899 2779 4498 3836 5626 2702

bring back to the Lord their God. **17** And he will go on before the Lord, in the spirit and power
ἐπιστρέψει ← ἐπὶ κύριον αὐτῶν ⌊τὸν θεὸν⌋ καὶ αὐτὸς → προελεύσεται ← ἐνώπιον αὐτοῦ ἐν πνεύματι καὶ δυνάμει
v.fai.3s p.a n.asm r.gpm.3 d.asm n.asm cj r.nsm v.fmi.3s p.g r.gsm.3 p.d n.dsn cj n.dsf
2188 2093 3261 899 3836 2536 2779 899 4601 1967 899 1877 4460 2779 1539

of Elijah, to turn the hearts of the fathers to their children and the disobedient to the wisdom of the
→ Ἠλίου → ἐπιστρέψαι καρδίας → πατέρων ἐπὶ τέκνα καὶ ἀπειθεῖς ἐν φρονήσει →
n.gsm f.aa n.apf n.gpm p.a n.apn cj a.apm p.d n.dsf
2460 2188 2840 4252 2093 5451 2779 579 1877 5860

righteous – to make ready a people prepared for the Lord." ¶ **18** Zechariah asked the angel,
δικαίων → → ἑτοιμάσαι λαὸν κατεσκευασμένον → κυρίῳ καὶ Ζαχαρίας εἶπεν πρὸς τὸν ἄγγελον
a.gpm f.aa n.asm pt.rp.asm n.dsm cj n.nsm v.aai.3s p.a d.asm n.asm
1465 2286 3295 2941 3261 2779 2408 3306 4639 3836 34

"How can I be sure of this? I am an old man and my wife is well along in
⌊κατὰ τί⌋ γνώσομαι ← τοῦτο γὰρ ἐγὼ εἰμι πρεσβύτης ← καὶ μου ⌊ἡ γυνή⌋ προβεβηκυῖα ἐν
p.a r.asn v.fmi.1s r.asn cj r.ns.1 v.pai.1s n.nsm cj r.gs.1 d.nsf n.nsf pt.ra.nsf p.d
2848 5515 1182 4047 1142 1609 1639 4566 2779 1609 3836 1222 4581 1877

years." **19** The angel answered, "I am Gabriel. I stand in the presence of
⌊ταῖς ἡμέραις αὐτῆς⌋ καὶ ὁ ἄγγελος ἀποκριθεὶς εἶπεν αὐτῷ ἐγὼ εἰμι Γαβριὴλ → ⌊ὁ παρεστηκὼς⌋ → ἐνώπιον ←
d.dpf n.dpf r.gsf.3 cj d.nsm n.nsm pt.ap.nsm v.aai.3s r.dsm.3 r.ns.1 v.pai.1s n.nsm d.nsm pt.ra.nsm p.g
3836 2465 899 2779 3836 34 646 3306 899 1609 1639 1120 3836 4225 1967

God, and I have been sent to speak to you and to tell you this good news. **20** And now you
⌊τοῦ θεοῦ⌋ καὶ → ἀπεστάλην λαλῆσαι πρὸς σὲ καὶ εὐαγγελίσασθαι σοι ταῦτα ← καὶ ἰδοὺ →
d.gsm n.gsm cj v.api.1s f.aa p.a r.as.2 cj f.am r.ds.2 r.apn cj j
3836 2536 2779 690 3281 4639 5148 2779 2294 5148 4047 2294 2294 2779 2627

will be silent and not able to speak until the day this happens, because you did not believe my
→ ἔσῃ σιωπῶν καὶ μὴ δυνάμενος → λαλῆσαι ἄχρι ⌊ἧς⌋ ἡμέρας ταῦτα γένηται ἀνθ᾽ ὧν → οὐκ ἐπίστευσας μου
v.fmi.2s pt.pa.nsm cj pl pt.pp.nsm f.aa p.g r.gsf n.gsf r.npn v.ams.3s p.g r.gpn pl v.aai.2s r.gs.1
1639 4995 2779 3590 1538 3281 948 4005 2465 4047 1181 505 4005 4024 4409 1609

words, which will come true at their proper time." ¶ **21** Meanwhile, the people were waiting
⌊τοῖς λόγοις⌋ οἵτινες → → πληρωθήσονται εἰς αὐτῶν → ⌊τὸν καιρόν⌋ Καὶ ὁ λαὸς ἦν προσδοκῶν
d.dpm n.dpm r.npm v.fpi.3p p.a r.gpm.3 d.asm n.asm cj d.nsm n.nsm v.iai.3s pt.pa.nsm
3836 3364 4015 1650 899 3836 2789 2779 3836 3295 1639 4659

θυσιαστηρίου τοῦ θυμιάματος. **12** καὶ ἐταράχθη Ζαχαρίας ἰδὼν καὶ φόβος ἐπέπεσεν ἐπ᾽ αὐτόν. **13** εἶπεν δὲ πρὸς αὐτὸν ὁ ἄγγελος, Μὴ φοβοῦ, Ζαχαρία, διότι εἰσηκούσθη ἡ δέησίς σου, καὶ ἡ γυνή σου Ἐλισάβετ γεννήσει υἱόν σοι καὶ καλέσεις τὸ ὄνομα αὐτοῦ Ἰωάννην. **14** καὶ ἔσται χαρά σοι καὶ ἀγαλλίασις καὶ πολλοὶ ἐπὶ τῇ γενέσει αὐτοῦ χαρήσονται. **15** ἔσται γὰρ μέγας ἐνώπιον [τοῦ] κυρίου, καὶ οἶνον καὶ σίκερα οὐ μὴ πίῃ, καὶ πνεύματος ἁγίου πλησθήσεται ἔτι ἐκ κοιλίας μητρὸς αὐτοῦ, **16** καὶ πολλοὺς τῶν υἱῶν Ἰσραὴλ ἐπιστρέψει ἐπὶ κύριον τὸν θεὸν αὐτῶν· **17** καὶ αὐτὸς προελεύσεται ἐνώπιον αὐτοῦ ἐν πνεύματι καὶ δυνάμει Ἠλίου, ἐπιστρέψαι καρδίας πατέρων ἐπὶ τέκνα καὶ ἀπειθεῖς ἐν φρονήσει δικαίων, ἑτοιμάσαι κυρίῳ λαὸν κατεσκευασμένον. ¶ **18** Καὶ εἶπεν Ζαχαρίας πρὸς τὸν ἄγγελον, Κατὰ τί γνώσομαι τοῦτο; ἐγὼ γάρ εἰμι πρεσβύτης καὶ ἡ γυνή μου προβεβηκυῖα ἐν ταῖς ἡμέραις αὐτῆς. **19** καὶ ἀποκριθεὶς ὁ ἄγγελος εἶπεν αὐτῷ, Ἐγώ εἰμι Γαβριὴλ ὁ παρεστηκὼς ἐνώπιον τοῦ θεοῦ καὶ ἀπεστάλην λαλῆσαι πρὸς σὲ καὶ εὐαγγελίσασθαί σοι ταῦτα· **20** καὶ ἰδοὺ ἔσῃ σιωπῶν καὶ μὴ δυνάμενος λαλῆσαι ἄχρι ἧς ἡμέρας γένηται ταῦτα, ἀνθ᾽ ὧν οὐκ ἐπίστευσας τοῖς λόγοις μου, οἵτινες πληρωθήσονται εἰς τὸν καιρὸν αὐτῶν. ¶ **21** Καὶ ἦν ὁ λαὸς προσδοκῶν τὸν Ζαχαρίαν

for Zechariah	and	wondering	why	he	stayed	so long	in	the	temple.	**22**		When	he	came	out,	he
⸆τὸν Ζαχαρίαν⸆	καὶ	ἐθαύμαζον		αὐτὸν	ἐν τῷ χρονίζειν⸆	←	ἐν	τῷ	ναῷ		δὲ			ἐξελθὼν		→
d.asm n.asm	cj	v.iai.3p		r.asm.3	p.d d.dsn f.pa		p.d	d.dsm	n.dsm		cj			pt.aa.nsm		
3836 2408	2779	2513		899	1877 3836 5988		1877	3836	3724		1254			2002		

could	not	speak	to	them.		They	realized	he	had	seen	a vision	in	the	temple,	for	he	kept	making
ἐδύνατο	οὐκ	λαλῆσαι	→	αὐτοῖς	καὶ	→	ἐπέγνωσαν	ὅτι	→	ἑώρακεν	ὀπτασίαν	ἐν	τῷ	ναῷ	καὶ	αὐτὸς	→	
v.ipi.3s	pl	f.aa		r.dpm.3	cj		v.aai.3p	cj		v.rai.3s	n.asf	p.d	d.dsm	n.dsm	cj	r.nsm		
1538	4024	3281		899	2779		2105	4022		3972	3965	1877	3836	3724	2779	899		

signs		to them	but	remained		unable to speak.	¶	**23**		When	his	time		of service	
⸆ἦν διανεύων⸆	→	αὐτοῖς	καὶ	διέμενεν	→	→ κωφός			καὶ	ἐγένετο ὡς		αὐτοῦ ⸆αἱ ἡμέραι⸆	→	⸆τῆς λειτουργίας⸆	
v.iai.3s pt.pa.nsm		r.dpm.3	cj	v.iai.3s		a.nsm			cj	v.ami.3s cj		r.gsm.3 d.npf n.npf		d.gsf n.gsf	
1639 1377		899	2779	1373		3273			2779	1181 6055		899 3836 2465		3836 3311	

was completed,	he returned		home.	**24**	After this				his	wife	Elizabeth	became	pregnant
→ ἐπλήσθησαν	→ ἀπῆλθεν	εἰς	τὸν οἶκον αὐτοῦ	δὲ	Μετὰ ⸆ταύτας τὰς ἡμέρας⸆				αὐτοῦ	⸆ἡ γυνὴ	Ἐλισάβετ	→	συνέλαβεν
v.api.3p	v.aai.3s	p.a	d.asm n.asm r.gsm.3	cj	p.a r.apf d.apf n.apf				r.gsm.3	d.nsf n.nsf	n.nsf		v.aai.3s
4398	599	1650	3836 3875 899	1254	3552 4047 2465				899	3836 1222	1810		5197

and	for	five	months	remained	in	seclusion.	**25**	"The	Lord	has	done	this	for	me,"	she	said.	"In	these
καὶ	→	πέντε	μῆνας	→	→	⸆περιέκρυβεν ἑαυτὴν⸆	ὅτι		κύριος	→	πεποίηκεν	οὕτως	→	μοι		λέγουσα	ἐν	
cj		a.apm	n.apm			v.iai.3s r.asf.3	cj		n.nsm		v.rai.3s	adv		r.ds.1		pt.pa.nsf	p.d	
2779		3604 4297	3604			4332 1571	4022		3261		4472	4048		1609		3306	1877	

days		he has	shown	his favor	and	taken away	my	disgrace	among	the people."	
ἡμέραις	αἷς	→	ἐπεῖδεν	←		ἀφελεῖν	μου	ὄνειδος	ἐν	ἀνθρώποις	
n.dpf	r.dpf		v.aai.3s			f.aa	r.gs.1	n.asn	p.d	n.dpm	
2465	4005		2078			904	1609	3945	1877	476	

The Birth of Jesus Foretold

1:26	In the	sixth	month,		God	sent	the	angel	Gabriel	to		Nazareth,	a town in
δὲ	Ἐν τῷ	⸆τῷ ἕκτῳ⸆	μηνὶ	ἀπὸ	⸆τοῦ θεοῦ	ἀπεστάλη	ὁ	ἄγγελος	Γαβριὴλ	εἰς	ᾗ ὄνομα	Ναζαρὲθ	πόλιν →
cj	p.d d.dsm	d.dsm a.dsm	n.dsm	p.g	d.gsm n.gsm	v.api.3s	d.nsm	n.nsm	n.nsm	p.a	r.dsf n.nsf	n.nsf	n.asf
1254	1877 3836	3836 1761	3604	608	3836 2536	34	3836	34	1120	1650	4005 3950	3714	4484

Galilee,	**27**	to	a virgin	pledged to be	married		to a man	named	Joseph,	a descendant	of David.
⸆τῆς Γαλιλαίας⸆		πρὸς	παρθένον →	→	ἐμνηστευμένην →		ἀνδρὶ	ᾧ ὄνομα	Ἰωσὴφ	⸆ἐξ οἴκου⸆	→ Δαυὶδ καὶ
d.gsf n.gsf		p.a	n.asf		pt.rp.asf		n.dsm	r.dsm n.nsn	n.nsm	p.g n.gsm	n.gsm cj
3836 1133		4639	4221		3650		467	4005 3950	2737	1666 3875	1253 2779

The	virgin's	name	was	Mary.	**28**	The	angel	went		to	her	and	said,	"Greetings,	you who	are	highly
τὸ	⸆τῆς παρθένου⸆	ὄνομα		Μαριάμ	καὶ			εἰσελθὼν	πρὸς	αὐτὴν		εἶπεν	χαῖρε		→	→	
d.nsn	d.gsf n.gsf	n.nsn		n.nsf	cj			pt.aa.nsm	p.a	r.asf.3		v.aai.3s	v.pam.2s				
3836	3836 4221	3950		3452	2779			1656	4639	899		3306	5897				

favored!	The	Lord	is	with	you."	¶	**29**		Mary	was	greatly	troubled	at	his	words	and	wondered	what
κεχαριτωμένη	ὁ	κύριος	μετὰ	σοῦ				δὲ	ἡ	→	→	διεταράχθη	ἐπὶ	τῷ	λόγῳ	καὶ	διελογίζετο	ποταπὸς
pt.rp.vsf	d.nsm	n.nsm	p.g	r.gs.2				cj	d.nsf			v.api.3s	p.d	d.dsm	n.dsm	cj	v.imi.3s	r.nsm
5923	3836	3261	3552	5148				1254	3836			1410	2093	3836	3364	2779	1368	4534

kind of	greeting		this	might be.	**30**	But	the	angel	said	to	her,	"Do not		be afraid,	Mary,		you have	found
←	⸆ὁ ἀσπασμὸς⸆	οὗτος		εἴη		καὶ	ὁ	ἄγγελος	εἶπεν		αὐτῇ	μὴ	→	φοβοῦ	Μαριάμ	γὰρ	→	εὗρες
	d.nsm n.nsm	r.nsm		v.pao.3s		cj	d.nsm	n.nsm	v.aai.3s		r.dsf.3	pl		v.ppm.2s	n.vsf	cj		v.aai.2s
	3836 833	4047		1639		2779	3836	34	3306		899	3590		5828	3452	1142		2351

favor	with	God.	**31**		You will	*be*		*with*	*child*	and	give	birth	to a son,	and	you are to	give		him	the
χάριν	παρὰ	⸆τῷ θεῷ⸆		καὶ ἰδοὺ	→	→	συλλήμψῃ	ἐν	γαστρὶ	καὶ	→	τέξῃ	υἱὸν	καὶ	→	→ καλέσεις	αὐτοῦ	τὸ	
n.asf	p.d	d.dsm n.dsm		cj			v.fmi.2s	p.d	n.dsf	cj		v.fmi.2s	n.asm	cj		v.fai.2s	r.gsm.3	d.asn	
5921	4123	3836 2536		2779 2627			5197	1877	1143	2779		5503	5626	2779		2813	899	3836	

name	Jesus.	**32**	He	will be	great	and	will be	called		the	Son	of the	Most	High.		The	Lord	God	will
ὄνομα	Ἰησοῦν		οὗτος	→ ἔσται	μέγας	καὶ	→	κληθήσεται			υἱὸς		ὑψίστου	καὶ			κύριος	ὁ θεὸς	→
n.asn	n.asm		r.nsm	v.fmi.3s	a.nsm	cj		v.fpi.3s			n.nsm		a.gsm.s	cj			n.nsm	d.nsm n.nsm	
3950	2652		4047	1639	3489	2779		2813			5626		5736	2779			3261	3836 2536	

give	him	the	throne	of	his	father	David,	**33**	and	he will	reign		over	the	house	of Jacob	forever;	
δώσει	αὐτῷ	τὸν	θρόνον	→	αὐτοῦ	⸆τοῦ πατρὸς⸆	Δαυὶδ		καὶ	→	βασιλεύσει	ἐπὶ	τὸν	οἶκον		Ἰακὼβ	⸆εἰς τοὺς αἰῶνας⸆	καὶ
v.fai.3s	r.dsm.3	d.asm	n.asm		r.gsm.3	d.gsm n.gsm	n.gsm		cj		v.fai.3s	p.a	d.asm	n.asm		n.gsm	p.a d.apm n.apm	cj
1443	899	3836	2585		899	3836 4252	1253		2779		996	2093	3836	3875		1253	1650 3836 172	2779

καὶ ἐθαύμαζον ἐν τῷ χρονίζειν ἐν τῷ ναῷ αὐτόν. **22** ἐξελθὼν δὲ οὐκ ἐδύνατο λαλῆσαι αὐτοῖς, καὶ ἐπέγνωσαν ὅτι ὀπτασίαν ἑώρακεν ἐν τῷ ναῷ· καὶ αὐτὸς ἦν διανεύων αὐτοῖς καὶ διέμενεν κωφός. ¶ **23** καὶ ἐγένετο ὡς ἐπλήσθησαν αἱ ἡμέραι τῆς λειτουργίας αὐτοῦ, ἀπῆλθεν εἰς τὸν οἶκον αὐτοῦ. **24** Μετὰ δὲ ταύτας τὰς ἡμέρας συνέλαβεν Ἐλισάβετ ἡ γυνὴ αὐτοῦ καὶ περιέκρυβεν ἑαυτὴν μῆνας πέντε λέγουσα **25** ὅτι Οὕτως μοι πεποίηκεν κύριος ἐν ἡμέραις αἷς ἐπεῖδεν ἀφελεῖν ὄνειδός μου ἐν ἀνθρώποις.

1:26 Ἐν δὲ τῷ μηνὶ τῷ ἕκτῳ ἀπεστάλη ὁ ἄγγελος Γαβριὴλ ἀπὸ τοῦ θεοῦ εἰς πόλιν τῆς Γαλιλαίας ᾗ ὄνομα Ναζαρὲθ **27** πρὸς παρθένον ἐμνηστευμένην ἀνδρὶ ᾧ ὄνομα Ἰωσὴφ ἐξ οἴκου Δαυὶδ καὶ τὸ ὄνομα τῆς παρθένου Μαριάμ. **28** καὶ εἰσελθὼν ὁ ἄγγελος πρὸς αὐτὴν εἶπεν, Χαῖρε, κεχαριτωμένη, ὁ κύριος μετὰ σοῦ. ¶ **29** ἡ δὲ ἐπὶ τῷ λόγῳ διεταράχθη καὶ διελογίζετο ποταπὸς εἴη ὁ ἀσπασμὸς οὗτος. **30** καὶ εἶπεν ὁ ἄγγελος αὐτῇ, Μὴ φοβοῦ, Μαριάμ, εὗρες γὰρ χάριν παρὰ τῷ θεῷ. **31** καὶ ἰδοὺ συλλήμψῃ ἐν γαστρὶ καὶ τέξῃ υἱὸν καὶ καλέσεις τὸ ὄνομα αὐτοῦ Ἰησοῦν. **32** οὗτος ἔσται μέγας καὶ υἱὸς ὑψίστου κληθήσεται καὶ δώσει αὐτῷ κύριος ὁ θεὸς τὸν θρόνον Δαυὶδ τοῦ πατρὸς αὐτοῦ, **33** καὶ βασιλεύσει ἐπὶ τὸν οἶκον Ἰακὼβ εἰς τοὺς αἰῶνας καὶ τῆς

his kingdom will never end." **34** "How will this be," Mary asked the angel, "since I am a
αὐτοῦ τῆς βασιλείας ἔσται οὐκ τέλος δὲ πῶς → τοῦτο ἔσται Μαριὰμ εἶπεν πρὸς τὸν ἄγγελον ἐπεὶ
r.gsn.3 d.gsf n.gsf v.fmi.3s pl n.nsn cj pl r.nsn v.fmi.3s n.nsf v.aai.3s p.a d.asm n.asm cj
899 3836 993 1639 4024 5465 1254 4802 1639 4047 3452 3306 4639 34 2075

virgin?" **35** The angel answered, "The Holy Spirit will come upon you, and the power of
ἄνδρα οὐ γινώσκω καὶ ὁ ἄγγελος ἀποκριθεὶς εἶπεν αὐτῇ ἅγιον πνεῦμα → ἐπελεύσεται ἐπὶ → καὶ δύναμις
n.asm pl v.pai.1s cj d.nsm n.nsm pt.ap.nsn v.aai.3s r.dsf.3 a.nsn n.nsn v.fmi.3s p.a r.as.2 cj n.nsf
467 4024 1182 2779 3836 34 646 3306 899 41 4460 2088 2093 5148 2779 1539

the Most High will overshadow you. So the holy one to be born will be called the Son of God.
→ ὑψίστου → ἐπισκιάσει σοι διὸ καὶ ἅγιον ← → τὸ γεννώμενον → → κληθήσεται υἱὸς → θεοῦ
a.gsm.s v.fai.3s r.ds.2 cj adv a.nsn d.nsn pt.pp.nsn v.fpi.3s n.nsm n.gsm
5736 2173 5148 1475 2779 41 3836 1164 2813 5626 2536

36 Even Elizabeth your relative is going to have a child in her old age, and she who was
καὶ ἰδοὺ Ἐλισάβετ σου ἡ συγγενίς καὶ αὐτὴ → → → συνείληφεν υἱὸν ἐν αὐτῆς γήρει ← καὶ οὗτος τῇ →
cj j n.nsf r.gs.2 d.nsf n.nsf adv r.nsf v.rai.3s n.asm p.d r.gsf.3 n.dsn cj r.nsm d.dsf
2779 2627 1810 5148 3836 5151 2779 899 5197 5626 1877 899 1179 2779 4047 3836

said to be barren is in her sixth month. **37** For nothing is impossible with God." ¶ **38** "I am
καλουμένη στείρα ἐστιν αὐτῇ ἕκτος μὴν ὅτι οὐκ πᾶν ῥῆμα → ἀδυνατήσει παρὰ τοῦ θεοῦ δὲ ἰδοὺ
pt.pp.dsf a.dsf v.pai.3s r.dsf.3 a.nsm n.nsm cj pl a.nsn n.nsn v.fai.3s p.g d.gsm n.gsm cj j
2813 5096 1639 899 1761 3604 4022 4024 4246 4839 104 4123 3836 2536 1254 2627

the Lord's servant," Mary answered. "May it be to me as you have said." Then the angel left her.
ἡ κυρίου δούλη Μαριὰμ εἶπεν → → γένοιτο → μοι κατὰ σου τὸ ῥῆμα καὶ ὁ ἄγγελος ἀπῆλθεν ἀπ᾽ αὐτῆς
d.nsf n.gsf n.nsf n.nsf v.aai.3s v.amo.3s r.ds.1 p.a r.gs.2 d.asn n.asn cj d.nsm n.nsm v.aai.3s p.g r.gsf.3
3836 3261 1527 3452 3306 1181 1609 2848 5148 3836 4839 2779 3836 34 599 608 899

Mary Visits Elizabeth

1:39 At that time Mary got ready and hurried to a town in the hill country
δὲ ἐν ταύταις ταῖς ἡμέραις Μαριὰμ → Ἀναστᾶσα ἐπορεύθη μετὰ σπουδῆς εἰς πόλιν εἰς τὴν ὀρεινὴν ←
cj p.d r.dpf d.dpf n.dpf n.nsf pt.aa.nsf v.api.3s p.g n.gsf p.a n.asf p.a d.asf n.asf
1254 1877 4047 3836 2465 3452 482 4513 3552 5082 1650 4484 1650 3836 3978

of Judea, **40** where she entered Zechariah's home and greeted Elizabeth. **41** When Elizabeth
→ Ἰούδα καὶ → εἰσῆλθεν εἰς Ζαχαρίου τὸν οἶκον καὶ ἠσπάσατο τὴν Ἐλισάβετ καὶ ἐγένετο ὡς ἡ Ἐλισάβετ
n.gsm cj v.aai.3s p.a n.asm d.asm n.asm cj v.ami.3s d.asf n.asf cj v.ami.3s cj d.nsf n.nsf
2683 2779 1656 1650 2408 3836 3875 2779 832 3836 1810 2779 1181 6055 3836 1810

heard Mary's greeting, the baby leaped in her womb, and Elizabeth was filled with the Holy
ἤκουσεν τῆς Μαρίας τὸν ἀσπασμὸν τὸ βρέφος ἐσκίρτησεν ἐν αὐτῆς τῇ κοιλίᾳ καὶ ἡ Ἐλισάβετ → ἐπλήσθη → ἁγίου
v.aai.3s d.gsf n.gsf d.asm n.asm d.nsn n.nsn v.aai.3s p.d r.gsf.3 d.dsf n.dsf cj d.nsf n.nsf v.api.3s a.gsn
201 3836 3451 3836 833 3836 1100 5015 1877 899 3836 3120 2779 3836 1810 4398 41

Spirit. **42** In a loud voice she exclaimed: "Blessed are you among women, and blessed is the child
πνεύματος καὶ → μεγάλῃ κραυγῇ → ἀνεφώνησεν καὶ εἶπεν εὐλογημένη σὺ ἐν γυναιξὶν καὶ εὐλογημένος ὁ καρπὸς
n.gsn cj a.dsf n.dsf v.aai.3s cj v.aai.3s pt.rp.nsf r.ns.2 p.d n.dpf cj pt.rp.nsm d.nsm n.nsm
4460 2779 3489 3199 430 2779 3306 2328 5148 1877 1222 2779 2328 3836 2843

you will bear! **43** But why am I so favored, that the mother of my Lord should come to me? **44**
σου τῆς κοιλίας καὶ πόθεν μοι τοῦτο ἵνα ἡ μήτηρ → μου τοῦ κυρίου → ἔλθῃ πρὸς ἐμέ γὰρ ἰδοὺ
r.gs.2 d.gsf n.gsf cj pl r.ds.1 r.nsn cj d.nsf n.nsf r.gs.1 d.gsm n.gsm v.aas.3s p.a r.as.1 cj j
5148 3836 3120 2779 4470 1609 4047 2671 3836 3613 3261 3836 3261 2262 4639 1609 1142 2627

As soon as the sound of your greeting reached my ears, the baby in my womb leaped for
ὡς → ἡ φωνὴ → σου τοῦ ἀσπασμοῦ ἐγένετο εἰς μου τὰ ὦτα τὸ βρέφος ἐν μου τῇ κοιλίᾳ ἐσκίρτησεν ἐν
cj d.nsf n.nsf r.gs.2 d.gsm n.gsm v.ami.3s p.a r.gs.1 d.apn n.apn d.nsn n.nsn p.d r.gs.1 d.dsf n.dsf v.aai.3s p.d
6055 3836 5889 833 5148 3836 833 1181 1650 1609 3836 4044 3836 1100 1877 1609 3836 3120 5015 1877

joy. **45** Blessed is she who has believed that what the Lord has said to her will be
ἀγαλλιάσει καὶ μακαρία ἡ → πιστεύσασα ὅτι τοῖς παρὰ κυρίου → λελαλημένοις → αὐτῇ ἔσται
n.dsf cj a.nsf d.nsf pt.aa.nsf cj d.dpn p.g n.gsm pt.rp.dpn r.dsf.3 v.fmi.3s
21 2779 3421 3836 4409 4022 3836 4123 3261 3281 899 1639

accomplished!"
τελείωσις
n.nsf
5459

βασιλείας αὐτοῦ οὐκ ἔσται τέλος. **34** εἶπεν δὲ Μαριὰμ πρὸς τὸν ἄγγελον, Πῶς ἔσται τοῦτο, ἐπεὶ ἄνδρα οὐ γινώσκω; **35** καὶ ἀποκριθεὶς ὁ ἄγγελος εἶπεν αὐτῇ, Πνεῦμα ἅγιον ἐπελεύσεται ἐπὶ σὲ καὶ δύναμις ὑψίστου ἐπισκιάσει σοι· διὸ καὶ τὸ γεννώμενον ἅγιον κληθήσεται υἱὸς θεοῦ. **36** καὶ ἰδοὺ Ἐλισάβετ ἡ συγγενίς σου καὶ αὐτὴ συνείληφεν υἱὸν ἐν γήρει αὐτῆς καὶ οὗτος μὴν ἕκτος ἐστιν αὐτῇ τῇ καλουμένῃ στείρα· **37** ὅτι οὐκ ἀδυνατήσει παρὰ τοῦ θεοῦ πᾶν ῥῆμα. ¶ **38** εἶπεν δὲ Μαριάμ, Ἰδοὺ ἡ δούλη κυρίου· γένοιτο μοι κατὰ τὸ ῥῆμά σου. καὶ ἀπῆλθεν ἀπ᾽ αὐτῆς ὁ ἄγγελος.

1:39 Ἀναστᾶσα δὲ Μαριὰμ ἐν ταῖς ἡμέραις ταύταις ἐπορεύθη εἰς τὴν ὀρεινὴν μετὰ σπουδῆς εἰς πόλιν Ἰούδα, **40** καὶ εἰσῆλθεν εἰς τὸν οἶκον Ζαχαρίου καὶ ἠσπάσατο τὴν Ἐλισάβετ. **41** καὶ ἐγένετο ὡς ἤκουσεν τὸν ἀσπασμὸν τῆς Μαρίας ἡ Ἐλισάβετ, ἐσκίρτησεν τὸ βρέφος ἐν τῇ κοιλίᾳ αὐτῆς, καὶ ἐπλήσθη πνεύματος ἁγίου ἡ Ἐλισάβετ, **42** καὶ ἀνεφώνησεν κραυγῇ μεγάλῃ καὶ εἶπεν, Εὐλογημένη σὺ ἐν γυναιξὶν καὶ εὐλογημένος ὁ καρπὸς τῆς κοιλίας σου. **43** καὶ πόθεν μοι τοῦτο ἵνα ἔλθῃ ἡ μήτηρ τοῦ κυρίου μου πρὸς ἐμέ; **44** ἰδοὺ γὰρ ὡς ἐγένετο ἡ φωνὴ τοῦ ἀσπασμοῦ σου εἰς τὰ ὦτά μου, ἐσκίρτησεν ἐν ἀγαλλιάσει τὸ βρέφος ἐν τῇ κοιλίᾳ μου. **45** καὶ μακαρία ἡ πιστεύσασα ὅτι ἔσται τελείωσις τοῖς λελαλημένοις αὐτῇ παρὰ κυρίου.

Mary's Song

1:46 And Mary said: "My soul glorifies the Lord **47** and my spirit rejoices in God my Savior,
Καὶ Μαριὰμ εἶπεν μου ἡ ψυχή Μεγαλύνει τὸν κύριον καὶ μου τὸ πνεῦμα ἠγαλλίασεν ἐπὶ τῷ θεῷ μου τῷ σωτῆρι
cj n.nsf v.aai.3s r.gs.1 d.nsf n.nsf v.pai.3s d.asm n.asm cj r.gs.1 d.nsn n.nsn v.aai.3s p.d d.dsm n.dsm r.gs.1 d.dsm n.dsm
2779 3452 3306 1609 3836 6034 3486 3836 3261 2779 1609 3836 4460 22 2093 3836 2536 1609 3836 5400

48 for he has been mindful of the humble state of his servant. From now on all generations will
ὅτι → → ἐπέβλεψεν ἐπὶ τὴν ταπείνωσιν ← αὐτοῦ τῆς δούλης γὰρ ἰδοὺ ἀπὸ τοῦ νῦν ← πᾶσαι αἱ γενεαί →
cj v.aai.3s p.a d.asf n.asf r.gsf.3 d.gsf n.gsf cj j p.g d.gsn adv a.npf d.npf n.npf
4022 2098 2093 3836 5428 899 3836 1527 1142 2627 608 3836 3814 4246 3836 1155 3420

call me blessed, **49** for the Mighty One has done great things for me — holy is his name. **50** His
μακαριοῦσιν ὅτι ὁ δυνατός ἐποίησεν μεγάλα μοι καὶ ἅγιον αὐτοῦ τὸ ὄνομα καὶ αὐτοῦ
με
r.as.1 v.fai.3p cj d.nsm a.nsm v.aai.3s a.apn r.ds.1 cj a.nsn r.gsm.3 d.nsn n.nsn cj r.gsm.3
3420 1609 3420 4022 3836 1543 4472 3489 1609 2779 41 899 3836 3950 2779 899

mercy extends to those who fear him, *from generation to generation.* **51** He has performed mighty deeds with
τὸ ἔλεος → τοῖς ← φοβουμένοις αὐτόν εἰς γενεὰς καὶ γενεὰς → Ἐποίησεν κράτος ← ἐν
d.nsn n.nsn d.dpm pt.pp.dpm r.asm.3 p.a n.apf cj n.apf v.aai.3s n.asn p.d
3836 1799 3836 5828 899 1650 1155 2779 1155 4472 3197 1877

his arm; he has scattered those who are proud in their inmost thoughts. **52** He has brought down rulers
αὐτοῦ βραχίονι → διεσκόρπισεν → → ὑπερηφάνους → αὐτῶν καρδίας διανοίᾳ ← καθεῖλεν δυνάστας
r.gsm.3 n.dsm v.aai.3s a.apm r.gsm.3 n.gsf n.dsf v.aai.3s n.apm
899 1098 1399 5662 899 2840 1379 2747 1541

from their thrones but has lifted up the humble. **53** He has filled the hungry with good things but has
ἀπὸ θρόνων καὶ → ὕψωσεν ταπεινούς → ἐνέπλησεν πεινῶντας → ἀγαθῶν καὶ →
p.g n.gpm cj v.aai.3s a.apm v.aai.3s pt.pa.apm a.gpn cj
608 2585 2779 5738 5424 1858 4277 19 2779

sent the rich away empty. **54** He has helped his servant Israel, remembering to be merciful **55** to
ἐξαπέστειλεν πλουτοῦντας ↰ κενούς → ἀντελάβετο αὐτοῦ παιδὸς Ἰσραὴλ μνησθῆναι ἐλέους →
v.aai.3s pt.pa.apm a.apm v.ami.3s r.gsm.3 n.gsm n.gsm f.ap n.gsn
1990 4456 1990 3031 514 899 4090 2702 3630 1799

Abraham and his descendants forever, even as he said to our fathers." **56** Mary stayed with
τῷ Ἀβραὰμ καὶ αὐτοῦ τῷ σπέρματι εἰς τὸν αἰῶνα καθὼς ← ἐλάλησεν πρὸς ἡμῶν τοὺς πατέρας δὲ Μαριὰμ Ἔμεινεν σὺν
d.dsm n.dsm cj r.gsm.3 d.dsn n.dsn p.a d.asm n.asm cj v.aai.3s p.a r.gp.1 d.apm n.apm cj n.nsf v.aai.3s p.d
3836 11 2779 899 3836 5065 1650 3836 172 2777 3281 4639 7005 3836 4252 1254 3452 3531 5250

Elizabeth for about three months and then returned home.
αὐτῇ → ὡς τρεῖς μῆνας καὶ ὑπέστρεψεν εἰς τὸν οἶκον αὐτῆς
r.dsf.3 pl a.apm n.apm cj v.aai.3s p.a d.asm n.asm r.gsf.3
899 5552 6055 5552 3604 2779 5715 1650 3836 3875 899

The Birth of John the Baptist

1:57 When it was time for Elizabeth to have her baby, she gave birth to a son. **58**
δὲ → → ἐπλήσθη ὁ χρόνος → Τῇ Ἐλισάβετ → τοῦ τεκεῖν αὐτὴν καὶ → ἐγέννησεν ← υἱόν καὶ
cj v.api.3s d.nsm n.nsm d.dsf n.dsf d.gsn f.aa r.asf.3 cj v.aai.3s n.asm cj
1254 4398 3836 5080 3836 1810 3836 5503 899 2779 1164 5626 2779

Her neighbors and relatives heard that the Lord had shown her great mercy, and they
αὐτῆς οἱ περίοικοι καὶ οἱ συγγενεῖς ἤκουσαν ὅτι κύριος → ἐμεγάλυνεν μετ᾽ αὐτῆς τὸ ἔλεος αὐτοῦ καὶ
r.gsf.3 d.npm n.npm cj d.npm n.npm v.aai.3p cj n.nsm v.iai.3s p.g r.gsf.3 d.asn n.asn r.gsm.3 cj
899 3836 4341 2779 3836 5150 201 4022 3261 3486 3552 899 3836 1799 899 2779 5176

shared her joy. ¶ **59** On the eighth day they came to circumcise the child, and they were
αὐτῇ συνέχαιρον Καὶ ἐγένετο ἐν τῇ τῇ ὀγδόῃ ἡμέρᾳ → ἦλθον περιτεμεῖν τὸ παιδίον καὶ →
r.dsf.3 v.iai.3p cj v.ami.3s p.d d.dsf d.dsf a.dsf n.dsf v.aai.3p f.aa d.asn n.asn cj
5176 899 5176 2779 1181 1877 3836 3836 3838 2465 4362 3836 4086 2779

going to name him after his father Zechariah, **60** but his mother spoke up and said, "No!
→ ἐκάλουν αὐτὸ ἐπὶ τῷ ὀνόματι αὐτοῦ τοῦ πατρὸς Ζαχαρίαν καὶ αὐτοῦ ἡ μήτηρ ἀποκριθεῖσα ← εἶπεν οὐχί
v.iai.3p r.asn.3 p.d d.dsn n.dsn r.gsm.3 d.gsm n.gsm n.asm cj r.gsm.3 d.nsf n.nsf pt.ap.nsf v.aai.3s pl
2813 899 2093 3836 3950 899 3836 4252 2408 2779 899 3836 3613 646 3306 4049

1:46 Καὶ εἶπεν Μαριάμ, Μεγαλύνει ἡ ψυχή μου τὸν κύριον, **47** καὶ ἠγαλλίασεν τὸ πνεῦμά μου ἐπὶ τῷ θεῷ τῷ σωτῆρί μου, **48** ὅτι ἐπέβλεψεν ἐπὶ τὴν ταπείνωσιν τῆς δούλης αὐτοῦ. ἰδοὺ γὰρ ἀπὸ τοῦ νῦν μακαριοῦσίν με πᾶσαι αἱ γενεαί, **49** ὅτι ἐποίησέν μοι μεγάλα ὁ δυνατός. καὶ ἅγιον τὸ ὄνομα αὐτοῦ, **50** καὶ τὸ ἔλεος αὐτοῦ εἰς γενεὰς καὶ γενεὰς τοῖς φοβουμένοις αὐτόν. **51** Ἐποίησεν κράτος ἐν βραχίονι αὐτοῦ, διεσκόρπισεν ὑπερηφάνους διανοίᾳ καρδίας αὐτῶν· **52** καθεῖλεν δυνάστας ἀπὸ θρόνων καὶ ὕψωσεν ταπεινούς, **53** πεινῶντας ἐνέπλησεν ἀγαθῶν καὶ πλουτοῦντας ἐξαπέστειλεν κενούς. **54** ἀντελάβετο Ἰσραὴλ παιδὸς αὐτοῦ, μνησθῆναι ἐλέους, **55** καθὼς ἐλάλησεν πρὸς τοὺς πατέρας ἡμῶν, τῷ Ἀβραὰμ καὶ τῷ σπέρματι αὐτοῦ εἰς τὸν αἰῶνα. **56** Ἔμεινεν δὲ Μαριὰμ σὺν αὐτῇ ὡς μῆνας τρεῖς, καὶ ὑπέστρεψεν εἰς τὸν οἶκον αὐτῆς.

1:57 Τῇ δὲ Ἐλισάβετ ἐπλήσθη ὁ χρόνος τοῦ τεκεῖν αὐτὴν καὶ ἐγέννησεν υἱόν. **58** καὶ ἤκουσαν οἱ περίοικοι καὶ οἱ συγγενεῖς αὐτῆς ὅτι ἐμεγάλυνεν κύριος τὸ ἔλεος αὐτοῦ μετ᾽ αὐτῆς καὶ συνέχαιρον αὐτῇ. ¶ **59** Καὶ ἐγένετο ἐν τῇ ἡμέρᾳ τῇ ὀγδόῃ ἦλθον περιτεμεῖν τὸ παιδίον καὶ ἐκάλουν αὐτὸ ἐπὶ τῷ ὀνόματι τοῦ πατρὸς αὐτοῦ Ζαχαρίαν. **60** καὶ ἀποκριθεῖσα ἡ μήτηρ αὐτοῦ εἶπεν,

He is to be called   John."   ¶   **61**   They said   to   her,   "There   is   no one   among   your
ἀλλὰ → → → κληθήσεται Ἰωάννης   καὶ   εἶπαν πρὸς αὐτὴν ὅτι   ἐστιν → οὐδείς ἐκ σου
cj   v.fpi.3s   n.nsm   cj   v.aai.3p p.a r.asf.3 cj   v.pai.3s a.nsm p.g r.gs.2
247   2813   2722   2779 3306   4639 899 4022 1639   4029 1666 5148

relatives   who has   that name."   ¶   **62** Then they made   signs   to   his   father,   to find out   what
⸀τῆς συγγενείας⸣ ὃς καλεῖται τούτῳ ⸀τῷ ὀνόματι⸣   δὲ → → ἐνένευον → αὐτοῦ τῷ πατρὶ   ⸀τί ἂν⸣
d.gsf n.gsf   r.nsm v.ppi.3s r.dsn d.dsn n.dsn   cj   v.iai.3p   r.gsm.3 d.dsm n.dsm   r.asn pl
3836 5149   4005 2813   4047 3836 3950   1254   1935   899   3836 4252   5515 323

he would like to name   the child. **63** He asked for a writing tablet,   and to everyone's astonishment he
→ → θέλοι → τὸ καλεῖσθαι αὐτό   καὶ → αἰτήσας ← → πινακίδιον καὶ πάντες ἐθαύμασαν →
v.pao.3s d.asn f.pp   r.asn.3   cj   pt.aa.nsm   n.asn   cj a.npm   v.aai.3p
2527   3836 2813   899   2779   160   4400   2779 4246   2513

wrote,   "His name is   John." **64** Immediately his mouth was opened and his tongue   was loosed,
ἔγραψεν λέγων αὐτοῦ ὄνομα ἐστὶν Ἰωάννης δὲ   παραχρῆμα αὐτοῦ ⸀τὸ στόμα⸣ → ἀνεῴχθη καὶ αὐτοῦ ἡ γλῶσσα
v.aai.3s pt.pa.nsm r.gsm.3 n.nsn v.pai.3s n.nsm cj   adv   r.gsm.3 d.nsn n.nsn v.api.3s cj r.gsm.3 d.nsf n.nsf
1211   3306   899   3950 1639   2722   1254   4202   899   3836 5125   487   2779 899   3836 1185

and he began to speak, praising God. **65**   The neighbors   were   all   filled with awe,   and
καὶ → → → ἐλάλει εὐλογῶν τὸν θεόν   Καὶ ἐγένετο τοὺς περιοικοῦντας αὐτούς, ἐπὶ πάντας   φόβος καὶ
cj   v.iai.3s pt.pa.nsm d.asm n.asm   cj   v.ami.3s d.apm pt.pa.apm r.apm.3 p.a a.apm   n.nsm cj
2779   3281   2328   3836 2536   2779 1181   3836 4340   899   2093 4246   5832 2779

throughout the hill country of Judea   people were talking about all   these things. **66** Everyone who
⸀ἐν ὅλῃ⸣ τῇ ὀρεινῇ ← → ⸀τῆς Ἰουδαίας⸣ → → διελαλεῖτο ← πάντα ταῦτα ⸀τὰ ῥήματα⸣ καὶ πάντες οἱ
p.d a.dsf d.dsf n.dsf   d.gsf n.gsf   v.ipi.3s   a.npn r.npn d.npn n.npn   cj a.npm d.npm
1877 3910 3836 3978   3836 2677   1362   4246 4047 3836 4839   2779 4246 3836

heard   this wondered   about it, asking, "What then is this child   going to be?" For the Lord's
ἀκούσαντες ἔθεντο ἐν τῇ αὐτῶν⸣   λέγοντες τί ἄρα τοῦτο τὸ παιδίον⸣ → → ἔσται γὰρ ἀδ   κυρίου
pt.aa.npm v.ami.3p p.d d.dsf r.gpm.3   pt.pa.npm r.nsn   r.nsn r.asn d.nsn n.nsn   v.fmi.3s cj adv n.gsm
201   5502   1877 3836 899   3306   5515 726 4047 3836 4086   1639 1142 2779 3261

hand was with him.
χεὶρ ἦν μετ' αὐτοῦ
n.nsf v.iai.3s p.g r.gsm.3
5931 1639 3552 899

Zechariah's Song

1:67   His father   Zechariah was filled with the Holy Spirit   and prophesied: **68** "Praise   be to the
Καὶ αὐτοῦ ὁ πατὴρ Ζαχαρίας → ἐπλήσθη → ἁγίου πνεύματος καὶ ἐπροφήτευσεν λέγων   Εὐλογητὸς
cj r.gsm.3 d.nsm n.nsm n.nsm   v.api.3s   a.gsn n.gsn cj v.aai.3s pt.pa.nsm   a.nsm
2779 899 3836 4252 2408   4398   41   4460 2779 4736   3306   2329

Lord, the God of Israel,   because he has come   and has redeemed   his people. **69** He has raised
κύριος ὁ θεὸς → ⸀τοῦ Ἰσραὴλ⸣ ὅτι → ἐπεσκέψατο καὶ → ⸀ἐποίησεν λύτρωσιν⸣ αὐτοῦ ⸀τῷ λαῷ⸣ καὶ → ἤγειρεν
n.nsm d.nsm n.nsm d.gsm n.gsm cj   v.ami.3s   cj   v.aai.3s n.asf   r.gsm.3 d.dsm n.dsm cj   v.aai.3s
3261 3836 2536 3836 2702 4022   2170   2779   4472   3391   899   3836 3295 2779   1586

up a horn of salvation for us in the house of his servant David **70** (as he said through   his
← κέρας → σωτηρίας → ἡμῖν ἐν οἴκῳ → αὐτοῦ παιδὸς Δαυὶδ   καθὼς → ἐλάλησεν διὰ στόματος αὐτοῦ
n.asn n.gsf   r.dp.1 p.d n.dsm r.gsm.3 n.gsm n.gsm   cj   v.aai.3s p.g n.gsn   r.gsm.3
3043 5401   7005 1877 3875   899   4090 1253   2777   3281   1328 5125   899

holy   prophets of long ago), salvation from our enemies and from the hand of all   who hate   us
⸀τῶν ἁγίων⸣ προφητῶν → ⸀ἀπ' αἰῶνος⸣ ← σωτηρίαν ἐξ ἡμῶν ἐχθρῶν καὶ ἐκ   χειρὸς → πάντων τῶν μισούντων ἡμᾶς
d.gpm a.gpm n.gpm   p.g n.gsm   n.asf ἐξ r.gp.1 a.gpm cj p.g   n.gsf   a.gpm d.gpm pt.pa.gpm r.ap.1
3836 41   4737   608 172   5401 1666 7005 2398 2779 1666   5931   4246 3836 3631   7005

– **72** to show mercy to our fathers   and to remember his holy covenant, **73** the oath   he swore to our
→ ποιῆσαι ἔλεος μετὰ ἡμῶν ⸀τῶν πατέρων⸣ καὶ → μνησθῆναι αὐτοῦ ἁγίας διαθήκης ὅρκον ὃν → ὤμοσεν πρὸς ἡμῶν
f.aa n.asn p.g r.gp.1 d.gpm n.gpm   cj   f.ap   r.gsm.3 a.gsf n.gsf   n.asm r.asm v.aai.3s p.a r.gp.1
4472 1799 3552 7005 3836 4252   2779   3630   899 41   1347   3992 4005   3923 4639 7005

father Abraham: **74** to rescue us from the hand of our enemies, and to enable us to serve him without
⸀τὸν πατέρα⸣ Ἀβραὰμ → ῥυσθέντας ἐκ χειρὸς → ἐχθρῶν → ⸀τοῦ δοῦναι⸣ ἡμῖν → λατρεύειν αὐτῷ →
d.asm n.asm n.asm   pt.ap.apm p.g n.gsf   a.gpm   d.gsn f.aa   r.dp.1 f.pa   r.dsm.3
3836 4252   11   4861   1666 5931   2398   3836 1443   7005 3302   899

Οὐχί, ἀλλὰ κληθήσεται Ἰωάννης. ¶ 61 καὶ εἶπαν πρὸς αὐτὴν ὅτι Οὐδείς ἐστιν ἐκ τῆς συγγενείας σου ὃς καλεῖται τῷ ὀνόματι τούτῳ. ¶ 62 ἐνένευον δὲ τῷ πατρὶ αὐτοῦ τὸ τί ἂν θέλοι καλεῖσθαι αὐτό. 63 καὶ αἰτήσας πινακίδιον ἔγραψεν λέγων, Ἰωάννης ἐστὶν ὄνομα αὐτοῦ. καὶ ἐθαύμασαν πάντες. 64 ἀνεῴχθη δὲ τὸ στόμα αὐτοῦ παραχρῆμα καὶ ἡ γλῶσσα αὐτοῦ, καὶ ἐλάλει εὐλογῶν τὸν θεόν. 65 καὶ ἐγένετο ἐπὶ πάντας φόβος τοὺς περιοικοῦντας αὐτούς, καὶ ἐν ὅλῃ τῇ ὀρεινῇ τῆς Ἰουδαίας διελαλεῖτο πάντα τὰ ῥήματα ταῦτα, 66 καὶ ἔθεντο πάντες οἱ ἀκούσαντες ἐν τῇ καρδίᾳ αὐτῶν λέγοντες, Τί ἄρα τὸ παιδίον τοῦτο ἔσται; καὶ γὰρ χεὶρ κυρίου ἦν μετ' αὐτοῦ.

1:67 Καὶ Ζαχαρίας ὁ πατὴρ αὐτοῦ ἐπλήσθη πνεύματος ἁγίου καὶ ἐπροφήτευσεν λέγων, 68 Εὐλογητὸς κύριος ὁ θεὸς τοῦ Ἰσραήλ, ὅτι ἐπεσκέψατο καὶ ἐποίησεν λύτρωσιν τῷ λαῷ αὐτοῦ, 69 καὶ ἤγειρεν κέρας σωτηρίας ἡμῖν ἐν οἴκῳ Δαυὶδ παιδὸς αὐτοῦ, 70 καθὼς ἐλάλησεν διὰ στόματος τῶν ἁγίων ἀπ' αἰῶνος προφητῶν αὐτοῦ, 71 σωτηρίαν ἐξ ἐχθρῶν ἡμῶν καὶ ἐκ χειρὸς πάντων τῶν μισούντων ἡμᾶς, 72 ποιῆσαι ἔλεος μετὰ τῶν πατέρων ἡμῶν καὶ μνησθῆναι διαθήκης ἁγίας αὐτοῦ, 73 ὅρκον ὃν ὤμοσεν πρὸς Ἀβραὰμ τὸν πατέρα ἡμῶν, τοῦ δοῦναι ἡμῖν 74 ἀφόβως ἐκ χειρὸς ἐχθρῶν ῥυσθέντας λατρεύειν αὐτῷ 75 ἐν ὁσιότητι καὶ δικαιοσύνῃ

fear	[75] in	holiness	and	righteousness	before	him	all	our	days.		[76]	And	you,	my child,	will be called	a
ἀφόβως	ἐν	ὁσιότητι	καὶ	δικαιοσύνῃ	ἐνώπιον	αὐτοῦ	πάσαις	ἡμῶν	⸂ταῖς ἡμέραις⸃		δὲ	Καὶ	σὺ	→ παιδίον →	→ κληθήσῃ	
adv	p.d	n.dsf	cj	n.dsf	p.g	r.gsm.3	a.dpf	r.gp.1	d.dpf n.dpf		cj	cj	r.ns.2	n.vsn	v.fpi.2s	
925	1877	4009	2779	1466	1967	899	4246	7005	3836 2465		1254	2779	5148	4086	2813	

prophet	of the Most High;	for	you will	go		on before	the Lord	to prepare	the way	for him,	[77] to give
προφήτης	→ → ὑψίστου	γὰρ	→	προπορεύσῃ	←	ἐνώπιον	κυρίου	ἑτοιμάσαι	ὁδοὺς	αὐτοῦ	⸂τοῦ δοῦναι⸃
n.nsm	a.gsm.s	cj		v.fmi.2s		p.g	n.gsm	f.aa	n.apf	r.gsm.3	d.gsn f.aa
4737	5736	1142		4638		1967	3261	2286	3847	899	3836 1443

his	people	the knowledge	of salvation	through	the	forgiveness	of their	sins,	[78] because	of the	tender	mercy	of
αὐτοῦ	τῷ λαῷ	γνῶσιν	→ σωτηρίας	ἐν		ἀφέσει	⸀ αὐτῶν	ἁμαρτιῶν	διὰ	←	σπλάγχνα	ἐλέους	→
r.gsm.3	d.dsm n.dsm	n.asf	n.gsf	p.d		n.dsf	r.gpm.3	n.gpf	p.a		n.apn	n.gsn	
899	3836 3295	1194	5401	1877		912	281 899	281	1328		5073	1799	2536

our	God,	by	which	the rising	sun	will come		to us	from	heaven	[79] to shine	on	those	living	in	darkness
ἡμῶν	θεοῦ	ἐν	οἷς	ἀνατολὴ	←	→ ἐπισκέψεται		ἡμᾶς ἐξ		ὕψους	→ ἐπιφᾶναι	→	τοῖς	καθημένοις	ἐν	σκότει
r.gp.1	n.gsm	p.d	r.dpn	n.nsf		v.fmi.3s		r.ap.1		n.gsn	f.aa		d.dpm	pt.pm.dpm	p.d	n.dsn
7005	2536	1877	4005	424		2170		7005 1666		5737	2210		3836	2764	1877	5030

and	in	the	shadow	of death,	to guide		our	feet	into	the	path	of peace."	¶	[80] And	the child
καὶ	→	σκιᾷ	→	θανάτου	⸂τοῦ κατευθῦναι⸃		ἡμῶν	⸂τοὺς πόδας⸃	εἰς		ὁδὸν	εἰρήνης		δὲ	Τὸ παιδίον
cj		n.dsf		n.gsm	d.gsn f.aa		r.gp.1	d.apm n.apm	p.a		n.asf	n.gsf		cj	d.nsn n.nsn
2779		5014		2505	3836 2985		7005	3836 4546	1650		3847	1645		1254	3836 4086

grew	and	became strong	in spirit;	and	he lived	in	the	desert	until		he	appeared publicly	to	Israel.
ηὔξανεν	καὶ	→ ἐκραταιοῦτο	→ πνεύματι	καὶ	→ ἦν	ἐν	ταῖς	ἐρήμοις	ἕως		ἡμέρας αὐτοῦ	ἀναδείξεως ←	πρὸς	⸂τὸν Ἰσραήλ⸃
v.iai.3s	cj	v.ipi.3s	n.dsn	cj	v.iai.3s	p.d	d.dpf	a.dpf	p.g		n.gsf r.gsm.3	n.gsf	p.a	d.asmn.asm
889	2779	3194	4460	2779	1639	1877	3836	2245	2401		2465 899	345	4639	38362702

The Birth of Jesus

[2:1]		In	those	days		Caesar	Augustus	issued	a	decree	that	a census		should be taken
δὲ	Ἐγένετο	ἐν	ἐκείναις	⸂ταῖς ἡμέραις⸃	παρὰ	Καίσαρος	Αὐγούστου	ἐξῆλθεν		δόγμα		ἀπογράφεσθαι ←	←	←
cj	v.ami.3s	p.d	r.dpf	d.dpf n.dpf	p.g	n.gsm	n.gsm	v.aai.3s		n.nsn		f.pp		
1254	1181	1877	1697	3836 2465	4123	2790	880	2002		1504		616		

of the	entire	Roman	world.	[2] (This	was	the	first	census	that	took place	while	Quirinius	was	governor	of
τὴν	πᾶσαν	οἰκουμένην		αὕτη	ἐγένετο		πρώτη	ἀπογραφὴ				Κυρηνίου	→	ἡγεμονεύοντος	→
d.asf	a.asf	n.asf		r.nsf	v.ami.3s		a.nsf	n.nsf				n.gsm		pt.pa.gsm	
3836	4246	3876		4047	1181		4/55	615				2448		3256	2448

Syria.)	[3] And	everyone	went		to	his	own	town	to register.	¶	[4] So	Joseph	also	went	up	from
⸂τῆς Συρίας⸃	καὶ	πάντες	ἐπορεύοντο	ἕκαστος	εἰς	ἑαυτοῦ	τὴν	πόλιν	ἀπογράφεσθαι		δὲ	Ἰωσὴφ	καὶ	Ἀνέβη ←		ἀπὸ
d.gsf n.gsf	cj	a.npm	v.imi.3p	n.nsm	p.a	r.gsm.3	d.asf	n.asf	f.pm		cj	n.nsm	adv	v.aai.3s		p.g
3836 5353	2779	4246	4513	1667	1650	1571	3836	4484	616		1254	2737	2779	326		608

	the town	of Nazareth	in Galilee		to	Judea,		to		Bethlehem	the town	of David,	because
ἐκ	πόλεως →	Ναζαρὲθ	⸂τῆς Γαλιλαίας⸃	εἰς	⸂τὴν Ἰουδαίαν⸃		εἰς	ἥτις	καλεῖται	Βηθλέεμ	πόλιν	Δαυὶδ	διὰ
p.g	n.gsf	n.gsf	d.gsf n.gsf	p.a	d.asf n.asf		p.a	r.nsf	v.ppi.3s	n.nsf	n.asf	n.gsm	p.a
1666	4484	3714	3836 1133	1650	3836 2677		1650	4015	2813	1033	4484	1253	1328

he	belonged	to the	house	and	line	of David.	[5] He went	there	to register	with	Mary,	who	was	pledged
αὐτὸν	⸂τὸ εἶναι ἐξ⸃	←	οἴκου	καὶ	πατριᾶς	→ Δαυὶδ		→	ἀπογράψασθαι	σὺν	Μαριὰμ	τῇ	→	→
r.asm.3	d.asn f.pa p.g		n.gsm	cj	n.gsf	n.gsm			f.am	p.d	n.dsf	d.dsf		
899	3836 1639 1666		3875	2779	4255	1253			616	5250	3452	3836		

to be married	to him	and	was	expecting	a child.	[6]	While	they	were		there,	the	time	came	for
→ ἐμνηστευμένῃ	αὐτῷ	οὔσῃ	→		ἐγκύῳ	δὲ	Ἐγένετο	ἐν	αὐτοὺς	⸂τῷ εἶναι⸃	ἐκεῖ	αἱ	ἡμέραι	ἐπλήσθησαν	→
pt.rp.dsf	r.dsm.3	pt.pa.dsf			a.dsf	cj	v.ami.3s	p.d	r.apm.3	d.dsn f.pa	adv	d.npf	n.npf	v.api.3p	
3650	899	1639			1607	1254	1181	1877	899	3836 1639	1695	3836	2465	4398	

the baby	to be born,		[7] and	she gave	birth	to	her	firstborn,	a	son.		She	wrapped	him	in
→	⸂τοῦ τεκεῖν⸃	αὐτήν	καὶ	→	ἔτεκεν		αὐτῆς	⸂τὸν πρωτότοκον⸃		⸂τὸν υἱόν⸃	καὶ		ἐσπαργάνωσεν	αὐτὸν	←
	d.gsn f.aa	r.asf.3	cj		v.aai.3s		r.gsf.3	d.asm a.asm		d.asm n.asm	cj		v.aai.3s	r.asm.3	
	3836 5503	899	2779		5503		899	3836 4758		3836 5626	2779		5058	899	5058

cloths	and	placed	him	in	a manger,	because	there	was	no	room	for them	in	the	inn.
←	καὶ	ἀνέκλινεν	αὐτὸν	ἐν	φάτνῃ	διότι	→	ἦν	οὐκ	τόπος	→ αὐτοῖς	ἐν	τῷ	καταλύματι
5058	cj	v.aai.3s	r.asm.3	p.d	n.dsf	cj		v.iai.3s	pl	n.nsm	r.dpm.3	p.d	d.dsn	n.dsn
	2779	369	899	1877	5764	1484		1639	4024	5536	899	1877	3836	2906

ἐνώπιον αὐτοῦ πάσαις ταῖς ἡμέραις ἡμῶν. [76] Καὶ σὺ δέ, παιδίον, προφήτης ὑψίστου κληθήσῃ· προπορεύσῃ γὰρ ἐνώπιον κυρίου ἑτοιμάσαι ὁδοὺς αὐτοῦ, [77] τοῦ δοῦναι γνῶσιν σωτηρίας τῷ λαῷ αὐτοῦ ἐν ἀφέσει ἁμαρτιῶν αὐτῶν, [78] διὰ σπλάγχνα ἐλέους θεοῦ ἡμῶν, ἐν οἷς ἐπισκέψεται ἡμᾶς ἀνατολὴ ἐξ ὕψους, [79] ἐπιφᾶναι τοῖς ἐν σκότει καὶ σκιᾷ θανάτου καθημένοις, τοῦ κατευθῦναι τοὺς πόδας ἡμῶν εἰς ὁδὸν εἰρήνης. ¶ [80] Τὸ δὲ παιδίον ηὔξανεν καὶ ἐκραταιοῦτο πνεύματι, καὶ ἦν ἐν ταῖς ἐρήμοις ἕως ἡμέρας ἀναδείξεως αὐτοῦ πρὸς τὸν Ἰσραήλ.

[2:1] Ἐγένετο δὲ ἐν ταῖς ἡμέραις ἐκείναις ἐξῆλθεν δόγμα παρὰ Καίσαρος Αὐγούστου ἀπογράφεσθαι πᾶσαν τὴν οἰκουμένην. [2] αὕτη ἀπογραφὴ πρώτη ἐγένετο ἡγεμονεύοντος τῆς Συρίας Κυρηνίου. [3] καὶ ἐπορεύοντο πάντες ἀπογράφεσθαι, ἕκαστος εἰς τὴν ἑαυτοῦ πόλιν. ¶ [4] Ἀνέβη δὲ καὶ Ἰωσὴφ ἀπὸ τῆς Γαλιλαίας ἐκ πόλεως Ναζαρὲθ εἰς τὴν Ἰουδαίαν εἰς πόλιν Δαυὶδ ἥτις καλεῖται Βηθλέεμ, διὰ τὸ εἶναι αὐτὸν ἐξ οἴκου καὶ πατριᾶς Δαυίδ, [5] ἀπογράψασθαι σὺν Μαριὰμ τῇ ἐμνηστευμένῃ αὐτῷ, οὔσῃ ἐγκύῳ. [6] ἐγένετο δὲ ἐν τῷ εἶναι αὐτοὺς ἐκεῖ ἐπλήσθησαν αἱ ἡμέραι τοῦ τεκεῖν αὐτήν, [7] καὶ ἔτεκεν τὸν υἱὸν αὐτῆς τὸν πρωτότοκον, καὶ ἐσπαργάνωσεν αὐτὸν καὶ ἀνέκλινεν αὐτὸν ἐν φάτνῃ, διότι οὐκ ἦν αὐτοῖς τόπος ἐν τῷ καταλύματι.

The Sheperds and the Angles

2:8 And there were shepherds living out in the fields nearby, keeping watch over their flocks
Καὶ → ἦσαν ποιμένες ἀγραυλοῦντες ← ἐν τῇ χώρᾳ ⌜τῇ αὐτῇ⌝ καὶ φυλάσσοντες φυλακὰς ἐπὶ αὐτῶν ⌜τὴν ποίμνην⌝
cj v.iai.3p n.npm pt.pa.npm p.d d.dsf n.dsf d.dsf r.dsf cj pt.pa.npm n.apf p.a r.gpm.3 d.asf n.asf
2779 1639 4478 64 1877 3836 6001 3836 899 2779 5875 5871 2093 899 3836 4479

at night. **9** An angel of the Lord appeared to them, and the glory of the Lord shone around them, and
τῆς νυκτὸς καὶ ἄγγελος → κυρίου ἐπέστη → αὐτοῖς καὶ δόξα κυρίου περιέλαμψεν ← αὐτούς καὶ
d.gsf n.gsf cj n.nsm n.gsm v.aai.3s r.dpm.3 cj n.nsf n.gsm v.aai.3s r.apm.3 cj
3836 3816 2779 34 3261 2392 899 2779 1518 3261 4334 899 2779

they were terrified. **10** But the angel said to them, "Do not be afraid. I bring you good
→ → ἐφοβήθησαν φόβον μέγαν. καὶ ὁ ἄγγελος εἶπεν αὐτοῖς μὴ → φοβεῖσθε γὰρ ἰδοὺ εὐαγγελίζομαι ὑμῖν ←
v.api.3p n.asm a.asm cj d.nsm n.nsm v.aai.3s r.dpm.3 pl v.ppm.2p cj v.pmi.1s r.dp.2
5828 5832 3489 2779 3836 34 3306 899 5828 3590 5828 1142 2627 2294 7007 2294

news of great joy that will be for all the people. **11** Today in the town of David a Savior has been born
μεγάλην χαρὰν ἥτις ἔσται → παντὶ τῷ λαῷ ὅτι σήμερον ἐν πόλει → Δαυίδ σωτὴρ → → ἐτέχθη
a.asf n.asf r.nsf v.fmi.3s a.dsm d.dsm n.dsm cj adv p.d n.dsf n.gsm n.nsm v.api.3s
2294 3489 5915 4015 1639 4246 3836 3295 4022 4958 1877 4484 1253 5400 5503

to you; he is Christ the Lord. **12** This will be a sign to you: You will find a baby wrapped in
ὑμῖν ὅς ἐστιν χριστὸς κύριος καὶ τοῦτο ⌜τὸ σημεῖον⌝ → ὑμῖν → εὑρήσετε βρέφος ἐσπαργανωμένον ←
r.dp.2 r.nsm v.pai.3s n.nsm n.nsm cj r.nsn d.nsn n.nsn r.dp.2 v.fai.2p n.asn pt.rp.asn
7007 4005 1639 5986 3261 2779 4047 3836 4956 7007 2351 1100 5058

cloths and lying in a manger." ¶ **13** Suddenly a great company of the heavenly host appeared with
← καὶ κείμενον ἐν φάτνῃ καὶ ἐξαίφνης πλῆθος ← οὐρανίου στρατιᾶς ἐγένετο σὺν
cj pt.pm.asn p.d n.dsf cj adv n.nsn a.gsf n.gsf v.ami.3s p.d
2779 3023 1877 5764 2779 1978 4436 4039 5131 1181 5250

the angel, praising God and saying, **14** "Glory to God in the highest, and on earth peace to men on whom
τῷ ἀγγέλῳ αἰνούντων ⌜τὸν θεὸν⌝ καὶ λεγόντων, δόξα → θεῷ ἐν ὑψίστοις καὶ ἐπὶ γῆς εἰρήνη ἐν ἀνθρώποις
d.dsm n.dsm pt.pa.gpm d.asm n.asm cj pt.pa.gpm n.nsf n.dsm p.d a.dpn.s cj p.g n.gsf n.nsf p.d n.dpm
3836 34 140 3836 2536 2779 3306 1518 2536 1877 5736 2779 2093 1178 1645 1877 476

his favor rests." **15** When the angels had left them and gone into heaven, the shepherds
εὐδοκίας. Καὶ ἐγένετο ὡς οἱ ἄγγελοι → ἀπῆλθον ἀπ' αὐτῶν εἰς ⌜τὸν οὐρανὸν⌝ οἱ ποιμένες
n.gsf cj v.ami.3s cj d.npm n.npm v.aai.3p p.g r.gpm.3 p.a d.asm n.asm d.npm n.npm
2306 2779 1181 6055 3836 34 599 608 899 1650 3836 4041 3836 4478

said to one another, "Let's go to Bethlehem and see this thing that has happened, which
ἐλάλουν πρὸς ἀλλήλους ← δὴ διέλθωμεν ἕως Βηθλέεμ καὶ ἴδωμεν τοῦτο ⌜τὸ ῥῆμα⌝ → ⌜τὸ γεγονὸς⌝ ὃ
v.iai.3p p.a r.apm pl v.aas.1p p.g n.gsf cj v.aas.1p r.asn d.asn n.asn d.asn pt.ra.asn r.asn
3281 4639 253 1314 1451 2401 1033 2779 1625 4047 3836 4839 3836 1181 4005

the Lord has told us about." ¶ **16** So they hurried off and found Mary and Joseph, and
ὁ κύριος → ἐγνώρισεν ἡμῖν ← καὶ σπεύσαντες ἦλθαν καὶ ἀνεῦραν τε ⌜τὴν Μαριὰμ⌝ καὶ ⌜τὸν Ἰωσὴφ⌝ καὶ
d.nsm n.nsm v.aai.3s r.dp.1 cj pt.aa.npm v.aai.3p cj v.aai.3p cj d.asf n.asf cj d.asm n.asm cj
3836 3261 1192 7005 1192 2779 5067 2262 2779 461 5445 3836 3452 2779 3836 2737 2779

the baby, who was lying in the manger. **17** When they had seen him, they spread the word concerning
τὸ βρέφος → → κείμενον ἐν τῇ φάτνῃ δὲ → → → ἰδόντες → ἐγνώρισαν ← περὶ
d.asn n.asn pt.pm.asn p.d d.dsf n.dsf cj pt.aa.npm v.aai.3p p.g
3836 1100 3023 1877 3836 5764 1254 1625 1192 4309

what had been told them about this child, **18** and all who heard it were amazed at
⌜τοῦ ῥήματος⌝ → ⌜τοῦ λαληθέντος⌝ αὐτοῖς περὶ τούτου ⌜τοῦ παιδίου⌝ καὶ πάντες οἱ ἀκούσαντες → ἐθαύμασαν περὶ
d.gsn n.gsn d.gsn pt.ap.gsn r.dpm.3 p.g r.gsn d.gsn n.gsn cj a.npm d.npm pt.aa.npm v.aai.3p p.g
3836 4839 3836 3281 899 4309 4047 3836 4086 2779 4246 3836 201 2513 4309

what the shepherds said to them. **19** But Mary treasured up all these things and pondered
τῶν ὑπὸ τῶν ποιμένων λαληθέντων πρὸς αὐτούς δὲ ἡ Μαριὰμ συνετήρει ← πάντα ταῦτα ⌜τὰ ῥήματα⌝ συμβάλλουσα
d.gpn p.g d.gpm n.gpm pt.ap.gpn p.a r.apm.3 cj d.nsf n.nsf v.iai.3s a.apn r.apn d.apn n.apn pt.pa.nsf
3836 5679 3836 4478 3281 4639 899 1254 3836 3452 5337 4246 4047 3836 4839 5202

them in her heart. **20** The shepherds returned, glorifying and praising God for all the things they had
ἐν αὐτῆς ⌜τῇ καρδίᾳ⌝ καὶ οἱ ποιμένες ὑπέστρεψαν δοξάζοντες καὶ αἰνοῦντες ⌜τὸν θεὸν⌝ ἐπὶ πᾶσιν οἷς → →
p.d r.gsf.3 d.dsf n.dsf cj d.npm n.npm v.aai.3p pt.pa.npm cj pt.pa.npm d.asm n.asm p.d a.dpn r.dpn
1877 899 3836 2840 2779 3836 4478 5715 1519 2779 140 3836 2536 2093 4246 4005

2:8 Καὶ ποιμένες ἦσαν ἐν τῇ χώρᾳ τῇ αὐτῇ ἀγραυλοῦντες καὶ φυλάσσοντες φυλακὰς τῆς νυκτὸς ἐπὶ τὴν ποίμνην αὐτῶν. **9** καὶ ἄγγελος κυρίου ἐπέστη αὐτοῖς καὶ δόξα κυρίου περιέλαμψεν αὐτούς, καὶ ἐφοβήθησαν φόβον μέγαν. **10** καὶ εἶπεν αὐτοῖς ὁ ἄγγελος, Μὴ φοβεῖσθε, ἰδοὺ γὰρ εὐαγγελίζομαι ὑμῖν χαρὰν μεγάλην ἥτις ἔσται παντὶ τῷ λαῷ, **11** ὅτι ἐτέχθη ὑμῖν σήμερον σωτὴρ ὅς ἐστιν Χριστὸς κύριος ἐν πόλει Δαυίδ. **12** καὶ τοῦτο ὑμῖν τὸ σημεῖον, εὑρήσετε βρέφος ἐσπαργανωμένον καὶ κείμενον ἐν φάτνῃ. ¶ **13** καὶ ἐξαίφνης ἐγένετο σὺν τῷ ἀγγέλῳ πλῆθος στρατιᾶς οὐρανίου αἰνούντων τὸν θεὸν καὶ λεγόντων, **14** Δόξα ἐν ὑψίστοις θεῷ καὶ ἐπὶ γῆς εἰρήνη ἐν ἀνθρώποις εὐδοκίας. **15** Καὶ ἐγένετο ὡς ἀπῆλθον ἀπ' αὐτῶν εἰς τὸν οὐρανὸν οἱ ἄγγελοι, οἱ ποιμένες ἐλάλουν πρὸς ἀλλήλους, Διέλθωμεν δὴ ἕως Βηθλέεμ καὶ ἴδωμεν τὸ ῥῆμα τοῦτο τὸ γεγονὸς ὃ ὁ κύριος ἐγνώρισεν ἡμῖν. ¶ **16** καὶ ἦλθαν σπεύσαντες καὶ ἀνεῦραν τήν τε Μαριὰμ καὶ τὸν Ἰωσὴφ καὶ τὸ βρέφος κείμενον ἐν τῇ φάτνῃ. **17** ἰδόντες δὲ ἐγνώρισαν περὶ τοῦ ῥήματος τοῦ λαληθέντος αὐτοῖς περὶ τοῦ παιδίου τούτου. **18** καὶ πάντες οἱ ἀκούσαντες ἐθαύμασαν περὶ τῶν λαληθέντων ὑπὸ τῶν ποιμένων πρὸς αὐτούς· **19** ἡ δὲ Μαριὰμ πάντα συνετήρει τὰ ῥήματα ταῦτα συμβάλλουσα ἐν τῇ καρδίᾳ αὐτῆς. **20** καὶ ὑπέστρεψαν οἱ

heard and seen, which were just as they had been told.
ἤκουσαν καὶ εἶδον καθὼς ← πρὸς αὐτούς → → ἐλαλήθη
v.aai.3p cj v.aai.3p cj p.a r.apm.3 v.api.3s
201 2779 1625 2777 4639 899 3281

Jesus Presented in the Temple

2:21 On the eighth day, when it was time to circumcise him, he was named
Καὶ ὀκτὼ ἡμέραι ὅτε → → ἐπλήσθησαν → ⌐τοῦ περιτεμεῖν᾽ αὐτὸν καὶ → → ⌐ἐκλήθη τὸ ὄνομα αὐτοῦ᾽
cj a.npf n.npf cj v.aai.3p d.gsn f.aa r.asm.3 cj v.api.3s d.nsn n.nsn r.gsm.3
2779 3893 2465 4021 4398 3836 4362 899 2779 2813 3836 3950 899

Jesus, the name the angel had given him before he had been conceived. ¶
Ἰησοῦς ὑπὸ τοῦ ἀγγέλου → ⌐τὸ κληθὲν᾽ πρὸ αὐτὸν → ⌐τοῦ συλλημφθῆναι᾽ ἐν τῇ κοιλίᾳ.
n.nsm p.g d.gsm n.gsm d.nsn pt.ap.nsn p.g r.asm.3 d.gsn f.ap p.d d.dsf n.dsf
2652 5679 3836 34 3836 2813 4574 899 3836 5197 1877 3836 3120

22 When the time of their purification according to the Law of Moses had been completed, Joseph and
Καὶ ὅτε αἱ ἡμέραι → αὐτῶν ⌐τοῦ καθαρισμοῦ᾽ κατὰ ← τὸν νόμον Μωϋσέως → → ἐπλήσθησαν
cj cj d.npf n.npf r.gpm.3 d.gsm n.gsm p.a d.asm n.asm n.gsm v.api.3p
2779 4021 3836 2465 2752 899 3836 2752 2848 3836 3795 3707 4398

Mary took him to Jerusalem to present him to the Lord **23** (as it is written in the Law of the Lord,
ἀνήγαγον αὐτὸν εἰς Ἱεροσόλυμα παραστῆσαι → τῷ κυρίῳ καθὼς → → γέγραπται ἐν νόμῳ → κυρίου ὅτι
v.aai.3p r.asm.3 p.a n.apn f.aa d.dsm n.dsm cj v.rpi.3s p.d n.dsm n.gsm r.gsm
343 899 1650 2642 4225 3836 3261 2777 1211 1877 3795 3261 4022

"Every firstborn male is to be consecrated to the Lord"), **24** and to offer a sacrifice in keeping
πᾶν ⌐διανοῖγον μήτραν᾽ ἄρσεν → → ⌐κληθήσεται ἅγιον᾽ → τῷ κυρίῳ καὶ ⌐τοῦ δοῦναι᾽ θυσίαν κατὰ ←
a.nsn pt.pa.nsn n.asf a.nsn v.fpi.3s a.nsn d.dsm n.dsm cj d.gsn f.aa n.asf p.a
4246 1380 3616 781 2813 41 3836 3261 2779 3836 1443 2602 2848

with what is said in the Law of the Lord: "a pair of doves or two young pigeons." ¶ **25** Now
← τὸ → εἰρημένον ἐν τῷ νόμῳ → κυρίου ζεῦγος → τρυγόνων ἢ δύο νοσσοὺς περιστερῶν Καὶ ἰδοὺ
d.asn pt.rp.asn p.d d.dsm n.dsm n.gsm n.gpf n.gpf cj a.apm n.apm n.gpf cj
3836 3306 1877 3836 3795 3261 2414 5583 2445 1545 3801 4361 2779 2627

there was a man in Jerusalem called Simeon, who was righteous and devout. He was
ἦν ἄνθρωπος ἐν Ἱερουσαλὴμ ᾧ ὄνομα Συμεὼν καὶ ὁ ἄνθρωπος οὗτος δίκαιος καὶ εὐλαβὴς → →
v.iai.3s n.nsm p.d n.dsf r.dsm n.nsn n.nsm cj d.nsm n.nsm r.nsm a.nsm cj a.nsm
1639 476 1877 2647 4005 3950 5208 2779 3836 476 4047 1465 2779 2327

waiting for the consolation of Israel, and the Holy Spirit was upon him. **26** It had been
προσδεχόμενος ← παράκλησιν → ⌐τοῦ Ἰσραήλ᾽ καὶ ἅγιον πνεῦμα ἦν ἐπ᾽ αὐτὸν καὶ
pt.pm.nsm n.asf d.gsn n.gsm cj a.nsn n.nsn v.iai.3s p.a r.asm.3 cj
4657 4155 3836 2702 2779 41 4460 1639 2093 899 2779

revealed to him by the Holy Spirit that he would not die before he had
⌐ἦν κεχρηματισμένον᾽ → αὐτῷ ὑπὸ τοῦ ⌐τοῦ ἁγίου᾽ πνεύματος ↦ μὴ ἰδεῖν θάνατον πρὶν [ἢ] ἂν →
v.iai.3s pt.rp.nsn r.dsm.3 p.g d.gsn d.gsn a.gsn n.gsn pl v.aa.inf n.asm cj pl
1639 5976 899 5679 3836 3836 41 4460 1625 1625 3590 1625 2505 4570 2445 323

seen the Lord's Christ. **27** Moved by the Spirit, he went into the temple courts. When the parents
ἤδη τὸν κυρίου χριστὸν καὶ → ἐν τῷ πνεύματι → ἦλθεν εἰς τὸ ἱερόν καὶ ἐν τοὺς γονεῖς
v.aas.3s d.asm n.gsm n.asm cj p.d d.dsn n.dsn v.aai.3s p.a d.asn n.asn cj p.d d.apm n.apm
1625 3836 3261 5986 2779 1877 3836 4460 2262 1650 3836 2639 2779 1877 3836 1204

brought in the child Jesus to do for him what the custom of the Law required, **28**
⌐τῷ εἰσαγαγεῖν᾽ ← τὸ παιδίον Ἰησοῦν αὐτοὺς → ⌐τοῦ ποιῆσαι᾽ περὶ αὐτοῦ κατὰ τὸ εἰθισμένον → τοῦ νόμου ↩ καὶ
d.dsn f.aa d.asn n.asn n.asm r.apm.3 d.gsn f.aa p.g r.gsm.3 p.a d.asn pt.rp.asn d.gsm n.gsm cj
3836 1652 3836 4086 2652 899 3836 4472 4309 899 2848 3836 1616 3836 3795 2779

Simeon took him in his arms and praised God, saying: **29** "Sovereign Lord, as you have promised, you
αὐτὸς ἐδέξατο αὐτὸ εἰς τὰς ἀγκάλας καὶ εὐλόγησεν ⌐τὸν θεὸν᾽ καὶ εἶπεν → δέσποτα κατὰ σου ⌐τὸ ῥῆμα᾽
r.nsm v.ami.3s r.asn.3 p.a d.apf n.apf cj v.aai.3s d.asm n.asm cj v.aai.3s n.vsm p.a r.gs.2 d.asn n.asn
899 1312 899 1650 3836 44 2779 2328 3836 2536 2779 3306 1305 2848 5148 3836 4839 668

now dismiss your servant in peace. **30** For my eyes have seen your salvation, **31** which you have prepared
νῦν ἀπολύεις σου ⌐τὸν δοῦλον᾽ ἐν εἰρήνῃ ὅτι μου ⌐οἱ ὀφθαλμοί᾽ εἶδον σου ⌐τὸ σωτήριον᾽ ὃ → → ἡτοίμασας
adv v.pai.2s r.gs.2 d.asm n.asm p.d n.dsf cj r.gs.1 d.npm n.npm v.aai.3p r.gs.2 d.asn n.asn r.asn v.aai.2s
3814 668 5148 3836 1529 1877 1645 4022 1609 3836 4057 1625 5148 3836 5402 4005 2286

ποιμένες δοξάζοντες καὶ αἰνοῦντες τὸν θεὸν ἐπὶ πᾶσιν οἷς ἤκουσαν καὶ εἶδον καθὼς ἐλαλήθη πρὸς αὐτούς.
2:21 Καὶ ὅτε ἐπλήσθησαν ἡμέραι ὀκτὼ τοῦ περιτεμεῖν αὐτὸν καὶ ἐκλήθη τὸ ὄνομα αὐτοῦ Ἰησοῦς, τὸ κληθὲν ὑπὸ τοῦ ἀγγέλου πρὸ τοῦ συλλημφθῆναι αὐτὸν ἐν τῇ κοιλίᾳ. ¶ **22** Καὶ ὅτε ἐπλήσθησαν αἱ ἡμέραι τοῦ καθαρισμοῦ αὐτῶν κατὰ τὸν νόμον Μωϋσέως, ἀνήγαγον αὐτὸν εἰς Ἱεροσόλυμα παραστῆσαι τῷ κυρίῳ, **23** καθὼς γέγραπται ἐν νόμῳ κυρίου ὅτι Πᾶν ἄρσεν διανοῖγον μήτραν ἅγιον τῷ κυρίῳ κληθήσεται, **24** καὶ τοῦ δοῦναι θυσίαν κατὰ τὸ εἰρημένον ἐν τῷ νόμῳ κυρίου, ζεῦγος τρυγόνων ἢ δύο νοσσοὺς περιστερῶν. ¶ **25** Καὶ ἰδοὺ ἄνθρωπος ἦν ἐν Ἱερουσαλὴμ ᾧ ὄνομα Συμεὼν καὶ ὁ ἄνθρωπος οὗτος δίκαιος καὶ εὐλαβὴς προσδεχόμενος παράκλησιν τοῦ Ἰσραήλ, καὶ πνεῦμα ἦν ἅγιον ἐπ᾽ αὐτόν· **26** καὶ ἦν αὐτῷ κεχρηματισμένον ὑπὸ τοῦ πνεύματος τοῦ ἁγίου μὴ ἰδεῖν θάνατον πρὶν [ἢ] ἂν ἴδῃ τὸν Χριστὸν κυρίου. **27** καὶ ἦλθεν ἐν τῷ πνεύματι εἰς τὸ ἱερόν· καὶ ἐν τῷ εἰσαγαγεῖν τοὺς γονεῖς τὸ παιδίον Ἰησοῦν τοῦ ποιῆσαι αὐτοὺς κατὰ τὸ εἰθισμένον τοῦ νόμου περὶ αὐτοῦ **28** καὶ αὐτὸς ἐδέξατο αὐτὸ εἰς τὰς ἀγκάλας καὶ εὐλόγησεν τὸν θεὸν καὶ εἶπεν, **29** Νῦν ἀπολύεις τὸν δοῦλόν σου, δέσποτα, κατὰ τὸ ῥῆμά σου ἐν εἰρήνῃ· **30** ὅτι εἶδον οἱ ὀφθαλμοί μου τὸ σωτήριόν σου, **31** ὃ ἡτοίμασας κατὰ πρόσωπον πάντων τῶν λαῶν, **32** φῶς

in　the sight　of all　people,　³² a light for revelation　to the Gentiles and for glory to　your people Israel."　¶
κατὰ　πρόσωπον　→ πάντων ⌐τῶν λαῶν┐　φῶς εἰς ἀποκάλυψιν →　ἐθνῶν　καὶ　δόξαν ↱ σου λαοῦ Ἰσραήλ
p.a　n.asn　a.gpm d.gpm n.gpm　n.asn p.a n.asf　n.gpn　cj　n.asf r.gs.2 n.gsm n.gsm
2848　4725　4246 3836 3295　5890 1650 637　1620　2779　1518 3295 5148 3295 2702

³³ The child's father　and mother　marveled　at what was said　about him.　³⁴ Then Simeon blessed
καὶ　αὐτοῦ ⌐ὁ πατὴρ┐ καὶ ⌐ἡ μήτηρ┐ ἦν θαυμάζοντες ἐπὶ τοῖς →　λαλουμένοις περὶ αὐτοῦ καὶ Συμεὼν εὐλόγησεν
cj　r.gsm.3 d.nsm n.nsm cj d.nsf n.nsf v.iai.3s pt.pa.npm p.d d.dpn　pt.pp.dpn p.g r.gsm.3 cj n.nsm v.aai.3s
2779　899 3836 4252 2779 3836 3613 1639 2513 2093 3836　3281 4309 899 2779 5208 2328

them and said to　Mary,　his　mother:　"This child is destined to cause the falling and rising　of many
αὐτοὺς καὶ εἶπεν πρὸς Μαριὰμ αὐτοῦ ⌐τὴν μητέρα┐ ἰδοὺ οὗτος ← → κεῖται εἰς → πτῶσιν καὶ ἀνάστασιν → πολλῶν
r.apm.3 cj v.aai.3s p.a n.asf r.gsm.3 d.asf n.asf j r.nsm v.pmi.3s p.a n.asf cj n.asf a.gpm
899 2779 3306 4639 3452 899 3836 3613 2627 4047 3023 1650 4774 2779 414 4498

in Israel,　and to be a sign　that will be spoken　against,　³⁵ so that　the thoughts　of many hearts
ἐν τῷ Ἰσραὴλ καὶ εἰς ← σημεῖον → → → ἀντιλεγόμενον ← ὅπως ← ἂν διαλογισμοὶ ἐκ πολλῶν καρδιῶν
p.d d.dsm n.dsm cj p.a n.asn pt.pp.asn cj pl n.npm p.g a.gpf n.gpf
1877 3836 2702 2779 1650 4956 515 3968 323 1369 1666 4498 2840

will be revealed.　And　a sword　will pierce　your own soul　too."　¶　³⁶ There was also a prophetess,
→ → ἀποκαλυφθῶσιν [δὲ] ῥομφαία → διελεύσεται σου αὐτῆς ⌐τὴν ψυχήν┐ καὶ → ἦν Καὶ προφῆτις
v.aps.3p cj n.nsf v.fmi.3s r.gs.2 r.gsf d.asf n.asf adv v.iai.3s cj n.nsf
636 1254 4855 1451 5148 899 3836 6034 2779 1639 2779 4739

Anna, the daughter of Phanuel, of the tribe of Asher. She was very old;　she had lived
Ἄννα θυγάτηρ → Φανουήλ ἐκ φυλῆς → Ἀσήρ αὕτη → ⌐προβεβηκυῖα ἐν ἡμέραις πολλαῖς┐ → ζήσασα
n.nsf n.nsf n.gsm p.g n.gsf n.gsf r.nsf pt.ra.nsf p.d n.dpf a.dpf pt.aa.nsf
483 2588 5750 1666 5876 818 4047 4581 1877 2465 4498 2409

with her husband seven years after her　marriage,　³⁷ and　then was a widow until she was
μετὰ ἀνδρὸς ἑπτὰ ἔτη ἀπὸ αὐτῆς ⌐τῆς παρθενίας┐ καὶ αὐτὴ χήρα ἕως
p.g n.gsm a.apn n.apn p.g r.gsf.3 d.gsf n.gsf cj r.nsf n.nsf p.g
3552 467 2231 2291 608 899 3836 4220 2779 899 5939 2401

eighty-four.　She never left　the temple but worshiped night and day,　fasting and praying.　³⁸
⌐ὀγδοήκοντα τεσσάρων ἐτῶν┐ ἣ οὐκ ἀφίστατο τοῦ ἱεροῦ λατρεύουσα νύκτα καὶ ἡμέραν νηστείαις καὶ δεήσεσιν καὶ
a.gpn a.gpn n.gpn r.nsf pl v.imi.3s d.gsn n.gsn pt.pa.nsf n.asf cj n.asf n.dpf cj n.dpf cj
3837 5475 2291 4005 4024 923 3836 2639 3302 3816 2779 2465 3763 2779 1255 2779

Coming up to them at that very moment, she gave thanks　to God　and spoke about the child to all　who
ἐπιστᾶσα ← → τῇ αὐτῇ ὥρᾳ → ἀνθωμολογεῖτο ⌐τῷ θεῷ┐ καὶ ἐλάλει περὶ αὐτοῦ → πᾶσιν τοῖς
pt.aa.nsf d.dsf r.dsf n.dsf v.imi.3s d.dsm n.dsm cj v.iai.3s p.g r.gsm.3 a.dpm d.dpm
2392 3836 899 6052 469 3836 2536 2779 3281 4309 899 4246 3836

were looking　forward to the redemption of Jerusalem.　¶　³⁹　When Joseph and Mary had done
→ προσδεχομένοις ← ← λύτρωσιν → Ἰερουσαλήμ Καὶ ὡς → ἐτέλεσαν
pt.pm.dpm n.asf n.gsf cj cj v.aai.3p
4657 3391 2647 2779 6055 5464

everything　required by　the Law of the Lord, they returned to Galilee　to their　own town of Nazareth.
πάντα τὰ → κατὰ τὸν νόμον → κυρίου ἐπέστρεψαν εἰς ⌐τὴν Γαλιλαίαν┐ εἰς ἑαυτῶν → πόλιν → Ναζαρέθ
a.apn d.apn p.a d.asm n.asm n.gsm v.aai.3p p.a d.asf n.asf p.a r.gpm.3 n.asf n.asf
4246 3836 2848 3836 3795 3261 2188 1650 3836 1133 1650 1571 4484 3714

⁴⁰ And the child　grew　and became strong;　he was filled　with wisdom, and the grace of God was upon him.
δὲ Τὸ παιδίον ηὔξανεν καὶ → ἐκραταιοῦτο → πληρούμενον → σοφίᾳ καὶ χάρις → θεοῦ ἦν ἐπ᾽ αὐτό
cj d.nsn n.nsn v.iai.3s cj v.ipi.3s pt.pp.nsn n.dsf cj n.nsf n.gsm v.iai.3s p.a r.asn.3
1254 3836 4086 889 2779 3194 4444 5053 2779 5921 2536 1639 2093 899

The Boy Jesus at the Temple

2:41 Every year his　parents　went　to Jerusalem for the Feast of the Passover.　⁴² When he was
Καὶ κατ᾽ ἔτος αὐτοῦ οἱ γονεῖς ἐπορεύοντο εἰς Ἰερουσαλήμ → τῇ ἑορτῇ τοῦ πάσχα Καὶ ὅτε → ἐγένετο
cj p.a n.asn r.gsm.3 d.npm n.npm v.imi.3p p.a n.asf d.dsf n.dsf d.gsn n.gsn cj cj v.ami.3s
2779 2848 2291 899 3836 1204 4513 1650 2647 3836 2038 3836 4247 2779 4021 1181

twelve years old, they went up　to the Feast, according to the custom.　⁴³ After the Feast was over,
δώδεκα ἐτῶν αὐτῶν → ἀναβαινόντων → τῆς ἑορτῆς κατὰ ← τὸ ἔθος καὶ → τὰς ἡμέρας → τελειωσάντων
a.gpn n.gpn r.gpm.3 pt.pa.gpm d.gsf n.gsf p.a d.asn n.asn cj d.apf n.apf pt.aa.gpm
1557 2291 899 326 3836 2038 2848 3836 1621 2779 5457 3836 2465 5457

εἰς ἀποκάλυψιν ἐθνῶν καὶ δόξαν λαοῦ σου Ἰσραήλ. ¶ ³³ καὶ ἦν ὁ πατὴρ αὐτοῦ καὶ ἡ μήτηρ θαυμάζοντες ἐπὶ τοῖς λαλουμένοις περὶ αὐτοῦ. ³⁴ καὶ εὐλόγησεν αὐτοὺς Συμεὼν καὶ εἶπεν πρὸς Μαριὰμ τὴν μητέρα αὐτοῦ, Ἰδοὺ οὗτος κεῖται εἰς πτῶσιν καὶ ἀνάστασιν πολλῶν ἐν τῷ Ἰσραὴλ καὶ εἰς σημεῖον ἀντιλεγόμενον ³⁵ —καὶ σοῦ [δὲ] αὐτῆς τὴν ψυχὴν διελεύσεται ῥομφαία—, ὅπως ἂν ἀποκαλυφθῶσιν ἐκ πολλῶν καρδιῶν διαλογισμοί. ¶ ³⁶ Καὶ ἦν Ἄννα προφῆτις, θυγάτηρ Φανουήλ, ἐκ φυλῆς Ἀσήρ· αὕτη προβεβηκυῖα ἐν ἡμέραις πολλαῖς, ζήσασα μετὰ ἀνδρὸς ἔτη ἑπτὰ ἀπὸ τῆς παρθενίας αὐτῆς ³⁷ καὶ αὐτὴ χήρα ἕως ἐτῶν ὀγδοήκοντα τεσσάρων, ἣ οὐκ ἀφίστατο τοῦ ἱεροῦ νηστείαις καὶ δεήσεσιν λατρεύουσα νύκτα καὶ ἡμέραν. ³⁸ καὶ αὐτὴ τῇ ὥρᾳ ἐπιστᾶσα ἀνθωμολογεῖτο τῷ θεῷ καὶ ἐλάλει περὶ αὐτοῦ πᾶσιν τοῖς προσδεχομένοις λύτρωσιν Ἰερουσαλήμ. ¶ ³⁹ Καὶ ὡς ἐτέλεσαν πάντα τὰ κατὰ τὸν νόμον κυρίου, ἐπέστρεψαν εἰς τὴν Γαλιλαίαν εἰς πόλιν ἑαυτῶν Ναζαρέθ. ⁴⁰ Τὸ δὲ παιδίον ηὔξανεν καὶ ἐκραταιοῦτο πληρούμενον σοφίᾳ, καὶ χάρις θεοῦ ἦν ἐπ᾽ αὐτό.

²:⁴¹ Καὶ ἐπορεύοντο οἱ γονεῖς αὐτοῦ κατ᾽ ἔτος εἰς Ἰερουσαλὴμ τῇ ἑορτῇ τοῦ πάσχα. ⁴² καὶ ὅτε ἐγένετο ἐτῶν δώδεκα,

while   his   parents   were   returning   home,   the   boy   Jesus   stayed   behind   in   Jerusalem,   but   they   were
ἐν   αὐτοὺς   →   τῷ ὑποστρέφειν   ὁ   παῖς   Ἰησοῦς   ὑπέμεινεν ←   ἐν   Ἰερουσαλήμ   καὶ   οἱ   γονεῖς αὐτοῦ   →
p.d   r.apm.3   t.dsn f.pa   d.nsm   n.nsm   n.nsm   v.aai.3s   p.d   n.dsf   cj   d.npm   n.npm   r.gsm.3
1877   899   3836 5715   3836   4090   2652   5702   1877   2647   2779   3836   1204   899

unaware   of it. ⁴⁴   Thinking   he   was   in   their   company,   they   traveled   on for a day.   Then   they
⸤οὐκ ἔγνωσαν⸥   δὲ   νομίσαντες   αὐτὸν   εἶναι   ἐν   τῇ   συνοδίᾳ   →   ἦλθον ←   →   ⸤ἡμέρας ὁδὸν⸥   καὶ   →
pl   v.aai.3p   cj   pt.aa.npm   r.asm.3   f.pa   p.d   d.dsf   n.dsf   v.aai.3p   n.gsf   n.asf   cj
4024   1182   1254   3787   899   1639   1877   3836   5322   2262   2465   3847   2779

began   looking   for   him   among   their   relatives   and   friends.   ⁴⁵   When   they   did   not   find   him,   they
→   ἀνεζήτουν ←   αὐτὸν   ἐν   τοῖς   συγγενεῦσιν   καὶ   ⸤τοῖς γνωστοῖς⸥   καὶ   →   →   →   μὴ   εὑρόντες   →
     v.iai.3p   r.asm.3   p.d   d.dpm   n.dpm   cj   d.dpm   a.dpm   cj   pl   pt.aa.npm
     349   899   1877   3836   5150   2779   3836   1196   2779   2351   2351   2351   3590   2351

went   back   to   Jerusalem   to   look   for him.   ⁴⁶   After   three   days   they   found   him   in   the   temple
ὑπέστρεψαν ←   εἰς   Ἰερουσαλὴμ   ἀναζητοῦντες ←   αὐτόν   καὶ   ἐγένετο   μετὰ   τρεῖς   ἡμέρας   →   εὗρον   αὐτὸν   ἐν   τῷ   ἱερῷ
v.aai.3p   p.a   n.asf   pt.pa.npm   r.asm.3   cj   v.ami.3s   p.a   a.apf   n.apf   v.aai.3p   r.asm.3   p.d   d.dsn   n.dsn
5715   1650   2647   349   899   2779   1181   3552   5552   2465   2351   899   1877   3836   2639

courts,   sitting   among   the   teachers,   listening   to   them   and   asking   them   questions.   ⁴⁷   Everyone   who
←   καθεζόμενον   ἐν   μέσῳ   τῶν   διδασκάλων   καὶ   ἀκούοντα ←   αὐτῶν   καὶ   ἐπερωτῶντα αὐτούς ←   δὲ   πάντες   οἱ
     pt.pm.asm   p.d   n.dsn   d.gpm   n.gpm   cj   pt.pa.asm   r.gpm.3   cj   pt.pa.asm   r.apm.3   cj   a.npm   d.npm
     2757   1877   3545   3836   1437   2779   201   899   2779   2089   899   2089   1254   4246   3836

heard   him   was   amazed   at   his   understanding   and   his   answers.   ⁴⁸   When   his   parents   saw   him,   they
ἀκούοντες   αὐτοῦ   →   ἐξίσταντο   ἐπὶ   τῇ   συνέσει   καὶ   αὐτοῦ   ⸤ταῖς ἀποκρίσεσιν⸥   καὶ   →   →   ἰδόντες   αὐτὸν   →
pt.pa.npm   r.gsm.3   v.imi.3p   p.d   d.dsf   n.dsf   cj   r.gsm.3   d.dpf   n.dpf   cj   pt.aa.npm   r.asm.3
201   899   2014   2093   3836   5304   2779   899   3836   647   2779   1625   899

were   astonished.   His   mother   said   to   him,   "Son,   why   have   you   treated   us   like   this?   Your   father
→   ἐξεπλάγησαν   καὶ   αὐτοῦ   ⸤ἡ   μήτηρ⸥   εἶπεν   πρὸς   αὐτὸν   τέκνον   τί   →   →   ἐποίησας   ἡμῖν   οὕτως ←   ἰδοὺ   σου   ⸤ὁ   πατήρ⸥
     v.api.3p   cj   r.gsm.3   d.nsf   n.nsf   v.aai.3s   p.a   r.asm.3   n.vsn   r.asn   v.aai.2s   r.dp.1   adv   2627   r.gs.2   d.nsm   n.nsm
     1742   2779   899   3836   3613   3306   4639   899   5451   5515   4472   7005   4048   2627   5148   3836   4252

and   I have been   anxiously   searching   for you."   ¶   ⁴⁹   "Why   were   you   searching   for me?"   he asked.
κἀγὼ ←   →   ὀδυνώμενοι   ἐζητοῦμεν ←   σε   →   →   καὶ   τί   ὅτι   →   ἐζητεῖτε ←   με   →   εἶπεν   πρὸς
crasis   pt.pp.npm   v.iai.1p   r.as.2   cj   r.asn   ὅτι   v.iai.2p   r.as.1   v.aai.3s   p.a
2743   2426   2426   3849   2426   5148   2779   5515   4022   2426   1609   3306   4639

"Didn't   you   know   I   had   to   be   in   my   Father's   house?"   ¶   ⁵⁰   But   they   did   not   understand
αὐτούς   οὐκ   →   ᾔδειτε   ὅτι   με   δεῖ   →   εἶναι   ἐν   μου   ⸤τοῦ πατρός⸥   τοῖς   καὶ   αὐτοὶ   →   οὐ   συνῆκαν
r.apm.3   pl   v.lai.2p   cj   r.as.1   v.pai.3s   f.pa   p.d   r.gs.1   d.gsm   n.gsm   d.dpn   cj   r.npm   pl   v.aai.3p
899   4024   3857   4022   1609   1256   1639   1877   1609   3836   4252   3836   2779   5317   4024   5317

what   he   was   saying   to them. ⁵¹   Then   he   went   down   to   Nazareth   with   them   and   was   obedient   to
⸤τὸ ῥῆμα⸥   ὃ   →   ἐλάλησεν   →   αὐτοῖς   καὶ   →   κατέβη   καὶ   ἦλθεν   εἰς   Ναζαρὲθ   μετ'   αὐτῶν   καὶ   ἦν   ὑποτασσόμενος   →
d.asn   n.asn   r.asn   v.aai.3s   r.dpm.3   cj   v.aai.3s   cj   v.aai.3s   p.a   n.asf   p.g   r.gpm.3   cj   v.iai.3s   pt.pp.nsm
3836   4839   4005   3281   899   2779   2849   2779   2262   1650   3714   3552   899   2779   1639   5718

them.   But   his   mother   treasured   all   these   things   in   her   heart.   ⁵²   And   Jesus   grew   in   wisdom   and
αὐτοῖς   καὶ   αὐτοῦ   ⸤ἡ   μήτηρ⸥   διετήρει   πάντα   τὰ   ῥήματα   ἐν   αὐτῆς   ⸤τῇ   καρδίᾳ⸥   Καὶ   Ἰησοῦς   προέκοπτεν   ἐν   ⸤τῇ   σοφίᾳ⸥   καὶ
r.dpm.3   cj   r.gsm.3   d.nsf   n.nsf   v.iai.3s   a.apn   d.apn   n.apn   p.d   r.gsf.3   d.dsf   n.dsf   cj   n.nsm   v.iai.3s   p.d   d.dsf   n.dsf   cj
899   2779   899   3836   3613   1413   4246   3836   4839   1877   899   3836   2840   2779   2652   4621   1877   3836   5053   2779

stature,   and   in   favor   with   God   and   men.
ἡλικίᾳ   καὶ   →   χάριτι   παρὰ   θεῷ   καὶ   ἀνθρώποις
n.dsf   cj   n.dsf   p.d   n.dsm   cj   n.dpm
2461   2779   5921   4123   2536   2779   476

John the Baptist Prepares the Way

⁴³·¹   In   the   fifteenth   year   of the   reign   of   Tiberius   Caesar   – when   Pontius   Pilate   was   governor   of
δὲ   Ἐν   πεντεκαιδεκάτῳ   ἔτει   →   τῆς   ἡγεμονίας   →   Τιβερίου   Καίσαρος   ↱   Ποντίου   Πιλάτου   →   ἡγεμονεύοντος   →
cj   p.d   a.dsn   n.dsn   d.gsf   n.gsf   n.gsm   n.gsm   n.gsm   n.gsm   pt.pa.gsm
1254   1877   4298   2291   3836   2449   5501   2790   2448   4508   4397   2448

ἀναβαινόντων αὐτῶν κατὰ τὸ ἔθος τῆς ἑορτῆς ⁴³ καὶ τελειωσάντων τὰς ἡμέρας, ἐν τῷ ὑποστρέφειν αὐτοὺς ὑπέμεινεν Ἰησοῦς ὁ παῖς ἐν Ἰερουσαλήμ, καὶ οὐκ ἔγνωσαν οἱ γονεῖς αὐτοῦ. ⁴⁴ νομίσαντες δὲ αὐτὸν εἶναι ἐν τῇ συνοδίᾳ ἦλθον ἡμέρας ὁδὸν καὶ ἀνεζήτουν αὐτὸν ἐν τοῖς συγγενεῦσιν καὶ τοῖς γνωστοῖς, ⁴⁵ καὶ μὴ εὑρόντες ὑπέστρεψαν εἰς Ἰερουσαλὴμ ἀναζητοῦντες αὐτόν. ⁴⁶ καὶ ἐγένετο μετὰ ἡμέρας τρεῖς εὗρον αὐτὸν ἐν τῷ ἱερῷ καθεζόμενον ἐν μέσῳ τῶν διδασκάλων καὶ ἀκούοντα αὐτῶν καὶ ἐπερωτῶντα αὐτούς· ⁴⁷ ἐξίσταντο δὲ πάντες οἱ ἀκούοντες αὐτοῦ ἐπὶ τῇ συνέσει καὶ ταῖς ἀποκρίσεσιν αὐτοῦ. ⁴⁸ καὶ ἰδόντες αὐτὸν ἐξεπλάγησαν, καὶ εἶπεν πρὸς αὐτὸν ἡ μήτηρ αὐτοῦ, Τέκνον, τί ἐποίησας ἡμῖν οὕτως; ἰδοὺ ὁ πατήρ σου κἀγὼ ὀδυνώμενοι ἐζητοῦμέν σε. ¶ ⁴⁹ καὶ εἶπεν πρὸς αὐτούς, Τί ὅτι ἐζητεῖτέ με; οὐκ ᾔδειτε ὅτι ἐν τοῖς τοῦ πατρός μου δεῖ εἶναί με; ¶ ⁵⁰ καὶ αὐτοὶ οὐ συνῆκαν τὸ ῥῆμα ὃ ἐλάλησεν αὐτοῖς. ⁵¹ καὶ κατέβη μετ' αὐτῶν καὶ ἦλθεν εἰς Ναζαρὲθ καὶ ἦν ὑποτασσόμενος αὐτοῖς. καὶ ἡ μήτηρ αὐτοῦ διετήρει πάντα τὰ ῥήματα ἐν τῇ καρδίᾳ αὐτῆς. ⁵² Καὶ Ἰησοῦς προέκοπτεν [ἐν τῇ] σοφίᾳ καὶ ἡλικίᾳ καὶ χάριτι παρὰ θεῷ καὶ ἀνθρώποις.

³·¹ Ἐν ἔτει δὲ πεντεκαιδεκάτῳ τῆς ἡγεμονίας Τιβερίου Καίσαρος, ἡγεμονεύοντος Ποντίου Πιλάτου τῆς Ἰουδαίας, καὶ

Judea,		Herod	tetrarch		of	Galilee,		his	brother	Philip	tetrarch		of
ιτῆς Ἰουδαίας,	καὶ	Ἡρῴδου	τετρααρχοῦντος	→	ιτῆς Γαλιλαίας,		δὲ	αὐτοῦ	τοῦ ἀδελφοῦ,	Φιλίππου	τετραρχοῦντος	χώρας	→
d.gsf n.gsf	cj	n.gsm	pt.pa.gsm		d.gsf n.gsf		cj	r.gsm.3	d.gsm n.gsm	n.gsm	pt.pa.gsm		n.gsf
3836 2677	2779	2476	5489		3836 1133		1254	899	3836 81	5805	5489		6001

Iturea		and	Traconitis,		and	Lysanias	tetrarch		of	Abilene	–	2 during the high priesthood of
ιτῆς Ἰτουραίας,	καὶ		Τραχωνίτιδος	χώρας	καὶ	Λυσανίου	τετραρχοῦντος	→	ιτῆς Ἀβιληνῆς,		ἐπὶ	→	ἀρχιερέως	→
d.gsf n.gsf	cj		n.gsf	n.gsf	cj	n.gsm	pt.pa.gsm		d.gsf n.gsf		p.g		n.gsm
3836 2714	2779		5551	6001	2779	3384	5489		3836 9		2093		797

Annas	and	Caiaphas,	the	word	of	God	came	to	John	son		of	Zechariah	in	the	desert.	3		He	went	into
Ἅννα	καὶ	Καϊάφα		ῥῆμα	→	θεοῦ	ἐγένετο	ἐπὶ	Ἰωάννην	ιτὸν υἱόν,	→		Ζαχαρίου	ἐν	τῇ	ἐρήμῳ	καὶ	→	ἦλθεν	εἰς
n.gsm	cj	n.gsm		n.nsn		n.gsm	v.ami.3s	p.a	n.asm	d.asm n.asm			n.gsm	p.d	d.dsf	n.dsf	cj		v.aai.3s	p.a
484	2779	2780		4839		2536	1181	2093	2722	3836 5626			2408	1877	3836	2245	2779		2262	1650

all	the	country	around	the	Jordan,	preaching	a	baptism	of	repentance	for	the	forgiveness	of	sins.	4 As	is
πᾶσαν	τὴν	περίχωρον	←	τοῦ	Ἰορδάνου	κηρύσσων		βάπτισμα	→	μετανοίας	εἰς		ἄφεσιν	→	ἁμαρτιῶν	ὡς	→
a.asf	d.asf	a.asf		d.gsm	n.gsm	pt.pa.nsm		n.asn		n.gsf	p.a		n.asf		n.gpf	cj
4246	3836	4369		3836	2674	3062		967		3567	1650		912		281	6055

written	in	the	book	of	the	words	of	Isaiah	the	prophet:	"A	voice	of	one	calling	in	the	desert,	'Prepare	the	way
γέγραπται	ἐν		βίβλῳ	→		λόγων	→	Ἠσαίου	τοῦ	προφήτου		φωνὴ	→		βοῶντος	ἐν	τῇ	ἐρήμῳ	ἑτοιμάσατε	τὴν	ὁδὸν
v.rpi.3s	p.d		n.dsf			n.gpm		n.gpm	d.gsm	n.gsm		n.nsf			pt.pa.gsm	p.d	d.dsf	n.dsf	v.aam.2p	d.asf	n.asf
1211	1877		1047			3364		2480	3836	4737		5889			1066	1877	3836	2245	2286	3836	3847

for	the	Lord,	make	straight	paths		for	him.	5 Every	valley	shall	be	filled		in,	every	mountain	and	hill
→		κυρίου	ποιεῖτε	εὐθείας	ιτὰς τρίβους,	→		αὐτοῦ	πᾶσα	φάραγξ	→		πληρωθήσεται	←		καὶ	πᾶν	ὄρος	καὶ	βουνὸς
		n.gsm	v.pam.2p	a.apf	d.apf n.apf			r.gsm.3	a.nsf	n.nsf			v.fpi.3s			cj	a.nsn	n.nsn	cj	n.nsm
		3261	4472	2318	3836 5561			899	4246	5754			4444			2779	4246	4001	2779	1090

made	low.		The	crooked	roads	shall	become		straight,		the	rough		ways	smooth.	6 And	all
→	ταπεινωθήσεται	καὶ	τὰ	σκολιὰ	→		ἔσται	εἰς	εὐθείαν	καὶ	αἱ	τραχεῖαι	εἰς	ὁδοὺς	λείας	καὶ	πᾶσα
	v.fpi.3s	cj	d.npn	a.npn			v.fmi.3s	p.a	a.asf	cj	d.npf	a.npf	p.a	n.apf	a.apf	cj	a.nsf
	5427	2779	3836	5021			1639	1650	2318	2779	3836	5550	1650	3847	3308	2779	4246

mankind	will	see	God's	salvation.'"	¶	7		John	said		to	the	crowds	coming		out	to	be	baptized
σάρξ	→	ὄψεται	ιτοῦ θεοῦ,	ιτὸ σωτήριον,			οὖν		Ἔλεγεν	→	τοῖς	ὄχλοις	ἐκπορευομένοις	←	→	βαπτισθῆναι
n.nsf		v.fmi.3s	d.gsm n.gsm	d.asn n.asn			cj		v.iai.3s		d.dpm	n.dpm	pt.pm.dpm			f.ap
4922		3972	3836 2536	3836 5402			4036		3306		3836	4063	1744			966

by	him,	"You	brood		of	vipers!	Who	warned	you	to	flee		from	the	coming	wrath?	8		Produce	fruit	in
ὑπ'	αὐτοῦ	→	γεννήματα	→	ἐχιδνῶν	τίς	ὑπέδειξεν	ὑμῖν	→	φυγεῖν	ἀπὸ	τῆς	μελλούσης	ὀργῆς		οὖν	ποιήσατε	καρποὺς	→
p.g	r.gsm.3		n.vpn		n.gpf	r.nsm	v.aai.3s	r.dp.2		f.aa	p.g	d.gsf	pt.pa.gsf	n.gsf		cj	v.aam.2p	n.apm
5679	899		1165		2399	5515	5683	7007		5771	608	3836	3516	3973		4036	4472	2843

keeping	with	repentance.	And	do	not	begin	to	say	to	yourselves,	'We	have	Abraham		as	our	father.'	For	I
ἀξίους	←	ιτῆς μετανοίας,	καὶ	→	μὴ	ἄρξησθε	→	λέγειν	ἐν	ἑαυτοῖς	→	ἔχομεν	ιτὸν Ἀβραάμ,			πατέρα		γὰρ	
a.apm		d.gsf n.gsf	cj		pl	v.ams.2p		f.pa	p.d	r.dpm.2		v.pai.1p	d.asm n.asm			n.asm		cj	
545		3836 3567	2779		3590	806		3306	1877	1571		2400	3836 11			4252		1142	

tell	you	that	out	of	these	stones	God		can		raise	up	children	for	Abraham.	9		The	ax	is
λέγω	ὑμῖν	ὅτι	ἐκ	←	τούτων	ιτῶν λίθων,	ὁ	θεὸς	δύναται	ἐγεῖραι	←		τέκνα	→	ιτῷ Ἀβραάμ,		δὲ	καὶ ἡ	ἀξίνη	κεῖται
v.pai.1s	r.dp.2	cj	p.g		r.gpm	d.gpm n.gpm	d.nsm	n.nsm	v.ppi.3s	f.aa			n.apn		d.dsm n.dsm		cj	adv d.nsf	n.nsf	v.pmi.3s
3306	7007	4022	1666		4047	3836 3345	3836	2536	1538	1586			5451		3836 11		1254	2779 3836	544	3023

already	at	the	root	of	the	trees,	and	every	tree	that	does	not	produce	good	fruit	will	be	cut		down	and
ἤδη	πρὸς	τὴν	ῥίζαν	→	τῶν	δένδρων	οὖν	πᾶν	δένδρον			μὴ	ποιοῦν	καλὸν	καρπὸν	→		ἐκκόπτεται	←		καὶ
adv	p.a	d.asf	n.asf		d.gpn	n.gpn	cj	a.nsn	n.nsn			pl	pt.pa.nsn	a.asm	n.asm			v.ppi.3s			cj
2453	4639	3836	4844		3836	1285	4036	4246	1285			4472	3590	2819	2843			1716			2779

thrown	into	the	fire."	¶	10		"What	should	we	do		then?"	the	crowd	asked.		11		John
βάλλεται	εἰς		πῦρ			Καὶ	τί	→	→	ποιήσωμεν	οὖν	οἱ	ὄχλοι	ἐπηρώτων	αὐτὸν	λέγοντες		δὲ	
v.ppi.3s	p.a		n.asn			cj	r.asn			v.aas.1p	cj	d.npm	n.npm	v.iai.3p	r.asm.3	pt.pa.npm		cj	
965	1650		4786			2779	5515			4472	4036	3836	4063	2089	899	3306		1254	

answered,		"The	man	with	two	tunics	should	share	with	him	who	has		none,	and	the	one	who
ἀποκριθεὶς	ἔλεγεν	αὐτοῖς	ὁ		ἔχων	δύο	χιτῶνας	→	μεταδότω	τῷ	←		ἔχοντι	μὴ	καὶ	ὁ	←	
pt.ap.nsm	v.iai.3s	r.dpm.3	d.nsm		pt.pa.nsm	a.apm	n.apm		v.aam.3s	d.dsm			pt.pa.dsm	pl	cj	d.nsm	
646	3306	899	3836		2400	1545	5945		3556	3836			2400	3590	2779	3836	

τετρααρχοῦντος τῆς Γαλιλαίας Ἡρῴδου, Φιλίππου δὲ τοῦ ἀδελφοῦ αὐτοῦ τετρααρχοῦντος τῆς Ἰτουραίας καὶ Τραχωνίτιδος χώρας, καὶ Λυσανίου τῆς Ἀβιληνῆς τετρααρχοῦντος, ² ἐπὶ ἀρχιερέως Ἅννα καὶ Καϊάφα, ἐγένετο ῥῆμα θεοῦ ἐπὶ Ἰωάννην τὸν Ζαχαρίου υἱὸν ἐν τῇ ἐρήμῳ. ³ καὶ ἦλθεν εἰς πᾶσαν [τὴν] περίχωρον τοῦ Ἰορδάνου κηρύσσων βάπτισμα μετανοίας εἰς ἄφεσιν ἁμαρτιῶν, ⁴ ὡς γέγραπται ἐν βίβλῳ λόγων Ἠσαίου τοῦ προφήτου, Φωνὴ βοῶντος ἐν τῇ ἐρήμῳ, Ἑτοιμάσατε τὴν ὁδὸν κυρίου, εὐθείας ποιεῖτε τὰς τρίβους αὐτοῦ· ⁵ πᾶσα φάραγξ πληρωθήσεται καὶ πᾶν ὄρος καὶ βουνὸς ταπεινωθήσεται, καὶ ἔσται τὰ σκολιὰ εἰς εὐθείαν καὶ αἱ τραχεῖαι εἰς ὁδοὺς λείας· ⁶ καὶ ὄψεται πᾶσα σὰρξ τὸ σωτήριον τοῦ θεοῦ. ¶ ⁷ Ἔλεγεν οὖν τοῖς ἐκπορευομένοις ὄχλοις βαπτισθῆναι ὑπ' αὐτοῦ, Γεννήματα ἐχιδνῶν, τίς ὑπέδειξεν ὑμῖν φυγεῖν ἀπὸ τῆς μελλούσης ὀργῆς; ⁸ ποιήσατε οὖν καρποὺς ἀξίους τῆς μετανοίας καὶ μὴ ἄρξησθε λέγειν ἐν ἑαυτοῖς, Πατέρα ἔχομεν τὸν Ἀβραάμ. λέγω γὰρ ὑμῖν ὅτι δύναται ὁ θεὸς ἐκ τῶν λίθων τούτων ἐγεῖραι τέκνα τῷ Ἀβραάμ. ⁹ ἤδη δὲ καὶ ἡ ἀξίνη πρὸς τὴν ῥίζαν τῶν δένδρων κεῖται· πᾶν οὖν δένδρον μὴ ποιοῦν καρπὸν καλὸν ἐκκόπτεται καὶ εἰς πῦρ βάλλεται. ¶ ¹⁰ Καὶ ἐπηρώτων αὐτὸν οἱ ὄχλοι λέγοντες, Τί οὖν ποιήσωμεν; ¹¹ ἀποκριθεὶς δὲ ἔλεγεν αὐτοῖς, Ὁ ἔχων δύο χιτῶνας μεταδότω τῷ μὴ ἔχοντι, καὶ ὁ ἔχων βρώματα ὁμοίως ποιείτω. ¶ ¹² ἦλθον δὲ καὶ τελῶναι βαπτισθῆναι

has food should do the same." ¶ **12** Tax collectors also came to be baptized. "Teacher," they
ἔχων βρώματα → ποιείτω → ὁμοίως δὲ τελῶναι καὶ ἦλθον → βαπτισθῆναι καὶ διδάσκαλε →
pt.pa.nsm n.apn v.pam.3s adv cj n.npm adv v.aai.3p f.ap cj n.vsm
2400 1109 4472 3931 1254 5467 2779 2262 966 2779 1437

asked, "what should we do?" **13** "Don't collect any more than you are required to,"
εἶπαν πρὸς αὐτόν τί → → ποιήσωμεν δὲ μηδὲν πράσσετε πλέον → ὑμῖν παρὰ τὸ διατεταγμένον
v.aai.3p p.a r.asm.3 r.asn v.aas.1p cj a.asn v.pam.2p a.asn.c r.dp.2 p.a d.asn pt.rp.asn
3306 4639 899 5515 4472 1254 3594 4556 4498 4123 7007 4123 3836 1411

he told them. ¶ **14** Then some soldiers asked him, "And what should we do?"
ὁ εἶπεν πρὸς αὐτούς δὲ καὶ στρατευόμενοι ἐπηρώτων αὐτὸν λέγοντες καὶ τί → ἡμεῖς ποιήσωμεν καὶ
d.nsm v.aai.3s p.a r.apm.3 cj adv pt.pm.npm v.iai.3p r.asm.3 pt.pa.npm adv r.asn r.np.1 v.aas.1p cj
3836 3306 4639 899 1254 2779 5129 2089 899 3306 2779 5515 4472 7005 4472 2779

He replied, "Don't extort money and don't accuse people falsely – be content with your
→ εἶπεν αὐτοῖς μηδένα διασείσητε ← μηδὲ ← συκοφαντήσητε ← καὶ → ἀρκεῖσθε → ὑμῶν
v.aai.3s r.dpm.3 a.asm v.aas.2p cj v.aas.2p cj v.ppm.2p r.gp.2
3306 899 3594 1398 3593 5193 2779 758 4072 7007

pay." ¶ **15** The people were waiting expectantly and were all wondering in their
τοῖς ὀψωνίοις δὲ τοῦ λαοῦ → Προσδοκῶντος ← καὶ → πάντων διαλογιζομένων ἐν αὐτῶν
d.dpn n.dpn cj d.gsm n.gsm pt.pa.gsm cj a.gpm pt.pm.gpm p.d r.gpm.3
3836 4072 1254 3836 3295 4659 2779 1368 4246 1368 1877 899

hearts if John might possibly be the Christ. **16** John answered them all,
ταῖς καρδίαις περὶ τοῦ Ἰωάννου αὐτὸς μήποτε εἴη ὁ χριστός ὁ Ἰωάννης ἀπεκρίνατο λέγων πᾶσιν λέγων μὲν
d.dpf n.dpf p.g d.gsm n.gsm r.nsm v.pao.3s d.nsm n.nsm d.nsm n.nsm v.ami.3s pt.pa.nsm a.dpm pt.pa.nsm pl
3836 2840 4309 3836 2722 899 1639 3607 1639 3836 5986 3836 2722 646 3306 4246 3306 3525

"I baptize you with water. But one more powerful than I will come, the thongs of whose sandals I
ἐγὼ βαπτίζω ὑμᾶς → ὕδατι δὲ ὁ → ἰσχυρότερος μου → ἔρχεται τὸν ἱμάντα → οὗ τῶν ὑποδημάτων αὐτοῦ
r.ns.1 v.pai.1s r.ap.2 n.dsn cj d.nsm a.nsm.c r.gs.1 v.pmi.3s d.asm n.asm r.gsm d.gpn n.gpn r.gsm.3
1609 966 7007 5623 1254 3836 2708 1609 2262 3836 2666 4005 3836 5687 899

am not worthy to untie. He will baptize you with the Holy Spirit and with fire. **17** His winnowing fork is in
εἰμὶ οὐκ ἱκανὸς → λῦσαι αὐτὸς → βαπτίσει ὑμᾶς ἐν ἁγίῳ πνεύματι καὶ → πυρί οὗ → τὸ πτύον ἐν
v.pai.1s pl a.nsm f.aa r.nsm v.fai.3s r.ap.2 p.d a.dsn n.dsn cj n.dsn r.gsm d.nsn n.nsn p.d
1639 4024 2653 3395 899 966 7007 1877 41 4460 2779 4786 4005 3836 4768 1877

his hand to clear his threshing floor and to gather the wheat into his barn, but he
αὐτοῦ τῇ χειρὶ → διακαθᾶραι αὐτοῦ τὴν ἅλωνα καὶ → συναγαγεῖν τὸν σῖτον εἰς αὐτοῦ τὴν ἀποθήκην δὲ →
r.gsm.3 d.dsf n.dsf f.aa r.gsm.3 d.asf n.asf cj f.aa d.asm n.asm p.a r.gsm.3 d.asf n.asf cj
899 3836 5931 1350 899 3836 272 2779 5251 3836 4992 1650 899 3836 630 1254

will burn up the chaff with unquenchable fire." **18** And with many other words John exhorted the
→ κατακαύσει τὸ ἄχυρον → ἀσβέστῳ πυρὶ οὖν μὲν καὶ Πολλὰ ἕτερα παρακαλῶν τὸν
v.fai.3s d.asn n.asn a.dsn n.dsn pl pl cj a.apn a.apn pt.pa.nsm d.asm
2876 3836 949 812 4786 4036 3525 2779 4498 2283 4151 3836

people and preached the good news to them. ¶ **19** But when John rebuked Herod the tetrarch
λαόν εὐηγγελίζετο δὲ ὑπ᾽ αὐτοῦ ἐλεγχόμενος Ὁ Ἡρῴδης ὁ τετραάρχης
n.asm v.imi.3s cj p.g r.gsm.3 pt.pp.nsm d.nsm n.nsm d.nsm n.nsm
3295 2294 1254 1794 5679 899 1794 3836 2476 3836 5490

because of Herodias, his brother's wife, and all the other evil things he had
περὶ Ἡρῳδιάδος αὐτοῦ τοῦ ἀδελφοῦ τῆς γυναικὸς καὶ περὶ πάντων πονηρῶν ὁ Ἡρῴδης ὧν
p.g n.gsf r.gsm.3 d.gsm n.gsm d.gsf n.gsf cj p.g a.gpn a.gpn d.nsm n.nsm r.gpn
4309 2478 899 3836 81 3836 1222 2779 4309 4246 4505 3836 2476 4005

done, **20** Herod added this to them all: He locked John up in prison.
ἐποίησεν καὶ προσέθηκεν τοῦτο ἐπὶ πᾶσιν [καὶ] → κατέκλεισεν τὸν Ἰωάννην ἐν φυλακῇ
v.aai.3s cj v.aai.3s r.asn p.d a.dpn cj v.aai.3s d.asm n.asm p.d n.dsf
4472 2779 4707 4047 2093 4246 2779 2881 3836 2722 1877 5871

The Baptism and Genealogy of Jesus

3:21 When all the people were being baptized, Jesus was baptized too. And as he was
δὲ Ἐγένετο ἐν ἅπαντα τὸν λαὸν → → τῷ βαπτισθῆναι Ἰησοῦ βαπτισθέντος καὶ καὶ → →
cj v.ami.3s p.d a.asm d.asm n.asm d.dsn f.ap n.gsm pt.ap.gsm cj cj
1254 1181 1877 570 3836 3295 3836 966 2652 966 2779 2779

καὶ εἶπαν πρὸς αὐτόν, Διδάσκαλε, τί ποιήσωμεν; ¹³ ὁ δὲ εἶπεν πρὸς αὐτούς, Μηδὲν πλέον παρὰ τὸ διατεταγμένον ὑμῖν
πράσσετε. ¶ ¹⁴ ἐπηρώτων δὲ αὐτὸν καὶ στρατευόμενοι λέγοντες, Τί ποιήσωμεν καὶ ἡμεῖς; καὶ εἶπεν αὐτοῖς, Μηδένα διασείσητε
μηδὲ συκοφαντήσητε καὶ ἀρκεῖσθε τοῖς ὀψωνίοις ὑμῶν. ¶ ¹⁵ Προσδοκῶντος δὲ τοῦ λαοῦ καὶ διαλογιζομένων πάντων ἐν ταῖς
καρδίαις αὐτῶν περὶ τοῦ Ἰωάννου, μήποτε αὐτὸς εἴη ὁ Χριστός, ¹⁶ ἀπεκρίνατο λέγων πᾶσιν ὁ Ἰωάννης, Ἐγὼ μὲν ὕδατι βαπτίζω
ὑμᾶς· ἔρχεται δὲ ὁ ἰσχυρότερός μου, οὗ οὐκ εἰμὶ ἱκανὸς λῦσαι τὸν ἱμάντα τῶν ὑποδημάτων αὐτοῦ· αὐτὸς ὑμᾶς βαπτίσει ἐν
πνεύματι ἁγίῳ καὶ πυρί· ¹⁷ οὗ τὸ πτύον ἐν τῇ χειρὶ αὐτοῦ διακαθᾶραι τὴν ἅλωνα αὐτοῦ καὶ συναγαγεῖν τὸν σῖτον εἰς τὴν
ἀποθήκην αὐτοῦ, τὸ δὲ ἄχυρον κατακαύσει πυρὶ ἀσβέστῳ. ¹⁸ Πολλὰ μὲν οὖν καὶ ἕτερα παρακαλῶν εὐηγγελίζετο τὸν λαόν ¶
¹⁹ ὁ δὲ Ἡρῴδης ὁ τετραάρχης, ἐλεγχόμενος ὑπ᾽ αὐτοῦ περὶ Ἡρῳδιάδος τῆς γυναικὸς τοῦ ἀδελφοῦ αὐτοῦ καὶ περὶ πάντων ὧν
ἐποίησεν πονηρῶν ὁ Ἡρῴδης, ²⁰ προσέθηκεν καὶ τοῦτο ἐπὶ πᾶσιν [καὶ] κατέκλεισεν τὸν Ἰωάννην ἐν φυλακῇ.
3:21 Ἐγένετο δὲ ἐν τῷ βαπτισθῆναι ἅπαντα τὸν λαὸν καὶ Ἰησοῦ βαπτισθέντος καὶ προσευχομένου ἀνεῳχθῆναι τὸν οὐρανὸν

praying, | heaven | was | opened | **22** and | the | Holy | Spirit | descended | on | him | in | bodily | form | like | a
προσευχομένου | τὸν οὐρανὸν | → | ἀνεῳχθῆναι | καὶ | τὸ | τὸ ἅγιον | πνεῦμα | καταβῆναι | ἐπ' | αὐτόν | → | σωματικῷ | εἴδει | ὡς
pt.pm.gsm | d.asm n.asm | | f.ap | cj | d.asn | d.asn a.asn | n.asn | f.aa | p.a | r.asm.3 | | a.dsn | n.dsn | pl
4667 | 3836 4041 | | 487 | 2779 | 3836 | 3836 41 | 4460 | 2849 | 2093 | 899 | | 5394 | 1626 | 6055

dove. | And | a | voice | came | from | heaven: | "You | are | my | Son, | whom | I love; | with | you | I am | well
περιστερὰν | καὶ | | φωνὴν | γενέσθαι | ἐξ | οὐρανοῦ | σὺ | εἶ | μου | ὁ υἱός, | ὁ | ἀγαπητός, | ἐν | σοὶ | → | →
n.asf | cj | | n.asf | f.am | p.g | n.gsm | r.ns.2 | v.pai.2s | r.gs.1 | d.nsm n.nsm | d.nsm | a.nsm | p.d | r.ds.2 | |
4361 | 2779 | | 5889 | 1181 | 1666 | 4041 | 5148 | 1639 | 1609 | 3836 5626 | 3836 | 28 | 1877 | 5148 | |

pleased." | ¶ | **23** Now | Jesus | himself | was | about | thirty | years old | when he began | his ministry. | He was | the
εὐδόκησα | | Καὶ | Ἰησοῦς | αὐτὸς | ἦν | ὡσεὶ | τριάκοντα | ἐτῶν | → ἀρχόμενος | | ὢν |
v.aai.1s | | cj | n.nsm | r.nsm | v.iai.3s | pl | a.gpn | n.gpn | pt.pm.nsm | | pt.pa.nsm |
2305 | | 2779 | 2652 | 899 | 1639 | 6059 | 5558 | 2291 | 806 | | 1639 |

son, | so | it was | thought, | of Joseph, | the son of Heli, | the son of Matthat, | the son of Levi, | the son of
υἱός, | ὡς | → | ἐνομίζετο | → Ἰωσὴφ | → τοῦ Ἡλὶ | → τοῦ Μαθθὰτ | → τοῦ Λευὶ | →
n.nsm | cj | | v.ipi.3s | n.gsm | d.gsm n.gsm | d.gsm n.gsm | d.gsm n.gsm |
5626 | 6055 | | 3787 | 2737 | 3836 2459 | 3836 3415 | 3836 3322 |

Melki, | the son of Jannai, | the son of Joseph, | **25** the son of Mattathias, | the son of Amos, | the son of
τοῦ Μελχὶ | → τοῦ Ἰανναὶ | → τοῦ Ἰωσὴφ | → τοῦ Ματταθίου, | → τοῦ Ἀμὼς | →
d.gsm n.gsm | d.gsm n.gsm | d.gsm n.gsm | d.gsm n.gsm | d.gsm n.gsm |
3836 3518 | 3836 2613 | 3836 2737 | 3836 3478 | 3836 322 |

Nahum, | the son of Esli, | the son of Naggai, | the son of Maath, | the son of Mattathias, | the son of
τοῦ Ναοὺμ | → τοῦ Ἑσλὶ | → τοῦ Ναγγαὶ | → τοῦ Μάαθ | → τοῦ Ματταθίου | →
d.gsm n.gsm | d.gsm n.gsm | d.gsm n.gsm | d.gsm n.gsm | d.gsm n.gsm |
3836 3725 | 3836 2268 | 3836 3710 | 3836 3399 | 3836 3478 |

Semein, | the son of Josech, | the son of Joda, | **27** the son of Joanan, | the son of Rhesa, | the son of
τοῦ Σεμεῒ | → τοῦ Ἰωσὴχ | → τοῦ Ἰωδὰ | → τοῦ Ἰωανὰν | → τοῦ Ῥησὰ | →
d.gsm n.gsm | d.gsm n.gsm | d.gsm n.gsm | d.gsm n.gsm | d.gsm n.gsm |
3836 4946 | 3836 2738 | 3836 2726 | 3836 2720 | 3836 4840 |

Zerubbabel, | the son of Shealtiel, | the son of Neri, | the son of Melki, | the son of Addi, | the son of
τοῦ Ζοροβαβὲλ | → τοῦ Σαλαθιὴλ | → τοῦ Νηρὶ | → τοῦ Μελχὶ | → τοῦ Ἀδδὶ | →
d.gsm n.gsm | d.gsm n.gsm | d.gsm n.gsm | d.gsm n.gsm | d.gsm n.gsm |
3836 2431 | 3836 4886 | 3836 3760 | 3836 3518 | 3836 79 |

Cosam, | the son of Elmadam, | the son of Er, | **29** the son of Joshua, | the son of Eliezer, | the son of
τοῦ Κωσὰμ | → τοῦ Ἐλμαδὰμ | → τοῦ Ἢρ | → τοῦ Ἰησοῦ | → τοῦ Ἐλιέζερ | →
d.gsm n.gsm | d.gsm n.gsm | d.gsm n.gsm | d.gsm n.gsm | d.gsm n.gsm |
3836 3272 | 3836 1825 | 3836 2474 | 3836 2652 | 3836 1808 |

Jorim, | the son of Matthat, | the son of Levi, | the son of Simeon, | the son of Judah, | the son
τοῦ Ἰωρὶμ | → Μαθθὰτ τοῦ Μαθθὰτ | → τοῦ Λευὶ | → τοῦ Συμεὼν | → τοῦ Ἰούδα | →
d.gsm n.gsm | n.gsm d.gsm n.gsm | d.gsm n.gsm | d.gsm n.gsm | d.gsm n.gsm |
3836 2733 | 3415 3836 3415 | 3836 3322 | 3836 5208 | 3836 2683 |

of Joseph, | the son of Jonam, | the son of Eliakim, | **31** the son of Melea, | the son of Menna, | the son of
→ τοῦ Ἰωσὴφ | → τοῦ Ἰωνὰμ | → τοῦ Ἐλιακὶμ | → τοῦ Μελεὰ | → τοῦ Μεννὰ | →
d.gsm n.gsm | d.gsm n.gsm | d.gsm n.gsm | d.gsm n.gsm | d.gsm n.gsm |
3836 2737 | 3836 2729 | 3836 1806 | 3836 3507 | 3836 3527 |

Mattatha, | the son of Nathan, | the son of David, | the son of Jesse, | the son of Obed, | the son of
τοῦ Ματταθὰ | → τοῦ Ναθὰμ | → τοῦ Δαυὶδ | → τοῦ Ἰεσσαὶ | → τοῦ Ἰωβὴδ | →
d.gsm n.gsm | d.gsm n.gsm | d.gsm n.gsm | d.gsm n.gsm | d.gsm n.gsm |
3836 3477 | 3836 3718 | 3836 1253 | 3836 2649 | 3836 2725 |

Boaz, | the son of Salmon, | the son of Nahshon, | **33** the son of Amminadab, | the son of Ram, | the
τοῦ Βόος | → τοῦ Σαλὰ | → τοῦ Ναασσὼν | → τοῦ Ἀμιναδὰβ | τοῦ Ἀδμὶν | → τοῦ Ἀρνὶ | →
d.gsm n.gsm | d.gsm n.gsm | d.gsm n.gsm | d.gsm n.gsm | d.gsm n.gsm | d.gsm n.gsm |
3836 1078 | 3836 4885 | 3836 3709 | 3836 300 | 3836 98 | 3836 747 |

son of Hezron, | the son of Perez, | the son of Judah, | the son of Jacob, | the son of Isaac, | the son of
→ τοῦ Ἑσρὼμ | → τοῦ Φάρες | → τοῦ Ἰούδα | → τοῦ Ἰακὼβ | → τοῦ Ἰσαὰκ | →
d.gsm n.gsm | d.gsm n.gsm | d.gsm n.gsm | d.gsm n.gsm | d.gsm n.gsm |
3836 2272 | 3836 5756 | 3836 2683 | 3836 2609 | 3836 2693 |

Abraham, | the son of Terah, | the son of Nahor, | **35** the son of Serug, | the son of Reu, | the son of
τοῦ Ἀβραὰμ | → τοῦ Θάρα | → τοῦ Ναχὼρ | → τοῦ Σεροὺχ | → τοῦ Ῥαγαὺ | →
d.gsm n.gsm | d.gsm n.gsm | d.gsm n.gsm | d.gsm n.gsm | d.gsm n.gsm |
3836 11 | 3836 2508 | 3836 3732 | 3836 4952 | 3836 4814 |

---

22 καὶ καταβῆναι τὸ πνεῦμα τὸ ἅγιον σωματικῷ εἴδει ὡς περιστερὰν ἐπ' αὐτόν, καὶ φωνὴν ἐξ οὐρανοῦ γενέσθαι, Σὺ εἶ ὁ υἱός μου ὁ ἀγαπητός, ἐν σοὶ εὐδόκησα. ¶ 23 Καὶ αὐτὸς ἦν Ἰησοῦς ἀρχόμενος ὡσεὶ ἐτῶν τριάκοντα, ὢν υἱός, ὡς ἐνομίζετο, Ἰωσὴφ τοῦ Ἡλὶ 24 τοῦ Μαθθὰτ τοῦ Λευὶ τοῦ Μελχὶ τοῦ Ἰανναὶ τοῦ Ἰωσὴφ 25 τοῦ Ματταθίου τοῦ Ἀμὼς τοῦ Ναοὺμ τοῦ Ἑσλὶ τοῦ Ναγγαὶ 26 τοῦ Μάαθ τοῦ Ματταθίου τοῦ Σεμεῒν τοῦ Ἰωσὴχ τοῦ Ἰωδὰ 27 τοῦ Ἰωανὰν τοῦ Ῥησὰ τοῦ Ζοροβαβὲλ τοῦ Σαλαθιὴλ τοῦ Νηρὶ 28 τοῦ Μελχὶ τοῦ Ἀδδὶ τοῦ Κωσὰμ τοῦ Ἐλμαδὰμ τοῦ Ἢρ 29 τοῦ Ἰησοῦ τοῦ Ἐλιέζερ τοῦ Ἰωρὶμ τοῦ Μαθθὰτ τοῦ Λευὶ 30 τοῦ Συμεὼν τοῦ Ἰούδα τοῦ Ἰωσὴφ τοῦ Ἰωνὰμ τοῦ Ἐλιακὶμ 31 τοῦ Μελεὰ τοῦ Μεννὰ τοῦ Ματταθὰ τοῦ Ναθὰμ τοῦ Δαυὶδ 32 τοῦ Ἰεσσαὶ τοῦ Ἰωβὴδ τοῦ Βόος τοῦ Σαλμὼν «Σαλὰ» τοῦ Ναασσὼν 33 τοῦ Ἀμιναδὰβ τοῦ Ἀρὰμ «Ἀδμὶν» τοῦ Ἀρνὶ τοῦ Ἑσρὼμ τοῦ Φάρες τοῦ Ἰούδα 34 τοῦ Ἰακὼβ τοῦ Ἰσαὰκ τοῦ Ἀβραὰμ τοῦ Θάρα τοῦ Ναχὼρ 35 τοῦ Σεροὺχ τοῦ Ῥαγαὺ τοῦ Φάλεκ τοῦ Ἔβερ

Peleg,   the son of Eber,   the son of Shelah,   the son of Cainan,   the son of Arphaxad,   the son of
τοῦ Φάλεκ → τοῦ Ἔβερ → τοῦ Σαλά → τοῦ Καϊνάμ → τοῦ Ἀρφαξάδ →
d.gsm n.gsm   d.gsm n.gsm   d.gsm n.gsm   d.gsm n.gsm   d.gsm n.gsm
3836 5744   3836 1576   3836 4885   3836 2783   3836 790

Shem,   the son of Noah,   the son of Lamech,   **37** the son of Methuselah,   the son of Enoch,   the son of
τοῦ Σήμ → τοῦ Νῶε → τοῦ Λάμεχ → τοῦ Μαθουσαλά → τοῦ Ἑνώχ →
d.gsm n.gsm   d.gsm n.gsm   d.gsm n.gsm   d.gsm n.gsm   d.gsm n.gsm
3836 4954   3836 3820   3836 3285   3836 3417   3836 1970

Jared,   the son of Mahalalel,   the son of Kenan,   the son of Enosh,   the son of Seth,   the son of
τοῦ Ἰάρετ → τοῦ Μαλελεήλ → τοῦ Καϊνάμ → τοῦ Ἑνώς → τοῦ Σήθ →
d.gsm n.gsm   d.gsm n.gsm   d.gsm n.gsm   d.gsm n.gsm   d.gsm n.gsm
3836 2616   3836 3435   3836 2783   3836 1968   3836 4953

Adam,   the son of God.
τοῦ Ἀδάμ → τοῦ θεοῦ
d.gsm n.gsm   d.gsm n.gsm
3836 77   3836 2536

The Temptation of Jesus

4:1   Jesus, full   of the Holy Spirit,   returned from the Jordan   and was led   by the Spirit   in the desert,
δὲ Ἰησοῦς πλήρης →   ἁγίου πνεύματος ὑπέστρεψεν ἀπὸ   τοῦ Ἰορδάνου   καὶ →   ἤγετο ἐν τῷ πνεύματι ἐν τῇ ἐρήμῳ
cj n.nsm a.nsm →   a.gsn n.gsn v.aai.3s p.g   d.gsm n.gsm   cj   v.ipi.3s p.d d.dsn n.dsn p.d d.dsf n.dsf
1254 2652 4441   41 4460 5715 608   3836 2674   2779   72 1877 3836 4460 1877 3836 2245

2 where for forty   days   he was tempted   by the devil.   He ate   nothing during those
→ τεσσεράκοντα ἡμέρας → → πειραζόμενος ὑπὸ τοῦ διαβόλου Καὶ οὐκ → ἔφαγεν οὐδὲν ἐν ἐκείναις
a.apf n.apf → → pt.pp.nsm p.g d.gsm n.gsm cj pl v.aai.3s a.asn p.d r.dpf
5477 2465 4279 5679 3836 1333 2779 4024 2266 4029 1877 1697

days,   and at the end   of them he was hungry. ¶   **3**   The devil   said to him, "If you are the
ταῖς ἡμέραις καὶ → συντελεσθεισῶν → αὐτῶν → ἐπείνασεν   δὲ ὁ διάβολος εἶπεν αὐτῷ εἰ → εἶ
d.dpf n.dpf cj pt.ap.gpf r.gpf.3 v.aai.3s   cj d.nsm n.nsm v.aai.3s r.dsm.3 cj v.pai.2s
3836 2465 2779 5334 899 4277   1254 3836 1333 3306 899 1623 1639

Son of God,   tell this stone   to become bread."   **4**   Jesus   answered,   "It is written:
υἱὸς → τοῦ θεοῦ εἰπὲ τούτῳ τῷ λίθῳ ἵνα γένηται ἄρτος καὶ ὁ Ἰησοῦς ἀπεκρίθη πρὸς αὐτόν → γέγραπται ὅτι
n.nsm d.gsm n.gsm v.aam.2s r.dsm d.dsm n.dsm cj v.ams.3s n.nsm cj d.nsm n.nsm v.api.3s p.a r.asm.3 v.rpi.3s cj
5626 3836 2536 3306 4047 3836 3345 2671 1181 788 2779 3836 2652 646 4639 899 1211 4022

'Man   does not live   on bread alone.'" ¶   **5**   The devil led   him up to a high place and
ὁ ἄνθρωπος → οὐκ ζήσεται ἐπ' ἄρτῳ μόνῳ   Καὶ → ἀναγαγὼν αὐτὸν ←
d.nsm n.nsm → pl v.fmi.3s p.d n.dsm a.dsm   cj pt.aa.nsm r.asm.3
3836 476 2409 4024 2409 2093 788 3668   2779 1333 343 899 343

showed him in an instant   all   the kingdoms of the world.   **6** And he   said to him, "I will give
ἔδειξεν αὐτῷ ἐν στιγμῇ χρόνου πάσας τὰς βασιλείας → τῆς οἰκουμένης καὶ ὁ διάβολος εἶπεν αὐτῷ → δώσω
v.aai.3s r.dsm.3 p.d n.dsf n.gsm a.apf d.apf n.apf d.gsf n.gsf cj d.nsm n.nsm v.aai.3s r.dsm.3 v.fai.1s
1259 899 1877 5117 5989 4246 3836 993 3836 3876 2779 3836 1333 3306 899 1443

you all   their authority   and splendor, for it has been given   to me, and I can give it   to
σοὶ ἅπασαν αὐτῶν τὴν ἐξουσίαν ταύτην καὶ τὴν δόξαν ὅτι → → παραδέδοται ἐμοὶ καὶ → δίδωμι αὐτὴν →
r.ds.2 a.asf r.gpf.3 d.asf n.asf r.asf cj d.asf n.asf cj v.rpi.3s r.ds.1 cj v.pai.1s r.asf.3
5148 570 899 3836 2026 4047 2779 3836 1518 4022 4140 1609 2779 1443 899

anyone I want to.   **7** So if   you worship   me, it will all   be   yours."   **8**   Jesus   answered,
ᾧ ἐὰν → θέλω οὖν ἐὰν σὺ προσκυνήσῃς ἐνώπιον ἐμοῦ → πᾶσα ἔσται σοῦ καὶ ὁ Ἰησοῦς ἀποκριθεὶς εἶπεν αὐτῷ
r.dsm pl → v.pas.1s cj pl r.ns.2 v.aas.2s p.g r.gs.1 a.nsf v.fmi.3s r.gs.2 cj d.nsm n.nsm pt.ap.nsm v.aai.3s r.dsm.3
4005 1569 2527 4036 1569 5148 4686 1967 1609 1639 1639 4246 1639 5148 2779 3836 2652 646 3306 899

"It is written: 'Worship   the Lord your God and serve   him only.'" ¶   **9**   The devil led   him to
→ → γέγραπται προσκυνήσεις τὸν κύριον σου θεόν καὶ λατρεύσεις αὐτῷ μόνῳ   δὲ   Ἤγαγεν αὐτὸν εἰς
v.rpi.3s v.fai.2s d.asm n.asm r.gs.2 n.asm cj v.fai.2s r.dsm.3 a.dsm   cj   v.aai.3s r.asm.3 p.a
1211 4686 3836 3261 5148 2536 2779 3302 899 3668   1254   72 899 1650

Jerusalem and had him stand on the highest   point of the temple.   "If you are   the Son of God,"   he said,
Ἰερουσαλήμ καὶ → → ἔστησεν ἐπὶ τὸ πτερύγιον ← → τοῦ ἱεροῦ καὶ εἰ → εἶ υἱός → τοῦ θεοῦ → εἶπεν
n.asf cj v.aai.3s p.a d.asn n.asn d.gsn n.gsn cj cj v.pai.2s n.nsm d.gsm n.gsm v.aai.3s
2647 2779 2705 2093 3836 4762 3836 2639 2779 1623 1639 5626 3836 2536 3306

τοῦ Σαλά   **36** τοῦ Καϊνάμ τοῦ Ἀρφαξάδ τοῦ Σήμ τοῦ Νῶε τοῦ Λάμεχ   **37** τοῦ Μαθουσαλά τοῦ Ἑνώχ τοῦ Ἰάρετ τοῦ Μαλελεήλ τοῦ Καϊνάμ   **38** τοῦ Ἑνώς τοῦ Σήθ τοῦ Ἀδάμ τοῦ θεοῦ.

4:1 Ἰησοῦς δὲ πλήρης πνεύματος ἁγίου ὑπέστρεψεν ἀπὸ τοῦ Ἰορδάνου καὶ ἤγετο ἐν τῷ πνεύματι ἐν τῇ ἐρήμῳ **2** ἡμέρας τεσσεράκοντα πειραζόμενος ὑπὸ τοῦ διαβόλου. καὶ οὐκ ἔφαγεν οὐδὲν ἐν ταῖς ἡμέραις ἐκείναις καὶ συντελεσθεισῶν αὐτῶν ἐπείνασεν. ¶ **3** Εἶπεν δὲ αὐτῷ ὁ διάβολος, Εἰ υἱὸς εἶ τοῦ θεοῦ, εἰπὲ τῷ λίθῳ τούτῳ ἵνα γένηται ἄρτος. **4** καὶ ἀπεκρίθη πρὸς αὐτὸν ὁ Ἰησοῦς, Γέγραπται ὅτι Οὐκ ἐπ' ἄρτῳ μόνῳ ζήσεται ὁ ἄνθρωπος. ¶ **5** Καὶ ἀναγαγὼν αὐτὸν ὁ διάβολος εἰς ὄρος ὑψηλὸν ἔδειξεν αὐτῷ πάσας τὰς βασιλείας τῆς οἰκουμένης ἐν στιγμῇ χρόνου **6** καὶ εἶπεν αὐτῷ ὁ διάβολος, Σοὶ δώσω τὴν ἐξουσίαν ταύτην ἅπασαν καὶ τὴν δόξαν αὐτῶν, ὅτι ἐμοὶ παραδέδοται καὶ ᾧ ἐὰν θέλω δίδωμι αὐτήν· **7** σὺ οὖν ἐὰν προσκυνήσῃς ἐνώπιον ἐμοῦ, ἔσται σοῦ πᾶσα. **8** καὶ ἀποκριθεὶς ὁ Ἰησοῦς εἶπεν αὐτῷ, Γέγραπται, Κύριον τὸν θεόν σου προσκυνήσεις καὶ αὐτῷ μόνῳ λατρεύσεις. ¶ **9** Ἤγαγεν δὲ αὐτὸν εἰς Ἰερουσαλὴμ καὶ ἔστησεν ἐπὶ τὸ πτερύγιον τοῦ ἱεροῦ καὶ εἶπεν αὐτῷ, Εἰ υἱὸς εἶ τοῦ

"throw yourself down from   here. **10** For it is written: "'He will command his   angels   concerning
αὐτῷ βάλε   σεαυτὸν κάτω ἐντεῦθεν ←   γὰρ → γέγραπται ὅτι →   ἐντελεῖται αὐτοῦ ˻τοῖς ἀγγέλοις˼ περὶ
r.dsm.3 v.aam.2s r.asm.2 adv   adv   cj   v.rpi.3s   cj   v.fmi.3s   r.gsm.3 d.dpm n.dpm   p.g
899   965   4932   3004 1949   1142   1211   4022   1948   899   3836 34   4309

you to guard   you carefully; **11**   they will lift   you up in their hands, so that you will not   strike
σοῦ → ˻τοῦ διαφυλάξαι˼ σε ←   καὶ ὅτι →   → ἀροῦσιν σε ← ἐπὶ χειρῶν ˹ ˹ ˹   ˹   μήποτε προσκόψῃς
r.gs.2 d.gsn f.aa   r.as.2   cj   cj   v.fai.3p r.as.2 p.g n.gpf   v.aas.2s
5148 3836 1428   5148 3836   2779 4022   149   149 2093 5931 3607 3607 4684 4684 3607 4684

your foot   against a stone.'" **12** Jesus   answered,   "It says: 'Do not put the Lord your
σοῦ ˻τὸν πόδα˼ πρὸς   λίθον   καὶ ὁ Ἰησοῦς, ἀποκριθεὶς εἶπεν αὐτῷ ὅτι → εἴρηται   οὐκ ˹   κύριον σου
r.gs.2 d.asm n.asm p.a   n.asm   cj d.nsm n.nsm   pt.ap.nsm   v.aai.3s r.dsm.3 cj   v.rpi.3s   pl   n.asm   r.gs.2
5148 3836 4546 4639 3345   2779 3836 2652   646   3306 899 4022 3306   1733 4024 1733 3261   5148

God   to the test.'" ¶ **13** When the devil   had finished   all   this tempting, he left   him until
˻τὸν θεόν˼ → → ἐκπειράσεις Καὶ ˹   ὁ διάβολος → συντελέσας πάντα   πειρασμὸν → ἀπέστη ἀπ᾿ αὐτοῦ ἄχρι
d.asm n.asm v.fai.2s   cj   d.nsm n.nsm   pt.aa.nsm a.asm   n.asm   v.aai.3s p.g r.gsm.3 p.g
3836 2536 1733   2779 5334   3836 1333   5334   4246   4280   923   608 899   948

an opportune time.
→ καιροῦ
n.gsm
2789

Jesus Rejected at Nazareth

4:14 Jesus   returned to Galilee   in the power of the Spirit,   and news about him spread
Καὶ ὁ Ἰησοῦς, ὑπέστρεψεν εἰς ˻τὴν Γαλιλαίαν˼ ἐν τῇ δυνάμει → τοῦ πνεύματος καὶ φήμη περὶ αὐτοῦ ἐξῆλθεν
cj d.nsm n.nsm   v.aai.3s   p.a d.asf n.asf   p.d d.dsf n.dsf   d.gsn n.gsn   cj   n.nsf p.g   r.gsm.3 v.aai.3s
2779 3836 2652   5715   1650 3836 1133   1877 3836 1539   3836 4460   2779 5773 4309 899   2002

through the whole countryside. **15** He   taught in their synagogues,   and   everyone praised him. ¶
καθ᾿   ὅλης ˻τῆς περιχώρου˼ καὶ αὐτὸς ἐδίδασκεν ἐν αὐτῶν ˻ταῖς συναγωγαῖς˼ ὑπὸ πάντων δοξαζόμενος
p.g   a.gsf d.gsf a.gsf   cj r.nsm v.iai.3s   p.d r.gpm.3 d.dpf n.dpf   p.g a.gpm   pt.pp.nsm
2848   3910 3836 4369   2779 899   1438   1877 899   3836 5252   5679 4246   1519

16 He went to Nazareth, where he had been brought   up, and on the Sabbath   day he went   into
Καὶ ἦλθεν εἰς Ναζαρά   οὗ   →   ἦν τεθραμμένος, ← καὶ ἐν τῇ ˻τῶν σαββάτων˼ ἡμέρᾳ → εἰσῆλθεν εἰς
cj v.aai.3s p.a n.asf   adv   v.iai.3s pt.rp.nsm   cj p.d d.dsf d.gpn n.gpn   n.dsf   v.aai.3s p.a
2779 2262 1650 3711   4023   1639 5555   2779 1877 3836 3836 4879   2465   1656   1650

the synagogue, as was his custom.   And he stood up to read.   **17** The scroll of the prophet Isaiah
τὴν συναγωγὴν   αὐτῷ ˻κατὰ τὸ εἰωθὸς˼ καὶ → ἀνέστη ← → ἀναγνῶναι καὶ   βιβλίον → τοῦ προφήτου Ἡσαΐου
d.asf n.asf   r.dsm.3 p.a d.asn pt.ra.asn cj v.aai.3s   f.aa   cj   n.nsn   d.gsm n.gsm   n.gsm
3836 5252   899   2848 3836 1665   2779 482   336   2779   1046   3836 4737   2480

was handed to him.   Unrolling it,   he found the place where it is written: **18** "The Spirit of the
→ ἐπεδόθη   αὐτῷ ˹ καὶ ἀναπτύξας ˻τὸ βιβλίον˼ → εὗρεν τὸν τόπον οὗ   ˻ἦν γεγραμμένον˼ πνεῦμα
v.api.3s   r.dsm.3 cj pt.aa.nsm d.asn n.asn   v.aai.3s d.asm n.asm adv v.iai.3s pt.rp.nsn   n.nsn
2113   899   2779 408   3836 1046   2351 3836 5536 4023 1639 1211   4460

Lord is on me, because   he has anointed me to preach   good news to the poor. He has sent   me to
κυρίου ἐπ᾿ ἐμὲ ˻οὗ εἴνεκεν˼ → → ἔχρισεν με → εὐαγγελίσασθαι ← →   → πτωχοῖς → ἀπέσταλκεν με →
n.gsm p.a r.as.1 r.gsn p.g   v.aai.3s r.as.1 f.am   a.dpm   v.rai.3s   r.as.1
3261 2093 1609 4005 1641   5987   1609 2294   4777   690   1609

proclaim freedom for the prisoners and recovery of sight for the blind, to release   the oppressed,
κηρύξαι ἄφεσιν → αἰχμαλώτοις καὶ ἀνάβλεψιν ←   →   τυφλοῖς ˻ἀποστεῖλαι ἐν ἀφέσει˼ τεθραυσμένους
f.aa   n.asf   n.dpm   cj n.asf   a.dpm   f.aa   p.d n.dsf   pt.rp.apm
3062   912   171   2779 330   5603   690   1877 912   2575

19 to proclaim the year   of the Lord's favor." **20** Then he rolled up the scroll, gave   it back to the attendant and
→ κηρύξαι ἐνιαυτὸν →   κυρίου δεκτόν   καὶ →   πτύξας ← τὸ βιβλίον ἀποδοὺς → → τῷ ὑπηρέτῃ
   f.aa   n.asm   n.gsm a.asm   cj   pt.aa.nsm   d.asn n.asn pt.aa.nsm   d.dsm n.dsm
   3062   1929   3261 1283   2779   4771   3836 1046 625   3836 5677

sat   down.   The eyes   of everyone in the synagogue were fastened on him, **21** and he began by saying to
ἐκάθισεν ← καὶ οἱ ὀφθαλμοὶ πάντων ἐν τῇ συναγωγῇ ἦσαν ἀτενίζοντες → αὐτῷ δὲ → ἤρξατο λέγειν πρὸς
v.aai.3s   cj d.npm n.npm   a.gpm   p.d d.dsf n.dsf   v.iai.3p pt.pa.npm   r.dsm.3 cj   v.ami.3s f.pa   p.a
2767   2779 3836 4057   4246   1877 3836 5252   1639 867   899   1254 806   3306   4639

θεοῦ, βάλε σεαυτὸν ἐντεῦθεν κάτω· **10** γέγραπται γὰρ ὅτι Τοῖς ἀγγέλοις αὐτοῦ ἐντελεῖται περὶ σοῦ τοῦ διαφυλάξαι σε, **11** καὶ ὅτι Ἐπὶ χειρῶν ἀροῦσίν σε, μήποτε προσκόψῃς πρὸς λίθον τὸν πόδα σου. **12** καὶ ἀποκριθεὶς εἶπεν αὐτῷ ὁ Ἰησοῦς ὅτι Εἴρηται, Οὐκ ἐκπειράσεις κύριον τὸν θεόν σου. ¶ **13** Καὶ συντελέσας πάντα πειρασμὸν ὁ διάβολος ἀπέστη ἀπ᾿ αὐτοῦ ἄχρι καιροῦ.

4:14 Καὶ ὑπέστρεψεν ὁ Ἰησοῦς ἐν τῇ δυνάμει τοῦ πνεύματος εἰς τὴν Γαλιλαίαν. καὶ φήμη ἐξῆλθεν καθ᾿ ὅλης τῆς περιχώρου περὶ αὐτοῦ. **15** καὶ αὐτὸς ἐδίδασκεν ἐν ταῖς συναγωγαῖς αὐτῶν δοξαζόμενος ὑπὸ πάντων. ¶ **16** Καὶ ἦλθεν εἰς Ναζαρά, οὗ ἦν τεθραμμένος, καὶ εἰσῆλθεν κατὰ τὸ εἰωθὸς αὐτῷ ἐν τῇ ἡμέρᾳ τῶν σαββάτων εἰς τὴν συναγωγὴν καὶ ἀνέστη ἀναγνῶναι. **17** καὶ ἐπεδόθη αὐτῷ βιβλίον τοῦ προφήτου Ἡσαΐου καὶ ἀναπτύξας τὸ βιβλίον εὗρεν τὸν τόπον οὗ ἦν γεγραμμένον, **18** Πνεῦμα κυρίου ἐπ᾿ ἐμὲ οὗ εἴνεκεν ἔχρισέν με εὐαγγελίσασθαι πτωχοῖς, ἀπέσταλκέν με, κηρύξαι αἰχμαλώτοις ἄφεσιν καὶ τυφλοῖς ἀνάβλεψιν, ἀποστεῖλαι τεθραυσμένους ἐν ἀφέσει, **19** κηρύξαι ἐνιαυτὸν κυρίου δεκτόν. **20** καὶ πτύξας τὸ βιβλίον ἀποδοὺς τῷ ὑπηρέτῃ ἐκάθισεν· καὶ πάντων οἱ ὀφθαλμοὶ ἐν τῇ συναγωγῇ ἦσαν ἀτενίζοντες αὐτῷ. **21** ἤρξατο δὲ λέγειν πρὸς αὐτοὺς ὅτι Σήμερον πεπλήρωται ἡ

them,   "Today   this   scripture   is fulfilled   in   your   hearing."   ¶   **22**   All   spoke   well of him   and were
αὐτοὺς ὅτι σήμερον αὕτη ἡ γραφὴ → πεπλήρωται ἐν ὑμῶν ｒτοῖς ὠσὶνˌ   Καὶ πάντες ἐμαρτύρουν ← αὐτῷ καὶ →
r.apm.3 cj adv r.nsf d.nsf n.nsf v.rpi.3s p.d r.gp.2 d.dpn n.dpn   cj a.npm v.iai.3p r.dsm.3 cj
899 4022 4958 4047 3836 1210 4444 1877 7007 3836 4044   2779 4246 3455 899 2779

amazed   at   the   gracious   words   that   came   from   his   lips.   "Isn't   this   Joseph's   son?"   they
ἐθαύμαζον ἐπὶ τοῖς ｒτῆς χάριτοςˌ λόγοις τοῖς ἐκπορευομένοις ἐκ αὐτοῦ ｒτοῦ στόματοςˌ καὶ ｒοὐχὶ ἐστιν οὗτος Ἰωσὴφ υἱός →
v.iai.3p p.d d.dpm d.gsf n.gsf n.dpm d.dpm pt.dm.dpm p.g r.gsm.3 d.gsn n.gsn cj r.nsm v.pai.3s r.nsm n.gsm n.nsm
2513 2093 3836 3836 5921 3364 3836 1744 1666 899 3836 5125 2779 4049 1639 4047 2737 5626

asked.   ¶   **23**   Jesus   said   to   them, "Surely   you will   quote   this   proverb   to me: 'Physician,   heal
ἔλεγον   καὶ   εἶπεν πρὸς αὐτούς πάντως → ἐρεῖτε ταύτην ｒτὴν παραβολὴνˌ → μοι ἰατρέ θεράπευσον
v.iai.3p cj v.aai.3s p.a r.apm.3 adv v.fai.2p r.asf d.asf n.asf r.ds.1 n.vsm v.aam.2s
3306 2779 3306 4639 899 4122 3306 4047 3836 4130 1609 2620 2543

yourself!   Do   here   in   your   hometown   what   we have   heard   that you did   in   Capernaum.'"   ¶
σεαυτόν ποίησον καὶ ὧδε ἐν σου ｒτῇ πατρίδιˌ ὅσα → → ἠκούσαμεν → γενόμενα εἰς ｒτὴν Καφαρναοὺμˌ
r.asm.2 v.aam.2s cj adv p.d r.gs.2 d.dsf n.dsf r.apn v.aai.1p pt.am.apn p.a d.asf n.asf
4932 4472 2779 6045 1877 5148 3836 4258 4012 201 1181 1650 3836 3019

24   "I tell   you the truth,"   he continued,   "no   prophet is   accepted   in   his   hometown.   **25**   I
δὲ   λέγω ὑμῖν   ἀμὴν   εἶπεν ὅτι οὐδεὶς προφήτης ἐστιν δεκτός ἐν αὐτοῦ ｒτῇ πατρίδιˌ δὲ →
cj v.pai.1s r.dp.2 pl v.aai.3s cj a.nsm n.nsm v.pai.3s a.nsm p.d r.gsm.3 d.dsf n.dsf cj
1254 3306 7007 297 3306 4022 4029 4737 1639 1283 1877 899 3836 4258 1254

assure   you that there   were   many   widows in   Israel   in   Elijah's   time,   when   the   sky   was
ｒἐπ᾽ ἀληθείας λέγωˌ ὑμῖν → ἦσαν πολλαὶ χῆραι ἐν ｒτῷ Ἰσραήλˌ ἐν Ἠλίου ｒταῖς ἡμέραιςˌ ὅτε ὁ οὐρανὸς →
p.g n.gsf v.pai.1s r.dp.2 v.iai.3p a.npf n.npf p.d d.dsm n.dsm p.d n.gsm d.dpf n.dpf cj d.nsm n.nsm
2093 237 3306 7007 1639 4498 5939 1877 3836 2702 1877 2460 3836 2465 4021 3836 4041

shut   for   three   and a half   years   and   there was   a severe   famine   throughout   the   land.   **26**   Yet   Elijah   was   not
ἐκλείσθη ἐπὶ τρία καὶ μῆνας ἕξ ἔτη ὡς → ἐγένετο μέγας λιμὸς ｒἐπὶ πᾶσανˌ τὴν γῆν καὶ Ἠλίας → →
v.api.3s p.a a.apn cj n.apm a.apm n.apn cj v.ami.3s a.nsm n.nsm p.a a.asf d.asf n.asf cj n.nsm
3091 2093 5552 2779 3604 1971 2291 6055 1181 3489 3350 2093 4246 3836 1178 2779 2460 4287 4029

sent   to   any   of them, but   to   a widow   in   Zarephath   in   the region of   Sidon.   **27**   And   there   were
ἐπέμφθη πρὸς οὐδεμίαν → αὐτῶν ｒεἰ μήˌ πρὸς γυναῖκα χήραν εἰς Σάρεπτα → τῆς → Σιδωνίας καὶ → ἦσαν
v.api.3s p.a a.asf r.gpf.3 cj pl p.a n.asf n.asf p.a n.asf d.gsf a.gsf cj v.iai.3p
4287 4639 4029 899 1623 3590 4639 1222 5939 1650 4919 3836 4973 2779 1639

many in   Israel   with   leprosy   in   the time of   Elisha   the   prophet,   yet   not one   of them   was   cleansed   –
πολλοὶ ἐν ｒτῷ Ἰσραήλˌ → λεπροὶ ἐπὶ ← ← Ἐλισαίου τοῦ προφήτου καὶ → οὐδεὶς → αὐτῶν ἐκαθαρίσθη
a.npm p.d d.dsm n.dsm a.npm p.g n.gsm d.gsm n.gsm cj a.nsm r.gpm.3 v.api.3s
4498 1877 3836 2702 3370 2093 1811 3836 4737 2779 4029 899 2751

only   Naaman   the   Syrian."   ¶   **28**   All   the people   in   the   synagogue   were   furious   when   they
ｒεἰ μήˌ Ναιμὰν ὁ Σύρος   καὶ πάντες   ἐν τῇ συναγωγῇ → ｒἐπλήσθησαν θυμοῦˌ → →
cj pl n.nsm d.nsm n.nsm cj a.npm p.d d.dsf n.dsf v.api.3p n.gsm
1623 3590 3722 3836 5354 2779 4246 1877 3836 5252 4398 2596

heard   this.   **29**   They   got   up,   drove   him   out   of the   town,   and   took   him   to   the   brow   of   the   hill   on
ἀκούοντες ταῦτα καὶ → ἀναστάντες ἐξέβαλον αὐτὸν ἔξω τῆς πόλεως καὶ ἤγαγον αὐτὸν ἕως ὀφρύος → τοῦ ὄρους ἐφ᾽
pt.pa.npm r.apn cj pt.aa.npm v.aai.3p r.asm.3 p.g d.gsf n.gsf cj v.aai.3p r.asm.3 p.g n.gsf d.gsn n.gsn p.g
201 4047 2779 482 1675 899 2032 3836 4484 2779 72 899 2401 4059 3836 4001 2093

which   the   town   was   built,   in   order to   throw   him   down   the cliff.   **30**   But   he   walked   right
οὗ ἡ πόλις αὐτῶν ᾠκοδόμητο ὥστε → κατακρημνίσαι αὐτὸν δὲ αὐτὸς διελθὼν
r.gsn d.nsf n.nsf r.gpm.3 v.lpi.3s cj f.aa r.asm.3 cj r.nsm pt.aa.nsm
4005 3836 4484 899 3868 6063 2889 899 1254 899 1451

through   the   crowd   and   went   on his way.
ｒδιὰ μέσουˌ αὐτῶν ἐπορεύετο ←
p.g n.gsn r.gpm.3 v.imi.3s
1328 3545 899 4513

Jesus Drives Out an Evil Spirit

4:31 Then   he   went   down   to   Capernaum,   a town   in   Galilee,   and   on the   Sabbath   began   to teach
Καὶ → κατῆλθεν ← εἰς Καφαρναοὺμ πόλιν ｒτῆς Γαλιλαίαςˌ καὶ ἐν τοῖς σάββασιν → → ｒἦν διδάσκωνˌ
cj v.aai.3s p.a n.asf n.asf d.gsf n.gsf cj p.d d.dpn n.dpn v.iai.3s pt.pa.nsm
2779 2982 1650 3019 4484 3836 1133 2779 1877 3836 4879 1639 1438

γραφὴ αὕτη ἐν τοῖς ὠσὶν ὑμῶν. ¶ 22 Καὶ πάντες ἐμαρτύρουν αὐτῷ καὶ ἐθαύμαζον ἐπὶ τοῖς λόγοις τῆς χάριτος τοῖς ἐκπορευομένοις ἐκ τοῦ στόματος αὐτοῦ καὶ ἔλεγον, Οὐχὶ υἱός ἐστιν Ἰωσὴφ οὗτος; ¶ 23 καὶ εἶπεν πρὸς αὐτούς, Πάντως ἐρεῖτέ μοι τὴν παραβολὴν ταύτην· Ἰατρέ, θεράπευσον σεαυτόν· ὅσα ἠκούσαμεν γενόμενα εἰς τὴν Καφαρναοὺμ ποίησον καὶ ὧδε ἐν τῇ πατρίδι σου. ¶ 24 εἶπεν δέ, Ἀμὴν λέγω ὑμῖν ὅτι οὐδεὶς προφήτης δεκτός ἐστιν ἐν τῇ πατρίδι αὐτοῦ. 25 ἐπ᾽ ἀληθείας δὲ λέγω ὑμῖν, πολλαὶ χῆραι ἦσαν ἐν ταῖς ἡμέραις Ἠλίου ἐν τῷ Ἰσραήλ, ὅτε ἐκλείσθη ὁ οὐρανὸς ἐπὶ ἔτη τρία καὶ μῆνας ἕξ, ὡς ἐγένετο λιμὸς μέγας ἐπὶ πᾶσαν τὴν γῆν, 26 καὶ πρὸς οὐδεμίαν αὐτῶν ἐπέμφθη Ἠλίας εἰ μὴ εἰς Σάρεπτα τῆς Σιδωνίας πρὸς γυναῖκα χήραν. 27 καὶ πολλοὶ λεπροὶ ἦσαν ἐν τῷ Ἰσραὴλ ἐπὶ Ἐλισαίου τοῦ προφήτου, καὶ οὐδεὶς αὐτῶν ἐκαθαρίσθη εἰ μὴ Ναιμὰν ὁ Σύρος. ¶ 28 καὶ ἐπλήσθησαν πάντες θυμοῦ ἐν τῇ συναγωγῇ ἀκούοντες ταῦτα 29 καὶ ἀναστάντες ἐξέβαλον αὐτὸν ἔξω τῆς πόλεως καὶ ἤγαγον αὐτὸν ἕως ὀφρύος τοῦ ὄρους ἐφ᾽ οὗ ἡ πόλις ᾠκοδόμητο αὐτῶν ὥστε κατακρημνίσαι αὐτόν· 30 αὐτὸς δὲ διελθὼν διὰ μέσου αὐτῶν ἐπορεύετο.

4:31 Καὶ κατῆλθεν εἰς Καφαρναοὺμ πόλιν τῆς Γαλιλαίας. καὶ ἦν διδάσκων αὐτοὺς ἐν τοῖς σάββασιν· 32 καὶ ἐξεπλήσσοντο

the people. **32** They were amazed   at his   teaching,   because his   message   had   authority.   ¶   **33**   In
αὐτούς   καὶ   →   ἐξεπλήσσοντο ἐπὶ αὐτοῦ τῇ διδαχῇ   ὅτι   αὐτοῦ ὁ   λόγος   ἦν ἐν ἐξουσίᾳ   Καὶ ἐν
r.apm.3   cj   v.ipi.3p   p.d r.gsm.3 d.dsf n.dsf   cj   r.gsm.3 d.nsm n.nsm   v.iai.3s p.d n.dsf   cj p.d
899   2779   1742   2093 899 3836 1439   4022   899 3836 3364   1639 1877 2026   2779 1877

the synagogue there was a man   possessed by a demon, an evil   spirit.   He cried   out *at the top*   of
τῇ συναγωγῇ   →   ἦν   ἄνθρωπος ἔχων   ←   δαιμονίου   ἀκαθάρτου πνεῦμα καὶ →   ἀνέκραξεν ←   μεγάλῃ
d.dsf n.dsf   v.iai.3s n.nsm   pt.pa.nsm   n.gsn   a.gsn   n.asn cj   v.aai.3s   a.dsf
3836 5252   1639 476   2400   1228   176   4460 2779   371   3489

his voice, **34** "Ha! What do you want with   us, Jesus of Nazareth? Have you come to destroy us? I know   who
φωνῇ   ἔα   τί   What ἡμῖν   καὶ σοί Ἰησοῦ → Ναζαρηνέ   →   ἦλθες   → ἀπολέσαι ἡμᾶς   οἶδα σε τίς
n.dsf   j   r.nsn   r.dp.1   cj r.ds.2 n.vsm   a.vsm   v.aai.2s   f.aa   r.ap.1   v.rai.1s r.as.2 r.nsm
5889   1568   5515   7005   2779 5148 2652   3716   2262   660   7005   3857 5148 5515

you are – the Holy One of God!" **35**   "Be quiet!" Jesus   said   sternly.   "Come out of
→   εἶ   ὁ   ἅγιος ←   → τοῦ θεοῦ   καὶ →   φιμώθητι ὁ Ἰησοῦς   ἐπετίμησεν ←   αὐτῷ λέγων καὶ ἔξελθε ←   ἀπ
v.pai.2s   d.nsm   a.nsm   d.gsm n.gsm   cj   v.apm.2s d.nsm n.nsm   v.aai.3s   r.dsn.3 pt.pa.nsm cj v.aam.2s   p.g
1639   3836   41   3836 2536   2779   5821 3836 2652   2203   899 3306 2779 2002   608

him!" Then the demon   threw the man down *before*   *them all* and came   out   without injuring him.
αὐτοῦ   καὶ   τὸ   δαιμόνιον ῥίψαν   αὐτὸν ←   εἰς τὸ   μέσον   ἐξῆλθεν   ἀπ αὐτοῦ μηδὲν   βλάψαν αὐτόν
r.gsm.3   cj   d.nsn n.nsn   pt.aa.nsn   r.asm.3   p.a d.asn n.asn   v.aai.3s   p.g r.gsm.3 a.asn   pt.aa.nsn r.asm.3
899   2779   3836 1228   4849   899 4849   1650 3836 3545   2002   608 899 3594   1055 899

¶ **36**   All   the people were   amazed and said   to each   other,   "What is this   teaching?
καὶ ἐπὶ πάντας   ἐγένετο θάμβος   καὶ συνελάλουν πρὸς ἀλλήλους ←   λέγοντες τίς   οὗτος ὁ λόγος ὅτι
cj p.a a.apm   v.ami.3s n.nsn   cj v.iai.3p   p.a r.apm   pt.pa.npm r.nsm   r.nsm d.nsm n.nsm cj
2779 2093 4246   1181 2502   2779 5196   4639 253   3306 5515   4047 3836 3364 4022

With authority and power he gives orders   to evil   spirits   and they come   out!" **37** And the news about
ἐν ἐξουσίᾳ καὶ δυνάμει →   →   ἐπιτάσσει   ἀκαθάρτοις πνεύμασιν καὶ →   ἐξέρχονται ←   καὶ   ἦχος περὶ
p.d n.dsf cj n.dsf   v.pai.3s   a.dpn n.dpn cj   v.pmi.3p   cj   n.nsm p.g
1877 2026 2779 1539   2199   4460 176   4460 2779   2002   2779   2491 4309

him spread   throughout the surrounding area.
αὐτοῦ ἐξεπορεύετο εἰς πάντα   τῆς περιχώρου   τόπον
r.gsm.3 v.imi.3s   p.a a.asm   d.gsf a.gsf   n.asm
899 1744   1650 4246   3836 4369   5536

Jesus Heals Many

4:38   Jesus left   the synagogue and went   to the home of Simon. Now Simon's   mother-in-law was
δὲ   Ἀναστὰς ἀπὸ τῆς συναγωγῆς   εἰσῆλθεν εἰς τὴν οἰκίαν → Σίμωνος δὲ   τοῦ Σίμωνος πενθερὰ   ἦν
cj   pt.aa.nsm p.g d.gsf n.gsf   v.aai.3s p.a d.asf n.asf   n.gsm cj   d.gsm n.gsm n.nsf   v.iai.3s
1254   482   608 3836 5252   1656 1650 3836 3864   4981 1254   3836 4981 4289   1639

suffering from a high   fever, and they asked   Jesus   to help her. **39**   So he bent   over her   and rebuked
συνεχομένη →   μεγάλῳ πυρετῷ καὶ →   ἠρώτησαν αὐτὸν περὶ   αὐτῆς   καὶ →   ἐπιστὰς ἐπάνω αὐτῆς   ἐπετίμησεν
pt.pp.nsf   a.dsm n.dsm cj   v.aai.3p   r.asm.3 p.g   r.gsf.3   cj   pt.aa.nsm p.g r.gsf.3   v.aai.3s
5309   3489 4790 2779   2263   899 4309   899   2779   2392 2062 899   2203

the fever, and it left   her.   She got   up at once   and began to wait   on them.   ¶   **40**   When the
τῷ πυρετῷ καὶ   ἀφῆκεν αὐτήν δὲ   →   ἀναστᾶσα ←   παραχρῆμα   → διηκόνει   αὐτοῖς   δὲ →   τοῦ
d.dsm n.dsm cj   v.aai.3s r.asf.3 cj   pt.aa.nsf   adv   v.iai.3s   r.dpm.3   cj   d.gsm
3836 4790 2779   918 899 1254   482   4202   1354   899   1254 1544   3836

sun was setting, the people brought to Jesus all   who had   various kinds of sickness, and laying
ἡλίου →   Δύνοντος   αὐτοὺς ἤγαγον   πρὸς αὐτὸν ἅπαντες ὅσοι   εἶχον ἀσθενοῦντας ποικίλαις ←   νόσοις   δὲ ἐπιτιθεὶς
n.gsm   pt.pa.gsm   r.apm.3 v.aai.3p   p.a r.asm.3 a.npm r.npm   v.iai.3p pt.pa.apm   a.dpf   n.dpf   cj pt.pa.nsm
2463   1544   899 72   4639 899 570 4012   2400 4476   3798   1254 2202

his hands on each   one,   he healed   them. **41** Moreover, demons came   out of many people, shouting,
τὰς χεῖρας ←   ἑκάστῳ ἑνὶ   αὐτῶν ὁ   ἐθεράπευεν αὐτούς   δὲ καὶ   δαιμόνια ἐξήρχετο ←   ἀπὸ πολλῶν   κραυγάζοντα
d.apf n.apf   r.dsm a.dsm   r.gpm.3 d.nsm   v.iai.3s   r.apm.3   cj adv   n.npn v.imi.3s   p.g a.gpm   pt.pa.npn
3836 5931   2202 1667   1651 899   2543   899   1254 2779   1228 2002   608 4498   3198

"You are   the Son of God!" But he rebuked them and would not allow them to speak, because
καὶ λέγοντα ὅτι σὺ   εἶ   ὁ   υἱὸς → τοῦ θεοῦ καὶ →   ἐπιτιμῶν   οὐκ εἴα   αὐτὰ → λαλεῖν ὅτι
cj pt.pa.npn cj r.ns.2   v.pai.2s d.nsm n.nsm   d.gsm n.gsm cj   pt.pa.nsm   pl   v.iai.3s   r.apn.3   f.pa cj
2779 3306 4022 5148   1639 3836 5626   3836 2536 2779   2203   1572   4024 1572   899   3281 4022

ἐπὶ τῇ διδαχῇ αὐτοῦ, ὅτι ἐν ἐξουσίᾳ ἦν ὁ λόγος αὐτοῦ. ¶ 33 καὶ ἐν τῇ συναγωγῇ ἦν ἄνθρωπος ἔχων πνεῦμα δαιμονίου ἀκαθάρτου
καὶ ἀνέκραξεν φωνῇ μεγάλῃ, 34 Ἔα, τί ἡμῖν καὶ σοί, Ἰησοῦ Ναζαρηνέ; ἦλθες ἀπολέσαι ἡμᾶς; οἶδά σε τίς εἶ, ὁ ἅγιος τοῦ θεοῦ.
35 καὶ ἐπετίμησεν αὐτῷ ὁ Ἰησοῦς λέγων, Φιμώθητι καὶ ἔξελθε ἀπ᾽ αὐτοῦ. καὶ ῥίψαν αὐτὸν τὸ δαιμόνιον εἰς τὸ μέσον ἐξῆλθεν ἀπ᾽
αὐτοῦ μηδὲν βλάψαν αὐτόν. ¶ 36 καὶ ἐγένετο θάμβος ἐπὶ πάντας καὶ συνελάλουν πρὸς ἀλλήλους λέγοντες, Τίς ὁ λόγος οὗτος
ὅτι ἐν ἐξουσίᾳ καὶ δυνάμει ἐπιτάσσει τοῖς ἀκαθάρτοις πνεύμασιν καὶ ἐξέρχονται; 37 καὶ ἐξεπορεύετο ἦχος περὶ αὐτοῦ εἰς πάντα
τόπον τῆς περιχώρου.
4:38 Ἀναστὰς δὲ ἀπὸ τῆς συναγωγῆς εἰσῆλθεν εἰς τὴν οἰκίαν Σίμωνος. πενθερὰ δὲ τοῦ Σίμωνος ἦν συνεχομένη πυρετῷ μεγάλῳ
καὶ ἠρώτησαν αὐτὸν περὶ αὐτῆς. 39 καὶ ἐπιστὰς ἐπάνω αὐτῆς ἐπετίμησεν τῷ πυρετῷ καὶ ἀφῆκεν αὐτήν· παραχρῆμα δὲ ἀναστᾶσα
διηκόνει αὐτοῖς. ¶ 40 Δύνοντος δὲ τοῦ ἡλίου ἅπαντες ὅσοι εἶχον ἀσθενοῦντας νόσοις ποικίλαις ἤγαγον αὐτοὺς πρὸς αὐτόν· ὁ
δὲ ἑνὶ ἑκάστῳ αὐτῶν τὰς χεῖρας ἐπιτιθεὶς ἐθεράπευεν αὐτούς. 41 ἐξήρχετο δὲ καὶ δαιμόνια ἀπὸ πολλῶν κρ[αυγ]άζοντα καὶ λέγοντα
ὅτι Σὺ εἶ ὁ υἱὸς τοῦ θεοῦ. καὶ ἐπιτιμῶν οὐκ εἴα αὐτὰ λαλεῖν, ὅτι ᾔδεισαν τὸν Χριστὸν αὐτὸν εἶναι. ¶ 42 Γενομένης δὲ ἡμέρας

they knew he was the Christ. ¶ **42** At daybreak   Jesus went out   to a solitary place.
→ ἤδεισαν αὐτὸν εἶναι τὸν χριστὸν | δὲ ⌐Γενομένης ἡμέρας⌐ | ἐξελθὼν ← ἐπορεύθη εἰς ἔρημον τόπον καὶ
v.lai.3p r.asm.3 f.pa d.asm n.asm | cj pt.am.gsf n.gsf | pt.aa.nsm v.api.3s p.a a.asm n.asm cj
3857 899 1639 3836 5986 | 1254 1181 2465 | 2002 4513 1650 2245 5536 2779

The people were looking for him and when they came to where he was, they tried to keep him from
οἱ ὄχλοι → ἐπεζήτουν ← αὐτὸν καὶ → ἦλθον ἕως ← αὐτοῦ καὶ → → → κατεῖχον αὐτὸν →
d.npm n.npm v.iai.3p r.asm.3 cj v.aai.3p p.a r.gsm.3 cj v.iai.3p r.asm.3
3836 4063 2118 899 2779 2262 2401 899 2779 2988 899

leaving   them. **43** But he said, "I must preach   the good news of the kingdom of
⌐τοῦ μὴ πορεύεσθαι⌐ ἀπ᾽ αὐτῶν δὲ ὁ εἶπεν πρὸς αὐτοὺς ὅτι με δεῖ εὐαγγελίσασθαι ← → τὴν βασιλείαν →
d.gsn pl f.pm r.gpm.3 cj d.nsm v.aai.3s p.a r.apm.3 rapm.3 r.as.1 v.pai.3s f.am d.asf n.asf
3836 3590 4513 608 899 1254 3836 3306 4639 899 4022 1609 1256 2294 3836 993

God   to the other towns also, because that   is why I was sent." **44** And he kept on preaching   in the
⌐τοῦ θεοῦ⌐ → ταῖς ἑτέραις πόλεσιν καὶ ὅτι → ⌐ἐπὶ τοῦτο⌐ ← ← → ἀπεστάλην Καὶ → → → ⌐ἦν κηρύσσων⌐ εἰς τὰς
d.gsm n.gsm d.dpf r.dpf n.dpf adv cj p.a r.asn v.api.1s cj v.iai.3s pt.pa.nsm p.a d.apf
3836 2536 3836 2283 4484 2779 4022 2093 4047 690 2779 1639 3062 1650 3836

synagogues of Judea.
συναγωγὰς ⌐τῆς Ἰουδαίας⌐
n.apf d.gsf n.gsf
5252 3836 2677

The Calling of the First Disciples

5:1 One day as Jesus was standing by the Lake of Gennesaret, with the people crowding
δὲ Ἐγένετο ← καὶ → αὐτὸς ἦν ἑστὼς παρὰ τὴν λίμνην → Γεννησαρὲτ τὸν ὄχλον ⌐ἐν τῷ ἐπικεῖσθαι⌐
cj v.ami.3s cj r.nsm v.iai.3s pt.ra.nsm p.a d.asf n.asf n.gsf d.asm n.asm p.d d.dsn f.pm
1254 1181 2779 2705 899 1639 2705 4123 3836 3349 1166 3836 4063 1877 3836 2130

around him and listening to the word of God, **2** he saw at the water's edge two boats, left
← αὐτῷ καὶ ἀκούειν → τὸν λόγον → ⌐τοῦ θεοῦ⌐ καὶ → εἶδεν παρὰ τὴν λίμνην ← δύο πλοῖα ἑστῶτα δὲ ἀποβάντες
r.dsm.3 cj f.pa d.asm n.asm d.gsm n.gsm cj v.aai.3s p.a d.asf n.asf a.apn n.apn pt.ra.apn cj pt.aa.npm
899 2779 201 3836 3364 3836 2536 2779 1625 4123 3836 3349 4123 1545 4450 2705 1254 650

there by the fishermen, who were washing their nets. **3** He got into one of the boats, the one belonging
ἀπ᾽ αὐτῶν οἱ ἁλιεῖς → ἔπλυνον τὰ δίκτυα δὲ ἐμβὰς εἰς ἓν → τῶν πλοίων ὃ ἦν
p.g r.gpm.3 d.npm n.npm v.iai.3p d.apn n.apn cj pt.aa.nsm p.a a.asn d.gpn n.gpn r.nsn v.iai.3s
608 899 3836 243 4459 3836 1473 1254 1832 1650 1651 3836 4450 4005 1639

to Simon, and asked him to put out a little from shore. Then he sat down and taught the people
→ Σίμωνος ἠρώτησεν αὐτὸν → ἐπαναγαγεῖν ← ὀλίγον ἀπὸ ⌐τῆς γῆς⌐ δὲ → καθίσας ← ἐδίδασκεν ⌐τοὺς ὄχλους⌐
n.gsm v.aai.3s r.asm.3 f.aa adv p.g d.gsf n.gsf cj pt.aa.nsm v.iai.3s d.apm n.apm
4981 2263 899 2056 3900 608 3836 1178 1254 2767 1438 3836 4063

from the boat. ¶ **4** When he had finished speaking, he said to Simon, "Put out into deep
ἐκ τοῦ πλοίου δὲ Ὡς → → ἐπαύσατο λαλῶν, → εἶπεν πρὸς ⌐τὸν Σίμωνα⌐ ἐπανάγαγε ← εἰς τὸ βάθος ⌐
p.g d.gsn n.gsn cj cj v.ami.3s pt.pa.nsm v.aai.3s p.a d.asm n.asm v.aam.2s p.a d.asn n.asn
1666 3836 4450 1254 6055 4264 3281 3306 4639 3836 4981 2056 1650 3836 958

water, and let down the nets for a catch." **5** Simon answered, "Master, we've worked hard
καὶ χαλάσατε ← τὰ δίκτυα ὑμῶν εἰς ἄγραν καὶ Σίμων ἀποκριθεὶς εἶπεν ἐπιστάτα → κοπιάσαντες ← δι᾽
cj v.aam.2p d.apn n.apn r.gp.2 p.a n.asf cj n.nsm pt.ap.nsm v.aai.3s n.vsm pt.aa.npm p.g
2779 5899 3836 1473 7007 1650 62 2779 4981 646 3306 2181 3159 1328

all night and haven't caught anything. But because you say so, I will let down the nets." ¶ **6**
ὅλης νυκτὸς → ἐλάβομεν οὐδὲν δὲ ἐπὶ σου ⌐τῷ ῥήματι⌐ → χαλάσω τὰ δίκτυα καὶ
a.gsf n.gsf v.aai.1p a.asn cj p.d r.gs.2 d.dsn n.dsn v.fai.1s d.apn n.apn cj
3910 3816 4029 4029 1254 2093 5148 3836 4839 5899 3836 1473 2779

When they had done so, they caught such a large number of fish that their nets began to
→ ποιήσαντες τοῦτο → συνέκλεισαν πολὺ πλῆθος → ἰχθύων δὲ αὐτῶν ⌐τὰ δίκτυα⌐ began to
pt.aa.npm r.asn v.aai.3p a.asn n.asn n.gpm cj r.gpm.3 d.npn n.npn
4472 4047 5168 4498 4436 2716 1254 899 3836 1473

break. **7** So they signaled their partners in the other boat to come and help them, and they came
διερρήσσετο καὶ → κατένευσαν τοῖς μετόχοις ἐν τῷ ἑτέρῳ πλοίῳ → ⌐τοῦ ἐλθόντας⌐ συλλαβέσθαι αὐτοῖς καὶ → ἦλθον
v.ipi.3s cj v.aai.3p d.dpm n.dpm p.d d.dsn r.dsn n.dsn d.gsn pt.aa.apm f.am r.dpm.3 cj v.aai.3p
1393 2779 2916 3836 3581 1877 3836 2283 4450 3836 2262 5197 899 2779 2262

ἐξελθὼν ἐπορεύθη εἰς ἔρημον τόπον· καὶ οἱ ὄχλοι ἐπεζήτουν αὐτὸν καὶ ἦλθον ἕως αὐτοῦ καὶ κατεῖχον αὐτὸν τοῦ μὴ πορεύεσθαι ἀπ᾽ αὐτῶν. 43 ὁ δὲ εἶπεν πρὸς αὐτοὺς ὅτι Καὶ ταῖς ἑτέραις πόλεσιν εὐαγγελίσασθαί με δεῖ τὴν βασιλείαν τοῦ θεοῦ, ὅτι ἐπὶ τοῦτο ἀπεστάλην. 44 καὶ ἦν κηρύσσων εἰς τὰς συναγωγὰς τῆς Ἰουδαίας.

5:1 Ἐγένετο δὲ ἐν τῷ τὸν ὄχλον ἐπικεῖσθαι αὐτῷ καὶ ἀκούειν τὸν λόγον τοῦ θεοῦ καὶ αὐτὸς ἦν ἑστὼς παρὰ τὴν λίμνην Γεννησαρὲτ 2 καὶ εἶδεν δύο πλοῖα ἑστῶτα παρὰ τὴν λίμνην· οἱ δὲ ἁλιεῖς ἀπ᾽ αὐτῶν ἀποβάντες ἔπλυνον τὰ δίκτυα. 3 ἐμβὰς δὲ εἰς ἓν τῶν πλοίων, ὃ ἦν Σίμωνος, ἠρώτησεν αὐτὸν ἀπὸ τῆς γῆς ἐπαναγαγεῖν ὀλίγον, καθίσας δὲ ἐκ τοῦ πλοίου ἐδίδασκεν τοὺς ὄχλους. ¶ 4 ὡς δὲ ἐπαύσατο λαλῶν, εἶπεν πρὸς τὸν Σίμωνα, Ἐπανάγαγε εἰς τὸ βάθος καὶ χαλάσατε τὰ δίκτυα ὑμῶν εἰς ἄγραν. 5 καὶ ἀποκριθεὶς Σίμων εἶπεν, Ἐπιστάτα, δι᾽ ὅλης νυκτὸς κοπιάσαντες οὐδὲν ἐλάβομεν· ἐπὶ δὲ τῷ ῥήματί σου χαλάσω τὰ δίκτυα. ¶ 6 καὶ τοῦτο ποιήσαντες συνέκλεισαν πλῆθος ἰχθύων πολύ, διερρήσσετο δὲ τὰ δίκτυα αὐτῶν. 7 καὶ κατένευσαν τοῖς μετόχοις ἐν τῷ ἑτέρῳ πλοίῳ τοῦ ἐλθόντας συλλαβέσθαι αὐτοῖς· καὶ ἦλθον καὶ ἔπλησαν ἀμφότερα τὰ πλοῖα ὥστε βυθίζεσθαι

and	filled	both	boats		so	full	that	they began	to sink.	¶	8		When	Simon	Peter	saw	this, he
καὶ	ἔπλησαν	ἀμφότερα	⸤τὰ πλοῖα⸥	←	ὥστε	αὐτὰ	→	→	βυθίζεσθαι			δὲ		Σίμων	Πέτρος	ἰδὼν
cj	v.aai.3p	a.apn	d.apn n.apn		cj	r.apn.3			f.pp			cj		n.nsm	n.nsm	pt.aa.nsm
2779	4398	317	3836 4450	4398 4398	6063	899			1112			1254 1625		4981	4377	1625

fell		at	Jesus'	knees		and said,	"Go	away	from	me,	Lord;		I	am	a sinful	man!"	9	For	he	and
προσέπεσεν	→		Ἰησοῦ	⸤τοῖς γόνασιν⸥		λέγων	ἔξελθε	←	ἀπ᾽	ἐμοῦ	κύριε	ὅτι	→	εἰμι	ἁμαρτωλός	ἀνὴρ		γὰρ	αὐτὸν	καὶ
v.aai.3s				d.dpn n.dpn		pt.pa.nsm	v.aam.2s		p.g	r.gs.1	n.vsm	cj		v.pai.1s	a.nsm	n.nsm		cj	r.asm.3	cj
4700		1205 2652		3836 1205		3306	2002		608	1609	3261	4022		1639	283	467		1142	899	2779

all	his	companions		were	astonished		at	the	catch	of fish			they had taken,	10	and so			were
πάντας	→	⸤τοὺς σὺν αὐτῷ⸥	→		θάμβος	περιέσχεν	ἐπὶ	τῇ	ἄγρᾳ	⸤τῶν ἰχθύων⸥	ὧν	→	συνέλαβον		δὲ	ὁμοίως	καὶ
a.apm		d.apm p.d r.dsm.3			n.nsn	v.aai.3s	p.d	d.dsf	n.dsf	d.gpm n.gpm	r.gpm		v.aai.3p		cj	adv	adv
4246	899	3836 5250 899			2502	4321	2093	3836	62	3836 2716	4005		5197		1254	3931	2779

James	and	John,	the sons	of Zebedee,		Simon's		partners.	¶	Then	Jesus		said to
Ἰάκωβον	καὶ	Ἰωάννην	υἱοὺς	→ Ζεβεδαίου	οἳ	ἦσαν	⸤τῷ Σίμωνι⸥	κοινωνοὶ		καὶ	ὁ	Ἰησοῦς	εἶπεν πρὸς
n.asm	cj	n.asm	n.apm	n.gsm	r.npm	v.iai.3p	d.dsm n.dsm	n.npm		cj	d.nsm n.nsm		v.aai.3s p.a
2610	2779	2722	5626	2411	4005	1639	3836 4981	3128		2779	3836 2652		3306 4639

Simon,		"Don't be afraid;	from	now	on you	will	catch		men."	11	So	they pulled		their	boats	up	on
⸤τὸν Σίμωνα⸥	μὴ	→ φοβοῦ	ἀπὸ	⸤τοῦ νῦν⸥		→	ἔσῃ	ζωγρῶν	ἀνθρώπους		καὶ		καταγαγόντες	τὰ	πλοῖα	↑	ἐπὶ
d.asm n.asm	pl	v.ppm.2s	p.g	d.gsm adv			v.fmi.2s	pt.pa.nsm	n.apm		cj		pt.aa.npm	d.apn	n.apn		p.a
3836 4981	3590	5828	608	3836 3814			1639	2436	476		2779		2864	3836	4450	2864	2093

shore,	left	everything	and	followed	him.
⸤τὴν γῆν⸥	ἀφέντες	πάντα		ἠκολούθησαν	αὐτῷ
d.asf n.asf	pt.aa.npm	a.apn		v.aai.3p	r.dsm.3
3836 1178	918	4246		199	899

The Man With Leprosy

5:12

While	Jesus	was		in	one	of the towns,		a man	came along	who was	covered	with
Καὶ	ἐγένετο	ἐν	αὐτὸν	⸤τῷ εἶναι⸥	ἐν	μιᾷ	→ τῶν πόλεων	καὶ	ἰδοὺ	ἀνὴρ		πλήρης	→
cj	v.ami.3s	p.d	r.asm.3	d.dsn f.pa	p.d	a.dsf	d.gpf n.gpf	cj		n.nsm		a.nsm
2779	1181	1877	899	3836 1639	1877	1651	3836 4484	2779	2627	467		4441

leprosy.	When	he	saw	Jesus,		he fell	with his	face		to the	ground	and	begged	him,		"Lord,	if
λέπρας	δὲ	→	ἰδὼν	⸤τὸν Ἰησοῦν⸥	→	πεσὼν	ἐπὶ	πρόσωπον					ἐδεήθη	αὐτοῦ	λέγων	κύριε	ἐὰν
n.gsf	cj		pt.aa.nsm	d.asm n.asm		pt.aa.nsm	p.a	n.asn					v.api.3s	r.gsm.3	pt.pa.nsm	n.vsm	cj
3319	1254		1625	3836 2652		4406	2093	4725	4406	4406	4406		1289	899	3306	3261	1569

you	are	willing,	you	can	make	me	clean."	13	Jesus	reached out	his	hand	and	touched	the man.	"I am willing,"
→	→	θέλῃς	→	δύνασαι	↑	με	καθαρίσαι		καὶ	ἐκτείνας	← τὴν	χεῖρα		ἥψατο	αὐτοῦ	→ → θέλω
		v.pas.2s		v.ppi.2s		r.as.1	v.aan		cj	pt.aa.nsm	d.asf n.asf			v.ami.3s	r.gsm.3	v.pai.1s
		2527		1538		2751	1609 2751		2779	1753	3836 5931			721	899	2527

he	said.	"Be clean!"	And	immediately	the	leprosy	left		him.	¶	14	Then	Jesus	ordered	him,	"Don't
→	λέγων	καθαρίσθητι	καὶ	εὐθέως	ἡ	λέπρα	ἀπῆλθεν	ἀπ᾽	αὐτοῦ			καὶ	αὐτὸς	παρήγγειλεν	αὐτῷ	μηδενὶ
	pt.pa.nsm	v.apm.2s	cj	adv	d.nsf	n.nsf	v.aai.3s	p.g	r.gsm.3			cj	r.nsm	v.aai.3s	r.dsm.3	a.dsm
	3306	2751	2779	2311	3836	3319	599	608	899			2779	899	4133	899	3594

tell	anyone,	but	go,		show	yourself	to the	priest	and	offer		the	sacrifices	that	Moses	commanded	for
εἰπεῖν	↑	ἀλλὰ	ἀπελθὼν	δεῖξον	σεαυτὸν	→	τῷ	ἱερεῖ	καὶ	προσένεγκε				καθὼς	Μωϋσῆς	προσέταξεν	περὶ
f.aa		cj	pt.aa.nsm	v.aam.2s	r.asm.2		d.dsm	n.dsm	cj	v.aam.2s				cj	n.nsm	v.aai.3s	p.g
3306	3594	247	599	1259	4932		3836	2636	2779	4712				2777	3707	4705	4309

your	cleansing,		as	a	testimony	to them."	15	Yet	the	news	about	him	spread	all	the more,		so that	crowds	of
σου	⸤τοῦ καθαρισμοῦ⸥	εἰς	μαρτύριον	→	αὐτοῖς		δὲ	ὁ	λόγος	περὶ	αὐτοῦ	διήρχετο	→	→	μᾶλλον	καὶ		ὄχλοι
r.gs.2	d.gsm n.gsm	p.a	n.asn		r.dpm.3		cj	d.nsm	n.nsm	p.g	r.gsm.3	v.imi.3s			adv.c	cj		n.npm
5148	3836 2752	1650	3457		899		1254	3836	3364	4309	899	1451			3437	2779		4063

people	came		to hear	him	and	to be healed		of	their	sicknesses.	16	But	Jesus	often	withdrew		to
πολλοὶ	συνήρχοντο	→	ἀκούειν	καὶ	→	→ θεραπεύεσθαι	ἀπὸ	αὐτῶν	⸤τῶν	ἀσθενειῶν⸥		δὲ	αὐτὸς	→	ἦν	ὑποχωρῶν	ἐν
a.npm	v.imi.3p		f.pa	cj		f.pp	p.g	r.gpm.3	d.gpf	n.gpf		cj	r.nsm		v.iai.3s	pt.pa.nsm	p.d
4498	5302		201	2779		2543	608	899	3836	819		1254	899		1639	5723	1877

lonely	places		and	prayed.
→	⸤ταῖς ἐρήμοις⸥	καὶ	προσευχόμενος
	d.dpf a.dpf	cj	pt.pm.nsm
	3836 2245	2779	4667

αὐτά. ¶ 8 ἰδὼν δὲ Σίμων Πέτρος προσέπεσεν τοῖς γόνασιν Ἰησοῦ λέγων, Ἔξελθε ἀπ᾽ ἐμοῦ, ὅτι ἀνὴρ ἁμαρτωλός εἰμι, κύριε. 9 θάμβος γὰρ περιέσχεν αὐτὸν καὶ πάντας τοὺς σὺν αὐτῷ ἐπὶ τῇ ἄγρᾳ τῶν ἰχθύων ὧν συνέλαβον, 10 ὁμοίως δὲ καὶ Ἰάκωβον καὶ Ἰωάννην υἱοὺς Ζεβεδαίου, οἳ ἦσαν κοινωνοὶ τῷ Σίμωνι. ¶ καὶ εἶπεν πρὸς τὸν Σίμωνα ὁ Ἰησοῦς, Μὴ φοβοῦ· ἀπὸ τοῦ νῦν ἀνθρώπους ἔσῃ ζωγρῶν. 11 καὶ καταγαγόντες τὰ πλοῖα ἐπὶ τὴν γῆν ἀφέντες πάντα ἠκολούθησαν αὐτῷ.

5:12 Καὶ ἐγένετο ἐν τῷ εἶναι αὐτὸν ἐν μιᾷ τῶν πόλεων καὶ ἰδοὺ ἀνὴρ πλήρης λέπρας· ἰδὼν δὲ τὸν Ἰησοῦν, πεσὼν ἐπὶ πρόσωπον ἐδεήθη αὐτοῦ λέγων, Κύριε, ἐὰν θέλῃς δύνασαί με καθαρίσαι. 13 καὶ ἐκτείνας τὴν χεῖρα ἥψατο αὐτοῦ λέγων, Θέλω, καθαρίσθητι· καὶ εὐθέως ἡ λέπρα ἀπῆλθεν ἀπ᾽ αὐτοῦ. ¶ 14 καὶ αὐτὸς παρήγγειλεν αὐτῷ μηδενὶ εἰπεῖν, ἀλλὰ ἀπελθὼν δεῖξον σεαυτὸν τῷ ἱερεῖ καὶ προσένεγκε περὶ τοῦ καθαρισμοῦ σου καθὼς προσέταξεν Μωϋσῆς, εἰς μαρτύριον αὐτοῖς. 15 διήρχετο δὲ μᾶλλον ὁ λόγος περὶ αὐτοῦ, καὶ συνήρχοντο ὄχλοι πολλοὶ ἀκούειν καὶ θεραπεύεσθαι ἀπὸ τῶν ἀσθενειῶν αὐτῶν· 16 αὐτὸς δὲ ἦν ὑποχωρῶν ἐν ταῖς ἐρήμοις καὶ προσευχόμενος.

Jesus Heals the Paralytic

5:17

One day		as he	was	teaching,	Pharisees	and teachers		of the law,	who
Καὶ ἐγένετο ἐν	μιᾷ ⌜τῶν ἡμερῶν⌝	καὶ →	αὐτὸς	ἦν διδάσκων	καὶ Φαρισαῖοι	καὶ νομοδιδάσκαλοι	← ←	←	οἳ
cj v.ami.3s p.d	a.dsf d.gpf n.gpf	cj	r.nsm	v.iai.3s pt.pa.nsm	cj n.npm	cj n.npm			r.npm
2779 1181 1877	1651 3836 2465	2779	1438 899	1639 1438	2779 5757	2779 3791			4005

had come		from every village	of Galilee		and from	Judea	and	Jerusalem,	were sitting		there.
→	⌜ἦσαν ἐληλυθότες⌝	ἐκ πάσης κώμης	→ ⌜τῆς Γαλιλαίας⌝	καὶ		Ἰουδαίας	καὶ	Ἰερουσαλήμ	→ ⌜ἦσαν καθήμενοι⌝		
v.iai.3p	pt.ra.npm	p.g a.gsf n.gsf	d.gsf n.gsf	cj		n.gsf	cj	n.gsf	v.iai.3p pt.pm.npm		
1639	2262	1666 4246 3267	3836 1133	2779		2677	2779	2647	1639 2764		

And the power	of the Lord	was present	for him	to heal	the sick.	[18]	Some men	came	carrying a
καὶ δύναμις	→ κυρίου	ἦν	εἰς αὐτὸν	→ ⌜τὸ ἰᾶσθαι⌝		καὶ ἰδοὺ	ἄνδρες		φέροντες
cj n.nsf	n.gsm	v.iai.3s	p.a r.asm.3	d.asn f.pm		cj	n.npm		pt.pa.npm
2779 1539	3261 1639		1650 899	3836 2615		2779 2627	467		5770

paralytic		on a mat	and tried	to take	him	into the house	to lay	him	before
⌜ἄνθρωπον⌝	ὃς ἦν παραλελυμένος	ἐπὶ κλίνης	καὶ ἐζήτουν	→ εἰσενεγκεῖν	αὐτὸν ⤶		καὶ → θεῖναι	αὐτὸν	ἐνώπιον
n.asm	r.nsm v.iai.3s pt.rp.nsm	p.g n.gsf	cj v.iai.3p	f.aa	r.asm.3		cj f.aa	r.asm.3	p.g
476	4005 1639 4168	2093 3109	2779 2426	1662	899 1662		2779 5502	899	1967

Jesus.	[19]	When they could	not find	a way	to do		this	because of the crowd,	they went		up	on the
αὐτοῦ	καὶ →	→ →	μὴ εὑρόντες	ποίας	εἰσενέγκωσιν	αὐτὸν διὰ		← τὸν ὄχλον	→ ἀναβάντες	←	ἐπὶ	τὸ
r.gsm.3	cj		pl pt.aa.npm	r.gsf	v.aas.3p	r.asm.3 p.a		d.asm n.asm	pt.aa.npm		p.a	d.asn
899	2779 2351	2351 2351	3590 2351	4481	1662	899 1328		3836 4063	326		2093	3836

roof	and lowered	him	on	his mat	through	the tiles	into	the middle	of the crowd,	right in front	of
δῶμα	καθῆκαν	αὐτὸν	σὺν τῷ	κλινιδίῳ	διὰ	τῶν κεράμων	εἰς	τὸ μέσον		→ ἔμπροσθεν	←
n.asn	v.aai.3p	r.asm.3	p.d d.dsn	n.dsn	p.g	d.gpm n.gpm	p.a	d.asn n.asn		p.g	
1560	2768	899	5250 3836	3110	1328	3836 3041	1650	3836 3545		1869	

Jesus.	[20]	When Jesus	saw	their	faith,		he said,	"Friend,	your	sins		are forgiven."		[21]	
⌜τοῦ Ἰησοῦ⌝	καὶ		ἰδὼν	αὐτῶν	⌜τὴν πίστιν⌝	→	εἶπεν	ἄνθρωπε	σου	⌜αἱ ἁμαρτίαι⌝	→	ἀφέωνται	σοι	¶	καὶ
d.gsm n.gsm	cj		pt.aa.nsm	r.gpm.3	d.asf n.asf		v.aai.3s	n.vsm	r.gs.2	d.npf n.npf		v.rpi.3p	r.ds.2		cj
3836 2652	2779		1625	899	3836 4411		3306	4411	5148	3836 281		918	5148		2779

The Pharisees	and the teachers		of the law	began	thinking		to themselves,	"Who is	this	fellow who
οἱ Φαρισαῖοι	καὶ οἱ γραμματεῖς	← ←	←	ἤρξαντο	διαλογίζεσθαι	←	λέγοντες	τίς ἐστιν	οὗτος	ὃς
d.npm n.npm	cj d.npm n.npm			v.ami.3p	f.pm		pt.pa.npm	r.nsm v.pai.3s	r.nsm	r.nsm
3836 5757	2779 3836 1208			806	1368		3306	5515 1639	4047	4005

speaks blasphemy?	Who can	forgive	sins	but	God	alone?"	¶	[22]	Jesus	knew	what they
λαλεῖ βλασφημίας	τίς δύναται	ἀφεῖναι	ἁμαρτίας	εἰ μὴ	ὁ θεός	μόνος			δὲ ὁ Ἰησοῦς	ἐπιγνοὺς	τοὺς αὐτῶν
v.pai.3s n.apf	r.nsm v.ppi.3s	f.aa	n.apf	cj pl	d.nsm n.nsm	a.nsm			cj d.nsm n.nsm	pt.aa.nsm	d.apm r.gpm.3
3281 1060	5515 1538	918	281	1623 3590	3836 2536	3668			1254 3836 2652	2105	3836 899

were thinking	and	asked,		"Why are you thinking	these things	in	your hearts?
διαλογισμοὺς	ἀποκριθεὶς	εἶπεν	πρὸς αὐτούς τί	→ →	διαλογίζεσθε	ἐν ὑμῶν	⌜ταῖς καρδίαις⌝
n.apm	pt.ap.nsm	v.aai.3s	p.a r.apm.3 r.asn		v.pmi.2p	p.d r.gp.2	d.dpf n.dpf
1369	646	3306	4639 899 5515		1368	1877 7007	3836 2840

[23] Which is	easier:	to say,	'Your	sins		are forgiven,'	or to say,	'Get up	and walk'?	[24] But that you
τί ἐστιν	εὐκοπώτερον	→ εἰπεῖν	σου	⌜αἱ ἁμαρτίαι⌝	→	ἀφέωνται	σοι ἢ → εἰπεῖν	ἔγειρε	καὶ περιπάτει	δὲ ἵνα
r.nsn v.pai.3s	a.nsn.c	f.aa	r.gs.2	d.npf n.npf		v.rpi.3p	r.ds.2 cj f.aa	v.pam.2s	cj v.pam.2s	cj cj
5515 1639	2324	3306	5148	3836 281		918	5148 2445 3306	1586	2779 4344	1254 2671

may know	that the Son	of Man	has authority	on earth	to forgive	sins...."	He said	to the paralyzed
→ εἰδῆτε	ὅτι ὁ υἱὸς	⌜τοῦ ἀνθρώπου⌝	ἔχει ἐξουσίαν	ἐπὶ ⌜τῆς γῆς⌝	→ ἀφιέναι	ἁμαρτίας	εἶπεν	τῷ παραλελυμένῳ
v.ras.2p	cj d.nsm n.nsm	d.gsm n.gsm	v.pai.3s n.asf	p.g d.gsf n.gsf	f.pa	n.apf	v.aai.3s	d.dsm pt.rp.dsm
3857	4022 3836 5626	3836 476	2400 2026	2093 3836 1178	918	281	3306	4168

man, "I tell	you,	get	up,	take	your mat	and go	home."	[25]	Immediately he stood	up
λέγω	σοὶ	ἔγειρε	καὶ	ἄρας	σου ⌜τὸ κλινίδιον⌝	πορεύου	εἰς ⌜τὸν οἶκον⌝	σου	καὶ παραχρῆμα	ἀναστὰς
v.pai.1s	r.ds.2	v.pam.2s	cj	pt.aa.nsm	r.gs.2 d.asn n.asn	v.pmm.2s	p.a d.asm n.asm	r.gs.2	cj adv	pt.aa.nsm
3306	5148	1586	2779	149	5148 3836 3110	4513	1650 3836 3875	5148	2779 4202	482

in front	of them,	took	what he had been lying	on	and went	home	praising God.	[26]
→ ἐνώπιον	αὐτῶν	ἄρας ἐφ' ὃ	→ → → κατέκειτο		ἀπῆλθεν εἰς	⌜τὸν οἶκον⌝ αὐτοῦ	δοξάζων ⌜τὸν θεόν⌝	καὶ
p.g	r.gpm.3	pt.aa.nsm p.a r.asn	v.imi.3s		v.aai.3s p.a	d.asm n.asm r.gsm.3	pt.pa.nsm d.asm n.asm	cj
1967	899	149 2093 4005	2879		599 1650	3836 3875 1519	3836 2536	2779

5:17 Καὶ ἐγένετο ἐν μιᾷ τῶν ἡμερῶν καὶ αὐτὸς ἦν διδάσκων, καὶ ἦσαν καθήμενοι Φαρισαῖοι καὶ νομοδιδάσκαλοι οἳ ἦσαν ἐληλυθότες ἐκ πάσης κώμης τῆς Γαλιλαίας καὶ Ἰουδαίας καὶ Ἰερουσαλήμ· καὶ δύναμις κυρίου ἦν εἰς τὸ ἰᾶσθαι αὐτόν. [18] καὶ ἰδοὺ ἄνδρες φέροντες ἐπὶ κλίνης ἄνθρωπον ὃς ἦν παραλελυμένος καὶ ἐζήτουν αὐτὸν εἰσενεγκεῖν καὶ θεῖναι [αὐτὸν] ἐνώπιον αὐτοῦ. [19] καὶ μὴ εὑρόντες ποίας εἰσενέγκωσιν αὐτὸν διὰ τὸν ὄχλον, ἀναβάντες ἐπὶ τὸ δῶμα διὰ τῶν κεράμων καθῆκαν αὐτὸν σὺν τῷ κλινιδίῳ εἰς τὸ μέσον ἔμπροσθεν τοῦ Ἰησοῦ. [20] καὶ ἰδὼν τὴν πίστιν αὐτῶν εἶπεν, Ἄνθρωπε, ἀφέωνταί σοι αἱ ἁμαρτίαι σου. ¶ [21] καὶ ἤρξαντο διαλογίζεσθαι οἱ γραμματεῖς καὶ οἱ Φαρισαῖοι λέγοντες, Τίς ἐστιν οὗτος ὃς λαλεῖ βλασφημίας; τίς δύναται ἁμαρτίας ἀφεῖναι εἰ μὴ μόνος ὁ θεός; ¶ [22] ἐπιγνοὺς δὲ ὁ Ἰησοῦς τοὺς διαλογισμοὺς αὐτῶν ἀποκριθεὶς εἶπεν πρὸς αὐτούς, Τί διαλογίζεσθε ἐν ταῖς καρδίαις ὑμῶν; [23] τί ἐστιν εὐκοπώτερον, εἰπεῖν, Ἀφέωνταί σοι αἱ ἁμαρτίαι σου, ἢ εἰπεῖν, Ἔγειρε καὶ περιπάτει; [24] ἵνα δὲ εἰδῆτε ὅτι ὁ υἱὸς τοῦ ἀνθρώπου ἐξουσίαν ἔχει ἐπὶ τῆς γῆς ἀφιέναι ἁμαρτίας— εἶπεν τῷ παραλελυμένῳ, Σοί λέγω, ἔγειρε καὶ ἄρας τὸ κλινίδιόν σου πορεύου εἰς τὸν οἶκόν σου. [25] καὶ παραχρῆμα ἀναστὰς ἐνώπιον αὐτῶν, ἄρας ἐφ' ὃ κατέκειτο, ἀπῆλθεν εἰς τὸν οἶκον αὐτοῦ δοξάζων τὸν θεόν. [26] καὶ ἔκστασις ἔλαβεν ἅπαντας καὶ ἐδόξαζον

Everyone was amazed and gave praise to God.   They were filled with awe and said, "We have
ἅπαντας ἔλαβεν ἔκστασις καὶ → ἐδόξαζον ← τὸν θεὸν καὶ → → ἐπλήσθησαν → φόβου λέγοντες ὅτι →
a.apm v.aai.3s n.nsf cj   v.iai.3p   d.asm n.asm cj   v.api.3p   n.gsm pt.pa.npm cj
570 3284 1749 2779   1519   3836 2536 2779   4398   5832 3306 4022

seen remarkable things today."
εἴδομεν παράδοξα → σήμερον
v.aai.1p a.apn   adv
1625 4141   4958

The Calling of Levi

5:27 After this, Jesus went out and saw a tax collector by the name of Levi sitting at his tax
Καὶ μετὰ ταῦτα ἐξῆλθεν ← καὶ ἐθεάσατο τελώνην ← → → ὀνόματι ← Λευὶν καθήμενον ἐπὶ τὸ τελώνιον
cj p.a r.apn v.aai.3s cj v.ami.3s n.asm   n.dsn   n.asn pt.pm.asm p.a d.asn n.asn
2779 3552 4047 2002 2779 2517 5467   3950   3322 2764 2093 3836 5468

booth. "Follow me," Jesus said to him, [28] and Levi got up, left everything and followed him. ¶
← καὶ ἀκολούθει μοι εἶπεν → αὐτῷ καὶ ἀναστὰς ← καταλιπὼν πάντα ἠκολούθει αὐτῷ
cj v.pam.2s r.ds.1 v.aai.3s r.dsm.3 cj pt.aa.nsm pt.aa.nsm a.apn v.iai.3s r.dsm.3
2779 199 1609 3306 899 2779 482 2901 4246 199 899

[29] Then Levi held a great banquet for Jesus at his house, and a large crowd of tax collectors and
Καὶ Λευὶς ἐποίησεν μεγάλην δοχὴν → αὐτῷ ἐν αὐτοῦ τῇ οἰκίᾳ καὶ ἦν πολὺς ὄχλος → τελωνῶν ← καὶ
cj n.nsm v.aai.3s a.asf n.asf   r.dsm.3 p.d r.gsm.3 d.dsf n.dsf cj v.iai.3s a.nsm n.nsm   n.gpm   cj
2779 3322 4472 3489 1531   899 1877 899 3836 3864 2779 1639 4498 4063   5467   2779

others were eating with them. [30] But the Pharisees and the teachers of the law who belonged to their
ἄλλων οἳ → ἦσαν κατακείμενοι μετ' αὐτῶν καὶ οἱ Φαρισαῖοι καὶ οἱ γραμματεῖς ← ← ← → αὐτῶν
r.gpm r.npm   v.iai.3p pt.pm.npm p.g r.gpm.3 cj d.npm n.npm cj d.npm n.npm   r.gpm.3
257 4005   1639 2879 3552 899 2779 3836 5757 2779 3836 1208   899

sect complained to his disciples, "Why do you eat and drink with tax collectors and
ἐγόγγυζον πρὸς αὐτοῦ τοὺς μαθητὰς λέγοντες διὰ τί → ἐσθίετε καὶ πίνετε μετὰ τῶν τελωνῶν ← καὶ
v.iai.3p p.a r.gsm.3 d.apm n.apm pt.pa.npm p.a r.asn   v.pai.2p cj v.pai.2p p.g d.gpm n.gpm   cj
1197 4639 899 3836 3412 3306 1328 5515   2266 2779 4403 3552 3836 5467   2779

'sinners'?" ¶ [31] Jesus answered them, "It is not the healthy who need a doctor,
ἁμαρτωλῶν καὶ ὁ Ἰησοῦς ἀποκριθεὶς εἶπεν πρὸς αὐτούς οὐ οἱ ὑγιαίνοντες → χρείαν ἔχουσιν ἰατροῦ
a.gpm cj d.nsm n.nsm pt.ap.nsm v.aai.3s p.a r.apm.3 pl d.npm pt.pa.npm   n.asf v.pai.3p n.gsm
283 2779 3836 2652 646 3306 4639 899 4024 3836 5617   5970 2400 2620

but the sick. [32] I have not come to call the righteous, but sinners to repentance." [33] They said
ἀλλὰ οἱ κακῶς ἔχοντες → → οὐκ ἐλήλυθα → καλέσαι δικαίους ἀλλὰ ἁμαρτωλοὺς εἰς μετάνοιαν δὲ Οἱ εἶπαν
cj d.npm adv pt.pa.npm pl v.rai.1s f.aa a.apm cj a.apm p.a n.asf cj d.npm v.aai.3p
247 3836 2809 2400 2262 2262 4024 2262 2813 1465 247 283 1650 3567 1254 3836 3306

to him, "John's disciples often fast and pray, and so do the disciples of the Pharisees, but
πρὸς αὐτόν Ἰωάννου οἱ μαθηταὶ πυκνὰ νηστεύουσιν καὶ δεήσεις ποιοῦνται καὶ ὁμοίως οἱ → τῶν Φαρισαίων δὲ
p.a r.asm.3 n.gsm d.npm n.npm adv v.pai.3p cj n.apf v.pmi.3p adv adv d.npm d.gpm n.gpm cj
4639 899 2722 3836 3412 4781 3764 2779 1255 4472 2779 3931 3836 3836 5757 1254

yours go on eating and drinking." ¶ [34] Jesus answered, "Can you make the
οἱ σοὶ → → ἐσθίουσιν καὶ πίνουσιν δὲ ὁ Ἰησοῦς εἶπεν πρὸς αὐτούς μὴ δύνασθε ← ποιῆσαι τοὺς
d.npm r.npm.2   v.pai.3p cj v.pai.3p cj d.nsm n.nsm v.aai.3s p.a r.apm.3 pl v.ppi.2p f.aa d.apm
3836 5050   2266 2779 4403 1254 3836 2652 3306 4639 899 3590 1538 4472 3836

guests of the bridegroom fast while he is with them? [35] But the time will come when the
υἱοὺς → τοῦ νυμφῶνος νηστεῦσαι ἐν ᾧ ὁ νυμφίος ἐστιν μετ' αὐτῶν δὲ ἡμέραι → ἐλεύσονται καὶ ὅταν ὁ
n.apm d.gsm n.gsm f.aa p.d r.dsm d.nsm n.nsm v.pai.3s p.g r.gpm.3 cj n.npf v.fmi.3p cj cj d.nsm
5626 3836 3813 3764 1877 4005 3836 3812 1639 3552 899 1254 2465 2262 2779 4020 3836

bridegroom will be taken from them; in those days they will fast." ¶ [36] He told and
νυμφίος → → ἀπαρθῇ ἀπ' αὐτῶν τότε ἐν ἐκείναις ταῖς ἡμέραις → νηστεύσουσιν δὲ → Ἔλεγεν καὶ
n.nsm v.aps.3s p.g r.gpm.3 adv p.d r.dpf d.dpf n.dpf v.fai.3p cj v.iai.3s adv
3812 554 608 899 5538 1877 1697 3836 2465 3764 1254 3306 2779

them this parable: "No one tears a patch from a new garment and sews it on an old one.
πρὸς αὐτούς παραβολὴν ὅτι → οὐδεὶς σχίσας ἐπίβλημα ἀπὸ καινοῦ ἱματίου ἐπιβάλλει ἐπὶ παλαιὸν ἱμάτιον
p.a r.apm.3 n.asf cj a.nsm pt.aa.nsm n.asn p.g a.gsn n.gsn v.pai.3s p.a a.asn n.asn
4639 899 4130 4022 4029 5387 2099 608 2785 2668 2095 2093 4094 2668

τὸν θεὸν καὶ ἐπλήσθησαν φόβου λέγοντες ὅτι Εἴδομεν παράδοξα σήμερον.
    [5:27] Καὶ μετὰ ταῦτα ἐξῆλθεν καὶ ἐθεάσατο τελώνην ὀνόματι Λευὶν καθήμενον ἐπὶ τὸ τελώνιον, καὶ εἶπεν αὐτῷ, Ἀκολούθει
μοι. [28] καὶ καταλιπὼν πάντα ἀναστὰς ἠκολούθει αὐτῷ. ¶ [29] Καὶ ἐποίησεν δοχὴν μεγάλην Λευὶς αὐτῷ ἐν τῇ οἰκίᾳ αὐτοῦ, καὶ
ἦν ὄχλος πολὺς τελωνῶν καὶ ἄλλων οἳ ἦσαν μετ' αὐτῶν κατακείμενοι. [30] καὶ ἐγόγγυζον οἱ Φαρισαῖοι καὶ οἱ γραμματεῖς αὐτῶν
πρὸς τοὺς μαθητὰς αὐτοῦ λέγοντες, Διὰ τί μετὰ τῶν τελωνῶν καὶ ἁμαρτωλῶν ἐσθίετε καὶ πίνετε; ¶ [31] καὶ ἀποκριθεὶς ὁ Ἰησοῦς
εἶπεν πρὸς αὐτούς, Οὐ χρείαν ἔχουσιν οἱ ὑγιαίνοντες ἰατροῦ ἀλλὰ οἱ κακῶς ἔχοντες· [32] οὐκ ἐλήλυθα καλέσαι δικαίους ἀλλὰ
ἁμαρτωλοὺς εἰς μετάνοιαν. [33] Οἱ δὲ εἶπαν πρὸς αὐτόν, Οἱ μαθηταὶ Ἰωάννου νηστεύουσιν πυκνὰ καὶ δεήσεις ποιοῦνται ὁμοίως
καὶ οἱ τῶν Φαρισαίων, οἱ δὲ σοὶ ἐσθίουσιν καὶ πίνουσιν. ¶ [34] ὁ δὲ Ἰησοῦς εἶπεν πρὸς αὐτούς, Μὴ δύνασθε τοὺς υἱοὺς τοῦ
νυμφῶνος ἐν ᾧ ὁ νυμφίος μετ' αὐτῶν ἐστιν ποιῆσαι νηστεῦσαι; [35] ἐλεύσονται δὲ ἡμέραι, καὶ ὅταν ἀπαρθῇ ἀπ' αὐτῶν ὁ νυμφίος,
τότε νηστεύσουσιν ἐν ἐκείναις ταῖς ἡμέραις. ¶ [36] Ἔλεγεν δὲ καὶ παραβολὴν πρὸς αὐτοὺς ὅτι Οὐδεὶς ἐπίβλημα ἀπὸ ἱματίου
καινοῦ σχίσας ἐπιβάλλει ἐπὶ ἱμάτιον παλαιόν· εἰ δὲ μή γε, καὶ τὸ καινὸν σχίσει καὶ τῷ παλαιῷ οὐ συμφωνήσει τὸ ἐπίβλημα τὸ

If	he does,			he will have	torn	the	new	garment,	and	the	patch		from	the	new	will not
δὲ	εἰ μὴ γε·	←	καὶ	→	σχίσει	τὸ	καινὸν		καὶ	τὸ	ἐπίβλημα	τὸ	ἀπὸ	τοῦ	καινοῦ	→ οὐ
cj	cj pl pl		cj		v.fai.3s	d.asn	a.asn		cj	d.nsn	n.nsn	d.nsn	p.g	d.gsn	a.gsn	pl
1254 1623 3590 1145			2779		5387	3836	2785		2779	3836	2099	3836	608	3836	2785	5244 4024

match	the old.	**37** And	no one		pours	new	wine	into	old		wineskins.	If	he does,	the	new
συμφωνήσει	τῷ παλαιῷ	καὶ →	οὐδεὶς	βάλλει	νέον	οἶνον	εἰς	παλαιούς	ἀσκούς·	δὲ	εἰ μὴ γε·	← ←	ὁ ὁ	νέος
v.fai.3s	d.dsn a.dsn	cj	a.nsm	v.pai.3s	a.asm	n.asm	p.a	a.apm	n.apm	cj	cj pl pl		d.nsm d.nsm	a.nsm
5244	3836 4094	2779	4029	965	3742	3885	1650	4094	829	1254 1623 3590 1145		3836 3836	3742

wine will burst	the	skins,		the	wine will	run	out	and	the	wineskins	will be ruined.	**38** No,	new	wine must
οἶνος →	ῥήξει	τοὺς	ἀσκοὺς	καὶ	αὐτὸς →	ἐκχυθήσεται	←	καὶ	οἱ	ἀσκοὶ	→ ἀπολοῦνται	ἀλλὰ	νέον	οἶνον →
n.nsm	v.fai.3s	d.apm	n.apm	cj	r.nsm	v.fpi.3s		cj	d.npm	n.npm	v.fmi.3p	cj	a.asm	n.asm
3885	4838	3836	829	2779	899	1773		2779	3836	829	660	247	3742	3885

be poured	into	new	wineskins.	**39** And	no one		after drinking	old		wine wants	the new,	for	he says,	'The	old
→ βλητέον	εἰς	καινοὺς	ἀσκούς.	καὶ →	οὐδεὶς	→	πιὼν	παλαιὸν		θέλει	νέον·	γὰρ →	λέγει	ὁ	παλαιὸς
a.nsn	p.a	a.apm	n.apm	cj	a.nsm		pt.aa.nsm	a.asn		v.pai.3s	a.asm	cj	v.pai.3s	d.nsm	a.nsm
1064	1650	2785	829	2779	4029		4403	4094		2527	3742	1142	3306	3836	4094

is	better.'"
ἐστιν	χρηστός
v.pai.3s	a.nsm
1639	5982

Lord of the Sabbath

6:1

	One Sabbath		Jesus was	going		through	the grainfields,	and	his		disciples	began to
δὲ	Ἐγένετο ἐν	σαββάτῳ	αὐτὸν →	διαπορεύεσθαι	διὰ		σπορίμων	καὶ	αὐτοῦ	οἱ	μαθηταὶ	→
cj	v.ami.3s p.d	n.dsn	r.asm.3	v.fpm	p.g		n.gpn	cj	r.gsm.3	d.npm	n.npm	
1254 1181	1877	4879	899	1388	1328		5077	2779	899	3836	3412	

pick	some heads of grain,	rub		them	in their	hands	and	eat	the	kernels.	**2**	Some of		the	Pharisees	asked,
ἔτιλλον	ψώχοντες	→	ταῖς	χερσίν	καὶ	ἤσθιον	τοὺς	στάχυας	δὲ	τινὲς	→	τῶν	Φαρισαίων	εἶπαν
v.iai.3p	pt.pa.npm		d.dpf	n.dpf	cj	v.iai.3p	d.apm	n.apm	cj	r.npm		d.gpm	n.gpm	v.aai.3p
5504	6041		3836	5931	2779	2266	3836	5092	1254	5516		3836	5757	3306

"Why	are you	doing	what	is	unlawful		on the	Sabbath?"	¶	**3**		Jesus	answered		them,	"Have
τί	→	ποιεῖτε	ὃ	→	οὐκ ἔξεστιν	→	τοῖς	σάββασιν;			καὶ ὁ	Ἰησοῦς,	ἀποκριθεὶς	πρὸς	αὐτοὺς	εἶπεν
r.asn		v.pai.2p	r.nsn	pl	v.pai.3s		d.dpn	n.dpn			cj d.nsm	n.nsm	pt.ap.nsm	p.a	r.apm	v.aai.3s
5515		4472	4005	4024	1997		3836	4879			2779 3836	2652	646	4639	899	3306 336

you	never	read		what	David	did	when	he	and	his	companions		were	hungry?	**4**		He
→	οὐδὲ	ἀνέγνωτε	τοῦτο	ὃ	Δαυὶδ	ἐποίησεν	ὅτε	αὐτὸς	καὶ →	οἱ	μετ᾽ αὐτοῦ,	[ὄντες]	→	ἐπείνασεν	[ὡς]	→
adv	v.aai.2p	r.asn	r.asn	n.nsm	v.aai.3s	cj	r.nsm	cj	d.npm	p.g	r.gsm.3	pt.pa.npm	v.aai.3s	cj		
336	4028	336	4047	4005	1253	4472	4021	899	2779	899	3836	3552	899	1639	4277	6055

entered		the house of God,		and	taking	the	consecrated	bread,	he ate	what		is lawful			only	for
εἰσῆλθεν	εἰς	τὸν οἶκον	→	τοῦ θεοῦ,	καὶ	λαβὼν	τοὺς	τῆς προθέσεως,	ἄρτους	→	ἔφαγεν	οὓς	οὐκ	ἔξεστιν	εἰ μὴ	μόνους	←
v.aai.3s	p.a	d.asm n.asm		d.gsm n.gsm	cj	pt.aa.nsm	d.apm	d.gsf n.gsf	n.apm		v.aai.3s	r.apm	pl	v.pai.3s	cj pl	a.apm	
1656	1650	3836 3875		3836 2536	2779	3284	3836	3836 4606	788		2266	4005	4024	1997	1623 3590	3668

priests	to eat.	And	he also gave	some	to	his	companions."	**5**	Then	Jesus	said		to them,	"The	Son of
τοὺς ἱερεῖς,	φαγεῖν	καὶ	ἔδωκεν	→	τοῖς	μετ᾽ αὐτοῦ,	καὶ	ἔλεγεν	αὐτοῖς ὁ	υἱὸς →
d.apm n.apm	f.aa	cj	v.aai.3s		d.dpm	p.g r.gsm.3	cj	v.iai.3s	r.dpm.3 d.nsm	n.nsm
3836 2636	2266	2779	1443		3836	3836 3552 899	2779	3306	899 3836	5626

Man		is	Lord	of the	Sabbath."	¶	**6**		On another	Sabbath	he	went		into	the	synagogue
τοῦ ἀνθρώπου,	ἐστιν	κύριος	→	τοῦ σαββάτου.		δὲ	Ἐγένετο ἐν	ἑτέρῳ	σαββάτῳ	αὐτὸν	εἰσελθεῖν	εἰς	τὴν	συναγωγὴν
d.gsm n.gsm	v.pai.3s	n.nsm		d.gsn n.gsn		cj	v.ami.3s p.d	r.dsn	n.dsn	r.asm.3	f.aa	p.a	d.asf	n.asf
3836 476	1639	3261		3836 4879		1254 1181	1877	2283	4879	899	1656	1650	3836	5252

and	was teaching,	and	a man	was	there	whose	right	hand	was	shriveled.	**7**		The	Pharisees	and	the
καὶ	διδάσκειν	καὶ	ἄνθρωπος	ἦν	ἐκεῖ	καὶ αὐτοῦ	ἡ δεξιὰ	ἡ χεὶρ	ἦν	ξηρά.	δὲ	οἱ	Φαρισαῖοι	καὶ	οἱ
cj	f.pa	cj	n.nsm	v.iai.3s	adv	cj r.gsm.3	d.nsf a.nsf	d.nsf n.nsf	v.iai.3s	a.nsf	cj	d.npm	n.npm	cj	d.npm
2779	1438	2779	476	1639	1695	2779 899	3836 1288	3836 5931	1639	3831	1254	3836	5757	2779	3836

teachers	of the law		were	looking for a reason	to accuse		Jesus,	so they	watched		him	closely	to see if	he
γραμματεῖς	← ←	ἵνα →	εὕρωσιν	→	κατηγορεῖν	αὐτοῦ	παρετηροῦντο	αὐτὸν	←	εἰ →
n.npm		cj	v.aas.3p		f.pa	r.gsm.3	v.imi.3p	r.asm.3		cj
1208		2671	2351		2989	899	4190	899 4190		1623

ἀπὸ τοῦ καινοῦ. ³⁷ καὶ οὐδεὶς βάλλει οἶνον νέον εἰς ἀσκοὺς παλαιούς· εἰ δὲ μή γε, ῥήξει ὁ οἶνος ὁ νέος τοὺς ἀσκοὺς καὶ αὐτὸς ἐκχυθήσεται καὶ οἱ ἀσκοὶ ἀπολοῦνται· ³⁸ ἀλλὰ οἶνον νέον εἰς ἀσκοὺς καινοὺς βλητέον. ³⁹ [καὶ] οὐδεὶς πιὼν παλαιὸν θέλει νέον· λέγει γάρ, Ὁ παλαιὸς χρηστότερος «χρηστός» ἐστιν.

⁶:¹ Ἐγένετο δὲ ἐν σαββάτῳ διαπορεύεσθαι αὐτὸν διὰ σπορίμων, καὶ ἔτιλλον οἱ μαθηταὶ αὐτοῦ καὶ ἤσθιον τοὺς στάχυας ψώχοντες ταῖς χερσίν. ² τινὲς δὲ τῶν Φαρισαίων εἶπαν, Τί ποιεῖτε ὃ οὐκ ἔξεστιν τοῖς σάββασιν; ¶ ³ καὶ ἀποκριθεὶς πρὸς αὐτοὺς εἶπεν ὁ Ἰησοῦς, Οὐδὲ τοῦτο ἀνέγνωτε ὃ ἐποίησεν Δαυὶδ ὅτε ἐπείνασεν αὐτὸς καὶ οἱ μετ᾽ αὐτοῦ [ὄντες], ⁴ [ὡς] εἰσῆλθεν εἰς τὸν οἶκον τοῦ θεοῦ καὶ τοὺς ἄρτους τῆς προθέσεως λαβὼν ἔφαγεν καὶ ἔδωκεν τοῖς μετ᾽ αὐτοῦ, οὓς οὐκ ἔξεστιν φαγεῖν εἰ μὴ μόνους τοὺς ἱερεῖς; ⁵ καὶ ἔλεγεν αὐτοῖς, Κύριός ἐστιν τοῦ σαββάτου ὁ υἱὸς τοῦ ἀνθρώπου. ¶ ⁶ Ἐγένετο δὲ ἐν ἑτέρῳ σαββάτῳ εἰσελθεῖν αὐτὸν εἰς τὴν συναγωγὴν καὶ διδάσκειν. καὶ ἦν ἄνθρωπος ἐκεῖ καὶ ἡ χεὶρ αὐτοῦ ἡ δεξιὰ ἦν ξηρά. ⁷ παρετηροῦντο δὲ αὐτὸν οἱ γραμματεῖς καὶ οἱ Φαρισαῖοι εἰ ἐν τῷ σαββάτῳ θεραπεύει, ἵνα εὕρωσιν κατηγορεῖν αὐτοῦ. ⁸ αὐτὸς δὲ ᾔδει τοὺς

would heal   on the Sabbath. **8** But Jesus knew what they   were thinking   and said to the man with
→   θεραπεύει ἐν   τῷ   σαββάτῳ   δὲ   αὐτὸς ᾔδει   αὐτῶν   ⌐τοὺς διαλογισμοὺς⌐   δὲ   εἶπεν → τῷ   ἀνδρὶ ⌐τῷ ἔχοντι⌐
v.pai.3s   p.d d.dsn n.dsn   cj   r.nsm v.iai.3s   r.gpm.3   d.apm n.apm   cj   v.aai.3s   d.dsm n.dsm   d.dsm pt.pa.dsm
2543   1877 3836 4879   1254 899 3857   1369 899   3836 1369   1254   3306   3836 467   3836 2400

the shriveled hand,   "Get up and stand in front   of everyone."   So he got   up and stood there.   ¶
τὴν   ξηρὰν   χεῖρα   ἔγειρε   καὶ   στῆθι   ⌐εἰς τὸ   μέσον⌐   ←   καὶ →   ἀναστὰς   ἔστη
d.asf   a.asf   n.asf   v.pam.2s   cj   v.aam.2s   p.a d.asn   n.asn   cj   pt.aa.nsm   v.aai.3s
3836   3831   5931   1586   2779   2705   1650 3836   3545   2779   482   2705

9 Then Jesus   said to   them, "I ask   you, which   is lawful on the Sabbath: to do good   or to do
δὲ   ὁ   Ἰησοῦς,   εἶπεν πρὸς αὐτούς   ⌐ἐπερωτῶ ὑμᾶς εἰ   →   ἔξεστιν   τῷ   σαββάτῳ   ἀγαθοποιῆσαι ἢ   →
cj   d.nsm n.nsm   v.aai.3s p.a   r.apm.3   v.pai.1s   r.ap.2 cj   v.pai.3s   d.dsn n.dsn   f.aa   cj
1254   3836 2652   3306 4639   899   2089   7007 1623   1997   3836 4879   16   2445

evil,   to save life   or to destroy it?" **10**   He looked   around at them all,   and then said to the man,
κακοποιῆσαι →   σῶσαι ψυχὴν ἢ   →   ἀπολέσαι   καὶ →   περιβλεψάμενος ←   αὐτοὺς πάντας   εἶπεν →   αὐτῷ
f.aa   f.aa   n.asf   cj   f.aa   cj   pt.am.nsm   r.apm.3   a.apm   v.aai.3s   r.dsm.3
2803   5392   6034   2445   660   2779   4315   899   4246   3306   899

"Stretch out your hand."   He did   so, and his   hand   was completely restored.   **11** But they were
ἔκτεινον ←   σου   ⌐τὴν χεῖρα⌐   δὲ   ὁ   ἐποίησεν   καὶ   αὐτοῦ ⌐ἡ   χείρ⌐   →   ἀπεκατεστάθη   δὲ   αὐτοὶ →
v.aam.2s   r.gs.2   d.asf n.asf   cj   d.nsm v.aai.3s   cj   r.gsm.3   d.nsf n.nsf   v.api.3s   cj   r.npm
1753   5148   3836 5931   1254 3836 4472   2779   899   3836 5931   635   1254   899

furious   and began to discuss   with one   another what   they might do   to Jesus.
⌐ἐπλήσθησαν ἀνοίας⌐   καὶ   →   διελάλουν πρὸς   ἀλλήλους ←   τί   ἂν   →   ποιήσαιεν →   ⌐τῷ   Ἰησοῦ⌐
v.api.3p   n.gsf   cj   v.iai.3p   p.a   r.apm   r.asn pl   v.aao.3p   d.dsm n.dsm
4398   486   2779   1362   4639 253   5515 323   4472   3836 2652

The Twelve Apostles

6:12   One of those   days   Jesus went   out to a mountainside to pray,   and
δὲ   Ἐγένετο ἐν   ταύταις ⌐ταῖς ἡμέραις⌐   αὐτὸν ἐξελθεῖν ←   εἰς   ⌐τὸ ὄρος⌐   →   προσεύξασθαι καὶ
cj   v.ami.3s   p.d   r.dpf   d.dpf n.dpf   r.asm.3 f.aa   p.a d.asn n.asn   f.am   cj
1254 1181   1877   4047   3836 2465   899 2002   1650 3836 4001   4667   2779

spent   the night   praying   to God.   **13**   When morning came, he called   his   disciples
⌐ἦν διανυκτερεύων⌐   ἐν   ⌐τῇ προσευχῇ⌐   ⌐τοῦ θεοῦ⌐   καὶ ὅτε   ἡμέρα   ἐγένετο   προσεφώνησεν αὐτοῦ ⌐τοὺς μαθητὰς⌐
v.iai.3s   pt.pa.nsm   p.d d.dsf n.dsf   d.gsm n.gsm   cj cj   n.nsf   v.ami.3s   v.aai.3s   r.gsm.3 d.apm n.apm
1639 1381   1877 3836 4666   3836 2536   2779 4021   2465   1181   4715   899 3836 3412

to   him and chose   twelve of   them, whom he   also designated apostles: **14** Simon (whom he   named Peter),
←   καὶ   ἐκλεξάμενος δώδεκα ἀπ'   αὐτῶν οὓς   →   καὶ ὠνόμασεν   ἀποστόλους   Σίμωνα ὃν   →   καὶ ὠνόμασεν Πέτρον
cj   pt.am.nsm   a.apm   p.g   r.gpm.3 r.apm   adv v.aai.3s   n.apm   n.asm r.asm   adv v.aai.3s   n.asm
4715   2779   1721   1557   899 4005   3951 2779 3951   693   4981 4005   3951 2779   4377

his   brother   Andrew,   James,   John,   Philip,   Bartholomew,   **15**   Matthew,   Thomas,
καὶ   αὐτοῦ ⌐τὸν ἀδελφὸν⌐   Ἀνδρέαν   καὶ Ἰάκωβον καὶ Ἰωάννην καὶ Φίλιππον καὶ Βαρθολομαῖον   καὶ Μαθθαῖον   καὶ Θωμᾶν   καὶ
cj   r.gsm.3   d.asm n.asm   n.asm   cj n.asm   cj n.asm   cj n.asm   cj n.asm   cj n.asm   cj n.asm   cj
2779   899   3836 81   436   2779 2610   2779 2722   2779 5805   2779 978   2779 3414   2779 2605   2779

James   son of Alphaeus,   Simon who was called   the Zealot,   **16** Judas   son of James,   and Judas Iscariot,
Ἰάκωβον   →   Ἀλφαίου   καὶ Σίμωνα τὸν   →   καλούμενον   ζηλωτὴν καὶ   Ἰούδαν   →   Ἰακώβου καὶ   Ἰούδαν Ἰσκαριὼθ
n.asm   n.gsm   cj n.asm d.asm   pt.pp.asm   n.asm   cj   n.asm   n.gsm   cj   n.asm n.asm
2610   271   2779 4981 3836   2813   2421   2779   2683   2610   2779 2683   2696

who became a traitor.
ὃς   ἐγένετο   προδότης
r.nsm   v.ami.3s   n.nsm
4005   1181   4595

Blessings and Woes

6:17   He went   down with   them and stood on a level   place.   A large crowd of his   disciples was there
Καὶ →   καταβὰς ←   μετ'   αὐτῶν   ἔστη ἐπὶ   πεδινοῦ   τόπου   καὶ   πολὺς ὄχλος   →   αὐτοῦ μαθητῶν
cj   pt.aa.nsm   p.g   r.gpm.3   v.aai.3s p.d   a.gsm   n.gsm   cj   a.nsm n.nsm   r.gsm.3 n.gpm
2779   2849   3552   899   2705 2093   4268   5536   2779   4498 4063   3412 899 3412

and a great number of people   from all   over Judea,   from Jerusalem, and from the coast   of Tyre
καὶ   πολὺ πλῆθος   →   ⌐τοῦ λαοῦ⌐ ἀπὸ   πάσης →   ⌐τῆς Ἰουδαίας⌐ καὶ   Ἰερουσαλὴμ καὶ   τῆς παραλίου   Τύρου
cj   a.nsn n.nsn   d.gsm n.gsm   p.g   a.gsf   d.gsf n.gsf   cj   n.gsf   cj   d.gsf n.gsf   n.gsf
2779   4498 4436   3836 2677   608   4024   3836 2647   2779   2647   2779   3836 4163   5602

διαλογισμοὺς αὐτῶν, εἶπεν δὲ τῷ ἀνδρὶ τῷ ξηρὰν ἔχοντι τὴν χεῖρα, Ἔγειρε καὶ στῆθι εἰς τὸ μέσον· καὶ ἀναστὰς ἔστη. ¶ **9** εἶπεν
δὲ ὁ Ἰησοῦς πρὸς αὐτούς, Ἐπερωτῶ ὑμᾶς εἰ ἔξεστιν τῷ σαββάτῳ ἀγαθοποιῆσαι ἢ κακοποιῆσαι, ψυχὴν σῶσαι ἢ ἀπολέσαι; **10** καὶ
περιβλεψάμενος πάντας αὐτοὺς εἶπεν αὐτῷ, Ἔκτεινον τὴν χεῖρά σου. ὁ δὲ ἐποίησεν καὶ ἀπεκατεστάθη ἡ χεὶρ αὐτοῦ. **11** αὐτοὶ
δὲ ἐπλήσθησαν ἀνοίας καὶ διελάλουν πρὸς ἀλλήλους τί ἂν ποιήσαιεν τῷ Ἰησοῦ.

6:12 Ἐγένετο δὲ ἐν ταῖς ἡμέραις ταύταις ἐξελθεῖν αὐτὸν εἰς τὸ ὄρος προσεύξασθαι, καὶ ἦν διανυκτερεύων ἐν τῇ προσευχῇ τοῦ
θεοῦ. **13** καὶ ὅτε ἐγένετο ἡμέρα, προσεφώνησεν τοὺς μαθητὰς αὐτοῦ, καὶ ἐκλεξάμενος ἀπ' αὐτῶν δώδεκα, οὓς καὶ ἀποστόλους
ὠνόμασεν, **14** Σίμωνα ὃν καὶ ὠνόμασεν Πέτρον, καὶ Ἀνδρέαν τὸν ἀδελφὸν αὐτοῦ, καὶ Ἰάκωβον καὶ Ἰωάννην καὶ Φίλιππον καὶ
Βαρθολομαῖον **15** καὶ Μαθθαῖον καὶ Θωμᾶν καὶ Ἰάκωβον Ἀλφαίου καὶ Σίμωνα τὸν καλούμενον Ζηλωτὴν **16** καὶ Ἰούδαν
Ἰακώβου καὶ Ἰούδαν Ἰσκαριώθ, ὃς ἐγένετο προδότης.

6:17 Καὶ καταβὰς μετ' αὐτῶν ἔστη ἐπὶ τόπου πεδινοῦ, καὶ ὄχλος πολὺς μαθητῶν αὐτοῦ, καὶ πλῆθος πολὺ τοῦ λαοῦ ἀπὸ πάσης
τῆς Ἰουδαίας καὶ Ἰερουσαλὴμ καὶ τῆς παραλίου Τύρου καὶ Σιδῶνος, **18** οἳ ἦλθον ἀκοῦσαι αὐτοῦ καὶ ἰαθῆναι ἀπὸ τῶν νόσων

and Sidon, **18** who had come to hear　him　and to be healed of　their　diseases.　　Those troubled　by
καὶ　Σιδῶνος　οἳ　→　ἦλθον　ἀκοῦσαι　αὐτοῦ καὶ　→　→　ἰαθῆναι ἀπὸ αὐτῶν τῶν νόσων καὶ οἱ　ἐνοχλούμενοι ἀπὸ
cj　n.gsf　r.npm　　v.aai.3p f.aa　r.gsm.3 cj　　　f.ap　p.g r.gpm.3 d.gpf n.gpf cj d.npm pt.pp.npm　p.g
2779　4972　4005　　2262　201　899　2779　　　2615　608 899 3836 3798 2779 3836 1943　608

evil　　spirits　were cured,　**19** and the people all tried　to touch　him, because power　was coming from
ἀκαθάρτων πνευμάτων　ἐθεραπεύοντο　καὶ ὁ ὄχλος πᾶς ἐζήτουν →　ἅπτεσθαι αὐτοῦ ὅτι δύναμις → ἐξήρχετο παρ᾽
a.gpn　n.gpn　v.ipi.3p　cj d.nsm n.nsm a.nsm v.iai.3p　f.pm　r.gsm.3 cj n.nsf　v.imi.3s p.g
176　4460　2543　2779 3836 4063 4246 2426　721　899 4022 1539　2002　4123

him　and healing them all.　¶　**20**　　Looking　　　　at his　disciples,　he　said: "Blessed
αὐτοῦ καὶ ἰᾶτο → πάντας　Καὶ ἐπάρας τοὺς ὀφθαλμοὺς αὐτοῦ εἰς αὐτοῦ τοὺς μαθητὰς αὐτὸς ἔλεγεν Μακάριοι
r.gsm.3 cj v.imi.3s　a.apm　cj pt.aa.nsm d.apm n.apm r.gsm.3 p.a r.gsm.3 d.apm n.apm r.nsm v.iai.3s a.npm
899 2779 2615　4246　2779 2048 3836 4057 899 1650 899 3836 3412 899 3306 3421

are you who are poor, for yours is　the kingdom of God.　**21** Blessed are you who hunger now, for you will be
οἱ πτωχοί ὅτι ὑμετέρα ἐστὶν ἡ βασιλεία → τοῦ θεοῦ μακάριοι　οἱ πεινῶντες νῦν ὅτι → →
d.vpm a.vpm cj r.nsf.2 v.pai.3s d.nsf n.nsf d.gsm n.gsm a.npm　d.vpm pt.pa.vpm adv cj
3836 4777 4022 5629 1639 3836 993 3836 2536 3421　3836 4277 3814 4022

satisfied.　Blessed are you who weep　now, for you will laugh. **22** Blessed are you when men　　hate
χορτασθήσεσθε μακάριοι　οἱ κλαίοντες νῦν ὅτι → → γελάσετε μακάριοι ἐστε ← ὅταν οἱ ἄνθρωποι μισήσωσιν
v.fpi.2p a.npm　d.vpm pt.pa.vpm adv cj　v.fai.2p a.npm v.pai.2p cj d.npm n.npm v.aas.3p
5963 3421　3836 3081 3814 4022　1151 3421 1639 4020 3836 476 3631

you,　when they exclude　you and insult　you and reject　your name　as evil,　because of the Son of
ὑμᾶς καὶ ὅταν → ἀφορίσωσιν ὑμᾶς καὶ ὀνειδίσωσιν καὶ ἐκβάλωσιν ὑμῶν τὸ ὄνομα ὡς πονηρὸν ἕνεκα ← τοῦ υἱοῦ
r.ap.2 cj cj　v.aas.3p r.ap.2 cj v.aas.3p cj v.aas.3p r.gp.2 d.asn n.asn pl a.asn p.g d.gsm n.gsm
7007 2779 4020　928 7007 2779 3943 2779 1675 7007 3836 3950 6055 4505 1914 3836 5626

Man.　¶　**23** "Rejoice in that day　and leap　for joy, because　great is your reward　in
τοῦ ἀνθρώπου χάρητε ἐν ἐκείνῃ τῇ ἡμέρᾳ καὶ σκιρτήσατε ← → γὰρ ἰδοὺ πολὺς ὑμῶν ὁ μισθὸς ἐν
d.gsm n.gsm v.apm.2p p.d r.dsf d.dsf n.dsf cj v.aam.2p cj ij a.nsm r.gp.2 d.nsm n.nsm p.d
3836 476 5897 1877 1697 3836 2465 2779 5015 1142 2627 4498 7007 3836 3635 1877

heaven.　For *that is how*　their fathers　treated the prophets. **24** "But woe to you who are rich,　for you
τῷ οὐρανῷ γὰρ κατὰ τὰ αὐτὰ αὐτῶν οἱ πατέρες ἐποίουν τοῖς προφήταις Πλὴν οὐαὶ → ὑμῖν τοῖς πλουσίοις ὅτι →
d.dsm n.dsm cj p.a d.apn r.apn r.gpm.3 d.npm n.npm v.iai.3p d.dpm n.dpm cj j r.dp.2 d.dpm a.dpm cj
3836 4041 1142 2848 3836 899 899 3836 4252 4472 3836 4737 4440 4026 7007 3836 4454 4022

have already received your comfort.　**25** Woe to you who are well fed　　now, for you will go hungry. Woe
→ ἀπέχετε ὑμῶν τὴν παράκλησιν οὐαὶ → ὑμῖν οἱ → ἐμπεπλησμένοι νῦν ὅτι → → → πεινάσετε οὐαὶ
v.pai.2p r.gp.2 d.asf n.asf j r.dp.2 d.vpm pt.rp.vpm adv cj v.fai.2p j
600 7007 3836 4155 4026 7007 3836 1858 3814 4022 4277 4026

to you who laugh　now, for you will mourn and weep. **26** Woe to you when all　men　speak well of
οἱ γελῶντες νῦν ὅτι → → πενθήσετε καὶ κλαύσετε οὐαὶ ὅταν πάντες οἱ ἄνθρωποι εἴπωσιν καλῶς
d.vpm pt.pa.vpm adv cj v.fai.2p cj v.fai.2p j cj a.npm d.npm n.npm v.aas.3p adv
3836 1151 3814 4022 4291 2779 3081 4026 4020 4246 3836 476 3306 2822

you, for *that is how*　their fathers　treated the false prophets.
ὑμᾶς γὰρ κατὰ τὰ αὐτὰ αὐτῶν οἱ πατέρες ἐποίουν τοῖς → ψευδοπροφήταις
r.ap.2 cj p.a d.apn r.apn r.gpm.3 d.npm n.npm v.iai.3p d.dpm n.dpm
7007 1142 2848 3836 899 899 3836 4252 4472 3836 6021

Love for Enemies

6:27 "But I tell you who hear　me: Love　your enemies,　do　good to those who hate　you,
Ἀλλὰ → λέγω ὑμῖν τοῖς ἀκούουσιν ἀγαπᾶτε ὑμῶν τοὺς ἐχθροὺς ποιεῖτε καλῶς → τοῖς ← μισοῦσιν ὑμᾶς
cj v.pai.1s r.dp.2 d.dpm pt.pa.dpm v.pam.2p r.gp.2 d.apm a.apm v.pam.2p adv d.dpm pt.pa.dpm r.ap.2
247 3306 7007 3836 201 26 7007 3836 2398 4472 2822 3836 3631 7007

28 bless　those who curse　you, pray　for those who mistreat　you. **29** If someone strikes　you on one
εὐλογεῖτε τοὺς ← καταρωμένους ὑμᾶς προσεύχεσθε περὶ τῶν ← ἐπηρεαζόντων ὑμᾶς τῷ τύπτοντι σε ἐπὶ τὴν
v.pam.2p d.apm pt.pm.apm r.ap.2 v.pmm.2p p.g d.gpm pt.pa.gpm r.ap.2 d.dsm pt.pa.dsm r.as.2 p.a d.asf
2328 3836 2933 7007 4667 4309 3836 2092 7007 3836 5597 5148 2093 3836

cheek, turn to him the other also. If　someone takes　your cloak,　do not stop　him from
σιαγόνα πάρεχε τὴν ἄλλην καὶ καὶ ἀπὸ → τοῦ αἴροντος σου τὸ ἱμάτιον καὶ → μὴ κωλύσῃς
n.asf v.pam.2s d.asf r.asf adv cj cj p.g d.gsm pt.pa.gsm r.gs.2 d.asn n.asn adv cj pl v.aas.2s
4965 4218 3836 257 2779 2779 608 3836 149 5148 3836 2668 2779 3266 3590 3266

αὐτῶν· καὶ οἱ ἐνοχλούμενοι ἀπὸ πνευμάτων ἀκαθάρτων ἐθεραπεύοντο, ¹⁹ καὶ πᾶς ὁ ὄχλος ἐζήτουν ἅπτεσθαι αὐτοῦ, ὅτι δύναμις παρ᾽ αὐτοῦ ἐξήρχετο καὶ ἰᾶτο πάντας. ¶ ²⁰ Καὶ αὐτὸς ἐπάρας τοὺς ὀφθαλμοὺς αὐτοῦ εἰς τοὺς μαθητὰς αὐτοῦ ἔλεγεν, Μακάριοι οἱ πτωχοί, ὅτι ὑμετέρα ἐστὶν ἡ βασιλεία τοῦ θεοῦ. ²¹ μακάριοι οἱ πεινῶντες νῦν, ὅτι χορτασθήσεσθε. μακάριοι οἱ κλαίοντες νῦν, ὅτι γελάσετε. ²² μακάριοί ἐστε ὅταν μισήσωσιν ὑμᾶς οἱ ἄνθρωποι καὶ ὅταν ἀφορίσωσιν ὑμᾶς καὶ ὀνειδίσωσιν καὶ ἐκβάλωσιν τὸ ὄνομα ὑμῶν ὡς πονηρὸν ἕνεκα τοῦ υἱοῦ τοῦ ἀνθρώπου· ¶ ²³ χάρητε ἐν ἐκείνῃ τῇ ἡμέρᾳ καὶ σκιρτήσατε, ἰδοὺ γὰρ ὁ μισθὸς ὑμῶν πολὺς ἐν τῷ οὐρανῷ· κατὰ τὰ αὐτὰ γὰρ ἐποίουν τοῖς προφήταις οἱ πατέρες αὐτῶν. ²⁴ Πλὴν οὐαὶ ὑμῖν τοῖς πλουσίοις, ὅτι ἀπέχετε τὴν παράκλησιν ὑμῶν. ²⁵ οὐαὶ ὑμῖν, οἱ ἐμπεπλησμένοι νῦν, ὅτι πεινάσετε. οὐαί, οἱ γελῶντες νῦν, ὅτι πενθήσετε καὶ κλαύσετε. ²⁶ οὐαὶ ὅταν ὑμᾶς καλῶς εἴπωσιν πάντες οἱ ἄνθρωποι· κατὰ τὰ αὐτὰ γὰρ ἐποίουν τοῖς ψευδοπροφήταις οἱ πατέρες αὐτῶν.

²⁷ Ἀλλὰ ὑμῖν λέγω τοῖς ἀκούουσιν, ἀγαπᾶτε τοὺς ἐχθροὺς ὑμῶν, καλῶς ποιεῖτε τοῖς μισοῦσιν ὑμᾶς, ²⁸ εὐλογεῖτε τοὺς καταρωμένους ὑμᾶς, προσεύχεσθε περὶ τῶν ἐπηρεαζόντων ὑμᾶς. ²⁹ τῷ τύπτοντί σε ἐπὶ τὴν σιαγόνα πάρεχε καὶ τὴν ἄλλην, καὶ

taking your tunic. **30** Give to everyone who asks you, and if anyone takes what belongs to you, do not
τὸν χιτῶνα δίδου → παντὶ → αἰτοῦντί σε καὶ ἀπὸ ⌞τοῦ αἴροντος⌟ τὰ → → σὰ ⌐ μὴ
d.asm n.asm v.pam.2s a.dsm pt.pa.dsm r.as.2 cj p.g d.gsm pt.pa.gsm d.apn r.ap.2 pl
3836 5945 1443 4246 160 5148 2779 608 3836 149 3836 5050 555 3590

demand it back. **31** Do to others as you would have them do to you. ¶ **32** "If
ἀπαίτει ← Καὶ ποιεῖτε → αὐτοῖς ὁμοίως καθὼς → θέλετε ἵνα ⌐ οἱ ἄνθρωποι ποιῶσιν → ὑμῖν καὶ εἰ
v.pam.2s cj v.pam.2p r.dpm.3 adv cj v.pai.2p cj d.npm n.npm v.pas.3p r.dp.2 cj cj
555 2779 4472 899 3931 2777 2527 2671 4472 3836 476 4472 7007 2779 1623

you love those who love you, what credit is that to you? Even 'sinners' love those who
→ ἀγαπᾶτε τοὺς ← ἀγαπῶντας ὑμᾶς ποία χάρις ἐστίν ← → ὑμῖν γὰρ καὶ ⌞οἱ ἁμαρτωλοὶ⌟ ἀγαπῶσιν τοὺς ←
v.pai.2p d.apm pt.pa.apm r.ap.2 r.nsf n.nsf v.pai.3s r.dp.2 cj adv d.npm a.npm v.pai.3p d.apm
26 3836 26 7007 4481 5921 1639 7007 1142 2779 3836 283 26 3836

love them. **33** And if you do good to those who are good to you, what credit is that to
ἀγαπῶντας αὐτούς [γὰρ] καὶ ἐὰν → → ἀγαθοποιῆτε τοὺς ← → ἀγαθοποιοῦντας ὑμᾶς ποία χάρις ἐστίν →
pt.pa.apm r.apm.3 cj cj cj v.pas.2p d.asn pt.pa.apm r.ap.2 r.nsf n.nsf v.pai.3s
26 899 1142 2779 1569 16 3836 16 7007 4481 5921 1639

you? Even 'sinners' do that. **34** And if you lend to those from whom you expect repayment, what
ὑμῖν καὶ ⌞οἱ ἁμαρτωλοὶ⌟ ποιοῦσιν ⌞τὸ αὐτό⌟ καὶ ἐὰν → δανίσητε παρ' ὧν → ἐλπίζετε λαβεῖν ποία
r.dp.2 adv d.npm a.npm v.pai.3p d.asn r.asn cj cj v.aas.2p p.g r.gpm v.pai.2p f.aa r.nsf
7007 2779 3836 283 4472 3836 899 2779 1569 1244 4123 4005 1827 3284 4481

credit is that to you? Even 'sinners' lend to 'sinners,' expecting to be repaid in full. **35** But love
χάρις ἐστίν ← ὑμῖν καὶ ἁμαρτωλοὶ δανίζουσιν ἁμαρτωλοῖς ἵνα → → ἀπολάβωσιν τὰ ἴσα πλὴν ἀγαπᾶτε
n.nsf v.pai.3s r.dp.2 adv a.npm v.pai.3p n.npm cj v.aas.3p d.apn a.apn cj v.pam.2p
5921 1639 7007 2779 283 1244 283 2671 655 3836 2698 4440 26

your enemies, do good to them, and lend to them without expecting to get anything back.
ὑμῶν ⌞τοὺς ἐχθρούς⌟ καὶ → ἀγαθοποιεῖτε → → καὶ δανίζετε → → μηδὲν → ἀπελπίζοντες ← ←
r.gp.2 d.apm a.apm cj v.pam.2p cj v.pam.2p a.asn pt.pa.npm
7007 3836 2398 2779 16 2779 1244 3594 594 3594 594

Then your reward will be great, and you will be sons of the Most High, because he is kind to the
καὶ ὑμῶν ὁ μισθός → ἔσται πολύς καὶ → → ἔσεσθε υἱοὶ → ὑψίστου ὅτι αὐτός ἐστιν χρηστός ἐπὶ τοὺς
cj r.gp.2 d.nsm n.nsm v.fmi.3s a.nsm cj v.fmi.2p n.npm a.gsm.s cj r.nsm v.pai.3s a.nsm p.a d.apm
2779 7007 3836 3635 1639 4498 2779 1639 5626 5736 4022 899 1639 5982 2093 3836

ungrateful and wicked. **36** Be merciful, just as your Father is merciful.
ἀχαρίστους καὶ πονηρούς Γίνεσθε οἰκτίρμονες καθὼς ← [καὶ] ὑμῶν ὁ πατήρ ἐστιν οἰκτίρμων
a.apm cj a.apm v.pmm.2p a.npm cj adv r.gp.2 d.nsm n.nsm v.pai.3s a.npm
940 2779 4505 1181 3881 2777 2779 7007 3836 4252 1639 3881

Judging Others

6:37 "Do not judge, and you will not be judged. Do not condemn, and you will not be
Καὶ ⌐ μὴ κρίνετε καὶ → → ⌞οὐ μή⌟ → κριθῆτε καὶ μὴ καταδικάζετε καὶ → → ⌞οὐ μή⌟ →
cj pl v.pam.2p cj pl pl v.aps.2p cj pl v.pam.2p cj pl pl
2779 3212 3590 3212 2779 3212 3212 4024 3590 3212 2779 2868 3590 2868 2779 2868 2868 4024 3590

condemned. Forgive, and you will be forgiven. **38** Give, and it will be given to you. A good measure, pressed
καταδικασθῆτε ἀπολύετε καὶ → → ἀπολυθήσεσθε δίδοτε καὶ → → δοθήσεται → ὑμῖν καλὸν μέτρον πεπιεσμένον
v.aps.2p v.pam.2p cj v.fpi.2p v.pam.2p cj v.fpi.3s r.dp.2 a.asn n.asn pt.rp.asn
2868 668 2779 668 1443 2779 1443 7007 2819 3586 4390

down, shaken together and running over, will be poured into your lap. For with the measure you
← σεσαλευμένον ← ὑπερεκχυννόμενον → → δώσουσιν εἰς ὑμῶν ⌞τὸν κόλπον⌟ γὰρ → ⌞ᾧ μέτρῳ⌟
pt.rp.asn pt.pp.asn v.fai.3p p.a r.gp.2 d.asn n.asn cj r.dsn n.dsn
4888 5658 1443 1650 7007 3836 3146 1142 4005 3586

use, it will be measured to you." ¶ **39** He also told them this parable: "Can a blind man
μετρεῖτε → → ἀντιμετρηθήσεται → ὑμῖν δὲ καὶ Εἶπεν αὐτοῖς παραβολὴν μήτι δύναται τυφλὸς
v.pai.2p v.fpi.3s r.dp.2 cj adv v.aai.3s r.dpm.3 n.asf pl v.ppi.3s a.nsm
3582 520 7007 1254 3306 2779 3306 899 4130 3614 1538 5603

lead a blind man? Will they not both fall into a pit? **40** A student is not above his teacher, but
ὁδηγεῖν τυφλόν ⌐ οὐχὶ ἀμφότεροι ἐμπεσοῦνται εἰς βόθυνον μαθητὴς ἔστιν οὐκ ὑπὲρ τὸν διδάσκαλον δὲ
f.pa a.asm pl a.npm v.fmi.3p p.a n.asm n.nsm v.pai.3s pl p.a d.asm n.asm cj
3842 5603 1860 1860 4049 317 1860 1650 1073 3412 1639 4024 5642 3836 1437 1254

ἀπὸ τοῦ αἴροντός σου τὸ ἱμάτιον καὶ τὸν χιτῶνα μὴ κωλύσῃς. ³⁰ παντὶ αἰτοῦντί σε δίδου, καὶ ἀπὸ τοῦ αἴροντος τὰ σὰ μὴ ἀπαίτει. ³¹ καὶ καθὼς θέλετε ἵνα ποιῶσιν ὑμῖν οἱ ἄνθρωποι ποιεῖτε αὐτοῖς ὁμοίως. ¶ ³² καὶ εἰ ἀγαπᾶτε τοὺς ἀγαπῶντας ὑμᾶς, ποία ὑμῖν χάρις ἐστίν; καὶ γὰρ οἱ ἁμαρτωλοὶ τοὺς ἀγαπῶντας αὐτοὺς ἀγαπῶσιν. ³³ καὶ [γὰρ] ἐὰν ἀγαθοποιῆτε τοὺς ἀγαθοποιοῦντας ὑμᾶς, ποία ὑμῖν χάρις ἐστίν; καὶ οἱ ἁμαρτωλοὶ τὸ αὐτὸ ποιοῦσιν. ³⁴ καὶ ἐὰν δανίσητε παρ' ὧν ἐλπίζετε λαβεῖν, ποία ὑμῖν χάρις [ἐστίν]; καὶ ἁμαρτωλοὶ ἁμαρτωλοῖς δανίζουσιν ἵνα ἀπολάβωσιν τὰ ἴσα. ³⁵ πλὴν ἀγαπᾶτε τοὺς ἐχθροὺς ὑμῶν καὶ ἀγαθοποιεῖτε καὶ δανίζετε μηδὲν ἀπελπίζοντες· καὶ ἔσται ὁ μισθὸς ὑμῶν πολύς, καὶ ἔσεσθε υἱοὶ ὑψίστου, ὅτι αὐτὸς χρηστός ἐστιν ἐπὶ τοὺς ἀχαρίστους καὶ πονηρούς. ³⁶ Γίνεσθε οἰκτίρμονες καθὼς [καὶ] ὁ πατὴρ ὑμῶν οἰκτίρμων ἐστίν.

⁶ᐟ³⁷ Καὶ μὴ κρίνετε, καὶ οὐ μὴ κριθῆτε· καὶ μὴ καταδικάζετε, καὶ οὐ μὴ καταδικασθῆτε. ἀπολύετε, καὶ ἀπολυθήσεσθε· ³⁸ δίδοτε, καὶ δοθήσεται ὑμῖν· μέτρον καλὸν πεπιεσμένον σεσαλευμένον ὑπερεκχυννόμενον δώσουσιν εἰς τὸν κόλπον ὑμῶν· ᾧ γὰρ μέτρῳ μετρεῖτε ἀντιμετρηθήσεται ὑμῖν. ¶ ³⁹ Εἶπεν δὲ καὶ παραβολὴν αὐτοῖς· Μήτι δύναται τυφλὸς τυφλὸν ὁδηγεῖν; οὐχὶ ἀμφότεροι εἰς βόθυνον ἐμπεσοῦνται; ⁴⁰ οὐκ ἔστιν μαθητὴς ὑπὲρ τὸν διδάσκαλον· κατηρτισμένος δὲ πᾶς ἔσται ὡς ὁ διδάσκαλος αὐτοῦ. ¶

everyone who is fully trained · · will be · like his · teacher. ¶ **41** "Why do you look · at the speck
πᾶς → → κατηρτισμένος → ἔσται ὡς αὐτοῦ ὁ διδάσκαλος δὲ Τί → → βλέπεις ← τὸ κάρφος
a.nsm pt.rp.nsm v.fmi.3s pl r.gsm.3 d.nsm n.nsm cj r.asn v.pai.2s d.asn n.asn
4246 2936 1639 6055 899 3836 1437 1254 5515 1063 3836 2847

of sawdust · in your brother's · eye · and pay no attention to the plank · in your own eye? **42** How
τὸ ἐν σου ιτοῦ ἀδελφοῦ, ιτῷ ὀφθαλμῷ, δὲ → οὐ κατανοεῖς ← τὴν δοκὸν τὴν ἐν τῷ ἰδίῳ ὀφθαλμῷ πῶς
d.asn p.d r.gs.2 d.gsm n.gsm d.dsm n.dsm cj pl v.pai.2s d.asf n.asf d.asf p.d d.dsm a.dsm n.dsm cj
3836 1877 5148 3836 81 3836 4057 1254 2917 4024 2917 3836 1512 3836 1877 3836 2625 4057 4802

can · you say · to your brother, 'Brother, let · me take · the speck out · of your eye,' · when you
δύνασαι ← λέγειν → σου ιτῷ ἀδελφῷ, ἀδελφέ ἄφες → ἐκβάλω τὸ κάρφος τὸ ἐν σου ιτῷ ὀφθαλμῷ, →
v.ppi.2s f.pa r.gs.2 d.dsm n.dsm n.vsm v.aam.2s v.aas.1s d.asn n.asn d.asn p.d r.gs.2 d.dsm n.dsm
1538 3306 81 5148 3836 81 81 918 1675 3836 2847 1675 3836 1877 5148 3836 4057 1063

yourself fail to see · the plank in your own eye? · You hypocrite, first · take · the plank out of your
αὐτὸς οὐ βλέπων τὴν δοκὸν ἐν σου τῷ ὀφθαλμῷ, → ὑποκριτά πρῶτον ἔκβαλε τὴν δοκὸν ἐκ ← σου
r.nsm pl pt.pa.nsm d.asf n.asf p.d r.gs.2 d.dsm n.dsm n.vsm adv v.aam.2s d.asf n.asf p.g r.gs.2
899 4024 1063 3836 1512 1877 5148 3836 4057 5695 4754 1675 3836 1512 1666 5148

eye, · and then you will see · clearly to remove the speck · from your brother's · eye.
ιτοῦ ὀφθαλμοῦ, καὶ τότε → διαβλέψεις → ἐκβαλεῖν τὸ κάρφος τὸ ἐν σου ιτοῦ ἀδελφοῦ, ιτῷ ὀφθαλμῷ,
d.gsm n.gsm cj adv v.fai.2s f.aa d.asn n.asn d.asn p.d r.gs.2 d.gsm n.gsm d.dsm n.dsm
3836 4057 2779 5538 1332 1675 3836 2847 3836 1877 5148 3836 81 3836 4057

A Tree and Its Fruit

6:43 "No good tree bears · bad fruit, nor · does a bad · tree bear good fruit. **44** Each
γὰρ Οὐ καλὸν δένδρον ιἐστιν ποιοῦν, σαπρὸν καρπὸν οὐδὲ πάλιν σαπρὸν δένδρον ποιοῦν καλόν καρπὸν γὰρ ἕκαστον
cj pl a.nsn n.nsn v.pai.3s pt.pa.nsn a.asm n.asm cj adv a.nsn n.nsn pt.pa.nsn a.asm n.asm cj r.nsn
1142 4024 2819 1285 1639 4472 4911 2843 4028 4099 4911 1285 4472 2819 2843 1142 1667

tree · is recognized by its own fruit. · People do not pick · figs from thornbushes, or · grapes
δένδρον → γινώσκεται ἐκ τοῦ ἰδίου καρποῦ γὰρ → → οὐ συλλέγουσιν σῦκα ἐξ ἀκανθῶν οὐδὲ τρυγῶσιν σταφυλὴν
n.nsn v.ppi.3s p.g d.gsm a.gsm n.gsm cj pl v.pai.3p n.apn p.g n.gpf cj v.pai.3p n.asf
1285 1182 1666 3836 2625 2843 1142 5198 5198 4024 5198 5192 1666 180 4028 5582 5091

from briers. **45** The good · man · brings good · things out of the good · stored · up in his heart, and the
ἐκ βάτου ὁ ἀγαθὸς ἄνθρωπος προφέρει ιτὸ ἀγαθόν, → ἐκ ← τοῦ ἀγαθοῦ θησαυροῦ → τῆς καρδίας καὶ ὁ
p.g n.gsf d.nsm a.nsm n.nsm v.pai.3s d.asn a.asn p.g d.gsm a.gsm n.gsm d.gsf n.gsf cj d.nsm
1666 1004 3836 19 476 4734 3836 19 1666 3836 19 2565 3836 2840 2779 3836

evil · man brings evil · things out of the evil · stored up in his heart. For out of the overflow · of his
πονηρὸς προφέρει ιτὸ πονηρόν, ← ἐκ ← τοῦ πονηροῦ → γὰρ ἐκ ← περισσεύματος →
a.nsm v.pai.3s d.asn a.asn p.g d.gsm a.gsm cj p.g n.gsn
4505 4734 3836 4505 1666 3836 4505 1142 1666 4354

heart · his mouth · speaks.
καρδίας αὐτοῦ ιτὸ στόμα, λαλεῖ
n.gsf r.gsm.3 d.nsn n.nsn v.pai.3s
2840 899 3836 5125 3281

The Wise and Foolish Builders

6:46 "Why do you call · me, 'Lord, Lord,' · and do not do · what I say? **47** I will show · you what he is
δὲ Τί → → καλεῖτε με κύριε κύριε καὶ → οὐ ποιεῖτε ἃ → λέγω ὑποδείξω ὑμῖν τίνι → ἐστιν
cj r.asn v.pai.2p r.as.1 n.vsm n.vsm cj pl v.pai.2p r.apn v.pai.1s v.fai.1s r.dp.2 r.dsm v.pai.3s
1254 5515 2813 1609 3261 3261 2779 4472 4024 4472 4005 3306 5683 7007 5515 1639

like · who comes · to · me and hears my words · and puts them · into practice. **48** He is · like · a man
ὅμοιος Πᾶς ὁ ἐρχόμενος πρός με καὶ ἀκούων μου ιτῶν λόγων, καὶ → αὐτούς → ποιῶν → ἐστιν ὅμοιος ἀνθρώπῳ
a.nsm a.nsm d.nsm pt.pm.nsm p.a r.as.1 cj pt.pa.nsm r.gs.1 d.gpm n.gpm cj r.apm.3 pt.pa.nsm v.pai.3s a.nsm n.dsm
3927 4246 3836 2262 4639 1609 2779 201 1609 3836 3364 2779 899 4472 1639 3927 476

building · a house, who dug · down · deep · and laid · the foundation on rock. · When a flood
οἰκοδομοῦντι οἰκίαν ὃς ἔσκαψεν ← καὶ ἐβάθυνεν καὶ ἔθηκεν θεμέλιον ἐπὶ ιτὴν πέτραν, δὲ → πλημμύρης
pt.pa.dsm n.asf r.nsm v.aai.3s cj v.aai.3s cj v.aai.3s n.asm p.a d.asf n.asf cj n.gsf
3868 3864 4005 4999 2779 959 2779 5502 2529 2093 3836 4376 1254 1181 4439

---

[41] Τί δὲ βλέπεις τὸ κάρφος τὸ ἐν τῷ ὀφθαλμῷ τοῦ ἀδελφοῦ σου, τὴν δὲ δοκὸν τὴν ἐν τῷ ἰδίῳ ὀφθαλμῷ οὐ κατανοεῖς; [42] πῶς δύνασαι λέγειν τῷ ἀδελφῷ σου, Ἀδελφέ, ἄφες ἐκβάλω τὸ κάρφος τὸ ἐν τῷ ὀφθαλμῷ σου, αὐτὸς τὴν ἐν τῷ ὀφθαλμῷ σοῦ δοκὸν οὐ βλέπων; ὑποκριτά, ἔκβαλε πρῶτον τὴν δοκὸν ἐκ τοῦ ὀφθαλμοῦ σοῦ, καὶ τότε διαβλέψεις τὸ κάρφος τὸ ἐν τῷ ὀφθαλμῷ τοῦ ἀδελφοῦ σου ἐκβαλεῖν.

[43] Οὐ γάρ ἐστιν δένδρον καλὸν ποιοῦν καρπὸν σαπρόν, οὐδὲ πάλιν δένδρον σαπρὸν ποιοῦν καρπὸν καλόν. [44] ἕκαστον γὰρ δένδρον ἐκ τοῦ ἰδίου καρποῦ γινώσκεται· οὐ γὰρ ἐξ ἀκανθῶν συλλέγουσιν σῦκα οὐδὲ ἐκ βάτου σταφυλὴν τρυγῶσιν. [45] ὁ ἀγαθὸς ἄνθρωπος ἐκ τοῦ ἀγαθοῦ θησαυροῦ τῆς καρδίας προφέρει τὸ ἀγαθόν, καὶ ὁ πονηρὸς ἐκ τοῦ πονηροῦ θησαυροῦ τῆς καρδίας αὐτοῦ προφέρει τὸ πονηρόν· ἐκ γὰρ περισσεύματος καρδίας λαλεῖ τὸ στόμα αὐτοῦ.

[46] Τί δέ με καλεῖτε, Κύριε κύριε, καὶ οὐ ποιεῖτε ἃ λέγω; [47] πᾶς ὁ ἐρχόμενος πρός με καὶ ἀκούων μου τῶν λόγων καὶ ποιῶν αὐτούς, ὑποδείξω ὑμῖν τίνι ἐστιν ὅμοιος· [48] ὅμοιός ἐστιν ἀνθρώπῳ οἰκοδομοῦντι οἰκίαν ὃς ἔσκαψεν καὶ ἐβάθυνεν καὶ

came,   the torrent struck that house   but could not shake it, because it   was well built.
γενομένης ὁ ποταμὸς προσέρηξεν ἐκείνῃ τῇ οἰκίᾳ καὶ ἴσχυσεν οὐκ σαλεῦσαι αὐτὴν διὰ αὐτὴν → καλῶς τὸ οἰκοδομῆσθαι
pt.am.gsf d.nsm n.nsm v.aai.3s r.dsf d.dsf n.dsf cj v.aai.3s pl f.aa r.asf.3 p.a r.asf.3 adv d.asn f.rp
1181 3836 4532 4704 1697 3836 3864 2779 2710 4024 4888 899 1328 899 3868 2822 3836 3868

49 But the one who hears   my words and does not put them into practice is   like a man who built   a
δὲ ὁ ← ← ἀκούσας καὶ ↑ μὴ → → ποιήσας ἐστιν ὅμοιος ἀνθρώπῳ οἰκοδομήσαντι
cj d.nsm pt.aa.nsm cj pl pt.aa.nsm v.pai.3s a.nsm n.dsm pt.aa.dsm
1254 3836 201 2779 4472 3590 4472 1639 3927 476 3868

house on the ground without a foundation.   The moment   the torrent struck that house,   it collapsed
οἰκίαν ἐπὶ τὴν γῆν χωρὶς θεμελίου καὶ εὐθὺς ᾗ ὁ ποταμὸς προσέρηξεν ἐκείνης τῆς οἰκίας → συνέπεσεν
n.asf p.a d.asf n.asf p.g n.gsm cj adv r.dsf d.nsm n.nsm v.aai.3s r.gsf d.gsf n.gsf v.aai.3s
3864 2093 3836 1178 6006 2529 2779 2318 4005 3836 4532 4704 1697 3836 3864 5229

and its destruction was   complete."
καὶ τὸ ῥῆγμα ἐγένετο μέγα
cj d.nsn n.nsn v.ami.3s a.nsn
2779 3836 4837 1181 3489

The Faith of the Centurion

7:1 When Jesus had finished saying   all   this in the hearing of the people, he entered   Capernaum.
Ἐπειδὴ → ἐπλήρωσεν τὰ ῥήματα αὐτοῦ πάντα ← εἰς τὰς ἀκοὰς → τοῦ λαοῦ → εἰσῆλθεν εἰς Καφαρναούμ
v.aai.3s d.apn n.apn r.gsm.3 a.apn p.a d.apf n.apf d.gsm n.gsm v.aai.3s p.a n.asf
2076 4444 3836 4839 899 4246 1650 3836 198 3836 3295 1656 1650 3019

2 There a centurion's servant, whom   his master valued highly, was sick and about to die. **3** The
δέ τινος Ἑκατοντάρχου δοῦλος ὃς ἦν αὐτῷ ἔντιμος ← ἔχων κακῶς ἤμελλεν → τελευτᾶν δὲ
cj r.gsm n.gsm n.nsm r.nsm v.iai.3s r.dsm.3 a.nsm pt.pa.nsm adv v.iai.3s f.pa cj
1254 5516 1672 1529 4005 1639 899 1952 2400 2809 3516 5462 1254

centurion heard of Jesus   and sent   some elders of the Jews   to him, asking him to come
ἀκούσας περὶ τοῦ Ἰησοῦ ἀπέστειλεν πρεσβυτέρους → τῶν Ἰουδαίων πρὸς αὐτὸν ἐρωτῶν αὐτὸν ὅπως ἐλθὼν
pt.aa.nsm p.g d.gsm n.gsm v.aai.3s a.apm d.gpm a.gpm p.a r.asm.3 pt.pa.nsm r.asm.3 cj pt.aa.nsm
201 4309 3836 2652 690 4565 3836 2681 4639 899 2263 899 3968 2262

and heal his servant. **4** When they came   to Jesus,   they pleaded earnestly with him,
διασώσῃ αὐτοῦ τὸν δοῦλον δὲ οἱ παραγενόμενοι πρὸς τὸν Ἰησοῦν παρεκάλουν σπουδαίως αὐτὸν λέγοντες
v.aas.3s r.gsm.3 d.asm n.asm cj d.npm pt.am.npm p.a d.asm n.asm v.iai.3p adv r.asm.3 pt.pa.npm
1407 899 3836 1529 1254 4134 3836 4134 4639 3836 2652 4151 5081 4151 899 3306

"This man deserves to have you do this, **5** because he loves our nation and has built our
ὅτι → ἄξιός ἐστιν → → → παρέξῃ τοῦτο ᾧ γὰρ → ἀγαπᾷ ἡμῶν τὸ ἔθνος καὶ αὐτὸς → ᾠκοδόμησεν ἡμῖν
cj a.nsm v.pai.3s v.fmi.2s r.asn r.dsm cj v.pai.3s r.gp.1 d.asn n.asn cj r.nsm v.aai.3s r.dp.1
4022 545 1639 4218 4047 4005 1142 26 7005 3836 1620 2779 899 3868 7005

synagogue." **6** So Jesus   went   with them. ¶   He was not far   from the house
τὴν συναγωγήν δὲ ὁ Ἰησοῦς ἐπορεύετο σὺν αὐτοῖς δὲ ἤδη αὐτοῦ ↑ οὐ μακρὰν ἀπέχοντος ἀπὸ τῆς οἰκίας
d.asf n.asf cj d.nsm n.nsm v.imi.3s p.d r.dpm.3 cj adv r.gsm.3 pl adv pt.pa.gsm p.g d.gsf n.gsf
3836 5252 1254 3836 2652 4513 5250 899 1254 2453 899 600 4024 3426 600 608 3836 3864

when the centurion sent   friends to say to him: "Lord, don't trouble yourself, for I do not deserve to have
↑ ὁ ἑκατοντάρχης ἔπεμψεν φίλους → λέγων αὐτῷ κύριε μὴ σκύλλου ← γὰρ → εἰμι οὐ ἱκανός ἵνα →
d.nsm n.nsm v.aai.3s a.apm pt.pa.nsm r.dsm.3 n.vsm pl v.ppm.2s cj v.pai.1s pl a.nsm cj
600 3836 1672 4287 5813 3306 899 3261 3590 5035 1142 1639 4024 2653 2671

you come under my roof. **7** *That is why* I did not even consider myself worthy to come to you. But say
→ εἰσέλθῃς ὑπὸ μου τὴν στέγην διὸ ↑ → οὐδὲ ← → ἐμαυτὸν ἠξίωσα → ἐλθεῖν πρὸς σὲ ἀλλὰ εἰπὲ
v.aas.2s p.a r.gs.1 d.asf n.asf cj pl r.asm.1 v.aai.1s f.aa p.as r.as.2 v.aam.2s
1656 5679 1609 3836 5094 1475 546 546 4028 546 1831 546 2262 4639 5148 247 3306

the word, and my servant will be healed. **8** For I myself am a man   under authority,   with
λόγῳ καὶ μου ὁ παῖς → → ἰαθήτω γὰρ καὶ ἐγὼ εἰμι ἄνθρωπος ὑπὸ ἐξουσίαν τασσόμενος ἔχων
n.dsm cj r.gs.1 d.nsm n.nsm v.apm.3s cj adv r.ns.1 v.pai.1s n.nsm p.a n.asf pt.pp.nsm pt.pa.nsm
3364 2779 1609 3836 4090 2615 1142 2779 1639 1609 1639 476 5679 2026 5435 2400

soldiers under me. I tell this one, 'Go,' and he goes; and that one, 'Come,' and he comes.   I say
στρατιώτας ὑπ' ἐμαυτὸν καὶ → λέγω τούτῳ πορεύθητι καὶ → πορεύεται καὶ ἄλλῳ ← ἔρχου καὶ → ἔρχεται καὶ
n.apm p.a r.asm.1 cj v.pai.1s r.dsm v.apm.2s cj v.pmi.3s cj r.dsm v.pmm.2s cj v.pmi.3s cj
5132 5679 1831 2779 3306 4047 4513 2779 4513 2779 257 2262 2779 2262 2779

ἔθηκεν θεμέλιον ἐπὶ τὴν πέτραν· πλημμύρης δὲ γενομένης προσέρηξεν ὁ ποταμὸς τῇ οἰκίᾳ ἐκείνῃ, καὶ οὐκ ἴσχυσεν σαλεῦσαι αὐτὴν διὰ τὸ καλῶς οἰκοδομῆσθαι αὐτήν. **49** ὁ δὲ ἀκούσας καὶ μὴ ποιήσας ὅμοιός ἐστιν ἀνθρώπῳ οἰκοδομήσαντι οἰκίαν ἐπὶ τὴν γῆν χωρὶς θεμελίου, ᾗ προσέρηξεν ὁ ποταμός, καὶ εὐθὺς συνέπεσεν καὶ ἐγένετο τὸ ῥῆγμα τῆς οἰκίας ἐκείνης μέγα.

7:1 Ἐπειδὴ ἐπλήρωσεν πάντα τὰ ῥήματα αὐτοῦ εἰς τὰς ἀκοὰς τοῦ λαοῦ, εἰσῆλθεν εἰς Καφαρναούμ. **2** Ἑκατοντάρχου δέ τινος δοῦλος κακῶς ἔχων ἤμελλεν τελευτᾶν, ὃς ἦν αὐτῷ ἔντιμος. **3** ἀκούσας δὲ περὶ τοῦ Ἰησοῦ ἀπέστειλεν πρὸς αὐτὸν πρεσβυτέρους τῶν Ἰουδαίων ἐρωτῶν αὐτὸν ὅπως ἐλθὼν διασώσῃ τὸν δοῦλον αὐτοῦ. **4** οἱ δὲ παραγενόμενοι πρὸς τὸν Ἰησοῦν παρεκάλουν αὐτὸν σπουδαίως λέγοντες ὅτι Ἄξιός ἐστιν ᾧ παρέξῃ τοῦτο· **5** ἀγαπᾷ γὰρ τὸ ἔθνος ἡμῶν καὶ τὴν συναγωγὴν αὐτὸς ᾠκοδόμησεν ἡμῖν. **6** ὁ δὲ Ἰησοῦς ἐπορεύετο σὺν αὐτοῖς. ἤδη δὲ αὐτοῦ οὐ μακρὰν ἀπέχοντος ἀπὸ τῆς οἰκίας ἔπεμψεν φίλους ὁ ἑκατοντάρχης λέγων αὐτῷ, Κύριε, μὴ σκύλλου, οὐ γὰρ ἱκανός εἰμι ἵνα ὑπὸ τὴν στέγην μου εἰσέλθῃς· **7** διὸ οὐδὲ ἐμαυτὸν ἠξίωσα πρὸς σὲ ἐλθεῖν· ἀλλὰ εἰπὲ λόγῳ, καὶ ἰαθήτω ὁ παῖς μου. **8** καὶ γὰρ ἐγὼ ἄνθρωπός εἰμι ὑπὸ ἐξουσίαν τασσόμενος ἔχων ὑπ' ἐμαυτὸν στρατιώτας, καὶ

to my servant, 'Do this,' and he does it." ¶ **9** When Jesus heard this, he was amazed at him,
→ μου ᾿τῷ δούλῳ ποίησον τοῦτο καὶ → ποιεῖ δὲ ὁ Ἰησοῦς ἀκούσας ταῦτα → ἐθαύμασεν ← αὐτὸν
→ r.gs.1 d.dsm n.dsm v.aam.2s r.asn cj v.pai.3s cj d.nsm n.nsm pt.aa.nsm r.apn v.aai.3s r.asm.3
1529 1609 3836 1529 4472 4047 2779 4472 1254 201 3836 2652 201 4047 2513 899

and turning to the crowd following him, he said, "I tell you, I have not found such great faith even in
καὶ στραφεὶς → τῷ ὄχλῳ ἀκολουθοῦντι αὐτῷ εἶπεν λέγω ὑμῖν → → εὗρον → τοσαύτην πίστιν οὐδὲ ἐν
cj pt.ap.nsm d.dsm n.dsm pt.pa.dsm r.dsm.3 v.aai.3s v.pai.1s r.dp.2 v.aai.1s r.asf n.asf adv p.d
2779 5138 3836 4063 199 899 3306 3306 7007 2351 2351 4028 2351 5537 4411 4028 1877

Israel." **10** Then the men who had been sent returned to the house and found the servant well.
᾿τῷ Ἰσραὴλ, Καὶ οἱ ← ← ← → πεμφθέντες ὑποστρέψαντες εἰς τὸν οἶκον εὗρον τὸν δοῦλον ὑγιαίνοντα
d.dsm n.dsm cj d.npm pt.ap.npm pt.aa.npm p.a d.asm n.asm v.aai.3p d.asm n.asm pt.pa.asm
3836 2702 2779 3836 4287 5715 1650 3836 3875 2351 3836 1529 5617

Jesus Raises a Widow's Son

7:11 Soon afterward, Jesus went to a town called Nain, and his disciples and a large
Καὶ ἐγένετο → ᾿ἐν τῷ ἑξῆς, ἐπορεύθη εἰς πόλιν καλουμένην Ναΐν καὶ αὐτοῦ οἱ μαθηταὶ καὶ πολύς
cj v.ami.3s p.d d.dsm adv v.api.3s p.a n.asf pt.pp.asf n.asf cj r.gsm.3 d.npm n.npm cj a.nsm
2779 1181 1877 3836 2009 4513 1650 4484 2813 3723 2779 899 3836 3412 2779 4498

crowd went along with him. **12** As he approached the town gate, a dead person was being
ὄχλος συνεπορεύοντο ← αὐτῷ δὲ ὡς → ἤγγισεν τῇ ᾿τῆς πόλεως, πύλῃ καὶ ἰδοὺ τεθνηκὼς ←
n.nsm v.imi.3p r.dsm.3 cj cj v.aai.3s d.dsf ᾿d.gsf n.gsf n.dsf cj ᾿ἰδοὺ pt.ra.nsm
4063 5233 899 1254 6055 1581 3836 3836 4484 4783 2779 2627 2569

carried out – the only son of his mother, and she was a widow. And a large crowd from the town was
ἐξεκομίζετο ← μονογενὴς υἱὸς → αὐτοῦ ᾿τῇ μητρὶ, καὶ αὐτὴ ἦν χήρα καὶ ἱκανὸς ὄχλος → τῆς πόλεως ἦν
v.ipi.3s a.nsm n.nsm r.gsm.3 d.dsf n.dsf cj r.nsf v.iai.3s n.nsf cj a.nsm n.nsm d.gsf n.gsf v.iai.3s
1714 3666 5626 3613 899 3836 3613 2779 899 1639 5939 2779 2653 4063 3836 4484 1639

with her. **13** When the Lord saw her, his heart went out to her and he said, "Don't cry." ¶
σὺν αὐτῇ καὶ ὁ κύριος ἰδὼν αὐτὴν → ἐσπλαγχνίσθη ← ἐπ᾿ αὐτῇ καὶ → εἶπεν αὐτῇ μὴ κλαῖε
p.d r.dsf.3 cj d.nsm n.nsm pt.aa.nsm r.asf.3 v.api.3s p.d r.dsf.3 cj v.aai.3s r.dsf.3 pl v.pam.2s
5250 899 2779 1625 3261 1625 899 5072 2093 899 2779 3306 899 3590 3081

14 Then he went up and touched the coffin, and those carrying it stood still. He said, "Young man, I
καὶ → → προσελθὼν ← ἥψατο τῆς σοροῦ δὲ οἱ βαστάζοντες ἔστησαν ← καὶ → εἶπεν νεανίσκε
cj pt.aa.nsm v.ami.3s d.gsf n.gsf cj d.npm pt.pa.npm v.aai.3p cj v.aai.3s n.vsm
2779 4665 721 3836 5049 1254 3836 1002 2705 2779 3306 3734

say to you, get up!" **15** The dead man sat up and began to talk, and Jesus gave him back to his
λέγω → σοὶ ἐγέρθητι → καὶ ὁ νεκρὸς ← ἀνεκάθισεν καὶ ἤρξατο → λαλεῖν καὶ → ἔδωκεν αὐτὸν → αὐτοῦ
v.pai.1s r.ds.2 v.apm.2s cj d.nsm a.nsm v.aai.3s cj v.ami.3s f.pa cj v.aai.3s r.asm.3 r.gsm.3
3306 5148 1586 2779 3836 3738 361 2779 806 3281 2779 1443 899 3613 899

mother. ¶ **16** They were all filled with awe and praised God. "A great prophet has appeared
᾿τῇ μητρὶ, δὲ → πάντας ἔλαβεν ← φόβος καὶ ἐδόξαζον ᾿τὸν θεόν, ὅτι μέγας προφήτης → ἠγέρθη
d.dsf n.dsf cj a.apm v.aai.3s n.nsm cj v.iai.3p d.asm n.asm cj a.nsm n.nsm v.api.3s
3836 3613 1254 3284 3284 4246 5832 2779 1519 3836 2536 4022 3489 4737 1586

among us," they said. "God has come to help his people." **17** This news about Jesus
ἐν ἡμῖν, λέγοντες καὶ ὅτι ᾿ὁ θεός, → → ἐπεσκέψατο αὐτοῦ ᾿τὸν λαόν, καὶ οὗτος ὁ λόγος, περὶ αὐτοῦ
p.d r.dp.1 pt.pa.npm cj cj d.nsm n.nsm v.ami.3s r.gsm.3 d.asm n.asm cj r.nsm d.nsm n.nsm p.g r.gsm.3
1877 7005 3306 2779 4022 3836 2536 2170 899 3836 3295 2779 4047 3836 3364 4309 899

spread throughout Judea and the surrounding country.
ἐξῆλθεν ἐν ὅλῃ ᾿τῇ Ἰουδαίᾳ, καὶ πάσῃ τῇ → περιχώρῳ
v.aai.3s p.d a.dsf d.dsf n.dsf cj a.dsf d.dsf a.dsf
2002 1877 3910 3836 2677 2779 4246 3836 4369

Jesus and John the Baptist

7:18 John's disciples told him about all these things. Calling two of them,
Καὶ Ἰωάννῃ οἱ μαθηταὶ αὐτοῦ ἀπήγγειλαν περὶ πάντων τούτων ← καὶ προσκαλεσάμενος δύο τινὰς τῶν
cj n.dsm d.npm n.npm r.gsm.3 v.aai.3p p.g a.gpn r.gpn cj pt.am.nsm a.apm r.apm d.gpm
2779 2722 3836 3412 899 550 4309 4246 4047 2779 4673 1545 5516 3836

λέγω τούτῳ, Πορεύθητι, καὶ πορεύεται, καὶ ἄλλῳ, Ἔρχου, καὶ ἔρχεται, καὶ τῷ δούλῳ μου, Ποίησον τοῦτο, καὶ ποιεῖ. ¶
9 ἀκούσας δὲ ταῦτα ὁ Ἰησοῦς ἐθαύμασεν αὐτὸν καὶ στραφεὶς τῷ ἀκολουθοῦντι αὐτῷ ὄχλῳ εἶπεν, Λέγω ὑμῖν, οὐδὲ ἐν τῷ Ἰσραὴλ
τοσαύτην πίστιν εὗρον. **10** καὶ ὑποστρέψαντες εἰς τὸν οἶκον οἱ πεμφθέντες εὗρον τὸν δοῦλον ὑγιαίνοντα.
7:11 Καὶ ἐγένετο ἐν τῷ ἑξῆς ἐπορεύθη εἰς πόλιν καλουμένην Ναΐν καὶ συνεπορεύοντο αὐτῷ οἱ μαθηταὶ αὐτοῦ καὶ ὄχλος
πολύς. **12** ὡς δὲ ἤγγισεν τῇ πύλῃ τῆς πόλεως, καὶ ἰδοὺ ἐξεκομίζετο τεθνηκὼς μονογενὴς υἱὸς τῇ μητρὶ αὐτοῦ καὶ αὐτὴ ἦν χήρα,
καὶ ὄχλος τῆς πόλεως ἱκανὸς ἦν σὺν αὐτῇ. **13** καὶ ἰδὼν αὐτὴν ὁ κύριος ἐσπλαγχνίσθη ἐπ᾿ αὐτῇ καὶ εἶπεν αὐτῇ, Μὴ κλαῖε. ¶
14 καὶ προσελθὼν ἥψατο τῆς σοροῦ, οἱ δὲ βαστάζοντες ἔστησαν, καὶ εἶπεν, Νεανίσκε, σοὶ λέγω, ἐγέρθητι. **15** καὶ ἀνεκάθισεν ὁ
νεκρὸς καὶ ἤρξατο λαλεῖν, καὶ ἔδωκεν αὐτὸν τῇ μητρὶ αὐτοῦ. ¶ **16** ἔλαβεν δὲ φόβος πάντας καὶ ἐδόξαζον τὸν θεὸν λέγοντες ὅτι
Προφήτης μέγας ἠγέρθη ἐν ἡμῖν καὶ ὅτι Ἐπεσκέψατο ὁ θεὸς τὸν λαὸν αὐτοῦ. **17** καὶ ἐξῆλθεν ὁ λόγος οὗτος ἐν ὅλῃ τῇ Ἰουδαίᾳ
περὶ αὐτοῦ καὶ πάσῃ τῇ περιχώρῳ.
7:18 Καὶ ἀπήγγειλαν Ἰωάννῃ οἱ μαθηταὶ αὐτοῦ περὶ πάντων τούτων. καὶ προσκαλεσάμενος δύο τινὰς τῶν μαθητῶν αὐτοῦ

19 he | sent | them to | the Lord | to ask, | "Are | you | the | one who was | to come, | or | should we
μαθητῶν αὐτοῦ | ὁ | Ἰωάννης | ἔπεμψεν | πρὸς | τὸν | κύριον → | λέγων | εἰ | σὺ | ὁ | ἐρχόμενος | ἢ | →
n.gpm r.gsm.3 | d.nsm | n.nsm | v.aai.3s | p.a | d.asm | n.asm | pt.pa.nsm | v.pai.2s | r.ns.2 | d.nsm | pt.pm.nsm | cj
3412 899 | 3836 | 2722 | 4287 | 4639 | 3836 | 3261 | 3306 | 1639 | 5148 | 3836 | 2262 | 2445

expect | someone else?" | ¶ | **20** When | the | men | came | to | Jesus, | they said, | "John | the | Baptist
προσδοκῶμεν → | ἄλλον | δὲ → | οἱ | ἄνδρες | παραγενόμενοι | πρὸς | αὐτὸν → | εἶπαν | Ἰωάννης | ὁ | βαπτιστὴς
v.pai.1p | r.asm | cj | d.npm | n.npm | pt.am.npm | p.a | r.asm.3 | v.aai.3p | n.nsm | d.nsm | n.nsm
4659 | 257 | 1254 4134 | 3836 | 467 | 4134 | 4639 | 899 | 3306 | 2722 | 3836 | 969

sent | us | to | you | to ask, | 'Are | you | the | one who was | to come, | or | should we | expect | someone else?'" | ¶
ἀπέστειλεν | ἡμᾶς | πρὸς | σὲ → | λέγων | εἰ | σὺ | ὁ | → ← | ἐρχόμενος | ἢ | → | προσδοκῶμεν → | ἄλλον
v.aai.3s | r.ap.1 | p.a | r.as.2 | pt.pa.nsm | v.pai.2s | r.ns.2 | d.nsm | | pt.pm.nsm | cj | | v.pai.1p | r.asm
690 | 7005 | 4639 | 5148 | 3306 | 1639 | 5148 | 3836 | | 2262 | 2445 | | 4659 | 257

21 At that | very | time | Jesus | cured | many | who had | diseases, | sicknesses | and | evil | spirits, | and | gave
ἐν | ἐκείνῃ τῇ | ὥρᾳ | | ἐθεράπευσεν | πολλοὺς | ἀπὸ | νόσων | καὶ | μαστίγων | καὶ | πονηρῶν | πνευμάτων | καὶ | ἐχαρίσατο
p.d | r.dsf d.dsf | n.dsf | | v.aai.3s | a.apm | p.g | n.gpf | cj | n.gpf | cj | a.gpn | n.gpn | cj | v.ami.3s
1877 | 1697 3836 | 6052 | | 2543 | 4498 | 608 | 3798 | 2779 | 3465 | 2779 | 4505 | 4460 | 2779 | 5919

sight | to many | who were blind. | **22** So | he replied | | to the messengers, | "Go | back | and report | | to | John
βλέπειν → | πολλοῖς | τυφλοῖς | καὶ → | ἀποκριθεὶς | εἶπεν → | αὐτοῖς | πορευθέντες | | ἀπαγγείλατε → | Ἰωάννῃ
f.pa | a.dpm | a.dpm | cj | pt.ap.nsm | v.aai.3s | r.dpm.3 | pt.ap.npm | | v.aam.2p | n.dsm
1063 | 4498 | 5603 | 2779 | 646 | 3306 | 899 | 4513 | | 550 | 2722

what | you have | seen | and | heard: | The blind | receive sight, | the lame | walk, | those who have | leprosy are
ἃ → | → | εἴδετε | καὶ | ἠκούσατε | τυφλοὶ → | ἀναβλέπουσιν | χωλοὶ | περιπατοῦσιν → | → | λεπροὶ
r.apn | | v.aai.2p | cj | v.aai.2p | a.npm | v.pai.3p | a.npm | v.pai.3p | | a.npm
4005 | | 1625 | 2779 | 201 | 5603 | 329 | 6000 | 4344 | | 3320

cured, | | the deaf | hear, | the dead | are raised, | and | the good news is preached | | to the poor. | **23**
καθαρίζονται καὶ | | κωφοὶ | ἀκούουσιν | νεκροὶ | ἐγείρονται | | εὐαγγελίζονται ← | πτωχοὶ | καὶ
v.ppi.3p | cj | | a.npm | v.pai.3p | a.npm | v.ppi.3p | | v.ppi.3p | a.dpm | cj
2751 | 2779 | | 3273 | 201 | 3738 | 1586 | | 2294 | 4777 | 2779

Blessed | is | the man | who | does | not | fall | | away | on account of me." | ¶ | **24** | After | John's | messengers
μακάριος | ἐστιν | ὃς | ἐὰν → | μὴ | σκανδαλισθῇ | ἐν | ← ἐμοί | | δὲ | Ἰωάννου | τῶν ἀγγέλων
a.nsm | v.pai.3s | r.nsm | pl | pl | v.aps.3s | p.d | r.ds.1 | | cj | n.gsm | d.gpm n.gpm
3421 | 1639 | 4005 | 1569 4997 | 3590 | 4997 | 1877 | 1609 | | 1254 599 | 2722 | 3836 34

left, | Jesus | began | to speak | to | the | crowd | about | John: | "What | did you | go | out into | the | desert | to
Ἀπελθόντων | | ἤρξατο → | λέγειν | πρὸς | τοὺς | ὄχλους | περὶ | Ἰωάννου | τί | → | → | ἐξήλθατε ← | εἰς | τὴν | ἔρημον →
pt.aa.gpm | | v.ami.3s | f.pa | p.a | d.apm | n.apm | p.g | n.gsm | r.asn | | | v.aai.2p | p.a | d.asf | n.asf
599 | | 806 | 3306 | 4639 | 3836 | 4063 | 4309 | 2722 | 5515 | | | 2002 | 1650 | 3836 | 2245

see? | A reed | swayed | by | the wind? | **25** If not, | what | did you | go | out | to see? | A man | dressed | in
θεάσασθαι | κάλαμον | σαλευόμενον | ὑπὸ | ἀνέμου | ἀλλὰ | τί | → | → | ἐξήλθατε ← | ἰδεῖν | ἄνθρωπον | ἠμφιεσμένον | ἐν
f.am | n.asm | pt.pp.asm | p.g | n.gsm | cj | r.asn | | | v.aai.2p | f.aa | n.asm | pt.rp.asm | p.d
2517 | 2812 | 4888 | 5679 | 449 | 247 | 5515 | | | 2002 | 1625 | 476 | 314 | 1877

fine | clothes? | No, | those who | wear | | expensive | clothes | and | indulge | in | luxury | are | in | palaces. | **26** But
μαλακοῖς | ἱματίοις | ἰδοὺ | οἱ | ← | ἐν | ἐνδόξῳ | ἱματισμῷ | καὶ | ὑπάρχοντες → | τρυφῇ | εἰσίν | ἐν | τοῖς βασιλείοις | ἀλλὰ
a.dpn | n.dpn | j | d.npm | | p.d | a.dsn | n.dsm | cj | pt.pa.npm | n.dsf | v.pai.3p | p.d | d.dpn a.dpn | cj
3434 | 2668 | 2627 | 3836 | | 1877 | 1902 | 2669 | 2779 | 5639 | 5588 | 1639 | 1877 | 3836 994 | 247

what | did you | go | out to see? | A prophet? | Yes, | I tell | you, | and | more | | than a prophet. | **27** This | is | the one
τί | → | → | ἐξήλθατε ← | ἰδεῖν | προφήτην | ναὶ | → λέγω | ὑμῖν | καὶ | περισσότερον → | προφήτου | οὗτός | ἐστιν
r.asn | | | v.aai.2p | f.aa | n.asm | pl | v.pai.1s | r.dp.2 | cj | adv.c | n.gsm | r.nsm | v.pai.3s
5515 | | | 2002 | 1625 | 4737 | 3721 | 3306 | 7007 | 2779 | 4358 | 4737 | 4047 | 1639

about | whom | it is written: | "'I | will send | my | messenger | ahead | | of you, | who | will prepare | | your
περὶ | οὗ | → → γέγραπται | ἰδοὺ | ἀποστέλλω | μου | τὸν ἄγγελον | πρὸ προσώπου | ← | σου | ὃς | κατασκευάσει | σου
p.g | r.gsm | v.rpi.3s | j | v.pai.1s | r.gs.1 | d.asm n.asm | p.g n.gsn | | r.gs.2 | r.nsm | v.fai.3s | r.gs.2
4309 | 4005 | 1211 | 2627 | 690 | 1609 | 3836 34 | 4574 4725 | | 5148 | 4005 | 2941 | 5148

way | before | you.' | **28** I tell | you, | among | those born | of | women | there is | no one | greater | than | John; | yet | the
τὴν ὁδόν | ἔμπροσθεν | σου | → λέγω | ὑμῖν | ἐν | → γεννητοῖς | → | γυναικῶν | → | ἐστιν | οὐδεὶς | μείζων | → | Ἰωάννου | δὲ | ὁ
d.asf n.asf | p.g | r.gs.2 | v.pai.1s | r.dp.2 | p.d | n.dpm | | n.gpf | | v.pai.3s | a.nsm | a.nsm.c | | n.gsm | cj | d.nsm
3836 3847 | 1869 | 5148 | 3306 | 7007 | 1877 | 1168 | | 1222 | | 1639 | 4029 | 3489 | | 2722 | 1254 | 3836

ὁ Ἰωάννης ¹⁹ ἔπεμψεν πρὸς τὸν κύριον λέγων, Σὺ εἶ ὁ ἐρχόμενος ἢ ἄλλον προσδοκῶμεν; ¶ ²⁰ παραγενόμενοι δὲ πρὸς αὐτὸν οἱ ἄνδρες εἶπαν, Ἰωάννης ὁ βαπτιστὴς ἀπέστειλεν ἡμᾶς πρὸς σὲ λέγων, Σὺ εἶ ὁ ἐρχόμενος ἢ ἄλλον προσδοκῶμεν; ¶ ²¹ ἐν ἐκείνῃ τῇ ὥρᾳ ἐθεράπευσεν πολλοὺς ἀπὸ νόσων καὶ μαστίγων καὶ πνευμάτων πονηρῶν καὶ τυφλοῖς πολλοῖς ἐχαρίσατο βλέπειν. ²² καὶ ἀποκριθεὶς εἶπεν αὐτοῖς, Πορευθέντες ἀπαγγείλατε Ἰωάννῃ ἃ εἴδετε καὶ ἠκούσατε· τυφλοὶ ἀναβλέπουσιν, χωλοὶ περιπατοῦσιν, λεπροὶ καθαρίζονται καὶ κωφοὶ ἀκούουσιν, νεκροὶ ἐγείρονται, πτωχοὶ εὐαγγελίζονται· ²³ καὶ μακάριός ἐστιν ὃς ἐὰν μὴ σκανδαλισθῇ ἐν ἐμοί. ¶ ²⁴ Ἀπελθόντων δὲ τῶν ἀγγέλων Ἰωάννου ἤρξατο λέγειν πρὸς τοὺς ὄχλους περὶ Ἰωάννου, Τί ἐξήλθατε εἰς τὴν ἔρημον θεάσασθαι; κάλαμον ὑπὸ ἀνέμου σαλευόμενον; ²⁵ ἀλλὰ τί ἐξήλθατε ἰδεῖν; ἄνθρωπον ἐν μαλακοῖς ἱματίοις ἠμφιεσμένον; ἰδοὺ οἱ ἐν ἱματισμῷ ἐνδόξῳ καὶ τρυφῇ ὑπάρχοντες ἐν τοῖς βασιλείοις εἰσίν. ²⁶ ἀλλὰ τί ἐξήλθατε ἰδεῖν; προφήτην; ναὶ λέγω ὑμῖν, καὶ περισσότερον προφήτου. ²⁷ οὗτός ἐστιν περὶ οὗ γέγραπται, Ἰδοὺ ἀποστέλλω τὸν ἄγγελόν μου πρὸ προσώπου σου, ὃς κατασκευάσει τὴν ὁδόν σου ἔμπροσθέν σου. ²⁸ λέγω ὑμῖν, μείζων ἐν γεννητοῖς γυναικῶν Ἰωάννου οὐδείς ἐστιν· ὁ δὲ

one who is least   in the kingdom of God   is   greater than he."   ¶   **29**   (All the people, even the
←   μικρότερος ἐν τῇ βασιλείᾳ → τοῦ θεοῦ ἐστιν μείζων → αὐτοῦ   Καὶ πᾶς ὁ λαὸς καὶ οἱ
     a.nsm.c   d.p d.dsf n.dsf   d.gsm n.gsm v.pai.3s a.nsm.c   r.gsm.3   cj a.nsm d.nsm n.nsm cj d.npm
     3625   1877 3836 993   3836 2536   1639 3489   899   2779 4246 3836 3295 2779 3836

tax   collectors, when they heard   Jesus' words, acknowledged that God's   way was right,   because they had
τελῶναι ←   →   → ἀκούσας   τὸν θεόν   → ἐδικαίωσαν →   →
n.npm   pt.aa.nsm   d.asm n.asm   v.aai.3p
5467   201   1467   3836 2536   1467

been baptized   by John.   **30** But the Pharisees and experts in the law   rejected God's
→ βαπτισθέντες τὸ βάπτισμα → Ἰωάννου δὲ οἱ Φαρισαῖοι καὶ   →   οἱ νομικοὶ ἠθέτησαν τοῦ θεοῦ
   pt.ap.npm   d.asn n.asn   n.gsm   cj d.npm n.npm   cj   d.npm n.npm   v.aai.3p d.gsm n.gsm
   966   3836 967   2722   1254 3836 5757   2779   3836 3788   119   3836 2536

purpose for themselves, because they had not been baptized   by John.)   ¶   **31** "To what, then, can I compare
τὴν βουλὴν εἰς ἑαυτοὺς   →   →   μὴ → βαπτισθέντες ὑπ' αὐτοῦ   →   Τίνι οὖν → → ὁμοιώσω
d.asf n.asf p.a r.apm.3   pl   pt.ap.npm   p.g r.gsm.3   r.dsn cj   v.fai.1s
3836 1087 1650 1571   966   966 966 3590   966   5679 899   5515 4036   3929

the people   of this   generation? What are they like? **32** They are   like   children sitting   in the
τοὺς ἀνθρώπους → ταύτης τῆς γενεᾶς καὶ τίνι εἰσὶν   ὅμοιοι   εἰσὶν ὅμοιοι παιδίοις τοῖς καθημένοις ἐν
d.apm n.apm   r.gsf   d.gsf n.gsf cj r.dsn v.pai.3p   a.npm   v.pai.3p a.npm n.dpn   d.dpn pt.pm.dpn   p.d
3836 476   1155 4047 3836 1155 2779 5515 1639   3927   1639 3927   4086   3836 2764   1877

marketplace and calling   out to each   other: "'We played the flute for you, and you did not
ἀγορᾷ   καὶ προσφωνοῦσιν → ἀλλήλοις ← ἃ λέγει   ηὐλήσαμεν ←   → ὑμῖν καὶ →   οὐκ
n.dsf   cj pt.pa.dpn   r.dpn   r.npn v.pai.3s v.aai.1p   r.dp.2 cj   pl
59   2779 4715   253   4005 3306   884   7007 2779 4004 4004 4024

dance;   we sang   a dirge, and you did not cry.'   **33** For John   the Baptist came   neither eating bread nor
ὠρχήσασθε ἐθρηνήσαμεν ← καὶ   → οὐκ ἐκλαύσατε γὰρ Ἰωάννης ὁ βαπτιστὴς ἐλήλυθεν μὴ   ἐσθίων ἄρτον μήτε
v.ami.2p   v.aai.1p   cj   → pl v.aai.2p   cj   n.nsm   d.nsm n.nsm   v.rai.3s   pl   pt.pa.nsm n.asm cj
4004   2577   2779 3081 3081 4024 3081   1142 2722   3836 969   2262   3590   2266   788   3612

drinking wine, and you say, 'He has a demon.' **34** The Son of Man   came   eating and drinking, and you
πίνων οἶνον καὶ → λέγετε   ἔχει δαιμόνιον ὁ υἱὸς → τοῦ ἀνθρώπου ἐλήλυθεν ἐσθίων καὶ πίνων   καὶ →
pt.pa.nsm n.asm cj   v.pai.2p   v.pai.3s n.asn   d.nsm n.nsm   d.gsm n.gsm   v.rai.3s   pt.pa.nsm cj pt.pa.nsm cj
4403   3885 2779   3306   2400 1228   3836 5626   3836 476   2262   2266   2779 4403   2779

say,   'Here is a glutton   and a drunkard, a friend of tax   collectors and "sinners."' **35** But wisdom   is
λέγετε ἰδοὺ   ἄνθρωπος φάγος καὶ οἰνοπότης φίλος → τελωνῶν ←   καὶ ἁμαρτωλῶν καὶ ἡ σοφία   →
v.pai.2p j   n.nsm   n.nsm   cj   n.nsm   a.nsm   n.gpm   cj a.gpm   cj d.nsf n.nsf
3306   2627   476   5741   2779 3884   5813   5467   2779 283   2779 3836 5053

proved right   by all   her children."
→ ἐδικαιώθη ἀπὸ πάντων αὐτῆς τῶν τέκνων
   v.api.3s   p.g a.gpn   r.gsf.3 d.gpn n.gpn
   1467   608 4246   899   3836 5451

Jesus Anointed by a Sinful Woman

7:36 Now one of the Pharisees invited Jesus to have dinner with him, so he went   to the Pharisee's
δὲ τις   τῶν Φαρισαίων Ἠρώτα αὐτὸν ἵνα   → φάγῃ   μετ' αὐτοῦ καὶ → εἰσελθὼν εἰς τὸν τοῦ Φαρισαίου
cj r.nsm d.gpm n.gpm   v.iai.3s r.asm.3 cj   v.aas.3s p.g r.gsm.3 cj   pt.aa.nsm p.a d.asm d.gsm n.gsm
1254 5516 3836 5757   2263   899   2671   2266   3552 899   2779   1656   1650 3836 3836 5757

house and reclined at the table. **37**   When a woman who had lived a sinful   life in that town   learned
οἶκον κατεκλίθη ← ←   καὶ ἰδοὺ   γυνὴ ἥτις → ἦν ἁμαρτωλός ←   ἐν τῇ πόλει καὶ ἐπιγνοῦσα
n.asm v.api.3s   cj j   n.nsf r.nsf   v.iai.3s a.nsf   p.d d.dsf n.dsf cj pt.aa.nsf
3875   2884   2779 2627   1222 4015   1639   283   1877 3836 4484 2779 2105

that Jesus was eating   at the Pharisee's   house, she brought an alabaster   jar of perfume, **38** and as she stood
ὅτι → κατάκειται ἐν τῇ τοῦ Φαρισαίου οἰκίᾳ → κομίσασα ἀλάβαστρον ← μύρου   καὶ → στᾶσα
cj   v.pmi.3s   p.d d.dsf d.gsm n.gsm   n.dsf   pt.aa.nsf n.asn   n.gsn   cj   pt.aa.nsf
4022   2879   1877 3836 3836 5757   3864 3152   223   3693   2779   2705

behind him at his feet   weeping, she began to wet his feet   with her tears.   Then she
ὀπίσω   παρὰ αὐτοῦ τοὺς πόδας κλαίουσα → ἤρξατο → βρέχειν αὐτοῦ τοὺς πόδας → τοῖς δάκρυσιν καὶ →
adv   p.a   r.gsm.3 d.apm n.apm pt.pa.nsf   v.ami.3s   f.pa   r.gsm.3 d.apm n.apm   d.dpn n.dpn   cj
3958   4123 899   3836 4546 3081   806   1101   899   3836 4546   3836 1232   2779

μικρότερος ἐν τῇ βασιλείᾳ τοῦ θεοῦ μείζων αὐτοῦ ἐστιν. ¶ **29** Καὶ πᾶς ὁ λαὸς ἀκούσας καὶ οἱ τελῶναι ἐδικαίωσαν τὸν θεὸν βαπτισθέντες τὸ βάπτισμα Ἰωάννου· **30** οἱ δὲ Φαρισαῖοι καὶ οἱ νομικοὶ τὴν βουλὴν τοῦ θεοῦ ἠθέτησαν εἰς ἑαυτοὺς μὴ βαπτισθέντες ὑπ' αὐτοῦ. ¶ **31** Τίνι οὖν ὁμοιώσω τοὺς ἀνθρώπους τῆς γενεᾶς ταύτης καὶ τίνι εἰσὶν ὅμοιοι; **32** ὅμοιοί εἰσιν παιδίοις τοῖς ἐν ἀγορᾷ καθημένοις καὶ προσφωνοῦσιν ἀλλήλοις ἃ λέγει, Ηὐλήσαμεν ὑμῖν καὶ οὐκ ὠρχήσασθε, ἐθρηνήσαμεν καὶ οὐκ ἐκλαύσατε. **33** ἐλήλυθεν γὰρ Ἰωάννης ὁ βαπτιστὴς μὴ ἐσθίων ἄρτον μήτε πίνων οἶνον, καὶ λέγετε, Δαιμόνιον ἔχει. **34** ἐλήλυθεν ὁ υἱὸς τοῦ ἀνθρώπου ἐσθίων καὶ πίνων, καὶ λέγετε, Ἰδοὺ ἄνθρωπος φάγος καὶ οἰνοπότης, φίλος τελωνῶν καὶ ἁμαρτωλῶν. **35** καὶ ἐδικαιώθη ἡ σοφία ἀπὸ πάντων τῶν τέκνων αὐτῆς.

7:36 Ἠρώτα δέ τις αὐτὸν τῶν Φαρισαίων ἵνα φάγῃ μετ' αὐτοῦ, καὶ εἰσελθὼν εἰς τὸν οἶκον τοῦ Φαρισαίου κατεκλίθη. **37** καὶ ἰδοὺ γυνὴ ἥτις ἦν ἐν τῇ πόλει ἁμαρτωλός, καὶ ἐπιγνοῦσα ὅτι κατάκειται ἐν τῇ οἰκίᾳ τοῦ Φαρισαίου, κομίσασα ἀλάβαστρον μύρου **38** καὶ στᾶσα ὀπίσω παρὰ τοὺς πόδας αὐτοῦ κλαίουσα τοῖς δάκρυσιν ἤρξατο βρέχειν τοὺς πόδας αὐτοῦ καὶ ταῖς θριξὶν

wiped them with her hair,   kissed them   and poured perfume on them. ¶
ἐξέμασσεν → αὐτῆς ⌊ταῖς θριξὶν⌋ τῆς κεφαλῆς κατεφίλει ⌊τοὺς πόδας⌋ αὐτοῦ καὶ ἤλειφεν ⌊τῷ μύρῳ⌋ ←
v.iai.3s | r.gsf.3 d.dpf n.dpf d.gsf n.gsf v.iai.3s d.apm n.apm r.gsm.3 cj v.iai.3s d.dsn n.dsn
1726 | 2582 899 2582 3836 3051 3836 2968 3836 4546 899 2779 230 3836 3693 230

39 When the Pharisee who had invited him saw this, he said to himself, "If this man were a prophet, he
δὲ → ὁ Φαρισαῖος ὁ → καλέσας αὐτὸν ἰδὼν → εἶπεν ἐν ἑαυτῷ λέγων εἰ οὗτος ← ἦν προφήτης →
cj | d.nsm n.nsm d.nsm pt.aa.nsm r.asm.3 pt.aa.nsm v.aai.3s p.d r.dsm.3 pt.pa.nsm cj r.nsm v.iai.3s n.nsm
1254 1625 3836 5757 3836 2813 899 1625 3306 1877 1571 3306 1623 4047 1639 4737 1182

would know who is touching him and what kind of woman she is – that she is a sinner." ¶
ἂν ἐγίνωσκεν τίς ἥτις → ἅπτεται αὐτοῦ καὶ ποταπὴ ← ← ἡ γυνὴ ὅτι → ἐστιν ἁμαρτωλός
pl v.iai.3s r.nsf r.nsf v.pmi.3s r.gsm.3 cj r.nsf d.nsf n.nsf cj v.pai.3s a.nsf
323 1182 5515 4015 721 899 2779 4534 3836 1222 4022 1639 283

40 Jesus answered him, "Simon, I have something to tell you." "Tell me, teacher," he said.
καὶ ὁ Ἰησοῦς ἀποκριθεὶς εἶπεν πρὸς αὐτόν Σίμων → ἔχω τι → εἰπεῖν σοί δὲ εἰπέ διδάσκαλε ὁ φησίν
cj d.nsm n.nsm pt.ap.nsm v.aai.3s p.a r.asm.3 n.vsm v.pai.1s r.asn f.aa r.ds.2 cj v.aam.2s n.vsm d.nsm v.pai.3s
2779 3836 2652 646 3306 4639 899 4981 2400 5516 3306 5148 1254 3306 1437 3836 5774

¶ **41** "Two men owed money to a certain moneylender. One owed him five hundred denarii,
δύο → ἦσαν χρεοφειλέται → τινι δανιστῇ ὁ εἷς ὤφειλεν πεντακόσια ← δηνάρια
a.npm v.iai.3p n.npm r.dsm n.dsm d.nsm a.nsm v.iai.3s a.apn n.apn
1545 1639 5971 5516 1250 3836 1651 4053 4296 1324

and the other fifty. **42** Neither of them had the money to pay him back, so he canceled the debts of
δὲ ὁ ἕτερος πεντήκοντα μὴ αὐτῶν ἐχόντων → ἀποδοῦναι ← → ἐχαρίσατο
pl d.nsm r.nsm a.apn pl r.gpm.3 pt.pa.gpm f.aa v.ami.3s
1254 3836 2283 4299 3590 899 2400 625 5919

both. Now which of them will love him more?" **43** Simon replied, "I suppose the one who had
ἀμφοτέροις οὖν τίς αὐτῶν → ἀγαπήσει αὐτὸν πλεῖον Σίμων ἀποκριθεὶς εἶπεν → ὑπολαμβάνω ὅτι ᾧ ←
a.dpm cj r.nsm r.gpm.3 v.fai.3s r.asm.3 adv.c n.nsm pt.ap.nsm v.aai.3s v.pai.1s cj r.dsm
317 4036 5515 899 26 899 4498 4981 646 3306 5696 4022 4005

the bigger debt canceled." "You have judged correctly," Jesus said. ¶ **44** Then he turned toward the
τὸ πλεῖον ἐχαρίσατο δὲ → ἔκρινας ὀρθῶς ὁ εἶπεν αὐτῷ καὶ → στραφεὶς πρὸς τὴν
d.asn a.asn.c v.ami.3s cj v.aai.2s adv d.nsm v.aai.3s r.dsm.3 cj pt.ap.nsm p.a d.asf
3836 4498 5919 1254 3212 3987 3836 3306 899 2779 5138 4639 3836

woman and said to Simon, "Do you see this woman? I came into your house. You did not give
γυναῖκα ἔφη → ⌊τῷ Σίμωνι⌋ βλέπεις ταύτην ⌊τὴν γυναῖκα⌋ → εἰσῆλθον εἰς σου ⌊τὴν οἰκίαν⌋ → → οὐκ ἔδωκας
n.asf v.iai.3s d.dsm n.dsm v.pai.2s r.asf d.asf n.asf v.aai.1s p.a r.gs.2 d.asf n.asf pl v.aai.2s
1222 5774 3836 4981 1063 4047 3836 1222 1656 1650 5148 3836 3864 1443 1443 4024 1443

me any water for my feet, but she wet my feet with her tears and wiped them with her hair.
μοι ὕδωρ ἐπὶ πόδας δὲ αὐτη ἔβρεξεν μου ⌊τοὺς πόδας⌋ → τοῖς δάκρυσιν καὶ ἐξέμαξεν → αὐτῆς ⌊ταῖς θριξὶν⌋
r.ds.1 n.asn p.a n.apm cj r.nsf v.aai.3s r.gs.1 d.apm n.apm d.dpn n.dpn cj v.aai.3s r.gsf.3 d.dpf n.dpf
1609 5623 2093 4546 1254 4047 1101 1609 3836 4546 3836 1232 2779 1726 2582 899 3836 2582

45 You did not give me a kiss, but this woman, from the time I entered, has not stopped kissing my
→ → οὐκ ἔδωκας μοι φίλημα δὲ αὐτη ← ἀφ' ἧς → εἰσῆλθον → οὐ διέλιπεν καταφιλοῦσά μου
pl v.aai.2s r.ds.1 n.asn cj r.nsf p.g r.gsf v.aai.1s pl v.aai.3s pt.pa.nsf r.gs.1
1443 1443 4024 1443 1609 5799 1254 4047 608 4005 1656 1364 4024 1364 2968 1609

feet. **46** You did not put oil on my head, but she has poured perfume on my feet.
⌊τοὺς πόδας⌋ → → οὐκ ἤλειψας ἐλαίῳ μου ⌊τὴν κεφαλήν⌋ δὲ αὐτη → ἤλειψεν μύρῳ → μου ⌊τοὺς πόδας⌋
d.apm n.apm pl v.aai.2s n.dsn r.gs.1 d.asf n.asf cj r.nsf v.aai.3s n.dsn r.gs.1 d.apm n.apm
3836 4546 230 230 4024 230 1778 230 1609 3836 3051 1254 4047 230 3693 230 1609 3836 4546

47 Therefore, I tell you, her many sins have been forgiven – for she loved much. But he who has
⌊οὗ χάριν⌋ → λέγω σοι αὐτῆς αἱ πολλαὶ αἱ ἁμαρτίαι → ἀφέωνται ὅτι → ἠγάπησεν πολύ δὲ ᾧ
r.gsn p.g v.pai.1s r.ds.2 r.gsf.3 d.npf a.npf d.npf n.npf v.rpi.3p cj v.aai.3s adv cj r.dsm
4005 5920 3306 5148 899 3836 4498 3836 281 918 4022 26 4498 1254 4005

been forgiven little loves little." ¶ **48** Then Jesus said to her, "Your sins are forgiven." **49** The other
→ ἀφίεται ὀλίγον ἀγαπᾷ ὀλίγον δὲ → εἶπεν αὐτη σου ⌊αἱ ἁμαρτίαι⌋ → ἀφέωνται καὶ οἱ
v.ppi.3s a.nsn v.pai.3s adv cj v.aai.3s r.dsf.3 r.gs.2 d.npf n.npf v.rpi.3p cj d.npm
918 3900 26 3900 1254 3306 899 5148 3836 281 918 2779 3836

τῆς κεφαλῆς αὐτῆς ἐξέμασσεν καὶ κατεφίλει τοὺς πόδας αὐτοῦ καὶ ἤλειφεν τῷ μύρῳ. ¶ **39** ἰδὼν δὲ ὁ Φαρισαῖος ὁ καλέσας αὐτὸν εἶπεν ἐν ἑαυτῷ λέγων, Οὗτος εἰ ἦν προφήτης, ἐγίνωσκεν ἂν τίς καὶ ποταπὴ ἡ γυνὴ ἥτις ἅπτεται αὐτοῦ, ὅτι ἁμαρτωλός ἐστιν. ¶ **40** καὶ ἀποκριθεὶς ὁ Ἰησοῦς εἶπεν πρὸς αὐτόν, Σίμων, ἔχω σοί τι εἰπεῖν. ὁ δέ, Διδάσκαλε, εἰπέ, φησίν. ¶ **41** δύο χρεοφειλέται ἦσαν δανιστῇ τινι· ὁ εἷς ὤφειλεν δηνάρια πεντακόσια, ὁ δὲ ἕτερος πεντήκοντα. **42** μὴ ἐχόντων αὐτῶν ἀποδοῦναι ἀμφοτέροις ἐχαρίσατο. τίς οὖν αὐτῶν πλεῖον ἀγαπήσει αὐτόν; **43** ἀποκριθεὶς Σίμων εἶπεν, Ὑπολαμβάνω ὅτι ᾧ τὸ πλεῖον ἐχαρίσατο. ὁ δὲ εἶπεν αὐτῷ, Ὀρθῶς ἔκρινας. ¶ **44** καὶ στραφεὶς πρὸς τὴν γυναῖκα τῷ Σίμωνι ἔφη, Βλέπεις ταύτην τὴν γυναῖκα; εἰσῆλθόν σου εἰς τὴν οἰκίαν, ὕδωρ μοι ἐπὶ πόδας οὐκ ἔδωκας· αὐτη δὲ τοῖς δάκρυσιν ἔβρεξέν μου τοὺς πόδας καὶ ταῖς θριξὶν αὐτῆς ἐξέμαξεν. **45** φίλημά μοι οὐκ ἔδωκας· αὐτη δὲ ἀφ' ἧς εἰσῆλθον οὐ διέλιπεν καταφιλοῦσά μου τοὺς πόδας. **46** ἐλαίῳ τὴν κεφαλήν μου οὐκ ἤλειψας· αὐτη δὲ μύρῳ ἤλειψεν τοὺς πόδας μου. **47** οὗ χάριν λέγω σοι, ἀφέωνται αἱ ἁμαρτίαι αὐτῆς αἱ πολλαί, ὅτι ἠγάπησεν πολύ· ᾧ δὲ ὀλίγον ἀφίεται, ὀλίγον ἀγαπᾷ. ¶ **48** εἶπεν δὲ αὐτῇ, Ἀφέωνταί σου αἱ ἁμαρτίαι. **49** καὶ ἤρξαντο οἱ συνανακείμενοι λέγειν ἐν ἑαυτοῖς,

guests	began to say	among	themselves,	"Who is	this	who even	forgives sins?"	[50]	Jesus said to	the
συνανακείμενοι	ἤρξαντο → λέγειν	ἐν	ἑαυτοῖς	τίς ἐστιν	οὗτος	ὃς καὶ	ἀφίησιν ἁμαρτίας	δὲ	εἶπεν πρὸς	τὴν
pt.pm.npm	v.ami.3p f.pa	p.d	r.dpm.3	r.nsm v.pai.3s	r.nsm	r.nsm adv	v.pai.3s n.apf	cj	v.aai.3s p.a	d.asf
5263	806 3306	1877	1571	5515 1639	4047	4005 2779	918 281	1254	3306 4639	3836

woman,	"Your	faith	has saved you;	go	in	peace."
γυναῖκα	σου	ἡ πίστις,	σέσωκεν σε	πορεύου	εἰς	εἰρήνην
n.asf	r.gs.2	d.nsf n.nsf	v.rai.3s r.as.2	v.pmm.2s	p.a	n.asf
1222	5148	3836 4411	5392 5148	4513	1650	1645

The Parable of the Sower

8:1

After this,	Jesus traveled about from one town	and	village to	another,	proclaiming	and
Καὶ ἐγένετο ἐν	τῷ καθεξῆς, καὶ αὐτὸς διώδευεν ←	κατὰ	πόλιν καὶ	κώμην ←	κηρύσσων	καὶ
cj v.ami.3s p.d	d.dsm adv cj r.nsm v.iai.3s	p.a	n.asf cj	n.asf	pt.pa.nsm	cj
2779 1181 1877	3836 2759 2779 899 1476	2848	4484 2779	3267 2848	3062	2779

the good news	of the kingdom	of God.	The Twelve	were with him,	[2] and also	some	women
εὐαγγελιζόμενος ←	τὴν βασιλείαν →	τοῦ θεοῦ,	καὶ οἱ δώδεκα	σὺν αὐτῷ	καὶ	τινες	γυναῖκες
pt.pm.nsm	d.asf n.asf	d.gsm n.gsm	cj d.npm a.npm	p.d r.dsm.3	cj	r.npf	n.npf
2294	3836 993	3836 2536	2779 3836 1557	5250 899	2779	5516	1222

who	had been	cured	of	evil	spirits	and	diseases: Mary	(called	Magdalene)	from whom
αἳ → →	ἦσαν	τεθεραπευμέναι	ἀπὸ	πονηρῶν	πνευμάτων	καὶ	ἀσθενειῶν Μαρία	ἡ καλουμένη	Μαγδαληνή	ἀφ᾽ ἧς
r.npf	v.iai.3p	pt.rp.npf	p.g	a.gpn	n.gpn	cj	n.gpf n.nsf	d.nsf pt.pp.nsf	n.nsf	p.g r.gsf
4005	1639	2543	608	4505	4460	2779	819 3451	3836 2813	3402	608 4005

seven	demons	had come out;	[3]	Joanna	the wife	of Cuza,	the manager	of Herod's household;	Susanna; and
ἑπτὰ	δαιμόνια →	ἐξελήλυθει	καὶ	Ἰωάννα	γυνὴ →	Χουζᾶ	ἐπιτρόπου →	Ἡρώδου	καὶ Σουσάννα καὶ
a.npn	n.npn	v.iai.3s	cj	n.nsf	n.nsf	n.gsm	n.gsm	n.gsm	cj n.nsf cj
2231	1228	2002	2779	2721	1222	5966	2207	2476	2779 5052 2779

many	others.	These	women	were	helping to	support	them	out of	their	own	means.	¶	[4]	While a	large
πολλαί	ἕτεραι	αἵτινες ←	→	→	→	διηκόνουν	αὐτοῖς	ἐκ	αὐταῖς	τῶν	ὑπαρχόντων		δὲ		πολλοῦ
a.npf	r.npf	r.npf				v.iai.3p	r.dpm.3	p.g	r.dpf.3	d.gpn	pt.pa.gpn		cj		a.gsm
4498	2283	4015				1354	899	1666	899	3836	5639		1254		4498

crowd	was gathering	and	people	were coming	to	Jesus	*from*	*town*	*after*	*town,*	he told	this	parable:	[5] "A
ὄχλου →	Συνιόντος	καὶ	τῶν	→	ἐπιπορευομένων	πρὸς	αὐτὸν	κατὰ	πόλιν	→	εἶπεν διὰ		παραβολῆς	
n.gsm	pt.pa.gsm	cj	d.gpm		pt.pm.gpm	p.a	r.asm.3	p.a	n.asf		v.aai.3s p.g		n.gsf	
4063	5290	2779	3836		2164	4639	899	2848	4484		3306 1328		4130	

farmer	went out to	sow	his	seed.	As	he	was scattering	the seed,	some	fell	along
ὁ σπείρων	ἐξῆλθεν ←	τοῦ σπεῖραι	αὐτοῦ	τὸν σπόρον	καὶ ἐν	αὐτὸν	τῷ σπείρειν ←	←	μὲν ὃ	ἔπεσεν	παρὰ
d.nsm pt.pa.nsm	v.aai.3s	d.gsn f.aa	r.gsm.3	d.asm n.asm	cj p.d	r.asm.3	d.dsn f.pa		pl r.nsn	v.aai.3s	p.a
3836 5062	2002	3836 5062	899	3836 5062	2779 1877	899	3836 5062		3525 4005	4406	4123

the path;	it was	trampled on,	and	the	birds	of the air	ate	it	up.	[6]	Some	fell	on rock,
τὴν ὁδὸν	καὶ →	κατεπατήθη	καὶ	τὰ	πετεινὰ →	τοῦ οὐρανοῦ	κατέφαγεν	αὐτό			καὶ ἕτερον	κατέπεσεν ἐπὶ	τὴν πέτραν,
d.asf n.asf	cj	v.api.3s	cj	d.npn	n.npn	d.gsm n.gsm	v.aai.3s	r.asn.3			cj r.nsn	v.aai.3s p.a	d.asf n.asf
3836 3847	2779	2922	2779	3836	4374	3836 4041	2983	899			2779 2283	2928 2093	3836 4376

and	when it	came up,	the plants	withered	because	they had	no	moisture.	[7]	Other seed	fell	among
καὶ →	φυὲν	ἐξηράνθη	διὰ	τὸ ἔχειν,	μὴ	ἰκμάδα			καὶ ἕτερον	ἔπεσεν ἐν	μέσῳ
cj	pt.ap.nsn	v.api.3s	p.a	d.asn f.pa	pl	n.asf			cj r.nsn	v.aai.3s p.d	n.dsn
2779	5886	3830	1328	3836 2400	3590	2657			2779 2283	4406 1877	3545

thorns,	which	grew	up with it and	choked	the plants.	[8] Still	other seed	fell	on	good
τῶν ἀκανθῶν,	καὶ	αἱ ἄκανθαι	συμφυεῖσαι ←	←	ἀπέπνιξαν	αὐτό	καὶ	ἕτερον	ἔπεσεν εἰς	τὴν ἀγαθὴν,
d.gpf n.gpf	cj	d.npf n.npf	pt.ap.npf		v.aai.3p	r.asn.3	cj	r.nsn	v.aai.3s p.a	d.asf a.asf
3836 180	2779	3836 180	5243		678	899	2779	2283	4406 1650	3836 19

soil.	It came up	and	yielded	a crop,	a hundred	times more than was sown."	¶	When he said
τὴν γῆν,	καὶ	φυὲν	ἐποίησεν	καρπὸν	ἑκατονταπλασίονα			→ λέγων
d.asf n.asf	cj	pt.ap.nsn	v.aai.3s	n.asm	a.asm			pt.pa.nsm
3836 1178	2779	5886	4472	2843	1671			3306

this,	he called out,	"He who has	ears	to hear,	let him hear."	¶	[9]	His	disciples	asked	him	what
ταῦτα →	ἐφώνει ←	ὁ ←	ἔχων ὦτα →	ἀκούειν →	→ ἀκουέτω			δὲ αὐτοῦ	οἱ μαθηταὶ,	Ἐπηρώτων	αὐτὸν	τίς
r.apn	v.iai.3s	d.nsm	pt.pa.nsm n.apn	f.pa	v.pam.3s			cj r.gsm.3	d.npm n.npm	v.iai.3p	r.asm.3	r.nsf
4047	5888	3836	2400 4044	201	201			1254 899	3836 3412	2089	899	5515

Τίς οὗτός ἐστιν ὃς καὶ ἁμαρτίας ἀφίησιν; 50 εἶπεν δὲ πρὸς τὴν γυναῖκα, Ἡ πίστις σου σέσωκέν σε· πορεύου εἰς εἰρήνην.
   8:1 Καὶ ἐγένετο ἐν τῷ καθεξῆς καὶ αὐτὸς διώδευεν κατὰ πόλιν καὶ κώμην κηρύσσων καὶ εὐαγγελιζόμενος τὴν βασιλείαν τοῦ θεοῦ καὶ οἱ δώδεκα σὺν αὐτῷ, 2 καὶ γυναῖκες τινες αἳ ἦσαν τεθεραπευμέναι ἀπὸ πνευμάτων πονηρῶν καὶ ἀσθενειῶν, Μαρία ἡ καλουμένη Μαγδαληνή, ἀφ᾽ ἧς δαιμόνια ἑπτὰ ἐξελήλυθει, 3 καὶ Ἰωάννα γυνὴ Χουζᾶ ἐπιτρόπου Ἡρώδου καὶ Σουσάννα καὶ ἕτεραι πολλαί, αἵτινες διηκόνουν αὐτοῖς ἐκ τῶν ὑπαρχόντων αὐταῖς. ¶ 4 Συνιόντος δὲ ὄχλου πολλοῦ καὶ τῶν κατὰ πόλιν ἐπιπορευομένων πρὸς αὐτὸν εἶπεν διὰ παραβολῆς, 5 Ἐξῆλθεν ὁ σπείρων τοῦ σπεῖραι τὸν σπόρον αὐτοῦ. καὶ ἐν τῷ σπείρειν αὐτὸν ὃ μὲν ἔπεσεν παρὰ τὴν ὁδὸν καὶ κατεπατήθη, καὶ τὰ πετεινὰ τοῦ οὐρανοῦ κατέφαγεν αὐτό. 6 καὶ ἕτερον κατέπεσεν ἐπὶ τὴν πέτραν, καὶ φυὲν ἐξηράνθη διὰ τὸ μὴ ἔχειν ἰκμάδα. 7 καὶ ἕτερον ἔπεσεν ἐν μέσῳ τῶν ἀκανθῶν, καὶ συμφυεῖσαι αἱ ἄκανθαι ἀπέπνιξαν αὐτό. 8 καὶ ἕτερον ἔπεσεν εἰς τὴν γῆν τὴν ἀγαθὴν καὶ φυὲν ἐποίησεν καρπὸν ἑκατονταπλασίονα. ¶ ταῦτα λέγων ἐφώνει, Ὁ ἔχων ὦτα ἀκούειν ἀκουέτω. ¶ 9 Ἐπηρώτων δὲ αὐτὸν οἱ μαθηταὶ αὐτοῦ τίς αὕτη εἴη ἡ παραβολή. 10 ὁ

this parable   meant. **10**   He said, "The knowledge of the secrets   of the kingdom of God   has been   given
αὕτη ἡ παραβολὴ εἴη   δὲ ὁ εἶπεν   γνῶναι   τὰ μυστήρια → τῆς βασιλείας → ‚τοῦ θεοῦ‚ → →   δέδοται
r.nsf d.nsf n.nsf v.pao.3s cj d.nsm v.aai.3s f.aa   d.apn n.apn   d.gsf n.gsf   d.gsm n.gsm   v.rpi.3s
4047 3836 4130   1639   1254 3836 3306   1182   3836 3696   3836 993   3836 2536   1443

to you, but to others   I speak in parables,   so that, "'though seeing, they may not see;   though
→ ὑμῖν δὲ → ‚τοῖς λοιποῖς‚ ἐν παραβολαῖς ἵνα ← →   βλέποντες → → μὴ βλέπωσιν καὶ →
→ r.dp.2 cj → d.dpm a.dpm   ἐν n.dpf   cj   pt.pa.npm   pl v.pas.3p cj
7007 1254 3836 3370   1877 4130 2671   1063   1063 1063 3590 1063 2779

hearing, they may not understand.'   ¶   **11**   "This is   the meaning of the parable: The seed is   the word
ἀκούοντες → → μὴ συνιῶσιν   δὲ αὕτη Ἔστιν   ἡ παραβολὴ ὁ σπόρος ἐστὶν ὁ λόγος
pt.pa.npm   pl v.pas.3p   cj r.nsf v.pai.3s   d.nsf n.nsf   d.nsm n.nsm v.pai.3s d.nsm n.nsm
201   5317 5317 3590 5317   1254 4047 1639   3836 4130   3836 5078 1639 3836 3364

of God. **12**   Those along the path are the ones who hear,   and then the devil   comes and takes away the
→ ‚τοῦ θεοῦ‚ δὲ οἱ παρὰ τὴν ὁδόν εἰσιν οἱ ← ἀκούσαντες εἶτα ὁ διάβολος ἔρχεται καὶ αἴρει ← τὸν
d.gsm n.gsm   cj d.npm παρὰ d.asf n.asf v.pai.3p d.npm   pt.aa.npm   adv d.nsm n.nsm v.pmi.3s cj v.pai.3s   d.asm
3836 2536   1254 3836 4123 3836 3847 1639 3836   201   1663 3836 1333 2262 2779 149   3836

word from their hearts,   so that they may not believe   and be saved. **13**   Those on the rock are the ones
λόγον ἀπὸ αὐτῶν ‚τῆς καρδίας‚ ἵνα ← → μὴ πιστεύσαντες → σωθῶσιν δὲ οἱ ἐπὶ τῆς πέτρας οἳ ←
n.asm p.g r.gpm.3 d.gsf n.gsf   cj   pl pt.aa.npm   v.aps.3p cj d.npm p.g d.gsf n.gsf r.npm
3364 608 899 3836 2840   2671   5392 5392 3590 4409   5392   1254 3836 2093 3836 4376 4005

who receive the word with joy   when they hear   it, but they have   no root. They believe   for a while, but
← δέχονται τὸν λόγον μετὰ χαρᾶς ὅταν ἀκούσωσιν καὶ οὗτοι ἔχουσιν οὐκ ῥίζαν οἳ πιστεύουσιν πρὸς καιρὸν καὶ
v.pmi.3p d.asm n.asm p.g n.gsf cj   v.aas.3p cj r.npm v.pai.3p pl n.asf r.npm v.pai.3p p.a n.asm cj
1312 3836 3364 3552 5915 4020   201   2779 4047 2400 4024 4844 4005 4409   4639 2789 2779

in the time of testing   they fall   away. **14**   The seed that fell among thorns   stands for those who
ἐν καιρῷ → πειρασμοῦ → ἀφίστανται ← δὲ τὸ πεσὸν εἰς ‚τὰς ἀκάνθας‚ οὗτοί εἰσιν ← οἱ
p.d καιρῷ n.gsm   v.pmi.3p   cj d.nsn pt.aa.nsn p.a d.apf n.apf r.npm v.pai.3p   d.npm
1877 2789 4280   923   1254 3836 4406 1650 3836 180   4047 1639   3836

hear,   but as they go   on their way they are choked   by life's   worries,   riches and pleasures,
ἀκούσαντες καὶ → πορευόμενοι ← → συμπνίγονται ὑπὸ ‚τοῦ βίου‚ μεριμνῶν καὶ πλούτου καὶ ἡδονῶν
pt.aa.npm cj → pt.pm.npm   v.ppi.3p p.g d.gsm n.gsm n.gpf cj n.gsm cj n.gpf
201   2779   4513   5231 5679 3836 1050 3533 2779 4458 2779 2454

and they do not mature. **15** But the seed on good soil   stands for those with a noble and good heart, who
καὶ → → οὐ τελεσφοροῦσιν δὲ τὸ ἐν καλῇ ‚τῇ γῇ‚ οὗτοί εἰσιν ← οἵτινες ἐν καλῇ καὶ ἀγαθῇ καρδίᾳ ←
cj   pl v.pai.3p   cj d.nsn p.d d.dsf d.dsf n.dsf r.npm v.pai.3p   r.npm p.d a.dsf cj a.dsf n.dsf
2779 5461 5461 4024 5461   1254 3836 1877 2819 3836 1178 4047 1639   4015 1877 2819 2779 19 2840 4015

hear   the word, retain   it, and by persevering produce   a crop.
ἀκούσαντες τὸν λόγον κατέχουσιν καὶ ἐν ὑπομονῇ καρποφοροῦσιν ←
pt.aa.npm d.asm n.asm v.pai.3p   cj p.d n.dsf v.pai.3p
201 3836 3364 2988   2779 1877 5705 2844

A Lamp on a Stand

8:16 "No one   lights a lamp and hides   it   in a jar   or puts it under a bed. Instead, he puts it
δὲ → Οὐδεὶς ἅψας λύχνον καλύπτει αὐτὸν σκεύει ἢ τίθησιν ὑποκάτω κλίνης ἀλλ' → τίθησιν
cj   a.nsm pt.aa.nsm n.asm v.pai.3s r.asm.3 n.dsn cj v.pai.3s p.g n.gsf cj   v.pai.3s
1254   4029 721 3394 2821 899 5007 2445 5502 5691 3109 247   5502

on a stand, so that those who come   in can see   the light. **17** For there is nothing hidden that will not
ἐπὶ λυχνίας ἵνα ← οἱ ← εἰσπορευόμενοι → βλέπωσιν τὸ φῶς γὰρ → ἐστιν οὐ κρυπτὸν ὃ → οὐ
p.g n.gsf cj   d.npm   pt.pm.npm   v.pas.3p d.asn n.asn cj   v.pai.3s pl a.nsn r.nsn   pl
2093 3393 2671   3836   1660   1063 3836 5890 1142   1639 4024 3220 4005 1181 4024

be   disclosed, and nothing concealed that will not   be known or brought out into the open. **18** Therefore
γενήσεται φανερὸν οὐδὲ ← ἀπόκρυφον ὃ → οὐ μὴ → γνωσθῇ καὶ ἔλθῃ ← εἰς φανερὸν οὖν
v.fmi.3s a.nsn cj   a.nsn r.nsn   pl pl v.aps.3s cj v.aas.3p   p.a a.asn cj
1181 5745   4028   649   4005 1182 4024 3590 1182 2779 2262   1650 5745 4036

consider carefully how you listen.   Whoever has will be given   more;   whoever does not have, even
Βλέπετε   πῶς → ἀκούετε γὰρ ὃς ἂν ἔχῃ → → δοθήσεται   αὐτῷ καὶ ὃς ἂν → μὴ ἔχῃ καὶ
v.pam.2p   cj   v.pai.2p cj r.nsm pl v.pas.3s   v.fpi.3s   r.dsm.3 cj r.nsm pl   pl v.pas.3s adv
1063   4802   201 1142 4005 323 2400   1443   899 2779 4005 323 2400 3590 2400 2779

δὲ εἶπεν, Ὑμῖν δέδοται γνῶναι τὰ μυστήρια τῆς βασιλείας τοῦ θεοῦ, τοῖς δὲ λοιποῖς ἐν παραβολαῖς, ἵνα βλέποντες μὴ βλέπωσιν καὶ ἀκούοντες μὴ συνιῶσιν. ¶ **11** Ἔστιν δὲ αὕτη ἡ παραβολή· Ὁ σπόρος ἐστὶν ὁ λόγος τοῦ θεοῦ. **12** οἱ δὲ παρὰ τὴν ὁδόν εἰσιν οἱ ἀκούσαντες, εἶτα ἔρχεται ὁ διάβολος καὶ αἴρει τὸν λόγον ἀπὸ τῆς καρδίας αὐτῶν, ἵνα μὴ πιστεύσαντες σωθῶσιν. **13** οἱ δὲ ἐπὶ τῆς πέτρας οἳ ὅταν ἀκούσωσιν μετὰ χαρᾶς δέχονται τὸν λόγον, καὶ οὗτοι ῥίζαν οὐκ ἔχουσιν, οἳ πρὸς καιρὸν πιστεύουσιν καὶ ἐν καιρῷ πειρασμοῦ ἀφίστανται. **14** τὸ δὲ εἰς τὰς ἀκάνθας πεσόν, οὗτοί εἰσιν οἱ ἀκούσαντες, καὶ ὑπὸ μεριμνῶν καὶ πλούτου καὶ ἡδονῶν τοῦ βίου πορευόμενοι συμπνίγονται καὶ οὐ τελεσφοροῦσιν. **15** τὸ δὲ ἐν τῇ καλῇ γῇ, οὗτοί εἰσιν οἵτινες ἐν καρδίᾳ καλῇ καὶ ἀγαθῇ ἀκούσαντες τὸν λόγον κατέχουσιν καὶ καρποφοροῦσιν ἐν ὑπομονῇ.

8:16 Οὐδεὶς δὲ λύχνον ἅψας καλύπτει αὐτὸν σκεύει ἢ ὑποκάτω κλίνης τίθησιν, ἀλλ' ἐπὶ λυχνίας τίθησιν, ἵνα οἱ εἰσπορευόμενοι βλέπωσιν τὸ φῶς. **17** οὐ γάρ ἐστιν κρυπτὸν ὃ οὐ φανερὸν γενήσεται οὐδὲ ἀπόκρυφον ὃ οὐ μὴ γνωσθῇ καὶ εἰς φανερὸν ἔλθῃ. **18** βλέπετε οὖν πῶς ἀκούετε· ὃς ἂν γὰρ ἔχῃ, δοθήσεται αὐτῷ· καὶ ὃς ἂν μὴ ἔχῃ, καὶ ὃ δοκεῖ ἔχειν ἀρθήσεται ἀπ' αὐτοῦ.

what he thinks he has will be taken from him."
ὁ → δοκεῖ → ἔχειν → → ἀρθήσεται ἀπ᾽ αὐτοῦ
r.asn v.pai.3s f.pa v.fpi.3s p.g r.gsm.3
4005 1506 2400 149 608 899

Jesus' Mother and Brothers

8:19 Now Jesus' mother and brothers came to see him, but they were not able to get near him
δὲ αὐτοῦ ἡ μήτηρ καὶ οἱ ἀδελφοὶ Παρεγένετο πρὸς αὐτὸν καὶ → → οὐκ ἠδύναντο → συντυχεῖν αὐτῷ
cj r.gsm.3 d.nsf n.nsf cj d.npm n.npm v.ami.3s p.a r.asm.3 cj pl v.ipi.3p f.aa r.dsm.3
1254 899 3836 3613 2779 3836 81 4134 4639 899 2779 1538 1538 4024 1538 5344 899

because of the crowd. **20** Someone told him, "Your mother and brothers are standing outside, wanting
διὰ ← τὸν ὄχλον δὲ ἀπηγγέλη αὐτῷ σου ἡ μήτηρ καὶ σου οἱ ἀδελφοί → ἑστήκασιν ἔξω θέλοντες
p.a d.asm n.asm cj v.api.3s r.dsm.3 r.gs.2 d.nsf n.nsf cj r.gs.2 d.npm n.npm v.rai.3p adv pt.pa.npm
1328 3836 4063 1254 550 899 5148 3836 3613 2779 5148 3836 81 2705 2032 2527

to see you." **21** He replied, "My mother and brothers are those who hear God's
→ ἰδεῖν σε δὲ ὁ ἀποκριθεὶς εἶπεν πρὸς αὐτούς μου μήτηρ καὶ μου ἀδελφοί οὗτοι εἰσιν οἱ ἀκούοντες τοῦ θεοῦ
f.aa r.as.2 cj d.nsm pt.ap.nsm v.aai.3s p.a r.apm.3 r.gs.1 n.nsf cj r.gs.1 n.npm r.npm v.pai.3p d.npm pt.pa.npm d.gsm n.gsm
1625 5148 1254 3836 646 3306 4639 899 1609 3613 2779 1609 81 4047 1639 3836 201 3836 2536

word and put it into practice."
τὸν λόγον καὶ → → ποιοῦντες
d.asm n.asm cj pt.pa.npm
3836 3364 2779 4472

Jesus Calms the Storm

8:22 One day Jesus said to his disciples, "Let's go over to the other side of the
δὲ Ἐγένετο ἐν μιᾷ τῶν ἡμερῶν καὶ εἶπεν πρὸς αὐτούς διέλθωμεν εἰς τὸ πέραν τῆς
cj v.ami.3s p.d a.dsf d.gpf n.gpf cj v.aai.3s p.a r.apm.3 v.aas.1p p.a d.asn p.g d.gsf
1254 1181 1877 1651 3836 2465 2779 3306 4639 899 1451 1650 3836 4305 3836

lake." So they got into a boat and set out. **23** As they sailed, he fell asleep.
λίμνης καὶ αὐτὸς καὶ οἱ μαθηταὶ αὐτοῦ ἐνέβη εἰς πλοῖον καὶ ἀνήχθησαν ← δὲ αὐτῶν πλεόντων → ἀφύπνωσεν καὶ
n.gsf cj r.nsm cj d.npm n.npm r.gsm.3 v.aai.3s p.a n.asn cj v.api.3p cj r.gpm.3 pt.pa.gpm v.aai.3s cj
3349 2779 899 2779 3836 3412 899 1832 1650 4450 2779 343 1254 4434 4434 934 2779

A squall came down on the lake, so that the boat was being swamped, and they were in great
λαῖλαψ ἀνέμου κατέβη → εἰς τὴν λίμνην καὶ → → συνεπληροῦντο καὶ
n.nsf n.gsm v.aai.3s p.a d.asf n.asf cj v.ipi.3p cj
3278 449 2849 1650 3836 3349 2779 5230 2779

danger. ¶ **24** The disciples went and woke him, saying, "Master, Master, we're going to
ἐκινδύνευον δὲ προσελθόντες διήγειραν αὐτὸν λέγοντες ἐπιστάτα ἐπιστάτα → →
v.iai.3p cj pt.aa.npm v.aai.3s r.asm.3 pt.pa.npm n.vsm n.vsm
3073 1254 4665 1444 899 3306 2181 2181

drown!" He got up and rebuked the wind and the raging waters; the storm subsided, and all
ἀπολλύμεθα δὲ ὁ διεγερθεὶς ← ἐπετίμησεν τῷ ἀνέμῳ καὶ τῷ κλύδωνι τοῦ ὕδατος καὶ ἐπαύσαντο καὶ
v.pmi.1p cj d.nsm pt.ap.nsm v.aai.3s d.dsm n.dsm cj d.dsm n.dsm d.gsn n.gsn cj v.ami.3p cj
660 1254 3836 1444 2203 3836 449 2779 3836 3114 3836 5623 2779 4264 2779

was calm. **25** "Where is your faith?" he asked his disciples. ¶ In fear and amazement they
ἐγένετο γαλήνη δὲ ποῦ ὑμῶν ἡ πίστις → εἶπεν αὐτοῖς δὲ → φοβηθέντες ἐθαύμασαν →
v.ami.3s n.nsf cj adv r.gp.2 d.nsf n.nsf v.aai.3s r.dpm.3 cj pt.ap.npm v.aai.3p
1181 1132 1254 4543 7007 3836 4411 3306 899 1254 5828 2513

asked one another, "Who is this? He commands even the winds and the water, and they
λέγοντες πρὸς ἀλλήλους ← τίς ἄρα ἐστὶν οὗτος ὅτι → ἐπιτάσσει καὶ τοῖς ἀνέμοις καὶ τῷ ὕδατι καὶ →
pt.pa.npm p.a r.apm r.nsm cj v.pai.3s r.nsm cj v.pai.3s adv d.dpm n.dpm cj d.dsn n.dsn cj
3306 4639 253 5515 726 1639 4047 4022 2199 2779 3836 449 2779 3836 5623 2779

obey him."
ὑπακούουσιν αὐτῷ
v.pai.3p r.dsm.3
5634 899

8:19 Παρεγένετο δὲ πρὸς αὐτὸν ἡ μήτηρ καὶ οἱ ἀδελφοὶ αὐτοῦ καὶ οὐκ ἠδύναντο συντυχεῖν αὐτῷ διὰ τὸν ὄχλον. **20** ἀπηγγέλη δὲ αὐτῷ, Ἡ μήτηρ σου καὶ οἱ ἀδελφοί σου ἑστήκασιν ἔξω ἰδεῖν θέλοντές σε. **21** ὁ δὲ ἀποκριθεὶς εἶπεν πρὸς αὐτούς, Μήτηρ μου καὶ ἀδελφοί μου οὗτοί εἰσιν οἱ τὸν λόγον τοῦ θεοῦ ἀκούοντες καὶ ποιοῦντες.

8:22 Ἐγένετο δὲ ἐν μιᾷ τῶν ἡμερῶν καὶ αὐτὸς ἐνέβη εἰς πλοῖον καὶ οἱ μαθηταὶ αὐτοῦ καὶ εἶπεν πρὸς αὐτούς, Διέλθωμεν εἰς τὸ πέραν τῆς λίμνης, καὶ ἀνήχθησαν. **23** πλεόντων δὲ αὐτῶν ἀφύπνωσεν. καὶ κατέβη λαῖλαψ ἀνέμου εἰς τὴν λίμνην καὶ συνεπληροῦντο καὶ ἐκινδύνευον. ¶ **24** προσελθόντες δὲ διήγειραν αὐτὸν λέγοντες, Ἐπιστάτα ἐπιστάτα, ἀπολλύμεθα. ὁ δὲ διεγερθεὶς ἐπετίμησεν τῷ ἀνέμῳ καὶ τῷ κλύδωνι τοῦ ὕδατος· καὶ ἐπαύσαντο καὶ ἐγένετο γαλήνη. **25** εἶπεν δὲ αὐτοῖς, Ποῦ ἡ πίστις ὑμῶν; ¶ φοβηθέντες δὲ ἐθαύμασαν λέγοντες πρὸς ἀλλήλους, Τίς ἄρα οὗτός ἐστιν ὅτι καὶ τοῖς ἀνέμοις ἐπιτάσσει καὶ τῷ ὕδατι, καὶ ὑπακούουσιν αὐτῷ;

The Healing of a Demon-Possessed Man

8:26 They sailed | | to | the | region of | the | Gerasenes, | which | is | across | | the lake from Galilee. | **27**
Καὶ → | κατέπλευσαν εἰς | τὴν | χώραν | τῶν | Γερασηνῶν | ἥτις | ἐστὶν | ἀντιπέρα | → | ⸃τῆς Γαλιλαίας⸃ | δὲ
cj | v.aai.3p | p.a | d.asf | n.asf | d.gpm | a.gpm | r.nsf | v.pai.3s | p.g | | d.gsf n.gsf | cj
2779 | 2929 | 1650 | 3836 | 6001 | 3836 | 1170 | 4015 | 1639 | 527 | | 3836 1133 | 1254

When | Jesus | stepped ashore, | | he was met | by a | demon-possessed | man | from | the | town. | For a long | time
→ | αὐτῷ | ἐξελθόντι | ἐπὶ τὴν γῆν⸃ → | ὑπήντησεν ← | τις | ἔχων δαιμόνια⸃ | ἀνὴρ | ἐκ | τῆς | πόλεως | καὶ → | ἱκανῷ χρόνῳ
2002 | r.dsm.3 | pt.aa.dsm | p.a d.asf n.asf | v.aai.3s | r.nsm | pt.pa.nsm n.apn | n.nsm | p.g | d.gsf | n.gsf | cj | a.dsm n.dsm
| 899 | 2002 | 2093 3836 1178 | 5636 | 5516 | 2400 1228 | 467 | 1666 | 3836 | 4484 | 2779 | 2653 5989

this man | had not | worn | clothes | or | | lived | in | a house, | but | had lived | in | the | tombs. | **28** | When he saw
→ | οὐκ | ἐνεδύσατο | ἱμάτιον | καὶ | οὐκ | ἔμενεν | ἐν | οἰκίᾳ | ἀλλ᾽ | | ἐν | τοῖς | μνήμασιν | δὲ → | → ἰδὼν
| pl | v.ami.3s | n.asn | cj | pl | v.iai.3s | p.d | n.dsf | cj | | p.d | d.dpn | n.dpn | cj | pt.aa.nsm
| 1907 | 4024 | 1907 | 2668 | 2779 | 4024 | 3531 | 1877 | 3864 | 247 | | 1877 | 3836 | 3645 | 1254 | 1625

Jesus, | | he cried | out and fell | | at his | feet, | | shouting | at the | top | of his | voice, | "What | do you
⸃τὸν Ἰησοῦν⸃ → | ἀνακράξας ← | | προσέπεσεν | αὐτῷ | καὶ | εἶπεν | μεγάλῃ | | φωνῇ | τί | | σοί | καὶ
d.asm n.asm | pt.aa.nsm | | v.aai.3s | r.dsm.3 | cj | v.aai.3s | a.dsf | | n.dsf | r.nsn | | r.ds.2 | cj
3836 2652 | 371 | | 4700 | 899 | 2779 | 3306 | 3489 | | 5889 | 5515 | | 5148 | 2779

want | with | me, | Jesus, | Son | of the | Most High | | God? | I beg | you, | don't | torture | me!" | **29** | For Jesus had commanded
⸃ἐμοὶ | Ἰησοῦ | υἱὲ | → | τοῦ | ὑψίστου | ⸃τοῦ θεοῦ⸃ | → | δέομαι | σου | μὴ | βασανίσῃς | με | γὰρ | → | παρήγγειλεν
r.ds.1 | n.vsm | n.vsm | | d.gsm | a.gsm.s | d.gsm n.gsm | | v.pmi.1s | r.gs.2 | pl | v.aas.2s | r.as.1 | cj | | v.aai.3s
1609 | 2652 | 5626 | 3836 | 5736 | 3836 2536 | | 1289 | 5148 | 3590 | 989 | 1609 | 1142 | | 4133

the evil | | spirit | to come out of | the | man. | | Many | times | it had seized | | him, | and though he was
τῷ | ⸃τῷ ἀκαθάρτῳ⸃ | πνεύματι | → ἐξελθεῖν ← | ἀπὸ τοῦ | ἀνθρώπου | γὰρ | πολλοῖς | χρόνοις | → | συνηρπάκει αὐτὸν | καὶ | → →
d.dsn | d.dsn a.dsn | n.dsn | f.aa | p.g d.gsm | n.gsm | cj | a.dpm | n.dpm | | v.lai.3s | r.asm.3 | cj
3836 | 3836 176 | 4460 | 2002 | 608 3836 | 476 | 1142 | 4498 | 5989 | | 5275 | 899 | 2779

chained | hand | and foot | and kept under | guard, | | he had broken | his chains | and had been | driven | by
ἐδεσμεύετο | ἁλύσεσιν | καὶ | πέδαις | → → | φυλασσόμενος | καὶ | → | διαρρήσσων | τὰ | δεσμὰ | → → | ἠλαύνετο ὑπὸ
v.ipi.3s | n.dpf | cj | n.dpf | | pt.pp.nsm | cj | | pt.pa.nsm | d.apn | n.apn | | v.ipi.3s p.g
1297 | 268 | 2779 | 4267 | | 5875 | 2779 | | 1393 | 3836 | 1301 | | 1785 5679

the | demon | into | solitary | places. | ¶ | **30** | Jesus | | asked | him, | "What | is | your | name?" | | "Legion,"
τοῦ | δαιμονίου | εἰς | ⸃τὰς ἐρήμους⸃ ← | | | δὲ | ὁ | Ἰησοῦς⸃ | ἐπηρώτησεν | αὐτὸν | τί | | ἐστιν | σοι | ὄνομα | δὲ | λεγιὼν
d.gsn | n.gsn | p.a | d.apf a.apf | | | cj | d.nsm | n.nsm | v.aai.3s | r.asm.3 | r.nsn | | v.pai.3s | r.ds.2 | n.nsn | cj | n.nsf
3836 | 1228 | 1650 | 3836 2245 | | | 1254 | 3836 | 2652 | 2089 | 899 | 5515 | | 1639 | 5148 | 3950 | 1254 | 3305

he | replied, | because | many | demons | had gone | into | him. | **31** | And they begged | | him | repeatedly | | not | to order
ὁ | εἶπεν | ὅτι | πολλὰ | δαιμόνια | → εἰσῆλθεν | εἰς | αὐτόν | καὶ | → | παρεκάλουν | αὐτὸν | ← | ἵνα | μὴ | → ἐπιτάξῃ
d.nsm | v.aai.3s | cj | a.npn | n.npn | v.aai.3s | p.a | r.asm.3 | cj | | v.iai.3p | r.asm.3 | | cj | pl | v.aas.3s
3836 | 3306 | 4022 | 4498 | 1228 | 1656 | 1650 | 899 | 2779 | | 4151 | 899 | 4151 | 2671 | 3590 | 2199

them | to go | into | the | Abyss. | ¶ | **32** | A large | herd | of pigs | was | feeding | there | on | the | hillside. | | The
αὐτοῖς | → ἀπελθεῖν | εἰς | τὴν | ἄβυσσον | | | δὲ | ἱκανῶν | ἀγέλη | χοίρων | ἦν | βοσκομένη | ἐκεῖ | ἐν | τῷ | ὄρει | καὶ
r.dpn.3 | f.aa | p.a | d.asf | n.asf | | | cj | a.gpm | n.nsf | n.gpm | v.iai.3s | pt.pp.nsf | adv | p.d | d.dsn | n.dsn | cj
899 | 599 | 1650 | 3836 | 12 | | | 1254 | 2653 | 36 | 5956 | 1639 | 1081 | 1695 | 1877 | 3836 | 4001 | 2779

demons | begged | Jesus | to | let | them | go | into | them, | and he gave | them | permission. | **33** | When the
παρεκάλεσαν | αὐτὸν | ἵνα | ἐπιτρέψῃ | αὐτοῖς | εἰσελθεῖν | εἰς | ἐκείνους | καὶ | → → | αὐτοῖς | ἐπέτρεψεν | δὲ | → τὰ
v.aai.3p | r.asm.3 | cj | v.aas.3s | r.dpn.3 | f.aa | p.a | r.apm | cj | | r.dpn.3 | v.aai.3s | cj | d.npn
4151 | 899 | 2671 | 2205 | 899 | 1656 | 1697 | 2205 | 2779 | 2205 2205 | 899 | 2205 | 1254 2002 | 3836

demons | came | out of | the | man, | | they went | into | the pigs, | and the | herd | rushed | down | the | steep | bank | into
δαιμόνια | ἐξελθόντα ← | ἀπὸ τοῦ | ἀνθρώπου | → | εἰσῆλθον | εἰς | τοὺς χοίρους | καὶ ἡ | ἀγέλη | ὥρμησεν | κατὰ | τοῦ | | κρημνοῦ εἰς
n.npn | pt.aa.npn | p.g d.gsm | n.gsm | | v.aai.3p | p.a | d.apm n.apm | cj d.nsf | n.nsf | v.aai.3s | p.a | d.gsm | | n.gsm p.a
1228 | 2002 | 608 3836 | 476 | | 1656 | 1650 | 3836 5956 | 2779 3836 | 36 | 3994 | 2848 | 3836 | | 3204 1650

the | lake | and was | drowned. | ¶ | **34** | When those | tending | the pigs | saw | what | had | happened, | they ran | off
τὴν | λίμνην | καὶ | → ἀπεπνίγη | | | δὲ | οἱ | βόσκοντες | ἰδόντες | τὸ | → | γεγονὸς | ἔφυγον | →
d.asf | n.asf | cj | v.api.3s | | | cj | d.npm | pt.pa.npm | pt.aa.npm | d.asn | | pt.ra.asn | v.aai.3p
3836 | 3349 | 2779 | 678 | | | 1254 1625 | 3836 | 1081 | 1625 | 3836 | | 1181 | 5771

and | reported | this | in | the | town and | | countryside, | **35** | and the | people | went | | out | to see | what | had | happened. | When
καὶ | ἀπήγγειλαν | | εἰς | τὴν | πόλιν | καὶ | εἰς | ⸃τοὺς ἀγρούς⸃ | δὲ | | → | ἐξῆλθον ← | → ἰδεῖν | τὸ | → | γεγονὸς | καὶ
cj | v.aai.3p | | p.a | d.asf | n.asf | cj | p.a | d.apm n.apm | cj | | | v.aai.3p | f.aa | d.asn | | pt.ra.asn | cj
2779 | 550 | | 1650 | 3836 | 4484 | 2779 | 1650 | 3836 1067 | 1254 | | | 2002 | 1625 | 3836 | | 1181 | 2779

8:26 Καὶ κατέπλευσαν εἰς τὴν χώραν τῶν Γερασηνῶν, ἥτις ἐστὶν ἀντιπέρα τῆς Γαλιλαίας. **27** ἐξελθόντι δὲ αὐτῷ ἐπὶ τὴν γῆν ὑπήντησεν ἀνήρ τις ἐκ τῆς πόλεως ἔχων δαιμόνια καὶ χρόνῳ ἱκανῷ οὐκ ἐνεδύσατο ἱμάτιον καὶ ἐν οἰκίᾳ οὐκ ἔμενεν ἀλλ᾽ ἐν τοῖς μνήμασιν. **28** ἰδὼν δὲ τὸν Ἰησοῦν ἀνακράξας προσέπεσεν αὐτῷ καὶ φωνῇ μεγάλῃ εἶπεν, Τί ἐμοὶ καὶ σοί, Ἰησοῦ υἱὲ τοῦ θεοῦ τοῦ ὑψίστου; δέομαί σου, μή με βασανίσῃς. **29** παρήγγειλεν γὰρ τῷ πνεύματι τῷ ἀκαθάρτῳ ἐξελθεῖν ἀπὸ τοῦ ἀνθρώπου. πολλοῖς γὰρ χρόνοις συνηρπάκει αὐτὸν καὶ ἐδεσμεύετο ἁλύσεσιν καὶ πέδαις φυλασσόμενος καὶ διαρρήσσων τὰ δεσμὰ ἠλαύνετο ὑπὸ τοῦ δαιμονίου εἰς τὰς ἐρήμους. ¶ **30** ἐπηρώτησεν δὲ αὐτὸν ὁ Ἰησοῦς, Τί σοι ὄνομά ἐστιν; ὁ δὲ εἶπεν, Λεγιών, ὅτι εἰσῆλθεν δαιμόνια πολλὰ εἰς αὐτόν. **31** καὶ παρεκάλουν αὐτὸν ἵνα μὴ ἐπιτάξῃ αὐτοῖς εἰς τὴν ἄβυσσον ἀπελθεῖν. ¶ **32** Ἦν δὲ ἐκεῖ ἀγέλη χοίρων ἱκανῶν βοσκομένη ἐν τῷ ὄρει· καὶ παρεκάλεσαν αὐτὸν ἵνα ἐπιτρέψῃ αὐτοῖς εἰς ἐκείνους εἰσελθεῖν· καὶ ἐπέτρεψεν αὐτοῖς. **33** ἐξελθόντα δὲ τὰ δαιμόνια ἀπὸ τοῦ ἀνθρώπου εἰσῆλθον εἰς τοὺς χοίρους, καὶ ὥρμησεν ἡ ἀγέλη κατὰ τοῦ κρημνοῦ εἰς τὴν λίμνην καὶ ἀπεπνίγη. ¶ **34** ἰδόντες δὲ οἱ βόσκοντες τὸ γεγονὸς ἔφυγον καὶ ἀπήγγειλαν εἰς τὴν πόλιν καὶ εἰς τοὺς ἀγρούς. **35** ἐξῆλθον δὲ

they came to Jesus, they found the man from whom the demons had gone out, sitting at
ἦλθον πρὸς τὸν Ἰησοῦν καὶ εὗρον τὸν ἄνθρωπον ἀφ' οὗ τὰ δαιμόνια ἐξῆλθεν καθήμενον παρὰ
v.aai.3p p.a d.asm n.asm cj v.aai.3p d.asm n.asm p.g r.gsm d.npn n.npn v.aai.3s pt.pm.asm p.a
2262 4639 3836 2652 2779 2351 3836 476 608 4005 3836 1228 2002 2764 4123

Jesus' feet, dressed and in his right mind; and they were afraid. **36** Those who had seen it
τοῦ Ἰησοῦ τοὺς πόδας ἱματισμένον καὶ σωφρονοῦντα καὶ ἐφοβήθησαν δὲ οἱ ἰδόντες
d.gsm n.gsm d.apm n.apm pt.rp.asm cj pt.pa.asm cj v.api.3p cj d.nsm pt.aa.npm
3836 2652 3836 4546 2667 2779 5404 2779 5828 1254 3836 1625

told the people how the demon-possessed man had been cured. **37** Then all the people of the region of the
ἀπήγγειλαν αὐτοῖς πῶς ὁ δαιμονισθεὶς ἐσώθη καὶ ἅπαν τὸ πλῆθος τῆς περιχώρου τῶν
v.aai.3p r.dpm.3 cj d.nsm pt.ap.nsm v.api.3s cj a.nsn d.nsn n.nsn d.gsf a.gsf d.gpm
550 899 4802 3836 1227 5392 2779 570 3836 4436 3836 4369 3836

Gerasenes asked Jesus to leave them, because they were overcome with fear. So he got into the
Γερασηνῶν ἠρώτησεν αὐτὸν ἀπελθεῖν ἀπ' αὐτῶν ὅτι συνείχοντο φόβῳ μεγάλῳ δὲ αὐτὸς ἐμβὰς εἰς
a.gpm v.aai.3s r.asm.3 f.aa p.g r.gpm.3 cj v.ipi.3p n.dsm a.dsm cj r.nsm pt.aa.nsm p.a
1170 2263 899 599 608 899 4022 5309 5832 3489 1254 899 1832 1650

boat and left. ¶ **38** The man from whom the demons had gone out begged to go with him,
πλοῖον ὑπέστρεψεν δὲ ὁ ἀνὴρ ἀφ' οὗ τὰ δαιμόνια ἐξεληλύθει ἐδεῖτο αὐτοῦ εἶναι σὺν αὐτῷ
n.asn v.aai.3s cj d.nsm n.nsm p.g r.gsm d.npn n.npn v.lai.3s v.imi.3s r.gsm.3 f.pa p.d r.dsm.3
4450 5715 1254 3836 467 608 4005 3836 1228 2002 1289 899 1639 5250 899

but Jesus sent him away, saying, **39** "Return home and tell how much God has done for you."
δὲ ἀπέλυσεν αὐτὸν λέγων ὑπόστρεφε εἰς τὸν οἶκον σου καὶ διηγοῦ ὅσα ὁ θεός ἐποίησεν σοι
cj v.aai.3s r.asm.3 pt.pa.nsm v.pam.2s p.a d.asm n.asm r.gs.2 cj v.pmm.2s r.apn d.nsm n.nsm v.aai.3s r.ds.2
1254 668 899 668 3306 5715 1650 3836 3875 5148 2779 1455 4012 3836 2536 4472 5148

So the man went away and told *all over* town how much Jesus had done for him.
καὶ ἀπῆλθεν κηρύσσων καθ' ὅλην τὴν πόλιν ὅσα ὁ Ἰησοῦς ἐποίησεν αὐτῷ
cj v.aai.3s pt.pa.nsm p.a a.asf d.asf n.asf r.apn d.nsm n.nsm v.aai.3s r.dsm.3
2779 599 3062 2848 3910 3836 4484 4012 3836 2652 4472 899

A Dead Girl and a Sick Woman

8:40 Now when Jesus returned, a crowd welcomed him, for they were all expecting him.
δὲ Ἐν τὸν Ἰησοῦν τῷ ὑποστρέφειν ὁ ὄχλος ἀπεδέξατο αὐτὸν γὰρ ἦσαν πάντες προσδοκῶντες αὐτόν
cj p.d d.asm n.asm d.dsn f.pa d.nsm n.nsm v.ami.3s r.asm.3 cj v.iai.3p a.npm pt.pa.npm r.asm.3
1254 1877 3836 2652 3836 5715 3836 4063 622 899 1142 1639 4246 4659 899

41 Then a man named Jairus, a ruler of the synagogue, came and fell at Jesus'
καὶ ἰδοὺ ἀνὴρ ᾧ ὄνομα Ἰάϊρος καὶ οὗτος ἄρχων τῆς συναγωγῆς ὑπῆρχεν ἦλθεν καὶ πεσὼν παρὰ τοῦ Ἰησοῦ
cj j n.nsm r.dsm n.nsn n.nsm cj r.nsm n.nsm d.gsf n.gsf v.iai.3s v.aai.3s cj pt.aa.nsm p.a d.gsm n.gsm
2779 2627 467 4005 3950 2608 2779 4047 807 3836 5639 5639 2262 2779 4406 4123 3836 2652

feet, pleading with him to come to his house **42** because his only daughter, a girl of about
τοὺς πόδας παρεκάλει αὐτὸν εἰσελθεῖν εἰς αὐτοῦ τὸν οἶκον ὅτι ἦν αὐτῷ μονογενὴς θυγάτηρ ὡς
d.apm n.apm v.iai.3s r.asm.3 f.aa p.a r.gsm.3 d.asm n.asm cj v.iai.3s r.dsm.3 a.nsf n.nsf pl
3836 4546 4151 899 1656 1650 899 3836 3875 4022 1639 899 3666 2588 6055

twelve, was dying. ¶ As Jesus was on his way, the crowds almost crushed him.
δώδεκα ἐτῶν καὶ αὐτὴ ἀπέθνησκεν δὲ Ἐν αὐτὸν τῷ ὑπάγειν οἱ ὄχλοι συνέπνιγον αὐτόν
a.gpn n.gpn cj r.nsf v.iai.3s cj p.d r.asm.3 d.dsn f.pa d.npm n.npm v.iai.3p r.asm.3
1557 2291 2779 899 633 1254 1877 899 3836 5632 3836 4063 5231 899

43 And a woman was there who had been subject to bleeding for twelve years, but [ἰατροῖς προσαναλώσασα
Καὶ γυνὴ οὖσα ἐν ῥύσει αἵματος ἀπὸ δώδεκα ἐτῶν [ἰατροῖς προσαναλώσασα
cj n.nsf pt.pa.nsf p.d n.dsf n.gsn p.g a.gpn n.gpn n.dpm pt.aa.nsf
2779 1222 1639 1877 4868 135 608 1557 2291 2620 4649

no one could heal her. **44** She came up behind him and touched the edge of
ὅλον τὸν βίον] οὐκ ἀπ' οὐδενὸς ἴσχυσεν θεραπευθῆναι ἥτις προσελθοῦσα ὄπισθεν ἥψατο τοῦ κρασπέδου
a.asm d.asm n.asm pl p.g a.gsm v.aai.3s f.ap r.nsf pt.aa.nsf adv v.ami.3s d.gsn n.gsn
3910 3836 1050 4024 608 4029 2710 2543 4015 4665 3957 721 3836 3192

his cloak, and immediately her bleeding stopped. ¶ **45** "Who touched me?"
αὐτοῦ τοῦ ἱματίου καὶ παραχρῆμα αὐτῆς ἡ ῥύσις τοῦ αἵματος ἔστη καὶ τίς ὁ ἁψάμενος μου
r.gsm.3 d.gsn n.gsn cj adv r.gsf.3 d.nsf n.nsf d.gsn n.gsn v.aai.3s cj r.nsm d.nsm pt.am.nsm r.gs.1
899 3836 2668 2779 4202 899 3836 4868 3836 135 2705 2779 5515 3836 721 1609

ἰδεῖν τὸ γεγονὸς καὶ ἦλθον πρὸς τὸν Ἰησοῦν καὶ εὗρον καθήμενον τὸν ἄνθρωπον ἀφ' οὗ τὰ δαιμόνια ἐξῆλθεν ἱματισμένον καὶ σωφρονοῦντα παρὰ τοὺς πόδας τοῦ Ἰησοῦ, καὶ ἐφοβήθησαν. **36** ἀπήγγειλαν δὲ αὐτοῖς οἱ ἰδόντες πῶς ἐσώθη ὁ δαιμονισθείς. **37** καὶ ἠρώτησεν αὐτὸν ἅπαν τὸ πλῆθος τῆς περιχώρου τῶν Γερασηνῶν ἀπελθεῖν ἀπ' αὐτῶν, ὅτι φόβῳ μεγάλῳ συνείχοντο· αὐτὸς δὲ ἐμβὰς εἰς πλοῖον ὑπέστρεψεν. ¶ **38** ἐδεῖτο δὲ αὐτοῦ ὁ ἀνὴρ ἀφ' οὗ ἐξεληλύθει τὰ δαιμόνια εἶναι σὺν αὐτῷ· ἀπέλυσεν δὲ αὐτὸν λέγων, **39** Ὑπόστρεφε εἰς τὸν οἶκόν σου καὶ διηγοῦ ὅσα σοι ἐποίησεν ὁ θεός. καὶ ἀπῆλθεν καθ' ὅλην τὴν πόλιν κηρύσσων ὅσα ἐποίησεν αὐτῷ ὁ Ἰησοῦς.
8:40 Ἐν δὲ τῷ ὑποστρέφειν τὸν Ἰησοῦν ἀπεδέξατο αὐτὸν ὁ ὄχλος· ἦσαν γὰρ πάντες προσδοκῶντες αὐτόν. **41** καὶ ἰδοὺ ἦλθεν ἀνὴρ ᾧ ὄνομα Ἰάϊρος καὶ οὗτος ἄρχων τῆς συναγωγῆς ὑπῆρχεν, καὶ πεσὼν παρὰ τοὺς πόδας [τοῦ] Ἰησοῦ παρεκάλει αὐτὸν εἰσελθεῖν εἰς τὸν οἶκον αὐτοῦ, **42** ὅτι θυγάτηρ μονογενὴς ἦν αὐτῷ ὡς ἐτῶν δώδεκα καὶ αὐτὴ ἀπέθνησκεν. ¶ Ἐν δὲ τῷ ὑπάγειν αὐτὸν οἱ ὄχλοι συνέπνιγον αὐτόν. **43** καὶ γυνὴ οὖσα ἐν ῥύσει αἵματος ἀπὸ ἐτῶν δώδεκα, ἥτις [ἰατροῖς προσαναλώσασα ὅλον τὸν βίον] οὐκ ἴσχυσεν ἀπ' οὐδενὸς θεραπευθῆναι, **44** προσελθοῦσα ὄπισθεν ἥψατο τοῦ κρασπέδου τοῦ ἱματίου αὐτοῦ καὶ

Jesus   asked.   When they all   denied   it, Peter   said, "Master, the people are crowding and
ὁ Ἰησοῦς, εἶπεν δὲ → πάντων ἀρνουμένων ὁ Πέτρος, εἶπεν ἐπιστάτα οἱ ὄχλοι → συνέχουσιν καὶ
d.nsm n.nsm v.aai.3s cj | a.gpm pt.pm.gpm | d.nsm n.nsm v.aai.3s n.vsm | d.npm n.npm | v.pai.3p cj
3836 2652 3306 1254 766 | 4246 766 | 3836 4377 3306 2181 | 3836 4063 | 5309 2779

pressing   against you." **46** But Jesus   said, "Someone touched me;   I   know that power has gone
ἀποθλίβουσιν ← σε δὲ ὁ Ἰησοῦς, εἶπεν τις ἥψατο μού γὰρ ἐγὼ ἔγνων δύναμιν →
v.pai.3p r.as.2 | cj d.nsm n.nsm v.aai.3s r.nsm | v.ami.3s r.gs.1 cj r.ns.1 v.aai.1s | n.asf
632 5148 | 1254 3836 2652 3306 5516 | 721 1609 1142 1609 1182 | 1539

out   from me." ¶ **47** Then the woman, seeing that she could not go unnoticed, came trembling and
ἐξεληλυθυῖαν ἀπ' ἐμοῦ δὲ ἡ γυνὴ ἰδοῦσα ὅτι → οὐκ → ἔλαθεν ἦλθεν τρέμουσα καὶ
pt.ra.asf p.g r.gs.1 | cj d.nsf n.nsf pt.aa.nsf cj → pl → v.aai.3s | v.aai.3s pt.pa.nsf cj
2002 608 1609 | 1254 3836 1222 1625 4022 3291 3291 4024 3291 | 2262 5554 2779

fell   at his feet. In the presence of all   the people, she told   why   she had touched him and
προσπεσοῦσα ← αὐτῷ → ἐνώπιον ← παντὸς τοῦ λαοῦ → ἀπήγγειλεν δι' ἣν αἰτίαν → ἥψατο αὐτοῦ καὶ
pt.aa.nsf r.dsm.3 | p.g a.gsm d.gsm n.gsm | v.aai.3s p.a r.asf n.asf | v.ami.3s r.gsm.3 cj
4700 899 | 1967 4246 3836 3295 | 550 1328 4005 162 | 721 899 2779

how she had been instantly healed. **48** Then he   said to her, "Daughter, your faith   has healed you. Go   in
ὡς → → → παραχρῆμα ἰάθη δὲ ὁ εἶπεν αὐτῇ θυγάτηρ σου ἡ πίστις, σέσωκεν σε πορεύου εἰς
cj adv v.api.3s | cj d.nsm v.aai.3s r.dsf.3 n.vsf | r.gs.2 d.nsf n.nsf | v.rai.3s r.as.2 v.pmm.2s p.a
6055 2615 2615 2615 4202 2615 | 1254 3836 3306 899 2588 | 5148 3836 4411 | 5392 5148 4513 1650

peace." ¶ **49** While Jesus was still speaking, someone came from the house of Jairus, the synagogue
εἰρήνην → αὐτοῦ → Ἔτι λαλοῦντος τις ἔρχεται παρὰ τοῦ
n.asf r.gsm.3 adv pt.pa.gsm r.nsm v.pmi.3s p.g d.gsm
1645 899 3281 3281 5516 2262 4123 3836

ruler.   "Your daughter is dead," he said. "Don't bother the teacher   any more." **50** Hearing this,
ἀρχισυναγώγου ὅτι σου ἡ θυγάτηρ, → τέθνηκεν λέγων μηκέτι σκύλλε τὸν διδάσκαλον ← ← δὲ ἀκούσας
n.gsm cj r.gs.2 d.nsf n.nsf | v.rai.3s pt.pa.nsm adv v.pam.2s d.asm n.asm | cj pt.aa.nsm
801 4022 5148 3836 2588 | 2569 3306 3600 5035 3836 1437 3600 3600 | 1254 201

Jesus   said   to Jairus, "Don't be afraid; just believe, and she will be healed." ¶ **51** When he arrived
ὁ Ἰησοῦς, ἀπεκρίθη αὐτῷ μὴ → φοβοῦ μόνον πίστευσον καὶ → → → σωθήσεται δὲ → ἐλθὼν
d.nsm n.nsm v.api.3s r.dsm.3 pl → v.ppm.2s adv v.aam.2s cj v.fpi.3s | cj pt.aa.nsm
3836 2652 646 899 3590 5828 3667 4409 2779 5392 | 1254 2262

at the house of Jairus, he did not let   anyone go   in with him except Peter,   John   and James, and
εἰς τὴν οἰκίαν → → οὐκ ἀφῆκεν τινα εἰσελθεῖν σὺν αὐτῷ εἰ μὴ Πέτρον καὶ Ἰωάννην καὶ Ἰάκωβον καὶ
p.a d.asf n.asf | pl v.aai.3s pl f.aa | p.d r.dsm.3 cj pl n.asm cj n.asm cj n.asm cj
1650 3836 3864 | 918 918 4024 5516 1656 | 5250 899 1623 3590 4377 2779 2722 2779 2610 2779

the child's   father and mother. **52** Meanwhile, all   the people were wailing and mourning for her.   "Stop
τὸν τῆς παιδὸς, πατέρα καὶ τὴν μητέρα, δὲ πάντες → ἔκλαιον καὶ ἐκόπτοντο αὐτήν δὲ μὴ
d.asm d.gsf n.gsf n.asm cj d.asf n.asf | cj a.npm | v.iai.3p cj v.imi.3p r.asf.3 cj pl
3836 3836 4090 4252 2779 3836 3613 | 1254 4246 | 3081 2779 3164 899 1254 3590

wailing," Jesus said.   "She is not dead   but asleep." ¶ **53** They laughed at him, knowing that she was
κλαίετε ὁ εἶπεν γὰρ → → οὐ ἀπέθανεν ἀλλὰ καθεύδει καὶ → κατεγέλων αὐτοῦ εἰδότες ὅτι →
v.pam.2p d.nsm v.aai.3s cj | pl v.aai.3s cj v.pai.3s | cj v.iai.3p r.gsm.3 pt.ra.npm cj
3081 3836 3306 1142 633 | 633 4024 633 247 2761 | 2779 2860 899 4022

dead. **54** But he took   her by the hand   and said,   "My child, get up!" **55** Her spirit
ἀπέθανεν δὲ αὐτὸς κρατήσας → τῆς χειρὸς αὐτῆς ἐφώνησεν λέγων ἡ παῖς, ἔγειρε καὶ αὐτῆς τὸ πνεῦμα,
v.aai.3s cj r.nsm pt.aa.nsm d.gsf n.gsf r.gsf.3 v.aai.3s pt.pa.nsm d.vsf n.vsf v.pam.2s cj r.gsf.3 d.nsn n.nsn
633 1254 899 3195 899 3836 5931 899 5888 3306 3836 4090 1586 2779 899 3836 4460

returned, and at once   she stood up. Then Jesus told   them to give   her something to eat. **56** Her
ἐπέστρεψεν καὶ → παραχρῆμα → ἀνέστη καὶ διέταξεν → δοθῆναι αὐτῇ → φαγεῖν καὶ αὐτῆς
v.aai.3s cj adv v.aai.3s cj v.aai.3s f.ap r.dsf.3 f.aa cj r.gsf.3
2188 2779 4202 482 2779 1411 1443 899 2266 2779 899

parents   were astonished, but he ordered   them not to tell   anyone what had happened.
οἱ γονεῖς, ἐξέστησαν δὲ ὁ παρήγγειλεν αὐτοῖς μηδενὶ → εἰπεῖν ← τὸ γεγονός
d.npm n.npm v.aai.3p cj d.nsm v.aai.3s r.dpm.3 a.dsm f.aa d.asn pt.ra.asn
3836 1204 2014 1254 3836 4133 899 3594 3306 3594 3836 1181

παραχρῆμα ἔστη ἡ ῥύσις τοῦ αἵματος αὐτῆς. ¶ **45** καὶ εἶπεν ὁ Ἰησοῦς, Τίς ὁ ἁψάμενός μου; ἀρνουμένων δὲ πάντων εἶπεν ὁ Πέτρος, Ἐπιστάτα, οἱ ὄχλοι συνέχουσίν σε καὶ ἀποθλίβουσιν. **46** ὁ δὲ Ἰησοῦς εἶπεν, Ἥψατό μού τις, ἐγὼ γὰρ ἔγνων δύναμιν ἐξεληλυθυῖαν ἀπ' ἐμοῦ. ¶ **47** ἰδοῦσα δὲ ἡ γυνὴ ὅτι οὐκ ἔλαθεν, τρέμουσα ἦλθεν καὶ προσπεσοῦσα αὐτῷ δι' ἣν αἰτίαν ἥψατο αὐτοῦ ἀπήγγειλεν ἐνώπιον παντὸς τοῦ λαοῦ καὶ ὡς ἰάθη παραχρῆμα. **48** ὁ δὲ εἶπεν αὐτῇ, Θυγάτηρ, ἡ πίστις σου σέσωκέν σε· πορεύου εἰς εἰρήνην. ¶ **49** Ἔτι αὐτοῦ λαλοῦντος ἔρχεταί τις παρὰ τοῦ ἀρχισυναγώγου λέγων ὅτι Τέθνηκεν ἡ θυγάτηρ σου· μηκέτι σκύλλε τὸν διδάσκαλον. **50** ὁ δὲ Ἰησοῦς ἀκούσας ἀπεκρίθη αὐτῷ, Μὴ φοβοῦ, μόνον πίστευσον, καὶ σωθήσεται. ¶ **51** ἐλθὼν δὲ εἰς τὴν οἰκίαν οὐκ ἀφῆκεν εἰσελθεῖν τινα σὺν αὐτῷ εἰ μὴ Πέτρον καὶ Ἰωάννην καὶ Ἰάκωβον καὶ τὸν πατέρα τῆς παιδὸς καὶ τὴν μητέρα. **52** ἔκλαιον δὲ πάντες καὶ ἐκόπτοντο αὐτήν. ὁ δὲ εἶπεν, Μὴ κλαίετε, οὐ γὰρ ἀπέθανεν ἀλλὰ καθεύδει. ¶ **53** καὶ κατεγέλων αὐτοῦ εἰδότες ὅτι ἀπέθανεν. **54** αὐτὸς δὲ κρατήσας τῆς χειρὸς αὐτῆς ἐφώνησεν λέγων, Ἡ παῖς, ἔγειρε. **55** καὶ ἐπέστρεψεν τὸ πνεῦμα αὐτῆς καὶ ἀνέστη παραχρῆμα καὶ διέταξεν αὐτῇ δοθῆναι φαγεῖν. **56** καὶ ἐξέστησαν οἱ γονεῖς αὐτῆς· ὁ δὲ παρήγγειλεν αὐτοῖς μηδενὶ εἰπεῖν τὸ γεγονός.

Jesus Sends Out the Twelve

9:1 When Jesus had called   the Twelve together, he gave them power and authority *to drive out*
δὲ → → Συγκαλεσάμενος τοὺς δώδεκα ← ἔδωκεν αὐτοῖς δύναμιν καὶ ἐξουσίαν ἐπὶ
cj   pt.am.nsm   d.apm a.apm   v.aai.3s r.dpm.3 n.asf cj n.asf p.a
1254   5157   3836 1557 5157   1443 899 1539 2779 2026 2093

all demons   and to cure   diseases, **2** and he sent   them out to preach the kingdom of God   and to
πάντα τὰ δαιμόνια καὶ → θεραπεύειν νόσους καὶ → ἀπέστειλεν αὐτοὺς ← → κηρύσσειν τὴν βασιλείαν → τοῦ θεοῦ καὶ
a.apn d.apn n.apn cj f.pa n.apf cj v.aai.3s r.apm.3 f.pa d.asf n.asf d.gsm n.gsm cj
4246 3836 1228 2779 2543 3798 2779 690 899 690 3062 3836 993 3836 2536 2779

heal the sick. **3** He told   them: "Take nothing for the journey – no staff, no bag, no bread, no
ἰᾶσθαι τοὺς ἀσθενεῖς καὶ → εἶπεν πρὸς αὐτούς αἴρετε μηδὲν εἰς τὴν ὁδόν μήτε ῥάβδον μήτε πήραν μήτε ἄρτον μήτε
f.pm d.apm a.apm cj v.aai.3s p.a r.apm.3 v.pam.2p a.asn p.a d.asf n.asf cj n.asf cj n.asf cj n.asm cj
2615 3836 822 2779 3306 4639 899 149 3594 1650 3836 3847 3612 4811 3612 4385 3612 788 3612

money, no   extra tunic. **4** Whatever house you enter, stay there until you leave that
ἀργύριον μήτε [ἀνὰ] δύο χιτῶνας ἔχειν καὶ εἰς ἣν ἂν οἰκίαν → εἰσέλθητε μένετε ἐκεῖ καὶ → ἐξέρχεσθε ἐκεῖθεν
n.asn cj p.a a.apm n.apm f.pa cj p.a r.asf pl n.asf v.aas.2p v.pam.2p adv cj v.pmm.2p adv
736 3612 324 1545 5945 2400 2779 1650 4005 323 3864 1656 3531 1695 2779 2002 1696

town. **5** If people do not welcome you, shake   the dust   off your feet   when you leave
← καὶ → ὅσοι ἂν → μὴ δέχωνται ὑμᾶς ἀποτινάσσετε τὸν κονιορτὸν ἀπὸ ὑμῶν τῶν ποδῶν → ἐξερχόμενοι ἀπὸ
cj r.npm pl pl v.pms.3p r.ap.2 v.pam.2p d.asm n.asm p.g r.gp.2 d.gpm n.gpm pt.pm.npm p.g
2779 4012 323 1312 3590 1312 7007 701 3836 3155 608 7007 3836 4546 2002 608

their town, as a testimony against them." **6** So they set   out and went *from village*   *to village,*
ἐκείνης τῆς πόλεως εἰς μαρτύριον ἐπ' αὐτούς δὲ → ἐξερχόμενοι ← διήρχοντο κατὰ τὰς κώμας
r.gsf d.gsf n.gsf p.a n.asn p.a r.apm.3 cj pt.pm.npm v.imi.3p p.a d.apf n.apf
1697 3836 4484 1650 3457 2093 899 1254 2002 1451 2848 3836 3267

preaching   the gospel and healing   people everywhere. ¶ **7** Now Herod the tetrarch heard   about all
εὐαγγελιζόμενοι ← ← καὶ θεραπεύοντες πανταχοῦ δὲ Ἡρῴδης ὁ τετραάρχης Ἤκουσεν ← πάντα
pt.pm.npm cj pt.pa.npm adv cj n.nsm d.nsm n.nsm v.aai.3s a.apn
2294 2779 2543 4116 1254 2476 3836 5490 201 4246

that was going on. And he was perplexed, because some were saying that John had been raised from
τὰ → γινόμενα καὶ → διηπόρει διὰ ὑπό τινων τὸ λέγεσθαι ὅτι Ἰωάννης → ἠγέρθη ἐκ
d.apn pt.pm.apn cj v.iai.3s p.a p.g r.gpm d.asn f.pp cj n.nsm v.api.3s p.g
3836 1181 2779 1389 1328 5679 5516 3836 3306 4022 2722 1586 1666

the dead, **8** others that Elijah had appeared, and still others that one of the prophets of long   ago had
νεκρῶν δὲ ὑπό τινων ὅτι Ἠλίας → ἐφάνη δὲ ἄλλων ὅτι τις προφήτης → τῶν ἀρχαίων ←
a.gpm pl p.g r.gpm cj n.nsm v.api.3s pl r.gpm cj r.gsm n.nsm d.gpm a.gpm
3738 1254 5679 5516 4022 2460 5743 1254 257 4022 5516 4737 3836 792

come back to life. **9** But Herod said, "I beheaded John. Who, then, is this I hear such things about?"
→ → ἀνέστη δὲ Ἡρῴδης εἶπεν ἐγὼ ἀπεκεφάλισα Ἰωάννην τίς δὲ ἐστιν οὗτος ἀκούω τοιαῦτα περὶ οὗ
v.aai.3s pl n.nsm v.aai.3s r.ns.1 v.aai.1s n.asm r.nsm cj v.pai.3s r.nsm v.pai.1s r.apn p.g r.gsm
482 1254 2476 3306 1609 642 2722 5515 1254 1639 4047 201 5525 4309 4005

And he tried to see him.
καὶ → ἐζήτει ἰδεῖν αὐτόν
cj v.iai.3s f.aa r.asm.3
2779 2426 1625 899

Jesus Feeds the Five Thousand

9:10 When the apostles returned, they reported to Jesus what they had done. Then he took   them
Καὶ → οἱ ἀπόστολοι ὑποστρέψαντες → διηγήσαντο αὐτῷ ὅσα → ἐποίησαν Καὶ → παραλαβὼν αὐτοὺς
cj d.npm n.npm pt.aa.npm v.ami.3p r.dsm.3 r.apn v.aai.3p cj pt.aa.nsm r.apm.3
2779 5715 3836 693 5715 1455 899 4012 4472 2779 4161 899

with him and they withdrew *by themselves* to a town called   Bethsaida, **11** but the crowds learned about it and
← → → ὑπεχώρησεν κατ' ἰδίαν εἰς πόλιν καλουμένην Βηθσαϊδά δὲ οἱ ὄχλοι γνόντες
v.aai.3s p.a a.asf p.a n.asf pt.pp.asf n.asf cj d.npm n.npm pt.aa.npm
4161 4161 5723 2848 2625 1650 4484 2813 1034 1254 3836 4063 1182

9:1 Συγκαλεσάμενος δὲ τοὺς δώδεκα ἔδωκεν αὐτοῖς δύναμιν καὶ ἐξουσίαν ἐπὶ πάντα τὰ δαιμόνια καὶ νόσους θεραπεύειν **2** καὶ ἀπέστειλεν αὐτοὺς κηρύσσειν τὴν βασιλείαν τοῦ θεοῦ καὶ ἰᾶσθαι [τοὺς ἀσθενεῖς], **3** καὶ εἶπεν πρὸς αὐτούς, Μηδὲν αἴρετε εἰς τὴν ὁδόν, μήτε ῥάβδον μήτε πήραν μήτε ἄρτον μήτε ἀργύριον μήτε [ἀνὰ] δύο χιτῶνας ἔχειν. **4** καὶ εἰς ἣν ἂν οἰκίαν εἰσέλθητε, ἐκεῖ μένετε καὶ ἐκεῖθεν ἐξέρχεσθε. **5** καὶ ὅσοι ἂν μὴ δέχωνται ὑμᾶς, ἐξερχόμενοι ἀπὸ τῆς πόλεως ἐκείνης τὸν κονιορτὸν ἀπὸ τῶν ποδῶν ὑμῶν ἀποτινάσσετε εἰς μαρτύριον ἐπ' αὐτούς. **6** ἐξερχόμενοι δὲ διήρχοντο κατὰ τὰς κώμας εὐαγγελιζόμενοι καὶ θεραπεύοντες πανταχοῦ. ¶ **7** Ἤκουσεν δὲ Ἡρῴδης ὁ τετραάρχης τὰ γινόμενα πάντα καὶ διηπόρει διὰ τὸ λέγεσθαι ὑπό τινων ὅτι Ἰωάννης ἠγέρθη ἐκ νεκρῶν, **8** ὑπό τινων δὲ ὅτι Ἠλίας ἐφάνη, ἄλλων δὲ ὅτι προφήτης τις τῶν ἀρχαίων ἀνέστη. **9** εἶπεν δὲ Ἡρῴδης, Ἰωάννην ἐγὼ ἀπεκεφάλισα· τίς δέ ἐστιν οὗτος περὶ οὗ ἀκούω τοιαῦτα; καὶ ἐζήτει ἰδεῖν αὐτόν.

9:10 Καὶ ὑποστρέψαντες οἱ ἀπόστολοι διηγήσαντο αὐτῷ ὅσα ἐποίησαν. καὶ παραλαβὼν αὐτοὺς ὑπεχώρησεν κατ' ἰδίαν εἰς πόλιν καλουμένην Βηθσαϊδά. **11** οἱ δὲ ὄχλοι γνόντες ἠκολούθησαν αὐτῷ· καὶ ἀποδεξάμενος αὐτοὺς ἐλάλει αὐτοῖς περὶ τῆς

followed   him.   He welcomed   them   and spoke to them   about   the   kingdom of God,   and healed those who
ἠκολούθησαν αὐτῷ καὶ → ἀποδεξάμενος αὐτοὺς   ἐλάλει → αὐτοῖς περὶ   τῆς βασιλείας   ˻τοῦ θεοῦ˼ καὶ ἰᾶτο   τοὺς →
v.aai.3p r.dsm.3 cj   pt.am.nsm   r.apm.3   v.iai.3s   r.dpm.3 p.g   d.gsf n.gsf   d.gsm n.gsm cj v.imi.3s d.apm
199   899   2779   622   899   3281   899   4309   3836 993   3836 2536 2779 2615   3836

needed   healing.   ¶   12   *Late*   *in the afternoon*   the   Twelve   came   to him and said,
˻χρείαν ἔχοντας˼ θεραπείας   δὲ ˻ἤρξατο κλίνειν˼ Ἡ ἡμέρα   δὲ οἱ δώδεκα προσελθόντες ←   →   εἶπαν αὐτῷ
n.asf pt.pa.apm n.gsf   cj v.ami.3s f.pa   d.nsf n.nsf   cj d.npm a.npm pt.aa.npm   v.aai.3p r.dsm.3
5970 2400 2542   1254 806 3111   3836 2465   1254 3836 1557 4665   899 3306 899

"Send   the crowd away so   they can go   to the surrounding   villages and countryside and find   food
ἀπόλυσον τὸν ὄχλον ← ἵνα → → πορευθέντες εἰς τὰς κύκλῳ   κώμας καὶ ἀγροὺς   καὶ εὕρωσιν ἐπισιτισμὸν
v.aam.2s d.asm n.asm   cj   pt.ap.npm p.a d.apf adv   n.apf cj n.apm   cj v.aas.3p n.asm
668 3836 4063   668 2671   4513   1650 3836 3241   3267 2779 69   2779 2351 2169

and lodging,   because we are   in a remote place here."   13   He replied,   "You give them something to
καταλύσωσιν ὅτι   → ἐσμέν ἐν   ἐρήμῳ τόπῳ ὧδε   δὲ → εἶπεν   πρὸς αὐτούς ὑμεῖς δότε αὐτοῖς   →
v.aas.3p cj   v.pai.1p p.d   a.dsm n.dsm adv   cj v.aai.3s   p.a r.apm.3 r.np.2 v.aam.2p r.dpm.3
2907 4022   1639 1877   2245 5536 6045   1254 3306   4639 899 7007 1443 899

eat."   They answered, "We   have only   five loaves of bread and two fish   — unless   we   go
φαγεῖν δὲ οἱ   εἶπαν   ἡμῖν οὐκ εἰσὶν ˻πλεῖον ἢ˼   πέντε →   → ἄρτοι καὶ δύο ἰχθύες   εἰ μήτι ἡμεῖς πορευθέντες
f.aa cj d.npm v.aai.3p   r.dp.1 pl v.pai.3p adv.c pl   a.npm   n.npm cj a.npm n.npm   cj cj r.np.1 pt.ap.npm
2266 1254 3836 3306   7005 4024 1639 4498 2445   4297   788 2779 1545 2716   1623 3614 7005 4513

and buy   food   for all   this crowd."   14   (About five   thousand men   were there.) But he said
ἀγοράσωμεν βρώματα εἰς πάντα τοῦτον ˻τὸν λαὸν˼   γὰρ ὡσεὶ πεντακισχίλιοι ←   ˻ἄνδρες ἦσαν ←   δὲ → εἶπεν
v.aas.1p   n.apn   p.a a.asm r.asm d.asm n.asm   cj pl   a.npm   n.npm v.iai.3p   cj   v.aai.3s
60   1109   1650 4246 4047 3836 3295   1142 6059   4295   467 1639   1254   3306

to his   disciples,   "Have them sit   down in groups of about fifty   each."   15   The disciples did
πρὸς αὐτοῦ ˻τοὺς μαθητάς˼   αὐτοὺς κατακλίνατε   → κλισίας   ὡσεὶ πεντήκοντα ἀνὰ   καὶ   ἐποίησαν
p.a r.gsm.3 d.apm n.apm   r.apm.3 v.aam.2p   n.apf   pl   a.apm   p.a   cj   v.aai.3p
4639 899 3836 3412   899 2884   3112   6059 4299 324   2779   4472

so,   and everybody sat   down.   16   Taking the five loaves and the two fish   and looking   up to
οὕτως καὶ ἅπαντας κατέκλιναν ←   δὲ λαβὼν τοὺς πέντε ἄρτους καὶ τοὺς δύο ἰχθύας   ἀναβλέψας ←   εἰς
adv cj a.apm v.aai.3p   cj pt.aa.nsm d.apm a.apm n.apm cj d.apm a.apm n.apm   pt.aa.nsm   p.a
4048 2779 570 2884   1254 3284 3836 4297 788 2779 3836 1545 2716   329   1650

heaven,   he gave thanks   and broke   them. Then he gave   them to the disciples to set   before the
˻τὸν οὐρανὸν˼ → → εὐλόγησεν καὶ κατέκλασεν αὐτοὺς καὶ → ἐδίδου   → τοῖς μαθηταῖς → παραθεῖναι ←   τῷ
d.asm n.asm   v.aai.3s cj v.aai.3s r.apm.3 cj v.iai.3s   d.dpm n.dpm f.aa   d.dsm
3836 4041   2328 2779 2880 899 2779 1443   3836 3412 4192   3836

people.   17   They all   ate   and were satisfied,   and the disciples picked up twelve basketfuls of broken
ὄχλῳ   καὶ   πάντες ἔφαγον καὶ → ἐχορτάσθησαν καὶ   αὐτοῖς   ἤρθη → δώδεκα κόφινοι → κλασμάτων
n.dsm   cj   a.npm v.aai.3p cj   v.api.3p cj   r.dpm.3   v.api.3s a.npm n.npm   n.gpn
4063   2779   4246 2266 2779   5963 2779   899   149 1557 3186   3083

pieces that were left over.
← → → → ˻τὸ περισσεῦσαν˼
d.nsn pt.aa.nsn
3836 4355

Peter's Confession of Christ

9:18 Once   when Jesus was   praying   in   private and his disciples were   with him,   he
˻Καὶ ἐγένετο ἐν   αὐτὸν ˻τῷ εἶναι˼ προσευχόμενον κατὰ μόνας   οἱ μαθηταί συνῆσαν ←   αὐτῷ καὶ →
cj v.ami.3s p.d   r.asm.3 d.dsn f.pa   pt.pm.acc   p.a a.apf   d.npm n.npm v.iai.3p   r.dsm.3 cj
2779 1181 1877   899 3836 1639   4667   2848 3668   3836 3412 5289   899 2779

asked   them,   "Who do the crowds say   I am?"   19   They replied,   "Some say John   the
ἐπηρώτησεν αὐτοὺς λέγων τίνα → οἱ ὄχλοι λέγουσιν με εἶναι   δὲ οἱ   ἀποκριθέντες εἶπαν   Ἰωάννην τὸν
v.aai.3s r.apm.3 pt.pa.nsm r.asm d.npm n.npm v.pai.3p r.as.1 f.pa   cj d.npm pt.ap.npm v.aai.3p   n.asm d.asm
2089 899 3306 5515   3836 4063 3306 1609 1639   1254 3836 646 3306   2722 3836

Baptist;   others say Elijah; and still others,   that one   of the prophets of long   ago has come back to life."   ¶
βαπτιστήν δὲ ἄλλοι   Ἠλίαν δὲ   ἄλλοι ὅτι τις   προφήτης → ˻τῶν ἀρχαίων˼ ← → → → ἀνέστη
n.asm pl r.npm   n.asm pl   r.npm cj r.nsm   n.nsm   d.gpm a.gpm   v.aai.3s
969 1254 257   2460 1254   257 4022 5516   4737   3836 792   482

βασιλείας τοῦ θεοῦ, καὶ τοὺς χρείαν ἔχοντας θεραπείας ἰᾶτο. ¶ 12 Ἡ δὲ ἡμέρα ἤρξατο κλίνειν· προσελθόντες δὲ οἱ δώδεκα εἶπαν αὐτῷ, Ἀπόλυσον τὸν ὄχλον, ἵνα πορευθέντες εἰς τὰς κύκλῳ κώμας καὶ ἀγροὺς καταλύσωσιν καὶ εὕρωσιν ἐπισιτισμόν, ὅτι ὧδε ἐν ἐρήμῳ τόπῳ ἐσμέν. 13 εἶπεν δὲ πρὸς αὐτούς, Δότε αὐτοῖς ὑμεῖς φαγεῖν. οἱ δὲ εἶπαν, Οὐκ εἰσὶν ἡμῖν πλεῖον ἢ ἄρτοι πέντε καὶ ἰχθύες δύο, εἰ μήτι πορευθέντες ἡμεῖς ἀγοράσωμεν εἰς πάντα τὸν λαὸν τοῦτον βρώματα. 14 ἦσαν γὰρ ὡσεὶ ἄνδρες πεντακισχίλιοι. εἶπεν δὲ πρὸς τοὺς μαθητὰς αὐτοῦ, Κατακλίνατε αὐτοὺς κλισίας [ὡσεὶ] ἀνὰ πεντήκοντα. 15 καὶ ἐποίησαν οὕτως καὶ κατέκλιναν ἅπαντας. 16 λαβὼν δὲ τοὺς πέντε ἄρτους καὶ τοὺς δύο ἰχθύας ἀναβλέψας εἰς τὸν οὐρανὸν εὐλόγησεν αὐτοὺς καὶ κατέκλασεν καὶ ἐδίδου τοῖς μαθηταῖς παραθεῖναι τῷ ὄχλῳ. 17 καὶ ἔφαγον καὶ ἐχορτάσθησαν πάντες, καὶ ἤρθη τὸ περισσεῦσαν αὐτοῖς κλασμάτων κόφινοι δώδεκα.

9:18 Καὶ ἐγένετο ἐν τῷ εἶναι αὐτὸν προσευχόμενον κατὰ μόνας συνῆσαν αὐτῷ οἱ μαθηταί, καὶ ἐπηρώτησεν αὐτοὺς λέγων, Τίνα με λέγουσιν οἱ ὄχλοι εἶναι; 19 οἱ δὲ ἀποκριθέντες εἶπαν, Ἰωάννην τὸν βαπτιστήν, ἄλλοι δὲ Ἠλίαν, ἄλλοι δὲ ὅτι προφήτης τις τῶν ἀρχαίων ἀνέστη. ¶ 20 εἶπεν δὲ αὐτοῖς, Ὑμεῖς δὲ τίνα με λέγετε εἶναι; Πέτρος δὲ ἀποκριθεὶς εἶπεν, Τὸν Χριστὸν τοῦ

20　　"But what about you?" he asked.　　"Who do you say I am?"　　Peter answered,　"The
　δὲ　δὲ　　　　　εἶπεν　αὐτοῖς　τίνα　　ὑμεῖς λέγετε εἶναι με　δὲ　Πέτρος ἀποκριθεὶς εἶπεν τὸν
　cj　cj　　　　　v.aai.3s r.dpm.3 r.asm　　r.np.2 v.pai.2p f.pa r.as.1 cj　n.nsm　pt.ap.nsm v.aai.3s d.asm
　1254 1254　　　　3306　899　5515　　7007　3306 1639 1609 1254 4377　646　3306 3836

Christ of God."　¶　**21**　Jesus strictly　warned　them not　to tell　this to anyone.　**22** And he said,
χριστὸν　τοῦ θεοῦ　　δὲ ὁ ἐπιτιμήσας παρήγγειλεν αὐτοῖς μηδενὶ　λέγειν τοῦτο　　　　εἶπεν ὅτι
n.asm　　d.gsm n.gsm　cj d.nsm pt.aa.nsm v.aai.3s r.dpm.3 a.dsm　f.pa r.asn　　　　pt.aa.nsm cj
5986　　3836 2536　1254 3836 2203　4133　899 3594　3306 4047 3594 3594　3306 4022

"The Son of Man　　must suffer many things and be rejected　　by the elders,　chief priests and
τὸν　υἱὸν　τοῦ ἀνθρώπου δεῖ παθεῖν πολλὰ　καὶ ἀποδοκιμασθῆναι ἀπὸ τῶν πρεσβυτέρων καὶ　ἀρχιερέων καὶ
d.asm n.asm d.gsm n.gsm v.pai.3s f.aa a.apn　cj　f.ap　　　μ.g d.gpm a.gpm　cj　n.gpm　cj
3836 5626 3836 476　1256 4248 4498　2779 627　　　608 3836 4565　2779　797　2779

teachers of the law, and he must be killed　and on the third day be raised　to life."　¶　**23** Then he
γραμματέων　　　καὶ　　ἀποκτανθῆναι καὶ　τῇ τρίτῃ ἡμέρᾳ ἐγερθῆναι　　　　δὲ
n.gpm　　　　cj　　f.ap　　　cj　d.dsf a.dsf n.dsf f.ap　　　　cj
1208　　　　2779　650　　　2779 3836 5569 2465 1586　　　　1254

said to them all: "If anyone would come after me, he must deny himself and take up his
Ἔλεγεν πρὸς　πάντας εἴ τις θέλει ἔρχεσθαι ὀπίσω μου　　ἀρνησάσθω ἑαυτὸν καὶ ἀράτω　αὐτοῦ
v.iai.3s p.a　a.apm cj r.nsm v.pai.3s f.pm p.g r.gs.1　　v.amm.3s r.asm.3 cj v.aam.3s r.gsm.3
3306　4639　4246 1623 5516 2527 2262 3958 1609　　766　1571　2779 149　899

cross daily　and follow me.　**24** For whoever wants to save his life　will lose it,　but
τὸν σταυρὸν καθ' ἡμέραν καὶ ἀκολουθείτω μοι　γὰρ ὃς ἂν θέλῃ　σῶσαι αὐτοῦ τὴν ψυχὴν　ἀπολέσει αὐτήν δ'
d.asm n.asm p.a n.asf cj v.pam.3s r.ds.1　cj r.nsm pl v.pas.3s f.aa r.gsm.3 d.asf n.asf　v.fai.3s r.asf.3 cj
3836 5089 2848 2465 2779 199　1609　1142 4005 323 2527 5392 899 3836 6034　660　899 1254

whoever loses his life　for me　will save it.　**25**　What good　is it for a man　to gain　the
ὃς ἂν ἀπολέσῃ αὐτοῦ τὴν ψυχὴν ἕνεκεν ἐμοῦ οὗτος σώσει αὐτήν　γὰρ τί ὠφελεῖται　ἄνθρωπος κερδήσας τὸν
r.nsm pl v.aas.3s r.gsm.3 d.asf n.asf p.g r.gs.1 r.nsm v.fai.3s r.asf.3　cj r.asn v.ppi.3s　n.nsm pt.aa.nsm d.asm
4005 323 660 899 3836 6034 1914 1609 4047 5392 899　1142 5515 6067　476 3045 3836

whole world, and yet lose or forfeit his very self?　**26**　If anyone is ashamed of me and my words,
ὅλον κόσμον δὲ ἀπολέσας ἢ ζημιωθεὶς ἑαυτὸν　　γὰρ ὃς ἂν ἐπαισχυνθῇ με καὶ ἐμοὺς τοὺς λόγους
a.asm n.asm cj pt.aa.nsm cj pt.ap.nsm r.asm.3　　cj r.nsm pl v.aps.3s r.as.1 cj r.apm.1 d.apm n.apm
3910 3180 1254 660 2445 2423 1571　　1142 4005 323 2049 1609 2779 1847 3836 3364

the Son of Man　　will be ashamed　of him when he comes in his glory　and in the glory of the
ὁ υἱὸς τοῦ ἀνθρώπου　ἐπαισχυνθήσεται τοῦτον ὅταν ἔλθῃ ἐν αὐτοῦ τῇ δόξῃ καὶ　　τοῦ
d.nsm n.nsm d.gsm n.gsm　v.fpi.3s r.asn cj v.aas.3s p.d r.gsm.3 d.dsf n.dsf cj　　d.gsm
3836 5626 3836 476　2049 4047 4020 2262 1877 899 3836 1518 2779　　3836

Father and of the holy angels.　**27** I tell you the truth,　some who are standing here　will not　taste
πατρὸς καὶ τῶν ἁγίων ἀγγέλων δὲ λέγω ὑμῖν ἀληθῶς εἰσίν τινες τῶν ἑστηκότων αὐτοῦ οἳ οὐ μὴ γεύσωνται
n.gsm cj d.gpm a.gpm n.gpm cj v.pai.1s r.dp.2 adv v.pai.3p r.npm d.gpm pt.ra.gpm adv r.npm pl pl v.ams.3p
4252 2779 3836 41 34 1254 3306 7007 242 1639 5516 3836 2705 7008 4005 1174 4024 3590 1174

death before they see the kingdom of God."
θανάτου ἕως ἂν ἴδωσιν τὴν βασιλείαν τοῦ θεοῦ
n.gsm cj pl v.aas.3p d.asf n.asf d.gsm n.gsm
2505 2401 323 1625 3836 993 3836 2536

The Transfiguration

9:28　About eight days after Jesus said this,　he took Peter, John and
δὲ Ἐγένετο ὡσεὶ ὀκτὼ ἡμέραι μετὰ τοὺς λόγους τούτους [καὶ] παραλαβὼν Πέτρον καὶ Ἰωάννην καὶ
cj v.ami.3s pl a.npf n.npf p.a d.apm n.apm r.apm cj pt.aa.nsm n.asm cj n.asm cj
1254 1181 6059 3893 2465 3552 3836 3364 4047 2779 4161 4377 2779 2722 2779

James with him and went up onto a mountain to pray.　**29** As he was praying, the
Ἰάκωβον　ἀνέβη εἰς τὸ ὄρος προσεύξασθαι καὶ ἐγένετο ἐν αὐτὸν τῷ προσεύχεσθαι τὸ
n.asm　v.aai.3s p.a d.asn n.asn f.am cj v.ami.3s p.d r.asm.3 d.dsn f.pm d.nsn
2610 4161 4161 326 1650 3836 4001 4667 2779 1181 1877 899 3836 4667 3836

appearance of his face changed, and his clothes became as bright as a flash of lightning.
εἶδος　αὐτοῦ τοῦ προσώπου ἕτερον καὶ αὐτοῦ ὁ ἱματισμὸς λευκὸς ἐξαστράπτων
n.nsn　r.gsm.3 d.gsn n.gsn r.nsn cj r.gsm.3 d.nsm n.nsm a.nsm pt.pa.nsm
1626　4725 3836 4725 2283 2779 899 3836 2669 1993 3328 1993

θεου ¶ 21 Ὁ δὲ ἐπιτιμήσας αὐτοῖς παρήγγειλεν μηδενὶ λέγειν τοῦτο 22 εἰπὼν ὅτι Δεῖ τὸν υἱὸν τοῦ ἀνθρώπου πολλὰ παθεῖν καὶ ἀποδοκιμασθῆναι ἀπὸ τῶν πρεσβυτέρων καὶ ἀρχιερέων καὶ γραμματέων καὶ ἀποκτανθῆναι καὶ τῇ τρίτῃ ἡμέρᾳ ἐγερθῆναι. ¶ 23 Ἔλεγεν δὲ πρὸς πάντας, Εἴ τις θέλει ὀπίσω μου ἔρχεσθαι, ἀρνησάσθω ἑαυτὸν καὶ ἀράτω τὸν σταυρὸν αὐτοῦ καθ' ἡμέραν καὶ ἀκολουθείτω μοι. 24 ὃς γὰρ ἂν θέλῃ τὴν ψυχὴν αὐτοῦ σῶσαι ἀπολέσει αὐτήν· ὃς δ' ἂν ἀπολέσῃ τὴν ψυχὴν αὐτοῦ ἕνεκεν ἐμοῦ οὗτος σώσει αὐτήν. 25 τί γὰρ ὠφελεῖται ἄνθρωπος κερδήσας τὸν κόσμον ὅλον ἑαυτὸν δὲ ἀπολέσας ἢ ζημιωθείς; 26 ὃς γὰρ ἂν ἐπαισχυνθῇ με καὶ τοὺς ἐμοὺς λόγους, τοῦτον ὁ υἱὸς τοῦ ἀνθρώπου ἐπαισχυνθήσεται, ὅταν ἔλθῃ ἐν τῇ δόξῃ αὐτοῦ καὶ τοῦ πατρὸς καὶ τῶν ἁγίων ἀγγέλων. 27 λέγω δὲ ὑμῖν ἀληθῶς, εἰσίν τινες τῶν αὐτοῦ ἑστηκότων οἳ οὐ μὴ γεύσωνται θανάτου ἕως ἂν ἴδωσιν τὴν βασιλείαν τοῦ θεοῦ.
　9:28 Ἐγένετο δὲ μετὰ τοὺς λόγους τούτους ὡσεὶ ἡμέραι ὀκτὼ [καὶ] παραλαβὼν Πέτρον καὶ Ἰωάννην καὶ Ἰάκωβον ἀνέβη εἰς τὸ ὄρος προσεύξασθαι. 29 καὶ ἐγένετο ἐν τῷ προσεύχεσθαι αὐτὸν τὸ εἶδος τοῦ προσώπου αὐτοῦ ἕτερον καὶ ὁ ἱματισμὸς αὐτοῦ λευκὸς ἐξαστράπτων. 30 καὶ ἰδοὺ ἄνδρες δύο συνελάλουν αὐτῷ, οἵτινες ἦσαν Μωϋσῆς καὶ Ἡλίας, 31 οἳ ὀφθέντες ἐν δόξῃ

30 Two men, Moses and Elijah, **31** appeared in glorious splendor, talking with Jesus. They
καὶ ἰδοὺ δύο ἄνδρες οἵτινες ἦσαν Μωϋσῆς καὶ Ἠλίας οἳ ὀφθέντες ἐν δόξῃ συνελάλουν ← αὐτῷ
cj j a.npm n.npm r.npm v.iai.3p n.nsm cj n.nsm r.npm pt.ap.npm p.d n.dsf v.iai.3p r.dsm.3
2779 2627 1545 467 4015 1639 3707 2779 2460 4005 3972 1877 1518 5196 899

spoke about his departure, which he was about to bring to fulfillment at Jerusalem. **32** Peter and his
ἔλεγον αὐτοῦ τὴν ἔξοδον, ἣν → → ἤμελλεν → → → πληροῦν ἐν Ἰερουσαλήμ δὲ ὁ Πέτρος καὶ αὐτῷ
v.iai.3p r.gsm.3 d.asf n.asf r.asf v.iai.3s f.pa p.d n.dsf cj d.nsm n.nsm cj r.dsm.3
3306 899 3836 2016 4005 3516 4444 1877 2647 1254 3836 4377 2779 899

companions were very sleepy, but when they became fully awake, they saw his glory and
οἱ σὺν ἦσαν → βεβαρημένοι ὕπνῳ δὲ → → → διαγρηγορήσαντες εἶδον αὐτοῦ τὴν δόξαν, καὶ
d.npm p.d v.iai.3p pt.rp.npm n.dsm cj pt.aa.npm v.aai.3p r.gsm.3 d.asf n.asf cj
3836 5250 1639 976 5678 1254 1340 1625 899 3836 1518 2779

the two men standing with him. **33** As the men were leaving Jesus, Peter said
τοὺς δύο ἄνδρας τοὺς συνεστῶτας ← αὐτῷ καὶ ἐγένετο ἐν αὐτοὺς → τῷ διαχωρίζεσθαι ἀπ᾽ αὐτοῦ ὁ Πέτρος, εἶπεν
d.apm a.npm n.apm d.apm pt.ra.apm r.dsm.3 cj v.ami.3s p.d r.apm.3 d.dsn f.pm p.g r.gsm.3 d.nsm n.nsm v.aai.3s
3836 1545 467 3836 5319 899 2779 1181 1877 899 3836 1431 608 899 3836 4377 3306

to him, "Master, it is good for us to be here. Let us put up three shelters – one for you,
πρὸς τὸν Ἰησοῦν, ἐπιστάτα → ἔστιν καλὸν ἡμᾶς εἶναι ὧδε καὶ → ποιήσωμεν τρεῖς σκηνὰς μίαν σοὶ καὶ
p.a d.asm n.asm n.vsm v.pai.3s a.nsn r.ap.1 f.pa adv cj v.aas.1p a.apf n.apf a.asf r.ds.2 cj
4639 3836 2652 2181 1639 2819 7005 1639 6045 2779 4472 5552 5008 1651 5148 2779

one for Moses and one for Elijah." (He did not know what he was saying.) ¶ **34** While he was speaking,
μίαν → Μωϋσεῖ καὶ μίαν → Ἠλίᾳ → μὴ εἰδὼς ὃ → λέγει δὲ αὐτοῦ → λέγοντος
a.asf n.dsm cj a.asf n.dsm pl pt.ra.nsm r.asn v.pai.3s cj r.gsm.3 pt.pa.gsm
1651 3707 2779 1651 2460 3857 3857 3590 3857 4005 3306 1254 3306 899 3306

a cloud appeared and enveloped them, and they were afraid as they entered the cloud. **35** A
ταῦτα νεφέλη ἐγένετο καὶ ἐπεσκίαζεν αὐτούς δὲ → ἐφοβήθησαν ἐν αὐτοὺς τῷ εἰσελθεῖν εἰς τὴν νεφέλην καὶ
r.apn n.nsf v.ami.3s cj v.iai.3s r.apm.3 cj v.api.3p p.d r.apm.3 d.dsn f.aa p.a d.asf n.asf cj
4047 3749 1181 2779 2173 899 1254 5828 1877 899 3836 1656 1650 3836 3749 2779

voice came from the cloud, saying, "This is my Son, whom I have chosen; listen to him." **36** When the
φωνὴ ἐγένετο ἐκ τῆς νεφέλης λέγουσα οὗτός ἐστιν μου ὁ υἱός, ὁ ἐκλελεγμένος ἀκούετε ← αὐτοῦ καὶ ἐν τὴν
n.nsf v.ami.3s p.g d.gsf n.gsf pt.pa.nsf r.nsm v.pai.3s r.gs.1 d.nsm n.nsm d.nsm pt.rp.nsm v.pam.2p r.gsm.3 cj p.d d.asf
5889 1181 1666 3836 3749 3306 4047 1639 1609 3836 5626 3836 1721 201 899 2779 1877 3836

voice had spoken, they found that Jesus was alone. The disciples kept this to themselves, and told
φωνὴν → τῷ γενέσθαι → εὑρέθη Ἰησοῦς μόνος καὶ αὐτοὶ ἐσίγησαν ← ← καὶ ἀπήγγειλαν
n.asf d.dsn f.am v.api.3s n.nsm a.nsm cj r.npm v.aai.3p cj v.aai.3p
5889 3836 1181 2351 2652 3668 2779 899 4967 2779 550

no one at that time what they had seen.
→ οὐδενὶ ἐν ἐκείναις ταῖς ἡμέραις οὐδὲν ὧν → → → ἑώρακαν.
a.dsm p.d r.dpf d.dpf n.dpf a.asn r.gpn v.rai.3p
4029 1877 1697 3836 2465 4029 4005 3972

The Healing of a Boy With an Evil Spirit

9:37 The next day, when they came down from the mountain, a large crowd met him.
δὲ Ἐγένετο τῇ ἑξῆς ἡμέρᾳ → αὐτῶν κατελθόντων ← ἀπὸ τοῦ ὄρους πολὺς ὄχλος συνήντησεν αὐτῷ
cj v.ami.3s d.dsf adv n.dsf r.gpm.3 pt.aa.gpm p.g d.gsn n.gsn a.nsm n.nsm v.aai.3s r.dsm.3
1254 1181 3836 2009 2465 2982 899 2982 608 3836 4001 4498 4063 5267 899

38 A man in the crowd called out, "Teacher, I beg you to look at my son, for he is my
καὶ ἰδοὺ ἀνὴρ ἀπὸ τοῦ ὄχλου ἐβόησεν ← λέγων διδάσκαλε → δέομαί σου → ἐπιβλέψαι ἐπὶ μου τὸν υἱόν, ὅτι → ἔστιν μοί
cj j n.nsm p.g d.gsm n.gsm v.aai.3s pt.pa.nsm n.vsm v.pmi.1s r.gs.2 f.aa p.a r.gs.1 d.asm n.asm cj v.pai.3s r.ds.1
2779 2627 467 608 3836 4063 1066 3306 1437 1289 5148 2098 2093 1609 3836 5626 4022 1639 1609

only child. **39** A spirit seizes him and he suddenly screams; it throws him into convulsions so that
→ μονογενής καὶ ἰδοὺ πνεῦμα λαμβάνει αὐτὸν καὶ ἐξαίφνης κράζει καὶ → αὐτὸν → σπαράσσει
a.nsm cj j n.nsn v.pai.3s r.asm.3 cj adv v.pai.3s cj r.asm.3 v.pai.3s
3666 2779 2627 4460 3284 899 2779 1978 3189 2779 5057 5057 899 5057

he foams at the mouth. It scarcely ever leaves him and is destroying him. **40** I begged your
μετὰ ἀφροῦ καὶ μόγις ἀποχωρεῖ ἀπ᾽ αὐτοῦ → συντρῖβον αὐτόν καὶ → ἐδεήθην σου
p.g n.gsm cj adv v.pai.3s p.g r.gsm.3 pt.pa.nsn r.asm.3 cj v.api.1s r.gs.2
3552 931 2779 713 3653 713 608 899 5341 899 2779 1289 5148

ἔλεγον τὴν ἔξοδον αὐτοῦ, ἣν ἤμελλεν πληροῦν ἐν Ἰερουσαλήμ. ³² ὁ δὲ Πέτρος καὶ οἱ σὺν αὐτῷ ἦσαν βεβαρημένοι ὕπνῳ· διαγρηγορήσαντες δὲ εἶδον τὴν δόξαν αὐτοῦ καὶ τοὺς δύο ἄνδρας τοὺς συνεστῶτας αὐτῷ. ³³ καὶ ἐγένετο ἐν τῷ διαχωρίζεσθαι αὐτοὺς ἀπ᾽ αὐτοῦ εἶπεν ὁ Πέτρος πρὸς τὸν Ἰησοῦν, Ἐπιστάτα, καλόν ἐστιν ἡμᾶς ὧδε εἶναι, καὶ ποιήσωμεν σκηνὰς τρεῖς, μίαν σοὶ καὶ μίαν Μωϋσεῖ καὶ μίαν Ἠλίᾳ, μὴ εἰδὼς ὃ λέγει. ¶ ³⁴ ταῦτα δὲ αὐτοῦ λέγοντος ἐγένετο νεφέλη καὶ ἐπεσκίαζεν αὐτούς· ἐφοβήθησαν δὲ ἐν τῷ εἰσελθεῖν αὐτοὺς εἰς τὴν νεφέλην. ³⁵ καὶ φωνὴ ἐγένετο ἐκ τῆς νεφέλης λέγουσα, Οὗτός ἐστιν ὁ υἱός μου ὁ ἐκλελεγμένος, αὐτοῦ ἀκούετε. ³⁶ καὶ ἐν τῷ γενέσθαι τὴν φωνὴν εὑρέθη Ἰησοῦς μόνος. καὶ αὐτοὶ ἐσίγησαν καὶ οὐδενὶ ἀπήγγειλαν ἐν ἐκείναις ταῖς ἡμέραις οὐδὲν ὧν ἑώρακαν.

⁹:³⁷ Ἐγένετο δὲ τῇ ἑξῆς ἡμέρᾳ κατελθόντων αὐτῶν ἀπὸ τοῦ ὄρους συνήντησεν αὐτῷ ὄχλος πολύς. ³⁸ καὶ ἰδοὺ ἀνὴρ ἀπὸ τοῦ ὄχλου ἐβόησεν λέγων, Διδάσκαλε, δέομαί σου ἐπιβλέψαι ἐπὶ τὸν υἱόν μου, ὅτι μονογενής μοί ἐστιν, ³⁹ καὶ ἰδοὺ πνεῦμα λαμβάνει αὐτὸν καὶ ἐξαίφνης κράζει καὶ σπαράσσει αὐτὸν μετὰ ἀφροῦ καὶ μόγις ἀποχωρεῖ ἀπ᾽ αὐτοῦ συντρῖβον αὐτόν· ⁴⁰ καὶ ἐδεήθην τῶν

disciples   to   drive   it   out, but they could   not." [41]   "O unbelieving and perverse   generation,"
⌐τῶν μαθητῶν⌐ ἵνα ἐκβάλωσιν αὐτό ←   καὶ → ἠδυνήθησαν οὐκ   δὲ ὦ ἄπιστος καὶ διεστραμμένη γενεὰ
d.gpm n.gpm   cj   v.aas.3p r.asn.3   cj   v.api.3p   pl   cj j   a.vsf   cj   pt.rp.vsf   n.vsf
3836 3412   2671 1675   899   1675 2779   1538   4024 1254 6043 603   2779 1406   1155

Jesus   replied,   "how long shall I stay   with you and put   up with you? Bring   your son
⌐ὁ Ἰησοῦς⌐ ἀποκριθεὶς εἶπεν ἕως πότε → → ἔσομαι πρὸς ὑμᾶς καὶ ἀνέξομαι ←   ὑμῶν προσάγαγε σου ⌐τὸν υἱόν⌐
d.nsm n.nsm   pt.ap.nsm v.aai.3s p.g adv   v.fmi.1s p.a r.ap.2 cj v.fmi.1s   r.gp.2 v.aam.2s r.gs.2 d.asm n.asm
3836 2652   646   3306   2401 4537   1639   4639 7007 2779 462   7007   4642   5148 3836 5626

here." ¶   [42] Even while the boy was coming,   the demon   threw him to the ground in a
ὧδε   δὲ ἔτι →   αὐτοῦ → προσερχομένου τὸ δαιμόνιον ἔρρηξεν αὐτὸν ←   καὶ
adv   cj adv   r.gsm.3   pt.pm.gsm   d.nsn n.nsn   v.aai.3s r.asm.3   cj
6045   1254 2285   4665   4665   3836 1228   4838   899   4838 4838 4838 2779

convulsion. But Jesus   rebuked the evil   spirit,   healed the boy and gave   him back to his
συνεσπάραξεν δὲ ⌐ὁ Ἰησοῦς⌐ ἐπετίμησεν τῷ ⌐τῷ ἀκαθάρτῳ πνεύματι καὶ ἰάσατο τὸν παῖδα καὶ ἀπέδωκεν αὐτὸν ←   → αὐτοῦ
v.aai.3s   cj d.nsm n.nsm   v.aai.3s d.dsn d.dsn a.dsn   n.dsn   cj v.ami.3s d.asm n.asm cj v.aai.3s r.asm.3   r.gsm.3
5360   1254 3836 2652   2203   3836 3836 176   4460   2779 2615   3836 4090 2779 625   899   625 176 899

father. [43] And they were all   amazed   at the greatness of God.   ¶   While everyone was marveling
⌐τῷ πατρὶ⌐ δὲ → → πάντες ἐξεπλήσσοντο ἐπὶ τῇ μεγαλειότητι → ⌐τοῦ θεοῦ⌐ δὲ →   Πάντων → θαυμαζόντων
d.dsm n.dsm   cj   a.npm v.ipi.3p   p.d d.dsf n.dsf   d.gsm n.gsm   cj   a.gpm   pt.pa.gpm
3836 4252   1254 1742 1742 4246 1742   2093 3836 3484   3836 2536   1254 2513 4246   2513

at all   that Jesus did, he said to his   disciples,   [44] "Listen   carefully   to what   I am about
ἐπὶ πᾶσιν οἷς   ἐποίει → εἶπεν πρὸς αὐτοῦ ⌐τοὺς μαθητὰς⌐   ⌐θέσθε ὑμεῖς⌐ ⌐εἰς τὰ ὦτα ὑμῶν⌐ ⌐τοὺς λόγους τούτους⌐
p.d a.dpn r.dpn   v.iai.3s v.aai.3s p.a r.gsm.3 d.apm n.apm   v.amm.2p r.np.2 p.a d.apn n.apn r.gp.2 d.apm n.apm r.apm
2093 4246 4005   4472   3306   4639 899 3836 3412   5502   7007 1650 3836 4044 7007 3836 3364 4047

to tell you: The Son of Man   is going to be betrayed   into the hands of men." [45] But they did not
γὰρ ὁ υἱὸς → ⌐τοῦ ἀνθρώπου⌐ → μέλλει → παραδίδοσθαι εἰς χεῖρας → ἀνθρώπων δὲ οἱ
cj d.nsm n.nsm   d.gsm n.gsm   v.pai.3s   v.pp   p.a n.apf   n.gpm   cj d.npm
1142 3836 5626   3836 476   3516   4140   1650 5931   476   1254 3836

understand what   this meant.   It was hidden   from them, so that they did not grasp   it, and they
ἠγνόουν ⌐τὸ ῥῆμα⌐ τοῦτο   καὶ → ἦν παρακεκαλυμμένον ἀπ᾽ αὐτῶν ἵνα ←   they → μὴ αἴσθωνται αὐτὸ καὶ
v.iai.3p d.asn n.asn r.asn   cj v.iai.3s pt.rp.nsn   p.g r.gpm.3 cj   pl v.ams.3p r.asn.3 cj
51   3836 4839 4047   2779 1639   4152   608 899   2671 150 150 3590 150   899   2779

were afraid to ask   him about it.
→ ἐφοβοῦντο → ἐρωτῆσαι αὐτὸν περὶ ⌐τοῦ ῥήματος τούτου⌐
v.ipi.3p   f.aa   r.asm.3 p.g d.gsn n.gsn r.gsn
5828   2263   899   4309 3836 4839 4047

Who Will Be the Greatest

9:46 An argument   started   among the disciples as to   which of them would be   the greatest. [47]
δὲ   διαλογισμὸς Εἰσῆλθεν ἐν   αὐτοῖς   τὸ ⌐τίς ἂν⌐ → αὐτῶν →   εἴη   μείζων   δὲ
cj   n.nsm   v.aai.3s p.d   r.dpm.3   d.nsn pl r.gpm.3   v.pao.3s a.nsm.c cj
1254 1369   1656   1877   899   3836 5515 323 899   1639   3489   1254

Jesus,   knowing their thoughts,   took   a little child and had him stand beside him.
⌐ὁ Ἰησοῦς⌐ εἰδὼς αὐτῶν ⌐τὸν διαλογισμόν⌐ τῆς καρδίας ἐπιλαβόμενος → παιδίον → αὐτὸ ἔστησεν παρ᾽ ἑαυτῷ
d.nsm n.nsm   pt.ra.nsm r.gpm.3 d.asm n.asm   d.gsf n.gsf pt.am.nsm   n.asn   r.asn.3 v.aai.3s p.d r.dsm.3
3836 2652   3857   899   3836 1369   3836 2840 2138   4086   2705 899 2705   4123 1571

[48] Then he said to them, "Whoever welcomes this little child   in my name   welcomes me; and whoever
καὶ → εἶπεν αὐτοῖς ⌐ὃς ἐάν⌐ δέξηται τοῦτο → ⌐τὸ παιδίον⌐ ἐπὶ μου ⌐τῷ ὀνόματι⌐ δέχεται ἐμὲ καὶ ⌐ὃς ἂν⌐
cj   v.aai.3s r.dpm.3 pl   v.ams.3s r.asn   d.asn n.asn   p.d r.gs.1 d.dsn n.dsn   v.pmi.3s r.as.1 cj r.nsm pl
2779   3306   899   4005 1569 1312   4047   3836 4086   2093 1609 3836 3950   1312   1609 2779 4005 323

welcomes me welcomes the one who sent   me. For he who is   least   among you all – he   is
δέξηται ἐμὲ δέχεται τὸν ←   ἀποστείλαντα με γὰρ ὁ   ὑπάρχων μικρότερος ἐν ὑμῖν πᾶσιν οὗτος ἐστιν
v.ams.3s r.as.1 v.pmi.3s d.asm   pt.aa.asm r.as.1 cj d.nsm pt.pa.nsm a.nsm.c   p.d r.dp.2 a.dpm r.nsm v.pai.3s
1312   1609 1312   3836   690   1609 1142 3836 5639   3625   1877 7007 4246 4047 1639

the greatest." ¶ [49] "Master," said   John,   "we saw a man driving out demons in your
μέγας   δὲ ἐπιστάτα Ἀποκριθεὶς εἶπεν Ἰωάννης → εἴδομεν τινα ἐκβάλλοντα ←   δαιμόνια ἐν σου
a.nsm   cj n.vsm   pt.ap.nsm v.aai.3s n.nsm   v.aai.1p r.asm pt.pa.asm   n.apn   p.d r.gs.2
3489   1254 2181   646   3306   2722   1625   5516 1675   1228   1877 5148

μαθητῶν σου ἵνα ἐκβάλωσιν αὐτό, καὶ οὐκ ἠδυνήθησαν. [41] ἀποκριθεὶς δὲ ὁ Ἰησοῦς εἶπεν, Ὦ γενεὰ ἄπιστος καὶ διεστραμμένη, ἕως πότε ἔσομαι πρὸς ὑμᾶς καὶ ἀνέξομαι ὑμῶν; προσάγαγε ὧδε τὸν υἱόν σου. ¶ [42] ἔτι δὲ προσερχομένου αὐτοῦ ἔρρηξεν αὐτὸν τὸ δαιμόνιον καὶ συνεσπάραξεν· ἐπετίμησεν δὲ ὁ Ἰησοῦς τῷ πνεύματι τῷ ἀκαθάρτῳ καὶ ἰάσατο τὸν παῖδα καὶ ἀπέδωκεν αὐτὸν τῷ πατρὶ αὐτοῦ. [43] ἐξεπλήσσοντο δὲ πάντες ἐπὶ τῇ μεγαλειότητι τοῦ θεοῦ. ¶ Πάντων δὲ θαυμαζόντων ἐπὶ πᾶσιν οἷς ἐποίει εἶπεν πρὸς τοὺς μαθητὰς αὐτοῦ, [44] Θέσθε ὑμεῖς εἰς τὰ ὦτα ὑμῶν τοὺς λόγους τούτους· ὁ γὰρ υἱὸς τοῦ ἀνθρώπου μέλλει παραδίδοσθαι εἰς χεῖρας ἀνθρώπων. [45] οἱ δὲ ἠγνόουν τὸ ῥῆμα τοῦτο καὶ ἦν παρακεκαλυμμένον ἀπ᾽ αὐτῶν ἵνα μὴ αἴσθωνται αὐτό, καὶ ἐφοβοῦντο ἐρωτῆσαι αὐτὸν περὶ τοῦ ῥήματος τούτου.

[9:46] Εἰσῆλθεν δὲ διαλογισμὸς ἐν αὐτοῖς, τὸ τίς ἂν εἴη μείζων αὐτῶν. [47] ὁ δὲ Ἰησοῦς εἰδὼς τὸν διαλογισμὸν τῆς καρδίας αὐτῶν, ἐπιλαβόμενος παιδίον ἔστησεν αὐτὸ παρ᾽ ἑαυτῷ [48] καὶ εἶπεν αὐτοῖς, Ὃς ἐὰν δέξηται τοῦτο τὸ παιδίον ἐπὶ τῷ ὀνόματί μου, ἐμὲ δέχεται· καὶ ὃς ἂν ἐμὲ δέξηται, δέχεται τὸν ἀποστείλαντά με· ὁ γὰρ μικρότερος ἐν πᾶσιν ὑμῖν ὑπάρχων οὗτός ἐστιν μέγας. ¶ [49] Ἀποκριθεὶς δὲ Ἰωάννης εἶπεν, Ἐπιστάτα, εἴδομέν τινα ἐν τῷ ὀνόματί σου ἐκβάλλοντα δαιμόνια καὶ ἐκωλύομεν

name and we tried to stop him, because he is not one of us." 50 "Do not stop him," Jesus
ⸯτῷ ὀνόματιⸯ καὶ → → ἐκωλύομεν αὐτόν ὅτι ↱ ↱ οὐκ ἀκολουθεῖ μεθ᾽ ἡμῶν δὲ → μὴ κωλύετε ὁ Ἰησοῦςⸯ
d.dsn n.dsn cj   v.iai.1p   r.asm.3 cj   pl v.pai.3s p.g r.gp.1 cj   pl v.pam.2p d.nsm n.nsm
3836 3950 2779   3266   899 4022   199 199 4024 199   3552 7005 1254 3590 3266 3836 2652

said, "for whoever is not against you is for you."
εἶπεν πρὸς αὐτὸν γὰρ ὃς ἔστιν οὐκ καθ᾽ ὑμῶν ἐστιν ὑπὲρ ὑμῶν
v.aai.3s p.a r.asm.3 cj r.nsm v.pai.3s pl r.gp.2 v.pai.3s p.g r.gp.2
3306 4639 899 1142 4005 1639 4024 2848 7007 1639 5642 7007

Samaritan Opposition

9:51 As the time approached for him to be taken up to heaven, Jesus
δὲ Ἐγένετο ἐν τὰς ἡμέρας ⸯτῷ συμπληροῦσθαιⸯ αὐτοῦ ⸯτῆς ἀναλήμψεωςⸯ ← καὶ αὐτὸς
cj v.ami.3s p.d d.apf n.apf d.dsn f.pp r.gsm.3 d.gsf n.gsf cj r.nsm
1254 1181 1877 3836 2465 3836 5230 899 3836 378 2779 899

resolutely set out for Jerusalem. 52 And he sent messengers on ahead, who
ⸯτὸ πρόσωπον ἐστήρισενⸯ ⸯτοῦ πορεύεσθαιⸯ ← εἰς Ἰερουσαλήμ καὶ → ἀπέστειλεν ἀγγέλους → ⸯπρὸ προσώπου αὐτοῦⸯ καὶ
d.asn n.asn v.aai.3s d.gsn f.pm p.a n.asf cj v.aai.3s n.apm p.g n.gsn r.gsm.3 cj
3836 4725 5114 3836 4513 1650 2647 2779 690 34 4574 4725 899 2779

went into a Samaritan village to get things ready for him; 53 but the people there did not welcome
πορευθέντες εἰσῆλθον εἰς Σαμαριτῶν κώμην ὡς → ἑτοιμάσαι αὐτῷ καὶ ↱ οὐκ ἐδέξαντο
pt.ap.npm v.aai.3p p.a n.gpm n.asf cj → f.aa r.dsm.3 cj pl v.ami.3p
4513 1656 1650 4901 3267 6055 2286 899 2779 1312 4024 1312

him, because he was heading for Jerusalem. 54 When the disciples James and John saw
αὐτόν ὅτι ⸯτὸ πρόσωπον αὐτοῦⸯ ἦν πορευόμενον εἰς Ἰερουσαλήμ δὲ οἱ μαθηταὶ Ἰάκωβος καὶ Ἰωάννης ἰδόντες
r.asm.3 cj d.nsn n.nsn r.gsm.3 v.iai.3s pt.pm.nsn p.a n.asf cj d.npm n.npm n.nsm cj n.nsm pt.aa.npm
899 4022 3836 4725 899 1639 4513 1650 2647 1254 1625 3836 3412 2610 2779 2722 1625

this, they asked, "Lord, do you want us to call fire down from heaven to destroy them?" 55 But Jesus
→ εἶπαν κύριε → → θέλεις → εἴπωμεν πῦρ καταβῆναι ἀπὸ ⸯτοῦ οὐρανοῦⸯ καὶ → ἀναλῶσαι αὐτούς δὲ
v.aai.3p n.vsm v.pai.2s v.aas.1p n.asn f.aa p.g d.gsm n.gsm cj f.aa r.apm.3 cj
3306 3261 2527 3306 4786 2849 608 3836 4041 2779 384 899 1254

turned and rebuked them,
στραφεὶς ἐπετίμησεν αὐτοῖς
pt.ap.nsm v.aai.3s r.dpm.3
5138 2203 899

The Cost of Following Jesus

9:56 and they went to another village. 57 As they were walking along the road, a man said to him,
καὶ → ἐπορεύθησαν εἰς ἑτέραν κώμην Καὶ ↱ αὐτῶν → πορευομένων ἐν τῇ ὁδῷ τις εἶπεν πρὸς αὐτόν
cj v.api.3p p.a r.asf n.asf cj r.gpm.3 pt.pm.gpm p.d d.dsf n.dsf r.nsm v.aai.3s p.a r.asm.3
2779 4513 1650 2283 3267 2779 4513 899 4513 1877 3836 3847 5516 3306 4639 899

"I will follow you wherever you go." 58 Jesus replied, "Foxes have holes and birds of
→ → ἀκολουθήσω σοι ὅπου ἐὰν → ἀπέρχῃ καὶ ὁ Ἰησοῦςⸯ εἶπεν αὐτῷ αἱ ἀλώπεκες ἔχουσιν φωλεοὺς καὶ ⸯτὰ πετεινὰⸯ
v.fai.1s r.ds.2 adv pl v.pms.2s cj d.nsm n.nsm v.aai.3s r.dsm.3 d.npf n.npf v.pai.3p n.apm cj d.npn n.npn
199 5148 3963 1569 599 2779 3836 2652 3306 899 3836 273 2400 5887 2779 3836 4374

the air have nests, but the Son of Man has no place to lay his head." ¶ 59 He said
τοῦ οὐρανοῦ → κατασκηνώσεις δὲ ὁ υἱὸς → ⸯτοῦ ἀνθρώπουⸯ ἔχει οὐκ ποῦ → κλίνῃ τὴν κεφαλὴν δὲ → Εἶπεν
d.gsm n.gsm n.apf cj d.nsm n.nsm d.gsm n.gsm v.pai.3s pl adv v.pas.3s d.asf n.asf cj v.aai.3s
3836 4041 2943 1254 3836 5626 3836 476 2400 4024 4543 3111 3836 3051 1254 3306

to another man, "Follow me." But the man replied, "Lord, first let me go and bury my father."
πρὸς ἕτερον ἀκολούθει μοι δὲ ὁ εἶπεν κύριε πρῶτον ἐπίτρεψον μοι ἀπελθόντι θάψαι μου ⸯτὸν πατέραⸯ
p.a r.asm v.pam.2s r.ds.1 cj d.nsm v.aai.3s n.vsm adv v.aam.2s r.ds.1 pt.aa.dsm f.aa r.gs.1 d.asm n.asm
4639 2283 199 1609 1254 3836 3306 3261 4754 2205 1609 599 2507 1609 3836 4252

60 Jesus said to him, "Let the dead bury their own dead, but you go and proclaim the kingdom of
δὲ εἶπεν → αὐτῷ ἄφες τοὺς νεκροὺς θάψαι τοὺς ἑαυτῶν νεκρούς δὲ σὺ ἀπελθὼν διάγγελλε τὴν βασιλείαν →
cj v.aai.3s r.dsm.3 v.aam.2s d.apm a.apm f.aa d.apm r.gpm.3 a.apm cj r.ns.2 pt.aa.nsm v.pam.2s d.asf n.asf
1254 3306 899 918 3836 3738 2507 3836 1571 3738 1254 5148 599 1334 3836 993

God." ¶ 61 Still another said, "I will follow you, Lord; but first let me go back and say
ⸯτοῦ θεοῦⸯ δὲ καὶ ἕτερος Εἶπεν → → ἀκολουθήσω σοι κύριε δὲ πρῶτον ἐπίτρεψον μοι →
d.gsm n.gsm cj adv r.nsm v.aai.3s v.fai.1s r.ds.2 n.vsm cj adv v.aam.2s r.ds.1
3836 2536 1254 2779 2283 3306 199 5148 3261 1254 4754 2205 1609

αὐτόν, ὅτι οὐκ ἀκολουθεῖ μεθ᾽ ἡμῶν. 50 εἶπεν δὲ πρὸς αὐτὸν ὁ Ἰησοῦς, Μὴ κωλύετε· ὃς γὰρ οὐκ ἔστιν καθ᾽ ὑμῶν, ὑπὲρ ὑμῶν ἐστιν.
9:51 Ἐγένετο δὲ ἐν τῷ συμπληροῦσθαι τὰς ἡμέρας τῆς ἀναλήμψεως αὐτοῦ καὶ αὐτὸς τὸ πρόσωπον ἐστήρισεν τοῦ πορεύεσθαι εἰς Ἰερουσαλήμ. 52 καὶ ἀπέστειλεν ἀγγέλους πρὸ προσώπου αὐτοῦ. καὶ πορευθέντες εἰσῆλθον εἰς κώμην Σαμαριτῶν ὡς ἑτοιμάσαι αὐτῷ· 53 καὶ οὐκ ἐδέξαντο αὐτόν, ὅτι τὸ πρόσωπον αὐτοῦ ἦν πορευόμενον εἰς Ἰερουσαλήμ. 54 ἰδόντες δὲ οἱ μαθηταὶ Ἰάκωβος καὶ Ἰωάννης εἶπαν, Κύριε, θέλεις εἴπωμεν πῦρ καταβῆναι ἀπὸ τοῦ οὐρανοῦ καὶ ἀναλῶσαι αὐτούς; 55 στραφεὶς δὲ ἐπετίμησεν αὐτοῖς.
9:56 καὶ ἐπορεύθησαν εἰς ἑτέραν κώμην. 57 Καὶ πορευομένων αὐτῶν ἐν τῇ ὁδῷ εἶπέν τις πρὸς αὐτόν, Ἀκολουθήσω σοι ὅπου ἐὰν ἀπέρχῃ. 58 καὶ εἶπεν αὐτῷ ὁ Ἰησοῦς, Αἱ ἀλώπεκες φωλεοὺς ἔχουσιν καὶ τὰ πετεινὰ τοῦ οὐρανοῦ κατασκηνώσεις, ὁ δὲ υἱὸς τοῦ ἀνθρώπου οὐκ ἔχει ποῦ τὴν κεφαλὴν κλίνῃ. ¶ 59 Εἶπεν δὲ πρὸς ἕτερον, Ἀκολούθει μοι. ὁ δὲ εἶπεν, [Κύριε,] ἐπίτρεψόν μοι ἀπελθόντι πρῶτον θάψαι τὸν πατέρα μου. 60 εἶπεν δὲ αὐτῷ, Ἄφες τοὺς νεκροὺς θάψαι τοὺς ἑαυτῶν νεκρούς, σὺ δὲ ἀπελθὼν διάγγελλε τὴν βασιλείαν τοῦ θεοῦ. ¶ 61 Εἶπεν δὲ καὶ ἕτερος, Ἀκολουθήσω σοι, κύριε· πρῶτον δὲ ἐπίτρεψόν μοι ἀποτάξασθαι τοῖς

good-by   to   my   family."   [62]   Jesus   replied,   "No one   who puts   his hand   to the
ἀποτάξασθαι → τοῖς εἰς μου τὸν οἶκον. δὲ ὁ Ἰησοῦς, εἶπεν [πρὸς αὐτόν] → οὐδεὶς → ἐπιβαλὼν τὴν χεῖρα ἐπ'
f.am   d.dpm p.a r.gs.1 d.asm n.asm cj d.nsm n.nsm v.aai.3s p.a r.asm.3   a.nsm pt.aa.nsm d.asf n.asf p.a
698   3836 1650 1609 3836 3875   1254 3836 2652   3306   4639 899   4029   2095   3836 5931   2093

plow   and looks back   is   fit   for service in the kingdom   of God."
ἄροτρον καὶ βλέπων εἰς τὰ ὀπίσω ἔστιν εὔθετος → τῇ βασιλείᾳ → τοῦ θεοῦ.
n.asn   cj   pt.pa.nsm p.a d.apn adv v.pai.3s a.nsm   d.dsf n.dsf   d.gsm n.gsm
770   2779 1063   1650 3836 3958 1639   2310   3836 993   3836 2536

Jesus Sends Out the Seventy-two

[10:1]   After this   the   Lord   appointed   seventy-two   others and sent   them   two   by two ahead
δὲ Μετὰ ταῦτα ὁ κύριος ἀνέδειξεν ἑβδομήκοντα δύο ἑτέρους καὶ ἀπέστειλεν αὐτοὺς [δύο] ἀνὰ δύο πρὸ προσώπου
cj   p.a r.apn d.nsm n.nsm v.aai.3s a.apm   a.apm r.apm   cj   v.aai.3s r.apm.3   a.apm p.a a.apm p.g n.gsn
1254 3552 4047 3836 3261 344   1573   1545 2283   2779 690   899   1545   324 1545 4574 4725

of him to every town and place where he   was about to go.   [2]   He told   them,   "The harvest is
← αὐτοῦ εἰς πᾶσαν πόλιν καὶ τόπον οὗ αὐτὸς → ἤμελλεν → ἔρχεσθαι δὲ → ἔλεγεν πρὸς αὐτοὺς μὲν ὁ θερισμὸς
r.gsm.3 p.a a.asf n.asf cj n.asm adv r.nsm   v.iai.3s   f.pm   cj v.iai.3s p.a r.apm.3 pl d.nsm n.nsm
899   1650 4246 4484 2779 5536 4023 899   3516   2262   1254 3306   4639 899   3525 3836 2546

plentiful, but the workers are few.   Ask   the Lord of the harvest, therefore, to   send out workers into his
πολύς δὲ οἱ ἐργάται ὀλίγοι δεήθητε τοῦ κυρίου → τοῦ θερισμοῦ οὖν ὅπως ἐκβάλῃ ← ἐργάτας εἰς αὐτοῦ
a.nsm cj d.npm n.npm a.npm v.apm.2p d.gsm n.gsm   d.gsm n.gsm   cj   adv v.aas.3s   n.apm   p.a r.gsm.3
4498   1254 3836 2239 3900   1289   3836 3261   3836 2546   4036 3968 1675   2239   1650 899

harvest   field. [3] Go!   I am sending you out like lambs among wolves. [4] Do not take   a purse   or
τὸν θερισμὸν ὑπάγετε ἰδού → ἀποστέλλω ὑμᾶς ← ὡς ἄρνας ἐν μέσῳ λύκων   μὴ βαστάζετε βαλλάντιον μὴ
d.asm n.asm   v.pam.2p j   v.pai.1s r.ap.2   pl n.apm p.d n.dsn n.gpm   pl v.pam.2p   n.asn   pl
3836 2546   5632   2627   690   690   6055 748   1877 3545 3380   3590 1002   1002   3590 964

bag   or sandals; and do not   greet   anyone on the road.   ¶   [5]   "When   you enter   a house, first
πήραν μὴ ὑποδήματα καὶ μηδένα ἀσπάσησθε ← κατὰ τὴν ὁδὸν   δ' εἰς ἣν ἂν → εἰσέλθητε οἰκίαν πρῶτον
n.asf pl n.apn cj a.asm v.ams.2p   p.a d.asf n.asf   cj p.a r.asf pl v.aas.2p n.asf   adv
4385 3590 5687 2779 3594 832   3594 2848 3836 3847   1254 1650 4005 323 1656   3864   4754

say,   'Peace to this house.'   [6]   If a man of peace is   there, your peace   will rest   on him; if
λέγετε εἰρήνη → τούτῳ τῷ οἴκῳ καὶ ἐὰν υἱὸς → εἰρήνης ᾖ ἐκεῖ ὑμῶν ἡ εἰρήνη ἐπαναπαήσεται ἐπ' αὐτόν δὲ εἰ
v.pam.2p n.nsf r.dsm d.dsm n.dsm cj cj   n.nsm   n.gsf   v.pas.3s adv r.gp.2 d.nsf n.nsf v.fpi.3s   p.a r.asm.3 cj cj
3306   1645   3875 4047 3836 3875 2779 1569 5626   1645 1639 1695 7007 3836 1645   2058   2093 899   1254 1623

not,   it will return   to you. [7] Stay in   that house,   eating   and drinking whatever   they give you, for
μή γε → ἀνακάμψει ἐφ' ὑμᾶς δὲ μένετε ἐν αὐτῇ τῇ οἰκίᾳ ἐσθίοντες καὶ πίνοντες τὰ   παρ' αὐτῶν   γὰρ
pl pl   v.fai.3s p.a r.ap.2 cj v.pam.2p p.d r.dsf d.dsf n.dsf pt.pa.npm cj pt.pa.npm d.apn   p.g r.gpm.3   cj
3590 1145 2093   7007   1254 3531 1877 899 3836 3864 2266   2779 4403   3836   4123 899   1142

the worker deserves his   wages.   Do not move   around from house to house.   ¶   [8] "When you
ὁ ἐργάτης ἄξιος αὐτοῦ τοῦ μισθοῦ μὴ μεταβαίνετε ← ἐξ οἰκίας εἰς οἰκίαν   καὶ εἰς ἣν ἂν
d.nsm n.nsm a.nsm r.gsm.3 d.gsm n.gsm pl v.pam.2p   p.g n.gsf p.a n.asf   cj   p.a r.asf pl
3836 2239 545   899   3836 3635   3553 3553   1666 3864 1650 3864   2779 1650 4005 323

enter   a town and are welcomed,   eat   what is set   before you. [9] Heal   the sick   who are
εἰσέρχησθε πόλιν καὶ δέχωνται ὑμᾶς ἐσθίετε τὰ → παρατιθέμενα ← ὑμῖν καὶ θεραπεύετε τοὺς ἀσθενεῖς
v.pms.2p n.asf cj v.pms.3p r.ap.2 v.pam.2p d.apn pt.pp.apn   r.dp.2 cj v.pam.2p d.apm a.apm
1656   4484 2779 1312   7007   2266   3836   4192   7007   2779 2543   3836 822

there   and tell them, 'The kingdom of God   is near   you.' [10] But when   you enter   a town and are
ἐν αὐτῇ καὶ λέγετε αὐτοῖς ἡ βασιλεία → τοῦ θεοῦ ἤγγικεν ἐφ' ὑμᾶς δ' εἰς ἣν ἂν → εἰσέλθητε πόλιν καὶ
p.d r.dsf.3 cj v.pam.2p r.dpm.3 d.nsf n.nsf d.gsm n.gsm v.rai.3s p.a r.ap.2 cj p.a r.asf pl v.aas.2p n.asf cj
1877 899   2779 3306   899   3836 993   3836 2536 1581   2093 7007 1254 1650 4005 323 1656   4484 2779 1312

not welcomed,   go   into its   streets   and say, [11] 'Even the dust   of your town   that sticks
μὴ δέχωνται ὑμᾶς ἐξελθόντες εἰς αὐτῆς τὰς πλατείας εἴπατε καὶ τὸν κονιορτὸν ἐκ ὑμῶν τῆς πόλεως τὸν κολληθέντα
pl v.pms.3p r.ap.2 pt.aa.npm p.a r.gsf.3 d.apf n.apf v.aam.2p cj d.asm n.asm   p.g r.gp.2 d.gsf n.gsf d.asm pt.ap.asm
3590 1312   7007 2002   1650 899 3836 4426   3306   2779 3836 3155   1666 7007 3836 4484   3836 3140

εἰς τὸν οἶκόν μου. [62] εἶπεν δὲ [πρὸς αὐτὸν] ὁ Ἰησοῦς, Οὐδεὶς ἐπιβαλὼν τὴν χεῖρα ἐπ' ἄροτρον καὶ βλέπων εἰς τὰ ὀπίσω εὔθετός ἐστιν τῇ βασιλείᾳ τοῦ θεοῦ.

[10:1] Μετὰ δὲ ταῦτα ἀνέδειξεν ὁ κύριος ἑτέρους ἑβδομήκοντα [δύο], καὶ ἀπέστειλεν αὐτοὺς ἀνὰ δύο [δύο] πρὸ προσώπου αὐτοῦ εἰς πᾶσαν πόλιν καὶ τόπον οὗ ἤμελλεν αὐτὸς ἔρχεσθαι. [2] ἔλεγεν δὲ πρὸς αὐτούς, Ὁ μὲν θερισμὸς πολύς, οἱ δὲ ἐργάται ὀλίγοι· δεήθητε οὖν τοῦ κυρίου τοῦ θερισμοῦ ὅπως ἐργάτας ἐκβάλῃ εἰς τὸν θερισμὸν αὐτοῦ. [3] ὑπάγετε· ἰδοὺ ἀποστέλλω ὑμᾶς ὡς ἄρνας ἐν μέσῳ λύκων. [4] μὴ βαστάζετε βαλλάντιον, μὴ πήραν, μὴ ὑποδήματα, καὶ μηδένα κατὰ τὴν ὁδὸν ἀσπάσησθε. ¶ [5] εἰς ἣν δ' ἂν εἰσέλθητε οἰκίαν, πρῶτον λέγετε, Εἰρήνη τῷ οἴκῳ τούτῳ. [6] καὶ ἐὰν ἐκεῖ ᾖ υἱὸς εἰρήνης, ἐπαναπαήσεται ἐπ' αὐτὸν ἡ εἰρήνη ὑμῶν· εἰ δὲ μή γε, ἐφ' ὑμᾶς ἀνακάμψει. [7] ἐν αὐτῇ δὲ τῇ οἰκίᾳ μένετε ἐσθίοντες καὶ πίνοντες τὰ παρ' αὐτῶν· ἄξιος γὰρ ὁ ἐργάτης τοῦ μισθοῦ αὐτοῦ. μὴ μεταβαίνετε ἐξ οἰκίας εἰς οἰκίαν. ¶ [8] καὶ εἰς ἣν ἂν πόλιν εἰσέρχησθε καὶ δέχωνται ὑμᾶς, ἐσθίετε τὰ παρατιθέμενα ὑμῖν [9] καὶ θεραπεύετε τοὺς ἐν αὐτῇ ἀσθενεῖς καὶ λέγετε αὐτοῖς, Ἤγγικεν ἐφ' ὑμᾶς ἡ βασιλεία τοῦ θεοῦ. [10] εἰς ἣν δ' ἂν πόλιν εἰσέλθητε καὶ μὴ δέχωνται ὑμᾶς, ἐξελθόντες εἰς τὰς πλατείας αὐτῆς εἴπατε, [11] Καὶ τὸν κονιορτὸν τὸν κολληθέντα ἡμῖν ἐκ τῆς πόλεως ὑμῶν εἰς τοὺς πόδας ἀπομασσόμεθα ὑμῖν· πλὴν τοῦτο γινώσκετε ὅτι ἤγγικεν ἡ βασιλεία

to our feet we wipe off against you. Yet be sure of this: The kingdom of God is near.'
ἡμῖν εἰς τοὺς πόδας → ἀπομασσόμεθα ← → ὑμῖν πλὴν → γινώσκετε → τοῦτο ὅτι ἡ βασιλεία → ⌐τοῦ θεοῦ⌐ → ἤγγικεν
r.dp.1   p.a   d.apm   n.apm   v.pmi.1p   r.dp.2   cj   v.pam.2p   r.asn   cj   d.nsf   n.nsf   d.gsm   n.gsm   v.rai.3s
7005   1650   3836   4546   669   7007   4440   1182   4047   4022   3836   993   3836   2536   1581

12 I tell you, it will be more bearable on that day for Sodom than for that town. ¶ **13** "Woe to
→ λέγω ὑμῖν, ὅτι → → ἔσται → ἀνεκτότερον ἐν ἐκείνῃ τῇ ἡμέρᾳ⌐ → Σοδόμοις ἢ → ἐκείνῃ ⌐τῇ πόλει⌐ Οὐαί →
v.pai.1s   r.dp.2   cj   v.fmi.3s   a.nsn.c   p.d   r.dsf   d.dsf   n.dsf   n.dpn   cj   r.dsf   d.dsf   n.dsf   j
3306   7007   4022   1639   445   1877   1697   3836   2465   5047   2445   4484   1697   3836   4484   4026

you, Korazin! Woe to you, Bethsaida! For if the miracles that were performed in you had been performed in
σοι Χοραζίν οὐαί → σοι Βηθσαϊδά ὅτι εἰ αἱ δυνάμεις αἱ → γενόμεναι ἐν ὑμῖν → ἐγενήθησαν ἐν
r.ds.2   n.vsf   j   r.ds.2   n.vsf   cj   cj   d.npf   n.npf   d.npf   pt.am.npf   p.d   r.dp.2   v.api.3p   p.d
5148   5960   4026   5148   1034   4022   1623   3836   1539   3836   1181   1877   7007   1181   1877

Tyre and Sidon, they would have repented long ago, sitting in sackcloth and ashes. **14** But it will be more
Τύρῳ καὶ Σιδῶνι → ἂν → μετενόησαν πάλαι ← καθήμενοι ἐν σάκκῳ καὶ σποδῷ πλὴν → → ἔσται →
n.dsf   cj   n.dsf   pl   v.aai.3p   adv   pt.pm.npm   p.d   n.dsm   cj   n.dsf   cj   v.fmi.3s
5602   2779   4972   3566   323   3566   4093   2764   1877   4884   2779   5075   4440   1639

bearable for Tyre and Sidon at the judgment than for you. **15** And you, Capernaum, will you be lifted up to the
ἀνεκτότερον → Τύρῳ καὶ Σιδῶνι ἐν τῇ κρίσει ἢ → ὑμῖν καὶ σὺ Καφαρναούμ → → → ὑψωθήσῃ ← ἕως
a.nsn.c   n.dsf   cj   n.dsf   p.d   d.dsf   n.dsf   pl   r.dp.2   cj   r.ns.2   n.vsf   v.fpi.2s   p.g
445   5602   2779   4972   1877   3836   3213   2445   7007   2779   5148   3019   5738   2401

skies? No, you will go down to the depths. ¶ **16** "He who listens to you listens to me; he who
οὐρανοῦ μὴ → καταβήσῃ ← ἕως τοῦ ᾅδου Ὁ ← ἀκούων ← ὑμῶν ἀκούει ← ἐμοῦ καὶ ὁ ←
n.gsm   pl   v.fmi.2s   p.g   d.gsm   n.gsm   d.nsm   pt.pa.nsm   r.gp.2   v.pai.3s   r.gs.1   cj   d.nsm
4041   3590   2849   2401   3836   87   3836   201   7007   201   1609   2779   3836

rejects you rejects me; but he who rejects me rejects him who sent me." ¶ **17** The seventy-two
ἀθετῶν ὑμᾶς ἀθετεῖ ἐμὲ δὲ ὁ ← ἀθετῶν ἐμὲ ἀθετεῖ τὸν ἀποστείλαντά με → δὲ οἱ ⌐ἑβδομήκοντα δύο⌐
pt.pa.nsm   r.ap.2   v.pai.3s   r.as.1   cj   d.nsm   pt.pa.nsm   r.as.1   v.pai.3s   d.asm   pt.aa.asm   r.as.1   cj   d.npm   a.npm   a.npm
119   7007   119   1609   1254   3836   119   1609   119   3836   690   1609   1254   3836   1573   1545

returned with joy and said, "Lord, even the demons submit to us in your name." **18** He replied,
Ὑπέστρεψαν μετὰ χαρᾶς λέγοντες κύριε καὶ τὰ δαιμόνια ὑποτάσσεται → ἡμῖν ἐν σου ⌐τῷ ὀνόματι⌐ δὲ → εἶπεν
v.aai.3p   p.g   n.gsf   pt.pa.npm   n.vsm   adv   d.npn   n.npn   v.ppi.3s   r.dp.1   p.d   r.gs.2   d.dsn   n.dsn   cj   v.aai.3s
5715   3552   5915   3306   3261   2779   3836   1228   5718   7005   1877   5148   3836   3950   1254   3306

"I saw Satan fall like lightning from heaven. **19** I have given you authority to trample
αὐτοῖς → ἐθεώρουν ⌐τὸν σατανᾶν⌐ πεσόντα ὡς ἀστραπὴν ἐκ ⌐τοῦ οὐρανοῦ⌐ ἰδοὺ → → δέδωκα ὑμῖν ⌐τὴν ἐξουσίαν⌐ → ⌐τοῦ πατεῖν⌐
r.dpm.3   v.iai.1s   d.asm   n.asm   pt.aa.asm   cj   n.asf   p.g   d.gsm   n.gsm   j   v.rai.1s   r.dp.2   d.asf   n.asf   d.gsm   f.pa
899   2555   3836   4928   4406   6055   847   1666   3836   4041   2627   1443   7007   3836   2026   3836   4251

on snakes and scorpions and to overcome all the power of the enemy; nothing will harm you.
ἐπάνω ὄφεων καὶ σκορπίων καὶ ἐπὶ πᾶσαν τὴν δύναμιν → τοῦ ἐχθροῦ καὶ οὐδὲν οὐ μὴ⌐ → ἀδικήσῃ ὑμᾶς
p.g   n.gpm   cj   n.gpm   cj   p.a   a.asf   d.asf   n.asf   d.gsm   A.gsm   cj   a.nsn   pl   pl   v.aas.3s   r.ap.2
2062   4058   2779   5026   2779   2093   4246   3836   1539   3836   2398   2779   4029   4024   3590   92   7007

20 However, do not rejoice that the spirits submit to you, but rejoice that your names are
πλὴν →⌐ μὴ χαίρετε ἐν τούτῳ ὅτι τὰ πνεύματα ὑποτάσσεται → ὑμῖν δὲ χαίρετε ὅτι ὑμῶν ⌐τὰ ὀνόματα⌐ →
cj   pl   v.pam.2p   p.d   r.dsn   cj   d.npn   n.npn   v.ppi.3s   r.dp.2   cj   v.pam.2p   cj   r.gp.2   d.npn   n.npn
4440   5897   3590   5897   1877   4047   4022   3836   4460   5718   7007   1254   5897   4022   3836   3950

written in heaven." ¶ **21** At that time Jesus, full of joy through the Holy Spirit, said,
ἐγγέγραπται ἐν ⌐τοῖς οὐρανοῖς⌐ Ἐν αὐτῇ ⌐τῇ ὥρᾳ⌐ → ἠγαλλιάσατο ἐν τῷ ⌐τῷ ἁγίῳ⌐ πνεύματι καὶ εἶπεν
v.rpi.3s   p.d   d.dpm   n.dpm   p.d   r.dsf   d.dsf   n.dsf   v.ami.3s   p.d   d.dsn   d.dsn   a.dsn   n.dsn   cj   v.aai.3s
1582   1877   3836   4041   1877   899   3836   6052   22   1877   3836   3836   41   4460   2779   3306

"I praise you, Father, Lord of heaven and earth, because you have hidden these things from the wise
→ ἐξομολογοῦμαι σοι πάτερ κύριε ⌐τοῦ οὐρανοῦ⌐ καὶ ⌐τῆς γῆς⌐ ὅτι → ἀπέκρυψας ταῦτα ← ἀπὸ σοφῶν
v.pmi.1s   r.ds.2   n.vsm   n.vsm   d.gsm   n.gsm   cj   d.gsf   n.gsf   cj   v.aai.2s   r.apn   p.g   a.gpm
2018   5148   4252   3261   3836   4041   2779   3836   1178   4022   648   4047   608   5055

and learned, and revealed them to little children. Yes, Father, for this was your good pleasure.
καὶ συνετῶν καὶ ἀπεκάλυψας αὐτὰ → νηπίοις ναὶ ὁ πατήρ, ὅτι οὕτως ἐγένετο ἔμπροσθεν σου εὐδοκία →
cj   a.gpm   cj   v.aai.2s   r.apn.3   n.dpm   pl   d.vsm   n.vsm   cj   adv   v.ami.3s   p.g   r.gs.2   n.nsf
2779   5305   2779   636   899   3758   3721   3836   4252   4022   4048   1181   1869   5148   2306

τοῦ θεοῦ. **12** λέγω ὑμῖν ὅτι Σοδόμοις ἐν τῇ ἡμέρᾳ ἐκείνῃ ἀνεκτότερον ἔσται ἢ τῇ πόλει ἐκείνῃ. ¶ **13** Οὐαί σοι, Χοραζίν, οὐαί σοι, Βηθσαϊδά· ὅτι εἰ ἐν Τύρῳ καὶ Σιδῶνι ἐγενήθησαν αἱ δυνάμεις αἱ γενόμεναι ἐν ὑμῖν, πάλαι ἂν ἐν σάκκῳ καὶ σποδῷ καθήμενοι μετενόησαν. **14** πλὴν Τύρῳ καὶ Σιδῶνι ἀνεκτότερον ἔσται ἐν τῇ κρίσει ἢ ὑμῖν. **15** καὶ σύ, Καφαρναούμ, μὴ ἕως οὐρανοῦ ὑψωθήσῃ; ἕως τοῦ ᾅδου καταβήσῃ. ¶ **16** Ὁ ἀκούων ὑμῶν ἐμοῦ ἀκούει, καὶ ὁ ἀθετῶν ὑμᾶς ἐμὲ ἀθετεῖ· ὁ δὲ ἐμὲ ἀθετῶν ἀθετεῖ τὸν ἀποστείλαντά με. ¶ **17** Ὑπέστρεψαν δὲ οἱ ἑβδομήκοντα [δύο] μετὰ χαρᾶς λέγοντες, Κύριε, καὶ τὰ δαιμόνια ὑποτάσσεται ἡμῖν ἐν τῷ ὀνόματί σου. **18** εἶπεν δὲ αὐτοῖς, Ἐθεώρουν τὸν Σατανᾶν ὡς ἀστραπὴν ἐκ τοῦ οὐρανοῦ πεσόντα. **19** ἰδοὺ δέδωκα ὑμῖν τὴν ἐξουσίαν τοῦ πατεῖν ἐπάνω ὄφεων καὶ σκορπίων, καὶ ἐπὶ πᾶσαν τὴν δύναμιν τοῦ ἐχθροῦ, καὶ οὐδὲν ὑμᾶς οὐ μὴ ἀδικήσῃ. **20** πλὴν ἐν τούτῳ μὴ χαίρετε ὅτι τὰ πνεύματα ὑμῖν ὑποτάσσεται, χαίρετε δὲ ὅτι τὰ ὀνόματα ὑμῶν ἐγγέγραπται ἐν τοῖς οὐρανοῖς. ¶ **21** Ἐν αὐτῇ τῇ ὥρᾳ ἠγαλλιάσατο [ἐν] τῷ πνεύματι τῷ ἁγίῳ καὶ εἶπεν, Ἐξομολογοῦμαί σοι, πάτερ, κύριε τοῦ οὐρανοῦ καὶ τῆς γῆς, ὅτι ἀπέκρυψας ταῦτα ἀπὸ σοφῶν καὶ συνετῶν καὶ ἀπεκάλυψας αὐτὰ νηπίοις· ναὶ ὁ πατήρ, ὅτι οὕτως εὐδοκία ἐγένετο ἔμπροσθέν

22 "All things have been committed to me by my Father. No one knows who the Son is except the
πάντα ← → → παρεδόθη → μοι ὑπό μου ⌐τοῦ πατρός⌐ καὶ → οὐδεὶς γινώσκει τίς ὁ υἱός ἐστιν εἰ μὴ ὁ
a.npn v.api.3s r.ds.1 p.g r.gs.1 d.gsm n.gsm cj a.nsm v.pai.3s r.nsm d.nsm n.nsm v.pai.3s cj pl d.nsm
4246 4140 1609 5679 1609 3836 4252 2779 4029 1182 5515 3836 5626 1639 1623 3590 3836

Father, and no one knows who the Father is except the Son and those to whom the Son chooses to
πατήρ καὶ → → τίς ὁ πατήρ ἐστιν εἰ μὴ ὁ υἱός καὶ → ᾧ ἐὰν ὁ υἱὸς βούληται →
n.nsm cj r.nsm d.nsm n.nsm v.pai.3s cj pl d.nsm n.nsm cj r.dsm pl d.nsm n.nsm v.pms.3s
4252 2779 5515 3836 4252 1639 1623 3590 3836 5626 2779 4005 1569 3836 5626 1089

reveal him." ¶ **23** Then he turned to his disciples and said privately, "Blessed are the eyes that
ἀποκαλύψαι Καὶ → στραφεὶς πρὸς τοὺς μαθητὰς εἶπεν κατ᾽ ἰδίαν μακάριοι οἱ ὀφθαλμοὶ οἱ
f.aa cj pt.ap.nsm p.a d.apm n.apm v.aai.3s p.a a.asf a.npm d.npm n.npm d.npm
636 2779 5138 4639 3836 3412 3306 2848 2625 3421 3836 4057 3836

see what you see. **24** For I tell you that many prophets and kings wanted to see what you see but did
βλέποντες ἃ → βλέπετε γὰρ → λέγω ὑμῖν ὅτι πολλοὶ προφῆται καὶ βασιλεῖς ἠθέλησαν → ἰδεῖν ἃ ὑμεῖς βλέπετε καὶ →
pt.pa.npm r.apn v.pai.2p cj v.pai.1s r.dp.2 cj a.npm n.npm cj n.npm v.aai.3p f.aa r.apn r.np.2 v.pai.2p cj
1063 4005 1063 1142 3306 7007 4022 4498 4737 2779 995 2527 1625 4005 7007 1063 2779 1625

not see it, and to hear what you hear but did not hear it."
οὐκ εἶδαν καὶ → ἀκοῦσαι ἃ → ἀκούετε καὶ → οὐκ ἤκουσαν
pl v.aai.3p cj f.aa r.apn v.pai.2p cj pl v.aai.3p
4024 1625 2779 201 4005 201 2779 201 4024 201

The Parable of the Good Samaritan

10:25 On one occasion an expert in the law stood up to test Jesus. "Teacher," he asked, "what must I
Καὶ ἰδοὺ τις → → → νομικός ἀνέστη ← ἐκπειράζων αὐτὸν διδάσκαλε → λέγων τί
cj j r.nsm n.nsm v.aai.3s pt.pa.nsm r.asm.3 n.vsm pt.pa.nsm r.asn
2779 2627 5516 3788 482 1733 899 1437 3306 5515

do to inherit eternal life?" **26** "What is written in the Law?" he replied. "How do you
ποιήσας → κληρονομήσω αἰώνιον ζωήν δὲ τί → γέγραπται ἐν τῷ νόμῳ ὁ εἶπεν πρὸς αὐτόν πῶς →
pt.aa.nsm v.fai.1s a.asf n.asf cj r.nsn v.rpi.3s p.d d.dsm n.dsm d.nsm v.aai.3s p.a r.asm.3 adv
4472 3099 173 2437 1254 5515 1211 1877 3836 3795 3836 3306 4639 899 4802

read it?" **27** He answered: "Love the Lord your God with all your heart and with all
ἀναγινώσκεις δὲ ὁ ἀποκριθεὶς εἶπεν ἀγαπήσεις κύριον σου τὸν θεόν ἐξ ὅλης σου ⌐τῆς καρδίας⌐ καὶ ἐν ὅλῃ
v.pai.2s cj d.nsm pt.ap.nsm v.aai.3s v.fai.2s n.asm r.gs.2 d.asm n.asm p.g a.gsf r.gs.2 d.gsf n.gsf cj p.d a.dsf
336 1254 3836 646 3306 26 3261 5148 3836 2536 1666 3910 5148 3836 2840 2779 1877 3910

your soul and with all your strength and with all your mind'; and, 'Love your neighbor as yourself.'"
σου ⌐τῇ ψυχῇ⌐ καὶ ἐν ὅλῃ σου ⌐τῇ ἰσχύϊ⌐ καὶ ἐν ὅλῃ σου ⌐τῇ διανοίᾳ⌐ καὶ σου ⌐τὸν πλησίον⌐ ὡς σεαυτόν
r.gs.2 d.dsf n.dsf cj p.d a.dsf r.gs.2 d.dsf n.dsf cj p.d a.dsf r.gs.2 d.dsf n.dsf cj r.gs.2 d.asm adv r.asm.2
5148 3836 6034 2779 1877 3910 5148 3836 2709 2779 1877 3910 5148 3836 1379 2779 5148 3836 4446 6055 4932

28 "You have answered correctly," Jesus replied. "Do this and you will live." ¶ **29** But he wanted to
δὲ → → ἀπεκρίθης ὀρθῶς εἶπεν αὐτῷ ποίει τοῦτο καὶ → ζήσῃ δὲ ὁ θέλων
cj v.api.2s adv v.aai.3s r.dsm.3 v.pam.2s r.asn cj v.fmi.2s cj d.nsm pt.pa.nsm
1254 646 3987 3306 899 4472 4047 2779 2409 1254 3836 2527

justify himself, so he asked Jesus, "And who is my neighbor?" **30** In reply Jesus said: "A
δικαιῶσαι ἑαυτὸν → εἶπεν πρὸς τὸν Ἰησοῦν καὶ τίς ἐστίν μου πλησίον Ὑπολαβὼν ὁ Ἰησοῦς εἶπεν τις
f.aa r.asm.3 v.aai.3s p.a d.asm n.asm cj r.nsm v.pai.3s r.gs.1 adv pt.aa.nsm d.nsm n.nsm v.aai.3s r.nsm
1467 1571 3306 4639 3836 2652 2779 5515 1639 1609 4446 5696 3836 2652 3306 5516

man was going down from Jerusalem to Jericho, when he fell into the hands of robbers. They
ἄνθρωπος → κατέβαινεν ← ἀπὸ Ἰερουσαλὴμ εἰς Ἰεριχὼ καὶ → περιέπεσεν ← λῃσταῖς οἳ καὶ
n.nsm v.iai.3s p.g n.asf p.a n.asf cj v.aai.3s n.dpm r.npm adv
476 2849 608 2647 1650 2637 2779 4346 3334 4005 2779

stripped him of his clothes, beat him and went away, leaving him half dead. **31** A priest
ἐκδύσαντες αὐτὸν ← καὶ ⌐πληγὰς ἐπιθέντες⌐ ἀπῆλθον ← ἀφέντες ἡμιθανῆ δὲ τις ἱερεύς
pt.aa.npm r.asm.3 cj n.apf pt.aa.npm v.aai.3p pt.aa.npm a.asm cj r.nsm n.nsm
1694 899 1694 1694 1694 2779 4435 2202 599 918 2467 1254 5516 2636

happened to be going down the same road, and when he saw the man, he passed by on the
⌐κατὰ συγκυρίαν⌐ → κατέβαινεν ἐν τῇ ἐκείνῃ ὁδῷ καὶ → ἰδὼν αὐτὸν ἀντιπαρῆλθεν ← ←
p.a n.asf v.iai.3s p.d d.dsf r.dsf n.dsf cj pt.aa.nsm r.asm.3 v.aai.3s
2848 5175 2849 1877 3836 1697 3847 2779 1625 899 524

σου. **22** Πάντα μοι παρεδόθη ὑπὸ τοῦ πατρός μου, καὶ οὐδεὶς γινώσκει τίς ἐστιν ὁ υἱὸς εἰ μὴ ὁ πατήρ, καὶ τίς ἐστιν ὁ πατὴρ εἰ μὴ ὁ υἱὸς καὶ ᾧ ἐὰν βούληται ὁ υἱὸς ἀποκαλύψαι. ¶ **23** Καὶ στραφεὶς πρὸς τοὺς μαθητὰς κατ᾽ ἰδίαν εἶπεν, Μακάριοι οἱ ὀφθαλμοὶ οἱ βλέποντες ἃ βλέπετε. **24** λέγω γὰρ ὑμῖν ὅτι πολλοὶ προφῆται καὶ βασιλεῖς ἠθέλησαν ἰδεῖν ἃ ὑμεῖς βλέπετε καὶ οὐκ εἶδαν, καὶ ἀκοῦσαι ἃ ἀκούετε καὶ οὐκ ἤκουσαν.

10:25 Καὶ ἰδοὺ νομικός τις ἀνέστη ἐκπειράζων αὐτὸν λέγων, Διδάσκαλε, τί ποιήσας ζωὴν αἰώνιον κληρονομήσω; **26** ὁ δὲ εἶπεν πρὸς αὐτόν, Ἐν τῷ νόμῳ τί γέγραπται; πῶς ἀναγινώσκεις; **27** ὁ δὲ ἀποκριθεὶς εἶπεν, Ἀγαπήσεις κύριον τὸν θεόν σου ἐξ ὅλης [τῆς] καρδίας σου καὶ ἐν ὅλῃ τῇ ψυχῇ σου καὶ ἐν ὅλῃ τῇ ἰσχύϊ σου καὶ ἐν ὅλῃ τῇ διανοίᾳ σου, καὶ τὸν πλησίον σου ὡς σεαυτόν. **28** εἶπεν δὲ αὐτῷ, Ὀρθῶς ἀπεκρίθης· τοῦτο ποίει καὶ ζήσῃ. ¶ **29** ὁ δὲ θέλων δικαιῶσαι ἑαυτὸν εἶπεν πρὸς τὸν Ἰησοῦν, Καὶ τίς ἐστίν μου πλησίον; **30** ὑπολαβὼν ὁ Ἰησοῦς εἶπεν, Ἄνθρωπός τις κατέβαινεν ἀπὸ Ἰερουσαλὴμ εἰς Ἰεριχὼ καὶ λῃσταῖς περιέπεσεν, οἳ καὶ ἐκδύσαντες αὐτὸν καὶ πληγὰς ἐπιθέντες ἀπῆλθον ἀφέντες ἡμιθανῆ. **31** κατὰ συγκυρίαν δὲ ἱερεύς τις κατέβαινεν ἐν τῇ ὁδῷ ἐκείνῃ καὶ ἰδὼν αὐτὸν ἀντιπαρῆλθεν· **32** ὁμοίως δὲ καὶ Λευίτης [γενόμενος] κατὰ τὸν τόπον ἐλθὼν καὶ

other side. **32** So too, a Levite, when he came to the place and saw him, passed by on the
δὲ καὶ ὁμοίως Λευίτης [γενόμενος] → ἐλθὼν κατὰ τὸν τόπον καὶ ἰδὼν ἀντιπαρῆλθεν ←
cj adv adv n.nsm pt.am.nsm pt.aa.nsm p.a d.asm n.asm cj pt.aa.nsm v.aai.3s
1254 2779 3931 3324 1181 2262 2848 3836 5536 2779 1625 524

other side. **33** But a Samaritan, as he traveled, came *where* *the man was;* and when he saw him, he took
δέ τις Σαμαρίτης → ὁδεύων ἦλθεν ‹κατ᾽ αὐτόν› καὶ → → ἰδὼν → →
cj r.nsm n.nsm pt.pa.nsm v.aai.3s p.a r.asm.3 cj pt.aa.nsm
1254 5516 4901 3841 2262 2848 899 2779 1625

pity on him. **34** He went to him and bandaged his wounds, pouring on oil and wine. Then he
ἐσπλαγχνίσθη καὶ → προσελθὼν ← κατέδησεν αὐτοῦ ‹τὰ τραύματα› ἐπιχέων ← ἔλαιον καὶ οἶνον δὲ →
v.api.3s cj pt.aa.nsm v.aai.3s r.gsm.3 d.apn n.apn pt.pa.nsm n.asn cj n.asm cj
5072 2779 4665 2866 899 3836 5546 2219 1778 2779 3885 1254

put the man on his own donkey, took him to an inn and took care of him. **35** The next
ἐπιβιβάσας αὐτὸν ἐπὶ τὸ ἴδιον κτῆνος ἤγαγεν αὐτὸν εἰς πανδοχεῖον καὶ → ἐπεμελήθη ← αὐτοῦ καὶ ἐπὶ τὴν αὔριον
pt.aa.nsm r.asm.3 p.a d.asn a.asn n.asn v.aai.3s r.asm.3 p.a n.asn cj v.api.3s r.gsm.3 cj p.a d.asf adv
2097 899 2093 3836 2625 3229 72 899 1650 4106 2779 2150 899 2779 2093 3836 892

day he took out two silver coins and gave them to the innkeeper. 'Look after him,' he said, 'and when
← → ἐκβαλὼν δύο → δηνάρια ἔδωκεν → τῷ πανδοχεῖ καὶ ἐπιμελήθητι ← αὐτοῦ εἶπεν καὶ ἐν
pt.aa.nsm a.apn n.apn v.aai.3s d.dsm n.dsm cj v.amp.2s r.gsm.3 v.aai.3s cj p.d
1675 1545 1324 1443 3836 4107 2779 2150 899 3306 2779 1877

I return, I will reimburse you for any extra expense you may have.' **36** "Which of these
με ‹τῷ ἐπανέρχεσθαι› ἐγὼ → ἀποδώσω σοι ‹ὅ τι ἂν› προσδαπανήσῃς ← τίς → τούτων
r.as.1 d.dsn f.pm r.ns.1 v.fai.1s r.ds.2 r.asn r.asn pl v.aas.2s r.nsm r.gpm
1609 3836 2059 1609 625 5148 4005 5516 323 4655 5515 4047

three do you think was a neighbor to the man who fell into the hands of robbers?" **37** The expert in
‹τῶν τριῶν› → σοι δοκεῖ γεγονέναι πλησίον τοῦ ← → ἐμπεσόντος εἰς τοὺς λῃστάς δὲ ὁ
d.gpm a.gpm r.ds.2 v.pai.3s f.ra adv d.gsm pt.aa.gsm p.a d.apm n.apm cj d.nsm
3836 5552 5148 1506 1181 4446 3836 1860 1650 3836 3334 1254 3836

the law replied, "The one who had mercy on him." Jesus told him, "Go and do likewise."
εἶπεν ὁ → ποιήσας ‹τὸ ἔλεος› μετ᾽ αὐτοῦ δὲ ὁ Ἰησοῦς εἶπεν αὐτῷ πορεύου καὶ σὺ ποίει ὁμοίως
v.aai.3s d.nsm pt.aa.nsm d.asn n.asn p.g r.gsm.3 cj d.nsm n.nsm v.aai.3s r.dsm.3 v.pmm.2s cj r.ns.2 v.pam.2s adv
3306 3836 4472 3836 1799 3552 899 1254 3836 2652 3306 899 4513 2779 5148 4472 3931

At the Home of Martha and Mary

10:38 As Jesus and his disciples were on their way, he came to a village where a woman
δὲ Ἐν αὐτοὺς ← ‹τῷ πορεύεσθαι› αὐτὸς εἰσῆλθεν εἰς τινὰ κώμην δέ τις γυνή
cj p.d r.apm.3 d.dsn f.pm r.nsm v.aai.3s p.a r.asf n.asf cj r.nsf n.nsf
1254 1877 899 3836 4513 899 1656 1650 5516 3267 1254 5516 1222

named Martha opened her home to him. **39** She had a sister called Mary, who sat at the
ὀνόματι Μάρθα ὑπεδέξατο ← ← αὐτόν καὶ τῇδε ἦν ἀδελφὴ καλουμένη Μαριάμ ἣ καὶ παρακαθεσθεῖσα πρὸς τοὺς
n.dsn n.nsf v.ami.3s r.asm.3 cj r.dsf v.iai.3s n.nsf pt.pp.nsf n.nsf r.nsf cj pt.ap.nsf p.a d.apm
3950 3450 5685 899 2779 3840 1639 80 2813 3452 4005 2779 4149 4639 3836

Lord's feet listening to what he said. **40** But Martha was distracted by all the preparations that had to
‹τοῦ κυρίου› πόδας ἤκουεν τὸν αὐτοῦ λόγον δὲ ἡ Μάρθα → περιεσπᾶτο περὶ πολλὴν διακονίαν
d.gsm n.gsm n.apm v.iai.3s d.asm r.gsm.3 n.asm cj d.nsf n.nsf v.ipi.3s p.a a.asf n.asf
3836 3261 4546 201 3836 899 3364 1254 3836 3450 4352 4309 4498 1355

be made. She came to him and asked, "Lord, don't you care that my sister has left me to do the
δὲ → ἐπιστᾶσα ← εἶπεν κύριε οὐ σοι μέλει ὅτι μου ἡ ἀδελφή → κατέλιπεν με → → →
cj pt.aa.nsf v.aai.3s n.vsm pl r.ds.2 v.pai.3s cj r.gs.1 d.nsf n.nsf v.aai.3s r.as.1
1254 2392 3306 3261 4024 5148 3508 4022 1609 3836 80 2901 1609

work by myself? Tell her to help me!" **41** "Martha, Martha," the Lord answered, "you
διακονεῖν → μόνην οὖν εἰπὲ αὐτῇ ἵνα συναντιλάβηταί μοι δὲ Μάρθα Μάρθα ὁ κύριος ἀποκριθεὶς εἶπεν αὐτῇ →
f.pa a.asf cj v.aam.2s r.dsf.3 cj v.ams.3s r.ds.1 cj n.vsf n.vsf d.nsm n.nsm pt.ap.nsm v.aai.3s r.dsf.3
1354 3668 4036 3306 899 2671 5269 1609 1254 3450 3450 3836 3261 646 3306 899

are worried and upset about many things, **42** but only one thing is needed. Mary has chosen what is
→ μεριμνᾷς καὶ θορυβάζῃ περὶ πολλά ← δέ → ἑνός ← ἐστιν χρεία γὰρ Μαριὰμ → ἐξελέξατο μερίδα →
v.pai.2s cj v.ppi.2s p.a a.apn cj a.gsn v.pai.3s n.nsf cj n.nsf v.ami.3s n.asf
3534 2779 2571 4309 4498 1254 1651 1639 5970 1142 3452 1721 3535

ἰδὼν ἀντιπαρῆλθεν. **33** Σαμαρίτης δέ τις ὁδεύων ἦλθεν κατ᾽ αὐτὸν καὶ ἰδὼν ἐσπλαγχνίσθη, **34** καὶ προσελθὼν κατέδησεν τὰ τραύματα αὐτοῦ ἐπιχέων ἔλαιον καὶ οἶνον, ἐπιβιβάσας δὲ αὐτὸν ἐπὶ τὸ ἴδιον κτῆνος ἤγαγεν αὐτὸν εἰς πανδοχεῖον καὶ ἐπεμελήθη αὐτοῦ. **35** καὶ ἐπὶ τὴν αὔριον ἐκβαλὼν ἔδωκεν δύο δηνάρια τῷ πανδοχεῖ καὶ εἶπεν, Ἐπιμελήθητι αὐτοῦ, καὶ ὅ τι ἂν προσδαπανήσῃς ἐγὼ ἐν τῷ ἐπανέρχεσθαί με ἀποδώσω σοι. **36** τίς τούτων τῶν τριῶν πλησίον δοκεῖ σοι γεγονέναι τοῦ ἐμπεσόντος εἰς τοὺς λῃστάς; **37** ὁ δὲ εἶπεν, Ὁ ποιήσας τὸ ἔλεος μετ᾽ αὐτοῦ. εἶπεν δὲ αὐτῷ ὁ Ἰησοῦς, Πορεύου καὶ σὺ ποίει ὁμοίως.

10:38 Ἐν δὲ τῷ πορεύεσθαι αὐτοὺς αὐτὸς εἰσῆλθεν εἰς κώμην τινά· γυνὴ δέ τις ὀνόματι Μάρθα ὑπεδέξατο αὐτόν. **39** καὶ τῇδε ἦν ἀδελφὴ καλουμένη Μαριάμ, [ἣ] καὶ παρακαθεσθεῖσα πρὸς τοὺς πόδας τοῦ κυρίου ἤκουεν τὸν λόγον αὐτοῦ. **40** ἡ δὲ Μάρθα περιεσπᾶτο περὶ πολλὴν διακονίαν· ἐπιστᾶσα δὲ εἶπεν, Κύριε, οὐ μέλει σοι ὅτι ἡ ἀδελφή μου μόνην με κατέλιπεν διακονεῖν; εἰπὲ οὖν αὐτῇ ἵνα μοι συναντιλάβηται. **41** ἀποκριθεὶς δὲ εἶπεν αὐτῇ ὁ κύριος, Μάρθα Μάρθα, μεριμνᾷς καὶ θορυβάζῃ περὶ πολλά,

better,   and it   will not be taken   away from her."
⸤τὴν ἀγαθὴν⸥   ἥτις →   οὐκ →   ἀφαιρεθήσεται ←   ←   αὐτῆς
d.asf a.asf   r.nsf   pl   v.fpi.3s   r.gsf.3
3836 19   4015 904 4024 904   899

Jesus' Teaching on Prayer

11:1 One   day Jesus was   praying   in a certain place. When he finished, one of his
⸤Καὶ ἐγένετο⸥   αὐτὸν ⸤ἐν τῷ εἶναι⸥ προσευχόμενον ἐν   τινὶ   τόπῳ ὡς   → ἐπαύσατο τις ↱ αὐτοῦ
cj   v.ami.3s   r.asm.3   p.d d.dsn f.pa   pt.pm.asm   p.d   r.dsn   n.dsm cj   v.ami.3s   r.nsm   r.gsm.3
2779 1181   899   1877 3836 1639   4667   1877 5516   5536 6055   4264   5516 3412 899

disciples   said to   him, "Lord, teach   us   to pray,   just as   John   taught his disciples."   ¶
⸤τῶν μαθητῶν⸥ εἶπεν πρὸς αὐτὸν κύριε δίδαξον ἡμᾶς → προσεύχεσθαι καθὼς ← καὶ Ἰωάννης ἐδίδαξεν αὐτοῦ ⸤τοὺς μαθητὰς⸥
d.gpm n.gpm   v.aai.3s p.a r.asm.3 n.vsm v.aam.2s r.ap.1   f.pm   cj   adv r.nsm   v.aai.3s r.gsm.3 d.apm n.apm
3836 3412   3306 4639 899 3261 1438   7005   4667   2777   2779 2722   1438   899 3836 3412

2 He said to them, "When you pray,   say: "'Father, hallowed be your name,   your kingdom   come.
δὲ → εἶπεν   αὐτοῖς ὅταν →   προσεύχησθε λέγετε Πάτερ   ἁγιασθήτω → σου ⸤τὸ ὄνομα⸥ σου ⸤ἡ βασιλεία⸥ ἐλθέτω
cj → v.aai.3s   r.dpm.3 cj →   v.pms.2p   v.pam.2p n.vsm   v.apm.3s   r.gs.2 d.nsn n.nsn   r.gs.2 d.nsf n.nsf   v.aam.3s
1254 3306   899 4020   4667   3306 4252   39   5148 3836 3950   5148 3836 993   2262

3 Give us   each day   our daily   bread.   **4**   Forgive us   our sins,   for we   also forgive
δίδου ἡμῖν → ⸤τὸ καθ᾽ ἡμέραν⸥ ἡμῶν ⸤τὸν ἐπιούσιον⸥ ⸤τὸν ἄρτον⸥ καὶ ἄφες   ἡμῖν ἡμῶν ⸤τὰς ἁμαρτίας⸥ γὰρ αὐτοὶ καὶ ἀφίομεν
v.pam.2s r.dp.1   d.asn p.a n.asf   r.gp.1 d.asn a.asm   d.asn n.asm   cj   v.aam.2s r.dp.1 r.gp.1 d.apf n.apf   cj   r.npm adv   v.pai.1p
1443 7005   3836 2848 2465   7005 3836 2157   3836 788   2779 918   7005 7005 3836 281   1142 899 2779 918

everyone who sins   against us. And lead   us   not into temptation.'"   ¶   **5** Then he said to   them,
παντὶ →   ὀφείλοντι ←   ἡμῖν καὶ εἰσενέγκῃς ἡμᾶς μὴ εἰς   πειρασμόν   Καὶ →   εἶπεν πρὸς αὐτούς
a.dsm →   pt.pa.dsm   r.dp.1 cj   v.aas.2s   r.ap.1 pl   p.a   n.asm   cj   v.aai.3s p.a   r.apm.3
4246   4053   7005 2779 1662   7005 3590 1650   4280   2779   3306 4639 899

"Suppose one of you has a friend, and he goes   to   him at midnight and says,   'Friend, lend   me three
→ τίς ἐξ ὑμῶν ἕξει   φίλον καὶ → πορεύσεται πρὸς αὐτὸν μεσονυκτίου καὶ εἴπῃ αὐτῷ φίλε   χρῆσον μοι τρεῖς
r.nsm p.g r.gp.2 v.fai.3s   a.asm cj   v.fmi.3s   p.a r.asm.3   n.gsn   cj   v.aas.3s r.dsm.3 n.vsm   v.aam.2s r.ds.1 a.apm
5515 1666 7005 2400   5813 2779   4513   4639 899   3543   2779 3306   899 5813   3079   1609 5552

loaves of bread,   **6** because a friend of mine on a journey has come   to   me, and I have nothing to set
→ ἄρτους   ἐπειδὴ   φίλος → μου ἐξ ὁδοῦ   παρεγένετο πρός με   καὶ → ἔχω ⸤οὐκ ὃ⸥ → παραθήσω
n.apm   cj   a.nsm   r.gs.1 p.g n.gsf   v.ami.3s   p.a r.as.1 cj   v.pai.1s pl   r.asn   v.fai.1s
788   2076   5813   1609 1666 3847   4134   4639 1609 2779   2400 4024 4005   4192

before him.'   ¶   **7** "Then the one inside answers,   'Don't bother   me. The door is   already locked,
← αὐτῷ   κἀκεῖνος ←   ← ἔσωθεν ἀποκριθεὶς εἴπῃ μὴ   ⸤κόπους πάρεχε⸥ μοι ἡ θύρα → ἤδη   κέκλεισται
r.dsm.3   crasis   adv   pt.ap.nsm   v.aas.3s pl   n.apm   v.pam.2s   r.ds.1 d.nsf n.nsf   adv   v.rpi.3s
899   2797   2277   646   3306 3590   3160   4218   1609 3836 2598   3091 2453   3091

and my children   are   with me in bed.   I can't   get   up and give   you anything.'   **8** I tell you,
καὶ μου ⸤τὰ παιδία⸥ εἰσίν μετ᾽ ἐμοῦ εἰς ⸤τὴν κοίτην⸥ → οὐ δύναμαι ἀναστὰς ←   δοῦναι σοι   → λέγω ὑμῖν
cj   r.gs.1 d.npn n.npn   v.pai.3p p.g r.gs.1 p.a d.asf n.asf   → v.ppi.1s pt.aa.nsm ←   f.aa   r.ds.2   v.pai.1s r.dp.2
2779 1609 3836 4086   1639 3552   1609 1650 3836 3130   4024 1538   482   1443   5148   3306 7007

though he will not get   up and give him the bread because he is   his   friend, yet because of the man's
⸤εἰ καὶ⸥ → → οὐ ἀναστὰς ←   δώσει αὐτῷ   διὰ   ⸤τὸ εἶναι⸥ αὐτοῦ φίλον γε διὰ   ← τὴν αὐτοῦ
cj   adv   pl   pt.aa.nsm   v.fai.3s r.dsm.3   p.a   d.asn f.pa   r.gsm.3 a.asm   pl   p.a   d.asf r.gsm.3
1623 2779   4024 482   1443 899   1328   3836 1639   899 5813   1145 1328   3836 899

boldness he will get   up and give him as   much as he needs.   ¶   **9** "So I say to you: Ask   and it will be
ἀναίδειαν → → ἐγερθεὶς ←   δώσει αὐτῷ ὅσων ←   ← χρῄζει   Κἀγὼ → λέγω   ὑμῖν αἰτεῖτε καὶ → →
n.asf   pt.ap.nsm   v.fai.3s r.dsm.3 r.gpn   v.pai.3s   crasis   v.pai.1s r.dp.2 v.pam.2p cj
357   1586   1443 899 4012   5974   2743   3306 7007 160   2779

given   to you; seek and you will find;   knock and the door will be opened   to you.   **10** For everyone who asks
δοθήσεται → ὑμῖν   ζητεῖτε καὶ →   εὑρήσετε κρούετε καὶ   ἀνοιγήσεται → ὑμῖν   γὰρ πᾶς   αἰτῶν
v.fpi.3s → r.dp.2   v.pam.2p cj   v.fai.2p   v.pam.2p cj   v.fpi.3s   r.dp.2   cj   a.nsm   d.nsm pt.pa.nsm
1443   7007   2426 2779   2351   3218 2779   487   7007   1142 4246   3836 160

receives;   he who seeks finds; and to him who knocks, the door will be opened.   ¶   **11**   "Which of you
λαμβάνει καὶ ὁ →   ζητῶν εὑρίσκει καὶ → τῷ   κρούοντι   → ἀνοιγήσεται   δὲ τίνα   ἐξ ὑμῶν
v.pai.3s cj   d.nsm   pt.pa.nsm v.pai.3s cj → d.dsm   pt.pa.dsm   v.fpi.3s   cj   r.asm   p.g r.gp.2
3284 2779 3836   2426 2351 2779   3836   3218   487   1254 5515   1666 7007

---

42 ἑνὸς δέ ἐστιν χρεία· Μαριὰμ γὰρ τὴν ἀγαθὴν μερίδα ἐξελέξατο ἥτις οὐκ ἀφαιρεθήσεται αὐτῆς.

11:1 Καὶ ἐγένετο ἐν τῷ εἶναι αὐτὸν ἐν τόπῳ τινὶ προσευχόμενον, ὡς ἐπαύσατο, εἶπέν τις τῶν μαθητῶν αὐτοῦ πρὸς αὐτόν, Κύριε, δίδαξον ἡμᾶς προσεύχεσθαι, καθὼς καὶ Ἰωάννης ἐδίδαξεν τοὺς μαθητὰς αὐτοῦ. ¶ 2 εἶπεν δὲ αὐτοῖς, Ὅταν προσεύχησθε λέγετε, Πάτερ, ἁγιασθήτω τὸ ὄνομά σου· ἐλθέτω ἡ βασιλεία σου· 3 τὸν ἄρτον ἡμῶν τὸν ἐπιούσιον δίδου ἡμῖν τὸ καθ᾽ ἡμέραν· 4 καὶ ἄφες ἡμῖν τὰς ἁμαρτίας ἡμῶν, καὶ γὰρ αὐτοὶ ἀφίομεν παντὶ ὀφείλοντι ἡμῖν· καὶ μὴ εἰσενέγκῃς ἡμᾶς εἰς πειρασμόν. ¶ 5 Καὶ εἶπεν πρὸς αὐτούς, Τίς ἐξ ὑμῶν ἕξει φίλον καὶ πορεύσεται πρὸς αὐτὸν μεσονυκτίου καὶ εἴπῃ αὐτῷ, Φίλε, χρῆσόν μοι τρεῖς ἄρτους, 6 ἐπειδὴ φίλος μου παρεγένετο ἐξ ὁδοῦ πρός με καὶ οὐκ ἔχω ὃ παραθήσω αὐτῷ· ¶ 7 κἀκεῖνος ἔσωθεν ἀποκριθεὶς εἴπῃ, Μή μοι κόπους πάρεχε· ἤδη ἡ θύρα κέκλεισται καὶ τὰ παιδία μου μετ᾽ ἐμοῦ εἰς τὴν κοίτην εἰσίν· οὐ δύναμαι ἀναστὰς δοῦναί σοι. 8 λέγω ὑμῖν, εἰ καὶ οὐ δώσει αὐτῷ ἀναστὰς διὰ τὸ εἶναι φίλον αὐτοῦ, διά γε τὴν ἀναίδειαν αὐτοῦ ἐγερθεὶς δώσει αὐτῷ ὅσων χρῄζει. ¶ 9 κἀγὼ ὑμῖν λέγω, αἰτεῖτε καὶ δοθήσεται ὑμῖν, ζητεῖτε καὶ εὑρήσετε, κρούετε καὶ ἀνοιγήσεται ὑμῖν· 10 πᾶς γὰρ ὁ αἰτῶν λαμβάνει καὶ ὁ ζητῶν εὑρίσκει καὶ τῷ κρούοντι ἀνοιγ[ήσ]εται. ¶ 11 τίνα δὲ ἐξ ὑμῶν τὸν πατέρα αἰτήσει ὁ υἱὸς

fathers, if your son asks for a fish, will give him a snake instead? **12** Or if he asks for an egg,
ⸯτὸν πατέραⸯ ὁ υἱὸς αἰτήσει ← ἰχθὺν καὶ → ἐπιδώσει αὐτῷ ὄφιν ἀντὶ ἰχθύος ἢ καὶ αἰτήσει ← ᾠόν
d.asm n.asm d.nsm n.nsm v.fai.3s n.asn cj v.fai.3s r.dsm.3 n.asm p.g n.gsm cj adv v.fai.3s n.asn
3836 4252 3836 5626 160 2716 2779 2113 899 4058 505 2716 2445 2779 160 6051

will give him a scorpion? **13** If you then, though you are evil, know how to give good gifts to your
→ ἐπιδώσει αὐτῷ σκορπίον εἰ ὑμεῖς οὖν → → ὑπάρχοντες πονηροὶ οἴδατε ← → διδόναι ἀγαθὰ δόματα → ὑμῶν
v.fai.3s r.dsm.3 n.asm cj r.np.2 cj pt.pa.npm a.npm v.rai.2p f.pa a.apn n.apn r.gp.2
2113 899 5026 1623 7007 4036 5639 4505 3857 1443 19 1517 5451 7007

children, how much more will your Father in heaven give the Holy Spirit to those who ask him!"
ⸯτοῖς τέκνοιςⸯ πόσῳ ← μᾶλλον → ὁ πατὴρ [ὁ] ἐξ οὐρανοῦ δώσει ἅγιον πνεῦμα → τοῖς ← αἰτοῦσιν αὐτόν
d.dpn n.dpn r.dsn adv.c d.nsm n.nsm d.nsm p.g n.gsm v.fai.3s a.asn n.asn d.dpm pt.pa.dpm r.asm.3
3836 5451 4531 3437 1443 3836 4252 3836 1666 4041 1443 41 4460 3836 160 899

Jesus and Beelzebub

11:14 Jesus was driving out a demon that was mute. When the demon left, the man
Καὶ ἦν ἐκβάλλων ← δαιμόνιον καὶ αὐτὸ ἦν κωφόν δὲ ἐγένετο τοῦ δαιμονίου ἐξελθόντος ὁ
cj v.iai.3s pt.pa.nsm n.asn cj r.nsn v.iai.3s a.nsn cj v.ami.3s d.gsn n.gsn pt.aa.gsn d.nsm
2779 1639 1675 1228 2779 899 1639 3273 1254 1181 2002 3836 1228 2002 3836

who had been mute spoke, and the crowd was amazed. **15** But some of them said, "By Beelzebub, the prince of
κωφὸς ἐλάλησεν καὶ οἱ ὄχλοι → ἐθαύμασαν δὲ τινὲς ἐξ αὐτῶν εἶπον ἐν Βεελζεβοὺλ τῷ ἄρχοντι →
a.nsm v.aai.3s cj d.npm n.npm v.aai.3p cj r.npm.3 p.g r.gpm.3 v.aai.3p p.d n.dsm d.dsm n.dsm
3273 3281 2779 3836 4063 2513 1254 5516 1666 899 3306 1877 1015 3836 807

demons, he is driving out demons." **16** Others tested him by asking for a sign from heaven.
ⸯτῶν δαιμονίωνⸯ → → ἐκβάλλει ← ⸯτὰ δαιμόνιαⸯ δὲ ἕτεροι πειράζοντες ἐζήτουν παρ' αὐτοῦ σημεῖον ἐξ οὐρανοῦ
d.gpn n.gpn v.pai.3s d.apn n.apn cj r.npm pt.pa.npm v.iai.3p p.g r.gsm.3 n.asn p.g n.gsm
3836 1228 1675 3836 1228 1254 2283 4279 2426 4123 899 4956 1666 4041

¶ **17** Jesus knew their thoughts and said to them: "Any kingdom divided against itself will be ruined,
δὲ αὐτὸς εἰδὼς αὐτῶν ⸯτὰ διανοήματαⸯ εἶπεν → αὐτοῖς πᾶσα βασιλεία διαμερισθεῖσα ἐφ' ἑαυτὴν → ἐρημοῦται
cj r.nsm pt.ra.nsm r.gpm.3 d.apn n.apn v.aai.3s r.dpm.3 a.nsf n.nsf pt.ap.nsf p.a r.asf.3 v.ppi.3s
1254 899 3857 899 3836 1378 3306 899 4246 993 1374 2093 1571 2246

and a house divided against itself will fall. **18** If Satan is divided against himself, how can his
καὶ οἶκος ἐπὶ οἶκον → πίπτει δὲ εἰ καὶ ὁ σατανᾶς → διεμερίσθη ἐφ' ἑαυτὸν πῶς → αὐτοῦ
cj n.nsm p.a n.asm v.pai.3s cj cj adv d.nsm n.nsm v.api.3s p.a r.asm.3 adv r.gsm.3
2779 3875 2093 3875 4406 1254 1623 2779 3836 4928 1374 2093 1571 4802 2705 899

kingdom stand? I say this because you claim that I drive out demons by Beelzebub. **19** Now if I
ⸯἡ βασιλείαⸯ σταθήσεται ὅτι → λέγετε με ἐκβάλλειν ← ⸯτὰ δαιμόνιαⸯ ἐν Βεελζεβοὺλ δὲ εἰ ἐγὼ
d.nsf n.nsf v.fpi.3s cj v.pai.2p r.as.1 f.pa d.apn n.apn p.d n.dsm cj cj r.ns.1
3836 993 2705 4022 3306 1609 1675 3836 1228 1877 1015 1254 1623 1609

drive out demons by Beelzebub, by whom do your followers drive them out? So then, they will
ἐκβάλλω ← ⸯτὰ δαιμόνιαⸯ ἐν Βεελζεβοὺλ ἐν τίνι → ὑμῶν οἱ υἱοὶ ἐκβάλλουσιν ← ⸯδιὰ τοῦτοⸯ αὐτοὶ
v.pai.1s d.apn n.apn p.d n.dsm p.d r.dsn r.gp.2 d.npm n.npm v.pai.3p p.a r.asn r.npm
1675 3836 1228 1877 1015 1877 5515 7007 3836 5626 1675 1328 4047 899

be your judges. **20** But if I drive out demons by the finger of God, then the kingdom of God has
ἔσονται ὑμῶν κριταὶ δὲ εἰ ἐγὼ ἐκβάλλω ← ⸯτὰ δαιμόνιαⸯ ἐν δακτύλῳ θεοῦ ἄρα ἡ βασιλεία → ⸯτοῦ θεοῦⸯ →
v.fmi.3p r.gp.2 n.npm cj cj r.ns.1 v.pai.1s d.apn n.apn p.d n.dsm n.gsm cj d.nsf n.nsf d.gsm n.gsm
1639 7007 3216 1254 1623 1609 1675 3836 1228 1877 1235 2536 726 3836 993 3836 2536

come to you. ¶ **21** "When a strong man, fully armed, guards his own house, his possessions
ἔφθασεν ἐφ' ὑμᾶς ὅταν ⸯὁ ἰσχυρὸςⸯ → καθωπλισμένος φυλάσσῃ τὴν ἑαυτοῦ αὐλήν αὐτοῦ ⸯτὰ ὑπάρχονταⸯ
v.aai.3s p.a r.ap.2 cj d.nsm a.nsm pt.rm.nsm v.pas.3s d.asf r.gsm.3 n.asf r.gsm.3 d.npn pt.pa.npn
5777 2093 7007 4020 3836 2708 2774 5875 3836 1571 885 899 3836 5639

are safe. **22** But when someone stronger attacks and overpowers him, he takes away the armor in
ἐστὶν ἐν εἰρήνῃ δὲ ἐπὰν αὐτοῦ ἰσχυρότερος ἐπελθὼν νικήσῃ αὐτόν αἴρει τὴν πανοπλίαν αὐτοῦ ἐφ'
v.pai.3s p.d n.dsf cj cj r.gsm.3 a.nsm.c pt.aa.nsm v.aas.3s r.asm.3 v.pai.3s d.asf n.asf r.gsm.3 p.d
1639 1877 1645 1254 2054 899 2708 2088 3771 899 149 3836 4110 899 2093

which the man trusted and divides up the spoils. ¶ **23** "He who is not with me is against me,
ᾗ ἐπεποίθει καὶ διαδίδωσιν ← τὰ σκῦλα αὐτοῦ Ὁ ← ὢν μὴ μετ' ἐμοῦ ἐστιν κατ' ἐμοῦ
r.dsf v.lai.3s cj v.pai.3s d.apn n.apn r.gsm.3 d.nsm pt.pa.nsm pl p.g r.gs.1 v.pai.3s p.g r.gs.1
4005 4275 2779 1344 3836 5036 899 3836 1639 3590 3552 1609 1639 2848 1609

ἰχθύν, καὶ ἀντὶ ἰχθύος ὄφιν αὐτῷ ἐπιδώσει; ¹² ἢ καὶ αἰτήσει ᾠόν, ἐπιδώσει αὐτῷ σκορπίον; ¹³ εἰ οὖν ὑμεῖς πονηροὶ ὑπάρχοντες οἴδατε δόματα ἀγαθὰ διδόναι τοῖς τέκνοις ὑμῶν, πόσῳ μᾶλλον ὁ πατὴρ [ὁ] ἐξ οὐρανοῦ δώσει πνεῦμα ἅγιον τοῖς αἰτοῦσιν αὐτόν.

¹¹:¹⁴ Καὶ ἦν ἐκβάλλων δαιμόνιον [καὶ αὐτὸ ἦν] κωφόν· ἐγένετο δὲ τοῦ δαιμονίου ἐξελθόντος ἐλάλησεν ὁ κωφὸς καὶ ἐθαύμασαν οἱ ὄχλοι. ¹⁵ τινὲς δὲ ἐξ αὐτῶν εἶπον, Ἐν Βεελζεβοὺλ τῷ ἄρχοντι τῶν δαιμονίων ἐκβάλλει τὰ δαιμόνια· ¹⁶ ἕτεροι δὲ πειράζοντες σημεῖον ἐξ οὐρανοῦ ἐζήτουν παρ' αὐτοῦ. ¶ ¹⁷ αὐτὸς δὲ εἰδὼς αὐτῶν τὰ διανοήματα εἶπεν αὐτοῖς, Πᾶσα βασιλεία ἐφ' ἑαυτὴν διαμερισθεῖσα ἐρημοῦται καὶ οἶκος ἐπὶ οἶκον πίπτει. ¹⁸ εἰ δὲ καὶ ὁ Σατανᾶς ἐφ' ἑαυτὸν διεμερίσθη, πῶς σταθήσεται ἡ βασιλεία αὐτοῦ; ὅτι λέγετε ἐν Βεελζεβοὺλ ἐκβάλλειν με τὰ δαιμόνια. ¹⁹ εἰ δὲ ἐγὼ ἐν Βεελζεβοὺλ ἐκβάλλω τὰ δαιμόνια, οἱ υἱοὶ ὑμῶν ἐν τίνι ἐκβάλλουσιν; διὰ τοῦτο αὐτοὶ ὑμῶν κριταὶ ἔσονται. ²⁰ εἰ δὲ ἐν δακτύλῳ θεοῦ [ἐγὼ] ἐκβάλλω τὰ δαιμόνια, ἄρα ἔφθασεν ἐφ' ὑμᾶς ἡ βασιλεία τοῦ θεοῦ. ¶ ²¹ ὅταν ὁ ἰσχυρὸς καθωπλισμένος φυλάσσῃ τὴν ἑαυτοῦ αὐλήν, ἐν εἰρήνῃ ἐστὶν τὰ ὑπάρχοντα αὐτοῦ· ²² ἐπὰν δὲ ἰσχυρότερος αὐτοῦ ἐπελθὼν νικήσῃ αὐτόν, τὴν πανοπλίαν αὐτοῦ αἴρει ἐφ' ᾗ ἐπεποίθει καὶ τὰ σκῦλα αὐτοῦ διαδίδωσιν. ¶ ²³ ὁ μὴ ὢν μετ' ἐμοῦ κατ' ἐμοῦ ἐστιν, καὶ ὁ μὴ συνάγων μετ' ἐμοῦ σκορπίζει. ¶ ²⁴ Ὅταν τὸ ἀκάθαρτον πνεῦμα ἐξέλθῃ ἀπὸ

and he who does not gather with me, scatters. ¶ **24** "When an evil spirit comes out of a
καὶ ὁ ← → μὴ συνάγων μετ᾽ ἐμοῦ σκορπίζει | Ὅταν ἀκάθαρτον τὸ πνεῦμα ἐξέλθη ← ἀπὸ
cj d.nsm pl pt.pa.nsm p.g r.gs.1 v.pai.3s | cj a.nsn d.nsn n.nsn v.aas.3s p.g
2779 3836 5251 3590 5251 3552 1609 5025 | 4020 176 3836 4460 2002 608

man, it goes through arid places seeking rest and does not find it. Then it says, 'I will
τοῦ ἀνθρώπου → διέρχεται δι᾽ ἀνύδρων τόπων ζητοῦν ἀνάπαυσιν καὶ → μὴ εὑρίσκον τότε → λέγει →
d.gsm n.gsm v.pmi.3s p.g a.gpm n.gpm pt.pa.nsn n.asf cj pl pt.pa.nsn adv v.pai.3s
3836 476 1451 1328 536 5536 2426 398 2779 2351 3590 2351 5538 3306

return to the house I left.' **25** When it arrives, it finds the house swept clean and put
ὑποστρέψω εἰς τὸν οἶκον μου ὅθεν → ἐξῆλθον καὶ → → ἐλθὸν → εὑρίσκει σεσαρωμένον ← καὶ κεκοσμημένον
v.fai.1s p.a d.asm n.asm r.gs.1 cj v.aai.1s cj pt.aa.nsn v.pai.3s pt.rp.asm cj pt.rp.asm
5715 1650 3836 3875 1609 3854 2002 2779 2262 2351 4924 2779 3175

in order. **26** Then it goes and takes seven other spirits more wicked than itself, and they go in
← ← τότε → πορεύεται καὶ παραλαμβάνει ἑπτὰ ἕτερα πνεύματα → πονηρότερα → ἑαυτοῦ καὶ → εἰσελθόντα ←
adv v.pmi.3s cj v.pai.3s a.apn r.apn n.apn a.apn.c r.gsn.3 cj pt.aa.npn
5538 4513 2779 4161 2231 2283 4460 4505 1571 2779 1656

and live there. And the final condition of that man is worse than the first." ¶ **27**
κατοικεῖ ἐκεῖ καὶ τὰ ἔσχατα ← → ἐκείνου τοῦ ἀνθρώπου γίνεται χείρονα τῶν πρώτων δὲ Ἐγένετο
v.pai.3s adv cj d.npn a.npn r.gsn d.gsm n.gsm v.pmi.3s a.npn.c d.gpm a.gpn cj v.ami.3s
2997 1695 2779 3836 2274 476 1697 3836 476 1181 5937 3836 4755 1254 1181

As Jesus was saying these things, a woman in the crowd called out, "Blessed is the mother
ἐν αὐτὸν → τῷ λέγειν ταῦτα ← τις γυνὴ ἐκ τοῦ ὄχλου ἐπάρασα φωνὴν ← εἶπεν αὐτῷ μακαρία ἡ κοιλία
p.d r.asm.3 d.dsn f.pa r.apn r.nsf n.nsf p.g d.gsm n.gsm pt.aa.nsf n.asf v.aai.3s r.dsm.3 a.nsf d.nsf n.nsf
1877 899 3836 3306 4047 5516 1222 1666 3836 4063 2048 5889 3306 899 3421 3836 3120

who gave you birth and *nursed you.*" **28** He replied, "Blessed rather are those who hear the
ἡ → σε βαστάσασα καὶ μαστοὶ οὓς ἐθήλασας δὲ αὐτὸς εἶπεν μακάριοι μενοῦν οἱ ← ἀκούοντες τὸν
d.nsf r.as.2 pt.aa.nsf cj n.npm r.apm v.aai.2s cj r.nsm v.aai.3s a.npm pl d.npm pt.pa.npm d.asm
3836 1002 1002 5148 2779 3466 4005 2558 1254 899 3306 3421 3528 3836 201 3836

word of God and obey it."
λόγον → τοῦ θεοῦ καὶ φυλάσσοντες
n.asm d.gsm n.gsm cj pt.pa.npm
3364 3836 2536 2779 5875

The Sign of Jonah

11:29 As the crowds increased, Jesus said, "This is a wicked generation. It asks for a
δὲ → Τῶν ὄχλων ἐπαθροιζομένων ἤρξατο λέγειν αὕτη ἡ γενεὰ ἐστιν πονηρά γενεὰ → ζητεῖ ←
cj d.gpm n.gpm pt.pp.gpm v.ami.3s f.pa r.nsf d.nsf n.nsf v.pai.3s a.nsf n.nsf v.pai.3s
1254 2044 3836 4063 2044 806 3306 4047 3836 1155 1639 4505 1155 2426

miraculous sign, but none will be given it except the sign of Jonah. **30** For as Jonah was a
→ σημεῖον καὶ οὐ σημεῖον → → δοθήσεται αὐτῇ εἰ μὴ τὸ σημεῖον → Ἰωνᾶ γὰρ καθὼς Ἰωνᾶς ἐγένετο
n.asn cj pl n.nsn v.fpi.3s r.dsf.3 cj pl d.nsn n.nsn n.gsm cj adv n.nsm v.ami.3s
4956 2779 4024 4956 1443 899 1623 3590 3836 4956 2731 1142 2777 2731 1181

sign to the Ninevites, so also will the Son of Man be to this generation. **31** The Queen of the South
σημεῖον → τοῖς Νινευίταις οὕτως καὶ → ὁ υἱὸς → τοῦ ἀνθρώπου ἔσται → ταύτῃ τῇ γενεᾷ βασίλισσα → νότου
n.nsn d.dpm n.dpm adv adv d.nsm n.nsm d.gsm n.gsm v.fmi.3s r.dsf d.dsf n.dsf n.nsf n.gsm
4956 3836 3780 4048 2779 1639 3836 5626 3836 476 1639 1155 4047 3836 1155 999 3803

will rise at the judgment with the men of this generation and condemn them; for she came from the
→ ἐγερθήσεται ἐν τῇ κρίσει μετὰ τῶν ἀνδρῶν → ταύτης τῆς γενεᾶς καὶ κατακρινεῖ αὐτοὺς ὅτι → ἦλθεν ἐκ τῶν
v.fpi.3s p.d d.dsf n.dsf p.g d.gpm n.gpm r.gsf d.gsf n.gsf cj v.fai.3s r.apm.3 cj v.aai.3s p.g d.gpm
1586 1877 3836 3213 3552 3836 467 1155 4047 3836 1155 2779 2891 899 4022 2262 1666 3836

ends of the earth to listen to Solomon's wisdom, and now one greater than Solomon is here. **32** The men of
περάτων τῆς γῆς → ἀκοῦσαι ← Σολομῶνος τὴν σοφίαν καὶ ἰδοὺ → πλεῖον Σολομῶνος ὧδε → ἄνδρες →
n.gpn d.gsf n.gsf f.aa n.gsm d.asf n.asf cj pl a.nsn.c n.gsm adv n.npm
4306 3836 1178 201 5048 3836 5053 2779 2627 4498 5048 6045 467

Nineveh will stand up at the judgment with this generation and condemn it; for they repented at
Νινευῖται → ἀναστήσονται ← ἐν τῇ κρίσει μετὰ ταύτης τῆς γενεᾶς καὶ κατακρινοῦσιν αὐτὴν ὅτι → μετενόησαν εἰς
n.npm v.fmi.3p p.d d.dsf n.dsf p.g r.gsf d.gsf n.gsf cj v.fai.3p r.asf.3 cj v.aai.3p p.a
3780 482 1877 3836 3213 3552 4047 3836 1155 2779 2891 899 4022 3566 1650

τοῦ ἀνθρώπου, διέρχεται δι᾽ ἀνύδρων τόπων ζητοῦν ἀνάπαυσιν καὶ μὴ εὑρίσκον· [τότε] λέγει, Ὑποστρέψω εἰς τὸν οἶκόν μου ὅθεν ἐξῆλθον· **25** καὶ ἐλθὸν εὑρίσκει σεσαρωμένον καὶ κεκοσμημένον. **26** τότε πορεύεται καὶ παραλαμβάνει ἕτερα πνεύματα πονηρότερα ἑαυτοῦ ἑπτὰ καὶ εἰσελθόντα κατοικεῖ ἐκεῖ· καὶ γίνεται τὰ ἔσχατα τοῦ ἀνθρώπου ἐκείνου χείρονα τῶν πρώτων. ¶ **27** Ἐγένετο δὲ ἐν τῷ λέγειν αὐτὸν ταῦτα ἐπάρασά τις φωνὴν γυνὴ ἐκ τοῦ ὄχλου εἶπεν αὐτῷ, Μακαρία ἡ κοιλία ἡ βαστάσασά σε καὶ μαστοὶ οὓς ἐθήλασας. **28** αὐτὸς δὲ εἶπεν, Μενοῦν μακάριοι οἱ ἀκούοντες τὸν λόγον τοῦ θεοῦ καὶ φυλάσσοντες.

11:29 Τῶν δὲ ὄχλων ἐπαθροιζομένων ἤρξατο λέγειν, Ἡ γενεὰ αὕτη γενεὰ πονηρά ἐστιν· σημεῖον ζητεῖ, καὶ σημεῖον οὐ δοθήσεται αὐτῇ εἰ μὴ τὸ σημεῖον Ἰωνᾶ. **30** καθὼς γὰρ ἐγένετο Ἰωνᾶς τοῖς Νινευίταις σημεῖον, οὕτως ἔσται καὶ ὁ υἱὸς τοῦ ἀνθρώπου τῇ γενεᾷ ταύτῃ. **31** βασίλισσα νότου ἐγερθήσεται ἐν τῇ κρίσει μετὰ τῶν ἀνδρῶν τῆς γενεᾶς ταύτης καὶ κατακρινεῖ αὐτούς, ὅτι ἦλθεν ἐκ τῶν περάτων τῆς γῆς ἀκοῦσαι τὴν σοφίαν Σολομῶνος, καὶ ἰδοὺ πλεῖον Σολομῶνος ὧδε. **32** ἄνδρες Νινευῖται ἀναστήσονται ἐν τῇ κρίσει μετὰ τῆς γενεᾶς ταύτης καὶ κατακρινοῦσιν αὐτήν· ὅτι μετενόησαν εἰς τὸ κήρυγμα Ἰωνᾶ, καὶ ἰδοὺ

the preaching of Jonah, and now one greater than Jonah is here.
τὸ κήρυγμα → Ἰωνᾶ καὶ ἰδοὺ → πλεῖον → Ἰωνᾶ ὧδε
d.asn n.asn   n.gsm cj j   a.nsn.c   n.gsm adv
3836 3060   2731 2779 2627   4498   2731 6045

The Lamp of the Body

11:33 "No one lights a lamp and puts it in a place where it will be hidden, or under a bowl. Instead
→ Οὐδεὶς ἅψας λύχνον τίθησιν εἰς   κρύπτην οὐδὲ ὑπὸ ⌜τὸν μόδιον⌝ ἀλλ'
a.nsm pt.aa.nsm n.asn v.pai.3s p.a   n.asf cj p.g d.asm n.asm cj
4029 721 3394 5502 1650   3219 4028 5679 3836 3654 247

he puts it on its stand, so that those who come in may see the light. **34** Your eye is the lamp
ἐπὶ τὴν λυχνίαν ἵνα οἱ εἰσπορευόμενοι ← βλέπωσιν τὸ φῶς σου ὁ ὀφθαλμός, ἐστιν Ὁ λύχνος
p.a d.asf n.asf cj d.npm pt.pm.npm   v.pas.3p d.asn n.asn r.gs.2 d.nsm n.nsm v.pai.3s d.nsm n.nsm
2093 3836 3393 2671 3836 1660   1063 3836 5890 5148 3836 4057 1639 3836 3394

of your body. When your eyes are good, your whole body also is full of light. But when they
→ τοῦ σώματος ὅταν σου ὁ ὀφθαλμός, ᾖ ἁπλοῦς σου ὅλον ⌜τὸ σῶμα⌝ καὶ ἐστιν → φωτεινόν δὲ ἐπὰν →
d.gsn n.gsn cj r.gs.2 d.nsm n.nsm v.pas.3s a.nsm r.gs.2 a.nsn d.nsn n.nsn adv v.pai.3s a.nsn cj cj
3836 5393 4020 5148 3836 4057 1639 606 5148 3910 3836 5393 2779 1639 5893 1254 2054

are bad, your body also is full of darkness. **35** See to it, then, that the light within you is not darkness.
ᾖ πονηρός σου ⌜τὸ σῶμα⌝ καὶ → σκοτεινόν σκόπει ← οὖν τὸ φῶς τὸ ἐν σοὶ ἐστίν μὴ σκότος
v.pas.3s a.nsm r.gs.2 d.nsn n.nsn adv a.nsn v.pam.2s cj d.nsn n.nsn d.nsn p.d r.ds.2 v.pai.3s pl n.nsn
1639 4505 5148 3836 5393 2779 5027 5023 4036 3836 5890 3836 1877 5148 1639 3590 5030

36 Therefore, if your whole body is full of light, and no part of it dark, it will be completely
οὖν εἰ σου ὅλον ⌜τὸ σῶμα⌝ → → φωτεινόν μὴ ⌜μέρος τι⌝ ἔχον σκοτεινόν → → ἔσται ὅλον
cj cj r.gs.2 a.nsn d.nsn n.nsn a.nsn pl n.asn r.asn pt.pa.nsn a.asn v.fmi.3s a.nsn
4036 1623 5148 3910 3836 5393 5893 3590 3538 5516 2400 5027 1639 3910

lighted, as when the light of a lamp shines on you."
φωτεινόν ὡς ὅταν τῇ ἀστραπῇ ὁ λύχνος, φωτίζῃ ← σε
a.nsn cj cj d.dsf n.dsf d.nsm n.nsm v.pas.3s r.as.2
5893 6055 4020 3836 847 3836 3394 5894 5148

Six Woes

11:37 When Jesus had finished speaking, a Pharisee invited him to eat with him; so he went in
δὲ Ἐν ↱ ↱ ⌜τῷ λαλῆσαι⌝ Φαρισαῖος ἐρωτᾷ αὐτὸν ὅπως ἀριστήσῃ παρ' αὐτῷ δὲ → εἰσελθὼν
cj p.d d.dsn f.aa n.nsm v.pai.3s r.asm.3 cj v.aas.3s p.d r.dsm.3 cj pt.aa.nsm
1254 1877 3281 3281 3836 3281 5757 2263 899 3968 753 4123 899 1254 1656

and reclined at the table. **38** But the Pharisee, noticing that Jesus did not first wash before the meal, was
ἀνέπεσεν ← ← ← δὲ ὁ Φαρισαῖος ἰδὼν ὅτι → οὐ πρῶτον ἐβαπτίσθη πρὸ τοῦ ἀρίστου →
v.aai.3s cj d.nsm n.nsm pt.aa.nsm cj pl adv v.api.3s p.g d.gsn n.gsn
404 1254 3836 5757 1625 4022 966 4024 4754 966 4574 3836 756

surprised. ¶ **39** Then the Lord said to him, "Now then, you Pharisees clean the outside of the
ἐθαύμασεν δὲ ὁ κύριος εἶπεν πρὸς αὐτὸν νῦν ← ὑμεῖς οἱ Φαρισαῖοι καθαρίζετε τὸ ἔξωθεν → τοῦ
v.aai.3s cj d.nsm n.nsm v.aai.3s p.a r.asm.3 adv r.np.2 d.npm n.npm v.pai.2p d.asn p.g p.g d.gsn
2513 1254 3836 3261 3306 4639 899 3814 7007 3836 5757 2751 3836 2033 3836

cup and dish, but inside you are full of greed and wickedness. **40** You foolish people! Did not the
ποτηρίου καὶ ⌜τοῦ πίνακος⌝ δὲ ⌜τὸ ἔσωθεν⌝ ὑμῶν → γέμει ἁρπαγῆς καὶ πονηρίας ἄφρονες → οὐχ ὁ
n.gsn cj d.gsm n.gsm cj d.nsn adv r.gp.2 v.pai.3s n.gsf cj n.gsf a.vpm pl d.nsm
4539 2779 3836 4402 1254 3836 2277 7007 1154 771 2779 4504 933 4024 3836

one who made the outside make the inside also? **41** But give what is inside the dish to the poor, and
← ← ποιήσας τὸ ἔξωθεν ἐποίησεν τὸ ἔσωθεν καὶ πλὴν δότε τὰ ἐνόντα ← ἐλεημοσύνην καὶ ἰδοὺ
pt.aa.nsm d.asn adv v.aai.3s d.asn adv adv cj v.aam.2p d.apn pt.pa.apn n.asf cj j
4472 3836 2033 4472 3836 2277 2779 4440 1443 3836 1913 1797 2779 2627

everything will be clean for you. ¶ **42** "Woe to you Pharisees, because you give God a tenth
πάντα → ἐστιν καθαρὰ → ὑμῖν ἀλλὰ οὐαὶ → ὑμῖν ⌜τοῖς Φαρισαίοις⌝ ὅτι → ἀποδεκατοῦτε
a.npn v.pai.3s a.npn r.dp.2 cj j r.dp.2 d.dpm n.dpm cj v.pai.2p
4246 1639 2754 7007 247 4026 7007 3836 5757 4022 620

of your mint, rue and all other kinds of garden herbs, but you neglect justice and the love
← τὸ ἡδύοσμον καὶ ⌜τὸ πήγανον⌝ καὶ πᾶν ← ← λάχανον καὶ → παρέρχεσθε ⌜τὴν κρίσιν⌝ καὶ τὴν ἀγάπην
d.asn n.asn cj d.asn n.asn cj a.asn n.asn cj v.pmi.2p d.asf n.asf cj d.asf n.asf
3836 2455 2779 3836 4379 2779 4246 3303 2779 4216 3836 3213 2779 3836 27

πλεῖον Ἰωνᾶ ὧδε.
  11:33 Οὐδεὶς λύχνον ἅψας εἰς κρύπτην τίθησιν [οὐδὲ ὑπὸ τὸν μόδιον] ἀλλ' ἐπὶ τὴν λυχνίαν, ἵνα οἱ εἰσπορευόμενοι τὸ φῶς βλέπωσιν. **34** ὁ λύχνος τοῦ σώματός ἐστιν ὁ ὀφθαλμός σου. ὅταν ὁ ὀφθαλμός σου ἁπλοῦς ᾖ, καὶ ὅλον τὸ σῶμά σου φωτεινόν ἐστιν· ἐπὰν δὲ πονηρὸς ᾖ, καὶ τὸ σῶμά σου σκοτεινόν. **35** σκόπει οὖν μὴ τὸ φῶς τὸ ἐν σοὶ σκότος ἐστίν. **36** εἰ οὖν τὸ σῶμά σου ὅλον φωτεινόν, μὴ ἔχον μέρος τι σκοτεινόν, ἔσται φωτεινὸν ὅλον ὡς ὅταν ὁ λύχνος τῇ ἀστραπῇ φωτίζῃ σε.
  11:37 Ἐν δὲ τῷ λαλῆσαι ἐρωτᾷ αὐτὸν Φαρισαῖος ὅπως ἀριστήσῃ παρ' αὐτῷ· εἰσελθὼν δὲ ἀνέπεσεν. **38** ὁ δὲ Φαρισαῖος ἰδὼν ἐθαύμασεν ὅτι οὐ πρῶτον ἐβαπτίσθη πρὸ τοῦ ἀρίστου. ¶ **39** εἶπεν δὲ ὁ κύριος πρὸς αὐτόν, Νῦν ὑμεῖς οἱ Φαρισαῖοι τὸ ἔξωθεν τοῦ ποτηρίου καὶ τοῦ πίνακος καθαρίζετε, τὸ δὲ ἔσωθεν ὑμῶν γέμει ἁρπαγῆς καὶ πονηρίας. **40** ἄφρονες, οὐχ ὁ ποιήσας τὸ ἔξωθεν καὶ τὸ ἔσωθεν ἐποίησεν; **41** πλὴν τὰ ἐνόντα δότε ἐλεημοσύνην, καὶ ἰδοὺ πάντα καθαρὰ ὑμῖν ἐστιν. ¶ **42** ἀλλὰ οὐαὶ ὑμῖν τοῖς Φαρισαίοις, ὅτι ἀποδεκατοῦτε τὸ ἡδύοσμον καὶ τὸ πήγανον καὶ πᾶν λάχανον καὶ παρέρχεσθε τὴν κρίσιν καὶ τὴν ἀγάπην τοῦ

of God.　　You should have practiced the latter without leaving the former undone.　¶　[43] "Woe to you
→ ⌐τοῦ θεοῦ⌐ δὲ → ἔδει → ποιῆσαι ταῦτα μὴ παρεῖναι κἀκεῖνα ← 　　Οὐαὶ → ὑμῖν
d.gsm n.gsm cj 　v.iai.3s 　f.aa 　r.apn pl f.aa 　cj 　　j → r.dp.2
3836 2536 1254 　1256 　4472 　4047 3590 4223 　2797 　　4026 7007

Pharisees,　　because you love 　the most important 　seats in the synagogues and greetings 　in the
⌐τοῖς Φαρισαίοις⌐ ὅτι → ἀγαπᾶτε τὴν → πρωτοκαθεδρίαν ← ἐν ταῖς συναγωγαῖς καὶ ⌐τοὺς ἀσπασμοὺς⌐ ἐν ταῖς
d.dpm n.dpm 　cj v.pai.2p d.asf n.asf 　p.d d.dpf n.dpf cj d.apm n.apm 　p.d d.dpf
3836 5757 　4022 26 3836 4751 　1877 3836 5252 2779 3836 833 　1877 3836

marketplaces.　¶　[44] "Woe to you, because you are 　like unmarked graves, 　　which men
ἀγοραῖς 　　Οὐαὶ → ὑμῖν ὅτι → ἐστὲ ὡς τὰ ἄδηλα ⌐τὰ μνημεῖα⌐ καὶ 　⌐οἱ ἄνθρωποι⌐
n.dpf 　　j → r.dp.2 cj 　v.pai.2p pl d.npn a.npn d.npn n.npn cj 　d.npm n.npm
59 　　4026 7007 4022 　1639 6055 3836 83 3836 3646 2779 　3836 476

walk 　　over without knowing it."　¶　[45] One of the experts in the law 　answered 　him,
⌐οἱ περιπατοῦντες⌐ ἐπάνω οὐκ 　οἴδασιν 　　δέ τις → τῶν → → → νομικῶν Ἀποκριθεὶς λέγει αὐτῷ
d.npm pt.pa.npm 　adv pl 　v.rai.3p 　　cj r.nsm d.gpm 　n.gpm pt.ap.nsm v.pai.3s r.dsm.3
3836 4344 　2062 4024 　3857 　　1254 5516 3836 　3788 646 3306 899

"Teacher, when you say 　these things, you insult us 　also."　¶　[46] Jesus replied, "And you experts in the
διδάσκαλε → → λέγων ταῦτα ← → ὑβρίζεις ἡμᾶς καὶ 　　δὲ ὁ.nsm εἶπεν καὶ ὑμῖν → τοῖς
n.vsm → → pt.pa.nsm r.apn ← → v.pai.2s r.ap.1 adv 　　cj d.nsm v.aai.3s adv r.dp.2 → d.dpm
1437 　　3306 4047 　5614 7005 2779 　　1254 3836 3306 2779 7007 　3836

law, 　woe to you, because you load 　people 　　down with burdens they can hardly carry, 　and you
νομικοῖς οὐαί 　ὅτι → φορτίζετε ⌐τοὺς ἀνθρώπους⌐ ⁔ φορτία → → δυσβάστακτα καὶ →
n.dpm j 　cj → v.pai.2p d.apm n.apm 　　n.apn → → a.apn cj →
3788 4026 　4022 5844 3836 476 5844 5845 1546 2779 4718

yourselves will not lift 　one finger 　*to help* 　*them.*　¶　[47] "Woe to you, because you
αὐτοὶ → οὐ προσψαύετε ἑνὶ ⌐τῶν δακτύλων⌐ ὑμῶν → ⌐τοῖς φορτίοις⌐ 　　Οὐαὶ → ὑμῖν ὅτι
r.npm → pl v.pai.2p a.dsm d.gpm n.gpm r.gp.2 → d.dpn n.dpn 　　j → r.dp.2 cj
899 　4718 4024 4718 1651 3836 1235 7007 3836 5845 　　4026 7007 4022

build 　tombs 　for the prophets, and it was your forefathers who killed 　them. [48] So you testify
οἰκοδομεῖτε ⌐τὰ μνημεῖα⌐ → τῶν προφητῶν δὲ ⌐ὑμῶν οἱ πατέρες⌐ ἀπέκτειναν αὐτούς ἄρα → ⌐ἐστε μάρτυρες⌐ καὶ
v.pai.2p d.apn n.apn → d.gpm n.gpm cj r.gp.2 d.npm n.npm v.aai.3p r.apm.3 cj → v.pai.2p n.npm cj
3868 3836 3646 　3836 4737 1254 7007 3836 4252 650 899 726 　1639 3459 2779

that you approve 　of what your forefathers did; 　　they killed 　the prophets, and you build
→ συνευδοκεῖτε ← ὑμῶν ⌐τῶν πατέρων⌐ ⌐τοῖς ἔργοις⌐ ὅτι μὲν αὐτοὶ ἀπέκτειναν αὐτούς δὲ ὑμεῖς οἰκοδομεῖτε
v.pai.2p ← r.gp.2 d.gpm n.gpm d.dpn n.dpn cj pl r.npm v.aai.3p r.apm.3 cj r.np.2 v.pai.2p
5306 　7007 3836 4752 3836 2240 4022 3525 899 650 899 1254 7007 3868

their tombs. [49] Because 　of this, 　God 　in his wisdom said, 'I will send 　them prophets and apostles,
→ ⌐διὰ τοῦτο⌐ ← καὶ ⌐τοῦ θεοῦ⌐ ἡ σοφία εἶπεν → ἀποστελῶ εἰς αὐτοὺς προφήτας καὶ ἀποστόλους καὶ
p.a r.asn ← adv d.gsm n.gsm d.nsf n.nsf v.aai.3s → v.fai.1s p.a r.apm.3 n.apm cj n.apm cj
1328 4047 2779 3836 2536 3836 5053 3306 690 1650 899 4737 2779 693 2779

some of 　whom they will kill 　　and others they will persecute.' [50] Therefore 　this 　generation will be held
ἐξ αὐτῶν → → ἀποκτενοῦσιν καὶ → → διώξουσιν ἵνα 　ἀπὸ ταύτης ⌐τῆς γενεᾶς⌐ → → →
p.g r.gpm.3 → → v.fai.3p cj → → v.fai.3p cj 　p.g r.gsf d.gsf n.gsf
1666 899 　650 2779 1503 2671 　608 4047 3836 1155

responsible for the blood of all 　the prophets that has been shed 　since the beginning of the world, [51] from the
ἐκζητηθῇ → τὸ αἷμα → πάντων τῶν προφητῶν τὸ → ἐκκεχυμένον ἀπὸ καταβολῆς → κόσμου ἀπὸ
v.aps.3s → d.nsn n.nsn → a.gpm d.gpm n.gpm d.nsn → pt.rp.nsn p.g n.gsf → n.gsm p.g
1699 3836 135 4246 3836 4737 3836 1773 608 2856 3180 608

blood 　of Abel to 　the blood of Zechariah, who was killed 　between the altar 　and the sanctuary. Yes, I
αἷματος → Ἄβελ ἕως 　αἵματος → Ζαχαρίου τοῦ → ἀπολομένου μεταξὺ τοῦ θυσιαστηρίου καὶ τοῦ οἴκου ναὶ →
n.gsn → n.gsm p.g 　n.gsn → n.gsm d.gsm → pt.am.gsm p.g d.gsn n.gsn cj d.gsm n.gsm pl →
135 6 2401 　135 2408 3836 660 3568 3836 2603 2779 3836 3875 3721

tell you, 　this generation will be held responsible for it all.　¶　[52] "Woe to you experts in the law,
λέγω ὑμῖν ἀπὸ ταύτης ⌐τῆς γενεᾶς⌐ → → → ἐκζητηθήσεται 　　Οὐαὶ → ὑμῖν → τοῖς νομικοῖς
v.pai.1s r.dp.2 p.g r.gsf d.gsf n.gsf → → → v.fpi.3s 　　j → r.dp.2 → d.dpm n.dpm
3306 7007 608 4047 3836 1155 1699 　　4026 7007 3836 3788

θεοῦ· ταῦτα δὲ ἔδει ποιῆσαι κἀκεῖνα μὴ παρεῖναι. ¶ [43] οὐαὶ ὑμῖν τοῖς Φαρισαίοις, ὅτι ἀγαπᾶτε τὴν πρωτοκαθεδρίαν ἐν ταῖς συναγωγαῖς καὶ τοὺς ἀσπασμοὺς ἐν ταῖς ἀγοραῖς. ¶ [44] οὐαὶ ὑμῖν, ὅτι ἐστὲ ὡς τὰ μνημεῖα τὰ ἄδηλα, καὶ οἱ ἄνθρωποι [οἱ] περιπατοῦντες ἐπάνω οὐκ οἴδασιν. ¶ [45] Ἀποκριθεὶς δέ τις τῶν νομικῶν λέγει αὐτῷ, Διδάσκαλε, ταῦτα λέγων καὶ ἡμᾶς ὑβρίζεις. ¶ [46] ὁ δὲ εἶπεν, Καὶ ὑμῖν τοῖς νομικοῖς οὐαί, ὅτι φορτίζετε τοὺς ἀνθρώπους φορτία δυσβάστακτα, καὶ αὐτοὶ ἑνὶ τῶν δακτύλων ὑμῶν οὐ προσψαύετε τοῖς φορτίοις. ¶ [47] οὐαὶ ὑμῖν, ὅτι οἰκοδομεῖτε τὰ μνημεῖα τῶν προφητῶν, οἱ δὲ πατέρες ὑμῶν ἀπέκτειναν αὐτούς. [48] ἄρα μάρτυρές ἐστε καὶ συνευδοκεῖτε τοῖς ἔργοις τῶν πατέρων ὑμῶν, ὅτι αὐτοὶ μὲν ἀπέκτειναν αὐτούς, ὑμεῖς δὲ οἰκοδομεῖτε. [49] διὰ τοῦτο καὶ ἡ σοφία τοῦ θεοῦ εἶπεν, Ἀποστελῶ εἰς αὐτοὺς προφήτας καὶ ἀποστόλους, καὶ ἐξ αὐτῶν ἀποκτενοῦσιν καὶ διώξουσιν, [50] ἵνα ἐκζητηθῇ τὸ αἷμα πάντων τῶν προφητῶν τὸ ἐκκεχυμένον ἀπὸ καταβολῆς κόσμου ἀπὸ τῆς γενεᾶς ταύτης, [51] ἀπὸ τοῦ αἵματος Ἄβελ ἕως τοῦ αἵματος Ζαχαρίου τοῦ ἀπολομένου μεταξὺ τοῦ θυσιαστηρίου καὶ τοῦ οἴκου·

because you have taken away the key   to knowledge. You yourselves have not entered, and you have hindered
ὅτι → → ἤρατε ← τὴν κλεῖδα → ⸢τῆς γνώσεως⸣ → αὐτοὶ → οὐκ εἰσήλθατε καὶ → → ἐκωλύσατε
cj   v.aai.2p   d.asf n.asf   d.gsf n.gsf   r.npm   pl v.aai.2p   cj   v.aai.2p
4022   149   3836 3090   3836 1194   1656   899   1656   4024 1656   2779   3266

those who were entering." ¶ 53 When Jesus left   there, the Pharisees and the teachers of the law
τοὺς ← → εἰσερχομένους → αὐτοῦ ἐξελθόντος Κἀκεῖθεν οἱ Φαρισαῖοι καὶ οἱ γραμματεῖς ← ← →
d.apm   pt.pm.apm   r.gsm.3 pt.aa.gsm crasis   d.npm n.npm   cj d.npm n.npm
3836   1656   2002 899   2002   2796   3836 5757   2779 3836 1208

began to oppose him fiercely and to besiege   him with questions, 54 waiting to catch him in
ἤρξαντο ἐνέχειν δεινῶς καὶ → ἀποστοματίζειν περὶ πλειόνων αὐτὸν ← → ἐνεδρεύοντες → θηρεῦσαι αὐτὸν
v.ami.3p f.pa   adv   cj   f.pa   p.g a.gpn.c   r.asm.3   pt.pa.npm   f.aa   r.asm.3
806   1923   1267 2779   694   4309 4498   899 694 694   1910   2561 899

something he   might say.
τι αὐτοῦ ⸢ἐκ τοῦ στόματος⸣
r.asn r.gsm.3   p.g d.gsn n.gsn
5516 899   1666 3836 5125

Warnings and Encouragements

12:1 Meanwhile, when a   crowd of many thousands   had gathered,   so that they were trampling on one
⸢Ἐν οἷς⸣ → τοῦ ὄχλου → ⸢τῶν μυριάδων⸣ → ἐπισυναχθεισῶν ὥστε → → καταπατεῖν ← →
p.d r.dpn   d.gsm n.gsm   d.gpf n.gpf   pt.ap.gpf   cj   f.pa
1877 4005   2190   3836 4063   3836 3689   2190   6063   2922

another, Jesus began to speak first to his disciples,   saying: "Be on your guard against the yeast of the
ἀλλήλους ἤρξατο → λέγειν πρῶτον πρὸς αὐτοῦ ⸢τοὺς μαθητὰς⸣ → ἑαυτοῖς προσέχετε ἀπὸ τῆς ζύμης → τῶν
r.apm   v.ami.3s   f.pa   adv   p.a r.gsm.3 d.apm n.apm   r.dpm.2 v.pam.2p p.g   d.gsf n.gsf   d.gpm
253   806   3306 4754   4639 899   3836 3412   4668 4668 1571   4668 608   3836 2434   3836

Pharisees, which is hypocrisy. 2 There is nothing concealed   that will not be disclosed,   or hidden
Φαρισαίων ἥτις ἐστὶν ὑπόκρισις δὲ → ἐστὶν Οὐδὲν συγκεκαλυμμένον ὃ → οὐκ → ἀποκαλυφθήσεται καὶ κρυπτὸν
n.gpm   r.nsf v.pai.3s n.nsf   cj   v.pai.3s a.nsn pt.rp.nsn   r.nsn   pl   v.fpi.3s   cj a.nsn
5757   4015 1639   5694   1254   1639   4029 5158   4005 636 4024 636   2779 3220

that will not be made known. 3 What you have said in the dark will be heard   in the daylight,
ὃ → οὐ → γνωσθήσεται ἀνθ᾽ ὧν ὅσα → εἴπατε ἐν τῇ σκοτίᾳ → ἀκουσθήσεται ἐν τῷ φωτὶ
r.nsn pl v.fpi.3s   p.g r.gpn r.apn   v.aai.2p p.d d.dsf n.dsf   v.fpi.3s   p.d d.dsn n.dsn
4005 1182 4024   1182   505 4005 4012   3306 1877 3836 5028   201   1877 3836 5890

and what you have whispered in the ear in the inner rooms will be proclaimed from the roofs. ¶ 4 "I
καὶ ὃ → → ἐλαλήσατε πρὸς τὸ οὖς ἐν τοῖς ταμείοις → κηρυχθήσεται ἐπὶ τῶν δωμάτων δὲ →
cj r.asn   v.aai.2p   p.a d.asn n.asn p.d d.dpn   n.dpn   v.fpi.3s   p.g d.gpn n.gpn   cj
2779 4005   3281   4639 3836 4044 1877 3836 5421   3062   2093 3836 1560   1254

tell you, my friends,   do not be afraid of those who kill   the body and after that can   do no
Λέγω ὑμῖν μου ⸢τοῖς φίλοις⸣ μὴ → φοβηθῆτε ἀπὸ τῶν ἀποκτεινόντων τὸ σῶμα καὶ μετὰ ταῦτα τι ποιῆσαι μὴ
v.pai.1s r.dp.2 r.gs.1 d.dpm a.dpm   pl   v.aps.2p   p.g d.gpm pt.pa.gpm   d.asn n.asn cj p.a r.apn   r.asn f.aa   pl
3306   7007 1609 3836 5813   5828 5828   608 3836 650   3836 5393 2779 3552 4047   5516 4472 3590

more. 5 But I will show you whom you should fear: Fear him who, after the killing of the
ἐχόντων περισσότερον δὲ → ὑποδείξω ὑμῖν τίνα → → φοβηθῆτε φοβήθητε τὸν ← μετὰ → ⸢τὸ ἀποκτεῖναι⸣
pt.pa.gpm a.asn.c   cj   v.fai.1s   r.dp.2 r.asm   v.aps.2p v.apm.2p d.asm   p.a   d.asn f.aa
2400 4358   1254   5683   7007 5515   5828   5828   3836   3552   3836 650

body, has power to throw you into hell.   Yes, I tell you, fear   him. 6 Are not five sparrows sold
ἔχοντα ἐξουσίαν → ἐμβαλεῖν εἰς ⸢τὴν γέενναν⸣ ναὶ → λέγω ὑμῖν φοβήθητε τοῦτον → οὐχὶ πέντε στρουθία πωλοῦνται
pt.pa.asn n.asf   f.aa   p.a d.asf n.asf   pl   v.pai.1s r.dp.2 v.apm.2p r.asm   pl   a.npn n.npn   v.ppi.3p
2400 2026   1833   1650 3836 1147   3721   3306 7007 5828   4047   4797 4049 4297   5141   4797

for two pennies? Yet not one of them is forgotten by   God. 7 Indeed,   the very hairs of your
→ δύο ἀσσαρίων καὶ οὐκ ἓν ἐξ αὐτῶν ἔστιν ἐπιλελησμένον ἐνώπιον ⸢τοῦ θεοῦ⸣ ἀλλὰ καὶ αἱ τρίχες ὑμῶν
a.gpn n.gpn   cj pl a.nsn p.g r.gpn.3 v.pai.3s pt.rp.nsn   p.g   d.gsm n.gsm cj   adv d.npf n.npf   r.gp.2
837 1545   837 2779 4024 1651 1666 899   1639   2140   1967   3836 2536 247   2779 3836 2582 3051 7007

head are all numbered. Don't be afraid; you are worth more than many sparrows. ¶ 8 "I tell
⸢τῆς κεφαλῆς⸣ πᾶσαι ἠρίθμηνται μὴ → φοβεῖσθε → διαφέρετε πολλῶν στρουθίων δὲ Λέγω
d.gsf n.gsf   a.npf v.rpi.3p   pl   v.ppm.2p   v.pai.2p a.gpn   n.gpn   cj v.pai.1s
3836 3051   749   4246   3590   5828   1422   4498   5141   1254 3306

ναὶ λέγω ὑμῖν, ἐκζητηθήσεται ἀπὸ τῆς γενεᾶς ταύτης. ¶ 52 οὐαὶ ὑμῖν τοῖς νομικοῖς, ὅτι ἤρατε τὴν κλεῖδα τῆς γνώσεως· αὐτοὶ οὐκ εἰσήλθατε καὶ τοὺς εἰσερχομένους ἐκωλύσατε. ¶ 53 Κἀκεῖθεν ἐξελθόντος αὐτοῦ ἤρξαντο οἱ γραμματεῖς καὶ οἱ Φαρισαῖοι δεινῶς ἐνέχειν καὶ ἀποστοματίζειν αὐτὸν περὶ πλειόνων, 54 ἐνεδρεύοντες αὐτὸν θηρεῦσαί τι ἐκ τοῦ στόματος αὐτοῦ.

12:1 Ἐν οἷς ἐπισυναχθεισῶν τῶν μυριάδων τοῦ ὄχλου, ὥστε καταπατεῖν ἀλλήλους, ἤρξατο λέγειν πρὸς τοὺς μαθητὰς αὐτοῦ πρῶτον. Προσέχετε ἑαυτοῖς ἀπὸ τῆς ζύμης, ἥτις ἐστὶν ὑπόκρισις, τῶν Φαρισαίων. 2 οὐδὲν δὲ συγκεκαλυμμένον ἐστὶν ὃ οὐκ ἀποκαλυφθήσεται καὶ κρυπτὸν ὃ οὐ γνωσθήσεται. 3 ἀνθ᾽ ὧν ὅσα ἐν τῇ σκοτίᾳ εἴπατε ἐν τῷ φωτὶ ἀκουσθήσεται, καὶ ὃ πρὸς τὸ οὖς ἐλαλήσατε ἐν τοῖς ταμείοις κηρυχθήσεται ἐπὶ τῶν δωμάτων. ¶ 4 Λέγω δὲ ὑμῖν τοῖς φίλοις μου, μὴ φοβηθῆτε ἀπὸ τῶν ἀποκτεινόντων τὸ σῶμα καὶ μετὰ ταῦτα μὴ ἐχόντων περισσότερόν τι ποιῆσαι. 5 ὑποδείξω δὲ ὑμῖν τίνα φοβηθῆτε· φοβήθητε τὸν μετὰ τὸ ἀποκτεῖναι ἔχοντα ἐξουσίαν ἐμβαλεῖν εἰς τὴν γέενναν. ναὶ λέγω ὑμῖν, τοῦτον φοβήθητε. 6 οὐχὶ πέντε στρουθία πωλοῦνται ἀσσαρίων δύο; καὶ ἓν ἐξ αὐτῶν οὐκ ἔστιν ἐπιλελησμένον ἐνώπιον τοῦ θεοῦ. 7 ἀλλὰ καὶ αἱ τρίχες τῆς κεφαλῆς ὑμῶν πᾶσαι ἠρίθμηνται. μὴ φοβεῖσθε· πολλῶν στρουθίων διαφέρετε. ¶ 8 Λέγω δὲ ὑμῖν, πᾶς ὃς ἂν ὁμολογήσῃ ἐν ἐμοὶ ἔμπροσθεν τῶν ἀνθρώπων,

you,	whoever	acknowledges		me	before	men,		the	Son	of Man			will	also	acknowledge		him
ὑμῖν	πᾶς	ὃς	ἂν	ὁμολογήσῃ	ἐν	ἐμοὶ	ἔμπροσθεν	τῶν ἀνθρώπων	ὁ	υἱὸς →	τοῦ ἀνθρώπου		καὶ	ὁμολογήσει		ἐν	αὐτῷ
r.dp.2	a.nsm	r.nsm	pl	v.aas.3s	p.d	r.ds.1	p.g	d.gpm n.gpm	d.nsm	n.nsm	d.gsm n.gsm		adv	v.fai.3s		p.d	r.dsm.3
7007	4246	4005	323	3933	1877	1609	1869	3836 476	3836	5626	3836 476		3933	2779 3933		1877	899

before	the	angels	of God.	**9** But	he	who	disowns		me	before	men			will be	disowned		before	the
ἔμπροσθεν	τῶν	ἀγγέλων →	τοῦ θεοῦ.	δὲ	ὁ ←		ἀρνησάμενος		με	ἐνώπιον	τῶν ἀνθρώπων		→	→	ἀπαρνηθήσεται		ἐνώπιον	τῶν
p.g	d.gpm	n.gpm	d.gsm n.gsm	cj	d.nsm		pt.am.nsm		r.as.1	p.g	d.gpm n.gpm				v.fpi.3s		p.g	d.gpm
1869	3836	34	3836 2536	1254	3836		766		1609	1967	3836 476				565		1967	3836

angels	of God.	**10** And	everyone	who	speaks	a	word	against	the	Son	of Man			will be	forgiven,		but
ἀγγέλων →	τοῦ θεοῦ.	Καὶ	πᾶς	ὃς	ἐρεῖ		λόγον	εἰς	τὸν	υἱὸν →	τοῦ ἀνθρώπου,		→	ἀφεθήσεται	αὐτῷ	δὲ
n.gpm	d.gsm n.gsm	cj	a.nsm	r.nsm	v.fai.3s		n.asm	p.a	d.asm	n.asm	d.gsm n.gsm			v.tpi.3s	r.dsm.3	cj
34	3836 2536	2779	4246	4005	3306		3364	1650	3836	5626	3836 476			918	899	1254

anyone	who	blasphemes		against	the	Holy	Spirit		will	not	be forgiven.	¶	**11**	"When	you	are brought	before
τῷ ←		βλασφημήσαντι	εἰς		τὸ	ἅγιον	πνεῦμα →		οὐκ →		ἀφεθήσεται		δὲ	Ὅταν	ὑμᾶς →	εἰσφέρωσιν	ἐπὶ
d.dsm		pt.aa.dsm	p.a		d.asn	a.asn	n.asn		pl		v.fpi.3s		cj	c.tam	r.ap.2	v.pas.3p	p.a
3836		1059	1650		3836	41	4460		4024		918		1254	4020	7007	1662	2093

synagogues,		rulers		and	authorities,		do	not	worry		about how			you	will defend		yourselves
τὰς συναγωγὰς,	καὶ	τὰς	ἀρχὰς,	καὶ	τὰς	ἐξουσίας, →	μὴ		μεριμνήσητε		πῶς	ἢ	τί →	→	ἀπολογήσησθε ←	
d.apf n.apf	cj	d.apf	n.apf	cj	d.apf	n.apf	pl		v.aas.2p		cj	cj	r.asn		v.ams.2p	
3836 5252	2779	3836	794	2779	3836	2026	3534		3590	3534	4802	2445	5515		664	

or	what	you	will say,	**12**	for	the	Holy	Spirit		will teach	you	at	that	time		what	you should say."
ἢ	τί →	→	εἴπητε		γὰρ	τὸ	ἅγιον	πνεῦμα →		διδάξει	ὑμᾶς	ἐν	αὐτῇ	τῇ ὥρᾳ	ἃ →	→	δεῖ εἰπεῖν
cj	r.asn		v.aas.2p		cj	d.nsn	a.nsn	n.nsn		v.fai.3s	r.ap.2	p.d	r.dsf	d.dsf n.dsf	r.apn		v.pai.3s f.aa
2445	5515		3306		1142	3836	41	4460		1438	7007	1877	899	3836 6052	4005		1256 3306

The Parable of the Rich Fool

12:13	Someone	in	the	crowd	said	to	him,	"Teacher,	tell	my	brother		to divide	the	inheritance	with
δέ	τις	ἐκ	τοῦ	ὄχλου	Εἶπεν →		αὐτῷ	διδάσκαλε	εἰπὲ	μου	τῷ ἀδελφῷ,	→	μερίσασθαι	τὴν	κληρονομίαν	μετ'
cj	r.nsm	p.g	d.gsm	n.gsm	v.aai.3s		r.dsm.3	n.vsm	v.aam.2s	r.gs.1	d.dsm n.dsm		f.am	d.asf	n.asf	p.g
1254	5516	1666	3836	4063	3306		899	1437	1609	3836 81		3532	3836	3100	3552

me."	¶	**14**	Jesus	replied,		"Man,	who	appointed	me	a judge	or	an arbiter	between	you?"	**15**	Then	he	said
ἐμοῦ		δὲ	ὁ	εἶπεν	αὐτῷ	ἄνθρωπε	τίς	κατέστησεν	με	κριτὴν	ἢ	μεριστὴν	ἐφ'	ὑμᾶς	δὲ	→	εἶπεν
r.gs.1		cj	d.nsm	v.aai.3s	r.dsm.3	n.vsm	r.nsm	v.aai.3s	r.as.1	n.asm	cj	n.asm	p.a	r.ap.2	cj		v.aai.3s
1609		1254	3836	3306	899	476	5515	2770	1609	3216	2445	3537	2093	7007	1254		3306

to	them,	"Watch out!		Be on your guard		against	all		kinds of greed;		a man's	life			does	not
πρὸς	αὐτούς	ὁρᾶτε ←	καὶ	→	φυλάσσεσθε	ἀπὸ	πάσης	←	πλεονεξίας	ὅτι	αὐτοῦ	ἡ ζωὴ		ἐστιν	οὐκ
p.a	r.apm.3	v.pam.2p	cj		v.pmm.2p	p.g	a.gsf		n.gsf	cj	r.gsm.3	d.nsf n.nsf		v.pai.3s	pl
4639	899	3972	2779		5875	608	4246		4432	4022	899	3836 2437		1639	4024

consist	in	the	abundance		of	his	possessions."	¶	**16** And		he	told		them	this	parable:	"The
ἐν	τῷ	περισσεύειν	τινι	ἐκ	αὐτῷ	τῶν ὑπαρχόντων,		δὲ	→	Εἶπεν	πρὸς	αὐτούς	παραβολὴν	λέγων	ἡ
p.d	d.dsn	f.pa	r.dsm	p.g	r.dsm.3	d.gpn pt.pa.gpn		cj		v.aai.3s	p.a	r.apm.3	n.asf	pt.pa.nsm	d.nsf
1639	1877 3836	4355	5516	1666	899	3836 5639		1254		3306	4639	899	4130	3306	3836

ground	of a	certain	rich	man	produced	a	good	crop.	**17**		He	thought	to	himself,		'What	shall I	do?
χώρα	→	τινὸς	πλουσίου	ἀνθρώπου	εὐφόρησεν				καὶ	→	διελογίζετο	ἐν	ἑαυτῷ	λέγων	τί	→	→	ποιήσω
n.nsf		r.gsm	a.gsm	n.gsm	v.aai.3s				cj		v.imi.3s	p.d	r.dsm.3	pt.pa.nsm	r.asn			v.aas.1s
6001		5516	4454	476	2369				2779		1368	1877	1571	3306	5515			4472

I	have	no	place	to store		my	crops.'	**18** "Then		he	said,	'This is what I'll do.			I	will	tear	down	my
ὅτι	ἔχω	οὐκ	ποῦ →	συνάξω	μου	τοὺς	καρπούς	καὶ		εἶπεν	τοῦτο	→	ποιήσω →	→	καθελῶ ←		μου
cj	v.pai.1s	pl	adv	v.aas.1s	r.gs.1	d.apm	n.apm	cj		v.aai.3s	r.asn		v.fai.1s		v.fai.1s		r.gs.1
4022	2400	4024	4543	5251	1609	3836	2843	2779		3306	4047		4472		2747		1609

barns		and build	bigger	ones, and	there	I	will store	all		my	grain	and	my	goods.	**19** And	I'll	say	to
τὰς ἀποθήκας,	καὶ	οἰκοδομήσω	μείζονας	καὶ	ἐκεῖ	→	συνάξω	πάντα	τὸν	σῖτον	καὶ	μου	τὰ ἀγαθά,		καὶ	→	ἐρῶ →	
d.apf n.apf	cj	v.fai.1s	a.apf.c	cj	adv		v.fai.1s	a.asm	d.asm	n.asm	cj	r.gs.1	d.apn a.apn		cj		v.fai.1s	
3836 630	2779	3868	3489	2779	1695		5251	4246	3836	4992	2779	1609	3836 19		2779		3306	

myself,	"You	have	plenty of	good	things	laid	up	for	many	years. Take	life	easy;		eat,	drink and be
τῇ ψυχῇ μου,	Ψυχή →	ἔχεις	πολλὰ →	ἀγαθὰ →		κείμενα ←		εἰς	πολλὰ	ἔτη	→	→	ἀναπαύου	φάγε	πίε
d.dsf n.dsf	r.gs.1	n.vsf	v.pai.2s	a.apn	a.apn		pt.pm.apn		p.a	a.apn	n.apn			v.pmm.2s	v.aam.2s v.aam.2s
3836 6034	1609	6034	2400	4498	19		3023		1650	4498	2291			399	2266 4403

καὶ ὁ υἱὸς τοῦ ἀνθρώπου ὁμολογήσει ἐν αὐτῷ ἔμπροσθεν τῶν ἀγγέλων τοῦ θεοῦ· 9 ὁ δὲ ἀρνησάμενός με ἐνώπιον τῶν ἀνθρώπων ἀπαρνηθήσεται ἐνώπιον τῶν ἀγγέλων τοῦ θεοῦ. 10 καὶ πᾶς ὃς ἐρεῖ λόγον εἰς τὸν υἱὸν τοῦ ἀνθρώπου, ἀφεθήσεται αὐτῷ· τῷ δὲ εἰς τὸ ἅγιον πνεῦμα βλασφημήσαντι οὐκ ἀφεθήσεται. ¶ 11 ὅταν δὲ εἰσφέρωσιν ὑμᾶς ἐπὶ τὰς συναγωγὰς καὶ τὰς ἀρχὰς καὶ τὰς ἐξουσίας, μὴ μεριμνήσητε πῶς ἢ τί ἀπολογήσησθε ἢ τί εἴπητε· 12 τὸ γὰρ ἅγιον πνεῦμα διδάξει ὑμᾶς ἐν αὐτῇ τῇ ὥρᾳ ἃ δεῖ εἰπεῖν.

12:13 Εἶπεν δέ τις ἐκ τοῦ ὄχλου αὐτῷ, Διδάσκαλε, εἰπὲ τῷ ἀδελφῷ μου μερίσασθαι μετ' ἐμοῦ τὴν κληρονομίαν. ¶ 14 ὁ δὲ εἶπεν αὐτῷ, Ἄνθρωπε, τίς με κατέστησεν κριτὴν ἢ μεριστὴν ἐφ' ὑμᾶς; 15 εἶπεν δὲ πρὸς αὐτούς, Ὁρᾶτε καὶ φυλάσσεσθε ἀπὸ πάσης πλεονεξίας, ὅτι οὐκ ἐν τῷ περισσεύειν τινι ἡ ζωὴ αὐτοῦ ἐστιν ἐκ τῶν ὑπαρχόντων αὐτῷ. ¶ 16 Εἶπεν δὲ παραβολὴν πρὸς αὐτοὺς λέγων, Ἀνθρώπου τινὸς πλουσίου εὐφόρησεν ἡ χώρα. 17 καὶ διελογίζετο ἐν ἑαυτῷ λέγων, Τί ποιήσω, ὅτι οὐκ ἔχω ποῦ συνάξω τοὺς καρπούς μου; 18 καὶ εἶπεν, Τοῦτο ποιήσω, καθελῶ μου τὰς ἀποθήκας καὶ μείζονας οἰκοδομήσω καὶ συνάξω ἐκεῖ πάντα τὸν σῖτον καὶ τὰ ἀγαθά μου 19 καὶ ἐρῶ τῇ ψυχῇ μου, Ψυχή, ἔχεις πολλὰ ἀγαθὰ κείμενα εἰς ἔτη πολλά· ἀναπαύου, φάγε,

merry.'" **20** "But God said to him, 'You fool! This very night your life will be demanded from you. Then
εὐφραίνου δὲ ὁ θεός εἶπεν → αὐτῷ → ἄφρων ταύτῃ τῇ νυκτὶ σου ⌜τὴν ψυχήν⌝ → → ἀπαιτοῦσιν ἀπὸ σοῦ δὲ
v.ppm.2s cj d.nsm n.nsm v.aai.3s r.dsm.3 a.vsm r.dsf d.dsf n.dsf r.gs.2 d.asf n.asf v.pai.3p p.g r.gs.2 cj
2370 1254 3836 2536 3306 899 933 4047 3836 3816 5148 3836 6034 555 608 5148 1254

who will get what you have prepared for yourself?' ¶ **21** "This is how it will be with anyone who stores up
τίνι → ἔσται ἃ → → ἡτοίμασας οὕτως ὁ ← θησαυρίζων ←
r.dsm v.fmi.3s r.apn v.aai.2s adv d.nsm pt.pa.nsm
5515 1639 4005 2286 4048 3836 2564

things for himself but is not rich toward God."
→ ἑαυτῷ καὶ μὴ πλουτῶν εἰς θεόν
r.dsm.3 cj pl pt.pa.nsm p.a n.asm
1571 2779 3590 4456 1650 2536

Do Not Worry

12:22 Then Jesus said to his disciples: "Therefore I tell you, do not worry about your life, what you
δὲ Εἶπεν πρὸς αὐτοῦ ⌜τοὺς μαθητάς⌝ διὰ τοῦτο → λέγω ὑμῖν → μὴ μεριμνᾶτε → τῇ ψυχῇ τί →
cj v.aai.3s p.a r.gsm.3 d.apm n.apm p.a r.asn v.pai.1s r.dp.2 pl v.pam.2p d.dsf n.dsf r.asn
1254 3306 4639 899 3836 3412 1328 4047 3306 7007 3534 3590 3534 3836 6034 5515

will eat; or about your body, what you will wear. **23** Life is more than food, and the body more
→ φάγητε μηδὲ → τῷ σώματι τί → → ἐνδύσησθε γὰρ ἡ ψυχή ἐστιν πλεῖόν → ⌜τῆς τροφῆς⌝ καὶ τὸ σῶμα
v.aas.2p d.dsn n.dsn r.asn v.ams.2p cj d.nsf n.nsf v.pai.3s a.nsn.c d.gsf n.gsf cj d.nsn n.nsn
2266 3593 3836 5393 5515 1907 1142 3836 6034 1639 4498 3836 5575 2779 3836 5393

than clothes. **24** Consider the ravens: They do not sow or reap, they have no storeroom or
→ ⌜τοῦ ἐνδύματος⌝ κατανοήσατε τοὺς κόρακας ὅτι → οὐ σπείρουσιν οὐδὲ θερίζουσιν οἷς ἔστιν οὐκ ταμεῖον οὐδὲ
d.gsn n.gsn v.aam.2p d.apm n.apm cj pl v.pai.3p cj v.pai.3p r.dpm v.pai.3s pl n.nsn cj
3836 1903 2917 3836 3165 4022 5062 5062 4024 5062 4028 2545 4005 1639 4024 5421 4028

barn; yet God feeds them. And how much more valuable you are than birds! **25** Who of you by
ἀποθήκη καὶ ὁ θεός τρέφει αὐτούς πόσῳ μᾶλλον διαφέρετε ὑμεῖς ← → ⌜τῶν πετεινῶν⌝ δὲ τίς ἐξ ὑμῶν
n.nsf cj d.nsm n.nsm v.pai.3s r.apm.3 r.dpn adv.c v.pai.2p r.np.2 d.gpn n.gpn cj r.nsm p.g r.gp.2
630 2779 3836 2536 5555 899 4531 3437 1422 7007 1422 3836 4374 1254 5515 1666 7007

worrying can add a single hour to his life? **26** Since you cannot do this very little thing,
μεριμνῶν δύναται προσθεῖναι πῆχυν ἐπὶ αὐτοῦ ⌜τὴν ἡλικίαν⌝ οὖν εἰ → οὐδὲ δύνασθε → ἐλάχιστον ←
pt.pa.nsm v.ppi.3s f.aa n.asm p.a r.gsm.3 d.asf n.asf cj cj adv v.ppi.2p a.asn.s
3534 1538 4707 4388 2093 899 3836 2461 4036 1623 1538 4028 1538 1788

why do you worry about the rest? ¶ **27** "Consider how the lilies grow. They do not labor or spin. Yet I
τί → → μεριμνᾶτε περὶ τῶν λοιπῶν κατανοήσατε πῶς τὰ κρίνα αὐξάνει → οὐ κοπιᾷ οὐδὲ νήθει δὲ →
r.asn v.pai.2p p.g d.gpn a.gpn v.aam.2p adv d.apn n.apn v.pai.3s pl v.pai.3s cj v.pai.3s cj
5515 3534 4309 3836 3370 2917 4802 3836 3211 889 3159 3159 4024 3159 4028 3756 1254

tell you, not even Solomon in all his splendor was dressed like one of these. **28** If that is how God
λέγω ὑμῖν οὐδὲ Σολομὼν ἐν πάσῃ αὐτοῦ ⌜τῇ δόξῃ⌝ περιεβάλετο ὡς ἓν τούτων δὲ εἰ → οὕτως ὁ θεός
v.pai.1s r.dp.2 adv n.nsm p.d a.dsf r.gsm.3 d.dsf n.dsf v.ami.3s cj a.nsn r.gpn cj cj adv d.nsm n.nsm
3306 7007 4028 5048 1877 4246 899 3836 1518 4314 6055 1651 4047 1254 1623 4048 3836 2536

clothes the grass of the field, which is here today, and tomorrow is thrown into the fire, how much
ἀμφιέζει τὸν χόρτον ἐν ἀγρῷ ὄντα σήμερον καὶ αὔριον → βαλλόμενον εἰς κλίβανον → πόσῳ
v.pai.3s d.asm n.asm p.d n.dsm pt.pa.asm adv cj adv pt.pp.asm p.a n.asm r.dpn
313 3836 5965 1877 69 1639 4958 2779 892 965 1650 3106 4531

more will he clothe you, O you of little faith! **29** And do not set your heart on what you will eat or
μᾶλλον ὑμᾶς → → → ὀλιγόπιστοι καὶ ὑμεῖς μὴ ζητεῖτε ← τί → φάγητε καὶ τί
adv.c r.ap.2 a.vpm cj r.np.2 pl v.pam.2p r.asn v.aas.2p cj r.asn
3437 7007 3899 2779 7007 2426 3590 2426 5515 2266 2779 5515

drink; do not worry about it. **30** For the pagan world runs after all such things, and your
πίητε καὶ μὴ μετεωρίζεσθε γὰρ τὰ ἔθνη ⌜τοῦ κόσμου⌝ ἐπιζητοῦσιν πάντα ταῦτα ← δὲ ὑμῶν
v.aas.2p cj pl v.ppm.2p cj d.npn n.npn d.gsn n.gsm v.pai.3p a.apn r.apn cj r.gp.2
4403 2779 3577 3590 3577 1142 3836 1620 3836 3180 2118 4246 4047 1254 7007

Father knows that you need them. **31** But seek his kingdom, and these things will be given to you as
ὁ πατήρ οἶδεν ὅτι → χρῄζετε τούτων πλὴν ζητεῖτε αὐτοῦ ⌜τὴν βασιλείαν⌝ καὶ ταῦτα ← → προστεθήσεται → ὑμῖν
d.nsm n.nsm v.rai.3s cj v.pai.2p r.gpn cj v.pam.2p r.gsm.3 d.asf n.asf cj r.npn v.fpi.3s r.dp.2
3836 4252 3857 4022 5974 4047 4440 2426 899 3836 993 2779 4047 4707 7007

πίε, εὐφραίνου. **20** εἶπεν δὲ αὐτῷ ὁ θεός, Ἄφρων, ταύτῃ τῇ νυκτὶ τὴν ψυχήν σου ἀπαιτοῦσιν ἀπὸ σοῦ· ἃ δὲ ἡτοίμασας, τίνι ἔσται; ¶ **21** οὕτως ὁ θησαυρίζων ἑαυτῷ καὶ μὴ εἰς θεὸν πλουτῶν.

12:22 Εἶπεν δὲ πρὸς τοὺς μαθητάς [αὐτοῦ], Διὰ τοῦτο λέγω ὑμῖν· μὴ μεριμνᾶτε τῇ ψυχῇ τί φάγητε, μηδὲ τῷ σώματι τί ἐνδύσησθε. **23** ἡ γὰρ ψυχὴ πλεῖόν ἐστιν τῆς τροφῆς καὶ τὸ σῶμα τοῦ ἐνδύματος. **24** κατανοήσατε τοὺς κόρακας ὅτι οὐ σπείρουσιν οὐδὲ θερίζουσιν, οἷς οὐκ ἔστιν ταμεῖον οὐδὲ ἀποθήκη, καὶ ὁ θεὸς τρέφει αὐτούς· πόσῳ μᾶλλον ὑμεῖς διαφέρετε τῶν πετεινῶν. **25** τίς δὲ ἐξ ὑμῶν μεριμνῶν δύναται ἐπὶ τὴν ἡλικίαν αὐτοῦ προσθεῖναι πῆχυν «πῆχυν;» ἕνα; **26** εἰ οὖν οὐδὲ ἐλάχιστον δύνασθε, τί περὶ τῶν λοιπῶν μεριμνᾶτε; ¶ **27** κατανοήσατε τὰ κρίνα πῶς αὐξάνει· οὐ κοπιᾷ οὐδὲ νήθει· λέγω δὲ ὑμῖν, οὐδὲ Σολομὼν ἐν πάσῃ τῇ δόξῃ αὐτοῦ περιεβάλετο ὡς ἓν τούτων. **28** εἰ δὲ ἐν ἀγρῷ τὸν χόρτον ὄντα σήμερον καὶ αὔριον εἰς κλίβανον βαλλόμενον ὁ θεὸς οὕτως ἀμφιέζει, πόσῳ μᾶλλον ὑμᾶς, ὀλιγόπιστοι. **29** καὶ ὑμεῖς μὴ ζητεῖτε τί φάγητε καὶ τί πίητε καὶ μὴ μετεωρίζεσθε· **30** ταῦτα γὰρ πάντα τὰ ἔθνη τοῦ κόσμου ἐπιζητοῦσιν, ὑμῶν δὲ ὁ πατὴρ οἶδεν ὅτι χρῄζετε τούτων. **31** πλὴν ζητεῖτε τὴν βασιλείαν αὐτοῦ,

well. ¶ ³² "Do not be afraid, little flock, for your Father has been pleased to give you the kingdom.
→ Μὴ φοβοῦ μικρὸν ˌτὸ ποίμνιονˌ ὅτι ὑμῶν ὁ πατήρˌ → → εὐδόκησεν → δοῦναι ὑμῖν τὴν βασιλείαν
pl v.ppm.2s a.vsn d.vsn n.vsn cj r.gp.2 d.nsm n.nsm v.aai.3s f.aa r.dp.2 d.asf n.asf
5828 3590 5828 3625 3836 4480 4022 7007 3836 4252 2305 1443 7007 3836 993

³³ Sell your possessions and give to the poor. Provide purses for yourselves that will not wear out,
Πωλήσατε ὑμῶν ˌτὰ ὑπάρχονταˌ καὶ δότε ἐλεημοσύνην ποιήσατε βαλλάντια → ἑαυτοῖς → → μὴ παλαιούμενα ←
v.aam.2p r.gp.2 d.apn pt.pa.apn cj v.aam.2p n.asf v.aam.2p n.apn r.dpm.2 pl pt.pp.apn
4797 7007 3836 5639 2779 1443 1797 4472 964 1571 4096 4096 3590 4096

a treasure in heaven that will not be exhausted, where no thief comes near and no moth destroys. ³⁴ For
θησαυρὸν ἐν ˌτοῖς οὐρανοῖςˌ → ἀνέκλειπτον ὅπου οὐκ κλέπτης → ἐγγίζει οὐδὲ ← σὴς διαφθείρει γάρ
n.asm p.d d.dpm n.dpm a.asm cj pl n.nsm v.pai.3s cj n.nsm v.pai.3s cj
2565 1877 3836 4041 444 3963 4024 3095 1581 4028 4962 1425 1142

where your treasure is, there your heart will be also.
ὅπου ὑμῶν ˌὁ θησαυρόςˌ ἐστιν ἐκεῖ ὑμῶν ἡ καρδίαˌ → ἔσται καὶ
cj r.gp.2 d.nsm n.nsm v.pai.3s adv r.gp.2 d.nsf n.nsf v.fmi.3s adv
3963 7007 3836 2565 1639 1695 7007 3836 2840 1639 2779

Watchfulness

12:35 "Be dressed ready for service and keep your lamps burning, ³⁶ like men
Ἔστωσαν ὑμῶν αἱ ὀσφύες περιεζωσμέναι ← ← ← καὶ → οἱ λύχνοι καιόμενοι καὶ ὑμεῖς ὅμοιοι ἀνθρώποις
v.pam.3p r.gp.2 d.npf n.npf pt.rp.npf cj d.npm n.npm pt.pp.npm cj r.np.2 a.npm n.dpm
1639 7007 3836 4019 4322 2779 2794 3836 3394 2794 2779 7007 3927 476

waiting for their master to return from a wedding banquet, so that when he comes and knocks
προσδεχομένοις ← ἑαυτῶν ˌτὸν κύριονˌ πότε ἀναλύσῃ ἐκ ˌτῶν γάμωνˌ ἵνα → → ἐλθόντος καὶ κρούσαντος
pt.pm.dpm r.gpm.3 d.asm n.asm cj v.aas.3s p.g d.gpm n.gpm cj pt.aa.gsm cj pt.aa.gsm
4657 1571 3836 3261 4537 386 1666 3836 1141 2671 2262 2779 3218

they can immediately open the door for him. ³⁷ It will be good for those servants whose master finds
→ → εὐθέως ἀνοίξωσιν → αὐτῷ μακάριοι ἐκεῖνοι ˌοἱ δοῦλοιˌ οὓς ˌὁ κύριοςˌ εὑρήσει
adv v.aas.3p r.dsm.3 a.npm r.npm d.npm n.npm r.apm d.nsm n.nsm v.fai.3s
487 487 2311 487 899 3421 1697 3836 1529 4005 3836 3261 2351

them watching when he comes. I tell you the truth, he will dress himself to serve, will have them
γρηγοροῦντας ← ἐλθὼν λέγω ὑμῖν ἀμὴν ὅτι → περιζώσεται καὶ → → αὐτοὺς
pt.pa.apm pt.aa.nsm v.pai.1s r.dp.2 pl cj v.fmi.3s cj r.apm.3
4005 1213 2262 3306 7007 297 4022 4322 2779 369 369 899

recline at the table and will come and wait on them. ³⁸ It will be good for those servants whose
ἀνακλινεῖ ← ← καὶ → παρελθὼν διακονήσει ← αὐτοῖς → εἰσιν μακάριοι ἐκεῖνοι καὶ
v.fai.3s cj pt.aa.nsm v.fai.3s r.dpm.3 v.pai.3p a.npm r.npm cj
369 2779 4216 1354 899 1639 3421 1697 2779

master finds them ready, even if he comes in the second or third watch of the night. ³⁹ But understand this:
εὕρῃ οὕτως κἂν ← ἔλθῃ ἐν τῇ δευτέρᾳ κἂν ἐν ˌτῇ τρίτῃ φυλακῇ ← ← δὲ γινώσκετε τοῦτο
v.aas.3s adv crasis v.aas.3s p.d d.dsf n.dsf crasis p.d d.dsf a.dsf n.dsf cj v.pam.2p r.asn
2351 4048 2829 2262 1877 3836 1311 2829 1877 3836 5569 5871 1254 1182 4047

If the owner of the house had known at what hour the thief was coming, he would not have let his
ὅτι εἰ ὁ οἰκοδεσπότης ← ← → ᾔδει → ποίᾳ ὥρᾳ ὁ κλέπτης → ἔρχεται → ἂν οὐκ → ἀφῆκεν αὐτοῦ
cj cj d.nsm n.nsm v.lai.3s r.dsf n.dsf d.nsm n.nsm v.pmi.3s pl pl v.aai.3s r.gsm.3
4022 1623 3836 3867 3857 4481 6052 3836 3095 2262 918 323 4024 918 899

house be broken into. ⁴⁰ You also must be ready, because the Son of Man will come at an hour
ˌτὸν οἶκονˌ διορυχθῆναι ← ὑμεῖς καὶ → γίνεσθε ἕτοιμοι ὅτι → ὁ υἱὸς → ˌτοῦ ἀνθρώπουˌ → ἔρχεται ᾗ ὥρᾳ
d.asm n.asm f.ap r.np.2 cj v.pmm.2p a.npm cj d.nsm n.nsm d.gsm n.gsm v.pmi.3s r.dsf n.dsf
3836 3875 1482 7007 2779 1181 2289 4022 3836 5626 3836 476 2262 4005 6052

when you do not expect him." ¶ ⁴¹ Peter asked, "Lord, are you telling this parable to us,
→ → οὐ δοκεῖτε δὲ ὁ Πέτρος, Εἶπεν κύριε λέγεις ταύτην ˌτὴν παραβολήνˌ πρὸς ἡμᾶς
pl v.pai.2p cj d.nsm n.nsm v.aai.3s n.vsm v.pai.2s r.asf d.asf n.asf p.a r.ap.1
1506 1506 4024 1506 1254 3836 4377 3306 3261 3306 4047 3836 4130 4639 7005

or to everyone?" ⁴² The Lord answered, "Who then is the faithful and wise manager, whom the
ἢ καὶ πρὸς πάντας καὶ ὁ κύριος εἶπεν τίς ἄρα ἐστὶν ὁ πιστὸς ˌὁ φρόνιμοςˌ οἰκονόμος ὃν ὁ
cj adv p.a a.apm cj d.nsm n.nsm v.aai.3s r.nsm cj v.pai.3s d.nsm a.nsm d.nsm a.nsm n.nsm r.asm d.nsm
2445 2779 4639 4246 2779 3836 3261 3306 5515 726 1639 3836 4412 3836 5861 3874 4005 3836

καὶ ταῦτα προστεθήσεται ὑμῖν. ¶ ³² Μὴ φοβοῦ, τὸ μικρὸν ποίμνιον, ὅτι εὐδόκησεν ὁ πατὴρ ὑμῶν δοῦναι ὑμῖν τὴν βασιλείαν.
³³ Πωλήσατε τὰ ὑπάρχοντα ὑμῶν καὶ δότε ἐλεημοσύνην· ποιήσατε ἑαυτοῖς βαλλάντια μὴ παλαιούμενα, θησαυρὸν ἀνέκλειπτον ἐν τοῖς οὐρανοῖς, ὅπου κλέπτης οὐκ ἐγγίζει οὐδὲ σὴς διαφθείρει· ³⁴ ὅπου γάρ ἐστιν ὁ θησαυρὸς ὑμῶν, ἐκεῖ καὶ ἡ καρδία ὑμῶν ἔσται.
12:35 Ἔστωσαν ὑμῶν αἱ ὀσφύες περιεζωσμέναι καὶ οἱ λύχνοι καιόμενοι· ³⁶ καὶ ὑμεῖς ὅμοιοι ἀνθρώποις προσδεχομένοις τὸν κύριον ἑαυτῶν πότε ἀναλύσῃ ἐκ τῶν γάμων, ἵνα ἐλθόντος καὶ κρούσαντος εὐθέως ἀνοίξωσιν αὐτῷ. ³⁷ μακάριοι οἱ δοῦλοι ἐκεῖνοι, οὓς ἐλθὼν ὁ κύριος εὑρήσει γρηγοροῦντας· ἀμὴν λέγω ὑμῖν ὅτι περιζώσεται καὶ ἀνακλινεῖ αὐτοὺς καὶ παρελθὼν διακονήσει αὐτοῖς. ³⁸ κἂν ἐν τῇ δευτέρᾳ κἂν ἐν τῇ τρίτῃ φυλακῇ ἔλθῃ καὶ εὕρῃ οὕτως, μακάριοί εἰσιν ἐκεῖνοι. ³⁹ τοῦτο δὲ γινώσκετε ὅτι εἰ ᾔδει ὁ οἰκοδεσπότης ποίᾳ ὥρᾳ ὁ κλέπτης ἔρχεται, οὐκ ἂν ἀφῆκεν διορυχθῆναι τὸν οἶκον αὐτοῦ. ⁴⁰ καὶ ὑμεῖς γίνεσθε ἕτοιμοι, ὅτι ᾗ ὥρᾳ οὐ δοκεῖτε ὁ υἱὸς τοῦ ἀνθρώπου ἔρχεται. ¶ ⁴¹ Εἶπεν δὲ ὁ Πέτρος, Κύριε, πρὸς ἡμᾶς τὴν παραβολὴν

master puts in charge of his servants to give them their food allowance at the proper time?
κύριος → → καταστήσει ἐπὶ αὐτοῦ ⌐τῆς θεραπείας⌐ → ⌐τοῦ διδόναι⌐ ⌐τὸ σιτομέτριον⌐ ἐν → καιρῷ
n.nsm v.fai.3s p.g r.gsm.3 d.gsf n.gsf d.gsn f.pa d.asn n.asn p.d n.dsm
3261 2770 2093 899 3836 2542 3836 1443 3836 4991 1877 2789

43 It will be good for that servant whom the master finds doing so when he returns. **44** I tell you the
μακάριος ἐκεῖνος ὁ δοῦλος ὃν ὁ κύριος αὐτοῦ εὑρήσει ποιοῦντα οὕτως → → ἐλθὼν → λέγω ὑμῖν
a.nsm r.nsm d.nsm n.nsm r.asm d.nsm n.nsm r.gsm.3 v.fai.3s pt.pa.asm adv pt.aa.nsm v.pai.1s r.dp.2
3421 1697 3836 1529 4005 3836 3261 899 2351 4472 4048 2262 3306 7007

truth, he will put him in charge of all his possessions. **45** But suppose the servant says to
ἀληθῶς ὅτι → → καταστήσει αὐτὸν ← ἐπὶ πᾶσιν αὐτοῦ ⌐τοῖς ὑπάρχουσιν⌐ δὲ ἐὰν ἐκεῖνος ὁ δοῦλος εἴπῃ
adv cj v.fai.3s r.asm.3 p.d a.dpn r.gsm.3 d.dpn pt.pa.dpn cj cj r.nsm d.nsm n.nsm v.aas.3s
242 4022 2770 899 2770 2770 2093 4246 899 3836 5639 1254 1569 1697 3836 1529 3306

himself, 'My master is taking a long time in coming,' and he then begins to beat the
⌐ἐν τῇ καρδίᾳ αὐτοῦ⌐ μου ὁ κύριος, → → → → χρονίζει ἔρχεσθαι καὶ → ἄρξηται → τύπτειν τοὺς
p.d d.dsf n.dsf r.gsm.3 r.gs.1 d.nsm n.nsm v.pai.3s f.pm cj v.ams.3s f.pa d.apm
1877 3836 2840 899 1609 3836 3261 5988 2262 2779 806 5597 3836

menservants and maidservants and to eat and drink and get drunk. **46** The master of that servant will
παῖδας καὶ ⌐τὰς παιδίσκας⌐ τε → ἐσθίειν καὶ πίνειν καὶ → μεθύσκεσθαι ὁ κύριος → ἐκείνου ⌐τοῦ δούλου⌐ →
n.apm cj d.apf n.apf cj f.pa cj f.pa cj f.pp d.nsm n.nsm r.gsm d.gsm n.gsm
4090 2779 3836 4087 5445 2266 2779 4403 2779 3499 3836 3261 1529 1697 3836 1529

come on a day when he does not expect him and at an hour he is not aware of. He will cut
ἥξει ἐν ἡμέρᾳ ᾗ → → οὐ προσδοκᾷ καὶ ἐν ὥρᾳ ᾗ → οὐ γινώσκει ← καὶ → διχοτομήσει
v.fai.3s p.d n.dsf r.dsf pl v.pai.3s cj p.d n.dsf r.dsf pl v.pai.3s cj v.fai.3s
2457 1877 2465 4005 4659 4659 4024 4659 2779 1877 6052 4005 1182 1182 4024 1182 2779 1497

him to pieces and assign him a place with the unbelievers. ¶ **47** "That servant who knows his
αὐτὸν ← ← καὶ θήσει αὐτοῦ ⌐τὸ μέρος⌐ μετὰ τῶν ἀπίστων δὲ Ἐκεῖνος ὁ δοῦλος ὁ γνοὺς αὐτοῦ
r.asm.3 cj v.fai.3s r.gsm.3 d.asn n.asn p.g d.gpm a.gpm cj r.nsm d.nsm n.nsm d.nsm pt.aa.nsm r.gsm.3
899 1497 1497 2779 5502 899 3836 3538 3552 3836 603 1254 1697 3836 1529 3836 1182 899

master's will and does not get ready or does not do what his master wants will be beaten
⌐τοῦ κυρίου⌐ ⌐τὸ θέλημα⌐ καὶ → μὴ → ἑτοιμάσας ἢ → ποιήσας πρὸς αὐτοῦ ⌐τὸ θέλημα⌐ → δαρήσεται
d.gsm n.gsm d.asn n.asn cj pl pt.aa.nsm cj pt.aa.nsm p.a r.gsm.3 d.asn n.asn v.fpi.3s
3836 3261 3836 2525 2779 2286 2286 2445 4472 4639 899 3836 2525 1296

with many blows. **48** But the one who does not know and does things deserving punishment will be beaten with
πολλάς δὲ ὁ ← → μὴ γνοὺς δὲ ποιήσας ἄξια πληγῶν → δαρήσεται
a.apf cj d.nsm pl pt.aa.nsm cj pt.aa.nsm a.apn n.gpf v.fpi.3s
4498 1254 3836 1182 3590 1182 1254 4472 545 4435 1296

few blows. From everyone who has been given much, much will be demanded; and from the one who
ὀλίγας δὲ παρ' αὐτοῦ παντὶ ᾧ → → ἐδόθη πολὺ πολὺ → ζητηθήσεται καὶ → → ᾧ
a.apf cj p.g r.gsm.3 a.dsm r.dsm v.api.3s a.nsn a.nsn v.fpi.3s cj r.dsm
3900 1254 4123 899 4246 4005 1443 4498 4498 2426 2779 4005

has been entrusted with much, much more will be asked.
→ → παρέθεντο πολύ → περισσότερον → → αἰτήσουσιν αὐτόν
v.ami.3p a.asn a.asn.c v.fai.3p r.asm.3
4192 4498 4358 160 899

Not Peace but Division

12:49 "I have come to bring fire on the earth, and how I wish it were already kindled! **50** But I have a baptism
→ → ἦλθον → βαλεῖν Πῦρ ἐπὶ τὴν γῆν καὶ τί → θέλω εἰ → → ἤδη ἀνήφθη δὲ → ἔχω βάπτισμα
v.aai.1s f.aa n.asn p.a d.asf n.asf cj r.asn v.pai.1s cj adv v.api.3s cj v.pai.1s n.asn
2262 965 4786 2093 3836 1178 2779 5515 2527 1623 409 409 2453 409 1254 2400 967

to undergo, and how distressed I am until it is completed! **51** Do you think I came to bring peace on
→ βαπτισθῆναι καὶ πῶς συνέχομαι ← ⌐ἕως ὅτου⌐ → τελεσθῇ δοκεῖτε ὅτι → παρεγενόμην → δοῦναι εἰρήνην ἐν
f.ap cj pl v.ppi.1s p.g r.gsn v.aps.3s v.pai.2p cj v.ami.1s f.aa n.asf p.d
966 2779 4802 5309 2401 4015 5464 1506 4022 4134 1443 1645 1877

earth? No, I tell you, but division. **52** From now on there will be five in one family divided
⌐τῇ γῇ⌐ οὐχὶ → λέγω ὑμῖν ἀλλ' ἢ διαμερισμόν γὰρ ἀπὸ ⌐τοῦ νῦν⌐ ← → ἔσονται πέντε ἐν ἑνὶ οἴκῳ διαμεμερισμένοι
d.dsf n.dsf pl v.pai.1s r.dp.2 cj pl n.asm cj p.g d.gsm adv v.fmi.3p a.npm p.d a.dsm n.dsm pt.rp.npm
3836 1178 4049 3306 7007 247 2445 1375 1142 608 3836 3814 1639 4297 1877 1651 3875 1374

ταύτην λέγεις ἢ καὶ πρὸς πάντας; **42** καὶ εἶπεν ὁ κύριος, Τίς ἄρα ἐστὶν ὁ πιστὸς οἰκονόμος ὁ φρόνιμος, ὃν καταστήσει ὁ κύριος ἐπὶ τῆς θεραπείας αὐτοῦ τοῦ διδόναι ἐν καιρῷ [τὸ] σιτομέτριον; **43** μακάριος ὁ δοῦλος ἐκεῖνος, ὃν ἐλθὼν ὁ κύριος αὐτοῦ εὑρήσει ποιοῦντα οὕτως. **44** ἀληθῶς λέγω ὑμῖν ὅτι ἐπὶ πᾶσιν τοῖς ὑπάρχουσιν αὐτοῦ καταστήσει αὐτόν. **45** ἐὰν δὲ εἴπῃ ὁ δοῦλος ἐκεῖνος ἐν τῇ καρδίᾳ αὐτοῦ, Χρονίζει ὁ κύριός μου ἔρχεσθαι, καὶ ἄρξηται τύπτειν τοὺς παῖδας καὶ τὰς παιδίσκας, ἐσθίειν τε καὶ πίνειν καὶ μεθύσκεσθαι, **46** ἥξει ὁ κύριος τοῦ δούλου ἐκείνου ἐν ἡμέρᾳ ᾗ οὐ προσδοκᾷ καὶ ἐν ὥρᾳ ᾗ οὐ γινώσκει, καὶ διχοτομήσει αὐτὸν καὶ τὸ μέρος αὐτοῦ μετὰ τῶν ἀπίστων θήσει. ¶ **47** ἐκεῖνος δὲ ὁ δοῦλος ὁ γνοὺς τὸ θέλημα τοῦ κυρίου αὐτοῦ καὶ μὴ ἑτοιμάσας ἢ ποιήσας πρὸς τὸ θέλημα αὐτοῦ δαρήσεται πολλάς· **48** ὁ δὲ μὴ γνούς, ποιήσας δὲ ἄξια πληγῶν δαρήσεται ὀλίγας. παντὶ δὲ ᾧ ἐδόθη πολύ, πολὺ ζητηθήσεται παρ' αὐτοῦ, καὶ ᾧ παρέθεντο πολύ, περισσότερον αἰτήσουσιν αὐτόν.

12:49 Πῦρ ἦλθον βαλεῖν ἐπὶ τὴν γῆν, καὶ τί θέλω εἰ ἤδη ἀνήφθη. **50** βάπτισμα δὲ ἔχω βαπτισθῆναι, καὶ πῶς συνέχομαι ἕως ὅτου τελεσθῇ. **51** δοκεῖτε ὅτι εἰρήνην παρεγενόμην δοῦναι ἐν τῇ γῇ; οὐχί, λέγω ὑμῖν, ἀλλ' ἢ διαμερισμόν. **52** ἔσονται γὰρ ἀπὸ

against each other, three against two and two against three. **53** They will be divided,   father against son and son
τρεῖς ἐπὶ δυσὶν καὶ δύο ἐπὶ τρισίν   διαμερισθήσονται πατὴρ ἐπὶ υἱῷ καὶ υἱὸς
a.npm p.d a.dpm cj a.npm p.d a.dpm   v.fpi.3p n.nsm p.d n.dsm cj n.nsm
5552 2093 1545 2779 1545 2093 5552   1374 4252 2093 5626 2779 5626

against father, mother against daughter   and daughter against mother,   mother-in-law against daughter-in-law
ἐπὶ πατρί μήτηρ ἐπὶ ⌜τὴν θυγατέρα⌝   καὶ θυγάτηρ ἐπὶ ⌜τὴν μητέρα⌝ πενθερὰ   ἐπὶ ⌜τὴν νύμφην⌝
p.d n.dsm n.nsf p.a d.asf n.asf   cj n.nsf p.a d.asf n.asf n.nsf   p.a d.asf n.asf
2093 4252 3613 2093 3836 2588   2779 2588 2093 3836 3613 4289   2093 3836 3811

and daughter-in-law against mother-in-law."
αὐτῆς καὶ νύμφη ἐπὶ ⌜τὴν πενθεράν⌝
r.gsf.3 cj n.nsf p.a d.asf n.asf
899 2779 3811 2093 3836 4289

Interpreting the Times

12:54 He said   to the crowd: "When you see a cloud   rising   in the west, immediately you
δὲ → Ἔλεγεν καὶ → τοῖς ὄχλοις ὅταν → ἴδητε ⌜τὴν νεφέλην⌝ ἀνατέλλουσαν ἐπὶ δυσμῶν εὐθέως →
cj v.iai.3s adv d.dpm n.dpm cj v.aas.2p d.asf n.asf pt.pa.asf p.g n.gpf adv
1254 3306 2779 3836 4063 4020 1625 3836 3749 422 2093 1553 2311

say, 'It's going to rain,' and it does. **55** And when the south wind blows, you say, 'It's going to be
λέγετε ὅτι → ἔρχεται ← ὄμβρος καὶ → γίνεται οὕτως καὶ ὅταν → νότον ← πνέοντα → λέγετε ὅτι → → ἔσται
v.pai.2p cj v.pmi.3s n.nsm cj v.pmi.3s adv cj cj n.asm pt.pa.asm v.pai.2p cj v.fmi.3s
3306 4022 2262 3915 2779 1181 4048 2779 4020 3803 4463 3306 4022 1639

hot,' and it is. **56** Hypocrites! You know how to interpret the appearance of the earth and the sky.   How is
καύσων καὶ → γίνεται ὑποκριταί → οἴδατε → δοκιμάζειν τὸ πρόσωπον → τῆς γῆς καὶ τοῦ οὐρανοῦ δὲ πῶς ←
n.nsm cj v.pmi.3s n.vpm v.rai.2p f.pa d.asn n.asn d.gsf n.gsf cj d.gsm n.gsm cj adv
3014 2779 1181 5695 3857 1507 3836 4725 3836 1178 2779 3836 4041 1254 4802

it that you don't know how to interpret this present time?   ¶   **57**   "Why   don't you judge for
← ↱ οὐκ οἴδατε → δοκιμάζειν τούτον ⌜τὸν καιρὸν⌝   δὲ Τί καὶ οὐ → κρίνετε ἀφ'
pl v.rai.2p f.pa r.asm d.asm n.asm   cj r.asm adv pl v.pai.2p p.g
3857 4024 3857 1507 4047 3836 2789   1254 5515 2779 4024 3212 608

yourselves what is right? **58** As you are going with your adversary to the magistrate, try   hard   to be
ἑαυτῶν τὸ δίκαιον γὰρ ὡς → → ὑπάγεις μετὰ σου ⌜τοῦ ἀντιδίκου⌝ ἐπ' ἄρχοντα δὸς ἐργασίαν → →
r.gpm.2 d.asn a.asn cj cj v.pai.2s p.g r.gs.2 d.gsm n.gsm p.a n.asm v.aam.2s n.asf
1571 3836 1465 1142 6055 5632 3557 5148 3836 508 2093 807 1443 2238

reconciled to him on the way, or   he may drag   you off to the judge, and the judge turn   you over to
ἀπηλλάχθαι ἀπ' αὐτοῦ ἐν τῇ ὁδῷ μήποτε → → κατασύρῃ σε ← πρὸς τὸν κριτὴν καὶ ὁ κριτής παραδώσει σε → ←
f.rp p.g r.gsm.3 p.d d.dsf n.dsf cj v.pas.3s r.as.2 p.a d.asm n.asm cj d.nsm n.nsm v.fai.3s r.as.2
557 608 899 1877 3836 3847 3607 2955 5148 2955 4639 3836 3216 2779 3836 3216 4140 5148 4140

the officer, and the officer throw you into prison. **59** I tell you, you will not   get   out   until   you have
τῷ πράκτορι καὶ ὁ πράκτωρ βαλεῖ σε εἰς φυλακήν → λέγω σοι ⌜οὐ μὴ⌝ ἐξέλθῃς ← ἐκεῖθεν ἕως καὶ → →
d.dsm n.dsm cj d.nsm n.nsm v.fai.3s r.as.2 p.a n.asf v.pai.1s r.ds.2 pl pl v.aas.2s adv cj adv
3836 4551 2779 3836 4551 965 5148 1650 5871 3306 5148 2002 2002 4024 3590 2002 1696 2401 2779

paid   the last   penny."
ἀποδῷς τὸ ἔσχατον λεπτὸν
v.aas.2s d.asn a.asn n.asn
625 3836 2274 3321

Repent or Perish

13:1 Now there were some present at that time   who told   Jesus about the Galileans whose blood
δὲ ↱ ↱ τινες Παρῆσαν ἐν αὐτῷ ⌜τῷ καιρῷ⌝ → ἀπαγγέλλοντες αὐτῷ περὶ τῶν Γαλιλαίων ὧν ⌜τὸ αἷμα⌝
cj r.npm v.iai.3p p.d r.dsm d.dsm n.dsm pt.pa.npm r.dsm.3 p.g d.gpm a.gpm r.gpm d.asn n.asn
1254 4205 4205 5516 4205 1877 899 3836 2789 550 899 4309 3836 1134 4005 3836 135

Pilate   had mixed with their sacrifices.   **2**   Jesus answered,   "Do you think that these Galileans
Πιλᾶτος → ἔμιξεν μετὰ αὐτῶν ⌜τῶν θυσιῶν⌝ καὶ → ἀποκριθεὶς εἶπεν αὐτοῖς → δοκεῖτε ὅτι οὗτοι ⌜οἱ Γαλιλαῖοι⌝
n.nsm v.aai.3s p.g r.gpm.3 d.gpf n.gpf cj pt.ap.nsm v.aai.3s r.dpm.3 v.pai.2p cj r.npm d.npm a.npm
4397 3624 3552 899 3836 2602 2779 646 3306 899 1506 4022 4047 3836 1134

were   worse sinners   than all   the other Galileans because they suffered this way? **3** I tell you, no! But
ἐγένοντο → ἁμαρτωλοὶ παρὰ πάντας τοὺς Γαλιλαίους ὅτι → πεπόνθασιν ταῦτα ← → λέγω ὑμῖν οὐχί ἀλλ'
v.ami.3p a.npm p.a a.apm d.apm a.apm cj v.rai.3p r.apn v.pai.1s r.dp.2 pl pl
1181 4123 283 4123 4246 3836 1134 4022 4248 4047 3306 7007 4049 247

τοῦ νῦν πέντε ἐν ἑνὶ οἴκῳ διαμεμερισμένοι, τρεῖς ἐπὶ δυσὶν καὶ δύο ἐπὶ τρισίν, **53** διαμερισθήσονται πατὴρ ἐπὶ υἱῷ καὶ υἱὸς ἐπὶ πατρί, μήτηρ ἐπὶ τὴν θυγατέρα καὶ θυγάτηρ ἐπὶ τὴν μητέρα, πενθερὰ ἐπὶ τὴν νύμφην αὐτῆς καὶ νύμφη ἐπὶ τὴν πενθεράν. **12:54** Ἔλεγεν δὲ καὶ τοῖς ὄχλοις, Ὅταν ἴδητε [τὴν] νεφέλην ἀνατέλλουσαν ἐπὶ δυσμῶν, εὐθέως λέγετε ὅτι Ὄμβρος ἔρχεται, καὶ γίνεται οὕτως· **55** καὶ ὅταν νότον πνέοντα, λέγετε ὅτι Καύσων ἔσται, καὶ γίνεται. **56** ὑποκριταί, τὸ πρόσωπον τῆς γῆς καὶ τοῦ οὐρανοῦ οἴδατε δοκιμάζειν, τὸν καιρὸν δὲ τοῦτον πῶς οὐκ οἴδατε δοκιμάζειν; ¶ **57** Τί δὲ καὶ ἀφ' ἑαυτῶν οὐ κρίνετε τὸ δίκαιον; **58** ὡς γὰρ ὑπάγεις μετὰ τοῦ ἀντιδίκου σου ἐπ' ἄρχοντα, ἐν τῇ ὁδῷ δὸς ἐργασίαν ἀπηλλάχθαι ἀπ' αὐτοῦ, μήποτε κατασύρῃ σε πρὸς τὸν κριτήν, καὶ ὁ κριτής σε παραδώσει τῷ πράκτορι, καὶ ὁ πράκτωρ σε βαλεῖ εἰς φυλακήν. **59** λέγω σοι, οὐ μὴ ἐξέλθῃς ἐκεῖθεν, ἕως καὶ τὸ ἔσχατον λεπτὸν ἀποδῷς.

13:1 Παρῆσαν δέ τινες ἐν αὐτῷ τῷ καιρῷ ἀπαγγέλλοντες αὐτῷ περὶ τῶν Γαλιλαίων ὧν τὸ αἷμα Πιλᾶτος ἔμιξεν μετὰ τῶν θυσιῶν αὐτῶν. **2** καὶ ἀποκριθεὶς εἶπεν αὐτοῖς, Δοκεῖτε ὅτι οἱ Γαλιλαῖοι οὗτοι ἁμαρτωλοὶ παρὰ πάντας τοὺς Γαλιλαίους

unless | you repent, | you too | will all | perish. | ⁴Or those | eighteen | | who | died | when the tower | in
ἐὰν μή → | μετανοῆτε → | ὁμοίως → | πάντες ἀπολεῖσθε | | ἤ ἐκεῖνοι οἱ | δεκαοκτὼ | καὶ αὐτοὺς | ἀπέκτεινεν | | ὁ πύργος ἐν
cj pl | v.pas.2p | adv | a.npm v.fmi.2p | | cj r.npm d.npm | a.npm | cj r.apm.3 | v.aai.3s | | d.nsm n.nsm p.d
1569 3590 | 3566 | 660 | 3931 660 | | 2445 1697 3836 | 1277 | 2779 899 | 650 | | 3836 4788 1877

Siloam | fell | on | them | – do you | think | | they | were | more | guilty | than | all | the others
τῷ Σιλωὰμ | ἔπεσεν | ἐφ᾿ | οὓς | → → | δοκεῖτε ὅτι | | αὐτοὶ | ἐγένοντο | | ὀφειλέται | παρὰ | πάντας | τοὺς ἀνθρώπους
d.dsm n.dsm | v.aai.3s | p.a | r.apm | | v.pai.2p cj | | r.npm | v.ami.3p | | n.npm | p.a | a.apm | d.apm n.apm
3836 4978 | 4406 | 2093 | 4005 | | 1506 4022 | | 899 | 1181 | | 4123 | 4050 | 4123 4246 | 3836 476

living | | in Jerusalem? | ⁵I tell | you, | no! | But | unless | you repent, | you too | | will all | perish.” | ¶
ᵗτοὺς κατοικοῦντας | Ἰερουσαλήμ | ← λέγω | ὑμῖν | οὐχί | ἀλλ᾿ | ἐὰν μή | → μετανοῆτε → | ὡσαύτως → | | πάντες ἀπολεῖσθε
d.apm pt.pa.apm | n.asf | v.pai.1s | r.dp.2 | pl | cj | cj pl | v.pas.2p | adv | | a.npm v.fmi.2p
3836 2997 | 2647 | 3306 | 7007 | 4049 | 247 | 1569 3590 | 3566 | 660 | | 6058 660 4246 660

⁶Then | he | told | this | parable: | “A man | had | a fig tree, | planted | in | his | vineyard, | and he | went | to look
δὲ | → | Ἔλεγεν | ταύτην | ᵗτὴν παραβολήν᾿ | τις | εἶχεν | → συκῆν | πεφυτευμένην | ἐν | αὐτοῦ | ᵗτῷ ἀμπελῶνι | καὶ → | ἦλθεν | ζητῶν
cj | | v.iai.3s | r.asf | d.asf n.asf | r.nsm | v.iai.3s | n.asf | pt.rp.asf | p.d | r.gsm.3 | d.dsm n.dsm | cj | v.aai.3s | pt.pa.nsm
1254 | | 3306 | 4047 | 3836 4130 | 5516 | 2400 | 5190 | 5885 | 1877 | 899 | 3836 308 | 2779 | 2262 | 2426

for fruit | on it, | but | did not | find | any. | ⁷So he | said | to | the | man | who took care of the vineyard, | | ‘For
← καρπὸν | ἐν αὐτῇ | καὶ → | οὐχ | εὗρεν | | δὲ → | εἶπεν | πρὸς | τὸν | ἀμπελουργόν | | ἰδοὺ
n.asm | p.d r.dsf.3 | cj | pl | v.aai.3s | | cj | v.aai.3s | p.a | d.asm | n.asm | | j
2843 | 1877 899 | 2779 2351 | 4024 | 2351 | | 1254 | 3306 | 4639 | 3836 | 307 | | 2627

three | years | now | I’ve been | coming | to look | for fruit | on | this | fig tree | and | haven’t | found | any.
τρία | ἔτη | ἀφ᾿ οὗ | → | ἔρχομαι | ζητῶν ← | καρπὸν | ἐν | ταύτῃ | ᵗτῇ συκῇ | καὶ | οὐχ | εὑρίσκω | [οὖν]
a.npn | n.npn | p.g r.gsm | | v.pmi.1s | pt.pa.nsm | n.asm | p.d | r.dsf | d.dsf n.dsf | cj | pl | v.pai.1s | cj
5552 | 2291 | 608 4005 | | 2262 | 2426 | 2843 | 1877 | 4047 | 3836 5190 | 2779 | 4024 | 2351 | 4036

Cut | it | down! | Why | | should it use | | up the soil?’ | ⁸ | “‘Sir,’ | the | man replied, | | ‘leave | it | alone
ἔκκοψον | αὐτήν | | ἱνατί καὶ → | → | καταργεῖ ← | τὴν γῆν | δὲ | κύριε | ὁ | ἀποκριθεὶς | λέγει αὐτῷ | ἄφες | αὐτήν →
v.aam.2s | r.asf.3 | | cj adv cj | | v.pai.3s | d.asf n.asf | cj | n.vsm | d.nsm | pt.ap.nsm | v.pai.3s r.dsm.3 | v.aam.2s | r.asf.3
1716 | 899 | | 2672 2779 | | 2934 | 3836 1178 | 1254 | 3261 | 3836 | 646 | 3306 918 | 918 | 899

for | *one* | *more* | *year,* | | and | | I’ll | dig | around | it | and | fertilize | it. | ⁹If | | it bears | fruit
→ | καὶ | ᵗτοῦτο | τὸ ἔτος᾿ | ἕως ὅτου | | σκάψω | περὶ | αὐτὴν | καὶ | βάλω | κόπρια | | κἂν μὲν | → ποιήσῃ | καρπὸν
adv | r.asn | d.asn n.asn | p.g r.gsn | | v.aas.1s | p.a | r.asf.3 | cj | v.aas.1s | n.apn | | crasis pl | v.aas.3s | n.asm
2291 2291 | 2779 | 4047 | 3836 2291 | 2401 4015 | | 4999 | 4309 | 899 | 2779 | 965 | 3162 | | 2829 3525 | 4472 | 2843

next | | year, fine! | If | not, then | cut | | it | down.’”
ᵗεἰς τὸ | μέλλον᾿ ← | | δὲ εἰ | μὴ | γε | ἐκκόψεις | αὐτήν →
p.a d.asn | pt.pa.asn | | cj | pl | | v.fai.2s | r.asf.3
1650 3836 | 3516 | | 1254 1623 | 3590 | 1145 | 1716 | 1716

The Crippled Woman Healed on the Sabbath

^{13:10} On a | Sabbath | | Jesus was | teaching | in | one | of the synagogues, | ¹¹and | | a woman | was there who
δὲ ἐν | ᵗτοῖς σάββασιν᾿ | | Ἦν | διδάσκων | ἐν | μιᾷ | → τῶν συναγωγῶν | καὶ | ἰδοὺ | γυνή
cj p.d | d.dpn n.dpn | | v.iai.3s | pt.pa.nsm | p.d | a.dsf | d.gpf n.gpf | cj | ! | n.nsf
1254 1877 | 3836 4879 | | 1639 | 1438 | 1877 | 1651 | 3836 5252 | 2779 | 2627 | 1222

had | been | crippled | by a | spirit | for | eighteen | years. | | She was | bent | | over | and | could | | not | straighten up
ἔχουσα | | ἀσθενείας | | πνεῦμα | → | δεκαοκτὼ | ἔτη | καὶ → | ἦν | συγκύπτουσα ← | | καὶ | δυναμένη | μὴ | ἀνακύψαι ←
pt.pa.nsf | | n.gsf | | n.asn | | a.apn | n.apn | cj | v.iai.3s | pt.pa.nsf | | cj | pt.pp.nsf | pl | f.aa
2400 | | 819 | | 4460 | | 1277 | 2291 | 2779 | 1639 | 5174 | | 2779 | 1538 | 3590 | 376

at | | *all.* | ¹² | When | Jesus | | saw | her, | he called | | her forward | and | said | to her, | “Woman, | you are
ᵗεἰς τὸ | παντελές᾿ | | δὲ → | ὁ | Ἰησοῦς᾿ | ἰδὼν | αὐτὴν | προσεφώνησεν | | καὶ | εἶπεν | αὐτῇ | γύναι
p.a d.asn | a.asn | | cj | d.nsm | n.nsm | pt.aa.nsm | r.asf.3 | v.aai.3s | | cj | v.aai.3s | r.dsf.3 | n.vsf
1650 3836 | 4117 | | 1254 | 1625 | 3836 2652 | 1625 | 899 | 4715 | | 2779 | 3306 | 899 | 1222

set | | free | from your | infirmity.” | ¹³Then | he put | | his | hands | on her, | and | immediately | | she | straightened | up | and
ἀπολέλυσαι ← | | σου | ᵗτῆς ἀσθενείας᾿ | καὶ | → | ἐπέθηκεν | τὰς χεῖρας | αὐτῇ | καὶ | παραχρῆμα | → | ἀνωρθώθη | | καὶ
v.rpi.2s | | r.gs.2 | d.gsf n.gsf | cj | | v.aai.3s | d.apf n.apf | r.dsf.3 | cj | adv | | v.api.3s | | cj
668 | | 819 | 5148 3836 819 | 2779 | | 2202 | 3836 5931 | 2202 899 | 2779 | 4202 | | 494 | | 2779

praised | God. | ¶ | ¹⁴ | Indignant | because | Jesus | | had healed | | on the | Sabbath, | the | synagogue
ἐδόξαζεν | ᵗτὸν θεόν᾿ | | δὲ | ἀγανακτῶν | ὅτι | ὁ | Ἰησοῦς᾿ | ἐθεράπευσεν | → | τῷ σαββάτῳ | ὁ | →
v.iai.3s | d.asm n.asm | | cj | pt.pa.nsm | cj | d.nsm n.nsm | | v.aai.3s | | d.dsn n.dsn | d.nsm
1519 | 3836 2536 | | 1254 24 | 4022 | 3836 2652 | 2543 | | 3836 4879 | 3836

ἐγένοντο, ὅτι ταῦτα πεπόνθασιν; ³ οὐχί, λέγω ὑμῖν, ἀλλ᾿ ἐὰν μὴ μετανοῆτε πάντες ὁμοίως ἀπολεῖσθε. ⁴ ἢ ἐκεῖνοι οἱ δεκαοκτὼ ἐφ᾿ οὓς ἔπεσεν ὁ πύργος ἐν τῷ Σιλωὰμ καὶ ἀπέκτεινεν αὐτούς, δοκεῖτε ὅτι αὐτοὶ ὀφειλέται ἐγένοντο παρὰ πάντας τοὺς ἀνθρώπους τοὺς κατοικοῦντας Ἰερουσαλήμ; ⁵ οὐχί, λέγω ὑμῖν, ἀλλ᾿ ἐὰν μὴ μετανοῆτε πάντες ὡσαύτως ἀπολεῖσθε. ¶ ⁶ Ἔλεγεν δὲ ταύτην τὴν παραβολήν· Συκῆν εἶχέν τις πεφυτευμένην ἐν τῷ ἀμπελῶνι αὐτοῦ, καὶ ἦλθεν ζητῶν καρπὸν ἐν αὐτῇ καὶ οὐχ εὗρεν. ⁷ εἶπεν δὲ πρὸς τὸν ἀμπελουργόν, Ἰδοὺ τρία ἔτη ἀφ᾿ οὗ ἔρχομαι ζητῶν καρπὸν ἐν τῇ συκῇ ταύτῃ καὶ οὐχ εὑρίσκω· ἔκκοψον [οὖν] αὐτήν, ἱνατί καὶ τὴν γῆν καταργεῖ; ⁸ ὁ δὲ ἀποκριθεὶς λέγει αὐτῷ, Κύριε, ἄφες αὐτὴν καὶ τοῦτο τὸ ἔτος, ἕως ὅτου σκάψω περὶ αὐτὴν καὶ βάλω κόπρια, ⁹ κἂν μὲν ποιήσῃ καρπὸν εἰς τὸ μέλλον· εἰ δὲ μή γε, ἐκκόψεις αὐτήν.

^{13:10} Ἦν δὲ διδάσκων ἐν μιᾷ τῶν συναγωγῶν ἐν τοῖς σάββασιν. ¹¹ καὶ ἰδοὺ γυνὴ πνεῦμα ἔχουσα ἀσθενείας ἔτη δεκαοκτὼ καὶ ἦν συγκύπτουσα καὶ μὴ δυναμένη ἀνακύψαι εἰς τὸ παντελές. ¹² ἰδὼν δὲ αὐτὴν ὁ Ἰησοῦς προσεφώνησεν καὶ εἶπεν αὐτῇ, Γύναι, ἀπολέλυσαι τῆς ἀσθενείας σου, ¹³ καὶ ἐπέθηκεν αὐτῇ τὰς χεῖρας· καὶ παραχρῆμα ἀνωρθώθη καὶ ἐδόξαζεν τὸν θεόν. ¶

ruler | said | to | the people, | "There | are | six | days | for | work. | So | come | and be
ἀρχισυνάγωγος | ἀποκριθεὶς | ἔλεγεν | τῷ ὄχλῳ | ὅτι → | εἰσὶν | ἓξ | ἡμέραι | ἐν αἷς | ⸤δεῖ ἐργάζεσθαι⸥ | οὖν | ἐρχόμενοι | καὶ →
n.nsm | pt.ap.nsm | v.iai.3s | d.dsm n.dsm | cj | v.pai.3p | a.npf | n.npf | p.d r.dpf | v.pai.3s f.pm | cj | pt.pm.npm | cj
801 | 646 | 3306 | 3836 4063 | 4022 | 1639 | 1971 | 2465 | 1877 4005 | 1256 2237 | 4036 | 2262 | 2779

healed | on those | days, | not on | the Sabbath." | ¶ | 15 | The | Lord | answered | him, | "You
θεραπεύεσθε | ἐν αὐταῖς | μὴ → | τῇ ἡμέρᾳ | τοῦ σαββάτου | | | δὲ ὁ | κύριος | ἀπεκρίθη | αὐτῷ καὶ | εἶπεν →
v.ppm.2p | p.d r.dpf.3 | pl | d.dsf n.dsf | d.gsn n.gsn | | | cj d.nsm | n.nsm | v.api.3s | r.dsm.3 cj | v.aai.3s
2543 | 1877 899 | 3590 | 3836 2465 | 3836 4879 | | | 1254 3836 | 3261 | 646 | 899 2779 | 3306

hypocrites! | Doesn't | each | of you | on the | Sabbath | untie | his | ox | or | donkey | from the | stall | and | lead | it
ὑποκριταί | οὐ | ἕκαστος → | ὑμῶν → | τῷ | σαββάτῳ | λύει | αὐτοῦ | ⸤τὸν βοῦν⸥ | ἢ | ⸤τὸν ὄνον⸥ | ἀπὸ | τῆς φάτνης | καὶ | ἀπαγαγὼν
n.vpm | pl | r.nsm | r.gp.2 | d.dsn | n.dsn | v.pai.3s | r.gsm.3 | d.asm n.asm | cj | d.asm n.asm | p.g | d.gsf n.gsf | cj | pt.aa.nsm
5695 | 4024 | 1667 | 7007 | 3836 | 4879 | 3395 | 899 | 3836 1091 | 2445 | 3836 3952 | 608 | 3836 5764 | 2779 | 552

out | to give | it water? | 16 | Then | should | not | this | woman, | a daughter | of Abraham, | whom | Satan | has kept
↶ | ποτίζει | ← | δὲ | ἔδει | οὐκ | ταύτην ← | οὖσαν | θυγατέρα → | Ἀβραὰμ | ἣν | ⸤ὁ σατανᾶς⸥ | →
| v.pai.3s | | cj | v.iai.3s | pl | r.asf | pt.pa.asf | n.asf | n.gsm | r.asf | d.nsm n.nsm
552 | 4540 | | 1254 | 1256 | 4024 | 4047 | 1639 | 2588 | 11 | 4005 | 3836 4928

bound | for eighteen | long years, | be set | free on the | Sabbath | day | from | what | bound | her?"
ἔδησεν | ⸤ἰδοὺ → δέκα καὶ ὀκτὼ⸥ | ἔτη → | λυθῆναι ← | τοῦ | σαββάτου | ⸤τῇ ἡμέρᾳ⸥ | ἀπὸ | ⸤τοῦ δεσμοῦ τούτου⸥
v.aai.3s | j a.apn cj a.npn | n.npn | f.ap | d.gsn | n.gsn | d.dsf n.dsf | p.g | d.gsm n.gsm r.gsm
1313 | 2627 1274 2779 3893 | 2291 | 3395 | 3836 | 4879 | 3836 2465 | 608 | 3836 1301 4047

¶ | 17 | When he | said | this, | all | his | opponents | were humiliated, | but | the | people were | delighted
καὶ → | αὐτοῦ | λέγοντος | ταῦτα | πάντες | αὐτῷ | ⸤οἱ ἀντικείμενοι⸥ | → κατῃσχύνοντο | καὶ | πᾶς ὁ | ὄχλος → | ἔχαιρεν
cj | r.gsm.3 | pt.pa.gsm | r.apn | a.npm | r.dsm.3 | d.npm pt.pm.npm | v.ipi.3p | cj | a.nsm d.nsm | n.nsm | v.iai.3s
2779 | 3306 | 899 | 3306 | 4047 | 4246 | 899 3836 512 | 2875 | 2779 | 4246 3836 | 4063 | 5897

with all | the | wonderful | things | he | was doing.
ἐπὶ | πᾶσιν | τοῖς | ἐνδόξοις | τοῖς | ὑπ' αὐτοῦ → | γινομένοις
p.d | a.dpn | d.dpn | a.dpn | d.dpn | p.g r.gsm.3 | pt.pm.dpn
2093 | 4246 | 3836 | 1902 | 3836 | 5679 899 | 1181

The Parables of the Mustard Seed and the Yeast

13:18 | Then | Jesus | asked, | "What | is | the | kingdom | of God | like? | What | shall I | compare | it | to? | 19 | It is
οὖν | | | Ἔλεγεν | τίνι | ἐστὶν ἡ | βασιλεία → | ⸤τοῦ θεοῦ⸥ | ὁμοία | καὶ | τίνι | → | ὁμοιώσω | αὐτήν | → | ἐστὶν
cj | | | v.iai.3s | r.dsn | v.pai.3s d.nsf | n.nsf | d.gsm n.gsm | a.nsf | cj | r.dsn | | v.fai.1s | r.asf.3 | | v.pai.3s
4036 | | | 3306 | 5515 | 1639 3836 | 993 | 3836 2536 | 3927 | 2779 | 5515 | | 3929 | 899 | 5515 | 1639

like | a mustard | seed, | which | a man | took | and planted | in | his | garden. | It grew | and | became | a tree,
ὁμοία | σινάπεως | κόκκῳ | ὃν | ἄνθρωπος | λαβὼν | ἔβαλεν | εἰς | ἑαυτοῦ | κῆπον | καὶ → ηὔξησεν | καὶ | ἐγένετο | εἰς δένδρον
a.nsf | n.gsn | n.dsm | r.asm | n.nsm | pt.aa.nsm | v.aai.3s | p.a | r.gsm.3 | n.asm | cj v.aai.3s | cj | v.ami.3s | p.a n.asn
3927 | 4983 | 3133 | 4005 | 476 | 3284 | 965 | 1650 | 1571 | 3057 | 2779 889 | 2779 | 1181 | 1650 1285

and | the | birds | of the | air | perched | in | its | branches." | ¶ | 20 | Again | he asked, | "What | shall I | compare
καὶ | τὰ | πετεινὰ | τοῦ | οὐρανοῦ | κατεσκήνωσεν | ἐν | αὐτοῦ | ⸤τοῖς κλάδοις⸥ | | | Καὶ πάλιν | εἶπεν | τίνι | → | ὁμοιώσω
cj | d.npn | n.npn | d.gsm | n.gsm | v.aai.3s | p.d | r.gsn.3 | d.dpm n.dpm | | | cj adv | v.aai.3s | r.dsn | | v.fai.1s
2779 | 3836 | 4374 | 3836 | 4041 | 2942 | 1877 | 899 | 3836 3080 | | | 2779 4099 | 3306 | 5515 | | 3929

the | kingdom | of God | to? | 21 | It is | like | yeast | that | a woman | took | and mixed | into a | large | amount | of flour
τὴν | βασιλείαν → | ⸤τοῦ θεοῦ⸥ | | | ἐστὶν | ὁμοία | ζύμῃ | ἣν | γυνὴ | λαβοῦσα | ἐνέκρυψεν | εἰς | τρία | σάτα | → ἀλεύρου
d.asf | n.asf | d.gsm n.gsm | | | v.pai.3s | a.nsf | n.dsf | r.asf | n.nsf | pt.aa.nsf | v.aai.3s | p.a | a.apn | n.apn | n.gsn
3836 | 993 | 3836 2536 | 5515 | | 1639 | 3927 | 2434 | 4005 | 1222 | 3284 | 1606 | 1650 | 5552 | 4929 | 236

until | it worked | all | through | the dough."
⸤ἕως οὗ⸥ | → ἐζυμώθη | ὅλον | ← | ←
p.g r.gsm | v.api.3s | a.nsn | | |
2401 4005 | 2435 | 3910 | 2435 | 2435 2435

The Narrow Door

13:22 | Then | Jesus | went | through | the | towns | and | villages, | teaching | as | he made | his | way | to | Jerusalem.
Καὶ | | | διεπορεύετο | κατὰ | | πόλεις | καὶ | κώμας | διδάσκων | καὶ → | ποιούμενος | πορείαν | | εἰς | Ἱεροσόλυμα
cj | | | v.imi.3s | p.a | | n.apf | cj | n.apf | pt.pa.nsm | cj | pt.pm.nsm | n.asf | | p.a | n.apn
2779 | | | 1388 | 2848 | | 4484 | 2779 | 3267 | 1438 | 2779 | 4472 | 4512 | | 1650 | 2642

---

14 ἀποκριθεὶς δὲ ὁ ἀρχισυνάγωγος, ἀγανακτῶν ὅτι τῷ σαββάτῳ ἐθεράπευσεν ὁ Ἰησοῦς, ἔλεγεν τῷ ὄχλῳ ὅτι Ἓξ ἡμέραι εἰσὶν ἐν αἷς δεῖ ἐργάζεσθαι· ἐν αὐταῖς οὖν ἐρχόμενοι θεραπεύεσθε καὶ μὴ τῇ ἡμέρᾳ τοῦ σαββάτου. ¶ 15 ἀπεκρίθη δὲ αὐτῷ ὁ κύριος καὶ εἶπεν, Ὑποκριταί, ἕκαστος ὑμῶν τῷ σαββάτῳ οὐ λύει τὸν βοῦν αὐτοῦ ἢ τὸν ὄνον ἀπὸ τῆς φάτνης καὶ ἀπαγαγὼν ποτίζει; 16 ταύτην δὲ θυγατέρα Ἀβραὰμ οὖσαν, ἣν ἔδησεν ὁ Σατανᾶς ἰδοὺ δέκα καὶ ὀκτὼ ἔτη, οὐκ ἔδει λυθῆναι ἀπὸ τοῦ δεσμοῦ τούτου τῇ ἡμέρᾳ τοῦ σαββάτου; ¶ 17 καὶ ταῦτα λέγοντος αὐτοῦ κατῃσχύνοντο πάντες οἱ ἀντικείμενοι αὐτῷ, καὶ πᾶς ὁ ὄχλος ἔχαιρεν ἐπὶ πᾶσιν τοῖς ἐνδόξοις τοῖς γινομένοις ὑπ' αὐτοῦ.

13:18 Ἔλεγεν οὖν, Τίνι ὁμοία ἐστὶν ἡ βασιλεία τοῦ θεοῦ καὶ τίνι ὁμοιώσω αὐτήν; 19 ὁμοία ἐστὶν κόκκῳ σινάπεως, ὃν λαβὼν ἄνθρωπος ἔβαλεν εἰς κῆπον ἑαυτοῦ, καὶ ηὔξησεν καὶ ἐγένετο εἰς δένδρον, καὶ τὰ πετεινὰ τοῦ οὐρανοῦ κατεσκήνωσεν ἐν τοῖς κλάδοις αὐτοῦ. ¶ 20 Καὶ πάλιν εἶπεν, Τίνι ὁμοιώσω τὴν βασιλείαν τοῦ θεοῦ; 21 ὁμοία ἐστὶν ζύμῃ, ἣν λαβοῦσα γυνὴ [ἐν]έκρυψεν εἰς ἀλεύρου σάτα τρία ἕως οὗ ἐζυμώθη ὅλον.

23 Someone asked him, "Lord, are only a few people going to be saved?" ¶ He said to them,
δέ τις　Εἶπεν αὐτῷ κύριε εἰ ὀλίγοι → → οἱ σωζόμενοι δὲ ὁ εἶπεν πρὸς αὐτούς
cj r.nsm　v.aai.3s r.dsm.3 n.vsm cj a.npm d.npm pt.pp.npm cj d.nsm v.aai.3s p.a r.apm.3
1254 5516　3306 899 3261 1623 3900 3836 5392 1254 3836 3306 4639 899

24 "Make every effort to enter through the narrow door, because many, I tell you, will try to enter and
→ → ἀγωνίζεσθε εἰσελθεῖν διὰ τῆς στενῆς θύρας ὅτι πολλοί → λέγω ὑμῖν ζητήσουσιν → εἰσελθεῖν καὶ
v.pmm.2p f.aa p.g d.gsf a.gsf n.gsf cj a.npm v.pai.1s r.dp.2 v.fai.3p f.aa cj
76 1656 1328 3836 5101 2598 4022 4498 3306 7007 2426 1656 2779

will not be able to. **25** Once the owner of the house gets up and closes the door, you will
→ οὐκ → ἰσχύσουσιν ἀφ᾽ οὗ ἂν ὁ οἰκοδεσπότης ← ἐγερθῇ καὶ ἀποκλείσῃ τὴν θύραν καὶ → ἄρξησθε
pl v.fai.3p p.g r.gsm pl d.nsm n.nsm v.aps.3s cj v.aas.3s d.asf n.asf cj v.ams.2p
2710 4024 2710 608 4005 323 3836 3867 1586 2779 643 3836 2598 2779 806

stand outside knocking and pleading, 'Sir, open the door for us.' "But he will answer, 'I
ἑστάναι ἔξω καὶ κρούειν τὴν θύραν λέγοντες κύριε ἄνοιξον → ἡμῖν καὶ → ἀποκριθεὶς ἐρεῖ ὑμῖν →
f.ra adv cj f.pia d.asf n.asf pt.pa.npm n.vsm v.aam.2s r.dp.1 cj pt.ap.nsm v.fai.3s r.dp.2
2705 2032 2779 3218 3836 2598 3306 3261 487 7005 2779 646 3306 7007 3857

don't know you or where you come from.' **26** "Then you will say, 'We ate and drank with you, and you
οὐκ οἶδα ὑμᾶς πόθεν → ἐστέ τότε → ἄρξεσθε λέγειν → ἐφάγομεν καὶ ἐπίομεν ἐνώπιόν σου καὶ
pl v.rai.1s r.ap.2 cj v.pai.2p adv v.fmi.2p f.pa v.aai.1p cj v.aai.1p p.g r.gs.2 cj
4024 3857 7007 4470 1639 4470 5538 806 3306 2266 2779 4403 1967 5148 2779

taught in our streets.' **27** "But he will reply, 'I don't know you or where you come from. Away
ἐδίδαξας ἐν ἡμῶν ταῖς πλατείαις καὶ → → ἐρεῖ λέγων ὑμῖν → οὐκ οἶδα ὑμᾶς πόθεν → ἐστέ ← ἀπόστητε
v.aai.2s p.d r.gp.1 d.dpf n.dpf cj v.fai.3s pt.pa.nsm r.dp.2 pl v.rai.1s r.ap.2 cj v.pai.2p v.aam.2p
1438 1877 7005 3836 4426 2779 3306 3306 7007 3857 4024 3857 7007 4470 1639 4470 923

from me, all you evildoers!' ¶ **28** "There will be weeping there, and gnashing of teeth,
ἀπ᾽ ἐμοῦ πάντες → ἐργάται ἀδικίας → → → ἔσται ὁ κλαυθμὸς ἐκεῖ καὶ ὁ βρυγμὸς → τῶν ὀδόντων
p.g r.gs.1 a.vpm n.npm n.gsf v.fmi.3s d.nsm n.nsm adv cj d.nsm n.nsm d.gpm n.gpm
608 1609 4246 2239 94 1639 3836 3088 1695 2779 3836 1106 3836 3848

when you see Abraham, Isaac and Jacob and all the prophets in the kingdom of God, but you
ὅταν → ὄψησθε Ἀβραὰμ καὶ Ἰσαὰκ καὶ Ἰακὼβ καὶ πάντας τοὺς προφήτας ἐν τῇ βασιλείᾳ → τοῦ θεοῦ δὲ ὑμᾶς
cj v.ams.2p n.asm cj n.asm cj n.asm cj a.apm d.apm n.apm p.d d.dsf n.dsf d.gsm n.gsm cj r.ap.2
4020 3972 11 2779 2693 2779 2609 2779 4246 3836 4737 1877 3836 993 3836 2536 1254 7007

yourselves thrown out. **29** People will come from east and west and north and south, and will
ἐκβαλλομένους ἔξω καὶ → → ἥξουσιν ἀπὸ ἀνατολῶν καὶ δυσμῶν καὶ ἀπὸ βορρᾶ καὶ νότου καὶ
pt.pp.apm adv cj v.fai.3p p.g n.gpf cj n.gpf cj p.g n.gsm cj n.gsm cj
1675 2032 2779 2457 608 424 2779 1553 2779 608 1080 2779 3803 2779

take their places at the feast in the kingdom of God. **30** Indeed there are those who are last who
ἀνακλιθήσονται ← ← ← ἐν τῇ βασιλείᾳ → τοῦ θεοῦ καὶ ἰδοὺ → εἰσὶν ἔσχατοι οἳ
v.fpi.3p p.d d.dsf n.dsf d.gsm n.gsm cj j v.pai.3p a.npm r.npm
369 1877 3836 993 3836 2536 2779 2627 1639 2274 4005

will be first, and first who will be last."
→ ἔσονται πρῶτοι καὶ εἰσὶν πρῶτοι οἳ → ἔσονται ἔσχατοι
v.fmi.3p a.npm cj v.pai.3p a.npm r.npm v.fmi.3p a.npm
1639 4755 2779 1639 4755 4005 1639 2274

Jesus' Sorrow for Jerusalem

13:31 At that time some Pharisees came to Jesus and said to him, "Leave this place and go
Ἐν αὐτῇ τῇ ὥρᾳ τινες Φαρισαῖοι προσῆλθαν ← λέγοντες αὐτῷ Ἔξελθε καὶ πορεύου
p.d r.dsf d.dsf n.dsf r.npm n.npm v.aai.3p pt.pa.npm r.dsm.3 v.aam.2s cj v.pmm.2s
1877 899 3836 6052 5516 5757 4665 3306 899 2002 2779 4513

somewhere else. Herod wants to kill you." **32** He replied, "Go tell that fox, 'I
ἐντεῦθεν ← ὅτι Ἡρῴδης θέλει → ἀποκτεῖναι σε καὶ → εἶπεν αὐτοῖς πορευθέντες εἴπατε ταύτῃ τῇ ἀλώπεκι ἰδοὺ →
adv cj n.nsm v.pai.3s f.aa r.as.2 cj v.aai.3s r.dpm.3 pt.ap.npm v.aam.2p r.dsf d.dsf n.dsf j
1949 4022 2476 2527 650 5148 2779 3306 899 4513 3306 4047 3836 273 2627

will drive out demons and heal people today and tomorrow, and on the third day I will reach my
→ ἐκβάλλω δαιμόνια καὶ ἰάσεις ἀποτελῶ σήμερον καὶ αὔριον καὶ → τῇ τρίτῃ → → → →
v.pai.1s n.apn cj n.apf v.pai.1s adv cj adv cj d.dsf a.dsf
1675 1228 2779 2617 699 4958 2779 892 2779 3836 5569

13:22 Καὶ διεπορεύετο κατὰ πόλεις καὶ κώμας διδάσκων καὶ πορείαν ποιούμενος εἰς Ἱεροσόλυμα. 23 εἶπεν δέ τις αὐτῷ, Κύριε, εἰ ὀλίγοι οἱ σωζόμενοι; ¶ ὁ δὲ εἶπεν πρὸς αὐτούς, 24 Ἀγωνίζεσθε εἰσελθεῖν διὰ τῆς στενῆς θύρας, ὅτι πολλοί, λέγω ὑμῖν, ζητήσουσιν εἰσελθεῖν καὶ οὐκ ἰσχύσουσιν. 25 ἀφ᾽ οὗ ἂν ἐγερθῇ ὁ οἰκοδεσπότης καὶ ἀποκλείσῃ τὴν θύραν καὶ ἄρξησθε ἔξω ἑστάναι καὶ κρούειν τὴν θύραν λέγοντες, Κύριε, ἄνοιξον ἡμῖν, καὶ ἀποκριθεὶς ἐρεῖ ὑμῖν, Οὐκ οἶδα ὑμᾶς πόθεν ἐστέ. 26 τότε ἄρξεσθε λέγειν, Ἐφάγομεν ἐνώπιόν σου καὶ ἐπίομεν καὶ ἐν ταῖς πλατείαις ἡμῶν ἐδίδαξας· 27 καὶ ἐρεῖ λέγων ὑμῖν, Οὐκ οἶδα [ὑμᾶς] πόθεν ἐστέ· ἀπόστητε ἀπ᾽ ἐμοῦ πάντες ἐργάται ἀδικίας. ¶ 28 ἐκεῖ ἔσται ὁ κλαυθμὸς καὶ ὁ βρυγμὸς τῶν ὀδόντων, ὅταν ὄψησθε Ἀβραὰμ καὶ Ἰσαὰκ καὶ Ἰακὼβ καὶ πάντας τοὺς προφήτας ἐν τῇ βασιλείᾳ τοῦ θεοῦ, ὑμᾶς δὲ ἐκβαλλομένους ἔξω. 29 καὶ ἥξουσιν ἀπὸ ἀνατολῶν καὶ δυσμῶν καὶ ἀπὸ βορρᾶ καὶ νότου καὶ ἀνακλιθήσονται ἐν τῇ βασιλείᾳ τοῦ θεοῦ. 30 καὶ ἰδοὺ εἰσὶν ἔσχατοι οἳ ἔσονται πρῶτοι καὶ εἰσὶν πρῶτοι οἳ ἔσονται ἔσχατοι.

13:31 Ἐν αὐτῇ τῇ ὥρᾳ προσῆλθάν τινες Φαρισαῖοι λέγοντες αὐτῷ, Ἔξελθε καὶ πορεύου ἐντεῦθεν, ὅτι Ἡρῴδης θέλει σε ἀποκτεῖναι. 32 καὶ εἶπεν αὐτοῖς, Πορευθέντες εἴπατε τῇ ἀλώπεκι ταύτῃ, Ἰδοὺ ἐκβάλλω δαιμόνια καὶ ἰάσεις ἀποτελῶ σήμερον

goal.' **33** *In any case,* I must keep going today and tomorrow and the next day – for surely no prophet
τελειοῦμαι πλὴν με δεῖ → πορεύεσθαι σήμερον καὶ αὔριον καὶ τῇ ἐχομένῃ ὅτι οὐκ προφήτην
v.ppi.1s cj r.as.1 v.pai.3s f.pm adv cj adv cj d.dsf pt.pm.dsf cj pl n.asm
5457 4440 1609 1256 4513 4958 2779 892 2779 3836 2400 4022 4024 4737

can die outside Jerusalem! ¶ **34** "O Jerusalem, Jerusalem, you who kill the prophets and
ἐνδέχεται ἀπολέσθαι ἔξω Ἰερουσαλήμ → Ἰερουσαλήμ Ἰερουσαλήμ ἡ → ἀποκτείνουσα τοὺς προφήτας καὶ
v.pmi.3s f.am p.g n.gsf n.vsf n.vsf d.vsf pt.pa.vsf d.apm n.apm cj
1896 660 2032 2647 2647 2647 3836 650 3836 4737 2779

stone those sent to you, how often I have longed to gather your children together, as a
λιθοβολοῦσα τοὺς ἀπεσταλμένους πρὸς αὐτήν → ποσάκις → ἠθέλησα → ἐπισυνάξαι σου τὰ τέκνα ← ὃν τρόπον
pt.pa.vsf d.apm pt.rp.apm p.a r.asf.3 adv v.aai.1s f.aa r.gs.2 d.apn n.apn r.asm n.asm
3344 3836 690 4639 899 4529 2527 2190 5148 3836 5451 2190 4005 5573

hen gathers her chicks under her wings, but you were not willing! **35** Look, your house is left to you
ὄρνις ἑαυτῆς τὴν νοσσιὰν ὑπὸ τὰς πτέρυγας καὶ → → οὐκ ἠθελήσατε ἰδοὺ ὑμῶν ὁ οἶκος ἀφίεται → ὑμῖν
n.nsf r.gsf.3 d.asf n.asf p.a d.apf n.apf cj pl v.aai.2p j r.gp.2 d.nsm n.nsm v.ppi.3s r.dp.2
3998 1571 3836 3799 5679 3836 4763 2779 2527 2527 4024 2527 2627 7007 3836 3875 918 7007

desolate. I tell you, you will not see me again until you say, 'Blessed is he who comes
← [δὲ] λέγω ὑμῖν → οὐ μὴ ἴδητέ με ἕως ἥξει ὅτε εἴπητε εὐλογημένος ὁ ἐρχόμενος
cj v.pai.1s r.dp.2 pl pl v.aas.2p r.as.1 cj v.fai.3s cj v.aas.2p pt.rp.nsm d.nsm pt.pm.nsm
918 1254 3306 7007 1625 1625 4024 3590 1625 1609 2401 2457 4021 3306 2328 3836 2262

in the name of the Lord.'"
ἐν ὀνόματι → κυρίου
p.d n.dsn n.gsm
1877 3950 3261

Jesus at a Pharisee's House

14:1 One Sabbath, when Jesus went to eat in the house of a prominent
Καὶ ἐγένετο σαββάτῳ ἐν αὐτὸν τῷ ἐλθεῖν → φαγεῖν ἄρτον εἰς οἶκον → τινος τῶν ἀρχόντων
cj v.ami.3s n.dsn p.d r.asn.3 d.dsn f.aa f.aa n.asm p.a n.asm r.gsm d.gpm n.gpm
2779 1181 4879 1877 899 3836 2262 2266 788 1650 3875 5516 3836 807

Pharisee, he was being carefully watched. **2** There in front of him was a
τῶν Φαρισαίων καὶ αὐτὸν → → ἦσαν παρατηρούμενοι αὐτοὶ Καὶ ἰδοὺ → ἔμπροσθεν → αὐτοῦ ἦν τις
d.gpm n.gpm cj r.asm.3 v.iai.3p pt.pm.npm r.npm cj j p.g r.gsm.3 v.iai.3s r.nsm
3836 5757 2779 899 1639 4190 899 2779 2627 1869 899 1639 5516

man suffering from dropsy. **3** Jesus asked the Pharisees and experts in the law,
ἄνθρωπος → → ὑδρωπικὸς καὶ ὁ Ἰησοῦς ἀποκριθεὶς εἶπεν πρὸς Φαρισαίους καὶ → τοὺς νομικοὺς λέγων
n.nsm a.nsm cj d.nsm n.nsm pt.ap.nsm v.aai.3s p.a n.apm cj d.apm n.apm pt.pa.nsm
476 5622 2779 3836 2652 646 3306 4639 5757 2779 3836 3788 3306

"Is it lawful to heal on the Sabbath or not?" **4** But they remained silent. So taking hold of the man,
→ ἔξεστιν → θεραπεῦσαι τῷ σαββάτῳ ἢ οὔ δὲ οἱ → ἡσύχασαν καὶ → ἐπιλαβόμενος ←
v.pai.3s f.aa d.dsn n.dsn cj pl cj d.npm v.aai.3p cj pt.am.nsm
1997 2543 3836 4879 2445 4024 1254 3836 2483 2779 2138

he healed him and sent him away. ¶ **5** Then he asked them, "If one of you has a son or an ox
→ ἰάσατο αὐτὸν καὶ ἀπέλυσεν ← καὶ → εἶπεν πρὸς αὐτοὺς τίνος → ὑμῶν υἱὸς ἢ βοῦς
v.ami.3s r.asm.3 cj v.aai.3s cj v.aai.3s p.a r.apm.3 r.gsm r.gp.2 n.nsm cj n.nsm
2615 899 2779 668 2779 3306 4639 899 5515 5626 2445 1091

that falls into a well on the Sabbath day, will you not immediately pull him out?" **6** And they had
πεσεῖται εἰς φρέαρ καὶ ἐν τοῦ σαββάτου ἡμέρα οὐκ εὐθέως ἀνασπάσει αὐτὸν → καὶ → ἴσχυσαν
v.fmi.3s p.a n.asn cj p.d d.gsn n.gsn n.dsf pl adv v.fai.3s r.asm.3 cj v.aai.3p
4406 1650 5853 2779 1877 3836 4879 2465 4024 2311 413 899 413 2779 2710

nothing to say. ¶ **7** When he noticed how the guests picked the places of honor
οὐκ → ἀνταποκριθῆναι πρὸς ταῦτα δὲ → ἐπέχων πῶς → ἐξελέγοντο τὰς → πρωτοκλισίας
pl f.ap p.a r.apn cj pt.pa.nsm cj v.imi.3p d.apf n.apf
4024 503 4639 4047 1254 2091 4802 2813 1721 3836 4752

at the table, he told them this parable: **8** "When someone invites you to a
→ Ἔλεγεν πρὸς τοὺς κεκλημένους παραβολὴν λέγων πρὸς αὐτοὺς ὅταν ὑπό τινος κληθῇς ← εἰς
v.iai.3s p.a d.apm pt.rp.apm n.asf pt.pa.nsm p.a r.apm.3 cj p.g r.gsm v.aps.2s p.a
3306 4639 3836 2813 4130 3306 4639 899 4020 5679 5516 2813 1650

καὶ αὔριον καὶ τῇ τρίτῃ τελειοῦμαι. ³³ πλὴν δεῖ με σήμερον καὶ αὔριον καὶ τῇ ἐχομένῃ πορεύεσθαι, ὅτι οὐκ ἐνδέχεται προφήτην ἀπολέσθαι ἔξω Ἰερουσαλήμ. ¶ ³⁴ Ἰερουσαλὴμ Ἰερουσαλήμ, ἡ ἀποκτείνουσα τοὺς προφήτας καὶ λιθοβολοῦσα τοὺς ἀπεσταλμένους πρὸς αὐτήν, ποσάκις ἠθέλησα ἐπισυνάξαι τὰ τέκνα σου ὃν τρόπον ὄρνις τὴν ἑαυτῆς νοσσιὰν ὑπὸ τὰς πτέρυγας, καὶ οὐκ ἠθελήσατε. ³⁵ ἰδοὺ ἀφίεται ὑμῖν ὁ οἶκος ὑμῶν «ὑμῶν.» ἔρημος. λέγω [δὲ] ὑμῖν, οὐ μὴ ἴδητέ με ἕως [ἥξει ὅτε] εἴπητε, Εὐλογημένος ὁ ἐρχόμενος ἐν ὀνόματι κυρίου.

¹⁴:¹ Καὶ ἐγένετο ἐν τῷ ἐλθεῖν αὐτὸν εἰς οἶκόν τινος τῶν ἀρχόντων [τῶν] Φαρισαίων σαββάτῳ φαγεῖν ἄρτον καὶ αὐτοὶ ἦσαν παρατηρούμενοι αὐτόν. ² καὶ ἰδοὺ ἄνθρωπός τις ἦν ὑδρωπικὸς ἔμπροσθεν αὐτοῦ. ³ καὶ ἀποκριθεὶς ὁ Ἰησοῦς εἶπεν πρὸς τοὺς νομικοὺς καὶ Φαρισαίους λέγων, Ἔξεστιν τῷ σαββάτῳ θεραπεῦσαι ἢ οὔ; ⁴ οἱ δὲ ἡσύχασαν. καὶ ἐπιλαβόμενος ἰάσατο αὐτὸν καὶ ἀπέλυσεν. ¶ ⁵ καὶ πρὸς αὐτοὺς εἶπεν, Τίνος ὑμῶν υἱὸς ἢ βοῦς εἰς φρέαρ πεσεῖται, καὶ οὐκ εὐθέως ἀνασπάσει αὐτὸν ἐν ἡμέρᾳ τοῦ σαββάτου; ⁶ καὶ οὐκ ἴσχυσαν ἀνταποκριθῆναι πρὸς ταῦτα. ¶ ⁷ Ἔλεγεν δὲ πρὸς τοὺς κεκλημένους παραβολήν,

wedding feast, do not take the place of honor, for a person more distinguished than you may have
γάμους μὴ κατακλιθῇς εἰς τὴν πρωτοκλισίαν μήποτε ἐντιμότερος σου
n.apm pl v.aps.2s p.a d.asf n.asf cj a.nsm.c r.gs.2
1141 2884 3590 2884 1650 3836 4752 3607 1952 5148

been invited. **9** If so, the host who invited both of you will come and say to you, 'Give this man
ἦ κεκλημένος ὑπ' αὐτοῦ καὶ ὁ καλέσας σὲ καὶ αὐτὸν ἐλθὼν ἐρεῖ σοι δὸς τούτῳ
v.pas.3s pt.rp.nsm p.g r.gsm.3 cj d.nsm pt.aa.nsm r.as.2 cj r.asm.3 pt.aa.nsm v.fai.3s r.ds.2 v.aam.2s r.dsm
1639 2813 5679 899 2779 3836 2813 5148 2779 899 3306 2262 3306 5148 1443 4047

your seat.' Then, humiliated, you will have to take the least important place. **10** But when you are
τόπον καὶ τότε ἄρξῃ μετὰ αἰσχύνης κατέχειν τὸν ἔσχατον τόπον ἀλλ' ὅταν
n.asm cj adv v.fmi.2s p.g n.gsf f.pa d.asm a.asm n.asm cj cj
5536 2779 5538 806 3552 158 2988 3836 2274 5536 247 4020

invited, take the lowest place, so that when your host comes, he will say to you, 'Friend,
κληθῇς πορευθεὶς ἀνάπεσε εἰς τὸν ἔσχατον τόπον ἵνα ὅταν σε ὁ κεκληκώς ἔλθῃ ἐρεῖ σοι φίλε
v.aps.2s pt.ap.nsm v.aam.2s p.a d.asm a.asm n.asm cj cj r.as.2 d.nsm pt.ra.nsm v.aas.3s v.fai.3s r.ds.2 a.vsm
2813 4513 404 1650 3836 2274 5536 2671 4020 5148 3836 2262 2262 3306 5148 5813

move up to a better place.' Then you will be honored in the presence of all your fellow
προσανάβηθι ἀνώτερον τότε σοι ἔσται δόξα ἐνώπιον πάντων σοι
v.aam.2s adv.c adv r.ds.2 v.fmi.3s n.nsf p.g a.gpm r.ds.2
4646 542 5538 5148 1639 1518 1967 4246 5148

guests. **11** For everyone who exalts himself will be humbled, and he who humbles himself will be
τῶν συνανακειμένων ὅτι πᾶς ὁ ὑψῶν ἑαυτὸν ταπεινωθήσεται καὶ ὁ ταπεινῶν ἑαυτὸν
d.gpm pt.pm.gpm cj a.nsm d.nsm pt.pa.nsm r.asm.3 v.fpi.3s cj d.nsm pt.pa.nsm r.asm.3
3836 5263 4022 4246 3836 5738 1571 5427 2779 3836 5427 1571

exalted." ¶ **12** Then Jesus said to his host, "When you give a luncheon or dinner, do not
ὑψωθήσεται δὲ καὶ Ἔλεγεν αὐτῷ τῷ κεκληκότι ὅταν ποιῇς ἄριστον ἢ δεῖπνον μὴ
v.fpi.3s cj adv v.iai.3s r.asm.3 d.dsm pt.ra.dsm cj v.pas.2s n.asn cj n.asn pl
5738 1254 2779 3306 2813 899 3836 2813 4020 4472 756 2445 1270 5888 3590

invite your friends, your brothers or relatives, or your rich neighbors; if you
φώνει σου τοὺς φίλους μηδὲ σου τοὺς ἀδελφοὺς μηδὲ σου τοὺς συγγενεῖς μηδὲ πλουσίους γείτονας μήποτε καὶ
v.pam.2s r.gs.2 d.apm a.apm cj r.gs.2 d.apm n.apm cj r.gs.2 d.apm n.apm cj a.apm n.apm cj adv
5888 5148 3836 5813 3593 5148 3836 81 3593 5148 3836 5150 3593 4454 1150 3607 2779

do, they may invite you back and so you will be repaid. **13** But when you give a banquet, invite the
αὐτοὶ ἀντικαλέσωσιν σε καὶ σοι γένηται ἀνταπόδομα ἀλλ' ὅταν ποιῇς δοχὴν κάλει
r.npm v.aas.3p r.as.2 cj r.ds.2 v.ams.3s n.nsn cj cj v.pas.2s n.asf v.pam.2s
899 511 5148 511 2779 5148 1181 501 247 4020 4472 1531 2813

poor, the crippled, the lame, the blind, **14** and you will be blessed. Although they cannot repay
πτωχούς ἀναπείρους χωλούς τυφλούς καὶ ἔσῃ μακάριος ὅτι οὐκ ἔχουσιν ἀνταποδοῦναι
a.apm n.apm a.apm a.apm cj v.fmi.2s a.nsm cj pl v.pai.3p f.aa
4777 401 6000 5603 2779 1639 3421 4022 4024 2400 500

you, you will be repaid at the resurrection of the righteous."
σοι γάρ σοι ἀνταποδοθήσεται ἐν τῇ ἀναστάσει τῶν δικαίων
r.ds.2 cj r.ds.2 v.fpi.3s p.d d.dsf n.dsf d.gpm a.gpm
5148 1142 5148 1877 3836 414 3836 1465

The Parable of the Great Banquet

14:15 When one of those at the table with him heard this, he said to Jesus, "Blessed is the man
δὲ τις τῶν συνανακειμένων Ἀκούσας ταῦτα εἶπεν αὐτῷ μακάριος
cj r.nsm d.gpm pt.pm.gpm pt.aa.nsm r.apn v.aai.3s r.dsm.3 a.nsm
1254 201 5516 3836 5263 201 4047 3306 899 3421

who will eat at the feast in the kingdom of God." ¶ **16** Jesus replied: "A certain man
ὅστις φάγεται ἄρτον ἐν τῇ βασιλείᾳ τοῦ θεοῦ δὲ Ὁ εἶπεν αὐτῷ τις ἄνθρωπος
r.nsm v.fmi.3s n.asm p.d d.dsf n.dsf d.gsm n.gsm cj d.nsm v.aai.3s r.dsm.3 r.nsm n.nsm
4015 2266 788 1877 3836 993 3836 2536 1254 3836 3306 899 5516 476

was preparing a great banquet and invited many guests. **17** At the time of the banquet he sent his
ἐποίει μέγα δεῖπνον καὶ ἐκάλεσεν πολλούς καὶ τῇ ὥρᾳ τοῦ δείπνου ἀπέστειλεν αὐτοῦ
v.iai.3s a.asn n.asn cj v.aai.3s a.apm cj d.dsf n.dsf d.gsn n.gsn v.aai.3s r.gsm.3
4472 3489 1270 2779 2813 4498 2779 3836 6052 3836 1270 690 899

ἐπέχων πῶς τὰς πρωτοκλισίας ἐξελέγοντο, λέγων πρὸς αὐτούς, 8 Ὅταν κληθῇς ὑπό τινος εἰς γάμους, μὴ κατακλιθῇς εἰς τὴν πρωτοκλισίαν, μήποτε ἐντιμότερός σου ᾖ κεκλημένος ὑπ' αὐτοῦ, 9 καὶ ἐλθὼν ὁ σὲ καὶ αὐτὸν καλέσας ἐρεῖ σοι, Δὸς τούτῳ τόπον, καὶ τότε ἄρξῃ μετὰ αἰσχύνης τὸν ἔσχατον τόπον κατέχειν. 10 ἀλλ' ὅταν κληθῇς, πορευθεὶς ἀνάπεσε εἰς τὸν ἔσχατον τόπον, ἵνα ὅταν ἔλθῃ ὁ κεκληκώς σε ἐρεῖ σοι, Φίλε, προσανάβηθι ἀνώτερον· τότε ἔσται σοι δόξα ἐνώπιον πάντων τῶν συνανακειμένων σοι. 11 ὅτι πᾶς ὁ ὑψῶν ἑαυτὸν ταπεινωθήσεται, καὶ ὁ ταπεινῶν ἑαυτὸν ὑψωθήσεται. ¶ 12 Ἔλεγεν δὲ καὶ τῷ κεκληκότι αὐτόν, Ὅταν ποιῇς ἄριστον ἢ δεῖπνον, μὴ φώνει τοὺς φίλους σου μηδὲ τοὺς ἀδελφούς σου μηδὲ τοὺς συγγενεῖς σου μηδὲ γείτονας πλουσίους, μήποτε καὶ αὐτοὶ ἀντικαλέσωσίν σε καὶ γένηται ἀνταπόδομά σοι. 13 ἀλλ' ὅταν δοχὴν ποιῇς, κάλει πτωχούς, ἀναπείρους, χωλούς, τυφλούς· 14 καὶ μακάριος ἔσῃ, ὅτι οὐκ ἔχουσιν ἀνταποδοῦναί σοι, ἀνταποδοθήσεται γάρ σοι ἐν τῇ ἀναστάσει τῶν δικαίων.

14:15 Ἀκούσας δέ τις τῶν συνανακειμένων ταῦτα εἶπεν αὐτῷ, Μακάριος ὅστις φάγεται ἄριστον «ἄρτον» ἐν τῇ βασιλείᾳ τοῦ θεοῦ. ¶ 16 ὁ δὲ εἶπεν αὐτῷ, Ἄνθρωπός τις ἐποίει δεῖπνον μέγα, καὶ ἐκάλεσεν πολλούς 17 καὶ ἀπέστειλεν τὸν δοῦλον αὐτοῦ τῇ

servant to tell those who had been invited, 'Come, for everything is now ready.' **18** "But *they* all
τὸν δοῦλον εἰπεῖν τοῖς κεκλημένοις ἔρχεσθε ὅτι ἐστιν ἤδη ἔτοιμα καὶ ἀπὸ μιᾶς πάντες
d.asm n.asm f.aa d.dpm pt.rp.dpm v.pmm.2p cj v.pai.3s adv a.npn cj p.g a.gsf a.npm
3836 1529 3306 3836 2813 2262 4022 1639 2453 2289 2779 608 1651 4246

alike began to make excuses. The first said, 'I have just bought a field, and I must go and
ἤρξαντο παραιτεῖσθαι ὁ πρῶτος εἶπεν αὐτῷ ἠγόρασα ἀγρὸν καὶ ἔχω ἀνάγκην ἐξελθὼν
v.ami.3p f.pm d.nsm a.nsm v.aai.3s r.dsm.3 v.aai.1s n.asm cj v.pai.1s n.asf pt.aa.nsm
806 4148 3836 4755 3306 899 60 69 2779 2400 340 2002

see it. *Please excuse* me.' **19** "Another said, 'I have just bought five yoke of oxen, and I'm on my
ἰδεῖν αὐτόν ἐρωτῶ σε ἔχε παρῃτημένον με καὶ ἕτερος εἶπεν ἠγόρασα πέντε ζεύγη βοῶν καὶ
f.aa r.asm.3 v.pai.1s r.as.2 v.pam.2s pt.rp.asm r.as.1 cj r.nsm v.aai.3s v.aai.1s a.apn n.apn n.gpm cj
1625 899 2263 5148 2400 4148 1609 2779 2283 3306 60 4297 2414 1091 2779

way to try them out. *Please excuse* me.' **20** "Still another said, 'I just got married,
πορεύομαι δοκιμάσαι αὐτά ἐρωτῶ σε ἔχε παρῃτημένον με καὶ ἕτερος εἶπεν γυναῖκα ἔγημα καὶ
v.pmi.1s f.aa r.apn.3 v.pai.1s r.as.2 v.pam.2s pt.rp.asm r.as.1 cj r.nsm v.aai.3s n.asf v.aai.1s cj
4513 1507 899 1507 2263 5148 2400 4148 1609 2779 2283 3306 1222 1138 2779

so I can't come.' ¶ **21** "The servant came back and reported this to his master.
ἰδιὰ τοῦτο οὐ δύναμαι ἐλθεῖν καὶ ὁ δοῦλος παραγενόμενος ἀπήγγειλεν ταῦτα αὐτοῦ τῷ κυρίῳ
p.a r.asn pl v.ppi.1s f.aa cj d.nsm n.nsm pt.am.nsm v.aai.3s r.apn r.gsm.3 d.dsm n.dsm
1328 4047 4024 1538 2262 2779 3836 1529 4134 550 4047 3261 899 3836 3261

Then the owner of the house became angry and ordered his servant, 'Go out quickly into the streets
τότε ὁ οἰκοδεσπότης ὀργισθεὶς εἶπεν αὐτοῦ τῷ δούλῳ ἔξελθε ταχέως εἰς τὰς πλατείας
adv d.nsm n.nsm pt.ap.nsm v.aai.3s r.gsm.3 d.dsm n.dsm v.aam.2s adv p.a d.apf n.apf
5538 3836 3867 3974 3306 899 3836 1529 2002 5441 1650 3836 4426

and alleys of the town and bring in the poor, the crippled, the blind and the lame.' **22** "'Sir,'
καὶ ῥύμας τῆς πόλεως καὶ εἰσάγαγε ὧδε τοὺς πτωχοὺς καὶ ἀναπείρους καὶ τυφλοὺς καὶ χωλοὺς καὶ κύριε
cj n.apf d.gsf n.gsf cj v.aam.2s adv d.apm a.apm cj n.apm cj a.apm cj a.apm cj n.vsm
2779 4860 3836 4484 2779 1652 6045 3836 4777 2779 401 2779 5603 2779 6000 2779 3261

the servant said, 'what you ordered has been done, but there is still room.' ¶ **23** "Then the master told
ὁ δοῦλος εἶπεν ὃ ἐπέταξας γέγονεν καὶ ἐστίν ἔτι τόπος καὶ ὁ κύριος εἶπεν πρὸς
d.nsm n.nsm v.aai.3s r.asn v.aai.2s v.rai.3s cj v.pai.3s adv n.nsm cj d.nsm n.nsm v.aai.3s p.a
3836 1529 3306 4005 2199 1181 2779 1639 2285 5536 2779 3836 3261 3306 4639

his servant, 'Go out to the roads and country lanes and make them come in, so that my house will
τὸν δοῦλον ἔξελθε εἰς τὰς ὁδοὺς καὶ φραγμοὺς καὶ ἀνάγκασον εἰσελθεῖν ἵνα μου ὁ οἶκος
d.asm n.asm v.aam.2s p.a d.apf n.apf cj n.apm cj v.aam.2s f.aa cj r.gs.1 d.nsm n.nsm
3836 1529 2002 1650 3836 3847 2779 5850 2779 337 1656 2671 1609 3836 3875

be full. **24** I tell you, not one of those men who were invited will get a taste of my
γεμισθῇ γὰρ λέγω ὑμῖν ὅτι οὐδεὶς ἐκείνων τῶν ἀνδρῶν τῶν κεκλημένων γεύσεται μου
v.aps.3s cj v.pai.1s r.dp.2 cj a.nsm r.gpm d.gpm n.gpm d.gpm pt.rp.gpm v.fmi.3s r.gs.1
1153 1142 3306 7007 4022 4029 1697 3836 467 3836 2813 1174 1270

banquet.'"
τοῦ δείπνου
d.gsn n.gsn
3836 1270

The Cost of Being a Disciple

14:25 Large crowds were traveling with Jesus, and turning to them he said: **26** "If anyone comes to me
δὲ πολλοί ὄχλοι Συνεπορεύοντο αὐτῷ καὶ στραφεὶς πρὸς αὐτούς εἶπεν εἴ τις ἔρχεται πρός με
cj a.npm n.npm v.imi.3p r.dsm.3 cj pt.ap.nsm p.a r.apm.3 v.aai.3s cj r.nsm v.pmi.3s p.a r.as.1
1254 4498 4063 5233 899 2779 5138 4639 899 3306 1623 5516 2262 4639 1609

and does not hate his father and mother, his wife and children, his brothers and sisters –
καὶ οὐ μισεῖ ἑαυτοῦ τὸν πατέρα καὶ τὴν μητέρα καὶ τὴν γυναῖκα καὶ τὰ τέκνα καὶ τοὺς ἀδελφοὺς καὶ τὰς ἀδελφὰς
cj pl v.pai.3s r.gsm.3 d.asm n.asm cj d.asf n.asf cj d.asf n.asf cj d.apn n.apn cj d.apm n.apm cj d.apf n.apf
2779 3631 4024 3631 1571 3836 4252 2779 3836 3613 2779 3836 1222 2779 3836 5451 2779 3836 81 2779 3836 80

yes, even his own life – he cannot be my disciple. **27** And anyone who does not carry his
καὶ ἔτι τε ἑαυτοῦ τὴν ψυχὴν οὐ δύναται εἶναι μου μαθητής ὅστις οὐ βαστάζει ἑαυτοῦ
adv adv cj r.gsm.3 d.asf n.asf pl v.ppi.3s f.pa r.gs.1 n.nsm r.nsm pl v.pai.3s r.gsm.3
2779 2285 5445 1571 3836 6034 4024 1538 1639 1609 3412 4015 1002 4024 1002 1571

ὥρα τοῦ δείπνου εἰπεῖν τοῖς κεκλημένοις, Ἔρχεσθε, ὅτι ἤδη ἔτοιμά ἐστιν. 18 καὶ ἤρξαντο ἀπὸ μιᾶς πάντες παραιτεῖσθαι. ὁ πρῶτος εἶπεν αὐτῷ, Ἀγρὸν ἠγόρασα καὶ ἔχω ἀνάγκην ἐξελθὼν ἰδεῖν αὐτόν· ἐρωτῶ σε, ἔχε με παρῃτημένον. 19 καὶ ἕτερος εἶπεν, Ζεύγη βοῶν ἠγόρασα πέντε καὶ πορεύομαι δοκιμάσαι αὐτά· ἐρωτῶ σε, ἔχε με παρῃτημένον. 20 καὶ ἕτερος εἶπεν, Γυναῖκα ἔγημα καὶ διὰ τοῦτο οὐ δύναμαι ἐλθεῖν. ¶ 21 καὶ παραγενόμενος ὁ δοῦλος ἀπήγγειλεν τῷ κυρίῳ αὐτοῦ ταῦτα. τότε ὀργισθεὶς ὁ οἰκοδεσπότης εἶπεν τῷ δούλῳ αὐτοῦ, Ἔξελθε ταχέως εἰς τὰς πλατείας καὶ ῥύμας τῆς πόλεως καὶ τοὺς πτωχοὺς καὶ ἀναπείρους καὶ τυφλοὺς καὶ χωλοὺς εἰσάγαγε ὧδε. 22 καὶ εἶπεν ὁ δοῦλος, Κύριε, γέγονεν ὃ ἐπέταξας, καὶ ἔτι τόπος ἐστίν. ¶ 23 καὶ εἶπεν ὁ κύριος πρὸς τὸν δοῦλον, Ἔξελθε εἰς τὰς ὁδοὺς καὶ φραγμοὺς καὶ ἀνάγκασον εἰσελθεῖν, ἵνα γεμισθῇ μου ὁ οἶκος· 24 λέγω γὰρ ὑμῖν ὅτι οὐδεὶς τῶν ἀνδρῶν ἐκείνων τῶν κεκλημένων γεύσεταί μου τοῦ δείπνου.

14:25 Συνεπορεύοντο δὲ αὐτῷ ὄχλοι πολλοί, καὶ στραφεὶς εἶπεν πρὸς αὐτούς, 26 Εἴ τις ἔρχεται πρός με καὶ οὐ μισεῖ τὸν πατέρα ἑαυτοῦ καὶ τὴν μητέρα καὶ τὴν γυναῖκα καὶ τὰ τέκνα καὶ τοὺς ἀδελφοὺς καὶ τὰς ἀδελφὰς ἔτι τε καὶ τὴν ψυχὴν ἑαυτοῦ, οὐ δύναται εἶναί μου μαθητής. 27 καὶ ὅστις οὐ βαστάζει τὸν σταυρὸν ἑαυτοῦ καὶ ἔρχεται ὀπίσω μου, οὐ δύναται εἶναί μου

cross | and follow | me cannot | be | my disciple. ¶ | **28** | "Suppose one of you wants to
ⲧὸν σταυρὸν | καὶ | ἔρχεται ὀπίσω | μου | οὐ δύναται | εἶναι | μου μαθητής | | γὰρ → | Τίς ἐξ ὑμῶν θέλων →
d.asm n.asm | cj | v.pmi.3s p.g | r.gs.1 | pl v.ppi.3s | f.pa | r.gs.1 n.nsm | | cj | r.nsm p.g r.gp.2 pt.pa.nsm
3836 5089 | 2779 | 2262 3958 | 1609 | 4024 1538 | 1639 | 1609 3412 | | 1142 | 5515 1666 7007 2527

build | a tower. Will he not first sit | down and estimate the cost | to see if | he has | enough money to
οἰκοδομῆσαι | πύργον → | → οὐχὶ πρῶτον καθίσας | | ψηφίζει τὴν δαπάνην | εἰ → | ἔχει | | εἰς
f.aa | n.asm | | pl adv pt.aa.nsm | v.pai.3s d.asf n.asf | cj | v.pai.3s | | p.a
3868 | 4788 | 6028 6028 4049 4754 2767 | | 6028 3836 1252 | 1623 | 2400 | | 1650

complete it? **29** For if | he lays | the foundation and is not able | to finish | it, everyone who sees | it
ἀπαρτισμόν | ἵνα μήποτε αὐτοῦ θέντος | θεμέλιον | καὶ → μὴ ἰσχύοντος → ἐκτελέσαι | πάντες οἱ θεωροῦντες →
n.asm | cj pl r.gsm.3 pt.aa.gsm | n.asm | cj pl pt.pa.gsm f.aa | a.npm d.npm pt.pa.npm
568 | 2671 3607 899 5502 | 2529 | 2779 1754 3590 2710 1754 | 4246 3836 2555

will ridicule him, **30** saying, 'This fellow | began to build | and was not able | to finish.' ¶
ἄρξωνται ἐμπαίζειν αὐτῷ | λέγοντες ὅτι οὗτος ὁ ἄνθρωπος | ἤρξατο | οἰκοδομεῖν καὶ → οὐκ ἴσχυσεν → ἐκτελέσαι
v.ams.3p f.pa r.dsm.3 | pt.pa.npm cj r.nsm d.nsm n.nsm | v.ami.3s | f.pa cj pl v.aai.3s f.aa
806 1850 899 | 3306 4022 4047 3836 476 | 2262 | 3868 2779 2710 4024 2710 1754

31 "Or suppose a king | is about | to go | to war | against another king. | Will he not first sit | down
Ἢ | τίς βασιλεὺς → πορευόμενος → συμβαλεῖν εἰς πόλεμον → ἑτέρῳ βασιλεῖ → οὐχὶ πρῶτον καθίσας →
cj | r.nsm n.nsm pt.pm.nsm f.aa p.a n.asm r.dsm n.dsm pl adv pt.aa.nsm
2445 | 5515 995 4513 5202 1650 4483 2283 995 1086 1086 4049 4754 2767

and consider whether he is | able | with ten thousand men to oppose | the one coming against him with
βουλεύσεται εἰ → ἔστιν δυνατός | ἐν δέκα χιλιάσιν | → ὑπαντῆσαι τῷ ← | ἐρχομένῳ ἐπ᾽ αὐτὸν μετὰ
v.fmi.3s cj v.pai.3s a.nsm | p.d a.dpf n.dpf | f.aa d.dsm | pt.pm.dsm p.a r.asm.3 p.g
1086 1623 1639 1543 1877 1274 5942 5636 3836 2262 2093 899 3552

twenty thousand? **32** If he is not able, | he will send | a delegation while the other is | still a long way off
εἴκοσι χιλιάδων | δὲ εἰ μὴ γε → → ἀποστείλας | πρεσβείαν → | αὐτοῦ ὄντος ἔτι | πόρρω ←
a.gpf a.gpf | cj cj pl pl pt.aa.nsm | n.asf | r.gsm.3 pt.pa.gsm adv | adv
1633 5942 | 1254 1623 3590 1145 690 | 4561 | 899 1639 2285 | 4522

and will ask for terms of peace. **33** In the same way, any of you who does not give | up everything he
→ ἐρωτᾷ τὰ πρὸς εἰρήνην | οὖν → οὕτως → πᾶς ἐξ ὑμῶν ὃς → οὐκ ἀποτάσσεται | πᾶσιν ἑαυτοῦ
v.pai.3s d.apn p.a n.asf | cj adv a.nsm p.g r.gp.2 r.nsm pl v.pmi.3s | a.dpn r.gsm.3
2263 3836 4639 1645 | 4036 4048 4246 1666 7007 4005 698 4024 698 | 4246 1571

has | cannot | be | my disciple. ¶ | **34** | "Salt | is good, but if | it loses | its saltiness,
ⲧοῖς ὑπάρχουσιν | οὐ δύναται | εἶναι | μου μαθητής | | οὖν | ⲧὸ ἅλας | Καλὸν δὲ ἐὰν καὶ → μωρανθῇ | τὸ ἅλας
d.dpn pt.pa.dpn | pl v.ppi.3s | f.pa | r.gs.1 n.nsm | | cj | d.nsn n.nsn | a.nsn cj cj cj v.aps.3s | d.nsn n.nsn
3836 5639 | 4024 1538 | 1639 | 1609 3412 | | 4036 | 3836 229 | 2819 1254 1569 2779 3701 | 3836 229

how can it be made salty | again? **35** It is | fit | neither for the soil nor for the manure pile; it | is thrown
ἐν τίνι → → → ἀρτυθήσεται | → ἐστιν | εὔθετον | οὔτε εἰς γῆν οὔτε εἰς κοπρίαν | αὐτό → βάλλουσιν
p.d r.dsn v.fpi.3s | v.pai.3s | a.nsn | cj p.a n.asf cj p.a n.asf | r.asn.3 v.pai.3p
1877 5515 789 | 1639 | 2310 | 4046 1650 1178 4046 1650 3161 | 899 965

out. ¶ | "He who has | ears to hear, | let him hear."
ἔξω | ὁ ← ἔχων ὦτα → ἀκούειν → ἀκουέτω
adv | d.nsm pt.pa.nsm n.apn f.pa v.pam.3s
2032 | 3836 2400 2400 201 201

The Parable of the Lost Sheep

15:1 Now the tax | collectors and "sinners" | were all | gathering around | to hear him. **2** But | the
δὲ οἱ τελῶναι ← | καὶ οἱ ἁμαρτωλοὶ | Ἦσαν πάντες ἐγγίζοντες ← | αὐτῷ → ἀκούειν αὐτοῦ | καὶ τε | οἱ
cj d.npm n.npm | cj d.npm a.npm | v.iai.3p a.npm pt.pa.npm | r.dsm.3 f.pa r.gsm.3 | cj cj | d.npm
1254 3836 5467 | 2779 3836 283 | 1639 4246 1581 | 899 201 899 | 2779 5445 | 3836

Pharisees and the teachers | of the law muttered, | "This man welcomes sinners | and eats with
Φαρισαῖοι καὶ οἱ γραμματεῖς ← ← | διεγόγγυζον λέγοντες ὅτι οὗτος | προσδέχεται ἁμαρτωλοὺς καὶ συνεσθίει ←
n.npm cj d.npm n.npm | v.iai.3p pt.pa.npm cj r.nsm | v.pmi.3s a.apm cj v.pai.3s
5757 2779 3836 1208 | 1339 3306 4022 4047 | 4657 283 2779 5303

them." ¶ **3** Then Jesus told | them this parable: | **4** "Suppose one | of you has a
αὐτοῖς | δὲ | Εἶπεν πρὸς αὐτοὺς ταύτην | τὴν παραβολὴν λέγων → | τίς ἄνθρωπος ἐξ ὑμῶν ἔχων
r.dpm.3 | cj | v.aai.3s p.a r.apm.3 r.asf | d.asf n.asf pt.pa.nsm | r.nsm n.nsm p.g r.gp.2 pt.pa.nsm
899 | 1254 | 3306 4639 899 4047 | 3836 4130 3306 | 2400 5515 476 1666 7007 2400

μαθητής. ¶ ²⁸ τίς γὰρ ἐξ ὑμῶν θέλων πύργον οἰκοδομῆσαι οὐχὶ πρῶτον καθίσας ψηφίζει τὴν δαπάνην, εἰ ἔχει εἰς ἀπαρτισμόν; ²⁹ ἵνα μήποτε θέντος αὐτοῦ θεμέλιον καὶ μὴ ἰσχύοντος ἐκτελέσαι πάντες οἱ θεωροῦντες ἄρξωνται αὐτῷ ἐμπαίζειν ³⁰ λέγοντες ὅτι Οὗτος ὁ ἄνθρωπος ἤρξατο οἰκοδομεῖν καὶ οὐκ ἴσχυσεν ἐκτελέσαι. ¶ ³¹ ἢ τίς βασιλεὺς πορευόμενος ἑτέρῳ βασιλεῖ συμβαλεῖν εἰς πόλεμον οὐχὶ καθίσας πρῶτον βουλεύσεται εἰ δυνατός ἐστιν ἐν δέκα χιλιάσιν ὑπαντῆσαι τῷ μετὰ εἴκοσι χιλιάδων ἐρχομένῳ ἐπ᾽ αὐτόν; ³² εἰ δὲ μή γε, ἔτι αὐτοῦ πόρρω ὄντος πρεσβείαν ἀποστείλας ἐρωτᾷ τὰ πρὸς εἰρήνην. ³³ οὕτως οὖν πᾶς ἐξ ὑμῶν ὃς οὐκ ἀποτάσσεται πᾶσιν τοῖς ἑαυτοῦ ὑπάρχουσιν οὐ δύναται εἶναί μου μαθητής. ¶ ³⁴ Καλὸν οὖν τὸ ἅλας· ἐὰν δὲ καὶ τὸ ἅλας μωρανθῇ, ἐν τίνι ἀρτυθήσεται; ³⁵ οὔτε εἰς γῆν οὔτε εἰς κοπρίαν εὔθετόν ἐστιν, ἔξω βάλλουσιν αὐτό. ¶ ὁ ἔχων ὦτα ἀκούειν ἀκουέτω.

¹⁵:¹ Ἦσαν δὲ αὐτῷ ἐγγίζοντες πάντες οἱ τελῶναι καὶ οἱ ἁμαρτωλοὶ ἀκούειν αὐτοῦ. ² καὶ διεγόγγυζον οἵ τε Φαρισαῖοι καὶ οἱ γραμματεῖς λέγοντες ὅτι Οὗτος ἁμαρτωλοὺς προσδέχεται καὶ συνεσθίει αὐτοῖς. ¶ ³ εἶπεν δὲ πρὸς αὐτοὺς τὴν παραβολὴν ταύτην

hundred	sheep	and	loses	one	of	them.	Does he	not	leave	the	ninety-nine		in	the	open country	and
ἑκατὸν	πρόβατα	καὶ	ἀπολέσας	ἓν	ἐξ	αὐτῶν	→	οὐ	καταλείπει	τὰ	ἐνενήκοντα	ἐννέα	ἐν	τῇ	ἐρήμῳ ←	καὶ
a.apn	n.apn	cj	pt.aa.nsm	a.asn	p.g	r.gpn.3		pl	v.pai.3s	d.apn	a.apn	a.apn	p.d	d.dsf	n.dsf	cj
1669	4585	2779	660	1651	1666	899	2901	2901	4024	2901	3836	1916	1933	1877	3836	2245	2779

go	after	the	lost		sheep	until	he	finds it?	[5] And	when	he	finds it,	he	joyfully	puts		it	on	his
πορεύεται	ἐπὶ	τὸ	ἀπολωλὸς			ἕως	→	εὕρῃ	αὐτό	καὶ	→	→	εὑρὼν	→	χαίρων	ἐπιτίθησιν	ἐπὶ	αὐτοῦ
v.pmi.3s	p.a	d.asn	pt.ra.asn			cj		v.aas.3s	r.asn.3	cj			pt.aa.nsm		v.pa.nsm	v.pai.3s	p.a	r.gsm.3
4513	2093	3836	660			2401		2351	899	2779			2351		2202	5897	2202	2093	899

shoulders	[6] and	goes		home.	Then	he calls		his	friends	and	neighbors		together	and says,		'Rejoice
τοὺς ὤμους	καὶ	ἐλθὼν	εἰς	τὸν οἶκον	→	συγκαλεῖ	τοὺς	φίλους	καὶ	τοὺς γείτονας			λέγων	αὐτοῖς	συγχάρητε
d.apm n.apm	cj	pt.aa.nsm	p.a	d.asm n.asm		v.pai.3s	d.apm	a.apm	cj	d.apm n.apm			pt.pa.nsm	r.dpm.3	v.apm.2p
3836 6049	2779	2262	1650	3836 3875		5157	3836	5813	2779	3836 1150		5157	3306	899	5176

with me;	I	have	found	my	lost		sheep.'	[7] I tell	you	that	in the	same way	there	will be	more
←	μοι	ὅτι	→	→	εὗρον	μου	τὸ ἀπολωλός	τὸ	πρόβατον	→	λέγω	ὑμῖν	ὅτι	→	→	οὕτως ←	→	ἔσται
	r.ds.1	cj			v.aai.1s	r.gs.1	d.asn pt.ra.asn	d.asn	n.asn		v.pai.1s	r.dp.2	cj			adv		v.fmi.3s
	1609	4022			2351	1609	3836 660	3836	4585		3306	7007	4022			4048		1639

rejoicing	in	heaven		over	one	sinner	who repents	than	over	ninety-nine		righteous	persons	who		do	not
χαρὰ	ἐν	τῷ	οὐρανῷ	ἐπὶ	ἑνὶ	ἁμαρτωλῷ →	μετανοοῦντι	ἢ	ἐπὶ	ἐνενήκοντα	ἐννέα	δικαίοις	←		οἵτινες	→	οὐ
n.nsf	p.d	d.dsm	n.dsm	p.d	a.dsm	n.dsm	pt.pa.dsm	cj	p.d	a.dpn	a.dpn	a.dpm			r.npm		pl
5915	1877	3836	4041	2093	1651	283	3566	2445	2093	1916	1933	1465			4015	2400	4024

need		to repent.
χρείαν	ἔχουσιν	μετανοίας
n.asf	v.pai.3p	n.gsf
5970	2400	3567

The Parable of the Lost Coin

[15:8] "Or	suppose	a	woman	has	ten	silver	coins		and	loses		one.	Does	she	not	light	a lamp,
Ἢ		τίς	γυνὴ	ἔχουσα	δέκα →		δραχμὰς		ἐὰν	ἀπολέσῃ	δραχμὴν	μίαν →		→	οὐχὶ	ἅπτει	λύχνον	καὶ
cj		r.nsf	n.nsf	pt.pa.nsf	a.apf		n.apf		cj	v.aas.3s	n.asf	a.asf			pl	v.pai.3s	n.asm	cj
2445	2400	5515	1222	2400	1274		1534		1569	660	1534	1651		721	721	4049	721	3394	2779

sweep	the	house	and	search	carefully	until		she finds it?	[9] And	when	she finds		it,	she calls		her	friends	and
σαροῖ	τὴν	οἰκίαν	καὶ	ζητεῖ	ἐπιμελῶς	ἕως	οὗ	εὕρῃ	καὶ	→	→	εὑροῦσα		συγκαλεῖ	τὰς	φίλας	καὶ
v.pai.3s	d.asf	n.asf	cj	v.pai.3s	adv	p.g	r.gsm	v.aas.3s	cj			pt.aa.nsf		v.pai.3s	d.apf	a.apf	cj
4924	3836	3864	2779	2426	2151	2401	4005	2351	2779			2351		5157	3836	5813	2779

neighbors	together	and says,		'Rejoice	with me;		I	have	found	my		lost	coin.'	[10] In the	same way,	I tell
γείτονας	↰		λέγουσα	συγχάρητε ←	μοι	ὅτι	→	εὗρον	τὴν	ἣν	ἀπώλεσα	δραχμήν		→	οὕτως	→ λέγω
n.apf			pt.pa.nsf	v.apm.2p	r.ds.1	cj		v.aai.1s	d.asf	r.asf	v.aai.1s	n.asf			adv	v.pai.1s
1150	5157		3306	5176	1609	4022		2351	3836	4005	660	1534			4048	3306

you,	there is		rejoicing	in the	presence	of the	angels	of God		over	one	sinner	who repents."
ὑμῖν	γίνεται	χαρὰ	→	→	ἐνώπιον	τῶν	ἀγγέλων	→ τοῦ θεοῦ	ἐπὶ	ἑνὶ	ἁμαρτωλῷ	→	μετανοοῦντι
r.dp.2	v.pmi.3s	n.nsf			p.g	d.gpm	n.gpm	d.gsm n.gsm	p.d	a.dsm	a.dsm		pt.pa.dsm
7007	1181	5915		1967	3836	34	3836 2536	2093	1651	283		3566

The Parable of the Lost Son

[15:11]	Jesus	continued:	"There	was	a	man		who had	two	sons.	[12] The	younger	one		said	to	his
	δὲ	Εἶπεν			τις	ἄνθρωπος		εἶχεν	δύο	υἱούς	καὶ	ὁ	νεώτερος ←	αὐτῶν	εἶπεν	→	τῷ
	cj	v.aai.3s			r.nsm	n.nsm		v.iai.3s	a.apm	n.apm	cj	d.nsm	a.nsm.c	r.gpm.3	v.aai.3s		d.dsm
	1254	3306			5516	476		2400	1545	5626	2779	3836	3742	899	3306		3836

father,	'Father,	give	me	my	share		of the estate.'	So	he	divided	his	property	between	them.	¶	[13]
πατρί	πάτερ	δός	μοι	τὸ	ἐπιβάλλον	μέρος	→ τῆς οὐσίας	δὲ	ὁ	διεῖλεν	τὸν	βίον	→	αὐτοῖς		καὶ
n.dsm	n.vsm	v.aam.2s	r.ds.1	d.asn	pt.pa.asn	n.asn	d.gsf n.gsf	cj	d.nsm	v.aai.3s	d.asm	n.asm		r.dpm.3		cj
4252	1443	1443	1609	3836	2095	3538	3836 4045	1254	3836	1349	3836	1050		899		2779

"Not	long	after	that,	the	younger	son	got		together	all		he had,	set		off	for a	distant	country
οὐ	πολλὰς	ἡμέρας	μετ'	ὁ	νεώτερος	υἱὸς	συναγαγὼν			πάντα			ἀπεδήμησεν ←	εἰς	μακρὰν	χώραν
pl	a.apf	n.apf	p.a	d.nsm	a.nsm.c	n.nsm	pt.aa.nsm			a.apn			v.aai.3s		p.a	a.asf	n.asf
4024	4498	2465	3552	3836	3742	5626	5251			4246			623		1650	3431	6001

λέγων, ⁴ Τίς ἄνθρωπος ἐξ ὑμῶν ἔχων ἑκατὸν πρόβατα καὶ ἀπολέσας ἐξ αὐτῶν ἓν οὐ καταλείπει τὰ ἐνενήκοντα ἐννέα ἐν τῇ ἐρήμῳ καὶ πορεύεται ἐπὶ τὸ ἀπολωλὸς ἕως εὕρῃ αὐτό; ⁵ καὶ εὑρὼν ἐπιτίθησιν ἐπὶ τοὺς ὤμους αὐτοῦ χαίρων ⁶ καὶ ἐλθὼν εἰς τὸν οἶκον συγκαλεῖ τοὺς φίλους καὶ τοὺς γείτονας λέγων αὐτοῖς, Συγχάρητέ μοι, ὅτι εὗρον τὸ πρόβατόν μου τὸ ἀπολωλός. ⁷ λέγω ὑμῖν ὅτι οὕτως χαρὰ ἐν τῷ οὐρανῷ ἔσται ἐπὶ ἑνὶ ἁμαρτωλῷ μετανοοῦντι ἢ ἐπὶ ἐνενήκοντα ἐννέα δικαίοις οἵτινες οὐ χρείαν ἔχουσιν μετανοίας.

¹⁵:⁸ Ἢ τίς γυνὴ δραχμὰς ἔχουσα δέκα ἐὰν ἀπολέσῃ δραχμὴν μίαν, οὐχὶ ἅπτει λύχνον καὶ σαροῖ τὴν οἰκίαν καὶ ζητεῖ ἐπιμελῶς ἕως οὗ εὕρῃ; ⁹ καὶ εὑροῦσα συγκαλεῖ τὰς φίλας καὶ γείτονας λέγουσα, Συγχάρητέ μοι, ὅτι εὗρον τὴν δραχμὴν ἣν ἀπώλεσα. ¹⁰ οὕτως, λέγω ὑμῖν, γίνεται χαρὰ ἐνώπιον τῶν ἀγγέλων τοῦ θεοῦ ἐπὶ ἑνὶ ἁμαρτωλῷ μετανοοῦντι.

¹⁵:¹¹ Εἶπεν δέ, Ἄνθρωπός τις εἶχεν δύο υἱούς. ¹² καὶ εἶπεν ὁ νεώτερος αὐτῶν τῷ πατρί, Πάτερ, δός μοι τὸ ἐπιβάλλον μέρος τῆς οὐσίας. ὁ δὲ διεῖλεν αὐτοῖς τὸν βίον. ¶ ¹³ καὶ μετ' οὐ πολλὰς ἡμέρας συναγαγὼν πάντα ὁ νεώτερος υἱὸς ἀπεδήμησεν εἰς

and there squandered his wealth in wild living. **14** After he had spent everything, there was a
καὶ ἐκεῖ διεσκόρπισεν αὐτοῦ ⌞τὴν οὐσίαν⌟ → ἀσώτως ζῶν δὲ → αὐτοῦ → δαπανήσαντος πάντα → ἐγένετο
cj adv v.aai.3s r.gsm.3 d.asf n.asf adv adv cj r.gsm.3 pt.aa.gsm a.apn v.ami.3s
2779 1695 1399 899 3836 4045 2409 862 2409 1254 1251 899 1251 4246 1181

severe famine in that whole country, and he began to be in need. **15** So he went and hired himself
ἰσχυρὰ λιμὸς κατὰ ἐκείνην ↵ ⌞τὴν χώραν⌟ καὶ αὐτὸς ἤρξατο → → ὑστερεῖσθαι καὶ → πορευθεὶς ἐκολλήθη ←
a.nsf n.nsf p.a r.asf d.asf n.asf cj r.nsm v.ami.3s f.pp cj pt.ap.nsm v.api.3s
2708 3350 2848 1697 2848 3836 6001 2779 899 806 5728 2779 4513 3140

out to a citizen of that country, who sent him to his fields to feed pigs. **16** He
← ἑνὶ ⌞τῶν πολιτῶν⌟ ἐκείνης ⌞τῆς χώρας⌟ καὶ ἔπεμψεν αὐτὸν εἰς αὐτοῦ ⌞τοὺς ἀγρούς⌟ → βόσκειν χοίρους καὶ
a.dsm d.gpm n.gpm r.gsf d.gsf n.gsf cj v.aai.3s r.asm.3 p.a r.gsm.3 d.apm n.apm f.pa n.apm cj
1651 3836 4489 6001 1697 3836 6001 2779 4287 899 1650 899 3836 69 1081 5956 2779

longed to fill his stomach with the pods that the pigs were eating, but no one gave him anything. ¶
ἐπεθύμει χορτασθῆναι ← ← ἐκ τῶν κερατίων ὧν οἱ χοῖροι → ἤσθιον καὶ → οὐδεὶς ἐδίδου αὐτῷ
v.iai.3s f.ap p.g d.gpn n.gpn r.gpn d.npm n.npm v.iai.3p cj a.nsm v.iai.3s r.dsm.3
2121 5963 1666 3836 3044 4005 3836 5956 2266 2779 4029 1443 899

17 "When he came to his senses, he said, 'How many of my father's hired men have food to spare,
δὲ → → ἐλθὼν εἰς ἑαυτὸν → → ἔφη → πόσοι μου ⌞τοῦ πατρός⌟ μίσθιοι → ἄρτων περισσεύονται
cj pt.aa.nsm p.a r.asm.3 v.iai.3s r.npm r.gs.1 d.gsm n.gsm n.npm n.gpm v.pmi.3p
1254 2262 1650 1571 5774 4531 1609 3836 4252 3634 4355 788 4355

and here I am starving to death! **18** I will set out and go back to my father and say to him:
δὲ ὧδε ἐγὼ → λιμῷ ἀπόλλυμαι ἀναστὰς → πορεύσομαι πρὸς μου ⌞τὸν πατέρα⌟ καὶ ἐρῶ αὐτῷ
cj adv r.ns.1 n.dsf v.pmi.1s pt.aa.nsm v.fmi.1s p.a r.gs.1 d.asm n.asm cj v.fai.1s r.dsm.3
1254 6045 1609 3350 660 482 4513 4639 1609 3836 4252 2779 3306 899

Father, I have sinned against heaven and against you. **19** I am no longer worthy to be called your son;
πάτερ → ἥμαρτον εἰς ⌞τὸν οὐρανὸν⌟ καὶ ἐνώπιον σου → εἰμὶ οὐκέτι ← ἄξιος → κληθῆναι σου υἱός
n.vsm v.aai.1s p.a d.asm n.asm cj p.g r.gs.2 v.pai.1s adv a.nsm f.ap r.gs.2 n.nsm
4252 279 1650 3836 4041 2779 1967 5148 1639 4033 545 2813 5148 5626

make me like one of your hired men.' **20** So he got up and went to his father. ¶ "But
ποίησον με ὡς ἕνα → σου ⌞τῶν μισθίων⌟ καὶ → ἀναστὰς ἦλθεν πρὸς ἑαυτοῦ ⌞τὸν πατέρα⌟ δὲ
v.aam.2s r.as.1 pl a.asm r.gs.2 d.gpm n.gpm cj pt.aa.nsm v.aai.3s p.a r.gsm.3 d.asm n.asm cj
4472 1609 6055 1651 3634 5148 3836 3634 2779 482 2262 4639 1571 3836 4252 1254

while he was still a long way off, his father saw him and was filled with compassion for him; he
→ αὐτοῦ → Ἔτι μακρὰν ἀπέχοντος ← αὐτοῦ ὁ πατὴρ εἶδεν αὐτὸν καὶ → → → ἐσπλαγχνίσθη καὶ →
r.gsm.3 adv adv pt.pa.gsm r.gsm.3 d.nsm n.nsm v.aai.3s r.asm.3 cj v.api.3s cj
600 899 600 2285 3426 600 899 3836 4252 1625 899 2779 5072 2779

ran to his son, threw his arms around him and kissed him. **21** "The son said to him, 'Father,
δραμὼν ἐπέπεσεν ἐπὶ τὸν τράχηλον αὐτοῦ καὶ κατεφίλησεν αὐτόν δὲ ὁ υἱός εἶπεν → αὐτῷ πάτερ
pt.aa.nsm v.aai.3s p.a d.asm n.asm r.gsm.3 cj v.aai.3s r.asm.3 cj d.nsm n.nsm v.aai.3s r.dsm.3 n.vsm
5556 2158 2093 3836 5549 899 2779 2968 899 1254 3836 5626 3306 899 4252

I have sinned against heaven and against you. I am no longer worthy to be called your son.' **22** "But the
→ → ἥμαρτον εἰς ⌞τὸν οὐρανὸν⌟ καὶ ἐνώπιον σου εἰμὶ οὐκέτι ← ἄξιος → κληθῆναι σου υἱός δὲ ὁ
v.aai.1s p.a d.asm n.asm cj p.g r.gs.2 v.pai.1s adv a.nsm f.ap r.gs.2 n.nsm cj d.nsm
279 1650 3836 4041 2779 1967 5148 1639 4033 545 2813 5148 5626 1254 3836

father said to his servants, 'Quick! Bring the best robe and put it on him. Put a ring
πατὴρ εἶπεν πρὸς αὐτοῦ ⌞τοὺς δούλους⌟ ταχὺ ἐξενέγκατε ⌞τὴν πρώτην⌟ στολὴν καὶ ἐνδύσατε ← αὐτόν καὶ δότε δακτύλιον
n.nsm v.aai.3s p.a r.gsm.3 d.apm n.apm adv v.aam.2p d.asf a.asf n.asf cj v.aam.2p r.asm.3 cj v.aam.2p n.asm
4252 3306 4639 899 3836 1529 5444 1766 3836 4755 5124 2779 1907 899 2779 1443 1234

on his finger and sandals on his feet. **23** Bring the fattened calf and kill it. Let's have a
εἰς αὐτοῦ ⌞τὴν χεῖρα⌟ καὶ ὑποδήματα εἰς τοὺς πόδας καὶ φέρετε τὸν ⌞τὸν σιτευτὸν⌟ μόσχον θύσατε καὶ →
p.a r.gsm.3 d.asf n.asf cj n.apn p.a d.apm n.apm cj v.pam.2p d.asm d.asm a.asm n.asm v.aam.2p cj
1650 899 3836 5931 2779 5687 1650 3836 4546 2779 5770 3836 3836 4988 3675 2604 2779

feast and celebrate. **24** For this son of mine was dead and is alive again; he was lost and is found.'
φαγόντες εὐφρανθῶμεν ὅτι οὗτος ὁ υἱός μου ἦν νεκρὸς καὶ → ἀνέζησεν → ἦν ἀπολωλὼς καὶ εὑρέθη
pt.aa.npm v.aps.1p cj r.nsm d.nsm n.nsm r.gs.1 v.iai.3s a.nsm cj v.aai.3s v.iai.3s pt.ra.nsm cj v.api.3s
2266 2370 4022 4047 3836 5626 1609 1639 3738 2779 348 1639 660 2779 2351

χώραν μακρὰν καὶ ἐκεῖ διεσκόρπισεν τὴν οὐσίαν αὐτοῦ ζῶν ἀσώτως. **14** δαπανήσαντος δὲ αὐτοῦ πάντα ἐγένετο λιμὸς ἰσχυρὰ κατὰ τὴν χώραν ἐκείνην, καὶ αὐτὸς ἤρξατο ὑστερεῖσθαι. **15** καὶ πορευθεὶς ἐκολλήθη ἑνὶ τῶν πολιτῶν τῆς χώρας ἐκείνης, καὶ ἔπεμψεν αὐτὸν εἰς τοὺς ἀγροὺς αὐτοῦ βόσκειν χοίρους, **16** καὶ ἐπεθύμει γεμίσαι «χορτασθῆναι» τὴν κοιλίαν αὐτοῦ ἀπὸ «ἐκ» τῶν κερατίων ὧν ἤσθιον οἱ χοῖροι, καὶ οὐδεὶς ἐδίδου αὐτῷ. ¶ **17** εἰς ἑαυτὸν δὲ ἐλθὼν ἔφη, Πόσοι μίσθιοι τοῦ πατρός μου περισσεύονται ἄρτων, ἐγὼ δὲ λιμῷ ὧδε ἀπόλλυμαι. **18** ἀναστὰς πορεύσομαι πρὸς τὸν πατέρα μου καὶ ἐρῶ αὐτῷ, Πάτερ, ἥμαρτον εἰς τὸν οὐρανὸν καὶ ἐνώπιόν σου, **19** οὐκέτι εἰμὶ ἄξιος κληθῆναι υἱός σου· ποίησόν με ὡς ἕνα τῶν μισθίων σου. **20** καὶ ἀναστὰς ἦλθεν πρὸς τὸν πατέρα ἑαυτοῦ. ¶ ἔτι δὲ αὐτοῦ μακρὰν ἀπέχοντος εἶδεν αὐτὸν ὁ πατὴρ αὐτοῦ καὶ ἐσπλαγχνίσθη καὶ δραμὼν ἐπέπεσεν ἐπὶ τὸν τράχηλον αὐτοῦ καὶ κατεφίλησεν αὐτόν. **21** εἶπεν δὲ ὁ υἱὸς αὐτῷ, Πάτερ, ἥμαρτον εἰς τὸν οὐρανὸν καὶ ἐνώπιόν σου, οὐκέτι εἰμὶ ἄξιος κληθῆναι υἱός σου. **22** εἶπεν δὲ ὁ πατὴρ πρὸς τοὺς δούλους αὐτοῦ, Ταχὺ ἐξενέγκατε στολὴν τὴν πρώτην καὶ ἐνδύσατε αὐτόν, καὶ δότε δακτύλιον εἰς τὴν χεῖρα αὐτοῦ καὶ ὑποδήματα εἰς τοὺς πόδας, **23** καὶ φέρετε τὸν μόσχον τὸν σιτευτόν, θύσατε, καὶ φαγόντες εὐφρανθῶμεν, **24** ὅτι οὗτος ὁ υἱός μου νεκρὸς ἦν καὶ ἀνέζησεν, ἦν ἀπολωλὼς καὶ εὑρέθη. καὶ ἤρξαντο εὐφραίνεσθαι. ¶

So they began to celebrate. ¶ **25** "Meanwhile, the older son was in the field. When he
καὶ → ἤρξαντο → εὐφραίνεσθαι δὲ ὁ ὁ πρεσβύτερος υἱὸς αὐτοῦ Ἦν ἐν ἀγρῷ καὶ ὡς
cj v.ami.3p f.pp cj d.nsm d.nsm a.nsm n.nsm n.gsm.3 v.iai.3s p.d n.dsm cj cj
2779 806 2370 1254 3836 3836 4565 5626 899 1639 1877 69 2779 6055

came near the house, he heard music and dancing. **26** So he called one of the servants and asked
ἐρχόμενος ἤγγισεν τῇ οἰκίᾳ → ἤκουσεν συμφωνίας καὶ χορῶν καὶ → προσκαλεσάμενος ἕνα → τῶν παίδων ἐπυνθάνετο
pt.pm.nsm v.aai.3s d.dsf n.dsf v.aai.3s n.gsf cj n.gpm cj pt.am.nsm a.asm d.gpm n.gpm v.imi.3s
2262 1581 3836 3864 201 5246 2779 5962 2779 4673 1651 3836 4090 4785

him *what was going on.* **27** 'Your brother has come,' he replied, 'and your father has
⸂τί ἂν ⸃εἴη ταῦτα δὲ ὅτι σου ὁ ἀδελφός⸃ → ἥκει ὁ εἶπεν αὐτῷ καὶ σου ⸃ὁ πατήρ⸃ →
r.nsn pl v.pao.3s r.npn cj cj r.gs.2 d.nsm n.nsm v.rai.3s d.nsm v.aai.3s r.dsm.3 cj r.gs.2 d.nsm n.nsm
5515 323 1639 4047 1254 4022 5148 3836 81 2457 3836 3306 899 2779 5148 3836 4252

killed the fattened calf because he has him back safe and sound.' ¶ **28** "The older brother
ἔθυσεν τὸν ⸂τὸν σιτευτόν⸃ μόσχον ὅτι → ἀπέλαβεν αὐτὸν ↵ ὑγιαίνοντα ← ← δὲ
v.aai.3s d.asm d.asm a.asm n.asm cj v.aai.3s r.asm.3 pt.pa.asm cj
2604 3836 3836 4988 3675 4022 655 899 655 5617 1254

became angry and refused to go in. So his father went out and pleaded with him. **29** But he
→ ὠργίσθη καὶ ⸂οὐκ ἤθελεν⸃ → εἰσελθεῖν ← δὲ αὐτοῦ ὁ πατὴρ ἐξελθὼν → παρεκάλει ← αὐτόν δὲ ὁ
v.api.3s cj pl v.iai.3s f.aa cj r.gsm.3 d.nsm n.nsm pt.aa.nsm v.iai.3s r.asm.3 cj d.nsm
3974 2779 4024 2527 1656 1254 899 3836 4252 2002 4151 899 1254 3836

answered his father, 'Look! All these years I've been slaving for you and never disobeyed your
ἀποκριθεὶς εἶπεν αὐτοῦ ⸂τῷ πατρὶ⸃ ἰδοὺ τοσαῦτα → ἔτη → δουλεύω → σοι καὶ οὐδέποτε παρῆλθον σου
pt.ap.nsm v.aai.3s r.gsm.3 d.dsm n.dsm j r.apn n.apn v.pai.1s r.ds.2 cj adv v.aai.1s r.gs.2
646 3306 899 3836 4252 2627 5537 2291 1526 5148 2779 4030 4216 5148

orders. Yet you never gave me even a young goat so I could celebrate with my friends. **30** But when this
ἐντολήν καὶ ↵ οὐδέποτε ἔδωκας ἐμοὶ → ἔριφον ἵνα → → εὐφρανθῶ μετὰ μου ⸂τῶν φίλων⸃ δὲ ὅτε οὗτος
n.asf cj adv v.aai.2s r.ds.1 n.asm cj v.aps.1s p.g r.gs.1 d.gpm a.gpm cj cj r.nsm
1953 2779 1443 4030 1443 1609 2253 2671 2370 3552 1609 3836 5813 1254 4021 4047

son of yours who has squandered your property with prostitutes comes home, you kill the fattened calf for
⸂ὁ υἱός⸃ σου ὁ → καταφαγών σου ⸂τὸν βίον⸃ μετὰ πορνῶν ἦλθεν → → ἔθυσας τὸν σιτευτὸν μόσχον →
d.nsm n.nsm r.gs.2 d.nsm pt.aa.nsm r.gs.2 d.asm n.asm p.g n.gpf v.aai.3s v.aai.2s d.asm a.asm n.asm
3836 5626 5148 3836 2983 5148 3836 1050 3552 4520 2262 2604 3836 4988 3675

him!' ¶ **31** "'My son,' the father said, 'you are always with me, and everything I have is
αὐτῷ δὲ → τέκνον ὁ εἶπεν αὐτῷ σὺ εἶ πάντοτε μετ' ἐμοῦ καὶ πάντα ⸂τὰ ἐμὰ⸃ ← ἐστιν
r.dsm.3 cj n.vsn d.nsm v.aai.3s r.dsm.3 r.ns.2 v.pai.2s adv p.g r.gs.1 cj a.npn d.npn r.npn.1 v.pai.3s
899 1254 5451 3836 3306 899 5148 1639 4121 3552 1609 2779 4246 3836 1847 1639

yours. **32** But we had to celebrate and be glad, because this brother of yours was dead and is alive again;
σά δὲ → ἔδει εὐφρανθῆναι καὶ → χαρῆναι ὅτι οὗτος ὁ ἀδελφός⸃ → σου ἦν νεκρὸς καὶ → ἔζησεν καὶ
r.npn.2 cj v.iai.3s f.ap cj f.ap cj r.nsm d.nsm n.nsm r.gs.2 v.iai.3s a.nsm cj v.aai.3s cj
5050 1254 2370 1256 2370 2779 5897 4022 4047 3836 81 5148 1639 3738 2409 2779

he was lost and is found.'"
→ → ἀπολωλὼς καὶ → εὑρέθη
pt.ra.nsm cj v.api.3s
660 2779 2351

The Parable of the Shrewd manager

16:1 Jesus told his disciples: "There was a rich man whose manager was
δὲ Ἔλεγεν καὶ πρὸς τοὺς μαθητάς → ἦν τις πλούσιος ἄνθρωπος ὃς εἶχεν οἰκονόμον καὶ οὗτος →
cj v.iai.3s adv p.a d.apm n.apm v.iai.3s r.nsm a.nsm n.nsm r.nsm v.iai.3s n.asm cj r.nsm
1254 3306 2779 4639 3836 3412 1639 5516 4454 476 4005 2400 3874 2779 4047

accused of wasting his possessions. **2** So he called him in and asked him, 'What is this I hear
διεβλήθη αὐτῷ ὡς διασκορπίζων αὐτοῦ ⸂τὰ ὑπάρχοντα⸃ καὶ → φωνήσας αὐτὸν ↵ εἶπεν αὐτῷ τί τοῦτο → ἀκούω
v.api.3s r.dsm.3 pl pt.pa.nsm r.gsm.3 d.apn pt.pa.apn cj pt.aa.nsm r.asm.3 v.aai.3s r.dsm.3 r.nsn r.nsn v.pai.1s
1330 899 6055 1399 899 3836 5639 2779 5888 899 5888 3306 899 5515 4047 201

about you? Give an account of your management, because you cannot be manager any longer.' ¶ **3**
περὶ σοῦ ἀπόδος ⸂τὸν λόγον⸃ ↵ σου ⸂τῆς οἰκονομίας⸃ γὰρ → ⸃οὐ δύνῃ⸃ οἰκονομεῖν ἔτι ← δὲ
p.g r.gs.2 v.aam.2s d.asm n.asm r.gs.2 d.gsf n.gsf cj pl v.ppi.2s f.pa adv cj
4309 5148 625 3836 3364 5148 3836 3873 1142 4024 1538 3872 2285 1254

---

²⁵ Ἦν δὲ ὁ υἱὸς αὐτοῦ ὁ πρεσβύτερος ἐν ἀγρῷ· καὶ ὡς ἐρχόμενος ἤγγισεν τῇ οἰκίᾳ, ἤκουσεν συμφωνίας καὶ χορῶν, ²⁶ καὶ προσκαλεσάμενος ἕνα τῶν παίδων ἐπυνθάνετο τί ἂν εἴη ταῦτα. ²⁷ ὁ δὲ εἶπεν αὐτῷ ὅτι Ὁ ἀδελφός σου ἥκει, καὶ ἔθυσεν ὁ πατήρ σου τὸν μόσχον τὸν σιτευτόν, ὅτι ὑγιαίνοντα αὐτὸν ἀπέλαβεν. ¶ ²⁸ ὠργίσθη δὲ καὶ οὐκ ἤθελεν εἰσελθεῖν, ὁ δὲ πατὴρ αὐτοῦ ἐξελθὼν παρεκάλει αὐτόν. ²⁹ ὁ δὲ ἀποκριθεὶς εἶπεν τῷ πατρὶ αὐτοῦ, Ἰδοὺ τοσαῦτα ἔτη δουλεύω σοι καὶ οὐδέποτε ἐντολήν σου παρῆλθον, καὶ ἐμοὶ οὐδέποτε ἔδωκας ἔριφον ἵνα μετὰ τῶν φίλων μου εὐφρανθῶ· ³⁰ ὅτε δὲ ὁ υἱός σου οὗτος ὁ καταφαγών σου τὸν βίον μετὰ πορνῶν ἦλθεν, ἔθυσας αὐτῷ τὸν σιτευτὸν μόσχον. ¶ ³¹ ὁ δὲ εἶπεν αὐτῷ, Τέκνον, σὺ πάντοτε μετ' ἐμοῦ εἶ, καὶ πάντα τὰ ἐμὰ σά ἐστιν· ³² εὐφρανθῆναι δὲ καὶ χαρῆναι ἔδει, ὅτι ὁ ἀδελφός σου οὗτος νεκρὸς ἦν καὶ ἀνέζησεν, «ἔζησεν,» καὶ ἀπολωλὼς καὶ εὑρέθη.

^{16:1} Ἔλεγεν δὲ καὶ πρὸς τοὺς μαθητάς, Ἄνθρωπός τις ἦν πλούσιος ὃς εἶχεν οἰκονόμον, καὶ οὗτος διεβλήθη αὐτῷ ὡς διασκορπίζων τὰ ὑπάρχοντα αὐτοῦ. ² καὶ φωνήσας αὐτὸν εἶπεν αὐτῷ, Τί τοῦτο ἀκούω περὶ σοῦ; ἀπόδος τὸν λόγον τῆς

"The manager said to himself, 'What shall I do   now?   My master   is taking   away   my
ὁ   οἰκονόμος   εἶπεν ἐν ἑαυτῷ   τί   → ποιήσω   ὅτι μου ὁ   κύριος   ἀφαιρεῖται   ἀπ᾽ ἐμοῦ
d.nsm   n.nsm   v.aai.3s p.d r.dsm.3   r.asn   v.aas.1s   cj r.gs.1 d.nsm   n.nsm   v.pmi.3s   p.g r.gs.1
3836   3874   3306   1877 1571   5515   4472   4022 1609 3836   3261   904   608 1609

job.   I'm not strong enough to dig,   and I'm ashamed   to beg   — ⁴I know what I'll do   so that,
τὴν οἰκονομίαν   οὐκ ἰσχύω   → σκάπτειν   → αἰσχύνομαι   ἐπαιτεῖν   → ἔγνων τί   → ποιήσω ἵνα
d.asf n.asf   pl v.pai.1s   f.pa   v.pmi.1s   f.pa   v.aai.1s r.asn   v.aas.1s cj
3836 3873   4024 2710   4999   159   2050   1182 5515   4472 2671

when I lose   my job   here, people will welcome me into their houses.'   ¶   ⁵"So he
ὅταν → μετασταθῶ ἐκ τῆς οἰκονομίας   → → δέξωνται με εἰς αὐτῶν τοὺς οἴκους   καὶ →
cj   v.aps.1s p.g d.gsf n.gsf   v.ams.3p r.as.1 p.a r.gpm.3 d.apm n.apm   cj
4020 3496   1666 3836 3873   1312 1609 1650 899 3836 3875   2779

called   in each   one of his   master's   debtors.   He asked the first, 'How much do you owe
προσκαλεσάμενος ← ἕκαστον ἕνα → ἑαυτοῦ τοῦ κυρίου   τῶν χρεοφειλετῶν → ἔλεγεν τῷ πρώτῳ   → πόσον → ὀφείλεις
pt.am.nsm   r.asn a.asm   r.gsm.3 d.gsm n.gsm   d.gpm n.gpm   v.iai.3s d.dsm a.dsm   r.asn   v.pai.2s
4673   1667 1651   5971 1571 3836 3261   3836 5971   3306 3836 4755   4531   4053

my master?'   ⁶   "Eight hundred gallons of olive oil,' he replied.   "The manager told him, 'Take your
μου τῷ κυρίῳ   δὲ   ἑκατὸν βάτους → → ἐλαίου ὁ   εἶπεν   δὲ ὁ   εἶπεν αὐτῷ δέξαι σου
r.gs.1 d.dsm n.dsm   cj   a.apm n.apm   n.gsn d.nsm   v.aai.3s   cj d.nsm   v.aai.3s r.dsm.3 v.amm.2s r.gs.2
1609 3836 3261   1254   1669 1003   1778 3836   3306   1254 3836   3306 899 1312 5148

bill,   sit   down quickly, and make it four   hundred.'   ⁷ "Then he asked the second, 'And how
τὰ γράμματα καὶ καθίσας ← ταχέως γράψον πεντήκοντα   ἔπειτα → εἶπεν ἑτέρῳ δὲ
d.apn n.apn   cj pt.aa.nsm   adv   v.aam.2s a.apm   adv   v.aai.3s r.dsm cj
3836 1207   2779 2767   5441   1211 4299   2083   3306 2283 1254

much do you owe?'   'A thousand bushels of wheat,' he replied.   "He told him, 'Take your bill   and
πόσον → σὺ ὀφείλεις δὲ   ἑκατὸν κόρους → σίτου ὁ   εἶπεν   → λέγει αὐτῷ δέξαι σου τὰ γράμματα καὶ
r.asn   r.ns.2 v.pai.2s cj   a.apm n.apm   n.gsn d.nsm v.aai.3s   v.pai.3s r.dsm.3 v.amm.2s r.gs.2 d.apn n.apn cj
4531   4053 5148 4053 1254   1669 3174   4992 3836 3306   3306 899 1312 5148 3836 1207 2779

make it eight   hundred.'   ¶   ⁸   "The master commended the dishonest   manager because he had acted
γράψον ὀγδοήκοντα   καὶ ὁ   κύριος ἐπήνεσεν   τὸν τῆς ἀδικίας   οἰκονόμον ὅτι   → → ἐποίησεν
v.aam.2s   a.apm   cj d.nsm   n.nsm v.aai.3s   d.asm d.gsf n.gsf   n.asm cj   v.aai.3s
1211   3837   2779 3836   3261 2046   3836 3836 94   3874 4022   4472

shrewdly. For the people of this   world   are more shrewd   in dealing with   their own kind   than
φρονίμως ὅτι οἱ υἱοὶ → τούτου τοῦ αἰῶνος   εἰσιν →   φρονιμώτεροι →   εἰς τὴν ἑαυτῶν   τὴν γενεὰν ὑπὲρ
adv   cj d.npm n.npm   r.gsm d.gsm n.gsm   v.pai.3p   a.npm.c   p.a d.asf r.gpm.3   d.asf n.asf p.a
5862   4022 3836 5626   4047 3836 172   1639   5861   1650 3836 1571   3836 1155 5642

are the people of the light.   ⁹   I tell you, use worldly   wealth   to gain   friends for yourselves, so
τοὺς υἱοὺς → τοῦ φωτός   Καὶ ἐγὼ λέγω ὑμῖν   ἐκ τῆς ἀδικίας   τοῦ μαμωνᾶ   ποιήσατε φίλους   ἑαυτοῖς   ἵνα
d.apm n.apm   d.gsn n.gsn   cj r.ns.1 v.pai.1s r.dp.2   p.g d.gsf n.gsf   d.gsm n.gsm   v.aam.2p a.apm   r.dpm.2   cj
3836 5626   3836 5890   2779 1609 3306 7007   1666 3836 94   3836 3440   4472 5813   1571   2671

that when it is gone, you will be welcomed into eternal   dwellings.   ¶   ¹⁰ "Whoever can be trusted with very
← ὅταν → ἐκλίπῃ ὑμᾶς → → δέξωνται εἰς αἰωνίους τὰς σκηνάς   Ὁ   πιστὸς ἐν
cj   v.aas.3s r.ap.2   v.ams.3p p.a a.apf d.apf n.apf   d.nsm   a.nsm p.d
4020   1722 7007   1312 1650 173 3836 5008   3836   4412 1877

little   can also be trusted with much, and whoever is dishonest with very little   will also be dishonest with
ἐλαχίστῳ → καὶ ἐστιν πιστός ἐν πολλῷ καὶ ὁ   ἄδικος ἐν → ἐλαχίστῳ   καὶ ἐστιν ἄδικος ἐν
a.dsn.s   cj v.pai.3s a.nsm p.d a.dsn cj d.nsm   a.nsm p.d   a.dsn.s   adv v.pai.3s a.nsm p.d
1788   1639 2779 1639 4412 1877 4498 2779 3836   96 1877   1788   1639 2779 1639 96 1877

much. ¹¹ So if you have not been   trustworthy in handling worldly wealth,   who will trust   you with
πολλῷ   οὖν εἰ → → οὐκ ἐγένεσθε πιστοί   ἐν   ἀδίκῳ τῷ μαμωνᾷ   τίς →   πιστεύσει ὑμῖν
a.dsn   cj cj   pl v.ami.2p a.npm   p.d   a.dsm d.dsm n.dsm   r.nsm   v.fai.3s r.dp.2
4498   4036 1623 1181 1181 4024 1181   4412   1877   96 3836 3440   5515   4409 7007

true   riches? ¹² And if you have not been   trustworthy with someone else's   property, who will give
τὸ ἀληθινόν   καὶ εἰ → → οὐκ ἐγένεσθε πιστοί   ἐν →   τῷ ἀλλοτρίῳ ←   τίς → δώσει
d.asn a.asn   cj cj   pl v.ami.2p a.npm   p.d   d.dsn d.dsn   r.nsm   v.fai.3s
3836 240   2779 1623 1181 1181 4024 1181 4412   1877   3836 259   5515   1443

you property of your   own?   ¶   ¹³ "No servant can   serve   two masters.   Either he will hate   the
ὑμῖν   τὸ ὑμέτερον ←   Οὐδεὶς οἰκέτης δύναται δουλεύειν δυσὶ κυρίοις   γὰρ ἢ   μισήσει τὸν
r.dp.2   d.asn r.asn.2   a.nsm n.nsm v.ppi.3s f.pa   a.dpm n.dpm   cj cj   v.fai.3s d.asm
7007   3836 5629   4029 3860 1538 1526   1545 3261   1142 2445   3631 3836

οἰκονομίας σου, οὐ γὰρ δύνῃ ἔτι οἰκονομεῖν. ¶ ³ εἶπεν δὲ ἐν ἑαυτῷ ὁ οἰκονόμος, Τί ποιήσω, ὅτι ὁ κύριός μου ἀφαιρεῖται τὴν οἰκονομίαν ἀπ᾽ ἐμοῦ; σκάπτειν οὐκ ἰσχύω, ἐπαιτεῖν αἰσχύνομαι. ⁴ ἔγνων τί ποιήσω, ἵνα ὅταν μετασταθῶ ἐκ τῆς οἰκονομίας δέξωνταί με εἰς τοὺς οἴκους αὐτῶν. ¶ ⁵ καὶ προσκαλεσάμενος ἕνα ἕκαστον τῶν χρεοφειλετῶν τοῦ κυρίου ἑαυτοῦ ἔλεγεν τῷ πρώτῳ, Πόσον ὀφείλεις τῷ κυρίῳ μου; ⁶ ὁ δὲ εἶπεν, Ἑκατὸν βάτους ἐλαίου. ὁ δὲ εἶπεν αὐτῷ, Δέξαι σου τὰ γράμματα καὶ καθίσας ταχέως γράψον πεντήκοντα. ⁷ ἔπειτα ἑτέρῳ εἶπεν, Σὺ δὲ πόσον ὀφείλεις; ὁ δὲ εἶπεν, Ἑκατὸν κόρους σίτου. λέγει αὐτῷ, Δέξαι σου τὰ γράμματα καὶ γράψον ὀγδοήκοντα. ¶ ⁸ καὶ ἐπῄνεσεν ὁ κύριος τὸν οἰκονόμον τῆς ἀδικίας ὅτι φρονίμως ἐποίησεν· ὅτι οἱ υἱοὶ τοῦ αἰῶνος τούτου φρονιμώτεροι ὑπὲρ τοὺς υἱοὺς τοῦ φωτὸς εἰς τὴν γενεὰν τὴν ἑαυτῶν εἰσιν. ⁹ Καὶ ἐγὼ ὑμῖν λέγω, ἑαυτοῖς ποιήσατε φίλους ἐκ τοῦ μαμωνᾶ τῆς ἀδικίας, ἵνα ὅταν ἐκλίπῃ δέξωνται ὑμᾶς εἰς τὰς αἰωνίους σκηνάς. ¶ ¹⁰ ὁ πιστὸς ἐν ἐλαχίστῳ καὶ ἐν πολλῷ πιστός ἐστιν, καὶ ὁ ἐν ἐλαχίστῳ ἄδικος καὶ ἐν πολλῷ ἄδικός ἐστιν. ¹¹ εἰ οὖν ἐν τῷ ἀδίκῳ μαμωνᾷ πιστοὶ οὐκ ἐγένεσθε, τὸ ἀληθινὸν τίς ὑμῖν πιστεύσει; ¹² καὶ εἰ ἐν τῷ ἀλλοτρίῳ πιστοὶ οὐκ ἐγένεσθε, τὸ ὑμέτερον τίς ὑμῖν δώσει; ¶ ¹³ Οὐδεὶς

one and love   the other, or   he will be   devoted   to the one and despise   the other. You cannot   serve
ἕνα   καὶ ἀγαπήσει τὸν ἕτερον ἢ   →   →   ἀνθέξεται ←   ἑνὸς καὶ καταφρονήσει τοῦ ἑτέρου   →   οὐ δύνασθε δουλεύειν
a.asm cj   v.fai.3s   d.asm r.asm   cj   v.fmi.3s   a.gsm cj   v.fai.3s   d.gsm r.gsm   pl v.ppi.2p f.pa
1651 2779   26   3836 2283   2445   504   1651 2779 2969   3836 2283   4024 1538   1526

both God and Money." ¶ 14   The Pharisees, who loved   money,   heard   all   this   and were
θεῷ   καὶ μαμωνᾷ   δὲ οἱ Φαρισαῖοι → φιλάργυροι ὑπάρχοντες Ἤκουον πάντα ταῦτα καὶ →
n.dsm cj   n.dsm   cj d.npm n.npm   a.npm   pt.pa.npm   v.iai.3p a.apn r.apn   cj
2536 2779 3440   1254 3836 5757   5795   5639   201   4246 4047   2779

sneering   at Jesus. 15   He said to them, "You are the ones who justify   yourselves in the eyes   of
ἐξεμυκτήριζον ← αὐτὸν καὶ   εἶπεν αὐτοῖς ὑμεῖς ἐστε οἱ   ← δικαιοῦντες ἑαυτοὺς   → ἐνώπιον
v.iai.3p   r.asm.3 cj   v.aai.3s r.dpm.3 r.np.2 v.pai.2p d.npm   pt.pa.npm   r.apm.2   p.g
1727   899   2779 3306 899   7007   1639 3836   1467   1571   1967

men,   but God   knows your hearts.   What is highly valued among men   is detestable in
⸢τῶν ἀνθρώπων⸣ δὲ ⸢ὁ θεὸς⸣ γινώσκει ὑμῶν ⸢τὰς καρδίας⸣ ὅτι τὸ   ὑψηλὸν ←   ἐν ἀνθρώποις βδέλυγμα   →
d.gpm n.gpm   cj   d.nsm n.nsm v.pai.3s   r.gp.2 d.apf n.apf   ὅτι d.nsn a.nsn   p.d n.dpm   n.nsn
3836 476   1254 3836 2536 1182   7007 3836 2840 4022 3836 5734   1877 476   1007   1967

God's   sight.
⸢τοῦ θεοῦ⸣ ἐνώπιον
d.gsm n.gsm p.g
3836 2536 1967

Additional Teachings

16:16 "The Law and the Prophets were proclaimed until John.   Since   that time, the good news of the
      Ὁ   νόμος καὶ οἱ προφῆται   μέχρι Ἰωάννου ⸢ἀπὸ τότε⸣ ←   →   →   ἡ
      d.nsm n.nsm cj d.npm n.npm   p.g   n.gsm   p.g adv   d.nsf
      3836 3795 2779 3836 4737   3588 2722   608 5538   2294 2294   3836

kingdom of God   is being preached, and everyone is forcing his way into it. 17   It is   easier   for
βασιλεία → ⸢τοῦ θεοῦ⸣ → εὐαγγελίζεται καὶ πᾶς → βιάζεται εἰς αὐτὴν δὲ → ἐστιν εὐκοπώτερον
n.nsf   d.gsm n.gsm   v.ppi.3s   cj a.nsm   v.pmi.3s p.a r.asf.3 cj v.pai.3s a.nsn.c
993   3836 2536   2294   2779 4246   1041   1650 899   1254 1639 2324

heaven   and earth   to disappear than for the least stroke of a pen to drop out of the Law. ¶
⸢τὸν οὐρανὸν⸣ καὶ ⸢τὴν γῆν⸣ → παρελθεῖν ἢ   γὰρ μίαν κεραίαν ← ←   → πεσεῖν → τοῦ νόμου
d.asm n.asm   cj   d.asf n.asf f.aa   pl   a.asf n.asf   f.aa   d.gsm n.gsm
3836 4041   2779 3836 1178 4216   2445   1651 3037   4406   3836 3795

18 "Anyone who divorces his   wife   and marries another woman commits adultery, and the man who marries a
   Πᾶς   ὁ   ἀπολύων αὐτοῦ ⸢τὴν γυναῖκα⸣ καὶ γαμῶν ἑτέραν ‹   ›   μοιχεύει καὶ ὁ   ←   γαμῶν
   a.nsm d.nsm pt.pa.nsm r.gsm.3 d.asf n.asf cj pt.pa.nsm r.asf   v.pai.3s cj d.nsm   pt.pa.nsm
   4246 3836 668   899   3836 1222 2779 1138   2283   3658   2779 3836   1138

divorced   woman commits adultery.
⸢ἀπολελυμένην⸣ ἀπὸ ἀνδρὸς⸣   →   μοιχεύει
pt.rp.asf   p.g n.gsm   v.pai.3s
668   608 467   3658

The Rich Man and Lazarus

16:19   "There was a rich   man   who was dressed   in purple and fine linen and lived   in
        δὲ → ἦν τις πλούσιος Ἄνθρωπος καὶ → ἐνεδιδύσκετο ← πορφύραν καὶ → βύσσον εὐφραινόμενος →
        cj   v.iai.3s r.nsm a.nsm   n.nsm cj   v.imi.3s   n.asf   cj   n.asf   pt.pp.nsm
        1254   1639 5516 4454   476   2779   1898   4525   2779   1116   2370

luxury every day. 20   At his   gate   was laid   a beggar named Lazarus, covered with sores   21 and
λαμπρῶς καθ' ἡμέραν δὲ πρὸς αὐτοῦ ⸢τὸν πυλῶνα⸣ → ἐβέβλητο τις πτωχὸς ὀνόματι Λάζαρος → → εἱλκωμένος καὶ
adv   p.a   n.asf   cj p.a   r.gsm.3 d.asm n.asm   v.lpi.3s r.nsm a.nsm   n.dsn   n.nsm   pt.rp.nsm   cj
3289 2848 2465   1254 4639 899   3836 4784   965   5516 4777   3950   3276   1815   2779

longing to eat   what fell   from the rich   man's table.   Even the dogs came   and
ἐπιθυμῶν → χορτασθῆναι ἀπὸ τῶν πιπτόντων ἀπὸ τῆς ⸢τοῦ πλουσίου⸣ → τραπέζης ἀλλὰ καὶ οἱ κύνες ἐρχόμενοι
pt.pa.nsm   f.ap   p.g d.gpn pt.pa.gpn p.g d.gsf d.gsm a.gsm   n.gsf   cj   adv d.npm n.npm pt.pm.npm
2121   5963   608 3836 4406   608 3836 3836 4454   5544   247 2779 3836 3264 2262

licked his   sores.   ¶   22   "The time came when the beggar died   and   the angels carried   him
ἐπέλειχον αὐτοῦ ⸢τὰ ἕλκη⸣   δὲ → ἐγένετο ← τὸν πτωχὸν ἀποθανεῖν καὶ ὑπὸ τῶν ἀγγέλων ἀπενεχθῆναι αὐτὸν
v.iai.3p r.gsm.3 d.apn n.apn   cj   v.ami.3s   d.asm a.asm   f.aa   cj   p.g d.gpm n.gpm   f.ap   r.asm.3
2143   899   3836 1814   1254   1181   3836 4777   633   2779 5679 3836   34   708   899

οἰκέτης δύναται δυσὶ κυρίοις δουλεύειν· ἢ γὰρ τὸν ἕνα μισήσει καὶ τὸν ἕτερον ἀγαπήσει, ἢ ἑνὸς ἀνθέξεται καὶ τοῦ ἑτέρου
καταφρονήσει. οὐ δύνασθε θεῷ δουλεύειν καὶ μαμωνᾷ. ¶ 14 Ἤκουον δὲ ταῦτα πάντα οἱ Φαρισαῖοι φιλάργυροι ὑπάρχοντες
καὶ ἐξεμυκτήριζον αὐτόν. 15 καὶ εἶπεν αὐτοῖς, Ὑμεῖς ἐστε οἱ δικαιοῦντες ἑαυτοὺς ἐνώπιον τῶν ἀνθρώπων, ὁ δὲ θεὸς γινώσκει
τὰς καρδίας ὑμῶν· ὅτι τὸ ἐν ἀνθρώποις ὑψηλὸν βδέλυγμα ἐνώπιον τοῦ θεοῦ.

16:16 Ὁ νόμος καὶ οἱ προφῆται μέχρι Ἰωάννου· ἀπὸ τότε ἡ βασιλεία τοῦ θεοῦ εὐαγγελίζεται καὶ πᾶς εἰς αὐτὴν βιάζεται.
17 Εὐκοπώτερον δέ ἐστιν τὸν οὐρανὸν καὶ τὴν γῆν παρελθεῖν ἢ τοῦ νόμου μίαν κεραίαν πεσεῖν. ¶ 18 Πᾶς ὁ ἀπολύων τὴν
γυναῖκα αὐτοῦ καὶ γαμῶν ἑτέραν μοιχεύει, καὶ ὁ ἀπολελυμένην ἀπὸ ἀνδρὸς γαμῶν μοιχεύει.

16:19 Ἄνθρωπος δέ τις ἦν πλούσιος, καὶ ἐνεδιδύσκετο πορφύραν καὶ βύσσον εὐφραινόμενος καθ' ἡμέραν λαμπρῶς. 20 πτωχὸς
δέ τις ὀνόματι Λάζαρος ἐβέβλητο πρὸς τὸν πυλῶνα αὐτοῦ εἱλκωμένος 21 καὶ ἐπιθυμῶν χορτασθῆναι ἀπὸ τῶν πιπτόντων ἀπὸ
τῆς τραπέζης τοῦ πλουσίου· ἀλλὰ καὶ οἱ κύνες ἐρχόμενοι ἐπέλειχον τὰ ἕλκη αὐτοῦ. ¶ 22 ἐγένετο δὲ ἀποθανεῖν τὸν πτωχὸν καὶ

to   Abraham's side.   The rich   man also died   and was buried. **23** In hell,   where he was   in
εἰς Ἀβραάμ ⸤τὸν κόλπον⸥ δὲ ὁ πλούσιος ← καὶ ἀπέθανεν καὶ → ἐτάφη   καὶ ἐν τῷ ᾅδῃ →   ὑπάρχων ἐν
p.a n.gsm   d.asm n.asm   cj d.nsm a.nsm   adv v.aai.3s cj   v.api.3s   cj   p.d d.dsm n.dsm   pt.pa.nsm p.d
1650 11   3836 3146   1254 3836 4454   2779 633   2779   2507   2779 1877 3836 87   5639   1877

torment, he looked   up and saw Abraham *far away,*   with Lazarus by his side. **24** So
βασάνοις → ⸤ἐπάρας τοὺς ὀφθαλμοὺς αὐτοῦ⸥ ← ὁρᾷ Ἀβραάμ ἀπὸ μακρόθεν καὶ Λάζαρον ἐν αὐτοῦ ⸤τοῖς κόλποις⸥ καὶ
n.dpf   pt.aa.nsm d.apm n.apm   r.gsm.3   v.pai.3s n.asm   p.g adv   cj   n.asm   p.d r.gsm.3 d.dsm n.dpm   cj
992   2048   3836 4057   899   3972 11   608 3427   2779 3276   1877 899   3836 3146   2779

he   called   to him, 'Father Abraham, have pity   on me and send   Lazarus to dip   the tip   of   his
αὐτός φωνήσας εἶπεν   πάτερ Ἀβραάμ → ἐλέησον με καὶ πέμψον Λάζαρον ἵνα βάψῃ τὸ ἄκρον → αὐτοῦ
r.nsm pt.aa.nsm v.aai.3s   n.vsm n.vsm   v.aam.2s r.as.1 cj v.aam.2s n.asm   cj v.aas.3s d.asn n.asn   r.gsm.3
899   5888   3306   4252   11   1796   1609 2779 4287   3276   970 3836 216   1235 899

finger   in water and cool   my tongue,   because I am in agony   in this   fire.' **25** "But Abraham
⸤τοῦ δακτύλου⸥ ὕδατος καὶ καταψύξῃ μου ⸤τὴν γλῶσσαν⸥ ὅτι → → ὀδυνῶμαι ἐν ταύτῃ ⸤τῇ φλογί⸥ δὲ Ἀβραάμ
d.gsn n.gsn   n.gsn   cj v.aas.3s r.gs.1 d.asf n.asf   cj   v.ppi.1s p.d r.dsf d.dsf n.dsf   cj   n.nsm
3836 1235   5623   2779 2976 1609 3836 1185   4022   3849   1877 4047 3836 5825   1254 11

replied, 'Son,   remember that in your lifetime you received your good   things, while Lazarus received bad
εἶπεν τέκνον μνήσθητι ὅτι ἐν σου ⸤τῇ ζωῇ⸥ → ἀπέλαβες σου ⸤τὰ ἀγαθά⸥ ← καὶ Λάζαρος ὁμοίως ⸤τὰ κακά⸥
v.aai.3s n.vsn v.apm.2s cj p.d r.gs.2 d.dsf n.dsf v.aai.2s r.gs.2 d.apn a.apn   cj n.nsm   adv   d.apn a.apn
3306   5451   3630   4022 1877 5148 3836 2437   655   5148 3836 19   2779 3276   3931   3836 2805

things, but now he is comforted   here and you are in agony. **26** And besides all   this,   between us   and you a
← δὲ νῦν → → παρακαλεῖται ὧδε δὲ σὺ → → ὀδυνᾶσαι καὶ ἐν   πᾶσι τούτοις μεταξὺ ἡμῶν καὶ ὑμῶν
cj adv v.ppi.3s   adv cj r.ns.2   v.ppi.2s cj   p.d a.dpn r.dpn n.pg r.gp.1 cj r.gp.2
1254 3814 4151   6045 1254 5148   3849   2779 1877 4246 4047 3568 7005 2779 7007

great chasm has been fixed,   so   that those who want   to go   from here to you cannot,   nor can
μέγα χάσμα → → ἐστήρικται ὅπως ← οἱ ← θέλοντες διαβῆναι → ἔνθεν πρὸς ὑμᾶς μὴ δύνωνται μηδὲ
a.nsn n.nsn   v.rpi.3s   cj   d.npm   pt.pa.npm f.aa   adv p.a r.ap.2 pl v.pps.3p cj
3489 5926   5114   3968   3836   2527   1329   1925 4639 7007 3590 1538   3593

anyone cross   over from there to us.' ¶ **27** "He answered, 'Then I beg you, father,   send Lazarus
→ διαπερῶσιν ← → ἐκεῖθεν πρὸς ἡμᾶς   δὲ εἶπεν   οὖν ἐρωτῶ σε πάτερ ἵνα πέμψῃς αὐτὸν
v.pas.3p   adv p.a r.ap.1   cj   v.aai.3s   cj   v.pai.1s r.as.2 n.vsm   cj v.aas.2s r.asm.3
1385   1696 4639 7005   1254 3306   4036 2263 5148 4252   2671 4287   899

to my father's   house,   **28** for I have five brothers.   Let him warn   them, so that they will not also
εἰς μου ⸤τοῦ πατρός⸥ ⸤τὸν οἶκον⸥ γὰρ → ἔχω πέντε ἀδελφούς ὅπως → → διαμαρτύρηται αὐτοῖς ἵνα ← αὐτοὶ → μὴ καὶ
p.a r.gs.1 d.gsm n.gsm d.asm n.asm   cj v.pai.1s a.apm n.apm   cj   v.pms.3s   r.dpm.3 cj   r.npm   adv
1650 1609 3836 4252 3836 3875   1142 2400 4297 81   3968   1371   899   2671   899   3590 2779

come to this   place   of torment.' **29** "Abraham replied, 'They have Moses and the Prophets; let them
ἔλθωσιν εἰς τοῦτον ⸤τὸν τόπον⸥ → ⸤τῆς βασάνου⸥ δὲ Ἀβραάμ λέγει   ἔχουσι Μωϋσέα καὶ τοὺς προφήτας
v.aas.3p p.a r.asm d.asm n.asm   d.gsf n.gsf   cj   n.nsm   v.pai.3s   v.pai.3p n.asm   cj d.apm n.apm
2262   1650 4047 3836 5536   3836 992   1254 11   3306   2400   3707   2779 3836 4737

listen   to them.' ¶ **30** "'No, father Abraham,' he said, 'but if someone from the dead goes   to
ἀκουσάτωσαν ← αὐτῶν   δὲ οὐχί πάτερ Ἀβραάμ ὁ εἶπεν ἀλλ' ἐάν τις   ἀπὸ   νεκρῶν πορευθῇ πρὸς
v.aam.3p   r.gpm.3   cj pl   n.vsm n.vsm   d.nsm v.aai.3s cj cj   r.nsm   p.g   a.gpm v.aps.3s p.a
201   899   1254 4049 4252   11   3836 3306 247 1569 5516   608   3738 4513   4639

them, they will repent.' **31** "He said to him, 'If they do not listen   to Moses   and the Prophets, they will
αὐτούς → μετανοήσουσιν δὲ εἶπεν → αὐτῷ εἰ → οὐκ ἀκούουσιν ← Μωϋσέως καὶ τῶν προφητῶν
r.apm.3   v.fai.3p   cj v.aai.3s   r.dsm.3 cj   pl v.pai.3p   n.gsm   cj d.gpm n.gpm
899   3566   1254 3306   899 1623 201   201 4024 201   3707   2779 3836 4737   4275 4275

not be convinced even if someone rises   from the dead.'"
οὐδ' → πεισθήσονται ἐάν τις ἀναστῇ ἐκ νεκρῶν
adv v.fpi.3p   cj r.nsm v.aas.3s p.g a.gpm
4028 4275   1569 5516 482   1666 3738

Sin, Faith, Duty

17:1 Jesus said to his   disciples: "Things that cause people to sin   are bound   to come,
δὲ Εἶπεν πρὸς αὐτοῦ ⸤τοὺς μαθητὰς⸥ τοῦ τὰ ←   →   σκάνδαλα ἐστιν ⸤ἀνένδεκτον μὴ⸥ → ἐλθεῖν
cj v.aai.3s p.a r.gsm.3 d.apm n.apm   d.gsn d.apn   n.apn   v.pai.3s a.nsn   pl   f.aa
1254 3306 4639 899   3836 3412   3836 3836   4998   1639 450   3590   2262

ἀπενεχθῆναι αὐτὸν ὑπὸ τῶν ἀγγέλων εἰς τὸν κόλπον Ἀβραάμ· ἀπέθανεν δὲ καὶ ὁ πλούσιος καὶ ἐτάφη. 23 καὶ ἐν τῷ ᾅδῃ ἐπάρας τοὺς ὀφθαλμοὺς αὐτοῦ, ὑπάρχων ἐν βασάνοις, ὁρᾷ Ἀβραὰμ ἀπὸ μακρόθεν καὶ Λάζαρον ἐν τοῖς κόλποις αὐτοῦ. 24 καὶ αὐτὸς φωνήσας εἶπεν, Πάτερ Ἀβραάμ, ἐλέησόν με καὶ πέμψον Λάζαρον ἵνα βάψῃ τὸ ἄκρον τοῦ δακτύλου αὐτοῦ ὕδατος καὶ καταψύξῃ τὴν γλῶσσάν μου, ὅτι ὀδυνῶμαι ἐν τῇ φλογὶ ταύτῃ. 25 εἶπεν δὲ Ἀβραάμ, Τέκνον, μνήσθητι ὅτι ἀπέλαβες τὰ ἀγαθά σου ἐν τῇ ζωῇ σου, καὶ Λάζαρος ὁμοίως τὰ κακά· νῦν δὲ ὧδε παρακαλεῖται, σὺ δὲ ὀδυνᾶσαι. 26 καὶ ἐν πᾶσι τούτοις μεταξὺ ἡμῶν καὶ ὑμῶν χάσμα μέγα ἐστήρικται, ὅπως οἱ θέλοντες διαβῆναι ἔνθεν πρὸς ὑμᾶς μὴ δύνωνται, μηδὲ ἐκεῖθεν πρὸς ἡμᾶς διαπερῶσιν. ¶ 27 εἶπεν δέ, Ἐρωτῶ σε οὖν, πάτερ, ἵνα πέμψῃς αὐτὸν εἰς τὸν οἶκον τοῦ πατρός μου, 28 ἔχω γὰρ πέντε ἀδελφούς, ὅπως διαμαρτύρηται αὐτοῖς, ἵνα μὴ καὶ αὐτοὶ ἔλθωσιν εἰς τὸν τόπον τοῦτον τῆς βασάνου. 29 λέγει δὲ Ἀβραάμ, Ἔχουσι Μωϋσέα καὶ τοὺς προφήτας· ἀκουσάτωσαν αὐτῶν. ¶ 30 ὁ δὲ εἶπεν, Οὐχί, πάτερ Ἀβραάμ, ἀλλ' ἐάν τις ἀπὸ νεκρῶν πορευθῇ πρὸς αὐτοὺς μετανοήσουσιν. 31 εἶπεν δὲ αὐτῷ, Εἰ Μωϋσέως καὶ τῶν προφητῶν οὐκ ἀκούουσιν, οὐδ' ἐάν τις ἐκ νεκρῶν ἀναστῇ πεισθήσονται.

17:1 Εἶπεν δὲ πρὸς τοὺς μαθητὰς αὐτοῦ, Ἀνένδεκτόν ἐστιν τοῦ τὰ σκάνδαλα μὴ ἐλθεῖν, πλὴν οὐαὶ δι' οὗ ἔρχεται· 2 λυσιτελεῖ

but woe to that person through whom they come. ² It would be better for him to be thrown into the sea
πλὴν οὐαὶ   δι᾿   οὗ → ἔρχεται → → → λυσιτελεῖ → αὐτῷ εἰ → → ἔρριπται εἰς τὴν θάλασσαν
cj   j   p.g   r.gsm   v.pmi.3s   v.pai.3s   r.dsm.3   v.rpi.3s   p.a   d.asf   n.asf
4440   4026   1328   4005   2262   3387   899   1623   4849   1650   3836   2498

with a millstone tied around his neck than for him to cause one of these little ones to
καὶ   λίθος μυλικὸς   περίκειται περὶ   αὐτοῦ τὸν τράχηλον   ἢ   ἵνα → →   ἕνα   τούτων τῶν μικρῶν ←
cj   n.nsm n.nsm   v.pmi.3s p.a   r.gsm.3 d.asm n.asm   pl   cj   a.asm   r.gpm   d.gpm a.gpm
2779   3345 3683   4329   4309   899   3836 5549   2445   2671 4997 4997 4997   1651   3625   4047   3836 3625

sin. ³ So watch yourselves. "If your brother sins, rebuke him, and if he repents, forgive him. ⁴
σκανδαλίσῃ   προσέχετε ἑαυτοῖς   Ἐὰν σου ὁ   ἀδελφός, ἁμάρτῃ ἐπιτίμησον αὐτῷ καὶ ἐὰν → μετανοήσῃ ἄφες   αὐτῷ καὶ
v.aas.3s   v.pam.2p r.dpm.2   cj r.gs.2 d.nsm n.nsm   v.aas.3s v.aam.2s r.dsm.3 cj cj   v.aas.3s v.aam.2s r.dsm.3 cj
4997   4668   1571   1569 5148 3836 81   279   2203   899   2779 1569   3566   918   899   2779

If he sins against you seven times in a day, and seven times comes back to you and says, 'I repent,'
ἐὰν → ἁμαρτήσῃ εἰς   σὲ   ἑπτάκις ← → τῆς ἡμέρας καὶ ἑπτάκις ← → ἐπιστρέψῃ ←   πρὸς σὲ   λέγων → μετανοῶ
cj   v.aas.3s   p.a   r.as.2   adv   d.gsf n.gsf   cj   adv   v.aas.3s   p.a   r.as.2   pt.pa.nsm v.pai.1s
1569   279   1650   5148   2232   3836 2465   2779 2232   2188   4639 5148   3306   3566

forgive him." ¶ ⁵ The apostles said to the Lord, "Increase our faith!" ⁶ He replied, "If you have
ἀφήσεις αὐτῷ   Καὶ οἱ   ἀπόστολοι εἶπαν → τῷ κυρίῳ πρόσθες ἡμῖν πίστιν δὲ ὁ κύριος, εἶπεν εἰ → ἔχετε
v.fai.2s r.dsm.3   cj d.npm   n.npm   v.aai.3p   d.dsm n.dsm v.aam.2s r.dp.1 n.asf cj d.nsm n.nsm v.aai.3s cj   v.pai.2p
918   899   2779 3836   693   3306   3836 3261   4707   7005 4411   1254 3836 3261   3306   1623   2400

faith as small as a mustard seed, you can say to this mulberry tree, 'Be uprooted and planted in the
πίστιν ὡς   σινάπεως κόκκον → → ἐλέγετε ἂν → ταύτῃ τῇ συκαμίνῳ ← → ἐκριζώθητι καὶ φυτεύθητι ἐν τῇ
n.asf pl   n.gsn   n.asm   v.iai.2p pl   r.dsf d.dsf n.dsf   v.apm.2s   cj   v.apm.2s   p.d d.dsf
4411 6055   4983   3133   3306   323 5189   4047 3836 5189   1748   2779   5885   1877 3836

sea,' and it will obey you. ¶ ⁷ "Suppose one of you had a servant plowing or looking after
θαλάσσῃ καὶ → → ὑπήκουσεν ἂν ὑμῖν   δὲ →   Τίς ἐξ ὑμῶν ἔχων δοῦλον ἀροτριῶντα ἢ   ποιμαίνοντα ←
n.dsf   cj   v.aai.3s   pl r.dp.2   cj   r.nsm p.g r.gp.2 pt.pa.nsm n.asm pt.pa.asm pl   pt.pa.asm
2498   2779   5634   323 7007   1254 2400   5515 1666 7007 2400   1529   769   2445 4477

the sheep. Would he say to the servant when he comes in from the field, 'Come along now and sit
   → ἐρεῖ   αὐτῷ ὃς → εἰσελθόντι ← ἐκ τοῦ ἀγροῦ παρελθὼν ← εὐθέως ἀνάπεσε
     v.fai.3s   r.dsm.3 r.nsm   pt.aa.dsm   p.g d.gsm n.gsm pt.aa.nsm   adv   v.aam.2s
     3306   899   4005   1656   1666 3836 69   4216   2311   404

down to eat'? ⁸ Would he not rather say, 'Prepare my supper, get yourself ready and wait on
← ← → οὐχὶ ἀλλ᾿ ἐρεῖ αὐτῷ ἑτοίμασον τί → δειπνήσω καὶ →   περιζωσάμενος   διακόνει ←
      pl   cj   v.fai.3s r.dsm.3 v.aam.1s r.asn   v.aas.1s   cj   pt.am.nsm   v.pam.2s
   3306   3306 4049 247   3306 899   2286   5515   1268   2779   4322   1354

me while I eat and drink; after that you may eat and drink'? ⁹ Would he thank the servant because
μοι ἕως → φάγω καὶ πίω   καὶ μετὰ ταῦτα σύ → φάγεσαι καὶ πίεσαι μὴ → ἔχει χάριν τῷ δούλῳ ὅτι
r.ds.1 cj   v.aas.1s cj v.aas.1s   cj p.a r.apn r.ns.2 → v.fmi.2s   cj v.fmi.2s pl   v.pai.3s n.asf d.dsm n.dsm cj
1609 2401   2266 2779 4403   2779 3552 4047 5148   2266   2779 4403 3590   2400 5921 3836 1529 4022

he did what he was told to do? ¹⁰ So you also, when you have done everything you were
→ ἐποίησεν τὰ → διαταχθέντα   οὕτως ὑμεῖς καὶ ὅταν → → ποιήσητε πάντα ὑμῖν →
  v.aai.3s d.apn   pt.ap.apn   adv r.np.2 cj adv   v.aas.2p a.apn   r.dp.2
  4472   3836   1411   4048 7007 2779 4020   4472   4246   7007

told to do, should say, 'We are unworthy servants; we have only done our duty.'"
τὰ διαταχθέντα → λέγετε ὅτι   ἐσμὲν ἀχρεῖοι δοῦλοι   πεποιήκαμεν → ὃ ὠφείλομεν ποιῆσαι
d.apn pt.ap.apn   v.pam.2p cj   v.pai.1p a.npm   n.npm   v.rai.1p   r.asn v.iai.1p   f.aa
3836 1411   3306 4022   1639 945   1529   4472   4005 4053   4472

Ten Healed of Leprosy

17:11 Now on his way to Jerusalem, Jesus traveled along the border between Samaria and
Καὶ ἐγένετο ἐν τῷ πορεύεσθαι εἰς Ἰερουσαλὴμ καὶ αὐτὸς διήρχετο ← ← διὰ μέσον Σαμαρείας καὶ
cj   v.ami.3s p.d d.dsn f.pm   p.a n.asf   cj r.nsm v.imi.3s   p.a n.asn   n.gsf   cj
2779 1181   1877 3836 4513   1650 2647   2779 899   1451   1328 3545   4899   2779

Galilee. ¹² As he was going into a village, ten men who had leprosy met him. They stood at a
Γαλιλαίας Καὶ → αὐτοῦ → εἰσερχομένου εἰς τινα κώμην δέκα ἄνδρες   λεπροὶ ἀπήντησαν αὐτῷ οἱ   ἔστησαν → →
n.gsf   cj   r.gsm.3   pt.pm.gsm   p.a r.asf n.asf a.npm n.npm   a.npm   v.aai.3p   r.dsm.3 r.npm v.aai.3p
1133   2779   1656 899   1656   1650 5516 3267 1274 467   3320   560   899   4005 2705

αὐτῷ εἰ λίθος μυλικὸς περίκειται περὶ τὸν τράχηλον αὐτοῦ καὶ ἔρριπται εἰς τὴν θάλασσαν ἢ ἵνα σκανδαλίσῃ τῶν μικρῶν τούτων ἕνα. ³ προσέχετε ἑαυτοῖς. ἐὰν ἁμάρτῃ ὁ ἀδελφός σου ἐπιτίμησον αὐτῷ, καὶ ἐὰν μετανοήσῃ ἄφες αὐτῷ. ⁴ καὶ ἐὰν ἑπτάκις τῆς ἡμέρας ἁμαρτήσῃ εἰς σὲ καὶ ἑπτάκις ἐπιστρέψῃ πρὸς σὲ λέγων, Μετανοῶ, ἀφήσεις αὐτῷ. ¶ ⁵ Καὶ εἶπαν οἱ ἀπόστολοι τῷ κυρίῳ, Πρόσθες ἡμῖν πίστιν. ⁶ εἶπεν δὲ ὁ κύριος, Εἰ ἔχετε πίστιν ὡς κόκκον σινάπεως, ἐλέγετε ἂν τῇ συκαμίνῳ [ταύτῃ], Ἐκριζώθητι καὶ φυτεύθητι ἐν τῇ θαλάσσῃ· καὶ ὑπήκουσεν ἂν ὑμῖν. ¶ ⁷ Τίς δὲ ἐξ ὑμῶν δοῦλον ἔχων ἀροτριῶντα ἢ ποιμαίνοντα, ὃς εἰσελθόντι ἐκ τοῦ ἀγροῦ ἐρεῖ αὐτῷ, Εὐθέως παρελθὼν ἀνάπεσε, ⁸ ἀλλ᾿ οὐχὶ ἐρεῖ αὐτῷ, Ἑτοίμασον τί δειπνήσω καὶ περιζωσάμενος διακόνει μοι ἕως φάγω καὶ πίω, καὶ μετὰ ταῦτα φάγεσαι καὶ πίεσαι σύ; ⁹ μὴ ἔχει χάριν τῷ δούλῳ ὅτι ἐποίησεν τὰ διαταχθέντα; ¹⁰ οὕτως καὶ ὑμεῖς, ὅταν ποιήσητε πάντα τὰ διαταχθέντα ὑμῖν, λέγετε ὅτι Δοῦλοι ἀχρεῖοι ἐσμεν, ὃ ὠφείλομεν ποιῆσαι πεποιήκαμεν.

¹⁷:¹¹ Καὶ ἐγένετο ἐν τῷ πορεύεσθαι εἰς Ἰερουσαλὴμ καὶ αὐτὸς διήρχετο διὰ μέσον Σαμαρείας καὶ Γαλιλαίας. ¹² καὶ

distance ¹³ and called out in a loud voice, "Jesus, Master, have pity on us!" ¹⁴ When he saw
πόρρωθεν καὶ αὐτοὶ ἦραν φωνὴν ← ← ← ← λέγοντες Ἰησοῦ ἐπιστάτα → ἐλέησον → ἡμᾶς καὶ → → ἰδὼν
adv cj r.npm v.aai.3p n.asf pt.pa.npm n.vsm n.vsm v.aam.2s r.ap.1 cj pt.aa.nsm
4523 2779 899 149 5889 3306 2652 2181 1796 7005 2779 1625

them, he said, "Go, show yourselves to the priests." And as they went, they were
εἶπεν αὐτοῖς πορευθέντες ἐπιδείξατε ἑαυτοὺς → τοῖς ἱερεῦσιν καὶ ἐγένετο ἐν αὐτοὺς τῷ ὑπάγειν →
v.aai.3s r.dpm.3 pt.ap.npm v.aam.2p r.apm.2 d.dpm n.dpm cj v.ami.3s p.d r.apm.3 d.dsn f.pa
3306 899 4513 2109 1571 3836 2636 2779 1181 1877 899 3836 5632

cleansed. ¶ ¹⁵ One of them, when he saw he was healed, came back, praising God in a
ἐκαθαρίσθησαν δὲ εἷς ἐξ αὐτῶν → ἰδὼν ὅτι → → ἰάθη ὑπέστρεψεν ← δοξάζων ⌐τὸν θεὸν μετὰ
v.api.3p cj a.nsm p.g r.gpm.3 pt.aa.nsm cj v.api.3s v.aai.3s pt.pa.nsm d.asm n.asm p.g
2751 1254 1651 1666 899 1625 4022 2615 5715 1519 3836 2536 3552

loud voice. ¹⁶ He threw himself at Jesus' feet and thanked him — and he was a
μεγάλης φωνῆς καὶ → ἔπεσεν ἐπὶ πρόσωπον παρὰ αὐτοῦ ⌐τοὺς πόδας⌐ εὐχαριστῶν αὐτῷ καὶ αὐτὸς ἦν
a.gsf n.gsf cj v.aai.3s p.a n.asn p.g r.gsm.3 d.apm n.apm pt.pa.nsm r.dsm.3 cj r.nsm v.iai.3s
3489 5889 2779 4406 2093 4725 4123 899 3836 4546 2373 899 2779 899 1639

Samaritan. ¹⁷ Jesus asked, "Were not all ten cleansed? Where are the other nine? ¹⁸ Was no
Σαμαρίτης δὲ ὁ Ἰησοῦς ἀποκριθεὶς εἶπεν → οὐχὶ οἱ δέκα ἐκαθαρίσθησαν δὲ ποῦ οἱ ἐννέα οὐχ
n.nsm cj d.nsm n.nsm pt.ap.nsm v.aai.3s pl d.npm a.npm v.api.3p cj adv d.npm a.npm pl
4901 1254 3836 2652 646 3306 4049 3836 1274 2751 1254 4543 3836 1933 2351 4024

one found to return and give praise to God except this foreigner?" ¹⁹ Then he said to him, "Rise
εὑρέθησαν ὑποστρέψαντες δοῦναι δόξαν → ⌐τῷ θεῷ⌐ εἰ μὴ οὗτος ὁ ἀλλογενής καὶ → εἶπεν → αὐτῷ ἀναστὰς
v.api.3p pt.aa.npm f.aa n.asf d.dsm n.dsm cj pl r.nsm d.nsm n.nsm cj v.aai.3s r.dsm.3 pt.aa.nsm
2351 5715 1443 1518 3836 2536 1623 3590 4047 3836 254 2779 3306 899 482

and go; your faith has made you well."
πορεύου σου ἡ πίστις⌐ σε σέσωκεν
v.pmm.2s r.gs.2 d.nsf n.nsf r.as.2 v.rai.3s
4513 5148 3836 4411 5392 5392 5148 5392

The Coming of the Kingdom of God

^{17:20}Once, having been asked by the Pharisees when the kingdom of God would come, Jesus replied,
δὲ → Ἐπερωτηθεὶς ὑπὸ τῶν Φαρισαίων πότε ἡ βασιλεία → ⌐τοῦ θεοῦ⌐ ἔρχεται ἀπεκρίθη
cj pt.ap.nsm p.g d.gpm n.gpm cj d.nsf n.nsf d.gsm n.gsm v.pmi.3s v.api.3s
1254 2089 5679 3836 5757 4537 3836 993 3836 2536 2262 646

"The kingdom of God does not come with your careful observation, ²¹ nor will people say,
αὐτοῖς καὶ εἶπεν ἡ βασιλεία → ⌐τοῦ θεοῦ⌐ οὐκ ἔρχεται μετὰ → παρατηρήσεως οὐδὲ → → ἐροῦσιν ἰδοὺ
r.dpm.3 cj v.aai.3s d.nsf n.nsf d.gsm n.gsm pl v.pmi.3s p.g n.gsf cj v.fai.3p j
899 2779 3306 3836 993 3836 2536 2262 4024 2262 3552 4191 4028 3306 2627

'Here it is,' or 'There it is,' because the kingdom of God is within you." ¶ ²² Then he said to his
ὧδε ἤ ἐκεῖ γὰρ ἰδοὺ ἡ βασιλεία → ⌐τοῦ θεοῦ⌐ ἐστιν ἐντὸς ὑμῶν δὲ → Εἶπεν πρὸς τοὺς
adv cj adv cj j d.nsf n.nsf d.gsm n.gsm v.pai.3s p.g r.gp.2 cj v.aai.3s p.a d.apm
6045 2445 1695 1142 2627 3836 993 3836 2536 1955 1639 7007 1254 3306 4639 3836

disciples, "The time is coming when you will long to see one of the days of the Son of Man, but
μαθητάς ἡμέραι ἐλεύσονται ὅτε → → ἐπιθυμήσετε ἰδεῖν μίαν τῶν ἡμερῶν → τοῦ υἱοῦ ⌐τοῦ ἀνθρώπου⌐ καὶ
n.apm n.npf v.fmi.3p cj v.fai.2p f.aa a.asf d.gpf n.gpf d.gsm n.gsm d.gsm n.gsm cj
3412 2465 2262 4021 2121 1625 1651 3836 2465 3836 5626 3836 476 2779

you will not see it. ²³ Men will tell you, 'There he is!' or 'Here he is!' Do not go running
→ οὐκ ὄψεσθε καὶ → ἐροῦσιν ὑμῖν ἰδοὺ ἐκεῖ ← ἤ ἰδοὺ ὧδε μὴ ἀπέλθητε μηδὲ διώξητε
pl v.fmi.2p cj v.fai.3p r.dp.2 j adv cj j adv pl v.aas.2p cj v.aas.2p
3972 3972 4024 3972 2779 3306 7007 2627 1695 2445 2627 6045 599 3590 599 3593 1503

off after them. ²⁴ For the Son of Man in his day will be like the lightning, which flashes
γὰρ οὕτως ὁ υἱὸς → ⌐τοῦ ἀνθρώπου⌐ ἐν αὐτοῦ ⌐τῇ ἡμέρᾳ⌐ → ἔσται ὥσπερ ἡ ἀστραπὴ → ἀστράπτουσα
cj adv d.nsm n.nsm d.gsm n.gsm p.d r.gsm.3 d.dsf n.dsf v.fmi.3s cj d.nsf n.nsf pt.pa.nsf
1142 4048 3836 5626 3836 476 1877 899 3836 2465 1639 6061 3836 847 848

and lights up the sky from one end to the other. ²⁵ But first he must suffer many things
λάμπει ← ἐκ τῆς ⌐ὑπὸ τὸν οὐρανὸν⌐ εἰς τὴν ὑπ' οὐρανὸν δὲ πρῶτον αὐτὸν δεῖ παθεῖν πολλὰ ←
v.pai.3s p.g d.gsf p.a d.asm n.asm p.a d.asf p.a n.asm cj adv r.asm.3 v.pai.3s f.aa a.apn
3290 1666 3836 5679 3836 4041 1650 3836 5679 4041 1254 4754 899 1256 4248 4498

εἰσερχομένου αὐτοῦ εἴς τινα κώμην ἀπήντησαν [αὐτῷ] δέκα λεπροὶ ἄνδρες, οἳ ἔστησαν πόρρωθεν ¹³ καὶ αὐτοὶ ἦραν φωνὴν λέγοντες, Ἰησοῦ ἐπιστάτα, ἐλέησον ἡμᾶς. ¹⁴ καὶ ἰδὼν εἶπεν αὐτοῖς, Πορευθέντες ἐπιδείξατε ἑαυτοὺς τοῖς ἱερεῦσιν. καὶ ἐγένετο ἐν τῷ ὑπάγειν αὐτοὺς ἐκαθαρίσθησαν. ¶ ¹⁵ εἷς δὲ ἐξ αὐτῶν, ἰδὼν ὅτι ἰάθη, ὑπέστρεψεν μετὰ φωνῆς μεγάλης δοξάζων τὸν θεόν, ¹⁶ καὶ ἔπεσεν ἐπὶ πρόσωπον παρὰ τοὺς πόδας αὐτοῦ εὐχαριστῶν αὐτῷ· καὶ αὐτὸς ἦν Σαμαρίτης. ¹⁷ ἀποκριθεὶς δὲ ὁ Ἰησοῦς εἶπεν, Οὐχὶ οἱ δέκα ἐκαθαρίσθησαν; οἱ δὲ ἐννέα ποῦ; ¹⁸ οὐχ εὑρέθησαν ὑποστρέψαντες δοῦναι δόξαν τῷ θεῷ εἰ μὴ ὁ ἀλλογενὴς οὗτος; ¹⁹ καὶ εἶπεν αὐτῷ, Ἀναστὰς πορεύου· ἡ πίστις σου σέσωκέν σε.

^{17:20} Ἐπερωτηθεὶς δὲ ὑπὸ τῶν Φαρισαίων πότε ἔρχεται ἡ βασιλεία τοῦ θεοῦ ἀπεκρίθη αὐτοῖς καὶ εἶπεν, Οὐκ ἔρχεται ἡ βασιλεία τοῦ θεοῦ μετὰ παρατηρήσεως, ²¹ οὐδὲ ἐροῦσιν, Ἰδοὺ ὧδε ἤ, Ἐκεῖ, ἰδοὺ γὰρ ἡ βασιλεία τοῦ θεοῦ ἐντὸς ὑμῶν ἐστιν. ¶ ²² Εἶπεν δὲ πρὸς τοὺς μαθητάς, Ἐλεύσονται ἡμέραι ὅτε ἐπιθυμήσετε μίαν τῶν ἡμερῶν τοῦ υἱοῦ τοῦ ἀνθρώπου ἰδεῖν καὶ οὐκ ὄψεσθε. ²³ καὶ ἐροῦσιν ὑμῖν, Ἰδοὺ ἐκεῖ, [ἤ,] Ἰδοὺ ὧδε· μὴ ἀπέλθητε μηδὲ διώξητε. ²⁴ ὥσπερ γὰρ ἡ ἀστραπὴ ἀστράπτουσα ἐκ τῆς ὑπὸ τὸν οὐρανὸν εἰς τὴν ὑπ' οὐρανὸν λάμπει, οὕτως ἔσται ὁ υἱὸς τοῦ ἀνθρώπου [ἐν τῇ ἡμέρᾳ αὐτοῦ]. ²⁵ πρῶτον δὲ δεῖ αὐτὸν πολλὰ παθεῖν καὶ

and be rejected by this generation. ¶ **26** "Just as it was in the days of Noah, so also will
καὶ → ἀποδοκιμασθῆναι ἀπὸ ταύτης ⌐τῆς γενεᾶς⌐ καὶ → καθὼς → ἐγένετο ἐν ταῖς ἡμέραις → Νῶε οὕτως καὶ →
cj f.ap p.g r.gsf d.gsf n.gsf cj cj v.ami.3s p.d d.dpf n.dpf n.gsm adv adv
2779 627 608 4047 3836 1155 2779 2777 1181 1877 3836 2465 3820 4048 2779

it be in the days of the Son of Man. **27** People were eating, drinking, marrying and being given in
→ ἔσται ἐν ταῖς ἡμέραις → τοῦ υἱοῦ ⌐τοῦ ἀνθρώπου⌐ ἤσθιον ἔπινον ἐγάμουν
v.fmi.3s p.d d.dpf n.dpf d.gsm n.gsm d.gsm n.gsm v.iai.3p v.iai.3p v.iai.3p
1639 1877 3836 2465 3836 5626 3836 476 2266 4403 1138

marriage up to the day Noah entered the ark. Then the flood came and destroyed them all.
ἐγαμίζοντο ἄχρι ἧς ← ἡμέρας Νῶε εἰσῆλθεν εἰς τὴν κιβωτὸν καὶ ὁ κατακλυσμὸς ἦλθεν καὶ ἀπώλεσεν πάντας
v.ipi.3p p.g r.gsf n.gsf n.nsm v.aai.3s p.a d.asf n.asf cj d.nsm n.nsm v.aai.3s cj v.aai.3s a.apm
1139 948 4005 2465 3820 1656 1650 3836 3066 2779 3836 2886 2262 2779 660 4246

¶ **28** "It was the same in the days of Lot. People were eating and drinking, buying and selling, planting
καθὼς → ἐγένετο → ὁμοίως ἐν ταῖς ἡμέραις → Λώτ → ἤσθιον ἔπινον ἠγόραζον ἐπώλουν ἐφύτευον
cj v.ami.3s adv p.d d.dpf n.dpf n.gsn v.iai.3p v.iai.3p v.iai.3p v.iai.3p v.iai.3p
2777 1181 3931 1877 3836 2465 3397 2266 4403 60 4797 5885

and building. **29** But the day Lot left Sodom, fire and sulfur rained down from heaven and destroyed them
ᾠκοδόμουν δὲ ᾗ ἡμέρα Λώτ ἐξῆλθεν ἀπὸ Σοδόμων πῦρ καὶ θεῖον ἔβρεξεν ← ἀπ᾽ οὐρανοῦ καὶ ἀπώλεσεν
v.iai.3p cj r.dsf n.dsf n.nsm v.aai.3s p.g n.gpn n.asn cj n.asn v.aai.3s p.g n.gsm cj v.aai.3s
3868 1254 4005 2465 3397 2002 608 5047 4786 2779 2520 1101 608 4041 2779 660

all. ¶ **30** "It will be just like this on the day the Son of Man is revealed. **31** On that
πάντας → ἔσται κατὰ ← ⌐τὰ αὐτά⌐ → ᾗ ἡμέρᾳ ὁ υἱὸς ⌐τοῦ ἀνθρώπου⌐ → ἀποκαλύπτεται ἐν ἐκείνῃ
a.apm v.fmi.3s p.a d.apn r.apn r.dsf n.dsf d.nsm n.nsm d.gsm n.gsm v.ppi.3s p.d r.dsf
4246 1639 2848 3836 899 4005 2465 3836 5626 3836 476 636 1877 1697

day no one who is on the roof of his house, with his goods inside, should go down to
⌐τῇ ἡμέρᾳ⌐ μὴ ὃς ἔσται ἐπὶ τοῦ δώματος ← ← καὶ αὐτοῦ ⌐τὰ σκεύη⌐ ἐν τῇ οἰκίᾳ → καταβάτω ← →
d.dsf n.dsf pl r.nsm v.fmi.3s p.g d.gsn n.gsn cj r.gsm.3 d.apn n.npn p.d d.dsf n.dsf v.aam.3s
3836 2465 3590 4005 1639 2093 3836 1560 2779 899 3836 5007 1877 3836 3864 2849

get them. Likewise, no one in the field should go back for anything. **32** Remember Lot's wife!
ἆραι αὐτά καὶ ὁμοίως μὴ ὁ ἐν ἀγρῷ ἐπιστρεψάτω ← εἰς ⌐τὰ ὀπίσω⌐ μνημονεύετε Λώτ ⌐τῆς γυναικὸς⌐
f.aa r.apn.3 cj adv pl d.nsm p.d n.dsm v.aam.3s p.a d.apn adv v.pam.2p n.gsm d.gsf n.gsf
149 899 2779 3931 3590 3836 1877 69 2188 1650 3836 3958 3648 3397 3836 1222

33 Whoever tries to keep his life will lose it, and whoever loses his life will preserve it.
⌐ὃς ἐὰν⌐ ζητήσῃ → περιποιήσασθαι αὐτοῦ ⌐τὴν ψυχὴν⌐ → ἀπολέσει αὐτήν δ᾽ ⌐ὃς ἂν⌐ ἀπολέσῃ → ζῳογονήσει αὐτήν
r.nsm r.nsm v.aas.3s f.am r.gsm.3 d.asf n.asf v.fai.3s r.asf.3 cj r.nsm pl v.aas.3s v.fai.3s r.asf.3
4005 1569 2426 4347 899 3836 6034 660 899 1254 4005 323 660 2441 899

34 I tell you, on that night two people will be in one bed; one will be taken and the other
→ λέγω ὑμῖν → ταύτῃ ⌐τῇ νυκτὶ⌐ δύο ← → ἔσονται ἐπὶ μιᾶς κλίνης ὁ εἷς → → παραλημφθήσεται καὶ ὁ ἕτερος
v.pai.1s r.dp.2 r.dsf d.dsf n.dsf a.npm v.fmi.3p p.g a.gsf n.gsf d.nsm a.nsm v.fpi.3s cj d.nsm r.nsm
3306 7007 3816 4047 3836 3816 1545 1639 2093 1651 3109 3836 1651 4161 2779 3836 2283

left. **35** Two women will be grinding grain together; one will be taken and the other left."
ἀφεθήσεται δύο ← → ἔσονται ἀλήθουσαι ⌐ἐπὶ τὸ αὐτό⌐ ἡ μία → → παραλημφθήσεται δὲ ἡ ἑτέρα ἀφεθήσεται
v.fpi.3s a.npf v.fmi.3p pt.pa.npf p.a d.asn r.asn d.nsf a.nsf v.fpi.3s cj d.nsf r.nsf v.fpi.3s
918 1545 1639 241 2093 3836 899 3836 1651 4161 1254 3836 2283 918

¶ **37** "Where, Lord?" they asked. He replied, "Where there is a dead body, there
καὶ ποῦ κύριε → ἀποκριθέντες λέγουσιν αὐτῷ δὲ → εἶπεν αὐτοῖς ὅπου ⌐τὸ σῶμα⌐ ἐκεῖ
cj cj n.vsm pt.ap.npm v.pai.3p r.dsm.3 cj d.nsm v.aai.3s r.dpm.3 adv d.nsn n.nsn adv
2779 4543 3261 646 3306 899 1254 3836 3306 899 3963 3836 5393 1695

the vultures will gather."
καὶ οἱ ἀετοὶ → ἐπισυναχθήσονται
adv d.npm n.npm v.fpi.3p
2779 3836 108 2190

The Parable of the Persistent Widow

18:1 Then Jesus told his disciples a parable to show them that they should always pray and not
δὲ Ἔλεγεν αὐτοῖς παραβολὴν πρὸς ← ← αὐτοὺς ⌐τὸ δεῖν⌐ πάντοτε προσεύχεσθαι καὶ μὴ
cj v.iai.3s r.dpm.3 n.asf p.a r.apm.3 d.asn f.pa adv f.pm cj pl
1254 3306 899 4130 4639 899 3836 1256 4121 4667 2779 3590

ἀποδοκιμασθῆναι ἀπὸ τῆς γενεᾶς ταύτης. ¶ ²⁶ καὶ καθὼς ἐγένετο ἐν ταῖς ἡμέραις Νῶε, οὕτως ἔσται καὶ ἐν ταῖς ἡμέραις τοῦ υἱοῦ τοῦ ἀνθρώπου· ²⁷ ἤσθιον, ἔπινον, ἐγάμουν, ἐγαμίζοντο, ἄχρι ἧς ἡμέρας εἰσῆλθεν Νῶε εἰς τὴν κιβωτὸν καὶ ἦλθεν ὁ κατακλυσμὸς καὶ ἀπώλεσεν πάντας. ¶ ²⁸ ὁμοίως καθὼς ἐγένετο ἐν ταῖς ἡμέραις Λώτ· ἤσθιον, ἔπινον, ἠγόραζον, ἐπώλουν, ἐφύτευον, ᾠκοδόμουν· ²⁹ ᾗ δὲ ἡμέρᾳ ἐξῆλθεν Λώτ ἀπὸ Σοδόμων, ἔβρεξεν πῦρ καὶ θεῖον ἀπ᾽ οὐρανοῦ καὶ ἀπώλεσεν πάντας. ¶ ³⁰ κατὰ τὰ αὐτὰ ἔσται ᾗ ἡμέρᾳ ὁ υἱὸς τοῦ ἀνθρώπου ἀποκαλύπτεται. ³¹ ἐν ἐκείνῃ τῇ ἡμέρᾳ ὃς ἔσται ἐπὶ τοῦ δώματος καὶ τὰ σκεύη αὐτοῦ ἐν τῇ οἰκίᾳ, μὴ καταβάτω ἆραι αὐτά, καὶ ὁ ἐν ἀγρῷ ὁμοίως μὴ ἐπιστρεψάτω εἰς τὰ ὀπίσω. ³² μνημονεύετε τῆς γυναικὸς Λώτ. ³³ ὃς ἐὰν ζητήσῃ τὴν ψυχὴν αὐτοῦ περιποιήσασθαι ἀπολέσει αὐτήν, ὃς δ᾽ ἂν ἀπολέσῃ ζῳογονήσει αὐτήν. ³⁴ λέγω ὑμῖν, ταύτῃ τῇ νυκτὶ ἔσονται δύο ἐπὶ κλίνης μιᾶς, ὁ εἷς παραλημφθήσεται καὶ ὁ ἕτερος ἀφεθήσεται· ³⁵ ἔσονται δύο ἀλήθουσαι ἐπὶ τὸ αὐτό, ἡ μία παραλημφθήσεται, ἡ δὲ ἑτέρα ἀφεθήσεται. ¶ ³⁷ καὶ ἀποκριθέντες λέγουσιν αὐτῷ, Ποῦ, κύριε; ὁ δὲ εἶπεν αὐτοῖς, Ὅπου τὸ σῶμα, ἐκεῖ καὶ οἱ ἀετοὶ ἐπισυναχθήσονται.

18:1 Ἔλεγεν δὲ παραβολὴν αὐτοῖς πρὸς τὸ δεῖν πάντοτε προσεύχεσθαι αὐτοὺς καὶ μὴ ἐγκακεῖν, ² λέγων, Κριτής τις ἦν ἔν

give up. ² He said: "In a certain town there was a judge who neither feared God nor cared
ἐγκακεῖν   λέγων ἕν τινι πόλει   ἦν τις κριτής   μὴ φοβούμενος ⸆τὸν θεὸν⸃ ⸆καὶ μὴ⸃ ἐντρεπόμενος
f.pa   pt.pa.nsm p.d r.dsf n.dsf   v.iai.3s r.nsm n.nsm   pl pt.pp.nsm d.asm n.asm   pl pt.pp.nsm
1591   3306 1877 5516 4484   1639 5516 3216   5828 5828 3836 2536   2779 3590 1956

about men. ³ And there was a widow in that town who kept coming to him with the plea, 'Grant
← ἄνθρωπον δὲ → ἦν χήρα ἐν ἐκείνῃ ⸆τῇ πόλει⸃ καὶ → ἤρχετο πρὸς αὐτὸν λέγουσα →
n.asm cj   v.iai.3s n.nsf p.d d.dsf n.dsf d.dsf n.dsf cj   v.imi.3s p.a r.asm.3 pt.pa.nsf
476 1254   1639 5939 1877 1697 3836 4484 2779   2262 4639 899 3306   1688

me justice against my adversary.' ¶ ⁴ "For some time he refused. But finally he said to
με ἐκδίκησον ἀπὸ μου ⸆τοῦ ἀντιδίκου⸃ καὶ ἐπὶ χρόνον ⸆οὐκ ἤθελεν⸃ δὲ ⸆μετὰ ταῦτα⸃ → εἶπεν ἐν
r.as.1 v.aam.2s p.g r.gs.1 d.gsm n.gsm cj p.a n.asm pl v.iai.3s cj p.a r.apn   v.aai.3s p.d
1609 1688 608 1609 3836 508   2779 2093 5989 4024 2527 1254 3552 4047   3306 1877

himself, 'Even though I don't fear God or care about men, ⁵ yet because this widow
ἑαυτῷ καὶ εἰ → οὐ φοβοῦμαι ⸆τὸν θεὸν⸃ οὐδὲ ἐντρέπομαι ← ἄνθρωπον γε διὰ ταύτην ⸆τὴν χήραν⸃
r.dsm.3 adv cj   pl v.ppi.1s d.asm n.asm cj v.ppi.1s   n.asm pl p.a r.asf d.asf n.asf
1571 2779 1623   4024 5828 3836 2536 4028 1956   476 1145 1328 4047 3836 5939

keeps bothering me, I will see that she gets justice, so that she won't eventually wear me out with her
⸆τὸ παρέχειν⸃ κόπον μοι → ⸆ αὐτὴν → ἐκδικήσω ἵνα → μὴ ⸆εἰς τέλος⸃ ὑπωπιάζῃ ⸆με⸃ →
d.asn f.pa n.asm r.ds.1   r.asf.3   v.fai.1s cj   pl p.a n.asn v.pas.3s r.as.1
3836 4218 3160 1609 1688 1688 1688   899   1688 2671   5724 3590 1650 5465 5724 1609 5724

coming!'" ¶ ⁶ And the Lord said, "Listen to what the unjust judge says. ⁷ And will not God bring
ἐρχομένη δὲ ὁ κύριος Εἶπεν ἀκούσατε τί ὁ ⸆τῆς ἀδικίας⸃ κριτὴς λέγει δὲ → ⸆οὐ μὴ⸃ ὁ θεὸς ποιήσῃ
pt.pm.nsf cj d.nsm n.nsm v.aai.3s v.aam.2p   r.asn d.nsm d.gsf n.gsf n.nsm v.pai.3s cj   pl pl d.nsm n.nsm v.aas.3s
2262 1254 3836 3261 3306 201   5515 3836 3836 94 3216 3306 1254   4472 4024 3590 3836 2536 4472

about justice for his chosen ones, who cry out to him day and night? Will he keep putting
← ⸆τὴν ἐκδίκησιν⸃ → αὐτοῦ ⸆τῶν ἐκλεκτῶν⸃ τῶν βοώντων → αὐτῷ ἡμέρας καὶ νυκτός καὶ → → μακροθυμεῖ
d.asf n.asf   r.gsm.3 d.gpm a.gpm d.gpm pt.pa.gpm   r.dsm.3 n.gsf cj n.gsf cj   v.pai.3s
3836 1689   1723 899 3836 1723 3836 1066   899 2465 2779 3816 2779   3428

them off? ⁸ I tell you, he will see that they get justice, and quickly. However, when the Son of
ἐπ' αὐτοῖς → λέγω ὑμῖν ὅτι → → αὐτῶν ποιήσει ⸆τὴν ἐκδίκησιν⸃ ἐν τάχει πλὴν → → ὁ υἱὸς
p.d r.dpm.3   v.pai.1s r.dp.2 cj   r.gpm.3 v.fai.3s d.asf n.asf p.d n.dsn cj   d.nsm n.nsm
2093 899 3428   3306 7007 4022 4472 4472 4472   899 4472 3836 1689 1877 5443 4440   2262 3836 5626

Man comes, will he find faith on the earth?"
⸆τοῦ ἀνθρώπου⸃ ἐλθὼν ἆρα → → εὑρήσει ⸆τὴν πίστιν⸃ ἐπὶ τῆς γῆς
d.gsm n.gsm pt.aa.nsm pl   v.fai.3s d.asf n.asf p.g d.gsf n.gsf
3836 476 2262 727   2351 3836 4411 2093 3836 1178

The Parable of the Pharisee and the Tax Collector

18:9 To some who were confident of their own righteousness and looked down on
δὲ πρός τινας τοὺς → πεποιθότας ἐφ' ἑαυτοῖς ← ὅτι εἰσὶν δίκαιοι καὶ ἐξουθενοῦντας ← ←
cj p.a r.apm d.apm   pt.ra.apm p.d r.dpm.3   cj v.pai.3p a.npm   cj pt.pa.apm
1254 4639 5516 3836   4275 2093 1571   4022 1639 1465   2779 2024

everybody else, Jesus told this parable: ¹⁰ "Two men went up to the temple to pray,
⸆τοὺς λοιπούς⸃ καὶ Εἶπεν ταύτην ⸆τὴν παραβολὴν⸃ δύο Ἄνθρωποι ἀνέβησαν ← εἰς τὸ ἱερὸν → προσεύξασθαι
d.apm a.apm adv v.aai.3s r.asf d.asf n.asf   a.npm n.npm v.aai.3p   p.a d.asn n.asn   f.am
3836 3370 2779 3306 4047 3836 4130   1545 476 326   1650 3836 2639   4667

one a Pharisee and the other a tax collector. ¹¹ The Pharisee stood up and prayed about himself:
ὁ εἷς⸃ Φαρισαῖος καὶ ὁ ἕτερος τελώνης ← ὁ Φαρισαῖος σταθεὶς ← προσηύχετο πρὸς ἑαυτὸν ταῦτα
d.nsm a.nsm n.nsm cj d.nsm a.nsm n.nsm   d.nsm n.nsm pt.ap.nsm   v.imi.3s p.a r.asm.3 r.apn
3836 1651 5757 2779 3836 2283 5467   3836 5757 2705   4667 4639 1571 4047

'God, I thank you that I am not like other men – robbers, evildoers, adulterers – or even like
ὁ θεός, → εὐχαριστῶ σοι ὅτι → εἰμὶ οὐκ ὥσπερ οἱ λοιποὶ ⸆τῶν ἀνθρώπων⸃ ἅρπαγες ἄδικοι μοιχοί ἢ καὶ ὡς
d.vsm n.vsm v.pai.1s r.ds.2 cj   v.pai.1s pl pl d.npm a.npm d.gpm n.gpm a.npm a.npm n.npm cj adv pl
3836 2536 2373 5148 4022   1639 4024 6061 3836 3370 3836 476 774 94 3659 2445 2779 6055

this tax collector. ¹² I fast twice a week and give a tenth of all I get.' ¶ ¹³ "But
οὗτος ὁ τελώνης⸃ → νηστεύω δὶς ⸆τοῦ σαββάτου⸃ ἀποδεκατῶ ← → πάντα ὅσα → κτῶμαι δὲ
r.nsm d.nsm n.nsm   v.pai.1s adv d.gsn n.gsn v.pai.1s   a.apn r.apn v.pmi.1s cj
4047 3836 5467   3764 1489 3836 4879 620   4246 4012 3227 1254

τινι πόλει τὸν θεὸν μὴ φοβούμενος καὶ ἄνθρωπον μὴ ἐντρεπόμενος. ³ χήρα δὲ ἦν ἐν τῇ πόλει ἐκείνῃ καὶ ἤρχετο πρὸς αὐτὸν λέγουσα, Ἐκδίκησόν με ἀπὸ τοῦ ἀντιδίκου μου. ¶ ⁴ καὶ οὐκ ἤθελεν ἐπὶ χρόνον. μετὰ δὲ ταῦτα εἶπεν ἐν ἑαυτῷ, Εἰ καὶ τὸν θεὸν οὐ φοβοῦμαι οὐδὲ ἄνθρωπον ἐντρέπομαι, ⁵ διά γε τὸ παρέχειν μοι κόπον τὴν χήραν ταύτην ἐκδικήσω αὐτήν, ἵνα μὴ εἰς τέλος ἐρχομένη ὑπωπιάζῃ με. ¶ ⁶ Εἶπεν δὲ ὁ κύριος, Ἀκούσατε τί ὁ κριτὴς τῆς ἀδικίας λέγει· ⁷ ὁ δὲ θεὸς οὐ μὴ ποιήσῃ τὴν ἐκδίκησιν τῶν ἐκλεκτῶν αὐτοῦ τῶν βοώντων αὐτῷ ἡμέρας καὶ νυκτός, καὶ μακροθυμεῖ ἐπ' αὐτοῖς; ⁸ λέγω ὑμῖν ὅτι ποιήσει τὴν ἐκδίκησιν αὐτῶν ἐν τάχει. πλὴν ὁ υἱὸς τοῦ ἀνθρώπου ἐλθὼν ἆρα εὑρήσει τὴν πίστιν ἐπὶ τῆς γῆς;

18:9 Εἶπεν δὲ καὶ πρός τινας τοὺς πεποιθότας ἐφ' ἑαυτοῖς ὅτι εἰσὶν δίκαιοι καὶ ἐξουθενοῦντας τοὺς λοιποὺς τὴν παραβολὴν ταύτην· ¹⁰ Ἄνθρωποι δύο ἀνέβησαν εἰς τὸ ἱερὸν προσεύξασθαι, ὁ εἷς Φαρισαῖος καὶ ὁ ἕτερος τελώνης. ¹¹ ὁ Φαρισαῖος σταθεὶς πρὸς ἑαυτὸν ταῦτα προσηύχετο, Ὁ θεός, εὐχαριστῶ σοι ὅτι οὐκ εἰμὶ ὥσπερ οἱ λοιποὶ τῶν ἀνθρώπων, ἅρπαγες, ἄδικοι, μοιχοί, ἢ καὶ ὡς οὗτος ὁ τελώνης· ¹² νηστεύω δὶς τοῦ σαββάτου, ἀποδεκατῶ πάντα ὅσα κτῶμαι. ¶ ¹³ ὁ δὲ τελώνης μακρόθεν ἑστὼς οὐκ

the	tax	collector	stood	at	a distance.	He would	not	even	look		up	to	heaven,	but	beat
ὁ	τελώνης ←		ἑστὼς →	μακρόθεν	→	ἤθελεν	οὐκ	οὐδὲ	⸢τοὺς ὀφθαλμοὺς ἐπᾶραι ←		εἰς	⸢τὸν οὐρανόν,		ἀλλ᾽	ἔτυπτεν
d.nsm	n.nsm		pt.ra.nsm	adv		v.iai.3s	pl	adv	d.apm n.apm f.aa		p.a	d.asm n.asm		cj	v.iai.3s
3836	5467		2705	3427		2527	4024	4028	3836 4057 2048		1650	3836 4041		247	5597

his	breast	and said,	'God,	have	mercy	on me, a sinner.'	¶	14 "I tell	you	that	this man,	rather
αὐτοῦ	⸢τὸ στῆθος⸣	λέγων,	ὁ θεός,	→	ἱλάσθητι	μοι ⸢τῷ ἁμαρτωλῷ.		→ λέγω	ὑμῖν		οὗτος ←	παρ᾽
r.gsm.3	d.asn n.asn	pt.pa.nsm	d.vsm n.vsm		v.apm.2s	r.ds.1 d.dsm n.dsm		v.pai.1s	r.dp.2		r.nsm	p.a
899	3836 5111	3306	3836 2536		2661	1609 3836 283		3306	7007		4047	4123

than	the other,	went	home	justified	before God.	For	everyone	who	exalts	himself	will be
←	ἐκεῖνον	κατέβη εἰς	⸢τὸν οἶκον	αὐτοῦ	δεδικαιωμένος	ὅτι	πᾶς	ὁ	ὑψῶν	ἑαυτὸν	→
	r.asm	v.aai.3s p.a	d.asm n.asm	r.gsm.3	pt.rp.nsm	cj	a.nsm	d.nsm	pt.pa.nsm	r.asm.3	
	1697	2849 1650	3836 3875	899	1467	4022	4246	3836	5738	1571	

humbled,	and	he	who	humbles	himself	will be exalted."
ταπεινωθήσεται	δὲ	ὁ	←	ταπεινῶν	ἑαυτὸν	→ ὑψωθήσεται
v.fpi.3s	cj	d.nsm		pt.pa.nsm	r.asm.3	v.fpi.3s
5427	1254	3836		5427	1571	5738

The Little Children and Jesus

18:15

People	were also	bringing	babies	to Jesus	to	have him touch	them.	When	the	disciples	saw
δὲ →	καὶ	Προσέφερον	⸢τὰ βρέφη	αὐτῷ	ἵνα	ἅπτηται αὐτῶν		δὲ	οἱ	μαθηταὶ	ἰδόντες
cj →	adv	v.iai.3p	d.apn n.apn	r.dsm.3	cj	v.pms.3s r.gpn.3		cj	d.npm	n.npm	pt.aa.npm
1254 4712	4712	2779	3836 1100	899	2671	721 899		1254	1625	3836 3412	1625

this,	they rebuked	them.	16 But	Jesus	called	the children	to him	and said,	"Let	the	little	children	come
→	ἐπετίμων	αὐτοῖς	δὲ	ὁ Ἰησοῦς	προσεκαλέσατο	αὐτὰ	←	λέγων	ἄφετε	τὰ	→	παιδία	ἔρχεσθαι
	v.iai.3p	r.dpm.3	cj	d.nsm n.nsm	v.ami.3s	r.apn.3		pt.pa.nsm	v.aam.2p	d.apn		n.apn	f.pm
	2203	899	1254	3836 2652	4673	899	4673 4673	3306	918	3836		4086	2262

to	me,	and	do	not	hinder	them,	for	the	kingdom	of God	belongs	to	such	as these.	17 I tell	you	the truth,
πρός	με	καὶ	→	μὴ	κωλύετε	αὐτά	γὰρ	ἡ	βασιλεία	⸢τοῦ θεοῦ⸣	ἐστιν	←	→	⸢τῶν τοιούτων⸣	→ λέγω	ὑμῖν	ἀμὴν
p.a	r.as.1	cj		pl	v.pam.2p	r.apn.3	cj	d.nsf	n.nsf	d.gsm n.gsm	v.pai.3s			d.gpn r.gpn	v.pai.1s	r.dp.2	pl
4639	1609	2779		3590	3266	899	1142	3836	993	3836 2536	1639			3836 5525	3306	7007	297

anyone	who	will	not	receive	the	kingdom	of God	like	a little	child	will	never	enter	it."
ὃς	ἂν	←	→ μὴ	δέξηται	τὴν	βασιλείαν	→ ⸢τοῦ θεοῦ⸣	ὡς	→	παιδίον	→	οὐ μὴ	εἰσέλθῃ εἰς	αὐτήν
r.nsm	pl		pl	v.ams.3s	d.asf	n.asf	d.gsm n.gsm	cj		n.nsn		pl pl	v.aas.3s p.a	r.asf.3
4005	323		3590	1312	3836	993	3836 2536	6055		4086		1656 4024 3590	1656 1650	899

The Rich Ruler

18:18

A	certain	ruler	asked	him,	"Good	teacher,	what	must	I	do	to inherit	eternal	life?"
Καὶ	τις	ἄρχων	ἐπηρώτησεν	αὐτὸν	λέγων	ἀγαθέ	διδάσκαλε	τί	→	→ ποιήσας	→ κληρονομήσω	αἰώνιον	ζωὴν
cj	r.nsm	n.nsm	v.aai.3s	r.asm.3	pt.pa.nsm	a.vsm	n.vsm	r.asn		pt.aa.nsm	v.fai.1s	a.asf	n.asf
2779	5516	807	2089	899	3306	19	1437	5515		3099 3099 4472	3099	173	2437

19	"Why	do you call	me	good?"	Jesus	answered.	"No one	is	good	— except	God	alone.	20 You
δὲ	τί	→ λέγεις	με	ἀγαθόν	ὁ Ἰησοῦς	εἶπεν	αὐτῷ	→	οὐδεὶς	ἀγαθὸς	εἰ μὴ	⸢ὁ θεός⸣	εἷς
cj	r.asn	v.pai.2s	r.as.1	a.asm	d.nsm n.nsm	v.aai.3s	r.dsm.3		a.nsm	a.nsm	cj pl	d.nsm n.nsm	a.nsm
1254	5515	3306	1609	19	3836 2652	3306	899		4029	19	1623 3590	3836 2536	1651

know	the	commandments:	'Do not commit	adultery,	do not	murder,	do not	steal,	do not	give false
οἶδας	τὰς	ἐντολὰς	μὴ	μοιχεύσῃς	μὴ	φονεύσῃς	μὴ	κλέψῃς	μὴ	ψευδομαρτυρήσῃς
v.rai.2s	d.apf	n.apf	pl	v.aas.2s	pl	v.aas.2s	pl	v.aas.2s	pl	v.aas.2s
3857	3836	1953	3658 3590	3658	5839 3590	5839	3096 3590	3096	6018 3590	6018

testimony,	honor	your	father	and	mother.'"	¶	21	"All	these	I have	kept	since	I was a boy,"	he
←	τίμα	σου	⸢τὸν πατέρα	καὶ	⸢τὴν μητέρα⸣			δὲ	πάντα	ταῦτα →	→ ἐφύλαξα	ἐκ	νεότητος	ὁ
	v.pam.2s	r.gs.2	d.asm n.asm	cj	d.asf n.asf			cj	a.apn	r.apn	v.aai.1s	p.g	n.gsf	d.nsm
	5506	5148	3836 4252	2779	3836 3613			1254	4246	4047	5875	1666	3744	3836

said.	22	When	Jesus	heard	this,	he said	to him,	"You	still	lack	one	thing.	Sell	everything	you have	and
εἶπεν	δὲ	→	ὁ Ἰησοῦς	ἀκούσας	→	εἶπεν	αὐτῷ	σοι	ἔτι	λείπει	ἕν		πώλησον	⸢πάντα ὅσα	→ ἔχεις	καὶ
v.aai.3s	cj		d.nsm n.nsm	pt.aa.nsm		v.aai.3s	r.dsm.3	r.ds.2	adv	v.pai.3s	a.nsn		v.aam.2s	a.apn r.apn	v.pai.2s	cj
3306	1254	201	3836 2652	201		3306	899	5148	2285	3309	1651		4797	4246 4012	2400	2779

ἤθελεν οὐδὲ τοὺς ὀφθαλμοὺς ἐπᾶραι εἰς τὸν οὐρανόν, ἀλλ᾽ ἔτυπτεν τὸ στῆθος αὐτοῦ λέγων, Ὁ θεός, ἱλάσθητί μοι τῷ ἁμαρτωλῷ. ¶ 14 λέγω ὑμῖν, κατέβη οὗτος δεδικαιωμένος εἰς τὸν οἶκον αὐτοῦ παρ᾽ ἐκεῖνον· ὅτι πᾶς ὁ ὑψῶν ἑαυτὸν ταπεινωθήσεται, ὁ δὲ ταπεινῶν ἑαυτὸν ὑψωθήσεται.

18:15 Προσέφερον δὲ αὐτῷ καὶ τὰ βρέφη ἵνα αὐτῶν ἅπτηται· ἰδόντες δὲ οἱ μαθηταὶ ἐπετίμων αὐτοῖς. 16 ὁ δὲ Ἰησοῦς προσεκαλέσατο αὐτὰ λέγων, Ἄφετε τὰ παιδία ἔρχεσθαι πρός με καὶ μὴ κωλύετε αὐτά, τῶν γὰρ τοιούτων ἐστὶν ἡ βασιλεία τοῦ θεοῦ. 17 ἀμὴν λέγω ὑμῖν, ὃς ἂν μὴ δέξηται τὴν βασιλείαν τοῦ θεοῦ ὡς παιδίον, οὐ μὴ εἰσέλθῃ εἰς αὐτήν.

18:18 Καὶ ἐπηρώτησέν τις αὐτὸν ἄρχων λέγων, Διδάσκαλε ἀγαθέ, τί ποιήσας ζωὴν αἰώνιον κληρονομήσω; 19 εἶπεν δὲ αὐτῷ ὁ Ἰησοῦς, Τί με λέγεις ἀγαθόν; οὐδεὶς ἀγαθὸς εἰ μὴ εἷς ὁ θεός. 20 τὰς ἐντολὰς οἶδας· Μὴ μοιχεύσῃς, Μὴ φονεύσῃς, Μὴ κλέψῃς, Μὴ ψευδομαρτυρήσῃς, Τίμα τὸν πατέρα σου καὶ τὴν μητέρα. ¶ 21 ὁ δὲ εἶπεν, Ταῦτα πάντα ἐφύλαξα ἐκ νεότητος. 22 ἀκούσας δὲ ὁ Ἰησοῦς εἶπεν αὐτῷ, Ἔτι ἕν σοι λείπει· πάντα ὅσα ἔχεις πώλησον καὶ διάδος πτωχοῖς, καὶ ἕξεις θησαυρὸν ἐν [τοῖς] οὐρανοῖς,

give | to the poor, | and | you will have | treasure | in | heaven. | | Then | come, | follow | me." | ¶ | 23 | | When he
διάδος → | πτωχοῖς καί | → | → ἕξεις | θησαυρὸν | ἐν | ⌐τοῖς οὐρανοῖς | καί | δεῦρο | ἀκολούθει μοι | | δέ | →
v.aam.2s | a.dpm cj | | v.fai.2s | n.asm | p.d | d.dpm n.dpm | cj | j | v.pam.2s r.ds.1 | | cj
1344 | 4777 2779 | | 2400 | 2565 | 1877 | 3836 4041 | 2779 | 199 | 1306 1609 | | 1254

heard | this, | he | became | very sad, | | because | he was | a man of | great | wealth. | 24 | Jesus | | looked at | him
ἀκούσας | ταῦτα | ὁ | ἐγενήθη | → περίλυπος | γάρ | → ἦν | | σφόδρα | πλούσιος | δέ ⌐ὁ Ἰησοῦς⌐ | ἰδών → | αὐτόν
pt.aa.nsm | r.apn | d.nsm | v.api.3s | a.nsm | cj | v.iai.3s | | adv | a.nsm | cj d.nsm n.nsm | pt.aa.nsm | r.asm.3
201 | 4047 | 3836 | 1181 | 4337 | 1142 | 1639 | | 5379 | 4454 | 1254 3836 2652 | 1625 | 899

| | and said, "How | hard | | it is for the rich | | | to enter | | the kingdom of
[περίλυπον | γενόμενον] | εἶπεν πῶς | δυσκόλως | | οἱ | ⌐τὰ χρήματα ἔχοντες⌐ | → | εἰσπορεύονται | εἰς | τὴν | βασιλείαν →
a.asm | pt.am.asm | v.aai.3s pl | adv | | d.npm | d.apn n.apn pt.pa.npm | | v.pmi.3p | p.a | d.asf | n.asf
4337 | 1181 | 3306 4802 | 1552 | | 3836 | 3836 5975 2400 | | 1660 | 1650 | 3836 | 993

God! | 25 | Indeed, | it is | easier | | for a camel | to go | through | the eye | | of a needle | than | for a rich | | man
⌐τοῦ θεοῦ⌐ | γάρ | → ἔστιν | εὐκοπώτερον | | κάμηλον | εἰσελθεῖν | διά | τρήματος | → | βελόνης | ἤ | | πλούσιον
d.gsm | cj | v.pai.3s | a.nsn.c | | n.asm | f.aa | p.g | n.gsn | | n.gsf | pl | | a.asm
3836 2536 | 1142 | 1639 | 2324 | | 2823 | 1656 | 1328 | 5557 | | 1017 | 2445 | | 4454

to enter | | the kingdom of God." | | ¶ | 26 | | Those who heard | | this asked, | | "Who | then | can | | be
→ εἰσελθεῖν | εἰς | τὴν | βασιλείαν → | ⌐τοῦ θεοῦ⌐ | | δέ | οἱ | → | ἀκούσαντες | εἶπαν | καί | τίς | | δύναται →
f.aa | p.a | d.asf | n.asf | d.gsm n.gsm | | cj | d.npm | | pt.aa.npm | v.aai.3p | cj | r.nsm | | v.ppi.3s
1656 | 1650 | 3836 | 993 | 3836 2536 | | 1254 | 3836 | | 201 | 3306 | 2779 | 5515 | | 1538

saved?" | 27 | | Jesus | replied, | "What | is impossible | with | men | is | possible | with | God." | | ¶ | 28 | | Peter | | said
σωθῆναι | δέ | ὁ | | εἶπεν | τά | → ἀδύνατα | παρά | ἀνθρώποις | ἔστιν | δυνατά | παρά | ⌐τῷ θεῷ⌐ | | δέ | ὁ | Πέτρος | Εἶπεν
f.ap | cj | d.nsm | | v.aai.3s | d.npn | a.npn | p.d | n.dpm | v.pai.3s | a.npn | p.d | d.dsm n.dsm | | cj | d.nsm | n.nsm | v.aai.3s
5392 | 1254 | 3836 | | 3306 | 3836 | 105 | 4123 | 476 | 1639 | 1543 | 4123 | 3836 2536 | | 1254 3836 | 4377 | 3306

to him, | | "We | have left | all | we | had | to follow | | you!" | 29 | | "I | tell | you | the truth," | | Jesus | said | to them, | that
ἰδού | ἡμεῖς | → | ἀφέντες | τά | ἴδια | ἠκολουθήσαμεν | σοι | | δέ | → | λέγω | ὑμῖν | ἀμήν | ὁ | | εἶπεν → | αὐτοῖς | ὅτι
j | r.np.1 | | pt.aa.npm | d.apn | a.apn | v.aai.1p | r.ds.2 | | cj | | v.pai.1s | r.dp.2 | pl | d.nsm | | v.aai.3s | r.dpm.3 | cj
2627 | 7005 | | 918 | 3836 | 2625 | 199 | 5148 | | 1254 | | 3306 | 7007 | 297 | 3836 | | 3306 | 899 | 4022

"no one | | who | has left | home | or | wife | or | brothers | or | parents | or | children | for | the sake of the | kingdom
οὐδείς | ἐστιν | ὅς | → | ἀφῆκεν | οἰκίαν | ἤ | γυναῖκα | ἤ | ἀδελφούς | ἤ | γονεῖς | ἤ | τέκνα | ἕνεκεν ← | → τῆς | βασιλείας
a.nsm | v.pai.3s | r.nsm | | v.aai.3s | n.asf | cj | n.asf | cj | n.apm | cj | n.apm | cj | n.apn | p.g | d.gsf | n.gsf
4029 | 1639 | 4005 | | 918 | 3864 | 2445 | 1222 | 2445 | 81 | 2445 | 1204 | 2445 | 5451 | 1914 | 3836 | 993

of God | 30 | | will fail | | to receive | many | | times as much | in | this | age | | and, | in | the | age | to
→ ⌐τοῦ θεοῦ⌐ | ὅς | ⌐οὐχὶ μή⌐ | | ἀπολάβη | πολλαπλασίονα ← | | ← | ἐν | τούτῳ | ⌐τῷ καιρῷ⌐ | καί | ἐν | ⌐τῷ αἰῶνι⌐ | →
d.gsm n.gsm | r.nsm | pl pl | | v.aas.3s | a.apn | | | p.d | r.dsm | d.dsm n.dsm | cj | p.d | d.dsm n.dsm
3836 2536 | 4005 | 655 4049 | | 655 | 4491 | | | 1877 | 4047 | 3836 2789 | 2779 | 1877 | 3836 172

come, | | eternal | life."
⌐τῷ ἐρχομένῳ⌐ | αἰώνιον | ζωήν
d.dsm pt.pm.dsm | a.asf | n.asf
3836 2262 | 173 | 2437

Jesus Again Predicts His Death

18:31 | | Jesus | took | | the | Twelve | aside and | told | | them, | | "We | are going | | up to | Jerusalem, | and
δέ | Παραλαβών | τούς | δώδεκα | ← | | εἶπεν | πρός | αὐτούς | ἰδού | | → | ἀναβαίνομεν | ← | εἰς | Ἰερουσαλήμ | καί
cj | pt.aa.nsm | d.apm | a.apm | | | v.aai.3s | p.a | r.apm.3 | j | | | v.pai.1p | | p.a | n.asf | cj
1254 | 4161 | 3836 | 1557 | 4161 | | 3306 | 4639 | 899 | 2627 | | | 326 | | 1650 | 2647 | 2779

everything | that | is | written | | by | the | prophets | about | the | Son | of Man | | will be fulfilled. | 32 | | He will be
πάντα | τά | → | γεγραμμένα | διά | τῶν | προφητῶν | | τῷ | υἱῷ | ⌐τοῦ ἀνθρώπου⌐ | → | → τελεσθήσεται | γάρ | → →
a.npn | d.npn | | pt.rp.npn | p.g | d.gpm | n.gpm | | d.dsm | n.dsm | d.gsm n.gsm | | v.fpi.3s | cj
4246 | 3836 | | 1211 | 1328 | 3836 | 4737 | | 3836 | 5626 | 3836 476 | | 5464 | 1142

handed | | over to | the | Gentiles. | They will | mock | | him, | insult | | him, | spit | | on him, | and
παραδοθήσεται ← | → τοῖς | ἔθνεσιν | καί | → | ἐμπαιχθήσεται | | καί | ὑβρισθήσεται | | καί | ἐμπτυσθήσεται ← | | καί
v.fpi.3s | d.dpn | n.dpn | cj | | v.fpi.3s | | cj | v.fpi.3s | | cj | v.fpi.3s | | cj
4140 | 3836 | 1620 | 2779 | | 1850 | | 2779 | 5614 | | 2779 | 1870 | | 2779

flog | | him and | kill | | him. | 33 | On the | third | | day | he will | rise | | again." | ¶ | 34 | | The
μαστιγώσαντες | | ἀποκτενοῦσιν | αὐτόν | καί | → τῇ | ⌐τῇ τρίτῃ⌐ | ἡμέρᾳ | → | → ἀναστήσεται | ← | | καί
pt.aa.npm | | v.fai.3p | r.asm.3 | cj | d.dsf | d.dsf a.dsf | n.dsf | | v.fmi.3s | | | cj
3463 | | 650 | 899 | 2779 | 3836 | 3836 5569 | 2465 | | 482 | | | 2779

καὶ δεῦρο ἀκολούθει μοι. ¶ 23 ὁ δὲ ἀκούσας ταῦτα περίλυπος ἐγενήθη· ἦν γὰρ πλούσιος σφόδρα. 24 Ἰδὼν δὲ αὐτὸν ὁ Ἰησοῦς [περίλυπον γενόμενον] εἶπεν, Πῶς δυσκόλως οἱ τὰ χρήματα ἔχοντες εἰς τὴν βασιλείαν τοῦ θεοῦ εἰσπορεύονται· 25 εὐκοπώτερον γάρ ἐστιν κάμηλον διὰ τρήματος βελόνης εἰσελθεῖν ἢ πλούσιον εἰς τὴν βασιλείαν τοῦ θεοῦ εἰσελθεῖν. ¶ 26 εἶπαν δὲ οἱ ἀκούσαντες, Καὶ τίς δύναται σωθῆναι; 27 ὁ δὲ εἶπεν, Τὰ ἀδύνατα παρὰ ἀνθρώποις δυνατὰ παρὰ τῷ θεῷ ἐστιν. ¶ 28 Εἶπεν δὲ ὁ Πέτρος, Ἰδοὺ ἡμεῖς ἀφέντες τὰ ἴδια ἠκολουθήσαμέν σοι. 29 ὁ δὲ εἶπεν αὐτοῖς, Ἀμὴν λέγω ὑμῖν ὅτι οὐδείς ἐστιν ὃς ἀφῆκεν οἰκίαν ἢ γυναῖκα ἢ ἀδελφοὺς ἢ γονεῖς ἢ τέκνα ἕνεκεν τῆς βασιλείας τοῦ θεοῦ, 30 ὃς οὐχὶ μὴ [ἀπο]λάβῃ πολλαπλασίονα ἐν τῷ καιρῷ τούτῳ καὶ ἐν τῷ αἰῶνι τῷ ἐρχομένῳ ζωὴν αἰώνιον.

18:31 Παραλαβὼν δὲ τοὺς δώδεκα εἶπεν πρὸς αὐτούς, Ἰδοὺ ἀναβαίνομεν εἰς Ἰερουσαλήμ, καὶ τελεσθήσεται πάντα τὰ γεγραμμένα διὰ τῶν προφητῶν τῷ υἱῷ τοῦ ἀνθρώπου· 32 παραδοθήσεται γὰρ τοῖς ἔθνεσιν καὶ ἐμπαιχθήσεται καὶ ὑβρισθήσεται καὶ ἐμπτυσθήσεται 33 καὶ μαστιγώσαντες ἀποκτενοῦσιν αὐτόν, καὶ τῇ ἡμέρᾳ τῇ τρίτῃ ἀναστήσεται. ¶ 34 καὶ αὐτοὶ οὐδὲν τούτων

disciples did not understand any of this.   Its meaning was hidden   from them, and they did not know
αὐτοὶ ↱ οὐδὲν συνῆκαν ↰ → τούτων καὶ τοῦτο τὸ ῥῆμα ἦν κεκρυμμένον ἀπ᾽ αὐτῶν καὶ ↱ ↱ οὐκ ἐγίνωσκον
r.npm a.asn v.aai.3p r.gpn cj r.nsn d.nsn n.nsn v.iai.3s pt.rp.nsn p.g r.gpm.3 cj pl v.iai.3p
899 5317 4029 5317 4029 4047 2779 4047 3836 4839 1639 3221 608 899 2779 1182 1182 4024 1182

what he was talking about.
τὰ → → λεγόμενα ←
d.apn pt.pp.apn
3836 3306

A Blind Beggar Receives His Sight

18:35   As Jesus approached   Jericho, a   blind man was sitting by   the roadside begging. **36** When
δὲ Ἐγένετο ἐν αὐτὸν ⸤τῷ ἐγγίζειν⸥ εἰς Ἰεριχὼ τις τυφλός ← ἐκάθητο παρὰ τὴν ὁδὸν ἐπαιτῶν δὲ →
cj v.ami.3s p.d r.asm.3 d.dsn f.pa p.a n.asf r.nsm a.nsm v.imi.3s p.a d.asf n.asf pt.pa.nsm cj
1254 1181 1877 899 3836 1581 1650 2637 5516 5603 2764 4123 3836 3847 2050 1254

he heard the crowd going   by, he asked   what was happening. **37** They told   him,   "Jesus of
→ ἀκούσας ὄχλου διαπορευομένου ← → ἐπυνθάνετο τί εἴη τοῦτο δὲ ἀπήγγειλαν αὐτῷ ὅτι Ἰησοῦς →
pt.aa.nsm n.gsm pt.pm.gsm v.imi.3s r.nsn v.pao.3s r.nsn cj v.aai.3p r.dsm.3 cj n.nsm
201 4063 1388 4785 5515 1639 4047 1254 550 899 4022 2652

Nazareth is passing by." **38** He called out,   "Jesus, Son of David, have mercy on me!" ¶ **39**
⸤ὁ Ναζωραῖος⸥ παρέρχεται ← καὶ → ἐβόησεν ← λέγων Ἰησοῦ υἱὲ → Δαυίδ ἐλέησον με καὶ
d.nsm n.nsm v.pmi.3s cj v.aai.3s pt.pa.nsm n.vsm n.vsm n.gsm v.aam.2s r.as.1 cj
3836 3717 4216 2779 1066 3306 2652 5626 1253 1796 1609 2779

Those who led   the way rebuked him and told him to be quiet, but he shouted all   the more, "Son of
οἱ ← προάγοντες ← ἐπετίμων αὐτῷ ἵνα → σιγήσῃ δὲ αὐτὸς ἔκραζεν πολλῷ μᾶλλον υἱὲ →
d.npm pt.pa.npm v.iai.3p r.dsm.3 cj v.aas.3s cj r.nsm v.iai.3s a.dsn adv.c n.vsm
3836 4575 2203 899 2671 4967 1254 899 3189 4498 3437 5626

David, have mercy on me!" **40** Jesus   stopped and ordered the man to be brought to him.   When he
Δαυίδ → ἐλέησον με δὲ ὁ Ἰησοῦς σταθεὶς ἐκέλευσεν αὐτὸν → ἀχθῆναι πρὸς αὐτόν δὲ ↱ αὐτοῦ
n.gsm v.aam.2s r.as.1 cj d.nsm n.nsm pt.ap.nsm v.aai.3s r.asm.3 f.ap p.a r.asm.3 cj r.gsm.3
1253 1796 1609 1254 3836 2652 2705 3027 899 72 4639 899 1254 1581 899

came   near, Jesus asked   him, **41** "What do you want me to do   for you?"   "Lord, I want to see,"   he
ἐγγίσαντος ← ἐπηρώτησεν αὐτὸν τί → θέλεις → ποιήσω σοι δὲ κύριε ἵνα ἀναβλέψω ὁ
pt.aa.gsm v.aai.3s r.asm.3 r.asn v.pai.2s v.aas.1s r.ds.2 cj n.vsm cj v.aas.1s d.nsm
1581 2089 899 5515 2527 4472 5148 1254 3261 2671 329 3836

replied. ¶ **42** Jesus   said to him, "Receive your sight;   your faith   has healed you." **43**
εἶπεν καὶ ὁ Ἰησοῦς εἶπεν → αὐτῷ ⸃ ἀνάβλεψον σου ⸤ἡ πίστις⸥ → σέσωκέν σε καὶ
v.aai.3s cj d.nsm n.nsm v.aai.3s r.dsm.3 v.aam.2s r.gs.2 d.nsf n.nsf v.rai.3s r.as.2 cj
3306 2779 3836 2652 3306 899 329 5148 3836 4411 5392 5148 2779

Immediately he received his sight   and followed Jesus, praising God.   When all the people saw it, they
παραχρῆμα → → ἀνέβλεψεν καὶ ἠκολούθει αὐτῷ δοξάζων ⸤τὸν θεόν⸥ καὶ → πᾶς ὁ λαὸς ἰδὼν
adv v.aai.3s cj v.iai.3s r.dsm.3 pt.pa.nsm d.asm n.asm cj a.nsm d.nsm n.nsm pt.aa.nsm
4202 329 2779 199 899 1519 3836 2536 2779 1625 4246 3836 3295 1625

also praised   God.
⸤ἔδωκεν αἶνον⸥ ⸤τῷ θεῷ⸥
v.aai.3s n.asm d.dsm n.dsm
1443 142 3836 2536

Zacchaeus the Tax Collector

19:1   Jesus entered Jericho   and was passing through. **2**   A man was there by the name   of
Καὶ εἰσελθὼν ⸤τὴν Ἰεριχώ⸥ → διήρχετο ← Καὶ ἰδοὺ ἀνὴρ → → ⸤ὀνόματι καλούμενος⸥
cj pt.aa.nsm d.asf n.asf v.imi.3s cj j n.nsm n.dsn pt.pp.nsm
2779 1656 3836 2637 1451 2779 2627 467 3950 2813

Zacchaeus;   he   was a chief tax   collector and   was wealthy. **3**   He wanted to see who Jesus
Ζακχαῖος καὶ αὐτὸς ἦν → ἀρχιτελώνης ← καὶ αὐτὸς πλούσιος καὶ → ἐζήτει → ἰδεῖν τίς ⸤τὸν Ἰησοῦν⸥
n.nsm cj r.nsm v.iai.3s n.nsm cj r.nsm a.nsm cj v.iai.3s f.aa r.nsm d.asm n.asm
2405 2779 899 1639 803 2779 899 4454 2779 2426 1625 5515 3836 2652

was, but being a short   man he could not, because of the crowd. **4** So he ran   ahead
ἐστιν καὶ ὅτι ἦν ⸤τῇ ἡλικίᾳ μικρός⸥ ← → ἠδύνατο οὐκ ἀπὸ ← τοῦ ὄχλου καὶ → προδραμὼν ⸤εἰς τὸ ἔμπροσθεν⸥
v.pai.3s cj cj v.iai.3s d.dsf n.dsf a.nsm v.ipi.3s pl p.g d.gsm n.gsm cj pt.aa.nsm p.a d.asn adv
1639 2779 4022 1639 3836 2461 3625 1538 4024 608 3836 4063 2779 4731 1650 3836 1869

συνῆκαν καὶ ἦν τὸ ῥῆμα τοῦτο κεκρυμμένον ἀπ᾽ αὐτῶν καὶ οὐκ ἐγίνωσκον τὰ λεγόμενα.
18:35 Ἐγένετο δὲ ἐν τῷ ἐγγίζειν αὐτὸν εἰς Ἰεριχὼ τυφλός τις ἐκάθητο παρὰ τὴν ὁδὸν ἐπαιτῶν. **36** ἀκούσας δὲ ὄχλου διαπορευομένου ἐπυνθάνετο τί εἴη τοῦτο. **37** ἀπήγγειλαν δὲ αὐτῷ ὅτι Ἰησοῦς ὁ Ναζωραῖος παρέρχεται. **38** καὶ ἐβόησεν λέγων, Ἰησοῦ υἱὲ Δαυίδ, ἐλέησόν με. ¶ **39** καὶ οἱ προάγοντες ἐπετίμων αὐτῷ ἵνα σιγήσῃ, αὐτὸς δὲ πολλῷ μᾶλλον ἔκραζεν, Υἱὲ Δαυίδ, ἐλέησόν με. **40** σταθεὶς δὲ ὁ Ἰησοῦς ἐκέλευσεν αὐτὸν ἀχθῆναι πρὸς αὐτόν. ἐγγίσαντος δὲ αὐτοῦ ἐπηρώτησεν αὐτόν, **41** Τί σοι θέλεις ποιήσω; ὁ δὲ εἶπεν, Κύριε, ἵνα ἀναβλέψω. ¶ **42** καὶ ὁ Ἰησοῦς εἶπεν αὐτῷ, Ἀνάβλεψον· ἡ πίστις σου σέσωκέν σε. **43** καὶ παραχρῆμα ἀνέβλεψεν καὶ ἠκολούθει αὐτῷ δοξάζων τὸν θεόν. καὶ πᾶς ὁ λαὸς ἰδὼν ἔδωκεν αἶνον τῷ θεῷ.

19:1 Καὶ εἰσελθὼν διήρχετο τὴν Ἰεριχώ. **2** καὶ ἰδοὺ ἀνὴρ ὀνόματι καλούμενος Ζακχαῖος, καὶ αὐτὸς ἦν ἀρχιτελώνης καὶ αὐτὸς πλούσιος· **3** καὶ ἐζήτει ἰδεῖν τὸν Ἰησοῦν τίς ἐστιν καὶ οὐκ ἠδύνατο ἀπὸ τοῦ ὄχλου, ὅτι τῇ ἡλικίᾳ μικρὸς ἦν. **4** καὶ προδραμὼν εἰς τὸ ἔμπροσθεν ἀνέβη ἐπὶ συκομορέαν ἵνα ἴδῃ αὐτὸν ὅτι ἐκείνης ἤμελλεν διέρχεσθαι. ¶ **5** καὶ ὡς ἦλθεν ἐπὶ τὸν

and climbed   a sycamore-fig tree   to   see   him, since Jesus was   coming   that   way.   ¶   **5** When Jesus
ἀνέβη   ἐπὶ   συκομορέαν ←   ἵνα ἴδῃ αὐτὸν ὅτι   ἤμελλεν διέρχεσθαι ἐκείνης ←   καὶ ὡς
v.aai.3s   p.a   n.asf   cj   v.aas.3s r.asm.3 cj   v.iai.3s f.pm   r.gsf   cj cj
326   2093   5191   2671 1625 899   4022   3516   1451   1697   2779 6055

reached   the spot, he   looked   up and said to   him, "Zacchaeus, come   down immediately. I
ἦλθεν   ἐπὶ τὸν τόπον ὁ Ἰησοῦς ἀναβλέψας ←   εἶπεν πρὸς αὐτόν Ζακχαῖε   κατάβηθι ←   σπεύσας   γάρ με
v.aai.3s   p.a r.asm n.asm r.nsm n.nsm pt.aa.nsm   v.aai.3s p.a r.asm.3 n.vsm   v.aam.2s   pt.aa.nsm   cj r.as.1
2262   2093 3836 5536 3836 2652 329   3306 4639 899   2405   2849   5067   1142 1609

must stay   at your house   today." **6** So he came down at once   and welcomed him gladly.   ¶   **7**   All
δεῖ μεῖναι ἐν σου τῷ οἴκῳ σήμερον καὶ → κατέβη ←   → σπεύσας καὶ ὑπεδέξατο αὐτὸν χαίρων   καὶ πάντες
v.pai.3s f.aa p.d r.gs.2 r.dsm n.dsm adv   cj   v.aai.3s   pt.aa.nsm cj v.ami.3s r.asm.3 pt.pa.nsm   cj a.npm
1256 3531 1877 5148 3836 3875 3875 adv   2779 2849   5067   2779 5685   899   5897   2779 4246

the people saw   this and began to mutter,   "He has gone   to be the guest   of a
ἰδόντες   →   → διεγόγγυζον λέγοντες ὅτι →   → εἰσῆλθεν → →   καταλῦσαι παρὰ
pt.aa.npm   v.iai.3p   pt.pa.npm cj   v.aai.3s   f.aa   p.d
1625   1339   3306   4022   1656   2907   4123

'sinner.'"   ¶   **8** But Zacchaeus stood up and said to   the Lord, "Look, Lord! Here and now I give
ἁμαρτωλῷ ἀνδρὶ   δὲ Ζακχαῖος σταθεὶς ←   εἶπεν πρὸς τὸν κύριον ἰδοὺ κύριε   → δίδωμι
a.dsm   n.dsm   cj n.nsm   pt.ap.nsm   v.aai.3s p.a r.asm n.asm j   n.vsm   v.pai.1s
283   467   1254 2405   2705   3306 4639 3836 3261 2627 3261   1443

half   of my possessions   to the poor, and if I have cheated   anybody out of anything, I will pay
τὰ ἡμίσια → μου τῶν ὑπαρχόντων → τοῖς πτωχοῖς καὶ εἰ → → ἐσυκοφάντησα τινός →   → τι   → ἀποδίδωμι
d.apn a.apn r.gs.1 d.gpn pt.pa.gpn   d.dpm a.dpm cj cj   v.aai.1s   r.gsm   r.asn   v.pai.1s
3836 2468   5639 1609 3836 5639   3836 4777 2779 1623   5193   5516   5516   625

back four   times the amount." **9**   Jesus   said to   him, "Today salvation has come to this house,
← τετραπλοῦν ←   δὲ ὁ Ἰησοῦς εἶπεν πρὸς αὐτὸν ὅτι σήμερον σωτηρία → ἐγένετο → τούτῳ τῷ οἴκῳ
adv   cj r.nsm n.nsm v.aai.3s p.a r.asm.3 cj adv   n.nsf   v.ami.3s   r.dsm r.dsm n.dsm
5487   1254 3836 2652 3306 4639 899 4022 4958   5401   1181   4047 3836 3875

because this man, too, is   a son of Abraham. **10** For the Son of Man   came to seek and to save what was
καθότι αὐτὸς καὶ ἔστιν υἱὸς → Ἀβραάμ   γὰρ ὁ υἱὸς → τοῦ ἀνθρώπου ἦλθεν → ζητῆσαι καὶ → σῶσαι τὸ →
cj   r.nsm adv v.pai.3s n.nsm n.gsm   cj d.nsm n.nsm d.gsm n.gsm   v.aai.3s f.aa   cj   f.aa d.asn
2776   899   2779 1639 5626 11   1142 3836 5626 3836 476   2262   2426   2779 5392 3836

lost."
ἀπολωλός
pt.ra.asn
660

The Parable of the Ten Minas

19:11 While they were listening to this, he went on to tell them a parable, because he was   near
δὲ →   αὐτῶν → Ἀκουόντων ← ταῦτα προσθεὶς ← → εἶπεν   παραβολὴν διὰ   αὐτὸν τὸ εἶναι ἔγγυς
cj   r.gpm.3   pt.pa.gpm   r.apn   pt.aa.nsm   v.aai.3s   n.asf   p.a   r.asm.3 d.asn f.pa p.g
1254 201   899   201   4047   4707   3306   4130   1328 899   3836 1639 1584

Jerusalem and the people thought that the kingdom of God   was going to appear   at once. **12** He said:
Ἰερουσαλὴμ καὶ   αὐτοὺς δοκεῖν ὅτι ἡ βασιλεία → τοῦ θεοῦ → μέλλει → ἀναφαίνεσθαι → παραχρῆμα οὖν → εἶπεν
n.gsf   cj   r.apm.3 f.pa cj d.nsf n.nsf   d.gsm n.gsm v.pai.3s f.pp   adv   cj   v.aai.3s
2647   2779   899   1506 4022 3836 993   3836 2536 3516   428   4202   4036 3306

"A man   of noble birth went   to a distant country to have himself appointed king   and then to return.
τις ἄνθρωπος εὐγενὴς ← ἐπορεύθη εἰς μακρὰν χώραν → → ἑαυτῷ λαβεῖν βασιλείαν καὶ → ὑποστρέψαι
r.nsm n.nsm a.nsm   v.api.3s p.a a.asf n.asf   r.dsm.3 f.aa n.asf   cj   f.aa
5516 476   2302   4513   1650 3431 6001   3284 3284 1571 3284 993   2779   5715

13 So he called ten of his   servants and gave them ten minas. 'Put this money to work,'   he said,
δὲ → καλέσας δέκα ἑαυτοῦ δούλους   ἔδωκεν αὐτοῖς δέκα μνᾶς καὶ   → πραγματεύσασθε → εἶπεν πρὸς
cj   pt.aa.nsm a.apm r.gsm.3 n.apm   v.aai.3s r.dpm.3 a.apf n.apf cj   v.amm.2p   v.aai.3s p.a
1254 2813   1274 1571 1529   1443   899   1274 3641 2779   4549   3306 4639

'until I come back.' **14** "But his   subjects hated him and sent   a delegation after him to say,
αὐτοὺς ἐν ᾧ → ἔρχομαι   δὲ αὐτοῦ οἱ πολῖται ἐμίσουν αὐτὸν καὶ ἀπέστειλαν πρεσβείαν ὀπίσω αὐτοῦ → λέγοντες
r.apm.3 p.d r.dsm v.pmi.1s cj r.gsm.3 d.npm n.npm v.iai.3p r.asm.3 cj v.aai.3p n.asf   p.g   r.gsm.3 pt.pa.npm
899   1877 4005 2262   1254 899 3836 4489   3631   899   2779 690   4561   3958 899   3306

τόπον, ἀναβλέψας ὁ Ἰησοῦς εἶπεν πρὸς αὐτόν, Ζακχαῖε, σπεύσας κατάβηθι, σήμερον γὰρ ἐν τῷ οἴκῳ σου δεῖ με μεῖναι. **6** καὶ σπεύσας κατέβη καὶ ὑπεδέξατο αὐτὸν χαίρων. ¶ **7** καὶ ἰδόντες πάντες διεγόγγυζον λέγοντες ὅτι Παρὰ ἁμαρτωλῷ ἀνδρὶ εἰσῆλθεν καταλῦσαι. ¶ **8** σταθεὶς δὲ Ζακχαῖος εἶπεν πρὸς τὸν κύριον, Ἰδοὺ τὰ ἡμίσιά μου τῶν ὑπαρχόντων, κύριε, τοῖς πτωχοῖς δίδωμι, καὶ εἴ τινός τι ἐσυκοφάντησα ἀποδίδωμι τετραπλοῦν. **9** εἶπεν δὲ πρὸς αὐτὸν ὁ Ἰησοῦς ὅτι Σήμερον σωτηρία τῷ οἴκῳ τούτῳ ἐγένετο, καθότι καὶ αὐτὸς υἱὸς Ἀβραάμ ἐστιν· **10** ἦλθεν γὰρ ὁ υἱὸς τοῦ ἀνθρώπου ζητῆσαι καὶ σῶσαι τὸ ἀπολωλός.

19:11 Ἀκουόντων δὲ αὐτῶν ταῦτα προσθεὶς εἶπεν παραβολὴν διὰ τὸ ἐγγὺς εἶναι Ἰερουσαλὴμ αὐτὸν καὶ δοκεῖν αὐτοὺς ὅτι παραχρῆμα μέλλει ἡ βασιλεία τοῦ θεοῦ ἀναφαίνεσθαι. **12** εἶπεν οὖν, Ἄνθρωπός τις εὐγενὴς ἐπορεύθη εἰς χώραν μακρὰν λαβεῖν ἑαυτῷ βασιλείαν καὶ ὑποστρέψαι. **13** καλέσας δὲ δέκα δούλους ἑαυτοῦ ἔδωκεν αὐτοῖς δέκα μνᾶς καὶ εἶπεν πρὸς αὐτούς, Πραγματεύσασθε ἐν ᾧ ἔρχομαι. **14** οἱ δὲ πολῖται αὐτοῦ ἐμίσουν αὐτὸν καὶ ἀπέστειλαν πρεσβείαν ὀπίσω αὐτοῦ λέγοντες, Οὐ

'We don't want this man to be   our king.'   ¶   15   "He was made king,   however,
→   οὐ   θέλομεν τοῦτον ←   → →   ἐφ' ἡμᾶς βασιλεῦσαι   καὶ ἐγένετο αὐτὸν → λαβόντα ⌜τὴν βασιλείαν⌝
     pl   v.pai.1p r.asm   p.a r.ap.1 f.aa   cj   v.ami.3s r.asm.3   pt.aa.asm d.asf n.asf
2527 4024 2527   4047   996 996 2093 7005 996   2779 1181   899   3284   3836 993

and returned   home. Then he sent   for the servants   to whom he had given the
ἐν τῷ ἐπανελθεῖν⌝   καὶ   εἶπεν φωνηθῆναι αὐτῷ ←   τοὺς δούλους τούτους → οἷς   δεδώκει τὸ
p.d d.dsn f.aa   cj   v.aai.3s f.ap   r.dsm.3   d.apm n.apm r.apm   r.dpm   v.lai.3s d.asn
1877 3836 2059   2779   3306   5888   899   3836 1529 4047   4005   1443   3836

money, in order to find out what they had gained   with it. ¶   16   "The first one came   and
ἀργύριον ἵνα ←   ← γνοῖ ← τί   →   → διεπραγματεύσαντο   δὲ ὁ   πρῶτος   παρεγένετο
n.asn   cj   v.aas.3s r.asn   v.ami.3p   cj d.nsm a.nsm   v.ami.3s
736   2671   1182   5515   1390   1254 3836 4755   4134

said, 'Sir, your mina   has earned   ten more.' 17   "'Well done, my good servant!' his master replied.
λέγων κύριε σου ⌜ἡ μνᾶ⌝ → προσηργάσατο δέκα μνᾶς καὶ → εὖγε ἀγαθὲ δοῦλε   εἶπεν αὐτῷ
pt.pa.nsm n.vsm r.gs.2 d.nsf n.nsf v.ami.3s a.apf n.apf cj   adv a.vsm n.vsm   v.aai.3s r.dsm.3
3306 3261 5148 3836 3641   4664   1274 3641 2779   2301 19   1529   3306 899

'Because you have been trustworthy in a very small matter, take   charge of ten cities.' ¶   18
ὅτι   →   →   ἐγένου πιστὸς   ἐν → ἐλαχίστῳ ←   ἴσθι ἔχων⌝ ἐξουσίαν ἐπάνω δέκα πόλεων   καὶ
cj   v.ami.2s a.nsm   p.d   a.dsn.s   v.pam.2s pt.pa.nsm n.asf p.g a.gpf n.gpf   cj
4022   1181   4412   1877   1788   1639 2400 2026   2062 1274 4484   2779

"The second came and said, 'Sir, your mina   has earned five more.' 19   "His master answered,   'You
ὁ   δεύτερος ἦλθεν   λέγων κύριε σου ⌜ἡ μνᾶ⌝ → ἐποίησεν πέντε μνᾶς   δὲ   εἶπεν καὶ τούτῳ σὺ καὶ
d.nsm a.nsm v.aai.3s pt.pa.nsm n.vsm r.gs.2 d.nsf n.nsf v.aai.3s a.apf n.apf cj   v.aai.3s adv r.dsm r.ns.2 adv
3836 1311   2262   3306 3261 5148 3836 3641   4472   4297 3641 1254   3306 2779 4047 5148 2779

take charge of   five cities.' ¶   20 "Then another   servant came and said, 'Sir, here is your mina; I have
γίνου   ἐπάνω πέντε πόλεων   καὶ   ὁ ἕτερος⌝   ἦλθεν λέγων κύριε ἰδοὺ σου ⌜ἡ μνᾶ⌝ →
v.pmm.2s p.g a.gpf n.gpf   cj   d.nsm r.nsm   v.aai.3s pt.pa.nsm n.vsm j   r.gs.2 d.nsf n.nsf
1181   2062 4297 4484   2779 3836 2283   2262   3306 3261 2627 5148 3836 3641

kept it laid   away in a piece of cloth.   21   I was afraid   of you, because you are a hard man.   You
εἶχον ἦν ἀποκειμένην ←   ἐν → σουδαρίῳ   γάρ → ἐφοβούμην ← σε ὅτι → εἶ αὐστηρὸς ἄνθρωπος →
v.iai.1s r.asf pt.pm.asf   p.d   n.dsn   cj   v.ipi.1s   r.as.2 cj   v.pai.2s a.nsm n.nsm
2400 4005 641   1877   5051   1142   5828   5148 4022   1639 893 476

take out what you did not put   in and reap what you did not sow.' 22 "His master replied,   'I will judge
αἴρεις ← ὃ → οὐκ ἔθηκας καὶ θερίζεις ὃ → → οὐκ ἔσπειρας   λέγει αὐτῷ → κρινῶ
v.pai.2s   r.asn   pl v.aai.2s cj v.pai.2s r.asn   pl v.aai.2s   v.pai.3s r.dsm.3   v.fai.1s
149   4005   5502 5502 4024 5502 2779 2545 4005   5062 5062 4024 5062   3306 899   3212

you by your own words, you wicked servant! You knew, did you, that I   am a hard   man,   taking out what
σε ἐκ σου τοῦ στόματος πονηρὲ δοῦλε → ἤδεις   ὅτι ἐγώ εἰμι αὐστηρός ἄνθρωπος αἴρων ← ὃ
r.as.2 p.g r.gs.2 d.gsn n.gsn   a.vsm n.vsm   v.lai.2s cj r.ns.1 v.pai.1s a.nsm n.nsm pt.pa.nsm r.asn
5148 1666 5148 3836 5125 4505   1529   3857   4022 1609 1639 893   476   149   4005

I   did not put in, and reaping what I   did not sow?   23 Why   then didn't you put my money   on deposit,
→ → οὐκ ἔθηκα καὶ θερίζων ὃ   → → οὐκ ἔσπειρα   ⌜διὰ τί⌝ καὶ οὐκ → ἔδωκας μου ⌜τὸ ἀργύριον⌝ ἐπὶ τράπεζαν
     pl v.aai.1s cj pt.pa.nsm r.asn   pl v.aai.1s   p.a r.asn cj   pl   v.aai.2s r.gs.1 d.asn n.asn   p.a n.asf
5502 5502 4024 4755 2779 2545 4005   5062 5062 4024 5062   1328 5515 2779 4024   1443 1609 3836 736   2093 5544

so that when I came back, I could have collected it with interest?' ¶   24 "Then he said to those standing
κἀγὼ ←   → → ἐλθὼν   ἂν → ἔπραξα   αὐτὸ σὺν τόκῳ   καὶ → εἶπεν → τοῖς παρεστῶσιν
crasis   pt.aa.nsm pl   v.aai.1s   r.asn.3 p.d n.dsm   cj   v.aai.3s d.dpm pt.ra.dpm
2743   2262   4556 323 4556   899 5250 5527   2779   3306 3836 4225

by, 'Take his mina away from him and give it to the one who has   ten minas.'   25 "'Sir,' they said,   'he
← ἄρατε τὴν μνᾶν ←   ἀπ' αὐτοῦ καὶ δότε   → τῷ ← → ἔχοντι δέκα ⌜τὰς μνᾶς⌝ καὶ κύριε → εἶπαν αὐτῷ
v.aam.2p d.asf n.asf   p.g r.gsm.3 cj v.aam.2p   d.dsm   pt.pa.dsm a.apf d.apf n.apf   cj n.vsm   v.aai.3p r.dsm.3
149   3836 3641   608 899 2779 1443   3836   2400 1274 3836 3641   2779 3261   3306 899

already has ten!'   26 "He replied, 'I tell you that to everyone who has, more will be given,   but as for the one
ἔχει δέκα μνᾶς   → λέγω ὑμῖν ὅτι   → παντὶ τῷ ἔχοντι   δοθήσεται   δὲ ← ἀπὸ τοῦ
v.pai.3s a.apf n.apf   v.pai.1s r.dp.2 cj   a.dsm d.dsm pt.pa.dsm   v.fpi.3s   cj   p.g d.gsm
2400 1274 3641   3306 7007 4022   4246 3836 2400   1443   1254   608 3836

θέλομεν τοῦτον βασιλεῦσαι ἐφ' ἡμᾶς. ¶ 15 Καὶ ἐγένετο ἐν τῷ ἐπανελθεῖν αὐτὸν λαβόντα τὴν βασιλείαν καὶ εἶπεν φωνηθῆναι
αὐτῷ τοὺς δούλους τούτους οἷς δεδώκει τὸ ἀργύριον, ἵνα γνοῖ τί διεπραγματεύσαντο. ¶ 16 παρεγένετο δὲ ὁ πρῶτος λέγων,
Κύριε, ἡ μνᾶ σου δέκα προσηργάσατο μνᾶς. 17 καὶ εἶπεν αὐτῷ, Εὖγε, ἀγαθὲ δοῦλε, ὅτι ἐν ἐλαχίστῳ πιστὸς ἐγένου, ἴσθι ἐξουσίαν
ἔχων ἐπάνω δέκα πόλεων. ¶ 18 καὶ ἦλθεν ὁ δεύτερος λέγων, Ἡ μνᾶ σου, κύριε, ἐποίησεν πέντε μνᾶς. 19 εἶπεν δὲ καὶ τούτῳ,
Καὶ σὺ ἐπάνω γίνου πέντε πόλεων. ¶ 20 καὶ ἕτερος ἦλθεν λέγων, Κύριε, ἰδοὺ ἡ μνᾶ σου ἣν εἶχον ἀποκειμένην ἐν σουδαρίῳ·
21 ἐφοβούμην γάρ σε, ὅτι ἄνθρωπος αὐστηρὸς εἶ, αἴρεις ὃ οὐκ ἔθηκας καὶ θερίζεις ὃ οὐκ ἔσπειρας. 22 λέγει αὐτῷ, Ἐκ τοῦ
στόματός σου κρίνω σε, πονηρὲ δοῦλε. ᾔδεις ὅτι ἐγὼ ἄνθρωπος αὐστηρός εἰμι, αἴρων ὃ οὐκ ἔθηκα καὶ θερίζων ὃ οὐκ ἔσπειρα;
23 καὶ διὰ τί οὐκ ἔδωκάς μου τὸ ἀργύριον ἐπὶ τράπεζαν; κἀγὼ ἐλθὼν σὺν τόκῳ ἂν αὐτὸ ἔπραξα. ¶ 24 καὶ τοῖς παρεστῶσιν
εἶπεν, Ἄρατε ἀπ' αὐτοῦ τὴν μνᾶν καὶ δότε τῷ τὰς δέκα μνᾶς ἔχοντι 25 —καὶ εἶπαν αὐτῷ, Κύριε, ἔχει δέκα μνᾶς— 26 λέγω

who has	nothing,	even	what	he	has	will be taken	away.	**27** But	those	enemies		of mine	who	did	not
← ἔχοντος	μὴ	καὶ	ὃ	→	ἔχει	→ → ἀρθήσεται	←	πλὴν	τούτους	⸢τοὺς ἐχθρούς⸣	→	μου	τοὺς	⸢	μὴ
pt.pa.gsm	adv	cj	r.asn		v.pai.3s	v.fpi.3s		cj	r.apm	d.apm a.apm		r.gs.1	d.apm		pl
2400	3590	2779	4005		2400	149		4440	4047	3836 2398		1609	3836	2527	3590

want	me	to be king	over	them	– bring	them	here	and	kill		them	in front		of me.'"
θελήσαντάς	με	→ → βασιλεῦσαι	ἐπ᾽	αὐτοὺς	ἀγάγετε		ὧδε	καὶ	κατασφάξατε	αὐτοὺς		ἔμπροσθεν	←	μου
pt.aa.apm	r.as.1	f.aa	r.a	r.apm.3	v.aam.2p		adv	cj	v.aam.2p	r.apm.3		p.g		r.gs.1
2527	1609	996	2093	899	72		6045	2779	2956	899		1869		1609

The Triumphal Entry

19:28	After Jesus had said	this,	he went	on ahead,	going	up to	Jerusalem.	**29**		As he
Καὶ →	→ → εἰπὼν	ταῦτα	→ ἐπορεύετο	→ ἔμπροσθεν	ἀναβαίνων	← εἰς	Ἱεροσόλυμα	Καὶ	ἐγένετο	ὡς
cj	pt.aa.nsm	r.apn	v.imi.3s	adv	pt.pa.nsm	p.a	n.apn	cj	v.ami.3s	cj
2779	3306	4047	4513	1869	326	1650	2642	2779	1181	6055

approached	Bethphage	and	Bethany	at	the	hill	called		the Mount of Olives,	he sent	two	of his
ἤγγισεν	εἰς Βηθφαγὴ	καὶ	Βηθανίαν	πρὸς	τὸ	ὄρος	⸢τὸ καλούμενον⸣	→	→ Ἐλαιῶν	ἀπέστειλεν	δύο	→ τῶν
v.aai.3s	p.a n.asf	cj	n.asf	p.a	d.asn	n.asn	d.asn pt.pp.asn		n.gpf	v.aai.3s	a.apm	d.gpm
1581	1650 1036	2779	1029	4639	3836	4001	3836 2813		1777	690	1545	3836

disciples,	saying	to them,	**30** "Go	to	the	village	ahead	of you,	and as		you enter		it, you will find	a
μαθητῶν	λέγων		ὑπάγετε	εἰς	τὴν	κώμην	κατέναντι	←	ἐν	ᾗ	→ εἰσπορευόμενοι	→	εὑρήσετε	
n.gpm	pt.pa.nsm		v.pam.2p	p.a	d.asf	n.asf	adv		p.d	r.dsf	pt.pm.npm		v.fai.2p	
3412	3306		5632	1650	3836	3267	2978		1877	4005	1660		2351	

colt	tied	there,	which	no	one	has ever	ridden.	Untie	it	and	bring	it here.	**31**	If	anyone
πῶλον	δεδεμένον	ἐφ᾽	ὃν	οὐδεὶς	ἀνθρώπων	⸢ πώποτε	ἐκάθισεν	καὶ	λύσαντες	αὐτὸν	ἀγάγετε			καὶ	ἐάν τις
n.asn	pt.rp.asm	p.a	r.asm	a.nsm	n.gpm	adv	v.aai.3s	cj	pt.aa.npm	r.asm.3	v.aam.2p			cj	cj r.nsm
4798	1313	2093	4005	4029	476	2767	4799	2779	3395	899	72			2779 1569 5516

asks	you,	'Why		are you untying it?'		tell	him,	'The	Lord	needs	it.'"	¶	**32**	Those who
ἐρωτᾷ	ὑμᾶς	⸢ διὰ τί⸣	→	λύετε		οὕτως	ἐρεῖτε	ὅτι	ὁ κύριος	⸢χρείαν	ἔχει⸣	αὐτοῦ	δὲ	οἱ ←
v.pas.3s	r.ap.2	p.a r.asn		v.pai.2p		adv	v.fai.2p	cj	d.nsm n.nsm	n.asf	v.pai.3s	r.gsm.3	cj	d.npm
2263	7007	1328 5515		3395		4048	3306	4022	3836 3261	5970	2400	899	1254	3836

were sent	ahead	went		and found	it just as		he had told	them.	**33**	As they	were untying	the colt,
→ ἀπελθόντες	←	ἀπεσταλμένοι	εὗρον	→	καθὼς	→	εἶπεν	αὐτοῖς	δὲ	⸢ αὐτῶν⸣ →	λυόντων	τὸν πῶλον
pt.aa.npm		pt.rp.npm	v.aai.3p		cj		v.aai.3s	r.dpm.3	cj	r.gpm.3	pt.pa.gpm	d.asm n.asm
599		690	2351		2777		3306	899	1254	3395 899	3395	3836 4798

its	owners	asked		them,	"Why	are you	untying	the colt?"	**34**	They replied,		"The	Lord	needs
αὐτοῦ	⸢οἱ κύριοι⸣	εἶπαν	πρὸς	αὐτοὺς	τί	→ →	λύετε	τὸν πῶλον	δὲ	οἱ	εἶπαν	ὅτι ὁ	κύριος	⸢χρείαν ἔχει⸣
r.gsm.3	d.npm n.npm	v.aai.3p	p.a	r.apm.3	r.asn		v.pai.2p	d.asm n.asm	cj	d.npm	v.aai.3p	cj d.nsm	n.nsm	n.asf v.pai.3s
899	3836 3261	3306	4639	899	5515		3395	3836 4798	1254	3836	3306	4022 3836	3261	5970 2400

it."	¶	**35**	They brought	it	to	Jesus,		threw	their	cloaks	on	the colt	and	put
αὐτοῦ	καὶ		ἤγαγον	αὐτὸν	πρὸς	⸢τὸν Ἰησοῦν⸣	καὶ	ἐπιρίψαντες	αὐτῶν	⸢τὰ ἱμάτια⸣	ἐπὶ	τὸν πῶλον		ἐπεβίβασαν
r.gsm.3	cj		v.aai.3p	r.asm.3	p.a	d.asm n.asm	cj	pt.aa.npm	r.gpm.3	d.apn n.apn	p.a	d.asm n.asm		v.aai.3p
899	2779		72	899	4639	3836 2652	2779	2166	899	3836 2668	2093	3836 4798		2097

Jesus	on it.	**36**	As he	went	along,	people	spread	their	cloaks	on	the road.	¶	**37**	When
⸢τὸν Ἰησοῦν⸣	←	δὲ	⸢ αὐτοῦ⸣	πορευομένου	←	→	ὑπεστρώννυον	αὐτῶν	⸢τὰ ἱμάτια⸣	ἐν	τῇ ὁδῷ		δὲ	
d.asm n.asm		cj	r.gsm.3	pt.pm.gsm			v.iai.3p	r.gpm.3	d.apn n.apn	p.d	d.dsf n.dsf		cj	
3836 2652		2097	899	4513			5716	899	3836 2668	1877	3836 3847		1254 1581	

he	came	near		the place	where	the road	goes	down	the	Mount of Olives,		the whole	crowd of
αὐτοῦ	→	ἐγγίζοντος	ἤδη		πρὸς	τῇ	→	καταβάσει	τοῦ	ὄρους	⸢τῶν ἐλαιῶν⸣	τὸ ἄπαν	πλῆθος →
r.gsm.3		pt.pa.gsm	adv		p.d	d.dsf		n.dsf	d.gsn	n.gsn	d.gpf n.gpf	d.nsn a.nsn	n.nsn
899		1581	2453		4639	3836		2853	3836	4001	3836 1777	3836 570	4436

disciples	began	joyfully	to praise	God		in	loud	voices	for	all	the miracles		they had	seen:
⸢τῶν μαθητῶν⸣	ἤρξαντο	χαίροντες	→ αἰνεῖν	⸢τὸν θεόν⸣	→	μεγάλῃ	φωνῇ		περὶ	πασῶν	δυνάμεων	ὧν →	→ εἶδον	λέγοντες
d.gpm n.gpm	v.ami.3p	pt.pa.npm	f.pa	d.asm n.asm		a.dsf	n.dsf		p.g	a.gpf	n.gpf	r.gpf	v.aai.3p	pt.pa.npm
3836 3412	806	5897	140	3836 2536		3489	5889		4309	4246	1539	4005	1625	3306

38 "Blessed	is	the	king	who comes	in	the	name		of the Lord!"	"Peace	in	heaven	and	glory	in	the highest!"
εὐλογημένος	ὁ		βασιλεὺς ὁ	ἐρχόμενος	ἐν		ὀνόματι	→	κυρίου	εἰρήνη	ἐν	οὐρανῷ	καὶ	δόξα	ἐν	ὑψίστοις
pt.rp.nsm	d.nsm		n.nsm d.nsm	pt.pm.nsm	p.d		n.dsn		n.gsm	n.nsf	p.d	n.dsm	cj	n.nsf	p.d	a.dpm.s
2328	3836		995 3836	2262	1877		3950		3261	1645	1877	4041	2779	1518	1877	5736

ὑμῖν ὅτι παντὶ τῷ ἔχοντι δοθήσεται, ἀπὸ δὲ τοῦ μὴ ἔχοντος καὶ ὃ ἔχει ἀρθήσεται. 27 πλὴν τοὺς ἐχθρούς μου τούτους τοὺς μὴ θελήσαντάς με βασιλεῦσαι ἐπ᾽ αὐτοὺς ἀγάγετε ὧδε καὶ κατασφάξατε αὐτοὺς ἔμπροσθέν μου.

19:28 Καὶ εἰπὼν ταῦτα ἐπορεύετο ἔμπροσθεν ἀναβαίνων εἰς Ἱεροσόλυμα. 29 Καὶ ἐγένετο ὡς ἤγγισεν εἰς Βηθφαγὴ καὶ Βηθανία[ν] πρὸς τὸ ὄρος τὸ καλούμενον Ἐλαιῶν, ἀπέστειλεν δύο τῶν μαθητῶν 30 λέγων, Ὑπάγετε εἰς τὴν κατέναντι κώμην, ἐν ᾗ εἰσπορευόμενοι εὑρήσετε πῶλον δεδεμένον, ἐφ᾽ ὃν οὐδεὶς πώποτε ἀνθρώπων ἐκάθισεν, καὶ λύσαντες αὐτὸν ἀγάγετε. 31 καὶ ἐάν τις ὑμᾶς ἐρωτᾷ, Διὰ τί λύετε; οὕτως ἐρεῖτε ὅτι Ὁ κύριος αὐτοῦ χρείαν ἔχει. ¶ 32 ἀπελθόντες δὲ οἱ ἀπεσταλμένοι εὗρον καθὼς εἶπεν αὐτοῖς. 33 λυόντων δὲ αὐτῶν τὸν πῶλον εἶπαν οἱ κύριοι αὐτοῦ πρὸς αὐτούς, Τί λύετε τὸν πῶλον; 34 οἱ δὲ εἶπαν ὅτι Ὁ κύριος αὐτοῦ χρείαν ἔχει. ¶ 35 καὶ ἤγαγον αὐτὸν πρὸς τὸν Ἰησοῦν καὶ ἐπιρίψαντες αὐτῶν τὰ ἱμάτια ἐπὶ τὸν πῶλον ἐπεβίβασαν τὸν Ἰησοῦν. 36 πορευομένου δὲ αὐτοῦ ὑπεστρώννυον τὰ ἱμάτια αὐτῶν ἐν τῇ ὁδῷ. ¶ 37 Ἐγγίζοντος δὲ αὐτοῦ ἤδη πρὸς τῇ καταβάσει τοῦ Ὄρους τῶν Ἐλαιῶν ἤρξαντο ἅπαν τὸ πλῆθος τῶν μαθητῶν χαίροντες αἰνεῖν τὸν θεὸν φωνῇ μεγάλῃ περὶ πασῶν

39 Some of the Pharisees in the crowd said to Jesus, "Teacher, rebuke your disciples!" **40** "I tell you,"
καὶ τινες → τῶν Φαρισαίων ἀπὸ τοῦ ὄχλου εἶπαν πρὸς αὐτὸν διδάσκαλε ἐπιτίμησον σου ⌜τοῖς μαθηταῖς⌝ καὶ → λέγω ὑμῖν
cj r.npm d.gpm n.gpm p.g d.gsm n.gsm v.aai.3p p.a r.asm.3 n.vsm v.aam.2s r.gs.2 d.dpm n.dpm cj v.pai.1s r.dp.2
2779 5516 3836 5757 608 3836 4063 3306 4639 899 1437 2203 5148 3836 3412 2779 3306 7007

he replied, "if they keep quiet, the stones will cry out." ¶ **41** As he approached Jerusalem
→ ἀποκριθεὶς εἶπεν ἐὰν οὗτοι → σιωπήσουσιν οἱ λίθοι → κράξουσιν ← Καὶ ὡς → ἤγγισεν
pt.ap.nsm v.aai.3s cj r.npm v.fai.3p d.npm n.npm v.fai.3p cj adv v.aai.3s
646 3306 1569 4047 4995 3836 3345 3189 2779 6055 1581

and saw the city, he wept over it **42** and said, "If you, even you, had only known on this day what
ἰδὼν τὴν πόλιν ἔκλαυσεν ἐπ᾽ αὐτὴν λέγων ὅτι εἰ καὶ σὺ → ἔγνως ἐν ταύτῃ ⌜τῇ ἡμέρᾳ⌝ τὰ
pt.aa.nsm d.asf n.asf v.aai.3s p.a r.asf.3 pt.pa.nsm cj cj adv r.ns.2 v.aai.2s p.d r.dsf d.dsf n.dsf d.apn
1625 3836 4484 3081 2093 899 3306 4022 1623 1182 2779 5148 1182 1877 4047 3836 2465 3836

would bring you peace – but now it is hidden from your eyes. **43** The days will come upon you when your
πρὸς εἰρήνην δὲ νῦν → ἐκρύβη ἀπὸ σοῦ ὀφθαλμῶν ὅτι ἡμέραι → ἥξουσιν ἐπὶ σὲ καὶ σου
p.a n.asf cj adv v.api.3s p.g r.gs.2 n.gpm cj n.npf v.fai.3p p.a r.as.2 cj r.gs.2
4639 1645 1254 3814 3221 608 5148 4057 4022 2465 2457 2093 5148 2779 5148

enemies will build an embankment against you and encircle you and hem you in on every
⌜οἱ ἐχθροί⌝ → παρεμβαλοῦσιν χάρακα → σοι καὶ περικυκλώσουσιν σε καὶ συνέξουσιν σε ← πάντοθεν
d.npm a.npm v.fai.3p n.asm r.ds.2 cj v.fai.3p r.as.2 cj v.fai.3p r.as.2 adv
3836 2398 4212 5918 5148 2779 4333 5148 2779 5309 5148 5309 4119

side. **44** They will dash you to the ground, you and the children within your walls. They will not
← καὶ → ἐδαφιοῦσιν σε ← ← ← καὶ τὰ τέκνα σου ἐν σοί καὶ → → οὐκ
cj v.fai.3p r.as.2 cj d.apn n.apn r.gs.2 p.d r.ds.2 cj pl
2779 1610 5148 1610 1610 1610 5148 2779 3836 5451 5148 1877 5148 2779 918 918 4024

leave one stone on another, because you did not recognize the time of God's coming to you."
ἀφήσουσιν λίθον ἐπὶ λίθον ἐν σοί ⌜ἀνθ᾽ ὧν⌝ → → οὐκ ἔγνως τὸν καιρὸν → ⌜τῆς ἐπισκοπῆς⌝ σου
v.fai.3p n.asm p.a n.asm p.d r.ds.2 p.g r.gpn pl v.aai.2s d.asm n.asm d.gsf n.gsf r.gs.2
918 3345 2093 3345 1877 5148 505 4005 1182 1182 4024 1182 3836 2789 3836 2175 5148

Jesus at the Temple

19:45 Then he entered the temple area and began driving out those who were selling. **46** "It is written," he
Καὶ → εἰσελθὼν εἰς τὸ ἱερὸν ← ἤρξατο ἐκβάλλειν ← τοὺς ← πωλοῦντας → γέγραπται
cj pt.aa.nsm p.a d.asn n.asn v.ami.3s f.pa d.apm pt.pa.apm v.rpi.3s
2779 1656 1650 3836 2639 806 1675 3836 4797 1211

said to them, "'My house will be a house of prayer'; but you have made it 'a den of
λέγων αὐτοῖς καὶ μου ⌜ὁ οἶκος⌝ → ἔσται οἶκος → προσευχῆς δὲ ὑμεῖς → ἐποιήσατε αὐτὸν σπήλαιον →
pt.pa.nsm r.dpm.3 cj r.gs.1 d.nsm n.nsm v.fmi.3s n.nsm n.gsf cj r.np.2 v.aai.2p r.asm.3 n.asn
3306 899 2779 1609 3836 3875 1639 3875 4666 1254 7007 4472 899 5068

robbers.'" ¶ **47** Every day he was teaching at the temple. But the chief priests, the teachers of
λῃστῶν → Καὶ τὸ καθ᾽ ἡμέραν → ἦν διδάσκων ἐν τῷ ἱερῷ δὲ οἱ ἀρχιερεῖς καὶ οἱ γραμματεῖς ←
n.gpm cj d.asn p.a n.asf v.iai.3s pt.pa.nsm p.d d.dsn n.dsn cj d.npm n.npm cj d.npm n.npm
3334 2779 3836 2848 2465 1639 1438 1877 3836 2639 1254 3836 797 2779 3836 1208

the law and the leaders among the people were trying to kill him. **48** Yet they could not find any way to
← καὶ οἱ πρῶτοι → τοῦ λαοῦ → ἐζήτουν ἀπολέσαι αὐτὸν καὶ → → οὐχ εὕρισκον τὸ τί
cj d.npm a.npm d.gsm n.gsm v.iai.3p f.aa r.asm.3 cj pl v.iai.3p d.asn r.asn
2779 3836 4755 3836 3295 2426 660 899 2779 2351 2351 4024 2351 3836 5515

do it, because all the people hung on his words.
ποιήσωσιν γὰρ ἅπας ὁ λαὸς ἐξεκρέματο ← αὐτοῦ ἀκούων
v.aas.3p cj a.nsm d.nsm n.nsm v.imi.3s r.gsm.3 pt.pa.nsm
4472 1142 570 3836 3295 1717 899 201

The Authority of Jesus Questioned

20:1 One day as he was teaching the people in the temple courts and preaching
Καὶ ἐγένετο ἐν μιᾷ ⌜τῶν ἡμερῶν⌝ → αὐτοῦ → διδάσκοντος τὸν λαὸν ἐν τῷ ἱερῷ καὶ εὐαγγελιζομένου
cj v.ami.3s p.d a.dsf d.gpf n.gpf r.gsm.3 pt.pa.gsm d.asm n.asm p.d d.dsn n.dsn cj pt.pm.gsm
2779 1181 1877 1651 3836 2465 899 1438 3836 3295 1877 3836 2639 2779 2294

ὧν εἶδον δυνάμεων, **38** λέγοντες, Εὐλογημένος ὁ ἐρχόμενος, ὁ βασιλεὺς ἐν ὀνόματι κυρίου· ἐν οὐρανῷ εἰρήνη καὶ δόξα ἐν ὑψίστοις. **39** καὶ τινες τῶν Φαρισαίων ἀπὸ τοῦ ὄχλου εἶπαν πρὸς αὐτόν, Διδάσκαλε, ἐπιτίμησον τοῖς μαθηταῖς σου. **40** καὶ ἀποκριθεὶς εἶπεν, Λέγω ὑμῖν, ἐὰν οὗτοι σιωπήσουσιν, οἱ λίθοι κράξουσιν. ¶ **41** Καὶ ὡς ἤγγισεν ἰδὼν τὴν πόλιν ἔκλαυσεν ἐπ᾽ αὐτὴν **42** λέγων ὅτι Εἰ ἔγνως ἐν τῇ ἡμέρᾳ ταύτῃ καὶ σὺ τὰ πρὸς εἰρήνην· νῦν δὲ ἐκρύβη ἀπὸ ὀφθαλμῶν σου. **43** ὅτι ἥξουσιν ἡμέραι ἐπὶ σὲ καὶ παρεμβαλοῦσιν οἱ ἐχθροί σου χάρακά σοι καὶ περικυκλώσουσίν σε καὶ συνέξουσίν σε πάντοθεν, **44** καὶ ἐδαφιοῦσίν σε καὶ τὰ τέκνα σου ἐν σοί, καὶ οὐκ ἀφήσουσιν λίθον ἐπὶ λίθον ἐν σοί, ἀνθ᾽ ὧν οὐκ ἔγνως τὸν καιρὸν τῆς ἐπισκοπῆς σου. **19:45** Καὶ εἰσελθὼν εἰς τὸ ἱερὸν ἤρξατο ἐκβάλλειν τοὺς πωλοῦντας **46** λέγων αὐτοῖς, Γέγραπται, Καὶ ἔσται ὁ οἶκός μου οἶκος προσευχῆς, ὑμεῖς δὲ αὐτὸν ἐποιήσατε σπήλαιον λῃστῶν. ¶ **47** Καὶ ἦν διδάσκων τὸ καθ᾽ ἡμέραν ἐν τῷ ἱερῷ. οἱ δὲ ἀρχιερεῖς καὶ οἱ γραμματεῖς ἐζήτουν αὐτὸν ἀπολέσαι καὶ οἱ πρῶτοι τοῦ λαοῦ, **48** καὶ οὐχ εὕρισκον τὸ τί ποιήσωσιν, ὁ λαὸς γὰρ ἅπας ἐξεκρέματο αὐτοῦ ἀκούων.
20:1 Καὶ ἐγένετο ἐν μιᾷ τῶν ἡμερῶν διδάσκοντος αὐτοῦ τὸν λαὸν ἐν τῷ ἱερῷ καὶ εὐαγγελιζομένου ἐπέστησαν οἱ ἀρχιερεῖς

the gospel, the chief priests and the teachers of the law, together with the elders, came up to him. ²
← οἱ ἀρχιερεῖς καὶ οἱ γραμματεῖς ← ← σὺν ← τοῖς πρεσβυτέροις ἐπέστησαν ← πρὸς αὐτὸν καὶ
  d.npm n.npm cj d.npm n.npm   p.d   d.dpm a.dpm v.aai.3p   p.a r.asm.3 cj
  3836 797 2779 3836 1208   5250   3836 4565 2392   4639 899 2779

"Tell us by what authority you are doing these things," they said. "Who gave you this
εἶπον ἡμῖν ἐν ποίᾳ ἐξουσίᾳ → → ποιεῖς ταῦτα ← εἶπαν λέγοντες τίς ἢ ἐστιν ὁ δούς, σοι ταύτην
v.aam.2s r.dp.1 p.d r.dsf n.dsf   v.pai.2s r.apn   v.aai.3p pt.pa.npm r.nsm cj v.pai.3s d.nsm n.nsm r.ds.2 r.asf
3306 7005 1877 4481 2026   4472 4047   3306 3306 5515 2445 1639 3836 1443 5148 4047

authority?" ³ He replied, "I will also ask you a question. Tell me, ⁴ John's
τὴν ἐξουσίαν δὲ → ἀποκριθεὶς εἶπεν πρὸς αὐτούς κἀγὼ → ἐρωτήσω ὑμᾶς λόγον καὶ εἴπατε μοι Ἰωάννου
d.asf n.asf cj pt.ap.nsm v.aai.3s p.a r.apm.3 crasis v.fai.1s r.ap.2 n.asm cj v.aam.2p r.ds.1 n.gsm
3836 2026 1254 646 3306 4639 899 2743 2263 2743 2263 7007 3364 2779 3306 1609 2722

baptism — was it from heaven, or from men?" ¶ ⁵ They discussed it among themselves and said,
τὸ βάπτισμα ἦν ← ἐξ οὐρανοῦ ἢ ἐξ ἀνθρώπων δὲ οἱ συνελογίσαντο πρὸς ἑαυτοὺς λέγοντες
d.nsn n.nsn v.iai.3s p.g n.gsm cj p.g n.gpm cj d.npm v.ami.3p p.a r.apm.3 pt.pa.npm
3836 967 1639 1666 4041 2445 1666 476 1254 3836 5199 4639 1571

"If we say, 'From heaven,' he will ask, 'Why didn't you believe him?' ⁶ But if we say, 'From men,'
ὅτι ἐὰν εἴπωμεν ἐξ οὐρανοῦ → ἐρεῖ διὰ τί οὐκ ἐπιστεύσατε αὐτῷ δὲ ἐὰν εἴπωμεν ἐξ ἀνθρώπων
cj cj v.aas.1p p.g n.gsm v.fai.3s p.a r.asn pl v.aai.2p r.dsm.3 cj cj v.aas.1p p.g n.gpm
4022 1569 3306 1666 4041 3306 1328 5515 4024 4409 899 1254 1569 3306 1666 476

all the people will stone us, because they are persuaded that John was a prophet." ⁷ So they answered,
ἅπας ὁ λαὸς → καταλιθάσει ἡμᾶς γὰρ → ἐστιν πεπεισμένος Ἰωάννην εἶναι προφήτην καὶ → ἀπεκρίθησαν
a.nsm d.nsm n.nsm v.fai.3s r.ap.1 cj v.pai.3s pt.rp.nsm n.asm f.pa n.asm cj v.api.3p
570 3836 3295 2902 7005 1142 1639 4275 2722 1639 4737 2779 646

"We don't know where it was from." ⁸ Jesus said, "Neither will I tell you by what authority I am
μὴ εἰδέναι πόθεν ← καὶ ὁ Ἰησοῦς εἶπεν αὐτοῖς οὐδὲ → ἐγὼ λέγω ὑμῖν ἐν ποίᾳ ἐξουσίᾳ → →
pl f.ra pl cj d.nsm n.nsm v.aai.3s r.dpm.3 cj r.ns.1 v.pai.1s r.dp.2 p.d r.dsf n.dsf
3590 3857 4470 2779 3836 2652 3306 899 4028 3306 1609 3306 7007 1877 4481 2026

doing these things."
ποιῶ ταῦτα ←
v.pai.1s r.apn
4472 4047

The Parable of the Tenants

20:9 He went on to tell the people this parable: "A man planted a vineyard, rented
δὲ → Ἤρξατο ← λέγειν πρὸς τὸν λαὸν ταύτην τὴν παραβολὴν τις ἄνθρωπος ἐφύτευσεν ἀμπελῶνα καὶ ἐξέδετο
cj v.ami.3s f.pa p.a d.asm n.asm r.asf d.asf n.asf r.nsm n.nsm v.aai.3s n.asm cj v.ami.3s
1254 806 3306 4639 3836 3295 4047 3836 4130 5516 476 5885 308 2779 1686

it to some farmers and went away for a long time. ¹⁰ At harvest time he sent a servant to the
αὐτὸν → γεωργοῖς καὶ ἀπεδήμησεν ← ἱκανούς χρόνους καὶ → καιρῷ → ἀπέστειλεν δοῦλον πρὸς τοὺς
r.asm.3 n.dpm cj v.aai.3s a.apm n.apm cj n.dsm v.aai.3s n.asm p.a d.apm
899 1177 2779 623 2653 5989 2779 2789 690 1529 4639 3836

tenants so they would give him some of the fruit of the vineyard. But the tenants beat him and
γεωργούς ἵνα → → δώσουσιν αὐτῷ ἀπὸ τοῦ καρποῦ → τοῦ ἀμπελῶνος δὲ οἱ γεωργοὶ δείραντες
n.apm cj v.fai.3p r.dsm.3 p.g d.gsm n.gsm d.gsm n.gsm cj d.npm n.npm pt.aa.npm
1177 2671 1443 899 608 3836 2843 3836 308 1254 3836 1177 1296

sent him away empty-handed. ¹¹ He sent another servant, but that one also they beat and
ἐξαπέστειλαν αὐτὸν ← κενόν καὶ προσέθετο πέμψαι ἕτερον δοῦλον δὲ κἀκεῖνον ← οἱ δείραντες καὶ
v.aai.3p r.asm.3 a.asm cj v.ami.3s f.aa r.asm n.asm cj adv d.npm pt.aa.npm cj
1990 899 1990 3031 2779 4707 4287 2283 1529 1254 2797 3836 1296 2779

treated shamefully and sent away empty-handed. ¹² He sent still a third, and they
ἀτιμάσαντες ← ἐξαπέστειλαν κενόν καὶ → προσέθετο πέμψαι τρίτον δὲ οἱ καὶ
pt.aa.npm v.aai.3p a.asm cj v.ami.3s f.aa a.asm cj d.npm adv
869 1990 3031 2779 4707 4287 5569 1254 3836 2779

wounded him and threw him out. ¶ ¹³ "Then the owner of the vineyard said, 'What shall I do? I will
τραυματίσαντες τοῦτον ἐξέβαλον ← δὲ ὁ κύριος τοῦ ἀμπελῶνος εἶπεν τί → → ποιήσω → →
pt.aa.npm r.asm v.aai.3p cj d.nsm n.nsm d.gsm n.gsm v.aai.3s r.asn v.aas.1s
5547 4047 1675 1254 3836 3261 3836 308 3306 5515 4472

καὶ οἱ γραμματεῖς σὺν τοῖς πρεσβυτέροις ² καὶ εἶπαν λέγοντες πρὸς αὐτόν, Εἰπὸν ἡμῖν ἐν ποίᾳ ἐξουσίᾳ ταῦτα ποιεῖς, ἢ τίς ἐστιν ὁ δούς σοι τὴν ἐξουσίαν ταύτην; ³ ἀποκριθεὶς δὲ εἶπεν πρὸς αὐτούς, Ἐρωτήσω ὑμᾶς κἀγὼ λόγον, καὶ εἴπατέ μοι· ⁴ Τὸ βάπτισμα Ἰωάννου ἐξ οὐρανοῦ ἦν ἢ ἐξ ἀνθρώπων; ¶ ⁵ οἱ δὲ συνελογίσαντο πρὸς ἑαυτοὺς λέγοντες ὅτι Ἐὰν εἴπωμεν, Ἐξ οὐρανοῦ, ἐρεῖ, Διὰ τί οὐκ ἐπιστεύσατε αὐτῷ; ⁶ ἐὰν δὲ εἴπωμεν, Ἐξ ἀνθρώπων, ὁ λαὸς ἅπας καταλιθάσει ἡμᾶς, πεπεισμένος γάρ ἐστιν Ἰωάννην προφήτην εἶναι. ⁷ καὶ ἀπεκρίθησαν μὴ εἰδέναι πόθεν. ⁸ καὶ ὁ Ἰησοῦς εἶπεν αὐτοῖς, Οὐδὲ ἐγὼ λέγω ὑμῖν ἐν ποίᾳ ἐξουσίᾳ ταῦτα ποιῶ.

20:9 Ἤρξατο δὲ πρὸς τὸν λαὸν λέγειν τὴν παραβολὴν ταύτην· Ἄνθρωπός [τις] ἐφύτευσεν ἀμπελῶνα καὶ ἐξέδετο αὐτὸν γεωργοῖς καὶ ἀπεδήμησεν χρόνους ἱκανούς. ¹⁰ καὶ καιρῷ ἀπέστειλεν πρὸς τοὺς γεωργοὺς δοῦλον ἵνα ἀπὸ τοῦ καρποῦ τοῦ ἀμπελῶνος δώσουσιν αὐτῷ· οἱ δὲ γεωργοὶ ἐξαπέστειλαν αὐτὸν δείραντες κενόν. ¹¹ καὶ προσέθετο ἕτερον πέμψαι δοῦλον· οἱ δὲ κἀκεῖνον δείραντες καὶ ἀτιμάσαντες ἐξαπέστειλαν κενόν. ¹² καὶ προσέθετο τρίτον πέμψαι· οἱ δὲ καὶ τοῦτον τραυματίσαντες ἐξέβαλον. ¶

send my son, whom I love; perhaps they will respect him.' **14** "But when the tenants saw him, they
πέμψω μου τὸν υἱόν, τὸν ἀγαπητόν ἴσως → → ἐντραπήσονται τοῦτον δὲ οἱ γεωργοὶ ἰδόντες αὐτὸν
v.fai.1s r.gs.1 d.asm n.asm d.asm a.asm adv v.fpi.3p r.asm cj d.npm n.npm pt.aa.npm r.asm.3
4287 1609 3836 5626 3836 28 2711 1956 4047 1254 1625 3836 1177 1625 899

talked the matter over. 'This is the heir,' they said. 'Let's kill him, and the
διελογίζοντο ← ← ← πρὸς ἀλλήλους οὗτος ἐστιν ὁ κληρονόμος → λέγοντες → ἀποκτείνωμεν αὐτὸν ἵνα ἡ
v.imi.3p p.a r.apm r.nsm v.pai.3s d.nsm n.nsm pt.pa.npm v.aas.1p r.asm.3 cj d.nsf
1368 4639 253 4047 1639 3836 3101 3306 650 899 2671 3836

inheritance will be ours.' **15** So they threw him out of the vineyard and killed him. ¶ "What then
κληρονομία → γένηται ἡμῶν καὶ ἐκβαλόντες αὐτὸν ἔξω → τοῦ ἀμπελῶνος ἀπέκτειναν τί οὖν
n.nsf v.ams.3s r.gp.1 cj pt.aa.npm r.asm.3 p.g d.gsm n.gsm v.aai.3p r.asn cj
3100 1181 7005 2779 1675 899 2032 3836 308 650 5515 4036

will the owner of the vineyard do to them? **16** He will come and kill those tenants and give the
→ ὁ κύριος τοῦ ἀμπελῶνος ποιήσει → αὐτοῖς → ἐλεύσεται καὶ ἀπολέσει τούτους τοὺς γεωργοὺς καὶ δώσει τὸν
d.nsm n.nsm d.gsm n.gsm v.fai.3s r.dpm.3 v.fmi.3s cj v.fai.3s r.apm d.apm n.apm cj v.fai.3s d.asm
4472 3836 3261 3836 308 4472 899 2262 2779 660 4047 3836 1177 2779 1443 3836

vineyard to others." When the people heard this, they said, *"May this never be!"* ¶ **17** Jesus looked
ἀμπελῶνα → ἄλλοις δὲ → → → ἀκούσαντες → εἶπαν μὴ γένοιτο δὲ ὁ ἐμβλέψας
n.asm r.dpm cj pt.aa.npm v.aai.3p pl v.amo.3s cj d.nsm pt.aa.nsm
308 257 1254 201 3306 3590 1181 1254 3836 1838

directly at them and asked, "Then what is the meaning of that which is written: "'The stone the
← → αὐτοῖς εἶπεν οὖν τί ἐστιν τοῦτο τὸ → γεγραμμένον λίθον ὃν οἱ
r.dpm.3 v.aai.3s cj r.nsn v.pai.3s r.nsn d.nsn pt.rp.nsn n.asm r.asm d.npm
899 3306 4036 5515 1639 4047 3836 1211 3345 4005 3836

builders rejected has become the capstone'? **18** Everyone who falls on that stone will be
οἰκοδομοῦντες ἀπεδοκίμασαν οὗτος → ἐγενήθη εἰς κεφαλὴν γωνίας, πᾶς ὁ πεσὼν ἐπ' ἐκεῖνον τὸν λίθον → →
pt.pa.npm v.aai.3p r.nsm v.api.3s p.a n.asf n.gsf a.nsm d.nsm pt.aa.nsm p.a r.asm d.asm n.asm
3868 627 4047 1181 1650 3051 1224 4246 3836 4406 2093 1697 3836 3345

broken to pieces, but he on whom it falls will be crushed." ¶ **19** The teachers of the law and
συνθλασθήσεται δ' αὐτὸν ἐφ' ὃν ἂν → πέσῃ → λικμήσει Καὶ οἱ γραμματεῖς ← καὶ
v.fpi.3s cj r.asm.3 p.a r.asm pl v.aas.3s v.fai.3s cj d.npm n.npm cj
5314 1254 899 2093 4005 323 4406 3347 2779 3836 1208 2779

the chief priests looked for a way to arrest him immediately, because they knew he
οἱ ἀρχιερεῖς ἐζήτησαν → ← → ἐπιβαλεῖν τὰς χεῖρας ἐπ' αὐτὸν ἐν αὐτῇ τῇ ὥρᾳ γὰρ → ἔγνωσαν ὅτι →
d.npm n.npm v.aai.3p f.aa d.apf n.apf p.a r.asm.3 p.d r.dsf d.dsf n.dsf cj v.aai.3p cj
3836 797 2426 2095 3836 5931 2093 899 1877 899 3836 6052 1142 1182 4022

had spoken this parable against them. But they were afraid of the people.
→ εἶπεν ταύτην τὴν παραβολὴν πρὸς αὐτοὺς καὶ → ἐφοβήθησαν ← τὸν λαόν
v.aai.3s r.asf d.asf n.asf p.a r.apm.3 cj v.api.3p d.asm n.asm
3306 4047 3836 4130 4639 899 2779 5828 3836 3295

Paying Taxes to Caesar

20:20 Keeping a close watch on him, they sent spies, who pretended to be
Καὶ → παρατηρήσαντες → ἀπέστειλαν ἐγκαθέτους → ὑποκρινομένους ἑαυτοὺς → εἶναι
cj pt.aa.npm v.aai.3p n.apm pt.pm.apm r.apm.3 f.pa
2779 4190 690 1588 5693 1571 1639

honest. They hoped to catch Jesus in something he said so that they might hand him over to the
δικαίους ἵνα ἐπιλάβωνται αὐτοῦ λόγου ὥστε ← → → παραδοῦναι αὐτὸν ← → τῇ
a.apm cj v.ams.3p r.gsm.3 n.gsm cj f.aa r.asm.3 d.dsf
1465 2671 2138 899 3364 6063 4140 899 4140 3836

power and authority of the governor. **21** So the spies questioned him: "Teacher, we know that you speak
ἀρχῇ καὶ τῇ ἐξουσίᾳ → τοῦ ἡγεμόνος καὶ ἐπηρώτησαν αὐτὸν λέγοντες διδάσκαλε → οἴδαμεν ὅτι → λέγεις
n.dsf cj d.dsf n.dsf d.gsm n.gsm cj v.aai.3p r.asm.3 pt.pa.npm n.vsm v.rai.1p cj v.pai.2s
794 2779 3836 2026 3836 2450 2779 2089 899 3306 1437 3857 4022 3306

and teach what is right, and that you do not *show* *partiality* but teach the way of God in accordance
καὶ διδάσκεις ὀρθῶς καὶ → → οὐ λαμβάνεις πρόσωπον ἀλλ' διδάσκεις τὴν ὁδὸν → τοῦ θεοῦ ἐπ'
cj v.pai.2s adv cj pl v.pai.2s n.asn cj v.pai.2s d.asf n.asf d.gsm n.gsm p.g
2779 1438 3987 2779 3284 3284 4024 3284 4725 247 1438 3836 3847 3836 2536 2093

¹³ εἶπεν δὲ ὁ κύριος τοῦ ἀμπελῶνος, Τί ποιήσω; πέμψω τὸν υἱόν μου τὸν ἀγαπητόν· ἴσως τοῦτον ἐντραπήσονται. ¹⁴ ἰδόντες δὲ αὐτὸν οἱ γεωργοὶ διελογίζοντο πρὸς ἀλλήλους λέγοντες, Οὗτός ἐστιν ὁ κληρονόμος· ἀποκτείνωμεν αὐτόν, ἵνα ἡμῶν γένηται ἡ κληρονομία. ¹⁵ καὶ ἐκβαλόντες αὐτὸν ἔξω τοῦ ἀμπελῶνος ἀπέκτειναν. ¶ τί οὖν ποιήσει αὐτοῖς ὁ κύριος τοῦ ἀμπελῶνος; ¹⁶ ἐλεύσεται καὶ ἀπολέσει τοὺς γεωργοὺς τούτους καὶ δώσει τὸν ἀμπελῶνα ἄλλοις. ἀκούσαντες δὲ εἶπαν, Μὴ γένοιτο. ¶ ¹⁷ ὁ δὲ ἐμβλέψας αὐτοῖς εἶπεν, Τί οὖν ἐστιν τὸ γεγραμμένον τοῦτο· Λίθον ὃν ἀπεδοκίμασαν οἱ οἰκοδομοῦντες, οὗτος ἐγενήθη εἰς κεφαλὴν γωνίας; ¹⁸ πᾶς ὁ πεσὼν ἐπ' ἐκεῖνον τὸν λίθον συνθλασθήσεται· ἐφ' ὃν δ' ἂν πέσῃ, λικμήσει αὐτόν. ¶ ¹⁹ Καὶ ἐζήτησαν οἱ γραμματεῖς καὶ οἱ ἀρχιερεῖς ἐπιβαλεῖν ἐπ' αὐτὸν τὰς χεῖρας ἐν αὐτῇ τῇ ὥρᾳ, καὶ ἐφοβήθησαν τὸν λαόν, ἔγνωσαν γὰρ ὅτι πρὸς αὐτοὺς εἶπεν τὴν παραβολὴν ταύτην.

²⁰·²⁰ Καὶ παρατηρήσαντες ἀπέστειλαν ἐγκαθέτους ὑποκρινομένους ἑαυτοὺς δικαίους εἶναι, ἵνα ἐπιλάβωνται αὐτοῦ λόγου, ὥστε παραδοῦναι αὐτὸν τῇ ἀρχῇ καὶ τῇ ἐξουσίᾳ τοῦ ἡγεμόνος. ²¹ καὶ ἐπηρώτησαν αὐτὸν λέγοντες, Διδάσκαλε, οἴδαμεν ὅτι

with the truth. **22** Is it right for us   to pay   taxes to Caesar or not?" ¶ **23**   He saw   through their
←   ἀληθείας ᾽Ις → ἔξεστιν ἡμᾶς δοῦναι φόρον → Καίσαρι ἢ οὐ   δὲ → κατανοήσας ←   αὐτῶν
   n.gsf   v.pai.3s r.ap.1 f.aa   n.asm n.dsm cj pl   cj   pt.aa.nsm   r.gpm.3
   237   1997   7005   1443   5843   2790   2445 4024   1254 2917   899

duplicity   and said to   them, **24** "Show me a denarius. Whose portrait and inscription are on it?" **25** "Caesar's,"
ᴛὴν πανουργίαν εἶπεν πρὸς αὐτούς   δείξατε μοι δηνάριον τίνος εἰκόνα καὶ ἐπιγραφήν → ἔχει ←   δὲ Καίσαρος
d.asf 4111   v.aai.3s p.a r.apm.3   v.aam.2p r.ds.1 n.asn r.gsm n.asf cj n.asf   v.pai.3s   cj n.gsm
3836 4111   3306   4639 899   1259   1609   1324   5515 1635 2779 2107   2400   1254 2790

they replied. ¶   He said to   them, "Then give   to Caesar what is Caesar's, and to God   what is
οἱ εἶπαν   δὲ ὁ εἶπεν πρὸς αὐτούς τοίνυν ἀπόδοτε → Καίσαρι τὰ Καίσαρος καὶ → ᴛῷ θεῷ᷎ τὰ
d.npm v.aai.3p   cj d.nsm v.aai.3s p.a r.apm.3 cj   v.aam.2p   n.dsm   d.apn n.gsm cj   d.dsm n.dsm d.apn
3836 3306   1254 3836 3306 4639 899   625   5523   2790   3836 2790 2779 3836 2536 3836

God's." ¶ **26**   They were unable   to trap   him in what he had said   there in   public.   And
ᴛοῦ θεοῦ᷎   καὶ → → οὐκ ἴσχυσαν → ἐπιλαβέσθαι αὐτοῦ   ῥήματος   ἐναντίον ᴛοῦ λαοῦ᷎ καὶ
d.gsm n.gsm cj   pl v.aai.3p   f.am   r.gsm.3   n.gsn   p.g   d.gsm n.gsm cj
3836 2536   2779   4024 2710   2138   899   4839   1883   3836 3295 2779

astonished by his answer,   they became silent.
θαυμάσαντες ἐπὶ αὐτοῦ ᴛῇ ἀποκρίσει᷎ → ἐσίγησαν
pt.aa.npm p.d r.gsm.3 d.dsf n.dsf   v.aai.3p
2513   2093 899   3836 647   4967

The Resurrection and Marriage

20:27   Some of the Sadducees, who say   there is   no resurrection, came   to Jesus with a
δέ τινες → ᴛῶν Σαδδουκαίων οἱ ἀντιλέγοντες εἶναι μὴ ἀνάστασιν Προσελθόντες ← αὐτὸν
cj r.npm   d.gpm n.gpm   d.npm pt.pa.npm   f.pa pl n.asf   pt.aa.npm   r.asm.3
1254 5516 3836 4881   3836 515   1639 3590 414   4665   899

question. **28** "Teacher," they said, "Moses wrote for us that if a man's brother dies   and leaves a wife but
ἐπηρώτησαν διδάσκαλε → λέγοντες Μωϋσῆς ἔγραψεν → ἡμῖν ἐάν τινος ἀδελφὸς ἀποθάνῃ ἔχων γυναῖκα καὶ
v.aai.3p n.vsm   pt.pa.npm n.nsm v.aai.3s r.dp.1 cj r.gsm n.nsm v.aas.3s pt.pa.nsm n.asf cj
2089   1437   3306   3707   1211   7005   1569 5516 81   633   2400   1222 2779

no children,   the man   must marry the widow and have   children for his   brother.
οὗτος ᾖ → ἄτεκνος ἵνα ὁ ἀδελφὸς αὐτοῦ → λάβῃ τὴν γυναῖκα καὶ ἐξαναστήσῃ σπέρμα → αὐτοῦ ᴛῷ ἀδελφῷ
r.nsm v.pas.3s a.nsm cj d.nsm n.nsm r.gsm.3 v.aas.3s d.asf n.asf cj v.aas.3s n.asn   r.gsm.3 d.dsm n.dsm
4047 1639 866 2671 3836 81   899   3284 3836 1222 2779 1985   5065   81 899   3836 81

29 Now there were seven brothers. The first one married a woman and died   childless. **30** The second **31** and
οὖν → ἦσαν ἑπτὰ ἀδελφοὶ καὶ ὁ πρῶτος ← λαβὼν γυναῖκα ἀπέθανεν ἄτεκνος καὶ ὁ δεύτερος καὶ
cj   v.iai.3p a.npm n.npm cj d.nsm a.nsm pt.aa.nsm n.asf v.aai.3s a.nsm   cj d.nsm a.nsm   cj
4036 1639 2231 81   2779 3836 4755 3284 1222   633   866   2779 3836 1311   2779

then the third married her, and in the same   way   the seven   died,   leaving no children. **32** Finally, the
ὁ τρίτος ἔλαβεν αὐτήν δὲ   ὡσαύτως καὶ οἱ ἑπτὰ καὶ ἀπέθανον κατέλιπον οὐ τέκνα ὕστερον ἡ
d.nsm a.nsm v.aai.3s r.asf.3 cj adv   adv d.npm a.npm cj v.aai.3p v.aai.3p pl n.apn adv.c   d.nsf
3836 5569 3284   899   1254 6058   2779 3836 2231 2779 633   2901   4024 5451   5731   3836

woman died too. **33** Now then, at the resurrection whose   wife will she   be, since the seven were
γυνὴ ἀπέθανεν καὶ → οὖν ἐν τῇ ἀναστάσει ᴛίνος αὐτῶν᷎ γυνὴ ᴛῇ γυνὴ᷎ γίνεται γὰρ οἱ ἑπτὰ ἔσχον
n.nsf v.aai.3s adv cj   p.d d.dsf n.dsf r.gsm r.gpm.3 n.nsf d.nsf n.nsf v.pmi.3s cj d.npm a.npm v.aai.3p
1222 633   2779 4036 1877 3836 414   5515 899   1222 3836 1222 1142   1142 3836 2231 2400

married to her?" ¶ **34**   Jesus replied,   "The people of this age   marry and are given in
γυναῖκα αὐτήν   καὶ ὁ Ἰησοῦς εἶπεν αὐτοῖς οἱ υἱοὶ → τούτου ᴛοῦ αἰῶνος᷎ γαμοῦσιν καὶ → αὐτῶ
n.asf r.asf.3   cj d.nsm n.nsm v.aai.3s r.dpm.3 d.npm n.npm r.gsm d.gsm n.gsm v.pai.3p cj
1222 899   2779 3836 2652 3306 899   3836 5626 172 4047 3836 172   1138   2779

marriage. **35** But those who are considered worthy   of taking part in that   age   and in the resurrection
γαμίσκονται δὲ οἱ ← ←   καταξιωθέντες ← τυχεῖν ← → ἐκείνου ᴛοῦ αἰῶνος᷎ καὶ → τῆς ἀναστάσεως τῆς
v.ppi.3p cj d.npm   pt.ap.npm   f.aa   r.gsm d.gsm n.gsm cj   d.gsf n.gsf   d.gsf
1140   1254 3836   2921   5593   1697 3836 172   2779 3836 414   3836

from the dead will neither marry nor be given in marriage, **36** and they can   no longer die;   for they are
ἐκ νεκρῶν → οὔτε γαμοῦσιν οὔτε → → → γαμίζονται γὰρ → δύνανται οὐδὲ ἔτι ἀποθανεῖν γὰρ → εἰσιν
p.g a.gpm   cj   v.pai.3p cj   v.ppi.3p   cj   v.ppi.3p cj adv f.aa   cj   v.pai.3p
1666 3738   4046 1138   4046   1139   1142   1538   4028 2285 633   1142 1639

ὀρθῶς λέγεις καὶ διδάσκεις καὶ οὐ λαμβάνεις πρόσωπον, ἀλλ᾽ ἐπ᾽ ἀληθείας τὴν ὁδὸν τοῦ θεοῦ διδάσκεις· ²² ἔξεστιν ἡμᾶς Καίσαρι φόρον δοῦναι ἢ οὔ; ¶ ²³ κατανοήσας δὲ αὐτῶν τὴν πανουργίαν εἶπεν πρὸς αὐτούς, ²⁴ Δείξατέ μοι δηνάριον· τίνος ἔχει εἰκόνα καὶ ἐπιγραφήν; οἱ δὲ εἶπαν, Καίσαρος. ¶ ²⁵ ὁ δὲ εἶπεν πρὸς αὐτούς, Τοίνυν ἀπόδοτε τὰ Καίσαρος Καίσαρι καὶ τὰ τοῦ θεοῦ τῷ θεῷ. ¶ ²⁶ καὶ οὐκ ἴσχυσαν ἐπιλαβέσθαι αὐτοῦ ῥήματος ἐναντίον τοῦ λαοῦ καὶ θαυμάσαντες ἐπὶ τῇ ἀποκρίσει αὐτοῦ ἐσίγησαν.

²⁰·²⁷ Προσελθόντες δέ τινες τῶν Σαδδουκαίων, οἱ [ἀντι]λέγοντες ἀνάστασιν μὴ εἶναι, ἐπηρώτησαν αὐτὸν ²⁸ λέγοντες, Διδάσκαλε, Μωϋσῆς ἔγραψεν ἡμῖν, ἐάν τινος ἀδελφὸς ἀποθάνῃ ἔχων γυναῖκα, καὶ οὗτος ἄτεκνος ᾖ, ἵνα λάβῃ ὁ ἀδελφὸς αὐτοῦ τὴν γυναῖκα καὶ ἐξαναστήσῃ σπέρμα τῷ ἀδελφῷ αὐτοῦ. ²⁹ ἑπτὰ οὖν ἀδελφοὶ ἦσαν· καὶ ὁ πρῶτος λαβὼν γυναῖκα ἀπέθανεν ἄτεκνος· ³⁰ καὶ ὁ δεύτερος ³¹ καὶ ὁ τρίτος ἔλαβεν αὐτήν, ὡσαύτως δὲ καὶ οἱ ἑπτὰ οὐ κατέλιπον τέκνα καὶ ἀπέθανον. ³² ὕστερον καὶ ἡ γυνὴ ἀπέθανεν. ³³ ἡ γυνὴ οὖν ἐν τῇ ἀναστάσει τίνος αὐτῶν γίνεται γυνή; οἱ γὰρ ἑπτὰ ἔσχον αὐτὴν γυναῖκα. ¶ ³⁴ καὶ εἶπεν αὐτοῖς ὁ Ἰησοῦς, Οἱ υἱοὶ τοῦ αἰῶνος τούτου γαμοῦσιν καὶ γαμίσκονται, ³⁵ οἱ δὲ καταξιωθέντες τοῦ αἰῶνος ἐκείνου τυχεῖν καὶ τῆς ἀναστάσεως τῆς ἐκ νεκρῶν οὔτε γαμοῦσιν οὔτε γαμίζονται· ³⁶ οὐδὲ γὰρ ἀποθανεῖν ἔτι δύνανται, ἰσάγγελοι γάρ εἰσιν

like the angels.   They are   God's children, since they are   children of the resurrection. **37** But in the account of
→   ἰσάγγελοι   καὶ →   εἰσιν   θεοῦ   υἱοί →   ὄντες   υἱοί →   τῆς ἀναστάσεως   δὲ   ἐπὶ ←
   a.npm   cj   v.pai.3p   n.gsm   n.npm   pt.pa.npm   n.npm   d.gsf   n.gsf   cj   p.g
   2694   2779   1639   2536   5626   1639   5626   3836   414   1254   2093

the bush, even Moses showed that the dead rise,   for he calls the Lord   'the God of Abraham, and the God of
τῆς βάτου   καὶ   Μωϋσῆς ἐμήνυσεν ὅτι   οἱ   νεκροὶ   ἐγείρονται ὡς →   λέγει   κύριον   τὸν   θεὸν →   Ἀβραὰμ   καὶ   θεὸν →
d.gsf   n.gsf   adv   n.nsm   v.aai.3s   cj   d.npm   a.npm   v.ppi.3p   cj   v.pai.3s   n.asm   d.asm   n.asm   n.gsm   cj   n.asm
3836   1004   2779   3707   3606   4022   3836   3738   1586   6055   3306   3261   3836   2536   11   2779   2536

Isaac, and the God of Jacob.' **38** He is   not the God of the dead, but   of the living, for to him all   are alive."
Ἰσαὰκ   καὶ   θεὸν →   Ἰακώβ   δὲ →   ἔστιν οὐκ   θεὸς → νεκρῶν ἀλλὰ → ζώντων   γὰρ → αὐτῷ πάντες →   ζῶσιν
n.gsm   cj   n.asm   n.gsm   cj →   v.pai.3s   pl   n.nsm   a.gpm   cj   pt.pa.gpm   cj   r.dsm.3   a.npm   v.pai.3p
2693   2779   2536   2609   1254   1639   4024   2536   3738   247   2409   1142   899   4246   2409

¶   **39**   Some of the teachers   of the law responded,   "Well said, teacher!" **40** And no one dared   to ask
   δέ   τινες → τῶν γραμματέων ← ←   Ἀποκριθέντες εἶπαν καλῶς   εἶπας διδάσκαλε   γὰρ →   ἐτόλμων → ἐπερωτᾶν
   cj   r.npm   d.gpm   n.gpm   pt.ap.npm   v.aai.3p   adv   v.aai.2s   n.vsm   cj   v.iai.3p   f.pa
   1254   5516   3836   1208   646   3306   2822   3306   1437   1142   4029   4029   5528   2089

him   any   more questions.
αὐτὸν   οὐδὲν   οὐκέτι ←
r.asm.3   a.asn   adv
899   4029   4033   2089

Whose Son Is the Christ?

20:41 Then Jesus said to   them, "How is it that they say   the Christ is   the Son of David? **42**   David
   δὲ   Εἶπεν πρὸς αὐτούς   πῶς   ←   →   λέγουσιν τὸν χριστὸν εἶναι   υἱόν →   Δαυὶδ   γὰρ   Δαυὶδ
   cj   v.aai.3s   p.a   r.apm.3   adv   v.pai.3p   d.asm   n.asm   f.pa   n.asm   n.gsm   cj   n.nsm
   1254   3306   4639   899   4802   3306   3836   5986   1639   5626   1253   1142   1253

himself declares in   the Book of Psalms: "'The Lord   said to   my Lord: "Sit   at   my right hand **43** until   I make
αὐτὸς   λέγει   ἐν   βίβλῳ → ψαλμῶν   κύριος εἶπεν →   μου ⌜τῷ κυρίῳ⌝ κάθου ἐκ   μου δεξιῶν ←   ἕως ἂν → θῶ
r.nsm   v.pai.3s   p.d   n.dsf   n.gpm   n.nsm   v.aai.3s   r.gs.1   d.dsm   n.dsm   v.pmm.2s   p.g   r.gs.1   a.gpf   cj   pl   v.aas.1s
899   3306   1877   1047   6011   3261   3306   1609   3836   3261   2764   1666   1609   1288   2401   323   5502

your enemies   a footstool for your feet.'" **44**   David   calls him 'Lord.' How then can he be   his   son?" ¶
σου   ⌜τοὺς ἐχθρούς⌝   ὑποπόδιον → σου   ⌜τῶν ποδῶν⌝   οὖν   Δαυὶδ   καλεῖ αὐτὸν κύριον   πῶς   καὶ   →   ἐστιν αὐτοῦ υἱός
r.gs.2   d.apm   a.apm   n.asn   r.gs.2   d.gpm   n.gpm   cj   n.nsm   v.pai.3s   r.asm.3   n.asm   adv   cj   v.pai.3s   r.gsm.3   n.nsm
5148   3836   2398   5711   4546   5148   3836   4546   4036   1253   2813   899   3261   4802   2779   1639   899   5626

45   While all   the people were listening, Jesus said to his   disciples,   **46** "Beware of   the teachers   of the law.
   δὲ →   παντὸς τοῦ λαοῦ →   Ἀκούοντος   εἶπεν →   αὐτοῦ ⌜τοῖς μαθηταῖς⌝   προσέχετε ἀπὸ τῶν γραμματέων ← ←
   cj   a.gsm   d.gsm   n.gsm   pt.pa.gsm   v.aai.3s   r.gsm.3   d.dpm   n.dpm   v.pam.2p   p.g   d.gpm   n.gpm
   1254   201   4246   3836   3295   201   3306   3412   899   3836   3412   4668   608   3836   1208

They like   to walk   around in flowing robes and love   to be greeted   in the marketplaces and have
τῶν   θελόντων → περιπατεῖν →   ἐν →   στολαῖς καὶ φιλούντων →   ἀσπασμοὺς ἐν   ταῖς ἀγοραῖς   καὶ
d.gpm   pt.pa.gpm   f.pa   p.d   n.dpf   cj   pt.pa.gpm   n.apm   p.d   d.dpf   n.dpf   cj
3836   2527   4344   1877   5124   2779   5797   833   1877   3836   59   2779

the most important seats   in the synagogues and the places of honor   at   banquets. **47** They
   πρωτοκαθεδρίας   ἐν ταῖς συναγωγαῖς καὶ →   πρωτοκλισίας   ἐν ⌜τοῖς δείπνοις⌝   οἳ
   n.apf   p.d   d.dpf   n.dpf   cj   n.apf   p.d   d.dpn   n.dpn   r.npm
   4751   1877   3836   5252   2779   4752   1877   3836   1270   4005

devour   widows'   houses   and for a show   make lengthy prayers.   Such men will be punished
κατεσθίουσιν ⌜τῶν χηρῶν⌝ ⌜τὰς οἰκίας⌝   καὶ →   προφάσει →   μακρὰ   προσεύχονται οὗτοι →   → ⌜λήμψονται κρίμα⌝
v.pai.3p   d.gpf   n.gpf   d.apf   n.apf   cj   n.dsf   adv   v.pmi.3p   r.npm   v.fmi.3p   n.asn
2983   3836   5939   3836   3864   2779   4733   3431   4667   4047   3284   3210

most severely."
→   περισσότερον
   a.asn.c
   4358

The Widow's Offering

21:1   As he looked   up, Jesus saw   the rich   putting   their gifts   into the temple treasury.   **2** He
   δὲ → → Ἀναβλέψας ←   εἶδεν τοὺς πλουσίους βάλλοντας αὐτῶν ⌜τὰ δῶρα⌝   εἰς   τὸ   γαζοφυλάκιον
   cj   pt.aa.nsm   v.aai.3s   d.apm   a.apm   pt.pa.apm   r.gpm.3   d.apn   n.apn   p.a   d.asn   n.asn
   1254   329   1625   3836   4454   965   899   3836   1565   1650   3836   1126   1625

καὶ υἱοί εἰσιν θεοῦ τῆς ἀναστάσεως υἱοὶ ὄντες. **37** ὅτι δὲ ἐγείρονται οἱ νεκροί, καὶ Μωϋσῆς ἐμήνυσεν ἐπὶ τῆς βάτου, ὡς λέγει κύριον τὸν θεὸν Ἀβραὰμ καὶ θεὸν Ἰσαὰκ καὶ θεὸν Ἰακώβ. **38** θεὸς δὲ οὐκ ἔστιν νεκρῶν ἀλλὰ ζώντων, πάντες γὰρ αὐτῷ ζῶσιν. ¶ **39** ἀποκριθέντες δέ τινες τῶν γραμματέων εἶπαν, Διδάσκαλε, καλῶς εἶπας. **40** οὐκέτι γὰρ ἐτόλμων ἐπερωτᾶν αὐτὸν οὐδέν.

20:41 Εἶπεν δὲ πρὸς αὐτούς, Πῶς λέγουσιν τὸν Χριστὸν εἶναι Δαυὶδ υἱόν; **42** αὐτὸς γὰρ Δαυὶδ λέγει ἐν βίβλῳ ψαλμῶν, Εἶπεν κύριος τῷ κυρίῳ μου, Κάθου ἐκ δεξιῶν μου, **43** ἕως ἂν θῶ τοὺς ἐχθρούς σου ὑποπόδιον τῶν ποδῶν σου. **44** Δαυὶδ οὖν κύριον αὐτὸν καλεῖ, καὶ πῶς αὐτοῦ υἱός ἐστιν; ¶ **45** Ἀκούοντος δὲ παντὸς τοῦ λαοῦ εἶπεν τοῖς μαθηταῖς [αὐτοῦ], **46** Προσέχετε ἀπὸ τῶν γραμματέων τῶν θελόντων περιπατεῖν ἐν στολαῖς καὶ φιλούντων ἀσπασμοὺς ἐν ταῖς ἀγοραῖς καὶ πρωτοκαθεδρίας ἐν ταῖς συναγωγαῖς καὶ πρωτοκλισίας ἐν τοῖς δείπνοις, **47** οἳ κατεσθίουσιν τὰς οἰκίας τῶν χηρῶν καὶ προφάσει μακρὰ προσεύχονται· οὗτοι λήμψονται περισσότερον κρίμα.

21:1 Ἀναβλέψας δὲ εἶδεν τοὺς βάλλοντας εἰς τὸ γαζοφυλάκιον τὰ δῶρα αὐτῶν πλουσίους. **2** εἶδεν δέ τινα χήραν πενιχρὰν

also saw a poor widow put in two *very small copper coins.* [3] "I tell you the truth," he said, "this
δὲ εἶδεν τινα πενιχρὰν χήραν βάλλουσαν ἐκεῖ δύο λεπτὰ καὶ → λέγω ὑμῖν ἀληθῶς → εἶπεν ὅτι αὕτη
cj v.aai.3s r.asf a.asf n.asf pt.pa.asf adv a.apn n.apn cj v.pai.1s r.dp.2 adv v.aai.3s cj r.nsf
1254 1625 5516 4293 5939 965 1695 1545 3321 2779 3306 7007 242 3306 4022 4047

poor widow has put in more than all the others. [4] All these people gave their gifts out of
ἡ πτωχὴ ἡ χήρα → ἔβαλεν ← πλεῖον → πάντων γὰρ πάντες οὗτοι ← ἔβαλον εἰς τὰ δῶρα ἐκ ←
d.nsf a.nsf d.nsf n.nsf v.aai.3s a.asn.c a.gpn cj a.npm r.npm v.aai.3p p.a d.apn n.apn p.g
3836 4777 3836 5939 965 4498 4246 1142 4246 4047 965 1650 3836 1565 1666

their wealth; but she out of her poverty put in all she had to live on."
αὐτοῖς ⸤τοῦ περισσεύοντος⸥ δὲ αὕτη ἐκ ← αὐτῆς ⸤τοῦ ὑστερήματος⸥ ἔβαλεν ← πάντα ὃν → εἶχεν ⸤τὸν βίον⸥ ←
r.dpm.3 d.gsn pt.pa.gsn cj r.nsf p.g r.gsf.3 d.gsn n.gsn v.aai.3s a.asm r.asm v.iai.3s d.asm n.asm
899 3836 4355 1254 4047 1666 899 3836 5729 965 4246 4005 2400 3836 1050

Signs of the End of the Age

21:5 Some of his disciples were remarking about how the temple was adorned with beautiful stones and
Καὶ τινων → λεγόντων περὶ τοῦ ἱεροῦ ὅτι → κεκόσμηται → καλοῖς λίθοις καὶ
cj r.gpm pt.pa.gpm p.g d.gsn n.gsn cj v.rpi.3s a.dpm n.dpm cj
2779 5516 3306 4309 3836 2639 4022 3175 2819 3345 2779

with gifts dedicated to God. But Jesus said, [6] "As for what you see here, the time will come
→ ἀναθήμασιν ← εἶπεν ταῦτα ἃ → θεωρεῖτε ἡμέραι → ἐλεύσονται
n.dpn v.aai.3s r.apn r.apn v.pai.2p n.npf v.fmi.3p
356 3306 4047 4005 2555 2465 2262

when not one stone will be left on another; every one of them will be thrown down." ¶ [7]
ἐν αἷς οὐκ λίθος → → ἀφεθήσεται ἐπὶ λίθῳ ὃς οὐ → καταλυθήσεται ← δὲ
p.d r.dpf pl n.nsm v.fpi.3s p.d n.dsm r.nsm pl v.fpi.3s cj
1877 4005 4024 3345 918 2093 3345 4005 4024 2907 1254

"Teacher," they asked, "when will these things happen? And what will be the sign that they
διδάσκαλε → Ἐπηρώτησαν αὐτὸν λέγοντες οὖν πότε → ταῦτα ἔσται καὶ τί τὸ σημεῖον ὅταν ταῦτα
n.vsm v.aai.3p r.asm.3 pt.pa.npm cj adv r.npn v.fmi.3s cj r.nsn d.nsn n.nsn r.nsn r.npn
1437 2089 899 3306 4036 4537 1639 4047 1639 2779 5515 3836 4956 4020 4047

are about to take place?" ¶ [8] He replied: "Watch out that you are not deceived. For many will come
→ μέλλῃ → γίνεσθαι ← δὲ ὁ εἶπεν βλέπετε ← → μὴ πλανηθῆτε γὰρ πολλοὶ → ἐλεύσονται
v.pas.3s f.pm cj d.nsm v.aai.3s v.pam.2p pl v.aps.2p cj a.npm v.fmi.3p
3516 1181 1254 3836 3306 1063 4414 4414 3590 4414 1142 4498 2262

in my name, claiming, 'I am he,' and, 'The time is near.' Do not follow them. [9] When you
ἐπὶ μου ⸤τῷ ὀνόματι⸥ λέγοντες ἐγώ εἰμι ← καὶ ὁ καιρὸς → ἤγγικεν → μὴ ⸤πορευθῆτε ὀπίσω⸥ αὐτῶν δὲ ὅταν →
p.d r.gs.1 d.dsn n.dsn pt.pa.npm r.ns.1 v.pai.1s cj d.nsm n.nsm v.rai.3s pl v.aps.2p p.g r.gpm.3 cj cj
2093 1609 3836 3950 3306 1609 1639 2779 3836 2789 1581 3590 4513 3958 899 1254 4020

hear of wars and revolutions, do not be frightened. These things must happen first, but the end will
ἀκούσητε πολέμους καὶ ἀκαταστασίας → μὴ → πτοηθῆτε γὰρ ταῦτα δεῖ γενέσθαι πρῶτον ἀλλ᾽ τὸ τέλος
v.aas.2p n.apm cj n.apf pl v.aps.2p cj r.apn v.pai.3s f.am adv d.nsn n.nsn
201 4483 2779 189 4765 3590 4765 1142 4047 1256 1181 4754 247 3836 5465

not come right away." ¶ [10] Then he said to them: "Nation will rise against nation, and kingdom against
οὐκ εὐθέως ← Τότε → ἔλεγεν → αὐτοῖς ἔθνος → ἐγερθήσεται ἐπ᾽ ἔθνος καὶ βασιλεία ἐπὶ
pl adv adv v.iai.3s r.dpm.3 n.nsn v.fpi.3s p.a n.asn cj n.nsf p.a
4024 2311 5538 3306 899 1620 1586 2093 1620 2779 993 2093

kingdom. [11] There will be great earthquakes, famines and pestilences in various places, and fearful
βασιλείαν τε → → ἔσονται μεγάλοι σεισμοὶ καὶ λιμοὶ καὶ λοιμοὶ κατὰ τόπους τε ἔσται φόβητρά
n.asf cj v.fmi.3p a.npm n.npm cj n.npm cj n.npm p.a n.apm cj v.fmi.3s n.npn
993 5445 1639 3489 4939 2779 3350 2779 3369 2848 5536 5445 1639 5831

events and great signs from heaven. ¶ [12] "But before all this, they will lay hands on
← καὶ μεγάλα σημεῖα ἀπ᾽ οὐρανοῦ δὲ Πρὸ πάντων τούτων → → ἐπιβαλοῦσιν ⸤τὰς χεῖρας αὐτῶν⸥ ἐφ᾽
cj a.npn n.npn p.g n.gsn cj p.g a.gpn r.gpn v.fai.3p d.apf n.apf r.gpm.3 p.a
2779 3489 4956 608 4041 1254 4574 4246 4047 2095 3836 5931 899 2093

you and persecute you. They will deliver you to synagogues and prisons, and you will be brought before
ὑμᾶς καὶ διώξουσιν → → παραδιδόντες εἰς ⸤τὰς συναγωγὰς⸥ καὶ φυλακάς → → → ἀπαγομένους ἐπὶ
r.ap.2 cj v.fai.3p pt.pa.npm p.a d.apf n.apf cj n.apf pt.pp.apm p.a
7007 2779 1503 4140 1650 3836 5252 2779 5871 552 2093

βάλλουσαν ἐκεῖ λεπτὰ δύο, [3] καὶ εἶπεν, Ἀληθῶς λέγω ὑμῖν ὅτι ἡ χήρα αὕτη ἡ πτωχὴ πλεῖον πάντων ἔβαλεν· [4] πάντες γὰρ οὗτοι ἐκ τοῦ περισσεύοντος αὐτοῖς ἔβαλον εἰς τὰ δῶρα, αὕτη δὲ ἐκ τοῦ ὑστερήματος αὐτῆς πάντα τὸν βίον ὃν εἶχεν ἔβαλεν.

21:5 Καί τινων λεγόντων περὶ τοῦ ἱεροῦ ὅτι λίθοις καλοῖς καὶ ἀναθήμασιν κεκόσμηται εἶπεν, [6] Ταῦτα ἃ θεωρεῖτε, ἐλεύσονται ἡμέραι ἐν αἷς οὐκ ἀφεθήσεται λίθος ἐπὶ λίθῳ ὃς οὐ καταλυθήσεται. ¶ [7] Ἐπηρώτησαν δὲ αὐτὸν λέγοντες, Διδάσκαλε, πότε οὖν ταῦτα ἔσται καὶ τί τὸ σημεῖον ὅταν μέλλῃ ταῦτα γίνεσθαι; ¶ [8] ὁ δὲ εἶπεν, Βλέπετε μὴ πλανηθῆτε· πολλοὶ γὰρ ἐλεύσονται ἐπὶ τῷ ὀνόματί μου λέγοντες, Ἐγώ εἰμι, καί, Ὁ καιρὸς ἤγγικεν. μὴ πορευθῆτε ὀπίσω αὐτῶν. [9] ὅταν δὲ ἀκούσητε πολέμους καὶ ἀκαταστασίας, μὴ πτοηθῆτε· δεῖ γὰρ ταῦτα γενέσθαι πρῶτον, ἀλλ᾽ οὐκ εὐθέως τὸ τέλος. ¶ [10] Τότε ἔλεγεν αὐτοῖς, Ἐγερθήσεται ἔθνος ἐπ᾽ ἔθνος καὶ βασιλεία ἐπὶ βασιλείαν, [11] σεισμοί τε μεγάλοι καὶ κατὰ τόπους λιμοὶ καὶ λοιμοὶ ἔσονται, φόβητρά τε καὶ ἀπ᾽ οὐρανοῦ σημεῖα μεγάλα ἔσται. ¶ [12] πρὸ δὲ τούτων πάντων ἐπιβαλοῦσιν ἐφ᾽ ὑμᾶς τὰς χεῖρας αὐτῶν καὶ διώξουσιν,

kings   and governors, and all on   account of my name.   **13** This will result   in your being witnesses to them.
βασιλεῖς καὶ ἡγεμόνας   ἕνεκεν ←   ← μου ⸢τοῦ ὀνόματος⸣   ἀποβήσεται εἰς ὑμῖν   μαρτύριον
n.apm   cj   n.apm   p.g   r.gs.1 d.gsn n.gsn   v.fmi.3s   p.a r.dp.2 n.asn
995   2779 2450   1914   1609   3836 3950   609   1650 7007   3457

14 But make up your mind   not to worry   beforehand how you will defend   yourselves.   **15** For I   will
οὖν θέτε ← ὑμῶν ⸤ἐν ταῖς καρδίαις⸥ μὴ → προμελετᾶν ←   →   →   →   ἀπολογηθῆναι ←   γὰρ ἐγὼ →
cj v.aam.2p r.gp.2 p.d d.dpf n.dpf pl f.pa   f.ap   cj   r.ns.1
4036 5502   7007   1877 3836 2840 3590 4627   664   1142 1609

give you words and wisdom that none   of your adversaries   will be able   to resist   or contradict.
δώσω ὑμῖν στόμα καὶ σοφίαν ᾗ   οὐ ἅπαντες   ὑμῖν οἱ ἀντικείμενοι   →   →   δυνήσονται → ἀντιστῆναι ἢ ἀντειπεῖν
v.fai.1s r.dp.2 n.asn cj n.asf r.dsf pl a.npm   r.dp.2 d.npm pt.pm.npm   v.fpi.3p   f.aa   cj f.aa
1443   7007   5125 2779 5053 4005 4024 570   7007 3836 512   1538   468   2445 515

16   You will be betrayed   even by parents,   brothers,   relatives and friends, and they will put some of   you
δὲ → → → παραδοθήσεσθε καὶ   ὑπὸ γονέων   καὶ ἀδελφῶν   καὶ συγγενῶν καὶ φίλων   καὶ ⸢   →   →   ⸣   ἐξ ὑμῶν
cj   v.fpi.2p   adv   p.g n.gpm   cj n.gpm   cj n.gpm   cj a.gpm   cj   p.g r.gp.2
1254   4140   2779   5679 1204   2779 81   2779 5150   2779 5813   2779 2506 2506 2506   1666 7007

to death.   **17**   All   men will   hate   you because of me.   **18** But not   a hair of your
→ θανατώσουσιν   καὶ ὑπὸ πάντων   ἔσεσθε μισούμενοι   διὰ   ← ⸤τὸ ὄνομα μου⸥   καὶ ⸤οὐ μὴ⸥   θρὶξ ἐκ ὑμῶν
v.fai.3p   cj p.g a.gpm   v.fmi.2p pt.pp.npm   p.a   d.asn n.asn r.gs.1 cj pl pl   n.nsf p.g r.gp.2
2506   2779 5679 4246   1639   3631   1328   3836 3950 1609   2779 4024 3590 2582 1666 7007

head   will perish.   **19** By standing firm   you will gain   life.   ¶   **20** "When you see
⸤τῆς κεφαλῆς⸥   ἀπόληται   ἐν   ⸤τῇ ὑπομονῇ ὑμῶν⸥   →   κτήσασθε ⸤τὰς ψυχὰς⸥ ὑμῶν   δὲ Ὅταν   →   ἴδητε
d.gsf n.gsf   v.ams.3s   p.d   d.dsf n.dsf r.gp.2   v.amm.2p d.apf n.apf r.gp.2   cj cj   v.aas.2p
3836 3051   660   1877 3836 5705 7007   3227   3836 6034 7007   1254 4020   1625

Jerusalem being surrounded by armies,   you will know that its   desolation   is near.   **21** Then let those who
Ἰερουσαλήμ →   κυκλουμένην ὑπὸ στρατοπέδων τότε →   → γνῶτε ὅτι αὐτῆς ἡ ἐρήμωσις   → ἤγγικεν   τότε ⸢ οἱ
n.asf   pt.pp.asf   p.g n.gpn   adv   v.aam.2p cj r.gsf.3 d.nsf n.nsf   v.rai.3s   adv   d.npm
2647   3240   5679 5136   5538   1182   4022 899   3836 2247   1581   5538 3836

are in Judea   flee   to the mountains,   let those in the city   get   out, and let those in
ἐν ⸤τῇ Ἰουδαίᾳ   φευγέτωσαν εἰς τὰ ὄρη   καὶ ⸢ οἱ ἐν   ⸤μέσῳ αὐτῆς⸥ ἐκχωρείτωσαν ←   καὶ ⸢ οἱ ἐν
p.d d.dsf n.dsf   v.pam.3p   p.a d.apn n.apn cj   d.npm p.d n.dsn r.gsf.3 v.pam.3p   cj   d.npm p.d
1877 3836 2677   5771   1650 3836 4001 2779 3836 1877 3545 899   1774   2779 3836 1877

the country not enter   the city.   **22** For this is   the time of punishment in fulfillment   of all   that has
ταῖς χώραις μὴ εἰσερχέσθωσαν εἰς   αὐτήν   ὅτι αὐται εἰσιν   ἡμέραι → ἐκδικήσεως   ⸤τοῦ πλησθῆναι⸥   ← πάντα τὰ   →
d.dpf n.dpf pl v.pmm.3p   p.a   r.asf.3 cj r.npf v.pai.3p n.npf   n.gsf   d.gsn f.ap   a.apn d.apn
3836 6001   3590 1656   1650   899   4022 4047 1639   2465   1689   3836 4398   4246 3836

been written.   **23** How dreadful it will be in those   days   for pregnant   women and
→ γεγραμμένα   οὐαὶ   ἐν ἐκείναις ⸤ταῖς ἡμέραις⸥   ⸤ταῖς ἐν γαστρὶ ἐχούσαις⸥   ←   καὶ
pt.rp.apn   j   p.d r.dpf   d.dpf n.dpf   d.dpf p.d n.dsf pt.pa.dpf   cj
1211   4026   1877 1697   3836 2465   3836 1877 1143 2400   2779

nursing   mothers! There will be   great distress in the land and wrath against this people.   **24**   They
⸤ταῖς θηλαζούσαις⸥   ←   γὰρ →   → ἔσται μεγάλη ἀνάγκη ἐπὶ τῆς γῆς καὶ ὀργὴ   → τούτῳ ⸤τῷ λαῷ⸥   καὶ →
d.dpf pt.pa.dpf   cj   v.fmi.3s a.nsf n.nsf p.g d.gsf n.gsf cj n.nsf   r.dsm d.dsm n.dsm   cj
3836 2558   1142   1639   3489 340   2093 3836 1178 2779 3973   4047 3836 3295   2779

will fall   by the   sword   and will be taken   as prisoners to all   the nations.   Jerusalem
→ πεσοῦνται →   στόματι μαχαίρης καὶ →   → αἰχμαλωτισθήσονται ←   εἰς πάντα τὰ ἔθνη   καὶ Ἰερουσαλὴμ
v.fmi.3p   n.dsn n.gsf   cj   v.fpi.3p   p.a a.apn d.apn n.apn cj n.nsf
4406   5125 3479   2779   170   1650 4246 3836 1620   2779 2647

will be   trampled on by the Gentiles until   the times of the Gentiles are fulfilled.   ¶   **25** "There will
→ ἔσται πατουμένη ←   ὑπὸ   ἐθνῶν ⸤ἄχρι οὗ⸥   καιροὶ   ἐθνῶν   → πληρωθῶσιν   Καὶ
v.fmi.3s pt.pp.nsf   p.g   n.gpn p.g r.gsm   n.npm   n.gpn   v.aps.3p   cj
1639   4251   5679   1620 948 4005   2789   1620   4444   2779

be   signs in the sun,   moon and stars.   On the earth, nations will be in anguish and   perplexity at the
ἔσονται σημεῖα ἐν   ἡλίῳ καὶ σελήνῃ καὶ ἄστροις καὶ ἐπὶ τῆς γῆς ἐθνῶν   συνοχῇ   ἐν ἀπορίᾳ   →
v.fmi.3p n.npn p.d   n.dsm cj n.dsf cj n.dpn   cj p.g d.gsf n.gsf n.gpn   n.nsf   p.d n.dsf
1639   4956 1877   2463 2779 4943   2779 849   2779 2093 3836 1178 1620   5330   1877 680

παραδιδόντες εἰς τὰς συναγωγὰς καὶ φυλακάς, ἀπαγομένους ἐπὶ βασιλεῖς καὶ ἡγεμόνας ἕνεκεν τοῦ ὀνόματός μου· **13** ἀποβήσεται ὑμῖν εἰς μαρτύριον. **14** θέτε οὖν ἐν ταῖς καρδίαις ὑμῶν μὴ προμελετᾶν ἀπολογηθῆναι· **15** ἐγὼ γὰρ δώσω ὑμῖν στόμα καὶ σοφίαν ᾗ οὐ δυνήσονται ἀντιστῆναι ἢ ἀντειπεῖν ἅπαντες οἱ ἀντικείμενοι ὑμῖν. **16** παραδοθήσεσθε δὲ καὶ ὑπὸ γονέων καὶ ἀδελφῶν καὶ συγγενῶν καὶ φίλων, καὶ θανατώσουσιν ἐξ ὑμῶν, **17** καὶ ἔσεσθε μισούμενοι ὑπὸ πάντων διὰ τὸ ὄνομά μου. **18** καὶ θρὶξ ἐκ τῆς κεφαλῆς ὑμῶν οὐ μὴ ἀπόληται. **19** ἐν τῇ ὑπομονῇ ὑμῶν κτήσασθε τὰς ψυχὰς ὑμῶν. ¶ **20** Ὅταν δὲ ἴδητε κυκλουμένην ὑπὸ στρατοπέδων Ἰερουσαλημ, τότε γνῶτε ὅτι ἤγγικεν ἡ ἐρήμωσις αὐτῆς. **21** τότε οἱ ἐν τῇ Ἰουδαίᾳ φευγέτωσαν εἰς τὰ ὄρη καὶ οἱ ἐν μέσῳ αὐτῆς ἐκχωρείτωσαν καὶ οἱ ἐν ταῖς χώραις μὴ εἰσερχέσθωσαν εἰς αὐτήν, **22** ὅτι ἡμέραι ἐκδικήσεως αὗταί εἰσιν τοῦ πλησθῆναι πάντα τὰ γεγραμμένα. **23** οὐαὶ ταῖς ἐν γαστρὶ ἐχούσαις καὶ ταῖς θηλαζούσαις ἐν ἐκείναις ταῖς ἡμέραις· ἔσται γὰρ ἀνάγκη μεγάλη ἐπὶ τῆς γῆς καὶ ὀργὴ τῷ λαῷ τούτῳ, **24** καὶ πεσοῦνται στόματι μαχαίρης καὶ αἰχμαλωτισθήσονται εἰς τὰ ἔθνη πάντα, καὶ Ἰερουσαλὴμ ἔσται πατουμένη ὑπὸ ἐθνῶν, ἄχρι οὗ πληρωθῶσιν καιροὶ ἐθνῶν. ¶ **25** Καὶ ἔσονται σημεῖα ἐν ἡλίῳ καὶ

roaring and tossing of the sea. **26** Men will faint from terror, apprehensive of what is coming on
ἤχους καὶ σάλου → θαλάσσης ἀνθρώπων → ἀποψυχόντων ἀπὸ φόβου καὶ προσδοκίας → τῶν → ἐπερχομένων ←
n.gsn cj n.gsm n.gsf n.gpm pt.pa.gpm p.g n.gsm cj n.gsf d.gpn pt.pm.gpn
2492 2779 4893 2498 476 715 608 5832 2779 4660 3836 2088

the world, for the heavenly bodies will be shaken. **27** At that time they will see the Son of
τῇ οἰκουμένῃ γὰρ αἱ ⌐τῶν οὐρανῶν¬ δυνάμεις → → σαλευθήσονται καὶ → → τότε → → ὄψονται τὸν υἱὸν →
d.dsf n.dsf cj d.npf d.gpm n.gpm n.npf v.fpi.3p cj adv v.fmi.3p d.asm n.asm
3836 3876 1142 3836 3836 4041 1539 4888 2779 5538 3972 3836 5626

Man coming in a cloud with power and great glory. **28** When these things begin to take place,
⌐τοῦ ἀνθρώπου¬ ἐρχόμενον ἐν νεφέλῃ μετὰ δυνάμεως καὶ πολλῆς δόξης δὲ → τούτων ← ἀρχομένων → γίνεσθαι ←
d.gsm n.gsm pt.pm.asm p.d n.dsf p.g n.gsf cj a.gsf n.gsf cj r.gpn pt.pm.gpn f.pm
3836 476 2262 1877 3749 3552 1539 2779 4498 1518 1254 806 4047 806 1181

stand up and lift up your heads, because your redemption is drawing near." ¶ **29** He told
ἀνακύψατε ← καὶ ἐπάρατε ← ὑμῶν ⌐τὰς κεφαλάς¬ διότι ὑμῶν ἡ ἀπολύτρωσις, → → ἐγγίζει Καὶ → εἶπεν
v.aam.2p cj v.aam.2p r.gp.2 d.apf n.apf cj r.gp.2 d.nsf n.nsf v.pai.3s cj v.aai.3s
376 2779 2048 7007 3836 3051 1484 7007 3836 667 1581 2779 3306

them this parable: "Look at the fig tree and all the trees. **30** When they sprout leaves, you can see
αὐτοῖς παραβολὴν ἴδετε τὴν → συκῆν καὶ πάντα τὰ δένδρα ὅταν → προβάλωσιν ← ἤδη → βλέποντες
r.dpm.3 n.asf v.aam.2p d.asf n.asf cj a.apn d.apn n.apn cj v.aas.3p adv pt.pa.npm
899 4130 1625 3836 5190 2779 4246 3836 1285 4020 4582 2453 1063

for yourselves and know that summer is near. **31** Even so, when you see these things happening, you
ἀφ' ἑαυτῶν γινώσκετε ὅτι ⌐τὸ θέρος¬ ἐστίν ἤδη ἐγγύς καὶ οὕτως ὅταν ὑμεῖς ἴδητε ταῦτα ← γινόμενα →
p.g r.gpm.2 v.pai.2p cj d.nsn n.nsn v.pai.3s adv adv cj adv cj r.np.2 v.aas.2p r.apn pt.pm.apn
608 1571 1182 4022 3836 2550 1639 2453 1584 2779 4048 4020 7007 1625 4047 1181

know that the kingdom of God is near. ¶ **32** "I tell you the truth, this generation will certainly
γινώσκετε ὅτι ἡ βασιλεία → ⌐τοῦ θεοῦ¬ ἐστίν ἐγγύς → λέγω ὑμῖν ἀμὴν ὅτι αὕτη ἡ γενεὰ →
v.pam.2p cj d.nsf n.nsf d.gsm n.gsm v.pai.3s adv v.pai.1s r.dp.2 pl cj r.nsf d.nsf n.nsf
1182 4022 3836 993 3836 2536 1639 1584 3306 7007 297 4022 4047 3836 1155 4216

not pass away until all these things have happened. **33** Heaven and earth will pass away, but my
⌐οὐ μὴ¬ παρέλθῃ ← ⌐ἕως ἂν¬ πάντα ← γένηται ὁ οὐρανὸς, καὶ ⌐ἡ γῆ¬ → παρελεύσονται ← δὲ μου
pl pl v.aas.3s cj pl a.npn v.ams.3s d.nsm n.nsm cj d.nsf n.nsf v.fmi.3p cj r.gs.1
4024 3590 4216 2401 323 4246 1181 3836 4041 2779 3836 1178 4216 1254 1609

words will never pass away. ¶ **34** "Be careful, or your hearts will be weighed
⌐οἱ λόγοι¬ → ⌐οὐ μὴ¬ παρελεύσονται ← δὲ → Προσέχετε ἑαυτοῖς μήποτε ὑμῶν ⌐αἱ καρδίαι¬ → → βαρηθῶσιν
d.npm n.npm pl pl v.fmi.3p cj v.pam.2p r.dpm.2 cj r.gp.2 d.npf n.npf v.aps.3p
3836 3364 4216 4024 3590 4216 1254 4668 1571 3607 7007 3836 2840 976

down with dissipation, drunkenness and the anxieties of life, and that day will close on you
← ἐν κραιπάλῃ καὶ μέθῃ καὶ μερίμναις → βιωτικαῖς καὶ ἐκείνη ⌐ἡ ἡμέρα¬ → ἐπιστῇ ἐφ' ὑμᾶς
p.d n.dsf cj n.dsf cj n.dpf a.dpf cj r.nsf d.nsf n.nsf v.aas.3s r.ap.2
1877 3190 2779 3494 2779 3533 1053 2779 1697 3836 2465 2392 2093 7007

unexpectedly like a trap. **35** For it will come upon all those who live on the face of the whole
αἰφνίδιος ὡς παγίς γὰρ → → ἐπεισελεύσεται ἐπὶ πάντας τοὺς → καθημένους ἐπὶ πρόσωπον → τῆς πάσης
a.nsf pl n.nsf cj v.fmi.3s p.a a.apm d.apm pt.pm.apm p.a n.asn d.gsf a.gsf
167 6055 4075 1142 2082 2093 4246 3836 2764 2093 4725 3836 4246

earth. **36** Be always on the watch, and pray that you may be able to escape all that is
γῆς δὲ → ἐν παντὶ καιρῷ, → → ἀγρυπνεῖτε δεόμενοι ἵνα → → κατισχύσητε ἐκφυγεῖν πάντα ταῦτα τὰ →
n.gsf cj p.d a.dsm n.dsm v.pam.2p pt.pm.npm cj v.aas.2p f.aa r.apn r.apn d.apn
1178 1254 70 1877 4246 2789 70 1289 2671 2996 1767 4246 4047 3836

about to happen, and that you may be able to stand before the Son of Man." ¶ **37** Each
μέλλοντα → γίνεσθαι καὶ → σταθῆναι ἔμπροσθεν τοῦ υἱοῦ → ⌐τοῦ ἀνθρώπου¬ δὲ
pt.pa.apn f.pm cj f.ap p.g d.gsm n.gsm d.gsm n.gsm cj
3516 1181 2779 2705 1869 3836 5626 3836 476 1254

day Jesus was teaching at the temple, and each evening he went out to spend the night on the
⌐τὰς ἡμέρας¬ ⁵Ἦν διδάσκων ἐν τῷ ἱερῷ δὲ → ⌐τὰς νύκτας¬ → ἐξερχόμενος ← → ηὐλίζετο ← εἰς τὸ
d.apf n.apf v.iai.3s pt.pa.nsm p.d d.dsn n.dsn cj d.apf n.apf pt.pm.nsm v.imi.3s p.a d.asn
3836 2465 1639 1438 1877 3836 2639 1254 3836 3816 2002 887 1650 3836

σελήνῃ καὶ ἄστροις, καὶ ἐπὶ τῆς γῆς συνοχὴ ἐθνῶν ἐν ἀπορίᾳ ἤχους θαλάσσης καὶ σάλου, **26** ἀποψυχόντων ἀνθρώπων ἀπὸ φόβου καὶ προσδοκίας τῶν ἐπερχομένων τῇ οἰκουμένῃ. αἱ γὰρ δυνάμεις τῶν οὐρανῶν σαλευθήσονται. **27** καὶ τότε ὄψονται τὸν υἱὸν τοῦ ἀνθρώπου ἐρχόμενον ἐν νεφέλῃ μετὰ δυνάμεως καὶ δόξης πολλῆς. **28** ἀρχομένων δὲ τούτων γίνεσθαι ἀνακύψατε καὶ ἐπάρατε τὰς κεφαλὰς ὑμῶν, διότι ἐγγίζει ἡ ἀπολύτρωσις ὑμῶν. ¶ **29** Καὶ εἶπεν παραβολὴν αὐτοῖς· Ἴδετε τὴν συκῆν καὶ πάντα τὰ δένδρα· **30** ὅταν προβάλωσιν ἤδη, βλέποντες ἀφ' ἑαυτῶν γινώσκετε ὅτι ἤδη ἐγγὺς τὸ θέρος ἐστίν· **31** οὕτως καὶ ὑμεῖς, ὅταν ἴδητε ταῦτα γινόμενα, γινώσκετε ὅτι ἐγγύς ἐστιν ἡ βασιλεία τοῦ θεοῦ. ¶ **32** ἀμὴν λέγω ὑμῖν ὅτι οὐ μὴ παρέλθῃ ἡ γενεὰ αὕτη ἕως ἂν πάντα γένηται. **33** ὁ οὐρανὸς καὶ ἡ γῆ παρελεύσονται, οἱ δὲ λόγοι μου οὐ μὴ παρελεύσονται. ¶ **34** Προσέχετε δὲ ἑαυτοῖς μήποτε βαρηθῶσιν ὑμῶν αἱ καρδίαι ἐν κραιπάλῃ καὶ μέθῃ καὶ μερίμναις βιωτικαῖς καὶ ἐπιστῇ ἐφ' ὑμᾶς αἰφνίδιος ἡ ἡμέρα ἐκείνη **35** ὡς παγίς· ἐπεισελεύσεται γὰρ ἐπὶ πάντας τοὺς καθημένους ἐπὶ πρόσωπον πάσης τῆς γῆς. **36** ἀγρυπνεῖτε δὲ ἐν παντὶ καιρῷ δεόμενοι ἵνα κατισχύσητε ἐκφυγεῖν ταῦτα πάντα τὰ μέλλοντα γίνεσθαι καὶ σταθῆναι ἔμπροσθεν τοῦ υἱοῦ τοῦ ἀνθρώπου. ¶ **37** ⁵Ἦν δὲ τὰς

hill	called		the Mount of Olives, [38]	and	all	the	people	came	early in the morning		to hear	him
ὄρος	τὸ καλούμενον	→	Ἐλαιῶν	καὶ	πᾶς	ὁ	λαὸς	ὤρθριζεν			πρὸς αὐτὸν →	ἀκούειν αὐτοῦ
n.asn	d.asn pt.pp.asn		n.gpf	cj	a.nsm	d.nsm	n.nsm	v.iai.3s			p.a r.asm.3	f.pa r.gsm.3
4001	3836 2813		1777	2779	4246	3836	3295	3983			4639 899	201 899

at	the	temple.
ἐν	τῷ	ἱερῷ
p.d	d.dsn	n.dsn
1877	3836	2639

Judas Agrees to Betray Jesus

[22:1]Now	the	Feast	of Unleavened Bread,	called		the Passover,	was approaching,	[2] and	the	chief	priests	and
δὲ	ἡ	ἑορτὴ	τῶν ἀζύμων	ἡ λεγομένη		πάσχα	Ἤγγιζεν	καὶ	οἱ	→	ἀρχιερεῖς	καὶ
cj	d.nsf	n.nsf	d.gpn n.gpn	d.nsf pt.pp.nsf		n.nsf	v.iai.3s	cj	d.npm		n.npm	cj
1254	3836	2038	3836 109	3836 3306		4247	1581	2779	3836		797	2779

the	teachers	of the law	were	looking	for some way		to get rid	of Jesus,	for	they	were	afraid	of the
οἱ	γραμματεῖς	←	→	ἐζήτουν	←	τὸ πῶς	ἀνέλωσιν	αὐτόν	γὰρ	→	→	ἐφοβοῦντο	τὸν
d.npm	n.npm			v.iai.3p		d.asn cj	v.aas.3p	r.asm.3	cj			v.ipi.3p	d.asm
3836	1208			2426		3836 4802	359	899	1142			5828	3836

people.	[3] Then	Satan	entered	Judas,	called		Iscariot,	one		of the	Twelve.	[4] And	Judas
λαόν	δὲ	σατανᾶς	Εἰσῆλθεν εἰς	Ἰούδαν	τὸν καλούμενον		Ἰσκαριώτην	ὄντα	ἐκ τοῦ ἀριθμοῦ	→	τῶν δώδεκα	καὶ	
n.asm	cj	n.nsm	v.aai.3s p.a	n.asm	d.asm pt.pp.asm		n.asm	pt.pa.asm	p.g d.gsm n.gsm		d.gpm a.gpm	cj	
3295	1254	4928	1656 1650	2683	3836 2813		2697	1639	1666 3836 750		3836 1557	2779	

went	to the	chief	priests	and	the	officers	of the temple guard	and	discussed	with them	how	he	might
ἀπελθὼν	→	τοῖς	ἀρχιερεῦσιν	καὶ		στρατηγοῖς	←	→	συνελάλησεν	←	τὸ πῶς		
pt.aa.nsm		d.dpm	n.dpm	cj		n.dpm			v.aai.3s		d.asn cj		
599		3836	797	2779		5130			5196		3836 4802		

betray	Jesus.	[5]	They	were	delighted	and	agreed	to	give	him	money.	[6]	He	consented,	and	watched for
παραδῷ	αὐτόν	αὐτοῖς	καὶ	→	→	ἐχάρησαν	καὶ	συνέθεντο	δοῦναι	αὐτῷ	ἀργύριον	καὶ	→	ἐξωμολόγησεν	καὶ	ἐζήτει ←
v.aas.3s	r.asm.3	r.dpm.3	cj			v.api.3p	cj	v.ami.3p	f.aa	r.dsm.3	n.asn	cj		v.aai.3s	cj	v.iai.3s
4140	899	899	2779			5897	2779	5338	1443	899	736	2779		2018	2779	2426

an opportunity	to hand		Jesus	over to	them	when no	crowd	was present.	
εὐκαιρίαν	τοῦ παραδοῦναι		αὐτὸν	→	αὐτοῖς	ἄτερ	ὄχλου		
n.asf	d.gsn f.aa		r.asm.3		r.dpm.3		n.gsm		
2321	3836 4140		899		899	868	4063	868 868	

The Last Supper

[22:7]Then	came	the	day	of Unleavened Bread	on	which	the	Passover lamb	had to	be sacrificed.	[8]	Jesus
δὲ	Ἦλθεν	ἡ	ἡμέρα	τῶν ἀζύμων	ἐν	ᾗ	τὸ	πάσχα	ἔδει →	θύεσθαι	καὶ	
cj	v.aai.3s	d.nsf	n.nsf	d.gpn n.gpn	p.d	r.dsf	d.asn	n.asn	v.iai.3s	f.pp	cj	
1254	2262	3836	2465	3836 109	1877	4005	3836	4247	1256	2604	2779	

sent	Peter	and	John,	saying,	"Go	and	make preparations	for us	to	eat	the	Passover."	[9]	"Where
ἀπέστειλεν	Πέτρον	καὶ	Ἰωάννην	εἰπών	πορευθέντες	→	ἑτοιμάσατε	ἡμῖν ἵνα	φάγωμεν	τὸ	πάσχα	δὲ	ποῦ	
v.aai.3s	n.asm	cj	n.asm	pt.aa.nsm	pt.ap.npm		v.aam.2p	r.dp.1 cj	v.aas.1p	d.asn	n.asn	cj	adv	
690	4377	2779	2722	3306	4513		2286	7005 2671	2266	3836	4247	1254	4543	

do	you	want	us	to	prepare	for it?"	they	asked.	¶	[10]		He	replied,		"As	you	enter	the
→	→	θέλεις	→	→	ἑτοιμάσωμεν		οἱ	εἶπαν	αὐτῷ		δὲ	ὁ	εἶπεν	αὐτοῖς ἰδοὺ	→	ὑμῶν	εἰσελθόντων εἰς	τὴν
		v.pai.2s			v.aas.1p		d.npm	v.aai.3p	r.dsm.3		cj	d.nsm	v.aai.3s	r.dpm.3 j		r.gp.2	pt.aa.gpm	p.a d.asf
		2527			2286		3836	3306	899		1254	3836	3306	899 2627	1656	7007	1656	1650 3836

city,	a man	carrying a jar		of water	will	meet		you.	Follow		him	to the	house	that	he enters,
πόλιν	ἄνθρωπος	βαστάζων	κεράμιον	ὕδατος	→	συναντήσει	ὑμῖν	ἀκολουθήσατε		αὐτῷ	εἰς	τὴν	οἰκίαν	εἰς	ἣν → εἰσπορεύεται
n.asf	n.nsm	pt.pa.nsm	n.asn	n.gsn		v.fai.3s	r.dp.2	v.aam.2p		r.dsm.3	p.a	d.asf	n.asf	p.a	r.asf v.pmi.3s
4484	476	1002	3040	5623		5267	7007	199		899	1650	3836	3864	1650	4005 1660

[11] and	say	to the	owner	of the	house,	'The	Teacher	asks:	Where	is	the	guest room,	where I may	eat
καὶ	ἐρεῖτε	τῷ	οἰκοδεσπότῃ	τῆς	οἰκίας	ὁ	διδάσκαλος	λέγει	σοι ποῦ	ἐστιν	τὸ	κατάλυμα ὅπου	→	φάγω
cj	v.fai.2p	d.dsm	n.dsm	d.gsf	n.gsf	d.nsm	n.nsm	v.pai.3s	r.ds.2 adv	v.pai.3s	d.nsn	n.nsn adv		v.aas.1s
2779	3306	3836	3867	3836	3864	3836	1437	3306	5148 4543	1639	3836	2906 3963		2266

the	Passover	with	my	disciples?'	[12] He		will	show	you	a large	upper	room,	all furnished.	Make preparations
τὸ	πάσχα	μετὰ	μου	τῶν μαθητῶν	κἀκεῖνος	→	δείξει	ὑμῖν	μέγα	→	ἀνάγαιον	→	ἐστρωμένον	ἑτοιμάσατε
d.asn	n.asn	p.g	r.gs.1	d.gpm n.gpm	crasis		v.fai.3s	r.dp.2	a.asn		n.asn		pt.rp.asn	v.aam.2p
3836	4247	3552	1609	3836 3412	2797		1259	7007	3489		333		5143	2286

ἡμέρας ἐν τῷ ἱερῷ διδάσκων, τὰς δὲ νύκτας ἐξερχόμενος ηὐλίζετο εἰς τὸ ὄρος τὸ καλούμενον Ἐλαιῶν· [38] καὶ πᾶς ὁ λαὸς ὤρθριζεν πρὸς αὐτὸν ἐν τῷ ἱερῷ ἀκούειν αὐτοῦ.

[22:1] Ἤγγιζεν δὲ ἡ ἑορτὴ τῶν ἀζύμων ἡ λεγομένη πάσχα. [2] καὶ ἐζήτουν οἱ ἀρχιερεῖς καὶ οἱ γραμματεῖς τὸ πῶς ἀνέλωσιν αὐτόν, ἐφοβοῦντο γὰρ τὸν λαόν. [3] Εἰσῆλθεν δὲ Σατανᾶς εἰς Ἰούδαν τὸν καλούμενον Ἰσκαριώτην, ὄντα ἐκ τοῦ ἀριθμοῦ τῶν δώδεκα· [4] καὶ ἀπελθὼν συνελάλησεν τοῖς ἀρχιερεῦσιν καὶ στρατηγοῖς τὸ πῶς αὐτοῖς παραδῷ αὐτόν. [5] καὶ ἐχάρησαν καὶ συνέθεντο αὐτῷ ἀργύριον δοῦναι. [6] καὶ ἐξωμολόγησεν, καὶ ἐζήτει εὐκαιρίαν τοῦ παραδοῦναι αὐτὸν ἄτερ ὄχλου αὐτοῖς.

[22:7] Ἦλθεν δὲ ἡ ἡμέρα τῶν ἀζύμων, [ἐν] ᾗ ἔδει θύεσθαι τὸ πάσχα· [8] καὶ ἀπέστειλεν Πέτρον καὶ Ἰωάννην εἰπών, Πορευθέντες ἑτοιμάσατε ἡμῖν τὸ πάσχα ἵνα φάγωμεν. [9] οἱ δὲ εἶπαν αὐτῷ, Ποῦ θέλεις ἑτοιμάσωμεν; ¶ [10] ὁ δὲ εἶπεν αὐτοῖς, Ἰδοὺ εἰσελθόντων ὑμῶν εἰς τὴν πόλιν συναντήσει ὑμῖν ἄνθρωπος κεράμιον ὕδατος βαστάζων· ἀκολουθήσατε αὐτῷ εἰς τὴν οἰκίαν εἰς ἣν εἰσπορεύεται [11] καὶ ἐρεῖτε τῷ οἰκοδεσπότῃ τῆς οἰκίας, Λέγει σοι ὁ διδάσκαλος, Ποῦ ἐστιν τὸ κατάλυμα ὅπου τὸ πάσχα

there." ¶ 13 They left and found things just as Jesus had told them. So they prepared the
ἐκεῖ δὲ → ἀπελθόντες εὗρον → καθὼς εἰρήκει αὐτοῖς καὶ ἡτοίμασαν τὸ
adv cj pt.aa.npm v.aai.3p cj v.lai.3s r.dpm.3 cj v.aai.3p d.asn
1695 1254 599 2351 2777 3306 899 2779 2286 3836

Passover. ¶ 14 When the hour came, Jesus and his apostles reclined at the table. 15 And he said to
πάσχα Καὶ ὅτε ἡ ὥρα ἐγένετο σὺν αὐτῷ καὶ οἱ ἀπόστολοι ἀνέπεσεν ← ← ← καὶ → εἶπεν πρὸς
n.asn cj cj d.nsf n.nsf v.ami.3s r.dsm.3 cj d.npm n.npm v.aai.3s cj v.aai.3s p.a
4247 2779 4021 3836 6052 1181 5250 899 2779 3836 693 404 2779 3306 4639

them, "I have eagerly desired to eat this Passover with you before I suffer. 16 For I tell you, I will
αὐτούς ' ↱ ἐπιθυμίᾳ ἐπεθύμησα φαγεῖν τοῦτο ↳τὸ πάσχα μεθ' ὑμῶν πρὸ με ↳τοῦ παθεῖν↲ γὰρ → λέγω ὑμῖν ὅτι ↱ ↱
r.apm.3 n.dsf v.aai.1s f.aa r.asn d.asn n.asn r.gp.2 p.g r.as.1 d.gsn f.aa cj v.pai.1s r.dp.2
899 2121 2121 2123 2121 2266 4047 3836 4247 3552 7007 4574 1609 3836 4248 1142 3306 7007 4022 2266 2266

not eat it again until it finds fulfillment in the kingdom of God." ¶ 17 After taking the
↳οὐ μὴ φάγω αὐτὸ ↳ἕως ὅτου↲ → → πληρωθῇ ἐν τῇ βασιλείᾳ → ↳τοῦ θεοῦ↲ καὶ δεξάμενος
pl pl v.aas.1s r.asn.3 p.g r.gsn v.aps.3s p.d d.dsf n.dsf d.gsm n.gsm cj pt.am.nsm
4024 3590 2266 899 2401 4015 4444 1877 3836 993 3836 2536 2779 1312

cup, he gave thanks and said, "Take this and divide it among you. 18 For I tell you I will not
ποτήριον → εὐχαριστήσας εἶπεν λάβετε τοῦτο καὶ διαμερίσατε εἰς ἑαυτούς γὰρ → λέγω ὑμῖν ὅτι ↱ ↳οὐ μὴ
n.asn pt.aa.nsm v.aai.3s v.aam.2p r.asn cj v.aam.2p p.a r.apm.2 cj v.pai.1s r.dp.2 cj pl pl
4539 2373 3306 3284 4047 2779 1374 1650 1571 1142 3306 7007 4022 4403 4403 4024 3590

drink again of the fruit of the vine until the kingdom of God comes." ¶ 19 And he took
πίω ↳ἀπὸ τοῦ νῦν ἀπὸ τοῦ γενήματος → τῆς ἀμπέλου ἕως οὗ ἡ βασιλεία → ↳τοῦ θεοῦ↲ ἔλθῃ καὶ → λαβὼν
v.aas.1s p.g d.gsn adv p.g d.gsn n.gsn d.gsf n.gsf p.g r.gsm d.nsf n.nsf d.gsm n.gsm v.aas.3s cj pt.aa.nsm
4403 608 3836 3814 608 3836 1163 3836 306 2401 4005 3836 993 3836 2536 2262 2779 3284

bread, gave thanks and broke it, and gave it to them, saying, "This is my body given for you;
ἄρτον → εὐχαριστήσας ἔκλασεν καὶ ἔδωκεν → αὐτοῖς λέγων τοῦτο ἐστιν μου ↳τὸ σῶμα↲ ↳τὸ διδόμενον↲ ὑπὲρ ὑμῶν
n.asn pt.aa.nsm v.aai.3s cj v.aai.3s r.dpm.3 pt.pa.nsm r.nsn v.pai.3s r.gs.1 d.nsn n.nsn d.nsn pt.pp.nsn p.g r.gp.2
788 2373 3089 2779 1443 899 3306 4047 1639 1609 3836 5393 3836 1443 5642 7007

do this in remembrance of me." ¶ 20 In the same way, after the supper he took the cup,
ποιεῖτε τοῦτο εἰς ↳τὴν ἀνάμνησιν↲ ἐμὴν καὶ → ὡσαύτως ← μετὰ ↳τὸ δειπνῆσαι↲ τὸ ποτήριον
v.pam.2p r.asn p.a d.asf n.asf r.asf.1 cj adv p.a d.asn f.aa d.asn n.asn
4472 4047 1650 3836 390 1847 2779 6058 3552 3836 1268 3836 4539

saying, "This cup is the new covenant in my blood, which is poured out for you. 21 But the
λέγων τοῦτο ↳τὸ ποτήριον↲ ἡ καινὴ διαθήκη ἐν μου ↳τῷ αἵματι↲ τὸ → ἐκχυννόμενον ← ὑπὲρ ὑμῶν Πλὴν ἰδοὺ ἡ
pt.pa.nsm r.nsn d.nsn n.nsn d.nsf a.nsf n.nsf p.d r.gs.1 d.dsn n.dsn d.nsn pt.pp.nsn p.g r.gp.2 cj j d.nsf
3306 4047 3836 4539 3836 2785 1347 1877 1609 3836 135 3836 1773 5642 7007 4440 2627 3836

hand of him who is going to betray me is with mine on the table. 22 The Son of Man will
χεὶρ → τοῦ ← → → παραδιδόντος με μετ' ἐμοῦ ἐπὶ τῆς τραπέζης ὅτι μὲν ὁ υἱὸς → ↳τοῦ ἀνθρώπου↲ →
n.nsf d.gsm pt.pa.gsm r.as.1 p.g r.gs.1 p.g d.gsf n.gsf cj pl d.nsm n.nsm d.gsm n.gsm
5931 3836 4140 1609 3552 1609 2093 3836 5544 4022 3525 3836 5626 3836 476

go as it has been decreed, but woe to that man who betrays him." 23 They began to
πορεύεται κατὰ τὸ → → ὡρισμένον πλὴν οὐαὶ → ἐκείνῳ ↳τῷ ἀνθρώπῳ δι' οὗ παραδίδοται ← καὶ αὐτοὶ ἤρξαντο →
v.pmi.3s p.a d.asn pt.rp.asn cj j r.dsm d.dsm n.dsm p.g r.gsm v.ppi.3s cj r.npm v.ami.3p
4513 2848 3836 3988 4440 4026 1697 3836 476 1328 4005 4140 2779 899 806

question among themselves which of them it might be who would do this. ¶ 24 Also a
συζητεῖν πρὸς ἑαυτοὺς τὸ τίς ἐξ αὐτῶν ἄρα → → εἴη ὁ μέλλων πράσσειν τοῦτο δὲ καὶ
f.pa p.a r.apm.3 d.asn r.nsm p.g r.gpm.3 cj v.pao.3s d.nsm pt.pa.nsm f.pa r.asn cj adv
5184 4639 1571 3836 5515 1666 899 726 1639 3836 3516 4556 4047 1254 2779

dispute arose among them as to which of them was considered to be greatest. 25 Jesus said to them, "The
φιλονεικία Ἐγένετο ἐν αὐτοῖς τὸ ← τίς → αὐτῶν → δοκεῖ → εἶναι μείζων δὲ ὁ εἶπεν αὐτοῖς οἱ
n.nsf v.ami.3s p.d r.dpm.3 d.nsn r.nsm r.gpm.3 v.pai.3s f.pa a.nsm.c cj d.nsm v.aai.3s r.dpm.3 d.npm
5808 1181 1877 899 3836 5515 899 1506 1639 3489 1254 3836 3306 899 3836

kings of the Gentiles lord it over them; and those who exercise authority over them call themselves
βασιλεῖς τῶν ἐθνῶν κυριεύουσιν ← αὐτῶν καὶ οἱ ← ἐξουσιάζοντες ← αὐτῶν καλοῦνται ←
n.npm d.gpn n.gpn v.pai.3p r.gpn.3 cj d.npm pt.pa.npm r.gpn.3 v.ppi.3p
995 3836 1620 3259 899 2779 3836 2027 899 2813

μετὰ τῶν μαθητῶν μου φάγω; 12 κἀκεῖνος ὑμῖν δείξει ἀνάγαιον μέγα ἐστρωμένον· ἐκεῖ ἑτοιμάσατε. ¶ 13 ἀπελθόντες δὲ εὗρον καθὼς εἰρήκει αὐτοῖς καὶ ἡτοίμασαν τὸ πάσχα. ¶ 14 Καὶ ὅτε ἐγένετο ἡ ὥρα, ἀνέπεσεν καὶ οἱ ἀπόστολοι σὺν αὐτῷ. 15 καὶ εἶπεν πρὸς αὐτούς, Ἐπιθυμίᾳ ἐπεθύμησα τοῦτο τὸ πάσχα φαγεῖν μεθ' ὑμῶν πρὸ τοῦ με παθεῖν· 16 λέγω γὰρ ὑμῖν ὅτι οὐ μὴ φάγω αὐτὸ ἕως ὅτου πληρωθῇ ἐν τῇ βασιλείᾳ τοῦ θεοῦ. ¶ 17 καὶ δεξάμενος ποτήριον εὐχαριστήσας εἶπεν, Λάβετε τοῦτο καὶ διαμερίσατε εἰς ἑαυτούς· 18 λέγω γὰρ ὑμῖν, [ὅτι] οὐ μὴ πίω ἀπὸ τοῦ νῦν ἀπὸ τοῦ γενήματος τῆς ἀμπέλου ἕως οὗ ἡ βασιλεία τοῦ θεοῦ ἔλθῃ. ¶ 19 καὶ λαβὼν ἄρτον εὐχαριστήσας ἔκλασεν καὶ ἔδωκεν αὐτοῖς λέγων, Τοῦτο ἐστιν τὸ σῶμά μου τὸ ὑπὲρ ὑμῶν διδόμενον· τοῦτο ποιεῖτε εἰς τὴν ἐμὴν ἀνάμνησιν. ¶ 20 καὶ τὸ ποτήριον ὡσαύτως μετὰ τὸ δειπνῆσαι, λέγων, Τοῦτο τὸ ποτήριον ἡ καινὴ διαθήκη ἐν τῷ αἵματί μου τὸ ὑπὲρ ὑμῶν ἐκχυννόμενον. 21 πλὴν ἰδοὺ ἡ χεὶρ τοῦ παραδιδόντος με μετ' ἐμοῦ ἐπὶ τῆς τραπέζης. 22 ὅτι ὁ υἱὸς μὲν τοῦ ἀνθρώπου κατὰ τὸ ὡρισμένον πορεύεται, πλὴν οὐαὶ τῷ ἀνθρώπῳ ἐκείνῳ δι' οὗ παραδίδοται. 23 καὶ αὐτοὶ ἤρξαντο συζητεῖν πρὸς ἑαυτοὺς τὸ τίς ἄρα εἴη ἐξ αὐτῶν ὁ τοῦτο μέλλων πράσσειν. ¶ 24 Ἐγένετο δὲ καὶ φιλονεικία ἐν αὐτοῖς, τὸ τίς αὐτῶν δοκεῖ εἶναι μείζων. 25 ὁ δὲ εἶπεν αὐτοῖς, Οἱ βασιλεῖς τῶν ἐθνῶν κυριεύουσιν αὐτῶν καὶ οἱ ἐξουσιάζοντες αὐτῶν εὐεργέται

Benefactors. **26** But you are not to be like that. Instead, the greatest among you should be like the youngest, and
εὐεργέται δὲ ὑμεῖς οὐχ οὕτως ἀλλ᾽ ὁ μείζων ἐν ὑμῖν → γινέσθω ὡς ὁ νεώτερος καὶ
n.npm cj r.np.2 pl adv cj d.nsm a.nsm.c p.d r.dp.2 v.pmm.3s pl d.nsm a.nsm.c cj
2309 1254 7007 4024 4048 247 3836 3489 1877 7007 1181 6055 3836 3742 2779

the one who rules like the one who serves. **27** For who is greater, the one who is at the table or the one
ὁ ← ← ἡγούμενος ὡς ὁ ← διακονῶν γὰρ τίς μείζων ὁ ← ← ← ἀνακείμενος ἢ ὁ
d.nsm pt.pm.nsm pl d.nsm pt.pa.nsm cj r.nsm a.nsm.c d.nsm pt.pm.nsm d.nsm
3836 2451 6055 3836 1354 1142 5515 3489 3836 367 2445 3836

who serves? Is it not the one who is at the table? But I am among you as one who serves. **28** You
← διακονῶν οὐχὶ ὁ ← ← → ἀνακείμενος δὲ ἐγώ εἰμι ἐν μέσῳ ὑμῶν ὡς ὁ ← διακονῶν δέ ὑμεῖς
pt.pa.nsm pl d.nsm pt.pm.nsm cj r.ns.1 v.pai.1s p.d n.dsn r.gp.2 pl d.nsm pt.pa.nsm cj r.np.2
1354 4049 3836 367 1254 1609 1639 1877 3545 7007 6055 3836 1354 1254 7007

are those who have stood by me in my trials. **29** And I confer on you a kingdom, just as
ἐστε οἱ ← → διαμεμενηκότες μετ᾽ ἐμοῦ ἐν μου τοῖς πειρασμοῖς → κἀγὼ διατίθεμαι → ὑμῖν βασιλείαν → καθὼς
v.pai.2p d.npm pt.ra.npm p.g r.gs.1 p.d r.gs.1 d.dpm n.dpm crasis v.pmi.1s r.dp.2 n.asf cj
1639 3836 1373 3552 1609 1877 1609 3836 4280 2743 1416 7007 993 2777

my Father conferred one on me, **30** so that you may eat and drink at my table in my kingdom and
μου ὁ πατήρ διέθετο → μοι ἵνα → → ἔσθητε καὶ πίνητε ἐπὶ μου τῆς τραπέζης ἐν μου τῇ βασιλείᾳ καὶ
r.gs.1 d.nsm n.nsm v.ami.3s r.ds.1 cj v.pas.2p cj v.pas.2p p.g r.gs.1 d.gsf n.gsf p.d r.gs.1 d.dsf n.dsf cj
1609 3836 4252 1416 1609 2671 2266 2779 4403 2093 1609 3836 5544 1877 1609 3836 993 2779

sit on thrones, judging the twelve tribes of Israel. ¶ **31** "Simon, Simon, Satan has asked
καθήσεσθε ἐπὶ θρόνων κρίνοντες τὰς δώδεκα φυλὰς → τοῦ Ἰσραήλ Σίμων Σίμων ἰδοὺ ὁ σατανᾶς → ἐξητήσατο
v.fmi.2p p.g n.gpm pt.pa.npm d.apf a.apf n.apf d.gsm n.gsm n.vsm n.vsm j d.nsm n.nsm v.ami.3s
2764 2093 2585 3212 3836 1557 3836 2702 3836 4981 4981 2627 3836 4928 1977

to sift you as wheat. **32** But I have prayed for you, Simon, that your faith may not fail. And when
→ τοῦ σινιάσαι ὑμᾶς ὡς τὸν σῖτον δὲ ἐγώ → ἐδεήθην περὶ σοῦ ἵνα σου ἡ πίστις → μὴ ἐκλίπῃ καὶ ποτε
d.gsn f.aa r.ap.2 pl d.asm n.asm cj r.ns.1 v.api.1s p.g r.gs.2 cj r.gs.2 d.nsf n.nsf pl v.aas.3s cj adv
3836 4985 7007 6055 3836 4992 1254 1609 1289 4309 5148 2671 5148 3836 4411 1722 3590 1722 2779 4537

you have turned back, strengthen your brothers." **33** But he replied, "Lord, I am ready to go
→ ἐπιστρέψας ← σύ στήρισον σου τοὺς ἀδελφούς δὲ ὁ εἶπεν αὐτῷ κύριε → εἰμι ἕτοιμος → πορεύεσθαι
pt.aa.nsm r.ns.2 v.aam.2s r.gs.2 d.apm n.apm cj d.nsm v.aai.3s r.dsm.3 n.vsm v.pai.1s a.nsm f.pm
2188 5148 5114 5148 3836 81 1254 3836 3306 899 3261 1639 2289 4513

with you to prison and to death." ¶ **34** Jesus answered, "I tell you, Peter, before the rooster crows
μετὰ σοῦ καὶ εἰς φυλακὴν καὶ εἰς θάνατον δὲ ὁ εἶπεν → λέγω σοι Πέτρε ἕως οὗ ἀλέκτωρ φωνήσει
p.g r.gs.2 cj p.a n.asf cj p.a n.asm cj d.nsm v.aai.3s v.pai.1s r.ds.2 n.vsm p.g n.nsm v.fai.3s
3552 5148 2779 1650 5871 2779 1650 2505 1254 3836 3306 3306 5148 4377 2401 4024 232 5888

today, you will deny three times that you know me." ¶ **35** Then Jesus asked them, "When I sent
σήμερον → → ἀπαρνήσῃ ἕως τρίς ← εἰδέναι με Καὶ εἶπεν αὐτοῖς ὅτε → ἀπέστειλα
adv v.ams.2s cj adv f.ra r.as.1 cj v.aai.3s r.dpm.3 cj v.aai.1s
4958 565 2401 5565 3857 1609 2779 3306 899 4021 690

you without purse, bag or sandals, did you lack anything?" "Nothing," they answered. ¶
ὑμᾶς ἄτερ βαλλαντίου καὶ πήρας καὶ ὑποδημάτων μὴ → → ὑστερήσατε τινος δὲ οὐθενός οἱ εἶπαν
r.ap.2 p.g n.gsn cj n.gsf cj n.gpn pl v.aai.2p r.gsn cj a.gsn d.npm v.aai.3p
7007 868 964 2779 4385 2779 5687 3590 5728 5516 1254 4032 3836 3306

36 He said to them, "But now if you have a purse, take it, and also a bag; and if you don't have
δὲ → εἶπεν αὐτοῖς ἀλλὰ νῦν → ← ὁ ἔχων βαλλάντιον ἀράτω καὶ ὁμοίως πήραν καὶ → μὴ ὁ ἔχων
cj v.aai.3s r.dpm.3 cj adv d.nsm pt.pa.nsm n.asn v.aam.3s adv adv n.asf cj pl d.nsm pt.pa.nsm
1254 3306 899 247 3814 3836 2400 964 149 2779 3931 4385 2779 3590 3836 2400

a sword, sell your cloak and buy one. **37** It is written: 'And he was numbered with the
μάχαιραν πωλησάτω αὐτοῦ τὸ ἱμάτιον καὶ ἀγορασάτω γὰρ → τὸ γεγραμμένον καὶ → → ἐλογίσθη μετὰ
n.asf v.aam.3s r.gsm.3 d.asn n.asn cj v.aam.3s cj d.asn pt.rp.asn cj v.api.3s p.g
3479 4797 899 3836 2668 2779 60 1142 3836 1211 2779 3357 3552

transgressors'; and I tell you that this must be fulfilled in me. Yes, what is written about me is reaching its
ἀνόμων → λέγω ὑμῖν ὅτι τοῦτο δεῖ → τελεσθῆναι ἐν ἐμοί γὰρ καὶ τὸ περὶ ἐμοῦ → ἔχει
a.gpm v.pai.1s r.dp.2 cj r.asn v.pai.3s f.ap p.d r.ds.1 cj adv d.nsn p.g r.gs.1 v.pai.3s
491 3306 7007 4022 4047 1256 5464 1877 1609 1142 2779 3836 4309 1609 2400

καλοῦνται. ²⁶ ὑμεῖς δὲ οὐχ οὕτως, ἀλλ᾽ ὁ μείζων ἐν ὑμῖν γινέσθω ὡς ὁ νεώτερος καὶ ὁ ἡγούμενος ὡς ὁ διακονῶν. ²⁷ τίς γὰρ μείζων, ὁ ἀνακείμενος ἢ ὁ διακονῶν; οὐχὶ ὁ ἀνακείμενος; ἐγὼ δὲ ἐν μέσῳ ὑμῶν εἰμι ὡς ὁ διακονῶν. ²⁸ ὑμεῖς δέ ἐστε οἱ διαμεμενηκότες μετ᾽ ἐμοῦ ἐν τοῖς πειρασμοῖς μου· ²⁹ κἀγὼ διατίθεμαι ὑμῖν καθὼς διέθετό μοι ὁ πατήρ μου βασιλείαν, ³⁰ ἵνα ἔσθητε καὶ πίνητε ἐπὶ τῆς τραπέζης μου ἐν τῇ βασιλείᾳ μου, καὶ καθήσεσθε ἐπὶ θρόνων τὰς δώδεκα φυλὰς κρίνοντες τοῦ Ἰσραήλ. ¶ ³¹ Σίμων Σίμων, ἰδοὺ ὁ Σατανᾶς ἐξητήσατο ὑμᾶς τοῦ σινιάσαι ὡς τὸν σῖτον· ³² ἐγὼ δὲ ἐδεήθην περὶ σοῦ ἵνα μὴ ἐκλίπῃ ἡ πίστις σου· καὶ σύ ποτε ἐπιστρέψας στήρισον τοὺς ἀδελφούς σου. ¶ ³³ ὁ δὲ εἶπεν αὐτῷ, Κύριε, μετὰ σοῦ ἕτοιμός εἰμι καὶ εἰς φυλακὴν καὶ εἰς θάνατον πορεύεσθαι. ¶ ³⁴ ὁ δὲ εἶπεν, Λέγω σοι, Πέτρε, οὐ φωνήσει σήμερον ἀλέκτωρ ἕως τρίς με ἀπαρνήσῃ εἰδέναι. ¶ ³⁵ Καὶ εἶπεν αὐτοῖς, Ὅτε ἀπέστειλα ὑμᾶς ἄτερ βαλλαντίου καὶ πήρας καὶ ὑποδημάτων, μή τινος ὑστερήσατε; οἱ δὲ εἶπαν, Οὐθενός. ¶ ³⁶ εἶπεν δὲ αὐτοῖς, Ἀλλὰ νῦν ὁ ἔχων βαλλάντιον ἀράτω, ὁμοίως καὶ πήραν, καὶ ὁ μὴ ἔχων πωλησάτω τὸ ἱμάτιον αὐτοῦ καὶ ἀγορασάτω μάχαιραν. ³⁷ λέγω γὰρ ὑμῖν ὅτι τοῦτο τὸ γεγραμμένον δεῖ τελεσθῆναι ἐν

fulfillment." **38** The disciples said, "See, Lord, here are two swords." ¶ "That is enough," he replied.
τέλος δὲ οἱ εἶπαν ἰδοὺ κύριε ὧδε δύο μάχαιραι δὲ → ἐστιν ἱκανόν ὁ εἶπεν αὐτοῖς
n.asn cj d.npm v.aai.3p j n.vsm adv a.npf n.npf cj v.pai.3s a.nsn d.nsm v.aai.3s r.dpm.3
5465 1254 3836 3306 2627 3261 6045 1545 3479 1254 1639 2653 3836 3306 899

Jesus Prays on the Mount of Olives

22:39 Jesus went out as usual to the Mount of Olives, and his disciples followed him.
Καὶ ἐπορεύθη ἐξελθὼν ⸂κατὰ τὸ ἔθος⸃ εἰς τὸ ὄρος ⸂τῶν Ἐλαιῶν⸃ δὲ καὶ οἱ μαθηταί ἠκολούθησαν αὐτῷ
cj v.api.3s pt.aa.nsm p.a d.asn n.asn p.a d.asn n.asn d.gpf n.gpf cj adv d.npm n.npm v.aai.3p r.dsm.3
2779 4513 2002 2848 3836 1621 1650 3836 4001 3836 1777 1254 2779 3836 3412 199 899

40 On reaching the place, he said to them, "Pray that you will not fall into temptation." **41** He
δὲ → γενόμενος ἐπὶ τοῦ τόπου → εἶπεν → αὐτοῖς προσεύχεσθε ↱ → μὴ εἰσελθεῖν εἰς πειρασμόν καὶ αὐτὸς
cj pt.am.nsm p.g d.gsm n.gsm v.aai.3s r.dpm.3 v.pmm.2p pl f.aa p.a n.asm cj r.nsm
1254 1181 2093 3836 5536 3306 899 4667 1656 1656 3590 1656 1650 4280 2779 899

withdrew about a stone's throw beyond them, knelt down and prayed, **42** "Father, if you are
ἀπεσπάσθη ὡσεὶ λίθου βολὴν ἀπ᾽ αὐτῶν καὶ ⸂θεὶς τὰ γόνατα⸃ ← προσηύχετο λέγων πάτερ εἰ →
v.api.3s pl n.gsm n.asf p.g r.gpm.3 cj pt.aa.nsm d.apn n.apn v.imi.3s pt.pa.nsm n.vsm cj
685 6059 3345 1074 608 899 2779 5502 3836 1205 4667 3306 4252 1623

willing, take this cup from me; yet not my will, but yours be done." **43** An angel from
βούλει παρένεγκε τοῦτο ⸂τὸ ποτήριον⸃ ἀπ᾽ ἐμοῦ πλὴν μὴ μου ⸂τὸ θέλημα⸃ ἀλλὰ ⸂τὸ σὸν⸃ → γινέσθω 〚δὲ ἄγγελος ἀπ᾽
v.pmi.2s v.aam.2s r.asn d.asn n.asn p.g r.gs.1 cj pl r.gs.1 d.nsn n.nsn cj d.nsn r.nsn.2 v.pmm.3s cj n.nsm p.g
1089 4195 4047 3836 4539 608 1609 4440 3590 1609 3836 2525 247 3836 5050 1181 1254 34 608

heaven appeared to him and strengthened him. **44** And being in anguish, he prayed more earnestly, and his
οὐρανοῦ ὤφθη → αὐτῷ ἐνισχύων αὐτόν καὶ γενόμενος ἐν ἀγωνίᾳ → προσηύχετο → ἐκτενέστερον καὶ αὐτοῦ
n.gsm v.api.3s r.dsm.3 pt.pa.nsm r.asm.3 cj pt.am.nsm p.d n.dsf v.imi.3s adv.c cj r.gsm.3
4041 3972 899 1932 899 2779 1181 1877 75 4667 1757 2779 899

sweat was like drops of blood falling to the ground. ¶ **45** When he rose from
⸂ὁ ἱδρὼς⸃ ἐγένετο ὡσεὶ θρόμβοι → αἵματος καταβαίνοντες ἐπὶ τὴν γῆν〛 καὶ → → ἀναστὰς ἀπὸ
d.nsm n.nsm v.ami.3s pl n.npm n.gsm pt.pa.gsn p.a d.asf n.asf cj pt.aa.nsm p.g
3836 2629 1181 6059 2584 135 2849 2093 3836 1178 2779 482 608

prayer and went back to the disciples, he found them asleep, exhausted from sorrow. **46** "Why are
⸂τῆς προσευχῆς⸃ ἐλθὼν πρὸς τοὺς μαθητὰς → εὗρεν αὐτοὺς κοιμωμένους ἀπὸ ⸂τῆς λύπης⸃ καὶ τί →
d.gsf n.gsf pt.aa.nsm p.a d.apm n.apm v.aai.3s r.apm.3 pt.pp.apm p.g d.gsf n.gsf cj r.asn
3836 4666 2262 4639 3836 3412 2351 899 3121 608 3836 3383 2779 5515

you sleeping?" he asked them. "Get up and pray so that you will not fall into temptation."
→ καθεύδετε → εἶπεν αὐτοῖς ἀναστάντες ← προσεύχεσθε ἵνα ← → μὴ εἰσέλθητε εἰς πειρασμόν
v.pai.2p v.aai.3s r.dpm.3 pt.aa.npm v.pmm.2p cj pl v.aas.2p p.a n.asm
2761 3306 899 482 4667 2671 1656 1656 3590 1656 1650 4280

Jesus Arrested

22:47 While he was still speaking a crowd came up, and the man who was called Judas, one of the
↱ αὐτοῦ → Ἔτι λαλοῦντος ἰδοὺ ὄχλος καὶ ὁ ← λεγόμενος Ἰούδας εἷς → τῶν
r.gsm.3 adv pt.pa.gsm j n.nsm cj d.nsm pt.pp.nsm n.nsm a.nsm d.gpm
3281 899 3281 2285 3281 2627 4063 2779 3836 3306 2683 1651 3836

Twelve, was leading them. He approached Jesus to kiss him, **48** but Jesus asked him, "Judas, are you
δώδεκα → προήρχετο αὐτοὺς καὶ → ἤγγισεν ⸂τῷ Ἰησοῦ⸃ → φιλῆσαι αὐτόν δὲ Ἰησοῦς εἶπεν αὐτῷ Ἰούδα → →
a.gpm v.imi.3s r.apm.3 cj v.aai.3s d.dsm n.dsm f.aa r.asm.3 cj n.nsm v.aai.3s r.dsm.3 n.vsm
1557 4601 899 2779 1581 3836 2652 5797 899 1254 2652 3306 899 2683

betraying the Son of Man with a kiss?" ¶ **49** When Jesus' followers saw what was going to
παραδίδως τὸν υἱὸν → ⸂τοῦ ἀνθρώπου⸃ φιλήματι δὲ → αὐτὸν οἱ περὶ ἰδόντες τὸ → → →
v.pai.2s d.asm n.asm d.gsm n.gsm n.dsn cj r.asm.3 d.npm p.a pt.aa.npm d.asn
4140 3836 5626 3836 476 5799 1254 1625 3836 4309 1625 3836

happen, they said, "Lord, should we strike with our swords?" **50** And one of them struck the servant of the
ἐσόμενον → εἶπαν κύριε εἰ → πατάξομεν ἐν μαχαίρῃ καὶ εἷς τις ἐξ αὐτῶν ἐπάταξεν τὸν δοῦλον → τοῦ
pt.fm.asn v.aai.3p n.vsm cj v.fai.1p p.d n.dsf cj a.nsm r.nsm p.g r.gpm.3 v.aai.3s d.asm n.asm d.gsm
1639 3306 3261 1623 4250 1877 3479 2779 1651 5516 1666 899 4250 3836 1529 3836

ἐμοί, τὸ Καὶ μετὰ ἀνόμων ἐλογίσθη· καὶ γὰρ τὸ περὶ ἐμοῦ τέλος ἔχει. ³⁸ οἱ δὲ εἶπαν, Κύριε, ἰδοὺ μάχαιραι ὧδε δύο. ¶ ὁ δὲ εἶπεν αὐτοῖς, Ἱκανόν ἐστιν.

²²·³⁹ Καὶ ἐξελθὼν ἐπορεύθη κατὰ τὸ ἔθος εἰς τὸ Ὄρος τῶν Ἐλαιῶν, ἠκολούθησαν δὲ αὐτῷ καὶ οἱ μαθηταί. ⁴⁰ γενόμενος δὲ ἐπὶ τοῦ τόπου εἶπεν αὐτοῖς, Προσεύχεσθε μὴ εἰσελθεῖν εἰς πειρασμόν. ⁴¹ καὶ αὐτὸς ἀπεσπάσθη ἀπ᾽ αὐτῶν ὡσεὶ λίθου βολὴν καὶ θεὶς τὰ γόνατα προσηύχετο ⁴² λέγων, Πάτερ, εἰ βούλει παρένεγκε τοῦτο τὸ ποτήριον ἀπ᾽ ἐμοῦ· πλὴν μὴ τὸ θέλημά μου ἀλλὰ τὸ σὸν γινέσθω. ⁴³ 〚ὤφθη δὲ αὐτῷ ἄγγελος ἀπ᾽ οὐρανοῦ ἐνισχύων αὐτόν. ⁴⁴ καὶ γενόμενος ἐν ἀγωνίᾳ ἐκτενέστερον προσηύχετο· καὶ ἐγένετο ὁ ἱδρὼς αὐτοῦ ὡσεὶ θρόμβοι αἵματος καταβαίνοντες ἐπὶ τὴν γῆν.〛 ¶ ⁴⁵ καὶ ἀναστὰς ἀπὸ τῆς προσευχῆς ἐλθὼν πρὸς τοὺς μαθητὰς εὗρεν κοιμωμένους αὐτοὺς ἀπὸ τῆς λύπης, ⁴⁶ καὶ εἶπεν αὐτοῖς, Τί καθεύδετε; ἀναστάντες προσεύχεσθε, ἵνα μὴ εἰσέλθητε εἰς πειρασμόν.

²²·⁴⁷ Ἔτι αὐτοῦ λαλοῦντος ἰδοὺ ὄχλος, καὶ ὁ λεγόμενος Ἰούδας εἷς τῶν δώδεκα προήρχετο αὐτοὺς καὶ ἤγγισεν τῷ Ἰησοῦ φιλῆσαι αὐτόν. ⁴⁸ Ἰησοῦς δὲ εἶπεν αὐτῷ, Ἰούδα, φιλήματι τὸν υἱὸν τοῦ ἀνθρώπου παραδίδως; ¶ ⁴⁹ ἰδόντες δὲ οἱ περὶ αὐτὸν τὸ ἐσόμενον εἶπαν, Κύριε, εἰ πατάξομεν ἐν μαχαίρῃ; ⁵⁰ καὶ ἐπάταξεν εἷς τις ἐξ αὐτῶν τοῦ ἀρχιερέως τὸν δοῦλον καὶ ἀφεῖλεν τὸ οὖς

high priest,   cutting off his   right   ear. **51** But Jesus   answered,   "No more   of this!" And he
→ ἀρχιερέως καὶ ἀφεῖλεν ← αὐτοῦ ⌐τὸ δεξιόν⌐ ⌐τὸ οὖς⌐ δὲ ὁ Ἰησοῦς, ἀποκριθεὶς εἶπεν → ⌐Ἐᾶτε ἕως⌐ τούτου καὶ →
n.gsm   cj   v.aai.3s   r.gsm.3 d.asn a.asn   d.asn n.asn   cj   d.nsm n.nsm   pt.ap.nsm   v.aai.3s   v.pam.2p r.gsm cj
797   2779 904   899   3836 1288   3836 4044   1254 3836 2652   646   3306   1572 2401   4047 2779

touched the man's ear   and healed him. ¶ **52** Then Jesus   said   to   the chief priests,   the officers   of the
ἀψάμενος τοῦ   ὠτίου ἰάσατο αὐτόν   δὲ   Ἰησοῦς Εἶπεν πρὸς → ἀρχιερεῖς καὶ   στρατηγοὺς → τοῦ
pt.am.nsm d.gsn   n.gsn   v.ami.3s r.asm.3   cj   n.nsm   v.aai.3s p.a   n.apm   cj   n.apm   d.gsn
721   3836   6065   2615   899   1254 2652   3306 4639   797   2779   5130   3836

temple guard, and the elders,   who had come   for him, *"Am I leading a rebellion,*   that you have
ἱεροῦ   καὶ   πρεσβυτέρους τοὺς → παραγενομένους ἐπ᾽ αὐτόν   ⌐ὡς ἐπὶ λῃστὴν⌐ → →
n.gsn   cj   a.apm   d.apm   pt.am.apm   p.a r.asm.3   pl p.a n.asm
2639   2779   4565   3836   4134   2093 899   6055 2093 3334

come with swords and clubs? **53** Every day   I   was with you in the temple courts, and you did not lay   a
ἐξήλθατε μετὰ μαχαιρῶν καὶ ξύλων   καθ᾽ ἡμέραν μου ὄντος μεθ᾽ ὑμῶν ἐν τῷ ἱερῷ → → οὐκ ἐξετείνατε
v.aai.2p μετὰ   n.gpf   cj   n.gpn   p.a   n.asf   r.gs.1 pt.pa.gsm p.g   r.gp.2 p.d d.dsn n.dsn   pl   v.aai.2p
2002   3552   3479   2779 3833   2848   2465   1609 1639   3552 7007 1877 3836 2639   1753 1753 4024 1753

hand   on me. But this is   your hour   — when darkness   reigns."
⌐τὰς χεῖρας⌐ ἐπ᾽ ἐμέ ἀλλ᾽ αὕτη ἐστὶν ὑμῶν ἡ ὥρα   καὶ   τοῦ σκότους ἡ ἐξουσία
d.apf n.apf   p.a r.as.1 cj   r.nsf v.pai.3s r.gp.2 d.nsf n.nsf cj   d.gsn n.gsn   d.nsf n.nsf
3836 5931   2093 1609 247   4047 1639   7007 3836 6052 2779   3836 5030   3836 2026

Peter Disowns Jesus

22:54 Then seizing   him, they led   him away and took   him into the house of the high priest.
δὲ Συλλαβόντες αὐτὸν → ἤγαγον   καὶ εἰσήγαγον   εἰς τὴν οἰκίαν τοῦ → ἀρχιερέως δὲ
cj pt.aa.npm   r.asm.3   v.aai.3p   cj   v.aai.3p   p.a d.asf n.asf   d.gsm   n.gsm   cj
1254 5197   899   1652   2779 1652   1650 3836 3864   3836   797   1254

Peter   followed at a distance. **55** But when they had kindled   a fire in the middle of the courtyard and had
ὁ Πέτρος, ἠκολούθει → μακρόθεν   δὲ → → → περιαψάντων πῦρ ἐν   μέσῳ   τῆς αὐλῆς καὶ →
d.nsm n.nsm   v.iai.3s   adv   cj   pt.aa.gpm   n.asn p.d   n.dsn   d.gsf n.gsf cj
3836 4377   199   3427   1254   4312   4786 1877 3545   3836 885   2779

sat   down together, Peter   sat   down with them. **56** A servant girl saw   him seated   there in
συγκαθισάντων ←   ὁ Πέτρος ἐκάθητο ← μέσος αὐτῶν δὲ τις παιδίσκη ← ἰδοῦσα αὐτὸν καθήμενον   πρὸς
pt.aa.gpm   d.nsm n.nsm v.imi.3s   a.nsm r.gpm.3 cj r.nsf n.nsf   pt.aa.nsf r.asm.3 pt.pm.asm   p.a
5154   3836 4377 2764   3545 899   1254 5516 4087   1625 899   2764   4639

the firelight.   She looked   closely at him and said,   "This man was with him." **57** But he denied it. "Woman,
τὸ φῶς   καὶ → ἀτενίσασα   αὐτῷ εἶπεν καὶ οὗτος ← ἦν σὺν αὐτῷ δὲ ὁ ἠρνήσατο γύναι
d.asn n.asn cj   pt.aa.nsf   r.dsm.3 v.aai.3s adv r.nsm   v.iai.3s p.d r.dsm.3 cj d.nsm v.ami.3s   n.vsf
3836 5890 2779   867   899   3306   2779 4047   1639 5250 899   1254 3836 766   1222

I   don't know him," he said. ¶ **58** A little   later someone else saw   him and said, "You also are one
→ οὐκ οἶδα αὐτὸν → λέγων   καὶ   μετὰ βραχὺ   ἕτερος ← ἰδὼν αὐτὸν ἔφη σὺ καὶ εἶ
pl v.rai.1s r.asm.3   pt.pa.nsm   cj   p.a a.asn   r.nsm   pt.aa.nsm r.asm.3 v.iai.3s r.ns.2 adv v.pai.2s
3857 4024 3857 899   3306   2779   3552 1099   2283   1625 899   5774 5148 2779 1639

of them." "Man, I am not!" Peter   replied. ¶ **59** About an hour later   another   asserted,
ἐξ αὐτῶν δὲ ἄνθρωπε εἰμί οὐκ ὁ Πέτρος, ἔφη   καὶ ὡσεὶ μιᾶς ὥρας διαστάσης ἄλλος τις διϊσχυρίζετο
p.g r.gpm.3 cj n.vsm   v.pai.1s pl d.nsm n.nsm   v.iai.3s   cj ὡσεὶ a.gsf n.gsf pt.aa.gsf   r.nsm r.nsm v.imi.3s
1666 899   1254 476   1639 4024 3836 4377   5774   2779 6059 1651 6052 1460   257 5516 1462

"Certainly   this fellow was with him, for   he is   a Galilean." **60** Peter   replied, "Man, I
λέγων ἐπ᾽ ἀληθείας, καὶ οὗτος ← ἦν μετ᾽ αὐτοῦ γὰρ καὶ → ἐστιν Γαλιλαῖος δὲ ὁ Πέτρος, εἶπεν ἄνθρωπε
pt.pa.nsm p.g n.gsf   adv r.nsm   v.iai.3s p.g r.gsm.3 cj adv   v.pai.3s a.nsm   cj d.nsm n.nsm   v.aai.3s n.vsm
3306 2093 237   2779 4047   1639 3552 899   1142 2779   1639   1134   1254 3836 4377   3306   476

don't know what you're talking about!" Just   as he   was   speaking, the rooster crowed. **61** The Lord
οὐκ οἶδα ὃ → λέγεις ← καὶ παραχρῆμα ← αὐτοῦ ἔτι λαλοῦντος ἀλέκτωρ ἐφώνησεν καὶ ὁ κύριος
pl v.rai.1s r.asn   v.pai.2s   cj παραχρῆμα   r.gsm.3 adv pt.pa.gsm   n.nsm   v.aai.3s   cj d.nsm n.nsm
4024 3857 4005   3306   2779 4202   899   2285 3281   232   5888   2779 3836 3261

turned and looked   straight at Peter.   Then Peter   remembered the word the Lord   had spoken to
στραφεὶς ἐνέβλεψεν ← → ⌐τῷ Πέτρῳ⌐ καὶ ὁ Πέτρος, ὑπεμνήσθη τοῦ ῥήματος τοῦ κυρίου ὡς → εἶπεν
pt.ap.nsm v.aai.3s   d.dsm n.dsm   cj d.nsm n.nsm   v.api.3s   d.gsn n.gsn   d.gsm n.gsm   cj   v.aai.3s
5138   1838   3836 4377   2779 3836 4377   5703   3836 4839   3836 3261   6055   3306

αὐτοῦ τὸ δεξιόν. ⁵¹ ἀποκριθεὶς δὲ ὁ Ἰησοῦς εἶπεν, Ἐᾶτε ἕως τούτου· καὶ ἁψάμενος τοῦ ὠτίου ἰάσατο αὐτόν. ¶ ⁵² εἶπεν δὲ
Ἰησοῦς πρὸς τοὺς παραγενομένους ἐπ᾽ αὐτὸν ἀρχιερεῖς καὶ στρατηγοὺς τοῦ ἱεροῦ καὶ πρεσβυτέρους, Ὡς ἐπὶ λῃστὴν ἐξήλθατε
μετὰ μαχαιρῶν καὶ ξύλων; ⁵³ καθ᾽ ἡμέραν ὄντος μου μεθ᾽ ὑμῶν ἐν τῷ ἱερῷ οὐκ ἐξετείνατε τὰς χεῖρας ἐπ᾽ ἐμέ, ἀλλ᾽ αὕτη ἐστὶν
ὑμῶν ἡ ὥρα καὶ ἡ ἐξουσία τοῦ σκότους.

²²·⁵⁴ Συλλαβόντες δὲ αὐτὸν ἤγαγον καὶ εἰσήγαγον εἰς τὴν οἰκίαν τοῦ ἀρχιερέως· ὁ δὲ Πέτρος ἠκολούθει μακρόθεν.
⁵⁵ περιαψάντων δὲ πῦρ ἐν μέσῳ τῆς αὐλῆς καὶ συγκαθισάντων ἐκάθητο ὁ Πέτρος μέσος αὐτῶν. ⁵⁶ ἰδοῦσα δὲ αὐτὸν παιδίσκη
τις καθήμενον πρὸς τὸ φῶς καὶ ἀτενίσασα αὐτῷ εἶπεν, Καὶ οὗτος σὺν αὐτῷ ἦν. ⁵⁷ ὁ δὲ ἠρνήσατο λέγων, Οὐκ οἶδα αὐτόν,
γύναι. ¶ ⁵⁸ καὶ μετὰ βραχὺ ἕτερος ἰδὼν αὐτὸν ἔφη, Καὶ σὺ ἐξ αὐτῶν εἶ. ὁ δὲ Πέτρος ἔφη, Ἄνθρωπε, οὐκ εἰμί. ¶ ⁵⁹ καὶ
διαστάσης ὡσεὶ ὥρας μιᾶς ἄλλος τις διϊσχυρίζετο λέγων, Ἐπ᾽ ἀληθείας καὶ οὗτος μετ᾽ αὐτοῦ ἦν, καὶ γὰρ Γαλιλαῖός ἐστιν.
⁶⁰ εἶπεν δὲ ὁ Πέτρος, Ἄνθρωπε, οὐκ οἶδα ὃ λέγεις. καὶ παραχρῆμα ἔτι λαλοῦντος αὐτοῦ ἐφώνησεν ἀλέκτωρ. ⁶¹ καὶ στραφεὶς
ὁ κύριος ἐνέβλεψεν τῷ Πέτρῳ, καὶ ὑπεμνήσθη ὁ Πέτρος τοῦ ῥήματος τοῦ κυρίου ὡς εἶπεν αὐτῷ ὅτι Πρὶν ἀλέκτορα φωνῆσαι

him: "Before the rooster crows today, you will disown me three times." **62** And he went outside and wept
αὐτῷ ὅτι πρὶν ἀλέκτορα φωνῆσαι σήμερον → → ἀπαρνήσῃ με τρίς ← καὶ → ἐξελθὼν ἔξω ἔκλαυσεν
r.dsm.3 cj cj n.asm f.aa adv v.fmi.2s r.as.1 adv cj pt.aa.nsm adv v.aai.3s
899 4022 4570 232 5888 4958 565 1609 5565 2779 2002 2032 3081

bitterly.
πικρῶς
adv
4396

The Guards Mock Jesus

22:63 The men who were guarding Jesus began mocking and beating him. **64** They blindfolded him and
Καὶ οἱ ἄνδρες οἱ → συνέχοντες αὐτόν → ἐνέπαιζον δέροντες αὐτῷ καὶ → περικαλύψαντες αὐτόν
cj d.npm n.npm d.npm pt.pa.npm r.asm.3 v.iai.3p pt.pa.npm r.dsm.3 cj pt.aa.npm r.asm.3
2779 3836 467 3836 5309 899 1850 1296 899 2779 4328 899

demanded, "Prophesy! Who hit you?" **65** And they said many other insulting things to him.
ἐπηρώτων λέγοντες προφήτευσον τίς ἐστιν ὁ παίσας σε καὶ → ἔλεγον πολλὰ ἕτερα βλασφημοῦντες ← εἰς αὐτόν
v.iai.3p pt.pa.npm v.aam.2s r.nsm v.pai.3s d.nsm pt.aa.nsm r.as.2 cj v.iai.3p a.apn r.apn pt.pa.npm p.a r.asm.3
2089 3306 4736 5515 1639 3836 4091 5148 2779 3306 4498 2283 1059 1650 899

Jesus Before Pilate and Herod

22:66 At daybreak the council of the elders of the people, both the chief priests and teachers
Καὶ ὡς ἐγένετο ἡμέρα τὸ πρεσβυτέριον → τοῦ λαοῦ τε ἀρχιερεῖς καὶ γραμματεῖς
cj cj v.ami.3s n.nsf d.nsn n.nsn d.gsm n.gsm cj n.npm cj n.npm
2779 6055 1181 2465 3836 4564 3836 3295 5445 797 2779 1208

of the law, met together, and Jesus was led before them. **67** "If you are the Christ," they said,
← ← συνήχθη ← καὶ αὐτὸν → ἀπήγαγον εἰς τὸ συνέδριον αὐτῶν εἰ σὺ εἶ ὁ χριστός → λέγοντες
v.api.3s cj r.asm.3 v.aai.3p p.a d.asn n.asn r.gpm.3 cj r.ns.2 v.pai.2s d.nsm n.nsm pt.pa.npm
5251 2779 899 552 1650 3836 5284 899 1623 5148 1639 3836 5986 3306

"tell us." Jesus answered, "If I tell you, you will not believe me, **68** and if I asked you, you would
εἰπὸν ἡμῖν δὲ εἶπεν αὐτοῖς ἐὰν → εἴπω ὑμῖν ↱ → οὐ μὴ πιστεύσητε δὲ ἐὰν → ἐρωτήσω ↱ →
v.aam.2s r.dp.1 cj v.aai.3s r.dpm.3 cj v.aas.1s r.dp.2 pl pl v.aas.2p cj cj v.aas.1s
3306 7005 1254 3306 899 1569 3306 7007 4409 4409 4024 3590 4409 1254 1569 2263 646 646

not answer. **69** But from now on, the Son of Man will be seated at the right hand of the
οὐ μὴ ἀποκριθῆτε δὲ ἀπὸ τοῦ νῦν ← ὁ υἱὸς τοῦ ἀνθρώπου → ἔσται καθήμενος ἐκ δεξιῶν → τοῦ
pl pl v.aps.2p cj p.g d.gsn adv d.nsm n.nsm d.gsm n.gsm v.fmi.3s pt.pm.nsm p.g a.gpf d.gsm
4024 3590 646 1254 608 3836 3814 3836 5626 3836 476 1639 2764 1666 1288 3836

mighty God." ¶ **70** They all asked, "Are you then the Son of God?" He replied,
τῆς δυνάμεως θεοῦ δὲ πάντες εἶπαν εἰ σὺ οὖν ὁ υἱὸς τοῦ θεοῦ δὲ ὁ ἔφη πρὸς αὐτούς
d.gsf n.gsf n.gsn cj a.npm v.aai.3p cj r.ns.2 cj d.nsm n.nsm d.gsm n.gsm cj d.nsm v.iai.3s p.a r.apm.3
3836 1539 2536 1254 4246 3306 1623 5148 4036 3836 5626 3836 2536 1254 3836 5774 4639 899

"You are right in saying I am." ¶ **71** Then they said, "Why do we need any more testimony?
ὑμεῖς λέγετε ὅτι ἐγώ εἰμι δὲ οἱ εἶπαν τί ἔχομεν χρείαν ἔτι μαρτυρίας γὰρ
r.np.2 v.pai.2p cj r.ns.1 v.pai.1s cj d.npm v.aai.3p r.asn v.pai.1p n.asf adv n.gsf cj
7007 3306 4022 1609 1639 1254 3836 3306 5515 2400 5970 2285 3456 1142

We have heard it from his own lips." **23:1** Then the whole assembly rose and led him off
αὐτοὶ → ἠκούσαμεν ἀπὸ αὐτοῦ τοῦ στόματος Καὶ τὸ ἅπαν πλῆθος αὐτῶν ἀναστὰν ἤγαγον αὐτὸν
r.npm v.aai.1p p.g r.gsm.3 d.gsn n.gsn cj d.nsn a.nsn n.nsn r.gpm.3 pt.aa.nsn v.aai.3p r.asm.3
899 201 608 899 3836 5125 2779 3836 570 4436 899 482 72 899

to Pilate. **2** And they began to accuse him, saying, "We have found this man subverting our nation.
ἐπὶ τὸν Πιλᾶτον δὲ → Ἤρξαντο κατηγορεῖν αὐτοῦ λέγοντες → → εὕραμεν τοῦτον ← διαστρέφοντα ἡμῶν τὸ ἔθνος
p.a d.asm n.asm cj v.ami.3p f.pa r.gsm.3 pt.pa.npm v.aai.1p r.asm.3 pt.pa.asm r.gp.1 d.asn n.asn
2093 3836 4397 1254 806 2989 899 3306 2351 4047 1406 7005 3836 1620

He opposes payment of taxes to Caesar and claims to be Christ, a king." ¶ **3** So Pilate
καὶ → κωλύοντα διδόναι φόρους → Καίσαρι καὶ λέγοντα ἑαυτὸν → εἶναι χριστὸν βασιλέα δὲ ὁ Πιλᾶτος
cj pt.pa.asm f.pa n.apm n.dsm cj pt.pa.asm r.asm.3 f.pa n.asm n.asm cj d.nsm n.nsm
2779 3266 1443 5843 2790 2779 3306 1571 1639 5986 995 1254 3836 4397

asked Jesus, "Are you the king of the Jews?" "Yes, it is as you say," Jesus replied. ¶
ἠρώτησεν αὐτὸν λέγων εἰ σὺ ὁ βασιλεὺς → τῶν Ἰουδαίων δὲ σὺ λέγεις ὁ ἀποκριθεὶς αὐτῷ ἔφη
v.aai.3s r.asm.3 pt.pa.nsm v.pai.2s r.ns.2 d.nsm n.nsm d.gpm a.gpm cj r.ns.2 v.pai.2s d.nsm pt.ap.nsm r.dsm.3 v.iai.3s
2263 899 3306 1639 5148 3836 995 3836 2681 1254 5148 3306 3836 646 899 5774

σήμερον ἀπαρνήσῃ με τρίς. **62** καὶ ἐξελθὼν ἔξω ἔκλαυσεν πικρῶς.
22:63 Καὶ οἱ ἄνδρες οἱ συνέχοντες αὐτὸν ἐνέπαιζον αὐτῷ δέροντες, **64** καὶ περικαλύψαντες αὐτὸν ἐπηρώτων λέγοντες, Προφήτευσον, τίς ἐστιν ὁ παίσας σε; **65** καὶ ἕτερα πολλὰ βλασφημοῦντες ἔλεγον εἰς αὐτόν.
22:66 Καὶ ὡς ἐγένετο ἡμέρα, συνήχθη τὸ πρεσβυτέριον τοῦ λαοῦ, ἀρχιερεῖς τε καὶ γραμματεῖς, καὶ ἀπήγαγον αὐτὸν εἰς τὸ συνέδριον αὐτῶν **67** λέγοντες, Εἰ σὺ εἶ ὁ Χριστός, εἰπὸν ἡμῖν. εἶπεν δὲ αὐτοῖς, Ἐὰν ὑμῖν εἴπω, οὐ μὴ πιστεύσητε· **68** ἐὰν δὲ ἐρωτήσω, οὐ μὴ ἀποκριθῆτε. **69** ἀπὸ τοῦ νῦν δὲ ἔσται ὁ υἱὸς τοῦ ἀνθρώπου καθήμενος ἐκ δεξιῶν τῆς δυνάμεως τοῦ θεοῦ. ¶ **70** εἶπαν δὲ πάντες, Σὺ οὖν εἶ ὁ υἱὸς τοῦ θεοῦ; ὁ δὲ πρὸς αὐτοὺς ἔφη, Ὑμεῖς λέγετε ὅτι ἐγώ εἰμι. ¶ **71** οἱ δὲ εἶπαν, Τί ἔτι ἔχομεν μαρτυρίας χρείαν; αὐτοὶ γὰρ ἠκούσαμεν ἀπὸ τοῦ στόματος αὐτοῦ. **23:1** Καὶ ἀναστὰν ἅπαν τὸ πλῆθος αὐτῶν ἤγαγον αὐτὸν ἐπὶ τὸν Πιλᾶτον. **2** ἤρξαντο δὲ κατηγορεῖν αὐτοῦ λέγοντες, Τοῦτον εὕραμεν διαστρέφοντα τὸ ἔθνος ἡμῶν καὶ κωλύοντα φόρους Καίσαρι διδόναι καὶ λέγοντα ἑαυτὸν Χριστὸν βασιλέα εἶναι. ¶ **3** ὁ δὲ Πιλᾶτος ἠρώτησεν αὐτὸν λέγων, Σὺ εἶ ὁ βασιλεὺς τῶν

4 Then Pilate announced to the chief priests and the crowd, "I find no basis for a charge against this
δὲ ὁ Πιλᾶτος εἶπεν πρὸς τοὺς → ἀρχιερεῖς καὶ τοὺς ὄχλους → εὑρίσκω οὐδὲν ← αἴτιον ἐν τούτῳ
cj d.nsm n.nsm v.aai.3s p.a d.apm n.apm cj d.apm n.apm v.pai.1s a.asn n.asn p.d r.dsm
1254 3836 4397 3306 4639 3836 797 2779 3836 4063 2351 4029 165 1877 4047

man." **5** But they insisted, "He stirs up the people *all over* Judea by his teaching. He
ιτῷ ἀνθρώπῳ δὲ οἱ ἐπίσχυον λέγοντες ὅτι → ἀνασείει ← τὸν λαὸν καθ᾽ ὅλης τῆς Ἰουδαίας, → → διδάσκων καὶ →
d.dsm n.dsm cj d.npm v.iai.3p pt.pa.npm cj v.pai.3s d.asm n.asm p.g a.gsf d.gsf n.gsf pt.pa.nsm cj
3836 476 1254 3836 2196 3306 4022 411 3836 3295 2848 3910 3836 2677 1438 2779

started in Galilee and has come all the way here." ¶ **6** On hearing this, Pilate asked if the
ἀρξάμενος ἀπὸ τῆς Γαλιλαίας, ἕως ← ← ὧδε δὲ → ἀκούσας Πιλᾶτος ἐπηρώτησεν εἰ ὁ
pt.am.nsm p.g d.gsf n.gsf p.g adv cj pt.aa.nsm n.nsm v.aai.3s cj d.nsm
806 608 3836 1133 2401 6045 1254 201 4397 2089 1623 3836

man was a Galilean. **7** When he learned that Jesus was under Herod's jurisdiction, he sent him to
ἄνθρωπος ἐστιν Γαλιλαῖος καὶ → → ἐπιγνοὺς ὅτι ἐστιν ἐκ Ἡρώδου ιτῆς ἐξουσίας, → ἀνέπεμψεν αὐτὸν πρὸς
n.nsm v.pai.3s a.nsm cj pt.aa.nsm cj v.pai.3s p.g n.gsm d.gsf n.gsf v.aai.3s r.asm.3 p.a
476 1639 1134 2779 2105 4022 1639 1666 2476 3836 2026 402 899 4639

Herod, who was also in Jerusalem at that time. ¶ **8** When Herod saw Jesus, he
Ἡρώδην αὐτὸν ὄντα καὶ ἐν Ἰεροσολύμοις ἐν ταύταις ιταῖς ἡμέραις, δὲ ↱ Ὁ Ἡρώδης ἰδὼν τὸν Ἰησοῦν ↱
n.asm r.asm.3 pt.pa.asm adv p.d n.dpn p.d r.dpf d.dpf n.dpf cj d.nsm n.nsm pt.aa.nsm d.asm n.asm
2476 899 1639 2779 1877 2642 1877 4047 3836 2465 1254 1625 3836 2476 1625 3836 2652 5897

was greatly pleased, because for a long time he had been wanting to see him. From what he had heard
↱ λίαν ἐχάρη γὰρ ἐξ ἱκανῶν χρόνων → → ἦν θέλων → ἰδεῖν αὐτὸν διὰ → → ιτὸ ἀκούειν,
adv v.api.3s cj p.g a.gpm n.gpm v.iai.3s pt.pa.nsm f.aa r.asm.3 p.a d.asn f.pa
5897 5897 3336 1142 1666 2653 5989 1639 2527 1625 899 1328 3836 201

about him, he hoped to see him perform some miracle. **9** He plied him with many questions, but
περὶ αὐτοῦ καὶ → ἤλπιζεν ἰδεῖν ὑπ᾽ αὐτοῦ γινόμενον τι σημεῖον δὲ → ἐπηρώτα αὐτὸν ἐν ἱκανοῖς λόγοις δὲ
p.g r.gsm.3 cj v.iai.3s f.aa p.g r.gsm.3 pt.pm.asn r.asn n.asn cj v.iai.3s r.asm.3 p.d a.dpm n.dpm cj
4309 899 2779 1827 1625 5679 899 1181 5516 4956 1254 2089 899 1877 2653 3364 1254

Jesus gave him no answer. **10** The chief priests and the teachers of the law were standing there,
αὐτὸς αὐτῷ οὐδὲν ἀπεκρίνατο δὲ οἱ ἀρχιερεῖς καὶ οἱ γραμματεῖς ← ← εἱστήκεισαν ←
r.nsm r.dsm.3 a.asn v.ami.3s cj d.npm n.npm cj d.npm n.npm v.lai.3p
899 646 899 4029 646 1254 3836 797 2779 3836 1208 2705

vehemently accusing him. **11** Then Herod and his soldiers ridiculed and mocked him.
εὐτόνως κατηγοροῦντες αὐτοῦ δὲ ὁ Ἡρώδης, καὶ σὺν αὐτοῦ ιτοῖς στρατεύμασιν, ἐξουθενήσας καὶ ἐμπαίξας αὐτὸν
adv pt.pa.npm r.gsm.3 cj d.nsm n.nsm adv p.d r.gsm.3 d.dpn n.dpn pt.aa.nsm cj pt.aa.nsm r.asm.3
2364 2989 899 1254 3836 2476 2779 5250 899 3836 5128 2024 2779 1850 899

Dressing him in an elegant robe, they sent him back to Pilate. **12** That day Herod and
περιβαλὼν ← λαμπρὰν ἐσθῆτα → ἀνέπεμψεν αὐτὸν ← → ιτῷ Πιλάτῳ δὲ ἐν αὐτῇ ιτῇ ἡμέρᾳ ὅ τε Ἡρώδης καὶ
pt.aa.nsm a.asf n.asf v.aai.3s r.asm.3 d.dsm n.dsm cj p.d r.dsf d.dsf n.dsf r.nsm cj n.nsm cj
4314 3287 2264 402 899 402 3836 4397 1254 1877 899 3836 2465 3836 5445 2476 2779

Pilate became friends – before this they had been enemies. ¶ **13** Pilate
ὁ Πιλᾶτος ἐγένοντο φίλοι μετ᾽ ἀλλήλων γὰρ προϋπῆρχον πρὸς αὐτούς → ὄντες ιἐν ἔχθρᾳ, δὲ Πιλᾶτος
d.nsm n.nsm v.ami.3p a.npm p.g r.gpm cj v.iai.3p p.a r.apm.3 pt.pa.npm p.d n.dsf cj n.nsm
3836 4397 1181 5813 3552 253 1142 4732 4639 899 1639 1877 2397 1254 4397

called together the chief priests, the rulers and the people, **14** and said to them, "You brought me
συγκαλεσάμενος ← τοὺς → ἀρχιερεῖς καὶ τοὺς ἄρχοντας καὶ τὸν λαόν → εἶπεν πρὸς αὐτούς → προσηνέγκατε μοι
pt.am.nsm d.apm n.apm cj d.apm n.apm cj d.asm n.asm v.aai.3s p.a r.apm.3 v.aai.2p r.ds.1
5157 3836 797 2779 3836 807 2779 3836 3295 3306 4639 899 4712 1609

this man as one who was inciting the people to rebellion. I have examined
τοῦτον τὸν ἄνθρωπον, ὡς → → ἀποστρέφοντα τὸν λαόν ← καὶ ἰδοὺ ἐγὼ → ἀνακρίνας ἐν
r.asm d.asm n.asm pl pt.pa.asm d.asm n.asm cj j r.ns.1 pt.aa.nsm p.d
4047 3836 476 6055 695 3836 3295 695 695 2779 2627 1609 373 1877

him in your presence and have found no basis for your charges against him. **15**
ιτῷ ἀνθρώπῳ τούτῳ, ὑμῶν ἐνώπιον καὶ ἔχουσι εὗρον οὐδὲν αἴτιον ὧν κατηγορεῖτε κατ᾽ αὐτοῦ ἀλλ᾽
d.dsm n.dsm r.dsm r.gp.2 p.g v.aai.1s a.asn n.asn r.gpn v.pai.2p p.g r.gsm.3 cj
3836 476 4047 7007 1967 2351 4032 165 4005 2989 2848 899 247

Ἰουδαίων; ὁ δὲ ἀποκριθεὶς αὐτῷ ἔφη, Σὺ λέγεις. ¶ **4** ὁ δὲ Πιλᾶτος εἶπεν πρὸς τοὺς ἀρχιερεῖς καὶ τοὺς ὄχλους, Οὐδὲν εὑρίσκω αἴτιον ἐν τῷ ἀνθρώπῳ τούτῳ. **5** οἱ δὲ ἐπίσχυον λέγοντες ὅτι Ἀνασείει τὸν λαὸν διδάσκων καθ᾽ ὅλης τῆς Ἰουδαίας, καὶ ἀρξάμενος ἀπὸ τῆς Γαλιλαίας ἕως ὧδε. ¶ **6** Πιλᾶτος δὲ ἀκούσας ἐπηρώτησεν εἰ ὁ ἄνθρωπος Γαλιλαῖός ἐστιν, **7** καὶ ἐπιγνοὺς ὅτι ἐκ τῆς ἐξουσίας Ἡρώδου ἐστὶν ἀνέπεμψεν αὐτὸν πρὸς Ἡρώδην, ὄντα καὶ αὐτὸν ἐν Ἰεροσολύμοις ἐν ταύταις ταῖς ἡμέραις. ¶ **8** ὁ δὲ Ἡρώδης ἰδὼν τὸν Ἰησοῦν ἐχάρη λίαν, ἦν γὰρ ἐξ ἱκανῶν χρόνων θέλων ἰδεῖν αὐτὸν διὰ τὸ ἀκούειν περὶ αὐτοῦ καὶ ἤλπιζέν τι σημεῖον ἰδεῖν ὑπ᾽ αὐτοῦ γινόμενον. **9** ἐπηρώτα δὲ αὐτὸν ἐν λόγοις ἱκανοῖς, αὐτὸς δὲ οὐδὲν ἀπεκρίνατο αὐτῷ. **10** εἱστήκεισαν δὲ οἱ ἀρχιερεῖς καὶ οἱ γραμματεῖς εὐτόνως κατηγοροῦντες αὐτοῦ. **11** ἐξουθενήσας δὲ αὐτὸν [καὶ] ὁ Ἡρώδης σὺν τοῖς στρατεύμασιν αὐτοῦ καὶ ἐμπαίξας περιβαλὼν ἐσθῆτα λαμπρὰν ἀνέπεμψεν αὐτὸν τῷ Πιλάτῳ. **12** ἐγένοντο δὲ φίλοι ὅ τε Ἡρώδης καὶ ὁ Πιλᾶτος ἐν αὐτῇ τῇ ἡμέρᾳ μετ᾽ ἀλλήλων· προϋπῆρχον γὰρ ἐν ἔχθρᾳ ὄντες πρὸς αὐτούς. ¶ **13** Πιλᾶτος δὲ συγκαλεσάμενος τοὺς ἀρχιερεῖς καὶ τοὺς ἄρχοντας καὶ τὸν λαὸν **14** εἶπεν πρὸς αὐτούς, Προσηνέγκατέ μοι τὸν ἄνθρωπον τοῦτον ὡς ἀποστρέφοντα τὸν λαόν, καὶ ἰδοὺ ἐγὼ ἐνώπιον ὑμῶν ἀνακρίνας οὐθὲν εὗρον ἐν τῷ ἀνθρώπῳ τούτῳ αἴτιον ὧν κατηγορεῖτε

Neither has Herod, for he sent　　him back to　us;　as you can see, he　has　done　　nothing to deserve
οὐδὲ　　Ἡρῴδης γὰρ → ἀνέπεμψεν αὐτὸν ←　πρὸς ἡμᾶς καὶ　　ἰδοὺ αὐτῷ ἐστιν πεπραγμένον οὐδὲν　ἄξιον
cj　　n.nsm　　cj　v.aai.3s　r.asm.3　　p.a　r.ap.1 cj　　j　r.dsm.3 v.pai.3s pt.rp.nsn　a.nsn　a.nsn
4028　　2476　1142　402　　899　402　4639　7005 2779　　2627　899　1639　4556　4029　545

death. **16** Therefore, I will punish　him and then release him."　¶　**18** *With one*　*voice* they cried　out,
θανάτου οὖν　→　παιδεύσας αὐτὸν　　ἀπολύσω　　　δὲ　πάμπληθεὶ　→　Ἀνέκραγον ←
n.gsm　cj　　　pt.aa.nsm r.asm.3　　v.fai.1s　　　cj　adv　　　　v.aai.3p
2505　4036　　4084　899　　668　　　1254　4101　　　371

"Away with this man!　Release Barabbas　to us!" **19** (Barabbas had been thrown into prison　for
λέγοντες αἶρε ← τοῦτον ←　δὲ ἀπόλυσον ⸤τὸν Βαραββᾶν⸥　→ ἡμῖν ὅστις　→　ἦν βληθεὶς ἐν ⸤τῇ φυλακῇ⸥ διὰ
pt.pa.npm v.pam.2s r.asm　　cj v.aam.2s d.asm n.asm　　　r.dp.1 r.nsm　　v.iai.3s pt.ap.nsm p.d d.dsf n.dsf p.a
3306　149　4047　　1254 668　3836 972　　　7005 4015　　1639 965　1877 3836 5871 1328

an insurrection　　in the city, and for murder.)　¶　**20** Wanting to release　Jesus,　Pilate
τινὰ στάσιν　　γενομένην ἐν τῇ πόλει καὶ　φόνου　　δὲ θέλων　→ ἀπολῦσαι ⸤τὸν Ἰησοῦν⸥ ὁ Πιλᾶτος⸥
r.asf n.asf　　pt.am.asf p.d d.dsf n.dsf cj n.asm　　cj pt.pa.nsm　f.aa　d.asm n.asm　d.nsm n.nsm
5516 5087　　1181　1877 3836 4484 2779 5840　　1254 668　　668　3836 2652　3836 4397

appealed　to them again. **21** But they kept shouting,　"Crucify him! Crucify him!" ¶ **22** For the third time
προσεφώνησεν → αὐτοῖς πάλιν　δὲ οἱ　→ ἐπεφώνουν λέγοντες σταύρου σταύρου αὐτὸν　δὲ ὁ τρίτον →
v.aai.3s　　r.dpm.3 adv　cj d.npm　v.iai.3p pt.pa.npm v.pam.2s v.pam.2s r.asm.3　cj d.nsm adv
4715　　　899　4099　1254 3836　2215　3306　5090　5090　899　　1254 3836 5568

he spoke to　them: "Why? What crime has this man committed? I have found in him no　grounds for the
→ εἶπεν πρὸς αὐτούς γὰρ τί κακὸν οὗτος ← ἐποίησεν　εὗρον ἐν αὐτῷ οὐδὲν αἴτιον →
v.aai.3s p.a r.apm.3 cj r.asn a.asn r.nsm ← v.aai.3s　v.aai.1s p.d r.dsm.3 a.asn n.asn
3306　4639 899　1142 5515 2805 4472 4047　4472　　2351　1877 899 4029 165

death penalty. Therefore I will have him punished and then release him." ¶ **23** But with loud　shouts they
θανάτου οὖν → → → παιδεύσας　ἀπολύσω αὐτὸν　δὲ → μεγάλαις φωναῖς οἱ
n.gsm cj　　　pt.aa.nsm　v.fai.1s r.asm.3　cj　a.dpf n.dpf d.npm
2505 4036　　4084　　　668 899　1254　3489 5889 3836

insistently demanded that he　be crucified,　and their shouts　prevailed. **24** So Pilate decided to grant their
ἐπέκειντο αἰτούμενοι　αὐτὸν → σταυρωθῆναι καὶ αὐτῶν ⸤αἱ φωναί⸥ κατίσχυον　Καὶ Πιλᾶτος ἐπέκρινεν → γενέσθαι αὐτῶν
v.imi.3p pt.pm.npm　r.asm.3　f.ap　　cj r.gpm.3 d.npf n.npf v.iai.3p　cj n.nsm v.aai.3s　f.am r.gpm.3
2130　160　　899　5090　　2779 899 3836 5889 2996　　2779 4397 2137　　1181 899

demand. **25**　He released the man who had been thrown　into prison for insurrection and murder, the one they
⸤τὸ αἴτημα⸥ δὲ → ἀπέλυσεν τὸν ← → → βεβλημένον εἰς φυλακὴν διὰ στάσιν　καὶ φόνον　ὃν →
d.asn n.asn cj　v.aai.3s d.asm　　　pt.rp.asm p.a n.asf p.a n.asf　cj n.asm　r.asm
3836 161 1254　668 3836　　　965　1650 5871 1328 5087　2779 5840　4005

asked for, and surrendered Jesus　to their will.
ᾐτοῦντο ← δὲ παρέδωκεν ⸤τὸν Ἰησοῦν⸥ → αὐτῶν ⸤τῷ θελήματι⸥
v.imi.3p cj v.aai.3s d.asm n.asm　r.gpm.3 d.dsn n.dsn
160　1254 4140 3836 2652　2525 899 3836 2525

The Crucifixion

23:26　As they led　him away, they seized　Simon　from Cyrene,　who was on his way　in
Καὶ ὡς → ἀπήγαγον αὐτὸν ← ἐπιλαβόμενοι Σίμωνά τινα → Κυρηναῖον → → ὡς ἐρχόμενον ←
cj cj　v.aai.3p r.asm.3　pt.am.npm n.asm r.asm　n.asm　　pt.pm.asm
2779 6055　552 899 552　2138 4981 5516　3254　　2262

from the country, and put　the cross　on him and made him carry it behind Jesus.　**27**　A large number of
ἀπ'　ἀγροῦ　ἐπέθηκαν τὸν σταυρὸν αὐτῷ　φέρειν ὄπισθεν ⸤τοῦ Ἰησοῦ⸥ δὲ πολὺ πλῆθος →
p.g n.gsm　v.aai.3p d.asm n.asm r.dsm.3　f.pa p.g d.gsm n.gsm　cj a.nsn n.nsn
608 69　2202 3836 5089 899　5770 3957 3836 2652　1254 4498 4436

people followed him, including women who mourned and wailed for him. **28** Jesus　turned and said to
⸤τοῦ λαοῦ⸥ Ἠκολούθει αὐτῷ καὶ　γυναικῶν αἱ ἐκόπτοντο καὶ ἐθρήνουν ← αὐτόν δὲ ὁ Ἰησοῦς⸥ στραφεὶς　εἶπεν πρὸς
d.gsm n.gsm v.iai.3s r.dsm.3 cj　n.gpf r.npf v.imi.3p cj v.iai.3p　r.asm.3 cj d.nsm n.nsm pt.ap.nsm　v.aai.3s p.a
3836 3295 199 899 2779　1222 4005 3164 2779 2577　899 1254 3836 2652 5138　3306 4639

them, "Daughters of Jerusalem, do not weep for me;　weep for yourselves and for your children. **29** For　the
αὐτάς θυγατέρες → Ἰερουσαλήμ μὴ κλαίετε ἐπ' ἐμὲ πλὴν κλαίετε ἐφ' ἑαυτὰς καὶ ἐπὶ ὑμῶν ⸤τὰ τέκνα⸥ ὅτι ἰδοὺ
r.apf.3 n.vpf　n.gsf　pl v.pam.2p p.a r.as.1 cj v.pam.2p p.a r.apf.2 cj p.a r.gp.2 d.apn n.apn cj j
899 2588　2647 3081 3590 3081 2093 1609 4440 3081 2093 1571 2779 2093 7007 3836 5451 4022 2627

κατ' αὐτοῦ. **15** ἀλλ' οὐδὲ Ἡρῴδης, ἀνέπεμψεν γὰρ αὐτὸν πρὸς ἡμᾶς, καὶ ἰδοὺ οὐδὲν ἄξιον θανάτου ἐστιν πεπραγμένον αὐτῷ· **16** παιδεύσας οὖν αὐτὸν ἀπολύσω. ¶ **18** ἀνέκραγον δὲ παμπληθεὶ λέγοντες, Αἶρε τοῦτον, ἀπόλυσον δὲ ἡμῖν τὸν Βαραββᾶν· **19** ὅστις ἦν διὰ στάσιν τινὰ γενομένην ἐν τῇ πόλει καὶ φόνον βληθεὶς ἐν τῇ φυλακῇ. ¶ **20** πάλιν δὲ ὁ Πιλᾶτος προσεφώνησεν αὐτοῖς θέλων ἀπολῦσαι τὸν Ἰησοῦν. **21** οἱ δὲ ἐπεφώνουν λέγοντες, Σταύρου σταύρου αὐτόν. ¶ **22** ὁ δὲ τρίτον εἶπεν πρὸς αὐτούς, Τί γὰρ κακὸν ἐποίησεν οὗτος; οὐδὲν αἴτιον θανάτου εὗρον ἐν αὐτῷ· παιδεύσας οὖν αὐτὸν ἀπολύσω. ¶ **23** οἱ δὲ ἐπέκειντο φωναῖς μεγάλαις αἰτούμενοι αὐτὸν σταυρωθῆναι, καὶ κατίσχυον αἱ φωναὶ αὐτῶν. **24** καὶ Πιλᾶτος ἐπέκρινεν γενέσθαι τὸ αἴτημα αὐτῶν· **25** ἀπέλυσεν δὲ τὸν διὰ στάσιν καὶ φόνον βεβλημένον εἰς φυλακὴν ὃν ᾐτοῦντο, τὸν δὲ Ἰησοῦν παρέδωκεν τῷ θελήματι αὐτῶν.

23:26 Καὶ ὡς ἀπήγαγον αὐτόν, ἐπιλαβόμενοι Σίμωνά τινα Κυρηναῖον ἐρχόμενον ἀπ' ἀγροῦ ἐπέθηκαν αὐτῷ τὸν σταυρὸν φέρειν ὄπισθεν τοῦ Ἰησοῦ. **27** Ἠκολούθει δὲ αὐτῷ πολὺ πλῆθος τοῦ λαοῦ καὶ γυναικῶν αἱ ἐκόπτοντο καὶ ἐθρήνουν αὐτόν. **28** στραφεὶς δὲ πρὸς αὐτὰς [ὁ] Ἰησοῦς εἶπεν, Θυγατέρες Ἰερουσαλήμ, μὴ κλαίετε ἐπ' ἐμέ· πλὴν ἐφ' ἑαυτὰς κλαίετε καὶ ἐπὶ τὰ τέκνα ὑμῶν, **29** ὅτι ἰδοὺ ἔρχονται ἡμέραι ἐν αἷς ἐροῦσιν, Μακάριαι αἱ στεῖραι καὶ αἱ κοιλίαι αἱ οὐκ ἐγέννησαν καὶ μαστοὶ οἳ οὐκ ἔθρεψαν.

time	will come	when	you will say,	'Blessed	are	the	barren	women,		the	wombs	that	never	bore	and
ἡμέραι →	ἔρχονται	ἐν αἷς, →	→ ἐροῦσιν	μακάριαι		αἱ	στεῖραι ←		καὶ	αἱ	κοιλίαι	αἱ	οὐκ	ἐγέννησαν	καὶ
n.npf	v.pmi.3p	p.d r.dpf	v.fai.3p	a.npf		d.npf	n.npf		cj	d.npf	n.npf	r.npf	pl	v.aai.3p	cj
2465	2262	1877 4005	3306	3421		3836	5096		2779	3836	3120	4005	4024	1164	2779

the	breasts	that	never	nursed!'	30 Then	"'they will		say	to	the	mountains,	"Fall on us!"	and	to	the	hills,
μαστοὶ		οἳ	οὐκ	ἔθρεψαν	τότε →	ἄρξονται	λέγειν →		τοῖς	ὄρεσιν		πέσετε ἐφ'	ἡμᾶς	καὶ →	τοῖς	βουνοῖς
n.npm		r.npm	pl	v.aai.3p	adv	v.fmi.3p	f.pa		d.dpn	n.dpn		v.aam.2p	p.a	r.ap.1	cj	d.dpm	n.dpm
3466		4005	4024	5555	5538	806	3306		3836	4001		4406	7005	2779	3836	1090

"Cover us!"'	31 For	if	men	do		these	things	when	the	tree	is	green,	what	will happen	when	it is	dry?"	¶
καλύψατε ἡμᾶς	ὅτι	εἰ		ποιοῦσιν	ταῦτα ←		ἐν	τῷ	ὑγρῷ	ὑγρῷ	τί	→	γένηται	ἐν	⌐τῷ ξηρῷ⌐	
v.aam.2p r.ap.1	cj	cj		v.pai.3p	r.apn		p.d	d.dsn	a.dsn	a.dsn	r.nsn		v.ams.3s	p.d	d.dsn a.dsn	
2821 7005	7005	4022		1623	4472	4047		1877	3836	5619	5619	5515		1181	1877	3836 3831	

32	Two	other	men,	both	criminals,	were		also	led	out	with	him	to be executed.	33		When	they	came	to	the
	δὲ	δύο	ἕτεροι ←		κακοῦργοι	Ἤγοντο	καὶ			σὺν	αὐτῷ →	→ ἀναιρεθῆναι	Καὶ	ὅτε		→	ἦλθον	ἐπὶ	τὸν
	cj	a.npm	r.npm		n.npm	v.ipi.3p	adv			p.d	r.dsm.3	f.ap		cj	cj		v.aai.3p	p.a	d.asm
	1254	1545	2283		2806	72	2779			5250	899	359		2779	4021		2262	2093	3836

place	called		the Skull,	there	they	crucified	him,	along	with		the	criminals	—	one	on	his	right,	the
τόπον	⌐τὸν καλούμενον⌐		Κρανίον	ἐκεῖ	→	ἐσταύρωσαν	αὐτὸν	καὶ	←		τοὺς	κακούργους		μὲν	ὃν	ἐκ	δεξιῶν	δὲ →
n.asm	d.asm pt.pp.asm		n.asn	adv		v.aai.3p	r.asm.3	cj			d.apm	n.apm		pl	r.asm	p.g	a.gpf	pl
5536	3836 2813		3191	1695		5090	899	2779			3836	2806		3525	4005	1666	1288	1254

other	on	his	left.	34		Jesus		said,	"Father,	forgive	them,	for	they	do not	know	what	they are doing."
ὃν	ἐξ	ἀριστερῶν		⟦ δὲ	ὁ	Ἰησοῦς		ἔλεγεν	πάτερ	ἄφες	αὐτοῖς	γὰρ →	→	οὐ	οἴδασιν	τί	→ → ποιοῦσιν ⟧
r.asm	p.g	a.gpf		cj	d.nsm	n.nsm		v.iai.3s	n.vsm	v.aam.2s	r.dpm.3	cj		pl	v.rai.3p	r.asn	v.pai.3p
4005	1666	754		1254	3836	2652		4252	3306	918	899	1142	3857	3857	4024	3857	5515	4472

And	they	divided	up	his	clothes	by casting	lots.	¶	35		The	people	stood	watching,	and the
δὲ	→	διαμεριζόμενοι ←		αὐτοῦ	⌐τὰ ἱμάτια⌐	ἔβαλον	κλήρους		Καὶ	ὁ	λαὸς	εἱστήκει	θεωρῶν	δὲ	οἱ
cj		pt.pm.npm		r.gsm.3	d.apn n.apn	v.aai.3p	n.apm		cj	d.nsm	n.nsm	v.lai.3s	pt.pa.nsm	cj	d.npm
1254		1374		899	3836 2668	965	3102		2779	3836	3295	2705	2555	1254	3836

rulers	even	sneered	at him.	They said,		"He saved	others;	let him	save		himself	if	he	is	the	Christ	of
ἄρχοντες	καὶ	ἐξεμυκτήριζον		λέγοντες →		ἔσωσεν	ἄλλους	→	σωσάτω	ἑαυτόν		εἰ	οὗτος	ἐστιν	ὁ	χριστὸς
n.npm	adv	v.iai.3p		pt.pa.npm		v.aai.3s	r.apm		v.aam.3s	r.asm.3		cj	r.nsm	v.pai.3s	d.nsm	n.nsm
807	2779	1727		3306		5392	257		5392	1571		1623	4047	1639	3836	5986

God,	the	Chosen One."	¶	36		The	soldiers	also	came		up and mocked	him.	They offered		him
⌐τοῦ θεοῦ⌐	ὁ	ἐκλεκτός ←			δὲ	οἱ	στρατιῶται	καὶ	προσερχόμενοι ←		ἐνέπαιξαν	αὐτῷ →	προσφέροντες		αὐτῷ
d.gsm n.gsm	d.nsm	a.nsm			cj	d.npm	n.npm	adv	pt.pm.npm		v.aai.3p	r.dsm.3	pt.pa.npm		r.dsm.3
3836 2536	3836	1723			1254	3836	5132	2779	4665		1850	899	4712		899

wine vinegar	37	and	said,	"If	you	are	the	king	of	the	Jews,	save	yourself."	¶	38		There	was	a
→	ὄξος	καὶ	λέγοντες	εἰ	σὺ	εἶ	ὁ	βασιλεὺς →		τῶν	Ἰουδαίων	σῶσον	σεαυτόν			δὲ	καὶ →		ἦν
	n.asn	cj	pt.pa.npm	cj	r.ns.2	v.pai.2s	d.nsm	n.nsm		d.gpm	a.gpm	v.aam.2s	r.asm.2			cj	adv		v.iai.3s
	3954	2779	3306	1623	5148	1639	3836	995		3836	2681	5392	4932			1254	2779		1639

written	notice	above	him,	which read:	THIS	IS	THE	KING	OF	THE	JEWS.	¶	39		One	of	the	criminals
→	ἐπιγραφὴ	ἐπ'	αὐτῷ		οὗτος	ὁ	βασιλεὺς →		τῶν	Ἰουδαίων			δὲ	Εἷς	→	τῶν	κακούργων
	n.nsf	p.d	r.dsm.3		r.nsm	d.nsm	n.nsm		d.gpm	a.gpm			cj	a.nsm		d.gpm	n.gpm
	2107	2093	899		4047	3836	995		3836	2681			1254	1651		3836	2806

who	hung		there	hurled	insults	at him:	"Aren't		you	the	Christ?	Save	yourself	and	us!"	40 But	the
→	κρεμασθέντων	→		ἐβλασφήμει	αὐτὸν	λέγων	⌐οὐχὶ	εἶ	σὺ	ὁ	χριστός	σῶσον	σεαυτὸν	καὶ	ἡμᾶς	δὲ	ὁ
	pt.ap.gpm			v.iai.3s	r.asm.3	pt.pa.nsm	pl		r.ns.2	d.nsm	n.nsm	v.aam.2s	r.asm.2	cj	r.ap.1	cj	d.nsm
	3203			1059	899	3306	4049	1639	5148	3836	5986	5392	4932	2779	7005	1254	3836

other	criminal		rebuked	him.	"Don't	you	fear	God,"		he said,	"since	you	are	under	the	same	sentence?
ἕτερος		ἀποκριθεὶς	ἐπιτιμῶν	αὐτῷ	οὐδὲ	σὺ	φοβῇ	⌐τὸν θεόν⌐		ἔφη	ὅτι	→	εἶ	ἐν	τῷ	αὐτῷ	κρίματι
r.nsm		pt.ap.nsm	pt.pa.nsm	r.dsm.3	adv	r.ns.2	v.ppi.2s	d.asm n.asm		v.iai.3s	cj		v.pai.2s	p.d	d.dsn	r.dsn	n.dsn
2283		646	2203	899	4028	5148	5828	3836 2536		5774	4022		1639	1877	3836	899	3210

41	We		are punished	justly,	for	we are getting		what	our	deeds		deserve.	But	this	man	has done
	καὶ	ἡμεῖς	μὲν	δικαίως	γὰρ →	→ ἀπολαμβάνομεν	ὧν	→	ἐπράξαμεν	ἄξια		δὲ	οὗτος ←		→	ἔπραξεν
	cj	r.np.1	pl	adv	cj	v.pai.1p	r.gpn		v.aai.1p	a.apn		cj	r.nsm			v.aai.3s
	2779	7005	3525	1469	1142	655	4005		4556	545		1254	4047			4556

---

30 τότε ἄρξονται λέγειν τοῖς ὄρεσιν, Πέσετε ἐφ' ἡμᾶς, καὶ τοῖς βουνοῖς, Καλύψατε ἡμᾶς· 31 ὅτι εἰ ἐν τῷ ὑγρῷ ξύλῳ ταῦτα ποιοῦσιν, ἐν τῷ ξηρῷ τί γένηται; ¶ 32 Ἤγοντο δὲ καὶ ἕτεροι κακοῦργοι δύο σὺν αὐτῷ ἀναιρεθῆναι. 33 καὶ ὅτε ἦλθον ἐπὶ τὸν τόπον τὸν καλούμενον Κρανίον, ἐκεῖ ἐσταύρωσαν αὐτὸν καὶ τοὺς κακούργους, ὃν μὲν ἐκ δεξιῶν ὃν δὲ ἐξ ἀριστερῶν. 34 ⟦ὁ δὲ Ἰησοῦς ἔλεγεν, Πάτερ, ἄφες αὐτοῖς, οὐ γὰρ οἴδασιν τί ποιοῦσιν.⟧ διαμεριζόμενοι δὲ τὰ ἱμάτια αὐτοῦ ἔβαλον κλήρους. ¶ 35 καὶ εἱστήκει ὁ λαὸς θεωρῶν. ἐξεμυκτήριζον δὲ καὶ οἱ ἄρχοντες λέγοντες, Ἄλλους ἔσωσεν, σωσάτω ἑαυτόν, εἰ οὗτός ἐστιν ὁ Χριστὸς τοῦ θεοῦ ὁ ἐκλεκτός. ¶ 36 ἐνέπαιξαν δὲ αὐτῷ καὶ οἱ στρατιῶται προσερχόμενοι, ὄξος προσφέροντες αὐτῷ 37 καὶ λέγοντες, Εἰ σὺ εἶ ὁ βασιλεὺς τῶν Ἰουδαίων, σῶσον σεαυτόν. ¶ 38 ἦν δὲ καὶ ἐπιγραφὴ ἐπ' αὐτῷ, Ὁ βασιλεὺς τῶν Ἰουδαίων οὗτος. ¶ 39 Εἷς δὲ τῶν κρεμασθέντων κακούργων ἐβλασφήμει αὐτὸν λέγων, Οὐχὶ σὺ εἶ ὁ Χριστός; σῶσον σεαυτὸν καὶ ἡμᾶς. 40 ἀποκριθεὶς δὲ ὁ ἕτερος ἐπιτιμῶν αὐτῷ ἔφη, Οὐδὲ φοβῇ σὺ τὸν θεόν, ὅτι ἐν τῷ αὐτῷ κρίματι εἶ; 41 καὶ ἡμεῖς μὲν δικαίως, ἄξια γὰρ ὧν ἐπράξαμεν

nothing wrong." ¶ **42** Then he said, "Jesus, remember me when you come into your kingdom." **43** Jesus
οὐδὲν ἄτοπον　　　καὶ → ἔλεγεν Ἰησοῦ μνήσθητί μου ὅταν → ἔλθῃς εἰς σου ⸤τὴν βασιλείαν⸥ καὶ
a.asn a.asn　　　cj　　v.iai.3s n.vsm v.apm.2s r.gs.1 cj　　v.aas.2s p.a r.gs.2 d.asf n.asf cj
4029 876　　　2779 →　3306 2652 3630 1609 4020 →　2262 1650 5148 3836 993 2779

answered him, "I tell you the truth, today you will be with me in paradise."
εἶπεν αὐτῷ　λέγω σοι　ἀμὴν σήμερον → → ἔσῃ μετ' ἐμοῦ ἐν τῷ παραδείσῳ
v.aai.3s r.dsm.3　v.pai.1s r.ds.2　pl adv　　v.fmi.2s p.g r.gs.1 p.d d.dsn n.dsm
3306 899　3306 5148　297 4958 → →　1639 3552 1609 1877 3836 4137

Jesus' Death

23:44 It was now about the sixth hour, and darkness came over the whole land until the ninth hour, **45** for the
Καὶ → ἦν ἤδη ὡσεὶ　ἕκτη ὥρα καὶ σκότος ἐγένετο ἐφ' τὴν ὅλην γῆν ἕως ἐνάτης ὥρας → τοῦ
cj　v.iai.3s adv pl　a.nsf n.nsf cj n.nsn v.ami.3s p.a d.asf a.asf n.asf p.g a.gsf n.gsf d.gsm
2779 1639 2453 6059　1761 6052 2779 5030 1181 2093 3836 3910 1178 2401 1888 6052 1722 3836

sun stopped shining. And the curtain of the temple was torn in two. **46** Jesus called out with a
ἡλίου → ἐκλιπόντος δὲ τὸ καταπέτασμα → τοῦ ναοῦ → ἐσχίσθη μέσον καὶ ὁ Ἰησοῦς φωνήσας ← →
n.gsm　pt.aa.gsm cj d.nsn n.nsn　d.gsm n.gsm　v.api.3s adv cj d.nsm n.nsm pt.aa.nsm
2463 →　1722 1254 3836 2925　3836 3724　5387 3545 2779 3836 2652 5888

loud voice, "Father, into your hands I commit my spirit." When he had said this, he breathed his
μεγάλῃ φωνῇ εἶπεν πάτερ εἰς σου χεῖρας → παρατίθεμαι μου τὸ πνεῦμα δὲ → τοῦτο ← → ἐξέπνευσεν ←
a.dsf n.dsf v.aai.3s n.vsm p.a r.gs.2 n.apf v.pmi.1s r.gs.1 d.asn n.asn cj pt.aa.nsm r.asn v.aai.3s
3489 5889 3306 4252 1650 5148 5931 4192 1609 3836 4460 1254 3306 4047 1743

last. ¶ **47** The centurion, seeing what had happened, praised God and said, "Surely this was a
← δὲ ὁ ἑκατοντάρχης ἰδὼν τὸ → γενόμενον ἐδόξαζεν ⸤τὸν θεὸν⸥ λέγων ὄντως οὗτος ἦν
cj d.nsm n.nsm pt.aa.nsm d.asn pt.am.asn v.iai.3s d.asm n.asm pt.pa.nsm adv r.nsm v.iai.3s
1254 3836 1672 1625 3836 1181 1519 3836 2536 3306 3953 4047 1639

righteous man." **48** When all the people who had gathered to witness this sight
δίκαιος ⸤ὁ ἄνθρωπος⸥ καὶ → πάντες οἱ ὄχλοι → → συμπαραγενόμενοι ἐπὶ ταύτην ⸤τὴν θεωρίαν⸥
a.nsm d.nsm n.nsm cj a.npm d.npm n.npm pt.am.npm p.a r.asf d.asf n.asf
1465 3836 476 2779 2555 4246 3836 4063 5219 2093 4047 3836 2556

saw what took place, they beat their breasts and went away. **49** But all those who knew him,
θεωρήσαντες τὰ γενόμενα ← τύπτοντες τὰ στήθη ὑπέστρεφον ← δὲ πάντες οἱ ← γνωστοὶ αὐτῷ
pt.aa.npm d.apn pt.am.apn pt.pa.npm d.apn n.apn v.iai.3p cj a.npm d.npm a.npm r.dsm.3
2555 3836 1181 5597 3836 5111 5715 1254 4246 3836 1196 899

including the women who had followed him from Galilee, stood at a distance, watching these things.
καὶ γυναῖκες αἱ → συνακολουθοῦσαι αὐτῷ ἀπὸ ⸤τῆς Γαλιλαίας⸥ Εἱστήκεισαν ἀπὸ μακρόθεν ὁρῶσαι ταῦτα ←
cj n.npf d.npf pt.pa.npf r.dsm.3 p.g d.gsf n.gsf v.iai.3p p.g adv pt.pa.npf r.apn
2779 1222 3836 5258 899 608 3836 1133 2705 608 3427 3972 4047

Jesus' Burial

23:50 Now there was a man named Joseph, a member of the Council, a good and upright man,
⸤Καὶ ἰδοὺ⸥ → ὑπάρχων ἀνὴρ ὀνόματι Ἰωσὴφ βουλευτὴς ← ← ← [καὶ] ἀγαθὸς καὶ δίκαιος ἀνὴρ
cj j pt.pa.nsm n.nsm n.dsn n.nsm n.nsm cj a.nsm cj a.nsm n.nsm
2779 2627 5639 467 3950 2737 1085 2779 19 2779 1465 467

51 who had not consented to their decision and action. He came from the Judean town of Arimathea
οὗτος ἦν οὐκ συγκατατεθειμένος ← αὐτῶν ⸤τῇ βουλῇ⸥ καὶ ⸤τῇ πράξει⸥ ἀπὸ ⸤τῶν Ἰουδαίων⸥ πόλεως → Ἀριμαθαίας
r.nsm v.iai.3s pl pt.rp.nsm r.gpm.3 d.dsf n.dsf cj d.dsf n.dsf p.g d.gpm a.gpm n.gsf n.gsf
4047 1639 4024 5163 899 3836 1087 2779 3836 4552 608 3836 2681 4484 751

and he was waiting for the kingdom of God. **52** Going to Pilate, he asked for Jesus' body.
ὃς → προσεδέχετο ← τὴν βασιλείαν → ⸤τοῦ θεοῦ⸥ προσελθὼν ← ⸤τῷ Πιλάτῳ⸥ οὗτος ᾐτήσατο ← ⸤τοῦ Ἰησοῦ⸥ ⸤τὸ σῶμα⸥
r.nsm v.imi.3s d.asf n.asf d.gsm n.gsm pt.aa.nsm d.dsm n.dsm r.nsm v.ami.3s d.gsm n.gsm d.asn n.asn
4005 4657 3836 993 3836 2536 4665 3836 4397 4047 160 3836 2652 3836 5393

53 Then he took it down, wrapped it in linen cloth and placed it in a tomb cut in the rock, one in
καὶ → καθελὼν ἐνετύλιξεν αὐτὸ → σινδόνι καὶ ἔθηκεν αὐτὸν ἐν μνήματι λαξευτῷ
cj pt.aa.nsm v.aai.3s r.asn.3 n.dsf cj v.aai.3s r.asm.3 p.d n.dsn a.dsn
2779 2747 1962 899 4984 2779 5502 899 1877 3645 3292

which no one had yet been laid. **54** It was Preparation Day, and the Sabbath was about to begin. ¶
οὗ οὐκ οὐδεὶς → οὔπω ἦν κείμενος καὶ → ἦν παρασκευῆς ἡμέρα καὶ σάββατον → → → ἐπέφωσκεν
adv pl a.nsm adv v.iai.3s pt.pm.nsm cj v.iai.3s n.gsf n.nsf cj n.nsn v.iai.3s
4023 4024 4029 1639 4037 1639 2779 1639 4187 2465 2779 4879 2216

ἀπολαμβάνομεν· οὗτος δὲ οὐδὲν ἄτοπον ἔπραξεν. ¶ **42** καὶ ἔλεγεν, Ἰησοῦ, μνήσθητί μου ὅταν ἔλθῃς εἰς τὴν βασιλείαν σου. **43** καὶ εἶπεν αὐτῷ, Ἀμήν σοι λέγω, σήμερον μετ' ἐμοῦ ἔσῃ ἐν τῷ παραδείσῳ.

23:44 Καὶ ἦν ἤδη ὡσεὶ ὥρα ἕκτη καὶ σκότος ἐγένετο ἐφ' ὅλην τὴν γῆν ἕως ὥρας ἐνάτης **45** τοῦ ἡλίου ἐκλιπόντος, ἐσχίσθη δὲ τὸ καταπέτασμα τοῦ ναοῦ μέσον. **46** καὶ φωνήσας φωνῇ μεγάλῃ ὁ Ἰησοῦς εἶπεν, Πάτερ, εἰς χεῖράς σου παρατίθεμαι τὸ πνεῦμά μου. τοῦτο δὲ εἰπὼν ἐξέπνευσεν. ¶ **47** Ἰδὼν δὲ ὁ ἑκατοντάρχης τὸ γενόμενον ἐδόξαζεν τὸν θεὸν λέγων, Ὄντως ὁ ἄνθρωπος οὗτος δίκαιος ἦν. **48** καὶ πάντες οἱ συμπαραγενόμενοι ὄχλοι ἐπὶ τὴν θεωρίαν ταύτην, θεωρήσαντες τὰ γενόμενα, τύπτοντες τὰ στήθη ὑπέστρεφον. **49** εἱστήκεισαν δὲ πάντες οἱ γνωστοὶ αὐτῷ ἀπὸ μακρόθεν καὶ γυναῖκες αἱ συνακολουθοῦσαι αὐτῷ ἀπὸ τῆς Γαλιλαίας ὁρῶσαι ταῦτα.

23:50 Καὶ ἰδοὺ ἀνὴρ ὀνόματι Ἰωσὴφ βουλευτὴς ὑπάρχων [καὶ] ἀνὴρ ἀγαθὸς καὶ δίκαιος **51** —οὗτος οὐκ ἦν συγκατατεθειμένος τῇ βουλῇ καὶ τῇ πράξει αὐτῶν— ἀπὸ Ἀριμαθαίας πόλεως τῶν Ἰουδαίων, ὃς προσεδέχετο τὴν βασιλείαν τοῦ θεοῦ, **52** οὗτος προσελθὼν τῷ Πιλάτῳ ᾐτήσατο τὸ σῶμα τοῦ Ἰησοῦ **53** καὶ καθελὼν ἐνετύλιξεν αὐτὸ σινδόνι καὶ ἔθηκεν αὐτὸ «αὐτὸν» ἐν μνήματι

55 The women who had come with Jesus from Galilee followed Joseph and saw the
δὲ αἱ γυναῖκες αἵτινες ἦσαν συνεληλυθυῖαι ← αὐτῷ ἐκ ⌐τῆς Γαλιλαίας⌐ Κατακολουθήσασαι ἐθεάσαντο τὸ
cj d.npf n.npf r.npf v.iai.3p pt.ra.npf r.dsm.3 p.g d.gsf n.gsf pt.aa.npf v.ami.3p d.asn
1254 3836 1222 4015 1639 5302 899 1666 3836 1133 2887 2517 3836

tomb and how his body was laid in it. **56** Then they went home and prepared spices and perfumes.
μνημεῖον καὶ ὡς αὐτοῦ ⌐τὸ σῶμα⌐ → ἐτέθη δὲ → ὑποστρέψασαι ← ἡτοίμασαν ἀρώματα καὶ μύρα
n.asn cj cj r.gsm.3 d.asn n.nsn v.api.3s cj pt.aa.npf v.aai.3p n.apn cj n.apn
3646 2779 6055 899 3836 5393 5502 1254 5715 2286 808 2779 3693

But they rested on the Sabbath in obedience to the commandment.
καὶ μὲν → ἡσύχασαν τὸ σάββατον κατὰ ← τὴν ἐντολήν
cj pl v.aai.3p d.asn n.asn p.a d.asf n.asf
2779 3525 2483 3836 4879 2848 3836 1953

The Resurrection

24:1 On the first day of the week, very early in the morning, the women took the spices they had
δὲ → Τῇ μιᾷ → τῶν σαββάτων βαθέως → → → ὄρθρου → φέρουσαι ἀρώματα ἃ →
cj d.dsf a.dsf d.gpn n.gpn a.gsm n.gsm pt.pa.npf n.apn r.apn
1254 3836 1651 3836 4879 960 3986 5770 808 4005

prepared and went to the tomb. **2** They found the stone rolled away from the tomb, **3** but when they
ἡτοίμασαν ἦλθον ἐπὶ τὸ μνῆμα δὲ → εὗρον τὸν λίθον ἀποκεκυλισμένον ← ἀπὸ τοῦ μνημείου δὲ →
v.aai.3p v.aai.3p p.a d.asn n.asn cj v.aai.3p d.asm n.asm pt.rp.asm p.g d.gsn n.gsn cj
2286 2262 2093 3836 3645 1254 2351 3836 3345 653 608 3836 3646 1254

entered, they did not find the body of the Lord Jesus. **4** While they were wondering about this,
εἰσελθοῦσαι ↱ ↱ οὐχ εὗρον τὸ σῶμα → τοῦ κυρίου Ἰησοῦ καὶ ἐγένετο ἐν αὐτὰς → ⌐τῷ ἀπορεῖσθαι⌐ περὶ τούτου καὶ
pt.aa.npf pl v.aai.3p d.asn n.asn d.gsm n.gsm n.gsm cj v.ami.3s p.d r.apf.3 d.dsn f.pm p.g r.gsn cj
1656 2351 2351 4024 2351 3836 5393 3836 3261 2652 2779 1181 1877 899 3836 679 4309 4047 2779

suddenly two men in clothes that gleamed like lightning stood beside them. **5** In their fright
ἰδοὺ δύο ἄνδρες ἐν ἐσθῆτι ἀστραπτούσῃ ← ← ← ἐπέστησαν ← αὐταῖς δὲ γενομένων αὐτῶν ἐμφόβων καὶ
j a.npm n.npm p.d n.dsf pt.pa.dsf v.aai.3p r.dpf.3 cj pt.am.gpf r.gpf.3 a.gpf cj
2627 1545 467 1877 2264 848 2392 899 1254 1181 899 1873 2779

the women bowed down with their faces to the ground, but the men said to them, "Why do you look for
→ κλινουσῶν ← τὰ πρόσωπα εἰς τὴν γῆν εἶπαν πρὸς αὐτάς τί → → ζητεῖτε ←
pt.pa.gpf d.apn n.apn p.a d.asf n.asf v.aai.3p p.a r.apf.3 r.asn v.pai.2p
3111 3836 4725 1650 3836 1178 3306 4639 899 5515 2426

the living among the dead? **6** He is not here; he has risen! Remember how he told you, while he was still
τὸν ζῶντα μετὰ τῶν νεκρῶν → ἔστιν οὐκ ὧδε ἀλλὰ → ἠγέρθη μνήσθητε ὡς → ἐλάλησεν ὑμῖν → → ὢν ἔτι
d.asm pt.pa.asm p.g d.gpm a.gpm v.pai.3s pl adv cj v.api.3s v.apm.2p cj v.aai.3s r.dp.2 pt.pa.nsm adv
3836 2409 3552 3836 3738 1639 4024 6045 247 1586 3630 6055 3281 7007 1639 2285

with you in Galilee: **7** 'The Son of Man must be delivered into the hands of sinful
ἐν ⌐τῇ Γαλιλαίᾳ⌐ λέγων τὸν υἱὸν → ⌐τοῦ ἀνθρώπου⌐ ὅτι → παραδοθῆναι εἰς χεῖρας → ἁμαρτωλῶν
p.d d.dsf n.dsf pt.pa.nsm d.asm n.asm d.gsm n.gsm cj f.ap p.a n.apf a.gpm
1877 3836 1133 3306 3836 5626 3836 476 4022 1256 4140 1650 5931 283

men, be crucified and on the third day be raised again.'" **8** Then they remembered his words.
ἀνθρώπων καὶ → σταυρωθῆναι καὶ → τῇ τρίτῃ ἡμέρᾳ → ἀναστῆναι καὶ → ἐμνήσθησαν αὐτοῦ ⌐τῶν ῥημάτων⌐
n.gpm cj f.ap cj d.dsf a.dsf n.dsf f.aa cj v.api.3p r.gsm.3 d.gpn n.gpn
476 2779 5090 2779 3836 5569 2465 482 2779 3630 899 3836 4839

¶ **9** When they came back from the tomb, they told all these things to the Eleven and to all
Καὶ → → ὑποστρέψασαι ← ἀπὸ τοῦ μνημείου ἀπήγγειλαν πάντα ταῦτα ← → τοῖς ἕνδεκα καὶ → πᾶσιν
cj pt.aa.npf p.g d.gsn n.gsn v.aai.3p a.apn r.apn d.dpm a.dpm cj a.dpm
2779 5715 608 3836 3646 550 4246 4047 3836 1894 2779 4246

the others. **10** It was Mary Magdalene, Joanna, Mary the mother of James, and the others with them
τοῖς λοιποῖς δὲ → ἦσαν Μαρία ἡ Μαγδαληνὴ καὶ Ἰωάννα καὶ Μαρία ἡ → Ἰακώβου καὶ αἱ λοιπαὶ σὺν αὐταῖς
d.dpm a.dpm cj v.iai.3p n.nsf d.nsf n.nsf cj n.nsf cj n.nsf d.nsf n.gsm cj d.npf a.npf p.d r.dpf.3
3836 3370 1254 1639 3451 3836 3402 2779 2721 2779 3451 3836 2610 2779 3836 3370 5250 899

who told this to the apostles. **11** But they did not believe the women, because their words seemed
ἔλεγον ταῦτα πρὸς τοὺς ἀποστόλους καὶ → → ἠπίστουν αὐταῖς καὶ → ταῦτα ⌐τὰ ῥήματα⌐ ἐφάνησαν
v.iai.3p r.apn p.a d.apm n.apm cj v.iai.3p r.dpf.3 cj r.npn d.npn n.npn v.api.3p
3306 4047 4639 3836 693 2779 601 899 2779 4047 3836 4839 5743

λαξευτῷ οὗ οὐκ ἦν οὐδεὶς οὔπω κείμενος. **54** καὶ ἡμέρα ἦν παρασκευῆς καὶ σάββατον ἐπέφωσκεν. ¶ **55** Κατακολουθήσασαι δὲ αἱ γυναῖκες, αἵτινες ἦσαν συνεληλυθυῖαι ἐκ τῆς Γαλιλαίας αὐτῷ, ἐθεάσαντο τὸ μνημεῖον καὶ ὡς ἐτέθη τὸ σῶμα αὐτοῦ, **56** ὑποστρέψασαι δὲ ἡτοίμασαν ἀρώματα καὶ μύρα. Καὶ τὸ μὲν σάββατον ἡσύχασαν κατὰ τὴν ἐντολήν.

24:1 τῇ δὲ μιᾷ τῶν σαββάτων ὄρθρου βαθέως ἐπὶ τὸ μνῆμα ἦλθον φέρουσαι ἃ ἡτοίμασαν ἀρώματα. **2** εὗρον δὲ τὸν λίθον ἀποκεκυλισμένον ἀπὸ τοῦ μνημείου, **3** εἰσελθοῦσαι δὲ οὐχ εὗρον τὸ σῶμα τοῦ κυρίου Ἰησοῦ. **4** καὶ ἐγένετο ἐν τῷ ἀπορεῖσθαι αὐτὰς περὶ τούτου καὶ ἰδοὺ ἄνδρες δύο ἐπέστησαν αὐταῖς ἐν ἐσθῆτι ἀστραπτούσῃ. **5** ἐμφόβων δὲ γενομένων αὐτῶν καὶ κλινουσῶν τὰ πρόσωπα εἰς τὴν γῆν εἶπαν πρὸς αὐτάς, Τί ζητεῖτε τὸν ζῶντα μετὰ τῶν νεκρῶν· **6** οὐκ ἔστιν ὧδε, ἀλλὰ ἠγέρθη. μνήσθητε ὡς ἐλάλησεν ὑμῖν ἔτι ὢν ἐν τῇ Γαλιλαίᾳ **7** λέγων τὸν υἱὸν τοῦ ἀνθρώπου ὅτι δεῖ παραδοθῆναι εἰς χεῖρας ἀνθρώπων ἁμαρτωλῶν καὶ σταυρωθῆναι καὶ τῇ τρίτῃ ἡμέρᾳ ἀναστῆναι. **8** καὶ ἐμνήσθησαν τῶν ῥημάτων αὐτοῦ. ¶ **9** καὶ ὑποστρέψασαι ἀπὸ τοῦ μνημείου ἀπήγγειλαν ταῦτα πάντα τοῖς ἕνδεκα καὶ πᾶσιν τοῖς λοιποῖς. **10** ἦσαν δὲ ἡ Μαγδαληνὴ Μαρία καὶ Ἰωάννα καὶ Μαρία ἡ Ἰακώβου καὶ αἱ λοιπαὶ σὺν αὐταῖς. ἔλεγον πρὸς τοὺς ἀποστόλους ταῦτα, **11** καὶ ἐφάνησαν ἐνώπιον αὐτῶν ὡσεὶ

to them like nonsense. **12** Peter, however, got up and ran to the tomb. Bending over, he saw
ἐνώπιον αὐτῶν ὡσεὶ λῆρος ⸂Ὁ Πέτρος⸃ δὲ ἀναστὰς ← ἔδραμεν ἐπὶ τὸ μνημεῖον καὶ παρακύψας ← → βλέπει
p.g r.gpm.3 pl n.nsm d.nsm n.nsm cj pt.aa.nsm v.aai.3s p.a d.asn n.asn cj pt.aa.nsm v.pai.3s
1967 899 6059 3333 3836 4377 1254 482 5556 2093 3836 3646 2779 4160 1063

the strips of linen lying by themselves, and he went away, wondering to himself what had happened.
τὰ ὀθόνια ← → μόνα καὶ → ἀπῆλθεν ← θαυμάζων πρὸς ἑαυτὸν τὸ → γεγονός
d.apn n.apn a.apn cj v.aai.3s pt.pa.nsm p.a r.asm.3 d.asn pt.ra.asn
3836 3856 3668 2779 599 2513 4639 1571 3836 1181

On the Road to Emmaus

24:13 Now that same day two of them were going to a village called Emmaus, about
⸂Καὶ ἰδοὺ⸃ ἐν τῇ αὐτῇ ἡμέρᾳ δύο ἐξ αὐτῶν ἦσαν πορευόμενοι εἰς κώμην ᾗ ὄνομα Ἐμμαοῦς ἀπέχουσαν
cj j p.d d.dsf r.dsf n.dsf a.npm p.g r.gpm.3 v.iai.3p pt.pm.npm p.a n.asf r.dsf n.nsn n.nsf pt.pa.asf
2779 2627 1877 3836 899 2465 1545 1666 899 1639 4513 1650 3267 4005 3950 1843 600

seven miles from Jerusalem. **14** They were talking with each other about everything that had happened.
ἑξήκοντα σταδίους ἀπὸ Ἰερουσαλήμ καὶ αὐτοὶ ὡμίλουν πρὸς → ἀλλήλους περὶ πάντων τῶν → συμβεβηκότων
a.apm n.apm p.g n.gsf cj r.npm v.iai.3p p.a r.apm p.g a.gpn d.gpn pt.ra.gpn
2008 5084 608 2647 2779 899 3917 4639 253 4309 4246 3836 5201

15 As they talked and discussed these things with each other, Jesus himself came up and
τούτων καὶ ἐγένετο ἐν αὐτοὺς ⸂τῷ ὁμιλεῖν⸃ καὶ συζητεῖν ← καὶ Ἰησοῦς αὐτὸς ἐγγίσας ←
r.gpn cj v.ami.3s p.d r.apm.3 d.dsn f.pa cj f.pa cj n.nsm r.nsm pt.aa.nsm
4047 2779 1181 1877 899 3836 3917 2779 5184 2779 2652 899 1581

walked along with them; **16** but they were kept from recognizing him. ¶ **17** He asked
συνεπορεύετο ← → αὐτοῖς δὲ οἱ ὀφθαλμοὶ αὐτῶν → ἐκρατοῦντο ⸂τοῦ μὴ ἐπιγνῶναι⸃ αὐτόν δὲ → εἶπεν
v.imi.3s r.dpm.3 cj d.npm n.npm r.gpm.3 v.ipi.3p d.gsn pl f.aa r.asm.3 cj v.aai.3s
5233 899 1254 3836 4057 899 3195 3836 3590 2105 899 1254 3306

them, "What are you discussing together as you walk along?" They
πρὸς αὐτούς τίνες ⸂οἱ λόγοι οὗτοι οὓς⸃ → → ἀντιβάλλετε ⸂πρὸς ἀλλήλους⸃ → περιπατοῦντες ← καὶ →
p.a r.apm.3 r.npm d.npm n.npm r.npm r.apm v.pai.2p p.a r.apm pt.pa.npm cj
4639 899 5515 3836 3364 4047 4005 506 4639 253 4344 2779

stood still, their faces downcast. **18** One of them, named Cleopas, asked him, "Are you only a
ἐστάθησαν ← σκυθρωποί δὲ εἷς ὀνόματι Κλεοπᾶς ἀποκριθεὶς εἶπεν πρὸς αὐτόν "Αρε σὺ μόνος
v.api.3p a.npm cj a.nsm n.dsn n.nsm pt.ap.nsm v.aai.3s p.a r.asm.3 r.ns.2 a.nsm
2705 5034 1254 1651 3950 3093 646 3306 4639 899 4228 5148 3668

visitor to Jerusalem and do not know the things that have happened there in these days?" ¶
παροικεῖς Ἰερουσαλήμ καὶ → οὐκ ἔγνως τὰ ← → → γενόμενα ⸂ἐν αὐτῇ⸃ ἐν ταύταις ⸂ταῖς ἡμέραις⸃
v.pai.2s n.asf cj pl v.aai.2s d.apn pt.am.apn p.d r.dsf.3 p.d r.dpf d.dpf n.dpf
4228 2647 2779 4024 1182 3836 1181 1877 899 1877 4047 3836 2465

19 "What things?" he asked. "About Jesus of Nazareth," they replied. "He was a
καὶ ποῖα → εἶπεν αὐτοῖς δὲ τὰ περὶ Ἰησοῦ ⸂τοῦ Ναζαρηνοῦ⸃ οἱ εἶπαν αὐτῷ ὃς ἐγένετο ἀνήρ
cj r.apn v.aai.3s r.dpm.3 cj d.apn p.g n.gsm d.gsm a.gsm d.npm v.aai.3p r.dsm.3 r.nsm v.ami.3s n.nsm
2779 4481 3306 899 1254 3836 4309 2652 3836 3716 3836 3306 899 4005 1181 467

prophet, powerful in word and deed before God and all the people. **20** The chief priests and our
προφήτης δυνατὸς ἐν λόγῳ καὶ ἔργῳ ἐναντίον ⸂τοῦ θεοῦ⸃ καὶ παντὸς τοῦ λαοῦ τε ὅπως οἱ → ἀρχιερεῖς καὶ ἡμῶν
n.nsm a.nsm p.d n.dsm cj n.dsn p.g d.gsm n.gsm cj a.gsm d.gsm n.gsm cj cj d.npm n.npm cj r.gp.1
4737 1543 1877 3364 2779 2240 1883 3836 2536 2779 4246 3836 3295 5445 3968 3836 797 2779 7005

rulers handed him over to be sentenced to death, and they crucified him; **21** but we had hoped that
⸂οἱ ἄρχοντες⸃ παρέδωκαν αὐτὸν ⸄ εἰς κρίμα → θανάτου καὶ → ἐσταύρωσαν αὐτόν δὲ ἡμεῖς → ἠλπίζομεν ὅτι
d.npm n.npm v.aai.3p r.asm.3 p.a n.asn n.gsm cj v.aai.3p r.asm.3 cj r.np.1 v.iai.1p cj
3836 807 4140 899 4140 1650 3210 2505 2779 5090 899 1254 7005 1827 4022

he was the one who was going to redeem Israel. *And* *what is more,* it is the third day
αὐτός ἐστιν ὁ ← ← → μέλλων λυτροῦσθαι ⸂τὸν Ἰσραήλ⸃ ἀλλά γε καὶ σὺν ⸂πᾶσιν τούτοις⸃ ταύτην τρίτην ἡμέραν
r.nsm v.pai.3s d.nsm pt.pa.nsm f.pm d.asm n.asm cj pl adv p.d a.dpn r.dpn r.asf a.asf n.asf
899 1639 3836 3516 3390 3836 2702 247 1145 2779 5250 4246 4047 4047 5569 2465

since all this took place. **22** *In* *addition,* some of our women amazed us. They went to the tomb
ἄγει ⸂ἀφ᾽ οὗ⸃ ταῦτα ἐγένετο ← ἀλλὰ καὶ τινες ἐξ ἡμῶν γυναῖκες ἐξέστησαν ἡμᾶς → γενόμεναι ἐπὶ τὸ μνημεῖον
v.pai.3s p.g r.gsn r.npn v.ami.3s cj adv r.npf p.g r.gp.1 n.npf v.aai.3p r.ap.1 pt.am.npf p.a d.asn n.asn
72 608 4005 1181 247 2779 5516 1666 7005 1222 2014 7005 1181 2093 3836 3646

λῆρος τὰ ῥήματα ταῦτα, καὶ ἠπίστουν αὐταῖς. **12** Ὁ δὲ Πέτρος ἀναστὰς ἔδραμεν ἐπὶ τὸ μνημεῖον καὶ παρακύψας βλέπει τὰ ὀθόνια μόνα, καὶ ἀπῆλθεν πρὸς ἑαυτὸν θαυμάζων τὸ γεγονός.

24:13 Καὶ ἰδοὺ δύο ἐξ αὐτῶν ἐν αὐτῇ τῇ ἡμέρᾳ ἦσαν πορευόμενοι εἰς κώμην ἀπέχουσαν σταδίους ἑξήκοντα ἀπὸ Ἰερουσαλήμ, ᾗ ὄνομα Ἐμμαοῦς, **14** καὶ αὐτοὶ ὡμίλουν πρὸς ἀλλήλους περὶ πάντων τῶν συμβεβηκότων τούτων. **15** καὶ ἐγένετο ἐν τῷ ὁμιλεῖν αὐτοὺς καὶ συζητεῖν καὶ αὐτὸς Ἰησοῦς ἐγγίσας συνεπορεύετο αὐτοῖς, **16** οἱ δὲ ὀφθαλμοὶ αὐτῶν ἐκρατοῦντο τοῦ μὴ ἐπιγνῶναι αὐτόν. ¶ **17** εἶπεν δὲ πρὸς αὐτούς, Τίνες οἱ λόγοι οὗτοι οὓς ἀντιβάλλετε πρὸς ἀλλήλους περιπατοῦντες; καὶ ἐστάθησαν σκυθρωποί. **18** ἀποκριθεὶς δὲ εἷς ἐξ αὐτῶν ὀνόματι Κλεοπᾶς εἶπεν πρὸς αὐτόν, Σὺ μόνος παροικεῖς Ἰερουσαλὴμ καὶ οὐκ ἔγνως τὰ γενόμενα ἐν αὐτῇ ἐν ταῖς ἡμέραις ταύταις; ¶ **19** καὶ εἶπεν αὐτοῖς, Ποῖα; οἱ δὲ εἶπαν αὐτῷ, Τὰ περὶ Ἰησοῦ τοῦ Ναζαρηνοῦ, ὃς ἐγένετο ἀνὴρ προφήτης δυνατὸς ἐν ἔργῳ καὶ λόγῳ ἐναντίον τοῦ θεοῦ καὶ παντὸς τοῦ λαοῦ, **20** ὅπως τε παρέδωκαν αὐτὸν οἱ ἀρχιερεῖς καὶ οἱ ἄρχοντες ἡμῶν εἰς κρίμα θανάτου καὶ ἐσταύρωσαν αὐτόν. **21** ἡμεῖς δὲ ἠλπίζομεν ὅτι αὐτός ἐστιν ὁ μέλλων λυτροῦσθαι τὸν Ἰσραήλ· ἀλλά γε καὶ σὺν πᾶσιν τούτοις τρίτην ταύτην ἡμέραν ἄγει ἀφ᾽ οὗ ταῦτα ἐγένετο. **22** ἀλλὰ καὶ γυναῖκές τινες ἐξ ἡμῶν

early	this morning	23	but	didn't	find	his	body.	They came	and	told	us	that	they had seen	a
ὀρθριναὶ	←	←	καὶ	μὴ	εὑροῦσαι	αὐτοῦ	τὸ σῶμα	ἦλθον	λέγουσαι	καὶ	→	→	ἑωρακέναι	
a.npf			cj	pt.aa.npf	r.gsm.3	d.asn n.asn	v.aai.3p	pt.pa.npf	adv			f.ra	
3984			2779	3590	2351	899	3836 5393	2262		2779		3972	

vision	of angels,	who	said	he	was alive.	24	Then	some	of	our	companions	went	to the	tomb	and	found it
ὀπτασίαν	→ ἀγγέλων	οἳ	λέγουσιν	αὐτὸν	→ ζῆν	καὶ	τινες	→ ἡμῖν	τῶν σὺν	ἀπῆλθον ἐπὶ τὸ	μνημεῖον καὶ	εὗρον
n.asf	n.gpm	r.npm	v.pai.3p	r.asm.3	f.pa	cj	r.npm	r.dp.1	d.gpm p.d	v.aai.3p p.a d.asn	n.asn cj	v.aai.3p
3965	34	4005	3306	899	2409	2779	5516	3836 7005	3836 5250	599 2093 3836	3646 2779	2351

	just	as	the	women	had said,	but	him	they did not see."	¶	25	He	said	to	them,	"How	foolish
	οὕτως	καθὼς	← καὶ	αἱ γυναῖκες	→ εἶπον	δὲ	αὐτὸν	→ οὐκ εἶδον	καὶ	αὐτὸς	εἶπεν πρὸς	αὐτούς	ὦ	ἀνόητοι
	adv	cj	adv	d.npf n.npf	v.aai.3p	cj	r.asm.3	pl v.aai.3p	cj	r.nsm	v.aai.3s p.a	r.apm.3	j	a.vpm
	4048	2777	2779	3836 1222	3306	1254	899	4024 1625	2779	899	3306 4639	899	6043	485

you are,	and	how	slow	of heart	to believe	all	that	the	prophets	have	spoken!	26	Did not	the	Christ
←	καὶ		βραδεῖς →	τῇ καρδίᾳ	‿τοῦ πιστεύειν‿	ἐπὶ	πᾶσιν	οἷς	οἱ προφῆται	→	ἐλάλησαν	→	οὐχὶ	τὸν χριστὸν
	cj		a.vpm	d.dsf n.dsf	d.gsn v.pan	p.d	a.dpn	r.dpn	d.npm n.npm		v.aai.3p		pl	d.asm n.asm
	2779		1096	3836 2840	3836 4409	2093	4246	4005	3836 4737		3281		1256 4049	3836 5986

have to	suffer	these	things	and	then enter	his	glory?"	27	And	beginning	with	Moses	and	all	the
ἔδει	→ παθεῖν	ταῦτα		καὶ	εἰσελθεῖν εἰς	αὐτοῦ	τὴν δόξαν	καὶ	ἀρξάμενος	ἀπὸ	Μωϋσέως καὶ	ἀπὸ	πάντων τῶν
v.iai.3s	f.aa	r.apn		cj	f.aa	p.a	r.gsm.3 d.asf n.asf	cj	pt.am.nsm	p.g	n.gsm	cj	p.g	a.gpm d.gpm
1256	4248	4047		2779	1656	1650	899 3836 1518	2779	806	608	3707 2779	608	4246 3836

Prophets,	he explained	to them	what	was said in	all	the	Scriptures	concerning	himself.	¶	28	As	they
προφητῶν	διερμήνευσεν	αὐτοῖς	τὰ	ἐν	πάσαις	ταῖς γραφαῖς	περὶ	ἑαυτοῦ			Καὶ	→
n.gpm	v.aai.3s	r.dpm.3	d.apn	p.d	a.dpf	d.dpf n.dpf	p.g	r.gsm.3			cj	
4737	1450	899	3836	1877	4246	3836 1210	4309	1571			2779	

approached	the	village	to which	they were going,	Jesus	acted	as if he were going	farther.
ἤγγισαν	εἰς τὴν	κώμην	οὗ	ἐπορεύοντο	καὶ αὐτὸς	προσεποιήσατο	← ← ← πορεύεσθαι	πορρώτερον
v.aai.3p	p.a d.asf	n.asf	adv	v.imi.3p	cj r.nsm	v.ami.3s	f.pm	adv.c
1581	1650 3836	3267	4023	4513	2779 899	4701	4513	4522

29	But	they	urged	him	strongly,	"Stay	with us,	for	it is	nearly	evening;	the	day	is	almost
καὶ	→		παρεβιάσαντο	αὐτὸν	←	λέγοντες	μεῖνον μεθ'	ἡμῶν	ὅτι	→ ἐστὶν	πρὸς	ἑσπέραν	καὶ ἡ	ἡμέρα	→ ἤδη
cj			v.ami.3p	r.asm.3		pt.pa.npm	v.aam.2s p.g	r.gp.1	cj	v.pai.3s	p.a	n.asf	cj d.nsf	n.nsf	adv
2779			4128	899	4128	3306	3531 3552	7005	4022	1639	4639	2270	2779 3836	2465	3111 2453

over."	So	he went	in	to stay	with	them.	¶	30		When	he	was	at the	table	with
κέκλικεν	καὶ	→ εἰσῆλθεν	←	‿τοῦ μεῖναι‿	σὺν	αὐτοῖς		καὶ	ἐγένετο ἐν	αὐτὸν	→ →	τῷ κατακλιθῆναι	μετ'
v.rai.3s	cj	v.aai.3s		d.gsn f.aa	p.d	r.dpm.3		cj	v.ami.3s p.d	r.asm.3		d.dsn f.ap	p.g
3111	2779	1656		3836 3531	5250	899		2779	1181 1877	899		3836 2884	3552

them,	he took	bread,	gave thanks,	broke	it	and	began to give	it	to them.	31	Then	their	eyes	were
αὐτῶν	→ λαβὼν	τὸν ἄρτον	εὐλόγησεν	καὶ κλάσας	→	→	ἐπεδίδου	→	αὐτοῖς	δὲ	αὐτῶν	οἱ ὀφθαλμοὶ	→
r.gpm.3	pt.aa.nsm	d.asm n.asm	v.aai.3s	cj pt.aa.nsm			v.iai.3s		r.dpm.3	cj	r.gpm.3	d.npm n.npm	
899	3284	3836 788	2328	2779 3089			2113		899	1254	899	3836 4057	

opened	and	they recognized	him,	and	he	disappeared	from	their	sight.	32	They	asked	each	other,
διηνοίχθησαν	καὶ	→ ἐπέγνωσαν	αὐτόν	καὶ	αὐτὸς	‿ἄφαντος ἐγένετο‿	ἀπ'	αὐτῶν		καὶ	→	εἶπαν	πρὸς →	ἀλλήλους
v.api.3p	cj	v.aai.3p	r.asm.3	cj	r.nsm	a.nsm v.ami.3s	p.g	r.gpm.3		cj		v.aai.3p	p.a	r.apm
1380	2779	2105	899	2779	899	908 1181	608	899		2779		3306	4639	253

"Were	not	our	hearts	burning	within	us	while	he talked	with	us	on	the	road	and	opened	the	Scriptures
ἦν	οὐχὶ	ἡμῶν	ἡ καρδία	καιομένη	ἐν	ἡμῖν	ὡς	→ ἐλάλει	→	ἡμῖν	ἐν	τῇ	ὁδῷ	ὡς	διήνοιγεν	τὰς	γραφάς
v.iai.3s	pl	r.gp.1	d.nsf n.nsf	pt.pp.nsf	p.d	r.dp.1	cj	v.iai.3s		r.dp.1	p.d	d.dsf	n.dsf	cj	v.iai.3s	d.apf	n.apf
1639	4049	7005	3836 2840	2794	1877	7005	6055	3281		7005	1877	3836	3847	6055	1380	3836	1210

to us?"	¶	33	They	got	up	and	returned	at once	to	Jerusalem.	There	they found	the
→ ἡμῖν			Καὶ	ἀναστάντες	←		ὑπέστρεψαν	‿αὐτῇ τῇ ὥρᾳ‿	εἰς	Ἰερουσαλὴμ	καὶ	→ εὗρον	τοὺς
r.dp.1			cj	pt.aa.npm			v.aai.3p	r.dsf d.dsf n.dsf	p.a	n.asf	cj	v.aai.3p	d.apm
7005			2779	482			5715	899 3836 6052	1650	2647	2779	2351	3836

Eleven	and	those	with	them,	assembled	together	34	and	saying,	"It is true!	The	Lord	has risen	and	has appeared
ἕνδεκα	καὶ	τοὺς	σὺν	αὐτοῖς	ἠθροισμένους	←		λέγοντας	ὅτι	→ ὄντως	ὁ	κύριος	ἠγέρθη	καὶ	ὤφθη
a.apm	cj	d.apm	p.d	r.dpm.3	pt.rp.apm			pt.pa.apm	cj	adv	d.nsm	n.nsm	v.api.3s	cj	v.api.3s
1894	2779	3836	5250	899	125			3306	4022	3953	3836	3261	1586	2779	3972

ἐξέστησαν ἡμᾶς, γενόμεναι ὀρθριναὶ ἐπὶ τὸ μνημεῖον, ²³ καὶ μὴ εὑροῦσαι τὸ σῶμα αὐτοῦ ἦλθον λέγουσαι καὶ ὀπτασίαν ἀγγέλων ἑωρακέναι, οἳ λέγουσιν αὐτὸν ζῆν. ²⁴ καὶ ἀπῆλθόν τινες τῶν σὺν ἡμῖν ἐπὶ τὸ μνημεῖον καὶ εὗρον οὕτως καθὼς καὶ αἱ γυναῖκες εἶπον, αὐτὸν δὲ οὐκ εἶδον. ¶ ²⁵ καὶ αὐτὸς εἶπεν πρὸς αὐτούς, Ὦ ἀνόητοι καὶ βραδεῖς τῇ καρδίᾳ τοῦ πιστεύειν ἐπὶ πᾶσιν οἷς ἐλάλησαν οἱ προφῆται· ²⁶ οὐχὶ ταῦτα ἔδει παθεῖν τὸν Χριστὸν καὶ εἰσελθεῖν εἰς τὴν δόξαν αὐτοῦ; ²⁷ καὶ ἀρξάμενος ἀπὸ Μωϋσέως καὶ ἀπὸ πάντων τῶν προφητῶν διερμήνευσεν αὐτοῖς ἐν πάσαις ταῖς γραφαῖς τὰ περὶ ἑαυτοῦ. ¶ ²⁸ Καὶ ἤγγισαν εἰς τὴν κώμην οὗ ἐπορεύοντο, καὶ αὐτὸς προσεποιήσατο πορρώτερον πορεύεσθαι. ²⁹ καὶ παρεβιάσαντο αὐτὸν λέγοντες, Μεῖνον μεθ' ἡμῶν, ὅτι πρὸς ἑσπέραν ἐστὶν καὶ κέκλικεν ἤδη ἡ ἡμέρα. καὶ εἰσῆλθεν τοῦ μεῖναι σὺν αὐτοῖς. ¶ ³⁰ καὶ ἐγένετο ἐν τῷ κατακλιθῆναι αὐτὸν μετ' αὐτῶν λαβὼν τὸν ἄρτον εὐλόγησεν καὶ κλάσας ἐπεδίδου αὐτοῖς, ³¹ αὐτῶν δὲ διηνοίχθησαν οἱ ὀφθαλμοὶ καὶ ἐπέγνωσαν αὐτόν· καὶ αὐτὸς ἄφαντος ἐγένετο ἀπ' αὐτῶν. ³² καὶ εἶπαν πρὸς ἀλλήλους, Οὐχὶ ἡ καρδία ἡμῶν καιομένη ἦν [ἐν ἡμῖν] ὡς ἐλάλει ἡμῖν ἐν τῇ ὁδῷ, ὡς διήνοιγεν ἡμῖν τὰς γραφάς; ¶ ³³ καὶ ἀναστάντες αὐτῇ τῇ ὥρᾳ ὑπέστρεψαν εἰς Ἰερουσαλὴμ καὶ εὗρον ἠθροισμένους τοὺς ἕνδεκα καὶ τοὺς σὺν αὐτοῖς, ³⁴ λέγοντας ὅτι ὄντως ἠγέρθη ὁ κύριος καὶ ὤφθη

to Simon." **35** Then the two told what had happened on the way, and how Jesus was recognized by them when
Σίμωνι καὶ αὐτοὶ ἐξηγοῦντο τὰ ← ← ἐν τῇ ὁδῷ καὶ ὡς ἐγνώσθη αὐτοῖς ἐν
n.dsm / cj / r.npm / v.imi.3p / d.apn / p.d / d.dsf / n.dsf / cj / cj / v.api.3s / r.dpm.3 / p.d
4981 2779 899 2007 3836 1877 3836 3847 2779 6055 1182 899 1877

he broke the bread.
τῇ κλάσει τοῦ ἄρτου
d.dsf / n.dsf / d.gsm / n.gsm
3836 3082 3836 788

Jesus Appears to the Disicples

24:36 While they were still talking about this, Jesus himself stood among them and said to them, "Peace
δὲ αὐτῶν λαλούντων Ταῦτα αὐτὸς ἔστη ἐν μέσῳ αὐτῶν καὶ λέγει αὐτοῖς εἰρήνη
cj / r.gpm.3 / pt.pa.gpm / r.apn / r.nsm / v.aai.3s / p.d / n.dsn / r.gpm.3 / cj / v.pai.3s / r.dpm.3 / n.nsf
1254 3281 899 3281 4047 899 2705 1877 3545 899 2779 3306 899 1645

be with you." ¶ **37** They were startled and frightened, thinking they saw a ghost. **38** He said to
ὑμῖν δὲ πτοηθέντες καὶ ἔμφοβοι γενόμενοι ἐδόκουν θεωρεῖν πνεῦμα καὶ εἶπεν
r.dp.2 / cj / pt.ap.npm / cj / a.npm / pt.am.npm / v.iai.3p / f.pa / n.asn / cj / v.aai.3s
7007 1254 4765 2779 1873 1181 1506 2555 4460 2779 3306

them, "Why are you troubled, and why do doubts rise in your minds? **39** Look at my hands
αὐτοῖς τί ἐστε τεταραγμένοι καὶ διὰ τί διαλογισμοὶ ἀναβαίνουσιν ἐν ὑμῶν τῇ καρδίᾳ ἴδετε μου τὰς χεῖρας
r.dpm.3 / r.asn / v.pai.2p / pt.rp.npm / cj / p.a / r.asn / n.npm / v.pai.3p / p.d / r.gp.2 / d.dsf / n.dsf / v.aam.2p / r.gs.1 / d.apf / n.apf
899 5515 1639 5429 2779 1328 5515 326 1369 326 1877 7007 3836 2840 1625 1609 3836 5931

and my feet. It is I myself! Touch me and see; a ghost does not have flesh and bones, as
καὶ μου τοὺς πόδας ὅτι εἰμι ἐγὼ αὐτός ψηλαφήσατε με καὶ ἴδετε ὅτι πνεῦμα οὐκ ἔχει σάρκα καὶ ὀστέα καθὼς
cj / r.gs.1 / d.apm / n.apm / cj / v.pai.1s / r.ns.1 / r.nsm / v.aam.2p / r.as.1 / cj / v.aam.2p / cj / n.nsn / pl / v.pai.3s / n.asf / cj / n.apn / cj
2779 1609 3836 4546 4022 1639 1609 899 6027 1609 2779 1625 4022 4460 4024 2400 4922 2779 4014 2777

you see I have." ¶ **40** When he had said this, he showed them his hands and feet. **41** And while
θεωρεῖτε ἐμὲ ἔχοντα καὶ εἶπεν τοῦτο ἔδειξεν αὐτοῖς τὰς χεῖρας καὶ τοὺς πόδας δὲ
v.pai.2p / r.as.1 / pt.pa.asm / cj / pt.aa.nsm / r.asn / v.aai.3s / r.dpm.3 / d.apf / n.apf / cj / d.apm / n.apm / cj
2555 1609 2400 2779 3306 4047 1259 899 3836 5931 2779 3836 4546 1254 601

they still did not believe it because of joy and amazement, he asked them, "Do you have anything here
αὐτῶν ἔτι ἀπιστούντων ἀπὸ τῆς χαρᾶς καὶ θαυμαζόντων εἶπεν αὐτοῖς ἔχετε τι ἐνθάδε
r.gpm.3 / adv / pt.pa.gpm / p.g / d.gsf / n.gsf / cj / pt.pa.gpm / v.aai.3s / r.dpm.3 / v.pai.2p / r.asn / adv
899 2285 601 608 3836 5915 2779 2513 3306 899 2400 5516 1924

to eat?" **42** They gave him a piece of broiled fish, **43** and he took it and ate it in their presence. ¶
βρώσιμον δὲ οἱ ἐπέδωκαν αὐτῷ μέρος ὀπτοῦ ἰχθύος καὶ λαβὼν ἔφαγεν αὐτῶν ἐνώπιον
n.asn / cj / d.npm / v.aai.3p / r.dsm.3 / n.asn / a.gsm / n.gsm / cj / pt.aa.nsm / v.aai.3s / r.gpm.3 / p.g
1110 1254 3836 2113 899 3538 3966 2716 2779 3284 2266 1967 1967

44 He said to them, "This is what I told you while I was still with you: Everything
δὲ Εἶπεν πρὸς αὐτούς οὗτοι οἱ λόγοι μου οὓς ἐλάλησα πρὸς ὑμᾶς ὢν ἔτι σὺν ὑμῖν ὅτι πάντα
cj / v.aai.3s / p.a / r.apm.3 / r.npm / d.npm / n.npm / r.gs.1 / r.apm / v.aai.1s / p.a / r.ap.2 / pt.pa.nsm / adv / p.d / r.dp.2 / cj / a.apn
1254 3306 4639 899 4047 3836 3364 1609 4005 3281 4639 7007 1639 2285 5250 7007 4022 4246

must be fulfilled that is written about me in the Law of Moses, the Prophets and the Psalms." ¶
δεῖ πληρωθῆναι τὰ γεγραμμένα περὶ ἐμοῦ ἐν τῷ νόμῳ Μωϋσέως καὶ τοῖς προφήταις καὶ ψαλμοῖς
v.pai.3s / f.ap / d.apn / pt.rp.apn / p.g / r.gs.1 / p.d / d.dsm / n.dsm / n.gsm / cj / d.dpm / n.dpm / cj / n.dpm
1256 4444 3836 1211 4309 1609 1877 3836 3795 3707 2779 3836 4737 2779 6011

45 Then he opened their minds so they could understand the Scriptures. **46** He told them, "This is what is
τότε διήνοιξεν αὐτῶν τὸν νοῦν τοῦ συνιέναι τὰς γραφάς καὶ εἶπεν αὐτοῖς ὅτι οὕτως
adv / v.aai.3s / r.gpm.3 / d.asm / n.asm / d.gsn / f.pa / d.apf / n.apf / cj / v.aai.3s / r.dpm.3 / cj / adv
5538 1380 899 3836 3808 3836 5317 3836 1210 2779 3306 899 4022 4048

written: The Christ will suffer and rise from the dead on the third day, **47** and repentance and forgiveness of
γέγραπται τὸν χριστὸν παθεῖν καὶ ἀναστῆναι ἐκ νεκρῶν τῇ τρίτῃ ἡμέρᾳ καὶ μετάνοιαν εἰς ἄφεσιν
v.rpi.3s / d.asm / n.asm / f.aa / cj / f.aa / p.g / a.gpm / d.dsf / a.dsf / n.dsf / cj / n.asf / p.a / n.asf
1211 3836 5986 4248 2779 482 1666 3738 3836 5569 2465 2779 3567 1650 912

sins will be preached in his name to all nations, beginning at Jerusalem. **48** You are witnesses of
ἁμαρτιῶν κηρυχθῆναι ἐπὶ αὐτοῦ τῷ ὀνόματι εἰς πάντα τὰ ἔθνη ἀρξάμενοι ἀπὸ Ἰερουσαλὴμ ὑμεῖς μάρτυρες
n.gpf / f.ap / p.d / r.gsm.3 / d.dsn / n.dsn / p.a / a.apn / d.apn / n.apn / pt.am.npm / p.g / n.gsf / r.np.2 / n.npm
281 3062 2093 899 3836 3950 1650 4246 3836 1620 806 608 2647 7007 3459

Σίμωνι. 35 καὶ αὐτοὶ ἐξηγοῦντο τὰ ἐν τῇ ὁδῷ καὶ ὡς ἐγνώσθη αὐτοῖς ἐν τῇ κλάσει τοῦ ἄρτου.

24:36 Ταῦτα δὲ αὐτῶν λαλούντων αὐτὸς ἔστη ἐν μέσῳ αὐτῶν καὶ λέγει αὐτοῖς, Εἰρήνη ὑμῖν. ¶ 37 πτοηθέντες δὲ καὶ ἔμφοβοι γενόμενοι ἐδόκουν πνεῦμα θεωρεῖν. 38 καὶ εἶπεν αὐτοῖς, Τί τεταραγμένοι ἐστὲ καὶ διὰ τί διαλογισμοὶ ἀναβαίνουσιν ἐν τῇ καρδίᾳ ὑμῶν; 39 ἴδετε τὰς χεῖράς μου καὶ τοὺς πόδας μου ὅτι ἐγώ εἰμι αὐτός· ψηλαφήσατέ με καὶ ἴδετε, ὅτι πνεῦμα σάρκα καὶ ὀστέα οὐκ ἔχει καθὼς ἐμὲ θεωρεῖτε ἔχοντα. ¶ 40 καὶ τοῦτο εἰπὼν ἔδειξεν αὐτοῖς τὰς χεῖρας καὶ τοὺς πόδας. 41 ἔτι δὲ ἀπιστούντων αὐτῶν ἀπὸ τῆς χαρᾶς καὶ θαυμαζόντων εἶπεν αὐτοῖς, Ἔχετέ τι βρώσιμον ἐνθάδε; 42 οἱ δὲ ἐπέδωκαν αὐτῷ ἰχθύος ὀπτοῦ μέρος· 43 καὶ λαβὼν ἐνώπιον αὐτῶν ἔφαγεν. ¶ 44 Εἶπεν δὲ πρὸς αὐτούς, Οὗτοι οἱ λόγοι μου οὓς ἐλάλησα πρὸς ὑμᾶς ἔτι ὢν σὺν ὑμῖν, ὅτι δεῖ πληρωθῆναι πάντα τὰ γεγραμμένα ἐν τῷ νόμῳ Μωϋσέως καὶ τοῖς προφήταις καὶ ψαλμοῖς περὶ ἐμοῦ. ¶ 45 τότε διήνοιξεν αὐτῶν τὸν νοῦν τοῦ συνιέναι τὰς γραφάς· 46 καὶ εἶπεν αὐτοῖς ὅτι Οὕτως γέγραπται παθεῖν τὸν Χριστὸν καὶ ἀναστῆναι ἐκ νεκρῶν τῇ τρίτῃ ἡμέρᾳ, 47 καὶ κηρυχθῆναι ἐπὶ τῷ ὀνόματι αὐτοῦ μετάνοιαν καὶ «εἰς» ἄφεσιν ἁμαρτιῶν εἰς πάντα τὰ ἔθνη. ἀρξάμενοι

these	things.	**49**		I	am going	to	send		you	what	my	Father		has	promised;	but		stay	in
τούτων ←			καὶ	[ἰδοὺ]	ἐγὼ →	→	→ ἀποστέλλω	ἐφ᾽	ὑμᾶς	τὴν	μου	⌐τοῦ πατρός⌐		ἐπαγγελίαν		δὲ	ὑμεῖς	καθίσατε	ἐν
r.gpn			cj	j	r.ns.1		v.pai.1s	p.a	r.ap.2	d.asf	r.gs.1	d.gsm n.gsm		n.asf		cj	r.np.2	v.aam.2p	p.d
4047			2779	2627	1609		690	2093	7007	3836	1609	3836 4252		2039		1254	7007	2767	1877

the	city	until		you have	been	clothed	with	power	from	on high."
τῇ	πόλει	ἕως οὗ	→	→ →	→	ἐνδύσησθε		δύναμιν	ἐξ	→ ὕψους
d.dsf	n.dsf	p.g r.gsm		v.ams.2p				n.asf	p.g	n.gsn
3836	4484	2401 4005		1907				1539	1666	5737

The Ascension

24:50 When	he	had	led		them	out	to	the	vicinity of	Bethany,		he	lifted	up	his	hands		and
δὲ	→	→	Ἐξήγαγεν		αὐτοὺς	ἔξω	ἕως		πρὸς ←	Βηθανίαν	καὶ	→	ἐπάρας	←	αὐτοῦ	⌐τὰς χεῖρας⌐		
cj			v.aai.3s		r.apm.3	adv	p.g		p.a	n.asf	cj		pt.aa.nsm		r.gsm.3	d.apf n.apf		
1254			1974		899	2032	2401		4639	1029	2779		2048		899	3836 5931		

blessed	them.	**51**		While	he	was	blessing		them,	he	left		them	and	was	taken	up	into
εὐλόγησεν	αὐτούς		καὶ	ἐγένετο	ἐν		αὐτὸν →	⌐τῷ εὐλογεῖν⌐	αὐτοὺς	→	διέστη	ἀπ᾽	αὐτῶν	καὶ	→	ἀνεφέρετο ←		εἰς
v.aai.3s	r.apm.3		cj	v.ami.3s	p.d		r.asm.3	d.dsn f.pa	r.apm.3		v.aai.3s	p.g	r.gpm.3	cj		v.ipi.3s		p.a
2328	899		2779	1181	1877		899	3836 2328	899		1460	608	899	2779		429		1650

heaven.	**52**	Then	they	worshiped		him	and	returned	to	Jerusalem	with	great	joy.	**53**	And	they	stayed
⌐τὸν οὐρανόν⌐		Καὶ	αὐτοὶ	προσκυνήσαντες		αὐτὸν		ὑπέστρεψαν	εἰς	Ἰερουσαλὴμ	μετὰ	μεγάλης	χαρᾶς		καὶ	→	ἦσαν
d.asm n.asm		cj	r.np.m	pt.aa.npm		r.asm.3		v.aai.3p	p.a	n.asf	p.g	a.gsf	n.gsf		cj		v.iai.3p
3836 4041		2779	899	4686		899		5715	1650	2647	3552	3489	5915		2779		1639

continually	at	the	temple,	praising	God.
⌐διὰ παντὸς⌐	ἐν	τῷ	ἱερῷ	εὐλογοῦντες	⌐τὸν θεόν⌐
p.g	a.gsm	p.d	d.dsn	n.dsn	pt.pa.npm	d.asm n.asm
1328	4246	1877	3836	2639	2328	3836 2536

ἀπὸ Ἰερουσαλήμ ⁴⁸ ὑμεῖς μάρτυρες τούτων. ⁴⁹ καὶ [ἰδοὺ] ἐγὼ ἀποστέλλω τὴν ἐπαγγελίαν τοῦ πατρός μου ἐφ᾽ ὑμᾶς· ὑμεῖς δὲ καθίσατε ἐν τῇ πόλει ἕως οὗ ἐνδύσησθε ἐξ ὕψους δύναμιν.

²⁴:⁵⁰ Ἐξήγαγεν δὲ αὐτοὺς [ἔξω] ἕως πρὸς Βηθανίαν, καὶ ἐπάρας τὰς χεῖρας αὐτοῦ εὐλόγησεν αὐτούς. ⁵¹ καὶ ἐγένετο ἐν τῷ εὐλογεῖν αὐτὸν αὐτοὺς διέστη ἀπ᾽ αὐτῶν καὶ ἀνεφέρετο εἰς τὸν οὐρανόν. ⁵² καὶ αὐτοὶ προσκυνήσαντες αὐτὸν ὑπέστρεψαν εἰς Ἰερουσαλὴμ μετὰ χαρᾶς μεγάλης ⁵³ καὶ ἦσαν διὰ παντὸς ἐν τῷ ἱερῷ εὐλογοῦντες τὸν θεόν.

John

The Word Became Flesh

1:1 In the beginning was the Word, and the Word was with God, and the Word was God. **2** He was with
Ἐν ἀρχῇ ἦν ὁ λόγος καὶ ὁ λόγος ἦν πρὸς τὸν θεόν καὶ ὁ λόγος ἦν θεός οὗτος ἦν πρὸς
p.d n.dsf v.iai.3s d.nsm n.nsm cj d.nsm n.nsm v.iai.3s p.a d.asm n.asm cj d.nsm n.nsm v.iai.3s n.nsm r.nsm v.iai.3s p.a
1877 794 1639 3836 3364 2779 3836 3364 1639 4639 3836 2536 2779 3836 3364 1639 2536 4047 1639 4639

God in the beginning. ¶ **3** Through him all things were made; without him nothing was made
τὸν θεόν ἐν ἀρχῇ δι᾽ αὐτοῦ πάντα ἐγένετο καὶ χωρὶς αὐτοῦ οὐδὲ ἕν ἐγένετο
d.asm n.asm p.d n.dsf p.g r.gsm.3 a.npn v.ami.3s cj p.g r.gsm.3 adv a.nsn v.ami.3s
3836 2536 1877 794 1328 899 4246 1181 2779 6006 899 4028 1651 1181

that has been made. **4** In him was life, and that life was the light of men. **5** The light shines in the
ὃ γέγονεν ἐν αὐτῷ ἦν ζωὴ καὶ ἡ ζωὴ ἦν τὸ φῶς τῶν ἀνθρώπων καὶ τὸ φῶς φαίνει ἐν τῇ
r.nsn v.rai.3s p.d r.dsm.3 v.iai.3s n.nsf cj d.nsf n.nsf v.iai.3s d.nsn n.nsn d.gpm n.gpm cj d.nsn n.nsn v.pai.3s p.d d.dsf
4005 1181 1877 899 1639 2437 2779 3836 2437 1639 3836 5890 3836 476 2779 3836 5890 5743 1877 3836

darkness, but the darkness has not understood it. ¶ **6** There came a man who was sent from
σκοτίᾳ καὶ ἡ σκοτία οὐ κατέλαβεν αὐτό Ἐγένετο ἄνθρωπος ἀπεσταλμένος παρὰ
n.dsf cj d.nsf n.nsf pl v.aai.3s r.asn.3 v.ami.3s n.nsm pt.rp.nsm p.g
5028 2779 3836 5028 4024 2898 899 1181 476 690 4123

God; his name was John. **7** He came as a witness to testify concerning that light, so that through him
θεοῦ αὐτῷ ὄνομα Ἰωάννης οὗτος ἦλθεν εἰς μαρτυρίαν ἵνα μαρτυρήσῃ περὶ τοῦ φωτός ἵνα δι᾽ αὐτοῦ
n.gsm r.dsm.3 n.nsn n.nsm r.nsm v.aai.3s p.a n.asf cj v.aas.3s p.a d.gsn n.gsn cj p.g r.gsm.3
2536 899 3950 2722 4047 2262 1650 3456 2671 3455 4309 3836 5890 2671 1328 899

all men might believe. **8** He himself was not the light; he came only as a witness to the light. **9** The true
πάντες πιστεύσωσιν ἐκεῖνος ἦν οὐκ τὸ φῶς ἵνα ἀλλ᾽ μαρτυρήσῃ περὶ τοῦ φωτός τὸ ἀληθινόν
a.npm v.aas.3p r.nsm v.iai.3s pl d.nsn n.nsn cj cj v.aas.3s p.g d.gsn n.gsn d.nsn a.nsn
4246 4409 1697 1639 4024 3836 5890 2671 247 3455 4309 3836 5890 3836 240

light that gives light to every man was coming into the world. ¶ **10** He was in the world, and though
τὸ φῶς ὃ φωτίζει πάντα ἄνθρωπον Ἦν ἐρχόμενον εἰς τὸν κόσμον ἦν ἐν τῷ κόσμῳ καὶ
d.nsn n.nsn r.nsn v.pai.3s a.asm n.asm v.iai.3s v.pmp.nsm p.a d.asm n.asm v.iai.3s p.d d.dsm n.dsm cj
3836 5890 4005 5894 4246 476 1639 2262 1650 3836 3180 1639 1877 3836 3180 2779

the world was made through him, the world did not recognize him. **11** He came to that which was his own, but
ὁ κόσμος ἐγένετο δι᾽ αὐτοῦ καὶ ὁ κόσμος οὐκ ἔγνω αὐτόν ἦλθεν εἰς τὰ ἴδια καὶ
d.nsm n.nsm v.ami.3s p.g r.gsm.3 cj d.nsm n.nsm pl v.aai.3s r.asm.3 v.aai.3s p.a d.apn a.apn cj
3836 3180 1181 1328 899 2779 3836 3180 1182 4024 1182 899 2262 1650 3836 2625 2779

his own did not receive him. **12** Yet to all who received him, to those who believed in his name, he gave
οἱ ἴδιοι οὐ παρέλαβον αὐτόν δὲ ὅσοι ἔλαβον αὐτόν τοῖς πιστεύουσιν εἰς αὐτοῦ τὸ ὄνομα ἔδωκεν
d.npm a.npm pl v.aai.3p r.asm.3 cj r.npm v.aai.3p r.asm.3 d.dpm pt.pa.dpm p.a r.gsm.3 d.asn n.asn v.aai.3s
3836 2625 4161 4024 4161 899 1254 4012 3284 899 3836 4409 1650 899 3836 3950 1443

the right to become children of God – **13** children born not of natural descent, nor of human decision or
αὐτοῖς ἐξουσίαν γενέσθαι τέκνα θεοῦ οἳ οὐκ ἐξ αἱμάτων οὐδὲ ἐκ σαρκὸς θελήματος οὐδὲ
r.dpm.3 n.asf f.am n.apn n.gsm r.npm pl p.g n.gpn cj p.g n.gsf n.gsn cj
899 2026 1181 5451 2536 4005 4024 1666 135 4028 1666 4922 2525 4028

a husband's will, but born of God. ¶ **14** The Word became flesh and made his dwelling
ἐκ ἀνδρὸς θελήματος ἀλλ᾽ ἐγεννήθησαν ἐκ θεοῦ Καὶ ὁ λόγος ἐγένετο σὰρξ καὶ ἐσκήνωσεν
p.g n.gsm n.gsn cj v.api.3p p.g n.gsm cj d.nsm n.nsm v.ami.3s n.nsf cj v.aai.3s
1666 467 2525 247 1164 1666 2536 2779 3836 3364 1181 4922 2779 5012

among us. We have seen his glory, the glory of the One and Only, who came from the
ἐν ἡμῖν καὶ ἐθεασάμεθα αὐτοῦ τὴν δόξαν δόξαν ὡς μονογενοῦς παρὰ
p.d r.dp.1 cj v.ami.1p r.gsm.3 d.asf n.asf n.asf pl a.gsm p.g
1877 7005 2779 2517 899 3836 1518 1518 6055 3666 4123

Father, full of grace and truth. ¶ **15** John testifies concerning him. He cries out, saying, "This
πατρός πλήρης χάριτος καὶ ἀληθείας Ἰωάννης μαρτυρεῖ περὶ αὐτοῦ καὶ κέκραγεν λέγων οὗτος
n.gsm n.gsf n.gsf cj n.gsf n.nsm v.pai.3s p.g r.gsm.3 cj v.rai.3s pt.pa.nsm r.nsm
4252 4441 5921 2779 237 2722 3455 4309 899 2779 3189 3306 4047

1:1 Ἐν ἀρχῇ ἦν ὁ λόγος, καὶ ὁ λόγος ἦν πρὸς τὸν θεόν, καὶ θεὸς ἦν ὁ λόγος. **2** οὗτος ἦν ἐν ἀρχῇ πρὸς τὸν θεόν. ¶ **3** πάντα δι᾽ αὐτοῦ ἐγένετο, καὶ χωρὶς αὐτοῦ ἐγένετο οὐδὲ ἕν. ὃ γέγονεν **4** ἐν αὐτῷ ζωὴ ἦν, καὶ ἡ ζωὴ ἦν τὸ φῶς τῶν ἀνθρώπων· **5** καὶ τὸ φῶς ἐν τῇ σκοτίᾳ φαίνει, καὶ ἡ σκοτία αὐτὸ οὐ κατέλαβεν. ¶ **6** Ἐγένετο ἄνθρωπος, ἀπεσταλμένος παρὰ θεοῦ, ὄνομα αὐτῷ Ἰωάννης· **7** οὗτος ἦλθεν εἰς μαρτυρίαν ἵνα μαρτυρήσῃ περὶ τοῦ φωτός, ἵνα πάντες πιστεύσωσιν δι᾽ αὐτοῦ. **8** οὐκ ἦν ἐκεῖνος τὸ φῶς, ἀλλ᾽ ἵνα μαρτυρήσῃ περὶ τοῦ φωτός. **9** Ἦν τὸ φῶς τὸ ἀληθινόν, ὃ φωτίζει πάντα ἄνθρωπον, ἐρχόμενον εἰς τὸν κόσμον. ¶ **10** ἐν τῷ κόσμῳ ἦν, καὶ ὁ κόσμος δι᾽ αὐτοῦ ἐγένετο, καὶ ὁ κόσμος αὐτὸν οὐκ ἔγνω. **11** εἰς τὰ ἴδια ἦλθεν, καὶ οἱ ἴδιοι αὐτὸν οὐ παρέλαβον. **12** ὅσοι δὲ ἔλαβον αὐτόν, ἔδωκεν αὐτοῖς ἐξουσίαν τέκνα θεοῦ γενέσθαι, τοῖς πιστεύουσιν εἰς τὸ ὄνομα αὐτοῦ, **13** οἳ οὐκ ἐξ αἱμάτων οὐδὲ ἐκ θελήματος σαρκὸς οὐδὲ ἐκ θελήματος ἀνδρὸς ἀλλ᾽ ἐκ θεοῦ ἐγεννήθησαν. ¶ **14** Καὶ ὁ λόγος σὰρξ ἐγένετο καὶ ἐσκήνωσεν ἐν ἡμῖν, καὶ ἐθεασάμεθα τὴν δόξαν αὐτοῦ, δόξαν ὡς μονογενοῦς παρὰ πατρός, πλήρης χάριτος καὶ ἀληθείας. ¶ **15** Ἰωάννης μαρτυρεῖ περὶ αὐτοῦ καὶ κέκραγεν λέγων, Οὗτος ἦν ὃν εἶπον, Ὁ ὀπίσω μου ἐρχόμενος ἔμπροσθέν μου

was	he	of whom	I	said,	'He who	comes	after	me	*has*	*surpassed*	me	because	he	was	before	me.'"	**16**		From	the
ἦν	ὃν		εἶπον	ὁ	ἐρχόμενος		ὀπίσω	μου	γέγονεν	ἔμπροσθεν	μου	ὅτι		ἦν	πρῶτός	μου		ὅτι	ἐκ	τοῦ
v.iai.3s	r.asm		v.aai.1s	d.nsm	pt.pm.nsm		p.g	r.gs.1	v.rai.3s		r.gs.1	cj		v.iai.3s	a.nsm	r.gs.1		cj	p.g	d.gsn
1639	4005		3306	3836	2262		3958	1609	1181	1869	1609	4022		1639	4755	1609		4022	1666	3836

fullness	of his		grace	we	have	all	received	*one*	blessing	*after*	*another.*	**17**	For	the	law	was	given	through
πληρώματος	αὐτοῦ			ἡμεῖς		πάντες	ἐλάβομεν	καὶ	χάριν	ἀντὶ	χάριτος	ὅτι	ὁ		νόμος		ἐδόθη	διὰ
n.gsn	r.gsm.3			r.np.1		a.npm	v.aai.1p	cj	n.asf	p.g	n.gsf	cj	d.nsm		n.nsm		v.api.3s	p.g
4445	899			7005		4246	3284	2779	5921	505	5921	4022	3836		3795		1443	1328

Moses;	grace	and	truth		came	through	Jesus	Christ.	**18**	No	one	has	ever	seen		God,	but	God	the
Μωϋσέως	ἡ	χάρις	καὶ	ἡ	ἀλήθεια	ἐγένετο	διὰ	Ἰησοῦ	Χριστοῦ	οὐδεὶς			πώποτε	ἑώρακεν		Θεὸν		θεὸς
n.gsm	d.nsf	n.nsf	cj	d.nsf	n.nsf	v.ami.3s	p.g	n.gsm	n.gsm	a.nsm			adv	v.rai.3s		n.asm		n.nsm
3707	3836	5921	2779	3836	237	1181	1328	2652	5986	4029			4799	3972		2536		2536

One	and Only,	who	is		at	the	Father's	side,		has made him known.
μονογενὴς		ὁ	ὢν	εἰς	τὸν	τοῦ πατρός,	κόλπον	ἐκεῖνος		ἐξηγήσατο
a.nsm		d.nsm	pt.pa.nsm	p.a	d.asm	d.gsm n.gsm	n.asm	r.nsm		v.ami.3s
3666		3836	1639	1650	3836	3836 4252	3146	1697		2007

John the Baptist Denies Being the Christ

1:19 Now	this	was	John's		testimony	when	the	Jews	of	Jerusalem	sent			priests	and
Καὶ	αὕτη	ἐστὶν	τοῦ Ἰωάννου,	ἡ	μαρτυρία,	ὅτε	οἱ	Ἰουδαῖοι	ἐξ	Ἱεροσολύμων	ἀπέστειλαν	πρὸς	αὐτὸν	ἱερεῖς	καὶ
cj	r.nsf	v.pai.3s	d.gsm d.gsm	d.nsf	n.nsf	cj	d.npm	a.npm	p.g	n.gpn	v.aai.3p	p.a	r.asm.3	n.apm	cj
2779	4047	1639	3836	3836	2722	3456	4021	3836	2681	1666	2642	690	4639	899	2636	2779

Levites	to	ask	him	who	he	was.	**20**		He did	not	fail		to confess,	but	confessed freely,		"I	am
Λευίτας	ἵνα	ἐρωτήσωσιν	αὐτόν	τίς	σὺ	εἶ		καὶ		οὐκ	ἠρνήσατο	καὶ	ὡμολόγησεν	καὶ	ὡμολόγησεν		ὅτι	ἐγώ	εἰμι
n.apm	cj	v.aas.3p	r.asm.3	r.nsm	r.ns.2	v.pai.2s		cj		pl	v.ami.3s	cj	v.aai.3s	cj	v.aai.3s		cj	r.ns.1	v.pai.1s
3324	2671	2263	899	5515	5148	1639		2779	766	766	4024 766	2779	3933	2779	3933		4022	1609	1639

not	the	Christ."	¶	**21**		They	asked	him,	"Then	who	are	you?	Are	you	Elijah?"		He said,	"I am	not."
οὐκ	ὁ	χριστός			καὶ		ἠρώτησαν	αὐτόν	οὖν	τί			εἶ	σὺ	Ἠλίας	καὶ	λέγει	εἰμὶ	οὐκ
pl	d.nsm	n.nsm			cj		v.aai.3p	r.asm.3	cj	r.nsn			v.pai.2s	r.ns.2	n.nsm	cj	v.pai.3s	v.pai.1s	pl
4024	3836	5986			2779		2263	899	4036	5515			1639	5148	2460	2779	3306	1639	4024

"Are	you	the	Prophet?"		He answered,	"No."	**22**	Finally	they	said,		"Who	are	you?		Give us	an	answer	to
εἰ	σὺ	ὁ	προφήτης	καὶ	ἀπεκρίθη	οὔ		εἶπαν	αὐτῷ	τίς		εἶ		ἵνα				ἀπόκρισιν
v.pai.2s	r.ns.2	d.nsm	n.nsm	cj	v.api.3s	pl		cj	v.aai.3p	r.dsm.3	r.nsn		v.pai.2s		cj				n.asf
1639	5148	3836	4737	2779	646	4024		4036	3306	899	5515	1639		2671					647

take	back	to those	who	sent	us.	What	do	you	say	about	yourself?"	**23**	John	replied	in		the	words	of	Isaiah
δῶμεν		τοῖς		πέμψασιν	ἡμᾶς	τί			λέγεις	περὶ	σεαυτοῦ		ἔφη		καθὼς			εἶπεν		Ἡσαΐας
v.aas.1p		d.dpm		pt.aa.dpm	r.ap.1	r.asn			v.pai.2s	p.g	r.gsm.2		v.iai.3s		cj			v.aai.3s		n.nsm
1443		3836		4287	7005	5515			3306	4309	4932		5774		2777			3306		2480

the	prophet,	"I	am	the	voice	of one	calling	in	the	desert,	'Make	straight	the	way	for the	Lord.'"	¶		**24** Now
ὁ	προφήτης	ἐγώ			φωνὴ		βοῶντος	ἐν	τῇ	ἐρήμῳ		εὐθύνατε	τὴν	ὁδὸν		κυρίου			Καὶ
d.nsm	n.nsm	r.ns.1			n.nsf		pt.pa.gsm	p.d	d.dsf	n.dsf		v.aam.2p	d.asf	n.asf		n.gsm			cj
3836	4737	1609			5889		1066	1877	3836	2245		2316	3836	3847		3261			2779

some	Pharisees		who	had	been	sent	**25**	questioned	him,			"Why	then	do	you	baptize	if
	ἐκ	τῶν Φαρισαίων,		ἦσαν	ἀπεσταλμένοι	καὶ	ἠρώτησαν	αὐτὸν	καὶ	εἶπαν	αὐτῷ	τί		οὖν		βαπτίζεις	εἰ
	p.g	d.gpm n.gpm		v.iai.3p	pt.rp.npm	cj	v.aai.3p	r.asm.3	cj	v.aai.3p	r.dsm.3	r.asn		cj		v.pai.2s	cj
	1666	3836 5757		1639	690	2779	2263	899	2779	3306	899	5515		4036		966	1623

you	are	not	the	Christ,	nor	Elijah,	nor	the	Prophet?"	**26** "I	baptize	with	water,"	John		replied,
σὺ	εἶ	οὐκ	ὁ	χριστός	οὐδὲ	Ἠλίας	οὐδὲ	ὁ	προφήτης	ἐγώ	βαπτίζω	ἐν	ὕδατι	ὁ Ἰωάννης,	ἀπεκρίθη	αὐτοῖς λέγων
r.ns.2	v.pai.2s	pl	d.nsm	n.nsm	cj	n.nsm	cj	d.nsm	n.nsm	r.ns.1	v.pai.1s	p.d	n.dsn	d.nsm n.nsm	v.api.3s	r.dpm.3 pt.pa.nsm
5148	1639	4024	3836	5986	4028	2460	4028	3836	4737	1609	966	1877	5623	3836 2722	646	899 3306

"but	among	you	stands	one	you	do	not	know.	**27** He	is	the	one	who	comes	after	me,		the	thongs	of	whose
μέσος	ὑμῶν		ἕστηκεν	ὃν	ὑμεῖς		οὐκ	οἴδατε	ὁ					ἐρχόμενος	ὀπίσω	μου	οὗ	τὸν	ἱμάντα		αὐτοῦ
a.nsm	r.gp.2		v.rai.3s	r.asm	r.np.2		pl	v.rai.2p	d.nsm					pt.pm.nsm	p.g	r.gs.1	r.gsm	d.asm	n.asm		r.gsm.3
3545	7007		2705	4005	7007		3857	4024 3857	3836					2262	3958	1609	4005	3836	2666	5687	899

sandals	I	am	not worthy	to	untie."	¶	**28** This	all	happened	at	Bethany			on the other side	of	the
τοῦ ὑποδήματος,	ἐγὼ	εἰμὶ	οὐκ ἄξιος	ἵνα	λύσω		ταῦτα		ἐγένετο	ἐν	Βηθανίᾳ			πέραν	τοῦ
d.gsn n.gsn	r.ns.1	v.pai.1s	pl a.nsm	cj	v.aas.1s		r.npn		v.ami.3s	p.d	n.dsf			p.g	d.gsm
3836 5687	1609	1639	4024 545	2671	3395		4047		1181	1877	1029			4305	3836

γέγονεν, ὅτι πρῶτός μου ἦν. ¹⁶ ὅτι ἐκ τοῦ πληρώματος αὐτοῦ ἡμεῖς πάντες ἐλάβομεν καὶ χάριν ἀντὶ χάριτος· ¹⁷ ὅτι ὁ νόμος διὰ Μωϋσέως ἐδόθη, ἡ χάρις καὶ ἡ ἀλήθεια διὰ Ἰησοῦ Χριστοῦ ἐγένετο. ¹⁸ θεὸν οὐδεὶς ἑώρακεν πώποτε· μονογενὴς θεὸς ὁ ὢν εἰς τὸν κόλπον τοῦ πατρὸς ἐκεῖνος ἐξηγήσατο.

¹:¹⁹ Καὶ αὕτη ἐστὶν ἡ μαρτυρία τοῦ Ἰωάννου, ὅτε ἀπέστειλαν [πρὸς αὐτὸν] οἱ Ἰουδαῖοι ἐξ Ἱεροσολύμων ἱερεῖς καὶ Λευίτας ἵνα ἐρωτήσωσιν αὐτόν, Σὺ τίς εἶ; ²⁰ καὶ ὡμολόγησεν καὶ οὐκ ἠρνήσατο, καὶ ὡμολόγησεν ὅτι Ἐγὼ οὐκ εἰμὶ ὁ Χριστός. ¶ ²¹ καὶ ἠρώτησαν αὐτόν, Τί οὖν; Σὺ Ἠλίας εἶ; καὶ λέγει, Οὐκ εἰμί. Ὁ προφήτης εἶ σύ; καὶ ἀπεκρίθη, Οὔ. ²² εἶπαν οὖν αὐτῷ, Τίς εἶ; ἵνα ἀπόκρισιν δῶμεν τοῖς πέμψασιν ἡμᾶς· τί λέγεις περὶ σεαυτοῦ; ²³ ἔφη, Ἐγὼ φωνὴ βοῶντος ἐν τῇ ἐρήμῳ, Εὐθύνατε τὴν ὁδὸν κυρίου, καθὼς εἶπεν Ἡσαΐας ὁ προφήτης. ¶ ²⁴ Καὶ ἀπεσταλμένοι ἦσαν ἐκ τῶν Φαρισαίων. ²⁵ καὶ ἠρώτησαν αὐτὸν καὶ εἶπαν αὐτῷ, Τί οὖν βαπτίζεις εἰ σὺ οὐκ εἶ ὁ Χριστὸς οὐδὲ Ἠλίας οὐδὲ ὁ προφήτης; ²⁶ ἀπεκρίθη αὐτοῖς ὁ Ἰωάννης λέγων, Ἐγὼ βαπτίζω ἐν ὕδατι· μέσος δὲ ὑμῶν ἕστηκεν ὃν ὑμεῖς οὐκ οἴδατε, ²⁷ ὁ ὀπίσω μου ἐρχόμενος, οὗ οὐκ εἰμὶ [ἐγὼ] ἄξιος ἵνα λύσω αὐτοῦ τὸν ἱμάντα τοῦ ὑποδήματος. ¶ ²⁸ Ταῦτα ἐν Βηθανίᾳ ἐγένετο πέραν τοῦ Ἰορδάνου, ὅπου ἦν ὁ Ἰωάννης βαπτίζων.

Jordan,   where   John   was   baptizing.
Ἰορδάνου ὅπου   ὁ Ἰωάννης   ἦν   βαπτίζων
n.gsm   cj   d.nsm n.nsm   v.iai.3s pt.pa.nsm
2674   3963   3836 2722   1639 966

Jesus the Lamb of God

1:29 The next day   John saw Jesus   coming   toward him   and said, "Look, the Lamb of God,   who
Τῇ → ἐπαύριον   βλέπει ₍τὸν Ἰησοῦν₎ ἐρχόμενον πρὸς   αὐτὸν καὶ λέγει ἴδε   ὁ ἀμνὸς → ₍τοῦ θεοῦ₎ ὁ
d.dsf   adv   v.pai.3s d.asm n.asm pt.pm.asm p.a   r.asm.3 cj   v.pai.3s pl   d.nsm n.nsm   d.gsm n.gsm d.nsm
3836   2069   1063 3836 2652   2262   4639   899   2779 3306 3306 2623 3836 303   3836 2536 3836

takes away the sin   of the world! **30** This is   the   one I meant when I   said, 'A man who comes after me
αἴρων ←   τὴν ἁμαρτίαν → τοῦ κόσμου   οὗτός ἐστιν τὸ   ὑπὲρ οὗ   ἐγὼ εἶπον   ἀνήρ →   ἔρχεται ὀπίσω μου
pt.pa.nsm   d.asf n.asf   d.gsm n.gsm   r.nsm v.pai.3s   p.g r.gsm   r.ns.1 v.aai.1s n.nsm   v.pmi.3s p.g r.gs.1
149   3836 281   3836 3180   4047 1639   5642 4005   1609 3306   467   2262   3958 1609

has   surpassed me because he was before me.' **31** I   myself did not know him, but the reason I   came
ὃς   γέγονεν ἔμπροσθεν μου ὅτι →   ἦν πρῶτος μου   κἀγὼ → οὐκ ᾔδειν αὐτόν ἀλλ' ₍διὰ τοῦτο₎ ἐγὼ ἦλθον
r.nsm v.rai.3s p.g   r.gs.1 cj   v.iai.3s a.nsm r.gs.1   crasis adv v.lai.1s r.asm.3 cj   p.a r.asn r.ns.1 v.aai.1s
4005 1181   1869   1609 4022 1639   4755   1609   3857   4024 3857 899   247 1328 4047 1609 2262

baptizing with water was that he might be   revealed to Israel."   ¶   **32** Then John   gave this testimony:
βαπτίζων ἐν   ὕδατι ἵνα → →   → φανερωθῇ ₍τῷ Ἰσραήλ₎   Καὶ Ἰωάννης →   ἐμαρτύρησεν λέγων
pt.pa.nsm p.d n.dsn cj   v.aps.3s d.dsm n.dsn   cj   n.nsm   v.aai.3s   pt.pa.nsm
966   1877 5623   2671   5746   3836 2702   2779 2722   3455   3306

"I saw   the Spirit come   down from heaven as a dove   and remain on him. **33** I   would not have
ὅτι → τεθέαμαι τὸ πνεῦμα καταβαῖνον ←   ἐξ οὐρανοῦ ὡς περιστερὰν καὶ ἔμεινεν ἐπ' αὐτόν κἀγὼ   οὐκ
cj   v.rmi.1s d.asn n.asn pt.pa.asn   p.g n.gsm   pl   n.asf   cj   v.aai.3s p.a r.asm.3 crasis   adv
4022 2517   3836 4460 2849   1666 4041   6055 4361   2779 3531   2093 899   2743   4024

known him, except that the one who sent me to baptize with water   told me, 'The man on whom you
ᾔδειν αὐτόν ἀλλ' → ὁ   ←   ← πέμψας   με → βαπτίζειν ἐν   ὕδατι ἐκεῖνος εἶπεν μοι οὗτος ἐφ' ὃν ἂν →
v.lai.1s r.asm.3 cj   d.nsm   pt.aa.nsm r.as.1 f.pa   p.d n.dsn r.nsm   v.aai.3s r.ds.1 r.nsm p.a r.asm pl
3857 899   247   3836   4287   1609 966   1877 5623 1697   3306 1609 4047 2093 3836 323

see the Spirit come   down and remain on him   is   he who will baptize with the Holy Spirit.' **34** I   have
ἴδῃς τὸ πνεῦμα καταβαῖνον ←   καὶ μένον ἐπ' αὐτόν ἐστιν ὁ   who   βαπτίζων ἐν   ἁγίῳ πνεύματι κἀγὼ
v.aas.2s d.asn n.asn pt.pa.asn   cj   pt.pa.asn p.a r.asm.3 v.pai.3s d.nsm   pt.pa.nsm p.d a.dsn n.dsn crasis
1625 3836 4460 2849   2779 3531   2093 899   1639 3836   966   1877 41   4460 2743

seen and I testify   that this is   the Son of God."
ἑώρακα καὶ → μεμαρτύρηκα ὅτι οὗτός ἐστιν ὁ υἱὸς → ₍τοῦ θεοῦ₎
v.rai.1s cj   v.rai.1s   cj   r.nsm v.pai.3s d.nsm n.nsm d.gsm n.gsm
3972 2779   3455   4022 4047 1639 3836 5626 3836 2536

Jesus' First Disciples

1:35 The next day   John   was there again   with two of his   disciples.   **36** When he saw
Τῇ → ἐπαύριον   ὁ Ἰωάννης →   εἱστήκει πάλιν καὶ   δύο →   αὐτοῦ ἐκ τῶν μαθητῶν   καὶ →   → ἐμβλέψας
d.dsf   adv   d.nsm n.nsm   v.lai.3s adv   cj   a.npm   r.gsm.3 p.g d.gpm n.gpm   cj   pt.aa.nsm
3836   2069   3836 2722   2705   4099 2779 1545   899   1666 3836 3412   2779   1838

Jesus   passing   by, he said, "Look, the Lamb of God!"   **37** When the two disciples heard him   say   this,
₍τῷ Ἰησοῦ₎ περιπατοῦντι ← λέγει ἴδε   ὁ ἀμνὸς → ₍τοῦ θεοῦ₎ καὶ οἱ δύο μαθηταὶ ἤκουσαν αὐτοῦ λαλοῦντος
d.dsm n.dsm pt.pa.dsm   v.pai.3s pl   d.nsm n.nsm   d.gsm n.gsm cj   d.npm a.npm n.npm v.aai.3p r.gsm.3 pt.pa.gsm
3836 2652 4344   3306   2623 3836 303   3836 2536   2779 3836 1545 3412   201   899   3281

they followed   Jesus.   **38** Turning around, Jesus   saw   them following   and asked,
καὶ →   ἠκολούθησαν ₍τῷ Ἰησοῦ₎ δὲ στραφεὶς ←   ὁ Ἰησοῦς καὶ θεασάμενος αὐτοὺς ἀκολουθοῦντας λέγει αὐτοῖς
cj   v.aai.3p   d.dsm n.dsm   cj   pt.ap.nsm   d.nsm n.nsm cj pt.am.nsm r.apm.3 pt.pa.apm   v.pai.3s r.dpm.3
2779 199   3836 2652   1254 5138   3836 2652   2779 2517   899   199   3306   899

"What do you want?" They said,   "Rabbi" (which means   Teacher),   "where are you
τί →   ζητεῖτε δὲ οἱ εἶπαν αὐτῷ ῥαββί ὃ ₍λέγεται μεθερμηνευόμενον₎ διδάσκαλε ποῦ →   →
r.asn   v.pai.2p cj d.npm v.aai.3p r.dsm.3 n.vsm r.nsn v.ppi.3s pt.pp.nsn   n.vsm   adv
5515   2426   1254 3836 3306 899   4806   4005 3306   3493   1437   4543

staying?" **39** "Come," he replied,   "and you will see." So they went and saw where he was staying, and spent
μένεις   ἔρχεσθε →   λέγει αὐτοῖς καὶ →   → ὄψεσθε οὖν → ἦλθαν καὶ εἶδαν ποῦ →   → μένει καὶ ἔμειναν
v.pai.2s v.pmm.2p   v.pai.3s r.dpm.3 cj   v.fmi.2p cj   v.aai.3p cj v.aai.3p adv   v.pai.3s cj v.aai.3p
3531   2262   3306 899   2779   3972   4036 2262 2779 1625 4543   3531 2779 3531

1:29 Τῇ ἐπαύριον βλέπει τὸν Ἰησοῦν ἐρχόμενον πρὸς αὐτὸν καὶ λέγει, Ἴδε ὁ ἀμνὸς τοῦ θεοῦ ὁ αἴρων τὴν ἁμαρτίαν τοῦ κόσμου. **30** οὗτός ἐστιν ὑπὲρ οὗ ἐγὼ εἶπον, Ὀπίσω μου ἔρχεται ἀνὴρ ὃς ἔμπροσθέν μου γέγονεν, ὅτι πρῶτός μου ἦν. **31** κἀγὼ οὐκ ᾔδειν αὐτόν, ἀλλ' ἵνα φανερωθῇ τῷ Ἰσραὴλ διὰ τοῦτο ἦλθον ἐγὼ ἐν ὕδατι βαπτίζων. ¶ **32** Καὶ ἐμαρτύρησεν Ἰωάννης λέγων ὅτι Τεθέαμαι τὸ πνεῦμα καταβαῖνον ὡς περιστερὰν ἐξ οὐρανοῦ καὶ ἔμεινεν ἐπ' αὐτόν. **33** κἀγὼ οὐκ ᾔδειν αὐτόν, ἀλλ' ὁ πέμψας με βαπτίζειν ἐν ὕδατι ἐκεῖνός μοι εἶπεν, Ἐφ' ὃν ἂν ἴδῃς τὸ πνεῦμα καταβαῖνον καὶ μένον ἐπ' αὐτόν, οὗτός ἐστιν ὁ βαπτίζων ἐν πνεύματι ἁγίῳ. **34** κἀγὼ ἑώρακα καὶ μεμαρτύρηκα ὅτι οὗτός ἐστιν ὁ υἱὸς τοῦ θεοῦ.

1:35 Τῇ ἐπαύριον πάλιν εἱστήκει ὁ Ἰωάννης καὶ ἐκ τῶν μαθητῶν αὐτοῦ δύο **36** καὶ ἐμβλέψας τῷ Ἰησοῦ περιπατοῦντι λέγει, Ἴδε ὁ ἀμνὸς τοῦ θεοῦ. **37** καὶ ἤκουσαν οἱ δύο μαθηταὶ αὐτοῦ λαλοῦντος καὶ ἠκολούθησαν τῷ Ἰησοῦ. **38** στραφεὶς δὲ ὁ Ἰησοῦς καὶ θεασάμενος αὐτοὺς ἀκολουθοῦντας λέγει αὐτοῖς, Τί ζητεῖτε; οἱ δὲ εἶπαν αὐτῷ, Ῥαββί, ὃ λέγεται μεθερμηνευόμενον Διδάσκαλε, ποῦ μένεις; **39** λέγει αὐτοῖς, Ἔρχεσθε καὶ ὄψεσθε. ἦλθαν οὖν καὶ εἶδαν ποῦ μένει καὶ παρ' αὐτῷ ἔμειναν τὴν ἡμέραν

that day with him. It was about the tenth hour. ¶ **40** Andrew, Simon Peter's brother, was one of
ἐκείνην ⌐τὴν ἡμέραν παρ' αὐτῷ → ἦν ὡς δεκάτη ὥρα Ἀνδρέας Σίμωνος Πέτρου ⌐ὁ ἀδελφός⌐ Ἦν εἷς ἐκ
r.asf d.asf n.asf p.d r.dsm.3 v.iai.3s pl a.nsf n.nsf n.nsm n.gsm n.gsm d.nsm n.nsm v.iai.3s a.nsm p.g
1697 3836 2465 4123 899 1639 6055 1281 6052 436 4981 4377 3836 81 1639 1651 1666

the two who heard what John had said and who had followed Jesus. **41** The first thing Andrew did
τῶν δύο τῶν ἀκουσάντων παρὰ Ἰωάννου καὶ → → ἀκολουθησάντων αὐτῷ πρῶτον ← οὗτος
d.gpm a.gpm d.gpm pt.aa.gpm n.gsm cj pt.aa.gpm r.dsm.3 adv r.nsm
3836 1545 3836 201 4123 2722 2779 199 899 4754 4047

was to find his brother Simon and tell him, "We have found the Messiah" (that
εὑρίσκει ⌐τὸν ἴδιον⌐ ⌐τὸν ἀδελφόν⌐ Σίμωνα καὶ λέγει αὐτῷ εὑρήκαμεν τὸν Μεσσίαν ὅ
v.pai.3s d.asm a.asm d.asm n.asm n.asm cj v.pai.3s r.dsm.3 v.rai.1p d.asm n.asm r.nsn
2351 3836 2625 3836 81 4981 2779 3306 899 2351 3836 3549 4005

is, the Christ). **42** And he brought him to Jesus. Jesus looked at him and said, "You
⌐ἐστιν μεθερμηνευόμενον⌐ χριστός → ἤγαγεν αὐτὸν πρὸς ⌐τὸν Ἰησοῦν⌐ ὁ Ἰησοῦς ἐμβλέψας ← αὐτῷ εἶπεν σὺ
v.pai.3s pt.pp.nsn n.nsm v.aai.3s r.asm.3 p.a d.asm n.asm d.nsm n.nsm pt.aa.3s r.dsm.3 v.aai.3s r.ns.2
1639 3493 5986 72 899 4639 3836 2652 3836 2652 1838 899 3306 5148

are Simon son of John. You will be called Cephas" (which, when translated, is Peter).
εἶ Σίμων ὁ υἱός⌐ ⌐Ἰωάννου σὺ → κληθήσῃ Κηφᾶς ὃ → ἑρμηνεύεται Πέτρος
v.pai.2s n.nsm d.nsm n.nsm n.gsm r.ns.2 v.fpi.2s n.nsm r.nsn v.ppi.3s n.nsm
1639 4981 3836 5626 2722 5148 2813 3064 4005 2257 4377

Jesus Calls Philip and Nathanael

1:43 The next day Jesus decided to leave for Galilee. Finding Philip, he said to him,
Τῇ → ἐπαύριον ἠθέλησεν → ἐξελθεῖν εἰς ⌐τὴν Γαλιλαίαν⌐ καὶ εὑρίσκει Φίλιππον καὶ ὁ Ἰησοῦς λέγει → αὐτῷ
d.dsf adv v.aai.3s f.aa p.a d.asf n.asf cj v.pai.3s n.asm cj d.nsm n.nsm v.pai.3s r.dsm.3
3836 2069 2527 2002 1650 3836 1133 2779 2351 5805 2779 3836 2652 3306 899

"Follow me." ¶ **44** Philip, like Andrew and Peter, was from the town of Bethsaida. **45** Philip found
ἀκολούθει μοι δὲ ὁ Φίλιππος, Ἀνδρέου καὶ Πέτρου ἦν ἀπὸ ἐκ τῆς πόλεως → Βηθσαϊδά Φίλιππος εὑρίσκει
v.pam.2s r.ds.1 cj d.nsm n.nsm n.gsm cj n.gsm v.iai.3s p.g p.g d.gsf n.gsf n.gsf n.nsm v.pai.3s
199 1609 1254 3836 5805 436 2779 4377 1639 608 1666 3836 4484 1034 5805 2351

Nathanael and told him, "We have found the one Moses wrote about in the Law, and about whom the
⌐τὸν Ναθαναήλ⌐ καὶ λέγει αὐτῷ εὑρήκαμεν ὃν Μωϋσῆς ἔγραψεν ἐν τῷ νόμῳ καὶ οἱ
d.asm n.asm cj v.pai.3s r.dsm.3 v.rai.1p r.asm n.nsm v.aai.3s p.d d.dsm n.dsm cj d.npm
3836 3720 2779 3306 899 2351 4005 3707 1211 1877 3836 3795 2779 3836

prophets also wrote – Jesus of Nazareth, the son of Joseph." **46** "Nazareth! Can anything good come
προφῆται Ἰησοῦν τὸν ἀπὸ Ναζαρέτ υἱὸν → ⌐τοῦ Ἰωσήφ⌐ καὶ δύναταί τι ἀγαθὸν εἶναι
n.npm n.asm d.asm p.g n.gsf n.asm d.gsm n.gsm cj v.ppi.3s r.asn a.asn f.pa
4737 2652 3836 608 3715 5626 3836 2737 2779 1538 5516 19 1639

from there?" Nathanael asked. "Come and see," said Philip. **47** When Jesus saw Nathanael
ἐκ Ναζαρὲτ Ναθαναήλ εἶπεν αὐτῷ ἔρχου καὶ ἴδε λέγει ὁ Φίλιππος, αὐτῷ ὁ Ἰησοῦς, εἶδεν Ναθαναὴλ
p.g n.gsf n.nsm v.aai.3s r.dsm.3 v.pmm.2s cj v.aam.2s v.pai.3s d.nsm n.nsm r.dsm.3 d.nsm n.nsm v.aai.3s n.asm
1666 3715 3720 3306 899 2262 2779 2623 3306 3836 5805 899 3836 2652 1625 3720

approaching, he said of him, "Here is a true Israelite, in whom there is nothing false."
⌐τὸν ἐρχόμενον⌐ πρὸς αὐτὸν καὶ → λέγει περὶ αὐτοῦ ἴδε ← ἀληθῶς Ἰσραηλίτης ἐν ᾧ → ἔστιν οὐκ δόλος
d.asm pt.pm.asm p.a r.asm.3 cj v.pai.3s p.g r.gsm.3 pl adv n.nsm p.d r.dsm v.pai.3s pl n.nsm
3836 2262 4639 899 2779 3306 4309 899 2623 242 2703 1877 4005 1639 4024 1515

48 "How do you know me?" Nathanael asked. Jesus answered, "I saw you while you were still
πόθεν → → γινώσκεις με Ναθαναήλ λέγει αὐτῷ Ἰησοῦς ἀπεκρίθη καὶ εἶπεν αὐτῷ → εἶδόν σε → ὄντα
cj v.pai.2s r.as.1 n.nsm v.pai.3s r.dsm.3 n.nsm v.api.3s cj v.aai.3s r.dsm.3 v.aai.1s r.as.2 pt.pa.asm
4470 1182 1609 3720 3306 899 2652 646 2779 3306 899 1625 5148 1639

under the fig tree before Philip called you." **49** Then Nathanael declared, "Rabbi, you are the Son of
ὑπὸ τὴν συκῆν πρὸ Φίλιππον ⌐τοῦ φωνῆσαι⌐ σε Ναθαναήλ ἀπεκρίθη αὐτῷ ῥαββί σὺ εἶ ὁ υἱὸς
p.a d.asf n.asf p.g n.asm d.gsn f.aa r.as.2 n.nsm v.api.3s r.dsm.3 n.vsm r.ns.2 v.pai.2s d.nsm n.nsm
5679 3836 5190 4574 5805 3836 5888 5148 3720 646 899 4806 5148 1639 3836 5626

God; you are the King of Israel." **50** Jesus said, "You believe because I told you I
⌐τοῦ θεοῦ⌐ σὺ εἶ βασιλεὺς → ⌐τοῦ Ἰσραήλ⌐ Ἰησοῦς ἀπεκρίθη καὶ εἶπεν αὐτῷ πιστεύεις ὅτι → εἶπόν σοι ὅτι →
d.gsm n.gsm r.ns.2 v.pai.2s n.nsm d.gsn n.gsn n.nsm v.api.3s cj v.aai.3s r.dsm.3 v.pai.2s cj v.aai.1s r.ds.2 cj
3836 2536 5148 1639 995 3836 2702 2652 646 2779 3306 899 4409 4022 3306 5148 4022

ἐκείνην· ὥρα ἦν ὡς δεκάτη. ¶ **40** ⸀Ἦν Ἀνδρέας ὁ ἀδελφὸς Σίμωνος Πέτρου εἷς ἐκ τῶν δύο τῶν ἀκουσάντων παρὰ Ἰωάννου καὶ ἀκολουθησάντων αὐτῷ· **41** εὑρίσκει οὗτος πρῶτον τὸν ἀδελφὸν τὸν ἴδιον Σίμωνα καὶ λέγει αὐτῷ, Εὑρήκαμεν τὸν Μεσσίαν, ὅ ἐστιν μεθερμηνευόμενον Χριστός· **42** ἤγαγεν αὐτὸν πρὸς τὸν Ἰησοῦν. ἐμβλέψας αὐτῷ ὁ Ἰησοῦς εἶπεν, Σὺ εἶ Σίμων ὁ υἱὸς Ἰωάννου, σὺ κληθήσῃ Κηφᾶς, ὃ ἑρμηνεύεται Πέτρος.
1:43 Τῇ ἐπαύριον ἠθέλησεν ἐξελθεῖν εἰς τὴν Γαλιλαίαν καὶ εὑρίσκει Φίλιππον. καὶ λέγει αὐτῷ ὁ Ἰησοῦς, Ἀκολούθει μοι. **44** ἦν δὲ ὁ Φίλιππος ἀπὸ Βηθσαϊδά, ἐκ τῆς πόλεως Ἀνδρέου καὶ Πέτρου. **45** εὑρίσκει Φίλιππος τὸν Ναθαναὴλ καὶ λέγει αὐτῷ, Ὃν ἔγραψεν Μωϋσῆς ἐν τῷ νόμῳ καὶ οἱ προφῆται εὑρήκαμεν, Ἰησοῦν υἱὸν τοῦ Ἰωσὴφ τὸν ἀπὸ Ναζαρέτ. **46** καὶ εἶπεν αὐτῷ Ναθαναήλ, Ἐκ Ναζαρὲτ δύναταί τι ἀγαθὸν εἶναι; λέγει αὐτῷ [ὁ] Φίλιππος, Ἔρχου καὶ ἴδε. **47** εἶδεν ὁ Ἰησοῦς τὸν Ναθαναὴλ ἐρχόμενον πρὸς αὐτὸν καὶ λέγει περὶ αὐτοῦ, Ἴδε ἀληθῶς Ἰσραηλίτης ἐν ᾧ δόλος οὐκ ἔστιν. **48** λέγει αὐτῷ Ναθαναήλ, Πόθεν με γινώσκεις; ἀπεκρίθη Ἰησοῦς καὶ εἶπεν αὐτῷ, Πρὸ τοῦ σε Φίλιππον φωνῆσαι ὄντα ὑπὸ τὴν συκῆν εἶδόν σε. **49** ἀπεκρίθη αὐτῷ Ναθαναήλ, Ῥαββί, σὺ εἶ ὁ υἱὸς τοῦ θεοῦ, σὺ βασιλεὺς εἶ τοῦ Ἰσραήλ. **50** ἀπεκρίθη Ἰησοῦς καὶ εἶπεν αὐτῷ, Ὅτι εἶπόν σοι ὅτι

saw you under the fig tree. You shall see greater things than that." **51** He then added, "I tell you the
εἶδον σε ὑποκάτω τῆς → συκῆς → → ὄψῃ μείζω ← τούτων ⸂ καὶ λέγει αὐτῷ → λέγω ὑμῖν
v.aai.1s r.as.2 p.g d.gsf n.gsf v.fmi.2s a.apn.c r.gpn cj v.pai.3s r.dsm.3 v.pai.1s r.dp.2
1625 5148 5691 3836 5190 3972 3489 4047 3306 2779 3306 899 3306 7007

truth, you shall see heaven open, and the angels of God ascending and descending on the
⸃ἀμὴν ἀμὴν → → ὄψεσθε τὸν οὐρανὸν ἀνεῳγότα καὶ τοὺς ἀγγέλους → ⸂τοῦ θεοῦ⸃ ἀναβαίνοντας καὶ καταβαίνοντας ἐπὶ τὸν
pl pl v.fmi.2p d.asm n.asm pt.ra.asm cj d.apm n.apm d.gsm n.gsm pt.pa.apm cj pt.pa.apm p.a d.asm
297 297 3972 3836 4041 487 2779 3836 34 3836 2536 326 2779 2849 2093 3836

Son of Man."
υἱὸν ⸂τοῦ ἀνθρώπου⸃
n.asm d.gsm n.gsm
5626 3836 476

Jesus Changes Water to Wine

2:1 On the third day a wedding took place at Cana in Galilee. Jesus' mother was
Καὶ → τῇ ⸂τῇ τρίτῃ⸃ ἡμέρᾳ γάμος ἐγένετο ← ἐν Κανὰ → ⸂τῆς Γαλιλαίας⸃ καὶ ⸂τοῦ Ἰησοῦ⸃ ἡ μήτηρ ἦν
cj d.dsf d.dsf a.dsf n.dsf n.nsm v.ami.3s p.d n.dsf d.gsf n.gsf cj d.gsm n.gsm d.nsf n.nsf v.iai.3s
2779 3836 3836 5569 2465 1141 1181 1877 2830 3836 1133 2779 3836 2652 3836 3613 1639

there, **2** and Jesus and his disciples had also been invited to the wedding. **3** When the wine was
ἐκεῖ δὲ ὁ Ἰησοῦς καὶ αὐτοῦ οἱ μαθηταὶ ⸂ καὶ → ἐκλήθη εἰς τὸν γάμον καὶ → οἴνου →
adv cj d.nsm n.nsm cj r.gsm.3 d.npm n.npm cj v.api.3s p.a d.asm n.asm cj n.gsm
1695 1254 3836 2652 2779 899 3836 3412 2813 2779 2813 1650 3836 1141 2779 5728 3885

gone, Jesus' mother said to him, "They have no more wine." **4** "Dear woman, *why do you*
ὑστερήσαντος τοῦ Ἰησοῦ ἡ μήτηρ λέγει πρὸς αὐτόν· ἔχουσιν οὐκ ← οἶνον [καὶ] → γύναι τί σοί καὶ
pt.aa.gsm d.gsm n.gsm d.nsf n.nsf v.pai.3s p.a r.asm.3 v.pai.3p pl n.asm cj n.vsf r.nsn r.ds.2 cj
5728 3836 2652 3836 3613 3306 4639 899 2400 4024 3885 2779 1222 5515 5148 2779

involve me?" Jesus replied. "My time has not yet come." **5** His mother said to the servants, "Do
ἐμοὶ ὁ Ἰησοῦς λέγει αὐτῇ μου ἡ ὥρα· → οὔπω ← ἥκει αὐτοῦ ἡ μήτηρ λέγει → τοῖς διακόνοις ποιήσατε
r.ds.1 d.nsm n.nsm v.pai.3s r.dsf.3 r.gs.1 d.nsf n.nsf adv v.rai.3s r.gsm.3 d.nsf n.nsf v.pai.3s d.dpm n.dpm v.aam.2p
1609 3836 2652 3306 899 1609 3836 6052 2457 4037 2457 899 3836 3613 3306 3836 1356 4472

whatever he tells you." **6** Nearby stood six stone water jars, the kind used by the Jews for ceremonial
ὅ τι ἂν λέγῃ ὑμῖν δὲ ἐκεῖ ἦσαν ἓξ λίθιναι ὑδρίαι κείμεναι → τῶν Ἰουδαίων κατὰ →
r.asn r.asn pl v.pas.3s r.dp.2 cj adv v.iai.3p a.npf a.npf n.npf pt.pm.npf d.gpm a.gpm p.a
4005 5516 3306 323 3306 7007 1254 1695 1639 1971 3343 5620 3023 3836 2681 2848

washing, each holding *from twenty to thirty gallons.* **7** Jesus said to the servants, "Fill the jars
⸂τὸν καθαρισμὸν⸃ χωροῦσαι δύο ἢ τρεῖς ⸂ἀνὰ μετρητὰς⸃ ὁ Ἰησοῦς λέγει → αὐτοῖς γεμίσατε τὰς ὑδρίας
d.asm n.asm pt.pa.npf a.apm cj a.apm p.a n.apm d.nsm n.nsm v.pai.3s r.dpm.3 v.aam.2p d.apf n.apf
3836 2752 6003 1545 2445 5552 324 3583 3836 2652 3306 899 1153 3836 5620

with water"; so they filled them to the brim. **8** Then he told them, "Now draw some out and take it to the
→ ὕδατος καὶ → ἐγέμισαν αὐτὰς ἕως → ἄνω καὶ → λέγει αὐτοῖς νῦν ἀντλήσατε ← καὶ φέρετε → τῷ
→ n.gsn cj v.aai.3p r.apf.3 p.g adv cj v.pai.3s r.dpm.3 adv v.aam.2p cj v.pam.2p d.dsn
5623 2779 1153 899 2401 539 2779 3306 899 3814 533 2779 5770 3836

master of the banquet." They did so, **9** and the master of the banquet tasted the water that had
ἀρχιτρικλίνῳ ← δὲ οἱ ἤνεγκαν δὲ ὡς ὁ ἀρχιτρίκλινος ← ← ἐγεύσατο τὸ ὕδωρ
n.dsm cj d.npm v.aai.3p cj cj d.nsm n.nsm v.ami.3s d.asn n.asn
804 1254 3836 5770 1254 6055 3836 804 1174 3836 5623

been turned into wine. He did not realize where it had come from, though the servants who had drawn
→ γεγενημένον ← οἶνον καὶ → → οὐκ ᾔδει πόθεν → ἐστίν ← δὲ οἱ διάκονοι οἱ → ἠντληκότες
pt.rp.asn n.asn cj pl v.lai.3s adv v.pai.3s cj d.npm n.npm d.npm pt.ra.npm
1181 3885 2779 3857 3857 4024 3857 4470 1639 4470 1254 3836 1356 3836 533

the water knew. Then he called the bridegroom aside **10** and said, "Everyone brings out the
τὸ ὕδωρ ᾔδεισαν ὁ ἀρχιτρίκλινος φωνεῖ τὸν νυμφίον καὶ λέγει αὐτῷ ⸂πᾶς ἄνθρωπος⸃ τίθησιν ← τὸν
d.asn n.asn v.lai.3p d.nsm n.nsm v.pai.3s d.asm n.asm cj v.pai.3s r.dsm.3 a.nsm n.nsm v.pai.3s d.asm
3836 5623 3857 3836 804 5888 3836 3812 2779 3306 899 4246 476 5502 3836

choice wine first and then the cheaper wine after the guests have had too much to drink; but you have
καλὸν οἶνον πρῶτον καὶ τὸν ἐλάσσω ὅταν → → → → μεθυσθῶσιν σὺ →
a.asm n.asm adv cj d.asm a.asm.c cj v.aps.3p r.ns.2
2819 3885 4754 2779 3836 1781 4020 3499 5148

εἶδόν σε ὑποκάτω τῆς συκῆς, πιστεύεις; μείζω τούτων ὄψῃ. **51** καὶ λέγει αὐτῷ, Ἀμὴν ἀμὴν λέγω ὑμῖν, ὄψεσθε τὸν οὐρανὸν ἀνεῳγότα καὶ τοὺς ἀγγέλους τοῦ θεοῦ ἀναβαίνοντας καὶ καταβαίνοντας ἐπὶ τὸν υἱὸν τοῦ ἀνθρώπου. **2:1** Καὶ τῇ ἡμέρᾳ τῇ τρίτῃ γάμος ἐγένετο ἐν Κανὰ τῆς Γαλιλαίας, καὶ ἦν ἡ μήτηρ τοῦ Ἰησοῦ ἐκεῖ· **2** ἐκλήθη δὲ καὶ ὁ Ἰησοῦς καὶ οἱ μαθηταὶ αὐτοῦ εἰς τὸν γάμον. **3** καὶ ὑστερήσαντος οἴνου λέγει ἡ μήτηρ τοῦ Ἰησοῦ πρὸς αὐτόν, Οἶνον οὐκ ἔχουσιν. **4** [καὶ] λέγει αὐτῇ ὁ Ἰησοῦς, Τί ἐμοὶ καὶ σοί, γύναι; οὔπω ἥκει ἡ ὥρα μου. **5** λέγει ἡ μήτηρ αὐτοῦ τοῖς διακόνοις, Ὅ τι ἂν λέγῃ ὑμῖν ποιήσατε. **6** ἦσαν δὲ ἐκεῖ λίθιναι ὑδρίαι ἓξ κατὰ τὸν καθαρισμὸν τῶν Ἰουδαίων κείμεναι, χωροῦσαι ἀνὰ μετρητὰς δύο ἢ τρεῖς. **7** λέγει αὐτοῖς ὁ Ἰησοῦς, Γεμίσατε τὰς ὑδρίας ὕδατος. καὶ ἐγέμισαν αὐτὰς ἕως ἄνω. **8** καὶ λέγει αὐτοῖς, Ἀντλήσατε νῦν καὶ φέρετε τῷ ἀρχιτρικλίνῳ· οἱ δὲ ἤνεγκαν. **9** ὡς δὲ ἐγεύσατο ὁ ἀρχιτρίκλινος τὸ ὕδωρ οἶνον γεγενημένον καὶ οὐκ ᾔδει πόθεν ἐστίν, οἱ δὲ διάκονοι ᾔδεισαν οἱ ἠντληκότες τὸ ὕδωρ, φωνεῖ τὸν νυμφίον ὁ ἀρχιτρίκλινος **10** καὶ λέγει αὐτῷ, Πᾶς ἄνθρωπος πρῶτον τὸν καλὸν οἶνον τίθησιν καὶ ὅταν μεθυσθῶσιν τὸν ἐλάσσω· σὺ τετήρηκας τὸν καλὸν οἶνον ἕως ἄρτι. ¶ **11** Ταύτην

saved | the | best | | till | now." | ¶ | **11** This, | the | first | of his | miraculous | signs, | Jesus | | performed | at | Cana
τετήρηκας | τὸν | καλὸν | οἶνον | ἕως | ἄρτι | | Ταύτην | | ἀρχὴν → | τῶν → | σημείων | ὁ | Ἰησοῦς, | ἐποίησεν | ἐν | Κανὰ
v.rai.2s | d.asm | a.asm | n.asm | p.g | adv | | r.asf | | n.asf | d.gpn | n.gpn | d.nsm | n.nsm | v.aai.3s | p.d | n.dsf
5498 | 3836 | 2819 | 3885 | 2401 | 785 | | 4047 | | 794 | 3836 | 4956 | 3836 | 2652 | 4472 | 1877 | 2830

in Galilee. | | He thus revealed | his | glory, | and | his | disciples | | put their faith | in | him.
→ | ⸤τῆς Γαλιλαίας⸥ | καὶ ↱ | ἐφανέρωσεν | αὐτοῦ | ⸤τὴν δόξαν⸥ | καὶ | αὐτοῦ | οἱ | μαθηταὶ⸥ → → | ἐπίστευσαν | εἰς | αὐτὸν
d.gsf | n.gsf | cj | v.aai.3s | r.gsm.3 | d.asf n.asf | cj | r.gsm.3 | d.npm | n.npm | v.aai.3p | p.a | r.asm.3
3836 | 1133 | 2779 5746 | 5746 | 899 | 3836 1518 | 2779 | 899 | 3836 | 3412 | 4409 | 1650 | 899

Jesus Clears the Temple

2:12 After | this | he | went down to | | Capernaum | with | his | mother | and | | brothers | and his
Μετὰ | τοῦτο | αὐτὸς | κατέβη → | εἰς | Καφαρναοὺμ | καὶ | αὐτοῦ | ἡ μήτηρ⸥ | καὶ | [αὐτοῦ] | ⸤οἱ ἀδελφοὶ⸥ | καὶ | αὐτοῦ
p.a | r.asn | r.nsm | v.aai.3s | p.a | n.asf | cj | r.gsm.3 | d.nsf n.nsf | cj | r.gsm.3 | d.npm n.npm | cj | r.gsm.3
3552 | 4047 | 899 | 2849 | 1650 | 3019 | 2779 | 899 | 3836 3613 | 2779 | 899 | 3836 81 | 2779 | 899

disciples. | | There | they stayed | for a few | | days. | ¶ | **13** When it was | *almost* | *time* | *for* | the | Jewish
⸤οἱ | μαθηταὶ⸥ καὶ | ἐκεῖ → | ἔμειναν | ⸤οὐ πολλὰς⸥ | ἡμέρας | | Καὶ | → ἦν | ἐγγὺς | | τὸ | ⸤τῶν Ἰουδαίων⸥
d.npm | n.npm | cj | adv | v.aai.3p | pl | a.apf | n.apf | cj | v.iai.3s | adv | d.nsn | d.gpm a.gpm
3836 | 3412 | 2779 | 1695 | 3531 | 4024 | 4498 | 2465 | 2779 | 1639 | 1584 | 3836 | 3836 2681

Passover, | | Jesus | | went up to | Jerusalem. | **14** | In | the | temple | courts | he found | men | selling | | cattle, | sheep
πάσχα | καὶ | ὁ | Ἰησοῦς, | ἀνέβη ← | εἰς Ἰεροσόλυμα | Καὶ | ἐν | τῷ | ἱερῷ | ← | → εὗρεν | τοὺς | πωλοῦντας | βόας | καὶ | πρόβατα
n.nsn | cj | d.nsm | n.nsm | v.aai.3s | p.a | n.apn | cj | p.d | d.dsn | n.dsn | v.aai.3s | d.apm | pt.pa.apm | n.apm | cj | n.apn
4247 | 2779 | 3836 | 2652 | 326 | 1650 | 2642 | 2779 | 1877 | 3836 | 2639 | 2351 | 3836 | 4797 | 1091 | 2779 | 4585

and doves, | and others | sitting | at tables | exchanging money. | **15** So | he | made | a whip | | out of cords, | and
καὶ περιστερὰς | καὶ τοὺς | καθημένους ← | | κερματιστὰς ← | καὶ | → ποιήσας | φραγέλλιον | ἐκ | ← σχοινίων
cj n.apf | cj d.apm | pt.pm.apm | | n.apm | cj | pt.aa.nsm | n.asn | p.g | n.gpn
2779 4361 | 2779 3836 | 2764 | | 3048 | 2779 | 4472 | 5848 | 1666 | 5389

drove | all | from | the | temple | area, | both | sheep | and | cattle; | | he | scattered | the | coins | of the money
ἐξέβαλεν | πάντας | ἐκ | τοῦ | ἱεροῦ | ← | τε | ⸤τά πρόβατα⸥ | καὶ | ⸤τοὺς βόας⸥ | καὶ | → ἐξέχεεν | τὸ | κέρμα | → τῶν →
v.aai.3s | a.apm | p.g | d.gsn | n.gsn | | cj | d.apn n.apn | cj | d.apm n.apm | cj | v.aai.3s | d.asn | n.asn | d.gpm
1675 | 4246 | 1666 | 3836 | 2639 | | 5445 | 3836 4585 | 2779 | 3836 1091 | 2779 | 1772 | 3836 | 3047 | 3836

changers | and | overturned | their | tables. | **16** | To those who | sold | | doves | | he said, | "Get | these | out | of
κολλυβιστῶν | καὶ | ἀνέτρεψεν | τὰς | τραπέζας | καὶ | → τοῖς | ← πωλοῦσιν | ⸤τὰς περιστερὰς⸥ | → | εἶπεν | ἄρατε | ταῦτα | ἐντεῦθεν
n.gpm | cj | v.aai.3s | d.apf | n.apf | cj | d.dpm | pt.pa.dpm | d.apf n.apf | | v.aai.3s | v.aam.2p | r.apn | adv
3142 | 2779 | 426 | 3836 | 5544 | 2779 | 3836 | 4797 | 3836 4361 | | 3306 | 149 | 4047 | 1949

here! | *How* | *dare* | *you* | *turn* | | my | Father's | | house | | into a market!" | **17** His | disciples | | remembered | that | it
← | μὴ | ποιεῖτε | μου | ⸤τοῦ πατρός⸥ | ⸤τὸν οἶκον⸥ | | οἶκον ἐμπορίου⸥ | αὐτοῦ | ⸤οἱ μαθηταὶ⸥ | ἐμνήσθησαν | ὅτι → | cj
 | pl | v.pam.2p | r.gs.1 | d.gsm n.gsm | d.asm n.asm | | n.asm n.gsn | r.gsm.3 | d.npm n.npm | v.api.3p | cj
 | 3590 | 4472 | 1609 | 3836 4252 | 3836 3875 | | 3875 1866 | 899 | 3836 3412 | 3630 | 4022

is | written: | "Zeal | for | your | house | | will consume | me." | ¶ | **18** Then | the | Jews | demanded | | of
ἐστὶν | γεγραμμένον | ὁ | ζῆλος⸥ | → σου | ⸤τοῦ οἴκου⸥ | → | καταφάγεται | με | | οὖν | οἱ | Ἰουδαῖοι | Ἀπεκρίθησαν | καὶ | εἶπαν
v.pai.3s | pt.rp.nsn | d.nsm | n.nsm | r.gs.2 | d.gsm n.gsm | | v.fmi.3s | r.as.1 | | cj | d.npm | n.npm | v.api.3p | cj | v.aai.3p
1639 | 1211 | 3836 | 2419 | 3875 5148 | 3836 3875 | | 2983 | 1609 | | 4036 | 3836 | 2681 | 646 | 2779 | 3306

him, | "What | miraculous | sign | can you | show | us | to prove | your | authority | | to do | all | this?" | **19** Jesus | answered
αὐτῷ | τί | → | σημεῖον | → | δεικνύεις | ἡμῖν | | | | ὅτι | ποιεῖς | ταῦτα | Ἰησοῦς | ἀπεκρίθη
r.dsm.3 | r.asn | | n.asn | | v.pai.2s | r.dp.1 | | | | cj | v.pai.2s | r.apn | n.nsm | v.api.3s
899 | 5515 | | 4956 | | 1260 | 7005 | | | | 4022 | 4472 | 4047 | 2652 | 646

them, | "Destroy | this | temple, | and | I will | raise | it | | again | in | three | days." | **20** | The | Jews | | replied, | "It has
καὶ | εἶπεν αὐτοῖς | λύσατε | τοῦτον | ⸤τὸν ναὸν⸥ | καὶ | → | ἐγερῶ | αὐτόν | | ἐν | τρισὶν | ἡμέραις | | οὖν | οἱ | Ἰουδαῖοι | εἶπαν
cj | v.aai.3s | r.dpm.3 | v.aam.2p | r.asm | d.asm n.asm | cj | | v.fai.1s | r.asm.3 | | p.d | a.dpf | n.dpf | | cj | d.npm | n.npm | v.aai.3p
2779 | 3306 | 899 | 3395 | 4047 | 3836 3724 | 2779 | | 1586 | 899 | | 1877 | 5552 | 2465 | | 4036 | 3836 | 2681 | 3306

taken | forty-six | | years | to build | | this | temple, | and | you | are going to | raise | it | | in | three | days?" | **21** But
⸤τεσσεράκοντα | καὶ | ἕξ | ἔτεσιν | οἰκοδομήθη | | οὗτος | ὁ | ναὸς⸥ | καὶ | σὺ | → | ἐγερεῖς | αὐτόν | ἐν | τρισὶν | ἡμέραις | δὲ
a.dpn | cj | a.dpn | n.dpn | v.api.3s | | r.nsm | d.nsm | n.nsm | cj | r.ns.2 | | v.fai.2s | r.asm.3 | p.d | a.dpf | n.dpf | cj
5477 | 2779 | 1971 | 2291 | 3868 | | 4047 | 3836 | 3724 | 2779 | 5148 | | 1586 | 899 | 1877 | 5552 | 2465 | 1254

the | temple | he | | had spoken | of | was | his | body. | **22** | After | he was | raised | from | the dead, | his | | disciples
περὶ | τοῦ | ναοῦ | ἐκεῖνος | → | ἔλεγεν | ← | αὐτοῦ | ⸤τοῦ σώματος⸥ | οὖν | ὅτε | → → | ἠγέρθη | ἐκ | νεκρῶν | αὐτοῦ | ⸤οἱ μαθηταὶ⸥
p.g | d.gsm | n.gsm | r.nsm | | v.iai.3s | | r.gsm.3 | d.gsn n.gsn | cj | cj | | v.api.3s | p.g | a.gpm | r.gsm.3 | d.npm n.npm
4309 | 3836 | 3724 | 1697 | | 3306 | | 899 | 3836 5393 | 4036 | 4021 | | 1586 | 1666 | 3738 | 899 | 3836 3412

ἐποίησεν ἀρχὴν τῶν σημείων ὁ Ἰησοῦς ἐν Κανὰ τῆς Γαλιλαίας καὶ ἐφανέρωσεν τὴν δόξαν αὐτοῦ, καὶ ἐπίστευσαν εἰς αὐτὸν οἱ μαθηταὶ αὐτοῦ.

2:12 Μετὰ τοῦτο κατέβη εἰς Καφαρναοὺμ αὐτὸς καὶ ἡ μήτηρ αὐτοῦ καὶ οἱ ἀδελφοὶ [αὐτοῦ] καὶ οἱ μαθηταὶ αὐτοῦ καὶ ἐκεῖ ἔμειναν οὐ πολλὰς ἡμέρας. ¶ **13** Καὶ ἐγγὺς ἦν τὸ πάσχα τῶν Ἰουδαίων, καὶ ἀνέβη εἰς Ἰεροσόλυμα ὁ Ἰησοῦς. **14** καὶ εὗρεν ἐν τῷ ἱερῷ τοὺς πωλοῦντας βόας καὶ πρόβατα καὶ περιστερὰς καὶ τοὺς κερματιστὰς καθημένους, **15** καὶ ποιήσας φραγέλλιον ἐκ σχοινίων πάντας ἐξέβαλεν ἐκ τοῦ ἱεροῦ τά τε πρόβατα καὶ τοὺς βόας, καὶ τῶν κολλυβιστῶν ἐξέχεεν τὸ κέρμα καὶ τὰς τραπέζας ἀνέτρεψεν, **16** καὶ τοῖς τὰς περιστερὰς πωλοῦσιν εἶπεν, Ἄρατε ταῦτα ἐντεῦθεν, μὴ ποιεῖτε τὸν οἶκον τοῦ πατρός μου οἶκον ἐμπορίου. **17** Ἐμνήσθησαν οἱ μαθηταὶ αὐτοῦ ὅτι γεγραμμένον ἐστίν, Ὁ ζῆλος τοῦ οἴκου σου καταφάγεταί με. ¶ **18** ἀπεκρίθησαν οὖν οἱ Ἰουδαῖοι καὶ εἶπαν αὐτῷ, Τί σημεῖον δεικνύεις ἡμῖν ὅτι ταῦτα ποιεῖς; **19** ἀπεκρίθη Ἰησοῦς καὶ εἶπεν αὐτοῖς, Λύσατε τὸν ναὸν τοῦτον καὶ ἐν τρισὶν ἡμέραις ἐγερῶ αὐτόν. **20** εἶπαν οὖν οἱ Ἰουδαῖοι, Τεσσεράκοντα καὶ ἓξ ἔτεσιν οἰκοδομήθη ὁ ναὸς οὗτος, καὶ σὺ ἐν τρισὶν ἡμέραις ἐγερεῖς αὐτόν; **21** ἐκεῖνος δὲ ἔλεγεν περὶ τοῦ ναοῦ τοῦ σώματος αὐτοῦ. **22** ὅτε οὖν ἠγέρθη ἐκ νεκρῶν,

recalled	what he had said.	Then they believed	the Scripture	and the words	that Jesus	had spoken. ¶
ἐμνήσθησαν ὅτι	τοῦτο → → ἔλεγεν καί	ἐπίστευσαν τῇ	γραφῇ	καί τῷ λόγῳ	ὅν ὁ Ἰησοῦς →	εἶπεν
v.api.3p	r.asn v.iai.3s cj	v.aai.3p d.dsf	n.dsf	cj d.dsm n.dsm	r.asm d.nsm n.nsm	v.aai.3s
3630 4022 4047	3306 2779	4409 3836	1210	2779 3836 3364	4005 3836 2652	3306

23 Now	while	he was in	Jerusalem	at the	Passover	Feast,	many people	saw	the	miraculous signs
δέ	Ὡς →	ἦν ἐν	τοῖς Ἰεροσολύμοις	ἐν τῷ	πάσχα	ἐν τῇ ἑορτῇ	πολλοί ←	θεωροῦντες	τά →	σημεῖα
cj	cj	v.iai.3s p.d	d.dpn n.dpn	p.d d.dsn	n.dsn	p.d d.dsf n.dsf	a.npm	pt.pa.npm	d.apn	n.apn
1254	6055	1639 1877	3836 2642	1877 3836	4247	1877 3836 2038	4498	2555	3836	4956

| he was doing | and believed | in | his | name. | **24** But | Jesus | | would not | entrust | himself to them, | for
--- | --- | --- | --- | --- | --- | --- | --- | --- | --- | --- | --- | ---
αὐτοῦ ἅ → → | ἐποίει | ἐπίστευσαν εἰς | αὐτοῦ τὸ | ὄνομα | δέ | Ἰησοῦς αὐτός → | | οὐκ ἐπίστευεν αὐτόν | → | αὐτοῖς | διά
r.gsm.3 r.apn | v.iai.3s | v.aai.3p p.a | r.gsm.3 d.asn | n.asn | cj | n.nsm r.nsm | | pl v.iai.3s | r.asm.3 | r.dpm.3 | p.a
899 4005 | 4472 | 4409 1650 | 899 3836 | 3950 | 1254 | 2652 899 | 4409 | 4024 4409 | 899 | 899 | 1328

he	knew	all	men.	**25**		He did not need		man's	testimony	about man,		for	he
αὐτόν	τὸ γινώσκειν	πάντας		καί ὅτι → →	οὐ	χρείαν εἶχεν ἵνα	τις		μαρτυρήσῃ	περί	τοῦ ἀνθρώπου	γάρ	αὐτός
r.asm.3	d.asn f.pa	a.apm		cj cj	pl	n.asf v.iai.3s cj	r.nsm		v.aas.3s	p.g	d.gsm n.gsm	cj	r.nsm
899	3836 1182	4246		2779 4022	2400 2400 4024	5970	2400 2671 5516	5516		3455	4309	3836 476	1142	899

knew	what was	in	a man.
ἐγίνωσκεν τί	ἦν	ἐν	τῷ ἀνθρώπῳ
v.iai.3s r.nsn	v.iai.3s	p.d	d.dsm n.dsm
1182 5515	1639	1877	3836 476

Jesus Teaches Nicodemus

3:1 Now	there was	a man	of	the Pharisees	named	Nicodemus,	a member of the	Jewish	ruling council.
δέ →	Ἦν	ἄνθρωπος ἐκ	τῶν Φαρισαίων	ὄνομα αὐτῷ	Νικόδημος		→ τῶν Ἰουδαίων	ἄρχων ←
cj	v.iai.3s	n.nsm p.g	d.gpm n.gpm	n.nsn r.dsm.3	n.nsm		d.gpm a.gpm	n.nsm
1254	1639	476 1666	3836 5757	3950 899	3773		3836 2681	807

2 He	came to	Jesus at	night	and said,	"Rabbi,	we know		you are	a teacher		who has come	from God.
οὗτος ἦλθεν	πρός αὐτόν →	νυκτός καί	εἶπεν αὐτῷ ῥαββί	→	οἴδαμεν ὅτι	→ →		διδάσκαλος →	→	ἐλήλυθας ἀπό	θεοῦ
r.nsm v.aai.3s	p.a r.asm.3	n.gsf cj	v.aai.3s r.dsm.3 n.vsm		v.rai.1p cj			n.nsm		v.rai.2s p.g	n.gsm
4047 2262	4639 899	3816 2779	3306 899 4806		3857 4022	2262 2262		1437		2262 608	2536

For	no one	could	perform		the	miraculous signs		you are doing	if	God		were not	with him."	**3** In
γάρ →	οὐδείς	δύναται	ποιεῖν	ταῦτα τά		σημεῖα ἅ	σύ	ποιεῖς ἐάν	ὁ	θεός	ἦ	μή μετ'	αὐτοῦ
cj	a.nsm	v.ppi.3s	f.pa	r.apn d.apn		n.apn r.apn	r.ns.2	v.pai.2s cj	d.nsm	n.nsm	v.pas.3s	pl p.g	r.gsm.3
1142	4029	1538	4472	4047 3836		4956 4005	5148	4472 1569	3836	2536	1639	3590 3552	899

reply	Jesus	declared,	"I	tell	you	the truth,		no one	can		see	the kingdom	of God		unless
ἀπεκρίθη	Ἰησοῦς καί	εἶπεν	αὐτῷ →	λέγω σοι		ἀμήν ἀμήν	οὐ	→	δύναται	ἰδεῖν	τήν	βασιλείαν →	τοῦ θεοῦ	ἐάν μή
v.api.3s	n.nsm cj v.aai.3s		r.dsm.3	v.pai.1s r.ds.2		pl	pl	pl	v.ppi.3s	f.aa	d.asf	n.asf	d.gsm n.gsm	cj pl
646	2652 2779 3306		899	3306 5148		297 297	4024		1538	1625	3836	2536	3836 2536	1569 3590

he is born	again."	**4** "How	can	a	man	be born		when he is	old?"	Nicodemus	asked.
τις γεννηθῇ	ἄνωθεν	πῶς	δύναται	ἄνθρωπος	→	γεννηθῆναι →		ὤν γέρων		Νικόδημος	λέγει πρός αὐτόν
r.nsm v.aps.3s	adv	cj	v.ppi.3s	n.nsm		f.ap		pt.pa.nsm a.nsm		n.nsm	v.pai.3s p.a r.asm.3
5516 1164	540	4802	1538	476		1164		1639 1173		3836 3773	3306 4639 899

"Surely he cannot	enter	a second time	into	his	mother's	womb		to be born!"	**5** Jesus	answered,
μή δύναται	εἰσελθεῖν	δεύτερον	εἰς	αὐτοῦ	τῆς μητρός	τήν κοιλίαν	καί →	γεννηθῆναι	Ἰησοῦς	ἀπεκρίθη
pl v.ppi.3s	f.aa	adv	p.a	r.gsm.3	d.gsf n.gsf	d.asf n.asf	cj	f.ap	n.nsm	v.api.3s
1538 3590 1538	1656	1311	1650	899	3836 3613	3836 3120	2779	1164	2652	646

"I tell	you	the truth,		no one	can	enter		the kingdom	of God		unless	he is	born	of	water	and
→ λέγω σοι		ἀμήν ἀμήν	οὐ	→	δύναται	εἰσελθεῖν εἰς	τήν	βασιλείαν	→ τοῦ θεοῦ	ἐάν μή	τις	→ γεννηθῇ	ἐξ	ὕδατος	καί
v.pai.1s r.ds.2		pl	pl	pl	v.ppi.3s	f.aa		d.asf	n.asf		d.gsm n.gsm	cj pl	r.nsm	v.aps.3s	p.g	n.gsn	cj
3306 5148		297 297	4024		1538	1656 1650	3836	993		3836 2536	1569 3590	5516	1164	1666	5623	2779

the Spirit.	**6**		Flesh		gives birth	to flesh, but			the Spirit		gives
πνεύματος	τὸ γεγεννημένον	ἐκ τῆς σαρκός		σάρξ	καί	τὸ γεγεννημένον		ἐκ τοῦ πνεύματος	ἐστιν
n.gsn	d.nsn pt.rp.nsn	p.g d.gsf n.gsf		n.nsf	cj	d.nsn pt.rp.nsn		p.g d.gsn n.gsn	v.pai.3s
4460	3836 1164	1666 3836 4922	1164	1164 1164 4922	2779	3836 1164		3836 1666 3836 4460	1639 1164

birth to spirit.	**7** You should	not	be surprised	at	my saying,	'You	must	be born		again.'	**8** The	wind	blows
→ πνεῦμα		μή →	θαυμάσῃς ὅτι	→	εἶπον	σοι ὑμᾶς	δεῖ	→ γεννηθῆναι	ἄνωθεν	τό	πνεῦμα πνεῖ
n.nsn		pl	v.aas.2s cj		v.aai.1s	r.ds.2 r.ap.2	v.pai.3s	f.ap	adv	d.nsn	n.nsn v.pai.3s
1164	1164 4460	2513 2513	3590		4022	3306	5148 7007	1256	1164	540	3836	4460 4463

ἐμνήσθησαν οἱ μαθηταὶ αὐτοῦ ὅτι τοῦτο ἔλεγεν, καὶ ἐπίστευσαν τῇ γραφῇ καὶ τῷ λόγῳ ὃν εἶπεν ὁ Ἰησοῦς. ¶ **23** Ὡς δὲ ἦν ἐν τοῖς Ἰεροσολύμοις ἐν τῷ πάσχα ἐν τῇ ἑορτῇ, πολλοὶ ἐπίστευσαν εἰς τὸ ὄνομα αὐτοῦ θεωροῦντες αὐτοῦ τὰ σημεῖα ἃ ἐποίει· **24** αὐτὸς δὲ Ἰησοῦς οὐκ ἐπίστευεν αὐτὸν αὐτοῖς διὰ τὸ αὐτὸν γινώσκειν πάντας **25** καὶ ὅτι οὐ χρείαν εἶχεν ἵνα τις μαρτυρήσῃ περὶ τοῦ ἀνθρώπου· αὐτὸς γὰρ ἐγίνωσκεν τί ἦν ἐν τῷ ἀνθρώπῳ.

3:1 Ἦν δὲ ἄνθρωπος ἐκ τῶν Φαρισαίων, Νικόδημος ὄνομα αὐτῷ, ἄρχων τῶν Ἰουδαίων· **2** οὗτος ἦλθεν πρὸς αὐτὸν νυκτὸς καὶ εἶπεν αὐτῷ, Ῥαββί, οἴδαμεν ὅτι ἀπὸ θεοῦ ἐλήλυθας διδάσκαλος· οὐδεὶς γὰρ δύναται ταῦτα τὰ σημεῖα ποιεῖν ἃ σὺ ποιεῖς, ἐὰν μὴ ᾖ ὁ θεὸς μετ' αὐτοῦ. **3** ἀπεκρίθη Ἰησοῦς καὶ εἶπεν αὐτῷ, Ἀμὴν ἀμὴν λέγω σοι, ἐὰν μή τις γεννηθῇ ἄνωθεν, οὐ δύναται ἰδεῖν τὴν βασιλείαν τοῦ θεοῦ. **4** λέγει πρὸς αὐτὸν [ὁ] Νικόδημος, Πῶς δύναται ἄνθρωπος γεννηθῆναι γέρων ὤν; μὴ δύναται εἰς τὴν κοιλίαν τῆς μητρὸς αὐτοῦ δεύτερον εἰσελθεῖν καὶ γεννηθῆναι; **5** ἀπεκρίθη Ἰησοῦς, Ἀμὴν ἀμὴν λέγω σοι, ἐὰν μή τις γεννηθῇ ἐξ ὕδατος καὶ πνεύματος, οὐ δύναται εἰσελθεῖν εἰς τὴν βασιλείαν τοῦ θεοῦ. **6** τὸ γεγεννημένον ἐκ τῆς σαρκὸς σάρξ ἐστιν, καὶ τὸ γεγεννημένον ἐκ τοῦ πνεύματος πνεῦμά ἐστιν. **7** μὴ θαυμάσῃς ὅτι εἶπόν σοι, Δεῖ ὑμᾶς γεννηθῆναι ἄνωθεν. **8** τὸ

wherever it pleases.   You hear   its   sound,   but you cannot tell   where it comes from or   where it is going.
ὅπου → θέλει καὶ → ἀκούεις αὐτοῦ ⌜τὴν φωνὴν⌝ ἀλλ᾽ → οὐκ οἶδας πόθεν → ἔρχεται καὶ ποῦ → → ὑπάγει
cj v.pai.3s cj v.pai.2s r.gsn.3 d.asf n.asf cj cj v.rai.2s cj v.pmi.3s cj adv v.pai.3s
3963 2527 2779 201 899 3836 5889 247 3857 4024 3857 4470 2262 2779 4543 5632

So   it is   with everyone born   of the Spirit."   9 "How can   this be?"   Nicodemus asked.
οὕτως → ἐστὶν πᾶς ὁ γεγεννημένος ἐκ τοῦ πνεύματος πῶς δύναται ταῦτα γενέσθαι Νικόδημος ἀπεκρίθη καὶ
adv v.pai.3s a.nsm d.nsm pt.rp.nsm p.g d.gsn n.gsn adv v.ppi.3s r.apn f.am n.nsm v.api.3s cj
4048 1639 4246 3836 1164 1666 3836 4460 4802 1538 4047 1181 3773 646 2779

   10 "You are Israel's   teacher,"   said   Jesus,   "and do you not understand these
εἶπεν αὐτῷ σὺ εἶ ⌜τοῦ Ἰσραὴλ⌝ ὁ διδάσκαλος ἀπεκρίθη Ἰησοῦς καὶ εἶπεν αὐτῷ καὶ → → οὐ γινώσκεις ταῦτα
v.aai.3s r.dsm.3 r.ns.2 v.pai.2s d.gsm n.gsm d.nsm n.nsm v.api.3s n.nsm cj v.aai.3s r.dsm.3 cj pl v.pai.2s r.apn
3306 899 5148 1639 3836 2702 3836 1437 646 2652 2779 3306 899 2779 1182 1182 4024 1182 4047

things?   11 I tell   you the truth,   we speak   of what we know,   and we testify   to what we have seen,
← → → λέγω σοι ⌜ἀμὴν ἀμὴν⌝ ὅτι → λαλοῦμεν ὃ → οἴδαμεν καὶ → μαρτυροῦμεν ← → → ἑωράκαμεν
v.pai.1s r.ds.2 pl pl cj v.rai.1p r.asn v.rai.1p cj v.rai.1p r.asn v.rai.1p
3306 5148 297 297 4022 3281 4005 3857 2779 3455 4005 3972

but still you people do not accept   our testimony.   12   I have spoken to you of earthly   things and you do
καὶ → → οὐ λαμβάνετε ἡμῶν ⌜τὴν μαρτυρίαν⌝ εἰ → εἶπον → ὑμῖν ⌜τὰ ἐπίγεια⌝ ← καὶ →
cj pl v.pai.2p r.gp.1 d.asf n.asf cj v.aai.1s r.dp.2 d.apn a.apn cj
2779 3284 3284 4024 3284 7005 3836 3456 1623 3306 7007 3836 2103 2779 4409 4409

not believe; how then will you believe if I speak   of heavenly   things? 13   No one   has ever gone
οὐ πιστεύετε πῶς → → πιστεύσετε ἐὰν → εἴπω ὑμῖν ⌜τὰ ἐπουράνια⌝ ← καὶ → οὐδεὶς ἀναβέβηκεν
pl v.pai.2p cj v.fai.2p cj v.aas.1s r.dp.2 d.apn a.apn cj a.nsm v.rai.3s
4024 4409 4802 4409 1569 3306 7007 3836 2230 2779 4029 326

into heaven   except the one who came   from heaven   – the Son of Man.   14   Just as Moses
εἰς τὸν οὐρανὸν εἰ μὴ ὁ καταβάς ἐκ τοῦ οὐρανοῦ ὁ υἱὸς ⌜τοῦ ἀνθρώπου⌝ Καὶ καθὼς ← Μωϋσῆς
p.a d.asm n.asm cj pl d.nsm pt.aa.nsm p.g d.gsm n.gsm d.nsm n.nsm d.gsm n.gsm cj cj n.nsm
1650 3836 4041 1623 3590 3836 2849 1666 3836 4041 3836 5626 3836 476 2779 2777 3707

lifted up the snake in the desert, so   the Son of Man   must be lifted   up, 15 that everyone who believes
ὕψωσεν ← τὸν ὄφιν ἐν τῇ ἐρήμῳ οὕτως τὸν υἱὸν → ⌜τοῦ ἀνθρώπου⌝ δεῖ → ὑψωθῆναι ← ἵνα πᾶς ὁ πιστεύων
v.aai.3s d.asm n.asm p.d d.dsf n.dsf adv d.asm n.asm d.gsm n.gsm v.pai.3s f.ap cj a.nsm d.nsm pt.pa.nsm
5738 3836 4058 1877 3836 2245 4048 3836 5626 3836 476 1256 5738 2671 4246 3836 4409

in him may have eternal life. ¶   16 "For God   so   loved   the world that he gave   his one   and only
ἐν αὐτῷ → ἔχῃ αἰώνιον ζωήν γὰρ ὁ θεὸς οὕτως ἠγάπησεν τὸν κόσμον ὥστε → ἔδωκεν τὸν μονογενῆ ← ←
p.d r.dsm.3 v.pas.3s a.asf n.asf cj d.nsm n.nsm adv v.aai.3s d.asm n.asm cj v.aai.3s d.asm a.asm
1877 899 2400 173 2437 1142 3836 2536 4048 26 3836 3180 6063 1443 3836 3666

Son,   that whoever believes in him shall not perish but have eternal life. 17 For God   did not send   his
τὸν υἱόν ἵνα πᾶς ὁ πιστεύων εἰς αὐτὸν → μὴ ἀπόληται ἀλλ᾽ ἔχῃ αἰώνιον ζωήν γὰρ ὁ θεὸς → οὐ ἀπέστειλεν τὸν
d.asm n.asm cj a.nsm d.nsm pt.pa.nsm p.a r.asm.3 pl v.ams.3s cj v.pas.3s a.asf n.asf cj d.nsm n.nsm pl v.aai.3s d.asm
3836 5626 2671 4246 3836 4409 1650 899 660 3590 660 247 2400 173 2437 1142 3836 2536 690 4024 690 3836

Son into the world to   condemn the world, but to   save the world through him. 18 Whoever believes in him is not
υἱὸν εἰς τὸν κόσμον ἵνα κρίνῃ τὸν κόσμον ἀλλ᾽ ἵνα σωθῇ ὁ κόσμος δι᾽ αὐτοῦ ὁ πιστεύων εἰς αὐτὸν → οὐ
n.asm p.a d.asm n.asm cj v.aas.3s d.asm n.asm cj cj v.aps.3s d.nsm n.nsm p.g r.gsm.3 d.nsm pt.pa.nsm p.a r.asm.3 pl
5626 1650 3836 3180 2671 3212 3836 3180 247 2671 5392 3836 3180 1328 899 3836 4409 1650 899 3212 4024

condemned, but whoever does not believe stands condemned already because he has not believed   in the name of
κρίνεται δὲ ὁ μὴ πιστεύων → κέκριται ἤδη ὅτι → μὴ πεπίστευκεν εἰς τὸ ὄνομα
v.ppi.3s cj d.nsm pl pt.pa.nsm v.rpi.3s adv cj pl v.rai.3s p.a d.asn n.asn
3212 1254 3836 4409 3590 4409 3212 2453 4022 4409 4409 3590 4409 1650 3836 3950

God's   one   and only Son.   19   This is   the verdict: Light   has come   into the world, but
⌜τοῦ θεοῦ⌝ μονογενοῦς ← ← ⌜τοῦ υἱοῦ⌝ δὲ αὕτη ἐστὶν ἡ κρίσις ὅτι ⌜τὸ φῶς⌝ → ἐλήλυθεν εἰς τὸν κόσμον καὶ
d.gsm n.gsm a.gsm d.gsm n.gsm cj r.nsf v.pai.3s d.nsf n.nsf cj d.nsn n.nsn v.rai.3s p.a d.asm n.asm cj
3836 2536 3666 3836 5626 1254 4047 1639 3836 3213 4022 3836 5890 2262 1650 3836 3180 2779

men   loved   darkness instead of light   because their deeds   were evil. 20   Everyone who does
⌜οἱ ἄνθρωποι⌝ ἠγάπησαν ⌜τὸ σκότος⌝ μᾶλλον ἢ ⌜τὸ φῶς⌝ γὰρ αὐτῶν ⌜τὰ ἔργα⌝ ἦν πονηρὰ γὰρ πᾶς ὁ πράσσων
d.npm n.npm v.aai.3p d.nsn n.nsn adv.c pl d.nsn n.nsn cj r.gpm.3 d.npn n.npn v.iai.3s a.npn cj a.nsm d.nsm pt.pa.nsm
3836 476 26 3836 5030 3437 2445 3836 3836 1142 899 3836 2240 1639 4505 1142 4246 3836 4556

πνεῦμα ὅπου θέλει πνεῖ καὶ τὴν φωνὴν αὐτοῦ ἀκούεις, ἀλλ᾽ οὐκ οἶδας πόθεν ἔρχεται καὶ ποῦ ὑπάγει· οὕτως ἐστὶν πᾶς ὁ γεγεννημένος ἐκ τοῦ πνεύματος. ⁹ ἀπεκρίθη Νικόδημος καὶ εἶπεν αὐτῷ, Πῶς δύναται ταῦτα γενέσθαι; ¹⁰ ἀπεκρίθη Ἰησοῦς καὶ εἶπεν αὐτῷ, Σὺ εἶ ὁ διδάσκαλος τοῦ Ἰσραὴλ καὶ ταῦτα οὐ γινώσκεις; ¹¹ ἀμὴν ἀμὴν λέγω σοι ὅτι ὃ οἴδαμεν λαλοῦμεν καὶ ὃ ἑωράκαμεν μαρτυροῦμεν, καὶ τὴν μαρτυρίαν ἡμῶν οὐ λαμβάνετε. ¹² εἰ τὰ ἐπίγεια εἶπον ὑμῖν καὶ οὐ πιστεύετε, πῶς ἐὰν εἴπω ὑμῖν τὰ ἐπουράνια πιστεύσετε; ¹³ καὶ οὐδεὶς ἀναβέβηκεν εἰς τὸν οὐρανὸν εἰ μὴ ὁ ἐκ τοῦ οὐρανοῦ καταβάς, ὁ υἱὸς τοῦ ἀνθρώπου. ¹⁴ καὶ καθὼς Μωϋσῆς ὕψωσεν τὸν ὄφιν ἐν τῇ ἐρήμῳ, οὕτως ὑψωθῆναι δεῖ τὸν υἱὸν τοῦ ἀνθρώπου, ¹⁵ ἵνα πᾶς ὁ πιστεύων ἐν αὐτῷ ἔχῃ ζωὴν αἰώνιον. ¶ ¹⁶ Οὕτως γὰρ ἠγάπησεν ὁ θεὸς τὸν κόσμον, ὥστε τὸν υἱὸν τὸν μονογενῆ ἔδωκεν, ἵνα πᾶς ὁ πιστεύων εἰς αὐτὸν μὴ ἀπόληται ἀλλ᾽ ἔχῃ ζωὴν αἰώνιον. ¹⁷ οὐ γὰρ ἀπέστειλεν ὁ θεὸς τὸν υἱὸν εἰς τὸν κόσμον ἵνα κρίνῃ τὸν κόσμον, ἀλλ᾽ ἵνα σωθῇ ὁ κόσμος δι᾽ αὐτοῦ. ¹⁸ ὁ πιστεύων εἰς αὐτὸν οὐ κρίνεται· ὁ δὲ μὴ πιστεύων ἤδη κέκριται, ὅτι μὴ πεπίστευκεν εἰς τὸ ὄνομα τοῦ μονογενοῦς υἱοῦ τοῦ θεοῦ. ¹⁹ αὕτη δέ ἐστιν ἡ κρίσις ὅτι τὸ φῶς ἐλήλυθεν εἰς τὸν κόσμον καὶ ἠγάπησαν οἱ ἄνθρωποι μᾶλλον τὸ σκότος ἢ τὸ φῶς· ἦν γὰρ αὐτῶν πονηρὰ τὰ ἔργα. ²⁰ πᾶς γὰρ ὁ φαῦλα πράσσων μισεῖ τὸ φῶς καὶ οὐκ ἔρχεται πρὸς τὸ

evil hates the light, and will not come into the light *for fear that* his deeds → → will be exposed. **21** But whoever

φαῦλα	μισεῖ	τὸ	φῶς	καὶ	→	οὐκ	ἔρχεται	πρὸς	τὸ	φῶς	ἵνα	μὴ		αὐτοῦ	τὰ	ἔργα			ἐλεγχθῇ	δὲ	ὁ
a.apn	v.pai.3s	d.asn	n.nsn	cj		pl	v.pmi.3s	p.a	d.asn	n.asn	cj	pl		r.gsm.3	d.npn	n.npn			v.aps.3s	cj	d.nsm
5765	3631	3836	5890	2779		4024	2262	4639	3836	5890	2671	3590		899	3836	2240			1794	1254	3836

lives by the truth comes into the light, so that it may be seen plainly that what he has done has been

ποιῶν	←	τὴν	ἀλήθειαν	ἔρχεται	πρὸς	τὸ	φῶς,	ἵνα	←	→	→	φανερωθῇ		ὅτι		αὐτοῦ	τὰ	ἔργα	→	→	
pt.pa.nsm		d.asf	n.asf	v.pmi.3s	p.a	d.asn	n.asn	cj				v.aps.3s		cj		r.gsm.3	d.npn	n.npn			
4472		3836	237	2262	4639	3836	5890	2671				5746		4022		899	3836	2240			

done through God."

ἐστιν	εἰργασμένα	ἐν	θεῷ
v.pai.3s	pt.rp.npn	p.d	n.dsm
1639	2237	1877	2536

John the Baptist's Testimony About Jesus

3:22 After this, Jesus and his disciples went out into the Judean countryside, where he spent

Μετὰ	ταῦτα	ὁ	Ἰησοῦς	καὶ	αὐτοῦ	οἱ	μαθηταὶ	ἦλθεν	εἰς	τὴν	Ἰουδαίαν	γῆν	καὶ	ἐκεῖ	→	διέτριβεν
p.a	r.apn	d.nsm	n.nsm	cj	r.gsm.3	d.npm	n.npm	v.aai.3s	p.a	d.asf	a.asf	n.asf	cj	adv		v.iai.3s
3552	4047	3836	2652	2779	899	3836	3412	2262	1650	3836	2681	1178	2779	1695		1417

some time with them, and baptized. **23** Now John also was baptizing at Aenon near Salim, because there

	μετ'	αὐτῶν	καὶ	ἐβάπτιζεν	δὲ	ὁ	Ἰωάννης	καὶ	Ἦν	βαπτίζων	ἐν	Αἰνὼν	ἐγγὺς	τοῦ Σαλείμ,	ὅτι	→
	p.g	r.gpm.3	cj	v.iai.3s	cj	d.nsm	n.nsm	adv	v.iai.3s	pt.pa.nsm	p.d	n.dsf	p.g	d.gsn n.gsn	cj	
	3552	899	2779	966	1254	3836	2722	2779	1639	966	1877	143	1584	3836 4887.5	4022	

was plenty of water, and people were constantly coming to be baptized. **24** (This was before

ἦν	πολλὰ	←	ὕδατα	ἐκεῖ	καὶ	→	→	παρεγίνοντο	καὶ	ἐβαπτίζοντο	γὰρ	→	οὔπω
v.iai.3s	a.npn		n.npn	adv	cj			v.imi.3p	cj	v.ipi.3p	cj		adv
1639	4498		5623	1695	2779			4134	2779	966	1142		4037

John was put in prison.) **25** An argument developed between some of John's disciples and a

ὁ	Ἰωάννης	ἦν	βεβλημένος	εἰς	τὴν φυλακὴν	οὖν	ζήτησις	Ἐγένετο	→	ἐκ	Ἰωάννου	τῶν μαθητῶν	μετὰ
d.nsm	n.nsm	v.iai.3s	pt.rp.nsm	p.a	d.asf n.asf	cj	n.nsf	v.ami.3s		p.g	n.gsm	d.gpm n.gpm	p.a
3836	2722	1639	965	1650	3836 5871	4036	2428	1181		1666	2722	3836 3412	3552

certain Jew over the matter of ceremonial washing. **26** They came to John and said to him, "Rabbi,

Ἰουδαίου	περὶ	←	←	←	καθαρισμοῦ	καὶ	→	ἦλθον	πρὸς	τὸν Ἰωάννην	καὶ	εἶπαν	→	αὐτῷ	ῥαββί
a.gsm	p.g				n.gsm	cj		v.aai.3p	p.a	d.asm n.asm	cj	v.aai.3p		r.dsm.3	n.vsm
2681	4309				2752	2779		2262	4639	3836 2722	2779	3306		899	4806

that man who was with you on the other side of the Jordan — the one you testified about — well, he is

ὃς	ἦν	μετὰ	σοῦ	→	→	πέραν	←	τοῦ	Ἰορδάνου	ᾧ	σὺ	μεμαρτύρηκας		ἴδε	οὗτος	→
r.nsm	v.iai.3s	p.g	r.gs.2			p.g		d.gsm	n.gsm	r.dsm	r.ns.2	v.rai.2s		pl	r.nsm	
4005	1639	3552	5148			4305		3836	2674	4005	5148	3455		2623	4047	

baptizing, and everyone is going to him." **27** To this John replied, "A man can receive

βαπτίζει	καὶ	πάντες	→	ἔρχονται	πρὸς	αὐτόν		Ἰωάννης	ἀπεκρίθη	καὶ	εἶπεν	ἄνθρωπος	οὐ	δύναται	λαμβάνειν
v.pai.3s	cj	a.npm		v.pmi.3p	p.a	r.asm.3		n.nsm	v.api.3s	cj	v.aai.3s	n.nsm	pl	v.ppi.3s	f.pa
966	2779	4246		2262	4639	899		2722	646	2779	3306	476	4024	1538	3284

only what is given him from heaven. **28** You yourselves can testify that I said, 'I

οὐδὲ	ἓν	ἐὰν	μὴ	ᾖ	→	δεδομένον	αὐτῷ	ἐκ	τοῦ οὐρανοῦ	ὑμεῖς	αὐτοὶ	μαρτυρεῖτε	μοι	ὅτι	→	εἶπον	[ὅτι]	ἐγὼ
adv	a.asn	cj	pl	v.pas.3s		pt.rp.nsm	r.dsm.3	p.g	d.gsm n.gsm	r.np.2	r.npm	v.pai.2p	r.ds.1	cj		v.aai.1s	cj	r.ns.1
4028	1651	1569	3590	1639		1443	899	1666	3836 4041	7007	899	3455	1609	4022		3306	4022	1609

am not the Christ but am sent ahead of him.' **29** The bride belongs to the bridegroom.

εἰμι	οὐκ	ὁ	Χριστός	ἀλλ'	ὅτι	εἰμὶ	ἀπεσταλμένος	ἔμπροσθεν	←	ἐκείνου	ὁ	ἔχων	τὴν	νύμφην	ἐστίν	←	νυμφίος	δὲ
v.pai.1s	pl	d.nsm	n.nsm	cj	cj	v.pai.1s	pt.rp.nsm	p.g		r.gsm	d.nsm	pt.pa.nsm	d.asf	n.asf	v.pai.3s		n.nsm	cj
1639	4024	3836	5986	247	4022	1639	690	1869		1697	3836	2400	3836	3811	1639		3812	1254

The friend who attends the bridegroom waits and listens for him, and *is full* of *joy* when he hears the

ὁ	φίλος	→	τοῦ	νυμφίου	ὁ	ἑστηκὼς	καὶ	ἀκούων	αὐτοῦ	χαίρει	χαρᾷ	διὰ	←	←	τὴν
d.nsm	a.nsm		d.gsm	n.gsm	d.nsm	pt.ra.nsm	cj	pt.pa.nsm	r.gsm.3	v.pai.3s	n.dsf	p.a			d.asf
3836	5813		3836	3812	3836	2705	2779	201	899	5897	5915	1328			3836

bridegroom's voice. That joy is mine, and it is now complete. **30** He must become greater; I must

τοῦ νυμφίου	φωνὴν	οὖν	αὕτη	ἡ	χαρὰ	ἡ	ἐμὴ	→	→	πεπλήρωται	ἐκεῖνον	δεῖ	→	αὐξάνειν	δὲ	ἐμὲ
d.gsm n.gsm	n.asf	cj	r.nsf	d.nsf	n.nsf	d.nsf	r.nsf.1			v.rpi.3s	r.asm	v.pai.3s		f.pa	cj	r.as.1
3836 3812	5889	4036	4047	3836	5915	3836	1847			4444	1697	1256		889	1254	1609

φῶς, ἵνα μὴ ἐλεγχθῇ τὰ ἔργα αὐτοῦ· ²¹ ὁ δὲ ποιῶν τὴν ἀλήθειαν ἔρχεται πρὸς τὸ φῶς, ἵνα φανερωθῇ αὐτοῦ τὰ ἔργα ὅτι ἐν θεῷ ἐστιν εἰργασμένα.

³:²² Μετὰ ταῦτα ἦλθεν ὁ Ἰησοῦς καὶ οἱ μαθηταὶ αὐτοῦ εἰς τὴν Ἰουδαίαν γῆν καὶ ἐκεῖ διέτριβεν μετ' αὐτῶν καὶ ἐβάπτιζεν. ²³ ἦν δὲ καὶ ὁ Ἰωάννης βαπτίζων ἐν Αἰνὼν ἐγγὺς τοῦ Σαλείμ, ὅτι ὕδατα πολλὰ ἦν ἐκεῖ, καὶ παρεγίνοντο καὶ ἐβαπτίζοντο· ²⁴ οὔπω γὰρ ἦν βεβλημένος εἰς τὴν φυλακὴν ὁ Ἰωάννης. ²⁵ Ἐγένετο οὖν ζήτησις ἐκ τῶν μαθητῶν Ἰωάννου μετὰ Ἰουδαίου περὶ καθαρισμοῦ. ²⁶ καὶ ἦλθον πρὸς τὸν Ἰωάννην καὶ εἶπαν αὐτῷ, Ῥαββί, ὃς ἦν μετὰ σοῦ πέραν τοῦ Ἰορδάνου, ᾧ σὺ μεμαρτύρηκας, ἴδε οὗτος βαπτίζει καὶ πάντες ἔρχονται πρὸς αὐτόν. ²⁷ ἀπεκρίθη Ἰωάννης καὶ εἶπεν, Οὐ δύναται ἄνθρωπος λαμβάνειν οὐδὲ ἓν ἐὰν μὴ ᾖ δεδομένον αὐτῷ ἐκ τοῦ οὐρανοῦ. ²⁸ αὐτοὶ ὑμεῖς μοι μαρτυρεῖτε ὅτι εἶπον [ὅτι] Οὐκ εἰμὶ ἐγὼ ὁ Χριστός, ἀλλ' ὅτι Ἀπεσταλμένος εἰμὶ ἔμπροσθεν ἐκείνου. ²⁹ ὁ ἔχων τὴν νύμφην νυμφίος ἐστίν· ὁ δὲ φίλος τοῦ νυμφίου ὁ ἑστηκὼς καὶ ἀκούων αὐτοῦ χαρᾷ χαίρει διὰ τὴν φωνὴν τοῦ νυμφίου. αὕτη οὖν ἡ χαρὰ ἡ ἐμὴ πεπλήρωται. ³⁰ ἐκεῖνον δεῖ αὐξάνειν, ἐμὲ δὲ

become less. ¶ **31** "The one who comes from above is above all; the one who is from the earth
ἐλαττοῦσθαι Ὁ ἐρχόμενος ἄνωθεν ἐστίν ἐπάνω πάντων ὁ ὢν ἐκ τῆς γῆς
f.pp d.nsm pt.pm.nsm adv v.pai.3s p.g a.gpn d.nsm pt.pa.nsm p.g d.gsf n.gsf
1783 3836 2262 540 1639 2062 4246 3836 1639 1666 3836 1178

belongs to the earth, and speaks as one from the earth. The one who comes from heaven is above all.
ἐστιν ἐκ τῆς γῆς καὶ λαλεῖ ἐκ τῆς γῆς ὁ ἐρχόμενος ἐκ τοῦ οὐρανοῦ ἐστίν ἐπάνω πάντων
v.pai.3s p.g d.gsf n.gsf cj v.pai.3s p.g d.gsf n.gsf d.nsm pt.pm.nsm ἐκ d.gsm n.gsm v.pai.3s p.g a.gpn
1639 1666 3836 1178 2779 3281 1666 3836 1178 3836 2262 1666 3836 4041 1639 2062 4246

32 He testifies to what he has seen and heard, but no one accepts his testimony. **33** The man who has
μαρτυρεῖ τοῦτο ὃ ἑώρακεν καὶ ἤκουσεν καὶ οὐδεὶς λαμβάνει αὐτοῦ τὴν μαρτυρίαν ὁ
v.pai.3s r.asn r.asn v.rai.3s cj v.aai.3s cj a.nsm v.pai.3s r.gsm.3 d.asf n.asf d.nsm
3455 4047 4005 3972 2779 201 2779 4029 3284 899 3836 3456 3836

accepted it has certified that God is truthful. **34** For the one whom God has sent
λαβὼν αὐτοῦ τὴν μαρτυρίαν ἐσφράγισεν ὅτι ὁ θεὸς ἐστιν ἀληθής γὰρ ὃν ὁ θεὸς ἀπέστειλεν
pt.aa.nsm r.gsm.3 d.asf n.asf v.aai.3s cj d.nsm n.nsm v.pai.3s a.nsm cj r.asm d.nsm n.nsm v.aai.3s
3284 899 3836 3456 5381 4022 3836 2536 1639 239 1142 4005 3836 2536 690

speaks the words of God, for God gives the Spirit without limit. **35** The Father loves the Son and has
λαλεῖ τὰ ῥήματα τοῦ θεοῦ γὰρ δίδωσιν τὸ πνεῦμα οὐ ἐκ μέτρου ὁ πατὴρ ἀγαπᾷ τὸν υἱὸν καὶ
v.pai.3s d.apn n.apn d.gsm n.gsm cj v.pai.3s d.asn n.asn pl p.g n.gsn d.nsm n.nsm v.pai.3s d.asm n.asm cj
3281 3836 4839 3836 2536 1142 1443 3836 4460 4024 1666 3586 3836 4252 26 3836 5626 2779

placed everything in his hands. **36** Whoever believes in the Son has eternal life, but whoever rejects the Son will
δέδωκεν πάντα ἐν αὐτοῦ τῇ χειρὶ ὁ πιστεύων εἰς τὸν υἱὸν ἔχει αἰώνιον ζωὴν δὲ ὁ ἀπειθῶν τῷ υἱῷ
v.rai.3s a.apn p.d r.gsm.3 d.dsf n.dsf d.nsm pt.pa.nsm p.a d.asm n.asm v.pai.3s a.asf n.asf cj d.nsm pt.pa.nsm d.dsm n.dsm
1443 4246 1877 899 3836 5931 3836 4409 1650 3836 5626 2400 173 2437 1254 3836 578 3836 5626 3972

not see life, for God's wrath remains on him."
οὐκ ὄψεται ζωήν ἀλλ' τοῦ θεοῦ ἡ ὀργὴ μένει ἐπ' αὐτόν
pl v.fmi.3s n.asf cj d.gsm n.gsm d.nsf n.nsf v.pai.3s p.a r.asm.3
4024 3972 2437 247 3836 2536 3836 3973 3531 2093 899

Jesus Talks With a Samaritan Woman

4:1 The Pharisees heard that Jesus was gaining and baptizing more disciples than John, **2** although in fact
ὅτι οἱ Φαρισαῖοι ἤκουσαν ὅτι Ἰησοῦς ποιεῖ καὶ βαπτίζει πλείονας μαθητὰς ἢ Ἰωάννης καίτοιγε
cj d.npm n.npm v.aai.3p cj n.nsm v.pai.3s cj v.pai.3s a.apm.c n.apm pl n.nsm cj
4022 3836 5757 201 4022 2652 4472 2779 966 4498 3412 2445 2722 2793

it was not Jesus who baptized, but his disciples. **3** When the Lord learned of this, he left
οὐκ Ἰησοῦς αὐτὸς ἐβάπτιζεν ἀλλ' αὐτοῦ οἱ μαθηταὶ οὖν Ὡς ὁ Ἰησοῦς ἔγνω ἀφῆκεν
pl n.nsm r.nsm v.iai.3s cj r.gsm.3 d.npm n.npm cj cj d.nsm n.nsm v.aai.3s v.aai.3s
4024 2652 899 966 247 899 3836 3412 4036 6055 3836 2652 1182 918

Judea and went back once more to Galilee. ¶ **4** Now he had to go through
τὴν Ἰουδαίαν καὶ ἀπῆλθεν πάλιν εἰς τὴν Γαλιλαίαν δὲ αὐτὸν Ἔδει διέρχεσθαι διὰ
d.asf n.asf cj v.aai.3s adv p.a d.asf n.asf cj r.asm.3 v.iai.3s f.pm p.g
3836 2677 2779 599 4099 1650 3836 1133 1254 899 1256 1451 1328

Samaria. **5** So he came to a town in Samaria called Sychar, near the plot of ground Jacob had
τῆς Σαμαρείας οὖν ἔρχεται εἰς πόλιν τῆς Σαμαρείας λεγομένην Συχὰρ πλησίον τοῦ χωρίου ὃ Ἰακὼβ
d.gsf n.gsf cj v.pmi.3s p.a n.asf d.gsf n.gsf pt.pp.asf n.asf p.g d.gsn n.gsn r.asn n.nsm
3836 4899 4036 2262 1650 4484 3836 4899 3306 5373 4446 3836 6005 4005 2609

given to his son Joseph. **6** Jacob's well was there, and Jesus, tired as he was from the
ἔδωκεν αὐτοῦ τῷ υἱῷ τῷ Ἰωσὴφ δὲ τοῦ Ἰακὼβ πηγὴ ἦν ἐκεῖ οὖν ὁ Ἰησοῦς κεκοπιακὼς ἐκ τῆς
v.aai.3s r.gsm.3 d.dsm n.dsm d.dsm n.dsm cj d.gsm n.gsm n.nsf v.iai.3s adv cj d.nsm n.nsm pt.ra.nsm p.g d.gsf
1443 899 3836 5626 3836 2737 1254 3836 2609 4380 1639 1695 4036 3836 2652 3159 1666 3836

journey, sat down by the well. It was about the sixth hour. ¶ **7** When a Samaritan woman
ὁδοιπορίας ἐκαθέζετο οὕτως ἐπὶ τῇ πηγῇ ἦν ὡς ἕκτη ὥρα ἐκ τῆς Σαμαρείας γυνὴ
n.gsf v.imi.3s adv p.d d.dsf n.dsf v.iai.3s pl a.nsf n.nsf p.g d.gsf n.gsf n.nsf
3845 2757 4048 2093 3836 4380 1639 6055 1761 6052 1666 3836 4899 1222

came to draw water, Jesus said to her, "Will you give me a drink?" **8** (His disciples had gone
ἔρχεται ἀντλῆσαι ὕδωρ ὁ Ἰησοῦς λέγει αὐτῇ δός μοι πεῖν γὰρ αὐτοῦ οἱ μαθηταὶ ἀπεληλύθεισαν
v.pmi.3s f.aa n.asn d.nsm n.nsm v.pai.3s r.dsf.3 v.aam.2s r.ds.1 f.aa cj r.gsm.3 d.npm n.npm v.lai.3p
2262 533 5623 3836 2652 3306 899 1443 1609 4403 1142 899 3836 3412 599

ἐλαττοῦσθαι. ¶ **31** Ὁ ἄνωθεν ἐρχόμενος ἐπάνω πάντων ἐστίν· ὁ ὢν ἐκ τῆς γῆς ἐκ τῆς γῆς ἐστιν καὶ ἐκ τῆς γῆς λαλεῖ. ὁ ἐκ τοῦ οὐρανοῦ ἐρχόμενος [ἐπάνω πάντων ἐστίν·] **32** ὃ ἑώρακεν καὶ ἤκουσεν τοῦτο μαρτυρεῖ, καὶ τὴν μαρτυρίαν αὐτοῦ οὐδεὶς λαμβάνει. **33** ὁ λαβὼν αὐτοῦ τὴν μαρτυρίαν ἐσφράγισεν ὅτι ὁ θεὸς ἀληθής ἐστιν. **34** ὃν γὰρ ἀπέστειλεν ὁ θεὸς τὰ ῥήματα τοῦ θεοῦ λαλεῖ, οὐ γὰρ ἐκ μέτρου δίδωσιν τὸ πνεῦμα. **35** ὁ πατὴρ ἀγαπᾷ τὸν υἱὸν καὶ πάντα δέδωκεν ἐν τῇ χειρὶ αὐτοῦ. **36** ὁ πιστεύων εἰς τὸν υἱὸν ἔχει ζωὴν αἰώνιον· ὁ δὲ ἀπειθῶν τῷ υἱῷ οὐκ ὄψεται ζωήν, ἀλλ' ἡ ὀργὴ τοῦ θεοῦ μένει ἐπ' αὐτόν.

4:1 Ὡς οὖν ἔγνω ὁ κύριος «Ἰησοῦς» ὅτι ἤκουσαν οἱ Φαρισαῖοι ὅτι Ἰησοῦς πλείονας μαθητὰς ποιεῖ καὶ βαπτίζει ἢ Ἰωάννης **2** — καίτοιγε Ἰησοῦς αὐτὸς οὐκ ἐβάπτιζεν ἀλλ' οἱ μαθηταὶ αὐτοῦ — **3** ἀφῆκεν τὴν Ἰουδαίαν καὶ ἀπῆλθεν πάλιν εἰς τὴν Γαλιλαίαν. ¶ **4** ἔδει δὲ αὐτὸν διέρχεσθαι διὰ τῆς Σαμαρείας. **5** ἔρχεται οὖν εἰς πόλιν τῆς Σαμαρείας λεγομένην Συχὰρ πλησίον τοῦ χωρίου ὃ ἔδωκεν Ἰακὼβ [τῷ] Ἰωσὴφ τῷ υἱῷ αὐτοῦ· **6** ἦν δὲ ἐκεῖ πηγὴ τοῦ Ἰακὼβ. ὁ οὖν Ἰησοῦς κεκοπιακὼς ἐκ τῆς ὁδοιπορίας ἐκαθέζετο οὕτως ἐπὶ τῇ πηγῇ· ὥρα ἦν ὡς ἕκτη. ¶ **7** Ἔρχεται γυνὴ ἐκ τῆς Σαμαρείας ἀντλῆσαι ὕδωρ. λέγει αὐτῇ ὁ Ἰησοῦς, Δός μοι πεῖν· **8** οἱ γὰρ μαθηταὶ αὐτοῦ ἀπεληλύθεισαν εἰς τὴν πόλιν ἵνα τροφὰς ἀγοράσωσιν. **9** λέγει οὖν αὐτῷ ἡ γυνὴ

into the town to buy　　food.) **9** The Samaritan　woman said to him, "You are　a Jew　and I am　a
εἰς τὴν πόλιν ἵνα ἀγοράσωσιν τροφάς οὖν ἡ ᾐ Σαμαρῖτις γυνὴ λέγει → αὐτῷ σὺ ὢν Ἰουδαῖος οὔσης
p.a d.asf n.asf cj v.aas.3p n.apf cj d.nsf d.nsf n.nsf n.nsf v.pai.3s r.dsm.3 r.ns.2 pt.pa.nsm a.nsm pt.pa.gsf
1650 3836 4484 2671 60 5575 4036 3836 3836 4902 1222 3306 899 5148 1639 2681 1639

Samaritan woman. How can you ask　me for a drink?" (For Jews　do not associate with Samaritans.)
Σαμαρίτιδος γυναικὸς πῶς → αἰτεῖς παρ᾽ ἐμοῦ πεῖν γὰρ Ἰουδαῖοι → οὐ συγχρῶνται ← Σαμαρίταις
n.gsf n.gsf cj v.pai.2s r.gs.1 f.aa cj a.npm v.pmi.3p n.dpm
4902 1222 4802 160 4123 1609 4403 1142 2681 5178 4024 5178 4901

10 Jesus answered　her, "If you knew the gift　of God　and who it is　that asks　you　for a
Ἰησοῦς ἀπεκρίθη καὶ εἶπεν αὐτῇ εἰ → ᾔδεις τὴν δωρεάν → ⸤τοῦ θεοῦ⸥ καὶ τίς ἐστιν ὁ λέγων σοι δός μοι
n.nsm v.api.3s cj v.aai.3s r.dsf.3 cj v.lai.2s d.asf n.asf d.gsm n.gsm cj r.nsm v.pai.3s d.nsm pt.pa.nsm r.ds.2 v.aam.2s r.ds.1
2652 646 2779 3306 899 1623 3857 3836 1561 3836 2536 2779 5515 1639 3836 3306 5148 1443 1609

drink, you would have asked him and he would have given you living water." **11** "Sir," the woman said, "you
πεῖν σὺ ἂν → ᾔτησας αὐτὸν καὶ → ἂν → ἔδωκεν σοι ζῶν ὕδωρ κύριε ἡ γυνή λέγει αὐτῷ →
f.aa r.ns.1 pl v.aai.2s r.asm.3 cj pl v.aai.3s r.ds.2 pt.pa.asn n.asn n.vsm d.nsf n.nsf v.pai.3s r.dsm.3
4403 5148 323 160 899 2779 1443 323 1443 5148 2409 5623 3261 3836 1222 3306 899

have nothing to draw with and the well is deep. Where can you get this living water? **12** Are you
ἔχεις οὔτε → ἄντλημα ← καὶ τὸ φρέαρ ἐστὶν βαθύ οὖν πόθεν → → ἔχεις τὸ ⸤τὸ ζῶν⸥ ὕδωρ μὴ εἰ σύ
v.pai.2s cj n.asn cj d.nsn n.nsn v.pai.3s a.nsn cj cj v.pai.2s d.asn d.asn pt.pa.asn n.asn pl v.pai.2s r.ns.2
2400 4046 534 2779 3836 5853 1639 960 4036 4470 2400 3836 3836 2409 5623 3590 1639 5148

greater than our father Jacob, who gave us the well and drank from it himself, as did also his sons
μείζων ← ἡμῶν ⸤τοῦ πατρός⸥ Ἰακώβ ὃς ἔδωκεν ἡμῖν τὸ φρέαρ καὶ ἔπιεν ἐξ αὐτοῦ αὐτὸς καὶ αὐτοῦ ⸤οἱ υἱοὶ⸥
a.nsm.c r.gp.1 d.gsm n.gsm n.gsm r.nsm v.aai.3s r.dp.1 d.asn n.asn cj v.aai.3s p.g r.gsn.3 r.nsm cj r.gsm.3 d.npm n.npm
3489 7005 3836 4252 2609 4005 1443 7005 3836 5853 2779 4403 1666 899 899 2779 899 3836 5626

and his flocks　and herds?" **13** Jesus answered,　"Everyone who drinks　this water　will be
καὶ αὐτοῦ ⸤τὰ θρέμματα⸥ ← ← Ἰησοῦς ἀπεκρίθη καὶ εἶπεν αὐτῇ πᾶς ὁ πίνων ἐκ τούτου ⸤τοῦ ὕδατος⸥ →
cj r.gsm.3 d.npn n.npn n.nsm v.api.3s cj v.aai.3s r.dsf.3 a.nsm d.nsm pt.pa.nsm p.g r.gsn d.gsn n.gsn
2779 899 3836 2576 2652 646 2779 3306 899 4246 3836 4403 1666 4047 3836 5623

thirsty again, **14** but whoever drinks　the water　I give him will never　thirst. Indeed, the water
διψήσει πάλιν δ᾽ ὃς ἂν πίῃ ἐκ τοῦ ὕδατος οὗ ἐγὼ δώσω αὐτῷ → ⸤οὐ μὴ⸥ εἰς τὸν αἰῶνα διψήσει ἀλλὰ τὸ ὕδωρ
v.fai.3s adv cj r.nsm pl v.aas.3s p.g d.gsn n.gsn r.gsn r.ns.1 v.fai.1s r.dsm.3 pl pl p.a d.asm n.asm v.fai.3s cj d.nsn n.nsn
1498 4099 1254 4005 323 4403 1666 3836 5623 4005 1609 1443 899 4024 3590 1650 3836 172 1498 247 3836 5623

I give him will become in him a spring of water welling　up to eternal life." **15** The woman said to him,
ὃ → δώσω αὐτῷ → γενήσεται ἐν αὐτῷ πηγὴ → ὕδατος ἁλλομένου ← εἰς αἰώνιον ζωήν ἡ γυνὴ λέγει πρὸς αὐτὸν
r.asn v.fai.1s r.dsm.3 v.fmi.3s p.d r.dsm.3 n.nsf n.gsn pt.pm.gsn p.a a.asf n.asf d.nsf n.nsf v.pai.3s p.a r.asm.3
4005 1443 899 1181 1877 899 4380 5623 256 1650 173 2437 3836 1222 3306 4639 899

"Sir, give me this water　so that I　won't get thirsty and have to keep coming here to draw water." **16** He
κύριε δός μοι τοῦτο τὸ ὕδωρ ἵνα ← μὴ → διψῶ μηδὲ → διέρχωμαι ἐνθάδε → ἀντλεῖν →
n.vsm v.aam.2s r.ds.1 r.asn d.asn n.asn cj pl v.pas.1s cj v.pms.1s adv f.pa
3261 1443 1609 4047 3836 5623 2671 1498 3590 1498 3593 1451 1924 533

told her, "Go, call　your husband　and come back." **17** "I have no husband," she　replied.
λέγει αὐτῇ ὕπαγε φώνησον σου ⸤τὸν ἄνδρα⸥ καὶ ἐλθὲ ἐνθάδε → ἔχω οὐκ ἄνδρα ⸤ἡ γυνὴ⸥ ἀπεκρίθη καὶ εἶπεν αὐτῷ
v.pai.3s r.dsf.3 v.pam.2s v.aam.2s r.gs.2 d.asm n.asm cj v.aam.2s adv v.pai.1s pl n.asm d.nsf n.nsf v.api.3s cj v.aai.3s r.dsm.3
3306 899 5632 5888 5148 3836 467 2779 2262 1924 2400 4024 467 3836 1222 646 2779 3306 899

Jesus　said to her, "You are right when you say　you have no husband. **18** The fact is, you have had five
⸤ὁ Ἰησοῦς⸥ λέγει → αὐτῇ καλῶς → εἶπας ὅτι → ἔχω οὐκ ἄνδρα → γὰρ ← → ἔσχες πέντε
d.nsm n.nsm v.pai.3s r.dsf.3 adv v.aai.2s cj v.pai.1s pl n.asm cj v.aai.2s a.apm
3836 2652 3306 899 2822 3306 4022 2400 4024 467 1142 2400 4297

husbands, and the man you now have is　not your husband. What you have just said　is quite true." **19** "Sir," the
ἄνδρας καὶ ὃν → νῦν ἔχεις ἐστιν οὐκ σου ἀνήρ τοῦτο εἴρηκας ἀληθὲς κύριε ἡ
n.apm cj r.asm adv v.pai.2s v.pai.3s pl r.gs.2 n.nsm r.asn v.rai.2s a.asn n.vsm d.nsf
467 2779 4005 2400 3814 2400 1639 4024 5148 467 4047 3306 239 3261 3836

woman said,　"I can see　that you are a prophet. **20** Our fathers　worshiped　on this mountain, but you
γυνὴ λέγει αὐτῷ → θεωρῶ ὅτι σὺ εἶ προφήτης ἡμῶν ⸤οἱ πατέρες⸥ προσεκύνησαν ἐν τούτῳ ⸤τῷ ὄρει⸥ καὶ ὑμεῖς
n.nsf v.pai.3s r.dsm.3 v.pai.1s cj r.ns.2 v.pai.2s n.nsm r.gp.1 d.npm n.npm v.aai.3p p.d r.dsn d.dsn n.dsn cj r.np.2
1222 3306 899 2555 4022 5148 1639 4737 7005 3836 4252 4686 1877 4047 3836 4001 2779 7007

ἡ Σαμαρῖτις, Πῶς σὺ Ἰουδαῖος ὢν παρ᾽ ἐμοῦ πεῖν αἰτεῖς γυναικὸς Σαμαρίτιδος οὔσης; οὐ γὰρ συγχρῶνται Ἰουδαῖοι Σαμαρίταις. **10** ἀπεκρίθη Ἰησοῦς καὶ εἶπεν αὐτῇ, Εἰ ᾔδεις τὴν δωρεὰν τοῦ θεοῦ καὶ τίς ἐστιν ὁ λέγων σοι, Δός μοι πεῖν, σὺ ἂν ᾔτησας αὐτὸν καὶ ἔδωκεν ἄν σοι ὕδωρ ζῶν. **11** λέγει αὐτῷ [ἡ γυνή], Κύριε, οὔτε ἄντλημα ἔχεις καὶ τὸ φρέαρ ἐστὶν βαθύ· πόθεν οὖν ἔχεις τὸ ὕδωρ τὸ ζῶν; **12** μὴ σὺ μείζων εἶ τοῦ πατρὸς ἡμῶν Ἰακώβ, ὃς ἔδωκεν ἡμῖν τὸ φρέαρ καὶ αὐτὸς ἐξ αὐτοῦ ἔπιεν καὶ οἱ υἱοὶ αὐτοῦ καὶ τὰ θρέμματα αὐτοῦ; **13** ἀπεκρίθη Ἰησοῦς καὶ εἶπεν αὐτῇ, Πᾶς ὁ πίνων ἐκ τοῦ ὕδατος τούτου διψήσει πάλιν· **14** ὃς δ᾽ ἂν πίῃ ἐκ τοῦ ὕδατος οὗ ἐγὼ δώσω αὐτῷ, οὐ μὴ διψήσει εἰς τὸν αἰῶνα, ἀλλὰ τὸ ὕδωρ ὃ δώσω αὐτῷ γενήσεται ἐν αὐτῷ πηγὴ ὕδατος ἁλλομένου εἰς ζωὴν αἰώνιον. **15** λέγει πρὸς αὐτὸν ἡ γυνή, Κύριε, δός μοι τοῦτο τὸ ὕδωρ, ἵνα μὴ διψῶ μηδὲ διέρχωμαι ἐνθάδε ἀντλεῖν. **16** Λέγει αὐτῇ, Ὕπαγε φώνησον τὸν ἄνδρα σου καὶ ἐλθὲ ἐνθάδε. **17** ἀπεκρίθη ἡ γυνὴ καὶ εἶπεν αὐτῷ, Οὐκ ἔχω ἄνδρα. λέγει αὐτῇ ὁ Ἰησοῦς, Καλῶς εἶπας ὅτι Ἄνδρα οὐκ ἔχω· **18** πέντε γὰρ ἄνδρας ἔσχες καὶ νῦν ὃν ἔχεις οὐκ ἔστιν σου ἀνήρ· τοῦτο ἀληθὲς εἴρηκας. **19** λέγει αὐτῷ ἡ γυνή, Κύριε, θεωρῶ ὅτι προφήτης εἶ σύ. **20** οἱ πατέρες ἡμῶν ἐν τῷ ὄρει τούτῳ

Jews claim that the place where we must worship is in Jerusalem." **21** Jesus declared, "Believe me, woman,
λέγετε ὅτι ὁ τόπος ὅπου δεῖ προσκυνεῖν ἐστιν ἐν Ἱεροσολύμοις ὁ Ἰησοῦς λέγει αὐτῇ πίστευε μοι γύναι
v.pai.2p cj d.nsm n.nsm cj v.pai.3s f.pa v.pai.3s p.d n.dpn d.nsm n.nsm v.pai.3s r.dsf.3 v.pam.2s r.ds.1 n.vsf
3306 4022 3836 5536 3963 1256 4686 1639 1877 2642 3836 2652 3306 899 4409 1609 1222

a time is coming when you will worship the Father neither on this mountain nor in Jerusalem. **22** You
ὅτι ὥρα → ἔρχεται ὅτε → → προσκυνήσετε τῷ πατρί οὔτε ἐν τούτῳ τῷ ὄρει οὔτε ἐν Ἱεροσολύμοις ὑμεῖς
cj n.nsf v.pmi.3s cj v.fai.2p d.dsm n.dsm p.d r.dsn d.dsn n.dsn cj p.d n.dpn r.np.2
4022 6052 2262 4021 4686 3836 4252 4046 1877 4047 3836 4001 4046 1877 2642 7007

Samaritans worship what you do not know; we worship what we do know, for salvation is from the
προσκυνεῖτε ὃ ↗ → οὐκ οἴδατε ἡμεῖς προσκυνοῦμεν ὃ → → οἴδαμεν ὅτι ἡ σωτηρία ἐστιν ἐκ τῶν
v.pai.2p r.asn pl v.rai.2p r.np.1 v.pai.1p r.asn v.rai.1p cj d.nsf n.nsf v.pai.3s p.g d.gpm
4686 4005 3857 3857 4024 3857 7005 4686 4005 3857 4022 3836 5401 1639 1666 3836

Jews. **23** Yet a time is coming and has now come when the true worshipers will worship the Father in
Ἰουδαίων ἀλλὰ ὥρα → ἔρχεται καὶ ↗ νῦν ἐστιν ὅτε οἱ ἀληθινοὶ προσκυνηταὶ → προσκυνήσουσιν τῷ πατρὶ ἐν
a.gpm cj n.nsf v.pmi.3s cj adv v.pai.3s cj d.npm a.npm n.npm v.fai.3p d.dsm n.dsm p.d
2681 247 6052 2262 2779 1639 3814 1639 4021 3836 240 4687 4686 3836 4252 1877

spirit and truth, for they are the kind of worshipers the Father seeks. **24** God is spirit, and
πνεύματι καὶ ἀληθείᾳ γὰρ καὶ τοιούτους τοὺς προσκυνοῦντας αὐτὸν ὁ πατὴρ ζητεῖ ὁ θεός πνεῦμα καὶ
n.dsn cj n.dsf cj adv r.apm d.apm pt.pa.apm r.asm.3 d.nsm n.nsm v.pai.3s d.nsm n.nsm n.nsn cj
4460 2779 237 1142 2779 5525 3836 4686 899 3836 4252 2426 3836 2536 4460 2779

his worshipers must worship in spirit and in truth." **25** The woman said, "I know that Messiah"
τοὺς προσκυνοῦντας δεῖ προσκυνεῖν αὐτὸν ἐν πνεύματι καὶ → ἀληθείᾳ ἡ γυνή λέγει αὐτῷ οἶδα ὅτι Μεσσίας
d.apm pt.pa.apm v.pai.3s f.pa r.asm.3 p.d n.dsn cj n.dsf d.nsf n.nsf v.pai.3s r.dsm.3 v.rai.1s cj n.nsm
3836 4686 1256 4686 899 1877 4460 2779 237 3836 1222 3306 899 3857 4022 3549

(called Christ) "is coming. When he comes, he will explain everything to us." **26** Then Jesus declared,
ὁ λεγόμενος χριστός → ἔρχεται ὅταν ἐκεῖνος ἔλθῃ → → ἀναγγελεῖ ἅπαντα → ἡμῖν ὁ Ἰησοῦς λέγει
d.nsm pt.pp.nsm n.nsm v.pmi.3s cj r.nsm v.aas.3s v.fai.3s a.apn r.dp.1 d.nsm n.nsm v.pai.3s
3836 3306 5986 2262 4020 1697 2262 334 570 7005 3836 2652 3306

"I who speak to you am he."
αὐτῇ ἐγώ ὁ λαλῶν → σοι εἰμι
r.dsf.3 r.ns.1 d.nsm pt.pa.nsm r.ds.2 v.pai.1s
899 1609 3836 3281 5148 1639

The Disciples Rejoin Jesus

4:27 Just then his disciples returned and were surprised to find him talking with a woman. But no
Καὶ ἐπὶ τούτῳ αὐτοῦ οἱ μαθηταί ἦλθαν καὶ → ἐθαύμαζον ὅτι → ἐλάλει μετὰ γυναικὸς μέντοι →
cj p.d r.dsn r.gsm.3 d.npm n.npm v.aai.3p cj v.iai.3p cj v.iai.3s p.g n.gsf cj
2779 2093 4047 899 3836 3412 2262 2779 2513 4022 3281 3552 1222 3530

one asked, "What do you want?" or "Why are you talking with her?" ¶ **28** Then, leaving her water
οὐδεὶς εἶπεν τί → → ζητεῖς ἢ τί → → λαλεῖς μετ' αὐτῆς οὖν ἀφῆκεν αὐτῆς →
a.nsm v.aai.3s r.asn v.pai.2s cj r.asn v.pai.2s p.g r.gsf.3 cj v.aai.3s r.gsf.3
4029 3306 5515 2426 2445 5515 3281 3552 899 4036 918 899

jar, the woman went back to the town and said to the people, **29** "Come, see a man who told me
τὴν ὑδρίαν ἡ γυνή καὶ ἀπῆλθεν ← εἰς τὴν πόλιν καὶ λέγει τοῖς ἀνθρώποις δεῦτε ἴδετε ἄνθρωπον ὃς εἶπεν μοι
d.asf n.asf d.nsf n.nsf cj v.aai.3s p.a d.asf n.asf cj v.pai.3s d.dpm n.dpm adv v.aam.2p n.asm r.nsm v.aai.3s r.ds.1
3836 5620 3836 1222 2779 599 1650 3836 4484 2779 3306 3836 476 1307 1625 476 4005 3306 1609

everything I ever did. Could this be the Christ?" **30** They came out of the town and made their way
πάντα ↗ ὅσα ἐποίησα μήτι οὗτος ἐστιν ὁ χριστός → ἐξῆλθον ἐκ τῆς πόλεως καὶ → → ἤρχοντο
a.apn r.apn v.aai.1s pl r.nsm v.pai.3s d.nsm n.nsm v.aai.3p p.g d.gsf n.gsf cj v.imi.3p
4246 4472 4012 4472 3614 4047 1639 3836 5986 2002 1666 3836 4484 2779 2262

toward him. ¶ **31** Meanwhile his disciples urged him, "Rabbi, eat something." **32** But he said to them,
πρὸς αὐτόν Ἐν τῷ μεταξὺ οἱ μαθηταὶ ἠρώτων αὐτὸν λέγοντες ῥαββί φάγε δὲ ὁ εἶπεν αὐτοῖς
p.a r.asm.3 p.d d.dsn adv d.npm n.npm v.iai.3p r.asm.3 pt.pa.npm n.vsm v.aam.2s cj d.nsm v.aai.3s r.dpm.3
4639 899 1877 3836 3568 3836 3412 2263 899 3306 4806 2266 1254 3836 3306 899

"I have food to eat that you know nothing about." **33** Then his disciples said to each other, "Could
ἐγὼ ἔχω βρῶσιν φαγεῖν ἣν ὑμεῖς οἴδατε οὐκ οὖν οἱ μαθηταὶ ἔλεγον πρὸς ἀλλήλους ← μὴ
r.ns.1 v.pai.1s n.asf f.aa r.asf r.np.2 v.rai.2p pl cj d.npm n.npm v.iai.3p p.a r.apm pl
1609 2400 1111 2266 4005 7007 3857 4024 4036 3836 3412 3306 4639 253 3590 5770

προσεκύνησαν· καὶ ὑμεῖς λέγετε ὅτι ἐν Ἱεροσολύμοις ἐστὶν ὁ τόπος ὅπου προσκυνεῖν δεῖ. **21** λέγει αὐτῇ ὁ Ἰησοῦς, Πίστευέ μοι, γύναι, ὅτι ἔρχεται ὥρα ὅτε οὔτε ἐν τῷ ὄρει τούτῳ οὔτε ἐν Ἱεροσολύμοις προσκυνήσετε τῷ πατρί. **22** ὑμεῖς προσκυνεῖτε ὃ οὐκ οἴδατε· ἡμεῖς προσκυνοῦμεν ὃ οἴδαμεν, ὅτι ἡ σωτηρία ἐκ τῶν Ἰουδαίων ἐστίν. **23** ἀλλὰ ἔρχεται ὥρα καὶ νῦν ἐστιν, ὅτε οἱ ἀληθινοὶ προσκυνηταὶ προσκυνήσουσιν τῷ πατρὶ ἐν πνεύματι καὶ ἀληθείᾳ· καὶ γὰρ ὁ πατὴρ τοιούτους ζητεῖ τοὺς προσκυνοῦντας αὐτόν. **24** πνεῦμα ὁ θεός, καὶ τοὺς προσκυνοῦντας αὐτὸν ἐν πνεύματι καὶ ἀληθείᾳ δεῖ προσκυνεῖν. **25** λέγει αὐτῷ ἡ γυνή, Οἶδα ὅτι Μεσσίας ἔρχεται ὁ λεγόμενος Χριστός· ὅταν ἔλθῃ ἐκεῖνος, ἀναγγελεῖ ἡμῖν ἅπαντα. **26** λέγει αὐτῇ ὁ Ἰησοῦς, Ἐγώ εἰμι, ὁ λαλῶν σοι.

4:27 Καὶ ἐπὶ τούτῳ ἦλθαν οἱ μαθηταὶ αὐτοῦ καὶ ἐθαύμαζον ὅτι μετὰ γυναικὸς ἐλάλει· οὐδεὶς μέντοι εἶπεν, Τί ζητεῖς; «ζητεῖς» ἢ, «ἢ» Τί «τί» λαλεῖς μετ' αὐτῆς; ¶ **28** ἀφῆκεν οὖν τὴν ὑδρίαν αὐτῆς ἡ γυνὴ καὶ ἀπῆλθεν εἰς τὴν πόλιν καὶ λέγει τοῖς ἀνθρώποις, **29** Δεῦτε ἴδετε ἄνθρωπον ὃς εἶπέν μοι πάντα ὅσα ἐποίησα, μήτι οὗτός ἐστιν ὁ Χριστός; **30** ἐξῆλθον ἐκ τῆς πόλεως καὶ ἤρχοντο πρὸς αὐτόν. ¶ **31** Ἐν τῷ μεταξὺ ἠρώτων αὐτὸν οἱ μαθηταὶ λέγοντες, Ῥαββί, φάγε. **32** ὁ δὲ εἶπεν αὐτοῖς, Ἐγὼ βρῶσιν ἔχω φαγεῖν ἣν ὑμεῖς οὐκ οἴδατε. **33** ἔλεγον οὖν οἱ μαθηταὶ πρὸς ἀλλήλους, Μή τις ἤνεγκεν αὐτῷ φαγεῖν; **34** λέγει αὐτοῖς ὁ Ἰησοῦς, Ἐμὸν

someone have brought him food?" **34** "My food," said Jesus,   "is   to do   the will   of him who
τις   →   ἤνεγκεν αὐτῷ φαγεῖν ἐμὸν βρῶμα λέγει ὁ Ἰησοῦς αὐτοῖς ἐστιν ἵνα ποιήσω τὸ θέλημα → τοῦ ←
r.nsm   v.aai.3s r.dsm.3 f.aa r.nsn.1 n.nsn v.pai.3s d.nsm n.nsm r.dpm.3 v.pai.3s cj v.aas.1s d.asn n.asn d.gsm
5516   5770   899   2266   1847 1109 3306 3836 2652   899   1639   2671 4472   3836 2525   3836

sent   me and to finish his work. **35** Do you not say,   'Four months more and then the harvest'?
πέμψαντος με καὶ → τελειώσω αὐτοῦ ⌐τὸ ἔργον⌐ → ὑμεῖς οὐχ λέγετε ὅτι ἐστιν → τετράμηνος ἔτι καὶ ὁ θερισμὸς
pt.aa.gsm r.as.1 cj v.aas.1s r.gsm.3 d.asn n.asn   r.np.2 v.pai.2p cj v.pai.3s n.nsf adv cj d.nsm n.nsm
4287   1609 2779   5457   899 3836 2240   3306 7007 4024 3306 4022 1639   5485 2285 2779 3836 2546

         I tell you, open your eyes   and look   at the fields! They are ripe for harvest.
ἔρχεται ἰδοὺ λέγω ὑμῖν ἐπάρατε ὑμῶν ⌐τοὺς ὀφθαλμοὺς⌐ καὶ θεάσασθε ← τὰς χώρας ὅτι εἰσιν λευκαί πρὸς θερισμόν
v.pmi.3s j v.pai.1s r.dp.2 v.aam.2p r.gp.2 d.apm n.apm   cj v.amm.2p   d.apf n.apf cj v.pai.3p a.npf p.a n.asm
2262   2627 3306 7007 2048 /007 3836 4057   2779 2517   3836 6001 4022 1639 3328 4639 2546

36 Even now the reaper draws his wages, even now he harvests the crop for eternal life, so that the sower and
→ ἤδη ὁ θερίζων λαμβάνει μισθὸν καὶ → συνάγει καρπὸν εἰς αἰώνιον ζωὴν ἵνα ὁ σπείρων καὶ
adv d.nsm pt.pa.nsm v.pai.3s n.asm cj v.pai.3s n.asm p.a a.asf n.asf cj d.nsm pt.pa.nsm cj
2453 3836 2545   3284 3635 2779   5251   2843 1650 173 2437 2671 3836 5062 2779

the reaper may be glad together. **37** Thus   the saying 'One   sows   and another reaps' is
ὁ θερίζων → → χαίρῃ ὁμοῦ ⌐γὰρ ἐν τούτῳ⌐ ὁ λόγος ὅτι ἄλλος ἐστιν ὁ σπείρων καὶ ἄλλος ⌐ὁ θερίζων⌐ ἐστιν
d.nsm pt.pa.nsm v.pas.3s adv cj p.d r.dsn d.nsm n.nsm cj r.nsm v.pai.3s d.nsm pt.pa.nsm cj r.nsm d.nsm pt.pa.nsm v.pai.3s
3836 2545   5897 3938 1142 1877 4047 3836 3364 4022 257 1639 3836 5062 2779 257 3836 2545 1639

true. **38** I sent   you to reap what you have not worked for. Others have done the hard work, and
ἀληθινός ἐγὼ ἀπέστειλα ὑμᾶς → θερίζειν ὃ ὑμεῖς ↱ οὐχ κεκοπιάκατε ← ἄλλοι → → → κεκοπιάκασιν καὶ
a.nsm r.ns.1 v.aai.1s r.ap.2 f.pa r.asn r.np.2 pl v.rai.2p r.npm   v.rai.3p cj
240 1609 690 7007 2545 4005 7007 4024 3159   257   3159 2779

you have reaped   the benefits of their labor."
ὑμεῖς → εἰσεληλύθατε → → εἰς αὐτῶν ⌐τὸν κόπον⌐
r.np.2 v.rai.2p   p.a r.gpm.3 d.asm n.asm
7007 1656   1650 899 3836 3160

Many Samaritans Believe

4:39 Many of the Samaritans from that town   believed in him because of the woman's
δὲ πολλοὶ → τῶν Σαμαριτῶν Ἐκ ἐκείνης ⌐τῆς πόλεως⌐ ἐπίστευσαν εἰς αὐτὸν διὰ ← τὸν ⌐τῆς γυναικὸς⌐
cj a.npm d.gpm n.gpm p.g r.gsf d.gsf n.gsf v.aai.3p p.a r.asm.3 p.a d.asm d.gsf n.gsf
1254 4498 3836 4901 1666 1697 3836 4484 4409 1650 899 1328 3836 3836 1222

testimony,   "He told me everything I ever did." **40** So when the Samaritans came to him, they urged
⌐λόγον μαρτυρούσης⌐ ὅτι → εἶπεν μοι πάντα ἃ → ἐποίησα οὖν ὡς οἱ Σαμαρῖται ἦλθον πρὸς αὐτὸν → ἠρώτων
n.asm pt.pa.gsf cj v.aai.3s r.ds.1 a.apn r.apn v.aai.1s cj cj d.npm n.npm v.aai.3p p.a r.asm.3 v.iai.3p
3364 3455 4022 3306 1609 4246 4005 4472 4036 6055 3836 4901 2262 4639 899 2263

him to stay with them, and he stayed two days. **41** And because of his words many more became
αὐτὸν → μεῖναι παρ' αὐτοῖς καὶ → ἔμεινεν ἐκεῖ δύο ἡμέρας καὶ διὰ ← αὐτοῦ ⌐τὸν λόγον⌐ πολλῷ πλείους
r.asm.3 f.aa p.d r.dpm.3 cj v.aai.3s adv a.apf n.apf cj p.a r.gsm.3 d.asm n.asm a.npm.c
899 3531 4123 899 2779 3531 1695 1545 2465 2779 1328 899 3836 3364 4498 4498

believers. ¶ **42** They said to the woman, "We no longer believe just because of what you said;
ἐπίστευσαν τε ἔλεγον → τῇ γυναικὶ ὅτι → οὐκέτι ← πιστεύομεν διὰ ← σὴν ⌐τὴν λαλιὰν⌐
v.aai.3p cj v.iai.3p d.dsf n.dsf cj adv   v.pai.1p p.a r.asf.2 d.asf n.asf
4409 5445 3306 3836 1222 4022 4409 4033   4409 1328 5050 3836 3282

now we have heard for ourselves, and we know that this man really is the Savior of the world."
γὰρ → → ἀκηκόαμεν αὐτοὶ καὶ → οἴδαμεν ὅτι οὗτος ← ἀληθῶς ἐστιν ὁ σωτὴρ → τοῦ κόσμου
cj v.rai.1p r.npm cj v.rai.1p cj r.nsm adv v.pai.3s d.nsm n.nsm d.gsm n.gsm
1142 201 899 2779 3857 4022 4047 242 1639 3836 5400 3836 3180

Jesus Heals the Official's Son

4:43 After the two days he left for Galilee. **44** (Now Jesus himself had pointed out that a
δὲ Μετὰ τὰς δύο ἡμέρας → ἐξῆλθεν ἐκεῖθεν εἰς τὴν Γαλιλαίαν γὰρ Ἰησοῦς αὐτὸς → ἐμαρτύρησεν ← ὅτι
cj p.a d.apf a.apf n.apf v.aai.3s adv p.a d.asf n.asf cj n.nsm r.nsm v.aai.3s cj
1254 3552 3836 1545 2465 2002 1696 1650 3836 1133 1142 2652 899 3455 4022

βρῶμά ἐστιν ἵνα ποιήσω τὸ θέλημα τοῦ πέμψαντός με καὶ τελειώσω αὐτοῦ τὸ ἔργον. 35 οὐχ ὑμεῖς λέγετε ὅτι Ἔτι τετράμηνός ἐστιν καὶ ὁ θερισμὸς ἔρχεται; ἰδοὺ λέγω ὑμῖν, ἐπάρατε τοὺς ὀφθαλμοὺς ὑμῶν καὶ θεάσασθε τὰς χώρας ὅτι λευκαί εἰσιν πρὸς θερισμόν. ἤδη 36 ὁ θερίζων μισθὸν λαμβάνει καὶ συνάγει καρπὸν εἰς ζωὴν αἰώνιον, ἵνα ὁ σπείρων ὁμοῦ χαίρῃ καὶ ὁ θερίζων. 37 ἐν γὰρ τούτῳ ὁ λόγος ἐστὶν ἀληθινὸς ὅτι Ἄλλος ἐστὶν ὁ σπείρων καὶ ἄλλος ὁ θερίζων. 38 ἐγὼ ἀπέστειλα ὑμᾶς θερίζειν ὃ οὐχ ὑμεῖς κεκοπιάκατε· ἄλλοι κεκοπιάκασιν καὶ ὑμεῖς εἰς τὸν κόπον αὐτῶν εἰσεληλύθατε.

4:39 Ἐκ δὲ τῆς πόλεως ἐκείνης πολλοὶ ἐπίστευσαν εἰς αὐτὸν τῶν Σαμαριτῶν διὰ τὸν λόγον τῆς γυναικὸς μαρτυρούσης ὅτι Εἶπέν μοι πάντα ἃ ἐποίησα 40 ὡς οὖν ἦλθον πρὸς αὐτὸν οἱ Σαμαρῖται, ἠρώτων αὐτὸν μεῖναι παρ' αὐτοῖς· καὶ ἔμεινεν ἐκεῖ δύο ἡμέρας. 41 καὶ πολλῷ πλείους ἐπίστευσαν διὰ τὸν λόγον αὐτοῦ, ¶ 42 τῇ τε γυναικὶ ἔλεγον ὅτι Οὐκέτι διὰ τὴν σὴν λαλιὰν πιστεύομεν, αὐτοὶ γὰρ ἀκηκόαμεν καὶ οἴδαμεν ὅτι οὗτός ἐστιν ἀληθῶς ὁ σωτὴρ τοῦ κόσμου.

4:43 Μετὰ δὲ τὰς δύο ἡμέρας ἐξῆλθεν ἐκεῖθεν εἰς τὴν Γαλιλαίαν· 44 αὐτὸς γὰρ Ἰησοῦς ἐμαρτύρησεν ὅτι προφήτης ἐν τῇ ἰδίᾳ

prophet has no honor in his own country.) **45** When he arrived in Galilee, the Galileans welcomed him.
προφήτης ἔχει οὐκ τιμὴν ἐν τῇ ἰδίᾳ πατρίδι   οὖν ὅτε → ἦλθεν εἰς ⸃τὴν Γαλιλαίαν⸂ οἱ Γαλιλαῖοι ἐδέξαντο αὐτὸν
n.nsm v.pai.3s pl n.asf p.d d.dsf a.dsf n.dsf   cj cj   v.aai.3s p.a d.asf n.asf d.npm a.npm v.ami.3p r.asm.3
4737 2400 4024 5507 1877 3836 2625 4258   4036 4021   2262 1650 3836 1133 3836 1134 1312 899

They had seen all that he had done in Jerusalem at the Passover Feast, for they also had been
→ → ἑωρακότες πάντα ὅσα → → ἐποίησεν ἐν Ἰεροσολύμοις ἐν τῇ → ἑορτῇ γὰρ αὐτοὶ καὶ → ἦλθον
  pt.ra.npm a.apn r.apn   v.aai.3s p.d n.dsf p.d d.dsf n.dsf cj r.npm adv v.aai.3p
3972 4246 4012 4472 1877 2642 1877 3836 2038 1142 899 2779 2262

there. ¶ **46** Once more he visited Cana in Galilee, where he had turned the water into
⸃εἰς τὴν ἑορτήν⸂ οὖν → πάλιν → Ἦλθεν εἰς ⸃τὴν Κανὰ⸂ → ⸃τῆς Γαλιλαίας⸂ ὅπου → ἐποίησεν τὸ ὕδωρ
p.a d.asf n.asf   cj   adv v.aai.3s p.a d.asf n.asf d.gsf n.gsf adv v.aai.3s d.asn n.asn
1650 3836 2038   4036 4099 2262 1650 3836 2830 3836 1133 3963 4472 3836 5623

wine. And there was a certain royal official whose son lay sick at Capernaum. **47** When this man heard
οἶνον Καὶ → ἦν τις → βασιλικὸς οὗ ὁ υἱός⸂ ἠσθένει ἐν Καφαρναούμ ↱ οὗτος ⟵ ἀκούσας
n.asm cj v.iai.3s r.nsm a.nsm r.gsm d.nsm n.nsm v.iai.3s p.d n.dsf r.nsm pt.aa.nsm
3885 2779 1639 5516 997 4005 3836 5626 820 1877 3019 201 4047 201

that Jesus had arrived in Galilee from Judea, he went to him and begged him to come and
ὅτι Ἰησοῦς → ἥκει εἰς ⸃τὴν Γαλιλαίαν⸂ ἐκ ⸃τῆς Ἰουδαίας⸂ → ἀπῆλθεν πρὸς αὐτὸν καὶ ἠρώτα ἵνα καταβῇ καὶ
cj n.nsm v.rai.3s p.a d.asf n.asf p.g d.gsf n.gsf v.aai.3s p.a r.asm.3 cj v.iai.3s cj v.aas.3s cj
4022 2652 2457 1650 3836 1133 1666 3836 2677 599 4639 899 2779 2263 2671 2849 2779

heal his son, who was close to death. **48** "Unless you people see miraculous signs and
ἰάσηται αὐτοῦ τὸν υἱὸν γὰρ → ἤμελλεν ἀποθνῄσκειν οὖν ⸃ἐὰν μὴ⸂ → ἴδητε → σημεῖα καὶ
v.ams.3s r.gsm.3 d.asm n.asm cj v.iai.3s f.pa cj cj pl v.aas.2p n.apn cj
2615 899 3836 5626 1142 3516 633 4036 1569 3590 1625 4956 2779

wonders," Jesus told him, "you will never believe." **49** The royal official said, "Sir, come
τέρατα ⸃ὁ Ἰησοῦς⸂ εἶπεν πρὸς αὐτὸν ⸃οὐ μὴ⸂ πιστεύσητε ὁ → βασιλικὸς λέγει πρὸς αὐτὸν κύριε κατάβηθι
n.apn d.nsm n.nsm v.aai.3s p.a r.asm.3 pl pl v.aas.2p d.nsm a.nsm v.pai.3s p.a r.asm.3 n.vsm v.aam.2s
5469 3836 2652 3306 4639 899 4409 4409 4024 3590 4409 3836 997 3306 4639 899 3261 2849

down before my child dies." **50** Jesus replied, "You may go. Your son will live." The man
← πρὶν μου ⸃τὸ παιδίον⸂ ἀποθανεῖν ὁ Ἰησοῦς⸂ λέγει αὐτῷ → πορεύου σου ὁ υἱός⸂ → ζῇ ὁ ἄνθρωπος
cj r.gs.1 d.asn n.asn f.aa d.nsm n.nsm v.pai.3s r.dsm.3 v.pmm.2s r.gs.2 d.nsm n.nsm v.pai.3s d.nsm n.nsm
4570 1609 3836 4086 633 3836 2652 3306 899 4513 5148 3836 5626 2409 3836 476

took Jesus at his word and departed. **51** While he was still on the way, his
ἐπίστευσεν ὁ Ἰησοῦς⸂ τῷ λόγῳ ὃν εἶπεν αὐτῷ καὶ ἐπορεύετο δὲ ↱ αὐτοῦ ↱ ἤδη → καταβαίνοντος αὐτοῦ
v.aai.3s d.nsm n.nsm d.dsm n.dsm r.asm v.aai.3s r.dsm.3 cj v.imi.3s cj r.gsm.3 adv pt.pa.gsm r.gsm.3
4409 3836 2652 3836 3364 4005 3306 899 2779 4513 1254 2849 899 2849 2453 2849 899

servants met him with the news that his boy was living. **52** When he inquired as
⸃οἱ δοῦλοι⸂ ὑπήντησαν αὐτῷ → λέγοντες ὅτι αὐτοῦ ὁ παῖς⸂ → ζῇ οὖν → ἐπύθετο παρ' αὐτῶν
d.npm n.npm v.aai.3p r.dsm.3 pt.pa.npm cj r.gsm.3 d.nsm n.nsm v.pai.3s cj v.ami.3s p.g r.gpm.3
3836 1529 5636 899 3306 4022 899 3836 4090 2409 4036 4785 4123 899

to the time when his son got better, they said to him, "The fever left him yesterday at the
τὴν ὥραν ⸃ἐν ᾗ⸂ ἔσχεν κομψότερον οὖν → εἶπαν → αὐτῷ ὅτι ὁ πυρετός ἀφῆκεν αὐτὸν ἐχθὲς
d.asf n.asf p.d r.dsf v.aai.3s adv.c cj v.aai.3p r.dsm.3 cj d.nsm n.nsm v.aai.3s r.asm.3 adv
3836 6052 1877 4005 2400 3153 4036 3306 899 4022 3836 4790 918 899 2396

seventh hour." **53** Then the father realized that this was the exact time at which Jesus had said to him,
ἑβδόμην ὥραν οὖν ὁ πατὴρ ἔγνω ὅτι ⸃ἐν ἐκείνῃ τῇ ὥρᾳ⸂ ἐν ᾗ ὁ Ἰησοῦς⸂ → εἶπεν → αὐτῷ
a.asf n.asf cj d.nsm n.nsm v.aai.3s cj p.d r.dsf d.dsf n.dsf p.d r.dsf d.nsm n.nsm v.aai.3s r.dsm.3
1575 6052 4036 3836 4252 1182 4022 1877 1697 3836 6052 1877 4005 3836 2652 3306 899

"Your son will live." So he and all his household believed. ¶ **54** This was the second
σου ⸃ὁ υἱός⸂ → ζῇ καὶ αὐτὸς καὶ ὅλη αὐτοῦ ἡ οἰκία ἐπίστευσεν δὲ Τοῦτο πάλιν δεύτερον
r.gs.2 d.nsm n.nsm v.pai.3s cj r.nsm cj a.nsf r.gsm.3 d.nsf n.nsf v.aai.3s cj r.asn adv a.asn
5148 3836 5626 2409 2779 899 2779 3910 899 3836 3864 4409 1254 4047 4099 1311

miraculous sign that Jesus performed, having come from Judea to Galilee.
→ σημεῖον ⸃ὁ Ἰησοῦς⸂ ἐποίησεν → ἐλθὼν ἐκ ⸃τῆς Ἰουδαίας⸂ εἰς ⸃τὴν Γαλιλαίαν⸂
n.asn d.nsm n.nsm v.aai.3s pt.aa.nsm p.g d.gsf n.gsf p.a d.asf n.asf
4956 3836 2652 4472 2262 1666 3836 2677 1650 3836 1133

πατρίδι τιμὴν οὐκ ἔχει. ⁴⁵ ὅτε οὖν ἦλθεν εἰς τὴν Γαλιλαίαν, ἐδέξαντο αὐτὸν οἱ Γαλιλαῖοι πάντα ἑωρακότες ὅσα ἐποίησεν ἐν Ἰεροσολύμοις ἐν τῇ ἑορτῇ, καὶ αὐτοὶ γὰρ ἦλθον εἰς τὴν ἑορτήν. ¶ ⁴⁶ Ἦλθεν οὖν πάλιν εἰς τὴν Κανὰ τῆς Γαλιλαίας, ὅπου ἐποίησεν τὸ ὕδωρ οἶνον. καὶ ἦν τις βασιλικὸς οὗ ὁ υἱὸς ἠσθένει ἐν Καφαρναούμ. ⁴⁷ οὗτος ἀκούσας ὅτι Ἰησοῦς ἥκει ἐκ τῆς Ἰουδαίας εἰς τὴν Γαλιλαίαν ἀπῆλθεν πρὸς αὐτὸν καὶ ἠρώτα ἵνα καταβῇ καὶ ἰάσηται αὐτοῦ τὸν υἱόν, ἤμελλεν γὰρ ἀποθνῄσκειν. ⁴⁸ εἶπεν οὖν ὁ Ἰησοῦς πρὸς αὐτόν, Ἐὰν μὴ σημεῖα καὶ τέρατα ἴδητε, οὐ μὴ πιστεύσητε. ⁴⁹ λέγει πρὸς αὐτὸν ὁ βασιλικός, Κύριε, κατάβηθι πρὶν ἀποθανεῖν τὸ παιδίον μου. ⁵⁰ λέγει αὐτῷ ὁ Ἰησοῦς, Πορεύου, ὁ υἱός σου ζῇ. ἐπίστευσεν ὁ ἄνθρωπος τῷ λόγῳ ὃν εἶπεν αὐτῷ ὁ Ἰησοῦς καὶ ἐπορεύετο. ⁵¹ ἤδη δὲ αὐτοῦ καταβαίνοντος οἱ δοῦλοι αὐτοῦ ὑπήντησαν αὐτῷ λέγοντες ὅτι ὁ παῖς αὐτοῦ ζῇ. ⁵² ἐπύθετο οὖν τὴν ὥραν παρ' αὐτῶν ἐν ᾗ κομψότερον ἔσχεν· εἶπαν οὖν αὐτῷ ὅτι Ἐχθὲς ὥραν ἑβδόμην ἀφῆκεν αὐτὸν ὁ πυρετός. ⁵³ ἔγνω οὖν ὁ πατὴρ ὅτι [ἐν] ἐκείνῃ τῇ ὥρᾳ ἐν ᾗ εἶπεν αὐτῷ ὁ Ἰησοῦς, Ὁ υἱός σου ζῇ, καὶ ἐπίστευσεν αὐτὸς καὶ ἡ οἰκία αὐτοῦ ὅλη. ¶ ⁵⁴ Τοῦτο [δὲ] πάλιν δεύτερον σημεῖον ἐποίησεν ὁ Ἰησοῦς ἐλθὼν ἐκ τῆς Ἰουδαίας εἰς τὴν Γαλιλαίαν.

The Healing at the Pool

5:1 *Some time later,* Jesus went up to Jerusalem for a feast of the Jews. **2** Now there is in

Μετὰ ταῦτα καὶ Ἰησοῦς ἀνέβη εἰς Ἱεροσόλυμα ἦν ἑορτὴ τῶν Ἰουδαίων δὲ Ἔστιν ἐν
r.pa r.apn cj n.nsm v.aai.3s pa n.apn v.iai.3s n.nsf d.gpm a.gpm cj v.pai.3s pd
3552 4047 2779 2652 326 1650 2642 1639 2038 3836 2681 1254 1639 1877

Jerusalem near the Sheep Gate a pool, which in Aramaic is called Bethesda and which is

τοῖς Ἱεροσολύμοις ἐπὶ τῇ προβατικῇ κολυμβήθρα ἡ Ἑβραϊστὶ ἐπιλεγομένη Βηθζαθὰ
d.dpn n.dpn pd d.dsf a.dsf n.nsf d.nsf adv pt.pp.nsf n.nsf
3836 2642 2093 3836 4583 3148 3836 1580 2141 1032

surrounded by five covered colonnades. **3** Here a great number of disabled people used to lie — the

ἔχουσα πέντε στοὰς ἐν ταύταις πλῆθος τῶν ἀσθενούντων κατέκειτο
pt.pa.nsf a.apf n.apf pd r.dpf n.nsn d.gpm pt.pa.gpm v.imi.3s
2400 4297 5119 1877 4047 4436 3836 820 2879

blind, the lame, the paralyzed. **5** One who was there had been an invalid for

τυφλῶν χωλῶν ξηρῶν δέ τις ἄνθρωπος ἦν ἐκεῖ ἔχων ἐν τῇ ἀσθενείᾳ αὐτοῦ
a.gpm a.gpm a.gpm cj r.nsm n.nsm v.iai.3s adv pt.pa.nsm pd d.dsf n.dsf r.gsm.3
5603 6000 3831 1254 5516 476 1639 1695 2400 1877 3836 819 899

thirty-eight years. **6** When Jesus saw him lying there and learned that he had been in this

τριάκοντα καὶ ὀκτὼ ἔτη ὁ Ἰησοῦς τοῦτον κατακείμενον καὶ γνοὺς ὅτι ἔχει
a.apn cj a.apn n.apn d.nsm n.nsm r.asm pt.pm.asm cj pt.aa.nsm cj v.pai.3s
5558 2779 3893 2291 1625 3836 2652 1625 4047 2879 2779 1182 4022 2400

condition for a long time, he asked him, "Do you want to get well?" **7** "Sir," the invalid replied, "I

πολὺν ἤδη χρόνον λέγει αὐτῷ θέλεις γενέσθαι ὑγιὴς κύριε ὁ ἀσθενῶν ἀπεκρίθη αὐτῷ
a.asm adv n.asm v.pai.3s r.dsm.3 v.pai.2s f.am a.nsm n.vsm d.nsm pt.pa.nsm v.api.3s r.dsm.3
4498 2453 5989 3306 899 2527 1181 5618 3261 3836 820 646 899

have no one to help me into the pool when the water is stirred. While I am trying to get in,

ἔχω οὐκ ἄνθρωπον ἵνα βάλῃ με εἰς τὴν κολυμβήθραν ὅταν τὸ ὕδωρ ταραχθῇ δὲ ἐν ᾧ ἐγώ ἔρχομαι
v.pai.1s pl n.asm cj v.aas.3s r.as.1 pa d.asf n.asf cj d.nsn n.nsn v.aps.3s cj pd r.ns.1 r.ns.1 v.pmi.1s
2400 4024 476 2671 965 1609 1650 3836 3148 4020 3836 5623 5429 1254 1877 4005 1609 2262

someone else goes down ahead of me." **8** Then Jesus said to him, "Get up! Pick up your mat and

ἄλλος καταβαίνει πρὸ ἐμοῦ ὁ Ἰησοῦς λέγει αὐτῷ ἔγειρε ἆρον σου τὸν κράβαττον καὶ
r.nsm v.pai.3s pg r.gs.1 d.nsm n.nsm v.pai.3s r.dsm.3 v.pam.2s v.aam.2s r.gs.2 d.asm n.asm cj
257 2849 4574 1609 3836 2652 3306 899 1586 149 5148 3836 3187 2779

walk." **9** At once the man was cured; he picked up his mat and walked. ¶ The

περιπάτει καὶ εὐθέως ὁ ἄνθρωπος ἐγένετο ὑγιὴς καὶ ἦρεν αὐτοῦ τὸν κράβαττον καὶ περιεπάτει δὲ τῇ
v.pam.2s cj adv d.nsm n.nsm v.ami.3s a.nsm cj v.aai.3s r.gsm.3 d.asm n.asm cj v.iai.3s cj d.dsf
4344 2779 2311 3836 476 1181 5618 2779 149 899 3836 3187 2779 4344 1254 3836

day on which this took place was a Sabbath, **10** and so the Jews said to the man who had been healed, "It

ἡμέρα ἐν ἐκείνῃ Ἦν σάββατον οὖν οἱ Ἰουδαῖοι ἔλεγον τῷ τεθεραπευμένῳ
n.dsf pd r.dsf v.iai.3s n.nsn cj d.npm a.npm v.iai.3p d.dsm pt.rp.dsm
2465 1877 1697 1639 4879 4036 3836 2681 3306 3836 2543

is the Sabbath; *the law forbids* you to carry your mat." **11** But he replied, "The man who

ἐστιν σάββατον καὶ ἔξεστιν οὐκ σοι ἆραι σου τὸν κράβαττον δὲ ὁ ἀπεκρίθη αὐτοῖς ὁ
v.pai.3s n.nsn cj v.pai.3s pl r.ds.2 f.aa r.gs.2 d.asm n.asm cj d.nsm v.api.3s r.dpm.3 d.nsm
1639 4879 2779 1997 4024 5148 149 5148 3836 3187 1254 3836 646 899 3836

made me well said to me, 'Pick up your mat and walk.'" **12** So they asked him, "Who is this

ποιήσας με ὑγιῆ ἐκεῖνος εἶπεν μοι ἆρον σου τὸν κράβαττον καὶ περιπάτει ἠρώτησαν αὐτόν τίς ἐστιν ὁ
pt.aa.nsm r.as.1 a.asm r.nsm v.aai.3s r.ds.1 v.aam.2s r.gs.2 d.asm n.asm cj v.pam.2s v.aai.3p r.asm.3 r.nsm v.pai.3s d.nsm
4472 1609 5618 1697 3306 1609 149 5148 3836 3187 2779 4344 2263 899 5515 1639 3836

fellow who told you to pick it up and walk?" **13** The man who was healed had no idea who it was, for

ἄνθρωπος ὁ εἰπών σοι ἆρον καὶ περιπάτει δὲ ὁ ἰαθεὶς οὐκ ᾔδει τίς ἐστιν γὰρ
n.nsm d.nsm pt.aa.nsm r.ds.2 v.aam.2s cj v.pam.2s cj d.nsm pt.ap.nsm pl v.lai.3s r.nsm v.pai.3s cj
476 3836 3306 5148 149 2779 4344 1254 3836 2615 3857 4024 3857 5515 1639 1142

Jesus had slipped away into the crowd that was there. ¶ **14** Later Jesus found him at

ὁ Ἰησοῦς ἐξένευσεν ὄχλου ὄντος ἐν τῷ τόπῳ μετὰ ταῦτα ὁ Ἰησοῦς εὑρίσκει αὐτὸν ἐν
d.nsm n.nsm v.aai.3s n.gsm pt.pa.gsm pd d.dsm n.dsm pa r.apn d.nsm n.nsm v.pai.3s r.asm.3 pd
3836 2652 1728 4063 1639 1877 3836 5536 3552 4047 3836 2652 2351 899 1877

5:1 Μετὰ ταῦτα ἦν ἑορτὴ τῶν Ἰουδαίων καὶ ἀνέβη Ἰησοῦς εἰς Ἱεροσόλυμα. **2** ἔστιν δὲ ἐν τοῖς Ἱεροσολύμοις ἐπὶ τῇ προβατικῇ κολυμβήθρα ἡ ἐπιλεγομένη Ἑβραϊστὶ Βηθεσδά, «Βηθζαθὰ» πέντε στοὰς ἔχουσα. **3** ἐν ταύταις κατέκειτο πλῆθος τῶν ἀσθενούντων, τυφλῶν, χωλῶν, ξηρῶν. **5** ἦν δέ τις ἄνθρωπος ἐκεῖ τριάκοντα [καὶ] ὀκτὼ ἔτη ἔχων ἐν τῇ ἀσθενείᾳ αὐτοῦ· **6** τοῦτον ἰδὼν ὁ Ἰησοῦς κατακείμενον καὶ γνοὺς ὅτι πολὺν ἤδη χρόνον ἔχει, λέγει αὐτῷ, Θέλεις ὑγιὴς γενέσθαι; **7** ἀπεκρίθη αὐτῷ ὁ ἀσθενῶν, Κύριε, ἄνθρωπον οὐκ ἔχω ἵνα ὅταν ταραχθῇ τὸ ὕδωρ βάλῃ με εἰς τὴν κολυμβήθραν· ἐν ᾧ δὲ ἔρχομαι ἐγώ, ἄλλος πρὸ ἐμοῦ καταβαίνει. **8** λέγει αὐτῷ ὁ Ἰησοῦς, Ἔγειρε ἆρον τὸν κράβαττόν σου καὶ περιπάτει. **9** καὶ εὐθέως ἐγένετο ὑγιὴς ὁ ἄνθρωπος καὶ ἦρεν τὸν κράβαττον αὐτοῦ καὶ περιεπάτει. ¶ Ἦν δὲ σάββατον ἐν ἐκείνῃ τῇ ἡμέρᾳ. **10** ἔλεγον οὖν οἱ Ἰουδαῖοι τῷ τεθεραπευμένῳ, Σάββατόν ἐστιν, καὶ οὐκ ἔξεστίν σοι ἆραι τὸν κράβαττόν σου. **11** ὁ δὲ ἀπεκρίθη αὐτοῖς, Ὁ ποιήσας με ὑγιῆ ἐκεῖνός μοι εἶπεν, Ἆρον τὸν κράβαττόν σου καὶ περιπάτει. **12** ἠρώτησαν αὐτόν, Τίς ἐστιν ὁ ἄνθρωπος ὁ εἰπών σοι, Ἆρον καὶ περιπάτει; **13** ὁ δὲ ἰαθεὶς οὐκ ᾔδει τίς ἐστιν, ὁ γὰρ Ἰησοῦς ἐξένευσεν ὄχλου ὄντος ἐν τῷ τόπῳ. ¶ **14** μετὰ ταῦτα εὑρίσκει αὐτὸν

the	temple	and	said	to him,	"See,	you	are		well	again.	Stop	sinning	or		something	worse	may	happen	to
τῷ	ἱερῷ	καὶ	εἶπεν	αὐτῷ	ἴδε		γέγονας	ὑγιής			μηκέτι	ἁμάρτανε	ἵνα	μὴ	τι			χεῖρον →	γένηται →
d.dsn	n.dsn	cj	v.aai.3s	r.dsm.3	pl		v.rai.2s	a.nsm			adv	v.pam.2s	cj	pl	r.nsn			a.nsn.c	v.ams.3s
3836	2639	2779	3306	899	2623		1181	5618			3600	279	2671	3590	5516			5937	1181

you."	¹⁵ The	man		went	away	and	told		the	Jews		that	it	was	Jesus	who	had	made	him	well.
σοί	ὁ	ἄνθρωπος	ἀπῆλθεν ←			καὶ	ἀνήγγειλεν		τοῖς	Ἰουδαίοις		ὅτι		→ ἔστιν	Ἰησοῦς	ὁ	→	ποιήσας	αὐτὸν	ὑγιῆ
r.ds.2	d.nsm	n.nsm	v.aai.3s			cj	v.aai.3s		d.dpm	a.dpm		cj		v.pai.3s	n.nsm	d.nsm		pt.aa.nsm	r.asm.3	a.asm
5148	3836	476	599			2779	334		3836	2681		4022		1639	2652	3836		4472	899	5618

Life Through the Son

5:16	So,		because	Jesus	was	doing	these	things	on	the	Sabbath,	the	Jews		persecuted	him.	¹⁷
	καὶ	⌐διὰ τοῦτο¬	ὅτι		→	ἐποίει	ταῦτα ←		ἐν		σαββάτῳ	οἱ	Ἰουδαῖοι		ἐδίωκον	⌐τὸν Ἰησοῦν¬	δὲ
	cj	p.a r.asn	cj			v.iai.3s	r.apn		p.d		n.dsn	d.npm	a.npm		v.iai.3p	d.asm n.asm	cj
	2779	1328 4047	4022			4472	4047		1877		4879	3836	2681		1503	3836 2652	1254

Jesus		said	to them,	"My	Father		is	always	at his	work	to		this	very	day,	and	I,	too,	am
⌐Ὁ Ἰησοῦς¬		ἀπεκρίνατο →	αὐτοῖς	μου	⌐ὁ πατήρ¬		ἐργάζεται	ἕως				ἄρτι ←	←		←			κἀγὼ	
d.nsm n.nsm		v.ami.3s	r.dpm.3	r.gs.1	d.nsm n.nsm		v.pmi.3s	p.g				adv						crasis	
3836 2652		646	899	1609	3836 4252		2237	2401				785						2743	

working."	¹⁸	For this reason			the	Jews	tried	all	the	harder	to	kill	him;		not	only	was	he	breaking
ἐργάζομαι	οὖν →		⌐διὰ τοῦτο¬	οἱ	Ἰουδαῖοι	ἐζήτουν →		→	μᾶλλον	→	ἀποκτεῖναι	αὐτὸν	ὅτι	οὐ	μόνον	→	ἔλυεν
v.pmi.1s	cj		p.a r.asn	d.npm	a.npm	v.iai.3p			adv.c		f.aa	r.asm.3	cj	pl	adv		v.iai.3s
2237	4036		1328 4047	3836	2681	2426			3437		650	899	4022	4024	3667		3395

the	Sabbath,	but	he	was	even	calling	God		his	own	Father,	making	himself	equal	with	God.	¶	¹⁹
τὸ	σάββατον	ἀλλὰ	→		καὶ	ἔλεγεν	⌐τὸν θεὸν¬	ἴδιον ←			πατέρα	ποιῶν	ἑαυτὸν	ἴσον	→	⌐τῷ θεῷ¬		οὖν
d.asn	n.asn	cj			adv	v.iai.3s	d.asm n.asm	a.asm			n.asm	pt.pa.nsm	r.asm.3	a.asm		d.dsm n.dsm		cj
3836	4879	247			2779	3306	3836 2536	2625			4252	4472	1571	2698		3836 2536		4036

Jesus		gave		them	this answer:	"I	tell	you	the	truth,		the	Son	can		do	nothing	by
⌐ὁ Ἰησοῦς¬		Ἀπεκρίνατο	καὶ	ἔλεγεν	αὐτοῖς	↰	→ λέγω	ὑμῖν	⌐ἀμὴν	ἀμὴν¬	ὁ	υἱὸς	δύναται	ποιεῖν	οὐ	ἀφ
d.nsm n.nsm		v.ami.3s	cj	v.iai.3s	r.dpm.3		v.pai.1s	r.dp.2	pl	pl	d.nsm	n.nsm	v.ppi.3s	f.pa	pl	p.g
3836 2652		646	2779	3306	899		3306	7007	297	297	3836	5626	1538	4472	4024	608

himself;	he	can	do		only	what	he	sees	his	Father	doing,	because	whatever	the	Father	does		the	Son
ἑαυτοῦ			οὐδὲν	⌐ἐὰν	μὴ¬	τι	→	βλέπῃ	τὸν	πατέρα	ποιοῦντα	γὰρ	⌐ἃ ἂν¬		ἐκεῖνος	ποιῇ	ταῦτα	ὁ	υἱὸς
r.gsm.3			a.asn	cj	pl	r.asn		v.pas.3s	d.asm	n.asm	pt.pa.asm	cj	r.apn pl		r.nsm	v.pas.3s	r.apn	d.nsm	n.nsm
1571			4029	1569	3590	5516		1063	3836	4252	4472	1142	4005 323		1697	4472	4047	3836	5626

also	does.	²⁰ For	the	Father	loves	the	Son	and	shows	him	all		he	does.	Yes,	to your	amazement	he
καὶ	ποιεῖ	ὁμοίως	γὰρ	ὁ	πατὴρ	φιλεῖ	τὸν	υἱὸν	καὶ	δείκνυσιν	αὐτῷ	πάντα	ἃ	αὐτὸς	ποιεῖ	ἵνα	⌐ὑμεῖς	θαυμάζητε →
adv	v.pai.3s	adv	cj	d.nsm	n.nsm	v.pai.3s	d.asm	n.asm	cj	v.pai.3s	r.dsm.3	a.apn	r.apn	r.nsm	v.pai.3s	cj	r.np.2	v.pas.2p
2779	4472	3931	1142	3836	4252	5797	3836	5626	2779	1259	899	4246	4005	899	4472	2671	7007	2513

will	show	him	even	greater	things	than	these.	²¹ For	just	as	the	Father	raises	the	dead	and	gives them	life,	even
→	δείξει	αὐτῷ	καὶ	μείζονα	ἔργα	→	τούτων	γὰρ	ὥσπερ ←		ὁ	πατὴρ	ἐγείρει	τοὺς	νεκροὺς	καὶ	→		ζωοποιεῖ
	v.fai.3s	r.dsm.3	adv	a.apn.c	n.apn		r.gpn	cj			d.nsm	n.nsm	v.pai.3s	d.apm	a.apm	cj			v.pai.3s
	1259	899	2779	3489	2240		4047	1142	6061		3836	4252	1586	3836	3738	2779			2443

so	the	Son		gives life	to whom	he	is pleased	to give it.	²² Moreover,		the	Father	judges	no one,	but	has
οὕτως	ὁ	υἱὸς	καὶ	→ ζωοποιεῖ	οὓς	→	θέλει		γὰρ		οὐδὲ ὁ	πατὴρ	κρίνει	→ οὐδένα	ἀλλὰ	
adv	d.nsm	n.nsm	adv	v.pai.3s	r.apm		v.pai.3s		cj		adv d.nsm n.nsm		v.pai.3s	a.asm	cj	
4048	3836	5626	2779	2443	4005		2527		1142		4028 3836 4252		3212	4029	247	

entrusted	all	judgment	to the Son,	²³ that	all		may	honor	the	Son	just	as	they	honor	the	Father.	He	who	does
δέδωκεν	πᾶσαν	⌐τὴν κρίσιν¬	→ τῷ υἱῷ	ἵνα	πάντες		→	τιμῶσι	τὸν	υἱὸν	καθὼς ←		→	τιμῶσι	τὸν	πατέρα	ὁ ←	→	
v.rai.3s	a.asf	d.asf n.asf	d.dsm n.dsm	cj	a.npm			v.pas.3p	d.asm	n.asm	cj			v.pai.3p	d.asm	n.asm	d.nsm		5506
1443	4246	3836 3213	3836 5626	2671	4246			5506	3836	5626	2777			5506	3836	4252	3836		

not	honor	the	Son	does	not	honor	the	Father,	who	sent		him.	¶	²⁴ "I	tell	you	the	truth,		whoever
μὴ	τιμῶν	τὸν	υἱὸν		οὐ	τιμᾷ	τὸν	πατέρα	τὸν	πέμψαντα	αὐτόν			→ λέγω	ὑμῖν	⌐Ἀμὴν	ἀμὴν¬	ὅτι	ὁ
pl	pt.pa.nsm	d.asm	n.asm		pl	v.pai.3s	d.asm	n.asm	d.asm	pt.aa.asm	r.asm.3			v.pai.1s	r.dp.2	pl	pl	cj	d.nsm
3590	5506	3836	5626		4024	5506	3836	4252	3836	4287	899			3306	7007	297	297	4022	3836

hears	my	word		and	believes	him	who sent		me	has	eternal	life	and	will	not	be		condemned;		he	has
ἀκούων	μου	⌐τὸν λόγον¬	καὶ	πιστεύων	τῷ	←	πέμψαντι	με	ἔχει	αἰώνιον	ζωὴν	καὶ	→		οὐκ	ἔρχεται	⌐εἰς κρίσιν¬	ἀλλὰ →	→
pt.pa.nsm	r.gs.1	d.asm n.asm	cj	pt.pa.nsm	d.dsm		pt.aa.asm	r.as.1	v.pai.3s	a.asf	n.asf	cj			pl	v.pmi.3s	p.a n.asf	cj	
201	1609	3836 3364	2779	4409	3836		4287	1609	2400	173	2437	2779			4024	2262	1650 3213	247	

ὁ Ἰησοῦς ἐν τῷ ἱερῷ καὶ εἶπεν αὐτῷ, Ἴδε ὑγιὴς γέγονας, μηκέτι ἁμάρτανε, ἵνα μὴ χεῖρόν σοί τι γένηται. ¹⁵ ἀπῆλθεν ὁ ἄνθρωπος καὶ ἀνήγγειλεν τοῖς Ἰουδαίοις ὅτι Ἰησοῦς ἐστιν ὁ ποιήσας αὐτὸν ὑγιῆ.

5:16 καὶ διὰ τοῦτο ἐδίωκον οἱ Ἰουδαῖοι τὸν Ἰησοῦν, ὅτι ταῦτα ἐποίει ἐν σαββάτῳ. ¹⁷ ὁ δὲ [Ἰησοῦς] ἀπεκρίνατο αὐτοῖς, Ὁ πατήρ μου ἕως ἄρτι ἐργάζεται κἀγὼ ἐργάζομαι· ¹⁸ διὰ τοῦτο οὖν μᾶλλον ἐζήτουν αὐτὸν οἱ Ἰουδαῖοι ἀποκτεῖναι, ὅτι οὐ μόνον ἔλυεν τὸ σάββατον, ἀλλὰ καὶ πατέρα ἴδιον ἔλεγεν τὸν θεὸν ἴσον ἑαυτὸν ποιῶν τῷ θεῷ. ¶ ¹⁹ Ἀπεκρίνατο οὖν ὁ Ἰησοῦς καὶ ἔλεγεν αὐτοῖς, Ἀμὴν ἀμὴν λέγω ὑμῖν, οὐ δύναται ὁ υἱὸς ποιεῖν ἀφ᾽ ἑαυτοῦ οὐδὲν ἐὰν μή τι βλέπῃ τὸν πατέρα ποιοῦντα· ἃ γὰρ ἂν ἐκεῖνος ποιῇ, ταῦτα καὶ ὁ υἱὸς ὁμοίως ποιεῖ. ²⁰ ὁ γὰρ πατὴρ φιλεῖ τὸν υἱὸν καὶ πάντα δείκνυσιν αὐτῷ ἃ αὐτὸς ποιεῖ, καὶ μείζονα τούτων δείξει αὐτῷ ἔργα, ἵνα ὑμεῖς θαυμάζητε. ²¹ ὥσπερ γὰρ ὁ πατὴρ ἐγείρει τοὺς νεκροὺς καὶ ζωοποιεῖ, οὕτως καὶ ὁ υἱὸς οὓς θέλει ζωοποιεῖ. ²² οὐδὲ γὰρ ὁ πατὴρ κρίνει οὐδένα, ἀλλὰ τὴν κρίσιν πᾶσαν δέδωκεν τῷ υἱῷ, ²³ ἵνα πάντες τιμῶσι τὸν υἱὸν καθὼς τιμῶσι τὸν πατέρα. ὁ μὴ τιμῶν τὸν υἱὸν οὐ τιμᾷ τὸν πατέρα τὸν πέμψαντα αὐτόν. ¶ ²⁴ Ἀμὴν ἀμὴν λέγω ὑμῖν ὅτι ὁ τὸν λόγον μου ἀκούων καὶ πιστεύων τῷ πέμψαντί με ἔχει ζωὴν αἰώνιον καὶ εἰς κρίσιν οὐκ ἔρχεται, ἀλλὰ μεταβέβηκεν ἐκ τοῦ

crossed   over from death   to life.   **25** I tell you the truth,   a time is coming and has now come
μεταβέβηκεν ←   ἐκ ⌐τοῦ θανάτου⌐ εἰς ⌐τὴν ζωήν⌐   → λέγω ὑμῖν   ⌐ἀμὴν ἀμὴν⌐ ὅτι   ὥρα → ἔρχεται καὶ → νῦν ἐστιν
v.rai.3s   p.g d.gsm n.gsm   p.a d.asf n.asf   v.pai.1s r.dp.2 pl   pl   cj   n.nsf v.pmi.3s cj   adv v.pai.3s
3553   1666 3836 2505   1650 3836 2437   3306 7007   297 297 4022 6052   2262   2779   3814 1639

when the dead will hear   the voice of the Son of God   and those who hear   will live.   **26** For as   the
ὅτε οἱ νεκροὶ → ἀκούσουσιν τῆς φωνῆς → τοῦ υἱοῦ → ⌐τοῦ θεοῦ⌐ καὶ οἱ ← ἀκούσαντες → ζήσουσιν   γὰρ ὥσπερ ὁ
cj   d.npm a.npm v.fai.3p   d.gsf n.gsf d.gsm n.gsm d.gsm n.gsm cj d.npm pt.aa.npm   v.fai.3p   cj   cj   d.nsm
4021 3836 3738   201   3836 5889   3836 5626   3836 2536 2779 3836   201   2409   1142 6061 3836

Father has life in himself, so   he has granted the Son to have life in himself. **27** And he has given him
πατὴρ ἔχει ζωὴν ἐν ἑαυτῷ οὕτως καὶ → ἔδωκεν τῷ υἱῷ → ἔχειν ζωὴν ἐν ἑαυτῷ   καὶ → ἔδωκεν αὐτῷ
n.nsm v.pai.3s n.asf p.d r.dsm.3 adv adv   v.aai.3s d.dsm n.dsm f.pa n.asf p.d r.dsm.3 cj   v.aai.3s r.dsm.3
4252 2400 2437 1877 1571 4048 2779   1443   3836 5626 2400 2437 1877 1571   2779 1443   899

authority to judge   because he is   the Son of Man.   ¶   **28** "Do not be amazed at this, for a time is
ἐξουσίαν → ⌐ποιεῖν κρίσιν⌐ ὅτι → ἐστίν υἱὸς → ἀνθρώπου   μὴ   θαυμάζετε ← τοῦτο ὅτι ὥρα →
n.asf   f.pa n.asf   cj   v.pai.3s n.nsm n.gsm   pl   v.pam.2p   r.asn cj   n.nsf
2026   4472 3213   4022   1639   5626   476   3590 2513   4047 4022 6052

coming when all who are in their graves   will hear   his voice   **29** and come   out – those who
ἔρχεται ἐν ᾗ πάντες οἱ → ἐν τοῖς μνημείοις → ἀκούσουσιν αὐτοῦ ⌐τῆς φωνῆς⌐ καὶ ἐκπορεύσονται ← οἱ
v.pmi.3s p.d r.dsf a.npm d.npm p.d d.dpn n.dpn   v.fai.3p   r.gsm.3 d.gsf n.gsf cj   v.fmi.3p   d.npm
2262   1877 4005 4246 3836   1877 3836 3646   201   899   3836 5889 2779 1744   3836

have done   good   will rise   to live, and those who have done   evil   will rise   to be
→ ποιήσαντες ⌐τὰ ἀγαθὰ⌐ εἰς ἀνάστασιν⌐ ζωῆς δὲ οἱ ← πράξαντες ⌐τὰ φαῦλα⌐ εἰς ἀνάστασιν⌐
pt.aa.npm   d.apn a.apn p.a n.asf   n.gsf cj d.npm pt.aa.npm d.apn a.apn p.a n.asf
4472   3836 19   1650 414   2437 1254 3836   4556   3836 5765 1650 414

condemned. **30** By myself I   can   do   nothing; I judge only as   I hear, and my   judgment is   just,
κρίσεως   ἀπ’ ἐμαυτοῦ ἐγὼ Οὐ δύναμαι ποιεῖν οὐδέν· → κρίνω → καθὼς → ἀκούω καὶ ⌐ἡ ἐμὴ⌐ ⌐ἡ κρίσις⌐ ἐστίν δικαία
n.gsf   p.g r.gsm.1 r.ns.1 pl v.pmi.1s f.pa a.asn   v.pai.1s   cj   v.pai.1s cj d.nsf r.nsf.1 d.nsf n.nsf v.pai.3s a.nsf
3213   608 1831 1609 4024 1538 4472 4029   3212   2777   201   2779 3836 1847 3836 3213 1639   1465

for I seek not to *please* *myself* but him who sent   me.
ὅτι → ζητῶ οὐ ⌐τὸ θέλημα⌐ ⌐τὸ ἐμὸν⌐ ἀλλὰ ⌐τὸ θέλημα⌐ τοῦ ← πέμψαντος με
cj   v.pai.1s pl d.asn n.asn   d.asn r.asn.1 cj d.asn n.asn d.gsm   pt.aa.gsm r.as.1
4022 2426 4024 3836 2525   3836 1847 247 3836 2525 3836   4287   1609

Testimonies About Jesus

5:31 "If I   testify about myself, my testimony is   not valid. **32** There is   another who testifies in   my
Ἐὰν ἐγὼ μαρτυρῶ περὶ ἐμαυτοῦ μου ⌐ἡ μαρτυρία⌐ ἔστιν οὐκ ἀληθής   ἐστιν ἄλλος ὁ μαρτυρῶν περὶ ἐμοῦ
cj   r.ns.1 v.pas.1s p.g r.gsm.1 r.gs.1 d.nsf n.nsf v.pai.3s pl a.nsf   v.pai.3s r.nsm d.nsm pt.pa.nsm p.g r.gs.1
1569 1609 3455 4309 1831 1609 3836 3456 1639 4024 239   1639 257   3836 3455   4309 1609

favor, and I know that his testimony   about me is   valid. ¶   **33** "You have sent   to John
← καὶ → οἶδα ὅτι ἡ μαρτυρία ἦν μαρτυρεῖ περὶ ἐμοῦ ἐστιν ἀληθής   ὑμεῖς → ἀπεστάλκατε πρὸς Ἰωάννην
← cj   v.rai.1s cj d.nsf n.nsf r.asf v.pai.3s p.g r.gs.1 v.pai.3s a.nsf   r.np.2 v.rai.2p   p.a n.asm
4309 2779 3857 4022 3836 3456 4005 3455 4309 1609 1639 239   7007   690   4639 2722

and he has testified   to the truth. **34** Not that I   accept   human testimony; but I mention it
καὶ → μεμαρτύρηκεν → τῇ ἀληθείᾳ δὲ οὐ ἐγὼ λαμβάνω παρὰ ἀνθρώπου ⌐τὴν μαρτυρίαν⌐ ἀλλὰ → λέγω ταῦτα
cj   v.rai.3s   d.dsf n.dsf cj pl r.ns.1 v.pai.1s p.g n.gsm   d.asf n.asf   cj   v.pai.1s r.apn
2779 3455   3836 237   1254 4024 1609 3284 4123 476   3836 3456   247   3306 4047

that you may be saved. **35** John was a lamp   that burned and gave light, and you chose   for a time to
ἵνα ὑμεῖς → → σωθῆτε ἐκεῖνος ἦν ⌐ὁ λύχνος⌐ ὁ καιόμενος καὶ φαίνων δὲ ὑμεῖς ἠθελήσατε πρὸς ὥραν →
cj r.np.2   v.aps.2p r.nsm v.iai.3s d.nsm n.nsm d.nsm pt.pp.nsm cj pt.pa.nsm cj r.np.2 v.aai.2p   p.a n.asf
2671 7007   5392 1697   2400 3836 3394 3836 2794   2779 5743   1254 7007 2527   4639 6052

enjoy   his light.   ¶ **36** "I have testimony   weightier than that of John.   For the very
ἀγαλλιαθῆναι ἐν αὐτοῦ ⌐τῷ φωτὶ⌐ δὲ Ἐγὼ ἔχω ⌐τὴν μαρτυρίαν⌐ μείζω   ⌐τοῦ Ἰωάννου⌐ γὰρ τὰ
f.ap   p.d r.gsm.3 d.dsn n.dsn cj r.ns.1 v.pai.1s d.asf n.asf a.asf.c   d.gsm n.gsm cj d.npn
22   1877 899 3836 5890 1254 1609 2400 3836 3456 3489   3836 2722   1142 3836

work that the Father has given   me to finish,   and   which I am doing, testifies   that the
ἔργα ἃ ὁ πατὴρ → δέδωκεν μοι ἵνα τελειώσω αὐτά   αὐτὰ τὰ ἔργα ἃ → ποιῶ μαρτυρεῖ περὶ ἐμοῦ ὅτι ὁ
n.npn r.apn d.nsm n.nsm v.rai.3s r.ds.1 cj v.aas.1s r.apn.3 r.npn d.npn n.npn r.apn v.pai.1s v.pai.3s p.g r.gs.1 cj d.nsm
2240 4005 3836 4252   1443 1609 2671 5457 899   899 3836 2240 4005   4472 3455 4309 1609 4022 3836

θανάτου εἰς τὴν ζωήν. **25** ἀμὴν ἀμὴν λέγω ὑμῖν ὅτι ἔρχεται ὥρα καὶ νῦν ἐστιν ὅτε οἱ νεκροὶ ἀκούσουσιν τῆς φωνῆς τοῦ υἱοῦ τοῦ θεοῦ καὶ οἱ ἀκούσαντες ζήσουσιν. **26** ὥσπερ γὰρ ὁ πατὴρ ἔχει ζωὴν ἐν ἑαυτῷ, οὕτως καὶ τῷ υἱῷ ἔδωκεν ζωὴν ἔχειν ἐν ἑαυτῷ. **27** καὶ ἐξουσίαν ἔδωκεν αὐτῷ κρίσιν ποιεῖν, ὅτι υἱὸς ἀνθρώπου ἐστίν. ¶ **28** μὴ θαυμάζετε τοῦτο, ὅτι ἔρχεται ὥρα ἐν ᾗ πάντες οἱ ἐν τοῖς μνημείοις ἀκούσουσιν τῆς φωνῆς αὐτοῦ **29** καὶ ἐκπορεύσονται οἱ τὰ ἀγαθὰ ποιήσαντες εἰς ἀνάστασιν ζωῆς, οἱ δὲ τὰ φαῦλα πράξαντες εἰς ἀνάστασιν κρίσεως. **30** Οὐ δύναμαι ἐγὼ ποιεῖν ἀπ’ ἐμαυτοῦ οὐδέν· καθὼς ἀκούω κρίνω, καὶ ἡ κρίσις ἡ ἐμὴ δικαία ἐστίν, ὅτι οὐ ζητῶ τὸ θέλημα τὸ ἐμὸν ἀλλὰ τὸ θέλημα τοῦ πέμψαντός με.

5:31 ἐὰν ἐγὼ μαρτυρῶ περὶ ἐμαυτοῦ, ἡ μαρτυρία μου οὐκ ἔστιν ἀληθής· **32** ἄλλος ἐστιν ὁ μαρτυρῶν περὶ ἐμοῦ, καὶ οἶδα ὅτι ἀληθής ἐστιν ἡ μαρτυρία ἣν μαρτυρεῖ περὶ ἐμοῦ. ¶ **33** ὑμεῖς ἀπεστάλκατε πρὸς Ἰωάννην, καὶ μεμαρτύρηκεν τῇ ἀληθείᾳ· **34** ἐγὼ δὲ οὐ παρὰ ἀνθρώπου τὴν μαρτυρίαν λαμβάνω, ἀλλὰ ταῦτα λέγω ἵνα ὑμεῖς σωθῆτε. **35** ἐκεῖνος ἦν ὁ λύχνος ὁ καιόμενος καὶ φαίνων, ὑμεῖς δὲ ἠθελήσατε ἀγαλλιαθῆναι πρὸς ὥραν ἐν τῷ φωτὶ αὐτοῦ. ¶ **36** ἐγὼ δὲ ἔχω τὴν μαρτυρίαν μείζω τοῦ Ἰωάννου· τὰ γὰρ ἔργα ἃ δέδωκέν μοι ὁ πατὴρ ἵνα τελειώσω αὐτά, αὐτὰ τὰ ἔργα ἃ ποιῶ μαρτυρεῖ περὶ ἐμοῦ ὅτι ὁ πατήρ με ἀπέσταλκεν.

Father has sent me. **37** And the Father who sent me has himself testified concerning me. You have
πατήρ → ἀπέσταλκεν με καὶ ὁ πατὴρ πέμψας με ᾿ ἐκεῖνος μεμαρτύρηκεν περὶ . ἐμοῦ .
n.nsm   v.rai.3s r.as.1 cj d.nsm n.nsm pt.aa.nsm r.as.1 r.nsm v.rai.3s p.g r.gs.1 r.gs.1
4252   690 1609 2779 3836 4252 4287 1609 3455 1697 3455 4309 1609 201 201

never heard his voice nor seen his form, **38** nor does his word dwell in you, for you do not
ιοὔτε πώποτε, ἀκηκόατε αὐτοῦ φωνὴν οὔτε ἑωράκατε αὐτοῦ εἶδος ικαὶ οὐκ, ἔχετε αὐτοῦ ιτὸν λόγον, μένοντα ἐν ὑμῖν ὅτι ὑμεῖς → οὐ
cj adv v.rai.2p r.gsm.3 n.asf cj v.rai.2p r.gsm.3 n.asn cj pl v.pai.2p r.gsm.3 d.asm n.asm pt.pa.asm p.d r.dp.2 cj r.np.2 pl
4046 4799 201 899 5889 4046 3972 899 1626 2779 4024 2400 899 3836 3364 3531 1877 7007 4022 7007 4409 4024

believe the one he sent. **39** You diligently study the Scriptures because you think that by them you
πιστεύετε τούτῳ ὃν ἐκεῖνος ἀπέστειλεν → ἐραυνᾶτε τὰς γραφάς ὅτι ὑμεῖς δοκεῖτε ἐν αὐταῖς →
v.pai.2p r.dsm r.asm r.nsm v.aai.3s d.apf n.apf cj r.np.2 v.pai.2p p.d r.dpf.3
4409 4047 4005 1697 690 2236 3836 1210 4022 7007 1506 1877 899

possess eternal life. These are the Scriptures that testify about me, **40** yet you refuse to come to me to
ἔχειν αἰώνιον ζωὴν καὶ ἐκεῖναι εἰσιν αἱ → μαρτυροῦσαι περὶ ἐμοῦ καὶ → ιοὐ θέλετε, → ἐλθεῖν πρός με ἵνα
f.pa a.asf n.asf cj r.npf v.pai.3p d.npf pt.pa.npf p.g r.gs.1 cj pl v.pai.2p f.aa p.a r.as.1 cj
2400 173 2437 2779 1697 1639 3836 3455 4309 1609 2779 4024 2527 2262 4639 1609 2671

have life. ¶ **41** "I do not accept praise from men, **42** but I know you. I know that you do not have the
ἔχητε ζωὴν → οὐ λαμβάνω Δόξαν παρὰ ἀνθρώπων ἀλλὰ ᾿ ἔγνωκα ὑμᾶς ὅτι → οὐκ ἔχετε τὴν
v.pas.2p n.asf pl v.pai.1s n.asf p.g n.gpm cj v.rai.1s r.ap.2 cj pl v.pai.2p d.asf
2400 2437 3284 3284 4024 3284 1518 4123 476 247 1182 7007 4022 2400 2400 4024 2400 3836

love of God in your hearts. **43** I have come in my Father's name, and you do not accept me;
ἀγάπην → ιτοῦ θεοῦ, ἐν ἑαυτοῖς ἐγὼ → ἐλήλυθα ἐν μου ιτοῦ πατρός, ιτῷ ὀνόματι, καὶ ᾿ → οὐ λαμβάνετε με
n.asf d.gsm n.gsm p.d r.dpm.2 r.ns.1 v.rai.1s p.d r.gs.1 d.gsm n.gsm d.dsn n.dsn cj pl v.pai.2p r.as.1
27 3836 2536 1877 1571 1609 2262 1877 1609 3836 4252 3836 3950 2779 3284 3284 4024 3284 1609

but if someone else comes in his own name, you will accept him. **44** How can you believe if you
ἐὰν ἄλλος ← ἔλθῃ ἐν τῷ ιτῷ ἰδίῳ, ὀνόματι → → λήμψεσθε ἐκεῖνον πῶς δύνασθε ὑμεῖς πιστεῦσαι → →
cj r.nsm v.aas.3s p.d d.dsn d.dsn a.dsn n.dsn v.fmi.2p r.asm pl v.ppi.2p r.np.2 f.aa
1569 257 2262 1877 3836 3836 2625 3950 v.fmi.2p 1697 4802 1538 7007 4409

accept praise from one another, yet make no effort to obtain the praise that comes from the only God? ¶
λαμβάνοντες δόξαν παρὰ ἀλλήλων ← καὶ οὐ → ζητεῖτε τὴν δόξαν τὴν παρὰ τοῦ μόνου θεοῦ
pt.pa.npm n.asf p.g r.gpm cj pl v.pai.2p d.asf n.asf d.asf p.g d.gsm a.gsm n.gsm
3284 1518 4123 253 2779 4024 2426 3836 1518 3836 4123 3836 3668 2536

45 "But do not think I will accuse you before the Father. Your accuser is Moses, on whom your
᾿ Μὴ δοκεῖτε ὅτι ἐγὼ κατηγορήσω ὑμῶν πρὸς τὸν πατέρα ὑμῶν ὁ κατηγορῶν ἔστιν Μωϋσῆς εἰς ὃν ὑμεῖς
pl v.pam.2p cj r.ns.1 v.fai.1s r.gp.2 p.a d.asm n.asm r.gp.2 d.nsm pt.pa.nsm v.pai.3s n.nsm p.a r.asm r.np.2
1506 3590 1506 4022 1609 2989 7007 4639 3836 4252 7007 3836 2989 1639 3707 1650 4005 7007

hopes are set. **46** If you believed Moses, you would believe me, for he wrote about me. **47** But since you do
ἠλπίκατε ← γὰρ εἰ → ἐπιστεύετε Μωϋσεῖ ᾿ ἂν ἐπιστεύετε ἐμοὶ γὰρ ἐκεῖνος ἔγραψεν περὶ ἐμοῦ δὲ εἰ
v.rai.2p cj cj v.iai.2p n.dsm pl v.iai.2p r.ds.1 cj r.nsm v.aai.3s p.g r.gs.1 cj cj
1827 1142 1623 4409 3707 4409 323 4409 1609 1142 1697 1211 4309 1609 1254 1623 4409 4409

not believe what he wrote, how are you going to believe what I say?"
οὐ πιστεύετε τοῖς ἐκείνου γράμμασιν πῶς → → → πιστεύσετε τοῖς ἐμοῖς ῥήμασιν
pl v.pai.2p d.dpn r.gsm n.dpn cj v.fai.2p d.dpn r.dpn.1 n.dpn
4024 4409 3836 1697 1207 4802 4409 3836 1847 4839

Jesus Feeds the Five Thousand

6:1 Some time after this, Jesus crossed to the far shore of the Sea of Galilee (that is, the Sea
Μετὰ ταῦτα ὁ Ἰησοῦς ἀπῆλθεν → πέραν ← → τῆς θαλάσσης ιτῆς Γαλιλαίας,
p.a r.apn d.nsm n.nsm v.aai.3s p.g d.gsf n.gsf d.gsf n.gsf
3552 4047 3836 2652 599 4305 3836 2498 3836 1133

of Tiberias), **2** and a great crowd of people followed him because they saw the miraculous signs he had
→ ιτῆς Τιβεριάδος, δὲ πολύς ὄχλος ἠκολούθει αὐτῷ ὅτι ἐθεώρουν τὰ σημεῖα ἃ
d.gsf n.gsf cj a.nsm n.nsm v.iai.3s r.dsm.3 cj v.iai.3p d.apn n.apn r.apn
3836 5500 1254 4498 4063 199 899 4022 2555 3836 4956 4005

performed on the sick. **3** Then Jesus went up on a mountainside and sat down with his
ἐποίει ἐπὶ τῶν ἀσθενούντων δὲ Ἰησοῦς ἀνῆλθεν εἰς ιτὸ ὄρος, καὶ ἐκεῖ ἐκάθητο ← μετὰ αὐτοῦ
v.iai.3s p.g d.gpm pt.pa.gpm cj n.nsm v.aai.3s p.a d.asn n.asn cj adv v.imi.3s p.g r.gsm.3
4472 2093 3836 820 1254 2652 456 1650 3836 4001 2779 1695 2764 3552 899

---

37 καὶ ὁ πέμψας με πατὴρ ἐκεῖνος μεμαρτύρηκεν περὶ ἐμοῦ. οὔτε φωνὴν αὐτοῦ πώποτε ἀκηκόατε οὔτε εἶδος αὐτοῦ ἑωράκατε,
38 καὶ τὸν λόγον αὐτοῦ οὐκ ἔχετε ἐν ὑμῖν μένοντα, ὅτι ὃν ἀπέστειλεν ἐκεῖνος, τούτῳ ὑμεῖς οὐ πιστεύετε. 39 ἐραυνᾶτε τὰς γραφάς,
ὅτι ὑμεῖς δοκεῖτε ἐν αὐταῖς ζωὴν αἰώνιον ἔχειν· καὶ ἐκεῖναί εἰσιν αἱ μαρτυροῦσαι περὶ ἐμοῦ· 40 καὶ οὐ θέλετε ἐλθεῖν πρός με
ἵνα ζωὴν ἔχητε. ¶ 41 Δόξαν παρὰ ἀνθρώπων οὐ λαμβάνω, 42 ἀλλὰ ἔγνωκα ὑμᾶς ὅτι τὴν ἀγάπην τοῦ θεοῦ οὐκ ἔχετε ἐν ἑαυτοῖς.
43 ἐγὼ ἐλήλυθα ἐν τῷ ὀνόματι τοῦ πατρός μου, καὶ οὐ λαμβάνετέ με· ἐὰν ἄλλος ἔλθῃ ἐν τῷ ὀνόματι τῷ ἰδίῳ, ἐκεῖνον λήμψεσθε.
44 πῶς δύνασθε ὑμεῖς πιστεῦσαι δόξαν παρὰ ἀλλήλων λαμβάνοντες, καὶ τὴν δόξαν τὴν παρὰ τοῦ μόνου θεοῦ οὐ ζητεῖτε; ¶ 45 μὴ
δοκεῖτε ὅτι ἐγὼ κατηγορήσω ὑμῶν πρὸς τὸν πατέρα· ἔστιν ὁ κατηγορῶν ὑμῶν Μωϋσῆς, εἰς ὃν ὑμεῖς ἠλπίκατε. 46 εἰ γὰρ ἐπιστεύετε
Μωϋσεῖ, ἐπιστεύετε ἂν ἐμοί· περὶ γὰρ ἐμοῦ ἐκεῖνος ἔγραψεν. 47 εἰ δὲ τοῖς ἐκείνου γράμμασιν οὐ πιστεύετε, πῶς τοῖς ἐμοῖς ῥήμασιν
πιστεύσετε;

6:1 Μετὰ ταῦτα ἀπῆλθεν ὁ Ἰησοῦς πέραν τῆς θαλάσσης τῆς Γαλιλαίας τῆς Τιβεριάδος. 2 ἠκολούθει δὲ αὐτῷ ὄχλος πολύς,
ὅτι ἐθεώρουν τὰ σημεῖα ἃ ἐποίει ἐπὶ τῶν ἀσθενούντων. 3 ἀνῆλθεν δὲ εἰς τὸ ὄρος Ἰησοῦς καὶ ἐκεῖ ἐκάθητο μετὰ τῶν μαθητῶν

disciples. **4** The Jewish Passover Feast was near. ¶ **5** When Jesus looked
ⸯτῶν μαθητῶνˏ δὲ ἡ ⸯτῶν Ἰουδαίωνˏ ⸯτὸ πάσχαˏ ἑορτὴ ἦν ἐγγὺς οὖν → ὁ Ἰησοῦςˏ Ἐπάρας τοὺς ὀφθαλμοὺςˏ
d.gpm n.gpm / cj d.nsf / d.gpm a.gpm / d.nsn n.nsn / n.nsf v.iai.3s adv / cj / d.nsm n.nsm pt.aa.nsm d.apm n.apm
3836 3412 / 1254 3836 / 3836 2681 / 3836 4247 / 2038 1639 1584 / 4036 / 2048 3836 2652 2048 3836 4057

up and saw a great crowd coming toward him, he said to Philip, "Where shall we buy bread for
← καὶ θεασάμενος ὅτι πολὺς ὄχλος ἔρχεται πρὸς αὐτόν → λέγει πρὸς Φίλιππον πόθεν → → ἀγοράσωμεν ἄρτους ἵνα
cj pt.am.nsm cj / a.nsm n.nsm / v.pmi.3s p.a r.asm.3 / v.pai.3s p.a n.asm / adv / v.aas.1p n.apm cj
2779 2517 4022 / 4498 4063 / 2262 4639 899 / 3306 4639 5805 / 4470 / 60 788 2671

these people to eat?" **6** He asked this only to test him, for he already had in mind what he was going
οὗτοι ← φάγωσιν δὲ → ἔλεγεν τοῦτο → πειράζων αὐτόν γὰρ αὐτὸς → → ᾔδει τί → → ἔμελλεν
r.npm v.aas.3p / cj v.iai.3s r.asn / pt.pa.nsm r.asm.3 cj r.nsm / v.lai.3s r.asn v.iai.3s
4047 2266 / 1254 3306 4047 / 4279 899 1142 899 / 3857 5515 3516

to do. **7** Philip answered him, "Eight months' wages would not buy enough bread for
→ ποιεῖν ὁ Φίλιππος, ἀπεκρίθη αὐτῷ ⸯδιακοσίων δηναρίωνˏ → οὐκ ἀρκοῦσιν αὐτοῖς ἄρτοι ἵνα
f.pa d.nsm n.nsm / v.api.3s r.dsm.3 a.gpn n.gpn / pl v.pai.3p / r.dpm.3 n.npm cj
4472 3836 5805 / 646 899 1357 1324 / 758 4024 758 / 899 788 2671

each one to have a bite!" **8** Another of his disciples, Andrew, Simon Peter's brother, spoke up,
ἕκαστος ← → λάβῃ βραχύ τι εἷς ἐκ αὐτοῦ ⸯτῶν μαθητῶνˏ Ἀνδρέας Σίμωνος Πέτρου ὁ ἀδελφός, λέγει ← αὐτῷ
r.nsm v.aas.3s a.asn r.asn / a.nsm p.g r.gsm.3 d.gpm n.gpm / n.nsm n.gsm n.gsm d.nsm n.nsm / v.pai.3s r.dsm.3
1667 3284 1099 5516 / 1651 1666 899 3836 3412 / 436 4981 4377 3836 81 / 3306 899

9 "Here is a boy with five small barley loaves and two small fish, but how far will they go among so
ὧδε ἐστιν παιδάριον ὃς ἔχει πέντε κριθίνους ἄρτους καὶ δύο → ὀψάρια ἀλλὰ ταῦτα τί ἐστιν εἰς →
adv v.pai.3s n.nsn r.nsm v.pai.3s a.apm a.apm n.apm cj a.apn n.apn cj r.npn r.nsn v.pai.3s p.a
6045 1639 4081 4005 2400 4297 3209 788 2779 1545 4066 247 4047 5515 1639 1650

many?" **10** Jesus said, "Have the people sit down." There was plenty of grass in that place, and the
τοσούτους ὁ Ἰησοῦςˏ εἶπεν ποιήσατε τοὺς ἀνθρώπους ἀναπεσεῖν ← δὲ → ἦν πολὺς ← χόρτος ἐν τῷ τόπῳ οὖν οἱ
r.apm d.nsm n.nsm v.aai.3s v.aam.2p d.apm n.apm f.aa / cj v.iai.3s a.nsm n.nsm p.d d.dsm n.dsm cj d.npm
5537 3836 2652 3306 4472 3836 476 404 / 1254 1639 4498 5965 1877 3836 5536 4036 3836

men sat down, about five thousand of them. **11** Jesus then took the loaves, gave
ἄνδρες ἀνέπεσαν ← τὸν ἀριθμὸν ὡς πεντακισχίλιοι ← ὁ Ἰησοῦςˏ οὖν ἔλαβεν τοὺς ἄρτους καὶ
n.npm v.aai.3p d.asm n.asm pl a.npm / d.nsm n.nsm cj v.aai.3s d.apm n.apm cj
467 404 3836 750 6055 4295 / 3836 2652 4036 3284 3836 788 2779

thanks, and distributed to those who were seated as much as they wanted. He did the same with the
εὐχαριστήσας διέδωκεν → τοῖς → ἀνακειμένοις ὅσον ← → ἤθελον καὶ ὁμοίως ἐκ τῶν
pt.aa.nsm v.aai.3s d.dpm pt.pm.dpm r.asn v.iai.3p adv adv p.g d.gpm
2373 1344 3836 367 4012 2527 2779 3931 1666 3836

fish. ¶ **12** When they had all had enough to eat, he said to his disciples, "Gather the pieces
ὀψαρίων δὲ ὡς ἐνεπλήσθησαν ← → λέγει αὐτοῦ τοῖς μαθηταῖς, συναγάγετε τὰ κλάσματα
n.gpn cj cj v.api.3p / v.pai.3s r.gsm.3 d.dpm n.dpm v.aam.2p d.apn n.apn
4066 1254 6055 1858 / 3306 3412 899 3836 3412 5251 3836 3083

that are left over. Let nothing be wasted." **13** So they gathered them and filled twelve baskets with the
→ → περισσεύσαντα ← ἵνα → μή τι → ἀπόληται οὖν → συνήγαγον καὶ ἐγέμισαν δώδεκα κοφίνους →
pt.aa.apn cj pl r.nsn v.ams.3s cj v.aai.3p cj v.aai.3p a.apm n.apm
4355 2671 660 3590 4005 5251 5251 4036 4355 / 2779 1153 1557 3186

pieces of the five barley loaves left over by those who had eaten. ¶ **14** After the
κλασμάτων ἐκ τῶν πέντε ⸯτῶν κριθίνωνˏ ἄρτων ἃ ἐπερίσσευσαν ← τοῖς ← → βεβρωκόσιν οὖν → Οἱ
n.gpn p.g d.gpm a.gpm d.gpm a.gpm n.gpm r.npn v.aai.3p d.dpm pt.ra.dpm cj d.npm
3083 1666 3836 4297 3836 3209 788 4005 4355 3836 1048 4036 1625 3836

people saw the miraculous sign that Jesus did, they began to say, "Surely this is the Prophet who
ἄνθρωποι ἰδόντες → σημεῖον ὃ ἐποίησεν → → ἔλεγον ὅτι ἀληθῶς οὗτος ἐστιν ὁ προφήτης ὁ
n.npm pt.aa.npm n.asn r.asn v.aai.3s v.iai.3p cj adv r.nsm v.pai.3s d.nsm n.nsm d.nsm
476 1625 4956 4005 4472 3306 4022 242 4047 1639 3836 4737 3836

is to come into the world." **15** Jesus, knowing that they intended to come and make him king by
→ ἐρχόμενος εἰς τὸν κόσμον οὖν Ἰησοῦς γνοὺς ὅτι → μέλλουσιν → ἔρχεσθαι καὶ ἵνα ποιήσωσιν βασιλέα
pt.pm.nsm p.a d.asm n.asm cj n.nsm pt.aa.nsm cj v.pai.3p f.pm cj cj v.aas.3p n.asm
2262 1650 3836 3180 4036 2652 1182 4022 3516 2262 2779 2671 4472 995

αὐτοῦ. ⁴ ἦν δὲ ἐγγὺς τὸ πάσχα, ἡ ἑορτὴ τῶν Ἰουδαίων. ¶ ⁵ ἐπάρας οὖν τοὺς ὀφθαλμοὺς ὁ Ἰησοῦς καὶ θεασάμενος ὅτι πολὺς ὄχλος ἔρχεται πρὸς αὐτὸν λέγει πρὸς Φίλιππον, Πόθεν ἀγοράσωμεν ἄρτους ἵνα φάγωσιν οὗτοι; ⁶ τοῦτο δὲ ἔλεγεν πειράζων αὐτόν· αὐτὸς γὰρ ᾔδει τί ἔμελλεν ποιεῖν. ⁷ ἀπεκρίθη αὐτῷ [ὁ] Φίλιππος, Διακοσίων δηναρίων ἄρτοι οὐκ ἀρκοῦσιν αὐτοῖς ἵνα ἕκαστος βραχύ [τι] λάβῃ. ⁸ λέγει αὐτῷ εἷς ἐκ τῶν μαθητῶν αὐτοῦ, Ἀνδρέας ὁ ἀδελφὸς Σίμωνος Πέτρου, ⁹ Ἔστιν παιδάριον ὧδε ὃς ἔχει πέντε ἄρτους κριθίνους καὶ δύο ὀψάρια· ἀλλὰ ταῦτα τί ἐστιν εἰς τοσούτους; ¹⁰ εἶπεν ὁ Ἰησοῦς, Ποιήσατε τοὺς ἀνθρώπους ἀναπεσεῖν. ἦν δὲ χόρτος πολὺς ἐν τῷ τόπῳ. ἀνέπεσαν οὖν οἱ ἄνδρες τὸν ἀριθμὸν ὡς πεντακισχίλιοι. ¹¹ ἔλαβεν οὖν τοὺς ἄρτους ὁ Ἰησοῦς καὶ εὐχαριστήσας διέδωκεν τοῖς ἀνακειμένοις ὁμοίως καὶ ἐκ τῶν ὀψαρίων ὅσον ἤθελον. ¶ ¹² ὡς δὲ ἐνεπλήσθησαν, λέγει τοῖς μαθηταῖς αὐτοῦ, Συναγάγετε τὰ περισσεύσαντα κλάσματα, ἵνα μή τι ἀπόληται. ¹³ συνήγαγον οὖν καὶ ἐγέμισαν δώδεκα κοφίνους κλασμάτων ἐκ τῶν πέντε ἄρτων τῶν κριθίνων ἃ ἐπερίσσευσαν τοῖς βεβρωκόσιν. ¶ ¹⁴ Οἱ οὖν ἄνθρωποι ἰδόντες ὃ ἐποίησεν σημεῖον ἔλεγον ὅτι Οὗτός ἐστιν ἀληθῶς ὁ προφήτης ὁ ἐρχόμενος εἰς τὸν κόσμον. ¹⁵ Ἰησοῦς οὖν

force,   withdrew again to a mountain by himself.
ἁρπάζειν αὐτὸν ἀνεχώρησεν πάλιν εἰς ⌐τὸ ὄρος⌐ ⌐αὐτὸς μόνος⌐
f.pa   r.asm.3 v.aai.3s adv   p.a d.asn n.asn r.nsm a.nsm
773   899   432   4099 1650 3836 4001   899   3668

Jesus Walks on the Water

6:16 When evening came, his disciples went down to the lake, **17** where they got into a
δὲ Ὡς   ὀψία ἐγένετο αὐτοῦ ⌐οἱ μαθηταὶ⌐ κατέβησαν ← ἐπὶ τὴν θάλασσαν καὶ   ἐμβάντες εἰς
cj cj   n.nsf v.ami.3s r.gsm.3 d.npm n.npm v.aai.3p   p.a d.asf n.asf   cj   pt.aa.npm p.a
1254 6055 4068 1181   899   3836 3412 2849   2093 3836 2498   2779   1832   1650

boat and set off across the lake   for Capernaum.   By now it was   dark, and Jesus   had not yet
πλοῖον ἤρχοντο ← πέραν τῆς θαλάσσης εἰς Καφαρναούμ καὶ → ἤδη → ἐγεγόνει σκοτία καὶ ⌐ὁ Ἰησοῦς⌐ → οὔπω →
n.asn v.imi.3p p.g   d.gsf n.gsf   p.a n.asf   cj   adv   v.lai.3s n.nsf cj d.nsm n.nsm   adv
4450   2262   4305 3836 2498   1650 3019   2779 2453 5028   2652 2779 3836 2652   4037

joined   them. **18** A strong wind was blowing and the waters grew rough. **19** When they had rowed
⌐ἐληλύθει πρὸς⌐ αὐτοὺς μεγάλου ἀνέμου → πνέοντος τε ἡ θάλασσα διεγείρετο οὖν → → → ἐληλακότες ὡς
v.lai.3s p.a   r.apm.3   a.gsm   n.gsm   pt.pa.gsm cj d.nsf n.nsf v.ipi.3s   cj   pt.ra.npm pl
2262   4639 899   3489   449   4463   5445 3836 2498   1444   4036   1785   6055

three   or three   and a half miles, they saw Jesus   approaching the boat, walking   on
⌐εἴκοσι πέντε⌐ ἢ τριάκοντα ← ← ← σταδίους → θεωροῦσιν τὸν Ἰησοῦν καὶ γινόμενον ἐγγὺς τοῦ πλοίου περιπατοῦντα ἐπὶ
a.apm a.apm cj a.apm   n.apm   v.pai.3p d.asm n.asm cj pt.pm.asm p.g   d.gsn n.gsn pt.pa.asn   p.g
1633   4297   2445 5558   5084   2555   3836 2652 2779 1181   1584 3836 4450   4344   2093

the water; and they were terrified. **20** But he said to them, "It is I; don't be afraid." **21** Then they were willing to
τῆς θαλάσσης καὶ → → ἐφοβήθησαν δὲ ὁ λέγει → αὐτοῖς εἰμι ἐγώ μὴ → φοβεῖσθε οὖν → → → ἤθελον →
d.gsf n.gsf   cj   v.api.3p   cj d.nsm v.pai.3s r.dpm.3 v.pai.1s r.ns.1 pl   v.ppm.2p cj   v.iai.3p
3836 2498   2779   5828   1254 3836 3306   899   1639   1609 3590   5828   4036   2527

take him into the boat, and immediately the boat reached the shore where they were heading. ¶
λαβεῖν αὐτὸν εἰς τὸ πλοῖον καὶ εὐθέως τὸ πλοῖον ⌐ἐγένετο ἐπὶ⌐ τῆς γῆς ⌐εἰς ἣν⌐ → → ὑπῆγον
f.aa   r.asm.3 p.a d.asn n.asn cj adv   d.nsn n.nsn v.ami.3s p.g d.gsf n.gsf p.a r.asf   v.iai.3p
3284   899   1650 3836 4450 2779 2311   3836 4450 1181   2093 3836 1178   1650 4005   5632

22 The next day the crowd that had stayed on the opposite shore of the lake realized that only one
Τῇ ἐπαύριον ← ὁ ὄχλος ὁ ἑστηκὼς → πέραν   τῆς θαλάσσης εἶδον ὅτι ⌐εἰ μὴ⌐ ἓν ἄλλο
d.dsf adv   d.nsm n.nsm d.nsm pt.ra.nsm p.g   d.gsf n.gsf   v.aai.3p cj cj pl a.nsn r.nsn
3836 2069   3836 4063 3836 2705   4305   3836 2498   1625 4022 1623 3590 1651 257

boat had been there, and that Jesus   had not entered it   with his disciples, but
πλοιάριον οὐκ → ἦν ἐκεῖ καὶ ὅτι ⌐ὁ Ἰησοῦς⌐ → οὐ συνεισῆλθεν εἰς ⌐τὸ πλοῖον⌐ → αὐτοῦ ⌐τοῖς μαθηταῖς⌐ ἀλλὰ
n.nsn   pl   v.iai.3s adv cj cj d.nsm n.nsm   pl v.aai.3s   p.a d.asn n.asn   r.gsm.3 d.dpm n.dpm   cj
4449   4024   1639 1695 2779 4022 3836 2652   5291 4024 5291   1650 3836 4450   3412   899 3836 3412   247

that they   had gone away alone. **23** Then some boats from Tiberias landed near the place where the
⌐οἱ μαθηταὶ αὐτοῦ⌐ → ἀπῆλθον ← μόνοι ἄλλα πλοιάρια ἐκ Τιβεριάδος ἦλθεν ἐγγὺς τοῦ τόπου ὅπου
d.npm n.npm r.gsm.3   v.aai.3p   a.npm r.npn   n.apn p.g n.gsf   v.aai.3s p.g d.gsm n.gsm cj
3836 3412 899   599   3668 257   4449 1666 5500   2262   1584 3836 5536 3963

people had eaten the bread after the Lord had given thanks. **24** Once the crowd realized that neither Jesus
→ ἔφαγον τὸν ἄρτον → τοῦ κυρίου → εὐχαριστήσαντος οὖν ὅτε ὁ ὄχλος εἶδεν ὅτι οὐκ Ἰησοῦς
v.aai.3p d.asm n.asm   d.gsm n.gsm   pt.aa.gsm   cj cj d.nsm n.nsm v.aai.3s cj pl n.nsm
2266 3836 788   2373 3836 3261   2373   4036 4021 3836 4063 1625 4022 4024 2652

nor his disciples were there, they got into the boats and went to Capernaum in search of Jesus.
οὐδὲ αὐτοῦ ⌐οἱ μαθηταὶ⌐ ἔστιν ἐκεῖ αὐτοὶ ἐνέβησαν εἰς τὰ πλοιάρια καὶ ἦλθον εἰς Καφαρναούμ ζητοῦντες ← ⌐τὸν Ἰησοῦν⌐
cj r.gsm.3 d.npm n.npm v.pai.3s adv r.npm v.aai.3p p.a d.apn n.apn cj v.aai.3p p.a n.asf   pt.pa.npm   d.asm n.asm
4028 899 3836 3412   1639 1695 899 1832   1650 3836 4449 2779 2262 1650 3019   2426   3836 2652

Jesus the Bread of Life

6:25 When they found him on the other side of the lake, they asked him, "Rabbi, when did you get
καὶ → → εὑρόντες αὐτὸν → πέραν τῆς θαλάσσης → εἶπον αὐτῷ ῥαββί πότε → → γέγονας
cj   pt.aa.npm r.asm.3 p.g   d.gsf n.gsf   v.aai.3p r.dsm.3 n.vsm adv   v.rai.2s
2779   2351   899   4305   3836 2498   3306 899   4806 4537   1181

here?" **26** Jesus   answered,   "I tell you the truth, you are looking for me, not because you saw
ὧδε ὁ Ἰησοῦς Ἀπεκρίθη αὐτοῖς καὶ εἶπεν λέγω ὑμῖν ⌐ἀμὴν ἀμὴν⌐ → ζητεῖτε ← με οὐχ ὅτι → εἴδετε
adv d.nsm n.nsm v.api.3s r.dpm.3 cj v.aai.3s v.pai.1s r.dp.2 pl   pl   v.pai.2p r.as.1 pl cj   v.aai.2p
6045 3836 2652 646   899 2779 3306 3306 7007 297 297   2426   1609 4024 4022   1625

γνοὺς ὅτι μέλλουσιν ἔρχεσθαι καὶ ἁρπάζειν αὐτὸν ἵνα ποιήσωσιν βασιλέα, ἀνεχώρησεν πάλιν εἰς τὸ ὄρος αὐτὸς μόνος.
⁶·¹⁶ Ὡς δὲ ὀψία ἐγένετο κατέβησαν οἱ μαθηταὶ αὐτοῦ ἐπὶ τὴν θάλασσαν ¹⁷ καὶ ἐμβάντες εἰς πλοῖον ἤρχοντο πέραν τῆς
θαλάσσης εἰς Καφαρναούμ. καὶ σκοτία ἤδη ἐγεγόνει καὶ οὔπω ἐληλύθει πρὸς αὐτοὺς ὁ Ἰησοῦς, ¹⁸ ἥ τε θάλασσα ἀνέμου μεγάλου
πνέοντος διεγείρετο. ¹⁹ ἐληλακότες οὖν ὡς σταδίους εἴκοσι πέντε ἢ τριάκοντα θεωροῦσιν τὸν Ἰησοῦν περιπατοῦντα ἐπὶ τῆς
θαλάσσης καὶ ἐγγὺς τοῦ πλοίου γινόμενον, καὶ ἐφοβήθησαν. ²⁰ ὁ δὲ λέγει αὐτοῖς, Ἐγώ εἰμι· μὴ φοβεῖσθε. ²¹ ἤθελον οὖν λαβεῖν
αὐτὸν εἰς τὸ πλοῖον, καὶ εὐθέως ἐγένετο τὸ πλοῖον ἐπὶ τῆς γῆς εἰς ἣν ὑπῆγον. ¶ ²² Τῇ ἐπαύριον ὁ ὄχλος ὁ ἑστηκὼς πέραν τῆς
θαλάσσης εἶδον ὅτι πλοιάριον ἄλλο οὐκ ἦν ἐκεῖ εἰ μὴ ἓν καὶ ὅτι οὐ συνεισῆλθεν τοῖς μαθηταῖς αὐτοῦ ὁ Ἰησοῦς εἰς τὸ πλοῖον
ἀλλὰ μόνοι οἱ μαθηταὶ αὐτοῦ ἀπῆλθον· ²³ ἄλλα ἦλθεν πλοιά[ρια] ἐκ Τιβεριάδος ἐγγὺς τοῦ τόπου ὅπου ἔφαγον τὸν ἄρτον
εὐχαριστήσαντος τοῦ κυρίου. ²⁴ ὅτε οὖν εἶδεν ὁ ὄχλος ὅτι Ἰησοῦς οὐκ ἔστιν ἐκεῖ οὐδὲ οἱ μαθηταὶ αὐτοῦ, ἐνέβησαν αὐτοὶ εἰς τὰ
πλοιάρια καὶ ἦλθον εἰς Καφαρναούμ ζητοῦντες τὸν Ἰησοῦν.
⁶·²⁵ καὶ εὑρόντες αὐτὸν πέραν τῆς θαλάσσης εἶπον αὐτῷ, Ῥαββί, πότε ὧδε γέγονας; ²⁶ ἀπεκρίθη αὐτοῖς ὁ Ἰησοῦς καὶ εἶπεν,

miraculous signs but because you ate   the loaves and had your fill.   **²⁷** Do not work   for food   that
→   σημεῖα ἀλλ' ὅτι   →   ἐφάγετε ἐκ τῶν ἄρτων καὶ →   →   ἐχορτάσθητε → μὴ ἐργάζεσθε ← ⌐τὴν βρῶσιν⌐ τὴν
          n.apn cj   cj   v.aai.2p p.g d.gpm n.gpm cj   v.api.2p   pl v.pmm.2p   d.asf n.asf   d.asf
          4956   247 4022   2266   1666 3836 788   2779   5963   2237 3590 2237   3836 1111   3836

spoils,   but for food   that endures to eternal life, which the Son of Man   will give you.   On
ἀπολλυμένην ἀλλὰ ⌐τὴν βρῶσιν⌐ τὴν μένουσαν εἰς αἰώνιον ζωὴν ἣν ὁ   υἱὸς →⌐τοῦ ἀνθρώπου⌐ δώσει ὑμῖν γὰρ →
pt.pm.asf   cj   d.asf n.asf   d.asf pt.pa.asf p.a a.asf n.asf r.asf d.nsm n.nsm d.gsm n.gsm v.fai.3s r.dp.2 cj
660   247 3836 1111   3836 3531   1650 173   2437 4005 3836 5626 3836 476   1443 7007 1142 5381

him   God   the Father has placed his seal   of approval." **²⁸** Then they asked   him, "What must we do
τοῦτον ὁ θεός, ὁ   πατὴρ →   ἐσφράγισεν ←   ←   οὖν →   εἶπον πρὸς αὐτόν τί →   ποιῶμεν
r.asm d.nsm n.nsm d.nsm n.nsm   v.aai.3s   cj   v.aai.3p p.a r.asm.3 r.asn   v.pas.1p
4047   3836 2536 3836 4252   5381   4036   3306   4639 899   5515   4472

to do   the works God   requires?" **²⁹** Jesus   answered,   "The work of God   is   this: to
ἵνα ἐργαζώμεθα τὰ ἔργα ⌐τοῦ θεοῦ⌐←   ὁ   Ἰησοῦς ἀπεκρίθη καὶ εἶπεν αὐτοῖς τὸ ἔργον →⌐τοῦ θεοῦ⌐ ἐστιν τοῦτο ἵνα
cj v.pms.1p   d.apn n.apn d.gsm n.gsm   d.nsm n.nsm v.api.3s cj v.aai.3s r.dpm.3 d.nsn n.nsn d.gsm n.gsm v.pai.3s r.asn cj
2671 2237   3836 2240 3836 2536   3836 2652 646   2779 3306   899   3836 2240 3836 2536 1639 4047 2671

believe in the one he   has sent." **³⁰** So they asked him, "What miraculous sign   then will you give that we
πιστεύητε εἰς ὃν ἐκεῖνος ἀπέστειλεν οὖν → Εἶπον αὐτῷ τί →   σημεῖον οὖν → σὺ ποιεῖς ἵνα
v.pas.2p p.a r.asm r.nsm v.aai.3s   cj   v.aai.3p r.dsm.3 r.asn   n.nsn   cj   r.ns.2 v.pai.2s cj
4409   1650 4005 4005   690   4036   3306   899   5515   4956   4036   5148 4472   2671

may see   it and believe you? What will you do? **³¹** Our forefathers ate   the manna in the desert; as   it is
→   ἴδωμεν καὶ πιστεύσωμεν σοι τί →   ἐργάζῃ ἡμῶν οἱ πατέρες ἔφαγον τὸ μάννα ἐν τῇ ἐρήμῳ καθώς → ἐστιν
     v.aas.1p cj v.aas.1p   r.ds.2 r.asn   v.pmi.2s r.gp.1 d.npm n.npm v.aai.3p d.asn n.asn p.d d.dsf n.dsf cj   v.pai.3s
     1625   2779 4409   5148 5515   2237   7005 3836 4252 2266   3836 3445 1877 3836 2245 2777   1639

written: 'He gave them bread from heaven   to eat.'" ¶ **³²** Jesus   said to them, "I tell you the
γεγραμμένον → ἔδωκεν αὐτοῖς ἄρτον ἐκ ⌐τοῦ οὐρανοῦ⌐ φαγεῖν   οὖν ⌐ὁ Ἰησοῦς⌐ εἶπεν → αὐτοῖς → λέγω ὑμῖν
pt.rp.nsn   v.aai.3s r.dpm.3 n.asm p.g d.gsm n.gsm   f.aa   cj d.nsm n.nsm v.aai.3s r.dpm.3 v.pai.1s r.dp.2
1211   1443   899   788   1666 3836 4041   2266   4036 3836 2652   3306   899   3306 7007

truth,   it is not Moses who has given you the bread from heaven,   but it is my Father   who gives you
ἀμὴν ἀμὴν ⌐οὐ⌐ Μωϋσῆς → δέδωκεν ὑμῖν τὸν ἄρτον ἐκ ⌐τοῦ οὐρανοῦ⌐ ἀλλ'   μου ὁ πατήρ → δίδωσιν ὑμῖν
pl   pl   pl n.nsm   v.rai.3s r.dp.2 d.asm n.asm p.g d.gsm n.gsm cj   r.gs.1 d.nsm n.nsm   v.pai.3s r.dp.2
297 297   4024 3707   1443   7007 3836 788 1666 3836 4041   247   1609 3836 4252   1443   7007

the true   bread from heaven. **³³** For the bread of God   is he who comes   down from heaven
τὸν ⌐τὸν ἀληθινόν⌐ ἄρτον ἐκ ⌐τοῦ οὐρανοῦ⌐ γὰρ ὁ ἄρτος →⌐τοῦ θεοῦ⌐ ἐστιν ὁ ←   καταβαίνων ← ἐκ ⌐τοῦ οὐρανοῦ⌐
d.asm d.asm d.asm n.asm p.g d.gsm n.gsm   cj d.nsm n.nsm d.gsm n.gsm v.pai.3s d.nsm   pt.pa.nsm   p.g d.gsm n.gsm
3836 3836 240   788   1666 3836 4041   1142 3836 788   3836 2536 1639 3836   2849   1666 3836 4041

and gives life to the world." **³⁴** "Sir," they said,   "from now on give us this bread." ¶
καὶ διδοὺς ζωὴν → τῷ κόσμῳ   οὖν κύριε →   εἶπον πρὸς αὐτόν πάντοτε ← δὸς ἡμῖν τοῦτον ⌐τὸν ἄρτον⌐
cj pt.pa.nsm n.asf d.dsm n.dsm cj n.vsm   v.aai.3p p.a r.asm.3 adv   v.aam.2s r.dp.1 r.asm d.asm n.asm
2779 1443   2437 3836 3180   4036 3261   3306   4639 899   4121   1443 7005 4047 3836 788

³⁵ Then Jesus   declared,   "I am the bread of life.   He who comes   to me will never go hungry,
ὁ Ἰησοῦς⌐ εἶπεν αὐτοῖς ἐγώ εἰμι ὁ ἄρτος ⌐τῆς ζωῆς⌐ ὁ ← ἐρχόμενος πρὸς ἐμέ →⌐οὐ μὴ⌐ → πεινάσῃ
d.nsm n.nsm v.aai.3s r.dpm.3 r.ns.1 v.pai.1s d.nsm n.nsm d.gsf n.gsf d.nsm   pt.pm.nsm p.a r.as.1 pl pl   v.aas.3s
3836 2652   3306   899   1609 1639 3836 788 3836 2437 3836   2262   4639 1609 4277 4024 3590   4277

and he who believes in me will never   be thirsty. **³⁶** But as I told you,   you have seen me and still
καὶ ὁ → πιστεύων εἰς ἐμὲ ⌐οὐ μὴ⌐ πώποτε⌐ διψήσει Ἀλλ' → εἶπον ὑμῖν ὅτι καὶ →   ἑωράκατέ με καὶ
cj d.nsm pt.pa.nsm p.a r.as.1 pl pl adv   v.fai.3s cj   v.aai.1s r.dp.2 cj cj   v.rai.3s r.as.1 cj
2779 3836 4409   1650 1609 1498 4024 3590 4799   1498   247   3306 7007 4022 2779   3972   1609 2779

you do not believe. **³⁷** All that the Father gives me will come to me, and whoever comes   to me I will never
→   οὐ πιστεύετε πᾶν ὃ ὁ πατὴρ δίδωσιν μοι →   ἥξει προς ἐμὲ καὶ τὸν ἐρχόμενον πρὸς ἐμέ → ⌐οὐ μὴ⌐
    pl v.pai.2p a.nsn r.asn d.nsm n.nsm v.pai.3s r.ds.1   v.fai.3s p.a r.as.1 cj d.asn pt.pm.asm   p.a r.as.1   pl pl
4409 4409 4024   4409 4005 3836 4252   1443   1609   2457 4639 1609 2779 3836 2262   4639 1609 1675 1675 4024 3590

drive away. **³⁸** For I have come down from heaven   not to do my   will   but to do the will   of
ἐκβάλω ἔξω   ὅτι → καταβέβηκα ← ἀπὸ ⌐τοῦ οὐρανοῦ⌐ οὐχ ἵνα ποιῶ ⌐τὸ ἐμὸν⌐ ⌐τὸ θέλημα⌐ ἀλλὰ   τὸ θέλημα
v.aas.1s adv   cj   v.rai.1s   p.g d.gsm n.gsm   pl cj v.pas.1s d.asn r.asn.1 d.asn n.asn   cj   d.asn n.asn
1675   2032   4022   2849   608 3836 4041   4024 2671 4472 3836 1847 3836 2525   247   3836 2525

Ἀμὴν ἀμὴν λέγω ὑμῖν, ζητεῖτέ με οὐχ ὅτι εἴδετε σημεῖα, ἀλλ' ὅτι ἐφάγετε ἐκ τῶν ἄρτων καὶ ἐχορτάσθητε. **²⁷** ἐργάζεσθε μὴ τὴν βρῶσιν τὴν ἀπολλυμένην ἀλλὰ τὴν βρῶσιν τὴν μένουσαν εἰς ζωὴν αἰώνιον, ἣν ὁ υἱὸς τοῦ ἀνθρώπου ὑμῖν δώσει· τοῦτον γὰρ ὁ πατὴρ ἐσφράγισεν ὁ θεός. **²⁸** εἶπον οὖν πρὸς αὐτόν, Τί ποιῶμεν ἵνα ἐργαζώμεθα τὰ ἔργα τοῦ θεοῦ; **²⁹** ἀπεκρίθη [ὁ] Ἰησοῦς καὶ εἶπεν αὐτοῖς, Τοῦτό ἐστι τὸ ἔργον τοῦ θεοῦ, ἵνα πιστεύητε εἰς ὃν ἀπέστειλεν ἐκεῖνος. **³⁰** εἶπον οὖν αὐτῷ, Τί οὖν ποιεῖς σὺ σημεῖον, ἵνα ἴδωμεν καὶ πιστεύσωμέν σοι; τί ἐργάζῃ; **³¹** οἱ πατέρες ἡμῶν τὸ μάννα ἔφαγον ἐν τῇ ἐρήμῳ, καθώς ἐστιν γεγραμμένον, Ἄρτον ἐκ τοῦ οὐρανοῦ ἔδωκεν αὐτοῖς φαγεῖν. ¶ **³²** εἶπεν οὖν αὐτοῖς ὁ Ἰησοῦς, Ἀμὴν ἀμὴν λέγω ὑμῖν, οὐ Μωϋσῆς δέδωκεν ὑμῖν τὸν ἄρτον ἐκ τοῦ οὐρανοῦ, ἀλλ' ὁ πατήρ μου δίδωσιν ὑμῖν τὸν ἄρτον ἐκ τοῦ οὐρανοῦ τὸν ἀληθινόν· **³³** ὁ γὰρ ἄρτος τοῦ θεοῦ ἐστιν ὁ καταβαίνων ἐκ τοῦ οὐρανοῦ καὶ ζωὴν διδοὺς τῷ κόσμῳ. **³⁴** Εἶπον οὖν πρὸς αὐτόν, Κύριε, πάντοτε δὸς ἡμῖν τὸν ἄρτον τοῦτον. ¶ **³⁵** εἶπεν οὖν αὐτοῖς ὁ Ἰησοῦς, Ἐγώ εἰμι ὁ ἄρτος τῆς ζωῆς· ὁ ἐρχόμενος πρὸς ἐμὲ οὐ μὴ πεινάσῃ, καὶ ὁ πιστεύων εἰς ἐμὲ οὐ μὴ διψήσει πώποτε. **³⁶** ἀλλ' εἶπον ὑμῖν ὅτι καὶ ἑωράκατέ [με] καὶ οὐ πιστεύετε. **³⁷** Πᾶν ὃ δίδωσίν μοι ὁ πατὴρ πρὸς ἐμὲ ἥξει, καὶ τὸν ἐρχόμενον πρὸς ἐμὲ οὐ μὴ ἐκβάλω ἔξω, **³⁸** ὅτι καταβέβηκα ἀπὸ τοῦ οὐρανοῦ οὐχ ἵνα ποιῶ τὸ θέλημα τὸ ἐμὸν

him who sent me. **39** And this is the will of him who sent me, that I shall lose none of all
τοῦ ← πέμψαντος με δέ τοῦτό ἐστιν τὸ θέλημα → τοῦ ← πέμψαντος με ἵνα → → ἀπολέσω μὴ ἐξ αὐτοῦ, πᾶν
d.gsm　pt.aa.gsm　r.as.1　cj　r.nsn　v.pai.3s　d.nsn　n.nsn　d.gsm　pt.aa.gsm　r.as.1　cj　v.aas.1s　pl　p.g　r.gsn.3　a.asn
3836　4287　1609　1254　4047　1639　3836　2525　3836　4287　1609　2671　660　3590　1666　899　4246

that he has given me, but raise them up at the last day. **40** For my Father's will is that
ὃ → → δέδωκέν μοι ἀλλὰ ἀναστήσω αὐτὸ ← [ἐν] τῇ ἐσχάτῃ ἡμέρα γάρ μου τοῦ πατρός, τὸ θέλημα, ἐστιν τοῦτό ἵνα
r.asn　v.rai.3s　r.ds.1　cj　v.fai.1s　r.asn.3　p.d　d.dsf　a.dsf　n.dsf　cj　r.gs.1　d.gsm　n.gsm　d.nsn　n.nsn　v.pai.3s　r.nsn　cj
4005　1443　1609　247　482　899　482　1877　3836　2274　2465　1142　1609　3836　4252　3836　2525　1639　4047　2671

everyone who looks to the Son and believes in him shall have eternal life, and I will raise him up at the
πᾶς ὁ θεωρῶν ← τὸν υἱὸν καὶ πιστεύων εἰς αὐτὸν → ἔχῃ αἰώνιον ζωὴν καὶ ἐγὼ ἀναστήσω αὐτὸν ← ἐν τῇ
a.nsm　d.nsm　pt.pa.nsm　d.asm　n.asm　cj　pt.pa.nsm　p.a　r.asm.3　v.pas.3s　a.asf　n.asf　cj　r.ns.1　v.fai.1s　r.asm.3　p.d　d.dsf
4246　3836　2555　3836　5626　2779　4409　1650　899　2400　173　2437　2779　1609　482　899　482　1877　3836

last day." ¶ **41** At this the Jews began to grumble about him because he said, "I am the bread that
ἐσχάτῃ ἡμέρα οὖν οἱ Ἰουδαῖοι → Ἐγόγγυζον περὶ αὐτοῦ ὅτι → εἶπεν ἐγὼ εἰμι ὁ ἄρτος ὁ
a.dsf　n.dsf　cj　d.npm　n.nsm　v.iai.3p　p.g　r.gs.3　cj　v.aai.3s　r.ns.1　v.pai.1s　d.nsm　n.nsm　d.nsm
2274　2465　4036　3836　2681　1197　4309　899　4022　3306　1609　1639　3836　788　3836

came down from heaven." **42** They said, "Is this not Jesus, the son of Joseph, whose father and
καταβὰς ← ἐκ τοῦ οὐρανοῦ, καὶ ἔλεγον ἐστιν οὗτος οὐχ Ἰησοῦς ὁ υἱὸς → Ἰωσήφ οὗ τὸν πατέρα, καὶ
pt.aa.nsm　p.g　d.gsm　n.gsm　cj　v.iai.3p　v.pai.3s　r.nsm　pl　n.nsm　d.nsm　n.nsm　n.gsm　r.gsm　d.asm　n.asm　cj
2849　1666　3836　4041　2779　3306　1639　4047　4024　2652　3836　5626　2737　4005　3836　4252　2779

mother we know? How can he now say, 'I came down from heaven'?" **43** "Stop grumbling among
τὴν μητέρα, ἡμεῖς οἴδαμεν πῶς → → νῦν λέγει ὅτι → καταβέβηκα ← ἐκ τοῦ οὐρανοῦ, μὴ γογγύζετε μετ'
d.asf　n.asf　r.np.1　v.rai.1p　cj　adv　v.pai.3s　cj　v.rai.1s　p.g　d.gsm　n.gsm　pl　v.pam.2p　p.g
3836　3613　7005　3857　4802　3306　3306　3814　3306　4022　2849　1666　3836　4041　3590　1197　3552

yourselves," Jesus answered. **44** "No one can come to me unless the Father who sent me
ἀλλήλων, Ἰησοῦς ἀπεκρίθη καὶ εἶπεν αὐτοῖς → οὐδεὶς δύναται ἐλθεῖν πρός με ἐὰν μὴ ὁ πατὴρ ὁ πέμψας με
r.gpm　n.nsm　v.api.3s　cj　v.aai.3s　r.dpm.3　r.nsm　v.ppi.3s　f.aa　p.a　r.as.1　cj　pl　d.nsm　n.nsm　d.nsm　pt.aa.nsm　r.as.1
253　2652　646　2779　3306　899　4029　1538　2262　4639　1609　1569　3590　3836　4252　3836　4287　1609

draws him, and I will raise him up at the last day. **45** It is written in the Prophets: 'They will
ἑλκύσῃ αὐτόν καγὼ ← ἀναστήσω αὐτὸν ← ἐν τῇ ἐσχάτῃ ἡμέρα → ἐστιν γεγραμμένον ἐν τοῖς προφήταις καὶ ἔσονται
v.aas.3s　r.asm.3　crasis　v.fai.1s　r.asm.3　p.d　d.dsf　a.dsf　n.dsf　v.pai.3s　pt.rp.nsm　p.d　d.dpm　n.dpm　cj　v.fmi.3p
1816　899　2743　482　899　482　1877　3836　2274　2465　1639　1211　1877　3836　4737　2779　1639

all be taught by God.' Everyone who listens to the Father and learns from him comes to me. **46** No one
πάντες ← διδακτοὶ θεοῦ πᾶς ὁ ἀκούσας παρὰ τοῦ πατρὸς καὶ μαθὼν ἔρχεται πρὸς ἐμέ οὐχ ὅτι τις
a.npm　a.npm　n.gsm　a.nsm　d.nsm　pt.aa.nsm　p.g　d.gsm　n.gsm　cj　pt.aa.nsm　v.pmi.3s　p.a　r.as.1　pl　cj　r.nsm
4246　1639　1435　2536　4246　3836　201　4123　3836　4252　2779　3443　2262　4639　1609　4024　4022　5516

has seen the Father except the one who is from God; only he has seen the Father. **47** I tell you the
→ ἑώρακεν τὸν πατέρα εἰ μὴ ὁ ← ὢν παρὰ τοῦ θεοῦ, οὗτος → ἑώρακεν τὸν πατέρα → λέγω ὑμῖν
v.rai.3s　d.asm　n.asm　cj　pl　d.nsm　pt.pa.nsm　p.g　d.gsm　n.gsm　r.nsm　v.rai.3s　d.asm　n.asm　v.pai.1s　r.dp.2
3972　3836　4252　1623　3590　3836　1639　4123　3836　2536　4047　3972　3836　4252　3306　7007

truth, he who believes has everlasting life. **48** I am the bread of life. **49** Your forefathers ate the manna
ἀμὴν ἀμὴν, ὁ ← πιστεύων ἔχει αἰώνιον ζωήν Ἐγώ εἰμι ὁ ἄρτος → τῆς ζωῆς, ὑμῶν οἱ πατέρες, ἔφαγον τὸ μάννα
pl　pl　d.nsm　pt.pa.nsm　v.pai.3s　a.asf　n.asf　r.ns.1　v.pai.1s　d.nsm　n.nsm　d.gsf　n.gsf　r.gp.2　d.npm　n.npm　v.aai.3p　d.asn　n.asn
297　297　3836　4409　2400　2437　1609　1639　3836　788　3836　2437　7007　3836　4252　2266　3836　3445

in the desert, yet they died. **50** But here is the bread that comes down from heaven, which a
ἐν τῇ ἐρήμῳ καὶ ἀπέθανον οὗτός ἐστιν ὁ ἄρτος ὁ καταβαίνων ἐκ τοῦ οὐρανοῦ, ἵνα ἐξ αὐτοῦ
p.d　d.dsf　n.dsf　cj　v.aai.3p　r.nsm　v.pai.3s　d.nsm　n.nsm　d.nsm　pt.pa.nsm　p.g　d.gsm　n.gsm　cj　p.g　r.gsn.3
1877　3836　2245　2779　633　4047　1639　3836　788　3836　2849　1666　3836　4041　2671　1666　899

man may eat and not die. **51** I am the living bread that came down from heaven. If anyone eats of
τις → φάγῃ καὶ μὴ ἀποθάνῃ ἐγώ εἰμι ὁ ζῶν ὁ ἄρτος ὁ καταβὰς ← ἐκ τοῦ οὐρανοῦ, ἐάν τις φάγῃ ἐκ
r.nsm　v.aas.3s　cj　pl　v.aas.3s　r.ns.1　v.pai.1s　d.nsm　pt.pa.nsm　d.nsm　n.nsm　d.nsm　pt.aa.nsm　p.g　d.gsm　n.gsm　cj　r.nsm　v.aas.3s　p.g
5516　2266　2779　3590　633　1609　1639　3836　2409　3836　788　3836　2849　1666　3836　4041　1569　5516　2266　1666

this bread, he will live forever. This bread is my flesh, which I will give for the life of
τούτου τοῦ ἄρτου, → → ζήσει εἰς τὸν αἰῶνα δὲ ὁ καὶ ἄρτος ἐστιν μού ἡ σάρξ, ὃν ἐγὼ → δώσω ὑπὲρ τῆς ζωῆς →
r.gsm　d.gsm　n.gsm　v.fai.3s　p.a　d.asm　n.asm　cj　d.nsm　cj　n.nsm　v.pai.3s　r.gs.1　d.nsf　n.nsf　r.asm　r.ns.1　v.fai.1s　p.g　d.gsf　n.gsf
4047　3836　788　2409　1650　3836　172　1254　3836　2779　788　1639　1609　4922　4005　1609　1443　5642　3836　2437

ἀλλὰ τὸ θέλημα τοῦ πέμψαντός με. **39** τοῦτο δέ ἐστιν τὸ θέλημα τοῦ πέμψαντός με, ἵνα πᾶν ὃ δέδωκέν μοι μὴ ἀπολέσω ἐξ αὐτοῦ, ἀλλὰ ἀναστήσω αὐτὸ [ἐν] τῇ ἐσχάτῃ ἡμέρα. **40** τοῦτο γάρ ἐστιν τὸ θέλημα τοῦ πατρός μου, ἵνα πᾶς ὁ θεωρῶν τὸν υἱὸν καὶ πιστεύων εἰς αὐτὸν ἔχῃ ζωὴν αἰώνιον, καὶ ἀναστήσω αὐτὸν ἐγὼ [ἐν] τῇ ἐσχάτῃ ἡμέρα. **¶** **41** Ἐγόγγυζον οὖν οἱ Ἰουδαῖοι περὶ αὐτοῦ ὅτι εἶπεν, Ἐγώ εἰμι ὁ ἄρτος ὁ καταβὰς ἐκ τοῦ οὐρανοῦ, **42** καὶ ἔλεγον, Οὐχ οὗτός ἐστιν Ἰησοῦς ὁ υἱὸς Ἰωσήφ, οὗ ἡμεῖς οἴδαμεν τὸν πατέρα καὶ τὴν μητέρα; πῶς νῦν λέγει ὅτι Ἐκ τοῦ οὐρανοῦ καταβέβηκα; **43** ἀπεκρίθη Ἰησοῦς καὶ εἶπεν αὐτοῖς, Μὴ γογγύζετε μετ' ἀλλήλων. **44** οὐδεὶς δύναται ἐλθεῖν πρός με ἐὰν μὴ ὁ πατὴρ ὁ πέμψας με ἑλκύσῃ αὐτόν, καγὼ ἀναστήσω αὐτὸν ἐν τῇ ἐσχάτῃ ἡμέρα. **45** ἔστιν γεγραμμένον ἐν τοῖς προφήταις, Καὶ ἔσονται πάντες διδακτοὶ θεοῦ· πᾶς ὁ ἀκούσας παρὰ τοῦ πατρὸς καὶ μαθὼν ἔρχεται πρὸς ἐμέ. **46** οὐχ ὅτι τὸν πατέρα ἑώρακέν τις εἰ μὴ ὁ ὢν παρὰ τοῦ θεοῦ, οὗτος ἑώρακεν τὸν πατέρα. **47** ἀμὴν ἀμὴν λέγω ὑμῖν, ὁ πιστεύων ἔχει ζωὴν αἰώνιον. **48** ἐγώ εἰμι ὁ ἄρτος τῆς ζωῆς. **49** οἱ πατέρες ὑμῶν ἔφαγον ἐν τῇ ἐρήμῳ τὸ μάννα καὶ ἀπέθανον· **50** οὗτός ἐστιν ὁ ἄρτος ὁ ἐκ τοῦ οὐρανοῦ καταβαίνων, ἵνα τις ἐξ αὐτοῦ φάγῃ καὶ μὴ ἀποθάνῃ. **51** ἐγώ εἰμι ὁ ἄρτος ὁ ζῶν ὁ ἐκ τοῦ οὐρανοῦ καταβάς· ἐάν τις φάγῃ ἐκ τούτου τοῦ ἄρτου ζήσει εἰς τὸν αἰῶνα, καὶ ὁ ἄρτος δὲ ὃν ἐγὼ δώσω ἡ

the world." ¶ **52** Then the Jews began to argue sharply among themselves, "How can this man
τοῦ κόσμου οὖν οἱ Ἰουδαῖοι → → Ἐμάχοντο ← πρὸς ἀλλήλους λέγοντες πῶς δύναται οὗτος ←
d.gsm n.gsm cj d.npm a.npm v.imi.3p p.a r.apm pt.pa.npm pt v.ppi.3s r.nsm
3836 3180 4036 3836 2681 3481 4639 253 3306 4802 1538 4047

give us his flesh to eat?" **53** Jesus said to them, "I tell you the truth, unless you eat the
δοῦναι ἡμῖν αὐτοῦ ⌐τὴν σάρκα⌐ → φαγεῖν οὖν ὁ Ἰησοῦς⌐ εἶπεν αὐτοῖς → λέγω ὑμῖν ἀμὴν ἀμὴν ἐὰν μὴ → φάγητε τὴν
f.aa r.dp.1 r.gsm.3 d.asf n.asf f.aa cj d.nsm n.nsm v.aai.3s r.dpm.3 v.pai.1s r.dp.2 pl pl cj pl v.aas.2p d.asf
1443 7005 899 3836 4922 2266 4036 3836 2652 3306 899 3306 7007 297 297 1569 3590 2266 3836

flesh of the Son of Man and drink his blood, you have no life in you. **54** Whoever eats my
σάρκα → τοῦ υἱοῦ → ⌐τοῦ ἀνθρώπου⌐ καὶ πίητε αὐτοῦ ⌐τὸ αἷμα⌐ → ἔχετε οὐκ ζωὴν ἐν ἑαυτοῖς ὁ τρώγων μου
n.asf d.gsm n.gsm d.gsm n.gsm cj v.aas.2p r.gsm.3 d.asn n.asn v.pai.2p pl n.asf p.d r.dpm.2 d.nsm pt.pa.nsm r.gs.1
4922 3836 5626 3836 476 2779 4403 899 3836 135 2400 4024 2437 1877 1571 3836 5592 1609

flesh and drinks my blood has eternal life, and I will raise him up at the last day. **55** For my flesh
⌐τὴν σάρκα⌐ καὶ πίνων μου ⌐τὸ αἷμα⌐ ἔχει αἰώνιον ζωὴν κἀγὼ ← ← ἀναστήσω αὐτὸν → → τῇ ἐσχάτῃ ἡμέρᾳ γὰρ μου ἡ σάρξ
d.asf n.asf cj pt.pa.nsm r.gs.1 d.asn n.asn v.pai.3s a.asf n.asf crasis v.fai.1s r.asm.3 d.dsf a.dsf n.dsf cj r.gs.1 d.nsf n.nsf
3836 4922 2779 4403 1609 3836 135 2400 173 2437 2743 482 899 482 3836 2274 2465 1142 1609 3836 4922

is real food and my blood is real drink. **56** Whoever eats my flesh and drinks my blood remains
ἐστιν ἀληθὴς βρῶσις καὶ μου ⌐τὸ αἷμα⌐ ἐστιν ἀληθής πόσις ὁ τρώγων μου ⌐τὴν σάρκα⌐ καὶ πίνων μου ⌐τὸ αἷμα⌐ μένει
v.pai.3s a.nsf n.nsf cj r.gs.1 d.nsn n.nsn v.pai.3s a.nsf n.nsf d.nsm pt.pa.nsm r.gs.1 d.asf n.asf cj pt.pa.nsm r.gs.1 d.asn n.asn v.pai.3s
1639 239 1111 2779 1609 3836 135 1639 239 4530 3836 5592 1609 3836 4922 2779 4403 1609 3836 135 3531

in me, and I in him. **57** Just as the living Father sent me and I live because of the Father, so the one who
ἐν ἐμοὶ κἀγὼ ← ἐν αὐτῷ καθὼς ← ὁ ζῶν πατὴρ ἀπέστειλεν με κἀγὼ ← ζῶ διὰ ← τὸν πατέρα καὶ ὁ ← ← ←
p.d r.ds.1 crasis p.d r.dsm.3 cj d.nsm pt.pa.nsm n.nsm v.aai.3s r.as.1 crasis v.pai.1s p.a d.asm n.asm cj d.nsm
1877 1609 2743 1877 899 2777 3836 2409 4252 690 1609 2743 2409 1328 3836 4252 2779 3836

feeds on me will live because of me. **58** This is the bread that came down from heaven. Your
τρώγων ← με κἀκεῖνος → ζήσει δι᾽ ← ἐμέ οὗτος ἐστιν ὁ ἄρτος ὁ καταβάς → ἐξ οὐρανοῦ οὐ καθὼς οἱ
pt.pa.nsm r.as.1 crasis v.fai.3s p.a r.as.1 r.nsm v.pai.3s d.nsm n.nsm d.nsm pt.aa.nsm p.g n.gsm pl cj d.npm
5592 1609 2797 2409 1328 1609 4047 1639 3836 788 3836 2849 1666 4041 4024 2777 3836

forefathers ate manna and died, but he who feeds on this bread will live forever." **59** He said this
πατέρες ἔφαγον καὶ ἀπέθανον ὁ ← τρώγων ← τοῦτον ⌐τὸν ἄρτον⌐ → ζήσει εἰς τὸν αἰῶνα⌐ → εἶπεν Ταῦτα
n.npm v.aai.3p cj v.aai.3p d.nsm pt.pa.nsm r.asm d.asm n.asm v.fai.3s p.a d.asm n.asm v.aai.3s r.apn
4252 2266 2779 633 3836 5592 4047 3836 788 2409 1650 3836 172 3306 4047

while teaching in the synagogue in Capernaum.
→ διδάσκων ἐν συναγωγῇ ἐν Καφαρναούμ
pt.pa.nsm p.d n.dsf p.d n.dsf
1438 1877 5252 1877 3019

Many Disciples Desert Jesus

6:60 On hearing it, many of his disciples said, "This is a hard teaching. Who can accept
οὖν → ἀκούσαντες Πολλοὶ ἐκ αὐτοῦ ⌐τῶν μαθητῶν⌐ εἶπαν οὗτος ἐστιν σκληρός ὁ λόγος⌐ τίς δύναται ἀκούειν
cj pt.aa.npm a.npm p.g r.gsm.3 d.gpm n.gpm v.aai.3p r.nsm v.pai.3s a.nsm d.nsm n.nsm r.nsm v.ppi.3s f.pa
4036 201 4498 1666 899 3836 3412 3306 4047 1639 5017 3836 3364 5515 1538 201

it?" ¶ **61** Aware that his disciples were grumbling about this, Jesus said to them, "Does
αὐτοῦ δὲ ⌐εἰδὼς ἐν ἑαυτῷ⌐ ὅτι αὐτοῦ οἱ μαθηταὶ → γογγύζουσιν περὶ τούτου ὁ Ἰησοῦς εἶπεν → αὐτοῖς ←
r.gsm.3 cj pt.ra.nsm p.d r.dsm.3 cj r.gsm.3 d.npm n.npm v.pai.3p p.g r.gsn d.nsm n.nsm v.aai.3s r.dpm.3
899 1254 3857 1877 1571 4022 899 3836 3412 1197 4309 4047 3836 2652 3306 899 4997

this offend you? **62** What if you see the Son of Man ascend to where he was before!
τοῦτο σκανδαλίζει ὑμᾶς οὖν ἐὰν → θεωρῆτε τὸν υἱὸν → ⌐τοῦ ἀνθρώπου⌐ ἀναβαίνοντα ὅπου → ἦν ⌐τὸ πρότερον⌐
r.nsn v.pai.3s r.ap.2 cj cj v.pas.2p d.asm n.asm d.gsm n.gsm pt.pa.asm r.adv v.iai.3s d.asn adv.c
4047 4997 7007 4036 1569 2555 3836 5626 3836 476 326 3963 1639 3836 4728

63 The Spirit gives life; the flesh counts for nothing. The words I have spoken to you are
τὸ πνεῦμα ἐστιν → ⌐τὸ ζῳοποιοῦν⌐ ἡ σὰρξ οὐκ ὠφελεῖ → οὐδέν τὰ ῥήματα ἃ ἐγὼ → λελάληκα ὑμῖν ἐστιν
d.nsn n.nsn v.pai.3s d.nsn pt.pa.nsn d.nsf n.nsf pl v.pai.3s a.asn d.npn n.npn r.apn r.ns.1 v.rai.1s r.dp.2 v.pai.3s
3836 4460 1639 3836 2443 3836 4922 4024 6067 4029 3836 4839 4005 1609 3281 7007 1639

σάρξ μού ἐστιν ὑπὲρ τῆς τοῦ κόσμου ζωῆς. ¶ **52** Ἐμάχοντο οὖν πρὸς ἀλλήλους οἱ Ἰουδαῖοι λέγοντες, Πῶς δύναται οὗτος ἡμῖν δοῦναι τὴν σάρκα [αὐτοῦ] φαγεῖν; **53** εἶπεν οὖν αὐτοῖς ὁ Ἰησοῦς, Ἀμὴν ἀμὴν λέγω ὑμῖν, ἐὰν μὴ φάγητε τὴν σάρκα τοῦ υἱοῦ τοῦ ἀνθρώπου καὶ πίητε αὐτοῦ τὸ αἷμα, οὐκ ἔχετε ζωὴν ἐν ἑαυτοῖς. **54** ὁ τρώγων μου τὴν σάρκα καὶ πίνων μου τὸ αἷμα ἔχει ζωὴν αἰώνιον, κἀγὼ ἀναστήσω αὐτὸν τῇ ἐσχάτῃ ἡμέρᾳ. **55** ἡ γὰρ σάρξ μου ἀληθής ἐστιν βρῶσις, καὶ τὸ αἷμά μου ἀληθής ἐστιν πόσις. **56** ὁ τρώγων μου τὴν σάρκα καὶ πίνων μου τὸ αἷμα ἐν ἐμοὶ μένει κἀγὼ ἐν αὐτῷ. **57** καθὼς ἀπέστειλέν με ὁ ζῶν πατὴρ κἀγὼ ζῶ διὰ τὸν πατέρα, καὶ ὁ τρώγων με κἀκεῖνος ζήσει δι᾽ ἐμέ. **58** οὗτός ἐστιν ὁ ἄρτος ὁ ἐξ οὐρανοῦ καταβάς, οὐ καθὼς ἔφαγον οἱ πατέρες ὑμῶν τὸ μάννα καὶ ἀπέθανον· ὁ τρώγων τοῦτον τὸν ἄρτον ζήσει εἰς τὸν αἰῶνα. **59** Ταῦτα εἶπεν ἐν συναγωγῇ διδάσκων ἐν Καφαρναούμ.

6:60 Πολλοὶ οὖν ἀκούσαντες ἐκ τῶν μαθητῶν αὐτοῦ εἶπαν, Σκληρός ἐστιν ὁ λόγος οὗτος· τίς δύναται αὐτοῦ ἀκούειν; ¶ **61** εἰδὼς δὲ ὁ Ἰησοῦς ἐν ἑαυτῷ ὅτι γογγύζουσιν περὶ τούτου οἱ μαθηταὶ αὐτοῦ εἶπεν αὐτοῖς, Τοῦτο ὑμᾶς σκανδαλίζει; **62** ἐὰν οὖν θεωρῆτε τὸν υἱὸν τοῦ ἀνθρώπου ἀναβαίνοντα ὅπου ἦν τὸ πρότερον; **63** τὸ πνεῦμά ἐστιν τὸ ζῳοποιοῦν, ἡ σὰρξ οὐκ ὠφελεῖ

spirit and they are life. **64** Yet there are some of you who do not believe." For Jesus had known from the
πνεῦμα καὶ → ἐστιν ζωή ἀλλ' → εἰσιν τινες ἐξ ὑμῶν οἳ → οὐ πιστεύουσιν γὰρ ὁ Ἰησοῦς → ᾔδει ἐξ
n.nsn cj v.pai.3s n.nsf cj v.pai.3p r.npm p.g r.gp.2 pl v.pai.3p cj d.nsm n.nsm v.lai.3s p.g
4460 2779 1639 2437 247 1666 5516 1666 7007 4005 4409 4409 1142 3836 2652 3857 1666

beginning which of them did not believe and who would betray him. **65** He went on to say,
ἀρχῆς τίνες εἰσὶν μὴ οἱ πιστεύοντες καὶ τίς ἐστιν ὁ παραδώσων αὐτόν καὶ → → → ἔλεγεν
n.gsf r.npm v.pai.3p pl d.npm pt.pa.npm cj r.nsm v.pai.3s d.nsm pt.fa.nsm r.asm.3 cj v.iai.3s
794 5515 1639 3590 3836 4409 2779 5515 1639 3836 4140 899 2779 3306

"This is why I told you that no one can come to me unless the Father has enabled him."
διὰ τοῦτο ← → εἴρηκα ὑμῖν ὅτι οὐδεὶς δύναται ἐλθεῖν πρός με ἐὰν μὴ ἐκ τοῦ πατρός → ᾖ δεδομένον αὐτῷ
p.a r.asn v.rai.1s r.dp.2 cj a.nsm v.ppi.3s f.aa p.a r.as.1 cj pl p.g d.gsm n.gsm v.pas.3s pt.rp.nsn r.dsm.3
1328 4047 3306 7007 4022 4029 1538 2262 4639 1609 1569 3590 1666 3836 4252 1639 1443 899

¶ **66** From this time many of his disciples turned back and no longer followed him. ¶
Ἐκ τούτου ← πολλοὶ ἐκ αὐτοῦ τῶν μαθητῶν ἀπῆλθον εἰς τὰ ὀπίσω καὶ οὐκέτι ← περιεπάτουν μετ' αὐτοῦ
p.g r.gsn a.npm p.g r.gsm.3 d.gpm n.gpm v.aai.3p p.a d.apn adv cj adv v.iai.3p p.g r.gsm.3
1666 4047 4498 1666 899 3836 3412 599 1650 3836 3958 2779 4033 4344 3552 899

67 "You do not want to leave too, do you?" Jesus asked the Twelve. **68** Simon Peter answered him, "Lord,
ὑμεῖς → ← θέλετε → ὑπάγειν καὶ μὴ → οὖν ὁ Ἰησοῦς εἶπεν τοῖς δώδεκα Σίμων Πέτρος ἀπεκρίθη αὐτῷ κύριε
r.np.2 v.pai.2p f.pa adv pl cj d.nsm n.nsm v.aai.3s d.dpm a.dpm n.nsm n.nsm v.api.3s r.dsm.3 n.vsm
7007 2527 3590 2527 5632 2779 3590 4036 3836 2652 3306 3836 1557 4981 4377 646 899 3261

to whom shall we go? You have the words of eternal life. **69** We believe and know that you are
πρός τίνα → → ἀπελευσόμεθα → ἔχεις ῥήματα → αἰωνίου ζωῆς καὶ ἡμεῖς πεπιστεύκαμεν καὶ ἐγνώκαμεν ὅτι σὺ εἶ
p.a r.asm v.fmi.1p v.pai.2s n.apn a.gsf n.gsf cj r.np.1 v.rai.1p cj v.rai.1p cj r.ns.2 v.pai.2s
4639 5515 2400 2400 4839 173 2437 2779 7005 4409 2779 1182 4022 5148 1639

the Holy One of God." **70** Then Jesus replied, "Have I not chosen you, the Twelve? Yet one of
ὁ ἅγιος → τοῦ θεοῦ ὁ Ἰησοῦς ἀπεκρίθη αὐτοῖς → ἐγὼ οὐκ ἐξελεξάμην ὑμᾶς τοὺς δώδεκα καὶ εἷς ἐξ
d.nsm a.nsm d.gsm n.gsm d.nsm n.nsm v.api.3s r.dpm.3 r.ns.1 pl v.ami.1s r.ap.2 d.apm a.apm cj a.nsm p.g
3836 41 3836 2536 3836 2652 646 899 1721 1609 4024 1721 7007 3836 1557 2779 1651 1666

you is a devil!" **71** (He meant Judas, the son of Simon Iscariot, who, though one of the Twelve,
ὑμῶν ἐστιν διάβολος δὲ → ἔλεγεν τὸν Ἰούδαν → Σίμωνος Ἰσκαριώτου γὰρ οὗτος εἷς ἐκ τῶν δώδεκα
r.gp.2 v.pai.3s n.nsm cj v.iai.3s d.asm n.asm n.gsm n.gsm cj r.nsm a.nsm p.g d.gpm a.gsm
7007 1639 1333 1254 3306 3836 2683 4981 2697 1142 4047 1651 1666 3836 1557

was later to betray him.)
→ ἔμελλεν → παραδιδόναι αὐτόν
v.iai.3s f.pa r.asm.3
3516 4140 899

Jesus Goes to the Feast of Tabernacles

7:1 After this, Jesus went around in Galilee, *purposely staying away from Judea*
Καὶ μετὰ ταῦτα ὁ Ἰησοῦς περιεπάτει ← ἐν τῇ Γαλιλαίᾳ γὰρ οὐ ἤθελεν περιπατεῖν ἐν τῇ Ἰουδαίᾳ
cj p.a r.apn d.nsm n.nsm v.iai.3s p.d d.dsf n.dsf cj pl v.iai.3s f.pa p.d d.dsf n.dsf
2779 3552 4047 3836 2652 4344 1877 3836 1133 1142 4024 2527 4344 1877 3836 2677

because the Jews there were waiting to take his life. **2** But when the Jewish Feast of Tabernacles
ὅτι οἱ Ἰουδαῖοι → ἐζήτουν ἀποκτεῖναι → αὐτόν δὲ ἡ τῶν Ἰουδαίων ἑορτὴ ἡ σκηνοπηγία
cj d.npm n.npm v.iai.3p f.aa r.asm.3 cj d.nsf d.gpm a.gpm n.nsf d.nsf n.nsf
4022 3836 2681 2426 650 899 1254 3836 3836 2681 2038 3836 5009

was near, **3** Jesus' brothers said to him, "You ought to leave here and go to Judea, so that
Ἦν ἐγγὺς οὖν αὐτοῦ οἱ ἀδελφοὶ εἶπον πρὸς αὐτόν → μετάβηθι ἐντεῦθεν καὶ ὕπαγε εἰς τὴν Ἰουδαίαν ἵνα
v.iai.3s adv cj r.gsm.3 d.npm n.npm v.aai.3p p.a r.asm.3 v.aam.2s adv cj v.pam.2s p.a d.asf n.asf cj
1639 1584 4036 899 3836 81 3306 4639 899 3553 1949 2779 5632 1650 3836 2677 2671

your disciples may see the miracles you do. **4** No one who wants *to become* a
σου οἱ μαθηταί καὶ → θεωρήσουσιν σοῦ τὰ ἔργα ἃ → ποιεῖς γὰρ → οὐδεὶς καὶ αὐτὸς ζητεῖ → εἶναι
r.gs.2 d.npm n.npm adv v.fai.3p r.gs.2 d.apn n.apn r.apn v.pai.2s cj a.nsm cj r.nsm v.pai.3s f.pa
5148 3836 3412 2779 2555 5148 3836 2240 4005 4472 1142 4029 2779 899 2426 1639

public figure acts in secret. Since you are doing these things, show yourself to the world." **5** For even
ἐν παρρησίᾳ τι ποιεῖ ἐν κρυπτῷ εἰ → → ποιεῖς ταῦτα ← φανέρωσον σεαυτὸν → τῷ κόσμῳ γὰρ →
p.d n.dsf r.asn v.pai.3s p.d a.dsn cj v.pai.2s r.apn v.aam.2s r.asm.2 d.dsm n.dsm cj
1877 4244 5516 4472 1877 1623 1623 4472 4047 5746 4932 3836 3180 1142 4028

οὐδέν· τὰ ῥήματα ἃ ἐγὼ λελάληκα ὑμῖν πνεῦμά ἐστιν καὶ ζωή ἐστιν. **64** ἀλλ' εἰσὶν ἐξ ὑμῶν τινες οἳ οὐ πιστεύουσιν. ᾔδει γὰρ ἐξ ἀρχῆς ὁ Ἰησοῦς τίνες εἰσὶν οἱ μὴ πιστεύοντες καὶ τίς ἐστιν ὁ παραδώσων αὐτόν. **65** καὶ ἔλεγεν, Διὰ τοῦτο εἴρηκα ὑμῖν ὅτι οὐδεὶς δύναται ἐλθεῖν πρός με ἐὰν μὴ ᾖ δεδομένον αὐτῷ ἐκ τοῦ πατρός. ¶ **66** Ἐκ τούτου πολλοὶ [ἐκ] τῶν μαθητῶν αὐτοῦ ἀπῆλθον εἰς τὰ ὀπίσω καὶ οὐκέτι μετ' αὐτοῦ περιεπάτουν. ¶ **67** εἶπεν οὖν ὁ Ἰησοῦς τοῖς δώδεκα, Μὴ καὶ ὑμεῖς θέλετε ὑπάγειν; **68** ἀπεκρίθη αὐτῷ Σίμων Πέτρος, Κύριε, πρὸς τίνα ἀπελευσόμεθα; ῥήματα ζωῆς αἰωνίου ἔχεις, **69** καὶ ἡμεῖς πεπιστεύκαμεν καὶ ἐγνώκαμεν ὅτι σὺ εἶ ὁ ἅγιος τοῦ θεοῦ. **70** ἀπεκρίθη αὐτοῖς ὁ Ἰησοῦς, Οὐκ ἐγὼ ὑμᾶς τοὺς δώδεκα ἐξελεξάμην; καὶ ἐξ ὑμῶν εἷς διάβολός ἐστιν. **71** ἔλεγεν δὲ τὸν Ἰούδαν Σίμωνος Ἰσκαριώτου· οὗτος γὰρ ἔμελλεν παραδιδόναι αὐτόν, εἷς ὢν ἐκ τῶν δώδεκα.

7:1 Καὶ μετὰ ταῦτα περιεπάτει ὁ Ἰησοῦς ἐν τῇ Γαλιλαίᾳ· οὐ γὰρ ἤθελεν ἐν τῇ Ἰουδαίᾳ περιπατεῖν, ὅτι ἐζήτουν αὐτὸν οἱ Ἰουδαῖοι ἀποκτεῖναι. **2** ἦν δὲ ἐγγὺς ἡ ἑορτὴ τῶν Ἰουδαίων ἡ σκηνοπηγία. **3** εἶπον οὖν πρὸς αὐτὸν οἱ ἀδελφοὶ αὐτοῦ, Μετάβηθι ἐντεῦθεν καὶ ὕπαγε εἰς τὴν Ἰουδαίαν, ἵνα καὶ οἱ μαθηταί σου θεωρήσουσιν σοῦ τὰ ἔργα ἃ ποιεῖς· **4** οὐδεὶς γάρ τι ἐν κρυπτῷ ποιεῖ καὶ ζητεῖ αὐτὸς ἐν παρρησίᾳ εἶναι. εἰ ταῦτα ποιεῖς, φανέρωσον σεαυτὸν τῷ κόσμῳ. **5** οὐδὲ γὰρ οἱ ἀδελφοὶ αὐτοῦ ἐπίστευον

his own brothers did not believe in him. ¶ **6** Therefore Jesus told them, "The right time for
αὐτοῦ οἱ ἀδελφοὶ → οὐδὲ ἐπίστευον εἰς αὐτόν οὖν ὁ Ἰησοῦς λέγει αὐτοῖς ὁ → καιρὸς
r.gsm.3 d.npm n.npm adv v.iai.3p p.a r.asm.3 cj d.nsm n.nsm v.pai.3s r.dpm.3 d.nsm n.nsm
899 3836 81 4409 4028 4409 1650 899 4036 3836 2652 3306 899 3836 2789

me has not yet come; for you any time is right. **7** The world cannot hate you,
ὁ ἐμὸς → οὔπω ← πάρεστιν δὲ ὁ ὑμέτερος πάντοτε ὁ καιρὸς ἐστιν ἕτοιμος ὁ κόσμος οὐ δύναται μισεῖν ὑμᾶς
d.nsm r.nsm.1 adv v.pai.3s cj d.nsm r.nsm.2 adv d.nsm n.nsm v.pai.3s a.nsm d.nsm n.nsm pl v.ppi.3s f.pa r.ap.2
3836 1847 4205 4037 4205 1254 3836 5629 4121 3836 2789 1639 2289 3836 3180 4024 1538 3631 7007

but it hates me because I testify that what it does is evil. **8** You go to the Feast. I am
δὲ → μισεῖ ἐμὲ ὅτι ἐγὼ μαρτυρῶ περὶ αὐτοῦ ὅτι → αὐτοῦ τὰ ἔργα ἐστιν πονηρά ὑμεῖς ἀνάβητε εἰς τὴν ἑορτὴν ἐγὼ
cj v.pai.3s r.as.1 cj r.ns.1 v.pai.1s p.g r.gsm.3 cj r.gsm.3 d.npn n.npn v.pai.3s a.npn r.np.2 v.aam.2p p.a d.asf n.asf r.ns.1
1254 3631 1609 4022 1609 3455 4309 899 4022 2240 899 3836 2240 1639 4505 7007 326 1650 3836 2038 1609 326

not yet going up to this Feast, because for me the right time has not yet come." **9** Having said
οὐκ ἀναβαίνω ← εἰς ταύτην τὴν ἑορτὴν ὅτι ἐμὸς ὁ → καιρὸς → οὔπω ← πεπλήρωται δὲ → εἰπὼν
pl v.pai.1s p.a r.asf d.asf n.asf cj r.nsm.1 d.nsm n.nsm adv v.rpi.3s cj pt.aa.nsm
4024 326 1650 4047 3836 2038 4022 1847 3836 2789 4444 4037 4444 1254 3306

this, he stayed in Galilee. ¶ **10** However, after his brothers had left for the Feast, he
ταῦτα αὐτὸς ἔμεινεν ἐν τῇ Γαλιλαίᾳ δὲ Ὡς αὐτοῦ οἱ ἀδελφοὶ → ἀνέβησαν εἰς τὴν ἑορτήν τότε αὐτὸς
r.apn r.nsm v.aai.3s p.d d.dsf n.dsf cj cj r.gsm.3 d.npm n.npm v.aai.3p p.a d.asf n.asf adv r.nsm
4047 899 3531 1877 3836 1133 1254 6055 899 3836 81 326 1650 3836 2038 5538 899

went also, not publicly, but in secret. **11** Now at the Feast the Jews were watching for him and asking,
ἀνέβη καὶ οὐ φανερῶς ἀλλὰ [ὡς] ἐν κρυπτῷ οὖν ἐν τῇ ἑορτῇ οἱ Ἰουδαῖοι → ἐζήτουν ← αὐτὸν καὶ ἔλεγον
v.aai.3s adv pl adv cj pl p.d a.dsn cj p.d d.dsf n.dsf d.npm a.npm v.iai.3p r.asm.3 cj v.iai.3p
326 2779 4024 5747 247 6055 1877 3220 4036 1877 3836 2038 3836 2681 2426 899 2779 3306

"Where is that man?" ¶ **12** Among the crowds there was widespread whispering about him. Some
ποῦ ἐστιν ἐκεῖνος ← καὶ ἐν τοῖς ὄχλοις → ἦν πολὺς γογγυσμὸς περὶ αὐτοῦ μὲν οἱ
adv v.pai.3s r.nsm cj p.d d.dpm n.dpm v.iai.3s a.nsm n.nsm p.g r.gsm.3 cj d.npm
4543 1639 1697 2779 1877 3836 4063 1639 4498 1198 4309 899 3525 3836

said, "He is a good man." Others replied, "No, he deceives the people." **13** But no one would
ἔλεγον ὅτι → ἐστιν ἀγαθός ← [δὲ] ἄλλοι ἔλεγον οὐ ἀλλὰ πλανᾷ τὸν ὄχλον μέντοι → οὐδεὶς
v.iai.3p cj v.pai.3s a.nsm pl a.npm v.iai.3p pl cj v.pai.3s d.asm n.asm cj a.nsm
3306 4022 1639 19 1254 257 3306 4024 247 4414 3836 4063 3530 4029

say anything publicly about him for fear of the Jews.
ἐλάλει παρρησίᾳ περὶ αὐτοῦ διὰ τὸν φόβον τῶν Ἰουδαίων
v.iai.3s n.dsf p.g r.gsm.3 p.a d.asm n.asm d.gpm a.gpm
3281 4244 4309 899 1328 3836 5832 3836 2681

Jesus Teaches at the Feast

7:14 Not until halfway through the Feast did Jesus go up to the temple courts and begin to teach.
δὲ → Ἤδη μεσούσης ← τῆς ἑορτῆς → Ἰησοῦς ἀνέβη ← εἰς τὸ ἱερὸν ← καὶ → ἐδίδασκεν
cj adv pt.pa.gsf d.gsf n.gsf n.nsm v.aai.3s p.a d.asn n.asn cj v.iai.3s
1254 2453 3548 3836 2038 2652 326 1650 3836 2639 2779 1438

15 The Jews were amazed and asked, "How did this man get such learning without having studied?" **16**
οὖν οἱ Ἰουδαῖοι ἐθαύμαζον λέγοντες πῶς → οὗτος οἶδεν μεμαθηκὼς μὴ μεμαθηκώς οὖν
cj d.npm a.npm v.iai.3p pt.pa.npm cj r.nsm v.rai.3s pt.ra.nsm pl pt.ra.nsm cj
4036 3836 2681 2513 3306 4802 4047 3857 3443 3590 3443 4036

Jesus answered, "My teaching is not my own. It comes from him who sent me.
ὁ Ἰησοῦς ἀπεκρίθη αὐτοῖς καὶ εἶπεν ἐμὴ ἡ διδαχὴ ἐστιν οὐκ ἐμή ← ἀλλὰ τοῦ ← πέμψαντος με
d.nsm n.nsm v.api.3s r.dpm.3 cj v.aai.3s r.nsf.1 d.nsf n.nsf v.pai.3s pl r.nsf.1 cj d.gsm pt.aa.gsm r.as.1
3836 2652 646 899 2779 3306 1847 3836 1439 1639 4024 1847 247 3836 4287 1609

17 If anyone chooses to do God's will, he will find out whether my teaching comes from God or
ἐάν τις θέλῃ → ποιεῖν αὐτοῦ τὸ θέλημα → γνώσεται ← πότερον περὶ τῆς διδαχῆς ἐστιν ἐκ τοῦ θεοῦ ἢ
cj r.nsm v.pas.3s f.pa r.gsm.3 d.asn n.asn v.fmi.3s cj p.g d.gsf n.gsf v.pai.3s p.g d.gsm n.gsm cj
1569 5516 2527 4472 899 3836 2525 1182 4538 4309 3836 1439 1639 1666 3836 2536 2445

whether I speak on my own. **18** He who speaks on his own does so to gain honor for himself, but he
ἐγὼ λαλῶ ἀπ᾽ ἐμαυτοῦ ← ὁ ← λαλῶν ἀφ᾽ ἑαυτοῦ ← ζητεῖ τὴν δόξαν → τὴν ἰδίαν δὲ ὁ
r.ns.1 v.pai.1s p.g r.gsm.1 d.nsm pt.pa.nsm p.g r.gsm.3 v.pai.3s d.asf n.asf d.asf a.asf cj d.nsm
1609 3281 608 1831 3836 3281 608 1571 2426 3836 1518 2426 3836 2625 1254 3836

εἰς αὐτόν. ¶ **6** λέγει οὖν αὐτοῖς ὁ Ἰησοῦς, Ὁ καιρὸς ὁ ἐμὸς οὔπω πάρεστιν, ὁ δὲ καιρὸς ὁ ὑμέτερος πάντοτέ ἐστιν ἕτοιμος. **7** οὐ δύναται ὁ κόσμος μισεῖν ὑμᾶς, ἐμὲ δὲ μισεῖ, ὅτι ἐγὼ μαρτυρῶ περὶ αὐτοῦ ὅτι τὰ ἔργα αὐτοῦ πονηρά ἐστιν. **8** ὑμεῖς ἀνάβητε εἰς τὴν ἑορτήν· ἐγὼ οὔπω «οὐκ» ἀναβαίνω εἰς τὴν ἑορτὴν ταύτην, ὅτι ὁ ἐμὸς καιρὸς οὔπω πεπλήρωται. **9** ταῦτα δὲ εἰπὼν αὐτὸς ἔμεινεν ἐν τῇ Γαλιλαίᾳ. ¶ **10** Ὡς δὲ ἀνέβησαν οἱ ἀδελφοὶ αὐτοῦ εἰς τὴν ἑορτήν, τότε καὶ αὐτὸς ἀνέβη οὐ φανερῶς ἀλλὰ [ὡς] ἐν κρυπτῷ. **11** οἱ οὖν Ἰουδαῖοι ἐζήτουν αὐτὸν ἐν τῇ ἑορτῇ καὶ ἔλεγον, Ποῦ ἐστιν ἐκεῖνος; ¶ **12** καὶ γογγυσμὸς περὶ αὐτοῦ ἦν πολὺς ἐν τοῖς ὄχλοις· οἱ μὲν ἔλεγον ὅτι Ἀγαθός ἐστιν, ἄλλοι [δὲ] ἔλεγον, Οὔ, ἀλλὰ πλανᾷ τὸν ὄχλον. **13** οὐδεὶς μέντοι παρρησίᾳ ἐλάλει περὶ αὐτοῦ διὰ τὸν φόβον τῶν Ἰουδαίων.

7:14 Ἤδη δὲ τῆς ἑορτῆς μεσούσης ἀνέβη Ἰησοῦς εἰς τὸ ἱερὸν καὶ ἐδίδασκεν. **15** ἐθαύμαζον οὖν οἱ Ἰουδαῖοι λέγοντες, Πῶς οὗτος γράμματα οἶδεν μὴ μεμαθηκώς; **16** ἀπεκρίθη οὖν αὐτοῖς [ὁ] Ἰησοῦς καὶ εἶπεν, Ἡ ἐμὴ διδαχὴ οὐκ ἔστιν ἐμὴ ἀλλὰ τοῦ πέμψαντός με· **17** ἐάν τις θέλῃ τὸ θέλημα αὐτοῦ ποιεῖν, γνώσεται περὶ τῆς διδαχῆς πότερον ἐκ τοῦ θεοῦ ἐστιν ἢ ἐγὼ ἀπ᾽ ἐμαυτοῦ λαλῶ. **18** ὁ ἀφ᾽ ἑαυτοῦ λαλῶν τὴν δόξαν τὴν ἰδίαν ζητεῖ· ὁ δὲ ζητῶν τὴν δόξαν τοῦ πέμψαντος αὐτὸν οὗτος ἀληθής ἐστιν καὶ

who	works	for	the	honor	of	the one	who	sent		him		is		a man of truth;		there is		nothing	false
←	ζητῶν	←	τὴν	δόξαν	τοῦ	←	←	πέμψαντος	αὐτὸν	οὗτος	ἐστιν		ἀληθής	καὶ	→		ἔστιν	οὐκ	ἀδικία
	pt.pa.nsm		d.asf	n.asf	d.gsm			pt.aa.gsm	r.asm.3	r.nsm	v.pai.3s		a.nsm	cj			v.pai.3s	pl	n.nsf
	2426		3836	1518	3836			4287	899	4047	1639		239	2779			1639	4024	94

about	him.	[19] Has	not	Moses	given	you	the	law?	Yet	not	one	of	you	keeps	the	law.	Why	are you	trying to
ἐν	αὐτῷ		Οὐ	Μωϋσῆς	δέδωκεν	ὑμῖν	τὸν	νόμον	καὶ	→	οὐδεὶς	ἐξ	ὑμῶν	ποιεῖ	τὸν	νόμον	τί	→	ζητεῖτε
p.d	r.dsm.3		pl	n.nsm	v.rai.3s	r.dp.2	d.asm	n.asm	cj		a.nsm	p.g	r.gp.2	v.pai.3s	d.asm	n.asm	r.asn		v.pai.2p
1877	899		4024	3707	1443	7007	3836	3795	2779		4029	1666	7007	4472	3836	3795	5515		2426

kill	me?"	¶	[20] "You	are	demon-possessed,"		the	crowd	answered.	"Who	is	trying to kill		you?"
ἀποκτεῖναι	με			ἔχεις	δαιμόνιον		ὁ	ὄχλος	ἀπεκρίθη	τίς	→	ζητεῖ	ἀποκτεῖναι	σε
f.aa	r.as.1			v.pai.2s	n.asn		d.nsm	n.nsm	v.api.3s	r.nsm		v.pai.3s	f.aa	r.as.2
650	1609			2400	1228		3836	4063	646	5515		2426	650	5148

[21] Jesus	said			to them,	"I did	one	miracle,	and	you	are	all	astonished.	[22] Yet,	because		Moses	gave
Ἰησοῦς	ἀπεκρίθη	καὶ	εἶπεν	αὐτοῖς	ἐποίησα	ἓν	ἔργον	καὶ	→	→	πάντες	θαυμάζετε		διὰ	τοῦτο	Μωϋσῆς	δέδωκεν
n.nsm	v.api.3s	cj	v.aai.3s	r.dpm.3	v.aai.1s	a.nsn	n.nsn	cj			a.npm	v.pai.2p		p.a	r.asn	n.nsm	v.rai.3s
2652	646	2779	3306	899	4472	1651	2240	2779			4246	2513		1328	4047	3707	1443

you	circumcision	(though	actually		it	did	not	come	from	Moses,		but	from	the	patriarchs),		you
ὑμῖν	τὴν περιτομήν			ὅτι	→		οὐχ	ἐστιν	ἐκ	τοῦ Μωϋσέως	ἀλλ'		ἐκ	τῶν	πατέρων	καὶ	→
r.dp.2	d.asf n.asf			cj			pl	v.pai.3s	p.g	d.gsm n.gsm	cj		p.g	d.gpm	n.gpm	cj	
7007	3836 4364			4022	1639	1639	4024	1639	1666	3836 3707	247		1666	3836	4252	2779	

circumcise	a child		on the	Sabbath.	[23] Now if	a	child	can be		circumcised	on the	Sabbath	so that	the
περιτέμνετε	ἄνθρωπον	ἐν		σαββάτῳ	εἰ		ἄνθρωπος	→	λαμβάνει	περιτομήν	ἐν	σαββάτῳ	ἵνα	ὁ
v.pai.2p	n.asm	p.d		n.dsn	cj		n.nsm		v.pai.3s	n.asf	p.d	n.dsn	cj	d.nsm
4362	476	1877		4879	1623		476		3284	4364	1877	4879	2671	3836

law	of Moses	may	not	be broken,	why	are	you	angry with	me	for	healing		the	whole	man		on	the
νόμος	Μωϋσέως		μὴ	λυθῇ	→			χολᾶτε	→	ἐμοὶ	ὅτι	ὑγιῆ	ἐποίησα	ὅλον	ἄνθρωπον	ἐν
n.nsm	n.gsm		pl	v.aps.3s				v.pai.2p		r.ds.1	cj	a.asn	v.aai.1s	a.asn	n.asm	p.d
3795	3707		3395	3590				5957		1609	4022	5618	4472	3910	476	1877

Sabbath?	[24] Stop	judging	by	mere	appearances,	and	make	a	right	judgment."
σαββάτῳ	μὴ	κρίνετε	κατ'		ὄψιν	ἀλλὰ	κρίνετε		δικαίαν	τὴν κρίσιν
n.dsn	pl	v.pam.2p	p.a		n.asf	cj	v.pam.2p		a.asf	d.asf n.asf
4879	3590	3212	2848		4071	247	3212		1465	3836 3213

Is Jesus the Christ?

[7:25] At	that	point	some	of	the	people of Jerusalem		began to ask,	"Isn't		this	the man	they are	trying
οὖν	←	←	τινες	ἐκ	τῶν	Ἰεροσολυμιτῶν	→	Ἔλεγον	οὐχ	ἐστιν	οὗτος	ὃν	→	ζητοῦσιν
cj			r.npm	p.g	d.gpm	n.gpm		v.iai.3p	pl	v.pai.3s	r.nsm	r.asm		v.pai.3p
4036			5516	1666	3836	2643		3306	4024	1639	4047	4005		2426

to kill?	[26]		Here he is,	speaking	publicly,	and	they	are	not	saying	a word	to him.		Have	the	authorities
→	ἀποκτεῖναι	καὶ	ἴδε	←	λαλεῖ	παρρησίᾳ	καὶ	→	→	οὐδὲν	λέγουσιν		αὐτῷ	μήποτε	οἱ	ἄρχοντες
	f.aa	cj	pl		v.pai.3s	n.dsf	cj			a.asn	v.pai.3p		r.dsm.3	pl	d.npm	n.npm
	650	2779	2623		3281	4244	2779			4029	3306		899	3607	3836	807

really	concluded	that	he	is	the	Christ?	[27] But	we	know	where	this	man	is	from;		when	the	Christ
ἀληθῶς	ἔγνωσαν	ὅτι	οὗτός	ἐστιν	ὁ	χριστός	ἀλλὰ	→	οἴδαμεν	πόθεν	τοῦτον	←	ἐστίν		δὲ	ὅταν	ὁ	χριστός
adv	v.aai.3p	cj	r.nsm	v.pai.3s	d.nsm	n.nsm	cj		v.rai.1p	cj	r.asm		v.pai.3s		cj	cj	d.nsm	n.nsm
242	1182	4022	4047	1639	3836	5986	247		4470	3857	4047		1639		1254	4020	3836	5986

comes,	no one	will	know	where	he	is	from."	¶	[28] Then	Jesus,		still	teaching	in	the	temple courts,
ἔρχηται	οὐδεὶς	→	γινώσκει	πόθεν	→	ἐστίν	←			οὖν	ὁ	Ἰησοῦς	διδάσκων	ἐν	τῷ	ἱερῷ
v.pms.3s	a.nsm		v.pai.3s	cj		v.pai.3s				cj	d.nsm	n.nsm	pt.pa.nsm	p.d	d.dsn	n.dsn
2262	4029		1182	4470		1639	4470			4036	3836	2652	1438	1877	3836	2639

cried	out,		"Yes, you	know	me,	and	you	know	where	I	am	from.		I	am	not	here	on	my	own,
ἔκραξεν		καὶ	λέγων		οἴδατε	κἀμὲ	καὶ		οἴδατε	πόθεν	→	εἰμί	←	καὶ			οὐκ	ἐλήλυθα	ἀπ'	ἐμαυτοῦ
v.aai.3s		cj	pt.pa.nsm		v.rai.2p	crasis	cj		v.rai.2p	cj		v.pai.1s		cj			pl	v.rai.1s	p.g	r.gsm.1
3189		2779	3306		3857	2743	2779		3857	4470		1639	4470	2779	2262	2262	4024	2262	608	1831

but	he	who	sent	me	is	true.	You	do	not	know	him,	[29] but	I	know	him	because	I	am	from	him	and
ἀλλ'	ὁ	←	πέμψας	με	ἐστιν	ἀληθινός	ὑμεῖς	→	οὐκ	οἴδατε	ὃν		ἐγὼ	οἶδα	αὐτόν	ὅτι	→	εἰμι	παρ'	αὐτοῦ	→
cj	d.nsm		pt.aa.nsm	r.as.1	v.pai.3s	a.nsm	r.np.2		pl	v.rai.2p	r.asm		r.ns.1	v.rai.1s	r.asm.3	cj		v.pai.1s	p.g	r.gsm.3	
247	3836		4287	1609	1639	240	7007		3857	4024	4005		1609	3857	899	4022		1639	4123	899	

ἀδικία ἐν αὐτῷ οὐκ ἔστιν. ¹⁹ οὐ Μωϋσῆς δέδωκεν ὑμῖν τὸν νόμον; καὶ οὐδεὶς ἐξ ὑμῶν ποιεῖ τὸν νόμον. τί με ζητεῖτε ἀποκτεῖναι; ¶ ²⁰ ἀπεκρίθη ὁ ὄχλος, Δαιμόνιον ἔχεις· τίς σε ζητεῖ ἀποκτεῖναι; ²¹ ἀπεκρίθη Ἰησοῦς καὶ εἶπεν αὐτοῖς, Ἓν ἔργον ἐποίησα καὶ πάντες θαυμάζετε. ²² διὰ τοῦτο Μωϋσῆς δέδωκεν ὑμῖν τὴν περιτομὴν — οὐχ ὅτι ἐκ τοῦ Μωϋσέως ἐστὶν ἀλλ' ἐκ τῶν πατέρων — καὶ ἐν σαββάτῳ περιτέμνετε ἄνθρωπον. ²³ εἰ περιτομὴν λαμβάνει ἄνθρωπος ἐν σαββάτῳ ἵνα μὴ λυθῇ ὁ νόμος Μωϋσέως, ἐμοὶ χολᾶτε ὅτι ὅλον ἄνθρωπον ὑγιῆ ἐποίησα ἐν σαββάτῳ; ²⁴ μὴ κρίνετε κατ' ὄψιν, ἀλλὰ τὴν δικαίαν κρίσιν κρίνετε.

⁷:²⁵ Ἔλεγον οὖν τινες ἐκ τῶν Ἰεροσολυμιτῶν, Οὐχ οὗτός ἐστιν ὃν ζητοῦσιν ἀποκτεῖναι; ²⁶ καὶ ἴδε παρρησίᾳ λαλεῖ καὶ οὐδὲν αὐτῷ λέγουσιν. μήποτε ἀληθῶς ἔγνωσαν οἱ ἄρχοντες ὅτι οὗτός ἐστιν ὁ Χριστός; ²⁷ ἀλλὰ τοῦτον οἴδαμεν πόθεν ἐστίν· ὁ δὲ Χριστὸς ὅταν ἔρχηται οὐδεὶς γινώσκει πόθεν ἐστίν. ¶ ²⁸ ἔκραξεν οὖν ἐν τῷ ἱερῷ διδάσκων ὁ Ἰησοῦς καὶ λέγων, Κἀμὲ οἴδατε καὶ οἴδατε πόθεν εἰμί· καὶ ἀπ' ἐμαυτοῦ οὐκ ἐλήλυθα, ἀλλ' ἔστιν ἀληθινὸς ὁ πέμψας με, ὃν ὑμεῖς οὐκ οἴδατε· ²⁹ ἐγὼ οἶδα αὐτόν, ὅτι παρ'

he sent me." ¶ **30** *At this* they tried to seize him, but no one laid a hand on him,
κἀκεῖνος ἀπέστειλεν με   οὖν → Ἐζήτουν → πιάσαι αὐτὸν καὶ → οὐδεὶς ἐπέβαλεν ⌐τὴν χεῖρα⌐ ἐπ᾿ αὐτὸν
crasis v.aai.3s r.as.1   cj   v.iai.3p   f.aa r.asm.3 cj   a.nsm v.aai.3s d.asf n.asf p.a r.asm.3
2778   690   1609   4036   2426   4389 899 2779   4029 2095 3836 5931 2093 899

because his time had not yet come. **31** Still, many in the crowd put their faith in him. They said,
ὅτι αὐτοῦ ἡ ὥρα → οὔπω ἐληλύθει δὲ πολλοὶ Ἐκ τοῦ ὄχλου → → ἐπίστευσαν εἰς αὐτὸν καὶ → ἔλεγον
cj r.gsm.3 d.nsf n.nsf   adv v.lai.3s cj a.npm p.g d.gsm n.gsm   v.aai.3p p.a r.asm.3 cj   v.iai.3p
4022 899 3836 6052   2262 4037 2262 1254 4498 1666 3836 4063   4409 1650 899 2779   3306

"When the Christ comes, will he do more miraculous signs than this man?" ¶ **32** The
ὅταν ὁ χριστὸς ἔλθῃ μὴ → ποιήσει πλείονα σημεῖα ὧν οὗτος ← ἐποίησεν οἱ
cj d.nsm n.nsm v.aas.3s pl → v.fai.3s a.apn.c n.apn r.gpn r.nsm   v.aai.3s d.npm
4020 3836 5986 2262 3590   4472 4498 4956 4005 4047   4472 3836

Pharisees heard the crowd whispering such things about him. Then the chief priests and the Pharisees sent
Φαρισαῖοι ἤκουσαν τοῦ ὄχλου γογγύζοντος ταῦτα περὶ αὐτοῦ καὶ οἱ → ἀρχιερεῖς καὶ οἱ Φαρισαῖοι ἀπέστειλαν
n.npm v.aai.3p d.gsm n.gsm pt.pa.gsm r.apn p.g r.gsm.3 cj d.npm   n.npm cj d.npm n.npm v.aai.3p
5757 201 3836 4063 1197 4047 4309 899 2779 3836   797 2779 3836 5757 690

temple guards to arrest him. ¶ **33** Jesus said, "I am with you for only a short time, and then I
→ ὑπηρέτας ἵνα πιάσωσιν αὐτόν   οὖν ὁ Ἰησοῦς, εἶπεν → εἰμι μεθ᾿ ὑμῶν ἔτι μικρὸν χρόνον καὶ →
  n.apm cj v.aas.3p r.asm.3   cj d.nsm n.nsm v.aai.3s   v.pai.1s p.g r.gp.2 adv a.asm n.asm cj
  5677 2671 4389 899   4036 3836 2652 3306   1639 3552 7007 2285 3625 5989 2779

go to the one who sent me. **34** You will look for me, but you will not find me; and where I am, you
ὑπάγω πρὸς τὸν ← πέμψαντά με → ζητήσετε με καὶ → → οὐχ εὑρήσετε με καὶ ὅπου ἐγώ εἰμι ὑμεῖς
v.pai.1s p.a d.asm pt.aa.asm r.as.1   v.fai.2p r.as.1 cj → pl v.fai.2p r.as.1 cj cj r.ns.1 v.pai.1s r.np.2
5632 4639 3836 4287 1609   2426 1609 2779 2351 2351 4024 2351 1609 2779 3963 1609 1639 7007

cannot come." ¶ **35** The Jews said to one another, "Where does this man intend to go that
⌐οὐ δύνασθε⌐ ἐλθεῖν → οὖν οἱ Ἰουδαῖοι εἶπον πρὸς → ἑαυτούς ποῦ → οὗτος ← μέλλει → πορεύεσθαι ὅτι
pl v.ppi.2p f.aa   cj d.npm n.npm v.aai.3p p.a → r.apm.3 adv → r.nsm ← v.pai.3s → f.pm cj
4024 1538 2262   4036 3836 2681 3306 4639 1571 4543 3516 4047 3516 4513 4022

we cannot find him? Will he go where our people live scattered among the Greeks, and
ἡμεῖς οὐχ εὑρήσομεν αὐτόν μὴ μέλλει ← πορεύεσθαι εἰς ⌐τὴν διασπορὰν⌐ → τῶν Ἑλλήνων καὶ
r.np.1 pl v.fai.1p r.asm.3 pl v.pai.3s ← f.pm p.a d.asf n.asf → d.gpm n.gpm cj
7005 4024 2351 899 3590 3516 4513 1650 3836 1402   3836 1818 2779

teach the Greeks? **36** What *did he mean* when he said, 'You will look for me, but you will not
διδάσκειν τοὺς Ἕλληνας τίς ἐστιν ὁ λόγος οὗτος ὃν → εἶπεν → → ζητήσετε ← με καὶ → οὐχ
f.pa d.apm n.apm r.nsm v.pai.3s d.nsm n.nsm r.nsm r.asm → v.aai.3s → → v.fai.2p r.as.1 cj → pl
1438 3836 1818 5515 1639 3836 3364 4047 4005 3306 2426 1609 2779 2351 2351 4024

find me,' and 'Where I am, you cannot come'?" ¶ **37** On the last and greatest day of the
εὑρήσετε με καὶ ὅπου ἐγώ εἰμι ὑμεῖς ⌐οὐ δύνασθε⌐ ἐλθεῖν δὲ Ἐν τῇ ἐσχάτῃ ⌐τῇ μεγάλῃ⌐ ἡμέρᾳ → τῆς
v.fai.2p r.as.1 cj cj r.ns.1 v.pai.1s r.np.2 pl v.ppi.2p f.aa cj p.d d.dsf a.dsf d.dsf a.dsf n.dsf d.gsf
2351 1609 2779 3963 1609 1639 7007 4024 1538 2262 1254 1877 3836 2274 3836 3489 2465 3836

Feast, Jesus stood and said in a loud voice, "If anyone is thirsty, let him come to me and drink.
ἑορτῆς ὁ Ἰησοῦς, εἱστήκει καὶ λέγων → → → ἔκραζεν ἐάν τις → διψᾷ → → ἐρχέσθω πρός με καὶ πινέτω
n.gsf d.nsm n.nsm v.lai.3s cj pt.pa.nsm   v.iai.3s cj r.nsm → v.pas.3s → → v.pmm.3s p.a r.as.1 cj v.pam.3s
2038 3836 2652 2705 2779 3306   3189 1569 5516 1498 2262 4639 1609 2779 4403

38 Whoever believes in me, as the Scripture has said, streams of living water will flow from within him."
ὁ πιστεύων εἰς ἐμέ καθὼς ἡ γραφή → εἶπεν ποταμοὶ → ζῶντος ὕδατος → ῥεύσουσιν ἐκ ⌐τῆς κοιλίας⌐ αὐτοῦ
d.nsm pt.pa.nsm p.a r.as.1 cj d.nsf n.nsf → v.aai.3s n.npm → pt.pa.gsn n.gsn → v.fai.3p p.g d.gsf n.gsf r.gsm.3
3836 4409 1650 1609 2777 3836 1210 3306 4532 2409 5623 4835 1666 3836 3120 899

39 By this he meant the Spirit, whom those who believed in him were later to receive. *Up to*
δὲ → τοῦτο εἶπεν περὶ τοῦ πνεύματος ὃ οἱ → πιστεύσαντες εἰς αὐτόν → ἔμελλον → λαμβάνειν γὰρ
cj → r.asn v.aai.3s p.g d.gsn n.gsn r.asn d.npm → pt.aa.npm p.a r.asm.3 → v.iai.3p → f.pa cj
1254 4047 3306 4309 3836 4460 4005 3836 4409 1650 899 3516 3284 1142

that time the Spirit had not been given, since Jesus had not yet been glorified. ¶ **40** On hearing his
οὔπω πνεῦμα → → ἦν ὅτι Ἰησοῦς → οὐδέπω → ἐδοξάσθη οὖν → ἀκούσαντες τούτων
adv n.nsn → → v.iai.3s cj n.nsm → adv → v.api.3s cj → pt.aa.npm r.gpm
4037 4460 1639 4037 1639 4022 2652 1519 4031 1519 4036 201 4047

αὐτοῦ εἰμι κἀκεῖνός με ἀπέστειλεν. ¶ 30 Ἐζήτουν οὖν αὐτὸν πιάσαι, καὶ οὐδεὶς ἐπέβαλεν ἐπ᾿ αὐτὸν τὴν χεῖρα, ὅτι οὔπω ἐληλύθει ἡ ὥρα αὐτοῦ. 31 Ἐκ τοῦ ὄχλου δὲ πολλοὶ ἐπίστευσαν εἰς αὐτὸν καὶ ἔλεγον, Ὁ Χριστὸς ὅταν ἔλθῃ μὴ πλείονα σημεῖα ποιήσει ὧν οὗτος ἐποίησεν; ¶ 32 Ἤκουσαν οἱ Φαρισαῖοι τοῦ ὄχλου γογγύζοντος περὶ αὐτοῦ ταῦτα, καὶ ἀπέστειλαν οἱ ἀρχιερεῖς καὶ οἱ Φαρισαῖοι ὑπηρέτας ἵνα πιάσωσιν αὐτόν. ¶ 33 εἶπεν οὖν ὁ Ἰησοῦς, Ἔτι χρόνον μικρὸν μεθ᾿ ὑμῶν εἰμι καὶ ὑπάγω πρὸς τὸν πέμψαντά με. 34 ζητήσετέ με καὶ οὐχ εὑρήσετέ [με], καὶ ὅπου εἰμὶ ἐγὼ ὑμεῖς οὐ δύνασθε ἐλθεῖν. ¶ 35 εἶπον οὖν οἱ Ἰουδαῖοι πρὸς ἑαυτούς, Ποῦ οὗτος μέλλει πορεύεσθαι ὅτι ἡμεῖς οὐχ εὑρήσομεν αὐτόν; μὴ εἰς τὴν διασπορὰν τῶν Ἑλλήνων μέλλει πορεύεσθαι καὶ διδάσκειν τοὺς Ἕλληνας; 36 τίς ἐστιν ὁ λόγος οὗτος ὃν εἶπεν, Ζητήσετέ με καὶ οὐχ εὑρήσετέ [με], καὶ ὅπου εἰμὶ ἐγὼ ὑμεῖς οὐ δύνασθε ἐλθεῖν; ¶ 37 Ἐν δὲ τῇ ἐσχάτῃ ἡμέρᾳ τῇ μεγάλῃ τῆς ἑορτῆς εἱστήκει ὁ Ἰησοῦς καὶ ἔκραξεν λέγων, Ἐάν τις διψᾷ ἐρχέσθω πρός με καὶ πινέτω. 38 ὁ πιστεύων εἰς ἐμέ, καθὼς εἶπεν ἡ γραφή, ποταμοὶ ἐκ τῆς κοιλίας αὐτοῦ ῥεύσουσιν ὕδατος ζῶντος. 39 τοῦτο δὲ εἶπεν περὶ τοῦ πνεύματος ὃ ἔμελλον λαμβάνειν οἱ πιστεύσαντες εἰς αὐτόν· οὔπω γὰρ ἦν πνεῦμα, δεδομένον ὅτι Ἰησοῦς οὐδέπω ἐδοξάσθη. ¶ 40 Ἐκ τοῦ ὄχλου οὖν ἀκούσαντες τῶν λόγων τούτων ἔλεγον, Οὗτός ἐστιν ἀληθῶς

words,   some of the people said,   "Surely this man is   the Prophet." **41** Others said, "He is   the   Christ." Still
⸤τῶν λόγων⸥ → Ἐκ τοῦ ὄχλου ἔλεγον ἀληθῶς οὗτος ← ἐστιν ὁ προφήτης ἄλλοι ἔλεγον οὗτος ἐστιν ὁ χριστός δὲ
d.gpm n.gpm   p.g d.gsm n.gsm v.iai.3p adv r.nsm   v.pai.3s d.nsm n.nsm r.npm v.iai.3p r.nsm v.pai.3s d.nsm n.nsm pl
3836 3364   1666 3836 4063 3306 242 4047   1639 3836 4737 257 3306 4047 1639 3836 5986 1254

others asked,   "How can the Christ come from Galilee? **42** Does not the Scripture say that the Christ
οἱ ἔλεγον γὰρ μὴ   ὁ χριστὸς ἔρχεται ἐκ ⸤τῆς Γαλιλαίας⸥   οὐχ ἡ γραφὴ εἶπεν ὅτι ὁ χριστός
d.npm v.iai.3p cj pl   d.nsm n.nsm v.pmi.3s p.g d.gsf n.gsf   pl d.nsf n.nsf v.aai.3s cj d.nsm n.nsm
3836 3306 1142 3590   3836 5986 2262 1666 3836 1133   4024 3836 1210 3306 4022 3836 5986

will come from David's family   and from Bethlehem, the town where David lived?" **43** Thus   the people
→ ἔρχεται ἐκ Δαυὶδ ⸤τοῦ σπέρματος⸥ καὶ ἀπὸ Βηθλέεμ τῆς κώμης ὅπου Δαυὶδ ἦν οὖν ἐν τῷ ὄχλῳ
  v.pmi.3s p.g n.gsm d.gsn n.gsn cj p.g n.gsf d.gsf n.gsf cj n.nsm v.iai.3s cj p.d d.dsm n.dsm
  2262 1666 1253 3836 5065 2779 608 1033 3836 3267 3963 1253 1639 4036 1877 3836 4063

were divided because of Jesus. **44** Some   wanted to seize   him, but no one   laid   a hand   on him.
ἐγένετο σχίσμα δι' ← αὐτόν δὲ τινὲς ἐξ αὐτῶν ἤθελον → πιάσαι αὐτόν ἀλλ' → οὐδεὶς ἐπέβαλεν ⸤τὰς χεῖρας⸥ ἐπ' αὐτόν
v.ami.3s n.nsn   p.a r.asm.3 cj r.npm p.g r.gpm.3 v.iai.3p   f.aai r.asm.3 cj   a.nsm v.aai.3s   d.apf n.apf p.a r.asm.3
1181 5388 1328   899 1254 5516 1666 899 2527   4389 899 247   4029 2095 3836 5931 2093 899

Unbelief of the Jewish Leaders

7:45 Finally the temple guards went back to   the chief priests and Pharisees,   who   asked them, "Why
οὖν οἱ → ὑπηρέται Ἦλθον πρὸς τοὺς → ἀρχιερεῖς καὶ Φαρισαίους καὶ ἐκεῖνοι εἶπον αὐτοῖς ⸤διὰ τί⸥
cj d.npm   n.npm v.aai.3p p.a d.apm   n.apm cj n.apm cj r.npm v.aai.3p r.dpm.3   r.asn
4036 3836   5677 2262 4639 3836   797 2779 5757 2779 1697 3306 899 1328 5515

didn't you bring him in?" **46** "No one ever   spoke the way this man   does," the guards declared. **47**   "You
οὐκ → ἠγάγετε αὐτόν   οὐδέποτε ἐλάλησεν οὕτως ἄνθρωπος οἱ ὑπηρέται ἀπεκρίθησαν μὴ
pl   v.aai.2p r.asm.3   adv v.aai.3s adv n.nsm d.npm n.npm v.api.3p pl
4024   72 899   4030 3281 4030 476 3836 5677 646 3590

mean he has deceived you also?"   the Pharisees retorted. **48** "Has any of the rulers   or of the
→ → πεπλάνησθε ὑμεῖς καὶ οὖν οἱ Φαρισαῖοι ἀπεκρίθησαν αὐτοῖς → τις ἐκ τῶν ἀρχόντων ἢ ἐκ τῶν
    v.rpi.2p r.np.2 cj cj d.npm n.npm v.api.3p r.dpm.3   r.nsm p.g d.gpm n.gpm cj p.g d.gpm
    4414 7007 2779 4036 3836 5757 646 899   5516 1666 3836 807 2445 1666 3836

Pharisees believed in him? **49** No! But this mob   that knows nothing of the law — there is   a curse   on
Φαρισαίων ἐπίστευσεν εἰς αὐτόν μὴ ἀλλὰ οὗτος ὁ ὄχλος ὁ γινώσκων μὴ τὸν νόμον → εἰσὶν ἐπάρατοι
n.gpm v.aai.3s p.a r.asm.3 pl cj r.nsm d.nsm n.nsm d.nsm pt.pa.nsm pl d.asm n.asm   v.pai.3p a.npm
5757 4409 1650 899 3590 247 4047 3836 4063 3836 1182 3590 3836 3795   1639 2063

them." ¶ **50** Nicodemus, who had gone to   Jesus earlier   and who was   one of their own number, asked,
Νικόδημος ὁ → ἐλθὼν πρὸς αὐτὸν ⸤τὸ πρότερον⸥ → ὢν εἰς ἐξ αὐτῶν ← λέγει
n.nsm d.nsm   pt.aa.nsm p.a r.asm.3 d.asn adv   pt.pa.nsm a.nsm p.g r.gpm.3   v.pai.3s
3773 3836   2262 4639 899 3836 4728   1639 1651 1666 899   3306

51 "Does our law   condemn anyone   without first hearing   him   to find out what
πρὸς αὐτούς μὴ ἡμῶν ὁ νόμος κρίνει ⸤τὸν ἄνθρωπον⸥ ⸤ἐὰν μὴ⸥ πρῶτον ἀκούσῃ παρ' αὐτοῦ καὶ → γνῷ ← τί
p.a r.apm.3 pl r.gp.1 d.nsm n.nsm v.pai.3s d.asm n.asm cj pl a.asn v.aas.3s p.g r.gsm.3 cj   v.aas.3s r.asn
4639 899 3590 7005 3836 3795 3212 3836 476 1569 3590 4754 201 4123 899 2779   1182 5515

he is doing?" **52** They replied,   "Are you from Galilee,   too? Look   into it, and you will
→ ποιεῖ → ἀπεκρίθησαν καὶ εἶπαν αὐτῷ μὴ εἰ σὺ ἐκ ⸤τῆς Γαλιλαίας⸥ καὶ ἐραύνησον ← ← καὶ →
  v.pai.3s   v.api.3p cj v.aai.3p r.dsm.3 pl v.pai.2s r.ns.2 p.g d.gsf n.gsf adv v.aam.2s   cj
  4472   646 2779 3306 899 3590 1639 5148 1666 3836 1133 2779 2236   2779

find that a prophet does not come   out of Galilee."
ἴδε ὅτι προφήτης → οὐκ ἐγείρεται ἐκ → ⸤τῆς Γαλιλαίας⸥
v.aam.2s cj n.nsm   pl v.ppi.3s p.g   d.gsf n.gsf
2623 4022 4737   1586 4024 1586 1666   3836 1133

Woman Caught in Adultery

7:53 Then each   went   to his   own home. ¶ **8:1** But Jesus went   to the Mount of Olives.
⟦καὶ ἕκαστος ἐπορεύθησαν εἰς αὐτοῦ ⸤τὸν οἶκον⸥ δὲ Ἰησοῦς ἐπορεύθη εἰς τὸ ὄρος → ⸤τῶν ἐλαιῶν⸥
cj r.nsm v.api.3p p.a r.gsm.3 d.asm n.asm cj n.nsm v.api.3s p.a d.asn n.asn   d.gpf n.gpf
2779 1667 4513 1650 899 3836 3875 1254 2652 4513 1650 3836 4001   3836 1777

2 At dawn   he appeared again in the temple courts, where all the people gathered around him, and he sat
δὲ → Ὄρθρου → παρεγένετο πάλιν εἰς τὸ ἱερὸν ← καὶ πᾶς ὁ λαὸς ἤρχετο πρὸς αὐτὸν καὶ → καθίσας
cj   n.gsm   v.ami.3s adv p.a d.asn n.asn   cj a.nsm d.nsm n.nsm v.imi.3s p.a r.asm.3 cj   pt.aa.nsm
1254   3986   4134 4099 1650 3836 2639   2779 4246 3836 3295 2262 4639 899 2779   2767

ὁ προφήτης. **41** ἄλλοι ἔλεγον, Οὗτός ἐστιν ὁ Χριστός, οἱ δὲ ἔλεγον, Μὴ γὰρ ἐκ τῆς Γαλιλαίας ὁ Χριστὸς ἔρχεται; **42** οὐχ ἡ γραφὴ εἶπεν ὅτι ἐκ τοῦ σπέρματος Δαυὶδ καὶ ἀπὸ Βηθλέεμ τῆς κώμης ὅπου ἦν Δαυὶδ ἔρχεται ὁ Χριστός; **43** σχίσμα οὖν ἐγένετο ἐν τῷ ὄχλῳ δι' αὐτόν· **44** τινὲς δὲ ἤθελον ἐξ αὐτῶν πιάσαι αὐτόν, ἀλλ' οὐδεὶς ἐπέβαλεν ἐπ' αὐτὸν τὰς χεῖρας.

7:45 ³Ἦλθον οὖν οἱ ὑπηρέται πρὸς τοὺς ἀρχιερεῖς καὶ Φαρισαίους, καὶ εἶπον αὐτοῖς ἐκεῖνοι, Διὰ τί οὐκ ἠγάγετε αὐτόν; **46** ἀπεκρίθησαν οἱ ὑπηρέται, Οὐδέποτε ἐλάλησεν οὕτως ἄνθρωπος. **47** ἀπεκρίθησαν οὖν αὐτοῖς οἱ Φαρισαῖοι, Μὴ καὶ ὑμεῖς πεπλάνησθε; **48** μή τις ἐκ τῶν ἀρχόντων ἐπίστευσεν εἰς αὐτὸν ἢ ἐκ τῶν Φαρισαίων; **49** ἀλλὰ ὁ ὄχλος οὗτος ὁ μὴ γινώσκων τὸν νόμον ἐπάρατοί εἰσιν. ¶ **50** λέγει Νικόδημος πρὸς αὐτούς, ὁ ἐλθὼν πρὸς αὐτὸν [τὸ] πρότερον, εἷς ὢν ἐξ αὐτῶν, **51** Μὴ ὁ νόμος ἡμῶν κρίνει τὸν ἄνθρωπον ἐὰν μὴ ἀκούσῃ πρῶτον παρ' αὐτοῦ καὶ γνῷ τί ποιεῖ; **52** ἀπεκρίθησαν καὶ εἶπαν αὐτῷ, Μὴ καὶ σὺ ἐκ τῆς Γαλιλαίας εἶ; ἐραύνησον καὶ ἴδε ὅτι ἐκ τῆς Γαλιλαίας προφήτης οὐκ ἐγείρεται.

7:53 ⟦Καὶ ἐπορεύθησαν ἕκαστος εἰς τὸν οἶκον αὐτοῦ, ¶ **8:1** Ἰησοῦς δὲ ἐπορεύθη εἰς τὸ Ὄρος τῶν Ἐλαιῶν. **2** Ὄρθρου δὲ πάλιν παρεγένετο εἰς τὸ ἱερὸν καὶ πᾶς ὁ λαὸς ἤρχετο πρὸς αὐτόν, καὶ καθίσας ἐδίδασκεν αὐτούς. **3** ἄγουσιν δὲ οἱ γραμματεῖς καὶ οἱ

down to teach　　them.　³　The teachers　of the law and the Pharisees brought in a woman caught　　in
←　　ἐδίδασκεν αὐτούς δὲ οἱ γραμματεῖς　←　　καὶ οἱ Φαρισαῖοι Ἄγουσιν ←　γυναῖκα κατειλημμένην ἐπὶ
　　v.iai.3s　r.apm.3 cj d.npm n.npm　　　　cj d.npm n.npm v.pai.3p　n.asf pt.rp.asf p.d
　　1438　　899 1254 3836 1208　　　　2779 3836 5757 72　　1222 2898 2093

adultery.　　They made her　　stand　　*before the group*　⁴ and said　　to Jesus, "Teacher, this woman was
μοιχείᾳ　καὶ　→　　αὐτὴν στήσαντες ἐν　μέσῳ　λέγουσιν →　αὐτῷ διδάσκαλε αὕτη ἡ γυνὴ →
n.dsf　cj　　　　r.asf.3 pt.aa.npm p.d n.dsn v.pai.3p　r.dsm.3 n.vsm r.nsf d.nsf n.nsf
3657　2779 2705 2705 899 2705 1877 3545 3306　　899 1437 4047 3836 1222

caught　in the act　　of adultery.　⁵　In the Law Moses commanded us to stone such　　women.
κατείληπται ἐπ᾽ αὐτοφώρῳ μοιχευομένη δὲ ἐν τῷ νόμῳ Μωϋσῆς ἐνετείλατο ἡμῖν → λιθάζειν ιτὰς τοιαύτας, ←
v.rpi.3s　p.d a.dsn pt.pp.nsf cj p.d d.dsn n.dsm n.nsm v.ami.3s r.dp.1 f.pa d.apf r.apf
2898　2093 900 3658 1254 1877 3836 3795 3707 1948 7005 3342 3836 5525

Now what do you say?" ⁶　They were using this question as a trap,　　　in order to have a basis for
οὖν τί → σὺ λέγεις δὲ → → ἔλεγον τοῦτο　　πειράζοντες αὐτὸν ἵνα ←　　ἔχωσιν
cj r.asn　r.ns.2 v.pai.2s cj　v.iai.3p r.asn　　pt.pa.npm r.asm.3 cj　　v.pas.3p
4036 5515 5148 3306 1254　3306 4047　　4279 899 2671　　2400

accusing him.　¶　But Jesus　bent down and started to write　on the ground with his finger.　⁷
κατηγορεῖν αὐτοῦ δὲ ὁ Ἰησοῦς, κύψας κάτω → κατέγραφεν εἰς τὴν γῆν → τῷ δακτύλῳ δὲ
f.pa r.gsm.3 cj d.nsm n.nsm pt.aa.nsm adv　v.iai.3s p.a d.asf n.asf　d.dsm n.dsm cj
2989 899 1254 3836 2652 3252 3004　2863 1650 3836 1178　3836 1235 1254

When they kept　on questioning him, he straightened up and said to them, "If any one of you is without
ὡς → ἐπέμενον ἐρωτῶντες αὐτόν → ἀνέκυψεν ← καὶ εἶπεν αὐτοῖς ὁ → ὑμῶν
cj　v.iai.3p pt.pa.npm r.asm.3 v.aai.3s cj v.aai.3s r.dpm.3 d.nsm r.gp.2
6055 2152 2263 899 376 2779 3306 899 3836 7007

sin,　　let him be the first　to throw a stone at her." ⁸　Again he stooped　down and wrote　on the ground.
ἀναμάρτητος → → πρῶτος βαλέτω λίθον ἐπ᾽ αὐτὴν καὶ πάλιν → κατακύψας ← ἔγραφεν εἰς τὴν γῆν
a.nsm　　　a.nsm v.aam.3s n.asm p.d r.asf.3 cj adv　pt.aa.nsm　v.iai.3s p.a d.asf n.asf
387 965 965 4755 965 3345 2093 899 2779 4099 2893　1211 1650 3836 1178

¶　⁹ At this, those who heard　began to go　away *one*　　*at a time,*　the older　ones first,
δὲ οἱ ἀκούσαντες → ἐξήρχοντο → εἷς καθ᾽ εἷς　ἀπὸ τῶν πρεσβυτέρων ἀρξάμενοι
cj d.npm pt.aa.npm　v.imi.3p　a.nsm p.a a.nsm　p.g d.gpm a.gpm　pt.am.npm
1254 3836 201　2002　1651 2848 1651　608 3836 4565　806

until only Jesus was left,　with the woman still standing there.　¹⁰　Jesus　straightened up and asked
καὶ μόνος → κατελείφθη καὶ ἡ γυνὴ οὖσα ιἐν μέσῳ, δὲ ὁ Ἰησοῦς, ἀνακύψας ← εἶπεν
cj a.nsm　v.api.3s cj d.nsf n.nsf pt.pa.nsf p.d n.dsn cj d.nsm n.nsm pt.aa.nsm　v.aai.3s
2779 3668　2901 2779 3836 1222 1639 1877 3545 1254 3836 2652 376　3306

her, "Woman, where are they? Has no　one condemned you?" ¹¹　"No one, sir," she said.　"Then neither
αὐτῇ γύναι ποῦ εἰσιν ← οὐδείς ← κατέκρινεν σε δὲ οὐδεὶς κύριε ἡ εἶπεν δὲ οὐδὲ
r.dsf.3 n.vsf adv v.pai.3p　a.nsm　v.aai.3s r.as.2 cj a.nsm n.vsm d.nsf v.aai.3s cj cj
899 1222 4543 1639 2891 4029 2891 5148 1254 4029 3261 3836 3306 1254 4028

do I　condemn you," Jesus　declared. "Go　now and *leave*　　*your life* of sin."
→ ἐγὼ κατακρίνω σε ὁ Ἰησοῦς, εἶπεν πορεύου καὶ ιἀπὸ τοῦ νῦν μηκέτι ἁμάρτανε]
r.ns.1 v.pai.1s r.as.2 d.nsm n.nsm v.aai.3s v.pmm.2s cj p.g d.gsn adv adv v.pam.2s
2891 1609 2891 5148 3836 2652 3306 4513 2779 608 3836 3814 3600 279

The Validity of Jesus' Testimony

8:12　When Jesus　spoke　again to the people, he said, "I am the light of the world. Whoever
οὖν ὁ Ἰησοῦς, ἐλάλησεν Πάλιν → αὐτοῖς → λέγων ἐγὼ εἰμι τὸ φῶς τοῦ κόσμου ὁ
cj d.nsm n.nsm v.aai.3s adv　r.dpm.3　pt.pa.nsm r.ns.1 v.pai.1s d.nsn n.nsn d.gsm n.gsm d.nsm
4036 3836 2652 3281 4099　899　3306 1609 1639 3836 5890 3836 3180 3836

follows　me will never　walk　in darkness,　but will have the light of life." ¹³　The Pharisees challenged
ἀκολουθῶν ἐμοὶ → ιοὐ μὴ περιπατήσῃ ἐν ιτῇ σκοτίᾳ ἀλλ᾽ → ἕξει τὸ φῶς → ιτῆς ζωῆς, οὖν οἱ Φαρισαῖοι εἶπον
pt.pa.nsm r.ds.1 pl pl v.aas.3s p.d d.dsf n.dsf cj　v.fai.3s d.asn n.asn d.gsf n.gsf cj d.npm n.npm v.aai.3p
199 1609 4344 4024 3590 4344 1877 3836 5028 247　2400 3836 5890 3836 2437 4036 3836 5757 3306

Φαρισαῖοι γυναῖκα ἐπὶ μοιχείᾳ κατειλημμένην καὶ στήσαντες αὐτὴν ἐν μέσῳ ⁴ λέγουσιν αὐτῷ, Διδάσκαλε, αὕτη ἡ γυνὴ κατείληπται ἐπ᾽ αὐτοφώρῳ μοιχευομένη· ⁵ ἐν δὲ τῷ νόμῳ ἡμῖν Μωϋσῆς ἐνετείλατο τὰς τοιαύτας λιθάζειν. σὺ οὖν τί λέγεις; ⁶ τοῦτο δὲ ἔλεγον πειράζοντες αὐτόν, ἵνα ἔχωσιν κατηγορεῖν αὐτοῦ. ¶ ὁ δὲ Ἰησοῦς κάτω κύψας τῷ δακτύλῳ κατέγραφεν εἰς τὴν γῆν. ⁷ ὡς δὲ ἐπέμενον ἐρωτῶντες αὐτόν, ἀνέκυψεν καὶ εἶπεν αὐτοῖς, Ὁ ἀναμάρτητος ὑμῶν πρῶτος ἐπ᾽ αὐτὴν βαλέτω λίθον. ⁸ καὶ πάλιν κατακύψας ἔγραφεν εἰς τὴν γῆν. ¶ ⁹ οἱ δὲ ἀκούσαντες ἐξήρχοντο εἷς καθ᾽ εἷς ἀρξάμενοι ἀπὸ τῶν πρεσβυτέρων καὶ κατελείφθη μόνος καὶ ἡ γυνὴ ἐν μέσῳ οὖσα. ¹⁰ ἀνακύψας δὲ ὁ Ἰησοῦς εἶπεν αὐτῇ, Γύναι, ποῦ εἰσιν; οὐδείς σε κατέκρινεν; ¹¹ ἡ δὲ εἶπεν, Οὐδείς, κύριε. εἶπεν δὲ ὁ Ἰησοῦς, Οὐδὲ ἐγώ σε κατακρίνω· πορεύου, [καὶ] ἀπὸ τοῦ νῦν μηκέτι ἁμάρτανε.]

8:12 Πάλιν οὖν αὐτοῖς ἐλάλησεν ὁ Ἰησοῦς λέγων, Ἐγώ εἰμι τὸ φῶς τοῦ κόσμου· ὁ ἀκολουθῶν ἐμοὶ οὐ μὴ περιπατήσῃ ἐν τῇ σκοτίᾳ, ἀλλ᾽ ἕξει τὸ φῶς τῆς ζωῆς. ¹³ εἶπον οὖν αὐτῷ οἱ Φαρισαῖοι, Σὺ περὶ σεαυτοῦ μαρτυρεῖς· ἡ μαρτυρία σου οὐκ ἔστιν ἀληθής. ¹⁴ ἀπεκρίθη Ἰησοῦς καὶ εἶπεν αὐτοῖς, Κἂν ἐγὼ μαρτυρῶ περὶ ἐμαυτοῦ, ἀληθής ἐστιν ἡ μαρτυρία μου, ὅτι οἶδα πόθεν

him, "Here you are, appearing as your own witness; your testimony is not valid." **14** Jesus answered,
αὐτῷ σὺ ↱ περὶ σεαυτοῦ ← μαρτυρεῖς σου ἡ μαρτυρία ἔστιν οὐκ ἀληθής Ἰησοῦς ἀπεκρίθη καὶ εἶπεν
r.dsm.3   r.ns.2   p.g   r.gsm.2   v.pai.2s   r.gs.2   d.nsf   n.nsf   v.pai.3s   pl   a.nsf   n.nsm   v.api.3s   cj   v.aai.1s
899   5148   3455   4309   4932   3455   5148   3836   3456   1639   4024   239   2652   646   2779   3306

"Even if I testify on my own behalf, my testimony is valid, for I know where I came from and
αὐτοῖς κἂν ← ἐγὼ μαρτυρῶ περὶ ἐμαυτοῦ ← μου ἡ μαρτυρία ἔστιν ἀληθής ὅτι → οἶδα πόθεν → ἦλθον ← καὶ
r.dpm.3   crasis   r.ns.1   v.pas.1s   p.g   r.gsm.1   r.gs.1   d.nsf   n.nsf   v.pai.3s   a.nsf   cj   v.rai.1s   cj   v.aai.1s   cj
899   2829   1609   3455   4309   1831   4309   1609   3836   3456   1639   239   4022   3857   4470   2262   4470   2779

where I am going. But you have no idea where I come from or where I am going. **15** You judge by human
ποῦ → → ὑπάγω δὲ ὑμεῖς ↱ οὐκ οἴδατε πόθεν → ἔρχομαι ← ἢ ποῦ → → ὑπάγω ὑμεῖς κρίνετε κατὰ τὴν σάρκα
adv   v.pai.1s   cj   r.np.2   pl   v.rai.2p   cj   v.pmi.1s   cj   cj   v.pai.1s   r.np.2   v.pai.2p   p.a   d.asf   n.asf
4543   5632   1254   7007   3857   4024   3857   4470   2262   4470   2445   4543   5632   7007   3212   2848   3836   4922

standards; I pass judgment on no one. **16** But if I do judge, my decisions are right, because I
← ἐγὼ οὐ → κρίνω ← οὐδένα δὲ καὶ ἐὰν ἐγὼ κρίνω ἡ ἐμὴ κρίσις ἐστιν ἀληθινή ὅτι →
r.ns.1   pl   v.pai.1s   a.asm   cj   cj   cj   r.ns.1   v.pas.1s   d.nsf   r.nsf.1   d.nsf   n.nsf   v.pai.3s   a.nsf   cj
1609   4024   3212   4029   1254   2779   1569   1609   3212   3836   1847   3836   3213   1639   240   4022

am not alone. I stand with the Father, who sent me. **17** In your own Law it is written that
εἰμὶ οὐκ μόνος ἀλλ' ἐγὼ καὶ πατήρ ὁ πέμψας με δὲ καὶ ἐν τῷ ὑμετέρῳ τῷ νόμῳ → γέγραπται ὅτι
v.pai.1s   pl   a.nsm   cj   r.ns.1   cj   n.nsm   d.nsm   pt.aa.nsm   r.as.1   cj   adv   p.d   d.dsm   r.dsm.2   d.dsm   n.dsm   v.rpi.3s   cj
1639   4024   3668   247   1609   2779   4252   3836   4287   1609   1254   2779   1877   3836   5629   3836   3795   1211   4022

the testimony of two men is valid. **18** I am one who testifies for myself; my other witness is the
ἡ μαρτυρία → δύο ἀνθρώπων ἐστιν ἀληθής ἐγώ εἰμι ὁ ← μαρτυρῶν περὶ ἐμαυτοῦ καὶ ἐμοῦ περὶ μαρτυρεῖ
d.nsf   n.nsf   a.gpm   n.gpm   v.pai.3s   a.nsf   r.ns.1   v.pai.1s   d.nsm   pt.aa.nsm   p.g   r.gsm.1   cj   r.gs.1   p.g   v.pai.3s
3836   3456   1545   476   1639   239   1609   1639   3836   3455   4309   1831   2779   1609   4309   3455

Father, who sent me." **19** Then they asked him, "Where is your father?" "You do not know me or my
πατήρ ὁ πέμψας με οὖν → ἔλεγον αὐτῷ ποῦ → ἐστιν σου ὁ πατήρ ↱ οὔτε οἴδατε ἐμὲ οὔτε μου
n.nsm   d.nsm   pt.aa.nsm   r.as.1   adv   v.iai.3p   r.dsm.3   cj   v.pai.3s   r.gs.2   d.nsm   n.nsm   cj   v.rai.2p   r.as.1   cj   r.gs.1
4252   3836   4287   1609   4036   3306   899   4543   1639   5148   3836   4252   3857   3857   4046   3857   1609   4046   1609

Father," Jesus replied. "If you knew me, you would know my Father also." **20** He spoke these words
τὸν πατέρα Ἰησοῦς ἀπεκρίθη εἰ → ᾔδειτε ἐμὲ ↱ ἂν ᾔδειτε μου τὸν πατέρα καὶ → ἐλάλησεν Ταῦτα τὰ ῥήματα
d.asm   n.asm   n.nsm   v.api.3s   cj   v.lai.2p   r.as.1   pl   v.lai.2p   r.gs.1   d.asm   n.asm   adv   v.aai.3s   r.apn   d.apn   n.apn
3836   4252   2652   646   1623   3857   1609   3857   323   3857   1609   3836   4252   2779   3281   4047   3836   4839

while teaching in the temple area near the place where the offerings were put. Yet no one seized him,
διδάσκων ἐν τῷ ἱερῷ ἐν τῷ γαζοφυλακίῳ ← ← καὶ οὐδεὶς ἐπίασεν αὐτὸν
pt.pa.nsm   p.d   d.dsn   n.dsn   p.d   d.dsn   n.dsn   cj   a.nsm   v.aai.3s   r.asm.3
1438   1877   3836   2639   1877   3836   1126   2779   4029   4389   899

because his time had not yet come. ¶ **21** Once more Jesus said to them, "I am going away, and you
ὅτι αὐτοῦ ἡ ὥρα → οὔπω ἐληλύθει οὖν πάλιν Εἶπεν αὐτοῖς ἐγὼ → ὑπάγω καὶ →
cj   r.gsm.3   d.nsf   n.nsf   adv   v.lai.3s   cj   adv   v.aai.3s   r.dpm.3   r.ns.1   v.pai.1s   cj
4022   899   3836   6052   2262   4037   2262   4036   4099   3306   899   1609   5632   2779

will look for me, and you will die in your sin. Where I go, you cannot come." **22** This made
→ ζητήσετε ← με καὶ → ἀποθανεῖσθε ἐν ὑμῶν τῇ ἁμαρτίᾳ ὅπου ἐγὼ ὑπάγω ὑμεῖς οὐ δύνασθε ἐλθεῖν οὖν
v.fai.2p   r.as.1   cj   v.fmi.2p   p.d   r.gp.2   d.dsf   n.dsf   cj   r.ns.1   v.pai.1s   r.np.2   pl   v.ppi.2p   f.aa   cj
2426   1609   2779   633   1877   7007   3836   281   3963   1609   5632   7007   4024   1538   2262   4036

the Jews ask, "Will he kill himself? Is that why he says, 'Where I go, you cannot come'?"
οἱ Ἰουδαῖοι ἔλεγον μήτι ἀποκτενεῖ ἑαυτόν ὅτι → λέγει ὅπου ἐγὼ ὑπάγω ὑμεῖς οὐ δύνασθε ἐλθεῖν
d.npm   a.npm   v.iai.3p   pl   v.fai.3s   r.asm.3   cj   v.pai.3s   cj   r.ns.1   v.pai.1s   r.np.2   pl   v.ppi.2p   f.aa
3836   2681   3306   3614   650   650   1571   4022   3306   3963   1609   5632   7007   4024   1538   2262

23 But he continued, "You are from below; I am from above. You are of this world; I am not
καὶ → ἔλεγεν αὐτοῖς ὑμεῖς ἐστέ ἐκ τῶν κάτω ἐγώ εἰμί ἐκ τῶν ἄνω ὑμεῖς ἐστέ ἐκ τούτου τοῦ κόσμου ἐγώ εἰμι οὐκ
cj   v.iai.3s   r.dpm.3   r.np.2   v.pai.2p   p.g   d.gpn   adv   r.ns.1   v.pai.1s   p.g   d.gpn   adv   r.np.2   v.pai.2p   p.g   r.gsm   d.gsm   n.gsm   r.ns.1   v.pai.1s   pl
2779   3306   899   7007   1639   1666   3836   3004   1609   1639   1666   3836   539   7007   1639   1666   4047   3836   3180   1609   1639   4024

of this world. **24** I told you that you would die in your sins; if you do not believe
ἐκ τούτου τοῦ κόσμου οὖν → εἶπον ὑμῖν ὅτι → → ἀποθανεῖσθε ἐν ὑμῶν ταῖς ἁμαρτίαις γὰρ ἐὰν → → μὴ πιστεύσητε
p.g   r.gsm   d.gsm   n.gsm   cj   v.aai.1s   r.dp.2   cj   v.fmi.2p   p.d   r.gp.2   d.dpf   n.dpf   cj   cj   pl   v.aas.2p
1666   4047   3836   3180   4036   3306   7007   4022   633   1877   7007   3836   281   1142   1569   4409   4409   3590   4409

ἦλθον καὶ ποῦ ὑπάγω· ὑμεῖς δὲ οὐκ οἴδατε πόθεν ἔρχομαι ἢ ποῦ ὑπάγω. **15** ὑμεῖς κατὰ τὴν σάρκα κρίνετε, ἐγὼ οὐ κρίνω οὐδένα. **16** καὶ ἐὰν κρίνω δὲ ἐγώ, ἡ κρίσις ἡ ἐμὴ ἀληθινή ἐστιν, ὅτι μόνος οὐκ εἰμί, ἀλλ' ἐγὼ καὶ ὁ πέμψας με πατήρ. **17** καὶ ἐν τῷ νόμῳ δὲ τῷ ὑμετέρῳ γέγραπται ὅτι δύο ἀνθρώπων ἡ μαρτυρία ἀληθής ἐστιν. **18** ἐγώ εἰμι ὁ μαρτυρῶν περὶ ἐμαυτοῦ καὶ μαρτυρεῖ περὶ ἐμοῦ ὁ πέμψας με πατήρ. **19** ἔλεγον οὖν αὐτῷ, Ποῦ ἐστιν ὁ πατήρ σου; ἀπεκρίθη Ἰησοῦς, Οὔτε ἐμὲ οἴδατε οὔτε τὸν πατέρα μου· εἰ ἐμὲ ᾔδειτε, καὶ τὸν πατέρα μου ἂν ᾔδειτε. **20** Ταῦτα τὰ ῥήματα ἐλάλησεν ἐν τῷ γαζοφυλακίῳ διδάσκων ἐν τῷ ἱερῷ· καὶ οὐδεὶς ἐπίασεν αὐτόν, ὅτι οὔπω ἐληλύθει ἡ ὥρα αὐτοῦ. ¶ **21** Εἶπεν οὖν πάλιν αὐτοῖς, Ἐγὼ ὑπάγω καὶ ζητήσετέ με, καὶ ἐν τῇ ἁμαρτίᾳ ὑμῶν ἀποθανεῖσθε· ὅπου ἐγὼ ὑπάγω ὑμεῖς οὐ δύνασθε ἐλθεῖν. **22** ἔλεγον οὖν οἱ Ἰουδαῖοι, Μήτι ἀποκτενεῖ ἑαυτόν, ὅτι λέγει, Ὅπου ἐγὼ ὑπάγω ὑμεῖς οὐ δύνασθε ἐλθεῖν; **23** καὶ ἔλεγεν αὐτοῖς, Ὑμεῖς ἐκ τῶν κάτω ἐστέ, ἐγὼ ἐκ τῶν ἄνω εἰμί· ὑμεῖς ἐκ τούτου τοῦ κόσμου ἐστέ, ἐγὼ οὐκ εἰμὶ ἐκ τοῦ κόσμου τούτου. **24** εἶπον οὖν ὑμῖν ὅτι ἀποθανεῖσθε ἐν ταῖς ἁμαρτίαις ὑμῶν· ἐὰν γὰρ μὴ πιστεύσητε ὅτι ἐγώ εἰμι, ἀποθανεῖσθε ἐν ταῖς ἁμαρτίαις ὑμῶν. **25** ἔλεγον οὖν αὐτῷ, Σὺ τίς εἶ; εἶπεν αὐτοῖς ὁ Ἰησοῦς, Τὴν ἀρχὴν

that I   am   the one I claim to be,   you will indeed die   in your sins."   25 "Who are you?" they
ὅτι ἐγώ εἰμι   ἀποθανεῖσθε ἐν ὑμῶν ⌐ταῖς ἁμαρτίαις⌐   οὖν τίς εἶ σὺ →
cj   r.ns.1 v.pai.1s   v.fmi.2p   p.d r.gp.2 d.dpf n.dpf   cj   r.nsm   1639 r.ns.2
4022 1609 1639   633   1877 7007 3836 281   4036 5515   5148

asked.   "Just what   I have been claiming *all along,"*   Jesus   replied.   26 "I have much to
ἔλεγον αὐτῷ   ὅ τι καὶ →   →   λαλῶ ὑμῖν ⌐τὴν ἀρχήν⌐ ὁ Ἰησοῦς, εἶπεν αὐτοῖς → ἔχω πολλὰ →
v.iai.3p r.dsm.3 r.asn r.asn adv   v.pai.1s r.dp.2 d.asf n.asf d.nsm n.nsm v.aai.3s r.dpm.3   v.pai.1s a.apn
3306   899   4005 5516 2779   3281   7007   3836 794   3836 2652   3306   899   2400 4498

say   in judgment of you. But he who sent me is   reliable, and what I have heard from him   I
λαλεῖν καὶ κρίνειν περὶ ὑμῶν ἀλλ᾽ ὁ ← πέμψας με ἐστιν ἀληθής κἀγὼ ἃ → → ἤκουσα παρ᾽ αὐτοῦ ταῦτα →
f.pa   cj   f.pa   p.g r.gp.2 cj d.nsm   pt.aa.nsm r.as.1 v.pai.3s a.nsm crasis r.apn   v.aai.1s p.g r.gsm.3 r.apn
3281   2779 3212   4309 7007 247 3836   4287   1609 1639 239   2743 4005   201   4123 899   4047

tell   the world." 27 They did not understand that he was telling them about his Father. 28 So Jesus   said,
λαλῶ εἰς τὸν κόσμον   → οὐκ ἔγνωσαν ὅτι → → ἔλεγεν αὐτοῖς   τὸν πατέρα οὖν ὁ Ἰησοῦς, εἶπεν
v.pai.1s p.a d.asm n.asm   ou v.aai.3p cj   v.iai.3s r.dpm.3 d.asm n.asm   cj d.nsm n.nsm   v.aai.3s
3281   1650 3836 3180   1182 4024 1182   4022   3306   899   3836 4252   4036 3836 2652   3306

        "When you have lifted up the Son of Man,   then you will know   that I am the one I claim
[αὐτοῖς] ὅταν →   → ὑψώσητε← τὸν υἱὸν ⌐τοῦ ἀνθρώπου⌐ τότε → → γνώσεσθε ὅτι ἐγώ εἰμι
r.dpm.3   cj   v.aas.2p   d.asm n.asm d.gsm n.gsm   adv   v.fmi.2p   cj   r.ns.1 v.pai.1s
899   4020   5738   3836 5626 3836 476   5538   1182   4022 1609 1639

to be and that I do nothing on my   own but   speak just what the Father has taught me. 29   The one
καὶ → ποιῶ οὐδέν ἀπ᾽ ἐμαυτοῦ← ἀλλὰ ταῦτα λαλῶ καθὼς ταῦτα ὁ πατήρ → ἐδίδαξεν με   καὶ ὁ ←
cj   v.pai.1s a.asn p.g r.gsm.1   cj   r.apn v.pai.1s r.apn r.apn d.nsm n.nsm   v.aai.3s r.as.1 cj d.nsm
2779   4472   4029 608 1831   247 4047 3281   2777 4047 3836 4252   1438   1609 2779 3836

who sent me is   with me; he has not left me alone, for I always do what pleases him." 30 Even as he
← πέμψας με ἐστιν μετ᾽ ἐμοῦ ← οὐκ ἀφῆκεν με μόνον ὅτι ἐγὼ πάντοτε ποιῶ τὰ ἀρεστὰ αὐτῷ → αὐτοῦ
pt.aa.nsm r.as.1 v.pai.3s p.g r.gs.1 pl v.aai.3s r.as.1 a.asm cj r.ns.1 adv v.pai.1s d.apn a.apn r.dsm.3   r.gsm.3
4287   1609 1639 3552 1609 918 4024 918   918 1609 3668 4022 1609 4121 4472 3836 744   899   3281 899

spoke,   many put their faith   in him.
λαλοῦντος Ταῦτα πολλοὶ → → ἐπίστευσαν εἰς αὐτόν
pt.pa.gsm r.apn a.npm   v.aai.3p p.a r.asm.3
3281   4047 4498   4409   1650 899

The Children of Abraham

8:31   To the Jews   who had believed   him, Jesus   said, "If you hold to my   teaching, you
οὖν πρὸς τοὺς Ἰουδαίους → → πεπιστευκότας αὐτῷ ὁ Ἰησοῦς ἔλεγεν ἐὰν ὑμεῖς μείνητε ἐν ⌐τῷ ἐμῷ⌐ ⌐τῷ λόγῳ⌐ →
cj   p.a d.apm a.apm   pt.ra.apm r.dsm.3 d.nsm n.nsm v.iai.3s cj r.np.2 v.aas.2p p.d d.dsm r.dsm.1 d.dsm n.dsm
4036 4639 3836 2681   4409   899 3836 2652   3306 1569 7007 3531   1877 3836 1847 3836 3364

are really my disciples. 32 Then you will know the truth, and the truth will set you free." 33 They answered
ἐστε ἀληθῶς μού μαθηταί καὶ → → γνώσεσθε τὴν ἀλήθειαν καὶ ἡ ἀλήθεια → ὑμᾶς ἐλευθερώσει → ἀπεκρίθησαν
v.pai.2p adv r.gs.1 n.npm cj   v.fmi.2p d.asf n.asf cj d.nsf n.nsf   r.ap.2 v.fai.3s   v.api.3p
1639   242 1609 3412   2779   1182   3836 237   2779 3836 237   1802 7007 1802   646

him, "We are Abraham's descendants and have never been slaves of anyone. How can you say that
πρὸς αὐτόν → ἐσμεν Ἀβραὰμ σπέρμα καὶ → πώποτε → δεδουλεύκαμεν οὐδενὶ πῶς ↱ σὺ λέγεις ὅτι
p.a r.asm.3 v.pai.1p n.gsm n.nsn   cj   adv   v.rai.1p   a.dsm   cj   r.ns.2 v.pai.2s cj
4639 899   1639 11   5065   2779 1526 4799   1526   4029   4802   3306 3306   4022

we shall be set free?" 34 Jesus   replied, "I tell you the truth, everyone who sins
→ γενήσεσθε ἐλεύθεροι ὁ Ἰησοῦς, ἀπεκρίθη αὐτοῖς → λέγω ὑμῖν ⌐ἀμὴν ἀμὴν⌐ ὅτι πᾶς ⌐ποιῶν τὴν ἁμαρτίαν⌐
v.fmi.2p a.npm   d.nsm n.nsm v.api.3s r.dpm.3   v.pai.1s r.dp.2 pl   cj a.nsm d.nsm pt.pa.nsm d.asf n.asf
1181   1801   3836 2652 646   899   3306 7007 297   4022 4246 3836 4472   3836 281

is a slave to sin. 35 Now a slave has no *permanent*   *place* in the family, but a son   belongs to it
ἐστιν δοῦλος → ⌐τῆς ἁμαρτίας⌐ δὲ ὁ δοῦλος μένει οὐ ⌐εἰς τὸν αἰῶνα⌐   ἐν τῇ οἰκίᾳ   ὁ υἱὸς μένει
v.pai.3s n.nsm   d.gsf n.gsf   cj d.nsm n.nsm v.pai.3s pl p.a d.asm n.asm   p.d d.dsf n.dsf d.nsm n.nsm v.pai.3s
1639   1529   3836 281   1254 3836 1529 3531 4024 1650 3836 172   1877 3836 3864   3836 5626 3531

forever. 36 So if the Son sets you free,   you will be free   indeed. 37 I know   you are Abraham's
⌐εἰς τὸν αἰῶνα⌐ οὖν ἐὰν ὁ υἱὸς ὑμᾶς ἐλευθερώσῃ → → ἔσεσθε ἐλεύθεροι ὄντως → Οἶδα ὅτι → ἐστε Ἀβραὰμ
p.a d.asm n.asm   cj cj d.nsm n.nsm r.ap.2 v.aas.3s   v.fmi.2p a.npm   adv   v.rai.1s cj   v.pai.2p n.gsm
1650 3836 172   4036 1569 3836 5626 1802 1802   1639   1801   3953   3857 4022   1639 11

ὅ τι καὶ λαλῶ ὑμῖν; ²⁶ πολλὰ ἔχω περὶ ὑμῶν λαλεῖν καὶ κρίνειν, ἀλλ᾽ ὁ πέμψας με ἀληθής ἐστιν, κἀγὼ ἃ ἤκουσα παρ᾽ αὐτοῦ ταῦτα λαλῶ εἰς τὸν κόσμον. ²⁷ οὐκ ἔγνωσαν ὅτι τὸν πατέρα αὐτοῖς ἔλεγεν. ²⁸ εἶπεν οὖν [αὐτοῖς] ὁ Ἰησοῦς, Ὅταν ὑψώσητε τὸν υἱὸν τοῦ ἀνθρώπου, τότε γνώσεσθε ὅτι ἐγώ εἰμι, καὶ ἀπ᾽ ἐμαυτοῦ ποιῶ οὐδέν, ἀλλὰ καθὼς ἐδίδαξέν με ὁ πατὴρ ταῦτα λαλῶ. ²⁹ καὶ ὁ πέμψας με μετ᾽ ἐμοῦ ἐστιν· οὐκ ἀφῆκέν με μόνον, ὅτι ἐγὼ τὰ ἀρεστὰ αὐτῷ ποιῶ πάντοτε. ³⁰ Ταῦτα αὐτοῦ λαλοῦντος πολλοὶ ἐπίστευσαν εἰς αὐτόν.

8:31 Ἔλεγεν οὖν ὁ Ἰησοῦς πρὸς τοὺς πεπιστευκότας αὐτῷ Ἰουδαίους, Ἐὰν ὑμεῖς μείνητε ἐν τῷ λόγῳ τῷ ἐμῷ, ἀληθῶς μαθηταί μού ἐστε ³² καὶ γνώσεσθε τὴν ἀλήθειαν, καὶ ἡ ἀλήθεια ἐλευθερώσει ὑμᾶς. ³³ ἀπεκρίθησαν πρὸς αὐτόν, Σπέρμα Ἀβραάμ ἐσμεν καὶ οὐδενὶ δεδουλεύκαμεν πώποτε· πῶς σὺ λέγεις ὅτι Ἐλεύθεροι γενήσεσθε; ³⁴ ἀπεκρίθη αὐτοῖς ὁ Ἰησοῦς, Ἀμὴν ἀμὴν λέγω ὑμῖν ὅτι πᾶς ὁ ποιῶν τὴν ἁμαρτίαν δοῦλός ἐστιν τῆς ἁμαρτίας. ³⁵ ὁ δὲ δοῦλος οὐ μένει ἐν τῇ οἰκίᾳ εἰς τὸν αἰῶνα, ὁ δὲ υἱὸς μένει εἰς τὸν αἰῶνα. ³⁶ ἐὰν οὖν ὁ υἱὸς ὑμᾶς ἐλευθερώσῃ, ὄντως ἐλεύθεροι ἔσεσθε. ³⁷ οἶδα ὅτι σπέρμα Ἀβραάμ ἐστε· ἀλλὰ

descendants. Yet you are ready to kill me, because you have no room for my word. [38] I am
σπέρμα ἀλλὰ → → ζητεῖτε ἀποκτεῖναι με ὅτι → → οὐ χωρεῖ ἐν ὑμῖν ὁ ἐμὸς ὁ λόγος
n.nsn · cj · v.pai.2p · f.aa · r.as.1 · cj · pl · v.pai.3s · p.d · r.dp.2 · d.nsm · r.nsm.1 · d.nsm · n.nsm
5065 · 247 · 2426 · 650 · 1609 · 4022 · 6003 · 6003 · 4024 · 6003 · 1877 · 7007 · 3836 · 1847 · 3836 · 3364

telling you what I have seen in the Father's presence, and you do what you have heard from your
λαλῶ ἃ ἐγὼ → ἑώρακα παρὰ τῷ πατρὶ ← οὖν καὶ ὑμεῖς ποιεῖτε ἃ → → ἠκούσατε παρὰ τοῦ
v.pai.1s · r.apn · r.ns.1 · v.rai.1s · p.g · d.dsm · n.dsm · cj · cj · r.np.2 · v.pai.2p · r.apn · v.aai.2p · p.g · d.gsm
3281 · 4005 · 1609 · 3972 · 4123 · 3836 · 4252 · 4123 · 4036 · 2779 · 7007 · 4472 · 4005 · 201 · 4123 · 3836

father." [39] "Abraham is our father," they answered. "If you were Abraham's children," said
πατρὸς Ἀβραάμ ἐστιν ἡμῶν ὁ πατήρ → ἀπεκρίθησαν καὶ εἶπαν αὐτῷ εἰ → ἐστε τοῦ Ἀβραάμ τέκνα λέγει
n.gsm · n.nsm · v.pai.3s · r.gp.1 · d.nsm · n.nsm · v.api.3p · cj · v.aai.3p · r.dsm.3 · cj · v.pai.2p · d.gsm · n.gsm · n.npn · v.pai.3s
4252 · 11 · 1639 · 7005 · 3836 · 4252 · 646 · 2779 · 3306 · 899 · 1623 · 1639 · 3836 · 11 · 5451 · 3306

Jesus, "then you would do the things Abraham did. [40] As it is, you are determined to kill
ὁ Ἰησοῦς, αὐτοῖς → → ἐποιεῖτε τὰ ἔργα τοῦ Ἀβραάμ δὲ νῦν ← → ζητεῖτε → ἀποκτεῖναι
d.nsm · n.nsm · r.dpm.3 · v.iai.2p · d.apn · n.apn · d.gsm · n.gsm · cj · adv · v.pai.2p · f.aa
3836 · 2652 · 899 · 4472 · 3836 · 2240 · 3836 · 11 · 2240 · 1254 · 3814 · 2426 · 650

me, a man who has told you the truth that I heard from God. Abraham did not do such things.
με ἄνθρωπον ὃς → λελάληκα ὑμῖν τὴν ἀλήθειαν ἣν → ἤκουσα παρὰ τοῦ θεοῦ Ἀβραάμ ← οὐκ ἐποίησεν τοῦτο ←
r.as.1 · n.asm · r.nsm · v.rai.1s · r.dp.2 · d.asf · n.asf · r.asf · v.aai.1s · p.g · d.gsm · n.gsm · n.nsm · pl · v.aai.3s · r.asn
1609 · 476 · 4005 · 3281 · 7007 · 3836 · 237 · 4005 · 201 · 4123 · 3836 · 2536 · 11 · 4472 · 4024 · 4472 · 4047

[41] You are doing the things your own father does." "We are not illegitimate children," they protested. "The
ὑμεῖς → ποιεῖτε τὰ ἔργα ὑμῶν τοῦ πατρὸς ← οὖν ἡμεῖς → οὐ ἐκ πορνείας, γεγεννήμεθα → εἶπαν αὐτῷ
r.np.2 · v.pai.2p · d.apn · n.apn · r.gp.2 · d.gsm · n.gsm · cj · r.np.1 · pl · p.g · n.gsf · v.rpi.1p · v.aai.3p · r.dsm.3
7007 · 4472 · 3836 · 2240 · 7007 · 3836 · 4252 · 2240 · 4036 · 7005 · 1164 · 4024 · 1666 · 4518 · 1164 · 3306 · 899

only Father we have is God himself."
ἕνα πατέρα → ἔχομεν τὸν θεόν.
a.asm · n.asm · v.pai.1p · d.asm · n.asm
1651 · 4252 · 2400 · 3836 · 2536

The Children of the Devil

8:42 Jesus said to them, "If God were your Father, you would love me, for I came from God
ὁ Ἰησοῦς, εἶπεν → αὐτοῖς εἰ ὁ θεὸς, ἦν ὑμῶν πατὴρ → ἂν ἠγαπᾶτε ἐμέ γὰρ ἐγὼ ἐξῆλθον ἐκ τοῦ θεοῦ
d.nsm · n.nsm · v.aai.3s · r.dpm.3 · cj · d.nsm · n.nsm · v.iai.3s · r.gp.2 · n.nsm · pl · v.iai.2p · r.as.1 · cj · r.ns.1 · v.aai.1s · p.g · d.gsm · n.gsm
3836 · 2652 · 3306 · 899 · 1623 · 3836 · 2536 · 1639 · 7007 · 4252 · 26 · 323 · 26 · 1609 · 1142 · 1609 · 2002 · 1666 · 3836 · 2536

and now am here. I have not come on my own; but he sent me. [43] Why is my language
καὶ → ἥκω γὰρ → οὐδὲ ἐλήλυθα ἀπ' ἐμαυτοῦ ← ἀλλ' ἐκεῖνος ἀπέστειλεν με διὰ τί → τὴν ἐμὴν τὴν λαλιὰν
cj · v.rai.1s · cj · adv · v.rai.1s · p.g · r.gsm.1 · cj · r.nsm · v.aai.3s · r.as.1 · p.a · r.asn · d.asf · r.asf.1 · d.asf · n.asf
2779 · 2457 · 1142 · 2262 · 2262 · 4028 · 2262 · 608 · 1831 · 247 · 1697 · 690 · 1609 · 1328 · 5515 · 1182 · 3836 · 1847 · 3836 · 3282

not clear to you? Because you are unable to hear what I say. [44] You belong to your father, the
οὐ γινώσκετε ← ← ὅτι → → οὐ δύνασθε, ἀκούειν τὸν ἐμόν, τὸν λόγον, ὑμεῖς ἐστε ἐκ τοῦ πατρὸς τοῦ
pl · v.pai.2p · cj · pl · v.ppi.2p · f.pa · d.asm · r.asm.1 · d.asm · n.asm · r.np.2 · v.pai.2p · p.g · d.gsm · n.gsm · d.gsm
4024 · 1182 · 4022 · 4024 · 1538 · 201 · 3836 · 1847 · 3836 · 3364 · 7007 · 1639 · 1666 · 3836 · 4252 · 3836

devil, and you want to carry out your father's desire. He was a murderer from the beginning,
διαβόλου καὶ → θέλετε → ποιεῖν ← ὑμῶν τοῦ πατρὸς, τὰς ἐπιθυμίας, ἐκεῖνος ἦν ἀνθρωποκτόνος ἀπ' ἀρχῆς καὶ
n.gsm · cj · v.pai.2p · f.pa · r.gp.2 · d.gsm · n.gsm · d.apf · n.apf · r.nsm · v.iai.3s · n.nsm · p.g · n.gsf · cj
1333 · 2779 · 2527 · 4472 · 7007 · 3836 · 4252 · 3836 · 2123 · 1697 · 1639 · 475 · 608 · 794 · 2779

not holding to the truth, for there is no truth in him. When he lies, he speaks his native
οὐκ ἔστηκεν ἐν τῇ ἀληθείᾳ ὅτι → ἔστιν οὐκ ἀλήθεια ἐν αὐτῷ ὅταν → λαλῇ τὸ ψεῦδος, → λαλεῖ ἐκ τῶν ἰδίων,
pl · v.iai.3s · p.d · d.dsf · n.dsf · cj · v.pai.3s · pl · n.nsf · p.d · r.dsm.3 · cj · v.pas.3s · d.asn · n.asn · v.pai.3s · p.g · d.gpn · a.gpn
4024 · 5112 · 1877 · 3836 · 237 · 4022 · 1639 · 4024 · 237 · 1877 · 899 · 4020 · 3281 · 3836 · 6022 · 3281 · 1666 · 3836 · 2625

language, for he is a liar and the father of lies. [45] Yet because I tell the truth, you do not believe me!
ὅτι → ἐστὶν ψεύστης καὶ ὁ πατὴρ αὐτοῦ δὲ ὅτι ἐγὼ λέγω τὴν ἀλήθειαν → οὐ πιστεύετε μοι
cj · v.pai.3s · n.nsm · cj · d.nsm · n.nsm · r.gsn.3 · cj · cj · r.ns.1 · v.pai.1s · d.asf · n.asf · pl · v.pai.2p · r.ds.1
4022 · 1639 · 6026 · 2779 · 3836 · 4252 · 899 · 1254 · 4022 · 1609 · 3306 · 3836 · 237 · 4409 · 4409 · 4024 · 4409 · 1609

[46] Can any of you prove me guilty of sin? If I am telling the truth, why don't you believe me? [47] He who
→ τίς ἐξ ὑμῶν ἐλέγχει με ← περὶ ἁμαρτίας εἰ → λέγω ἀλήθειαν διὰ τί οὐ ὑμεῖς πιστεύετε μοι ὁ ←
r.nsm · p.g · r.gp.2 · v.pai.3s · r.as.1 · p.g · n.gsf · cj · v.pai.1s · n.asf · p.a · r.asn · pl · r.np.2 · v.pai.2p · r.ds.1 · d.nsm
1794 · 5515 · 1666 · 7007 · 1794 · 1609 · 1794 · 4309 · 1623 · 3306 · 237 · 1328 · 5515 · 4024 · 7007 · 4409 · 1609 · 3836

ζητεῖτέ με ἀποκτεῖναι, ὅτι ὁ λόγος ὁ ἐμὸς οὐ χωρεῖ ἐν ὑμῖν. [38] ἃ ἐγὼ ἑώρακα παρὰ τῷ πατρὶ λαλῶ· καὶ ὑμεῖς οὖν ἃ ἠκούσατε παρὰ τοῦ πατρὸς ὑμῶν ποιεῖτε. [39] Ἀπεκρίθησαν καὶ εἶπαν αὐτῷ, Ὁ πατὴρ ἡμῶν Ἀβραάμ ἐστιν. λέγει αὐτοῖς ὁ Ἰησοῦς, Εἰ τέκνα τοῦ Ἀβραὰμ ἦτε, «ἐστε,» τὰ ἔργα τοῦ Ἀβραὰμ ἐποιεῖτε· [40] νῦν δὲ ζητεῖτέ με ἀποκτεῖναι ἄνθρωπον ὃς τὴν ἀλήθειαν ὑμῖν λελάληκα ἣν ἤκουσα παρὰ τοῦ θεοῦ· τοῦτο Ἀβραὰμ οὐκ ἐποίησεν. [41] ὑμεῖς ποιεῖτε τὰ ἔργα τοῦ πατρὸς ὑμῶν. εἶπαν [οὖν] αὐτῷ, Ἡμεῖς ἐκ πορνείας οὐ γεγεννήμεθα· ἕνα πατέρα ἔχομεν τὸν θεόν.

[8:42] εἶπεν αὐτοῖς ὁ Ἰησοῦς, Εἰ ὁ θεὸς πατὴρ ὑμῶν ἦν ἠγαπᾶτε ἂν ἐμέ, ἐγὼ γὰρ ἐκ τοῦ θεοῦ ἐξῆλθον καὶ ἥκω· οὐδὲ γὰρ ἀπ' ἐμαυτοῦ ἐλήλυθα, ἀλλ' ἐκεῖνός με ἀπέστειλεν. [43] διὰ τί τὴν λαλιὰν τὴν ἐμὴν οὐ γινώσκετε; ὅτι οὐ δύνασθε ἀκούειν τὸν λόγον τὸν ἐμόν. [44] ὑμεῖς ἐκ τοῦ πατρὸς τοῦ διαβόλου ἐστὲ καὶ τὰς ἐπιθυμίας τοῦ πατρὸς ὑμῶν θέλετε ποιεῖν. ἐκεῖνος ἀνθρωποκτόνος ἦν ἀπ' ἀρχῆς καὶ ἐν τῇ ἀληθείᾳ οὐκ ἔστηκεν, ὅτι οὐκ ἔστιν ἀλήθεια ἐν αὐτῷ. ὅταν λαλῇ τὸ ψεῦδος, ἐκ τῶν ἰδίων λαλεῖ, ὅτι ψεύστης ἐστὶν καὶ ὁ πατὴρ αὐτοῦ. [45] ἐγὼ δὲ ὅτι τὴν ἀλήθειαν λέγω, οὐ πιστεύετέ μοι. [46] τίς ἐξ ὑμῶν ἐλέγχει με περὶ ἁμαρτίας;

belongs to God hears what God says. The reason you do not hear is that you do not belong to
ὢν ἐκ ⌐τοῦ θεοῦ⌐ ἀκούει τὰ ⌐τοῦ θεοῦ⌐ ῥήματα → ⌐διὰ τοῦτο⌐ ὑμεῖς → οὐκ ἀκούετε ὅτι → ἐστέ οὐκ ← ἐκ
pt.pa.nsm d.p.g d.gsm n.gsm v.pai.3s d.apn d.gsm n.gsm n.apn p.a r.asn r.np.2 pl v.pai.2p cj v.pai.2p pl p.g
1639 1666 3836 2536 201 3836 3836 2536 4839 1328 4047 7007 201 4024 201 4022 1639 4024 1639 1666

God."
⌐τοῦ θεοῦ⌐
d.gsm n.gsm
3836 2536

The Claims of Jesus About Himself

8:48 The Jews answered him, "Aren't we right in saying that you are a Samaritan and
οἱ Ἰουδαῖοι Ἀπεκρίθησαν καὶ εἶπαν αὐτῷ οὐ ἡμεῖς καλῶς λέγομεν ὅτι σὺ εἶ Σαμαρίτης καὶ
d.npm a.npm v.api.3p cj v.aai.3p r.dsm.3 pl r.np.1 adv v.pai.1p cj r.ns.2 v.pai.2s n.nsm cj
3836 2681 646 2779 3306 899 4024 7005 2822 3306 4022 5148 1639 4901 2779

demon-possessed?" **49** "I am not possessed by a demon," said Jesus, "but I honor my Father and you
⌐δαιμόνιον ἔχεις⌐ ἐγὼ → οὐκ ἔχω δαιμόνιον ἀπεκρίθη Ἰησοῦς ἀλλὰ → τιμῶ μου ⌐τὸν πατέρα⌐ καὶ ὑμεῖς
n.asn v.pai.2s r.ns.1 pl v.pai.1s n.asn v.api.3s n.nsm cj v.pai.1s r.gs.1 d.asm n.asm cj r.np.2
1228 2400 1609 2400 4024 2400 1228 646 2652 247 5506 1609 3836 4252 2779 7007

dishonor me. **50** I am not seeking glory for myself; but there is one who seeks it, and he is the judge. **51** I
ἀτιμάζετε με δὲ ἐγὼ → οὐ ζητῶ ⌐τὴν δόξαν⌐ → μου → ἔστιν ὁ ← ζητῶν καὶ → → κρίνων →
v.pai.2p r.as.1 cj r.ns.1 pl v.pai.1s d.asf n.asf r.gs.1 v.pai.3s d.nsm pt.pa.nsm cj pt.pa.nsm
869 1609 1254 1609 4024 2426 3836 1518 1609 1639 3836 2426 2779 3212

tell you the truth, if anyone keeps my word, he will never see death." **52** At this the
λέγω ὑμῖν ⌐ἀμὴν ἀμὴν⌐ ἐάν τις τηρήσῃ ἐμὸν ⌐τὸν λόγον⌐ → → ⌐οὐ μὴ⌐ εἰς τὸν αἰῶνα θεωρήσῃ θάνατον οὖν οἱ
v.pai.1s r.dp.2 pl pl cj r.nsm v.aas.3s r.asm.1 d.asm n.asm pl pl p.a d.asm n.asm v.aas.3s n.asm cj d.npm
3306 7007 297 297 1569 5516 5498 1847 3836 3364 2555 2555 4024 3590 1650 3836 172 2555 2505 4036 3836

Jews exclaimed, "Now we know that you are demon-possessed! Abraham died and so did the
Ἰουδαῖοι εἶπον αὐτῷ νῦν → ἐγνώκαμεν ὅτι → → ⌐δαιμόνιον ἔχεις⌐ Ἀβραὰμ ἀπέθανεν καὶ οἱ
a.npm v.aai.3p r.dsm.3 adv v.rai.1p cj n.asn v.pai.2s n.nsm v.aai.3s cj d.npm
2681 3306 899 3814 1182 4022 1228 2400 11 633 2779 3836

prophets, yet you say that if anyone keeps your word, he will never taste death. **53** Are
προφῆται καὶ σὺ λέγεις ἐάν τις τηρήσῃ μου ⌐τὸν λόγον⌐ → → ⌐οὐ μὴ⌐ εἰς τὸν αἰῶνα γεύσηται θανάτου μὴ εἶ
n.npm cj r.ns.2 v.pai.2s cj r.nsm v.aas.3s r.gs.1 d.asm n.asm pl pl p.a d.asm n.asm v.ams.3s n.gsm pl v.pai.2s
4737 2779 5148 3306 1569 5516 5498 1609 3836 3364 1174 1174 4024 3590 1650 3836 172 1174 2505 3590 1639

you greater than our father Abraham? He died, and so did the prophets. Who do you think you
σὺ μείζων → ἡμῶν ⌐τοῦ πατρὸς⌐ Ἀβραάμ ὅστις ἀπέθανεν καὶ ἀπέθανον οἱ προφῆται τίνα → → ποιεῖς σεαυτὸν
r.ns.2 a.nsm.c r.gp.1 d.gsm n.gsm n.gsm r.nsm v.aai.3s cj v.aai.3p d.npm n.npm r.asm v.pai.2s r.asm.2
5148 3489 7005 3836 4252 11 4015 633 2779 633 3836 4737 5515 4472 4932

are?" **54** Jesus replied, "If I glorify myself, my glory means nothing. My Father, whom you claim as
→ Ἰησοῦς ἀπεκρίθη ἐὰν ἐγὼ δοξάσω ἐμαυτὸν μου ἡ δόξα ἐστιν οὐδέν μου ὁ πατήρ ὃν ὑμεῖς λέγετε ⌐ὅτι ἐστιν⌐
n.nsm v.api.3s cj r.ns.1 v.aas.1s r.asm.1 r.gs.1 d.nsf n.nsf v.pai.3s a.nsn r.gs.1 d.nsm n.nsm r.asm r.np.2 v.pai.2p v.pai.3s
4472 2652 646 1569 1609 1519 1831 1609 3836 1518 1639 4029 1609 3836 4252 4005 7007 3306 4022 1639

your God, is the one who glorifies me. **55** Though you do not know him, I know him. If I said I did
ἡμῶν θεὸς ἔστιν ὁ ← δοξάζων με καὶ → οὐκ ἐγνώκατε αὐτόν δὲ ἐγὼ οἶδα αὐτόν κἂν → εἴπω ὅτι → →
r.gp.1 n.nsm v.pai.3s d.nsm pt.pa.nsm r.as.1 cj pl v.rai.2p r.asm.3 cj r.ns.1 v.rai.1s r.asm.3 crasis v.aas.1s cj
7005 2536 1639 3836 1519 1609 2779 1182 1182 4024 1182 899 1254 1609 3857 899 2829 3306 4022 3857 3857

not, I would be a liar like you, but I do know him and keep his word. **56** Your father
οὐκ οἶδα αὐτόν → ἔσομαι ψεύστης ὅμοιος ὑμῖν ἀλλὰ → οἶδα αὐτὸν καὶ τηρῶ αὐτοῦ ⌐τὸν λόγον⌐ ὑμῶν ὁ πατὴρ
pl v.rai.1s r.asm.3 v.fmi.1s n.nsm a.nsm r.dp.2 cj v.rai.1s r.asm.3 cj v.pai.1s r.gsm.3 d.asm n.asm r.gp.2 d.nsm n.nsm
4024 3857 899 1639 6026 3927 247 3857 899 2779 5498 899 3836 3364 7007 3836 4252

Abraham rejoiced at the thought of seeing my day; he saw it and was glad." **57** "You are
Ἀβραὰμ ἠγαλλιάσατο ἵνα ἴδῃ ⌐τὴν ἐμὴν⌐ ⌐τὴν ἡμέραν⌐ καὶ → εἶδεν καὶ → ἐχάρη οὖν → ἔχεις
n.nsm v.ami.3s cj v.aas.3s d.asf r.asf.1 d.asf n.asf cj v.aai.3s cj v.api.3s cj v.pai.2s
11 22 2671 1625 3836 1847 3836 2465 2779 1625 2779 5897 4036 2400

εἰ ἀλήθειαν λέγω, διὰ τί ὑμεῖς οὐ πιστεύετέ μοι; ⁴⁷ ὁ ὢν ἐκ τοῦ θεοῦ τὰ ῥήματα τοῦ θεοῦ ἀκούει· διὰ τοῦτο ὑμεῖς οὐκ ἀκούετε,
ὅτι ἐκ τοῦ θεοῦ οὐκ ἐστέ.
    8:48 Ἀπεκρίθησαν οἱ Ἰουδαῖοι καὶ εἶπαν αὐτῷ, Οὐ καλῶς λέγομεν ἡμεῖς ὅτι Σαμαρίτης εἶ σὺ καὶ δαιμόνιον ἔχεις;
⁴⁹ ἀπεκρίθη Ἰησοῦς, Ἐγὼ δαιμόνιον οὐκ ἔχω, ἀλλὰ τιμῶ τὸν πατέρα μου, καὶ ὑμεῖς ἀτιμάζετέ με. ⁵⁰ ἐγὼ δὲ οὐ ζητῶ τὴν δόξαν
μου· ἔστιν ὁ ζητῶν καὶ κρίνων. ⁵¹ ἀμὴν ἀμὴν λέγω ὑμῖν, ἐάν τις τὸν ἐμὸν λόγον τηρήσῃ, θάνατον οὐ μὴ θεωρήσῃ εἰς τὸν αἰῶνα.
⁵² εἶπον [οὖν] αὐτῷ οἱ Ἰουδαῖοι, Νῦν ἐγνώκαμεν ὅτι δαιμόνιον ἔχεις. Ἀβραὰμ ἀπέθανεν καὶ οἱ προφῆται, καὶ σὺ λέγεις, Ἐάν
τις τὸν λόγον μου τηρήσῃ, οὐ μὴ γεύσηται θανάτου εἰς τὸν αἰῶνα. ⁵³ μὴ σὺ μείζων εἶ τοῦ πατρὸς ἡμῶν Ἀβραάμ, ὅστις ἀπέθανεν;
καὶ οἱ προφῆται ἀπέθανον. τίνα σεαυτὸν ποιεῖς; ⁵⁴ ἀπεκρίθη Ἰησοῦς, Ἐὰν ἐγὼ δοξάσω ἐμαυτόν, ἡ δόξα μου οὐδέν ἐστιν· ἔστιν
ὁ πατήρ μου ὁ δοξάζων με, ὃν ὑμεῖς λέγετε ὅτι θεὸς ἡμῶν ἐστιν, ⁵⁵ καὶ οὐκ ἐγνώκατε αὐτόν, ἐγὼ δὲ οἶδα αὐτόν. κἂν εἴπω ὅτι
οὐκ οἶδα αὐτόν, ἔσομαι ὅμοιος ὑμῖν ψεύστης· ἀλλὰ οἶδα αὐτὸν καὶ τὸν λόγον αὐτοῦ τηρῶ. ⁵⁶ Ἀβραὰμ ὁ πατὴρ ὑμῶν
ἠγαλλιάσατο ἵνα ἴδῃ τὴν ἡμέραν τὴν ἐμήν, καὶ εἶδεν καὶ ἐχάρη. ⁵⁷ εἶπον οὖν οἱ Ἰουδαῖοι πρὸς αὐτόν, Πεντήκοντα ἔτη οὔπω

not yet fifty years old," the Jews said to him, "and you have seen Abraham!" **58** "I tell you the
οὔπω πεντήκοντα ἔτη οἱ Ἰουδαῖοι εἶπον πρὸς αὐτόν καὶ → → ἑώρακας Ἀβραάμ → λέγω ὑμῖν
adv a.apn n.apn d.npm a.npm v.aai.3p p.a r.asm.3 cj v.rai.2s n.asm v.pai.1s r.dp.2
4037 4299 2291 3836 2681 3306 4639 2779 3972 11 3306 7007

truth," Jesus answered, "before Abraham was born, I am!" **59** At this, they picked up stones to
ἀμὴν ἀμήν Ἰησοῦς εἶπεν αὐτοῖς πρὶν Ἀβραάμ γενέσθαι ἐγὼ εἰμι οὖν ἦραν λίθους ἵνα
pl pl n.nsm v.aai.3s r.dpm.3 cj n.asm v.fam r.ns.1 v.pai.1s cj v.aai.3p n.apm cj
297 297 2652 3306 899 4570 11 1181 1609 1639 4036 149 3345 2671

stone him, but Jesus hid himself, slipping away from the temple grounds.
βάλωσιν ἐπ' αὐτόν δὲ Ἰησοῦς ἐκρύβη → καὶ ἐξῆλθεν → ἐκ τοῦ ἱεροῦ
v.aas.3p p.a r.asm.3 cj n.nsm v.api.3s cj v.aai.3s p.g d.gsn n.gsn
965 2093 899 1254 2652 3221 2779 2002 1666 3836 2639

Jesus Heals a Man Born Blind

9:1 As he went along, he saw a man blind from birth. **2** His disciples asked him,
Καὶ → → παράγων ← → εἶδεν ἄνθρωπον τυφλὸν ἐκ γενετῆς καὶ αὐτοῦ οἱ μαθηταί ἠρώτησαν αὐτόν λέγοντες
cj pt.pa.nsm v.aai.3s n.asm a.asm p.g n.gsf cj r.gsm.3 d.npm n.npm v.aai.3p r.asm.3 pt.pa.npm
2779 4135 1625 476 5603 1666 1162 2779 899 3836 3412 2263 899 3306

"Rabbi, who sinned, this man or his parents, that he was born blind?" **3** "Neither this man nor his
ῥαββί τίς ἥμαρτεν οὗτος ← ἢ αὐτοῦ οἱ γονεῖς ἵνα → γεννηθῇ τυφλὸς οὔτε οὗτος ← οὔτε αὐτοῦ
n.vsm r.nsm v.aai.3s r.nsm cj r.gsm.3 d.npm n.npm cj v.aps.3s a.nsm cj r.nsm cj r.gsm.3
4806 5515 279 4047 2445 899 3836 1204 2671 1164 5603 4046 4047 4046 899

parents sinned," said Jesus, "but this happened so that the work of God might be displayed in his life.
οἱ γονεῖς ἥμαρτεν ἀπεκρίθη Ἰησοῦς ἀλλ' ἵνα → τὰ ἔργα → τοῦ θεοῦ → → φανερωθῇ ἐν αὐτῷ
d.npm n.npm v.aai.3s v.api.3s n.nsm cj cj d.npn n.npn d.gsm n.gsm v.aps.3s p.d r.dsm.3
3836 1204 646 646 2652 247 2671 3836 2240 3836 2536 5746 1877 899

4 As long as it is day, we must do the work of him who sent me. Night is coming, when no one
ἕως ← → ἐστίν ἡμέρα ἡμᾶς δεῖ ἐργάζεσθαι τὰ ἔργα → τοῦ → πέμψαντος με νὺξ → ἔρχεται ὅτε → οὐδεὶς
cj v.pai.3s n.nsf r.ap.1 v.pai.3s f.pm d.apn n.apn d.gsm pt.aa.gsm r.as.1 n.nsf v.pmi.3s cj a.nsm
2401 1639 2465 7005 1256 2237 3836 2240 3836 4287 1609 3816 2262 4021 4029

can work. **5** While I am in the world, I am the light of the world." **6** Having said this, he spit on the
δύναται ἐργάζεσθαι ὅταν → ὦ ἐν τῷ κόσμῳ → εἰμι φῶς → τοῦ κόσμου εἰπὼν ταῦτα → ἔπτυσεν → ἐπὶ
v.ppi.3s f.pm cj v.pas.1s p.d d.dsm n.dsm v.pai.1s n.nsn d.gsm n.gsm pt.aa.nsm r.apn v.aai.3s
1538 2237 4020 1639 1877 3836 3180 1639 5890 3836 3180 3306 4047 4772

ground, made some mud with the saliva, and put it on the man's eyes. **7** "Go," he told
χαμαὶ καὶ ἐποίησεν πηλὸν ἐκ τοῦ πτύσματος καὶ ἐπέχρισεν τὸν πηλὸν ἐπὶ τοὺς αὐτοῦ ὀφθαλμοὺς καὶ ὕπαγε → εἶπεν
adv cj v.aai.3s n.asm p.g d.gsn n.gsn cj v.aai.3s d.asm n.asm p.a d.apm r.gsm.3 n.apm cj v.pam.2s v.aai.3s
5912 2779 4472 4384 1666 3836 4770 2779 2222 3836 4384 2093 3836 899 4057 2779 5632 3306

him, "wash in the Pool of Siloam" (this word means Sent). So the man went and washed, and
αὐτῷ νίψαι εἰς τὴν κολυμβήθραν → τοῦ Σιλωάμ ὃ ἑρμηνεύεται ἀπεσταλμένος οὖν → ἀπῆλθεν καὶ ἐνίψατο καὶ
r.dsm.3 v.amm.2s p.a d.asf n.asf d.gsn n.gsn r.nsn v.ppi.3s pt.rp.nsm cj v.aai.3s cj v.ami.3s cj
899 3782 1650 3836 3148 3836 4978 4005 2257 690 4036 599 2779 3782 2779

came home seeing. **8** His neighbors and those who had formerly seen him begging asked,
ἦλθεν βλέπων οὖν Οἱ γείτονες καὶ οἱ ← → τὸ πρότερον θεωροῦντες αὐτὸν ὅτι ἦν προσαίτης ἔλεγον
v.aai.3s pt.pa.nsm cj d.npm n.npm cj d.npm d.asn adv.c pt.pa.npm r.asm.3 cj v.iai.3s n.nsm v.iai.3p
2262 1063 4036 3836 1150 2779 3836 2555 3836 4728 2555 899 4022 1639 4645 3306

"Isn't this the same man who used to sit and beg?" **9** Some claimed that he was. Others said, "No,
οὐχ ἐστιν οὗτος ὁ → καθήμενος καὶ προσαιτῶν ἄλλοι ἔλεγον ὅτι → οὗτος ἐστιν ἄλλοι ἔλεγον οὐχί
pl v.pai.3s r.nsm d.nsm pt.pm.nsm cj pt.pa.nsm r.npm v.iai.3p cj r.nsm v.pai.3s r.npm v.iai.3p pl
4024 1639 4047 3836 2764 2779 4644 257 3306 4022 4047 1639 257 3306 4049

he only looks like him." But he himself insisted, "I am the man." **10** "How then were your eyes
→ ἀλλὰ ἐστιν ὅμοιος αὐτῷ → ἐκεῖνος ἔλεγεν ὅτι ἐγὼ εἰμι οὖν πῶς οὖν → σου οἱ ὀφθαλμοί
cj v.pai.3s a.nsm r.dsm.3 r.nsm v.iai.3s cj r.ns.1 v.pai.1s cj v.pai.3s cj r.gs.2 d.npm n.npm
1639 247 1639 3927 899 3306 1697 3306 4022 1609 1639 4036 4802 4036 5148 3836 4057

opened?" they demanded. **11** He replied, "The man they call Jesus made some mud and
ἠνεῴχθησαν → ἔλεγον αὐτῷ ἐκεῖνος ἀπεκρίθη ὁ ἄνθρωπος ὁ λεγόμενος Ἰησοῦς ἐποίησεν πηλὸν καὶ
v.api.3p v.iai.3p r.dsm.3 r.nsm v.api.3s d.nsm n.nsm d.nsm pt.pp.nsm n.nsm v.aai.3s n.asm cj
487 3306 899 1697 646 3836 476 3836 3306 2652 4472 4384 2779

ἔχεις καὶ Ἀβραὰμ ἑώρακας; **58** εἶπεν αὐτοῖς Ἰησοῦς, Ἀμὴν ἀμὴν λέγω ὑμῖν, πρὶν Ἀβραὰμ γενέσθαι ἐγὼ εἰμι. **59** ἦραν οὖν λίθους ἵνα βάλωσιν ἐπ' αὐτόν. Ἰησοῦς δὲ ἐκρύβη καὶ ἐξῆλθεν ἐκ τοῦ ἱεροῦ.

9:1 Καὶ παράγων εἶδεν ἄνθρωπον τυφλὸν ἐκ γενετῆς. **2** καὶ ἠρώτησαν αὐτὸν οἱ μαθηταὶ αὐτοῦ λέγοντες, Ῥαββί, τίς ἥμαρτεν, οὗτος ἢ οἱ γονεῖς αὐτοῦ, ἵνα τυφλὸς γεννηθῇ; **3** ἀπεκρίθη Ἰησοῦς, Οὔτε οὗτος ἥμαρτεν οὔτε οἱ γονεῖς αὐτοῦ, ἀλλ' ἵνα φανερωθῇ τὰ ἔργα τοῦ θεοῦ ἐν αὐτῷ. **4** ἡμᾶς δεῖ ἐργάζεσθαι τὰ ἔργα τοῦ πέμψαντός με ἕως ἡμέρα ἐστίν· ἔρχεται νὺξ ὅτε οὐδεὶς δύναται ἐργάζεσθαι. **5** ὅταν ἐν τῷ κόσμῳ ὦ, φῶς εἰμι τοῦ κόσμου. **6** ταῦτα εἰπὼν ἔπτυσεν χαμαὶ καὶ ἐποίησεν πηλὸν ἐκ τοῦ πτύσματος καὶ ἐπέχρισεν αὐτοῦ τὸν πηλὸν ἐπὶ τοὺς ὀφθαλμοὺς **7** καὶ εἶπεν αὐτῷ, Ὕπαγε νίψαι εἰς τὴν κολυμβήθραν τοῦ Σιλωάμ (ὃ ἑρμηνεύεται Ἀπεσταλμένος). ἀπῆλθεν οὖν καὶ ἐνίψατο καὶ ἦλθεν βλέπων. **8** Οἱ οὖν γείτονες καὶ οἱ θεωροῦντες αὐτὸν τὸ πρότερον ὅτι προσαίτης ἦν ἔλεγον, Οὐχ οὗτός ἐστιν ὁ καθήμενος καὶ προσαιτῶν; **9** ἄλλοι ἔλεγον ὅτι Οὗτός ἐστιν, ἄλλοι ἔλεγον, Οὐχί, ἀλλὰ ὅμοιος αὐτῷ ἐστιν. ἐκεῖνος ἔλεγεν ὅτι Ἐγώ εἰμι. **10** ἔλεγον οὖν αὐτῷ, Πῶς [οὖν] ἠνεῴχθησάν σου οἱ ὀφθαλμοί; **11** ἀπεκρίθη ἐκεῖνος, Ὁ ἄνθρωπος ὁ λεγόμενος Ἰησοῦς πηλὸν ἐποίησεν καὶ ἐπέχρισέν μου τοὺς ὀφθαλμοὺς καὶ εἶπέν μοι ὅτι Ὕπαγε εἰς τὸν

put   it on my eyes.   He told me   to go   to Siloam   and wash. So I went   and washed,
ἐπέχρισεν   μου ⸢τοὺς ὀφθαλμούς⸥ καὶ → εἶπέν μοι ὅτι   ὕπαγε εἰς ⸢τὸν Σιλωάμ⸥ καὶ νίψαι οὖν → ἀπελθὼν καὶ νιψάμενος
v.aai.3s   r.gs.1 d.apm n.apm   cj   v.aai.3s r.ds.1 cj   v.pam.2s p.a d.asm n.asm   cj v.amm.2s cj   pt.aa.nsm cj pt.am.nsm
2222   1609 3836 4057   2779   3306 1609 4022   5632 1650 3836 4978   2779 3782 4036   599 2779 3782

and then I could see."   12   "Where is   this   man?" they asked him. "I don't know," he said.
→ → ἀνέβλεψα   καὶ ποῦ   ἐστιν ἐκεῖνος ←   → εἶπαν αὐτῷ   οὐκ οἶδα   → λέγει
v.aai.1s   cj adv   v.pai.3s r.nsm   v.aai.3p r.dsm.3   pl v.rai.1s   v.pai.3s
329   2779 4543   1639 1697   3306 899   3857 4024   3857 3306

The Pharisees Investigate the Healing

9:13 They brought   to   the Pharisees   the man who had been blind.   14 Now the day   on which Jesus
Ἄγουσιν αὐτὸν πρὸς τοὺς Φαρισαίους τόν   ποτε τυφλόν   δὲ   ἡμέρα ἐν ᾗ   ὁ Ἰησοῦς
v.pai.3p r.asm.3 p.a d.apm n.apm d.asm   adv a.asm   cj   n.dsf p.d r.dsf   d.nsm n.nsm
72   899 4639 3836 5757   3836   4537 5603   1254   2465 1877 4005   3836 2652

had made   the mud and opened the man's eyes   was a Sabbath.   15 Therefore   the Pharisees also asked
→ ἐποίησεν τὸν πηλὸν καὶ ἀνέῳξεν τοὺς αὐτοῦ ὀφθαλμούς   ἦν σάββατον   οὖν   πάλιν οἱ Φαρισαῖοι καὶ ἠρώτων
v.aai.3s d.asm n.asm cj v.aai.3s d.apm r.gsm.3 n.apm   v.iai.3s n.nsn   cj   adv d.npm n.npm adv v.iai.3p
4472   3836 4384 2779 487 3836 899 4057   1639 4879   4036   4099 3836 5757 2779 2263

him how he had received his sight.   "He put   mud on my eyes,"   the man replied,   "and I
αὐτὸν πῶς → → →   ἀνέβλεψεν δὲ →   ἐπέθηκεν πηλὸν ἐπὶ μου ⸢τοὺς ὀφθαλμούς⸥ ὁ ←   εἶπεν αὐτοῖς καὶ
r.asm.3 r.asn   v.aai.3s cj   v.aai.3s n.asm p.a r.gs.1 d.apm n.apm   d.nsm   v.aai.3s r.dpm.3 cj
899 4802   329 1254   2202 4384 2093 1609 3836 4057   3836   3306 899 2779

washed, and now I see."   16   Some of the Pharisees said, "This man   is   not from God, for he does not
ἐνιψάμην καὶ   βλέπω   οὖν τινες ἐκ τῶν Φαρισαίων ἔλεγον οὗτος ὁ ἄνθρωπος   ἐστιν οὐκ παρὰ θεοῦ ὅτι →   → οὐ
v.ami.1s cj   v.pai.1s   cj r.npm p.g d.gpm n.gpm v.iai.3p r.nsm d.nsm n.nsm   v.pai.3s pl p.g n.gsm cj   pl
3782 2779   1063   4036 5516 1666 3836 5757 3306 4047 3836 476   1639 4024 4123 2536 4022 5498 5498 4024

keep the Sabbath." But others asked, "How can   a sinner   do   such   miraculous signs?" So they
τηρεῖ τὸ σάββατον δὲ ἄλλοι ἔλεγον πῶς   δύναται ⸢ἄνθρωπος ἁμαρτωλὸς⸥ ποιεῖν τοιαῦτα →   σημεῖα καὶ →
v.pai.3s d.asn n.asn cj r.npm v.iai.3p adv   v.ppi.3s a.nsm a.nsm f.pa r.apn   n.apn cj
5498 3836 4879 1254 257 3306 4802   1538 476 283 4472 5525   4956 2779

were divided.   17 Finally they turned again to the blind man, "What have you to say   about him?   It was
ἦν σχίσμα ἐν αὐτοῖς οὖν →   λέγουσιν πάλιν τῷ τυφλῷ   τί   σὺ λέγεις περὶ αὐτοῦ ὅτι   It was
v.iai.3s n.nsn p.d r.dpm.3 cj   v.pai.3p adv d.dsm a.dsm   r.asn   r.ns.2 v.pai.2s p.g r.gsm.3 cj
1639 5388 1877 899 4036   3306 4099 3836 5603   5515   5148 3306 4309 899 4022

your eyes   he opened." The man replied,   "He is   a prophet."   18 The Jews   still did not believe
σου ⸢τοὺς ὀφθαλμούς⸥ → ἠνέῳξεν δὲ ὁ ←   εἶπεν ὅτι   ἐστίν προφήτης   οἱ Ἰουδαῖοι οὖν →   Οὐκ ἐπίστευσαν
r.gs.2 d.apm n.apm   v.aai.3s cj d.nsm   v.aai.3s cj   v.pai.3s n.nsm   d.npm a.npm cj   pl v.aai.3p
5148 3836 4057   487 1254 3836   3306 4022   1639 4737   3836 2681 4036   4024 4409

that he had been blind and had received his sight   until   they sent   for the man's
περὶ αὐτοῦ ὅτι → → ἦν τυφλὸς καὶ →   ἀνέβλεψεν ἕως ὅτου   ἐφώνησαν ←   τοὺς ⸢τοῦ ἀναβλέψαντος⸥
p.g r.gsm.3 cj   v.iai.3s a.nsm cj   v.aai.3s p.g r.gsn   v.aai.3p   d.apm d.gsm pt.aa.gsm
4309 899 4022   1639 5603 2779   329 2401 4015   5888   3836 3836 329

parents.   19   "Is this your son?"   they asked.   "Is this the one   you say   was born
γονεῖς αὐτοῦ καὶ ἐστιν οὗτος ὑμῶν ὁ υἱός →   ἠρώτησαν αὐτοὺς λέγοντες   ὃν ὑμεῖς λέγετε ὅτι →   ἐγεννήθη
n.apm r.gsm.3 cj v.pai.3s r.nsm r.gp.2 d.nsm n.nsm   v.aai.3p r.apm.3 pt.pa.npm   r.asm r.np.2 v.pai.2p cj   v.api.3s
1204 899 2779 1639 4047 7007 3836 5626   2263 899 3306   4005 7007 3306 4022   1164

blind?   How is it that now he can see?"   20   "We know   he is   our son,"   the parents   answered,
τυφλὸς οὖν πῶς   ἄρτι → → βλέπει οὖν →   οἴδαμεν ὅτι οὗτός ἐστιν ἡμῶν ὁ υἱός οἱ γονεῖς αὐτοῦ ἀπεκρίθησαν
a.nsm cj adv   adv v.pai.3s cj   v.rai.1p cj r.nsm v.pai.3s r.gp.1 d.nsm n.nsm d.npm n.npm r.gsm.3 v.api.3p
5603 4036 4802   785 1063 4036   3857 4022 4047 1639 7005 3836 5626 3836 1204 899 646

"and we know   he was born   blind. 21 But how he can see   now,   or who opened his
καὶ εἶπαν καὶ   ὅτι   ἐγεννήθη τυφλὸς δὲ πῶς →   βλέπει νῦν   οὐκ οἴδαμεν ἢ τίς ἤνοιξεν αὐτοῦ
cj v.aai.3p cj   cj   v.api.3s a.nsm cj cj   v.pai.3s adv   pl v.rai.1p r.nsm v.aai.3s r.gsm.3
2779 3306 2779   4022   1164 5603 1254 4802   1063 3814   4024 3857 2445 5515 487 899

Σιλωάμ· καὶ νίψαι· ἀπελθὼν οὖν καὶ νιψάμενος ἀνέβλεψα. ¹² καὶ εἶπαν αὐτῷ, Ποῦ ἐστιν ἐκεῖνος; λέγει, Οὐκ οἶδα.
    9:13 Ἄγουσιν αὐτὸν πρὸς τοὺς Φαρισαίους τόν ποτε τυφλόν. ¹⁴ ἦν δὲ σάββατον ἐν ᾗ ἡμέρᾳ τὸν πηλὸν ἐποίησεν ὁ Ἰησοῦς καὶ ἀνέῳξεν αὐτοῦ τοὺς ὀφθαλμούς. ¹⁵ πάλιν οὖν ἠρώτων αὐτὸν καὶ οἱ Φαρισαῖοι πῶς ἀνέβλεψεν. ὁ δὲ εἶπεν αὐτοῖς, Πηλὸν ἐπέθηκέν μου ἐπὶ τοὺς ὀφθαλμούς, καὶ ἐνιψάμην καὶ βλέπω. ¹⁶ ἔλεγον οὖν ἐκ τῶν Φαρισαίων τινές, Οὐκ ἔστιν οὗτος παρὰ θεοῦ ὁ ἄνθρωπος, ὅτι τὸ σάββατον οὐ τηρεῖ. ἄλλοι [δὲ] ἔλεγον, Πῶς δύναται ἄνθρωπος ἁμαρτωλὸς τοιαῦτα σημεῖα ποιεῖν; καὶ σχίσμα ἦν ἐν αὐτοῖς. ¹⁷ λέγουσιν οὖν τῷ τυφλῷ πάλιν, Τί σὺ λέγεις περὶ αὐτοῦ, ὅτι ἠνέῳξέν σου τοὺς ὀφθαλμούς; ὁ δὲ εἶπεν ὅτι Προφήτης ἐστίν. ¹⁸ Οὐκ ἐπίστευσαν οὖν οἱ Ἰουδαῖοι περὶ αὐτοῦ ὅτι ἦν τυφλὸς καὶ ἀνέβλεψεν ἕως ὅτου ἐφώνησαν τοὺς γονεῖς αὐτοῦ τοῦ ἀναβλέψαντος ¹⁹ καὶ ἠρώτησαν αὐτοὺς λέγοντες, Οὗτός ἐστιν ὁ υἱὸς ὑμῶν, ὃν ὑμεῖς λέγετε ὅτι τυφλὸς ἐγεννήθη; πῶς οὖν βλέπει ἄρτι; ²⁰ ἀπεκρίθησαν οὖν οἱ γονεῖς αὐτοῦ καὶ εἶπαν, Οἴδαμεν ὅτι οὗτός ἐστιν ὁ υἱὸς ἡμῶν καὶ ὅτι τυφλὸς ἐγεννήθη· ²¹ πῶς δὲ νῦν βλέπει οὐκ οἴδαμεν, ἢ τίς ἤνοιξεν αὐτοῦ τοὺς ὀφθαλμούς ἡμεῖς οὐκ οἴδαμεν· αὐτὸν ἐρωτήσατε,

eyes, we don't know. Ask him. He is of age; he will speak for himself." 22 His parents
⌞τοὺς ὀφθαλμοὺς⌟ ἡμεῖς οὐκ οἴδαμεν ἐρωτήσατε αὐτὸν → ἔχει → ἡλικίαν αὐτὸς → λαλήσει περὶ ἑαυτοῦ αὐτοῦ ⌞οἱ γονεῖς⌟
d.apm n.apm r.np.1 pl v.rai.1p v.aam.2p r.asm.3 v.pai.3s n.asf r.nsm v.fai.3s p.g r.gsm.3 r.gsm.3 d.npm n.npm
3836 4057 7005 4024 3857 2263 899 2400 2461 899 3281 4309 1571 899 3836 1204

said this because they were afraid of the Jews, for already the Jews had decided that anyone who
εἶπαν ταῦτα ὅτι → → ἐφοβοῦντο ← τοὺς Ἰουδαίους γὰρ ἤδη οἱ Ἰουδαῖοι → συνετέθειντο ἵνα ἐάν τις
v.aai.3p r.apn cj v.ipi.3p d.apm a.apm cj adv d.npm a.npm v.lmi.3p cj cj r.nsm
3306 4047 4022 5828 3836 2681 1142 2453 3836 2681 5338 2671 1569 5516

acknowledged that Jesus was the Christ would be put out of the synagogue. 23 That was why his
ὁμολογήσῃ αὐτὸν χριστόν → γένηται → → → ἀποσυνάγωγος → ⌞διὰ τοῦτο⌟ αὐτοῦ
v.aas.3s r.asm.3 n.asm v.ams.3s a.nsm p.a r.asn r.gsm.3
3933 899 5986 1181 697 1328 4047 899

parents said, "He is of age; ask him." 24 A second time they summoned the man who
⌞οἱ γονεῖς⌟ εἶπαν ὅτι → ἔχει → ἡλικίαν ἐπερωτήσατε αὐτὸν οὖν ⌞ἐκ δευτέρου⌟ ← → Ἐφώνησαν τὸν ἄνθρωπον ὃς
d.npm n.npm v.aai.3p cj v.pai.3s n.asf v.aam.2p r.asm.3 cj p.g a.gsn v.aai.3p d.asm n.asm r.nsm
3836 1204 3306 4022 2400 2461 2089 899 4036 1666 1311 5888 3836 476 4005

had been blind. "Give glory to God," they said. "We know this man is a sinner." 25
→ ἦν τυφλὸς καὶ δὸς δόξαν → ⌞τῷ θεῷ⌟ → εἶπαν αὐτῷ ἡμεῖς οἴδαμεν ὅτι οὗτος ⌞ὁ ἄνθρωπος⌟ ἐστιν ἁμαρτωλός οὖν
v.iai.3s a.nsm cj v.aam.2s n.asf d.dsm n.dsm v.aai.3p r.dsm.3 r.np.1 v.rai.1p cj r.nsm d.nsm n.nsm v.pai.3s a.nsm cj
1639 5603 2779 1443 1518 3836 2536 3306 899 7005 3857 4022 4047 3836 476 1639 283 4036

He replied, "Whether he is a sinner or not, I don't know. One thing I do know. I was blind but
ἐκεῖνος ἀπεκρίθη εἰ → ἐστιν ἁμαρτωλός ↱ οὐκ οἶδα ἓν ← → → οἶδα ὅτι → ὢν τυφλὸς
r.nsm v.api.3s cj v.pai.3s a.nsm pl v.rai.1s a.asn v.rai.1s cj pt.pa.nsm a.nsm
1697 646 1623 1639 283 3857 4024 3857 1651 3857 4022 1639 5603

now I see!" 26 Then they asked him, "What did he do to you? How did he open your eyes?" 27 He
ἄρτι → βλέπω οὖν → εἶπον αὐτῷ τί → → ἐποίησεν → σοι πῶς → → ἤνοιξεν σου ⌞τοὺς ὀφθαλμούς⌟ →
adv v.pai.1s cj v.aai.3p r.dsm.3 r.asn v.aai.3s r.ds.2 cj v.aai.3s r.gs.2 d.apm n.apm
785 1063 4036 3306 899 5515 4472 5148 4802 487 5148 3836 4057

answered, "I have told you already and you did not listen. Why do you want to hear it again? Do
ἀπεκρίθη αὐτοῖς → → εἶπον ὑμῖν ἤδη καὶ ↱ ↱ οὐκ ἠκούσατε τί → → θέλετε → ἀκούειν πάλιν μὴ ↱
v.api.3s r.dpm.3 v.aai.1s r.dp.2 adv cj pl v.aai.2p r.asn v.pai.2p f.pa adv pl
646 899 3306 7007 2453 2779 201 201 4024 201 5515 2527 201 4099 3590 2527

you want to become his disciples, too?" 28 Then they hurled insults at him and said, "You are this fellow's
ὑμεῖς θέλετε → γενέσθαι αὐτοῦ μαθηταὶ καὶ καὶ → → ἐλοιδόρησαν ← αὐτὸν καὶ εἶπον σὺ εἶ ἐκείνου ←
r.np.2 v.pai.2p f.am r.gsm.3 n.npm adv cj v.aai.3p r.asm.3 cj v.aai.3p r.ns.2 v.pai.2s r.gsm
7007 2527 1181 899 3412 2779 2779 3366 899 2779 3306 5148 1639 1697

disciple! We are disciples of Moses! 29 We know that God spoke to Moses, but as for this fellow,
μαθητὴς δὲ ἡμεῖς ἐσμὲν μαθηταί ⌞τοῦ Μωϋσέως⌟ ἡμεῖς οἴδαμεν ὅτι ⌞ὁ θεός⌟ λελάληκεν → Μωϋσεῖ δὲ τοῦτον ←
n.nsm cj r.np.1 v.pai.1p n.npm d.gsm n.gsm r.np.1 v.rai.1p cj d.nsm n.nsm v.rai.3s n.dsm cj r.asm
3412 1254 7005 1639 3412 3836 3707 7005 3857 4022 3836 2536 3281 3707 1254 4047

we don't even know where he comes from." 30 The man answered, "Now that is
↱ οὐκ οἴδαμεν πόθεν → ἐστίν ὁ ἄνθρωπος ἀπεκρίθη καὶ εἶπεν αὐτοῖς γὰρ ⌞ἐν τούτῳ⌟ ἐστιν
pl v.rai.1p cj v.pai.3s d.nsm n.nsm v.api.3s cj v.aai.3s r.dpm.3 cj p.d r.dsn v.pai.3s
3857 4024 3857 4470 1639 4470 3836 476 646 2779 3306 899 1142 1877 4047 1639

remarkable! You don't know where he comes from, yet he opened my eyes. 31 We know that God
⌞τὸ θαυμαστόν⌟ ὅτι ὑμεῖς οὐκ οἴδατε πόθεν → ἐστίν καὶ → ἤνοιξεν μου ⌞τοὺς ὀφθαλμούς⌟ → οἴδαμεν ὅτι ⌞ὁ θεὸς⌟
d.nsn a.nsn cj r.np.2 pl v.rai.2p cj v.pai.3s cj v.aai.3s r.gs.1 d.apm n.apm v.rai.1p cj d.nsm n.nsm
3836 2515 4022 7007 4024 3857 4470 1639 4470 2779 487 1609 3836 4057 3857 4022 3836 2536

does not listen to sinners. He listens to the godly man who does his will.
↱ οὐκ ἀκούει ← ἁμαρτωλῶν ἀλλ' → ἀκούει ← τούτου ἐάν τις θεοσεβὴς ᾖ καὶ ποιῇ αὐτοῦ ⌞τὸ θέλημα⌟
pl v.pai.3s a.gpm cj v.pai.3s r.gsm cj r.nsm a.nsm v.pas.3s cj v.pas.3s r.gsm.3 d.asn n.asn
201 4024 201 283 247 201 4047 1569 5516 2538 1639 2779 4472 899 3836 2525

32 Nobody has ever heard of opening the eyes of a man born blind. 33 If this man were
οὐκ ↱ ⌞ἐκ τοῦ αἰῶνος⌟ ἠκούσθη ὅτι τις ἠνέῳξεν ὀφθαλμοὺς γεγεννημένου τυφλοῦ εἰ οὗτος ← ἦν
pl p.g d.gsm n.gsm v.api.3s cj r.nsm v.aai.3s n.apm pt.rp.gsm a.gsm cj r.nsm v.iai.3s
4024 201 1666 3836 172 201 4022 5516 487 4057 1164 5603 1623 4047 1639

ἡλικίαν ἔχει, αὐτὸς περὶ ἑαυτοῦ λαλήσει. 22 ταῦτα εἶπαν οἱ γονεῖς αὐτοῦ ὅτι ἐφοβοῦντο τοὺς Ἰουδαίους· ἤδη γὰρ συνετέθειντο
οἱ Ἰουδαῖοι ἵνα ἐάν τις αὐτὸν ὁμολογήσῃ Χριστόν, ἀποσυνάγωγος γένηται. 23 διὰ τοῦτο οἱ γονεῖς αὐτοῦ εἶπαν ὅτι Ἡλικίαν ἔχει,
αὐτὸν ἐπερωτήσατε. 24 Ἐφώνησαν οὖν τὸν ἄνθρωπον ἐκ δευτέρου ὃς ἦν τυφλὸς καὶ εἶπαν αὐτῷ, Δὸς δόξαν τῷ θεῷ· ἡμεῖς οἴδαμεν
ὅτι οὗτος ὁ ἄνθρωπος ἁμαρτωλός ἐστιν. 25 ἀπεκρίθη οὖν ἐκεῖνος, Εἰ ἁμαρτωλός ἐστιν οὐκ οἶδα· ἓν οἶδα ὅτι τυφλὸς ὢν ἄρτι
βλέπω. 26 εἶπον οὖν αὐτῷ, Τί ἐποίησέν σοι; πῶς ἤνοιξέν σου τοὺς ὀφθαλμούς; 27 ἀπεκρίθη αὐτοῖς, Εἶπον ὑμῖν ἤδη καὶ οὐκ
ἠκούσατε· τί πάλιν θέλετε ἀκούειν; μὴ καὶ ὑμεῖς θέλετε αὐτοῦ μαθηταὶ γενέσθαι; 28 καὶ ἐλοιδόρησαν αὐτὸν καὶ εἶπον, Σὺ μαθητὴς
εἶ ἐκείνου, ἡμεῖς δὲ τοῦ Μωϋσέως ἐσμὲν μαθηταί· 29 ἡμεῖς οἴδαμεν ὅτι Μωϋσεῖ λελάληκεν ὁ θεός, τοῦτον δὲ οὐκ οἴδαμεν πόθεν
ἐστίν. 30 ἀπεκρίθη ὁ ἄνθρωπος καὶ εἶπεν αὐτοῖς, Ἐν τούτῳ γὰρ τὸ θαυμαστόν ἐστιν, ὅτι ὑμεῖς οὐκ οἴδατε πόθεν ἐστίν, καὶ ἤνοιξέν
μου τοὺς ὀφθαλμούς. 31 οἴδαμεν ὅτι ἁμαρτωλῶν ὁ θεὸς οὐκ ἀκούει, ἀλλ' ἐάν τις θεοσεβὴς ᾖ καὶ τὸ θέλημα αὐτοῦ ποιῇ τούτου
ἀκούει. 32 ἐκ τοῦ αἰῶνος οὐκ ἠκούσθη ὅτι ἠνέῳξέν τις ὀφθαλμοὺς τυφλοῦ γεγεννημένου· 33 εἰ μὴ ἦν οὗτος παρὰ θεοῦ, οὐκ

not from God,   he could   do   nothing." **34** To this they replied,   "You were steeped in sin
μὴ παρὰ θεοῦ οὐκ → ἠδύνατο ποιεῖν οὐδέν   →   ἀπεκρίθησαν καὶ εἶπαν αὐτῷ σὺ ↱ ὅλος ἐν ἁμαρτίαις
pl p.g n.gsm pl v.ipi.3s f.pa a.asn   v.api.3p cj v.aai.3p r.dsm.3 r.ns.2 a.nsm p.d n.dpf
3590 4123 2536 4024 1538 4472 4029   646 2779 3306 899 5148 1164 3910 1877 281

at birth;   how dare you lecture   us!" And they threw   him out.
→ ἐγεννήθης καὶ   σὺ διδάσκεις ἡμᾶς καὶ → ἐξέβαλον αὐτὸν ἔξω
v.api.2s cj   r.ns.2 v.pai.2s r.ap.1 cj   v.aai.3p r.asm.3 adv
1164 2779   5148 1438 7005 2779   1675 899 2032

Spiritual Blindness

9:35 Jesus   heard   that they had thrown him   out, and when he found him,   he said, "Do you believe in the
Ἰησοῦς Ἤκουσεν ὅτι → ἐξέβαλον αὐτὸν ἔξω καὶ → → εὑρὼν αὐτὸν → εἶπεν σὺ πιστεύεις εἰς τὸν
n.nsm v.aai.3s cj   v.aai.3p r.asm.3 adv cj   pt.aa.nsm r.asm.3 v.aai.3s r.ns.2 v.pai.2s p.a d.asm
2652 201 4022   1675 899 2032 2779   2351 899 3306 4409 5148 4409 1650 3836

Son of Man?" **36**   "Who is   he, sir?" the man   asked.   "Tell me so that I may believe in him."
υἱὸν τοῦ ἀνθρώπου καὶ τίς ἐστιν ← κύριε ἐκεῖνος ἀπεκρίθη καὶ εἶπεν   ἵνα ← → πιστεύσω εἰς αὐτόν
n.asm d.gsm n.gsm cj r.nsm v.pai.3s n.vsm r.nsm v.api.3s cj v.aai.3s   cj   v.aas.1s p.a r.asm.3
5626 3836 476 2779 5515 1639 3261 1697 646 2779 3306   2671   4409 1650 899

37 Jesus   said,   "You have now seen   him; *in fact,* he   is   the one speaking with you." **38** Then the man
ὁ Ἰησοῦς εἶπεν αὐτῷ →   καὶ ἑώρακας αὐτὸν καὶ ἐκεῖνος ἐστιν ὁ λαλῶν μετὰ σοῦ δὲ ὁ
d.nsm n.nsm v.aai.3s r.dsm.3   cj v.rai.2s r.asm.3 cj r.nsm v.pai.3s d.nsm pt.pa.nsm p.g r.gs.2 cj d.nsm
3836 2652 3306 899 3972   2779 3972 899 2779 1697 1639 3836 3281 3552 5148 1254 3836

said, "Lord, I believe," and he worshiped him. **39**   Jesus   said, "For judgment I   have come into this
ἔφη κύριε → πιστεύω καὶ → προσεκύνησεν αὐτῷ Καὶ ὁ Ἰησοῦς εἶπεν εἰς κρίμα ἐγὼ → ἦλθον εἰς τοῦτον
v.iai.3s n.vsm v.pai.1s cj v.aai.3s r.dsm.3 cj d.nsm n.nsm v.aai.3s p.a n.asn r.ns.1 v.aai.1s p.a r.asm
5774 3261 4409 2779 4686 899 2779 3836 2652 3306 1650 3210 1609 2262 1650 4047

world,   so that the blind   will see   and those who see   will become blind." **40** Some
τὸν κόσμον ἵνα οἱ μὴ βλέποντες βλέπωσιν καὶ οἱ ← βλέποντες → γένωνται τυφλοὶ → ἐκ
d.asm n.asm cj d.npm pl pt.pa.npm v.pas.3p cj d.npm pt.pa.npm v.ams.3p a.npm p.g
3836 3180 2671 3836 3590 1063 1063 2779 3836 1063 1181 5603 1666

Pharisees   who were   with him   heard   him say this   and asked,   "What? Are we   blind too?"
τῶν Φαρισαίων οἱ ὄντες μετ' αὐτοῦ ἤκουσαν ταῦτα καὶ εἶπον αὐτῷ μὴ ἐσμεν ἡμεῖς τυφλοὶ καὶ
d.gpm n.gpm d.npm pt.pa.npm p.g r.gsm.3 v.aai.3p r.apn cj v.aai.3p r.dsm.3 pl v.pai.1p r.np.1 a.npm adv
3836 5757 3836 1639 3552 899 201 4047 2779 3306 899 3590 1639 7005 5603 2779

41 Jesus   said,   "If you were blind, you would not be guilty of sin;   but now that you claim   you can
ὁ Ἰησοῦς εἶπεν αὐτοῖς εἰ → ἦτε τυφλοὶ ↱ ἂν οὐκ → εἴχετε ἁμαρτίαν δὲ νῦν → λέγετε ὅτι → →
d.nsm n.nsm v.aai.3s r.dpm.3 cj v.iai.2p a.npm pl pl v.iai.2p n.asf cj adv v.pai.2p cj
3836 2652 3306 899 1623 1639 5603 323 4024 2400 281 1254 3814 3306 4022

see,   your guilt   remains.
βλέπομεν ὑμῶν ἡ ἁμαρτία μένει
v.pai.1p r.gp.2 d.nsf n.nsf v.pai.3s
1063 7007 3836 281 3531

The Shepherd and His Flock

10:1 "I tell you the truth,   the man who does not enter   the sheep   pen by the gate, but
λέγω ὑμῖν Ἀμὴν ἀμὴν ὁ ← μὴ εἰσερχόμενος εἰς τὴν τῶν προβάτων αὐλὴν διὰ τῆς θύρας ἀλλὰ
v.pai.1s r.dp.2 pl pl d.nsm pl pt.pm.nsm p.a d.asf d.gpn n.gpn n.asf p.g d.gsf n.gsf cj
3306 7007 297 297 3836 3590 1656 1650 3836 3836 4585 885 1328 3836 2598 247

climbs   in by some other way,   is a thief and a robber. **2**   The man who enters   by the gate
ἀναβαίνων ← → → ἀλλαχόθεν ἐκεῖνος ἐστιν κλέπτης καὶ λῃστής δὲ ὁ ← εἰσερχόμενος διὰ τῆς θύρας
pt.pa.nsm adv r.nsm v.pai.3s n.nsm cj n.nsm cj d.nsm pt.pm.nsm p.g d.gsf n.gsf
326 249 1697 1639 3095 2779 3334 1254 3836 1656 1328 3836 2598

is   the shepherd of his sheep. **3** The watchman opens the gate for him, and the sheep   listen to his   voice.
ἐστιν ποιμήν → τῶν προβάτων ὁ θυρωρὸς ἀνοίγει → τούτῳ καὶ τὰ πρόβατα ἀκούει ← αὐτοῦ τῆς φωνῆς
v.pai.3s n.nsm d.gpn n.gpn d.nsm n.nsm v.pai.3s r.dsm cj d.npn n.npn v.pai.3s r.gsm.3 d.gsf n.gsf
1639 4478 3836 4585 3836 2601 487 4047 2779 3836 4585 201 899 3836 5889

ἠδύνατο ποιεῖν οὐδέν. ³⁴ ἀπεκρίθησαν καὶ εἶπαν αὐτῷ, Ἐν ἁμαρτίαις σὺ ἐγεννήθης ὅλος καὶ σὺ διδάσκεις ἡμᾶς; καὶ ἐξέβαλον αὐτὸν ἔξω.

9:35 Ἤκουσεν Ἰησοῦς ὅτι ἐξέβαλον αὐτὸν ἔξω καὶ εὑρὼν αὐτὸν εἶπεν, Σὺ πιστεύεις εἰς τὸν υἱὸν τοῦ ἀνθρώπου; ³⁶ ἀπεκρίθη ἐκεῖνος καὶ εἶπεν, Καὶ τίς ἐστιν, κύριε, ἵνα πιστεύσω εἰς αὐτόν; ³⁷ εἶπεν αὐτῷ ὁ Ἰησοῦς, Καὶ ἑώρακας αὐτὸν καὶ ὁ λαλῶν μετὰ σοῦ ἐκεῖνός ἐστιν. ³⁸ ὁ δὲ ἔφη, Πιστεύω, κύριε· καὶ προσεκύνησεν αὐτῷ. ³⁹ καὶ εἶπεν ὁ Ἰησοῦς, Εἰς κρίμα ἐγὼ εἰς τὸν κόσμον τοῦτον ἦλθον, ἵνα οἱ μὴ βλέποντες βλέπωσιν καὶ οἱ βλέποντες τυφλοὶ γένωνται. ⁴⁰ Ἤκουσαν ἐκ τῶν Φαρισαίων ταῦτα οἱ μετ' αὐτοῦ ὄντες καὶ εἶπον αὐτῷ, Μὴ καὶ ἡμεῖς τυφλοί ἐσμεν; ⁴¹ εἶπεν αὐτοῖς ὁ Ἰησοῦς, Εἰ τυφλοὶ ἦτε, οὐκ ἂν εἴχετε ἁμαρτίαν· νῦν δὲ λέγετε ὅτι Βλέπομεν, ἡ ἁμαρτία ὑμῶν μένει.

10:1 Ἀμὴν ἀμὴν λέγω ὑμῖν, ὁ μὴ εἰσερχόμενος διὰ τῆς θύρας εἰς τὴν αὐλὴν τῶν προβάτων ἀλλὰ ἀναβαίνων ἀλλαχόθεν ἐκεῖνος κλέπτης ἐστὶν καὶ λῃστής· ² ὁ δὲ εἰσερχόμενος διὰ τῆς θύρας ποιμήν ἐστιν τῶν προβάτων. ³ τούτῳ ὁ θυρωρὸς ἀνοίγει,

He calls his own sheep   by name and leads them out. **4** When   he has brought out   all   his own,   he goes   on
καὶ → φωνεῖ τὰ ἴδια πρόβατα κατ᾽ ὄνομα καὶ ἐξάγει αὐτά ↩   ὅταν →   ἐκβάλῃ ← πάντα τὰ ἴδια → πορεύεται ←
cj   v.pai.3s d.apn a.apn n.apn p.a n.asn cj v.pai.3s r.apn.3   cj   v.aas.3s   a.apn d.apn a.apn v.pmi.3s
2779 5888 3836 2625 4585 2848 3950 2779 1974 899 1974   4020   1675   4246 3836 2625 4513

ahead of them, and his sheep   follow   him because they know his voice. **5** But they will never
ἔμπροσθεν → αὐτῶν καὶ τὰ πρόβατα ἀκολουθεῖ αὐτῷ ὅτι → οἴδασιν αὐτοῦ ⌜τὴν φωνήν⌝ δὲ ↩ → ⌜οὐ μὴ
p.g   r.gpn.3 cj d.npn n.npn v.pai.3s r.apn.3 cj   v.rai.3p r.gsm.3 d.asf n.asf dsm pl pl
1869   899 2779 3836 4585 199 899 4022   3857 899 3836 5889 1254 199 199 4024 3590

follow   a stranger; in fact, they will run   away from him because they do not recognize a stranger's
ἀκολουθήσουσιν ἀλλοτρίῳ ἀλλὰ → φεύξονται ← ἀπ᾽ αὐτοῦ ὅτι → → οὐκ οἴδασιν ⌜τῶν ἀλλοτρίων⌝
v.fai.3p   n.dsm   cj   v.fmi.3p p.g r.gsm.3 cj   pl v.rai.3p d.gpm n.gpm
199   259   247   5771   608 899 4022   4024 3857 3836 259

voice." **6** Jesus   used   this figure   of speech, but they did not understand what he was telling
⌜τὴν φωνήν⌝ ὁ Ἰησοῦς εἶπεν αὐτοῖς Ταύτην ⌜τὴν παροιμίαν⌝ ← ← δὲ ἐκεῖνοι → οὐκ ἔγνωσαν τίνα → ἦν ἃ ἐλάλει
d.asf n.asf d.nsm n.nsm v.aai.3s r.dpm.3 r.asf d.asf n.asf   cj r.npm   pl v.aai.3p r.npn   v.iai.3s r.apn v.iai.3s
3836 5889 3836 2652 3306 899 4047 3836 4231   1254 1697   4024 1182 5515   1639 4005 3281

them. ¶ **7** Therefore Jesus   said again, "I tell you the truth,   I am the gate for the sheep.
αὐτοῖς οὖν ὁ Ἰησοῦς Εἶπεν πάλιν → λέγω ὑμῖν ⌜ἀμὴν ἀμὴν⌝ ὅτι ἐγώ εἰμι ἡ θύρα → τῶν προβάτων
r.dpm.3 cj d.nsm n.nsm v.aai.3s adv v.pai.1s r.dp.2 pl pl cj r.ns.1 v.pai.1s d.nsf n.nsf d.gpn n.gpn
899 4036 3836 2652 3306 4099 3306 7007 297 297 4022 1609 1639 3836 2598 3836 4585

8 All who ever came before me were thieves and robbers, but the sheep did not listen to them. **9** I am the
πάντες ὅσοι ← ἦλθον πρὸ ἐμοῦ εἰσιν κλέπται καὶ λῃσταί ἀλλ᾽ τὰ πρόβατα ↪ οὐκ ἤκουσαν ← αὐτῶν ἐγώ εἰμι ἡ
a.npm r.npm v.aai.3p p.g r.gs.1 v.pai.3p n.npm cj n.npm cj d.npn n.npn pl v.aai.3p r.gpm.3 r.ns.1 v.pai.1s d.nsf
4246 4012   2262 4574 1609 1639 3095 2779 3334 247 3836 4585 201 4024 201 899 1609 1639 3836

gate; whoever enters through me will be saved. He will come in and go out, and find   pasture.
θύρα ⌜ἐάν τις⌝ εἰσέλθῃ δι᾽ ἐμοῦ → σωθήσεται καὶ → εἰσελεύσεται ← καὶ ἐξελεύσεται ← καὶ εὑρήσει νομήν
n.nsf r.nsm v.aas.3s p.g r.gs.1 v.fpi.3s cj v.fmi.3s cj v.fmi.3s cj v.fai.3s n.asf
2598 1569 5516 1656 1328 1609 5392 2779 1656 2779 2002 2779 2351 3786

10 The thief   comes only to steal and kill and destroy; I have come that they may have life, and have it
ὁ κλέπτης οὐκ ἔρχεται εἰ μὴ ἵνα κλέψῃ καὶ θύσῃ καὶ ἀπολέσῃ ἐγώ → ἦλθον ἵνα → ἔχωσιν ζωὴν καὶ ἔχωσιν
d.nsm n.nsm pl v.pmi.3s cj pl cj v.aas.3s cj v.aas.3s cj v.aas.3s r.ns.1 v.aai.1s cj v.pas.3p n.asf cj v.pas.3p
3836 3095 4024 2262 1623 3590 2671 3096 2779 2604 2779 660 1609 2262 2671 2400 2437 2779 2400

to the full. ¶ **11** "I am the good   shepherd. The good   shepherd lays down his life for
→ περισσὸν Ἐγώ εἰμι ὁ ⌜ὁ καλός⌝ ποιμὴν ὁ ⌜ὁ καλός⌝ ποιμὴν τίθησιν ← αὐτοῦ ⌜τὴν ψυχήν⌝ ὑπὲρ
adv   r.ns.1 v.pai.1s d.nsm d.nsm a.nsm n.nsm d.nsm d.nsm a.nsm n.nsm v.pai.3s r.gsm.3 d.asf n.asf p.g
4356   1609 1639 3836 3836 2819 4478 3836 3836 2819 4478 5502 899 3836 6034 5642

the sheep. **12** The hired hand   is   not the shepherd who owns   the sheep. So when he sees the
τῶν προβάτων ὁ μισθωτὸς ← καὶ ὢν οὐκ ποιμήν οὐ ⌜οὐκ ἔστιν ἴδια⌝ τὰ πρόβατα → θεωρεῖ τὸν
d.gpn n.gpn d.nsm n.nsm cj pt.pa.nsm pl n.nsm r.gsm pl v.pai.3s a.npn d.npn n.npn v.pai.3s d.asm
3836 4585 3836 3638 2779 1639 4024 4478 4005 4024 1639 2625 3836 4585 2262 2555 3836

wolf coming,   he abandons the sheep and runs away. Then the wolf attacks the flock and scatters it. **13** The
λύκον ἐρχόμενον καὶ → ἀφίησιν τὰ πρόβατα καὶ φεύγει ← καὶ ὁ λύκος ἁρπάζει αὐτὰ καὶ σκορπίζει
n.asm pt.pm.asm cj v.pai.3s d.apn n.apn cj v.pai.3s cj d.nsm n.nsm v.pai.3s r.apn.3 cj v.pai.3s
3380 2262 2779 918 3836 4585 2779 5771 2779 3836 3380 773 899 2779 5025

man runs away because he is a hired hand and cares nothing for the sheep. ¶ **14** "I am the
ὅτι → ἐστιν μισθωτὸς ← καὶ μέλει οὐ αὐτῷ περὶ τῶν προβάτων Ἐγώ εἰμι ὁ
cj v.pai.3s n.nsm cj v.pai.3s pl r.dsm.3 p.g d.gpn n.gpn r.ns.1 v.pai.1s d.nsm
4022 1639 3638 2779 3508 4024 899 4309 3836 4585 1609 1639 3836

good   shepherd; I know my sheep and my sheep know me – **15** just as the Father knows me
ὁ ⌜καλός⌝ ποιμὴν καὶ → γινώσκω τὰ ἐμά καὶ ⌜τὰ ἐμά⌝ γινώσκουσι με καθὼς ← ὁ πατὴρ γινώσκει με
d.nsm a.nsm n.nsm cj v.pai.1s d.apn r.apn.1 cj d.npn r.npn.1 v.pai.3p r.as.1 cj d.nsm n.nsm v.pai.3s r.as.1
3836 2819 4478 2779 1182 3836 1847 2779 3836 1847 1182 1609 2777 3836 4252 1182 1609

and I know the Father – and I lay   down my life for the sheep. **16** I have other sheep that are not
κἀγὼ → γινώσκω τὸν πατέρα καὶ → τίθημι ← μου ⌜τὴν ψυχήν⌝ ὑπὲρ τῶν προβάτων καὶ → ἔχω ἄλλα πρόβατα ἃ ἐστιν οὐκ
crasis v.pai.1s d.asm n.asm cj v.pai.1s r.gs.1 d.asf n.asf p.g d.gpn n.gpn cj v.pai.1s r.apn n.apn r.npn v.pai.3s pl
2743 1182 3836 4252 2779 5502 1609 3836 6034 5642 3836 4585 2779 2400 257 4585 4005 1639 4024

καὶ τὰ πρόβατα τῆς φωνῆς αὐτοῦ ἀκούει καὶ τὰ ἴδια πρόβατα φωνεῖ κατ᾽ ὄνομα καὶ ἐξάγει αὐτά. **4** ὅταν τὰ ἴδια πάντα ἐκβάλῃ, ἔμπροσθεν αὐτῶν πορεύεται, καὶ τὰ πρόβατα αὐτῷ ἀκολουθεῖ, ὅτι οἴδασιν τὴν φωνὴν αὐτοῦ· **5** ἀλλοτρίῳ δὲ οὐ μὴ ἀκολουθήσουσιν, ἀλλὰ φεύξονται ἀπ᾽ αὐτοῦ, ὅτι οὐκ οἴδασιν τῶν ἀλλοτρίων τὴν φωνήν. **6** Ταύτην τὴν παροιμίαν εἶπεν αὐτοῖς ὁ Ἰησοῦς, ἐκεῖνοι δὲ οὐκ ἔγνωσαν τίνα ἦν ἃ ἐλάλει αὐτοῖς. ¶ **7** Εἶπεν οὖν πάλιν ὁ Ἰησοῦς, Ἀμὴν ἀμὴν λέγω ὑμῖν ὅτι ἐγώ εἰμι ἡ θύρα τῶν προβάτων. **8** πάντες ὅσοι ἦλθον [πρὸ ἐμοῦ] κλέπται εἰσὶν καὶ λῃσταί, ἀλλ᾽ οὐκ ἤκουσαν αὐτῶν τὰ πρόβατα. **9** ἐγώ εἰμι ἡ θύρα· δι᾽ ἐμοῦ ἐάν τις εἰσέλθῃ σωθήσεται καὶ εἰσελεύσεται καὶ ἐξελεύσεται καὶ νομὴν εὑρήσει. **10** ὁ κλέπτης οὐκ ἔρχεται εἰ μὴ ἵνα κλέψῃ καὶ θύσῃ καὶ ἀπολέσῃ· ἐγὼ ἦλθον ἵνα ζωὴν ἔχωσιν καὶ περισσὸν ἔχωσιν. ¶ **11** Ἐγώ εἰμι ὁ ποιμὴν ὁ καλός. ὁ ποιμὴν ὁ καλὸς τὴν ψυχὴν αὐτοῦ τίθησιν ὑπὲρ τῶν προβάτων· **12** ὁ μισθωτὸς καὶ οὐκ ὢν ποιμήν, οὗ οὐκ ἔστιν τὰ πρόβατα ἴδια, θεωρεῖ τὸν λύκον ἐρχόμενον καὶ ἀφίησιν τὰ πρόβατα καὶ φεύγει — καὶ ὁ λύκος ἁρπάζει αὐτὰ καὶ σκορπίζει — **13** ὅτι μισθωτός ἐστιν καὶ οὐ μέλει αὐτῷ περὶ τῶν προβάτων. ¶ **14** Ἐγώ εἰμι ὁ ποιμὴν ὁ καλὸς καὶ γινώσκω τὰ ἐμὰ καὶ γινώσκουσί με τὰ ἐμά, **15** καθὼς γινώσκει με ὁ πατὴρ κἀγὼ γινώσκω τὸν πατέρα, καὶ τὴν ψυχήν μου τίθημι ὑπὲρ τῶν προβάτων. **16** καὶ ἄλλα πρόβατα

of this   sheep pen.   I   must bring them also. They too will listen   to my voice,   and there shall
ἐκ ταύτης   ⌐τῆς αὐλῆς⌐ με   δεῖ ἀγαγεῖν κἀκεῖνα ←   καὶ → ἀκούσουσιν ← μου ⌐τῆς φωνῆς⌐ καὶ
p.g r.gsf   d.gsf n.gsf   r.as.1 v.pai.3s f.aa   adv   cj   v.fai.3p   r.gs.1 d.gsf n.gsf   cj
1666 4047   3836 885   1609 1256   72   201   2779   201   1609 3836 5889   2779

be   one flock and one shepherd. [17] The reason   my Father loves me is that I   lay   down my life
γενήσονται μία ποίμνη εἰς ποιμήν.   ⌐Διὰ τοῦτο⌐ ὁ πατὴρ ἀγαπᾷ με   ὅτι ἐγὼ τίθημι ←   μου ⌐τὴν ψυχήν⌐
v.fmi.3p   a.nsf n.nsf a.nsf n.nsm   p.a   r.asn   d.nsm n.nsm v.pai.3s r.as.1 cj r.ns.1 v.pai.1s   r.gs.1 d.asf n.asf
1181   1651 4479 1651 4478   1328 4047 3836 4252 26   1609 4022 1609 5502   1609 3836 6034

only to take it   up again. [18] No one takes it   from me, but I   lay it down of my   own accord. I
ἵνα λάβω αὐτήν ←   πάλιν   οὐδεὶς αἴρει αὐτὴν ἀπ᾽ ἐμοῦ ἀλλ᾽ ἐγὼ τίθημι αὐτὴν ← ἀπ᾽ ἐμαυτοῦ ←   →
cj   v.aas.1s r.asf.3   adv   a.nsm v.pai.3s r.asf.3 p.g r.gs.1 cj r.ns.1 v.pai.1s r.asf.3   p.g r.gsm.1
2671 3284 899   4099   4029 149   899   608 1609 247 1609 5502   899   608 1831

have authority to lay   it   down and   authority to take it   up again. This command   I received from my
ἔχω ἐξουσίαν → θεῖναι αὐτήν ←   καὶ ἔχω ἐξουσίαν → λαβεῖν αὐτὴν ← πάλιν ταύτην ⌐τὴν ἐντολὴν⌐ → ἔλαβον παρὰ μου
v.pai.1s n.asf   f.aa   r.asf.3   cj v.pai.1s n.asf   f.aa r.asf.3   adv r.asf   d.asf n.asf   v.aai.1s p.g r.gs.1
2400 2026   5502 899   5502 2779 2400 2026   3284 899   3284 4099 4047 3836 1953   3284   4123 1609

Father." ¶   [19] At these words   the Jews   were again divided. [20]   Many of them said, "He is
⌐τοῦ πατρός⌐   διὰ τούτους ⌐τοὺς λόγους⌐ ἐν τοῖς Ἰουδαίοις ἐγένετο πάλιν Σχίσμα   δὲ πολλοὶ ἐξ αὐτῶν ἔλεγον → ἔχει
d.gsm n.gsm   p.a r.apm d.apm n.apm   p.d d.dpm a.dpm   v.ami.3s adv n.nsn   cj a.npm p.g r.gpm.3 v.iai.3p   v.pai.3s
3836 4252   1328 4047 3836 3364   1877 3836 2681   1181 4099 5388   1254 4498 1666 899   3306   2400

demon-possessed and raving mad. Why listen to him?" [21] But others said, "These are not the sayings of a man
δαιμόνιον   καὶ μαίνεται ← τί ἀκούετε ← αὐτοῦ   ἄλλοι ἔλεγον ταῦτα ἔστιν οὐκ τὰ ῥήματα →
n.asn   cj v.pmi.3s   r.asn v.pai.2p r.gsn.3   r.npm v.iai.3p r.npn v.pai.3s pl d.npn n.npn
1228   2779 3419   5515 201   899   257   3306 4047 1639 4024 3836 4839

possessed   by a demon. Can   a demon open   the eyes   of the blind?"
δαιμονιζομένου ← ← ←   μὴ δύναται δαιμόνιον ἀνοῖξαι ὀφθαλμοὺς → τυφλῶν
pt.pp.gsm   pl v.ppi.3s n.nsn   f.aa n.apm   a.gpm
1227   3590 1538   1228 487 4057   5603

The Unbelief of the Jews

10:22 Then came the Feast of Dedication at Jerusalem.   It was winter, [23] and Jesus   was in the temple
τότε Ἐγένετο τὰ → ἐγκαίνια ἐν τοῖς Ἱεροσολύμοις → ἦν χειμών καὶ ὁ Ἰησοῦς ἐν τῷ ἱερῷ
adv   v.ami.3s d.npn   n.npn p.d d.dpn n.dpn   v.iai.3s n.nsm cj d.nsm n.nsm p.d d.dsn n.dsn
5538 1181   3836   1589   1877 3836 2642   1639 5930 7779 3836 2652 1877 3836 2639

area walking in Solomon's   Colonnade. [24] The Jews   gathered around him,   saying, "How long
← περιεπάτει ἐν ⌐τοῦ Σολομῶνος⌐ ⌐τῇ στοᾷ⌐ οὖν οἱ Ἰουδαῖοι ἐκύκλωσαν ← αὐτὸν καὶ ἔλεγον αὐτῷ ⌐ἕως πότε⌐
v.iai.3s   p.d d.gsm n.gsm   d.dsf n.dsf cj d.npm a.npm   v.aai.3p   r.asm.3 cj v.iai.3p r.dsm.3 p.g adv
4344   1877 3836 5048   3836 5119 4036 3836 2681   3240   899   2779 3306 899 2401 4537

will you keep us   in suspense? If you are the Christ, tell us   plainly ¶ [25] Jesus   answered,
⌐τὴν ψυχὴν ἡμῶν⌐ αἴρεις εἰ σὺ εἶ ὁ χριστός, εἰπὲ ἡμῖν παρρησίᾳ   ⌐ὁ Ἰησοῦς⌐ ἀπεκρίθη
d.asf n.asf r.gp.1   v.pai.2s cj r.ns.2 v.pai.2s d.nsm n.nsm v.aam.2s r.dp.1 n.dsf   d.nsm n.nsm v.api.3s
3836 6034 7005   149   1623 5148 1639 3836 5986   3306 7005 4244   3836 2652 646

"I did tell you, but you do not believe. The miracles   I   do in my Father's   name   speak
αὐτοῖς → εἶπον ὑμῖν καὶ → οὐ πιστεύετε τὰ ἔργα ἃ ἐγὼ ποιῶ ἐν μου τοῦ πατρός ⌐τῷ ὀνόματι⌐ ταῦτα μαρτυρεῖ
r.dpm.3   v.aai.1s r.dp.2 cj   pl v.pai.2p d.npn n.npn r.apn r.ns.1 v.pai.1s p.d r.gs.1 d.gsm n.gsm d.dsn n.dsn r.npn v.pai.3s
899   3306 7007 2779 4409 4024 4409   3836 2240 4005 1609 4472 1877 1609 3836 4252 3836 3950 4047 3455

for me, [26] but you do not believe because you are not   my   sheep. [27] My   sheep   listen   to my
περὶ ἐμοῦ ἀλλὰ ὑμεῖς → οὐ πιστεύετε ὅτι → ἐστὲ οὐκ ἐκ ⌐τῶν ἐμῶν⌐ ⌐τῶν προβάτων⌐ τὰ ἐμὰ ⌐τὰ πρόβατα⌐ ἀκούσουσιν μου
p.g r.gs.1 cj r.np.2   pl v.pai.2p cj   v.pai.2p pl p.g d.gpn r.gpn.1 d.gpn n.gpn d.npn r.npn.1 d.npn n.npn v.pai.3p   r.gs.1
4309 1609 247 7007 4409 4024 4409   4022   1639 4024 1666 3836 1847 3836 4585   3836 1847 3836 4585   201   1609

voice; I know them, and they follow me. [28] I give them eternal life, and they shall never
⌐τῆς φωνῆς⌐ κἀγὼ γινώσκω αὐτὰ καὶ → ἀκολουθοῦσιν μοι   κἀγὼ δίδωμι αὐτοῖς αἰώνιον ζωὴν καὶ →   οὐ μὴ
d.gsf n.gsf crasis v.pai.1s r.apn.3 cj v.pai.3p   r.ds.1   crasis v.pai.1s r.dpn.3 a.asf n.asf cj   pl pl
3836 5889   2743 1182   899 2779   199   1609   2743 1443 899   173   2437 2779   4024 3590

ἔχω ἃ οὐκ ἔστιν ἐκ τῆς αὐλῆς ταύτης· κἀκεῖνα δεῖ με ἀγαγεῖν καὶ τῆς φωνῆς μου ἀκούσουσιν, καὶ γενήσονται μία ποίμνη, εἷς
ποιμήν. [17] διὰ τοῦτό με ὁ πατὴρ ἀγαπᾷ ὅτι ἐγὼ τίθημι τὴν ψυχήν μου, ἵνα πάλιν λάβω αὐτήν. [18] οὐδεὶς αἴρει αὐτὴν ἀπ᾽ ἐμοῦ,
ἀλλ᾽ ἐγὼ τίθημι αὐτὴν ἀπ᾽ ἐμαυτοῦ. ἐξουσίαν ἔχω θεῖναι αὐτήν, καὶ ἐξουσίαν ἔχω πάλιν λαβεῖν αὐτήν· ταύτην τὴν ἐντολὴν
ἔλαβον παρὰ τοῦ πατρός μου. ¶ [19] Σχίσμα πάλιν ἐγένετο ἐν τοῖς Ἰουδαίοις διὰ τοὺς λόγους τούτους. [20] ἔλεγον δὲ πολλοὶ ἐξ
αὐτῶν, Δαιμόνιον ἔχει καὶ μαίνεται· τί αὐτοῦ ἀκούετε; [21] ἄλλοι δὲ ἔλεγον, Ταῦτα τὰ ῥήματα οὐκ ἔστιν δαιμονιζομένου· μὴ
δαιμόνιον δύναται τυφλῶν ὀφθαλμοὺς ἀνοῖξαι;

[10:22] Ἐγένετο τότε τὰ ἐγκαίνια ἐν τοῖς Ἱεροσολύμοις, χειμὼν ἦν. [23] καὶ περιεπάτει ὁ Ἰησοῦς ἐν τῷ ἱερῷ ἐν τῇ στοᾷ τοῦ
Σολομῶνος. [24] ἐκύκλωσαν οὖν αὐτὸν οἱ Ἰουδαῖοι καὶ ἔλεγον αὐτῷ, Ἕως πότε τὴν ψυχὴν ἡμῶν αἴρεις; εἰ σὺ εἶ ὁ Χριστός, εἰπὲ
ἡμῖν παρρησίᾳ. ¶ [25] ἀπεκρίθη αὐτοῖς ὁ Ἰησοῦς, Εἶπον ὑμῖν καὶ οὐ πιστεύετε· τὰ ἔργα ἃ ἐγὼ ποιῶ ἐν τῷ ὀνόματι τοῦ πατρός
μου ταῦτα μαρτυρεῖ περὶ ἐμοῦ· [26] ἀλλὰ ὑμεῖς οὐ πιστεύετε, ὅτι οὐκ ἐστὲ ἐκ τῶν προβάτων τῶν ἐμῶν. [27] τὰ πρόβατα τὰ ἐμὰ
τῆς φωνῆς μου ἀκούουσιν, κἀγὼ γινώσκω αὐτὰ καὶ ἀκολουθοῦσίν μοι, [28] κἀγὼ δίδωμι αὐτοῖς ζωὴν αἰώνιον καὶ οὐ μὴ

perish;   no one can snatch   them out of my hand.   **29** My Father,   who has given   them to
εἰς τὸν αἰῶνα ἀπόλωνται καὶ οὐχ τις → ἁρπάσει αὐτὰ ἐκ ← μου ⌐τῆς χειρός⌐ μου ⌐ὁ πατήρ⌐ ὃ → δέδωκεν →
p.a d.asm n.asm v.ams.3p cj pl r.nsm   v.fai.3s r.apn.3 p.g r.gs.1 d.gsf n.gsf r.gs.1 d.nsm n.nsm r.asn v.rai.3s
1650 3836 172 660 2779 4024 5516   773 899 1666 1609 3836 5931 1609 3836 4252 4005 1443

me, is   greater than all;   no one can   snatch   them out of my Father's   hand.   **30** I   and the Father are
μοι ἐστιν μεῖζον → πάντων καὶ → οὐδεὶς δύναται ἁρπάζειν   ἐκ ← τῆς ⌐τοῦ πατρός⌐ χειρός ἐγὼ καὶ ὁ πατὴρ ἐσμεν
r.ds.1 v.pai.3s a.nsm.c a.gpm cj a.nsm v.ppi.3s f.pa   p.g d.gsf d.gsm n.gsm n.gsf r.ns.1 cj d.nsm n.nsm v.pai.1p
1609 1639 3489 4246 2779 4029 1538 773   1666 3836 3836 4252 5931 1609 2779 3836 4252 1639

one."   ¶   **31** Again the Jews   picked   up stones to stone   him,   **32** but Jesus   said   to them, "I have
ἕν   πάλιν οἱ Ἰουδαῖοι Ἐβάστασαν ← λίθους ἵνα λιθάσωσιν αὐτόν   ὁ Ἰησοῦς ἀπεκρίθη → αὐτοῖς → →
a.nsn   adv d.npm a.npm v.aai.3p   n.apm cj v.aas.3p r.asm.3   d.nsm n.nsm v.api.3s r.dpm.3
1651   4099 3836 2681 1002   3345 2671 3342 899   3836 2652 646 899

shown you many great miracles from the Father. For which of these   do you stone   me?" **33** "We are not stoning
ἔδειξα ὑμῖν πολλὰ καλὰ ἔργα   ἐκ τοῦ πατρός διὰ ποῖον → αὐτῶν ἔργον → → λιθάζετε ἐμὲ   ↱   ↱ οὐ λιθάζομεν
v.aai.1s r.dp.2 a.apn a.apn n.apn   p.g d.gsm n.gsm p.a r.asn   r.gpn.3 n.asn   v.pai.2p r.as.1   pl v.pai.1p
1259 7007 4498 2819 2240   1666 3836 4252 1328 4481   3836 3342   3342 1609   3342 3342 4024 3342

you for any of these,"   replied   the Jews,   "but for blasphemy,   because you,   a mere
σε περὶ   ⌐καλοῦ ἔργου⌐ ἀπεκρίθησαν οἱ Ἰουδαῖοι αὐτῷ ἀλλὰ περὶ βλασφημίας καὶ ὅτι σὺ ὢν
r.as.2 p.g   a.gsn n.gsn v.api.3p d.npm a.npm r.dsm.3 cj p.g n.gsf cj cj r.ns.2 pt.pa.nsm
5148 4309   2819 2240 646 3836 2681 899 247 4309 1060   2779 4022 5148 1639

man,   claim   to be God."   ¶   **34** Jesus   answered them, "Is   it not written   in   your Law,
ἄνθρωπος ⌐ποιεῖς σεαυτὸν⌐   θεόν   ὁ Ἰησοῦς ἀπεκρίθη αὐτοῖς ἔστιν ← οὐκ γεγραμμένον ἐν ὑμῖν ⌐τῷ νόμῳ⌐ ὅτι
n.nsm v.pai.2s r.asm.2   n.asm   d.nsm n.nsm v.api.3s r.dpm.3 v.pai.3s pl pt.rp.nsn p.d r.gp.2 d.dsm n.dsm cj
476 4472 4932   2536   3836 2652 646 899 1639 4024 1211 1877 7007 3836 3795 4022

'I   have said you are gods'? **35** If he called them   'gods,' to   whom the word of God   came – and the
ἐγὼ → εἶπα → ἐστε θεοί εἰ → εἶπεν ἐκείνους θεοὺς πρὸς οὓς ὁ λόγος → ⌐τοῦ θεοῦ⌐ ἐγένετο καὶ ἡ
r.ns.1 v.aai.1s v.pai.2p n.npm cj v.aai.3s r.apm n.apm p.a r.apm d.nsm n.nsm d.gsm n.gsm v.ami.3s cj d.nsf
1609 3306 1639 2536 1623 3306 1697 2536 4639 4005 3836 3364 3836 2536 1181 2779 3836

Scripture cannot   be broken – **36** what about the one whom the Father set   apart as his very own and sent
γραφή ⌐οὐ δύναται⌐ → λυθῆναι   ὃν ὁ πατὴρ ἡγίασεν ←   καὶ ἀπέστειλεν
n.nsf pl v.ppi.3s f.ap   r.asm d.nsm n.nsm v.aai.3s   cj v.aai.3s
1210 4024 1538 3395   4005 3836 4252 39   2779 690

into the world? Why then do you accuse me   of blasphemy because I said, 'I am God's   Son'? **37** Do not
εἰς τὸν κόσμον   ὑμεῖς λέγετε   ὅτι βλασφημεῖς ὅτι → εἶπον → εἰμι ⌐τοῦ θεοῦ⌐ υἱός   ↱ μὴ
p.a d.asm n.asm   r.np.2 v.pai.2p   cj v.pai.2s cj   v.aai.1s v.pai.1s d.gsm n.gsm n.nsm   pl
1650 3836 3180   7007 3306   4022 1059 4022   3306 1639 3836 2536 5626   4409 3590

believe me unless I do   what my Father   does. **38** But if   I → do it, even though you do not believe me, believe
πιστεύετε μοι ⌐εἰ οὐ⌐ → ποιῶ τὰ   μου ⌐τοῦ πατρός⌐ ἔργα   δὲ εἰ → ποιῶ κἂν ← → μὴ πιστεύητε ἐμοὶ πιστεύετε
v.pam.2p r.ds.1 cj pl   v.pai.1s d.apn r.gs.1 d.gsm n.gsm n.apn   cj cj v.pai.1s crasis   pl v.pas.2p r.ds.1 v.pam.2p
4409 1609 1623 4024   4472 3836 1609 3836 4252 2240   1254 1623 4472 2829   4409 4409 3590 4409 1609 4409

the miracles, that you may know and understand that the Father is in me, and I in the Father." **39**   Again they
τοῖς ἔργοις ἵνα → → γνῶτε καὶ γινώσκητε ὅτι ὁ πατὴρ ἐν ἐμοὶ κἀγὼ ← ἐν τῷ πατρί [οὖν] πάλιν →
d.dpn n.dpn cj   v.aas.2p cj v.pas.2p cj d.nsm n.nsm p.d r.ds.1 crasis p.d d.dsm n.dsm   cj adv
3836 2240 2671   1182 2779 1182 4022 3836 4252 1877 1609 2743 1877 3836 4252   4036 4099

tried   to seize him, but he escaped   their grasp.   ¶   **40** Then Jesus went   back across the Jordan   to
Ἐζήτουν → πιάσαι αὐτὸν καὶ → ἐξῆλθεν ἐκ αὐτῶν ⌐τῆς χειρός⌐   Καὶ   ἀπῆλθεν πάλιν πέραν τοῦ Ἰορδάνου εἰς
v.iai.3p f.aa r.asm.3 cj v.aai.3s p.g r.gpm.3 d.gsf n.gsf   cj   v.aai.3s adv p.g d.gsm n.gsm p.a
2426 4389 899 2779 2002 1666 899 3836 5931   2779   599 4099 4305 3836 2674 1650

the place where John   had been baptizing in the early   days.   Here he stayed **41** and many people came to
τὸν τόπον ὅπου Ἰωάννης → ἦν βαπτίζων → ⌐τὸ πρῶτον⌐ days. καὶ ἐκεῖ → ἔμεινεν καὶ πολλοὶ ← ἦλθον πρὸς
d.asm n.asm cj n.nsm v.iai.3s pt.pa.nsm d.asn adv   cj adv v.aai.3s cj a.npm v.aai.3p p.g
3836 5536 3963 2722 1639 966 3836 4754   2779 1695 3531 2779 4498 2262 4639

him.   They said,   "Though John   never performed a miraculous sign,   all   that John   said about
αὐτὸν καὶ → ἔλεγον ὅτι μὲν   Ἰωάννης οὐδέν ἐποίησεν → σημεῖον δὲ πάντα ὅσα Ἰωάννης εἶπεν περὶ
r.asm.3 cj v.iai.3p cj pl   n.nsm a.asn v.aai.3s   n.asn cj a.npn a.rpn n.nsm v.aai.3s p.g
899 2779 3306 4022 3525   2722 4029 4472   4956 1254 4246 4012 2722 3306 4309

ἀπόλωνται εἰς τὸν αἰῶνα καὶ οὐχ ἁρπάσει τις αὐτὰ ἐκ τῆς χειρός μου. ²⁹ ὁ πατήρ μου ὃς «ὃ» δέδωκέν μοι αὐτὰ μείζων «μεῖζόν» πάντων ἐστίν, «ἐστιν,» καὶ οὐδεὶς δύναται ἁρπάζειν ἐκ τῆς χειρὸς τοῦ πατρός. ³⁰ ἐγὼ καὶ ὁ πατὴρ ἕν ἐσμεν. ¶ ³¹ Ἐβάστασαν πάλιν λίθους οἱ Ἰουδαῖοι ἵνα λιθάσωσιν αὐτόν. ³² ἀπεκρίθη αὐτοῖς ὁ Ἰησοῦς, Πολλὰ ἔργα καλὰ ἔδειξα ὑμῖν ἐκ τοῦ πατρός· διὰ ποῖον αὐτῶν ἔργον ἐμὲ λιθάζετε; ³³ ἀπεκρίθησαν αὐτῷ οἱ Ἰουδαῖοι, Περὶ καλοῦ ἔργου οὐ λιθάζομέν σε ἀλλὰ περὶ βλασφημίας, καὶ ὅτι σὺ ἄνθρωπος ὢν ποιεῖς σεαυτὸν θεόν. ¶ ³⁴ ἀπεκρίθη αὐτοῖς [ὁ] Ἰησοῦς, Οὐκ ἔστιν γεγραμμένον ἐν τῷ νόμῳ ὑμῶν ὅτι Ἐγὼ εἶπα, Θεοί ἐστε; ³⁵ εἰ ἐκείνους εἶπεν θεοὺς πρὸς οὓς ὁ λόγος τοῦ θεοῦ ἐγένετο, καὶ οὐ δύναται λυθῆναι ἡ γραφή, ³⁶ ὃν ὁ πατὴρ ἡγίασεν καὶ ἀπέστειλεν εἰς τὸν κόσμον ὑμεῖς λέγετε ὅτι Βλασφημεῖς, ὅτι εἶπον, Υἱός τοῦ θεοῦ εἰμι; ³⁷ εἰ οὐ ποιῶ τὰ ἔργα τοῦ πατρός μου, μὴ πιστεύετέ μοι· ³⁸ εἰ δὲ ποιῶ, κἂν ἐμοὶ μὴ πιστεύητε, τοῖς ἔργοις πιστεύετε, ἵνα γνῶτε καὶ γινώσκητε ὅτι ἐν ἐμοὶ ὁ πατὴρ κἀγὼ ἐν τῷ πατρί. ³⁹ Ἐζήτουν [οὖν] αὐτὸν πάλιν πιάσαι, καὶ ἐξῆλθεν ἐκ τῆς χειρὸς αὐτῶν. ¶ ⁴⁰ Καὶ ἀπῆλθεν πάλιν πέραν τοῦ Ἰορδάνου εἰς τὸν τόπον ὅπου ἦν Ἰωάννης τὸ πρῶτον βαπτίζων καὶ ἔμεινεν ἐκεῖ. ⁴¹ καὶ πολλοὶ ἦλθον πρὸς αὐτὸν καὶ ἔλεγον ὅτι Ἰωάννης μὲν σημεῖον ἐποίησεν οὐδέν, πάντα δὲ ὅσα εἶπεν Ἰωάννης περὶ τούτου ἀληθῆ ἦν. ⁴² καὶ πολλοὶ

this	man	was	true."	⁴² And	in	that	place	many	believed	in	Jesus.
τούτου	←	ἦν	ἀληθῆ	καὶ	→	ἐκεῖ		πολλοὶ	ἐπίστευσαν	εἰς	αὐτὸν
r.gsm		v.iai.3s	a.npn	cj		adv		a.npm	v.aai.3p	p.a	r.asm.3
4047		1639	239	2779		1695		4498	4409	1650	899

The Death of Lazarus

¹¹:¹ Now	a	man	named	Lazarus	was	sick.	He	was	from	Bethany,	the	village	of	Mary	and	her	sister
δὲ		τις		Λάζαρος	Ἦν	ἀσθενῶν			ἀπὸ	Βηθανίας	ἐκ	τῆς κώμης	→	Μαρίας	καὶ	αὐτῆς	˻τῆς ἀδελφῆς˼
cj		r.nsm		n.nsm	v.iai.3s	pt.pa.nsm			p.g	n.gsf	p.g	d.gsf n.gsf		n.gsf	cj	r.gsf.3	d.gsf n.gsf
1254		5516		3276	1639	820			608	1029	1666	3836 3267		3451	2779	899	3836 80

Martha.	²	This	Mary,	whose	brother	Lazarus	now	lay	sick,	was	the	same	one	who	poured	perfume	on	the
Μάρθας	δὲ		Μαριὰμ	ἧς	˻ὁ ἀδελφὸς˼	Λάζαρος	→	→	ἠσθένει	ἦν	ἡ				ἀλείψασα	μύρῳ	←	τὸν
n.gsf	cj		n.nsf	r.gsf	d.nsm n.nsm	n.nsm			v.iai.3s	v.iai.3s	d.nsf				pt.aa.nsf	n.dsn		d.asm
3450	1254		3452	4005	3836 81	3276			820	1639	3836				230	3693	230	3836

Lord	and	wiped	his	feet	with	her	hair.	³ So	the	sisters	sent	word	to	Jesus,	"Lord,
κύριον	καὶ	ἐκμάξασα	αὐτοῦ	˻τοὺς πόδας˼	→	αὐτῆς	˻ταῖς θριξὶν˼	οὖν	αἱ	ἀδελφαὶ	ἀπέστειλαν	←	πρὸς	αὐτὸν	λέγουσαι	κύριε
n.asm	cj	pt.aa.nsf	r.gsm.3	d.apm n.apm		r.gsf.3	d.dpf n.dpf	cj	d.npf	n.npf	v.aai.3p		p.a	r.asm.3	pt.pa.npf	n.vsm
3261	2779	1726	899	3836 4546		899	3836 2582	4036	3836	80	690		4639	899	3306	3261

the	one	you	love	is sick."	¶	⁴	When	he	heard	this,	Jesus	said,	"This	sickness	will	not	end
ἴδε	ὃν	→	φιλεῖς	ἀσθενεῖ			δὲ	→	→ ἀκούσας		ὁ Ἰησοῦς	εἶπεν	αὕτη	ἡ ἀσθένεια	ἔστιν	οὐκ	πρὸς
pl	r.asm		v.pai.2s	v.pai.3s			cj		pt.aa.nsm		d.nsm n.nsm	v.aai.3s	r.nsf	d.nsf n.nsf	v.pai.3s	pl	p.a
2623	4005		5797	820			1254		201		3836 2652	3306	4047	3836 819	1639	4024	4639

in death.	No,	it is	for	God's	glory	so that	God's	Son	may be	glorified	through	it."	⁵	Jesus
← θάνατον	ἀλλ'		ὑπὲρ	˻τοῦ θεοῦ˼	˻τῆς δόξης˼	ἵνα	˻τοῦ θεοῦ˼	ὁ υἱὸς	→	δοξασθῇ	δι'	αὐτῆς	δὲ	ὁ Ἰησοῦς
n.asm	cj		p.g	d.gsm n.gsm	d.gsf n.gsf	cj	d.gsm n.gsm	d.nsm n.nsm		v.aps.3s	p.g	r.gsf.3	cj	d.nsm n.nsm
2505	247		5642	3836 2536	3836 1518	2671	3836 2536	3836 5626		1519	1328	899	1254	3836 2652

loved	Martha	and	her	sister	and	Lazarus.	⁶	Yet	when	he	heard	that	Lazarus	was sick,	he
ἠγάπα	˻τὴν Μάρθαν˼	καὶ	αὐτῆς	˻τὴν ἀδελφὴν˼	καὶ	˻τὸν Λάζαρον˼		οὖν	ὡς	→	ἤκουσεν	ὅτι	→	ἀσθενεῖ	μὲν τότε
v.iai.3s	d.asf n.asf	cj	r.gsf.3	d.asf n.asf	cj	d.asm n.asm		cj	cj		v.aai.3s	cj		v.pai.3s	pl adv
26	3836 3450	2779	899	3836 80	2779	3836 3276		4036	6055		201	4022		820	3525 5538

stayed	where		he	was	two	more	days.	¶	⁷ Then		he	said	to his	disciples,	"Let us go	back	to
ἔμεινεν	ἐν	τόπῳ ᾧ		ἦν	δύο		ἡμέρας		ἔπειτα	μετὰ τοῦτο	→	λέγει	τοῖς	μαθηταῖς	→ → ἄγωμεν	πάλιν	εἰς
v.aai.3s	p.d	n.dsm r.dsm		v.iai.3s	a.apf		n.apf		adv	p.a r.asn		v.pai.3s	d.dpm	n.dpm	v.pas.1p	adv	p.a
3531	1877	5536 4005		1639	1545		2465		2083	3552 4047		3306	3836	3412	72	4099	1650

Judea."	⁸	"But	Rabbi,"	they	said,	"a	short	while	ago	the	Jews	tried	to	stone	you,	and yet
˻τὴν Ἰουδαίαν˼		ῥαββί		οἱ μαθηταί	λέγουσιν αὐτῷ	νῦν				οἱ	Ἰουδαῖοι	ἐζήτουν	→	λιθάσαι	σε	καὶ
d.asf n.asf		n.vsm		d.npm n.npm	v.pai.3p r.dsm.3	adv				d.npm	a.npm	v.iai.3p		f.aa	r.as.2	cj
3836 2677		4806		3836 3412	3306 899	3814				3836	2681	2426		3342	5148	2779

you	are going	back	there?"	⁹ Jesus	answered,	"Are there	not	twelve	hours	of daylight?	A	man	who	walks	by
→ →	ὑπάγεις	πάλιν	ἐκεῖ	Ἰησοῦς	ἀπεκρίθη	εἰσιν ←	οὐχὶ	δώδεκα	ὧραι	˻τῆς ἡμέρας˼	ἐάν	τις		περιπατῇ	ἐν
	v.pai.2s	adv	adv	n.nsm	v.api.3s	v.pai.3p	pl	a.npf	n.npf	d.gsf n.gsf	cj	r.nsm		v.pas.3s	p.d
	5632	4099	1695	2652	646	1639	4049	1557	6052	3836 2465	1569	5516		4344	1877

day		will not stumble,	for	he sees	by this	world's	light.	¹⁰	It is	when	he	walks	by	night	that he
˻τῇ ἡμέρᾳ˼	→	οὐ προσκόπτει	ὅτι →	βλέπει	τούτου	˻τοῦ κόσμου˼	˻τὸ φῶς˼		δὲ		ἐάν	τις περιπατῇ	ἐν	˻τῇ νυκτί˼	→
d.dsf n.dsf		pl v.pai.3s	cj	v.pai.3s	r.gsm	d.gsm n.gsm	d.asn n.asn		cj		cj	r.nsm v.pas.3s	p.d	d.dsf n.dsf	
3836 2465		4684 4024 4684	4022	1063	4047	3836 3180	3836 5890		1254		1569	5516 4344	1877	3836 3816	

stumbles,	for	he has	no	light."	¶	¹¹	After	he	had said	this,	he went on to tell	them,	"Our
προσκόπτει	ὅτι	→ ἔστιν	οὐκ	˻τὸ φῶς˼	ἐν	αὐτῷ		καὶ	˻μετὰ τοῦτο˼	→ →	εἶπεν Ταῦτα →	λέγει αὐτοῖς	ἡμῶν
v.pai.3s	cj	v.pai.3s	pl	d.nsn n.nsn	p.d	r.dsm.3		cj	p.a r.asn		v.aai.3s r.apn	v.pai.3s r.dpm.3	r.gp.1
4684	4022	1639	4024	3836 5890	1877	899		2779	3552 4047		3306 4047	3306 899	7005

friend	Lazarus	has fallen asleep;	but	I am	going	there	to	wake	him	up."	¹²	His	disciples	replied,
ὁ φίλος˼	Λάζαρος	κεκοίμηται	ἀλλὰ	→	πορεύομαι		ἵνα	ἐξυπνίσω	αὐτόν			οὖν	οἱ μαθηταὶ	εἶπαν	αὐτῷ
d.nsm a.nsm	n.nsm	v.rpi.3s			v.pmi.1s		cj	v.aas.1s	r.asm.3			cj	d.npm n.npm	v.aai.3p	r.dsm.3
3836 5813	3276	3121	247		4513		2671	2030	899			4036	3836 3412	3306	899

"Lord,	if	he sleeps,	he will get better."	¹³	Jesus		had been speaking	of	his	death,	but	his
κύριε	εἰ	→ κεκοίμηται	→ → σωθήσεται	δὲ	ὁ Ἰησοῦς˼	→	εἰρήκει	περὶ	αὐτοῦ	˻τοῦ θανάτου˼	δὲ	
n.vsm	cj	v.rpi.3s	v.fpi.3s	cj	d.nsm n.nsm		v.lai.3s	p.g	r.gsm.3	d.gsm n.gsm	cj	
3261	1623	3121	5392	1254	3836 2652		3306	4309	899	3836 2505	1254	

ἐπίστευσαν εἰς αὐτὸν ἐκεῖ.

¹¹:¹ Ἦν δέ τις ἀσθενῶν, Λάζαρος ἀπὸ Βηθανίας, ἐκ τῆς κώμης Μαρίας καὶ Μάρθας τῆς ἀδελφῆς αὐτῆς. ² ἦν δὲ Μαριὰμ ἡ ἀλείψασα τὸν κύριον μύρῳ καὶ ἐκμάξασα τοὺς πόδας αὐτοῦ ταῖς θριξὶν αὐτῆς, ἧς ὁ ἀδελφὸς Λάζαρος ἠσθένει. ³ ἀπέστειλαν οὖν αἱ ἀδελφαὶ πρὸς αὐτὸν λέγουσαι, Κύριε, ἴδε ὃν φιλεῖς ἀσθενεῖ. ¶ ⁴ ἀκούσας δὲ ὁ Ἰησοῦς εἶπεν, Αὕτη ἡ ἀσθένεια οὐκ ἔστιν πρὸς θάνατον ἀλλ' ὑπὲρ τῆς δόξης τοῦ θεοῦ, ἵνα δοξασθῇ ὁ υἱὸς τοῦ θεοῦ δι' αὐτῆς. ⁵ ἠγάπα δὲ ὁ Ἰησοῦς τὴν Μάρθαν καὶ τὴν ἀδελφὴν αὐτῆς καὶ τὸν Λάζαρον. ⁶ ὡς οὖν ἤκουσεν ὅτι ἀσθενεῖ, τότε μὲν ἔμεινεν ἐν ᾧ ἦν τόπῳ δύο ἡμέρας, ¶ ⁷ ἔπειτα μετὰ τοῦτο λέγει τοῖς μαθηταῖς, Ἄγωμεν εἰς τὴν Ἰουδαίαν πάλιν. ⁸ λέγουσιν αὐτῷ οἱ μαθηταί, Ῥαββί, νῦν ἐζήτουν σε λιθάσαι οἱ Ἰουδαῖοι, καὶ πάλιν ὑπάγεις ἐκεῖ; ⁹ ἀπεκρίθη Ἰησοῦς, Οὐχὶ δώδεκα ὧραί εἰσιν τῆς ἡμέρας; ἐάν τις περιπατῇ ἐν τῇ ἡμέρᾳ, οὐ προσκόπτει, ὅτι τὸ φῶς τοῦ κόσμου τούτου βλέπει· ¹⁰ ἐὰν δέ τις περιπατῇ ἐν τῇ νυκτί, προσκόπτει, ὅτι τὸ φῶς οὐκ ἔστιν ἐν αὐτῷ. ¶ ¹¹ ταῦτα εἶπεν, καὶ μετὰ τοῦτο λέγει αὐτοῖς, Λάζαρος ὁ φίλος ἡμῶν κεκοίμηται· ἀλλὰ πορεύομαι ἵνα ἐξυπνίσω αὐτόν. ¹² εἶπαν οὖν οἱ μαθηταὶ αὐτῷ, Κύριε, εἰ κεκοίμηται σωθήσεται. ¹³ εἰρήκει δὲ ὁ Ἰησοῦς περὶ τοῦ θανάτου αὐτοῦ, ἐκεῖνοι δὲ

disciples thought he meant natural sleep. **14** So then he told them plainly, "Lazarus is
ἐκεῖνοι ἔδοξαν ὅτι → λέγει περὶ ˻τοῦ ὕπνου˼ ˻τῆς κοιμήσεως˼ οὖν τότε ὁ Ἰησοῦς εἶπεν αὐτοῖς παρρησίᾳ Λάζαρος →
r.npm v.aai.3p cj v.pai.3s p.g d.gsm n.gsm d.gsf n.gsf cj adv d.nsm n.nsm v.aai.3s r.dpm.3 n.dsf n.nsm
1697 1506 4022 3306 4309 3836 5678 3836 3122 4036 5538 3836 2652 3306 899 4244 3276

dead, **15** and for your sake I am glad I was not there, so that you may believe. But let us go to him."
ἀπέθανεν καὶ δι᾽ ὑμᾶς ← → χαίρω ὅτι → ἤμην οὐκ ἐκεῖ ἵνα ← → πιστεύσητε ἀλλὰ → → ἄγωμεν πρὸς αὐτόν
v.aai.3s cj p.a r.ap.2 v.pai.1s cj v.iai.1s pl adv cj v.aas.2p cj v.pas.1p p.a r.asm.3
633 2779 1328 7007 1328 5897 4022 1639 4024 1695 2671 4409 247 72 4639 899

16 Then Thomas (called Didymus) said to the rest of the disciples, "Let us also go, that we may
οὖν Θωμᾶς ὁ λεγόμενος˼ Δίδυμος εἶπεν → τοῖς → → ← συμμαθηταῖς ˻ ἡμεῖς καὶ ἄγωμεν ἵνα
cj n.nsm d.nsm pt.pp.nsm n.nsm v.aai.3s d.dpm n.dpm r.np.1 adv v.pas.1p cj
4036 2605 3836 3306 1441 3306 3836 5209 72 7005 2779 72 2671

die with him."
ἀποθάνωμεν μετ᾽ αὐτοῦ
v.aas.1p p.g r.gsm.3
633 3552 899

Jesus Comforts the Sisters

11:17 On his arrival, Jesus found that Lazarus had already been in the tomb for four days. **18**
οὖν → → Ἐλθὼν ὁ Ἰησοῦς˼ εὗρεν αὐτὸν → ἤδη ἔχοντα ἐν τῷ μνημείῳ → τέσσαρας ἡμέρας δὲ
cj pt.aa.nsm d.nsm n.nsm v.aai.3s r.asm.3 adv pt.pa.asm p.d d.dsn n.dsn a.apf n.apf cj
4036 2262 3836 2652 2351 899 2400 2453 2400 1877 3836 3646 5475 2465 1254

Bethany was *less than two miles* from Jerusalem, **19** and many Jews had come to
˻ἡ Βηθανία˼ ἦν ἐγγὺς ὡς ἀπὸ δεκαπέντε σταδίων τῶν Ἱεροσολύμων δὲ πολλοὶ ἐκ ˻τῶν Ἰουδαίων˼ → ἐληλύθεισαν πρὸς
d.nsf n.nsf v.iai.3s p.g pl p.g a.gpm n.gpm d.gpn n.gpn cj a.npm p.g d.gpm a.gpm v.lai.3p p.a
3836 1029 1639 1584 6055 608 1278 5084 3836 2642 1254 4498 1666 3836 2681 2262 4639

Martha and Mary to comfort them in the loss of their brother. **20** When Martha heard that
˻τὴν Μάρθαν˼ καὶ Μαριὰμ ἵνα παραμυθήσωνται αὐτὰς περὶ ← ← ← τοῦ ἀδελφοῦ οὖν ὡς ἡ Μάρθα ἤκουσεν ὅτι
d.asf n.asf cj n.asf cj v.ams.3p r.apf.3 p.g d.gsm n.gsm cj cj d.nsf n.nsf v.aai.3s cj
3836 3450 2779 3452 2671 4170 899 4309 3836 81 4036 6055 3836 3450 201 4022

Jesus was coming, she went out to meet him, but Mary stayed at home. ¶ **21** "Lord," Martha
Ἰησοῦς → ἔρχεται → ὑπήντησεν αὐτῷ δὲ Μαριὰμ ἐκαθέζετο ἐν ˻τῷ οἴκῳ˼ οὖν κύριε ἡ Μάρθα˼
n.nsm v.pmi.3s v.aai.3s r.dsm.3 cj n.nsf v.imi.3s p.d d.dsm n.dsm cj n.vsm d.nsf n.nsf
2652 2262 5636 899 1254 3452 2757 1877 3836 3875 4036 3261 3836 3450

said to Jesus, "if you had been here, my brother would not have died. **22** But I know that even now
εἶπεν πρὸς ˻τὸν Ἰησοῦν˼ εἰ → → ἦς ὧδε μου ὁ ἀδελφός˼ ἄν οὐκ ἀπέθανεν ἀλλὰ → οἶδα ὅτι καὶ νῦν
v.aai.3s p.a d.asm n.asm cj v.iai.2s adv r.gs.1 d.nsm n.nsm pl pl v.aai.3s cj v.rai.1s cj adv adv
3306 4639 3836 2652 1623 1639 6045 1609 3836 81 323 4024 633 247 4022 3857 2779 3814

God will give you whatever you ask." **23** Jesus said to her, "Your brother will rise again."
ὁ θεός˼ δώσει σοι ˻ὅσα ἂν˼ → αἰτήσῃ τὸν θεὸν ὁ Ἰησοῦς˼ λέγει → αὐτῇ σου ὁ ἀδελφός˼ → ἀναστήσεται ←
d.nsm n.nsm v.fai.3s r.ds.2 r.apn pl v.ams.2s d.asm n.asm d.nsm n.nsm v.pai.3s r.dsf.3 r.gs.2 d.nsm n.nsm v.fmi.3s
3836 2536 1443 5148 4012 323 160 3836 2536 3836 2652 3306 899 5148 3836 81 482

24 Martha answered, "I know he will rise again in the resurrection at the last day." **25** Jesus said
ἡ Μάρθα˼ λέγει αὐτῷ ὅτι → οἶδα → → ἀναστήσεται ← ἐν τῇ ἀναστάσει ἐν τῇ ἐσχάτῃ ἡμέρᾳ ὁ Ἰησοῦς˼ εἶπεν
d.nsf n.nsf v.pai.3s r.dsm.3 cj v.rai.1s v.fmi.3s p.d d.dsf n.dsf p.d d.dsf a.dsf n.dsf d.nsm n.nsm v.aai.3s
3836 3450 3306 899 4022 3857 482 1877 3836 414 1877 3836 2274 2465 3836 2652 3306

to her, "I am the resurrection and the life. He who believes in me will live, even though he dies; **26** and
→ αὐτῇ ἐγώ εἰμι ἡ ἀνάστασις καὶ ἡ ζωή ὁ πιστεύων εἰς ἐμὲ → ζήσεται κἂν ← ἀποθάνῃ καὶ
r.dsf.3 r.ns.1 v.pai.1s d.nsf n.nsf cj d.nsf n.nsf d.nsm pt.pa.nsm p.a r.as.1 v.fmi.3s crasis v.aas.3s cj
899 1609 1639 3836 414 2779 3836 2437 3836 4409 1650 1609 2409 2829 633 2779

whoever lives and believes in me will never die. Do you believe this?" **27** "Yes, Lord," she told
˻πᾶς ὁ ζῶν καὶ πιστεύων εἰς ἐμὲ˼ → ˻οὐ μὴ˼ εἰς τὸν αἰῶνα˼ ἀποθάνῃ → πιστεύεις τοῦτο ναὶ κύριε → λέγει
a.nsm d.nsm pt.pa.nsm cj pt.pa.nsm p.a r.as.1 pl pl p.a d.asm n.asm v.aas.3s v.pai.2s r.asn pl n.vsm v.pai.3s
4246 3836 2409 2779 4409 1650 1609 4024 3590 1650 3836 172 633 4409 4047 3721 3261 3306

him, "I believe that you are the Christ, the Son of God, who was to come into the world." ¶
αὐτῷ ἐγὼ πεπίστευκα ὅτι σὺ εἶ ὁ χριστὸς ὁ υἱὸς → ˻τοῦ θεοῦ˼ ὁ → → ἐρχόμενος εἰς τὸν κόσμον
r.dsm.3 r.ns.1 v.rai.1s cj r.ns.2 v.pai.2s d.nsm n.nsm d.nsm n.nsm d.gsm n.gsm d.nsm pt.pm.nsm p.a d.asm n.asm
899 1609 4409 4022 5148 1639 3836 5986 3836 5626 3836 2536 3836 2262 1650 3836 3180

ἔδοξαν ὅτι περὶ τῆς κοιμήσεως τοῦ ὕπνου λέγει. ¹⁴ τότε οὖν εἶπεν αὐτοῖς ὁ Ἰησοῦς παρρησίᾳ, Λάζαρος ἀπέθανεν, ¹⁵ καὶ χαίρω δι᾽ ὑμᾶς ἵνα πιστεύσητε, ὅτι οὐκ ἤμην ἐκεῖ· ἀλλὰ ἄγωμεν πρὸς αὐτόν. ¹⁶ εἶπεν οὖν Θωμᾶς ὁ λεγόμενος Δίδυμος τοῖς συμμαθηταῖς, Ἄγωμεν καὶ ἡμεῖς ἵνα ἀποθάνωμεν μετ᾽ αὐτοῦ.

¹¹:¹⁷ Ἐλθὼν οὖν ὁ Ἰησοῦς εὗρεν αὐτὸν τέσσαρας ἤδη ἡμέρας ἔχοντα ἐν τῷ μνημείῳ. ¹⁸ ἦν δὲ ἡ Βηθανία ἐγγὺς τῶν Ἱεροσολύμων ὡς ἀπὸ σταδίων δεκαπέντε. ¹⁹ πολλοὶ δὲ ἐκ τῶν Ἰουδαίων ἐληλύθεισαν πρὸς τὴν Μάρθαν καὶ Μαριὰμ ἵνα παραμυθήσωνται αὐτὰς περὶ τοῦ ἀδελφοῦ. ²⁰ ἡ οὖν Μάρθα ὡς ἤκουσεν ὅτι Ἰησοῦς ἔρχεται ὑπήντησεν αὐτῷ· Μαριὰμ δὲ ἐν τῷ οἴκῳ ἐκαθέζετο. ¶ ²¹ εἶπεν οὖν ἡ Μάρθα πρὸς τὸν Ἰησοῦν, Κύριε, εἰ ἦς ὧδε οὐκ ἂν ἀπέθανεν ὁ ἀδελφός μου· ²² [ἀλλὰ] καὶ νῦν οἶδα ὅτι ὅσα ἂν αἰτήσῃ τὸν θεὸν δώσει σοι ὁ θεός. ²³ λέγει αὐτῇ ὁ Ἰησοῦς, Ἀναστήσεται ὁ ἀδελφός σου. ²⁴ λέγει αὐτῷ ἡ Μάρθα, Οἶδα ὅτι ἀναστήσεται ἐν τῇ ἀναστάσει ἐν τῇ ἐσχάτῃ ἡμέρᾳ. ²⁵ εἶπεν αὐτῇ ὁ Ἰησοῦς, Ἐγώ εἰμι ἡ ἀνάστασις καὶ ἡ ζωή· ὁ πιστεύων εἰς ἐμὲ κἂν ἀποθάνῃ ζήσεται, ²⁶ καὶ πᾶς ὁ ζῶν καὶ πιστεύων εἰς ἐμὲ οὐ μὴ ἀποθάνῃ εἰς τὸν αἰῶνα. πιστεύεις τοῦτο; ²⁷ λέγει αὐτῷ, Ναὶ κύριε, ἐγὼ πεπίστευκα ὅτι σὺ εἶ ὁ Χριστὸς ὁ υἱὸς τοῦ θεοῦ ὁ εἰς τὸν κόσμον ἐρχόμενος. ¶ ²⁸ Καὶ τοῦτο

28 And after she had said this, she went back and called her sister Mary aside. "The Teacher is
Καὶ → → εἰποῦσα τοῦτο → ἀπῆλθεν ← καὶ ἐφώνησεν αὐτῆς τὴν ἀδελφὴν Μαριὰμ λάθρα ὁ διδάσκαλος
cj → → pt.aa.nsf r.asn → v.aai.3s ← cj v.aai.3s r.gsf.3 d.asf n.asf n.asf adv d.nsm n.nsm
2779   3306 4047   599   2779 5888 899 3836 80 3452 3277 3836 1437

here," she said, "and is asking for you." **29** When Mary heard this, she got up quickly and went to him.
πάρεστιν → εἰποῦσα καὶ → φωνεῖ ← σε δὲ ὡς ἐκείνη ἤκουσεν → ἠγέρθη ← ταχὺ καὶ ἤρχετο πρὸς αὐτόν
v.pai.3s → pt.aa.nsf cj → v.pai.3s ← r.as.2 cj cj r.nsf v.aai.3s → v.api.3s ← adv cj v.imi.3s p.a r.asm.3
4205   3306 2779   5888   5148 1254 6055 1697 201   1586   5444 2779 2262 4639 899

30 Now Jesus had not yet entered the village, but was still at the place where Martha had met him.
δὲ ὁ Ἰησοῦς → οὔπω ἐληλύθει εἰς τὴν κώμην ἀλλ' ἦν ἔτι ἐν τῷ τόπῳ ὅπου ἡ Μάρθα → ὑπήντησεν αὐτῷ
cj d.nsm n.nsm → adv v.lai.3s p.a d.asf n.asf cj v.iai.3s adv p.d d.dsm n.dsm cj d.nsf n.nsf → v.aai.3s r.dsm.3
1254 3836 2652 2262 4037 2262 1650 3836 3267 247 1639 2285 1877 3836 5536 3963 3836 3450 5636 899

31 When the Jews who had been with Mary in the house, comforting her, noticed how quickly
οὖν οἱ Ἰουδαῖοι οἱ → ὄντες μετ' αὐτῆς ἐν τῇ οἰκίᾳ καὶ παραμυθούμενοι αὐτὴν ἰδόντες ὅτι ταχέως
cj d.npm a.npm d.npm → pt.pa.npm p.g r.gsf.3 p.d d.dsf n.dsf cj pt.pm.npm r.asf.3 pt.aa.npm cj adv
4036 1625 2681 3836 1639 3552 899 1877 3836 3864 2779 4170 899 1625 4022 5441

she got up and went out, they followed her, supposing she was going to the tomb to mourn
τὴν Μαριὰμ ἀνέστη καὶ ἐξῆλθεν ← ἠκολούθησαν αὐτῇ δόξαντες ὅτι → → ὑπάγει εἰς τὸ μνημεῖον ἵνα κλαύσῃ
d.asf n.asf v.aai.3s cj v.aai.3s ← v.aai.3p r.dsf.3 pt.aa.npm cj → → v.pai.3s p.a d.asn n.asn cj v.aas.3s
3836 3452 482 2779 2002 199 899 1506 4022 5632 1650 3836 3646 2671 3081

¶ **32** When Mary reached the place where Jesus was and saw him, she fell at his
ἐκεῖ οὖν ὡς Ἡ Μαριὰμ ἦλθεν ὅπου Ἰησοῦς ἦν ἰδοῦσα αὐτὸν → ἔπεσεν πρὸς αὐτοῦ
adv cj cj d.nsf n.nsf v.aai.3s cj n.nsm v.iai.3s pt.aa.nsf r.asm.3 → v.aai.3s p.a r.gsm.3
1695 4036 6055 3836 3452 2262 3963 2652 1639 1625 899 4406 4639 899

feet and said, "Lord, if you had been here, my brother would not have died." **33** When
τοὺς πόδας λέγουσα αὐτῷ κύριε εἰ → → ἦς ὧδε μου ὁ ἀδελφός ἂν οὐκ → ἀπέθανεν οὖν ὡς
d.apm n.apm pt.pa.nsf r.dsm.3 n.vsm cj → → v.iai.2s adv r.gs.1 d.nsm n.nsm pl pl → v.aai.3s cj cj
3836 4546 3306 899 3261 1623 1639 6045 1609 3836 81 323 4024 633 4036 6055

Jesus saw her weeping, and the Jews who had come along with her also weeping, he was deeply
Ἰησοῦς εἶδεν αὐτὴν κλαίουσαν καὶ τοὺς Ἰουδαίους → → συνελθόντας ← ← αὐτῇ κλαίοντας
n.nsm v.aai.3s r.asf.3 pt.pa.asf cj d.apm a.apm → → pt.aa.apm ← ← r.dsf.3 pt.pa.apm
2652 1625 899 3081 2779 3836 2681 5302 899 3081

moved in spirit and troubled. **34** "Where have you laid him?" he asked. "Come and see,
ἐνεβριμήσατο → τῷ πνεύματι καὶ ἐτάραξεν ἑαυτὸν καὶ ποῦ → → τεθείκατε αὐτόν → εἶπεν ἔρχου καὶ ἴδε
v.ami.3s → d.dsn n.dsn cj v.aai.3s r.asm.3 cj pl → → v.rai.2p r.asm.3 → v.aai.3s v.pmm.2s cj v.aam.2s
1839 3836 4460 2779 5429 1571 2779 4543 5502 899 3306 2262 2779 2623

Lord," they replied. **35** Jesus wept. **36** Then the Jews said, "See how he loved him!" **37** But some of them
κύριε → λέγουσιν αὐτῷ ὁ Ἰησοῦς ἐδάκρυσεν οὖν οἱ Ἰουδαῖοι ἔλεγον ἴδε πῶς → ἐφίλει αὐτόν δὲ τινὲς ἐξ αὐτῶν
n.vsm → v.pai.3p r.dsm.3 d.nsm n.nsm v.aai.3s cj d.npm a.npm v.iai.3p pl pl → v.iai.3s r.asm.3 cj r.npm p.g r.gpm.3
3261 3306 899 3836 2652 1233 4036 3836 2681 3306 2623 4802 5797 899 1254 5516 1666 899

said, "Could not he who opened the eyes of the blind man have kept this man from dying?"
εἶπαν ἐδύνατο οὐκ οὗτος ὁ ἀνοίξας τοὺς ὀφθαλμοὺς τοῦ τυφλοῦ → ποιῆσαι καὶ οὗτος ← ἵνα μὴ ἀποθάνῃ
v.aai.3p v.ipi.3s pl r.nsm d.nsm pt.aa.nsm d.apm n.apm d.gsm a.gsm → f.aa adv r.nsm ← cj pl v.aas.3s
3306 1538 4024 4047 3836 487 3836 4057 3836 5603 4472 2779 4047 2671 3590 633

Jesus Raises Lazarus From the Dead

11:38 Jesus, once more deeply moved, came to the tomb. It was a cave with a
οὖν Ἰησοῦς πάλιν → ἐμβριμώμενος ἐν ἑαυτῷ ἔρχεται εἰς τὸ μνημεῖον δὲ → ἦν σπήλαιον καὶ
cj n.nsm adv → pt.pm.nsm p.d r.dsm.3 v.pmi.3s p.a d.asn n.asn cj → v.iai.3s n.nsn cj
4036 2652 4099 1839 1877 1571 1650 3836 3646 1254 1639 5068 2779

stone laid across the entrance. **39** "Take away the stone," he said. "But, Lord," said Martha, the sister
λίθος ἐπέκειτο ἐπ' αὐτῷ ἄρατε τὸν λίθον ὁ Ἰησοῦς λέγει κύριε λέγει αὐτῷ Μάρθα ἡ ἀδελφὴ
n.nsm v.imi.3s p.d r.dsn.3 v.aam.2p d.asm n.asm d.nsm n.nsm v.pai.3s n.vsm v.pai.3s r.dsm.3 n.nsf d.nsf n.nsf
3345 2130 2093 899 149 3836 3345 3836 2652 3306 3261 3306 899 3450 3836 80

of the dead man, "by this time there is a bad odor, for he has been there four days." **40** Then Jesus
→ τοῦ τετελευτηκότος ἤδη ← ← → ὄζει γάρ → ἐστιν τεταρταῖος ← ὁ Ἰησοῦς
→ d.gsm pt.ra.gsm adv ← ← → v.pai.3s cj → v.pai.3s a.nsm ← d.nsm n.nsm
3836 5462 2453 3853 1142 1639 5479 3836 2652

εἰποῦσα ἀπῆλθεν καὶ ἐφώνησεν Μαριὰμ τὴν ἀδελφὴν αὐτῆς λάθρα εἰποῦσα, Ὁ διδάσκαλος πάρεστιν καὶ φωνεῖ σε. ²⁹ ἐκείνη δὲ ὡς ἤκουσεν ἠγέρθη ταχὺ καὶ ἤρχετο πρὸς αὐτόν. ³⁰ οὔπω δὲ ἐληλύθει ὁ Ἰησοῦς εἰς τὴν κώμην, ἀλλ' ἦν ἔτι ἐν τῷ τόπῳ ὅπου ὑπήντησεν αὐτῷ ἡ Μάρθα. ³¹ οἱ οὖν Ἰουδαῖοι οἱ ὄντες μετ' αὐτῆς ἐν τῇ οἰκίᾳ καὶ παραμυθούμενοι αὐτήν, ἰδόντες τὴν Μαριὰμ ὅτι ταχέως ἀνέστη καὶ ἐξῆλθεν, ἠκολούθησαν αὐτῇ δόξαντες ὅτι ὑπάγει εἰς τὸ μνημεῖον ἵνα κλαύσῃ ἐκεῖ. ¶ ³² ἡ οὖν Μαριὰμ ὡς ἦλθεν ὅπου ἦν Ἰησοῦς ἰδοῦσα αὐτὸν ἔπεσεν αὐτοῦ πρὸς τοὺς πόδας λέγουσα αὐτῷ, Κύριε, εἰ ἦς ὧδε οὐκ ἄν μου ἀπέθανεν ὁ ἀδελφός. ³³ Ἰησοῦς οὖν ὡς εἶδεν αὐτὴν κλαίουσαν καὶ τοὺς συνελθόντας αὐτῇ Ἰουδαίους κλαίοντας, ἐνεβριμήσατο τῷ πνεύματι καὶ ἐτάραξεν ἑαυτὸν ³⁴ καὶ εἶπεν, Ποῦ τεθείκατε αὐτόν; λέγουσιν αὐτῷ, Κύριε, ἔρχου καὶ ἴδε. ³⁵ ἐδάκρυσεν ὁ Ἰησοῦς. ³⁶ ἔλεγον οὖν οἱ Ἰουδαῖοι, Ἴδε πῶς ἐφίλει αὐτόν. ³⁷ τινὲς δὲ ἐξ αὐτῶν εἶπαν, Οὐκ ἐδύνατο οὗτος ὁ ἀνοίξας τοὺς ὀφθαλμοὺς τοῦ τυφλοῦ ποιῆσαι ἵνα καὶ οὗτος μὴ ἀποθάνῃ;

¹¹:³⁸ Ἰησοῦς οὖν πάλιν ἐμβριμώμενος ἐν ἑαυτῷ ἔρχεται εἰς τὸ μνημεῖον· ἦν δὲ σπήλαιον καὶ λίθος ἐπέκειτο ἐπ' αὐτῷ. ³⁹ λέγει ὁ Ἰησοῦς, Ἄρατε τὸν λίθον. λέγει αὐτῷ ἡ ἀδελφὴ τοῦ τετελευτηκότος Μάρθα, Κύριε, ἤδη ὄζει, τεταρταῖος γάρ ἐστιν. ⁴⁰ λέγει

said, "Did I not tell you that if you believed, you would see the glory of God?" ¶ **41** So they took
λέγει αὐτῇ → → οὐκ εἶπόν σοι ὅτι ἐὰν → πιστεύσῃς → → ὄψῃ τὴν δόξαν → ⸂τοῦ θεοῦ⸃ οὖν → ἦραν
v.pai.3s r.dsf.3   pl v.aai.1s rds.2 cj v.aas.2s   v.fmi.3s d.asf n.asf d.gsm n.gsm cj v.aai.3p
3306 899   3306 3306 4024 4022 5148 4022 1569 4409   3972 3836 1518 3836 2536 4036 149

away the stone. Then Jesus looked up and said, "Father, I thank you that you have heard
← τὸν λίθον δὲ ὁ Ἰησοῦς, ἦρεν τοὺς ὀφθαλμοὺς ἄνω καὶ εἶπεν πάτερ → εὐχαριστῶ σοι ὅτι → → ἤκουσας
← d.asm n.asm cj d.nsm n.nsm v.aai.3s d.apm n.apm adv cj v.aai.3s n.vsm → v.pai.1s rds.2 cj → → v.aai.2s
3836 3345 1254 3836 2652 149 3836 4057 539 2779 3306 4252 2373 5148 4022 201

me. **42** I knew that you always hear me, but I said this for the benefit of the people standing here, that
μου δὲ ἐγὼ ᾔδειν ὅτι → πάντοτε ἀκούεις μου ἀλλὰ → εἶπον διὰ ← → ← τὸν ὄχλον ⸂τὸν περιεστῶτα⸃ ← ἵνα
r.gs.1 cj r.ns.1 v.lai.1s cj → adv v.pai.2s r.gs.1 cj → v.aai.1s p.a ←   ← d.asm n.asm d.asm pt.ra.asm ← cj
1609 1254 1609 3857 4022 → 4121 201 1609 247 → 1328 1328   3836 4063 3836 4325 2671

they may believe that you sent me." **43** When he had said this, Jesus called in a loud voice,
→ πιστεύσωσιν ὅτι σύ ἀπέστειλας με καὶ → → → εἰπὼν ταῦτα ἐκραύγασεν → μεγάλῃ φωνῇ
→ v.aas.3p cj r.ns.2 v.aai.2s r.as.1 cj → → → pt.aa.nsm r.apn v.aai.3s → a.dsf n.dsf
4409 4022 5148 690 1609 2779   3306 4047 3198   3489 5889

"Lazarus, come out!" **44** The dead man came out, his hands and feet wrapped with strips of linen, and a
Λάζαρε δεῦρο ἔξω ὁ τεθνηκὼς ← ἐξῆλθεν ← τὰς χεῖρας καὶ ⸂τοὺς πόδας⸃ δεδεμένος → κειρίαις ← καὶ
n.vsm j adv d.nsm pt.ra.nsm ← v.aai.3s ← d.apf n.apf cj d.apm n.apm pt.rp.nsm → n.dpf ← cj
3276 1306 2032 3836 2569 2002 3836 5931 2779 3836 4546 1313 3024 2779

cloth around his face. Jesus said to them, "Take off the grave clothes and let him go."
σουδαρίῳ περιεδέδετο αὐτοῦ ⸂ἡ ὄψις⸃ ὁ Ἰησοῦς, λέγει αὐτοῖς λύσατε ← αὐτὸν καὶ ἄφετε αὐτὸν ὑπάγειν
n.dsn v.lpi.3s r.gsm.3 d.nsf n.nsf d.nsm n.nsm v.pai.3s r.dpm.3 v.aam.2p ← r.asm.3 cj v.aam.2p r.asm.3 f.pa
5051 4317 899 3836 4071 3836 2652 3306 899 3395 899 2779 918 899 5632

The Plot to Kill Jesus

11:45 Therefore many of the Jews who had come to visit Mary, and had seen what Jesus
οὖν Πολλοὶ ἐκ τῶν Ἰουδαίων οἱ → ἐλθόντες πρὸς ⸂τὴν Μαριὰμ⸃ καὶ → θεασάμενοι ἃ
cj a.npm p.g d.gpm a.gpm d.npm → pt.aa.npm p.a d.asf n.asf cj → pt.am.npm r.apn
4036 4498 1666 3836 2681 3836 2262 4639 3836 3452 2779 2517 4005

did, put their faith in him. **46** But some of them went to the Pharisees and told them what Jesus had
ἐποίησεν → → ἐπίστευσαν εἰς αὐτόν δὲ τινὲς ἐξ αὐτῶν ἀπῆλθον πρὸς τοὺς Φαρισαίους καὶ εἶπαν αὐτοῖς ἃ Ἰησοῦς →
v.aai.3s → → v.aai.3p p.a r.asm.3 cj r.npm p.g r.gpm.3 v.aai.3p p.a d.apm n.apm cj v.aai.3p r.dpm.3 r.apn n.nsm →
4472 4409 1650 899 1254 5516 1666 899 599 4639 3836 5757 2779 899 4005 2652

done. **47** Then the chief priests and the Pharisees called a meeting of the Sanhedrin. "What are we
ἐποίησεν οὖν οἱ → ἀρχιερεῖς καὶ οἱ Φαρισαῖοι → Συνήγαγον συνέδριον καὶ τί → →
v.aai.3s cj d.npm → n.npm cj d.npm n.npm → v.aai.3p n.asn cj r.asn
4472 4036 3836 797 2779 3836 5757 5251 5284 2779 5515

accomplishing?" they asked. "Here is this man performing many miraculous signs. **48** If we let him
ποιοῦμεν → ἔλεγον ὅτι οὗτος ὁ ἄνθρωπος ποιεῖ πολλὰ σημεῖα ἐὰν → ἀφῶμεν αὐτὸν
v.pai.1p → v.iai.3p cj r.nsm d.nsm n.nsm v.pai.3s a.apn n.apn cj → v.aas.1p r.asm.3
4472 3306 4022 4047 3836 476 4472 4498 4956 1569 918 899

go on like this, everyone will believe in him, and then the Romans will come and take away both our
οὕτως πάντες → πιστεύσουσιν εἰς αὐτόν καὶ → οἱ Ῥωμαῖοι → ἐλεύσονται καὶ ἀροῦσιν ← καὶ ἡμῶν
adv a.npm → v.fai.3p p.a r.asm.3 cj → d.npm n.npm → v.fmi.3p cj v.fai.3p ← cj r.gp.1
4048 4246 4409 1650 899 2779 3836 4871 2262 2779 808 2779 7005

place and our nation." ¶ **49** Then one of them, named Caiaphas, who was high priest that
⸂τὸν τόπον⸃ καὶ ⸂τὸ ἔθνος⸃ δὲ εἷς τις ἐξ αὐτῶν Καϊάφας → ὢν → ἀρχιερεὺς ἐκείνου
d.asm n.asm cj d.asn n.asn cj a.nsm r.nsm p.g r.gpm.3 n.nsm → pt.pa.nsm n.nsm n.gsm
3836 5536 2779 3836 1620 1254 1651 5516 1666 899 2780 1639 797 1697

year, spoke up, "You know nothing at all! **50** You do not realize that it is better for you that one
⸂τοῦ ἐνιαυτοῦ⸃ εἶπεν ← αὐτοῖς ὑμεῖς οὐκ οἴδατε οὐδέν → οὐδὲ λογίζεσθε ὅτι → → συμφέρει → ὑμῖν ἵνα εἷς
d.gsm n.gsm v.aai.3s ← r.dpm.3 r.np.2 pl v.rai.2p a.asn cj v.pmi.2p cj → v.pai.3s r.dp.2 cj a.nsm
3836 1929 3306 899 7007 4024 3857 4029 3357 3357 4028 3357 4022 5237 7007 2671 1651

man die for the people than that the whole nation perish." ¶ **51** He did not say this on
ἄνθρωπος ἀποθάνῃ ὑπὲρ τοῦ λαοῦ καὶ μὴ ὅλον ⸂τὸ ἔθνος⸃ ἀπόληται δὲ → → οὐκ εἶπεν τοῦτο ἀφ'
n.nsm v.aas.3s p.g d.gsm n.gsm cj pl a.nsn d.nsn n.nsn v.ams.3s cj → → pl v.aai.3s r.asn p.g
476 633 5642 3836 3295 2779 3590 3910 3836 1620 660 1254 3306 3306 4024 3306 4047 608

αὐτὴ ὁ Ἰησοῦς, Οὐκ εἶπόν σοι ὅτι ἐὰν πιστεύσῃς ὄψῃ τὴν δόξαν τοῦ θεοῦ; ¶ ⁴¹ ἦραν οὖν τὸν λίθον. ὁ δὲ Ἰησοῦς ἦρεν τοὺς ὀφθαλμοὺς ἄνω καὶ εἶπεν, Πάτερ, εὐχαριστῶ σοι ὅτι ἤκουσάς μου. ⁴² ἐγὼ δὲ ᾔδειν ὅτι πάντοτέ μου ἀκούεις, ἀλλὰ διὰ τὸν ὄχλον τὸν περιεστῶτα εἶπον, ἵνα πιστεύσωσιν ὅτι σύ με ἀπέστειλας. ⁴³ καὶ ταῦτα εἰπὼν φωνῇ μεγάλῃ ἐκραύγασεν, Λάζαρε, δεῦρο ἔξω. ⁴⁴ ἐξῆλθεν ὁ τεθνηκὼς δεδεμένος τοὺς πόδας καὶ τὰς χεῖρας κειρίαις καὶ ἡ ὄψις αὐτοῦ σουδαρίῳ περιεδέδετο. λέγει αὐτοῖς ὁ Ἰησοῦς, Λύσατε αὐτὸν καὶ ἄφετε αὐτὸν ὑπάγειν.

⁴⁵ Πολλοὶ οὖν ἐκ τῶν Ἰουδαίων οἱ ἐλθόντες πρὸς τὴν Μαριὰμ καὶ θεασάμενοι ἃ ἐποίησεν ἐπίστευσαν εἰς αὐτόν· ⁴⁶ τινὲς δὲ ἐξ αὐτῶν ἀπῆλθον πρὸς τοὺς Φαρισαίους καὶ εἶπαν αὐτοῖς ἃ ἐποίησεν Ἰησοῦς. ⁴⁷ συνήγαγον οὖν οἱ ἀρχιερεῖς καὶ οἱ Φαρισαῖοι συνέδριον καὶ ἔλεγον, Τί ποιοῦμεν ὅτι οὗτος ὁ ἄνθρωπος πολλὰ ποιεῖ σημεῖα; ⁴⁸ ἐὰν ἀφῶμεν αὐτὸν οὕτως, πάντες πιστεύσουσιν εἰς αὐτόν, καὶ ἐλεύσονται οἱ Ῥωμαῖοι καὶ ἀροῦσιν ἡμῶν καὶ τὸν τόπον καὶ τὸ ἔθνος. ¶ ⁴⁹ εἷς δέ τις ἐξ αὐτῶν Καϊάφας, ἀρχιερεὺς ὢν τοῦ ἐνιαυτοῦ ἐκείνου, εἶπεν αὐτοῖς, Ὑμεῖς οὐκ οἴδατε οὐδέν, ⁵⁰ οὐδὲ λογίζεσθε ὅτι συμφέρει ὑμῖν ἵνα εἷς ἄνθρωπος ἀποθάνῃ ὑπὲρ τοῦ λαοῦ καὶ μὴ ὅλον τὸ ἔθνος ἀπόληται. ¶ ⁵¹ τοῦτο δὲ ἀφ' ἑαυτοῦ οὐκ εἶπεν, ἀλλὰ ἀρχιερεὺς ὢν τοῦ ἐνιαυτοῦ ἐκείνου

his   own,   but   as   high priest   that   year   he prophesied that   Jesus   would   die   for the Jewish
ἑαυτοῦ ←   ἀλλὰ   ὢν   ἀρχιερεὺς ἐκείνου ˻τοῦ ἐνιαυτοῦ˼   ἐπροφήτευσεν ὅτι   Ἰησοῦς   ἔμελλεν   ἀποθνήσκειν   ὑπὲρ τοῦ
r.gsm.3   cj   pt.pa.nsm   n.nsm   r.gsm   d.gsn n.gsm   v.aai.3s   cj   n.nsm   v.iai.3s   f.pa   p.g   d.gsn
1571   247   1639   797   1697   3836 1929   4736   4022   2652   3516   633   5642   3836

nation, 52 and not only for that nation but   also for the scattered   children of God,   to bring   them
ἔθνους   καὶ   οὐχ μόνον   ὑπὲρ τοῦ   ἔθνους   ἀλλ᾽ ἵνα καὶ   τὰ ˻τὰ διεσκορπισμένα˼   τέκνα   → ˻τοῦ θεοῦ˼   συναγάγῃ
n.gsn   cj   pl   adv   p.g   d.gsn   n.gsn   cj   cj   adv   d.apn   d.apn pt.rp.apn   n.apn   d.gsn n.gsm   v.aas.3s
1620   2779   4024   3667   5642   3836   1620   247   2671   2779   3836   3836 1399   5451   3836 2536   5251

together and make them   one. 53 So from that   day   on they plotted   to take his   life.   ¶
←   εἰς ἓν   οὖν ἀπ᾽ ἐκείνης τῆς ἡμέρας,   → ἐβουλεύσαντο ἵνα   → αὐτὸν ἀποκτείνωσιν
p.a a.asn   cj   p.g   r.gsf   d.gsf n.gsf   v.ami.3p   cj   r.asm.3   v.aas.3p
1650 1651   4036 608   1697   3836 2465   1086   2671 650   899   650

54 Therefore Jesus   no   longer moved   about publicly among the Jews.   Instead he withdrew   to a
οὖν   ˻Ὁ Ἰησοῦς˼   οὐκέτι ←   περιεπάτει ←   παρρησίᾳ ἐν   τοῖς Ἰουδαίοις ἀλλὰ   → ˻ἀπῆλθεν ἐκεῖθεν˼ εἰς
cj   d.nsm n.nsm   adv   v.iai.3s   n.dsf   p.d   d.dpm adj.dpm   cj   v.aai.3s   adv   p.a
4036   3836 2652   4033   4344   4244   1877   3836 2681   247   599   1696   1650

region   near the desert, to a village called   Ephraim, where he stayed with his disciples.   ¶   55 When it was
˻τὴν χώραν˼ ἐγγὺς τῆς ἐρήμου, εἰς   πόλιν λεγομένην   Ἐφραὶμ   κἀκεῖ   → ἔμεινεν μετὰ τῶν μαθητῶν   δὲ   → Ἦν
d.asf n.asf   p.g   d.gsf n.gsf   p.a   n.asf   pt.pp.asf   n.asm   crasis   v.aai.3s   p.g   d.gpm n.gpm   cj   v.iai.3s
3836 6001   1584   3836 2245   1650   4484   3306   2394   2795   3531   3552   3836 3412   1254   1639

almost time for the Jewish   Passover,   many went   up from the country to Jerusalem for their
ἐγγὺς   τὸ ˻τῶν Ἰουδαίων˼ πάσχα   καὶ πολλοὶ ἀνέβησαν   ← ἐκ τῆς χώρας   εἰς Ἱεροσόλυμα ἵνα ἑαυτοὺς
adv   d.nsn   d.gpm a.gpm   n.nsn   cj   a.npm   v.aai.3p   p.g   d.gsf n.gsf   p.a   n.apn   cj   r.apm.3
1584   3836   3836 2681   4247   2779 4498   326   1666   3836 6001   1650   2642   2671 1571

ceremonial cleansing before the Passover. 56   They kept looking for Jesus,   and as they stood   in the temple
→   ἁγνίσωσιν πρὸ   τοῦ πάσχα   οὖν   →   → ἐζήτουν   ˻τὸν Ἰησοῦν˼ καὶ   → ἑστηκότες ἐν   τῷ ἱερῷ
v.aas.3p   p.g   d.gsn n.gsn   cj   v.iai.3p   d.asm n.asm   cj   pt.ra.npm   p.d   d.dsn n.dsn
49   4574   3836 4247   4036   2426   3836 2652   2779   2705   1877   3836 2639

area they asked   one   another, "What do you think?   Isn't   he coming to the Feast at all?" 57 But the chief
→   ἔλεγον μετ᾽ ἀλλήλων ←   τί   → ὑμῖν δοκεῖ   ὅτι ˻οὐ μὴ˼   → ἔλθῃ   εἰς τὴν ἑορτήν   δὲ   οἱ
v.iai.3p   p.g   r.gpm   r.asn   r.dp.2 v.pai.3s   cj   pl   pl   v.aas.3s   p.a   d.asf n.asf   cj   d.npm
3306   3552   253   5515   7007 1506   4022 4024   3590   2262   1650 3836 2038   1254   3836

priests and Pharisees   had given   orders that if   anyone found out where Jesus was, he should report it
ἀρχιερεῖς καὶ ˻οἱ Φαρισαῖοι˼ → δεδώκεισαν ἐντολὰς ἵνα   ἐάν τις   γνῷ ←   ποῦ   ἐστιν → →   μηνύσῃ
n.npm   cj   d.npm n.npm   v.lai.3p   n.apf   cj   cj   r.nsm   v.aas.3s   adv   v.pai.3s   v.aas.3s
797   2779   3836 5757   1443   1953   2671   1569   5516   1182   4543   1639   3606

so   that they might arrest   him.
ὅπως ←   → πιάσωσιν αὐτόν
cj   v.aas.3p   r.asm.3
3968   4389   899

Jesus Anointed at Bethany

12:1   Six days before the Passover, Jesus   arrived at Bethany, where Lazarus lived, whom Jesus had
οὖν ˻ἓξ ἡμερῶν πρὸ   τοῦ πάσχα ˻Ὁ Ἰησοῦς˼ ἦλθεν   εἰς Βηθανίαν ὅπου   Λάζαρος ἦν   ὃν   Ἰησοῦς →
cj   a.gpf   n.gpf   p.g   d.gsn n.gsn   d.nsm n.nsm   v.aai.3s   p.a   n.asf   cj   n.nsm   v.iai.3s   r.asm   n.nsm
4036 1971   2465   4574   3836 4247   3836 2652   2262   1650 1029   3963   3276   1639   4005   2652

raised from the dead. 2   Here a dinner was given   in Jesus' honor.   Martha   served, while Lazarus   was
ἤγειρεν ἐκ   νεκρῶν   οὖν ἐκεῖ   δεῖπνον   → ἐποίησαν → αὐτῷ   καὶ ἡ Μάρθα   διηκόνει δὲ   ὁ Λάζαρος, ἦν
v.aai.3s   p.g   a.gpm   cj   adv   n.asn   v.aai.3p   r.dsm.3   cj   d.nsf n.nsf   v.iai.3s   cj   d.nsm n.nsm   v.iai.3s
1586   1666   3738   4036   1695   1270   4472   899   2779   3836 3450   1354   1254   3836 3276   1639

among those reclining   at the table with him. 3 Then Mary   took   about a pint of pure   nard,   an
˻εἷς ἐκ   τῶν ἀνακειμένων ← ←   σὺν αὐτῷ   οὖν ˻Ἡ Μαριὰμ˼ λαβοῦσα   λίτραν → πιστικῆς νάρδου
a.nsm p.g   d.gpm pt.pm.gpm   p.d   r.dsm.3   cj   d.nsf n.nsf   pt.aa.nsf   n.asf   a.gsf   n.gsf
1651 1666   3836   367   5250   899   4036   3836 3452   3284   3354   4410   3726

expensive perfume; she poured it on Jesus'   feet   and wiped his   feet   with her   hair.   And
πολυτίμου μύρου   → ἤλειψεν   ← ˻τοῦ Ἰησοῦ˼ ˻τοὺς πόδας˼ καὶ ἐξέμαξεν αὐτοῦ ˻τοὺς πόδας,˼ →   αὐτῆς ˻ταῖς θριξὶν˼ δὲ
n.gsf   n.gsn   v.aai.3s   d.gsn n.gsm   d.apm n.apm   cj   v.aai.3s   r.gsm.3   d.apm n.apm   r.gsf.3   d.dpf n.dpf   cj
4501   3693   230   3836 2652   3836 4546   2779   1726   899   3836 4546   2582   3836 2582   1254

ἐπροφήτευσεν ὅτι ἔμελλεν Ἰησοῦς ἀποθνήσκειν ὑπὲρ τοῦ ἔθνους, 52 καὶ οὐχ ὑπὲρ τοῦ ἔθνους μόνον ἀλλ᾽ ἵνα καὶ τὰ τέκνα τοῦ θεοῦ τὰ διεσκορπισμένα συναγάγῃ εἰς ἕν. 53 ἀπ᾽ ἐκείνης οὖν τῆς ἡμέρας ἐβουλεύσαντο ἵνα ἀποκτείνωσιν αὐτόν. ¶ 54 Ὁ οὖν Ἰησοῦς οὐκέτι παρρησίᾳ περιεπάτει ἐν τοῖς Ἰουδαίοις, ἀλλὰ ἀπῆλθεν ἐκεῖθεν εἰς τὴν χώραν ἐγγὺς τῆς ἐρήμου, εἰς Ἐφραὶμ λεγομένην πόλιν, κἀκεῖ ἔμεινεν μετὰ τῶν μαθητῶν. ¶ 55 Ἦν δὲ ἐγγὺς τὸ πάσχα τῶν Ἰουδαίων, καὶ ἀνέβησαν πολλοὶ εἰς Ἱεροσόλυμα ἐκ τῆς χώρας πρὸ τοῦ πάσχα ἵνα ἁγνίσωσιν ἑαυτούς. 56 ἐζήτουν οὖν τὸν Ἰησοῦν καὶ ἔλεγον μετ᾽ ἀλλήλων ἐν τῷ ἱερῷ ἑστηκότες, Τί δοκεῖ ὑμῖν; ὅτι οὐ μὴ ἔλθῃ εἰς τὴν ἑορτήν; 57 δεδώκεισαν δὲ οἱ ἀρχιερεῖς καὶ οἱ Φαρισαῖοι ἐντολὰς ἵνα ἐάν τις γνῷ ποῦ ἐστιν μηνύσῃ, ὅπως πιάσωσιν αὐτόν.

12:1 Ὁ οὖν Ἰησοῦς πρὸ ἓξ ἡμερῶν τοῦ πάσχα ἦλθεν εἰς Βηθανίαν, ὅπου ἦν Λάζαρος, ὃν ἤγειρεν ἐκ νεκρῶν Ἰησοῦς. 2 ἐποίησαν οὖν αὐτῷ δεῖπνον ἐκεῖ, καὶ ἡ Μάρθα διηκόνει, ὁ δὲ Λάζαρος εἷς ἦν ἐκ τῶν ἀνακειμένων σὺν αὐτῷ. 3 ἡ οὖν Μαριὰμ λαβοῦσα λίτραν μύρου νάρδου πιστικῆς πολυτίμου ἤλειψεν τοὺς πόδας τοῦ Ἰησοῦ καὶ ἐξέμαξεν ταῖς θριξὶν αὐτῆς τοὺς πόδας

the house	was filled		with	the	fragrance		of the perfume.	¶	**4** But	one	of	his	disciples,	Judas
ἡ οἰκία	ἐπληρώθη	→	ἐκ	τῆς	ὀσμῆς	→	τοῦ μύρου		δὲ	εἷς	ἐκ	αὐτοῦ	⌐τῶν μαθητῶν₌	Ἰούδας
d.nsf n.nsf	v.api.3s		p.g	d.gsf	n.gsf		d.gsn n.gsn		cj	a.nsm	p.g	r.gsm.3	d.gpm n.gpm	n.nsm
3836 3864	4444		1666	3836	4011		3836 3693		1254	1651	1666	899	3836 3412	2683

Iscariot,		who was later	to betray	him,	objected,	**5** "Why		wasn't	this	perfume	sold	and	the money
ὁ Ἰσκαριώτης	ὁ	μέλλων	→ παραδιδόναι	αὐτὸν	λέγει	⌐διὰ τί₌		οὐκ	τοῦτο	⌐τὸ μύρον₌	ἐπράθη	καὶ	
d.nsm n.nsm	d.nsm	pt.pa.nsm	f.pa	r.asm.3	v.pai.3s	p.a r.asn		pl	r.nsn	d.nsn n.nsn	v.api.3s	cj	
3836 2697	3836	3516	4140	899	3306	1328 5515		4024	4047	3836 3693	4405	2779	

given	to the poor?	It was worth	a	*year's*	*wages.*"	**6**	He	did not	say	this	because	he	cared	about	the poor
ἐδόθη	→ πτωχοῖς			τριακοσίων	δηναρίων	δὲ		οὐχ	εἶπεν	τοῦτο	ὅτι		αὐτῷ	ἔμελεν	περὶ	τῶν πτωχῶν
v.api.3s	a.dpm			a.gpn	n.gpn	cj		pl	v.aai.3s	r.asn	cj		r.dsm.3	v.iai.3s	p.g	d.gpm a.gpm
1443	4777			5559	1324	1254		3306	3306	4024	3306 4047		4022	899	3508 4309	3836 4777

but	because	he was	a thief;	as	keeper	of the	money bag,		he used to help		himself	to	what was
ἀλλ'	ὅτι	→ ἦν	κλέπτης	καὶ	ἔχων	← τὸ	γλωσσόκομον	→	→ ἐβάσταζεν			τὰ	→
cj	cj	v.iai.3s	n.nsm	cj	pt.pa.nsm	d.asn	n.asn		v.iai.3s			d.apn	
247	4022	1639	3095	2779	2400	3836	1186		1002			3836	

put	into it.	¶	**7**	"Leave	her	alone,"	Jesus		replied.	"It was intended	that	she should	save	this
βαλλόμενα	←			οὖν ἄφες	αὐτήν		ὁ Ἰησοῦς	εἶπεν		ἵνα	→ →		τηρήσῃ	αὐτό
pt.pp.apn				cj v.aam.2s	r.asf.3		d.nsm n.nsm	v.aai.3s		cj			v.aas.3s	r.asn.3
965				4036 918	899	918	3836 2652	3306		2671			5498	899

perfume	for	the	day	of	my	burial.	**8**		You	will always have	the	poor	among	you,	but	you will	not
	εἰς	τὴν	ἡμέραν	μου	⌐τοῦ ἐνταφιασμοῦ₌		γὰρ →		→	πάντοτε ἔχετε	τοὺς	πτωχοὺς	μεθ'	ἑαυτῶν	δὲ	→ →	οὐ
	p.a	d.asf	n.asf	r.gs.1	d.gsm n.gsm		cj			adv v.pai.2p	d.apm	a.apm	p.g	r.gpm.2	cj		pl
	1650	3836	2465	1947	1609 3836 1947		1142			2400 4121	3836	4777	3552	1571	1254	2400 2400	4024

always have	me."	¶	**9** Meanwhile	a large	crowd		of Jews		found out	that	Jesus	was	there	and	came,
πάντοτε ἔχετε	ἐμὲ		οὖν	πολὺς ὁ	ὄχλος	ἐκ	⌐τῶν Ἰουδαίων₌	Ἔγνω	←	ὅτι		ἔστιν	ἐκεῖ	καὶ	ἦλθον
adv v.pai.2p	r.as.1		cj	a.nsm d.nsm	n.nsm	p.g	d.gpm a.gpm	v.aai.3s		cj		v.pai.3s	adv	cj	v.aai.3p
4121 2400	1609		4036	4498 3836	4063	1666	3836 2681	1182		4022		1639	1695	2779	2262

not	only	because of him		but	also	to	see	Lazarus,		whom	he had	raised	from	the dead.	**10** So	the chief
οὐ	μόνον	διὰ	← ⌐τὸν Ἰησοῦν₌	ἀλλ'	καὶ	ἵνα	ἴδωσιν	⌐τὸν Λάζαρον₌		ὃν	→ →	ἤγειρεν	ἐκ	νεκρῶν	δὲ	οἱ
pl	adv	p.a	d.asm n.asm	cj	adv	cj	v.aas.3p	d.asm n.asm		r.asm		v.aai.3s	p.g	a.gpm	cj	d.npm
4024	3667	1328	3836 2652	247	2779	2671	1625	3836 3276		4005		1586	1666	3738	1254	3836

priests	made plans		to kill	Lazarus	*as*	*well,*	**11**	for	on account of	him	many	of	the Jews		were
ἀρχιερεῖς	→ ἐβουλεύσαντο	ἵνα	ἀποκτείνωσιν	⌐τὸν Λάζαρον₌	καὶ			ὅτι	δι'	←	← αὐτὸν	πολλοὶ	→	⌐τῶν Ἰουδαίων₌	→
n.npm	v.ami.3p	cj	v.aas.3p	d.asm n.asm	adv			cj	p.a		r.asm.3	a.npm		d.gpm a.gpm	
797	1086	2671	650	3836 3276	2779			4022	1328		899	4498		3836 2681	

going	over	to Jesus	and	putting	their	faith		in	him.
ὑπῆγον	←	←	καὶ	→	ἐπίστευον	εἰς	⌐τὸν Ἰησοῦν₌		
v.iai.3p			cj		v.iai.3p	p.a	d.asm n.asm		
5632		2652	2779		4409	1650	3836 2652		

The Triumphal Entry

12:12 The	next	day	the	great	crowd	that	had	come	for	the	Feast	heard		that	Jesus		was	on his way
Τῇ	ἐπαύριον	ὁ	πολὺς	ὄχλος	ὁ	→	ἐλθὼν	εἰς	τὴν	ἑορτὴν	ἀκούσαντες	ὅτι		ὁ Ἰησοῦς		ἔρχεται	← ←
d.dsf	adv	d.nsm	a.nsm	n.nsm	d.nsm		pt.aa.nsm	p.a	d.asf	n.asf	pt.aa.npm	cj		d.nsm n.nsm		v.pmi.3s	
3836	2069	3836	4498	4063	3836		2262	1650	3836	2038	201	4022		3836 2652		2262	

to Jerusalem.	**13** They	took	palm		branches	and	went	out	to	meet	him,	and	shouting,	"Hosanna!"
εἰς Ἱεροσόλυμα	→	ἔλαβον	⌐τῶν φοινίκων₌	⌐τὰ	βαΐα₌	καὶ	ἐξῆλθον	←	εἰς	ὑπάντησιν	αὐτῷ	καὶ	ἐκραύγαζον	ὡσαννά
p.a n.apn		v.aai.3p	d.gpm n.gpm	d.apn	n.apn	cj	v.aai.3p		p.a	n.asf	r.dsm.3	cj	v.iai.3p	
1650 2642		3284	3836 5836	3836	961	2779	2002		1650	5637	899	2779	3198	6057

"Blessed	is he	who comes	in	the	name	→	of the Lord!"		"Blessed	is	the	King	of Israel!"	**14**
εὐλογημένος	ὁ	← ἐρχόμενος	ἐν		ὀνόματι	→	κυρίου	[καὶ]		ὁ	βασιλεὺς	→ ⌐τοῦ Ἰσραήλ₌		δὲ
pt.rp.nsm	d.nsm	pt.pm.nsm	p.d		n.dsn		n.gsm	cj		d.nsm	n.nsm	d.gsm n.gsm		cj
2328	3836	2262	1877		3950		3261	2779		3836	995	3836 2702		1254

Jesus		found	a	young	donkey	and	sat		upon it,	as		it is	written,	**15** "Do	not	be afraid,	O	Daughter	of
ὁ Ἰησοῦς	εὑρὼν	→		ὀνάριον	ἐκάθισεν	ἐπ'		αὐτό	καθὼς	→ ἔστιν	γεγραμμένον		→	μὴ	→	φοβοῦ	→	θυγάτηρ	→
d.nsm n.nsm	pt.aa.nsm			n.asn	v.aai.3s	p.a		r.asn.3	cj	v.pai.3s	pt.rp.nsn			pl		v.ppm.2s		n.vsf	
3836 2652	2351			3942	2767	2093		899	2777	1639	1211			5828		3590	5828	2588	

αὐτοῦ· ἡ δὲ οἰκία ἐπληρώθη ἐκ τῆς ὀσμῆς τοῦ μύρου. ¶ 4 λέγει δὲ Ἰούδας ὁ Ἰσκαριώτης εἷς [ἐκ] τῶν μαθητῶν αὐτοῦ, ὁ μέλλων αὐτὸν παραδιδόναι, 5 Διὰ τί τοῦτο τὸ μύρον οὐκ ἐπράθη τριακοσίων δηναρίων καὶ ἐδόθη πτωχοῖς; 6 εἶπεν δὲ τοῦτο οὐχ ὅτι περὶ τῶν πτωχῶν ἔμελεν αὐτῷ, ἀλλ' ὅτι κλέπτης ἦν καὶ τὸ γλωσσόκομον ἔχων τὰ βαλλόμενα ἐβάσταζεν. ¶ 7 εἶπεν οὖν ὁ Ἰησοῦς, Ἄφες αὐτήν, ἵνα εἰς τὴν ἡμέραν τοῦ ἐνταφιασμοῦ μου τηρήσῃ αὐτό· 8 τοὺς πτωχοὺς γὰρ πάντοτε ἔχετε μεθ' ἑαυτῶν, ἐμὲ δὲ οὐ πάντοτε ἔχετε. ¶ 9 Ἔγνω οὖν [ὁ] ὄχλος πολὺς ἐκ τῶν Ἰουδαίων ὅτι ἐκεῖ ἐστιν καὶ ἦλθον οὐ διὰ τὸν Ἰησοῦν μόνον, ἀλλ' ἵνα καὶ τὸν Λάζαρον ἴδωσιν ὃν ἤγειρεν ἐκ νεκρῶν. 10 ἐβουλεύσαντο δὲ οἱ ἀρχιερεῖς ἵνα καὶ τὸν Λάζαρον ἀποκτείνωσιν, 11 ὅτι πολλοὶ δι' αὐτὸν ὑπῆγον τῶν Ἰουδαίων καὶ ἐπίστευον εἰς τὸν Ἰησοῦν.

12:12 Τῇ ἐπαύριον ὁ ὄχλος πολὺς ὁ ἐλθὼν εἰς τὴν ἑορτήν, ἀκούσαντες ὅτι ἔρχεται ὁ Ἰησοῦς εἰς Ἱεροσόλυμα 13 ἔλαβον τὰ βαΐα τῶν φοινίκων καὶ ἐξῆλθον εἰς ὑπάντησιν αὐτῷ καὶ ἐκραύγαζον, Ὡσαννά· εὐλογημένος ὁ ἐρχόμενος ἐν ὀνόματι κυρίου, [καὶ] ὁ βασιλεὺς τοῦ Ἰσραήλ. 14 εὑρὼν δὲ ὁ Ἰησοῦς ὀνάριον ἐκάθισεν ἐπ' αὐτό, καθώς ἐστιν γεγραμμένον, 15 Μὴ φοβοῦ, θυγάτηρ

Zion; see, your king | is coming, seated | on a donkey's colt." **16** At first | his | disciples | did not
Σιών ἰδοὺ σου ὁ βασιλεύς → ἔρχεται καθήμενος ἐπὶ ὄνου πῶλον ⸤τὸ πρῶτον⸥ αὐτοῦ ⸤οἱ μαθηταὶ⸥ ↦ οὐκ
n.gsf j r.gs.2 d.nsm n.nsm   v.pmi.3s pt.pm.nsm p.a n.gsf n.asm   d.asn adv r.gs.3 d.npm n.npm   pl
4994 2627 5148 3836 995   2262 2764 2093 3952 4798   3836 4754 899 3836 3412   1182 4024

understand all this. Only after Jesus | was glorified | did they realize | that these things had been written
ἔγνωσαν ταῦτα ἀλλ' ὅτε Ἰησοῦς → ἐδοξάσθη τότε → → ἐμνήσθησαν ὅτι ταῦτα ← → ἦν γεγραμμένα
v.aai.3p r.apn cj cj n.nsm   v.api.3s adv   v.aai.3p cj r.npn   v.iai.3s pt.rp.npn
1182 4047 247 4021 2652   1519 5538   3630 4022 4047   1639 1211

about him and that | they had done | these things to him. ¶ **17** Now the crowd that was | with him when he
ἐπ' αὐτῷ καὶ → ἐποίησαν ταῦτα ← → αὐτῷ   οὖν ὁ ὄχλος ὁ ὢν μετ' αὐτοῦ ὅτε →
p.d r.dsm.3 cj   v.aai.3p r.apn   r.dsm.3   cj d.nsm n.nsm d.nsm pt.pa.nsm p.g r.gsm.3 cj
2093 899 2779   4472 4047   899   4036 3836 4063 3836 1639 3552 899 4021

called Lazarus | from the tomb | and raised him | from the dead continued to spread the word. **18**
ἐφώνησεν τὸν Λάζαρον ἐκ τοῦ μνημείου καὶ ἤγειρεν αὐτὸν ἐκ νεκρῶν → ἐμαρτύρει ← ← διὰ τοῦτο
v.aai.3s d.asm n.asm p.g d.gsn n.gsn cj v.aai.3s r.asm.3 p.g a.gpm   v.iai.3s   p.a r.asn
5888 3836 3276 1666 3836 3646 2779 1586 899 1666 3738   3455   1328 4047

Many people, | because they had heard | that he | had given | this miraculous sign, | went out to
[καὶ] ὁ ὄχλος ὅτι → ἤκουσαν αὐτὸν πεποιηκέναι τοῦτο ⸤τὸ σημεῖον⸥ → →
adv d.nsm n.nsm cj   v.aai.3p r.asm.3 f.ra r.asn d.asn n.asn
2779 3836 4063 4022   201 899 4472 4047 3836 4956

meet him. **19** So the Pharisees said to one another, "See, | this is getting us nowhere. Look how the
ὑπήντησεν αὐτῷ οὖν οἱ Φαρισαῖοι εἶπαν πρὸς ἑαυτούς ← Θεωρεῖτε ὅτι οὐκ → ὠφελεῖτε οὐδέν ἴδε ὁ
v.aai.3s r.dsm.3 cj d.npm n.npm v.aai.3p p.a r.apm.3   v.pai.2p cj pl v.pai.2p a.asn pl d.nsm
5636 899 4036 3836 5757 3306 4639 1571   2555 4022 4024 6067 4029 2623 3836

whole world has gone after him!"
κόσμος → ἀπῆλθεν ὀπίσω αὐτοῦ
n.nsm   v.aai.3s p.g r.gsm.3
3180 599 3958 899

Jesus Predicts His Death

12:20 Now there were some Greeks among those who went | up to worship | at the Feast. **21** They
δὲ → Ἦσαν τινες Ἕλληνες ἐκ τῶν ἀναβαινόντων ← ἵνα προσκυνήσωσιν ἐν τῇ ἑορτῇ οὖν οὗτοι
cj   v.iai.3p r.npm n.npm p.g d.gpm pt.pa.gpm   cj v.aas.3p p.d d.dsf n.dsf cj r.npm
1254 1639 5516 1818 1666 3836 326   2671 4686 1877 3836 2038 4036 4047

came to Philip, who was from Bethsaida in Galilee, | with a request. "Sir," they said, "we
προσῆλθον ← Φιλίππῳ τῷ ἀπὸ Βηθσαϊδὰ ⸤τῆς Γαλιλαίας⸥ καὶ ἠρώτων αὐτὸν κύριε → λέγοντες
v.aai.3p n.dsm d.dsm p.g n.gsf d.gsf n.gsf cj v.iai.3p r.asm.3 n.vsm pt.pa.npm
4665 5805 3836 608 1034 3836 1133 2779 2263 899 3261 3306

would like to see Jesus." **22** Philip | went | to tell Andrew; | Andrew and Philip | in turn
→ θέλομεν → ἰδεῖν ⸤τὸν Ἰησοῦν⸥ ὁ Φίλιππος ἔρχεται καὶ → λέγει ⸤τῷ Ἀνδρέᾳ⸥ Ἀνδρέας καὶ Φίλιππος ἔρχεται καὶ
v.pai.1p f.aa d.asm n.asm d.nsm n.nsm v.pmi.3s cj v.pai.3s d.dsm n.dsm n.nsm cj n.nsm v.pmi.3s cj
2527 1625 3836 2652 3836 5805 2262 2779 3306 3836 436 436 2779 5805 2262 2779

told Jesus. ¶ **23** Jesus | replied, | "The hour has come | for the Son of Man
λέγουσιν ⸤τῷ Ἰησοῦ⸥ δὲ ὁ Ἰησοῦς ἀποκρίνεται αὐτοῖς λέγων ἡ ὥρα → ἐλήλυθεν ἵνα ὁ υἱὸς → ⸤τοῦ ἀνθρώπου⸥
v.pai.3p d.dsm n.dsm cj d.nsm n.nsm v.pmi.3s r.dpm.3 pt.pa.nsm d.nsf n.nsf v.rai.3s cj d.nsm n.nsm d.gsm n.gsm
3306 3836 2652 1254 3836 2652 646 899 3306 3836 6052 2262 2671 3836 5626 3836 476

to be glorified. **24** I tell you the truth, | unless a kernel | of wheat | falls to the ground and dies, | it
→ δοξασθῇ → λέγω ὑμῖν ⸤ἀμὴν ἀμὴν⸥ ⸤ἐὰν μὴ⸥ ⸤ὁ κόκκος⸥ → ⸤τοῦ σίτου⸥ πεσὼν εἰς τὴν γῆν ἀποθάνῃ αὐτός
v.aps.3s v.pai.1s r.dp.2 pl pl cj pl d.nsm n.nsm d.gsm n.gsm pt.aa.nsm p.a d.asf n.asf v.aas.3s r.nsm
1519 3306 7007 297 297 1569 3590 3836 3133 3836 4992 4406 1650 3836 1178 633 899

remains only a single seed. But if it dies, | it produces many seeds. **25** The man who loves his life | will
μένει → μόνος δὲ ἐὰν ἀποθάνῃ → φέρει πολὺν καρπόν ὁ φιλῶν αὐτοῦ ⸤τὴν ψυχὴν⸥
v.pai.3s a.nsm cj cj v.aas.3s v.pai.3s a.asm n.asm d.nsm pt.pa.nsm r.gsm.3 d.asf n.asf
3531 3668 1254 1569 633 5770 4498 2843 3836 5797 899 3836 6034

lose it, while the man who hates his life | in this world | will keep it | for eternal life.
ἀπολλύει αὐτήν καὶ ὁ ← μισῶν αὐτοῦ ⸤τὴν ψυχὴν⸥ ἐν τούτῳ ⸤τῷ κόσμῳ⸥ → φυλάξει αὐτήν εἰς αἰώνιον ζωήν
v.pai.3s r.asf.3 cj d.nsm pt.pa.nsm r.gsm.3 d.asf n.asf p.d r.dsm d.dsm n.dsm v.fai.3s r.asf.3 p.a a.asf n.asf
660 899 2779 3836 3631 899 3836 6034 1877 4047 3836 3180 5875 899 1650 173 2437

Σιών· ἰδοὺ ὁ βασιλεύς σου ἔρχεται, καθήμενος ἐπὶ πῶλον ὄνου. **16** ταῦτα οὐκ ἔγνωσαν αὐτοῦ οἱ μαθηταὶ τὸ πρῶτον, ἀλλ' ὅτε ἐδοξάσθη Ἰησοῦς τότε ἐμνήσθησαν ὅτι ταῦτα ἦν ἐπ' αὐτῷ γεγραμμένα καὶ ταῦτα ἐποίησαν αὐτῷ. ¶ **17** ἐμαρτύρει οὖν ὁ ὄχλος ὁ ὢν μετ' αὐτοῦ ὅτε τὸν Λάζαρον ἐφώνησεν ἐκ τοῦ μνημείου καὶ ἤγειρεν αὐτὸν ἐκ νεκρῶν. **18** διὰ τοῦτο [καὶ] ὑπήντησεν αὐτῷ ὁ ὄχλος, ὅτι ἤκουσαν τοῦτο αὐτὸν πεποιηκέναι τὸ σημεῖον. **19** οἱ οὖν Φαρισαῖοι εἶπαν πρὸς ἑαυτούς, Θεωρεῖτε ὅτι οὐκ ὠφελεῖτε οὐδέν· ἴδε ὁ κόσμος ὅλος ὀπίσω αὐτοῦ ἀπῆλθεν.

12:20 Ἦσαν δὲ Ἕλληνές τινες ἐκ τῶν ἀναβαινόντων ἵνα προσκυνήσωσιν ἐν τῇ ἑορτῇ· **21** οὗτοι οὖν προσῆλθον Φιλίππῳ τῷ ἀπὸ Βηθσαϊδὰ τῆς Γαλιλαίας καὶ ἠρώτων αὐτὸν λέγοντες, Κύριε, θέλομεν τὸν Ἰησοῦν ἰδεῖν. **22** ἔρχεται ὁ Φίλιππος καὶ λέγει τῷ Ἀνδρέᾳ, ἔρχεται Ἀνδρέας καὶ Φίλιππος καὶ λέγουσιν τῷ Ἰησοῦ. ¶ **23** ὁ δὲ Ἰησοῦς ἀποκρίνεται αὐτοῖς λέγων, Ἐλήλυθεν ἡ ὥρα ἵνα δοξασθῇ ὁ υἱὸς τοῦ ἀνθρώπου. **24** ἀμὴν ἀμὴν λέγω ὑμῖν, ἐὰν μὴ ὁ κόκκος τοῦ σίτου πεσὼν εἰς τὴν γῆν ἀποθάνῃ, αὐτὸς μόνος μένει· ἐὰν δὲ ἀποθάνῃ, πολὺν καρπὸν φέρει. **25** ὁ φιλῶν τὴν ψυχὴν αὐτοῦ ἀπολλύει αὐτήν, καὶ ὁ μισῶν τὴν ψυχὴν

26 Whoever serves me must follow me; and where I am, my servant also will be. My Father
ἐὰν τις, διακονῇ ἐμοί → ἀκολουθείτω ἐμοί καὶ ὅπου ἐγὼ εἰμι ὁ ἐμός, ὁ διάκονος καὶ → ἔσται ἐκεῖ ὁ πατήρ
cj r.nsm v.pas.3s r.ds.1 v.pam.3s r.ds.1 cj adv r.ns.1 v.pai.1s d.nsm r.nsm.1 d.nsm n.nsm adv v.fmi.3s adv d.nsm n.nsm
1569 5516 1354 1609 199 1609 2779 3963 1609 1639 3836 1847 3836 1356 2779 1639 1695 3836 4252

will honor the one who serves me. ¶ **27** "Now my heart is troubled, and what shall I say? 'Father,
→ τιμήσει αὐτόν → ἐὰν τις, διακονῇ ἐμοί Νῦν μου ἡ ψυχή → τετάρακται καὶ τί → εἴπω πάτερ
v.fai.3s r.asm.3 cj r.nsm v.pas.3s r.ds.1 adv r.gs.1 d.nsf n.nsf v.rpi.3s cj r.asn v.aas.1s n.vsm
5506 899 1569 5516 1354 1609 3814 1609 3836 6034 5429 2779 5515 3306 4252

save me from this hour'? No, it was for this very reason I came to this hour. **28** Father, glorify your
σῶσον με ἐκ ταύτης ,τῆς ὥρας, ἀλλὰ διὰ τοῦτο ← → ἦλθον εἰς ταύτην ,τὴν ὥραν, πάτερ δόξασόν σου
v.aam.2s r.as.1 p.g r.gsf d.gsf n.gsf cj p.a r.asn v.aai.1s p.a r.asf d.asf n.asf n.vsm v.aam.2s r.gs.2
5392 1609 1666 4047 3836 6052 247 1328 4047 2262 1650 4047 3836 6052 4252 1519 5148

name!" Then a voice came from heaven, "I have glorified it, and will glorify it again." **29** The crowd that
,τὸ ὄνομα, οὖν φωνὴ ἦλθεν ἐκ ,τοῦ οὐρανοῦ, καὶ → ἐδόξασα καὶ → δοξάσω πάλιν οὖν ὁ ὄχλος ὁ
d.asn n.asn cj n.nsf v.aai.3s p.g d.gsm n.gsm cj v.aai.1s cj v.fai.1s adv cj d.nsm n.nsm d.nsm
3836 3950 4036 5889 2262 1666 3836 4041 2779 1519 2779 1519 4099 4036 3836 4063 3836

was there and heard it said it had thundered; others said an angel had spoken to him. **30** Jesus said,
→ ἑστὼς καὶ ἀκούσας ἔλεγεν → γεγονέναι βροντὴν ἄλλοι ἔλεγον ἄγγελος → λελάληκεν → αὐτῷ Ἰησοῦς ἀπεκρίθη καὶ
pt.ra.nsm cj pt.aa.nsm v.iai.3s f.ra n.asf n.npm v.iai.3p n.nsm v.rai.3s r.dsm.3 n.nsm v.api.3s cj
2705 2779 201 3306 1181 1103 257 3306 34 3281 899 2652 646 2779

"This voice was for your benefit, not mine. **31** Now is the time for judgment on this world;
εἶπεν αὕτη ἡ φωνὴ γέγονεν ἀλλὰ δι' ὑμᾶς ← οὐ δι' ἐμέ νῦν ἐστιν κρίσις → τούτου ,τοῦ κόσμου,
v.aai.3s r.nsf d.nsf n.nsf v.rai.3s cj p.a r.ap.2 pl p.a r.as.1 adv v.pai.3s n.nsf r.gsm d.gsm n.gsm
3306 4047 3836 5889 1181 247 1328 7007 4024 1328 1609 3814 1639 3213 4047 3836 3180

now the prince of this world will be driven out. **32** But I, when I am lifted up from the earth, will draw
νῦν ὁ ἄρχων → τούτου ,τοῦ κόσμου, → ἐκβληθήσεται ἔξω κἀγὼ ἐὰν → ὑψωθῶ ἐκ τῆς γῆς → ἑλκύσω
adv d.nsm n.nsm r.gsm d.gsm n.gsm v.fpi.3s adv crasis cj v.aps.1s p.g d.gsf n.gsf v.fai.1s
3814 3836 807 3180 4047 3836 3180 1675 2032 2743 1569 5738 1666 3836 1178 1816

all men to myself." **33** He said this to show the kind of death he was going to die. ¶ **34**
πάντας πρὸς ἐμαυτόν δὲ → ἔλεγεν τοῦτο σημαίνων ποίῳ → θανάτῳ → ἤμελλεν ἀποθνήσκειν οὖν
a.apm p.a r.asm.1 cj v.iai.3s r.asn pt.pa.nsm r.dsm n.dsm v.iai.3s f.pa cj
4246 4639 1831 1254 3306 4047 4955 4481 2505 3516 633 4036

The crowd spoke up, "We have heard from the Law that the Christ will remain forever, so how
ὁ ὄχλος Ἀπεκρίθη ← αὐτῷ ἡμεῖς → ἠκούσαμεν ἐκ τοῦ νόμου ὅτι ὁ χριστὸς → μένει ,εἰς τὸν αἰῶνα, καὶ πῶς
d.nsm n.nsm v.api.3s r.dsm.3 r.np.1 v.aai.1p p.g d.gsm n.gsm cj d.nsm n.nsm v.pai.3s p.a d.asm n.asm cj adv
3836 4063 646 899 7005 201 1666 3836 3795 4022 3836 5986 3531 1650 3836 172 2779 4802

can you say, 'The Son of Man must be lifted up'? Who is this 'Son of Man'? **35** Then
↱ σὺ λέγεις ὅτι τὸν υἱὸν ,τοῦ ἀνθρώπου, δεῖ → ὑψωθῆναι τίς ἐστιν οὗτος ὁ υἱὸς ,τοῦ ἀνθρώπου, οὖν
r.ns.2 v.pai.2s cj d.asm n.asm d.gsm n.gsm v.pai.3s f.ap r.nsm v.pai.3s r.nsm d.nsm n.nsm d.gsm n.gsm adv
3306 5148 3306 4022 3836 5626 3836 476 1256 5738 5515 1639 4047 3836 5626 3836 476 4036

Jesus told them, "You are going to have the light just a little while longer. Walk while you have the
ὁ Ἰησοῦς, εἶπεν αὐτοῖς ,ἐν ὑμῖν, ἐστιν τὸ φῶς ἔτι μικρὸν χρόνον ← περιπατεῖτε ὡς → ἔχετε τὸ
d.nsm n.nsm v.aai.3s r.dpm.3 p.d r.dp.2 v.pai.3s d.nsn n.nsn adv a.asm n.asm v.pam.2p cj v.pai.2p d.asn
3836 2652 3306 899 1877 7007 1639 3836 5890 2285 3625 5989 4344 6055 2400 3836

light, before darkness overtakes you. The man who walks in the dark does not know where he is going.
φῶς, ἵνα μὴ σκοτία καταλάβῃ ὑμᾶς καὶ ὁ περιπατῶν ἐν τῇ σκοτίᾳ ↱ οὐκ οἶδεν ποῦ → ὑπάγει
n.asn pl pl n.nsf v.aas.3s r.ap.2 cj d.nsm pt.pa.nsm p.d d.dsf n.dsf v.rai.3s pl adv v.pai.3s
5890 2671 3590 5028 2898 7007 2779 3836 4344 1877 3836 5028 3857 4024 3857 4543 5632

36 Put your trust in the light while you have it, so that you may become sons of light." When he had
→ πιστεύετε εἰς τὸ φῶς ὡς → ἔχετε ,τὸ φῶς, ἵνα → γένησθε υἱοὶ → φωτός Ἰησοῦς
v.pam.2p p.a d.asn n.asn cj v.pai.2p d.asn n.asn cj v.ams.2p n.npm n.gsn n.nsm
4409 1650 3836 5890 6055 2400 3836 5890 2671 1181 5626 5890 2652

finished speaking, Jesus left and hid himself from them.
ἐλάλησεν ταῦτα καὶ ↱ ἀπελθὼν ἐκρύβη → ἀπ' αὐτῶν
v.aai.3s r.apn cj pt.aa.nsm v.api.3s p.g r.gpm.3
3281 4047 2779 2652 599 3221 608 899

αὐτοῦ ἐν τῷ κόσμῳ τούτῳ εἰς ζωὴν αἰώνιον φυλάξει αὐτήν. **26** ἐὰν ἐμοί τις διακονῇ, ἐμοὶ ἀκολουθείτω, καὶ ὅπου εἰμὶ ἐγὼ ἐκεῖ καὶ ὁ διάκονος ὁ ἐμὸς ἔσται· ἐάν τις ἐμοὶ διακονῇ τιμήσει αὐτὸν ὁ πατήρ. ¶ **27** Νῦν ἡ ψυχή μου τετάρακται, καὶ τί εἴπω; Πάτερ, σῶσόν με ἐκ τῆς ὥρας ταύτης; ἀλλὰ διὰ τοῦτο ἦλθον εἰς τὴν ὥραν ταύτην. **28** πάτερ, δόξασόν σου τὸ ὄνομα. ἦλθεν οὖν φωνὴ ἐκ τοῦ οὐρανοῦ, Καὶ ἐδόξασα καὶ πάλιν δοξάσω. **29** ὁ οὖν ὄχλος ὁ ἑστὼς καὶ ἀκούσας ἔλεγεν βροντὴν γεγονέναι, ἄλλοι ἔλεγον, Ἄγγελος αὐτῷ λελάληκεν. **30** ἀπεκρίθη Ἰησοῦς καὶ εἶπεν, Οὐ δι' ἐμὲ ἡ φωνὴ αὕτη γέγονεν ἀλλὰ δι' ὑμᾶς. **31** νῦν κρίσις ἐστὶν τοῦ κόσμου τούτου, νῦν ὁ ἄρχων τοῦ κόσμου τούτου ἐκβληθήσεται ἔξω· **32** κἀγὼ ἐὰν ὑψωθῶ ἐκ τῆς γῆς, πάντας ἑλκύσω πρὸς ἐμαυτόν. **33** τοῦτο δὲ ἔλεγεν σημαίνων ποίῳ θανάτῳ ἤμελλεν ἀποθνήσκειν. ¶ **34** ἀπεκρίθη οὖν αὐτῷ ὁ ὄχλος, Ἡμεῖς ἠκούσαμεν ἐκ τοῦ νόμου ὅτι ὁ Χριστὸς μένει εἰς τὸν αἰῶνα, καὶ πῶς λέγεις σὺ ὅτι δεῖ ὑψωθῆναι τὸν υἱὸν τοῦ ἀνθρώπου; τίς ἐστιν οὗτος ὁ υἱὸς τοῦ ἀνθρώπου; **35** εἶπεν οὖν αὐτοῖς ὁ Ἰησοῦς, Ἔτι μικρὸν χρόνον τὸ φῶς ἐν ὑμῖν ἐστιν. περιπατεῖτε ὡς τὸ φῶς ἔχετε, ἵνα μὴ σκοτία ὑμᾶς καταλάβῃ· καὶ ὁ περιπατῶν ἐν τῇ σκοτίᾳ οὐκ οἶδεν ποῦ ὑπάγει. **36** ὡς τὸ φῶς ἔχετε, πιστεύετε εἰς τὸ φῶς, ἵνα υἱοὶ φωτὸς γένησθε. Ταῦτα ἐλάλησεν Ἰησοῦς, καὶ ἀπελθὼν ἐκρύβη ἀπ' αὐτῶν.

The Jews Continue in Their Unbelief

12:37 Even after Jesus had done all these miraculous signs in their presence, they still would not
δὲ → → αὐτοῦ πεποιηκότος → Τοσαῦτα → σημεῖα αὐτῶν ἔμπροσθεν οὐκ
cj → → r.gsm.3 pt.ra.gsm r.apn n.apn r.gpm.3 p.g pl
1254 4472 4472 899 4472 5537 4956 1869 899 1869 4409 4409 4024

believe in him. **38** This was to fulfill the word of Isaiah the prophet: "Lord, who has believed our
ἐπίστευον εἰς αὐτόν ἵνα πληρωθῇ ὁ λόγος Ἠσαΐου τοῦ προφήτου ὃν εἶπεν κύριε τίς ἐπίστευσεν ἡμῶν
v.iai.3p p.a r.asm.3 cj v.aps.3s d.nsm n.nsm n.gsm d.gsm n.gsm r.asm v.aai.3s n.vsm r.nsm v.aai.3s r.gp.1
4409 1650 899 2671 4444 3836 3364 2480 3836 4737 4005 3306 3261 5515 4409 7005

message and to whom has the arm of the Lord been revealed?" **39** For this reason they could not believe,
ἀκοῇ καὶ τίνι ὁ βραχίων κυρίου ἀπεκαλύφθη διὰ τοῦτο ἠδύναντο οὐκ πιστεύειν
d.dsf n.dsf cj r.dsm d.nsm n.nsm n.gsm v.api.3s p.a r.asn v.ipi.3p pl f.pa
3836 198 2779 5515 636 3836 1098 3261 636 1328 4047 1538 4024 4409

because, as Isaiah says elsewhere: **40** "He has blinded their eyes and deadened their hearts, so they
ὅτι Ἠσαΐας εἶπεν πάλιν τετύφλωκεν αὐτῶν τοὺς ὀφθαλμοὺς καὶ ἐπώρωσεν αὐτῶν τὴν καρδίαν ἵνα
cj n.nsm v.aai.3s adv v.rai.3s r.gpm.3 d.apm n.apm cj v.aai.3s r.gpm.3 d.asf n.asf cj
4022 2480 3306 4099 5604 899 3836 4057 2779 4800 899 3836 2840 2671 1625

can neither see with their eyes, nor understand with their hearts, nor turn — and I would heal them."
μὴ ἴδωσιν τοῖς ὀφθαλμοῖς καὶ νοήσωσιν τῇ καρδίᾳ καὶ στραφῶσιν καὶ ἰάσομαι αὐτούς
pl v.aas.3p d.dpm n.dpm cj v.aas.3p d.dsf n.dsf cj v.aps.3p cj v.fmi.1s r.apm.3
1625 3590 1625 3836 4057 2779 3783 3836 2840 2779 5138 2779 2615 899

41 Isaiah said this because he saw Jesus' glory and spoke about him. ¶ **42** Yet at the same
Ἠσαΐας εἶπεν ταῦτα ὅτι εἶδεν αὐτοῦ τὴν δόξαν καὶ ἐλάλησεν περὶ αὐτοῦ καὶ ὅμως μέντοι
n.nsm v.aai.3s r.apn cj v.aai.3s r.gsm.3 d.asf n.asf cj v.aai.3s p.g r.gsm.3 adv adv adv
2480 3306 4047 4022 1625 899 3836 1518 2779 3281 4309 899 2779 3940 3530

time many even among the leaders believed in him. But because of the Pharisees they would not confess
πολλοὶ ἐκ τῶν ἀρχόντων ἐπίστευσαν εἰς αὐτόν ἀλλὰ διὰ τοὺς Φαρισαίους οὐχ ὡμολόγουν
a.npm p.g d.gpm n.gpm v.aai.3p p.a r.asm.3 cj p.a d.apm n.apm pl v.iai.3p
4498 1666 3836 807 4409 1650 899 247 1328 3836 5757 3933 3933 4024 3933

their faith for fear they would be put out of the synagogue; **43** for they loved praise from men
ἵνα μὴ γένωνται ἀποσυνάγωγοι γὰρ ἠγάπησαν τὴν δόξαν τῶν ἀνθρώπων
cj pl v.ams.3p v.aai.3p d.asf n.asf d.gpm n.gpm
2671 3590 1181 697 1142 26 3836 1518 3836 476

more than praise from God. ¶ **44** Then Jesus cried out, "When a man believes in me, he
μᾶλλον ἤπερ τὴν δόξαν τοῦ θεοῦ δὲ Ἰησοῦς ἔκραξεν καὶ εἶπεν ὁ πιστεύων εἰς ἐμὲ
adv.c pl d.asf n.asf d.gsm n.gsm cj n.nsm v.aai.3s cj v.aai.3s d.nsm pt.pa.nsm p.a r.as.1
3437 2472 3836 1518 3836 2536 1254 2652 3189 2779 3306 4409 3836 4409 1650 1609 4409

does not believe in me only, but in the one who sent me. **45** When he looks at me, he sees the one who
οὐ πιστεύει εἰς ἐμὲ ἀλλὰ εἰς τὸν πέμψαντά με καὶ ὁ θεωρῶν ἐμὲ θεωρεῖ τὸν
pl v.pai.3s p.a r.as.1 cj p.a d.asm pt.aa.asm r.as.1 cj d.nsm pt.pa.nsm r.as.1 v.pai.3s d.asm
4409 4024 4409 1650 1609 247 1650 3836 4287 1609 2779 3836 2555 1609 2555 3836

sent me. **46** I have come into the world as a light, so that no one who believes in me should stay in
πέμψαντά με ἐγὼ ἐλήλυθα εἰς τὸν κόσμον φῶς ἵνα μὴ πᾶς ὁ πιστεύων εἰς ἐμὲ μείνῃ ἐν
pt.aa.asm r.as.1 r.ns.1 v.rai.1s p.a d.asm n.asm n.nsn cj pl a.nsm d.nsm pt.pa.nsm p.a r.as.1 v.aas.3s p.d
4287 1609 1609 2262 1650 3836 3180 5890 2671 3590 4246 3836 4409 1650 1609 3531 1877

darkness. ¶ **47** "As for the person who hears my words but does not keep them, I do not judge
τῇ σκοτίᾳ καὶ ἐάν τίς ἀκούσῃ μου τῶν ῥημάτων καὶ μὴ φυλάξῃ ἐγὼ οὐ κρίνω
d.dsf n.dsf cj cj r.nsm v.aas.3s r.gs.1 d.gpn n.gpn cj pl v.aas.3s r.ns.1 pl v.pai.1s
3836 5028 2779 1569 5516 201 1609 4839 2779 5875 3590 5875 1609 3212 4024 3212

him. For I did not come to judge the world, but to save it. **48** There is a judge for the one
αὐτόν γὰρ οὐ ἦλθον ἵνα κρίνω τὸν κόσμον ἀλλ' ἵνα σώσω τὸν κόσμον ἔχει τὸν κρίνοντα αὐτόν ὁ
r.asm.3 cj pl v.aai.1s cj v.pas.1s d.asm n.asm cj cj v.aas.1s d.asm n.asm v.pai.3s d.asm pt.pa.asm r.asm.3 d.nsm
899 1142 2262 2262 4024 2262 2671 3212 3836 3180 247 2671 5392 3836 3180 2400 3836 3212 899 3836

who rejects me and does not accept my words; that very word which I spoke will condemn him at
ἀθετῶν ἐμὲ καὶ μὴ λαμβάνων μου τὰ ῥήματα ἐκεῖνος ὁ λόγος ὃν ἐλάλησα κρινεῖ αὐτὸν ἐν
pt.pa.nsm r.as.1 cj pl pt.pa.nsm r.gs.1 d.apn n.apn r.nsm d.nsm n.nsm r.asm v.aai.1s v.fai.3s r.asm.3 p.d
119 1609 2779 3590 3284 1609 3836 4839 1697 3836 3364 4005 3281 3212 899 1877

12:37 Τοσαῦτα δὲ αὐτοῦ σημεῖα πεποιηκότος ἔμπροσθεν αὐτῶν οὐκ ἐπίστευον εἰς αὐτόν, **38** ἵνα ὁ λόγος Ἠσαΐου τοῦ προφήτου πληρωθῇ ὃν εἶπεν, Κύριε, τίς ἐπίστευσεν τῇ ἀκοῇ ἡμῶν; καὶ ὁ βραχίων κυρίου τίνι ἀπεκαλύφθη; **39** διὰ τοῦτο οὐκ ἠδύναντο πιστεύειν, ὅτι πάλιν εἶπεν Ἠσαΐας, **40** Τετύφλωκεν αὐτῶν τοὺς ὀφθαλμοὺς καὶ ἐπώρωσεν αὐτῶν τὴν καρδίαν, ἵνα μὴ ἴδωσιν τοῖς ὀφθαλμοῖς καὶ νοήσωσιν τῇ καρδίᾳ καὶ στραφῶσιν, καὶ ἰάσομαι αὐτούς. **41** ταῦτα εἶπεν Ἠσαΐας ὅτι εἶδεν τὴν δόξαν αὐτοῦ, καὶ ἐλάλησεν περὶ αὐτοῦ. ¶ **42** ὅμως μέντοι καὶ ἐκ τῶν ἀρχόντων πολλοὶ ἐπίστευσαν εἰς αὐτόν, ἀλλὰ διὰ τοὺς Φαρισαίους οὐχ ὡμολόγουν ἵνα μὴ ἀποσυνάγωγοι γένωνται· **43** ἠγάπησαν γὰρ τὴν δόξαν τῶν ἀνθρώπων μᾶλλον ἤπερ τὴν δόξαν τοῦ θεοῦ. ¶ **44** Ἰησοῦς δὲ ἔκραξεν καὶ εἶπεν, Ὁ πιστεύων εἰς ἐμὲ οὐ πιστεύει εἰς ἐμὲ ἀλλὰ εἰς τὸν πέμψαντά με, **45** καὶ ὁ θεωρῶν ἐμὲ θεωρεῖ τὸν πέμψαντά με. **46** ἐγὼ φῶς εἰς τὸν κόσμον ἐλήλυθα, ἵνα πᾶς ὁ πιστεύων εἰς ἐμὲ ἐν τῇ σκοτίᾳ μὴ μείνῃ. ¶ **47** καὶ ἐάν τίς μου ἀκούσῃ τῶν ῥημάτων καὶ μὴ φυλάξῃ, ἐγὼ οὐ κρίνω αὐτόν· οὐ γὰρ ἦλθον ἵνα κρίνω τὸν κόσμον, ἀλλ' ἵνα σώσω τὸν κόσμον. **48** ὁ ἀθετῶν ἐμὲ καὶ μὴ λαμβάνων τὰ ῥήματά μου ἔχει τὸν κρίνοντα αὐτόν· ὁ λόγος ὃν ἐλάλησα ἐκεῖνος

the last day. **49** For I did not speak of my own accord, but the Father who sent me commanded
τῇ ἐσχάτῃ ἡμέρᾳ ὅτι ἐγὼ → οὐκ ἐλάλησα ἐξ ἐμαυτοῦ ← ἀλλ' πατὴρ ὁ πέμψας με αὐτός ἐντολὴν δέδωκεν
d.dsf a.dsf n.dsf cj r.ns.1 pl v.aai.1s p.g r.gsm.1 cj n.nsm d.nsm pt.aa.nsm r.as.1 r.nsm n.asf v.rai.3s
3836 2274 2465 4022 1609 3281 4024 3281 1666 1831 247 4252 3836 4287 1609 899 1953 1443

me what to say and how to say it. **50** I know that his command leads to eternal life. So whatever I say is
μοι τί → εἴπω καὶ τί → λαλήσω καὶ οἶδα ὅτι αὐτοῦ ἡ ἐντολὴ ἐστιν αἰώνιος ζωὴ οὖν ἃ ἐγὼ λαλῶ
r.ds.1 r.asn v.aas.1s cj r.asn v.aas.1s cj v.rai.1s cj r.gsm.3 d.nsf n.nsf v.pai.3s a.nsf n.nsf cj r.apn r.ns.1 v.pai.1s
1609 5515 3306 2779 5515 3281 2779 3857 4022 899 3836 1953 1639 173 2437 4036 4005 1609 3281

just what the Father has told me to say."
καθὼς ← ὁ πατὴρ → εἴρηκεν μοι οὕτως → λαλῶ
cj d.nsm n.nsm v.rai.3s r.ds.1 adv v.pai.1s
2777 3836 4252 3306 1609 4048 3281

Jesus Washes his Disciples' Feet

13:1 It was just before the Passover Feast. Jesus knew that the time had come for him to leave
δὲ Πρὸ τῆς τοῦ πάσχα ἑορτῆς ὁ Ἰησοῦς εἰδὼς ὅτι ἡ ὥρα → ἦλθεν αὐτοῦ ἵνα μεταβῇ ἐκ
cj p.g d.gsf d.gsn n.gsn n.gsf d.nsm n.nsm pt.ra.nsm cj d.nsf n.nsf v.aai.3s r.gsm.3 cj v.aas.3s p.g
1254 4574 3836 3836 4247 2038 3836 2652 3857 4022 3836 6052 2262 899 2671 3553 1666

this world and go to the Father. Having loved his own who were in the world, he now showed them
τούτου τοῦ κόσμου πρὸς τὸν πατέρα → ἀγαπήσας τοὺς ἰδίους τοὺς ἐν τῷ κόσμῳ αὐτούς
r.gsn d.gsm n.gsm p.a d.asm n.asm pt.aa.nsm d.apm a.apm d.apm p.d d.dsm n.dsm r.apm.3
4047 3836 3180 4639 3836 4252 26 3836 2625 3836 1877 3836 3180 899

the full extent of his love. **2** The evening meal was being served, and the devil had already
εἰς τέλος → ἠγάπησεν καὶ δείπνου → γινομένου τοῦ διαβόλου ἤδη
p.a n.asn v.aai.3s cj n.gsn pt.pm.gsn d.gsm n.gsm adv
1650 5465 26 2779 1270 1181 3836 1333 965 2453

prompted Judas Iscariot, son of Simon, to betray Jesus. ¶ **3** Jesus knew that the Father had
βεβληκότος εἰς τὴν καρδίαν Ἰούδας Ἰσκαριώτου → Σίμωνος ἵνα παραδοῖ αὐτὸν εἰδὼς ὅτι ὁ πατὴρ →
pt.ra.gsm p.a d.asf n.asf n.nsm n.gsm n.gsm cj v.aas.3s r.asm.3 pt.ra.nsm cj d.nsm n.nsm
965 1650 3836 2840 2683 2697 4981 2671 4140 899 3857 4022 3836 4252

put all things *under his power*, and that he had come from God and was returning to God; **4** so
ἔδωκεν αὐτῷ πάντα αὐτῷ εἰς τὰς χεῖρας καὶ ὅτι ἐξῆλθεν ἀπὸ θεοῦ καὶ ὑπάγει πρὸς τὸν θεὸν
v.aai.3s r.dsm.3 a.apn r.dsm.3 p.a d.apf n.apf cj cj v.aai.3s p.g n.gsm cj v.pai.3s p.a d.asm n.asm
1443 899 4246 899 1650 3836 5931 2779 4022 2002 608 2536 2779 5632 4639 3836 2536

he got up from the meal, took off his outer clothing, and wrapped a towel around his waist.
→ ἐγείρεται ← ἐκ τοῦ δείπνου καὶ τίθησιν τὰ → ἱμάτια καὶ λαβὼν διέζωσεν λέντιον ἑαυτόν
v.ppi.3s p.g d.gsn n.gsn cj v.pai.3s d.apn n.apn cj pt.aa.nsm v.aai.3s n.asn r.asm.3
1586 1666 3836 1270 2779 5502 3836 2668 2779 3284 1346 3317 1346 1571

5 After that, he poured water into a basin and began to wash his disciples' feet, drying them with
εἶτα ← → βάλλει ὕδωρ εἰς τὸν νιπτῆρα καὶ ἤρξατο → νίπτειν τῶν μαθητῶν τοὺς πόδας καὶ ἐκμάσσειν
adv v.pai.3s n.asn p.a d.asm n.asm cj v.ami.3s f.pa d.gpm n.gpm d.apm n.apm cj f.pa
1663 965 5623 1650 3836 3781 2779 806 3782 3836 3412 3836 4546 2779 1726

the towel that was wrapped around him. ¶ **6** He came to Simon Peter, who said to him, "Lord, are you
τῷ λεντίῳ ᾧ ἦν διεζωσμένος ← οὖν ἔρχεται πρὸς Σίμωνα Πέτρον λέγει αὐτῷ κύριε → σὺ
d.dsn n.dsn r.dsn v.iai.3s pt.rp.nsm cj v.pmi.3s p.a n.asm n.asm v.pai.3s r.dsm.3 n.vsm r.ns.2
3836 3317 4005 1639 1346 4036 2262 4639 4981 4377 3306 899 3261 3782 5148

going to wash my feet?" **7** Jesus replied, "You do not realize now what I am doing, but
→ → νίπτεις μου τοὺς πόδας Ἰησοῦς ἀπεκρίθη καὶ εἶπεν αὐτῷ σὺ → οὐκ οἶδας ἄρτι ὃ ἐγὼ → ποιῶ δὲ
v.pai.2s r.gs.1 d.apm n.apm n.nsm v.api.3s cj v.aai.3s r.dsm.3 r.ns.2 pl v.rai.2s adv r.asn r.ns.1 v.pai.1s cj
3782 1609 3836 4546 2652 646 2779 3306 899 5148 3857 4024 3857 785 4005 1609 4472 1254

later you will understand." **8** "No," said Peter, "you shall never wash my feet."
μετὰ ταῦτα → → γνώσῃ λέγει Πέτρος αὐτῷ οὐ μὴ εἰς τὸν αἰῶνα νίψῃς μου τοὺς πόδας
p.a r.apn v.fmi.2s v.pai.3s n.nsm r.dsm.3 pl pl p.a d.asm n.asm v.aas.2s r.gs.1 d.apm n.apm
3552 4047 1182 3306 4377 899 4024 3590 1650 3836 172 3782 1609 3836 4546

Jesus answered, "Unless I wash you, you have no part with me." **9** "Then, Lord," Simon Peter replied,
Ἰησοῦς ἀπεκρίθη αὐτῷ ἐὰν μὴ → νίψω σε → ἔχεις οὐκ μέρος μετ' ἐμοῦ κύριε Σίμων Πέτρος λέγει αὐτῷ
n.nsm v.api.3s r.dsm.3 cj pl v.aas.1s r.as.2 v.pai.2s pl n.asn p.g r.gs.1 n.vsm n.nsm n.nsm v.pai.3s r.dsm.3
2652 646 899 1569 3590 3782 5148 2400 4024 3538 3552 1609 3261 4981 4377 3306 899

κρινεῖ αὐτὸν ἐν τῇ ἐσχάτῃ ἡμέρᾳ. **49** ὅτι ἐγὼ ἐξ ἐμαυτοῦ οὐκ ἐλάλησα, ἀλλ' ὁ πέμψας με πατὴρ αὐτός μοι ἐντολὴν δέδωκεν τί εἴπω καὶ τί λαλήσω. **50** καὶ οἶδα ὅτι ἡ ἐντολὴ αὐτοῦ ζωὴ αἰώνιός ἐστιν. ἃ οὖν ἐγὼ λαλῶ, καθὼς εἴρηκέν μοι ὁ πατήρ, οὕτως λαλῶ. **13:1** Πρὸ δὲ τῆς ἑορτῆς τοῦ πάσχα εἰδὼς ὁ Ἰησοῦς ὅτι ἦλθεν αὐτοῦ ἡ ὥρα ἵνα μεταβῇ ἐκ τοῦ κόσμου τούτου πρὸς τὸν πατέρα, ἀγαπήσας τοὺς ἰδίους τοὺς ἐν τῷ κόσμῳ εἰς τέλος ἠγάπησεν αὐτούς. **2** καὶ δείπνου γινομένου, τοῦ διαβόλου ἤδη βεβληκότος εἰς τὴν καρδίαν ἵνα παραδοῖ αὐτὸν Ἰούδας Σίμωνος Ἰσκαριώτου, ¶ **3** εἰδὼς ὅτι πάντα ἔδωκεν αὐτῷ ὁ πατὴρ εἰς τὰς χεῖρας καὶ ὅτι ἀπὸ θεοῦ ἐξῆλθεν καὶ πρὸς τὸν θεὸν ὑπάγει, **4** ἐγείρεται ἐκ τοῦ δείπνου καὶ τίθησιν τὰ ἱμάτια καὶ λαβὼν λέντιον διέζωσεν ἑαυτόν· **5** εἶτα βάλλει ὕδωρ εἰς τὸν νιπτῆρα καὶ ἤρξατο νίπτειν τοὺς πόδας τῶν μαθητῶν καὶ ἐκμάσσειν τῷ λεντίῳ ᾧ ἦν διεζωσμένος. ¶ **6** ἔρχεται οὖν πρὸς Σίμωνα Πέτρον· λέγει αὐτῷ, Κύριε, σύ μου νίπτεις τοὺς πόδας; **7** ἀπεκρίθη Ἰησοῦς καὶ εἶπεν αὐτῷ, Ὃ ἐγὼ ποιῶ σὺ οὐκ οἶδας ἄρτι, γνώσῃ δὲ μετὰ ταῦτα. **8** λέγει αὐτῷ Πέτρος, Οὐ μὴ νίψῃς μου τοὺς πόδας εἰς τὸν αἰῶνα. ἀπεκρίθη Ἰησοῦς αὐτῷ, Ἐὰν μὴ νίψω σε, οὐκ ἔχεις μέρος μετ' ἐμοῦ. **9** λέγει αὐτῷ Σίμων Πέτρος, Κύριε, μὴ τοὺς πόδας μου μόνον

"not just   my   feet   but   my   hands   and   my   head   *as   well!*"   ¹⁰ Jesus   answered,   "A person who has had
μὴ   μόνον   μου   ⸂τοὺς   πόδας⸃   ἀλλὰ   τὰς   χεῖρας   καὶ   τὴν   κεφαλήν   καὶ   ὁ   Ἰησοῦς   λέγει   αὐτῷ   ὁ ←
pl   adv   r.gs.1   r.dpm   n.apm   cj   d.apf   n.apf   cj   d.asf   n.asf   adv   d.nsm   n.nsm   v.pai.3s   r.dsm.3   d.nsm
3590   3667   1609   3836   4546   247   3836   5931   2779   3836   3051   2779   3836   2652   3306   899   3836

a bath   needs   only   to wash   his feet;   his whole body is   clean.   And you   are   clean,
λελουμένος   ἔχει   χρείαν   ⸂οὐκ   εἰ   μὴ⸃   →   νίψασθαι   τοὺς   πόδας   ἀλλ'   ὅλος   ἔστιν   καθαρὸς   καὶ   ὑμεῖς   ἐστε   καθαροί
pt.rp.nsm   v.pai.3s   n.asf   pl   cj   pl   f.am   d.apm   n.apm   cj   a.nsm   v.pai.3s   a.nsm   cj   r.np.2   v.pai.2p   a.npm
3374   2400   5970   4024   1623   3590   3782   3836   4546   247   3910   1639   2754   2779   7007   1639   2754

though not every one of you."   ¹¹ For he knew   who was going to betray   him,   and *that was why*   he said
ἀλλ'   οὐχὶ   πάντες ←   γὰρ   →   ᾔδει   τὸν   →   →   παραδιδόντα   αὐτόν   ⸂διὰ   τοῦτο⸃   →   εἶπεν   ὅτι
cj   pl   a.npm   cj   v.lai.3s   d.asm   pt.pa.asm   r.asm.3   p.a   r.asn   v.aai.3s   cj
247   4049   4246   1142   3857   3836   4140   899   1328   4047   3306   4022

not every one was clean.   ¶   ¹²   When he had finished washing their feet,   he put   on his
οὐχὶ   πάντες ←   ἐστε   καθαροί   οὖν   Ὅτε   →   →   →   ἔνιψεν   αὐτῶν   ⸂τοὺς   πόδας⸃   [καὶ]   →   ἔλαβεν   αὐτοῦ
pl   a.npm   v.pai.2p   a.npm   cj   cj   v.aai.3s   r.gpm.3   d.apm   n.apm   cj   v.aai.3s   r.gsm.3
4049   4246   1639   2754   4036   4021   3782   899   3836   4546   2779   3284   899

clothes   and returned   to his place. "Do you understand what I have done   for you?" he asked them.
⸂τὰ   ἱμάτια⸃   καὶ   ⸂ἀνέπεσεν   πάλιν⸃ ←   ←   →   γινώσκετε   τί   →   πεποίηκα   →   ὑμῖν   εἶπεν   αὐτοῖς
d.apn   n.apn   cj   v.aai.3s   adv   v.pai.2p   r.asn   v.rai.1s   r.dp.2   v.aai.3s   r.dpm.3
3836   2668   2779   404   4099   1182   5515   4472   7007   3306   899

¹³ "You call   me 'Teacher'   and 'Lord,'   and rightly so,   for that is what I am. ¹⁴ Now that I,   your Lord
ὑμεῖς   φωνεῖτε   με   ὁ   διδάσκαλος   καὶ   ὁ   κύριος   καὶ   καλῶς   λέγετε   γάρ   →   εἰμι   οὖν   εἰ   ἐγὼ ὁ   κύριος
r.np.2   v.pai.2p   r.as.1   d.nsm   n.nsm   cj   d.nsm   n.nsm   cj   adv   v.pai.2p   cj   v.pai.1s   cj   cj   r.ns.1   d.nsmn.nsm
7007   5888   1609   3836   1437   2779   3836   3261   2779   2822   3306   1142   1639   4036   1623   1609   38363261

and Teacher,   have washed your feet,   you also should wash one   another's feet.   ¹⁵   I have
καὶ   ὁ   διδάσκαλος   →   ἔνιψα   ὑμῶν   ⸂τοὺς   πόδας⸃   ὑμεῖς   καὶ   ὀφείλετε   νίπτειν   ἀλλήλων ←   ⸂τοὺς   πόδας⸃   γάρ →
cj   d.nsm   n.nsm   v.aai.1s   r.gp.2   d.apm   n.apm   r.np.2   adv   v.pai.2p   f.pa   r.gpm   d.apm   n.apm   cj
2779   3836   1437   3782   7007   3836   4546   7007   2779   4053   3782   253   3836   4546   1142

set   you an example that   you should do   as   I   have done for you. ¹⁶ I   tell you the truth,   no
ἔδωκα   ὑμῖν   ὑπόδειγμα   ἵνα   καὶ   ὑμεῖς →   ποιῆτε   καθὼς   ἐγὼ   →   ἐποίησα   ὑμῖν   λέγω   ὑμῖν   ⸂ἀμὴν   ἀμὴν⸃ οὐκ
v.aai.1s   r.dp.2   n.asn   cj   adv   r.np.2   v.pas.2p   cj   r.ns.1   v.aai.1s   r.dp.2   v.pai.1s   r.dp.2   pl   plpl
1443   7007   5682   2671   2779   7007   4472   2777   1609   4472   7007   3306   7007   297   2974024

servant is   greater than his   master,   nor is a messenger greater than the one who sent   him. ¹⁷ Now that you
δοῦλος   ἔστιν   μείζων   αὐτοῦ   ⸂τοῦ   κυρίου⸃   οὐδὲ   ἀπόστολος   μείζων ←   τοῦ ←   πέμψαντος   αὐτόν   εἰ   →
n.nsm   v.pai.3s   a.nsm.c   r.gsm.3   d.gsm   n.gsm   cj   n.nsm   a.nsm.c   d.gsm   pt.aa.gsm   r.asm.3   cj
1529   1639   3489   899   3836   3261   4028   693   3489   3836   4287   899   1623

know these things, you will be   blessed if   you do   them.
οἴδατε   ταῦτα   →   →   ἐστε   μακάριοι   ἐὰν   →   ποιῆτε   αὐτά
v.rai.2p   r.apn   v.pai.2p   a.npm   cj   v.pas.2p   r.apn
3857   4047   1639   3421   1569   4472   899

Jesus Predicts His Betrayal

13:18 "I   am not referring to   all   of you;   I know those I have chosen. But this is to   fulfill   the scripture:
→   →   Οὐ   λέγω   περὶ   πάντων →   ὑμῶν   ἐγὼ   οἶδα   τίνας   →   →   ἐξελεξάμην   ἀλλ'   ἵνα   πληρωθῇ   ἡ   γραφή
pl   v.pai.1s   p.g   a.gpm   r.gp.2   r.ns.1   v.rai.1s   r.apm   v.ami.1s   cj   cj   v.aps.3s   d.nsf   n.nsf
3306   3306   4024   3306   4309   4246   7007   1609   3857   5515   1721   247   2671   4444   3836   1210

'He who shares my bread   has lifted up his   heel   against me.' ¹⁹ "I am telling you now   before it
ὁ   τρώγων   μου   τὸν   ἄρτον⸃   →   ἐπῆρεν   αὐτοῦ   ⸂τὴν   πτέρναν⸃   ἐπ'   ἐμέ   λέγω   ὑμῖν   ⸂ἀπ'   ἄρτι⸃   πρὸ   →
d.nsm   pt.pa.nsm   r.gs.1   d.asm   n.asm   v.aai.3s   r.gsm.3   d.asf   n.asf   p.a   r.as.1   v.pai.1s   r.dp.2   p.g   adv   p.g
3836   5592   1609   3836   788   2048   899   3836   4761   2093   1609   3306   7007   608   785   4574

happens,   so that when it does happen you will believe   that I am He. ²⁰ I tell you the truth,   whoever
⸂τοῦ   γενέσθαι⸃   ἵνα ←   ὅταν   →   γένηται   →   πιστεύσητε ὅτι   ἐγώ   εἰμι   λέγω   ὑμῖν   ⸂ἀμὴν   ἀμὴν⸃   ὁ   ἄν
d.gsn   f.am   cj   cj   v.ams.3s   v.aas.2p   cj   r.ns.1   v.pai.1s   v.pai.1s   r.dp.2   pl   pl   d.nsm   pl
3836   1181   2671   4020   1181   4409   4022   1609   1639   3306   7007   297   297   3836   323

accepts anyone I send   accepts me; and whoever accepts   me accepts the one who sent   me."   ¶   ²¹ After
λαμβάνων   τινα   →   πέμψω   λαμβάνει   ἐμέ   δὲ   ὁ   λαμβάνων   ἐμέ   λαμβάνει   τὸν ←   ←   πέμψαντα   με
pt.pa.nsm   r.asm   v.aas.1s   v.pai.3s   r.as.1   cj   d.nsm   pt.pa.nsm   r.as.1   v.pai.3s   d.asm   pt.aa.asm   r.as.1
3284   5516   4287   3284   1609   1254   3836   3284   1609   3284   3836   4287   1609

ἀλλὰ καὶ τὰς χεῖρας καὶ τὴν κεφαλήν. ¹⁰ λέγει αὐτῷ ὁ Ἰησοῦς, Ὁ λελουμένος οὐκ ἔχει χρείαν εἰ μὴ τοὺς πόδας νίψασθαι, ἀλλ' ἔστιν καθαρὸς ὅλος· καὶ ὑμεῖς καθαροί ἐστε, ἀλλ' οὐχὶ πάντες. ¹¹ ᾔδει γὰρ τὸν παραδιδόντα αὐτόν· διὰ τοῦτο εἶπεν ὅτι Οὐχὶ πάντες καθαροί ἐστε. ¶ ¹² Ὅτε οὖν ἔνιψεν τοὺς πόδας αὐτῶν [καὶ] ἔλαβεν τὰ ἱμάτια αὐτοῦ καὶ ἀνέπεσεν πάλιν, εἶπεν αὐτοῖς, Γινώσκετε τί πεποίηκα ὑμῖν; ¹³ ὑμεῖς φωνεῖτέ με Ὁ διδάσκαλος καὶ Ὁ κύριος, καὶ καλῶς λέγετε, εἰμὶ γάρ. ¹⁴ εἰ οὖν ἐγὼ ἔνιψα ὑμῶν τοὺς πόδας ὁ κύριος καὶ ὁ διδάσκαλος, καὶ ὑμεῖς ὀφείλετε ἀλλήλων νίπτειν τοὺς πόδας· ¹⁵ ὑπόδειγμα γὰρ ἔδωκα ὑμῖν ἵνα καθὼς ἐγὼ ἐποίησα ὑμῖν καὶ ὑμεῖς ποιῆτε. ¹⁶ ἀμὴν ἀμὴν λέγω ὑμῖν, οὐκ ἔστιν δοῦλος μείζων τοῦ κυρίου αὐτοῦ οὐδὲ ἀπόστολος μείζων τοῦ πέμψαντος αὐτόν. ¹⁷ εἰ ταῦτα οἴδατε, μακάριοί ἐστε ἐὰν ποιῆτε αὐτά.

13:18 οὐ περὶ πάντων ὑμῶν λέγω· ἐγὼ οἶδα τίνας ἐξελεξάμην· ἀλλ' ἵνα ἡ γραφὴ πληρωθῇ, Ὁ τρώγων μου τὸν ἄρτον ἐπῆρεν ἐπ' ἐμὲ τὴν πτέρναν αὐτοῦ. ¹⁹ ἀπ' ἄρτι λέγω ὑμῖν πρὸ τοῦ γενέσθαι, ἵνα πιστεύσητε ὅταν γένηται ὅτι ἐγώ εἰμι. ²⁰ ἀμὴν ἀμὴν λέγω ὑμῖν, ὁ λαμβάνων ἄν τινα πέμψω ἐμὲ λαμβάνει, ὁ δὲ ἐμὲ λαμβάνων λαμβάνει τὸν πέμψαντά με. ¶ ²¹ Ταῦτα εἰπὼν [ὁ]

he had said this, Jesus was troubled in spirit and testified, "I tell you the truth,
→ → εἰπὼν Ταῦτα ὁ Ἰησοῦς, → ἐταράχθη ˌτῷ πνεύματιˌ καὶ ἐμαρτύρησεν καὶ εἶπεν λέγω ὑμῖν ˌἀμὴν ἀμὴν ὅτι
pt.aa.nsm r.apn d.nsm n.nsm v.api.3s d.dsn n.dsn cj v.aai.3s cj v.aai.3s v.pai.1s r.dp.2 pl pl cj
3306 4047 3836 2652 5429 3836 4460 2779 3455 2779 3306 3306 7007 297 297 4022

one of you is going to betray me." 22 His disciples stared at one another, at a loss to know which
εἷς ἐξ ὑμῶν → → παραδώσει με οἱ μαθηταὶ ἔβλεπον εἰς ἀλλήλους ← ἀπορούμενοι ← ← περὶ τίνος
a.nsm p.g r.gp.2 v.fai.3s r.as.1 d.npm n.npm v.iai.3p p.a r.apm pt.pm.npm p.g r.gsm
1651 1666 7007 4140 1609 3836 3412 1063 1650 253 679 4309 5515

of them he meant. 23 One of them, the disciple whom Jesus loved, was reclining next to
← ← → λέγει εἷς ἐκ ˌτῶν μαθητῶν αὐτοῦˌ ὃν ὁ Ἰησοῦς ἠγάπα ἦν ἀνακείμενος ˌἐν τῷ κόλπῳˌ
v.pai.3s a.nsm p.g d.gpm n.gpm r.gsm.3 r.asm d.nsm n.nsm v.iai.3s v.iai.3s pt.pm.nsm p.d d.dsm n.dsm
3306 1651 1666 3836 3412 899 4005 3836 2652 26 1639 367 1877 3836 3146

him. 24 Simon Peter motioned to this disciple and said, "Ask him which one he means."
ˌτοῦ Ἰησοῦˌ οὖν Σίμων Πέτρος νεύει → τούτῳ πυθέσθαι τίς ἂν → εἴη περὶ οὗ λέγει
d.gsm n.gsm cj n.nsm n.nsm v.pai.3s r.dsm f.am r.nsm pl v.pao.3s p.g r.gsm v.pai.3s
3836 2652 4036 4981 4377 3748 4047 4785 5515 323 1639 4309 4005 3306

¶ 25 Leaning back against Jesus, he asked him, "Lord, who is it?" 26 Jesus answered, "It
οὖν ἀναπεσὼν ← ˌἐπὶ τὸ στῆθοςˌ ˌτοῦ Ἰησοῦˌ ἐκεῖνος οὕτως λέγει αὐτῷ κύριε τίς ἐστιν ὁ Ἰησοῦς ἀποκρίνεται
cj pt.aa.nsm p.a d.asn n.asn d.gsm n.gsm r.nsm adv v.pai.3s r.dsm.3 n.vsm r.nsm v.pai.3s d.nsm n.nsm v.pmi.3s
4036 404 2093 3836 5111 3836 2652 1697 4048 3306 899 3261 5515 1639 3836 2652 646

is the one to whom I will give this piece of bread when I have dipped it in the dish." Then, dipping
ἐστιν → ἐκεῖνος → ᾧ ἐγὼ → δώσω αὐτῷ τὸ ψωμίον ← καὶ → βάψω οὖν βάψας
v.pai.3s r.nsm r.dsm r.ns.1 v.fai.1s r.dsm.3 d.asn n.asn cj v.fai.1s cj pt.aa.nsm
1639 1697 4005 1609 1443 899 3836 6040 2779 970 4036 970

the piece of bread, he gave it to Judas Iscariot, son of Simon. 27 As soon as Judas took the
τὸ ψωμίον ← [λαμβάνει καὶ] → δίδωσιν → Ἰούδα Ἰσκαριώτου → Σίμωνος καὶ μετὰ τὸ
d.asn n.asn v.pai.3s cj v.pai.3s n.dsm n.dsm n.gsm cj p.a d.asn
3836 6040 3284 2779 1443 2683 2697 4981 2779 3552 3836

bread, Satan entered into him. "What you are about to do, do quickly," Jesus told him,
ψωμίον τότε ὁ σατανᾶς, εἰσῆλθεν εἰς ἐκεῖνον οὖν ὃ → → → ποιεῖς ποίησον τάχιον ὁ Ἰησοῦς, λέγει αὐτῷ
n.asn adv d.nsm n.nsm v.aai.3s p.a r.asm cj r.asn v.pai.2s v.aam.2s adv.c d.nsm n.nsm v.pai.3s r.dsm.3
6040 5538 3836 4928 1656 1650 1697 4036 4005 4472 4472 5441 3836 2652 3306 899

28 but no one at the meal understood why Jesus said this to him. 29 Since Judas had charge of the
δὲ → οὐδεὶς ˌτῶν ἀνακειμένωνˌ ἔγνω ˌπρὸς τίˌ εἶπεν τοῦτο αὐτῷ γὰρ ἐπεὶ Ἰούδας → εἶχεν τὸ
cj a.nsm d.gpm pt.pm.gpm v.aai.3s p.a r.asn v.aai.3s r.asn r.dsm.3 cj cj n.nsm v.iai.3s d.asn
1254 4029 3836 367 1182 4639 5515 3306 4047 899 1142 2075 2683 2400 3836

money, some thought Jesus was telling him to buy what was needed for the Feast, or to give
γλωσσόκομον τινὲς ἐδόκουν ὅτι ὁ Ἰησοῦς, → λέγει αὐτῷ ἀγόρασον ὧν ἔχομεν χρείαν εἰς τὴν ἑορτὴν ἢ ἵνα δῷ
n.asn r.npm v.iai.3p cj d.nsm n.nsm v.pai.3s r.dsm.3 v.aam.2s r.gpn v.pai.1p n.asf p.a d.asf n.asf cj cj v.aas.3s
1186 5516 1506 4022 3836 2652 3306 899 60 4005 2400 5970 1650 3836 2038 2445 2671 1443

something to the poor. 30 As soon as Judas had taken the bread, he went out. And it was night.
τι → τοῖς πτωχοῖς οὖν εὐθύς → λαβὼν τὸ ψωμίον ἐκεῖνος ἐξῆλθεν ← δὲ → ἦν νύξ.
r.asn d.dpm a.dpm cj adv pt.aa.nsm d.asn n.asn r.nsm v.aai.3s cj v.iai.3s n.nsf
5516 3836 4777 4036 2318 3284 3836 6040 1697 2002 1254 1639 3816

Jesus Predicts Peter's Denial

13:31 When he was gone, Jesus said, "Now is the Son of Man glorified and God is glorified in
οὖν Ὅτε → ἐξῆλθεν Ἰησοῦς λέγει νῦν → ὁ υἱὸς ˌτοῦ ἀνθρώπουˌ ἐδοξάσθη καὶ ὁ θεός, → ἐδοξάσθη ἐν
cj cj v.aai.3s n.nsm v.pai.3s adv d.nsm n.nsm d.gsm n.gsm v.api.3s cj d.nsm n.nsm v.api.3s p.d
4036 4021 2002 2652 3306 3814 1519 3836 5626 3836 476 1519 2779 3836 2536 1519 1877

him. 32 If God is glorified in him, God will glorify the Son in himself, and will glorify him at once. ¶
αὐτῷ εἰ ὁ θεός, ἐδοξάσθη ἐν αὐτῷ καὶ ὁ θεός, → δοξάσει αὐτὸν ἐν αὐτῷ καὶ → δοξάσει αὐτόν → εὐθύς
r.dsm.3 cj d.nsm n.nsm v.api.3s p.d r.dsm.3 cj d.nsm n.nsm v.fai.3s r.asm.3 p.d r.dsm.3 cj v.fai.3s r.asm.3 adv
899 1623 3836 2536 1519 1877 899 2779 3836 2536 1519 899 1877 899 2779 1519 899 2318

33 "My children, I will be with you only a little longer. You will look for me, and just as I told the Jews,
τεκνία → → εἰμι μεθ' ὑμῶν ἔτι μικρὸν → → ζητήσετε ← με καὶ καθὼς → εἶπον τοῖς Ἰουδαίοις
n.vpn v.pai.1s p.g r.gp.2 adv a.asn v.fai.2p r.as.1 cj cj v.aai.1s d.dpm a.dpm
5448 1639 3552 7007 2285 3625 2426 1609 2779 2777 3306 3836 2681

Ἰησοῦς ἐταράχθη τῷ πνεύματι καὶ ἐμαρτύρησεν καὶ εἶπεν, Ἀμὴν ἀμὴν λέγω ὑμῖν ὅτι εἷς ἐξ ὑμῶν παραδώσει με. 22 ἔβλεπον εἰς ἀλλήλους οἱ μαθηταὶ ἀπορούμενοι περὶ τίνος λέγει. 23 ἦν ἀνακείμενος εἷς ἐκ τῶν μαθητῶν αὐτοῦ ἐν τῷ κόλπῳ τοῦ Ἰησοῦ, ὃν ἠγάπα ὁ Ἰησοῦς. 24 νεύει οὖν τούτῳ Σίμων Πέτρος πυθέσθαι τίς ἂν εἴη περὶ οὗ λέγει. ¶ 25 ἀναπεσὼν οὖν ἐκεῖνος οὕτως ἐπὶ τὸ στῆθος τοῦ Ἰησοῦ λέγει αὐτῷ, Κύριε, τίς ἐστιν; 26 ἀποκρίνεται [ὁ] Ἰησοῦς, Ἐκεῖνός ἐστιν ᾧ ἐγὼ βάψω τὸ ψωμίον καὶ δώσω αὐτῷ. βάψας οὖν τὸ ψωμίον [λαμβάνει καὶ] δίδωσιν Ἰούδα Σίμωνος Ἰσκαριώτου. 27 καὶ μετὰ τὸ ψωμίον τότε εἰσῆλθεν εἰς ἐκεῖνον ὁ Σατανᾶς. λέγει οὖν αὐτῷ ὁ Ἰησοῦς, Ὃ ποιεῖς ποίησον τάχιον. 28 τοῦτο [δὲ] οὐδεὶς ἔγνω τῶν ἀνακειμένων πρὸς τί εἶπεν αὐτῷ· 29 τινὲς γὰρ ἐδόκουν, ἐπεὶ τὸ γλωσσόκομον εἶχεν Ἰούδας, ὅτι λέγει αὐτῷ [ὁ] Ἰησοῦς, Ἀγόρασον ὧν χρείαν ἔχομεν εἰς τὴν ἑορτήν, ἢ τοῖς πτωχοῖς ἵνα τι δῷ. 30 λαβὼν οὖν τὸ ψωμίον ἐκεῖνος ἐξῆλθεν εὐθύς. ἦν δὲ νύξ.

13:31 Ὅτε οὖν ἐξῆλθεν, λέγει Ἰησοῦς, Νῦν ἐδοξάσθη ὁ υἱὸς τοῦ ἀνθρώπου, καὶ ὁ θεὸς ἐδοξάσθη ἐν αὐτῷ· 32 [εἰ ὁ θεὸς ἐδοξάσθη ἐν αὐτῷ,] καὶ ὁ θεὸς δοξάσει αὐτὸν ἐν αὐτῷ, καὶ εὐθὺς δοξάσει αὐτόν. ¶ 33 τεκνία, ἔτι μικρὸν μεθ' ὑμῶν εἰμι· ζητήσετέ με, καὶ

so I tell you now: Where I   am going, you   cannot   come. ¶ **34** "A new   command I give   you:
καὶ → λέγω ὑμῖν ἄρτι ὅτι ὅπου ἐγὼ → ὑπάγω ὑμεῖς οὐ δύνασθε ἐλθεῖν   καινὴν Ἐντολὴν → δίδωμι ὑμῖν ἵνα
adv → v.pai.1s r.dp.2 adv cj cj r.ns.1 v.pai.1s r.np.2 pl v.ppi.2p f.aa   a.asf n.asf   v.pai.1s r.dp.2 cj
2779 3306 7007 785 4022 3963 1609 5632 7007 4024 1538 2262   2785 1953   1443 7007 2671

Love   one   another. As   I have loved   you, so   you   must love   one   another. **35** By this all   men
ἀγαπᾶτε ἀλλήλους ←   καθὼς → → ἠγάπησα ὑμᾶς ἵνα ὑμεῖς καὶ → ἀγαπᾶτε ἀλλήλους ←   ἐν τούτῳ πάντες
v.pas.2p r.apm   cj   v.aai.1s r.ap.2 cj r.np.2 adv → v.pas.2p r.apm   p.d r.dsn a.npm
26 253   2777   26 7007 2671 7007 2779   26 253   1877 4047 4246

will know   that you are my disciples, if   you love   one   another." ¶ **36** Simon Peter asked
→ γνώσονται ὅτι → ἐστε ἐμοὶ μαθηταί ἐὰν → ἀγάπην ἔχητε ἐν ἀλλήλοις ←   Σίμων Πέτρος Λέγει
v.fmi.3p cj   v.pai.2p a.npm n.npm cj   n.asf v.pas.2p p.d r.dpm   n.nsm n.nsm v.pai.3s
1182 4022   1639 1847 3412 1569   27 2400 1877 253   4981 4377 3306

him, "Lord, where are you going?" Jesus replied,   "Where I am going, you cannot   follow
αὐτῷ κύριε ποῦ → → ὑπάγεις Ἰησοῦς ἀπεκρίθη [αὐτῷ] ὅπου → → ὑπάγω   οὐ δύνασαι ἀκολουθῆσαι μοι
r.dsm.3 n.vsm adv   v.pai.2s n.nsm v.api.3s r.dsm.3 cj   v.pai.1s   pl v.ppi.2s f.aa r.ds.1
899 3261 4543   5632 2652 646 899 3963   5632   4024 1538 199 1609

now, but you will follow   later." **37** Peter   asked,   "Lord, why   can't   I follow   you now? I will
νῦν δὲ → → ἀκολουθήσεις ὕστερον ὁ Πέτρος λέγει αὐτῷ κύριε ιδιὰ τί ιοὐ δύναμαι ← ἀκολουθῆσαι σοι ἄρτι
adv cj   v.fai.2s adv.c d.nsm n.nsm v.pai.3s r.dsm.3 n.vsm p.a r.asn pl v.ppi.1s f.aa r.ds.2 adv
3814 1254   199 5731 3836 4377 3306 899 3261 1328 5515 4024 1538 199 5148 785

lay   down my life   for you." **38** Then Jesus   answered, "Will you really lay   down your life   for me? I
θήσω ← μου ιτὴν ψυχήνι ὑπὲρ σοῦ   Ἰησοῦς ἀποκρίνεται → → θήσεις ← σοῦ ιτὴν ψυχήνι ὑπὲρ ἐμοῦ →
v.fai.1s r.gs.1 d.asf n.asf p.g r.gs.2   n.nsm v.pmi.3s   v.fai.2s   r.gs.2 d.asf n.asf p.g r.gs.1
5502 1609 3836 6034 5642 5148   2652 646   5502   5148 3836 6034 5642 1609

tell you the truth,   before   the rooster   crows, you will disown me three times!
λέγω σοι   ιἀμὴν ἀμήνι ἕως οὗ   ἀλέκτωρ οὐ μὴ φωνήσῃ → ἀρνήσῃ με τρίς ←
v.pai.1s r.ds.2 pl pl p.g r.gsm   n.nsm pl pl v.aas.3s → v.ams.2s r.as.1 adv
3306 5148 297 297 2401 4005   232 4024 3590 5888   766 1609 5565

Jesus Comforts His Disciples

14:1 "Do not let your hearts   be troubled. Trust in God;   trust   also in me. **2** In my Father's
     Μὴ → ὑμῶν ἡ καρδία → ταρασσέσθω πιστεύετε εἰς ιτὸν θεόνι πιστεύετε καὶ εἰς ἐμέ ἐν μου ιτοῦ πατρόςι
     pl   r.gp.2 d.nsf n.nsf → v.ppm.3s v.pai.2p p.a d.asm n.asm v.pam.2p adv p.a r.as.1 p.d r.gs.1 d.gsm n.gsm
     5429 3590 5429 7007 3836 2840   5429 4409 1650 3836 2536 4409 2779 1650 1609 1877 1609 3836 4252

house   are many rooms;   if it were not so, I   would have told you.   I am going   there to prepare a
ιτῇ οἰκίαι εἰσιν πολλαί μοναὶ δὲ εἰ   μή ιἂν → εἶπον ὑμῖν ὅτι → → πορεύομαι → ἑτοιμάσαι
d.dsf n.dsf v.pai.3p a.npf n.npf cj cj   pl pl → v.aai.1s r.dp.2 cj   v.pmi.1s f.aa
3836 3864 1639 4498 3665 1254 1623   3590 323   3306 7007 4022   4513 2286

place for you. **3** And if I go   and prepare a place for you, I will come back and take   you to be with
τόπον → ὑμῖν καὶ ἐὰν → πορευθῶ καὶ ἑτοιμάσω τόπον → ὑμῖν → ἔρχομαι πάλιν καὶ παραλήμψομαι ὑμᾶς πρὸς
n.asm → r.dp.2 cj cj → v.aps.1s cj v.aas.1s n.asm r.dp.2 → v.pmi.1s adv cj v.fmi.1s r.ap.2 p.a
5536   7007 2779 1569   4513 2779 2286 5536 7007   2262 4099 2779 4161 7007 4639

me that you also may be where I am. **4**   You know the way to the place where I   am going."
ἐμαυτόν ἵνα ὑμεῖς καὶ → ἦτε ὅπου ἐγὼ εἰμι   καὶ → οἴδατε τὴν ὁδόν   ὅπου ἐγὼ → ὑπάγω
r.asm.1 cj r.np.2 adv → v.pas.2p cj r.ns.1 v.pai.1s cj → v.rai.2p d.asf n.asf   cj r.ns.1 v.pai.1s
1831 2671 7007 2779   1639 3963 1609 1639 2779   3857 3836 3847   3963 1609 5632

Jesus the Way to the Father

14:5 Thomas said to him, "Lord, we don't know where you are going, so how can   we know the way?"
     Θωμᾶς Λέγει → αὐτῷ κύριε → οὐκ οἴδαμεν ποῦ → → ὑπάγεις πῶς δυνάμεθα ← εἰδέναι τὴν ὁδὸν
     n.nsm v.pai.3s r.dsm.3 n.vsm → pl v.rai.1p adv   v.pai.2s cj v.ppi.1p f.ra d.asf n.asf
     2605 3306 899 3261 3857 4024 3857 4543   5632 4802 1538 3857 3836 3847

6 Jesus   answered,   "I am the way and the truth   and the life. No one   comes to   the Father except
ιὸ Ἰησοῦςι λέγει   αὐτῷ ἐγὼ εἰμι ἡ ὁδὸς καὶ ἡ ἀλήθεια καὶ ἡ ζωή   οὐδεὶς ἔρχεται πρὸς τὸν πατέρα ιεἰ μὴ
d.nsm n.nsm v.pai.3s r.dsm.3 r.ns.1 v.pai.1s d.nsf n.nsf cj d.nsf n.nsf cj d.nsf n.nsf   a.nsm v.pmi.3s p.a d.asm n.asm cj pl
3836 2652 3306 899 1609 1639 3836 3847 2779 3836 237 2779 3836 2437   4029 2262 4639 3836 4252 1623 3590

καθὼς εἶπον τοῖς Ἰουδαίοις ὅτι Ὅπου ἐγὼ ὑπάγω ὑμεῖς οὐ δύνασθε ἐλθεῖν, καὶ ὑμῖν λέγω ἄρτι. ¶ **34** ἐντολὴν καινὴν δίδωμι ὑμῖν, ἵνα ἀγαπᾶτε ἀλλήλους, καθὼς ἠγάπησα ὑμᾶς ἵνα καὶ ὑμεῖς ἀγαπᾶτε ἀλλήλους. **35** ἐν τούτῳ γνώσονται πάντες ὅτι ἐμοὶ μαθηταί ἐστε, ἐὰν ἀγάπην ἔχητε ἐν ἀλλήλοις. ¶ **36** Λέγει αὐτῷ Σίμων Πέτρος, Κύριε, ποῦ ὑπάγεις; ἀπεκρίθη [αὐτῷ] Ἰησοῦς, Ὅπου ὑπάγω οὐ δύνασαί μοι νῦν ἀκολουθῆσαι, ἀκολουθήσεις δὲ ὕστερον. **37** λέγει αὐτῷ ὁ Πέτρος, Κύριε, διὰ τί οὐ δύναμαί σοι ἀκολουθῆσαι ἄρτι; τὴν ψυχήν μου ὑπὲρ σοῦ θήσω. **38** ἀποκρίνεται Ἰησοῦς, Τὴν ψυχήν σου ὑπὲρ ἐμοῦ θήσεις; ἀμὴν ἀμὴν λέγω σοι, οὐ μὴ ἀλέκτωρ φωνήσῃ ἕως οὗ ἀρνήσῃ με τρίς.

14:1 Μὴ ταρασσέσθω ὑμῶν ἡ καρδία· πιστεύετε εἰς τὸν θεὸν καὶ εἰς ἐμὲ πιστεύετε. **2** ἐν τῇ οἰκίᾳ τοῦ πατρός μου μοναὶ πολλαί εἰσιν· εἰ δὲ μή, εἶπον ἂν ὑμῖν ὅτι πορεύομαι ἑτοιμάσαι τόπον ὑμῖν; **3** καὶ ἐὰν πορευθῶ καὶ ἑτοιμάσω τόπον ὑμῖν, πάλιν ἔρχομαι καὶ παραλήμψομαι ὑμᾶς πρὸς ἐμαυτόν, ἵνα ὅπου εἰμὶ ἐγὼ καὶ ὑμεῖς ἦτε. **4** καὶ ὅπου [ἐγὼ] ὑπάγω οἴδατε τὴν ὁδόν.

14:5 Λέγει αὐτῷ Θωμᾶς, Κύριε, οὐκ οἴδαμεν ποῦ ὑπάγεις· πῶς δυνάμεθα τὴν ὁδὸν εἰδέναι; **6** λέγει αὐτῷ [ὁ] Ἰησοῦς, Ἐγώ εἰμι ἡ ὁδὸς καὶ ἡ ἀλήθεια καὶ ἡ ζωή· οὐδεὶς ἔρχεται πρὸς τὸν πατέρα εἰ μὴ δι' ἐμοῦ. **7** εἰ ἐγνώκειτέ «ἐγνώκατέ» με, καὶ τὸν

through me. **7** If you really knew me, you would know my Father *as well.* From now on, you do
δι'   ἐμοῦ   εἰ   ἐγνώκατε με   γνώσεσθε μου τὸν πατέρα καὶ   καὶ ἀπ' ἄρτι
p.g   r.gs.1   cj   v.rai.2p r.as.1   v.fmi.2p r.gs.1 d.asm n.asm adv   cj p.g adv
1328   1609   1623   1182   1609   1182   1609 3836 4252   2779   2779 608 785

know   him and have seen   him."   ¶   **8** Philip   said,   "Lord, show us   the Father and that will be
γινώσκετε αὐτόν καὶ   ἑωράκατε αὐτόν   Φίλιππος Λέγει αὐτῷ κύριε δεῖξον ἡμῖν τὸν πατέρα καὶ
v.pai.2p r.asm.3 cj   v.rai.2p r.asm.3   n.nsm   v.pai.3s r.dsm.3 n.vsm v.aam.2s r.dp.1 d.asm n.asm cj
1182   899   2779   3972   899   5805   3306   899   3261 1259   7005 3836 4252 2779

enough for us." **9** Jesus   answered: "Don't you know me, Philip, even after I have been among you
ἀρκεῖ   ἡμῖν ὁ   Ἰησοῦς λέγει   αὐτῷ καὶ οὐκ   ἔγνωκάς με Φίλιππε   εἰμι μεθ' ὑμῶν
v.pai.3s r.dp.1 d.nsm n.nsm v.pai.3s   r.dsm.3 cj pl   v.rai.2s r.as.1 n.vsm   v.pai.1s p.g r.gp.2
758   7005 3836 2652 3306   899 2779 4024   1182   1609 5805   1639 3552 7007

such a long time? Anyone who has seen   me has seen   the Father. How can you say, 'Show us the Father'?
         τοσούτῳ χρόνῳ ὁ   ἑωρακὼς ἐμὲ ἑώρακεν τὸν πατέρα πῶς   σὺ λέγεις δεῖξον ἡμῖν τὸν πατέρα
         r.dsm n.dsm d.nsm   pt.ra.nsm r.as.1 v.rai.3s d.asm n.asm cj   r.ns.2 v.pai.2s v.aam.2s r.dp.1 d.asm n.asm
         5537   5989 3836   3972   1609 3972   3836 4252   4802   5148   3306   1259   7005 3836 4252

10 Don't you believe that I am in the Father, and that the Father is in me? The words I say to you are
οὐ   πιστεύεις ὅτι ἐγὼ ἐν τῷ πατρὶ καὶ   ὁ πατὴρ ἐστιν ἐν ἐμοί τὰ ῥήματα ἃ ἐγὼ λέγω   ὑμῖν λαλῶ
pl   v.pai.2s cj r.ns.1 p.d d.dsm n.dsm cj   d.nsm n.nsm v.pai.3s p.d r.ds.1 d.apn n.apn r.apn r.ns.1 v.pai.1s r.dp.2 v.pai.1s
4024   4409   4022 1609 1877 3836 4252 2779   3836 4252 1639 1877 1609 3836 4839 4005 1609 3306 7007 3281

not just my   own. Rather, it is the Father, living in me, who is doing his   work. **11** Believe me when I say
οὐ   ἀπ' ἐμαυτοῦ   δὲ   ὁ πατὴρ μένων ἐν ἐμοί   ποιεῖ αὐτοῦ τὰ ἔργα πιστεύετε μοι
pl   p.g r.gsm.1   cj   d.nsm n.nsm pt.pa.nsm p.d r.ds.1   v.pai.3s r.gsm.3 d.apn n.apn v.pam.2p r.ds.1
4024   608 1831   1254   3836 4252 3531 1877 1609   4472 899 3836 2240 4409   1609

that I am in the Father and the Father is in me; or at least believe on the evidence of the miracles
ὅτι ἐγὼ   ἐν τῷ πατρὶ καὶ ὁ πατὴρ ἐν ἐμοί δὲ εἰ μή πιστεύετε διὰ   τὰ ἔργα
cj r.ns.1   p.d d.dsm n.dsm cj d.nsm n.nsm p.d r.ds.1 cj p.p   v.pam.2p p.a   d.apn n.apn
4022 1609   1877 3836 4252 2779 3836 4252 1877 1609 1254 1623 3590 4409   1328   3836 2240

themselves. **12** I tell you the truth,   anyone who has faith in me   will do   what I have
αὐτὰ   λέγω ὑμῖν ⌐Ἀμὴν ἀμὴν⌐ ὁ   πιστεύων εἰς ἐμὲ κἀκεῖνος   ποιήσει ⌐τὰ ἔργα⌐ ἃ ἐγὼ
r.apn   v.pai.1s r.dp.2 pl   pl   d.nsm   pt.pa.nsm p.a r.as.1 crasis   v.fai.3s d.apn n.apn r.apn r.ns.1
899   3306 7007 297   297   3836   4409   1650 1609 2797   4472   3836 2240 4005 1609

been doing. He will do   even greater things than these, because I am going   to the Father. **13** And I will
    ποιῶ   ποιήσει καὶ μείζονα   τούτων ὅτι   ἐγὼ   πορεύομαι πρὸς τὸν πατέρα καὶ
    v.pai.1s   v.fai.3s cj a.apn.c   r.gpn cj   r.ns.1   v.pmi.1s p.a d.asm n.asm cj
    4472   4472   2779 3489   4047   4022   1609   4513   4639 3836 4252 2779

do   whatever you ask   in my name,   so that the Son may bring glory to the Father. **14** You may
ποιήσω τοῦτο ὅ τι ἂν   αἰτήσητε ἐν μου ⌐τῷ ὀνόματι⌐ ἵνα   ἐν τῷ υἱῷ   δοξασθῇ ὁ πατήρ
v.fai.1s r.asn r.asn r.asn pl v.aas.2p p.d r.gs.1 d.dsn n.dsn cj   p.d d.dsm n.dsm v.aps.3s d.nsm n.nsm
4472   4047 4005 5516 323   160   1877 1609 3836 3950 2671   1877 3836 5626   1519   3836 4252

ask   me for anything in my name,   and I will do   it.
αἰτήσητε με ⌐ἐάν τι ἐν μου ⌐τῷ ὀνόματι⌐ ἐγὼ   ποιήσω
v.aas.2p r.as.1 cj r.asn p.d r.gs.1 d.dsn n.dsn r.ns.1   v.fai.1s
160   1609 1569 5516 1877 1609 3836 3950 1609   4472

Jesus Promises the Holy Spirit

14:15 "If you love me, you will obey what I   command. **16** And I will ask   the Father, and he will
Ἐὰν   ἀγαπᾶτέ με   τηρήσετε ⌐τὰς ἐμάς⌐ ⌐τὰς ἐντολάς⌐ κἀγὼ   ἐρωτήσω τὸν πατέρα καὶ
cj   v.pas.2p r.as.1   v.fai.2p d.apf r.apf.1 d.apf n.apf crasis   v.fai.1s d.asm n.asm cj
1569   26   1609   5498   3836 1847 3836 1953   2743   2263   3836 4252 2779

give you another Counselor to be   with you forever – **17** the Spirit of truth.   The world cannot
δώσει ὑμῖν ἄλλον παράκλητον ἵνα ᾖ μεθ' ὑμῶν εἰς τὸν αἰῶνα   τὸ πνεῦμα ⌐τῆς ἀληθείας⌐ ὁ κόσμος ⌐οὐ δύναται⌐
v.fai.3s r.dp.2 r.asm n.asm cj v.pas.3s p.g r.gp.2 p.a d.asm n.asm   d.asn n.asn d.gsf n.gsf d.nsm n.nsm pl v.ppi.3s
1443 7007 257 4156   2671 1639 3552 7007 1650 3836 172   3836 4460 3836 237 3836 3180 4024 1538

accept him, because it neither sees him nor knows him. But you know   him, for he lives with you and will
λαβεῖν ὃ   ὅτι   οὐ θεωρεῖ αὐτὸ οὐδὲ γινώσκει   ὑμεῖς γινώσκετε αὐτό ὅτι μένει παρ' ὑμῖν καὶ
f.aa r.asn cj   pl v.pai.3s r.asn.3 cj v.pai.3s   r.np.2 v.pai.2p r.asn.3 cj v.pai.3s p.d r.dp.2 cj
3284 4005 4022   4024 2555 899   4028 1182   7007 1182   899 4022 3531 4123 7007 2779

πατέρα μου ἂν ᾔδειτε. «γνώσεσθε.» καὶ ἀπ' ἄρτι γινώσκετε αὐτὸν καὶ ἑωράκατε αὐτόν. ¶ **8** λέγει αὐτῷ Φίλιππος, Κύριε, δεῖξον ἡμῖν τὸν πατέρα, καὶ ἀρκεῖ ἡμῖν. **9** λέγει αὐτῷ ὁ Ἰησοῦς, Τοσούτῳ χρόνῳ μεθ' ὑμῶν εἰμι καὶ οὐκ ἔγνωκάς με, Φίλιππε; ὁ ἑωρακὼς ἐμὲ ἑώρακεν τὸν πατέρα· πῶς σὺ λέγεις, Δεῖξον ἡμῖν τὸν πατέρα; **10** οὐ πιστεύεις ὅτι ἐγὼ ἐν τῷ πατρὶ καὶ ὁ πατὴρ ἐν ἐμοί ἐστιν; τὰ ῥήματα ἃ ἐγὼ λέγω ὑμῖν ἀπ' ἐμαυτοῦ οὐ λαλῶ, ὁ δὲ πατὴρ ἐν ἐμοὶ μένων ποιεῖ τὰ ἔργα αὐτοῦ. **11** πιστεύετέ μοι ὅτι ἐγὼ ἐν τῷ πατρὶ καὶ ὁ πατὴρ ἐν ἐμοί· εἰ δὲ μή, διὰ τὰ ἔργα αὐτὰ πιστεύετε. **12** ἀμὴν ἀμὴν λέγω ὑμῖν, ὁ πιστεύων εἰς ἐμὲ τὰ ἔργα ἃ ἐγὼ ποιῶ κἀκεῖνος ποιήσει καὶ μείζονα τούτων ποιήσει, ὅτι ἐγὼ πρὸς τὸν πατέρα πορεύομαι· **13** καὶ ὅ τι ἂν αἰτήσητε ἐν τῷ ὀνόματί μου τοῦτο ποιήσω, ἵνα δοξασθῇ ὁ πατὴρ ἐν τῷ υἱῷ· **14** ἐάν τι αἰτήσητέ με ἐν τῷ ὀνόματί μου ἐγὼ ποιήσω.

14:15 Ἐὰν ἀγαπᾶτέ με, τὰς ἐντολὰς τὰς ἐμὰς τηρήσετε· **16** κἀγὼ ἐρωτήσω τὸν πατέρα καὶ ἄλλον παράκλητον δώσει ὑμῖν, ἵνα μεθ' ὑμῶν εἰς τὸν αἰῶνα ᾖ, **17** τὸ πνεῦμα τῆς ἀληθείας, ὃ ὁ κόσμος οὐ δύναται λαβεῖν, ὅτι οὐ θεωρεῖ αὐτὸ οὐδὲ γινώσκει· ὑμεῖς

be | in | you. | ¹⁸ I | will | not | leave | you | as | orphans; | I | will | come | to | you. | ¹⁹ Before | long, | the world | will | not | see
ἔσται | ἐν | ὑμῖν | | | Οὐκ | ἀφήσω | ὑμᾶς | | ὀρφανούς | → | → | ἔρχομαι | πρὸς | ὑμᾶς | ἔτι | μικρὸν | καὶ | ὁ | κόσμος | → | οὐκέτι | θεωρεῖ
v.fmi.3s | p.d | r.dp.2 | | | pl | v.fai.1s | r.ap.2 | | a.apm | | | v.pmi.1s | p.a | r.ap.2 | adv | a.asn | cj | d.nsm | n.nsm | | adv | v.pai.3s
1639 | 1877 | 7007 | 918 918 | | 4024 | 918 | 7007 | | 4003 | | | 2262 | 4639 | 7007 | 2285 | 3625 | 2779 | 3836 | 3180 | | 2555 | 4033 | 2555

me anymore, | but | you | will see | me. | Because | I | live, | you | also | will live. | ²⁰ On | that | day | you | will realize
με | ↞ | δὲ | ὑμεῖς | → | θεωρεῖτέ με | ὅτι | ἐγὼ | ζῶ | ὑμεῖς | καὶ | → | ζήσετε | ἐν | ἐκείνῃ | τῇ ἡμέρᾳ | ὑμεῖς | → | γνώσεσθε
r.as.1 | | cj | r.np.2 | | v.pai.2p | r.as.1 | r.ns.1 | v.pai.1s | r.np.2 | cj | | v.fai.2p | p.d | r.dsf | d.dsf n.dsf | r.np.2 | | v.fmi.2p
1609 | 4033 | 1254 | 7007 | | 2555 | 1609 | 1609 | 2409 | 7007 | 2779 | | 2409 | 1877 | 1697 | 3836 2465 | 7007 | | 1182

that | I | am | in | my Father, | and you | are | in | me, | and | I | am | in | you. | ²¹ Whoever | has | my | commands | and | obeys
ὅτι | ἐγὼ | ἐν | μου | τῷ πατρί | καὶ | ὑμεῖς | ἐν | ἐμοὶ | κἀγὼ | ἐν | ὑμῖν | ὁ | ἔχων | μου | τὰς ἐντολάς | καὶ | τηρῶν
cj | r.ns.1 | p.d | r.gs.1 | d.dsm n.dsm | cj | r.np.2 | p.d | r.ds.1 | crasis | p.d | r.dp.2 | d.nsm | pt.pa.nsm | r.gs.1 | d.apf n.apf | cj | pt.pa.nsm
4022 | 1609 | 1877 | 1609 | 3836 4252 | 2779 | 7007 | 1877 | 1609 | 2743 | 1877 | 7007 | 3836 | 2400 | 1609 | 3836 1953 | 2779 | 5498

them, | he | is | the | one who | loves | me. | He who | loves | me | will be loved | by | my | Father, | and | I too
αὐτάς | ἐκεῖνος | ἐστιν | ὁ | ← | ἀγαπῶν | με | δὲ ὁ | ← | ἀγαπῶν | με | → | ἀγαπηθήσεται | ὑπὸ | μου | τοῦ πατρός | κἀγὼ
r.apf.3 | r.nsm | v.pai.3s | d.nsm | | pt.pa.nsm | r.as.1 | cj d.nsm | | pt.pa.nsm | r.as.1 | | v.fpi.3s | p.g | r.gs.1 | d.gsm n.gsm | crasis
899 | 1697 | 1639 | 3836 | | 26 | 1609 | 1254 3836 | | 26 | 1609 | | 26 | 5679 | 1609 | 3836 4252 | 2743

will love | him | and | show | myself | to him." | ¶ | ²² Then | Judas | (not | Judas | Iscariot) | said, | "But,
→ | ἀγαπήσω | αὐτὸν | καὶ | ἐμφανίσω | ἐμαυτόν | αὐτῷ | | | Ἰούδας | οὐχ | ὁ | Ἰσκαριώτης | Λέγει | αὐτῷ | καὶ
| v.fai.1s | r.asm.3 | cj | v.fai.1s | r.asm.1 | r.dsm.3 | | | n.nsm | pl | d.nsm | n.nsm | v.pai.3s | r.dsm.3 | cj
| 26 | 899 | 2779 | 1872 | 1831 | 899 | | | 2683 | 4024 | 3836 | 2697 | 3306 | 899 | 2779

Lord, | why | do you intend | to show | yourself | to us | and | not | to the world?" | ²³ Jesus | replied,
κύριε | τί | γέγονεν ὅτι | → | μέλλεις | ἐμφανίζειν | σεαυτὸν | → | ἡμῖν | καὶ | οὐχὶ | → | τῷ κόσμῳ | Ἰησοῦς | ἀπεκρίθη | καὶ | εἶπεν αὐτῷ
n.vsm | r.nsn | v.rai.3s cj | | v.pai.2s | f.pa | r.asm.2 | | r.dp.1 | cj | pl | | d.dsm n.dsm | n.nsm | v.api.3s | cj | v.aai.3s r.dsm.3
3261 | 5515 | 1181 4022 | | 3516 | 1872 | 4932 | | 7005 | 2779 | 4049 | | 3836 3180 | 2652 | 646 | 2779 | 3306 899

"If | anyone | loves | me, | he will obey | my | teaching. | My | Father | will love | him, | and | we will come | to
ἐάν | τις | ἀγαπᾷ | με | → | τηρήσει | μου | τὸν λόγον | καὶ | μου | ὁ | πατήρ | → | ἀγαπήσει | αὐτὸν | καὶ | → | ἐλευσόμεθα | πρὸς
cj | r.nsm | v.pas.3s | r.as.1 | | v.fai.3s | r.gs.1 | d.asm n.asm | cj | r.gs.1 | d.nsm | n.nsm | | v.fai.3s | r.asm.3 | cj | | v.fmi.1p | p.a
1569 | 5516 | 26 | 1609 | | 5498 | 1609 | 3836 3364 | 2779 | 1609 | 3836 | 4252 | | 26 | 899 | 2779 | | 2262 | 4639

him | and | make | our home | with | him. | ²⁴ He who | does | not | love | me | will | not | obey | my | teaching. | These | words
αὐτὸν | καὶ | ποιησόμεθα | μονὴν | παρ' | αὐτῷ | ὁ | ← | μὴ | ἀγαπῶν | με | → | οὐ | τηρεῖ | μου | τοὺς λόγους | καὶ ὁ | λόγος
r.asm.3 | cj | v.fmi.1p | n.asf | p.d | r.dsm.3 | d.nsm | | pl | pt.pa.nsm | r.as.1 | | pl | v.pai.3s | r.gs.1 | d.apm n.apm | cj d.nsm | n.nsm
899 | 2779 | 4472 | 3665 | 4123 | 899 | 3836 | | 3590 | 26 | 1609 | | 4024 | 5498 | 1609 | 3836 3364 | 2779 3836 | 3364

you | hear | are | not | my | own; | they belong | to the | Father | who | sent | me. | ¶ | ²⁵ "All | this | I have
ὃν | → | ἀκούετε | ἔστιν | οὐκ | ἐμός | ← | ἀλλὰ | → | → | πατρός | τοῦ | πέμψαντός | με | | Ταῦτα | → | →
r.asm | | v.pai.2p | v.pai.3s | pl | r.nsm.1 | | cj | | | n.gsm | d.gsm | pt.aa.nsm | r.as.1 | | r.apn
4005 | 201 | 1639 | 4024 | 1847 | | 247 | | | 4252 | 3836 | 4287 | 1609 | | 4047

spoken | while | still | with you. | ²⁶ But | the | Counselor, | the | Holy | Spirit, | whom | the | Father | will send | in | my
λελάληκα | ὑμῖν | → | μένων | παρ' | ὑμῖν | δὲ | ὁ | παράκλητος | τὸ | τὸ ἅγιον | πνεῦμα | ὃ | ὁ | πατὴρ | → | πέμψει | ἐν | μου
v.rai.1s | r.dp.2 | | pt.pa.nsm | p.d | r.dp.2 | cj | d.nsm | n.nsm | d.nsn | d.nsn a.nsn | n.nsn | r.asn | d.nsm | n.nsm | | v.fai.3s | p.d | r.gs.1
3281 | 7007 | 3531 | 4123 | 7007 | 1254 | 3836 | 4156 | 3836 | 3836 41 | 4460 | 4005 | 3836 | 4252 | | 4287 | 1877 | 1609

name, | will teach | you | all | things | and | will remind | you | of everything | I | have | said | to you.
τῷ ὀνόματι | ἐκεῖνος | → | διδάξει | ὑμᾶς | πάντα | ← | καὶ | → | ὑπομνήσει | ὑμᾶς | πάντα | ἃ | ἐγὼ | → | εἶπον | → | ὑμῖν
d.dsn n.dsn | r.nsm | | v.fai.3s | r.ap.2 | a.apn | | cj | | v.fai.3s | r.ap.2 | a.apn | r.apn | r.ns.1 | | v.aai.1s | | r.dp.2
3836 3950 | 1697 | | 1438 | 7007 | 4246 | | 2779 | | 5703 | 7007 | 4246 | 4005 | 1609 | | 3306 | | 7007

²⁷ Peace | I | leave | with you; | my | peace | I | give | you. | I | do | not | give | to you | as | the | world | gives. | Do not | let
Εἰρήνην | ἐγὼ | ἀφίημι | ὑμῖν | τὴν ἐμὴν | εἰρήνην | → | δίδωμι | ὑμῖν | ἐγὼ | → | οὐ | δίδωμι | ὑμῖν | καθὼς | ὁ | κόσμος | δίδωσιν | → | μὴ | →
n.asf | r.ns.1 | v.pai.1s | r.dp.2 | d.asf r.asf.1 | n.asf | | v.pai.1s | r.dp.2 | r.ns.1 | | pl | v.pai.1s | r.dp.2 | cj | d.nsm | n.nsm | v.pai.3s | | pl |
1645 | 1609 | 918 | 7007 | 3836 1847 | 1645 | | 1443 | 7007 | 1609 | | 4024 | 1443 | 7007 | 2777 | 3836 | 3180 | 1443 | | 5429 3590 | 5429

your | hearts | be troubled | and | do not | be afraid. | ¶ | ²⁸ "You | heard | me | say, | 'I | am going | away | and
ὑμῶν | ἡ | καρδία | → | ταρασσέσθω | → | μηδὲ | δειλιάτω | | ἠκούσατε | ὅτι | ἐγὼ | εἶπον | ὑμῖν | → | ὑπάγω | καὶ
r.gp.2 | d.nsf | n.nsf | | v.ppm.3s | | cj | v.pam.3s | | v.aai.2p | cj | r.ns.1 | v.aai.1s | r.dp.2 | | v.pai.1s | cj
7007 | 3836 | 2840 | | 5429 | 3593 | 1262 | 3593 1262 | | 201 | 4022 | 1609 | 3306 | 7007 | | 5632 | 2779

I | am coming | back | to | you.' | If | you | loved | me, | you | would | be glad | that | I | am going | to | the Father, | for the
→ | → | ἔρχομαι | πρὸς | ὑμᾶς | εἰ | → | ἠγαπᾶτέ | με | → | ἂν | → | ἐχάρητε | ὅτι | → | πορεύομαι | πρὸς | τὸν | πατέρα | ὅτι ὁ
| | v.pmi.1s | p.a | r.ap.2 | cj | | v.iai.2p | r.as.1 | | pl | | v.api.2p | cj | | v.pmi.1s | p.a | d.asm | n.asm | cj d.nsm
| | 2262 | 4639 | 7007 | 1623 | | 26 | 1609 | | 323 | | 5897 | 4022 | | 4513 | 4639 | 3836 | 4252 | 4022 3836

γινώσκετε αὐτό, ὅτι παρ᾽ ὑμῖν μένει καὶ ἐν ὑμῖν ἔσται. ¹⁸ Οὐκ ἀφήσω ὑμᾶς ὀρφανούς, ἔρχομαι πρὸς ὑμᾶς. ¹⁹ ἔτι μικρὸν καὶ ὁ κόσμος με οὐκέτι θεωρεῖ, ὑμεῖς δὲ θεωρεῖτέ με, ὅτι ἐγὼ ζῶ καὶ ὑμεῖς ζήσετε. ²⁰ ἐν ἐκείνῃ τῇ ἡμέρᾳ γνώσεσθε ὑμεῖς ὅτι ἐγὼ ἐν τῷ πατρί μου καὶ ὑμεῖς ἐν ἐμοὶ κἀγὼ ἐν ὑμῖν. ²¹ ὁ ἔχων τὰς ἐντολάς μου καὶ τηρῶν αὐτὰς ἐκεῖνός ἐστιν ὁ ἀγαπῶν με· ὁ δὲ ἀγαπῶν με ἀγαπηθήσεται ὑπὸ τοῦ πατρός μου, κἀγὼ ἀγαπήσω αὐτὸν καὶ ἐμφανίσω αὐτῷ ἐμαυτόν. ¶ ²² Λέγει αὐτῷ Ἰούδας, οὐχ ὁ Ἰσκαριώτης, Κύριε, [καὶ] τί γέγονεν ὅτι ἡμῖν μέλλεις ἐμφανίζειν σεαυτὸν καὶ οὐχὶ τῷ κόσμῳ; ²³ ἀπεκρίθη Ἰησοῦς καὶ εἶπεν αὐτῷ, Ἐάν τις ἀγαπᾷ με τὸν λόγον μου τηρήσει, καὶ ὁ πατήρ μου ἀγαπήσει αὐτὸν καὶ πρὸς αὐτὸν ἐλευσόμεθα καὶ μονὴν παρ᾽ αὐτῷ ποιησόμεθα. ²⁴ ὁ μὴ ἀγαπῶν με τοὺς λόγους μου οὐ τηρεῖ· καὶ ὁ λόγος ὃν ἀκούετε οὐκ ἔστιν ἐμὸς ἀλλὰ τοῦ πέμψαντός με πατρός. ¶ ²⁵ Ταῦτα λελάληκα ὑμῖν παρ᾽ ὑμῖν μένων· ²⁶ ὁ δὲ παράκλητος, τὸ πνεῦμα τὸ ἅγιον, ὃ πέμψει ὁ πατὴρ ἐν τῷ ὀνόματί μου, ἐκεῖνος ὑμᾶς διδάξει πάντα καὶ ὑπομνήσει ὑμᾶς πάντα ἃ εἶπον ὑμῖν [ἐγώ]. ²⁷ Εἰρήνην ἀφίημι ὑμῖν, εἰρήνην τὴν ἐμὴν δίδωμι ὑμῖν· οὐ καθὼς ὁ κόσμος δίδωσιν ἐγὼ δίδωμι ὑμῖν. μὴ ταρασσέσθω ὑμῶν ἡ καρδία μηδὲ δειλιάτω. ¶
²⁸ ἠκούσατε ὅτι ἐγὼ εἶπον ὑμῖν, Ὑπάγω καὶ ἔρχομαι πρὸς ὑμᾶς. εἰ ἠγαπᾶτέ με ἐχάρητε ἂν ὅτι πορεύομαι πρὸς τὸν πατέρα, ὅτι

Father is greater than I. ²⁹ I have told you now before it happens, so that when it does happen you will
πατὴρ ἐστιν μείζων → μού καὶ εἴρηκα ὑμῖν νῦν πρὶν → γενέσθαι ἵνα ← ὅταν → → γένηται →
n.nsm v.pai.3s a.nsm.c r.gs.1 cj v.rai.1s r.dp.2 adv cj f.am cj cj cj v.ams.3s
4252 1639 3489 1609 2779 3306 7007 3814 4570 1181 2671 4020 1181

believe. ³⁰ I will not speak with you much longer, for the prince of this world is coming. He has no hold
πιστεύσητε → → οὐκέτι λαλήσω μεθ' ὑμῶν πολλὰ ← γὰρ ὁ ἄρχων → τοῦ κόσμου ἔρχεται καὶ → οὐκ ἔχει
v.aas.2p adv v.fai.1s p.g r.gp.2 a.apn cj d.nsm n.nsm d.gsm n.gsm v.pmi.3s cj pl v.pai.3s
4409 3281 3281 4033 3281 3552 7007 4498 4033 1142 3836 807 3836 3180 2262 2779 2400 2400 4024 2400

on me, ³¹ but the world must learn that I love the Father and that I do exactly what my Father has
οὐδέν ἐν ἐμοί ἀλλ' ἵνα ὁ κόσμος γνῶ ὅτι → ἀγαπῶ τὸν πατέρα καὶ → ποιῶ καθὼς οὕτως ὁ πατήρ →
a.asn p.d r.ds.1 cj cj d.nsm n.nsm v.aas.3s cj v.pai.1s d.asm n.asm cj v.pai.1s cj adv d.nsm n.nsm
4029 1877 1609 247 2671 3836 3180 1182 4022 26 3836 4252 2779 4472 2777 4048 3836 4252

commanded me. "Come now; let us leave.
ἐνετείλατο μοι ἐγείρεσθε → → ἄγωμεν ἐντεῦθεν
v.ami.3s r.ds.1 v.ppm.2p v.pas.1p adv
1948 1609 1586 72 1949

The Vine and the Branches

^{15:1}"I am the true vine, and my Father is the gardener. ² He cuts off every branch in me
Ἐγώ εἰμι ἡ ἀληθινή ἄμπελος καὶ μου ὁ πατήρ ἐστιν ὁ γεωργός → αἴρει ← αὐτό πᾶν κλῆμα ἐν ἐμοὶ
r.ns.1 v.pai.1s d.nsf d.nsf a.nsf n.nsf cj r.gs.1 d.nsm n.nsm v.pai.3s d.nsm n.nsm v.pai.3s r.asn.3 a.asn n.asn p.d r.ds.1
1609 1639 3836 3836 240 306 2779 1609 3836 4252 1639 3836 1177 149 899 4246 3097 1877 1609

that bears no fruit, while every branch that does bear fruit he prunes so that it will be even more
φέρον μὴ καρπὸν καὶ πᾶν τὸ καρπὸν φέρον → καθαίρει αὐτό ἵνα ← → φέρῃ πλείονα
pt.pa.asn pl n.asm cj a.asn d.asn n.asm pt.pa.asn v.pai.3s r.asn.3 cj v.pas.3s a.asm.c
5770 3590 2843 2779 4246 3836 2843 5770 2748 899 2671 5770 4498

fruitful. ³ You are already clean because of the word I have spoken to you. ⁴ Remain in me, and I will remain
καρπὸν ὑμεῖς ἐστε ἤδη καθαροί διὰ ← τὸν λόγον ὃν → λελάληκα → ὑμῖν μείνατε ἐν ἐμοὶ κἀγὼ ←
n.asm r.np.2 v.pai.2p adv a.npm p.a d.asm n.asm r.asm v.rai.1s r.dp.2 v.aam.2p p.d r.ds.1 crasis
2843 7007 1639 2453 2754 1328 3836 3364 4005 3281 7007 3531 1877 1609 2743

in you. No branch can bear fruit by itself; it must remain in the vine. Neither can you
ἐν ὑμῖν καθὼς οὐ τὸ κλῆμα δύναται φέρειν καρπὸν ἀφ' ἑαυτοῦ ἐὰν μὴ μένῃ ἐν τῇ ἀμπέλῳ οὕτως οὐδὲ ὑμεῖς
p.d r.dp.2 cj pl d.nsn n.nsn v.ppi.3s f.pa n.asm p.g r.gsn.3 cj pl v.pas.3s p.d d.dsf n.dsf adv cj r.np.2
1877 7007 2777 4024 3836 3097 1538 5770 2843 608 1571 1569 3590 3531 1877 3836 306 4048 4028 7007

bear fruit unless you remain in me. ¶ ⁵ "I am the vine; you are the branches. If a man remains in
ἐὰν μὴ → μένητε ἐν ἐμοὶ ἐγώ εἰμι ἡ ἄμπελος ὑμεῖς τὰ κλήματα ὁ μένων ἐν
cj pl v.pas.2p p.d r.ds.1 r.ns.1 v.pai.1s d.nsf n.nsf r.np.2 d.npn n.npn d.nsm pt.pa.nsm p.d
1569 3590 3531 1877 1609 1609 1639 3836 306 7007 3836 3097 3836 3531 1877

me and I in him, he will bear much fruit; apart from me you can do nothing. ⁶ If anyone does
ἐμοὶ κἀγὼ ← ἐν αὐτῷ οὗτος → φέρει πολὺν καρπὸν ὅτι χωρὶς ← ἐμοῦ → οὐ δύνασθε ποιεῖν οὐδέν ἐὰν τις →
r.ds.1 crasis p.d r.dsm.3 r.nsm v.pai.3s a.asm n.asm cj p.g r.gs.1 pl v.ppi.2p f.pa a.asn cj r.nsm
1609 2743 1877 899 4047 5770 4498 2843 4022 6006 1609 1538 4024 1538 4472 4029 1569 5516 3531

not remain in me, he is like a branch that is thrown away and withers; such branches are picked up,
μὴ μένῃ ἐν ἐμοί ὡς τὸ κλῆμα → ἐβλήθη ἔξω καὶ ἐξηράνθη καὶ αὐτὰ ← → συνάγουσιν ← καὶ
pl v.pas.3s p.d r.ds.1 pl d.nsn n.nsn v.api.3s adv cj v.api.3s cj r.apn.3 v.pai.3p cj
3590 3531 1877 1609 6055 3836 3097 965 2032 2779 3830 2779 899 5251 2779

thrown into the fire and burned. ⁷ If you remain in me and my words remain in you, ask whatever you
βάλλουσιν εἰς τὸ πῦρ καὶ καίεται ἐὰν → μείνητε ἐν ἐμοὶ καὶ μου τὰ ῥήματα μείνῃ ἐν ὑμῖν αἰτήσασθε ὃ ἐὰν →
v.pai.3p p.a d.asn n.asn cj v.ppi.3s cj v.aas.2p p.d r.ds.1 cj r.gs.1 d.npn n.npn v.aas.3s p.d r.dp.2 v.amm.2p r.asn cj
965 1650 3836 4786 2779 2794 1569 3531 1877 1609 2779 1609 3836 4839 3531 1877 7007 160 4005 1569

wish, and it will be given you. ⁸ This is to my Father's glory, that you bear much fruit, showing
θέλητε καὶ → → γενήσεται ὑμῖν ἐν τούτῳ μου ὁ πατήρ ἐδοξάσθη ἵνα → φέρητε πολὺν καρπὸν καὶ
v.pas.2p cj v.fmi.3s r.dp.2 p.d r.dsn r.gs.1 d.nsm n.nsm v.api.3s cj v.pas.2p a.asm n.asm cj
2527 2779 1181 7007 1877 4047 1609 3836 4252 1519 2671 5770 4498 2843 2779

yourselves to be my disciples. ¶ ⁹ "As the Father has loved me, so have I loved you. Now
→ → γένεσθε ἐμοὶ μαθηταί Καθὼς ὁ πατήρ → ἠγάπησεν με κἀγὼ → ← ἠγάπησα ὑμᾶς
v.ams.2p a.dsm n.npm cj d.nsm n.nsm v.aai.3s r.as.1 crasis v.aai.1s r.ap.2
1181 1847 3412 2777 3836 4252 26 2743 26 2743 26 7007

ὁ πατὴρ μείζων μού ἐστιν. ²⁹ καὶ νῦν εἴρηκα ὑμῖν πρὶν γενέσθαι, ἵνα ὅταν γένηται πιστεύσητε. ³⁰ οὐκέτι πολλὰ λαλήσω μεθ᾽ ὑμῶν, ἔρχεται γὰρ ὁ τοῦ κόσμου ἄρχων· καὶ ἐν ἐμοὶ οὐκ ἔχει οὐδέν, ³¹ ἀλλ᾽ ἵνα γνῷ ὁ κόσμος ὅτι ἀγαπῶ τὸν πατέρα, καὶ καθὼς ἐνετείλατό μοι ὁ πατήρ, οὕτως ποιῶ. Ἐγείρεσθε, ἄγωμεν ἐντεῦθεν.

¹⁵:¹ Ἐγώ εἰμι ἡ ἄμπελος ἡ ἀληθινὴ καὶ ὁ πατήρ μου ὁ γεωργός ἐστιν. ² πᾶν κλῆμα ἐν ἐμοὶ μὴ φέρον καρπὸν αἴρει αὐτό, καὶ πᾶν τὸ καρπὸν φέρον καθαίρει αὐτὸ ἵνα καρπὸν πλείονα φέρῃ. ³ ἤδη ὑμεῖς καθαροί ἐστε διὰ τὸν λόγον ὃν λελάληκα ὑμῖν· ⁴ μείνατε ἐν ἐμοί, κἀγὼ ἐν ὑμῖν. καθὼς τὸ κλῆμα οὐ δύναται καρπὸν φέρειν ἀφ᾽ ἑαυτοῦ ἐὰν μὴ μένῃ ἐν τῇ ἀμπέλῳ, οὕτως οὐδὲ ὑμεῖς ἐὰν μὴ ἐν ἐμοὶ μένητε. ¶ ⁵ ἐγώ εἰμι ἡ ἄμπελος, ὑμεῖς τὰ κλήματα. ὁ μένων ἐν ἐμοὶ κἀγὼ ἐν αὐτῷ οὗτος φέρει καρπὸν πολύν, ὅτι χωρὶς ἐμοῦ οὐ δύνασθε ποιεῖν οὐδέν. ⁶ ἐὰν μή τις μένῃ ἐν ἐμοί, ἐβλήθη ἔξω ὡς τὸ κλῆμα καὶ ἐξηράνθη καὶ συνάγουσιν αὐτὰ καὶ εἰς τὸ πῦρ βάλλουσιν καὶ καίεται. ⁷ ἐὰν μείνητε ἐν ἐμοὶ καὶ τὰ ῥήματά μου ἐν ὑμῖν μείνῃ, ὃ ἐὰν θέλητε αἰτήσασθε, καὶ γενήσεται ὑμῖν. ⁸ ἐν τούτῳ ἐδοξάσθη ὁ πατήρ μου, ἵνα καρπὸν πολὺν φέρητε καὶ γένησθε ἐμοὶ μαθηταί. ¶ ⁹ καθὼς ἠγάπησεν

remain in my love. **¹⁰ If** you obey my commands, you will remain in my love, just as I have
μείνατε ἐν ⌐τῇ ἐμῇ, ⌐τῇ ἀγάπῃ, ἐὰν → τηρήσητέ μου ⌐τὰς ἐντολάς, → μενεῖτε ἐν μου ⌐τῇ ἀγάπῃ, καθὼς ← ἐγὼ →
v.aam.2p p.d d.dsf d.dsf.1 d.dsf n.dsf cj v.aas.2p r.gs.1 d.apf n.apf v.fai.2p p.d r.gs.1 d.dsf n.dsf cj r.ns.1
3531 1877 3836 1847 3836 27 1569 5498 1609 3836 1953 3531 1877 1609 3836 27 2777 1609

obeyed my Father's commands and remain in his love. **¹¹ I** have told you this so that my
τετήρηκα μου ⌐τοῦ πατρός, ⌐τὰς ἐντολὰς, καὶ μένω ἐν αὐτοῦ.3 ⌐τῇ ἀγάπῃ, → → λελάληκα ὑμῖν Ταῦτα ἵνα ← ⌐ἡ ἐμὴ,
v.rai.1s r.gs.1 d.gsm n.gsm d.apf n.apf cj v.pai.1s p.d r.gsm.3 d.dsf n.dsf v.rai.1s r.dp.2 r.apn cj d.nsf r.nsf.1
5498 1609 3836 4252 3836 1953 2779 3531 1877 899 3836 27 3281 7007 4047 2671 3836 1847

joy may be in you and that your joy may be complete. **¹² My** command is this: Love each
⌐ἡ χαρὰ, → ᾖ ἐν ὑμῖν καὶ ὑμῶν ⌐ἡ χαρὰ, → πληρωθῇ ⌐ἡ ἐμή, ⌐ἡ ἐντολὴ, ἐστίν Αὕτη ἵνα ἀγαπᾶτε ἀλλήλους
d.nsf n.nsf v.pas.3s p.d r.dp.2 cj r.gp.2 d.nsf n.nsf v.aps.3s d.nsf r.nsf.1 d.nsf n.nsf v.pai.3s r.nsf cj v.pas.2p r.apm
3836 5915 1639 1877 7007 2779 7007 3836 5915 4444 3836 1847 3836 1953 1639 4047 2671 26 253

other as I have loved you. **¹³ Greater** love has no one than this, that he lay down his life for
← καθὼς → ἠγάπησα ὑμᾶς μείζονα ἀγάπην ἔχει → οὐδεὶς → ταύτης ἵνα τις θῇ ← αὐτοῦ ⌐τὴν ψυχὴν, ὑπὲρ
cj v.aai.1s r.ap.2 a.asf.c n.asf v.pai.3s a.nsm r.gsf cj r.nsm v.aas.3s r.gsm.3 d.asf n.asf p.g
2777 26 7007 3489 27 2400 4029 4047 2671 5516 5502 899 3836 6034 5642

his friends. **¹⁴ You** are my friends if you do what I command. **¹⁵ I** no longer call you servants,
αὐτοῦ ⌐τῶν φίλων, ὑμεῖς ἐστε μού φίλοι ἐὰν → ποιῆτε ἃ ἐγὼ ἐντέλλομαι ὑμῖν ┌ οὐκέτι ← λέγω ὑμᾶς δούλους,
r.gsm.3 d.gpm a.gpm r.np.2 v.pai.2p r.gs.1 a.npm cj v.pas.2p r.apn r.ns.1 v.pmi.1s r.dp.2 adv v.pai.1s r.ap.2 n.apm
899 3836 5813 7007 1639 1609 5813 1569 4472 4005 1609 1948 7007 3306 4033 3306 7007 1529

because a servant does not know his master's business. Instead, I have called you friends, for everything
ὅτι ὁ δοῦλος, οὐκ οἶδεν τί αὐτοῦ ὁ κύριος, ποιεῖ δὲ → → εἴρηκα ὑμᾶς φίλους, ὅτι πάντα
cj d.nsm n.nsm pl v.rai.3s r.asn r.gsm.3 d.nsm n.nsm v.pai.3s cj v.rai.1s r.ap.2 a.apm cj a.apn
4022 3836 1529 3857 4024 3857 5515 899 3836 3261 4472 1254 3306 7007 5813 4022 4246

that I learned from my Father I have made known to you. **¹⁶ You** did not choose me, but I chose you
ἃ → ἤκουσα παρὰ μου ⌐τοῦ πατρός, → → ἐγνώρισα → ὑμῖν ὑμεῖς ┌ οὐχ ἐξελέξασθε με ἀλλ' ἐγὼ ἐξελεξάμην ὑμᾶς
r.apn v.aai.1s p.g r.gs.1 d.gsm n.gsm v.aai.1s r.dp.2 r.np.2 pl v.ami.2p r.as.1 cj r.ns.1 v.ami.1s r.ap.2
4005 201 4123 1609 3836 4252 1192 7007 7007 1721 4024 1721 1609 247 1609 1721 7007

and appointed you to go and bear fruit → fruit that will last. Then the Father will give
καὶ ἔθηκα ὑμᾶς ἵνα ὑμεῖς ὑπάγητε καὶ φέρητε καρπὸν καὶ ὁ καρπὸς, ὑμῶν μένῃ ἵνα τὸν πατέρα → δῷ
cj v.aai.1s r.ap.2 cj r.np.2 v.pas.2p cj v.pas.2p n.asm cj d.nsm n.nsm r.gp.2 v.pas.3s cj d.asm n.asm v.aas.3s
2779 5502 7007 2671 7007 5632 2779 5770 2843 2779 3836 2843 7007 3531 2671 3836 4252 1443

you whatever you ask in my name. **¹⁷ This** is my command: Love each other.
ὑμῖν ὅ τι ἂν → αἰτήσητε ἐν μου ⌐τῷ ὀνόματι, ταῦτα → ἐντέλλομαι ὑμῖν ἵνα ἀγαπᾶτε ἀλλήλους ←
r.dp.2 r.asn r.asn cj v.aas.2p p.d r.gs.1 d.dsn n.dsn r.apn v.pmi.1s r.dp.2 cj v.pas.2p r.apm
7007 4005 5516 323 160 1877 1609 3836 3950 4047 1948 7007 2671 26 253

The World Hates the Disciples

15:18 "If the world hates you, keep in mind that it hated me first. **¹⁹ If** you belonged to the world,
Εἰ ὁ κόσμος μισεῖ ὑμᾶς → γινώσκετε ὅτι → μεμίσηκεν ἐμὲ πρῶτον ὑμῶν εἰ → ἦτε ἐκ τοῦ κόσμου
cj d.nsm n.nsm v.pai.3s r.ap.2 v.pai.2p cj v.rai.3s r.as.1 adv r.gp.2 cj v.iai.2p p.g d.gsm n.gsm
1623 3836 3180 3631 7007 1182 4022 3631 1609 4754 7007 1623 1639 1666 3836 3180

it would love you as its own. *As it is,* you do not belong to the world, but I have chosen you
⌐ὁ κόσμος, ἂν ἐφίλει τὸ ἴδιον ὅτι δὲ → οὐκ ἐστὲ ἐκ τοῦ κόσμου ἀλλ' ἐγὼ → ἐξελεξάμην ὑμᾶς
d.nsm n.nsm pl v.iai.3s d.asn a.asn cj cj pl v.pai.2p p.g d.gsm n.gsm cj r.ns.1 v.ami.1s r.ap.2
3836 3180 323 5797 3836 2625 4022 1254 1639 1639 4024 1639 1666 3836 3180 247 1609 1721 7007

out of the world. *That is why* the world hates you. **²⁰ Remember** the words I spoke to you: 'No servant is
ἐκ ⌐τοῦ κόσμου, διὰ τοῦτο, ὁ κόσμος μισεῖ ὑμᾶς μνημονεύετε τοῦ λόγου οὗ ἐγὼ εἶπον → ὑμῖν οὐκ δοῦλος ἔστιν
p.g d.gsm n.gsm p.a r.asn d.nsm n.nsm v.pai.3s r.ap.2 v.pam.2p d.gsm n.gsm r.gsm r.ns.1 v.aai.1s r.dp.2 pl n.nsm v.pai.3s
1666 3836 3180 1328 4047 3836 3180 3631 7007 3648 3836 3364 4005 1609 3306 7007 4024 1529 1639

greater than his master.' If they persecuted me, they will persecute you also. If they obeyed my teaching,
μείζων → αὐτοῦ ⌐τοῦ κυρίου, εἰ → ἐδίωξαν ἐμὲ → διώξουσιν ὑμᾶς καὶ εἰ → ἐτήρησαν μου ⌐τὸν λόγον,
a.nsm.c r.gsm.3 d.gsm n.gsm cj v.aai.3p r.as.1 v.fai.3p r.ap.2 adv cj v.aai.3p r.gs.1 d.asm n.asm
3489 3261 899 3836 3261 1623 1503 1609 1503 7007 2779 1623 5498 1609 3836 3364

they will obey yours also. **²¹** They will treat you *this way* because of my name, for they
→ τηρήσουσιν ⌐τὸν ὑμέτερον, καὶ ἀλλὰ → ποιήσουσιν εἰς ὑμᾶς ταῦτα πάντα διὰ ← μου ⌐τὸ ὄνομα, ὅτι →
v.fai.3p d.asm r.asm.2 adv cj v.fai.3p p.a r.ap.2 r.apn a.apn p.a r.gs.1 d.asn n.asn cj
5498 3836 5629 2779 247 4472 1650 7007 4047 4246 1328 1609 3836 3950 4022 3857

με ὁ πατήρ, κἀγὼ ὑμᾶς ἠγάπησα· μείνατε ἐν τῇ ἀγάπῃ τῇ ἐμῇ. ¹⁰ ἐὰν τὰς ἐντολάς μου τηρήσητε, μενεῖτε ἐν τῇ ἀγάπῃ μου, καθὼς ἐγὼ τὰς ἐντολὰς τοῦ πατρός μου τετήρηκα καὶ μένω αὐτοῦ ἐν τῇ ἀγάπῃ. ¹¹ Ταῦτα λελάληκα ὑμῖν ἵνα ἡ χαρὰ ἡ ἐμὴ ἐν ὑμῖν ᾖ καὶ ἡ χαρὰ ὑμῶν πληρωθῇ. ¹² αὕτη ἐστὶν ἡ ἐντολὴ ἡ ἐμή, ἵνα ἀγαπᾶτε ἀλλήλους καθὼς ἠγάπησα ὑμᾶς. ¹³ μείζονα ταύτης ἀγάπην οὐδεὶς ἔχει, ἵνα τις τὴν ψυχὴν αὐτοῦ θῇ ὑπὲρ τῶν φίλων αὐτοῦ. ¹⁴ ὑμεῖς φίλοι μού ἐστε ἐὰν ποιῆτε ἃ ἐγὼ ἐντέλλομαι ὑμῖν. ¹⁵ οὐκέτι λέγω ὑμᾶς δούλους, ὅτι ὁ δοῦλος οὐκ οἶδεν τί ποιεῖ αὐτοῦ ὁ κύριος· ὑμᾶς δὲ εἴρηκα φίλους, ὅτι πάντα ἃ ἤκουσα παρὰ τοῦ πατρός μου ἐγνώρισα ὑμῖν. ¹⁶ οὐχ ὑμεῖς με ἐξελέξασθε, ἀλλ' ἐγὼ ἐξελεξάμην ὑμᾶς καὶ ἔθηκα ὑμᾶς ἵνα ὑμεῖς ὑπάγητε καὶ καρπὸν φέρητε καὶ ὁ καρπὸς ὑμῶν μένῃ, ἵνα ὅ τι ἂν αἰτήσητε τὸν πατέρα ἐν τῷ ὀνόματί μου δῷ ὑμῖν. ¹⁷ ταῦτα ἐντέλλομαι ὑμῖν, ἵνα ἀγαπᾶτε ἀλλήλους.

15:18 Εἰ ὁ κόσμος ὑμᾶς μισεῖ, γινώσκετε ὅτι ἐμὲ πρῶτον ὑμῶν μεμίσηκεν. ¹⁹ εἰ ἐκ τοῦ κόσμου ἦτε, ὁ κόσμος ἂν τὸ ἴδιον ἐφίλει· ὅτι δὲ ἐκ τοῦ κόσμου οὐκ ἐστέ, ἀλλ' ἐγὼ ἐξελεξάμην ὑμᾶς ἐκ τοῦ κόσμου, διὰ τοῦτο μισεῖ ὑμᾶς ὁ κόσμος. ²⁰ μνημονεύετε τοῦ λόγου οὗ ἐγὼ εἶπον ὑμῖν, Οὐκ ἔστιν δοῦλος μείζων τοῦ κυρίου αὐτοῦ. εἰ ἐμὲ ἐδίωξαν, καὶ ὑμᾶς διώξουσιν· εἰ τὸν λόγον μου ἐτήρησαν, καὶ τὸν ὑμέτερον τηρήσουσιν. ²¹ ἀλλὰ ταῦτα πάντα ποιήσουσιν εἰς ὑμᾶς διὰ τὸ ὄνομά μου, ὅτι οὐκ οἴδασιν

do not know   the One who sent   me. ²² If I   had not come and spoken to them, they would not be guilty of
οὐκ οἴδασιν   τὸν   πέμψαντα με   εἰ   μὴ ἦλθον καὶ ἐλάλησα → αὐτοῖς   οὐκ → εἴχοσαν
pl v.rai.3p   d.asm   pt.aa.asm r.as.1 cj   pl v.aai.1s cj v.aai.1s   r.dpm.3   pl   v.iai.3p
3857 4024   3857   4287   1609   1623   2262 2262   2779 3281   899   4024 2400

sin.   Now, however, they have   no excuse   for their sin.   ²³ He who hates   me hates my Father   as   and
ἁμαρτίαν νῦν   δὲ   → ἔχουσιν   οὐκ πρόφασιν περὶ αὐτῶν ‹τῆς ἁμαρτίας›   ὁ   ← μισῶν   ἐμὲ μισεῖ μου ‹τὸν πατέρα› καὶ
n.asf   adv   cj   v.pai.3p pl n.asf   p.g r.gpn.3 d.gsf n.gsf   d.nsm   pt.pa.nsm r.as.1 v.pai.3s r.gs.1 d.asm n.asm cj
281   3814   1254   2400   4024 4733   4309 899   3836 281   3836   3631   1609 3631   1609 3836 4252   2779

well. ²⁴ If I had not done   among them what no one else did,   they would not be guilty of sin.
        εἰ   μὴ ἐποίησα τὰ ἔργα   ἐν   αὐτοῖς ἃ   → οὐδεὶς ἄλλος ἐποίησεν   οὐκ → εἴχοσαν ← ἁμαρτίαν
        cj   pl v.aai.1s d.apn n.apn p.d r.dpm.3 r.apn   a.nsm r.nsm v.aai.3s   pl   v.iai.3p   n.asf
        1623   4472 4472   3590 4472 1877 899   4005   4029   257   4472   4024 2400   281

But now they have   seen   these miracles, and yet they have hated   both me and my Father.   ²⁵ But
δὲ νῦν → →   καὶ ἑωράκασιν ←   καὶ   → →   μεμισήκασιν καὶ ἐμὲ καὶ μου ‹τὸν πατέρα› ἀλλ᾽ ἵνα
cj adv   καὶ v.rai.3p   cj   v.rai.3p   cj r.as.1 cj r.gs.1 d.asm n.asm cj   cj
1254 3814   2779 3972   2779   3631   2779 1609 2779 1609 3836 4252 247 2671

this is to fulfill what   is written   in their Law: 'They hated   me without reason.'   ¶
πληρωθῇ ὁ λόγος,   ὁ   γεγραμμένος,   ἐν   αὐτῶν ‹τῷ νόμῳ› ὅτι   ἐμίσησάν με →   δωρεάν
v.aps.3s d.nsm n.nsm   d.nsm pt.rp.nsm   p.d r.gpn.3 d.dsm n.dsm cj   v.aai.3p r.as.1   adv
4444   3836 3364   3836 1211   1877 899   3836 3795   4022 3631   1609   1562

²⁶ "When the Counselor comes, whom I   will send to you from the Father, the Spirit of truth   who goes
Ὅταν ὁ παράκλητος ἔλθη   ὃν ἐγὼ →   πέμψω → ὑμῖν παρὰ τοῦ πατρός τὸ πνεῦμα → ‹τῆς ἀληθείας› ὃ   ἐκπορεύεται
cj   d.nsm n.nsm   v.aas.3s r.asm r.ns.1   v.fai.1s r.dp.2 p.g d.gsm n.gsm d.nsn n.nsn   d.gsf n.gsf   r.nsn v.pmi.3s
4020 3836 4156   2262   4005 1609   4287   7007 4123 3836 4252   3836 4460   3836 237   4005 1744

out from the Father, he   will testify about me. ²⁷ And you also must testify, for you have been with me from
← παρὰ τοῦ πατρός ἐκεῖνος → μαρτυρήσει περὶ ἐμοῦ   δὲ ὑμεῖς καὶ   μαρτυρεῖτε ὅτι → → ἐστε μετ᾽ ἐμοῦ ἀπ᾽
  p.g d.gsm n.gsm r.nsm   v.fai.3s   p.g r.gs.1   cj r.np.2 adv   v.pai.2p cj   v.pai.2p p.g r.gs.1 p.g
  4123 3836 4252   1697   3455   4309 1609   1254 7007 2779   3455   4022   1639 3552 1609 608

the beginning. ¶   ^{16:1} All this I have told   you so that you will not go astray. ² They will put   you
ἀρχῆς   Ταῦτα →   λελάληκα ὑμῖν ἵνα ← →   μὴ σκανδαλισθῆτε   ποιήσουσιν ὑμᾶς
n.gsf   r.apn   v.rai.1s r.dp.2 cj   pl v.aps.2p   v.fai.3p   r.ap.2
794   4047   3281   7007 2671 4997 4997 3590 4997   4472   7007

out of the synagogue;   in fact, a time is coming when anyone who kills   you will think he is offering   a
→ → ἀποσυναγώγους ἀλλ᾽ ← ὥρα ἔρχεται ἵνα πᾶς ὁ ἀποκτείνας ὑμᾶς → δόξῃ   προσφέρειν
   a.apm   cj   n.nsf v.pmi.3s cj a.nsm d.nsm pt.aa.nsm r.ap.2   v.aas.3s f.pa
   697   247   6052 2262   2671 4246 3836 650   7007   1506   4712

service to God. ³ They will do   such things because they have not known the Father or me. ⁴ I
λατρείαν ‹τῷ θεῷ› καὶ → ποιήσουσιν → ταῦτα ὅτι   οὐκ ἔγνωσαν τὸν πατέρα οὐδὲ ἐμέ ἀλλὰ
n.asf   d.dsm n.dsm cj   v.fai.3p   r.apn cj   pl v.aai.3p d.asm n.asm r.as.1   cj
3301   3836 2536   2779   4472   4047 4022   4024 1182   3836 4252 4028 1609   247
                                                  1182 1182

have told   you this, so that when the time   comes you will remember   that I warned you.   I
→ λελάληκα ὑμῖν ταῦτα ἵνα ← ὅταν ἡ ὥρα αὐτῶν ἔλθη → → μνημονεύητε αὐτῶν ὅτι ἐγὼ εἶπον ὑμῖν δὲ →
  v.rai.1s r.dp.2 r.apn cj   cj   d.nsf n.nsf r.gpn.3 v.aas.3s   v.pas.2p   r.gpn.3 cj r.ns.1 v.aai.1s r.dp.2 cj
  3281   7007 4047 2671   4020 3836 6052 899   2262   3648   899   4022 1609 3306 7007 1254 3306

did not tell   you this at first because I was with you.
οὐκ εἶπον ὑμῖν Ταῦτα ἐξ ἀρχῆς ὅτι → ἤμην μεθ᾽ ὑμῶν
pl v.aai.1s r.dp.2 r.apn p.g n.gsf cj   v.imi.1s p.g r.gp.2
3306 4024   3306 7007 4047 1666 794 4022 1639 3552 7007

The Work of the Holy Spirit

^{16:5} "Now I am going to   him who sent   me, yet none of you asks me, 'Where are you going?' ⁶
δὲ Νῦν → ὑπάγω πρὸς τὸν   πέμψαντα με καὶ οὐδεὶς ἐξ ὑμῶν ἐρωτᾷ με   ποῦ   → ὑπάγεις ἀλλ᾽
cj adv   v.pai.1s p.a d.asm   pt.aa.asm r.as.1 cj a.nsm p.g r.gp.2 v.pai.3s r.as.1 adv   v.pai.2s cj
1254 3814 5632 4639 3836   4287   1609 2779 4029   1666 7007 4543 1609 2263   5632   247

Because I have said   these things,   you   are filled   with grief.   ⁷ But I tell you the
ὅτι → → λελάληκα ταῦτα ← ὑμῖν ‹ὑμῶν τὴν καρδίαν›   πεπλήρωκεν ← ‹ἡ λύπη› ἀλλ᾽ ἐγὼ λέγω ὑμῖν τὴν
cj   v.rai.1s r.apn   r.dp.2 r.gp.2 d.asf n.asf   v.rai.3s   d.nsf n.nsf cj   r.ns.1 v.pai.1s r.dp.2 d.asf
4022   3281   4047   7007 7007 3836 2840   4444   3836 3383 247 1609 3306 7007 3836

τὸν πέμψαντά με. ²² εἰ μὴ ἦλθον καὶ ἐλάλησα αὐτοῖς, ἁμαρτίαν οὐκ εἴχοσαν· νῦν δὲ πρόφασιν οὐκ ἔχουσιν περὶ τῆς ἁμαρτίας αὐτῶν. ²³ ὁ ἐμὲ μισῶν καὶ τὸν πατέρα μου μισεῖ. ²⁴ εἰ τὰ ἔργα μὴ ἐποίησα ἐν αὐτοῖς ἃ οὐδεὶς ἄλλος ἐποίησεν, ἁμαρτίαν οὐκ εἴχοσαν· νῦν δὲ καὶ ἑωράκασιν καὶ μεμισήκασιν καὶ ἐμὲ καὶ τὸν πατέρα μου. ²⁵ ἀλλ᾽ ἵνα πληρωθῇ ὁ λόγος ὁ ἐν τῷ νόμῳ αὐτῶν γεγραμμένος ὅτι Ἐμίσησάν με δωρεάν. ¶ ²⁶ Ὅταν ἔλθη ὁ παράκλητος ὃν ἐγὼ πέμψω ὑμῖν παρὰ τοῦ πατρός, τὸ πνεῦμα τῆς ἀληθείας ὃ παρὰ τοῦ πατρὸς ἐκπορεύεται, ἐκεῖνος μαρτυρήσει περὶ ἐμοῦ· ²⁷ καὶ ὑμεῖς δὲ μαρτυρεῖτε, ὅτι ἀπ᾽ ἀρχῆς μετ᾽ ἐμοῦ ἐστε.

¹⁶:¹ Ταῦτα λελάληκα ὑμῖν ἵνα μὴ σκανδαλισθῆτε. ² ἀποσυναγώγους ποιήσουσιν ὑμᾶς· ἀλλ᾽ ἔρχεται ὥρα ἵνα πᾶς ὁ ἀποκτείνας ὑμᾶς δόξῃ λατρείαν προσφέρειν τῷ θεῷ. ³ καὶ ταῦτα ποιήσουσιν ὅτι οὐκ ἔγνωσαν τὸν πατέρα οὐδὲ ἐμέ. ⁴ ἀλλὰ ταῦτα λελάληκα ὑμῖν ἵνα ὅταν ἔλθη ἡ ὥρα αὐτῶν μνημονεύητε αὐτῶν ὅτι ἐγὼ εἶπον ὑμῖν. Ταῦτα δὲ ὑμῖν ἐξ ἀρχῆς οὐκ εἶπον, ὅτι μεθ᾽ ὑμῶν ἤμην.

¹⁶:⁵ νῦν δὲ ὑπάγω πρὸς τὸν πέμψαντά με, καὶ οὐδεὶς ἐξ ὑμῶν ἐρωτᾷ με, Ποῦ ὑπάγεις; ⁶ ἀλλ᾽ ὅτι ταῦτα λελάληκα ὑμῖν ἡ λύπη πεπλήρωκεν ὑμῶν τὴν καρδίαν. ⁷ ἀλλ᾽ ἐγὼ τὴν ἀλήθειαν λέγω ὑμῖν, συμφέρει ὑμῖν ἵνα ἐγὼ ἀπέλθω. ἐὰν γὰρ μὴ ἀπέλθω,

truth: It is for your good that I am going away.   Unless I go   away, the Counselor will not come
ἀλήθειαν → → ὑμῖν συμφέρει ἵνα ἐγὼ → ἀπέλθω   γὰρ ἐὰν μὴ → ἀπέλθω   ὁ παράκλητος → οὐκ ἐλεύσεται
n.asf   r.dp.2 v.pai.3s cj r.ns.1 v.aas.1s   cj cj pl v.aas.1s   d.nsm n.nsm   pl v.fmi.3s
237   5237 5237 7007 5237 2671 1609 599   1142 1569 3590 599   3836 4156   2262 4024 2262

to you; but if I go,   I will send him to you. ⁸ When he comes, he will convict the world of guilt
πρὸς ὑμᾶς δὲ ἐὰν → πορευθῶ → πέμψω αὐτὸν πρὸς ὑμᾶς καὶ → → ἐλθὼν ἐκεῖνος → ἐλέγξει τὸν κόσμον
p.a r.ap.2 1254 1569 v.aps.1s v.fai.1s r.asm.3 p.a r.ap.2 2779 pt.aa.nsm r.nsm v.fai.3s d.asm n.asm
4639 7007 1254 1569 4513 4287 899 4639 7007 2779 2262 1697 1794 3836 3180

in regard to sin   and   righteousness and   judgment: ⁹ in regard to sin,   because men do not
περὶ ← ἁμαρτίας καὶ περὶ δικαιοσύνης καὶ περὶ κρίσεως μέν περὶ ← ἁμαρτίας ὅτι   οὐ
p.g n.gsf cj p.g n.gsf cj p.g n.gsf pl p.g n.gsf ὅτι pl
4309 281 2779 4309 1466 2779 4309 3213 3525 4309 281 4022 4409 4024

believe in me; ¹⁰ in regard to righteousness, because I am going to the Father,   where you can see
πιστεύουσιν εἰς ἐμέ δὲ περὶ ← δικαιοσύνης ὅτι → ὑπάγω πρὸς τὸν πατέρα καὶ → → θεωρεῖτε
v.pai.3p p.a r.as.1 cj p.g n.gsf cj v.pai.1s p.a d.asm n.asm cj v.pai.2p
4409 1650 1473 1254 4309 1466 4022 5632 4639 3836 4252 2779 2555

me no longer; ¹¹ and in regard to judgment, because the prince of this   world   now stands condemned. ¶
με οὐκέτι ← δὲ περὶ ← κρίσεως ὅτι ὁ ἄρχων τούτου τοῦ κόσμου   κέκριται
r.as.1 adv cj p.g n.gsf ὅτι d.nsm n.nsm r.gsm r.gsm n.gsm   v.rpi.3s
1609 4033 1254 4309 3213 4022 3836 807 3180 4047 3836 3180   3212

¹² "I have much more to say to you, more than you can   now bear. ¹³ But when he,   the Spirit of
Ἔτι → ἔχω → πολλὰ → λέγειν → ὑμῖν ἀλλ' οὐ → δύνασθε ἄρτι βαστάζειν δὲ ὅταν ἐκεῖνος τὸ πνεῦμα
adv v.pai.1s a.apn f.pa r.dp.2 cj pl v.ppi.2p adv f.pa cj cj r.nsm d.nsn n.nsn
2285 2400 4498 3306 7007 247 4024 1538 785 1002 1254 4020 1697 3836 4460

truth,   comes, he will guide you into all truth.   He will not speak on his   own;   he will
ιτῆς ἀληθείαςι ἔλθῃ → → ὁδηγήσει ὑμᾶς ἐν πάσῃ ιτῇ ἀληθείαι γὰρ → → οὐ λαλήσει ἀφ' ἑαυτοῦ← ἀλλ'
d.gsf n.gsf v.aas.3s v.fai.3s r.ap.2 p.d a.dsf d.dsf n.dsf cj pl v.fai.3s p.g r.gsm.3 cj
3836 237 2262 3842 7007 1877 4246 3836 237 1142 3281 3281 4024 3281 608 1571 247

speak only what he hears, and he will tell   you what is yet to come. ¹⁴ He will bring glory to me by
λαλήσει ὅσα → ἀκούσει καὶ → → ἀναγγελεῖ ὑμῖν τὰ → → ἐρχόμενα ἐκεῖνος → → δοξάσει → ἐμὲ ὅτι
v.fai.3s r.apn v.fai.3s cj v.fai.3s r.dp.2 d.apn pt.pm.apn r.nsm v.fai.3s r.as.1 cj
3281 4012 201 2779 334 7007 3836 2262 1697 1519 1609 4022

taking from what is mine and making it known   to you. ¹⁵ All   that belongs to the Father is   mine. That   is
λήμψεται ἐκ τοῦ ἐμοῦ καὶ → ἀναγγελεῖ ὑμῖν πάντα ὅσα ἔχει ← ὁ πατὴρ ἐστιν ἐμά ιδιὰ τοῦτοι
v.fmi.3s p.g d.gsn r.gsn.1 cj v.fai.3s r.dp.2 a.npn r.apn v.pai.3s d.nsm n.nsm v.pai.3s r.npn.1 p.a r.asn
3284 1666 3836 1847 2779 334 7007 4246 4012 2400 3836 4252 1639 1847 1328 4047

why I said   the Spirit will take   from what is mine and make it known   to you. ¶ ¹⁶ "In a little   while
εἶπον ὅτι → λαμβάνει ἐκ τοῦ ἐμοῦ καὶ → ἀναγγελεῖ → ὑμῖν → Μικρὸν
v.aai.1s cj v.pai.3s p.g d.gsn r.gsn.1 cj v.fai.3s r.dp.2 a.asn
3306 4022 3284 1666 3836 1847 2779 334 7007 3625

you will see   me no   more, and then after a little   while   you will see   me."
καὶ → θεωρεῖτε με οὐκέτι ← καὶ πάλιν → μικρὸν καὶ → ὄψεσθέ με
cj v.pai.2p r.as.1 adv cj adv a.asn cj v.fmi.2p r.as.1
2779 2555 1609 4033 2779 4099 3625 2779 3972 1609

The Disciples' Grief Will Turn to Joy

¹⁶:¹⁷ Some of his   disciples   said to one   another, "What does he mean   by saying,   'In a
οὖν ἐκ αὐτοῦ ιτῶν μαθητῶνι εἶπαν πρὸς ἀλλήλους ← τί   ιἐστιν τοῦτοι ὃ λέγει ἡμῖν → →
cj p.g r.gsm.3 d.gpm n.gpm v.aai.3p p.a r.apm r.nsn v.pai.3s r.nsn r.asn v.pai.3s r.dp.1
4036 1666 899 3836 3412 3306 4639 253 5515 1639 4047 4005 3306 7005

little while   you will see   me no more, and then after a little   while   you will see   me,' and 'Because I
μικρὸν ← καὶ → θεωρεῖτε με οὐ καὶ πάλιν → μικρὸν καὶ → ὄψεσθέ με καὶ ὅτι
a.asn cj v.pai.2p r.as.1 pl cj adv a.asn cj v.fmi.2p r.as.1 cj cj
3625 2779 2555 1609 4024 2779 4099 3625 2779 3972 1609 2779 4022

am going to   the Father'?" ¹⁸ They kept asking, "What does he mean   by   'a little   while'? We don't
→ ὑπάγω πρὸς τὸν πατέρα οὖν → ἔλεγον τί   ιἐστιν τοῦτοι ὃ λέγει ιτὸ μικρόνι ← → οὐκ
v.pai.1s p.a d.asm n.asm cj v.iai.3p r.nsn v.pai.3s r.nsn r.asn v.pai.3s d.nsn a.asn pl
5632 4639 3836 4252 4036 3306 5515 1639 4047 4005 3306 3836 3625 3857 4024

ὁ παράκλητος οὐκ ἐλεύσεται πρὸς ὑμᾶς· ἐὰν δὲ πορευθῶ, πέμψω αὐτὸν πρὸς ὑμᾶς. ⁸ καὶ ἐλθὼν ἐκεῖνος ἐλέγξει τὸν κόσμον περὶ ἁμαρτίας καὶ περὶ δικαιοσύνης καὶ περὶ κρίσεως· ⁹ περὶ ἁμαρτίας μέν, ὅτι οὐ πιστεύουσιν εἰς ἐμέ· ¹⁰ περὶ δικαιοσύνης δέ, ὅτι πρὸς τὸν πατέρα ὑπάγω καὶ οὐκέτι θεωρεῖτέ με· ¹¹ περὶ δὲ κρίσεως, ὅτι ὁ ἄρχων τοῦ κόσμου τούτου κέκριται. ¶ ¹² Ἔτι πολλὰ ἔχω ὑμῖν λέγειν, ἀλλ' οὐ δύνασθε βαστάζειν ἄρτι· ¹³ ὅταν δὲ ἔλθῃ ἐκεῖνος, τὸ πνεῦμα τῆς ἀληθείας, ὁδηγήσει ὑμᾶς ἐν τῇ ἀληθείᾳ πάσῃ· οὐ γὰρ λαλήσει ἀφ' ἑαυτοῦ, ἀλλ' ὅσα ἀκούσει λαλήσει καὶ τὰ ἐρχόμενα ἀναγγελεῖ ὑμῖν. ¹⁴ ἐκεῖνος ἐμὲ δοξάσει, ὅτι ἐκ τοῦ ἐμοῦ λήμψεται καὶ ἀναγγελεῖ ὑμῖν. ¹⁵ πάντα ὅσα ἔχει ὁ πατὴρ ἐμά ἐστιν· διὰ τοῦτο εἶπον ὅτι ἐκ τοῦ ἐμοῦ λαμβάνει καὶ ἀναγγελεῖ ὑμῖν. ¶ ¹⁶ Μικρὸν καὶ οὐκέτι θεωρεῖτέ με, καὶ πάλιν μικρὸν καὶ ὄψεσθέ με.

¹⁶:¹⁷ εἶπαν οὖν ἐκ τῶν μαθητῶν αὐτοῦ πρὸς ἀλλήλους, Τί ἐστιν τοῦτο ὃ λέγει ἡμῖν, Μικρὸν καὶ οὐ θεωρεῖτέ με, καὶ πάλιν μικρὸν καὶ ὄψεσθέ με; καί, Ὅτι ὑπάγω πρὸς τὸν πατέρα; ¹⁸ ἔλεγον οὖν, Τί ἐστιν τοῦτο [ὃ λέγει], τὸ μικρόν; οὐκ οἴδαμεν τί

understand what he is saying." ¶ **19** Jesus   saw that they wanted to ask him about this, so he said to
οἴδαμεν τί → → λαλεῖ ὁ Ἰησοῦς Ἔγνω ὅτι → ἤθελον → ἐρωτᾶν αὐτὸν καὶ → εἶπεν
v.rai.1p r.nsn v.pai.3s d.nsm n.nsm v.aai.3s cj v.iai.3p f.pa r.asm.3 cj v.aai.3s
3857 5515 3281 3836 2652 1182 4022 2527 2263 899 2779 3306

them, "Are you asking one another what I meant when I said, 'In a little while you will see
αὐτοῖς → → ζητεῖτε μετ' ἀλλήλων ← περὶ τούτου ὅτι → εἶπον → μικρὸν ← καὶ → θεωρεῖτε
r.dpm.3 v.pai.2p p.g r.gpm p.g r.gsn cj v.aai.1s a.asn cj v.pai.2p
899 2426 3552 253 4309 4047 4022 3306 3625 2779 2555

me no more, and then after a little while you will see me'? **20** I tell you the truth, you will weep
με οὐ ← καὶ πάλιν → μικρὸν καὶ → ὄψεσθε με → λέγω ὑμῖν ἀμὴν ἀμὴν ὅτι ὑμεῖς → κλαύσετε
r.as.1 pl cj adv a.asn cj v.fmi.2p r.as.1 v.pai.1s r.dp.2 pl pl cj r.np.2 v.fai.2p
1609 4024 2779 4099 3625 2779 3972 1609 3306 7007 297 297 4022 7007 3081

and mourn while the world rejoices. You will grieve, but your grief will turn to joy. **21** A woman
καὶ θρηνήσετε δὲ ὁ κόσμος χαρήσεται ὑμεῖς → λυπηθήσεσθε ἀλλ' ὑμῶν ἡ λύπη → γενήσεται εἰς χαρὰν ἡ γυνὴ ὅταν
cj v.fai.2p cj d.nsm n.nsm v.fpi.3s r.np.2 v.fpi.2p cj r.gp.2 d.nsf n.nsf v.fmi.3s p.a n.asf d.nsf n.nsf cj
2779 2577 1254 3836 3180 5897 7007 3382 247 7007 3836 3383 1181 1650 5915 3836 1222 4020

giving birth to a child has pain because her time has come; but when her baby is born she
→ τίκτῃ ἔχει λύπην ὅτι αὐτῆς ἡ ὥρα → ἦλθεν δὲ ὅταν τὸ παιδίον → γεννήσῃ →
v.pas.3s v.pai.3s n.asf cj r.gsf.3 d.nsf n.nsf v.aai.3s cj cj d.asn n.asn v.aas.3s
5503 2400 3383 4022 899 3836 6052 2262 1254 4020 3836 4086 1164

forgets the anguish because of her joy that a child is born into the world. **22** So with you:
οὐκέτι μνημονεύει τῆς θλίψεως διὰ ← τὴν χαρὰν ὅτι ἄνθρωπος → ἐγεννήθη εἰς τὸν κόσμον οὖν καὶ ὑμεῖς μὲν
adv v.pai.3s d.gsf n.gsf p.a d.asf n.asf cj n.nsm v.api.3s p.a d.asm n.asm cj cj r.np.2 pl
4033 3648 3836 2568 1328 3836 5915 4022 476 1164 1650 3836 3180 4036 2779 7007 3525

Now *is your time of* grief, but I will see you again and you will rejoice, and no one will take
νῦν ἔχετε λύπην δὲ → ὄψομαι ὑμᾶς πάλιν καὶ ὑμῶν ἡ καρδία → χαρήσεται καὶ → οὐδεὶς → αἴρει
adv v.pai.2p n.asf cj v.fmi.1s r.ap.2 adv cj r.gp.2 d.nsf n.nsf v.fpi.3s cj a.nsm v.pai.3s
3814 2400 3383 1254 3972 7007 4099 2779 7007 3836 2840 5897 2779 4029 149

away your joy. **23** In that day you will no longer ask me anything. I tell you the
← ἀφ' ὑμῶν ὑμῶν τὴν χαρὰν Καὶ ἐν ἐκείνῃ τῇ ἡμέρᾳ → → οὐκ ← ἐρωτήσετε ἐμὲ οὐδέν → λέγω ὑμῖν
p.g r.gp.2 r.gp.2 d.asf n.asf cj p.d r.dsf d.dsf n.dsf pl v.fai.2p r.as.1 a.asn v.pai.1s r.dp.2
608 7007 7007 3836 5915 2779 1877 1697 3836 2465 2263 2263 4024 2263 1609 4029 3306 7007

truth, my Father will give you whatever you ask in my name. **24** Until now you have not asked for
ἀμὴν ἀμὴν τὸν πατέρα → δώσει ὑμῖν ἄν τι → αἰτήσητε ἐν μου τῷ ὀνόματι ἕως ἄρτι → → οὐκ ἠτήσατε ←
pl pl d.asm n.asm v.fai.3s r.dp.2 cj r.asn v.aas.2p p.d r.gs.1 d.dsn n.dsn p.g adv pl v.aai.2p
297 297 3836 4252 1443 7007 323 5516 160 1877 1609 3836 3950 2401 785 160 160 4024 160

anything in my name. Ask and you will receive, and your joy will be complete. ¶ **25** "Though I
οὐδὲν ἐν μου τῷ ὀνόματι αἰτεῖτε καὶ → → λήμψεσθε ἵνα ὑμῶν ἡ χαρὰ → ᾖ πεπληρωμένη →
a.asn p.d r.gs.1 d.dsn n.dsn v.pam.2p cj v.fmi.2p cj r.gp.2 d.nsf n.nsf v.pas.3s pt.rp.nsf
4029 1877 1609 3836 3950 160 2779 3284 2671 7007 3836 5915 1639 4444

have been speaking figuratively, a time is coming when I will no longer use *this kind of*
λελάληκα Ταῦτα ἐν παροιμίαις ὑμῖν ὥρα → ἔρχεται ὅτε → → οὐκέτι → λαλήσω ὑμῖν
v.rai.1s r.apn p.d n.dpf r.dp.2 n.nsf v.pmi.3s cj adv v.fai.1s r.dp.2
3281 4047 1877 4231 7007 6052 2262 4021 3281 3281 4033 3281 7007

language but will tell you plainly about my Father. **26** In that day you will ask in my
ἐν παροιμίαις ἀλλὰ → ἀπαγγελῶ ὑμῖν παρρησίᾳ περὶ τοῦ πατρός ἐν ἐκείνῃ τῇ ἡμέρᾳ αἰτήσεσθε ἐν μου
p.d n.dpf cj v.fai.1s r.dp.2 n.dsf p.g d.gsm n.gsm p.d r.dsf d.dsf n.dsf v.fmi.2p p.d r.gs.1
1877 4231 247 550 7007 4244 4309 3836 4252 1877 1697 3836 2465 160 1877 1609

name. I am not saying that I will ask the Father on your behalf. **27** No, the Father himself loves
τῷ ὀνόματι καὶ → οὐ λέγω ὑμῖν ὅτι ἐγὼ → ἐρωτήσω τὸν πατέρα περὶ ὑμῶν γὰρ ὁ πατὴρ αὐτὸς φιλεῖ
d.dsn n.dsn cj pl v.pai.1s r.dp.2 cj r.ns.1 v.fai.1s d.asm n.asm p.g r.gp.2 cj d.nsm n.nsm r.nsm v.pai.3s
3836 3950 2779 3306 3306 4024 3306 7007 4022 1609 2263 3836 4252 4309 7007 1142 3836 4252 899 5797

you because you have loved me and have believed that I came from God. **28** I came from the Father
ὑμᾶς ὅτι ὑμεῖς → πεφιλήκατε ἐμὲ καὶ → πεπιστεύκατε ὅτι ἐγὼ ἐξῆλθον παρὰ τοῦ θεοῦ → ἐξῆλθον παρὰ τοῦ πατρὸς
r.ap.2 cj r.np.2 v.rai.2p r.as.1 cj v.rai.2p cj r.ns.1 v.aai.1s p.g d.gsm n.gsm v.aai.1s p.g d.gsm n.gsm
7007 4022 7007 5797 1609 2779 4409 4022 1609 2002 4123 3836 2536 2002 4123 3836 4252

λαλεῖ. ¶ **19** ἔγνω [ὁ] Ἰησοῦς ὅτι ἤθελον αὐτὸν ἐρωτᾶν, καὶ εἶπεν αὐτοῖς, Περὶ τούτου ζητεῖτε μετ' ἀλλήλων ὅτι εἶπον, Μικρὸν
καὶ οὐ θεωρεῖτέ με, καὶ πάλιν μικρὸν καὶ ὄψεσθέ με; **20** ἀμὴν ἀμὴν λέγω ὑμῖν ὅτι κλαύσετε καὶ θρηνήσετε ὑμεῖς, ὁ δὲ κόσμος
χαρήσεται· ὑμεῖς λυπηθήσεσθε, ἀλλ' ἡ λύπη ὑμῶν εἰς χαρὰν γενήσεται. **21** ἡ γυνὴ ὅταν τίκτῃ λύπην ἔχει, ὅτι ἦλθεν ἡ ὥρα αὐτῆς·
ὅταν δὲ γεννήσῃ τὸ παιδίον, οὐκέτι μνημονεύει τῆς θλίψεως διὰ τὴν χαρὰν ὅτι ἐγεννήθη ἄνθρωπος εἰς τὸν κόσμον. **22** καὶ ὑμεῖς
οὖν νῦν μὲν λύπην ἔχετε· πάλιν δὲ ὄψομαι ὑμᾶς, καὶ χαρήσεται ὑμῶν ἡ καρδία, καὶ τὴν χαρὰν ὑμῶν οὐδεὶς αἴρει ἀφ' ὑμῶν.
23 καὶ ἐν ἐκείνῃ τῇ ἡμέρᾳ ἐμὲ οὐκ ἐρωτήσετε οὐδέν. ἀμὴν ἀμὴν λέγω ὑμῖν, ἄν τι αἰτήσητε τὸν πατέρα ἐν τῷ ὀνόματί μου δώσει
ὑμῖν. **24** ἕως ἄρτι οὐκ ἠτήσατε οὐδὲν ἐν τῷ ὀνόματί μου· αἰτεῖτε καὶ λήμψεσθε, ἵνα ἡ χαρὰ ὑμῶν ᾖ πεπληρωμένη. ¶ **25** Ταῦτα
ἐν παροιμίαις λελάληκα ὑμῖν· ἔρχεται ὥρα ὅτε οὐκέτι ἐν παροιμίαις λαλήσω ὑμῖν, ἀλλὰ παρρησίᾳ περὶ τοῦ πατρὸς ἀπαγγελῶ
ὑμῖν. **26** ἐν ἐκείνῃ τῇ ἡμέρᾳ ἐν τῷ ὀνόματί μου αἰτήσεσθε, καὶ οὐ λέγω ὑμῖν ὅτι ἐγὼ ἐρωτήσω τὸν πατέρα περὶ ὑμῶν· **27** αὐτὸς
γὰρ ὁ πατὴρ φιλεῖ ὑμᾶς, ὅτι ὑμεῖς ἐμὲ πεφιλήκατε καὶ πεπιστεύκατε ὅτι ἐγὼ παρὰ [τοῦ] θεοῦ ἐξῆλθον. **28** ἐξῆλθον παρὰ τοῦ πατρὸς

and entered   the world; now I am leaving the world and going   back to   the Father."   ¶   29 Then Jesus'
καὶ   ἐλήλυθα εἰς¬ τὸν κόσμον πάλιν → ἀφίημι   τὸν κόσμον καὶ πορεύομαι   πρὸς τὸν πατέρα   αὐτοῦ
cj   v.rai.1s   p.a   d.asm n.asm adv   v.pai.1s   d.asm n.asm cj   v.pmi.1s   p.a   d.asm n.asm   r.gsm.3
2779 2262   1650 3836 3180 4099   918   3836 3180 2779 4513   4639 3836 4252   899

disciples   said,   "Now you are speaking clearly   and   without figures   of speech. 30 Now we can
ͺοἱ μαθηταὶ Λέγουσιν ἴδε νῦν →   → λαλεῖς ἐν παρρησίᾳ καὶ λέγεις οὐδεμίαν παροιμίαν ← ←   νῦν → →
d.npm n.npm   v.pai.3p pl adv   v.pai.2s p.d n.dsf   cj   v.pai.3s a.asf   n.asf   adv
3836 3412   3306   2623 3814   3281   1877 4244   2779 3306   4029   4231   3814

see   that you know all   things and that you do not even need   to have anyone ask you questions.
οἴδαμεν ὅτι → οἶδας πάντα ←   καὶ   ͺ→ → οὐ   ͺχρείαν ἔχεις ἵνα   τίς   ἐρωτᾷ σε ↵
v.rai.1p cj   v.rai.2s a.apn   cj   pl   pl n.asf v.pai.2s cj   r.nsm   v.pas.3s r.as.2
3857   4022   3857   4246   2779   2400 4024 5970   2400   2671   2263   2263   5148 2263

This   makes us believe   that you came from God."   ¶   31 "You believe at last!" Jesus   answered.
ͺἐν τούτῳ →   πιστεύομεν ὅτι → ἐξῆλθες ἀπὸ θεοῦ   πιστεύετε → ἄρτι Ἰησοῦς ἀπεκρίθη αὐτοῖς
p.d r.dsn   v.pai.1p   cj   v.aai.2s p.g n.gsm   v.pai.2p   adv n.nsm v.api.3s r.dpm.3
1877 4047   4409   4022   2002   608 2536   4409   785 2652   646   899

32 "But a time is coming, and has come,   when you will be scattered, each   to his own home. You will leave me   all
ἰδοὺ   ὥρα   ἔρχεται καὶ → ἐλήλυθεν ἵνα →   → σκορπισθῆτε ἕκαστος εἰς τὰ ἴδια ←   →   ἀφῆτε καμὲ →
j   n.nsf v.pmi.3s cj   v.rai.3s ἵνα   v.aps.2p   a.nsm   p.a d.apn a.apn   v.aas.2p crasis
2627   6052   2262   2779   2262   2671   5025   1667   1650 3836 2625   918   2743

alone. Yet I am not alone, for my Father is   with me.   ¶   33 "I have told   you these things, so that in me
μόνον καὶ → εἰμὶ οὐκ μόνος ὅτι ὁ πατὴρ ἐστὶν μετ' ἐμοῦ   →   λελάληκα ὑμῖν ταῦτα ←   ἵνα ←   ἐν ἐμοὶ
a.asm cj   v.pai.1s pl a.nsm ὅτι d.nsm n.nsm v.pai.3s p.g r.gs.1   v.rai.1s r.dp.2 r.apn   cj   p.d r.ds.1
3668   2779 1639 4024 3668 4022 3836 4252 1639 3552 1609   3281   7007   4047   2671   1877 1609

you may have peace. In this world you will have trouble. But take heart! I   have overcome the world."
→   →   ἔχητε εἰρήνην ἐν τῷ κόσμῳ → → ἔχετε θλῖψιν ἀλλὰ → θαρσεῖτε ἐγώ → νενίκηκα τὸν κόσμον
v.pas.2p n.asf   p.d d.dsm n.dsm   v.pai.2p n.asf   cj   v.pam.2p r.ns.1   v.rai.1s d.asm n.asm
2400   1645   1877 3836 3180   2400   2568   247   2510   1609   3771   3836 3180

Jesus Prays for Himself

17:1 After Jesus said   this, he looked   toward heaven   and prayed: "Father, the time
Ἰησοῦς ἐλάλησεν Ταῦτα → ἐπάρας τοὺς ὀφθαλμοὺς αὐτοῦ εἰς ͺτὸν οὐρανὸν καὶ εἶπεν πάτερ ἡ ὥρα
n.nsm v.aai.3s   r.apn   pt.aa.nsm d.apm n.apm   r.gsm.3 p.a d.asm n.asm   cj v.aai.3s n.vsm d.nsf n.nsf
2652   3281   4047   2048   3836 4057   899   1650 3836 4011   2779 3306   4252   3836 6052

has come.   Glorify your Son,   that your Son may glorify you. 2 For   you granted him authority over all   people
→   ἐλήλυθεν δόξασόν σου ͺτὸν υἱόν, ἵνα ὁ υἱὸς → δοξάσῃ σέ   καθὼς → ἔδωκας αὐτῷ ἐξουσίαν →   πάσης σαρκός
v.rai.3s   v.aam.2s r.gs.2 d.asm n.asm cj d.nsm n.nsm   v.aas.3s r.as.2 cj   v.aai.2s r.dsm.3 n.asf   a.gsf n.gsf
2262   1519   5148 3836 5626 2671 3836 5626   1519   5148 2777   1443   899   2026   4246   4922

that he might give eternal life to all those   you have given him. 3 Now this is   eternal life: that they may
ἵνα →   → δώσῃ αἰώνιον ζωὴν → πᾶν αὐτοῖς ὃ → δέδωκας αὐτῷ δὲ αὕτη ἐστὶν αἰώνιος ἡ ζωὴ ἵνα → →
cj   v.aas.3s a.asf   n.asf   a.asn r.dpm.3 r.asn   v.rai.2s r.dsm.3 cj r.nsf v.pai.3s a.nsf d.nsf n.nsf cj
2671   1443   173   2437   899 4246   899 4005   1443   899   1254 4047 1639 173   3836 2437 2671

know   you, the only true   God, and Jesus   Christ, whom you have sent.   4 I   have brought you glory
γινώσκωσιν σὲ τὸν μόνον ἀληθινὸν θεὸν καὶ Ἰησοῦν Χριστόν ὃν → ἀπέστειλας   ἐγώ → → σε ἐδόξασα
v.pas.3p r.as.2 d.asm a.asm a.asm   n.asm cj n.asm   n.asm   r.asm   v.aai.2s   r.ns.1   r.as.2 v.aai.1s
1182   5148 3836 3668 240   2536 2779 2652   5986   4005   690   1609 1519 1519 5148 1519

on earth by completing the work you gave   me to do.   5 And now, Father,   glorify me in   your
ἐπὶ τῆς γῆς → τελειώσας τὸ ἔργον ὃ → δέδωκας μοι ἵνα ποιήσω καὶ νῦν πάτερ σὺ δόξασόν με παρὰ σεαυτῷ
p.g d.gsf n.gsf   pt.aa.nsm d.asn n.asn r.asn v.rai.2s r.ds.1 cj v.aas.1s cj adv n.vsm r.ns.2 v.aam.2s r.as.1 p.d r.dsm.2
2093 3836 1178   5457   3836 2240 4005   1443 1609 2671 4472 2779 3814 4252 5148 1519 1609 4123 4932

presence with the glory   I had with you before the world began.
←   →   τῇ δόξῃ ᾗ → εἶχον παρὰ σοί πρὸ τὸν κόσμον ͺτοῦ εἶναι
        d.dsf n.dsf r.dsf v.iai.1s p.d r.ds.2 p.g d.asm n.asm   d.gsn f.pa
4123   3836 1518 4005 2400   4123 5148 4574 3836 3180   3836 1639

καὶ ἐλήλυθα εἰς τὸν κόσμον· πάλιν ἀφίημι τὸν κόσμον καὶ πορεύομαι πρὸς τὸν πατέρα. ¶ 29 Λέγουσιν οἱ μαθηταὶ αὐτοῦ, Ἴδε νῦν ἐν παρρησίᾳ λαλεῖς καὶ παροιμίαν οὐδεμίαν λέγεις. 30 νῦν οἴδαμεν ὅτι οἶδας πάντα καὶ οὐ χρείαν ἔχεις ἵνα τίς σε ἐρωτᾷ· ἐν τούτῳ πιστεύομεν ὅτι ἀπὸ θεοῦ ἐξῆλθες. ¶ 31 ἀπεκρίθη αὐτοῖς Ἰησοῦς, Ἄρτι πιστεύετε; 32 ἰδοὺ ἔρχεται ὥρα καὶ ἐλήλυθεν ἵνα σκορπισθῆτε ἕκαστος εἰς τὰ ἴδια κἀμὲ μόνον ἀφῆτε· καὶ οὐκ εἰμὶ μόνος, ὅτι ὁ πατὴρ μετ' ἐμοῦ ἐστιν. ¶ 33 ταῦτα λελάληκα ὑμῖν ἵνα ἐν ἐμοὶ εἰρήνην ἔχητε· ἐν τῷ κόσμῳ θλῖψιν ἔχετε· ἀλλὰ θαρσεῖτε, ἐγὼ νενίκηκα τὸν κόσμον.

17:1 Ταῦτα ἐλάλησεν Ἰησοῦς καὶ ἐπάρας τοὺς ὀφθαλμοὺς αὐτοῦ εἰς τὸν οὐρανὸν εἶπεν, Πάτερ, ἐλήλυθεν ἡ ὥρα· δόξασόν σου τὸν υἱόν, ἵνα ὁ υἱὸς δοξάσῃ σέ, 2 καθὼς ἔδωκας αὐτῷ ἐξουσίαν πάσης σαρκός, ἵνα πᾶν ὃ δέδωκας αὐτῷ δώσῃ αὐτοῖς ζωὴν αἰώνιον. 3 αὕτη δέ ἐστιν ἡ αἰώνιος ζωὴ ἵνα γινώσκωσιν σὲ τὸν μόνον ἀληθινὸν θεὸν καὶ ὃν ἀπέστειλας Ἰησοῦν Χριστόν. 4 ἐγώ σε ἐδόξασα ἐπὶ τῆς γῆς τὸ ἔργον τελειώσας ὃ δέδωκάς μοι ἵνα ποιήσω· 5 καὶ νῦν δόξασόν με σύ, πάτερ, παρὰ σεαυτῷ τῇ δόξῃ ᾗ εἶχον πρὸ τοῦ τὸν κόσμον εἶναι παρὰ σοί.

Jesus Prays for His Disciples

17:6 "I have revealed you to those whom you gave me out of the world. They were yours;
→ → Ἐφανέρωσα ⌞σου τὸ ὄνομα⌟ ⌞τοῖς ἀνθρώποις⌟ οὓς → ἔδωκας μοι ἐκ ← τοῦ κόσμου → ἦσαν σοὶ
v.aai.1s r.gs.2 d.asn n.asn d.dpm n.dpm r.apm v.aai.2s r.ds.1 p.g d.gsm n.gsm v.iai.3p r.ds.2
5746 5148 3836 3950 3836 476 4005 1443 1609 1666 3836 3180 1639 5050

you gave them to me and they have obeyed your word. 7 Now they know that everything you have given
→ ἔδωκας αὐτοὺς → καμοὶ καὶ → → τετήρηκαν σου ⌞τὸν λόγον⌟ νῦν → ἔγνωκαν ὅτι ⌞πάντα ὅσα⌟ → → δέδωκας
v.aai.2s r.apm.3 crasis cj v.rai.3p r.gs.2 d.asm n.asm adv v.rai.3p cj a.npn r.apn v.rai.2s
1443 899 2743 2779 5498 5148 3836 3364 3814 1182 4022 4246 4012 1443

me comes from you. 8 For I gave them the words you gave me and they accepted them. They knew
μοι εἰσιν παρὰ σοῦ ὅτι → δέδωκα αὐτοῖς τὰ ῥήματα ἃ → ἔδωκας μοι καὶ αὐτοὶ ἔλαβον καὶ → ἔγνωσαν
r.ds.1 v.pai.3p p.g r.gs.2 cj v.rai.1s r.dpm.3 d.apn n.apn r.apn v.aai.2s r.ds.1 cj r.npm v.aai.3p cj v.aai.3p
1609 1639 4123 5148 4022 1443 899 3836 4839 4005 1443 1609 2779 899 3284 2779 1182

with certainty that I came from you, and they believed that you sent me. 9 I pray for them. I am not
→ ἀληθῶς ὅτι → ἐξῆλθον παρὰ σοῦ καὶ → ἐπίστευσαν ὅτι σύ ἀπέστειλας με Ἐγὼ ἐρωτῶ περὶ αὐτῶν ↱ ↱ οὐ
adv cj v.aai.1s p.g r.gs.2 cj v.aai.3p cj r.ns.2 v.aai.2s r.as.1 r.ns.1 v.pai.1s p.g r.gpm.3 pl
242 4022 2002 4123 5148 2779 4409 4022 5148 690 1609 1609 2263 4309 899 2263 2263 4024

praying for the world, but for those you have given me, for they are yours. 10 All I have is yours,
ἐρωτῶ περὶ τοῦ κόσμου ἀλλὰ περὶ ὧν → → δέδωκας μοι ὅτι → εἰσιν σοί καὶ πάντα ⌞τὰ ἐμὰ⌟ ἐστιν σά
v.pai.1s p.g d.gsm n.gsm cj p.g r.gpm v.rai.2s r.ds.1 cj v.pai.3p r.ds.2 cj a.npn d.npn r.npn.1 v.pai.3s r.npn.2
2263 4309 3836 3180 247 4309 4005 1443 1609 4022 1639 5148 2779 4246 3836 1847 1639 5050

and all you have is mine. And glory has come to me through them. 11 I will remain in the world no
καὶ ⌞τὰ σὰ⌟ ἐμά καὶ δεδόξασμαι ← ← ← ← ἐν αὐτοῖς καὶ → → εἰμὶ ἐν τῷ κόσμῳ οὐκέτι
cj d.npn r.npn.2 r.npn.1 cj v.rpi.1s p.d r.dpm.3 cj v.pai.1s p.d d.dsm n.dsm adv
2779 3836 5050 1847 2779 1519 1877 899 2779 1639 1877 3836 3180 4033

longer, but they are still in the world, and I am coming to you. Holy Father, protect them by the power of
← καὶ αὐτοὶ εἰσίν ἐν τῷ κόσμῳ καγὼ ← → ἔρχομαι πρὸς σὲ ἅγιε πάτερ τήρησον αὐτοὺς ἐν
cj r.npm v.pai.3p p.d d.dsm n.dsm crasis v.pmi.1s p.a r.as.2 a.vsm n.vsm v.aam.2s r.apm.3 p.d
2779 899 1639 1877 3836 3180 2743 2262 4639 5148 41 4252 5498 899 1877

your name – the name you gave me – so that they may be one as we are one. 12 While I was with
σου ⌞τῷ ὀνόματι⌟ ᾧ ← → δέδωκας μοι ἵνα ← → ὦσιν ἓν καθὼς ἡμεῖς ὅτε → ἤμην μετ᾽
r.gs.2 d.dsn n.dsn r.dsn v.rai.2s r.ds.1 cj v.pas.3p a.nsn cj r.np.1 cj v.imi.1s p.g
5148 3836 3950 4005 1443 1609 2671 1639 1651 2777 7005 4021 1639 3552

them, I protected them and kept them safe by that name you gave me. None has
αὐτῶν ἐγὼ ἐτήρουν αὐτοὺς καὶ ἐφύλαξα ← ἐν σου ⌞τῷ ὀνόματι⌟ ᾧ → δέδωκας μοι καὶ οὐδεὶς ἐξ αὐτῶν →
r.gpm.3 r.ns.1 v.iai.1s r.apm.3 cj v.aai.1s p.d r.gs.2 d.dsn n.dsn r.dsn v.rai.2s r.ds.1 cj a.nsm p.g r.gpm.3
899 1609 5498 899 2779 5875 1877 5148 3836 3950 4005 1443 1609 2779 4029 1666 899

been lost except the one doomed to destruction so that Scripture would be fulfilled. ¶ 13 "I am
→ ἀπώλετο ⌞εἰ μὴ⌟ ὁ υἱὸς → → ⌞τῆς ἀπωλείας⌟ ἵνα ← ⌞ἡ γραφὴ⌟ → → πληρωθῇ δὲ → →
v.ami.3s cj pl d.nsm n.nsm d.gsf n.gsf cj d.nsf n.nsf v.aps.3s cj
660 1623 3590 3836 5626 3836 724 2671 3836 1210 4444 1254

coming to you now, but I say these things while I am still in the world, so that they may have the
ἔρχομαι πρὸς σὲ νῦν καὶ → λαλῶ ταῦτα ← ἐν τῷ κόσμῳ ἵνα ← → ἔχωσιν
v.pmi.1s p.a r.as.2 adv cj v.pai.1s r.apn p.d d.dsm n.dsm cj v.pas.3p
2262 4639 5148 3814 2779 3281 4047 1877 3836 3180 2671 2400

full measure of my joy within them. 14 I have given them your word and the world has
πεπληρωμένην ← ⌞τὴν ἐμὴν⌟ ⌞τὴν χαρὰν⌟ ἐν ἑαυτοῖς ἐγὼ δέδωκα αὐτοῖς σου ⌞τὸν λόγον⌟ καὶ ὁ κόσμος →
pt.rp.asf d.asf r.asf.1 d.asf n.asf p.d r.dpm.3 r.ns.1 v.rai.1s r.dpm.3 r.gs.2 d.asm n.asm cj d.nsm n.nsm
4444 3836 1847 3836 5915 1877 1571 1609 1443 899 5148 3836 3364 2779 3836 3180

hated them, for they are not of the world any more than I am of the world. 15 My prayer is not that you
ἐμίσησεν αὐτούς ὅτι → εἰσὶν οὐκ ἐκ τοῦ κόσμου καθὼς ← ← ἐγὼ εἰμὶ οὐκ ἐκ τοῦ κόσμου → ἐρωτῶ ← οὐκ ἵνα →
v.aai.3s r.apm.3 cj v.pai.3p pl p.g d.gsm n.gsm cj r.ns.1 v.pai.1s pl p.g d.gsm n.gsm v.pai.1s pl cj
3631 899 4022 1639 4024 1666 3836 3180 2777 1609 1639 4024 1666 3836 3180 2263 4024 2671

take them out of the world but that you protect them from the evil one. 16 They are not of the world, even as
ἄρῃς αὐτοὺς ἐκ ← τοῦ κόσμου ἀλλ᾽ ἵνα → τηρήσῃς αὐτοὺς ἐκ τοῦ πονηροῦ ← → εἰσὶν οὐκ ἐκ τοῦ κόσμου καθὼς ←
v.aas.2s r.apm.3 p.g d.gsm n.gsm cj cj v.aas.2s r.apm.3 p.g d.gsm a.gsm v.pai.3p pl p.g d.gsm n.gsm cj
149 899 1666 3836 3180 247 2671 5498 899 1666 3836 4505 1639 4024 1666 3836 3180 2777

17:6 Ἐφανέρωσά σου τὸ ὄνομα τοῖς ἀνθρώποις οὓς ἔδωκάς μοι ἐκ τοῦ κόσμου. σοὶ ἦσαν καμοὶ αὐτοὺς ἔδωκας καὶ τὸν λόγον
σου τετήρηκαν. 7 νῦν ἔγνωκαν ὅτι πάντα ὅσα δέδωκάς μοι παρὰ σοῦ εἰσιν· 8 ὅτι τὰ ῥήματα ἃ ἔδωκάς μοι δέδωκα αὐτοῖς, καὶ
αὐτοὶ ἔλαβον καὶ ἔγνωσαν ἀληθῶς ὅτι παρὰ σοῦ ἐξῆλθον, καὶ ἐπίστευσαν ὅτι σύ με ἀπέστειλας. 9 ἐγὼ περὶ αὐτῶν ἐρωτῶ, οὐ
περὶ τοῦ κόσμου ἐρωτῶ ἀλλὰ περὶ ὧν δέδωκάς μοι, ὅτι σοί εἰσιν, 10 καὶ τὰ ἐμὰ πάντα σά ἐστιν καὶ τὰ σὰ ἐμά, καὶ δεδόξασμαι
ἐν αὐτοῖς. 11 καὶ οὐκέτι εἰμὶ ἐν τῷ κόσμῳ, καὶ αὐτοὶ ἐν τῷ κόσμῳ εἰσίν, καγὼ πρὸς σὲ ἔρχομαι. Πάτερ ἅγιε, τήρησον αὐτοὺς
ἐν τῷ ὀνόματί σου ᾧ δέδωκάς μοι, ἵνα ὦσιν ἓν καθὼς ἡμεῖς. 12 ὅτε ἤμην μετ᾽ αὐτῶν ἐγὼ ἐτήρουν αὐτοὺς ἐν τῷ ὀνόματί σου ᾧ
δέδωκάς μοι, καὶ ἐφύλαξα, καὶ οὐδεὶς ἐξ αὐτῶν ἀπώλετο εἰ μὴ ὁ υἱὸς τῆς ἀπωλείας, ἵνα ἡ γραφὴ πληρωθῇ. ¶ 13 νῦν δὲ πρὸς σὲ
ἔρχομαι καὶ ταῦτα λαλῶ ἐν τῷ κόσμῳ ἵνα ἔχωσιν τὴν χαρὰν τὴν ἐμὴν πεπληρωμένην ἐν ἑαυτοῖς. 14 ἐγὼ δέδωκα αὐτοῖς τὸν λόγον
σου καὶ ὁ κόσμος ἐμίσησεν αὐτούς, ὅτι οὐκ εἰσὶν ἐκ τοῦ κόσμου καθὼς ἐγὼ οὐκ εἰμὶ ἐκ τοῦ κόσμου. 15 οὐκ ἐρωτῶ ἵνα ἄρῃς
αὐτοὺς ἐκ τοῦ κόσμου, ἀλλ᾽ ἵνα τηρήσῃς αὐτοὺς ἐκ τοῦ πονηροῦ. 16 ἐκ τοῦ κόσμου οὐκ εἰσὶν καθὼς ἐγὼ οὐκ εἰμὶ ἐκ τοῦ κόσμου.

I am not of it. **17** Sanctify them by the truth; your word is truth. **18** As you sent me
ἐγὼ εἰμι οὐκ ἐκ τοῦ κόσμου, ἁγίασον αὐτοὺς ἐν τῇ ἀληθείᾳ ὁ σὸς ὁ λόγος ἐστιν ἀλήθεια καθὼς → ἀπέστειλας ἐμὲ
r.ns.1 v.pai.1s pl p.g d.gsm n.gsm v.aam.2s r.apm.3 p.d d.dsf n.dsf d.nsm r.nsm.2 d.nsm n.nsm v.pai.3s n.nsf cj v.aai.2s r.as.1
1609 1639 4024 1666 3836 3180 39 899 1877 3836 237 3836 5050 3836 3364 1639 237 2777 690 1609

into the world, I have sent them into the world. **19** For them I sanctify myself, that they too may be
εἰς τὸν κόσμον κἀγὼ → ἀπέστειλα αὐτοὺς εἰς τὸν κόσμον καὶ ὑπὲρ αὐτῶν ἐγὼ ἁγιάζω ἐμαυτόν ἵνα αὐτοὶ ὦσιν
p.a d.asm n.asm crasis v.aai.1s r.apm.3 p.a d.asm n.asm cj p.g r.gpm.3 r.ns.1 v.pai.1s r.asm.1 cj r.npm adv v.pas.3p
1650 3836 3180 2743 690 899 1650 3836 3180 2779 5642 899 1609 39 1831 2671 899 2779 1639

truly sanctified.
ἐν ἀληθείᾳ ἡγιασμένοι
p.d n.dsf pt.rp.npm
1877 237 39

Jesus Prays for All Believers

17:20 "My prayer is not for them alone. I pray also for those who will believe in me through their
δὲ → ἐρωτῶ Οὐ περὶ τούτων μόνον ἀλλὰ καὶ περὶ τῶν ← πιστευόντων εἰς ἐμὲ διὰ αὐτῶν
cj v.pai.1s pl p.g r.gpm adv cj adv p.g d.gpm pt.pa.gpm p.a r.as.1 p.g r.gpm.3
1254 2263 4024 4309 4047 3667 247 2779 4309 3836 4409 1650 1609 1328 899

message, **21** that all of them may be one, Father, just as you are in me and I am in you. May they also
τοῦ λόγου, ἵνα πάντες ← → ὦσιν ἓν πάτερ καθὼς σύ ἐν ἐμοὶ κἀγὼ ἐν σοί ἵνα αὐτοὶ καὶ
d.gsm n.gsm cj a.npm v.pas.3p a.nsn n.vsm cj r.ns.2 p.d r.ds.1 crasis p.d r.ds.2 cj r.npm adv
3836 3364 2671 4246 1639 1651 4252 2777 5148 1877 1609 2743 1877 5148 2671 1639 899 2779

be in us so that the world may believe that you have sent me. **22** I have given them the glory that you
ὦσιν ἐν ἡμῖν ἵνα ← ὁ κόσμος → πιστεύῃ ὅτι σύ → ἀπέστειλας με κἀγὼ → δέδωκα αὐτοῖς τὴν δόξαν ἣν →
v.pas.3p p.d r.dp.1 cj d.nsm n.nsm v.pas.3s cj r.ns.2 v.aai.2s r.as.1 crasis v.rai.1s r.dpm.3 d.asf n.asf r.asf
1639 1877 7005 2671 3836 3180 4409 4022 5148 690 1609 2743 1443 899 3836 1518 4005

gave me, that they may be one as we are one: **23** I in them and you in me. May they be brought to
δέδωκας μοι ἵνα → → ὦσιν ἓν καθὼς ἡμεῖς ἕν ἐγὼ ἐν αὐτοῖς καὶ σὺ ἐν ἐμοί ἵνα → → ὦσιν →
v.rai.2s r.ds.1 cj v.pas.3p a.nsn cj r.np.1 a.nsn r.ns.1 p.d r.dpm.3 cj r.ns.2 p.d r.ds.1 cj v.pas.3p
1443 1609 2671 1639 1651 2777 7005 1651 1609 1877 899 2779 5148 1877 1609 2671 1639

complete unity to let the world know that you sent me and have loved them even as you have
τετελειωμένοι εἰς ἓν ἵνα ὁ κόσμος γινώσκῃ ὅτι σύ ἀπέστειλας με καὶ → ἠγάπησας αὐτοὺς καθὼς ← →
pt.rp.npm p.a a.asn cj d.nsm n.nsm v.pas.3s cj r.ns.2 v.aai.2s r.as.1 cj v.aai.2s r.apm.3 cj
5457 1650 1651 2671 3836 3180 1182 4022 5148 690 1609 2779 26 899 2777

loved me. ¶ **24** "Father, I want those you have given me to be with me where I am, and to
ἠγάπησας ἐμὲ Πάτερ → θέλω ὃ → → δέδωκας μοι ἵνα κἀκεῖνοι ὦσιν μετ᾽ ἐμοῦ ὅπου ἐγὼ εἰμι ἵνα
v.aai.2s r.as.1 n.vsm v.pai.1s r.asn v.rai.2s r.ds.1 cj adv v.pas.3p p.g r.gs.1 cj r.ns.1 v.pai.1s cj
26 1609 4252 2527 4005 1443 1609 2671 2797 1639 3552 1609 3963 1609 1639 2671

see my glory, the glory you have given me because you loved me before the creation of the
θεωρῶσιν τὴν ἐμὴν τὴν δόξαν, ἣν → → δέδωκας μοι ὅτι → ἠγάπησας με πρὸ καταβολῆς →
v.pas.3p d.asf r.asf.1 d.asf n.asf r.asf v.rai.2s r.ds.1 cj v.aai.2s r.as.1 p.g n.gsf
2555 3836 1847 3836 1518 4005 1443 1609 4022 26 1609 4574 2856

world. ¶ **25** "Righteous Father, though the world does not know you, I know you, and they know that
κόσμου δίκαιε πάτερ καὶ ὁ κόσμος → οὐκ ἔγνω σε δέ ἐγὼ ἔγνων σε καὶ οὗτοι ἔγνωσαν ὅτι
n.gsm a.vsm n.vsm adv d.nsm n.nsm pl v.aai.3s r.as.2 cj r.ns.1 v.aai.1s r.as.2 cj r.npm v.aai.3p cj
3180 1465 4252 2779 3836 3180 1182 4024 1182 5148 1254 1609 1182 5148 2779 4047 1182 4022

you have sent me. **26** I have made you known to them, and will continue to make you known in
σύ → ἀπέστειλας με καὶ → → τὸ ὄνομά σου ἐγνώρισα αὐτοῖς καὶ → → → → γνωρίσω ἵνα
r.ns.2 v.aai.2s r.as.1 cj d.asn n.asn r.gs.2 v.aai.1s r.dpm.3 cj v.fai.1s cj
5148 690 1609 2779 1192 1192 1192 3836 3950 5148 1192 899 2779 1192 2671

order that the love you have for me may be in them and that I myself may be in them."
← ← ἡ ἀγάπη ἣν → ἠγάπησας με ᾖ ἐν αὐτοῖς κἀγὼ ← ἐν αὐτοῖς
d.nsf n.nsf r.asf v.aai.2s r.as.1 v.pas.3s p.d r.dpm.3 crasis p.d r.dpm.3
3836 27 4005 26 1609 1639 1877 899 2743 1877 899

---

[17] ἁγίασον αὐτοὺς ἐν τῇ ἀληθείᾳ· ὁ λόγος ὁ σὸς ἀλήθειά ἐστιν. [18] καθὼς ἐμὲ ἀπέστειλας εἰς τὸν κόσμον, κἀγὼ ἀπέστειλα αὐτοὺς εἰς τὸν κόσμον· [19] καὶ ὑπὲρ αὐτῶν ἐγὼ ἁγιάζω ἐμαυτόν, ἵνα ὦσιν καὶ αὐτοὶ ἡγιασμένοι ἐν ἀληθείᾳ.

17:20 Οὐ περὶ τούτων δὲ ἐρωτῶ μόνον, ἀλλὰ καὶ περὶ τῶν πιστευόντων διὰ τοῦ λόγου αὐτῶν εἰς ἐμέ, [21] ἵνα πάντες ἓν ὦσιν, καθὼς σύ, πάτερ, ἐν ἐμοὶ κἀγὼ ἐν σοί, ἵνα καὶ αὐτοὶ ἐν ἡμῖν ὦσιν, ἵνα ὁ κόσμος πιστεύῃ ὅτι σύ με ἀπέστειλας. [22] κἀγὼ τὴν δόξαν ἣν δέδωκάς μοι δέδωκα αὐτοῖς, ἵνα ὦσιν ἓν καθὼς ἡμεῖς ἕν· [23] ἐγὼ ἐν αὐτοῖς καὶ σὺ ἐν ἐμοί, ἵνα ὦσιν τετελειωμένοι εἰς ἕν, ἵνα γινώσκῃ ὁ κόσμος ὅτι σύ με ἀπέστειλας καὶ ἠγάπησας αὐτοὺς καθὼς ἐμὲ ἠγάπησας. ¶ [24] Πάτερ, ὃ δέδωκάς μοι, θέλω ἵνα ὅπου εἰμὶ ἐγὼ κἀκεῖνοι ὦσιν μετ᾽ ἐμοῦ, ἵνα θεωρῶσιν τὴν δόξαν τὴν ἐμήν, ἣν δέδωκάς μοι ὅτι ἠγάπησάς με πρὸ καταβολῆς κόσμου. ¶ [25] πάτερ δίκαιε, καὶ ὁ κόσμος σε οὐκ ἔγνω, ἐγὼ δέ σε ἔγνων, καὶ οὗτοι ἔγνωσαν ὅτι σύ με ἀπέστειλας· [26] καὶ ἐγνώρισα αὐτοῖς τὸ ὄνομά σου καὶ γνωρίσω, ἵνα ἡ ἀγάπη ἣν ἠγάπησάς με ἐν αὐτοῖς ᾖ κἀγὼ ἐν αὐτοῖς.

Jesus Arrested

18:1 When he had finished praying, Jesus left with his disciples and crossed the Kidron
→ → → Ταῦτα εἰπὼν Ἰησοῦς ἐξῆλθεν σὺν αὐτοῦ τοῖς μαθηταῖς πέραν τοῦ Κεδρὼν
   r.apn pt.aa.nsm n.nsm v.aai.3s p.d r.gsm.3 d.dpm n.dpm p.g d.gsm d.gsm n.gsm
   4047 3306 2652 2002 5250 899 3836 3412 4305 3836 3836 3022

Valley. On the other side there was an olive grove, and he and his disciples went into it. ¶
χειμάρρου ὅπου → ἦν κῆπος αὐτὸς καὶ αὐτοῦ οἱ μαθηταί εἰσῆλθεν εἰς ὃν
n.gsm cj v.iai.3s n.nsm r.nsm cj r.gsm.3 d.npm n.npm v.aai.3s p.a r.asm
5929 3963 1639 3057 899 2779 899 3836 3412 1656 1650 4005

2 Now Judas, who betrayed him, knew the place, because Jesus had often met there with his
δὲ καὶ Ἰούδας ὁ παραδιδοὺς αὐτὸν Ἤιδει τὸν τόπον ὅτι Ἰησοῦς ↱ πολλάκις συνήχθη ἐκεῖ μετὰ αὐτοῦ
cj adv n.nsm d.nsm pt.pa.nsm r.asm.3 v.iai.3s d.asm n.asm cj n.nsm adv v.api.3s adv p.g r.gsm.3
1254 2779 2683 3836 4140 899 3857 3836 5536 4022 2652 5251 4490 5251 1695 3552 899

disciples. **3** So Judas came to the grove, guiding a detachment of soldiers and some officials from the chief
τῶν μαθητῶν οὖν ὁ Ἰούδας ἔρχεται → → ἐκεῖ λαβὼν τὴν σπεῖραν ← ← καὶ ὑπηρέτας ἐκ τῶν
d.gpm n.gpm cj d.nsm n.nsm v.pmi.3s adv pt.aa.nsm d.asf n.asf cj n.apm p.g d.gpm
3836 3412 4036 3836 2683 2262 1695 3284 3836 5061 2779 5677 1666 3836

priests and Pharisees. They were *carrying* torches, lanterns and weapons. ¶ **4** Jesus, knowing
ἀρχιερέων καὶ ἐκ τῶν Φαρισαίων μετὰ φανῶν καὶ λαμπάδων καὶ ὅπλων οὖν Ἰησοῦς εἰδὼς
n.gpm cj p.g d.gpm n.gpm p.g n.gpm cj n.gpf cj n.gpn cj n.nsm pt.ra.nsm
797 2779 1666 3836 5757 3552 5749 2779 3286 2779 3960 4036 2652 3857

all that was going to happen to him, went out and asked them, "Who is it you want?" **5** "Jesus of
πάντα τὰ → ἐρχόμενα ← ← ἐπ' αὐτὸν ἐξῆλθεν ← καὶ λέγει αὐτοῖς τίνα → ζητεῖτε Ἰησοῦν →
a.apn d.apn pt.pm.apn p.a r.asm.3 v.aai.3s cj v.pai.3s r.dpm.3 r.asm v.pai.2p n.asm
4246 3836 2262 2093 899 2002 2779 3306 899 5515 2426 2652

Nazareth," they replied. "I am he," Jesus said. (And Judas the traitor was
τὸν Ναζωραῖον → ἀπεκρίθησαν αὐτῷ ἐγώ εἰμι λέγει αὐτοῖς δὲ καὶ Ἰούδας ὁ παραδιδοὺς αὐτὸν →
d.asm n.asm v.api.3p r.dsm.3 r.ns.1 v.pai.1s v.pai.3s r.dpm.3 cj adv n.nsm d.nsm pt.pa.nsm r.asm.3
3836 3717 646 899 1609 1639 3306 899 1254 2779 2683 3836 4140 899

standing there with them.) **6** When Jesus said, "I am he," they drew back and fell to the
εἱστήκει μετ' αὐτῶν οὖν ὡς εἶπεν αὐτοῖς ἐγώ εἰμι → ἀπῆλθον εἰς τὰ ὀπίσω καὶ ἔπεσαν →
v.lai.3s p.g r.gpm.3 cj cj v.aai.3s r.dpm.3 r.ns.1 v.pai.1s v.aai.3p p.a d.apn adv cj v.aai.3p
2705 3552 899 4036 6055 3306 899 1609 1639 599 1650 3836 3958 2779 4406

ground. **7** Again he asked them, "Who is it you want?" And they said, "Jesus of Nazareth." **8** "I told you
χαμαί οὖν πάλιν → ἐπηρώτησεν αὐτούς τίνα → → ζητεῖτε δὲ οἱ εἶπαν Ἰησοῦν τὸν Ναζωραῖον → εἶπον ὑμῖν
adv cj adv v.aai.3s r.apm.3 r.asm v.pai.2p cj d.npm v.aai.3p n.asm d.asm n.asm v.aai.1s r.dp.2
5912 4036 4099 2089 899 5515 2426 1254 3836 3306 2652 3836 3717 3306 7007

that I am he," Jesus answered. "If you are looking for me, then let these men go." **9** This happened so
ὅτι ἐγώ εἰμι Ἰησοῦς ἀπεκρίθη οὖν εἰ → ζητεῖτε ← ἐμὲ ἄφετε τούτους ← ὑπάγειν → ἵνα
cj r.ns.1 v.pai.1s n.nsm v.api.3s cj cj v.pai.2p r.as.1 v.aam.2p r.apm f.pa cj
4022 1609 1639 2652 646 4036 1623 2426 1609 918 4047 5632 2671

that the words he had spoken would be fulfilled: "I have not lost one of those you gave me."
← ὁ λόγος ὃν → εἶπεν → πληρωθῇ ὅτι → → οὐκ ἀπώλεσα οὐδένα ἐξ αὐτῶν οὓς → δέδωκάς μοι
d.nsm n.nsm r.asm v.aai.3s v.aps.3s cj pl v.aai.1s a.asm p.g r.gpm.3 r.apm v.rai.2s r.ds.1
3836 3364 4005 3306 4444 4022 660 660 4024 660 4029 1666 899 4005 1443 1609

10 Then Simon Peter, who had a sword, drew it and struck the high priest's servant, cutting off
οὖν Σίμων Πέτρος → ἔχων μάχαιραν εἵλκυσεν αὐτὴν καὶ ἔπαισεν τὸν τοῦ ἀρχιερέως δοῦλον καὶ ἀπέκοψεν ←
cj n.nsm n.nsm pt.pa.nsm n.asf v.aai.3s r.asf.3 cj v.aai.3s d.asm d.gsm n.gsm n.asm cj v.aai.3s
4036 4981 4377 2400 3479 1816 899 2779 4091 3836 3836 797 1529 2779 644

his right ear. (The servant's name was Malchus.) **11** Jesus commanded Peter, "Put your
αὐτοῦ τὸ δεξιὸν τὸ ὠτάριον δὲ τῷ δούλῳ ὄνομα ἦν Μάλχος οὖν ὁ Ἰησοῦς εἶπεν τῷ Πέτρῳ βάλε τὴν
r.gsm.3 d.asn a.asn d.asn n.asn cj d.dsm n.dsm n.asn v.iai.3s n.nsm cj d.nsm n.nsm v.aai.3s d.dsm n.dsm v.aam.2s d.asf
899 3836 1288 3836 6064 1254 3836 1529 3950 1639 3438 4036 3836 2652 3306 3836 4377 965 3836

sword away! Shall I not drink the cup the Father has given me?"
μάχαιραν εἰς τὴν θήκην → → οὐ μὴ πίω αὐτὸ τὸ ποτήριον ὃ ὁ πατὴρ → δέδωκεν μοι
n.asf p.a d.asf n.asf pl pl v.aas.1s r.asn.3 d.asn n.asn r.asn d.nsm n.nsm v.rai.3s r.ds.1
3479 1650 3836 2557 4403 4403 4024 3590 4403 899 3836 4539 4005 3836 4252 1443 1609

18:1 Ταῦτα εἰπὼν Ἰησοῦς ἐξῆλθεν σὺν τοῖς μαθηταῖς αὐτοῦ πέραν τοῦ χειμάρρου τοῦ Κεδρὼν ὅπου ἦν κῆπος, εἰς ὃν εἰσῆλθεν αὐτὸς καὶ οἱ μαθηταὶ αὐτοῦ. ¶ **2** ᾔδει δὲ καὶ Ἰούδας ὁ παραδιδοὺς αὐτὸν τὸν τόπον, ὅτι πολλάκις συνήχθη Ἰησοῦς ἐκεῖ μετὰ τῶν μαθητῶν αὐτοῦ. **3** ὁ οὖν Ἰούδας λαβὼν τὴν σπεῖραν καὶ ἐκ τῶν ἀρχιερέων καὶ ἐκ τῶν Φαρισαίων ὑπηρέτας ἔρχεται ἐκεῖ μετὰ φανῶν καὶ λαμπάδων καὶ ὅπλων. ¶ **4** Ἰησοῦς οὖν εἰδὼς πάντα τὰ ἐρχόμενα ἐπ' αὐτὸν ἐξῆλθεν καὶ λέγει αὐτοῖς, Τίνα ζητεῖτε; **5** ἀπεκρίθησαν αὐτῷ, Ἰησοῦν τὸν Ναζωραῖον. λέγει αὐτοῖς, Ἐγώ εἰμι. εἱστήκει δὲ καὶ Ἰούδας ὁ παραδιδοὺς αὐτὸν μετ' αὐτῶν. **6** ὡς οὖν εἶπεν αὐτοῖς, Ἐγώ εἰμι, ἀπῆλθον εἰς τὰ ὀπίσω καὶ ἔπεσαν χαμαί. **7** πάλιν οὖν ἐπηρώτησεν αὐτούς, Τίνα ζητεῖτε; οἱ δὲ εἶπαν, Ἰησοῦν τὸν Ναζωραῖον. **8** ἀπεκρίθη Ἰησοῦς, Εἶπον ὑμῖν ὅτι ἐγώ εἰμι. εἰ οὖν ἐμὲ ζητεῖτε, ἄφετε τούτους ὑπάγειν· **9** ἵνα πληρωθῇ ὁ λόγος ὃν εἶπεν ὅτι Οὓς δέδωκάς μοι οὐκ ἀπώλεσα ἐξ αὐτῶν οὐδένα. **10** Σίμων οὖν Πέτρος ἔχων μάχαιραν εἵλκυσεν αὐτὴν καὶ ἔπαισεν τὸν τοῦ ἀρχιερέως δοῦλον καὶ ἀπέκοψεν αὐτοῦ τὸ ὠτάριον τὸ δεξιόν· ἦν δὲ ὄνομα τῷ δούλῳ Μάλχος. **11** εἶπεν οὖν ὁ Ἰησοῦς τῷ Πέτρῳ, Βάλε τὴν μάχαιραν εἰς τὴν θήκην· τὸ ποτήριον ὃ δέδωκέν μοι ὁ πατὴρ οὐ μὴ πίω αὐτό;

Jesus Taken to Annas

18:12 Then the detachment of soldiers with its commander and the Jewish officials arrested Jesus.
οὖν Ἡ σπεῖρα ← ← καὶ ὁ χιλίαρχος καὶ οἱ ⌐τῶν Ἰουδαίων⌐ ὑπηρέται συνέλαβον ⌐τὸν Ἰησοῦν⌐ καὶ
cj d.nsf n.nsf cj d.nsm n.nsm cj d.npm d.gpm a.gpm n.npm v.aai.3p d.asm n.asm cj
4036 3836 5061 2779 3836 5941 2779 3836 3836 2681 5677 5197 3836 2652 2779

They bound him ¹³ and brought him first to Annas, who was the father-in-law of Caiaphas, the
→ ἔδησαν αὐτὸν καὶ ἤγαγον πρῶτον πρὸς Ἄνναν γὰρ → ἦν πενθερὸς → ⌐τοῦ Καϊάφα⌐ ὃς ἦν
v.aai.3p r.asm.3 cj v.aai.3p adv p.a n.asm cj v.iai.3s n.nsm d.gsm n.gsm r.nsm v.iai.3s
1313 899 2779 72 4754 4639 484 1142 1639 4290 3836 2780 4005 1639

high priest that year. ¹⁴ Caiaphas was the one who had advised the Jews that it would be
→ ἀρχιερεὺς ἐκείνου ⌐τοῦ ἐνιαυτοῦ⌐ δὲ Καϊάφας ἦν ὁ ← → συμβουλεύσας τοῖς Ἰουδαίοις ὅτι → →
n.nsm r.gsm d.gsm n.gsm cj n.nsm v.iai.3s d.nsm pt.aa.nsm d.dpm a.dpm cj
797 1697 3836 1929 1254 2780 1639 3836 5205 3836 2681 4022

good if one man died for the people.
συμφέρει ἕνα ἄνθρωπον ἀποθανεῖν ὑπὲρ τοῦ λαοῦ
v.pai.3s a.asm n.asm f.aa p.g d.gsm n.gsm
5237 1651 476 633 5642 3836 3295

Peter's First Denial

18:15 Simon Peter and another disciple were following Jesus. Because this disciple was known
δὲ Σίμων Πέτρος καὶ ἄλλος μαθητής → Ἠκολούθει ⌐τῷ Ἰησοῦ⌐ δὲ ἐκεῖνος ὁ μαθητὴς ἦν γνωστὸς
cj n.nsm n.nsm cj r.nsm n.nsm v.iai.3s d.dsm n.dsm cj r.nsm d.nsm n.nsm v.iai.3s a.nsm
1254 4981 4377 2779 257 3412 199 3836 2652 1254 1697 3836 3412 1639 1196

to the high priest, he went with Jesus into the high priest's courtyard, ¹⁶ but Peter had to
→ τῷ → ἀρχιερεῖ καὶ → συνεισῆλθεν → ⌐τῷ Ἰησοῦ⌐ εἰς τὴν → ⌐τοῦ ἀρχιερέως⌐ αὐλὴν δὲ ὁ Πέτρος
d.dsm n.dsm cj v.aai.3s d.dsm n.dsm p.a d.asf d.gsm n.gsm n.asf cj d.nsm n.nsm
3836 797 2779 5291 3836 2652 1650 3836 3836 797 885 1254 3836 4377

wait outside at the door. The other disciple, who was known to the high priest, came back,
εἱστήκει ἔξω πρὸς τῇ θύρᾳ οὖν ὁ ὁ ἄλλος μαθητὴς ὁ → γνωστὸς τοῦ ἀρχιερέως ἐξῆλθεν ← καὶ
v.lai.3s adv p.d d.dsf n.dsf cj d.nsm d.nsm r.nsm n.nsm d.nsm a.nsm d.gsm n.gsm v.aai.3s cj
2705 2032 4639 3836 2598 4036 3836 3836 257 3412 3836 1196 3836 797 2002 2779

spoke to the girl on duty there and brought Peter in. ¹⁷ "You are not one of his
εἶπεν → τῇ θυρωρῷ καὶ εἰσήγαγεν ⌐τὸν Πέτρον⌐ οὖν σὺ καὶ μὴ ἐκ ⌐τοῦ ἀνθρώπου τούτου⌐
v.aai.3s d.dsf n.dsf cj v.aai.3s d.asm n.asm cj r.ns.2 cj pl p.g d.gsm n.gsm r.gsm
3306 3836 2601 2779 1652 3836 4377 1652 4036 5148 2779 3590 1666 3836 476 4047

disciples, are you?" the girl at the door asked Peter. He replied, "I am not." ¶ ¹⁸ It
⌐τῶν μαθητῶν⌐ εἶ ← ἡ παιδίσκη ἡ θυρωρὸς λέγει ⌐τῷ Πέτρῳ⌐ ἐκεῖνος λέγει → εἰμί οὐκ δὲ ὅτι →
d.gpm n.gpm v.pai.2s d.nsf n.nsf d.nsf n.nsf v.pai.3s d.dsm n.dsm r.nsm v.pai.3s v.pai.1s pl cj cj
3836 3412 1639 3836 4087 3836 2601 3306 3836 4377 1697 3306 1639 4024 1254 4022

was cold, and the servants and officials stood around a fire they had made to keep warm.
ἦν ψῦχος οἱ δοῦλοι καὶ οἱ ὑπηρέται εἱστήκεισαν ← ἀνθρακιὰν → πεποιηκότες καὶ → ἐθερμαίνοντο
v.iai.3s n.nsn d.npm n.npm cj d.npm n.npm v.lai.3p n.asf pt.ra.npm cj v.imi.3p
1639 6036 3836 1529 2779 3836 5677 2705 471 4472 2779 2548

Peter also was standing with them, warming himself.
δὲ ὁ Πέτρος καὶ ἦν ἑστὼς μετ' αὐτῶν καὶ θερμαινόμενος ←
cj d.nsm n.nsm adv v.iai.3s pt.ra.nsm p.g r.gpm.3 cj pt.pm.nsm
1254 3836 4377 2779 1639 2705 3552 899 2779 2548

The High Priest Questions Jesus

18:19 Meanwhile, the high priest questioned Jesus about his disciples and his teaching.
οὖν Ὁ → ἀρχιερεὺς ἠρώτησεν ⌐τὸν Ἰησοῦν⌐ περὶ αὐτοῦ ⌐τῶν μαθητῶν⌐ καὶ περὶ αὐτοῦ ⌐τῆς διδαχῆς⌐
cj d.nsm n.nsm v.aai.3s d.asm n.asm p.g r.gsm.3 d.gpm n.gpm cj p.g r.gsm.3 d.gsf n.gsf
4036 3836 797 2263 3836 2652 4309 899 3836 3412 2779 4309 899 3836 1439

²⁰ "I have spoken openly to the world," Jesus replied. "I always taught in synagogues or at the temple,
ἐγὼ → λελάληκα παρρησίᾳ → τῷ κόσμῳ Ἰησοῦς ἀπεκρίθη αὐτῷ ἐγὼ πάντοτε ἐδίδαξα ἐν συναγωγῇ καὶ ἐν τῷ ἱερῷ
r.ns.1 v.rai.1s n.dsf d.dsm n.dsm n.nsm v.api.3s r.dsm.3 r.ns.1 adv v.aai.1s p.d n.dsf cj p.d d.dsn n.dsn
1609 3281 4244 3836 3180 2652 646 899 1609 4121 1438 1877 5252 2779 1877 3836 2639

18:12 Ἡ οὖν σπεῖρα καὶ ὁ χιλίαρχος καὶ οἱ ὑπηρέται τῶν Ἰουδαίων συνέλαβον τὸν Ἰησοῦν καὶ ἔδησαν αὐτὸν ¹³ καὶ ἤγαγον πρὸς Ἄνναν πρῶτον· ἦν γὰρ πενθερὸς τοῦ Καϊάφα, ὃς ἦν ἀρχιερεὺς τοῦ ἐνιαυτοῦ ἐκείνου· ¹⁴ ἦν δὲ Καϊάφας ὁ συμβουλεύσας τοῖς Ἰουδαίοις ὅτι συμφέρει ἕνα ἄνθρωπον ἀποθανεῖν ὑπὲρ τοῦ λαοῦ.

18:15 Ἠκολούθει δὲ τῷ Ἰησοῦ Σίμων Πέτρος καὶ ἄλλος μαθητής. ὁ δὲ μαθητὴς ἐκεῖνος ἦν γνωστὸς τῷ ἀρχιερεῖ καὶ συνεισῆλθεν τῷ Ἰησοῦ εἰς τὴν αὐλὴν τοῦ ἀρχιερέως, ¹⁶ ὁ δὲ Πέτρος εἱστήκει πρὸς τῇ θύρᾳ ἔξω. ἐξῆλθεν οὖν ὁ μαθητὴς ὁ ἄλλος ὁ γνωστὸς τοῦ ἀρχιερέως καὶ εἶπεν τῇ θυρωρῷ καὶ εἰσήγαγεν τὸν Πέτρον. ¹⁷ λέγει οὖν τῷ Πέτρῳ ἡ παιδίσκη ἡ θυρωρός, Μὴ καὶ σὺ ἐκ τῶν μαθητῶν εἶ τοῦ ἀνθρώπου τούτου; λέγει ἐκεῖνος, Οὐκ εἰμί. ¶ ¹⁸ εἱστήκεισαν δὲ οἱ δοῦλοι καὶ οἱ ὑπηρέται ἀνθρακιὰν πεποιηκότες, ὅτι ψῦχος ἦν, καὶ ἐθερμαίνοντο· ἦν δὲ καὶ ὁ Πέτρος μετ' αὐτῶν ἑστὼς καὶ θερμαινόμενος.

18:19 Ὁ οὖν ἀρχιερεὺς ἠρώτησεν τὸν Ἰησοῦν περὶ τῶν μαθητῶν αὐτοῦ καὶ περὶ τῆς διδαχῆς αὐτοῦ. ²⁰ ἀπεκρίθη αὐτῷ Ἰησοῦς, Ἐγὼ παρρησίᾳ λελάληκα τῷ κόσμῳ, ἐγὼ πάντοτε ἐδίδαξα ἐν συναγωγῇ καὶ ἐν τῷ ἱερῷ, ὅπου πάντες οἱ Ἰουδαῖοι

where all the Jews come together. I said nothing in secret. ²¹ Why question me? Ask those who
ὅπου πάντες οἱ Ἰουδαῖοι συνέρχονται ← καὶ → ἐλάλησα οὐδέν ἐν κρυπτῷ τί ἐρωτᾷς με ἐρώτησον τοὺς ←
cj a.npm d.npm a.npm v.pmi.3p cj v.aai.1s a.asn p.d a.dsn r.asn v.pai.2s r.as.1 v.aam.2s d.apm
3963 4246 3836 2681 5302 2779 3281 4029 1877 3220 5515 2263 1609 2263 3836

heard me. Surely they know what I said." ¶ ²² When Jesus said this, one of the
ἀκηκοότας τί ἐλάλησα αὐτοῖς ἴδε οὗτοι οἴδασιν ἃ ἐγὼ εἶπον δὲ → αὐτοῦ εἰπόντος ταῦτα εἰς → τῶν
pt.ra.apm r.asn v.aai.1s r.dpm.3 pl r.npm v.rai.3p r.apn r.ns.1 v.aai.1s cj r.gsm.3 pt.aa.gsm r.apn a.nsm d.gpm
201 5515 3281 899 2623 4047 3857 4005 1609 3306 1254 3306 899 3306 4047 1651 3836

officials nearby struck him in the face. "Is this the way you answer the high priest?" he
ὑπηρετῶν παρεστηκὼς ἔδωκεν ῥάπισμα ˻τῷ Ἰησοῦ˼ οὕτως ← → → ἀποκρίνῃ τῷ → ἀρχιερεῖ →
n.gpm pt.ra.nsm v.aai.3s n.asn d.dsm n.dsm adv v.pmi.2s d.dsm n.dsm
5677 4225 1443 4825 3836 2652 4048 646 3836 797

demanded. ²³ "If I said something wrong," Jesus replied, "testify as to what is wrong. But if I spoke
εἰπών εἰ → ἐλάλησα → κακῶς Ἰησοῦς ἀπεκρίθη αὐτῷ μαρτύρησον περὶ ← ˻τοῦ κακοῦ˼ δὲ εἰ
pt.aa.nsm cj v.aai.1s adv n.nsm v.aai.3s r.dsm.3 v.aam.2s p.g d.gsn a.gsn cj cj
3306 1623 3281 2809 2652 646 899 3455 4309 3836 2805 1254 1623

the truth, why did you strike me?" ²⁴ Then Annas sent him, still bound, to Caiaphas the high priest.
καλῶς τί → → δέρεις με οὖν ὁ Ἅννας ἀπέστειλεν αὐτὸν → δεδεμένον πρὸς Καϊάφαν τὸν → ἀρχιερέα
adv r.asn v.pai.2s r.as.1 cj d.nsm n.nsm v.aai.3s r.asm.3 pt.rp.asm p.a n.asm d.asm n.asm
2822 5515 1296 1609 4036 3836 484 690 899 1313 4639 2780 3836 797

Peter's Second and Third Denials

^{18:25} As Simon Peter stood warming himself, he was asked, "You are not one of his
δὲ Σίμων Πέτρος ˻Ἦν ἑστὼς˼ καὶ θερμαινόμενος ← οὖν αὐτῷ εἶπον σὺ καὶ μὴ ἐκ αὐτοῦ
cj n.nsm n.nsm v.iai.3s pt.ra.nsm cj pt.pm.nsm cj r.dsm.3 v.aai.3p r.ns.2 adv pl p.g r.gsm.3
1254 4981 4377 1639 2705 2779 2548 4036 899 3306 5148 2779 3590 1666 899

disciples, are you?" He denied it, saying, "I am not." ²⁶ One of the high priest's servants, a
˻τῶν μαθητῶν˼ εἶ ← ἐκεῖνος ἠρνήσατο καὶ εἶπεν → εἰμὶ οὐκ εἷς ἐκ τῶν → ˻τοῦ ἀρχιερέως˼ δούλων ὢν
d.gpm n.gpm v.pai.2s r.nsm v.ami.3s cj v.aai.3s v.pai.1s pl a.nsm p.g d.gpm d.gsm n.gsm n.gpm pt.pa.nsm
3836 3412 1639 1697 766 2779 3306 1639 4024 1651 1666 3836 3836 797 1529 1639

relative of the man whose ear Peter had cut off, challenged him, "Didn't I see you with him in the
συγγενὴς → οὗ ˻τὸ ὠτίον˼ Πέτρος → ἀπέκοψεν ← λέγει οὐκ ἐγὼ εἶδον σε μετ' αὐτοῦ ἐν τῷ
n.nsm r.gsm d.asn n.asn n.nsm v.aai.3s v.pai.3s pl r.ns.1 v.aai.1s r.as.2 p.g r.gsm.3 p.d d.dsm
5150 4005 3836 6065 4377 644 3306 4024 1609 1625 5148 3552 899 1877 3836

olive grove?" ²⁷ Again Peter denied it, and at that moment a rooster began to crow.
κήπῳ οὖν πάλιν Πέτρος ἠρνήσατο καὶ εὐθέως ← ἀλέκτωρ → → ἐφώνησεν
n.dsm cj adv n.nsm v.ami.3s cj adv n.nsm v.aai.3s
3057 4036 4099 4377 766 2779 2311 232 5888

Jesus Before Pilate

^{18:28} Then the Jews led Jesus from Caiaphas to the palace of the Roman governor. By now it
οὖν ˻τὸν Ἰησοῦν˼ Ἄγουσιν ἀπὸ ˻τοῦ Καϊάφα˼ εἰς τὸ πραιτώριον δὲ →
cj d.asn n.asn v.pai.3p p.g d.gsm n.gsm p.a d.asn n.asn cj
4036 3836 2652 72 608 3836 2780 1650 3836 4550 1254

was early morning, and to avoid ceremonial uncleanness the Jews did not enter the palace; they
ἦν → πρωΐ καὶ ἵνα → ˻μὴ μιανθῶσιν˼ αὐτοὶ → οὐκ εἰσῆλθον εἰς τὸ πραιτώριον ἀλλὰ →
v.iai.3s adv cj cj pl v.aps.3p r.npm pl v.aai.3p p.a d.asn n.asn cj
1639 4745 2779 2671 3590 3620 899 1656 4024 1656 1650 3836 4550 247

wanted to be able to eat the Passover. ²⁹ So Pilate came out to them and asked, "What charges are
→ → → φάγωσιν τὸ πάσχα οὖν ὁ Πιλᾶτος, ἐξῆλθεν ἔξω πρὸς αὐτοὺς καὶ φησίν τίνα κατηγορίαν →
v.aas.3p d.asn n.asn cj d.nsm n.nsm v.aai.3s p.a r.apm.3 cj v.pai.3s r.asf n.asf
2266 3836 4247 4036 3836 4397 2002 2032 4639 899 2779 5774 5515 2990

you bringing against this man?" ³⁰ "If he were not a criminal," they replied, "we would
→ φέρετε κατὰ τούτου ˻τοῦ ἀνθρώπου˼ εἰ οὗτος ἦν μὴ ˻κακὸν ποιῶν˼ → ἀπεκρίθησαν καὶ εἶπαν αὐτῷ ἂν
v.pai.2p p.g r.gsm d.gsm n.gsm cj r.nsm v.iai.3s pl a.asn pt.pa.nsm v.api.3p cj v.aai.3p r.dsm.3 pl
5770 2848 4047 3836 476 1623 4047 1639 3590 2805 4472 646 2779 3306 899 323

not have handed him over to you." ³¹ Pilate said, "Take him yourselves and judge him by
οὐκ → παρεδώκαμεν αὐτόν ← → σοι οὖν ὁ Πιλᾶτος, εἶπεν αὐτοῖς λάβετε αὐτὸν ὑμεῖς καὶ κρίνατε αὐτὸν κατὰ
pl v.aai.1p r.asm.3 r.ds.2 cj d.nsm n.nsm v.aai.3s r.dpm.3 v.aam.2p r.asm.3 r.np.2 cj v.aam.2p r.asm.3 p.a
4024 4140 899 4140 5148 4036 3836 4397 3306 899 3284 899 7007 2779 3212 899 2848

συνέρχονται, καὶ ἐν κρυπτῷ ἐλάλησα οὐδέν. ²¹ τί με ἐρωτᾷς; ἐρώτησον τοὺς ἀκηκοότας τί ἐλάλησα αὐτοῖς· ἴδε οὗτοι οἴδασιν ἃ εἶπον ἐγώ. ¶ ²² ταῦτα δὲ αὐτοῦ εἰπόντος εἷς παρεστηκὼς τῶν ὑπηρετῶν ἔδωκεν ῥάπισμα τῷ Ἰησοῦ εἰπών, Οὕτως ἀποκρίνῃ τῷ ἀρχιερεῖ; ²³ ἀπεκρίθη αὐτῷ Ἰησοῦς, Εἰ κακῶς ἐλάλησα, μαρτύρησον περὶ τοῦ κακοῦ· εἰ δὲ καλῶς, τί με δέρεις; ²⁴ ἀπέστειλεν οὖν αὐτὸν ὁ Ἅννας δεδεμένον πρὸς Καϊάφαν τὸν ἀρχιερέα.

^{18:25} Ἦν δὲ Σίμων Πέτρος ἑστὼς καὶ θερμαινόμενος. εἶπον οὖν αὐτῷ, Μὴ καὶ σὺ ἐκ τῶν μαθητῶν αὐτοῦ εἶ; ἠρνήσατο ἐκεῖνος καὶ εἶπεν, Οὐκ εἰμί. ²⁶ λέγει εἷς ἐκ τῶν δούλων τοῦ ἀρχιερέως, συγγενὴς ὢν οὗ ἀπέκοψεν Πέτρος τὸ ὠτίον, Οὐκ ἐγώ σε εἶδον ἐν τῷ κήπῳ μετ' αὐτοῦ; ²⁷ πάλιν οὖν ἠρνήσατο Πέτρος, καὶ εὐθέως ἀλέκτωρ ἐφώνησεν.

^{18:28} Ἄγουσιν οὖν τὸν Ἰησοῦν ἀπὸ τοῦ Καϊάφα εἰς τὸ πραιτώριον· ἦν δὲ πρωΐ· καὶ αὐτοὶ οὐκ εἰσῆλθον εἰς τὸ πραιτώριον, ἵνα μὴ μιανθῶσιν ἀλλὰ φάγωσιν τὸ πάσχα. ²⁹ ἐξῆλθεν οὖν ὁ Πιλᾶτος ἔξω πρὸς αὐτοὺς καὶ φησίν, Τίνα κατηγορίαν φέρετε [κατὰ] τοῦ ἀνθρώπου τούτου; ³⁰ ἀπεκρίθησαν καὶ εἶπαν αὐτῷ, Εἰ μὴ ἦν οὗτος κακὸν ποιῶν, οὐκ ἄν σοι παρεδώκαμεν αὐτόν. ³¹ εἶπεν οὖν αὐτοῖς ὁ Πιλᾶτος, Λάβετε αὐτὸν ὑμεῖς καὶ κατὰ τὸν νόμον ὑμῶν κρίνατε αὐτόν. εἶπον αὐτῷ οἱ Ἰουδαῖοι, Ἡμῖν οὐκ ἔξεστιν

your own law." "But we have no right to execute anyone," the Jews objected. **32** This happened so
ὑμῶν ⌐τὸν νόμον⌐ ἡμῖν → οὐκ ἔξεστιν → ἀποκτεῖναι οὐδένα οἱ Ἰουδαῖοι εἶπον αὐτῷ ἵνα
r.gp.2 d.asm n.asm r.dp.1 pl v.pai.3s f.aa a.asm d.npm a.npm v.aai.3p r.dsm.3 cj
7007 3836 3795 7005 1997 4024 1997 650 4029 3836 2681 3306 899 2671

that the words Jesus had spoken indicating the kind of death he was going to die would be
← ὁ λόγος ⌐τοῦ Ἰησοῦ⌐ ὃν → εἶπεν σημαίνων → ποίῳ ← θανάτῳ → ἤμελλεν → ἀποθνῄσκειν →
d.nsm n.nsm d.gsm r.asm v.aai.3s pt.pa.nsm r.dsm n.dsm v.iai.3s f.pa
3836 3364 3836 2652 4005 3306 4955 4481 2505 3516 633

fulfilled. ¶ **33** Pilate then went back inside the palace, summoned Jesus and asked him, "Are
πληρωθῇ ὁ Πιλᾶτος οὖν Εἰσῆλθεν πάλιν εἰς τὸ πραιτώριον καὶ ἐφώνησεν ⌐τὸν Ἰησοῦν⌐ καὶ εἶπεν αὐτῷ εἰ
v.aps.3s d.nsm n.nsm cj v.aai.3s adv p.a d.asn n.asn cj v.aai.3s d.asm n.asm cj v.aai.3s r.dsm.3 v.pai.2s
4444 3836 4397 4036 1656 4099 1650 3836 4550 2779 5888 3836 2652 2779 3306 899 1639

you the king of the Jews?" **34** "Is that *your* *own* *idea*," Jesus asked, "or did others talk to you
σὺ ὁ βασιλεὺς → τῶν Ἰουδαίων σὺ λέγεις τοῦτο ⌐ἀπὸ σεαυτοῦ⌐ Ἰησοῦς ἀπεκρίθη ἢ → ἄλλοι εἶπον → σοι
r.ns.2 d.nsm n.nsm d.gpm a.gpm r.ns.2 v.pai.2s r.asn p.g r.gsm.2 n.nsm v.api.3s cj r.npm v.aai.3p r.ds.2
5148 3836 995 3836 2681 5148 3306 4047 608 4932 2652 646 2445 3306 257 3306 5148

about me?" **35** "Am I a Jew?" Pilate replied. "It was your people and your chief priests who
περὶ ἐμοῦ μήτι εἰμι ἐγὼ Ἰουδαῖος ὁ Πιλᾶτος ἀπεκρίθη ⌐τὸ σὸν⌐ ⌐τὸ ἔθνος⌐ καὶ → ⌐οἱ ἀρχιερεῖς⌐
p.g r.gs.1 pl v.pai.1s r.ns.1 a.nsm d.nsm n.nsm v.api.3s d.nsn r.nsn.2 d.nsn n.nsn cj d.npm n.npm
4309 1609 3614 1639 1609 2681 3836 4397 646 3836 5050 3836 1620 2779 3836 797

handed you over to me. What is it you have done?" **36** Jesus said, "My kingdom is not of this
παρέδωκαν σε ← → ἐμοί τί → → → ἐποίησας Ἰησοῦς ἀπεκρίθη ⌐ἡ ἐμὴ⌐ ⌐ἡ βασιλεία⌐ ἔστιν οὐκ ἐκ τούτου
v.aai.3p r.as.2 r.ds.1 r.asn v.aai.2s n.nsm v.api.3s d.nsf r.nsf.1 d.nsf n.nsf v.pai.3s pl p.g r.gsm
4140 5148 4140 1609 5515 4472 2652 646 3836 1847 3836 993 1639 4024 1666 4047

world. If it were, my servants would fight to *prevent* *my*
⌐τοῦ κόσμου⌐ εἰ ἡ βασιλεία ἡ ἐμὴ ἦν ἐκ τούτου ⌐τοῦ κόσμου⌐ ⌐οἱ ἐμοὶ⌐ ⌐οἱ ὑπηρέται⌐ ἂν ἠγωνίζοντο ἵνα μὴ
d.gsm n.gsm cj d.nsf n.nsf d.nsf r.nsf.1 v.iai.3s p.g r.gsm d.gsm n.gsm d.npm r.npm.1 d.npm n.npm pl v.imi.3p cj pl
3836 3180 1623 3836 993 3836 1847 1639 1666 4047 3836 3180 3836 1847 3836 5677 323 76 2671 3590

arrest by the Jews. But now my kingdom is *from* *another* *place*." **37** "You are a king, then!"
παραδοθῶ → τοῖς Ἰουδαίοις δὲ νῦν ⌐ἡ ἐμὴ⌐ ⌐ἡ βασιλεία⌐ ἔστιν οὐκ ἐντεῦθεν οὖν σύ εἶ βασιλεὺς οὐκοῦν
v.aps.1s d.dpm a.dpm cj adv d.nsf r.nsf.1 d.nsf n.nsf v.pai.3s pl adv cj r.ns.2 v.pai.2s n.nsm cj
4140 3836 2681 1254 3814 3836 1847 3836 993 1639 4024 1949 4036 5148 1639 995 4034

said Pilate. Jesus answered, "You are right in saying I am a king. In fact, for this reason I
εἶπεν ὁ Πιλᾶτος αὐτῷ ὁ Ἰησοῦς ἀπεκρίθη σὺ λέγεις ὅτι → εἰμι βασιλεύς εἰς τοῦτο ← ἐγὼ
v.aai.3s d.nsm n.nsm r.dsm.3 d.nsm n.nsm v.api.3s r.ns.2 v.pai.2s cj v.pai.1s n.nsm p.a r.asn r.ns.1
3306 3836 4397 899 3836 2652 646 5148 3306 4022 1639 995 1650 4047 1609

was born, and for this I came into the world, to testify to the truth. Everyone on the side of
→ γεγέννημαι καὶ εἰς τοῦτο ἐλήλυθα εἰς τὸν κόσμον ἵνα μαρτυρήσω → τῇ ἀληθείᾳ πᾶς ὁ ὢν ἐκ ←
v.rpi.1s cj p.a r.asn v.rai.1s p.a d.asm n.asm cj v.aas.1s d.dsf n.dsf a.nsm d.nsm pt.pa.nsm p.g
1164 2779 1650 4047 2262 1650 3836 3180 2671 3455 3836 237 4246 3836 1639 1666

truth listens to me." ¶ **38** "What is truth?" Pilate asked. *With* *this* he
⌐τῆς ἀληθείας⌐ ἀκούει ← μου τῆς φωνῆς τί ἔστιν ἀλήθεια ὁ Πιλᾶτος λέγει αὐτῷ ⌐Καὶ τοῦτο εἰπὼν⌐
d.gsf n.gsf v.pai.3s r.gs.1 d.gsf n.gsf r.nsn v.pai.3s n.nsf d.nsm n.nsm v.pai.3s r.dsm.3 cj r.asn pt.aa.nsm
3836 237 201 1609 3836 5889 5515 1639 237 3836 4397 3306 899 2779 4047 3306

went out again to the Jews and said, "I find no basis for a charge against him. **39** But it is
ἐξῆλθεν ← πάλιν πρὸς τοὺς Ἰουδαίους καὶ λέγει αὐτοῖς ἐγὼ εὑρίσκω οὐδεμίαν ← αἰτίαν ἐν αὐτῷ δὲ → ἔστιν
v.aai.3s adv p.a d.apm a.apm cj v.pai.3s r.dpm.3 r.ns.1 v.pai.1s a.asf n.asf p.d r.dsm.3 cj v.pai.3s
2002 4099 4639 3836 2681 2779 3306 899 1609 2351 4029 162 1877 899 1254 1639

your custom for me to release to you one prisoner at the time of the Passover. Do you want me to release
ὑμῖν συνήθεια → ἵνα ἀπολύσω ὑμῖν ἕνα ἐν ← → τῷ πάσχα οὖν → βούλεσθε → → ἀπολύσω
r.dp.2 n.nsf cj v.aas.1s r.dp.2 a.asm p.d d.dsn n.dsn cj v.pmi.2p v.aas.1s
7007 5311 668 2671 668 7007 1651 1877 3836 4247 4036 1089 668

'the king of the Jews'?" **40** They shouted back, "No, not him! Give us Barabbas!" Now
ὑμῖν τὸν βασιλέα → τῶν Ἰουδαίων οὖν → ἐκραύγασαν πάλιν λέγοντες μὴ τοῦτον ἀλλὰ ⌐τὸν Βαραββᾶν⌐ δὲ
r.dp.2 d.asm n.asm d.gpm a.gpm cj v.aai.3p adv pt.pa.npm pl r.asm cj d.asm n.asm cj
7007 3836 995 3836 2681 4036 3198 4099 3306 3590 4047 247 3836 972 1254

ἀποκτεῖναι οὐδένα· ³² ἵνα ὁ λόγος τοῦ Ἰησοῦ πληρωθῇ ὃν εἶπεν σημαίνων ποίῳ θανάτῳ ἤμελλεν ἀποθνῄσκειν. ¶ ³³ Εἰσῆλθεν οὖν πάλιν εἰς τὸ πραιτώριον ὁ Πιλᾶτος καὶ ἐφώνησεν τὸν Ἰησοῦν καὶ εἶπεν αὐτῷ, Σὺ εἶ ὁ βασιλεὺς τῶν Ἰουδαίων; ³⁴ ἀπεκρίθη Ἰησοῦς, Ἀπὸ σεαυτοῦ σὺ τοῦτο λέγεις ἢ ἄλλοι εἶπόν σοι περὶ ἐμοῦ; ³⁵ ἀπεκρίθη ὁ Πιλᾶτος, Μήτι ἐγὼ Ἰουδαῖός εἰμι; τὸ ἔθνος τὸ σὸν καὶ οἱ ἀρχιερεῖς παρέδωκάν σε ἐμοί· τί ἐποίησας; ³⁶ ἀπεκρίθη Ἰησοῦς, Ἡ βασιλεία ἡ ἐμὴ οὐκ ἔστιν ἐκ τοῦ κόσμου τούτου· εἰ ἐκ τοῦ κόσμου τούτου ἦν ἡ βασιλεία ἡ ἐμή, οἱ ὑπηρέται οἱ ἐμοὶ ἠγωνίζοντο [ἂν] ἵνα μὴ παραδοθῶ τοῖς Ἰουδαίοις· νῦν δὲ ἡ βασιλεία ἡ ἐμὴ οὐκ ἔστιν ἐντεῦθεν. ³⁷ εἶπεν οὖν αὐτῷ ὁ Πιλᾶτος, Οὐκοῦν βασιλεὺς εἶ σύ; ἀπεκρίθη ὁ Ἰησοῦς, Σὺ λέγεις ὅτι βασιλεύς εἰμι. ἐγὼ εἰς τοῦτο γεγέννημαι καὶ εἰς τοῦτο ἐλήλυθα εἰς τὸν κόσμον, ἵνα μαρτυρήσω τῇ ἀληθείᾳ· πᾶς ὁ ὢν ἐκ τῆς ἀληθείας ἀκούει μου τῆς φωνῆς. ¶ ³⁸ λέγει αὐτῷ ὁ Πιλᾶτος, Τί ἐστιν ἀλήθεια; Καὶ τοῦτο εἰπὼν πάλιν ἐξῆλθεν πρὸς τοὺς Ἰουδαίους καὶ λέγει αὐτοῖς, Ἐγὼ οὐδεμίαν εὑρίσκω ἐν αὐτῷ αἰτίαν. ³⁹ ἔστιν δὲ συνήθεια ὑμῖν ἵνα ἕνα ἀπολύσω ὑμῖν ἐν τῷ πάσχα· βούλεσθε οὖν ἀπολύσω ὑμῖν τὸν βασιλέα τῶν Ἰουδαίων; ⁴⁰ ἐκραύγασαν οὖν πάλιν λέγοντες, Μὴ τοῦτον ἀλλὰ

Barabbas   had taken part in a rebellion.
ὁ Βαραββᾶς,   ἦν ←   ←   λῃστής
d.nsm n.nsm   v.iai.3s   n.nsm
3836 972   1639   3334

Jesus Sentenced to be Crucified

19:1 Then Pilate   took Jesus   and had him flogged.   2   The soldiers   twisted   together a crown
οὖν Τότε   ὁ Πιλᾶτος, ἔλαβεν τὸν Ἰησοῦν καὶ →   ἐμαστίγωσεν καὶ οἱ στρατιῶται πλέξαντες ←   στέφανον
cj adv   d.nsm n.nsm v.aai.3s d.asm n.asm cj   v.aai.3s   cj d.npm n.npm pt.aa.npm   n.asm
4036 5538 3836 4397 3284 3836 2652 2779   3463   2779 3836 5132 4428   5109

of thorns and put   it   on his head.   They clothed   him in a purple robe   3 and went   up to
ἐξ ἀκανθῶν ἐπέθηκαν αὐτοῦ → αὐτοῦ τῇ κεφαλῇ καὶ → περιέβαλον αὐτὸν πορφυροῦν ἱμάτιον καὶ ἤρχοντο   πρὸς
p.g n.gpf   v.aai.3p r.gsm.3 r.gsm.3 d.dsf n.dsf cj   v.aai.3p   r.asm.3 a.asn   n.asn cj v.imi.3p   p.a
1666 180   2202   899   3051 899 3836 3051 2779   4314   899 4314 4528   2668   2779 2262   4639

him again and again,   saying, "Hail, king   of the Jews!" And they struck   him in the face.
αὐτὸν ←   ←   καὶ ἔλεγον χαῖρε ὁ βασιλεὺς → τῶν Ἰουδαίων καὶ →   ἐδίδοσαν ῥαπίσματα αὐτῷ
r.asm.3   cj v.iai.3p v.pam.2s d.vsm n.vsm d.gpm a.gpm cj   v.iai.3p n.apn   r.dsm.3
899 2262 2262 2262 2779 3306 5897 3836 995 3836 2681 2779   1443   4825   899

¶   4   Once more Pilate   came out and said to the Jews, "Look, I am bringing him out to you to let
Καὶ πάλιν ←   ὁ Πιλᾶτος, ἐξῆλθεν ἔξω καὶ λέγει   αὐτοῖς ἴδε → → ἄγω   αὐτὸν ἔξω → ὑμῖν ἵνα →
cj adv   d.nsm n.nsm v.aai.3s adv cj v.pai.3s   r.dpm.3 pl   v.pai.1s r.asm.3 adv r.dp.2 cj
2779 4099   3836 4397 2002 2032 2779 3306   899 2623   72   899 2032 7007 2671

you know that I find   no   basis for a charge against him." 5 When Jesus   came out wearing the crown of
→ γνῶτε ὅτι → εὑρίσκω οὐδεμίαν →   → αἰτίαν ἐν αὐτῷ οὖν ὁ Ἰησοῦς ἐξῆλθεν ἔξω φορῶν   τὸν στέφανον
v.aas.2p cj v.pai.1s a.asf   n.asf p.d r.dsm.3 cj d.nsm n.nsm v.aai.3s adv pt.pa.nsm d.asm n.asm
1182 4022   2351   4029   162 1877 899 4036 3836 2652 2002 2032 5841   3836 5109

thorns   and the purple   robe,   Pilate said to them, "Here is the man!"   6   As   soon as the chief priests
ἀκάνθινον καὶ τὸ πορφυροῦν ἱμάτιον καὶ λέγει αὐτοῖς ἰδοὺ ὁ ἄνθρωπος οὖν Ὅτε ←   ← οἱ ἀρχιερεῖς
a.asm   cj d.asn a.asn   n.asn cj v.pai.3s r.dpm.3 j   d.nsm n.nsm cj cj   d.npm n.npm
181   2779 3836 4528   2668   2779 3306 899 2627   3836 476   4036 4021   3836 797

and their officials saw him,   they shouted,   "Crucify! Crucify!" But Pilate   answered,   "You
καὶ οἱ ὑπηρέται εἶδον αὐτὸν → ἐκραύγασαν λέγοντες σταύρωσον σταύρωσον ὁ Πιλᾶτος, λέγει   αὐτοῖς ὑμεῖς
cj d.npm n.npm v.aai.3p r.asm.3 v.aai.3p   pt.pa.npm v.aam.2s v.aam.2s d.nsm n.nsm v.pai.3s r.dpm.3 r.np.2
2779 3836 5677   1625   899   3198   3306   5090   5090   3836 4397 3306   899   7007

take him and crucify him. As for me, I find   no basis for a charge against him." 7 The Jews   insisted,
λάβετε αὐτὸν καὶ σταυρώσατε γὰρ ← ← ἐγὼ εὑρίσκω οὐχ → → αἰτίαν ἐν αὐτῷ   οἱ Ἰουδαῖοι ἀπεκρίθησαν
v.aam.2p r.asm.3 cj v.aam.2p   cj   r.ns.1 v.pai.1s pl   n.asf p.d r.dsm.3 d.npm a.npm v.api.3p
3284 899   2779 5090   1142   1609 2351   4024   162 1877 899 3836 2681   646

"We have a law, and according to that law he must die,   because he claimed   to be the Son of
αὐτῷ ἡμεῖς ἔχομεν νόμον καὶ κατὰ ← τὸν νόμον ὀφείλει ἀποθανεῖν ὅτι → ἑαυτὸν ἐποίησεν υἱὸν
r.dsm.3 r.np.1 v.pai.1p n.asm cj p.a   d.asm n.asm v.pai.3s f.aa   cj   r.asm.3 v.aai.3s n.asm
899 7005 2400   3795 2779 2848   3836 3795 4053   633   4022   1571   4472   5626

God." ¶ 8 When Pilate   heard this,   he was even more afraid, 9 and he went   back inside
θεοῦ   οὖν Ὅτε ὁ Πιλᾶτος, ἤκουσεν τοῦτον τὸν λόγον →   → μᾶλλον ἐφοβήθη καὶ → εἰσῆλθεν πάλιν εἰς
n.gsm cj cj d.nsm n.nsm v.aai.3s r.asm d.asm n.asm   adv.c v.api.3s cj   v.aai.3s adv p.a
2536   4036 4021 3836 4397 201   4047 3836 3364   3437   5828   2779 1656   4099 1650

the palace.   "Where do you come from?" he asked Jesus,   but Jesus   gave   him no answer. 10   "Do
τὸ πραιτώριον καὶ πόθεν   σὺ εἶ →   λέγει τῷ Ἰησοῦ δὲ ὁ Ἰησοῦς ἔδωκεν αὐτῷ οὐκ ἀπόκρισιν οὖν →
d.asn n.asn   cj adv   r.ns.2 v.pai.2s   v.pai.3s d.dsm n.dsm cj d.nsm n.nsm v.aai.3s r.dsm.3 pl n.asf   cj
3836 4550   2779 4470   1639 1639   3306 3836 2652 1254 3836 2652 1443 899 4024 647   4036 3281

you refuse to speak to me?" Pilate   said.   "Don't you realize I have power either to free   you or
→ οὐ → λαλεῖς → ἐμοὶ ὁ Πιλᾶτος, λέγει αὐτῷ οὐκ → οἶδας ὅτι → ἔχω ἐξουσίαν   ἀπολῦσαι σε καὶ
pl v.pai.2s   r.ds.1 d.nsm n.nsm v.pai.3s r.dsm.3 pl   v.rai.2s cj v.pai.1s n.asf   f.aa   r.as.2 cj
3281 4024   3281 1609 3836 4397 3306 899 4024   3857 4022   2400 2026   668   5148 2779

to crucify you?" 11 Jesus answered,   "You would have no   power over me if it
ἔχω ἐξουσίαν → σταυρῶσαι σε Ἰησοῦς ἀπεκρίθη [αὐτῷ] →   → εἶχες οὐκ οὐδεμίαν ἐξουσίαν κατ' ἐμοῦ εἰ →
v.pai.1s n.asf f.aa   r.as.2 n.nsm v.api.3s   r.dsm.3   v.iai.2s pl a.asf n.asf   p.g r.gs.1 cj
2400 2026   5090 5148 2652 646   899   2400 4024 4029   2026   2848 1609 1623

τὸν Βαραββᾶν. ἦν δὲ ὁ Βαραββᾶς λῃστής.
   19:1 Τότε οὖν ἔλαβεν ὁ Πιλᾶτος τὸν Ἰησοῦν καὶ ἐμαστίγωσεν. 2 καὶ οἱ στρατιῶται πλέξαντες στέφανον ἐξ ἀκανθῶν ἐπέθηκαν αὐτοῦ τῇ κεφαλῇ καὶ ἱμάτιον πορφυροῦν περιέβαλον αὐτὸν 3 καὶ ἤρχοντο πρὸς αὐτὸν καὶ ἔλεγον, Χαῖρε ὁ βασιλεὺς τῶν Ἰουδαίων· καὶ ἐδίδοσαν αὐτῷ ῥαπίσματα. ¶ 4 Καὶ ἐξῆλθεν πάλιν ἔξω ὁ Πιλᾶτος καὶ λέγει αὐτοῖς, Ἴδε ἄγω ὑμῖν αὐτὸν ἔξω, ἵνα γνῶτε ὅτι οὐδεμίαν αἰτίαν εὑρίσκω ἐν αὐτῷ. 5 ἐξῆλθεν οὖν ὁ Ἰησοῦς ἔξω, φορῶν τὸν ἀκάνθινον στέφανον καὶ τὸ πορφυροῦν ἱμάτιον. καὶ λέγει αὐτοῖς, Ἰδοὺ ὁ ἄνθρωπος. 6 ὅτε οὖν εἶδον αὐτὸν οἱ ἀρχιερεῖς καὶ οἱ ὑπηρέται ἐκραύγασαν λέγοντες, Σταύρωσον σταύρωσον. λέγει αὐτοῖς ὁ Πιλᾶτος, Λάβετε αὐτὸν ὑμεῖς καὶ σταυρώσατε· ἐγὼ γὰρ οὐχ εὑρίσκω ἐν αὐτῷ αἰτίαν. 7 ἀπεκρίθησαν αὐτῷ οἱ Ἰουδαῖοι, Ἡμεῖς νόμον ἔχομεν καὶ κατὰ τὸν νόμον ὀφείλει ἀποθανεῖν, ὅτι υἱὸν θεοῦ ἑαυτὸν ἐποίησεν. ¶ 8 Ὅτε οὖν ἤκουσεν ὁ Πιλᾶτος τοῦτον τὸν λόγον, μᾶλλον ἐφοβήθη, 9 καὶ εἰσῆλθεν εἰς τὸ πραιτώριον πάλιν καὶ λέγει τῷ Ἰησοῦ, Πόθεν εἶ σύ; ὁ δὲ Ἰησοῦς ἀπόκρισιν οὐκ ἔδωκεν αὐτῷ. 10 λέγει οὖν αὐτῷ ὁ Πιλᾶτος, Ἐμοὶ οὐ λαλεῖς; οὐκ οἶδας ὅτι ἐξουσίαν ἔχω ἀπολῦσαί σε καὶ ἐξουσίαν ἔχω σταυρῶσαί σε; 11 ἀπεκρίθη [αὐτῷ] Ἰησοῦς, Οὐκ εἶχες ἐξουσίαν κατ' ἐμοῦ οὐδεμίαν εἰ μὴ ἦν δεδομένον σοι

were not given to you from above. Therefore the one who handed me over to you is guilty of a greater
ἦν μὴ δεδομένον → σοι → ἄνωθεν ⌊διὰ τοῦτο⌋ ὁ ← ← παραδούς μέ ↰ → σοι ἔχει ← ← μείζονα
v.iai.3s pl pt.rp.nsn r.ds.2 adv p.a r.asn d.nsm pt.aa.nsm r.as.1 r.ds.2 v.pai.3s a.asf.c
1639 3590 1443 5148 540 1328 4047 3836 4140 1609 4140 5148 2400 3489

sin." ¶ 12 From then on, Pilate tried to set Jesus free, but the Jews kept shouting, "If
ἁμαρτίαν ⌊ἐκ τούτου⌋ ← ← ⌊ὁ Πιλᾶτος⌋ ἐζήτει ↱ ↱ αὐτόν ἀπολῦσαι δὲ οἱ Ἰουδαῖοι → ἐκραύγασαν λέγοντες ἐὰν
n.asf p.g r.gsn d.nsm n.nsm v.iai.3s r.asm.3 f.aa cj d.npm a.npm v.aai.3p pt.pa.npm cj
281 1666 4047 3836 4397 2426 668 668 899 668 1254 3836 2681 3198 3306 1569

you let this man go, you are no friend of Caesar. Anyone who claims to be a king opposes
↱ ↱ τοῦτον ἀπολύσῃς → εἶ οὐκ φίλος → ⌊τοῦ Καίσαρος⌋ πᾶς ὁ ⌊ποιῶν ἑαυτὸν⌋ βασιλέα ἀντιλέγει
r.asm v.aas.2s v.pai.2s pl a.nsm d.gsm n.gsm a.nsm d.nsm pt.pa.nsm r.asm.3 n.asm v.pai.3s
668 668 4047 668 1639 4024 5813 3836 2790 4246 3836 4472 1571 995 515

Caesar." ¶ 13 When Pilate heard this, he brought Jesus out and sat down
⌊τῷ Καίσαρι⌋ οὖν ↱ ⌊ὁ Πιλᾶτος⌋ ἀκούσας ⌊τῶν λόγων τούτων⌋ → ἤγαγεν ⌊τὸν Ἰησοῦν⌋ ἔξω καὶ ἐκάθισεν ←
d.dsm n.dsm cj d.nsm n.nsm pt.aa.nsm d.gpm n.gpm r.gpm v.aai.3s d.asm n.asm adv cj v.aai.3s
3836 2790 4036 201 3836 4397 201 3836 3364 4047 72 3836 2652 2032 2779 2767

on the judge's seat at a place known as the Stone Pavement (which in Aramaic is Gabbatha). 14 It was
ἐπὶ βήματος εἰς τόπον λεγόμενον ← → λιθόστρωτον δὲ → Ἑβραϊστὶ Γαββαθα δὲ → ἦν
p.g n.gsn p.a n.asm pt.pp.asm n.asn cj adv n.asn cj v.iai.3s
2093 1037 1650 5536 3306 3346 1254 1580 1119 1254 1639

the day of Preparation of Passover Week, about the sixth hour. "Here is your king," Pilate said to
→ → παρασκευὴ → ⌊τοῦ πάσχα⌋ ἦν ὡς ἕκτη ὥρα καὶ ἴδε ὑμῶν ⌊ὁ βασιλεὺς⌋ λέγει →
n.nsf d.gsn n.gsn v.iai.3s pl a.nsf n.nsf cj pl r.gp.2 d.nsm n.nsm v.pai.3s
4187 3836 4247 1639 6055 1761 6052 2779 2623 7007 3836 995 3306

the Jews. 15 But they shouted, "Take him away! Take him away! Crucify him!" "Shall I crucify your
τοῖς Ἰουδαίοις οὖν ἐκεῖνοι ἐκραύγασαν ἆρον ← ἆρον ← σταύρωσον αὐτόν → → σταυρώσω ὑμῶν
d.dpm a.dpm cj r.npm v.aai.3p v.aam.2s v.aam.2s v.aam.2s r.asm.3 v.aas.1s r.gp.2
3836 2681 4036 1697 3198 149 149 5090 899 5090 7007

king?" Pilate asked. "We have no king but Caesar," the chief priests answered. 16
⌊τὸν βασιλέα⌋ ⌊ὁ Πιλᾶτος⌋ λέγει αὐτοῖς → ἔχομεν οὐκ βασιλέα ⌊εἰ μὴ⌋ Καίσαρα οἱ → ἀρχιερεῖς ἀπεκρίθησαν οὖν
d.asm n.asm d.nsm n.nsm v.pai.3s r.dpm.3 v.pai.1p pl n.asm cj pl n.asm d.npm n.npm v.api.3p cj
3836 995 3836 4397 3306 899 2400 4024 995 1623 3590 2790 3836 797 646 4036

Finally Pilate handed him over to them to be crucified.
Τότε παρέδωκεν αὐτὸν ↰ → αὐτοῖς ἵνα → σταυρωθῇ
adv v.aai.3s r.asm.3 r.dpm.3 cj v.aps.3s
5538 4140 899 4140 899 2671 5090

The Crucifixion

19:16 So the soldiers took charge of Jesus. 17 Carrying his own cross, he went out to the place
οὖν → Παρέλαβον ← ⌊τὸν Ἰησοῦν⌋ καὶ βαστάζων ἑαυτῷ ← ⌊τὸν σταυρὸν⌋ → ἐξῆλθεν ← εἰς τὸν Τόπον
cj v.aai.3p d.asm n.asm cj pt.pa.nsm r.dsm.3 d.asm n.asm v.aai.3s p.a d.asm n.asm
4036 4161 3836 2652 2779 1002 1571 3836 5089 2002 1650 3836 5536

of the Skull (which in Aramaic is called Golgotha). 18 Here they crucified him, and with him two others
λεγόμενον → Κρανίου ὃ → Ἑβραϊστὶ → λέγεται Γολγοθα ὅπου → ἐσταύρωσαν αὐτὸν καὶ μετ᾽ αὐτοῦ δύο ἄλλους
pt.pp.asm n.gsn r.nsn adv v.ppi.3s n.nsf cj v.aai.3p r.asm.3 cj p.g r.gsm.3 a.apm r.apm
3306 3191 4005 1580 3306 1201 3963 5090 899 2779 3552 899 1545 257

– *one on each side* and Jesus in the middle. ¶ 19 Pilate had a notice prepared
⌊ἐντεῦθεν καὶ ἐντεῦθεν⌋ δὲ ⌊τὸν Ἰησοῦν⌋ → μέσον δὲ ⌊ὁ Πιλᾶτος⌋ καὶ ↱ τίτλον ἔγραψεν
adv cj adv cj d.asm n.asm adv cj d.nsm n.nsm adv n.asm v.aai.3s
1949 2779 1949 1254 3836 2652 3545 1254 3836 4397 2779 1211 5518 1211

and fastened to the cross. It read: JESUS OF NAZARETH, THE KING OF THE JEWS. 20
καὶ ἔθηκεν ἐπὶ τοῦ σταυροῦ δὲ → ⌊ἦν γεγραμμένον⌋ Ἰησοῦς → ⌊ὁ Ναζωραῖος⌋ ὁ βασιλεὺς → τῶν Ἰουδαίων οὖν
cj v.aai.3s p.g d.gsm n.gsm cj v.iai.3s pt.rp.nsn n.nsm d.nsm n.nsm d.nsm n.nsm d.gpm a.gpm cj
2779 5502 2093 3836 5089 1254 1639 1211 2652 3836 3717 3836 995 3836 2681 4036

Many of the Jews read this sign, for the place where Jesus was crucified was near the city,
πολλοὶ → τῶν Ἰουδαίων ἀνέγνωσαν τοῦτον ⌊τὸν τίτλον⌋ ὅτι ὁ τόπος ὅπου ⌊ὁ Ἰησοῦς⌋ → ἐσταυρώθη ἦν ἐγγὺς τῆς πόλεως
a.npm d.gpm a.gpm v.aai.3p r.asm d.asm n.asm cj d.nsm n.nsm cj d.nsm n.nsm v.api.3s v.iai.3s p.g d.gsf n.gsf
4498 3836 2681 336 4047 3836 5518 4022 3836 5536 3963 3836 2652 5090 1639 1584 3836 4484

ἄνωθεν· διὰ τοῦτο ὁ παραδούς μέ σοι μείζονα ἁμαρτίαν ἔχει. ¶ 12 ἐκ τούτου ὁ Πιλᾶτος ἐζήτει ἀπολῦσαι αὐτόν· οἱ δὲ Ἰουδαῖοι
ἐκραύγασαν λέγοντες, Ἐὰν τοῦτον ἀπολύσῃς, οὐκ εἶ φίλος τοῦ Καίσαρος· πᾶς ὁ βασιλέα ἑαυτὸν ποιῶν ἀντιλέγει τῷ Καίσαρι ¶
13 Ὁ οὖν Πιλᾶτος ἀκούσας τῶν λόγων τούτων ἤγαγεν ἔξω τὸν Ἰησοῦν καὶ ἐκάθισεν ἐπὶ βήματος εἰς τόπον λεγόμενον
Λιθόστρωτον, Ἑβραϊστὶ δὲ Γαββαθα. 14 ἦν δὲ παρασκευὴ τοῦ πάσχα, ὥρα ἦν ὡς ἕκτη. καὶ λέγει τοῖς Ἰουδαίοις, Ἴδε ὁ βασιλεὺς
ὑμῶν. 15 ἐκραύγασαν οὖν ἐκεῖνοι, Ἆρον ἆρον, σταύρωσον αὐτόν. λέγει αὐτοῖς ὁ Πιλᾶτος, Τὸν βασιλέα ὑμῶν σταυρώσω;
ἀπεκρίθησαν οἱ ἀρχιερεῖς, Οὐκ ἔχομεν βασιλέα εἰ μὴ Καίσαρα.

19:16 τότε οὖν παρέδωκεν αὐτὸν αὐτοῖς ἵνα σταυρωθῇ. Παρέλαβον οὖν τὸν Ἰησοῦν, 17 καὶ βαστάζων ἑαυτῷ τὸν σταυρὸν
ἐξῆλθεν εἰς τὸν λεγόμενον Κρανίου Τόπον, ὃ λέγεται Ἑβραϊστὶ Γολγοθα, 18 ὅπου αὐτὸν ἐσταύρωσαν, καὶ μετ᾽ αὐτοῦ ἄλλους
δύο ἐντεῦθεν καὶ ἐντεῦθεν, μέσον δὲ τὸν Ἰησοῦν. ¶ 19 ἔγραψεν δὲ καὶ τίτλον ὁ Πιλᾶτος καὶ ἔθηκεν ἐπὶ τοῦ σταυροῦ· ἦν δὲ
γεγραμμένον, Ἰησοῦς ὁ Ναζωραῖος ὁ βασιλεὺς τῶν Ἰουδαίων. 20 τοῦτον οὖν τὸν τίτλον πολλοὶ ἀνέγνωσαν τῶν Ἰουδαίων, ὅτι
ἐγγὺς ἦν ὁ τόπος τῆς πόλεως ὅπου ἐσταυρώθη ὁ Ἰησοῦς· καὶ ἦν γεγραμμένον Ἑβραϊστί, Ῥωμαϊστί, Ἑλληνιστί. 21 ἔλεγον οὖν

and the sign was written　　in Aramaic, Latin　　and Greek.　²¹　The chief priests　of the Jews　　protested to
καὶ　　ἦν　γεγραμμένον　Ἑβραϊστί　Ῥωμαϊστί　Ἑλληνιστί　οὖν οἱ →　ἀρχιερεῖς →　τῶν Ἰουδαίων　ἔλεγον →
cj　v.iai.3s　pt.rp.nsn　adv　adv　adv　cj d.npm　n.npm　d.gpm a.gpm　v.iai.3p
2779　1639　1211　1580　4872　1822　4036 3836　797　3836 2681　3306

Pilate,　　"Do not write 'The King　of the Jews,'　but that this　man claimed to be　king　of the Jews."
τῷ Πιλάτῳ →　μὴ γράφε ὁ　βασιλεὺς →　τῶν Ἰουδαίων ἀλλ' ὅτι ἐκεῖνος ←　εἶπεν　εἰμι βασιλεύς →　τῶν Ἰουδαίων
d.dsm n.dsm　pl v.pam.2s d.nsm　n.nsm →　d.gpm a.gpm　cj cj　r.nsm ←　v.aai.3s　v.pai.1s n.nsm　d.gpm a.gpm
3836 4397　1211 3590 1211 3836　995　3836 2681　247 4022 1697　3306　1639 995　3836 2681

²²　Pilate　　answered,　"What I have written, I have written."　¶　²³　When the soldiers　crucified　Jesus,
ὁ　Πιλάτος, ἀπεκρίθη ὁ → →　γέγραφα → →　γέγραφα　οὖν ὅτε　Οἱ στρατιῶται ἐσταύρωσαν τὸν Ἰησοῦν,
d.nsm n.nsm　v.api.3s r.asn　v.rai.1s　v.rai.1s　cj cj　d.npm n.npm　v.aai.3p　d.asm n.asm
3836 4397　646 4005　1211　1211　4036 4021　3836 5132　5090　3836 2652

they took　his　clothes,　　dividing them into four　shares, one for each　of them,　with the undergarment
→　ἔλαβον αὐτοῦ τὰ ἱμάτια καὶ ἐποίησαν　τέσσαρα μέρη　μέρος →　ἑκάστῳ　στρατιώτῃ καὶ　τὸν χιτῶνα
v.aai.3p r.gsm.3 d.apn n.apn cj v.aai.3p　a.apn n.apn　n.asn →　r.dsm　n.dsm cj　d.asm n.asm
3284 899 3836 2668 2779 4472　5475 3538　3538 1667　5132 2779　3836 5945

remaining.　This garment was seamless, woven　in one piece from top　to bottom.　²⁴　"Let's not tear
δὲ ὁ　χιτὼν　ἦν ἄραφος ὑφαντὸς δι' ὅλου ←　ἐκ τῶν ἄνωθεν　οὖν →　μὴ σχίσωμεν
cj d.nsm　n.nsm　v.iai.3s a.nsm a.nsm p.g a.gsm ←　p.g d.gpn adv　cj →　pl v.aas.1p
1254 3836　5945　1639 731 5733 1328 3910　1666 3836 540　4036　3590 5387

it," they said to　one　another.　　"Let's decide by lot who will　get it." This happened that the
αὐτόν →　εἶπαν πρὸς ἀλλήλους ←　ἀλλὰ →　λάχωμεν ←　← τίνος ἔσται περὶ →　αὐτοῦ　ἵνα ἡ
r.asm.3 →　v.aai.3p p.a r.apm ←　cj →　v.aas.1p ←　r.gsm v.fmi.3s p.g　r.gsm.3　cj d.nsf
899 3306 4639 253　247　3275　5515 1639 4309 1639 899　2671 3836

scripture might be fulfilled which said,　"They divided　my garments among them and cast lots for my
γραφὴ → → πληρωθῇ ἡ λέγουσα →　διεμερίσαντο μου τὰ ἱμάτια →　ἑαυτοῖς καὶ ἔβαλον κλῆρον ἐπὶ μου
n.nsf → v.aps.3s d.nsf pt.pa.nsf →　v.ami.3p r.gs.1 d.apn n.apn →　r.dpm.3 cj v.aai.3p n.asm p.a r.gs.1
1210 4444 3836 3306　1374 1609 3836 2668　1571 2779 965 3102 2093 1609

clothing." So　　this is what the soldiers did.　¶　²⁵　Near the cross of Jesus　stood　his
τὸν ἱματισμόν, οὖν μὲν ταῦτα　Οἱ στρατιῶται ἐποίησαν　δὲ παρὰ τῷ σταυρῷ → τοῦ Ἰησοῦ, Εἱστήκεισαν αὐτοῦ
d.asm n.asm　cj pl r.apn　d.npm n.npm v.aai.3p　cj p.d d.dsm n.dsm　d.gsm n.gsm v.lai.3p r.gsm.3
3836 2669　4036 3525 4047　3836 5132 4472　1254 4123 3836 5089　3836 2652 2705 899

mother,　his　mother's　sister,　Mary the wife of Clopas,　and Mary Magdalene.　²⁶　When Jesus
ἡ μήτηρ καὶ αὐτοῦ τῆς μητρὸς ἡ ἀδελφὴ Μαρία ἡ →　τοῦ Κλωπᾶ καὶ Μαρία ἡ Μαγδαληνή,　οὖν →　Ἰησοῦς
d.nsf n.nsf cj r.gsm.3 d.gsf n.gsf d.nsf n.nsf n.nsf d.nsf →　d.gsm n.gsm cj n.nsf d.nsf n.nsf　cj →　n.nsm
3836 3613 2779 899 3836 3613 3836 80 3451 3836　3836 3116 2779 3451 3836 3402　4036 1625　2652

saw　his mother there, and the disciple whom he loved standing nearby, he said to his mother, "Dear woman, here
ἰδὼν τὴν μητέρα　καὶ τὸν μαθητὴν ὃν →　ἠγάπα παρεστῶτα ←　→　λέγει τῇ μητρί →　γύναι ἴδε
pt.aa.nsm d.asf n.asf　cj d.asm n.asm r.asm →　v.iai.3s pt.ra.asm ←　v.pai.3s d.dsf n.dsf　n.vsf pl
1625 3836 3613　2779 3836 3412 4005 →　26 4225　3306 3836 3613　1222 2623

is your son,"　²⁷　and to the disciple,　　"Here is your mother."　From that　time　on, this disciple took
σου ὁ υἱός,　εἶτα →　τῷ μαθητῇ λέγει ἴδε　σου ἡ μήτηρ καὶ ἀπ'　ἐκείνης τῆς ὥρας, ←　ὁ μαθητὴς ἔλαβεν
r.gs.2 d.nsm n.nsm　adv →　d.dsm n.dsm v.pai.3s pl　r.gs.2 d.nsf n.nsf cj p.g　r.gsf d.gsf n.gsf　d.nsm n.nsm v.aai.3s
5148 3836 5626　1663 →　3836 3412 3306 2623　5148 3836 3613 2779 608　1697 3836 6052　608 3836 3412 3284

her　into his home.
αὐτὴν εἰς τὰ ἴδια
r.asf.3 p.a d.apn a.apn
899 1650 3836 2625

The Death of Jesus

¹⁹:²⁸ Later,　　knowing that all　was now completed, and so that the Scripture would be fulfilled,
Μετὰ τοῦτο εἰδὼς　ὅτι πάντα →　ἤδη τετέλεσται　ἵνα ←　ἡ γραφὴ →　→ τελειωθῇ
p.a r.asn pt.ra.nsm　cj a.npn →　adv v.rpi.3s　cj ←　d.nsf n.nsf　v.aps.3s
3552 4047 3857　4022 4246 →　2453 5464　2671　3836 1210　5457

Jesus　　said, "I am thirsty."　²⁹ A jar　　of wine vinegar was there, so they soaked a sponge in it,
ὁ Ἰησοῦς λέγει → → διψῶ　σκεῦος μεστόν → →　ὄξους →　ἔκειτο οὖν　μεστὸν σπόγγον τοῦ ὄξους
d.nsm n.nsm v.pai.3s　v.pai.1s　n.nsn a.nsn → →　n.gsn →　v.imi.3s cj　a.asm n.asm d.gsn n.gsn
3836 2652 3306　1498　5007 3550 →　3954 →　3023 4036　3550 5074 3836 3954

τῷ Πιλάτῳ οἱ ἀρχιερεῖς τῶν Ἰουδαίων, Μὴ γράφε, Ὁ βασιλεὺς τῶν Ἰουδαίων, ἀλλ᾽ ὅτι ἐκεῖνος εἶπεν, Βασιλεύς εἰμι τῶν Ἰουδαίων. ²² ἀπεκρίθη ὁ Πιλάτος, Ὃ γέγραφα, γέγραφα. ¶ ²³ Οἱ οὖν στρατιῶται, ὅτε ἐσταύρωσαν τὸν Ἰησοῦν, ἔλαβον τὰ ἱμάτια αὐτοῦ καὶ ἐποίησαν τέσσαρα μέρη, ἑκάστῳ στρατιώτῃ μέρος, καὶ τὸν χιτῶνα. ἦν δὲ ὁ χιτὼν ἄραφος, ἐκ τῶν ἄνωθεν ὑφαντὸς δι᾽ ὅλου. ²⁴ εἶπαν οὖν πρὸς ἀλλήλους, Μὴ σχίσωμεν αὐτόν, ἀλλὰ λάχωμεν περὶ αὐτοῦ τίνος ἔσται· ἵνα ἡ γραφὴ πληρωθῇ [ἡ λέγουσα], Διεμερίσαντο τὰ ἱμάτιά μου ἑαυτοῖς καὶ ἐπὶ τὸν ἱματισμόν μου ἔβαλον κλῆρον. Οἱ μὲν οὖν στρατιῶται ταῦτα ἐποίησαν. ¶ ²⁵ εἱστήκεισαν δὲ παρὰ τῷ σταυρῷ τοῦ Ἰησοῦ ἡ μήτηρ αὐτοῦ καὶ ἡ ἀδελφὴ τῆς μητρὸς αὐτοῦ, Μαρία ἡ τοῦ Κλωπᾶ καὶ Μαρία ἡ Μαγδαληνή. ²⁶ Ἰησοῦς οὖν ἰδὼν τὴν μητέρα καὶ τὸν μαθητὴν παρεστῶτα ὃν ἠγάπα, λέγει τῇ μητρί, Γύναι, ἴδε ὁ υἱός σου. ²⁷ εἶτα λέγει τῷ μαθητῇ, Ἴδε ἡ μήτηρ σου. καὶ ἀπ᾽ ἐκείνης τῆς ὥρας ἔλαβεν ὁ μαθητὴς αὐτὴν εἰς τὰ ἴδια. ¹⁹:²⁸ Μετὰ τοῦτο εἰδὼς ὁ Ἰησοῦς ὅτι ἤδη πάντα τετέλεσται, ἵνα τελειωθῇ ἡ γραφή, λέγει, Διψῶ. ²⁹ σκεῦος ἔκειτο ὄξους μεστόν·

put   the sponge on a stalk of the hyssop plant, and lifted   it to Jesus' lips. **30** When he had received
περιθέντες   → → → ὑσσώπῳ ←   προσήνεγκαν αὐτοῦ → τῷ στόματι   οὖν ὅτε → → ἔλαβεν
pt.aa.npm   n.dsf   v.aai.3p r.gsm.3   d.dsn n.dsn   cj cj   v.aai.3s
4363   5727   4712 899 5125 3836 5125   4036 4021   3284

the drink, Jesus   said, "It is finished." *With that,* he bowed his head   and gave   up his spirit. ¶
τὸ ὄξος ὁ Ἰησοῦς, εἶπεν → → τετέλεσται καὶ → → κλίνας τὴν κεφαλὴν   παρέδωκεν ← τὸ πνεῦμα
d.asn n.asn d.nsm n.nsm v.aai.3s v.rpi.3s cj   pt.aa.nsm d.asf n.asf   v.aai.3s   d.asn n.asn
3836 3954 3836 2652 3306 5464 2779   3111 3836 3051   4140   3836 4460

31 Now it was the day of Preparation,   and the   next day was to be a special Sabbath.   Because the
οὖν ἐπεὶ → ἦν → → παρασκευὴ γὰρ ἡ ἐκείνου ἡμέρα ἦν   μεγάλη ⸂τοῦ σαββάτου⸃   Οἱ
cj cj v.iai.3s n.nsf cj d.nsf r.gsn n.nsf v.iai.3s   a.nsf d.gsn n.gsn   d.npm
4036 2075 1639 4187 1142 3836 1697 2465 1639   3489 3836 4879   3836

Jews   did not want the bodies left   on the crosses during the Sabbath, they asked   Pilate   to have the
Ἰουδαῖοι ἵνα μὴ → τὰ σώματα μείνῃ ἐπὶ τοῦ σταυροῦ ἐν τῷ σαββάτῳ → ἠρώτησαν τὸν Πιλᾶτον ἵνα → τὰ
a.npm cj pl d.npn n.npn v.aas.3s p.d d.gsm n.gsm p.d d.dsn n.dsn v.aai.3p d.asm n.asm cj   d.apn
2681 2671 3590 3836 5393 3531 2093 3836 5089 1877 3836 4879 2263 3836 4397 2671 2862 3836

legs   broken   and the bodies taken   down. **32** The soldiers therefore came and   broke   the legs of the
σκέλη αὐτῶν κατεαγῶσιν καὶ   ἀρθῶσιν ← οἱ στρατιῶται οὖν ἦλθον καὶ μὲν κατέαξαν τὰ σκέλη → τοῦ
n.apn r.gpm.3 v.aps.3p cj   v.aps.3p d.npm n.npm cj v.aai.3p cj pl v.aai.3p d.apn n.apn d.gsm
5003 899 2862 2779   149 3836 5132 4036 2262 2779 3525 2862 3836 5003 3836

first man who had been crucified   with Jesus, and then those of the other. **33** But when they came   to
πρώτου ← τοῦ → → συσταυρωθέντος ← αὐτῷ καὶ → τοῦ ἄλλου δὲ → → ἐλθόντες ἐπὶ
a.gsm   d.gsm   pt.ap.gsm   r.dsm.3 cj   d.gsm r.gsm cj   pt.aa.npm p.a
4755   3836   5365   899 2779   3836 257 1254   2262 2093

Jesus   and found that he   was already dead,   they did not break   his legs. **34** Instead, one of the
⸂τὸν Ἰησοῦν⸃ ὡς εἶδον αὐτὸν → ἤδη τεθνηκότα → οὐ κατέαξαν αὐτοῦ ⸂τὰ σκέλη⸃ ἀλλ' εἰς → τῶν
d.asm n.asm cj v.aai.3p r.asm.3 adv pt.ra.asm pl v.aai.3p r.gsm.3 d.apn n.apn cj a.nsm d.gpm
3836 2652 6055 1625 899 2453 2569 4024 2862 899 3836 5003 247 1651 3836

soldiers pierced Jesus' side   with a spear,   bringing a sudden flow   of blood and water. **35** The man
στρατιωτῶν ἔνυξεν αὐτοῦ ⸂τὴν πλευρὰν⸃ → λόγχῃ καὶ → → εὐθὺς ἐξῆλθεν αἷμα καὶ ὕδωρ καὶ ὁ
n.gpm v.aai.3s r.gsm.3 d.asf n.asf n.dsf cj   adv v.aai.3s n.nsn cj n.nsn cj d.nsm
5132 3817 899 3836 4433 3365 2779 2002   2318 2002 135 2779 5623 2779 3836

who saw   it has given testimony,   and his   testimony   is true.   He   knows that he tells the truth, and
← ἑωρακὼς → → μεμαρτύρηκεν καὶ αὐτοῦ ⸂ἡ μαρτυρία⸃ ἐστιν ἀληθινὴ καὶ ἐκεῖνος οἶδεν ὅτι → λέγει ἀληθῆ
pt.ra.nsm v.rai.3s cj r.gsm.3 d.nsf n.nsf v.pai.3s a.nsf cj r.nsm v.rai.3s cj   v.pai.3s a.apn
3972 3455 2779 899 3836 3456 1639 240 2779 1697 3857 4022   3306 239

he testifies so that you   also may believe. **36** These things happened so that the scripture would be fulfilled:
ἵνα ← ὑμεῖς καὶ → πιστεύσητε γὰρ ταῦτα → ἐγένετο ἵνα → ἡ γραφὴ → → πληρωθῇ
cj r.np.2 adv v.aas.2p cj r.npn v.ami.3s cj d.nsf n.nsf v.aps.3s
2671 7007 2779 4409 1142 4047 1181 2671 3836 1210 4444

"Not one of his   bones will be broken,"   **37** and,   as another scripture says, "They will look   on the one they
οὐ αὐτοῦ ὀστοῦν → → συντριβήσεται καὶ πάλιν ἑτέρα γραφὴ λέγει → → ὄψονται εἰς ὃν →
pl r.gsm.3 n.nsn v.fpi.3s cj adv r.nsf n.nsf v.pai.3s v.fmi.3p p.a r.asm
4024 899 4014 5341 2779 4099 2283 1210 3306 3972 1650 4005

have pierced."
→ ἐξεκέντησαν
v.aai.3p
1708

The Burial of Jesus

19:38 Later,   Joseph of   Arimathea   asked   Pilate   for   the body of Jesus. Now Joseph
δὲ ⸂Μετὰ ταῦτα⸃ Ἰωσὴφ ἀπὸ ὁ Ἁριμαθαίας, ἠρώτησεν τὸν Πιλᾶτον, ἵνα ἄρῃ τὸ σῶμα τοῦ Ἰησοῦ Ἰωσὴφ
cj p.a r.apn n.nsm p.g d.nsm n.gsf v.aai.3s d.asm n.asm cj v.aas.3s d.asn n.asn d.gsm n.gsm
1254 3552 4047 2737 608 3836 751 2263 3836 4397 2671 149 3836 5393 3836 2652

was a disciple of Jesus,   but secretly   because he feared   the Jews.   With Pilate's   permission,
ὢν μαθητὴς → ⸂τοῦ Ἰησοῦ⸃ δὲ κεκρυμμένος διὰ ⸂τὸν φόβον⸃ τῶν Ἰουδαίων καὶ → ὁ Πιλᾶτος, ἐπέτρεψεν οὖν
pt.pa.nsm n.nsm d.gsm n.gsm cj pt.rp.nsm p.a d.asm n.asm d.gpm a.gpm cj d.nsm n.nsm v.aai.3s cj
1639 3412 3836 2652 1254 3221 1328 3836 5832 3836 2681 2779 2205 3836 4397 2205 4036

σπόγγον οὖν μεστὸν τοῦ ὄξους ὑσσώπῳ περιθέντες προσήνεγκαν αὐτοῦ τῷ στόματι. 30 ὅτε οὖν ἔλαβεν τὸ ὄξος [ὁ] Ἰησοῦς εἶπεν, Τετέλεσται, καὶ κλίνας τὴν κεφαλὴν παρέδωκεν τὸ πνεῦμα. ¶ 31 Οἱ οὖν Ἰουδαῖοι, ἐπεὶ παρασκευὴ ἦν, ἵνα μὴ μείνῃ ἐπὶ τοῦ σταυροῦ τὰ σώματα ἐν τῷ σαββάτῳ, ἦν γὰρ μεγάλη ἡ ἡμέρα ἐκείνου τοῦ σαββάτου, ἠρώτησαν τὸν Πιλᾶτον ἵνα κατεαγῶσιν αὐτῶν τὰ σκέλη καὶ ἀρθῶσιν. 32 ἦλθον οὖν οἱ στρατιῶται καὶ τοῦ μὲν πρώτου κατέαξαν τὰ σκέλη καὶ τοῦ ἄλλου τοῦ συσταυρωθέντος αὐτῷ· 33 ἐπὶ δὲ τὸν Ἰησοῦν ἐλθόντες, ὡς εἶδον ἤδη αὐτὸν τεθνηκότα, οὐ κατέαξαν αὐτοῦ τὰ σκέλη, 34 ἀλλ' εἰς τῶν στρατιωτῶν λόγχῃ αὐτοῦ τὴν πλευρὰν ἔνυξεν, καὶ ἐξῆλθεν εὐθὺς αἷμα καὶ ὕδωρ. 35 καὶ ὁ ἑωρακὼς μεμαρτύρηκεν, καὶ ἀληθινὴ αὐτοῦ ἐστιν ἡ μαρτυρία, καὶ ἐκεῖνος οἶδεν ὅτι ἀληθῆ λέγει, ἵνα καὶ ὑμεῖς πιστεύ[σ]ητε. 36 ἐγένετο γὰρ ταῦτα ἵνα ἡ γραφὴ πληρωθῇ, Ὀστοῦν οὐ συντριβήσεται αὐτοῦ. 37 καὶ πάλιν ἑτέρα γραφὴ λέγει, Ὄψονται εἰς ὃν ἐξεκέντησαν.

19:38 Μετὰ δὲ ταῦτα ἠρώτησεν τὸν Πιλᾶτον Ἰωσὴφ [ὁ] ἀπὸ Ἁριμαθαίας, ὢν μαθητὴς τοῦ Ἰησοῦ κεκρυμμένος δὲ διὰ τὸν φόβον τῶν Ἰουδαίων, ἵνα ἄρῃ τὸ σῶμα τοῦ Ἰησοῦ· καὶ ἐπέτρεψεν ὁ Πιλᾶτος. ἦλθεν οὖν καὶ ἦρεν τὸ σῶμα αὐτοῦ. 39 ἦλθεν δὲ

he came and took the body   away. **39**   He was accompanied by Nicodemus,   the man who earlier   had
→ ἦλθεν καὶ ἦρεν τὸ σῶμα αὐτοῦ ↵   δὲ →   ἦλθεν   Νικόδημος καὶ ὁ   ↙τὸ πρῶτον· →
v.aai.3s cj v.aai.3s d.asn n.asn r.gsm.3   cj   v.aai.3s   n.nsm   adv d.nsm   d.asn adv
2262 2779 149 3836 5393 899 149   1254   2262   3773   2779 3836   3836 4754

visited   Jesus at night. Nicodemus brought a mixture of myrrh and aloes, about *seventy-five* *pounds.* **40**   Taking
ἐλθὼν πρὸς αὐτὸν → νυκτός   φέρων   μίγμα → σμύρνης καὶ ἀλόης ὡς ἑκατὸν   λίτρας   οὖν ἔλαβον
pt.aa.nsm p.a r.asn.3 n.gsf   pt.pa.nsm   n.asn   n.gsf cj n.gsf pl a.apf   n.apf   cj v.aai.3p
2262 4639 899 3816   5770   3623   5043 2779 264 6055 1669   3354   4036 3284

Jesus'   body,   the two of them wrapped it,   with the spices,   in strips of linen. This was in
↙τοῦ Ἰησοῦ· τὸ σῶμα καὶ   ἔδησαν αὐτὸ μετὰ τῶν ἀρωμάτων →   ὀθονίοις →   ἐστὶν καθὼς
d.gsm n.gsm d.asn n.asn cj   v.aai.3p r.asn.3 p.g d.gpn n.gpn   n.dpn   v.pai.3s cj
3836 2652 3836 5393 2779   1313 899 3552 3836 808   3856   1639 2777

accordance with Jewish   burial   customs. **41** At the place where Jesus was crucified, there was a garden,
←   ↙τοῖς Ἰουδαίοις· ἐνταφιάζειν ἔθος   δὲ ἐν τῷ τόπῳ ὅπου   →   ἐσταυρώθη →   ἦν κῆπος
d.dpm a.dpm f.pa n.nsn   cj p.d d.dsm n.dsm cj   v.api.3s   v.iai.3s n.nsm
3836 2681 1946 1621   1254 1877 3836 5536 3963   5090   1639 3057

and in the garden a new   tomb, in which no one had ever been laid.   **42** Because it was the
καὶ ἐν τῷ κήπῳ   καινὸν μνημεῖον ἐν ᾧ   →   οὐδεὶς   οὐδέπω ἦν τεθειμένος οὖν διὰ   τὴν
cj p.d d.dsm n.dsm a.nsn n.nsn p.d r.dsn   a.nsm   adv v.iai.3s pt.rp.nsm cj p.a   d.asf
2779 1877 3836 3057 2785 3646 1877 4005   4029   4031 1639 5502 4036 1328   3836

Jewish   day of Preparation and since the tomb was nearby, they laid Jesus   there.
↙τῶν Ἰουδαίων· →   παρασκευὴν   ὅτι τὸ μνημεῖον ἦν ἐγγὺς   →   ἔθηκαν τὸν Ἰησοῦν, ἐκεῖ
d.gpm a.gpm n.asf   cj d.nsn n.nsn v.iai.3s adv   v.aai.3p d.asm n.asn adv
3836 2681 4187   4022 3836 3646 1639 1584   5502 3836 2652 1695

The Empty Tomb

20:1 Early on the first day of the week,   while it was still dark, Mary Magdalene   went to the tomb
δὲ πρωῒ → Τῇ μιᾷ → τῶν σαββάτων →   → οὔσης ἔτι σκοτίας Μαρία ἡ Μαγδαληνὴ ἔρχεται εἰς τὸ μνημεῖον
cj adv d.dsf a.dsf d.gpn n.gpn   pt.pa.gsf adv n.gsf n.nsf d.nsf n.nsf v.pmi.3s p.a d.asn n.asn
1254 4745 3836 1651 3836 4879   1639 2285 5028 3451 3836 3402 2262 1650 3836 3646

and saw   that the stone had been removed from the entrance. **2** So she came   running to Simon Peter and
καὶ βλέπει   τὸν λίθον   ἠρμένον ἐκ τοῦ μνημείου   οὖν → ἔρχεται καὶ τρέχει   πρὸς Σίμωνα Πέτρον καὶ
cj v.pai.3s   d.asm n.asm   pt.rp.asm p.g d.gsn n.gsn   cj v.pmi.3s cj v.pai.3s   p.a n.asm n.asm cj
2779 1063   3836 3345   149 1666 3836 3646   4036 2262 2779 5556   4639 4981 4377 2779

the other disciple, the one Jesus   loved, and said,   "They have taken the Lord out of the tomb,
πρὸς τὸν ἄλλον μαθητὴν ὃν → ὁ Ἰησοῦς, ἐφίλει καὶ λέγει αὐτοῖς →   → ἦραν τὸν κύριον ἐκ ← τοῦ μνημείου
p.a d.asm r.asm n.asm r.asm d.nsm n.nsm v.iai.3s cj v.pai.3s r.dpm.3   v.aai.3p d.asm n.asm p.g d.gsn n.gsn
4639 3836 257 3412 4005 3836 2652 5797 2779 3306 899   149 3836 3261 1666 3836 3646

and we don't know where they have put him!" ¶ **3** So Peter and the other disciple started
καὶ → οὐκ οἴδαμεν ποῦ → ἔθηκαν αὐτόν →   οὖν ὁ Πέτρος, καὶ ὁ ἄλλος μαθητὴς ἐξῆλθεν καὶ ἤρχοντο
cj pl v.rai.1p adv → v.aai.3p r.asm.3   cj d.nsm n.nsm cj d.nsm r.nsm n.nsm v.aai.3s cj v.imi.3p
2779 3857 4024 3857 4543 5502 899   4036 3836 4377 2779 3836 257 3412 2002 2779 2262

for the tomb. **4** Both   were running, but the other disciple outran   Peter   and reached
εἰς τὸ μνημεῖον δὲ οἱ δύο, → ἔτρεχον ὁμοῦ καὶ ὁ ἄλλος μαθητὴς προέδραμεν τάχιον ↙τοῦ Πέτρου, καὶ ἦλθεν εἰς
p.a d.asn n.asn cj d.npm a.npm v.iai.3p adv cj d.nsm r.nsm n.nsm v.aai.3s adv.c d.gsm n.gsm cj v.aai.3s p.a
1650 3836 3646 1254 3836 1545 5556 3938 2779 3836 257 3412 4731 5441 3836 4377 2779 2262 1650

the tomb first. **5** He bent   over and looked in at the strips of linen lying there but did not go   in.
τὸ μνημεῖον πρῶτος καὶ → παρακύψας ← βλέπει ← τὰ → ὀθόνια κείμενα   μέντοι → οὐ εἰσῆλθεν
d.asn n.asn n.nsm cj pt.aa.nsm v.pai.3s d.apn n.apn pt.pm.apn   cj pl v.aai.3s
3836 3646 4755 2779 1063 3836 3856 3023   3530 4024 1656

6 Then   Simon Peter, who was behind him, arrived and went into the tomb.   He saw   the strips of linen
οὖν καὶ Σίμων Πέτρος, → ἀκολουθῶν αὐτῷ ἔρχεται καὶ εἰσῆλθεν εἰς τὸ μνημεῖον καὶ   θεωρεῖ τὰ → ὀθόνια
cj adv n.nsm n.nsm pt.pa.nsm r.dsm.3 v.pmi.3s cj v.aai.3s p.a d.asn n.asn cj   v.pai.3s d.apn n.apn
4036 2779 4981 4377 199 899 2262 2779 1656 1650 3836 3646 2779   2555 3836 3856

lying   there, **7** as well as the burial cloth   that had been around Jesus' head.   The cloth was folded   up
κείμενα   καὶ ← τὸ → σουδάριον ὃ → ἦν ἐπὶ αὐτοῦ ↙τῆς κεφαλῆς, →   ἐντετυλιγμένον ←
pt.pm.apn   cj d.asn n.asn r.nsn v.iai.3s p.g r.gsm.3 d.gsf n.gsf   pt.rp.asn
3023   2779 3836 5051 4005 1639 2093 899 3836 3051   1962

καὶ Νικόδημος, ὁ ἐλθὼν πρὸς αὐτὸν νυκτὸς τὸ πρῶτον, φέρων μίγμα σμύρνης καὶ ἀλόης ὡς λίτρας ἑκατόν. **40** ἔλαβον οὖν τὸ σῶμα τοῦ Ἰησοῦ καὶ ἔδησαν αὐτὸ ὀθονίοις μετὰ τῶν ἀρωμάτων, καθὼς ἔθος ἐστὶν τοῖς Ἰουδαίοις ἐνταφιάζειν. **41** ἦν δὲ ἐν τῷ τόπῳ ὅπου ἐσταυρώθη κῆπος, καὶ ἐν τῷ κήπῳ μνημεῖον καινὸν ἐν ᾧ οὐδέπω οὐδεὶς ἦν τεθειμένος· **42** ἐκεῖ οὖν διὰ τὴν παρασκευὴν τῶν Ἰουδαίων, ὅτι ἐγγὺς ἦν τὸ μνημεῖον, ἔθηκαν τὸν Ἰησοῦν.

20:1 Τῇ δὲ μιᾷ τῶν σαββάτων Μαρία ἡ Μαγδαληνὴ ἔρχεται πρωῒ σκοτίας ἔτι οὔσης εἰς τὸ μνημεῖον καὶ βλέπει τὸν λίθον ἠρμένον ἐκ τοῦ μνημείου. **2** τρέχει οὖν καὶ ἔρχεται πρὸς Σίμωνα Πέτρον καὶ πρὸς τὸν ἄλλον μαθητὴν ὃν ἐφίλει ὁ Ἰησοῦς καὶ λέγει αὐτοῖς, Ἦραν τὸν κύριον ἐκ τοῦ μνημείου καὶ οὐκ οἴδαμεν ποῦ ἔθηκαν αὐτόν. ¶ **3** Ἐξῆλθεν οὖν ὁ Πέτρος καὶ ὁ ἄλλος μαθητὴς καὶ ἤρχοντο εἰς τὸ μνημεῖον. **4** ἔτρεχον δὲ οἱ δύο ὁμοῦ· καὶ ὁ ἄλλος μαθητὴς προέδραμεν τάχιον τοῦ Πέτρου καὶ ἦλθεν πρῶτος εἰς τὸ μνημεῖον, **5** καὶ παρακύψας βλέπει κείμενα τὰ ὀθόνια, οὐ μέντοι εἰσῆλθεν. **6** ἔρχεται οὖν καὶ Σίμων Πέτρος ἀκολουθῶν αὐτῷ καὶ εἰσῆλθεν εἰς τὸ μνημεῖον, καὶ θεωρεῖ τὰ ὀθόνια κείμενα, **7** καὶ τὸ σουδάριον, ὃ ἦν ἐπὶ τῆς κεφαλῆς αὐτοῦ,

by	itself,			separate	from the	linen.	**8**	Finally	the	other	disciple,	who	had	reached		the
χωρὶς	⌐εἰς ἕνα	τόπον⌐	ἀλλὰ	⌐οὐ μετὰ ←		τῶν ὀθονίων	κείμενον	οὖν	τότε	ὁ	ἄλλος	μαθητὴς	ὁ	→	ἐλθὼν	εἰς τὸ
adv	p.a	a.asm	n.asm	cj	pl	p.g	d.gpn	n.gpn	pt.pm.asn	cj	adv	d.nsm	r.nsm	n.nsm	d.nsm	pt.aa.nsm	p.a	d.asn
6006	1650 1651	5536	247	4024	3552	3836 3856	3023	4036	5538	3836	257	3412	3836	2262	1650 3836

tomb	first,	also	went	inside.		He	saw	and	believed.	**9**	(They still	did	not	understand	from	Scripture
μνημεῖον	πρῶτος	καὶ	εἰσῆλθεν ←		καὶ →	εἶδεν	καὶ	ἐπίστευσεν	γὰρ ↱	→	→	οὐδέπω	ᾔδεισαν	⌐τὴν γραφὴν⌐
n.asn	a.nsm	adv	v.aai.3s		cj	v.aai.3s	cj	v.aai.3s	cj	adv	v.lai.3p	d.asf	n.asf
3646	4755	2779	1656		2779	1625	2779	4409	1142	3857	4031	3857	3857	3836 1210

that	Jesus	had	to rise		from	the dead.)
ὅτι	αὐτὸν	δεῖ	→	ἀναστῆναι	ἐκ	νεκρῶν
cj	r.asm.3	v.pai.3s		v.aa	p.g	a.gpm
4022	899	1256	482	1666	3738

Jesus Appears to Mary Magdalene

20:10 Then	the	disciples	went	back	to	their	homes,	**11** but	Mary	stood	outside		the	tomb	crying.		As
οὖν	οἱ	μαθηταί	ἀπῆλθον	πάλιν	πρὸς	αὑτούς		δὲ	Μαρία	εἱστήκει	ἔξω		πρὸς τῷ	μνημείῳ	κλαίουσα	οὖν	ὡς
cj	d.npm	n.npm	v.aai.3p	adv	p.a	r.apm.3		cj	n.nsf	v.lai.3s	adv		p.d	d.dsn	n.dsn	pt.pa.nsf	cj	cj
4036	3836	3412	599	4099	4639	899		1254	3451	2705	2032		4639	3836	3646	3081	4036	6055

she wept,	she bent		over to look	into the tomb	**12** and saw	two	angels	in	white,	seated		where	Jesus'
→ ἔκλαιεν	→ παρέκυψεν ←		εἰς τὸ	μνημεῖον	καὶ θεωρεῖ	δύο	ἀγγέλους	ἐν	λευκοῖς	καθεζομένους		ὅπου	⌐τοῦ Ἰησοῦ⌐
v.iai.3s	v.aai.3s		p.a	d.asn	n.asn	cj	v.pai.3s	a.apm	n.apm	p.d	a.dpn	pt.pm.apm		cj	d.gsm n.gsm
3081	4160		1650	3836	3646	2779	2555	1545	34	1877	3328	2757		3963	3836 2652

body	had been,	one	at	the	head	and	the	other	at	the	foot.	**13**	They	asked	her,	"Woman,	why	are you
⌐τὸ σῶμα⌐	→	ἔκειτο	ἕνα	πρὸς	τῇ	κεφαλῇ	καὶ	→	ἕνα	πρὸς	τοῖς	ποσίν	καὶ	ἐκεῖνοι	λέγουσιν	αὐτῇ	γύναι	τί
d.nsn n.nsn		v.imi.3s	a.asm	p.d	d.dsf	n.dsf	cj		a.asm	p.d	d.dpm	n.dpm	cj	r.npm	v.pai.3p	r.dsf.3	n.vsf	r.asn
3836 5393		3023	1651	4639	3836	3051	2779		1651	4639	3836	4546	2779	1697	3306	899	1222	5515

crying?"	"They	have	taken	my	Lord		away,"	she said,		"and I	don't	know	where	they have	put
κλαίεις	ὅτι	→	→	ἦραν	μου	⌐τὸν κύριον⌐	←	→	λέγει	αὐτοῖς	καὶ	⌐	οὐκ	οἶδα	ποῦ	→	→	ἔθηκαν
v.pai.2s	cj			v.aai.3p	r.gs.1	d.asm n.asm			v.pai.3s	r.dpm.3	cj		pl	v.rai.1s	adv			v.aai.3p
3081	4022			149	1609	3836 3261	149		3306	899	2779	3857	4024	3857	4543	5502

him."	**14** At this,		she turned around		and saw	Jesus		standing there,	but	she did not	realize	that	it
αὐτόν	ταῦτα	εἰποῦσα	→	ἐστράφη	⌐εἰς τὰ	ὀπίσω⌐	καὶ	θεωρεῖ	⌐τὸν Ἰησοῦν⌐	ἑστῶτα	καὶ	↱	→	οὐκ	ᾔδει	ὅτι
r.asm.3	r.apn	pt.aa.nsf		v.api.3s	p.a	d.apn adv	cj	v.pai.3s	d.asm n.asm	pt.ra.asm		cj			pl	v.lai.3s	cj
899	4047	3306		5138	1650	3836 3958	2779	2555	3836 2652	7705		2779	3857	3857	4024	3857	4022

was	Jesus.	**15** "Woman,"	he	said,		"why	are you	crying?	Who	is it	you are	looking for?"	Thinking		he	was
ἐστιν	Ἰησοῦς	γύναι		Ἰησοῦς	λέγει	αὐτῇ	τί	→	→	κλαίεις	τίνα	→	→	ζητεῖς	←	δοκοῦσα	ὅτι	→	ἐστιν
v.pai.3s	n.nsm	n.vsf		n.nsm	v.pai.3s	r.dsf.3	r.asn			v.pai.2s	r.asm			v.pai.2s		pt.pa.nsf	cj		v.pai.3s
1639	2652	1222		2652	3306	899	5515			3081	5515			2426		1506	4022		1639

the	gardener,	she	said,		"Sir,	if	you have	carried	him	away,	tell	me	where	you have	put		him,	and I
ὁ	κηπουρός	ἐκείνη	λέγει	αὐτῷ	κύριε	εἰ	σὺ	→	ἐβάστασας	αὐτόν	→	εἰπέ	μοι	ποῦ	→	→	ἔθηκας	αὐτόν	κἀγὼ
d.nsm	n.nsm	r.nsf	v.pai.3s	r.dsm.3	n.vsm	cj	r.ns.2	→	v.aai.2s	r.asm.3		v.aam.2s	r.ds.1	adv			v.aai.2s	r.asm.3	crasis
3836	3058	1697	3306	899	3261	1623	5148		1002	899	1002	3306	1609	4543			5502	899	2743

will get	him."	**16** Jesus	said	to her,	"Mary."	She	turned	toward him	and cried out		in	Aramaic,	"Rabboni!"
→ ἀρῶ	αὐτόν	Ἰησοῦς	λέγει	αὐτῇ	Μαριάμ	ἐκείνη	στραφεῖσα		λέγει	←	αὐτῷ	Ἑβραϊστί	ραββουνι
v.fai.1s	r.asm.3	n.nsm	v.pai.3s	r.dsf.3	n.vsf	r.nsf	pt.ap.nsf		v.pai.3s		r.dsm.3	adv	n.vsm
149	899	2652	3306	899	3452	1697	5138		3306		899	1580	4808

(which	means	Teacher).	**17** Jesus	said,		"Do not	hold on to	me,	for I	have	not	yet	returned	to	the	Father.
ὃ	λέγεται	διδάσκαλε	Ἰησοῦς	λέγει	αὐτῇ	μή	ἅπτου ←	μου	γάρ	↱	→	οὔπω	ἀναβέβηκα	πρὸς	τὸν	πατέρα
r.nsn	v.ppi.3s	n.vsm	n.nsm	v.pai.3s	r.dsf.3	pl	v.pmm.2s	r.gs.1	cj			adv	v.rai.1s	p.a	d.asm	n.asm
4005	3306	1437	2652	3306	899	721	3590	721	1609	1142	326	326	4037	326	4639	3836	4252

Go	instead	to	my brothers		and	tell	them,	'I am	returning	to	my	Father		and	your	Father,		to my
πορεύου	δὲ	πρὸς	μου	⌐τοὺς ἀδελφούς⌐	καὶ	εἰπὲ	αὐτοῖς	→	ἀναβαίνω	πρὸς	μου	⌐τὸν πατέρα⌐	καὶ	ὑμῶν	πατέρα	καὶ	μου
v.pmm.2s	cj	p.a	r.gs.1	d.apm n.apm	cj	v.aam.2s	r.dpm.3		v.pai.1s	p.a	r.gs.1	d.asm n.asm	cj	r.gp.2	n.asm	cj	r.gs.1
4513	1254	4639	1609	3836	2779	3306	899		326	4639	1609	3836 4252	2779	7007	4252	2779	1609

God	and	your	God.'"	¶	**18** Mary	Magdalene		went	to	the disciples	with the news:		"I have	seen
θεόν	καὶ	ὑμῶν	θεόν		Μαριάμ	ἡ	Μαγδαληνή	ἔρχεται	→	τοῖς μαθηταῖς	→	ἀγγέλλουσα	ὅτι →	→	ἑώρακα
n.asm	cj	r.gp.2	n.asm		n.nsf	d.nsf	n.nsf	v.pmi.3s		d.dpm n.dpm		pt.pa.nsf	cj		v.rai.1s
2536	2779	7007	2536		3452	3836	3402	2262		3836 3412		33	4022		3972

οὐ μετὰ τῶν ὀθονίων κείμενον ἀλλὰ χωρὶς ἐντετυλιγμένον εἰς ἕνα τόπον. ⁸ τότε οὖν εἰσῆλθεν καὶ ὁ ἄλλος μαθητὴς ὁ ἐλθὼν πρῶτος εἰς τὸ μνημεῖον καὶ εἶδεν καὶ ἐπίστευσεν· ⁹ οὐδέπω γὰρ ᾔδεισαν τὴν γραφὴν ὅτι δεῖ αὐτὸν ἐκ νεκρῶν ἀναστῆναι.

²⁰:¹⁰ ἀπῆλθον οὖν πάλιν πρὸς αὐτοὺς οἱ μαθηταί. ¹¹ Μαρία δὲ εἱστήκει πρὸς τῷ μνημείῳ ἔξω κλαίουσα. ὡς οὖν ἔκλαιεν, παρέκυψεν εἰς τὸ μνημεῖον ¹² καὶ θεωρεῖ δύο ἀγγέλους ἐν λευκοῖς καθεζομένους, ἕνα πρὸς τῇ κεφαλῇ καὶ ἕνα πρὸς τοῖς ποσίν, ὅπου ἔκειτο τὸ σῶμα τοῦ Ἰησοῦ. ¹³ καὶ λέγουσιν αὐτῇ ἐκεῖνοι, Γύναι, τί κλαίεις; λέγει αὐτοῖς ὅτι ῏Ηραν τὸν κύριόν μου, καὶ οὐκ οἶδα ποῦ ἔθηκαν αὐτόν. ¹⁴ ταῦτα εἰποῦσα ἐστράφη εἰς τὰ ὀπίσω καὶ θεωρεῖ τὸν Ἰησοῦν ἑστῶτα καὶ οὐκ ᾔδει ὅτι Ἰησοῦς ἐστιν. ¹⁵ λέγει αὐτῇ Ἰησοῦς, Γύναι, τί κλαίεις; τίνα ζητεῖς; ἐκείνη δοκοῦσα ὅτι ὁ κηπουρός ἐστιν λέγει αὐτῷ, Κύριε, εἰ σὺ ἐβάστασας αὐτόν, εἰπέ μοι ποῦ ἔθηκας αὐτόν, κἀγὼ αὐτὸν ἀρῶ. ¹⁶ λέγει αὐτῇ Ἰησοῦς, Μαριάμ. στραφεῖσα ἐκείνη λέγει αὐτῷ Ἑβραϊστί, Ραββουνι (ὃ λέγεται Διδάσκαλε). ¹⁷ λέγει αὐτῇ Ἰησοῦς, Μή μου ἅπτου, οὔπω γὰρ ἀναβέβηκα πρὸς τὸν πατέρα· πορεύου δὲ πρὸς τοὺς ἀδελφούς μου καὶ εἰπὲ αὐτοῖς, Ἀναβαίνω πρὸς τὸν πατέρα μου καὶ πατέρα ὑμῶν καὶ θεόν μου καὶ θεὸν ὑμῶν. ¶ ¹⁸ ἔρχεται Μαριὰμ ἡ Μαγδαληνὴ ἀγγέλλουσα τοῖς μαθηταῖς ὅτι Ἑώρακα τὸν κύριον, καὶ ταῦτα εἶπεν αὐτῇ.

the Lord!" And she told them that he had said these things to her.
τὸν κύριον καὶ   → → εἶπεν ταῦτα ← → αὐτῇ
d.asm n.asm cj   v.aai.3s r.apn r.dsf.3
3836 3261 2779   3306 4047 899

Jesus Appears to His Disciples

20:19 On the evening of that first day of the week, when the disciples were together, with the
οὖν Οὔσης ὀψίας ἐκείνη τῇ μιᾷ τῇ ἡμέρᾳ → σαββάτων ὅπου οἱ μαθηταὶ ἦσαν ← καὶ τῶν
cj pt.pa.gsf n.gsf r.dsf d.dsf a.dsf d.dsf n.dsf n.gpn d.npm n.npm v.iai.3p cj d.gpf
4036 1639 4068 1697 3836 1651 3836 2465 4879 3963 3836 3412 1639 3963 2779 3836

doors locked for fear of the Jews, Jesus came and stood among them and said,
θυρῶν κεκλεισμένων διὰ τὸν φόβον → τῶν Ἰουδαίων ὁ Ἰησοῦς ἦλθεν καὶ ἔστη εἰς τὸ μέσον ← καὶ λέγει αὐτοῖς
n.gpf pt.rp.gpf p.a d.asm n.asm d.gpm a.gpm d.nsm n.nsm v.aai.3s cj v.aai.3s p.a d.asn n.asn cj v.pai.3s r.dpm.3
2598 3091 1328 3836 5832 3836 2681 3836 2652 2262 2779 2705 1650 3836 3545 2779 3306 899

"Peace be with you!" **20** After he said this, he showed them his hands and side. The disciples were
εἰρήνη → ὑμῖν καὶ → εἰπὼν τοῦτο → ἔδειξεν αὐτοῖς τὰς χεῖρας καὶ τὴν πλευρὰν οὖν οἱ μαθηταὶ →
n.nsf r.dp.2 cj pt.aa.nsm r.asn v.aai.3s r.dpm.3 d.apf n.apf cj d.asf n.asf cj d.npm n.npm
1645 7007 2779 3306 4047 1259 899 3836 5931 2779 3836 4433 4036 3836 3412

overjoyed when they saw the Lord. ¶ **21** Again Jesus said, "Peace be with you! As the
ἐχάρησαν → ἰδόντες τὸν κύριον οὖν πάλιν ὁ Ἰησοῦς εἶπεν αὐτοῖς εἰρήνη → ὑμῖν καθὼς ὁ
v.api.3p pt.aa.npm d.asm n.asm cj adv d.nsm n.nsm v.aai.3s r.dpm.3 n.nsf r.dp.2 cj d.nsm
5897 1625 3836 3261 4036 4099 3836 2652 3306 899 1645 7007 2777 3836

Father has sent me, I am sending you." **22** And with that he breathed on them and said, "Receive the
πατήρ → ἀπέσταλκεν με κἀγὼ → πέμπω ὑμᾶς καὶ εἰπὼν τοῦτο ἐνεφύσησεν ← αὐτοῖς καὶ λέγει λάβετε
n.nsm v.rai.3s r.as.1 crasis v.pai.1s r.ap.2 cj pt.aa.nsm r.asn v.aai.3s r.dpm.3 cj v.pai.3s v.aam.2p
4252 690 1609 2743 4287 7007 2779 3306 4047 1874 899 2779 3306 3284

Holy Spirit. **23** If you forgive anyone his sins, they are forgiven; if you do not forgive them, they are not
ἅγιον πνεῦμα ἄν → ἀφῆτε ἄν τινων τὰς ἁμαρτίας → → ἀφέωνται αὐτοῖς ἄν → → κρατῆτε τινων → →
a.asn n.asn cj v.aas.2p cj r.gpm d.apf n.apf v.rpi.3p r.dpm.3 cj v.pas.2p r.gpm
41 4460 323 918 323 5516 3836 281 918 899 323 3195 5516

forgiven."
κεκράτηνται
v.rpi.3p
3195

Jesus Appears to Thomas

20:24 Now Thomas (called Didymus), one of the Twelve, was not with the disciples when Jesus came.
δὲ Θωμᾶς ὁ λεγόμενος Δίδυμος εἷς ἐκ τῶν δώδεκα ἦν οὐκ μετ᾽ αὐτῶν ὅτε Ἰησοῦς ἦλθεν
cj n.nsm d.nsm pt.pp.nsm n.nsm a.nsm p.g d.gpm a.gpm v.iai.3s pl p.g r.gpm.3 cj n.nsm v.aai.3s
1254 2605 3836 3306 1441 1651 1666 3836 1557 1639 4024 3552 899 4021 2652 2262

25 So the other disciples told him, "We have seen the Lord!" But he said to them, "Unless I see the nail
οὖν τοῖς ἄλλοι μαθηταὶ ἔλεγον αὐτῷ → → ἑωράκαμεν τὸν κύριον δὲ ὁ εἶπεν αὐτοῖς ἐὰν μὴ → ἴδω τὸν τῶν ἥλων
cj d.npm r.npm n.npm v.iai.3p r.dsm.3 v.rai.1p d.asm n.asm cj d.nsm v.aai.3s r.dpm.3 cj pl v.aas.1s d.asm d.gpm n.gpm
4036 3836 257 3412 3306 899 3972 3836 3261 1254 3836 3306 899 1569 3590 1625 3836 3836 2464

marks in his hands and put my finger where the nails were, and put my hand into his
τύπον ἐν αὐτοῦ ταῖς χερσὶν καὶ βάλω μου τὸν δάκτυλον εἰς τὸν τύπον τῶν ἥλων καὶ βάλω μου τὴν χεῖρα εἰς αὐτοῦ
n.asm p.d r.gsm.3 d.dpf n.dpf cj v.aas.1s r.gs.1 d.asm n.asm p.a d.asm n.asm d.gpm n.gpm cj v.aas.1s r.gs.1 d.asf n.asf p.a r.gsm.3
5596 1877 899 3836 5931 2779 965 1609 3836 1235 1650 3836 5596 3836 2464 2779 965 1609 3836 5931 1650 899

side, I will not believe it." ¶ **26** A week later his disciples were in the house
τὴν πλευρὰν → → οὐ μὴ πιστεύσω Καὶ μεθ᾽ ἡμέρας ὀκτὼ αὐτοῦ οἱ μαθηταὶ ἦσαν ἔσω
d.asf n.asf pl pl v.aas.1s cj p.a n.apf a.apf r.gsm.3 d.npm n.npm v.iai.3p adv
3836 4433 4409 4409 4024 3590 4409 2779 3552 2465 3893 3552 899 3836 3412 1639 2276

again, and Thomas was with them. Though the doors were locked, Jesus came and stood among
πάλιν καὶ Θωμᾶς μετ᾽ αὐτῶν → τῶν θυρῶν κεκλεισμένων ὁ Ἰησοῦς ἔρχεται καὶ ἔστη εἰς τὸ μέσον
adv cj n.nsm p.g r.gpm.3 d.gpf n.gpf pt.rp.gpf d.nsm n.nsm v.pmi.3s cj v.aai.3s p.a d.asn n.asn
4099 2779 2605 3552 899 3091 3836 2598 3091 3836 2652 2262 2779 2705 1650 3836 3545

them and said, "Peace be with you!" **27** Then he said to Thomas, "Put your finger here; see my
← καὶ εἶπεν εἰρήνη → ὑμῖν εἶτα → λέγει τῷ Θωμᾷ φέρε σου τὸν δάκτυλον ὧδε καὶ ἴδε μου
cj v.aai.3s n.nsf r.dp.2 adv v.pai.3s d.dsm n.dsm v.pam.2s r.gs.2 d.asm n.asm adv cj v.aam.2s r.gs.1
2779 3306 1645 7007 1663 3306 3836 2605 5770 5148 3836 1235 6045 2779 2623 1609

20:19 Οὔσης οὖν ὀψίας τῇ ἡμέρᾳ ἐκείνη τῇ μιᾷ σαββάτων καὶ τῶν θυρῶν κεκλεισμένων ὅπου ἦσαν οἱ μαθηταὶ διὰ τὸν φόβον τῶν Ἰουδαίων, ἦλθεν ὁ Ἰησοῦς καὶ ἔστη εἰς τὸ μέσον καὶ λέγει αὐτοῖς, Εἰρήνη ὑμῖν. **20** καὶ τοῦτο εἰπὼν ἔδειξεν τὰς χεῖρας καὶ τὴν πλευρὰν αὐτοῖς. ἐχάρησαν οὖν οἱ μαθηταὶ ἰδόντες τὸν κύριον. ¶ **21** εἶπεν οὖν αὐτοῖς [ὁ Ἰησοῦς] πάλιν, Εἰρήνη ὑμῖν· καθὼς ἀπέσταλκέν με ὁ πατήρ, κἀγὼ πέμπω ὑμᾶς. **22** καὶ τοῦτο εἰπὼν ἐνεφύσησεν καὶ λέγει αὐτοῖς, Λάβετε πνεῦμα ἅγιον· **23** ἄν τινων ἀφῆτε τὰς ἁμαρτίας ἀφέωνται αὐτοῖς, ἄν τινων κρατῆτε κεκράτηνται.

20:24 Θωμᾶς δὲ εἷς ἐκ τῶν δώδεκα, ὁ λεγόμενος Δίδυμος, οὐκ ἦν μετ᾽ αὐτῶν ὅτε ἦλθεν Ἰησοῦς. **25** ἔλεγον οὖν αὐτῷ οἱ ἄλλοι μαθηταί, Ἑωράκαμεν τὸν κύριον. ὁ δὲ εἶπεν αὐτοῖς, Ἐὰν μὴ ἴδω ἐν ταῖς χερσὶν αὐτοῦ τὸν τύπον τῶν ἥλων καὶ βάλω τὸν δάκτυλόν μου εἰς τὸν τύπον τῶν ἥλων καὶ βάλω μου τὴν χεῖρα εἰς τὴν πλευρὰν αὐτοῦ, οὐ μὴ πιστεύσω. ¶ **26** Καὶ μεθ᾽ ἡμέρας ὀκτὼ πάλιν ἦσαν ἔσω οἱ μαθηταὶ αὐτοῦ καὶ Θωμᾶς μετ᾽ αὐτῶν. ἔρχεται ὁ Ἰησοῦς τῶν θυρῶν κεκλεισμένων καὶ ἔστη εἰς τὸ μέσον καὶ εἶπεν, Εἰρήνη ὑμῖν. **27** εἶτα λέγει τῷ Θωμᾷ, Φέρε τὸν δάκτυλόν σου ὧδε καὶ ἴδε τὰς χεῖράς μου καὶ φέρε τὴν χεῖρά σου καὶ βάλε εἰς

hands.   Reach out your hand   and put   it into my side.   Stop doubting   and believe.”
ιτὰς χεῖρας, καὶ φέρε → σου ιτὴν χεῖρα, καὶ βάλε εἰς μου ιτὴν πλευράν, καὶ μὴ γίνου ἄπιστος, ἀλλὰ πιστός
d.apf n.apf cj v.pam.2s r.gs.2 d.asf n.asf cj v.aam.2s p.a r.gs.1 d.asf n.asf cj pl v.pmm.2s a.nsm cj a.nsm
3836 5931 2779 5770 5148 3836 5931 2779 965 1650 1609 3836 4433 2779 3590 1181 603 247 4412

28 Thomas   said to him, “My Lord   and my God!” **29** Then Jesus   told him, “Because you have → →
Θωμᾶς, ἀπεκρίθη καὶ εἶπεν → αὐτῷ, ὁ κύριος, καὶ μου ὁ θεός, ὁ Ἰησοῦς, λέγει αὐτῷ ὅτι → →
n.nsm v.api.3s cj v.aai.3s r.dsm.3 r.gs.1 d.vsm n.vsm cj r.gs.1 d.vsm n.vsm d.nsm n.nsm v.pai.3s r.dsm.3 cj
2605 646 2779 3306 899 1609 3836 3261 2779 1609 3836 2536 3836 2652 3306 899 4022

seen me, you have believed; blessed are those who have not seen and yet have believed.”   ¶   **30**
ἑώρακας με → → πεπίστευκας μακάριοι οἱ ← → μὴ ἰδόντες καὶ → → πιστεύσαντες   οὖν
v.rai.2s r.as.1 v.rai.2s a.npm d.npm pl pt.aa.npm cj pt.aa.npm cj
3972 1609 4409 3421 3836 1625 3590 1625 2779 4409 4036

Jesus   did   many other miraculous signs in the presence of his disciples,   which are not
ὁ Ἰησοῦς, μὲν ἐποίησεν καὶ Πολλὰ ἄλλα → σημεῖα → ἐνώπιον → αὐτοῦ ιτῶν μαθητῶν, ἃ ἔστιν οὐκ
d.nsm n.nsm pl v.aai.3s adv a.apn a.rpn n.apn p.g r.gsm.3 d.gpm n.gpm r.npn v.pai.3s pl
3836 2652 3525 4472 2779 4498 257 4956 1967 3412 899 3836 3412 4005 1639 4024

recorded in this book.   **31** But these are written   that you may believe that Jesus is the Christ, the Son of
γεγραμμένα ἐν τούτῳ ιτῷ βιβλίῳ, δὲ ταῦτα → γέγραπται ἵνα → → πιστεύσητε ὅτι Ἰησοῦς ἔστιν ὁ χριστὸς ὁ υἱὸς
pt.rp.npn p.d r.dsn d.dsn n.dsn cj r.npn v.rpi.3s cj v.aas.2p cj n.nsm v.pai.3s d.nsm n.nsm d.nsm n.nsm
1211 1877 4047 3836 1046 1254 4047 1211 2671 4409 4022 2652 1639 3836 5986 3836 5626

God,   and that by believing you may have life in his name.
ιτοῦ θεοῦ, καὶ ἵνα → πιστεύοντες → → ἔχητε ζωὴν ἐν αὐτοῦ ιτῷ ὀνόματι,
d.gsm n.gsm cj cj pt.pa.npm v.pas.2p n.asf p.d r.gsm.3 d.dsn n.dsn
3836 2536 2779 2671 4409 2400 2437 1877 899 3836 3950

Jesus and the Miraculous Catch of Fish

21:1 Afterward Jesus   appeared   again to his disciples, by the Sea   of Tiberias.   It
ιΜετὰ ταῦτα, ὁ Ἰησοῦς, ἐφανέρωσεν ἑαυτὸν πάλιν → τοῖς μαθηταῖς ἐπὶ τῆς θαλάσσης → ιτῆς Τιβεριάδος, δὲ →
p.a r.apn d.nsm n.nsm v.aai.3s r.asm.3 adv d.dpm n.dpm p.g d.gsf n.gsf d.gsf n.gsf cj
3552 4047 3836 2652 5746 1571 4099 3836 3412 2093 3836 2498 3836 5500 1254

happened this way: **2** Simon Peter,   Thomas (called   Didymus),   Nathanael   from Cana in
ἐφανέρωσεν οὕτως ← Σίμων Πέτρος καὶ Θωμᾶς ὁ λεγόμενος, Δίδυμος καὶ Ναθαναὴλ ὁ ἀπὸ Κανὰ
v.aai.3s adv n.nsm n.nsm cj n.nsm d.nsm pt.pp.nsm n.nsm cj n.nsm d.nsm p.g n.gsf
5746 4048 4981 4377 2779 2605 3836 3306 1441 2779 3720 3836 608 2830

Galilee,   the sons of Zebedee,   and two other disciples   were together. **3** “I’m going out to
ιτῆς Γαλιλαίας, καὶ οἱ → ιτοῦ Ζεβεδαίου, καὶ δύο ἄλλοι ἐκ ιτῶν μαθητῶν, αὐτοῦ ἦσαν ὁμοῦ → ὑπάγω ← →
d.gsf n.gsf cj d.npm d.gsm n.gsm cj a.npm a.rpn p.g d.gpm n.gpm r.gsm.3 v.iai.3p adv v.pai.1s
3836 1133 2779 3836 3836 2411 2779 1545 257 1666 3836 3412 899 1639 3938 5632

fish,” Simon Peter told them, and they said,   “We’ll go with you.” So they went out and
ἁλιεύειν Σίμων Πέτρος λέγει αὐτοῖς → λέγουσιν αὐτῷ ἡμεῖς καὶ ἐρχόμεθα σὺν σοί, καὶ → ἐξῆλθον ← →
f.pa n.nsm n.nsm v.pai.3s r.dpm.3 v.pai.3p r.dsm.3 r.np.1 cj v.pmi.1p p.d r.ds.2 cj v.aai.3p
244 4981 4377 3306 899 3306 899 7005 2779 2262 5250 5148 2779 2002

got   into the boat, but   that night   they caught nothing.   ¶   **4** Early   in the morning,
ἐνέβησαν εἰς τὸ πλοῖον καὶ ἐν ἐκείνῃ τῇ νυκτὶ → ἐπίασαν οὐδέν   δὲ πρωΐας ἤδη γενομένης,
v.aai.3p p.a d.asn n.asn cj p.d r.dsf d.dsf n.dsf v.aai.3p a.asn cj n.gsf adv pt.am.gsf
1832 1650 3836 4450 2779 1877 1697 3836 3816 4389 4029 1254 4746 2453 1181

Jesus stood on the shore,   but the disciples did not realize that it was Jesus. **5** He   called out to them,
Ἰησοῦς ἔστη εἰς τὸν αἰγιαλόν μέντοι οἱ μαθηταὶ → οὐ ᾔδεισαν ὅτι → ἔστιν Ἰησοῦς οὖν ὁ Ἰησοῦς, λέγει ← → αὐτοῖς
n.nsm v.aai.3s p.a d.asm n.asm cj d.npm n.npm pl v.lai.3p cj v.pai.3s n.nsm cj d.nsm n.nsm v.pai.3s r.dpm.3
2652 2705 1650 3836 129 3530 3836 3412 4024 3857 4022 1639 2652 4036 3836 2652 3306 899

“Friends, haven’t you any fish?”   “No,” they answered. **6** He said,   “Throw your net   on the
παιδία, μὴ ἔχετε ← τι προσφάγιον οὔ → ἀπεκρίθησαν αὐτῷ δὲ ὁ εἶπεν αὐτοῖς βάλετε τὸ δίκτυον εἰς τὰ
n.vpn pl v.pai.2p r.asn n.asn pl v.api.3p r.dsm.3 cj d.nsm v.aai.3s r.dpm.3 v.aam.2p d.asn n.asn p.a d.apn
4086 3590 2400 5516 4709 4024 646 899 1254 3836 3306 899 965 3836 1473 1650 3836

right side of the boat and you will find   some.” When they did,   they were unable   to haul the net
δεξιὰ μέρη → τοῦ πλοίου καὶ → → εὑρήσετε οὖν → ἔβαλον καὶ → → ιοὐκέτι ἴσχυον, → ἑλκύσαι αὐτὸ
a.apn n.apn d.gsn n.gsn cj v.fai.2p cj v.aai.3p cj adv v.iai.3p f.aa r.asn.3
1288 3538 3836 4450 2779 2351 4036 965 2779 4033 2710 1816 899

τὴν πλευράν μου, καὶ μὴ γίνου ἄπιστος ἀλλὰ πιστός. ²⁸ ἀπεκρίθη Θωμᾶς καὶ εἶπεν αὐτῷ, Ὁ κύριός μου καὶ ὁ θεός μου.
²⁹ λέγει αὐτῷ ὁ Ἰησοῦς, Ὅτι ἑώρακάς με πεπίστευκας; μακάριοι οἱ μὴ ἰδόντες καὶ πιστεύσαντες. ¶ ³⁰ Πολλὰ μὲν οὖν καὶ
ἄλλα σημεῖα ἐποίησεν ὁ Ἰησοῦς ἐνώπιον τῶν μαθητῶν [αὐτοῦ], ἃ οὐκ ἔστιν γεγραμμένα ἐν τῷ βιβλίῳ τούτῳ· ³¹ ταῦτα δὲ
γέγραπται ἵνα πιστεύ[σ]ητε ὅτι Ἰησοῦς ἐστιν ὁ Χριστὸς ὁ υἱὸς τοῦ θεοῦ, καὶ ἵνα πιστεύοντες ζωὴν ἔχητε ἐν τῷ ὀνόματι αὐτοῦ.
   ^{21:1} Μετὰ ταῦτα ἐφανέρωσεν ἑαυτὸν πάλιν ὁ Ἰησοῦς τοῖς μαθηταῖς ἐπὶ τῆς θαλάσσης τῆς Τιβεριάδος· ἐφανέρωσεν δὲ οὕτως.
² ἦσαν ὁμοῦ Σίμων Πέτρος καὶ Θωμᾶς ὁ λεγόμενος Δίδυμος καὶ Ναθαναὴλ ὁ ἀπὸ Κανὰ τῆς Γαλιλαίας καὶ οἱ τοῦ Ζεβεδαίου
καὶ ἄλλοι ἐκ τῶν μαθητῶν αὐτοῦ δύο. ³ λέγει αὐτοῖς Σίμων Πέτρος, Ὑπάγω ἁλιεύειν. λέγουσιν αὐτῷ, Ἐρχόμεθα καὶ ἡμεῖς
σὺν σοί. ἐξῆλθον καὶ ἐνέβησαν εἰς τὸ πλοῖον, καὶ ἐν ἐκείνῃ τῇ νυκτὶ ἐπίασαν οὐδέν. ¶ ⁴ πρωΐας δὲ ἤδη γενομένης ἔστη Ἰησοῦς
εἰς τὸν αἰγιαλόν, οὐ μέντοι ᾔδεισαν οἱ μαθηταὶ ὅτι Ἰησοῦς ἐστιν. ⁵ λέγει οὖν αὐτοῖς [ὁ] Ἰησοῦς, Παιδία, μή τι προσφάγιον
ἔχετε; ἀπεκρίθησαν αὐτῷ, Οὔ. ⁶ ὁ δὲ εἶπεν αὐτοῖς, Βάλετε εἰς τὰ δεξιὰ μέρη τοῦ πλοίου τὸ δίκτυον, καὶ εὑρήσετε. ἔβαλον οὖν,

in because of the large number of fish. ¶ **7** Then the disciple whom Jesus loved said to
↩ ἀπὸ → τοῦ πλήθους ← → ⸂τῶν ἰχθύων⸃ οὖν ὁ μαθητὴς ὃν ⸀ὁ Ἰησοῦς ἠγάπα ἐκεῖνος λέγει →
p.g | d.gsn n.gsn | d.gpm n.gpm | cj d.nsm n.nsm r.asm d.nsm n.nsm v.iai.3s r.nsm v.pai.3s
1816 | 608 | 3836 4436 | 3836 2716 | 4036 3836 3412 4005 3836 2652 26 1697 3306

Peter, "It is the Lord!" As soon as Simon Peter heard him say, "It is the Lord," he wrapped his
⸂τῷ Πέτρῳ⸃ → ἔστιν ὁ κύριος οὖν ← ← Σίμων Πέτρος ἀκούσας ὅτι → ἔστιν ὁ κύριος → διεζώσατο τὸν
d.dsm n.dsm | v.pai.3s d.nsm n.nsm | cj | n.nsm n.nsm pt.aa.nsm | cj | v.pai.3s d.nsm n.nsm | v.ami.3s d.asm
3836 4377 | 1639 3836 3261 | 4036 | 4981 4377 201 | 4022 | 1639 3836 3261 | 1346 3836

outer garment around him (for he had taken it off) and jumped into the water. **8** The other disciples
→ ἐπενδύτην ← γὰρ → ἦν γυμνός καὶ ἔβαλεν ἑαυτὸν εἰς τὴν θάλασσαν δὲ οἱ ἄλλοι μαθηταὶ
n.asm | cj v.iai.3s a.nsm | cj v.aai.3s r.asm.3 p.a d.asf n.asf | cj d.npm r.npm n.npm
2087 | 1346 1142 1639 1218 | 2779 965 1571 1650 3836 2498 | 1254 3836 257 3412

followed in the boat, towing the net full of fish, for they were not far from shore, about
ἦλθον → τῷ πλοιαρίῳ σύροντες τὸ δίκτυον → ⸂τῶν ἰχθύων⸃ γὰρ → ἦσαν οὐ μακρὰν ἀπὸ ⸂τῆς γῆς⸃ ἀλλὰ ὡς ἀπὸ
v.aai.3p | d.dsn n.dsn pt.pa.npm d.asn n.asn | d.gpm n.gpm cj | v.iai.3p pl adv p.g d.gsf n.gsf pl cj p.g
2262 | 3836 4449 5359 3836 1473 | 3836 2716 1142 | 1639 4024 3426 608 3836 1178 247 6055 608

a *hundred yards*. **9** When they landed, they saw a fire of burning coals there with fish
διακοσίων πηχῶν οὖν ὡς ⸂ἀπέβησαν εἰς τὴν γῆν⸃ βλέπουσιν ἀνθρακιὰν ← κειμένην καὶ ὀψάριον
a.gpm n.gpm cj cj v.aai.3p p.a d.asf n.asf | v.pai.3p n.asf | pt.pm.asf cj n.asn
1357 4388 4036 6055 609 1650 3836 1178 | 1063 471 | 3023 2779 4066

on it, and some bread. ¶ **10** Jesus said to them, "Bring some of the fish you have just
ἐπικείμενον καὶ ἄρτον ⸀ὁ Ἰησοῦς λέγει → αὐτοῖς ἐνέγκατε ἀπὸ τῶν ὀψαρίων ὧν ↱ ↱ νῦν
pt.pm.asn cj n.asm | d.nsm n.nsm v.pai.3s r.dpm.3 v.aam.2p | p.g d.gpn n.gpn r.gpn adv
2130 2779 788 | 3836 2652 3306 899 5770 | 608 3836 4066 4005 4389 4389 3814

caught." **11** Simon Peter climbed aboard and dragged the net ashore. It was full of large fish,
ἐπιάσατε οὖν Σίμων Πέτρος ἀνέβη ← καὶ εἵλκυσεν τὸ δίκτυον εἰς τὴν γῆν μεστὸν → μεγάλων ἰχθύων
v.aai.2p cj n.nsm n.nsm v.aai.3s | cj v.aai.3s d.asn n.asn p.a d.asf n.asf | a.asn | a.gpm n.gpm
4389 4036 4981 4377 326 | 2779 1816 3836 1473 1650 3836 1178 | 3550 | 3489 2716

153, but even with so many the net was not torn. **12** Jesus said to them, "Come and
⸂ἑκατὸν πεντήκοντα τριῶν⸃ καὶ → ὄντων τοσούτων ← τὸ δίκτυον ↱ οὐκ ἐσχίσθη ⸀ὁ Ἰησοῦς λέγει → αὐτοῖς δεῦτε
a.gpm a.gpm a.gpm cj | pt.pa.gpm r.gpm | d.nsn n.nsn pl v.api.3s | d.nsm n.nsm v.pai.3s r.dpm.3 adv
1669 4299 5552 2779 | 1639 5537 | 3836 1473 4024 5387 | 3836 2652 3306 899 1307

have breakfast." None of the disciples dared ask him, "Who are you?" They knew it was the Lord.
→ ἀριστήσατε δὲ οὐδεὶς → τῶν μαθητῶν ἐτόλμα ἐξετάσαι αὐτόν τίς εἶ σὺ ὅτι → εἰδότες → ἔστιν ὁ κύριος
v.aam.2p cj a.nsm d.gpm n.gpm v.iai.3s f.aa r.asm.3 r.nsm v.pai.2s r.ns.2 cj | pt.ra.npm v.pai.3s d.nsm n.nsm
753 1254 4029 3836 3412 5528 2004 899 5515 1639 5148 4022 | 3857 1639 3836 3261

13 Jesus came, took the bread and gave it to them, and did the same with the fish. **14** This was now the
Ἰησοῦς ἔρχεται καὶ λαμβάνει τὸν ἄρτον καὶ δίδωσιν → αὐτοῖς καὶ → → ὁμοίως ← τὸ ὀψάριον τοῦτο ἤδη
n.nsm v.pmi.3s cj v.pai.3s d.asm n.asm cj v.pai.3s r.dpm.3 cj adv d.asn n.asn r.asn adv
2652 2262 2779 3284 3836 788 2779 1443 899 2779 3931 3836 4066 4047 2453

third time Jesus appeared to his disciples after he was raised from the dead.
τρίτον ← Ἰησοῦς ἐφανερώθη τοῖς μαθηταῖς → → → ἐγερθεὶς ἐκ νεκρῶν
adv n.nsm v.api.3s d.dpm n.dpm pt.ap.nsm p.g a.gpm
5568 2652 5746 3836 3412 1586 1666 3738

Jesus Reinstates Peter

21:15 When they had finished eating, Jesus said to Simon Peter, "Simon son of John, do you
οὖν Ὅτε → → ἠρίστησαν ὁ Ἰησοῦς λέγει ⸂τῷ Σίμωνι⸃ Πέτρῳ Σίμων → Ἰωάννου ↱ ↱
cj cj | v.aai.3p d.nsm n.nsm v.pai.3s d.dsm n.dsm n.dsm n.vsm | n.gsm
4036 4021 | 753 3836 2652 3306 3836 4981 4377 4981 | 2722 26 26

truly love me more than these?" "Yes, Lord," he said, "you know that I love you." Jesus said, "Feed
ἀγαπᾷς με πλέον → τούτων ναὶ κύριε → λέγει αὐτῷ σὺ οἶδας ὅτι → φιλῶ σε λέγει αὐτῷ βόσκε
v.pai.2s r.as.1 adv.c r.gpm | pl n.vsm | v.pai.3s r.dsm.3 r.ns.2 v.rai.2s cj v.pai.1s r.as.2 | v.pai.3s r.dsm.3 v.pam.2s
26 1609 4498 4047 | 3721 3261 | 3306 899 5148 3857 4022 5797 5148 | 3306 899 1081

my lambs." ¶ **16** Again Jesus said, "Simon son of John, do you truly love me?" He answered,
μου ⸂τὰ ἀρνία⸃ πάλιν λέγει αὐτῷ δεύτερον Σίμων → Ἰωάννου → ἀγαπᾷς με → λέγει
r.gs.1 d.apn n.apn | adv v.pai.3s r.dsm.3 adv n.vsm n.gsm | v.pai.2s r.as.1 | v.pai.3s
1609 3836 768 | 4099 3306 899 1311 4981 2722 | 26 1609 | 3306

καὶ οὐκέτι αὐτὸ ἑλκύσαι ἴσχυον ἀπὸ τοῦ πλήθους τῶν ἰχθύων. ¶ ⁷ λέγει οὖν ὁ μαθητὴς ἐκεῖνος ὃν ἠγάπα ὁ Ἰησοῦς τῷ Πέτρῳ, Ὁ κύριός ἐστιν. Σίμων οὖν Πέτρος ἀκούσας ὅτι ὁ κύριός ἐστιν τὸν ἐπενδύτην διεζώσατο, ἦν γὰρ γυμνός, καὶ ἔβαλεν ἑαυτὸν εἰς τὴν θάλασσαν, ⁸ οἱ δὲ ἄλλοι μαθηταὶ τῷ πλοιαρίῳ ἦλθον, οὐ γὰρ ἦσαν μακρὰν ἀπὸ τῆς γῆς ἀλλὰ ὡς ἀπὸ πηχῶν διακοσίων, σύροντες τὸ δίκτυον τῶν ἰχθύων. ¶ ⁹ ὡς οὖν ἀπέβησαν εἰς τὴν γῆν βλέπουσιν ἀνθρακιὰν κειμένην καὶ ὀψάριον ἐπικείμενον καὶ ἄρτον. ¶ ¹⁰ λέγει αὐτοῖς ὁ Ἰησοῦς, Ἐνέγκατε ἀπὸ τῶν ὀψαρίων ὧν ἐπιάσατε νῦν. ¹¹ ἀνέβη οὖν Σίμων Πέτρος καὶ εἵλκυσεν τὸ δίκτυον εἰς τὴν γῆν μεστὸν ἰχθύων μεγάλων ἑκατὸν πεντήκοντα τριῶν· καὶ τοσούτων ὄντων οὐκ ἐσχίσθη τὸ δίκτυον. ¹² λέγει αὐτοῖς ὁ Ἰησοῦς, Δεῦτε ἀριστήσατε. οὐδεὶς δὲ ἐτόλμα τῶν μαθητῶν ἐξετάσαι αὐτόν, Σὺ τίς εἶ; εἰδότες ὅτι ὁ κύριός ἐστιν. ¹³ ἔρχεται Ἰησοῦς καὶ λαμβάνει τὸν ἄρτον καὶ δίδωσιν αὐτοῖς, καὶ τὸ ὀψάριον ὁμοίως. ¹⁴ τοῦτο ἤδη τρίτον ἐφανερώθη Ἰησοῦς τοῖς μαθηταῖς ἐγερθεὶς ἐκ νεκρῶν.

²¹:¹⁵ Ὅτε οὖν ἠρίστησαν λέγει τῷ Σίμωνι Πέτρῳ ὁ Ἰησοῦς, Σίμων Ἰωάννου, ἀγαπᾷς με πλέον τούτων; λέγει αὐτῷ, Ναὶ κύριε, σὺ οἶδας ὅτι φιλῶ σε. λέγει αὐτῷ, Βόσκε τὰ ἀρνία μου. ¶ ¹⁶ λέγει αὐτῷ πάλιν δεύτερον, Σίμων Ἰωάννου, ἀγαπᾷς με; λέγει

"Yes, Lord, you know that I love you." Jesus said, "Take care of my sheep." ¶ **17** The third
αὐτῷ ναὶ κύριε σὺ οἶδας ὅτι → φιλῶ σε λέγει αὐτῷ → ποίμαινε ← μου ⌐τὰ πρόβατα⌐ τὸ τρίτον
r.dsm.3 n.vsm r.ns.2 v.rai.2s cj v.pai.1s r.as.2 v.pai.3s r.dsm.3 v.pam.2s r.gs.1 d.apn n.apn d.asn adv
899 3721 3261 5148 3857 4022 5797 5148 3306 899 4477 1609 3836 4585 3836 5568

time he said to him, "Simon son of John, do you love me?" Peter was hurt because Jesus asked him the
← λέγει → αὐτῷ Σίμων → Ἰωάννου → → φιλεῖς με ὁ Πέτρος → ἐλυπήθη ὅτι → εἶπεν αὐτῷ τὸ
v.pai.3s r.dsm.3 n.vsm n.gsm v.pai.2s r.as.1 d.nsm n.nsm v.api.3s cj v.aai.3s r.dsm.3 d.asn
3306 899 4981 2722 5797 1609 3836 4377 3382 4022 3306 899 3836

third time, "Do you love me?" He said, "Lord, you know all things; you know that I love you."
τρίτον ← → φιλεῖς με καὶ → λέγει αὐτῷ κύριε σὺ οἶδας πάντα ← σὺ γινώσκεις ὅτι → φιλῶ σε
adv v.pai.2s r.as.1 cj v.pai.3s r.dsm.3 n.vsm r.ns.2 v.rai.2s a.apn r.ns.2 v.pai.2s cj v.pai.1s r.as.2
5568 5797 1609 2779 3306 899 3261 5148 3857 4246 5148 1182 4022 5797 5148

Jesus said, "Feed my sheep. **18** I tell you the truth, when you were younger you dressed yourself
ὁ Ἰησοῦς λέγει αὐτῷ βόσκε μου ⌐τὰ πρόβατα⌐ → λέγω σοι ⌐ἀμὴν ἀμὴν⌐ ὅτε → ἦς νεώτερος → ἐζώννυες σεαυτὸν
d.nsm n.nsm v.pai.3s r.dsm.3 v.pam.2s r.gs.1 d.apn n.apn v.pai.1s r.ds.2 pl pl cj v.iai.2s a.nsm.c v.iai.3s r.asm.2
3836 2652 3306 899 1081 1609 3836 4585 3306 5148 297 297 4021 1639 3742 2439 4932

and went where you wanted; but when you are old you will stretch out your hands, and someone else
καὶ περιεπάτεις ὅπου → ἤθελες δὲ ὅταν → γηράσῃς → ἐκτενεῖς ← σου ⌐τὰς χεῖρας⌐ καὶ ἄλλος
cj v.iai.2s cj v.iai.2s cj cj v.aas.2s v.fai.2s r.gs.2 d.apf n.apf cj r.nsm
2779 4344 3963 2527 1254 4020 1180 1753 5148 3836 5931 2779 257

will dress you and lead you where you do not want to go." **19** Jesus said this to indicate the kind of death by
→ ζώσει σε καὶ οἴσει ὅπου ⌐ → οὐ θέλεις δὲ εἶπεν τοῦτο → σημαίνων ποίῳ → θανάτῳ ⌐
v.fai.3s r.as.2 cj v.fai.3s cj pl v.pai.2s cj v.aai.3s r.asn pt.pa.nsm r.dsm n.dsm
2439 5148 2779 5770 3963 2527 2527 4024 2527 1254 3306 4047 4955 4481 2505 4481

which Peter would glorify God. Then he said to him, "Follow me!" ¶ **20** Peter turned and
← δοξάσει ⌐τὸν θεόν⌐ καὶ τοῦτο εἰπὼν → λέγει → αὐτῷ ἀκολούθει μοι ὁ Πέτρος Ἐπιστραφεὶς
v.fai.3s d.asm n.asm cj r.asn pt.aa.nsm v.pai.3s r.dsm.3 v.pam.2s r.ds.1 d.nsm n.nsm pt.ap.nsm
4481 1519 3836 2536 2779 4047 3306 3306 899 199 1609 3836 4377 2188

saw that the disciple whom Jesus loved was following them. (This was the one who had leaned back
βλέπει τὸν μαθητὴν ὃν ὁ Ἰησοῦς ἠγάπα → ἀκολουθοῦντα ὃς ← καὶ → ἀνέπεσεν ←
v.pai.3s d.asm n.asm r.asm d.nsm n.nsm v.iai.3s pt.pa.asm r.nsm adv v.aai.3s
1063 3836 3412 4005 3836 2652 26 199 4005 2779 404

against Jesus at the supper and had said, "Lord, who is going to betray you?") **21** When
ἐπὶ ⌐τὸ στῆθος αὐτοῦ⌐ ἐν τῷ δείπνῳ καὶ → εἶπεν κύριε τίς ἐστιν → → ὁ παραδιδούς⌐ σε οὖν →
p.a d.asn n.asn r.gsm.3 p.d d.dsn n.dsn cj v.aai.3s n.vsm r.nsm v.pai.3s d.nsm pt.pa.nsm r.as.2 cj
2093 3836 5111 899 1877 3836 1270 2779 3306 3261 5515 1639 3836 4140 5148 4036 1625

Peter saw him, he asked, "Lord, what about him?" **22** Jesus answered, "If I want him
ὁ Πέτρος ἰδὼν τοῦτον → λέγει τῷ Ἰησοῦ⌐ κύριε δὲ τί οὗτος ὁ Ἰησοῦς λέγει αὐτῷ ἐὰν → θέλω αὐτὸν
d.nsm n.nsm pt.aa.nsm r.asm v.pai.3s d.dsm n.dsm n.vsm cj r.asn r.nsm d.nsm n.nsm v.pai.3s r.dsm.3 cj v.pas.1s r.asm.3
3836 4377 1625 4047 3306 3836 2652 3261 1254 5515 4047 3836 2652 3306 899 1569 2527 899

to remain alive until I return, what is that to you? You must follow me." **23** Because of this, the rumor
→ μένειν ἕως → ἔρχομαι τί πρὸς σέ σὺ → ἀκολούθει μοι οὖν ← οὗτος ὁ λόγος
f.pa cj v.pmi.1s r.nsn p.a r.as.2 r.ns.2 v.pam.2s r.ds.1 cj r.nsm d.nsm n.nsm
3531 2401 2262 5515 4639 5148 5148 4036 4047 3836 3364

spread among the brothers that this disciple would not die. But Jesus did not say that he
ἐξῆλθεν εἰς τοὺς ἀδελφοὺς ὅτι ἐκεῖνος ὁ μαθητὴς⌐ → οὐκ ἀποθνήσκει δὲ ὁ Ἰησοῦς⌐ → οὐκ εἶπεν αὐτῷ ὅτι →
v.aai.3s p.a d.apm n.apm cj r.nsm d.nsm n.nsm pl v.pai.3s cj d.nsm n.nsm pl v.aai.3s r.dsm.3 cj
2002 1650 3836 81 4022 1697 3836 3412 633 4024 633 1254 3836 2652 4024 3306 899 4022 633

would not die; he only said, "If I want him to remain alive until I return, what is that to you?" ¶
→ οὐκ ἀποθνήσκει ἀλλ' ἐὰν → θέλω αὐτὸν → μένειν ἕως → ἔρχομαι τί πρὸς σέ
pl v.pai.3s cj cj v.pas.1s r.asm.3 f.pa cj v.pmi.1s r.nsn p.a r.as.2
633 4024 633 247 1569 2527 899 3531 2401 2262 5515 4639 5148

24 This is the disciple who testifies to these things and who wrote them down. We know that his
Οὗτος ἐστιν ὁ μαθητὴς ὁ μαρτυρῶν περὶ τούτων καὶ ὁ γράψας ταῦτα καὶ → οἴδαμεν ὅτι αὐτοῦ
r.nsm v.pai.3s d.nsm n.nsm d.nsm pt.pa.nsm p.g r.gpn cj d.nsm pt.aa.nsm r.apn cj v.rai.1p cj r.gsm.3
4047 1639 3836 3412 3836 3455 4309 4047 2779 3836 1211 4047 1211 2779 3857 4022 899

αὐτῷ, Ναὶ κύριε, σὺ οἶδας ὅτι φιλῶ σε. λέγει αὐτῷ, Ποίμαινε τὰ πρόβατά μου. ¶ **17** λέγει αὐτῷ τὸ τρίτον, Σίμων Ἰωάννου, φιλεῖς με; ἐλυπήθη ὁ Πέτρος ὅτι εἶπεν αὐτῷ τὸ τρίτον, Φιλεῖς με; καὶ λέγει αὐτῷ, Κύριε, πάντα σὺ οἶδας, σὺ γινώσκεις ὅτι φιλῶ σε. λέγει αὐτῷ [ὁ Ἰησοῦς], Βόσκε τὰ πρόβατά μου. **18** ἀμὴν ἀμὴν λέγω σοι, ὅτε ἦς νεώτερος, ἐζώννυες σεαυτὸν καὶ περιεπάτεις ὅπου ἤθελες· ὅταν δὲ γηράσῃς, ἐκτενεῖς τὰς χεῖράς σου, καὶ ἄλλος σε ζώσει καὶ οἴσει ὅπου οὐ θέλεις. **19** τοῦτο δὲ εἶπεν σημαίνων ποίῳ θανάτῳ δοξάσει τὸν θεόν. καὶ τοῦτο εἰπὼν λέγει αὐτῷ, Ἀκολούθει μοι. ¶ **20** Ἐπιστραφεὶς ὁ Πέτρος βλέπει τὸν μαθητὴν ὃν ἠγάπα ὁ Ἰησοῦς ἀκολουθοῦντα, ὃς καὶ ἀνέπεσεν ἐν τῷ δείπνῳ ἐπὶ τὸ στῆθος αὐτοῦ καὶ εἶπεν, Κύριε, τίς ἐστιν ὁ παραδιδούς σε; **21** τοῦτον οὖν ἰδὼν ὁ Πέτρος λέγει τῷ Ἰησοῦ, Κύριε, οὗτος δὲ τί; **22** λέγει αὐτῷ ὁ Ἰησοῦς, Ἐὰν αὐτὸν θέλω μένειν ἕως ἔρχομαι, τί πρὸς σέ; σύ μοι ἀκολούθει. **23** ἐξῆλθεν οὖν οὗτος ὁ λόγος εἰς τοὺς ἀδελφοὺς ὅτι ὁ μαθητὴς ἐκεῖνος οὐκ

testimony	is	true.	¶	25			Jesus	did	many	other	things	as	well.		If	every		one	
ἡ	μαρτυρία	ἐστίν	ἀληθής		δὲ	Ἔστιν	ἃ	ὁ	Ἰησοῦς	ἐποίησεν	πολλὰ	ἄλλα	←	καὶ	←	ἅτινα	ἐὰν	καθ᾽	ἕν	←
d.nsf	n.nsf	v.pai.3s	a.nsf		cj	v.pai.3s	r.apn	d.nsm	n.nsm	v.aai.3s	a.npn	r.npn		adv		r.npn	cj	p.a	a.asn
3836	3456	1639	239		1254	1639	4005	3836	2652	4472	4498	257		2779		4015	1569	2848	1651

of them	were written down,	I	suppose	that	even		the	whole	world		would	not	have	room	for	the	books	that
→	γράφηται	←	οἶμαι			τὸν	κόσμον	αὐτὸν			οὐδ᾽		χωρῆσαι	←	τὰ	βιβλία	
	v.pps.3s		v.pmi.1s			d.asm	n.asm	r.asm			adv		f.aa		d.apn	n.apn	
	1211		3887		4028	3836	3180	899	6003	4028		6003		3836	1046	

would be written.
→ → γραφόμενα
pt.pp.apn
1211

ἀποθνῄσκει· οὐκ εἶπεν δὲ αὐτῷ ὁ Ἰησοῦς ὅτι οὐκ ἀποθνῄσκει ἀλλ᾽, Ἐὰν αὐτὸν θέλω μένειν ἕως ἔρχομαι[, τί πρὸς σέ]; ¶ 24 Οὗτός ἐστιν ὁ μαθητὴς ὁ μαρτυρῶν περὶ τούτων καὶ ὁ γράψας ταῦτα, καὶ οἴδαμεν ὅτι ἀληθὴς αὐτοῦ ἡ μαρτυρία ἐστίν. ¶ 25 Ἔστιν δὲ καὶ ἄλλα πολλὰ ἃ ἐποίησεν ὁ Ἰησοῦς, ἅτινα ἐὰν γράφηται καθ᾽ ἕν, οὐδ᾽ αὐτὸν οἶμαι τὸν κόσμον χωρῆσαι τὰ γραφόμενα βιβλία.

Acts

Jesus Taken Up Into Heaven

1:1 In my former book, Theophilus, I wrote about all that Jesus began to do and to
μὲν Τὸν πρῶτον λόγον ᾧ Θεόφιλε →ἐποιησάμην περὶ πάντων ὧν ὁ Ἰησοῦς ἤρξατο τε →ποιεῖν καὶ →
pl d.asm a.asm n.asm j n.vsm v.ami.1s p.g a.gpn r.gpn d.nsm n.nsm v.ami.3s cj f.pa cj
3525 3836 4755 3364 6043 2541 4472 4309 4246 4005 3836 2652 806 5445 4472 2779

teach **2** until the day he was taken up to heaven, after giving instructions through the Holy Spirit to the
διδάσκειν ἄχρι ἧς ἡμέρας → → ἀνελήμφθη ← ἐντειλάμενος διὰ ἁγίου πνεύματος → τοῖς
f.pa p.g r.gsf n.gsf v.api.3s pt.am.nsm p.g a.gsn n.gsn d.dpm
1438 948 4005 2465 377 1948 1328 41 4460 3836

apostles he had chosen. **3** After his suffering, he showed himself to these men and gave many
ἀποστόλοις οὓς → ἐξελέξατο μετὰ αὐτὸν τὸ παθεῖν → παρέστησεν ἑαυτὸν καὶ → οἷς ἐν πολλοῖς
n.dpm r.apm v.ami.3s p.a r.asm.3 d.asn f.aa v.aai.3s r.asm.3 adv r.dpm p.d a.dpn
693 4005 1721 3552 899 3836 4248 4225 1571 2779 4005 1877 4498

convincing proofs that he was alive. He appeared to them over a period of forty days and spoke
→ τεκμηρίοις → → ζῶντα ὀπτανόμενος → αὐτοῖς δι᾽ ← ← τεσσεράκοντα ἡμερῶν καὶ λέγων τὰ
n.dpn pt.pa.asm pt.pm.nsm r.dpm.3 p.g a.gpf n.gpf cj pt.pa.nsm d.apn
5447 2409 3964 899 1328 5477 2465 2779 3306 3836

about the kingdom of God. **4** *On one occasion,* while he was eating with them, he gave them this
περὶ τῆς βασιλείας τοῦ θεοῦ καὶ → → → συναλιζόμενος → → αὐτοῖς
p.g d.gsf n.gsf d.gsm n.gsm cj pt.pm.nsm r.dpm.3
4309 3836 993 3836 2536 2779 5259 4133 4133 899

command: "Do not leave Jerusalem, but wait for the gift my Father promised, which you have
παρήγγειλεν →μὴ χωρίζεσθαι ἀπὸ Ἱεροσολύμων ἀλλὰ περιμένειν ← τοῦ πατρὸς τὴν ἐπαγγελίαν ἣν →
v.aai.3s pl f.pp p.g n.gpn cj f.pa d.gsm n.gsm d.asf n.asf r.asf
4133 6004 3590 6004 608 2642 247 4338 3836 4252 3836 2039 4005

heard me speak about. **5** For John baptized with water, but in a few days you will be
ἠκούσατε μου ὅτι μὲν Ἰωάννης ἐβάπτισεν → ὕδατι δὲ μετὰ οὐ πολλὰς ταύτας ἡμέρας ὑμεῖς → →
v.aai.2p r.gs.1 cj pl n.nsm v.aai.3s n.dsn cj p.a pl a.apf r.apf n.apf r.np.2
201 1609 4022 3525 2722 966 5623 1254 3552 4024 4498 4047 2465 7007

baptized with the Holy Spirit." ¶ **6** So when they met together, they asked him, "Lord,
βαπτισθήσεσθε ἐν ἁγίῳ πνεύματι οὖν μὲν → συνελθόντες ← Οἱ ἠρώτων αὐτὸν λέγοντες κύριε
v.fpi.2p p.d a.dsn n.dsn cj pl pt.aa.npm d.npm v.iai.3p r.asm.3 pt.pa.npm n.vsm
966 1877 41 4460 4036 3525 5302 3836 2263 899 3306 3261

are you at this time going to restore the kingdom to Israel?" ¶ **7** He said to them: "It
εἰ → ἐν τούτῳ τῷ χρόνῳ → ἀποκαθιστάνεις τὴν βασιλείαν → τῷ Ἰσραήλ δὲ → εἶπεν πρὸς αὐτούς →
cj p.d r.dsn d.dsm n.dsm v.pai.2s d.asf n.asf d.dsm n.dsm cj v.aai.3s p.a r.apm.3
1623 635 635 1877 4047 3836 5989 635 3836 993 3836 2702 1254 3306 4639 899

is not for you to know the times or dates the Father has set by his own authority. **8** But you will
ἐστιν οὐχ ὑμῶν → γνῶναι χρόνους ἢ καιροὺς οὓς ὁ πατὴρ → ἔθετο ἐν τῇ ἰδίᾳ ἐξουσίᾳ ἀλλὰ →
v.pai.3s pl r.gp.2 f.aa n.apm cj n.apm r.apm d.nsm n.nsm v.ami.3s p.d d.dsf a.dsf n.dsf cj
1639 4024 7007 1182 5989 2445 2789 4005 3836 4252 5502 1877 3836 2625 2026 247

receive power when the Holy Spirit comes on you; and you will be my witnesses in Jerusalem, and in
λήμψεσθε δύναμιν → τοῦ ἁγίου πνεύματος ἐπελθόντος ἐφ᾽ ὑμᾶς καὶ → ἔσεσθε μου μάρτυρες τε ἔν Ἱερουσαλὴμ καὶ ἐν
v.fmi.2p n.asf d.gsn a.gsn n.gsn pt.aa.gsn p.a r.ap.2 cj v.fmi.2p r.gs.1 n.npm cj p.d n.dsf cj p.d
3284 1539 2088 3836 41 4460 2088 2093 7007 2779 1639 1609 3459 5445 1877 2647 2779 1877

all Judea and Samaria, and to the ends of the earth." ¶ **9** After he said this, he was taken up
πάσῃ τῇ Ἰουδαίᾳ καὶ Σαμαρείᾳ καὶ ἕως ἐσχάτου → τῆς γῆς Καὶ → → εἰπὼν ταῦτα → ἐπήρθη ←
a.dsf d.dsf n.dsf cj n.dsf cj p.g a.gsn d.gsf n.gsf cj pt.aa.nsm r.apn v.api.3s
4246 3836 2677 2779 4899 2779 2401 2274 3836 1178 2779 3306 4047 2048

before their very eyes, and a cloud hid him from their sight. ¶ **10** They were looking
→ αὐτῶν βλεπόντων καὶ νεφέλη ὑπέλαβεν αὐτὸν ἀπὸ αὐτῶν τῶν ὀφθαλμῶν καὶ ὡς ἦσαν ἀτενίζοντες
r.gpm.3 pt.pa.npm cj n.nsf v.aai.3s r.asm.3 p.g r.gpm.3 d.gpm n.gpm cj cj v.iai.3p pt.pa.npm
1063 899 1063 2779 3749 5696 899 608 899 3836 4057 2779 6055 1639 867

1:1 Τὸν μὲν πρῶτον λόγον ἐποιησάμην περὶ πάντων, ὦ Θεόφιλε, ὧν ἤρξατο ὁ Ἰησοῦς ποιεῖν τε καὶ διδάσκειν, **2** ἄχρι ἧς ἡμέρας ἐντειλάμενος τοῖς ἀποστόλοις διὰ πνεύματος ἁγίου οὓς ἐξελέξατο ἀνελήμφθη· **3** οἷς καὶ παρέστησεν ἑαυτὸν ζῶντα μετὰ τὸ παθεῖν αὐτὸν ἐν πολλοῖς τεκμηρίοις, δι᾽ ἡμερῶν τεσσεράκοντα ὀπτανόμενος αὐτοῖς καὶ λέγων τὰ περὶ τῆς βασιλείας τοῦ θεοῦ· **4** καὶ συναλιζόμενος παρήγγειλεν αὐτοῖς ἀπὸ Ἱεροσολύμων μὴ χωρίζεσθαι ἀλλὰ περιμένειν τὴν ἐπαγγελίαν τοῦ πατρὸς ἣν ἠκούσατέ μου, **5** ὅτι Ἰωάννης μὲν ἐβάπτισεν ὕδατι, ὑμεῖς δὲ ἐν πνεύματι βαπτισθήσεσθε ἁγίῳ οὐ μετὰ πολλὰς ταύτας ἡμέρας. ¶ **6** Οἱ μὲν οὖν συνελθόντες ἠρώτων αὐτὸν λέγοντες, Κύριε, εἰ ἐν τῷ χρόνῳ τούτῳ ἀποκαθιστάνεις τὴν βασιλείαν τῷ Ἰσραήλ; ¶ **7** εἶπεν δὲ πρὸς αὐτούς, Οὐχ ὑμῶν ἐστιν γνῶναι χρόνους ἢ καιροὺς οὓς ὁ πατὴρ ἔθετο ἐν τῇ ἰδίᾳ ἐξουσίᾳ, **8** ἀλλὰ λήμψεσθε δύναμιν ἐπελθόντος τοῦ ἁγίου πνεύματος ἐφ᾽ ὑμᾶς καὶ ἔσεσθέ μου μάρτυρες ἔν τε Ἰερουσαλημ καὶ [ἐν] πάσῃ τῇ Ἰουδαίᾳ καὶ Σαμαρείᾳ καὶ ἕως ἐσχάτου τῆς γῆς. ¶ **9** καὶ ταῦτα εἰπὼν βλεπόντων αὐτῶν ἐπήρθη καὶ νεφέλη ὑπέλαβεν αὐτὸν ἀπὸ τῶν ὀφθαλμῶν αὐτῶν. ¶ **10** καὶ ὡς ἀτενίζοντες ἦσαν εἰς τὸν οὐρανὸν πορευομένου αὐτοῦ, καὶ ἰδοὺ ἄνδρες δύο παρειστήκεισαν

intently up into the sky as he was going, when suddenly two men dressed in white stood
εἰς τὸν οὐρανὸν αὐτοῦ πορευομένου καὶ ἰδοὺ δύο ἄνδρες ἐσθήσεσι ἐν λευκαῖς παρειστήκεισαν

beside them. **11** "Men of Galilee," they said, "why do you stand here looking into the sky? This same
αὐτοῖς καὶ ἄνδρες Γαλιλαῖοι οἳ εἶπαν τί ἑστήκατε ἐμβλέποντες εἰς τὸν οὐρανόν οὗτος

Jesus, who has been taken from you into heaven, will come back in the same way you
ὁ Ἰησοῦς ὁ ἀναλημφθεὶς ἀφ᾽ ὑμῶν εἰς τὸν οὐρανόν, ἐλεύσεται οὕτως ὃν τρόπον

have seen him go into heaven."
ἐθεάσασθε αὐτὸν πορευόμενον εἰς τὸν οὐρανόν,

Matthias Chosen to Replace Judas

1:12 Then they returned to Jerusalem from the hill called the Mount of Olives, a Sabbath day's
Τότε ὑπέστρεψαν εἰς Ἰερουσαλὴμ ἀπὸ ὄρους τοῦ καλουμένου Ἐλαιῶνος ἔχον σαββάτου

walk from the city. **13** When they arrived, they went upstairs to the room where they
ὁδὸν ὅ ἐστιν ἐγγὺς Ἰερουσαλὴμ καὶ ὅτε εἰσῆλθον ἀνέβησαν εἰς τὸ ὑπερῷον οὗ

were staying. Those present were Peter, John, James and Andrew; Philip and Thomas,
ἦσαν καταμένοντες ὅ τε Πέτρος καὶ Ἰωάννης καὶ Ἰάκωβος καὶ Ἀνδρέας Φίλιππος καὶ Θωμᾶς

Bartholomew and Matthew; James son of Alphaeus and Simon the Zealot, and Judas son of James. **14** They all
Βαρθολομαῖος καὶ Μαθθαῖος Ἰάκωβος Ἀλφαίου καὶ Σίμων ὁ ζηλωτὴς καὶ Ἰούδας Ἰακώβου οὗτοι πάντες

joined together constantly in prayer, along with the women and Mary the mother of Jesus, and
ἦσαν ὁμοθυμαδὸν προσκαρτεροῦντες τῇ προσευχῇ σὺν γυναιξὶν καὶ Μαριὰμ τῇ μητρὶ τοῦ Ἰησοῦ καὶ

with his brothers. ¶ **15** In those days Peter stood up among the believers (a group
αὐτοῦ τοῖς ἀδελφοῖς, Καὶ ἐν ταύταις ταῖς ἡμέραις Πέτρος ἀναστὰς ἐν μέσῳ τῶν ἀδελφῶν τε ὄχλος ἦν

numbering about a hundred and twenty) **16** and said, "Brothers, the Scripture had to be fulfilled
ὀνομάτων ἐπὶ τὸ αὐτὸ ὡσεὶ ἑκατὸν εἴκοσι εἶπεν ἄνδρες ἀδελφοί τὴν γραφὴν ἔδει πληρωθῆναι

which the Holy Spirit spoke long ago through the mouth of David concerning Judas, who served as guide
ἣν τὸ τὸ ἅγιον πνεῦμα προεῖπεν διὰ στόματος Δαυὶδ περὶ Ἰούδα τοῦ γενομένου ὁδηγοῦ

for those who arrested Jesus – **17** he was one of our number and shared in this ministry."
τοῖς συλλαβοῦσιν Ἰησοῦν ὅτι ἦν ἐν ἡμῖν κατηριθμημένος καὶ ἔλαχεν τὸν κλῆρον ταύτης τῆς διακονίας,

¶ **18** (With the reward he got for his wickedness, Judas bought a field; there he fell headlong, his
οὖν μὲν ἐκ μισθοῦ τῆς ἀδικίας οὗτος ἐκτήσατο χωρίον καὶ γενόμενος πρηνὴς

αὐτοῖς ἐν ἐσθήσεσι λευκαῖς, ¹¹ οἳ καὶ εἶπαν, Ἄνδρες Γαλιλαῖοι, τί ἑστήκατε [ἐμ]βλέποντες εἰς τὸν οὐρανόν; οὗτος ὁ Ἰησοῦς ὁ ἀναλημφθεὶς ἀφ᾽ ὑμῶν εἰς τὸν οὐρανὸν οὕτως ἐλεύσεται ὃν τρόπον ἐθεάσασθε αὐτὸν πορευόμενον εἰς τὸν οὐρανόν.

¹·¹² Τότε ὑπέστρεψαν εἰς Ἰερουσαλὴμ ἀπὸ ὄρους τοῦ καλουμένου Ἐλαιῶνος, ὅ ἐστιν ἐγγὺς Ἰερουσαλὴμ σαββάτου ἔχον ὁδόν. ¹³ καὶ ὅτε εἰσῆλθον, εἰς τὸ ὑπερῷον ἀνέβησαν οὗ ἦσαν καταμένοντες, ὅ τε Πέτρος καὶ Ἰωάννης καὶ Ἰάκωβος καὶ Ἀνδρέας, Φίλιππος καὶ Θωμᾶς, Βαρθολομαῖος καὶ Μαθθαῖος, Ἰάκωβος Ἀλφαίου καὶ Σίμων ὁ ζηλωτὴς καὶ Ἰούδας Ἰακώβου. ¹⁴ οὗτοι πάντες ἦσαν προσκαρτεροῦντες ὁμοθυμαδὸν τῇ προσευχῇ σὺν γυναιξὶν καὶ Μαριὰμ τῇ μητρὶ τοῦ Ἰησοῦ καὶ τοῖς ἀδελφοῖς αὐτοῦ ¶ ¹⁵ Καὶ ἐν ταῖς ἡμέραις ταύταις ἀναστὰς Πέτρος ἐν μέσῳ τῶν ἀδελφῶν εἶπεν· ἦν τε ὄχλος ὀνομάτων ἐπὶ τὸ αὐτὸ ὡσεὶ ἑκατὸν εἴκοσι· ¹⁶ Ἄνδρες ἀδελφοί, ἔδει πληρωθῆναι τὴν γραφὴν ἣν προεῖπεν τὸ πνεῦμα τὸ ἅγιον διὰ στόματος Δαυὶδ περὶ Ἰούδα τοῦ γενομένου ὁδηγοῦ τοῖς συλλαβοῦσιν Ἰησοῦν, ¹⁷ ὅτι κατηριθμημένος ἦν ἐν ἡμῖν καὶ ἔλαχεν τὸν κλῆρον τῆς διακονίας ταύτης. ¶ ¹⁸ Οὗτος μὲν οὖν ἐκτήσατο χωρίον ἐκ μισθοῦ τῆς ἀδικίας καὶ πρηνὴς γενόμενος ἐλάκησεν μέσος καὶ ἐξεχύθη πάντα τὰ σπλάγχνα

body burst open	and all	his	intestines	spilled out. [19]	Everyone in		Jerusalem
ἐλάκησεν ←	μέσος καὶ	πάντα αὐτοῦ	τὰ σπλάγχνα	ἐξεχύθη	καὶ πᾶσι	τοῖς κατοικοῦσιν	Ἰερουσαλήμ
v.aai.3s	a.nsm cj	a.npn r.gsm.3	d.npn n.npn	v.api.3s	cj a.dpm	d.dpm pt.pa.dpm	n.asf
3279	3545 2779	4246 899	3836 5073	1773	2779 4246	3836 2997	2647

heard		about this, so	they called	that field		in their language	Akeldama, that is,	Field
ἐγένετο γνωστὸν		ὥστε →	κληθῆναι	ἐκεῖνο τὸ χωρίον	→	αὐτῶν τῇ ἰδίᾳ διαλέκτῳ	Ἁκελδαμάχ τοῦτ᾽ ἔστιν	χωρίον
v.ami.3s a.nsn		cj	f.ap	r.asn d.asn n.asn		r.gpm.3 d.dsf a.dsf n.dsf	n.asn r.nsn v.pai.3s	n.asn
1181 1196		6063	2813	1697 3836 6005	1365	899 3836 2625 1365	192 4047 1639	6005

of Blood.) ¶	[20] "For," said Peter, "it is written	in	the book of Psalms, "'May his	place	be
→ αἵματος	γὰρ → γέγραπται	ἐν	βίβλῳ ψαλμῶν αὐτοῦ ἡ ἔπαυλις		γενηθήτω
n.gsn	cj v.rpi.3s	p.d	n.dsf n.gpm r.gsm.3 d.nsf n.nsf		v.apm.3s
135	1142 1211	1877	1047 6011 1181 899 3836 2068		1181

deserted;	let there be	no one to dwell	in it,' and, "'May another take	his	place of leadership.'
ἔρημος καὶ →	→ ἔστω μὴ ὁ	→ κατοικῶν ἐν αὐτῇ καὶ	→ ἕτερος λαβέτω αὐτοῦ →		→ τὴν ἐπισκοπήν
a.nsf cj	v.pam.3s pl d.nsm	pt.pa.nsm p.d r.dsf.3 cj	r.nsm v.aam.3s r.gsm.3		d.asf n.asf
2245 2779	1639 3590 3836	2997 1877 899 2779	3284 2283 3284 899		3836 2175

[21] Therefore it is necessary to choose one of the men	who have been	with us the whole	time	the
οὖν → δεῖ → ἀνδρῶν τῶν	συνελθόντων ←	ἡμῖν ἐν παντὶ χρόνῳ	ᾧ	ὁ
cj v.pai.3s	n.gpm d.gpm	pt.aa.gpm	r.dp.1 p.d a.dsm n.dsm	r.dsm d.nsm
4036 1256	467 3836	5302	7005 1877 4246 5989	4005 3836

Lord Jesus went in	and out	among us,	[22] beginning from John's	baptism	to the time when Jesus
κύριος Ἰησοῦς → εἰσῆλθεν	καὶ ἐξῆλθεν ἐφ᾽	ἡμᾶς	ἀρξάμενος ἀπὸ Ἰωάννου	τοῦ βαπτίσματος	ἕως τῆς ἡμέρας ἧς
n.nsm n.nsm v.aai.3s	cj v.aai.3s p.a	r.ap.1	pt.am.nsm p.g n.gsm	d.gsn n.gsn	p.g d.gsf n.gsf r.gsf
3261 2652 1656	2779 2002 2093	7005	806 608 2722	3836 967	2401 3836 2465 4005

was taken	up from us.	For one of these	must become a witness with us	of his	resurrection." ¶	[23] So
→ ἀνελήμφθη	ἀφ᾽ ἡμῶν	ἕνα → τούτων	→ γενέσθαι μάρτυρα σὺν ἡμῖν	αὐτοῦ	τῆς ἀναστάσεως	Καὶ
v.api.3s	p.g r.gp.1	a.asm r.gpm	f.am n.asm p.d r.dp.1	r.gsm.3	d.gsf n.gsf	cj
377	608 7005	1651 4047	1181 3459 5250 7005	414 899	3836 414	2779

they proposed two men: Joseph called	Barsabbas	(also known as Justus) and Matthias.	[24] Then they
ἔστησαν δύο Ἰωσὴφ τὸν καλούμενον	Βαρσαββᾶν ὃς	ἐπεκλήθη ← Ἰοῦστος καὶ Μαθθίαν	καὶ
v.aai.3p a.apm n.asm d.asm pt.pp.asm	n.asm r.nsm	v.api.3s n.nsm cj n.asm	cj
2705 1545 2737 3836 2813	984 4005	2126 2688 2779 3416	2779

prayed,	"Lord, you know everyone's heart.	Show	us which	of these two	you have
προσευξάμενοι εἶπαν κύριε σὺ	᾽ πάντων καρδιογνῶστα	ἀνάδειξον	ὃν ἕνα ἐκ	τούτων τῶν δύο	→
pt.am.npm v.aai.3p n.vsm r.ns.2	a.gpm n.vsm	v.aam.2s	r.asm a.asm p.g	r.gpm d.gpm a.gpm	
4667 3306 3261 5148	2841 4246 2841	344	4005 1651 1666	4047 3836 1545	

chosen [25] to take	over	this apostolic ministry,	which	Judas left	to go	where	he
ἐξελέξω λαβεῖν τὸν τόπον		ταύτης καὶ ἀποστολῆς τῆς διακονίας	ἀφ᾽ ἧς	Ἰούδας παρέβη	→ πορευθῆναι	εἰς τὸν τόπον	→
v.ami.2s f.aa d.asm n.asm		r.gsf cj n.gsf d.gsf n.gsf	p.g r.gsf	n.nsm v.aai.3s	f.ap	p.a d.asm n.asm	
1721 3284 3836 5536		4047 2779 692 3836 1355	608 4005	2683 4124	4513	1650 3836 5536	

belongs."	[26] Then they cast	lots,	and the lot	fell	to Matthias; so he was added	to the eleven
τὸν ἴδιον	καὶ ᾽ ἔδωκαν	κλήρους αὐτοῖς	καὶ ὁ κλῆρος	ἔπεσεν ἐπὶ	Μαθθίαν καὶ → → συγκατεψηφίσθη	μετὰ τῶν ἕνδεκα
d.asm a.asm	cj v.aai.3p	n.apm r.dpm.3	cj d.nsm n.nsm	v.aai.3s p.a	n.asm cj v.api.3s	p.g d.gpm a.gpm
3836 2625	2779 1443	3102 899	2779 3836 3102	4406 2093	3416 2779 5164	3552 3836 1894

apostles.
ἀποστόλων
n.gpm
693

The Holy Spirit Comes at Pentecost

[2:1]	When the day	of Pentecost	came,	they were all	together in one	place. [2]
Καὶ ἐν	τὴν ἡμέραν →	τῆς πεντηκοστῆς	τῷ συμπληροῦσθαι →	ἦσαν πάντες ὁμοῦ	ἐπὶ τὸ αὐτό ←	καὶ
cj p.d	d.asf n.asf	d.gsf n.gsf	d.dsn f.pp	v.iai.3p a.npm adv	p.a d.asn r.asn	cj
2779 1877	3836 2465	3836 4300	3836 5230	1639 4246 3938	2093 3836 899	2779

Suddenly a sound like	the blowing	of a violent wind	came from heaven	and filled	the whole house where
ἄφνω ἦχος ὥσπερ	φερομένης →	βιαίας πνοῆς	ἐγένετο ἐκ τοῦ οὐρανοῦ	καὶ ἐπλήρωσεν	τὸν ὅλον οἶκον οὗ
adv n.nsm pl	pt.pm.gsf	a.gsf n.gsf	v.ami.3s p.g d.gsn n.gsn	cj v.aai.3s	d.asm a.asm n.asm adv
924 2491 6061	5770	1042 4466	1181 1666 3836 4041	2779 4444	3836 3910 3875 4023

αὐτοῦ· [19] καὶ γνωστὸν ἐγένετο πᾶσι τοῖς κατοικοῦσιν Ἰερουσαλήμ, ὥστε κληθῆναι τὸ χωρίον ἐκεῖνο τῇ ἰδίᾳ διαλέκτῳ αὐτῶν Ἁκελδαμάχ, τοῦτ᾽ ἔστιν Χωρίον Αἵματος. ¶ [20] Γέγραπται γὰρ ἐν βίβλῳ ψαλμῶν, Γενηθήτω ἡ ἔπαυλις αὐτοῦ ἔρημος καὶ μὴ ἔστω ὁ κατοικῶν ἐν αὐτῇ, καί, Τὴν ἐπισκοπὴν αὐτοῦ λαβέτω ἕτερος. [21] δεῖ οὖν τῶν συνελθόντων ἡμῖν ἀνδρῶν ἐν παντὶ χρόνῳ ᾧ εἰσῆλθεν καὶ ἐξῆλθεν ἐφ᾽ ἡμᾶς ὁ κύριος Ἰησοῦς, [22] ἀρξάμενος ἀπὸ τοῦ βαπτίσματος Ἰωάννου ἕως τῆς ἡμέρας ἧς ἀνελήμφθη ἀφ᾽ ἡμῶν, μάρτυρα τῆς ἀναστάσεως αὐτοῦ σὺν ἡμῖν γενέσθαι ἕνα τούτων. ¶ [23] καὶ ἔστησαν δύο, Ἰωσὴφ τὸν καλούμενον Βαρσαββᾶν ὃς ἐπεκλήθη Ἰοῦστος, καὶ Μαθθίαν. [24] καὶ προσευξάμενοι εἶπαν, Σὺ κύριε καρδιογνῶστα πάντων, ἀνάδειξον ὃν ἐξελέξω ἐκ τούτων τῶν δύο ἕνα [25] λαβεῖν τὸν τόπον τῆς διακονίας ταύτης καὶ ἀποστολῆς ἀφ᾽ ἧς παρέβη Ἰούδας πορευθῆναι εἰς τὸν τόπον τὸν ἴδιον. [26] καὶ ἔδωκαν κλήρους αὐτοῖς καὶ ἔπεσεν ὁ κλῆρος ἐπὶ Μαθθίαν καὶ συγκατεψηφίσθη μετὰ τῶν ἕνδεκα ἀποστόλων.

[2:1] Καὶ ἐν τῷ συμπληροῦσθαι τὴν ἡμέραν τῆς πεντηκοστῆς ἦσαν πάντες ὁμοῦ ἐπὶ τὸ αὐτό. [2] καὶ ἐγένετο ἄφνω ἐκ τοῦ οὐρανοῦ ἦχος ὥσπερ φερομένης πνοῆς βιαίας καὶ ἐπλήρωσεν ὅλον τὸν οἶκον οὗ ἦσαν καθήμενοι [3] καὶ ὤφθησαν αὐτοῖς

they were sitting. **3** They saw   what seemed to be tongues of fire   that separated   and came to rest   on
→   ἦσαν καθήμενοι   καὶ αὐτοῖς ὤφθησαν →   ὡσεὶ   γλῶσσαι → πυρὸς   διαμεριζόμεναι καὶ → → ἐκάθισεν ἐφ᾽
    v.iai.3p pt.pm.npm   cj r.dpm.3 v.api.3p   pl   n.npf   n.gsn   pt.pp.npf   cj   v.aai.3s   p.a
    1639   2764   2779 899   3972   6059   1185   4786   1374   2779   2767   2093

each   of them. **4** All   of them were filled   with the Holy Spirit   and began to speak in other
ἕκαστον ἕνα → αὐτῶν καὶ πάντες ← → ἐπλήσθησαν →   ἁγίου πνεύματος καὶ ἤρξαντο → λαλεῖν → ἑτέραις
r.asm   a.asm r.gpm.3 cj a.npm   v.api.3p   a.gsn   n.gsn   cj v.ami.3p   f.pa   r.dpf
1667   1651   899   2779 4246   4398   41   4460   2779 806   3281   2283

tongues as   the Spirit enabled   them. ¶ **5** Now there were staying   in Jerusalem
γλώσσαις καθὼς τὸ πνεῦμα ἐδίδου ἀποφθέγγεσθαι αὐτοῖς   δὲ →   Ἦσαν κατοικοῦντες εἰς Ἰερουσαλὴμ
n.dpf   cj   d.nsn n.nsn v.iai.3s f.pm   r.dpm.3   cj   v.iai.3p pt.pa.npm   p.a n.asf
1185   2777 3836 4460   1443   710   899   1254   1639   2997   1650 2647

God-fearing   Jews   from every nation   under heaven. **6** When they heard   this   sound,   a crowd
ἄνδρες εὐλαβεῖς Ἰουδαῖοι ἀπὸ παντὸς ἔθνους τῶν ὑπὸ τὸν οὐρανόν. δὲ → → γενομένης ταύτης τῆς φωνῆς τὸ πλῆθος
n.npm a.npm   a.npm   p.g a.gsn n.gsn d.gpn p.a d.asm n.asm   cj   pt.am.gsf r.gsf d.gsf n.gsf d.nsn n.nsn
467   2327   2681   608 4246   1620   3836 5679 3836 4041   1254   1181   4047 3836 5889 3836 4436

came together   in bewilderment, because each   one heard   them speaking in his own language. **7** Utterly
→ συνῆλθεν καὶ συνεχύθη   ὅτι ἕκαστος εἰς ἤκουον αὐτῶν λαλούντων → τῇ ἰδίᾳ διαλέκτῳ δὲ →
   v.aai.3s cj v.api.3s   cj r.nsm   a.nsm v.iai.3p r.gpm.3 pt.pa.gpm   d.dsf a.dsf n.dsf   cj
   5302   2779 5177   4022 1667   1651 201   899   3281   3836 2625 1365   1254

amazed,   they asked: "Are not all   these men who are speaking Galileans? **8** Then how is it that
ἐξίσταντο καὶ ἐθαύμαζον → λέγοντες ἰδοὺ εἰσιν οὐχ ἅπαντες οὗτοι   οἱ → λαλοῦντες Γαλιλαῖοι καὶ πῶς →
v.imi.3p cj v.iai.3p   pt.pa.npm j   v.pai.3p a.npm   r.nsm   d.npm   pt.pa.npm a.npm   cj cj
2014   2779 2513   3306   2627 1639   4024 570   4047   3836   3281   1134   2779 4802

each   of us hears   them in his own native   language? **9** Parthians,   Medes and Elamites;
ἕκαστος ἡμεῖς ἀκούομεν → τῇ ἰδίᾳ ἐν ᾗ ἐγεννήθημεν διαλέκτῳ ἡμῶν Πάρθοι   καὶ Μῆδοι καὶ Ἐλαμῖται καὶ
r.nsm   r.np.1 v.pai.1p   d.dsf a.dsf p.d r.dsf v.api.1p   n.dsf   r.gp.1 n.npm   cj n.npm cj n.npm   cj
1667   7005 201   1365 3836 2625 1877 4005 1164   1365   7005   4222   2779 3597   2779 1780   2779

residents   of Mesopotamia,   Judea and Cappadocia, Pontus and Asia,   **10** Phrygia and Pamphylia,
οἱ κατοικοῦντες τὴν Μεσοποταμίαν τε Ἰουδαίαν καὶ Καππαδοκίαν Πόντον καὶ τὴν Ἀσίαν τε Φρυγίαν καὶ Παμφυλίαν
d.npm pt.pa.npm d.asf n.asf   cj n.asf   cj n.asf   n.asm cj d.asf n.asf   cj n.asf   cj n.asf
3836 2997   3836 3544   5445 2677   2779 2838   4509   2779 3836 823   5445 5867   2779 4103

Egypt   and the parts of Libya   near Cyrene;   visitors   from Rome **11** (both Jews   and converts
Αἴγυπτον καὶ τὰ μέρη → τῆς Λιβύης τῆς κατὰ Κυρήνην καὶ οἱ ἐπιδημοῦντες ← Ῥωμαῖοι τε Ἰουδαῖοι καὶ προσήλυτοι
n.asf   cj d.apn n.apn d.gsf n.gsf d.gsf p.a   n.asf   cj d.npm pt.pa.npm   n.npm te a.npm   cj n.npm
131   2779 3836 3538   3836 3340   3836 2848 3255   2779 3836 2111   4871   5445 2681   2779 4670

to Judaism); Cretans and Arabs – we hear them declaring the wonders of God in our own tongues!"
← Κρῆτες καὶ Ἄραβες ἀκούομεν αὐτῶν λαλούντων τὰ μεγαλεῖα → τοῦ θεοῦ → ἡμετέραις ταῖς γλώσσαις
  n.npm   cj n.npm   v.pai.1p r.gpm.3 pt.pa.gpm d.apn n.apn   d.gsm n.gsn   r.dpf.1 d.dpf n.dpf
  3205   2779 732   201   899   3281   3836 3483   3836 2536   2466   3836 1185

12 Amazed   and perplexed, they asked one   another, *"What does this mean?"* ¶ **13** Some, however,
δὲ ἐξίσταντο πάντες καὶ διηπόρουν → λέγοντες ἄλλος πρὸς ἄλλον τί   θέλει τοῦτο εἶναι   ἕτεροι δὲ
cj v.imi.3p a.npm   cj v.iai.3p   pt.pa.npm a.nsm p.a r.asm r.asn v.pai.3s r.asn f.pa   r.npm cj
1254 2014   4246   2779 1389   3306   257   4639 257   5515 2527   4047 1639   2283   1254

made fun   of them and said, "They have had too much   wine."
→ διαχλευάζοντες ←   ἔλεγον ὅτι   → εἰσίν → μεμεστωμένοι γλεύκους
  pt.pa.npm   v.iai.3p cj   v.pai.3p   pt.rp.npm   n.gsn
  1430   3306   4022   1639   3551   1183

Peter Addresses the Crowd

2:14 Then Peter   stood up with the Eleven, raised his   voice   and addressed the crowd: *"Fellow*
δὲ ὁ Πέτρος Σταθεὶς ← σὺν τοῖς ἕνδεκα ἐπῆρεν αὐτοῦ τὴν φωνὴν καὶ ἀπεφθέγξατο αὐτοῖς ἄνδρες
cj d.nsm n.nsm pt.ap.nsm p.d d.dpm a.dpm v.aai.3s r.gsm.3 d.asf n.asf cj v.ami.3s   r.dpm.3 n.vpm
1254 3836 4377 2705   5250 3836 1894   2048   899   3836 5889 2779 710   899   467

Jews   and all   of you who live   in Jerusalem, *let me explain* this to you; listen   carefully to what
Ἰουδαῖοι καὶ πάντες οἱ κατοικοῦντες ← Ἰερουσαλὴμ ἔστω γνωστὸν τοῦτο → ὑμῖν καὶ ἐνωτίσασθε ← τὰ
a.vpm   cj a.vpm   d.vpm pt.pa.vpm   n.asf   v.pam.3s a.nsn r.asn   r.dp.2 cj v.amm.2p   d.apn
2681   2779 4246   3836 2997   2647   1639   1196   4047   7007   2779 1969   3836

διαμεριζόμεναι γλῶσσαι ὡσεὶ πυρὸς καὶ ἐκάθισεν ἐφ᾽ ἕνα ἕκαστον αὐτῶν, ⁴ καὶ ἐπλήσθησαν πάντες πνεύματος ἁγίου καὶ ἤρξαντο λαλεῖν ἑτέραις γλώσσαις καθὼς τὸ πνεῦμα ἐδίδου ἀποφθέγγεσθαι αὐτοῖς. ¶ ⁵ Ἦσαν δὲ εἰς Ἰερουσαλὴμ κατοικοῦντες Ἰουδαῖοι, ἄνδρες εὐλαβεῖς ἀπὸ παντὸς ἔθνους τῶν ὑπὸ τὸν οὐρανόν. ⁶ γενομένης δὲ τῆς φωνῆς ταύτης συνῆλθεν τὸ πλῆθος καὶ συνεχύθη, ὅτι ἤκουον εἷς ἕκαστος τῇ ἰδίᾳ διαλέκτῳ λαλούντων αὐτῶν. ⁷ ἐξίσταντο δὲ καὶ ἐθαύμαζον λέγοντες, Οὐχ ἰδοὺ ἅπαντες οὗτοί εἰσιν οἱ λαλοῦντες Γαλιλαῖοι; ⁸ καὶ πῶς ἡμεῖς ἀκούομεν ἕκαστος τῇ ἰδίᾳ διαλέκτῳ ἡμῶν ἐν ᾗ ἐγεννήθημεν; ⁹ Πάρθοι καὶ Μῆδοι καὶ Ἐλαμῖται καὶ οἱ κατοικοῦντες τὴν Μεσοποταμίαν, Ἰουδαίαν τε καὶ Καππαδοκίαν, Πόντον καὶ τὴν Ἀσίαν, ¹⁰ Φρυγίαν τε καὶ Παμφυλίαν, Αἴγυπτον καὶ τὰ μέρη τῆς Λιβύης τῆς κατὰ Κυρήνην, καὶ οἱ ἐπιδημοῦντες Ῥωμαῖοι, ¹¹ Ἰουδαῖοί τε καὶ προσήλυτοι, Κρῆτες καὶ Ἄραβες, ἀκούομεν λαλούντων αὐτῶν ταῖς ἡμετέραις γλώσσαις τὰ μεγαλεῖα τοῦ θεοῦ. ¹² ἐξίσταντο δὲ πάντες καὶ διηπόρουν, ἄλλος πρὸς ἄλλον λέγοντες, Τί θέλει τοῦτο εἶναι; ¶ ¹³ ἕτεροι δὲ διαχλευάζοντες ἔλεγον ὅτι Γλεύκους μεμεστωμένοι εἰσίν.

²:¹⁴ Σταθεὶς δὲ ὁ Πέτρος σὺν τοῖς ἕνδεκα ἐπῆρεν τὴν φωνὴν αὐτοῦ καὶ ἀπεφθέγξατο αὐτοῖς, Ἄνδρες Ἰουδαῖοι καὶ οἱ

I say. **15** These men are not drunk, as you suppose. It's only nine in the morning! **16** No, this
μου ῥήματα   γὰρ οὗτοι   →   οὐ μεθύουσιν ὡς ὑμεῖς ὑπολαμβάνετε γὰρ ἔστιν   ὥρα τρίτη → τῆς ἡμέρας   ἀλλὰ τοῦτο
r.gs.1 n.apn   cj r.npm   pl v.pai.3p cj r.np.2 v.pai.2p   cj v.pai.3s   n.nsf a.nsf   d.gsf n.gsf   cj r.nsn
1609 4839   1142 4047   3501 4024 3501   6055 7007 5696   1142 1639   6052 5569   3836 2465   247 4047

is what was spoken by the prophet Joel: **17** "'In the last days, God says, I will pour out my
ἔστιν τὸ → εἰρημένον διὰ τοῦ προφήτου Ἰωήλ   καὶ ἔσται ἐν ταῖς ἐσχάταις ἡμέραις ὁ θεός, λέγει → → ἐκχεῶ ἀπὸ μου
v.pai.3s d.nsn   pt.rp.nsn p.g d.gsm n.gsm n.nsn   cj v.fmi.3s p.d d.dpf a.dpf n.dpf d.nsm n.nsm v.pai.3s   v.fai.1s p.g r.gs.1
1639 3836   3306 1328 3836 4737 2727   2779 1639 1877 3836 2274 2465 3836 2536 3306   1772 608 1609

Spirit on all people. Your sons and daughters will prophesy, your young men
τοῦ πνεύματος, ἐπὶ πᾶσαν σάρκα καὶ ὑμῶν οἱ υἱοὶ καὶ ὑμῶν αἱ θυγατέρες, → προφητεύσουσιν καὶ ὑμῶν οἱ νεανίσκοι
d.gsn n.gsn   p.a a.asf n.asf cj r.gp.2 d.npm n.npm cj r.gp.2 d.npf n.npf   v.fai.3p   cj r.gp.2 d.npm n.npm
3836 4460   2093 4246 4922 2779 7007 3836 5626 2779 7007 3836 2588   4736   2779 7007 3836 3734

will see visions, your old men will dream dreams. **18** Even on my servants, both
→ ὄψονται ὁράσεις καὶ ὑμῶν οἱ πρεσβύτεροι → ἐνυπνιασθήσονται ἐνυπνίοις καὶ γε ἐπὶ μου τοὺς δούλους,
  v.fmi.3p n.apf cj r.gp.2 d.npm n.npm   v.fpi.3p n.dpn cj pl p.a r.gs.1 d.apm n.apm
3972 3970 2779 7007 3836 4565   1965 1966 2779 1145 2093 1609 3836 1529

men and women, I will pour out my Spirit in those days, and they will prophesy.
← καὶ ἐπὶ μου τὰς δούλας, → → ἐκχεῶ ἀπὸ μου τοῦ πνεύματος, ἐν ἐκείναις ταῖς ἡμέραις, καὶ → προφητεύσουσιν
  cj p.a r.gs.1 d.apf n.apf   v.fai.1s p.g r.gs.1 d.gsn n.gsn p.d r.dpf d.dpf n.dpf cj   v.fai.3p
2779 2093 1609 3836 1527   1772 608 1609 3836 4460 1877 1697 3836 2465 2779   4736

19 I will show wonders in the heaven above and signs on the earth below, blood and fire and billows of smoke.
καὶ → → δώσω τέρατα ἐν τῷ οὐρανῷ ἄνω καὶ σημεῖα ἐπὶ τῆς γῆς κάτω αἷμα καὶ πῦρ καὶ ἀτμίδα → καπνοῦ
cj   v.fai.1s n.apn p.d d.dsm n.dsm adv cj n.apn p.g d.gsf n.gsf adv n.asn cj n.asn cj n.asf   n.gsm
2779   1443 5469 1877 3836 4041 539 2779 4956 2093 3836 1178 3004 135 2779 4786 2779 874   2837

20 The sun will be turned to darkness and the moon to blood before the coming of the great and
ὁ ἥλιος → → μεταστραφήσεται εἰς σκότος καὶ ἡ σελήνη εἰς αἷμα πρὶν → ἐλθεῖν ← τὴν μεγάλην, καὶ
d.nsm n.nsm   v.fpi.3s p.a n.asn cj d.nsf n.nsf p.a n.asn p.a   f.aa   d.asf a.asf cj
3836 2463   3570 1650 5030 2779 3836 4943 1650 135 4570   2262   3836 3489 2779

glorious day of the Lord. **21** And everyone who calls on the name of the Lord will be saved.'
ἐπιφανῆ ἡμέραν → κυρίου καὶ ἔσται πᾶς ὃς ἂν ἐπικαλέσηται ← τὸ ὄνομα → κυρίου → σωθήσεται
a.asf n.asf   n.gsm cj v.fmi.3s a.nsm r.nsm pl v.ams.3s   d.asn n.asn   n.gsm   v.fpi.3s
2212 2465   3261 2779 1639 4246 4005 323 2126   3836 3950   3261   5392

22 "Men of Israel, listen to this: Jesus of Nazareth was a man accredited by God
Ἄνδρες → Ἰσραηλῖται ἀκούσατε ← τοὺς λόγους τούτους, Ἰησοῦν → τὸν Ναζωραῖον, ἄνδρα ἀποδεδειγμένον ἀπὸ τοῦ θεοῦ,
n.vpm   n.vpm v.aam.2p   d.apm n.apm r.apm n.asm   d.asm n.asm n.asm pt.rp.asm p.g d.gsm n.gsm
467   2703 201   3836 3364 4047 2652   3836 3717 467 617   608 3836 2536

to you by miracles, wonders and signs, which God did among you through him, as you
εἰς ὑμᾶς → δυνάμεσι καὶ τέρασι καὶ σημείοις οἷς ὁ θεὸς ἐποίησεν ἐν μέσῳ ὑμῶν δι' αὐτοῦ καθὼς →
p.a r.ap.2   n.dpf cj n.dpn cj n.dpn r.dpn d.nsm n.nsm v.aai.3s p.d n.dsn r.gp.2 p.g r.gsm.3 cj
1650 7007   1539 2779 5469 2779 4956 4005 3836 2536 4472 1877 3545 7007 1328 899 2777 3857

yourselves know. **23** This man was handed over to you by God's set purpose and foreknowledge; and you,
αὐτοὶ οἴδατε τοῦτον ← ἔκδοτον ← → τοῦ θεοῦ, ὡρισμένῃ τῇ βουλῇ, καὶ προγνώσει →
r.npm v.rai.2p r.asm   a.asm   d.gsm n.gsm pt.rp.dsf d.dsf n.dsf cj n.dsf
899 3857 4047   1692   1087 3836 2536 3988 3836 1087 2779 4590   359

with the help of wicked men, put him to death by nailing him to the cross. **24** But God raised him from
διὰ χειρὸς → ἀνόμων → → ἀνείλατε → προσπήξαντες ← ← ← ὁ θεὸς, ἀνέστησεν ὃν ←
p.g n.gsf   a.gpm   v.aai.2p   pt.aa.npm   d.nsm n.nsm v.aai.3s r.asm
1328 5931   491   359   4699   3836 2536 482 4005 482

the dead, freeing him from the agony of death, because it was impossible for death to keep its hold
λύσας ← τὰς ὠδῖνας → τοῦ θανάτου, καθότι → ἦν οὐκ δυνατὸν ὑπ' αὐτοῦ → → κρατεῖσθαι
pt.aa.nsm   d.apf n.apf   d.gsm n.gsm cj   v.iai.3s pl a.nsn p.g r.gsm.3   f.pp
3395   3836 6047   3836 2505 2776   1639 4024 1543 5679 899   3195

on him. **25** David said about him: "'I saw the Lord always before me. Because he is at my right
← αὐτὸν γὰρ Δαυὶδ λέγει εἰς αὐτόν → προορώμην τὸν κύριον διὰ παντός, ἐνώπιον μου ὅτι → ἐστιν ἐκ μού δεξιῶν
r.asm.3 cj n.nsm v.pai.3s p.a r.asm.3   v.imi.1s d.asm n.asm p.g a.gsm p.g r.gs.1 cj   v.pai.3s p.g r.gs.1 a.gpf
899 1142 1253 3306 1650 899   4632 3836 3261 1328 4246 1967 1609 4022   1639 1666 1609 1288

κατοικοῦντες Ἰερουσαλὴμ πάντες, τοῦτο ὑμῖν γνωστὸν ἔστω καὶ ἐνωτίσασθε τὰ ῥήματά μου. ¹⁵ οὐ γὰρ ὡς ὑμεῖς ὑπολαμβάνετε οὗτοι μεθύουσιν, ἔστιν γὰρ ὥρα τρίτη τῆς ἡμέρας, ¹⁶ ἀλλὰ τοῦτό ἐστιν τὸ εἰρημένον διὰ τοῦ προφήτου Ἰωήλ· ¹⁷ Καὶ ἔσται ἐν ταῖς ἐσχάταις ἡμέραις, λέγει ὁ θεός, ἐκχεῶ ἀπὸ τοῦ πνεύματός μου ἐπὶ πᾶσαν σάρκα, καὶ προφητεύσουσιν οἱ υἱοὶ ὑμῶν καὶ αἱ θυγατέρες ὑμῶν καὶ οἱ νεανίσκοι ὑμῶν ὁράσεις ὄψονται καὶ οἱ πρεσβύτεροι ὑμῶν ἐνυπνίοις ἐνυπνιασθήσονται· ¹⁸ καί γε ἐπὶ τοὺς δούλους μου καὶ ἐπὶ τὰς δούλας μου ἐν ταῖς ἡμέραις ἐκείναις ἐκχεῶ ἀπὸ τοῦ πνεύματός μου, καὶ προφητεύσουσιν. ¹⁹ καὶ δώσω τέρατα ἐν τῷ οὐρανῷ ἄνω καὶ σημεῖα ἐπὶ τῆς γῆς κάτω, αἷμα καὶ πῦρ καὶ ἀτμίδα καπνοῦ· ²⁰ ὁ ἥλιος μεταστραφήσεται εἰς σκότος καὶ ἡ σελήνη εἰς αἷμα, πρὶν ἐλθεῖν ἡμέραν κυρίου τὴν μεγάλην καὶ ἐπιφανῆ. ²¹ καὶ ἔσται πᾶς ὃς ἂν ἐπικαλέσηται τὸ ὄνομα κυρίου σωθήσεται. ²² Ἄνδρες Ἰσραηλῖται, ἀκούσατε τοὺς λόγους τούτους· Ἰησοῦν τὸν Ναζωραῖον, ἄνδρα ἀποδεδειγμένον ἀπὸ τοῦ θεοῦ εἰς ὑμᾶς δυνάμεσι καὶ τέρασι καὶ σημείοις οἷς ἐποίησεν δι' αὐτοῦ ὁ θεὸς ἐν μέσῳ ὑμῶν καθὼς αὐτοὶ οἴδατε, ²³ τοῦτον τῇ ὡρισμένῃ βουλῇ καὶ προγνώσει τοῦ θεοῦ ἔκδοτον διὰ χειρὸς ἀνόμων προσπήξαντες ἀνείλατε, ²⁴ ὃν ὁ θεὸς ἀνέστησεν λύσας τὰς ὠδῖνας τοῦ θανάτου, καθότι οὐκ ἦν δυνατὸν κρατεῖσθαι αὐτὸν ὑπ' αὐτοῦ. ²⁵ Δαυὶδ γὰρ λέγει

hand,　I　will not be　shaken.　²⁶ Therefore　my heart　is glad　and my tongue　rejoices;　my
← ἵνα → → μὴ → σαλευθῶ διὰ τοῦτο, μου ἡ καρδία → ηὐφράνθη καὶ μου ἡ γλῶσσα ἠγαλλιάσατο δὲ ἔτι μου
cj pl v.aps.1s p.a r.asn r.gs.1 d.nsf n.nsf v.api.3s cj r.gs.1 d.nsf n.nsf v.ami.3s cj adv r.gs.1
2671 4888 4888 3590 4888 1328 4047 1609 3836 2840 2370 2779 1609 3836 1185 22 1254 2285 1609

body　also will live　in hope,　²⁷ because you will not abandon　me　to the grave, nor will you
ἡ σάρξ καὶ → κατασκηνώσει ἐπ᾽ ἐλπίδι ὅτι → → οὐκ ἐγκαταλείψεις τὴν ψυχήν μου εἰς ᾅδην οὐδὲ → →
d.nsf n.nsf adv v.fai.3s p.d n.dsf cj pl v.fai.2s d.asf n.asf r.gs.1 p.a n.asm
3836 4922 2779 2942 2093 1828 4022 1593 1593 4024 1593 3836 6034 1609 1650 87 4028

let　your Holy　One see　decay.　²⁸ You have made known　to me the paths of life; you will fill　me
δώσεις σου τὸν ὅσιον ← ἰδεῖν διαφθοράν ἐγνώρισας → μοι ὁδοὺς → ζωῆς → → πληρώσεις με
v.fai.2s r.gs.2 d.asm a.asm f.aa n.asf v.aai.2s r.ds.1 n.apf n.gsf v.fai.2s r.as.1
1443 5148 3836 4008 1625 1426 1192 1609 3847 2437 4444 1609

with joy　in　your presence.’　¶　²⁹　“Brothers, I can　tell　you confidently　that　the
→ εὐφροσύνης μετὰ σου τοῦ προσώπου Ἄνδρες ἀδελφοί → ἐξὸν εἰπεῖν πρὸς ὑμᾶς μετὰ παρρησίας περὶ τοῦ
n.gsf p.g r.gs.2 d.gsn n.gsn n.vpm n.vpm pt.pa.nsn f.aa r.ap.2 p.g n.gsf p.g d.gsm
2372 3552 5148 3836 4725 467 81 1997 3306 4639 7007 3552 4244 4309 3836

patriarch David　died　and was buried, and his　tomb　is　here　to this day.　³⁰ But he
πατριάρχου Δαυὶδ ὅτι καὶ ἐτελεύτησεν καὶ → ἐτάφη καὶ αὐτοῦ τὸ μνῆμα ἔστιν ἐν ἡμῖν ἄχρι ταύτης τῆς ἡμέρας, οὖν
n.gsm n.gsm cj cj v.aai.3s cj v.api.3s cj r.gsm.3 d.nsn n.nsn v.pai.3s p.d r.dp.1 p.g r.gsf d.gsf n.gsf cj
4256 1253 4022 2779 5462 2779 2507 2779 899 3836 3645 1639 1877 7005 948 4047 3836 2465 4036

was　a prophet and knew that God　had promised him on oath that he would place　one of his
ὑπάρχων προφήτης καὶ εἰδὼς ὅτι ὁ θεός, → ὤμοσεν αὐτῷ ὅρκῳ → καθίσαι ἐκ αὐτοῦ
pt.pa.nsm n.nsm cj pt.ra.nsm cj d.nsm n.nsm v.aai.3s r.dsm.3 n.dsm f.aa p.g r.gsm.3
5639 4737 2779 3857 4022 3836 2536 3923 899 3992 2767 1666 899

descendants　on his　throne.　³¹ Seeing what was ahead, he spoke　of　the resurrection of the Christ, that
καρποῦ τῆς ὀσφύος, ἐπ᾽ αὐτοῦ τὸν θρόνον. προϊδὼν → ἐλάλησεν περὶ τῆς ἀναστάσεως → τοῦ Χριστοῦ ὅτι
n.gsm d.gsf n.gsf p.a r.gsm.3 d.asm n.asm pt.aa.nsm v.aai.3s p.g d.gsf n.gsf d.gsm n.gsm cj
2843 3836 4019 2093 899 3836 2585 4632 3281 4309 3836 414 3836 5986 4022

he was not abandoned to the grave, nor did his　body　see decay.　³² God　has raised　this　Jesus　to
→ → οὔτε ἐγκατελείφθη εἰς ᾅδην οὔτε → αὐτοῦ ἡ σάρξ εἶδεν διαφθοράν. ὁ θεός, → ἀνέστησεν τοῦτον τὸν Ἰησοῦν ←
cj v.api.3s p.a n.asm cj r.gsm.3 d.nsf n.nsf v.aai.3s n.asf d.nsm n.nsm v.aai.3s r.asm d.asm n.asm
1593 1593 4046 1593 1650 87 4046 1625 899 3836 4922 1625 1426 3836 2536 482 4047 3836 2652 482

life, and we　are all　witnesses of the fact.　³³ Exalted to the right hand of God,　he has received from
← ἡμεῖς ἐσμεν πάντες μάρτυρες → οὗ οὖν ὑψωθεὶς → τῇ δεξιᾷ → τοῦ θεοῦ, τε → λαβὼν παρὰ
r.np.1 v.pai.1p a.npm n.npm r.gsm cj pt.ap.nsm d.dsf a.dsf d.gsm n.gsm cj pt.aa.nsm p.a
482 7005 1639 4246 3459 4005 4036 5738 3836 1288 3836 2536 5445 3284 4123

the Father the promised Holy　Spirit　and has poured out what　you now see　and hear.　³⁴ For
τοῦ πατρός τὴν ἐπαγγελίαν τοῦ ἁγίου τοῦ πνεύματος → ἐξέχεεν ← τοῦτο ὃ ὑμεῖς καὶ βλέπετε καὶ ἀκούετε γὰρ
d.gsm n.gsm d.asf n.asf d.gsn a.gsn d.gsn n.gsn v.aai.3s r.asn r.asn r.np.2 cj v.pai.2p cj v.pai.2p cj
3836 4252 3836 2039 3836 41 3836 4460 1772 4047 4005 7007 2779 1063 2779 201 1142

David did not ascend to heaven,　and yet he　said, “‘The Lord said to my Lord:　“Sit　at my right
Δαυὶδ → οὐ ἀνέβη εἰς τοὺς οὐρανούς, δὲ αὐτός λέγει ὁ κύριος εἶπεν → μου τῷ κυρίῳ, κάθου ἐκ μου δεξιῶν
n.nsm pl v.aai.3s p.a d.apm n.apm cj r.nsm v.pai.3s d.nsm n.nsm v.aai.3s r.gs.1 d.dsm n.dsm v.pmm.2s p.g r.gs.1 a.gpf
1253 326 4024 326 1650 3836 4041 1254 899 3306 3836 3261 3306 1609 3836 3261 2764 1666 1609 1288

hand ³⁵ until　I make your enemies　a footstool for your feet.”’　¶　³⁶ “Therefore let all Israel
← ἕως ἂν → θῶ σου τοὺς ἐχθρούς, ὑποπόδιον → σου τῶν ποδῶν. οὖν → πᾶς οἶκος Ἰσραὴλ
cj pl v.aas.1s r.gs.2 d.apm a.apm n.asn r.gs.2 d.gpm n.gpm cj a.nsm n.nsm n.gsm
2401 323 5502 5148 3836 2398 5711 4546 5148 3836 4546 4036 1182 4246 3875 2702

be　assured of this:　God　has made　this Jesus,　whom you crucified, both Lord　and
γινωσκέτω ἀσφαλῶς ὅτι ὁ θεός, → ἐποίησεν αὐτὸν τοῦτον τὸν Ἰησοῦν, ὃν ὑμεῖς ἐσταυρώσατε καὶ κύριον αὐτὸν καὶ
v.pam.3s adv cj d.nsm n.nsm v.aai.3s r.asm.3 r.asm d.asm n.asm r.asm r.np.2 v.aai.2p cj n.asm r.asm.3 cj
1182 857 4022 3836 2536 4472 899 4047 3836 2652 4005 7007 5090 2779 3261 899 2779

Christ.”　¶　³⁷ When the people heard　this, they were cut　to the heart　and said to　Peter
χριστόν δὲ → → → Ἀκούσαντες → → κατενύγησαν τὴν καρδίαν τε εἶπον πρὸς τὸν Πέτρον,
n.asm cj pt.aa.npm v.api.3p d.asf n.asf cj v.aai.3p p.a d.asm n.asm
5986 1254 201 2920 3836 2840 5445 3306 4639 3836 4377

εἰς αὐτόν, Προορώμην τὸν κύριον ἐνώπιόν μου διὰ παντός, ὅτι ἐκ δεξιῶν μού ἐστιν ἵνα μὴ σαλευθῶ. ²⁶ διὰ τοῦτο ηὐφράνθη ἡ
καρδία μου καὶ ἠγαλλιάσατο ἡ γλῶσσά μου, ἔτι δὲ καὶ ἡ σάρξ μου κατασκηνώσει ἐπ᾽ ἐλπίδι, ²⁷ ὅτι οὐκ ἐγκαταλείψεις τὴν
ψυχήν μου εἰς ᾅδην οὐδὲ δώσεις τὸν ὅσιόν σου ἰδεῖν διαφθοράν. ²⁸ ἐγνώρισάς μοι ὁδοὺς ζωῆς, πληρώσεις με εὐφροσύνης μετὰ
τοῦ προσώπου σου. ¶ ²⁹ Ἄνδρες ἀδελφοί, ἐξὸν εἰπεῖν μετὰ παρρησίας πρὸς ὑμᾶς περὶ τοῦ πατριάρχου Δαυὶδ ὅτι καὶ ἐτελεύτησεν
καὶ ἐτάφη, καὶ τὸ μνῆμα αὐτοῦ ἔστιν ἐν ἡμῖν ἄχρι τῆς ἡμέρας ταύτης. ³⁰ προφήτης οὖν ὑπάρχων, καὶ εἰδὼς ὅτι ὅρκῳ ὤμοσεν
αὐτῷ ὁ θεὸς ἐκ καρποῦ τῆς ὀσφύος αὐτοῦ καθίσαι ἐπὶ τὸν θρόνον αὐτοῦ, ³¹ προϊδὼν ἐλάλησεν περὶ τῆς ἀναστάσεως τοῦ Χριστοῦ
ὅτι οὔτε ἐγκατελείφθη εἰς ᾅδην οὔτε ἡ σὰρξ αὐτοῦ εἶδεν διαφθοράν. ³² τοῦτον τὸν Ἰησοῦν ἀνέστησεν ὁ θεός, οὗ πάντες ἡμεῖς
ἐσμεν μάρτυρες· ³³ τῇ δεξιᾷ οὖν τοῦ θεοῦ ὑψωθείς, τήν τε ἐπαγγελίαν τοῦ πνεύματος τοῦ ἁγίου λαβὼν παρὰ τοῦ πατρός, ἐξέχεεν
τοῦτο ὃ ὑμεῖς [καὶ] βλέπετε καὶ ἀκούετε. ³⁴ οὐ γὰρ Δαυὶδ ἀνέβη εἰς τοὺς οὐρανούς, λέγει δὲ αὐτός, Εἶπεν [ὁ] κύριος τῷ κυρίῳ
μου, Κάθου ἐκ δεξιῶν μου, ³⁵ ἕως ἂν θῶ τοὺς ἐχθρούς σου ὑποπόδιον τῶν ποδῶν σου. ¶ ³⁶ ἀσφαλῶς οὖν γινωσκέτω πᾶς οἶκος
Ἰσραὴλ ὅτι καὶ κύριον αὐτὸν καὶ Χριστὸν ἐποίησεν ὁ θεός, τοῦτον τὸν Ἰησοῦν ὃν ὑμεῖς ἐσταυρώσατε. ¶ ³⁷ Ἀκούσαντες δὲ

and the other apostles,   "Brothers, what shall we do?"   ¶   **38**   Peter replied,   "Repent
καὶ τοὺς λοιποὺς ἀποστόλους ἄνδρες ἀδελφοί τί → ποιήσωμεν δὲ Πέτρος φησὶν πρὸς αὐτούς μετανοήσατε
cj d.apm a.apm n.apm n.vpm n.vpm r.asn v.aas.1p cj n.nsm v.pai.3s p.a r.apm.3 v.aam.2p
2779 3836 3370 693 467 81 5515 4472 1254 4377 5774 4639 899 3566

and be baptized, every one of you, in the name of Jesus Christ for the forgiveness of your sins.   And
καὶ → βαπτισθήτω ἕκαστος ← → ὑμῶν ἐπὶ τῷ ὀνόματι Ἰησοῦ Χριστοῦ εἰς ἄφεσιν → ὑμῶν τῶν ἁμαρτιῶν καὶ
v.apm.3s r.nsm r.gp.2 p.d d.dsn n.dsn n.gsm n.gsm p.a n.asf r.gp.2 d.gpf n.gpf cj
2779 966 1667 7007 2093 3836 3950 2652 5986 1650 912 281 7007 3836 281 2779

you will receive the gift of the Holy Spirit.   **39**   The promise is for you and your children and for all
→ → λήμψεσθε τὴν δωρεὰν → τοῦ ἁγίου πνεύματος γὰρ ἡ ἐπαγγελία ἐστιν → ὑμῖν καὶ ὑμῶν τοῖς τέκνοις καὶ → πᾶσιν
v.fmi.2p d.asf n.asf d.gsn a.gsn n.gsn cj d.nsf n.nsf v.pai.3s r.dp.2 cj r.gp.2 d.dpn n.dpn cj a.dpm
3284 3836 1561 3836 41 4460 1142 3836 2039 1639 7007 2779 7007 3836 5451 2779 4246

who are far off – for all whom the Lord our God will call."   ¶   **40**   With many other
τοῖς εἰς μακρὰν ← ὅσους ἂν κύριος ἡμῶν ὁ θεὸς → προσκαλέσηται τε → πλείοσιν ἑτέροις
d.dpm p.a adv r.apm pl n.nsm r.gp.1 d.nsm n.nsm v.ams.3s cj a.dpm.c a.dpm
3836 1650 3426 4012 323 3261 7005 3836 2536 4673 5445 4498 2283

words he warned them; and he pleaded with them,   "Save yourselves from this corrupt generation."
λόγοις → διεμαρτύρατο καὶ → παρεκάλει ← αὐτοὺς λέγων σώθητε ← ἀπὸ ταύτης τῆς σκολιᾶς τῆς γενεᾶς
n.dpm v.ami.3s cj v.iai.3s r.apm.3 pt.pa.nsm v.apm.2p p.g r.gsf d.gsf a.gsf d.gsf n.gsf
3364 1371 2779 4151 899 3306 5392 608 4047 3836 5021 3836 1155

41   Those who accepted his message were baptized, and about three thousand were added
οὖν μὲν οἱ ← ἀποδεξάμενοι αὐτοῦ τὸν λόγον → ἐβαπτίσθησαν καὶ ὡσεὶ τρισχίλιαι ← ψυχαὶ → προσετέθησαν
cj pl d.npm pt.am.npm r.gsm.3 d.asm n.asm v.api.3p cj pl a.npf n.npf v.api.3p
4036 3525 3836 622 899 3836 3364 966 2779 6059 5567 6034 4707

to their number that day.
← ← ἐν ἐκείνῃ τῇ ἡμέρᾳ
p.d r.dsf d.dsf n.dsf
1877 1697 3836 2465

The Fellowship of the Believers

2:42   They devoted themselves to the apostles' teaching and to the fellowship, to the
δὲ → Ἦσαν προσκαρτεροῦντες ← → τῇ τῶν ἀποστόλων διδαχῇ καὶ → τῇ κοινωνίᾳ τῇ
cj v.iai.3p pt.pa.npm d.dsf d.gpm n.gpm n.dsf cj d.dsf n.dsf d.dsf
1254 1639 4674 3836 3836 693 1439 2779 3836 3126 3836

breaking of bread and to prayer.   **43**   Everyone was filled with awe, and many wonders and
κλάσει → τοῦ ἄρτου καὶ → ταῖς προσευχαῖς δὲ πάσῃ ψυχῇ → ἐγίνετο ← φόβος τε πολλά τέρατα καὶ
n.dsf d.gsm n.gsm cj d.dpf n.dpf cj a.dsf n.dsf v.imi.3s n.nsm cj a.npn n.npn cj
3082 3836 788 2779 3836 4666 1254 4246 6034 1181 5832 5445 4498 5469 2779

miraculous signs were done by the apostles.   **44**   All the believers were together and had everything in
σημεῖα → ἐγίνετο διὰ τῶν ἀποστόλων δὲ πάντες οἱ πιστεύοντες ἦσαν ἐπὶ τὸ αὐτὸ καὶ εἶχον ἅπαντα
n.npn v.imi.3s p.g d.gpm n.gpm cj a.npm d.npm pt.pa.npm v.iai.3p p.a d.asn r.asn cj v.iai.3p a.apn
4956 1181 1328 3836 693 1254 4246 3836 4409 1639 2093 3836 899 2779 2400 570

common.   **45**   Selling their possessions and goods, they gave to anyone as he had need.
κοινά καὶ ἐπίπρασκον τὰ κτήματα καὶ τὰς ὑπάρξεις καὶ → διεμέριζον αὐτὰ → πᾶσιν καθότι ἄν τις εἶχεν χρείαν
a.apn cj v.iai.3p d.apn n.apn cj d.apf n.apf cj v.iai.3p r.apn.3 a.dpm cj pl r.nsm v.iai.3s n.asf
3123 2779 4405 3836 3228 2779 3836 5638 2779 1374 899 4246 2776 323 5516 2400 5970

46   Every day they continued *to meet together* in the temple courts. They broke bread in their
τε καθ᾽ ἡμέραν → προσκαρτεροῦντες ὁμοθυμαδόν ἐν τῷ ἱερῷ τε → κλῶντες ἄρτον κατ᾽
cj p.a n.asf pt.pa.npm adv p.d d.dsn n.dsn cj pt.pa.npm n.asm p.a
5445 2848 2465 4674 3924 1877 3836 2639 5445 3089 788 2848

homes and ate together with glad and sincere hearts,   **47**   praising God and enjoying the favor
οἶκον μετελάμβανον τροφῆς → ἐν ἀγαλλιάσει καὶ ἀφελότητι καρδίας αἰνοῦντες τὸν θεὸν καὶ ἔχοντες χάριν
n.asm v.iai.3p n.gsf p.d n.dsf cj n.dsf n.gsf pt.pa.npm d.asm n.asm cj pt.pa.npm n.asf
3875 3561 5575 1877 21 2779 911 2840 140 3836 2536 2779 2400 5921

of all the people. And the Lord added to *their number* daily those who were being saved.
πρὸς ὅλον τὸν λαὸν δὲ ὁ κύριος προσετίθει ἐπὶ τὸ αὐτό καθ᾽ ἡμέραν τοὺς ← → σῳζομένους
p.a a.asm d.asm n.asm cj d.nsm n.nsm v.iai.3s p.a d.asn r.asn p.a n.asf d.apm pt.pp.apm
4639 3910 3295 1254 3836 3261 4707 2093 3836 899 2848 2465 3836 5392

κατενύγησαν τὴν καρδίαν εἶπόν τε πρὸς τὸν Πέτρον καὶ τοὺς λοιποὺς ἀποστόλους, Τί ποιήσωμεν, ἄνδρες ἀδελφοί; ¶ **38** Πέτρος δὲ πρὸς αὐτούς, Μετανοήσατε, [φησίν,] καὶ βαπτισθήτω ἕκαστος ὑμῶν ἐπὶ τῷ ὀνόματι Ἰησοῦ Χριστοῦ εἰς ἄφεσιν τῶν ἁμαρτιῶν ὑμῶν καὶ λήμψεσθε τὴν δωρεὰν τοῦ ἁγίου πνεύματος. **39** ὑμῖν γάρ ἐστιν ἡ ἐπαγγελία καὶ τοῖς τέκνοις ὑμῶν καὶ πᾶσιν τοῖς εἰς μακράν, ὅσους ἂν προσκαλέσηται κύριος ὁ θεὸς ἡμῶν. ¶ **40** ἑτέροις τε λόγοις πλείοσιν διεμαρτύρατο καὶ παρεκάλει αὐτοὺς λέγων, Σώθητε ἀπὸ τῆς γενεᾶς τῆς σκολιᾶς ταύτης. **41** οἱ μὲν οὖν ἀποδεξάμενοι τὸν λόγον αὐτοῦ ἐβαπτίσθησαν καὶ προσετέθησαν ἐν τῇ ἡμέρᾳ ἐκείνῃ ψυχαὶ ὡσεὶ τρισχίλιαι. **2:42** ἦσαν δὲ προσκαρτεροῦντες τῇ διδαχῇ τῶν ἀποστόλων καὶ τῇ κοινωνίᾳ, τῇ κλάσει τοῦ ἄρτου καὶ ταῖς προσευχαῖς. **43** Ἐγίνετο δὲ πάσῃ ψυχῇ φόβος, πολλά τε τέρατα καὶ σημεῖα διὰ τῶν ἀποστόλων ἐγίνετο. **44** πάντες δὲ οἱ πιστεύοντες ἦσαν ἐπὶ τὸ αὐτὸ καὶ εἶχον ἅπαντα κοινά **45** καὶ τὰ κτήματα καὶ τὰς ὑπάρξεις ἐπίπρασκον καὶ διεμέριζον αὐτὰ πᾶσιν καθότι ἄν τις χρείαν εἶχεν· **46** καθ᾽ ἡμέραν τε προσκαρτεροῦντες ὁμοθυμαδὸν ἐν τῷ ἱερῷ, κλῶντές τε κατ᾽ οἶκον ἄρτον, μετελάμβανον τροφῆς ἐν ἀγαλλιάσει καὶ ἀφελότητι καρδίας **47** αἰνοῦντες τὸν θεὸν καὶ ἔχοντες χάριν πρὸς ὅλον τὸν λαόν. ὁ δὲ κύριος προσετίθει

Peter Heals the Crippled Beggar

3:1 One day Peter and John were going up to the temple at the time of prayer – at three
δὲ Πέτρος καὶ Ἰωάννης → ἀνέβαινον ← εἰς τὸ ἱερὸν ἐπὶ τὴν ὥραν ⸤τῆς προσευχῆς⸥ ⸤τὴν ἐνάτην⸥
cj n.nsm cj n.nsm v.iai.3p p.a d.asn n.asn p.a d.asf n.asf d.gsf n.gsf d.asf a.asf
1254 4377 2779 2722 326 1650 3836 2639 2093 3836 6052 3836 4666 3836 1888

in the afternoon. **2** Now a man crippled from birth was being carried to the temple gate
← ← καὶ τις ἀνὴρ χωλὸς ἐκ ⸤κοιλίας μητρὸς αὐτοῦ⸥ → ὑπάρχων ἐβαστάζετο πρὸς τὴν ⸤τοῦ ἱεροῦ⸥ θύραν
cj r.nsm n.nsm a.nsm p.g n.gsf n.gsf r.gsm.3 pt.pa.nsm v.ipi.3s p.a d.asf d.gsn n.gsn n.asf
2779 5516 467 6000 1666 3120 3613 899 5639 1002 4639 3836 3836 2639 2598

called Beautiful, where he was put every day to beg from those going into the
⸤τὴν λεγομένην⸥ Ὡραίαν ὃν → → ἐτίθουν καθ᾽ ἡμέραν ⸤τοῦ αἰτεῖν ἐλεημοσύνην⸥ παρὰ τῶν εἰσπορευομένων εἰς τὸ
d.asf pt.pp.asf a.asf r.asm v.iai.3p p.a n.asf d.gsn f.pa n.asf p.g d.gpm pt.pm.gpm p.a d.asn
3836 3306 6053 4005 5502 2848 2465 3836 160 1797 4123 3836 1660 1650 3836

temple courts. **3** When he saw Peter and John about to enter, he asked them for
ἱερόν ← ὃς → → ἰδὼν Πέτρον καὶ Ἰωάννην μέλλοντας → εἰσιέναι εἰς τὸ ἱερὸν ἠρώτα ← λαβεῖν
n.asn r.nsm pt.aa.nsm n.asm cj n.asm pt.pa.apm f.pa p.a d.asn n.asn v.iai.3s f.aa
2639 4005 1625 4377 2779 2722 3516 1655 1650 3836 2639 2263 3284

money. **4** Peter looked straight at him, *as did* John. Then Peter said, "Look at us!" **5** So the man
ἐλεημοσύνην δὲ Πέτρος ἀτενίσας ← εἰς αὐτὸν σὺν ⸤τῷ Ἰωάννῃ⸥ εἶπεν βλέψον εἰς ἡμᾶς δὲ ὁ
n.asf cj n.nsm pt.aa.nsm p.a r.asm.3 p.d d.dsm n.dsm v.aai.3s v.aam.2s p.a r.ap.1 cj d.nsm
1797 1254 4377 867 1650 899 5250 3836 2722 3306 1063 1650 7005 1254 3836

gave them his attention, expecting to get something from them. ¶ **6** Then Peter said, "Silver or gold
ἐπεῖχεν αὐτοῖς προσδοκῶν → λαβεῖν τι παρ᾽ αὐτῶν δὲ Πέτρος εἶπεν ἀργύριον καὶ χρυσίον
v.iai.3s r.dpm.3 pt.pa.nsm f.aa r.asn p.g r.gpm.3 cj n.nsm v.aai.3s n.nsn cj n.nsn
2091 899 2091 4659 3284 5516 4123 899 1254 4377 3306 736 2779 5992

I do not have, but what I have I give you. In the name of Jesus Christ of Nazareth,
μοι → οὐχ ὑπάρχει δὲ ὃ → ἔχω τοῦτο → δίδωμι σοι ἐν τῷ ὀνόματι → Ἰησοῦ Χριστοῦ → ⸤τοῦ Ναζωραίου⸥ [ἔγειρε
r.ds.1 pl v.pai.3s cj r.asn v.pai.1s r.asn v.pai.1s r.ds.2 p.d d.dsn n.dsn n.gsm n.gsm d.gsm n.gsm v.pam.2s
1609 5639 4024 5639 1254 4005 2400 4047 1443 5148 1877 3836 3950 2652 5986 3836 3717 1586

walk." **7** Taking him by the right hand, he helped him up, and instantly the man's feet and
καὶ] περιπάτει καὶ πιάσας αὐτὸν → τῆς δεξιᾶς χειρὸς → ἤγειρεν αὐτόν ← δὲ παραχρῆμα αἱ αὐτοῦ βάσεις καὶ
cj v.pam.2s cj pt.aa.nsm r.asm.3 d.gsf a.gsf n.gsf v.aai.3s r.asm.3 cj adv d.npf r.gsm.3 n.npf cj
2779 4344 2779 4389 899 3836 1288 5931 1586 899 1586 1254 4202 3836 899 1000 2779

ankles became strong. **8** He jumped *to his feet* and began to walk. Then he went with them into
⸤τὰ σφυδρά⸥ → ἐστερεώθησαν καὶ → ἐξαλλόμενος ἔστη καὶ → → περιεπάτει καὶ → εἰσῆλθεν σὺν αὐτοῖς εἰς
d.npn n.npn v.api.3p cj pt.pm.nsm v.aai.3s cj v.iai.3s cj v.aai.3s p.d r.dpm.3 p.a
3836 5383 5105 2779 1982 2705 2779 4344 2779 1656 5250 899 1650

the temple courts, walking and jumping, and praising God. **9** When all the people saw him walking and
τὸ ἱερὸν ← περιπατῶν καὶ ἁλλόμενος καὶ αἰνῶν ⸤τὸν θεόν⸥ καὶ πᾶς ὁ λαὸς εἶδεν αὐτὸν περιπατοῦντα καὶ
d.asn n.asn pt.pa.nsm cj pt.pm.nsm cj pt.pa.nsm d.asm n.asm cj a.nsm d.nsm n.nsm v.aai.3s r.asm.3 pt.pa.asm cj
3836 2639 4344 2779 256 2779 140 3836 2536 2779 4246 3836 3295 1625 899 4344 2779

praising God, **10** they recognized him as the same man who used to sit begging at the
αἰνοῦντα ⸤τὸν θεόν⸥ δὲ → ἐπεγίνωσκον αὐτὸν ὅτι αὐτὸς ← ἦν ὁ → → καθήμενος πρὸς ⸤τὴν ἐλεημοσύνην⸥ ἐπὶ τῇ
pt.pa.asm d.asm n.asm cj v.iai.3p r.asm.3 cj r.nsm v.iai.3s d.nsm pt.pm.nsm p.a d.asf n.asf p.d d.dsf
140 3836 2536 1254 2105 899 4022 899 1639 3836 2764 4639 3836 1797 2093 3836

temple gate called Beautiful, and they were filled with wonder and amazement at what had happened to him.
⸤τοῦ ἱεροῦ⸥ πύλῃ ὡραίᾳ καὶ → ἐπλήσθησαν ← θάμβους καὶ ἐκστάσεως ἐπὶ τῷ → συμβεβηκότι → αὐτῷ
d.gsn n.gsn n.dsf a.dsf cj v.api.3p n.gsn cj n.gsf p.d d.dsn pt.ra.dsn r.dsm.3
3836 2639 4783 6053 2779 4398 2502 2779 1749 2093 3836 5201 899

Peter Speaks to the Onlookers

3:11 While the beggar held on to Peter and John, all the people were astonished and came
δὲ αὐτοῦ Κρατοῦντος ← ⸤τὸν Πέτρον⸥ καὶ ⸤τὸν Ἰωάννην⸥ πᾶς ὁ λαὸς ἔκθαμβοι →
cj r.gsm.3 pt.pa.gsm d.asm n.asm cj d.asm n.asm a.nsm d.nsm n.nsm n.npm
1254 3195 899 3195 3836 4377 2779 3836 2722 4246 3836 3295 1702

τοὺς σωζομένους καθ᾽ ἡμέραν ἐπὶ τὸ αὐτό.

³·¹ Πέτρος δὲ καὶ Ἰωάννης ἀνέβαινον εἰς τὸ ἱερὸν ἐπὶ τὴν ὥραν τῆς προσευχῆς τὴν ἐνάτην. ² καὶ τις ἀνὴρ χωλὸς ἐκ κοιλίας μητρὸς αὐτοῦ ὑπάρχων ἐβαστάζετο, ὃν ἐτίθουν καθ᾽ ἡμέραν πρὸς τὴν θύραν τοῦ ἱεροῦ τὴν λεγομένην Ὡραίαν τοῦ αἰτεῖν ἐλεημοσύνην παρὰ τῶν εἰσπορευομένων εἰς τὸ ἱερόν· ³ ὃς ἰδὼν Πέτρον καὶ Ἰωάννην μέλλοντας εἰσιέναι εἰς τὸ ἱερόν, ἠρώτα ἐλεημοσύνην λαβεῖν. ⁴ ἀτενίσας δὲ Πέτρος εἰς αὐτὸν σὺν τῷ Ἰωάννῃ εἶπεν, Βλέψον εἰς ἡμᾶς. ⁵ ὁ δὲ ἐπεῖχεν αὐτοῖς προσδοκῶν τι παρ᾽ αὐτῶν λαβεῖν. ¶ ⁶ εἶπεν δὲ Πέτρος, Ἀργύριον καὶ χρυσίον οὐχ ὑπάρχει μοι, ὃ δὲ ἔχω τοῦτό σοι δίδωμι· ἐν τῷ ὀνόματι Ἰησοῦ Χριστοῦ τοῦ Ναζωραίου [ἔγειρε καὶ] περιπάτει. ⁷ καὶ πιάσας αὐτὸν τῆς δεξιᾶς χειρὸς ἤγειρεν αὐτόν· παραχρῆμα δὲ ἐστερεώθησαν αἱ βάσεις αὐτοῦ καὶ τὰ σφυδρά, ⁸ καὶ ἐξαλλόμενος ἔστη καὶ περιεπάτει καὶ εἰσῆλθεν σὺν αὐτοῖς εἰς τὸ ἱερὸν περιπατῶν καὶ ἁλλόμενος καὶ αἰνῶν τὸν θεόν. ⁹ καὶ εἶδεν πᾶς ὁ λαὸς αὐτὸν περιπατοῦντα καὶ αἰνοῦντα τὸν θεόν· ¹⁰ ἐπεγίνωσκον δὲ αὐτὸν ὅτι αὐτὸς ἦν ὁ πρὸς τὴν ἐλεημοσύνην καθήμενος ἐπὶ τῇ Ὡραίᾳ Πύλῃ τοῦ ἱεροῦ καὶ ἐπλήσθησαν θάμβους καὶ ἐκστάσεως ἐπὶ τῷ συμβεβηκότι αὐτῷ.

³·¹¹ Κρατοῦντος δὲ αὐτοῦ τὸν Πέτρον καὶ τὸν Ἰωάννην συνέδραμεν πᾶς ὁ λαὸς πρὸς αὐτοὺς ἐπὶ τῇ στοᾷ τῇ καλουμένῃ

running	to	them	in	the place called		Solomon's	Colonnade.	**12**	When	Peter		saw	this,	he said
συνέδραμεν	πρὸς	αὐτοὺς	ἐπὶ	⸂τῇ καλουμένῃ	Σολομῶντος	⸄τῇ στοᾷ⸅		δὲ	→	ὁ Πέτρος	ἰδὼν	→	ἀπεκρίνατο
v.aai.3s	p.a	r.apm.3	p.d	d.dsf pt.pp.dsf	n.gsm	d.dsf n.dsf		cj		d.nsm n.nsm	pt.aa.nsm		v.ami.3s
5340	4639	899	2093	3836 2813	5048	3836 5119		1254 1625		3836 4377	1625		646

to	them:	"Men	of Israel,	why	does this		surprise you?		Why	do you stare		at us		as	if by	our
πρὸς	⸂τὸν λαόν⸃	ἄνδρες	⸃ Ἰσραηλῖται	τί	→	⸂ἐπὶ τούτῳ	θαυμάζετε	←	ἢ	τί	→	ἀτενίζετε	⸂ἡμῖν⸃	ὡς	←	ἰδίᾳ
p.a	d.asm n.vpm	n.vpm	n.vpm	r.asn		p.d r.dsn	v.pai.2p		cj	r.asn		v.pai.2p	r.dp.1	pl		a.dsf
4639	3836 3295	467	2703	5515	2513	2093 4047	2513		2445	5515		867	7005	6055		2625

own	power	or	godliness	we had made		this man	walk?		**13**	The	God	of Abraham,				Isaac
←	δυνάμει	ἢ	εὐσεβείᾳ	→	πεποιηκόσιν	αὐτόν	⸂τοῦ περιπατεῖν⸃			ὁ	θεὸς	Ἀβραὰμ	καὶ	[ὁ	θεὸς]	Ἰσαὰκ
	n.dsf	cj	n.dsf		pt.ra.dpm	r.asm.3	d.gsn f.pa			d.nsm	n.nsm	n.gsm	cj	d.nsm	n.nsm	n.gsm
	1539	2445	2354		4472	899	3836 4344			3836	2536	11	2779	3836	2536	2693

and			Jacob,	the	God	of our	fathers,		has glorified	his		servant	Jesus.		You	handed	him
καὶ	[ὁ	θεὸς]	Ἰακώβ	ὁ	θεὸς	→ ἡμῶν	⸂τῶν πατέρων⸃	→	ἐδόξασεν	αὐτοῦ	⸂τὸν παῖδα⸃		Ἰησοῦν	μὲν	ὑμεῖς	παρεδώκατε	ὃν
cj	d.nsm n.nsm	n.gsm	n.gsm	d.nsm n.nsm		r.gp.1	d.gpm n.gpm		v.aai.3s	r.gsm.3	d.asm n.nsm		n.asm	pl	r.np.2	v.aai.2p	r.asm
2779	3836 2536	2609	3836 2536	4252		7005	3836 4252		1519	899	3836 4090		2652	3525	7007	4140	4005

over to be killed,	and	you disowned	him	before			Pilate,	though	he	had decided	to let	him	go.		**14**
	καὶ	→	ἠρνήσασθε	⸂κατὰ πρόσωπον⸃	Πιλάτου	→		→		κρίναντος	←	ἐκείνου	ἀπολύειν		δὲ
	cj		v.ami.2p	p.a	n.gsm					pt.aa.gsm		r.gsm	f.pa		cj
4140	2779		766	2848 4725	4397					3212	668 668	1697	668		1254

You	disowned	the Holy	and	Righteous	One	and	asked		that a murderer		be released		to you.		**15**		You	killed
ὑμεῖς	ἠρνήσασθε	τὸν ἅγιον	καὶ	δίκαιον	←	καὶ	ᾐτήσασθε		⸂ἄνδρα φονέα⸃		χαρισθῆναι	→	ὑμῖν	δὲ	→		ἀπεκτείνατε
r.np.2	v.ami.2p	d.asm a.asm	cj	a.asm		cj	v.ami.2p		n.asm n.asm		f.ap		r.dp.2	cj			v.aai.2p
7007	766	3836 41	2779	1465		2779	160		467 5838		5919		7007	1254			650

the	author	of life,		but	God		raised	him	from the	dead.	We	are	witnesses	of this.	**16**		By	faith		in the
τὸν	ἀρχηγὸν	⸂τῆς ζωῆς⸃	→	⸃ ὁ	θεὸς	ἤγειρεν	ὃν	ἐκ	νεκρῶν	ἡμεῖς	ἐσμεν	μάρτυρες	→	οὗ		καὶ	ἐπὶ	⸂τῇ πίστει⸃	→	τοῦ
d.asm	n.asm	d.gsf n.gsf		d.nsm n.nsm		v.aai.3s	r.asm	p.g	a.gpm	r.np.1	v.pai.1p	n.npm		r.gsm		cj	p.d	d.dsf n.dsf		d.gsn
3836	795	3836 2437		3836 2536		1586	4005	1666	3738	7005	1639	3459		4005		2779	2093	3836 4411		3836

name	of Jesus,	this	man	whom	you	see		and	know	was made		strong.	It is	Jesus'	name		and	the	faith
ὀνόματος	→ αὐτοῦ	τοῦτον	←	ὃν	→	θεωρεῖτε	καὶ	οἴδατε	→	→	ἐστερέωσεν		αὐτοῦ	⸂τὸ ὄνομα⸃		καὶ	ἡ	πίστις
n.gsn	r.gsm.3	r.asm		r.asm		v.pai.2p	cj	v.rai.2p			v.aai.3s		r.gsm.3	d.nsn n.nsn		cj	d.nsf	n.nsf
3950	899	4047	4005		2555		2779	3857			5105		899	3836 3950		2779	3836	4411

that comes	through	him	that has	given	this	complete		healing	to him,			as	you	can	all	see.	¶
ἡ	δι'	αὐτοῦ	→	→ ἔδωκεν	ταύτην	⸂τὴν ὁλοκληρίαν⸃	←	→	αὐτῷ	ἀπέναντι	ὑμῶν	πάντων	↰
d.nsf	p.g	r.gsm.3		v.aai.3s	r.asf	d.asf n.asf			r.dsm.3	p.g	r.gp.2	a.gpm	
3836	1328	899		1443	4047	3836 3907			899	595	7007	4246	595

17	"Now,	brothers,	I	know	that	you	acted	in	ignorance,	as		did	your	leaders.		**18** But	this is	how
	Καὶ	νῦν	ἀδελφοί	οἶδα	ὅτι	→	ἐπράξατε	κατὰ	ἄγνοιαν	ὥσπερ	καὶ	⸃ ὑμῶν	οἱ ἄρχοντες		δὲ	→	οὕτως
	cj	adv	n.vpm	v.rai.1s	cj		v.aai.2p	p.a	n.asf	pl	adv	r.gp.2	d.npm n.npm		cj		adv
	2779	3814	81	3857	4022		4556	2848	53	6061	2779	7007	3836 807		1254		4048

God	fulfilled	what	he had foretold			through		all	the prophets,	saying that	his	Christ
⸃ ὁ θεὸς	ἐπλήρωσεν	ἃ	→	προκατήγγειλεν	διὰ		στόματος	πάντων	τῶν προφητῶν		αὐτοῦ	⸂τὸν χριστὸν⸃
d.nsm n.nsm	v.aai.3s	r.apn		v.aai.3s	p.g		n.gsn	a.gpm	d.gpm n.gpm		r.gsm.3	d.asm n.asm
3836 2536	4444	4005		4615	1328		5125	4246	3836 4737		899	3836 5986

would suffer.	**19** Repent,	then,	and	turn		to God,	so that	your	sins		may be wiped		out,
→ παθεῖν	μετανοήσατε	οὖν	καὶ	ἐπιστρέψατε		εἰς	←	ὑμῶν	⸂τὰς ἁμαρτίας⸃		→	⸂τὸ ἐξαλειφθῆναι⸃
f.aa	v.aam.2p	cj	cj	v.aam.2p		p.a		r.gp.2	d.apf n.apf			d.asn f.ap
4248	3566	4036	2779	2188		1650		7007	3836 281			3836 1981

that	times	of refreshing	may come		from		the Lord,	**20**	and that	he	may send		the Christ,	who has
ὅπως	ἂν	καιροὶ	→ ἀναψύξεως	→	ἔλθωσιν	ἀπὸ	προσώπου	τοῦ κυρίου		καὶ	→	ἀποστείλῃ		χριστόν	τὸν →
cj	pl	n.npm	n.gsf		v.aas.3p	p.g	n.gsn	d.gsm n.gsm		cj		v.aas.3s		n.asm	d.asm
3968	323	2789	433		2262	608	4725	3836 3261		2779		690		5986	3836

been appointed		for you	– even	Jesus.	**21**	He	must		remain	in heaven	until	the	time	comes for God to
→ προκεχειρισμένον		ὑμῖν	Ἰησοῦν	ὃν	δεῖ		μὲν	δέξασθαι	←	οὐρανὸν	ἄχρι		χρόνων	
pt.rm.asm		r.dp.2	n.asm	r.asm	v.pai.3s		pl	f.am		n.asm	p.g		n.gpm	
4741		7007	2652	4005	1256		3525	1312		4041	948		5989	

Σολομῶντος ἔκθαμβοι. 12 ἰδὼν δὲ ὁ Πέτρος ἀπεκρίνατο πρὸς τὸν λαόν, Ἄνδρες Ἰσραηλῖται, τί θαυμάζετε ἐπὶ τούτῳ ἢ ἡμῖν τί ἀτενίζετε ὡς ἰδίᾳ δυνάμει ἢ εὐσεβείᾳ πεποιηκόσιν τοῦ περιπατεῖν αὐτόν; 13 ὁ θεὸς Ἀβραὰμ καὶ [ὁ θεὸς] Ἰσαὰκ καὶ [ὁ θεὸς] Ἰακώβ, ὁ θεὸς τῶν πατέρων ἡμῶν, ἐδόξασεν τὸν παῖδα αὐτοῦ Ἰησοῦν ὃν ὑμεῖς μὲν παρεδώκατε καὶ ἠρνήσασθε κατὰ πρόσωπον Πιλάτου, κρίναντος ἐκείνου ἀπολύειν· 14 ὑμεῖς δὲ τὸν ἅγιον καὶ δίκαιον ἠρνήσασθε καὶ ᾐτήσασθε ἄνδρα φονέα χαρισθῆναι ὑμῖν, 15 τὸν δὲ ἀρχηγὸν τῆς ζωῆς ἀπεκτείνατε ὃν ὁ θεὸς ἤγειρεν ἐκ νεκρῶν, οὗ ἡμεῖς μάρτυρές ἐσμεν. 16 καὶ ἐπὶ τῇ πίστει τοῦ ὀνόματος αὐτοῦ τοῦτον ὃν θεωρεῖτε καὶ οἴδατε, ἐστερέωσεν τὸ ὄνομα αὐτοῦ, καὶ ἡ πίστις ἡ δι' αὐτοῦ ἔδωκεν αὐτῷ τὴν ὁλοκληρίαν ταύτην ἀπέναντι πάντων ὑμῶν. ¶ 17 καὶ νῦν, ἀδελφοί, οἶδα ὅτι κατὰ ἄγνοιαν ἐπράξατε ὥσπερ καὶ οἱ ἄρχοντες ὑμῶν· 18 ὁ δὲ θεός, ἃ προκατήγγειλεν διὰ στόματος πάντων τῶν προφητῶν παθεῖν τὸν Χριστὸν αὐτοῦ, ἐπλήρωσεν οὕτως. 19 μετανοήσατε οὖν καὶ ἐπιστρέψατε εἰς τὸ ἐξαλειφθῆναι ὑμῶν τὰς ἁμαρτίας, 20 ὅπως ἂν ἔλθωσιν καιροὶ ἀναψύξεως ἀπὸ προσώπου τοῦ κυρίου καὶ ἀποστείλῃ τὸν προκεχειρισμένον ὑμῖν Χριστόν Ἰησοῦν, 21 ὃν δεῖ οὐρανὸν μὲν δέξασθαι ἄχρι χρόνων

restore everything, as he promised long ago through his holy prophets. ²² For
ἀποκαταστάσεως πάντων ὧν ὁ θεός, ἐλάλησεν ⌐ἀπ᾽ αἰῶνος⌐ ← διὰ στόματος αὐτοῦ τῶν ἁγίων προφητῶν μὲν
n.gsf a.gpn r.gpn d.nsm n.nsm v.aai.3s p.g n.gsm p.g n.gsn r.gsm.3 d.gpm a.gpm n.gpm pl
640 4246 4005 3836 2536 3281 608 172 1328 5125 899 3836 41 4737 3525

Moses said, 'The Lord your God will raise up for you a prophet like me from among your own people;
Μωϋσῆς εἶπεν ὅτι κύριος ὑμῶν ὁ θεός, → ἀναστήσει ← → ὑμῖν προφήτην ὡς ἐμὲ ἐκ ← ὑμῶν τῶν ἀδελφῶν
n.nsm v.aai.3s cj n.nsm r.gp.2 d.nsm n.nsm v.fai.3s r.dp.2 n.asm pl r.as.1 p.g r.gp.2 d.gpm n.gpm
3707 3306 4022 3261 7007 3836 2536 482 7007 4737 6055 1609 1666 7007 3836 81

you must listen to everything he tells you. ²³ Anyone who does not listen to
→ → ἀκούσεσθε ← αὐτοῦ ⌐κατὰ πάντα ὅσα ἂν⌐ → λαλήσῃ πρὸς ὑμᾶς δὲ ⌐πᾶσα ψυχὴ⌐ ἥτις ἐὰν⌐ → μὴ ἀκούσῃ ←
v.fmi.2p r.gsm.3 p.a a.apn r.apn pl v.aas.3s p.a r.ap.2 cj a.nsf n.nsf r.nsf pl pl v.aas.3s
201 899 2848 4246 4012 323 3281 4639 7007 1254 4246 6034 4015 1569 201 3590 201

him will be completely cut off from among his people.' ¶ ²⁴ "Indeed, all the
⌐τοῦ προφήτου ἐκείνου⌐ → ἔσται ← ἐξολεθρευθήσεται ← ἐκ ← τοῦ λαοῦ ⌐δὲ καὶ⌐ πάντες οἱ
d.gsm n.gsm r.gsm v.fmi.3s v.fpi.3s p.g d.gsm n.gsm cj cj a.npm d.npm
3836 4737 1697 1639 2017 1666 3836 3295 1254 2779 4246 3836

prophets from Samuel on, as many as have spoken, have foretold these days. ²⁵ And you
προφῆται ἀπὸ Σαμουήλ ⌐καὶ τῶν καθεξῆς⌐ ὅσοι ← ← ἐλάλησαν καὶ → κατήγγειλαν ταύτας ⌐τὰς ἡμέρας⌐ ὑμεῖς
n.npm p.g n.gsm cj d.gpm adv r.npm v.aai.3p adv v.aai.3p r.apf d.apf n.apf r.np.2
4737 608 4905 2779 3836 2759 4012 3281 2779 2859 4047 3836 2465 7007

are heirs of the prophets and of the covenant God made with your fathers. He said to
ἐστε ⌐οἱ υἱοὶ⌐ → τῶν προφητῶν καὶ → τῆς διαθήκης ἧς ὁ θεός, διέθετο πρὸς ὑμῶν ⌐τοὺς πατέρας⌐ → λέγων πρὸς
v.pai.2p d.npm n.npm d.gpm n.gpm cj d.gsf n.gsf r.gsf d.nsm n.nsm v.ami.3s p.a r.gp.2 d.apm n.apm pt.pa.nsm p.a
1639 3836 5626 3836 4737 2779 3836 1347 4005 3836 2536 1416 4639 7007 3836 4252 3306 4639

Abraham, 'Through your offspring all peoples on earth will be blessed.' ²⁶ When God
Ἀβραάμ, καὶ ἐν σου ⌐τῷ σπέρματι⌐ πᾶσαι ⌐αἱ πατριαὶ⌐ → ⌐τῆς γῆς⌐ → ἐνευλογηθήσονται ⌐ ὁ θεός,
n.asm cj p.d r.gs.2 d.dsn n.dsn a.npf d.npf n.npf d.gsf n.gsf v.fpi.3p d.nsm n.nsm
11 2779 1877 5148 3836 5065 4246 3836 4255 3836 1178 1922 482 3836 2536

raised up his servant, he sent him first to you to bless you by turning each of you
ἀναστήσας αὐτοῦ ⌐τὸν παῖδα⌐ → ἀπέστειλεν αὐτὸν πρῶτον ὑμῖν εὐλογοῦντα ὑμᾶς ἐν ⌐τῷ ἀποστρέφειν⌐ ἕκαστον
pt.aa.nsm r.gsm.3 d.asm n.asm v.aai.3s r.asm.3 adv r.dp.2 pt.pa.asm r.ap.2 p.d d.dsn f.pa r.asm
482 899 3836 4090 690 899 4754 7007 2328 7007 1877 3836 695 1667

from your wicked ways."
ἀπὸ ὑμῶν ⌐τῶν πονηριῶν⌐ ←
p.g r.gp.2 d.gpf n.gpf
608 7007 3836 4504

Peter and John Before the Sanhedrin

⁴:¹ The priests and the captain of the temple guard and the Sadducees came up to Peter and John
δὲ οἱ ἱερεῖς καὶ ὁ στρατηγὸς → τοῦ ἱεροῦ καὶ οἱ Σαδδουκαῖοι ἐπέστησαν ← ← αὐτοῖς ← ←
cj d.npm n.npm cj d.nsm n.nsm d.gsn n.gsn cj d.npm n.npm v.aai.3p r.dpm.3
1254 3836 2636 2779 3836 5130 3836 2639 2779 3836 4881 2392 899

while they were speaking to the people. ² They were greatly disturbed because the apostles were teaching
↱ αὐτῶν → λαλούντων πρὸς τὸν λαόν → → greatly διαπονούμενοι διὰ αὐτοὺς → ⌐τὸ διδάσκειν⌐
r.gpm.3 pt.pa.gpm p.a d.asm n.asm pt.pm.npm p.a r.apm.3 d.asn f.pa
3281 899 3281 4639 3836 3295 1387 1328 899 3836 1438

the people and proclaiming in Jesus the resurrection of the dead. ³ They seized Peter and
τὸν λαὸν καὶ καταγγέλλειν ἐν ⌐τῷ Ἰησοῦ⌐ τὴν ἀνάστασιν τὴν ἐκ νεκρῶν καὶ → ⌐ἐπέβαλον τὰς χεῖρας⌐ αὐτοῖς ←
d.asm n.asm cj f.pa p.d d.dsm n.dsm d.asf n.asf d.asf p.g a.gpm cj v.aai.3p d.apf n.apf r.dpm.3
3836 3295 2779 2859 1877 3836 2652 3836 414 3836 1666 3738 2779 2095 3836 5931 899

John, and because it was evening, they put them in jail until the next day. ⁴ But many who heard the
καὶ γὰρ → ἦν ἤδη ἑσπέρα → ἔθεντο εἰς τήρησιν εἰς τὴν αὔριον δὲ πολλοὶ τῶν ἀκουσάντων τὸν
cj cj v.iai.3s adv n.nsf v.ami.3p p.a n.asf p.a d.asf adv cj a.npm d.gpm pt.aa.gpm d.asm
2779 1142 1639 2453 2270 5502 1650 5499 1650 3836 892 1254 4498 3836 201 3836

message believed, and the number of men grew to about five thousand. ¶ ⁵ The next
λόγον ἐπίστευσαν καὶ ὁ ἀριθμὸς ⌐τῶν ἀνδρῶν⌐ ἐγενήθη ὡς πέντε χιλιάδες δὲ Ἐγένετο ἐπὶ τὴν αὔριον
n.asm v.aai.3p cj d.nsm n.nsm d.gpm n.gpm v.api.3s pl a.npf n.npf cj v.ami.3s p.a d.asf adv
3364 4409 2779 3836 750 3836 467 1181 6055 4297 5942 1254 1181 2093 3836 892

ἀποκαταστάσεως πάντων ὧν ἐλάλησεν ὁ θεὸς διὰ στόματος τῶν ἁγίων ἀπ᾽ αἰῶνος αὐτοῦ προφητῶν. ²² Μωϋσῆς μὲν εἶπεν ὅτι Προφήτην ὑμῖν ἀναστήσει κύριος ὁ θεὸς ὑμῶν ἐκ τῶν ἀδελφῶν ὑμῶν ὡς ἐμέ· αὐτοῦ ἀκούσεσθε κατὰ πάντα ὅσα ἂν λαλήσῃ πρὸς ὑμᾶς. ²³ ἔσται δὲ πᾶσα ψυχὴ ἥτις ἐὰν μὴ ἀκούσῃ τοῦ προφήτου ἐκείνου ἐξολεθρευθήσεται ἐκ τοῦ λαοῦ. ¶ ²⁴ καὶ πάντες δὲ οἱ προφῆται ἀπὸ Σαμουὴλ καὶ τῶν καθεξῆς ὅσοι ἐλάλησαν καὶ κατήγγειλαν τὰς ἡμέρας ταύτας. ²⁵ ὑμεῖς ἐστε οἱ υἱοὶ τῶν προφητῶν καὶ τῆς διαθήκης ἧς διέθετο ὁ θεὸς πρὸς τοὺς πατέρας ὑμῶν λέγων πρὸς Ἀβραάμ, Καὶ ἐν τῷ σπέρματί σου [ἐν]ευλογηθήσονται πᾶσαι αἱ πατριαὶ τῆς γῆς. ²⁶ ὑμῖν πρῶτον ἀναστήσας ὁ θεὸς τὸν παῖδα αὐτοῦ ἀπέστειλεν αὐτὸν εὐλογοῦντα ὑμᾶς ἐν τῷ ἀποστρέφειν ἕκαστον ἀπὸ τῶν πονηριῶν ὑμῶν.

⁴:¹ Λαλούντων δὲ αὐτῶν πρὸς τὸν λαὸν ἐπέστησαν αὐτοῖς οἱ ἱερεῖς καὶ ὁ στρατηγὸς τοῦ ἱεροῦ καὶ οἱ Σαδδουκαῖοι, ² διαπονούμενοι διὰ τὸ διδάσκειν αὐτοὺς τὸν λαὸν καὶ καταγγέλλειν ἐν τῷ Ἰησοῦ τὴν ἀνάστασιν τὴν ἐκ νεκρῶν, ³ καὶ ἐπέβαλον αὐτοῖς τὰς χεῖρας καὶ ἔθεντο εἰς τήρησιν εἰς τὴν αὔριον· ἦν γὰρ ἑσπέρα ἤδη. ⁴ πολλοὶ δὲ τῶν ἀκουσάντων τὸν λόγον ἐπίστευσαν, καὶ ἐγενήθη [ὁ] ἀριθμὸς τῶν ἀνδρῶν [ὡς] χιλιάδες πέντε. ¶ ⁵ Ἐγένετο δὲ ἐπὶ τὴν αὔριον συναχθῆναι αὐτῶν τοὺς ἄρχοντας καὶ

day the rulers,   elders   and teachers   of the law met   in Jerusalem. ⁶ Annas the
← τοὺς ἄρχοντας καὶ τοὺς πρεσβυτέρους καὶ τοὺς γραμματεῖς ←   συναχθῆναι αὐτῶν ἐν Ἰερουσαλήμ καὶ Ἄννας ὁ
d.apm n.apm cj d.apm a.apm cj d.apm n.apm   f.ap r.gpm.3 p.d n.dsf cj n.nsm d.nsm
3836 807 2779 3836 4565 2779 3836 1208   5251 899 1877 2647 2779 484 3836

high priest was there, and so were Caiaphas,   John,   Alexander and the other men of the high
→ ἀρχιερεὺς   καὶ ἦσαν Καϊάφας καὶ Ἰωάννης καὶ Ἀλέξανδρος καὶ ὅσοι ← ἐκ →
n.nsm   cj v.iai.3p n.nsm cj n.nsm cj n.nsm cj r.npm p.g
797   2779 1639 2780 2779 2722 2779 235 2779 4012 1666

priest's   family. ⁷ They had Peter and John brought before   them and began to question   them: "By
ἀρχιερατικοῦ γένους καὶ ← αὐτοὺς ← στήσαντες ἐν τῷ μέσῳ ←   ἐπυνθάνοντο   ἐν
a.gsn n.gsn cj r.apm.3   pt.aa.npm p.d d.dsn n.dsn   v.imi.3p   p.d
796 1169 2779 2705 2705 899   2705 1877 3836 3545   4785   1877

what power or   what name did you do   this?" ¶   ⁸ Then Peter, filled   with the Holy Spirit,   said
ποίᾳ δυνάμει ἢ ἐν ποίῳ ὀνόματι → ὑμεῖς ἐποιήσατε τοῦτο   Τότε Πέτρος πλησθεὶς →   ἁγίου πνεύματος εἶπεν
r.dsf n.dsf cj p.d r.dsn n.dsn r.np.2 v.aai.2p r.asn   adv n.nsm pt.ap.nsm   a.gsn n.gsn v.aai.3s
4481 1539 2445 1877 4481 3950 4472 7007 4472 4047   5538 4377 4398   41 4460 3306

to them: "Rulers and elders   of the people! ⁹ If we   are being called to account   today for an act of
πρὸς αὐτούς ἄρχοντες καὶ πρεσβύτεροι τοῦ λαοῦ εἰ ἡμεῖς → ἀνακρινόμεθα σήμερον ἐπὶ εὐεργεσίᾳ ←
p.a r.apm.3 n.vpm cj a.vpm d.gsn n.gsm cj r.np.1   v.ppi.1p adv p.d n.dsf
4639 899 807 2779 4565 3836 3295 1623 7005   373 4958 2093 2307

kindness shown to a cripple   and are asked how   he   was healed, ¹⁰ then know   this,   you
←   ἀνθρώπου ἀσθενοῦς   ἐν τίνι οὗτος → σέσωται   γνωστὸν ἔστω   πᾶσιν ὑμῖν
n.gsm a.gsm   p.d r.dsn r.nsm v.rpi.3s   a.nsn v.pam.3s   a.dpm r.dp.2
476 822   1877 5515 4047 5392   1196 1639   4246 7007

and all the people of Israel: It is by the name   of Jesus Christ of Nazareth,   whom you crucified but
καὶ παντὶ τῷ λαῷ → Ἰσραὴλ ὅτι ἐν τῷ ὀνόματι Ἰησοῦ Χριστοῦ → τοῦ Ναζωραίου ὃν ὑμεῖς ἐσταυρώσατε
cj a.dsm d.dsm n.dsm n.gsm cj p.d d.dsn n.dsn n.gsm n.gsm d.gsm n.gsm r.asm r.np.2 v.aai.2p
2779 4246 3836 3295 2702 4022 1877 3836 3950 2652 5986 3836 3717 4005 7007 5090

whom God raised from the dead, that   this man stands   before you healed. ¹¹ He is "'the stone
ὃν ὁ θεὸς ἤγειρεν ἐκ νεκρῶν ἐν τούτῳ οὗτος ← παρέστηκεν ἐνώπιον ὑμῶν ὑγιής οὗτός ἐστιν ὁ λίθος
r.asm d.nsm n.nsm v.aai.3s p.g a.gpm p.d r.dsn r.nsm v.rai.3s p.g r.gp.2 a.nsm r.nsm v.pai.3s d.nsm n.nsm
4005 3836 2536 1586 1666 3738 1877 4047 4047 4225 1967 7007 5618 4047 1639 3836 3345

you builders   rejected,   which has become   the capstone.'   ¹² Salvation is   found in
ὑφ' ὑμῶν τῶν οἰκοδόμων ὁ ἐξουθενηθεὶς ὁ → γενόμενος εἰς κεφαλὴν γωνίας καὶ ἡ σωτηρία ἔστιν οὐκ   ἐν
p.g r.gp.2 d.gpm n.gpm d.nsm pt.ap.nsm d.nsm pt.am.nsm p.a n.asf n.gsf cj d.nsf n.nsf v.pai.3s pl   p.d
5679 7007 3836 3871 3836 2024 3836 1181 1650 3051 1224 2779 3836 5401 1639 4024   1877

no one   else, for there is   no other name under heaven   given   to men   by which we   must be
→ οὐδενὶ ἄλλῳ γὰρ → ἐστιν οὐδὲ ἕτερον ὄνομα ὑπὸ τὸν οὐρανὸν τὸ δεδομένον ἐν ἀνθρώποις ἐν ᾧ ἡμᾶς δεῖ →
a.dsm r.dsm cj v.pai.3s adv r.nsn n.nsn p.a d.asm n.asm d.nsn pt.rp.nsn p.d n.dpm p.d r.dsn r.ap.1 v.pai.3s
4029 257 1142 1639 4028 2283 3950 5679 3836 4041 3836 1443 1877 476 1877 4005 7005 1256

saved." ¶ ¹³ When they   saw   the courage of Peter   and John   and realized   that they
σωθῆναι δὲ ἄνθρωποι Θεωροῦντες τὴν παρρησίαν → τοῦ Πέτρου καὶ Ἰωάννου καὶ καταλαβόμενοι ὅτι ἄνθρωποι
f.ap cj n.npm pt.pa.npm d.asf n.asf d.gsm n.gsm cj n.gsm cj pt.am.npm cj n.npm
5392 1254 476 2555 3836 4244 3836 4377 2779 2722 2779 2898 4022 476

were unschooled,   ordinary men, they were astonished and they took note   that these men had been
εἰσιν ἀγράμματοι καὶ ἰδιῶται → → → ἐθαύμαζον τε → ἐπεγίνωσκον αὐτοὺς ὅτι ← → ἦσαν
v.pai.3p a.npm cj n.npm v.iai.3p cj v.iai.3p r.apm.3 cj v.iai.3p
1639 63 2779 2626 476 2513 5445 2105 899 4022 899 899 1639

with Jesus. ¹⁴ But since they could see   the man   who had been healed   standing there with them,
σὺν τῷ Ἰησοῦ τε → → βλέποντες τὸν ἄνθρωπον τὸν → τεθεραπευμένον ἑστῶτα   σὺν αὐτοῖς
p.d d.dsm n.dsm cj pt.pa.npm d.asm n.asm d.asm pt.rp.asm pt.ra.asm p.d r.dpm.3
5250 3836 2652 5445 1063 3836 476 3836 2543 2705 5250 899

there was nothing they could say. ¹⁵ So they ordered   them to withdraw from the Sanhedrin and then conferred
εἶχον οὐδὲν → → ἀντειπεῖν δὲ → κελεύσαντες αὐτοὺς → ἀπελθεῖν ἔξω τοῦ συνεδρίου   συνέβαλλον
v.iai.3p a.asn f.aa cj pt.aa.npm r.apm.3 f.aa p.g d.gsn n.gsn v.iai.3p
2400 4029 515 1254 3027 899 599 2032 3836 5284 5202

τοὺς πρεσβυτέρους καὶ τοὺς γραμματεῖς ἐν Ἰερουσαλήμ, ⁶ καὶ Ἄννας ὁ ἀρχιερεὺς καὶ Καϊάφας καὶ Ἰωάννης καὶ Ἀλέξανδρος
καὶ ὅσοι ἦσαν ἐκ γένους ἀρχιερατικοῦ, ⁷ καὶ στήσαντες αὐτοὺς ἐν τῷ μέσῳ ἐπυνθάνοντο, Ἐν ποίᾳ δυνάμει ἢ ἐν ποίῳ ὀνόματι
ἐποιήσατε τοῦτο ὑμεῖς; ¶ ⁸ τότε Πέτρος πλησθεὶς πνεύματος ἁγίου εἶπεν πρὸς αὐτούς, Ἄρχοντες τοῦ λαοῦ καὶ πρεσβύτεροι,
⁹ εἰ ἡμεῖς σήμερον ἀνακρινόμεθα ἐπὶ εὐεργεσίᾳ ἀνθρώπου ἀσθενοῦς ἐν τίνι οὗτος σέσωται, ¹⁰ γνωστὸν ἔστω πᾶσιν ὑμῖν καὶ
παντὶ τῷ λαῷ Ἰσραὴλ ὅτι ἐν τῷ ὀνόματι Ἰησοῦ Χριστοῦ τοῦ Ναζωραίου ὃν ὑμεῖς ἐσταυρώσατε, ὃν ὁ θεὸς ἤγειρεν ἐκ νεκρῶν,
ἐν τούτῳ οὗτος παρέστηκεν ἐνώπιον ὑμῶν ὑγιής. ¹¹ οὗτός ἐστιν ὁ λίθος, ὁ ἐξουθενηθεὶς ὑφ' ὑμῶν τῶν οἰκοδόμων, ὁ γενόμενος
εἰς κεφαλὴν γωνίας. ¹² καὶ οὐκ ἔστιν ἐν ἄλλῳ οὐδενὶ ἡ σωτηρία, οὐδὲ γὰρ ὄνομά ἐστιν ἕτερον ὑπὸ τὸν οὐρανὸν τὸ δεδομένον
ἐν ἀνθρώποις ἐν ᾧ δεῖ σωθῆναι ἡμᾶς. ¶ ¹³ Θεωροῦντες δὲ τὴν τοῦ Πέτρου παρρησίαν καὶ Ἰωάννου καὶ καταλαβόμενοι ὅτι
ἄνθρωποι ἀγράμματοί εἰσιν καὶ ἰδιῶται, ἐθαύμαζον ἐπεγίνωσκόν τε αὐτοὺς ὅτι σὺν τῷ Ἰησοῦ ἦσαν, ¹⁴ τόν τε ἄνθρωπον
βλέποντες σὺν αὐτοῖς ἑστῶτα τὸν τεθεραπευμένον οὐδὲν εἶχον ἀντειπεῖν. ¹⁵ κελεύσαντες δὲ αὐτοὺς ἔξω τοῦ συνεδρίου ἀπελθεῖν

together. **16** "What are we going to do with these men?" they asked. "Everybody
πρὸς ἀλλήλους, τί → → → ποιήσωμεν ⌐ τούτοις ⌐τοῖς ἀνθρώποις, → λέγοντες ὅτι γὰρ μὲν πᾶσιν
p.a r.apm r.asn v.aas.1p r.dpm d.dpm n.dpm pt.pa.npm cj cj pl a.dpm
4639 253 5515 4472 476 4047 3836 476 3306 4022 1142 3525 4246

living in Jerusalem knows they have done an outstanding miracle, and we cannot deny it.
⌐τοῖς κατοικοῦσιν ← Ἰερουσαλὴμ γνωστὸν δι' αὐτῶν → γέγονεν φανερὸν σημεῖον καὶ → ⌐οὐ δυνάμεθα, ἀρνεῖσθαι
d.dpm pt.pa.dpm n.asf a.nsn p.g r.gpm.3 v.rai.3s a.nsn n.nsn cj pl v.ppi.1p f.pm
3836 2997 2647 1196 1328 899 1181 5745 4956 2779 4024 1538 766

17 But to stop this thing from spreading *any further* among the people, we must warn these men to speak
ἀλλ' ἵνα μὴ διανεμηθῇ ἐπὶ πλεῖον εἰς τὸν λαὸν → ἀπειλησώμεθα αὐτοῖς → λαλεῖν
cj cj pl v.aps.3s p.a adv.c p.a d.asm n.asm v.ams.1p r.dpm.3 f.pa
247 2671 3590 1376 2093 4498 1650 3836 3295 580 899 3281

no longer to anyone in this name." ¶ **18** Then they called them in again and
μηκέτι ← → ⌐μηδενὶ ἀνθρώπων, ἐπὶ τούτῳ τῷ ὀνόματι, Καὶ → → καλέσαντες αὐτοὺς
adv a.dsm n.gpm p.d r.dsn d.dsn n.dsn cj pt.aa.npm r.apm.3
3600 3594 476 2093 4047 3836 3950 2779 2813 899

commanded them not to speak or teach at all in the name of Jesus. **19** But Peter and
παρήγγειλαν μὴ → φθέγγεσθαι μηδὲ διδάσκειν ⌐τὸ καθόλου, ἐπὶ τῷ ὀνόματι ⌐τοῦ Ἰησοῦ, δὲ ὁ Πέτρος καὶ
v.aai.3p pl f.pm cj f.pa d.asn adv p.d d.dsn n.dsn d.gsm n.gsm cj d.nsm n.nsm cj
4133 3590 5779 3593 1438 3836 2773 2093 3836 3950 3836 2652 1254 3836 4377 2779

John replied, "Judge for yourselves whether it is right in God's sight to obey you
Ἰωάννης ἀποκριθέντες εἶπον πρὸς αὐτούς κρίνατε ← ← εἰ → ἐστιν δίκαιον ⌐τοῦ θεοῦ, ἐνώπιον → ἀκούειν ὑμῶν
n.nsm pt.ap.npm v.aai.3p p.a r.apm.3 v.aam.2p cj v.pai.3s a.nsn d.gsm n.gsm p.g f.pa r.gp.2
2722 646 3306 4639 899 3212 1623 1639 1465 1967 3836 2536 1967 201 7007

rather than God. **20** For we cannot help speaking about what we have seen and heard." ¶ **21**
μᾶλλον ἢ ⌐τοῦ θεοῦ, γὰρ ἡμεῖς ⌐οὐ δυνάμεθα, μὴ λαλεῖν ἃ εἴδαμεν καὶ ἠκούσαμεν δὲ
adv.c pl d.gsm n.gsm cj r.np.1 pl v.ppi.1p pl f.pa r.apn v.aai.1p cj v.aai.1p cj
3437 2445 3836 2536 1142 7005 4024 1538 3590 3281 4005 1625 2779 201 1254

After further threats they let them go. They could not decide how to punish them,
→ → προσαπειλησάμενοι οἱ → αὐτοὺς ἀπέλυσαν μηδὲν εὑρίσκοντες τὸ πῶς → κολάσωνται αὐτούς
pt.am.npm d.npm r.apm.3 v.aai.3p a.asn pt.pa.npm d.asn cj v.ams.3p r.apm.3
4653 3836 668 899 668 3594 2351 3836 4802 3134 899

because all the people were praising God for what had happened. **22** For the man who was
ὅτι πάντες διὰ τὸν λαὸν → ἐδόξαζον ⌐τὸν θεόν, ἐπὶ τῷ → γεγονότι γὰρ ὁ ἄνθρωπος ἐφ' ὃν γεγόνει
cj a.npm p.a d.asm n.asm v.iai.3p d.asm n.asm p.d d.dsn pt.ra.dsn cj d.nsm n.nsm p.a r.asm v.lai.3s
4022 4246 1328 3836 3295 1519 3836 2536 2093 3836 1181 1142 3836 476 2093 4005 1181

miraculously healed was over forty years old.
⌐τὸ σημεῖον, τοῦτο ⌐τῆς ἰάσεως, ἦν πλειόνων τεσσεράκοντα ἐτῶν ←
d.nsn n.nsn r.nsn d.gsf n.gsf v.iai.3s a.gpn.c a.gpn n.gpn
3836 4956 4047 3836 2617 1639 4498 5477 2291

The Believers' Prayer

4:23 On their release, Peter and John went back to their own people and reported all that the chief
δὲ → → Ἀπολυθέντες ἦλθον πρὸς τοὺς ἰδίους ← καὶ ἀπήγγειλαν ὅσα οἱ →
cj pt.ap.npm v.aai.3p p.a d.apm a.apm cj v.aai.3p r.apn d.npm
1254 668 2262 4639 3836 2625 2779 550 4012 3836

priests and elders had said to them. **24** When they heard this, they raised their voices together in
ἀρχιερεῖς καὶ οἱ πρεσβύτεροι → εἶπαν πρὸς αὐτούς δὲ → → ἀκούσαντες οἱ ἦραν φωνὴν ὁμοθυμαδὸν
n.npm cj d.npm a.npm v.aai.3p p.a r.apm.3 cj pt.aa.npm d.npm v.aai.3p n.asf adv
797 2779 3836 4565 3306 4639 899 1254 201 3836 149 5889 3924

prayer to God. "Sovereign Lord," they said, "you made the heaven and the earth and the sea,
πρὸς ⌐τὸν θεόν, καὶ δέσποτα ← εἶπαν σὺ ὁ ποιήσας, τὸν οὐρανὸν καὶ τὴν γῆν καὶ τὴν θάλασσαν
p.a d.asm n.asm cj n.vsm v.aai.3p r.ns.2 d.nsm pt.aa.nsm d.asm n.asm cj d.asf n.asf cj d.asf n.asf
4639 3836 2536 2779 1305 3306 5148 3836 4472 3836 4041 2779 3836 1178 2779 3836 2498

and everything in them. **25** You spoke by the Holy Spirit through the mouth of your servant, our father
καὶ πάντα τὰ ἐν αὐτοῖς εἰπών διὰ ἁγίου πνεύματος → στόματος σου παιδός ἡμῶν ⌐τοῦ πατρὸς,
cj a.apn d.apn p.d r.dpm.3 pt.aa.nsm p.g a.gsn n.gsn n.gsn r.gs.2 n.gsm r.gp.1 d.gsm n.gsm
2779 4246 3836 1877 899 3306 1328 41 4460 5125 4090 5148 4090 7005 3836 4252

συνέβαλλον πρὸς ἀλλήλους ¹⁶ λέγοντες, Τί ποιήσωμεν τοῖς ἀνθρώποις τούτοις; ὅτι μὲν γὰρ γνωστὸν σημεῖον γέγονεν δι' αὐτῶν πᾶσιν τοῖς κατοικοῦσιν Ἰερουσαλὴμ φανερὸν καὶ οὐ δυνάμεθα ἀρνεῖσθαι· ¹⁷ ἀλλ' ἵνα μὴ ἐπὶ πλεῖον διανεμηθῇ εἰς τὸν λαὸν ἀπειλησώμεθα αὐτοῖς μηκέτι λαλεῖν ἐπὶ τῷ ὀνόματι τούτῳ μηδενὶ ἀνθρώπων. ¹⁸ καὶ καλέσαντες αὐτοὺς παρήγγειλαν τὸ καθόλου μὴ φθέγγεσθαι μηδὲ διδάσκειν ἐπὶ τῷ ὀνόματι τοῦ Ἰησοῦ. ¹⁹ ὁ δὲ Πέτρος καὶ Ἰωάννης ἀποκριθέντες εἶπον πρὸς αὐτούς, Εἰ δίκαιόν ἐστιν ἐνώπιον τοῦ θεοῦ ὑμῶν ἀκούειν μᾶλλον ἢ τοῦ θεοῦ, κρίνατε· ²⁰ οὐ δυνάμεθα γὰρ ἡμεῖς ἃ εἴδαμεν καὶ ἠκούσαμεν μὴ λαλεῖν. ¶ ²¹ οἱ δὲ προσαπειλησάμενοι ἀπέλυσαν αὐτούς, μηδὲν εὑρίσκοντες τὸ πῶς κολάσωνται αὐτούς, διὰ τὸν λαόν, ὅτι πάντες ἐδόξαζον τὸν θεὸν ἐπὶ τῷ γεγονότι· ²² ἐτῶν γὰρ ἦν πλειόνων τεσσεράκοντα ὁ ἄνθρωπος ἐφ' ὃν γεγόνει τὸ σημεῖον τοῦτο τῆς ἰάσεως.

^{4:23} Ἀπολυθέντες δὲ ἦλθον πρὸς τοὺς ἰδίους καὶ ἀπήγγειλαν ὅσα πρὸς αὐτοὺς οἱ ἀρχιερεῖς καὶ οἱ πρεσβύτεροι εἶπαν. ²⁴ οἱ δὲ ἀκούσαντες ὁμοθυμαδὸν ἦραν φωνὴν πρὸς τὸν θεὸν καὶ εἶπαν, Δέσποτα, σὺ ὁ ποιήσας τὸν οὐρανὸν καὶ τὴν γῆν καὶ τὴν θάλασσαν καὶ πάντα τὰ ἐν αὐτοῖς, ²⁵ ὁ τοῦ πατρὸς ἡμῶν διὰ πνεύματος ἁγίου στόματος Δαυὶδ παιδός σου εἰπών, Ἱνατί ἐφρύαξαν

David: "'Why do the nations rage and the peoples plot in vain? **26** The kings of the earth take their
ὁ Δαυὶδ ἱνατί → ἔθνη ἐφρύαξαν καὶ λαοὶ ἐμελέτησαν → κενά οἱ βασιλεῖς → τῆς γῆς → →
d.nsm n.gsm cj n.npn v.aai.3p cj n.npm v.aai.3p a.apn d.npm n.npm d.gsf n.gsf
3836 1253 2672 5865 1620 5865 2779 3295 3509 3031 3836 995 3836 1178

stand and the rulers gather together against the Lord and against his Anointed One.' **27**
παρέστησαν καὶ οἱ ἄρχοντες συνήχθησαν ἐπὶ τὸ αὐτὸ κατὰ τοῦ κυρίου καὶ κατὰ αὐτοῦ τοῦ χριστοῦ ← γὰρ
v.aai.3p cj d.npm n.npm v.api.3p p.a d.asn p.g d.gsm n.gsm cj p.a r.gsm.3 d.gsm n.gsm cj
4225 2779 3836 807 5251 2093 3836 899 2848 3836 3261 2779 2848 899 3836 5986 1142

Indeed Herod and Pontius Pilate met together with the Gentiles and the people of Israel in this
ἐπ' ἀληθείας, τε Ἡρῴδης καὶ Πόντιος Πιλᾶτος συνήχθησαν ← σὺν ἔθνεσιν καὶ λαοῖς → Ἰσραὴλ ἐν ταύτῃ
p.g n.gsf cj n.nsm cj n.nsm n.nsm v.api.3p p.d n.dpn cj n.dpm n.gsm p.d r.dsf
2093 237 5445 2476 2779 4508 4397 5251 5250 1620 2779 3295 2702 1877 4047

city to conspire against your holy servant Jesus, whom you anointed. **28** They did what your power and
τῇ πόλει ἐπὶ σου ἅγιον τὸν παῖδα, Ἰησοῦν ὃν → ἔχρισας, → ποιῆσαι ὅσα σου ἡ χεὶρ καὶ
d.dsf n.dsf p.a r.gs.2 a.asn d.asm n.asm n.asm r.asm v.aai.2s f.aa r.apn r.gs.2 d.nsf n.nsf cj
3836 4484 2093 5148 41 3836 4090 2652 4005 5987 4472 4012 5148 3836 5931 2779

will had decided beforehand should happen. **29** Now, Lord, consider their threats and
[σου] ἡ βουλή, → προώρισεν ← → γενέσθαι καὶ τὰ νῦν, κύριε ἔπιδε ἐπὶ αὐτῶν τὰς ἀπειλὰς, καὶ
r.gs.2 d.nsf n.nsf v.aai.3s f.am cj d.apn adv n.vsm v.aam.2s p.a r.gpm.3 d.apf n.apf cj
5148 3836 1087 4633 1181 2779 3836 3814 3261 2078 2093 899 3836 581 2779

enable your servants to speak your word with great boldness. **30** Stretch out your hand to
δὸς σου τοῖς δούλοις, → λαλεῖν σου τὸν λόγον, μετὰ πάσης παρρησίας σε ἐν τῷ ἐκτείνειν ← σου τὴν χεῖρα εἰς
v.aam.2s r.gs.2 d.dpm n.dpm f.pa r.gs.2 d.asm n.asm p.g a.gsf n.gsf r.as.2 p.d d.dsn f.pa r.gs.2 d.asf n.asf p.a
1443 5148 3836 1529 3281 5148 3836 3364 3552 4246 4244 5148 1877 3836 1753 5148 3836 5931 1650

heal and perform miraculous signs and wonders through the name of your holy servant Jesus." ¶
ἴασιν καὶ γίνεσθαι → σημεῖα καὶ τέρατα διὰ τοῦ ὀνόματος → σου ἁγίου τοῦ παιδός, Ἰησοῦ
n.asf cj f.pp n.apn cj n.apn p.g d.gsn n.gsn r.gs.2 a.gsm d.gsm n.gsm n.gsm
2617 2779 1181 4956 2779 5469 1328 3836 3950 4090 5148 41 3836 4090 2652

31 After they prayed, the place where they were meeting was shaken. And they were all filled with the
καὶ → αὐτῶν δεηθέντων ὁ τόπος ἐν ᾧ, → ἦσαν συνηγμένοι → ἐσαλεύθη καὶ → → ἅπαντες ἐπλήσθησαν → τοῦ
cj r.gpm.3 pt.ap.gpm d.nsm n.nsm p.d r.dsm v.iai.3p pt.rp.npm v.api.3s cj a.npm v.api.3p d.gsn
2779 1289 899 1289 3836 5536 1877 4005 1639 5251 4888 2779 4398 4398 570 4398 3836

Holy Spirit and spoke the word of God boldly.
ἁγίου πνεύματος καὶ ἐλάλουν τὸν λόγον → τοῦ θεοῦ μετὰ παρρησίας,
a.gsn n.gsn cj v.iai.3p d.asm n.asm d.gsn n.gsn p.g n.gsf
41 4460 2779 3281 3836 3364 3836 2536 3552 4244

The Believers Share Their Possessions

4:32 All the believers were one in heart and mind. No one claimed that any of his
δὲ Τοῦ πλήθους, τῶν πιστευσάντων ἦν μία καρδία καὶ ψυχὴ καὶ οὐδὲ εἷς ἔλεγεν τι → αὐτῷ
cj d.gsn n.gsn d.gpm pt.aa.gpm v.iai.3s a.nsf n.nsf cj n.nsf cj adv a.nsm v.iai.3s r.asn r.dsm.3
1254 3836 4436 3836 4409 1639 1651 2840 2779 6034 2779 4028 1651 3306 5516 5639 899

possessions was his own, but they shared everything they had. **33** With great power the apostles
τῶν ὑπαρχόντων, εἶναι ἴδιον ← ἀλλ' ἦν κοινά, ἅπαντα αὐτοῖς καὶ → μεγάλῃ δυνάμει οἱ ἀπόστολοι
d.gpn pt.pa.gpn f.pa a.asn cj v.iai.3s a.npn a.npn r.dpm.3 cj a.dsf n.dsf d.npm n.npm
3836 5639 1639 2625 247 1639 3123 570 899 2779 3489 1539 3836 693

continued to testify to the resurrection of the Lord Jesus, and much grace was upon them all.
→ ἀπεδίδουν τὸ μαρτύριον → τῆς ἀναστάσεως → τοῦ κυρίου Ἰησοῦ τε μεγάλη χάρις ἦν ἐπὶ αὐτούς πάντας
v.iai.3p d.asn n.asn d.gsf n.gsf d.gsm n.gsm n.gsm cj a.nsf n.nsf v.iai.3s p.a r.apm.3 a.apm
625 3836 3457 3836 414 3836 3261 2652 5445 3489 5921 1639 2093 899 4246

34 There were no needy persons among them. For *from time to time* those who owned lands or houses
γὰρ → ἦν οὐδὲ ἐνδεής τις ἐν αὐτοῖς γὰρ ὅσοι κτήτορες ← ὑπῆρχον χωρίων ἢ οἰκιῶν
cj v.iai.3s adv a.nsm r.nsm p.d r.dpm.3 cj r.npm n.npm v.iai.3p n.gpn cj n.gpf
1142 1639 4028 1890 5516 1877 899 1142 4012 3230 5639 6005 2445 3864

sold them, brought the money from the sales **35** and put it at the apostles' feet, and it was
πωλοῦντες ἔφερον τὰς τιμάς, → τῶν πιπρασκομένων καὶ ἐτίθουν παρὰ τοὺς τῶν ἀποστόλων, πόδας δὲ → →
pt.pa.npm v.iai.3p d.apf n.apf d.gpn pt.pp.gpn cj v.iai.3p p.a d.apm d.gpm n.gpm n.apm cj
4797 5770 3836 5507 3836 4405 2779 5502 4123 3836 3836 693 4546 1254

ἔθνη καὶ λαοὶ ἐμελέτησαν κενά; 26 παρέστησαν οἱ βασιλεῖς τῆς γῆς καὶ οἱ ἄρχοντες συνήχθησαν ἐπὶ τὸ αὐτὸ κατὰ τοῦ κυρίου καὶ κατὰ τοῦ Χριστοῦ αὐτοῦ. 27 συνήχθησαν γὰρ ἐπ' ἀληθείας ἐν τῇ πόλει ταύτῃ ἐπὶ τὸν ἅγιον παῖδά σου Ἰησοῦν ὃν ἔχρισας, Ἡρῴδης τε καὶ Πόντιος Πιλᾶτος σὺν ἔθνεσιν καὶ λαοῖς Ἰσραήλ, 28 ποιῆσαι ὅσα ἡ χείρ σου καὶ ἡ βουλὴ [σου] προώρισεν γενέσθαι. 29 καὶ τὰ νῦν, κύριε, ἔπιδε ἐπὶ τὰς ἀπειλὰς αὐτῶν καὶ δὸς τοῖς δούλοις σου μετὰ παρρησίας πάσης λαλεῖν τὸν λόγον σου, 30 ἐν τῷ τὴν χεῖρά [σου] ἐκτείνειν σε εἰς ἴασιν καὶ σημεῖα καὶ τέρατα γίνεσθαι διὰ τοῦ ὀνόματος τοῦ ἁγίου παιδός σου Ἰησοῦ. ¶ 31 καὶ δεηθέντων αὐτῶν ἐσαλεύθη ὁ τόπος ἐν ᾧ ἦσαν συνηγμένοι, καὶ ἐπλήσθησαν ἅπαντες τοῦ ἁγίου πνεύματος καὶ ἐλάλουν τὸν λόγον τοῦ θεοῦ μετὰ παρρησίας.

4:32 Τοῦ δὲ πλήθους τῶν πιστευσάντων ἦν καρδία καὶ ψυχὴ μία, καὶ οὐδὲ εἷς τι τῶν ὑπαρχόντων αὐτῷ ἔλεγεν ἴδιον εἶναι ἀλλ' ἦν αὐτοῖς ἅπαντα κοινά. 33 καὶ δυνάμει μεγάλῃ ἀπεδίδουν τὸ μαρτύριον οἱ ἀπόστολοι τῆς ἀναστάσεως τοῦ κυρίου Ἰησοῦ, χάρις τε μεγάλη ἦν ἐπὶ πάντας αὐτούς. 34 οὐδὲ γὰρ ἐνδεής τις ἦν ἐν αὐτοῖς· ὅσοι γὰρ κτήτορες χωρίων ἢ οἰκιῶν ὑπῆρχον, πωλοῦντες ἔφερον τὰς τιμὰς τῶν πιπρασκομένων 35 καὶ ἐτίθουν παρὰ τοὺς πόδας τῶν ἀποστόλων, διεδίδετο δὲ ἑκάστῳ καθότι

distributed	to anyone	as		he had	need.	¶	**36**	Joseph,	a Levite	from	Cyprus,	whom		the apostles
διεδίδετο	→ ἑκάστῳ	καθότι	ἄν	τις εἶχεν	χρείαν		δὲ	Ἰωσὴφ	Λευίτης	⸤τῷ γένει⸥	Κύπριος ὁ	ἀπὸ	τῶν	ἀποστόλων
v.ipi.3s	r.dsm	cj	pl	r.nsm v.iai.3s	n.asf		cj	n.nsm	n.nsm	d.dsn d.dsn	n.nsm d.nsm	p.g	d.gpm	n.gpm
1344	1667	2776	323	5516 2400	5970		1254	2737	3324	3836 1169	3250 3836	608	3836	693

called	Barnabas	(which		means		Son	of Encouragement),	**37**	sold	a field	he owned		and	brought
ἐπικληθεὶς	Βαρναβᾶς	ὃ	⸤ἐστιν	μεθερμηνευόμενον⸥	υἱὸς	→	παρακλήσεως		πωλήσας	ἀγροῦ	αὐτῷ ὑπάρχοντος			ἤνεγκεν
pt.ap.nsm	n.nsm	r.nsn	v.pai.3s	pt.pp.nsn	n.nsm		n.gsf		pt.aa.nsm	n.gsm	r.dsm.3 pt.pa.gsm			v.aai.3s
2126	982	4005	1639	3493	5626		4155		4797	69	899 5639			5770

the	money	and	put	it	at	the	apostles'	feet.
τὸ	χρῆμα	καὶ	ἔθηκεν		πρὸς	τοὺς	⸤τῶν ἀποστόλων⸥	πόδας
d.asn	n.asn	cj	v.aai.3s		p.a	d.apm	d.gpm n.gpm	n.apm
3836	5975	2779	5502		4639	3836	3836 693	4546

Ananias and Sapphira

5:1 Now	a	man	named	Ananias,	together	with	his	wife	Sapphira,	also	sold		a piece of property.	**2**
δὲ	τις	Ἀνὴρ	ὀνόματι	Ἀνανίας	→	σὺν	αὐτῷ	⸤τῇ γυναικὶ⸥	Σαπφίρῃ		ἐπώλησεν	→	→ κτῆμα	καὶ
cj	r.nsm	n.nsm	n.dsn	n.nsm		p.d	r.gsm.3	d.dsf n.dsf	n.dsf		v.aai.3s		n.asn	adv
1254	5516	467	3950	393		5250	899	3836 1222	4912		4797		3228	2779

With	his	wife's	full knowledge		he kept	back part	of the money	for himself,	but	brought	the rest	and
→	τῆς	γυναικός	συνειδυίης	καὶ	ἐνοσφίσατο	→ ἀπὸ	τῆς τιμῆς	←	καὶ	ἐνέγκας	⸤μέρος τι⸥	
	d.gsf	n.gsf	pt.ra.gsf	cj	v.ami.3s	p.g	d.gsf n.gsf		cj	pt.aa.nsm	n.asn r.asn	
	3836	1222	5323	2779	3802	608	3836 5507	3802	3802	2779 5770	3538 5516	

put	it	at	the	apostles'	feet.	¶	**3** Then	Peter		said,	"Ananias,	how		is it that	Satan		has so
ἔθηκεν		παρὰ	τῶν	ἀποστόλων	⸤τοὺς πόδας⸥		δὲ	ὁ	Πέτρος	εἶπεν	Ἀνανία	⸤διὰ	τί⸥ →	←	ὁ	σατανᾶς,	→
v.aai.3s		p.a	d.gpm	n.gpm	d.apm n.apm		cj	d.nsm	n.nsm	v.aai.3s	n.vsm	p.a	r.asn		d.nsm	n.nsm	
5502		4123	3836	693	3836 4546		1254	3836	4377	3306	393	1328	5515		3836	4928	

filled	your	heart		that	you have lied		to the	Holy	Spirit	and	have	kept		for yourself	some	of
ἐπλήρωσεν	σου	⸤τὴν καρδίαν⸥	σε	→	ψεύσασθαι	⸤τὸ	⸤τὸ	ἅγιον⸥	πνεῦμα	καὶ	→	νοσφίσασθαι	←		→	ἀπὸ
v.aai.3s	r.gs.2	d.asf n.asf	r.as.2		f.am	d.asn	d.asn	a.asn	n.asn	cj		f.am				p.g
4444	5148	3836 2840	5148		6017	3836	3836	41	4460	2779		3802				608

the	money	you received	for	the land?	**4** Didn't	it belong	to you	before	it was sold?	And	after it was sold,				wasn't the
τῆς	τιμῆς	→	τοῦ	χωρίου	οὐχὶ	→ ἔμενεν	→ σοὶ		μένον	καὶ	→	←		πραθὲν	ὑπῆρχεν
d.gsf	n.gsf		d.gsn	n.gsn	pl	v.iai.3s	r.ds.2		pt.pa.nsn	cj				pt.ap.nsn	v.iai.3s
3836	5507		3836	6005	4049	3531	5148		3531	2779				4405	5639

money	at	your	disposal?	What		made you think			of doing		such a thing?	You have not	lied
ἐν	σῇ	⸤τῇ ἐξουσίᾳ⸥	τί		ὅτι ἔθου		⸤ἐν τῇ καρδίᾳ	σου⸥	⸤τὸ πρᾶγμα⸥	τοῦτο ←		→	οὐκ ἐψεύσω
p.d	r.dsf.2	d.dsf n.dsf	r.asn		cj v.ami.2s		p.d d.dsf n.dsf	r.gs.2	d.asn n.asn	r.asn			pl v.ami.2s
1877	5050	3836 2026	5515		4022 5502		1877 3836 2840	5148	3836 4547	4047			6017 6017 4024 6017

to men		but		to God."	¶	**5**	When	Ananias	heard	this,			he fell	down and died.
→ ἀνθρώποις	ἀλλὰ		⸤τῷ θεῷ⸥			δὲ		ὁ Ἀνανίας	ἀκούων	⸤τοὺς λόγους	τούτους⸥	→	πεσὼν	← ἐξέψυξεν
n.dpm	d.dsm n.dsm					cj		d.nsm n.nsm	pt.pa.nsm	d.apm n.apm	r.apm		pt.aa.nsm	v.aai.3s
476	247		3836 2536			1254		201 3836 393	201	3836 3364	4047		4406	1775

And	great	fear	seized		all	who	heard	what had happened.	**6** Then	the	young	men	came		forward,
καὶ	μέγας	φόβος	⸤ἐγένετο ἐπὶ⸥	πάντας	τοὺς	ἀκούοντας			δὲ	οἱ	νεώτεροι	←	ἀναστάντες	←	
cj	a.nsm	n.nsm	v.ami.3s p.a	a.apm	d.apm	pt.pa.apm			cj	d.npm	a.npm.c		pt.aa.npm		
2779	3489	5832	1181 2093	4246	3836	201			1254	3836	3742		482		

wrapped	up	his	body,	and	carried		him	out and	buried	him.	¶	**7**		About three	hours	later
συνέστειλαν		αὐτὸν		καὶ	ἐξενέγκαντες	←			ἔθαψαν				δὲ	Ἐγένετο ὡς	τριῶν ὡρῶν	διάστημα
v.aai.3p		r.asm.3		cj	pt.aa.npm				v.aai.3p				cj	v.ami.3s pl	a.gpf n.gpf	n.nsn
5366		899		2779	1766				2507				1254 1181	6055	5552 6052	1404

	his	wife	came	in, not	knowing	what had	happened.	**8**	Peter	asked		her,	"Tell	me,		is	this
καὶ	αὐτοῦ	ἡ γυνὴ	εἰσῆλθεν	← μὴ	εἰδυῖα	τὸ	→ γεγονὸς		δὲ	Πέτρος	ἀπεκρίθη	πρὸς αὐτὴν	εἰπέ	μοι	εἰ		τοσούτου
cj	r.gsm.3	d.nsf n.nsf	v.aai.3s	pl	pt.ra.nsf	d.asn	pt.ra.asn		cj	n.nsm	v.api.3s	p.a r.asf.3	v.aam.2s	r.ds.1	cj		r.gsn
2779	899	3836 1222	1656	3590	3857	3836	1181		1254	4377	646	4639 899	3306	1609	1623		5537

the	price	you and	Ananias	got		for	the land?"		"Yes,"	she	said,	"that		is the price."	¶	**9**	Peter
→	→	→		ἀπέδοσθε	←	τὸ	χωρίον	δὲ	ναί	ἡ	εἶπεν	τοσούτου					δὲ ⸤ὁ Πέτρος⸥
				v.ami.2p		d.asn	n.asn	cj	pl	d.nsf	v.aai.3s	r.gsn					cj d.nsm n.nsm
				625		3836	6005	1254	3721	3836	3306	5537					1254 3836 4377

ἄν τις χρείαν εἶχεν. ¶ ³⁶ Ἰωσὴφ δὲ ὁ ἐπικληθεὶς Βαρναβᾶς ἀπὸ τῶν ἀποστόλων, ὅ ἐστιν μεθερμηνευόμενον υἱὸς παρακλήσεως, Λευίτης, Κύπριος τῷ γένει, ³⁷ ὑπάρχοντος αὐτῷ ἀγροῦ πωλήσας ἤνεγκεν τὸ χρῆμα καὶ ἔθηκεν πρὸς τοὺς πόδας τῶν ἀποστόλων.

5:1 Ἀνὴρ δέ τις Ἀνανίας ὀνόματι σὺν Σαπφίρῃ τῇ γυναικὶ αὐτοῦ ἐπώλησεν κτῆμα ² καὶ ἐνοσφίσατο ἀπὸ τῆς τιμῆς, συνειδυίης καὶ τῆς γυναικός, καὶ ἐνέγκας μέρος τι παρὰ τοὺς πόδας τῶν ἀποστόλων ἔθηκεν. ¶ ³ εἶπεν δὲ ὁ Πέτρος, Ἀνανία, διὰ τί ἐπλήρωσεν ὁ Σατανᾶς τὴν καρδίαν σου, ψεύσασθαί σε τὸ πνεῦμα τὸ ἅγιον καὶ νοσφίσασθαι ἀπὸ τῆς τιμῆς τοῦ χωρίου; ⁴ οὐχὶ μένον σοὶ ἔμενεν καὶ πραθὲν ἐν τῇ σῇ ἐξουσίᾳ ὑπῆρχεν; τί ὅτι ἔθου ἐν τῇ καρδίᾳ σου τὸ πρᾶγμα τοῦτο; οὐκ ἐψεύσω ἀνθρώποις ἀλλὰ τῷ θεῷ. ¶ ⁵ ἀκούων δὲ ὁ Ἀνανίας τοὺς λόγους τούτους πεσὼν ἐξέψυξεν, καὶ ἐγένετο φόβος μέγας ἐπὶ πάντας τοὺς ἀκούοντας. ⁶ ἀναστάντες δὲ οἱ νεώτεροι συνέστειλαν αὐτὸν καὶ ἐξενέγκαντες ἔθαψαν. ¶ ⁷ Ἐγένετο δὲ ὡς ὡρῶν τριῶν διάστημα καὶ ἡ γυνὴ αὐτοῦ μὴ εἰδυῖα τὸ γεγονὸς εἰσῆλθεν. ⁸ ἀπεκρίθη δὲ πρὸς αὐτὴν Πέτρος, Εἰπέ μοι, εἰ τοσούτου τὸ χωρίον ἀπέδοσθε; ἡ δὲ εἶπεν, Ναί, τοσούτου. ¶ ⁹ ὁ δὲ Πέτρος πρὸς αὐτήν, Τί ὅτι συνεφωνήθη ὑμῖν πειράσαι τὸ πνεῦμα κυρίου; ἰδοὺ οἱ πόδες τῶν θαψάντων

said to her, "How could you agree to test the Spirit of the Lord? Look! The feet of the men who
πρὸς αὐτήν τί ὅτι → ὑμῖν συνεφωνήθη → πειράσαι τὸ πνεῦμα → κυρίου ἰδοὺ οἱ πόδες → τῶν ← ←
p.a r.asf.3 r.asn cj   r.dp.2 v.api.3s   f.aa d.asn n.asn   n.gsm j d.npm n.npm   d.gpm
4639 899 5515 4022 5244 7007 5244   4279 3836 4460   3261 2627 3836 4546   3836

buried your husband are at the door, and they will carry you out also." ¶ 10 At that moment she
θαψάντων σου ⌐τὸν ἄνδρα⌐ ἐπὶ τῇ θύρᾳ → → ἐξοίσουσιν σε ⌐ καὶ → δὲ → → παραχρῆμα →
pt.aa.gpm r.gs.2 d.asm n.asm p.d d.dsf n.dsf   v.fai.3p r.as.2   cj   cj   adv
2507 5148 3836 467 2093 3836 2598   1766 5148 1766 2779   1254   4202

fell down at his feet and died. Then the young men came in and, finding her dead,
ἔπεσεν ← πρὸς αὐτοῦ ⌐τοὺς πόδας⌐ καὶ ἐξέψυξεν δὲ οἱ νεανίσκοι ← εἰσελθόντες ← εὗρον αὐτὴν νεκρὰν καὶ
v.aai.3s p.a r.gsm.3 d.apm n.apm cj v.aai.3s cj d.npm n.npm   pt.aa.npm   v.aai.3p r.asf.3 a.asf cj
4406 4639 899 3836 4546 2779 1775 1254 3836 3734   1656   2351 899 3738 2779

carried her out and buried her beside her husband. 11 Great fear seized the whole church and
ἐξενέγκαντες ← ἔθαψαν πρὸς αὐτῆς ⌐τὸν ἄνδρα⌐ καὶ μέγας φόβος ⌐ἐγένετο ἐφ᾽ τὴν ὅλην ἐκκλησίαν καὶ ἐπὶ
pt.aa.npm   v.aai.3p p.a r.gsf.3 d.asm n.asm cj a.nsm n.nsm v.ami.3s p.a d.asf a.asf n.asf cj p.a
1766   2507 4639 899 3836 467 2779 3489 5832 1181 2093 3836 3910 1711 2779 2093

all who heard about these events.
πάντας τοὺς ἀκούοντας ← ταῦτα ←
a.apm d.apm pt.pa.apm   r.apn
4246 3836 201   4047

The Apostles Heal Many

5:12 The apostles performed many miraculous signs and wonders among the people. And
δὲ Διὰ τῶν χειρῶν τῶν ἀποστόλων ἐγίνετο πολλὰ → σημεῖα καὶ τέρατα ἐν τῷ λαῷ καὶ
cj p.g d.gpf n.gpf d.gpm n.gpm v.imi.3s a.npn   n.npn cj n.npn p.d d.dsm n.dsm cj
1254 1328 3836 5931 3836 693 1181 4498   4956 2779 5469 1877 3836 3295 2779

all the believers used to meet together in Solomon's Colonnade. 13 No one else dared join
ἅπαντες → → ἦσαν ὁμοθυμαδὸν ἐν Σολομῶντος ⌐τῇ στοᾷ⌐ δὲ → οὐδεὶς ⌐τῶν λοιπῶν⌐ ἐτόλμα κολλᾶσθαι
a.npm   v.iai.3p adv p.d n.gsm d.dsf n.dsf cj   a.nsm d.gpm a.gpm v.iai.3s f.pp
570   1639 3924 1877 5048 3836 5119 1254   4029 3836 3370 5528 3140

them, even though they were highly regarded by the people. 14 Nevertheless, more and more men and women
αὐτοῖς ἀλλ᾽ ← αὐτοὺς ← ἐμεγάλυνεν ὁ λαός ⌐δὲ μᾶλλον⌐ πλήθη ← ← τε ἀνδρῶν καὶ γυναικῶν
r.dpm.3 cj   r.apm.3   v.iai.3s d.nsm n.nsm cj adv.c n.npn   cj n.gpm cj n.gpf
899 247   899   3486 3836 3295 1254 3437 4436   5445 467 2779 1222

believed in the Lord and were added to their number. 15 As a result, people brought the sick into the
πιστεύοντες τῷ κυρίῳ → προσετίθεντο → → ὥστε καὶ → ἐκφέρειν τοὺς ἀσθενεῖς εἰς τὰς
pt.pa.npm d.dsm n.dsm v.ipi.3p   crasis adv   f.pa d.apm a.apm p.a d.apf
4409 3836 3261 4707   6063 2779   1766 3836 822 1650 3836

streets and laid them on beds and mats so that at least Peter's shadow might fall on some of
πλατείας καὶ τιθέναι ἐπὶ κλιναρίων καὶ κραβάττων ἵνα ← κἂν ← Πέτρου ⌐ἡ σκιὰ⌐ → ἐπισκιάσῃ → τινὶ →
n.apf cj f.pa p.g n.gpn cj n.gpm cj   crasis   n.gsm d.nsf n.nsf v.aas.3s r.dsm
4426 2779 5502 2093 3108 2779 3187 2671   2829   4377 3836 5014 2173 5516

them as he passed by. 16 Crowds gathered also from the towns around Jerusalem, bringing their sick and
αὐτῶν → ἐρχομένου δὲ ⌐τὸ πλῆθος⌐ συνήρχετο καὶ → τῶν πόλεων πέριξ Ἰερουσαλὴμ φέροντες ἀσθενεῖς καὶ
r.gpm.3   pt.pm.gsm cj d.nsn n.nsn v.imi.3s adv   d.gpf n.gpf adv n.gsf pt.pa.npm a.apm cj
899   2262 1254 3836 4436 5302 2779   3836 4484 4339 2647 5770 822 2779

those tormented by evil spirits, and all of them were healed.
→ ὀχλουμένους ὑπὸ ἀκαθάρτων πνευμάτων ⌐ ἅπαντες οἵτινες → ἐθεραπεύοντο
pt.pp.apm p.g a.gpn n.gpn a.npm r.npm   v.ipi.3p
4061 5679 176 4460 570 4015   2543

The Apostles Persecuted

5:17 Then the high priest and all his associates, who were members of the party of the Sadducees,
δὲ ὁ → ἀρχιερεὺς καὶ πάντες αὐτῷ οἱ σὺν ἡ οὖσα αἵρεσις ← ← → τῶν Σαδδουκαίων
cj d.nsm n.nsm cj a.npm r.dsm.3 d.npm p.d d.nsf pt.pa.nsf n.nsf d.gpm n.gpm
1254 3836 797 2779 4246 899 3836 5250 3836 1639 146 3836 4881

τὸν ἄνδρα σου ἐπὶ τῇ θύρᾳ καὶ ἐξοίσουσίν σε. ¶ 10 ἔπεσεν δὲ παραχρῆμα πρὸς τοὺς πόδας αὐτοῦ καὶ ἐξέψυξεν· εἰσελθόντες δὲ οἱ νεανίσκοι εὗρον αὐτὴν νεκρὰν καὶ ἐξενέγκαντες ἔθαψαν πρὸς τὸν ἄνδρα αὐτῆς, 11 καὶ ἐγένετο φόβος μέγας ἐφ᾽ ὅλην τὴν ἐκκλησίαν καὶ ἐπὶ πάντας τοὺς ἀκούοντας ταῦτα.

5:12 Διὰ δὲ τῶν χειρῶν τῶν ἀποστόλων ἐγίνετο σημεῖα καὶ τέρατα πολλὰ ἐν τῷ λαῷ. καὶ ἦσαν ὁμοθυμαδὸν ἅπαντες ἐν τῇ Στοᾷ Σολομῶντος, 13 τῶν δὲ λοιπῶν οὐδεὶς ἐτόλμα κολλᾶσθαι αὐτοῖς, ἀλλ᾽ ἐμεγάλυνεν αὐτοὺς ὁ λαός. 14 μᾶλλον δὲ προσετίθεντο πιστεύοντες τῷ κυρίῳ, πλήθη ἀνδρῶν τε καὶ γυναικῶν, 15 ὥστε καὶ εἰς τὰς πλατείας ἐκφέρειν τοὺς ἀσθενεῖς καὶ τιθέναι ἐπὶ κλιναρίων καὶ κραβάττων, ἵνα ἐρχομένου Πέτρου κἂν ἡ σκιὰ ἐπισκιάσῃ τινὶ αὐτῶν. 16 συνήρχετο δὲ καὶ τὸ πλῆθος τῶν πέριξ πόλεων Ἰερουσαλὴμ φέροντες ἀσθενεῖς καὶ ὀχλουμένους ὑπὸ πνευμάτων ἀκαθάρτων, οἵτινες ἐθεραπεύοντο ἅπαντες.

5:17 Ἀναστὰς δὲ ὁ ἀρχιερεὺς καὶ πάντες οἱ σὺν αὐτῷ, ἡ οὖσα αἵρεσις τῶν Σαδδουκαίων, ἐπλήσθησαν ζήλου 18 καὶ ἐπέβαλον

were filled with jealousy. **18** They arrested the apostles and put them in the
Ἀναστὰς → ἐπλήσθησαν → ζήλου καὶ → ἐπέβαλον τὰς χεῖρας ἐπὶ τοὺς ἀποστόλους καὶ ἔθεντο αὐτοὺς ἐν
pt.aa.nsm v.api.3p n.gsm cj v.aai.3p d.apf n.apf p.a d.apm n.apm cj v.ami.3p r.apm.3 p.d
482 4398 2419 2779 2095 3836 5931 2093 3836 693 2779 5502 899 1877

public jail. **19** But during the night an angel of the Lord opened the doors of the jail and brought them
δημοσίᾳ τηρήσει δὲ διὰ νυκτὸς Ἄγγελος → κυρίου ἀνοίξας τὰς θύρας τῆς φυλακῆς τε ἐξαγαγών αὐτοὺς
a.dsf n.dsf cj p.g n.gsf n.nsm n.gsm pt.aa.nsm d.apf n.apf d.gsf n.gsf cj pt.aa.nsm r.apm.3
1323 5499 1254 1328 3816 34 3261 487 3836 2598 3836 5871 5445 1974 899

out. **20** "Go, stand in the temple courts," he said, "and tell the people the full message of this new
ἕ πορεύεσθε καὶ σταθέντες ἐν τῷ ἱερῷ → εἶπεν λαλεῖτε τῷ λαῷ τὰ πάντα ῥήματα → ταύτης
v.pmm.2p cj pt.ap.npm p.d d.dsn n.dsn v.aai.3s v.pam.2p d.dsm n.dsm d.apn a.apn n.apn r.gsf
1974 4513 2779 2705 1877 3836 2639 3306 3281 3836 3295 3836 4246 4839 2437 4047

life." ¶ **21** At daybreak they entered the temple courts, as they had been told, and began to
ἕτῆς ζωῆς δὲ → ὑπὸ τὸν ὄρθρον → εἰσῆλθον εἰς τὸ ἱερὸν ← ἀκούσαντες καὶ →
d.gsf n.gsf cj p.a d.asm n.asm v.aai.3p p.a d.asn n.asn pt.aa.npm cj
3836 2437 1254 5679 3836 3986 1656 1650 3836 2639 201 2779

teach the people. ¶ When the high priest and his associates arrived, they called together
ἐδίδασκον δὲ → ὁ → ἀρχιερεὺς καὶ αὐτῷ οἱ σὺν Παραγενόμενος → συνεκάλεσαν ←
v.iai.3p cj d.nsm n.nsm cj r.dsm.3 d.npm p.d pt.am.nsm v.aai.3p
1438 1254 4134 3836 797 2779 899 3836 5250 4134 5157

the Sanhedrin — the full assembly of the elders of Israel — and sent to the jail for the
τὸ συνέδριον καὶ τὴν πᾶσαν γερουσίαν → τῶν υἱῶν → Ἰσραὴλ καὶ ἀπέστειλαν εἰς τὸ δεσμωτήριον ἀχθῆναι
d.asn n.asn cj d.asf a.asf n.asf d.gpm n.gpm n.gsm cj v.aai.3p p.a d.asn n.asn f.ap
3836 5284 2779 3836 4246 1172 3836 5626 2702 2779 690 1650 3836 1303 72

apostles. **22** But on arriving at the jail, the officers did not find them there. So they went back and
αὐτούς δὲ → παραγενόμενοι ἐν τῇ φυλακῇ οἱ ὑπηρέται ͵ οὐχ εὗρον αὐτοὺς δὲ → → → ἀναστρέψαντες
r.apm.3 cj pt.am.npm p.d d.dsf n.dsf d.npm n.npm pl v.aai.3p r.apm.3 cj pt.aa.npm
899 1254 4134 1877 3836 5871 3836 2351 4024 2351 899 1254 418

reported, **23** "We found the jail securely locked, with the guards standing at the
ἀπήγγειλαν λέγοντες ὅτι → εὕρομεν τὸ δεσμωτήριον ἐν πάσῃ ἀσφαλείᾳ κεκλεισμένον καὶ τοὺς φύλακας ἑστῶτας ἐπὶ τῶν
v.aai.3p pt.pa.npm cj v.aai.1p d.asn n.asn p.d a.dsf n.dsf pt.rp.asn cj d.apm n.apm pt.ra.apm p.g d.gpf
550 3306 4022 2351 3836 1303 1877 4246 854 3091 2779 3836 5874 2705 2093 3836

doors; but when we opened them, we found no one inside." **24** On hearing this report, the captain
θυρῶν δὲ → → ἀνοίξαντες → εὕρομεν οὐδένα ἔσω δὲ ὡς ἤκουσαν τούτους ἕτοὺς λόγους τε ὁ στρατηγὸς
n.gpf cj pt.aa.npm v.aai.1p a.asm adv cj cj v.aai.3p r.apm d.apm n.apm cj d.nsm n.nsm
2598 1254 487 2351 4029 2276 1254 6055 201 4047 3836 3364 5445 3836 5130

of the temple guard and the chief priests were puzzled, wondering what would come of this. ¶
→ τοῦ ἱεροῦ ← καὶ οἱ → ἀρχιερεῖς → διηπόρουν περὶ αὐτῶν τί ἂν γένοιτο ← τοῦτο
d.gsn n.gsn cj d.npm n.npm v.iai.3p p.g r.gpm.3 r.nsn pl v.amo.3s r.nsn
3836 2639 5130 2779 3836 797 1389 4309 899 5515 323 1181 4047

25 Then someone came and said, "Look! The men you put in jail are standing
δέ τις παραγενόμενος ἀπήγγειλεν αὐτοῖς ὅτι ἰδοὺ οἱ ἄνδρες οὓς → ἔθεσθε ἐν ἕτῇ φυλακῇ εἰσὶν ἑστῶτες
cj r.nsm pt.am.nsm v.aai.3s r.dpm.3 cj j d.npm n.npm r.apm v.ami.2p p.d d.dsf n.dsf v.pai.3p pt.ra.npm
1254 5516 4134 550 899 4022 2627 3836 467 4005 5502 1877 3836 5871 1639 2705

in the temple courts teaching the people." **26** At that, the captain went with his officers and brought the
ἐν τῷ ἱερῷ ← καὶ διδάσκοντες τὸν λαόν Τότε ← ὁ στρατηγὸς ἀπελθὼν σὺν τοῖς ὑπηρέταις ἦγεν
p.d d.dsn n.dsn cj pt.pa.npm d.asm n.asm adv d.nsm n.nsm pt.aa.nsm p.d d.dpm n.dpm v.iai.3s
1877 3836 2639 2779 1438 3836 3295 5538 3836 5130 599 5250 3836 5677 72

apostles. They did not use force, because they feared that the people would stone them. ¶ **27** Having
αὐτούς οὐ μετὰ βίας γὰρ → ἐφοβοῦντο μὴ τὸν λαόν → λιθασθῶσιν δὲ
r.apm.3 pl p.g n.gsf cj v.imi.3p cj d.asm n.asm v.aps.3p cj
899 4024 3552 1040 1142 5828 3590 3836 3295 3342 1254

brought the apostles, they made them appear before the Sanhedrin to be questioned by the high
Ἀγαγόντες αὐτοὺς → → → ἔστησαν ἐν τῷ συνεδρίῳ καὶ → ἐπηρώτησεν αὐτοὺς ὁ →
pt.aa.npm r.apm.3 v.aai.3p p.d d.dsn n.dsn cj v.aai.3s r.apm.3 d.nsm
72 899 2705 1877 3836 5284 2779 2089 899 3836

τὰς χεῖρας ἐπὶ τοὺς ἀποστόλους καὶ ἔθεντο αὐτοὺς ἐν τηρήσει δημοσίᾳ. ¹⁹ ἄγγελος δὲ κυρίου διὰ νυκτὸς ἀνοίξας τὰς θύρας τῆς φυλακῆς ἐξαγαγών τε αὐτοὺς εἶπεν, ²⁰ Πορεύεσθε καὶ σταθέντες λαλεῖτε ἐν τῷ ἱερῷ τῷ λαῷ πάντα τὰ ῥήματα τῆς ζωῆς ταύτης. ¶ ²¹ ἀκούσαντες δὲ εἰσῆλθον ὑπὸ τὸν ὄρθρον εἰς τὸ ἱερὸν καὶ ἐδίδασκον. ¶ Παραγενόμενος δὲ ὁ ἀρχιερεὺς καὶ οἱ σὺν αὐτῷ συνεκάλεσαν τὸ συνέδριον καὶ πᾶσαν τὴν γερουσίαν τῶν υἱῶν Ἰσραὴλ καὶ ἀπέστειλαν εἰς τὸ δεσμωτήριον ἀχθῆναι αὐτούς. ²² οἱ δὲ παραγενόμενοι ὑπηρέται οὐχ εὗρον αὐτοὺς ἐν τῇ φυλακῇ· ἀναστρέψαντες δὲ ἀπήγγειλαν ²³ λέγοντες ὅτι Τὸ δεσμωτήριον εὕρομεν κεκλεισμένον ἐν πάσῃ ἀσφαλείᾳ καὶ τοὺς φύλακας ἑστῶτας ἐπὶ τῶν θυρῶν, ἀνοίξαντες δὲ ἔσω οὐδένα εὕρομεν. ²⁴ ὡς δὲ ἤκουσαν τοὺς λόγους τούτους ὅ τε στρατηγὸς τοῦ ἱεροῦ καὶ οἱ ἀρχιερεῖς, διηπόρουν περὶ αὐτῶν τί ἂν γένοιτο τοῦτο. ¶ ²⁵ παραγενόμενος δέ τις ἀπήγγειλεν αὐτοῖς ὅτι Ἰδοὺ οἱ ἄνδρες οὓς ἔθεσθε ἐν τῇ φυλακῇ εἰσὶν ἐν τῷ ἱερῷ ἑστῶτες καὶ διδάσκοντες τὸν λαόν. ²⁶ τότε ἀπελθὼν ὁ στρατηγὸς σὺν τοῖς ὑπηρέταις ἦγεν αὐτοὺς οὐ μετὰ βίας, ἐφοβοῦντο γὰρ τὸν λαὸν μὴ λιθασθῶσιν ¶ ²⁷ Ἀγαγόντες δὲ αὐτοὺς ἔστησαν ἐν τῷ συνεδρίῳ. καὶ ἐπηρώτησεν αὐτοὺς ὁ ἀρχιερεὺς ²⁸ λέγων, [Οὐ] Παραγγελίᾳ «παραγγελίᾳ»

priest. **28** "We gave you strict orders not to teach in this name," he said. "Yet you
ἀρχιερεὺς [οὐ] παρηγγείλαμεν ὑμῖν παραγγελίᾳ μὴ διδάσκειν ἐπὶ τούτῳ ‚τῷ ὀνόματι‚ λέγων ‚καὶ ἰδοὺ‚
n.nsm pl v.aai.1p r.dp.2 n.dsf pl f.pa p.d r.dsn d.dsn n.dsn pt.pa.nsm cj j
797 4024 4133 7007 4132 3590 1438 2093 4047 3836 3950 3306 2779 2627

have filled Jerusalem with your teaching and are determined to make us guilty of this
πεπληρώκατε ‚τὴν Ἰερουσαλὴμ‚ ὑμῶν ‚τῆς διδαχῆς‚ καὶ βούλεσθε ἐπαγαγεῖν ἐφ᾽ ἡμᾶς‚ τούτου
v.rai.2p d.asf n.asf r.gp.2 d.gsf n.gsf cj v.pmi.2p f.aa p.a r.ap.1 r.gsn
4444 3836 2647 1439 7007 3836 1439 2779 1089 2042 2093 7005 2042 135 4047

man's blood." ¶ **29** Peter and the other apostles replied: "We must obey God rather
‚τοῦ ἀνθρώπου‚ ‚τὸ αἷμα‚ δὲ Πέτρος καὶ οἱ ἀπόστολοι ἀποκριθεὶς εἶπαν δεῖ πειθαρχεῖν θεῷ μᾶλλον
d.gsm n.gsm d.asn n.asn cj n.nsm cj d.npm n.npm pt.ap.nsm v.aai.3p v.pai.3s f.pa n.dsm adv.c
3836 476 3836 135 1254 4377 2779 3836 693 646 3306 1256 4272 2536 3437

than men! **30** The God of our fathers raised Jesus from the dead – whom you had killed by
ἢ ἀνθρώποις ὁ θεὸς ἡμῶν ‚τῶν πατέρων‚ ἤγειρεν Ἰησοῦν ὃν ὑμεῖς διεχειρίσασθε
pl n.dpm d.nsm n.nsm r.gp.1 d.gpm n.gpm v.aai.3s n.asm r.asm r.np.2 v.ami.2p
2445 476 3836 2536 4252 3836 4252 1586 2652 4005 7007 1429

hanging him on a tree. **31** God exalted him to his own right hand as Prince and Savior that he might
κρεμάσαντες ἐπὶ ξύλου ὁ θεὸς ὕψωσεν τοῦτον αὐτοῦ τῇ δεξιᾷ ἀρχηγὸν καὶ σωτῆρα
pt.aa.npm p.g n.gsn d.nsm n.nsm v.aai.3s r.asm r.gsm.3 d.dsf a.dsf n.asm cj n.asm
3203 2093 3833 3836 2536 5738 4047 1288 899 3836 1288 795 2779 5400

give repentance and forgiveness of sins to Israel. **32** We are witnesses of these things, and so
‚τοῦ δοῦναι‚ μετάνοιαν καὶ ἄφεσιν ἁμαρτιῶν ‚τῷ Ἰσραὴλ‚ καὶ ἡμεῖς ἐσμεν μάρτυρες τούτων ‚τῶν ῥημάτων‚ καὶ
d.gsn f.aa n.asf cj n.asf n.gpf d.dsm n.dsm cj r.np.1 v.pai.1p n.npm r.gpn d.gpn n.gpn cj
3836 1443 3567 2779 912 281 3836 2702 2779 7005 1639 3459 4839 4047 3836 4839 2779

is the Holy Spirit, whom God has given to those who obey him." ¶ **33** When they heard
τὸ ‚τὸ ἅγιον‚ πνεῦμα ὃ ‚ὁ θεὸς‚ ἔδωκεν τοῖς πειθαρχοῦσιν αὐτῷ δὲ ἀκούσαντες
d.nsn d.nsn a.nsn n.nsn r.nsn d.nsm n.nsm v.aai.3s d.dpm pt.pa.dpm r.dsn.3 cj pt.aa.npm
3836 3836 41 4460 4005 3836 2536 1443 3836 4272 899 1254 201

this, they were furious and wanted to put them to death. **34** But a Pharisee named Gamaliel, a teacher of
Οἱ διεπρίοντο καὶ ἐβούλοντο αὐτοὺς ἀνελεῖν δέ τις Φαρισαῖος ὀνόματι Γαμαλιήλ νομοδιδάσκαλος
d.npm v.ipi.3p cj v.imi.3p r.apm.3 f.aa cj r.nsm n.nsm n.dsn n.nsm n.nsm
3836 1391 2779 1089 359 359 899 359 1254 5516 5757 3950 1137 3791

the law, who was honored by all the people, stood up in the Sanhedrin and ordered that the men be
τίμιος παντὶ ‚τῷ λαῷ‚ ἀναστὰς ἐν ‚τῷ συνεδρίῳ‚ ἐκέλευσεν τοὺς ἀνθρώπους
a.nsm a.dsm d.dsm n.dsm pt.aa.nsm p.d d.dsn n.dsn v.aai.3s d.apm n.apm
5508 4246 3836 3295 482 1877 3836 5284 3027 3836 476

put outside for a little while. **35** Then he addressed them: "Men of Israel, consider carefully what
ποιῆσαι ἔξω βραχὺ τε εἶπεν πρὸς αὐτοὺς ἄνδρες Ἰσραηλῖται προσέχετε ἑαυτοῖς‚ τί
f.aa adv adv cj v.aai.3s p.a r.apm.3 n.vpm n.vpm v.pam.2p r.dpm.3 r.asn
4472 2032 1099 5445 3306 4639 899 467 2703 4668 1571 5515

you intend to do to these men. **36** Some time ago Theudas appeared, claiming to
μέλλετε πράσσειν ἐπὶ τούτοις ‚τοῖς ἀνθρώποις‚ γὰρ ‚πρὸ τούτων τῶν ἡμερῶν‚ Θευδᾶς ἀνέστη λέγων
v.pai.2p f.pa p.d r.dpm d.dpm n.dpm cj p.g r.gpf d.gpf n.gpf n.nsm v.aai.3s pt.pa.nsm
3516 4556 2093 4047 3836 476 1142 4574 4047 2465 2554 482 3306

be somebody, and about four hundred men rallied to him. He was killed, all his
εἶναι ‚τινα ἑαυτόν‚ ἀριθμὸς ὡς τετρακοσίων ἀνδρῶν προσεκλίθη ‚τῷ‚ ἀνῃρέθη καὶ πάντες ὅσοι αὐτῷ
f.pa r.asm r.asm.3 n.nsm pl a.gpm n.gpm v.api.3s r.dsm r.nsm v.api.3s cj a.npm r.npm r.dsm.3
1639 5516 1571 750 6055 5484 467 4679 4005 4005 359 2779 4246 4012 899

followers were dispersed, and it all came to nothing. **37** After him, Judas the Galilean appeared in the days of
ἐπείθοντο διελύθησαν καὶ ἐγένοντο εἰς οὐδέν μετὰ τοῦτον Ἰούδας ὁ Γαλιλαῖος ἀνέστη ἐν ταῖς ἡμέραις
v.ipi.3p v.api.3p cj v.ami.3p p.a a.asn p.a r.asm n.nsm d.nsm a.nsm v.aai.3s p.d d.dpf n.dpf
4275 1370 2779 1181 1650 4029 3552 4047 2683 3836 1134 482 1877 3836 2465

the census and led a band of people in revolt. He too was killed, and all his
τῆς ἀπογραφῆς καὶ ἀπέστησεν ‚λαὸν‚ ὀπίσω αὐτοῦ‚ κἀκεῖνος ἀπώλετο καὶ πάντες ὅσοι αὐτῷ
d.gsf n.gsf cj v.aai.3s n.asm p.g r.gsm.3 crasis v.ami.3s cj a.npm r.npm r.dsm.3
3836 615 2779 923 3295 3958 899 923 923 2797 660 2779 4246 4012 899

παρηγγείλαμεν ὑμῖν μὴ διδάσκειν ἐπὶ τῷ ὀνόματι τούτῳ, καὶ ἰδοὺ πεπληρώκατε τὴν Ἰερουσαλὴμ τῆς διδαχῆς ὑμῶν καὶ βούλεσθε ἐπαγαγεῖν ἐφ᾽ ἡμᾶς τὸ αἷμα τοῦ ἀνθρώπου τούτου. ¶ **29** ἀποκριθεὶς δὲ Πέτρος καὶ οἱ ἀπόστολοι εἶπαν, Πειθαρχεῖν δεῖ θεῷ μᾶλλον ἢ ἀνθρώποις. **30** ὁ θεὸς τῶν πατέρων ἡμῶν ἤγειρεν Ἰησοῦν ὃν ὑμεῖς διεχειρίσασθε κρεμάσαντες ἐπὶ ξύλου· **31** τοῦτον ὁ θεὸς ἀρχηγὸν καὶ σωτῆρα ὕψωσεν τῇ δεξιᾷ αὐτοῦ [τοῦ] δοῦναι μετάνοιαν τῷ Ἰσραὴλ καὶ ἄφεσιν ἁμαρτιῶν. **32** καὶ ἡμεῖς ἐσμεν μάρτυρες τῶν ῥημάτων τούτων καὶ τὸ πνεῦμα τὸ ἅγιον ὃ ἔδωκεν ὁ θεὸς τοῖς πειθαρχοῦσιν αὐτῷ. ¶ **33** Οἱ δὲ ἀκούσαντες διεπρίοντο καὶ ἐβούλοντο ἀνελεῖν αὐτούς. **34** ἀναστὰς δέ τις ἐν τῷ συνεδρίῳ Φαρισαῖος ὀνόματι Γαμαλιήλ, νομοδιδάσκαλος τίμιος παντὶ τῷ λαῷ, ἐκέλευσεν ἔξω βραχὺ τοὺς ἀνθρώπους ποιῆσαι **35** εἶπέν τε πρὸς αὐτούς, Ἄνδρες Ἰσραηλῖται, προσέχετε ἑαυτοῖς ἐπὶ τοῖς ἀνθρώποις τούτοις τί μέλλετε πράσσειν. **36** πρὸ γὰρ τούτων τῶν ἡμερῶν ἀνέστη Θευδᾶς λέγων εἶναί τινα ἑαυτόν, ᾧ προσεκλίθη ἀνδρῶν ἀριθμὸς ὡς τετρακοσίων· ὃς ἀνῃρέθη, καὶ πάντες ὅσοι ἐπείθοντο αὐτῷ διελύθησαν καὶ ἐγένοντο εἰς οὐδέν. **37** μετὰ τοῦτον ἀνέστη Ἰούδας ὁ Γαλιλαῖος ἐν ταῖς ἡμέραις τῆς ἀπογραφῆς καὶ ἀπέστησεν λαὸν ὀπίσω αὐτοῦ·

followers were scattered. **38** Therefore, *in the present case* I advise you: Leave these men alone!
ἐπείθοντο → διεσκορπίσθησαν καὶ τὰ νῦν → λέγω ὑμῖν τούτων ἀπὸ ⌐τῶν ἀνθρώπων⌐ ἀπόστητε καὶ
v.ipi.3p v.api.3p cj d.apn adv v.pai.1s r.dp.2 r.gpm p.g d.gpm n.gpm v.aam.2p cj
4275 1399 2779 3836 3814 3306 7007 923 4047 608 3836 476 923 2779

Let them go! For if their purpose or activity is of human origin, it will fail. **39** But if it is
↱ αὐτούς ἄφετε ὅτι ἐὰν αὕτη ⌐ἡ βουλὴ⌐ ἢ ⌐τὸ ἔργον⌐ τοῦτο ᾖ ἐξ ἀνθρώπων ← → καταλυθήσεται δὲ εἰ → ἐστιν
r.apm.3 v.aam.2p cj cj r.nsf d.nsf n.nsf cj d.nsn n.nsn r.nsn v.pas.3s p.g n.gpm v.fpi.3s cj cj v.pai.3s
918 899 918 4022 1569 4047 3836 1087 2445 3836 2240 4047 1639 1666 476 1666 2907 1254 1623 1639

from God, you will not be able to stop these men; you will only find yourselves fighting against
ἐκ θεοῦ οὐ → δυνήσεσθε → καταλῦσαι αὐτούς ← καὶ → μήποτε εὑρεθῆτε θεομάχοι ←
p.g n.gsm pl v.fmi.2p f.aa r.apm.3 adv cj v.aps.2p a.npm
1666 2536 1538 1538 4024 1538 2907 899 2779 2351 2351 3607 2351 2534

God." ¶ **40** His speech persuaded them. They called the apostles in and had them flogged.
← δὲ αὐτῷ ἐπείσθησαν ← καὶ → προσκαλεσάμενοι τοὺς ἀποστόλους ⌐ → δείραντες
cj r.dsm.3 v.api.3p cj pt.am.npm d.apm n.apm pt.aa.npm
1254 899 4275 2779 4673 3836 693 4673 1296

Then they ordered them not to speak in the name of Jesus, and let them go. ¶ **41** The
παρήγγειλαν μὴ → λαλεῖν ἐπὶ τῷ ὀνόματι → τοῦ Ἰησοῦ καὶ → ἀπέλυσαν οὖν μὲν Οἱ
v.aai.3p pl f.pa p.d d.dsn n.dsn d.gsm n.gsm cj v.aai.3p cj cj d.npm
4133 3590 3281 2093 3836 3950 3836 2652 2779 668 4036 3525 3836

apostles left the Sanhedrin, rejoicing because they had been counted worthy of suffering
ἐπορεύοντο ἀπὸ προσώπου τοῦ συνεδρίου χαίροντες ὅτι → κατηξιώθησαν
v.imi.3p p.g n.gsn d.gsn n.gsn pt.pa.npm cj v.api.3p
4513 608 4725 3836 5284 5897 4022 2921

disgrace for the Name. **42** *Day after day,* in the temple courts and from house to house, they never
ἀτιμασθῆναι ὑπὲρ τοῦ ὀνόματος τε πᾶσαν ἡμέραν ἐν τῷ ἱερῷ ← καὶ ⌐κατ' οἶκον⌐ ← → οὐκ
f.ap p.g d.gsn n.gsn cj a.asf n.asf p.d d.dsn n.dsn cj n.asm pl
869 5642 3836 3950 5445 4246 2465 1877 3836 2639 2779 2848 3875 4264 4024

stopped teaching and proclaiming the good news that Jesus is the Christ.
ἐπαύοντο διδάσκοντες καὶ εὐαγγελιζόμενοι Ἰησοῦν τὸν χριστόν
v.imi.3p pt.pa.npm cj pt.pm.npm n.asm d.asm n.asm
4264 1438 2779 2294 2652 3836 5986

The Choosing of the Seven

6:1 In those days when the number of disciples was increasing, the Grecian Jews among them
δὲ Ἐν ταύταις ⌐ταῖς ἡμέραις⌐ → ⌐τῶν μαθητῶν⌐ πληθυνόντων τῶν Ἑλληνιστῶν ←
cj p.d r.dpf d.dpf n.dpf d.gpm n.gpm pt.pa.gpm d.gpm n.gpm
1254 1877 4047 3836 2465 4437 3836 3412 4437 3836 1821

complained against the Hebraic Jews because their widows were being overlooked in the daily
⌐ἐγένετο γογγυσμὸς⌐ πρὸς τοὺς Ἑβραίους ← ὅτι αὐτῶν ⌐αἱ χῆραι⌐ → παρεθεωροῦντο ἐν τῇ ⌐τῇ καθημερινῇ⌐
v.ami.3s n.nsm p.a d.apm n.apm cj r.gpm.3 d.npf n.npf v.ipi.3p p.d d.dsf d.dsf a.dsf
1181 1198 4639 3836 1578 4022 899 3836 5939 4145 1877 3836 3836 2766

distribution of food. **2** So the Twelve gathered all the disciples together and said, "It would not be
διακονία ← δὲ οἱ δώδεκα προσκαλεσάμενοι ⌐τὸ πλῆθος⌐ τῶν μαθητῶν ← εἶπαν οὐκ ἐστιν
n.dsf cj d.npm a.npm pt.am.npm d.asn n.asn d.gpm n.gpm v.aai.3p pl v.pai.3s
1355 1254 3836 1557 4673 3836 4436 3836 3412 4673 3306 1639 1639 4024 1639

right for us to neglect the ministry of the word of God in order to wait on tables. **3** Brothers,
ἀρεστόν ἡμᾶς καταλείψαντας τὸν λόγον → ⌐τοῦ θεοῦ⌐ → διακονεῖν τραπέζαις δὲ ἀδελφοί
a.nsn r.ap.1 pt.aa.apm d.asm n.asm d.gsm n.gsm f.pa n.dpf cj n.vpm
744 7005 2901 3836 3364 3836 2536 1354 5544 1254 81

choose seven men from among you who are known to be full of the Spirit and wisdom. We will
ἐπισκέψασθε ἑπτὰ ἄνδρας ἐξ ὑμῶν → μαρτυρουμένους πλήρεις → πνεύματος καὶ σοφίας →
v.amm.2p a.apm n.apm p.g r.gp.2 pt.pp.apm a.apm n.gsn cj n.gsf
2170 2231 467 1666 7007 3455 4441 4460 2779 5053

turn this responsibility over to them **4** and will give our attention to prayer and the
καταστήσομεν ταύτης ἐπὶ ⌐τῆς χρείας⌐ ⌐ ← οὓς δὲ ἡμεῖς → προσκαρτερήσομεν → ⌐τῇ προσευχῇ καὶ τῇ
v.fai.1p r.gsf p.g d.gsf n.gsf r.apm cj r.np.1 v.fai.1p d.dsf n.dsf cj d.dsf
2770 4047 2093 3836 5970 2770 2770 4005 1254 7005 4674 3836 4666 2779 3836

κἀκεῖνος ἀπώλετο καὶ πάντες ὅσοι ἐπείθοντο αὐτῷ διεσκορπίσθησαν. ³⁸ καὶ τὰ νῦν λέγω ὑμῖν, ἀπόστητε ἀπὸ τῶν ἀνθρώπων τούτων καὶ ἄφετε αὐτούς· ὅτι ἐὰν ᾖ ἐξ ἀνθρώπων ἡ βουλὴ αὕτη ἢ τὸ ἔργον τοῦτο, καταλυθήσεται, ³⁹ εἰ δὲ ἐκ θεοῦ ἐστιν, οὐ δυνήσεσθε καταλῦσαι αὐτούς, μήποτε καὶ θεομάχοι εὑρεθῆτε. ἐπείσθησαν δὲ αὐτῷ ¶ ⁴⁰ καὶ προσκαλεσάμενοι τοὺς ἀποστόλους δείραντες παρήγγειλαν μὴ λαλεῖν ἐπὶ τῷ ὀνόματι τοῦ Ἰησοῦ καὶ ἀπέλυσαν. ¶ ⁴¹ Οἱ μὲν οὖν ἐπορεύοντο χαίροντες ἀπὸ προσώπου τοῦ συνεδρίου, ὅτι κατηξιώθησαν ὑπὲρ τοῦ ὀνόματος ἀτιμασθῆναι, ⁴² πᾶσάν τε ἡμέραν ἐν τῷ ἱερῷ καὶ κατ᾽ οἶκον οὐκ ἐπαύοντο διδάσκοντες καὶ εὐαγγελιζόμενοι τὸν Χριστὸν Ἰησοῦν.
⁶˸¹ Ἐν δὲ ταῖς ἡμέραις ταύταις πληθυνόντων τῶν μαθητῶν ἐγένετο γογγυσμὸς τῶν Ἑλληνιστῶν πρὸς τοὺς Ἑβραίους, ὅτι παρεθεωροῦντο ἐν τῇ διακονίᾳ τῇ καθημερινῇ αἱ χῆραι αὐτῶν. ² προσκαλεσάμενοι δὲ οἱ δώδεκα τὸ πλῆθος τῶν μαθητῶν εἶπαν, Οὐκ ἀρεστόν ἐστιν ἡμᾶς καταλείψαντας τὸν λόγον τοῦ θεοῦ διακονεῖν τραπέζαις. ³ ἐπισκέψασθε δέ, ἀδελφοί, ἄνδρας ἐξ ὑμῶν μαρτυρουμένους ἑπτά, πλήρεις πνεύματος καὶ σοφίας, οὓς καταστήσομεν ἐπὶ τῆς χρείας ταύτης. ⁴ ἡμεῖς δὲ τῇ προσευχῇ καὶ τῇ

ministry of the word." ¶ **5** This proposal pleased the whole group. They chose Stephen, a
διακονίᾳ → τοῦ λόγου καὶ ὁ λόγος ἤρεσεν ἐνώπιον τοῦ παντὸς πλήθους καὶ → ἐξελέξαντο Στέφανον
n.dsf d.gsm n.gsm cj d.nsm n.nsm v.aai.3s p.g d.gsn a.gsn n.gsn cj v.ami.3p n.asm
1355 3836 3364 2779 3836 3364 743 1967 3836 4246 4436 2779 1721 5108

man full of faith and of the Holy Spirit; also Philip, Procorus, Nicanor, Timon, Parmenas,
ἄνδρα πλήρης → πίστεως καὶ → ἁγίου πνεύματος καὶ Φίλιππον καὶ Πρόχορον καὶ Νικάνορα καὶ Τίμωνα καὶ Παρμενᾶν
n.asm a.asm n.gsf cj a.gsn n.gsn cj n.asm cj n.asm cj n.asm cj n.asm cj n.asm
467 4441 4411 2779 41 4460 2779 5805 2779 4743 2779 3770 2779 5511 2779 4226

and Nicolas from Antioch, a convert to Judaism. **6** They presented these men to the apostles, who
καὶ Νικόλαον Ἀντιοχέα προσήλυτον ← ← → ἔστησαν οὓς ← ἐνώπιον τῶν ἀποστόλων καὶ
cj n.asm n.asm n.asm v.aai.3p r.apm p.g d.gpm n.gpm cj
2779 3775 523 4670 2705 4005 1967 3836 693 2779

prayed and laid their hands on them. ¶ **7** So the word of God spread. The number of
προσευξάμενοι ἐπέθηκαν τὰς χεῖρας → αὐτοῖς Καὶ ὁ λόγος → τοῦ θεοῦ ηὔξανεν καὶ ὁ ἀριθμὸς →
pt.am.npm v.aai.3p d.apf n.apf r.dpm.3 cj d.nsm n.nsm d.gsm n.gsm v.iai.3s cj d.nsm n.nsm
4667 2202 3836 5931 899 2779 3836 3364 3836 2536 889 2779 3836 750

disciples in Jerusalem increased rapidly, and a large number of priests became obedient to the faith.
τῶν μαθητῶν ἐν Ἰερουσαλὴμ ἐπληθύνετο σφόδρα τε πολὺς ὄχλος → τῶν ἱερέων → ὑπήκουον → τῇ πίστει
d.gpm n.gpm p.d n.dsf v.ipi.3s adv cj a.nsm n.nsm d.gpm n.gpm v.iai.3p d.dsf n.dsf
3836 3412 1877 2647 4437 5379 5445 4498 4063 3836 2636 5634 3836 4411

Stephen Seized

6:8 Now Stephen, a man full of God's grace and power, did great wonders and miraculous signs among
δὲ Στέφανος πλήρης → χάριτος καὶ δυνάμεως ἐποίει μεγάλα τέρατα καὶ σημεῖα ἐν
cj n.nsm a.nsm n.gsf cj n.gsf v.iai.3s a.apn n.apn cj n.apn p.d
1254 5108 4441 5921 2779 1539 4472 3489 5469 2779 4956 1877

the people. **9** Opposition arose, however, from members of the Synagogue of the Freedmen (as it was
τῷ λαῷ ἀνέστησαν δέ τινες τῶν ἐκ τῆς συναγωγῆς → Λιβερτίνων → →
d.dsm n.dsm v.aai.3p cj r.npm d.gpm p.g d.gsf n.gsf n.gpm
3836 3295 482 1254 5516 3836 1666 3836 5252 3339

called) – Jews of Cyrene and Alexandria as well as the provinces of Cilicia and Asia. These
τῆς λεγομένης καὶ → Κυρηναίων καὶ Ἀλεξανδρέων καὶ ← τῶν ἀπὸ → Κιλικίας καὶ Ἀσίας →
d.gsf pt.pp.gsf cj n.gpm cj n.gpm cj d.gpm p.g n.gsf cj n.gsf
3836 3306 2779 3254 2779 233 2779 3836 608 3070 2779 823

men began to argue with Stephen, **10** but they could not stand up against his wisdom or the Spirit by
→ → συζητοῦντες ← τῷ Στεφάνῳ καὶ → ἴσχυον οὐκ ἀντιστῆναι ← ← τῇ σοφίᾳ καὶ τῷ πνεύματι →
pt.pa.npm d.dsm n.dsm cj v.iai.3p pl f.aa d.dsf n.dsf cj d.dsn n.dsn
5184 3836 5108 2779 2710 4024 468 3836 5053 2779 3836 4460

whom he spoke. ¶ **11** Then they secretly persuaded some men to say, "We have heard Stephen
ᾧ → ἐλάλει τότε → ὑπέβαλον ἄνδρας → λέγοντας ὅτι → ἀκηκόαμεν αὐτοῦ
r.dsn v.iai.3s adv v.aai.3p n.apm pt.pa.apm cj v.rai.1p r.gsm.3
4005 3281 5538 5680 467 3306 4022 201 899

speak words of blasphemy against Moses and against God." ¶ **12** So they stirred up the people and
λαλοῦντος ῥήματα → βλάσφημα εἰς Μωϋσῆν καὶ τὸν θεόν τε → συνεκίνησαν ← τὸν λαὸν καὶ
pt.pa.gsm n.apn a.apn p.a n.asm cj d.asm n.asm cj v.aai.3p d.asm n.asm cj
3281 4839 1061 1650 3707 2779 3836 2536 5445 5167 3836 3295 2779

the elders and the teachers of the law. They seized Stephen and brought him before the
τοὺς πρεσβυτέρους καὶ τοὺς γραμματεῖς ← ← καὶ ἐπιστάντες συνήρπασαν αὐτὸν καὶ ἤγαγον εἰς τὸ
d.apm n.apm cj d.apm n.apm cj pt.aa.npm v.aai.3p r.asm.3 cj v.aai.3p p.a d.asn
3836 4565 2779 3836 1208 2779 2392 5275 899 2779 72 1650 3836

Sanhedrin. **13** They produced false witnesses, who testified, "This fellow never stops speaking
συνέδριον τε → ἔστησαν ψευδεῖς μάρτυρας → λέγοντας οὗτος ὁ ἄνθρωπος οὐ παύεται λαλῶν ῥήματα
n.asn cj v.aai.3p a.apm n.apm pt.pa.apm r.nsm d.nsm n.nsm pl v.pmi.3s pt.pa.nsm n.apn
5284 5445 2705 6014 3459 3306 4047 3836 476 4024 4264 3281 4839

διακονίᾳ τοῦ λόγου προσκαρτερήσομεν. ¶ ⁵ καὶ ἤρεσεν ὁ λόγος ἐνώπιον παντὸς τοῦ πλήθους καὶ ἐξελέξαντο Στέφανον, ἄνδρα πλήρης πίστεως καὶ πνεύματος ἁγίου, καὶ Φίλιππον καὶ Πρόχορον καὶ Νικάνορα καὶ Τίμωνα καὶ Παρμενᾶν καὶ Νικόλαον προσήλυτον Ἀντιοχέα, ⁶ οὓς ἔστησαν ἐνώπιον τῶν ἀποστόλων, καὶ προσευξάμενοι ἐπέθηκαν αὐτοῖς τὰς χεῖρας. ¶ ⁷ Καὶ ὁ λόγος τοῦ θεοῦ ηὔξανεν καὶ ἐπληθύνετο ὁ ἀριθμὸς τῶν μαθητῶν ἐν Ἰερουσαλὴμ σφόδρα, πολύς τε ὄχλος τῶν ἱερέων ὑπήκουον τῇ πίστει.

⁶:⁸ Στέφανος δὲ πλήρης χάριτος καὶ δυνάμεως ἐποίει τέρατα καὶ σημεῖα μεγάλα ἐν τῷ λαῷ. ⁹ ἀνέστησαν δέ τινες τῶν ἐκ τῆς συναγωγῆς τῆς λεγομένης Λιβερτίνων καὶ Κυρηναίων καὶ Ἀλεξανδρέων καὶ τῶν ἀπὸ Κιλικίας καὶ Ἀσίας συζητοῦντες τῷ Στεφάνῳ, ¹⁰ καὶ οὐκ ἴσχυον ἀντιστῆναι τῇ σοφίᾳ καὶ τῷ πνεύματι ᾧ ἐλάλει. ¶ ¹¹ τότε ὑπέβαλον ἄνδρας λέγοντας ὅτι Ἀκηκόαμεν αὐτοῦ λαλοῦντος ῥήματα βλάσφημα εἰς Μωϋσῆν καὶ τὸν θεόν· ¶ ¹² συνεκίνησάν τε τὸν λαὸν καὶ τοὺς πρεσβυτέρους καὶ τοὺς γραμματεῖς καὶ ἐπιστάντες συνήρπασαν αὐτὸν καὶ ἤγαγον εἰς τὸ συνέδριον, ¹³ ἔστησάν τε μάρτυρας ψευδεῖς λέγοντας, Ὁ ἄνθρωπος οὗτος οὐ παύεται λαλῶν ῥήματα κατὰ τοῦ τόπου τοῦ ἁγίου [τούτου] καὶ τοῦ νόμου·

against this holy   place   and against the law.   **14** For we have heard him   say   that this Jesus of
κατὰ   τούτου ⌐τοῦ ἁγίου⌐ ⌐τοῦ τόπου⌐ καὶ   τοῦ νόμου γὰρ →   ἀκηκόαμεν αὐτοῦ λέγοντος ὅτι οὗτος Ἰησοῦς →
p.g   r.gsm d.gsm a.gsm d.gsm n.gsm cj   d.gsm n.gsm cj   v.rai.1p r.gsm.3 pt.pa.gsm cj r.nsm n.nsm
2848   4047   3836 41   3836 5536   2779   3836 3795 1142   201   899   3306   4022 4047 2652

Nazareth   will destroy this   place   and change the customs   Moses handed down to us."   ¶
⌐ὁ Ναζωραῖος⌐ → καταλύσει τοῦτον ⌐τὸν τόπον⌐ καὶ ἀλλάξει τὰ ἔθη   ἃ   Μωϋσῆς παρέδωκεν ←   → ἡμῖν
d.nsm n.nsm   → v.fai.3s r.asm d.asm n.asm cj v.fai.3s d.apn n.apn r.apn n.nsm v.aai.3s   r.dp.1
3836 3717   2907   4047 3836 5536   2779 248   3836 1621 4005 3707   4140   7005

15   All   who were sitting   in the Sanhedrin   looked   intently at Stephen, and they saw that his
καὶ   πάντες οἱ   →   καθεζόμενοι ἐν τῷ συνεδρίῳ ἀτενίσαντες ←   εἰς αὐτὸν   εἶδον αὐτοῦ
cj   a.npm d.npm →   pt.pm.npm p.d d.dsn n.dsn   pt.aa.npm   p.a r.asm.3   v.aai.3p r.gsm.3
2779 4246   3836   2757   1877 3836 5284   867   1650 899   1625   899

face   was like the face   of an angel.
⌐τὸ πρόσωπον⌐ ὡσεὶ πρόσωπον →   ἀγγέλου
d.asn n.asn   pl   n.asn   n.gsm
3836 4725   6059   4725   34

Stephen's Speech to the Sanhedrin

7:1 Then the high priest asked him,   "Are these charges true?" ¶   **2**   To this he replied:
δὲ   ὁ   ἀρχιερεύς Εἶπεν   εἰ ἔχει ταῦτα οὕτως   δὲ   ὁ   ἔφη   Ἄνδρες
cj   d.nsm   n.nsm   v.aai.3s cj v.pai.3s r.npn adv   cj   d.nsm v.iai.3s n.vpm
1254 3836   797   3306   1623 2400 4047 4048   1254   3836 5774   467

"Brothers and fathers, listen   to me! The God of glory   appeared to our father Abraham while he was
ἀδελφοὶ καὶ πατέρες ἀκούσατε   Ὁ   θεός → ⌐τῆς δόξης⌐ ὤφθη   → ἡμῶν τῷ πατρὶ ⌐Ἀβραὰμ →   → ὄντι
n.vpm   cj n.vpm   v.aam.2p   d.nsm n.nsm d.gsf n.gsf v.api.3s r.gp.1 d.dsm n.dsm n.dsm   pt.pa.dsm
81   2779 4252   201   3836 2536   3836 1518 3972   7005 3836 4252   11   1639

still in Mesopotamia,   before   he lived   in Haran. **3** 'Leave   your country and   your
ἐν ⌐τῇ Μεσοποταμίᾳ⌐ ⌐πρὶν ἢ⌐ αὐτὸν κατοικῆσαι ἐν Χαρράν καὶ ἔξελθε ἐκ σου ⌐τῆς γῆς⌐ καὶ [ἐκ] σου
p.d d.dsf n.dsf   cj   pl αὐτὸν v.faa   p.d n.dsf cj v.aam.2s p.g r.gs.2 d.gsf n.gsf cj   p.g r.gs.2
1877 3836 3544   4570 2445 899 2997   1877 5924 2779 2002   1666 5148 3836 1178 2779   1666 5148

people,'   God said, 'and go to the land   I will show you.' ¶   **4** "So he left   the
⌐τῆς συγγενείας⌐ εἶπεν πρὸς αὐτόν καὶ δεῦρο εἰς τὴν γῆν ἣν ἄν → → δείξω σοι   τότε → ἐξελθὼν ἐκ
d.gsf n.gsf   v.aai.3s p.a r.asm.3 cj j   p.a d.asf n.asf r.asf pl v.aas.1s r.ds.2   adv   pt.aa.nsm p.g
3836 5149   3306   4639 899   2779 1306 1650 3836 1178 4005 323   1259   5148   5538   2002   1666

land of the Chaldeans and settled   in Haran.   After the death   of his father,   God sent
γῆς → Χαλδαίων   κατῴκησεν ἐν Χαρράν κἀκεῖθεν μετὰ → ⌐τὸ ἀποθανεῖν⌐ αὐτοῦ ⌐τὸν πατέρα⌐ μετῴκισεν
n.gsf → n.gpm   v.aai.3s p.d n.dsf crasis   p.a   d.asn f.aa   r.gsm.3 d.asm n.asm v.aai.3s
1178   5900   2997   1877 5924 2796   3552   3836 633   899   3836 4252   3579

him to this land   where   you are now living. **5** He gave   him no inheritance here, not even a
αὐτὸν εἰς ταύτην ⌐τὴν γῆν⌐ ⌐εἰς ἣν⌐ ὑμεῖς → νῦν κατοικεῖτε καὶ → ἔδωκεν αὐτῷ οὐκ κληρονομίαν ἐν αὐτῇ, οὐδὲ
r.asm.3 p.a r.asf d.asf n.asf p.a r.asf r.np.2 adv v.pai.2p cj   v.aai.3s r.dsm.3 pl n.asf   p.d r.dsf.3 cj
899   1650 4047 3836 1178 1650 4005 7007   3814 2997   2779 1443   899   4024 3100   1877 899   4028

foot   of ground. But God promised   him that he and his descendants after him would   possess
⌐βῆμα ποδός⌐ ←   καὶ   ἐπηγγείλατο δοῦναι αὐτῷ   καὶ αὐτοῦ ⌐τῷ σπέρματι⌐ μετ' αὐτόν   εἰς κατάσχεσιν
n.asn n.gsm ←   cj   v.ami.3s   f.aa   r.dsm.3   cj r.gsm.3 d.dsn n.dsn p.a r.asm.3   p.a n.asf
1037 4546   2779 2040   1443   899   2779 899   3836 5065   3552 899   1650 2959

the land, even though at that time Abraham had no child. **6** God   spoke to him in this way: 'Your
αὐτήν →   →   αὐτῷ   ὄντος οὐκ τέκνου δὲ ὁ θεός ἐλάλησεν →   →   οὕτως ὅτι αὐτοῦ
r.asf.3 →   →   r.dsm.3 pt.pa.gsn pl n.gsn cj d.nsm n.nsm v.aai.3s   adv   cj r.gsm.3
899   1639   1639   899   1639 4024 5451 1254 3836 2536 3281   4048 4022 899

descendants will be strangers in a country not   their own, and they will be enslaved   and mistreated
⌐τὸ σπέρμα⌐ → ἔσται πάροικον ἐν γῇ   ἀλλοτρίᾳ   καὶ → →   δουλώσουσιν αὐτὸ καὶ κακώσουσιν
d.nsn n.nsn → v.fmi.3s a.nsn p.d n.dsf a.dsf   cj   v.fai.3p r.asn.3 cj v.fai.3p
3836 5065   1639   4230   1877 1178 259   2779   1530   899   2779 2808

four   hundred years. **7** But I will punish the nation   they serve   as slaves,' God   said, 'and
τετρακόσια ←   ἔτη   καὶ ἐγώ → κρινῶ τὸ ἔθνος ᾧ ἐὰν → δουλεύσουσιν ←   ⌐ὁ θεός⌐ εἶπεν καὶ
a.apn   ←   n.apn cj r.ns.1 → v.fai.1s d.asn n.asn r.dsn pl   v.fai.3p   d.nsm n.nsm v.aai.3s cj
5484   2291   2779 1609   3212 3836 1620 4005 1569   1526   3836 2536 3306 2779

¹⁴ ἀκηκόαμεν γὰρ αὐτοῦ λέγοντος ὅτι Ἰησοῦς ὁ Ναζωραῖος οὗτος καταλύσει τὸν τόπον τοῦτον καὶ ἀλλάξει τὰ ἔθη ἃ παρέδωκεν
ἡμῖν Μωϋσῆς. ¶ ¹⁵ καὶ ἀτενίσαντες εἰς αὐτὸν πάντες οἱ καθεζόμενοι ἐν τῷ συνεδρίῳ εἶδον τὸ πρόσωπον αὐτοῦ ὡσεὶ πρόσωπον
ἀγγέλου.
⁷:¹ Εἶπεν δὲ ὁ ἀρχιερεύς, Εἰ ταῦτα οὕτως ἔχει; ¶ ² ὁ δὲ ἔφη. Ἄνδρες ἀδελφοὶ καὶ πατέρες, ἀκούσατε. Ὁ θεὸς τῆς δόξης ὤφθη
τῷ πατρὶ ἡμῶν Ἀβραὰμ ὄντι ἐν τῇ Μεσοποταμίᾳ πρὶν ἢ κατοικῆσαι αὐτὸν ἐν Χαρράν ³ καὶ εἶπεν πρὸς αὐτόν, Ἔξελθε ἐκ τῆς
γῆς σου καὶ [ἐκ] τῆς συγγενείας σου, καὶ δεῦρο εἰς τὴν γῆν ἣν ἄν σοι δείξω. ¶ ⁴ τότε ἐξελθὼν ἐκ γῆς Χαλδαίων κατῴκησεν ἐν
Χαρράν. κἀκεῖθεν μετὰ τὸ ἀποθανεῖν τὸν πατέρα αὐτοῦ μετῴκισεν αὐτὸν εἰς τὴν γῆν ταύτην εἰς ἣν ὑμεῖς νῦν κατοικεῖτε, ⁵ καὶ
οὐκ ἔδωκεν αὐτῷ κληρονομίαν ἐν αὐτῇ οὐδὲ βῆμα ποδός καὶ ἐπηγγείλατο δοῦναι αὐτῷ εἰς κατάσχεσιν αὐτὴν καὶ τῷ σπέρματι
αὐτοῦ μετ' αὐτόν, οὐκ ὄντος αὐτῷ τέκνου. ⁶ ἐλάλησεν δὲ αὐτῷ οὕτως ὁ θεὸς ὅτι ἔσται τὸ σπέρμα αὐτοῦ πάροικον ἐν γῇ ἀλλοτρίᾳ
καὶ δουλώσουσιν αὐτὸ καὶ κακώσουσιν ἔτη τετρακόσια· ⁷ καὶ τὸ ἔθνος ᾧ ἐὰν δουλεύσουσιν κρινῶ ἐγώ, ὁ θεὸς εἶπεν, καὶ μετὰ

afterward they will come   out of that country and worship   me in this place.'   ⁸ Then he gave Abraham
⸢μετὰ ταῦτα⸣ → → ἐξελεύσονται ←   καὶ λατρεύσουσιν μοι ἐν τούτῳ ⸢τῷ τόπῳ⸥ καὶ → ἔδωκεν αὐτῷ
p.a   r.apn   v.fmi.3p   cj   v.fai.3p   r.ds.1 p.d r.dsm d.dsm n.dsm   cj   v.aai.3s r.dsm.3
3552   4047   2002   2779 3302   1609 1877 4047 3836 5536   2779   1443   899

the covenant of circumcision. And   Abraham became the father of Isaac   and circumcised him eight
διαθήκην → περιτομῆς   καὶ οὕτως   ἐγέννησεν ← ←   ⸢τὸν Ἰσαὰκ⸥ καὶ περιέτεμεν αὐτὸν ⸢τῇ ὀγδόῃ⸥
n.asf   n.gsf   cj adv   v.aai.3s   d.asm n.asm   cj   v.aai.3s   r.asm.3 d.dsf d.dsf
1347   4364   2779 4048   1164   3836 2693   2779 4362   899   3836 3838

days   after his birth. Later Isaac became the father of Jacob,   and Jacob became the father of the twelve
⸢τῇ ἡμέρᾳ⸥   καὶ Ἰσαὰκ   ⸢τὸν Ἰακώβ⸥ καὶ Ἰακὼβ   τοὺς δώδεκα
d.dsf n.dsf   cj   n.nsm   d.asm n.asm   cj   n.nsm   d.apm a.apm
3836 2465   2779 2693   3836 2609   2779 2609   3836 1557

patriarchs. ¶ ⁹ "Because the patriarchs were jealous of Joseph,   they sold   him as a slave into
πατριάρχας   Καὶ ↱   οἱ πατριάρχαι → ζηλώσαντες ← ⸢τὸν Ἰωσὴφ⸥ → ἀπέδοντο   εἰς
n.apm   cj   d.npm n.npm   pt.aa.npm   d.asm n.asm   v.ami.3p   p.a
4256   2779 2420   3836 4256   2420   3836 2737   625   1650

Egypt. But God   was with him ¹⁰ and rescued him from all   his troubles.   He gave Joseph wisdom
Αἴγυπτον καὶ ὁ θεός, ἦν μετ᾽ αὐτοῦ καὶ ἐξείλατο αὐτὸν ἐκ πασῶν αὐτοῦ ⸢τῶν θλίψεων⸥ καὶ → ἔδωκεν αὐτῷ σοφίαν
n.asf   cj   d.nsm n.nsm v.iai.3s p.g r.gsm.3   cj   v.ami.3s r.asm.3 p.g a.gpf r.gsm.3 d.gpf n.gpf   cj   v.aai.3s r.dsm.3 n.asf
131   2779 3836 2536 1639 3552 899   2779 1975   899   1666 4246 899   3836 2568   2779   1443   899   5053

and enabled him to gain the goodwill of   Pharaoh king   of Egypt; so he made   him ruler   over
καὶ   χάριν ἐναντίον Φαραὼ βασιλέως → Αἰγύπτου καὶ → κατέστησεν αὐτὸν ἡγούμενον ἐπ᾽
cj   n.asf   p.g   n.gsm   n.gsm   n.gsf   cj   v.aai.3s   r.asm.3 pt.pm.asm   p.a
2779   5921   1883   5755   995   131   2779   2770   899   2451   2093

Egypt and   all his palace. ¶ ¹¹ "Then a famine struck   all Egypt   and Canaan,
Αἴγυπτον καὶ [ἐφ᾽] ὅλον αὐτοῦ ⸢τὸν οἶκον⸥   δὲ   λιμὸς ⸢ἦλθεν ἐφ᾽⸥ ὅλην ⸢τὴν Αἴγυπτον⸥ καὶ Χανάαν καὶ
n.asf   cj   p.a   a.asm r.gsm.3 d.asm n.asm   cj   n.nsm   v.aai.3s p.a   a.asf   d.asf n.asf   cj   n.asf   cj
131   2779   2093 3910 899   3836 3875   1254   3350   2262   2093 3910 3836 131   2779 5913   2779

bringing great suffering, and our fathers   could not find   food.   ¹² When Jacob heard that there was
    μεγάλη θλῖψις   καὶ ἡμῶν οἱ πατέρες, → οὐχ ηὕρισκον χορτάσματα δὲ → Ἰακὼβ ἀκούσας   ὄντα
    a.nsf   n.nsf   cj   r.gp.1 d.npm n.npm   pl   v.iai.3p   n.apn   cj   n.nsm   pt.aa.nsm   pt.pa.apn
    3489   2568   2779 7005 3836 4252   2351 4024 2351   5964   1254   2609   201   1639

grain in Egypt, he sent   our fathers   on their first   visit. ¹³ On their second visit, Joseph told
σιτία εἰς Αἴγυπτον → ἐξαπέστειλεν ἡμῶν ⸢τοὺς πατέρας⸥   πρῶτον   καὶ ἐν τῷ δευτέρῳ   Ἰωσὴφ ἀνεγνωρίσθη
n.apn p.a   n.asf   v.aai.3s   r.gp.1 d.apm n.apm   adv   cj p.d d.dsn a.dsn   n.nsm   v.api.3s
4989   1650 131   1990   7005 3836 4252   4754   2779 1877 3836 1311   2737   331

his brothers who he was, and Pharaoh   learned   about Joseph's family.   ¹⁴ After this, Joseph
αὐτοῦ ⸢τοῖς ἀδελφοῖς⸥   καὶ ⸢τῷ Φαραὼ⸥ ⸢φανερὸν ἐγένετο⸥   ⸢τοῦ Ἰωσὴφ⸥ ⸢τὸ γένος⸥   δὲ ←   Ἰωσὴφ
r.gsm.3 d.dpm n.dpm   cj   d.dsm n.dsm   a.nsn v.ami.3s   d.gsm n.gsm   d.nsn n.nsn   cj   n.nsm
899   3836 81   341 341 341   2779 3836 5755   5745 1181   3836 2737   3836 1169   1254   2737

sent   for his father   Jacob and his whole family, seventy-five   in all.   ¹⁵ Then Jacob
⸢ἀποστείλας μετεκαλέσατο⸥ ← αὐτοῦ ⸢τὸν πατέρα⸥ Ἰακὼβ καὶ τὴν πᾶσαν συγγένειαν ⸢ἑβδομήκοντα πέντε⸥ ἐν ψυχαῖς καὶ Ἰακὼβ
pt.aa.nsm   v.ami.3s   r.gsm.3 d.asm n.asm   n.asm   cj d.asf a.asf   n.asf   a.dpf   a.dpf   p.d n.dpf   cj n.nsm
690   3559   899   3836 4252   2609   2779 3836 4246   5149   4297   1573   1877 6034   2779 2609

went down to Egypt,   where he   and our fathers   died. ¹⁶ Their bodies were brought   back to
κατέβη εἰς Αἴγυπτον καὶ   αὐτὸς καὶ ἡμῶν οἱ πατέρες, ἐτελεύτησεν καὶ   μετετέθησαν ←   εἰς
v.aai.3s εἰς Αἴγυπτον καὶ   r.nsm καὶ r.gp.1 d.npm n.npm v.aai.3s καὶ   v.api.3p   p.a
2849   1650 131   2779   899   2779 7005 3836 4252   5462   2779   3572   1650

Shechem and placed in the tomb   that Abraham had bought from the sons of Hamor at Shechem for a certain
Συχὲμ καὶ ἐτέθησαν ἐν τῷ μνήματι ᾧ   Ἀβραὰμ → ὠνήσατο παρὰ τῶν υἱῶν → Ἐμμὼρ ἐν Συχέμ
n.asf   cj   v.api.3p   p.d d.dsn n.dsn r.dsn n.nsm   v.ami.3s p.g   d.gpm n.gpm   n.gsm   p.d n.dsf
5374   2779 5502   1877 3836 3645 4005 11   6050   4123 3836 5626   1846   1877 5374

sum of money. ¶ ¹⁷ "As   the time drew near for God   to fulfill   his promise to Abraham,
τιμῆς → ἀργυρίου   δὲ Καθὼς ὁ χρόνος → ἤγγιζεν ⸢ὁ θεός⸥ ἧς → ὡμολόγησεν τῆς ἐπαγγελίας → ⸢τῷ Ἀβραάμ⸥
n.gsf   n.gsn   cj cj   d.nsm n.nsm   v.iai.3s d.nsm n.nsm r.gsf   v.aai.3s   d.gsf n.gsf   d.dsm n.dsm
5507   736   1254 2777 3836 5989   1581   3836 2536 4005   3933   3836 2039   3836 11

ταῦτα ἐξελεύσονται καὶ λατρεύσουσίν μοι ἐν τῷ τόπῳ τούτῳ. ⁸ καὶ ἔδωκεν αὐτῷ διαθήκην περιτομῆς· καὶ οὕτως ἐγέννησεν τὸν Ἰσαὰκ καὶ περιέτεμεν αὐτὸν τῇ ἡμέρᾳ τῇ ὀγδόῃ, καὶ Ἰσαὰκ τὸν Ἰακώβ, καὶ Ἰακὼβ τοὺς δώδεκα πατριάρχας. ¶ ⁹ Καὶ οἱ πατριάρχαι ζηλώσαντες τὸν Ἰωσὴφ ἀπέδοντο εἰς Αἴγυπτον. καὶ ἦν ὁ θεὸς μετ᾽ αὐτοῦ ¹⁰ καὶ ἐξείλατο αὐτὸν ἐκ πασῶν τῶν θλίψεων αὐτοῦ καὶ ἔδωκεν αὐτῷ χάριν καὶ σοφίαν ἐναντίον Φαραὼ βασιλέως Αἰγύπτου καὶ κατέστησεν αὐτὸν ἡγούμενον ἐπ᾽ Αἴγυπτον καὶ [ἐφ᾽] ὅλον τὸν οἶκον αὐτοῦ. ¶ ¹¹ ἦλθεν δὲ λιμὸς ἐφ᾽ ὅλην τὴν Αἴγυπτον καὶ Χανάαν καὶ θλῖψις μεγάλη, καὶ οὐχ ηὕρισκον χορτάσματα οἱ πατέρες ἡμῶν. ¹² ἀκούσας δὲ Ἰακὼβ ὄντα σιτία εἰς Αἴγυπτον ἐξαπέστειλεν τοὺς πατέρας ἡμῶν πρῶτον. ¹³ καὶ ἐν τῷ δευτέρῳ ἀνεγνωρίσθη Ἰωσὴφ τοῖς ἀδελφοῖς αὐτοῦ καὶ φανερὸν ἐγένετο τῷ Φαραὼ τὸ γένος [τοῦ] Ἰωσήφ. ¹⁴ ἀποστείλας δὲ Ἰωσὴφ μετεκαλέσατο Ἰακὼβ τὸν πατέρα αὐτοῦ καὶ πᾶσαν τὴν συγγένειαν ἐν ψυχαῖς ἑβδομήκοντα πέντε. ¹⁵ καὶ κατέβη Ἰακὼβ εἰς Αἴγυπτον καὶ ἐτελεύτησεν αὐτὸς καὶ οἱ πατέρες ἡμῶν, ¹⁶ καὶ μετετέθησαν εἰς Συχὲμ καὶ ἐτέθησαν ἐν τῷ μνήματι ᾧ ὠνήσατο Ἀβραὰμ τιμῆς ἀργυρίου παρὰ τῶν υἱῶν Ἐμμὼρ ἐν Συχέμ. ¶ ¹⁷ Καθὼς δὲ ἤγγιζεν ὁ χρόνος τῆς ἐπαγγελίας

the number of our people in Egypt　greatly increased.　**18** Then　　another king,　who knew nothing about
ὁ λαὸς ἐν Αἰγύπτῳ → ηὔξησεν καὶ ἐπληθύνθη ‚ἄχρι οὗ‚ ἕτερος βασιλεὺς ὃς ᾔδει οὐκ →
d.nsm n.nsm p.d n.dsf　v.aai.3s cj v.api.3s　p.g r.gsm r.nsm n.nsm r.nsm v.lai.3s pl
3836 3295 1877 131　889 2779 4437　948 4005 2283 995 4005 3857 4024　3857

Joseph,　became ruler of Egypt.　**19** He dealt treacherously　with our people　and oppressed our forefathers
‚τὸν Ἰωσήφ‚　ἀνέστη ἐπ᾽ Αἴγυπτον οὗτος → κατασοφισάμενος ← ἡμῶν ‚τὸ γένος‚ ἐκάκωσεν ἡμῶν ‚τοὺς πατέρας‚
d.asm n.asm　v.aai.3s p.a n.asf r.nsm pt.am.nsm r.gp.1 d.asn n.asn v.aai.3s r.gp.1 d.apm n.apm
3836 2737　482 2093 131 4047 2947 7005 3836 1169 2808 7005 3836 4252

by forcing　them to throw out their newborn babies　so that they would die.　¶　**20** "At that
→ ‚τοῦ ποιεῖν‚　ἔκθετα ← αὐτῶν → ‚τὰ βρέφη‚ εἰς ← → ‚τὸ μὴ ζῳογονεῖσθαι‚　Ἐν ᾧ
d.gsn f.pa　a.apn r.gpm.3 d.apn n.apn p.a d.asn pl f.pp　p.d r.dsm
3836 4472　1704 899 3836 1100 1650 3836 3590 2441　1877 4005

time Moses was born,　and he was no ordinary　child. For three months he was cared　for in his
καιρῷ Μωϋσῆς → ἐγεννήθη καὶ → ἦν ‚ἀστεῖος τῷ θεῷ‚ ← τρεῖς μῆνας ὃς → ἀνετράφη ἐν τοῦ
n.dsm n.nsm　v.api.3s cj v.iai.3s a.nsm d.dsm n.dsm a.apm n.apm r.nsm v.api.3s p.d d.gsm
2789 3707　1164 2779 1639 842 3836 2536 5552 3604 4005 427 1877 3836

father's house.　**21** When he　was placed outside,　Pharaoh's daughter took　him and brought him up
πατρός ‚τῷ οἴκῳ‚ δὲ → αὐτοῦ ἐκτεθέντος ← Φαραὼ ἡ θυγάτηρ ἀνείλατο αὐτὸν καὶ ἀνεθρέψατο αὐτὸν →
n.gsm d.dsm n.dsm cj r.gsm.3 pt.ap.gsm　n.gsm d.nsf n.nsf v.ami.3s r.asm.3 cj v.ami.3s r.asm.3
4252 3836 3875 1254 1758 899 1758　5755 3836 2588 359 899 2779 427 899 427

as her own son.　**22** Moses was educated in all　the wisdom of the Egyptians and was powerful in speech
→ ἑαυτῇ εἰς υἱόν καὶ Μωϋσῆς → ἐπαιδεύθη ἐν πάσῃ σοφίᾳ → Αἰγυπτίων δὲ ἦν δυνατὸς ἐν λόγοις
r.dsf.3 p.a n.asm cj n.nsm v.api.3s p.d a.dsf n.dsf　n.gpm cj v.iai.3s a.nsm p.d n.dpm
1571 1650 5626 2779 3707 4084 1877 4246 5053　130 1254 1639 1543 1877 3364

and action.　¶　**23** "When Moses was forty　years *old*,　he decided
καὶ ἔργοις αὐτοῦ δὲ Ὡς αὐτῷ → τεσσαρακονταετὴς ← ἐπληροῦτο χρόνος → ‚ἀνέβη ἐπὶ τὴν καρδίαν αὐτοῦ‚
cj n.dpn r.gsm.3 cj r.dsm.3 a.nsm　v.ipi.3s n.nsm v.aai.3s p.a d.asf n.asf r.gsm.3
2779 2240 899 1254 6055 899 4444 5478　4444 5989 326 2093 3836 2840 899

to visit　his fellow　Israelites.　**24** He saw one of them being mistreated by an Egyptian, so
→ ἐπισκέψασθαι αὐτοῦ ‚τοὺς ἀδελφούς‚ ‚τοὺς υἱοὺς Ἰσραήλ‚ καὶ → ἰδών τινα → ἀδικούμενον
f.am r.gsm.3 d.apm n.apm d.apm n.apm n.gsm cj pt.aa.nsm r.asm pt.pp.asm
2170 899 3836 81 3836 5626 2702 2779 1625 5516 92

he went to his defense and avenged　him　by killing the Egyptian. **25** Moses thought that
→ ἠμύνατο καὶ ἐποίησεν ἐκδίκησιν ‚τῷ καταπονουμένῳ‚ → πατάξας τὸν Αἰγύπτιον δὲ ἐνόμιζεν
v.ami.3s cj v.aai.3s n.asf d.dsm pt.pp.dsm pt.aa.nsm d.asm n.asm cj v.iai.3s
310 2779 4472 1689 3836 2930 4250 3836 130 1254 3787

his own people would realize that God　was using　him to rescue　them, but they did
αὐτοῦ τοὺς ἀδελφοὺς → συνιέναι ὅτι ὁ θεὸς → ‚διὰ χειρὸς αὐτοῦ‚ → ‚δίδωσιν σωτηρίαν‚ αὐτοῖς δὲ οἱ →
r.gsm.3 d.apm n.apm f.pa cj d.nsm n.nsm p.g n.gsf r.gsm.3 v.pai.3s n.asf r.dpm.3 cj d.npm
899 3836 81 5317 4022 3836 2536 1328 5931 899 1443 5401 899 1254 3836 5317

not.　**26** The next　day Moses came upon two Israelites who were fighting.　He tried to reconcile
οὐ συνῆκαν τε τῇ ἐπιούσῃ ἡμέρα ὤφθη αὐτοῖς → → μαχομένοις καὶ → → → συνήλλασσεν
pl v.aai.3p cj d.dsf pt.pa.dsf n.dsf v.api.3s r.dpm.3 pt.pm.dpm cj v.iai.3s
4024 5317 5445 3836 2465 3972 899 3481 2779 5261

them　by saying, 'Men, you are brothers; why do you want to hurt each other?' ¶ **27** "But the
αὐτοὺς εἰς εἰρήνην εἰπών ἄνδρες ἐστε ἀδελφοί ἱνατί → → → ἀδικεῖτε ἀλλήλους ← δὲ ὁ
r.apm.3 p.a n.asf pt.aa.nsm n.vpm v.pai.2p n.npm cj v.pai.2p r.apm cj d.nsm
899 1650 1645 3306 467 1639 81 2672 92 253 1254 3836

man who was mistreating the other pushed Moses aside and said, 'Who made　you ruler and judge over
← ← → ἀδικῶν τὸν πλησίον ἀπώσατο αὐτὸν → εἰπών τίς κατέστησεν σε ἄρχοντα καὶ δικαστὴν ἐφ᾽
pt.pa.nsm d.asm adv v.ami.3s r.asm.3 pt.aa.nsm r.nsm v.aai.3s r.as.2 n.asm cj n.asm p.g
92 3836 4446 723 899 723 3306 5515 2770 5148 807 2779 1471 2093

us?　**28** Do you want to kill me as　you killed the Egyptian yesterday?' **29** When Moses heard　this,
ἡμῶν μὴ → σὺ θέλεις → ἀνελεῖν με ὃν τρόπον → ἀνεῖλες τὸν Αἰγύπτιον ἐχθές δὲ ἐν Μωϋσῆς ‚τῷ λόγῳ‚ τούτῳ
r.gp.1 pl r.ns.2 v.pai.2s f.aa r.as.1 r.asm n.asm v.aai.2s d.asm n.asm adv cj p.d n.nsm d.dsm n.dsm r.dsm
7005 3590 2527 5148 2527 359 1609 4005 5573 359 3836 130 2396 1254 1877 3707 3836 3364 4047

ἧς ὡμολόγησεν ὁ θεὸς τῷ Ἀβραάμ, ηὔξησεν ὁ λαὸς καὶ ἐπληθύνθη ἐν Αἰγύπτῳ ¹⁸ ἄχρι οὗ ἀνέστη βασιλεὺς ἕτερος [ἐπ᾽ Αἴγυπτον] ὃς οὐκ ᾔδει τὸν Ἰωσήφ. ¹⁹ οὗτος κατασοφισάμενος τὸ γένος ἡμῶν ἐκάκωσεν τοὺς πατέρας [ἡμῶν] τοῦ ποιεῖν τὰ βρέφη ἔκθετα αὐτῶν εἰς τὸ μὴ ζῳογονεῖσθαι. ¶ ²⁰ ἐν ᾧ καιρῷ ἐγεννήθη Μωϋσῆς καὶ ἦν ἀστεῖος τῷ θεῷ· ὃς ἀνετράφη μῆνας τρεῖς ἐν τῷ οἴκῳ τοῦ πατρός, ²¹ ἐκτεθέντος δὲ αὐτοῦ ἀνείλατο αὐτὸν ἡ θυγάτηρ Φαραὼ καὶ ἀνεθρέψατο αὐτὸν ἑαυτῇ εἰς υἱόν. ²² καὶ ἐπαιδεύθη Μωϋσῆς [ἐν] πάσῃ σοφίᾳ Αἰγυπτίων, ἦν δὲ δυνατὸς ἐν λόγοις καὶ ἔργοις αὐτοῦ. ¶ ²³ Ὡς δὲ ἐπληροῦτο αὐτῷ τεσσερακονταετὴς χρόνος, ἀνέβη ἐπὶ τὴν καρδίαν αὐτοῦ ἐπισκέψασθαι τοὺς ἀδελφοὺς αὐτοῦ τοὺς υἱοὺς Ἰσραήλ. ²⁴ καὶ ἰδών τινα ἀδικούμενον ἠμύνατο καὶ ἐποίησεν ἐκδίκησιν τῷ καταπονουμένῳ πατάξας τὸν Αἰγύπτιον. ²⁵ ἐνόμιζεν δὲ συνιέναι τοὺς ἀδελφοὺς [αὐτοῦ] ὅτι ὁ θεὸς διὰ χειρὸς αὐτοῦ δίδωσιν σωτηρίαν αὐτοῖς· οἱ δὲ οὐ συνῆκαν. ²⁶ τῇ τε ἐπιούσῃ ἡμέρᾳ ὤφθη αὐτοῖς μαχομένοις καὶ συνήλλασσεν αὐτοὺς εἰς εἰρήνην εἰπών, Ἄνδρες, ἀδελφοί ἐστε· ἱνατί ἀδικεῖτε ἀλλήλους; ¶ ²⁷ ὁ δὲ ἀδικῶν τὸν πλησίον ἀπώσατο αὐτὸν εἰπών, Τίς σε κατέστησεν ἄρχοντα καὶ δικαστὴν ἐφ᾽ ἡμῶν; ²⁸ μὴ ἀνελεῖν με σὺ θέλεις ὃν τρόπον ἀνεῖλες ἐχθὲς τὸν

he fled   to   Midian, where he settled as a foreigner and had   two sons. ¶ **30** "After forty
→ ἔφυγεν καὶ ἐν γῇ Μαδιάμ → ἐγένετο → πάροικος οὗ ἐγέννησεν δύο υἱούς   Καὶ → τεσσεράκοντα
v.aai.3s cj p.d n.dsf n.gsm   v.ami.3s   n.nsm adv v.aai.3s a.apm n.apm   cj   a.gpn
5771 2779 1877 1178 3409   1181   4230 4023 1164 1545 5626   2779 4444 5477

years had passed,   an angel   appeared to Moses in the flames of a burning bush in the desert near Mount
ἐτῶν → πληρωθέντων ἄγγελος ὤφθη → αὐτῷ ἐν φλογὶ πυρὸς βάτου ἐν τῇ ἐρήμῳ → ˻τοῦ ὄρους˼
n.gpn pt.ap.gpn n.nsm v.api.3s r.dsm.3 p.d n.dsf n.gsm n.gsm p.d d.dsf n.dsf d.gsn n.gsn
2291 4444 34 3972 899 1877 5825 4786 1004 1877 3836 2245 3836 4001

Sinai. **31** When he   saw this, he was amazed at the sight. As he   went over   to look
Σινᾶ δὲ → ὁ Μωϋσῆς ἰδὼν → ἐθαύμαζεν ← τὸ ὅραμα δὲ αὐτοῦ → προσερχομένου ← κατανοῆσαι
n.gsn cj d.nsm n.nsm pt.aa.nsm v.iai.3s d.asn n.asn cj r.gsm.3 pt.pm.gsm f.aa
4982 1254 1625 3836 3707 1625 2513 3836 3969 1254 4665 899 4665 2917

more closely, he heard the Lord's voice: **32** 'I am the God of your fathers,   the God of Abraham,   Isaac and
← ← ἐγένετο κυρίου φωνή ἐγώ ὁ θεὸς ˻ σου ˻τῶν πατέρων˼ ὁ θεὸς → Ἀβραὰμ καὶ Ἰσαὰκ καὶ
v.ami.3s n.gsn n.nsf r.ns.1 d.nsm n.nsm r.gs.2 d.gpm n.gpm d.nsm n.nsm n.gsm cj n.gsm cj
1181 3261 5889 1609 3836 2536 4252 5148 3836 4252 3836 2536 11 2779 2693 2779

Jacob.'   Moses trembled   with fear and did not dare to look. ¶ **33** "Then the Lord said to
Ἰακώβ δὲ Μωϋσῆς ἔντρομος γενόμενος ← → οὐκ ἐτόλμα κατανοῆσαι δὲ ὁ κύριος εἶπεν →
n.nsm cj n.nsm a.nsm pt.am.nsm pl v.iai.3s f.aa cj d.nsm n.nsm v.aai.3s
2609 1254 3707 1958 1181 5528 4024 5528 2917 1254 3836 3261 3306

him, 'Take off your sandals;   the   place where you are standing is   holy ground. **34** I   have indeed
αὐτῷ λῦσον ← σου ˻τὸ ὑπόδημα˼ τῶν ποδῶν ὁ γὰρ τόπος ἐφ᾿ ᾧ → → ἕστηκας ἐστίν ἁγία γῆ ˻ → idὼν
r.dsm.3 v.aam.2s r.gs.2 d.asn n.asn d.gpm n.gpm d.nsm cj n.nsm p.d r.dsm v.rai.2s v.pai.3s a.nsf n.nsf pt.aa.nsm
899 3395 5148 3836 5687 3836 4546 3836 1142 5536 2093 4005 2705 1639 41 1178 1625 1625 1625

seen the oppression of my people   in Egypt. I have heard their groaning   and have come   down to
εἶδον τὴν κάκωσιν → μου ˻τοῦ λαοῦ˼ τοῦ ἐν Αἰγύπτῳ καὶ → ἤκουσα αὐτῶν ˻τοῦ στεναγμοῦ˼ καὶ → κατέβην ← →
v.aai.1s d.asf n.asf r.gs.1 d.gsm n.gsm d.gsm p.d n.dsf cj v.aai.1s r.gpm.3 d.gsm n.gsm cj v.aai.1s
1625 3836 2810 3295 3836 3295 3836 1877 131 2779 201 899 3836 5099 2779 2849 1975

set them free.   Now come, I will send   you back to Egypt.' ¶ **35** "This is the same Moses whom
˻ αὐτούς ἐξελέσθαι καὶ νῦν δεῦρο ᾿ ᾿ ἀποστείλω σε εἰς Αἴγυπτον Τοῦτον τὸν Μωϋσῆν ὃν
r.apm.3 f.am cj adv j v.aas.1s r.as.2 p.a n.asf r.asm d.asm n.asm r.asm
1975 899 1975 2779 3814 1306 690 5148 1650 131 4047 3836 3707 4005

they had rejected with the words, 'Who made   you ruler   and judge?'   He was sent   to be their
→ → ἠρνήσαντο → → εἰπόντες τίς κατέστησεν σε ἄρχοντα καὶ δικαστήν [καὶ] τοῦτον → ἀπέσταλκεν
v.ami.3p pt.aa.npm r.nsm v.aai.3s r.as.2 n.asm cj n.asm cj r.asm v.rai.3s
766 3306 5515 2770 5148 807 2779 1471 2779 4047 690

ruler   and deliverer by God   himself, through the angel who appeared to him in the bush. **36** He led
ἄρχοντα καὶ λυτρωτὴν ὁ θεός   ˻σὺν χειρὶ˼ ἀγγέλου τοῦ ὀφθέντος → αὐτῷ ἐν τῇ βάτῳ οὗτος ἐξήγαγεν
n.asm cj n.asm d.nsm n.nsm p.d n.dsf n.gsm d.gsm pt.ap.gsm r.dsm.3 p.d d.dsf n.dsf r.nsm v.aai.3s
807 2779 3392 3836 2536 5250 5931 34 3836 3972 899 1877 3836 1004 4047 1974

them out of Egypt and did   wonders and miraculous signs in   Egypt,   at the Red Sea   and for
αὐτοὺς ← ποιήσας τέρατα καὶ → σημεῖα ἐν γῇ Αἰγύπτῳ καὶ ἐν ἐρυθρᾷ θαλάσσῃ καὶ →
r.apm.3 pt.aa.nsm n.apn cj n.apn p.d n.dsf n.dsf cj p.d a.dsf n.dsf cj
899 1974 4472 5469 2779 4956 1877 1178 131 2779 1877 2261 2498 2779

forty   years in the desert. ¶ **37** "This is   that Moses who told the Israelites,   'God   will send
τεσσεράκοντα ἔτη ἐν τῇ ἐρήμῳ οὗτός ἐστιν ὁ Μωϋσῆς ὁ εἴπας τοῖς ˻υἱοῖς Ἰσραήλ˼ ὁ θεὸς → ἀναστήσει
a.apn n.apn p.d d.dsf n.dsf r.nsm v.pai.3s d.nsm n.nsm d.nsm pt.aa.nsm d.dpm n.dpm d.nsm n.nsm v.fai.3s
5477 2291 1877 3836 2245 4047 1639 3836 3707 3836 3306 3836 5626 2702 3836 2536 482

you a prophet like me from your own people.' **38** He was   in the assembly in the desert, with the
ὑμῖν προφήτην ὡς ἐμὲ ἐκ ὑμῶν τῶν ἀδελφῶν οὗτός ἐστιν ὁ γενόμενος ἐν τῇ ἐκκλησίᾳ ἐν τῇ ἐρήμῳ μετὰ τοῦ
r.dp.2 n.asm pl r.as.1 p.g r.gp.2 d.gpm n.gpm r.nsm v.pai.3s d.nsm pt.am.nsm p.d d.dsf n.dsf p.d d.dsf n.dsf p.g d.gsm
7007 4737 6055 1609 1666 7007 3836 81 4047 1639 3836 1181 1877 3836 1711 1877 3836 2245 3552 3836

angel who spoke   to him on Mount Sinai, and with our fathers;   and he received living words to pass   on
ἀγγέλου τοῦ λαλοῦντος → αὐτῷ ἐν ˻τῷ ὄρει˼ Σινᾶ καὶ → ἡμῶν ˻τῶν πατέρων˼ ὃς ἐδέξατο ζῶντα λόγια → δοῦναι ←
n.gsm d.gsm pt.pa.gsm r.dsm.3 p.d d.dsn n.dsn n.gsn cj r.gp.1 d.gpm n.gpm r.nsm v.ami.3s pt.pa.apn n.apn f.aa
34 3836 3281 899 1877 3836 4001 4982 2779 7005 3836 4252 4005 1312 2409 3359 1443

Αἰγύπτιον; ²⁹ ἔφυγεν δὲ Μωϋσῆς ἐν τῷ λόγῳ τούτῳ καὶ ἐγένετο πάροικος ἐν γῇ Μαδιάμ, οὗ ἐγέννησεν υἱοὺς δύο. ¶ ³⁰ Καὶ
πληρωθέντων ἐτῶν τεσσεράκοντα ὤφθη αὐτῷ ἐν τῇ ἐρήμῳ τοῦ ὄρους Σινᾶ ἄγγελος ἐν φλογὶ πυρὸς βάτου. ³¹ ὁ δὲ Μωϋσῆς ἰδὼν
ἐθαύμαζεν τὸ ὅραμα, προσερχομένου δὲ αὐτοῦ κατανοῆσαι ἐγένετο φωνὴ κυρίου, ³² Ἐγὼ ὁ θεὸς τῶν πατέρων σου, ὁ θεὸς
Ἀβραὰμ καὶ Ἰσαὰκ καὶ Ἰακώβ. ἔντρομος δὲ γενόμενος Μωϋσῆς οὐκ ἐτόλμα κατανοῆσαι. ¶ ³³ εἶπεν δὲ αὐτῷ ὁ κύριος, Λῦσον
τὸ ὑπόδημα τῶν ποδῶν σου, ὁ γὰρ τόπος ἐφ᾿ ᾧ ἕστηκας γῆ ἁγία ἐστίν. ³⁴ ἰδὼν εἶδον τὴν κάκωσιν τοῦ λαοῦ μου τοῦ ἐν Αἰγύπτῳ
καὶ τοῦ στεναγμοῦ αὐτῶν ἤκουσα, καὶ κατέβην ἐξελέσθαι αὐτούς· καὶ νῦν δεῦρο ἀποστείλω σε εἰς Αἴγυπτον. ¶ ³⁵ Τοῦτον
τὸν Μωϋσῆν, ὃν ἠρνήσαντο εἰπόντες, Τίς σε κατέστησεν ἄρχοντα καὶ δικαστήν; τοῦτον ὁ θεὸς [καὶ] ἄρχοντα καὶ λυτρωτὴν
ἀπέσταλκεν σὺν χειρὶ ἀγγέλου τοῦ ὀφθέντος αὐτῷ ἐν τῇ βάτῳ. ³⁶ οὗτος ἐξήγαγεν αὐτοὺς ποιήσας τέρατα καὶ σημεῖα ἐν γῇ
Αἰγύπτῳ καὶ ἐν Ἐρυθρᾷ Θαλάσσῃ καὶ ἐν τῇ ἐρήμῳ ἔτη τεσσεράκοντα. ¶ ³⁷ οὗτός ἐστιν ὁ Μωϋσῆς ὁ εἴπας τοῖς υἱοῖς Ἰσραήλ,
Προφήτην ὑμῖν ἀναστήσει ὁ θεὸς ἐκ τῶν ἀδελφῶν ὑμῶν ὡς ἐμέ. ³⁸ οὗτός ἐστιν ὁ γενόμενος ἐν τῇ ἐκκλησίᾳ ἐν τῇ ἐρήμῳ μετὰ
τοῦ ἀγγέλου τοῦ λαλοῦντος αὐτῷ ἐν τῷ ὄρει Σινᾶ καὶ τῶν πατέρων ἡμῶν, ὃς ἐδέξατο λόγια ζῶντα δοῦναι ἡμῖν. ¶ ³⁹ ᾧ οὐκ

to us. ¶ **39** "But our fathers refused to obey him. Instead, they rejected him and in their
→ ἡμῖν ἡμῶν οἱ πατέρες ˌοὐκ ἠθέλησαν˺ → ὑπήκοοι γενέσθαι ᾧ ἀλλὰ ἀπώσαντο καὶ ἐν αὐτῶν
r.dp.1　　　　r.gp.1 d.npm n.npm　pl v.aai.3p　　→ a.npm f.am　r.dsm cj　　v.ami.3p　　cj p.d r.gpm.3
7005　　　　7005 3836 4252　4024 2527　　　5675 1181　4005 247　　723　　　2779 1877 899

hearts turned back to Egypt. **40** They told Aaron, 'Make us gods who will go before
ˌταῖς καρδίαις˺ ἐστράφησαν ← εἰς Αἴγυπτον → εἰπόντες ˌτῷ Ἀαρών˺ ποίησον ἡμῖν θεοὺς οἳ → προπορεύσονται ←
d.dpf n.dpf　v.api.3p　　p.a n.asf　　　pt.aa.npm d.dsm n　v.aam.2s r.dp.1 n.apm r.npm　v.fmi.3p
3836 2840　5138　　　1650 131　　　3306　　3836 2　4472　　7005 2536 4005　4638

us. As for this fellow Moses who led us out of Egypt — we don't know what has happened to
ἡμῶν γὰρ οὗτος ˌὁ Μωϋσῆς˺ ὃς ἐξήγαγεν ἡμᾶς ἐκ ← γῆς Αἰγύπτου οὐκ οἴδαμεν τί → ἐγένετο →
r.gp.1 cj r.nsm d.nsm n.nsm r.nsm v.aai.3s r.ap.1 p.g n.gsf n.gsf pl v.rai.1p r.nsn v.ami.3s
7005 1142 4047 3836 3707 4005 1974 7005 1666 1178 131 3857 4024 3857 5515 1181

him!' **41** *That was the time* they made an idol in the form of a calf. They brought sacrifices
αὐτῷ καὶ ἐν ταῖς ἡμέραις ἐκείναις → ἐμοσχοποίησαν ← → ← → ← ← καὶ → ἀνήγαγον θυσίαν
r.dsm.3 cj p.d d.dpf n.dpf r.dpf v.aai.3p cj v.aai.3p n.asf
899 2779 1877 3836 2465 1697 3674 2779 343 2602

to it and held a celebration in honor of what their hands had made. **42** But God turned
→ ˌτῷ εἰδώλῳ˺ καὶ → εὐφραίνοντο ἐν αὐτῶν ˌτῶν χειρῶν˺ → ˌτοῖς ἔργοις˺ δὲ ὁ θεός ἔστρεψεν
d.dsn n.dsn cj v.ipi.3p p.d r.gpm.3 d.gpf n.gpf d.dpn n.dpn cj d.nsm n.nsm v.aai.3s
3836 1631 2779 2370 1877 899 3836 5931 3836 2240 1254 3836 2536 5138

away and gave them over to the worship of the heavenly bodies. This agrees with what is written in the
← καὶ παρέδωκεν αὐτοὺς ↰ λατρεύειν → τῇ ˌτοῦ οὐρανοῦ˺ στρατιᾷ καθὼς ← → γέγραπται ἐν
cj v.aai.3s r.apm.3 f.pa d.dsf d.gsm n.gsm n.dsf cj v.rpi.3s p.d
2779 4140 899 4140 3302 3836 3836 4041 5131 2777 1211 1877

book of the prophets: "'Did you bring me sacrifices and offerings forty years in the desert, O house
βίβλῳ ˌτῶν προφητῶν˺ μὴ → → προσηνέγκατε μοι σφάγια καὶ θυσίας τεσσεράκοντα ἔτη ἐν τῇ ἐρήμῳ οἶκος
n.dsf d.gpm n.gpm pl v.aai.2p r.ds.1 n.apn cj n.apf a.apn n.apn p.d d.dsf n.dsf n.vsm
1047 3836 4737 3590 4712 1609 5376 2779 2602 5477 2291 1877 3836 2245 3875

of Israel? **43** You have lifted up the shrine of Molech and the star of your god Rephan, the idols
→ Ἰσραήλ καὶ → ἀνελάβετε τὴν σκηνὴν ˌτοῦ Μολὸχ˺ καὶ τὸ ἄστρον → ὑμῶν ˌτοῦ θεοῦ˺ Ῥαιφάν τοὺς τύπους οὓς
n.gsm cj v.aai.2p d.asf n.asf d.gsm n.gsm cj d.asn n.asn r.gp.2 d.gsm n.gsm n.gsm d.apm n.apm r.apm
2702 2779 377 3836 5008 3836 3661 2779 3836 849 7007 3836 2536 4818 3836 5596 4005

you made to worship. Therefore I will send you into exile' beyond Babylon. ¶ **44** "Our
→ ἐποιήσατε → προσκυνεῖν αὐτοῖς καὶ → μετοικιῶ ὑμᾶς ↰ ἐπέκεινα Βαβυλῶνος ἡμῶν
v.aai.2p f.pa r.dpm.3 cj v.fai.1s r.ap.2 p.g n.gsf r.gp.1
4472 4686 899 2779 3579 7007 3579 3579 2084 956 7005

forefathers had the tabernacle of the Testimony with them in the desert. It had been made as God
ˌτοῖς πατράσιν˺ ἦν Ἡ σκηνὴ → τοῦ μαρτυρίου ἐν τῇ ἐρήμῳ καθὼς ˌὁ λαλῶν˺
d.dpm n.dpm v.iai.3s d.nsf n.nsf d.gsn n.gsn p.d d.dsf n.dsf cj d.nsm pt.pa.nsm
3836 4252 1639 3836 5008 3836 3457 1877 3836 2245 2777 3836 3281

directed Moses, according to the pattern he had seen. **45** Having received the tabernacle,
διετάξατο ˌτῷ Μωϋσῇ˺ ποιῆσαι αὐτὴν κατὰ ← τὸν τύπον ὃν → ἑωράκει καὶ διαδεξάμενοι ἣν
v.ami.3s d.dsm n.dsm f.aa r.asf.3 p.a d.asm n.asm r.asm v.lai.3s adv pt.am.npm r.asf
1411 3836 3707 4472 899 2848 3836 5596 4005 3972 2779 1342 4005

our fathers under Joshua brought it with them when they took the land from the nations God
ἡμῶν ˌοἱ πατέρες˺ μετὰ Ἰησοῦ εἰσήγαγον ἐν ˌτῇ κατασχέσει˺ τῶν ἐθνῶν ὧν ὁ θεὸς
r.gp.1 d.npm n.npm p.g n.gsm v.aai.3p p.d d.dsf n.dsf d.gpn n.gpn r.gpn d.nsm n.nsm
7005 3836 4252 3552 2652 1652 1877 3836 2959 3836 1620 4005 3836 2536

drove out before them. It remained in the land until the time of David, **46** who enjoyed
ἐξῶσεν ← ἀπὸ προσώπου ˌτῶν πατέρων ἡμῶν˺ ἕως τῶν ἡμερῶν → Δαυίδ ὃς εὗρεν ἐνώπιον
v.aai.3s p.g n.gsn d.gpm n.gpm r.gp.1 p.g d.gpf n.gpf n.gsm r.nsm v.aai.3s p.g
2034 608 4725 3836 4252 7005 2401 3836 2465 1253 4005 2351 1967

God's favor and asked that he might provide a dwelling place for the God of Jacob. **47** But it was Solomon who
ˌτοῦ θεοῦ˺ χάριν καὶ ᾐτήσατο → → εὑρεῖν σκήνωμα → τῷ οἴκῳ → Ἰακώβ δὲ Σολομῶν
d.gsm n.gsm n.asf cj v.ami.3s f.aa n.asn d.dsm n.dsm n.gsm cj n.nsm
3836 2536 5921 2779 160 2351 5013 3836 3875 2609 1254 5048

built the house for him. ¶ **48** "However, the Most High does not live in houses made by men.
οἰκοδόμησεν οἶκον → αὐτῷ ἀλλ' ὁ ὕψιστος οὐχ κατοικεῖ ἐν χειροποιήτοις
v.aai.3s n.asm r.dsm.3 cj d.nsm a.nsm.s pl v.pai.3s p.d a.dpm
3868 3875 899 247 3836 5736 2997 4024 2997 1877 5935

ἠθέλησαν ὑπήκοοι γενέσθαι οἱ πατέρες ἡμῶν, ἀλλὰ ἀπώσαντο καὶ ἐστράφησαν ἐν ταῖς καρδίαις αὐτῶν εἰς Αἴγυπτον **40** εἰπόντες τῷ Ἀαρών, Ποίησον ἡμῖν θεοὺς οἳ προπορεύσονται ἡμῶν· ὁ γὰρ Μωϋσῆς οὗτος, ὃς ἐξήγαγεν ἡμᾶς ἐκ γῆς Αἰγύπτου, οὐκ οἴδαμεν τί ἐγένετο αὐτῷ. **41** καὶ ἐμοσχοποίησαν ἐν ταῖς ἡμέραις ἐκείναις καὶ ἀνήγαγον θυσίαν τῷ εἰδώλῳ καὶ εὐφραίνοντο ἐν τοῖς ἔργοις τῶν χειρῶν αὐτῶν. **42** ἔστρεψεν δὲ ὁ θεὸς καὶ παρέδωκεν αὐτοὺς λατρεύειν τῇ στρατιᾷ τοῦ οὐρανοῦ καθὼς γέγραπται ἐν βίβλῳ τῶν προφητῶν, Μὴ σφάγια καὶ θυσίας προσηνέγκατέ μοι ἔτη τεσσεράκοντα ἐν τῇ ἐρήμῳ, οἶκος Ἰσραήλ; **43** καὶ ἀνελάβετε τὴν σκηνὴν τοῦ Μολὸχ καὶ τὸ ἄστρον τοῦ θεοῦ [ὑμῶν] Ῥαιφάν, τοὺς τύπους οὓς ἐποιήσατε προσκυνεῖν αὐτοῖς, καὶ μετοικιῶ ὑμᾶς ἐπέκεινα Βαβυλῶνος. ¶ **44** Ἡ σκηνὴ τοῦ μαρτυρίου ἦν τοῖς πατράσιν ἡμῶν ἐν τῇ ἐρήμῳ καθὼς διετάξατο ὁ λαλῶν τῷ Μωϋσῇ ποιῆσαι αὐτὴν κατὰ τὸν τύπον ὃν ἑωράκει· **45** ἣν καὶ εἰσήγαγον διαδεξάμενοι οἱ πατέρες ἡμῶν μετὰ Ἰησοῦ ἐν τῇ κατασχέσει τῶν ἐθνῶν, ὧν ἐξῶσεν ὁ θεὸς ἀπὸ προσώπου τῶν πατέρων ἡμῶν ἕως τῶν ἡμερῶν Δαυίδ, **46** ὃς εὗρεν χάριν ἐνώπιον τοῦ θεοῦ καὶ ᾐτήσατο εὑρεῖν σκήνωμα τῷ θεῷ «οἴκῳ» Ἰακώβ. **47** Σολομῶν δὲ οἰκοδόμησεν αὐτῷ οἶκον. ¶ **48** ἀλλ' οὐχ ὁ ὕψιστος ἐν χειροποιήτοις

As   the prophet says: **49** "'Heaven   is my throne, and the earth is my footstool.   What kind of house will
καθὼς   ὁ   προφήτης λέγει   ὁ   οὐρανός,   μοι θρόνος   δὲ   ἡ   γῆ   μου ὑποπόδιον τῶν ποδῶν. ποῖον ← ← οἶκον →
cj   d.nsm n.nsm   v.pai.3s d.nsm n.nsm   r.ds.1 n.nsm cj   d.nsf n.nsf   r.gs.1 n.nsn   d.gpm n.gpm   r.asm   n.asm
2777   3836   4737   3306   3836 4041   1609 2585   1254 3836 1178   1609 5711   3836 4546   4481   3875

you build   for me? says the Lord. Or where   will my resting   place be? **50** Has not my hand   made
→ οἰκοδομήσετε   μοι λέγει   κύριος ἢ   τίς τόπος,   μου καταπαύσεως ←   → οὐχὶ μου ἡ   χεὶρ   ἐποίησεν
   v.fai.2p   r.ds.1 v.pai.3s n.nsm cj r.nsm n.nsm r.gs.1 n.gsf   pl   r.gs.1 d.nsf n.nsf v.aai.3s
   3868   1609 3306   3261   2445 5515 5536   1609   2923   4472 4049 1609 3836 5931 4472

all these things?' ¶ **51** "You stiff-necked   people, with uncircumcised hearts and ears!   You are just
πάντα ταῦτα ←   Σκληροτράχηλοι ←   καὶ ἀπερίτμητοι   καρδίαις καὶ τοῖς ὠσίν, καὶ ὑμεῖς →
a.apn r.apn   a.vpm   cj a.vpm   n.dpf   cj d.dpn n.dpn adv r.np.2
4246 4047   5019   2779 598   2840   2779 3836 4044 2779 7007

like your fathers: You always resist   the Holy Spirit! **52** Was there ever a prophet   your fathers   did
ὡς ὑμῶν οἱ πατέρες, ὑμεῖς ἀεὶ ἀντιπίπτετε τῷ τῷ ἁγίῳ πνεύματι   τίνα τῶν προφητῶν, ὑμῶν οἱ πατέρες. →
cj r.gp.2 d.npm n.npm r.np.2 adv v.pai.2p   d.dsn d.dsn a.dsn n.dsn   r.asm d.gpm n.gpm r.gp.2 d.npm n.npm   1503
6055 7007 3836 4252   7007 107 528   3836 3836 41 4460   5515 3836 4737   7007 3836 4252

not persecute? They even killed   those who predicted   the coming of the Righteous One. And now
οὐκ ἐδίωξαν καὶ ἀπέκτειναν τοὺς ← προκαταγγείλαντας περὶ τῆς ἐλεύσεως → τοῦ δικαίου   νῦν
pl   v.aai.3p cj   v.aai.3p   d.apm   pt.aa.apm   p.g d.gsf n.gsf   d.gsm a.gsm   adv
4024 1503   650 650   3836   4615   4309 3836 1803   3836 1465   3814

you have   betrayed and murdered him – **53** you who have received the law   that was put into effect   through
ὑμεῖς ἐγένεσθε προδόται καὶ φονεῖς   οὗ   → οἵτινες → ἐλάβετε τὸν νόμον   εἰς διαταγὰς →
r.np.2 v.ami.2p n.npm   cj n.npm   r.gsm   r.npm   v.aai.2p d.asm n.asm p.a n.apf
7007 1181   4595   2779 5838   4005   3284   3284 4015 3284   3836 3795   1650 1408

angels but have not obeyed it."
ἀγγέλων καὶ → οὐκ ἐφυλάξατε
n.gpm   cj   pl   v.aai.2p
34   2779 4024 5875 5875

The Stoning of Stephen

7:54   When they heard   this, they were furious   and gnashed their teeth at him.
δὲ →   → Ἀκούοντες ταῦτα →   →   διεπρίοντο ταῖς καρδίαις αὐτῶν καὶ ἔβρυχον τοὺς ὀδόντας ἐπ' αὐτόν
cj   pt.pa.npm r.apn   v.ipi.3p d.dpf n.dpf r.gpm.3 cj v.iai.3p d.apm n.apm p.a r.asm.3
1254   201   4047   1391   3836 2840   899   2779 1107   3848 2093 899

55 But Stephen,   full of the Holy Spirit,   looked up to heaven   and saw the glory of God, and Jesus
δὲ   ὑπάρχων πλήρης → ἁγίου πνεύματος ἀτενίσας ←   εἰς τὸν οὐρανὸν   εἶδεν   δόξαν θεοῦ καὶ Ἰησοῦν
cj   pt.pa.nsm a.nsm   a.gsn n.gsn   pt.aa.nsm   p.a d.asm n.asm   v.aai.3s n.asf n.gsm cj n.asm
1254   5639   4441   41   4460   867   1650 3836 4041   1625   1518 2536 2779 2652

standing at the right hand of God.   **56** "Look," he said, "I see heaven   open   and the Son of
ἑστῶτα ἐκ δεξιῶν ← → τοῦ θεοῦ.   καὶ ἰδοὺ   εἶπεν → θεωρῶ τοὺς οὐρανοὺς διηνοιγμένους καὶ τὸν υἱὸν
pt.ra.asm p.g a.gpf   d.gsm n.gsm cj j   v.aai.3s v.pai.1s d.apm n.apm   pt.rp.apm   cj d.asm n.asm
2705   1666 1288   3836 2536 2779 2627   3306   2555 3836 4041   1380   2779 3836 5626

Man   standing at the right hand of God." ¶ **57** At this they covered their ears   and, yelling   at
τοῦ ἀνθρώπου ἑστῶτα ἐκ δεξιῶν ← → τοῦ θεοῦ.   δὲ → συνέσχον αὐτῶν τὰ ὦτα καὶ κράξαντες →
d.gsm n.gsm pt.ra.asm p.g a.gpf   d.gsm n.gsm   cj   v.aai.3p r.gpm.3 d.apn n.apn cj pt.aa.npm
3836 476   2705   1666 1288   3836 2536   1254   5309   899   3836 4044 2779 3189

the top of their voices, they all   rushed at him, **58** dragged him out of the city and began to
μεγάλῃ   φωνῇ → ὁμοθυμαδὸν ὥρμησαν ἐπ' αὐτόν.   καὶ ἐκβαλόντες ἔξω τῆς πόλεως   and began to
a.dsf   n.dsf   adv   v.aai.3p p.a r.asm.3   cj pt.aa.npm p.g d.gsf n.gsf
3489   5889   3924   3994   2093 899   2779 1675   2032 3836 4484

stone   him. Meanwhile, the witnesses laid   their clothes   at the feet of a young man named   Saul.
ἐλιθοβόλουν καὶ   οἱ μάρτυρες ἀπέθεντο αὐτῶν τὰ ἱμάτια παρὰ τοὺς πόδας νεανίου ← καλουμένου Σαύλου.
v.iai.3p   cj   d.npm n.npm v.ami.3p r.gpm.3 d.apn n.apn p.a d.apm n.apm n.gsm   pt.pp.gsm n.gsm
3344   2779   3836 3459   700   899   3836 2668 4123 3836 4546   3733   2813   4930

¶ **59** While they were stoning   him,   Stephen prayed,   "Lord Jesus, receive my spirit."
καὶ →   →   ἐλιθοβόλουν τὸν Στέφανον ← ἐπικαλούμενον καὶ λέγοντα κύριε Ἰησοῦ δέξαι μου τὸ πνεῦμα
cj   v.iai.3p d.asm n.asm   pt.pm.asm   cj pt.pa.asm n.vsm n.vsm v.amm.2s r.gs.1 d.asn n.asn
2779   3344   3836 5108   2126   2779 3306   3261 2652 1312   1609 3836 4460

κατοικεῖ, καθὼς ὁ προφήτης λέγει, **49** Ὁ οὐρανός μοι θρόνος, ἡ δὲ γῆ ὑποπόδιον τῶν ποδῶν μου· ποῖον οἶκον οἰκοδομήσετέ μοι, λέγει κύριος, ἢ τίς τόπος τῆς καταπαύσεώς μου; **50** οὐχὶ ἡ χείρ μου ἐποίησεν ταῦτα πάντα; ¶ **51** Σκληροτράχηλοι καὶ ἀπερίτμητοι καρδίαις καὶ τοῖς ὠσίν, ὑμεῖς ἀεὶ τῷ πνεύματι τῷ ἁγίῳ ἀντιπίπτετε ὡς οἱ πατέρες ὑμῶν καὶ ὑμεῖς. **52** τίνα τῶν προφητῶν οὐκ ἐδίωξαν οἱ πατέρες ὑμῶν; καὶ ἀπέκτειναν τοὺς προκαταγγείλαντας περὶ τῆς ἐλεύσεως τοῦ δικαίου, οὗ νῦν ὑμεῖς προδόται καὶ φονεῖς ἐγένεσθε, **53** οἵτινες ἐλάβετε τὸν νόμον εἰς διαταγὰς ἀγγέλων καὶ οὐκ ἐφυλάξατε.

7:54 Ἀκούοντες δὲ ταῦτα διεπρίοντο ταῖς καρδίαις αὐτῶν καὶ ἔβρυχον τοὺς ὀδόντας ἐπ' αὐτόν. **55** ὑπάρχων δὲ πλήρης πνεύματος ἁγίου ἀτενίσας εἰς τὸν οὐρανὸν εἶδεν δόξαν θεοῦ καὶ Ἰησοῦν ἑστῶτα ἐκ δεξιῶν τοῦ θεοῦ **56** καὶ εἶπεν, Ἰδοὺ θεωρῶ τοὺς οὐρανοὺς διηνοιγμένους καὶ τὸν υἱὸν τοῦ ἀνθρώπου ἐκ δεξιῶν ἑστῶτα τοῦ θεοῦ. ¶ **57** κράξαντες δὲ φωνῇ μεγάλῃ συνέσχον τὰ ὦτα αὐτῶν καὶ ὥρμησαν ὁμοθυμαδὸν ἐπ' αὐτόν **58** καὶ ἐκβαλόντες ἔξω τῆς πόλεως ἐλιθοβόλουν. καὶ οἱ μάρτυρες ἀπέθεντο τὰ ἱμάτια αὐτῶν παρὰ τοὺς πόδας νεανίου καλουμένου Σαύλου, ¶ **59** καὶ ἐλιθοβόλουν τὸν Στέφανον ἐπικαλούμενον καὶ

60 Then he fell on his knees and cried out, "Lord, do not hold this sin against them."
δὲ θεὶς τὰ γόνατα ἔκραξεν φωνῇ μεγάλῃ κύριε μὴ στήσῃς ταύτην τὴν ἁμαρτίαν αὐτοῖς καὶ
cj pt.aa.nsm d.apn n.apn v.aai.3s n.dsf a.dsf n.vsm pl v.aas.2s r.asf d.asf n.asf r.dpm.3 cj
1254 5502 3836 1205 3189 5889 3489 3261 2705 3590 2705 4047 3836 281 899 2779

When he had said this, he fell asleep. **8:1** And Saul was there, giving approval to his death.
εἰπὼν τοῦτο ἐκοιμήθη δὲ Σαῦλος ἦν συνευδοκῶν αὐτοῦ ἀναιρέσει
pt.aa.nsm r.asn v.api.3s cj n.nsm v.iai.3s pt.pa.nsm r.gsm.3 d.dsf n.dsf
3306 4047 3121 1254 4930 1639 5306 358 899 3836 358

The Church Persecuted and Scattered

On that day a greatpersecutionbrokeout againstthe church at Jerusalem,and all
δὲ ἐν ἐκείνῃ τῇ ἡμέρᾳ μέγας διωγμὸς Ἐγένετο ἐπὶ τὴν ἐκκλησίαν τὴν ἐν Ἱεροσολύμοις δὲ πάντες
cj p.d r.dsf d.dsf n.dsf a.nsm n.nsm v.ami.3s p.a d.asf n.asf d.asf p.d n.dpn cj a.npm
1254 1877 1697 3836 2465 3489 1501 1181 2093 3836 1711 3836 1877 2642 1254 4246

except the apostles were scattered throughout Judea and Samaria. **2** Godly men buried
πλὴν τῶν ἀποστόλων διεσπάρησαν κατὰ τὰς χώρας τῆς Ἰουδαίας καὶ Σαμαρείας δὲ εὐλαβεῖς ἄνδρες συνεκόμισαν
p.g d.gpm n.gpm v.api.3p p.a d.apf n.apf d.gsf n.gsf cj n.gsf cj a.npm n.npm v.aai.3p
4440 3836 693 1401 2848 3836 6001 3836 2677 2779 4899 1254 2327 467 5172

Stephen and mourned deeply for him. **3** But Saul began to destroy the church. Going
τὸν Στέφανον καὶ ἐποίησαν κοπετὸν μέγαν ἐπ᾽ αὐτῷ δὲ Σαῦλος ἐλυμαίνετο τὴν ἐκκλησίαν εἰσπορευόμενος
d.asm n.asm cj v.aai.3p n.asm a.asm p.d r.dsm.3 cj n.nsm v.imi.3s d.asf n.asf pt.pm.nsm
3836 5108 2779 4472 3157 3489 2093 899 1254 4930 3381 3836 1711 1660

from house to house, he dragged off men and women and put them in prison.
κατὰ τοὺς οἴκους σύρων τε ἄνδρας καὶ γυναῖκας παρεδίδου εἰς φυλακήν
p.a d.apm n.apm pt.pa.nsm cj n.apm cj n.apf v.iai.3s p.a n.asf
2848 3836 3875 5359 5445 467 2779 1222 4140 1650 5871

Philip in Samaria

8:4 Those who had been scattered preached the word wherever they went. **5** Philip went
οὖν μὲν Οἱ διασπαρέντες εὐαγγελιζόμενοι τὸν λόγον διῆλθον δὲ Φίλιππος κατελθὼν
cj pl d.npm pt.ap.npm pt.pm.npm d.asm n.asm v.aai.3p cj n.nsm pt.aa.nsm
4036 3525 3836 1401 2294 3836 3364 1451 1254 5805 2982

down to a city in Samaria and proclaimed the Christ there. **6** When the crowds heard
εἰς τὴν πόλιν τῆς Σαμαρείας ἐκήρυσσεν αὐτοῖς τὸν Χριστόν δὲ ἐν αὐτοὺς τῷ ἀκούειν
p.a d.asf n.asf d.gsf n.gsf v.iai.3s r.dpm.3 d.asm n.asm cj p.d r.apm.3 d.dsn f.pa
1650 3836 4484 3836 4899 3062 899 3836 5986 1254 1877 899 3836 201

Philip and saw the miraculous signs he did, they all paid close attention to what
καὶ βλέπειν τὰ σημεῖα ἃ ἐποίει οἱ ὄχλοι ὁμοθυμαδὸν προσεῖχον τοῖς ὑπὸ
cj f.pa d.apn n.apn r.apn v.iai.3s d.npm n.npm adv v.iai.3p d.dpn p.g
2779 1063 3836 4956 4005 4472 3836 4063 3924 4668 3836 5679

he said. **7** With shrieks, evil spirits came out of many, and many
τοῦ Φιλίππου λεγομένοις γὰρ βοῶντα φωνῇ μεγάλῃ ἀκάθαρτα πνεύματα ἐξήρχοντο πολλοὶ τῶν ἐχόντων δὲ πολλοὶ
d.gsm n.gsm pt.pp.dpn cj pt.pa.apn n.dsf a.dsf a.apn n.apn v.imi.3p a.npm d.gpm pt.pa.gpm cj a.npm
3836 5805 3306 1142 1066 5889 3489 176 4460 2002 4498 3836 2400 1254 4498

paralytics and cripples were healed. **8** So there was great joy in that city.
παραλελυμένοι καὶ χωλοὶ ἐθεραπεύθησαν δὲ ἐγένετο πολλὴ χαρὰ ἐν ἐκείνῃ τῇ πόλει
pt.rp.npm cj a.npm v.api.3p cj v.ami.3s a.nsf n.nsf p.d r.dsf d.dsf n.dsf
4168 2779 6000 2543 1254 1181 4498 5915 1877 1697 3836 4484

Simon the Sorcerer

8:9 Now for some time a man named Simon had practiced sorcery in the city and amazed all the
δὲ προϋπῆρχεν τις Ἀνὴρ ὀνόματι Σίμων μαγεύων ἐν τῇ πόλει καὶ ἐξιστάνων τὸ
cj v.iai.3s r.nsm n.nsm n.dsn n.nsm pt.pa.nsm p.d d.dsf n.dsf cj pt.pa.nsm d.asn
1254 4732 5516 467 3950 4981 3405 1877 3836 4484 2779 2014 3836

people of Samaria. He boasted that he was someone great, **10** and all the people, both high and low,
ἔθνος τῆς Σαμαρείας λέγων ἑαυτὸν εἶναι τινα μέγαν πάντες ἀπὸ μεγάλου ἕως μικροῦ
n.asn d.gsf n.gsf pt.pa.nsm r.asm.3 f.pa r.asm a.asm a.npm p.g a.gsm p.g a.gsm
1620 3836 4899 3306 1571 1639 5516 3489 4246 608 3489 2401 3625

λέγοντα, Κύριε Ἰησοῦ, δέξαι τὸ πνεῦμά μου. ⁶⁰ θεὶς δὲ τὰ γόνατα ἔκραξεν φωνῇ μεγάλῃ, Κύριε, μὴ στήσῃς αὐτοῖς ταύτην τὴν ἁμαρτίαν. καὶ τοῦτο εἰπὼν ἐκοιμήθη. ⁸:¹ Σαῦλος δὲ ἦν συνευδοκῶν τῇ ἀναιρέσει αὐτοῦ.

Ἐγένετο δὲ ἐν ἐκείνῃ τῇ ἡμέρᾳ διωγμὸς μέγας ἐπὶ τὴν ἐκκλησίαν τὴν ἐν Ἱεροσολύμοις, πάντες δὲ διεσπάρησαν κατὰ τὰς χώρας τῆς Ἰουδαίας καὶ Σαμαρείας πλὴν τῶν ἀποστόλων. ² συνεκόμισαν δὲ τὸν Στέφανον ἄνδρες εὐλαβεῖς καὶ ἐποίησαν κοπετὸν μέγαν ἐπ᾽ αὐτῷ. ³ Σαῦλος δὲ ἐλυμαίνετο τὴν ἐκκλησίαν κατὰ τοὺς οἴκους εἰσπορευόμενος, σύρων τε ἄνδρας καὶ γυναῖκας παρεδίδου εἰς φυλακήν.

⁸:⁴ Οἱ μὲν οὖν διασπαρέντες διῆλθον εὐαγγελιζόμενοι τὸν λόγον. ⁵ Φίλιππος δὲ κατελθὼν εἰς [τὴν] πόλιν τῆς Σαμαρείας ἐκήρυσσεν αὐτοῖς τὸν Χριστόν. ⁶ προσεῖχον δὲ οἱ ὄχλοι τοῖς λεγομένοις ὑπὸ τοῦ Φιλίππου ὁμοθυμαδὸν ἐν τῷ ἀκούειν αὐτοὺς καὶ βλέπειν τὰ σημεῖα ἃ ἐποίει. ⁷ πολλοὶ γὰρ τῶν ἐχόντων πνεύματα ἀκάθαρτα βοῶντα φωνῇ μεγάλῃ ἐξήρχοντο, πολλοὶ δὲ παραλελυμένοι καὶ χωλοὶ ἐθεραπεύθησαν· ⁸ ἐγένετο δὲ πολλὴ χαρὰ ἐν τῇ πόλει ἐκείνῃ.

⁸:⁹ Ἀνὴρ δέ τις ὀνόματι Σίμων προϋπῆρχεν ἐν τῇ πόλει μαγεύων καὶ ἐξιστάνων τὸ ἔθνος τῆς Σαμαρείας, λέγων εἶναι τινα ἑαυτὸν μέγαν, ¹⁰ ᾧ προσεῖχον πάντες ἀπὸ μικροῦ ἕως μεγάλου λέγοντες, Οὗτός ἐστιν ἡ δύναμις τοῦ θεοῦ ἡ καλουμένη Μεγάλη.

gave him their attention and exclaimed, "This man is the divine power known as the Great Power."
→ ᾧ → προσεῖχον λέγοντες οὗτος ἐστιν ἡ ⌐τοῦ θεοῦ⌐ δύναμις ἡ καλουμένη ← μεγάλη
  r.dsm   v.iai.3p   pt.pa.npm r.nsm v.pai.3s d.nsf d.gsm n.gsm n.nsf   d.nsf pt.pp.nsf   a.nsf
4668 4005   4668   3306   4047   1639 3836 3836 2536 1539   3836 2813   3489

11 They followed him because he had amazed them for a long time with his magic. **12** But when they
δὲ → προσεῖχον αὐτῷ διὰ ⌐τὸ ἐξεστακέναι⌐ αὐτούς → ἱκανῷ χρόνῳ → ταῖς μαγείαις δὲ ὅτε →
cj   v.iai.3p   r.dsm.3 di   d.asn f.ra   r.apm.3   a.dsm n.dsm   d.dpf n.dpf   cj   cj
1254   4668   899 1328   3836 2014   899   2653 5989   3836 3404   1254 4021

believed Philip as he preached the good news of the kingdom of God and the name of Jesus
ἐπίστευσαν τῷ Φιλίππῳ → εὐαγγελιζομένῳ ← περὶ τῆς βασιλείας → ⌐τοῦ θεοῦ⌐ καὶ τοῦ ὀνόματος Ἰησοῦ
v.aai.3p d.dsm n.dsm   pt.pm.dsm   p.g d.gsf n.gsf   d.gsm n.gsm cj   d.gsn n.gsn   n.gsm
4409   3836 5805   2294   4309 3836 993   3836 2536 2779 3836 3950   2652

Christ, they were baptized, both men and women. **13** Simon himself believed and was baptized. And he
Χριστοῦ → → ἐβαπτίζοντο τε ἄνδρες καὶ γυναῖκες δὲ ὁ Σίμων καὶ αὐτὸς ἐπίστευσεν καὶ → βαπτισθεὶς
n.gsm   v.ipi.3p   cj n.npm cj n.npf   cj d.nsm n.nsm adv r.nsm v.aai.3s   cj   pt.ap.nsm
5986   966   5445 467   2779 1222   1254 3836 4981 2779 899 4409   2779   966

followed Philip everywhere, astonished by the great signs and miracles he saw. ¶
ἦν προσκαρτερῶν, τῷ Φιλίππῳ ⌐ τε ἐξίστατο γινομένας μεγάλας σημεῖα καὶ δυνάμεις → θεωρῶν
v.iai.3s pt.pa.nsm   d.dsm n.dsm   cj v.imi.3s pt.pm.apf a.apf   n.apn cj   n.apf   pt.pa.nsm
1639 4674   3836 5805   4674   5445 2014   1181   3489   4956 2779 1539   2555

14 When the apostles in Jerusalem heard that Samaria had accepted the word of God, they
δὲ → οἱ ἀπόστολοι ἐν Ἰεροσολύμοις Ἀκούσαντες ὅτι ἡ Σαμάρεια → δέδεκται τὸν λόγον → ⌐τοῦ θεοῦ⌐ →
cj   d.npm n.npm   p.d n.dpn   pt.aa.npm cj d.nsf n.nsf   v.rmi.3s d.asm n.asm   d.gsm n.gsm
1254   3836 693   1877 2642   201   4022 3836 4899   1312   3836 3364 3836 2536

sent Peter and John to them. **15** When they arrived, they prayed for them that they might receive
ἀπέστειλαν Πέτρον καὶ Ἰωάννην πρὸς αὐτοὺς → → καταβάντες οἵτινες προσηύξαντο περὶ αὐτῶν ὅπως → → λάβωσιν
v.aai.3p   n.asm cj n.asm   p.a r.apm.3   pt.aa.npm r.npm   v.ami.3p   p.g r.gpm.3 cj   v.aas.3p
690   4377 2779 2722   4639 899   2849   4015   4667   4309 899   3968   3284

the Holy Spirit, **16** because the Holy Spirit had not yet come upon any of them; they had simply
ἅγιον πνεῦμα γὰρ οὐδέπω ← ἦν ἐπιπεπτωκός, ἐπ᾽ οὐδενὶ → αὐτῶν δὲ → → μόνον
a.asn n.asn   cj   adv   v.iai.3s pt.ra.nsn   p.d a.dsm   r.gpm.3 cj   adv
41   4460   1142   4031   1639 2158   2093 4029   899   1254 5639 5639 3667

been baptized into the name of the Lord Jesus. **17** Then Peter and John placed their hands on them, and they
ὑπῆρχον βεβαπτισμένοι εἰς τὸ ὄνομα → τοῦ κυρίου Ἰησοῦ τότε ἐπετίθεσαν τὰς χεῖρας ἐπ᾽ αὐτοὺς καὶ →
v.iai.3p pt.rp.nprn   p.a d.asn n.asn   d.gsm n.gsm n.gsm adv   v.iai.3p d.apf n.apf p.a r.apm.3 cj
5639   966   1650 3836 3950   3836 3261 2652 5538   2202   3836 5931 2093 899   2779

received the Holy Spirit. ¶ **18** When Simon saw that the Spirit was given at the laying on of the
ἐλάμβανον πνεῦμα ἅγιον δὲ → ὁ Σίμων ἰδὼν ὅτι τὸ πνεῦμα → δίδοται διὰ τῆς ἐπιθέσεως ← → τῶν
v.iai.3p n.asn   a.asn   cj   d.nsm n.nsm pt.aa.nsm cj d.nsn n.nsn   v.ppi.3s p.g d.gsf n.gsf   d.gpm
3284   4460   41   1254 1625   3836 4981 1625   4022 3836 4460 1443   1328 3836 2120   3836

apostles' hands, he offered them money **19** and said, "Give me also this ability so that everyone on
ἀποστόλων ⌐τῶν χειρῶν⌐ → προσήνεγκεν αὐτοῖς χρήματα λέγων δότε κἀμοὶ ← ταύτην ⌐ἐξουσίαν⌐ ἵνα ← →
n.gpm   d.gpf n.gpf   v.aai.3s   r.dpm.3 n.apn   pt.pa.nsm v.aam.2p crasis   r.asf d.asf n.asf   cj
693   3836 5931   4712   899   5975   3306   1443 2743   4047 3836 2026   2671

whom I lay my hands may receive the Holy Spirit." ¶ **20** Peter answered: "May your
ᾧ ἐὰν ἐπιθῶ τὰς χεῖρας → λαμβάνῃ ἅγιον πνεῦμα δὲ Πέτρος εἶπεν πρὸς αὐτόν → σου
r.dsm pl   v.aas.1s d.apf n.apf   v.pas.3s a.asn n.asn   cj   n.nsm v.aai.3s   p.a r.asm.3   r.gs.2
4005 1569 2202   3836 5931   3284   41   4460   1254 4377 3306   4639 899   1639 5148

money perish with you, because you thought you could buy the gift of God with money!
⌐τὸ ἀργύριον⌐ εἴη εἰς ἀπώλειαν σὺν σοὶ ὅτι → ἐνόμισας → κτᾶσθαι τὴν δωρεὰν ⌐τοῦ θεοῦ⌐ διὰ χρημάτων
d.nsn n.nsn   v.pao.3s p.a n.asf   p.d r.ds.2 cj   v.aai.2s   f.pm   d.asf n.asf   d.gsm n.gsm p.g n.gpn
3836 736   1639   1650 724   5250 5148 4022   3787   3227   3836 1561   3836 2536 1328 5975

21 You have no part or share in this ministry, because your heart is not right before God. **22**
σοι ἐστιν οὐκ μερὶς οὐδὲ κλῆρος ἐν τούτῳ ⌐τῷ λόγῳ⌐ γὰρ σου ἡ καρδία ἐστιν οὐκ εὐθεῖα ἔναντι ⌐τοῦ θεοῦ⌐ οὖν
r.ds.2 v.pai.3s pl n.nsf cj   n.nsm p.d r.dsm d.dsm n.dsm   cj   r.gs.2 d.nsf n.nsf   v.pai.3s pl a.nsf   p.g   d.gsm n.gsm cj
5148 1639   4024 3535 4028 3102   1877 4047   3836 3364   1142   5148 3836 2840 1639   4024 2318   1882   3836 2536 4036

---

11 προσεῖχον δὲ αὐτῷ διὰ τὸ ἱκανῷ χρόνῳ ταῖς μαγείαις ἐξεστακέναι αὐτούς. 12 ὅτε δὲ ἐπίστευσαν τῷ Φιλίππῳ εὐαγγελιζομένῳ περὶ τῆς βασιλείας τοῦ θεοῦ καὶ τοῦ ὀνόματος Ἰησοῦ Χριστοῦ, ἐβαπτίζοντο ἄνδρες τε καὶ γυναῖκες. 13 ὁ δὲ Σίμων καὶ αὐτὸς ἐπίστευσεν καὶ βαπτισθεὶς ἦν προσκαρτερῶν τῷ Φιλίππῳ, θεωρῶν τε σημεῖα καὶ δυνάμεις μεγάλας γινομένας ἐξίστατο. ¶ 14 Ἀκούσαντες δὲ οἱ ἐν Ἰεροσολύμοις ἀπόστολοι ὅτι δέδεκται ἡ Σαμάρεια τὸν λόγον τοῦ θεοῦ, ἀπέστειλαν πρὸς αὐτοὺς Πέτρον καὶ Ἰωάννην, 15 οἵτινες καταβάντες προσηύξαντο περὶ αὐτῶν ὅπως λάβωσιν πνεῦμα ἅγιον· 16 οὐδέπω γὰρ ἦν ἐπ᾽ οὐδενὶ αὐτῶν ἐπιπεπτωκός, μόνον δὲ βεβαπτισμένοι ὑπῆρχον εἰς τὸ ὄνομα τοῦ κυρίου Ἰησοῦ. 17 τότε ἐπετίθεσαν τὰς χεῖρας ἐπ᾽ αὐτοὺς καὶ ἐλάμβανον πνεῦμα ἅγιον. ¶ 18 ἰδὼν δὲ ὁ Σίμων ὅτι διὰ τῆς ἐπιθέσεως τῶν χειρῶν τῶν ἀποστόλων δίδοται τὸ πνεῦμα, προσήνεγκεν αὐτοῖς χρήματα 19 λέγων, Δότε κἀμοὶ τὴν ἐξουσίαν ταύτην ἵνα ᾧ ἐὰν ἐπιθῶ τὰς χεῖρας λαμβάνῃ πνεῦμα ἅγιον ¶ 20 Πέτρος δὲ εἶπεν πρὸς αὐτόν, Τὸ ἀργύριόν σου σὺν σοὶ εἴη εἰς ἀπώλειαν ὅτι τὴν δωρεὰν τοῦ θεοῦ ἐνόμισας διὰ χρημάτων κτᾶσθαι. 21 οὐκ ἔστιν σοι μερὶς οὐδὲ κλῆρος ἐν τῷ λόγῳ τούτῳ, ἡ γὰρ καρδία σου οὐκ ἔστιν εὐθεῖα ἔναντι τοῦ θεοῦ.

Repent of this wickedness and pray to the Lord. Perhaps he will forgive you for having such a
μετανόησον ἀπὸ ταύτης τῆς κακίας σου καὶ δεήθητι ← τοῦ κυρίου εἰ ἄρα ἀφεθήσεται σοι ἡ
v.aam.2s p.g r.gsf d.gsf n.gsf r.gs.2 cj v.apm.2s d.gsm n.gsm cj cj v.fpi.3s r.ds.2 d.nsf
3566 608 4047 3836 2798 5148 2779 1289 3836 3261 1623 726 918 5148 3836

thought in your heart. 23 For I see that you are full of bitterness and captive to sin." ¶ 24 Then
ἐπίνοια → σου τῆς καρδίας γὰρ ὁρῶ σε ὄντα εἰς → χολὴν πικρίας καὶ σύνδεσμον ἀδικίας δὲ
n.nsf r.gs.2 d.gsf n.gsf cj v.pai.1s r.as.2 pt.pa.asm p.a n.asf n.gsf cj n.asm n.gsf cj
2154 2840 5148 3836 2840 1142 3972 5148 1639 1650 5958 4394 2779 5278 94 1254

Simon answered, "Pray to the Lord for me so that nothing you have said may happen
ὁ Σίμων ἀποκριθεὶς εἶπεν ὑμεῖς δεήθητε πρὸς τὸν κύριον ὑπὲρ ἐμοῦ ὅπως ← μηδὲν ὧν → → εἰρήκατε ἐπέλθῃ
d.nsm n.nsm pt.ap.nsm v.aai.3s r.np.2 v.apm.2p p.a d.asm n.asm p.g r.gs.1 3968 a.nsn r.gpn v.rai.2p v.aas.3s
3836 4981 646 3306 7007 1289 4639 3836 3261 5642 1609 3594 4005 3306 2088

to me." ¶ 25 When they had testified and proclaimed the word of the Lord, Peter and John
ἐπ᾽ ἐμὲ οὖν μὲν → → διαμαρτυράμενοι καὶ λαλήσαντες τὸν λόγον → τοῦ κυρίου Οἱ ← ←
p.a r.as.1 cj pl pt.am.npm cj pt.aa.npm d.asm n.asm d.gsm n.gsm d.npm
2093 1609 4036 3525 1371 2779 3364 3836 3261 3836 3836

returned to Jerusalem, preaching the gospel in many Samaritan villages.
ὑπέστρεφον εἰς Ἱεροσόλυμα τε εὐηγγελίζοντο ← ← πολλάς τῶν Σαμαριτῶν κώμας
v.iai.3p p.a n.apn cj v.imi.3p a.apf d.gpm n.gpm n.apf
5715 1650 2642 5445 2294 4498 3836 4901 3267

Philip and the Ethiopian

8:26 Now an angel of the Lord said to Philip, "Go south to the road –
δὲ Ἄγγελος → κυρίου ἐλάλησεν πρὸς Φίλιππον λέγων ἀνάστηθι καὶ πορεύου κατὰ μεσημβρίαν ἐπὶ τὴν ὁδὸν
cj n.nsm n.gsm v.aai.3s p.a n.asm pt.pa.nsm v.aam.2s cj v.pmm.2s p.a n.asf p.a d.asf n.asf
1254 34 3261 3281 4639 5805 3306 482 2779 4513 2848 3540 2093 3836 3847

the desert road – that goes down from Jerusalem to Gaza." 27 So he started out, and on
αὕτη ἐστὶν ἔρημος τὴν καταβαίνουσαν ← ἀπὸ Ἱερουσαλὴμ εἰς Γάζαν καὶ ἀναστὰς → ἐπορεύθη ← καὶ
r.nsf v.pai.3s a.nsf d.asf pt.pa.asf p.g n.gsf p.a n.asf cj pt.aa.nsm v.api.3s cj
4047 1639 2245 3836 2849 608 2647 1650 1124 2779 482 4513 2779

his way he met an Ethiopian eunuch, an important official in charge of all the treasury
ἰδοὺ ἀνὴρ Αἰθίοψ εὐνοῦχος δυνάστης ὃς ἦν ἐπὶ πάσης τῆς γάζης αὐτῆς
j n.nsm n.nsm n.nsm n.nsm r.nsm v.iai.3s p.g a.gsf d.gsf n.gsf r.gsf.3
2627 467 134 2336 1541 4005 1639 2093 4246 3836 1125 899

of Candace, queen of the Ethiopians. This man had gone to Jerusalem to worship, 28 and on his way
→ Κανδάκης βασιλίσσης → Αἰθιόπων ὃς ← → ἐληλύθει εἰς Ἱερουσαλὴμ → προσκυνήσων τε →
n.gsf n.gsf n.gpm r.nsm v.lai.3s p.a n.asf pt.fa.nsm cj
2833 999 134 4005 2262 1650 2647 4686 5445

home was sitting in his chariot reading the book of Isaiah the prophet. 29 The Spirit
ἦν ὑποστρέφων καὶ → καθήμενος ἐπὶ αὐτοῦ τοῦ ἅρματος καὶ ἀνεγίνωσκεν Ἡσαΐαν τὸν προφήτην δὲ τὸ πνεῦμα
v.iai.3s pt.pa.nsm cj pt.pm.nsm p.g r.gsm.3 d.gsn n.gsn cj v.iai.3s n.asm d.asm n.asm cj d.nsn n.nsn
1639 5715 2779 2764 2093 899 3836 761 2779 336 2480 3836 4737 1254 3836 4460

told Philip, "Go to that chariot and stay near it." ¶ 30 Then Philip ran up to the
εἶπεν τῷ Φιλίππῳ πρόσελθε τούτῳ τῷ ἅρματι καὶ → κολλήθητι δὲ ὁ Φίλιππος προσδραμὼν ←
v.aai.3s d.dsm n.dsm v.aam.2s r.dsn d.dsn n.dsn cj v.apm.2s cj d.nsm n.nsm pt.aa.nsm
3306 3836 5805 4665 4047 3836 761 2779 3140 1254 3836 5805 4708

chariot and heard the man reading Isaiah the prophet. "Do you understand what you are
ἤκουσεν αὐτοῦ ἀναγινώσκοντος Ἡσαΐαν τὸν προφήτην καὶ ἆρα γε → γινώσκεις ἃ →
v.aai.3s r.gsm.3 pt.pa.gsm n.asm d.asm n.asm cj pl pl v.pai.2s r.apn
201 899 336 2480 3836 4737 2779 727 1145 1182 4005

reading?" Philip asked. ¶ 31 "How can I," he said, "unless someone explains it to me?" So he
ἀναγινώσκεις εἶπεν δὲ γὰρ πῶς ἂν δυναίμην ὁ εἶπεν ἐὰν μή τις ὁδηγήσει ← με τε →
v.pai.2s v.aai.3s cj cj pl pl v.ppo.1s d.nsm v.aai.3s cj pl r.nsm v.fai.3s r.as.1 cj
336 3306 1254 1142 4802 323 1538 3836 3306 1569 3590 5516 3842 1609 5445

invited Philip to come up and sit with him. ¶ 32 The eunuch was reading this
παρεκάλεσεν τὸν Φίλιππον → ἀναβάντα ← καθίσαι σὺν αὐτῷ δὲ ἦν ἣν ἀνεγίνωσκεν αὕτη ἡ
v.aai.3s d.asm n.asm pt.aa.asm f.aa p.d r.dsm.3 cj r.asf r.asf v.iai.3s r.nsf d.nsf
4151 3836 5805 326 2767 5250 899 1254 4005 4005 336 4047 3836

22 μετανόησον οὖν ἀπὸ τῆς κακίας σου ταύτης καὶ δεήθητι τοῦ κυρίου, εἰ ἄρα ἀφεθήσεταί σοι ἡ ἐπίνοια τῆς καρδίας σου. 23 εἰς
γὰρ χολὴν πικρίας καὶ σύνδεσμον ἀδικίας ὁρῶ σε ὄντα. ¶ 24 ἀποκριθεὶς δὲ ὁ Σίμων εἶπεν, Δεήθητε ὑμεῖς ὑπὲρ ἐμοῦ πρὸς τὸν
κύριον ὅπως μηδὲν ἐπέλθῃ ἐπ᾽ ἐμὲ ὧν εἰρήκατε. ¶ 25 Οἱ μὲν οὖν διαμαρτυράμενοι καὶ λαλήσαντες τὸν λόγον τοῦ κυρίου
ὑπέστρεφον εἰς Ἱεροσόλυμα, πολλάς τε κώμας τῶν Σαμαριτῶν εὐηγγελίζοντο.
8:26 Ἄγγελος δὲ κυρίου ἐλάλησεν πρὸς Φίλιππον λέγων, Ἀνάστηθι καὶ πορεύου κατὰ μεσημβρίαν ἐπὶ τὴν ὁδὸν τὴν
καταβαίνουσαν ἀπὸ Ἱερουσαλὴμ εἰς Γάζαν, αὕτη ἐστὶν ἔρημος. 27 καὶ ἀναστὰς ἐπορεύθη. καὶ ἰδοὺ ἀνὴρ Αἰθίοψ εὐνοῦχος
δυνάστης Κανδάκης βασιλίσσης Αἰθιόπων, ὃς ἦν ἐπὶ πάσης τῆς γάζης αὐτῆς, ὃς ἐληλύθει προσκυνήσων εἰς Ἱερουσαλήμ, 28 ἦν
τε ὑποστρέφων καὶ καθήμενος ἐπὶ τοῦ ἅρματος αὐτοῦ καὶ ἀνεγίνωσκεν τὸν προφήτην Ἡσαΐαν. 29 εἶπεν δὲ τὸ πνεῦμα τῷ Φιλίππῳ,
Πρόσελθε καὶ κολλήθητι τῷ ἅρματι τούτῳ. ¶ 30 προσδραμὼν δὲ ὁ Φίλιππος ἤκουσεν αὐτοῦ ἀναγινώσκοντος Ἡσαΐαν τὸν
προφήτην καὶ εἶπεν, Ἆρά γε γινώσκεις ἃ ἀναγινώσκεις; ¶ 31 ὁ δὲ εἶπεν, Πῶς γὰρ ἂν δυναίμην ἐὰν μή τις ὁδηγήσει με;
παρεκάλεσέν τε τὸν Φίλιππον ἀναβάντα καθίσαι σὺν αὐτῷ. ¶ 32 ἡ δὲ περιοχὴ τῆς γραφῆς ἣν ἀνεγίνωσκεν ἦν αὕτη· Ὡς πρόβατον

passage of Scripture: "He was led like a sheep to the slaughter, and as a lamb before the shearer is
περιοχή → ⌐τῆς γραφῆς⌐ → → ἤχθη ὡς πρόβατον ἐπὶ σφαγὴν καὶ ὡς ἀμνὸς ἐναντίον τοῦ κείραντος αὐτὸν
n.nsf　d.gsf n.gsf　　　v.api.3s pl　n.nsm　p.a　n.asf　cj ὡς n.nsm p.g d.gsm pt.aa.gsm r.asm.3
4343　3836 1210　　72 6055 4585 2093 5375 2779 6055 303 1883 3025 899

silent, so he did not open his mouth. **33** In his humiliation he was deprived of justice. Who can
ἄφωνος οὕτως → → οὐκ ἀνοίγει αὐτοῦ ⌐τὸ στόμα⌐ Ἐν αὐτῷ ⌐τῇ ταπεινώσει⌐ → ἤρθη ← ⌐ἡ κρίσις⌐ αὐτοῦ τίς
a.nsm adv　　pl v.pai.3s r.gsm.3 d.asn n.asn　p.d r.gsm.3 d.dsf n.dsf　v.api.3s　d.nsf n.nsf r.gsm.3 r.nsm
936 4048　487 487 4024 487 899 3836 5125　1877 899 3836 5428　149　3836 3213 899 5515

speak of his descendants? For his life was taken from the earth." ¶ **34** The eunuch asked
διηγήσεται ← αὐτοῦ ⌐τὴν γενεάν⌐ ὅτι αὐτοῦ ⌐ἡ ζωὴ⌐ → αἴρεται ἀπὸ τῆς γῆς δὲ ὁ εὐνοῦχος ἀποκριθεὶς
v.fmi.3s　r.gsm.3 d.asf n.asf cj r.gsm.3 d.nsf n.nsf　v.ppi.3s p.g d.gsf n.gsf　cj d.nsm n.nsm pt.ap.nsm
1455　899 3836 1155 4022 899 3836 2437　149 608 3836 1178　1254 3836 2336 646

Philip, "Tell me, please, who is the prophet talking about, himself or someone else?"
εἶπεν ⌐τῷ Φιλίππῳ⌐ δέομαί σου τίνος → ὁ προφήτης τοῦτο λέγει ← περὶ ἑαυτοῦ ἢ περὶ τίνος ἑτέρου
v.aai.3s d.dsm n.dsm v.pmi.1s r.gs.2 r.gsm　d.nsm n.nsm r.asn v.pai.3s　p.g r.gsm.3 cj p.g r.gsm r.gsm
3306 3836 5805 1289 5148 5515　3836 4737 4047 3306　4309 1571 2445 4309 5516 2283

35 Then Philip began with that very passage of Scripture and told him
δὲ ⌐ὁ Φίλιππος⌐ ἀνοίξας τὸ στόμα αὐτοῦ καὶ ἀρξάμενος ἀπὸ ταύτης → → ⌐τῆς γραφῆς⌐ εὐηγγελίσατο αὐτῷ
cj d.nsm n.nsm pt.aa.nsm d.asn n.asn r.gsm.3 cj pt.am.nsm p.g r.gsf　d.gsf n.gsf v.ami.3s r.dsm.3
1254 3836 5805 487 3836 5125 899 2779 806 608 4047　3836 1210 2294 899

the good news about Jesus. ¶ **36** As they traveled along the road, they came to some water and the
← ← ⌐τὸν Ἰησοῦν⌐ δὲ ὡς → ἐπορεύοντο κατὰ τὴν ὁδόν → ἦλθον ἐπί τι ὕδωρ καὶ ὁ
d.asm n.asm cj ὡς v.imi.3p p.a d.asf n.asf v.aai.3p p.a r.asn n.asn cj d.nsm
2294 2294 2294 3836 2652 1254 6055 4513 2848 3836 3847 2262 2093 5516 5623 2779 3836

eunuch said, "Look, here is water. Why shouldn't I be baptized?" **38** And he gave orders to stop the chariot.
εὐνοῦχος φησιν ἰδοὺ ὕδωρ τί κωλύει με βαπτισθῆναι καὶ ἐκέλευσεν ← στῆναι τὸ ἅρμα
n.nsm v.pai.3s j n.nsn r.nsn v.pai.3s r.as.1 f.ap cj v.aai.3s f.aa d.asn n.asn
2336 5774 2627 5623 5515 3266 1609 966 2779 3027 2705 3836 761

Then both Philip and the eunuch went down into the water and Philip baptized him. **39** When
καὶ ἀμφότεροι ὅ τε Φίλιππος καὶ ὁ εὐνοῦχος κατέβησαν ← εἰς τὸ ὕδωρ καὶ ἐβάπτισεν αὐτόν δὲ ὅτε
cj a.nmm d.nsm cj n.nsm cj d.nsm n.nsm v.aai.3p p.a d.asn n.asn cj v.aai.3s r.asm.3 cj cj
2779 317 3836 5445 5805 2779 3836 2336 2849 1650 3836 5623 2779 966 899 1254 4021

they came up out of the water, the Spirit of the Lord suddenly took Philip away, and the eunuch did
→ ἀνέβησαν ← ἐκ ← τοῦ ὕδατος πνεῦμα κυρίου → ἥρπασεν ⌐τὸν Φίλιππον⌐ καὶ ὁ εὐνοῦχος →
v.aai.3p p.g d.gsn n.gsn n.nsn n.gsm v.aai.3s d.asm n.asm cj d.nsm n.nsm
326 1666 3836 5623 4460 3261 773 3836 5805 773 2779 3836 2336 1625

not see him again, but went on his way rejoicing. **40** Philip, however, appeared at Azotus and traveled
οὐκ εἶδεν αὐτὸν οὐκέτι γὰρ ἐπορεύετο ← αὐτοῦ ⌐τὴν ὁδόν⌐ χαίρων Φίλιππος δὲ εὑρέθη εἰς Ἄζωτον καὶ διερχόμενος
pl v.aai.3s r.asm.3 adv cj v.imi.3s r.gsm.3 d.asf n.asf pt.pa.nsm n.nsm cj v.api.3s p.a n.asf cj pt.pm.nsm
4024 1625 899 4033 1142 4513 899 3836 3847 5897 5805 1254 2351 1650 111 2779 1451

about, preaching the gospel in all the towns until he reached Caesarea.
← εὐηγγελίζετο ← πάσας τὰς πόλεις ἕως αὐτὸν ⌐τοῦ ἐλθεῖν⌐ εἰς Καισάρειαν
v.imi.3s a.apf d.apf n.apf p.g r.asm.3 d.gsn f.aa p.a n.asf
2294 4246 3836 4484 2401 899 3836 2262 1650 2791

Saul's Conversion

9:1 Meanwhile, Saul was still breathing out murderous threats against the Lord's disciples. He
δὲ ⌐Ὁ Σαῦλος⌐ ἔτι ἐμπνέων φόνου καὶ ἀπειλῆς εἰς τοὺς ⌐τοῦ κυρίου⌐ μαθητὰς →
cj d.nsm n.nsm adv pt.pa.nsm n.gsm cj n.gsf p.a d.apm d.gsm n.gsm n.apm
1254 3836 4930 1863 2285 5840 2779 581 1650 3836 3836 3261 3412

went to the high priest **2** and asked him for letters to the synagogues in Damascus, so that if he
προσελθὼν τῷ → ἀρχιερεῖ ἠτήσατο παρ' αὐτοῦ ἐπιστολὰς πρὸς τὰς συναγωγάς εἰς Δαμασκὸν ὅπως ← ἐάν →
pt.aa.nsm d.dsm n.dsm v.ami.3s p.g r.gsm.3 n.apf p.a d.apf n.apf p.a n.asf cj cj
4665 3836 797 160 4123 899 2186 4639 3836 5252 1650 1242 3968 1569

found any there who belonged to the Way, whether men or women, he might take them as prisoners to
εὕρη τινας → ὄντας ← τῆς ὁδοῦ τε ἄνδρας καὶ γυναῖκας → ἀγάγῃ → → δεδεμένους εἰς
v.aas.3s r.apm pt.pa.apm d.gsf n.gsf cj n.apm cj n.apf v.aas.3s pt.rp.apm p.a
2351 5516 1639 3836 3847 5445 467 2779 1222 72 1313 1650

ἐπὶ σφαγὴν ἤχθη καὶ ὡς ἀμνὸς ἐναντίον τοῦ κείραντος αὐτὸν ἄφωνος, οὕτως οὐκ ἀνοίγει τὸ στόμα αὐτοῦ. **33** Ἐν τῇ ταπεινώσει [αὐτοῦ] ἡ κρίσις αὐτοῦ ἤρθη· τὴν γενεὰν αὐτοῦ τίς διηγήσεται; ὅτι αἴρεται ἀπὸ τῆς γῆς ἡ ζωὴ αὐτοῦ. ¶ **34** Ἀποκριθεὶς δὲ ὁ εὐνοῦχος τῷ Φιλίππῳ εἶπεν, Δέομαί σου, περὶ τίνος ὁ προφήτης λέγει τοῦτο; περὶ ἑαυτοῦ ἢ περὶ ἑτέρου τινός; **35** ἀνοίξας δὲ ὁ Φίλιππος τὸ στόμα αὐτοῦ καὶ ἀρξάμενος ἀπὸ τῆς γραφῆς ταύτης εὐηγγελίσατο αὐτῷ τὸν Ἰησοῦν. ¶ **36** ὡς δὲ ἐπορεύοντο κατὰ τὴν ὁδόν, ἦλθον ἐπί τι ὕδωρ, καί φησιν ὁ εὐνοῦχος, Ἰδοὺ ὕδωρ, τί κωλύει με βαπτισθῆναι; **38** καὶ ἐκέλευσεν στῆναι τὸ ἅρμα καὶ κατέβησαν ἀμφότεροι εἰς τὸ ὕδωρ, ὅ τε Φίλιππος καὶ ὁ εὐνοῦχος, καὶ ἐβάπτισεν αὐτόν. **39** ὅτε δὲ ἀνέβησαν ἐκ τοῦ ὕδατος, πνεῦμα κυρίου ἥρπασεν τὸν Φίλιππον καὶ οὐκ εἶδεν αὐτὸν οὐκέτι ὁ εὐνοῦχος, ἐπορεύετο γὰρ τὴν ὁδὸν αὐτοῦ χαίρων. **40** Φίλιππος δὲ εὑρέθη εἰς Ἄζωτον· καὶ διερχόμενος εὐηγγελίζετο τὰς πόλεις πάσας ἕως τοῦ ἐλθεῖν αὐτὸν εἰς Καισάρειαν.

9:1 Ὁ δὲ Σαῦλος ἔτι ἐμπνέων ἀπειλῆς καὶ φόνου εἰς τοὺς μαθητὰς τοῦ κυρίου, προσελθὼν τῷ ἀρχιερεῖ **2** ἠτήσατο παρ' αὐτοῦ ἐπιστολὰς εἰς Δαμασκὸν πρὸς τὰς συναγωγάς, ὅπως ἐάν τινας εὕρη τῆς ὁδοῦ ὄντας, ἄνδρας τε καὶ γυναῖκας, δεδεμένους

Jerusalem. **3** As he neared Damascus on his journey, suddenly a light from heaven flashed
Ἰερουσαλήμ δὲ αὐτὸν ἐγγίζειν ⌐τῇ Δαμασκῷ Ἐν τῷ πορεύεσθαι ἐγένετο ἐξαίφνης τε φῶς ἐκ ⌐τοῦ οὐρανοῦ περιήστραψεν
n.asf | cj | r.asm.3 | f.pa | d.dsf | d.dsf | p.d | d.dsn | f.pm | v.ami.3s | adv | cj | n.nsn | p.g | d.gsm | n.gsm | v.aai.3s
2647 | 1254 | 899 | 1581 | 3836 | 1242 | 1877 | 3836 | 4513 | 1181 | 1978 | 5445 | 5890 | 1666 | 3836 | 4041 | 4313

around him. **4** He fell to the ground and heard a voice say to him, "Saul, Saul, why do you persecute
← αὐτὸν καὶ πεσὼν ἐπὶ τὴν γῆν ἤκουσεν φωνὴν λέγουσαν → αὐτῷ Σαοὺλ Σαοὺλ τί → → διώκεις
r.asm.3 | cj | pt.aa.nsm | p.a | d.asf | n.asf | v.aai.3s | n.asf | pt.pa.asf | r.dsm.3 | n.vsm | n.vsm | r.asn | v.pai.2s
899 | 2779 | 4406 | 2093 | 3836 | 1178 | 201 | 5889 | 3306 | 899 | 4910 | 4910 | 5515 | 1503

me?" ¶ **5** "Who are you, Lord?" Saul asked. ¶ "I am Jesus, whom you are persecuting," he
με δέ τίς εἶ ← κύριε εἶπεν δέ ἐγώ εἰμι Ἰησοῦς ὃν σὺ → διώκεις ὁ
r.as.1 | cj | r.nsm | v.pai.2s | n.vsm | v.aai.3s | cj | r.ns.1 | v.pai.1s | n.nsm | r.asm | r.ns.2 | v.pai.2s | d.nsm
1609 | 1254 | 5515 | 1639 | 3261 | 3306 | 1254 | 1609 | 1639 | 2652 | 4005 | 5148 | 1503 | 3836

replied. **6** "Now get up and go into the city, and you will be told what you must do." ¶ **7**
ἀλλὰ ἀνάστηθι ← καὶ εἴσελθε εἰς τὴν πόλιν καὶ σοι → → λαληθήσεται ὅ τί σε δεῖ ποιεῖν δέ
cj | v.aam.2s | cj | v.aam.2s | p.a | d.asf | n.asf | cj | r.ds.2 | v.fpi.3s | r.asn | r.asn | r.as.2 | v.pai.3s | f.pa | cj
247 | 482 | 2779 | 1656 | 1650 | 3836 | 4484 | 2779 | 5148 | 3281 | 4005 | 5515 | 5148 | 1256 | 4472 | 1254

The men traveling with Saul stood there speechless; they heard the sound but did not
οἱ ἄνδρες ⌐οἱ συνοδεύοντες ← αὐτῷ εἱστήκεισαν ἐνεοί μὲν → ἀκούοντες τῆς φωνῆς δέ → μηδένα
d.npm | n.npm | d.npm | pt.pa.npm | r.dsm.3 | v.lai.3p | a.npm | pl | pt.pa.npm | d.gsf | n.gsf | cj | a.asm
3836 | 467 | 3836 | 5321 | 899 | 2705 | 1917 | 3525 | 201 | 3836 | 5889 | 1254 | 3594

see anyone. **8** Saul got up from the ground, but when he opened his eyes he could see
θεωροῦντες ← δέ Σαῦλος ἠγέρθη ← ἀπὸ τῆς γῆς δέ → ἀνεῳγμένων αὐτοῦ ⌐τῶν ὀφθαλμῶν⌐ → → ἔβλεπεν
pt.pa.npm | cj | n.nsm | v.api.3s | p.g | d.gsf | n.gsf | cj | pt.rp.gpm | r.gsm.3 | d.gpm | n.gpm | v.iai.3s
2555 | 3594 | 1254 | 4930 | 1586 | 608 | 3836 | 1178 | 1254 | 487 | 899 | 3836 | 4057 | 1063

nothing. So they led him by the hand into Damascus. **9** For three days he was blind, and did
οὐδέν δέ → εἰσήγαγον αὐτὸν → → χειραγωγοῦντες εἰς Δαμασκόν καὶ → τρεῖς ἡμέρας → ἦν μὴ βλέπων καὶ →
a.asn | cj | v.aai.3p | r.asm.3 | pt.pa.npm | p.a | n.asf | cj | a.apf | n.apf | v.iai.3s | pl | pt.pa.nsm | cj
4029 | 1254 | 1652 | 899 | 5932 | 1650 | 1242 | 2779 | 5552 | 2465 | 1639 | 3590 | 1063 | 2779 | 2266

not eat or drink anything. ¶ **10** In Damascus there was a disciple named Ananias. The Lord called
οὐκ ἔφαγεν οὐδὲ ἔπιεν δέ ἐν Δαμασκῷ → Ἦν τις μαθητὴς ὀνόματι Ἁνανίας καὶ ὁ κύριος εἶπεν
pl | v.aai.3s | cj | v.aai.3s | cj | p.d | n.dsf | v.iai.3s | r.nsm | n.nsm | n.dsn | n.nsm | cj | d.nsm | n.nsm | v.aai.3s
4024 | 2266 | 4028 | 4403 | 1254 | 1877 | 1242 | 1639 | 5516 | 3412 | 3950 | 393 | 2779 | 3836 | 3261 | 3306

to him in a vision, "Ananias!" "Yes, Lord," he answered. ¶ **11** The Lord told him,
πρὸς αὐτὸν ἐν ὁράματι Ἁνανία δέ ἰδοὺ ἐγώ κύριε ὁ εἶπεν δέ ὁ κύριος πρὸς αὐτὸν ἀναστὰς
p.a | r.asm.3 | p.d | n.dsn | n.vsm | cj | j | r.ns.1 | n.vsm | d.nsm | v.aai.3s | cj | d.nsm | n.nsm | p.a | r.asm.3 | pt.aa.nsm
4639 | 899 | 1877 | 3969 | 393 | 1254 | 2627 | 1609 | 3261 | 3836 | 3306 | 1254 | 3836 | 3261 | 4639 | 899 | 482

"Go to the house of Judas on Straight Street and ask for a man from Tarsus named Saul,
πορεύθητι ἐν οἰκίᾳ → Ἰούδα ἐπὶ τὴν καλουμένην⌐ Εὐθεῖαν ⌐τὴν ῥύμην⌐ καὶ ζήτησον ← Ταρσέα ὀνόματι Σαῦλον
v.apm.2s | p.d | n.dsf | n.gsm | p.a | d.asf | pt.pp.asf | a.asf | d.asf | n.asf | cj | v.aam.2s | n.asm | n.dsn | n.asm
4513 | 1877 | 3864 | 2683 | 2093 | 3836 | 2813 | 2318 | 3836 | 4860 | 2779 | 2426 | 5432 | 3950 | 4930

for he is praying. **12** In a vision he has seen a man named Ananias come and place his hands on
γὰρ ἰδοὺ → προσεύχεται καὶ ἐν ὁράματι → → εἶδεν ἄνδρα ὀνόματι Ἁνανίαν εἰσελθόντα καὶ ἐπιθέντα τὰς χεῖρας →
cj | j | v.pmi.3s | cj | p.d | n.dsn | v.aai.3s | n.asm | n.dsn | n.asm | pt.aa.asm | cj | pt.aa.asm | d.apf | n.apf
1142 | 2627 | 4667 | 2779 | 1877 | 3969 | 1625 | 467 | 3950 | 393 | 1656 | 2779 | 2202 | 3836 | 5931

him to restore his sight." ¶ **13** "Lord," Ananias answered, "I have heard many reports about this
αὐτῷ ὅπως ἀναβλέψῃ ← δέ κύριε Ἁνανίας ἀπεκρίθη → ἤκουσα ἀπὸ πολλῶν περὶ τούτου
r.dsm.3 | cj | v.aas.3s | cj | n.vsm | n.nsm | v.api.3s | v.aai.1s | p.g | a.gpm | p.g | r.gsm
899 | 3968 | 329 | 1254 | 3261 | 393 | 646 | 201 | 608 | 4498 | 4309 | 4047

man and all the harm he has done to your saints in Jerusalem. **14** And he has come here with authority
⌐τοῦ ἀνδρὸς⌐ ὅσα κακὰ → ἐποίησεν σου ⌐τοῖς ἁγίοις⌐ ἐν Ἰερουσαλήμ καὶ → → ἔχει ὧδε ἐξουσίαν
d.gsm | n.gsm | r.apn | a.apn | v.aai.3s | r.gs.2 | d.dpm | a.dpm | p.d | n.dsf | cj | v.pai.3s | adv | n.asf
3836 | 467 | 4012 | 2805 | 4472 | 41 | 5148 | 3836 | 41 | 1877 | 2647 | 2779 | 2400 | 6045 | 2026

from the chief priests to arrest all who call on your name." ¶ **15** But the Lord said to
παρὰ τῶν → ἀρχιερέων → δῆσαι πάντας τοὺς ἐπικαλουμένους ← σου ⌐τὸ ὄνομα⌐ δέ ὁ κύριος εἶπεν πρὸς
p.g | d.gpm | n.gpm | f.aa | a.apm | d.apm | pt.pm.apm | r.gs.2 | d.asn | n.asn | cj | d.nsm | n.nsm | v.aai.3s | p.a
4123 | 3836 | 797 | 1313 | 4246 | 3836 | 2126 | 5148 | 3836 | 3950 | 1254 | 3836 | 3261 | 3306 | 4639

ἀγάγῃ εἰς Ἰερουσαλήμ. **3** ἐν δὲ τῷ πορεύεσθαι ἐγένετο αὐτὸν ἐγγίζειν τῇ Δαμασκῷ, ἐξαίφνης τε αὐτὸν περιήστραψεν φῶς ἐκ τοῦ οὐρανοῦ **4** καὶ πεσὼν ἐπὶ τὴν γῆν ἤκουσεν φωνὴν λέγουσαν αὐτῷ, Σαοὺλ Σαούλ, τί με διώκεις; ¶ **5** εἶπεν δέ, Τίς εἶ, κύριε; ¶ ὁ δέ, Ἐγώ εἰμι Ἰησοῦς ὃν σὺ διώκεις· **6** ἀλλὰ ἀνάστηθι καὶ εἴσελθε εἰς τὴν πόλιν καὶ λαληθήσεταί σοι ὅ τί σε δεῖ ποιεῖν. ¶ **7** οἱ δὲ ἄνδρες οἱ συνοδεύοντες αὐτῷ εἱστήκεισαν ἐνεοί, ἀκούοντες μὲν τῆς φωνῆς μηδένα δὲ θεωροῦντες. **8** ἠγέρθη δὲ Σαῦλος ἀπὸ τῆς γῆς, ἀνεῳγμένων δὲ τῶν ὀφθαλμῶν αὐτοῦ οὐδὲν ἔβλεπεν· χειραγωγοῦντες δὲ αὐτὸν εἰσήγαγον εἰς Δαμασκόν. **9** καὶ ἦν ἡμέρας τρεῖς μὴ βλέπων καὶ οὐκ ἔφαγεν οὐδὲ ἔπιεν. ¶ **10** Ἦν δέ τις μαθητὴς ἐν Δαμασκῷ ὀνόματι Ἁνανίας, καὶ εἶπεν πρὸς αὐτὸν ἐν ὁράματι ὁ κύριος, Ἁνανία. ὁ δὲ εἶπεν, Ἰδοὺ ἐγώ, κύριε. ¶ **11** ὁ δὲ κύριος πρὸς αὐτόν, Ἀναστὰς πορεύθητι ἐπὶ τὴν ῥύμην τὴν καλουμένην Εὐθεῖαν καὶ ζήτησον ἐν οἰκίᾳ Ἰούδα Σαῦλον ὀνόματι Ταρσέα· ἰδοὺ γὰρ προσεύχεται **12** καὶ εἶδεν ἄνδρα [ἐν ὁράματι] Ἁνανίαν ὀνόματι εἰσελθόντα καὶ ἐπιθέντα αὐτῷ [τὰς] χεῖρας ὅπως ἀναβλέψῃ. ¶ **13** ἀπεκρίθη δὲ Ἁνανίας, Κύριε, ἤκουσα ἀπὸ πολλῶν περὶ τοῦ ἀνδρὸς τούτου ὅσα κακὰ τοῖς ἁγίοις σου ἐποίησεν ἐν Ἰερουσαλήμ· **14** καὶ ὧδε ἔχει ἐξουσίαν παρὰ τῶν ἀρχιερέων δῆσαι πάντας τοὺς ἐπικαλουμένους τὸ ὄνομά σου. ¶ **15** εἶπεν δὲ πρὸς αὐτὸν ὁ κύριος, Πορεύου, ὅτι σκεῦος ἐκλογῆς ἐστίν μοι

Ananias, "Go!   This man is   my chosen instrument to carry   my name   before   the Gentiles and
αὐτὸν   πορεύου ὅτι   οὗτος ←   ἐστίν μοι ἐκλογῆς σκεῦος   →ιτοῦ βαστάσαι   μου ιτὸ ὄνομαι ἐνώπιον τε   ἐθνῶν   καὶ
r.asm.3 v.pmm.2s cj   r.nsm   v.pai.3s r.ds.1 n.gsf n.nsn   d.gsn f.aa   r.gs.1 d.asn n.asn   p.g   n.gpn   cj
899   4513   4022 4047   1639 1609 1724   3836 1002   1609 3836 3950 1967   5445 1620   2779

their kings   and before the people of Israel. 16 I   will show   him how much he   must suffer for my
βασιλέων τε   υἱῶν →   Ἰσραήλ γὰρ   ἐγὼ   ὑποδείξω αὐτῷ ὅσα ←   αὐτὸν δεῖ   παθεῖν ὑπὲρ μου
n.gpm   cj   n.gpm   n.gpm   cj   r.ns.1 v.fai.1s r.dsm.3 r.apn   r.asm.3 v.pai.3s f.aa   p.g r.gs.1
995   5445   5626   2702   1142 1609   5683   899 4012   899   1256   4248   5642 1609

name."   ¶ 17 Then Ananias went   to the house and entered it.   Placing his hands on Saul, he said,
ιτοῦ ὀνόματοςι   δὲ   Ἀνανίας Ἀπῆλθεν εἰς τὴν οἰκίαν καὶ εἰσῆλθεν   καὶ ἐπιθεὶς τὰς χεῖρας ἐπ᾽ αὐτὸν → εἶπεν
d.gsn n.gsn   cj   n.nsm v.aai.3s p.a d.asf n.asf cj v.aai.3s   cj pt.aa.nsm d.apf n.apf p.a r.asm.3 v.aai.3s
3836 3950   1254 393   599   1650 3836 3864 2779 1656   2779 2202   3836 5931 2093 899   3306

"Brother Saul, the Lord – Jesus, who appeared to you on the road as you were coming here – has sent   me
ἀδελφέ   Σαοὺλ ὁ   κύριος Ἰησοῦς ὁ   ὀφθείς   → σοι ἐν τῇ ὁδῷ ᾗ   →   →   ἤρχου   →   ἀπέσταλκεν με
n.vsm   n.nsm d.nsm n.nsm Ἰησοῦς d.nsm pt.aa.nsm r.ds.2 p.d d.dsf n.dsf r.dsf   v.imi.2s   v.rai.3s r.as.1
81   4910 3836 3261   2652 3836 3972   5148 1877 3836 3847 4005   2262   690   1609

so that you may see   again and be filled with the Holy Spirit."   18   Immediately, something like scales
ὅπως ←   ἀναβλέψῃς ←   καὶ   πλησθῇς →   ἁγίου πνεύματος   καὶ εὐθέως   ὡς λεπίδες
cj   v.aas.2s   cj   v.aps.2s   a.gsn n.gsn   cj adv   pl n.npf
3968   329   2779 4398   41   4460   2779 2311   6055 3318

fell   from Saul's eyes,   and he could see   again.   He got   up and was baptized, 19 and after
ἀπέπεσαν ἀπὸ αὐτοῦ ιτῶν ὀφθαλμῶνι τε →   ἀνέβλεψεν ←   καὶ → ἀναστὰς   →   ἐβαπτίσθη   καὶ →
v.aai.3p p.g r.gsm.3 d.gpm n.gpm   cj   v.aai.3s   cj   pt.aa.nsm   v.api.3s   cj
674   608 899   3836 4057   5445   329   2779   482   966   2779

taking some food, he regained his strength.
λαβὼν   τροφήν →   ἐνίσχυσεν
pt.aa.nsm n.asf   v.aai.3s
3284   5575   1932

Saul in Damascus and Jerusalem

9:19 Saul spent   several days   with the disciples in Damascus. 20   At   once he began to preach
      δὲ   Ἐγένετο τινὰς ἡμέρας μετὰ τῶν μαθητῶν ἐν Δαμασκῷ   καὶ εὐθέως ←   →   → ἐκήρυσσεν τὸν
      cj   v.ami.3s r.apf n.apf p.g d.gpm n.gpm p.d n.dsf   cj adv   v.iai.3s d.asm
      1254 1181   5516   2465   3557 3836 3412   1877 1242   2779 2311   3062   3836

in the synagogues that Jesus is   the Son of God.   21 All   those who heard   him were astonished
Ἰησοῦν ἐν ταῖς συναγωγαῖς ὅτι οὗτος ἐστιν ὁ   υἱὸς → ιτοῦ θεοῦι δὲ πάντες οἱ   ←   ἀκούοντες →   ἐξίσταντο
n.asm p.d d.dpf n.dpf   cj   r.nsm v.pai.3s d.nsm n.nsm d.gsm n.gsn cj a.npm d.npm   pt.pa.npm   v.imi.3p
2652   1877 3836 5252   4022 4047 1639   3836 5626 3836 2536   1254 4246 3836   201   2014

and asked, "Isn't   he   the man who raised havoc in Jerusalem among those who call   on this
καὶ ἔλεγον ιοὐχι ἐστιν οὗτος ὁ   πορθήσας   εἰς Ἰερουσαλὴμ   τοὺς   ἐπικαλουμένους τοῦτο
cj v.iai.3p r.nsm v.pai.3s r.nsm d.nsm   pt.aa.nsm p.a n.asf   d.apm   pt.pm.apm   r.asn
2779 3306 4024 1639 4047 3836   4514   1650 2647   3836   2126   4047

name? And hasn't he come   here   to take them as prisoners to the chief priests?" 22 Yet Saul
ιτὸ ὄνομαι καὶ → ἐλήλύθει ὧδε εἰς τοῦτο ἵνα ἀγάγῃ αὐτοὺς → δεδεμένους ἐπὶ τοὺς → ἀρχιερεῖς   δὲ Σαῦλος
d.asn n.asn cj   v.lai.3s adv p.a r.asn cj v.aas.3s r.apm.3   pt.rp.apm   p.a d.apm   n.apm   cj n.nsm
3836 3950 2779   2262   6045 1650 4047 2671 72   899   1313   2093 3836   797   1254 4930

grew   more and more powerful and baffled the Jews   living   in Damascus by proving   that
ἐνεδυναμοῦτο μᾶλλον ←   →   καὶ συνέχυννεν τοὺς Ἰουδαίους ιτοὺς κατοικοῦνταςι ἐν Δαμασκῷ → συμβιβάζων ὅτι
v.ipi.3s   adv.c   cj v.iai.3s   d.apm a.apm   d.apm pt.pa.apm   p.d n.dsf   pt.pa.nsm cj
1904   3437   1904   2779 5177   3836 2681   3836 2997   1877 1242   5204   4022

Jesus is   the Christ.   ¶ 23 After many days   had gone   by, the Jews conspired   to kill   him,
οὗτος ἐστιν ὁ   χριστός   δὲ Ὡς ἱκαναὶ ἡμέραι →   ἐπληροῦντο ← οἱ Ἰουδαῖοι συνεβουλεύσαντο → ἀνελεῖν αὐτὸν
r.nsm v.pai.3s d.nsm n.nsm   cj cj a.npf n.npf   v.ipi.3p   d.npm a.npm v.ami.3p   f.aa r.asm.3
4047 1639   3836 5986   1254 6055 2653 2465   4444   3836 2681   5205   359 899

24 but Saul   learned of their plan.   Day and night they kept close watch   on   the city gates
δὲ ιτῷ Σαύλῳι ἐγνώσθη ← αὐτῶν ἡ ἐπιβουλὴ δὲ τε ἡμέρας καὶ νυκτὸς →   →   παρετηροῦντο καὶ τὰς →   πύλας
cj d.dsm n.dsm v.api.3s   r.gpm.3 d.nsf n.nsf cj te n.gsf cj n.gsf   v.imi.3p   cj d.apf   n.apf
1254 3836 4930 1182   899   3836 2101 1254 5445 2465 2779 3816   4190   2779 3836   4783

οὗτος τοῦ βαστάσαι τὸ ὄνομά μου ἐνώπιον ἐθνῶν τε καὶ βασιλέων υἱῶν τε Ἰσραήλ· 16 ἐγὼ γὰρ ὑποδείξω αὐτῷ ὅσα δεῖ αὐτὸν ὑπὲρ τοῦ ὀνόματός μου παθεῖν. ¶ 17 Ἀπῆλθεν δὲ Ἀνανίας καὶ εἰσῆλθεν εἰς τὴν οἰκίαν καὶ ἐπιθεὶς ἐπ᾽ αὐτὸν τὰς χεῖρας εἶπεν, Σαοὺλ ἀδελφέ, ὁ κύριος ἀπέσταλκέν με, Ἰησοῦς ὁ ὀφθείς σοι ἐν τῇ ὁδῷ ᾗ ἤρχου, ὅπως ἀναβλέψῃς καὶ πλησθῇς πνεύματος ἁγίου. 18 καὶ εὐθέως ἀπέπεσαν αὐτοῦ ἀπὸ τῶν ὀφθαλμῶν ὡς λεπίδες, ἀνέβλεψέν τε καὶ ἀναστὰς ἐβαπτίσθη 9:19 καὶ λαβὼν τροφὴν ἐνίσχυσεν. Ἐγένετο δὲ μετὰ τῶν ἐν Δαμασκῷ μαθητῶν ἡμέρας τινὰς 20 καὶ εὐθέως ἐν ταῖς συναγωγαῖς ἐκήρυσσεν τὸν Ἰησοῦν ὅτι οὗτός ἐστιν ὁ υἱὸς τοῦ θεοῦ. 21 ἐξίσταντο δὲ πάντες οἱ ἀκούοντες καὶ ἔλεγον, Οὐχ οὗτός ἐστιν ὁ πορθήσας εἰς Ἰερουσαλὴμ τοὺς ἐπικαλουμένους τὸ ὄνομα τοῦτο, καὶ ὧδε εἰς τοῦτο ἐλήλύθει ἵνα δεδεμένους ἀγάγῃ ἐπὶ τοὺς ἀρχιερεῖς; 22 Σαῦλος δὲ μᾶλλον ἐνεδυναμοῦτο καὶ συνέχυννεν [τοὺς] Ἰουδαίους τοὺς κατοικοῦντας ἐν Δαμασκῷ συμβιβάζων ὅτι οὗτός ἐστιν ὁ Χριστός. ¶ 23 Ὡς δὲ ἐπληροῦντο ἡμέραι ἱκαναί, συνεβουλεύσαντο οἱ Ἰουδαῖοι ἀνελεῖν αὐτόν· 24 ἐγνώσθη δὲ τῷ Σαύλῳ ἡ ἐπιβουλὴ αὐτῶν. παρετηροῦντο δὲ καὶ τὰς πύλας ἡμέρας τε καὶ νυκτὸς ὅπως αὐτὸν ἀνέλωσιν·

in order to kill him. **25** But his followers took him by night and lowered him in a basket
ὅπως ←   → ἀνέλωσιν αὐτὸν δὲ αὐτοῦ οἱ μαθηταὶ˻ λαβόντες   → νυκτὸς καθῆκαν αὐτὸν χαλάσαντες ἐν σπυρίδι
cj   v.aas.3p r.asm.3 cj r.gsm.3 d.npm n.npm pt.aa.npm   n.gsf v.aai.3p r.asm.3 pt.aa.npm p.d n.dsf
3968   359   899   1254 899   3836 3412   3284   3816 2768   899   5899   1877 5083

through an opening in the wall. ¶ **26** When he came to Jerusalem, he tried to join the
διὰ   τοῦ τείχους   δὲ →   → Παραγενόμενος εἰς Ἰερουσαλὴμ → ἐπείραζεν κολλᾶσθαι τοῖς
p.g   d.gsn n.gsn   cj   pt.am.nsm   p.a n.asf   v.iai.3s f.pp   d.dpm
1328   3836 5446   1254   4134   1650 2647   4279   3140   3836

disciples, but they were all afraid of him, not believing that he really was a disciple. **27** But Barnabas
μαθηταῖς, καὶ ↱   ↱   πάντες ἐφοβοῦντο ← αὐτὸν μὴ πιστεύοντες ὅτι → ἐστὶν μαθητής δὲ Βαρναβᾶς
n.dpm   cj   a.npm v.ipi.3p   r.asm.3 pl pt.pa.npm cj   v.pai.3s n.nsm cj n.nsm
3412   2779 5828 5828 4246   5828   899   3590 4409   4022   1639   3412   1254 982

took him and brought him to the apostles. He told them how Saul on his journey had seen the
ἐπιλαβόμενος αὐτὸν ἤγαγεν πρὸς τοὺς ἀποστόλους καὶ → διηγήσατο αὐτοῖς πῶς ἐν τῇ ὁδῷ → εἶδεν τὸν
pt.am.nsm   r.asm.3 v.aai.3s p.a d.apm n.apm   cj   v.ami.3s r.dpm.3 cj p.d d.dsf n.dsf   v.aai.3s r.asm
2138   899   72   4639 3836 693   2779 1455   899   4802 1877 3836 3847   1625   3836

Lord and that the Lord had spoken to him, and how in Damascus he had preached fearlessly in the name of
κύριον καὶ ὅτι → ἐλάλησεν αὐτῷ καὶ πῶς ἐν Δαμασκῷ → ἐπαρρησιάσατο ← ἐν τῷ ὀνόματι →
n.asm cj cj   v.aai.3s r.dsm.3 cj cj p.d n.dsf   v.ami.3s   p.d d.dsn n.dsn
3261   2779 4022 3281   899   2779 4802 1877 1242   4245   1877 3836 3950

Jesus. **28** So Saul stayed with them and moved about freely in Jerusalem, speaking
˻τοῦ Ἰησοῦ. καὶ ἦν μετ' αὐτῶν ˻εἰσπορευόμενος καὶ ἐκπορευόμενος˼ ← ← εἰς Ἰερουσαλήμ παρρησιαζόμενος
d.gsn n.gsn cj v.iai.3s p.g r.gpm.3 pt.pm.nsm   cj pt.pm.nsm   p.a n.asf   pt.pm.nsm
3836 2652   2779 1639 3552 899   1660   2779 1744   1650 2647   4245

boldly in the name of the Lord. **29** He talked and debated with the Grecian Jews, but they tried to kill
← ἐν τῷ ὀνόματι → τοῦ κυρίου τε → ἐλάλει καὶ συνεζήτει πρὸς τοὺς Ἑλληνιστάς, δὲ οἱ ἐπεχείρουν → ἀνελεῖν
   p.d d.dsn n.dsn d.gsm n.gsm cj   v.iai.3s cj v.iai.3s   p.a d.apm n.apm   cj d.npm v.iai.3p   f.aa
   1877 3836 3950   3836 3261   5445 3281   2779 5184   4639 3836 1821   1254 3836 2217   359

him. **30** When the brothers learned of this, they took him down to Caesarea and sent him off to
αὐτόν δὲ ↱ οἱ ἀδελφοὶ ἐπιγνόντες → κατήγαγον αὐτὸν ← εἰς Καισάρειαν καὶ ἐξαπέστειλαν αὐτὸν ← εἰς
r.asm.3 cj d.npm n.npm pt.aa.npm   v.aai.3p r.asm.3   p.a n.asf   cj v.aai.3p   r.asm.3   p.a
899   1254 2105 3836 81 2105   2864   899   1650 2791   2779 1990   899   1990 1650

Tarsus. ¶ **31** Then the church throughout Judea, Galilee and Samaria enjoyed a time of peace.
Ταρσόν.   οὖν μὲν Ἡ ἐκκλησία ˻καθ' ὅλης˼ ˻τῆς Ἰουδαίας˼ καὶ Γαλιλαίας καὶ Σαμαρείας εἶχεν εἰρήνην
n.asf   cj pl d.nsf n.nsf p.g a.gsf d.gsf n.gsf   cj n.gsf   cj n.gsf   v.iai.3s n.asf
5433   4036 3525 3836 1711 2848 3910 3836 2677   2779 1133   2779 4899   2400   1645

It was strengthened; and encouraged by the Holy Spirit, it grew in numbers, living in the fear of
→ → οἰκοδομουμένη καὶ ˻τῇ παρακλήσει˼ τοῦ ἁγίου πνεύματος → ἐπληθύνετο ← καὶ πορευομένη → τῷ φόβῳ
    pt.pp.nsf   cj d.dsf n.dsf   d.gsn a.gsn n.gsn   v.ipi.3s   cj pt.pm.nsf   d.dsm n.dsm
    3868   2779 3836 4155   3836 41   4460   4437   2779 4513   3836 5832

the Lord.
τοῦ κυρίου
d.gsm n.gsm
3836 3261

Aeneas and Dorcas

9:32 As Peter traveled about the country, he went to visit the saints in
δὲ Ἐγένετο Πέτρον διερχόμενον διὰ πάντων → κατελθεῖν καὶ πρὸς τοὺς ἁγίους ˻τοὺς κατοικοῦντας˼
cj v.ami.3s n.asm pt.pm.asm   p.g a.gpn   f.aa   adv p.a d.apm a.apm d.apm pt.pa.apm
1254 1181   4377   1451   1328 4246   2982   2779 4639 3836 41   3836 2997

Lydda. **33** There he found a man named Aeneas, a paralytic who had been
Λύδδα δὲ ἐκεῖ → εὗρεν τινα ἄνθρωπον ὀνόματι Αἰνέαν, ὃς ἦν παραλελυμένος →
n.asf cj adv   v.aai.3s r.asm n.asm   n.dsn   n.asm   r.nsm v.iai.3s pt.rp.nsm
3375   1254 1695 2351   1695 476   3950   138   4005 1639   4168

bedridden for eight years. **34** "Aeneas," Peter said to him, "Jesus Christ heals you. Get up
˻κατακείμενον ἐπὶ κραβάττου˼ ἐξ ὀκτὼ ἐτῶν καὶ Αἰνέα ὁ Πέτρος, εἶπεν → αὐτῷ Ἰησοῦς Χριστὸς ἰᾶται σε ἀνάστηθι ←
pt.pm.asm   p.g n.gsm   p.g a.gpn n.gpn cj n.vsm d.nsm n.nsm v.aai.3s r.dsm.3 n.nsm n.nsm   v.pmi.3s r.as.2 v.aam.2s
2879   2093 3187   1666 3893 2291 2779 138   3836 4377 3306   899   2652   5986   2615   5148   482

---

²⁵ λαβόντες δὲ οἱ μαθηταὶ αὐτοῦ νυκτὸς διὰ τοῦ τείχους καθῆκαν αὐτὸν χαλάσαντες ἐν σπυρίδι. ¶ ²⁶ Παραγενόμενος δὲ εἰς Ἰερουσαλὴμ ἐπείραζεν κολλᾶσθαι τοῖς μαθηταῖς, καὶ πάντες ἐφοβοῦντο αὐτὸν μὴ πιστεύοντες ὅτι ἐστὶν μαθητής. ²⁷ Βαρναβᾶς δὲ ἐπιλαβόμενος αὐτὸν ἤγαγεν πρὸς τοὺς ἀποστόλους καὶ διηγήσατο αὐτοῖς πῶς ἐν τῇ ὁδῷ εἶδεν τὸν κύριον καὶ ὅτι ἐλάλησεν αὐτῷ καὶ πῶς ἐν Δαμασκῷ ἐπαρρησιάσατο ἐν τῷ ὀνόματι τοῦ Ἰησοῦ. ²⁸ καὶ ἦν μετ' αὐτῶν εἰσπορευόμενος καὶ ἐκπορευόμενος εἰς Ἰερουσαλήμ, παρρησιαζόμενος ἐν τῷ ὀνόματι τοῦ κυρίου, ²⁹ ἐλάλει τε καὶ συνεζήτει πρὸς τοὺς Ἑλληνιστάς, οἱ δὲ ἐπεχείρουν ἀνελεῖν αὐτόν. ³⁰ ἐπιγνόντες δὲ οἱ ἀδελφοὶ κατήγαγον αὐτὸν εἰς Καισάρειαν καὶ ἐξαπέστειλαν αὐτὸν εἰς Ταρσόν. ¶ ³¹ Ἡ μὲν οὖν ἐκκλησία καθ' ὅλης τῆς Ἰουδαίας καὶ Γαλιλαίας καὶ Σαμαρείας εἶχεν εἰρήνην οἰκοδομουμένη καὶ πορευομένη τῷ φόβῳ τοῦ κυρίου καὶ τῇ παρακλήσει τοῦ ἁγίου πνεύματος ἐπληθύνετο.

⁹:³² Ἐγένετο δὲ Πέτρον διερχόμενον διὰ πάντων κατελθεῖν καὶ πρὸς τοὺς ἁγίους τοὺς κατοικοῦντας Λύδδα. ³³ εὗρεν δὲ ἐκεῖ ἄνθρωπόν τινα ὀνόματι Αἰνέαν ἐξ ἐτῶν ὀκτὼ κατακείμενον ἐπὶ κραβάττου, ὃς ἦν παραλελυμένος. ³⁴ καὶ εἶπεν αὐτῷ ὁ Πέτρος,

and take care   of your   mat."   Immediately Aeneas got   up. [35]   All   those who lived   in Lydda and
καὶ →   στρῶσον   σεαυτῷ →   καὶ εὐθέως   ἀνέστη   καὶ πάντες οἱ   κατοικοῦντες ← Λύδδα καὶ
cj   v.aam.2s   r.dsm.2   cj   adv   v.aai.3s   cj   a.npm   d.npm   pt.pa.npm   n.asf   cj
2779   5143   4932   5143   2779 2311   482   2779 4246   3836   2997   3375   2779

Sharon   saw   him and   turned   to the Lord. ¶   [36]   In Joppa there was a   disciple named
ˌτὸν Σαρῶναˌ εἶδαν αὐτὸν   οἵτινες ἐπέστρεψαν ἐπὶ τὸν κύριον   δὲ Ἐν Ἰόππῃ →   ἦν   τις μαθήτρια ὀνόματι
d.asm n.asm   v.aai.3p r.asm.3   r.npm   v.aai.3p   p.a   d.asm n.asm   cj   p.d   n.dsf   v.iai.3s r.nsf n.nsf   n.dsn
3836 4926   1625   899   4015   2188   2093 3836   3261   1254 1877 2673   1639   5516 3413   3950

Tabitha (which, when translated,   is   Dorcas), who was always doing good   and helping   the poor.
Ταβιθά ἣ   →   διερμηνευομένη λέγεται Δορκάς   αὕτη ἦν   πλήρης ἔργων ἀγαθῶν καὶ ἐλεημοσυνῶν ←   ὧν ἐποίει
n.nsf   r.nsf   pt.pp.nsf   v.ppi.3s n.nsf   r.nsf v.iai.3s a.nsf   n.gpn a.gpn   cj   n.gpf   r.gpf v.iai.3s
5412   4005   1450   3306   1520   4047 1639 4441   2240 19   2779 1797   4005 4472

[37]   About that   time   she became sick   and died,   and her body was washed and
δὲ ἐγένετο ἐν   ἐκείναις ˌταῖς ἡμέραιςˌ αὐτὴν →   ἀσθενήσασαν   ἀποθανεῖν δὲ αὐτὴν ←   →   λούσαντες
cj v.ami.3s p.d   r.dpf   d.dpf n.dpf   r.asf.3   pt.aa.asf   f.aa   cj   r.asf.3   pt.aa.npm
1254 1181   1877   1697   3836 2465   899   820   633   1254 899   3374

placed in an upstairs room. [38]   Lydda was   near Joppa;   so when the disciples heard   that Peter was in
ἔθηκαν ἐν   ὑπερῴῳ ←   δὲ Λύδδας οὔσης ἐγγὺς ˌτῇ Ἰόππῃˌ   →   οἱ   μαθηταὶ ἀκούσαντες ὅτι   Πέτρος ἐστὶν ἐν
v.aai.3p en   n.dsn   cj   n.gsf   pt.pa.gsf adv   d.dsf n.dsf   d.npm n.npm   pt.aa.npm cj   n.nsm v.pai.3s p.d
5502   1877   5673   1254 3375   1639   1584   3836 2673   201   3836 3412   201   4022   4377 1639 1877

Lydda, they sent   two men   to him and urged   him, "Please come   at once!"   ¶
αὐτῇ   ἀπέστειλαν δύο ἄνδρας πρὸς αὐτὸν   παρακαλοῦντες   διελθεῖν → ˌμὴ ὀκνήσῃςˌ ἕως ἡμῶν
r.dsf.3   v.aai.3p a.apm n.apm p.a r.asm.3   pt.pa.npm   f.aa   pl v.aas.2s   p.g r.gp.1
899   690   1545 467   4639 899   4151   1451   3590 3890   2401 7005

[39]   Peter   went   with them, and   when he arrived   he was taken   upstairs to the room.
δὲ Πέτρος ἀναστὰς συνῆλθεν ←   αὐτοῖς   ὃν →   παραγενόμενον →   ἀνήγαγον →   εἰς τὸ ὑπερῷον καὶ
cj n.nsm n.nsm   pt.aa.nsm v.aai.3s   r.dpm.3   r.asm   pt.aa.asm   v.aai.3p   p.a d.asn n.asn   cj
1254 4377   482   5302   899   4005   4134   343   5673   1650 3836 5673   2779

All   the widows stood   around him, crying   and showing   him the robes   and other clothing that
πᾶσαι αἱ χῆραι   παρέστησαν ←   αὐτῷ κλαίουσαι καὶ ἐπιδεικνύμεναι   χιτῶνας καὶ   ἱμάτια   ὅσα
a.npf   d.npf n.npf   v.aai.3p   r.dsm.3 pt.pa.npf cj   pt.pm.npf   n.apm cj   n.apn   r.apn
4246   3836 5939   4225   899   3081 2779   2109   5945 2779   2668   4012

Dorcas had made while she was still with them. ¶   [40]   Peter   sent   them all   out of the room;
ˌἡ Δορκάςˌ ἐποίει →   →   οὖσα μετ' αὐτῶν   δὲ ὁ   Πέτροςˌ ἐκβαλὼν   πάντας ἔξω
d.nsf n.nsf   v.iai.3s   pt.pa.nsf p.g r.gpf.3   cj d.nsm n.nsm   pt.aa.nsm   a.apm   adv
3836 1520   4472   1639 3552   899   1254 3836 4377   1675   4246   2032

then he got   down on his knees and prayed.   Turning   toward the dead woman, he said, "Tabitha, get
καὶ θεὶς   →   τὰ γόνατα   προσηύξατο καὶ ἐπιστρέψας πρὸς   τὸ σῶμα   →   εἶπεν Ταβιθά →
cj pt.aa.nsm   d.apn n.apn   v.ami.3s cj pt.aa.nsm p.a   d.asn n.asn   v.aai.3s n.vsf
2779 5502   3836 1205   4667   2779 2188   4639   3836 5393   3306 5412

up."   She opened her eyes,   and seeing Peter   she sat   up. [41]   He took her by the hand
ἀνάστηθι δὲ ἡ   ἤνοιξεν αὐτῆς ˌτοὺς ὀφθαλμούςˌ καὶ ἰδοῦσα ˌτὸν Πέτρονˌ →   ἀνεκάθισεν ←   δὲ →   δοὺς αὐτῇ →   χεῖρα
v.aam.2s cj d.nsf v.aai.3s r.gsf.3   d.apm n.apm   cj pt.aa.nsf d.asm n.asm   v.aai.3s   cj   pt.aa.nsm r.dsf.3   n.asf
482   1254 3836 487   899   3836 4057   2779 1625 3836 4377   361   1254   1443 899   5931

and helped her to her feet. Then he called   the believers and the widows and presented her   to them alive.
ἀνέστησεν αὐτήν ←   δὲ   →   φωνήσας τοὺς ἁγίους   καὶ τὰς χήρας   παρέστησεν αὐτὴν   ζώσαν
v.aai.3s r.asf.3   cj   pt.aa.nsm d.apm a.apm   cj d.apf n.apf   v.aai.3s r.asf.3   pt.aa.asf
482   899   482 482 482   1254   5888   3836 41   2779 3836 5939   4225   899   2409

[42]   This became known all   over Joppa,   and many people believed in the Lord. [43]   Peter stayed
δὲ →   ἐγένετο γνωστὸν ˌκαθ' ὅλης,   ←   ˌτῆς Ἰόππης,   καὶ πολλοὶ ←   ἐπίστευσαν ἐπὶ τὸν κύριον   δὲ Ἐγένετο   μεῖναι
cj   v.ami.3s a.nsn   p.g a.gsf   d.gsf n.gsf   cj a.npm   v.aai.3p p.a d.asm n.asm   cj v.ami.3s   f.aa
1254   1181   1196   2848 3910   3836 2673   2779 4498   4409   2093 3836 3261   1254 1181   3531

in Joppa for some   time   with a   tanner named Simon.
ἐν Ἰόππῃ →   ἱκανὰς ἡμέρας παρὰ τινι βυρσεῖ   Σίμωνι
p.d n.dsf   a.apf   n.apf   p.d r.dsm n.dsm   n.dsm
1877 2673   2653   2465   4123 5516 1114   4981

Αἰνέα, ἰᾶταί σε Ἰησοῦς Χριστός· ἀνάστηθι καὶ στρῶσον σεαυτῷ. καὶ εὐθέως ἀνέστη. [35] καὶ εἶδαν αὐτὸν πάντες οἱ κατοικοῦντες Λύδδα καὶ τὸν Σαρῶνα, οἵτινες ἐπέστρεψαν ἐπὶ τὸν κύριον. ¶ [36] Ἐν Ἰόππῃ δέ τις ἦν μαθήτρια ὀνόματι Ταβιθά, ἣ διερμηνευομένη λέγεται Δορκάς· αὕτη ἦν πλήρης ἔργων ἀγαθῶν καὶ ἐλεημοσυνῶν ὧν ἐποίει. [37] ἐγένετο δὲ ἐν ταῖς ἡμέραις ἐκείναις ἀσθενήσασαν αὐτὴν ἀποθανεῖν· λούσαντες δὲ ἔθηκαν [αὐτὴν] ἐν ὑπερῴῳ. [38] ἐγγὺς δὲ οὔσης Λύδδας τῇ Ἰόππῃ οἱ μαθηταὶ ἀκούσαντες ὅτι Πέτρος ἐστὶν ἐν αὐτῇ ἀπέστειλαν δύο ἄνδρας πρὸς αὐτὸν παρακαλοῦντες, Μὴ ὀκνήσῃς διελθεῖν ἕως ἡμῶν. ¶ [39] ἀναστὰς δὲ Πέτρος συνῆλθεν αὐτοῖς· ὃν παραγενόμενον ἀνήγαγον εἰς τὸ ὑπερῷον καὶ παρέστησαν αὐτῷ πᾶσαι αἱ χῆραι κλαίουσαι καὶ ἐπιδεικνύμεναι χιτῶνας καὶ ἱμάτια ὅσα ἐποίει μετ' αὐτῶν οὖσα ἡ Δορκάς. ¶ [40] ἐκβαλὼν δὲ ἔξω πάντας ὁ Πέτρος καὶ θεὶς τὰ γόνατα προσηύξατο καὶ ἐπιστρέψας πρὸς τὸ σῶμα εἶπεν, Ταβιθά, ἀνάστηθι. ἡ δὲ ἤνοιξεν τοὺς ὀφθαλμοὺς αὐτῆς, καὶ ἰδοῦσα τὸν Πέτρον ἀνεκάθισεν. [41] δοὺς δὲ αὐτῇ χεῖρα ἀνέστησεν αὐτήν· φωνήσας δὲ τοὺς ἁγίους καὶ τὰς χήρας παρέστησεν αὐτὴν ζῶσαν. [42] γνωστὸν δὲ ἐγένετο καθ' ὅλης τῆς Ἰόππης καὶ ἐπίστευσαν πολλοὶ ἐπὶ τὸν κύριον. [43] Ἐγένετο δὲ ἡμέρας ἱκανὰς μεῖναι ἐν Ἰόππῃ παρά τινι Σίμωνι βυρσεῖ.

Cornelius Calls for Peter

10:1 At Caesarea there was a man named Cornelius, a centurion in what was known as the Italian
δέ ἐν Καισαρείᾳ τις Ἀνήρ ὀνόματι Κορνήλιος ἑκατοντάρχης ἐκ τῆς → καλουμένης ← Ἰταλικῆς
cj p.d n.dsf r.nsm n.nsm n.dsn n.nsm n.nsm p.g d.gsf pt.pp.gsf a.gsf
1254 1877 2791 5516 467 3950 3173 1672 1666 3836 2813 2713

Regiment. **2** He and all his family were devout and God-fearing; he gave generously to
σπείρης σὺν παντὶ αὐτοῦ τῷ οἴκῳ εὐσεβὴς καὶ φοβούμενος τὸν θεὸν → ποιῶν ἐλεημοσύνας πολλὰς →
n.gsf p.d a.dsm r.gsm.3 d.dsm n.dsm a.nsm cj pt.pp.nsm d.asm n.asm pt.pa.nsm n.apf a.apf
5061 5250 4246 899 3836 3875 2356 2779 5828 3836 2536 4472 1797 4498

those in need and prayed to God regularly. **3** One day at about three in the afternoon
τῷ λαῷ ← καὶ δεόμενος → τοῦ θεοῦ διὰ παντός, → ὡσεὶ περὶ ὥραν ἐνάτην τῆς ἡμέρας ←
d.dsm n.dsm cj pt.pp.nsm d.gsm n.gsm p.g a.gsm pl p.a n.asf a.asf d.gsf n.gsf
3836 3295 2779 1289 3836 2536 1328 4246 6059 4309 6052 1888 3836 2465

he had a vision. He distinctly saw an angel of God, who came to him and said, "Cornelius!"
ἐν ὁράματι → φανερῶς εἶδεν ἄγγελον τοῦ θεοῦ → εἰσελθόντα πρὸς αὐτὸν καὶ εἰπόντα αὐτῷ Κορνήλιε
p.d n.dsn adv v.aai.3s n.asm d.gsm n.gsm pt.aa.asm p.a r.asm.3 cj pt.aa.asm r.dsm.3 n.vsm
1877 3969 1625 5747 34 3836 2536 1656 4639 899 2779 3306 899 3173

¶ **4** Cornelius stared at him in fear. "What is it, Lord?" he asked. The angel answered,
δὲ ὁ ἀτενίσας αὐτῷ καὶ γενόμενος ἔμφοβος τί ἐστιν ← κύριε → εἶπεν δὲ εἶπεν
cj d.nsm pt.aa.nsm r.dsm.3 cj pt.am.nsm a.nsm r.nsm v.pai.3s n.vsm v.aai.3s cj v.aai.3s
1254 3836 867 899 2779 1181 1873 5515 1639 3261 3306 1254 3306

"Your prayers and gifts to the poor have come up as a memorial offering before
αὐτῷ σου αἱ προσευχαί καὶ αἱ ἐλεημοσύναι ← ← σου → ἀνέβησαν ← εἰς μνημόσυνον ← ἔμπροσθεν
r.dsm.3 r.gs.2 d.npf n.npf cj d.npf n.npf r.gs.2 v.aai.3p p.a n.asn p.g
899 5148 3836 4666 2779 3836 1797 5148 326 1650 3649 1869

God. **5** Now send men to Joppa to bring back a man named Simon who is called Peter.
τοῦ θεοῦ καὶ νῦν πέμψον ἄνδρας εἰς Ἰόππην καὶ μετάπεμψαι ← τινα Σίμωνα ὃς → ἐπικαλεῖται Πέτρος
d.gsm n.gsm cj adv v.aam.2s n.apm p.a n.asf cj v.amm.2s r.asm n.asm r.nsm v.ppi.3s n.nsm
3836 2536 2779 3814 4287 467 1650 2673 2779 3569 5516 4981 4005 2126 4377

6 He is staying with Simon the tanner, whose house is by the sea." ¶ **7** When the angel who
οὗτος → ξενίζεται παρά τινι Σίμωνι βυρσεῖ ᾧ οἰκία ἐστιν παρὰ θάλασσαν δὲ ὡς ὁ ἄγγελος ὁ
r.nsm v.ppi.3s p.d r.dsm n.dsm n.dsm r.dsm n.nsf v.pai.3s p.a n.asf cj cj d.nsm n.nsm d.nsm
4047 3826 4123 5516 4981 1114 4005 3864 1639 4123 2498 1254 6055 3836 34 3836

spoke to him had gone, Cornelius called two of his servants and a devout soldier who was one of his
λαλῶν → αὐτῷ ἀπῆλθεν φωνήσας δύο → τῶν οἰκετῶν καὶ εὐσεβῆ στρατιώτην → αὐτῷ
pt.pa.nsm r.dsm.3 v.aai.3s pt.aa.nsm a.apm d.gpm n.gpm cj a.asm n.asm r.dsm.3
3281 899 599 5888 1545 3836 3860 2779 2356 5132 3836 899

attendants. **8** He told them everything that had happened and sent them to Joppa
τῶν προσκαρτερούντων καὶ → ἐξηγησάμενος αὐτοῖς ἅπαντα ἀπέστειλεν αὐτοὺς εἰς τὴν Ἰόππην
d.gpm pt.pa.gpm cj pt.am.nsm r.dpm.3 a.apn v.aai.3s r.apm.3 p.a d.asf n.asf
3836 4674 2779 2007 899 570 690 899 1650 3836 2673

Peter's Vision

10:9 About noon the following day as they were on their journey and approaching the city,
δὲ περὶ ὥραν ἕκτην Τῇ ἐπαύριον → ἐκείνων → → ὁδοιπορούντων καὶ ἐγγιζόντων τῇ πόλει
cj p.a n.asf a.asf d.dsf adv r.gpm pt.pa.gpm cj pt.pa.gpm d.dsf n.dsf
1254 4309 6052 1761 3836 2069 3844 1697 3844 2779 1581 3836 4484

Peter went up on the roof to pray. **10** He became hungry and wanted something to eat, and while
Πέτρος ἀνέβη ← ἐπὶ τὸ δῶμα → προσεύξασθαι δὲ → ἐγένετο πρόσπεινος καὶ ἤθελεν → γεύσασθαι δὲ →
n.nsm v.aai.3s p.a d.asn n.asn f.am cj v.ami.3s a.nsm cj v.iai.3s f.am cj
4377 326 2093 3836 1560 4667 1254 1181 4698 2779 2527 1174 1254

the meal was being prepared, he fell into a trance. **11** He saw heaven opened and
→ → παρασκευαζόντων αὐτῶν ἐπ' αὐτὸν ἐγένετο ἔκστασις καὶ θεωρεῖ τὸν οὐρανὸν ἀνεῳγμένον καὶ
pt.pa.gpm r.gpm.3 p.a r.asm.3 v.ami.3s n.nsf cj v.pai.3s d.asm n.asm pt.rp.asm cj
4186 899 2093 899 1181 1749 2779 2555 3836 4041 487 2779

something like a large sheet being let down to earth by its four corners. **12** It contained
καταβαῖνον σκεῦός τι ὡς μεγάλην ὀθόνην → καθιέμενον ← ἐπὶ τῆς γῆς → τέσσαρσιν ἀρχαῖς ἐν ᾧ ὑπῆρχεν
pt.pa.asn n.asn r.asn pl a.asf n.asf pt.pp.asn p.g d.gsf n.gsf a.dpf n.dpf p.d r.dsn v.iai.3s
2849 5007 5516 6055 3489 2768 2768 2093 3836 1178 5475 794 1877 4005 5639

10:1 Ἀνὴρ δέ τις ἐν Καισαρείᾳ ὀνόματι Κορνήλιος, ἑκατοντάρχης ἐκ σπείρης τῆς καλουμένης Ἰταλικῆς, 2 εὐσεβὴς καὶ φοβούμενος τὸν θεὸν σὺν παντὶ τῷ οἴκῳ αὐτοῦ, ποιῶν ἐλεημοσύνας πολλὰς τῷ λαῷ καὶ δεόμενος τοῦ θεοῦ διὰ παντός, 3 εἶδεν ἐν ὁράματι φανερῶς ὡσεὶ περὶ ὥραν ἐνάτην τῆς ἡμέρας ἄγγελον τοῦ θεοῦ εἰσελθόντα πρὸς αὐτὸν καὶ εἰπόντα αὐτῷ, Κορνήλιε. ¶ 4 ὁ δὲ ἀτενίσας αὐτῷ καὶ ἔμφοβος γενόμενος εἶπεν, Τί ἐστιν, κύριε; εἶπεν δὲ αὐτῷ, Αἱ προσευχαί σου καὶ αἱ ἐλεημοσύναι σου ἀνέβησαν εἰς μνημόσυνον ἔμπροσθεν τοῦ θεοῦ. 5 καὶ νῦν πέμψον ἄνδρας εἰς Ἰόππην καὶ μετάπεμψαι Σίμωνά τινα ὃς ἐπικαλεῖται Πέτρος· 6 οὗτος ξενίζεται παρά τινι Σίμωνι βυρσεῖ, ᾧ ἐστιν οἰκία παρὰ θάλασσαν. ¶ 7 ὡς δὲ ἀπῆλθεν ὁ ἄγγελος ὁ λαλῶν αὐτῷ, φωνήσας δύο τῶν οἰκετῶν καὶ στρατιώτην εὐσεβῆ τῶν προσκαρτερούντων αὐτῷ 8 καὶ ἐξηγησάμενος ἅπαντα αὐτοῖς ἀπέστειλεν αὐτοὺς εἰς τὴν Ἰόππην.

10:9 Τῇ δὲ ἐπαύριον, ὁδοιπορούντων ἐκείνων καὶ τῇ πόλει ἐγγιζόντων, ἀνέβη Πέτρος ἐπὶ τὸ δῶμα προσεύξασθαι περὶ ὥραν ἕκτην. 10 ἐγένετο δὲ πρόσπεινος καὶ ἤθελεν γεύσασθαι. παρασκευαζόντων δὲ αὐτῶν ἐγένετο ἐπ' αὐτὸν ἔκστασις 11 καὶ θεωρεῖ τὸν οὐρανὸν ἀνεῳγμένον καὶ καταβαῖνον σκεῦός τι ὡς ὀθόνην μεγάλην τέσσαρσιν ἀρχαῖς καθιέμενον ἐπὶ τῆς γῆς, 12 ἐν ᾧ ὑπῆρχεν

all   kinds of four-footed   animals, as well as reptiles of the earth and birds of the air. ¹³ Then a voice told
πάντα   ← ⌐τὰ τετράποδα   καὶ ← ⌐ἑρπετὰ → τῆς γῆς καὶ πετεινὰ → τοῦ οὐρανοῦ καὶ   φωνὴ ἐγένετο
a.npn   d.npn n.npn   cj   n.npn   d.gsf n.gsf cj n.npn   d.gsm n.gsm   cj   n.nsf v.ami.3s
4246   3836 5488   2779   2260   3836 1178 2779 4374   3836 4041   2779 5889 1181

him, "Get   up, Peter. Kill and eat." ¶   ¹⁴   "Surely not,   Lord!"   Peter   replied. "I have
πρὸς αὐτόν ἀναστάς ← Πέτρε θῦσον καὶ φάγε   δὲ →   μηδαμῶς κύριε   ὁ Πέτρος εἶπεν   ὅτι ⌐ ⌐
p.a r.asm.3 pt.aa.nsm   n.vsm v.aam.2s cj v.aam.2s   cj   adv   n.vsm d.nsm n.nsm v.aai.3s cj
4639 899   482   4377 2604 2779 2266   1254   3592   3261 3836 4377 3306 4022 2266 2266

never eaten anything impure or unclean." ¹⁵   The voice spoke to him   a second   time,   "Do not
οὐδέποτε ἔφαγον πᾶν κοινὸν καὶ ἀκάθαρτον καὶ   φωνὴ   πρὸς αὐτόν πάλιν ⌐ἐκ δευτέρου⌐ σὺ   μὴ
adv   v.aai.1s a.asn a.asn cj a.asn   cj   n.nsf   p.a r.asm.3 adv   p.g a.gsn   r.ns.2 pl
4030   2266   4246 3123 2779 176   2779   5889   4639 899 4099 1666 1311   5148 3590

call   anything impure that God   has made clean."   ¶   ¹⁶   This happened   three times, and
κοίνου   ← ἃ ⌐ὁ θεός⌐ → → ἐκαθάρισεν   δὲ τοῦτο ἐγένετο   ἐπὶ τρίς ← καὶ
v.pam.2s   r.apn d.nsm n.nsm   v.aai.3s   cj r.nsn v.ami.3s   p.a adv   cj
3123   4005 3836 2536   2751   1254 4047 1181   2093 5565   2779

immediately the sheet was taken   back to heaven. ¶   ¹⁷   While Peter   was wondering
εὐθὺς   τὸ σκεῦος → ἀνελήμφθη εἰς ⌐τὸν οὐρανόν⌐   δὲ ⌐Ὡς ⌐ ὁ Πέτρος⌐ → διηπόρει ἐν ἑαυτῷ
adv   d.nsn n.nsn   v.api.3s   p.a d.asm n.asm   cj cj   d.nsm n.nsm   v.iai.3s p.d r.dsm.3
2318   3836 5007   377   1650 3836 4041   1254 6055   3836 4377   1389   1877 1571

about the meaning of the vision,   the men sent   by Cornelius   found   out where
⌐τί ἂν εἴη   τὸ ὅραμα ὃ εἶδεν ἰδοὺ οἱ ἄνδρες ⌐οἱ ἀπεσταλμένοι ὑπὸ ⌐τοῦ Κορνηλίου⌐ διερωτήσαντες ←
r.nsn pl   v.pao.3s d.nsn n.nsn r.asn v.aai.3s j d.npm n.npm d.npm pt.rp.npm   p.g d.gsm n.gsm   pt.aa.npm
5515 323 1639   3836 3969 4005 2627 1625 3836 467 3836 690   5679 3836 3173   1452

Simon's   house was and stopped at the gate. ¹⁸   They called   out, asking if Simon who was
⌐τοῦ Σίμωνος⌐ ⌐τὴν οἰκίαν⌐ ἐπέστησαν ἐπὶ τὸν πυλῶνα καὶ → φωνήσαντες ← ἐπυνθάνοντο εἰ Σίμων ὁ →
d.gsm n.gsm   d.asf n.asf   v.aai.3p p.a d.asm n.asm cj   pt.aa.npm   v.imi.3p cj n.nsm d.nsm
3836 4981   3836 3864   2392 2093 3836 4/84 2779   5888   4785   1623 4981 3836

known   as Peter was staying there. ¶   ¹⁹   While Peter   was still thinking   about the vision,   the
ἐπικαλούμενος ← Πέτρος → ξενίζεται ἐνθάδε   δὲ   ⌐τοῦ Πέτρου⌐ →   διενθυμουμένου περὶ τοῦ ὁράματος τὸ
pt.pp.nsm   n.nsm   v.ppi.3s adv   cj   d.gsm n.gsm   pt.pm.gsm   p.g d.gsn n.gsn   d.nsn
2126   4377   3826 1924   1254 1445 3836 4377   1445   4309 3836 3969   3836

Spirit said to him,   "Simon, three men are looking for you. ²⁰ So get   up and go   downstairs. Do
πνεῦμα εἶπεν αὐτῷ ἰδοὺ τρεῖς ἄνδρες → ζητοῦντές ← σε   ἀλλὰ ἀναστάς ←   κατάβηθι ←   καὶ ⌐
n.nsn v.aai.3s r.dsm.3 j a.npm n.npm   pt.pa.npm r.as.2 cj pt.aa.nsm   v.aam.2s   cj
4460 3306 899 2627   5552 467   2426   5148 247 482   2849   2779 1359

not hesitate   to go   with them, for I have sent   them." ¶ ²¹   Peter went   down and said to
μηδὲν διακρινόμενος πορεύου σὺν αὐτοῖς ὅτι ἐγὼ ἀπέσταλκα αὐτούς   δὲ Πέτρος καταβὰς ←   εἶπεν πρὸς
a.asn pt.pm.nsm   v.pmm.2s p.d r.dpm.3 cj r.ns.1 v.rai.1s r.apm.3   cj n.nsm pt.aa.nsm   v.aai.3s p.a
3594 1359   4513 5250 899 4022 1609 690   899   1254 4377 2849   3306 4639

the men,   "I'm   the one you're looking for. Why   have you come?" ¶   ²²   The men
τοὺς ἄνδρας ἰδοὺ ⌐ἐγώ εἰμι⌐ ὃν ← ζητεῖτε ← ⌐τίς ἡ αἰτία δι' ἣν → → πάρεστε   δὲ οἱ ←
d.apm n.apm j r.ns.1 v.pai.1s r.asm v.pai.2p r.nsf d.nsf n.nsf p.a r.asf v.pai.2p   cj d.npm
3836 467 2627 1609 1639 4005 2426   5515 3836 162 1328 4005 4205   1254 3836

replied, "We have come from Cornelius the centurion.   He is a righteous and God-fearing   man,   who is
εἶπαν   Κορνήλιος ἑκατοντάρχης   δίκαιος καὶ ⌐φοβούμενος τὸν θεόν⌐ ἀνὴρ τε →   →
v.aai.3p   n.nsm   n.nsm   a.nsm   cj pt.pm.nsm d.asm n.asm n.nsm cj
3306   3173   1672   1465   2779 5828 3836 2536 467   5445

respected   by all the Jewish   people. A holy angel told   him to have you come   to his
μαρτυρούμενος ὑπὸ ὅλου τοῦ ⌐τῶν Ἰουδαίων⌐ ἔθνους ὑπὸ ἁγίου ἀγγέλου ἐχρηματίσθη ← ⌐ → σε μεταπέμψασθαι εἰς αὐτοῦ
pt.pp.nsm   p.g a.gsn d.gsn d.gpm a.gpm n.gsn   p.g a.gsm n.gsm v.api.3s   r.as.2 f.am   p.a r.gsm.3
3455   5679 3910 3836 3836 2681 1620   5679 41 34   5976   3569 3569 5148 3569   1650 899

house   so that he could hear   what   you have to say." ²³ Then Peter invited   the men into the house
⌐τὸν οἶκον⌐ καὶ ⌐ → → ἀκοῦσαι παρὰ σοῦ   ῥήματα οὖν   εἰσκαλεσάμενος   αὐτοὺς ← ←
d.asm n.asm cj   f.aa   p.g r.gs.2 n.apn   cj   pt.am.nsm   r.apm.3
3836 3875 2779   201   4123 5148   4839   4036 1657   899 1657 1657 1657

πάντα τὰ τετράποδα καὶ ἑρπετὰ τῆς γῆς καὶ πετεινὰ τοῦ οὐρανοῦ. ¹³ καὶ ἐγένετο φωνὴ πρὸς αὐτόν, Ἀναστάς, Πέτρε, θῦσον καὶ φάγε. ¶ ¹⁴ ὁ δὲ Πέτρος εἶπεν, Μηδαμῶς, κύριε, ὅτι οὐδέποτε ἔφαγον πᾶν κοινὸν καὶ ἀκάθαρτον. ¹⁵ καὶ φωνὴ πάλιν ἐκ δευτέρου πρὸς αὐτόν, Ἃ ὁ θεὸς ἐκαθάρισεν, σὺ μὴ κοίνου. ¶ ¹⁶ τοῦτο δὲ ἐγένετο ἐπὶ τρὶς καὶ εὐθὺς ἀνελήμφθη τὸ σκεῦος εἰς τὸν οὐρανόν. ¶ ¹⁷ Ὡς δὲ ἐν ἑαυτῷ διηπόρει ὁ Πέτρος τί ἂν εἴη τὸ ὅραμα ὃ εἶδεν, ἰδοὺ οἱ ἄνδρες οἱ ἀπεσταλμένοι ὑπὸ τοῦ Κορνηλίου διερωτήσαντες τὴν οἰκίαν τοῦ Σίμωνος ἐπέστησαν ἐπὶ τὸν πυλῶνα, ¹⁸ καὶ φωνήσαντες ἐπυνθάνοντο εἰ Σίμων ὁ ἐπικαλούμενος Πέτρος ἐνθάδε ξενίζεται. ¶ ¹⁹ τοῦ δὲ Πέτρου διενθυμουμένου περὶ τοῦ ὁράματος εἶπεν [αὐτῷ] τὸ πνεῦμα, Ἰδοὺ ἄνδρες τρεῖς ζητοῦντές σε, ²⁰ ἀλλὰ ἀναστὰς κατάβηθι καὶ πορεύου σὺν αὐτοῖς μηδὲν διακρινόμενος ὅτι ἐγὼ ἀπέσταλκα αὐτούς. ¶ ²¹ καταβὰς δὲ Πέτρος πρὸς τοὺς ἄνδρας εἶπεν, Ἰδοὺ ἐγώ εἰμι ὃν ζητεῖτε· τίς ἡ αἰτία δι' ἣν πάρεστε; ¶ ²² οἱ δὲ εἶπαν, Κορνήλιος ἑκατοντάρχης, ἀνὴρ δίκαιος καὶ φοβούμενος τὸν θεόν, μαρτυρούμενός τε ὑπὸ ὅλου τοῦ ἔθνους τῶν Ἰουδαίων, ἐχρηματίσθη ὑπὸ ἀγγέλου ἁγίου μεταπέμψασθαί σε εἰς τὸν οἶκον αὐτοῦ καὶ ἀκοῦσαι ῥήματα παρὰ σοῦ. ²³ εἰσκαλεσάμενος οὖν αὐτοὺς ἐξένισεν.
Τῇ δὲ ἐπαύριον ἀναστὰς ἐξῆλθεν σὺν αὐτοῖς καί τινες τῶν ἀδελφῶν τῶν ἀπὸ Ἰόππης συνῆλθον αὐτῷ. ²⁴ τῇ δὲ ἐπαύριον

to be his guests.
→ → → ἐξένισεν
v.aai.3s
3826

Peter at Cornelius' House

The next day Peter started out with them, and some of the brothers from Joppa went
δὲ Τῇ ἐπαύριον ← ἀναστὰς ἐξῆλθεν ← σὺν αὐτοῖς καί τινες → τῶν ἀδελφῶν τῶν ἀπὸ Ἰόππης συνῆλθον
cj d.dsf adv pt.aa.nsm v.aai.3s p.d r.dpm.3 cj r.npm d.gpm n.gpm d.gpm p.g n.gsf v.aai.3p
1254 3836 2069 482 2002 5250 899 2779 5516 3836 81 3836 608 2673 5302

along. 24 The following day he arrived in Caesarea. Cornelius was expecting them and had
αὐτῷ δὲ τῇ ἐπαύριον εἰσῆλθεν εἰς τὴν Καισάρειαν. δὲ ὁ Κορνήλιος ἦν προσδοκῶν αὐτοὺς →
r.dsm.3 cj d.dsf adv v.aai.3s p.a d.asf n.asf cj d.nsm n.nsm v.iai.3s pt.pa.nsm r.apm.3
899 1254 3836 2069 1656 1650 3836 2791 1254 3836 3173 1639 4659 899

called together his relatives and close friends. 25 As Peter entered the
συγκαλεσάμενος ← αὐτοῦ τοὺς συγγενεῖς καὶ ἀναγκαίους τοὺς φίλους. δὲ ἐγένετο Ὡς τὸν Πέτρον τοῦ εἰσελθεῖν
pt.am.nsm r.gsm.3 d.apm n.apm cj a.apm d.apm a.apm cj v.ami.3s d.asm n.asm d.gsn f.aa
5157 899 3836 5150 2779 338 3836 5813 1254 1181 6055 3836 4377 3836 1656

house, Cornelius met him and fell at his feet in reverence. 26 But Peter made him get up.
ὁ Κορνήλιος συναντήσας αὐτῷ πεσὼν ἐπὶ τοὺς πόδας προσεκύνησεν δὲ ὁ Πέτρος, αὐτὸν ἤγειρεν ←
d.nsm n.nsm pt.aa.nsm r.dsm.3 pt.aa.nsm p.a d.apm n.apm v.aai.3s cj d.nsm n.nsm r.asm.3 v.aai.3s
3836 3173 5267 899 4406 2093 3836 4546 4686 1254 3836 4377 1586 899 1586

"Stand up," he said, "I am only a man myself." ¶ 27 Talking with him, Peter went inside and
ἀνάστηθι ← λέγων καὶ ἐγὼ εἰμι ἄνθρωπος αὐτός καὶ συνομιλῶν ← αὐτῷ εἰσῆλθεν καὶ
v.aam.2s pt.pa.nsm adv r.ns.1 v.pai.1s n.nsm r.nsm cj pt.pa.nsm r.dsm.3 v.aai.3s cj
482 3306 2779 1609 1639 476 899 2779 5326 899 1656 2779

found a large gathering of people. 28 He said to them: "You are well aware that it is against our law
εὑρίσκει πολλούς συνεληλυθότας ← τε → ἔφη πρὸς αὐτούς ὑμεῖς → ἐπίστασθε ὡς → ἐστιν ἀθέμιτον ←
v.pai.3s a.apm pt.ra.apm cj v.iai.3s p.a r.apm.3 r.np.2 v.ppi.2p cj v.pai.3s a.nsn
2351 4498 5302 5445 5774 4639 899 7007 2179 6055 1639 116

for a Jew to associate with a Gentile or visit him. But God has shown me that I should not
→ ἀνδρὶ Ἰουδαίῳ → κολλᾶσθαι ← ἀλλοφύλῳ ἢ προσέρχεσθαι καμοὶ ὁ θεὸς ἔδειξεν ←
n.dsm a.dsm f.pp a.dsm cj f.pm crasis d.nsm n.nsm v.aai.3s
467 2681 3140 260 2445 4665 2743 3836 2536 1259 2743 3306 3306 3594

call any man impure or unclean. 29 So when I was sent for, I came without raising any
λέγειν μηδένα ἄνθρωπον κοινὸν ἢ ἀκάθαρτον διὸ καὶ → → μεταπεμφθεὶς ← ἦλθον →
f.pa a.asm n.asm a.asm cj a.asm cj adv pt.ap.nsm v.aai.1s
3306 3594 476 3123 2445 176 1475 2779 3569 2262

objection. May I ask why you sent for me?" ¶ 30 Cornelius answered: ἀπὸ
ἀναντιρρήτως οὖν → πυνθάνομαι τίνι λόγῳ → μετεπέμψασθε με καὶ ὁ Κορνήλιος ἔφη ἀπὸ
adv cj v.pmi.1s r.dsn n.dsn v.ami.2p r.as.1 cj d.nsm n.nsm v.iai.3s p.g
395 4036 4785 5515 3364 3569 1609 2779 3836 3173 5774 608

"Four days ago I was in my house praying at this hour, at three in the afternoon. καὶ
τετάρτης ἡμέρας ← ἐγὼ ἤμην ἐν μου τῷ οἴκῳ προσευχόμενος μέχρι ταύτης τῆς ὥρας → τὴν ἐνάτην ← ← καὶ
a.gsf n.gsf v.imi.1s p.d r.gs.1 d.dsm n.dsm pt.pm.nsm p.g r.gsf d.gsf n.gsf d.asf a.asf cj
5480 2465 608 1639 1877 1609 3836 3875 4667 3588 4047 3836 6052 3836 1888 2779

Suddenly a man in shining clothes stood before me 31 and said, 'Cornelius, God has heard your
ἰδοὺ ἀνὴρ ἐν λαμπρᾷ ἐσθῆτι ἔστη ἐνώπιον μου καὶ φησίν Κορνήλιε ἐνώπιον τοῦ θεοῦ → εἰσηκούσθη σου
j n.nsm p.d a.dsf n.dsf v.aai.3s p.g r.gs.1 cj v.pai.3s n.vsm p.g d.gsm n.gsm v.api.3s r.gs.2
2627 467 1877 3287 2264 2705 1967 1609 2779 5774 3173 1967 3836 2536 1653 5148

prayer and remembered your gifts to the poor. 32 Send to Joppa for Simon who is
ἡ προσευχὴ καὶ ἐμνήσθησαν σου αἱ ἐλεημοσύναι ← ← οὖν πέμψον εἰς Ἰόππην καὶ μετακάλεσαι ← Σίμωνα ὃς
d.nsf n.nsf cj v.api.3p r.gs.2 d.npf n.npf cj v.aam.2s p.a n.asf cj v.amm.2s n.asm r.nsm
3836 4666 2779 3630 5148 3836 1797 4036 4287 1650 2673 2779 3559 4981 4005

called Peter. He is a guest in the home of Simon the tanner, who lives by the sea.' 33 So I sent for
ἐπικαλεῖται Πέτρος οὗτος → ξενίζεται ἐν οἰκίᾳ → Σίμωνος βυρσέως παρὰ θάλασσαν οὖν → ἔπεμψα πρὸς
v.ppi.3s n.nsm r.nsm v.ppi.3s p.d n.dsf n.gsm n.gsm p.a n.asf cj v.aai.1s p.a
2126 4377 4047 3826 1877 3864 4981 1114 4123 2498 4036 4287 4639

εἰσῆλθεν εἰς τὴν Καισάρειαν. ὁ δὲ Κορνήλιος ἦν προσδοκῶν αὐτοὺς συγκαλεσάμενος τοὺς συγγενεῖς αὐτοῦ καὶ τοὺς ἀναγκαίους φίλους. 25 ὡς δὲ ἐγένετο τοῦ εἰσελθεῖν τὸν Πέτρον, συναντήσας αὐτῷ ὁ Κορνήλιος πεσὼν ἐπὶ τοὺς πόδας προσεκύνησεν. 26 ὁ δὲ Πέτρος ἤγειρεν αὐτὸν λέγων, Ἀνάστηθι· καὶ ἐγὼ αὐτὸς ἄνθρωπός εἰμι. ¶ 27 καὶ συνομιλῶν αὐτῷ εἰσῆλθεν καὶ εὑρίσκει συνεληλυθότας πολλούς, 28 ἔφη τε πρὸς αὐτούς, Ὑμεῖς ἐπίστασθε ὡς ἀθέμιτόν ἐστιν ἀνδρὶ Ἰουδαίῳ κολλᾶσθαι ἢ προσέρχεσθαι ἀλλοφύλῳ· κἀμοὶ ὁ θεὸς ἔδειξεν μηδένα κοινὸν ἢ ἀκάθαρτον λέγειν ἄνθρωπον· 29 διὸ καὶ ἀναντιρρήτως ἦλθον μεταπεμφθείς. πυνθάνομαι οὖν τίνι λόγῳ μετεπέμψασθέ με; ¶ 30 καὶ ὁ Κορνήλιος ἔφη, Ἀπὸ τετάρτης ἡμέρας μέχρι ταύτης τῆς ὥρας ἤμην τὴν ἐνάτην προσευχόμενος ἐν τῷ οἴκῳ μου, καὶ ἰδοὺ ἀνὴρ ἔστη ἐνώπιόν μου ἐν ἐσθῆτι λαμπρᾷ 31 καὶ φησίν, Κορνήλιε, εἰσηκούσθη σου ἡ προσευχὴ καὶ αἱ ἐλεημοσύναι σου ἐμνήσθησαν ἐνώπιον τοῦ θεοῦ. 32 πέμψον οὖν εἰς Ἰόππην καὶ μετακάλεσαι Σίμωνα ὃς ἐπικαλεῖται Πέτρος, οὗτος ξενίζεται ἐν οἰκίᾳ Σίμωνος βυρσέως παρὰ θάλασσαν. 33 ἐξαυτῆς οὖν ἔπεμψα πρὸς σέ, σύ τε καλῶς ἐποίησας παραγενόμενος. νῦν οὖν πάντες ἡμεῖς ἐνώπιον τοῦ θεοῦ πάρεσμεν ἀκοῦσαι πάντα τὰ προστεταγμένα σοι ὑπὸ τοῦ κυρίου.

you immediately, and it was good of you to come.   Now we are all here in the presence
σέ ἐξαυτῆς τε καλῶς σύ → ἐποίησας παραγενόμενος‚ οὖν νῦν ἡμεῖς → πάντες πάρεσμεν → → ἐνώπιον
r.as.2 adv cj adv r.ns.2 v.aai.2s pt.am.nsm cj adv r.np.1 a.npm v.pai.1p p.g
5148 1994 5445 2822 5148 4472 4134 4036 3814 7005 4205 4246 4205 1967

of God to listen to everything the Lord has commanded you to tell us." ¶ **34** Then
→ ‚τοῦ θεοῦ‚ → ἀκοῦσαι ← πάντα ὑπὸ τοῦ κυρίου → ‚τὰ προστεταγμένα‚ σοι δὲ Ἀνοίξας τὸ
d.gsm n.gsm f.aa a.apn p.g d.gsm n.gsm d.apn v.rp.apn r.ds.2 cj pt.aa.nsm d.asn
3836 2536 201 4246 5679 3836 3261 3836 4705 5148 1254 487 3836

Peter began to speak: "I now realize how true it is that God does not show favoritism
στόμα Πέτρος → → εἶπεν καταλαμβάνομαι ἐπ᾽ ἀληθείας ὅτι ‚ὁ θεὸς‚ ἔστιν οὐκ → προσωπολήμπτης
n.asn n.nsm v.aai.3s v.pmi.1s p.g n.gsf cj d.nsm n.nsm v.pai.3s pl n.nsm
5125 4377 3306 2898 2093 237 4022 3836 2536 1639 4024 4720

35 but accepts men from every nation who fear him and do what is right. **36** You know the
ἀλλ᾽ ἔστιν δεκτὸς αὐτῷ ἐν παντὶ ἔθνει ὁ φοβούμενος αὐτὸν καὶ ἐργαζόμενος δικαιοσύνην τὸν
cj v.pai.3s a.nsm r.dsm.3 p.d a.dsn n.dsn d.nsm pt.pm.nsm r.asm.3 cj pt.pm.nsm n.asf d.asm
247 1639 1283 899 1877 4246 1620 3836 5828 899 2779 2237 1466 3836

message God sent to the people of Israel, telling the good news of peace through Jesus Christ,
λόγον [ὃν] ἀπέστειλεν τοῖς υἱοῖς → Ἰσραὴλ εὐαγγελιζόμενος ← εἰρήνην διὰ Ἰησοῦ Χριστοῦ
n.asm r.asm v.aai.3s d.dpm n.dpm n.gsm pt.pm.nsm n.asf p.g n.gsm n.gsm
3364 4005 690 3836 5626 2702 2294 1645 1328 2652 5986

who is Lord of all. **37** You know what has happened throughout Judea, beginning in Galilee
οὗτός ἐστιν κύριος → πάντων ὑμεῖς οἴδατε ‚τὸ ῥῆμα‚ → γενόμενον ‚καθ᾽ ὅλης‚ ‚τῆς Ἰουδαίας‚ ἀρξάμενος ἀπὸ ‚τῆς Γαλιλαίας‚
r.nsm v.pai.3s n.nsm a.gpn r.np.2 v.rai.2p d.asn n.asn pt.am.asn p.g a.gsf d.gsf n.gsf pt.am.nsm p.g d.gsf n.gsf
4047 1639 3261 4246 7007 3857 3836 4839 1181 2848 3910 3836 2677 806 608 3836 1133

after the baptism that John preached – **38** how God anointed Jesus of Nazareth with the Holy
μετὰ τὸ βάπτισμα ὃ Ἰωάννης ἐκήρυξεν ὡς ὁ θεὸς ἔχρισεν αὐτὸν Ἰησοῦν τὸν ἀπὸ Ναζαρέθ ἁγίῳ
p.a d.asn n.asn r.asn n.nsm v.aai.3s cj d.nsm n.nsm v.aai.3s r.asm.3 n.asm d.asm p.g n.gsf a.dsn
3552 3836 967 4005 2722 3062 6055 3836 2536 5987 899 2652 3836 608 3714 41

Spirit and power, and how he went around doing good and healing all who were under the
πνεύματι καὶ δυνάμει ὃς διῆλθεν ← → εὐεργετῶν καὶ ἰώμενος πάντας τοὺς → →
n.dsn cj n.dsf r.nsm v.aai.3s pt.pa.nsm cj pt.pm.nsm a.apm d.apm
4460 2779 1539 4005 1451 2308 2779 2615 4246 3836

power of the devil, because God was with him. ¶ **39** "We are witnesses of everything
καταδυναστευομένους ὑπὸ τοῦ διαβόλου ὅτι ‚ὁ θεὸς‚ ἦν μετ᾽ αὐτοῦ καὶ ἡμεῖς μάρτυρες → πάντων ὧν
pt.pp.apm p.g d.gsm n.gsm cj d.nsm n.nsm v.iai.3s p.g r.gsm.3 cj r.np.1 n.npm a.gpn r.gpn
2872 5679 3836 1333 4022 3836 2536 1639 3552 899 2779 7005 3459 4246 4005

he did in the country of the Jews and in Jerusalem. They killed him by hanging him on a tree,
→ ἐποίησεν τε ἐν τῇ χώρᾳ → τῶν Ἰουδαίων καὶ ἐν Ἰερουσαλήμ καὶ ἀνεῖλαν ὃν → κρεμάσαντες ἐπὶ ξύλου
v.aai.3s cj p.d d.dsf n.dsf d.gpm a.gpm cj p.d n.dsf adv v.aai.3p r.asm pt.aa.npm p.g n.gsn
4472 5445 1877 3836 6001 3836 2681 2779 1877 2647 2779 359 4005 3203 2093 3833

40 but God raised him from the dead on the third day and caused him to be seen. **41** He was not seen by
‚ὁ θεὸς‚ ἤγειρεν τοῦτον ἐν τῇ τρίτῃ ἡμέρᾳ καὶ ἔδωκεν αὐτὸν → γενέσθαι ἐμφανῆ οὐ →
d.nsm n.nsm v.aai.3s r.asm p.d d.dsf a.dsf n.dsf cj v.aai.3s r.asm.3 f.am a.asm pl
3836 2536 1586 4047 1877 3836 5569 2465 2779 1443 899 1181 1871 4024

all the people, but by witnesses whom God had already chosen – by us who ate and
παντὶ τῷ λαῷ ἀλλὰ → μάρτυσιν τοῖς ὑπὸ ‚τοῦ θεοῦ‚ προκεχειροτονημένοις → ἡμῖν οἵτινες συνεφάγομεν καὶ
a.dsm d.dsm n.dsm cj n.dpm d.dpm p.g d.gsm n.gsm pt.rp.dpm r.dp.1 r.npm v.aai.1p cj
4246 3836 3295 247 3459 3836 5679 3836 2536 4742 7005 4015 5303 2779

drank with him after he rose from the dead. **42** He commanded us to preach to the people and to
συνεπίομεν ← αὐτῷ μετὰ αὐτὸν ‚τὸ ἀναστῆναι‚ ἐκ νεκρῶν καὶ → παρήγγειλεν ἡμῖν κηρύξαι → τῷ λαῷ καὶ →
v.aai.1p r.dsm.3 p.a r.asm.3 d.asn f.aa p.g a.gpm cj v.aai.3s r.dp.1 f.aa d.dsm n.dsm cj
5228 899 3552 899 3836 482 1666 3738 2779 4133 7005 3062 3836 3295 2779

testify that he is the one whom God appointed as judge of the living and the dead. **43** All the
διαμαρτύρασθαι ὅτι οὗτός ἐστιν ὁ ← ὑπὸ ‚τοῦ θεοῦ‚ ὡρισμένος κριτὴς → ζώντων καὶ νεκρῶν πάντες οἱ
f.am cj r.nsm v.pai.3s d.nsm p.g d.gsm n.gsm pt.rp.nsm n.nsm pt.pa.gpm cj a.gpm a.npm d.npm
1371 4022 4047 1639 3836 5679 3836 2536 3988 3216 2409 2779 3738 4246 3836

¶ **34** Ἀνοίξας δὲ Πέτρος τὸ στόμα εἶπεν, Ἐπ᾽ ἀληθείας καταλαμβάνομαι ὅτι οὐκ ἔστιν προσωπολήμπτης ὁ θεός, **35** ἀλλ᾽ ἐν παντὶ ἔθνει ὁ φοβούμενος αὐτὸν καὶ ἐργαζόμενος δικαιοσύνην δεκτὸς αὐτῷ ἐστιν. **36** τὸν λόγον [ὃν] ἀπέστειλεν τοῖς υἱοῖς Ἰσραὴλ εὐαγγελιζόμενος εἰρήνην διὰ Ἰησοῦ Χριστοῦ, οὗτός ἐστιν πάντων κύριος, **37** ὑμεῖς οἴδατε τὸ γενόμενον ῥῆμα καθ᾽ ὅλης τῆς Ἰουδαίας, ἀρξάμενος ἀπὸ τῆς Γαλιλαίας μετὰ τὸ βάπτισμα ὃ ἐκήρυξεν Ἰωάννης, **38** Ἰησοῦν τὸν ἀπὸ Ναζαρέθ, ὡς ἔχρισεν αὐτὸν ὁ θεὸς πνεύματι ἁγίῳ καὶ δυνάμει, ὃς διῆλθεν εὐεργετῶν καὶ ἰώμενος πάντας τοὺς καταδυναστευομένους ὑπὸ τοῦ διαβόλου, ὅτι ὁ θεὸς ἦν μετ᾽ αὐτοῦ. ¶ **39** καὶ ἡμεῖς μάρτυρες πάντων ὧν ἐποίησεν ἔν τε τῇ χώρᾳ τῶν Ἰουδαίων καὶ [ἐν] Ἰερουσαλήμ. ὃν καὶ ἀνεῖλαν κρεμάσαντες ἐπὶ ξύλου, **40** τοῦτον ὁ θεὸς ἤγειρεν [ἐν] τῇ τρίτῃ ἡμέρᾳ καὶ ἔδωκεν αὐτὸν ἐμφανῆ γενέσθαι, **41** οὐ παντὶ τῷ λαῷ ἀλλὰ μάρτυσιν τοῖς προκεχειροτονημένοις ὑπὸ τοῦ θεοῦ, ἡμῖν, οἵτινες συνεφάγομεν καὶ συνεπίομεν αὐτῷ μετὰ τὸ ἀναστῆναι αὐτὸν ἐκ νεκρῶν· **42** καὶ παρήγγειλεν ἡμῖν κηρύξαι τῷ λαῷ καὶ διαμαρτύρασθαι ὅτι οὗτός ἐστιν ὁ ὡρισμένος ὑπὸ τοῦ θεοῦ κριτὴς ζώντων καὶ νεκρῶν. **43** τούτῳ πάντες οἱ προφῆται μαρτυροῦσιν ἄφεσιν ἁμαρτιῶν λαβεῖν διὰ τοῦ ὀνόματος

prophets testify → about him that everyone who believes in him receives forgiveness of sins → through his
προφῆται μαρτυροῦσιν → τούτῳ πάντα τὸν πιστεύοντα εἰς αὐτὸν λαβεῖν ἄφεσιν → ἁμαρτιῶν διὰ αὐτοῦ
n.npm v.pai.3p r.dsm a.asm d.asm pt.pa.asm p.a r.asm.3 f.aa n.asf n.gpf p.g r.gsm.3
4737 3455 4047 4246 3836 4409 1650 899 3284 912 281 1328 899

name." ¶ **44** While Peter → was still speaking these words, the Holy Spirit came on all who
τοῦ ὀνόματος → τοῦ Πέτρου → Ἔτι λαλοῦντος ταῦτα τὰ ῥήματα τὸ τὸ ἅγιον πνεῦμα ἐπέπεσεν ἐπὶ πάντας τοὺς
d.gsn n.gsn d.gsn n.gsm adv pt.pa.gsm r.apn d.apn n.apn d.nsn d.nsn a.nsn n.nsn v.aai.3s p.a a.apm d.apm
3836 3950 3281 3836 4377 3281 2285 3281 4047 3836 4839 3836 3836 41 4460 2158 2093 4246 3836

heard the message. **45** The circumcised believers who had come with Peter → were astonished that the
ἀκούοντας τὸν λόγον καὶ οἱ ἐκ περιτομῆς πιστοὶ ὅσοι → συνῆλθαν ← τῷ Πέτρῳ → ἐξέστησαν ὅτι ἡ
pt.pa.apm d.asm n.asm cj d.npm p.g n.gsf a.npm r.npm v.aai.3p d.dsm n.dsm v.aai.3p cj d.nsf
201 3836 3364 2779 3836 1666 4364 4412 4012 5302 3836 4377 2014 4022 3836

gift of the Holy Spirit → had been poured out even on the Gentiles. **46** For they heard them speaking in tongues
δωρεὰ τοῦ ἁγίου πνεύματος → → ἐκκέχυται ← καὶ ἐπὶ τὰ ἔθνη γὰρ → ἤκουον αὐτῶν λαλούντων → γλώσσαις
n.nsf d.gsn a.gsn n.gsn v.rpi.3s adv p.a d.apn n.apn cj v.iai.3p r.gpm.3 pt.pa.gpm n.dpf
1561 3836 41 4460 1773 2779 2093 3836 1620 1142 201 899 3281 1185

and praising God. ¶ Then Peter said, **47** "Can anyone keep these people from being
καὶ μεγαλυνόντων τὸν θεόν τότε Πέτρος ἀπεκρίθη μήτι δύναται τις κωλῦσαι τούτους ←
cj pt.pa.gpm d.asm n.asm adv n.nsm v.api.3s pl v.ppi.3s r.nsm f.aa r.apm
2779 3486 3836 2536 5538 4377 646 3614 1538 5516 3266 4047

baptized with water? They have received the Holy Spirit just as we have." **48** So he ordered
τοῦ μὴ βαπτισθῆναι → τὸ ὕδωρ οἵτινες → ἔλαβον τὸ τὸ ἅγιον πνεῦμα → ὡς ἡμεῖς καὶ δὲ → προσέταξεν
d.gsn pl f.ap d.asn n.asn r.npm v.aai.3p d.asn d.asn a.asn n.asn cj r.np.1 adv cj v.aai.3s
3836 3590 966 3836 5623 4015 3284 3836 3836 41 4460 6055 7005 2779 1254 4705

that they be baptized in the name of Jesus Christ. Then they asked Peter to stay with them for a few days.
αὐτοὺς βαπτισθῆναι ἐν τῷ ὀνόματι → Ἰησοῦ Χριστοῦ τότε → ἠρώτησαν αὐτὸν ἐπιμεῖναι → τινὰς ἡμέρας
r.apm.3 f.ap p.d d.dsn n.dsn n.gsm n.gsm adv v.aai.3p r.asm.3 f.aa r.apf n.apf
899 966 1877 3836 3950 2652 5986 5538 2263 899 2152 5516 2465

Peter Explains His Actions

11:1 The apostles and the brothers throughout Judea heard that the Gentiles also had
δὲ οἱ ἀπόστολοι καὶ οἱ ἀδελφοὶ οἱ ὄντες κατὰ τὴν Ἰουδαίαν Ἤκουσαν ὅτι τὰ ἔθνη καὶ →
cj d.npm n.npm cj d.npm n.npm d.npm pt.pa.npm p.a d.asf n.asf v.aai.3p cj d.npn n.npn adv
1254 3836 693 2779 3836 81 3836 1639 2848 3836 2677 201 4022 3836 1620 2779

received the word of God. **2** So when Peter went up to Jerusalem, the circumcised believers criticized
ἐδέξαντο τὸν λόγον τοῦ θεοῦ δὲ Ὅτε Πέτρος ἀνέβη ← εἰς Ἰερουσαλήμ οἱ ἐκ περιτομῆς διεκρίνοντο πρὸς
v.ami.3p d.asm n.asm d.gsn n.gsm cj cj n.nsm v.aai.3s p.a n.gsf d.npm p.g n.gsf v.imi.3p p.a
1312 3836 3364 3836 2536 1254 4021 4377 326 1650 2647 3836 1666 4364 1359 4639

him **3** and said, "You went into the house of uncircumcised men and ate with them." ¶
αὐτόν λέγοντες ὅτι Εἰσῆλθες πρὸς ἄνδρας ἔχοντας ἀκροβυστίαν καὶ συνέφαγες ← αὐτοῖς
r.asm.3 pt.pa.npm cj v.aai.2s p.a n.apm pt.pa.apm n.asf cj v.aai.2s r.dpm.3
899 3306 4022 1656 4639 467 2400 213 2779 5303 899

4 Peter began and explained everything to them precisely as it had happened: **5** "I was in the city of
δὲ Πέτρος Ἀρξάμενος ἐξετίθετο → αὐτοῖς → → → καθεξῆς λέγων ἐγὼ ἤμην ἐν πόλει
cj n.nsm pt.am.nsm v.imi.3s r.dpm.3 adv pt.pa.nsm r.ns.1 v.imi.1s p.d n.dsf
1254 4377 806 1758 899 2759 3306 1609 1639 1877 4484

Joppa praying, and in a trance I saw a vision. I saw something like a large sheet being let
Ἰόππῃ προσευχόμενος καὶ ἐν ἐκστάσει → εἶδον ὅραμα καταβαῖνον σκεῦος τι ὡς μεγάλην ὀθόνην → καθιεμένην
n.dsf pt.pm.nsm cj p.d n.dsf v.aai.1s n.asn pt.pa.asn n.asn r.asn cj a.asf a.asf pt.pp.asf
2673 4667 2779 1877 1749 1625 3969 2849 5007 5516 6055 3489 3855 2768

down from heaven by its four corners, and it came down to where I was. **6** I looked into it
← ἐκ τοῦ οὐρανοῦ → τέσσαρσιν ἀρχαῖς καὶ → ἦλθεν ἄχρι ἐμοῦ ἀτενίσας εἰς ἣν κατενόουν
p.g d.gsm n.gsm a.dpf n.dpf cj v.aai.3s p.g r.gs.1 pt.aa.nsm p.a r.asf v.iai.1s
1666 3836 4041 5475 794 2779 2262 948 1609 867 1650 4005 2917

αὐτοῦ πάντα τὸν πιστεύοντα εἰς αὐτόν. ¶ **44** Ἔτι λαλοῦντος τοῦ Πέτρου τὰ ῥήματα ταῦτα ἐπέπεσεν τὸ πνεῦμα τὸ ἅγιον ἐπὶ πάντας τοὺς ἀκούοντας τὸν λόγον. **45** καὶ ἐξέστησαν οἱ ἐκ περιτομῆς πιστοὶ ὅσοι συνῆλθαν τῷ Πέτρῳ, ὅτι καὶ ἐπὶ τὰ ἔθνη ἡ δωρεὰ τοῦ ἁγίου πνεύματος ἐκκέχυται· **46** ἤκουον γὰρ αὐτῶν λαλούντων γλώσσαις καὶ μεγαλυνόντων τὸν θεόν. ¶ τότε ἀπεκρίθη Πέτρος, **47** Μήτι τὸ ὕδωρ δύναται κωλῦσαί τις τοῦ μὴ βαπτισθῆναι τούτους, οἵτινες τὸ πνεῦμα τὸ ἅγιον ἔλαβον ὡς καὶ ἡμεῖς; **48** προσέταξεν δὲ αὐτοὺς ἐν τῷ ὀνόματι Ἰησοῦ Χριστοῦ βαπτισθῆναι. τότε ἠρώτησαν αὐτὸν ἐπιμεῖναι ἡμέρας τινάς.

11:1 Ἤκουσαν δὲ οἱ ἀπόστολοι καὶ οἱ ἀδελφοὶ οἱ ὄντες κατὰ τὴν Ἰουδαίαν ὅτι καὶ τὰ ἔθνη ἐδέξαντο τὸν λόγον τοῦ θεοῦ. **2** ὅτε δὲ ἀνέβη Πέτρος εἰς Ἰερουσαλήμ, διεκρίνοντο πρὸς αὐτὸν οἱ ἐκ περιτομῆς **3** λέγοντες ὅτι Εἰσῆλθες πρὸς ἄνδρας ἀκροβυστίαν ἔχοντας καὶ συνέφαγες αὐτοῖς. ¶ **4** ἀρξάμενος δὲ Πέτρος ἐξετίθετο αὐτοῖς καθεξῆς λέγων, **5** Ἐγὼ ἤμην ἐν πόλει Ἰόππῃ προσευχόμενος καὶ εἶδον ἐν ἐκστάσει ὅραμα, καταβαῖνον σκεῦός τι ὡς ὀθόνην μεγάλην τέσσαρσιν ἀρχαῖς καθιεμένην ἐκ τοῦ οὐρανοῦ, καὶ ἦλθεν ἄχρι ἐμοῦ. **6** εἰς ἣν ἀτενίσας κατενόουν καὶ εἶδον τὰ τετράποδα τῆς γῆς καὶ τὰ θηρία καὶ τὰ ἑρπετὰ καὶ

and saw   four-footed   animals of the earth,   wild beasts,   reptiles,   and birds   of the air.   ⁷ Then I
καὶ εἶδον ⸤τὰ τετράποδα⸥ ←   → τῆς γῆς   καὶ   ⸤τὰ θηρία⸥ καὶ ⸤τὰ ἑρπετὰ⸥ καὶ ⸤τὰ πετεινὰ⸥ → τοῦ οὐρανοῦ   δὲ →
cj   v.aai.1s d.apn n.apn   d.gsf n.gsf cj   d.apn n.apn cj d.apn n.apn cj d.apn n.apn   d.gsm n.gsm   cj
2779 1625   3836 5488   3836 1178   2779 3836 2563 2779 3836 2260 2779 3836 4374   3836 4041   1254

heard   a voice telling   me, 'Get   up, Peter. Kill   and eat.'   ¶   ⁸   "I replied, 'Surely not, Lord!
ἤκουσα καὶ   φωνῆς λεγούσης μοι ἀναστάς ← Πέτρε θῦσον καὶ φάγε   δὲ εἶπον →   μηδαμῶς κύριε ὅτι
v.aai.1s adv n.gsf pt.pa.gsf r.ds.1 pt.aa.nsm   n.vsm v.aam.2s cj v.aam.2s   cj v.aai.1s   adv   n.vsm cj
201   2779 5889 3306   1609 482   4377 2604 2779 2266   1254 3306   3592   3261   4022

Nothing impure or unclean has ever entered   my mouth.'   ⁹   "The voice spoke   from heaven   a
→   κοινὸν ἢ ἀκάθαρτον ⸤ οὐδέποτε εἰσῆλθεν εἰς μου ⸤τὸ στόμα⸥ δὲ φωνὴ ἀπεκρίθη ἐκ ⸤τοῦ οὐρανοῦ⸥
        a.nsn cj a.nsn   adv   v.aai.3s   p.a r.gs.1 d.asn n.asn cj n.nsf v.api.3s p.g d.gsm n.gsm
4030   3123 2445 176   1656   4030   1656   1650 1609 3836 5125 1254 5889 646   1666 3836 4041

second   time, 'Do not call   anything impure that God   has made clean.'   ¹⁰   This happened three
⸤ἐκ δευτέρου⸥ ← σὺ μὴ κοίνου ←   ἃ ὁ θεὸς⸥ → → ἐκαθάρισεν δὲ τοῦτο ἐγένετο   τρὶς
p.g a.gsn   r.ns.2 pl v.pam.2s   r.apn d.nsm n.nsm   v.aai.3s   cj r.nsn v.ami.3s   adv
1666 1311   5148 3590 3123   4005 3836 2536   2751   1254 4047 1181   5565

times, and then it was all   pulled up to heaven   again. ¶ ¹¹   "Right then three men   who had
ἐπὶ καὶ   →   ἅπαντα ἀνεσπάσθη ← εἰς ⸤τὸν οὐρανόν⸥ πάλιν   καὶ ἰδοὺ ἐξαυτῆς ← τρεῖς ἄνδρες →
p.a cj   a.npn v.api.3s   p.a d.asm n.asm   adv   cj adv adv   a.npm n.npm
2093 2779 413 413 570   413   1650 3836 4041   4099   2779 2627 1994   5552 467

been sent   to   me from Caesarea stopped at the house where I was staying. ¹² The Spirit told me to
→ ἀπεσταλμένοι πρός με ἀπὸ Καισαρείας ἐπέστησαν ἐπὶ τὴν οἰκίαν ἐν ᾗ → ἦμεν   δὲ τὸ πνεῦμα εἶπέν μοι ⸤
   pt.rp.npm   p.a r.as.1 p.g n.gsf   v.aai.3p   p.a d.asf n.asf p.d r.dsf v.iai.1p cj d.nsn n.nsn v.aai.3s r.ds.1
690   4639 1609 608 2791   2392   2093 3836 3864 1877 4005 1639   1254 3836 4460   3306 1609 1359

have no hesitation about going   with them.   These six brothers   also went with me, and we entered
→ μηδὲν διακρίναντα συνελθεῖν ← αὐτοῖς δὲ οὗτοι ἓξ ⸤οἱ ἀδελφοὶ⸥ καὶ ἦλθον σὺν ἐμοὶ καὶ → εἰσήλθομεν εἰς
   a.asn pt.aa.asm   f.aa   r.dpm.3 cj r.npm a.npm d.npm n.npm cj v.aai.3p p.d r.ds.1 cj v.aai.1p   p.a
1359 3594 1359   5302   899   1254 4047 1971 3836 81   2779 2262 5250 1609 2779 1656   1650

the man's   house. ¹³   He told   us how he had seen an angel   appear in his house   and say,
τὸν ⸤τοῦ ἀνδρός⸥ οἶκον δὲ → ἀπήγγειλεν ἡμῖν πῶς → → εἶδεν ⸤τὸν ἄγγελον⸥ σταθέντα ἐν αὐτοῦ ⸤τῷ οἴκῳ⸥ καὶ εἰπόντα
d.asm d.gsm n.gsm n.asm cj   v.aai.3s r.dp.1 cj   v.aai.3s d.asm n.asn pt.ap.asm p.d r.gsm.3 d.dsm n.dsm cj pt.aa.asm
3836 3836 467   3875   1254   550   7005 4802   1625 3836 34   2705   1877 899   3836 3875 2779 3306

'Send   to Joppa for Simon who is called   Peter. ¹⁴ He will bring   you a message through
ἀπόστειλον εἰς Ἰόππην καὶ μετάπεμψαι ← Σίμωνα τὸν → ἐπικαλούμενον Πέτρον ὃς → λαλήσει πρός σε   ῥήματα ἐν
v.aam.2s   p.a n.asf cj v.amm.2s   n.asm d.asm   pt.pp.asm   n.asm r.nsm v.fai.3s p.a r.as.2 n.apn p.d
690   1650 2673 2779 3569   4981 3836   2126   4377 4005   3281   4639 5148 4839   1877

which you and all your household will be saved.' ¶ ¹⁵ "As I began   to speak, the Holy   Spirit
οἷς σὺ καὶ πᾶς σου ὁ οἶκος⸥ → → σωθήσῃ   δὲ ἐν με ⸤τῷ ἄρξασθαι⸥ → λαλεῖν τὸ τὸ ἅγιον πνεῦμα
r.dpn r.ns.2 cj a.nsm r.gs.2 d.nsm n.nsm v.fpi.2s   cj p.d r.as.1 d.dsn f.am   f.pa d.nsn d.nsn a.nsn n.nsn
4005 5148 2779 4246 5148 3836 3875   5392   1254 1877 1609 3836 806   3281   3836 3836 41   4460

came on them as   he had come on us   at the beginning. ¹⁶ Then I remembered what   the Lord
ἐπέπεσεν ἐπ' αὐτοὺς ὥσπερ καὶ → ἐφ' ἡμᾶς ἐν ἀρχῇ   δὲ → ἐμνήσθην ⸤τοῦ ῥήματος⸥ τοῦ κυρίου ὡς
v.aai.3s p.a r.apm.3 adv   cj   p.a r.ap.1 p.d n.dsf   cj   v.api.1s d.gsn n.gsn   d.gsm n.gsm cj
2158   2093 899   6061 2779   2093 7005 1877 794   1254   3630   3836 4839   3836 3261 6055

had said: 'John   baptized with water, but you will be baptized with the Holy Spirit.' ¹⁷ So if God
→ ἔλεγεν μὲν Ἰωάννης ἐβάπτισεν → ὕδατι δὲ ὑμεῖς → βαπτισθήσεσθε ἐν   ἁγίῳ πνεύματι οὖν εἰ ὁ θεὸς
  v.iai.3s pl n.nsm v.aai.3s   n.dsn cj r.np.2   v.fpi.2p   p.d   a.dsn n.dsn   cj cj d.nsm n.nsm
3306 3525 2722 966   5623 1254 7007   966   1877   41   4460   4036 1623 3836 2536

gave them the same gift as   he gave us, who believed in the Lord Jesus   Christ, who was I   to think
ἔδωκεν αὐτοῖς τὴν ἴσην δωρεὰν ὡς καὶ ἡμῖν → πιστεύσασιν ἐπὶ τὸν κύριον Ἰησοῦν Χριστόν τίς ἤμην ἐγὼ
v.aai.3s r.dpm.3 d.asf a.asf n.asf cj adv r.dp.1   pt.aa.dpm p.a d.asm n.asm n.asm n.asm r.nsm v.imi.1s r.ns.1
1443   899   3836 2698 1561 6055 2779 7005   4409   2093 3836 3261 2652 5986   5515 1639 1609

that I could   oppose God?"   ¶ ¹⁸ When they heard   this, they had no further objections and praised
δυνατὸς κωλῦσαι ⸤τὸν θεόν⸥   δὲ → → Ἀκούσαντες ταῦτα → → → ἡσύχασαν καὶ ἐδόξασαν
a.nsm   f.aa   d.asm n.asm   cj   pt.aa.npm r.apn   v.aai.3p cj v.aai.3p
1543   3266   3836 2536   1254   201   4047   2483   2779 1519

τὰ πετεινὰ τοῦ οὐρανοῦ. ⁷ ἤκουσα δὲ καὶ φωνῆς λεγούσης μοι, Ἀναστάς, Πέτρε, θῦσον καὶ φάγε. ¶ ⁸ εἶπον δέ, Μηδαμῶς, κύριε, ὅτι κοινὸν ἢ ἀκάθαρτον οὐδέποτε εἰσῆλθεν εἰς τὸ στόμα μου. ⁹ ἀπεκρίθη δὲ φωνὴ ἐκ δευτέρου ἐκ τοῦ οὐρανοῦ, Ἃ ὁ θεὸς ἐκαθάρισεν, σὺ μὴ κοίνου. ¹⁰ τοῦτο δὲ ἐγένετο ἐπὶ τρίς, καὶ ἀνεσπάσθη πάλιν ἅπαντα εἰς τὸν οὐρανόν. ¶ ¹¹ καὶ ἰδοὺ ἐξαυτῆς τρεῖς ἄνδρες ἐπέστησαν ἐπὶ τὴν οἰκίαν ἐν ᾗ ἦμεν, «ἤμην,» ἀπεσταλμένοι ἀπὸ Καισαρείας πρός με. ¹² εἶπεν δὲ τὸ πνεῦμά μοι συνελθεῖν αὐτοῖς μηδὲν διακρίναντα. ἦλθον δὲ σὺν ἐμοὶ καὶ οἱ ἓξ ἀδελφοὶ οὗτοι καὶ εἰσήλθομεν εἰς τὸν οἶκον τοῦ ἀνδρός. ¹³ ἀπήγγειλεν δὲ ἡμῖν πῶς εἶδεν [τὸν] ἄγγελον ἐν τῷ οἴκῳ αὐτοῦ σταθέντα καὶ εἰπόντα, Ἀπόστειλον εἰς Ἰόππην καὶ μετάπεμψαι Σίμωνα τὸν ἐπικαλούμενον Πέτρον, ¹⁴ ὃς λαλήσει ῥήματα πρός σε ἐν οἷς σωθήσῃ σὺ καὶ πᾶς ὁ οἶκός σου. ¶ ¹⁵ ἐν δὲ τῷ ἄρξασθαί με λαλεῖν ἐπέπεσεν τὸ πνεῦμα τὸ ἅγιον ἐπ' αὐτοὺς ὥσπερ καὶ ἐφ' ἡμᾶς ἐν ἀρχῇ. ¹⁶ ἐμνήσθην δὲ τοῦ ῥήματος τοῦ κυρίου ὡς ἔλεγεν, Ἰωάννης μὲν ἐβάπτισεν ὕδατι, ὑμεῖς δὲ βαπτισθήσεσθε ἐν πνεύματι ἁγίῳ. ¹⁷ εἰ οὖν τὴν ἴσην δωρεὰν ἔδωκεν αὐτοῖς ὁ θεὸς ὡς καὶ ἡμῖν πιστεύσασιν ἐπὶ τὸν κύριον Ἰησοῦν Χριστόν, ἐγὼ τίς ἤμην δυνατὸς κωλῦσαι τὸν θεόν; ¶ ¹⁸ ἀκούσαντες δὲ ταῦτα ἡσύχασαν καὶ ἐδόξασαν τὸν θεὸν λέγοντες, Ἄρα καὶ τοῖς ἔθνεσιν ὁ θεὸς τὴν μετάνοιαν εἰς ζωὴν ἔδωκεν.

God,   saying,   "So then, God   has granted even the Gentiles repentance   unto life."
ⸯτὸν θεὸνⸯ λέγοντες ἄρα ←   ὁ   θεός → ἔδωκεν καὶ τοῖς ἔθνεσιν ⸯτὴν μετάνοιανⸯ εἰς   ζωήν
d.asm n.asm pt.pa.npm cj   d.nsm n.nsm v.aai.3s adv d.dpn n.dpn d.asf n.asf   p.a   n.asf
3836 2536   3306   726   3836 2536   1443   2779 3836 1620   3836 3567   1650 2437

The Church in Antioch

11:19 Now   those   who had been scattered   by   the persecution in connection   with Stephen traveled as   far
οὖν   μὲν   Οἱ   ←   →   →   διασπαρέντες ἀπὸ   τῆς θλίψεως   ⸯτῆς γενομένηςⸯ ἐπὶ Στεφάνῳ διῆλθον   ἕως ←
cj   pl   d.npm   pt.ap.npm   p.g   d.gsf n.gsf   d.gsf pt.am.gsf   p.d n.dsm   v.aai.3p p.g
4036 3525 3836   1401   608   3836 2568   3836 1181   2093 5108   1451   2401

as Phoenicia,   Cyprus and Antioch,   telling   the message   only to Jews.   **20** Some of them,
← Φοινίκης   καὶ Κύπρου καὶ Ἀντιοχείας μηδενὶ λαλοῦντες τὸν λόγον   εἰ μὴ μόνον → Ἰουδαίοις   τινες ἐξ αὐτῶν
n.gsf   cj   n.gsf   cj   n.gsf   a.dsm pt.pa.npm d.asm n.nsm cj pl adv   a.dpm   r.npm p.g r.gpm.3
5834   2779 3251   2779 522   3594   3281   3836 3364 1623 3590 3667   2681   1666 899

however,   men from Cyprus and Cyrene,   went   to Antioch   and began to speak to
δὲ   ⸯἮσαν ἄνδρες → Κύπριοι καὶ Κυρηναῖοι οἵτινες ἐλθόντες εἰς Ἀντιόχειαν →   → ἐλάλουν πρὸς
cj   v.iai.3p n.npm   n.npm   cj n.npm   r.npm   pt.aa.npm p.a n.asf   v.iai.3p p.a
1254 1639   467   3250   2779 3254   4015   2262   1650 522   3281   4639

Greeks   also, telling   them the good news about the Lord Jesus.   **21** The Lord's hand was with
ⸯτοὺς Ἑλληνιστάςⸯ καὶ εὐαγγελιζόμενοι ←   →   →   → τὸν κύριον Ἰησοῦν καὶ   κυρίου χεὶρ ἦν   μετ'
d.apm n.apm   adv pt.pm.npm   d.asm n.asm n.asm cj   n.gsm   n.nsf v.iai.3s p.g
3836 1821   2779 2294   3836 3261 2652   2779 3261   5931 1639 3552

them, and a great number of people believed   and turned   to the Lord. ¶   **22** News   of   this
αὐτῶν τε πολὺς ἀριθμὸς   ὁ   πιστεύσας ἐπέστρεψεν ἐπὶ τὸν κύριον   δὲ ὁ   λόγος περὶ αὐτῶν
r.gpm.3 cj a.nsm n.nsm   d.nsm pt.aa.nsm v.aai.3s   p.a d.asm n.asm   cj d.nsm n.nsm p.g r.gpm.3
899   5445 4498   750   3836 4409   2188   2093 3836 3261   1254 3836 3364   4309 899

reached   the ears of the church   at Jerusalem, and they sent   Barnabas   to Antioch.
Ἠκούσθη εἰς τὰ ὦτα → τῆς ἐκκλησίας τῆς οὔσης ἐν Ἰερουσαλὴμ καὶ → ἐξαπέστειλαν Βαρναβᾶν [διελθεῖν] ἕως Ἀντιοχείας
v.api.3s p.a d.apn n.apn d.gsf n.gsf   d.gsf pt.pa.gsf p.d n.dsf   cj   v.aai.3p   n.asm   f.aa   p.g n.gsf
201   1650 3836 4044   3836 1711   3836 1639   1877 2647   2779 1990   982   1451   2401 522

23 When he arrived   and saw the evidence of the grace   of God,   he was glad and encouraged them
→   → παραγενόμενος καὶ ἰδὼν   τὴν χάριν [τὴν]   ⸯτοῦ θεοῦⸯ ὃς → ἐχάρη καὶ παρεκάλει
pt.am.nsm cj pt.aa.nsm   d.asf n.asf d.asf   d.gsm n.gsm r.nsm   v.api.3s cj v.iai.3s
4134   2779 1625   3836 5921 3836   3836 2536   4005   5897   2779 4151

all   to remain true   to the Lord with all their hearts. **24** He was a good man,   full of the Holy
πάντας → προσμένειν ⸯτῇ προθέσειⸯ → τῷ κυρίῳ   τῆς καρδίας ὅτι → ἦν ἀγαθὸς ἀνὴρ καὶ πλήρης   ἁγίου
a.apm   f.pa   d.dsf n.dsf   d.dsm n.dsm   d.gsf n.gsf   cj   v.iai.3s a.nsm n.nsm cj a.nsm   a.gsn
4246   4693   3836 4606   3836 3261   3836 2840   4022 1639   19   467   2779 4441   41

Spirit   and faith, and a great number of people were brought to the Lord. ¶ **25** Then Barnabas went to
πνεύματος καὶ πίστεως καὶ ἱκανὸς   ὄχλος →   προσετέθη τῷ κυρίῳ   δὲ   ἐξῆλθεν εἰς
n.gsn   cj n.gsf   cj a.nsm   n.nsm   v.api.3s   d.dsm n.dsm   cj   v.aai.3s p.a
4460   2779 4411   2779 2653   4063   4707   3836 3261   1254   2002   1650

Tarsus to look   for Saul, **26** and when he found him, he brought him to Antioch. So   for a
Ταρσὸν → ἀναζητῆσαι Σαῦλον καὶ →   → εὑρὼν   → ἤγαγεν   εἰς Ἀντιόχειαν δὲ ἐγένετο αὐτοῖς καὶ →
n.asf   f.aa   n.asm   cj   pt.aa.nsm   v.aai.3s p.a n.asf   cj v.ami.3s r.dpm.3 adv
5433   349   4930   2779   2351   72   1650 522   1254 1181   899   2779

whole year   Barnabas and Saul met   with   the church and taught great numbers of people.   The
ὅλον ἐνιαυτὸν   → συναχθῆναι ← ἐν τῇ ἐκκλησίᾳ καὶ διδάξαι ἱκανόν   ὄχλον τε τοὺς
a.asm n.asm   f.ap   p.d d.dsf n.dsf   cj f.aa   a.asm   n.asm cj d.apm
3910 1929   5251   1877 3836 1711   2779 1438   2653   4063 5445 3836

disciples were called   Christians first at Antioch. ¶   **27** During this time   some prophets
μαθητὰς → χρηματίσαι Χριστιανοὺς πρώτως ἐν Ἀντιοχείᾳ   δὲ Ἐν ταύταις ⸯταῖς ἡμέραιςⸯ   προφῆται
n.apm   f.aa   n.apm   adv   p.d n.dsf   cj p.d r.dpf d.dpf n.dpf   n.npm
3412   5976   5985   4759   1877 522   1254 1877 4047 3836 2465   4737

came   down from Jerusalem to Antioch.   **28** One of them, named Agabus stood   up and through the Spirit
κατῆλθον ← ἀπὸ Ἰεροσολύμων εἰς Ἀντιόχειαν δὲ εἰς ἐξ αὐτῶν ὀνόματι Ἄγαβος ἀναστὰς ← διὰ τοῦ πνεύματος
v.aai.3p   p.g n.gpn   p.a n.asf   cj a.nsm p.g r.gpm.3 n.dsn n.nsm   pt.aa.nsm   p.g d.gsn n.gsn
2982   608 2642   1650 522   1254 1651 1666 899   3950   13   482   1328 3836 4460

11:19 Οἱ μὲν οὖν διασπαρέντες ἀπὸ τῆς θλίψεως τῆς γενομένης ἐπὶ Στεφάνῳ διῆλθον ἕως Φοινίκης καὶ Κύπρου καὶ Ἀντιοχείας μηδενὶ λαλοῦντες τὸν λόγον εἰ μὴ μόνον Ἰουδαίοις. **20** ἦσαν δέ τινες ἐξ αὐτῶν ἄνδρες Κύπριοι καὶ Κυρηναῖοι, οἵτινες ἐλθόντες εἰς Ἀντιόχειαν ἐλάλουν καὶ πρὸς τοὺς Ἕλληνας «Ἑλληνιστὰς» εὐαγγελιζόμενοι τὸν κύριον Ἰησοῦν. **21** καὶ ἦν χεὶρ κυρίου μετ' αὐτῶν, πολύς τε ἀριθμὸς ὁ πιστεύσας ἐπέστρεψεν ἐπὶ τὸν κύριον. ¶ **22** ἠκούσθη δὲ ὁ λόγος εἰς τὰ ὦτα τῆς ἐκκλησίας τῆς οὔσης ἐν Ἰερουσαλὴμ περὶ αὐτῶν καὶ ἐξαπέστειλαν Βαρναβᾶν [διελθεῖν] ἕως Ἀντιοχείας. **23** ὃς παραγενόμενος καὶ ἰδὼν τὴν χάριν [τὴν] τοῦ θεοῦ, ἐχάρη καὶ παρεκάλει πάντας τῇ προθέσει τῆς καρδίας προσμένειν τῷ κυρίῳ, **24** ὅτι ἦν ἀνὴρ ἀγαθὸς καὶ πλήρης πνεύματος ἁγίου καὶ πίστεως. καὶ προσετέθη ὄχλος ἱκανὸς τῷ κυρίῳ. ¶ **25** ἐξῆλθεν δὲ εἰς Ταρσὸν ἀναζητῆσαι Σαῦλον, **26** καὶ εὑρὼν ἤγαγεν εἰς Ἀντιόχειαν. ἐγένετο δὲ αὐτοῖς καὶ ἐνιαυτὸν ὅλον συναχθῆναι ἐν τῇ ἐκκλησίᾳ καὶ διδάξαι ὄχλον ἱκανόν, χρηματίσαι τε πρώτως ἐν Ἀντιοχείᾳ τοὺς μαθητὰς Χριστιανούς. ¶ **27** Ἐν ταύταις δὲ ταῖς ἡμέραις κατῆλθον ἀπὸ Ἰεροσολύμων προφῆται εἰς Ἀντιόχειαν. **28** ἀναστὰς δὲ εἷς ἐξ αὐτῶν ὀνόματι Ἄγαβος ἐσήμανεν διὰ τοῦ πνεύματος λιμὸν μεγάλην μέλλειν

predicted that a severe famine would spread over the entire Roman world. (This happened during the reign of →
ἐσήμανεν   μεγάλην λιμὸν μέλλειν ἔσεσθαι ἐφ' τὴν ὅλην   οἰκουμένην ἥτις ἐγένετο ἐπὶ
v.aai.3s   a.asf n.asf f.pa f.fm p.a d.asf a.asf   n.asf r.nsf v.ami.3s p.g
4955   3489 3350 3516 1639 2093 3836 3910   3876 4015 1181 2093

Claudius.) **29** The disciples, each   according to his ability, decided to provide help for the brothers
Κλαυδίου δὲ τῶν μαθητῶν ἔκαστος αὐτῶν καθὼς ← τις εὐπορεῖτό ὥρισαν → πέμψαι εἰς διακονίαν → τοῖς ἀδελφοῖς
n.gsm cj d.gpm n.gpm r.nsm r.gpm.3 cj   r.nsm v.imi.3s v.aai.3p f.aa p.a n.asf   d.dpm n.dpm
3087 1254 3836 3412 1667 899 2777   5516 2344 3988 4287 1650 1355   3836 81

living in Judea. **30** This they did, sending their gift to the elders by Barnabas and
κατοικοῦσιν ἐν τῇ Ἰουδαίᾳ ὃ καὶ → ἐποίησαν ἀποστείλαντες πρὸς τοὺς πρεσβυτέρους διὰ χειρὸς Βαρναβᾶ καὶ
pt.pa.dpm p.d d.dsf n.dsf r.asn adv v.aai.3p pt.aa.npm p.a d.apm a.apm p.g n.gsf n.gsm cj
2997 1877 3836 2677 4005 2779 4472 690 4639 3836 4565 1328 5931 982 2779

Saul.
Σαύλου
n.gsm
4930

Peter's Miraculous Escape From Prison

12:1 It was about this time that King Herod arrested some who belonged to the
δὲ Κατ' ἐκεῖνον τὸν καιρὸν ὁ βασιλεύς, Ἡρῴδης ἐπέβαλεν τὰς χεῖρας, τινας τῶν ἀπὸ ← τῆς
cj p.a r.asm d.asm n.asm d.nsm n.nsm n.nsm v.aai.3s d.apf n.apf r.apm d.gpm p.g d.gsf
1254 2848 1697 3836 2789 3836 995 2476 2095 3836 5931 5516 3836 608 3836

church, intending to persecute them. **2** He had James, the brother of John, put to death with the sword. **3**
ἐκκλησίας → κακῶσαι δὲ Ἰάκωβον τὸν ἀδελφὸν Ἰωάννου → ἀνεῖλεν → μαχαίρῃ δὲ
n.gsf f.aa cj n.asm d.asm n.asm n.gsm v.aai.3s n.dsf cj
1711 2808 1254 2610 3836 81 2722 359 3479 1254

When he saw that this pleased the Jews, he proceeded to seize Peter also. This happened
→ → ἰδὼν ὅτι → ἀρεστόν ἐστιν τοῖς Ἰουδαίοις → προσέθετο → συλλαβεῖν Πέτρον καὶ δὲ → ἦσαν
pt.aa.nsm cj a.nsn v.pai.3s d.dpm a.dpm v.ami.3s f.aa n.asm adv cj v.iai.3p
1625 4022 744 1639 3836 2681 4707 5197 4377 2779 1254 1639

during the Feast of Unleavened Bread. **4** After arresting him, he put him in prison, handing him over to be
αἱ ἡμέραι τῶν → ἀζύμων πιάσας ὃν καὶ ἔθετο εἰς φυλακὴν παραδοὺς ←
d.npf n.npf d.gpn n.gpn pt.aa.nsm r.asm adv v.ami.3s p.a n.asf pt.aa.nsm
3836 2465 3836 109 4389 4005 2779 5502 1650 5871 4140

guarded by four squads of four soldiers each. Herod intended to bring him out for public
φυλάσσειν αὐτόν → τέσσαρσιν → → τετραδίοις στρατιωτῶν βουλόμενος → ἀναγαγεῖν αὐτὸν ← → τῷ λαῷ
f.pa r.asm.3 a.dpn n.dpn n.gpm pt.pm.nsm f.aa r.asm.3 d.dsm n.dsm
5875 899 5475 5482 5132 1089 343 899 343 3836 3295

trial after the Passover. ¶ **5** So Peter was kept in prison, but the church was earnestly
μετὰ τὸ πάσχα οὖν μὲν ὁ Πέτρος, → ἐτηρεῖτο ἐν τῇ φυλακῇ, δὲ ὑπὸ τῆς ἐκκλησίας ἦν ἐκτενῶς
p.a d.asn n.asn cj pl d.nsm n.nsm v.ipi.3s p.d d.dsf n.dsf cj p.g d.gsf n.gsf v.iai.3s adv
3552 3836 4247 4036 3525 3836 4377 5498 1877 3836 5871 1254 5679 3836 1711 1639 1757

praying to God for him. ¶ **6** The night before Herod was to bring him to
γινομένη προσευχὴ πρὸς τὸν θεὸν περὶ αὐτοῦ δὲ ἐκείνῃ τῇ νυκτὶ Ὅτε ὁ Ἡρῴδης ἤμελλεν → προαγαγεῖν αὐτὸν ←
pt.pm.nsf n.nsf p.a d.asm n.asm p.g r.gsm.3 cj r.dsf d.dsf n.dsf cj d.nsm n.nsm v.iai.3s f.aa r.asm.3
1181 4666 4639 3836 2536 4309 899 1254 1697 3836 3816 4021 3836 2476 3516 4575 899 4575

trial, Peter was sleeping between two soldiers, bound with two chains, and sentries stood guard at
← ὁ Πέτρος, ἦν κοιμώμενος μεταξὺ δύο στρατιωτῶν δεδεμένος → δυσὶν ἁλύσεσιν τε φύλακες ἐτήρουν τὴν φυλακήν, πρὸ
d.nsm n.nsm v.iai.3s pt.pm.nsm p.g a.gpm n.gpm pt.rp.nsm a.dpf n.dpf cj n.npm v.iai.3p d.asf n.asf p.g
4575 3836 4377 1639 3121 3568 1545 5132 1313 1545 268 5445 5874 5498 3836 5871 4574

the entrance. **7** Suddenly an angel of the Lord appeared and a light shone in the cell. He struck
τῆς θύρας καὶ ἰδοὺ ἄγγελος → κυρίου ἐπέστη καὶ φῶς ἔλαμψεν ἐν τῷ οἰκήματι δὲ → πατάξας
d.gsf n.gsf cj n.nsm n.gsm v.aai.3s cj n.nsn v.aai.3s p.d d.dsn n.dsn cj pt.aa.nsm
3836 2598 2779 2627 34 3261 2392 2779 5890 3290 1877 3836 3862 1254 4250

Peter on the side and woke him up. "Quick, get up!" he said, and the chains fell off Peter's
τοῦ Πέτρου, τὴν πλευρὰν ἤγειρεν αὐτὸν ἐν τάχει ἀνάστα ← → λέγων καὶ αἱ ἁλύσεις ἐξέπεσαν ἐκ αὐτοῦ
d.gsm n.gsm d.asf n.asf v.aai.3s r.asm.3 p.d n.dsn v.aam.2s pt.pa.nsm cj d.npf n.npf v.aai.3p p.g r.gsm.3
3836 4377 3836 4433 1586 899 1877 5443 482 3306 2779 3836 268 1738 1666 899

ἔσεσθαι ἐφ' ὅλην τὴν οἰκουμένην, ἥτις ἐγένετο ἐπὶ Κλαυδίου. ²⁹ τῶν δὲ μαθητῶν, καθὼς εὐπορεῖτό τις ὥρισαν ἔκαστος αὐτῶν εἰς διακονίαν πέμψαι τοῖς κατοικοῦσιν ἐν τῇ Ἰουδαίᾳ ἀδελφοῖς· ³⁰ ὃ καὶ ἐποίησαν ἀποστείλαντες πρὸς τοὺς πρεσβυτέρους διὰ χειρὸς Βαρναβᾶ καὶ Σαύλου.

12:1 Κατ' ἐκεῖνον δὲ τὸν καιρὸν ἐπέβαλεν Ἡρῴδης ὁ βασιλεὺς τὰς χεῖρας κακῶσαί τινας τῶν ἀπὸ τῆς ἐκκλησίας. ² ἀνεῖλεν δὲ Ἰάκωβον τὸν ἀδελφὸν Ἰωάννου μαχαίρῃ ³ ἰδὼν δὲ ὅτι ἀρεστόν ἐστιν τοῖς Ἰουδαίοις προσέθετο συλλαβεῖν καὶ Πέτρον, ἦσαν δὲ [αἱ] ἡμέραι τῶν ἀζύμων ⁴ ὃν καὶ πιάσας ἔθετο εἰς φυλακὴν παραδοὺς τέσσαρσιν τετραδίοις στρατιωτῶν φυλάσσειν αὐτόν, βουλόμενος μετὰ τὸ πάσχα ἀναγαγεῖν αὐτὸν τῷ λαῷ. ¶ ⁵ ὁ μὲν οὖν Πέτρος ἐτηρεῖτο ἐν τῇ φυλακῇ· προσευχὴ δὲ ἦν ἐκτενῶς γινομένη ὑπὸ τῆς ἐκκλησίας πρὸς τὸν θεὸν περὶ αὐτοῦ. ¶ ⁶ Ὅτε δὲ ἤμελλεν προαγαγεῖν αὐτὸν ὁ Ἡρῴδης, τῇ νυκτὶ ἐκείνῃ ἦν ὁ Πέτρος κοιμώμενος μεταξὺ δύο στρατιωτῶν δεδεμένος ἁλύσεσιν δυσὶν φύλακές τε πρὸ τῆς θύρας ἐτήρουν τὴν φυλακήν. ⁷ καὶ ἰδοὺ ἄγγελος κυρίου ἐπέστη καὶ φῶς ἔλαμψεν ἐν τῷ οἰκήματι· πατάξας δὲ τὴν πλευρὰν τοῦ Πέτρου ἤγειρεν αὐτὸν λέγων, Ἀνάστα ἐν τάχει. καὶ ἐξέπεσαν αὐτοῦ αἱ ἁλύσεις ἐκ τῶν χειρῶν. ¶ ⁸ εἶπεν δὲ ὁ ἄγγελος πρὸς αὐτόν, Ζῶσαι καὶ

wrists. ¶ **8** Then the angel said to him, "Put on your clothes and sandals." And Peter
ⸯτῶν χειρῶνⸯ δὲ ὁ ἄγγελος εἶπεν πρὸς αὐτόν ζῶσαι ← σου ↰ καὶ ὑπόδησαι ⸯτὰ σανδάλιαⸯ δὲ
d.gpf n.gpf cj d.nsm n.nsm v.aai.3s r.asm.3 v.amm.2s r.gs.2 cj v.amm.2s d.apn n.apn cj
3836 5931 1254 3836 34 3306 4639 899 2439 5148 2439 2779 5686 3836 4908 1254

did so. "Wrap your cloak around you and follow me," the angel told him. **9** Peter followed
ἐποίησεν οὕτως καὶ περιβαλοῦ σου ⸯτὸ ἱμάτιονⸯ ↰ καὶ ἀκολούθει μοι λέγει αὐτῷ καὶ ἠκολούθει
v.aai.3s adv cj v.amm.2s r.gs.2 d.asn n.asn cj v.pam.2s r.ds.1 v.pai.3s r.dsm.3 cj v.iai.3s
4472 4048 2779 4314 5148 3836 2668 4314 2779 199 1609 3306 899 2779 199

him out of the prison, but he had no idea that what the angel was doing was really happening; he
ἐξελθών ← καὶ → → οὐκ ᾔδει ὅτι τὸ διὰ τοῦ ἀγγέλου → γινόμενον ↱ ἀληθές ἐστιν δὲ →
pt.aa.nsm cj pl v.iai.3s cj d.nsn p.g d.gsm n.gsm pt.pm.nsn a.nsn v.pai.3s cj
2002 2779 3857 3857 4024 3857 4022 3836 1328 3836 34 1181 1639 239 1639 1254

thought he was seeing a vision. **10** They passed the first and second guards and came to the iron gate
ἐδόκει → → βλέπειν ὅραμα δὲ διελθόντες πρώτην καὶ δευτέραν φυλακὴν ἦλθαν ἐπὶ τ. asf ⸯσιδηρᾶνⸯ πύλην
v.iai.3s f.pa n.asn cj pt.aa.npm a.asf cj a.asf n.asf v.aai.3p p.a d.asf d.asf n.asf
1506 1063 3969 1254 1451 4755 2779 1311 5871 2262 2093 3836 3836 4971 4783

leading to the city. It opened for them by itself, and they went through it. When they had walked
ⸯτὴν φέρουσανⸯ εἰς τὴν πόλιν ἥτις ἠνοίγη → αὐτοῖς αὐτομάτη → καὶ → ἐξελθόντες ← → → προῆλθον
d.asf pt.pa.asf p.a d.asf n.asf r.nsf v.api.3s r.dpm.3 a.nsf cj pt.aa.npm v.aai.3p
3836 5770 1650 3836 4484 4015 487 899 897 2779 2002 4601

the length of one street, suddenly the angel left him. ¶ **11** Then Peter came to himself and
μίαν ῥύμην καὶ εὐθέως ὁ ἄγγελος ἀπέστη ἀπ᾽ αὐτοῦ Καὶ ὁ Πέτρος γενόμενος ἐν ἑαυτῷ
a.asf n.asf cj adv d.nsm n.nsm v.aai.3s p.g r.gsm.3 cj d.nsm n.nsm pt.am.nsm p.d r.dsm.3
1651 4860 2779 2311 3836 34 923 608 899 2779 3836 4377 1181 1877 1571

said, "Now I know without a doubt that the Lord sent his angel and rescued me from Herod's
εἶπεν νῦν οἶδα → ἀληθῶς ὅτι ὁ κύριος ἐξαπέστειλεν αὐτοῦ ⸯτὸν ἄγγελονⸯ καὶ ἐξείλατο με ἐκ Ἡρῴδου
v.aai.3s adv v.rai.1s adv cj d.nsm n.nsm v.aai.3s r.gsm.3 d.asm n.asm cj v.ami.3s r.as.1 p.g
3306 3814 3857 242 4022 3836 3261 1990 899 3836 34 2779 1975 1609 1666 2476

clutches and from everything the Jewish people were anticipating." ¶ **12** When this had dawned on
χειρὸς καὶ πάσης τοῦ ⸯτῶν Ἰουδαίωνⸯ λαοῦ ⸯτῆς προσδοκίαςⸯ τε → → → συνιδών ←
n.gsf cj a.gsf d.gsm d.gpm a.gpm n.gsm d.gsf n.gsf cj pt.aa.nsm
5931 2779 4246 3836 3836 2681 3295 3836 4660 5445 5328

him, he went to the house of Mary the mother of John, also called Mark, where many people
← → ἦλθεν ἐπὶ τὴν οἰκίαν ⸯτῆς Μαρίαςⸯ τῆς μητρὸς → Ἰωάννου ⸯτοῦ ἐπικαλουμένουⸯ Μάρκου οὗ ἱκανοὶ ←
v.aai.3s p.a d.asf n.asf d.gsf n.gsf d.gsf n.gsf n.gsm d.gsm pt.pp.gsm n.gsm adv a.npm
2262 2093 3836 3864 3836 3451 3836 3613 2722 3836 2126 3453 4023 2653

had gathered and were praying. **13** Peter knocked at the outer entrance, and a servant girl named
ἦσαν συνηθροισμένοι καὶ → προσευχόμενοι δὲ αὐτοῦ κρούσαντος τὴν ⸯτοῦ πυλῶνοςⸯ θύραν παιδίσκη ὀνόματι
v.iai.3p pt.rp.npm cj pt.pm.npm cj r.gsm.3 pt.aa.gsm d.asf d.gsm n.gsm n.asf n.nsf n.dsn
1639 5255 2779 4667 1254 899 3218 3836 3836 4784 2598 4087 3950

Rhoda came to answer the door. **14** When she recognized Peter's voice, she was so overjoyed
Ῥόδη προσῆλθεν ← ὑπακοῦσαι καὶ → → ἐπιγνοῦσα ⸯτοῦ Πέτρουⸯ ⸯτὴν φωνὴνⸯ ⸯἀπὸ τῆς χαρᾶςⸯ δὲ
n.nsf v.aai.3s f.aa cj pt.aa.nsf d.gsm n.gsm d.asf n.asf p.g d.gsf n.gsf cj
4851 4665 5634 2779 2105 3836 4377 3836 5889 608 3836 5915 1254

she ran back without opening it and exclaimed, "Peter is at the door!" ¶ **15**
→ εἰσδραμοῦσα ← οὐκ ἤνοιξεν ⸯτὸν πυλῶναⸯ ἀπήγγειλεν ⸯτὸν Πέτρονⸯ ἑστάναι πρὸ τοῦ πυλῶνος δὲ
pt.aa.nsf pl v.aai.3s d.asm n.asm v.aai.3s d.asm n.asm f.ra p.g d.gsm n.gsm cj
1661 4024 487 3836 4784 550 3836 4377 2705 4574 3836 4784 1254

"You're out of your mind," they told her. When she kept insisting that it was so, they said, "It
→ → → μαίνῃ οἱ εἶπαν πρὸς αὐτὴν δὲ ἡ → διϊσχυρίζετο → → ⸯοὕτως ἔχεινⸯ δὲ οἱ ἔλεγον →
v.pmi.2s d.npm v.aai.3p p.a r.asf.3 cj d.nsf v.imi.3s adv f.pa cj d.npm v.iai.3p
3419 3836 3306 4639 899 1254 3836 1462 4048 2400 1254 3836 3306

must be his angel." ¶ **16** But Peter kept on knocking, and when they opened the door and
→ ἐστιν αὐτοῦ ὁ ἄγγελοςⸯ δὲ ὁ Πέτρος ἐπέμενεν ← κρούων δὲ → → ἀνοίξαντες
v.pai.3s r.gsm.3 d.nsm n.nsm cj d.nsm n.nsm v.iai.3s pt.pa.nsm cj pt.aa.npm
1639 899 3836 34 1254 3836 4377 2152 3218 1254 487

saw him, they were astonished. **17** Peter motioned with his hand for them to be quiet and described
εἶδαν αὐτὸν καὶ → ἐξέστησαν δὲ κατασείσας → τῇ χειρὶ → αὐτοῖς → σιγᾶν διηγήσατο
v.aai.3p r.asm.3 cj v.aai.3p cj pt.aa.nsm d.dsf n.dsf r.dpm.3 f.pa v.ami.3s
1625 899 2779 2014 1254 2715 3836 5931 899 4967 1455

ὑπόδησαι τὰ σανδάλιά σου. ἐποίησεν δὲ οὕτως. καὶ λέγει αὐτῷ, Περιβαλοῦ τὸ ἱμάτιόν σου καὶ ἀκολούθει μοι. **9** καὶ ἐξελθὼν ἠκολούθει καὶ οὐκ ᾔδει ὅτι ἀληθές ἐστιν τὸ γινόμενον διὰ τοῦ ἀγγέλου· ἐδόκει δὲ ὅραμα βλέπειν. **10** διελθόντες δὲ πρώτην φυλακὴν καὶ δευτέραν ἦλθαν ἐπὶ τὴν πύλην τὴν σιδηρᾶν τὴν φέρουσαν εἰς τὴν πόλιν, ἥτις αὐτομάτη ἠνοίγη αὐτοῖς καὶ ἐξελθόντες προῆλθον ῥύμην μίαν, καὶ εὐθέως ἀπέστη ὁ ἄγγελος ἀπ᾽ αὐτοῦ. ¶ **11** καὶ ὁ Πέτρος ἐν ἑαυτῷ γενόμενος εἶπεν, Νῦν οἶδα ἀληθῶς ὅτι ἐξαπέστειλεν [ὁ] κύριος τὸν ἄγγελον αὐτοῦ καὶ ἐξείλατό με ἐκ χειρὸς Ἡρῴδου καὶ πάσης τῆς προσδοκίας τοῦ λαοῦ τῶν Ἰουδαίων. ¶ **12** συνιδών τε ἦλθεν ἐπὶ τὴν οἰκίαν τῆς Μαρίας τῆς μητρὸς Ἰωάννου τοῦ ἐπικαλουμένου Μάρκου, οὗ ἦσαν ἱκανοὶ συνηθροισμένοι καὶ προσευχόμενοι. **13** κρούσαντος δὲ αὐτοῦ τὴν θύραν τοῦ πυλῶνος προσῆλθεν παιδίσκη ὑπακοῦσαι ὀνόματι Ῥόδη, **14** καὶ ἐπιγνοῦσα τὴν φωνὴν τοῦ Πέτρου ἀπὸ τῆς χαρᾶς οὐκ ἤνοιξεν τὸν πυλῶνα, εἰσδραμοῦσα δὲ ἀπήγγειλεν ἑστάναι τὸν Πέτρον πρὸ τοῦ πυλῶνος. ¶ **15** οἱ δὲ πρὸς αὐτὴν εἶπαν, Μαίνῃ. ἡ δὲ διϊσχυρίζετο οὕτως ἔχειν. οἱ δὲ ἔλεγον, Ὁ ἄγγελός ἐστιν αὐτοῦ. ¶ **16** ὁ δὲ Πέτρος ἐπέμενεν κρούων· ἀνοίξαντες δὲ εἶδαν αὐτὸν καὶ ἐξέστησαν. **17** κατασείσας δὲ αὐτοῖς τῇ χειρὶ σιγᾶν

how the Lord had brought him out of prison.   "Tell   James   and   the brothers   about this,"
[αὐτοῖς]   πῶς   ὁ   κύριος   →   ἐξήγαγεν   αὐτὸν   ἐκ   ←   τῆς φυλακῆς   τε   ἀπαγγείλατε   Ἰακώβῳ   καὶ   τοῖς ἀδελφοῖς   ταῦτα
r.dpm.3   cj   d.nsm n.nsm   v.aai.3s   r.asm.3   d.gsf n.gsf   cj   v.aam.2p   n.dsm   cj   d.dpm n.dpm   r.apn
899   4802 3836   3261   1974   899   1666   3836 5871   5445 550   2610   2779 3836   81   4047

he said, and then   he left   for another place.   ¶   18   In the morning,   there was no small
→   εἶπεν   καὶ   →   ἐξελθὼν   →   ἐπορεύθη   εἰς   ἕτερον   τόπον   δὲ   →   Γενομένης   ἡμέρας   →   ἦν   οὐκ   ὀλίγος
v.aai.3s   cj   pt.aa.nsm   v.api.3s   p.a   r.asm   n.asm   cj   pt.am.gsf   n.gsf   v.iai.3s pl   a.nsm
3306   2779   2002   4513   1650   2283   5536   1254   1181   2465   1639   4024   3900

commotion among the soldiers   as   to what had become of Peter.   19   After Herod had a thorough search
τάραχος   ἐν   τοῖς στρατιώταις   ἄρα   ←   τί   →   ἐγένετο   ὁ   Πέτρος   δὲ   Ἡρῴδης   →   →   →   ἐπιζητήσας
n.nsm   p.d   d.dpm n.dpm   cj   r.nsn   v.ami.3s   d.nsm n.nsm   cj   n.nsm   pt.aa.nsm
5431   1877   3836   5132   726   5515   1181   3836   4377   1254 2118   2118

made for him   and did not find   him, he cross-examined the guards   and ordered that they be executed.
←   αὐτὸν   καὶ   →   μὴ   εὑρών   →   ἀνακρίνας   τοὺς φύλακας   ἐκέλευσεν   →   ἀπαχθῆναι
     r.asm.3   cj   pl   pt.aa.nsm   pt.aa.nsm   d.apm n.apm   v.aai.3s   f.ap
     899   2779   3590 2351   373   3836   5874   3027   552

Herod's Death

12:19 Then Herod went   from Judea   to   Caesarea   and stayed   there a while.   20   He had been
καὶ   κατελθὼν   ἀπὸ   τῆς Ἰουδαίας   εἰς   Καισάρειαν   διέτριβεν   ←   δὲ   →   Ἦν
cj   pt.aa.nsm   p.g   d.gsf n.gsf   p.a   n.asf   v.iai.3s   cj   v.iai.3s
2779   2982   608   3836   2677   1650   2791   1417   1254   1639

quarreling with the people of Tyre   and Sidon;   they now joined   together and sought   an audience with
θυμομαχῶν   →   →   →   →   Τυρίοις   καὶ   Σιδωνίοις   δὲ   →   ὁμοθυμαδὸν   ←   παρῆσαν   ←   ←   πρὸς
pt.pa.nsm   n.dpm   cj   a.dpm   cj   adv   v.iai.3p   p.a
2595   5601   2779 4973   1254   3924   4205   4639

him.   Having secured the support of Blastus,   a trusted personal servant   of the king,   they asked
αὐτὸν   καὶ   →   →   →   πείσαντες   Βλάστον   τὸν   →   →   ἐπὶ τοῦ κοιτῶνος   →   τοῦ βασιλέως   →   ᾐτοῦντο
r.asm.3   cj   pt.aa.npm   n.asm   d.asm   p.g d.gsm n.gsm   d.gsm n.gsm   v.imi.3p
899   2779   4275   1058   3836   2093 3836   3131   3836   995   160

for peace, because they depended on the king's   country   for their food   supply.   ¶   21   On the
←   εἰρήνην   διὰ   →   →   →   ἀπὸ   τῆς βασιλικῆς   τὴν χώραν   αὐτῶν   τὸ   τρέφεσθαι   ←   δὲ
     n.asf   p.a   p.g   d.gsf a.gsf   d.asf n.asf   r.gpm.3 d.asn f.pp   cj
     1645   1328   608   3836   997   3836   6001   899   3836   5555   1254

appointed day Herod,   wearing   his royal   robes,   sat   on his throne   and delivered a public
τακτῇ   ἡμέρα   ὁ   Ἡρῴδης   ἐνδυσάμενος   βασιλικὴν   ἐσθῆτα   [καὶ]   καθίσας   ἐπὶ   τοῦ βήματος   ἐδημηγόρει   ←
a.dsf   n.dsf   d.nsm n.nsm   pt.am.nsm   a.asf   n.asf   cj   pt.aa.nsm   p.g   d.gsn n.gsn   v.iai.3s
5414   2465   3836   2476   1907   997   2264   2779   2767   2093   3836   1037   1319

address to   the people.   22   They   shouted, "This is the voice of a god,   not of a man."   23   Immediately,
←   πρὸς   αὐτούς   δὲ   ὁ   δῆμος   ἐπεφώνει   φωνὴ   →   θεοῦ   καὶ   οὐκ   ἀνθρώπου   δὲ   παραχρῆμα
     p.a   r.apm.3   cj   d.nsm n.nsm   v.iai.3s   n.nsf   n.gsm   cj   pl   n.gsm   cj   adv
     4639   899   1254 3836   1322   2215   5889   2536   2779 4024   476   1254 4202

because Herod did not give   praise   to God,   an angel of the Lord struck   him   down, and he was
ἀνθ᾽ ὧν   →   οὐκ   ἔδωκεν   τὴν δόξαν   →   τῷ θεῷ   ἄγγελος   →   κυρίου   ἐπάταξεν   αὐτὸν   ←   καὶ   →   γενόμενος
p.g r.gpn   pl   v.aai.3s   d.asf n.asf   d.dsm n.dsm   n.nsm   n.gsm   v.aai.3s   r.asm.3   cj   pt.am.nsm
505 4005   4024 1443   3836   1518   3836   2536   34   3261   4250   899   2779   1181

eaten   by worms and died.   ¶   24   But the word of God   continued to increase and spread.   ¶
σκωληκόβρωτος   ←   ←   ἐξέψυξεν   δὲ   Ὁ   λόγος   →   τοῦ θεοῦ   →   ηὔξανεν   καὶ   ἐπληθύνετο
a.nsm   v.aai.3s   cj   d.nsm n.nsm   d.gsm n.gsm   v.iai.3s   cj   v.ipi.3s
5037   1775   1254 3836   3364   3836   2536   889   2779 4437

25   When Barnabas and Saul   had finished   their mission,   they returned from Jerusalem, taking   with
δὲ   →   Βαρναβᾶς   καὶ   Σαῦλος   →   πληρώσαντες   τὴν διακονίαν   →   ὑπέστρεψαν εἰς   Ἰερουσαλὴμ   συμπαραλαβόντες   ←
cj   n.nsm   cj   n.nsm   pt.aa.npm   d.asf n.asf   v.aai.3p   p.a   n.asf   pt.aa.npm
1254 4444 982   2779 4930   4444   3836   1355   5715   1650   2647   5221

them John,   also called   Mark.
←   Ἰωάννην   τὸν ἐπικληθέντα   Μᾶρκον
     n.asm   d.asm pt.ap.asm   n.asm
     2722   3836   2126   3453

διηγήσατο [αὐτοῖς] πῶς ὁ κύριος αὐτὸν ἐξήγαγεν ἐκ τῆς φυλακῆς εἶπέν τε, Ἀπαγγείλατε Ἰακώβῳ καὶ τοῖς ἀδελφοῖς ταῦτα. καὶ ἐξελθὼν ἐπορεύθη εἰς ἕτερον τόπον. ¶ 18 Γενομένης δὲ ἡμέρας ἦν τάραχος οὐκ ὀλίγος ἐν τοῖς στρατιώταις τί ἄρα ὁ Πέτρος ἐγένετο.

12:19 Ἡρῴδης δὲ ἐπιζητήσας αὐτὸν καὶ μὴ εὑρών, ἀνακρίνας τοὺς φύλακας ἐκέλευσεν ἀπαχθῆναι, καὶ κατελθὼν ἀπὸ τῆς Ἰουδαίας εἰς Καισάρειαν διέτριβεν. 20 Ἦν δὲ θυμομαχῶν Τυρίοις καὶ Σιδωνίοις· ὁμοθυμαδὸν δὲ παρῆσαν πρὸς αὐτὸν καὶ πείσαντες Βλάστον, τὸν ἐπὶ τοῦ κοιτῶνος τοῦ βασιλέως, ᾐτοῦντο εἰρήνην διὰ τὸ τρέφεσθαι αὐτῶν τὴν χώραν ἀπὸ τῆς βασιλικῆς. ¶ 21 τακτῇ δὲ ἡμέρα ὁ Ἡρῴδης ἐνδυσάμενος ἐσθῆτα βασιλικὴν [καὶ] καθίσας ἐπὶ τοῦ βήματος ἐδημηγόρει πρὸς αὐτούς, 22 ὁ δὲ δῆμος ἐπεφώνει, Θεοῦ φωνὴ καὶ οὐκ ἀνθρώπου. 23 παραχρῆμα δὲ ἐπάταξεν αὐτὸν ἄγγελος κυρίου ἀνθ᾽ ὧν οὐκ ἔδωκεν τὴν δόξαν τῷ θεῷ, καὶ γενόμενος σκωληκόβρωτος ἐξέψυξεν. ¶ 24 Ὁ δὲ λόγος τοῦ θεοῦ ηὔξανεν καὶ ἐπληθύνετο. ¶ 25 Βαρναβᾶς δὲ καὶ Σαῦλος ὑπέστρεψαν ἀπὸ «εἰς» Ἰερουσαλὴμ πληρώσαντες τὴν διακονίαν, συμπαραλαβόντες Ἰωάννην τὸν ἐπικληθέντα Μᾶρκον.

Barnabas and Saul Sent Off

13:1

In	the		church	at	Antioch		there were		prophets	and	teachers:		Barnabas,		Simeon
	δὲ	κατὰ τὴν	οὖσαν	ἐκκλησίαν	ἐν	Ἀντιοχείᾳ →	Ἦσαν	προφῆται	καὶ	διδάσκαλοι τε	ὅ	Βαρναβᾶς	καὶ	Συμεὼν
	cj	p.a d.asf	pt.pa.asf	n.asf	p.d	n.dsf	v.iai.3p	n.npm	cj	n.npm	d.nsm	n.nsm	cj	n.nsm
	1254	2848 3836	1639	1711	1877	522	1639	4737	2779	1437	5445 3836	982	2779	5208

called		Niger,		Lucius	of Cyrene,			Manaen	(who	had	been	brought	up with	Herod	the
ὁ	καλούμενος	Νίγερ	καὶ	Λούκιος →	ὁ	Κυρηναῖος	τε	Μαναήν →		→		σύντροφος	← →	Ἡρῴδου τοῦ
d.nsm	pt.pp.nsm	n.nsm	cj	n.nsm	d.nsm	n.nsm	cj	n.nsm				n.nsm		d.gsm d.gsm
3836	2813	3769	2779	3372	3836	3254	5445	3441				5343		2476 3836

tetrarch)	and	Saul.	**2**	While	they	were	worshiping		the	Lord	and	fasting,		the	Holy		Spirit	said,	"Set
τετραάρχου	καὶ	Σαῦλος	δὲ	→	αὐτῶν →		Λειτουργούντων	τῷ	κυρίῳ	καὶ	νηστευόντων	τὸ	τὸ	ἅγιον	πνεῦμα	εἶπεν	δή	→
n.gsm	cj	n.nsm	cj		r.gpm.3		pt.pa.gpm	d.dsm	n.dsm	cj	pt.pa.gpm	d.nsn	d.nsn	a.nsn	n.nsn	v.aai.3s	pl	
5490	2779	4930	1254	3310	899		3310	3836	3261	2779	3764	3836	3836	41	4460	3306	1314	

apart	for me	Barnabas		and	Saul	for	the	work	to	which	I	have	called		them."	**3**	So	after they had
ἀφορίσατε →	μοι	τὸν Βαρναβᾶν	καὶ	Σαῦλον	εἰς	τὸ	ἔργον →	ὃ		→		προσκέκλημαι	αὐτούς	τότε →		→
v.aam.2p	r.ds.1	d.asm n.asm	cj	n.asm	p.a	d.asn	n.asn	r.asn				v.rmi.1s	r.apm.3	adv		
928	1609	3836 982	2779	4930	1650	3836	2240	4673	4005			4673	899	5538		

fasted	and	prayed,		they placed	their	hands	on	them	and	sent		them off.
νηστεύσαντες	καὶ	προσευξάμενοι	καὶ	ἐπιθέντες	τὰς	χεῖρας		αὐτοῖς		ἀπέλυσαν		←
pt.aa.npm	cj	pt.am.npm	cj	pt.aa.npm	d.apf	n.apf		r.dpm.3		v.aai.3p		
3764	2779	4667	2779	2202	3836	5931		899		668		

On Cyprus

13:4

The	two	of them,	sent		on their	way	by	the	Holy	Spirit,		went		down	to	Seleucia	and
οὖν	μὲν →		→ Αὐτοὶ	ἐκπεμφθέντες	←	←	ὑπὸ	τοῦ	ἁγίου	πνεύματος	κατῆλθον			εἰς	Σελεύκειαν	τε
cj	pl →		r.npm	pt.ap.npm			p.g	d.gsn	a.gsn	n.gsn	v.aai.3p			p.a	n.asf	cj
4036	3525		899	1734			5679	3836	41	4460	2982			1650	4942	5445

sailed	from	there	to	Cyprus.	**5**	When	they	arrived	at	Salamis,	they proclaimed	the	word	of God		in
ἀπέπλευσαν	ἐκεῖθεν	←	εἰς	Κύπρον	καὶ	→		γενόμενοι	ἐν	Σαλαμῖνι →	κατήγγελλον	τὸν	λόγον →	τοῦ θεοῦ	ἐν
v.aai.3p	adv		p.a	n.asf	cj			pt.am.npm	p.d	n.dsf	v.iai.3p	d.asm	n.asm	d.gsm n.gsm	p.d
676	1696		1650	3251	2779			1181	1877	4887	2859	3836	3364	3836 2536	1877

the	Jewish		synagogues.		John	was	with	them	as	their helper.	**6**	They	traveled	through	the	whole
ταῖς	τῶν Ἰουδαίων	συναγωγαῖς	δὲ	καὶ	Ἰωάννην →	εἶχον	←			ὑπηρέτην	δὲ	→	Διελθόντες	←		τὴν ὅλην
d.dpf	d.gpm a.gpm	n.dpf	cj	adv	n.asm	v.iai.3p				n.asm	cj		pt.aa.npm			d.asf a.asf
3836	3836 2681	5252	1254	2779	2722	2400				5677	1254		1451			3836 3910

island	until	they	came	to	Paphos.	There	they	met	a		Jewish	sorcerer	and false	prophet		named
νῆσον	ἄχρι				Πάφου	→		εὗρον	τινὰ	ἄνδρα	Ἰουδαῖον	μάγον	→	ψευδοπροφήτην	ᾧ	ὄνομα
n.asf	p.g				n.gsf			v.aai.3p	r.asm	n.asm	a.asm	n.asm		n.asm	r.dsm	n.nsn
3762	948				4265			2351	5516	467	2681	3407		6021	4005	3950

Bar-Jesus,	**7** who	was	an	attendant	of	the	proconsul,	Sergius	Paulus.	The	proconsul,	an	intelligent	man,	sent
Βαριησοῦ	ὃς	ἦν	σὺν			τῷ	ἀνθυπάτῳ	Σεργίῳ	Παύλῳ	οὗτος		συνετῷ	ἀνδρὶ	προσκαλεσάμενος
n.gsm	r.nsm	v.iai.3s	p.d			d.dsm	n.dsm	n.dsm	n.dsm	r.nsm		a.dsm	n.dsm	pt.am.nsm
979	4005	1639	5250			3836	478	4950	4263	4047		5305	467	4673

for	Barnabas	and	Saul		because	he	wanted	to	hear		the	word	of God.	**8**	But	Elymas	the	sorcerer	(for that	is
←	Βαρναβᾶν	καὶ	Σαῦλον		→		ἐπεζήτησεν	→	ἀκοῦσαι	τὸν	λόγον →	τοῦ θεοῦ	δὲ	Ἐλύμας	ὁ	μάγος	γὰρ	οὕτως
	n.asm	cj	n.asm				v.aai.3s		f.aa	d.asm	n.asm	d.gsm n.gsm	cj	n.nsm	d.nsm	n.nsm	cj	adv
982	2779	4930			2118		201	3836	3364	3836 2536	1254	1829	3836	3407	1142	4048		

what	his	name	means)	opposed	them	and tried	to	turn		the	proconsul	from	the	faith.	**9**	Then	Saul,
←	αὐτοῦ	τὸ ὄνομα	μεθερμηνεύεται	ἀνθίστατο	αὐτοῖς		ζητῶν →	διαστρέψαι	τὸν	ἀνθύπατον	ἀπὸ	τῆς	πίστεως	δὲ	Σαῦλος
	r.gsm.3	d.nsn n.nsn	v.ppi.3s	v.imi.3s	r.dpm.3		pt.pa.nsm	f.aa	d.asm	n.asm	p.g	d.gsf	n.gsf	cj	n.nsm
899	3836 3950	3493	468	899		2426	1406	3836	478	608	3836	4411	1254	4930		

who	was	also	called	Paul,	filled		with	the	Holy	Spirit,		looked	straight	at	Elymas	and	said,	**10**	"You	are	a	child of
ὁ		καὶ		Παῦλος	πλησθεὶς	→			ἁγίου	πνεύματος		ἀτενίσας		εἰς	αὐτὸν		εἶπεν	ὦ				υἱὲ →
d.nsm		adv		n.nsm	pt.ap.nsm				a.gsn	n.gsn		pt.aa.nsm		p.a	r.asm.3		v.aai.3s	j				n.vsm
3836		2779		4263	4398				41	4460		867		1650	899		3306	6043				5626

13:1 ⁵Ἦσαν δὲ ἐν Ἀντιοχείᾳ κατὰ τὴν οὖσαν ἐκκλησίαν προφῆται καὶ διδάσκαλοι ὅ τε Βαρναβᾶς καὶ Συμεὼν ὁ καλούμενος Νίγερ καὶ Λούκιος ὁ Κυρηναῖος, Μαναήν τε Ἡρῴδου τοῦ τετραάρχου σύντροφος καὶ Σαῦλος. ²λειτουργούντων δὲ αὐτῶν τῷ κυρίῳ καὶ νηστευόντων εἶπεν τὸ πνεῦμα τὸ ἅγιον, Ἀφορίσατε δή μοι τὸν Βαρναβᾶν καὶ Σαῦλον εἰς τὸ ἔργον ὃ προσκέκλημαι αὐτούς. ³τότε νηστεύσαντες καὶ προσευξάμενοι καὶ ἐπιθέντες τὰς χεῖρας αὐτοῖς ἀπέλυσαν.

13:4 Αὐτοὶ μὲν οὖν ἐκπεμφθέντες ὑπὸ τοῦ ἁγίου πνεύματος κατῆλθον εἰς Σελεύκειαν, ἐκεῖθέν τε ἀπέπλευσαν εἰς Κύπρον ⁵καὶ γενόμενοι ἐν Σαλαμῖνι κατήγγελλον τὸν λόγον τοῦ θεοῦ ἐν ταῖς συναγωγαῖς τῶν Ἰουδαίων. εἶχον δὲ καὶ Ἰωάννην ὑπηρέτην.
⁶διελθόντες δὲ ὅλην τὴν νῆσον ἄχρι Πάφου εὗρον ἄνδρα τινὰ μάγον ψευδοπροφήτην Ἰουδαῖον ᾧ ὄνομα Βαριησοῦ ⁷ὃς ἦν σὺν τῷ ἀνθυπάτῳ Σεργίῳ Παύλῳ, ἀνδρὶ συνετῷ. οὗτος προσκαλεσάμενος Βαρναβᾶν καὶ Σαῦλον ἐπεζήτησεν ἀκοῦσαι τὸν λόγον τοῦ θεοῦ. ⁸ἀνθίστατο δὲ αὐτοῖς Ἐλύμας ὁ μάγος, οὕτως γὰρ μεθερμηνεύεται τὸ ὄνομα αὐτοῦ, ζητῶν διαστρέψαι τὸν ἀνθύπατον ἀπὸ τῆς πίστεως. ⁹Σαῦλος δέ, ὁ καὶ Παῦλος, πλησθεὶς πνεύματος ἁγίου ἀτενίσας εἰς αὐτὸν ¹⁰εἶπεν, Ὦ πλήρης παντὸς δόλου καὶ

the devil   and an enemy of everything that is right!   You are full   of all   kinds of deceit and
διαβόλου   ἐχθρὲ → πάσης   → → δικαιοσύνης   πλήρης → παντὸς ←   ← δόλου καὶ πάσης
n.gsm   a.vsm   a.gsf   n.gsf   a.vsm   a.gsm   n.gsm cj a.gsf
1333   2398   4246   1466   4441   4246   1515 2779 4246

trickery.   Will you never stop   perverting the right   ways of the Lord? **11**   Now   the hand of the Lord
ῥᾳδιουργίας → → οὐ   παύσῃ διαστρέφων τὰς ⌜τὰς εὐθείας⌝ ὁδοὺς → τοῦ κυρίου καὶ νῦν ἰδοὺ χεὶρ → κυρίου
n.gsf   pl   v.fmi.2s pt.pa.nsm d.apf ⌜d.apf a.apf⌝ n.apf → d.gsm n.gsm cj adv j n.nsf → n.gsm
4816   4264 4264 pl   4024   4264 1406   3836 3836 2318   3847   3836 3261 2779 3814 2627 5931   3261

is against you.   You are going to be   blind, and for a time   you will be unable to see   the light of the sun."
ἐπὶ σὲ καὶ → → → ἔσῃ τυφλὸς ἄχρι καιροῦ → → → μὴ → βλέπων   τὸν ἥλιον
p.a r.as.2 cj   v.fmi.2s a.nsm p.g n.gsm   pl   pt.pa.nsm   d.asm n.asm
2093 5148 2779   1639 5603 948 2789   1063 1063 1063 3590   1063   3836 2463

¶   Immediately mist and darkness came over him, and he groped about, seeking someone to lead   him
τε παραχρῆμα ἀχλὺς καὶ σκότος ἔπεσεν ἐπ᾽ αὐτὸν καὶ → περιάγων ← ἐζήτει → → χειραγωγούς
cj adv   n.nsf cj n.nsn v.aai.3s p.a r.asm.3 cj   pt.pa.nsm   v.iai.3s   n.apm
5445 4202   944 2779 5030 4406 2093 899 2779   4310   2426   5933

by the hand. **12** When the proconsul saw   what had happened, he believed, for he was amazed   at the teaching
← ←   τότε ὁ ἀνθύπατος ἰδὼν τὸ → γεγονός ἐπίστευσεν → ἐκπλησσόμενος ἐπὶ τῇ διδαχῇ
    adv d.nsm n.nsm pt.aa.nsm d.asn   pt.ra.asn v.aai.3s   pt.pp.nsm p.d d.dsf n.dsf
    5538 3836 478 1625 3836   1181 4409   1742 2093 3836 1439

about the Lord.
→ τοῦ κυρίου
d.gsm n.gsm
3836 3261

In Pisidian Antioch

13:13   From Paphos,   Paul and his companions   sailed   to Perga in Pamphylia,   where
δὲ ἀπὸ ⌜τῆς Πάφου⌝ → ⌜οἱ περὶ Παῦλον⌝ Ἀναχθέντες ἦλθον εἰς Πέργην → ⌜τῆς Παμφυλίας⌝ δὲ
cj p.g d.gsf n.gsf   d.npm p.a n.asm   pt.ap.npm v.aai.3p p.a n.asf → d.gsf n.gsf   cj
1254 608 3836 4265   3836 4309 4263   343   2262 1650 n.asf 1308 → 3836 4103   1254

John left   them to return   to Jerusalem. **14**   From Perga   they went   on to
Ἰωάννης ἀποχωρήσας ἀπ᾽ αὐτῶν ὑπέστρεψεν εἰς Ἱεροσόλυμα δὲ ἀπὸ ⌜τῆς Πέργης⌝ Αὐτοὶ ⌜διελθόντες παρεγένοντο⌝ ← εἰς
n.nsm pt.aa.nsm p.g r.gpm.3 v.aai.3s p.a n.apsn   cj p.g d.gsf n.gsf r.npm pt.aa.npm v.ami.3p   p.a
2722 713 608 899 5715 1650 2642   1254 608 3836 4308 899 1451 4134   1650

Pisidian Antioch.   On   the Sabbath they entered   the synagogue and sat   down. **15**   After
⌜τὴν Πισιδίαν⌝ Ἀντιόχειαν καὶ → τῇ ἡμέρᾳ τῶν σαββάτων → εἰσελθόντες εἰς τὴν συναγωγὴν ἐκάθισαν ← δὲ μετὰ
d.asf a.asf n.asf cj → d.dsf n.dsf d.gpn n.gpn   pt.aa.npm p.a d.asf n.asf v.aai.3p   cj p.a
3836 4408 522 2779 → 3836 2465 3836 4879   1656 1650 3836 5252 2767   1254 3552

the reading   from the Law and the Prophets, the synagogue rulers   sent   word to   them, saying,
τὴν ἀνάγνωσιν → τοῦ νόμου καὶ τῶν προφητῶν οἱ   ἀρχισυνάγωγοι ἀπέστειλαν πρὸς αὐτοὺς λέγοντες ἄνδρες
d.asf n.asf → d.gsm n.gsm cj d.gpm n.gpm d.npm   n.npm v.aai.3p p.a r.apm.3 pt.pa.npm n.vpm
3836 342 → 3836 3795 2779 3836 4737 3836   801 690 4639 899 3306 467

"Brothers, if   you have a   message of encouragement for   the people, please speak." ¶ **16**   Standing up,
ἀδελφοί εἴ ἐν ὑμῖν ἐστιν τίς λόγος → παρακλήσεως πρὸς τὸν λαόν   λέγετε   δὲ Ἀναστὰς ←
n.vpm cj p.d r.dp.2 v.pai.3s r.nsm n.nsm → n.gsf   p.a d.asm n.asm   v.pam.2p   cj pt.aa.nsm
81 1623 1877 7007 1639 5516 3364 → 4155   4639 3836 3295   3306   1254 482

Paul   motioned with his hand and said: "Men of Israel   and you Gentiles who worship   God,   listen
Παῦλος καὶ κατασείσας → τῇ χειρὶ εἶπεν ἄνδρες → Ἰσραηλῖται καὶ οἱ φοβούμενοι ⌜τὸν θεόν⌝ ἀκούσατε
n.nsm cj pt.aa.nsm → d.dsf n.dsf v.aai.3s n.vpm → n.vpm cj d.vpm pt.pp.vpm d.asm n.asm v.aam.2p
4263 2779 2939 → 3836 5931 3306 467   2703 2779 3836 5828 3836 2536 201

to me! **17** The God of the people   of Israel chose   our fathers;   he made the people prosper during
ὁ θεὸς τοῦ λαοῦ τούτου → Ἰσραὴλ ἐξελέξατο ἡμῶν ⌜τοὺς πατέρας⌝ καὶ → → τὸν λαὸν ὕψωσεν ἐν
d.nsm n.nsm d.gsm n.gsm r.gsm → n.gsm v.ami.3s r.gp.1 d.apm n.apm cj   d.asm n.asm v.aai.3s p.d
3836 2536 4047 3836 3295 4047 → 2702 1721 7005 3836 4252 2779 5738 5738 3836 3295 5738 1877

their stay   in   Egypt,   with mighty power   he led   them out of that country, **18**   he endured
τῇ παροικίᾳ ἐν γῇ Αἰγύπτου καὶ μετὰ ὑψηλοῦ βραχίονος → ἐξήγαγεν αὐτοὺς ἐξ → αὐτῆς   καὶ → ἐτροποφόρησεν
d.dsf n.dsf p.d n.dsf n.gsf cj p.g a.gsm n.gsm → v.aai.3s r.apm.3 p.g r.gsf.3   cj → v.aai.3s
3836 4229 1877 1178 131 2779 3552 5734 1098 → 1974 899 1666 899   2779 5574

πάσης ῥᾳδιουργίας, υἱὲ διαβόλου, ἐχθρὲ πάσης δικαιοσύνης, οὐ παύσῃ διαστρέφων τὰς ὁδοὺς [τοῦ] κυρίου τὰς εὐθείας; 11 καὶ νῦν ἰδοὺ χεὶρ κυρίου ἐπὶ σὲ καὶ ἔσῃ τυφλὸς μὴ βλέπων τὸν ἥλιον ἄχρι καιροῦ. ¶ παραχρῆμά τε ἔπεσεν ἐπ᾽ αὐτὸν ἀχλὺς καὶ σκότος καὶ περιάγων ἐζήτει χειραγωγούς. 12 τότε ἰδὼν ὁ ἀνθύπατος τὸ γεγονὸς ἐπίστευσεν ἐκπλησσόμενος ἐπὶ τῇ διδαχῇ τοῦ κυρίου.

13:13 Ἀναχθέντες δὲ ἀπὸ τῆς Πάφου οἱ περὶ Παῦλον ἦλθον εἰς Πέργην τῆς Παμφυλίας, Ἰωάννης δὲ ἀποχωρήσας ἀπ᾽ αὐτῶν ὑπέστρεψεν εἰς Ἱεροσόλυμα. 14 αὐτοὶ δὲ διελθόντες ἀπὸ τῆς Πέργης παρεγένοντο εἰς Ἀντιόχειαν τὴν Πισιδίαν, καὶ [εἰσ]ελθόντες εἰς τὴν συναγωγὴν τῇ ἡμέρᾳ τῶν σαββάτων ἐκάθισαν. 15 μετὰ δὲ τὴν ἀνάγνωσιν τοῦ νόμου καὶ τῶν προφητῶν ἀπέστειλαν οἱ ἀρχισυνάγωγοι πρὸς αὐτοὺς λέγοντες, Ἄνδρες ἀδελφοί, εἴ τίς ἐστιν ἐν ὑμῖν λόγος παρακλήσεως πρὸς τὸν λαόν, λέγετε. ¶ 16 ἀναστὰς δὲ Παῦλος καὶ κατασείσας τῇ χειρὶ εἶπεν· Ἄνδρες Ἰσραηλῖται καὶ οἱ φοβούμενοι τὸν θεόν, ἀκούσατε. 17 ὁ θεὸς τοῦ λαοῦ τούτου Ἰσραὴλ ἐξελέξατο τοὺς πατέρας ἡμῶν καὶ τὸν λαὸν ὕψωσεν ἐν τῇ παροικίᾳ ἐν γῇ Αἰγύπτου καὶ μετὰ βραχίονος ὑψηλοῦ ἐξήγαγεν αὐτοὺς ἐξ αὐτῆς, 18 καὶ ὡς τεσσερακονταετῆ χρόνον ἐτροποφόρησεν αὐτοὺς ἐν τῇ ἐρήμῳ 19 καὶ καθελὼν

their	conduct	for	about	forty		years	in	the	desert,	**19**		he overthrew	seven	nations	in		Canaan	and	gave
αὐτοὺς	→	ὡς	τεσσερακονταετῆ	χρόνον	ἐν	τῇ	ἐρήμῳ	καὶ	→	καθελὼν	ἑπτὰ	ἔθνη	ἐν	γῇ	Χαναάν				
r.apm.3		pl	a.asm	n.asm	p.d	d.dsf	n.dsf	cj		pt.aa.nsm	a.apn	n.apn	p.d	n.dsf	n.gsf				
899		5478	6055	5478	5989	1877	3836	2245	2779	2747	2231	1620	1877	1178	5913		2883		

their	land		to his people	as	their	inheritance.	**20**	All this took		about	450			years.	¶	
αὐτῶν	⌊τὴν γῆν⌋	→	κατεκληρονόμησεν					ὡς	⌊τετρακοσίοις	καὶ	πεντήκοντα⌋	ἔτεσιν			καὶ	
r.gpn.3	d.asf n.asf		v.aai.3s					pl	a.dpn	cj	a.dpn	n.dpn			cj	
899	3836 1178		2883					6055	5484	2779	4299	2291			2779	

"After	this,	God	gave	them	judges	until	the	time of	Samuel	the	prophet.	**21**	Then	the people	asked		for a	king,
μετὰ	ταῦτα	ἔδωκεν	κριτὰς	ἕως	←	time of	→	Σαμουὴλ	τοῦ	προφήτου		κἀκεῖθεν		ᾐτήσαντο	←	βασιλέα		
p.a	r.apn	v.aai.3s	n.apm	p.g				n.gsm	d.gsm	n.gsm		crasis		v.ami.3p		n.asm		
3552	4047	1443	3216	2401				4905	3836	4737		2796		160		995		

and	he		gave	them	Saul		son of	Kish,		of	the	tribe	of	Benjamin,	who ruled	forty		years.
καὶ	ὁ	θεὸς	ἔδωκεν	αὐτοῖς	τὸν Σαοὺλ	υἱὸν	→	Κίς,	ἄνδρα	ἐκ		φυλῆς	→	Βενιαμίν,		τεσσεράκοντα	ἔτη	
cj	d.nsm	n.nsm	v.aai.3s	r.dpm.3	d.asm n.asm	n.asm		n.gsm	n.asm	p.g		n.gsf		n.gsm		a.apn	n.apn	
2779	3836	2536	1443	899	3836 4910	5626		3078	467	1666		5876		1021		5477	2291	

22	After removing	Saul,	he made	David	their		king.	He		testified	concerning him:	'I have	found
καὶ	→ μεταστήσας	αὐτὸν	ἤγειρεν	τὸν Δαυὶδ	αὐτοῖς	εἰς	βασιλέα	καὶ	→	εἶπεν μαρτυρήσας	→ ᾧ	→	εὗρον
cj	pt.aa.nsm	r.asm.3	v.aai.3s	d.asm n.asm	r.dpm.3	p.a	n.asm	cj		v.aai.3s pt.aa.nsm	r.dsm		v.aai.1s
2779	3496	899	1586	3836 1253	899	1650	995	2779		3306 3455	4005		2351

David	son of	Jesse	a man	after	my	own	heart;	he	will do	everything	I	want		him to do.'	¶
Δαυὶδ	τὸν	⌊τοῦ Ἰεσσαί⌋	ἄνδρα	κατὰ	μου	τὴν	καρδίαν	ὃς	→ ποιήσει	πάντα	μου	⌊τὰ θελήματα⌋			
n.asm	d.asm	d.gsm n.gsm	n.asm	p.a	r.gs.1	d.asf	n.asf	r.nsm	v.fai.3s	a.apn	r.gs.1	d.apn n.apn			
1253	3836	3836 2649	467	2848	1609	3836	2840	4005	4472	4246	1609	3836 2525			

23	"From	this	man's	descendants	God		has brought	to	Israel	the Savior	Jesus,	as	he promised.
ἀπὸ	τούτου	←	⌊τοῦ σπέρματος⌋	ὁ	θεὸς	→	ἤγαγεν	→	⌊τῷ Ἰσραὴλ⌋	σωτῆρα	Ἰησοῦν	κατ'	ἐπαγγελίαν
p.g	r.gsm		d.gsn n.gsn	d.nsm	n.nsm		v.aai.3s		d.dsm n.dsm	n.asm	n.asm	p.a	n.asf
608	4047		3836 5065	3836	2536		72		3836 2702	5400	2652	2848	2039

24	Before	the coming	of Jesus,	John	preached	repentance	and	baptism	to	all	the	people	of Israel.	**25**	As
⌊πρὸ προσώπου⌋		τῆς εἰσόδου	→ αὐτοῦ	Ἰωάννου	προκηρύξαντος	μετανοίας		βάπτισμα	→	παντὶ	τῷ	λαῷ	→ Ἰσραὴλ	δὲ	ὡς
p.g n.gsn		d.gsf n.gsf	r.gsm.3	n.gsm	pt.aa.gsm	n.gsf		n.asn		a.dsm	d.dsm	n.dsm	n.asm	cj	cj
4574 4725		3836 1658	899	2722	4619	3567		967		4246	3836	3295	2702	1254	6055

John	was	completing	his	work,	he said:	'Who	do you	think	I	am?	I	am	not	that one.	No,	but		he is
Ἰωάννης	→	ἐπλήρου	τὸν	δρόμον	→ ἔλεγεν	τί	→	ὑπονοεῖτε	ἐμὲ	εἶναι	ἐγὼ	εἰμι	οὐκ			ἀλλ'	ἰδοὺ	→
n.nsm		v.iai.3s	d.asm	n.asm	v.iai.3s	r.asn		v.pai.2p	r.as.1	f.pa	r.ns.1	v.pai.1s	pl			cj	j	
2722		4444	3836	1536	3306	5515		5706	1609	1639	1609	1639	4024			247	2627	

coming	after	me,	whose	sandals		I am	not	worthy	to untie.'	¶	**26**		"Brothers,	children
ἔρχεται	μετ'	ἐμὲ	οὗ	⌊τὸ ὑπόδημα⌋	τῶν ποδῶν	→ εἰμὶ	οὐκ	ἄξιος	→ λῦσαι			Ἄνδρες	ἀδελφοί	υἱοὶ	γένους
v.pmi.3s	p.a	r.as.1	r.gsm	d.asn n.asn	d.gpm n.gpm	v.pai.1s	pl	a.nsm	f.aa			n.vpm	n.vpm	n.vpm	n.gsn
2262	3552	1609	4005	3836 5687	3836 4546	1639	4024	545	3395			467	81	5626	1169

of Abraham,	and	you		God-fearing		Gentiles,	it is to us	that	this	message	of salvation	has been
→ Ἀβραὰμ	καὶ	⌊οἱ ἐν ὑμῖν⌋	⌊φοβούμενοι	τὸν θεόν⌋		→	ἡμῖν	ταύτης	ὁ	λόγος⌋	⌊τῆς σωτηρίας⌋	→ →
n.gsm	cj	d.vpm p.d r.dp.2	pt.pp.vpm	d.asm n.asm			r.dp.1	r.gsf	d.nsm	n.nsm	d.gsf n.gsf	
11	2779	3836 1877 7007	5828	3836 2536			7005	4047	3836	3364	3836 5401	

sent.	**27**	The people	of	Jerusalem	and	their	rulers		did not	recognize	Jesus,	yet in condemning	him
ἐξαπεστάλη	γὰρ	οἱ	κατοικοῦντες	ἐν	Ἰερουσαλὴμ	καὶ	αὐτῶν	⌊οἱ ἄρχοντες⌋	ἀγνοήσαντες		τοῦτον	καὶ →	κρίναντες
v.api.3s	cj	d.npm	pt.pa.npm	p.d	n.dsf	cj	r.gpm.3	d.npm n.npm	pt.aa.npm		r.asm	cj	pt.aa.npm
1990	1142	3836	2997	1877	2647	2779	899	3836 807	51		4047	2779	3212

they fulfilled		the words	of the	prophets	that	are read		every	Sabbath.	**28**	Though	they found
→ ἐπλήρωσαν	τὰς	φωνὰς	→ τῶν	προφητῶν	τὰς	→ ἀναγινωσκομένας	⌊κατὰ πᾶν⌋		σάββατον	καὶ	→	εὑρόντες
v.aai.3p	d.apf	n.apf	d.gpm	n.gpm	d.apf	pt.pp.apf	p.a a.asn		n.asn	cj		pt.aa.npm
4444	3836	5889	3836	4737	3836	336	2848 4246		4879	2779		2351

no		proper	ground	for a	death	sentence,	they asked	Pilate	to have	him	executed.	**29**	When	they had
μηδεμίαν		αἰτίαν	→		θανάτου		→ ᾐτήσαντο	Πιλᾶτον	→ →	αὐτόν	ἀναιρεθῆναι	δὲ	ὡς	→ →
a.asf		n.asf			n.gsm		v.ami.3p	n.asm		r.asm.3	f.ap	cj	cj	
3594		162			2505		160	4397	359 359	899	359	1254	6055	

ἔθνη ἑπτὰ ἐν γῇ Χαναάν κατεκληρονόμησεν τὴν γῆν αὐτῶν. ²⁰ ὡς ἔτεσιν τετρακοσίοις καὶ πεντήκοντα. ¶ καὶ μετὰ ταῦτα ἔδωκεν κριτὰς ἕως Σαμουὴλ [τοῦ] προφήτου. ²¹ κἀκεῖθεν ᾐτήσαντο βασιλέα καὶ ἔδωκεν αὐτοῖς ὁ θεὸς τὸν Σαοὺλ υἱὸν Κίς, ἄνδρα ἐκ φυλῆς Βενιαμίν, ἔτη τεσσεράκοντα, ²² καὶ μεταστήσας αὐτὸν ἤγειρεν τὸν Δαυὶδ αὐτοῖς εἰς βασιλέα ᾧ καὶ εἶπεν μαρτυρήσας. Εὗρον Δαυὶδ τὸν τοῦ Ἰεσσαί, ἄνδρα κατὰ τὴν καρδίαν μου, ὃς ποιήσει πάντα τὰ θελήματά μου. ¶ ²³ τούτου ὁ θεὸς ἀπὸ τοῦ σπέρματος κατ' ἐπαγγελίαν ἤγαγεν τῷ Ἰσραὴλ σωτῆρα Ἰησοῦν, ²⁴ προκηρύξαντος Ἰωάννου πρὸ προσώπου τῆς εἰσόδου αὐτοῦ βάπτισμα μετανοίας παντὶ τῷ λαῷ Ἰσραήλ. ²⁵ ὡς δὲ ἐπλήρου Ἰωάννης τὸν δρόμον, ἔλεγεν, Τί ἐμὲ ὑπονοεῖτε εἶναι; οὐκ εἰμὶ ἐγώ· ἀλλ' ἰδοὺ ἔρχεται μετ' ἐμὲ οὗ οὐκ εἰμὶ ἄξιος τὸ ὑπόδημα τῶν ποδῶν λῦσαι. ¶ ²⁶ Ἄνδρες ἀδελφοί, υἱοὶ γένους Ἀβραὰμ καὶ οἱ ἐν ὑμῖν φοβούμενοι τὸν θεόν, ἡμῖν ὁ λόγος τῆς σωτηρίας ταύτης ἐξαπεστάλη. ²⁷ οἱ γὰρ κατοικοῦντες ἐν Ἰερουσαλὴμ καὶ οἱ ἄρχοντες αὐτῶν τοῦτον ἀγνοήσαντες καὶ τὰς φωνὰς τῶν προφητῶν τὰς κατὰ πᾶν σάββατον ἀναγινωσκομένας κρίναντες ἐπλήρωσαν, ²⁸ καὶ μηδεμίαν αἰτίαν θανάτου εὑρόντες ᾐτήσαντο Πιλᾶτον ἀναιρεθῆναι αὐτόν. ²⁹ ὡς δὲ ἐτέλεσαν πάντα τὰ περὶ

carried out all that was written about him, they took him down from the tree and laid him in a
ἐτέλεσαν ← πάντα τὰ → γεγραμμένα περὶ αὐτοῦ καθελόντες ← ἀπὸ τοῦ ξύλου ἔθηκαν εἰς
v.aai.3p a.apn t.apn pt.rp.apn p.g r.gsm.3 pt.aa.npm p.g d.gsn n.gsn v.aai.3p p.a
5464 4246 3836 1211 4309 899 2747 608 3836 3833 5502 1650

tomb. **30** But God raised him from the dead, **31** and for many days he was seen by those who had traveled
μνημεῖον δὲ ὁ θεὸς ἤγειρεν αὐτὸν ἐκ νεκρῶν ἐπὶ πλείους ἡμέρας ὃς → ὤφθη → τοῖς ← συναναβᾶσιν
n.asn cj d.nsm n.nsm v.aai.3s r.asm.3 p.g a.gpm p.a a.apf.c n.apf r.nsm v.api.3s d.dpm pt.aa.dpm
3646 1254 3836 2536 1586 899 1666 3738 2093 4498 2465 4005 3972 3836 5262

with him from Galilee to Jerusalem. They are now his witnesses to our people. ¶ **32** "We
← αὐτῷ ἀπὸ τῆς Γαλιλαίας εἰς Ἰερουσαλήμ οἵτινες εἰσὶν νῦν αὐτοῦ μάρτυρες πρὸς τὸν λαόν Καὶ ἡμεῖς
r.dsm.3 p.g d.gsf n.gsf εἰς p.a n.asf r.npm v.pai.3p adv r.gsm.3 n.npm p.a d.asm n.asm cj r.np.1
899 608 3836 1133 1650 2647 4015 1639 3814 899 3459 4639 3836 3295 2779 7005

tell you the good news: What God promised our fathers **33** he has fulfilled
εὐαγγελιζόμεθα ὑμᾶς ← ← ← τὴν γενομένην ἐπαγγελίαν πρὸς τοὺς πατέρας ὅτι ὁ θεὸς → ἐκπεπλήρωκεν ταύτην
v.pmi.1p r.ap.2 d.asf pt.am.asf n.asf p.a d.apm n.apm cj d.nsm n.nsm v.rai.3s r.asf
2294 7007 2294 2294 2294 3836 1181 2039 4639 3836 4252 4022 3836 2536 1740 4047

for us, their children, by raising up Jesus. As it is written in the second Psalm: "'You are my Son;
→ ἡμῖν αὐτῶν τοῖς τέκνοις → ἀναστήσας ← Ἰησοῦν ὡς καὶ → γέγραπται ἐν τῷ τῷ δευτέρῳ ψαλμῷ σύ εἶ μου υἱός
r.dp.1 r.gpm.3 d.dpn n.dpn pt.aa.nsm n.asm cj adv v.rpi.3s p.d d.dsm d.dsm a.dsm n.dsm r.ns.2 v.pai.2s r.gs.1 n.nsm
7005 899 3836 5451 482 2652 6055 2779 1211 1877 3836 3836 1311 6011 5148 1639 1609 5626

today I have become your Father.' **34** The fact that God raised him from the dead, never to
σήμερον ἐγώ σε γεγέννηκα δὲ ὅτι ἀνέστησεν αὐτὸν ἐκ νεκρῶν μηκέτι →
adv r.ns.1 r.as.2 v.rai.1s cj cj v.aai.3s r.asm.3 p.g a.gpm adv
4958 1609 1164 1164 5148 1164 1254 4022 482 899 1666 3738 3600

decay, is stated in these words: "I will give you the holy and sure blessings
μέλλοντα ὑποστρέφειν εἰς διαφθοράν → εἴρηκεν → οὕτως ← ὅτι → δώσω ὑμῖν τὰ ὅσια τὰ πιστά
pt.pa.asm f.pa p.a n.asf v.rai.3s adv cj v.fai.1s r.dp.2 d.apn a.apn d.apn a.apn
3516 5715 1650 1426 3306 4048 4022 1443 7007 3836 4008 3836 4412

promised to David.' **35** So it is stated elsewhere: "'You will not let your Holy One see decay.' ¶
Δαυὶδ διότι καὶ → λέγει ἐν ἑτέρῳ οὐ δώσεις σου τὸν ὅσιον ← ἰδεῖν διαφθοράν
n.gsm cj adv v.pai.3s p.d r.dsn pl v.fai.2s r.gs.2 d.asm a.asm f.aa n.asf
1253 1484 2779 3306 1877 2283 1443 1443 4024 1443 5148 3836 4008 1625 1426

36 "For when David had served God's purpose in his own generation, he fell asleep; he was buried
γὰρ μὲν → Δαυὶδ → ὑπηρετήσας τοῦ θεοῦ τῇ βουλῇ → ἰδίᾳ ← γενεᾷ → → ἐκοιμήθη καὶ προσετέθη
cj pl n.nsm pt.aa.nsm d.gsn n.gsn d.dsf n.dsf a.dsf n.dsf v.api.3s cj v.api.3s
1142 3525 5676 1253 5676 3836 2536 3836 1087 2625 1155 3121 2779 4707

with his fathers and his body decayed. **37** But the one whom God raised from the dead did not see
πρὸς αὐτοῦ τοὺς πατέρας καὶ εἶδεν διαφθοράν δὲ → → ὃν ὁ θεὸς ἤγειρεν → οὐκ εἶδεν
p.a r.gsm.3 d.apm n.apm cj v.aai.3s n.asf cj r.asm d.nsm n.nsm v.aai.3s pl v.aai.3s
4639 899 3836 4252 2779 1625 1426 1254 4005 3836 2536 1586 1625 4024 1625

decay. ¶ **38** "Therefore, my brothers, I want you to know that through Jesus the forgiveness of
διαφθοράν οὖν → ἄνδρες ἀδελφοί ἔστω ὑμῖν γνωστὸν ὅτι διὰ τούτου ἄφεσις →
n.asf cj n.vpm n.vpm v.pam.3s r.dp.2 a.nsn cj p.g r.gsm n.nsf
1426 4036 467 81 1639 7007 1196 4022 1328 4047 912

sins is proclaimed to you. **39** Through him everyone who believes is justified from everything you
ἁμαρτιῶν → καταγγέλλεται → ὑμῖν [καὶ] ἐν τούτῳ πᾶς ὁ πιστεύων δικαιοῦται ἀπὸ πάντων ὧν →
n.gpf v.ppi.3s r.dp.2 adv p.d r.dsn a.nsm d.nsm pt.pa.nsm v.ppi.3s p.g a.gpn r.gpn
281 2859 7007 2779 1877 4047 4246 3836 4409 1467 608 4246 4005

could not be justified from by the law of Moses. **40** Take care that what the prophets have said
ἠδυνήθητε οὐκ → δικαιωθῆναι ἐν νόμῳ Μωϋσέως οὖν → βλέπετε τὸ ἐν τοῖς προφήταις → εἰρημένον
v.api.2p pl f.ap p.d n.dsm n.gsm cj v.pam.2p d.nsn p.d d.dpm n.dpm pt.rp.nsn
1538 4024 1467 1877 3795 3707 4036 1063 3836 1877 3836 4737 3306

does not happen to you: **41** "'Look, you scoffers, wonder and perish, for I am going to do
→ μὴ ἐπέλθῃ ἴδετε οἱ καταφρονηταί καὶ θαυμάσατε καὶ ἀφανίσθητε ὅτι ἐγώ → → → ἐργάζομαι
cj v.aas.3s v.aam.2p d.vpm n.vpm cj v.aam.2p cj v.apm.2p cj r.ns.1 v.pmi.1s
2088 3590 2088 1625 3836 2970 2779 2513 2779 906 4022 1609 2237

αὐτοῦ γεγραμμένα, καθελόντες ἀπὸ τοῦ ξύλου ἔθηκαν εἰς μνημεῖον. **30** ὁ δὲ θεὸς ἤγειρεν αὐτὸν ἐκ νεκρῶν, **31** ὃς ὤφθη ἐπὶ ἡμέρας πλείους τοῖς συναναβᾶσιν αὐτῷ ἀπὸ τῆς Γαλιλαίας εἰς Ἰερουσαλήμ, οἵτινες [νῦν] εἰσιν μάρτυρες αὐτοῦ πρὸς τὸν λαόν. ¶ **32** καὶ ἡμεῖς ὑμᾶς εὐαγγελιζόμεθα τὴν πρὸς τοὺς πατέρας ἐπαγγελίαν γενομένην, **33** ὅτι ταύτην ὁ θεὸς ἐκπεπλήρωκεν τοῖς τέκνοις [αὐτῶν] ἡμῖν ἀναστήσας Ἰησοῦν ὡς καὶ ἐν τῷ ψαλμῷ γέγραπται τῷ δευτέρῳ, Υἱός μου εἶ σύ, ἐγὼ σήμερον γεγέννηκά σε. **34** ὅτι δὲ ἀνέστησεν αὐτὸν ἐκ νεκρῶν μηκέτι μέλλοντα ὑποστρέφειν εἰς διαφθοράν, οὕτως εἴρηκεν ὅτι Δώσω ὑμῖν τὰ ὅσια Δαυὶδ τὰ πιστά. **35** διότι καὶ ἐν ἑτέρῳ λέγει, Οὐ δώσεις τὸν ὅσιόν σου ἰδεῖν διαφθοράν. ¶ **36** Δαυὶδ μὲν γὰρ ἰδίᾳ γενεᾷ ὑπηρετήσας τῇ τοῦ θεοῦ βουλῇ ἐκοιμήθη καὶ προσετέθη πρὸς τοὺς πατέρας αὐτοῦ καὶ εἶδεν διαφθοράν· **37** ὃν δὲ ὁ θεὸς ἤγειρεν, οὐκ εἶδεν διαφθοράν. ¶ **38** γνωστὸν οὖν ἔστω ὑμῖν, ἄνδρες ἀδελφοί, ὅτι διὰ τούτου ὑμῖν ἄφεσις ἁμαρτιῶν καταγγέλλεται[, καὶ] ἀπὸ πάντων ὧν οὐκ ἠδυνήθητε ἐν νόμῳ Μωϋσέως δικαιωθῆναι **39** ἐν τούτῳ πᾶς ὁ πιστεύων δικαιοῦται. **40** βλέπετε οὖν μὴ ἐπέλθῃ τὸ εἰρημένον ἐν τοῖς προφήταις, **41** Ἴδετε, οἱ καταφρονηταί, καὶ θαυμάσατε καὶ ἀφανίσθητε, ὅτι ἔργον ἐργάζομαι ἐγὼ

something in your days | | | that you would never believe, even if someone told you.'" ¶
ἔργον ἐν ὑμῶν ⌊ταῖς ἡμέραις⌋ ἔργον ὃ → → ⌊οὐ μὴ⌋ πιστεύσητε ἐάν τις ἐκδιηγῆται ὑμῖν
n.asn p.d r.gp.2 d.dpf n.dpf n.asn r.asn pl pl v.aas.2p cj r.nsm v.pms.3s r.dp.2
2240 1877 7007 3836 2465 2240 4005 4409 4409 4024 3590 4409 1569 5516 1687 7007

42 As Paul and Barnabas were leaving the synagogue, the people invited them to speak further about
δὲ → αὐτῶν ← ← → Ἐξιόντων → παρεκάλουν → λαληθῆναι αὐτοῖς
cj r.gpm.3 pt.pa.gpm v.iai.3p f.ap r.dpm.3
1254 899 1997 4151 3281 899

these things on the next Sabbath. **43** When the congregation was dismissed, many of the Jews and
ταῦτα ⌊τὰ ῥήματα⌋ εἰς τὸ μεταξὺ σάββατον δὲ → τῆς συναγωγῆς → λυθείσης πολλοὶ → τῶν Ἰουδαίων καὶ
r.apn d.apn n.apn p.a d.asn adv n.asn cj d.gsf n.gsf pt.ap.gsf a.npm d.gpm a.gpm cj
4047 3836 4839 1650 3836 3568 4879 1254 3395 3836 5252 3395 4498 3836 2681 2779

devout converts to Judaism followed Paul and Barnabas, who talked with them and
⌊τῶν σεβομένων⌋ προσηλύτων ἠκολούθησαν ⌊τῷ Παύλῳ⌋ καὶ ⌊τῷ Βαρναβᾷ⌋ οἵτινες προσλαλοῦντες → αὐτοῖς
d.gpm pt.pm.gpm n.gpm v.aai.3p d.dsm n.dsm cj d.dsm n.dsm r.npm pt.pa.npm r.dpm.3
3836 4936 4670 199 3836 4263 2779 3836 982 4015 4688 899

urged them to continue in the grace of God. ¶ **44** On the next Sabbath almost the whole city
ἔπειθον αὐτοὺς → προσμένειν → τῇ χάριτι → ⌊τοῦ θεοῦ⌋ δὲ ⌊Τῷ ἐρχομένῳ⌋ σαββάτῳ σχεδὸν ἡ πᾶσα πόλις
v.iai.3p r.apm.3 f.pa d.dsf n.dsf d.gsm n.gsm cj d.dsn pt.pm.dsn n.dsn adv d.nsf a.nsf n.nsf
4275 899 4693 3836 5921 3836 2536 1254 3836 2262 4879 5385 3836 4246 4484

gathered to hear the word of the Lord. **45** When the Jews saw the crowds, they were filled with
συνήχθη → ἀκοῦσαι τὸν λόγον → τοῦ κυρίου δὲ → οἱ Ἰουδαῖοι ἰδόντες τοὺς ὄχλους → ἐπλήσθησαν →
v.api.3s f.aa d.asm n.asm d.gsm n.gsm cj d.npm a.npm pt.aa.npm d.apm n.apm v.api.3p
5251 201 3836 3364 3836 3261 1254 1625 3836 2681 1625 3836 4063 4398

jealousy and talked abusively against what Paul was saying. ¶ **46** Then Paul and
ζήλου καὶ ἀντέλεγον βλασφημοῦντες ← τοῖς ὑπὸ Παύλου → λαλουμένοις τε ⌊ὁ Παῦλος⌋ καὶ
n.gsm cj v.iai.3p pt.pa.npm d.dpn p.g n.gsm pt.pp.dpn d.nsm.m.nsm cj
2419 2779 515 1059 515 3836 5679 4263 3281 5445 3836 4263 2779

Barnabas answered them boldly: "We had to speak the word of God to you first.
⌊ὁ Βαρναβᾶς⌋ παρρησιασάμενοι εἶπαν ἦν ἀναγκαῖον → λαληθῆναι τὸν λόγον → ⌊τοῦ θεοῦ⌋ → ὑμῖν πρῶτον
d.nsm n.nsm pt.am.npm v.aai.3p v.iai.3s a.nsn f.ap d.asm n.asm d.gsm n.gsm r.dp.2 adv
3836 982 4245 3306 1639 338 3281 3836 3364 3836 2536 7007 4754

Since you reject it and do not consider yourselves worthy of eternal life, we now turn to the
ἐπειδὴ → ἀπωθεῖσθε αὐτὸν καὶ οὐκ κρίνετε ἑαυτοὺς ἀξίους → αἰωνίου τῆς ζωῆς ἰδοὺ → στρεφόμεθα εἰς τὰ
cj v.pmi.2p r.asm.3 cj pl v.pai.2p r.apm.2 a.apm a.gsf d.gsf n.gsf j v.ppi.1p p.a d.apn
2076 723 899 2779 4024 3212 1571 545 2437 173 3836 2437 2627 5138 1650 3836

Gentiles. **47** For this is what the Lord has commanded us: "'I have made you a light for the Gentiles, that you
ἔθνη γὰρ οὕτως ← ὁ κύριος → ἐντέταλται ἡμῖν → τέθεικά σε εἰς φῶς → ἐθνῶν σε
n.apn cj adv d.nsm n.nsm v.rmi.3s r.dp.1 v.rai.1s r.as.2 p.a n.asn n.gpn r.as.2
1620 1142 4048 3836 3261 1948 7005 5502 5148 1650 5890 1620 5148

may bring salvation to the ends of the earth.'" ¶ **48** When the Gentiles heard this, they were
→ ⌊τοῦ εἶναι⌋ εἰς σωτηρίαν ἕως ἐσχάτου → τῆς γῆς δὲ → τὰ ἔθνη Ἀκούοντα → →
d.gsn f.pa p.a n.asf p.g a.gsn d.gsf n.gsf cj d.npn n.npn pt.pa.npn
3836 1639 1650 5401 2401 2274 3836 1178 1254 201 3836 1620 201

glad and honored the word of the Lord; and all who were appointed for eternal life believed. ¶ **49** The
ἔχαιρον καὶ ἐδόξαζον τὸν λόγον → τοῦ κυρίου καὶ ὅσοι ← ἦσαν τεταγμένοι εἰς αἰώνιον ζωὴν ἐπίστευσαν δὲ ὁ
v.iai.3p cj v.iai.3p d.asm n.asm d.gsm n.gsm cj r.npm v.iai.3p v.rp.npm p.a a.asf n.asf v.aai.3p cj d.nsm
5897 2779 1519 3836 3364 3836 3261 2779 4012 1639 5435 1650 173 2437 4409 1254 3836

word of the Lord spread through the whole region. **50** But the Jews incited the God-fearing women of high
λόγος → τοῦ κυρίου διεφέρετο δι' → τῆς ὅλης χώρας δὲ οἱ Ἰουδαῖοι παρώτρυναν τὰς σεβομένας γυναῖκας →
n.nsm d.gsm n.gsm v.ipi.3s p.g d.gsf a.gsf n.gsf cj d.npm a.npm v.aai.3p d.apf pt.pm.apf n.apf
3364 3836 3261 1422 1328 3836 3910 6001 1254 3836 2681 4241 3836 4936 1222

standing and the leading men of the city. They stirred up persecution against Paul and
⌊τὰς εὐσχήμονας⌋ καὶ τοὺς πρώτους ← → τῆς πόλεως καὶ → ἐπήγειραν διωγμὸν ἐπὶ ⌊τὸν Παῦλον⌋ καὶ
d.apf a.apf cj d.apm a.apm d.gsf n.gsf cj v.aai.3p n.asm p.a d.asm n.asm cj
3836 2363 2779 3836 4755 3836 4484 2779 2074 1501 2093 3836 4263 2779

ἐν ταῖς ἡμέραις ὑμῶν, ἔργον ὃ οὐ μὴ πιστεύσητε ἐάν τις ἐκδιηγῆται ὑμῖν. ¶ **42** Ἐξιόντων δὲ αὐτῶν ἐκ τῆς συναγωγῆς παρεκάλουν εἰς τὸ μεταξὺ σάββατον λαληθῆναι αὐτοῖς τὰ ῥήματα ταῦτα. **43** λυθείσης δὲ τῆς συναγωγῆς ἠκολούθησαν πολλοὶ τῶν Ἰουδαίων καὶ τῶν σεβομένων προσηλύτων τῷ Παύλῳ καὶ τῷ Βαρναβᾷ, οἵτινες προσλαλοῦντες αὐτοῖς ἔπειθον αὐτοὺς προσμένειν τῇ χάριτι τοῦ θεοῦ. ¶ **44** Τῷ δὲ ἐρχομένῳ σαββάτῳ σχεδὸν πᾶσα ἡ πόλις συνήχθη ἀκοῦσαι τὸν λόγον τοῦ κυρίου. **45** ἰδόντες δὲ οἱ Ἰουδαῖοι τοὺς ὄχλους ἐπλήσθησαν ζήλου καὶ ἀντέλεγον τοῖς ὑπὸ Παύλου λαλουμένοις βλασφημοῦντες. ¶ **46** παρρησιασάμενοί τε ὁ Παῦλος καὶ ὁ Βαρναβᾶς εἶπαν, Ὑμῖν ἦν ἀναγκαῖον πρῶτον λαληθῆναι τὸν λόγον τοῦ θεοῦ· ἐπειδὴ ἀπωθεῖσθε αὐτὸν καὶ οὐκ ἀξίους κρίνετε ἑαυτοὺς τῆς αἰωνίου ζωῆς, ἰδοὺ στρεφόμεθα εἰς τὰ ἔθνη. **47** οὕτως γὰρ ἐντέταλται ἡμῖν ὁ κύριος, Τέθεικά σε εἰς φῶς ἐθνῶν τοῦ εἶναί σε εἰς σωτηρίαν ἕως ἐσχάτου τῆς γῆς. ¶ **48** ἀκούοντα δὲ τὰ ἔθνη ἔχαιρον καὶ ἐδόξαζον τὸν λόγον τοῦ κυρίου καὶ ἐπίστευσαν ὅσοι ἦσαν τεταγμένοι εἰς ζωὴν αἰώνιον· ¶ **49** διεφέρετο δὲ ὁ λόγος τοῦ κυρίου δι' ὅλης τῆς χώρας. **50** οἱ δὲ Ἰουδαῖοι παρώτρυναν τὰς σεβομένας γυναῖκας τὰς εὐσχήμονας καὶ τοὺς πρώτους τῆς πόλεως καὶ ἐπήγειραν διωγμὸν ἐπὶ τὸν

Barnabas, and expelled them from their region. [51] So they shook the dust from their feet in protest
Βαρναβᾶν καὶ ἐξέβαλον αὐτοὺς ἀπὸ αὐτῶν ⌐τῶν ὁρίων⌐ δὲ οἱ ἐκτιναξάμενοι τὸν κονιορτὸν → τῶν ποδῶν
n.asm cj v.aai.3p r.apm.3 p.g r.gpm.3 d.gpn n.gpn cj d.npm pt.am.npm d.asm n.asm d.gpm n.gpm
982 2779 1675 899 608 899 3836 3990 1254 3836 1759 3836 3155 3836 4546

against them and went to Iconium. [52] And the disciples were filled with joy and with the Holy Spirit.
ἐπ' αὐτοὺς ἦλθον εἰς Ἰκόνιον τε οἱ μαθηταὶ → ἐπληροῦντο → χαρᾶς καὶ ἁγίου πνεύματος
p.a r.apm.3 v.aai.3p p.a n.asn cj d.npm n.npm v.ipi.3p n.gsf cj a.gsn n.gsn
2093 899 2262 1650 2658 5445 3836 3412 4444 5915 2779 41 4460

In Iconium
14:1 At Iconium Paul and Barnabas went as usual into the Jewish synagogue.
δὲ Ἐγένετο ἐν Ἰκονίῳ αὐτοὺς ← εἰσελθεῖν → ⌐κατὰ τὸ αὐτὸ⌐ εἰς τὴν ⌐τῶν Ἰουδαίων⌐ συναγωγὴν καὶ
cj v.ami.3s p.d n.dsn r.apm.3 f.aa p.a d.asn r.asn p.a d.asf d.gpm a.gpm n.asf cj
1254 1181 1877 2658 899 1656 2848 3836 899 1650 3836 3836 2681 5252 2779

There they spoke so effectively that a great number of Jews and Gentiles believed. [2] But the Jews who
→ λαλῆσαι οὕτως ← ὥστε πολὺ πλῆθος τε → Ἰουδαίων καὶ Ἑλλήνων πιστεῦσαι δὲ οἱ Ἰουδαῖοι →
f.aa adv cj a.asn n.asn cj a.gpm cj n.gpm f.aa cj d.npm a.npm
3281 4048 6063 4498 4436 5445 2681 2779 1818 4409 1254 3836 2681

refused to believe stirred up the Gentiles and poisoned their minds against the brothers. [3] So Paul and
→ ἀπειθήσαντες ἐπήγειραν ← τῶν ἐθνῶν καὶ ἐκάκωσαν τὰς ψυχὰς κατὰ τῶν ἀδελφῶν οὖν μὲν
pt.aa.npm v.aai.3p d.gpn n.gpn cj v.aai.3p d.apf n.apf p.g d.gpm n.gpm cj pl
578 2074 3836 1620 2779 2808 3836 6034 2848 3836 81 4036 3525

Barnabas spent considerable time there, speaking boldly for the Lord, who confirmed the message
διέτριψαν ἱκανὸν χρόνον παρρησιαζόμενοι ← ἐπὶ τῷ κυρίῳ τῷ μαρτυροῦντι [ἐπὶ] τῷ λόγῳ
v.aai.3p a.asm n.asm pt.pm.npm p.d d.dsm n.dsm d.dsm pt.pa.dsm p.d d.dsm n.dsm
1417 2653 5989 4245 2093 3836 3261 3836 3455 2093 3836 3364

of his grace by enabling them to do miraculous signs and wonders. [4] The people of
→ αὐτοῦ ⌐τῆς χάριτος⌐ → διδόντι ⌐διὰ τῶν χειρῶν αὐτῶν⌐ → γίνεσθαι → σημεῖα καὶ τέρατα δὲ τὸ πλῆθος →
r.gsm.3 d.gsf n.gsf pt.pa.dsm p.g d.gpf r.gpm.3 f.pm n.apn cj n.apn cj d.nsn n.nsn
5921 899 3836 5921 1443 1328 3836 5931 899 1181 4956 2779 5469 1254 3836 4436

the city were divided; some sided with the Jews, others with the apostles. [5] There was a
τῆς πόλεως → ἐσχίσθη καὶ μὲν οἱ ἦσαν σὺν τοῖς Ἰουδαίοις δὲ οἱ σὺν τοῖς ἀποστόλοις δὲ ὡς ἐγένετο
d.gsf n.gsf v.api.3s cj pl d.npm v.iai.3p p.d d.dpm a.dpm pl d.npm p.d d.dpm n.dpm cj cj v.ami.3s
3836 4484 5387 2779 3525 3836 1639 5250 3836 2681 1254 3836 5250 3836 693 1254 6055 1181

plot afoot among the Gentiles and Jews, together with their leaders, to mistreat them and stone
ὁρμὴ → τε τῶν ἐθνῶν καὶ Ἰουδαίων → σὺν αὐτῶν ⌐τοῖς ἄρχουσιν⌐ → ὑβρίσαι καὶ λιθοβολῆσαι
n.nsf cj d.gpn n.gpn cj a.gpm p.d r.gpm.3 d.dpm n.dpm f.aa cj f.aa
3995 5445 3836 1620 2779 2681 5250 899 3836 807 5614 2779 3344

them. [6] But they found out about it and fled to the Lycaonian cities of Lystra and Derbe and to the
αὐτοὺς → συνιδόντες ← κατέφυγον εἰς τὰς ⌐τῆς Λυκαονίας⌐ πόλεις Λύστραν καὶ Δέρβην καὶ τὴν
r.apm.3 pt.aa.npm v.aai.3p p.a d.apf d.gsf n.gsf n.apf n.asf cj n.asf cj d.asf
899 5328 2966 1650 3836 3836 3377 4484 3388 2779 1292 2779 3836

surrounding country, [7] where they continued to preach the good news.
→ περίχωρον κἀκεῖ → ἦσαν → εὐαγγελιζόμενοι ←
a.asf crasis v.iai.3p pt.pm.npm
4369 2795 1639 2294

In Lystra and Derbe
14:8 In Lystra there sat a man crippled in his feet, who was lame from birth and
Καὶ ἐν λύστροις → ἐκάθητο τις ἀνὴρ ἀδύνατος → τοῖς ποσίν → χωλὸς ἐκ ⌐κοιλίας μητρὸς αὐτοῦ⌐ ὃς
cj p.d n.dpn v.imi.3s r.nsm n.nsm a.nsm d.dpm n.dpm a.nsm p.g n.gsf n.gsf r.gsm.3 r.nsm
2779 1877 3388 2764 5516 467 105 3836 4005 6000 1666 3120 3613 899 4005

had never walked. [9] He listened to Paul as he was speaking. Paul looked directly at him, saw that
→ οὐδέποτε περιεπάτησεν οὗτος ἤκουσεν ← ⌐τοῦ Παύλου⌐ → λαλοῦντος ὃς ἀτενίσας ← → αὐτῷ καὶ ἰδὼν ὅτι
adv v.aai.3s r.nsm v.aai.3s d.gsm n.gsm pt.pa.gsm r.nsm pt.aa.nsm r.dsm.3 cj pt.aa.nsm cj
4344 4030 4344 4047 201 3836 4263 3281 4005 867 899 2779 1625 4022

Παῦλον καὶ Βαρναβᾶν καὶ ἐξέβαλον αὐτοὺς ἀπὸ τῶν ὁρίων αὐτῶν. ⁵¹ οἱ δὲ ἐκτιναξάμενοι τὸν κονιορτὸν τῶν ποδῶν ἐπ' αὐτοὺς ἦλθον εἰς Ἰκόνιον, ⁵² οἵ τε μαθηταὶ ἐπληροῦντο χαρᾶς καὶ πνεύματος ἁγίου.

¹⁴:¹ Ἐγένετο δὲ ἐν Ἰκονίῳ κατὰ τὸ αὐτὸ εἰσελθεῖν αὐτοὺς εἰς τὴν συναγωγὴν τῶν Ἰουδαίων καὶ λαλῆσαι οὕτως ὥστε πιστεῦσαι Ἰουδαίων τε καὶ Ἑλλήνων πολὺ πλῆθος. ² οἱ δὲ ἀπειθήσαντες Ἰουδαῖοι ἐπήγειραν καὶ ἐκάκωσαν τὰς ψυχὰς τῶν ἐθνῶν κατὰ τῶν ἀδελφῶν. ³ ἱκανὸν μὲν οὖν χρόνον διέτριψαν παρρησιαζόμενοι ἐπὶ τῷ κυρίῳ τῷ μαρτυροῦντι [ἐπὶ] τῷ λόγῳ τῆς χάριτος αὐτοῦ, διδόντι σημεῖα καὶ τέρατα γίνεσθαι διὰ τῶν χειρῶν αὐτῶν. ⁴ ἐσχίσθη δὲ τὸ πλῆθος τῆς πόλεως, καὶ οἱ μὲν ἦσαν σὺν τοῖς Ἰουδαίοις, οἱ δὲ σὺν τοῖς ἀποστόλοις. ⁵ ὡς δὲ ἐγένετο ὁρμὴ τῶν ἐθνῶν τε καὶ Ἰουδαίων σὺν τοῖς ἄρχουσιν αὐτῶν ὑβρίσαι καὶ λιθοβολῆσαι αὐτούς, ⁶ συνιδόντες κατέφυγον εἰς τὰς πόλεις τῆς Λυκαονίας Λύστραν καὶ Δέρβην καὶ τὴν περίχωρον, ⁷ κἀκεῖ εὐαγγελιζόμενοι ἦσαν.

¹⁴:⁸ Καί τις ἀνὴρ ἀδύνατος ἐν Λύστροις τοῖς ποσὶν ἐκάθητο, χωλὸς ἐκ κοιλίας μητρὸς αὐτοῦ ὃς οὐδέποτε περιεπάτησεν. ⁹ οὗτος ἤκουσεν τοῦ Παύλου λαλοῦντος· ὃς ἀτενίσας αὐτῷ καὶ ἰδὼν ὅτι ἔχει πίστιν τοῦ σωθῆναι, ¹⁰ εἶπεν μεγάλῃ φωνῇ,

he had faith to be healed **10** and called out, "Stand up on your feet!" At that, the man
ἔχει πίστιν τοῦ σωθῆναι εἶπεν μεγάλῃ φωνῇ ἀνάστηθι ὀρθός ἐπὶ σου τοὺς πόδας καὶ
v.pai.3s n.asf d.gsn f.ap v.aai.3s a.dsf n.dsf v.aam.2s a.nsm p.a r.gs.2 d.apm n.apm cj
2400 4411 3836 5392 3306 3489 5889 482 3981 2093 5148 3836 4546 2779

jumped up and began to walk. ¶ **11** When the crowd saw what Paul had done, they
ἥλατο καὶ περιεπάτει τε οἱ ὄχλοι ἰδόντες ὃ Παῦλος ἐποίησεν
v.ami.3s cj v.iai.3s cj d.npm n.npm pt.aa.npm r.asn n.nsm v.aai.3s
256 2779 4344 5445 1625 3836 4063 1625 4005 4263 4472

shouted in the Lycaonian language, "The gods have come down to us in human
ἐπῆραν τὴν φωνὴν αὐτῶν Λυκαονιστὶ λέγοντες οἱ θεοὶ κατέβησαν πρὸς ἡμᾶς ἀνθρώποις
v.aai.3p d.asf n.asf r.gpm.3 adv pt.pa.npm d.npm n.npm v.aai.3p p.a r.ap.1 n.dpm
2048 3836 5889 899 3378 3306 3836 2536 2849 4639 7005 3929 476

form!" **12** Barnabas they called Zeus, and Paul they called Hermes because he was the chief
ὁμοιωθέντες τε τὸν Βαρναβᾶν ἐκάλουν Δία δὲ τὸν Παῦλον Ἑρμῆν ἐπειδὴ αὐτὸς ἦν ὁ ἡγούμενος
pt.ap.npm cj d.asm n.asm v.iai.3p n.asm cj d.asm n.asm n.asm cj r.nsm v.iai.3s d.nsm pt.pm.nsm
3929 5445 3836 982 2813 2416 1254 3836 4263 2258 2076 1639 3836 2451

speaker. **13** The priest of Zeus, whose temple was just outside the city, brought bulls and wreaths to
τοῦ λόγου τε ὁ ἱερεὺς τοῦ Διὸς τοῦ ὄντος πρὸ τῆς πόλεως ἐνέγκας ταύρους καὶ στέμματα ἐπὶ
d.gsn n.gsn cj d.nsm n.nsm d.gsn n.gsn d.gsm pt.pa.gsm p.g d.gsf n.gsf pt.aa.nsm n.apm cj n.apn p.a
3836 3364 5445 3836 2636 3836 2416 3836 1639 4574 3836 4484 5770 5436 2779 5098 2093

the city gates because he and the crowd wanted to offer sacrifices to them. ¶ **14** But when the apostles
τοὺς πυλῶνας σὺν τοῖς ὄχλοις ἤθελεν θύειν δὲ οἱ ἀπόστολοι
d.apm n.apm p.d d.dpm n.dpm v.iai.3s f.pa cj d.npm n.npm
3836 4784 5250 3836 4063 2527 2604 1254 201 3836 693

Barnabas and Paul heard of this, they tore their clothes and rushed out into the crowd,
Βαρναβᾶς καὶ Παῦλος Ἀκούσαντες διαρρήξαντες αὐτῶν τὰ ἱμάτια ἐξεπήδησαν εἰς τὸν ὄχλον
n.nsm cj n.nsm pt.aa.npm pt.aa.npm r.gpm.3 d.apn n.apn v.aai.3p p.a d.asm n.asm
982 2779 4263 201 1396 899 3836 2668 1737 1650 3836 4063

shouting: **15** "Men, why are you doing this? We too are only men, human like you. We are
κράζοντες καὶ λέγοντες ἄνδρες τί ποιεῖτε ταῦτα ἡμεῖς καὶ ἐσμεν ἄνθρωποι ὁμοιοπαθεῖς ὑμῖν
pt.pa.npm cj pt.pa.npm n.vpm r.asn v.pai.2p r.apn r.np.1 adv v.pai.1p n.npm a.npm r.dp.2
3189 2779 3306 467 5515 4472 4047 7005 2779 1639 476 3926 7007

bringing you good news, telling you to turn from these worthless things to the living God, who made
εὐαγγελιζόμενοι ὑμᾶς ἐπιστρέφειν ἀπὸ τούτων τῶν ματαίων ἐπὶ ζῶντα θεὸν ὃς ἐποίησεν
pt.pm.npm r.ap.2 f.pa p.g r.gpn d.gpn a.gpn p.a pt.pa.asm n.asm r.nsm v.aai.3s
2294 7007 2294 2294 2188 608 4047 3836 3469 2093 2409 2536 4005 4472

heaven and earth and sea and everything in them. **16** In the past, he let
τὸν οὐρανὸν καὶ τὴν γῆν καὶ τὴν θάλασσαν καὶ πάντα τὰ ἐν αὐτοῖς ὃς ἐν ταῖς παρῳχημέναις γενεαῖς εἴασεν
d.asm n.asm cj d.asf n.asf cj d.asf n.asf cj a.apn d.apn p.d r.dpm.3 r.nsm p.d d.dpf pt.rp.dpf n.dpf v.aai.3s
3836 4041 2779 3836 1178 2779 3836 2498 2779 4246 3836 1877 899 4005 1877 3836 4233 1155 1572

all nations go their own way. **17** Yet he has not left himself without testimony: He has shown kindness
πάντα τὰ ἔθνη πορεύεσθαι αὐτῶν ταῖς ὁδοῖς καίτοι οὐκ ἀφῆκεν αὐτὸν ἀμάρτυρον ἀγαθουργῶν
a.apn d.apn n.apn f.pm r.gpn.3 d.dpf n.dpf cj pl v.aai.3s r.asm.3 a.asm pt.pa.nsm
4246 3836 1620 4513 899 3836 3847 2792 918 918 4024 918 899 282 14

by giving you rain from heaven and crops in their seasons; he provides you with plenty of food and fills
διδοὺς ὑμῖν ὑετοὺς οὐρανόθεν καὶ καρποφόρους καιροὺς ἐμπιπλῶν τροφῆς καὶ
pt.pa.nsm r.dp.2 n.apm adv cj a.apm n.apm pt.pa.nsm n.gsf cj
1443 7007 5624 4040 2779 2845 2789 1858 5575 2779

your hearts with joy." **18** Even with these words, they had difficulty keeping the crowd from sacrificing to
ὑμῶν τὰς καρδίας εὐφροσύνης καὶ ταῦτα λέγοντες μόλις κατέπαυσαν τοὺς ὄχλους μὴ τοῦ θύειν
r.gp.2 d.apf n.apf n.gsf cj r.apn pt.pa.npm adv v.aai.3p d.apm n.apm pl d.gsn f.pa
7007 3836 2840 2372 2779 4047 3306 2924 2924 3660 2924 3836 4063 3590 3836 2604

them. ¶ **19** Then some Jews came from Antioch and Iconium and won the crowd over. They
αὐτοῖς δὲ Ἰουδαῖοι Ἐπῆλθαν ἀπὸ Ἀντιοχείας καὶ Ἰκονίου καὶ πείσαντες τοὺς ὄχλους καὶ
r.dpm.3 cj a.npm v.aai.3p p.g n.gsf cj n.gsn cj pt.aa.npm d.apm n.apm cj
899 1254 2681 2088 608 522 2779 2658 2779 4275 3836 4063 4275 2779

Ἀνάστηθι ἐπὶ τοὺς πόδας σου ὀρθός. καὶ ἥλατο καὶ περιεπάτει. ¶ **11** οἵ τε ὄχλοι ἰδόντες ὃ ἐποίησεν Παῦλος ἐπῆραν τὴν φωνὴν αὐτῶν Λυκαονιστὶ λέγοντες, Οἱ θεοὶ ὁμοιωθέντες ἀνθρώποις κατέβησαν πρὸς ἡμᾶς, **12** ἐκάλουν τε τὸν Βαρναβᾶν Δία, τὸν δὲ Παῦλον Ἑρμῆν, ἐπειδὴ αὐτὸς ἦν ὁ ἡγούμενος τοῦ λόγου. **13** ὅ τε ἱερεὺς τοῦ Διὸς τοῦ ὄντος πρὸ τῆς πόλεως ταύρους καὶ στέμματα ἐπὶ τοὺς πυλῶνας ἐνέγκας σὺν τοῖς ὄχλοις ἤθελεν θύειν. ¶ **14** ἀκούσαντες δὲ οἱ ἀπόστολοι Βαρναβᾶς καὶ Παῦλος διαρρήξαντες τὰ ἱμάτια αὐτῶν ἐξεπήδησαν εἰς τὸν ὄχλον κράζοντες **15** καὶ λέγοντες, Ἄνδρες, τί ταῦτα ποιεῖτε; καὶ ἡμεῖς ὁμοιοπαθεῖς ἐσμεν ὑμῖν ἄνθρωποι εὐαγγελιζόμενοι ὑμᾶς ἀπὸ τούτων τῶν ματαίων ἐπιστρέφειν ἐπὶ θεὸν ζῶντα, ὃς ἐποίησεν τὸν οὐρανὸν καὶ τὴν γῆν καὶ τὴν θάλασσαν καὶ πάντα τὰ ἐν αὐτοῖς· **16** ὃς ἐν ταῖς παρῳχημέναις γενεαῖς εἴασεν πάντα τὰ ἔθνη πορεύεσθαι ταῖς ὁδοῖς αὐτῶν· **17** καίτοι οὐκ ἀμάρτυρον αὐτὸν ἀφῆκεν ἀγαθουργῶν, οὐρανόθεν ὑμῖν ὑετοὺς διδοὺς καὶ καιροὺς καρποφόρους, ἐμπιπλῶν τροφῆς καὶ εὐφροσύνης τὰς καρδίας ὑμῶν. **18** καὶ ταῦτα λέγοντες μόλις κατέπαυσαν τοὺς ὄχλους τοῦ μὴ θύειν αὐτοῖς. ¶ **19** Ἐπῆλθαν δὲ ἀπὸ Ἀντιοχείας καὶ Ἰκονίου Ἰουδαῖοι καὶ πείσαντες τοὺς ὄχλους καὶ λιθάσαντες τὸν Παῦλον ἔσυρον ἔξω τῆς

stoned | Paul | and dragged | him | outside | the | city, | thinking | he | was dead. | [20] But | after | the | disciples | had
λιθάσαντες | ⌐τὸν Παῦλον⌐ | ἔσυρον | ἔξω | τῆς | πόλεως | νομίζοντες | αὐτὸν → | τεθνηκέναι | δὲ → | τῶν | μαθητῶν →
pt.aa.npm | d.asm n.asm | v.iai.3p | p.g | d.gsf | n.gsf | pt.pa.npm | r.asm.3 | f.ra | cj | d.gpm | n.gpm
3342 | 3836 4263 | 5359 | 2032 | 3836 | 4484 | 3787 | 899 | 2569 | 1254 3240 | 3836 | 3412

gathered | around | him, | he got | up | and went | back | into | the | city. | The | next | day | he | and | Barnabas
κυκλωσάντων ← | αὐτὸν → | ἀναστὰς ← | εἰσῆλθεν | εἰς | τὴν | πόλιν | Καὶ | τῇ | ἐπαύριον | → | σὺν | ⌐τῷ Βαρναβᾷ⌐
pt.aa.gpm | r.asm.3 | pt.aa.nsm | v.aai.3s | p.a | d.asf | n.asf | cj | d.dsf | adv | p.d | d.dsm n.dsm
3240 | 899 | 482 | 1656 | 1650 | 3836 | 4484 | 2779 | 3836 | 2069 | 2002 5250 | 3836 982

left | for | Derbe.
ἐξῆλθεν | εἰς | Δέρβην·
v.aai.3s | p.a | n.asf
2002 | 1650 | 1292

The Return to Antioch in Syria

14:21 They | preached | the good news | in that | city | and won | a large | number | of disciples. | Then
τε → | εὐαγγελισάμενοι ← | ← | ← | ἐκείνην | ⌐τὴν πόλιν | καὶ → | ἱκανοὺς ← | | μαθητεύσαντες
cj | pt.am.npm | | | r.asf | d.asf n.asf | cj | a.apm | | pt.aa.npm
5445 | 2294 | | | 1697 | 3836 4484 | 2779 3411 | 2653 | | 3411

they returned | to Lystra, | Iconium | and | Antioch, | [22] strengthening | the disciples and
→ ὑπέστρεψαν | εἰς ⌐τὴν Λύστραν⌐ | καὶ εἰς Ἰκόνιον | καὶ | εἰς Ἀντιόχειαν | ἐπιστηρίζοντες | τὰς ψυχὰς τῶν μαθητῶν
v.aai.3p | p.a d.asf n.asf | cj p.a n.asn | cj | p.a n.asf | pt.pa.npm | d.apf n.apf d.gpm n.gpm
5715 | 1650 3836 3388 | 2779 1650 2658 | 2779 | 1650 522 | 2185 | 3836 6034 3836 3412

encouraging | them to remain | true to | the | faith. | "We | must go through | many | hardships | to enter | the
παρακαλοῦντες | → ἐμμένειν | → τῇ | πίστει | καὶ ὅτι | ἡμᾶς | δεῖ | διὰ | πολλῶν θλίψεων | → εἰσελθεῖν εἰς | τὴν
pt.pa.npm | f.pa | d.dsf | n.dsf | cj cj | r.ap.1 | v.pai.3s | p.g | a.gpf n.gpf | f.aa | p.a d.asf
4151 | 1844 | 3836 | 4411 | 2779 4022 | 7005 | 1256 | 1328 | 4498 2568 | 1656 | 1650 3836

kingdom | of God," | they said. | [23] | Paul and Barnabas | appointed | elders | for them | in each | church | and,
βασιλείαν → | ⌐τοῦ θεοῦ⌐ | | δὲ | | χειροτονήσαντες | πρεσβυτέρους → | αὐτοῖς → | κατ' | ἐκκλησίαν
n.asf | d.gsm n.gsm | | cj | | pt.aa.npm | n.apm | r.dpm.3 | p.a | n.asf
993 | 3836 2536 | | 1254 | | 5936 | 4565 | 899 | 2848 | 1711

with prayer | and fasting, | committed | them | to the | Lord, | in whom | they had | put their trust. | [24]
προσευξάμενοι μετὰ ← | νηστειῶν | παρέθεντο | αὐτοὺς | τῷ | κυρίῳ | εἰς ὃν | | πεπιστεύκεισαν | Καὶ
pt.am.npm p.g | n.gpf | v.ami.3p | r.apm.3 | d.dsm | n.dsm | p.a r.asm | | v.lai.3p | cj
4667 3552 | 4667 3763 | 4192 | 899 | 3836 | 3261 | 1650 4005 | | 4409 | 2779

After going | through | Pisidia, | they came | into | Pamphylia, | [25] and when | they had preached | the word | in | Perga,
→ διελθόντες ← | | ⌐τὴν Πισιδίαν⌐ | → ἦλθον | εἰς | ⌐τὴν Παμφυλίαν⌐ | καὶ → | → λαλήσαντες | τὸν λόγον | ἐν | Πέργῃ
pt.aa.npm | | d.asf n.asf | v.aai.3p | p.a | d.asf n.asf | cj | pt.aa.npm | d.asm n.asm | p.d | n.dsf
1451 | | 3836 4407 | 2262 | 1650 | 3836 4103 | 2779 | 3281 | 3836 3364 | 1877 | 4308

they went | down | to Attalia. | ¶ | [26] From | Attalia | they sailed | back to | Antioch, | where | they had been
→ κατέβησαν ← | εἰς | Ἀττάλειαν | | κἀκεῖθεν | | → ἀπέπλευσαν ← | εἰς | Ἀντιόχειαν | ὅθεν → | → ἦσαν
v.aai.3p | p.a | n.asf | | crasis | | v.aai.3p | p.a | n.asf | cj | v.iai.3p
2849 | 1650 | 877 | | 2796 | | 676 | 1650 | 522 | 3854 | 1639

committed | to the | grace | of God, | for | the | work | they had now | completed. | [27] On arriving | there, | they
παραδεδομένοι | → τῇ | χάριτι | ⌐τοῦ θεοῦ⌐ | εἰς | τὸ | ἔργον | ὃ → | ἐπλήρωσαν | δὲ → παραγενόμενοι | | καὶ →
pt.rp.npm | d.dsf | n.dsf | d.gsm n.gsm | p.a | d.asn | n.asn | r.asn | v.aai.3p | cj pt.am.npm | | cj
4140 | 3836 | 5921 | 3836 2536 | 1650 | 3836 | 2240 | 4005 | 4444 | 1254 4134 | | 2779

gathered | the | church | together | and reported | all that | God | had done | through them | and | how | he had
συναγόντες | τὴν | ἐκκλησίαν ← | | ἀνήγγελλον | ὅσα ← | ὁ θεὸς⌐ | → ἐποίησεν μετ' | αὐτῶν | καὶ | ὅτι → | →
pt.aa.npm | d.asf | n.asf | | v.iai.3p | r.apn | d.nsm n.nsm | v.aai.3s | r.gpm.3 | cj | cj
5251 | 3836 | 1711 | | 334 | 4012 | 3836 2536 | 4472 | 899 | 2779 | 4022

opened | the door | of faith | to the | Gentiles. | [28] And | they stayed | there | a long | time | with | the | disciples.
ἤνοιξεν | θύραν → | πίστεως → | τοῖς | ἔθνεσιν | δὲ → | διέτριβον | | ⌐οὐκ ὀλίγον⌐ | χρόνον | σὺν | τοῖς | μαθηταῖς·
v.aai.3s | n.asf | n.gsf | d.dpn | n.dpn | cj | v.iai.3p | | pl a.asm | n.asm | p.d | d.dpm | n.dpm
487 | 2598 | 4411 | 3836 | 1620 | 1254 | 1417 | | 4024 3900 | 5989 | 5250 | 3836 | 3412

The Council at Jerusalem

15:1 Some | men | came | down | from | Judea | to Antioch and | were teaching | the | brothers: | "Unless
Καὶ | τινες | κατελθόντες ← | | ἀπὸ | ⌐τῆς Ἰουδαίας⌐ | → | ἐδίδασκον | τοὺς | ἀδελφοὺς | ὅτι ἐὰν μὴ
cj | r.npm | pt.aa.npm | | p.g | d.gsf n.gsf | | v.iai.3p | d.apm | n.apm | cj cj pl
2779 | 5516 | 2982 | | 608 | 3836 2677 | | 1438 | 3836 | 81 | 4022 1569 3590

πόλεως νομίζοντες αὐτὸν τεθνηκέναι. 20 κυκλωσάντων δὲ τῶν μαθητῶν αὐτὸν ἀναστὰς εἰσῆλθεν εἰς τὴν πόλιν. καὶ τῇ ἐπαύριον ἐξῆλθεν σὺν τῷ Βαρναβᾷ εἰς Δέρβην. 14:21 Εὐαγγελισάμενοί τε τὴν πόλιν ἐκείνην καὶ μαθητεύσαντες ἱκανοὺς ὑπέστρεψαν εἰς τὴν Λύστραν καὶ εἰς Ἰκόνιον καὶ εἰς Ἀντιόχειαν 22 ἐπιστηρίζοντες τὰς ψυχὰς τῶν μαθητῶν, παρακαλοῦντες ἐμμένειν τῇ πίστει καὶ ὅτι διὰ πολλῶν θλίψεων δεῖ ἡμᾶς εἰσελθεῖν εἰς τὴν βασιλείαν τοῦ θεοῦ. 23 χειροτονήσαντες δὲ αὐτοῖς κατ' ἐκκλησίαν πρεσβυτέρους, προσευξάμενοι μετὰ νηστειῶν παρέθεντο αὐτοὺς τῷ κυρίῳ εἰς ὃν πεπιστεύκεισαν. 24 καὶ διελθόντες τὴν Πισιδίαν ἦλθον εἰς τὴν Παμφυλίαν 25 καὶ λαλήσαντες ἐν Πέργῃ τὸν λόγον κατέβησαν εἰς Ἀττάλειαν ¶ 26 κἀκεῖθεν ἀπέπλευσαν εἰς Ἀντιόχειαν, ὅθεν ἦσαν παραδεδομένοι τῇ χάριτι τοῦ θεοῦ εἰς τὸ ἔργον ὃ ἐπλήρωσαν. 27 παραγενόμενοι δὲ καὶ συναγαγόντες τὴν ἐκκλησίαν ἀνήγγελλον ὅσα ἐποίησεν ὁ θεὸς μετ' αὐτῶν καὶ ὅτι ἤνοιξεν τοῖς ἔθνεσιν θύραν πίστεως. 28 διέτριβον δὲ χρόνον οὐκ ὀλίγον σὺν τοῖς μαθηταῖς. 15:1 Καί τινες κατελθόντες ἀπὸ τῆς Ἰουδαίας ἐδίδασκον τοὺς ἀδελφοὺς ὅτι Ἐὰν μὴ περιτμηθῆτε τῷ ἔθει τῷ Μωϋσέως, οὐ

you are circumcised, according to the custom taught by Moses,   you cannot   be saved." **2**   This brought
→ → περιτμηθῆτε →   → τῷ ἔθει   ⸤τῷ Μωϋσέως⸥   ⸤οὐ δύνασθε⸥ → σωθῆναι δὲ   γενομένης
v.aps.2p   d.dsn n.dsn   d.dsn n.gsm   pl v.ppi.2p   f.ap   cj   pt.am.gsf
4362   3836 1621   3836 3707   4024 1538   5392   1254   1181

Paul   and Barnabas   into sharp   dispute and debate   with them. So Paul   and Barnabas were
⸤τῷ Παύλῳ⸥ καὶ ⸤τῷ Βαρναβᾷ⸥   ⸤οὐκ ὀλίγης⸥ στάσεως καὶ ζητήσεως πρὸς αὐτούς   Παῦλον καὶ Βαρναβᾶν →
d.dsm n.dsm cj d.dsm n.dsm   pl a.gsf n.gsf cj n.gsf p.a r.apm.3   n.asm cj n.asm
3836 4263 2779 3836 982   4024 3900 5087 2779 2428 4639 899   4263 2779 982

appointed, along with some other believers, to go   up to Jerusalem to   see the apostles   and elders
ἔταξαν καὶ ← τινας ἄλλους ⸤ἐξ αὐτῶν⸥ → ἀναβαίνειν ← εἰς Ἰερουσαλὴμ πρὸς   τοὺς ἀποστόλους καὶ πρεσβυτέρους
v.aai.3p cj r.apm r.apm p.g r.gpm.3 f.pa p.a n.asf p.a d.apm n.apm cj a.apm
5435 2779 5516 257 1666 899 326 1650 2647 4639 3836 693 2779 4565

about this   question. **3**   The church   sent   them on their way, and as they traveled through
περὶ τούτου ⸤τοῦ ζητήματος⸥ οὖν μὲν ὑπὸ τῆς ἐκκλησίας προπεμφθέντες ← ← ←   Οἱ διήρχοντο ← τε
p.g r.gsn d.gsn n.gsn cj cj p.g d.gsf n.gsf pt.ap.npm   d.npm v.imi.3p cj
4309 4047 3836 2427 4036 3525 5679 3836 1711 4636   3836 1451 5445

Phoenicia   and Samaria, they told   how the Gentiles had been converted.   This news made all   the
⸤τὴν Φοινίκην⸥ καὶ Σαμάρειαν → ἐκδιηγούμενοι ← τῶν ἐθνῶν   ⸤τὴν ἐπιστροφὴν⸥ καὶ   ἐποίουν πᾶσιν τοῖς
d.asf n.asf cj n.asf pt.pm.npm d.gpn n.gpn   d.asf n.asf cj   v.iai.3p a.dpm d.dpm
3836 5834 2779 4899 1687 3836 1620   3836 2189 2779   4472 4246 3836

brothers very   glad. **4**   When they came   to Jerusalem, they were welcomed   by the church   and the
ἀδελφοῖς μεγάλην χαρὰν δὲ → → παραγενόμενοι εἰς Ἰερουσαλὴμ → → παρεδέχθησαν ἀπὸ τῆς ἐκκλησίας καὶ τῶν
n.dpm a.asf n.asf cj pt.am.npm p.a n.asf v.api.3p p.g d.gsf n.gsf cj d.gpm
81 3489 5915 1254 4134 1650 2647 4138 608 3836 1711 2779 3836

apostles and elders,   to whom they reported everything God   had done   through them. ¶
ἀποστόλων καὶ ⸤τῶν πρεσβυτέρων⸥ τε → ἀνήγγειλαν ὅσα ⸤ὁ θεὸς⸥ → ἐποίησεν μετ᾽ αὐτῶν
n.gpm cj d.gpm a.gpm cj v.aai.3p r.apn d.nsm n.nsm v.aai.3s p.g r.gpm.3
693 2779 3836 4565 5445 334 4012 3836 2536 4472 3552 899

5 Then some of the believers   who belonged to the party   of the Pharisees stood   up and said,   "The
δὲ τινες πεπιστευκότες τῶν ἀπὸ ← τῆς αἱρέσεως → τῶν Φαρισαίων Ἐξανέστησαν ← λέγοντες ὅτι
cj r.npm pt.ra.npm d.gpm p.g d.gsf n.gsf d.gpm n.gpm v.aai.3p pt.pa.npm cj
1254 5516 4409 3836 608 3836 146 3836 5757 1985 3306 4022

Gentiles must be circumcised and required   to obey the law of Moses." ¶   **6**   The apostles and
αὐτοὺς δεῖ → περιτέμνειν τε παραγγέλλειν → τηρεῖν τὸν νόμον Μωϋσέως   τε οἱ ἀπόστολοι καὶ
r.apm.3 v.pai.3s f.pai cj f.pai f.pai d.asm n.asm n.gsm   cj d.npm n.npm cj
899 1256 4362 5445 4133 5498 3836 3795 3707   5445 3836 693 2779

elders   met   to consider   this question. **7**   After much discussion, Peter got   up and
⸤οἱ πρεσβύτεροι⸥ Συνήχθησαν → ἰδεῖν περὶ τούτου ⸤τοῦ λόγου⸥ δὲ γενομένης ← Πολλῆς ζητήσεως Πέτρος ἀναστὰς ←
d.npm a.npm v.api.3p f.aa p.g r.gsn d.gsm n.gsm cj pt.am.gsf a.gsf n.gsf n.nsm pt.aa.nsm
3836 4565 5251 1625 4309 4047 3836 3364 1254 1181 4498 2428 4377 482

addressed   them: "Brothers, you know   that some time ago   God   made a choice   among you
εἶπεν πρὸς αὐτούς ἄνδρες ἀδελφοί ὑμεῖς ἐπίστασθε ὅτι ἀφ᾽ ἡμερῶν ἀρχαίων ὁ θεὸς → ἐξελέξατο ἐν ὑμῖν
v.aai.3s p.a r.apm.3 n.vpm n.vpm r.np.2 v.ppi.2p cj p.g n.gpf a.gpf d.nsm n.nsm v.ami.3s p.d r.dp.2
3306 4639 899 467 81 7007 2179 4022 608 2465 792 3836 2536 1721 1877 7007

that the Gentiles might hear   from my lips   the message of the gospel   and believe. **8**   God,   who
τὰ ἔθνη → ἀκοῦσαι διὰ μου ⸤τοῦ στόματος⸥ τὸν λόγον → τοῦ εὐαγγελίου καὶ πιστεῦσαι καὶ ὁ θεὸς
d.apn n.npn f.aa p.g r.gs.1 d.gsn n.gsn d.asm n.asm d.gsn n.gsn cj f.aa cj d.nsm n.nsm
3836 1620 201 1328 1609 3836 5125 3836 3364 3836 2295 2779 4409 2779 3836 2536

knows   the heart, showed   that he accepted them by giving the Holy   Spirit to them, just as   he did
καρδιογνώστης ← ← ἐμαρτύρησεν αὐτοῖς → δοὺς τὸ ⸤τὸ ἅγιον⸥ πνεῦμα καθὼς ← καὶ
n.nsm v.aai.3s r.dpn.3 pt.aa.nsm d.asn d.asn a.asn n.asn pl adv
2841 3455 899 1443 3836 3836 41 4460 2777 2779

to us. **9**   He made no   distinction between   us and them, for he purified their hearts   by faith.
→ ἡμῖν καὶ → → οὐθὲν διέκρινεν μεταξὺ τε ἡμῶν καὶ αὐτῶν → καθαρίσας αὐτῶν ⸤τὰς καρδίας⸥ ⸤τῇ πίστει⸥
r.dp.1 cj a.asn v.aai.3s p.g cj r.gp.1 cj r.gpn.3 pt.aa.nsm r.gpn.3 d.apf n.apf d.dsf n.dsf
7005 2779 1359 1359 4032 1359 3568 5445 7005 2779 899 2751 899 3836 2840 3836 4411

δύνασθε σωθῆναι. ² γενομένης δὲ στάσεως καὶ ζητήσεως οὐκ ὀλίγης τῷ Παύλῳ καὶ τῷ Βαρναβᾷ πρὸς αὐτούς, ἔταξαν ἀναβαίνειν Παῦλον καὶ Βαρναβᾶν καί τινας ἄλλους ἐξ αὐτῶν πρὸς τοὺς ἀποστόλους καὶ πρεσβυτέρους εἰς Ἰερουσαλὴμ περὶ τοῦ ζητήματος τούτου. ³ Οἱ μὲν οὖν προπεμφθέντες ὑπὸ τῆς ἐκκλησίας διήρχοντο τήν τε Φοινίκην καὶ Σαμάρειαν ἐκδιηγούμενοι τὴν ἐπιστροφὴν τῶν ἐθνῶν καὶ ἐποίουν χαρὰν μεγάλην πᾶσιν τοῖς ἀδελφοῖς. ⁴ παραγενόμενοι δὲ εἰς Ἰερουσαλὴμ παρεδέχθησαν ἀπὸ τῆς ἐκκλησίας καὶ τῶν ἀποστόλων καὶ τῶν πρεσβυτέρων, ἀνήγγειλάν τε ὅσα ὁ θεὸς ἐποίησεν μετ᾽ αὐτῶν. ¶ ⁵ ἐξανέστησαν δέ τινες τῶν ἀπὸ τῆς αἱρέσεως τῶν Φαρισαίων πεπιστευκότες λέγοντες ὅτι δεῖ περιτέμνειν αὐτοὺς παραγγέλλειν τε τηρεῖν τὸν νόμον Μωϋσέως. ¶ ⁶ Συνήχθησάν τε οἱ ἀπόστολοι καὶ οἱ πρεσβύτεροι ἰδεῖν περὶ τοῦ λόγου τούτου. ⁷ πολλῆς δὲ ζητήσεως γενομένης ἀναστὰς Πέτρος εἶπεν πρὸς αὐτούς, Ἄνδρες ἀδελφοί, ὑμεῖς ἐπίστασθε ὅτι ἀφ᾽ ἡμερῶν ἀρχαίων ἐν ὑμῖν ἐξελέξατο ὁ θεὸς διὰ τοῦ στόματός μου ἀκοῦσαι τὰ ἔθνη τὸν λόγον τοῦ εὐαγγελίου καὶ πιστεῦσαι. ⁸ καὶ ὁ καρδιογνώστης θεὸς ἐμαρτύρησεν αὐτοῖς δοὺς αὐτοῖς τὸ πνεῦμα τὸ ἅγιον καθὼς καὶ ἡμῖν ⁹ καὶ οὐθὲν διέκρινεν μεταξὺ ἡμῶν τε καὶ αὐτῶν τῇ πίστει καθαρίσας τὰς καρδίας αὐτῶν.

10 Now then, why do you try to test God by putting on the necks of the disciples a yoke that neither we
νῦν οὖν τί → → πειράζετε τὸν θεὸν → ἐπιθεῖναι ἐπὶ τὸν τράχηλον → τῶν μαθητῶν ζυγὸν ὃν οὔτε ἡμεῖς
adv cj r.asn v.pai.2p d.asm n.asm f.aa p.a d.asm n.asm d.gpm n.gpm n.asm r.asm cj r.np.1
3814 4036 5515 4279 3836 2536 2202 2093 3836 5549 3836 3412 2433 4005 4046 7005

nor our fathers have been able to bear? **11** No! We believe it is through the grace of our Lord Jesus
οὔτε ἡμῶν οἱ πατέρες → → ἰσχύσαμεν → βαστάσαι ἀλλὰ → πιστεύομεν διὰ τῆς χάριτος → τοῦ κυρίου Ἰησοῦ
cj r.gp.1 d.npm n.npm v.aai.1p f.aa cj v.pai.1p p.g d.gsf n.gsf d.gsm n.gsm n.gsm
4046 7005 3836 4252 2710 1002 247 4409 1328 3836 5921 3836 3261 2652

that we are saved, just as they are." ¶ **12** The whole assembly became silent as they
→ → → σωθῆναι καθ' ὃν τρόπον κἀκεῖνοι δὲ τὸ πᾶν πλῆθος → Ἐσίγησεν καὶ →
f.ap p.a r.asm n.asm adv cj d.nsn a.nsn n.nsn v.aai.3s cj
5392 2848 4005 5573 2797 1254 3836 4246 4436 4967 2779

listened to Barnabas and Paul telling about the miraculous signs and wonders God had done
ἤκουον → Βαρναβᾶ καὶ Παύλου ἐξηγουμένων ← ὅσα → σημεῖα καὶ τέρατα ὁ θεὸς ἐποίησεν
v.iai.3p n.gsm cj n.gsm pt.pm.gpm r.apn n.apn cj n.apn d.nsm n.nsm v.aai.3s
201 982 2779 4263 2007 4012 4956 2779 5469 3836 2536 4472

among the Gentiles through them. **13** When they finished, James spoke up: "Brothers, listen
ἐν τοῖς ἔθνεσιν δι' αὐτῶν δὲ Μετὰ αὐτοὺς τὸ σιγῆσαι Ἰάκωβος ἀπεκρίθη ← λέγων ἄνδρες ἀδελφοί ἀκούσατε
p.d d.dpn n.dpn p.g r.gpm.3 cj p.a r.apm.3 d.asn f.aa n.nsm v.api.3s pt.pa.nsm n.vpm n.vpm v.aam.2p
1877 3836 1620 1328 899 1254 3552 899 3836 4967 2610 646 3306 467 81 201

to me. **14** Simon has described to us how God at first showed his concern by taking from the Gentiles a
← μου Συμεὼν → ἐξηγήσατο ὁ θεὸς καθὼς πρῶτον ἐπεσκέψατο ← ← → λαβεῖν ἐξ ἐθνῶν
r.gs.1 n.nsm v.ami.3s d.nsm n.nsm cj adv v.ami.3s f.aa p.g n.gpn
1609 5208 2007 3836 2536 2777 4754 2170 3284 1666 1620

people for himself. **15** The words of the prophets are in agreement with this, as it is written: **16**"'After
λαὸν → τῷ ὀνόματι αὐτοῦ καὶ οἱ λόγοι τῶν προφητῶν → συμφωνοῦσιν → τούτῳ καθὼς → γέγραπται μετὰ
n.asm d.dsn n.dsn r.gsm.3 cj d.npm n.npm d.gpm n.gpm v.pai.3p r.dsn cj v.rpi.3s p.a
3295 3836 3950 899 2779 3836 3364 3836 4737 5244 4047 2777 1211 3552

this I will return and rebuild David's fallen tent. Its ruins I will rebuild,
ταῦτα → ἀναστρέψω καὶ ἀνοικοδομήσω Δαυὶδ τὴν πεπτωκυῖαν τὴν σκηνὴν καὶ αὐτῆς τὰ κατεσκαμμένα → ἀνοικοδομήσω
r.apn v.fai.1s cj v.fai.1s n.gsm d.asf pt.ra.asf d.asf n.asf cj r.gsf.3 d.apn pt.rp.apn v.fai.1s
4047 418 2779 488 1253 3836 4406 3836 5008 2779 899 3836 2940 488

and I will restore it, **17** that the remnant of men may seek the Lord, and all the Gentiles
καὶ → ἀνορθώσω αὐτήν ὅπως ἂν οἱ κατάλοιποι τῶν ἀνθρώπων → ἐκζητήσωσιν τὸν κύριον καὶ πάντα τὰ ἔθνη ἐφ'
cj v.fai.1s r.asf.3 cj pl d.npm a.npm d.gpm n.gpm v.aas.3p d.asm n.asm cj a.npn d.npn n.npn p.a
2779 494 899 3968 323 3836 2905 3836 476 1699 3836 3261 2779 4246 3836 1620 2093

who bear my name, says the Lord, who does these things' **18** that have been known for ages. ¶
οὓς ἐπικέκληται μου τὸ ὄνομα ἐπ' αὐτούς λέγει κύριος → ποιῶν ταῦτα → → → γνωστὰ ἀπ' αἰῶνος
r.apm v.rpi.3s r.gs.1 d.nsn n.nsn p.a r.apm.3 v.pai.3s n.nsm pt.pa.nsm r.apn a.apn p.g n.gsm
4005 2126 1609 3836 3950 2093 899 3306 3261 4472 4047 1196 608 172

19 "It is my judgment, therefore, that we should not make it difficult for the Gentiles who are turning
→ ἐγὼ κρίνω διὸ → μὴ → → παρενοχλεῖν → τοῖς ἀπὸ τῶν ἐθνῶν → ἐπιστρέφουσιν
r.ns.1 v.pai.1s cj pl f.pa d.dpm p.g d.gpn n.gpn pt.pa.dpm
3212 3212 3212 1475 3590 4214 3836 608 3836 1620 2188

to God. **20** Instead we should write to them, telling them to abstain from food polluted by
ἐπὶ τὸν θεόν ἀλλὰ → → ἐπιστεῖλαι αὐτοῖς → τοῦ ἀπέχεσθαι ← τῶν ἀλισγημάτων
p.a d.asm n.asm cj f.aa r.dpm.3 d.gsn f.pm d.gpn n.gpn
2093 3836 2536 247 2182 899 3836 600 3836 246

idols, from sexual immorality, from the meat of strangled animals and from blood. **21** For Moses
τῶν εἰδώλων καὶ τῆς πορνείας καὶ τοῦ πνικτοῦ καὶ τοῦ αἵματος γὰρ Μωϋσῆς
d.gpn n.gpn cj d.gsf n.gsf cj d.gsn a.gsn cj d.gsn n.gsn cj n.nsm
3836 1631 2779 3836 4518 2779 3836 4465 2779 3836 135 1142 3707

has been preached in every city from the earliest times and is read in the synagogues
→ → τοὺς κηρύσσοντας αὐτὸν κατὰ ← πόλιν ἐκ ἀρχαίων γενεῶν ἔχει ἀναγινωσκόμενος ἐν ταῖς συναγωγαῖς
d.apm pt.pa.apm r.asm.3 p.a n.asf p.g a.gpf n.gpf v.pai.3s pt.pp.nsm p.d d.dpf n.dpf
3836 3062 899 2848 4484 1666 792 1155 2400 336 1877 3836 5252

---

10 νῦν οὖν τί πειράζετε τὸν θεὸν ἐπιθεῖναι ζυγὸν ἐπὶ τὸν τράχηλον τῶν μαθητῶν ὃν οὔτε οἱ πατέρες ἡμῶν οὔτε ἡμεῖς ἰσχύσαμεν βαστάσαι; **11** ἀλλὰ διὰ τῆς χάριτος τοῦ κυρίου Ἰησοῦ πιστεύομεν σωθῆναι καθ' ὃν τρόπον κἀκεῖνοι. ¶ **12** Ἐσίγησεν δὲ πᾶν τὸ πλῆθος καὶ ἤκουον Βαρναβᾶ καὶ Παύλου ἐξηγουμένων ὅσα ἐποίησεν ὁ θεὸς σημεῖα καὶ τέρατα ἐν τοῖς ἔθνεσιν δι' αὐτῶν. **13** Μετὰ δὲ τὸ σιγῆσαι αὐτοὺς ἀπεκρίθη Ἰάκωβος λέγων, Ἄνδρες ἀδελφοί, ἀκούσατέ μου. **14** Συμεὼν ἐξηγήσατο καθὼς πρῶτον ὁ θεὸς ἐπεσκέψατο λαβεῖν ἐξ ἐθνῶν λαὸν τῷ ὀνόματι αὐτοῦ. **15** καὶ τούτῳ συμφωνοῦσιν οἱ λόγοι τῶν προφητῶν καθὼς γέγραπται, **16** Μετὰ ταῦτα ἀναστρέψω καὶ ἀνοικοδομήσω τὴν σκηνὴν Δαυὶδ τὴν πεπτωκυῖαν καὶ τὰ κατεσκαμμένα αὐτῆς ἀνοικοδομήσω καὶ ἀνορθώσω αὐτήν, **17** ὅπως ἂν ἐκζητήσωσιν οἱ κατάλοιποι τῶν ἀνθρώπων τὸν κύριον καὶ πάντα τὰ ἔθνη ἐφ' οὓς ἐπικέκληται τὸ ὄνομά μου ἐπ' αὐτούς, λέγει κύριος ποιῶν ταῦτα **18** γνωστὰ ἀπ' αἰῶνος. ¶ **19** διὸ ἐγὼ κρίνω μὴ παρενοχλεῖν τοῖς ἀπὸ τῶν ἐθνῶν ἐπιστρέφουσιν ἐπὶ τὸν θεόν, **20** ἀλλὰ ἐπιστεῖλαι αὐτοῖς τοῦ ἀπέχεσθαι τῶν ἀλισγημάτων τῶν εἰδώλων καὶ τῆς πορνείας καὶ τοῦ πνικτοῦ καὶ τοῦ αἵματος. **21** Μωϋσῆς γὰρ ἐκ γενεῶν ἀρχαίων κατὰ πόλιν τοὺς κηρύσσοντας αὐτὸν ἔχει ἐν ταῖς συναγωγαῖς κατὰ πᾶν σάββατον ἀναγινωσκόμενος.

on   every   Sabbath.”
κατὰ   πᾶν   σάββατον
p.a   a.asn   n.asn
2848   4246   4879

The Council's Letter to Gentile Believers

15:22 Then the apostles   and elders,   with the whole church, decided to choose   some of their own
Τότε   τοῖς ἀποστόλοις καὶ τοῖς πρεσβυτέροις, σὺν   τῇ   ὅλῃ   ἐκκλησίᾳ ἔδοξε → ἐκλεξαμένους   ἐξ   αὐτῶν
adv   d.dpm n.dpm   cj   d.dpm a.dpm   p.d   d.dsf a.dsf n.dsf   v.aai.3s   pt.am.apm   p.g r.gpm.3
5538   3836   693   2779 3836   4565   5250 3836   3910   1711   1506   1721   1666 899

men   and send   them to Antioch   with Paul   and Barnabas. They chose Judas (called   Barsabbas)
ἄνδρας πέμψαι   εἰς Ἀντιόχειαν σὺν   τῷ Παύλῳ καὶ Βαρναβᾷ   Ἰούδαν τὸν καλούμενον Βαρσαββᾶν
n.apm   f.aa   p.a n.asf   p.d   d.dsm n.dsm cj   n.dsm   n.asm   d.asm pt.pp.asm   n.asm
467   4287   1650 522   5250 3836 4263   2779 982   2683   3836 2813   984

and Silas, two men   who were leaders   among the brothers. **23** With   them they sent the following letter:
καὶ Σίλαν   ἄνδρας → → ἡγουμένους ἐν   τοῖς ἀδελφοῖς   διὰ   χειρὸς αὐτῶν   γράψαντες
cj   n.asm   n.apm   pt.pm.apm   p.d d.dpm n.dpm   p.g   n.gsf   r.gpm.3   pt.aa.npm
2779 4976   467   2451   1877 3836   81   1328 5931   899   1211

The apostles and elders,   your brothers, To the Gentile   believers in Antioch,   Syria and
Οἱ   ἀπόστολοι καὶ οἱ πρεσβύτεροι, ἀδελφοὶ   τοῖς τοῖς ἐξ ἐθνῶν, ἀδελφοῖς κατὰ τὴν Ἀντιόχειαν καὶ Συρίαν καὶ
d.npm n.npm   cj   d.npm a.npm   n.npm   d.dpm d.dpm p.g n.gpn   n.dpm   p.a   d.asf n.asf   cj   n.asf cj
3836   693   2779 3836 4565   81   3836   3836 1666 1620   81   2848 3836 522   2779 5353   2779

Cilicia: Greetings. **24**   We have heard   that some went   out from us   without our authorization and
Κιλικίαν χαίρειν   Ἐπειδὴ → → ἠκούσαμεν ὅτι   τινὲς ἐξελθόντες ← ἐξ   ἡμῶν οἷς οὐ → διεστειλάμεθα
n.asf   f.pa   cj   v.aai.1p   cj   r.npm pt.aa.npm   p.g r.gp.1 r.dpm pl   v.ami.1p
3070   5897   2076   201   4022   5516   2002   1666 7005   4005   4024   1403

disturbed you, troubling   your minds   by what they said. **25** So we all   agreed   to
ἐτάραξαν   ὑμᾶς ἀνασκευάζοντες ὑμῶν τὰς ψυχάς, → → → λόγοις   ἡμῖν ἔδοξεν γενομένοις ὁμοθυμαδὸν →
v.aai.3p   r.ap.2 pt.pa.npm   r.gp.2 d.apf n.apf   n.dp.1 v.aai.3s pt.am.dpm   adv
5429   7007   412   7007   3836   6034   3364 7005   1506   1181   3924

choose   some men   and send them to you with our dear friends   Barnabas and Paul   **26** men
ἐκλεξαμένοις ἄνδρας πέμψαι   πρὸς ὑμᾶς σὺν ἡμῶν → τοῖς ἀγαπητοῖς, Βαρναβᾷ καὶ Παύλῳ   ἀνθρώποις
pt.am.dpm n.apm   f.aa   p.a   r.ap.2 p.d r.gp.1   d.dpm a.dpm   n.dsm   cj   n.dsm   n.dpm
1721   467   4287   4639 7007   5250 7005   3836   28   982   2779 4263   476

who have risked   their lives   for the name   of our Lord   Jesus Christ. **27** Therefore we are
→ → παραδεδωκόσι αὐτῶν τὰς ψυχάς, ὑπὲρ τοῦ ὀνόματος ἡμῶν τοῦ κυρίου Ἰησοῦ Χριστοῦ οὖν   → →
pt.ra.dpm r.gpm.3 d.apf n.apf   p.g   d.gsn n.gsn   r.gp.1 d.gsm n.gsm n.gsm n.gsm   cj
4140   899   3836   6034   5642 3836   3950   7005   3836 3261   2652   5986   4036

sending   Judas and Silas   to confirm   by word of mouth what   we are writing. **28** It seemed
ἀπεστάλκαμεν Ἰούδαν καὶ Σίλαν καὶ αὐτοὺς ἀπαγγέλλοντας διὰ λόγου   τὰ αὐτά,   γὰρ → ἔδοξεν
v.rai.1p   n.asm   cj   n.asm cj   r.apm.3   pt.pa.apm   p.g n.gsm   d.apn r.apn   cj   v.aai.3s
690   2683   2779 4976   2779 899   550   1328 3364   3836   899   1142   1506

good to the Holy   Spirit   and to us   not to burden   you with anything beyond the following
← → τῷ τῷ ἁγίῳ πνεύματι καὶ → ἡμῖν μηδὲν ἐπιτίθεσθαι βάρος, ὑμῖν πλέον πλὴν τούτων ←
d.dsn d.dsn a.dsn n.dsn   cj   r.dp.1 a.asn f.pm   n.asn   r.dp.2 a.asn.c p.g   r.gpn
3836   3836 41   4460   2779   7005   3594   2202   983   7007   4498   4440 4047

requirements: **29** You are to abstain   from food sacrificed to idols,   from blood,   from the meat of strangled
τῶν ἐπάναγκες, ἀπέχεσθαι ←   εἰδωλοθύτων καὶ αἵματος καὶ   → πνικτῶν
d.gpn adv   f.pm   n.gpn   cj   n.gsn   cj   a.gpn
3836 2055   600   1628   2779 135   2779   4465

animals and from sexual immorality. You will do   well to avoid   these things.   Farewell. ¶
καὶ   πορνείας,   → πράξετε εὖ διατηροῦντες ἐξ ὧν ἑαυτοὺς ἔρρωσθε
cj   n.gsf   v.fai.2p adv pt.pa.npm   p.g r.gpn r.apm.2 v.rpm.2p
2779 4518   4556   2292 1413   1666 4005   1571   4874

30   The men were sent   off and went   down to Antioch,   where they gathered   the church
οὖν μὲν Οἱ ← ἀπολυθέντες ← κατῆλθον ← εἰς Ἀντιόχειαν καὶ   συναγαγόντες τὸ πλῆθος
cj pl d.npm   pt.ap.npm   v.aai.3p   p.a n.asf   cj   pt.aa.npm   d.asn n.asn
4036 3525 3836   668   2982   1650 522   2779 5251   3836 4436

15:22 Τότε ἔδοξε τοῖς ἀποστόλοις καὶ τοῖς πρεσβυτέροις σὺν ὅλῃ τῇ ἐκκλησίᾳ ἐκλεξαμένους ἄνδρας ἐξ αὐτῶν πέμψαι εἰς Ἀντιόχειαν σὺν τῷ Παύλῳ καὶ Βαρναβᾷ, Ἰούδαν τὸν καλούμενον Βαρσαββᾶν καὶ Σιλᾶν, ἄνδρας ἡγουμένους ἐν τοῖς ἀδελφοῖς, **23** γράψαντες διὰ χειρὸς αὐτῶν, Οἱ ἀπόστολοι καὶ οἱ πρεσβύτεροι ἀδελφοὶ τοῖς κατὰ τὴν Ἀντιόχειαν καὶ Συρίαν καὶ Κιλικίαν ἀδελφοῖς τοῖς ἐξ ἐθνῶν χαίρειν. **24** Ἐπειδὴ ἠκούσαμεν ὅτι τινὲς ἐξ ἡμῶν [ἐξελθόντες] ἐτάραξαν ὑμᾶς λόγοις ἀνασκευάζοντες τὰς ψυχὰς ὑμῶν οἷς οὐ διεστειλάμεθα, **25** ἔδοξεν ἡμῖν γενομένοις ὁμοθυμαδὸν ἐκλεξαμένοις ἄνδρας πέμψαι πρὸς ὑμᾶς σὺν τοῖς ἀγαπητοῖς ἡμῶν Βαρναβᾷ καὶ Παύλῳ, **26** ἀνθρώποις παραδεδωκόσι τὰς ψυχὰς αὐτῶν ὑπὲρ τοῦ ὀνόματος τοῦ κυρίου ἡμῶν Ἰησοῦ Χριστοῦ. **27** ἀπεστάλκαμεν οὖν Ἰούδαν καὶ Σιλᾶν καὶ αὐτοὺς διὰ λόγου ἀπαγγέλλοντας τὰ αὐτά. **28** ἔδοξεν γὰρ τῷ πνεύματι τῷ ἁγίῳ καὶ ἡμῖν μηδὲν πλέον ἐπιτίθεσθαι ὑμῖν βάρος πλὴν τούτων τῶν ἐπάναγκες, **29** ἀπέχεσθαι εἰδωλοθύτων καὶ αἵματος καὶ πνικτῶν καὶ πορνείας, ἐξ ὧν διατηροῦντες ἑαυτοὺς εὖ πράξετε. Ἔρρωσθε. ¶ **30** Οἱ μὲν οὖν ἀπολυθέντες κατῆλθον εἰς Ἀντιόχειαν,

together and delivered the letter. **31** The people read it and were glad for its encouraging message. **32**
← ἐπέδωκαν τὴν ἐπιστολήν δὲ → ἀναγνόντες → ἐχάρησαν ἐπὶ τῇ παρακλήσει ← τε
      v.aai.3p d.asf n.asf cj pt.aa.npm v.api.3p p.d d.dsf n.dsf cj
5251 2113 3836 2186 1254 336 5897 2093 3836 4155 5445

Judas and Silas, who themselves were prophets, said much to encourage and strengthen the brothers.
Ἰούδας καὶ Σιλᾶς καὶ αὐτοὶ ὄντες προφῆται διὰ λόγου πολλοῦ παρεκάλεσαν καὶ ἐπεστήριξαν τοὺς ἀδελφοὺς
n.nsm cj n.nsm adv r.npm pt.pa.npm n.npm p.g n.gsm n.gsm v.aai.3p cj v.aai.3p d.apm n.apm
2683 2779 4976 2779 899 1639 4737 1328 3364 4498 4151 2779 2185 3836 81

33 After spending some time there, they were sent off by the brothers with the blessing of peace to return
δὲ → ποιήσαντες χρόνον → → ἀπελύθησαν ← ἀπὸ τῶν ἀδελφῶν μετ' εἰρήνης
cj pt.aa.npm n.asm v.api.3p p.g d.gpm n.gpm p.g n.gsf
1254 4472 5989 668 608 3836 81 3552 1645

to those who had sent them. **35** But Paul and Barnabas remained in Antioch, where they and many
πρὸς τοὺς ← → ἀποστείλαντας αὐτούς δὲ Παῦλος καὶ Βαρναβᾶς διέτριβον ἐν Ἀντιοχείᾳ → μετὰ καὶ πολλῶν
p.a d.apm pt.aa.apm r.apm.3 cj n.nsm cj n.nsm v.iai.3p p.d n.dsf p.a adv a.gpm
4639 3836 690 899 1254 4263 2779 982 1417 1877 522 1438 3552 2779 4498

others taught and preached the word of the Lord.
ἑτέρων διδάσκοντες καὶ εὐαγγελιζόμενοι τὸν λόγον → τοῦ κυρίου
r.gpm pt.pa.npm cj pt.pm.npm d.asm n.asm d.gsm n.gsm
2283 1438 2779 2294 3836 3364 3836 3261

Disagreement Between Paul and Barnabas

15:36 Some time later Paul said to Barnabas, "Let us go back and visit the brothers
δὲ τινας ἡμέρας Μετὰ Παῦλος εἶπεν πρὸς Βαρναβᾶν δὴ ⌐Let us go ἐπιστρέψαντες ← ἐπισκεψώμεθα τοὺς ἀδελφοὺς
cj r.apf n.apf p.a n.nsm v.aai.3s p.a n.asm pl   pt.aa.npm v.ams.1p d.apm n.apm
1254 5516 2465 3552 4263 3306 4639 982 1314 2170 2170 2188 2170 3836 81

in all the towns where we preached the word of the Lord and see how they are doing." **37** Barnabas
κατὰ πᾶσαν πόλιν ἐν αἷς⌐ κατηγγείλαμεν τὸν λόγον → τοῦ κυρίου πῶς → ἔχουσιν δὲ Βαρναβᾶς
p.a a.asf n.asf p.d r.dpf v.aai.1p d.asm n.asm d.gsm n.gsm cj v.pai.3p cj n.nsm
2848 4246 4484 1877 4005 2859 3836 3364 3836 3261 4802 2400 1254 982

wanted to take John, also called Mark, with them, **38** but Paul did not think it wise to
ἐβούλετο → συμπαραλαβεῖν καὶ ⌐τὸν Ἰωάννην⌐ ⌐τὸν καλούμενον⌐ Μᾶρκον ← δὲ Παῦλος → μὴ ἠξίου ← →
v.imi.3s f.aa adv d.asm n.asm d.asm pt.pp.asm n.asm cj n.nsm pl v.iai.3s
1089 5221 2779 3836 2722 3836 2813 3453 5221 1254 4263 546 3590 546

take him, because he had deserted them in Pamphylia and had not continued with them in
συμπαραλαμβάνειν τοῦτον → → ⌐τὸν ἀποστάντα⌐ ἀπ' αὐτῶν ἀπὸ Παμφυλίας καὶ → μὴ συνελθόντα ← αὐτοῖς εἰς
f.pa r.asm d.asm pt.aa.asm p.g r.gpm.3 p.g n.gsf cj pl pt.aa.asm r.dpm.3 p.a
5221 4047 3836 923 608 899 608 4103 2779 3590 5302 899 1650

the work. **39** They had such a sharp disagreement that they parted company. Barnabas
τὸ ἔργον δὲ → ἐγένετο παροξυσμός ὥστε αὐτοὺς ἀποχωρισθῆναι ἀπ' ἀλλήλων τε ⌐τὸν Βαρναβᾶν⌐
d.asn n.asn cj v.ami.3s n.nsm cj r.apm.3 f.ap p.g r.gpm cj d.asm n.asm
3836 2240 1254 1181 4237 6063 899 714 608 253 5445 3836 982

took Mark and sailed for Cyprus, **40** but Paul chose Silas and left, commended by the
παραλαβόντα ⌐τὸν Μᾶρκον⌐ ἐκπλεῦσαι εἰς Κύπρον δὲ Παῦλος ἐπιλεξάμενος Σιλᾶν ἐξῆλθεν παραδοθεὶς ὑπὸ τῶν
pt.aa.asm d.asm n.asm f.aa p.a n.asf cj n.nsm pt.am.nsm n.asm v.aai.3s pt.ap.nsm p.g d.gpm
4161 3836 3453 1739 1650 3251 1254 4263 2141 4976 2002 4140 5679 3836

brothers to the grace of the Lord. **41** He went through Syria and Cilicia, strengthening the churches.
ἀδελφῶν → τῇ χάριτι τοῦ κυρίου δὲ → διήρχετο ← ⌐τὴν Συρίαν⌐ καὶ ⌐τὴν Κιλικίαν⌐ ἐπιστηρίζων τὰς ἐκκλησίας
n.gpm d.dsf n.dsf d.gsm n.gsm cj v.imi.3s d.asf n.asf cj d.asf n.asf pt.pa.nsm d.apf n.apf
81 3836 5921 3836 3261 1254 1451 3836 5353 2779 3836 3070 2185 3836 1711

Timothy Joins Paul and Silas

16:1 He came to Derbe and then to Lystra, where a disciple named Timothy lived,
δὲ → Κατήντησεν [καὶ] εἰς Δέρβην καὶ εἰς Λύστραν καὶ ἰδοὺ ἐκεῖ τις μαθητής ὀνόματι Τιμόθεος ἦν
cj v.aai.3s adv p.a n.asf cj p.a n.asf cj j adv r.nsm n.nsm n.dsn n.nsm v.iai.3s
1254 2918 2779 1650 1292 2779 1650 3388 2779 2627 1695 5516 3412 3950 5510 1639

καὶ συναγόντες τὸ πλῆθος ἐπέδωκαν τὴν ἐπιστολήν. **31** ἀναγνόντες δὲ ἐχάρησαν ἐπὶ τῇ παρακλήσει. **32** Ἰούδας τε καὶ Σιλᾶς καὶ αὐτοὶ προφῆται ὄντες διὰ λόγου πολλοῦ παρεκάλεσαν τοὺς ἀδελφοὺς καὶ ἐπεστήριξαν, **33** ποιήσαντες δὲ χρόνον ἀπελύθησαν μετ' εἰρήνης ἀπὸ τῶν ἀδελφῶν πρὸς τοὺς ἀποστείλαντας αὐτούς. **35** Παῦλος δὲ καὶ Βαρναβᾶς διέτριβον ἐν Ἀντιοχείᾳ διδάσκοντες καὶ εὐαγγελιζόμενοι μετὰ καὶ ἑτέρων πολλῶν τὸν λόγον τοῦ κυρίου.

15:36 Μετὰ δέ τινας ἡμέρας εἶπεν πρὸς Βαρναβᾶν Παῦλος, Ἐπιστρέψαντες δὴ ἐπισκεψώμεθα τοὺς ἀδελφοὺς κατὰ πόλιν πᾶσαν ἐν αἷς κατηγγείλαμεν τὸν λόγον τοῦ κυρίου πῶς ἔχουσιν. **37** Βαρναβᾶς δὲ ἐβούλετο συμπαραλαβεῖν καὶ τὸν Ἰωάννην τὸν καλούμενον Μᾶρκον· **38** Παῦλος δὲ ἠξίου, τὸν ἀποστάντα ἀπ' αὐτῶν ἀπὸ Παμφυλίας καὶ μὴ συνελθόντα αὐτοῖς εἰς τὸ ἔργον μὴ συμπαραλαμβάνειν τοῦτον. **39** ἐγένετο δὲ παροξυσμὸς ὥστε ἀποχωρισθῆναι αὐτοὺς ἀπ' ἀλλήλων, τόν τε Βαρναβᾶν παραλαβόντα τὸν Μᾶρκον ἐκπλεῦσαι εἰς Κύπρον, **40** Παῦλος δὲ ἐπιλεξάμενος Σιλᾶν ἐξῆλθεν παραδοθεὶς τῇ χάριτι τοῦ κυρίου ὑπὸ τῶν ἀδελφῶν. **41** διήρχετο δὲ τὴν Συρίαν καὶ [τὴν] Κιλικίαν ἐπιστηρίζων τὰς ἐκκλησίας.

16:1 Κατήντησεν δὲ [καὶ] εἰς Δέρβην καὶ εἰς Λύστραν. καὶ ἰδοὺ μαθητής τις ἦν ἐκεῖ ὀνόματι Τιμόθεος, υἱὸς γυναικὸς

whose mother　　　was a Jewess　　and a believer,　but whose father was a Greek.　**2**　The brothers at Lystra
ᵥυἱὸς γυναικὸς₎　　Ἰουδαίας　　　　πιστῆς　　δὲ　　πατρὸς　　Ἕλληνος　ὑπὸ τῶν ἀδελφῶν ἐν λύστροις
n.nsm n.gsf　　　　a.gsf　　　　　　a.gsf　　　cj　　n.gsm　　　n.gsm　　　p.g d.gpm n.gpm　p.d n.dpn
5626 1222　　　　　2681　　　　　　4412　　　1254　　4252　　　　1818　　　5679 3836 81　　1877 3388

and Iconium spoke　well of him.　**3** Paul　　wanted to take　him　along　on the journey, so　　he
καὶ Ἰκονίῳ ἐμαρτυρεῖτο ←　←　ὃς　ὁ Παῦλος₎ ἠθέλησεν ← ἐξελθεῖν τοῦτον ₎σὺν αὐτῷ₎　　　　καὶ λαβὼν →
cj n.dsn v.ipi.3s　　　r.nsm　d.nsm n.nsm v.aai.3s　　f.aa　　r.asm r.dsm.3　　　　　　cj pt.aa.nsm
2779 2658 3455　　　4005　3836 4263 2527　　　2002 4047 5250 899　　　　　　　　　2779 3284

circumcised him because of the Jews　　who lived in　that　area,　　for they all　　knew　that his
περιέτεμεν αὐτὸν διὰ　← τοὺς Ἰουδαίους τοὺς ὄντας ἐν ἐκείνοις ₎τοῖς τόποις₎ γὰρ →　ἅπαντες ᾔδεισαν ὅτι　αὐτοῦ
v.aai.3s　r.asm.3 p.a　　d.apm a.apm　　d.apm pt.pa.apm p.d d.dpn　n.dpm　cj　　a.npm　v.lai.3p cj　r.gsm.3
4362　　899　　1328　　3836 2681　　　3836 1639 1877 1697　　3836 5536　1142　570　　3857　　3857 4022 899

father　was　a Greek.　**4**　As they traveled　from town　to town, they delivered　the decisions
ὁ πατὴρ ὑπῆρχεν Ἕλλην　δὲ Ὡς →　διεπορεύοντο ←　₎τὰς πόλεις₎　←　←　→　παρεδίδοσαν τὰ δόγματα
d.nsm n.nsm v.iai.3s n.nsm　cj　n.nsm　v.imi.3p　　　d.apf n.apf　　　　　　　　v.iai.3p　　d.apn n.apn
3836 4252 5639　1818　　1254 6055　1388　　　　3836 4484　　　1388 1388　　4140　　　3836 1504

reached　　by the apostles and elders　in Jerusalem for the people to obey.　**5** So　　the churches
₎τὰ κεκριμένα₎ ὑπὸ τῶν ἀποστόλων καὶ πρεσβυτέρων τῶν ἐν Ἱεροσολύμοις　αὐτοῖς　φυλάσσειν　οὖν μὲν Αἱ ἐκκλησίαι
d.apn pt.rp.apn　p.g d.gpm n.gpm　cj a.gpm　　d.gpm p.d n.dpn　　r.dpm.3　f.pa　　cj pl d.npf n.npf
3836 3212　　　5679 3836 693　　2779 4565　　3836 1877 2642　　899　　5875　　4036 3525 3836 1711

were strengthened in the faith and grew　daily　in numbers.
→ ἐστερεοῦντο → τῇ πίστει καὶ ἐπερίσσευον ₎καθ᾽ ἡμέραν₎ → ₎τῷ ἀριθμῷ₎
v.ipi.3p　　　d.dsf n.dsf cj　v.iai.3p　　p.a n.asf　　d.dsm n.dsm
5105　　　　3836 4411 2779 4355　　2848 2465　　3836 750

Paul's Vision of the Man of Macedonia
16:6　Paul and his companions　traveled throughout the region of Phrygia　and Galatia,　having been
δὲ　　　　　　　　　　　Διῆλθον ←　χώραν ₎τὴν Φρυγίαν₎ καὶ Γαλατικὴν →　→
cj　　　　　　　　　　　　v.aai.3p　n.asf d.asf n.asf　cj a.asf
1254　　　　　　　　　　　1451　　　6001 3836 5867　2779 1131

kept　by the Holy Spirit　from preaching the word in the province of Asia.　**7**　When they came　to　the
κωλυθέντες ὑπὸ τοῦ ἁγίου πνεύματος → λαλῆσαι τὸν λόγον ἐν τῇ → Ἀσίᾳ δὲ → ἐλθόντες κατὰ ←
pt.ap.npm p.g d.gsn a.gsn n.gsn　f.aa　　d.asm n.asm p.d d.dsf　n.dsf cj　pt.aa.npm p.a
3266　　5679 3836 41 4460　　　3281　　3836 3364 1877 3836　823 1254　2262　2848

border of Mysia,　they tried　to enter　Bithynia,　but the Spirit of Jesus would not allow them to.
←　← ₎τὴν Μυσίαν₎ → ἐπείραζον πορευθῆναι εἰς ₎τὴν Βιθυνίαν₎ καὶ τὸ πνεῦμα → Ἰησοῦ → οὐκ εἴασεν αὐτούς
d.asf n.asf　v.iai.3p　f.ap　p.a d.asf n.asf　cj d.nsn n.nsn　n.gsm　pl v.aai.3s r.apm.3
3836 3695　4279　4513 1650 3836 1049　2779 3836 4460　2652　1572　4024 1572 899

8 So they passed　by Mysia　and went　down to Troas.　**9**　During the night Paul　had a vision of
δὲ they παρελθόντες ← ₎τὴν Μυσίαν₎ κατέβησαν ←　εἰς Τρῳάδα Καὶ διὰ τῆς νυκτὸς ₎τῷ Παύλῳ₎ ὤφθη όραμα
cj　　pt.aa.npm　d.asf n.asf　v.aai.3p　　p.a n.asf　cj p.g d.gsf n.gsf d.dsm n.dsm v.api.3s n.nsn
1254　4216　　　3836 3695　2849　　　1650 5590 2779 1328 3836 3816 3836 4263 3972 3969

a man of Macedonia　standing and begging him,　　"Come over to Macedonia and help　us."
τις ἀνὴρ → Μακεδὼν ἦν ἑστὼς καὶ παρακαλῶν αὐτὸν καὶ λέγων διαβάς ← εἰς Μακεδονίαν βοήθησον ἡμῖν
r.nsm n.nsm　n.nsm　v.iai.3s pt.ra.nsm cj pt.pa.nsm r.asm.3 cj pt.pa.nsm pt.aa.nsm　p.a n.asf　v.aam.2s r.dp.1
5516 467　　3424　　1639 2705　2779 4151　899　2779 3306 1329　　1650 3423　　1070　7005

10　After Paul had　seen the vision, we got ready　at once to leave　for Macedonia, concluding that God　had
δὲ ὡς →　εἶδεν τὸ ὅραμα　ἐζητήσαμεν εὐθέως ἐξελθεῖν εἰς Μακεδονίαν συμβιβάζοντες ὅτι ὁ θεὸς₎
cj cj　　v.aai.3s d.asn n.asn　v.aai.1p　adv　f.aa　p.a n.asf　pt.pa.npm cj d.nsm n.nsm
1254 6055　1625 3836 3969　2426　2311　2002 1650 3423　5204　4022 3836 2536

called　us to preach　the gospel to them.
προσκέκληται ἡμᾶς → εὐαγγελίσασθαι ← αὐτούς
v.rmi.3s　r.ap.1　f.am　　　　r.apm.3
4673　7005　2294　　　　899

Lydia's Conversion in Philippi
16:11　From Troas　we put　out to sea and sailed　straight for Samothrace, and the next　day on
δὲ ἀπὸ Τρῳάδος → Ἀναχθέντες ← ← εὐθυδρομήσαμεν ← εἰς Σαμοθρᾴκην δὲ τῇ ἐπιούσῃ
cj p.g n.gsf　n.nsf pt.ap.npm　　v.aai.1p　　　p.a n.asf　cj d.dsf pt.pa.dsf
1254 608 5590　343　　　　2312　　　　1650 4903　　　1254 3836 2079

Ἰουδαίας πιστῆς, πατρὸς δὲ Ἕλληνος, ² ὃς ἐμαρτυρεῖτο ὑπὸ τῶν ἐν Λύστροις καὶ Ἰκονίῳ ἀδελφῶν. ³ τοῦτον ἠθέλησεν ὁ Παῦλος σὺν αὐτῷ ἐξελθεῖν, καὶ λαβὼν περιέτεμεν αὐτὸν διὰ τοὺς Ἰουδαίους τοὺς ὄντας ἐν τοῖς τόποις ἐκείνοις· ᾔδεισαν γὰρ ἅπαντες ὅτι Ἕλλην ὁ πατὴρ αὐτοῦ ὑπῆρχεν. ⁴ ὡς δὲ διεπορεύοντο τὰς πόλεις, παρεδίδοσαν αὐτοῖς φυλάσσειν τὰ δόγματα τὰ κεκριμένα ὑπὸ τῶν ἀποστόλων καὶ πρεσβυτέρων τῶν ἐν Ἱεροσολύμοις. ⁵ αἱ μὲν οὖν ἐκκλησίαι ἐστερεοῦντο τῇ πίστει καὶ ἐπερίσσευον τῷ ἀριθμῷ καθ᾽ ἡμέραν.
¹⁶:⁶ Διῆλθον δὲ τὴν Φρυγίαν καὶ Γαλατικὴν χώραν κωλυθέντες ὑπὸ τοῦ ἁγίου πνεύματος λαλῆσαι τὸν λόγον ἐν τῇ Ἀσίᾳ· ⁷ ἐλθόντες δὲ κατὰ τὴν Μυσίαν ἐπείραζον εἰς τὴν Βιθυνίαν πορευθῆναι, καὶ οὐκ εἴασεν αὐτοὺς τὸ πνεῦμα Ἰησοῦ· ⁸ παρελθόντες δὲ τὴν Μυσίαν κατέβησαν εἰς Τρῳάδα. ⁹ καὶ ὅραμα διὰ [τῆς] νυκτὸς τῷ Παύλῳ ὤφθη, ἀνὴρ Μακεδών τις ἦν ἑστὼς καὶ παρακαλῶν αὐτὸν καὶ λέγων, Διαβὰς εἰς Μακεδονίαν βοήθησον ἡμῖν. ¹⁰ ὡς δὲ τὸ ὅραμα εἶδεν, εὐθέως ἐζητήσαμεν ἐξελθεῖν εἰς Μακεδονίαν συμβιβάζοντες ὅτι προσκέκληται ἡμᾶς ὁ θεὸς εὐαγγελίσασθαι αὐτούς.
¹⁶:¹¹ Ἀναχθέντες δὲ ἀπὸ Τρῳάδος εὐθυδρομήσαμεν εἰς Σαμοθρᾴκην, τῇ δὲ ἐπιούσῃ εἰς Νέαν ¹² κἀκεῖθεν εἰς Φιλίππους, ἥτις

to Neapolis. **12** From there we traveled to Philippi, a Roman colony and the leading city of that district
εἰς ⸢Νέαν πόλιν⸣ κακεῖθεν ← εἰς Φιλίππους ἥτις ἐστὶν → κολωνία πρώτη πόλις → μερίδος
p.a a.asf n.asf crasis p.a n.apm r.nsf v.pai.3s n.nsf n.nsf n.gsf
1650 3742 4484 2796 1650 5804 4015 1639 3149 4755 4484 3535

of Macedonia. And we stayed there several days. ¶ **13** On the Sabbath
→ ⸤τῆς Μακεδονίας⸥ δὲ ⸢Ἦμεν διατρίβοντες⸣ ἐν ταύτῃ τῇ πόλει τινὰς ἡμέρας τε → τῇ ἡμέρᾳ τῶν σαββάτων
d.gsf n.gsf cj v.iai.1p pt.pa.npm p.d r.dsf d.dsf n.dsf r.apf n.apf cj d.dsf n.dsf d.gpn n.gpn
3836 3423 1254 1639 1417 1877 4047 3836 4484 5516 2465 5445 3836 2465 3836 4879

we went outside the city gate to the river, where we expected to find a place of prayer. We sat
→ ἐξήλθομεν ἔξω τῆς → πύλης παρὰ ποταμὸν οὗ → ἐνομίζομεν → εἶναι → προσευχὴν καὶ → καθίσαντες
v.aai.1p p.g d.gsf n.gsf p.a n.asm adv v.iai.1p f.pa n.asf cj pt.aa.npm
2002 2032 3836 4783 4123 4532 4023 3787 1639 4666 2779 2767

down and began to speak to the women who had gathered there. **14** One of those listening was a woman
← → → ἐλαλοῦμεν ταῖς γυναιξὶν → συνελθούσαις καὶ ἤκουεν τις γυνὴ
v.iai.1p d.dpf n.dpf pt.aa.dpf cj v.iai.3s r.nsf n.nsf
3281 3836 1222 5302 2779 201 5516 1222

named Lydia, a dealer in purple cloth from the city of Thyatira, who was a worshiper of God. The
ὀνόματι Λυδία → πορφυρόπωλις ← ← πόλεως → Θυατείρων → σεβομένη ⸤τὸν θεόν⸥ ὁ
n.dsn n.nsf n.nsf n.gsf n.gpn pt.pm.nsf d.asm n.asm d.nsm
3950 3376 4527 4484 2587 4936 3836 2536 3836

Lord opened her heart to respond to Paul's message. **15** When she and the members of
κύριος διήνοιξεν ἧς ⸤τὴν καρδίαν⸥ → προσέχειν ὑπὸ ⸤τοῦ Παύλου⸥ ⸤τοῖς λαλουμένοις⸥ δὲ ὡς → καὶ
n.nsf v.aai.3s r.gsf d.asf n.asf f.pa p.g d.gsm n.gsm d.dpn pt.pp.dpn cj cj cj
3261 1380 4005 3836 2840 4668 3281 5679 3836 4263 3836 3281 1254 6055 966 2779

her household were baptized, she invited us to her home. "If you consider me a believer in the Lord,"
αὐτῆς ὁ οἶκος, → ἐβαπτίσθη παρεκάλεσεν εἰ → κεκρίκατε με → εἶναι πιστὴν → τῷ κυρίῳ
r.gsf.3 d.nsm n.nsm v.api.3s v.aai.3s cj v.rai.2p r.as.1 f.pa a.asf d.dsm n.dsm
899 3836 3875 966 4151 1623 3212 1609 1639 4412 3836 3261

she said, "come and stay at my house." And she persuaded us.
→ λέγουσα εἰσελθόντες μένετε εἰς μου ⸤τὸν οἶκον⸥ καὶ → παρεβιάσατο ἡμᾶς
pt.pa.nsf pt.aa.npm v.pam.2p p.a r.gs.1 d.asm n.asm cj v.ami.3s r.ap.1
3306 1656 3531 1650 1609 3836 3875 2779 4128 7005

Paul and Silas in Prison

16:16 Once when we were going to the place of prayer, we were met by a slave girl
δὲ Ἐγένετο → ἡμῶν → πορευομένων εἰς τὴν → προσευχὴν ἡμῖν → ὑπαντῆσαι τινὰ → παιδίσκην
cj v.ami.3s r.gp.1 pt.pm.gpm p.a d.asf n.asf r.dp.1 f.aa r.asf n.asf
1254 1181 4513 7005 4513 1650 3836 4666 7005 5636 5516 4087

who had a spirit by which she predicted the future. She earned a great deal of money for her
→ ἔχουσαν πνεῦμα → → πύθωνα ἥτις παρεῖχεν πολλὴν ἐργασίαν ← → αὐτῆς
pt.pa.asf n.asn n.asm r.nsf v.iai.3s a.asf n.asf r.gsf.3
2400 4460 4780 4015 4218 4498 2238 3261 899

owners by fortune-telling. **17** This girl followed Paul and the rest of us, shouting, "These
⸤τοῖς κυρίοις⸥ → μαντευομένη αὕτη ← κατακολουθοῦσα ⸤τῷ Παύλῳ⸥ καὶ ἡμῖν ἔκραζεν λέγουσα οὗτοι
d.dpm n.dpm pt.pm.nsf r.nsf pt.pa.nsf d.dsm n.dsm cj r.dp.1 v.iai.3s pt.pa.nsf r.npm
3836 3261 3446 4047 2887 3836 4263 2779 7005 3189 3306 4047

men are servants of the Most High God, who are telling you the way to be saved." **18** She
⸤οἱ ἄνθρωποι⸥ εἰσὶν δοῦλοι → τοῦ → ⸤τοῦ ὑψίστου⸥ θεοῦ, οἵτινες → καταγγέλλουσιν ὑμῖν ὁδὸν → σωτηρίας δὲ →
d.npm n.npm v.pai.3p n.npm d.gsm d.gsm a.gsm.s n.gsm r.npm v.pai.3p r.dp.2 n.asf n.gsf cj
3836 476 1639 1529 3836 3836 5736 2536 4015 2859 7007 3847 5401 1254

kept this up for many days. Finally Paul became so troubled that he turned around and said to the
ἐποίει τοῦτο ↰ ἐπὶ πολλὰς ἡμέρας δὲ Παῦλος → διαπονηθεὶς καὶ → ἐπιστρέψας ← εἶπεν τῷ
v.iai.3s r.asn p.a a.apf n.apf cj n.nsm pt.ap.nsm cj pt.aa.nsm v.aai.3s d.dsn
4472 4047 4472 2093 4498 2465 1254 4263 1387 2779 2188 3306 3836

spirit, "In the name of Jesus Christ I command you to come out of her!" At that moment the spirit left
πνεύματι ἐν ὀνόματι → Ἰησοῦ Χριστοῦ → παραγγέλλω σοι → ἐξελθεῖν ἀπ' αὐτῆς καὶ → τῇ ὥρᾳ ἐξῆλθεν
n.dsn p.d n.dsn n.gsm n.gsm v.pai.1s r.ds.2 f.aa p.g r.gsf.3 cj d.dsf n.dsf v.aai.3s
4460 1877 3950 2652 5986 4133 5148 2002 608 899 2779 3836 6052 2002

ἐστὶν πρώτη «πρώτη[ς]» τῆς μερίδος Μακεδονίας πόλις, κολωνία. ἦμεν δὲ ἐν ταύτῃ τῇ πόλει διατρίβοντες ἡμέρας τινάς. ¶ **13** τῇ τε ἡμέρᾳ τῶν σαββάτων ἐξήλθομεν ἔξω τῆς πύλης παρὰ ποταμὸν οὗ ἐνομίζομεν προσευχὴν εἶναι, καὶ καθίσαντες ἐλαλοῦμεν ταῖς συνελθούσαις γυναιξίν. **14** καί τις γυνὴ ὀνόματι Λυδία, πορφυρόπωλις πόλεως Θυατείρων σεβομένη τὸν θεόν, ἤκουεν, ἧς ὁ κύριος διήνοιξεν τὴν καρδίαν προσέχειν τοῖς λαλουμένοις ὑπὸ τοῦ Παύλου. **15** ὡς δὲ ἐβαπτίσθη καὶ ὁ οἶκος αὐτῆς, παρεκάλεσεν λέγουσα, Εἰ κεκρίκατέ με πιστὴν τῷ κυρίῳ εἶναι, εἰσελθόντες εἰς τὸν οἶκόν μου μένετε· καὶ παρεβιάσατο ἡμᾶς.

16:16 Ἐγένετο δὲ πορευομένων ἡμῶν εἰς τὴν προσευχὴν παιδίσκην τινὰ ἔχουσαν πνεῦμα πύθωνα ὑπαντῆσαι ἡμῖν, ἥτις ἐργασίαν πολλὴν παρεῖχεν τοῖς κυρίοις αὐτῆς μαντευομένη. **17** αὕτη κατακολουθοῦσα τῷ Παύλῳ καὶ ἡμῖν ἔκραζεν λέγουσα, Οὗτοι οἱ ἄνθρωποι δοῦλοι τοῦ θεοῦ τοῦ ὑψίστου εἰσίν, οἵτινες καταγγέλλουσιν ὑμῖν ὁδὸν σωτηρίας. **18** τοῦτο δὲ ἐποίει ἐπὶ πολλὰς ἡμέρας. διαπονηθεὶς δὲ Παῦλος καὶ ἐπιστρέψας τῷ πνεύματι εἶπεν, Παραγγέλλω σοι ἐν ὀνόματι Ἰησοῦ Χριστοῦ ἐξελθεῖν

her. ¶ **19** When the owners of the slave girl realized that their hope of making money was gone,
αὐτῇ δὲ → οἱ κύριοι → αὐτῆς ἰδόντες ὅτι αὐτῶν ἡ ἐλπὶς ⌐τῆς ἐργασίας⌐ → → ἐξῆλθεν
r.dsf cj d.npm n.npm r.gsf.3 pt.aa.npm cj r.gpm.3 d.nsf n.nsf d.gsf n.gsf v.aai.3s
899 1254 1625 3836 3261 899 1625 4022 899 3836 1828 3836 2238 2002

they seized Paul and Silas and dragged them into the marketplace to face the authorities. **20** They
→ ἐπιλαβόμενοι ⌐τὸν Παῦλον⌐ καὶ ⌐τὸν Σιλᾶν⌐ εἵλκυσαν εἰς τὴν ἀγορὰν ἐπὶ ← τοὺς ἄρχοντας καὶ →
pt.am.npm d.asm n.asm cj d.asm n.asm v.aai.3p p.a d.asf n.asf p.a d.apm n.apm cj
2138 3836 4263 2779 3836 4976 1816 1650 3836 59 2093 3836 807 2779

brought them before the magistrates and said, "These men are Jews, and are throwing our
προσαγαγόντες αὐτοὺς → τοῖς στρατηγοῖς εἶπαν οὗτοι ⌐οἱ ἄνθρωποι⌐ ὑπάρχοντες Ἰουδαῖοι → → ἡμῶν
pt.aa.npm r.apm.3 d.dpm n.dpm v.aai.3p r.npm d.npm n.npm pt.pa.npm a.npm r.gp.1
4642 899 3836 5130 3306 4047 3836 476 5639 2681 1752 1752 7005

city into an uproar **21** by advocating customs unlawful for us Romans to accept or
⌐τὴν πόλιν⌐ → → ἐκταράσσουσιν καὶ καταγγέλλουσιν ἔθη ἃ ⌐οὐκ ἔξεστιν⌐ ἡμῖν οὖσιν Ῥωμαίοις → παραδέχεσθαι οὐδὲ
d.asf n.asf v.pai.3p cj v.pai.3p n.apn r.npn v.pai.3s r.dp.1 pt.pa.dpm a.dpm f.pm cj
3836 4484 1752 2779 2859 1621 4005 4024 1997 7005 1639 4871 4138 4028

practice." ¶ **22** The crowd joined in the attack against Paul and Silas, and the magistrates ordered them to
ποιεῖν καὶ ὁ ὄχλος συνεπέστη ← ← κατ᾽ αὐτῶν ← καὶ οἱ στρατηγοὶ ἐκέλευον
f.pa cj d.nsm n.nsm v.aai.3s p.g r.gpm.3 cj d.npm n.npm v.iai.3p
4472 2779 3836 4063 5308 2848 899 2779 3836 5130 3027

be stripped and beaten. **23** After they had been severely flogged, they were thrown
→ ⌐περιρήξαντες τὰ ἱμάτια αὐτῶν⌐ ῥαβδίζειν τε → αὐτοῖς → πολλὰς ⌐ἐπιθέντες πληγὰς⌐ → → ἔβαλον
pt.aa.npm d.apn n.apn r.gpm.3 f.pa cj r.dpm.3 a.apf pt.aa.npm n.apf v.aai.3p
4351 3836 2668 899 4810 5445 2202 899 2202 2202 4498 2202 4435 965

into prison, and the jailer was commanded to guard them carefully. **24** Upon receiving such orders, he
εἰς φυλακὴν τῷ δεσμοφύλακι → παραγγείλαντες → τηρεῖν αὐτοὺς ἀσφαλῶς → λαβὼν τοιαύτην παραγγελίαν ὃς
p.a n.asf d.dsm n.dsm pt.aa.npm f.pa r.apm.3 adv pt.aa.nsm r.asf n.asf r.nsm
1650 5871 3836 1302 4133 5498 899 857 3284 5525 4132 4005

put them in the inner cell and fastened their feet in the stocks. ¶ **25** About midnight
ἔβαλεν αὐτοὺς εἰς τὴν ἐσωτέραν φυλακὴν καὶ ἠσφαλίσατο αὐτῶν ⌐τοὺς πόδας⌐ εἰς τὸ ξύλον δὲ Κατὰ ⌐τὸ μεσονύκτιον⌐
v.aai.3s r.apm.3 p.a d.asf a.asf n.asf cj v.ami.3s r.gpm.3 d.apm n.apm p.a d.asn n.asn cj p.a d.asn n.asn
965 899 1650 3836 2278 5871 2779 856 899 3836 4546 1650 3836 3833 1254 2848 3836 3543

Paul and Silas were praying and singing hymns to God, and the other prisoners were listening to them.
Παῦλος καὶ Σιλᾶς → προσευχόμενοι ὕμνουν ← ⌐τὸν θεόν⌐ δὲ οἱ δέσμιοι → ἐπηκροῶντο ← αὐτῶν
n.nsm cj n.nsm pt.pm.npm v.iai.3p d.asm n.asm cj d.npm n.npm v.imi.3p r.gpm.3
4263 2779 4976 4667 5630 3836 2536 1254 3836 1300 2053 899

26 Suddenly there was such a violent earthquake that the foundations of the prison were shaken. At
δὲ ἄφνω ἐγένετο μέγας σεισμὸς ὥστε τὰ θεμέλια → τοῦ δεσμωτηρίου → σαλευθῆναι δὲ
cj adv v.ami.3s a.nsm n.nsm cj d.apn n.apn d.gsn n.gsn f.ap cj
1254 924 1181 3489 4939 6063 3836 2528 3836 1303 4888 1254

once all the prison doors flew open, and everybody's chains came loose. **27** The jailer
παραχρῆμα πᾶσαι αἱ θύραι → ἠνεῴχθησαν καὶ πάντων ⌐τὰ δεσμὰ⌐ → ἀνέθη δὲ ὁ δεσμοφύλαξ
adv a.npf d.npf n.npf v.api.3p cj a.gpm d.npn n.npn v.api.3s cj d.nsm n.nsm
4202 4246 3836 2598 487 2779 4246 3836 1301 479 1254 3836 1302

woke up, and when he saw the prison doors open, he drew his sword and was about
⌐ἔξυπνος γενόμενος⌐ καὶ ← ἰδὼν τὰς ⌐τῆς φυλακῆς⌐ θύρας ἀνεῳγμένας → σπασάμενος τὴν μάχαιραν → ἤμελλεν
a.nsm pt.am.nsm cj pt.aa.nsm d.apf d.gsf n.gsf n.apf pt.rp.apf pt.am.nsm d.asf n.asf v.iai.3s
2031 1181 2779 1625 3836 3836 5871 2598 487 5060 3836 3479 3516

to kill himself because he thought the prisoners had escaped. **28** But Paul shouted,
→ ἀναιρεῖν ἑαυτόν → → νομίζων τοὺς δεσμίους → ἐκπεφευγέναι δὲ ὁ Παῦλος ἐφώνησεν μεγάλῃ φωνῇ λέγων
f.pa r.asm.3 pt.pa.nsm d.apm n.apm f.ra cj d.nsm n.nsm v.aai.3s a.dsf n.dsf pt.pa.nsm
359 1571 3787 3836 1300 1767 1254 3836 4263 5888 3489 5889 3306

"Don't harm yourself! We are all here!" ¶ **29** The jailer called for lights, rushed in and
μηδὲν ⌐πράξῃς κακόν⌐ σεαυτῷ γὰρ → ἐσμεν ἅπαντες ἐνθάδε δὲ αἰτήσας ← φῶτα εἰσεπήδησεν ← καὶ
a.asn v.aas.2s a.asn r.dsm.2 cj v.pai.1p a.npm adv cj pt.aa.nsm n.apn v.aai.3s cj
3594 4556 2805 4932 1142 1639 570 1924 1254 160 5890 1659 2779

ἀπ᾽ αὐτῆς· καὶ ἐξῆλθεν αὐτῇ τῇ ὥρᾳ. ¶ **19** ἰδόντες δὲ οἱ κύριοι αὐτῆς ὅτι ἐξῆλθεν ἡ ἐλπὶς τῆς ἐργασίας αὐτῶν, ἐπιλαβόμενοι τὸν Παῦλον καὶ τὸν Σιλᾶν εἵλκυσαν εἰς τὴν ἀγορὰν ἐπὶ τοὺς ἄρχοντας **20** καὶ προσαγαγόντες αὐτοὺς τοῖς στρατηγοῖς εἶπαν, Οὗτοι οἱ ἄνθρωποι ἐκταράσσουσιν ἡμῶν τὴν πόλιν, Ἰουδαῖοι ὑπάρχοντες, **21** καὶ καταγγέλλουσιν ἔθη ἃ οὐκ ἔξεστιν ἡμῖν παραδέχεσθαι οὐδὲ ποιεῖν Ῥωμαίοις οὖσιν. ¶ **22** καὶ συνεπέστη ὁ ὄχλος κατ᾽ αὐτῶν καὶ οἱ στρατηγοὶ περιρήξαντες αὐτῶν τὰ ἱμάτια ἐκέλευον ῥαβδίζειν, **23** πολλάς τε ἐπιθέντες αὐτοῖς πληγὰς ἔβαλον εἰς φυλακὴν παραγγείλαντες τῷ δεσμοφύλακι ἀσφαλῶς τηρεῖν αὐτούς. **24** ὃς παραγγελίαν τοιαύτην λαβὼν ἔβαλεν αὐτοὺς εἰς τὴν ἐσωτέραν φυλακὴν καὶ τοὺς πόδας ἠσφαλίσατο αὐτῶν εἰς τὸ ξύλον. **25** Κατὰ δὲ τὸ μεσονύκτιον Παῦλος καὶ Σιλᾶς προσευχόμενοι ὕμνουν τὸν θεόν, ἐπηκροῶντο δὲ αὐτῶν οἱ δέσμιοι. **26** ἄφνω δὲ σεισμὸς ἐγένετο μέγας ὥστε σαλευθῆναι τὰ θεμέλια τοῦ δεσμωτηρίου· ἠνεῴχθησαν δὲ παραχρῆμα αἱ θύραι πᾶσαι καὶ πάντων τὰ δεσμὰ ἀνέθη. **27** ἔξυπνος δὲ γενόμενος ὁ δεσμοφύλαξ καὶ ἰδὼν ἀνεῳγμένας τὰς θύρας τῆς φυλακῆς, σπασάμενος [τὴν] μάχαιραν ἤμελλεν ἑαυτὸν ἀναιρεῖν νομίζων ἐκπεφευγέναι τοὺς δεσμίους. **28** ἐφώνησεν δὲ μεγάλῃ φωνῇ [ὁ] Παῦλος λέγων, Μηδὲν πράξῃς σεαυτῷ κακόν, ἅπαντες γάρ ἐσμεν ἐνθάδε. ¶ **29** αἰτήσας δὲ φῶτα εἰσεπήδησεν καὶ ἔντρομος γενόμενος προσέπεσεν τῷ Παύλῳ καὶ

fell trembling before Paul and Silas. 30 He then brought them out and asked, "Sirs, what
προσέπεσεν ⌊ἔντρομος γενόμενος⌋ → ⌊τῷ Παύλῳ⌋ καὶ ⌊τῷ Σιλᾷ⌋ ↱ καὶ προαγαγὼν αὐτοὺς ἔξω ἔφη κύριοι τί
v.aai.3s a.nsm pt.am.nsm d.dsm n.dsm cj d.dsm n.dsm cj pt.aa.nsm r.apm.3 adv v.iai.3s n.vpm r.asn
4700 1958 1181 3836 4263 2779 3836 4976 4575 2779 4575 899 2032 5774 3261 5515

must I do to be saved?" ¶ 31 They replied, "Believe in the Lord Jesus, and you will be saved – you
δεῖ με ποιεῖν ἵνα → σωθῶ δὲ οἱ εἶπαν πίστευσον ἐπὶ τὸν κύριον Ἰησοῦν καὶ → → → σωθήσῃ σὺ
v.pai.3s r.as.1 f.pa cj v.aps.1s cj d.npm v.aai.3p v.aam.2s p.a d.asm n.asm n.asm cj v.fpi.2s r.ns.2
1256 1609 4472 2671 5392 1254 3836 3306 4409 2093 3836 3261 2652 2779 5392 5148

and your household." 32 Then they spoke the word of the Lord to him and to all the others in his house.
καὶ σου ⌊ὁ οἶκος⌋ καὶ → ἐλάλησαν τὸν λόγον τοῦ κυρίου → αὐτῷ σὺν πᾶσιν τοῖς ἐν αὐτοῦ ⌊τῇ οἰκίᾳ⌋
cj r.gs.2 d.nsm n.nsm cj v.aai.3p d.asm n.asm d.gsm n.gsm r.dsm.3 p.d a.dpm d.dpm p.d r.gsm.3 d.dsf n.dsf
2779 5148 3836 3875 2779 3281 3836 3364 3836 3261 899 5250 4246 3836 1877 899 3836 3864

33 At that hour of the night the jailer took them and washed their wounds; then immediately he
καὶ ἐν ἐκείνῃ ⌊τῇ ὥρᾳ⌋ → τῆς νυκτὸς παραλαβὼν αὐτοὺς ἔλουσεν ἀπὸ τῶν πληγῶν καὶ παραχρῆμα αὐτὸς
cj p.d r.dsf d.dsf n.dsf d.gsf n.gsf pt.aa.nsm r.apm.3 v.aai.3s p.g d.gpf n.gpf cj adv r.nsm
2779 1877 1697 3836 6052 3836 3816 4161 899 3374 608 3836 4435 2779 4202 899

and all his family were baptized. 34 The jailer brought them into his house and set a meal
καὶ ⌊οἱ πάντες⌋ αὐτοῦ → ἐβαπτίσθη τε ἀναγαγών αὐτοὺς εἰς τὸν οἶκον παρέθηκεν τράπεζαν
cj d.npm a.npm r.gsm.3 v.api.3s cj pt.aa.nsm r.apm.3 p.a d.asm n.asm v.aai.3s n.asf
2779 3836 4246 899 966 5445 343 899 1650 3836 3875 4192 5544

before them; he was filled with joy because he had come to believe in God – he and his whole
↰ καὶ → → → ἠγαλλιάσατο → → → → πεπιστευκὼς → ⌊τῷ θεῷ⌋ → →
cj v.ami.3s pt.ra.nsm d.dsm n.dsm
4192 2779 22 4409 3836 2536

family. ¶ 35 When it was daylight, the magistrates sent their officers to the jailer with the
πανοικεὶ δὲ → → γενομένης Ἡμέρας οἱ στρατηγοὶ ἀπέστειλαν τοὺς ῥαβδούχους → →
adv cj pt.am.gsf n.gsf d.npm n.npm v.aai.3p d.apm n.apm
4109 1254 1181 2465 3836 5130 690 3836 4812

order: "Release those men." 36 The jailer told Paul, "The
λέγοντες ἀπόλυσον ἐκείνους ⌊τοὺς ἀνθρώπους⌋ δὲ ὁ δεσμοφύλαξ ἀπήγγειλεν τοὺς λόγους [τούτους] πρὸς ⌊τὸν Παῦλον⌋ ὅτι οἱ
pt.pa.npm v.aam.2s r.apm d.apm n.apm cj d.nsm n.nsm v.aai.3s d.apm n.apm r.apm p.a d.asm n.asm cj d.npm
3306 668 1697 3836 476 1254 3836 1302 550 3836 3364 4047 4639 3836 4263 4022 3836

magistrates have ordered that you and Silas be released. Now you can leave. Go in peace." ¶
στρατηγοὶ → ἀπέσταλκαν ἵνα → → ἀπολυθῆτε οὖν νῦν → → ἐξελθόντες πορεύεσθε ἐν εἰρήνῃ
n.npm v.rai.3p cj v.aps.2p cj adv pt.aa.npm v.pmm.2p p.d n.dsf
5130 690 2671 668 4036 3814 2002 4513 1877 1645

37 But Paul said to the officers: "They beat us publicly without a trial, even though we are
δὲ ⌊ὁ Παῦλος⌋ ἔφη πρὸς αὐτούς δείραντες ἡμᾶς δημοσίᾳ → → ἀκατακρίτους → → → ὑπάρχοντας
cj d.nsm n.nsm v.iai.3s p.a r.apm.3 pt.aa.npm r.ap.1 a.dsf a.apm pt.pa.apm
1254 3836 4263 5774 4639 899 1296 7005 1323 185 5639

Roman citizens, and threw us into prison. And now do they want to get rid of us quietly? No!
Ῥωμαίους ἀνθρώπους ἔβαλαν εἰς φυλακὴν καὶ νῦν → → → → ἐκβάλλουσιν ἡμᾶς λάθρᾳ γάρ οὐ ἀλλὰ
n.apm n.apm v.aai.3p p.a n.asf cj adv v.pai.3p r.ap.1 adv cj pl cj
4871 476 965 1650 5871 2779 3814 1675 7005 3277 1142 4024 247

Let them come themselves and escort us out." ¶ 38 The officers reported this to the
↱ ↱ ἐλθόντες αὐτοὶ ἐξαγαγέτωσαν ἡμᾶς ↰ δὲ τοῖς στρατηγοῖς ἀπήγγειλαν τὰ ῥήματα ταῦτα οἱ
pt.aa.npm r.npm v.aam.3p r.ap.1 cj d.dpm n.dpm v.aai.3p d.apn n.apn r.apn d.npm
1974 1974 2262 899 1974 7005 1974 1254 3836 5130 550 3836 4839 4047 3836

magistrates, and when they heard that Paul and Silas were Roman citizens, they were alarmed. 39 They came
ῥαβδοῦχοι δὲ → → ἀκούσαντες ὅτι εἰσιν Ῥωμαῖοι ← → ἐφοβήθησαν καὶ ἐλθόντες
n.npm cj pt.aa.npm cj v.pai.3p n.npm v.api.3p cj pt.aa.npm
4812 1254 201 4022 1639 4871 5828 2779 2262

to appease them and escorted them from the prison, requesting them to leave the city. 40 After Paul
→ παρεκάλεσαν αὐτοὺς καὶ ἐξαγαγόντες ἠρώτων → ἀπελθεῖν ἀπὸ τῆς πόλεως δὲ →
v.aai.3p r.apm.3 cj pt.aa.npm v.iai.3p f.aa p.g d.gsf n.gsf cj
4151 899 2779 1974 2263 599 608 3836 4484 1254

[τῷ] Σιλᾷ 30 καὶ προαγαγὼν αὐτοὺς ἔξω ἔφη, Κύριοι, τί με δεῖ ποιεῖν ἵνα σωθῶ; ¶ 31 οἱ δὲ εἶπαν, Πίστευσον ἐπὶ τὸν κύριον
Ἰησοῦν καὶ σωθήσῃ σὺ καὶ ὁ οἶκός σου. 32 καὶ ἐλάλησαν αὐτῷ τὸν λόγον τοῦ κυρίου σὺν πᾶσιν τοῖς ἐν τῇ οἰκίᾳ αὐτοῦ.
33 καὶ παραλαβὼν αὐτοὺς ἐν ἐκείνῃ τῇ ὥρᾳ τῆς νυκτὸς ἔλουσεν ἀπὸ τῶν πληγῶν, καὶ ἐβαπτίσθη αὐτὸς καὶ οἱ αὐτοῦ πάντες
παραχρῆμα, 34 ἀναγαγών τε αὐτοὺς εἰς τὸν οἶκον παρέθηκεν τράπεζαν καὶ ἠγαλλιάσατο πανοικεὶ πεπιστευκὼς τῷ θεῷ ¶
35 Ἡμέρας δὲ γενομένης ἀπέστειλαν οἱ στρατηγοὶ τοὺς ῥαβδούχους λέγοντες, Ἀπόλυσον τοὺς ἀνθρώπους ἐκείνους. 36 ἀπήγγειλεν
δὲ ὁ δεσμοφύλαξ τοὺς λόγους [τούτους] πρὸς τὸν Παῦλον ὅτι Ἀπέσταλκαν οἱ στρατηγοὶ ἵνα ἀπολυθῆτε· νῦν οὖν ἐξελθόντες
πορεύεσθε ἐν εἰρήνῃ. ¶ 37 ὁ δὲ Παῦλος ἔφη πρὸς αὐτούς, Δείραντες ἡμᾶς δημοσίᾳ ἀκατακρίτους, ἀνθρώπους Ῥωμαίους
ὑπάρχοντας, ἔβαλαν εἰς φυλακήν, καὶ νῦν λάθρᾳ ἡμᾶς ἐκβάλλουσιν; οὐ γάρ, ἀλλὰ ἐλθόντες αὐτοὶ ἡμᾶς ἐξαγαγέτωσαν. ¶
38 ἀπήγγειλαν δὲ τοῖς στρατηγοῖς οἱ ῥαβδοῦχοι τὰ ῥήματα ταῦτα. ἐφοβήθησαν δὲ ἀκούσαντες ὅτι Ῥωμαῖοί εἰσιν, 39 καὶ ἐλθόντες
παρεκάλεσαν αὐτοὺς καὶ ἐξαγαγόντες ἠρώτων ἀπελθεῖν ἀπὸ τῆς πόλεως. 40 ἐξελθόντες δὲ ἀπὸ τῆς φυλακῆς εἰσῆλθον πρὸς τὴν

and Silas came out of the prison, they went to Lydia's house, where they met with the brothers
ἐξελθόντες ← ἀπὸ τῆς φυλακῆς → εἰσῆλθον πρὸς ⌐τὴν Λυδίαν⌐ καὶ → ἰδόντες ← τοὺς ἀδελφοὺς
pt.aa.npm p.g d.gsf n.gsf v.aai.3p p.a d.asf n.asf cj pt.aa.npm d.apm n.apm
2002 608 3836 5871 1656 4639 3836 3376 2779 1625 3836 81

and encouraged them. Then they left.
παρεκάλεσαν ↰ καὶ → ἐξῆλθαν
v.aai.3p cj v.aai.3p
4151 81 2779 2002

In Thessalonica

17:1 When they had passed through Amphipolis and Apollonia, they came to Thessalonica, where
δὲ → → → Διοδεύσαντες ← ⌐τὴν Ἀμφίπολιν⌐ καὶ ⌐τὴν Ἀπολλωνίαν⌐ → ἦλθον εἰς Θεσσαλονίκην ὅπου
cj pt.aa.npm d.asf n.asf cj d.asf n.asf v.aai.3p p.a n.asf cj
1254 1476 3836 315 2779 3836 662 2262 1650 2553 3963

there was a Jewish synagogue. **2** As his custom was, Paul went into the synagogue, and on three
→ ἦν ⌐τῶν Ἰουδαίων⌐ συναγωγή δὲ κατὰ ⌐τῷ Παύλῳ⌐ εἰωθὸς ↰ εἰσῆλθεν πρὸς αὐτοὺς καὶ ἐπὶ τρία
v.iai.3s d.gpm a.gpm n.nsf cj p.a d.dsm n.dsm pt.ra.asn v.aai.3s p.a r.apm.3 cj p.a a.apn
1639 3836 2681 5252 1254 2848 3836 4263 1665 4263 1656 4639 899 2779 2093 5552

Sabbath days he reasoned with them from the Scriptures, **3** explaining and proving that the Christ had to suffer
σάββατα ← → διελέξατο → αὐτοῖς ἀπὸ τῶν γραφῶν διανοίγων καὶ παρατιθέμενος ὅτι τὸν χριστὸν ἔδει → παθεῖν
n.apn v.ami.3s r.dpm.3 p.g d.gpf n.gpf pt.pa.nsm cj pt.pm.nsm cj d.asm n.asm v.iai.3s f.aa
4879 1363 899 608 3836 1210 1380 2779 4192 4022 3836 5986 1256 4248

and rise from the dead. "This Jesus I am proclaiming to you is the Christ," he said. **4**
καὶ ἀναστῆναι ἐκ νεκρῶν καὶ ὅτι οὗτος ὁ Ἰησοῦς⌐ ὃν ἐγὼ → καταγγέλλω → ὑμῖν ἐστιν ὁ χριστὸς καὶ
cj f.aa p.g a.gpm cj cj r.nsm d.nsm n.nsm r.asm r.ns.1 v.pai.1s r.dp.2 v.pai.3s d.nsm n.nsm cj
2779 482 1666 3738 2779 4022 4047 3836 2652 4005 1609 2859 7007 1639 3836 5986 2779

Some of the Jews were persuaded and joined Paul and Silas, as did a large number of
τινες ἐξ αὐτῶν ἐπείσθησαν καὶ προσεκληρώθησαν ⌐τῷ Παύλῳ⌐ καὶ ⌐τῷ Σιλᾷ⌐ τε πολύ πλῆθος →
r.npm p.g r.gpm.3 v.api.3p cj v.api.3p d.dsm n.dsm cj d.dsm n.dsm cj a.nsn n.nsn
5516 1666 899 4275 2779 4677 3836 4263 2779 3836 4976 5445 4498 4436 1818

God-fearing Greeks and not a few prominent women. ¶ **5** But the Jews were jealous; so they
σεβομένων ⌐τῶν Ἑλλήνων⌐ τε οὐκ ὀλίγαι ⌐τῶν πρώτων⌐ γυναικῶν δὲ οἱ Ἰουδαῖοι → Ζηλώσαντες καὶ →
pt.pm.gpm d.gpm n.gpm cj pl a.npf d.gpf a.gpf n.gpf cj d.npm a.npm pt.aa.npm cj
4936 3836 1818 5445 4024 3900 3836 4755 1222 1254 3836 2681 2420 2779

rounded up some bad characters from the marketplace, formed a mob and started a riot in
προσλαβόμενοι ← τινὰς πονηροὺς ἄνδρας → τῶν ἀγοραίων καὶ → ὀχλοποιήσαντες → → ἐθορύβουν →
pt.am.npm r.apm a.apm n.apm d.gpm a.gpm cj pt.aa.npm v.iai.3p
4689 5516 4505 467 3836 61 2779 4062 2572

the city. They rushed to Jason's house in search of Paul and Silas in order to bring them out to
τὴν πόλιν καὶ → ἐπιστάντες → Ἰάσονος τῇ οἰκίᾳ⌐ ἐζήτουν αὐτοὺς → → προαγαγεῖν ← εἰς
d.asf n.asf cj pt.aa.npm n.gsm d.dsf n.dsf v.iai.3p r.apm.3 f.aa p.a
3836 4484 2779 2392 3864 2619 3836 3864 2426 899 4575 1650

the crowd. **6** But when they did not find them, they dragged Jason and some other brothers before the city
τὸν δῆμον δὲ → → μὴ εὑρόντες αὐτοὺς → ἔσυρον Ἰάσονα καὶ τινας ἀδελφοὺς ἐπὶ τοὺς →
d.asm n.asm cj pl pt.aa.npm r.apm.3 v.iai.3p n.asm cj r.apm n.apm p.a d.apm
3836 1322 1254 2351 2351 2351 3590 2351 899 5359 2619 2779 5516 81 2093 3836

officials, shouting: "These men who have caused trouble all over the world have now come here,
πολιτάρχας βοῶντες ὅτι οὗτοι οἱ ← → ἀναστατώσαντες τὴν οἰκουμένην → καὶ πάρεισιν ἐνθάδε
n.apm pt.pa.npm cj r.npm d.npm pt.aa.npm d.asf n.asf cj v.pai.3p adv
4485 1066 4022 4047 3836 415 3836 3876 4205 2779 4205 1924

7 and Jason has welcomed them into his house. They are all defying Caesar's decrees, saying
Ἰάσων → ὑποδέδεκται οὓς ← ← ← καὶ οὗτοι πάντες πράσσουσιν ἀπέναντι Καίσαρος ⌐τῶν δογμάτων⌐ λέγοντες
n.nsm v.rmi.3s r.apm cj r.npm a.npm v.pai.3p p.g n.gsm d.gpn n.gpn pt.pa.npm
2619 5685 4005 5685 5685 5685 2779 4047 4556 4246 4556 595 2790 3836 1504 3306

that there is another king, one called Jesus." **8** When they heard this, the crowd and the city officials
→ εἶναι ἕτερον βασιλέα Ἰησοῦν δὲ → → ἀκούοντας ταῦτα τὸν ὄχλον καὶ τοὺς → πολιτάρχας
f.pa r.asm n.asm n.asm cj pt.pa.apm r.apn d.asm n.asm cj d.apm n.apm
1639 2283 995 2652 1254 201 4047 3836 4063 2779 3836 4485

Λυδίαν καὶ ἰδόντες παρεκάλεσαν τοὺς ἀδελφοὺς καὶ ἐξῆλθαν.

17:1 Διοδεύσαντες δὲ τὴν Ἀμφίπολιν καὶ τὴν Ἀπολλωνίαν ἦλθον εἰς Θεσσαλονίκην ὅπου ἦν συναγωγὴ τῶν Ἰουδαίων. **2** κατὰ δὲ τὸ εἰωθὸς τῷ Παύλῳ εἰσῆλθεν πρὸς αὐτοὺς καὶ ἐπὶ σάββατα τρία διελέξατο αὐτοῖς ἀπὸ τῶν γραφῶν, **3** διανοίγων καὶ παρατιθέμενος ὅτι τὸν Χριστὸν ἔδει παθεῖν καὶ ἀναστῆναι ἐκ νεκρῶν καὶ ὅτι οὗτός ἐστιν ὁ Χριστὸς [ὁ] Ἰησοῦς ὃν ἐγὼ καταγγέλλω ὑμῖν. **4** καί τινες ἐξ αὐτῶν ἐπείσθησαν καὶ προσεκληρώθησαν τῷ Παύλῳ καὶ τῷ Σιλᾷ, τῶν τε σεβομένων Ἑλλήνων πλῆθος πολύ, γυναικῶν τε τῶν πρώτων οὐκ ὀλίγαι. ¶ **5** Ζηλώσαντες δὲ οἱ Ἰουδαῖοι καὶ προσλαβόμενοι τῶν ἀγοραίων ἄνδρας τινὰς πονηροὺς καὶ ὀχλοποιήσαντες ἐθορύβουν τὴν πόλιν καὶ ἐπιστάντες τῇ οἰκίᾳ Ἰάσονος ἐζήτουν αὐτοὺς προαγαγεῖν εἰς τὸν δῆμον· **6** μὴ εὑρόντες δὲ αὐτοὺς ἔσυρον Ἰάσονα καὶ τινας ἀδελφοὺς ἐπὶ τοὺς πολιτάρχας βοῶντες ὅτι Οἱ τὴν οἰκουμένην ἀναστατώσαντες οὗτοι καὶ ἐνθάδε πάρεισιν, **7** οὓς ὑποδέδεκται Ἰάσων· καὶ οὗτοι πάντες ἀπέναντι τῶν δογμάτων Καίσαρος πράσσουσι βασιλέα ἕτερον λέγοντες εἶναι Ἰησοῦν. **8** ἐτάραξαν δὲ τὸν ὄχλον καὶ τοὺς πολιτάρχας ἀκούοντας ταῦτα, **9** καὶ λαβόντες τὸ ἱκανὸν παρὰ

were thrown into turmoil. **9** Then they made Jason and the others post bond and let them go.
→ → → ἐτάραξαν καὶ   παρὰ ⸤τοῦ Ἰάσονος⸥ καὶ τῶν λοιπῶν λαβόντες ⸤τὸ ἱκανόν⸥ ἀπέλυσαν αὐτούς ↞
   v.aai.3p cj   p.g d.gsm n.gsm cj d.gpm a.gpm pt.aa.npm d.asn a.asn v.aai.3p r.apm.3
   5429 2779 3284 3284 4123 3836 2619 2779 3836 3370 3284 3836 2653 668 899 668

In Berea

17:10 As soon as it was night, the brothers sent Paul and Silas away to Berea.
δὲ εὐθέως ← ← → → ⸤διὰ νυκτός⸥ Οἱ ἀδελφοὶ ἐξέπεμψαν τε ⸤τὸν Παῦλον⸥ καὶ ⸤τὸν Σιλᾶν⸥ ↞ εἰς Βέροιαν
cj adv   p.g n.gsf d.npm n.npm v.aai.3p cj d.asm n.asm cj d.asm n.asm p.a n.asf
1254 2311   1328 3816 3836 81 1734 5445 3836 4263 2779 3836 4976 1734 1650 1023

On arriving there, they went to the Jewish synagogue. **11** Now the Bereans were of more noble
→ παραγενόμενοι οἵτινες ἀπῆεσαν εἰς τὴν ⸤τῶν Ἰουδαίων⸥ συναγωγήν δὲ οὗτοι ἦσαν → → εὐγενέστεροι
 pt.am.npm r.npm v.iai.3p p.a d.asf d.gpm a.gpm n.asf cj r.npm v.iai.3p a.npm.c
 4134 4015 583 1650 3836 3836 2681 5252 1254 4047 1639 2302

character than the Thessalonians, for they received the message with great eagerness and examined the
← → τῶν ἐν Θεσσαλονίκῃ⸥ οἵτινες ἐδέξαντο τὸν λόγον μετὰ πάσης προθυμίας ἀνακρίνοντες τὰς
  d.gpm p.d n.dsf r.npm v.ami.3p d.asm n.asm p.g a.gsf n.gsf pt.pa.npm d.apf
  3836 1877 2553 4015 1312 3836 3364 3552 4246 4608 373 3836

Scriptures every day to see if what Paul said was true. **12** Many of the Jews believed, as did also a
γραφὰς καθ᾽ ἡμέραν εἰ ταῦτα ἔχοι οὕτως οὖν μὲν πολλοὶ ἐξ αὐτῶν ἐπίστευσαν → → καὶ
n.apf p.a n.asf cj r.npn v.pao.3s cj pl a.npm p.g r.gpm.3 v.aai.3p cj
1210 2848 2465 1623 4047 2400 4048 4036 3525 4498 1666 899 4409 2779

number of prominent Greek women and many Greek men. ¶ **13** When the Jews in
→ ⸤τῶν εὐσχημόνων⸥ Ἑλληνίδων ⸤τῶν γυναικῶν⸥ καὶ ⸤οὐκ ὀλίγοι⸥ ἀνδρῶν δὲ Ὡς οἱ Ἰουδαῖοι ἀπὸ
 d.gpf a.gpf a.gpf d.gpf n.gpf cj pl a.npm n.gpm cj d.npm a.npm p.g
 3836 2363 1820 3836 1222 2779 4024 3900 467 1254 6055 3836 2681 608

Thessalonica learned that Paul was preaching the word of God at Berea, they went there
⸤τῆς Θεσσαλονίκης⸥ ἔγνωσαν ὅτι καὶ ὑπὸ ⸤τοῦ Παύλου⸥ → κατηγγέλη ὁ λόγος → ⸤τοῦ θεοῦ⸥ ἐν ⸤τῇ Βεροίᾳ⸥ → ἦλθον κἀκεῖ
d.gsf n.gsf v.aai.3p cj adv p.g d.gsm n.gsm v.api.3s d.nsm n.nsm d.gsm n.gsm p.d d.dsf n.dsf v.aai.3p crasis
3836 2553 1182 4022 2779 5679 3836 4263 2859 3836 3364 3836 2536 1877 3836 1023 2262 2795

too, agitating the crowds and stirring them up. **14** The brothers immediately sent Paul
← σαλεύοντες τοὺς ὄχλους καὶ ταράσσοντες δὲ τότε οἱ ἀδελφοὶ εὐθέως ἐξαπέστειλαν ⸤τὸν Παῦλον⸥
 pt.pa.npm d.apm n.apm cj pt.pa.npm cj adv d.npm n.npm adv v.aai.3p d.asm n.asm
 4888 3836 4063 2779 5429 1254 5538 3836 81 2311 1990 3836 4263

  to the coast, but Silas and Timothy stayed at Berea. **15** The men who escorted
πορεύεσθαι ἕως ἐπὶ τὴν θάλασσαν τε τε ⸤ὅ Σιλᾶς⸥ καὶ ὁ Τιμόθεος⸥ ὑπέμειναν ἐκεῖ δὲ οἱ → καθιστάνοντες
f.pm p.g p.a d.asf n.asf cj cj d.nsm n.nsm cj d.nsm n.nsm v.aai.3p adv cj d.npm pt.pa.npm
4513 2401 2093 3836 2498 5445 5445 3836 4976 2779 3836 5510 5702 1695 1254 3836 2770

Paul brought him to Athens and then left with instructions for Silas and Timothy to
⸤τὸν Παῦλον⸥ ἤγαγον ἕως Ἀθηνῶν καὶ → ἐξῆεσαν λαβόντες ἐντολὴν πρὸς ⸤τὸν Σιλᾶν⸥ καὶ ⸤τὸν Τιμόθεον⸥ ἵνα
d.asm n.asm v.aai.3p p.g n.gpf cj v.aai.3p pt.aa.npm n.asf p.a d.asm n.asm cj d.asm n.asm cj
3836 4263 72 2401 121 2779 3284 1997 3284 1953 4639 3836 4976 2779 3836 5510 2671

join him as soon as possible.
ἔλθωσιν πρὸς αὐτὸν ὡς τάχιστα ← ←
v.aas.3p p.a r.asm.3 pl adv.s
2262 4639 899 6055 5441

In Athens

17:16 While Paul was waiting for them in Athens, he   was greatly distressed
δὲ ⸤τοῦ Παύλου⸥ → ἐκδεχομένου ← αὐτούς Ἐν ⸤ταῖς Ἀθήναις⸥ ⸤τὸ πνεῦμα αὐτοῦ⸥ → → παρωξύνετο ἐν
cj d.gsm n.gsm pt.pm.gsm r.apm.3 p.d d.dpf n.dpf d.nsn n.nsn r.gsm.3 v.ipi.3s p.d
1254 3836 4263 1683 899 1877 3836 121 3836 4460 899 4236 1877

to see that the city was full of idols. **17** So he reasoned in the synagogue with the Jews and
αὐτῷ θεωροῦντος τὴν πόλιν οὖσαν → κατείδωλον οὖν μὲν διελέγετο ἐν τῇ συναγωγῇ → τοῖς Ἰουδαίοις καὶ
r.dsm.3 pt.pa.gsm d.asf n.asf pt.pa.asf a.asf cj pl v.imi.3s p.d d.dsf n.dsf d.dpm a.dpm cj
899 2555 3836 4484 1639 2977 4036 3525 1363 1877 3836 5252 3836 2681 2779

τοῦ Ἰάσονος καὶ τῶν λοιπῶν ἀπέλυσαν αὐτούς.
17:10 Οἱ δὲ ἀδελφοὶ εὐθέως διὰ νυκτὸς ἐξέπεμψαν τόν τε Παῦλον καὶ τὸν Σιλᾶν εἰς Βέροιαν, οἵτινες παραγενόμενοι εἰς τὴν συναγωγὴν τῶν Ἰουδαίων ἀπῇεσαν. **11** οὗτοι δὲ ἦσαν εὐγενέστεροι τῶν ἐν Θεσσαλονίκῃ, οἵτινες ἐδέξαντο τὸν λόγον μετὰ πάσης προθυμίας καθ᾽ ἡμέραν ἀνακρίνοντες τὰς γραφὰς εἰ ἔχοι ταῦτα οὕτως. **12** πολλοὶ μὲν οὖν ἐξ αὐτῶν ἐπίστευσαν καὶ τῶν Ἑλληνίδων γυναικῶν τῶν εὐσχημόνων καὶ ἀνδρῶν οὐκ ὀλίγοι. ¶ **13** Ὡς δὲ ἔγνωσαν οἱ ἀπὸ τῆς Θεσσαλονίκης Ἰουδαῖοι ὅτι καὶ ἐν τῇ Βεροίᾳ κατηγγέλη ὑπὸ τοῦ Παύλου ὁ λόγος τοῦ θεοῦ, ἦλθον κἀκεῖ σαλεύοντες καὶ ταράσσοντες τοὺς ὄχλους.
14 εὐθέως δὲ τότε τὸν Παῦλον ἐξαπέστειλαν οἱ ἀδελφοὶ πορεύεσθαι ἕως ἐπὶ τὴν θάλασσαν, ὑπέμεινάν τε ὅ τε Σιλᾶς καὶ ὁ Τιμόθεος ἐκεῖ. **15** οἱ δὲ καθιστάνοντες τὸν Παῦλον ἤγαγον ἕως Ἀθηνῶν, καὶ λαβόντες ἐντολὴν πρὸς τὸν Σιλᾶν καὶ τὸν Τιμόθεον ἵνα ὡς τάχιστα ἔλθωσιν πρὸς αὐτὸν ἐξῄεσαν.
17:16 Ἐν δὲ ταῖς Ἀθήναις ἐκδεχομένου αὐτοὺς τοῦ Παύλου παρωξύνετο τὸ πνεῦμα αὐτοῦ ἐν αὐτῷ θεωροῦντος κατείδωλον οὖσαν τὴν πόλιν. **17** διελέγετο μὲν οὖν ἐν τῇ συναγωγῇ τοῖς Ἰουδαίοις καὶ τοῖς σεβομένοις καὶ ἐν τῇ ἀγορᾷ κατὰ πᾶσαν ἡμέραν

the God-fearing Greeks, as   well as in   the marketplace *day*   *by day* with those who happened   to
τοῖς σεβομένοις   καὶ ←   ἐν τῇ ἀγορᾷ   ⌐κατὰ πᾶσαν ἡμέραν⌐   πρὸς τοὺς ⌐   παρατυγχάνοντας ←
d.dpm pt.pm.dpm   cj   p.d d.dsf n.dsf   p.a   a.asf   n.asf   p.a d.apm   pt.pa.apm
3836 4936   2779   1877 3836 59   2848 4246   2465   4639 3836   4193

be there. [18]   A group   of Epicurean   and Stoic   philosophers began to dispute   with him.   Some of
← ←   δὲ τινὲς καὶ ⌐τῶν Ἐπικουρείων⌐ καὶ Στοϊκῶν φιλοσόφων →   → συνέβαλλον ←   αὐτῷ καί τινες
              cj   n.npm   adv d.gpm n.gpm   cj   a.gpm   n.gpm   v.iai.3p   r.dsm.3 cj r.npm
             1254 5516   2779 3836 2134   2779 5121   5815   5202   899 2779 5516

them asked, "What is   this babbler   trying to say?"   Others remarked, "He seems to be   advocating
ἔλεγον τί ἄν, → οὗτος ὁ σπερμολόγος; θέλοι → λέγειν δέ οἱ   →   δοκεῖ   → εἶναι καταγγελεὺς
v.iai.3p r.asn pl   r.nsm d.nsm n.nsm   v.pao.3s f.pa pl d.npm   v.pai.3s f.pa n.nsm
3306   5515 323   2527 4047 5066   2527   3306 1254 3836   1506   1639 2858

foreign gods."   They said this because Paul was preaching the good news about Jesus   and the resurrection.
ξένων δαιμονίων   ὅτι →   εὐηγγελίζετο ← ← ←   ⌐τὸν Ἰησοῦν⌐ καὶ τὴν ἀνάστασιν
a.gpn n.gpn   cj   v.imi.3s   d.asm n.asm   cj d.asf n.asf
3828   1228   4022   2294   3836 2652   2779 3836 414

[19] Then they took   him and brought him to   a meeting of the Areopagus,   where they said   to him, "May
τε → ἐπιλαβόμενοι αὐτοῦ ἤγαγον ἐπὶ   τὸν Ἄρειον πάγον, →   λέγοντες   →
cj   pt.am.npm r.gsm.3 v.aai.3p p.a   d.asm a.asm n.asm   pt.pa.npm
5445   2138   899   72   2093   3836 740 4076   3306

we   know what this new   teaching is that   you are presenting? [20] You are bringing some strange
→ δυνάμεθα γνῶναι τίς αὕτη ἡ καινὴ ἡ διδαχή, ὑπὸ σοῦ → λαλουμένη γάρ → → εἰσφέρεις τινα ξενίζοντα
v.ppi.1p f.aa   r.nsf r.nsf d.nsf a.nsf d.nsf n.nsf p.g r.gs.2 pt.pp.nsf cj   v.pai.2s r.apn pt.pa.apn
1538   1182   5515 4047 3836 2785 3836 1439   5679 5148 3281   1142   1662   5516 3826

ideas to our ears,   and we want   to know what   they mean." [21] (All   the Athenians and the
← εἰς ἡμῶν ⌐τὰς ἀκοάς⌐ οὖν → βουλόμεθα → γνῶναι τίνα θέλει ταῦτα εἶναι δὲ πάντες Ἀθηναῖοι καὶ οἱ
p.a r.gp.1 d.apf n.apf cj   v.pmi.1p f.aa   r.apn v.pai.3s r.apn f.pa cj a.npm n.npm   cj d.npm
1650 7005 3836 198   4036   1089   1182   5515 2527 4047 1639 1254 4246 122   2779 3836

foreigners who lived   there spent their time   doing nothing   but talking about   and listening to
ξένοι → ἐπιδημοῦντες ←   → ηὐκαίρουν εἰς οὐδὲν ἕτερον ἢ λέγειν ← τι ἢ ἀκούειν ← τι
n.npm   pt.pa.npm   v.iai.3p p.a a.asn r.asn pl f.pa   r.asn cj f.pa   r.asn
3828   2111   2320   1650 4029 2283 2445 3306   5516 2445 201   5516

the latest ideas.) ¶ [22]   Paul   then stood up in the meeting of the Areopagus and said: "Men of
καινότερον   δὲ ὁ Παῦλος, → Σταθεὶς ← ἐν μέσῳ → τοῦ ⌐Ἀρείου πάγου⌐ ἔφη ἄνδρες →
a.asn.c   cj d.nsm n.nsm pt.ap.nsm p.d n.dsn   d.gsm a.gsm n.gsm   v.iai.3s n.vpm
2785   1254 3836 4263 2705   1877 3545   3836 740 4076   5774 467

Athens! I see   that in   every way   you are very religious. [23] For as I walked around and looked
Ἀθηναῖοι → θεωρῶ κατὰ πάντα ← ὡς ὑμᾶς → δεισιδαιμονεστέρους γάρ → I διερχόμενος καὶ ἀναθεωρῶν
n.vpm   v.pai.1s p.a a.apn   pl r.ap.2   a.apm.c   cj   pt.pm.nsm   cj pt.pa.nsm
122   2555   2848 4246   6055 7007   1273   1142   1451   2779 355

carefully at your objects   of worship, I   even found an altar with   this inscription: To An Unknown
← ← ὑμῶν ⌐τὰ σεβάσματα⌐ ← ← → καὶ εὗρον βωμὸν ἐν ᾧ ἐπεγέγραπτο → Ἀγνώστῳ
r.gp.2 d.apn n.apn   adv v.aai.1s n.asm p.d r.dsm v.lpi.3s   a.dsm
7007 3836 4934   2351 2779 2351 1117 1877 4005 2108   58

God. Now what you worship as something unknown   I am going to proclaim to you. ¶ [24] "The God
θεῷ οὖν ὃ → εὐσεβεῖτε → → ἀγνοοῦντες τοῦτο ἐγὼ →   καταγγέλλω → ὑμῖν   ὁ θεὸς
n.dsm cj r.asn v.pai.2p   pt.pa.npm r.asn r.ns.1   v.pai.1s r.dp.2   d.nsm n.nsm
2536 4036 4005 2355   51   4047 1609   2859   7007   3836 2536

who made the world and everything in it   is   the Lord of heaven and earth and does not live
ὁ ποιήσας τὸν κόσμον καὶ πάντα τὰ ἐν αὐτῷ οὗτος ὑπάρχων κύριος → οὐρανοῦ καὶ γῆς → οὐκ κατοικεῖ
d.nsm pt.aa.nsm d.asm n.asm cj a.apn d.apn p.d r.dsm.3 r.nsm pt.pa.nsm n.nsm n.gsm cj n.gsf pl v.pai.3s
3836 4472 3836 3180 2779 4246 3836 1877 899 4047 5639 3261 4041 2779 1178 2997 4024 2997

in temples built   by hands. [25] And he is not served   by human   hands, as if he needed   anything,
ἐν ναοῖς χειροποιήτοις ← ← → → → οὐδὲ θεραπεύεται ὑπὸ ἀνθρωπίνων χειρῶν → → προσδεόμενος τινος
p.d n.dpm a.dpm   4028 v.ppi.3s p.g a.gpf n.gpf   pt.pm.nsm r.gsn
1877 3724 5935   4028 2543 2543 2543 474 5931   4656   5516

because he himself gives all   men life and breath and everything else. [26] From one man he made every nation
→ → αὐτὸς διδοὺς πᾶσι ζωὴν καὶ πνοὴν καὶ ⌐τὰ πάντα⌐ τε ἐξ ἑνὸς → ἐποίησεν πᾶν ἔθνος
r.nsm pt.pa.nsm a.dpm n.asf cj n.asf cj d.apn a.apn cj p.g a.gsn v.aai.3s a.asn n.asn
1443 1443 899 1443 4246 2437 2779 4466 2779 3836 4246 5445 1666 1651 4472 4246 1620

πρὸς τοὺς παρατυγχάνοντας. ¹⁸ τινὲς δὲ καὶ τῶν Ἐπικουρείων καὶ Στοϊκῶν φιλοσόφων συνέβαλλον αὐτῷ, καί τινες ἔλεγον, Τί
ἂν θέλοι ὁ σπερμολόγος οὗτος λέγειν; οἱ δέ, Ξένων δαιμονίων δοκεῖ καταγγελεὺς εἶναι, ὅτι τὸν Ἰησοῦν καὶ τὴν ἀνάστασιν
εὐηγγελίζετο. ¹⁹ ἐπιλαβόμενοί τε αὐτοῦ ἐπὶ τὸν Ἄρειον ἤγαγον λέγοντες, Δυνάμεθα γνῶναι τίς ἡ καινὴ αὕτη ἡ ὑπὸ σοῦ
λαλουμένη διδαχή; ²⁰ ξενίζοντα γάρ τινα εἰσφέρεις εἰς τὰς ἀκοὰς ἡμῶν· βουλόμεθα οὖν γνῶναι τίνα θέλει ταῦτα εἶναι.
²¹ Ἀθηναῖοι δὲ πάντες καὶ οἱ ἐπιδημοῦντες ξένοι εἰς οὐδὲν ἕτερον ηὐκαίρουν ἢ λέγειν τι ἢ ἀκούειν τι καινότερον. ¶ ²² Σταθεὶς
δὲ [ὁ] Παῦλος ἐν μέσῳ τοῦ Ἀρείου ἔφη, Ἄνδρες Ἀθηναῖοι, κατὰ πάντα ὡς δεισιδαιμονεστέρους ὑμᾶς θεωρῶ. ²³ διερχόμενος γὰρ
καὶ ἀναθεωρῶν τὰ σεβάσματα ὑμῶν εὗρον καὶ βωμὸν ἐν ᾧ ἐπεγέγραπτο, Ἀγνώστῳ θεῷ. ὃ οὖν ἀγνοοῦντες εὐσεβεῖτε, τοῦτο ἐγὼ
καταγγέλλω ὑμῖν. ¶ ²⁴ ὁ θεὸς ὁ ποιήσας τὸν κόσμον καὶ πάντα τὰ ἐν αὐτῷ, οὗτος οὐρανοῦ καὶ γῆς ὑπάρχων κύριος οὐκ ἐν
χειροποιήτοις ναοῖς κατοικεῖ ²⁵ οὐδὲ ὑπὸ χειρῶν ἀνθρωπίνων θεραπεύεται προσδεόμενός τινος, αὐτὸς διδοὺς πᾶσι ζωὴν καὶ πνοὴν
καὶ τὰ πάντα· ²⁶ ἐποίησέν τε ἐξ ἑνὸς πᾶν ἔθνος ἀνθρώπων κατοικεῖν ἐπὶ παντὸς προσώπου τῆς γῆς, ὁρίσας προστεταγμένους

of men,   that they should inhabit   the whole   earth;   and he determined the times   set   for
→ ἀνθρώπων →   →   →   κατοικεῖν ἐπὶ   παντὸς προσώπου ⌐τῆς γῆς⌐   → ὁρίσας   καιροὺς προστεταγμένους ←
n.gpm   f.pa   p.g   a.gsn   n.gsn   d.gsf   n.gsf   pt.aa.nsm   n.apm   pt.rp.apm
476   2997   2093   4246   4725   3836   1178   3988   2789   4705

them and the exact   places where they should live.   **27** God did this so that men would seek him   and
← καὶ τὰς ὁροθεσίας ←   αὐτῶν ⌐τῆς κατοικίας⌐   →   →   →   ζητεῖν ⌐τὸν θεόν⌐
cj   d.apf   n.apf   r.gpm.3   d.gsf   n.gsf   f.pa   d.asm   n.asm
2779   3836   3999   899   3836   3000   2426   3836   2536

perhaps   reach   out for him and find   him, though   he is   not far   from each   one of us.
⌐εἰ ἄρα γε⌐ ψηλαφήσειαν ←   ← αὐτὸν καὶ εὕροιεν   ⌐καί γε⌐ → ὑπάρχοντα οὐ μακρὰν ἀπὸ ἑκάστου ἑνὸς   ἡμῶν
cj   cj   pl   v.aao.3p   r.asm.3   cj   v.aao.3p   cj   pl   pt.pa.asm   pl   adv   p.g   a.gsm   a.gsm   r.gp.1
1623   726   1145   6027   899   2779   2351   2779   1145   5639   4024   3426   608   1667   1651   7005

28 'For in him we live and move   and have our being.' As   some of your   own poets have said,
γὰρ ἐν αὐτῷ → ζῶμεν καὶ κινούμεθα καὶ →   → ἐσμέν ὡς καὶ τινες → ⌐καθ' ὑμᾶς⌐ τῶν ποιητῶν → εἰρήκασιν γὰρ
cj   p.d   r.dsm.3   v.pai.1p   cj   v.ppi.1p   cj   v.pai.1p   cj   adv   r.npm   p.a   r.ap.2   d.gpm   n.gpm   v.rai.3p   cj
1142   1877   899   2409   2779   3075   2779   1639   6055   2779   5516   4475   2848   7007   3836   4475   3306   1142

'We are   his offspring.' ¶   **29** "Therefore since we are   God's   offspring, we should   not think that
→ ἐσμέν καὶ τοῦ γένος   οὖν   → ὑπάρχοντες ⌐τοῦ θεοῦ⌐ γένος   → ὀφείλομεν οὐκ νομίζειν
v.pai.1p   adv   d.gsm   n.nsn   cj   pt.pa.npm   d.gsm   n.gsm   n.nsn   v.pai.1p   pl   f.pa
1639   2779   3836   1169   4036   5639   3836   2536   1169   4053   4024   3787

the divine being is   like   gold or silver or stone – an image   made by man's   design and skill.   **30**
τὸ θεῖον ←   εἶναι ὅμοιον χρυσῷ ἢ   ἀργύρῳ ἢ λίθῳ   χαράγματι →   → ἀνθρώπου τέχνης καὶ ἐνθυμήσεως   οὖν μὲν
d.asn   a.asn   f.pa   a.asn   n.dsm   cj   n.dsm   cj   n.dsm   n.dsn   n.gsm   n.gsf   cj   n.gsf   cj   pl
3836   2521   1639   3927   5996   2445   738   2445   3345   5916   5492   5492   476   5492   2779   1927   4036   3525

In the past God   overlooked such ignorance, but now   he commands all   people   everywhere to
→ τοὺς χρόνους ὁ θεός, ὑπεριδὼν τῆς ἀγνοίας   ⌐τὰ νῦν⌐ → παραγγέλλει πάντας ⌐τοῖς ἀνθρώποις⌐ πανταχοῦ   →
d.apm   n.apm   d.nsm   n.nsm   pt.aa.nsm   d.gsf   n.gsf   d.apn   adv   v.pai.3s   a.apm   d.dpm   n.dpm   adv
3836   5989   3836   2536   5666   3836   53   3836   3814   4133   4246   3836   476   4116

repent.   **31** For   he has set   a day   when   he will   judge the world   with justice   by the man   he has
μετανοεῖν καθότι →   → ἔστησεν ἡμέραν ἐν ᾗ → μέλλει κρίνειν τὴν οἰκουμένην ἐν δικαιοσύνῃ ἐν   ἀνδρὶ ᾧ
f.pa   cj   v.aai.3s   n.asf   p.d   r.dsf   v.pai.3s   f.pa   d.asf   n.asf   p.d   n.dsf   p.d   n.dsm   r.dsm
3566   2776   2705   2465   1877   4005   3516   3212   3836   3876   1877   1466   1877   467   4005

appointed. He has given   proof of this to all   men by raising   him from the dead." ¶   **32**   When they
ὥρισεν →   → παρασχὼν πίστιν → πᾶσιν   → ἀναστήσας αὐτὸν ἐκ   νεκρῶν   δὲ   →
v.aai.3s   pt.aa.nsm   n.asf   a.dpm   pt.aa.nsm   r.asm.3   p.g   a.gpm   cj
3988   4218   4411   4246   482   899   1666   3738   1254

heard   about the resurrection of the dead,   some of them sneered, but others said, "We want to hear
Ἀκούσαντες ←   ἀνάστασιν → νεκρῶν μὲν οἱ → ← ἐχλεύαζον δὲ οἱ   εἶπαν →   → ἀκουσόμεθα
pt.aa.npm   n.asf   a.gpm   pl   d.npm   v.iai.3p   pl   d.npm   v.aai.3p   v.fmi.1p
201   414   3738   3525   3836   5949   1254   3836   3306   201

you   again on   this   subject."   **33** At   that, Paul   left   the Council.   **34**   A few men became
σου καὶ πάλιν περὶ τούτου ←   οὕτως ←   ὁ Παῦλος, ἐξῆλθεν ἐκ   ⌐μέσου αὐτῶν⌐   δὲ   τινες ἄνδρες →
r.gs.2   adv   adv   p.g   r.gsn   adv   d.nsm   n.nsm   v.aai.3s   p.g   n.gsn   r.gpm.3   cj   r.npm   n.npm
5148   2779   4099   4309   4047   4048   3836   4263   2002   1666   3545   899   1254   5516   467

followers   of Paul and believed. Among them   was Dionysius, a member of the Areopagus, also a woman named
κολληθέντες → αὐτῷ ἐπίστευσαν ἐν   οἷς καὶ   Διονύσιος →   → ὁ Ἀρεοπαγίτης καὶ   γυνὴ   ὀνόματι
pt.ap.npm   r.dsm.3   v.aai.3p   p.d   r.dpm   cj   n.nsm   d.nsm   n.nsm   cj   n.nsf   n.dsn
3140   899   4409   1877   4005   2779   1477   3836   741   2779   1222   3950

Damaris, and a number of others.
Δάμαρις καὶ   ἕτεροι σὺν αὐτοῖς
n.nsf   cj   r.npm   p.d   r.dpm.3
1240   2779   2283   5250   899

In Corinth

18:1 After this, Paul left   Athens   and went to Corinth.   **2**   There he met   a   Jew   named
Μετὰ ταῦτα   χωρισθεὶς ἐκ ⌐τῶν Ἀθηνῶν⌐ ἦλθεν εἰς Κόρινθον καὶ   → εὑρών τινα Ἰουδαῖον ὀνόματι
p.a   r.apn   pt.ap.nsm   p.g   d.gpf   n.gpf   v.aai.3s   p.a   n.asf   cj   pt.aa.nsm   r.asn   a.asm   n.dsn
3552   4047   6004   1666   3836   121   2262   1650   3172   2779   2351   5516   2681   3950

καιροὺς καὶ τὰς ὁροθεσίας τῆς κατοικίας αὐτῶν   **27** ζητεῖν τὸν θεόν, εἰ ἄρα γε ψηλαφήσειαν αὐτὸν καὶ εὕροιεν, καί γε οὐ μακρὰν ἀπὸ ἑνὸς ἑκάστου ἡμῶν ὑπάρχοντα.   **28** Ἐν αὐτῷ γὰρ ζῶμεν καὶ κινούμεθα καὶ ἐσμέν, ὡς καί τινες τῶν καθ' ὑμᾶς ποιητῶν εἰρήκασιν, Τοῦ γὰρ καὶ γένος ἐσμέν. ¶ **29** γένος οὖν ὑπάρχοντες τοῦ θεοῦ οὐκ ὀφείλομεν νομίζειν χρυσῷ ἢ ἀργύρῳ ἢ λίθῳ, χαράγματι τέχνης καὶ ἐνθυμήσεως ἀνθρώπου, τὸ θεῖον εἶναι ὅμοιον.   **30** τοὺς μὲν οὖν χρόνους τῆς ἀγνοίας ὑπεριδὼν ὁ θεός, τὰ νῦν παραγγέλλει τοῖς ἀνθρώποις πάντας πανταχοῦ μετανοεῖν,   **31** καθότι ἔστησεν ἡμέραν ἐν ᾗ μέλλει κρίνειν τὴν οἰκουμένην ἐν δικαιοσύνῃ ἐν ἀνδρὶ ᾧ ὥρισεν, πίστιν παρασχὼν πᾶσιν ἀναστήσας αὐτὸν ἐκ νεκρῶν. ¶ **32** Ἀκούσαντες δὲ ἀνάστασιν νεκρῶν οἱ μὲν ἐχλεύαζον, οἱ δὲ εἶπαν, Ἀκουσόμεθά σου περὶ τούτου καὶ πάλιν.   **33** οὕτως ὁ Παῦλος ἐξῆλθεν ἐκ μέσου αὐτῶν.   **34** τινὲς δὲ ἄνδρες κολληθέντες αὐτῷ ἐπίστευσαν, ἐν οἷς καὶ Διονύσιος ὁ Ἀρεοπαγίτης καὶ γυνὴ ὀνόματι Δάμαρις καὶ ἕτεροι σὺν αὐτοῖς.

18:1 Μετὰ ταῦτα χωρισθεὶς ἐκ τῶν Ἀθηνῶν ἦλθεν εἰς Κόρινθον.   **2** καὶ εὑρών τινα Ἰουδαῖον ὀνόματι Ἀκύλαν, Ποντικὸν

Aquila,	a native		of	Pontus,	who	had	recently	come	from	Italy		with	his	wife	Priscilla,	because
Ἀκύλαν	τῷ	γένει	Ποντικὸν				προσφάτως	ἐληλυθότα	ἀπὸ	τῆς Ἰταλίας		καὶ	αὐτοῦ	γυναῖκα	Πρίσκιλλαν	διὰ
n.asm	d.dsn	n.dsn	a.asm				adv	pt.ra.asm	p.g	d.gsf n.gsf		cj	r.gsm.3	n.asf	n.asf	p.a
217	3836	1169	4507	2262	2262	4711	2262		608	3836 2712		2779	899	1222	4572	1328

Claudius	had ordered		all	the	Jews	to leave		Rome.	Paul	went	to see them,		³ and
Κλαύδιον	τὸ	διατεταχέναι	πάντας	τοὺς	Ἰουδαίους	χωρίζεσθαι	ἀπὸ	τῆς Ῥώμης		προσῆλθεν	αὐτοῖς	καὶ
n.asm	d.asn	f.ra	a.apm	d.apm	n.apm	f.pp	p.g	d.gsf n.gsf		v.aai.3s	r.dpm.3	cj
3087	3836	1411	4246	3836	2681	6004	608	3836 4873		4665	899	2779

because	he was		a tentmaker	as	they were,			he stayed	and	worked	with	them.	⁴		Every
διὰ	τὸ	εἶναι	ὁμότεχνον	σκηνοποιοὶ	γὰρ	ἦσαν	τῇ τέχνῃ	ἔμενεν	καὶ	ἠργάζετο	παρ᾽	αὐτοῖς	δὲ	κατὰ	πᾶν
p.a	d.asn	f.pa	a.asm	n.npm	cj	v.iai.3p	d.dsf n.dsf	v.iai.3s	cj	v.imi.3s	p.d	r.dpm.3	cj	p.a	a.asn
1328	3836	1639	3937	5010	1142	1639	3836 5492	3531	2779	2237	4123	899	1254	2848	4246

Sabbath	he reasoned	in	the	synagogue,	trying to persuade		Jews	and	Greeks.	¶	⁵	When		
σάββατον	διελέγετο	ἐν	τῇ	συναγωγῇ	ἔπειθεν	τε	Ἰουδαίους	καὶ	Ἕλληνας			δὲ Ὡς	ὅ	τε
n.asn	v.imi.3s	p.d	d.dsf	n.dsf	v.iai.3s		v.apm	cj	n.apm			d.nsm cj	cj
4879	1363	1877	3836	5252	4275	5445	2681	2779	1818			1254 6055	3836	5445

Silas	and	Timothy	came	from	Macedonia,	Paul		devoted himself	exclusively	to preaching,	
Σιλᾶς	καὶ	ὁ Τιμόθεος,	κατῆλθον	ἀπὸ	τῆς Μακεδονίας,	ὁ	Παῦλος	συνείχετο		τῷ	λόγῳ
n.nsm	cj	d.nsm n.nsm	v.aai.3p	p.g	d.gsf n.gsf	d.nsm	n.nsm	v.ipi.3s		d.dsm	n.dsm
4976	2779	3836 5510	2982	608	3836 3423	3836	4263	5309		3836	3364

testifying		to the	Jews	that	Jesus	was	the	Christ.	⁶ But	when	the	Jews	opposed		Paul and became
διαμαρτυρόμενος	τοῖς	Ἰουδαίοις	Ἰησοῦν	εἶναι	τὸν	χριστὸν	δὲ		αὐτῶν	ἀντιτασσομένων		καὶ
pt.pm.nsm	d.dpm	a.dpm	n.asm	f.pa	d.asm	n.asm	cj		r.gpm.3	pt.pm.gpm		cj
1371	3836	2681	2652	1639	3836	5986	1254	530	899	530		2779

abusive,		he shook		out	his	clothes	in protest	and	said	to	them,	"Your	blood	be	on	your	own	heads!
βλασφημούντων	ἐκτιναξάμενος	τὰ	ἱμάτια			εἶπεν	πρὸς	αὐτοὺς	ὑμῶν	τὸ	αἷμα	ἐπὶ	ὑμῶν	τὴν	κεφαλὴν
pt.pa.gpm	pt.am.nsm	d.apn	n.apn			v.aai.3s	p.a	r.apm.3	r.gp.2	d.nsn	n.nsn	p.a	r.gp.2	d.asf	n.asf
1059	1759	3836	2668			3306	4639	899	7007	3836	135	2093	7007	3836	3051

I	am clear	of my responsibility.	From now	on	I will go		to	the	Gentiles."	¶	⁷ Then	Paul	left
ἐγώ	καθαρὸς	ἀπὸ	τοῦ νῦν		πορεύσομαι	εἰς	τὰ	ἔθνη			καὶ		μεταβὰς
r.ns.1	a.nsm	p.g	d.gsm adv		v.fmi.1s	p.a	d.apn	n.apn			cj		pt.aa.nsm
1609	2754	608	3836 3814		4513	1650	3836	1620			2779		3553

	the synagogue	and went		next		door		to the	house		of	Titius
ἐκεῖθεν			εἰσῆλθεν	οὗ	ἡ	οἰκία	ἦν	συνομοροῦσα	τῇ	συναγωγῇ	εἰς	οἰκίαν	τινὸς	ὀνόματι	Τιτίου
adv			v.aai.3s	r.gsm	d.nsf	n.nsf	v.iai.3s	pt.pa.nsf	d.dsf	n.dsf	p.a	n.asf	r.gsm	n.dsn	n.gsm
1696	5252		1656	4005	3836	3864	1639	5327	3836	5252	1650	3864	5516	3950	5517

Justus,	a worshiper	of God.	⁸	Crispus,	the	synagogue ruler,		and	his	entire	household	believed	in the
Ἰούστου	σεβομένου	τὸν θεόν,	δὲ	Κρίσπος	ὁ	ἀρχισυνάγωγος	σὺν	αὐτοῦ	ὅλῳ	τῷ	οἴκῳ	ἐπίστευσεν	τῷ
n.gsm	pt.pm.gsm	d.asm n.asm	cj	n.nsm	d.nsm	n.nsm	p.d	r.gsm.3	a.dsm	d.dsm	n.dsm	v.aai.3s	d.dsm
2688	4936	3836 2536	1254	3214	3836	801	5250	899	3910	3836	3875	4409	3836

Lord;	and	many	of the	Corinthians	who	heard		him	believed	and	were	baptized.	¶	⁹	One	night	the	Lord
κυρίῳ	καὶ	πολλοὶ	τῶν	Κορινθίων	ἀκούοντες	ἐπίστευον	καὶ		ἐβαπτίζοντο				δὲ	ἐν	νυκτὶ	ὁ	κύριος
n.dsm	cj	a.npm	d.gpm	a.gpm	pt.pa.npm	v.iai.3p	cj		v.ipi.3p				cj	p.d	n.dsf	d.nsm n.nsm
3261	2779	4498	3836	3171	201	4409	2779	966				1254	1877	3816	3836	3261

spoke	to Paul		in	a vision:	"Do	not	be afraid;		keep on speaking,		do	not	be silent.	¹⁰ For	I	am
Εἶπεν	τῷ Παύλῳ	δι᾽	ὁράματος	μὴ	φοβοῦ	ἀλλὰ	λάλει	καὶ	μὴ	σιωπήσῃς	διότι	ἐγώ εἰμι
v.aai.3s	d.dsm n.dsm	p.g	n.gsn	pl	v.ppm.2s	cj	v.pam.2s	cj	pl	v.aas.2s	cj	r.ns.1 v.pai.1s
3306	3836 4263	1328	3969	5828	3590	5828	247	3281	2779	4995	3590	4995	1484	1609 1639

with	you,	and	no one		is going	to attack		and	harm		you,	because	I	have	many	people	in	this
μετὰ	σοῦ	καὶ	οὐδεὶς			ἐπιθήσεταί	σοι	τοῦ κακῶσαι		σε	διότι	μοι	ἐστί	πολὺς	λαὸς	ἐν	ταύτῃ
p.g	r.gs.2	cj	a.nsm			v.fmi.3s	r.ds.2	d.gsn f.aa		r.as.2	cj	r.ds.1	v.pai.3s	a.nsm	n.nsm	p.d	r.dsf
3552	5148	2779	4029		2202	5148	3836 2808		5148	1484	1609	1639	4498	3295	1877	4047

city."	¹¹ So	Paul	stayed	for a	year	and	a half,		teaching		them	the	word	of God.	¶	¹²	While
τῇ πόλει	δὲ	Ἐκάθισεν	ἐνιαυτὸν	καὶ	μῆνας	ἓξ	διδάσκων	ἐν	αὐτοῖς	τὸν	λόγον	τοῦ θεοῦ		δὲ
d.dsf n.dsf	cj	v.aai.3s	n.asm	cj	n.apm	a.apm	pt.pa.nsm	p.d	r.dpm.3	d.asm	n.asm	d.gsm n.gsm		cj
3836 4484	1254	2767	1929	2779	3604	1971	1438	1877	899	3836	3364	3836 2536		1254 1639

τῷ γένει προσφάτως ἐληλυθότα ἀπὸ τῆς Ἰταλίας καὶ Πρίσκιλλαν γυναῖκα αὐτοῦ, διὰ τὸ διατεταχέναι Κλαύδιον χωρίζεσθαι πάντας τοὺς Ἰουδαίους ἀπὸ τῆς Ῥώμης, προσῆλθεν αὐτοῖς ³ καὶ διὰ τὸ ὁμότεχνον εἶναι ἔμενεν παρ᾽ αὐτοῖς, καὶ ἠργάζετο· ἦσαν γὰρ σκηνοποιοὶ τῇ τέχνῃ. ⁴ διελέγετο δὲ ἐν τῇ συναγωγῇ κατὰ πᾶν σάββατον ἔπειθέν τε Ἰουδαίους καὶ Ἕλληνας. ¶ ⁵ Ὡς δὲ κατῆλθον ἀπὸ τῆς Μακεδονίας ὅ τε Σιλᾶς καὶ ὁ Τιμόθεος, συνείχετο τῷ λόγῳ ὁ Παῦλος διαμαρτυρόμενος τοῖς Ἰουδαίοις εἶναι τὸν Χριστὸν Ἰησοῦν. ⁶ ἀντιτασσομένων δὲ αὐτῶν καὶ βλασφημούντων ἐκτιναξάμενος τὰ ἱμάτια εἶπεν πρὸς αὐτούς, Τὸ αἷμα ὑμῶν ἐπὶ τὴν κεφαλὴν ὑμῶν· καθαρὸς ἐγὼ ἀπὸ τοῦ νῦν εἰς τὰ ἔθνη πορεύσομαι. ¶ ⁷ καὶ μεταβὰς ἐκεῖθεν εἰσῆλθεν εἰς οἰκίαν τινὸς ὀνόματι Τιτίου Ἰούστου σεβομένου τὸν θεόν, οὗ ἡ οἰκία ἦν συνομοροῦσα τῇ συναγωγῇ. ⁸ Κρίσπος δὲ ὁ ἀρχισυνάγωγος ἐπίστευσεν τῷ κυρίῳ σὺν ὅλῳ τῷ οἴκῳ αὐτοῦ, καὶ πολλοὶ τῶν Κορινθίων ἀκούοντες ἐπίστευον καὶ ἐβαπτίζοντο. ¶ ⁹ εἶπεν δὲ ὁ κύριος ἐν νυκτὶ δι᾽ ὁράματος τῷ Παύλῳ, Μὴ φοβοῦ, ἀλλὰ λάλει καὶ μὴ σιωπήσῃς, ¹⁰ διότι ἐγώ εἰμι μετὰ σοῦ καὶ οὐδεὶς ἐπιθήσεταί σοι τοῦ κακῶσαί σε, διότι λαός ἐστί μοι πολὺς ἐν τῇ πόλει ταύτῃ. ¹¹ Ἐκάθισεν δὲ ἐνιαυτὸν καὶ μῆνας ἓξ διδάσκων ἐν αὐτοῖς τὸν

Gallio was proconsul of Achaia, | the Jews | made a united attack | on Paul | and brought him
Γαλλίωνος ὄντος ἀνθυπάτου → ⌐τῆς Ἀχαΐας⌐ | οἱ Ἰουδαῖοι → | ὁμοθυμαδὸν κατεπέστησαν → | ⌐τῷ Παύλῳ⌐ | καὶ ἤγαγον αὐτὸν
n.gsm pt.pa.gsm n.gsm · d.gsf n.gsf · d.npm a.npm · adv · v.aai.3s · d.dsm n.dsm · cj v.aai.3p r.asm.3
1136 1639 478 · 3836 938 · 3836 2681 · 2987 · 3924 2987 · 3836 4263 · 2779 72 899

into court. **13** "This man," they charged, "is persuading the people to worship God in ways contrary to
ἐπὶ ⌐τὸ βῆμα⌐ οὗτος ← → λέγοντες ὅτι → ἀναπείθει τοὺς ἀνθρώπους σέβεσθαι ⌐τὸν θεόν⌐ παρὰ ←
p.a d.asn n.asn · r.nsm · pt.pa.npm cj · v.pai.3s · d.apm n.apm · f.pm · d.asm n.asm · p.a
2093 3836 1037 · 4047 · 3306 4022 · 400 · 3836 476 · 4936 · 3836 2536 · 4123

the law." ¶ **14** Just as Paul was about to speak, Gallio said to the Jews,
τὸν νόμον δὲ → → ⌐τοῦ Παύλου⌐ → μέλλοντος ⌐ἀνοίγειν τὸ στόμα⌐ ὁ Γαλλίων εἶπεν πρὸς τοὺς Ἰουδαίους μὲν
d.asm n.asm · cj · d.gsm n.gsm · pt.pa.gsm · f.pa d.asn n.asn · d.nsm n.nsm · v.aai.3s p.a · d.apm a.apm · pl
3836 3795 · 1254 3516 · 3516 3836 4263 · 3516 · 487 3836 5125 · 3836 1136 · 3306 4639 · 3836 2681 · 3525

"If you Jews were making a complaint about some misdemeanor or serious crime, it would be reasonable
εἰ ὦ Ἰουδαῖοι ἦν τι ἀδίκημα ἢ πονηρὸν ῥᾳδιούργημα ἂν ⌐κατὰ λόγον⌐
cj j n.vpm v.iai.3s · r.nsn n.nsn · cj a.nsn n.nsn · pl · p.a n.asn
1623 6043 2681 1639 · 5516 93 · 2445 4505 4815 · 323 · 2848 3364

for me to listen to you. **15** But since it involves questions about words and names and your own law –
→ → ἀνεσχόμην ὑμῶν δὲ εἰ → ἐστιν ζητήματα περὶ λόγου καὶ ὀνομάτων καὶ ⌐τοῦ καθ' ὑμᾶς⌐ ← νόμου
v.ami.1s r.gp.2 · cj cj · v.pai.3s · n.npn · p.g n.gsm · cj n.gpn · cj · d.gsm p.a r.ap.2 · n.gsm
462 7007 · 1254 1623 · 1639 · 2427 · 4309 3364 · 2779 3950 · 2779 · 3836 2848 7007 · 3795

settle the matter yourselves. I will not be a judge of such things." **16** So he had them ejected from the
ὄψεσθε ← ← αὐτοί ἐγὼ βούλομαι οὐ εἶναι κριτὴς → τούτων ← καὶ → → αὐτοὺς ἀπήλασεν ἀπὸ τοῦ
v.fmi.2p · r.npm · r.ns.1 v.pmi.1s · pl f.pa · n.nsm · r.gpn · cj · r.apm.3 v.aai.3s · p.g d.gsn
3972 · 899 · 1609 1089 · 4024 1639 · 3216 · 4047 · 2779 · 899 590 · 608 3836

court. **17** Then they all turned on Sosthenes the synagogue ruler and beat him in front of the
βήματος δὲ → πάντες ἐπιλαβόμενοι ← Σωσθένην τὸν → ἀρχισυνάγωγον ἔτυπτον ἔμπροσθεν ← τοῦ
n.gsn · cj · a.npm pt.am.npm · n.asm d.asm · n.asm · v.iai.3p · p.g · d.gsn
1037 · 1254 · 2138 4246 · 5398 3836 · 801 · 5597 · 1869 · 3836

court. But Gallio showed no concern whatever.
βήματος καὶ ⌐τῷ Γαλλίωνι⌐ → οὐδὲν ἔμελεν τούτων
n.gsn · cj · d.dsm n.dsm · a.nsn · v.iai.3s · r.gpn
1037 · 2779 · 3836 1136 · 3508 4029 · 3508 · 4047

Priscilla, Aquila and Apollos

18:18 Paul stayed on in Corinth for some time. Then he left the brothers and sailed
δὲ Ὁ Παῦλος ἔτι προσμείνας ← → ἱκανὰς ἡμέρας → ἀποταξάμενος τοῖς ἀδελφοῖς ἐξέπλει
cj d.nsm n.nsm · adv pt.aa.nsm · a.apf n.apf · pt.am.nsm · d.dpm n.dpm · v.iai.3s
1254 3836 4263 · 2285 4693 · 2653 2465 · 698 · 3836 81 · 1739

for Syria, accompanied by Priscilla and Aquila. Before he sailed, he had his hair cut off
εἰς ⌐τὴν Συρίαν⌐ καὶ ⌐σὺν αὐτῷ⌐ Πρίσκιλλα καὶ Ἀκύλας → → → κειράμενος ← ⌐τὴν κεφαλήν⌐
p.a d.asf n.asf · cj p.d r.dsm.3 · n.nsf · cj n.nsm · pt.am.nsm · d.asf n.asf
1650 3836 5353 · 2779 5250 899 · 4572 · 2779 217 · 3025 · 3836 3051

at Cenchrea because of a vow he had taken. **19** They arrived at Ephesus, where Paul left Priscilla and
ἐν Κεγχρεαῖς γὰρ εὐχήν → → εἶχεν δὲ κατήντησαν εἰς Ἔφεσον αὐτοῦ κατέλιπεν κἀκείνους ←
p.d n.dpf · cj · n.asf · v.iai.3s · cj · v.aai.3p · p.a n.asf · adv · v.aai.3s · cj
1877 3020 · 1142 · 2376 · 2400 · 1254 · 2918 · 1650 2387 · 7008 · 2901 · 2797

Aquila. He himself went into the synagogue and reasoned with the Jews. **20** When they asked him to
← δὲ → αὐτὸς εἰσελθὼν εἰς τὴν συναγωγὴν διελέξατο τοῖς Ἰουδαίοις δὲ → αὐτῶν ἐρωτώντων →
cj · r.nsm · pt.aa.nsm p.a · d.asf n.asf · v.ami.3s · d.dpm a.dpm · cj · r.gpm.3 pt.pa.gpm
1254 · 1656 899 · 1656 1650 · 3836 5252 · 1363 · 3836 2681 · 1254 · 2263 2263

spend more time with them, he declined. **21** But as he left, he promised, "I will come back
μεῖναι ἐπὶ πλείονα χρόνον → ⌐οὐκ ἐπένευσεν⌐ ἀλλὰ → → ἀποταξάμενος καὶ → εἰπών ἀνακάμψω πάλιν
f.aa p.a a.asm.c n.asm · pl v.aai.3s · cj · pt.am.nsm cj · pt.aa.nsm · v.fai.1s adv
3531 2093 4498 5989 · 4024 2153 · 247 · 698 2779 · 3306 · 366 4099

if it is God's will." Then he set sail from Ephesus. **22** When he landed at Caesarea, he
πρὸς ὑμᾶς → → ⌐τοῦ θεοῦ⌐ θέλοντος → ἀνήχθη ἀπὸ ⌐τῆς Ἐφέσου⌐ καὶ → κατελθὼν εἰς Καισάρειαν →
p.a r.ap.2 · d.gsm n.gsm pt.pa.gsm · v.api.3s · p.g d.gsf n.gsf · cj · pt.aa.nsm p.a n.asf
4639 7007 2527 2527 · 3836 2536 2527 · 343 · 608 3836 2387 · 2779 · 2982 1650 2791

λόγον τοῦ θεοῦ. ¶ 12 Γαλλίωνος δὲ ἀνθυπάτου ὄντος τῆς Ἀχαΐας κατεπέστησαν ὁμοθυμαδὸν οἱ Ἰουδαῖοι τῷ Παύλῳ καὶ ἤγαγον αὐτὸν ἐπὶ τὸ βῆμα 13 λέγοντες ὅτι Παρὰ τὸν νόμον ἀναπείθει οὗτος τοὺς ἀνθρώπους σέβεσθαι τὸν θεόν. ¶ 14 μέλλοντος δὲ τοῦ Παύλου ἀνοίγειν τὸ στόμα εἶπεν ὁ Γαλλίων πρὸς τοὺς Ἰουδαίους, Εἰ μὲν ἦν ἀδίκημά τι ἢ ῥᾳδιούργημα πονηρόν, ὦ Ἰουδαῖοι, κατὰ λόγον ἂν ἀνεσχόμην ὑμῶν, 15 εἰ δὲ ζητήματά ἐστιν περὶ λόγου καὶ ὀνομάτων καὶ νόμου τοῦ καθ' ὑμᾶς, ὄψεσθε αὐτοί· κριτὴς ἐγὼ τούτων οὐ βούλομαι εἶναι. 16 καὶ ἀπήλασεν αὐτοὺς ἀπὸ τοῦ βήματος. 17 ἐπιλαβόμενοι δὲ πάντες Σωσθένην τὸν ἀρχισυνάγωγον ἔτυπτον ἔμπροσθεν τοῦ βήματος· καὶ οὐδὲν τούτων τῷ Γαλλίωνι ἔμελεν.
18:18 Ὁ δὲ Παῦλος ἔτι προσμείνας ἡμέρας ἱκανὰς τοῖς ἀδελφοῖς ἀποταξάμενος ἐξέπλει εἰς τὴν Συρίαν, καὶ σὺν αὐτῷ Πρίσκιλλα καὶ Ἀκύλας, κειράμενος ἐν Κεγχρεαῖς τὴν κεφαλήν, εἶχεν γὰρ εὐχήν. 19 κατήντησαν δὲ εἰς Ἔφεσον, κἀκείνους κατέλιπεν αὐτοῦ, αὐτὸς δὲ εἰσελθὼν εἰς τὴν συναγωγὴν διελέξατο τοῖς Ἰουδαίοις. 20 ἐρωτώντων δὲ αὐτῶν ἐπὶ πλείονα χρόνον μεῖναι οὐκ ἐπένευσεν, 21 ἀλλὰ ἀποταξάμενος καὶ εἰπών, Πάλιν ἀνακάμψω πρὸς ὑμᾶς τοῦ θεοῦ θέλοντος, ἀνήχθη ἀπὸ τῆς Ἐφέσου, 22 καὶ κατελθὼν εἰς Καισάρειαν, ἀναβὰς καὶ ἀσπασάμενος τὴν ἐκκλησίαν κατέβη εἰς Ἀντιόχειαν. ¶ 23 καὶ ποιήσας

went up and greeted the church and then went down to Antioch. ¶ **23** After spending some time
ἀναβὰς ← καὶ ἀσπασάμενος τὴν ἐκκλησίαν κατέβη εἰς Ἀντιόχειαν Καὶ → ποιήσας τινὰ χρόνον
pt.aa.nsm cj pt.am.nsm d.asf n.asf v.aai.3s p.a n.asf cj pt.aa.nsm r.asm n.asm
326 2779 832 3836 1711 2849 1650 522 2779 4472 5516 5989

in Antioch, Paul set out from there and traveled from place to place throughout the region of Galatia and
ἐξῆλθεν ← διερχόμενος καθεξῆς ← ← ↑ τὴν χώραν Γαλατικὴν καὶ
v.aai.3s pt.pm.nsm adv d.asf n.asf a.asf cj
2002 1451 2759 1451 3836 6001 1131 2779

Phrygia, strengthening all the disciples. ¶ **24** Meanwhile a Jew named Apollos, a native of
Φρυγίαν ἐπιστηρίζων πάντας τοὺς μαθητάς δέ τις Ἰουδαῖος ὀνόματι Ἀπολλῶς τῷ γένει
n.asf pt.pa.nsm a.apm d.apm n.apm cj r.nsm n.nsm n.dsn n.nsm d.dsn n.dsn
5867 2185 4246 3836 3412 1254 5516 2681 3950 663 3836 1169

Alexandria, came to Ephesus. He was a learned man, with a thorough knowledge of the Scriptures. **25** He
Ἀλεξανδρεὺς κατήντησεν εἰς Ἔφεσον λόγιος ἀνὴρ δυνατὸς ὢν ἐν ταῖς γραφαῖς οὗτος
n.nsm v.aai.3s p.a n.asf a.nsm n.nsm a.nsm pt.pa.nsm p.d d.dpf n.dpf r.nsm
233 2918 1650 2387 3360 467 1543 1639 1877 3836 1210 4047

had been instructed in the way of the Lord, and he spoke with great fervor and taught about
→ ἦν κατηχημένος ← τὴν ὁδὸν → τοῦ κυρίου καὶ ἐλάλει ζέων τῷ πνεύματι καὶ ἐδίδασκεν τὰ περὶ
v.iai.3s pt.rp.nsm d.asf n.asf d.gsm n.gsm cj v.iai.3s pt.pa.nsm d.dsn n.dsn cj v.iai.3s d.apn p.g
1639 2994 3836 3847 3836 3261 2779 3281 2417 3836 4460 2779 1438 3836 4309

Jesus accurately, though he knew only the baptism of John. **26** He began to speak boldly in
τοῦ Ἰησοῦ ἀκριβῶς → → ἐπιστάμενος μόνον τὸ βάπτισμα → Ἰωάννου τε οὗτος ἤρξατο → παρρησιάζεσθαι ← ἐν
d.gsm n.gsm adv pt.pp.nsm adv d.asn n.asn n.gsm cj r.nsm v.ami.3s f.pm p.d
3836 2652 209 2179 3667 3836 967 2722 5445 4047 806 4245 1877

the synagogue. When Priscilla and Aquila heard him, they invited him to their home and explained
τῇ συναγωγῇ δέ → Πρίσκιλλα καὶ Ἀκύλας ἀκούσαντες αὐτοῦ → προσελάβοντο αὐτὸν ↑ ← καὶ ἐξέθεντο
d.dsf n.dsf cj n.nsf cj n.nsm pt.aa.npm r.gsm.3 v.ami.3p r.asm.3 cj v.ami.3p
3836 5252 1254 201 4572 2779 217 201 899 4689 899 4689 4689 4689 2779 1758

to him the way of God more adequately. ¶ **27** When Apollos wanted to go to Achaia, the
→ αὐτῷ τὴν ὁδὸν → τοῦ θεοῦ → ἀκριβέστερον δέ → αὐτοῦ βουλομένου → διελθεῖν εἰς τὴν Ἀχαΐαν οἱ
r.dsm.3 d.asf n.asf d.gsm n.gsm adv.c cj r.gsm.3 pt.pm.gsm f.aa p.a d.asf n.asf d.npm
899 3836 3847 3836 2536 209 1254 1089 899 1089 1451 1650 3836 938 3836

brothers encouraged him and wrote to the disciples there to welcome him. On arriving, he was a great
ἀδελφοὶ προτρεψάμενοι ἔγραψαν → τοῖς μαθηταῖς → ἀποδέξασθαι αὐτόν → παραγενόμενος ὃς → πολὺ
n.npm pt.am.npm v.aai.3p d.dpm n.dpm f.am r.asm.3 pt.am.nsm r.nsm adv
81 4730 1211 3836 3412 4134 4005 5202 4498

help to those who by grace had believed. **28** For he vigorously refuted the Jews in public
συνεβάλετο → τοῖς ← διὰ τῆς χάριτος → πεπιστευκόσιν γὰρ εὐτόνως διακατηλέγχετο τοῖς Ἰουδαίοις δημοσίᾳ
v.ami.3s d.dpm p.g d.gsf n.gsf pt.ra.dpm cj adv v.imi.3s d.dpm a.dpm a.dsf
5202 3836 1328 3836 5921 4409 1142 1352 2364 1352 3836 2681 1323

debate, proving from the Scriptures that Jesus was the Christ.
ἐπιδεικνὺς διὰ τῶν γραφῶν Ἰησοῦν εἶναι τὸν χριστὸν
pt.pa.nsm p.g d.gpf n.gpf n.asm f.pa d.asm n.asm
2109 1328 3836 1210 2652 1639 3836 5986

Paul in Ephesus

19:1 While Apollos was at Corinth, Paul took the road through the interior and
δέ Ἐγένετο ἐν τὸν Ἀπολλῶ τῷ εἶναι ἐν Κορίνθῳ Παῦλον διελθόντα ← τὰ ἀνωτερικὰ μέρη
cj v.ami.3s p.d d.asm n.asm d.dsn f.pa p.d n.dsf n.asm pt.aa.asm d.apn a.apn n.apn
1254 1181 1877 3836 663 3836 1639 1877 3172 4263 1451 3836 541 3538

arrived at Ephesus. There he found some disciples **2** and asked them, "Did you receive the Holy Spirit
κατελθεῖν εἰς Ἔφεσον καὶ εὑρεῖν τινας μαθητάς τε εἶπεν πρὸς αὐτοὺς εἰ → ἐλάβετε ἅγιον πνεῦμα
f.aa p.a n.asf cj f.aa r.apm n.apm cj v.aai.3s p.a r.apm.3 cj v.aai.2p a.asn n.asn
2982 1650 2387 2779 2351 5516 3412 5445 3306 4639 899 1623 3284 41 4460

when you believed?" They answered, "No, we have not even heard that there is a Holy Spirit."
→ → πιστεύσαντες δέ οἱ πρὸς αὐτὸν ἀλλ' → → οὐδ' ἠκούσαμεν εἰ → ἔστιν ἅγιον πνεῦμα
pt.aa.npm cj d.npm p.a r.asm.3 cj adv v.aai.1p cj v.pai.3s a.nsn n.nsn
4409 1254 3836 4639 899 247 201 201 4028 201 1623 1639 41 4460

χρόνον τινὰ ἐξῆλθεν διερχόμενος καθεξῆς τὴν Γαλατικὴν χώραν καὶ Φρυγίαν, ἐπιστηρίζων πάντας τοὺς μαθητάς. ¶ **24** Ἰουδαῖος δέ τις Ἀπολλῶς ὀνόματι, Ἀλεξανδρεὺς τῷ γένει, ἀνὴρ λόγιος, κατήντησεν εἰς Ἔφεσον, δυνατὸς ὢν ἐν ταῖς γραφαῖς. **25** οὗτος ἦν κατηχημένος τὴν ὁδὸν τοῦ κυρίου καὶ ζέων τῷ πνεύματι ἐλάλει καὶ ἐδίδασκεν ἀκριβῶς τὰ περὶ τοῦ Ἰησοῦ, ἐπιστάμενος μόνον τὸ βάπτισμα Ἰωάννου· **26** οὗτός τε ἤρξατο παρρησιάζεσθαι ἐν τῇ συναγωγῇ. ἀκούσαντες δὲ αὐτοῦ Πρίσκιλλα καὶ Ἀκύλας προσελάβοντο αὐτὸν καὶ ἀκριβέστερον αὐτῷ ἐξέθεντο τὴν ὁδὸν [τοῦ θεοῦ]. ¶ **27** βουλομένου δὲ αὐτοῦ διελθεῖν εἰς τὴν Ἀχαΐαν, προτρεψάμενοι οἱ ἀδελφοὶ ἔγραψαν τοῖς μαθηταῖς ἀποδέξασθαι αὐτόν, ὃς παραγενόμενος συνεβάλετο πολὺ τοῖς πεπιστευκόσιν διὰ τῆς χάριτος· **28** εὐτόνως γὰρ τοῖς Ἰουδαίοις διακατηλέγχετο δημοσίᾳ ἐπιδεικνὺς διὰ τῶν γραφῶν εἶναι τὸν Χριστὸν Ἰησοῦν.

19:1 Ἐγένετο δὲ ἐν τῷ τὸν Ἀπολλῶ εἶναι ἐν Κορίνθῳ Παῦλον διελθόντα τὰ ἀνωτερικὰ μέρη [κατ]ελθεῖν εἰς Ἔφεσον καὶ εὑρεῖν τινας μαθητάς **2** εἶπέν τε πρὸς αὐτούς, Εἰ πνεῦμα ἅγιον ἐλάβετε πιστεύσαντες; οἱ δὲ πρὸς αὐτόν, Ἀλλ' οὐδ' εἰ πνεῦμα ἅγιον ἔστιν

¶ **3** So Paul asked, "Then   what baptism   did you receive?"   "John's baptism,"   they replied. ¶
τε   εἶπεν   οὖν   εἰς   τί   ἐβαπτίσθητε ← ←   δὲ   εἰς   Ἰωάννου   ⌞τὸ βάπτισμα⌟   οἱ   εἶπαν
cj   v.aai.3s   cj   p.a   r.asn   v.api.2p   cj   p.a   n.gsm   d.asn n.asn   d.npm   v.aai.3p
5445   3306   4036   1650   5515   966   1254   1650   2722   3836 967   3836   3306

4 Paul   said, "John's   baptism was   a baptism   of repentance.   He told   the people   to   believe   in   the one
δὲ   Παῦλος   εἶπεν   Ἰωάννης   ἐβάπτισεν   βάπτισμα →   μετανοίας   →   λέγων   τῷ λαῷ   ἵνα   πιστεύσωσιν   εἰς   τὸν
cj   n.nsm   v.aai.3s   n.nsm   v.aai.3s   n.asn   n.gsf   pt.pa.nsm   d.dsm n.dsm   cj   v.aas.3p   p.a   d.asm
1254   4263   3306   2722   966   967   3567   3306   3836 3295   2671   4409   1650   3836

coming   after him,   that is,   in Jesus."   **5**   On hearing   this, they were baptized   into   the   name of the Lord
ἐρχόμενον   μετ᾽   αὐτὸν   τοῦτ᾽ ἔστιν   εἰς   ⌞τὸν Ἰησοῦν⌟   δὲ   ἀκούσαντες   ἐβαπτίσθησαν   εἰς   τὸ   ὄνομα →   τοῦ κυρίου
pt.pm.asm   p.a   r.asm.3   r.nsn v.pai.3s   p.a   d.asn n.asn   cj   pt.aa.npm   v.api.3p   p.a   d.asn   n.asn   d.gsm n.gsm
2262   3552   899   4047 1639   1650   3836 2652   1254   201   966   1650   3836   3950   3836 3261

Jesus.   **6**   When Paul   placed   his hands   on them,   the Holy   Spirit came   on them,   and they spoke   in
Ἰησοῦ   καὶ →   ⌞τοῦ Παύλου⌟   ἐπιθέντος   τὰς χεῖρας →   αὐτοῖς   τὸ ⌞τὸ ἅγιον⌟   πνεῦμα ἦλθε   ἐπ᾽ αὐτούς   τε   ἐλάλουν →
n.gsm   cj   d.gsm n.gsm   pt.aa.gsm   d.apf n.apf   r.dpm.3   d.nsn d.nsn a.nsn   n.nsn v.aai.3s   p.a r.apm.3   cj   v.iai.3p
2652   2779 2202   3836 4263   2202   3836 5931   899   3836 3836 41   4460 2093   899 5445   5445   3281

tongues   and prophesied.   **7**   There were about   twelve   men   in all.   ¶   **8**   Paul entered   the
γλώσσαις   καὶ   ἐπροφήτευον   δὲ →   ἦσαν ὡσεὶ   δώδεκα   ἄνδρες   ⌞οἱ πάντες⌟   δὲ   Εἰσελθὼν εἰς   τὴν
n.dpf   cj   v.iai.3p   cj   v.iai.3p ὡσεὶ   a.npm   n.npm   d.npm a.npm   cj   pt.aa.nsm   p.a   d.asf
1185   2779   4736   1254   1639 6059   1557   467   3836 4246   1254   1656   1650   3836

synagogue and spoke   boldly there for three months,   arguing   persuasively   about the kingdom of
συναγωγὴν   ἐπαρρησιάζετο ←   ἐπὶ τρεῖς   μῆνας   διαλεγόμενος   καὶ πείθων   [τὰ]   περὶ   τῆς βασιλείας →
n.asf   v.imi.3s   p.a a.apm   n.apm   pt.pm.nsm   cj pt.pa.nsm   d.apn   p.g   d.gsf n.gsf
5252   4245   2093 5552   3604   1363   2779 4275   3836   4309   3836 993

God.   **9** But   some of them became obstinate;   they refused to believe and publicly   maligned
⌞τοῦ θεοῦ⌟   δὲ ὡς   τινες ← ←   ἐσκληρύνοντο καὶ →   ἠπείθουν ← ←   ἐνώπιον τοῦ πλήθους   κακολογοῦντες
d.gsm n.gsm   cj r.npm   v.ipi.3p   cj   v.iai.3p   p.g   d.gsn n.gsn   pt.pa.npm
3836 2536   1254 6055 5516   5020   2779   578   1967   3836 4436   2800

the Way. So Paul left   them. He took   the disciples with him and had   discussions   daily   in   the
τὴν ὁδὸν   ἀποστὰς ἀπ᾽ αὐτῶν →   ἀφώρισεν τοὺς μαθητὰς   →   διαλεγόμενος   ⌞καθ᾽ ἡμέραν⌟   ἐν   τῇ
d.asf n.asf   pt.aa.nsm p.g r.gpm.3   v.aai.3s   d.apm n.apm   pt.pm.nsm   p.a n.asf   p.d   d.dsf
3836 3847   923 608 899   928   3836 3412   1363   2848 2465   1877   3836

lecture hall   of Tyrannus.   **10**   This went   on for two years, so   that all   the Jews   and Greeks who
→   σχολῇ →   Τυράννου   δὲ   τοῦτο ἐγένετο ←   ἐπὶ δύο   ἔτη   ὥστε ←   πάντας τε   Ἰουδαίους   καὶ Ἕλληνας τοὺς
n.dsf   n.gsm   cj   r.nsn v.ami.3s   p.a a.apn   n.apn   cj   a.apm τε   a.apm   cj n.apm   d.apm
5391   5598   1254   4047 1181   2093 1545   2291   6063   4246 5445   2681   2779 1818   3836

lived   in the province of Asia   heard   the word of the Lord.   ¶   **11**   God   did   extraordinary
κατοικοῦντας ←   τὴν →   Ἀσίαν   ἀκοῦσαι   τὸν λόγον →   τοῦ κυρίου   τε   ⌞ὁ θεὸς⌟   ἐποίει   ⌞οὐ τὰς τυχούσας⌟
pt.pa.apm   d.asf   n.asf   f.aa   d.asn n.asn   d.gsm n.gsm   cj   d.nsm n.nsm   v.iai.3s   pl   d.apf pt.aa.apf
2997   3836   823   201   3836 3364   3836 3261   5445   3836 2536   4472   4024 3836 5593

miracles through   Paul,   **12** so   that even handkerchiefs and aprons   that had touched   him   were
Δυνάμεις   διὰ   τῶν χειρῶν Παύλου   ὥστε ←   καὶ σουδάρια   ἢ σιμικίνθια   ⌞ἀπὸ τοῦ χρωτὸς⌟ αὐτοῦ →
n.apf   p.g   d.gpf n.gpf n.gsm   cj   adv n.apn   n.apn   p.g d.gsm n.gsm   r.gsm.3
1539   1328   3836 5931 4263   6063   2779 5051   2445 4980   608 3836 5999   899

taken   to the sick,   and their illnesses were cured   and the evil   spirits left   them.
ἀποφέρεσθαι   ἐπὶ τοὺς ἀσθενοῦντας   καὶ τὰς νόσους   →   ἀπαλλάσσεσθαι τε   τὰ ⌞τὰ πονηρὰ⌟ πνεύματα   ἐκπορεύεσθαι ἀπ᾽ αὐτῶν
f.pp   p.a d.apm pt.pa.apm   cj d.apf n.apf   f.pp   τε   d.apn d.apn a.apn n.apn   f.pm   p.g r.gpm.3
708   2093 3836 820   2779 3836 3798   557   5445   3836 3836 4505 4460   1744   608 899

¶   **13**   Some   Jews   who went   around   driving   out evil spirits   tried   to invoke   the name of
δὲ   τινες   καὶ Ἰουδαίων   →   περιερχομένων   ⌞τῶν ἐξορκιστῶν⌟   Ἐπεχείρησαν →   ὀνομάζειν   τὸ ὄνομα →
cj   r.npm   adv a.gpm   pt.pm.gpm   d.gpm n.gpm   v.aai.3p   f.pa   d.asn n.asn
1254   5516   2779 2681   4320   3836 2020   4505 4460   2217   3951   3836 3950

the Lord Jesus over those who were demon-possessed.   They would say,   "In the name of
τοῦ κυρίου Ἰησοῦ ἐπὶ τοὺς ← ←   ἔχοντας τὰ πνεύματα τὰ πονηρὰ →   →   λέγοντες
d.gsm n.gsm n.gsm p.a d.apm   pt.pa.apm d.apn n.apn d.apn a.apn   pt.pa.npm
3836 3261 2652 2093 3836   2400 3836 4460 3836 4505   3306

ἠκούσαμεν. ¶ **3** εἶπέν τε, Εἰς τί οὖν ἐβαπτίσθητε; οἱ δὲ εἶπαν, Εἰς τὸ Ἰωάννου βάπτισμα. ¶ **4** εἶπεν δὲ Παῦλος, Ἰωάννης ἐβάπτισεν βάπτισμα μετανοίας τῷ λαῷ λέγων εἰς τὸν ἐρχόμενον μετ᾽ αὐτὸν ἵνα πιστεύσωσιν, τοῦτ᾽ ἔστιν εἰς τὸν Ἰησοῦν. **5** ἀκούσαντες δὲ ἐβαπτίσθησαν εἰς τὸ ὄνομα τοῦ κυρίου Ἰησοῦ, **6** καὶ ἐπιθέντος αὐτοῖς τοῦ Παύλου [τὰς] χεῖρας ἦλθε τὸ πνεῦμα τὸ ἅγιον ἐπ᾽ αὐτούς, ἐλάλουν τε γλώσσαις καὶ ἐπροφήτευον. **7** ἦσαν δὲ οἱ πάντες ἄνδρες ὡσεὶ δώδεκα. ¶ **8** Εἰσελθὼν δὲ εἰς τὴν συναγωγὴν ἐπαρρησιάζετο ἐπὶ μῆνας τρεῖς διαλεγόμενος καὶ πείθων [τὰ] περὶ τῆς βασιλείας τοῦ θεοῦ. **9** ὡς δέ τινες ἐσκληρύνοντο καὶ ἠπείθουν κακολογοῦντες τὴν ὁδὸν ἐνώπιον τοῦ πλήθους, ἀποστὰς ἀπ᾽ αὐτῶν ἀφώρισεν τοὺς μαθητὰς καθ᾽ ἡμέραν διαλεγόμενος ἐν τῇ σχολῇ Τυράννου. **10** τοῦτο δὲ ἐγένετο ἐπὶ ἔτη δύο, ὥστε πάντας τοὺς κατοικοῦντας τὴν Ἀσίαν ἀκοῦσαι τὸν λόγον τοῦ κυρίου, Ἰουδαίους τε καὶ Ἕλληνας. ¶ **11** Δυνάμεις τε οὐ τὰς τυχούσας ὁ θεὸς ἐποίει διὰ τῶν χειρῶν Παύλου, **12** ὥστε καὶ ἐπὶ τοὺς ἀσθενοῦντας ἀποφέρεσθαι ἀπὸ τοῦ χρωτὸς αὐτοῦ σουδάρια ἢ σιμικίνθια καὶ ἀπαλλάσσεσθαι ἀπ᾽ αὐτῶν τὰς νόσους, τά τε πνεύματα τὰ πονηρὰ ἐκπορεύεσθαι. ¶ **13** ἐπεχείρησαν δέ τινες καὶ τῶν περιερχομένων Ἰουδαίων ἐξορκιστῶν ὀνομάζειν ἐπὶ τοὺς ἔχοντας τὰ πνεύματα τὰ πονηρὰ τὸ ὄνομα τοῦ κυρίου Ἰησοῦ λέγοντες, Ὁρκίζω ὑμᾶς τὸν Ἰησοῦν

Jesus, whom Paul preaches, I command you to come out." **14** Seven sons of Sceva, a Jewish chief
τὸν Ἰησοῦν, ὃν Παῦλος κηρύσσει → ὁρκίζω ὑμᾶς δὲ ἑπτὰ υἱοὶ → τινος Σκευᾶ Ἰουδαίου →
d.asm n.asm r.asm n.nsm v.pai.3s v.pai.1s r.ap.2 cj a.npm n.npm r.gsm n.gsm a.gsm
3836 2652 4005 4263 3062 3991 7007 1254 2231 5626 5516 5005 2681

priest, were doing this. **15** One day the evil spirit answered them, "Jesus I know,
ἀρχιερέως ἦσαν ποιοῦντες τοῦτο δὲ τὸ τὸ πονηρὸν πνεῦμα ἀποκριθὲν εἶπεν αὐτοῖς [μὲν] τὸν Ἰησοῦν, → γινώσκω
n.gsm v.iai.3p pt.pa.npm r.asn cj d.nsn d.nsn a.nsn n.nsn pt.ap.nsn v.aai.3s r.dpm.3 pl d.asm n.asm v.pai.1s
797 1639 4472 4047 1254 3836 3836 4505 4460 646 3306 899 3525 3836 2652 1182

and I know about Paul, but who are you?" **16** Then the man who had the evil spirit
καὶ → ἐπίσταμαι ← τὸν Παῦλον, δὲ τίνες ἐστέ ὑμεῖς καὶ ὁ ἄνθρωπος → ἐν ᾧ ἦν τὸ τὸ πονηρὸν πνεῦμα
cj v.ppi.1s d.asm n.asm cj r.npm v.pai.2p r.np.2 cj d.nsm n.nsm p.d r.dsm v.iai.3s d.nsn d.nsn a.nsn n.nsn
2779 2179 3836 4263 1254 5515 1639 7007 2779 3836 476 1877 4005 1639 3836 3836 4505 4460

jumped on them and overpowered them all. He gave them such a beating that they ran out of
ἐφαλόμενος ἐπ᾽ αὐτοὺς κατακυριεύσας ἀμφοτέρων → → κατ᾽ αὐτῶν ἴσχυσεν ὥστε → ἐκφυγεῖν ἐκ ←
pt.am.nsm p.a r.apm.3 pt.aa.nsm a.gpm p.g r.gpm.3 v.aai.3s cj f.aa p.g
2383 2093 899 2894 317 2710 2710 2848 899 2710 6063 1767 1666

the house naked and bleeding. ¶ **17** When this became known to the Jews and
ἐκείνου τοῦ οἴκου, γυμνοὺς καὶ τετραυματισμένους δὲ τοῦτο ἐγένετο γνωστὸν → πᾶσίν τε Ἰουδαίοις καὶ
r.gsm d.gsm n.gsm a.apm cj pt.rp.npm cj r.nsn v.ami.3s a.nsn a.dpm cj a.dpm cj
1697 3836 3875 1218 2779 5547 1254 4047 1181 1196 2681 4246 5445 2681 2779

Greeks living in Ephesus, they were all seized with fear, and the name of the Lord Jesus
Ἕλλησιν τοῖς κατοικοῦσιν ← τὴν Ἔφεσον καὶ αὐτοὺς → ἐπὶ πάντας ἐπέπεσεν φόβος καὶ τὸ ὄνομα → τοῦ κυρίου Ἰησοῦ
n.dpm d.dpm pt.pa.dpm d.asf n.asf cj r.apm.3 p.a a.apm v.aai.3s n.nsm cj d.nsn n.nsn d.gsm n.gsm n.gsm
1818 3836 2997 3836 2387 2779 899 2158 2093 4246 2158 5832 2779 3836 3950 3836 3261 2652

was held in high honor. **18** Many of those who believed now came and openly confessed
→ → → → ἐμεγαλύνετο τε Πολλοί → τῶν ← πεπιστευκότων ἤρχοντο ἀναγγέλλοντες καὶ ἐξομολογούμενοι
v.ipi.3s te a.npm d.gpm pt.ra.gpm v.imi.3p pt.pa.npm cj pt.pm.npm
3486 5445 4498 3836 4409 2262 334 2779 2018

their evil deeds. **19** A number who had practiced sorcery brought their scrolls together and burned
αὐτῶν τὰς πράξεις, δὲ ἱκανοὶ τῶν → πραξάντων τὰ περίεργα, συνενέγκαντες τὰς βίβλους ← κατέκαιον
r.gpm.3 d.apf n.apf cj a.npm d.gpm pt.aa.gpm d.apn n.apn pt.aa.npm d.apf n.apf v.iai.3p
899 3836 4552 1254 2653 3836 4556 3836 4319 5237 3836 1047 5237 2876

them publicly. When they calculated the value of the scrolls, the total came to fifty
ἐνώπιον πάντων, καὶ → συνεψήφισαν τὰς τιμὰς → αὐτῶν καὶ → εὗρον ἀργυρίου μυριάδας πέντε
p.g a.gpm cj v.aai.3p d.apf n.apf r.gpf.3 cj v.aai.3p n.gsn n.apf a.apf
1967 4246 2779 5248 3836 5507 899 2779 2351 736 3689 4297

thousand drachmas. **20** In this way the word of the Lord spread widely and grew in power. ¶ **21** After all
→ οὕτως ὁ λόγος → τοῦ κυρίου ηὔξανεν ← καὶ ἴσχυεν κατὰ κράτος δὲ Ὡς
adv d.nsm n.nsm d.gsm n.gsm v.iai.3s cj v.iai.3s p.a n.asn cj cj
4048 3836 3364 3836 3261 889 2779 2710 2848 3197 1254 6055

this had happened, Paul decided to go to Jerusalem, passing through Macedonia and
ταῦτα → ἐπληρώθη ὁ Παῦλος, ἔθετο ἐν τῷ πνεύματι → πορεύεσθαι εἰς Ἱεροσόλυμα διελθὼν ← τὴν Μακεδονίαν, καὶ
r.npn v.api.3s d.nsm n.nsm v.ami.3s p.d d.dsn n.dsn f.pm p.a n.apn pt.aa.nsm d.asf n.asf cj
4047 4444 3836 4263 5502 1877 3836 4460 4513 1650 2642 1451 3836 3423 2779

Achaia. "After I have been there," he said, "I must visit Rome also." **22** He sent two of his
Ἀχαΐαν ὅτι μετὰ με → τὸ γενέσθαι ἐκεῖ → εἰπὼν δεῖ ἰδεῖν Ῥώμην καὶ δὲ ἀποστείλας δύο → αὐτῷ
n.asf cj p.a r.as.1 d.asn f.am adv pt.aa.nsm r.as.1 v.pai.3s f.aa n.asf adv cj pt.aa.nsm a.apm r.dsm.3
938 4022 3552 1609 3836 1181 1695 3306 1609 1256 1625 4873 2779 1254 690 1545 1354 899

helpers, Timothy and Erastus, to Macedonia, while he stayed in the province of Asia a little longer.
τῶν διακονούντων, Τιμόθεον καὶ Ἔραστον εἰς τὴν Μακεδονίαν, αὐτὸς ἐπέσχεν εἰς τὴν → → Ἀσίαν χρόνον
d.gpm pt.pa.gpm n.asm cj n.asm p.a d.asf n.asf r.nsm v.aai.3s p.a d.asf n.asf n.asm
3836 1354 5510 2779 2235 1650 3836 3423 899 2091 1650 3836 823 5989

The Riot in Ephesus

19:23 About that time there arose a great disturbance about the Way. **24** A silversmith
δὲ κατὰ ἐκεῖνον τὸν καιρόν, → Ἐγένετο οὐκ ὀλίγος, τάραχος περὶ τῆς ὁδοῦ. γάρ τις ἀργυροκόπος
cj p.a r.asm d.asm n.asm v.ami.3s pl a.nsm n.nsm p.g d.gsf n.gsf cj r.nsm n.nsm
1254 2848 1697 3836 2789 1181 4024 3900 5431 4309 3836 3847 1142 5516 737

ὃν Παῦλος κηρύσσει. ¹⁴ ἦσαν δέ τινος Σκευᾶ Ἰουδαίου ἀρχιερέως ἑπτὰ υἱοὶ τοῦτο ποιοῦντες. ¹⁵ ἀποκριθὲν δὲ τὸ πνεῦμα τὸ πονηρὸν εἶπεν αὐτοῖς, Τὸν [μὲν] Ἰησοῦν γινώσκω καὶ τὸν Παῦλον ἐπίσταμαι, ὑμεῖς δὲ τίνες ἐστέ; ¹⁶ καὶ ἐφαλόμενος ὁ ἄνθρωπος ἐπ᾽ αὐτοὺς ἐν ᾧ ἦν τὸ πνεῦμα τὸ πονηρόν, κατακυριεύσας ἀμφοτέρων ἴσχυσεν κατ᾽ αὐτῶν ὥστε γυμνοὺς καὶ τετραυματισμένους ἐκφυγεῖν ἐκ τοῦ οἴκου ἐκείνου. ¶ ¹⁷ τοῦτο δὲ ἐγένετο γνωστὸν πᾶσιν Ἰουδαίοις τε καὶ Ἕλλησιν τοῖς κατοικοῦσιν τὴν Ἔφεσον καὶ ἐπέπεσεν φόβος ἐπὶ πάντας αὐτοὺς καὶ ἐμεγαλύνετο τὸ ὄνομα τοῦ κυρίου Ἰησοῦ. ¹⁸ πολλοί τε τῶν πεπιστευκότων ἤρχοντο ἐξομολογούμενοι καὶ ἀναγγέλλοντες τὰς πράξεις αὐτῶν. ¹⁹ ἱκανοὶ δὲ τῶν τὰ περίεργα πραξάντων συνενέγκαντες τὰς βίβλους κατέκαιον ἐνώπιον πάντων, καὶ συνεψήφισαν τὰς τιμὰς αὐτῶν καὶ εὗρον ἀργυρίου μυριάδας πέντε. ²⁰ Οὕτως κατὰ κράτος τοῦ κυρίου ὁ λόγος ηὔξανεν καὶ ἴσχυεν. ¶ ²¹ Ὡς δὲ ἐπληρώθη ταῦτα, ἔθετο ὁ Παῦλος ἐν τῷ πνεύματι διελθὼν τὴν Μακεδονίαν καὶ Ἀχαΐαν πορεύεσθαι εἰς Ἱεροσόλυμα εἰπὼν ὅτι Μετὰ τὸ γενέσθαι με ἐκεῖ δεῖ με καὶ Ῥώμην ἰδεῖν. ²² ἀποστείλας δὲ εἰς τὴν Μακεδονίαν δύο τῶν διακονούντων αὐτῷ, Τιμόθεον καὶ Ἔραστον, αὐτὸς ἐπέσχεν χρόνον εἰς τὴν Ἀσίαν.

19:23 Ἐγένετο δὲ κατὰ τὸν καιρὸν ἐκεῖνον τάραχος οὐκ ὀλίγος περὶ τῆς ὁδοῦ. ²⁴ Δημήτριος γάρ τις ὀνόματι, ἀργυροκόπος,

named Demetrius, who made silver shrines of Artemis, brought in no little business for the craftsmen. **25** He
ὀνόματι Δημήτριος → ποιῶν ἀργυροῦς ναοὺς → Ἀρτέμιδος παρείχετο ← οὐκ ὀλίγην ἐργασίαν → τοῖς τεχνίταις
n.dsn n.nsm   pt.pa.nsm a.apm n.apm   n.gsf v.imi.3s   pl a.asf n.asf   d.dpm n.dpm
3950 1320   4472 739 3724   783 4218   4024 3900 2238   3836 5493

called them together, along with the workmen in related trades, and said: "Men, you know we
συναθροίσας οὓς ← → καὶ ← τοὺς ἐργάτας περὶ τὰ τοιαῦτα → εἶπεν ἄνδρες → ἐπίστασθε ὅτι ἡμῖν
pt.aa.nsm r.apm   adv   d.apm n.apm p.a d.apn r.apn   v.aai.3s n.vpm   v.ppi.2p cj r.dp.1
5255 4005 5255 2779   3836 2239 4309 3836 5525   3306 467   2179 4022 7005

receive a good income from this business. **26** And you see and hear how this fellow Paul has
ἔστιν → ἡ εὐπορία ἐκ ταύτης τῆς ἐργασίας καὶ → θεωρεῖτε καὶ ἀκούετε ὅτι οὗτος ὁ Παῦλος →
v.pai.3s   d.nsf n.nsf p.g r.gsf d.gsf n.gsf cj   v.pai.2p cj v.pai.2p cj r.nsm d.nsm n.nsm
1639   3836 2345 1666 4047 3836 2238 2779   2555 2779 201 4022 4047 3836 4263

convinced and led astray large numbers of people here in Ephesus and in practically the whole
πείσας μετέστησεν ← ἱκανὸν ← ὄχλον οὐ μόνον → Ἐφέσου ἀλλὰ → σχεδὸν τῆς πάσης
pt.aa.nsm v.aai.3s   a.asm   n.asm pl adv   n.gsf cj   adv d.gsf a.gsf
4275 3496 2653 4063 4024 3667 2387 247 823 5385 3836 4246

province of Asia. He says that man-made gods are no gods at all. **27** There is danger not only
→ → Ἀσίας → λέγων ὅτι οἱ διὰ χειρῶν γινόμενοι εἰσὶν οὐκ θεοί δὲ → → κινδυνεύει οὐ μόνον
n.gsf   pt.pa.nsm cj d.npm p.g n.gpf pt.pm.npm v.pai.3p pl n.npm cj   v.pai.3s pl adv
823   3306 4022 3836 1328 5931 1181 1639 4024 2536 1254   3073 4024 3667

that our trade *will lose its good name,* but also that the temple of the great goddess
τοῦτο ἡμῖν τὸ μέρος εἰς ἀπελεγμὸν ἐλθεῖν ἀλλὰ καὶ τὸ ἱερὸν → τῆς μεγάλης θεᾶς
r.asn r.dp.1 d.asn n.asn p.a n.asm f.aa cj adv d.asn n.asn   d.gsf a.gsf n.gsf
4047 7005 3836 3538 1650 591 2262 247 2779 3836 2639   3836 3489 2516

Artemis *will be discredited,* and the goddess herself, who is worshiped throughout the province of
Ἀρτέμιδος εἰς οὐθὲν λογισθῆναι ἢν → σέβεται ὅλη ἡ →
n.gsf p.a a.asn f.ap r.asf v.pmi.3s a.nsf d.nsf
783 1650 4032 3357 4005 4936 3910 3836

Asia and the world, will be robbed of her divine majesty." ¶ **28** When they
Ἀσία καὶ ἡ οἰκουμένη τε μέλλειν καὶ → καθαιρεῖσθαι → τῆς αὐτῆς μεγαλειότητος δὲ
n.nsf cj d.nsf n.nsf cj f.pa adv f.pp d.gsf r.gsf.3 n.gsf cj
823 2779 3836 3876 5445 3516 2779 2747 3836 899 3484 1254

heard this, they were furious and began shouting: "Great is Artemis of the Ephesians!"
Ἀκούσαντες καὶ → γενόμενοι πλήρεις θυμοῦ → ἔκραζον λέγοντες μεγάλη ἡ Ἀρτεμις → Ἐφεσίων
pt.aa.npm cj   pt.am.npm a.npm n.gsm   v.iai.3p pt.pa.npm a.nsf d.nsf n.nsf   a.gpm
201 2779 1181 4441 2596 3189 3306 3489 783 2386

29 Soon the whole city was in an uproar. The people seized Gaius and Aristarchus, Paul's
καὶ ἡ πόλις → ἐπλήσθη τῆς συγχύσεως → → συναρπάσαντες Γάϊον καὶ Ἀρίσταρχον Παύλου
cj d.nsf n.nsf v.api.3s d.gsf n.gsf   pt.aa.npm n.asm cj n.asm n.gsm
2779 3836 4398 4484 4398 3836 5180 5275 1127 2779 752 4263

traveling companions from Macedonia, and rushed as one man into the theater. **30** Paul wanted to
→ συνεκδήμους Μακεδόνας τε ὥρμησαν ὁμοθυμαδὸν ← εἰς τὸ θέατρον δὲ Παύλου βουλομένου →
n.apm n.apm cj v.aai.3p adv p.a d.asn n.asn cj n.gsm pt.pm.gsm
5292 3424 5445 3994 3924 1650 3836 2519 1254 4263 1089

appear before the crowd, but the disciples would not let him. **31** Even some of the officials of the province,
εἰσελθεῖν εἰς τὸν δῆμον οἱ μαθηταί → οὐκ εἴων αὐτόν δὲ καὶ τινὲς → τῶν Ἀσιαρχῶν ← ←
f.aa p.a d.asm n.asm d.npm n.npm pl v.iai.3p r.asm.3 cj cj r.npm d.gpm n.gpm
1656 1650 3836 1322 3836 3412 1572 4024 1572 899 1254 2779 5516 3836 825

friends of Paul, sent him a message begging him not to venture into the theater. ¶
ὄντες φίλοι → αὐτῷ πέμψαντες πρὸς αὐτὸν παρεκάλουν μὴ δοῦναι ἑαυτὸν εἰς τὸ θέατρον
pt.pa.npm a.npm r.dsm.3 pt.aa.npm p.a r.asm.3 v.iai.3p pl f.aa r.asm.3 p.a d.asn n.asn
1639 5813 899 4287 4639 899 4151 1571 3590 1443 1571 1650 3836 2519

32 The assembly was in confusion: Some were shouting one thing, some another. Most of the
γὰρ ἡ ἐκκλησία ἦν συγκεχυμένη οὖν μὲν ἄλλοι → ἔκραζον τι ἄλλο καὶ οἱ πλείους ←
cj d.nsf n.nsf v.iai.3s pt.rp.nsf cj pl r.npm v.iai.3p r.asn r.asn cj d.npm a.npm.c
1142 3836 1711 1639 5177 4036 3525 257 3189 5516 257 2779 3836 4498

ποιῶν ναοὺς ἀργυροῦς Ἀρτέμιδος παρείχετο τοῖς τεχνίταις οὐκ ὀλίγην ἐργασίαν, **25** οὓς συναθροίσας καὶ τοὺς περὶ τὰ τοιαῦτα ἐργάτας εἶπεν, Ἄνδρες, ἐπίστασθε ὅτι ἐκ ταύτης τῆς ἐργασίας ἡ εὐπορία ἡμῖν ἐστιν **26** καὶ θεωρεῖτε καὶ ἀκούετε ὅτι οὐ μόνον Ἐφέσου ἀλλὰ σχεδὸν πάσης τῆς Ἀσίας ὁ Παῦλος οὗτος πείσας μετέστησεν ἱκανὸν ὄχλον λέγων ὅτι οὐκ εἰσὶν θεοὶ οἱ διὰ χειρῶν γινόμενοι. **27** οὐ μόνον δὲ τοῦτο κινδυνεύει ἡμῖν τὸ μέρος εἰς ἀπελεγμὸν ἐλθεῖν ἀλλὰ καὶ τὸ τῆς μεγάλης θεᾶς Ἀρτέμιδος ἱερὸν εἰς οὐθὲν λογισθῆναι, μέλλειν τε καὶ καθαιρεῖσθαι τῆς μεγαλειότητος αὐτῆς ἣν ὅλη ἡ Ἀσία καὶ ἡ οἰκουμένη σέβεται. ¶ **28** Ἀκούσαντες δὲ καὶ γενόμενοι πλήρεις θυμοῦ ἔκραζον λέγοντες, Μεγάλη ἡ Ἄρτεμις Ἐφεσίων. **29** καὶ ἐπλήσθη ἡ πόλις τῆς συγχύσεως, ὥρμησάν τε ὁμοθυμαδὸν εἰς τὸ θέατρον συναρπάσαντες Γάϊον καὶ Ἀρίσταρχον Μακεδόνας, συνεκδήμους Παύλου. **30** Παύλου δὲ βουλομένου εἰσελθεῖν εἰς τὸν δῆμον οὐκ εἴων αὐτὸν οἱ μαθηταί· **31** τινὲς δὲ καὶ τῶν Ἀσιαρχῶν, ὄντες αὐτῷ φίλοι, πέμψαντες πρὸς αὐτὸν παρεκάλουν μὴ δοῦναι ἑαυτὸν εἰς τὸ θέατρον. ¶ **32** ἄλλοι μὲν οὖν ἄλλο τι ἔκραζον· ἦν γὰρ ἡ

people did not even know   why   they were there.   33   The Jews   pushed   Alexander to the front,
←   ↱   οὐκ   ἤδεισαν ⌐τίνος ἕνεκα⌐ →   →   συνεληλύθεισαν δὲ τῶν Ἰουδαίων προβαλόντων αὐτὸν
pl   4024   v.lai.3p r.gsn p.g   v.lai.3p   cj d.gpm a.gpm pt.aa.gpm   r.asm.3
3857   3857   5515 1914   5302   1254 3836 2681   4582   899   4582 4582 4582

and some of the crowd shouted   instructions to him.   He   motioned   for silence in
ἐκ τοῦ ὄχλου συνεβίβασαν ←   ←   Ἀλέξανδρον δὲ ὁ Ἀλέξανδρος ⌐κατασείσας τὴν χεῖρα⌐ ←   ←
p.g d.gsn n.gsn v.aai.3p   n.asm   cj d.nsm n.nsm   pt.aa.nsm   d.asf n.asf
1666 3836 4063 5204   235   1254 3836 235   2939   3836 5931

order to make a defense   before the people. 34 But when they realized   he was a Jew,   they
ἤθελεν →   ἀπολογεῖσθαι →   τῷ δήμῳ   δὲ   ἐπιγνόντες ὅτι → ἐστιν Ἰουδαῖος φωνὴ ἐγένετο
v.iai.3s   f.pm   d.dsm n.dsm   cj   pt.aa.npm cj   v.pai.3s a.nsm   n.nsf v.ami.3s
2527   664   3836 1322   1254   2105   4022   1639   2681   5889 1181   3189

all shouted in unison   for about two hours: "Great is Artemis   of the Ephesians!" ¶   35 The city
↱ κραζόντων ⌐μία ἐκ πάντων⌐ ἐπὶ ὡς δύο ὥρας μεγάλη ⌐ἡ Ἄρτεμις⌐ → Ἐφεσίων   δὲ ὁ
pt.pa.gpm   a.nsf p.g a.gpm p.a pl a.apf n.apf a.nsf   d.nsf n.nsf   a.gpm   cj d.nsm
4246 3189   1651 1666 4246   2093 6055 1545 6052 3489   3836 783   2386   1254 3836

clerk   quieted   the crowd and said: "Men of Ephesus, doesn't all   the world   know
γραμματεὺς Καταστείλας τὸν ὄχλον   φησίν ἄνδρες Ἐφέσιοι γὰρ ⌐τίς ἐστιν ἀνθρώπων⌐   ὃς οὐ γινώσκει
n.nsm   pt.aa.nsm   d.asm n.asm   v.pai.3s n.vpm a.vpm cj   r.nsm v.pai.3s n.gpm   r.nsm pl v.pai.3s
1208   2948   3836 4063   5774   467   2386   1142 1182 5515 1639 476   4005 4024 1182

that the city of Ephesus is   the guardian of the temple of the great Artemis and of her image, which fell
τὴν πόλιν Ἐφεσίων οὖσαν   νεωκόρον   → τῆς μεγάλης Ἀρτέμιδος καὶ → τοῦ διοπετοῦς ←
d.asf n.asf a.gpm pt.pa.asf   n.asm   d.gsf a.gsm n.gsf   cj   d.gsn a.gsn
3836 4484 2386   1639   3753   3836 3489   783   2779   3836 1479

from heaven? 36 Therefore, since these facts are undeniable, you ought to be   quiet   and not
←   ←   οὖν   ↱ τούτων   ὄντων ἀναντιρρήτων ὑμᾶς ⌐δέον ἐστιν⌐ → ὑπάρχειν κατεσταλμένους καὶ μηδὲν
             cj   r.gpn   pt.pa.gpn a.gpn   r.ap.2 pt.pa.nsn v.pai.3s f.pa pt.rp.apm   cj cj
4036   1639   1639 394   7007 1256   1639 5639 2948   2779 3594

do anything rash. 37 You have brought these men   here, though they have neither robbed temples
πράσσειν ←   προπετές γὰρ   ἠγάγετε τούτους ⌐τοὺς ἄνδρας⌐   οὔτε ἱεροσύλους
f.pa   a.asn   cj   v.aai.2p r.apm   d.apm n.apm   cj   n.apm
4556 3594   4637   1142 72   4047   3836 467   4046 2645

nor blasphemed our goddess. 38 If, then, Demetrius and his fellow craftsmen have a grievance against
οὔτε βλασφημοῦντας ἡμῶν ⌐τὴν θεὸν⌐ μὲν εἰ οὖν Δημήτριος καὶ αὐτῷ σὺν ⌐οἱ τεχνῖται⌐ ἔχουσι λόγον πρός
cj   pt.pa.apm   r.gp.1 d.asf n.asf pl cj   cj   n.nsm   cj r.dsm.3 p.d d.npm n.npm v.pai.3p n.asm p.a
4046 1059   7005 3836 2536 3525 1623 4036 1320   2779 899 5250 3836 5493   2400   3364 4639

anybody, the courts are open   and there are proconsuls. They can press charges. 39 If there is
τινα   ἀγοραῖοι ἄγονται καὶ εἰσὶν ἀνθύπατοι   → ἐγκαλείτωσαν ἀλλήλοις δὲ εἰ
r.asm   n.npf   v.ppi.3p cj   v.pai.3p n.npm   v.pam.3p   r.dpm   cj cj
5516   61   772   2779 1639   478   1592   253   1254 1623

anything further you want to bring up, it must be settled in a legal assembly. 40 As it is, we are in
τι   περαιτέρω →   →   ἐπιζητεῖτε ←   →   ἐπιλυθήσεται ἐν ἐννόμῳ ⌐τῇ ἐκκλησίᾳ⌐ γὰρ καὶ ←   →   →
r.asn adv.c   v.pai.2p   v.fpi.3s   p.d a.dsf d.dsf n.dsf   cj adv
5516 4304   2118   2147   1877 1937 3836 1711   1142 2779

danger   of being charged with rioting because of today's   events. In that case we would not be able
κινδυνεύομεν → → ἐγκαλεῖσθαι → στάσεως περὶ ← ⌐τῆς σήμερον⌐   περὶ οὗ → ↱ οὐ → δυνησόμεθα
v.pai.1p   f.pp   n.gsf   p.g   d.gsf adv   p.g   r.gsn   pl   v.fmi.1p
3073   1592   5087   4309   3836 4958   4309 4005 1538 1538 4024 1538

to account   for this commotion, since there is no   reason for it." 41 After he had said this,
→ ἀποδοῦναι λόγον περὶ ταύτης ⌐τῆς συστροφῆς⌐   ὑπάρχοντος μηδενὸς αἰτίου   καὶ →   ↱   εἰπὼν ταῦτα
f.aa   n.asm p.g r.gsf d.gsf n.gsf   pt.pa.gsn a.gsn   n.gsn   cj   pt.aa.nsm r.apn
625   3364   4309 4047   3836 5371   5639   3594   165   2779   3306   4047

he dismissed the assembly.
→ ἀπέλυσεν τὴν ἐκκλησίαν
v.aai.3s   d.asf n.asf
668   3836 1711

ἐκκλησία συγκεχυμένη καὶ οἱ πλείους οὐκ ᾔδεισαν τίνος ἕνεκα συνεληλύθεισαν. ³³ ἐκ δὲ τοῦ ὄχλου συνεβίβασαν Ἀλέξανδρον, προβαλόντων αὐτὸν τῶν Ἰουδαίων· ὁ δὲ Ἀλέξανδρος κατασείσας τὴν χεῖρα ἤθελεν ἀπολογεῖσθαι τῷ δήμῳ. ³⁴ ἐπιγνόντες δὲ ὅτι Ἰουδαῖός ἐστιν, φωνὴ ἐγένετο μία ἐκ πάντων ὡς ἐπὶ ὥρας δύο κραζόντων, Μεγάλη ἡ Ἄρτεμις Ἐφεσίων. ¶ ³⁵ καταστείλας δὲ ὁ γραμματεὺς τὸν ὄχλον φησίν, Ἄνδρες Ἐφέσιοι, τίς γάρ ἐστιν ἀνθρώπων ὃς οὐ γινώσκει τὴν Ἐφεσίων πόλιν νεωκόρον οὖσαν τῆς μεγάλης Ἀρτέμιδος καὶ τοῦ διοπετοῦς; ³⁶ ἀναντιρρήτων οὖν ὄντων τούτων δέον ἐστὶν ὑμᾶς κατεσταλμένους ὑπάρχειν καὶ μηδὲν προπετὲς πράσσειν. ³⁷ ἠγάγετε γὰρ τοὺς ἄνδρας τούτους οὔτε ἱεροσύλους οὔτε βλασφημοῦντας τὴν θεὸν ἡμῶν. ³⁸ εἰ μὲν οὖν Δημήτριος καὶ οἱ σὺν αὐτῷ τεχνῖται ἔχουσι πρός τινα λόγον, ἀγοραῖοι ἄγονται καὶ ἀνθύπατοί εἰσιν, ἐγκαλείτωσαν ἀλλήλοις. ³⁹ εἰ δέ τι περαιτέρω ἐπιζητεῖτε, ἐν τῇ ἐννόμῳ ἐκκλησίᾳ ἐπιλυθήσεται. ⁴⁰ καὶ γὰρ κινδυνεύομεν ἐγκαλεῖσθαι στάσεως περὶ τῆς σήμερον, μηδενὸς αἰτίου ὑπάρχοντος περὶ οὗ [οὐ] δυνησόμεθα ἀποδοῦναι λόγον περὶ τῆς συστροφῆς ταύτης. καὶ ταῦτα εἰπὼν ἀπέλυσεν τὴν ἐκκλησίαν.

Through Macedonia and Greece

20:1

	When	the	uproar	had ended,		Paul		sent		for the	disciples	and,	after	encouraging
δὲ	Μετὰ	τὸν	θόρυβον	→	⌐τὸ παύσασθαι	ὁ	Παῦλος	μεταπεμψάμενος	←	τοὺς	μαθητὰς	καὶ		παρακαλέσας
cj	p.a	d.asm	n.asm		d.asn f.am	d.nsm	n.nsm	pt.am.nsm		d.apm	n.apm	cj		pt.aa.nsm
1254	3552	3836	2573		3836 4264	3836	4263	3569		3836	3412	2779		4151

them,	said good-by		and	set	out		for	Macedonia.	2	He	traveled	through	that	area,		speaking
→	ἀσπασάμενος	ἐξῆλθεν	←		πορεύεσθαι	εἰς	Μακεδονίαν	δὲ	διελθὼν			ἐκεῖνα	⌐τὰ μέρη	καὶ	→
	pt.am.nsm	v.aai.3s			f.pm	p.a	n.asf	cj	pt.aa.nsm			r.apn	d.apn n.apn	cj	
	832	2002			4513	1650	3423	1254	1451			1697	3836 3538	2779	4151

many	words	of encouragement	to the	people,	and	finally	arrived	in	Greece,	3	where	he	stayed	three	months.
πολλῷ	λόγῳ	παρακαλέσας	←	αὐτοὺς			ἦλθεν	εἰς	⌐τὴν Ἑλλάδα	τε	→		ποιήσας	τρεῖς	μῆνας
a.dsm	n.dsm	pt.aa.nsm		r.apm.3			v.aai.3s	p.a	d.asf n.asf	cj			pt.aa.nsm	a.apm	n.apm
4498	3364	4151		899			2262	1650	3836 1817	5445			4472	5552	3604

Because		the	Jews	made	a plot	against	him	just as he was	about	to sail		for	Syria,	he
→	ὑπὸ	τῶν	Ἰουδαίων	γενομένης	ἐπιβουλῆς	→	αὐτῷ	→ → →	μέλλοντι	→	ἀνάγεσθαι	εἰς	⌐τὴν Συρίαν	→
	p.g	d.gpm	a.gpm	pt.am.gsf	n.gsf		r.dsm.3		pt.pa.dsm		f.pm	p.a	d.asf n.asf	
1181	5679	3836	2681	1181	2101		899		3516		343	1650	3836 5353	

decided		to go		back through	Macedonia.	4	He	was	accompanied	by	Sopater	son of	Pyrrhus
⌐ἐγένετο γνώμης⌐		⌐τοῦ ὑποστρέφειν⌐	←	διὰ	Μακεδονίας	δὲ	αὐτῷ		συνείπετο	←	Σώπατρος	→	Πύρρου
v.ami.3s	n.gsf	d.gsn f.pa		p.g	n.gsf	cj	r.dsm.3		v.imi.3s		n.nsm		n.nsm
1181	1191	3836 5715		1328	3423	1254	899		5299		5396		4795

from Berea,		Aristarchus	and	Secundus	from	Thessalonica,		Gaius	from	Derbe,	Timothy	also,	and	Tychicus
→	Βεροιαῖος	δὲ	Ἀρίσταρχος	καὶ	Σεκοῦνδος	→	Θεσσαλονικέων	καὶ	Γάϊος	→	Δερβαῖος	Τιμόθεος	καὶ	δὲ	Τύχικος
	a.nsm	cj	n.nsm	cj	n.nsm		n.gpm	cj	n.nsm		a.nsm	n.nsm	cj	cj	n.nsm
	1024	1254	752	2779	4941		2552	2779	1127		1291	5510	2779	1254	5608

and	Trophimus	from	the	province	of Asia.	5	These	men	went	on ahead	and	waited	for	us	at	Troas.
καὶ	Τρόφιμος			→	Ἀσιανοὶ	δὲ	οὗτοι	←	προελθόντες	←		ἔμενον	←	ἡμᾶς	ἐν	Τρῳάδι
cj	n.nsm				n.npm	cj	r.npm		pt.aa.npm			v.iai.3p		r.ap.1	p.d	n.dsf
2779	5576				824	1254	4047		4601			3531		7005	1877	5590

6 But	we	sailed	from	Philippi	after		the	Feast	of Unleavened	Bread,	and	five	days	later	joined
δὲ	ἡμεῖς	ἐξεπλεύσαμεν ἀπὸ		Φιλίππων	μετὰ	τὰς	ἡμέρας	τῶν	→	ἀζύμων		καὶ	πέντε	ἡμερῶν	ἄχρι	⌐ἤλθομεν	πρὸς
cj	r.np.1	v.aai.1p	p.g	n.gpm	p.a	d.apf	n.apf	d.gpn		n.gpn		cj	a.gpf	n.gpf	p.g	v.aai.1p	μ.d
1254	7005	1739	608	5804	3552	3836	2465	3836		109		2779	4297	2465	948	2262	4639

the others	at	Troas,		where	we	stayed	seven	days.
αὐτοὺς	εἰς	⌐τὴν Τρῳάδα	ὅπου	→	διετρίψαμεν	ἑπτὰ	ἡμέρας
r.apm.3	p.a	d.asf n.asf	cj		v.aai.1p	a.apf	n.apf
899	1650	3836 5590	3963		1417	2231	2465

Eutychus Raised From the Dead at Troas

20:7

	On	the	first	day	of	the	week	we	came	together	to break	bread.	Paul		spoke	to the
δὲ	Ἐν	τῇ	μιᾷ	←	→	τῶν	σαββάτων	ἡμῶν	συνηγμένων	←	→	κλάσαι	ἄρτον	⌐ὁ	Παῦλος	διελέγετο	→
cj	p.d	d.dsf	a.dsf			d.gpn	n.gpn	r.gp.1	pt.rp.gpm			f.aa	n.asm	d.nsm	n.nsm	v.imi.3s	
1254	1877	3836	1651			3836	4879	7005	5251			3089	788	3836	4263	1363	

people	and,	because	he	intended	to leave	the	next	day,		kept	on	talking	until	midnight.	8	There
αὐτοῖς		→		μέλλων	→	ἐξιέναι	τῇ	ἐπαύριον	τε	παρέτεινεν	←	⌐τὸν λόγον⌐	μέχρι	μεσονυκτίου	δὲ	→
r.dpm.3				pt.pa.nsm		f.pa	d.dsf	adv	cj	v.iai.3s		d.asm n.asm	p.g	n.gsn	cj	
899				3516		1997	3836	2069	5445	4189		3836 3364	3588	3543	1254	

were	many	lamps	in	the	upstairs	room	where	we	were	meeting.	9	Seated		in	a window		was	a	young
ἦσαν	ἱκαναὶ	λαμπάδες	ἐν	τῷ	ὑπερῴῳ	←	οὗ	→	ἦμεν	συνηγμένοι	δέ	καθεζόμενος	ἐπὶ		⌐τῆς θυρίδος⌐		τις	νεανίας
v.iai.3p	a.npf	n.npf	p.d	d.dsn	n.dsn		adv		v.iai.1p	pt.rp.npm	cj	pt.pm.nsm	p.g		d.gsf n.gsf		r.nsm	n.nsm
1639	2653	3286	1877	3836	5673		4023		1639	5251	1254	2757	2093		3836 2600		5516	3733

man	named	Eutychus,	who	was	sinking	into a	deep	sleep	as	Paul		talked	on		and	on. When
ὀνόματι	Εὔτυχος		who	κατεφερόμενος		βαθεῖ	ὕπνῳ		⌐τοῦ Παύλου⌐	διαλεγομένου	⌐ἐπὶ πλεῖον⌐				When
ὀνόματι	Εὔτυχος		→	κατεφερόμενος		βαθεῖ	ὕπνῳ		⌐τοῦ Παύλου⌐	διαλεγομένου	⌐ἐπὶ πλεῖον⌐		
n.dsn	n.nsm			pt.pp.nsm		a.dsm	n.dsm		d.gsm n.gsm	pt.pm.gsm	p.a adv.c		
3950	2366			2965		960	5678	1363	3836 4263	1363	2093 4498		

20:1 Μετὰ δὲ τὸ παύσασθαι τὸν θόρυβον μεταπεμψάμενος ὁ Παῦλος τοὺς μαθητὰς καὶ παρακαλέσας, ἀσπασάμενος ἐξῆλθεν πορεύεσθαι εἰς Μακεδονίαν. 2 διελθὼν δὲ τὰ μέρη ἐκεῖνα καὶ παρακαλέσας αὐτοὺς λόγῳ πολλῷ ἦλθεν εἰς τὴν Ἑλλάδα 3 ποιήσας τε μῆνας τρεῖς· γενομένης ἐπιβουλῆς αὐτῷ ὑπὸ τῶν Ἰουδαίων μέλλοντι ἀνάγεσθαι εἰς τὴν Συρίαν, ἐγένετο γνώμης τοῦ ὑποστρέφειν διὰ Μακεδονίας. 4 συνείπετο δὲ αὐτῷ Σώπατρος Πύρρου Βεροιαῖος, Θεσσαλονικέων δὲ Ἀρίσταρχος καὶ Σεκοῦνδος, καὶ Γάϊος Δερβαῖος καὶ Τιμόθεος, Ἀσιανοὶ δὲ Τύχικος καὶ Τρόφιμος. 5 οὗτοι δὲ προελθόντες ἔμενον ἡμᾶς ἐν Τρῳάδι, 6 ἡμεῖς δὲ ἐξεπλεύσαμεν μετὰ τὰς ἡμέρας τῶν ἀζύμων ἀπὸ Φιλίππων καὶ ἤλθομεν πρὸς αὐτοὺς εἰς τὴν Τρῳάδα ἄχρι ἡμερῶν πέντε, ὅπου διετρίψαμεν ἡμέρας ἑπτά.

20:7 Ἐν δὲ τῇ μιᾷ τῶν σαββάτων συνηγμένων ἡμῶν κλάσαι ἄρτον, ὁ Παῦλος διελέγετο αὐτοῖς μέλλων ἐξιέναι τῇ ἐπαύριον, παρέτεινέν τε τὸν λόγον μέχρι μεσονυκτίου. 8 ἦσαν δὲ λαμπάδες ἱκαναὶ ἐν τῷ ὑπερῴῳ οὗ ἦμεν συνηγμένοι. 9 καθεζόμενος δέ τις νεανίας ὀνόματι Εὔτυχος ἐπὶ τῆς θυρίδος, καταφερόμενος ὕπνῳ βαθεῖ διαλεγομένου τοῦ Παύλου ἐπὶ πλεῖον, κατενεχθεὶς

he was sound — asleep, — he fell — to the ground from the third story — and was picked up dead. **10**
→ κατενεχθεὶς ἀπὸ ⌐τοῦ ὕπνου⌐ ἔπεσεν → κάτω ἀπὸ τοῦ τριστέγου καὶ → ἤρθη ← νεκρός δὲ
pt.ap.nsm p.g d.gsm n.gsm v.aai.3s adv p.g d.gsn n.gsn cj v.api.3s a.nsm δὲ
2965 608 3836 5678 4406 3004 608 3836 5566 2779 149 3738 1254

Paul went down, threw himself on the young man and put — his arms around him. "Don't be
ὁ Παῦλος καταβὰς ← ἐπέπεσεν — αὐτῷ ← καὶ συμπεριλαβὼν ← ← ← μὴ
d.nsm n.nsm pt.aa.nsm v.aai.3s r.dsm.3 cj pt.aa.nsm pl
3836 4263 2849 2158 899 2779 5227 3590

alarmed," he said. *"He's alive!"* **11** Then he went upstairs again and broke bread and
θορυβεῖσθε εἶπεν γὰρ ⌐ἐν αὐτῷ ἐστιν⌐ ἡ ψυχὴ αὐτοῦ· δὲ → ἀναβὰς καὶ κλάσας ⌐τὸν ἄρτον⌐ καὶ
v.ppm.2p v.aai.3s cj p.d r.dsm.3 v.pai.3s d.nsf n.nsf r.gsm.3 cj pt.aa.nsm cj pt.aa.nsm d.asm n.asm cj
2572 3306 1142 1877 899 1639 3836 6034 899 1254 326 2779 3089 3836 788 2779

ate. After talking until daylight, he left. **12** The people took the young man home
γευσάμενος τε → ὁμιλήσας ἐφ᾽ ἱκανόν ἄχρι αὐγῆς οὕτως ἐξῆλθεν δὲ ἤγαγον τὸν παῖδα ←
pt.am.nsm te pt.aa.nsm p.a a.asm p.g n.gsf adv v.aai.3s cj v.aai.3p d.asm n.asm
1174 5445 3917 2093 2653 948 879 4048 2002 1254 72 3836 4090

alive and were greatly comforted.
ζῶντα καὶ → ⌐οὐ μετρίως⌐ παρεκλήθησαν
pt.pa.asm cj pl adv v.api.3p
2409 2779 4151 4024 3585 4151

Paul's Farewell to the Ephesian Elders

20:13 We went on ahead to the ship and sailed for Assos, where we were going to
δὲ ἡμεῖς προελθόντες ← ἐπὶ τὸ πλοῖον ἀνήχθημεν ἐπὶ ⌐τὴν Ἆσσον⌐ ἐκεῖθεν → → μέλλοντες
cj r.np.1 pt.aa.npm p.a d.asn n.asn v.api.1p p.a d.asf n.asf adv pt.pa.npm
1254 7005 4601 2093 3836 4450 343 2093 3836 840 1696 3516

take Paul aboard. He had made this arrangement because he was going there on foot. **14**
ἀναλαμβάνειν ⌐τὸν Παῦλον⌐ ← γὰρ → → → οὕτως διατεταγμένος → αὐτὸς ἦν μέλλων → πεζεύειν δὲ
f.pa d.asm n.asm cj adv pt.rp.nsm r.nsm v.iai.3s pt.pa.nsm f.pa cj
377 3836 4263 377 1142 1411 1411 1411 4048 1411 3516 899 1639 3516 4269 1254

When he met us at Assos, we took him aboard and went on to Mitylene. **15** The next day we
ὡς → συνέβαλλεν ἡμῖν εἰς ⌐τὴν Ἆσσον⌐ → ἀναλαβόντες αὐτὸν ← → ἤλθομεν εἰς Μιτυλήνην τῇ ἐπιούσῃ
cj v.iai.3s r.dp.1 p.a d.asf n.asf pt.aa.npm r.asm.3 v.aai.1p p.a n.asf d.dsf pt.pa.dsf
6055 5202 7005 1650 3836 840 377 899 377 2262 1650 3639 3836 2079

set sail from there and arrived off Kios. The day after that we crossed over to Samos,
→ ἀποπλεύσαντες → κἀκεῖθεν κατηντήσαμεν ἄντικρυς Χίου δὲ τῇ → ἑτέρᾳ → παρεβάλομεν ← εἰς Σάμον
pt.aa.npm crasis v.aai.1p p.g n.gsf cj d.dsf r.dsf v.aai.1p p.a n.asf
676 2796 2918 513 5944 1254 3836 2283 4125 1650 4904

and on the following day arrived at Miletus. **16** Paul had decided to sail past Ephesus to
δὲ → τῇ ἐχομένῃ ← ἤλθομεν εἰς Μίλητον γὰρ ὁ Παῦλος → κεκρίκει → παραπλεῦσαι ← ⌐τὴν Ἔφεσον⌐ ὅπως
cj d.dsf pt.pm.dsf v.aai.1p p.a n.asf cj d.nsm n.nsm v.lai.3s f.aa d.asf n.asf cj
1254 3836 2400 2262 1650 3626 1142 3836 4263 3212 4179 3836 2387 3968

avoid spending time in the province of Asia, for he was in a hurry to reach Jerusalem, if
μὴ γένηται αὐτῷ χρονοτριβῆσαι ← ἐν τῇ → Ἀσίᾳ γὰρ → → → ἔσπευδεν → γενέσθαι εἰς Ἱεροσόλυμα εἰ
pl v.ams.3s r.dsm.3 f.aa p.d d.dsf n.dsf cj v.iai.3s f.am p.a n.apn cj
3590 1181 899 5990 1877 3836 823 1142 5067 1181 1650 2642 1623

possible, by the day of Pentecost. ¶ **17** From Miletus, Paul sent to Ephesus
δυνατὸν εἴη αὐτῷ → τὴν ἡμέραν ⌐τῆς πεντηκοστῆς⌐ δὲ Ἀπὸ ⌐τῆς Μιλήτου⌐ πέμψας μετεκαλέσατο εἰς Ἔφεσον
n.nsn v.pao.3s r.dsm.3 d.asf n.asf d.gsf n.gsf cj p.g d.gsf n.gsf pt.aa.nsm v.ami.3s p.a n.asf
1543 1639 899 3836 2465 3836 4300 1254 608 3836 3626 4287 3559 1650 2387

for the elders of the church. **18** When they arrived, he said to them: "You know how I
τοὺς πρεσβυτέρους → τῆς ἐκκλησίας δὲ ὡς → παρεγένοντο πρὸς αὐτὸν εἶπεν αὐτοῖς· ὑμεῖς ἐπίστασθε πῶς
d.apm a.apm d.gsf n.gsf cj cj v.ami.3p p.a r.asm.3 v.aai.3s r.dpm.3 r.np.2 v.ppi.2p cj
3836 4565 3836 1711 1254 6055 4134 4639 899 3306 899 7007 2179 4802

lived the whole time I was with you, from the first day I came into the province of Asia. **19** I served
ἐγενόμην τὸν πάντα χρόνον μεθ᾽ ὑμῶν ἀπὸ πρώτης ἡμέρας ἀφ᾽ ἧς → ἐπέβην εἰς τὴν → → Ἀσίαν → δουλεύων
v.ami.1s d.asm a.asm n.asm p.g r.gp.2 p.g a.gsf n.gsf p.g r.gsf v.aai.1s p.a d.asf n.asf pt.pa.nsm
1181 3836 4246 5989 3552 7007 608 4755 2465 608 4005 2094 1650 3836 823 1526

ἀπὸ τοῦ ὕπνου ἔπεσεν ἀπὸ τοῦ τριστέγου κάτω καὶ ἤρθη νεκρός. ¹⁰ καταβὰς δὲ ὁ Παῦλος ἐπέπεσεν αὐτῷ καὶ συμπεριλαβὼν εἶπεν, Μὴ θορυβεῖσθε, ἡ γὰρ ψυχὴ αὐτοῦ ἐν αὐτῷ ἐστιν. ¹¹ ἀναβὰς δὲ καὶ κλάσας τὸν ἄρτον καὶ γευσάμενος ἐφ᾽ ἱκανόν τε ὁμιλήσας ἄχρι αὐγῆς, οὕτως ἐξῆλθεν. ¹² ἤγαγον δὲ τὸν παῖδα ζῶντα καὶ παρεκλήθησαν οὐ μετρίως. ²⁰:¹³ Ἡμεῖς δὲ προελθόντες ἐπὶ τὸ πλοῖον ἀνήχθημεν ἐπὶ τὴν Ἆσσον ἐκεῖθεν μέλλοντες ἀναλαμβάνειν τὸν Παῦλον· οὕτως γὰρ διατεταγμένος ἦν μέλλων αὐτὸς πεζεύειν. ¹⁴ ὡς δὲ συνέβαλλεν ἡμῖν εἰς τὴν Ἆσσον, ἀναλαβόντες αὐτὸν ἤλθομεν εἰς Μιτυλήνην, ¹⁵ κἀκεῖθεν ἀποπλεύσαντες τῇ ἐπιούσῃ κατηντήσαμεν ἄντικρυς Χίου, τῇ δὲ ἑτέρᾳ παρεβάλομεν εἰς Σάμον, τῇ δὲ ἐχομένῃ ἤλθομεν εἰς Μίλητον. ¹⁶ κεκρίκει γὰρ ὁ Παῦλος παραπλεῦσαι τὴν Ἔφεσον, ὅπως μὴ γένηται αὐτῷ χρονοτριβῆσαι ἐν τῇ Ἀσίᾳ· ἔσπευδεν γὰρ εἰ δυνατὸν εἴη αὐτῷ τὴν ἡμέραν τῆς πεντηκοστῆς γενέσθαι εἰς Ἱεροσόλυμα. ¶ ¹⁷ Ἀπὸ δὲ τῆς Μιλήτου πέμψας εἰς Ἔφεσον μετεκαλέσατο τοὺς πρεσβυτέρους τῆς ἐκκλησίας. ¹⁸ ὡς δὲ παρεγένοντο πρὸς αὐτὸν εἶπεν αὐτοῖς, Ὑμεῖς ἐπίστασθε, ἀπὸ πρώτης ἡμέρας ἀφ᾽ ἧς ἐπέβην εἰς τὴν Ἀσίαν, πῶς μεθ᾽ ὑμῶν τὸν πάντα χρόνον ἐγενόμην, ¹⁹ δουλεύων τῷ κυρίῳ μετὰ πάσης

the Lord with great humility   and with tears,   although I   was   severely tested   by the plots
τῷ κυρίῳ μετὰ πάσης ταπεινοφροσύνης καὶ   δακρύων καὶ   μοι ⸂τῶν συμβάντων⸃ →   πειρασμῶν ἐν ταῖς ἐπιβουλαῖς
d.dsm n.dsm p.g a.gsf n.gsf cj n.gpn cj r.ds.1 d.gpm pt.aa.gpm n.gpm p.d d.dpf n.dpf
3836 3261 3552 4246 5425 2779 1232 2779 1609 3836 5201 4280 1877 3836 2101

of the Jews. **20**   You know that I   have not hesitated   to preach   anything that would be helpful
→ τῶν Ἰουδαίων ὡς   →   →   οὐδὲν ὑπεστειλάμην μὴ   ⸂τοῦ ἀναγγεῖλαι⸃   τῶν →   → συμφερόντων
d.gpm a.gpm cj a.asn v.ami.1s pl d.gsn f.aa d.gpn pt.pa.gpn
3836 2681 6055 5713 5713 4029 5713 3590 3836 334 3836 5237

to you but have taught you publicly and from house   to house. **21** I have declared   to both Jews   and
→ ὑμῖν καὶ →   διδάξαι ὑμᾶς δημοσίᾳ καὶ → ⸂κατ' οἴκους⸃ ←   διαμαρτυρόμενος τε   Ἰουδαίοις καὶ
r.dp.2 cj f.aa r.ap.2 a.dsf cj p.a n.apm pt.pm.nsm cj a.dpm cj
7007 2779 1438 7007 1323 2779 2848 3875 1371 5445 2681 2779

Greeks that they must turn to God in repentance   and have faith in   our   Lord   Jesus. ¶ **22** "And now,
Ἕλλησιν   εἰς θεὸν → ⸂τὴν μετάνοιαν⸃ καὶ   πίστιν εἰς ἡμῶν ⸂τὸν κύριον⸃ Ἰησοῦν   Καὶ νῦν
n.dpm p.a n.asm d.asf n.asf cj n.asf p.a r.gp.1 d.asm n.asm n.asm cj adv
1818 1650 2536 3836 3567 2779 4411 1650 7005 3836 3261 2652 2779 3814

    compelled by the Spirit, I   am going   to Jerusalem, not knowing what will happen   to me   there. **23** I
ἰδοὺ δεδεμένος → τῷ πνεύματι ἐγὼ → πορεύομαι εἰς Ἰερουσαλὴμ μὴ εἰδώς τὰ → συναντήσοντα → μοι ἐν αὐτῇ
j pt.rp.nsm d.dsn n.dsn r.ns.1 v.pmi.1s p.a n.asf pl pt.ra.nsm d.apn pt.fa.apn r.ds.1 p.d r.dsf.3
2627 1313 3836 4460 1609 4513 1650 2647 3590 3857 3836 5267 1609 1877 899

only know that in every city the Holy   Spirit warns   me   that prison and hardships are facing   me.
πλὴν ὅτι → κατὰ πόλιν τὸ ⸂τὸ ἅγιον⸃ πνεῦμα διαμαρτύρεταί μοι λέγον ὅτι δεσμὰ καὶ θλίψεις → μένουσιν με
cj cj p.a n.asf d.nsn d.nsn a.nsn n.nsn v.pmi.3s r.ds.1 pt.pa.nsn cj n.npn cj n.npf v.pai.3p r.as.1
4440 4022 2848 4484 3836 3836 41 4460 1371 1609 3306 4022 1301 2779 2568 3531 1609

24 However, I consider my life   worth nothing   to me,   if only I may finish   the race   and complete
ἀλλ'   → ποιοῦμαι τὴν ψυχὴν τιμίαν ⸂οὐδενὸς λόγου⸃ ἐμαυτῷ ὡς ←   → → τελειῶσαι τὸν δρόμον μου καὶ
cj v.pmi.1s d.asf n.asf a.asf a.gsm n.gsm r.dsm.1 cj f.aa d.asm n.asm r.gs.1 cj
247 4472 3836 6034 5508 4029 3364 1831 6055 5457 3836 1536 1609 2779

the task   the Lord Jesus has given me – the task of testifying   to the gospel   of God's
τὴν διακονίαν ἣν παρὰ τοῦ κυρίου Ἰησοῦ → ἔλαβον ←   διαμαρτύρασθαι ← τὸ εὐαγγέλιον → ⸂τοῦ θεοῦ⸃
d.asf n.asf r.asf p.g d.gsm n.gsm n.gsm v.aai.1s f.am d.asn n.asn d.gsn n.gsn
3836 1355 4005 4123 3836 3261 2652 3284 1371 3836 2295 5921 3836 2536

grace. ¶ **25**   "Now   I   know that *none* of you among whom I have gone   about preaching the
⸂τῆς χάριτος⸃   Καὶ νῦν ἰδοὺ ἐγὼ οἶδα ὅτι πάντες ὑμεῖς ἐν οἷς → → διῆλθον ← κηρύσσων τὴν
d.gsf n.gsf cj adv j r.ns.1 v.rai.1s cj a.npm r.np.2 p.d r.dpm v.aai.1s pt.pa.nsm d.asf
3836 5921 2779 3814 2627 1609 3857 4022 4246 7007 1877 4005 1451 3062 3836

kingdom will ever see   me   again. **26** Therefore, I declare   to you today   that I am
βασιλείαν →   ὄψεσθε ⸂τὸ πρόσωπον μου⸃ οὐκέτι διότι   → μαρτύρομαι → ὑμῖν ἐν τῇ σήμερον ἡμέρᾳ ὅτι → εἰμι
n.asf v.fmi.2p d.asn n.asn r.gs.1 adv cj v.pmi.1s r.dp.2 p.d d.dsf adv n.dsf cj v.pai.1s
993 3972 3836 4725 1609 4033 1484 3458 7007 1877 3836 4958 2465 4022 1639

innocent of the blood of all   men. **27** For I   have not hesitated   to proclaim   to you the whole will   of
καθαρός ἀπὸ τοῦ αἵματος → πάντων   γάρ → → οὐ ὑπεστειλάμην μὴ → ⸂τοῦ ἀναγγεῖλαι⸃ → ὑμῖν τὴν πᾶσαν βουλὴν →
a.nsm p.g d.gsn n.gsn a.gpm cj pl v.ami.1s pl d.gsn f.aa r.dp.2 d.asf a.asf n.asf
2754 608 3836 135 4246 1142 5713 5713 4024 5713 3590 3836 334 7007 3836 4246 1087

God. **28** Keep watch   over yourselves and all   the flock   of which the Holy   Spirit has made you overseers.
⸂τοῦ θεοῦ⸃   → προσέχετε ← ἑαυτοῖς καὶ παντὶ τῷ ποιμνίῳ ἐν ᾧ τὸ ⸂τὸ ἅγιον⸃ πνεῦμα → ἔθετο ὑμᾶς ἐπισκόπους
d.gsm n.gsm v.pam.2p r.dpm.2 cj a.dsn d.dsn n.dsn p.d r.dsn d.nsn d.nsn a.nsn n.nsn v.ami.3s r.ap.2 n.apm
3836 2536 4668 1571 2779 4246 3836 4480 1877 4005 3836 3836 41 4460 5502 7007 2176

Be shepherds of the church   of God,   which he bought   with his own   blood. **29** I   know that after I
→ ποιμαίνειν τὴν ἐκκλησίαν → ⸂τοῦ θεοῦ⸃ ἣν → περιεποιήσατο διὰ τοῦ ⸂τοῦ ἰδίου⸃ αἵματος   ἐγὼ οἶδα ὅτι μετὰ μου
f.pa d.asf n.asf d.gsm n.gsm r.asf v.ami.3s p.g d.gsn d.gsn a.gsn n.gsn r.ns.1 v.rai.1s cj p.a r.gs.1
4477 3836 1711 3836 2536 4005 4347 1328 3836 3836 2625 135 1609 3857 4022 3552 1609

leave,   savage wolves will come   in among you and will not spare   the flock. **30** Even from your own
⸂τὴν ἄφιξιν⸃ βαρεῖς λύκοι → εἰσελεύσονται ← εἰς ὑμᾶς → μὴ φειδόμενοι τοῦ ποιμνίου καὶ ἐξ ὑμῶν αὐτῶν
d.asf n.asf a.npm n.npm v.fmi.3p p.a r.ap.2 pl pt.pm.npm d.gsn n.gsn cj p.g r.gp.2 r.gpm
3836 922 987 3380 1656 1650 7007 3590 5767 3836 4480 2779 1666 7007 899

ταπεινοφροσύνης καὶ δακρύων καὶ πειρασμῶν τῶν συμβάντων μοι ἐν ταῖς ἐπιβουλαῖς τῶν Ἰουδαίων, ²⁰ ὡς οὐδὲν ὑπεστειλάμην τῶν συμφερόντων τοῦ μὴ ἀναγγεῖλαι ὑμῖν καὶ διδάξαι ὑμᾶς δημοσίᾳ καὶ κατ' οἴκους, ²¹ διαμαρτυρόμενος Ἰουδαίοις τε καὶ Ἕλλησιν τὴν εἰς θεὸν μετάνοιαν καὶ πίστιν εἰς τὸν κύριον ἡμῶν Ἰησοῦν. ¶ ²² καὶ νῦν ἰδοὺ δεδεμένος ἐγὼ τῷ πνεύματι πορεύομαι εἰς Ἰερουσαλὴμ τὰ ἐν αὐτῇ συναντήσοντά μοι μὴ εἰδώς, ²³ πλὴν ὅτι τὸ πνεῦμα τὸ ἅγιον κατὰ πόλιν διαμαρτύρεταί μοι λέγον ὅτι δεσμὰ καὶ θλίψεις με μένουσιν. ²⁴ ἀλλ' οὐδενὸς λόγου ποιοῦμαι τὴν ψυχὴν τιμίαν ἐμαυτῷ ὡς τελειῶσαι τὸν δρόμον μου καὶ τὴν διακονίαν ἣν ἔλαβον παρὰ τοῦ κυρίου Ἰησοῦ, διαμαρτύρασθαι τὸ εὐαγγέλιον τῆς χάριτος τοῦ θεοῦ. ¶ ²⁵ Καὶ νῦν ἰδοὺ ἐγὼ οἶδα ὅτι οὐκέτι ὄψεσθε τὸ πρόσωπόν μου ὑμεῖς πάντες ἐν οἷς διῆλθον κηρύσσων τὴν βασιλείαν. ²⁶ διότι μαρτύρομαι ὑμῖν ἐν τῇ σήμερον ἡμέρᾳ ὅτι καθαρός εἰμι ἀπὸ τοῦ αἵματος πάντων· ²⁷ οὐ γὰρ ὑπεστειλάμην τοῦ μὴ ἀναγγεῖλαι πᾶσαν τὴν βουλὴν τοῦ θεοῦ ὑμῖν. ²⁸ προσέχετε ἑαυτοῖς καὶ παντὶ τῷ ποιμνίῳ, ἐν ᾧ ὑμᾶς τὸ πνεῦμα τὸ ἅγιον ἔθετο ἐπισκόπους ποιμαίνειν τὴν ἐκκλησίαν τοῦ θεοῦ, ἣν περιεποιήσατο διὰ τοῦ αἵματος τοῦ ἰδίου. ²⁹ ἐγὼ οἶδα ὅτι εἰσελεύσονται μετὰ τὴν ἄφιξίν μου λύκοι βαρεῖς εἰς ὑμᾶς μὴ φειδόμενοι τοῦ ποιμνίου, ³⁰ καὶ ἐξ ὑμῶν αὐτῶν ἀναστήσονται ἄνδρες λαλοῦντες

number men will arise and distort the truth in order to draw away disciples after
ἄνδρες → ἀναστήσονται λαλοῦντες διεστραμμένα ← → ⌐τοῦ ἀποσπᾶν⌐ ← ⌐τοὺς μαθητὰς⌐ ὀπίσω
n.npm v.fmi.3p pt.pa.npm pt.rp.apn d.gsn f.pa d.apm n.apm p.g
467 482 3281 1406 3836 685 3836 3412 3958

them. ³¹ So be on your guard! Remember that for three years I never stopped warning each of you night
αὐτῶν διὸ → → γρηγορεῖτε μνημονεύοντες ὅτι → τριετίαν ← οὐκ ἐπαυσάμην νουθετῶν ἕκαστον ἕνα νύκτα
r.gpm.3 cj v.pam.2p pt.pa.npm cj n.asf pl v.ami.1s pt.pa.nsm r.asm a.asm n.asf
899 1475 1213 3648 4022 5562 4264 4024 4264 3805 1667 1651 3816

and day with tears. ¶ ³² "Now I commit you to God and to the word of his grace,
καὶ ἡμέραν μετὰ δακρύων Καὶ ⌐τὰ νῦν⌐ → παρατίθεμαι ὑμᾶς → ⌐τῷ θεῷ⌐ καὶ → τῷ λόγῳ ↗ αὐτοῦ τῆς χάριτος⌐
cj n.asf p.g n.gpn cj d.apn adv v.pmi.1s r.ap.2 d.dsm n.dsm cj d.dsm n.dsm r.gsm.3 d.gsf n.gsf
2779 2465 3552 1232 2779 3836 3814 4192 7007 3836 2536 2779 3836 3364 5921 899 3836 5921

which can build you up and give you an inheritance among all those who are sanctified. ³³ I have
τῷ δυναμένῳ οἰκοδομῆσαι ← καὶ δοῦναι ⌐τὴν κληρονομίαν⌐ ἐν πᾶσιν τοῖς ← ἡγιασμένοις → →
d.dsm pt.pp.dsm f.aa cj f.aa d.asf n.asf p.d a.dpm d.dpm pt.rp.dpm
3836 1538 3868 2779 1443 3836 3100 1877 4246 3836 39 2121 2121

not coveted anyone's silver or gold or clothing. ³⁴ You yourselves know that these hands of mine have
ἐπεθύμησα οὐδενὸς ἀργυρίου ἢ χρυσίου ἢ ἱματισμοῦ → αὐτοὶ γινώσκετε ὅτι αὗται ⌐αἱ χεῖρες⌐ →
v.aai.1s a.gsm n.gsn cj n.gsn cj n.gsm r.npm v.pai.2p cj r.npf d.npf n.npf
4029 2121 4029 736 2445 5992 2445 2669 1182 899 1182 4022 4047 3836 5931

supplied my own needs and the needs of my companions. ³⁵ In everything I did, I showed you that by this
ὑπηρέτησαν μου ταῖς χρείαις καὶ ⌐τοῖς οὖσιν μετ᾽ ἐμοῦ⌐ πάντα → ὑπέδειξα ὑμῖν ὅτι → →
v.aai.3p r.gs.1 d.dpf n.dpf cj d.dpm pt.pa.dpm p.g r.gs.1 a.apn v.aai.1s r.dp.2 cj
5676 1609 3836 5970 2779 1609 3836 1639 3552 1609 4246 5683 7007 4022

kind of hard work we must help the weak, remembering the words the Lord Jesus
οὕτως ← → κοπιῶντας δεῖ ἀντιλαμβάνεσθαι τῶν ἀσθενούντων τε μνημονεύειν τῶν λόγων τοῦ κυρίου Ἰησοῦ ὅτι
adv pt.pa.apm v.pai.3s f.pm d.gpm pt.pa.gpm cj f.pa d.gpm n.gpm d.gsm n.gsm n.gsm cj
4048 3159 1256 514 3836 820 5445 3648 3836 3364 3836 3261 2652 4022

himself said: 'It is more blessed to give than to receive.'" ¶ ³⁶ When he had said this, he
αὐτὸς εἶπεν ἔστιν μᾶλλον μακάριον → διδόναι ἢ → λαμβάνειν Καὶ → εἰπὼν ταῦτα αὐτοῦ
r.nsm v.aai.3s v.pai.3s adv.c a.nsn f.pa pl f.pa cj pt.aa.nsm r.apn r.gsm.3
899 3306 1639 3437 3421 1443 2445 3284 2779 3306 4047 899

knelt down with all of them and prayed. ³⁷ They all wept as they
⌐θεὶς τὰ γόνατα⌐ σὺν πᾶσιν αὐτοῖς προσηύξατο δὲ → πάντων ⌐ἱκανὸς κλαυθμὸς ἐγένετο⌐ καὶ → →
pt.aa.nsm d.apn n.apn p.d a.dpm r.dpm.3 v.ami.3s cj a.gpm a.nsm n.nsm v.ami.3s cj
5502 3836 1205 5250 4246 899 4667 1254 1181 4246 2653 3088 1181 2779

embraced him and kissed him. ³⁸ What grieved them most was his statement
⌐ἐπιπεσόντες ἐπὶ τὸν τράχηλον⌐ ⌐τοῦ Παύλου⌐ κατεφίλουν αὐτόν ὀδυνώμενοι μάλιστα ἐπὶ τῷ ⌐λόγῳ ᾧ εἰρήκει⌐
pt.aa.npm p.a d.asm n.asm d.gsm n.gsm v.iai.3p r.asm.3 pt.pp.npm adv.s p.d d.dsm n.dsm r.dsm v.lai.3s
2158 2093 3836 5549 3836 4263 2968 899 3849 3436 2093 3836 3364 4005 3306

that they would never see his face again. Then they accompanied him to the ship.
ὅτι → μέλλουσιν οὐκέτι θεωρεῖν αὐτοῦ ⌐τὸ πρόσωπον⌐ ↰ δὲ → προέπεμπον αὐτὸν εἰς τὸ πλοῖον
cj v.pai.3p adv f.pa r.gsm.3 d.asn n.asn cj v.iai.3p r.asm.3 p.a d.asn n.asn
4022 3516 4033 2555 899 3836 4725 4033 1254 4636 899 1650 3836 4450

On to Jerusalem

21:1 After we had torn ourselves away from them, we put out to sea and sailed
δὲ ἐγένετο Ὡς → → ἀποσπασθέντας ← ← ἀπ᾽ αὐτῶν ἡμᾶς ἀναχθῆναι ← ← εὐθυδρομήσαντες
cj v.ami.3s cj pt.ap.apm p.g r.gpm.3 r.ap.1 f.ap pt.aa.npm
1254 1181 6055 685 608 899 7005 343 2312

straight to Cos. The next day we went to Rhodes and from there to Patara. ² We found a
← ἤλθομεν εἰς ⌐τὴν Κῶ⌐ δὲ τῇ ἑξῆς → εἰς ⌐τὴν Ῥόδον⌐ κἀκεῖθεν ← ← εἰς Πάταρα καὶ εὑρόντες
v.aai.1p p.a d.asf n.asf cj d.dsf adv p.a d.asf n.asf crasis p.a n.apn cj pt.aa.npm
2262 1650 3836 3271 1254 3836 2009 1650 3836 4852 2796 1650 4249 2779 2351

ship crossing over to Phoenicia, went on board and set sail. ³ After sighting Cyprus and
πλοῖον διαπερῶν ← εἰς Φοινίκην → ἐπιβάντες → ἀνήχθημεν δὲ → ἀναφάναντες ⌐τὴν Κύπρον⌐ καὶ
n.asn pt.pa.asn p.a n.asf pt.aa.npm v.api.1p cj pt.aa.npm d.asf n.asf cj
4450 1385 1650 5834 2094 343 1254 428 3836 3251 2779

διεστραμμένα τοῦ ἀποσπᾶν τοὺς μαθητὰς ὀπίσω αὐτῶν. ³¹ διὸ γρηγορεῖτε μνημονεύοντες ὅτι τριετίαν νύκτα καὶ ἡμέραν οὐκ ἐπαυσάμην μετὰ δακρύων νουθετῶν ἕνα ἕκαστον. ¶ ³² καὶ τὰ νῦν παρατίθεμαι ὑμᾶς τῷ θεῷ καὶ τῷ λόγῳ τῆς χάριτος αὐτοῦ, τῷ δυναμένῳ οἰκοδομῆσαι καὶ δοῦναι τὴν κληρονομίαν ἐν τοῖς ἡγιασμένοις πᾶσιν. ³³ ἀργυρίου ἢ χρυσίου ἢ ἱματισμοῦ οὐδενὸς ἐπεθύμησα· ³⁴ αὐτοὶ γινώσκετε ὅτι ταῖς χρείαις μου καὶ τοῖς οὖσιν μετ᾽ ἐμοῦ ὑπηρέτησαν αἱ χεῖρες αὗται. ³⁵ πάντα ὑπέδειξα ὑμῖν ὅτι οὕτως κοπιῶντας δεῖ ἀντιλαμβάνεσθαι τῶν ἀσθενούντων, μνημονεύειν τε τῶν λόγων τοῦ κυρίου Ἰησοῦ ὅτι αὐτὸς εἶπεν, Μακάριόν ἐστιν μᾶλλον διδόναι ἢ λαμβάνειν. ¶ ³⁶ Καὶ ταῦτα εἰπὼν θεὶς τὰ γόνατα αὐτοῦ σὺν πᾶσιν αὐτοῖς προσηύξατο. ³⁷ ἱκανὸς δὲ κλαυθμὸς ἐγένετο πάντων καὶ ἐπιπεσόντες ἐπὶ τὸν τράχηλον τοῦ Παύλου κατεφίλουν αὐτόν, ³⁸ ὀδυνώμενοι μάλιστα ἐπὶ τῷ λόγῳ ᾧ εἰρήκει, ὅτι οὐκέτι μέλλουσιν τὸ πρόσωπον αὐτοῦ θεωρεῖν. προέπεμπον δὲ αὐτὸν εἰς τὸ πλοῖον.

²¹:¹ Ὡς δὲ ἐγένετο ἀναχθῆναι ἡμᾶς ἀποσπασθέντας ἀπ᾽ αὐτῶν, εὐθυδρομήσαντες ἤλθομεν εἰς τὴν Κῶ, τῇ δὲ ἑξῆς εἰς τὴν Ῥόδον κἀκεῖθεν εἰς Πάταρα, ² καὶ εὑρόντες πλοῖον διαπερῶν εἰς Φοινίκην ἐπιβάντες ἀνήχθημεν. ³ ἀναφάναντες δὲ τὴν Κύπρον καὶ

passing		to the south	of it,	we	sailed	on to	Syria.		We	landed	at	Tyre,	where	our	ship	was to
καταλιπόντες ←		εὐώνυμον	αὐτὴν →		ἐπλέομεν	εἰς	Συρίαν	καὶ →		κατήλθομεν	εἰς	Τύρον	γὰρ	ἐκεῖσε	τὸ	πλοῖον	ἦν →
pt.aa.npm		a.asf	r.asf.3		v.iai.1p	p.a	n.asf	cj		v.aai.1p	p.a	n.asf	cj	adv	d.nsn	n.nsn	v.iai.3s
2901		2381	899		4434	1650	5353	2779		2982	1650	5602	1142	1698	3836	4450	1639

unload		its	cargo.	**4**	Finding	the	disciples	there,	we	stayed		with	them	seven	days.	Through	the
ἀποφορτιζόμενον		τὸν	γόμον	δὲ	ἀνευρόντες	τοὺς	μαθητὰς	αὐτοῦ	→	ἐπεμείναμεν ←				ἑπτά	ἡμέρας	διὰ	τοῦ
pt.pm.nsn		d.asm	n.asm	cj	pt.aa.npm	d.apm	n.apm	adv		v.aai.1p				a.apf	n.apf	p.g	d.gsn
711		3836	1203	1254	461	3836	3412	7008		2152				2231	2465	1328	3836

Spirit	they	urged	Paul		not	to go		on to	Jerusalem.	**5** But	when	our	time		was	up,		we
πνεύματος	οἵτινες	ἔλεγον	τῷ	Παύλῳ	μὴ	→	ἐπιβαίνειν ←	εἰς	Ἰεροσόλυμα	δὲ	ὅτε	ἡμᾶς	τὰς	ἡμέρας	ἐγένετο	ἐξαρτίσαι	→
n.gsn	r.npm	v.iai.3p	d.dsm	n.dsm	pl		f.pa	p.a	n.apn	cj	cj	r.ap.1	d.apf	n.apf	v.ami.3s	f.aa	
4460	4015	3306	3836	4263	3590		2094	1650	2642	1254	4021	7005	3836	2465	1181	1992	

left		and continued	on our way.	All		the disciples	and their	wives	and	children	accompanied	us		out of
ἐξελθόντες		ἐπορευόμεθα ←	←	πάντων			σὺν	γυναιξὶ	καὶ	τέκνοις	προπεμπόντων	ἡμᾶς	ἕως	ἔξω ←
pt.aa.npm		v.imi.1p		a.gpm			p.d	n.dpf	cj	n.dpn	pt.pa.gpm	r.ap.1	p.g	p.g
2002		4513		4246			5250	1222	2779	5451	4636	7005	2401	2032

the city,		and there	on the beach		we	knelt			to pray.	**6** After	saying	good-by		to each		other,
τῆς	πόλεως	καὶ	ἐπὶ	τὸν	αἰγιαλὸν	θέντες	τὰ	γόνατα	προσευξάμενοι	→		ἀπησπασάμεθα ←	ἀλλήλους ←	
d.gsf	n.gsf	cj	p.a	d.asm	n.asm	pt.aa.npm	d.apn	n.apn	pt.am.npm			v.ami.1p	r.apm	
3836	4484	2779	2093	3836	129	5502	3836	1205	4667			571	253	

	we went		aboard	the	ship,	and	they	returned	home.	¶	**7**		We	continued	our	voyage	from
καὶ	→	ἀνέβημεν	εἰς	τὸ	πλοῖον	δὲ	ἐκεῖνοι	ὑπέστρεψαν	εἰς	τὰ	ἴδια	δὲ	ἡμεῖς	διανύσαντες	τὸν	πλοῦν	ἀπὸ
cj		v.aai.1p	p.a	d.asn	n.asn	cj	r.npm	v.aai.3p	p.a	d.apn	a.apn	cj	r.np.1	pt.aa.npm	d.asm	n.asm	p.g
2779		326	1650	3836	4450	1254	1697	5715	1650	3836	2625	1254	7005	1382	3836	4452	608

Tyre	and landed		at	Ptolemais,	where	we	greeted		the	brothers	and	stayed		with	them	for a	day.	**8**
Τύρου	κατηντήσαμεν	εἰς		Πτολεμαΐδα	καὶ	→	ἀσπασάμενοι	τοὺς	ἀδελφοὺς		ἐμείναμεν	παρ᾽	αὐτοῖς	μίαν	ἡμέραν	δὲ
n.gsf	v.aai.1p	p.a		n.asf	cj		pt.am.npm	d.apm	n.apm		v.aai.1p	p.d	r.dpm.3	a.asf	n.asf	cj
5602	2918	1650		4767	2779		832	3836	81		3531	4123	899	1651	2465	1254

Leaving	the	next	day,	we	reached		Caesarea	and		stayed		at	the	house	of	Philip	the
ἐξελθόντες	τῇ	ἐπαύριον		→	ἤλθομεν	εἰς	Καισάρειαν	καὶ	εἰσελθόντες	ἐμείναμεν	παρ᾽	αὐτῷ	εἰς	τὸν	οἶκον	→	Φιλίππου	τοῦ
pt.aa.npm	d.dsf	adv			v.aai.1p	p.a	n.asf	cj	pt.aa.npm	v.aai.1p	p.d	r.dsm.3	p.a	d.asm	n.asm		n.gsm	d.gsm
2002	3836	2069			2262	1650	2791	2779	1656	3531	4123	899	1650	3836	3875		5805	3836

evangelist,		one	of	the	Seven.	**9**	He	had		four	unmarried	daughters	who	prophesied.	¶	**10**
εὐαγγελιστοῦ	ὄντος	ἐκ	τῶν	ἑπτά		δὲ	→	τούτῳ	ἦσαν	τέσσαρες	παρθένοι	θυγατέρες	→	προφητεύουσαι		δὲ
n.gsm	pt.pa.gsm	p.g	d.gpm	a.gpm		cj		r.dsm	v.iai.3p	a.npf	n.npf	n.npf		pt.pa.npf		cj
2296	1639	1666	3836	2231		1254		4047	1639	5475	4221	2588		4736		1254

After	we	had	been		there	a number	of days,	a	prophet	named	Agabus	came	down	from	Judea.		**11**
→	→	→	Ἐπιμενόντων ←		πλείους		ἡμέρας	τις	προφήτης	ὀνόματι	Ἅγαβος	κατῆλθεν		ἀπὸ	τῆς Ἰουδαίας		καὶ
			pt.pa.gpm		a.apf.c		n.apf	r.nsm	n.nsm	n.dsn	n.nsm	v.aai.3s		p.g	d.gsf n.gsf		cj
			2152		4498		2465	5516	4737	3950	13	2982		608	3836 2677		2779

Coming	over	to	us,		he	took	Paul's		belt,	tied	his	own	hands		and	feet		with	it	and
ἐλθὼν	←	πρὸς	ἡμᾶς	καὶ	→	ἄρας	τοῦ Παύλου	τὴν ζώνην	δήσας	ἑαυτοῦ ←		τὰς χεῖρας		καὶ	τοὺς πόδας			
pt.aa.nsm		p.a	r.ap.1	cj		pt.aa.nsm	d.gsm n.gsm	d.asf n.asf	pt.aa.nsm	r.gsm.3		d.apf n.apf		cj	d.apm n.apm			
2262		4639	7005	2779		149	3836 4263	3836 2438	1313	1571		3836 5931		2779	3836 4546			

said, "The	Holy		Spirit	says,	'In	this	way	the	Jews	of	Jerusalem		will bind	the	owner	of		this
εἶπεν	τὸ ἅγιον	πνεῦμα	λέγει	τάδε →		→	οὕτως	οἱ	Ἰουδαῖοι	ἐν	Ἰερουσαλὴμ	→	δήσουσιν	τὸν	ἄνδρα	οὗ ἐστιν		αὕτη
v.aai.3s	d.nsn d.nsn	n.nsn	v.pai.3s	adv			adv	d.npm	a.npm	p.d	n.dsf		v.fai.3p	d.asm	n.asm	r.gsm v.pai.3s		r.nsf
3306	3836 3836 41	4460	3306	3840			4048	3836	2681	1877	2647		1313	3836	467	4005 1639		4047

belt		and will hand		him	over	to		the	Gentiles.'"	¶	**12**	When	we	heard	this,		we	and
τῇ ζώνῃ	καὶ	→	παραδώσουσιν			εἰς	χεῖρας	ἐθνῶν			δὲ	ὡς	→	ἠκούσαμεν	ταῦτα	τε	ἡμεῖς	καὶ
d.nsf n.nsf	cj		v.fai.3p			p.a	n.apf	n.gpn			cj	cj		v.aai.1p	r.apn	cj	r.np.1	cj
3836 2438	2779		4140			1650	5931	1620			1254	6055		201	4047	5445	7005	2779

the	people	there	pleaded		with	Paul	not	to go		up to	Jerusalem.	**13**	Then	Paul		answered,	"Why
οἱ	ἐντόπιοι		παρεκαλοῦμεν		αὐτὸν	μὴ		τοῦ ἀναβαίνειν		εἰς	Ἰερουσαλήμ		τότε	ὁ Παῦλος		ἀπεκρίθη	τί
d.npm	a.npm		v.iai.1p		r.asm.3	pl		d.gsn f.pa		p.a	n.asf		adv	d.nsm n.nsm		v.api.3s	r.asn
3836	1954		4151		899	3590		3836 326		1650	2647		5538	3836 4263		646	5515

καταλιπόντες αὐτὴν εὐώνυμον ἐπλέομεν εἰς Συρίαν καὶ κατήλθομεν εἰς Τύρον· ἐκεῖσε γὰρ τὸ πλοῖον ἦν ἀποφορτιζόμενον τὸν γόμον. ⁴ ἀνευρόντες δὲ τοὺς μαθητὰς ἐπεμείναμεν αὐτοῦ ἡμέρας ἑπτά, οἵτινες τῷ Παύλῳ ἔλεγον διὰ τοῦ πνεύματος μὴ ἐπιβαίνειν εἰς Ἰεροσόλυμα. ⁵ ὅτε δὲ ἐγένετο ἡμᾶς ἐξαρτίσαι τὰς ἡμέρας, ἐξελθόντες ἐπορευόμεθα προπεμπόντων ἡμᾶς πάντων σὺν γυναιξὶ καὶ τέκνοις ἕως ἔξω τῆς πόλεως, καὶ θέντες τὰ γόνατα ἐπὶ τὸν αἰγιαλὸν προσευξάμενοι ⁶ ἀπησπασάμεθα ἀλλήλους καὶ ἀνέβημεν εἰς τὸ πλοῖον, ἐκεῖνοι δὲ ὑπέστρεψαν εἰς τὰ ἴδια. ¶ ⁷ Ἡμεῖς δὲ τὸν πλοῦν διανύσαντες ἀπὸ Τύρου κατηντήσαμεν εἰς Πτολεμαΐδα καὶ ἀσπασάμενοι τοὺς ἀδελφοὺς ἐμείναμεν ἡμέραν μίαν παρ᾽ αὐτοῖς. ⁸ τῇ δὲ ἐπαύριον ἐξελθόντες ἤλθομεν εἰς Καισάρειαν καὶ εἰσελθόντες εἰς τὸν οἶκον Φιλίππου τοῦ εὐαγγελιστοῦ, ὄντος ἐκ τῶν ἑπτά, ἐμείναμεν παρ᾽ αὐτῷ. ⁹ τούτῳ δὲ ἦσαν θυγατέρες τέσσαρες παρθένοι προφητεύουσαι. ¶ ¹⁰ ἐπιμενόντων δὲ ἡμέρας πλείους κατῆλθέν τις ἀπὸ τῆς Ἰουδαίας προφήτης ὀνόματι Ἅγαβος, ¹¹ καὶ ἐλθὼν πρὸς ἡμᾶς καὶ ἄρας τὴν ζώνην τοῦ Παύλου, δήσας ἑαυτοῦ τοὺς πόδας καὶ τὰς χεῖρας εἶπεν. Τάδε λέγει τὸ πνεῦμα τὸ ἅγιον, Τὸν ἄνδρα οὗ ἐστιν ἡ ζώνη αὕτη, οὕτως δήσουσιν ἐν Ἰερουσαλὴμ οἱ Ἰουδαῖοι καὶ παραδώσουσιν εἰς χεῖρας ἐθνῶν. ¶ ¹² ὡς δὲ ἠκούσαμεν ταῦτα, παρεκαλοῦμεν ἡμεῖς τε καὶ οἱ ἐντόπιοι τοῦ μὴ ἀναβαίνειν αὐτὸν εἰς Ἰερουσαλήμ. ¹³ τότε ἀπεκρίθη ὁ Παῦλος, Τί ποιεῖτε κλαίοντες καὶ συνθρύπτοντές μου τὴν καρδίαν; ἐγὼ γὰρ οὐ μόνον δεθῆναι ἀλλὰ καὶ ἀποθανεῖν

are you weeping   and breaking   my heart?   I   am ready not only to be bound, but also to
→ →   ⌐ποιεῖτε κλαίοντες⌐   καὶ   συνθρύπτοντες μου   ⌐τὴν καρδίαν⌐   γὰρ ἐγὼ ἔχω   ἑτοίμως οὐ   μόνον → →   δεθῆναι   ἀλλὰ καὶ →
v.pai.2p   pt.pa.npm   cj   pt.pa.npm   r.gs.1   d.asf n.asf   cj   r.ns.1   v.pai.1s   adv   pl   adv   f.ap   cj   adv
4472   3081   2779   5316   1609   3836 2840   1142   1609   2400   2290   4024   3667   1313   247   2779

die   in Jerusalem for the name   of the Lord Jesus."   14   When he   would not be dissuaded, we gave
ἀποθανεῖν   εἰς Ἰερουσαλὴμ   ὑπὲρ τοῦ ὀνόματος →   τοῦ κυρίου Ἰησοῦ   δὲ →   αὐτοῦ →   μὴ →   πειθομένου →   ἡσυχάσαμεν
f.aa   p.a   n.asf   p.g   d.gsn n.gsn   d.gsn n.gsm   n.gsm   cj   r.gsm.3   pl   pt.pp.gsm   v.aai.1p
633   1650   2647   5642   3836 3950   3836 3261   2652   1254 4275   4275   3590   4275   2483

up and said, "The Lord's   will   be done." ¶   15   After   this,   we got ready   and
←   εἰπόντες τὸ   ⌐τοῦ κυρίου⌐ θέλημα →   γινέσθω   δὲ   Μετὰ τὰς ἡμέρας ταύτας →   ἐπισκευασάμενοι
pt.aa.npm   d.nsn   d.gsm n.gsm   n.nsn   v.pmm.3s   cj   p.a   d.apf n.apf   r.apf   pt.am.npm
3306   3836   3836 3261   2525   1181   1254 3552   3836 2465   4047   2171

went   up to Jerusalem.   16   Some of the disciples from Caesarea   accompanied   us   and brought us to
ἀνεβαίνομεν ←   εἰς Ἱεροσόλυμα   δὲ καὶ →   →   τῶν μαθητῶν ἀπὸ Καισαρείας συνῆλθον   σὺν ἡμῖν   ἄγοντες →
v.iai.1p   p.a   n.apn   cj   adv   d.gpm n.gpm   p.g   n.gsf   v.aai.3p   p.d r.dp.1   pt.pa.npm
326   1650   2642   1254 2779   3836 3412   608   2791   5302   5250 7005   72

the home of Mnason, where   we were to stay.   He was a man from Cyprus and one of the early   disciples.
Μνάσωνι ⌐παρ' ᾧ⌐ → →   ξενισθῶμεν   τινι   Κυπρίῳ   ἀρχαίῳ μαθητῇ
n.dsm   p.d r.dsm   v.aps.1p   r.dsm   n.dsm   a.dsm n.dsm
3643   4123 4005   3826   5516   3250   792 3412

Paul's Arrival at Jerusalem

21:17   When we   arrived   at Jerusalem, the brothers received   us   warmly.   18   The next   day Paul
δὲ →   ἡμῶν Γενομένων εἰς   Ἱεροσόλυμα οἱ   ἀδελφοὶ   ἀπεδέξαντο ἡμᾶς ἀσμένως   δὲ Τῇ   ἐπιούσῃ   ὁ   Παῦλος
cj   r.gp.1   pt.am.gpm   p.a   n.apn   d.npm n.npm   v.ami.3p   r.ap.1   adv   cj   d.dsf   pt.pa.dsf   d.nsm n.nsm
1254 1181   7005   1181   1650   2642   3836 81   622   7005   830   1254 3836   2079   3836 4263

and the rest of us   went to   see James,   and all   the elders   were present.   19   Paul greeted   them and
σὺν   ἡμῖν εἰσῄει πρὸς   Ἰάκωβον τε   πάντες οἱ   πρεσβύτεροι →   παρεγένοντο   καὶ   ἀσπασάμενος αὐτοὺς
p.d   r.dp.1   v.iai.3s   p.a   n.asm   cj   a.npm   d.npm a.npm   v.ami.3p   cj   pt.am.nsm   r.apm.3
5250   7005   1655   4639   2610   5445   4246   3836 4565   4134   2779   832   899

reported in   detail   what God   had done   among the Gentiles through his   ministry.   ¶   20
ἐξηγεῖτο καθ'   ἓν ἕκαστον, ὧν   ὁ   θεὸς →   ἐποίησεν ἐν   τοῖς ἔθνεσιν διὰ   αὐτοῦ ⌐τῆς διακονίας⌐   δὲ
v.imi.3s   p.a   a.asn r.asn   r.gpn   d.nsm n.nsm   v.aai.3s   p.d   d.dpn n.dpn   p.g   r.gsm.3   d.gsf n.gsf   cj
2007   2848   1651 1667   4005   3836 2536   4472   1877   3836 1620   1328   899   3836 1355   1254

When they heard   this, they praised God.   Then they said to Paul: "You see,   brother, how many
→ →   ἀκούσαντες   Οἱ   ἐδόξαζον ⌐τὸν θεόν⌐   τε →   εἶπόν   αὐτῷ   Θεωρεῖς ἀδελφέ →   πόσαι
pt.aa.npm   d.npm   v.iai.3p   d.asm n.asm   cj   v.aai.3p   r.dsm.3   v.pai.2s   n.vsm   r.npf
201   3836   1519   3836 2536   5445   3306   899   2555   81   4531

thousands   of Jews   have believed,   and all   of them are   zealous for the law.   21   They
μυριάδες   εἰσὶν ἐν ⌐τοῖς Ἰουδαίοις⌐   ⌐τῶν πεπιστευκότων⌐ καὶ   πάντες ←   ὑπάρχουσιν ζηλωταὶ →   τοῦ νόμου   δὲ →
n.npf   v.pai.3p   p.d   d.dpm a.dpm   d.gpm pt.ra.gpm   cj   a.npm   v.pai.3p   n.npm   d.gsm n.gsm   cj
3689   1639   1877   3836 2681   3836 4409   2779   4246   5639   2421   3836 3795   1254

have been informed   that you teach   all   the Jews   who live among the Gentiles to turn
→ →   κατηχήθησαν περὶ σοῦ ὅτι →   διδάσκεις πάντας τοὺς Ἰουδαίους   κατὰ   τὰ ἔθνη   ἀποστασίαν
v.api.3p   p.g   r.gs.2   cj   v.pai.2s   a.apm   d.apm a.apm   p.a   d.apn n.apn   n.asf
2994   4309 5148   4022   1438   4246   3836 2681   2848   3836 1620   686

away from Moses,   telling them not to circumcise their   children or   live   according to our customs.   22   What
←   ἀπὸ   Μωϋσέως λέγων   μὴ →   περιτέμνειν αὐτοὺς ⌐τὰ τέκνα⌐   μηδὲ περιπατεῖν ←   τοῖς ἔθεσιν   οὖν τί
p.g   n.gsm   pt.pa.nsm   pl   f.pa   r.apm.3   d.apn n.apn   cj   f.pa   d.dpn n.dpn   cj   r.nsn
608   3707   3306   3590   4362   899   3836 5451   3593   4344   3836 1621   4036 5515

shall we do? They will certainly hear   that you have come,   23   so do   what   we tell   you. There are
ἐστιν →   πάντως ἀκούσονται ὅτι →   ἐλήλυθας   οὖν ποίησον ⌐τοῦτο ὅ⌐ →   λέγομεν σοι   εἰσὶν
v.pai.3s   adv   v.fmi.3p   cj   v.rai.2s   cj   v.aam.2s   r.asn ó.asn   v.pai.1p   r.ds.2   v.pai.3p
1639   201   201   4122   201   4022   2262   4036 4472   4047 4005   3306   5148   1639

four   men   with us   who have made a vow.   24 Take   these   men, join in their   purification rites
τέσσαρες ἄνδρες →   ἡμῖν →   ἔχοντες   εὐχὴν ἐφ' ἑαυτῶν   παραλαβὼν τούτους ←   σὺν αὐτοῖς ἁγνίσθητι
a.npm   n.npm   r.dp.1   pt.pa.npm   n.asf   p.g   r.gpm.3   pt.aa.nsm   r.apm   p.d   r.dpm.3   v.apm.2s
5475   467   7005   2400   2376   2093   1571   4161   4047   5250   899   49

εἰς Ἰερουσαλὴμ ἑτοίμως ἔχω ὑπὲρ τοῦ ὀνόματος τοῦ κυρίου Ἰησοῦ. ¹⁴ μὴ πειθομένου δὲ αὐτοῦ ἡσυχάσαμεν εἰπόντες, Τοῦ κυρίου τὸ θέλημα γινέσθω. ¶ ¹⁵ Μετὰ δὲ τὰς ἡμέρας ταύτας ἐπισκευασάμενοι ἀνεβαίνομεν εἰς Ἱεροσόλυμα· ¹⁶ συνῆλθον δὲ καὶ τῶν μαθητῶν ἀπὸ Καισαρείας σὺν ἡμῖν, ἄγοντες παρ' ᾧ ξενισθῶμεν Μνάσωνί τινι Κυπρίῳ, ἀρχαίῳ μαθητῇ.

²¹:¹⁷ Γενομένων δὲ ἡμῶν εἰς Ἱεροσόλυμα ἀσμένως ἀπεδέξαντο ἡμᾶς οἱ ἀδελφοί. ¹⁸ τῇ δὲ ἐπιούσῃ εἰσῄει ὁ Παῦλος σὺν ἡμῖν πρὸς Ἰάκωβον, πάντες τε παρεγένοντο οἱ πρεσβύτεροι. ¹⁹ καὶ ἀσπασάμενος αὐτοὺς ἐξηγεῖτο καθ' ἓν ἕκαστον, ὧν ἐποίησεν ὁ θεὸς ἐν τοῖς ἔθνεσιν διὰ τῆς διακονίας αὐτοῦ. ¶ ²⁰ οἱ δὲ ἀκούσαντες ἐδόξαζον τὸν θεὸν εἶπόν τε αὐτῷ, Θεωρεῖς, ἀδελφέ, πόσαι μυριάδες εἰσὶν ἐν τοῖς Ἰουδαίοις τῶν πεπιστευκότων καὶ πάντες ζηλωταὶ τοῦ νόμου ὑπάρχουσιν· ²¹ κατηχήθησαν δὲ περὶ σοῦ ὅτι ἀποστασίαν διδάσκεις ἀπὸ Μωϋσέως τοὺς κατὰ τὰ ἔθνη πάντας Ἰουδαίους λέγων μὴ περιτέμνειν αὐτοὺς τὰ τέκνα μηδὲ τοῖς ἔθεσιν περιπατεῖν. ²² τί οὖν ἐστιν; πάντως ἀκούσονται ὅτι ἐλήλυθας. ²³ τοῦτο οὖν ποίησον ὅ σοι λέγομεν· εἰσὶν ἡμῖν ἄνδρες τέσσαρες εὐχὴν ἔχοντες ἐφ' ἑαυτῶν. ²⁴ τούτους παραλαβὼν ἁγνίσθητι σὺν αὐτοῖς καὶ δαπάνησον ἐπ' αὐτοῖς ἵνα ξυρήσονται τὴν κεφαλήν, καὶ γνώσονται πάντες ὅτι ὧν κατήχηνται περὶ σοῦ οὐδέν ἐστιν ἀλλὰ στοιχεῖς καὶ αὐτὸς φυλάσσων τὸν νόμον. ²⁵ περὶ

and pay | their expenses, so that | they | can have | their | heads | shaved. | Then | everybody | will know
καὶ δαπάνησον ἐπ᾽ αὐτοῖς ← ἵνα → → τὴν κεφαλὴν ξυρήσονται καὶ πάντες → γνώσονται ὅτι
cj v.aam.2s p.d r.dpm.3 cj d.asf n.asf v.fmi.3p cj a.npm v.fmi.3p cj
2779 1251 2093 899 1251 2671 3834 3834 3834 3836 3051 3834 2779 4246 1182 4022

there | is | no | truth | in | these | reports | about you, but | that | you | yourself | are living | in | obedience to the law.
→ ἔστιν οὐδὲν ← ὧν → κατήχηνται περὶ σοῦ ἀλλὰ → καὶ αὐτὸς → στοιχεῖς φυλάσσων ← τὸν νόμον
v.pai.3s a.nsn r.gpn v.rpi.3p p.g r.gs.2 cj adv r.nsm v.pai.2s pt.pa.nsm d.asm n.asm
1639 4029 4005 2994 4309 5148 247 5123 2779 899 5123 5875 3836 3795

25 As for | the Gentile believers, | we | have | written | to them | our | decision that | they | should | abstain | from
δὲ περὶ τῶν ἐθνῶν πεπιστευκότων ἡμεῖς → ἐπεστείλαμεν → κρίναντες αὐτοὺς → φυλάσσεσθαι ← τε
cj p.g d.gpn n.gpn pt.ra.gpn r.np.1 v.aai.1p pt.aa.npm r.apm.3 f.pm cj
1254 4309 3836 1620 4409 7005 2182 3212 899 5875 5445

food | sacrificed to idols, | from blood, | from the meat of | strangled | animals and | from | sexual
→ τὸ εἰδωλόθυτον καὶ αἷμα καὶ → → πνικτὸν ← καὶ πορνείαν
d.asn n.asn cj n.asn cj a.asn cj n.asf
3836 1628 2779 135 2779 4465 2779 4518

immorality." ¶ **26** The | next | day | Paul | took | the men | and purified himself along with | them.
← Τότε τῇ ἐχομένῃ ἡμέρᾳ ὁ Παῦλος παραλαβὼν τοὺς ἄνδρας ἁγνισθεὶς ← σὺν αὐτοῖς
adv d.dsf pt.pm.dsf n.dsf d.nsm n.nsm pt.aa.nsm d.apm n.apm pt.ap.nsm p.d r.dpm.3
5538 3836 2400 2465 3836 4263 4161 3836 467 49 5250 899

Then he | went to | the temple to give notice | of the date when the days | of purification | would end
→ εἰσῄει εἰς τὸ ἱερὸν → διαγγέλλων → τῶν ἡμερῶν τοῦ ἁγνισμοῦ → τὴν ἐκπλήρωσιν ἕως
v.iai.3s p.a d.asn n.asn pt.pa.nsm d.gpf n.gpf d.gsm n.gsm d.asf n.asf p.g
1655 1650 3836 2639 1334 3836 2465 3836 50 3836 1741 2401

and the offering | would be made | for | each | of them.
οὗ ἡ προσφορὰ → προσηνέχθη ὑπὲρ ἑκάστου ἑνὸς → αὐτῶν
r.gsm d.nsf n.nsf v.api.3s p.g r.gsm a.gsm r.gpm.3
4005 3836 4714 4712 5642 1667 1651 899

Paul Arrested

21:27 When | the | seven | days | were | nearly | over, | some | Jews | from | the province of | Asia | saw | Paul
δὲ Ὡς αἱ ἑπτὰ ἡμέραι → ἔμελλον συντελεῖσθαι οἱ Ἰουδαῖοι ἀπὸ τῆς Ἀσίας θεασάμενοι αὐτὸν
cj cj d.npf a.npf n.npf v.iai.3p f.pp d.npm a.npm p.g d.gsf n.gsf pt.am.npm r.asm.3
1254 6055 3836 2231 2465 3516 5334 3836 2681 608 3836 823 7517 899

at | the temple. | They | stirred up | the | whole | crowd and | seized | him, **28** shouting, "Men of Israel,
ἐν τῷ ἱερῷ → συνέχεον ← τὸν πάντα ὄχλον καὶ ἐπέβαλον τὰς χεῖρας ἐπ᾽ αὐτὸν κράζοντες ἄνδρες → Ἰσραηλῖται
p.d d.dsn n.dsn v.iai.3p d.asm a.asm n.asm cj v.aai.3p d.apf n.apf p.a r.asm.3 pt.pa.npm n.vpm n.vpm
1877 3836 2639 5177 3836 4246 4063 2779 2095 3836 5931 2093 899 3189 467 2703

help | us! This | is | the | man | who | teaches | all | men everywhere | against | our | people | and | our | law | and | this
βοηθεῖτε οὗτος ἐστιν ὁ ἄνθρωπος ὁ διδάσκων πάντας πανταχῇ κατὰ τοῦ λαοῦ καὶ τοῦ νόμου καὶ τούτου
v.pam.2p r.nsm v.pai.3s d.nsm n.nsm d.nsm pt.pa.nsm a.apm adv p.g d.gsm n.gsm cj d.gsm n.gsm cj r.gsm
1070 4047 1639 3836 476 3836 1438 4246 4114 2848 3836 3295 2779 3836 3795 2779 4047

place. | And besides, | he has | brought | Greeks | into | the | temple area | and | defiled | this | holy | place." **29**
τοῦ τόπου τε ἔτι καὶ εἰσήγαγεν Ἕλληνας εἰς τὸ ἱερὸν ← καὶ κεκοίνωκεν τοῦτον ἅγιον τὸν τόπον γὰρ
d.gsm n.gsm cj adv adv v.aai.3s n.apm p.a d.asn n.asn cj v.rai.3s r.asm a.asm d.asm n.asm cj
3836 5536 5445 2285 2779 1652 1818 1650 3836 2639 2779 3124 4047 41 3836 5536 1142

(They had | previously | seen | Trophimus | the | Ephesian | in | the | city | with | Paul | and | assumed that | Paul
→ ἦσαν → προεωρακότες Τρόφιμον τὸν Ἐφέσιον ἐν τῇ πόλει σὺν αὐτῷ ἐνόμιζον ὅτι ὁ Παῦλος
v.iai.3p pt.ra.npm n.asm d.asm a.asm p.d d.dsf n.dsf p.d r.dsm.3 v.iai.3p cj d.nsm n.nsm
1639 4632 5576 3836 2386 1877 3836 4484 5250 899 3787 4022 3836 4263

had brought | him | into | the | temple area.) ¶ **30** The | whole | city | was | aroused, | and | the | people | came | running
→ εἰσήγαγεν ὃν εἰς τὸ ἱερὸν ← τε ἡ ὅλη πόλις → ἐκινήθη καὶ τοῦ λαοῦ ἐγένετο συνδρομὴ
v.aai.3s r.asm p.a d.asn n.asn cj d.nsf a.nsf n.nsf v.api.3s cj d.gsm n.gsm v.ami.3s n.nsf
1652 4005 1650 3836 2639 5445 3836 3910 4484 3075 2779 3836 3295 1181 5282

from all directions. | Seizing | Paul, | they | dragged | him | from | the temple, | and | immediately | the | gates | were
← ← ← καὶ ἐπιλαβόμενοι τοῦ Παύλου → εἶλκον αὐτὸν ἔξω τοῦ ἱεροῦ καὶ εὐθέως αἱ θύραι →
cj pt.am.npm d.gsm n.gsm v.iai.3s r.asm.3 p.g d.gsm n.gsm cj adv d.npf n.npf
2779 2138 3836 4263 1816 899 2032 3836 2639 2779 2311 3836 2598

δὲ τῶν πεπιστευκότων ἐθνῶν ἡμεῖς ἐπεστείλαμεν κρίναντες φυλάσσεσθαι αὐτοὺς τό τε εἰδωλόθυτον καὶ αἷμα καὶ πνικτὸν καὶ πορνείαν. ¶ 26 τότε ὁ Παῦλος παραλαβὼν τοὺς ἄνδρας τῇ ἐχομένῃ ἡμέρᾳ σὺν αὐτοῖς ἁγνισθείς, εἰσῄει εἰς τὸ ἱερὸν διαγγέλλων τὴν ἐκπλήρωσιν τῶν ἡμερῶν τοῦ ἁγνισμοῦ ἕως οὗ προσηνέχθη ὑπὲρ ἑνὸς ἑκάστου αὐτῶν ἡ προσφορά.

21:27 Ὡς δὲ ἔμελλον αἱ ἑπτὰ ἡμέραι συντελεῖσθαι, οἱ ἀπὸ τῆς Ἀσίας Ἰουδαῖοι θεασάμενοι αὐτὸν ἐν τῷ ἱερῷ συνέχεον πάντα τὸν ὄχλον καὶ ἐπέβαλον ἐπ᾽ αὐτὸν τὰς χεῖρας 28 κράζοντες, Ἄνδρες Ἰσραηλῖται, βοηθεῖτε· οὗτός ἐστιν ὁ ἄνθρωπος ὁ κατὰ τοῦ λαοῦ καὶ τοῦ νόμου καὶ τοῦ τόπου τούτου πάντας πανταχῇ διδάσκων, ἔτι τε καὶ Ἕλληνας εἰσήγαγεν εἰς τὸ ἱερὸν καὶ κεκοίνωκεν τὸν ἅγιον τόπον τοῦτον. 29 ἦσαν γὰρ προεωρακότες Τρόφιμον τὸν Ἐφέσιον ἐν τῇ πόλει σὺν αὐτῷ, ὃν ἐνόμιζον ὅτι εἰς τὸ ἱερὸν εἰσήγαγεν ὁ Παῦλος. ¶ 30 ἐκινήθη τε ἡ πόλις ὅλη καὶ ἐγένετο συνδρομὴ τοῦ λαοῦ, καὶ ἐπιλαβόμενοι τοῦ Παύλου εἷλκον αὐτὸν ἔξω τοῦ ἱεροῦ καὶ εὐθέως ἐκλείσθησαν αἱ θύραι. 31 ζητούντων τε αὐτὸν ἀποκτεῖναι ἀνέβη φάσις τῷ χιλιάρχῳ

shut.　　**31**　While they were　trying　　to kill　　him,　news　reached　the commander　of the　Roman　troops that
ἐκλείσθησαν　τε　→　　　→　　Ζητούντων　→　ἀποκτεῖναι　αὐτὸν　φάσις　ἀνέβη　τῷ　χιλιάρχῳ　→　τῆς　　　σπείρης　ὅτι
v.api.3p　cj　　　　　　　pt.pa.gpm　　f.aa　　r.asm.3　n.nsf　v.aai.3s　d.dsm　n.dsm　　d.gsf　　　n.gsf　　cj
3091　　5445　　　　　　2426　　　650　　899　5762　326　3836　5941　　3836　　　5061　　4022

the whole　city　of Jerusalem　was　in an uproar.　**32** He at once　took　some officers　and　soldiers　and
ὅλη　→　　　→　Ἰερουσαλήμ　→　　→　　συγχύννεται　ὃς　ἐξαυτῆς　παραλαβὼν　στρατιώτας　καὶ　ἑκατοντάρχας
a.nsf　　　　　n.nsf　　　　　　　　v.ppi.3s　　r.nsm　adv　　pt.aa.nsm　　n.apm　　cj　　n.apm
3910　　　　2647　　　　　　　　　5177　　4005　1994　　4161　　　　　5132　2779　1672

ran　　down　to the crowd.　When the rioters saw　the commander　and　his　soldiers,　they stopped
κατέδραμεν　←　ἐπ'　αὐτούς　δὲ　→　οἱ　　ἰδόντες　τὸν　χιλίαρχον　καὶ　τοὺς στρατιώτας　→　ἐπαύσαντο
v.aai.3s　　p.a　r.apm.3　cj　　d.npm　pt.aa.npm　d.asm　n.asm　　cj　d.apm　n.apm　　　v.ami.3p
2963　　　　2093　899　1254 1625　3836　1625　3836　5941　2779　3836　5132　　　4264

beating　Paul.　¶ **33**　The commander　came　up and　arrested him　and ordered him to be bound with
τύπτοντες　ˌτὸν Παῦλονˌ　τότε ὁ　χιλίαρχος　ἐγγίσας　←　ἐπελάβετο αὐτοῦ　καὶ　ἐκέλευσεν　→　→　δεθῆναι　→
pt.pa.npm　d.asm　n.asm　adv　d.nsm　n.nsm　　pt.aa.nsm　　v.ami.3s　r.gsm.3　cj　v.aai.3s　　　f.ap
5597　　　3836　4263　5538 3836　5941　　1581　　　2138　　899　2779　3027　　　1313

two chains.　Then he asked　who he was　and what　he had done.　**34** Some in　the crowd shouted　one thing and
δυσὶ ἀλύσεσι καὶ　→　ἐπυνθάνετο τίς　→　εἴη　καὶ τί　→　ἐστιν πεποιηκώς　ἄλλοι　ἐν　τῷ ὄχλῳ　ἐπεφώνουν τι　←　δὲ
a.dpf n.dpf　cj　　v.imi.3s　　r.nsm　v.pao.3s cj　r.asn　v.pai.3s pt.ra.nsm　r.npm　p.d d.dsm n.dsm　v.iai.3p　r.asn　cj
1545 268　2779　　4785　　5515　　1639　2779 5515　1639　4472　　257　1877 3836 4063　2215　5516　1254

some another,　and since the commander　could　not get　at the truth　because　of the uproar,　he ordered that
ἄλλο　δὲ　→　　αὐτοῦ　δυναμένου μὴ　γνῶναι　←　τὸ ἀσφαλὲς διὰ　←　τὸν θόρυβον　→　ἐκέλευσεν
r.asn　cj　　r.gsm.3　pt.pp.gsm　pl　f.aa　　d.asn a.asn　p.a　　d.asm n.asm　　v.aai.3s
257　1254 1538　899　1538　3590 1182　3836 855　1328　　3836 2573　　3027

Paul be taken　into the barracks.　**35** When Paul reached　the steps,　the violence of the mob was so
αὐτὸν　→　ἄγεσθαι εἰς τὴν παρεμβολήν　δὲ　ὅτε　ἐγένετο ἐπὶ τοὺς ἀναβαθμούς διὰ τὴν βίαν　→　τοῦ ὄχλου　→
r.asm.3　　f.pp　p.a d.asf n.asf　　cj　cj　v.ami.3s p.a d.apm n.apm　　p.a d.asf n.asf　d.gsm n.gsm
899　　72　1650 3836 4213　1254 4021　1181　2093 3836 325　　1328 3836 1040　3836 4063

great he　had to be carried　by the soldiers.　**36** The crowd　that followed kept shouting, "Away
συνέβη αὐτὸν　→　→　βαστάζεσθαι ὑπὸ τῶν στρατιωτῶν　γὰρ τὸ ˌπλῆθος τοῦ λαοῦˌ　ἠκολούθει　κράζοντες　αἶρε
v.aai.3s r.asm.3　　　f.pp　　p.g d.gpm n.gpm　　cj d.nsn n.nsn d.gsm n.gsm　v.iai.3s　pt.pa.npm　v.pam.2s
5201　899　　　1002　　5679 3836 5132　　1142 3836 4436 3836 3295　199　　3189　　149

with him!"
→　αὐτόν
r.asm.3
899

Paul Speaks to the Crowd

21:37　As the soldiers were about　to take　Paul into the barracks,　he　　asked the commander,
τε　→　　→　Μέλλων →　εἰσάγεσθαι　εἰς τὴν παρεμβολὴν ὁ Παῦλος λέγει τῷ χιλιάρχῳ
cj　　　　pt.pa.nsm　f.pp　　　p.a d.asf n.asf　d.nsm n.nsm　v.pai.3s d.dsm n.dsm
5445　　3516　　1652　　　1650 3836 4213　3836 4263　3306　3836 5941

"May　I　say something to you?"　¶　"Do you speak　Greek?" he replied. **38**　"Aren't　you the
ˌεἰ ἔξεστινˌ μοι εἰπεῖν τι　πρός σέ　δὲ　→　γινώσκεις Ἑλληνιστὶ ὁ ἔφη　ἄρα ˌοὐκ εἶˌ σὺ ὁ
cj v.pai.3s r.ds.1 f.aa r.asn　p.a r.as.2　cj　　v.pai.2s　adv　d.nsm v.iai.3s　cj pl v.pai.2s r.ns.2 d.nsm
1623 1997 1609 3306 5516　4639 5148　1254　　1182　1822　3836 5774　726 4024 1639 5148 3836

Egyptian who started a revolt　and led　four　thousand terrorists　out into the
Αἰγύπτιος ὁ　→　ἀναστατώσας καὶ ἐξαγαγὼν ˌτοὺς τετρακισχιλίουςˌ ←　ˌἄνδρας τῶν σικαρίωνˌ ←　εἰς τὴν
n.nsm　d.nsm　　pt.aa.nsm　cj　pt.aa.nsm　d.apm　n.apm　　　n.apm d.gpm n.gpm　　p.a d.asf
130　3836　　415　2779 1974　3836 5483　　467 3836 4974　　1974 1650 3836

desert some time ago?"　¶ **39**　Paul　answered,　"I am a Jew,　from
ἔρημον →　　ˌπρὸ τούτων τῶν ἡμερῶνˌ δὲ ὁ Παῦλος εἶπεν μέν ἐγὼ εἰμι ˌἄνθρωπος Ἰουδαῖοςˌ →
n.asf　　p.g r.gpf d.gpf n.gpf　cj d.nsm n.nsm v.aai.3s pl r.ns.1 v.pai.1s n.nsm a.nsm
2245　　4574 4047 3836 2465　1254 3836 4263 3306　3525 1609 1639 476　2681

Tarsus in Cilicia,　a citizen of no ordinary city.　Please　let　me speak　to the people." ¶
Ταρσεὺς →　ˌτῆς Κιλικίαςˌ πολίτης οὐκ ἀσήμου πόλεως δὲ δέομαι σου ἐπίτρεψόν μοι λαλῆσαι πρὸς τὸν λαόν
n.nsm　d.gsf n.gsf　n.nsm pl a.gsf n.gsf cj v.ppi.1s r.gs.2 v.aam.2s r.ds.1 f.aa　p.a d.asm n.asm
5432　3836 3070　4489 4024 817 4484 1254 1289 5148 2205　1609 3281　4639 3836 3295

τῆς σπείρης ὅτι ὅλη συγχύννεται Ἰερουσαλήμ. **32** ὃς ἐξαυτῆς παραλαβὼν στρατιώτας καὶ ἑκατοντάρχας κατέδραμεν ἐπ' αὐτούς, οἱ δὲ ἰδόντες τὸν χιλίαρχον καὶ τοὺς στρατιώτας ἐπαύσαντο τύπτοντες τὸν Παῦλον. ¶ **33** τότε ἐγγίσας ὁ χιλίαρχος ἐπελάβετο αὐτοῦ καὶ ἐκέλευσεν δεθῆναι ἁλύσεσι δυσί, καὶ ἐπυνθάνετο τίς εἴη καὶ τί ἐστιν πεποιηκώς. **34** ἄλλοι δὲ ἄλλο τι ἐπεφώνουν ἐν τῷ ὄχλῳ. μὴ δυναμένου δὲ αὐτοῦ γνῶναι τὸ ἀσφαλὲς διὰ τὸν θόρυβον ἐκέλευσεν ἄγεσθαι αὐτὸν εἰς τὴν παρεμβολήν. **35** ὅτε δὲ ἐγένετο ἐπὶ τοὺς ἀναβαθμούς, συνέβη βαστάζεσθαι αὐτὸν ὑπὸ τῶν στρατιωτῶν διὰ τὴν βίαν τοῦ ὄχλου, **36** ἠκολούθει γὰρ τὸ πλῆθος τοῦ λαοῦ κράζοντες, Αἶρε αὐτόν.

21:37 Μέλλων τε εἰσάγεσθαι εἰς τὴν παρεμβολὴν ὁ Παῦλος λέγει τῷ χιλιάρχῳ, Εἰ ἔξεστίν μοι εἰπεῖν τι πρός σέ; ¶ ὁ δὲ ἔφη, Ἑλληνιστὶ γινώσκεις; **38** οὐκ ἄρα σὺ εἶ ὁ Αἰγύπτιος ὁ πρὸ τούτων τῶν ἡμερῶν ἀναστατώσας καὶ ἐξαγαγὼν εἰς τὴν ἔρημον τοὺς τετρακισχιλίους ἄνδρας τῶν σικαρίων; ¶ **39** εἶπεν δὲ ὁ Παῦλος, Ἐγὼ ἄνθρωπος μέν εἰμι Ἰουδαῖος, Ταρσεὺς τῆς Κιλικίας, οὐκ ἀσήμου πόλεως πολίτης· δέομαι δέ σου, ἐπίτρεψόν μοι λαλῆσαι πρὸς τὸν λαόν. ¶ **40** ἐπιτρέψαντος δὲ αὐτοῦ ὁ Παῦλος ἑστὼς ἐπὶ

40 Having received the commander's permission, Paul stood on the steps and motioned to the
δὲ ┌→ αὐτοῦ ἐπιτρέψαντος ὁ Παῦλος ἑστὼς ἐπὶ τῶν ἀναβαθμῶν ⌐κατέσεισεν τῇ χειρὶ → τῷ
cj r.gsm.3 pt.aa.gsm d.nsm n.nsm pt.ra.nsm p.g d.gpm n.gpm v.aai.3s d.dsf n.dsf d.dsm
1254 2205 2205 899 2205 3836 4263 2705 2093 3836 325 2939 3836 5931 3836

crowd. When they were all silent, he said to them in Aramaic: **22:1** "Brothers
λαῷ δὲ → → γενομένης πολλῆς σιγῆς → προσεφώνησεν ← → ⌐τῇ Ἑβραΐδι διαλέκτῳ λέγων ἄνδρες ἀδελφοὶ
n.dsm cj pt.am.gsf a.gsf n.gsf v.aai.3s d.dsf a.dsf n.dsf pt.pa.nsm n.vpm n.vpm
3295 1254 1181 4498 4968 4715 3836 1579 1365 3306 467 81

and fathers, listen now to my defense." ¶ **2** When they heard him speak to them
καὶ πατέρες ἀκούσατε νυνὶ ↰ μου ⌐τῆς ἀπολογίας⌐ πρὸς ὑμᾶς δὲ → ἀκούσαντες ὅτι προσεφώνει → αὐτοῖς
cj n.vpm v.aam.2p adv r.gs.1 d.gsf n.gsf p.a r.ap.2 cj pt.aa.npm cj v.iai.3s r.dpm.3
2779 4252 201 3815 201 1609 3836 665 4639 7007 1254 201 4022 4715 899

in Aramaic, they became very quiet. ¶ Then Paul said: **3** "I am a Jew, born in
┌→ ⌐τῇ Ἑβραΐδι διαλέκτῳ → παρέσχον μᾶλλον ἡσυχίαν καὶ φησίν ἐγώ εἰμι ⌐ἀνὴρ Ἰουδαῖος⌐ γεγεννημένος ἐν
d.dsf a.dsf n.dsf v.aai.3p adv.c n.asf cj v.pai.3s r.ns.1 v.pai.1s n.nsm a.nsm pt.rp.nsm p.d
3836 1579 1365 4218 3437 2484 2779 5774 1609 1639 467 2681 1164 1877

Tarsus of Cilicia, but brought up in this city. Under Gamaliel I was thoroughly
Ταρσῷ → ⌐τῆς Κιλικίας⌐ δὲ ἀνατεθραμμένος ← ἐν ταύτῃ ⌐τῇ πόλει⌐ παρὰ τοὺς πόδας Γαμαλιὴλ → → ⌐κατὰ ἀκρίβειαν⌐
n.dsf d.gsf n.gsf cj pt.rp.nsm p.d r.dsf d.dsf n.dsf p.a d.apm n.apm n.gsm p.a n.asf
5433 3836 3070 1254 427 1877 4047 3836 4484 4123 3836 4546 1137 2848 205

trained in the law of our fathers and was just as zealous for God as any of you are today. **4** I
πεπαιδευμένος → τοῦ νόμου → πατρῴου ὑπάρχων ζηλωτὴς → ⌐τοῦ θεοῦ⌐ καθὼς πάντες ὑμεῖς ἐστε σήμερον ὃς
pt.rp.nsm d.gsm n.gsm a.gsm pt.pa.nsm n.nsm d.gsm n.gsm cj a.npm r.np.2 v.pai.2p adv r.nsm
4084 3836 3795 4262 5639 2421 3836 2536 2777 4246 7007 1639 4958 4005

persecuted the followers of this Way to their death, arresting both men and women and throwing them
ἐδίωξα ταύτην ⌐τὴν ὁδὸν⌐ ἄχρι θανάτου δεσμεύων τε ἄνδρας καὶ γυναῖκας καὶ παραδιδοὺς
v.aai.1s r.asf d.asf n.asf p.g n.gsm pt.pa.nsm cj n.apm cj n.apf cj pt.pa.nsm
1503 4047 3836 3847 948 2505 1297 5445 467 2779 1222 2779 4140

into prison, **5** as also the high priest and all the Council can testify. I even obtained letters from them
εἰς φυλακὰς ὡς καὶ ὁ → ἀρχιερεὺς καὶ πᾶν τὸ πρεσβυτέριον → μαρτυρεῖ μοι ↱ καὶ δεξάμενος ἐπιστολὰς παρ' ὧν
p.a n.apf cj adv d.nsm n.nsm cj a.nsn d.nsn n.nsn v.pai.3s r.ds.1 adv pt.am.nsm n.apf p.g r.gpm
1650 5871 6055 2779 3836 797 2779 4246 3836 4564 3455 1609 1312 2779 1312 2186 4123 4005

to their brothers in Damascus, and went there to bring these people as prisoners to Jerusalem
πρὸς τοὺς ἀδελφοὺς εἰς Δαμασκὸν ἐπορευόμην → ἄξων καὶ → ⌐τοὺς ἐκεῖσε ὄντας⌐ δεδεμένους εἰς Ἰερουσαλὴμ
p.a d.apm n.apm p.a n.asf v.imi.1s pt.fa.nsm adv d.apm pt.pa.apm pt.rp.apm p.a n.asf
4639 3836 81 1650 1242 4513 72 2779 3836 1698 1639 1313 1650 2647

to be punished. ¶ **6** "About noon as I came near Damascus, suddenly a bright
ἵνα → τιμωρηθῶσιν δὲ Ἐγένετο περὶ μεσημβρίαν → μοι πορευομένῳ καὶ ἐγγίζοντι ⌐τῇ Δαμασκῷ⌐ ἐξαίφνης ἱκανὸν
cj v.aps.3p cj v.ami.3s p.a n.asf r.ds.1 pt.pm.dsm cj pt.pa.dsm d.dsf n.dsf adv a.asn
2671 5512 1254 1181 4309 3540 4513 4513 2779 1581 3836 1242 1978 2653

light from heaven flashed around me. **7** I fell to the ground and heard a voice say to me, 'Saul!
φῶς ἐκ ⌐τοῦ οὐρανοῦ⌐ περιαστράψαι περὶ ἐμέ τε → ἔπεσα εἰς τὸ ἔδαφος καὶ ἤκουσα φωνῆς λεγούσης → μοι Σαοὺλ
n.asn p.g d.gsm n.gsm f.aa p.a r.as.1 cj v.aai.1s p.a d.asn n.asn cj v.aai.1s n.gsf pt.pa.gsf r.ds.1 n.vsm
5890 1666 3836 4041 4313 4309 1609 5445 4406 1650 3836 1611 2779 201 5889 3306 1609 4910

Saul! Why do you persecute me?' ¶ **8** "'Who are you, Lord?' I asked. "'I am Jesus of
Σαούλ τί → διώκεις με δὲ τίς εἶ ← κύριε ἐγὼ ἀπεκρίθην τε ἐγώ εἰμι Ἰησοῦς →
n.vsm r.asn v.pai.2s r.as.1 cj r.nsm v.pai.2s n.vsm r.ns.1 v.api.1s cj r.ns.1 v.pai.1s n.nsm
4910 5515 1503 1609 1254 5515 1639 3261 1609 646 5445 1609 1639 2652

Nazareth, whom you are persecuting,' he replied. **9** My companions saw the light, but they
ὁ Ναζωραῖος⌐ ὃν σὺ → διώκεις εἶπεν πρός με δὲ ἐμοὶ ⌐οἱ ὄντες σὺν⌐ μὲν ἐθεάσαντο τὸ φῶς δὲ →
d.nsm n.nsm r.asm r.ns.2 v.pai.2s v.aai.3s p.a r.as.1 cj r.ds.1 d.npm pt.pa.npm p.d pl v.ami.3p d.asn n.asn cj
3836 3717 4005 5148 1503 3306 4639 1609 1254 1609 3836 1639 5250 3525 2517 3836 5890 1254 201

did not understand the voice of him who was speaking to me. ¶ **10** "'What shall I do, Lord?' I asked.
┌→ οὐκ ἤκουσαν τὴν φωνὴν τοῦ → λαλοῦντος → μοι δέ τί → ποιήσω κύριε → εἶπον δὲ
pl v.aai.3p d.asf n.asf d.gsm pt.pa.gsm r.ds.1 cj r.asn v.aas.1s n.vsm v.aai.1s cj
201 4024 201 3836 5889 3836 3281 1609 1254 5515 4472 3261 3306 1254

τῶν ἀναβαθμῶν κατέσεισεν τῇ χειρὶ τῷ λαῷ. πολλῆς δὲ σιγῆς γενομένης προσεφώνησεν τῇ Ἑβραΐδι διαλέκτῳ λέγων,
22:1 Ἄνδρες ἀδελφοὶ καὶ πατέρες, ἀκούσατέ μου τῆς πρὸς ὑμᾶς νυνὶ ἀπολογίας. ¶ **2** ἀκούσαντες δὲ ὅτι τῇ Ἑβραΐδι διαλέκτῳ
προσεφώνει αὐτοῖς, μᾶλλον παρέσχον ἡσυχίαν. ¶ καὶ φησίν, **3** Ἐγώ εἰμι ἀνὴρ Ἰουδαῖος, γεγεννημένος ἐν Ταρσῷ τῆς Κιλικίας,
ἀνατεθραμμένος δὲ ἐν τῇ πόλει ταύτῃ, παρὰ τοὺς πόδας Γαμαλιὴλ πεπαιδευμένος κατὰ ἀκρίβειαν τοῦ πατρῴου νόμου, ζηλωτὴς
ὑπάρχων τοῦ θεοῦ καθὼς πάντες ὑμεῖς ἐστε σήμερον· **4** ὃς ταύτην τὴν ὁδὸν ἐδίωξα ἄχρι θανάτου δεσμεύων καὶ παραδιδοὺς
εἰς φυλακὰς ἄνδρας τε καὶ γυναῖκας, **5** ὡς καὶ ὁ ἀρχιερεὺς μαρτυρεῖ μοι καὶ πᾶν τὸ πρεσβυτέριον, παρ' ὧν καὶ ἐπιστολὰς
δεξάμενος πρὸς τοὺς ἀδελφοὺς εἰς Δαμασκὸν ἐπορευόμην, ἄξων καὶ τοὺς ἐκεῖσε ὄντας δεδεμένους εἰς Ἰερουσαλὴμ ἵνα
τιμωρηθῶσιν. ¶ **6** Ἐγένετο δέ μοι πορευομένῳ καὶ ἐγγίζοντι τῇ Δαμασκῷ περὶ μεσημβρίαν ἐξαίφνης ἐκ τοῦ οὐρανοῦ
περιαστράψαι φῶς ἱκανὸν περὶ ἐμέ, **7** ἔπεσά τε εἰς τὸ ἔδαφος καὶ ἤκουσα φωνῆς λεγούσης μοι, Σαοὺλ Σαούλ, τί με διώκεις; ¶
8 ἐγὼ δὲ ἀπεκρίθην, Τίς εἶ, κύριε; εἶπέν τε πρός με, Ἐγώ εἰμι Ἰησοῦς ὁ Ναζωραῖος, ὃν σὺ διώκεις. **9** οἱ δὲ σὺν ἐμοὶ ὄντες τὸ
μὲν φῶς ἐθεάσαντο τὴν δὲ φωνὴν οὐκ ἤκουσαν τοῦ λαλοῦντός μοι. ¶ **10** εἶπον δέ, Τί ποιήσω, κύριε; ὁ δὲ κύριος εἶπεν πρός με,

"'Get up,' the Lord said, 'and go into Damascus. There you will be told all that you
ἀναστὰς ← ὁ κύριος εἶπεν πρός με πορεύου εἰς Δαμασκόν κἀκεῖ σοι → λαληθήσεται περὶ πάντων ὧν σοι
pt.aa.nsm d.nsm n.nsm v.aai.3s p.a r.as.1 v.pmm.2s p.a n.asf crasis r.ds.2 v.fpi.3s p.g a.gpn r.gpn r.ds.2
482 3836 3261 3306 4639 1609 4513 1650 1242 2795 5148 3281 4309 4246 4005 5148

have been assigned to do.' 11 My companions led me by the hand into Damascus,
→ τέτακται → ποιῆσαι δὲ ὡς μοι ὑπὸ τῶν συνόντων χειραγωγούμενος ← ← ← ἦλθον εἰς Δαμασκόν
v.rpi.3s f.aa cj r.ds.1 p.g d.gpm pt.pp.gpm pt.pp.nsm v.aai.1s p.a n.asf
5435 4472 1254 6055 1609 5679 3836 5289 5932 2262 1650 1242

because the brilliance of the light had blinded me. ¶ 12 "A man named Ananias came to see
ἀπὸ τῆς δόξης → ἐκείνου τοῦ φωτός, → οὐκ ἐνέβλεπον ← δέ τις ἀνὴρ Ἁνανίας ἐλθὼν πρός
p.g d.gsf n.gsf r.gsn d.gsn n.gsn pl v.iai.1s cj r.nsm n.nsm n.nsm pt.aa.nsm p.a
608 3836 1518 5890 1697 3836 5890 4024 1838 1254 5516 467 393 2262 4639

me. He was a devout observer of the law and highly respected by all the Jews living there.
με εὐλαβὴς κατὰ τὸν νόμον → μαρτυρούμενος ὑπὸ πάντων τῶν Ἰουδαίων κατοικούντων ←
r.as.1 a.nsm p.a d.asm n.asm pt.pp.nsm p.g a.gpm d.gpm a.gpm pt.pa.gpm
1609 2327 2848 3836 3795 3455 5679 4246 3836 2681 2997

13 He stood beside me and said, 'Brother Saul, receive your sight!' And at that very moment I was able to
καὶ → ἐπιστὰς ← εἶπεν μοι ἀδελφέ Σαοὺλ → ἀνάβλεψον κἀγὼ τῇ αὐτῇ ὥρᾳ → →
cj pt.aa.nsm v.aai.3s r.ds.1 n.vsm n.vsm v.aam.2s crasis d.dsf r.dsf n.dsf
2779 2392 3306 1609 81 4910 329 2743 3836 899 6052

see him. ¶ 14 "Then he said: 'The God of our fathers has chosen you to know his
ἀνέβλεψα εἰς αὐτόν δὲ ὁ εἶπεν ὁ θεὸς → ἡμῶν τῶν πατέρων, → προεχειρίσατό σε → γνῶναι αὐτοῦ
v.aai.1s p.a r.asm.3 cj d.nsm v.aai.3s d.nsm n.nsm r.gp.1 d.gpm n.gpm v.ami.3s r.as.2 f.aa r.gsm.3
329 1650 899 1254 3836 3306 3836 2536 4252 7005 3836 4252 4741 5148 1182 899

will and to see the Righteous One and to hear words from his mouth. 15 You will be his witness
τὸ θέλημα, καὶ → ἰδεῖν τὸν δίκαιον ← καὶ → ἀκοῦσαι φωνὴν ἐκ αὐτοῦ τοῦ στόματος, ὅτι → → ἔσῃ αὐτῷ μάρτυς
d.asn n.asn cj f.aa d.asm a.asm cj f.aa n.asf p.g r.gsm.3 d.gsn n.gsn cj v.fmi.2s r.dsm.3 n.nsm
3836 2525 2779 1625 3836 1465 2779 201 5889 1666 899 3836 5125 4022 1639 899 3459

to all men of what you have seen and heard. 16 And now what are you waiting for? Get up, be
πρὸς πάντας ἀνθρώπους → ὧν → ἑώρακας καὶ ἤκουσας καὶ νῦν τί → μέλλεις ἀναστὰς
p.a a.apm n.apm r.gpn v.rai.2s cj v.aai.2s cj adv r.asn v.pai.2s pt.aa.nsm
4639 4246 476 4005 3972 2779 201 2779 3814 5515 3516 482

baptized and wash your sins away, calling on his name.' ¶ 17 "When I
βάπτισαι καὶ ἀπόλουσαι σου ⸤τὰς ἁμαρτίας,⸥ ἐπικαλεσάμενος ← αὐτοῦ ⸤τὸ ὄνομα δὲ Ἐγένετο → μοι
v.amm.2s cj v.amm.2s r.gs.2 d.apf n.apf pt.am.nsm r.gsm.3 d.asn n.asn cj v.ami.3s r.ds.1
966 2779 666 5148 3836 281 2126 899 3836 3950 1254 1181 5715 1609

returned to Jerusalem and was praying at the temple, I fell into a trance 18 and saw the Lord
ὑποστρέψαντι εἰς Ἰερουσαλὴμ καὶ μου → προσευχομένου ἐν τῷ ἱερῷ με γενέσθαι ἐν ἐκστάσει καὶ ἰδεῖν αὐτὸν
pt.aa.dsm p.a n.asf cj r.gs.1 pt.pm.gsm p.d d.dsn n.dsn r.as.1 f.am p.d n.dsf cj f.aa r.asm.3
5715 1650 2647 2779 1609 4667 1877 3836 2639 1609 1181 1877 1749 2779 1625 899

speaking. 'Quick!' he said to me. 'Leave Jerusalem immediately, because they will not accept your
λέγοντα σπεῦσον → μοι καὶ ἔξελθε ἐξ Ἰερουσαλήμ ἐν τάχει διότι → → οὐ παραδέξονταί σου
pt.pa.asm v.aam.2s r.ds.1 cj v.aam.2s p.g n.gsf p.d n.dsn cj pl v.fmi.3p r.gs.2
3306 5067 1609 2779 2002 1666 2647 1877 5443 1484 4138 4138 4024 4138 5148

testimony about me.' ¶ 19 "'Lord,' I replied, 'these men know that I went from one
μαρτυρίαν περὶ ἐμοῦ κύριε κἀγὼ εἶπον αὐτοὶ ἐπίστανται ὅτι ἐγὼ ἤμην ⸤κατὰ τὰς συναγωγὰς, ←
n.asf p.g r.gs.1 n.vsm crasis v.aai.1s r.npm v.ppi.3p cj r.ns.1 v.imi.1s p.a d.apf n.apf
3456 4309 1609 3261 2743 3306 899 2179 4022 1609 1639 2848 3836 5252

synagogue to another to imprison and beat those who believe in you. 20 And when the blood of your martyr
→ φυλακίζων καὶ δέρων τοὺς → πιστεύοντας ἐπί σέ καὶ ὅτε τὸ αἷμα → σου ⸤τοῦ μάρτυρος,
pt.pa.nsm cj pt.pa.nsm d.apm pt.pa.apm p.a r.as.2 cj cj d.nsn n.nsn r.gs.2 d.gsm n.gsm
5872 2779 1296 3836 4409 2093 5148 2779 4021 3836 135 5108 5148 3836 3459

Stephen was shed, I stood there giving my approval and guarding the clothes of those who
Στεφάνου → ἐξεχύννετο καὶ αὐτὸς ⸤ἤμην ἐφεστὼς,⸥ καὶ → συνευδοκῶν καὶ φυλάσσων τὰ ἱμάτια → τῶν ←
n.gsm v.ipi.3s cj r.nsm v.imi.1s pt.ra.nsm cj pt.pa.nsm cj pt.pa.nsm d.apn n.apn d.gpm
5108 1773 2779 899 1639 2392 2779 5306 2779 5875 3836 2668 3836

Ἀναστὰς πορεύου εἰς Δαμασκὸν κἀκεῖ σοι λαληθήσεται περὶ πάντων ὧν τέτακταί σοι ποιῆσαι. 11 ὡς δὲ οὐκ ἐνέβλεπον ἀπὸ τῆς δόξης τοῦ φωτὸς ἐκείνου, χειραγωγούμενος ὑπὸ τῶν συνόντων μοι ἦλθον εἰς Δαμασκόν. ¶ 12 Ἁνανίας δέ τις, ἀνὴρ εὐλαβὴς κατὰ τὸν νόμον, μαρτυρούμενος ὑπὸ πάντων τῶν κατοικούντων Ἰουδαίων, 13 ἐλθὼν πρός με καὶ ἐπιστὰς εἶπέν μοι, Σαοὺλ ἀδελφέ, ἀνάβλεψον. κἀγὼ αὐτῇ τῇ ὥρᾳ ἀνέβλεψα εἰς αὐτόν. ¶ 14 ὁ δὲ εἶπεν, Ὁ θεὸς τῶν πατέρων ἡμῶν προεχειρίσατό σε γνῶναι τὸ θέλημα αὐτοῦ καὶ ἰδεῖν τὸν δίκαιον καὶ ἀκοῦσαι φωνὴν ἐκ τοῦ στόματος αὐτοῦ, 15 ὅτι ἔσῃ μάρτυς αὐτῷ πρὸς πάντας ἀνθρώπους ὧν ἑώρακας καὶ ἤκουσας. 16 καὶ νῦν τί μέλλεις; ἀναστὰς βάπτισαι καὶ ἀπόλουσαι τὰς ἁμαρτίας σου ἐπικαλεσάμενος τὸ ὄνομα αὐτοῦ ¶ 17 Ἐγένετο δέ μοι ὑποστρέψαντι εἰς Ἰερουσαλὴμ καὶ προσευχομένου μου ἐν τῷ ἱερῷ γενέσθαι με ἐν ἐκστάσει 18 καὶ ἰδεῖν αὐτὸν λέγοντά μοι, Σπεῦσον καὶ ἔξελθε ἐν τάχει ἐξ Ἰερουσαλήμ, διότι οὐ παραδέξονταί σου μαρτυρίαν περὶ ἐμοῦ. ¶ 19 κἀγὼ εἶπον, Κύριε, αὐτοὶ ἐπίστανται ὅτι ἐγὼ ἤμην φυλακίζων καὶ δέρων κατὰ τὰς συναγωγὰς τοὺς πιστεύοντας ἐπί σέ, 20 καὶ ὅτε ἐξεχύννετο τὸ αἷμα Στεφάνου τοῦ μάρτυρός σου, καὶ αὐτὸς ἤμην ἐφεστὼς καὶ συνευδοκῶν καὶ φυλάσσων τὰ ἱμάτια τῶν

were killing   him.'   ¶ **21** "Then the Lord said to me, 'Go;   I will send   you far   away to the
→ ἀναιρούντων αὐτόν   καὶ   εἶπεν πρός με πορεύου ὅτι ἐγώ → ἐξαποστελῶ σε μακρὰν ←   εἰς
pt.pa.gpm r.asm.3   cj   v.aai.3s p.a r.as.1 v.pmm.2s cj r.ns.1   v.fai.1s r.as.2 adv   p.a
359   899   2779   3306 4639 1609 4513 4022 1609   1990 5148 3426   1650

Gentiles.'"
ἔθνη
n.apn
1620

Paul the Roman Citizen

22:22   The crowd listened to Paul until he said   this. Then they raised their voices   and shouted,
δὲ   Ἤκουον ← αὐτοῦ ἄχρι ⌜τοῦ λόγου⌝ τούτου καὶ → ἐπῆραν αὐτῶν ⌜τὴν φωνὴν⌝   λέγοντες
cj   v.iai.3p   r.gsm.3 p.g d.gsm n.gsm r.gsn cj   v.aai.3p r.gpm.3 d.asf n.asf   pt.pa.npm
1254   201   899 948 3836 3364 4047 2779   2048 899 3836 5889   3306

"Rid   the earth of him!   He's not fit   to live!" ¶ **23** As they were shouting and
αἶρε ἀπὸ τῆς γῆς ⌜τὸν τοιοῦτον⌝ γὰρ αὐτὸν οὐ καθῆκεν → ζῆν   τε → αὐτῶν → κραυγαζόντων καὶ
v.pam.2s p.g d.gsf n.gsf d.asm r.asm cj r.asm.3 pl v.iai.3s f.pa   cj r.gpm.3   pt.pa.gpm cj
149 608 3836 1178 3836 5525 1142 899 4024 2763 2409   5445 3198 899   3198 2779

throwing off their cloaks and flinging dust   into the air, **24** the commander ordered Paul to be taken   into the
ῥιπτούντων ← τὰ ἱμάτια καὶ βαλλόντων κονιορτὸν εἰς τὸν ἀέρα ὁ χιλίαρχος ἐκέλευσεν αὐτόν → → εἰσάγεσθαι εἰς τὴν
pt.pa.gpm d.apn n.apn cj pt.pa.gpm n.asm p.a d.asm n.asm d.nsm n.nsm v.aai.3s r.asm.3   f.pp p.a d.asf
4848 3836 2668 2779 965 3155 1650 3836 113 3836 5941 3027 899   1652 1650 3836

barracks. He directed that he   be flogged and questioned in order to find   out why   the people were
παρεμβολήν → εἶπας   αὐτὸν μάστιξιν ἀνετάζεσθαι ἵνα ← → ἐπιγνῷ ⌜δι' ἣν αἰτίαν⌝   →
n.asf   pt.aa.nsm   r.asm.3 n.dpf f.pp cj   v.aas.3s p.a r.asf n.asf
4213   3306   899 3465 458 2671   2105 1328 4005 162

shouting at him like this. **25** As they stretched him out to flog   him, Paul   said to the centurion
ἐπεφώνουν → αὐτῷ οὕτως ← δὲ ὡς → προέτειναν αὐτὸν ← → ⌜τοῖς ἱμᾶσιν⌝ ὁ Παῦλος εἶπεν πρὸς τὸν ἑκατόνταρχον
v.iai.3p → r.dsm.3 adv ← cj cj → v.aai.3p r.asm.3 ← d.dpm n.dpm d.nsm n.nsm v.aai.3s p.a d.asm n.asm
2215   899 4048 1254 6055 4727 899 4727 3836 2666 3836 4263 3306 4639 3836 1672

standing there, "Is it legal for you to flog   a Roman citizen   who hasn't even been found
ἑστῶτα ← → ἔξεστιν → ὑμῖν → μαστίζειν εἰ ἄνθρωπον Ῥωμαῖον   καὶ
pt.ra.asm v.pai.3s r.dp.2 f.pa cj n.asm n.asm   cj
2705 1997 7007 3464 1623 476 4871   2779

guilty?" ¶ **26** When the centurion heard this, he went   to the commander and reported it. "What
ἀκατάκριτον δὲ ↱ ὁ ἑκατοντάρχης ἀκούσας → προσελθὼν ← τῷ χιλιάρχῳ ἀπήγγειλεν τί
a.asm cj d.nsm n.nsm pt.aa.nsm pt.aa.nsm d.dsm n.dsm v.aai.3s r.asn
185 1254 201 3836 1672 201 4665 3836 5941 550 5515

are you going to do?" he asked. "This man   is a Roman citizen." ¶ **27** The commander
μέλλεις → ποιεῖν λέγων γὰρ οὗτος ὁ ἄνθρωπος ἐστιν Ῥωμαῖος   δὲ ὁ χιλίαρχος
v.pai.2s f.pa pt.pa.nsm cj r.nsm d.nsm n.nsm v.pai.3s n.nsm   cj d.nsm n.nsm
3516 4472 3306 1142 4047 3836 476 1639 4871   1254 3836 5941

went   to Paul and asked,   "Tell me, are you a Roman citizen?"   "Yes, I am," he answered. ¶
προσελθὼν ← εἶπεν αὐτῷ λέγε μοι εἰ σὺ Ῥωμαῖος ← δὲ ναί ὁ ἔφη
pt.aa.nsm v.aai.3s r.dsm.3 v.pam.2s r.ds.1 v.pai.2s r.ns.2 n.nsm cj pl d.nsm v.iai.3s
4665 3306 899 3306 1609 1639 5148 4871 1254 3721 3836 5774

28 Then the commander said, "I had to pay   a big price   for my citizenship."   "But I   was
δὲ ὁ χιλίαρχος ἀπεκρίθη ἐγώ → → ἐκτησάμην πολλοῦ κεφαλαίου τὴν πολιτείαν ταύτην δὲ δὲ ἐγὼ καὶ →
cj d.nsm n.nsm v.aai.3s r.ns.1 v.ami.1s a.gsn n.gsn d.asf n.asf r.asf cj cj r.ns.1 adv
1254 3836 5941 646 1609 3227 4498 3049 3836 4486 4047 1254 1254 1609 2779

born   a citizen," Paul   replied. ¶ **29** Those who were about   to question him withdrew
γεγέννημαι ὁ Παῦλος ἔφη   οὖν οἱ ← → μέλλοντες → ἀνετάζειν αὐτὸν ἀπέστησαν ἀπ' αὐτοῦ
v.rpi.1s d.nsm n.nsm v.iai.3s   cj d.npm pt.pa.npm f.pa r.asm.3 v.aai.3p p.g r.gsm.3
1164 3836 4263 5774   4036 3836 3516 458 899 923 608 899

immediately. The commander himself was alarmed when he realized that he had put   Paul, a Roman citizen,
εὐθέως δὲ ὁ χιλίαρχος καὶ → ἐφοβήθη → → ἐπιγνοὺς ὅτι → ἦν δεδεκώς αὐτὸν Ῥωμαῖος ←
adv cj d.nsm n.nsm cj v.api.3s pt.aa.nsm cj v.iai.3s pt.ra.nsm r.asm.3 n.nsm
2311 1254 3836 5941 2779 5828 2105 4022 1639 1313 899 4871

ἀναιρούντων αὐτόν ¶ ²¹ καὶ εἶπεν πρός με, Πορεύου, ὅτι ἐγὼ εἰς ἔθνη μακρὰν ἐξαποστελῶ σε.

22:22 Ἤκουον δὲ αὐτοῦ ἄχρι τούτου τοῦ λόγου καὶ ἐπῆραν τὴν φωνὴν αὐτῶν λέγοντες, Αἶρε ἀπὸ τῆς γῆς τὸν τοιοῦτον, οὐ γὰρ καθῆκεν αὐτὸν ζῆν. ¶ ²³ κραυγαζόντων τε αὐτῶν καὶ ῥιπτούντων τὰ ἱμάτια καὶ κονιορτὸν βαλλόντων εἰς τὸν ἀέρα, ²⁴ ἐκέλευσεν ὁ χιλίαρχος εἰσάγεσθαι αὐτὸν εἰς τὴν παρεμβολήν, εἴπας μάστιξιν ἀνετάζεσθαι αὐτὸν ἵνα ἐπιγνῷ δι' ἣν αἰτίαν οὕτως ἐπεφώνουν αὐτῷ. ²⁵ ὡς δὲ προέτειναν αὐτὸν τοῖς ἱμᾶσιν, εἶπεν πρὸς τὸν ἑστῶτα ἑκατόνταρχον ὁ Παῦλος, Εἰ ἄνθρωπον Ῥωμαῖον καὶ ἀκατάκριτον ἔξεστιν ὑμῖν μαστίζειν; ²⁶ ἀκούσας δὲ ὁ ἑκατοντάρχης προσελθὼν τῷ χιλιάρχῳ ἀπήγγειλεν λέγων, Τί μέλλεις ποιεῖν; ὁ γὰρ ἄνθρωπος οὗτος Ῥωμαῖός ἐστιν. ¶ ²⁷ προσελθὼν δὲ ὁ χιλίαρχος εἶπεν αὐτῷ, Λέγε μοι, σὺ Ῥωμαῖος εἶ; ὁ δὲ ἔφη, Ναί. ¶ ²⁸ ἀπεκρίθη δὲ ὁ χιλίαρχος, Ἐγὼ πολλοῦ κεφαλαίου τὴν πολιτείαν ταύτην ἐκτησάμην. ὁ δὲ Παῦλος ἔφη, Ἐγὼ δὲ καὶ γεγέννημαι. ¶ ²⁹ εὐθέως οὖν ἀπέστησαν ἀπ' αὐτοῦ οἱ μέλλοντες αὐτὸν ἀνετάζειν, καὶ ὁ χιλίαρχος δὲ ἐφοβήθη ἐπιγνοὺς ὅτι Ῥωμαῖός ἐστιν καὶ ὅτι αὐτὸν ἦν δεδεκώς.

in　chains.
ἔστιν καὶ ὅτι ←┘
v.pai.3s cj cj
1639　2779　4022 1313 1313

Before the Sanhedrin

22:30 The　next　　　day, since the commander wanted　　to find　　out exactly　　why Paul was being
δὲ Τῇ ἐπαύριον ←　　　　　　　　βουλόμενος → γνῶναι ← ⌐τὸ ἀσφαλές⌐ τὸ τί → → →
cj d.dsf adv　　　　　　　　　　pt.pm.nsm　f.aa　d.asn a.asn　d.asn a.asn
1254 3836 2069　　　　　　　　　1089　　　1182　3836 855　　3836 5515

accused　　by the Jews,　　he released him and ordered the chief priests and all the Sanhedrin to assemble.
κατηγορεῖται ὑπὸ τῶν Ἰουδαίων → ἔλυσεν αὐτὸν καὶ ἐκέλευσεν τοὺς ἀρχιερεῖς καὶ πᾶν τὸ συνέδριον → συνελθεῖν
v.ppi.3s p.g d.gpm a.gpm　v.aai.3s r.asm.3 cj v.aai.3s d.apm n.apm cj a.asn d.asn n.asn f.aa
2989　5679 3836 2681　　3395　899　2779 3027　3836 797　　2779 4246 3836 5284　5302

Then he brought　　Paul　　and had him stand before them. **23:1** Paul　　looked　　straight at the Sanhedrin
καὶ → καταγαγὼν ⌐τὸν Παῦλον⌐ → → ἔστησεν εἰς αὐτούς δὲ ὁ Παῦλος Ἀτενίσας ← → τῷ συνεδρίῳ
cj pt.aa.nsm d.asm n.asm　　　v.aai.3s p.a r.apm.3 cj d.nsm n.nsm pt.aa.nsm　　d.dsn n.dsn
2779 2864 3836 4263　　　　2705 1650 899　1254 3836 4263 867　　　3836 5284

and said,　　"My brothers, I　have fulfilled　my duty to God　in all　good conscience to　this
εἶπεν ἄνδρες → ἀδελφοί ἐγὼ → πεπολίτευμαι ← → ⌐τῷ θεῷ⌐ → πάσῃ ἀγαθῇ συνειδήσει ἄχρι ταύτης
v.aai.3s n.vpm　n.vpm r.ns.1　v.rmi.1s　　　d.dsm n.dsm a.dsf a.dsf n.dsf p.g r.gsf
3306 467　　81　1609　4488　　　　3836 2536 4246 19 5287　948 4047

day."　　**2** At this the high priest　Ananias ordered those standing　near Paul to strike him on the mouth. **3** Then
⌐τῆς ἡμέρας⌐ δὲ ὁ ἀρχιερεὺς Ἁνανίας ἐπέταξεν τοῖς παρεστῶσιν ← αὐτῷ → τύπτειν αὐτοῦ τὸ στόμα τότε
d.gsf n.gsf cj d.nsm n.nsm n.nsm v.aai.3s d.dpm pt.ra.dpm r.dsm.3 f.pa r.gsm.3 d.asn n.asn adv
3836 2465 1254 3836 797 393 2199 3836 4225　899　5597 899 3836 5125 5538

Paul　　said to him, "God　will　strike you, you whitewashed wall!　You sit　there to judge me
ὁ Παῦλος εἶπεν πρὸς αὐτόν ὁ θεός μέλλει τύπτειν σε → κεκονιαμένε τοίχε καὶ σὺ κάθῃ → κρίνων με
d.nsm n.nsm v.aai.3s p.a r.asm.3 d.nsm n.nsm v.pai.3s f.pa r.as.2 pt.rp.vsm n.vsm cj r.ns.2 v.pmi.2s pt.pa.nsm r.as.1
3836 4263 3306 4639 899 3836 2536 3516 5597 5148　3154　5526 2779 5148 2764　3212 1609

according to the law,　yet you yourself violate　the law by commanding that I be struck!" ¶ **4** Those
κατὰ ← τὸν νόμον καὶ → παρανομῶν ← → κελεύεις με → τύπτεσθαι δὲ οἱ
p.a d.asm n.asm cj pt.pa.nsm v.pai.2s r.as.1 f.pp cj d.npm
2848 3836 3795 2779 4174 3027 1609 5597 1254 3836

who were standing　near Paul said, "You dare to insult　God's　high priest?" ¶ **5** Paul
← → παρεστῶτες ← εἶπαν → λοιδορεῖς ⌐τοῦ θεοῦ⌐ → ⌐τὸν ἀρχιερέα⌐ τε ὁ Παῦλος
pt.ra.npm v.aai.3p v.pai.2s d.gsm n.gsm d.asm n.asm cj d.nsm n.nsm
4225 3306 3366 3836 2536 3836 797 5445 3836 4263

replied, "Brothers, I did not realize that he was the high priest; for it is written: 'Do not speak evil about
ἔφη ἀδελφοί → οὐκ ᾔδειν ὅτι → ἐστὶν ἀρχιερεύς γὰρ → γέγραπται ὅτι → οὐκ ἐρεῖς κακῶς
v.iai.3s n.vpm pl v.lai.1s cj v.pai.3s n.nsm cj v.rpi.3s cj pl v.fai.2s adv
5774 81 3857 3857 4024 3857 4022 1639 797 1142 1211 4022 3306 4024 3306 2809

the ruler of your people.'" ¶ **6** Then Paul,　knowing that some　of them were Sadducees and
ἄρχοντα → σου ⌐τοῦ λαοῦ⌐ δὲ ὁ Παῦλος Γνοὺς ὅτι ⌐τὸ ἓν μέρος⌐ → ἐστὶν Σαδδουκαίων δὲ
n.asm r.gs.2 d.gsm n.gsm cj d.nsm n.nsm pt.aa.nsm cj d.nsn a.nsn n.nsn v.pai.3s n.gpm cj
807 5295 3836 3295 1254 3836 4263 1182 4022 3836 1651 3538　1639 4881 1254

the others Pharisees, called out in the Sanhedrin,　　"My brothers, I am a Pharisee, the son of a Pharisee.
τὸ ἕτερον Φαρισαίων ἔκραζεν ← ἐν τῷ συνεδρίῳ ἄνδρες → ἀδελφοί ἐγώ εἰμι Φαρισαῖος υἱὸς → Φαρισαίων
d.nsn a.nsn n.gpm v.iai.3s p.d d.dsn n.dsn n.vpm n.vpm r.ns.1 v.pai.1s n.nsm n.nsm n.gpm
3836 2283 5757 3189 1877 3836 5284 467　81　1609 1639 5757 5626 5757

I stand on trial because of my hope in the resurrection of the dead." **7** When he said this, a
ἐγὼ → κρίνομαι περὶ → ἐλπίδος καὶ ἀναστάσεως → νεκρῶν δὲ → αὐτοῦ εἰπόντος τοῦτο
r.ns.1 v.ppi.1s p.g n.gsf cj n.gsf a.gpm cj r.gsm.3 pt.aa.gsm r.asn
1609 3212 4309 1828 2779 414 3738 1254 899 3306 4047

dispute broke out between the Pharisees and the Sadducees, and the assembly was divided. **8** (The
στάσις ἐγένετο ← → τῶν Φαρισαίων καὶ Σαδδουκαίων καὶ τὸ πλῆθος → ἐσχίσθη γὰρ μὲν
n.nsf v.ami.3s d.gpm n.gpm cj n.gpm cj d.nsn n.nsn v.api.3s cj pl
5087 1181 3836 5757 2779 4881 2779 3836 4436 5387 1142 3525

22:30 Τῇ δὲ ἐπαύριον βουλόμενος γνῶναι τὸ ἀσφαλές, τὸ τί κατηγορεῖται ὑπὸ τῶν Ἰουδαίων, ἔλυσεν αὐτὸν καὶ ἐκέλευσεν συνελθεῖν τοὺς ἀρχιερεῖς καὶ πᾶν τὸ συνέδριον, καὶ καταγαγὼν τὸν Παῦλον ἔστησεν εἰς αὐτούς. **23:1** ἀτενίσας δὲ ὁ Παῦλος τῷ συνεδρίῳ εἶπεν, Ἄνδρες ἀδελφοί, ἐγὼ πάσῃ συνειδήσει ἀγαθῇ πεπολίτευμαι τῷ θεῷ ἄχρι ταύτης τῆς ἡμέρας. **2** ὁ δὲ ἀρχιερεὺς Ἁνανίας ἐπέταξεν τοῖς παρεστῶσιν αὐτῷ τύπτειν αὐτοῦ τὸ στόμα. **3** τότε ὁ Παῦλος πρὸς αὐτὸν εἶπεν, Τύπτειν σε μέλλει ὁ θεός, τοῖχε κεκονιαμένε· καὶ σὺ κάθῃ κρίνων με κατὰ τὸν νόμον καὶ παρανομῶν κελεύεις με τύπτεσθαι; ¶ **4** οἱ δὲ παρεστῶτες εἶπαν, Τὸν ἀρχιερέα τοῦ θεοῦ λοιδορεῖς; ¶ **5** ἔφη τε ὁ Παῦλος, Οὐκ ᾔδειν, ἀδελφοί, ὅτι ἐστὶν ἀρχιερεύς· γέγραπται γὰρ ὅτι Ἄρχοντα τοῦ λαοῦ σου οὐκ ἐρεῖς κακῶς. ¶ **6** Γνοὺς δὲ ὁ Παῦλος ὅτι τὸ ἓν μέρος ἐστὶν Σαδδουκαίων τὸ δὲ ἕτερον Φαρισαίων ἔκραζεν ἐν τῷ συνεδρίῳ, Ἄνδρες ἀδελφοί, ἐγὼ Φαρισαῖός εἰμι, υἱὸς Φαρισαίων, περὶ ἐλπίδος καὶ ἀναστάσεως νεκρῶν [ἐγὼ] κρίνομαι. **7** τοῦτο δὲ αὐτοῦ εἰπόντος ἐγένετο στάσις τῶν Φαρισαίων καὶ Σαδδουκαίων καὶ ἐσχίσθη τὸ πλῆθος. **8** Σαδδουκαῖοι μὲν γὰρ

Sadducees say that there is no resurrection, and that there are neither angels nor spirits, but the Pharisees
Σαδδουκαῖοι λέγουσιν → εἶναι μὴ ἀνάστασιν μήτε ἄγγελον μήτε πνεῦμα δὲ Φαρισαῖοι
n.npm v.pai.3p f.pa pl n.asf cj n.asm cj n.asn pl n.npm
4881 3306 1639 3590 414 3612 34 3612 4460 1254 5757

acknowledge them all.) ¶ 9 There was a great uproar, and some of the teachers of the law who
ὁμολογοῦσιν → ⸤τὰ ἀμφότερα⸥ δὲ → ἐγένετο μεγάλη κραυγή καὶ τινὲς τῶν γραμματέων ←
v.pai.3p d.apn a.apn cj v.ami.3s a.nsf n.nsf cj x.npm d.gpm n.gpm
3933 3836 317 1254 1181 3489 3199 2779 5516 3836 1208

were Pharisees stood up and argued vigorously. "We find nothing wrong with this
τοῦ μέρους ⸤τῶν Φαρισαίων⸥ ἀναστάντες ← διεμάχοντο εὑρίσκομεν οὐδὲν κακὸν ἐν τούτῳ
d.gsn n.gsn d.gpm n.gpm pt.aa.npm v.imi.3p v.pai.1p a.asn a.asn p.d r.dsm
3836 3538 3836 5757 482 1372 2351 4029 2805 1877 4047

man," they said. "What if a spirit or an angel has spoken to him?" 10 The dispute became so
⸤τῷ ἀνθρώπῳ⸥ → λέγοντες δὲ εἰ πνεῦμα ἢ ἄγγελος → ἐλάλησεν → αὐτῷ δὲ στάσεως γινομένης
d.dsm n.dsm pt.pa.npm cj cj n.nsn cj n.nsm v.aai.3s r.dsm.3 cj n.gsf pt.pm.gsf
3836 476 3306 1254 1623 4460 2445 34 3281 899 1254 5087 1181

violent that the commander was afraid Paul would be torn to pieces by them. He ordered the
Πολλῆς ὁ χιλίαρχος → φοβηθεὶς μὴ ὁ Παῦλος⸥ → → διασπασθῇ ← ὑπ' αὐτῶν ἐκέλευσεν τὸ
a.gsf d.nsm n.nsm pt.ap.nsm cj d.nsm n.nsm v.aps.3s p.g r.gpm.3 v.aai.3s d.asn
4498 3836 5941 5828 3590 3836 4263 1400 5679 899 3027 3836

troops to go down and take him away from them by force and bring him into the barracks. ¶
στράτευμα → καταβὰν ← ἁρπάσαι αὐτὸν ἐκ μέσου αὐτῶν ← τε ἄγειν εἰς τὴν παρεμβολήν
n.asn pt.aa.asn f.aa r.asm.3 p.g n.gsn r.gpm.3 cj f.pa p.a d.asf n.asf
5128 2849 773 899 773 1666 3545 899 773 773 5445 72 1650 3836 4213

11 The following night the Lord stood near Paul and said, "Take courage! As you have testified about
δὲ Τῇ ἐπιούσῃ νυκτὶ ὁ κύριος ἐπιστὰς ← αὐτῷ εἶπεν → θάρσει γὰρ ὡς → διαμαρτύρω τὰ περὶ
cj d.dsf pt.pa.dsf n.dsf d.nsm n.nsm pt.aa.nsm r.dsm.3 v.aai.3s v.pam.2s cj cj v.ami.2s d.apn p.g
1254 3836 2079 3816 3836 3261 2392 899 3306 2510 1142 6055 1371 3836 4309

me in Jerusalem, so you must also testify in Rome."
ἐμοῦ εἰς Ἰερουσαλήμ οὕτω σε δεῖ καὶ μαρτυρῆσαι εἰς Ῥώμην
r.gs.1 p.a n.asf adv r.as.2 v.pai.3s adv f.aa p.a n.asf
1609 1650 2647 4048 5148 1256 2779 3455 1650 4873

The Plot to Kill Paul

23:12 The next morning the Jews formed a conspiracy and bound themselves with an oath
δὲ Γενομένης ἡμέρας οἱ Ἰουδαῖοι ποιήσαντες συστροφὴν ἀνεθεμάτισαν ἑαυτοὺς ⸂ ← ⸄
cj pt.am.gsf n.gsf d.npm a.npm pt.aa.npm n.asf v.aai.3p r.apm.3
1254 1181 2465 3836 2681 4472 5371 354 1571 354 354 354

not to eat or drink until they had killed Paul. 13 More than forty men were
λέγοντες μήτε → φαγεῖν μήτε πιεῖν ἕως οὗ ἀποκτείνωσιν ⸤τὸν Παῦλον⸥ δὲ πλείους τεσσεράκοντα ← ἦσαν
pt.pa.npm cj f.aa cj f.aa p.g r.gsn v.aas.3p d.asm n.asm cj a.npm.c a.npm v.iai.3p
3306 3612 2266 3612 4403 2401 4005 650 3836 4263 1254 4498 5477 1639

involved in this plot. 14 They went to the chief priests and elders and said, "We
⸤οἱ ποιησάμενοι⸥ ← ταύτην ⸤τὴν συνωμοσίαν⸥ οἵτινες προσελθόντες ← τοῖς ἀρχιερεῦσιν καὶ ⸤τοῖς πρεσβυτέροις⸥ εἶπαν
d.npm pt.am.npm r.asf d.asf n.asf r.npm pt.aa.npm d.dpm n.dpm cj d.dpm a.dpm v.aai.3p
3836 4472 4047 3836 5350 4015 4665 3836 797 2779 3836 4565 3306

have taken a solemn oath not to eat anything until we have killed Paul.
→ ἀνεθεματίσαμεν → ἀναθέματι ἑαυτοὺς μηδενὸς → γεύσασθαι ⸤ἕως οὗ⸥ → ἀποκτείνωμεν ⸤τὸν Παῦλον⸥
v.aai.1p n.dsn r.apm.1 a.gsm f.am p.g r.gsn v.pai.1p d.asm n.asm
354 353 1571 3594 1174 3594 2401 4005 650 3836 4263

15 Now then, you and the Sanhedrin petition the commander to bring him before you on the pretext of
νῦν οὖν ὑμεῖς σὺν τῷ συνεδρίῳ ἐμφανίσατε τῷ χιλιάρχῳ ὅπως → καταγάγῃ αὐτὸν εἰς ὑμᾶς ὡς ←
adv cj r.np.2 p.d d.dsn n.dsn v.aam.2p d.dsm n.dsm cj v.aas.3s r.asm.3 p.a r.ap.2 pl
3814 4036 7007 5250 3836 5284 1872 3836 5941 3968 2864 899 1650 7007 6055

wanting more accurate information about his case. We are ready to kill him before he gets
μέλλοντας → ἀκριβέστερον διαγινώσκειν τὰ περὶ αὐτοῦ δὲ ἡμεῖς ἐσμεν ἕτοιμοι → ⸤τοῦ ἀνελεῖν⸥ αὐτὸν πρὸ αὐτὸν →
pt.pa.apm adv.c f.pa d.apn p.g r.gsm.3 cj r.np.1 v.pai.1p a.npm d.gsn f.aa r.asm.3 p.g r.asm.3
3516 209 1336 3836 4309 899 1254 7005 1639 2289 3836 359 899 4574 899

λέγουσιν μὴ εἶναι ἀνάστασιν μήτε ἄγγελον μήτε πνεῦμα, Φαρισαῖοι δὲ ὁμολογοῦσιν τὰ ἀμφότερα. ¶ 9 ἐγένετο δὲ κραυγὴ μεγάλη, καὶ ἀναστάντες τινὲς τῶν γραμματέων τοῦ μέρους τῶν Φαρισαίων διεμάχοντο λέγοντες, Οὐδὲν κακὸν εὑρίσκομεν ἐν τῷ ἀνθρώπῳ τούτῳ· εἰ δὲ πνεῦμα ἐλάλησεν αὐτῷ ἢ ἄγγελος; 10 Πολλῆς δὲ γινομένης στάσεως φοβηθεὶς ὁ χιλίαρχος μὴ διασπασθῇ ὁ Παῦλος ὑπ' αὐτῶν ἐκέλευσεν τὸ στράτευμα καταβὰν ἁρπάσαι αὐτὸν ἐκ μέσου αὐτῶν ἄγειν τε εἰς τὴν παρεμβολήν. ¶ 11 Τῇ δὲ ἐπιούσῃ νυκτὶ ἐπιστὰς αὐτῷ ὁ κύριος εἶπεν, Θάρσει· ὡς γὰρ διεμαρτύρω τὰ περὶ ἐμοῦ εἰς Ἰερουσαλήμ, οὕτω σε δεῖ καὶ εἰς Ῥώμην μαρτυρῆσαι.

23:12 Γενομένης δὲ ἡμέρας ποιήσαντες συστροφὴν οἱ Ἰουδαῖοι ἀνεθεμάτισαν ἑαυτοὺς λέγοντες μήτε φαγεῖν μήτε πιεῖν ἕως οὗ ἀποκτείνωσιν τὸν Παῦλον. 13 ἦσαν δὲ πλείους τεσσεράκοντα οἱ ταύτην τὴν συνωμοσίαν ποιησάμενοι, 14 οἵτινες προσελθόντες τοῖς ἀρχιερεῦσιν καὶ τοῖς πρεσβυτέροις εἶπαν, Ἀναθέματι ἀνεθεματίσαμεν ἑαυτοὺς μηδενὸς γεύσασθαι ἕως οὗ ἀποκτείνωμεν τὸν Παῦλον. 15 νῦν οὖν ὑμεῖς ἐμφανίσατε τῷ χιλιάρχῳ σὺν τῷ συνεδρίῳ ὅπως καταγάγῃ αὐτὸν εἰς ὑμᾶς ὡς μέλλοντας διαγινώσκειν

here." ¶ **16** But when the son of Paul's sister heard of this plot, he went into
⌐τοῦ ἐγγίσαι⌐ δὲ → ὁ υἱὸς → Παύλου ⌐τῆς ἀδελφῆς⌐ Ἀκούσας ← τὴν ἐνέδραν παραγενόμενος καὶ → εἰσελθὼν εἰς
d.gsn f.aa cj d.nsm n.nsm n.gsm d.gsf n.gsf pt.aa.nsm d.asf n.asf pt.am.nsm cj pt.aa.nsm p.a
3836 1581 1254 201 3836 5626 80 4263 3836 80 201 3836 1909 4134 2779 1656 1650

the barracks and told Paul. ¶ **17** Then Paul called one of the centurions and said,
τὴν παρεμβολὴν ἀπήγγειλεν ⌐τῷ Παύλῳ⌐ δὲ ⌐ὁ Παῦλος⌐ προσκαλεσάμενος ἕνα → τῶν ἑκατονταρχῶν ἔφη
d.asf n.asf v.aai.3s d.dsm n.dsm cj d.nsm n.nsm pt.am.nsm a.asm d.gpm n.gpm v.iai.3s
3836 4213 550 3836 4263 1254 3836 4263 4673 1651 3836 1672 5774

"Take this young man to the commander; he has something to tell him." **18** So he
ἀπάγαγε τοῦτον ⌐τὸν νεανίαν⌐ ← πρὸς τὸν χιλίαρχον γὰρ → ἔχει τι → ἀπαγγεῖλαι αὐτῷ οὖν μὲν ὁ παραλαβὼν⌐
v.aam.2s r.asm d.asm n.asm p.a d.asm n.asm cj v.pai.3s r.asn f.aa r.dsm.3 cj pl d.nsm pt.aa.nsm
552 4047 3836 3733 4639 3836 5941 1142 2400 5516 550 899 4036 3525 3836 4161

took him to the commander. ¶ The centurion said, "Paul, the prisoner, sent for me and
ἤγαγεν αὐτὸν πρὸς τὸν χιλίαρχον καὶ φησίν Παῦλος ὁ δέσμιος προσκαλεσάμενός ← με
v.aai.3s r.asm.3 p.a d.asm n.asm cj v.pai.3s n.nsm d.nsm n.nsm pt.am.nsm r.as.1
72 899 4639 3836 5941 2779 5774 4263 3836 1300 4673 1609

asked me to bring this young man to you because he has something to tell you." ¶ **19**
ἠρώτησεν → ἀγαγεῖν τοῦτον ⌐τὸν νεανίσκον⌐ ← πρὸς σὲ → ἔχοντα τι → λαλῆσαί σοι δὲ
v.aai.3s f.aa r.asm d.asm n.asm p.a r.as.2 pt.pa.asm r.asn f.aa r.ds.2 cj
2263 72 4047 3836 3734 4639 5148 2400 5516 3281 5148 1254

The commander took the young man by the hand, drew him aside and asked, "What is
ὁ χιλίαρχος ἐπιλαβόμενος αὐτοῦ ← → τῆς χειρὸς καὶ ἀναχωρήσας ⌐κατ' ἰδίαν⌐ ἐπυνθάνετο τί ἐστιν
d.nsm n.nsm pt.am.nsm r.gsm.3 d.gsf n.gsf cj pt.aa.nsm p.a a.asf v.imi.3s r.nsn v.pai.3s
3836 5941 2138 899 3836 5931 2779 432 2848 2625 4785 5515 1639

it you want to tell me?" ¶ **20** He said: "The Jews have agreed to ask you to
ὃ → ἔχεις → ἀπαγγεῖλαί μοι δὲ → εἶπεν ὅτι οἱ Ἰουδαῖοι → συνέθεντο ⌐τοῦ ἐρωτῆσαί⌐ σε ὅπως
r.asn v.pai.2s f.aa r.ds.1 cj v.aai.3s cj d.npm n.npm v.ami.3p d.gsn f.aa r.as.2 cj
4005 2400 550 1609 1254 3306 4022 3836 2681 5338 3836 2263 5148 3968

bring Paul before the Sanhedrin tomorrow *on the pretext* *of* wanting more accurate information
καταγάγῃς ⌐τὸν Παῦλον⌐ εἰς τὸ συνέδριον αὔριον ⌐ὡς μέλλον⌐ πυνθάνεσθαι → ἀκριβέστερόν τι
v.aas.2s d.asm n.asm p.a d.asn n.asn adv pl pt.pa.asn f.pm adv.c r.asn
2864 3836 4263 1650 3836 5284 892 6055 3516 4785 209 5516

about him. **21** Don't give in to them, because more than forty of them are waiting in
περὶ αὐτοῦ οὖν σὺ μὴ πεισθῇς ← αὐτοῖς γὰρ πλείους τεσσεράκοντα ἐξ αὐτῶν ἄνδρες → → →
p.g r.gsm.3 cj r.ns.2 cj v.aps.2s r.dpm.3 cj a.npm.c a.npm p.g r.gpm.3 n.npm
4309 899 4036 5148 3590 4275 899 1142 4498 5477 1666 899 467

ambush for him. They have taken an oath not to eat or drink until they have killed
ἐνεδρεύουσιν αὐτὸν οἵτινες → → ἀνεθεμάτισαν ἑαυτοὺς μήτε → φαγεῖν μήτε πιεῖν ἕως οὗ → → ἀνέλωσιν
v.pai.3p r.asm.3 r.npm v.aai.3p r.apm.3 cj f.aa cj f.aa p.g r.gsm v.aas.3p
1910 899 4015 354 1571 3612 2266 3612 4403 2401 4005 359

him. They are ready now, waiting for your consent to their request." ¶ **22** The
αὐτόν καὶ → εἰσιν ἕτοιμοι νῦν προσδεχόμενοι ← ἀπὸ σοῦ ⌐τὴν ἐπαγγελίαν⌐ οὖν μὲν ὁ
r.asm.3 cj v.pai.3p a.npm adv pt.pm.npm p.g r.gs.2 d.asf n.asf cj pl d.nsm
899 2779 2289 3814 4657 608 5148 2039 4036 3525 3836

commander dismissed the young man and cautioned him, "Don't tell anyone that you have reported this
χιλίαρχος ἀπέλυσε τὸν νεανίσκον παραγγείλας μηδενὶ ἐκλαλῆσαι ← ὅτι → → ἐνεφάνισας ταῦτα
n.nsm v.aai.3s d.asm n.asm pt.aa.nsm a.dsm f.aa cj v.aai.2s r.apn
5941 668 3836 3734 4133 3594 1718 3594 4022 1872 4047

to me."
πρός με
p.a r.as.1
4639 1609

Paul Transferred to Caesarea

23:23 Then he called two of his centurions and ordered them, "Get ready a detachment of
Καὶ → προσκαλεσάμενος δύο [τινὰς] → τῶν ἑκατονταρχῶν εἶπεν → ἑτοιμάσατε
cj pt.am.nsm a.apm r.apm d.gpm n.gpm v.aai.3s v.aam.2p
2779 4673 1545 5516 3836 1672 3306 2286

ἀκριβέστερον τὰ περὶ αὐτοῦ· ἡμεῖς δὲ πρὸ τοῦ ἐγγίσαι αὐτὸν ἕτοιμοί ἐσμεν τοῦ ἀνελεῖν αὐτόν. ¶ **16** Ἀκούσας δὲ ὁ υἱὸς τῆς ἀδελφῆς Παύλου τὴν ἐνέδραν, παραγενόμενος καὶ εἰσελθὼν εἰς τὴν παρεμβολὴν ἀπήγγειλεν τῷ Παύλῳ. ¶ **17** προσκαλεσάμενος δὲ ὁ Παῦλος ἕνα τῶν ἑκατονταρχῶν ἔφη, Τὸν νεανίαν τοῦτον ἀπάγαγε πρὸς τὸν χιλίαρχον, ἔχει γὰρ ἀπαγγεῖλαί τι αὐτῷ. **18** ὁ μὲν οὖν παραλαβὼν αὐτὸν ἤγαγεν πρὸς τὸν χιλίαρχον καὶ ¶ φησίν, Ὁ δέσμιος Παῦλος προσκαλεσάμενός με ἠρώτησεν τοῦτον τὸν νεανίσκον ἀγαγεῖν πρὸς σὲ ἔχοντά τι λαλῆσαί σοι. ¶ **19** ἐπιλαβόμενος δὲ τῆς χειρὸς αὐτοῦ ὁ χιλίαρχος καὶ ἀναχωρήσας κατ' ἰδίαν ἐπυνθάνετο, Τί ἐστιν ὃ ἔχεις ἀπαγγεῖλαί μοι; ¶ **20** εἶπεν δὲ ὅτι Οἱ Ἰουδαῖοι συνέθεντο τοῦ ἐρωτῆσαί σε ὅπως αὔριον τὸν Παῦλον καταγάγῃς εἰς τὸ συνέδριον ὡς μέλλον τι ἀκριβέστερον πυνθάνεσθαι περὶ αὐτοῦ. **21** σὺ οὖν μὴ πεισθῇς αὐτοῖς· ἐνεδρεύουσιν γὰρ αὐτὸν ἐξ αὐτῶν ἄνδρες πλείους τεσσεράκοντα, οἵτινες ἀνεθεμάτισαν ἑαυτοὺς μήτε φαγεῖν μήτε πιεῖν ἕως οὗ ἀνέλωσιν αὐτόν, καὶ νῦν εἰσιν ἕτοιμοι προσδεχόμενοι τὴν ἀπὸ σοῦ ἐπαγγελίαν. ¶ **22** ὁ μὲν οὖν χιλίαρχος ἀπέλυσε τὸν νεανίσκον παραγγείλας μηδενὶ ἐκλαλῆσαι ὅτι ταῦτα ἐνεφάνισας πρός με.
23:23 Καὶ προσκαλεσάμενος δύο [τινὰς] τῶν ἑκατονταρχῶν εἶπεν, Ἑτοιμάσατε στρατιώτας διακοσίους, ὅπως πορευθῶσιν ἕως

two	hundred	soldiers,		seventy	horsemen	and	two	hundred	spearmen	to	go		to
διακοσίους ←		στρατιώτας	καὶ	ἑβδομήκοντα	ἱππεῖς	καὶ	διακοσίους ←		δεξιολάβους	ὅπως	πορευθῶσιν		ἕως
a.apm		n.apm	cj	a.apm	n.apm	cj	a.apm		n.apm	cj	v.aps.3p		p.g
1357		5132	2779	1573	2689	2779	1357		1287	3968	4513		2401

Caesarea	at	nine		tonight.	[24]	Provide	mounts	for Paul	so	that		he		may be
Καισαρείας	ἀπὸ	τρίτης	ὥρας	τῆς νυκτός	τε	παραστῆσαι	κτήνη		ἵνα ←		ἐπιβιβάσαντες	τὸν Παῦλον →	→
n.gsf	p.g	a.gsf	n.gsf	d.gsf n.gsf		f.aa	n.apn		cj		pt.aa.npm	d.asm n.asm	
2791	608	5569	6052	3836 3816	5445	4225	3229		2671		2097	3836 4263	

taken	safely	to	Governor	Felix."	¶	[25] He	wrote	a letter		as follows:			[26] Claudius	Lysias, To
διασώσωσι ←		πρὸς	τὸν ἡγεμόνα	Φήλικα			γράψας	ἐπιστολὴν	ἔχουσαν	τὸν	τύπον	τοῦτον	Κλαύδιος	Λυσίας →
v.aas.3p		p.a	d.asm n.asm	n.asm			pt.aa.nsm	n.asf	pt.pa.asf	d.asm	n.asm	r.asm	n.nsm	n.nsm
1407		4639	3836 2450	5772			1211	2186	2400	3836	5596	4047	3087	3385

His Excellency,	Governor	Felix:	Greetings.	[27] This	man		was	seized		by the	Jews	and		they were
τῷ κρατίστῳ	ἡγεμόνι	Φήλικι	χαίρειν	τοῦτον	Τὸν ἄνδρα	→		συλλημφθέντα	ὑπὸ	τῶν	Ἰουδαίων	καὶ	ὑπ'	αὐτῶν →
d.dsm a.dsm.s	n.dsm	n.dsm	f.pa	r.asm	d.asm n.asm			pt.ap.asm	p.g	d.gpm	a.gpm	cj	p.g	r.gpm.3
3836 3196	2450	5772	5897	4047	3836 467			5197	5679	3836	2681	2779	5679	899

about	to kill		him, but	I came	with	my	troops	and	rescued	him, for	I had	learned	that	he	is	a
μέλλοντα →	ἀναιρεῖσθαι		→	ἐπιστὰς	σὺν	τῷ	στρατεύματι		ἐξειλάμην			μαθὼν	ὅτι		ἐστιν	
pt.pa.asm	f.pp			pt.aa.nsm	p.d	d.dsn	n.dsn		v.ami.1s			pt.aa.nsm	cj		v.pai.3s	
3516	359			2392	5250	3836	5128		1975			3443	4022		1639	

Roman	citizen.	[28]	I	wanted	to	know	why		they were	accusing	him, so	I brought	him	to	their
Ῥωμαῖος ←		τε	→	βουλόμενος	→	ἐπιγνῶναι	τὴν αἰτίαν	δι' ἣν	→	ἐνεκάλουν	αὐτῷ	→ κατήγαγον		εἰς	αὐτῶν
n.nsm		cj		pt.pm.nsm		f.aa	d.asf n.asf	p.a r.asf		v.iai.3p	r.dsm.3	v.aai.1s		p.a	r.gpm.3
4871		5445		1089		2105	3836 162	1328 4005		1592	899	2864		1650	899

Sanhedrin.	[29]	I	found	that	the	accusation		had to do with	questions	about	their	law,		but there was	no
τὸ συνέδριον		ὃν	εὗρον			ἐγκαλούμενον →	→	περὶ	ζητημάτων →		αὐτῶν	τοῦ νόμου	δὲ	→ ἔχοντα	μηδὲν
d.asn n.asn		r.asm	v.aai.1s			pt.pp.asm		p.gen	n.gpn		r.gpm.3	d.gsm n.gsm	cj	pt.pa.asm	a.asn
3836 5284		4005	2351			1592		4309	2427		899	3836 3795	1254	2400	3594

charge	against	him	that	deserved	death	or	imprisonment.	[30]	When	I	was	informed	of a	plot		to be	carried
ἔγκλημα				ἄξιον	θανάτου	ἢ	δεσμῶν		δὲ →	μοι	→	μηνυθείσης		ἐπιβουλῆς	→	→	ἔσεσθαι
n.asn				a.asn	n.gsm	cj	n.gpm		cj	r.ds.1		pt.ap.gsf		n.gsf			f.fm
1598				545	2505	2445	1301		1254 3606	1609		3606		2101			1639

out	against	the man,	I	sent		him	to	you	at once.	I	also	ordered	his	accusers	to	present		to you
←	εἰς	τὸν ἄνδρα →	ἔπεμψα		πρὸς	σὲ	→	ἐξαυτῆς	←	καὶ	παραγγείλας		τοῖς κατηγόροις	→	λέγειν	[τὰ]	ἐπὶ	σοῦ
	p.a	d.asm n.asm	v.aai.1s		p.a	r.as.2		adv		cj	pt.aa.nsm		d.dpm n.dpm		f.pa	d.apn	p.g	r.gs.2
	1650	3836 467	4287		4639	5148		1994		2779	4133		3836 2991		3306	3836	2093	5148

their	case	against	him.	¶	[31] So		the	soldiers,	carrying	out	their	orders,		took		Paul		with
πρὸς	αὐτὸν				οὖν μὲν	Οἱ		στρατιῶται	κατὰ	←	αὐτοῖς	τὸ διατεταγμένον		ἀναλαβόντες		τὸν Παῦλον		
p.a	r.asm.3				cj pl	d.npm		n.npm	p.a		r.dpm.3	d.asn pt.rp.asn		pt.aa.npm		d.asm n.asm		
4639	899				4036 3525	3836		5132	2848		899	3836 1411		377		3836 4263		

them	during	the	night	and	brought	him	as	far	as Antipatris.	[32]	The	next		day	they let		the	cavalry
διὰ		νυκτὸς		ἤγαγον		εἰς	←	←	τὴν Ἀντιπατρίδα		δὲ	τῇ	ἐπαύριον	←	→	ἐάσαντες	τοὺς	ἱππεῖς
p.g		n.gsf		v.aai.3p		p.a			d.asf n.asf		cj	d.dsf	adv			pt.aa.npm	d.apm	n.apm
1328		3816		72		1650			3836 526		1254	3836	2069			1572	3836	2689

go	on	with	him,	while	they	returned	to	the	barracks.	[33] When	the	cavalry	arrived		in	Caesarea,	
ἀπέρχεσθαι	←	σὺν	αὐτῷ	→		ὑπέστρεψαν	εἰς	τὴν	παρεμβολήν			οἵτινες	εἰσελθόντες	εἰς	τὴν Καισάρειαν		καὶ
f.pm		p.d	r.dsm.3			v.aai.3p	p.a	d.asf	n.asf			r.npm	pt.aa.npm	p.a	d.asf n.asf		cj
599		5250	899			5715	1650	3836	4213			4015	1656	1650	3836 2791		2779

they	delivered	the	letter		to the	governor	and	handed		Paul		over to	him.	[34]	The governor	read		the
ἀναδόντες		τὴν	ἐπιστολὴν	→	τῷ	ἡγεμόνι		παρέστησαν	καὶ	τὸν Παῦλον	←	→	αὐτῷ	δὲ		ἀναγνοὺς		
pt.aa.npm		d.asf	n.asf		d.dsm	n.dsm		v.aai.3p	cj	d.asm n.asm			r.dsm.3	cj		pt.aa.nsm		
347		3836	2186		3836	2450		4225	2779	3836 4263			899	1254		336		

letter	and	asked		what	province	he	was	from.		Learning	that	he was	from	Cilicia,		[35] he	said, "I will
	καὶ	ἐπερωτήσας	ἐκ	ποίας	ἐπαρχείας	→	ἐστίν	↩		καὶ	πυθόμενος	ὅτι		ἀπὸ	Κιλικίας	→	ἔφη →
	cj	pt.aa.nsm	p.g	r.gsf	n.gsf		v.pai.3s			cj	pt.am.nsm	cj		p.g	n.gsf		v.iai.3s
	2779	2089	1666	4481	2065		1639	1666		2779	4785	4022		608	3070		5774

Καισαρείας, καὶ ἱππεῖς ἑβδομήκοντα καὶ δεξιολάβους διακοσίους ἀπὸ τρίτης ὥρας τῆς νυκτός, [24] κτήνη τε παραστῆσαι ἵνα ἐπιβιβάσαντες τὸν Παῦλον διασώσωσι πρὸς Φήλικα τὸν ἡγεμόνα, ¶ [25] γράψας ἐπιστολὴν ἔχουσαν τὸν τύπον τοῦτον· [26] Κλαύδιος Λυσίας τῷ κρατίστῳ ἡγεμόνι Φήλικι χαίρειν. [27] Τὸν ἄνδρα τοῦτον συλλημφθέντα ὑπὸ τῶν Ἰουδαίων καὶ μέλλοντα ἀναιρεῖσθαι ὑπ' αὐτῶν ἐπιστὰς σὺν τῷ στρατεύματι ἐξειλάμην μαθὼν ὅτι Ῥωμαῖός ἐστιν. [28] βουλόμενός τε ἐπιγνῶναι τὴν αἰτίαν δι' ἣν ἐνεκάλουν αὐτῷ, κατήγαγον εἰς τὸ συνέδριον αὐτῶν· [29] ὃν εὗρον ἐγκαλούμενον περὶ ζητημάτων τοῦ νόμου αὐτῶν, μηδὲν δὲ ἄξιον θανάτου ἢ δεσμῶν ἔχοντα ἔγκλημα. [30] μηνυθείσης δέ μοι ἐπιβουλῆς εἰς τὸν ἄνδρα ἔσεσθαι ἐξαυτῆς ἔπεμψα πρὸς σὲ παραγγείλας καὶ τοῖς κατηγόροις λέγειν [τὰ] πρὸς αὐτὸν ἐπὶ σοῦ. ¶ [31] Οἱ μὲν οὖν στρατιῶται κατὰ τὸ διατεταγμένον αὐτοῖς ἀναλαβόντες τὸν Παῦλον ἤγαγον διὰ νυκτὸς εἰς τὴν Ἀντιπατρίδα, [32] τῇ δὲ ἐπαύριον ἐάσαντες τοὺς ἱππεῖς ἀπέρχεσθαι σὺν αὐτῷ ὑπέστρεψαν εἰς τὴν παρεμβολήν· [33] οἵτινες εἰσελθόντες εἰς τὴν Καισάρειαν καὶ ἀναδόντες τὴν ἐπιστολὴν τῷ ἡγεμόνι παρέστησαν καὶ τὸν Παῦλον αὐτῷ. [34] ἀναγνοὺς δὲ καὶ ἐπερωτήσας ἐκ ποίας ἐπαρχείας ἐστίν, καὶ πυθόμενος ὅτι ἀπὸ Κιλικίας, [35] Διακούσομαί σου, ἔφη, ὅταν καὶ οἱ κατήγοροί σου παραγένωνται· κελεύσας ἐν τῷ πραιτωρίῳ τοῦ Ἡρῴδου φυλάσσεσθαι

hear your case when your accusers get here." Then he ordered that Paul be kept under

διακούσομαι	σου	ὅταν	καὶ	σου	οἱ	κατήγοροι	παραγένωνται ←	→	κελεύσας	αὐτόν → →	
v.fmi.1s	r.gs.2	cj	adv	r.gs.2	d.npm	n.npm	v.ams.3p		pt.aa.nsm	r.asm.3	
1358	5148	4020	2779	5148	3836	2991	4134		3027	899	

guard in Herod's palace.

φυλάσσεσθαι	ἐν	⌐τοῦ Ἡρῴδου⌐	⌐τῷ πραιτωρίῳ⌐	
f.pp	p.d	d.gsm d.gsm	d.dsn n.dsn	
5875	1877	3836 2476	3836 4550	

The Trial Before Felix

24:1 Five days later the high priest Ananias went down to Caesarea with some of the elders and a

δὲ	πέντε	ἡμέρας	Μετὰ	ὁ →	ἀρχιερεὺς	Ἀνανίας →	κατέβη		μετὰ	τινῶν		πρεσβυτέρων	καὶ	τινός
cj	a.apf	n.apf	p.a	d.nsm	n.nsm	n.nsm	v.aai.3s		p.g	r.gpm		a.gpm	cj	r.gsm
1254	4297	2465	3552	3836	797	393	2849		3552	5516		4565	2779	5516

lawyer named Tertullus, and they brought their charges against Paul before the governor. **2** When Paul

ῥήτορος	Τερτύλλου	οἵτινες	ἐνεφάνισαν ←	←	κατὰ	⌐τοῦ Παύλου⌐ →	τῷ	ἡγεμόνι	δὲ →	αὐτοῦ
n.gsm	n.gsm	r.npm	v.aai.3p		p.g	d.gsm n.gsm	d.dsm	n.dsm	cj	r.gsm.3
4842	5472	4015	1872		2848	3836 4263	3836	2450	1254 2813	899

was called in, Tertullus presented his case before Felix: "We have enjoyed a long period of

→	κληθέντος	ὁ	Τέρτυλλος	ἤρξατο	κατηγορεῖν		λέγων →	→	τυγχάνοντες	πολλῆς ←
	pt.ap.gsm	d.nsm	n.nsm	v.ami.3s	f.pa		pt.pa.nsm		pt.pa.nsm	a.gsf
	2813	3836	5472	806	2989		3306		5593	4498

peace under you, and your foresight has brought about reforms in this nation. **3** Everywhere and in

εἰρήνης	διὰ	σοῦ	καὶ	διὰ	σῆς	⌐τῆς προνοίας⌐	→	γινομένων ←	διορθωμάτων →	τούτῳ	⌐τῷ ἔθνει⌐	τε	πάντη	καὶ →
n.gsf	p.g	r.gs.2	cj	p.g	r.gsf.2	d.gsf n.gsf		pt.pm.gpn	n.gpn	r.dsn	d.dsn n.dsn	cj	adv	cj
1645	1328	5148	2779	1328	5050	3836 4630		1181	1480	1620	4047 3836 1620	5445	4118	2779

every way, most excellent Felix, we acknowledge this with profound gratitude. **4** But in order not to weary you

πανταχοῦ ←	→	κράτιστε	Φῆλιξ →	ἀποδεχόμεθα	μετὰ	πάσης	εὐχαριστίας	δὲ	ἵνα ←		μὴ →	ἐγκόπτω	σε
adv		a.vsm.s	n.vsm	v.pmi.1p	p.g	a.gsf	n.gsf	cj	cj		pl	v.pas.1s	r.as.2
4116		3196	5772	622	3552	4246	2374	1254	2671		3590	1601	5148

further, I would request that you be kind enough to hear us briefly. ¶ **5** "We have

⌐ἐπὶ πλεῖον⌐	→	παρακαλῶ	σε →	⌐τῇ σῇ	ἐπιεικείᾳ⌐		ἀκοῦσαί	ἡμῶν	συντόμως	γὰρ → →
p.a adv.c		v.pai.1s	r.as.2	d.dsf r.dsf.2	n.dsf		f.aa	r.gp.1	adv	cj
2093 4498		4151	5148	3836 5050	2116		201	7005	5339	1142

found this man to be a troublemaker, stirring up riots among the Jews all over the

εὑρόντες	τοῦτον	⌐τὸν ἄνδρα⌐		λοιμὸν	καὶ	κινοῦντα ←	στάσεις →		πᾶσιν	τοῖς	Ἰουδαίοις	τοῖς →	κατὰ τὴν
pt.aa.npm	r.asm	d.asm n.asm		n.asm	cj	pt.pa.asm	n.apf		a.dpm	d.dpm	a.dpm	d.dpm	p.a d.asf
2351	4047	3836 467		3369	2779	3075	5087		4246	3836	2681	3836	2848 3836

world. He is a ringleader of the Nazarene sect **6** and even tried to desecrate the temple; so we

οἰκουμένην	τε		πρωτοστάτην →	τῆς	⌐τῶν Ναζωραίων⌐	αἱρέσεως	ὃς	καὶ	ἐπείρασεν →	βεβηλῶσαι	τὸ	ἱερὸν	καὶ →
n.asf	cj		n.asm	d.gsf	d.gpm n.gpm	n.gsf	r.nsm	adv	v.aai.3s	f.aa	d.asn	n.asn	adv
3876	5445		4756	3836	3836 3717	146	4005	2779	4279	1014	3836	2639	2779

seized him. **8** By examining him yourself you will be able to learn the truth about all these charges

ἐκρατήσαμεν	ὃν	→	ἀνακρίνας	⌐παρ' οὗ⌐	αὐτὸς	→ →	δυνήσῃ →	ἐπιγνῶναι		περὶ	πάντων	τούτων →
v.aai.1p	r.asm		pt.aa.nsm	p.g r.gsm	r.nsm		v.fpi.2s	f.aa		p.g	a.gpn	r.gpn
3195	4005		373	4123 4005	899		1538	2105		4309	4246	4047

we are bringing against him." ¶ **9** The Jews joined in the accusation, asserting that these

ὧν	ἡμεῖς →	κατηγοροῦμεν ←	αὐτοῦ	δὲ	καὶ	οἱ	Ἰουδαῖοι	συνεπέθεντο ←	←	φάσκοντες	ταῦτα
r.gpn	r.np.1	v.pai.1p	r.gsm.3	cj	adv	d.npm	a.npm	v.ami.3p		pt.pa.npm	r.apn
4005	7005	2989	899	1254	2779	3836	2681	5298		5763	4047

things were true. ¶ **10** When the governor motioned for him to speak, Paul replied: "I know that

←	ἔχειν	οὕτως	τε →	τοῦ	ἡγεμόνος	νεύσαντος →	αὐτῷ	λέγειν	ὁ	Παῦλος⌐	Ἀπεκρίθη →	ἐπιστάμενος
	f.pa	adv	cj	d.gsm	n.gsm	pt.aa.gsm	r.dsm.3	f.pa	d.nsm	n.nsm	v.api.3s	pt.pp.nsm
	2400	4048	5445	3836	2450	3748	899	3306	3836	4263	646	2179

for a number of years you have been a judge over this nation; so I gladly make my defense.

ἐκ	πολλῶν	→	ἐτῶν	σε	→	ὄντα	κριτὴν	τούτῳ	⌐τῷ ἔθνει⌐	→	εὐθύμως	↱	τὰ	περὶ	ἐμαυτοῦ	ἀπολογοῦμαι
p.g	a.gpn		n.gpn	r.as.2		pt.pa.asm	n.asm	r.dsn	d.dsn n.dsn		adv		d.apn	p.g	r.gsm.1	v.pmi.1s
1666	4498		2291	5148		1639	3216	1620	4047 3836 1620		664 2315		664	3836	4309 1831	664

αὐτόν.

24:1 Μετὰ δὲ πέντε ἡμέρας κατέβη ὁ ἀρχιερεὺς Ἀνανίας μετὰ πρεσβυτέρων τινῶν καὶ ῥήτορος Τερτύλλου τινός, οἵτινες ἐνεφάνισαν τῷ ἡγεμόνι κατὰ τοῦ Παύλου. **2** κληθέντος δὲ αὐτοῦ ἤρξατο κατηγορεῖν ὁ Τέρτυλλος λέγων, Πολλῆς εἰρήνης τυγχάνοντες διὰ σοῦ καὶ διορθωμάτων γινομένων τῷ ἔθνει τούτῳ διὰ τῆς σῆς προνοίας, **3** πάντη τε καὶ πανταχοῦ ἀποδεχόμεθα, κράτιστε Φῆλιξ, μετὰ πάσης εὐχαριστίας. **4** ἵνα δὲ μὴ ἐπὶ πλεῖόν σε ἐγκόπτω, παρακαλῶ ἀκοῦσαί σε ἡμῶν συντόμως τῇ σῇ ἐπιεικείᾳ. ¶ **5** εὑρόντες γὰρ τὸν ἄνδρα τοῦτον λοιμὸν καὶ κινοῦντα στάσεις πᾶσιν τοῖς Ἰουδαίοις τοῖς κατὰ τὴν οἰκουμένην πρωτοστάτην τε τῆς τῶν Ναζωραίων αἱρέσεως, **6** ὃς καὶ τὸ ἱερὸν ἐπείρασεν βεβηλῶσαι ὃν καὶ ἐκρατήσαμεν, **8** παρ' οὗ δυνήσῃ αὐτὸς ἀνακρίνας περὶ πάντων τούτων ἐπιγνῶναι ὧν ἡμεῖς κατηγοροῦμεν αὐτοῦ. ¶ **9** συνεπέθεντο δὲ καὶ οἱ Ἰουδαῖοι φάσκοντες ταῦτα οὕτως ἔχειν. ¶ **10** Ἀπεκρίθη τε ὁ Παῦλος νεύσαντος αὐτῷ τοῦ ἡγεμόνος λέγειν, Ἐκ πολλῶν ἐτῶν ὄντα σε κριτὴν τῷ ἔθνει

11 You can easily verify that no more than twelve days ago I went up to Jerusalem to
σου δυναμένου ἐπιγνῶναι ὅτι οὐ πλείους ← εἰσίν μοι δώδεκα ἡμέραι ἀφ᾽ ἧς → → ἀνέβην εἰς Ἰερουσαλήμ →
r.gs.2 pt.pp.gsm f.aa cj pl a.npf.c v.pai.3p r.ds.1 a.npf n.npf p.g r.gsf v.aai.1s p.a n.asf
5148 1538 2105 4022 4024 4498 1639 1609 1557 2465 608 4005 326 1650 2647

worship. **12** My accusers did not find me arguing with anyone at the temple, or stirring up a
προσκυνήσων καί οὔτε εὗρόν με διαλεγόμενον πρός τινα ἐν τῷ ἱερῷ ἤ ἐπίστασιν ποιοῦντα ←
pt.fa.nsm cj cj v.aai.3p r.as.1 pt.pm.asm p.a r.asm p.d d.dsn n.dsn cj n.asf pt.pa.asm
4686 2779 4046 2351 1609 1363 4639 5516 1877 3836 2639 2445 2180 4472

crowd in the synagogues or anywhere else in the city. **13** And they cannot prove to you the charges
ὄχλου οὔτε ἐν ταῖς συναγωγαῖς οὔτε → → κατὰ τὴν πόλιν οὐδὲ δύνανται παραστῆσαι → σοι περὶ ὧν
n.gsm cj p.d d.dpf n.dpf cj p.a d.asf n.asf cj v.ppi.3p f.aa r.ds.2 p.g r.gpn
4063 4046 1877 3836 5252 4046 2848 3836 4484 4028 1538 4225 5148 4309 4005

they are now making against me. **14** However, I admit that I worship the God of our fathers as a
→ → νυνὶ κατηγοροῦσιν ← μου δὲ → ὁμολογῶ τοῦτο σοι ὅτι οὕτως → λατρεύω τῷ θεῷ → → πατρῴῳ ←
adv v.pai.3p r.gs.1 cj v.pai.1s r.asn r.ds.2 cj adv v.pai.1s d.dsm n.dsm a.dsm
2989 2989 3815 2989 1609 1254 3933 4047 5148 4022 4048 3302 3836 2536 4262

follower of the Way, which they call a sect. I believe everything that agrees with the Law and that is
κατὰ ← τὴν ὁδὸν ἣν → λέγουσιν αἵρεσιν → πιστεύων πᾶσι τοῖς κατὰ τὸν νόμον καὶ τοῖς
p.a d.asf n.asf r.asf v.pai.3p n.asf pt.pa.nsm a.dpn d.dpn p.a d.asm n.asm cj d.dpn
2848 3836 3847 4005 3306 146 4409 4246 3836 2848 3836 3795 2779 3836

written in the Prophets, **15** and I have the same hope in God as these men, that there
γεγραμμένοις ἐν τοῖς προφήταις → ἔχων ἐλπίδα εἰς τὸν θεόν ἣν καὶ οὗτοι αὐτοὶ προσδέχονται →
pt.rp.dpn p.d d.dpm n.dpm pt.pa.nsm n.asf p.a d.asm n.asm r.asf adv r.npm r.npm v.pmi.3p
1211 1877 3836 4737 2400 1828 1650 3836 2536 4005 2779 4047 899 4657

will be a resurrection of both the righteous and the wicked. **16** So I strive always to keep my
μέλλειν ἔσεσθαι ἀνάστασιν τε δικαίων καὶ ἀδίκων ἐν τούτῳ καὶ αὐτὸς ἀσκῶ διὰ παντός → ἔχειν
f.pa f.fm n.asf cj a.gpm cj a.gpm p.d r.dsn adv r.nsm v.pai.1s p.g a.gsm f.pa
3516 1639 414 5445 1465 2779 96 1877 4047 2779 899 828 1328 4246 2400

conscience clear before God and man. ¶ **17** "After an absence of several years, I
συνείδησιν ἀπρόσκοπον πρός τὸν θεόν καὶ τοὺς ἀνθρώπους δὲ δι᾽ πλειόνων ἐτῶν →
n.asf a.asf p.a d.asm n.asm cj d.apm n.apm cj p.g a.gpn.c n.gpn
5287 718 4639 3836 2536 2779 3836 476 1254 1328 4498 2291

came to Jerusalem to bring my people gifts for the poor and to present offerings. **18** I was
παρεγενόμην → ποιήσων εἰς μου τὸ ἔθνος ἐλεημοσύνας ← ← καὶ → προσφοράς
v.ami.1s pt.fa.nsm p.a r.gs.1 d.asn n.asn n.apf cj n.apf
4134 4472 1650 1609 3836 1620 1797 2779 4/14

ceremonially clean when they found me in the temple courts doing this. There was no crowd with me, nor
→ ἡγνισμένον ἐν αἷς → εὗρόν με ἐν τῷ ἱερῷ οὐ ὄχλου μετὰ οὐδὲ
pt.rp.asm p.d r.dpf v.aai.3p r.as.1 p.d d.dsn n.dsn pl n.gsm p.g cj
49 1877 4005 2351 1609 1877 3836 2639 4024 4063 3552 4028

was I involved in any disturbance. **19** But there are some Jews from the province of Asia, who ought to be
μετὰ θορύβου δὲ τινὲς Ἰουδαῖοι ἀπὸ τῆς → → Ἀσίας οὓς ἔδει →
p.g n.gsm cj r.npm a.npm p.g d.gsf n.gsf r.apm v.iai.3s
3552 2573 1254 5516 2681 608 3836 823 4005 1256

here before you and bring charges if they have anything against me. **20** Or these who are here should state
παρεῖναι ἐπὶ σοῦ καὶ κατηγορεῖν εἴ → ἔχοιεν τι πρός ἐμέ ἢ οὗτοι αὐτοὶ ← ← εἰπάτωσαν
f.pa p.g r.gs.2 cj f.pa cj v.pao.3p r.asn p.a r.as.1 cj r.npm r.npm v.aam.3p
4205 2093 5148 2779 2989 1623 2400 5516 4639 1609 2445 4047 899 3306

what crime they found in me when I stood before the Sanhedrin – **21** unless it was this one thing I
τί ἀδίκημα → εὗρον μου στάντος ἐπὶ τοῦ συνεδρίου ἢ περὶ ταύτης μιᾶς φωνῆς ἧς →
r.asn n.asn v.aai.3p r.gs.1 pt.aa.gsm p.g d.gsn n.gsn pl p.g r.gsf a.gsf n.gsf r.gsf
5515 93 2351 1609 2705 2093 3836 5284 2445 4309 4047 1651 5889 4005

shouted as I stood in their presence: 'It is concerning the resurrection of the dead that I am on trial
ἐκέκραξα → ἑστὼς ἐν αὐτοῖς ὅτι περὶ ἀναστάσεως → νεκρῶν ἐγὼ → κρίνομαι
v.aai.1s pt.ra.nsm p.d r.dpm.3 cj p.g n.gsf a.gpm r.ns.1 v.ppi.1s
3189 2705 1877 899 4022 4309 414 3738 1609 3212

τούτῳ ἐπιστάμενος εὐθύμως τὰ περὶ ἐμαυτοῦ ἀπολογοῦμαι, **11** δυναμένου σου ἐπιγνῶναι ὅτι οὐ πλείους εἰσίν μοι ἡμέραι δώδεκα ἀφ᾽ ἧς ἀνέβην προσκυνήσων εἰς Ἰερουσαλήμ. **12** καὶ οὔτε ἐν τῷ ἱερῷ εὗρόν με πρός τινα διαλεγόμενον ἢ ἐπίστασιν ποιοῦντα ὄχλου οὔτε ἐν ταῖς συναγωγαῖς οὔτε κατὰ τὴν πόλιν, **13** οὐδὲ παραστῆσαι δύνανταί σοι περὶ ὧν νυνὶ κατηγοροῦσίν μου. **14** ὁμολογῶ δὲ τοῦτό σοι ὅτι κατὰ τὴν ὁδὸν ἣν λέγουσιν αἵρεσιν, οὕτως λατρεύω τῷ πατρῴῳ θεῷ πιστεύων πᾶσι τοῖς κατὰ τὸν νόμον καὶ τοῖς ἐν τοῖς προφήταις γεγραμμένοις, **15** ἐλπίδα ἔχων εἰς τὸν θεὸν ἣν καὶ αὐτοὶ οὗτοι προσδέχονται, ἀνάστασιν μέλλειν ἔσεσθαι δικαίων τε καὶ ἀδίκων. **16** ἐν τούτῳ καὶ αὐτὸς ἀσκῶ ἀπρόσκοπον συνείδησιν ἔχειν πρὸς τὸν θεὸν καὶ τοὺς ἀνθρώπους διὰ παντός. ¶ **17** δι᾽ ἐτῶν δὲ πλειόνων ἐλεημοσύνας ποιήσων εἰς τὸ ἔθνος μου παρεγενόμην καὶ προσφοράς, **18** ἐν αἷς εὗρόν με ἡγνισμένον ἐν τῷ ἱερῷ οὐ μετὰ ὄχλου οὐδὲ μετὰ θορύβου, **19** τινὲς δὲ ἀπὸ τῆς Ἀσίας Ἰουδαῖοι, οὓς ἔδει ἐπὶ σοῦ παρεῖναι καὶ κατηγορεῖν εἴ τι ἔχοιεν πρὸς ἐμέ. **20** ἢ αὐτοὶ οὗτοι εἰπάτωσαν τί εὗρον ἀδίκημα στάντος μου ἐπὶ τοῦ συνεδρίου, **21** ἢ περὶ μιᾶς ταύτης φωνῆς ἧς ἐκέκραξα ἐν αὐτοῖς ἑστὼς ὅτι Περὶ ἀναστάσεως νεκρῶν ἐγὼ κρίνομαι σήμερον ἐφ᾽ ὑμῶν. ¶

before you today.'" ¶ **22** Then Felix, who was well acquainted with the Way, adjourned the
ἐφ' ὑμῶν σήμερον δὲ ὁ Φῆλιξ → → ἀκριβέστερον εἰδὼς τὰ περὶ τῆς ὁδοῦ ἀνεβάλετο
p.g r.gp.2 adv cj d.nsm n.nsm adv.c pt.ra.nsm d.apn p.g d.gsf n.gsf v.ami.3s
2093 7007 4958 1254 3836 5772 3857 3857 209 3857 3836 4309 3836 3847 327

proceedings. "When Lysias the commander comes," he said, "I will decide your case." **23** He ordered the
αὐτοὺς ὅταν Λυσίας ὁ χιλίαρχος καταβῇ → εἴπας → διαγνώσομαι ὑμᾶς τὰ καθ' → διαταξάμενος τῷ
r.apm.3 cj n.nsm d.nsm n.nsm v.aas.3s pt.aa.nsm v.fmi.1s r.ap.2 d.apn p.a pt.am.nsm d.dsm
899 4020 3385 3836 5941 2849 3306 1336 7007 3836 2848 1411 3836

centurion to keep Paul under guard but to give him some freedom and permit his friends to take
ἑκατοντάρχῃ → τηρεῖσθαι αὐτὸν → → τε → ἔχειν → ἄνεσιν καὶ μηδένα κωλύειν αὐτοῦ τῶν ἰδίων → →
n.dsm f.pp r.asm.3 cj f.pa n.asf cj a.asm f.pa r.gsm.3 d.gpm a.gpm
1672 5498 899 5498 5498 5445 2400 457 2779 3594 3266 899 3836 2625

care of his needs. ¶ **24** Several days later Felix came with his wife Drusilla, who
ὑπηρετεῖν ← αὐτῷ ← δὲ τινὰς ἡμέρας Μετὰ ὁ Φῆλιξ, παραγενόμενος σὺν ἰδίᾳ τῇ γυναικί, Δρουσίλλῃ →
f.pa r.dsm.3 cj a.apf n.apf p.a d.nsm n.nsm pt.am.nsm p.d a.dsf d.dsf n.dsf n.dsf
5676 899 5676 1254 5516 2465 3552 3836 5772 4134 5250 2625 3836 1222 1537

was a Jewess. He sent for Paul and listened to him as he spoke about faith in Christ Jesus.
οὔσῃ Ἰουδαίᾳ → μετεπέμψατο ← τὸν Παῦλον καὶ ἤκουσεν → αὐτοῦ περὶ τῆς πίστεως, εἰς Χριστὸν Ἰησοῦν
pt.pa.dsf a.dsf v.ami.3s d.asm n.asm cj v.aai.3s r.gsm.3 p.g d.gsf n.gsf p.a n.asm n.asm
1639 2681 3569 3836 4263 2779 201 899 4309 3836 4411 1650 5986 2652

25 As Paul discoursed on righteousness, self-control and the judgment to come, Felix was
δὲ → αὐτοῦ διαλεγομένου περὶ δικαιοσύνης καὶ ἐγκρατείας καὶ τοῦ κρίματος → τοῦ μέλλοντος, ὁ Φῆλιξ, γενόμενος
cj r.gsm.3 pt.pm.gsm p.g n.gsf cj n.gsf cj d.gsn n.gsn d.gsn pt.pa.gsn d.nsm n.nsm pt.am.nsm
1254 1363 899 1363 4309 1466 2779 1602 2779 3836 3210 3836 3516 3836 5772 1181

afraid and said, *"That's enough for now!* You may leave. When I find it convenient, I will
ἔμφοβος ἀπεκρίθη ἔχον → τὸ νῦν, → → πορεύου δὲ → μεταλαβὼν καιρὸν
a.nsm v.api.3s pt.pa.asn d.asn adv v.pmm.2s cj pt.aa.nsm n.asm
1873 646 2400 3836 3814 4513 1254 3561 2789

send for you." **26** At the same time he was hoping that Paul would offer him a bribe, so
μετακαλέσομαι ← ἅμα ← ← καὶ → ἐλπίζων ὅτι ὑπὸ τοῦ Παύλου, → δοθήσεται αὐτῷ χρήματα διὸ
v.fmi.1s adv cj pt.pa.nsm cj p.g d.gsm n.gsm v.fpi.3s r.dsm.3 n.npn cj
3559 275 2779 1827 4022 5679 3836 4263 1443 899 5975 1475

he sent for him frequently and talked with him. ¶ **27** When two years had passed,
καὶ → μεταπεμπόμενος ← αὐτὸν πυκνότερον ὡμίλει → αὐτῷ δὲ → Διετίας ← → πληρωθείσης
adv pt.pm.nsm r.asm.3 adv.c v.iai.3s r.dsm.3 cj n.gsf pt.ap.gsf
2779 3569 899 4781 3917 899 1254 4444 1454 4444

Felix was succeeded by Porcius Festus, but because Felix wanted to grant a favor to the Jews,
ὁ Φῆλιξ, ἔλαβεν διάδοχον Πόρκιον Φῆστον τε → ὁ Φῆλιξ, θέλων → καταθέσθαι χάριτα → τοῖς Ἰουδαίοις
d.nsm n.nsm v.aai.3s n.asm n.asm n.asm cj d.nsm n.nsm pt.pa.nsm f.am n.asf d.dpm a.dpm
3836 5772 3284 1345 4517 5776 5445 2527 3836 5772 2527 2960 5921 3836 2681

he left Paul in prison.
→ κατέλιπε τὸν Παῦλον → δεδεμένον
v.aai.3s d.asm n.asm pt.rp.asm
2901 3836 4263 1313

The Trial Before Festus

25:1 Three days after arriving in the province, Festus went up from Caesarea to Jerusalem, **2** where the
οὖν τρεῖς ἡμέρας μετὰ ἐπιβὰς → τῇ ἐπαρχείᾳ Φῆστος ἀνέβη ← ἀπὸ Καισαρείας εἰς Ἱεροσόλυμα τε οἱ
cj a.apf n.apf p.a pt.aa.nsm d.dsf n.dsf n.nsm v.aai.3s p.g n.gsf p.a n.apn cj d.npm
4036 5552 2465 3552 2094 3836 2065 5776 326 608 2791 1650 2642 5445 3836

chief priests and Jewish leaders appeared before him and presented the charges against
ἀρχιερεῖς καὶ τῶν Ἰουδαίων, οἱ πρῶτοι, ἐνεφάνισαν → αὐτῷ καὶ παρεκάλουν ← ← αὐτὸν κατὰ
n.npm cj d.gpm a.gpm d.npm a.npm v.aai.3p r.dsm.3 cj v.iai.3p r.asm.3 p.g
797 2779 3836 2681 3836 4755 1872 899 2779 4151 899 2848

Paul. **3** They urgently requested Festus, as a favor to them, to have Paul transferred to Jerusalem, for
τοῦ Παύλου, → → αἰτούμενοι κατ' αὐτοῦ, χάριν ὅπως → αὐτὸν μεταπέμψηται εἰς Ἱερουσαλήμ →
d.gsm n.gsm pt.pm.npm p.g r.gsm.3 n.asf cj r.asm.3 v.ams.3s p.a n.asf
3836 4263 160 2848 899 5921 3968 3569 899 3569 1650 2647

---

22 Ἀνεβάλετο δὲ αὐτοὺς ὁ Φῆλιξ, ἀκριβέστερον εἰδὼς τὰ περὶ τῆς ὁδοῦ εἴπας, Ὅταν Λυσίας ὁ χιλίαρχος καταβῇ, διαγνώσομαι τὰ καθ' ὑμᾶς· **23** διαταξάμενος τῷ ἑκατοντάρχῃ τηρεῖσθαι αὐτὸν ἔχειν τε ἄνεσιν καὶ μηδένα κωλύειν τῶν ἰδίων αὐτοῦ ὑπηρετεῖν αὐτῷ. ¶ **24** Μετὰ δὲ ἡμέρας τινὰς παραγενόμενος ὁ Φῆλιξ σὺν Δρουσίλλῃ τῇ ἰδίᾳ γυναικὶ οὔσῃ Ἰουδαίᾳ μετεπέμψατο τὸν Παῦλον καὶ ἤκουσεν αὐτοῦ περὶ τῆς εἰς Χριστὸν Ἰησοῦν πίστεως. **25** διαλεγομένου δὲ αὐτοῦ περὶ δικαιοσύνης καὶ ἐγκρατείας καὶ τοῦ κρίματος τοῦ μέλλοντος, ἔμφοβος γενόμενος ὁ Φῆλιξ ἀπεκρίθη, Τὸ νῦν ἔχον πορεύου, καιρὸν δὲ μεταλαβὼν μετακαλέσομαί σε, **26** ἅμα καὶ ἐλπίζων ὅτι χρήματα δοθήσεται αὐτῷ ὑπὸ τοῦ Παύλου· διὸ καὶ πυκνότερον αὐτὸν μεταπεμπόμενος ὡμίλει αὐτῷ ¶ **27** Διετίας δὲ πληρωθείσης ἔλαβεν διάδοχον ὁ Φῆλιξ Πόρκιον Φῆστον, θέλων τε χάριτα καταθέσθαι τοῖς Ἰουδαίοις ὁ Φῆλιξ κατέλιπε τὸν Παῦλον δεδεμένον.

25:1 Φῆστος οὖν ἐπιβὰς τῇ ἐπαρχείᾳ μετὰ τρεῖς ἡμέρας ἀνέβη εἰς Ἱεροσόλυμα ἀπὸ Καισαρείας, **2** ἐνεφάνισάν τε αὐτῷ οἱ ἀρχιερεῖς καὶ οἱ πρῶτοι τῶν Ἰουδαίων κατὰ τοῦ Παύλου καὶ παρεκάλουν αὐτὸν **3** αἰτούμενοι χάριν κατ' αὐτοῦ ὅπως

they were preparing an ambush to kill him along the way. **4** Festus answered, "Paul is being
→ → ποιοῦντες ἐνέδραν → ἀνελεῖν αὐτὸν κατὰ τὴν ὁδόν. οὖν μὲν ὁ Φῆστος ἀπεκρίθη ⌐τὸν Παῦλον⌐ →
pt.pa.npm n.asf f.aa r.asm.3 p.a d.asf n.asf cj pl d.nsm n.nsm v.api.3s d.asm n.asm
4472 1909 359 899 2848 3836 3847 4036 3525 3836 5776 646 3836 4263

held at Caesarea, and I myself am going there soon. **5** Let some of your leaders
τηρεῖσθαι εἰς Καισάρειαν δὲ ἑαυτὸν μέλλειν ἐκπορεύεσθαι ἐν τάχει οὖν φησίν ⌐ ἐν ὑμῖν οἱ δυνατοὶ⌐
f.pp p.a n.asf cj r.asm.3 f.pa f.pm p.d n.dsn cj v.pai.3s p.d r.dp.2 d.npm a.npm
5498 1650 2791 1254 1571 3516 1744 1877 5443 4036 5774 2989 1877 7007 3836 1543

come with me and press charges against the man there, if he has done anything wrong." ¶
συγκαταβάντες ← κατηγορείτωσαν ← αὐτοῦ ἐν τῷ ἀνδρὶ εἴ → ἔστιν τί ἄτοπον
pt.aa.npm v.pam.3p r.gsm.3 p.d d.dsm n.dsm cj v.pai.3s r.nsn a.nsn
5160 2989 899 1877 3836 467 1623 1639 5516 876

6 After spending eight or ten days with them, he went down to Caesarea, and the next day he
δὲ → Διατρίψας οὐ πλείους ὀκτὼ ἢ δέκα ἡμέρας ἐν αὐτοῖς → καταβὰς ← εἰς Καισάρειαν τῇ ἐπαύριον ← →
cj pt.aa.nsm pl a.apf.c a.gpf cj a.gpf n.apf p.d r.dpm.3 pt.aa.nsm p.a n.asf d.dsf adv
1254 1417 4024 4498 3893 2445 1274 2465 1877 899 2849 1650 2791 3836 2069

convened the court and ordered that Paul be brought before him. **7** When Paul appeared, the
καθίσας ἐπὶ τοῦ βήματος ἐκέλευσεν ⌐τὸν Παῦλον⌐ → ἀχθῆναι δὲ ↑ αὐτοῦ παραγενομένου οἱ
pt.aa.nsm p.g d.gsn n.gsn v.aai.3s d.asm n.asm f.ap cj r.gsm.3 pt.am.gsm d.npm
2767 2093 3836 1037 3027 3836 4263 72 1254 4134 899 4134 3836

Jews who had come down from Jerusalem stood around him, bringing many serious charges
Ἰουδαῖοι → → καταβεβηκότες ← ἀπὸ Ἱεροσολύμων περιέστησαν ← αὐτὸν καταφέροντες πολλὰ καὶ βαρέα αἰτιώματα
a.npm pt.ra.npm p.g n.gpn v.aai.3p r.asm.3 pt.pa.npm a.apn cj a.apn n.apn
2681 2849 608 2642 4325 899 2965 4498 2779 987 166

against him, which they could not prove. ¶ **8** Then Paul made his defense: "I have done
ἃ → ἴσχυον οὐκ ἀποδεῖξαι ⌐τοῦ Παύλου⌐ → → ἀπολογουμένου ὅτι ↑ → →
r.apn v.iai.3p pl f.aa d.gsm n.gsm pt.pm.gsm cj
4005 2710 4024 617 664 3836 4263 664 4022 279 279 279

nothing wrong against the law of the Jews or against the temple or against Caesar." ¶ **9**
τι ἥμαρτον οὔτε εἰς τὸν νόμον ← τῶν Ἰουδαίων οὔτε εἰς τὸ ἱερὸν οὔτε εἰς Καίσαρα δὲ
r.asn v.aai.1s cj p.a d.asm n.asm d.gpm a.gpm cj p.a d.asn n.asn cj p.a n.asm cj
5516 279 4046 1650 3836 3795 3836 2681 4046 1650 3836 2639 4046 1650 2790 1254

Festus, wishing to do the Jews a favor, said to Paul, "Are you willing to go up
⌐Ὁ Φῆστος⌐ θέλων → καταθέσθαι τοῖς Ἰουδαίοις χάριν ἀποκριθεὶς εἶπεν → ⌐τῷ Παύλῳ⌐ → → θέλεις → ἀναβὰς ←
d.nsm n.nsm pt.pa.nsm f.am d.dpm a.dpm n.asf pt.ap.nsm v.aai.3s d.dsm n.dsm v.pai.2s pt.aa.nsm
3836 5776 2527 2960 3836 2681 5921 646 3306 3836 4263 2527 326

to Jerusalem and stand trial before me there on these charges?" ¶ **10** Paul answered: "I am
εἰς Ἱεροσόλυμα → κριθῆναι ἐπ' ἐμοῦ ἐκεῖ περὶ τούτων → δὲ ὁ Παῦλος εἶπεν εἰμι
p.a n.apn f.ap p.g r.gs.1 adv p.g r.gpn cj d.nsm n.nsm v.aai.3s v.pai.1s
1650 2642 3212 2093 1609 1695 4309 4047 1254 3836 4263 3306 1639

now standing before Caesar's court, where I ought to be tried. I have not done any wrong to the
ἑστώς ἐπὶ Καίσαρος ⌐τοῦ βήματος⌐ οὗ ⌐ιε δεῖ → → κρίνεσθαι ↑ → οὐδὲν ↓ ↑ ἠδίκησα ←
pt.ra.nsm p.g n.gsm d.gsn n.gsn adv r.as.1 v.pai.3s f.pp a.asn v.aai.1s
2705 2093 2790 3836 1037 4023 1609 1256 3212 92 92 4029 92 4029 92

Jews, as you yourself know very well. **11** If, however, I am guilty of doing anything deserving
Ἰουδαίους ὡς καὶ → σὺ ἐπιγινώσκεις → κάλλιον εἰ οὖν → μὲν → ἀδικῶ πέπραχα τι καὶ ἄξιον
a.apm cj adv r.ns.2 v.pai.2s adv.c cj cj pl v.pai.1s v.rai.1s r.asn cj a.asn
2681 6055 2779 2105 5148 2105 2822 1623 4036 3525 92 4556 5516 2779 545

death, I do not refuse to die. But if the charges brought against me by these Jews are
θανάτου → οὐ παραιτοῦμαι → ⌐τὸ ἀποθανεῖν⌐ δὲ εἰ ὧν κατηγοροῦσιν ← ← μου οὗτοι ἐστιν
n.gsn pl v.pmi.1s d.asn f.aa cj cj r.gpn v.pai.3p r.gs.1 r.npm v.pai.3s
2505 4148 4148 4024 4148 3836 633 1254 1623 4005 2989 1609 4047 1639

not true, no one has the right to hand me over to them. I appeal to Caesar!" ¶ **12** After
οὐδέν ← → οὐδείς → δύναται ← με χαρίσασθαι αὐτοῖς → ἐπικαλοῦμαι Καίσαρα τότε →
a.nsn a.nsm v.ppi.3s r.as.1 f.am r.dpm.3 v.pmi.1s n.asm adv
4029 4029 1538 5919 5919 1609 5919 899 2126 2790 5538 5196

μεταπέμψηται αὐτὸν εἰς Ἱερουσαλήμ, ἐνέδραν ποιοῦντες ἀνελεῖν αὐτὸν κατὰ τὴν ὁδόν. **4** ὁ μὲν οὖν Φῆστος ἀπεκρίθη τηρεῖσθαι τὸν Παῦλον εἰς Καισάρειαν, ἑαυτὸν δὲ μέλλειν ἐν τάχει ἐκπορεύεσθαι· **5** Οἱ οὖν ἐν ὑμῖν, φησίν, δυνατοὶ συγκαταβάντες εἴ τί ἐστιν ἐν τῷ ἀνδρὶ ἄτοπον κατηγορείτωσαν αὐτοῦ. ¶ **6** Διατρίψας δὲ ἐν αὐτοῖς ἡμέρας οὐ πλείους ὀκτὼ ἢ δέκα, καταβὰς εἰς Καισάρειαν, τῇ ἐπαύριον καθίσας ἐπὶ τοῦ βήματος ἐκέλευσεν τὸν Παῦλον ἀχθῆναι. **7** παραγενομένου δὲ αὐτοῦ περιέστησαν αὐτὸν οἱ ἀπὸ Ἱεροσολύμων καταβεβηκότες Ἰουδαῖοι πολλὰ καὶ βαρέα αἰτιώματα καταφέροντες ἃ οὐκ ἴσχυον ἀποδεῖξαι, ¶ **8** τοῦ Παύλου ἀπολογουμένου ὅτι Οὔτε εἰς τὸν νόμον τῶν Ἰουδαίων οὔτε εἰς τὸ ἱερὸν οὔτε εἰς Καίσαρά τι ἥμαρτον. ¶ **9** ὁ Φῆστος δὲ θέλων τοῖς Ἰουδαίοις χάριν καταθέσθαι ἀποκριθεὶς τῷ Παύλῳ εἶπεν, Θέλεις εἰς Ἱεροσόλυμα ἀναβὰς ἐκεῖ περὶ τούτων κριθῆναι ἐπ' ἐμοῦ; ¶ **10** εἶπεν δὲ ὁ Παῦλος, Ἐπὶ τοῦ βήματος Καίσαρος ἑστώς εἰμι, οὗ με δεῖ κρίνεσθαι. Ἰουδαίους οὐδὲν ἠδίκησα ὡς καὶ σὺ κάλλιον ἐπιγινώσκεις. **11** εἰ μὲν οὖν ἀδικῶ καὶ ἄξιον θανάτου πέπραχά τι, οὐ παραιτοῦμαι τὸ ἀποθανεῖν· εἰ δὲ οὐδέν ἐστιν ὧν οὗτοι κατηγοροῦσίν μου, οὐδείς με δύναται αὐτοῖς χαρίσασθαι· Καίσαρα ἐπικαλοῦμαι. ¶ **12** τότε ὁ Φῆστος

Festus	had conferred	with	his	council,	he declared:	"You have appealed	to	Caesar.	To	Caesar	you will go!"
ὁ Φῆστος⌐	→ συλλαλήσας	μετὰ	τοῦ	συμβουλίου	→ ἀπεκρίθη → →	ἐπικέκλησαι ←	Καίσαρα	ἐπὶ	Καίσαρα	→	πορεύσῃ
d.nsm n.nsm	pt.aa.nsm	p.g	d.gsn	n.gsn	v.api.3s	v.rmi.2s	n.asm	p.a	n.asm		v.fmi.2s
3836 5776	5196	5192	3552	5206	646	2126	2790	2093	2790		4513

Festus Consults King Agrippa

25:13	A few	days	later		King	Agrippa	and	Bernice	arrived	at	Caesarea	to pay their
	δὲ τινῶν	Ἡμερῶν	διαγενομένων	ὁ	βασιλεὺς⌐	Ἀγρίππας	καὶ	Βερνίκη	κατήντησαν	εἰς	Καισάρειαν → → →
	cj r.gpf	n.gpf	pt.am.gpf	d.nsm	n.nsm	n.nsm	cj	n.nsf	v.aai.3p	p.a	n.asf
	1254 5516	2465	1335	3836	995	68	2779	1022	2918	1650	2791

respects	to Festus.	[14]	Since they were	spending	many	days	there,	Festus	discussed	Paul's	case
ἀσπασάμενοι ←	⌐τὸν Φῆστον⌐	δὲ ὡς		διέτριβον	πλείους	ἡμέρας	ἐκεῖ	ὁ Φῆστος⌐	ἀνέθετο	⌐τὸν Παῦλον⌐	⌐τὰ κατὰ
pt.am.npm	d.asm n.asm	cj cj		v.iai.3p	a.apf.c	n.apf	adv	d.nsm n.nsm	v.ami.3s	d.asm n.asm	d.apn p.a
832	3836 5776	1254 6055		1417	4498	2465	1695	3836 5776	423	3836 4263	3836 2848

with	the	king.	He said:	"There	is	a	man	here whom	Felix	left	as a prisoner.	[15]	When	I
→	τῷ	βασιλεῖ	→ λέγων →	ἐστιν	τίς	ἀνήρ		ὑπὸ Φήλικος	καταλελειμμένος	δέσμιος	περὶ οὗ →	μου
	d.dsm	n.dsm	pt.pa.nsm	v.pai.3s	r.nsm	n.nsm		p.g n.gsm	pt.rp.nsm	n.nsm	p.g r.gs.1	r.gs.1
	3836	995	3306	1639	5516	467		5679 5772	2901	1300	4309 4005 1181	1609

went	to Jerusalem,	the chief	priests	and	elders	of the Jews	brought charges	against	him	and
γενομένου	εἰς Ἱεροσόλυμα	οἱ	ἀρχιερεῖς	καὶ	οἱ πρεσβύτεροι	→ τῶν Ἰουδαίων	→ ἐνεφάνισαν	κατ'	αὐτοῦ
pt.am.gsm	p.a n.apn	d.npm	n.npm	cj	d.npm a.npm	d.gpm a.gpm	v.aai.3p	p.g	r.gsm.3
1181	1650 2642	3836	797	2779	3836 4565	3836 2681	1872	2848	899

asked	that he be condemned.	¶	[16] "I	told		them that	it is	not the	Roman	custom to hand
αἰτούμενοι	καταδίκην			ἀπεκρίθην	πρὸς	οὓς	ὅτι →	ἔστιν οὐκ	Ῥωμαίοις ἔθος	→ →
pt.pm.npm	n.asf			v.api.1s	p.a	r.apm	cj	v.pai.3s pl	n.dpm n.nsn	
160	2869			646	4639	4005	4022	1639 4022	4871 1621	

over	any	man	before			he	has faced	his	accusers	and	has had	an
χαρίζεσθαι	τινα	ἄνθρωπον	πρὶν	ἢ ⌐ὁ	κατηγορούμενος⌐		ἔχοι	⌐κατὰ πρόσωπον⌐	τοὺς κατηγόρους	τε	←	λάβοι
f.pm	r.asm	n.asm	cj	pl d.nsm	pt.pp.nsm		v.pao.3s	p.a n.asn	d.apm n.apm	cj		v.aao.3s
5919	5516	476	4570	2445 3836	2989		2400	2848 4725	3836 2991	5445		3284

opportunity	to defend	himself	against	their	charges.	[17]	When they	came	here	with me,	I did
τόπον	ἀπολογίας	περὶ	τοῦ	ἐγκλήματος	οὖν →		αὐτῶν	συνελθόντων	ἐνθάδε ←	→	ποιησάμενος
n.asm	n.gsf	p.g	d.gsn	n.gsn	cj		r.gpm.3	pt.aa.gpm	adv		pt.am.nsm
5536	665	4309	3836	1598	4036		899 5302	5302	1924 5302		4472

not	delay	the case,	but	convened	the court		the next day	and	ordered	the	man	to be brought in.	[18]
μηδεμίαν	ἀναβολὴν			καθίσας	ἐπὶ τοῦ βήματος	τῇ	ἑξῆς ←		ἐκέλευσα	τὸν	ἄνδρα →	ἀχθῆναι	περὶ
a.asf	n.asf			pt.aa.nsm	p.g d.gsn n.gsn	d.dsf	adv		v.aai.1s	d.asm	n.asm	f.ap	p.g
3594	332			2767	2093 3836 1037	3836	2009		3027	3836	467	72	4309

	When	his	accusers	got	up to speak,	they did not		charge		him with any	of the	crimes	I	had
οὗ →		οἱ	κατήγοροι	σταθέντες ←		οὐδεμίαν	⌐αἰτίαν	ἔφερον⌐	→	πονηρῶν	ὧν	ἐγὼ →
r.gsm		d.npm	n.npm	pt.ap.npm		a.asf	n.asf	v.iai.3p		a.gpn	r.gpn	r.ns.1
4005 2705		3836	2991	2705		5770 5770	4029	162 5770		4505	4005	1609

expected.	[19]	Instead,	they had	some	points	of dispute	with	him	about	their	own	religion	and	about a
ὑπενόουν	δὲ	→	εἶχον	τινα	→	ζητήματα	πρὸς	αὐτὸν	περὶ	τῆς	ἰδίας	δεισιδαιμονίας	καὶ	περὶ τινος
v.iai.1s	cj		v.iai.3p	r.apn		n.apn	p.a	r.asm.3	p.g	d.gsf	a.gsf	n.gsf	cj	p.g r.gsm
5706	1254		2400	5516		2427	4639	899	4309	3836	2625	1272	2779	4309 5516

dead	man	named	Jesus	who	Paul	claimed	was	alive.	[20]	I	was	at a loss	how to	investigate	such
τεθνηκότος ←		Ἰησοῦ	ὃν	ὁ	Παῦλος⌐	ἔφασκεν	ζῆν		δὲ	ἐγὼ	→	ἀπορούμενος	⌐τὴν	ζήτησιν⌐	περὶ
pt.ra.gsm		n.gsm	r.asm	d.nsm	n.nsm	v.iai.3s	f.pa		cj	r.ns.1		pt.pm.nsm	d.asf	n.asf	p.g
2569		2652	4005	3836	4263	5763	2409		1254	1609		679	3836	2428	4309

matters;	so	I	asked	if	he	would be	willing	to go		to	Jerusalem	and	stand trial		there	on	these	charges.
τούτων	→		ἔλεγον	εἰ	→		βούλοιτο	πορεύεσθαι	εἰς	Ἱεροσόλυμα	κἀκεῖ →		κρίνεσθαι		περὶ	τούτων
r.gpn			v.iai.1s	cj			v.pmo.3s	f.pm	p.a	n.apn	crasis		f.pp		p.g	r.gpn
4047			3306	1623			1089	4513	1650	2642	2795		3212 2795		4309	4047

[21]	When	Paul	made his	appeal		to be held	over for	the	Emperor's	decision,	I	ordered
δὲ	→	⌐τοῦ Παύλου⌐	→	ἐπικαλεσαμένου	αὐτὸν →	→ τηρηθῆναι ←	εἰς	τὴν	⌐τοῦ Σεβαστοῦ⌐	διάγνωσιν	→	ἐκέλευσα
cj		d.gsm n.gsm		pt.am.gsm	r.asm.3	f.ap	p.a	d.asf	d.gsm n.gsm	n.asf		v.aai.1s
1254 2126		3836 4263		2126	899	5498	1650 3836	3836	4935	1338		3027

συλλαλήσας μετὰ τοῦ συμβουλίου ἀπεκρίθη, Καίσαρα ἐπικέκλησαι, ἐπὶ Καίσαρα πορεύσῃ.

 25:13 Ἡμερῶν δὲ διαγενομένων τινῶν Ἀγρίππας ὁ βασιλεὺς καὶ Βερνίκη κατήντησαν εἰς Καισάρειαν ἀσπασάμενοι τὸν Φῆστον. [14] ὡς δὲ πλείους ἡμέρας διέτριβον ἐκεῖ, ὁ Φῆστος τῷ βασιλεῖ ἀνέθετο τὰ κατὰ τὸν Παῦλον λέγων, Ἀνήρ τίς ἐστιν καταλελειμμένος ὑπὸ Φήλικος δέσμιος, [15] περὶ οὗ γενομένου μου εἰς Ἱεροσόλυμα ἐνεφάνισαν οἱ ἀρχιερεῖς καὶ οἱ πρεσβύτεροι τῶν Ἰουδαίων αἰτούμενοι κατ' αὐτοῦ καταδίκην. ¶ [16] πρὸς οὓς ἀπεκρίθην ὅτι οὐκ ἔστιν ἔθος Ῥωμαίοις χαρίζεσθαί τινα ἄνθρωπον πρὶν ἢ ὁ κατηγορούμενος κατὰ πρόσωπον ἔχοι τοὺς κατηγόρους τόπον τε ἀπολογίας λάβοι περὶ τοῦ ἐγκλήματος. [17] συνελθόντων οὖν [αὐτῶν] ἐνθάδε ἀναβολὴν μηδεμίαν ποιησάμενος τῇ ἑξῆς καθίσας ἐπὶ τοῦ βήματος ἐκέλευσα ἀχθῆναι τὸν ἄνδρα· [18] περὶ οὗ σταθέντες οἱ κατήγοροι οὐδεμίαν αἰτίαν ἔφερον ὧν ἐγὼ ὑπενόουν πονηρῶν, [19] ζητήματα δέ τινα περὶ τῆς ἰδίας δεισιδαιμονίας εἶχον πρὸς αὐτὸν καὶ περὶ τινος Ἰησοῦ τεθνηκότος ὃν ἔφασκεν ὁ Παῦλος ζῆν. [20] ἀπορούμενος δὲ ἐγὼ τὴν περὶ τούτων ζήτησιν ἔλεγον εἰ βούλοιτο πορεύεσθαι εἰς Ἱεροσόλυμα κἀκεῖ κρίνεσθαι περὶ τούτων. [21] τοῦ δὲ Παύλου ἐπικαλεσαμένου τηρηθῆναι αὐτὸν

him	held	until		I could send	him	to	Caesar."	¶	22 Then	Agrippa	said to	Festus,	"I would
αὐτὸν	τηρεῖσθαι	ἕως οὗ	→ →	ἀναπέμψω	αὐτὸν	πρὸς	Καίσαρα		δὲ	Ἀγρίππας		πρὸς ⌜τὸν Φῆστον⌝	→ →
r.asm.3	f.pp	p.g	r.gsm	v.aas.1s	r.asm.3	p.a	n.asm		cj	n.nsm		p.a d.asm n.asm	
899	5498	2401 4005		402	899	4639	2790		1254	68		4639 3836 5776	

like		to hear	this	man	myself."	He replied,	"Tomorrow	you will hear	him."
ἐβουλόμην	καὶ →	ἀκοῦσαι	τοῦ	ἀνθρώπου	αὐτὸς	→ φησίν	αὔριον	→ → ἀκούσῃ	αὐτοῦ
v.imi.1s	adv	f.aa	d.gsm	n.gsm	r.nsm	v.pai.3s	adv	v.fmi.2s	r.gsm.3
1089	2779	201	3836	476	899	5774	892	201	899

Paul Before Agrippa

25:23	The	next	day	Agrippa		and	Bernice	came	with	great	pomp	and	entered		the
	οὖν	Τῇ	ἐπαύριον ←	⌜τοῦ Ἀγρίππα⌝	καὶ		⌜τῆς Βερνίκης⌝	ἐλθόντος	μετὰ	πολλῆς	φαντασίας	καὶ	εἰσελθόντων	εἰς	τὸ
	cj	d.dsf	adv	d.gsm n.gsm	cj		d.gsf n.gsf	pt.aa.gsn	p.g	a.gsf	n.gsf	cj	pt.aa.gpn	p.a	d.asn
	4036	3836	2069	3836 68	2779		3836 1022	2262	3552	4498	5752	2779	1656	1650	3836

audience	room	with		the high	ranking	officers	and	the	leading		men	of the	city.		At the
ἀκροατήριον ←		σύν	τε → →		χιλιάρχοις	καὶ		⌜τοῖς κατ' ἐξοχὴν⌝		ἀνδράσιν	→	τῆς	πόλεως	καὶ → →
n.asn		p.d	cj		n.dpm	cj		d.dpm p.a n.asf		n.dpm		d.gsf	n.gsf	cj
211		5250	5445		5941	2779		3836 2848 2029		467		3836	4484	2779

command	of Festus,	Paul		was brought in.	24	Festus		said: "King	Agrippa,	and all		who are
κελεύσαντος →	⌜τοῦ Φήστου⌝	ὁ Παῦλος⌝	→	ἤχθη ←		καὶ ὁ	Φῆστος,	φησιν βασιλεῦ	Ἀγρίππα	καὶ πάντες	ἄνδρες	οἱ
pt.aa.gsm	d.gsm n.gsm	d.nsm n.nsm		v.api.3s		cj d.nsm	n.nsm	v.pai.3s n.vsm	n.vsm	cj a.vpm	n.vpm	d.vpm
3027	3836 5776	3836 4263		72		2779 3836	5776	5774 995	68	2779 4246	467	3836

present	with us,	you see		this	man!	The whole	Jewish	community	has petitioned	me	about	him		in
συμπαρόντες ←	ἡμῖν	θεωρεῖτε	τοῦτον ←	τῶν	ἅπαν	Ἰουδαίων	⌜τὸ πλῆθος⌝	→	ἐνέτυχον	μοι	περὶ	οὗ	τε	ἕν
pt.pa.vpm	r.dp.1	v.pai.2p	r.asm	d.gpm	a.nsn	a.gpm	d.nsn n.nsn		v.aai.3p	r.ds.1	p.g	r.gsm	cj	p.d
5223	7005	2555	4047	3836	570	2681	3836 4436		1961	1609	4309	4005	5445	1877

Jerusalem	and	here	in	Caesarea,	shouting	that	he	ought	not to	live	any longer.	25	I	found	he	had
Ἱεροσολύμοις	καὶ	ἐνθάδε		βοῶντες		αὐτὸν	δεῖν	μὴ →	ζῆν →	μηκέτι		δὲ	ἐγὼ	κατελαβόμην	αὐτὸν →
n.dpn	cj	adv		pt.pa.npm		r.asm.3	v.pa	pl	f.pa	adv		cj	r.ns.1	v.ami.1s	r.asm.3
2642	2779	1924		1066		899	1256	3590	2409	3600		1254	1609	2898	899

done	nothing	deserving	of death,	but	because	he		made his appeal		to the	Emperor	I	decided to
πεπραχέναι	μηδὲν	ἄξιον	→ θανάτου	δὲ	→	αὐτοῦ	τούτου	→ ἐπικαλεσαμένου ←		τὸν	Σεβαστὸν	→	ἔκρινα
f.ra	a.asn	a.asn	n.gsm	cj		r.gsm.3	r.gsm	pt.am.gsm		d.asm	a.asm		v.aai.1s
4556	3594	545	2505	1254	2126	899	4047	2126		3836	4935		3212

send	him	to Rome.	26	But	I	have	nothing	definite	to write		to His	Majesty	about	him.	Therefore	I have	brought
πέμπειν				ἔχω	οὐκ	τι		ἀσφαλές	→ γράψαι	→	τῷ	κυρίῳ	περὶ	οὗ	διὸ	→ →	προήγαγον
f.pa				v.pai.1s	pl	r.asn		a.asn	f.aa		d.dsm	n.dsm	p.g	r.gsm	cj		v.aai.1s
4287				2400	4024	5516		855	1211		3836	3261	4309	4005	1475		4575

him	before	all of you,	and	especially	before	you,	King	Agrippa,	so	that as a	result		of this	investigation	I	may
αὐτὸν	ἐφ'	→ ὑμῶν καὶ →		μάλιστα	ἐπὶ	σοῦ	βασιλεῦ	Ἀγρίππα	ὅπως	→ →	γενομένης	→	τῆς	ἀνακρίσεως	→ →
r.asm.3	p.g	r.gp.2 cj		adv.s	p.g	r.gs.2	n.vsm	n.vsm	cj		pt.am.gsf		d.gsf	n.gsf	
899	2093	7007 2779		3436	2093	5148	995	68	3968		1181		3836	374	

have	something	to write.	27	For	I	think	it is	unreasonable	to	send	on a	prisoner	without		specifying	the	charges
σχῶ	τι	→ γράψω		γάρ	μοι	δοκεῖ		ἄλογον	→	πέμποντα		δέσμιον	μὴ	καὶ	σημᾶναι	τὰς	αἰτίας
v.aas.1s	r.asn	v.aas.1s		cj	r.ds.1	v.pai.3s		a.nsn		pt.pa.asm		n.asm	pl	adv	f.aa	d.apf	n.apf
2400	5515	1211		1142	1609	1506		263		4287		1300	3590	2779	4955	3836	162

against	him."	26:1 Then	Agrippa	said to		Paul,	"You	have	permission to	speak	for yourself."	¶	So
κατ'	αὐτοῦ	δὲ	Ἀγρίππας	ἔφη	πρὸς	⌜τὸν Παῦλον⌝	σοι	→	ἐπιτρέπεται	→ λέγειν	περὶ σεαυτοῦ		τότε
p.g	r.gsm.3	cj	n.nsm	v.iai.3s	p.a	d.asm n.asm	r.ds.2		v.ppi.3s	f.pa	p.g r.gsm.2		adv
2848	899	1254	68	5774	4639	3836 4263	5148		2205	3306	4309 4932		5538

Paul		motioned	with	his	hand	and began	his	defense:	2 "King	Agrippa,	I	consider	myself	fortunate	to stand
ὁ	Παῦλος⌝	ἐκτείνας ←		τὴν	χεῖρα	→	→	ἀπελογεῖτο	βασιλεῦ	Ἀγρίππα	→	ἥγημαι	ἐμαυτὸν	μακάριον	
d.nsm	n.nsm	pt.aa.nsm		d.asf	n.asf			v.imi.3s	n.vsm	n.vsm		v.rmi.1s	r.asm.1	a.asm	
3836	4263	1753		3836	5931			664	995	68		2451	1831	3421	

before	you	today		as I	make	my	defense	against	all		the	accusations	of the	Jews,	3 and	especially
ἐπὶ	σοῦ	σήμερον	μέλλων →	→ →	→	ἀπολογεῖσθαι	Περὶ		πάντων	ὧν		ἐγκαλοῦμαι	ὑπὸ	Ἰουδαίων		μάλιστα
p.g	r.gs.2	adv	pt.pa.nsm			f.pm	p.g		a.gpn	r.gpn		v.ppi.1s	p.g	a.gpm		adv.s
2093	5148	4958	3516			664	4309		4246	4005		1592	5679	2681		3436

εἰς τὴν τοῦ Σεβαστοῦ διάγνωσιν, ἐκέλευσα τηρεῖσθαι αὐτὸν ἕως οὗ ἀναπέμψω αὐτὸν πρὸς Καίσαρα. ¶ 22 Ἀγρίππας δὲ πρὸς τὸν Φῆστον, Ἐβουλόμην καὶ αὐτὸς τοῦ ἀνθρώπου ἀκοῦσαι. Αὔριον, φησίν, ἀκούσῃ αὐτοῦ.

25:23 Τῇ οὖν ἐπαύριον ἐλθόντος τοῦ Ἀγρίππα καὶ τῆς Βερνίκης μετὰ πολλῆς φαντασίας καὶ εἰσελθόντων εἰς τὸ ἀκροατήριον σύν τε χιλιάρχοις καὶ ἀνδράσιν τοῖς κατ' ἐξοχὴν τῆς πόλεως καὶ κελεύσαντος τοῦ Φήστου ἤχθη ὁ Παῦλος. 24 καὶ φησιν ὁ Φῆστος, Ἀγρίππα βασιλεῦ καὶ πάντες οἱ συμπαρόντες ἡμῖν ἄνδρες, θεωρεῖτε τοῦτον περὶ οὗ ἅπαν τὸ πλῆθος τῶν Ἰουδαίων ἐνέτυχον μοι ἔν τε Ἱεροσολύμοις καὶ ἐνθάδε βοῶντες μὴ δεῖν αὐτὸν ζῆν μηκέτι. 25 ἐγὼ δὲ κατελαβόμην μηδὲν ἄξιον αὐτὸν θανάτου πεπραχέναι, αὐτοῦ δὲ τούτου ἐπικαλεσαμένου τὸν Σεβαστὸν ἔκρινα πέμπειν. 26 περὶ οὗ ἀσφαλές τι γράψαι τῷ κυρίῳ οὐκ ἔχω, διὸ προήγαγον αὐτὸν ἐφ' ὑμῶν καὶ μάλιστα ἐπὶ σοῦ, βασιλεῦ Ἀγρίππα, ὅπως τῆς ἀνακρίσεως γενομένης σχῶ τί γράψω· 27 ἄλογον γάρ μοι δοκεῖ πέμποντα δέσμιον μὴ καὶ τὰς κατ' αὐτοῦ αἰτίας σημᾶναι.

26:1 Ἀγρίππας δὲ πρὸς τὸν Παῦλον ἔφη, Ἐπιτρέπεταί σοι περὶ σεαυτοῦ λέγειν. ¶ τότε ὁ Παῦλος ἐκτείνας τὴν χεῖρα ἀπελογεῖτο, 2 Περὶ πάντων ὧν ἐγκαλοῦμαι ὑπὸ Ἰουδαίων, βασιλεῦ Ἀγρίππα, ἥγημαι ἐμαυτὸν μακάριον ἐπὶ σοῦ μέλλων σήμερον

so because you are well acquainted with all the Jewish customs and controversies. Therefore, I
σε ὄντα → γνώστην ← τε πάντων τῶν ⸆κατὰ Ἰουδαίους⸇ ἐθῶν καὶ ζητημάτων διὸ →
r.as.2 pt.pa.asm n.asm cj a.gpn d.gpn p.a a.apm n.gpn cj n.gpn cj
5148 1639 1195 5445 4246 3836 2848 2681 1621 2779 2427 1475

beg you to listen to me patiently. ¶ 4 "The Jews all know the way I have lived
δέομαι → ἀκοῦσαι μου μακροθύμως οὖν μὲν οἱ Ἰουδαῖοι πάντες ἴσασι Τὴν βίωσιν μου ← [τὴν]
v.pmi.1s f.aa n.gs.1 adv cj pl d.npm a.npm a.npm v.rai.3p d.asf n.asf r.gs.1 d.asf
1289 201 1609 3430 4036 3525 3836 2681 4246 3857 3836 1052 1609 1052 1052 3836

ever since I was a child, from the beginning of my life in my own country, and also in Jerusalem.
ἐκ ← νεότητος τὴν γενομένην ἀπ᾽ ἀρχῆς ἐν μου τῷ ἔθνει τε ἔν Ἱεροσολύμοις
p.g n.gsf d.asf pt.am.asf p.g n.gsf p.d r.gs.1 d.dsn n.dsn cj p.d n.dpn
1666 3744 3836 1181 608 794 1877 1609 3836 1620 5445 1877 2642

5 They have known me for a long time and can testify, if they are willing, that according to the
→ → προγινώσκοντες με → ἄνωθεν ← → μαρτυρεῖν ἐὰν → θέλωσι ὅτι κατὰ ← τὴν
pt.pa.npm r.as.1 adv f.pa v.pas.3p cj p.a d.asf
4589 1609 540 3455 1569 2527 4022 2848 3836

strictest sect of our religion, I lived as a Pharisee. 6 And now it is because of my hope in what
ἀκριβεστάτην αἵρεσιν → ἡμετέρας ⸂τῆς θρησκείας⸃ → ἔζησα ← Φαρισαῖος καὶ νῦν ἐπ᾽ ἐλπίδι ὑπὸ
a.asf.s n.asf r.gsf.1 d.gsf n.gsf v.aai.1s n.nsm cj adv p.d n.dsf p.g
207 146 2579 2466 3836 2579 2409 5757 2779 3814 2093 1828 5679

God has promised our fathers that I am on trial today. 7 This is the promise
⸂τοῦ θεοῦ⸃ ⸂τῆς γενομένης⸃ ἐπαγγελίας εἰς ἡμῶν ⸂τοὺς πατέρας⸃ → ἔστηκα κρινόμενος εἰς ἣν
d.gsm n.gsm d.gsf pt.am.gsf n.gsf p.a r.gp.1 d.apm n.apm v.rai.1s pt.pp.nsm p.a r.asf
3836 2536 3836 1181 2039 1650 7005 3836 4252 2705 3212 1650 4005

our twelve tribes are hoping to see fulfilled as they earnestly serve God day and night. O king,
ἡμῶν → ⸂τὸ δωδεκάφυλον⸃ → ἐλπίζει → → καταντῆσαι → → ἐν ἐκτενείᾳ λατρεῦον ἡμέραν καὶ νύκτα → βασιλεῦ
r.gp.1 d.nsn n.nsn v.pai.3s f.aa p.d n.dsf pt.pa.nsn n.asf cj n.asf n.vsm
7005 3836 1559 1827 2918 3302 3302 1877 1755 3302 2465 2779 3816 995

it is because of this hope that the Jews are accusing me. 8 Why should any of you consider it incredible
περὶ ← ἧς ἐλπίδος ὑπὸ Ἰουδαίων ἐγκαλοῦμαι ← τί → παρ᾽ ὑμῖν κρίνεται ἄπιστον
p.g r.gsf n.gsf p.g a.gpm v.ppi.1s r.asn p.d r.dp.2 v.ppi.3s a.nsn
4309 4005 1828 5679 2681 1592 5515 3212 4123 7007 3212 603

that God raises the dead? ¶ 9 "I too was convinced that I ought to do all that was
εἰ ὁ θεὸς ἐγείρει νεκροὺς οὖν μὲν Ἐγὼ ἐμαυτῷ → ἔδοξα δεῖν → πρᾶξαι πολλὰ
cj d.nsm n.nsm v.pai.3s a.apm cj pl r.ns.1 r.dsm.1 v.aai.1s f.pa f.aa a.apn
1623 3836 2536 1586 3738 4036 3525 1609 1831 1506 1256 4556 4498

possible to oppose the name of Jesus of Nazareth. 10 And that is just what I did in Jerusalem.
ἐναντία πρὸς τὸ ὄνομα → Ἰησοῦ ⸂τοῦ Ναζωραίου⸃ καὶ ὃ → ἐποίησα ἐν Ἱεροσολύμοις καὶ τε
a.apn p.a d.asn n.asn n.gsm d.gsm n.gsm adv r.asn v.aai.1s p.d n.dpn cj cj
1885 4639 3836 3950 2652 3836 3717 2779 4005 4472 1877 2642 2779 5445

On the authority of the chief priests I put many of the saints in prison, and when they were
λαβὼν παρὰ τὴν ἐξουσίαν → τῶν ἀρχιερέων ἐγὼ κατέκλεισα πολλούς → τῶν ἁγίων ἐν φυλακαῖς τε → αὐτῶν
pt.aa.nsm p.a d.asf n.asf d.gpm n.gpm r.ns.1 v.aai.1s a.apm d.gpm a.gpm p.d n.dpf cj r.gpm.3
3284 4123 3836 2026 3836 797 1609 2881 4498 3836 41 1877 5871 5445 359 899

put to death, I cast my vote against them. 11 Many a time I went from one
→ ἀναιρουμένων → κατήνεγκα ψῆφον καὶ πολλάκις ← ⸂κατὰ πάσας τὰς συναγωγάς⸃
pt.pp.gpm v.aai.1s n.asf cj adv p.a a.apf d.apf n.apf
359 2965 6029 2965 2779 4490 2848 4246 3836 5252

synagogue to another to have them punished, and I tried to force them to blaspheme. In my
αὐτοὺς τιμωρῶν → → ἠνάγκαζον → βλασφημεῖν τε → →
r.apm.3 pt.pa.nsm v.iai.1s f.pa cj
5512 5512 899 5512 337 1059 5445

obsession against them, I even went to foreign cities to persecute them. ¶ 12 "On one of
⸂περισσῶς ἐμμαινόμενος⸃ → αὐτοῖς ἕως καὶ εἰς ἔξω ⸂τὰς πόλεις⸃ → ἐδίωκον Ἐν → →
adv pt.pm.nsm r.dpm.3 cj adv p.a adv d.apf n.apf v.iai.1s p.d
4360 1841 899 2401 2779 1650 2032 3836 4484 1503 1877

ἀπολογεῖσθαι 3 μάλιστα γνωστὴν ὄντα σε πάντων τῶν κατὰ Ἰουδαίους ἐθῶν τε καὶ ζητημάτων, διὸ δέομαι μακροθύμως ἀκοῦσαί μου. ¶ 4 Τὴν μὲν οὖν βίωσίν μου [τὴν] ἐκ νεότητος τὴν ἀπ᾽ ἀρχῆς γενομένην ἐν τῷ ἔθνει μου ἔν τε Ἱεροσολύμοις ἴσασι πάντες [οἱ] Ἰουδαῖοι 5 προγινώσκοντές με ἄνωθεν, ἐὰν θέλωσι μαρτυρεῖν, ὅτι κατὰ τὴν ἀκριβεστάτην αἵρεσιν τῆς ἡμετέρας θρησκείας ἔζησα Φαρισαῖος. 6 καὶ νῦν ἐπ᾽ ἐλπίδι τῆς εἰς τοὺς πατέρας ἡμῶν ἐπαγγελίας γενομένης ὑπὸ τοῦ θεοῦ ἔστηκα κρινόμενος, 7 εἰς ἣν τὸ δωδεκάφυλον ἡμῶν ἐν ἐκτενείᾳ νύκτα καὶ ἡμέραν λατρεῦον ἐλπίζει καταντῆσαι, περὶ ἧς ἐλπίδος ἐγκαλοῦμαι ὑπὸ Ἰουδαίων, βασιλεῦ. 8 τί ἄπιστον κρίνεται παρ᾽ ὑμῖν εἰ ὁ θεὸς νεκροὺς ἐγείρει; ¶ 9 ἐγὼ μὲν οὖν ἔδοξα ἐμαυτῷ πρὸς τὸ ὄνομα Ἰησοῦ τοῦ Ναζωραίου δεῖν πολλὰ ἐναντία πρᾶξαι, 10 ὃ καὶ ἐποίησα ἐν Ἱεροσολύμοις, καὶ πολλούς τε τῶν ἁγίων ἐγὼ ἐν φυλακαῖς κατέκλεισα τὴν παρὰ τῶν ἀρχιερέων ἐξουσίαν λαβὼν ἀναιρουμένων τε αὐτῶν κατήνεγκα ψῆφον. 11 καὶ κατὰ πάσας τὰς συναγωγὰς πολλάκις τιμωρῶν αὐτοὺς ἠνάγκαζον βλασφημεῖν περισσῶς τε ἐμμαινόμενος αὐτοῖς ἐδίωκον ἕως καὶ εἰς τὰς ἔξω πόλεις. ¶ 12 Ἐν οἷς

these journeys I was going   to Damascus   with the authority and commission   of the chief priests.
οἷς → → πορευόμενος εἰς ⸤τὴν Δαμασκὸν⸥ μετ᾿ ἐξουσίας καὶ ἐπιτροπῆς τῆς → τῶν ἀρχιερέων
r.dpn   pt.pm.nsm   p.a d.asf n.asf   p.g   n.gsf   cj   n.gsf   d.gsf d.gpm n.gpm
4005   4513   1650 3836 1242   3552   2026   2779 2207   3836 3836 797

13 About noon,   O king,   as I was on the road, I saw a light from heaven,   brighter   than the sun,
→ ⸤ἡμέρας μέσης⸥ βασιλεῦ κατὰ ← ← τὴν ὁδὸν → εἶδον φῶς → οὐρανόθεν ⸤τὴν λαμπρότητα⸥ ὑπὲρ τοῦ ἡλίου
n.gsf n.gsf   n.vsm p.a   d.asf n.asf   v.aai.1s n.asn   adv   d.asf n.asf   p.a d.gsm n.gsm
2465 3545   995 2848   3836 3847   1625 5890   4040   3836 3288   5642 3836 2463

blazing   around me and my companions.   **14** We all fell   to the ground, and I heard a voice
περιλάμψαν ← με καὶ ἐμοὶ τοὺς σὺν πορευομένους τε ἡμῶν πάντων καταπεσόντων εἰς τὴν γῆν → ἤκουσα φωνὴν
pt.aa.asn   r.as.1 cj r.ds.1 d.apm p.d pt.pm.apm   cj r.gp.1 a.gpm pt.aa.gpm   p.a d.asf n.asf   v.aai.1s n.asf
4334   1609 2779 1609 3836 5250 4513   5445 7005 4246 2928   1650 3836 1178   201 5889

saying to me in Aramaic,   'Saul, Saul, why do you persecute me? It is hard   for you to kick
λέγουσαν πρός με → τῇ Ἑβραΐδι διαλέκτῳ Σαοὺλ Σαούλ τί → → διώκεις με σκληρόν → σοι → λακτίζειν
pt.pa.asf p.a r.as.1 d.dsf a.dsf n.dsf   n.vsm n.vsm r.asn   v.pai.2s r.as.1   a.nsn r.ds.2 f.pa
3306 4639 1609 3836 1579 1365   4910 4910 5515   1503 1609   5017 5148 3280

against the goads.' ¶ **15** "Then I asked, 'Who are you, Lord?'   "'I am Jesus, whom you are persecuting,'
πρὸς κέντρα   δὲ ἐγὼ εἶπα τίς εἶ ← κύριε δὲ ἐγώ εἰμι Ἰησοῦς ὃν σὺ → διώκεις
p.a n.apn   cj r.ns.1 v.aai.1s r.nsm v.pai.2s   n.vsm cj r.ns.1 v.pai.1s n.nsm r.asm r.ns.2 v.pai.2s
4639 3034   1254 1609 3306 5515 1639   3261 1254 1609 1639 2652 4005 5148 1503

the Lord replied. **16** 'Now get   up and stand on your feet.   I have appeared to you to
ὁ κύριος εἶπεν ἀλλὰ ἀνάστηθι ← καὶ στῆθι ἐπὶ σου ⸤τοὺς πόδας⸥ γὰρ εἰς τοῦτο → ὤφθην → σοι →
d.nsm n.nsm v.aai.3s cj v.aam.2s cj v.aam.2s p.a r.gs.2 d.apm n.apm cj p.a r.asn   v.api.1s r.ds.2
3836 3261 3306 247 482 2779 2705 2093 5148 3836 4546 1142 1650 4047   3972 5148

appoint   you as a servant and as a witness   of what you have seen of me and what I will show   you. **17** I
προχειρίσασθαι σε ὑπηρέτην καὶ μάρτυρα τε → ὧν → εἶδες ← με r.as.1 τε ὧν → ὀφθήσομαί σοι →
f.am   r.as.2 n.asm cj n.asm cj r.gpn v.aai.2s   r.as.1 cj r.gpn   v.fpi.1s r.ds.2
4741   5148 5677 2779 3459 5445 4005 1625   1609 5445 4005   3972 5148

will rescue   you from your own people and from the Gentiles. I am sending you to them **18** to open their
→ ἐξαιρούμενός σε ἐκ τοῦ λαοῦ καὶ ἐκ τῶν ἐθνῶν ἐγώ ἀποστέλλω σε εἰς οὓς → ἀνοῖξαι αὐτῶν
pt.pm.nsm r.as.2 p.g d.gsm n.gsm cj p.g d.gpn n.gpn r.ns.1 v.pai.1s r.as.2 p.a r.apm   f.aa r.gpm.3
1975 5148 1666 3836 3295 2779 1666 3836 1620 1609 690 5148 1650 4005   487 899

eyes   and turn   them from darkness to light, and from the power of Satan   to God,   so that
ὀφθαλμοὺς ⸤τοῦ ἐπιστρέψαι⸥ ἀπὸ σκότους εἰς φῶς καὶ τῆς ἐξουσίας → ⸤τοῦ σατανᾶ⸥ ἐπὶ ⸤τὸν θεόν⸥ → →
n.apm d.gsn f.aa   p.g n.gsn p.a n.asn cj d.gsf n.gsf d.gsm n.gsm p.a d.asm n.asm
4057 3836 2188   608 5030 1650 5890 2779 3836 2026 3836 4928 2093 3836 2536 3284 3284

they may receive   forgiveness of sins   and a place among those who are sanctified by faith in me.' ¶
αὐτοὺς → ⸤τοῦ λαβεῖν⸥ ἄφεσιν → ἁμαρτιῶν καὶ κλῆρον ἐν τοῖς → ἡγιασμένοις → πίστει τῇ εἰς ἐμέ
r.apm.3 d.gsn f.aa n.asf → n.gpf cj n.asm p.d d.dpm   pt.rp.dpm   n.dsf d.dsf p.a r.as.1
899 3836 3284 912 281 2779 3102 1877 3836   39   4411 3836 1650 1609

19 "So then, King Agrippa, I was   not disobedient to the vision from heaven. **20**   First to those in
Ὅθεν ← βασιλεῦ Ἀγρίππα → ἐγενόμην οὐκ ἀπειθὴς ᾿ τῇ ὁπτασίᾳ → οὐρανίῳ ἀλλὰ τε πρῶτον → τοῖς ἐν
cj n.vsm n.vsm v.ami.1s pl a.nsm d.dsf n.dsf a.dsf cj cj adv d.dpm p.d
3854 995 68 1181 4024 570 3836 3965 4039 247 5445 4754 3836 1877

Damascus, then to those in Jerusalem and in all   Judea,   and to the Gentiles also, I preached
Δαμασκῷ καὶ → Ἱεροσολύμοις τε → πᾶσαν τὴν χώραν τῆς Ἰουδαίας καὶ → τοῖς ἔθνεσιν → ἀπήγγελλον
n.dsf cj n.dpn cj a.asf d.asf n.asf d.gsf n.gsf cj d.dpn n.dpn v.iai.1s
1242 2779 2642 5445 4246 3836 6001 3836 2677 2779 3836 1620 550

that they should repent   and turn   to God   and prove their repentance by their   deeds.
→ μετανοεῖν καὶ ἐπιστρέφειν ἐπὶ ⸤τὸν θεόν⸥ ἄξια τῆς μετανοίας πράσσοντας ἔργα
f.pa cj f.pa p.a d.asm n.asm a.apn d.gsf n.gsf pt.pa.apm n.apn
3566 2779 2188 2093 3836 2536 545 3836 3567 4556 2240

21 That   is why the Jews   seized   me   in the temple courts and tried   to kill   me.
⸤ἕνεκα τούτων⸥ ← Ἰουδαῖοι συλλαβόμενοι με [ὄντα] ἐν τῷ ἱερῷ ← ἐπειρῶντο διαχειρίσασθαι
p.g r.gpn   a.npm pt.am.npm r.as.1 pt.pa.asm p.d d.dsn n.dsn   v.imi.3p f.am
1914 4047   2681 5197 1609 1639 1877 3836 2639   4281 1429

πορευόμενος εἰς τὴν Δαμασκὸν μετ᾿ ἐξουσίας καὶ ἐπιτροπῆς τῆς τῶν ἀρχιερέων ¹³ ἡμέρας μέσης κατὰ τὴν ὁδὸν εἶδον, βασιλεῦ, οὐρανόθεν ὑπὲρ τὴν λαμπρότητα τοῦ ἡλίου περιλάμψαν με φῶς καὶ τοὺς σὺν ἐμοὶ πορευομένους. ¹⁴ πάντων τε καταπεσόντων ἡμῶν εἰς τὴν γῆν ἤκουσα φωνὴν λέγουσαν πρός με τῇ Ἑβραΐδι διαλέκτῳ, Σαοὺλ Σαούλ, τί με διώκεις; σκληρόν σοι πρὸς κέντρα λακτίζειν. ¶ ¹⁵ ἐγὼ δὲ εἶπα, Τίς εἶ, κύριε; ὁ δὲ κύριος εἶπεν, Ἐγώ εἰμι Ἰησοῦς ὃν σὺ διώκεις. ¹⁶ ἀλλὰ ἀνάστηθι καὶ στῆθι ἐπὶ τοὺς πόδας σου· εἰς τοῦτο γὰρ ὤφθην σοι, προχειρίσασθαί σε ὑπηρέτην καὶ μάρτυρα ὧν τε εἶδές [με] ὧν τε ὀφθήσομαί σοι, ¹⁷ ἐξαιρούμενός σε ἐκ τοῦ λαοῦ καὶ ἐκ τῶν ἐθνῶν εἰς οὓς ἐγὼ ἀποστέλλω σε ¹⁸ ἀνοῖξαι ὀφθαλμοὺς αὐτῶν, τοῦ ἐπιστρέψαι ἀπὸ σκότους εἰς φῶς καὶ τῆς ἐξουσίας τοῦ Σατανᾶ ἐπὶ τὸν θεόν, τοῦ λαβεῖν αὐτοὺς ἄφεσιν ἁμαρτιῶν καὶ κλῆρον ἐν τοῖς ἡγιασμένοις πίστει τῇ εἰς ἐμέ. ¶ ¹⁹ Ὅθεν, βασιλεῦ Ἀγρίππα, οὐκ ἐγενόμην ἀπειθὴς τῇ οὐρανίῳ ὀπτασίᾳ ²⁰ ἀλλὰ τοῖς ἐν Δαμασκῷ πρῶτόν τε καὶ Ἱεροσολύμοις, πᾶσάν τε τὴν χώραν τῆς Ἰουδαίας καὶ τοῖς ἔθνεσιν ἀπήγγελλον μετανοεῖν καὶ ἐπιστρέφειν ἐπὶ τὸν θεόν, ἄξια τῆς μετανοίας ἔργα πράσσοντας. ²¹ ἕνεκα τούτων με Ἰουδαῖοι συλλαβόμενοι [ὄντα] ἐν τῷ ἱερῷ ἐπειρῶντο διαχειρίσασθαι.

22 But I have had   God's   help   to   this   very day,   and so I stand here and testify   to   small
οὖν → →   τυχὼν τῆς ἀπὸ .τοῦ θεοῦ. ἐπικουρίας ἄχρι ταύτης τῆς ἡμέρας → ἕστηκα μαρτυρόμενος → τε μικρῷ
cj   pt.aa.nsm d.gsf p.g d.gsm n.gsm n.gsf   p.g   r.gsf d.gsf n.gsf   v.rai.1s   pt.pm.nsm   cj a.dsm
4036   5593   3836 608 3836 2536 2135   948   4047 3836 2465   2705   3455   3625 5445 3625

and great alike. I am saying nothing beyond what   the prophets and Moses said   would   happen — **23** that
καὶ μεγάλῳ → →   λέγων οὐδὲν ἐκτὸς ὧν   τε οἱ προφῆται καὶ Μωϋσῆς ἐλάλησαν μελλόντων γίνεσθαι   εἰ
cj a.dsm   pt.pa.nsm a.nsn p.g   r.gpn cj d.npm n.npm cj n.nsm v.aai.3p pt.pa.gpn f.pm   cj
2779 3489   3306 4029 1760 4005   5445 3836 4737 2779 3707 3281   3516   1181   1623

the Christ would suffer and,   as the first   to rise   from the dead, would proclaim light to his
ὁ χριστός παθητὸς εἰ   πρῶτος ἐξ ἀναστάσεως →   νεκρῶν μέλλει καταγγέλλειν φῶς τε → τῷ
d.nsm n.nsm a.nsm   cj   a.nsm p.g n.gsf   a.gpm v.pai.3s f.pa   n.asn cj   d.dsm
3836 5986   4078   1623   4755 1666 414   3738   3516   2859   5890 5445   3836

own people and to the Gentiles."   ¶   **24** *At this point* Festus   interrupted Paul's defense.   "You are
λαῷ καὶ → τοῖς ἔθνεσιν   δὲ   ὁ Φῆστος,   αὐτοῦ Ταῦτα ἀπολογουμένου, → →
n.dsm cj   d.dpn n.dpn   cj   d.nsm n.nsm   r.gsm.3 r.apn pt.pm.gsm
3295 2779 3836 1620   1254   3836 5776   899   4047 664

out of your mind, Paul!" he shouted.   "Your great learning   is driving you insane."   ¶
→ →   μαίνῃ Παῦλε ,φησίν μεγάλῃ τῇ φωνῇ σε πολλά ,τὰ γράμματα, → περιτρέπει εἰς μανίαν,
       v.pmi.2s n.vsm v.pai.3s a.dsf d.dsf n.dsf r.as.2 a.npn d.npn n.npn   v.pai.3s   p.a n.asf
       3419   4263 5774   3489 3836 5889 5148 4498 3836 1207   4365   1650 3444

25 "I am not insane, most excellent Festus," Paul   replied.   "What I am saying   is true   and
δὲ → → οὐ μαίνομαι →   κράτιστε Φῆστε ὁ Παῦλος, φησίν ἀλλὰ ῥήματα → ἀποφθέγγομαι ἀληθείας καὶ
cj   pl v.pmi.1s   a.vsm.s n.vsm d.nsm n.nsm v.pai.3s cj n.apn   v.pmi.1s   n.gsf   cj
1254 3419 3419 4024 3419   3196   5776 3836 4263 5774   247 4839   710   237   2779

reasonable. **26** The king is familiar with these things, and I can speak freely   to him.   I am
σωφροσύνης γὰρ ὁ βασιλεὺς → ἐπίσταται περὶ τούτων ←   καὶ → λαλῶ παρρησιαζόμενος πρὸς ὃν γὰρ → → οὐ
n.gsf   cj d.nsm n.nsm   v.ppi.3s p.g r.gpn   adv   v.pai.1s pt.pm.nsm   p.a r.asm cj   pl
5408   1142 3836 995   2179   4309 4047   2779 3281   4245   4639 4005 1142 4275 4275 4024

convinced that none   of this has escaped his notice, because it was not done   in a corner.
πείθομαι ,οὐθέν τι, → τούτων ←   αὐτὸν λανθάνειν γὰρ τοῦτο ἐστιν οὐ πεπραγμένον ἐν γωνίᾳ
v.ppi.1s a.asn r.asn r.gpn   r.asn.3 f.pa   cj   r.nsn v.pai.3s pl pt.rp.nsn   p.d n.dsf
4275   4032 5516 4047   899   3291   1142 4047 1639   4024 4556   1877 1224

27 King Agrippa, do you believe the prophets? I know you do."   ¶   **28** Then Agrippa   said to
βασιλεῦ Ἀγρίππα → → πιστεύεις τοῖς προφήταις → οἶδα ὅτι → πιστεύεις   δὲ ὁ Ἀγρίππας πρὸς
n.vsm n.vsm   v.pai.2s d.dpm n.dpm   v.rai.1s cj v.pai.2s   cj d.nsm n.nsm   p.a
995   68   4409   3836 4737   3857 4022 4409   1254 3836 68   4639

Paul,   "Do you think that in such a short time you can persuade me to be a Christian?" ¶   **29**
,τὸν Παῦλον,   ἐν   ὀλίγῳ → → πείθεις με → ποιῆσαι Χριστιανόν   δὲ
d.asm n.asm   p.d   a.dsn   v.pai.2s r.as.1 f.aa   n.asn   cj
3836 4263   1877 3900   4275 1609 4472 5985   1254

Paul   replied,   "Short   time or long   — I pray   God   that not only you but   all   who
ὁ Παῦλος, καὶ ἐν ὀλίγῳ ← καὶ ἐν μεγάλῳ → εὐξαίμην ἂν τῷ θεῷ, οὐ μόνον σε ἀλλὰ καὶ πάντας τοὺς
d.nsm n.nsm cj p.d a.dsn   cj p.d a.dsn   v.amo.1s pl d.dsm n.dsm pl adv r.as.2 cj adv a.apm d.apm
3836 4263   2779 1877 3900 2779 1877 3489 2377   323 3836 2536 4024 3667 5148 247 2779 4246 3836

are listening to me today   may become   what   I am, except for these chains." ¶   **30** The
→ ἀκούοντας ← μου σήμερον → γενέσθαι τοιούτους ὁποῖος καὶ ἐγὼ εἰμι παρεκτὸς ← τούτων ,τῶν δεσμῶν,   τε ὁ
pt.pa.apm   r.gs.1 adv   f.am   r.apm   r.nsm adv r.ns.1 v.pai.1s adv   r.gpm d.gpm n.gpm   cj d.nsm
201   1609 4958   1181   5525   3961 2779 1609 1639 4211   4047 3836 1301   5445 3836

king   rose,   and with him the governor and Bernice and those sitting   with them. **31** They left
βασιλεὺς Ἀνέστη καὶ   ὁ ἡγεμὼν τε ἡ Βερνίκη καὶ οἱ συγκαθήμενοι ←   αὐτοῖς καὶ → ἀναχωρήσαντες
n.nsm   v.aai.3s cj   d.nsm n.nsm cj d.nsf n.nsf cj d.npm pt.pm.npm   r.dpm.3 cj   pt.aa.npm
995   482   2779   3836 2450 5445 3836 1022 2779 3836 5153   899   2779   432

the room, and while talking with one   another, they said, "This man   is not doing anything
ἐλάλουν πρὸς ἀλλήλους ←   → λέγοντες ὅτι οὗτος ὁ ἄνθρωπος, οὐδὲν πράσσει τι
v.iai.3p p.a r.apm   pt.pa.npm cj r.nsm d.nsm n.nsm   a.asn v.pai.3s r.asn
3281   4639 253   3306   4022 4047 3836 476   4556 4029   5516

---

²² ἐπικουρίας οὖν τυχὼν τῆς ἀπὸ τοῦ θεοῦ ἄχρι τῆς ἡμέρας ταύτης ἕστηκα μαρτυρόμενος μικρῷ τε καὶ μεγάλῳ οὐδὲν ἐκτὸς λέγων ὧν τε οἱ προφῆται ἐλάλησαν μελλόντων γίνεσθαι καὶ Μωϋσῆς, ²³ εἰ παθητὸς ὁ Χριστός, εἰ πρῶτος ἐξ ἀναστάσεως νεκρῶν φῶς μέλλει καταγγέλλειν τῷ τε λαῷ καὶ τοῖς ἔθνεσιν. ¶ ²⁴ Ταῦτα δὲ αὐτοῦ ἀπολογουμένου ὁ Φῆστος μεγάλῃ τῇ φωνῇ φησιν, Μαίνῃ, Παῦλε· τὰ πολλά σε γράμματα εἰς μανίαν περιτρέπει. ¶ ²⁵ ὁ δὲ Παῦλος, Οὐ μαίνομαι, φησίν, κράτιστε Φῆστε, ἀλλὰ ἀληθείας καὶ σωφροσύνης ῥήματα ἀποφθέγγομαι. ²⁶ ἐπίσταται γὰρ περὶ τούτων ὁ βασιλεὺς πρὸς ὃν καὶ παρρησιαζόμενος λαλῶ, λανθάνειν γὰρ αὐτὸν [τι] τούτων οὐ πείθομαι οὐθέν· οὐ γάρ ἐστιν ἐν γωνίᾳ πεπραγμένον τοῦτο. ²⁷ πιστεύεις, βασιλεῦ Ἀγρίππα, τοῖς προφήταις; οἶδα ὅτι πιστεύεις. ¶ ²⁸ ὁ δὲ Ἀγρίππας πρὸς τὸν Παῦλον, Ἐν ὀλίγῳ με πείθεις Χριστιανὸν ποιῆσαι. ¶ ²⁹ ὁ δὲ Παῦλος, Εὐξαίμην ἂν τῷ θεῷ καὶ ἐν ὀλίγῳ καὶ ἐν μεγάλῳ οὐ μόνον σὲ ἀλλὰ καὶ πάντας τοὺς ἀκούοντάς μου σήμερον γενέσθαι τοιούτους ὁποῖος καὶ ἐγὼ εἰμι παρεκτὸς τῶν δεσμῶν τούτων. ¶ ³⁰ Ἀνέστη τε ὁ βασιλεὺς καὶ ὁ ἡγεμὼν ἥ τε Βερνίκη καὶ οἱ συγκαθήμενοι αὐτοῖς, ³¹ καὶ ἀναχωρήσαντες ἐλάλουν πρὸς ἀλλήλους λέγοντες ὅτι Οὐδὲν θανάτου ἢ δεσμῶν ἄξιον [τι] πράσσει

that deserves death　or　imprisonment."　¶　**32**　Agrippa　said to Festus,　"This　man　could　have
ἄξιον θανάτου ἢ δεσμῶν　δὲ Ἀγρίππας ἔφη → τῷ Φήστῳ οὗτος ὁ ἄνθρωπος ἐδύνατο →
a.asn n.gsm cj n.gpm　cj n.nsm v.iai.3s d.dsm n.dsm r.nsm d.nsm n.nsm v.ipi.3s
545 2505 2445 1301　1254 68 5774 3836 5776 4047 3836 476 1538

been set free　if　he had not appealed to Caesar."
→ → ἀπολελύσθαι εἰ → → μὴ ἐπεκέκλητο ← Καίσαρα
f.rp cj pl v.lmi.3s n.asm
668 1623 2126 2126 3590 2126 2790

Paul Sails for Rome

27:1　When it was decided that we　would sail　for Italy,　Paul　and some other
δὲ Ὡς → → ἐκρίθη ἡμᾶς → τοῦ ἀποπλεῖν εἰς τὴν Ἰταλίαν τε τόν Παῦλον καί τινας ἑτέρους
cj cj v.api.3s r.ap.1 d.gsn f.pa p.a d.asf n.asf cj d.asm n.asm cj r.apm r.apm
1254 6055 3212 7005 3836 676 1650 3836 2712 5445 3836 4263 2779 5516 2283

prisoners were handed　over to a centurion　named Julius, who belonged to the Imperial Regiment.　**2**　We
δεσμώτας → παρεδίδουν ← ἑκατοντάρχῃ ὀνόματι Ἰουλίῳ → → Σεβαστῆς σπείρης δὲ
n.apm v.iai.3p n.dsm n.dsn n.dsm a.gsf n.gsf cj
1304 4140 1672 3950 2685 4935 5061 1254

boarded a ship from Adramyttium about　to sail　for ports　along the coast of the province of Asia,　and we
ἐπιβάντες πλοίῳ Ἀδραμυττηνῷ μέλλοντι → πλεῖν εἰς τοὺς τόπους κατὰ ← τὴν → Ἀσίαν →
pt.aa.npm n.dsn n.dsn pt.pa.dsn f.pa p.a d.apm n.apm p.a d.asf n.asf
2094 4450 101 3516 4434 1650 3836 5536 2848 3836 823

put　out to sea. Aristarchus, a Macedonian from Thessalonica,　was　with us.　¶　**3**　The next day we
ἀνήχθημεν ← ← Ἀριστάρχου Μακεδόνος → Θεσσαλονικέως ὄντος σὺν ἡμῖν τε τῇ ἑτέρᾳ
v.api.1p n.gsm n.gsm n.gsm pt.pa.gsm p.d r.dp.1 cj d.dsf r.dsf
343 752 3424 2552 1639 5250 7005 5445 3836 2283

landed　at Sidon; and Julius,　in kindness　to Paul,　allowed him to go　to his
κατήχθημεν εἰς Σιδῶνα τε ὁ Ἰούλιος χρησάμενος → φιλανθρώπως → τῷ Παύλῳ ἐπέτρεψεν → πορευθέντι πρὸς τοὺς
v.api.1p p.a n.asf cj d.nsm n.nsm pt.am.nsm adv d.dsm n.dsm v.aai.3s pt.ap.dsm p.a d.apm
2864 1650 4972 5445 3836 2685 5968 5793 3836 4263 2205 4513 4639 3836

friends so they might provide for his needs.　**4**　From there　we put　out to sea again and passed　to the lee
φίλους → → τυχεῖν ← ἐπιμελείας κἀκεῖθεν ἀναχθέντες ← ← ὑπεπλεύσαμεν
a.apm f.aa n.gsf crasis pt.ap.npm v.aai.1p
5813 5593 2149 2796 343 5709

of Cyprus　because the winds　were　against us.　**5**　When we had sailed　across the open sea
τὴν Κύπρον διὰ τοὺς ἀνέμους τὸ εἶναι ἐναντίους τε → → διαπλεύσαντες τό → πέλαγος τὸ
d.asf n.asf p.a d.apm n.apm d.asn f.pa a.apm cj pt.aa.npm d.asn n.asn d.asn
3836 3251 1328 3836 449 3836 1639 1885 5445 1386 3836 4283 3836

off　the coast of Cilicia　and Pamphylia, we landed　at Myra in Lycia.　**6**　There the centurion　found an
κατὰ ← ← τὴν Κιλικίαν καὶ Παμφυλίαν → κατήλθομεν εἰς Μύρα τῆς Λυκίας. Κἀκεῖ ὁ ἑκατοντάρχης εὑρὼν
p.a d.asf n.asf cj n.asf v.aai.1p p.a n.asf d.gsf n.gsf crasis d.nsm n.nsm pt.aa.nsm
2848 3836 3070 2779 4103 2982 1650 3688 3836 3379 2795 3836 1672 2351

Alexandrian ship sailing for Italy　and put　us on board.　**7**　We made slow　headway for
Ἀλεξανδρῖνον πλοῖον πλέον εἰς τὴν Ἰταλίαν ἐνεβίβασεν ἡμᾶς εἰς αὐτό δὲ → βραδυπλοοῦντες ἐν
a.asn n.asn pt.pa.asn p.a d.asf n.asf v.aai.3s r.ap.1 p.a r.asn.3 cj pt.pa.npm p.d
234 4450 4434 1650 3836 2712 1837 7005 1650 899 1254 1095 1877

many　days　and had　difficulty arriving off Cnidus.　When the wind　did not allow　us　to hold our
ἱκαναῖς ἡμέραις καὶ γενόμενοι μόλις κατὰ → τὴν Κνίδον τοῦ ἀνέμου μὴ προσεῶντος ἡμᾶς
a.dpf n.dpf cj pt.am.npm adv p.a d.asf n.asf d.gsm n.gsm pl pt.pa.gsm r.ap.1
2653 2465 2779 1181 3660 2848 3836 3118 3836 449 4661 3590 4661 7005 4661 4661 4661

course, we sailed　to the lee of Crete,　opposite Salmone.　**8**　We moved　along the coast with difficulty
← ὑπεπλεύσαμεν ← ← ← τὴν Κρήτην κατὰ Σαλμώνην τε → παραλεγόμενοι ← αὐτὴν → μόλις
v.aai.1p d.asf n.asf p.a n.asf cj pt.pm.npm r.asf.3 adv
4661 5709 3836 3207 2848 4892 5445 4162 899 3660

and came　to a　place called　Fair　Havens,　near the town of Lasea.　¶　**9**　Much time　had
ἤλθομεν εἰς τινα τόπον καλούμενον Καλοὺς λιμένας ᾧ ἦν ἐγγὺς πόλις Λασαία δὲ Ἱκανοῦ χρόνου →
v.aai.1p p.a r.asm n.asm pt.pp.asm a.apm n.apm r.dsm v.iai.3s adv n.nsf n.nsf cj a.gsm n.gsm
2262 1650 5516 5536 2813 2819 3348 4005 1639 1584 4484 3297 1254 2653 5989

ὁ ἄνθρωπος οὗτος. ¶ **32** Ἀγρίππας δὲ τῷ Φήστῳ ἔφη, Ἀπολελύσθαι ἐδύνατο ὁ ἄνθρωπος οὗτος εἰ μὴ ἐπεκέκλητο Καίσαρα.
27:1 Ὡς δὲ ἐκρίθη τοῦ ἀποπλεῖν ἡμᾶς εἰς τὴν Ἰταλίαν, παρεδίδουν τόν τε Παῦλον καί τινας ἑτέρους δεσμώτας ἑκατοντάρχῃ ὀνόματι Ἰουλίῳ σπείρης Σεβαστῆς. ² ἐπιβάντες δὲ πλοίῳ Ἀδραμυττηνῷ μέλλοντι πλεῖν εἰς τοὺς κατὰ τὴν Ἀσίαν τόπους ἀνήχθημεν ὄντος σὺν ἡμῖν Ἀριστάρχου Μακεδόνος Θεσσαλονικέως. ¶ ³ τῇ τε ἑτέρᾳ κατήχθημεν εἰς Σιδῶνα, φιλανθρώπως τε ὁ Ἰούλιος τῷ Παύλῳ χρησάμενος ἐπέτρεψεν πρὸς τοὺς φίλους πορευθέντι ἐπιμελείας τυχεῖν. ⁴ κἀκεῖθεν ἀναχθέντες ὑπεπλεύσαμεν τὴν Κύπρον διὰ τὸ τοὺς ἀνέμους εἶναι ἐναντίους, ⁵ τό τε πέλαγος τὸ κατὰ τὴν Κιλικίαν καὶ Παμφυλίαν διαπλεύσαντες κατήλθομεν εἰς Μύρα τῆς Λυκίας. ⁶ κἀκεῖ εὑρὼν ὁ ἑκατοντάρχης πλοῖον Ἀλεξανδρῖνον πλέον εἰς τὴν Ἰταλίαν ἐνεβίβασεν ἡμᾶς εἰς αὐτό. ⁷ ἐν ἱκαναῖς δὲ ἡμέραις βραδυπλοοῦντες καὶ μόλις γενόμενοι κατὰ τὴν Κνίδον, μὴ προσεῶντος ἡμᾶς τοῦ ἀνέμου ὑπεπλεύσαμεν τὴν Κρήτην κατὰ Σαλμώνην, ⁸ μόλις τε παραλεγόμενοι αὐτὴν ἤλθομεν εἰς τόπον τινὰ καλούμενον Καλοὺς ᾧ ἐγγὺς πόλις ἦν Λασαία. ¶ ⁹ Ἱκανοῦ δὲ χρόνου διαγενομένου καὶ ὄντος ἤδη ἐπισφαλοῦς τοῦ πλοὸς διὰ τὸ καὶ τὴν

been lost, and sailing had already become dangerous because by now it was after the
→ διαγενομένου καὶ ⌐τοῦ πλοὸς⌐ ἤδη ὄντος ἐπισφαλοῦς διὰ → ἤδη → ⌐τὸ παρεληλυθέναι⌐ καὶ τὴν
pt.am.gsm cj d.gsn n.gsn adv pt.pa.gsm a.gsn p.a adv d.asn f.ra adv d.asf
1335 2779 3836 4452 1639 2453 2195 1328 2453 3836 4216 2779 3836

Fast. So Paul warned them, 10 "Men, I can see that our voyage is going to be disastrous and
νηστείαν ὁ Παῦλος παρῄνει λέγων αὐτοῖς ἄνδρες, → → θεωρῶ ὅτι τὸν πλοῦν → μέλλειν → ἔσεσθαι μετὰ ὕβρεως, καὶ
n.asf d.nsm n.nsm v.iai.3s pt.pa.nsm r.dpm.3 n.vpm v.pai.1s cj d.asn n.asm f.pa f.fm p.g n.gsf cj
3763 3836 4263 4147 3306 899 467 2555 4022 3836 4452 3516 1639 3552 5615 2779

bring great loss to ship and cargo, and to our own lives also." 11 But the centurion, instead
πολλῆς ζημίας οὐ μόνον ⌐τοῦ πλοίου⌐ καὶ ⌐τοῦ φορτίου⌐ ἀλλὰ ἡμῶν τῶν ψυχῶν καὶ δὲ ὁ ἑκατοντάρχης μᾶλλον
a.gsf n.gsf pl adv d.gsn n.gsn cj d.gsn n.gsn cj r.gp.1 d.gpf n.gpf adv cj d.nsm n.nsm adv.c
4498 2422 4024 3667 3836 4450 2779 3836 5845 247 7005 3836 6034 2779 1254 3836 1672 3437

of listening to what Paul said, followed the advice of the pilot and of the owner of the ship. 12
ἢ → τοῖς ὑπὸ Παύλου λεγομένοις → → ἐπείθετο τῷ κυβερνήτῃ καὶ τῷ ναυκλήρῳ ← ← ← δὲ
pl d.dpn p.g n.gsm pt.pp.dpn v.ipi.3s d.dsm n.dsm cj d.dsm n.dsm cj
2445 3836 5679 4263 3306 4275 3836 3237 2779 3836 3729 1254

Since the harbor was unsuitable to winter in, the majority decided that we should sail on,
→ τοῦ λιμένος ὑπάρχοντος ἀνευθέτου πρὸς παραχειμασίαν ← οἱ πλείονες ἔθεντο βουλὴν, → → ἀναχθῆναι ←
d.gsm n.gsm pt.pa.gsm a.gsm p.a n.asf d.npm a.npm.c v.ami.3p n.asf f.ap
5639 3836 3348 5639 460 4639 4200 3836 4498 5502 1087 343

hoping to reach Phoenix and winter there. This was a harbor in Crete, facing
ἐκεῖθεν εἴ πως δύναιντο, → καταντήσαντες εἰς Φοίνικα παραχειμάσαι λιμένα → ⌐τῆς Κρήτης, βλέποντα
adv cj pl v.ppo.3p pt.aa.npm p.a n.asm f.aa n.asm d.gsf n.gsf pt.pa.asm
1696 1623 4803 1538 2870 1650 5837 4199 3348 3836 3207 1063

both southwest and northwest.
⌐κατὰ λίβα καὶ ⌐κατὰ χῶρον,
p.a n.asm cj p.a n.asm
2848 3355 2779 2848 6008

The Storm

27:13 When a gentle south wind began to blow, they thought they had obtained what they wanted;
δὲ → νότου → → Ὑποπνεύσαντος → δόξαντες → κεκρατηκέναι τῆς → προθέσεως
cj n.gsm pt.aa.gsm pt.aa.npm f.ra d.gsf n.gsf
1254 5710 5710 3803 5710 1506 3195 3836 4606

so they weighed anchor and sailed along the shore of Crete. 14 Before very long, a wind of
→ ἄραντες ← παρελέγοντο ἆσσον ← ← ⌐τὴν Κρήτην, δὲ ⌐μετ' οὐ πολύ, ← ← ἄνεμος →
pt.aa.npm v.imi.3p adv.c d.asf n.asf cj p.a pl a.asn n.nsm
149 4162 839 3836 3207 1254 3552 4024 4498 449

hurricane force, called the "northeaster," swept down from the island. 15 The ship was caught by
τυφωνικὸς ← ὁ καλούμενος, εὐρακύλων ἔβαλεν ← κατ' αὐτῆς δὲ τοῦ πλοίου συναρπασθέντος
a.nsm d.nsm pt.pp.nsm n.nsm v.aai.3s p.g r.gsf.3 cj d.gsn n.gsn pt.ap.gsn
5607 3836 2813 2350 965 2848 899 1254 3836 4450 5275

the storm and could not head into the wind; so we gave way to it and were driven along. 16 As we
καὶ δυναμένου μὴ ἀντοφθαλμεῖν ← τῷ ἀνέμῳ → ἐπιδόντες ← → ἐφερόμεθα ← δέ →
cj pt.pp.gsn pl f.pa d.dsm n.dsm pt.aa.npm v.ipi.1p cj
2779 1538 3590 535 3836 449 2113 5770 1254

passed to the lee of a small island called Cauda, we were hardly able to make the lifeboat
ὑποδραμόντες ← ← τι → νησίον καλούμενον Καῦδα → → μόλις ἰσχύσαμεν ← γενέσθαι τῆς σκάφης
pt.aa.npm r.asn n.asn pt.pp.asn n.asn adv v.aai.1p f.am d.gsf n.gsf
5720 5516 3761 2813 3007 2710 2710 3660 2710 1181 3836 5002

secure. 17 When the men had hoisted it aboard, they passed ropes under the ship itself to hold it
περικρατεῖς ἦν → → → ἄραντες → ὑποζωννύντες βοηθείαις → τὸ πλοῖον → ἐχρῶντο
a.npm r.asf pt.aa.npm pt.pa.npm n.dpf d.asn n.asn v.imi.3p
4331 4005 149 5690 1069 5690 3836 4450 5968

together. Fearing that they would run aground on the sandbars of Syrtis, they lowered the sea anchor
← . τε φοβούμενοι μὴ → → ἐκπέσωσιν εἰς ⌐τὴν Σύρτιν, → χαλάσαντες τὸ → σκεῦος
cj pt.pp.npm cj v.aas.3p p.a d.asf n.asf pt.aa.npm d.asn n.asn
5445 5828 3590 1738 1650 3836 5358 5899 3836 5007

νηστείαν ἤδη παρεληλυθέναι παρῄνει ὁ Παῦλος 10 λέγων αὐτοῖς, Ἄνδρες, θεωρῶ ὅτι μετὰ ὕβρεως καὶ πολλῆς ζημίας οὐ μόνον τοῦ φορτίου καὶ τοῦ πλοίου ἀλλὰ καὶ τῶν ψυχῶν ἡμῶν μέλλειν ἔσεσθαι τὸν πλοῦν. 11 ὁ δὲ ἑκατοντάρχης τῷ κυβερνήτῃ καὶ τῷ ναυκλήρῳ μᾶλλον ἐπείθετο ἢ τοῖς ὑπὸ Παύλου λεγομένοις. 12 ἀνευθέτου δὲ τοῦ λιμένος ὑπάρχοντος πρὸς παραχειμασίαν οἱ πλείονες ἔθεντο βουλὴν ἀναχθῆναι ἐκεῖθεν, εἴ πως δύναιντο καταντήσαντες εἰς Φοίνικα παραχειμάσαι λιμένα τῆς Κρήτης βλέποντα κατὰ λίβα καὶ κατὰ χῶρον. 27:13 Ὑποπνεύσαντος δὲ νότου δόξαντες τῆς προθέσεως κεκρατηκέναι, ἄραντες ἆσσον παρελέγοντο τὴν Κρήτην. 14 μετ' οὐ πολὺ δὲ ἔβαλεν κατ' αὐτῆς ἄνεμος τυφωνικὸς ὁ καλούμενος Εὐρακύλων· 15 συναρπασθέντος δὲ τοῦ πλοίου καὶ μὴ δυναμένου ἀντοφθαλμεῖν τῷ ἀνέμῳ ἐπιδόντες ἐφερόμεθα. 16 νησίον δέ τι ὑποδραμόντες καλούμενον Καῦδα ἰσχύσαμεν μόλις περικρατεῖς γενέσθαι τῆς σκάφης, 17 ἣν ἄραντες βοηθείαις ἐχρῶντο ὑποζωννύντες τὸ πλοῖον, φοβούμενοί τε μὴ εἰς τὴν Σύρτιν ἐκπέσωσιν,

and   let the ship be driven   along. **18**   We   took such a violent battering from the storm   that the next day
οὕτως   → ἐφέροντο ←   δὲ ἡμῶν   σφοδρῶς   →   → χειμαζομένων   τῇ ἑξῆς →
adv   v.ipi.3p   cj   r.gp.1   adv   pt.pp.gpm   d.dsf adv
4048   5770   1254 7005   5380   5928   3836 2009

they began   to throw   the cargo overboard. **19**   On the third day, they threw   the ship's   tackle overboard with
→ ἐποιοῦντο   ἐκβολὴν   καὶ   τῇ τρίτῃ ←   ἔρριψαν   τὴν ιτοῦ πλοίου, σκευὴν ←
v.imi.3p   n.asf   cj   d.dsf a.dsf   v.aai.3p   d.asf d.gsn n.gsn   n.asf
4472   1678   2779   3836 5569   4849   3836 3836 4450   5006   4849

their own hands. **20**   When neither sun   nor stars   appeared   for many   days   and the storm   continued
→ → αὐτόχειρες   δὲ →   μήτε   ἡλίου μήτε ἄστρων ἐπιφαινόντων   ἐπὶ πλείονας ἡμέρας τε   χειμῶνος ,οὐκ ὀλίγου,
n.npm   cj   cj   n.gsm cj   n.gpn   pt.pa.gpn   p.a a.apf.c   n.apf cj   n.gsm   pl   a.gsm
901   1254 2210   3612   2463 3612 849   2210   2093 4498   2465 5445   5930   4024 3900

raging,   we   finally gave   up all   hope of being saved.   ¶   **21**   After the men had gone   a long
ἐπικειμένου ἡμᾶς λοιπὸν περιῃρεῖτο ← πᾶσα ἐλπὶς →   ιτοῦ σῴζεσθαι,   τε →   →   →   → ὑπαρχούσης Πολλῆς
pt.pm.gsm   r.ap.1   adv   v.ipi.3s   a.nsf n.nsf   d.gsn f.pp   cj   pt.pa.gsf   a.gsf
2130   7005   3370   4311   4246 1828   3836 5392   5445   5639   4498

time without food,   Paul   stood up before   them and said: "Men,   you should have taken my
← ἀσιτίας τότε ὁ Παῦλος, σταθεὶς ← ἐν μέσῳ, αὐτῶν   εἶπεν ῶ ἄνδρες, μέν →   ἔδει →   μοι
n.gsf   adv d.nsm n.nsm   pt.ap.nsm   p.d n.dsn   r.gpm.3   v.aai.3s j   n.vpm   pl   v.iai.3s   r.ds.1
826   5538 3836 4263   2705   1877 3545   899   3306 6043 467   3525   1256   4272 4272   1609

advice   not to sail   from Crete;   then you would have spared   yourselves this   damage   and
πειθαρχήσαντας μὴ → ἀνάγεσθαι ἀπὸ ,τῆς Κρήτης, τε →   →   κερδῆσαι   ταύτην ,τὴν ὕβριν, καὶ
pt.aa.apm   pl   f.pp   p.g   d.gsf n.gsf   cj   f.aa   r.asf   d.asf n.asf   cj
4272   3590   343   608   3836 3207   5445   3045   4047   3836 5615   2779

loss.   **22** But now   I   urge   you to keep up your courage, because not one   of you will be   lost;
,τὴν ζημίαν, καὶ ,τὰ νῦν, → παραινῶ ὑμᾶς → →   εὐθυμεῖν γὰρ →   οὐδεμία ψυχῆς ἐξ ὑμῶν,   ἔσται ἀποβολὴ
d.asf n.asf   cj   d.apn adv → v.pai.1s r.ap.2   f.pa   cj   a.nsf   n.gsf p.g r.gp.2   v.fmi.3s n.nsf
3836 2422   2779 3836 3814   4147   7007   2313   1142   4029   6034 1666 7007   1639 613

only the ship   will be destroyed. **23**   Last night   an angel   of the God whose I   am   and whom   I serve
πλὴν τοῦ πλοίου   γὰρ ταύτῃ ,τῇ νυκτὶ, ἄγγελος → τοῦ θεοῦ οὗ   ἐγώ εἰμι   ᾧ   καὶ → λατρεύω
p.g d.gsn n.gsn   cj   r.dsf   d.dsf n.dsf   n.nsm   d.gsm n.gsm r.gsm   r.ns.1 v.pai.1s   r.dsm   cj   v.pai.1s
4440   3836 4450   1142 4047   3836 3816   34   3836 2536   4005   1609 1639   4005   2779 3302

stood beside me **24** and said, 'Do not be afraid, Paul. You must stand trial   before Caesar; and   God   has
παρέστη ←   μοι   λέγων → μὴ   φοβοῦ Παῦλε σε δεῖ →   παραστῆναι →   Καίσαρι καὶ ἰδοὺ ὁ   θεὸς, →
v.aai.3s   r.ds.1   pt.pa.nsm → μὴ   v.ppm.2s n.vsm   r.as.2 v.pai.3s   f.aa   n.dsm   cj   j   d.nsm n.nsm
4225   1609   3306   5828 3590   5828   4263 5148 1256   4225   2790   2779 2627 3836 2536

graciously given   you the lives of all   who sail   with you.' **25** So keep up your courage, men,   for I have
→ κεχάρισται σοι → → πάντας τοὺς πλέοντας μετὰ σοῦ → διὸ →   εὐθυμεῖτε ἄνδρες γὰρ →
v.rmi.3s   r.ds.2   a.apm d.apm pt.pa.apm   p.g   r.gs.2   cj   v.pam.2p   n.vpm   cj
5919   5148   4246   3836 4434   3552 5148   1475   2313   467   1142

faith   in God   that   it will happen just   as he told   me. **26** Nevertheless, we   must run
πιστεύω → τῷ θεῷ, ὅτι οὕτως ',   ἔσται ,καθ' ὃν τρόπον, ← λελάληται μοι   δὲ   ἡμᾶς δεῖ ἐκπεσεῖν
v.pai.1s   d.dsm n.dsm   cj   adv   v.fmi.3s   p.a   r.asm n.asm   v.rpi.3s   r.ds.1   cj   r.ap.1 v.pai.3s f.aa
4409   3836 2536   4022 4048   1639   2848 4005 5573   3281   1609   1254   7005 1256 1738

aground on some island."
← εἰς τινα νῆσον
p.a r.asf n.asf
1650 5516 3762

The Shipwreck

27:27   On the fourteenth   night we   were   still being driven   across the Adriatic Sea, when about
δὲ Ὡς   τεσσαρεσκαιδεκάτη νὺξ   ἡμῶν ἐγένετο → διαφερομένων ἐν   τῷ Ἀδρίᾳ
cj   cj   a.nsf   n.nsf   r.gp.1 v.ami.3s   pt.pp.gpm   p.d   d.dsm n.dsm
1254 6055   5476   3816   7005 1181   1422   1877   3836 102

midnight   the sailors sensed they   were approaching   land. **28**   They took soundings and found that
,κατὰ μέσον τῆς νυκτὸς, οἱ   ναῦται ὑπενόουν αὐτοῖς → προσάγειν   τινὰ χώραν καὶ →   βολίσαντες   εὗρον
p.a n.asn d.gsf n.gsf   d.npm n.npm v.iai.3p   r.dpm.3   f.pa   r.asf n.asf   cj   pt.aa.npm   v.aai.3p
2848 3545 3836 3816   3836 3731 5706   899   4642   5516 6001   2779   1075   2351

χαλάσαντες τὸ σκεῦος, οὕτως ἐφέροντο. ¹⁸ σφοδρῶς δὲ χειμαζομένων ἡμῶν τῇ ἑξῆς ἐκβολὴν ἐποιοῦντο ¹⁹ καὶ τῇ τρίτῃ αὐτόχειρες τὴν σκευὴν τοῦ πλοίου ἔρριψαν. ²⁰ μήτε δὲ ἡλίου μήτε ἄστρων ἐπιφαινόντων ἐπὶ πλείονας ἡμέρας, χειμῶνός τε οὐκ ὀλίγου ἐπικειμένου, λοιπὸν περιῃρεῖτο ἐλπὶς πᾶσα τοῦ σῴζεσθαι ἡμᾶς. ¶ ²¹ Πολλῆς τε ἀσιτίας ὑπαρχούσης τότε σταθεὶς ὁ Παῦλος ἐν μέσῳ αὐτῶν εἶπεν, Ἔδει μέν, ὦ ἄνδρες, πειθαρχήσαντάς μοι μὴ ἀνάγεσθαι ἀπὸ τῆς Κρήτης κερδῆσαί τε τὴν ὕβριν ταύτην καὶ τὴν ζημίαν. ²² καὶ τὰ νῦν παραινῶ ὑμᾶς εὐθυμεῖν· ἀποβολὴ γὰρ ψυχῆς οὐδεμία ἔσται ἐξ ὑμῶν πλὴν τοῦ πλοίου. ²³ παρέστη γάρ μοι ταύτῃ τῇ νυκτὶ τοῦ θεοῦ, οὗ εἰμι [ἐγὼ] ᾧ καὶ λατρεύω, ἄγγελος ²⁴ λέγων, Μὴ φοβοῦ, Παῦλε, Καίσαρί σε δεῖ παραστῆναι, καὶ ἰδοὺ κεχάρισταί σοι ὁ θεὸς πάντας τοὺς πλέοντας μετὰ σοῦ. ²⁵ διὸ εὐθυμεῖτε, ἄνδρες· πιστεύω γὰρ τῷ θεῷ ὅτι οὕτως ἔσται καθ' ὃν τρόπον λελάληταί μοι. ²⁶ εἰς νῆσον δέ τινα δεῖ ἡμᾶς ἐκπεσεῖν.

27:27 Ὡς δὲ τεσσαρεσκαιδεκάτη νὺξ ἐγένετο διαφερομένων ἡμῶν ἐν τῷ Ἀδρίᾳ, κατὰ μέσον τῆς νυκτὸς ὑπενόουν οἱ ναῦται προσάγειν τινὰ αὐτοῖς χώραν. ²⁸ καὶ βολίσαντες εὗρον ὀργυιὰς εἴκοσι, βραχὺ δὲ διαστήσαντες καὶ πάλιν βολίσαντες εὗρον

the water was a hundred | and twenty | feet | deep. | A short | time | later | they took soundings | again | and
ὀργυιὰς εἴκοσι ← | ← | ← | δὲ | βραχὺ | διαστήσαντες ← | καὶ → | βολίσαντες | πάλιν
n.apf a.apf | | | cj | adv | pt.aa.npm | cj | pt.aa.npm | adv
3976 1633 | | | 1254 | 1099 | 1460 | 2779 | 1075 | 4099

found | it was ninety | feet deep. | ²⁹ | Fearing | that | we would be dashed | against the rocks, | they
εὗρον | ὀργυιὰς δεκαπέντε ← | | τε | φοβούμενοι | μή που → | → ἐκπέσωμεν κατὰ | τραχεῖς τόπους → |
v.aai.3p | n.apf a.apf | | cj | pt.pp.npm | cj pl | v.aas.1p p.a | a.apm n.apm |
2351 | 3976 1278 | | 5445 | 5828 | 3590 4543 | 1738 2848 | 5550 5536 |

dropped | four | anchors | from | the stern | and prayed for | daylight. | ³⁰ | In an attempt | to escape | from | the ship,
ῥίψαντες | τέσσαρας | ἀγκύρας | ἐκ | πρύμνης | ηὔχοντο γενέσθαι | ἡμέραν | δὲ | ζητούντων → | φυγεῖν | ἐκ | τοῦ πλοίου
pt.aa.npm | a.apf | n.apf | p.g | n.gsf | v.imi.3p f.am | n.asf | cj | pt.pa.gpm | f.aa | p.g | d.gsn n.gsn
4849 | 5475 | 46 | 1666 | 4744 | 2377 1181 | 2465 | 1254 | 2426 | 5771 | 1666 | 3836 4450

the sailors | let | the lifeboat | down | into | the sea, | pretending | they were going | to lower | some
καὶ Τῶν ναυτῶν → | τὴν σκάφην | χαλασάντων εἰς | τὴν θάλασσαν | προφάσει | ὡς → | → μελλόντων | ἐκτείνειν |
cj d.gpm n.gpm | d.asf n.asf | pt.aa.gpm p.a | d.asf n.asf | n.dsf | pl | pt.pa.gpm | f.pa |
2779 3836 3731 | 5899 3836 5002 | 5899 1650 | 3836 2498 | 4733 | 6055 | 3516 | 1753 |

anchors | from the bow. | ³¹ Then Paul | said | to the centurion | and | the soldiers, | "Unless | these men | stay
ἀγκύρας | ἐκ πρῴρης | ὁ Παῦλος | εἶπεν → | τῷ ἑκατοντάρχῃ | καὶ | τοῖς στρατιώταις | ἐὰν μὴ | οὗτοι → | μείνωσιν
n.apf | p.g n.gsf | d.nsm n.nsm | v.aai.3s | d.dsm n.dsm | cj | d.dpm n.dpm | cj pl | r.npm | v.aas.3p
46 | 1666 4749 | 3836 4263 | 3306 | 3836 1672 | 2779 | 3836 5132 | 1569 3590 | 4047 | 3531

with | the ship, | you | cannot | be saved." | ³² So | the soldiers | cut | the ropes | that held the lifeboat | and let
ἐν | τῷ πλοίῳ | ὑμεῖς | οὐ δύνασθε | → σωθῆναι | τότε οἱ | στρατιῶται | ἀπέκοψαν | τὰ σχοινία | τῆς σκάφης | καὶ εἴασαν
p.d | d.dsn n.dsn | r.np.2 | pl v.ppi.2p | f.ap | adv d.npm | n.npm | v.aai.3p | d.apn n.apn | d.gsf n.gsf | cj v.aai.3p
1877 | 3836 4450 | 7007 | 4024 1538 | 5392 | 5538 3836 | 5132 | 644 | 3836 5389 | 3836 5002 | 2779 1572

it | fall | away. | ¶ | ³³ Just | before | dawn | Paul | urged | them all | to
αὐτὴν | ἐκπεσεῖν ← | | δὲ | Ἄχρι οὗ | ἤμελλεν γίνεσθαι | ἡμέρα | ὁ Παῦλος | παρεκάλει | ἅπαντας → |
r.asf.3 | f.aa | | cj | r.gsn | v.iai.3s f.pm | n.nsf | d.nsm n.nsm | v.iai.3s | a.apm |
899 | 1738 | | 1254 948 | 4005 | 3516 | 1181 | 2465 3836 4263 | 4151 | 570 |

eat. | "For the last | fourteen | days," he said, | "you have been | in constant suspense | and have
μεταλαβεῖν τροφῆς ← | σήμερον τεσσαρεσκαιδεκάτην | ἡμέραν → | λέγων → | → | → διατελεῖτε προσδοκῶντες |
f.aa n.gsf | adv a.asf | n.asf | pt.pa.nsm | | v.pai.2p pt.pa.npm |
3561 5575 | 4958 5476 | 2465 | 3306 | | 1412 4659 |

gone without food | – you haven't | eaten | anything. | ³⁴ Now I urge | you to take | some food. | You
→ ἄσιτοι → | προσλαβόμενοι μηθὲν | | διὸ → παρακαλῶ ὑμᾶς → | μεταλαβεῖν | τροφῆς γὰρ ὑμετέρας
a.npm | pt.am.npm a.asn | | cj v.pai.1s r.ap.2 | f.aa | n.gsf cj r.gsf.2
827 | 4689 3594 | | 1475 4151 7007 | 3561 | 5575 1142 5629

need | it | to | survive. | Not one | of you | will lose | a single hair | from his head." | ³⁵ | After he said
ὑπάρχει | τοῦτο | πρὸς | τῆς σωτηρίας | γὰρ → οὐδενὸς → | ὑμῶν → | ἀπολεῖται | θρὶξ ἀπὸ | τῆς κεφαλῆς | δὲ | εἴπας
v.pai.3s | r.nsn | p.g | d.gsf n.gsf | cj a.gsm | r.gp.2 | v.fmi.3s | n.nsf p.g | d.gsf n.gsf | cj | pt.aa.nsm
5639 | 4047 | 4639 | 3836 5401 | 1142 4029 | 7007 | 660 | 2582 608 | 3836 3051 | 1254 | 3306

this, | he took | some bread | and gave thanks | to God | in front | of them all. | Then he broke | it and
ταῦτα καὶ → | λαβὼν | ἄρτον | εὐχαρίστησεν → | τῷ θεῷ → | ἐνώπιον ← | πάντων καὶ → | κλάσας
r.apn cj | pt.aa.nsm | n.asm | v.aai.3s | d.dsm n.dsm | p.g | a.gpm cj | pt.aa.nsm
4047 2779 | 3284 | 788 | 2373 | 3836 2536 | 1967 | 4246 2779 | 3089

began to eat. | ³⁶ | They were | all | encouraged and ate | some food themselves. | ³⁷ | Altogether there
ἤρξατο → ἐσθίειν | δὲ | → γενόμενοι | πάντες εὔθυμοι | καὶ προσελάβοντο | τροφῆς αὐτοί | δὲ πᾶσαι | αἱ ψυχαὶ
v.ami.3s f.pa | cj | pt.am.npm | a.npm a.npm | adv v.ami.3p | n.gsf r.npm | a.npf | d.npf n.npf
806 2266 | 1254 | 1181 | 4246 2314 | 2779 4689 | 5575 899 | 1254 4246 | 3836 6034

were 276 | of us | on board. | ³⁸ | When they had eaten | as much as they wanted, | they
ἤμεθα διακόσιαι ἑβδομήκοντα ἕξ | ἐν | τῷ πλοίῳ | δὲ → | τροφῆς → | κορεσθέντες →
v.imi.1p a.npf a.npf a.npf | p.d | d.dsn n.dsn | cj | n.gsf | pt.ap.npm
1639 1357 1573 1971 | 1639 1877 | 3836 4450 | 1254 3170 | 5575 | 3170

lightened | the ship | by throwing | the grain | into | the sea. | ¶ | ³⁹ | When daylight | came, they did | not
ἐκούφιζον | τὸ πλοῖον → | ἐκβαλλόμενοι | τὸν σῖτον | εἰς | τὴν θάλασσαν | δὲ | Ὅτε | ἡμέρα | ἐγένετο → | οὐκ
v.iai.3p | d.asn n.asn | pt.pm.npm | d.asm n.asm | p.a | d.asf n.asf | cj | | n.nsf | v.ami.3s | pl
3185 | 3836 4450 | 1675 | 3836 4992 | 1650 | 3836 2498 | 1254 4021 | | 2465 | 1181 | 2105 2105 4024

ὀργυιὰς δεκαπέντε· ²⁹ φοβούμενοί τε μή που κατὰ τραχεῖς τόπους ἐκπέσωμεν, ἐκ πρύμνης ῥίψαντες ἀγκύρας τέσσαρας ηὔχοντο ἡμέραν γενέσθαι. ³⁰ τῶν δὲ ναυτῶν ζητούντων φυγεῖν ἐκ τοῦ πλοίου καὶ χαλασάντων τὴν σκάφην εἰς τὴν θάλασσαν προφάσει ὡς ἐκ πρῴρης ἀγκύρας μελλόντων ἐκτείνειν, ³¹ εἶπεν ὁ Παῦλος τῷ ἑκατοντάρχῃ καὶ τοῖς στρατιώταις, Ἐὰν μὴ οὗτοι μείνωσιν ἐν τῷ πλοίῳ, ὑμεῖς σωθῆναι οὐ δύνασθε. ³² τότε ἀπέκοψαν οἱ στρατιῶται τὰ σχοινία τῆς σκάφης καὶ εἴασαν αὐτὴν ἐκπεσεῖν ¶ ³³ Ἄχρι δὲ οὗ ἡμέρα ἤμελλεν γίνεσθαι, παρεκάλει ὁ Παῦλος ἅπαντας μεταλαβεῖν τροφῆς λέγων, Τεσσαρεσκαιδεκάτην σήμερον ἡμέραν προσδοκῶντες ἄσιτοι διατελεῖτε μηθὲν προσλαβόμενοι. ³⁴ διὸ παρακαλῶ ὑμᾶς μεταλαβεῖν τροφῆς· τοῦτο γὰρ πρὸς τῆς ὑμετέρας σωτηρίας ὑπάρχει, οὐδενὸς γὰρ ὑμῶν θρὶξ ἀπὸ τῆς κεφαλῆς ἀπολεῖται. ³⁵ εἴπας δὲ ταῦτα καὶ λαβὼν ἄρτον εὐχαρίστησεν τῷ θεῷ ἐνώπιον πάντων καὶ κλάσας ἤρξατο ἐσθίειν. ³⁶ εὔθυμοι δὲ γενόμενοι πάντες καὶ αὐτοὶ προσελάβοντο τροφῆς. ³⁷ ἤμεθα δὲ αἱ πᾶσαι ψυχαὶ ἐν τῷ πλοίῳ διακόσιαι ἑβδομήκοντα ἕξ. ³⁸ κορεσθέντες δὲ τροφῆς ἐκούφιζον τὸ πλοῖον ἐκβαλλόμενοι τὸν σῖτον εἰς τὴν θάλασσαν. ¶ ³⁹ Ὅτε δὲ ἡμέρα ἐγένετο, τὴν γῆν οὐκ ἐπεγίνωσκον, κόλπον δέ τινα κατενόουν ἔχοντα αἰγιαλὸν εἰς ὃν

recognize the land, but they saw a bay with a sandy beach, where they decided to run the ship
ἐπεγίνωσκον τὴν γῆν δὲ → κατενόουν τινα κόλπον ἔχοντα → αἰγιαλὸν εἰς ὃν → ἐβουλεύοντο → τὸ πλοῖον
v.iai.3p d.asf n.asf cj v.iai.3p r.asm n.asm pt.pa.asm n.asm r.asm v.imi.3p d.asn n.asn
2105 3836 1178 1254 2917 5516 3146 2400 129 1650 4005 1086 2034 2034 3836 4450

aground if they could. **40** Cutting loose the anchors, they left them in the sea and at the same time
ἐξῶσαι εἰ → δύναιντο καὶ περιελόντες ← τὰς ἀγκύρας → εἴων εἰς τὴν θάλασσαν ἅμα
f.aa cj v.ppo.3p cj pt.aa.npm d.apf n.apf v.iai.3p p.a d.asf n.asf adv
2034 1623 1538 2779 4311 3836 46 1572 1650 3836 2498 275

untied the ropes that held the rudders. Then they hoisted the foresail to the wind and made for the
ἀνέντες τὰς ζευκτηρίας τῶν πηδαλίων καὶ → ἐπάραντες τὸν ἀρτέμωνα τῇ πνεούσῃ κατεῖχον εἰς τὸν
pt.aa.npm d.apf n.apf d.gpn n.gpn cj pt.aa.npm d.asm n.asm d.dsf pt.pa.dsf v.iai.3p p.a d.asm
479 3836 2415 3836 4382 2779 2048 3836 784 3836 4463 2988 1650 3836

beach. **41** But the ship struck a sandbar and ran aground. The bow stuck fast and
αἰγιαλόν δὲ τὴν ναῦν περιπεσόντες εἰς τόπον διθάλασσον ἐπέκειλαν ← καὶ μὲν ἡ πρῷρα ἐρείσασα ←
n.asm cj d.asf n.asf pt.aa.npm p.a n.asm a.asm v.aai.3p cj pl d.nsf n.nsf pt.aa.nsf
129 1254 3836 3730 4346 1650 5536 1458 2131 2779 3525 3836 4749 2242

would not move, and the stern was broken to pieces by the pounding of the surf. ¶ **42** The
→ → ἔμεινεν ἀσάλευτος, δὲ ἡ πρύμνα → ἐλύετο ὑπὸ τῆς βίας → τῶν κυμάτων δὲ Τῶν
v.aai.3s a.nsf cj d.nsf n.nsf v.ipi.3s p.g d.gsf n.gsf d.gpn n.gpn cj d.gpm
3531 810 1254 3836 4744 3395 5679 3836 1040 3836 3246 1254 3836

soldiers planned to kill the prisoners to prevent any of them from swimming away and escaping.
στρατιωτῶν βουλὴ ἐγένετο ἵνα ἀποκτείνωσιν τοὺς δεσμώτας μὴ τις ἐκκολυμβήσας ← διαφύγῃ
n.gpm n.nsf v.ami.3s cj v.aas.3p d.apm n.apm cj r.nsm pt.aa.nsm v.aas.3s
5132 1087 1181 2671 650 3836 1304 3590 5516 1713 1423

43 But the centurion wanted to spare Paul's life and kept them from carrying out their plan.
δὲ ὁ ἑκατοντάρχης βουλόμενος → διασῶσαι τὸν Παῦλον ἐκώλυσεν αὐτοὺς → τοῦ βουλήματος τε
cj d.nsm n.nsm pt.pm.nsm f.aa d.asm n.asm v.aai.3s r.apm.3 d.gsn n.gsn cj
1254 3836 1672 1089 1407 3836 4263 3266 899 3836 1088 5445

He ordered those who could swim to jump overboard first and get to land. **44** The rest
→ ἐκέλευσεν τοὺς ← δυναμένους κολυμβᾶν ἀπορίψαντας πρώτους ἐξιέναι ἐπὶ τὴν γῆν καὶ τοὺς λοιποὺς
v.aai.3s d.apm pt.pp.apm f.pa pt.aa.apm a.apm f.pa p.a d.asf n.asf cj d.apm a.apm
3027 3836 1538 3147 681 4755 1997 2093 3836 1178 2779 3836 3370

were to get there on planks or on pieces of the ship. In this way everyone reached on
μὲν οὓς ἐπὶ σανίσιν δὲ οὓς ἐπί τινων τῶν ἀπὸ τοῦ πλοίου καὶ → → οὕτως πάντας ἐγένετο ἐπὶ
pl r.apm p.d n.dpf pl r.apm p.q r.qpn d.gpn p.g d.gsn n.gsn cj adv a.apm v.ami.3s p.a
3525 4005 2093 4909 1254 4005 2093 5516 3836 608 3836 4450 2779 4048 4246 1181 2093

land in safety.
τὴν γῆν → διασωθῆναι
d.asf n.asf f.ap
3836 1178 1407

Ashore on Malta

28:1 Once safely on shore, we found out that the island was called Malta. **2** The islanders showed
Καὶ τότε διασωθέντες ← → ἐπέγνωμεν ← ὅτι ἡ νῆσος → καλεῖται Μελίτη τε οἱ βάρβαροι παρεῖχον
cj adv pt.ap.npm v.aai.1p cj d.nsf n.nsf v.ppi.3s n.nsf cj d.npm n.npm v.iai.3p
2779 5538 1407 2105 4022 3836 3762 2813 3514 5445 3836 975 4218

us unusual kindness. They built a fire and welcomed us all because it was
ἡμῖν οὐ τὴν τυχοῦσαν φιλανθρωπίαν γὰρ → ἅψαντες πυρὰν προσελάβοντο ἡμᾶς πάντας διὰ τὸν ἐφεστῶτα
r.dp.1 d.asf pt.aa.asf n.asf cj pt.aa.npm n.asf v.ami.3p r.ap.1 a.apm p.a d.asm pt.ra.asm
7005 4024 3836 5593 5792 1142 721 4787 4689 7005 4246 1328 3836 2392

raining and cold. **3** Paul gathered a pile of brushwood and, as he put it on the fire, a
τὸν ὑετὸν καὶ διὰ τὸ ψῦχος, δὲ τοῦ Παύλου Συστρέψαντος τι πλῆθος → φρυγάνων καὶ → ἐπιθέντος ἐπὶ τὴν πυρὰν
d.asm n.asm cj p.a d.asn n.asn cj d.gsm n.gsm pt.aa.gsm r.asn n.asn n.gpn cj pt.aa.gsm p.a d.asf n.asf
3836 5624 2779 1328 3836 6036 1254 3836 4263 5370 5516 4436 5866 2779 2202 2093 3836 4787

viper, driven out by the heat, fastened itself on his hand. **4** When the islanders saw the snake hanging
ἔχιδνα ἐξελθοῦσα ← ἀπὸ τῆς θέρμης καθῆψεν ← αὐτοῦ τῆς χειρός, δὲ ὡς οἱ βάρβαροι εἶδον τὸ θηρίον κρεμάμενον
n.nsf pt.aa.nsf p.g d.gsf n.gsf v.aai.3s r.gsm.3 d.gsf n.gsf cj cj d.npm n.npm v.aai.3p d.asn n.asn pt.pm.asn
2399 2002 608 3836 2549 2750 899 3836 5931 1254 6055 3836 975 1625 3836 2563 3203

ἐβουλεύοντο εἰ δύναιντο ἐξῶσαι τὸ πλοῖον. ⁴⁰ καὶ τὰς ἀγκύρας περιελόντες εἴων εἰς τὴν θάλασσαν, ἅμα ἀνέντες τὰς ζευκτηρίας τῶν πηδαλίων καὶ ἐπάραντες τὸν ἀρτέμωνα τῇ πνεούσῃ κατεῖχον εἰς τὸν αἰγιαλόν. ⁴¹ περιπεσόντες δὲ εἰς τόπον διθάλασσον ἐπέκειλαν τὴν ναῦν καὶ ἡ μὲν πρῷρα ἐρείσασα ἔμεινεν ἀσάλευτος, ἡ δὲ πρύμνα ἐλύετο ὑπὸ τῆς βίας [τῶν κυμάτων ¶ ⁴² τῶν δὲ στρατιωτῶν βουλὴ ἐγένετο ἵνα τοὺς δεσμώτας ἀποκτείνωσιν, μή τις ἐκκολυμβήσας διαφύγῃ. ⁴³ ὁ δὲ ἑκατοντάρχης βουλόμενος διασῶσαι τὸν Παῦλον ἐκώλυσεν αὐτοὺς τοῦ βουλήματος, ἐκέλευσέν τε τοὺς δυναμένους κολυμβᾶν ἀπορίψαντας πρώτους ἐπὶ τὴν γῆν ἐξιέναι ⁴⁴ καὶ τοὺς λοιποὺς οὓς μὲν ἐπὶ σανίσιν, οὓς δὲ ἐπί τινων τῶν ἀπὸ τοῦ πλοίου. καὶ οὕτως ἐγένετο πάντας διασωθῆναι ἐπὶ τὴν γῆν.

²⁸:¹ Καὶ διασωθέντες τότε ἐπέγνωμεν ὅτι Μελίτη ἡ νῆσος καλεῖται. ² οἵ τε βάρβαροι παρεῖχον οὐ τὴν τυχοῦσαν φιλανθρωπίαν ἡμῖν, ἅψαντες γὰρ πυρὰν προσελάβοντο πάντας ἡμᾶς διὰ τὸν ὑετὸν τὸν ἐφεστῶτα καὶ διὰ τὸ ψῦχος. ³ συστρέψαντος δὲ τοῦ Παύλου φρυγάνων τι πλῆθος καὶ ἐπιθέντος ἐπὶ τὴν πυράν, ἔχιδνα ἀπὸ τῆς θέρμης ἐξελθοῦσα καθῆψεν τῆς χειρὸς αὐτοῦ. ⁴ ὡς δὲ εἶδον οἱ βάρβαροι κρεμάμενον τὸ θηρίον ἐκ τῆς χειρὸς αὐτοῦ, πρὸς ἀλλήλους ἔλεγον, Πάντως φονεύς

from his hand, they said to each other, "This man must be a murderer; for though he
ἐκ αὐτοῦ τῆς χειρός, → ἔλεγον πρὸς ἀλλήλους ← οὗτος ὁ ἄνθρωπος, πάντως ἐστιν φονεύς ὃν
p.g r.gsm.3 d.gsf n.gsf — v.iai.3p p.a r.apm — r.nsm d.nsm n.nsm adv v.pai.3s n.nsm — r.asm
1666 899 3836 5931 — 3306 4639 253 — 4047 3836 476 4122 1639 5838 — 4005

escaped from the sea, Justice has not allowed him to live." 5 But Paul shook the snake off into the fire
διασωθέντα ἐκ τῆς θαλάσσης ἡ δίκη οὐκ εἴασεν → ζῆν οὖν μὲν ὁ ἀποτινάξας τὸ θηρίον ← εἰς τὸ πῦρ
pt.ap.asm p.g d.gsf n.gsf d.nsf n.nsf pl v.aai.3s f.pa cj pl d.nsm pt.aa.nsm d.asn n.asn p.a d.asn n.asn
1407 1666 3836 2498 3836 1472 1572 4024 1572 2409 4036 3525 3836 701 3836 2563 701 1650 3836 4786

and suffered no ill effects. 6 The people expected him to swell up or suddenly fall dead,
ἔπαθεν οὐδὲν κακόν ← δὲ οἱ προσεδόκων αὐτὸν μέλλειν πίμπρασθαι ← ἢ ἄφνω καταπίπτειν νεκρόν
v.aai.3s a.asn a.asn cj d.npm v.iai.3p r.asm.3 f.pa f.pp cj adv f.pa a.asm
4248 4029 2805 1254 3836 4659 899 3516 4399 2445 924 2928 3738

but after waiting a long time and seeing nothing unusual happen to him, they changed their
δὲ αὐτῶν → προσδοκώντων ἐπὶ πολὺ ← καὶ θεωρούντων μηδὲν ἄτοπον γινόμενον εἰς αὐτὸν → μεταβαλόμενοι ←
cj r.gpm.3 pt.pa.gpm p.a a.asn cj pt.pa.gpm a.asn a.asn pt.pm.asn p.a r.asm.3 pt.am.npm
1254 899 4659 2093 4498 2779 2555 3594 876 1181 1650 899 3554

minds and said he was a god. ¶ 7 There was an estate nearby that
← ἔλεγον αὐτὸν εἶναι θεόν δὲ ὑπῆρχεν χωρία Ἐν τοῖς περὶ τὸν τόπον ἐκεῖνον ὀνόματι
v.iai.3p r.asm.3 f.pa n.asn cj v.iai.3s n.npn p.d d.dpn p.a d.asm n.asm r.asm n.dsn
3306 899 1639 2536 1254 5639 6005 1877 3836 4309 3836 5536 1697 3950

belonged to Publius, the chief official of the island. He welcomed us to his home and for three days
→ → Ποπλίῳ τῷ πρώτῳ ← τῆς νήσου ὃς ἀναδεξάμενος ἡμᾶς ← → → τρεῖς ἡμέρας
n.dsm d.dsm a.dsm d.gsf n.gsf r.nsm pt.am.nsm r.ap.1 a.apf n.apf
4511 3836 4755 3836 3762 4005 346 7005 346 346 5552 2465

entertained us hospitably. 8 His father was sick in bed, suffering from fever and dysentery.
ἐξένισεν φιλοφρόνως δὲ τοῦ Ποπλίου τὸν πατέρα ἐγένετο → κατακεῖσθαι συνεχόμενον → πυρετοῖς καὶ δυσεντερίῳ
v.aai.3s adv cj d.gsm n.gsm d.asm n.asm v.ami.3s f.pm pt.pp.asm n.dpm cj n.dsn
3826 5819 1254 3836 4511 3836 4252 1181 2879 5309 4790 2779 1548

Paul went in to see him and, after prayer, placed his hands on him and healed him. 9 When
ὁ Παῦλος εἰσελθὼν πρὸς ὃν καὶ προσευξάμενος ἐπιθεὶς τὰς χεῖρας αὐτῷ ἰάσατο αὐτὸν δὲ →
d.nsm n.nsm pt.aa.nsm p.a r.asm cj pt.am.nsm pt.aa.nsm d.apf n.apf r.dsm.3 v.ami.3s r.asm.3 cj
3836 4263 1656 4639 4005 2779 4667 2202 3836 5931 899 2615 899 1254 1181

this had happened, the rest of the sick on the island came and were cured. 10 They
τούτου → γενομένου καὶ οἱ λοιποὶ οἱ ἔχοντες ἀσθενείας ἐν τῇ νήσῳ προσήρχοντο καὶ → ἐθεραπεύοντο οἱ καὶ
r.gsn pt.am.gsn adv d.npm a.npm d.npm pt.pa.npm n.apf p.d d.dsf n.dsf v.imi.3p cj v.ipi.3p r.npm adv
4047 1181 2779 3836 3370 3836 2400 819 1877 3836 3762 4665 2779 2543 4005 2779

honored us in many ways and when we were ready to sail, they furnished us with the supplies we
ἐτίμησαν ἡμᾶς → πολλαῖς τιμαῖς καὶ → → → ἀναγομένοις → ἐπέθεντο → τὰ
v.aai.3p r.ap.1 a.dpf n.dpf cj pt.pp.dpm v.ami.3p d.apn
5506 7005 4498 5507 2779 343 2202 3836

needed.
πρὸς τὰς χρείας,
p.a d.apf n.apf
4639 3836 5970

Arrival at Rome

28:11 After three months we put out to sea in a ship that had wintered in the island. It was an
δὲ Μετὰ τρεῖς μῆνας → ἀνήχθημεν ← → ἐν πλοίῳ → παρακεχειμακότι ἐν τῇ νήσῳ
cj p.a a.apm n.apm v.api.1p p.d n.dsn pt.ra.dsn p.d d.dsf n.dsf
1254 3552 5552 3604 343 1877 4450 4199 1877 3836 3762

Alexandrian ship with the figurehead of the twin gods Castor and Pollux. 12 We put in at Syracuse
Ἀλεξανδρίνῳ → παρασήμῳ → Διοσκούροις καὶ → καταχθέντες ← εἰς Συρακούσας
a.dsn a.dsn n.dpm cj pt.ap.npm p.a
234 4185 1483 2779 2864 1650 5352

and stayed there three days. 13 From there we set sail and arrived at Rhegium. The next
ἐπεμείναμεν τρεῖς ἡμέρας ὅθεν ← → περιελόντες ← κατηντήσαμεν εἰς Ῥήγιον καὶ μετὰ μίαν
v.aai.1p a.apf n.apf cj pt.aa.npm v.aai.1p p.a n.asn cj p.a a.asf
2152 5552 2465 3854 4311 2918 1650 4836 2779 3552 1651

ἔστιν ὁ ἄνθρωπος οὗτος ὃν διασωθέντα ἐκ τῆς θαλάσσης ἡ δίκη ζῆν οὐκ εἴασεν. 5 ὁ μὲν οὖν ἀποτινάξας τὸ θηρίον εἰς τὸ πῦρ ἔπαθεν οὐδὲν κακόν, 6 οἱ δὲ προσεδόκων αὐτὸν μέλλειν πίμπρασθαι ἢ καταπίπτειν ἄφνω νεκρόν. ἐπὶ πολὺ δὲ αὐτῶν προσδοκώντων καὶ θεωρούντων μηδὲν ἄτοπον εἰς αὐτὸν γινόμενον μεταβαλόμενοι ἔλεγον αὐτὸν εἶναι θεόν. ¶ 7 Ἐν δὲ τοῖς περὶ τὸν τόπον ἐκεῖνον ὑπῆρχεν χωρία τῷ πρώτῳ τῆς νήσου ὀνόματι Ποπλίῳ, ὃς ἀναδεξάμενος ἡμᾶς τρεῖς ἡμέρας φιλοφρόνως ἐξένισεν. 8 ἐγένετο δὲ τὸν πατέρα τοῦ Ποπλίου πυρετοῖς καὶ δυσεντερίῳ συνεχόμενον κατακεῖσθαι, πρὸς ὃν ὁ Παῦλος εἰσελθὼν καὶ προσευξάμενος ἐπιθεὶς τὰς χεῖρας αὐτῷ ἰάσατο αὐτόν. 9 τούτου δὲ γενομένου καὶ οἱ λοιποὶ οἱ ἐν τῇ νήσῳ ἔχοντες ἀσθενείας προσήρχοντο καὶ ἐθεραπεύοντο, 10 οἳ καὶ πολλαῖς τιμαῖς ἐτίμησαν ἡμᾶς καὶ ἀναγομένοις ἐπέθεντο τὰ πρὸς τὰς χρείας.
28:11 Μετὰ δὲ τρεῖς μῆνας ἀνήχθημεν ἐν πλοίῳ παρακεχειμακότι ἐν τῇ νήσῳ, Ἀλεξανδρίνῳ, παρασήμῳ Διοσκούροις. 12 καὶ καταχθέντες εἰς Συρακούσας ἐπεμείναμεν ἡμέρας τρεῖς, 13 ὅθεν περιελόντες κατηντήσαμεν εἰς Ῥήγιον. καὶ μετὰ μίαν ἡμέραν

day the south wind came up, and on the following day we reached Puteoli. **14** There we found some
ἡμέραν → νότου ἐπιγενομένου ← → → δευτεραῖοι → ἤλθομεν εἰς Ποτιόλους οὗ → εὑρόντες
n.asf n.gsm pt.am.gsm a.npm v.aai.1p p.a n.apm adv pt.aa.npm
2465 3803 2104 1308 2262 1650 4541 4023 2351

brothers who invited us to spend a week with them. And so we came to Rome. **15** The brothers
ἀδελφοὺς παρεκλήθημεν ← ἐπιμεῖναι ἡμέρας ἑπτά, παρ᾽ αὐτοῖς καὶ οὕτως → ἤλθαμεν εἰς τὴν Ῥώμην οἱ ἀδελφοὶ
n.apm v.api.1p f.aa n.apf n.apf p.d r.dpm.3 cj adv v.aai.1p p.a d.asf n.asf d.npm n.npm
81 4151 2152 2465 2231 4123 899 2779 4048 2262 1650 3836 4873 3836 81

there had heard *that* *we were coming,* and they traveled as far as the Forum of Appius and the
κἀκεῖθεν → ἀκούσαντες ⸂τὰ περὶ ἡμῶν⸃ ← → ἦλθαν ἄχρι φόρου → Ἀππίου καὶ
crasis pt.aa.npm d.apn p.g r.gp.1 v.aai.3p p.g n.gsn n.gsm cj
2796 201 3836 4309 7005 2262 948 5842 716 2779

Three Taverns to meet us. At the sight of these men Paul thanked God and was encouraged.
Τριῶν ταβερνῶν εἰς ἀπάντησιν ἡμῖν → → ἰδὼν → οὓς ← ⸆ ὁ Παῦλος εὐχαριστήσας ⸂τῷ θεῷ⸃ ἔλαβε θάρσος
a.gpf n.gpf p.a n.asf r.dp.1 pt.aa.nsm r.apm d.nsm n.nsm pt.aa.nsm d.dsm n.dsm v.aai.3s n.asn
5552 5411 1650 561 7005 1625 4005 3836 4263 2373 3836 2536 3284 2511

16 When we got to Rome, Paul was allowed to live by himself, with a soldier to guard
δὲ Ὅτε → εἰσήλθομεν εἰς Ῥώμην ⸂τῷ Παύλῳ⸃ → ἐπετράπη → μένειν καθ᾽ ἑαυτὸν σὺν ⸂τῷ στρατιώτῃ⸃ → φυλάσσοντι
cj cj v.aai.1p p.a n.asf d.dsm n.dsm v.api.3s f.pa p.a r.asm.3 p.d d.dsm n.dsm pt.pa.dsm
1254 4021 1656 1650 4873 3836 4263 2205 3531 2848 1571 5250 3836 5132 5875

him.
αὐτόν
r.asm.3
899

Paul Preaches at Rome Under Guard

28:17 Three days later he called together the leaders of the Jews. When they
δὲ Ἐγένετο τρεῖς ἡμέρας μετὰ αὐτὸν συγκαλέσασθαι ← τοὺς ⸂ὄντας πρώτους⸃ → τῶν Ἰουδαίων δὲ ⸆ αὐτῶν
cj v.ami.3s a.apf n.apf p.a r.asm.3 f.am d.apm pt.pa.apm a.apm d.gpm n.gpm cj r.gpm.3
1254 1181 5552 2465 3552 899 5157 3836 1639 4755 3836 2681 1254 5302 899

had assembled, Paul said to them: "My brothers, although I have done nothing against our people or
→ συνελθόντων ἔλεγεν πρὸς αὐτούς ἄνδρες ⸀ ἀδελφοί ⸀ ἐγώ → ποιήσας οὐδὲν ἐναντίον τῷ λαῷ ἢ
pt.aa.gpm v.iai.3s p.a r.apm.3 n.vpm n.vpm r.ns.1 pt.aa.nsm a.asn p.g d.dsm n.dsm cj
5302 3306 4639 899 467 81 4472 1609 4472 4029 1883 3836 3295 2445

against the customs of our ancestors, I was arrested in Jerusalem and handed over to the Romans.
τοῖς ἔθεσι → τοῖς πατρῴοις δέσμιος ἐξ Ἱεροσολύμων παρεδόθην ← εἰς τὰς χεῖρας τῶν Ῥωμαίων
d.dpn n.dpn d.dpn a.dpn n.nsm p.g n.gpn v.api.1s p.a d.apf n.apf d.gpm n.gpm
3836 1621 3836 4262 1300 1666 2642 4140 1650 3836 5931 3836 4871

18 They examined me and wanted to release me, because I was not guilty of any crime
οἵτινες ἀνακρίναντές με ἐβούλοντο → ἀπολῦσαι με διὰ ἐν ἐμοὶ ⸂τὸ ὑπάρχειν⸃ μηδεμίαν αἰτίαν
r.npm pt.aa.npm r.as.1 v.imi.3p f.aa r.as.1 p.a p.d r.ds.1 d.asn f.pa a.asf n.asf
4015 373 1609 1089 668 1609 1328 1877 1609 3836 5639 3594 162

deserving death. **19** But when the Jews objected, I was compelled to appeal to Caesar – not that I had
→ θανάτου δὲ → τῶν Ἰουδαίων ἀντιλεγόντων → ἠναγκάσθην ἐπικαλέσασθαι ← Καίσαρα οὐχ ὡς → ἔχων
n.gsm cj d.gpm a.gpm pt.pa.gpm v.api.1s f.am n.asm pl pl pt.pa.nsm
2505 1254 515 3836 2681 515 337 2126 2790 4024 6055 2400

any charge to bring against my own people. **20** For this reason I have asked to see you and
τι κατηγορεῖν ← ← μου τοῦ ἔθνους ⸀ διὰ ταύτην ⸂τὴν αἰτίαν⸃ → παρεκάλεσα → ἰδεῖν ὑμᾶς καὶ
r.asn f.pa r.gs.1 d.gsn n.gsn cj p.a r.asf d.asf n.asf v.aai.1s f.aa r.ap.2 cj
5516 2989 1609 3836 1620 4036 1328 4047 3836 162 4151 1625 7007 2779

talk with you. It is because of the hope of Israel that I am bound with this chain." ¶
προσλαλῆσαι ← γὰρ ἕνεκεν ← τῆς ἐλπίδος → ⸂τοῦ Ἰσραὴλ⸃ → περίκειμαι ταύτην ⸂τὴν ἅλυσιν⸃
f.aa cj p.g d.gsf n.gsf d.gsm n.gsm v.pmi.1s r.asf d.asf n.asf
4688 1142 1914 3836 1828 3836 2702 4329 4047 3836 268

21 They replied, "We have not received any letters from Judea concerning you, and none of the
δὲ οἱ εἶπαν πρὸς αὐτόν ἡμεῖς ⸆ οὔτε ἐδεξάμεθα γράμματα ἀπὸ ⸂τῆς Ἰουδαίας⸃ περὶ σοῦ οὔτε τις → τῶν
cj d.npm v.aai.3p p.a r.asm.3 r.np.1 cj v.ami.1p n.apn p.g d.gsf n.gsf p.g r.gs.2 cj r.nsm d.gpm
1254 3836 3306 4639 899 7005 1312 4046 1312 1207 608 3836 2677 4309 5148 4046 5516 3836

ἐπιγενομένου νότου δευτεραῖοι ἤλθομεν εἰς Ποτιόλους, ¹⁴ οὗ εὑρόντες ἀδελφοὺς παρεκλήθημεν παρ᾽ αὐτοῖς ἐπιμεῖναι ἡμέρας ἑπτά· καὶ οὕτως εἰς τὴν Ῥώμην ἤλθαμεν. ¹⁵ κἀκεῖθεν οἱ ἀδελφοὶ ἀκούσαντες τὰ περὶ ἡμῶν ἦλθαν εἰς ἀπάντησιν ἡμῖν ἄχρι Ἀππίου Φόρου καὶ Τριῶν οὓς ἰδὼν ὁ Παῦλος εὐχαριστήσας τῷ θεῷ ἔλαβε θάρσος. ¹⁶ Ὅτε δὲ εἰσήλθομεν εἰς Ῥώμην, ἐπετράπη τῷ Παύλῳ μένειν καθ᾽ ἑαυτὸν σὺν τῷ φυλάσσοντι αὐτὸν στρατιώτῃ.

¹⁷ **28:17** Ἐγένετο δὲ μετὰ ἡμέρας τρεῖς συγκαλέσασθαι αὐτὸν τοὺς ὄντας τῶν Ἰουδαίων πρώτους· συνελθόντων δὲ αὐτῶν ἔλεγεν πρὸς αὐτούς, Ἐγώ, ἄνδρες ἀδελφοί, οὐδὲν ἐναντίον ποιήσας τῷ λαῷ ἢ τοῖς ἔθεσι τοῖς πατρῴοις δέσμιος ἐξ Ἱεροσολύμων παρεδόθην εἰς τὰς χεῖρας τῶν Ῥωμαίων, ¹⁸ οἵτινες ἀνακρίναντές με ἐβούλοντο ἀπολῦσαι διὰ τὸ μηδεμίαν αἰτίαν θανάτου ὑπάρχειν ἐν ἐμοί. ¹⁹ ἀντιλεγόντων δὲ τῶν Ἰουδαίων ἠναγκάσθην ἐπικαλέσασθαι Καίσαρα οὐχ ὡς τοῦ ἔθνους μου ἔχων τι κατηγορεῖν. ²⁰ διὰ ταύτην οὖν τὴν αἰτίαν παρεκάλεσα ὑμᾶς ἰδεῖν καὶ προσλαλῆσαι, ἕνεκεν γὰρ τῆς ἐλπίδος τοῦ Ἰσραὴλ τὴν ἅλυσιν ταύτην περίκειμαι. ¶ ²¹ οἱ δὲ πρὸς αὐτὸν εἶπαν, Ἡμεῖς οὔτε γράμματα περὶ σοῦ ἐδεξάμεθα ἀπὸ τῆς Ἰουδαίας οὔτε

brothers who have come   from there has reported or said   anything bad   about you. **22** But we want   to
ἀδελφῶν → → παραγενόμενος ← ← → ἀπήγγειλεν ἢ ἐλάλησεν τι   πονηρόν περὶ σοῦ δὲ → ἀξιοῦμεν →
n.gpm   pt.am.nsm   v.aai.3s cj v.aai.3s r.asn   a.asn περὶ r.gs.2 cj v.pai.1p
81   4134   550 2445 3281 5516   4505 4505 5148 1254 546

hear what   your views are, for   we know   that people everywhere are talking   against   this
ἀκοῦσαι ἃ παρὰ σοῦ φρονεῖς ← γὰρ μὲν ἡμῖν γνωστόν ἐστιν ὅτι   πανταχοῦ → ἀντιλέγεται ← περὶ ταύτης
f.aa r.apn p.g r.gs.2 v.pai.2s   cj pl r.dp.1 a.nsn v.pai.3s cj   adv   v.ppi.3s p.g r.gsf
201 4005 4123 5148 5858   1142 3525 7005 1196 1639 4022 515 4116   515 4309 4047

sect."   ¶   **23**   They arranged to meet Paul on a certain day,   and came   in even larger
ͺτῆς αἱρέσεωςͺ δὲ → Ταξάμενοι αὐτῷ   ἡμέραν ἦλθον πρὸς αὐτὸν → πλείονες
d.gsf n.gsf   cj   pt.am.npm r.dsm.3   n.asf v.aai.3p p.a r.asm.3   a.npm.c
3836 146   1254   5435 899   2465 2262 4639 899   4498

numbers to the place where he was staying. From morning till evening he explained and declared   to them
← εἰς τὴν ξενίαν ← ← ← ἀπὸ πρωῒ ἕως ἑσπέρας ἐξετίθετο διαμαρτυρόμενος οἷς
p.a d.asf n.asf   p.g adv p.g n.gsf v.imi.3s pt.pm.nsm r.dpn
1650 3836 3825   608 4745 2401 2270 1758 1371 4005

the kingdom of God   and tried to convince them about Jesus   from the Law of Moses   and from the
τὴν βασιλείαν → ͺτοῦ θεοῦͺ τε → πείθων αὐτοὺς περὶ ͺτοῦ Ἰησοῦͺ τε ἀπό τοῦ νόμου → Μωϋσέως καὶ   τῶν
d.asf n.asf   d.gsm n.gsm cj   pt.pa.nsm r.apm.3 p.g d.gsm n.gsm cj p.g d.gsm n.gsm   n.gsm cj   d.gpm
3836 993   3836 2536 5445   4275 899 4309 3836 2652 5445 608 3836 3795   3707 2779   3836

Prophets. **24**   Some were convinced by what he said,   but others would not believe. **25**   They
προφητῶν καὶ ͺμὲν οἱͺ → ἐπείθοντο → τοῖς → λεγομένοις δὲ οἱ → ἠπίστουν δὲ →
n.gpm cj pl d.npm   v.ipi.3p   d.dpn   pt.pp.dpn pl d.npm   v.iai.3p cj
4737 2779 3525 3836   4275   3836   3306 1254 3836   601 1254

disagreed   among themselves and began to leave   after Paul   had made   this final statement:
ͺἀσύμφωνοι ὄντες,ͺ πρὸς ἀλλήλους → → ἀπελύοντο ͺτοῦ Παύλου,ͺ → εἰπόντος ἓν ῥῆμα   ὅτι
a.npm pt.pa.npm p.a r.apm   v.imi.3p d.gsm n.gsm   pt.aa.gsm a.asn n.asn   cj
851 1639 4639 253   668 3306 3836 4263   3306 1651 4839   4022

"The Holy   Spirit spoke the truth to   your forefathers   when he said through Isaiah the prophet:
τὸ ͺτὸ ἅγιονͺ πνεῦμα ἐλάλησεν καλῶς πρὸς ὑμῶν ͺτοὺς πατέρας,ͺ → λέγων διὰ Ἡσαΐου τοῦ προφήτου
d.nsn d.nsn a.nsn n.nsn v.aai.3s adv p.a r.gp.2 d.apm n.apm   pt.pa.nsm p.a n.gsm d.gsm n.gsm
3836 3836 41 4460 3281 2822 4639 7007 3836 4252   3306 1328 2480 3836 4737

26 "'Go   to   this people   and say, "You will be ever hearing   but never understanding;   you will be
πορεύθητι πρὸς τοῦτον τὸν λαὸν καὶ εἰπόν, ͺἀκοῇ ἀκούσετε,ͺ καὶ ͺοὐ μὴͺ συνῆτε   καὶ → →
v.apm.2s p.a r.asm d.asm n.asm cj v.aam.2s   n.dsf v.fai.2p cj pl pl v.aas.2p   cj
4513 4639 4047 3836 3295 2779 3306   198 201 2779 4024 3590 5317   2779

ever seeing   but never perceiving." **27** For this people's heart   has become calloused;   they hardly
→ ͺβλέποντες βλέψετε,ͺ καὶ ͺοὐ μὴͺ ἴδητε γὰρ τούτου ͺτοῦ λαοῦͺ ͺἡ καρδίαͺ → → ἐπαχύνθη καὶ → βαρέως
pt.pa.npm v.fai.2p cj pl pl v.aas.2p cj r.gsm d.gsm n.gsm d.nsf n.nsf   v.api.3s cj adv
1063 1063 2779 4024 3590 1625 1142 4047 3836 3295 3836 2840   4266 2779 201 977

hear   with their ears, and they have closed   their eyes.   Otherwise they might see   with their eyes,
ἤκουσαν τοῖς ὠσὶν καὶ → ἐκάμμυσαν αὐτῶν ͺτοὺς ὀφθαλμούς,ͺ μήποτε → ἴδωσιν → τοῖς ὀφθαλμοῖς
v.aai.3p d.dpn n.dpn cj   v.aai.3p r.gpn.3 d.apm n.apm adv   v.aas.3p   d.dpm n.dpm
201 3836 4044 2779   2826 899 3836 4057 3607   1625   3836 4057

hear   with their ears,   understand with their hearts and turn,   and I would heal   them.' ¶
καὶ ἀκούσωσιν → τοῖς ὠσὶν καὶ συνῶσιν → τῇ καρδίᾳ καὶ ἐπιστρέψωσιν καὶ → → ἰάσομαι αὐτούς
cj v.aas.3p d.dpn n.dpn cj v.aas.3p d.dsf n.dsf cj v.aas.3p cj   v.fmi.1s r.apm.3
2779 201 3836 4044 2779 5317 3836 2840 2779 2188 2779   2615 899

28 "Therefore I want you to know that God's   salvation   has been sent   to the Gentiles, and they will
οὖν ἔστω ὑμῖν γνωστὸν ὅτι ͺτοῦ θεοῦͺ τοῦτο ͺτὸ σωτήριον,ͺ → ἀπεστάλη → τοῖς ἔθνεσιν καὶ αὐτοὶ →
cj v.pam.3s r.dp.2 a.nsn cj d.gsm n.gsm r.nsn d.nsn n.nsn   v.api.3s   d.dpn n.dpn cj r.npm
4036 1639 7007 1196 4022 3836 2536 4047 3836 5402   690   3836 1620 2779 899

listen!" ¶ **30**   For two   whole years Paul stayed   there in his own rented   house and welcomed all
ἀκούσονται δὲ → διετίαν ὅλην → Ἐνέμεινεν ἐν ἰδίῳ μισθώματι καὶ ἀπεδέχετο πάντας
v.fmi.3p cj n.asf a.asf v.aai.3s p.d a.dsn n.dsn cj v.imi.3s a.apm
201 1254 1454 3910 1454 1844 1877 2625 3637 2779 622 4246

παραγενόμενός τις τῶν ἀδελφῶν ἀπήγγειλεν ἢ ἐλάλησέν τι περὶ σοῦ πονηρόν. **22** ἀξιοῦμεν δὲ παρὰ σοῦ ἀκοῦσαι ἃ φρονεῖς, περὶ μὲν γὰρ τῆς αἱρέσεως ταύτης γνωστὸν ἡμῖν ἐστιν ὅτι πανταχοῦ ἀντιλέγεται. ¶ **23** Ταξάμενοι δὲ αὐτῷ ἡμέραν ἦλθον πρὸς αὐτὸν εἰς τὴν ξενίαν πλείονες οἷς ἐξετίθετο διαμαρτυρόμενος τὴν βασιλείαν τοῦ θεοῦ, πείθων τε αὐτοὺς περὶ τοῦ Ἰησοῦ ἀπό τε τοῦ νόμου Μωϋσέως καὶ τῶν προφητῶν, ἀπὸ πρωῒ ἕως ἑσπέρας. **24** καὶ οἱ μὲν ἐπείθοντο τοῖς λεγομένοις, οἱ δὲ ἠπίστουν· **25** ἀσύμφωνοι δὲ ὄντες πρὸς ἀλλήλους ἀπελύοντο εἰπόντος τοῦ Παύλου ῥῆμα ἕν, ὅτι Καλῶς τὸ πνεῦμα τὸ ἅγιον ἐλάλησεν διὰ Ἡσαΐου τοῦ προφήτου πρὸς τοὺς πατέρας ὑμῶν **26** λέγων, Πορεύθητι πρὸς τὸν λαὸν τοῦτον καὶ εἰπόν, Ἀκοῇ ἀκούσετε καὶ οὐ μὴ συνῆτε καὶ βλέποντες βλέψετε καὶ οὐ μὴ ἴδητε· **27** ἐπαχύνθη γὰρ ἡ καρδία τοῦ λαοῦ τούτου καὶ τοῖς ὠσὶν βαρέως ἤκουσαν καὶ τοὺς ὀφθαλμοὺς αὐτῶν ἐκάμμυσαν· μήποτε ἴδωσιν τοῖς ὀφθαλμοῖς καὶ τοῖς ὠσὶν ἀκούσωσιν καὶ τῇ καρδίᾳ συνῶσιν καὶ ἐπιστρέψωσιν, καὶ ἰάσομαι αὐτούς. ¶ **28** γνωστὸν οὖν ἔστω ὑμῖν ὅτι τοῖς ἔθνεσιν ἀπεστάλη τοῦτο τὸ σωτήριον τοῦ θεοῦ· αὐτοὶ καὶ ἀκούσονται ¶

who came   to   see him. ³¹   Boldly   and without hindrance he preached the kingdom of God
τοὺς εἰσπορευομένους πρὸς   αὐτόν   μετὰ πάσης παρρησίας   →   ἀκωλύτως   →   κηρύσσων   τὴν βασιλείαν   →   ⌐τοῦ θεοῦ⌐
d.apm pt.pm.apm   p.a   r.asm.3   p.g a.gsf n.gsf   adv   pt.pa.nsm   d.asf n.asf   d.gsm n.gsm
3836   1660   4639   899   3552 4246   4244   219   3062   3836 993   3836 2536

and taught   about the Lord Jesus Christ.
καὶ διδάσκων   τὰ   περὶ τοῦ κυρίου Ἰησοῦ Χριστοῦ
cj pt.pa.nsm d.apn p.g d.gsm n.gsm n.gsm n.gsm
2779 1438   3836 4309 3836 3261   2652   5986

³⁰ Ἐνέμεινεν δὲ διετίαν ὅλην ἐν ἰδίῳ μισθώματι καὶ ἀπεδέχετο πάντας τοὺς εἰσπορευομένους πρὸς αὐτόν, ³¹ κηρύσσων τὴν βασιλείαν τοῦ θεοῦ καὶ διδάσκων τὰ περὶ τοῦ κυρίου Ἰησοῦ Χριστοῦ μετὰ πάσης παρρησίας ἀκωλύτως.

Romans

1:1 Paul, a servant of Christ Jesus, called to be an apostle and set apart for the gospel of God —
Παῦλος δοῦλος → Χριστοῦ Ἰησοῦ κλητὸς ἀπόστολος ἀφωρισμένος ← εἰς εὐαγγέλιον → θεοῦ
n.nsm n.nsm n.gsm n.gsm a.nsm n.nsm pt.rp.nsm p.a n.asn n.gsm
4263 1529 5986 2652 3105 693 928 1650 2295 2536

2 the gospel he promised beforehand through his prophets in the Holy Scriptures **3** regarding his Son,
ὃ ← προεπηγγείλατο ← διὰ αὐτοῦ ⌐τῶν προφητῶν⌐ ἐν ἁγίαις γραφαῖς περὶ αὐτοῦ ⌐τοῦ υἱοῦ⌐
r.asn v.ami.3s p.g r.gsm.3 d.gpm n.gpm p.d a.dpf n.dpf p.g r.gsm.3 d.gsm n.gsm
4005 4600 1328 899 3836 4737 1877 41 1210 4309 899 3836 5626

who as to his human nature was a descendant of David, **4** and who through the Spirit of holiness was
τοῦ κατὰ ← σάρκα ← γενομένου ἐκ σπέρματος → Δαυὶδ τοῦ κατὰ πνεῦμα → ἁγιωσύνης →
d.gsm p.a n.asf pt.am.gsm p.g n.gsn n.gsm d.gsm p.a n.asn n.gsf
3836 2848 4922 1181 1666 5065 1253 3836 2848 4460 43

declared with power to be the Son of God by his resurrection from the dead: Jesus Christ our Lord.
ὁρισθέντος ἐν δυνάμει υἱοῦ → θεοῦ ἐξ ἀναστάσεως → νεκρῶν Ἰησοῦ Χριστοῦ ἡμῶν ⌐τοῦ κυρίου⌐
pt.ap.gsm p.d n.dsf n.gsm n.gsm p.g n.gsf a.gpm n.gsm n.gsm r.gp.1 d.gsm n.gsm
3988 1877 1539 5626 2536 1666 414 3738 2652 5986 7005 3836 3261

5 Through him and for his name's sake, we received grace and apostleship to call people from among all
δι᾽ οὗ ὑπὲρ αὐτοῦ ⌐τοῦ ὀνόματος⌐ ↵ → ἐλάβομεν χάριν καὶ ἀποστολὴν ἐν πᾶσιν
p.g r.gsm p.g r.gsm.3 d.gsn n.gsn v.aai.1p n.asf cj n.asf p.d a.dpn
1328 4005 5642 899 3836 3950 5642 3284 5921 2779 693 1877 4246

the Gentiles to the obedience that comes from faith. **6** And you also are among those who are called to belong to
τοῖς ἔθνεσιν εἰς ὑπακοὴν → πίστεως ὑμεῖς καὶ ἐστε ἐν οἷς → κλητοὶ → →
d.dpn n.dpn p.a n.asf n.gsf r.np.2 adv v.pai.2p p.d r.dpn a.npm
3836 1620 1650 5633 4411 7007 2779 1639 1877 4005 3105

Jesus Christ. ¶ **7** To all in Rome who are loved by God and called to be saints: ¶
Ἰησοῦ Χριστοῦ πᾶσιν τοῖς οὖσιν ἐν Ῥώμῃ ἀγαπητοῖς → θεοῦ κλητοῖς ἁγίοις
n.gsm n.gsm a.dpm d.dpm pt.pa.dpm p.d n.dsf a.dpm n.gsm a.dpm a.dpm
2652 5986 4246 3836 1639 1877 4873 28 2536 3105 41

Grace and peace to you from God our Father and from the Lord Jesus Christ.
χάρις καὶ εἰρήνη → ὑμῖν ἀπὸ θεοῦ ἡμῶν πατρὸς καὶ κυρίου Ἰησοῦ Χριστοῦ
n.nsf cj n.nsf r.dp.2 p.g n.gsm r.gp.1 n.gsm cj n.gsm n.gsm n.gsm
5921 2779 1645 7007 608 2536 7005 4252 2779 3261 2652 5986

Paul's Longing to Visit Rome

1:8 First, I thank my God through Jesus Christ for all of you, because your faith is being
μὲν Πρῶτον → εὐχαριστῶ μου ⌐τῷ θεῷ⌐ διὰ Ἰησοῦ Χριστοῦ περὶ πάντων ὑμῶν ὅτι ⌐ὑμῶν ἡ πίστις⌐ →
pl adv v.pai.1s r.gs.1 d.dsm n.dsm p.g n.gsm n.gsm p.g a.gpm r.gp.2 cj r.gp.2 d.nsf n.nsf
3525 4754 2373 1609 3836 2536 1328 2652 5986 4309 4246 7007 4022 7007 3836 4411

reported all over the world. **9** God, whom I serve with my whole heart in preaching the
καταγγέλλεται ἐν ὅλῳ ⌐τῷ κόσμῳ⌐ γὰρ ὁ θεός, ᾧ → λατρεύω ἐν μου ⌐τῷ πνεύματι⌐ ἐν ↵ τῷ
v.ppi.3s p.d a.dsm d.dsm n.dsm cj d.nsm n.nsm r.dsm v.pai.1s p.d r.gs.1 d.dsn n.dsn p.d d.dsn
2859 1877 3910 3836 3180 1142 3836 2536 4005 3302 1877 1609 3836 4460 1877 3836

gospel of his Son, is my witness how constantly I remember you **10** in my prayers at all
εὐαγγελίῳ → αὐτοῦ ⌐τοῦ υἱοῦ⌐ ἐστιν μού μάρτυς ὡς ἀδιαλείπτως → ⌐ποιοῦμαι μνείαν⌐ ὑμῶν ἐπὶ μου ⌐τῶν προσευχῶν⌐ → πάντοτε
n.dsn r.gsm.3 d.gsm n.gsm v.pai.3s r.gs.1 n.nsm cj adv v.pmi.1s n.asf r.gp.2 p.g r.gs.1 d.gpf n.gpf adv
2295 5626 899 3836 5626 1639 1609 3459 6055 90 4472 3644 7007 2093 1609 3836 4666 4121

times; and I pray that now at last by God's will the way may be opened for me to come
δεόμενος εἴ ἤδη πως ποτὲ ἐν ⌐τοῦ θεοῦ⌐ ⌐τῷ θελήματι⌐ εὐοδωθήσομαι ← ← ← → ἐλθεῖν
pt.pm.nsm cj adv pl adv p.d d.gsm n.gsm d.dsn n.dsn v.fpi.1s f.aa
1289 1623 2453 4803 4537 1877 3836 2536 3836 2525 2338 2262

to you. ¶ **11** I long to see you so that I may impart to you some spiritual gift to make you
πρὸς ὑμᾶς γὰρ → ἐπιποθῶ → ἰδεῖν ὑμᾶς ἵνα → → μεταδῶ → ὑμῖν τι πνευματικὸν χάρισμα εἰς → ὑμᾶς
p.a r.ap.2 cj v.pai.1s f.aa r.ap.2 cj v.aas.1s r.dp.2 r.asn a.asn n.asn p.a r.ap.2
4639 7007 1142 2160 1625 7007 2671 3356 7007 5516 4461 5922 1650 5114 7007

1:1 Παῦλος δοῦλος Χριστοῦ Ἰησοῦ, κλητὸς ἀπόστολος ἀφωρισμένος εἰς εὐαγγέλιον θεοῦ, **2** ὃ προεπηγγείλατο διὰ τῶν προφητῶν αὐτοῦ ἐν γραφαῖς ἁγίαις **3** περὶ τοῦ υἱοῦ αὐτοῦ τοῦ γενομένου ἐκ σπέρματος Δαυὶδ κατὰ σάρκα, **4** τοῦ ὁρισθέντος υἱοῦ θεοῦ ἐν δυνάμει κατὰ πνεῦμα ἁγιωσύνης ἐξ ἀναστάσεως νεκρῶν, Ἰησοῦ Χριστοῦ τοῦ κυρίου ἡμῶν, **5** δι᾽ οὗ ἐλάβομεν χάριν καὶ ἀποστολὴν εἰς ὑπακοὴν πίστεως ἐν πᾶσιν τοῖς ἔθνεσιν ὑπὲρ τοῦ ὀνόματος αὐτοῦ, **6** ἐν οἷς ἐστε καὶ ὑμεῖς κλητοὶ Ἰησοῦ Χριστοῦ, ¶ **7** πᾶσιν τοῖς οὖσιν ἐν Ῥώμῃ ἀγαπητοῖς θεοῦ, κλητοῖς ἁγίοις, ¶ χάρις ὑμῖν καὶ εἰρήνη ἀπὸ θεοῦ πατρὸς ἡμῶν καὶ κυρίου Ἰησοῦ Χριστοῦ.

1:8 Πρῶτον μὲν εὐχαριστῶ τῷ θεῷ μου διὰ Ἰησοῦ Χριστοῦ περὶ πάντων ὑμῶν ὅτι ἡ πίστις ὑμῶν καταγγέλλεται ἐν ὅλῳ τῷ κόσμῳ. **9** μάρτυς γάρ μού ἐστιν ὁ θεός, ᾧ λατρεύω ἐν τῷ πνεύματί μου ἐν τῷ εὐαγγελίῳ τοῦ υἱοῦ αὐτοῦ, ὡς ἀδιαλείπτως μνείαν ὑμῶν ποιοῦμαι **10** πάντοτε ἐπὶ τῶν προσευχῶν μου δεόμενος εἴ πως ἤδη ποτὲ εὐοδωθήσομαι ἐν τῷ θελήματι τοῦ θεοῦ ἐλθεῖν πρὸς ὑμᾶς. ¶ **11** ἐπιποθῶ γὰρ ἰδεῖν ὑμᾶς, ἵνα τι μεταδῶ χάρισμα ὑμῖν πνευματικὸν εἰς τὸ στηριχθῆναι ὑμᾶς, **12** τοῦτο

strong	– 12	that is,	that	you	and	I	may be mutually encouraged	by each	other's
⌜τὸ στηριχθῆναι⌝	δέ	τοῦτο ἐστιν	τε	ὑμῶν	καὶ	ἐμοῦ	συμπαρακληθῆναι ἐν ὑμῖν διὰ	⌜ἐν ἀλλήλοις⌝	←
d.asn f.ap	cj	r.nsn v.pai.3s	cj	r.gp.2	cj	r.gs.1	f.ap	p.d r.dp.2 p.g	p.d r.dpm
3836 5114	1254	4047 1639	5445	7007	2779	1609	5220	1877 7007 1328	1877 253

faith.	13	I	do not want	you	to be unaware,	brothers,	that	I	planned	many	times	to come	to	you	(but
⌜τῆς πίστεως⌝	δέ	→	οὐ θέλω	ὑμᾶς	→ ἀγνοεῖν	ἀδελφοί	ὅτι	→	προεθέμην	πολλάκις	←	→ ἐλθεῖν	πρὸς	ὑμᾶς	καὶ
d.gsf n.gsf	cj		pl v.pai.1s	r.ap.2	f.pa	n.vpm	cj		v.ami.1s	adv		f.aa	p.a	r.ap.2	cj
3836 4411	1254 2527 2527	4024 2527	7007	51		81	4022		4729	4490		2262	4639	7007	2779

have been prevented	from doing so until now)		in order that	I	might have	a	harvest	among you,	just	as
ἐκωλύθην	ἄχρι ⌜τοῦ δεῦρο⌝		ἵνα		σχῶ	τινὰ	καρπὸν	καὶ ἐν ὑμῖν	καθὼς	←
v.api.1s	p.g d.gsm adv		cj		v.aas.1s	r.asn	n.asm	adv p.d r.dp.2	pl	
3266	948 3836 1306		2671		2400	5516	2843	2779 1877 7007	2777	

I have had	among	the other	Gentiles. ¶	14 I	am	obligated	both	to Greeks	and	non-Greeks,	both	to the
καὶ ἐν	τοῖς	λοιποῖς	ἔθνεσιν	→ εἰμί		ὀφειλέτης	τε	→ Ἕλλησιν	καὶ	βαρβάροις	τε	→
adv p.d	d.dpn	a.dpn	n.dpn	v.pai.1s		n.nsm	cj	n.dpm	cj	n.dpm	cj	
2779 1877	3836	3370	1620	1639		4050	5445	1818	2779	975	5445	

wise	and	the foolish.	15 That is why	I	am so eager	to preach	the gospel also to you who are at
σοφοῖς	καὶ	ἀνοήτοις	οὕτως ←	⌜κατ᾽ ἐμὲ	⌜τὸ πρόθυμον⌝	εὐαγγελίσασθαι ←	← καὶ → ὑμῖν τοῖς ἐν
a.dpm	cj	a.dpm	adv	p.a r.as.1	d.nsn n.asn	f.am	adv r.dp.2 d.dpm p.d
5055	2779	485	4048	2848 1609	3836 4609	2294	2779 7007 3836 1877

Rome. ¶	16	I	am not	ashamed	of the gospel,	because	it is	the power	of God	for the salvation of
Ῥώμη	γὰρ	↱ →	Οὐ ἐπαισχύνομαι	←	τὸ εὐαγγέλιον	γὰρ	→ ἐστιν	δύναμις	⌜θεοῦ⌝	εἰς σωτηρίαν
n.dsf	cj	pl	v.pmi.1s		d.asn n.asn	cj	v.pai.3s	n.nsf	n.gsm	p.a n.asf
4873	1142 2049 2049	4024	2049		3836 2295	1142	1639	1539	2536	1650 5401

everyone	who believes:	first	for the Jew,	then	for the Gentile.	17 For	in	the gospel	a righteousness	from God is
παντὶ	τῷ πιστεύοντι	τε	πρῶτον →	Ἰουδαίῳ	καὶ →	Ἕλληνι	γὰρ ἐν	αὐτῷ	δικαιοσύνη	→ θεοῦ →
a.dsm	d.dsm pt.pa.dsm	cj	adv	n.dsm	cj	n.dsm	cj p.d	r.dsn.3	n.nsf	n.gsm
4246	3836 4409	5445	4754	2681	2779	1818	1142 1877	899	1466	2536

revealed,	a righteousness that is	by faith	from first to last,	just	as it is written:	"The righteous will
ἀποκαλύπτεται		ἐκ πίστεως	εἰς πίστιν	καθὼς	← → γέγραπται δὲ ὁ	δίκαιος →
v.ppi.3s		p.g n.gsf	p.a n.asf	pl	v.rpi.3s cj d.nsm	a.nsm
636		1666 4411	1650 4411	2777	1211 1254 3836	1465

live	by faith."
ζήσεται	ἐκ πίστεως
v.fmi.3s	p.g n.gsf
2409	1666 4411

God's Wrath Against Mankind

1:18	The wrath	of God	is being revealed	from heaven	against	all	the godlessness	and	wickedness of
γὰρ	ὀργὴ	→ θεοῦ →	Ἀποκαλύπτεται ἀπ᾽	οὐρανοῦ	ἐπὶ	πᾶσαν	ἀσέβειαν	καὶ	ἀδικίαν →
cj	n.nsf	n.gsm	v.ppi.3s p.g	n.gsm	p.a	a.asf	n.asf	cj	n.asf
1142	3973	2536	636 608	4041	2093	4246	813	2779	94

men	who suppress	the truth	by their wickedness,	19 since	what may be	known	about God	is	plain
ἀνθρώπων	τῶν κατεχόντων	τὴν ἀλήθειαν	ἐν ἀδικίᾳ	διότι	→ →	⌜τὸ γνωστὸν⌝	⌜τοῦ θεοῦ⌝	ἐστιν	φανερόν
n.gpm	d.gpm pt.pa.gpm	d.asf n.asf	p.d n.dsf	cj		d.nsn a.nsn	d.gsm n.gsm	v.pai.3s	a.nsn
476	3836 2988	3836 237	1877 94	1484		3836 1196	3836 2536	1639	5745

to them,	because	God	has made it plain	to them.	20 For since	the creation	of the world	God's	invisible
ἐν αὐτοῖς	γὰρ	⌜ὁ θεὸς⌝	→ → ἐφανέρωσεν →	αὐτοῖς	γὰρ ἀπὸ	κτίσεως →	κόσμου	αὐτοῦ	⌜τὰ ἀόρατα⌝
p.d r.dpm.3	cj	d.nsm n.nsm	v.aai.3s	r.dpm.3	cj p.g	n.gsf	n.gsm	r.gsm.3	d.npn a.npn
1877 899	1142	3836 2536	5746	899	1142 608	3232	3180	899	3836 548

qualities –	his	eternal	power	and	divine nature –	have been clearly seen,	being understood	from what
τε	αὐτοῦ	ἀΐδιος	⌜ἤ δύναμις⌝	καὶ	θειότης ←	καθορᾶται	νοούμενα →	τοῖς
cj	r.gsm.3	a.nsf	d.nsf n.nsf	cj	n.nsf	v.ppi.3s	pt.pp.npn	d.dpn
5445	899	132	3836 1539	2779	2522	2775	3783	3836

has been made,	so that	men	are	without excuse.	¶	21 For	although	they knew	God,	they
→ → ποιήμασιν	εἰς ←	αὐτοὺς	⌜τὸ εἶναι⌝	→ ἀναπολογήτους		διότι	→ →	γνόντες	⌜τὸν θεὸν⌝	↱
n.dpn	p.a	r.apm.3	d.asn f.pa	a.apm		cj		pt.aa.npm	d.asm n.asm	
4473	1650	899	3836 1639	406		1484		1182	3836 2536	1519

δέ ἐστιν συμπαρακληθῆναι ἐν ὑμῖν διὰ τῆς ἐν ἀλλήλοις πίστεως ὑμῶν τε καὶ ἐμοῦ. [13] οὐ θέλω δὲ ὑμᾶς ἀγνοεῖν, ἀδελφοί, ὅτι πολλάκις προεθέμην ἐλθεῖν πρὸς ὑμᾶς, καὶ ἐκωλύθην ἄχρι τοῦ δεῦρο, ἵνα τινὰ καρπὸν σχῶ καὶ ἐν ὑμῖν καθὼς καὶ ἐν τοῖς λοιποῖς ἔθνεσιν. ¶ [14] Ἕλλησίν τε καὶ βαρβάροις, σοφοῖς τε καὶ ἀνοήτοις ὀφειλέτης εἰμί, [15] οὕτως τὸ κατ᾽ ἐμὲ πρόθυμον καὶ ὑμῖν τοῖς ἐν Ῥώμῃ εὐαγγελίσασθαι. ¶ [16] Οὐ γὰρ ἐπαισχύνομαι τὸ εὐαγγέλιον, δύναμις γὰρ θεοῦ ἐστιν εἰς σωτηρίαν παντὶ τῷ πιστεύοντι, Ἰουδαίῳ τε πρῶτον καὶ Ἕλληνι. [17] δικαιοσύνη γὰρ θεοῦ ἐν αὐτῷ ἀποκαλύπτεται ἐκ πίστεως εἰς πίστιν, καθὼς γέγραπται, Ὁ δὲ δίκαιος ἐκ πίστεως ζήσεται.

[1:18] Ἀποκαλύπτεται γὰρ ὀργὴ θεοῦ ἀπ᾽ οὐρανοῦ ἐπὶ πᾶσαν ἀσέβειαν καὶ ἀδικίαν ἀνθρώπων τῶν τὴν ἀλήθειαν ἐν ἀδικίᾳ κατεχόντων, [19] διότι τὸ γνωστὸν τοῦ θεοῦ φανερόν ἐστιν ἐν αὐτοῖς· ὁ θεὸς γὰρ αὐτοῖς ἐφανέρωσεν. [20] τὰ γὰρ ἀόρατα αὐτοῦ ἀπὸ κτίσεως κόσμου τοῖς ποιήμασιν νοούμενα καθορᾶται, ἥ τε ἀΐδιος αὐτοῦ δύναμις καὶ θειότης, εἰς τὸ εἶναι αὐτοὺς ἀναπολογήτους, ¶ [21] διότι γνόντες τὸν θεὸν οὐχ ὡς θεὸν ἐδόξασαν ἢ ηὐχαρίστησαν, ἀλλ᾽ ἐματαιώθησαν ἐν τοῖς διαλογισμοῖς

neither glorified him as God nor gave thanks to him, but their thinking became futile and
οὐχ ἐδόξασαν ὡς θεὸν ἢ ηὐχαρίστησαν ἀλλ᾽ ἐν αὐτῶν ⌐τοῖς διαλογισμοῖς⌐ → ἐματαιώθησαν καὶ
pl v.aai.3p pl n.asm cj v.aai.3p cj p.d r.gpm.3 d.dpm n.dpm v.api.3p cj
4024 1519 6055 2536 2445 2373 247 1877 899 3836 1369 3471 2779

their foolish hearts were darkened. 22 Although they claimed to be wise, they became fools 23 and
αὐτῶν ἀσύνετος ἡ καρδία⌐ → ἐσκοτίσθη → → φάσκοντες εἶναι σοφοὶ → ἐμωράνθησαν καὶ
r.gpm.3 a.nsf d.nsf n.nsf v.api.3s pt.pa.npm f.pa a.npm v.api.3p cj
899 852 3836 2840 5029 5763 1639 5055 3701 2779

exchanged the glory of the immortal God for images made to look like mortal man and birds and
ἤλλαξαν τὴν δόξαν → τοῦ ἀφθάρτου θεοῦ εἰκόνος ἐν ὁμοιώματι φθαρτοῦ ἀνθρώπου καὶ πετεινῶν καὶ
v.aai.3p d.asf n.asf d.gsm a.gsm n.gsm n.gsf p.d n.dsn a.gsm n.gsm cj n.gpn cj
248 3836 1518 3836 915 2536 1635 1877 3930 5778 476 2779 4374 2779

animals and reptiles. ¶ 24 Therefore God gave them over in the sinful desires of their
τετραπόδων καὶ ἑρπετῶν Διὸ ⌐ὁ θεὸς⌐ παρέδωκεν αὐτοὺς ↰ ἐν ταῖς → ἐπιθυμίαις ↱ αὐτῶν
n.gpn cj n.gpn cj d.nsm n.nsm v.aai.3s r.apm.3 p.d d.dpf n.dpf r.gpm.3
5488 2779 2260 1475 3836 2536 4140 899 1877 3836 2123 2840 899

hearts to sexual impurity for the degrading of their bodies with one another. 25 They exchanged
⌐καρδιῶν⌐ εἰς ἀκαθαρσίαν → ⌐τοῦ ἀτιμάζεσθαι⌐ αὐτῶν ⌐τὰ σώματα⌐ ἐν αὐτοῖς ↰ οἵτινες μετήλλαξαν
d.gpf n.gpf p.a n.asf d.gsn n.fpp r.gpm.3 d.apn n.apn p.d r.dpm.3 r.npm v.aai.3p
3836 2840 1650 174 3836 869 899 3836 5393 1877 899 4015 3563

the truth of God for a lie, and worshiped and served created things rather than the Creator –
τὴν ἀλήθειαν → ⌐τοῦ θεοῦ⌐ ἐν τῷ ψεύδει καὶ ἐσεβάσθησαν καὶ ἐλάτρευσαν ⌐τῇ κτίσει⌐ ← παρὰ → τὸν κτίσαντα
d.asf n.asf d.gsm n.gsm p.d d.dsn n.dsn cj v.api.3p cj v.aai.3p d.dsf n.dsf p.a d.asm pt.aa.asm
3836 237 3836 2536 1877 3836 6022 2779 4933 2779 3302 3836 3232 4123 3836 3231

who is forever praised. Amen. ¶ 26 Because of this, God gave them over to shameful lusts.
ὅς ἐστιν εἰς τοὺς αἰῶνας εὐλογητὸς ἀμήν Διὰ ← τοῦτο ⌐ὁ θεὸς⌐ παρέδωκεν αὐτοὺς ↰ εἰς ἀτιμίας πάθη
r.nsm v.pai.3s p.a d.apm n.apm a.nsm pl r.asn d.nsm n.nsm v.aai.3s r.apm.3 p.a n.gsf n.apn
4005 1639 1650 3836 172 2329 297 1328 4047 3836 2536 4140 899 4140 1650 871 4079

Even their women exchanged natural relations for unnatural ones. 27 In the same way the men
γὰρ τε αὐτῶν αἵ θήλειαι μετήλλαξαν φυσικὴν ⌐τὴν χρῆσιν⌐ εἰς ⌐τὴν παρὰ φύσιν⌐ τε → → ὁμοίως οἱ ἄρσενες
cj cj r.gpm.3 d.npf a.npf v.aai.3p a.asf d.asf n.asf p.a d.asf p.a n.asf cj adv d.npm a.npm
1142 5445 899 3836 2559 3563 5879 3836 5979 1650 3836 4123 5882 5445 3931 3836 781

also abandoned natural relations with women and were inflamed with lust for one another.
καὶ ἀφέντες φυσικὴν ⌐τὴν χρῆσιν⌐ → ⌐τῆς θηλείας⌐ → ἐξεκαύθησαν ἐν αὐτῶν ⌐τῇ ὀρέξει⌐ εἰς ἀλλήλους ←
adv pt.aa.npm a.asf d.asf n.asf d.gsf a.gsf v.api.3p p.d r.gpm.3 d.dsf n.dsf p.a r.apm
2779 918 5879 3836 5979 3836 2559 1706 1877 899 3836 3979 1650 253

Men committed indecent acts with other men, and received in themselves the due penalty
ἄρσενες κατεργαζόμενοι ⌐τὴν ἀσχημοσύνην⌐ ← ἐν ἄρσεσιν καὶ ἀπολαμβάνοντες ἐν ἑαυτοῖς τὴν ἣν ἔδει ἀντιμισθίαν
a.npm pt.pm.npm d.asf n.asf p.d a.dpm cj pt.pa.npm p.d r.dpm.3 d.asf r.asf v.iai.3s n.asf
781 2981 3836 859 1877 781 2779 655 1877 1571 3836 4005 1256 521

for their perversion. ¶ 28 Furthermore, since they did not think it worthwhile to retain the knowledge of
↱ αὐτῶν ⌐τῆς πλάνης⌐ Καὶ καθὼς ↱ οὐκ ἐδοκίμασαν ← → ἔχειν ἐν ἐπιγνώσει →
r.gpm.3 d.gsf n.gsf cj cj pl v.aai.3p f.pa p.d n.dsf
4415 899 3836 4415 2779 2777 1507 1507 4024 1507 2400 1877 2106

God, he gave them over to a depraved mind, to do what ought not to be done. 29 They have
⌐τὸν θεὸν⌐ ⌐ὁ θεὸς⌐ παρέδωκεν αὐτοὺς ↰ εἰς ἀδόκιμον νοῦν → ποιεῖν τὰ → μὴ → καθήκοντα →
d.asm n.asm d.nsm n.nsm v.aai.3s r.apm.3 p.a a.asm n.asm f.pa d.apn pl pt.pa.apn
3836 2536 3836 2536 4140 899 4140 1650 99 3808 4472 3836 2763 3590 2763

become filled with every kind of wickedness, evil, greed and depravity. They are full of envy,
→ πεπληρωμένους → πάσῃ ← ἀδικίᾳ πονηρίᾳ πλεονεξίᾳ κακίᾳ → μεστοὺς → φθόνου
pt.rp.apm a.dsf n.dsf n.dsf n.dsf n.dsf a.apm n.gsm
4444 4246 94 4504 4432 2798 3550 5784

murder, strife, deceit and malice. They are gossips, 30 slanderers, God-haters, insolent, arrogant and boastful;
φόνου ἔριδος δόλου κακοηθείας ψιθυριστάς καταλάλους θεοστυγεῖς ὑβριστὰς ὑπερηφάνους ἀλαζόνας
n.gsm n.gsf n.gsm n.gsf n.apm n.apm a.apm n.apm a.apm n.apm
5840 2251 1515 2799 6031 2897 2539 5616 5662 225

αὐτῶν καὶ ἐσκοτίσθη ἡ ἀσύνετος αὐτῶν καρδία. 22 φάσκοντες εἶναι σοφοὶ ἐμωράνθησαν 23 καὶ ἤλλαξαν τὴν δόξαν τοῦ ἀφθάρτου θεοῦ ἐν ὁμοιώματι εἰκόνος φθαρτοῦ ἀνθρώπου καὶ πετεινῶν καὶ τετραπόδων καὶ ἑρπετῶν. ¶ 24 Διὸ παρέδωκεν αὐτοὺς ὁ θεὸς ἐν ταῖς ἐπιθυμίαις τῶν καρδιῶν αὐτῶν εἰς ἀκαθαρσίαν τοῦ ἀτιμάζεσθαι τὰ σώματα αὐτῶν ἐν αὐτοῖς· 25 οἵτινες μετήλλαξαν τὴν ἀλήθειαν τοῦ θεοῦ ἐν τῷ ψεύδει καὶ ἐσεβάσθησαν καὶ ἐλάτρευσαν τῇ κτίσει παρὰ τὸν κτίσαντα, ὅς ἐστιν εὐλογητὸς εἰς τοὺς αἰῶνας, ἀμήν. ¶ 26 διὰ τοῦτο παρέδωκεν αὐτοὺς ὁ θεὸς εἰς πάθη ἀτιμίας, αἵ τε γὰρ θήλειαι αὐτῶν μετήλλαξαν τὴν φυσικὴν χρῆσιν εἰς τὴν παρὰ φύσιν, 27 ὁμοίως τε καὶ οἱ ἄρσενες ἀφέντες τὴν φυσικὴν χρῆσιν τῆς θηλείας ἐξεκαύθησαν ἐν τῇ ὀρέξει αὐτῶν εἰς ἀλλήλους, ἄρσενες ἐν ἄρσεσιν τὴν ἀσχημοσύνην κατεργαζόμενοι καὶ τὴν ἀντιμισθίαν ἣν ἔδει τῆς πλάνης αὐτῶν ἐν ἑαυτοῖς ἀπολαμβάνοντες. ¶ 28 καὶ καθὼς οὐκ ἐδοκίμασαν τὸν θεὸν ἔχειν ἐν ἐπιγνώσει, παρέδωκεν αὐτοὺς ὁ θεὸς εἰς ἀδόκιμον νοῦν, ποιεῖν τὰ μὴ καθήκοντα, 29 πεπληρωμένους πάσῃ ἀδικίᾳ πονηρίᾳ πλεονεξίᾳ κακίᾳ, μεστοὺς φθόνου φόνου ἔριδος δόλου κακοηθείας, ψιθυριστὰς 30 καταλάλους θεοστυγεῖς ὑβριστὰς ὑπερηφάνους ἀλαζόνας, ἐφευρετὰς

they invent ways of doing evil; they disobey their parents; **31** they are senseless, faithless, heartless, ruthless.
ἐφευρετὰς κακῶν ἀπειθεῖς γονεῦσιν ἀσυνέτους ἀσυνθέτους ἀστόργους ἀνελεήμονας
n.apm a.gpn a.apm n.dpm a.apm a.apm a.apm a.apm
2388 2805 579 1204 852 853 845 446

32 Although they know God's righteous decree that those who do such things deserve
οἵτινες ἐπιγνόντες τοῦ θεοῦ τὸ δικαίωμα ὅτι οἱ πράσσοντες τὰ τοιαῦτα εἰσίν ἄξιοι
r.npm pt.aa.npm d.gsm n.gsm d.asn n.asn cj d.npm pt.pa.npm d.apn r.apn v.pai.3p a.npm
2105 4015 2105 3836 2536 3836 1468 4022 3836 4556 3836 5525 1639 545

death, they not only continue to do these very things but also approve of those who practice them.
θανάτου οὐ μόνον ποιοῦσιν αὐτὰ ἀλλὰ καὶ συνευδοκοῦσιν τοῖς πράσσουσιν
n.gsm pl adv v.pai.3p r.apn.3 cj adv v.pai.3p d.dpm pt.pa.dpm
2505 4472 4024 3667 4472 899 247 2779 5306 3836 4556

God's Righteous Judgment

2:1 You, therefore, have no excuse, you who pass judgment on someone else, for at whatever
Διὸ εἶ ἀναπολόγητος ὦ ἄνθρωπε πᾶς ὁ κρίνων γὰρ ἐν ᾧ
cj v.pai.2s a.nsm j n.vsm a.vsm d.nsm pt.pa.vsm cj p.d r.dsn
1639 1475 1639 406 6043 476 4246 3836 3212 1142 1877 4005

point you judge the other, you are condemning yourself, because you who pass judgment do the same things.
κρίνεις τὸν ἕτερον κατακρίνεις σεαυτὸν γὰρ ὁ κρίνων πράσσεις τὰ αὐτὰ
v.pai.2s d.asm r.asm v.pai.2s r.asm.2 cj d.nsm pt.pa.nsm v.pai.2s d.apn r.apn
3212 3836 2283 2891 4932 1142 4556 3836 3212 4556 3836 899

2 Now we know that God's judgment against those who do such things is based on truth. **3** So
δὲ οἴδαμεν ὅτι τοῦ θεοῦ τὸ κρίμα ἐπὶ τοὺς πράσσοντας τὰ τοιαῦτα ἐστιν κατὰ ἀλήθειαν δὲ
cj v.rai.1p cj d.gsm n.gsm d.nsn n.nsn p.a d.apm pt.pa.apm d.apn r.apn v.pai.3s p.a n.asf cj
1254 3857 4022 3836 2536 3836 3210 2093 3836 4556 3836 5525 1639 2848 237 1254

when you, a mere man, pass judgment on them and yet do the same things, do you
ὦ ἄνθρωπε ὁ κρίνων τοὺς τὰ τοιαῦτα πράσσοντας καὶ ποιῶν αὐτά
j n.vsm d.vsm pt.pa.vsm d.asm d.apn r.apn pt.pa.apm cj pt.pa.vsm r.apn
3212 3212 6043 476 3836 3212 3836 3836 5525 4556 2779 4472 899

think you will escape God's judgment? **4** Or do you show contempt for the riches of his
λογίζῃ τοῦτο ὅτι σὺ ἐκφεύξῃ τοῦ θεοῦ τὸ κρίμα ἤ καταφρονεῖς τοῦ πλούτου αὐτοῦ
v.pmi.2s r.asn cj r.ns.2 v.fmi.2s d.gsm n.gsm d.asn n.asn j v.pai.2s d.gsm n.gsm r.gsm.3
3357 4047 4022 5148 1767 3836 2536 3836 3210 2445 2969 3836 4458 5983 899

kindness, tolerance and patience, not realizing that God's kindness leads you toward
τῆς χρηστότητος καὶ τῆς ἀνοχῆς καὶ τῆς μακροθυμίας ἀγνοῶν ὅτι τοῦ θεοῦ τὸ χρηστὸν ἄγει σε εἰς
d.gsf n.gsf cj d.gsf n.gsf cj d.gsf n.gsf pt.pa.nsm cj d.gsm n.gsm d.nsn a.nsn v.pai.3s r.as.2 p.a
3836 5983 2779 3836 496 2779 3836 3429 51 4022 3836 2536 3836 5982 72 5148 1650

repentance? ¶ **5** But because of your stubbornness and your unrepentant heart, you are storing up wrath
μετάνοιαν δὲ κατὰ σου τὴν σκληρότητα καὶ ἀμετανόητον καρδίαν θησαυρίζεις ὀργὴν
n.asf cj p.a r.gs.2 d.asf n.asf cj a.asf n.asf v.pai.2s n.asf
3567 1254 2848 5148 3836 5018 2779 295 2840 2564 3973

against yourself for the day of God's wrath, when his righteous judgment will be revealed. **6** God "will
σεαυτῷ ἐν ἡμέρᾳ τοῦ θεοῦ ὀργῆς καὶ δικαιοκρισίας ἀποκαλύψεως ὃς
r.dsm.2 p.d n.dsf d.gsm n.gsm n.gsf cj n.gsf n.gsf r.nsm
4932 1877 2465 3973 3836 2536 3973 2779 1464 637 4005

give to each person according to what he has done." **7** To those who by persistence in doing good
ἀποδώσει ἑκάστῳ κατὰ τὰ ἔργα αὐτοῦ μὲν τοῖς καθ᾽ ὑπομονὴν ἔργου ἀγαθοῦ
v.fai.3s r.dsm p.a d.apn n.apn r.gsm.3 pl d.dpm p.a n.asf n.gsn a.gsn
625 1667 2848 3836 2240 899 2240 3525 3836 2848 5705 2240 19

seek glory, honor and immortality, he will give eternal life. **8** But for those who are self-seeking and who
ζητοῦσιν δόξαν καὶ τιμὴν καὶ ἀφθαρσίαν αἰώνιον ζωὴν δὲ τοῖς ἐξ ἐριθείας καὶ
pt.pa.dpm n.asf cj n.asf cj n.asf a.asf n.asf pl d.dpm p.g n.gsf cj
2426 1518 2779 5507 2779 914 173 2437 1254 3836 1666 2249 2779

reject the truth and follow evil, there will be wrath and anger. **9** There will be trouble and distress for
ἀπειθοῦσι τῇ ἀληθείᾳ δὲ πειθομένοις τῇ ἀδικίᾳ ὀργὴ καὶ θυμός θλῖψις καὶ στενοχωρία ἐπὶ
pt.pa.dpm d.dsf n.dsf cj pt.pm.dpm d.dsf n.dsf n.nsf cj n.nsm n.nsf cj n.nsf p.a
578 3836 237 1254 4275 3836 94 3973 2779 2596 2568 2779 5103 2093

κακῶν, γονεῦσιν ἀπειθεῖς, **31** ἀσυνέτους ἀσυνθέτους ἀστόργους ἀνελεήμονας· **32** οἵτινες τὸ δικαίωμα τοῦ θεοῦ ἐπιγνόντες ὅτι οἱ τὰ τοιαῦτα πράσσοντες ἄξιοι θανάτου εἰσίν, οὐ μόνον αὐτὰ ποιοῦσιν ἀλλὰ καὶ συνευδοκοῦσιν τοῖς πράσσουσιν.

2:1 Διὸ ἀναπολόγητος εἶ, ὦ ἄνθρωπε πᾶς ὁ κρίνων· ἐν ᾧ γὰρ κρίνεις τὸν ἕτερον, σεαυτὸν κατακρίνεις, τὰ γὰρ αὐτὰ πράσσεις ὁ κρίνων. **2** οἴδαμεν δὲ ὅτι τὸ κρίμα τοῦ θεοῦ ἐστιν κατὰ ἀλήθειαν ἐπὶ τοὺς τὰ τοιαῦτα πράσσοντας. **3** λογίζῃ δὲ τοῦτο, ὦ ἄνθρωπε ὁ κρίνων τοὺς τὰ τοιαῦτα πράσσοντας καὶ ποιῶν αὐτά, ὅτι σὺ ἐκφεύξῃ τὸ κρίμα τοῦ θεοῦ; **4** ἢ τοῦ πλούτου τῆς χρηστότητος αὐτοῦ καὶ τῆς ἀνοχῆς καὶ τῆς μακροθυμίας καταφρονεῖς, ἀγνοῶν ὅτι τὸ χρηστὸν τοῦ θεοῦ εἰς μετάνοιάν σε ἄγει; ¶ **5** κατὰ δὲ τὴν σκληρότητά σου καὶ ἀμετανόητον καρδίαν θησαυρίζεις σεαυτῷ ὀργὴν ἐν ἡμέρᾳ ὀργῆς καὶ ἀποκαλύψεως δικαιοκρισίας τοῦ θεοῦ **6** ὃς ἀποδώσει ἑκάστῳ κατὰ τὰ ἔργα αὐτοῦ· **7** τοῖς μὲν καθ᾽ ὑπομονὴν ἔργου ἀγαθοῦ δόξαν καὶ τιμὴν καὶ ἀφθαρσίαν ζητοῦσιν ζωὴν αἰώνιον, **8** τοῖς δὲ ἐξ ἐριθείας καὶ ἀπειθοῦσι τῇ ἀληθείᾳ πειθομένοις δὲ τῇ ἀδικίᾳ ὀργὴ καὶ θυμός. **9** θλῖψις καὶ στενοχωρία ἐπὶ πᾶσαν ψυχὴν ἀνθρώπου τοῦ κατεργαζομένου τὸ κακόν, Ἰουδαίου τε πρῶτον καὶ Ἕλληνος· **10** δόξα

every human being who does evil: first for the Jew, then for the Gentile; **10** but glory,
πᾶσαν ἀνθρώπου ψυχὴν τοῦ κατεργαζομένου ⌞τὸ κακόν⌟ τε πρῶτον → Ἰουδαίου καὶ → Ἕλληνος δὲ δόξα καὶ
a.asf n.gsm n.asf d.gsm pt.pm.gsm d.asn a.asn cj adv a.gsm cj n.gsm cj n.nsf cj
4246 476 6034 3836 2981 3836 2805 5445 4754 2681 2779 1818 1254 1518 2779

honor and peace for everyone who does good: first for the Jew, then for the Gentile. **11** For
τιμὴ καὶ εἰρήνη → παντὶ τῷ ἐργαζομένῳ ⌞τὸ ἀγαθόν⌟ τε πρῶτον → Ἰουδαίῳ καὶ → Ἕλληνι γὰρ παρὰ
n.nsf cj n.nsf a.dsm d.dsm pt.pm.dsm d.asn a.asn cj adv a.dsm cj n.dsm cj cj
5507 2779 1645 4246 3836 2237 3836 19 5445 4754 2681 2779 1818 1142 4123

God does not show favoritism. ¶ **12** All who sin apart from the law will also perish apart
⌞τῷ θεῷ⌟ ἐστιν οὐ προσωπολημψία γὰρ Ὅσοι ← ἥμαρτον → → ἀνόμως ← καὶ ἀπολοῦνται →
d.dsm n.dsm v.pai.3s pl n.nsf cj r.npm v.aai.3p adv adv v.fmi.3p
3836 2536 1639 4024 4721 1142 4012 279 492 660 2779 660

from the law, and all who sin under the law will be judged by the law. **13** For it is not those who hear
→ ἀνόμως καὶ ὅσοι ← ἥμαρτον ἐν νόμῳ → κριθήσονται διὰ νόμου γὰρ οὐ οἱ ← ἀκροαταὶ
adv cj r.npm v.aai.3p p.d n.dsm v.fpi.3p p.g n.gsm cj pl d.npm n.npm
492 2779 4012 279 1877 3795 3212 1328 3795 1142 4024 3836 212

the law who are righteous in God’s sight, but it is those who obey the law who will be declared
νόμου δίκαιοι παρὰ ⌞τῷ θεῷ⌟ ← ἀλλ’ οἱ ← ποιηταὶ νόμου → →
n.gsm a.npm p.d d.dsm n.dsm cj d.npm n.npm n.gsm
3795 1465 4123 3836 2536 4123 247 3836 4475 3795

righteous. **14** (Indeed, when Gentiles, who do not have the law, do by nature things required by the law,
δικαιωθήσονται γὰρ ὅταν ἔθνη τὰ → μὴ ἔχοντα νόμον ποιῶσιν → φύσει τὰ → → τοῦ νόμου
v.fpi.3p cj cj n.npn d.npn pl pt.pa.npn n.asm v.pas.3p n.dsf d.apn d.gsm n.gsm
1467 1142 4020 1620 3836 2400 3590 2400 3795 4472 5882 3836 3836 3795

they are a law for themselves, even though they do not have the law, **15** since they show that the
→ εἰσιν νόμος ἑαυτοῖς → οὗτοι → μὴ ἔχοντες νόμον οἵτινες ἐνδείκνυνται τὸ
v.pai.3p n.nsm r.dpm.3 r.npm pl pt.pa.npm n.asm r.npm v.pmi.3p d.asn
1639 3795 1571 2400 2400 4047 2400 3590 2400 3795 4015 1892 3836

requirements of the law are written on their hearts, their consciences also bearing witness, and
ἔργον → τοῦ νόμου γραπτὸν ἐν αὐτῶν ⌞ταῖς καρδίαις⌟ αὐτῶν ⌞τῆς συνειδήσεως⌟ → συμμαρτυρούσης καὶ
n.asn d.gsm n.gsm a.asn p.d r.gpm.3 d.dpf n.dpf r.gpm.3 d.gsf n.gsf pt.pa.gsf cj
2240 3836 3795 1209 1877 899 3836 2840 899 3836 5287 5210 2779

their thoughts now accusing, now even defending them.) **16** This will take place on the day when
μεταξὺ ἀλλήλων τῶν λογισμῶν κατηγορούντων ἢ καὶ ἀπολογουμένων ἐν ἡμέρᾳ ὅτε
p.g r.gpm d.gpm n.gpm pt.pa.gpm cj adv pt.pa.gpm p.d n.dsf cj
3568 253 3836 3361 2989 2445 2779 664 1877 2465 4021

God will judge men’s secrets through Jesus Christ, as my gospel declares.
ὁ θεὸς⌟ → κρίνει ⌞τῶν ἀνθρώπων⌟ ⌞τὰ κρυπτὰ⌟ διὰ Ἰησοῦ Χριστοῦ κατὰ μου ⌞τὸ εὐαγγέλιον⌟ ←
d.nsm n.nsm v.pai.3s d.gpm n.gpm d.apn a.apn p.g r.gs.1 d.asn n.asn
3836 2536 3212 3836 476 3836 3220 1328 2652 5986 2848 1609 3836 2295 2848

The Jews and the Law

2:17 Now you, if you call yourself a Jew; if you rely on the law and brag *about your*
δὲ σὺ Εἰ → ἐπονομάζῃ ← Ἰουδαῖος καὶ → ἐπαναπαύῃ ← νόμῳ καὶ καυχᾶσαι ἐν
cj r.ns.2 cj v.ppi.2s a.nsm cj v.pmi.2s n.dsm cj v.pmi.2s p.d
1254 5148 1623 2226 2681 2779 2058 3795 2779 3016 1877

relationship to God; **18** if you know his will and approve of what is superior because you are instructed by
→ θεῷ καὶ → γινώσκεις τὸ θέλημα καὶ δοκιμάζεις ← τὰ → διαφέροντα → → → κατηχούμενος ἐκ
n.dsm cj v.pai.2s d.asn n.asn cj v.pai.2s d.apn pt.pa.apn pt.pp.nsm p.g
2536 2779 1182 3836 2525 2779 1507 3836 1422 2994 1666

the law; **19** if you are convinced that you are a guide for the blind, a light for those who are in the dark,
τοῦ νόμου τε → πέποιθας σεαυτὸν εἶναι ὁδηγὸν → τυφλῶν φῶς → τῶν ← ἐν σκότει
d.gsm n.gsm cj v.rai.2s r.asm.2 f.pa n.asm n.gpm n.asn d.gpm p.d n.dsn
3836 3795 5445 4275 4932 1639 3843 5603 5890 3836 1877 5030

20 an instructor of the foolish, a teacher of infants, because you have in the law the embodiment of knowledge
παιδευτὴν → ἀφρόνων διδάσκαλον → νηπίων → → ἔχοντα ἐν τῷ νόμῳ τὴν μόρφωσιν → ⌞τῆς γνώσεως⌟
n.asm a.gpm n.asm a.gpm pt.pa.asm p.d d.dsm n.dsm d.asf n.asf d.gsf n.gsf
4083 933 1437 3758 2400 1877 3836 3795 3836 3673 3836 1194

δὲ καὶ τιμὴ καὶ εἰρήνη παντὶ τῷ ἐργαζομένῳ τὸ ἀγαθόν, Ἰουδαίῳ τε πρῶτον καὶ Ἕλληνι· **11** οὐ γὰρ ἐστιν προσωπολημψία παρὰ τῷ θεῷ. ¶ **12** ὅσοι γὰρ ἀνόμως ἥμαρτον, ἀνόμως καὶ ἀπολοῦνται, καὶ ὅσοι ἐν νόμῳ ἥμαρτον, διὰ νόμου κριθήσονται· **13** οὐ γὰρ οἱ ἀκροαταὶ νόμου δίκαιοι παρὰ [τῷ] θεῷ, ἀλλ’ οἱ ποιηταὶ νόμου δικαιωθήσονται. **14** ὅταν γὰρ ἔθνη τὰ μὴ νόμον ἔχοντα φύσει τὰ τοῦ νόμου ποιῶσιν, οὗτοι νόμον μὴ ἔχοντες ἑαυτοῖς εἰσιν νόμος· **15** οἵτινες ἐνδείκνυνται τὸ ἔργον τοῦ νόμου γραπτὸν ἐν ταῖς καρδίαις αὐτῶν, συμμαρτυρούσης αὐτῶν τῆς συνειδήσεως καὶ μεταξὺ ἀλλήλων τῶν λογισμῶν κατηγορούντων ἢ καὶ ἀπολογουμένων, **16** ἐν ἡμέρᾳ ὅτε κρίνει ὁ θεὸς τὰ κρυπτὰ τῶν ἀνθρώπων κατὰ τὸ εὐαγγέλιόν μου διὰ Ἰησοῦ «Ἰησοῦ.» Χριστοῦ. «Χριστοῦ»

2:17 Εἰ δὲ σὺ Ἰουδαῖος ἐπονομάζῃ καὶ ἐπαναπαύῃ νόμῳ καὶ καυχᾶσαι ἐν θεῷ **18** καὶ γινώσκεις τὸ θέλημα καὶ δοκιμάζεις τὰ διαφέροντα κατηχούμενος ἐκ τοῦ νόμου, **19** πέποιθάς τε σεαυτὸν ὁδηγὸν εἶναι τυφλῶν, φῶς τῶν ἐν σκότει, **20** παιδευτὴν

and truth   — ²¹ you, then, who teach   others, do you not teach   yourself? You who preach against stealing,
καὶ ⌐τῆς ἀληθείας⌐   οὖν ὁ διδάσκων ἕτερον   οὐ διδάσκεις σεαυτὸν   ὁ κηρύσσων μὴ   κλέπτειν
cj d.gsf n.gsf   cj d.vsm pt.pa.vsm r.asm   pl v.pai.2s r.asm.2   d.vsm pt.pa.vsm pl   f.pa
2779 3836 237   1438 4036 3836 1438 2283   1438 1438 4024 1438   4932   3096 3836 3062 3590   3096

do you steal? ²² You who say   that people should not commit adultery, do you commit adultery? You who
→ → κλέπτεις   → ὁ λέγων   → μὴ → μοιχεύειν → → μοιχεύεις → ὁ
v.pai.2s   d.vsm pt.pa.vsm   pl → f.pa   v.pai.2s   d.vsm
3096   3658 3836 3306   3658 3590   3658   3658 2644 3836

abhor idols,   do you rob temples? ²³ You who brag   about the law, do you dishonor God   by
βδελυσσόμενος ⌐τὰ εἴδωλα⌐ → ἱεροσυλεῖς ← ὃς καυχᾶσαι ἐν νόμῳ → ἀτιμάζεις ⌐τὸν θεὸν⌐ διὰ
pt.pm.vsm d.apn n.apn   v.pai.2s   r.nsm v.pmi.2s p.d n.dsm   v.pai.2s d.asm n.asm p.g
1009 3836 1631   2644   4005 3016 1877 3795   869 3836 2536 1328

breaking   the law? ²⁴   As   it is written: "God's   name   is blasphemed among the Gentiles because of
⌐τῆς παραβάσεως⌐ τοῦ νόμου γὰρ καθὼς → γέγραπται ⌐τοῦ θεοῦ⌐ ⌐τὸ ὄνομα⌐ βλασφημεῖται ἐν τοῖς ἔθνεσιν δι' ←
d.gsf n.gsf d.gsm n.gsm cj cj v.rpi.3s d.gsm n.gsm d.nsn n.nsn v.ppi.3s p.d d.dpn n.dpn p.a
3836 4126 3836 3795 1142 2777 1211 3836 2536 3836 3950 1059 1877 3836 1620 1328

you." ¶ ²⁵   Circumcision has value if   you observe the law, but if you break   the law, you
ὑμᾶς   γὰρ μὲν Περιτομὴ → ὠφελεῖ ἐὰν → πράσσῃς νόμον δὲ ἐὰν → ⌐παραβάτης ᾖς⌐ νόμου σου
r.ap.2   cj pl n.nsf   v.pai.3s cj   v.pas.2s n.asm cj cj   n.nsm v.pas.2s n.gsm r.gs.2
7007   1142 3525 4364   6067 1569 4556 3795 1254 1569 1639 4127 1639 3795 5148

   have become as though you had not been circumcised. ²⁶ If those who are not circumcised keep   the
ἡ περιτομὴ → γέγονεν   → ἀκροβυστία οὖν ἐὰν ἡ   → ἀκροβυστία φυλάσσῃ τὰ
d.nsf n.nsf   v.rai.3s   n.nsf   cj cj d.nsf   n.nsf v.pas.3s d.apn
3836 4364   1181   213   4036 1569 3836   213 5875 3836

law's   requirements, will   they not be regarded *as though* they were circumcised? ²⁷   The one
⌐τοῦ νόμου⌐ δικαιώματα → ἡ ἀκροβυστία αὐτοῦ οὐχ → λογισθήσεται εἰς → περιτομὴν καὶ ←
d.gsm n.gsm n.apn   d.nsf n.nsf r.gsm.3 pl v.fpi.3s p.a   n.asf cj d.nsf
3836 3795 1468   3357 3836 213 899 4024 3357 1650   4364 2779 3836

who is not circumcised physically and yet obeys the law   will condemn you who, even though you have the
← → ἀκροβυστία ⌐ἐκ φύσεως⌐ → τελοῦσα τὸν νόμον → κρινεῖ σὲ τὸν   διὰ
n.nsf p.g n.gsf   pt.pa.nsf d.asm n.asm v.fai.3s r.as.2 d.asm   p.g
213 1666 5882   5464 3836 3795 3212 5148 3836   1328

written code and circumcision, are a lawbreaker. ¶ ²⁸   A man is   not a Jew   if he is only one
γράμματος ← καὶ περιτομῆς ⌐παραβάτην νόμου⌐   γὰρ ἐστιν οὐ ⌐ὁ Ἰουδαῖος⌐
n.gsn cj n.gsf   n.asm n.gsm   cj v.pai.3s pl d.nsm n.nsm
1207 2779 4364   4127 3795   1142 1639 4024 3836 2681

outwardly,   nor is circumcision merely outward   and physical. ²⁹ No, a man is a Jew   if he is one
⌐ἐν τῷ φανερῷ⌐ οὐδὲ ⌐ἡ περιτομὴ⌐ ⌐ἐν τῷ φανερῷ⌐ ἐν σαρκὶ ἀλλ'   ὁ Ἰουδαῖος
p.d d.dsn a.dsn cj d.nsf n.nsf   p.d d.dsn a.dsn p.d n.dsf cj   d.nsm n.nsm
1877 3836 5745 4028 3836 4364   1877 3836 5745 1877 4922 247   3836 2681

inwardly;   and circumcision is circumcision of the heart, by the Spirit, not by the written code. Such a
⌐ἐν τῷ κρυπτῷ⌐ καὶ περιτομὴ   → καρδίας ἐν πνεύματι οὐ → γράμματι ← οὐ
p.d d.dsn n.dsn cj n.nsf   n.gsf p.d n.dsn pl n.dsn r.gsm
1877 3836 3220 2779 4364   2840 1877 4460 4024 1207 4005

man's praise   is not from men,   but from God.
⌐ὁ ἔπαινος⌐ οὐκ ἐξ ἀνθρώπων ἀλλ' ἐκ ⌐τοῦ θεοῦ⌐
d.nsm n.nsm pl p.g n.gpm cj p.g d.gsm n.gsm
3836 2047 4024 1666 476 247 1666 3836 2536

God's Faithfulness

^{3:1} What advantage, then, is there in being a Jew,   or what value   is there in circumcision? ² Much
Τί ⌐τὸ περισσὸν⌐ οὖν → → ⌐τοῦ Ἰουδαίου⌐ ἢ τίς ⌐ἡ ὠφέλεια⌐ → ⌐τῆς περιτομῆς⌐ πολὺ
r.nsn d.nsn a.nsn cj   d.gsm a.gsm cj r.nsf d.nsf n.nsf   d.gsf n.gsf a.nsn
5515 3836 4356 4036   3836 2681 2445 5515 3836 6066   3836 4364 4498

in every way!   First of all,   they have been entrusted   with the very words of God. ¶
κατὰ πάντα τρόπον [γὰρ] μὲν πρῶτον ← ὅτι → → → ἐπιστεύθησαν ← τὰ λόγια → ⌐τοῦ θεοῦ⌐
p.a a.asm n.asm cj pl adv cj   v.api.3p d.apn n.apn d.gsm n.gsm
2848 4246 5573 1142 3525 4754 4022   4409 3836 3359 3836 2536

ἀφρόνων, διδάσκαλον νηπίων, ἔχοντα τὴν μόρφωσιν τῆς γνώσεως καὶ τῆς ἀληθείας ἐν τῷ νόμῳ· ²¹ ὁ οὖν διδάσκων ἕτερον σεαυτὸν οὐ διδάσκεις; ὁ κηρύσσων μὴ κλέπτειν κλέπτεις; ²² ὁ λέγων μὴ μοιχεύειν μοιχεύεις; ὁ βδελυσσόμενος τὰ εἴδωλα ἱεροσυλεῖς; ²³ ὃς ἐν νόμῳ καυχᾶσαι, διὰ τῆς παραβάσεως τοῦ νόμου τὸν θεὸν ἀτιμάζεις· ²⁴ τὸ γὰρ ὄνομα τοῦ θεοῦ δι' ὑμᾶς βλασφημεῖται ἐν τοῖς ἔθνεσιν, καθὼς γέγραπται. ¶ ²⁵ περιτομὴ μὲν γὰρ ὠφελεῖ ἐὰν νόμον πράσσῃς· ἐὰν δὲ παραβάτης νόμου ᾖς, ἡ περιτομή σου ἀκροβυστία γέγονεν. ²⁶ ἐὰν οὖν ἡ ἀκροβυστία τὰ δικαιώματα τοῦ νόμου φυλάσσῃ, οὐχ ἡ ἀκροβυστία αὐτοῦ εἰς περιτομὴν λογισθήσεται; ²⁷ καὶ κρινεῖ ἡ ἐκ φύσεως ἀκροβυστία τὸν νόμον τελοῦσα σὲ τὸν διὰ γράμματος καὶ περιτομῆς παραβάτην νόμου. ¶ ²⁸ οὐ γὰρ ὁ ἐν τῷ φανερῷ Ἰουδαῖός ἐστιν οὐδὲ ἡ ἐν τῷ φανερῷ ἐν σαρκὶ περιτομή, ²⁹ ἀλλ' ὁ ἐν τῷ κρυπτῷ Ἰουδαῖος, καὶ περιτομὴ καρδίας ἐν πνεύματι οὐ γράμματι, οὗ ὁ ἔπαινος οὐκ ἐξ ἀνθρώπων ἀλλ' ἐκ τοῦ θεοῦ.

^{3:1} Τί οὖν τὸ περισσὸν τοῦ Ἰουδαίου ἢ τίς ἡ ὠφέλεια τῆς περιτομῆς; ² πολὺ κατὰ πάντα τρόπον. πρῶτον μὲν [γὰρ] ὅτι

3 What if some did not have faith?   Will their lack of faith   nullify   God's   faithfulness?
γὰρ τί εἰ τινες → → ἠπίστησαν μὴ → αὐτῶν → ἡ ἀπιστία κατάργησει τοῦ θεοῦ τὴν πίστιν
cj r.nsn cj r.npm   v.aai.3p pl   r.gpm.3   d.nsf n.nsf v.fai.3s d.gsm n.gsm d.asf n.asf
1142 5515 1623 5516   601 3590   2934 899   3836 602 2934 3836 2536 3836 4411

4 Not   at all! Let God   be   true, and every man   a liar.   As   it is written: "So that   you may
μὴ γένοιτο· ← δὲ → ὁ θεὸς· γινέσθω ἀληθής δὲ πᾶς ἄνθρωπος ψεύστης καθὼς → γέγραπται ὅπως ← ἂν →
pl v.amo.3s   cj   d.nsm n.nsm v.pmm.3s a.nsm cj a.nsm n.nsm n.nsm cj   v.rpi.3s cj   cj
3590 1181   1254 1181 3836 2536 1181 239 1254 4246 476 6026 2777   1211 3968   323

be proved right   when you speak   and prevail when you judge."   ¶ **5** But if our unrighteousness
→ δικαιωθῇς ἐν σου ⌐τοῖς λόγοις⌐ καὶ νικήσεις ἐν σε ⌐τῷ κρίνεσθαι⌐   δὲ εἰ ἡμῶν ἡ ἀδικία·
   v.aps.2s d.p r.gs.2 d.dpm n.dpm cj v.fai.2s d.p r.as.2 d.dsn f.pp   cj cj r.gp.1 d.nsf n.nsf
   1467 1877 5148 3836 3364 2779 3771 1877 5148 3836 3212   1254 1623 7005 3836 94

brings   out God's righteousness more clearly, what shall we say?   That God   is unjust in bringing   his
συνίστησιν ← θεοῦ δικαιοσύνην ← ← τί → → ἐροῦμεν μὴ ὁ θεὸς· ἄδικος ὁ ἐπιφέρων τὴν
v.pai.3s   n.gsm n.asf   r.asn   v.fai.1p pl d.nsm n.nsm a.nsm d.nsm pt.pa.nsm d.asf
5319   2536 1466   5319 5319 5515   3306 3590 3836 2536 96 3836 2214 3836

wrath on us? (I am using a human   argument.) **6** Certainly not!   If that were so, how could God
ὀργήν → → λέγω ⌐κατὰ ἄνθρωπον⌐   μὴ γένοιτο· ἐπεὶ πῶς → ὁ θεὸς
n.asf   v.pai.1s p.a n.asm   pl v.amo.3s cj   cj   d.nsm n.nsm
3973   3306 2848 476   3590 1181 2075   4802 3212 3836 2536

judge the world? **7** Someone might argue, "If my falsehood enhances God's truthfulness and so increases
κρινεῖ τὸν κόσμον   δὲ εἰ ἐν ἐμῷ τῷ ψεύσματι ἐπερίσσευσεν τοῦ θεοῦ ἡ ἀλήθεια εἰς
v.fai.3s d.asm n.asm   cj cj p.d r.dsn.1 d.dsn n.dsn v.aai.3s d.gsm n.gsm d.nsf n.nsf p.a
3212 3836 3180   1254 1623 1877 1847 3836 6025 4355 3836 2536 3836 237 1650

his glory,   why am I   still condemned as a sinner?" **8** Why not say – as   we are being slanderously
αὐτοῦ ⌐τὴν δόξαν⌐ τί → κἀγὼ ἔτι κρίνομαι ὡς ἁμαρτωλὸς καὶ μὴ καθὼς → → βλασφημούμεθα
r.gsm.3 d.asf n.asf r.asn crasis adv v.ppi.1s cj a.nsm cj pl cj   v.ppi.1p
899 3836 1518 5515 3212 2743 2285 3212 6055 283 2779 3590 2777   1059

reported as saying and as some claim that we say – "Let us do   evil   that good   may
←   καὶ καθὼς τινες φασίν ἡμᾶς λέγειν ὅτι → ποιήσωμεν τὰ κακά ἵνα τὰ ἀγαθά →
    cj cj r.npm v.pai.3p r.ap.1 f.pa cj   v.aas.1p d.apn a.apn cj d.npn a.npn
2779 2777 5516 5774 7005 3306 4022   4472 3836 2805 2671 3836 19

result"? Their condemnation is   deserved.
ἔλθῃ ὧν ⌐τὸ κρίμα⌐ ἐστιν ἔνδικον
v.aas.3s r.gpm d.nsn n.nsn v.pai.3s a.nsn
2262 4005 3836 3210 1639 1899

No One Is Righteous

3:9 What shall we conclude then? Are we any better? Not at all! We have already made the
Τί   οὖν   προεχόμεθα οὐ → πάντως γὰρ
r.nsn   cj   v.pmi.1p pl adv cj
5515   4036   4604 4024 4122 1142

charge   that Jews and Gentiles alike are all under sin. **10** As it is written: "There is no
προῃτιασάμεθα τε Ἰουδαίους καὶ Ἕλληνας εἶναι πάντας ὑφ' ἁμαρτίαν καθὼς → γέγραπται ὅτι ἔστιν οὐκ
v.ami.1p cj a.apm cj n.apm f.pa a.apm p.a n.asf cj v.rpi.3s cj v.pai.3s pl
4577 5445 2681 2779 1818 1639 4246 5679 281 2777 1211 4022 1639 4024

one righteous, not even one; **11** there is no one who understands, no one who seeks God. **12** All have
δίκαιος οὐδὲ εἷς ἔστιν οὐκ ὁ συνίων ἔστιν οὐκ ὁ ἐκζητῶν τὸν θεόν πάντες →
a.nsm adv a.nsm v.pai.3s pl d.nsm pt.pa.nsm v.pai.3s pl d.nsm pt.pa.nsm d.asm n.asm a.npm
1465 4028 1651 1639 4024 3836 5317 1639 4024 3836 1699 3836 2536 4246

turned away, they have together become worthless; there is no one who does good,   not even one."
ἐξέκλιναν ← → ἅμα → ἠχρεώθησαν ἔστιν οὐκ ὁ ποιῶν χρηστότητα [ἔστιν οὐκ] ἕως ἑνός
v.aai.3p adv adv v.api.3p v.pai.3s pl d.nsm pt.pa.nsm n.asf v.pai.3s pl p.g a.gsm
1712 946 946 275 946 1639 4024 3836 4472 5983 1639 4024 2401 1651

13 "Their throats are open graves; their tongues practice deceit." "The poison of vipers is on their
αὐτῶν ὁ λάρυγξ· ἀνεῳγμένος τάφος αὐτῶν ⌐ταῖς γλώσσαις⌐ → ἐδολιοῦσαν ἰὸς → ἀσπίδων ὑπὸ αὐτῶν
r.gpm.3 d.nsm n.nsm pt.rp.nsm n.nsm r.gpm.3 d.dpf n.dpf v.iai.3p n.nsm n.gpf p.a r.gpm.3
899 3836 3296 487 5439 899 3836 1185 1514 2675 835 5679 899

ἐπιστεύθησαν τὰ λόγια τοῦ θεοῦ. ¶ **3** τί γάρ; εἰ ἠπίστησάν τινες, μὴ ἡ ἀπιστία αὐτῶν τὴν πίστιν τοῦ θεοῦ καταργήσει; **4** μὴ γένοιτο· γινέσθω δὲ ὁ θεὸς ἀληθής, πᾶς δὲ ἄνθρωπος ψεύστης, καθὼς γέγραπται, Ὅπως ἂν δικαιωθῇς ἐν τοῖς λόγοις σου καὶ νικήσεις ἐν τῷ κρίνεσθαί σε. ¶ **5** εἰ δὲ ἡ ἀδικία ἡμῶν θεοῦ δικαιοσύνην συνίστησιν, τί ἐροῦμεν; μὴ ἄδικος ὁ θεὸς ὁ ἐπιφέρων τὴν ὀργήν; κατὰ ἄνθρωπον λέγω. **6** μὴ γένοιτο· ἐπεὶ πῶς κρινεῖ ὁ θεὸς τὸν κόσμον; **7** εἰ δὲ ἡ ἀλήθεια τοῦ θεοῦ ἐν τῷ ἐμῷ ψεύσματι ἐπερίσσευσεν εἰς τὴν δόξαν αὐτοῦ, τί ἔτι κἀγὼ ὡς ἁμαρτωλὸς κρίνομαι; **8** καὶ μὴ καθὼς βλασφημούμεθα καὶ καθὼς φασίν τινες ἡμᾶς λέγειν ὅτι Ποιήσωμεν τὰ κακά, ἵνα ἔλθῃ τὰ ἀγαθά; ὧν τὸ κρίμα ἔνδικόν ἐστιν.

3:9 Τί οὖν; προεχόμεθα; οὐ πάντως· προῃτιασάμεθα γὰρ Ἰουδαίους τε καὶ Ἕλληνας πάντας ὑφ' ἁμαρτίαν εἶναι, **10** καθὼς γέγραπται ὅτι Οὐκ ἔστιν δίκαιος οὐδὲ εἷς, **11** οὐκ ἔστιν ὁ συνίων, οὐκ ἔστιν ὁ ἐκζητῶν τὸν θεόν. **12** πάντες ἐξέκλιναν ἅμα ἠχρεώθησαν· οὐκ ἔστιν ὁ ποιῶν χρηστότητα, [οὐκ ἔστιν] ἕως ἑνός. **13** τάφος ἀνεῳγμένος ὁ λάρυγξ αὐτῶν, ταῖς γλώσσαις αὐτῶν

lips." **14** "Their mouths are full of cursing and bitterness." **15** "Their feet are swift to shed blood; **16** ruin

⸢τὰ χείλη⸣	ὧν	⸢τὸ στόμα⸣	→	γέμει	←	ἀρᾶς	καὶ	πικρίας		
d.apn n.apn	r.gpm	d.nsn n.nsn		v.pai.3s		n.gsf	cj	n.gsf		
3836 5927	4005	3836 5125		1154		725	2779	4394		

αὐτῶν	⸢οἱ πόδες⸣	ὀξεῖς	→	ἐκχέαι	αἷμα	σύντριμμα
r.gpm.3	d.npm n.npm	a.npm		f.aa	n.asn	n.nsn
899	3836 4546	3955		1772	135	5342

and misery mark their ways, **17** and the way of peace they do not know." **18** "There is no fear of God

καὶ	ταλαιπωρία	ἐν	αὐτῶν	⸢ταῖς ὁδοῖς⸣	καὶ	ὁδὸν	→	εἰρήνης	→
cj	n.nsf	p.d	r.gpm.3	d.dpf n.dpf	cj	n.asf		n.gsf	
2779	5416	1877	899	3836 3847	2779	3847		1645	

→	οὐκ	ἔγνωσαν	→	ἔστιν	οὐκ	φόβος	→	θεοῦ
		v.aai.3p		v.pai.3s		n.nsm		n.gsm
1182	4024	1182		1639	4024	5832		2536

before their eyes." ¶ **19** Now we know that whatever the law says, it says to those who are under the

ἀπέναντι	αὐτῶν	⸢τῶν ὀφθαλμῶν⸣	δὲ	→	οἴδαμεν	ὅτι	ὅσα	ὁ	νόμος	λέγει	→	λαλεῖ	→
p.g	r.gpm.3	d.gpm n.gpm	cj		v.rai.1p	cj	r.apn	d.nsm	n.nsm	v.pai.3s		v.pai.3s	
595	899	3836 4057	1254		3857	4022	4012	3836	3795	3306		3281	

τοῖς	←	ἐν	τῷ
d.dpm		p.d	d.dsm
3836		1877	3836

law, so that every mouth may be silenced and the whole world held accountable to God. **20** Therefore no

νόμῳ	ἵνα	←	πᾶν	στόμα	→	φραγῇ	καὶ	ὁ	πᾶς	κόσμος	γένηται	ὑπόδικος
n.dsm	cj		a.nsn	n.nsn		v.aps.3s	cj	d.nsm	a.nsm	n.nsm	v.ams.3s	a.nsm
3795	2671		4246	5125		5852	2779	3836	4246	3180	1181	5688

→	⸢τῷ θεῷ⸣	διότι	οὐ
	d.dsm n.dsm	cj	pl
	3836 2536	1484	4024

one will be declared righteous in his sight by observing the law; rather, through the law we

⸢πᾶσα σάρξ⸣	→	→	δικαιωθήσεται	ἐνώπιον	αὐτοῦ	ἐξ	ἔργων	νόμου	γὰρ	διὰ	νόμου
a.nsf n.nsf			v.fpi.3s	p.g	r.gsm.3	p.g	n.gpn	n.gsm	cj	p.g	n.gsm
4246 4922			1467	1967	899	1666	2240	3795	1142	1328	3795

become conscious of sin.

ἐπίγνωσις	→	ἁμαρτίας
n.nsf		n.gsf
2106		281

Righteousness Through Faith

3:21 But now a righteousness from God, apart from law, has been made known, to which the Law and

δὲ	Νυνὶ	δικαιοσύνη	→	θεοῦ	χωρὶς	←	νόμου	→	→	→	πεφανέρωται
cj	adv	n.nsf		n.gsm	p.g		n.gsm				v.rpi.3s
1254	3815	1466		2536	6006		3795				5746

ὑπὸ	τοῦ	νόμου	καὶ
p.g	d.gsm	n.gsm	cj
5679	3836	3795	2779

the Prophets testify. **22** This righteousness from God comes through faith in Jesus Christ to all who

τῶν	προφητῶν	μαρτυρουμένη	δὲ	δικαιοσύνη	→	θεοῦ	διὰ	πίστεως	→	Ἰησοῦ	Χριστοῦ	εἰς	πάντας	τοὺς
d.gpm	n.gpm	pt.pp.nsf	cj	n.nsf		n.gsm	p.g	n.gsf		n.gsm	n.gsm	p.a	a.apm	d.apm
3836	4737	3455	1254	1466		2536	1328	4411		2652	5986	1650	4246	3836

believe. There is no difference, **23** for all have sinned and fall short of the glory of God, **24** and are

πιστεύοντας	γάρ	→	ἔστιν	οὐ	διαστολή	γὰρ	πάντες	→	ἥμαρτον	καὶ	ὑστεροῦνται	←	→	τῆς	δόξης	⸢τοῦ θεοῦ⸣	→
pt.pa.apm	cj		v.pai.3s	pl	n.nsf	cj	a.npm		v.aai.3p	cj	v.pmi.3p			d.gsf	n.gsf	d.gsm n.gsm	
4409	1142		1639	4024	1405	1142	4246		279	2779	5728			3836	1518	3836 2536	

justified freely by his grace through the redemption that came by Christ Jesus. **25** God presented him as a

δικαιούμενοι	δωρεὰν	αὐτοῦ	⸢τῇ χάριτι⸣	διὰ	τῆς	ἀπολυτρώσεως	τῆς	ἐν	Χριστῷ	Ἰησοῦ	ὁ	θεὸς	προέθετο	ὃν
pt.pp.npm	adv	r.gsm.3	d.dsf n.dsf	p.g	d.gsf	n.gsf	d.gsf	p.d	n.dsm	n.dsm	d.nsm	n.nsm	v.ami.3s	r.asm
1467	1562	899	3836 5921	1328	3836	667	3836	1877	5986	2652	3836	2536	4729	4005

sacrifice of atonement, through faith in his blood. He did this to demonstrate his justice,

ἱλαστήριον	←	διὰ	⸢τῆς πίστεως⸣	ἐν	αὐτοῦ	⸢τῷ αἵματι⸣	εἰς	ἔνδειξιν	αὐτοῦ	⸢τῆς δικαιοσύνης⸣
n.asn		p.g	d.gsf n.gsf	p.d	r.gsm.3	d.dsn n.dsn	p.a	n.asf	r.gsm.3	d.gsf n.gsf
2663		1328	3836 4411	1877	899	3836 135	1650	1893	899	3836 1466

because in his forbearance he had left the sins committed beforehand unpunished – **26** he did it to

διὰ	ἐν	⸢τοῦ θεοῦ⸣	⸢τῇ ἀνοχῇ⸣	τῶν	ἁμαρτημάτων	προγεγονότων	←	⸢τὴν πάρεσιν⸣	πρὸς
p.a	p.d	d.gsm n.gsm	d.dsf n.dsf	d.gpn	n.gpn	pt.ra.gpn		d.asf n.asf	p.a
1328	1877	3836 2536	3836 496	3836	280	4588		3836 4217	4639

demonstrate his justice at the present time, so as to be just and the one who justifies

⸢τὴν ἔνδειξιν⸣	αὐτοῦ	⸢τῆς δικαιοσύνης⸣	ἐν	τῷ	νῦν	καιρῷ	εἰς	αὐτὸν	⸢τὸ εἶναι⸣	δίκαιον	καὶ	δικαιοῦντα
d.asf n.asf	r.gsm.3	d.gsf n.gsf	p.d	d.dsm	adv	n.dsm	p.a	r.asm.3	d.asn f.pa	n.asm	cj	pt.pa.asm
3836 1893	899	3836 1466	1877	3836	3814	2789	1650	899	3836 1639	1465	2779	1467

those who have faith in Jesus. ¶ **27** Where, then, is boasting? It is excluded. On what principle? On that

τὸν	←	ἐκ	πίστεως	→	Ἰησοῦ	Ποῦ	οὖν	ἡ	καύχησις	→	ἐξεκλείσθη	διὰ	ποίου	νόμου
d.asm		p.g	n.gsf		n.gsm	adv	cj	d.nsf	n.nsf		v.api.3s	p.g	r.gsm	n.gsm
3836		1666	4411		2652	4543	4036	3836	3018		1710	1328	4481	3795

ἐδολίουσαν, ἰὸς ἀσπίδων ὑπὸ τὰ χείλη αὐτῶν· **14** ὧν τὸ στόμα ἀρᾶς καὶ πικρίας γέμει, **15** ὀξεῖς οἱ πόδες αὐτῶν ἐκχέαι αἷμα, **16** σύντριμμα καὶ ταλαιπωρία ἐν ταῖς ὁδοῖς αὐτῶν, **17** καὶ ὁδὸν εἰρήνης οὐκ ἔγνωσαν. **18** οὐκ ἔστιν φόβος θεοῦ ἀπέναντι τῶν ὀφθαλμῶν αὐτῶν. ¶ **19** Οἴδαμεν δὲ ὅτι ὅσα ὁ νόμος λέγει τοῖς ἐν τῷ νόμῳ λαλεῖ, ἵνα πᾶν στόμα φραγῇ καὶ ὑπόδικος γένηται πᾶς ὁ κόσμος τῷ θεῷ· **20** διότι ἐξ ἔργων νόμου οὐ δικαιωθήσεται πᾶσα σὰρξ ἐνώπιον αὐτοῦ, διὰ γὰρ νόμου ἐπίγνωσις ἁμαρτίας.

3:21 Νυνὶ δὲ χωρὶς νόμου δικαιοσύνη θεοῦ πεφανέρωται μαρτυρουμένη ὑπὸ τοῦ νόμου καὶ τῶν προφητῶν, **22** δικαιοσύνη δὲ θεοῦ διὰ πίστεως Ἰησοῦ Χριστοῦ εἰς πάντας τοὺς πιστεύοντας. οὐ γάρ ἐστιν διαστολή, **23** πάντες γὰρ ἥμαρτον καὶ ὑστεροῦνται τῆς δόξης τοῦ θεοῦ **24** δικαιούμενοι δωρεὰν τῇ αὐτοῦ χάριτι διὰ τῆς ἀπολυτρώσεως τῆς ἐν Χριστῷ Ἰησοῦ **25** ὃν προέθετο ὁ θεὸς ἱλαστήριον διὰ [τῆς] πίστεως ἐν τῷ αὐτοῦ αἵματι εἰς ἔνδειξιν τῆς δικαιοσύνης αὐτοῦ διὰ τὴν πάρεσιν τῶν προγεγονότων ἁμαρτημάτων **26** ἐν τῇ ἀνοχῇ τοῦ θεοῦ, πρὸς τὴν ἔνδειξιν τῆς δικαιοσύνης αὐτοῦ ἐν τῷ νῦν καιρῷ, εἰς τὸ εἶναι αὐτὸν δίκαιον καὶ δικαιοῦντα τὸν ἐκ πίστεως Ἰησοῦ. ¶ **27** Ποῦ οὖν ἡ καύχησις; ἐξεκλείσθη. διὰ ποίου νόμου; τῶν ἔργων; οὐχί, ἀλλὰ διὰ νόμου

of observing the law? No, but on that of faith. ²⁸ For we maintain that a man is justified by faith apart from
⌐τῶν ἔργων⌐   οὐχί ἀλλὰ διὰ νόμου → πίστεως γὰρ → λογιζόμεθα ἄνθρωπον → δικαιοῦσθαι → πίστει χωρὶς ←
d.gpn n.gpn   pl   cj   p.g n.gsm   n.gsf   cj   v.pmi.1p   n.asm   f.pp   n.dsf p.g
3836 2240   4049 247 1328 3795   4411   1142   3357   476   1467   4411   6006

observing the law. ²⁹ Is God the God of Jews only? Is he not the God of Gentiles too? Yes, of Gentiles too,
ἔργων   νόμου   ἤ   ὁ θεὸς Ἰουδαίων μόνον οὐχὶ → ἐθνῶν καὶ ναὶ → ἐθνῶν καὶ
n.gpn   n.gsm   cj d.nsm n.nsm a.gpm   adv   pl   n.gpn   pl   pl   n.gpn   adv
2240   3795   2445 3836 2536 2681   3667   4049   1620   2779 3721   1620   2779

³⁰ since there is only one God, who will justify the circumcised by faith and the uncircumcised through that
εἴπερ   εἷς ὁ θεός ὃς → δικαιώσει περιτομὴν ἐκ πίστεως καὶ ἀκροβυστίαν διὰ
cj   a.nsm d.nsm n.nsm r.nsm v.fai.3s   n.asf   p.g n.gsf   cj   n.asf   p.g
1642   1651 3836 2536 4005   1467   4364   1666 4411   2779 213   1328

same faith. ³¹ Do we, then, nullify the law by this faith? Not at all! Rather, we uphold the law.
τῆς πίστεως ↱ ↱ οὖν καταργοῦμεν νόμον διὰ τῆς πίστεως μὴ γένοιτο ← ← ἀλλὰ → ἱστάνομεν νόμον
d.gsf n.gsf   cj   v.pai.1p   n.asm p.g d.gsf n.gsf pl v.amo.3s   cj   v.pai.1p   n.asm
3836 4411   2934 2934 4036 2934   3795 1328 3836 4411 3590 1181   247   2705   3795

Abraham Justified by Faith

^{4:1} What then shall we say that Abraham, our forefather, discovered in this matter? ² If, in
Τί   οὖν → → ἐροῦμεν Ἀβραὰμ ἡμῶν ⌐τὸν προπάτορα⌐ κατὰ σάρκα εὑρηκέναι γὰρ εἰ
r.asn 4036   v.fai.1p   n.asm   r.gp.1 d.asm n.asm   p.a n.asf f.ra   cj cj
5515   3306   11   7005 3836 4635   2848 4922 2351   1142 1623

fact, Abraham was justified by works, he had something to boast about – but not before God. ³ What does the
Ἀβραὰμ → ἐδικαιώθη ἐξ ἔργων → ἔχει → → καύχημα ← ἀλλ᾽ οὐ πρὸς θεόν γὰρ τί ↱ ἡ
n.nsm   v.api.3s p.g n.gpn   v.pai.3s   n.asn   cj pl p.a n.asm cj r.asn   d.nsf
11   1467   1666 2240   2400   3017   247 4024 4639 2536 1142 5515   3836

Scripture say? "Abraham believed God, and it was credited to him as righteousness." ¶ ⁴ Now when a
γραφὴ λέγει δὲ Ἀβραὰμ ἐπίστευσεν ⌐τῷ θεῷ⌐ καὶ → ἐλογίσθη αὐτῷ εἰς δικαιοσύνην δὲ →
n.nsf v.pai.3s cj n.nsm   v.aai.3s   d.dsm n.dsm cj   v.api.3s r.dsm.3 p.a n.asf   cj
1210   3306 1254 11   4409   3836 2536 2779   3357   899 1650 1466   1254

man works, his wages are not credited to him as a gift, but as an obligation. ⁵ However, to the man who
ἐργαζομένῳ ὁ μισθὸς → οὐ λογίζεται κατὰ χάριν ἀλλὰ κατὰ ὀφείλημα δὲ → τῷ
pt.pm.dsm d.nsm n.nsm   pl v.ppi.3s   p.a n.asf cj   p.a   n.asn   cj   d.dsm
2237   3836 3635   4024 3357   2848 5921 247 2848 4052   1254 3836

does not work but trusts God who justifies the wicked, his faith is credited as righteousness.
→ μὴ ἐργαζομένῳ δὲ πιστεύοντι ἐπὶ τὸν δικαιοῦντα τὸν ἀσεβῆ αὐτοῦ ⌐ἡ πίστις⌐ → λογίζεται εἰς δικαιοσύνην
pl pt.pm.dsm   cj pt.pa.dsm p.a d.asm pt.pa.asm d.asm a.asm r.gsm.3 d.nsf n.nsf   v.ppi.3s p.a n.asf
2237 3590 2237 1254 4409   2093 3836 1467   3836 815   899 3836 4411   3357   1650 1466

⁶ David says the same thing when he speaks of the blessedness of the man to whom God credits
καὶ Δαυὶδ λέγει καθάπερ ← τὸν μακαρισμὸν τοῦ ἀνθρώπου → ὁ θεὸς λογίζεται
adv n.nsm v.pai.3s adv   d.asm n.asm   d.gsm n.gsm   r.dsm d.nsm n.nsm v.pmi.3s
7779 1753 3306   2749   3836 3422   3836 476   4005 3836 2536 3357

righteousness apart from works: ⁷ "Blessed are they whose transgressions are forgiven, whose sins are
δικαιοσύνην χωρὶς ← ἔργων μακάριοι ὧν ⌐αἱ ἀνομίαι⌐ → ἀφέθησαν καὶ ὧν ⌐αἱ ἁμαρτίαι⌐ →
n.asf   p.g   n.gpn   a.npm   r.gpm d.npf n.npf   v.api.3p cj r.gpm d.npf n.npf
1466   6006   2240   3421   4005 3836 490   918   2779 4005 3836 281

covered. ⁸ Blessed is the man whose sin the Lord will never count against him." ¶ ⁹ Is this
ἐπεκαλύφθησαν μακάριος ἀνὴρ οὗ ἁμαρτίαν κύριος ↱ ⌐οὐ μὴ⌐ λογίσηται οὖν οὗτος
v.api.3p   a.nsm   n.nsm r.gsm n.asf   n.nsm   pl pl v.ams.3s   cj r.nsm
2128   3421   467 4005 281   3261   3357 4024 3590 3357   4036 4047

blessedness only for the circumcised, or also for the uncircumcised? We have been saying that Abraham's
⌐Ὁ μακαρισμὸς⌐ ἐπὶ τὴν περιτομὴν ἤ καὶ ἐπὶ τὴν ἀκροβυστίαν γὰρ → → λέγομεν ⌐τῷ Ἀβραὰμ⌐
d.nsm n.nsm   p.a d.asf n.asf   cj adv p.a d.asf n.asf   cj   v.pai.1p   d.dsm n.dsm
3836 3422   2093 3836 4364   2445 2779 2093 3836 213   1142   3306   3836 11

faith was credited to him as righteousness. ¹⁰ Under what circumstances was it credited? Was it after he was
⌐ἡ πίστις⌐ → ἐλογίσθη εἰς δικαιοσύνην οὖν πῶς ← ← → → ἐλογίσθη ↱ ὄντι
d.nsf n.nsf   v.api.3s   p.a n.asf   cj cj   v.api.3s   pt.pa.dsm
3836 4411   3357   1650 1466   4036 4802   3357   1639

πίστεως. ²⁸ λογιζόμεθα γὰρ δικαιοῦσθαι πίστει ἄνθρωπον χωρὶς ἔργων νόμου. ²⁹ ἤ Ἰουδαίων ὁ θεὸς μόνον; οὐχὶ καὶ ἐθνῶν; ναὶ καὶ ἐθνῶν, ³⁰ εἴπερ εἷς ὁ θεὸς ὃς δικαιώσει περιτομὴν ἐκ πίστεως καὶ ἀκροβυστίαν διὰ τῆς πίστεως. ³¹ νόμον οὖν καταργοῦμεν διὰ τῆς πίστεως; μὴ γένοιτο· ἀλλὰ νόμον ἱστάνομεν.

^{4:1} Τί οὖν ἐροῦμεν εὑρηκέναι Ἀβραὰμ τὸν προπάτορα ἡμῶν κατὰ σάρκα; ² εἰ γὰρ Ἀβραὰμ ἐξ ἔργων ἐδικαιώθη, ἔχει καύχημα, ἀλλ᾽ οὐ πρὸς θεόν. ³ τί γὰρ ἡ γραφὴ λέγει; Ἐπίστευσεν δὲ Ἀβραὰμ τῷ θεῷ καὶ ἐλογίσθη αὐτῷ εἰς δικαιοσύνην. ¶ ⁴ τῷ δὲ ἐργαζομένῳ ὁ μισθὸς οὐ λογίζεται κατὰ χάριν ἀλλὰ κατὰ ὀφείλημα, ⁵ τῷ δὲ μὴ ἐργαζομένῳ πιστεύοντι δὲ ἐπὶ τὸν δικαιοῦντα τὸν ἀσεβῆ λογίζεται ἡ πίστις αὐτοῦ εἰς δικαιοσύνην· ⁶ καθάπερ καὶ Δαυὶδ λέγει τὸν μακαρισμὸν τοῦ ἀνθρώπου ᾧ ὁ θεὸς λογίζεται δικαιοσύνην χωρὶς ἔργων, ⁷ Μακάριοι ὧν ἀφέθησαν αἱ ἀνομίαι καὶ ὧν ἐπεκαλύφθησαν αἱ ἁμαρτίαι· ⁸ μακάριος ἀνὴρ οὗ οὐ μὴ λογίσηται κύριος ἁμαρτίαν. ¶ ⁹ ὁ μακαρισμὸς οὖν οὗτος ἐπὶ τὴν περιτομὴν ἤ καὶ ἐπὶ τὴν ἀκροβυστίαν; λέγομεν γάρ, Ἐλογίσθη τῷ Ἀβραὰμ ἡ πίστις εἰς δικαιοσύνην. ¹⁰ πῶς οὖν ἐλογίσθη; ἐν περιτομῇ ὄντι ἤ ἐν

circumcised, or before?   It was not after,   but before!   **11** And he received the sign   of circumcision,
ἐν περιτομῇ ἢ ἐν ἀκροβυστίᾳ   οὐκ ἐν περιτομῇ ἀλλ᾽ ἐν ἀκροβυστίᾳ   καὶ → ἔλαβεν σημεῖον → περιτομῆς
p.d n.dsf   cj   p.d n.dsf   pl   p.d n.dsf   cj   p.d n.dsf   cj   v.aai.3s   n.asn   n.gsf
1877 4364   2445   1877 213   4024   1877 4364   247   1877 213   2779   3284   4956   4364

a seal   of the righteousness that he had by faith   while he was still uncircumcised.   So then, he
σφραγῖδα → τῆς δικαιοσύνης   ⌐τῆς πίστεως⌐   → ⌐τῆς ἐν τῇ ἀκροβυστίᾳ⌐ εἰς ← αὐτὸν
n.asf   d.gsf n.gsf   d.gsf n.gsf   d.gsf p.d d.dsf n.dsf   p.a   r.asm.3
5382   3836 1466   3836 4411   3836 1877 3836 213   1650   899

is   the father of all   who believe   but have not been circumcised,   in order that righteousness   might
⌐τὸ εἶναι⌐ πατέρα → πάντων τῶν πιστευόντων   → ⌐δι᾽ ἀκροβυστίας⌐ εἰς ← ⌐τὴν δικαιοσύνην⌐ →
d.asn f.pa   n.asm → a.gpm d.gpm pt.pa.gpm   p.g n.gsf   p.a   d.asf n.asf
3836 1639   4252   4246 3836 4409   213   1328 213   1650   3836 1466

be credited   to them. **12** And he is also the father of the circumcised who not only are   circumcised
→ ⌐τὸ λογισθῆναι⌐ [καὶ] → αὐτοῖς καὶ   πατέρα → περιτομῆς τοῖς οὐκ μόνον ἐκ περιτομῆς
d.asn f.ap   adv   r.dpm.3 cj   n.asm → n.gsf d.dpm pl adv p.g n.gsf
3836 3357   2779   899 2779   4252   4364 3836 4024 3667 1666 4364

but who also walk   in the footsteps of the faith   that our father   Abraham had *before he was circumcised.*
ἀλλὰ τοῖς καὶ στοιχοῦσιν → τοῖς ἴχνεσιν → τῆς πίστεως ἡμῶν τοῦ πατρὸς Ἀβραάμ ἐν ἀκροβυστίᾳ
cj   d.dpm adv pt.pa.dpm   d.dpn n.dpn   d.gsf n.gsf r.gp.1 d.gsm n.gsm n.gsm   p.d   n.dsf
247   3836 2779 5123   3836 2717   3836 4411 7005 3836 4252 11   1877   213

¶ **13**   It was not through law   that Abraham   and his   offspring   received the promise that he   would
γὰρ   Οὐ διὰ νόμου ⌐τῷ Ἀβραὰμ⌐ ἢ αὐτοῦ ⌐τῷ σπέρματι⌐   ἡ ἐπαγγελία αὐτὸν →
cj   pl p.g n.gsm   d.dsm n.gsm   cj r.gsm.3 d.dsn n.dsn   d.nsf n.nsf   r.asm.3
1142   4024 1328 3795   3836 11   2445 899 3836 5065   3836 2039   899

be heir   of the world, but   through the righteousness that comes by faith.   **14** For if   those who live by
εἶναι τὸ κληρονόμον⌐ → κόσμου ἀλλὰ διὰ δικαιοσύνης → πίστεως γὰρ εἰ οἱ ← ἐκ
f.pa d.nsn n.nsn   n.gsm cj p.g   n.gsf   n.gsf cj d.npm   p.g
1639 3836 3101   3180 247 1328   1466   4411 1142 1623 3836   1666

law are heirs,   faith   has no value   and the promise is worthless, **15** because law   brings   wrath.
νόμου κληρονόμοι ἡ πίστις⌐ → κεκένωται καὶ ἡ ἐπαγγελία → κατήργηται γὰρ ὁ νόμος⌐ κατεργάζεται ὀργὴν
n.gsm n.npm d.nsf n.nsf → v.rpi.3s cj d.nsf n.nsf v.rpi.3s   cj d.nsm n.nsm v.pmi.3s   n.asf
3795 3101 3836 4411   3033 2779 3836 2039 2934   1142 3836 3795 2981   3973

And where there is   no law   there is no transgression. ¶ **16** Therefore,   the promise   comes by faith, so
δὲ οὗ → ἔστιν οὐκ νόμος   οὐδὲ παράβασις   ⌐Διὰ τοῦτο⌐ τὴν ἐπαγγελίαν ἐκ πίστεως ἵνα
cj adv → v.pai.3s pl n.nsm   adv n.nsf   p.a r.asn   d.asf n.asf   p.g n.gsf cj
1254 4023   1639 4024 3795   4028 4126   1328 4047   3836 2039   1666 4411 2671

that it may be by   grace and may be   guaranteed to all   Abraham's offspring – not only to those who are
← κατὰ χάριν → ⌐εἰς τὸ εἶναι⌐ βεβαίαν → παντὶ τῷ σπέρματι οὐ μόνον → τῷ ←
p.a n.asf   p.a d.asn f.pa a.asf   a.dsn d.dsn n.dsn pl adv   d.dsn
2848 5921   1650 3836 1639 1010   4246 3836 5065 4024 3667   3836

of the law but   also to those who are of the faith   of Abraham. He is   the father of us   all.   **17** As   it is
ἐκ τοῦ νόμου ἀλλὰ καὶ → τῷ ← ἐκ πίστεως → Ἀβραάμ ὅς ἐστιν πατὴρ → ἡμῶν πάντων καθὼς → →
p.g d.gsm n.gsm cj adv d.dsn   p.g n.gsf   n.gsm r.nsm v.pai.3s n.nsm   r.gp.1 a.gpm cj
1666 3836 3795 247 2779 3836   1666 4411   11 4005 1639 4252   7005 4246 2777

written: "I have made you a father of many nations." He is our father in   the sight of God, in whom he
γέγραπται ὅτι → τέθεικα σε πατέρα → πολλῶν ἐθνῶν   κατέναντι ← → θεοῦ οὗ
v.rpi.3s cj → v.rai.1s r.as.2 n.asm → a.gpn n.gpn   p.g   n.gsm r.gsm
1211 4022   5502 5148 4252   4498 1620   2978   2536 4005

believed – the God who gives life   to the dead   and calls   things that are   not as though they were. ¶
ἐπίστευσεν τοῦ → ζωοποιοῦντος ← τοὺς νεκροὺς καὶ καλοῦντος τὰ → ὄντα μὴ ὡς → ὄντα
v.aai.3s d.gsm   pt.pa.gsm   d.apm a.apm cj pt.pa.gsm d.apn   pt.pa.apn pl pl   pt.pa.apn
4409 3836   2443   3836 3738 2779 2813 3836   1639 3590 6055   1639

18 Against all hope, Abraham in hope believed and   so became   the father of many nations, just as it had
παρ᾽ ἐλπίδα Ὃς ἐπ᾽ ἐλπίδι ἐπίστευσεν αὐτὸν εἰς ⌐τὸ γενέσθαι⌐ πατέρα → πολλῶν ἐθνῶν κατὰ ← τὸ
p.a n.asf r.nsm p.d n.dsf v.aai.3s r.asm.3 p.a d.asn f.am n.asm → a.gpn n.gpn p.a   d.asn
4123 1828 4005 2093 1828 4409 899 1650 3836 1181 4252   4498 1620 2848   3836

been said   to him, "So shall your offspring be." **19**   Without weakening in his faith, he faced   the fact that
→ εἰρημένον οὕτως σου ⌐τὸ σπέρμα⌐ ἔσται καὶ μὴ ἀσθενήσας → τῇ πίστει κατενόησεν
pt.rp.asn adv r.gs.2 d.nsn n.nsn v.fmi.3s cj pl pt.aa.nsm   d.dsf n.dsf → v.aai.3s
3306 4048 1639 5148 3836 5065 1639 2779 3590 820   3836 4411 2917

ἀκροβυστίᾳ; οὐκ ἐν περιτομῇ ἀλλ᾽ ἐν ἀκροβυστίᾳ· ¹¹ καὶ σημεῖον ἔλαβεν περιτομῆς σφραγῖδα τῆς δικαιοσύνης τῆς πίστεως τῆς ἐν τῇ ἀκροβυστίᾳ, εἰς τὸ εἶναι αὐτὸν πατέρα πάντων τῶν πιστευόντων δι᾽ ἀκροβυστίας, εἰς τὸ λογισθῆναι [καὶ] αὐτοῖς [τὴν] δικαιοσύνην, ¹² καὶ πατέρα περιτομῆς τοῖς οὐκ ἐκ περιτομῆς μόνον ἀλλὰ καὶ τοῖς στοιχοῦσιν τοῖς ἴχνεσιν τῆς ἐν ἀκροβυστίᾳ πίστεως τοῦ πατρὸς ἡμῶν Ἀβραάμ. ¶ ¹³ Οὐ γὰρ διὰ νόμου ἡ ἐπαγγελία τῷ Ἀβραὰμ ἢ τῷ σπέρματι αὐτοῦ, τὸ κληρονόμον αὐτὸν εἶναι κόσμου, ἀλλὰ διὰ δικαιοσύνης πίστεως. ¹⁴ εἰ γὰρ οἱ ἐκ νόμου κληρονόμοι, κεκένωται ἡ πίστις καὶ κατήργηται ἡ ἐπαγγελία· ¹⁵ ὁ γὰρ νόμος ὀργὴν κατεργάζεται· οὗ δὲ οὐκ ἔστιν νόμος οὐδὲ παράβασις. ¶ ¹⁶ διὰ τοῦτο ἐκ πίστεως, ἵνα κατὰ χάριν, εἰς τὸ εἶναι βεβαίαν τὴν ἐπαγγελίαν παντὶ τῷ σπέρματι, οὐ τῷ ἐκ τοῦ νόμου μόνον ἀλλὰ καὶ τῷ ἐκ πίστεως Ἀβραάμ, ὅς ἐστιν πατὴρ πάντων ἡμῶν, ¹⁷ καθὼς γέγραπται ὅτι Πατέρα πολλῶν ἐθνῶν τέθεικά σε, κατέναντι οὗ ἐπίστευσεν θεοῦ τοῦ ζωοποιοῦντος τοὺς νεκροὺς καὶ καλοῦντος τὰ μὴ ὄντα ὡς ὄντα· ¶ ¹⁸ ὃς παρ᾽ ἐλπίδα ἐπ᾽ ἐλπίδι ἐπίστευσεν εἰς τὸ γενέσθαι αὐτὸν πατέρα πολλῶν ἐθνῶν κατὰ τὸ εἰρημένον, Οὕτως ἔσται τὸ σπέρμα σου, ¹⁹ καὶ μὴ ἀσθενήσας τῇ πίστει κατενόησεν τὸ ἑαυτοῦ σῶμα [ἤδη]

his   body   was   *as good as* dead   — since he was   about a hundred   years old — and that Sarah's
ἑαυτοῦ ⌐τὸ σῶμα┐ →   ἤδη   νενεκρωμένον   →   ὑπάρχων που ἑκατονταετής ←   ←   καὶ   Σάρρας
r.gsn.3 d.asn n.asn   adv   pt.rp.asn   pt.pa.nsm   adv   a.nsm   cj   n.gsf
1571   3836 5393   3739   3739   5639   4543 1670   2779   4925

womb   was also dead.   **20** Yet he did not waver   through unbelief   regarding the promise   of God,   but
⌐τῆς μήτρας┐   ⌐τὴν νέκρωσιν┐ δὲ →   → οὐ διεκρίθη →   ⌐τῇ ἀπιστίᾳ┐ εἰς   τὴν ἐπαγγελίαν →   ⌐τοῦ θεοῦ┐ ἀλλ᾽
d.gsf n.gsf   d.asf n.asf   cj   pl v.api.3s   d.dsf n.dsf   p.a   d.asf n.asf   d.gsm n.gsm cj
3836 3616   3836 3740   1254 1359 1359 4024 1359   3836 602   1650   3836 2039   3836 2536 247

was strengthened in his faith and gave   glory to God,   **21**   being fully persuaded   that God had power   to
→ ἐνεδυναμώθη → τῇ πίστει δοὺς δόξαν ⌐τῷ θεῷ┐ καὶ   → πληροφορηθεὶς ὅτι   ἐστιν δυνατὸς καὶ   →
   v.api.3s   d.dsf n.dsf pt.aa.nsm n.asf d.dsm n.dsm cj   pt.ap.nsm   cj   v.pai.3s a.nsm   adv
   1904   3836 4411   1443 1518 3836 2536   2779   4442   4022   1639   1543   2779

do   what he had promised.   **22** This is why   "it was credited to him as righteousness."   **23** The words   "it
ποιῆσαι ὃ   →   → ἐπήγγελται διὸ ←   ←   [καὶ]   → ἐλογίσθη → αὐτῷ εἰς δικαιοσύνην   δὲ   ὅτι →
f.aa   r.asn   v.rmi.3s   cj   adv   v.api.3s   r.dsm.3 p.a n.asf   cj   cj
4472   4005   2040   1475   2779   3357   899   1650 1466   1254   4022

was credited to him" were written not for him   alone,   **24** but also for us,   to whom God will   credit   righteousness
→ ἐλογίσθη → αὐτῷ → ἐγράφη Οὐκ δι᾽ αὐτὸν μόνον   ἀλλὰ καὶ δι᾽ ἡμᾶς → οἷς   μέλλει λογίζεσθαι
   v.api.3s   r.dsm.3   v.api.3s   pl p.a r.asm.3 a.asm   cj adv p.a r.ap.1   r.dpm   v.pai.3s f.pp
   3357   899   1211   4024 1328 899   3667   247 2779 1328 7005   4005   3516   3357

— for us who believe   in him who raised Jesus our Lord   from the dead.   **25** He was delivered over to death
→   → τοῖς πιστεύουσιν ἐπὶ τὸν ← ἐγείραντα Ἰησοῦν ἡμῶν ⌐τὸν κύριον┐ ἐκ   νεκρῶν   ὃς → παρεδόθη ←
       d.dpm pt.pa.dpm   p.a d.asm   pt.aa.asm   n.asm r.gp.1 d.asm n.asm p.g a.gpm   r.nsm   v.api.3s
       3836 4409   2093 3836   1586   2652   7005 3836 3261   1666 3738   4005   4140

for our sins   and was raised to life for our justification.
διὰ ἡμῶν ⌐τὰ παραπτώματα┐ καὶ → ἠγέρθη   διὰ ἡμῶν ⌐τὴν δικαίωσιν┐
p.a r.gp.1 d.apn n.apn   cj   v.api.3s   p.a r.gp.1 d.asf n.asf
1328 7005 3836 4183   2779   1586   1328 7005 3836 1470

Peace and Joy

5:1 Therefore, since we have been justified   through faith,   we have peace with God   through our
οὖν   →   →   →   →   Δικαιωθέντες ἐκ   πίστεως ἔχομεν εἰρήνην πρὸς ⌐τὸν θεὸν┐ διὰ   ἡμῶν
cj   pt.ap.npm   p.g   n.gsf   v.pai.1p n.asf p.a d.asm n.asm p.g   r.gp.1
4036   1467   1666 4411   2400   1645   4639 3836 2536   1328 7005

Lord   Jesus Christ, **2** through whom   we have gained access   by faith   into this grace   in
⌐τοῦ κυρίου┐ Ἰησοῦ Χριστοῦ δι᾽   οὗ   καὶ → → ἐσχήκαμεν ⌐τὴν προσαγωγὴν┐ → ⌐τῇ πίστει┐ εἰς ταύτην ⌐τὴν χάριν┐ ἐν
d.gsm n.gsm n.gsm n.gsm   p.g   r.gsm adv   v.rai.1p   d.asf n.asf   d.dsf n.dsf p.a r.asf   d.asf n.asf p.d
3836 3261   2652 5986   1328 4005 2779   2400   3836 4643   3836 4411   1650 4047   3836 5921   1877

which we now stand.   And we rejoice   in the hope of the glory of God.   **3**   Not only so, but we also
ᾗ   → → ἑστήκαμεν καὶ → → καυχώμεθα ἐπ᾽ ἐλπίδι → τῆς δόξης → ⌐τοῦ θεοῦ┐ δὲ οὐ μόνον   ἀλλὰ → καὶ
r.dsf   v.rai.1p   cj   v.pmi.1p   p.d n.dsf   d.gsf n.gsf   d.gsm n.gsm cj adv adv   cj   adv
4005   2705   2779   3016   2093 1828   3836 1518   3836 2536   1254 4024 3667   247   3016 2779

rejoice   in our sufferings, because we know that suffering produces perseverance; **4**   perseverance, character;
καυχώμεθα ἐν ταῖς θλίψεσιν →   → εἰδότες ὅτι ⌐ἡ θλῖψις┐ κατεργάζεται ὑπομονὴν   δὲ ⌐ἡ ὑπομονὴ┐ δοκιμήν
v.pmi.1p   p.d d.dpf n.dpf   pt.ra.npm cj d.nsf n.nsf v.pmi.3s   n.asf   cj d.nsf n.nsf   n.asf
3016   1877 3836 2568   3857   4022 3836 2568   2981   5705   1254 3836 5705   1509

and character, hope. **5** And hope   does not disappoint us, because God has poured out his   love   into
δὲ ⌐ἡ δοκιμὴ┐ ἐλπίδα δὲ ⌐ἡ ἐλπίς┐ οὐ καταισχύνει ὅτι   → → ἐκκέχυται ⌐τοῦ θεοῦ┐ ἡ ἀγάπη ἐν
cj d.nsf n.nsf n.asf   cj d.nsf n.nsf   pl v.pai.3s   cj   v.rpi.3s   d.gsm n.gsm d.nsf n.nsf p.d
1254 3836 1509 1828   1254 3836 1828   2875 4024   2536   1773   3836 2536 3836 27 1877

our hearts   by the Holy Spirit,   whom he has given us. ¶ **6** You see, at just the right time,
ἡμῶν ⌐ταῖς καρδίαις┐ διὰ   ἁγίου πνεύματος τοῦ → δοθέντος ἡμῖν   γὰρ   κατὰ   → καιρὸν
r.gp.1 d.dpf n.dpf   p.g   a.gsn n.gsn   d.gsn   pt.ap.gsn r.dp.1   cj   p.a   n.asm
7005 3836 2840   1328 41   4460   3836   1443   7005   1142   2848   2789

when we were still powerless, Christ died   for the ungodly. **7** Very rarely will anyone die   for a
→ ἡμῶν ὄντων ἔτι ἀσθενῶν Χριστὸς ἀπέθανεν ὑπὲρ ἀσεβῶν   γὰρ μόλις → τις   ἀποθανεῖται ὑπὲρ
   r.gp.1 pt.pa.gpm adv a.gpm   n.nsm   v.aai.3s p.g a.gpm   cj   adv   r.nsm v.fmi.3s   p.g
1639 7005 1639   2285 822   5986   633   5642 815   1142 3660   5516   633   5642

νενεκρωμένον, ἑκατονταετής που ὑπάρχων, καὶ τὴν νέκρωσιν τῆς μήτρας Σάρρας· **20** εἰς δὲ τὴν ἐπαγγελίαν τοῦ θεοῦ οὐ διεκρίθη τῇ ἀπιστίᾳ ἀλλ᾽ ἐνεδυναμώθη τῇ πίστει, δοὺς δόξαν τῷ θεῷ **21** καὶ πληροφορηθεὶς ὅτι ὃ ἐπήγγελται δυνατός ἐστιν καὶ ποιῆσαι. **22** διὸ [καὶ] ἐλογίσθη αὐτῷ εἰς δικαιοσύνην. **23** Οὐκ ἐγράφη δὲ δι᾽ αὐτὸν μόνον ὅτι ἐλογίσθη αὐτῷ **24** ἀλλὰ καὶ δι᾽ ἡμᾶς, οἷς μέλλει λογίζεσθαι, τοῖς πιστεύουσιν ἐπὶ τὸν ἐγείραντα Ἰησοῦν τὸν κύριον ἡμῶν ἐκ νεκρῶν, **25** ὃς παρεδόθη διὰ τὰ παραπτώματα ἡμῶν καὶ ἠγέρθη διὰ τὴν δικαίωσιν ἡμῶν.
5:1 Δικαιωθέντες οὖν ἐκ πίστεως εἰρήνην ἔχομεν πρὸς τὸν θεὸν διὰ τοῦ κυρίου ἡμῶν Ἰησοῦ Χριστοῦ **2** δι᾽ οὗ καὶ τὴν προσαγωγὴν ἐσχήκαμεν [τῇ πίστει] εἰς τὴν χάριν ταύτην ἐν ᾗ ἑστήκαμεν καὶ καυχώμεθα ἐπ᾽ ἐλπίδι τῆς δόξης τοῦ θεοῦ. **3** οὐ μόνον δέ, ἀλλὰ καὶ καυχώμεθα ἐν ταῖς θλίψεσιν, εἰδότες ὅτι ἡ θλῖψις ὑπομονὴν κατεργάζεται, **4** ἡ δὲ ὑπομονὴ δοκιμήν, ἡ δὲ δοκιμὴ ἐλπίδα. **5** ἡ δὲ ἐλπὶς οὐ καταισχύνει, ὅτι ἡ ἀγάπη τοῦ θεοῦ ἐκκέχυται ἐν ταῖς καρδίαις ἡμῶν διὰ πνεύματος ἁγίου τοῦ δοθέντος ἡμῖν. ¶ **6** ἔτι γὰρ Χριστὸς ὄντων ἡμῶν ἀσθενῶν ἔτι κατὰ καιρὸν ὑπὲρ ἀσεβῶν ἀπέθανεν. **7** μόλις γὰρ ὑπὲρ δικαίου

righteous man, though for a good   man someone   might possibly dare to die.   **8** But God
δικαίου   γὰρ   ὑπὲρ ⌐τοῦ ἀγαθοῦ⌐   τις   καὶ   τάχα   τολμᾷ → ἀποθανεῖν δὲ ⌐ὁ θεός⌐
a.gsm   cj   p.g d.gsm a.gsm   r.nsm adv   adv   v.pai.3s f.aa   d.nsm n.nsm
1465   1142   5642 3836 19   5516   2779   5440   5528   633   1254 3836 2536

demonstrates his own   love   for us   in this: While we   were still sinners,   Christ died   for us.   ¶   **9**
συνίστησιν   τὴν ἑαυτοῦ ἀγάπην εἰς ἡμᾶς → ὅτι →   ἡμῶν ὄντων ἔτι ἁμαρτωλῶν Χριστὸς ἀπέθανεν ὑπὲρ ἡμῶν   οὖν
v.pai.3s   d.asf r.gsm.3 n.asf p.a r.ap.1   cj   r.gp.1 pt.pa.gpm adv n.gpm n.nsm   v.aai.3s p.g r.gp.1   cj
5319   3836 1571   27   1650 7005   4022   7005 1639   2285 283   5986   633   5642 7005   4036

Since we have now been justified   by his blood,   how much more   shall we be saved   from God's wrath
→   →   → νῦν → δικαιωθέντες ἐν αὐτοῦ ⌐τῷ αἵματι⌐ → πολλῷ μᾶλλον → →   → σωθησόμεθα ἀπὸ τῆς ὀργῆς
              adv   pt.ap.npm   p.d r.gsm.3 d.dsn n.dsn   a.dsn adv.c   v.fpi.1p   p.g d.gsf n.gsf
1467   1467 1467 3814   1467   1877 899   3836 135   4498 3437   5392   608 3836 3973

through him! **10** For if, when we were God's enemies, we were reconciled   to him   through the death   of his
δι'   αὐτοῦ   γὰρ εἰ → →   ὄντες → ἐχθροὶ →   κατηλλάγημεν ⌐τῷ θεῷ⌐ διὰ τοῦ θανάτου → αὐτοῦ
p.g   r.gsm.3 cj cj   pt.pa.npm a.nmp   v.api.1p   d.dsn n.dsn p.g d.gsm n.gsm   r.gsm.3
1328   899   1142 1623   1639   2536 2398   2904   3836 2536 1328 3836 2505   5626 899

Son,   how much more, having been reconciled,   shall we be saved   through his   life!   **11**   Not only is
⌐τοῦ υἱοῦ⌐ → πολλῷ μᾶλλον →   καταλλαγέντες   → → σωθησόμεθα ἐν αὐτοῦ ⌐τῇ ζωῇ⌐ δὲ οὐ μόνον
d.gsm n.gsm   a.dsn adv.c   pt.ap.npm   v.fpi.1p   p.d r.gsm.3 d.dsf n.dsf cj pl adv
3836 5626   4498 3437   2904   5392   1877 899   3836 2437 1254 4024 3667

this so, but we also rejoice   in God   through our Lord   Jesus Christ, through whom we have now
ἀλλὰ → καὶ καυχώμενοι ἐν ⌐τῷ θεῷ⌐ διὰ ἡμῶν ⌐τοῦ κυρίου⌐ Ἰησοῦ Χριστοῦ δι' οὗ → → νῦν
cj   adv pt.pm.npm p.d d.dsm n.dsm p.g r.gp.1 d.gsm n.gsm n.nsm n.gsm p.g r.gsm   adv
247   3016 2779 3016   1877 3836 2536 1328 7005 3836 3261 2652 5986 1328 4005 3284 3284 3814

received reconciliation.
ἐλάβομεν ⌐τὴν καταλλαγήν⌐
v.aai.1p d.asf n.asf
3284   3836 2903

Death Through Adam, Life Through Christ

5:12 Therefore, just as sin   entered   the world through one man,   and death   through
⌐Διὰ τοῦτο⌐ ὥσπερ ← ἡ ἁμαρτία εἰσῆλθεν εἰς τὸν κόσμον δι' ἑνὸς ἀνθρώπου καὶ ὁ θάνατος δια
p.a r.asn   cj   d.nsf n.nsf v.aai.3s p.a d.asm n.asm p.g a.gsm n.gsm cj d.nsm n.nsm p.g
1328 4047   6061   3836 281   1656   1650 3836 3180 1328 1651 476   2779 3836 2505 1328

sin,   and in this way death   came to all   men,   because all   sinned – **13** for before the law
⌐τῆς ἁμαρτίας⌐ καὶ οὕτως ← ← ὁ θάνατος⌐ διῆλθεν εἰς πάντας ἀνθρώπους ⌐ἐφ' ᾧ⌐ πάντες ἥμαρτον γὰρ ἄχρι νόμου
d.gsf n.gsf   cj adv   d.nsm n.nsm v.aai.3s p.a a.apm n.apm   p.d r.dsn a.npm v.aai.3p cj p.g n.gsm
3836 281   2779 4048   3836 2505   1451   1650 4246 476   2093 4005 4005 279   1142 948 3795

was given, sin   was in the world. But sin   is not taken into account when there is   no law.
ἁμαρτία ἦν ἐν κόσμῳ δὲ ἁμαρτία οὐκ → → ἐλλογεῖται → → ὄντος μὴ νόμου
n.nsf v.iai.3s p.d n.dsm cj n.nsf pl   v.ppi.3s   pt.pa.gsm pl n.gsm
281   1639   1877 3180 1254 281 1824 4024   1824   1639   3590 3795

14 Nevertheless, death   reigned   from the time of Adam to   the time of Moses, even over those who did not
ἀλλὰ   ὁ θάνατος⌐ ἐβασίλευσεν ἀπὸ   Ἀδὰμ μέχρι ← ← Μωϋσέως καὶ ἐπὶ τοὺς ← → μὴ
cj   d.nsm n.nsm v.aai.3s p.g   n.gsm p.g   n.gsm adv p.a d.apm   pl
247   3836 2505   996   608   77   3588   3707 2779 2093 3836   279 3590

sin   by breaking a command,   as   did Adam, who was a pattern of the one to come.   ¶
ἁμαρτήσαντας →   ⌐τῆς παραβάσεως⌐ ⌐ἐπὶ τῷ ὁμοιώματι⌐ Ἀδὰμ ὅς ἐστιν τύπος → τοῦ ← → μέλλοντος
pt.aa.apm   d.gsf n.gsf   p.d d.dsn n.dsn   n.gsm r.nsm v.pai.3s n.nsm   d.gsm   pt.pa.gsm
279   4126 4126   2093 3836 3930   77   4005 1639   5596   3836   3516

15 But   the gift   is not like the trespass. For if the many died   by the trespass   of the one man,
Ἀλλ' οὕτως καὶ τὸ χάρισμα οὐχ ὡς τὸ παράπτωμα γὰρ εἰ οἱ πολλοὶ ἀπέθανον → τῷ παραπτώματι τοῦ ἑνὸς ←
cj   adv   adv d.nsn n.nsn pl cj d.nsn n.nsn   cj cj d.npm a.npm v.aai.3p d.dsn n.dsn   d.gsm a.gsm
247   4048 2779 3836 5922   4024 6055 3836 4183 1142 1623 3836 4498 633   3836 4183   3836 1651

how much more   did God's   grace   and the gift   that came by the grace   of the one man,   Jesus Christ,
→ πολλῷ μᾶλλον → ⌐τοῦ θεοῦ⌐ ἡ χάρις καὶ ἡ δωρεὰ   ἐν χάριτι τῇ → τοῦ ἑνὸς ἀνθρώπου Ἰησοῦ Χριστοῦ
   a.dsn adv.c   d.gsm n.gsm d.nsf n.nsf cj d.nsf n.nsf p.d n.dsf d.dsf d.gsm a.gsm n.gsm n.gsm n.gsm
   4498 3437   3836 2536 3836 5921 2779 3836 1561   1877 5921 3836 3836 1651 476   2652 5986

τις ἀποθανεῖται· ὑπὲρ γὰρ τοῦ ἀγαθοῦ τάχα τις καὶ τολμᾷ ἀποθανεῖν· **8** συνίστησιν δὲ τὴν ἑαυτοῦ ἀγάπην εἰς ἡμᾶς ὁ θεός, ὅτι ἔτι ἁμαρτωλῶν ὄντων ἡμῶν Χριστὸς ὑπὲρ ἡμῶν ἀπέθανεν. ¶ **9** πολλῷ οὖν μᾶλλον δικαιωθέντες νῦν ἐν τῷ αἵματι αὐτοῦ σωθησόμεθα δι' αὐτοῦ ἀπὸ τῆς ὀργῆς. **10** εἰ γὰρ ἐχθροὶ ὄντες κατηλλάγημεν τῷ θεῷ διὰ τοῦ θανάτου τοῦ υἱοῦ αὐτοῦ, πολλῷ μᾶλλον καταλλαγέντες σωθησόμεθα ἐν τῇ ζωῇ αὐτοῦ· **11** οὐ μόνον δέ, ἀλλὰ καὶ καυχώμενοι ἐν τῷ θεῷ διὰ τοῦ κυρίου ἡμῶν Ἰησοῦ Χριστοῦ δι' οὗ νῦν τὴν καταλλαγὴν ἐλάβομεν.

5:12 Διὰ τοῦτο ὥσπερ δι' ἑνὸς ἀνθρώπου ἡ ἁμαρτία εἰς τὸν κόσμον εἰσῆλθεν καὶ διὰ τῆς ἁμαρτίας ὁ θάνατος, καὶ οὕτως εἰς πάντας ἀνθρώπους ὁ θάνατος διῆλθεν, ἐφ' ᾧ πάντες ἥμαρτον· **13** ἄχρι γὰρ νόμου ἁμαρτία ἦν ἐν κόσμῳ, ἁμαρτία δὲ οὐκ ἐλλογεῖται μὴ ὄντος νόμου, **14** ἀλλὰ ἐβασίλευσεν ὁ θάνατος ἀπὸ Ἀδὰμ μέχρι Μωϋσέως καὶ ἐπὶ τοὺς μὴ ἁμαρτήσαντας ἐπὶ τῷ ὁμοιώματι τῆς παραβάσεως Ἀδὰμ ὅς ἐστιν τύπος τοῦ μέλλοντος. ¶ **15** Ἀλλ' οὐχ ὡς τὸ παράπτωμα, οὕτως καὶ τὸ χάρισμα· εἰ γὰρ τῷ τοῦ ἑνὸς παραπτώματι οἱ πολλοὶ ἀπέθανον, πολλῷ μᾶλλον ἡ χάρις τοῦ θεοῦ καὶ ἡ δωρεὰ ἐν χάριτι τῇ τοῦ ἑνὸς ἀνθρώπου Ἰησοῦ

overflow to the many! **16** Again, the gift of God is not like the result of the one man's sin: The
ἐπερίσσευσεν εἰς τοὺς πολλούς καὶ τὸ δώρημα οὐχ ὡς → δι᾿ ← ἑνὸς → ἁμαρτήσαντος γὰρ μὲν τὸ
v.aai.3s p.a d.apm a.apm cj d.nsn n.nsn pl cj p.g pt.aa.gsm cj pl d.nsn
4355 1650 3836 4498 2779 3836 1564 4024 6055 1328 1651 279 1142 3525 3836

judgment followed one sin and brought condemnation, but the gift followed many trespasses and brought
κρίμα ἐξ ἑνὸς εἰς κατάκριμα δὲ τὸ χάρισμα ἐκ πολλῶν παραπτωμάτων εἰς
n.nsn p.g a.gsn p.a n.nsn cj d.nsn n.nsn p.g a.gpn n.gpn p.a
3210 1666 1651 1650 2890 1254 3836 5922 1666 4498 4183 1650

justification. **17** For if, by the trespass of the one man, death reigned through that one man, how much
δικαίωμα γὰρ εἰ τῷ παραπτώματι τοῦ ἑνὸς ← ὁ θάνατος ἐβασίλευσεν διὰ τοῦ ἑνὸς ← πολλῷ
n.asn cj cj d.dsn n.dsn d.gsm a.gsm d.nsm n.nsm v.aai.3s p.g d.gsm a.gsm a.dsn
1468 1142 1623 3836 4183 3836 1651 3836 2505 996 1328 3836 1651 4498

more will those who receive God's abundant provision of grace and of the gift of righteousness
μᾶλλον → οἱ ← λαμβάνοντες ⸢τὴν περισσείαν⸥ → ⸢τῆς χάριτος⸥ καὶ → τῆς δωρεᾶς ⸢τῆς δικαιοσύνης⸥
adv.c d.npm pt.pa.npm d.asf n.asf d.gsf n.gsf cj d.gsf n.gsf d.gsf n.gsf
3437 996 3836 3284 3836 4353 3836 5921 2779 3836 1561 3836 1466

reign in life through the one man, Jesus Christ. ¶ **18** Consequently, just as the result of one trespass
βασιλεύσουσιν ἐν ζωῇ διὰ τοῦ ἑνὸς ← Ἰησοῦ Χριστοῦ ⸢Ἄρα οὖν⸥ → ὡς → δι᾿ ← ἑνὸς παραπτώματος
v.fai.3p p.d n.dsf p.g d.gsm a.gsm n.gsm n.gsm cj cj cj p.g a.gsn n.gsn
996 1877 2437 1328 3836 1651 2652 5986 726 4036 6055 1328 1651 4183

was condemnation for all men, so also the result of one act of righteousness was justification that
εἰς κατάκριμα εἰς πάντας ἀνθρώπους οὕτως καὶ → δι᾿ ← ἑνὸς → δικαιώματος εἰς δικαίωσιν →
p.a n.asn p.a a.apm n.apm adv adv p.g a.gsn n.gsn p.a n.asf
1650 2890 1650 4246 476 4048 2779 1328 1651 1468 1650 1470

brings life for all men. **19** For just as through the disobedience of the one man the many were
→ ζωῆς εἰς πάντας ἀνθρώπους γὰρ ὥσπερ ← διὰ τῆς παρακοῆς → τοῦ ἑνὸς ἀνθρώπου οἱ πολλοί →
n.gsf p.a a.apm n.apm cj cj p.g d.gsf n.gsf d.gsm a.gsm n.gsm d.npm a.npm
2437 1650 4246 476 1142 6061 1328 3836 4157 3836 1651 476 3836 4498

made sinners, so also through the obedience of the one man the many will be made righteous.
κατεστάθησαν ἁμαρτωλοί οὕτως καὶ διὰ τῆς ὑπακοῆς → τοῦ ἑνὸς ← οἱ πολλοί → → κατασταθήσονται δίκαιοι
v.api.3p a.npm adv adv p.g d.gsf n.gsf d.gsm a.gsm d.npm a.npm v.fpi.3p a.npm
2770 283 4048 2779 1328 3836 5633 3836 1651 3836 4498 2770 1465

¶ **20** The law was added so that the trespass might increase. But where sin increased, grace
δὲ νόμος → παρεισῆλθεν ἵνα ← τὸ παράπτωμα πλεονάσῃ δὲ οὗ ⸢ἡ ἁμαρτία⸥ ἐπλεόνασεν ⸢ἡ χάρις⸥
cj n.nsm v.aai.3s cj d.nsn n.nsn v.aas.3s cj adv d.nsf n.nsf v.aai.3s d.nsf n.nsf
1254 3795 4209 2671 3836 4183 4429 1254 4023 3836 281 4429 3836 5921

increased all the more, **21** so that, just as sin reigned in death, so also grace might
ὑπερεπερίσσευσεν ← ← ἵνα ← ὥσπερ ⸢ἡ ἁμαρτία⸥ ἐβασίλευσεν ἐν ⸢τῷ θανάτῳ⸥ οὕτως καὶ ⸢ἡ χάρις⸥ →
v.aai.3s cj cj d.nsf n.nsf v.aai.3s p.d d.dsm n.dsm adv adv d.nsf n.nsf
5668 2671 6061 3836 281 996 1877 3836 2505 4048 2779 3836 5921

reign through righteousness to bring eternal life through Jesus Christ our Lord.
βασιλεύσῃ διὰ δικαιοσύνης εἰς ← αἰώνιον ζωὴν διὰ Ἰησοῦ Χριστοῦ ἡμῶν ⸢τοῦ κυρίου⸥
v.aas.3s p.g n.gsf p.a a.asf n.asf p.g n.gsm n.gsm r.gp.1 d.gsm n.gsm
996 1328 1466 1650 173 2437 1328 2652 5986 7005 3836 3261

Dead to Sin, Alive in Christ

6:1 What shall we say, then? Shall we go on sinning so that grace may increase? **2** By no
Τί → → ἐροῦμεν οὖν → → ἐπιμένωμεν ⸢τῇ ἁμαρτίᾳ⸥ ἵνα ⸢ἡ χάρις⸥ → πλεονάσῃ → ⸢μὴ γένοιτο⸥
r.asn v.fai.1p cj v.pas.1p d.dsf n.dsf cj d.nsf n.nsf v.aas.3s pl v.amo.3s
5515 3306 4036 2152 3836 281 2671 3836 5921 4429 3590 1181

means! We died to sin; how can we live in it any longer? **3** Or don't you know that all of us
οἵτινες ἀπεθάνομεν ⸢τῇ ἁμαρτίᾳ⸥ πῶς → ζήσομεν ἐν αὐτῇ ἔτι ἤ → → ἀγνοεῖτε ὅτι ὅσοι
r.npm v.aai.1p d.dsf n.dsf pl v.fai.1p p.d r.dsf.3 adv pl v.pai.2p cj r.npm
4015 633 3836 281 4802 2409 1877 899 2285 2445 51 4022 4012

who were baptized into Christ Jesus were baptized into his death? **4** We were therefore buried with
← ἐβαπτίσθημεν εἰς Χριστὸν Ἰησοῦν → ἐβαπτίσθημεν εἰς αὐτοῦ ⸢τὸν θάνατον⸥ → → οὖν συνετάφημεν ←
v.api.1p p.a n.asm n.asm v.api.1p p.a r.gsm.3 d.asm n.asm cj v.api.1p
966 1650 5986 2652 966 1650 899 3836 2505 5313 5313 4036 5313

Χριστοῦ εἰς τοὺς πολλοὺς ἐπερίσσευσεν. ⁱ⁶ καὶ οὐχ ὡς δι᾽ ἑνὸς ἁμαρτήσαντος τὸ δώρημα· τὸ μὲν γὰρ κρίμα ἐξ ἑνὸς εἰς κατάκριμα, τὸ δὲ χάρισμα ἐκ πολλῶν παραπτωμάτων εἰς δικαίωμα. ⁱ⁷ εἰ γὰρ τῷ τοῦ ἑνὸς παραπτώματι ὁ θάνατος ἐβασίλευσεν διὰ τοῦ ἑνός, πολλῷ μᾶλλον οἱ τὴν περισσείαν τῆς χάριτος καὶ τῆς δωρεᾶς τῆς δικαιοσύνης λαμβάνοντες ἐν ζωῇ βασιλεύσουσιν διὰ τοῦ ἑνὸς Ἰησοῦ Χριστοῦ. ¶ ¹⁸ Ἄρα οὖν ὡς δι᾽ ἑνὸς παραπτώματος εἰς πάντας ἀνθρώπους εἰς κατάκριμα, οὕτως καὶ δι᾽ ἑνὸς δικαιώματος εἰς πάντας ἀνθρώπους εἰς δικαίωσιν ζωῆς· ¹⁹ ὥσπερ γὰρ διὰ τῆς παρακοῆς τοῦ ἑνὸς ἀνθρώπου ἁμαρτωλοὶ κατεστάθησαν οἱ πολλοί, οὕτως καὶ διὰ τῆς ὑπακοῆς τοῦ ἑνὸς δίκαιοι κατασταθήσονται οἱ πολλοί. ¶ ²⁰ νόμος δὲ παρεισῆλθεν, ἵνα πλεονάσῃ τὸ παράπτωμα· οὗ δὲ ἐπλεόνασεν ἡ ἁμαρτία, ὑπερεπερίσσευσεν ἡ χάρις, ²¹ ἵνα ὥσπερ ἐβασίλευσεν ἡ ἁμαρτία ἐν τῷ θανάτῳ, οὕτως καὶ ἡ χάρις βασιλεύσῃ διὰ δικαιοσύνης εἰς ζωὴν αἰώνιον διὰ Ἰησοῦ Χριστοῦ τοῦ κυρίου ἡμῶν.

⁶:¹ Τί οὖν ἐροῦμεν; ἐπιμένωμεν τῇ ἁμαρτίᾳ, ἵνα ἡ χάρις πλεονάσῃ; ² μὴ γένοιτο. οἵτινες ἀπεθάνομεν τῇ ἁμαρτίᾳ, πῶς ἔτι ζήσομεν ἐν αὐτῇ; ³ ἢ ἀγνοεῖτε ὅτι, ὅσοι ἐβαπτίσθημεν εἰς Χριστὸν Ἰησοῦν, εἰς τὸν θάνατον αὐτοῦ ἐβαπτίσθημεν; ⁴ συνετάφημεν

him | through | baptism | into | death | in order that, just | as | Christ | was raised | from | the dead | through | the
αὐτῷ | διὰ | τοῦ βαπτίσματος | εἰς | τὸν θάνατον | ἵνα | ὥσπερ | Χριστὸς | ἠγέρθη | ἐκ | νεκρῶν | διὰ | τῆς
r.dsm.3 p.g | d.gsn n.gsn | p.a | d.asm n.asm | cj | cj | n.nsm | v.api.3s | p.g | a.gpm | p.g | d.gsf
899 1328 | 3836 967 | 1650 | 3836 2505 | 2671 | 6061 | 5986 | 1586 | 1666 | 3738 | 1328 | 3836

glory | of the Father, | we | too | may live | a new | life. ¶ **5** | If | we have been | united
δόξης | τοῦ πατρός | οὕτως ἡμεῖς | καὶ | περιπατήσωμεν ἐν | καινότητι ζωῆς | γὰρ εἰ | γεγόναμεν | σύμφυτοι
n.gsf | d.gsm n.gsm | r.np.1 | cj | v.aas.1p p.d | n.dsf n.gsf | cj cj | v.rai.1p | a.npm
1518 | 3836 4252 | 4048 7005 | 2779 | 4344 1877 | 2786 2437 | 1142 1623 | 1181 | 5242

with him | like | this | in | his | death, | we will certainly also be | united with him in his
τῷ ὁμοιώματι | αὐτοῦ | τοῦ θανάτου | ἀλλὰ | καὶ ἐσόμεθα | τῆς
d.dsn n.dsn | r.gsm.3 | d.gsm n.gsm | cj | adv v.fmi.1p | d.gsf
3836 3930 | 2505 899 | 3836 2505 | 247 1639 1639 | 2779 1639 | 3836

resurrection. **6** For we know | that our old | self | was crucified | with him so that the body of
ἀναστάσεως | γινώσκοντες τοῦτο ὅτι | ἡμῶν παλαιὸς ὁ | ἄνθρωπος | συνεσταυρώθη | ἵνα τὸ σῶμα
n.gsf | pt.pa.npm r.asn cj | r.gp.1 a.nsm d.nsm | n.nsm | v.api.3s | cj d.nsn n.nsn
414 | 1182 4047 4022 | 7005 4094 3836 | 476 | 5365 | 2671 3836 5393

sin | might be done | away with, that we | should no | longer be slaves | to sin | — **7** because
τῆς ἁμαρτίας | καταργηθῇ | ἡμᾶς | μηκέτι | τοῦ δουλεύειν | τῇ ἁμαρτίᾳ | γὰρ
d.gsf n.gsf | v.aps.3s | r.ap.1 | adv | d.gsn f.pa | d.dsf n.dsf | cj
3836 281 | 2934 | 1526 7005 1526 | 3600 | 3836 1526 | 3836 281 | 1142

anyone | who has died | has been freed | from sin. | ¶ **8** Now if | we died | with Christ, we
ὁ | ἀποθανὼν | δεδικαίωται | ἀπὸ τῆς ἁμαρτίας | δὲ εἰ | ἀπεθάνομεν | σὺν Χριστῷ
d.nsm | pt.aa.nsm | v.rpi.3s | p.g d.gsf n.gsf | cj cj | v.aai.1p | p.d n.dsm
3836 | 633 | 1467 | 608 3836 281 | 1254 1623 | 633 | 5250 5986

believe | that we will also live | with him. | **9** For we know that since | Christ | was raised | from the dead, | he cannot
πιστεύομεν | ὅτι καὶ συζήσομεν | αὐτῷ | εἰδότες ὅτι | Χριστὸς | ἐγερθεὶς | ἐκ νεκρῶν | οὐκέτι
v.pai.1p | cj cj v.fai.1p | r.dsm.3 | pt.ra.npm cj | n.nsm | pt.ap.nsm | p.g a.gpm | adv
4409 | 4022 5182 5182 2779 5182 | 899 | 3857 4022 | 1586 | 1586 | 1666 3738 | 633 4033

die | again; death | no | longer has mastery over | him. | **10** The | death he died, | he died | to sin
ἀποθνήσκει | θάνατος | οὐκέτι | κυριεύει | αὐτοῦ | γὰρ | ὃ | ἀπέθανεν | ἀπέθανεν | τῇ ἁμαρτίᾳ
v.pai.3s | n.nsm | adv | v.pai.3s | r.gsm.3 | cj | r.asn | v.aai.3s | v.aai.3s | d.dsf n.dsf
633 | 4033 | 2505 4033 | 3259 | 899 | 1142 | 4005 | 633 | 633 | 3836 281

once | for all; but the life he lives, | he lives | to God. | ¶ **11** | In | the same way, | count | yourselves
ἐφάπαξ | δὲ ὃ ζῇ | ζῇ | τῷ θεῷ | καὶ οὕτως | ὑμεῖς | λογίζεσθε | ἑαυτοὺς
adv | cj r.asn v.pai.3s | v.pai.3s | d.dsm n.dsm | adv adv | r.np.2 | v.pmm.2p | r.apm.2
2384 | 1254 4005 2409 | 2409 | 3836 2536 | 2779 4048 | 7007 | 3357 | 1571

dead | to sin | but | alive | to God | in | Christ Jesus. | **12** Therefore | do not let sin | reign
[εἶναι] μὲν νεκροὺς | τῇ ἁμαρτίᾳ | δὲ | ζῶντας | τῷ θεῷ | ἐν | Χριστῷ Ἰησοῦ | οὖν | Μὴ | ἡ ἁμαρτία | βασιλευέτω
f.pa pl a.apm | d.dsf n.dsf | cj | pt.pa.apm | d.dsm n.dsm | p.d | n.dsm n.dsm | cj | pl | d.nsf n.nsf | v.pam.3s
1639 3525 3738 | 3836 281 | 1254 | 2409 | 3836 2536 | 1877 | 5986 2652 | 4036 | 3590 | 996 3836 281 | 996

in | your | mortal | body | so that you obey | its | evil desires. | **13** Do not offer | the parts of your
ἐν | ὑμῶν | θνητῷ | τῷ σώματι | εἰς τὸ ὑπακούειν | αὐτοῦ | ταῖς ἐπιθυμίαις | μηδὲ παριστάνετε | τὰ μέλη ὑμῶν
p.d | r.gp.2 | a.dsn | d.dsn n.dsn | p.a d.asn f.pa | r.gsn.3 | d.dpf n.dpf | cj v.pam.2p | d.apn n.apn r.gp.2
1877 | 7007 | 2570 | 3836 5393 | 1650 3836 5634 | 899 | 3836 2123 | 4225 3593 | 3836 3517 7007

body to sin, | as instruments of wickedness, | but | rather offer | yourselves to God, | as | those who have
τῇ ἁμαρτίᾳ | ὅπλα | ἀδικίας | ἀλλὰ | παραστήσατε ἑαυτοὺς | τῷ θεῷ | ὡσεὶ
d.dsf n.dsf | n.apn | n.gsf | cj | v.aam.2p r.apm.2 | d.dsm n.dsm | pl
3836 281 | 3960 | 94 | 247 | 4225 1571 | 3836 2536 | 6059 2409

been brought | from | death | to life; | and offer | the parts of your | body | to him | as instruments of righteousness.
ἐκ | νεκρῶν | ζῶντας | καὶ | τὰ μέλη | ὑμῶν | τῷ θεῷ | ὅπλα | δικαιοσύνης
p.g | a.gpm | pt.pa.apm | cj | d.apn n.apn | r.gp.2 | d.dsm n.dsm | n.apn | n.gsf
2409 2409 | 1666 3738 | 2409 | 2779 | 3836 3517 | 7007 | 3836 2536 | 3960 | 1466

14 For sin | shall not be | your | master, | because | you | are | not | under | law, | but | under | grace.
γὰρ ἁμαρτία | οὐ | ὑμῶν | κυριεύσει | γὰρ | ἐστε | οὐ | ὑπὸ | νόμον | ἀλλὰ | ὑπὸ | χάριν
cj n.nsf | pl | r.gp.2 | v.fai.3s | cj | v.pai.2p | pl | p.a | n.asm | cj | p.a | n.asf
1142 281 | 3259 | 4024 3259 7007 | 3259 | 1142 | 1639 4024 | 5679 | 3795 | 247 | 5679 | 5921

οὖν αὐτῷ διὰ τοῦ βαπτίσματος εἰς τὸν θάνατον, ἵνα ὥσπερ ἠγέρθη Χριστὸς ἐκ νεκρῶν διὰ τῆς δόξης τοῦ πατρός, οὕτως καὶ ἡμεῖς ἐν καινότητι ζωῆς περιπατήσωμεν. ¶ 5 εἰ γὰρ σύμφυτοι γεγόναμεν τῷ ὁμοιώματι τοῦ θανάτου αὐτοῦ, ἀλλὰ καὶ τῆς ἀναστάσεως ἐσόμεθα· 6 τοῦτο γινώσκοντες ὅτι ὁ παλαιὸς ἡμῶν ἄνθρωπος συνεσταυρώθη, ἵνα καταργηθῇ τὸ σῶμα τῆς ἁμαρτίας, τοῦ μηκέτι δουλεύειν ἡμᾶς τῇ ἁμαρτίᾳ· 7 ὁ γὰρ ἀποθανὼν δεδικαίωται ἀπὸ τῆς ἁμαρτίας. ¶ 8 εἰ δὲ ἀπεθάνομεν σὺν Χριστῷ, πιστεύομεν ὅτι καὶ συζήσομεν αὐτῷ, 9 εἰδότες ὅτι Χριστὸς ἐγερθεὶς ἐκ νεκρῶν οὐκέτι ἀποθνήσκει, θάνατος αὐτοῦ οὐκέτι κυριεύει. 10 ὃ γὰρ ἀπέθανεν, τῇ ἁμαρτίᾳ ἀπέθανεν ἐφάπαξ· ὃ δὲ ζῇ, ζῇ τῷ θεῷ. ¶ 11 οὕτως καὶ ὑμεῖς λογίζεσθε ἑαυτοὺς [εἶναι] νεκροὺς μὲν τῇ ἁμαρτίᾳ ζῶντας δὲ τῷ θεῷ ἐν Χριστῷ Ἰησοῦ. 12 Μὴ οὖν βασιλευέτω ἡ ἁμαρτία ἐν τῷ θνητῷ ὑμῶν σώματι εἰς τὸ ὑπακούειν ταῖς ἐπιθυμίαις αὐτοῦ, 13 μηδὲ παριστάνετε τὰ μέλη ὑμῶν ὅπλα ἀδικίας τῇ ἁμαρτίᾳ, ἀλλὰ παραστήσατε ἑαυτοὺς τῷ θεῷ ὡσεὶ ἐκ νεκρῶν ζῶντας καὶ τὰ μέλη ὑμῶν ὅπλα δικαιοσύνης τῷ θεῷ. 14 ἁμαρτία γὰρ ὑμῶν οὐ κυριεύσει· οὐ γάρ ἐστε ὑπὸ νόμον ἀλλὰ ὑπὸ χάριν.

Slaves to Righteousness

6:15 What then? Shall we sin   because we are   not under law   but   under grace? By no   means!
Τί   οὖν   →   →   ἁμαρτήσωμεν ὅτι   →   ἐσμὲν οὐκ ὑπὸ νόμον ἀλλὰ ὑπὸ χάριν   →   ⸢μὴ γένοιτο⸣ ←
r.nsn   cj   v.aas.1p   cj   v.pai.1p pl p.a n.asm cj   p.a n.asf   pl v.amo.3s
5515   4036   279   4022   1639 4024 5679 3795 247 5679 5921   3590 1181

16 Don't you know that when you offer   yourselves to someone to obey   him as slaves,   you are slaves to the
ούκ   →   οἴδατε ὅτι   →   παριστάνετε ἑαυτοὺς   →   ᾧ   εἰς ὑπακοήν   δούλους →   ἐστε δοῦλοι → ᾧ
pl   v.rai.2p cj   v.pai.2p   r.apm.2   r.dsm p.a n.asf   n.apm   v.pai.2p n.npm r.dsm
4024   3857   4022   4225   1571   4005 1650 5633   1529   1639 1529 4005

one whom you obey   – whether you are slaves to sin,   which leads to death, or to obedience, which leads
←   ←   ὑπακούετε ἤτοι   →   →   ἁμαρτίας   →   εἰς θάνατον ἢ   →   ὑπακοῆς   →   →
         v.pai.2p cj   n.gsf   p.a n.asm   cj   n.gsf
         5634   2486   281   1650 2505 2445   5633

to righteousness? **17** But thanks be to God   that, though you used to be   slaves to sin,   you
εἰς δικαιοσύνην   δὲ χάρις   ←   ⸢τῷ θεῷ⸣ ὅτι   →   →   ἦτε δοῦλοι → ⸤τῆς ἁμαρτίας⸥ δὲ ⸢
p.a n.asf   cj n.nsf   d.dsm n.dsm cj   v.iai.2p n.npm d.gsf n.gsf   cj
1650 1466   1254 5921   3836 2536 4022   1639 1529 3836 281   1254 5634

wholeheartedly obeyed   the form of teaching to which you were entrusted. **18**   You have been set free
⸤ἐκ καρδίας⸥ ὑπηκούσατε τύπον → διδαχῆς εἰς ὃν   →   →   παρεδόθητε   δὲ →   →   →   ἐλευθερωθέντες
p.gsf   v.aai.2p   n.asm   n.gsf p.a r.asm   v.api.2p   cj   pt.ap.npm
1666 2840   5634   5596   1439 1650 4005   4140   1254   1802

from sin   and have become slaves   to righteousness. ¶ **19** I put this in human   terms because you
ἀπὸ ⸤τῆς ἁμαρτίας⸥ →   →   ἐδουλώθητε ⸤τῇ δικαιοσύνῃ⸥   →   λέγω   →   Ἀνθρώπινον ←   διὰ
p.g d.gsf n.gsf   v.api.2p   d.dsf n.dsf   v.pai.1s   a.asn   p.a
608 3836 281   1530   3836 1466   3306   474   1328

are weak   in your natural   selves.   Just as you used to offer   the parts of your body in slavery to
⸤τὴν ἀσθένειαν⸥ → ὑμῶν ⸤τῆς σαρκὸς⸥ ←   γὰρ ὥσπερ ← →   →   παρεστήσατε τὰ μέλη   ὑμῶν   δοῦλα   →
d.asf n.asf   r.gp.2 d.gsf n.gsf   cj cj   v.aai.2p d.apn n.apn r.gp.2   a.apn
3836 819   4922 7007 3836 4922   1142 6061   4225   3836 3517 7007   1529

impurity   and to *ever-increasing* wickedness, so now offer   them   in slavery to righteousness
⸤τῇ ἀκαθαρσίᾳ⸥ καὶ ⸢ εἰς τὴν ἀνομίαν⸥ ⸤τῇ ἀνομίᾳ⸥ οὕτως νῦν παραστήσατε ⸤τὰ μέλη ὑμῶν⸥ δοῦλα →   ⸤τῇ δικαιοσύνῃ
d.dsf n.dsf   cj   p.a d.asf n.asf   d.dsf n.dsf adv adv v.aam.2p d.apn n.apn r.gp.2 a.apn   d.dsf n.dsf
3836 174   2779 490 1650 3836 490   3836 490   4048 3814 4225   3836 3517 7007   1529   3836 1466

leading to holiness. **20**   When you were slaves to sin,   you were free   from the control of righteousness.
→   εἰς ἁγιασμόν γὰρ ὅτε   →   ἦτε δοῦλοι → ⸤τῆς ἁμαρτίας⸥ →   ἦτε ἐλεύθεροι →   ⸤τῇ δικαιοσύνῃ⸥
p.a n.asm   cj cj   v.iai.2p n.npm d.gsf n.gsf   v.iai.2p a.npm   d.dsf n.dsf
1650 40   1142 4021   1639 1529 3836 281   1639 1801   3836 1466

21 What benefit did you reap *at that time* from the things you are now ashamed of?   Those things result
οὖν τίνα καρπὸν → εἴχετε τότε ἐφ’ οἷς   →   →   νῦν ἐπαισχύνεσθε ← γὰρ ἐκείνων ←   ⸤τὸ τέλος⸥
cj r.asm n.asm   v.iai.2p adv p.d r.dpn   adv v.ppi.2p   cj r.gpn   d.nsn n.nsn
4036 5515 2843   2400   5538 2093 4005   3814 2049   1142 1697   3836 5465

in death! **22** But now that you have been set free   from sin   and have become slaves   to God,
θάνατος δὲ νννὶ →   →   →   ἐλευθερωθέντες ἀπὸ ⸤τῆς ἁμαρτίας⸥ δὲ →   →   δουλωθέντες → ⸤τῷ θεῷ⸥
n.nsm   cj adv   pt.ap.npm   p.g d.gsf n.gsf   cj   pt.ap.npm   d.dsm n.dsm
2505   1254 3815   1802   608 3836 281   1254   1530   3836 2536

the benefit   you reap leads to holiness, and the result is eternal life. **23** For the wages of sin   is death,
τὸν καρπὸν ὑμῶν →   ἔχετε →   εἰς ἁγιασμόν δὲ τὸ τέλος   αἰώνιον ζωὴν γὰρ τὰ ὀψώνια → ⸤τῆς ἁμαρτίας⸥ θάνατος
d.asm n.asm r.gp.2 v.pai.2p   p.a n.asm   cj d.asn n.asn a.asf n.asf cj d.npn n.npn d.gsf n.gsf   n.nsm
3836 2843 7007   2400   1650 40   1254 3836 5465   173   2437 1142 3836 4072   3836 281   2505

but the gift   of God   is eternal life in Christ Jesus our Lord.
δὲ τὸ χάρισμα → ⸤τοῦ θεοῦ⸥ αἰώνιος ζωὴ ἐν Χριστῷ Ἰησοῦ ἡμῶν ⸤τῷ κυρίῳ⸥
cj d.nsn n.nsn d.gsm n.gsm a.nsf n.nsf p.d n.dsm n.dsm r.gp.1 d.dsm n.dsm
1254 3836 5922 3836 2536   173   2437 1877 5986   2652 7005 3836 3261

An Illustration From Marriage

7:1   Do you not know, brothers – for I am speaking to men who know   the law – that the law has
Ἤ   →   →   ἀγνοεῖτε ἀδελφοί   γὰρ → λαλῶ   →   →   γινώσκουσιν νόμον ὅτι ὁ νόμος →
cj   v.pai.2p n.vpm   cj   v.pai.1s   pt.pa.dpm   n.asm cj d.nsm n.nsm
2445   51   81   1142 3281   1182   3795 4022 3836 3795

6:15 Τί οὖν; ἁμαρτήσωμεν, ὅτι οὐκ ἐσμὲν ὑπὸ νόμον ἀλλὰ ὑπὸ χάριν; μὴ γένοιτο. 16 οὐκ οἴδατε ὅτι ᾧ παριστάνετε ἑαυτοὺς δούλους εἰς ὑπακοήν, δοῦλοί ἐστε ᾧ ὑπακούετε, ἤτοι ἁμαρτίας εἰς θάνατον ἢ ὑπακοῆς εἰς δικαιοσύνην; 17 χάρις δὲ τῷ θεῷ ὅτι ἦτε δοῦλοι τῆς ἁμαρτίας ὑπηκούσατε δὲ ἐκ καρδίας εἰς ὃν παρεδόθητε τύπον διδαχῆς, 18 ἐλευθερωθέντες δὲ ἀπὸ τῆς ἁμαρτίας ἐδουλώθητε τῇ δικαιοσύνῃ. ¶ 19 ἀνθρώπινον λέγω διὰ τὴν ἀσθένειαν τῆς σαρκὸς ὑμῶν. ὥσπερ γὰρ παρεστήσατε τὰ μέλη ὑμῶν δοῦλα τῇ ἀκαθαρσίᾳ καὶ τῇ ἀνομίᾳ εἰς τὴν ἀνομίαν, οὕτως νῦν παραστήσατε τὰ μέλη ὑμῶν δοῦλα τῇ δικαιοσύνῃ εἰς ἁγιασμόν. 20 ὅτε γὰρ δοῦλοι ἦτε τῆς ἁμαρτίας, ἐλεύθεροι ἦτε τῇ δικαιοσύνῃ. 21 τίνα οὖν καρπὸν εἴχετε τότε; ἐφ’ οἷς νῦν ἐπαισχύνεσθε, τὸ γὰρ τέλος ἐκείνων θάνατος. 22 νυνὶ δὲ ἐλευθερωθέντες ἀπὸ τῆς ἁμαρτίας δουλωθέντες δὲ τῷ θεῷ ἔχετε τὸν καρπὸν ὑμῶν εἰς ἁγιασμόν, τὸ δὲ τέλος ζωὴν αἰώνιον. 23 τὰ γὰρ ὀψώνια τῆς ἁμαρτίας θάνατος, τὸ δὲ χάρισμα τοῦ θεοῦ ζωὴ αἰώνιος ἐν Χριστῷ Ἰησοῦ τῷ κυρίῳ ἡμῶν.

7:1 Ἤ ἀγνοεῖτε, ἀδελφοί, γινώσκουσιν γὰρ νόμον λαλῶ, ὅτι ὁ νόμος κυριεύει τοῦ ἀνθρώπου ἐφ’ ὅσον χρόνον ζῇ; 2 ἡ γὰρ

authority over a man   *only*   *as long as* he lives? **2** For example, by law a married woman is bound
κυριεύει → ⌊τοῦ ἀνθρώπου⌋ ⌊ἐφ' ὅσον χρόνον⌋ → ζῇ γὰρ → νόμῳ ὕπανδρος ἡ γυνὴ → δέδεται
v.pai.3s   d.gsm n.gsm   p.a r.asm n.asm   v.pai.3s cj   n.dsm a.nsf d.nsf n.nsf v.rpi.3s
3259   3836 476   2093 4012 5989   2409 1142   3795 5635 3836 1222 1313

to her husband as long as he is alive, but if her husband dies, she is released from the law of marriage.
→ τῷ ἀνδρὶ → → → → ζῶντι δὲ ἐὰν ὁ ἀνήρ ἀποθάνῃ → κατήργηται ἀπὸ τοῦ νόμου → ⌊τοῦ ἀνδρός⌋
d.dsm n.dsm   pt.pa.dsm cj cj d.nsm n.nsm v.aas.3s v.rpi.3s p.g d.gsm n.gsm d.gsm n.gsm
3836 467   2409 1254 1569 3836 467 633 2934 608 3836 3795 3836 467

3 So then, if she marries another man while her husband is still alive, she is called an adulteress. But if her
οὖν ἄρα ἐὰν → γένηται ἑτέρῳ ἀνδρὶ ↱ τοῦ ἀνδρὸς → ζῶντος → χρηματίσει μοιχαλὶς δὲ ἐὰν ὁ
cj cj cj v.ams.3s r.dsm n.dsm d.gsm n.gsm pt.pa.gsm v.fai.3s n.nsf cj cj d.nsm
4036 726 1569 1181 2283 467 3836 467 2409 5976 3655 1254 1569 3836

husband dies, she is released from that law and is not an adulteress, even though she marries
ἀνήρ ἀποθάνῃ → ἐστὶν ἐλευθέρα ἀπὸ τοῦ νόμου αὐτὴν ⌊τοῦ εἶναι⌋ μὴ μοιχαλίδα → → → γενομένην
n.nsm v.aas.3s v.pai.3s a.nsf p.g d.gsm n.gsm r.asf.3 d.gsn f.pai pl n.asf pt.am.asf
467 633 1639 1801 608 3836 3795 899 3836 1639 3590 3655 1181

another man. ¶ **4** So, my brothers, you also died to the law through the body of Christ, that you
ἑτέρῳ ἀνδρὶ ὥστε μου ἀδελφοί ὑμεῖς καὶ ἐθανατώθητε τῷ νόμῳ διὰ τοῦ σώματος → ⌊τοῦ Χριστοῦ⌋ εἰς ὑμᾶς
r.dsm n.dsm cj r.gs.1 n.vpm r.np.2 adv v.api.2p d.dsm n.dsm p.g d.gsn n.gsn d.gsm n.gsm p.a r.ap.2
2283 467 6063 1609 81 7007 2779 2506 3836 3795 1328 3836 5393 3836 5986 1650 7007

might belong to another, to him who was raised from the dead, in order that we might bear fruit
→ ⌊τὸ γενέσθαι⌋ → ἑτέρῳ → τῷ → ἐγερθέντι ἐκ νεκρῶν ἵνα ← → ← καρποφορήσωμεν ←
d.asn f.am r.dsm d.dsm pt.ap.dsm p.g a.gpm cj v.aas.1p
3836 1181 2283 3836 1586 1666 3738 2671 2844

to God. **5** For when we were controlled by the sinful nature, the sinful passions aroused by the law
→ ⌊τῷ θεῷ⌋ γὰρ ὅτε → ἦμεν ἐν τῇ σαρκί ← τὰ ⌊τῶν ἁμαρτιῶν⌋ παθήματα τὰ → διὰ τοῦ νόμου
d.dsm n.dsm cj cj v.iai.1p p.d d.dsf n.dsf d.npn d.gpf n.gpf n.npn d.npn p.g d.gsm n.gsm
3836 2536 1142 4021 1639 1877 3836 4922 3836 3836 281 4077 3836 1328 3836 3795

were at work in our bodies, so that we bore fruit for death. **6** But now, by dying to
→ → ἐνηργεῖτο ἐν ἡμῶν τοῖς μέλεσιν εἰς ← ⌊τὸ καρποφορῆσαι⌋ → ⌊τῷ θανάτῳ⌋ δὲ νυνὶ → ἀποθανόντες ἐν
v.imi.3s p.d r.gp.1 d.dpn n.dpn p.a d.asn f.aa d.dsm n.dsm cj adv pt.aa.npm p.d
1919 1877 7005 3836 3517 1650 3836 2844 3836 2505 1254 3815 633 1877

what once bound us, we have been released from the law so that we serve in the new way of the
ᾧ κατειχόμεθα ← → → → κατηργήθημεν ἀπὸ τοῦ νόμου ὥστε ← ἡμᾶς δουλεύειν ἐν καινότητι ← →
r.dsm v.ipi.1p v.api.1p p.g d.gsm n.gsm cj r.ap.1 f.pa p.d n.dsf
4005 2988 2934 608 3836 3795 6063 7005 1526 1877 2786

Spirit, and not in the old way of the written code.
πνεύματος καὶ οὐ → παλαιότητι ← γράμματος →
n.gsn cj pl n.dsf n.gsn
4460 2779 4024 4095 1207

Struggling With Sin

7:7 What shall we say, then? Is the law sin? Certainly not! Indeed I would not have known what
Τί → ἐροῦμεν οὖν ὁ νόμος ἁμαρτία → μὴ γένοιτο ἀλλὰ ↱ οὐκ → ἔγνων
r.asn v.fai.1p cj d.nsm n.nsm n.nsf pl v.amo.3s cj pl → v.aai.1s
5515 3306 4036 3836 3795 281 3590 1181 247 1182 1182 4024 1182

sin was except through the law. For I would not have known what coveting really was if the
⌊τὴν ἁμαρτίαν⌋ εἰ μὴ διὰ νόμου γὰρ τε → ↱ οὐκ → ᾔδειν ⌊τὴν ἐπιθυμίαν⌋ εἰ ὁ
d.asf n.asf cj pl p.g n.gsm cj cj pl → v.lai.1s d.asf n.asf cj d.nsm
3836 281 1623 3590 1328 3795 1142 5445 3857 3857 4024 3857 3836 2123 1623 3836

law had not said, "Do not covet." **8** But sin, seizing the opportunity afforded by the commandment,
νόμος ↱ μὴ ἔλεγεν οὐκ ἐπιθυμήσεις δὲ ἡ ἁμαρτία λαβοῦσα ἀφορμὴν ← διὰ τῆς ἐντολῆς
n.nsm pl v.iai.3s pl v.fai.2s cj d.nsf n.nsf pt.aa.nsf n.asf p.g d.gsf n.gsf
3795 3306 3590 3306 2121 4024 2121 1254 3836 281 3284 929 1328 3836 1953

produced in me every kind of covetous desire. For apart from law, sin is dead. **9** Once I was alive apart
κατειργάσατο ἐν ἐμοὶ πᾶσαν ← ← ἐπιθυμίαν γὰρ χωρὶς ← νόμου ἁμαρτία νεκρά δὲ ποτέ ἐγὼ → ἔζων χωρὶς
v.ami.3s p.d r.ds.1 a.asf n.asf cj p.g n.gsm n.nsf a.nsf cj adv r.ns.1 v.iai.1s p.g
2981 1877 1609 4246 2123 1142 6006 3795 281 3738 1254 4537 1609 2409 6006

ὕπανδρος γυνὴ τῷ ζῶντι ἀνδρὶ δέδεται νόμῳ· ἐὰν δὲ ἀποθάνῃ ὁ ἀνήρ, κατήργηται ἀπὸ τοῦ νόμου τοῦ ἀνδρός. **3** ἄρα οὖν ζῶντος τοῦ ἀνδρὸς μοιχαλὶς χρηματίσει ἐὰν γένηται ἀνδρὶ ἑτέρῳ· ἐὰν δὲ ἀποθάνῃ ὁ ἀνήρ, ἐλευθέρα ἐστὶν ἀπὸ τοῦ νόμου, τοῦ μὴ εἶναι αὐτὴν μοιχαλίδα γενομένην ἀνδρὶ ἑτέρῳ. ¶ **4** ὥστε, ἀδελφοί μου, καὶ ὑμεῖς ἐθανατώθητε τῷ νόμῳ διὰ τοῦ σώματος τοῦ Χριστοῦ, εἰς τὸ γενέσθαι ὑμᾶς ἑτέρῳ, τῷ ἐκ νεκρῶν ἐγερθέντι, ἵνα καρποφορήσωμεν τῷ θεῷ. **5** ὅτε γὰρ ἦμεν ἐν τῇ σαρκί, τὰ παθήματα τῶν ἁμαρτιῶν τὰ διὰ τοῦ νόμου ἐνηργεῖτο ἐν τοῖς μέλεσιν ἡμῶν, εἰς τὸ καρποφορῆσαι τῷ θανάτῳ· **6** νυνὶ δὲ κατηργήθημεν ἀπὸ τοῦ νόμου ἀποθανόντες ἐν ᾧ κατειχόμεθα, ὥστε δουλεύειν ἡμᾶς ἐν καινότητι πνεύματος καὶ οὐ παλαιότητι γράμματος.

7:7 Τί οὖν ἐροῦμεν; ὁ νόμος ἁμαρτία; μὴ γένοιτο· ἀλλὰ τὴν ἁμαρτίαν οὐκ ἔγνων εἰ μὴ διὰ νόμου· τήν τε γὰρ ἐπιθυμίαν οὐκ ᾔδειν εἰ μὴ ὁ νόμος ἔλεγεν, Οὐκ ἐπιθυμήσεις. **8** ἀφορμὴν δὲ λαβοῦσα ἡ ἁμαρτία διὰ τῆς ἐντολῆς κατειργάσατο ἐν ἐμοὶ πᾶσαν ἐπιθυμίαν· χωρὶς γὰρ νόμου ἁμαρτία νεκρά. **9** ἐγὼ δὲ ἔζων χωρὶς νόμου ποτέ, ἐλθούσης δὲ τῆς ἐντολῆς ἡ ἁμαρτία ἀνέζησεν, **10** ἐγὼ

from law; but when the commandment came, sin sprang to life and I died. **10** I found that
← νόμου δὲ → τῆς ἐντολῆς ἐλθούσης ἡ ἁμαρτία → → ἀνέζησεν δὲ ἐγὼ ἀπέθανον καὶ μοι εὑρέθη
n.gsm cj d.gsf n.gsf pt.aa.gsf d.nsf n.nsf v.aai.3s cj r.ns.1 v.aai.1s c.rds.1 v.api.3s
3795 1254 2262 3836 1953 2262 3836 281 348 1254 1609 633 2779 1609 2351

the very commandment that was intended to bring life actually brought death. **11** For sin, seizing the
ἡ ἐντολὴ ἡ → → εἰς ζωήν αὕτη εἰς θάνατον γὰρ ἡ ἁμαρτία λαβοῦσα
d.nsf n.nsf d.nsf p.a n.asf r.nsf p.a n.asm cj d.nsf n.nsf pt.aa.nsf
3836 1953 3836 1650 2437 4047 1650 2505 1142 3836 281 3284

opportunity afforded by the commandment, deceived me, and through the commandment put me to death.
ἀφορμὴν → διὰ τῆς ἐντολῆς ἐξηπάτησεν με καὶ δι' αὐτῆς → → ἀπέκτεινεν
n.asf p.g d.gsf n.gsf v.aai.3s r.as.1 cj p.g r.gsf.3 v.aai.3s
929 1328 3836 1953 1987 1609 2779 1328 899 650

12 So then, the law is holy, and the commandment is holy, righteous and good. ¶ **13** Did that which is
ὥστε μὲν ὁ νόμος ἅγιος καὶ ἡ ἐντολὴ ἁγία καὶ δικαία καὶ ἀγαθή
cj pl d.nsm n.nsm a.nsm cj d.nsf n.nsf a.nsf cj a.nsf cj a.nsf
6063 3525 3836 3795 41 2779 3836 1953 41 2779 1465 2779 19 1181

good, then, become death to me? By no means! But in order that sin might be recognized
Τὸ ἀγαθὸν οὖν ἐγένετο θάνατος → ἐμοὶ μὴ γένοιτο ← ἀλλὰ ἵνα ← ← ἡ ἁμαρτία → φανῇ
d.nsn a.nsn cj v.ami.3s n.nsm r.ds.1 pl v.amo.3s cj cj d.nsf n.nsf v.aps.3s
3836 19 4036 1181 2505 1609 3590 1181 247 2671 3836 281 5743

as sin, it produced death in me through what was good, so that through the commandment
← ἁμαρτία κατεργαζομένη θάνατον → μοι διὰ → τοῦ ἀγαθοῦ ἵνα ← διὰ τῆς ἐντολῆς
n.nsf pt.pm.nsf n.asm r.ds.1 p.g d.gsn a.gsn cj p.g d.gsf n.gsf
281 2981 2505 1609 1328 3836 19 2671 1328 3836 1953

sin might become utterly sinful. ¶ **14** We know that the law is spiritual; but I
ἡ ἁμαρτία → γένηται καθ' ὑπερβολὴν ἁμαρτωλός γὰρ → Οἴδαμεν ὅτι ὁ νόμος ἐστιν πνευματικός δὲ ἐγὼ
d.nsf n.nsf v.ams.3s p.a n.asf a.nsf cj v.rai.1p cj d.nsm n.nsm v.pai.3s a.nsm cj r.ns.1
3836 281 1181 2848 5651 283 1142 3857 4022 3836 3795 1639 4461 1254 1609

am unspiritual, sold as a slave to sin. **15** I do not understand what I do. For what I
εἰμι σάρκινος πεπραμένος ← ← ὑπὸ τὴν ἁμαρτίαν γὰρ → → οὐ γινώσκω ὃ → κατεργάζομαι γὰρ ὃ →
v.pai.1s a.nsm pt.rp.nsm p.a d.asf n.asf cj pl v.pai.1s r.asn v.pmi.1s cj r.asn
1639 4921 4405 5679 3836 281 1142 1182 1182 4024 1182 4005 2981 1142 4005

want to do I do not do, but what I hate I do. **16** And if I do what I do not want to do, I
θέλω τοῦτο → οὐ πράσσω ἀλλ' ὃ → μισῶ τοῦτο → ποιῶ δὲ εἰ → ποιῶ τοῦτο ὃ → → οὐ θέλω →
v.pai.1s r.asn pl v.pai.1s cj r.asn v.pai.1s r.asn v.pai.1s cj cj v.pai.1s r.asn r.asn pl v.pai.1s
2527 4047 4024 4556 247 4005 3631 4047 4472 1254 1623 4472 4047 4005 4024 2527

agree that the law is good. **17** As it is, it is no longer I myself who do it, but it is sin
σύμφημι ὅτι τῷ νόμῳ καλός δὲ νυνὶ ← ← οὐκέτι ← → ἐγὼ κατεργάζομαι αὐτὸ ἀλλὰ ἡ ἁμαρτία
v.pai.1s cj d.dsm n.dsm a.nsm cj adv adv r.ns.1 v.pmi.1s r.asn.3 cj d.nsf n.nsf
5238 4022 3836 3795 2819 1254 3815 4033 1609 2981 899 247 3836 281

living in me. **18** I know that nothing good lives in me, that is, in my sinful nature. For I have the
οἰκοῦσα ἐν ἐμοί γὰρ → Οἶδα ὅτι οὐκ ἀγαθὸν οἰκεῖ ἐν ἐμοί τοῦτ' ἔστιν ἐν μου τῇ σαρκί ← γὰρ μοι παράκειται
pt.pa.nsf p.d r.ds.1 cj v.rai.1s cj pl a.nsn v.pai.3s p.d r.ds.1 r.nsn v.pai.3s p.d r.gs.1 d.dsf n.dsf cj r.ds.1 v.pmi.3s
3861 1877 1609 1142 3857 4022 4024 19 3861 1877 1609 4047 1639 1877 1609 3836 4922 1142 1609 4154

desire to do what is good, but I cannot carry it out. **19** For what I do is not the good I want
τὸ θέλειν → τὸ καλὸν δὲ οὐ τὸ κατεργάζεσθαι ← γὰρ → ποιῶ οὐ ἀγαθὸν ὃ → θέλω
d.nsn f.pa d.asn a.asn cj pl d.nsn f.pm cj v.pai.1s pl a.asn r.asn v.pai.1s
3836 2527 3836 2819 1254 4024 3836 2981 1142 4472 4024 19 4005 2527

to do; no, the evil I do not want to do – this I keep on doing. **20** Now if I do what I do not
ἀλλὰ κακὸν ὃ → → οὐ θέλω τοῦτο → → πράσσω δὲ εἰ ἐγὼ ποιῶ τοῦτο ὃ → → οὐ
cj a.asn r.asn pl v.pai.1s r.asn v.pai.1s cj cj r.ns.1 v.pai.1s r.asn r.asn pl
247 2805 4005 4024 2527 4047 4556 1254 1623 1609 4472 4047 4005 2527 2527 4024

want to do, it is no longer I who do it, but it is sin living in me that does it. ¶
θέλω οὐκέτι ← ἐγὼ κατεργάζομαι αὐτὸ ἀλλὰ ἡ ἁμαρτία οἰκοῦσα ἐν ἐμοί
v.pai.1s adv r.ns.1 v.pmi.1s r.asn.3 cj d.nsf n.nsf pt.pa.nsf p.d r.ds.1
2527 4033 1609 2981 899 247 3836 281 3861 1877 1609

21 So I find this law at work: When I want to do good, evil is right there with me.
ἄρα εὑρίσκω τὸν νόμον → ἐμοὶ τῷ θέλοντι → ποιεῖν τὸ καλὸν ὅτι τὸ κακὸν → παράκειται → ἐμοί
cj v.pai.1s d.asm n.asm r.ds.1 d.dsm pt.pa.dsm f.pa d.asn a.asn cj d.nsn a.nsn v.pmi.3s r.ds.1
726 2351 3836 3795 2527 1609 3836 2527 4472 3836 2819 4022 3836 2805 4154 1609

δὲ ἀπέθανον καὶ εὑρέθη μοι ἡ ἐντολὴ ἡ εἰς ζωήν, αὕτη εἰς θάνατον· **11** ἡ γὰρ ἁμαρτία ἀφορμὴν λαβοῦσα διὰ τῆς ἐντολῆς ἐξηπάτησέν με καὶ δι' αὐτῆς ἀπέκτεινεν. **12** ὥστε ὁ μὲν νόμος ἅγιος καὶ ἡ ἐντολὴ ἁγία καὶ δικαία καὶ ἀγαθή. ¶ **13** Τὸ οὖν ἀγαθὸν ἐμοὶ ἐγένετο θάνατος; μὴ γένοιτο· ἀλλὰ ἡ ἁμαρτία, ἵνα φανῇ ἁμαρτία, διὰ τοῦ ἀγαθοῦ μοι κατεργαζομένη θάνατον, ἵνα γένηται καθ' ὑπερβολὴν ἁμαρτωλὸς ἡ ἁμαρτία διὰ τῆς ἐντολῆς. ¶ **14** οἴδαμεν γὰρ ὅτι ὁ νόμος πνευματικός ἐστιν, ἐγὼ δὲ σάρκινός εἰμι πεπραμένος ὑπὸ τὴν ἁμαρτίαν. **15** ὃ γὰρ κατεργάζομαι οὐ γινώσκω· οὐ γὰρ ὃ θέλω τοῦτο πράσσω, ἀλλ' ὃ μισῶ τοῦτο ποιῶ. **16** εἰ δὲ ὃ οὐ θέλω τοῦτο ποιῶ, σύμφημι τῷ νόμῳ ὅτι καλός. **17** νυνὶ δὲ οὐκέτι ἐγὼ κατεργάζομαι αὐτὸ ἀλλὰ ἡ οἰκοῦσα ἐν ἐμοὶ ἁμαρτία. **18** οἶδα γὰρ ὅτι οὐκ οἰκεῖ ἐν ἐμοί, τοῦτ' ἔστιν ἐν τῇ σαρκί μου, ἀγαθόν· τὸ γὰρ θέλειν παράκειταί μοι, τὸ δὲ κατεργάζεσθαι τὸ καλὸν οὔ· **19** οὐ γὰρ ὃ θέλω ποιῶ ἀγαθόν, ἀλλὰ ὃ οὐ θέλω κακὸν τοῦτο πράσσω. **20** εἰ δὲ ὃ οὐ θέλω [ἐγὼ] τοῦτο ποιῶ, οὐκέτι ἐγὼ κατεργάζομαι αὐτὸ ἀλλὰ ἡ οἰκοῦσα ἐν ἐμοὶ ἁμαρτία. ¶ **21** Εὑρίσκω ἄρα τὸν νόμον, τῷ θέλοντι ἐμοὶ

22 For in | my | inner being | I delight | in | God's | law; | **23** but | I see | another | law | at work in | the members of
γὰρ | κατὰ | τὸν ἔσω | ἄνθρωπον | → συνήδομαι ← | τοῦ θεοῦ | τῷ νόμῳ | δὲ | → βλέπω | ἕτερον | νόμον | ἐν | τοῖς μέλεσιν
cj | p.a | d.asm adv | n.asm | v.pmi.1s | d.gsm n.gsm | d.dsm n.dsm | cj | v.pai.1s | r.asm | n.asm | p.d | d.dpn n.dpn
1142 | 2848 | 3836 2276 | 476 | 5310 | 3836 2536 | 3836 3795 | 1254 | 1063 | 2283 | 3795 | 1877 | 3836 3517

my body, | waging war | | against | the law | of | my | mind | and | making | me | a prisoner | | of the law | of
μου | → ἀντιστρατευόμενον ← | τῷ νόμῳ | μου | τοῦ νοός | καὶ | → | με | αἰχμαλωτίζοντα | ἐν | τῷ νόμῳ
r.gs.1 | pt.pm.asm | | | d.dsm n.dsm | r.gs.1 | d.gsm n.gsm | cj | | r.as.1 | pt.pa.asm | p.d | d.dsm n.dsm
1609 | 529 | | | 3836 3795 | 1609 | 3836 3808 | 2779 | 170 | 1609 | 170 | 1877 | 3836 3795

sin | | at work | within | my members. | **24** What a | wretched | man | I | am! Who will | rescue | me | from | this
τῆς ἁμαρτίας | → τῷ ὄντι | ἐν | μου | τοῖς μέλεσιν | | Ταλαίπωρος | ἄνθρωπος | ἐγὼ | τίς | → ῥύσεται | με | ἐκ | τούτου
d.gsf n.gsf | | d.dsm pt.pa.dsm | p.d | r.gs.1 | d.dpn n.dpn | | a.nsm | n.nsm | r.ns.1 | r.nsm | v.fmi.3s | r.as.1 | p.g | r.gsm
3836 281 | | 3836 1639 | 1877 | 1609 | 3836 3517 | | 5417 | 476 | 1609 | 5515 | 4861 | 1609 | 1666 | 4047

body | of death? | **25** | Thanks | be to God | | – through | Jesus | Christ | our | Lord! | ¶ | So then, | I
τοῦ σώματος | → τοῦ θανάτου | δὲ | χάρις | → τῷ θεῷ | διὰ | Ἰησοῦ | Χριστοῦ | ἡμῶν | τοῦ κυρίου | | οὖν | Ἄρα | ἐγὼ
d.gsn n.gsn | d.gsm n.gsm | cj | n.nsf | d.dsm n.dsm | p.g | n.gsm | n.gsm | r.gp.1 | d.gsm n.gsm | | cj | cj | r.ns.1
3836 5393 | 3836 2505 | 1254 | 5921 | 3836 2536 | 1328 | 2652 | 5986 | 7005 | 3836 3261 | | 4036 | 726 | 1609

myself | in | my | mind am | a slave | to | God's | law, | but | in | the | sinful nature | a slave to | the | law | of sin.
αὐτὸς | μὲν | τῷ | νοΐ | δουλεύω | θεοῦ | νόμῳ | δὲ | → | τῇ | σαρκὶ ← | | νόμῳ | → ἁμαρτίας
r.nsm | pl | d.dsm | n.dsm | v.pai.1s | n.gsm | n.dsm | cj | | d.dsf | n.dsf | | n.dsm | n.gsf
899 | 3525 | 3836 | 3808 | 1526 | 3795 | 2536 | 3795 | 1254 | 3836 | 4922 | | 3795 | 281

Life Through the Spirit

8:1 Therefore, | there is | now | no | condemnation | for | those | who are | in | Christ | Jesus, | **2** because | through | Christ | Jesus
ἄρα | | νῦν | Οὐδὲν | κατάκριμα | → | τοῖς | ← | ἐν | Χριστῷ | Ἰησοῦ | γὰρ | ἐν | Χριστῷ | Ἰησοῦ
cj | | adv | a.nsn | n.nsn | | d.dpm | | p.d | n.dsm | n.dsm | cj | p.d | n.dsm | n.dsm
726 | | 3814 | 4029 | 2890 | | 3836 | | 1877 | 5986 | 2652 | 1142 | 1877 | 5986 | 2652

the law | of the Spirit | of life | set | me | free | | from | the law | of | sin | and | death. | **3** For what | the
ὁ νόμος | → τοῦ πνεύματος | τῆς ζωῆς | → σε | ἠλευθέρωσεν | ἀπὸ | τοῦ νόμου | → τῆς ἁμαρτίας | καὶ | τοῦ θανάτου | γὰρ | τοῦ
d.nsm n.nsm | d.gsn n.gsn | d.gsf n.gsf | r.as.2 | v.aai.3s | p.g | d.gsm n.gsm | d.gsf n.gsf | cj | d.gsm n.gsm | cj | d.gsm
3836 3795 | 3836 4460 | 3836 2437 | 1802 5148 | 1802 | 608 | 3836 3795 | 3836 281 | 2779 | 3836 2505 | 1142 | 3836

law | was powerless | to do in | that | it was | weakened | by | the | sinful | nature, | God | did | by sending | his own | Son
νόμου | Τὸ ἀδύνατον | ἐν | ᾧ | | ἠσθένει | διὰ | τῆς | σαρκός | | ὁ θεὸς | | → πέμψας | τὸν ἑαυτοῦ | υἱὸν
n.gsm | d.asn a.asn | p.d | r.dsn | | v.iai.3s | p.g | d.gsf | n.gsf | | d.nsm n.nsm | | pt.aa.nsm | d.asm r.gsm.3 | n.asm
3795 | 3836 105 | 1877 4005 | | 820 | 1328 3836 4922 | | 3836 2536 | | 4287 | 3836 1571 | 5626

in | the | likeness | of sinful | man | to be a | sin | | offering. | And so he | condemned | sin | | in | sinful
ἐν | ὁμοιώματι | → ἁμαρτίας | σαρκὸς | καὶ | περὶ ← | ἁμαρτίας ← | | → | κατέκρινεν | τὴν ἁμαρτίαν | ἐν | τῇ σαρκί
p.d | n.dsn | n.gsf | n.gsf | cj | p.g | n.gsf | | | v.aai.3s | d.asf n.asf | p.d | d.dsf n.dsf
1877 | 3930 | 281 | 4922 | 2779 | 4309 | 281 | | | 2891 | 3836 281 | 1877 | 3836 4922

man, | **4** in | order that | the | righteous | requirements | of | the law | might | be fully met | in | us, | who do | not | live
| ἵνα ← | | τὸ | δικαίωμα | | → | τοῦ νόμου | | πληρωθῇ | ἐν | ἡμῖν | τοῖς | μὴ | περιπατοῦσιν
| cj | | d.nsn | n.nsn | | | d.gsm n.gsm | | v.aps.3s | p.d | r.dp.1 | d.dpm | pl | pt.pa.dpm
| 2671 | | 3836 | 1468 | | | 3836 3795 | | 4444 | 1877 | 7005 | 3836 | 3590 | 4344

according | to the | sinful nature | but | according | to the | Spirit. | ¶ | **5** | Those who | live | according | to the sinful
κατὰ | ← | σάρκα ← | ἀλλὰ | κατὰ | ← | πνεῦμα | | | γὰρ οἱ | ← | ὄντες κατὰ | ← | σάρκα
p.a | | n.asf | cj | p.a | | n.asn | | | cj d.npm | | pt.pa.npm p.a | | n.asf
2848 | | 4922 | 247 | 2848 | | 4460 | | | 1142 3836 | | 1639 2848 | | 4922

nature have | their minds | set on what | that | nature | desires; | but | those who | live in | | accordance | with the | Spirit have
← | φρονοῦσιν | ← | τὰ | τῆς | σαρκὸς | δὲ | οἱ | ← | κατὰ | | | πνεῦμα
| v.pai.3p | | d.apn | d.gsf | n.gsf | cj | d.npm | | p.a | | | n.asn
| 5858 | | 3836 | 3836 | 4922 | 1254 | 3836 | | 2848 | | | 4460

their minds set on | what | the | Spirit | desires. | **6** | The mind | of sinful | | man | is death, | but | the | mind
τὰ | τοῦ | πνεύματος | | γὰρ | τὸ | φρόνημα | → τῆς σαρκὸς | | θάνατος | δὲ | τὸ | φρόνημα
d.apn | d.gsn | n.gsn | | cj | d.nsn | n.nsn | d.gsf n.gsf | | n.nsm | cj | d.nsn | n.nsn
3836 | 3836 | 4460 | | 1142 | 3836 | 5859 | 3836 4922 | | 2505 | 1254 | 3836 | 5859

controlled by | the | Spirit | is life | and | peace; | **7** | the | sinful | mind | is hostile | to | God. | It | does not
τοῦ | πνεύματος | ζωὴ | καὶ | εἰρήνη | διότι | τὸ | τῆς σαρκὸς | φρόνημα | ἔχθρα | εἰς | θεόν | γὰρ | → | οὐχ
d.gsn | n.gsn | n.nsf | cj | n.nsf | cj | d.nsn | d.gsf n.gsf | n.nsn | n.nsf | p.a | n.asm | cj | | pl
3836 | 4460 | 2437 | 2779 | 1645 | 1484 | 3836 | 3836 4922 | 5859 | 2397 | 1650 | 2536 | 1142 | 5718 5718 | 4024

ποιεῖν τὸ καλόν, ὅτι ἐμοὶ τὸ κακὸν παράκειται· **22** συνήδομαι γὰρ τῷ νόμῳ τοῦ θεοῦ κατὰ τὸν ἔσω ἄνθρωπον, **23** βλέπω δὲ ἕτερον νόμον ἐν τοῖς μέλεσίν μου ἀντιστρατευόμενον τῷ νόμῳ τοῦ νοός μου καὶ αἰχμαλωτίζοντά με ἐν τῷ νόμῳ τῆς ἁμαρτίας τῷ ὄντι ἐν τοῖς μέλεσίν μου. **24** ταλαίπωρος ἐγὼ ἄνθρωπος· τίς με ῥύσεται ἐκ τοῦ σώματος τοῦ θανάτου τούτου; **25** χάρις δὲ τῷ θεῷ διὰ Ἰησοῦ Χριστοῦ τοῦ κυρίου ἡμῶν. ¶ ἄρα οὖν αὐτὸς ἐγὼ τῷ μὲν νοΐ δουλεύω νόμῳ θεοῦ τῇ δὲ σαρκὶ νόμῳ ἁμαρτίας.

8:1 Οὐδὲν ἄρα νῦν κατάκριμα τοῖς ἐν Χριστῷ Ἰησοῦ. **2** ὁ γὰρ νόμος τοῦ πνεύματος τῆς ζωῆς ἐν Χριστῷ Ἰησοῦ ἠλευθέρωσέν με «σε» ἀπὸ τοῦ νόμου τῆς ἁμαρτίας καὶ τοῦ θανάτου. **3** τὸ γὰρ ἀδύνατον τοῦ νόμου ἐν ᾧ ἠσθένει διὰ τῆς σαρκός, ὁ θεὸς τὸν ἑαυτοῦ υἱὸν πέμψας ἐν ὁμοιώματι σαρκὸς ἁμαρτίας καὶ περὶ ἁμαρτίας κατέκρινεν τὴν ἁμαρτίαν ἐν τῇ σαρκί, **4** ἵνα τὸ δικαίωμα τοῦ νόμου πληρωθῇ ἐν ἡμῖν τοῖς μὴ κατὰ σάρκα περιπατοῦσιν ἀλλὰ κατὰ πνεῦμα. ¶ **5** οἱ γὰρ κατὰ σάρκα ὄντες τὰ τῆς σαρκὸς φρονοῦσιν, οἱ δὲ κατὰ πνεῦμα τὰ τοῦ πνεύματος. **6** τὸ γὰρ φρόνημα τῆς σαρκὸς θάνατος, τὸ δὲ φρόνημα τοῦ πνεύματος ζωὴ καὶ εἰρήνη· **7** διότι τὸ φρόνημα τῆς σαρκὸς ἔχθρα εἰς θεόν, τῷ γὰρ νόμῳ τοῦ θεοῦ οὐχ ὑποτάσσεται, οὐδὲ γὰρ δύναται· **8** οἱ δὲ ἐν

submit   to   God's   law,   nor can   it do so. ⁸ Those controlled by the sinful nature cannot
ὑποτάσσεται ˌτοῦ θεοῦˌ ˌτῷ νόμῳ γὰρ οὐδὲ δύναται ← ←   δὲ οἱ   ὄντες   ἐν σαρκὶ ←   οὐ δύνανται
v.ppi.3s   d.gsm n.gsm d.dsm n.dsm cj cj v.ppi.3s   cj d.npm pt.pa.npm p.d n.dsf   pl v.ppi.3p
5718   3795 3836 2536 3795 1142 4028 1538   1254 3836 1639   1877 4922   4024 1538

please God.   ¶ ⁹You, however, are controlled not by the sinful nature but   by the Spirit, if   the Spirit of
ἀρέσαι θεῷ   ὑμεῖς δὲ   ἐστε ←   οὐκ ἐν σαρκὶ ←   ἀλλὰ ἐν πνεύματι εἴπερ πνεῦμα →
f.aa   n.dsm   r.np.2 cj   v.pai.2p   pl p.d n.dsf   cj p.d n.dsn   cj   n.nsn
743   2536   7007 1254   1639   4024 1877 4922   247 1877 4460   1642   4460

God lives in you. And if anyone does not have the Spirit of Christ, he does not belong to Christ. ¹⁰But if
θεοῦ οἰκεῖ ἐν ὑμῖν δὲ εἰ τις   →   οὐκ ἔχει   πνεῦμα → Χριστοῦ οὗτος ἔστιν οὐκ →   →   αὐτοῦ   δὲ εἰ
n.gsm v.pai.3s p.d r.dp.2 cj cj r.nsm   pl v.pai.3s n.asn   n.gsm r.nsm v.pai.3s pl   r.gsm.3   cj cj
2536 3861 1877 7007 1254 1623 5516   4024 2400   4460   5986   4047 1639 4024   899   1254 1623

Christ is in you,   your body is dead because of sin,   yet your spirit is alive because of righteousness. ¹¹And
Χριστὸς ἐν ὑμῖν μὲν τὸ σῶμα νεκρὸν διὰ ← ἁμαρτίαν δὲ τὸ πνεῦμα ζωὴ διὰ ←   δικαιοσύνην   δὲ
n.nsm   p.d r.dp.2 cj d.nsn n.nsn a.nsn p.a   n.asf   cj d.nsn n.nsn n.nsf p.a   n.asf   cj
5986   1877 7007 3525 3836 5393 3738 1328   281   1254 3836 4460 2437 1328   1466   1254

if the Spirit of him who raised Jesus   from the dead is living in you, he who raised Christ from the
εἰ τὸ πνεῦμα → τοῦ ← ἐγείραντος ˌτὸν Ἰησοῦνˌ ἐκ   νεκρῶν → οἰκεῖ ἐν ὑμῖν ὁ   ← ἐγείρας Χριστὸν ἐκ
cj d.nsn n.nsn   d.gsm   pt.aa.gsm   d.asm n.asm   p.g   a.gpm   v.pai.3s p.d r.dp.2 d.nsm   pt.aa.nsm n.asm p.g
1623 3836 4460   3836   1586   3836 2652   1666 3738   3861 1877 7007 3836   1586   5986   1666

dead will also give life   to your mortal bodies   through his Spirit,   who lives   in you. ¶
νεκρῶν καὶ → ζωοποιήσει ← ὑμῶν θνητὰ ˌτὰ σώματαˌ διὰ αὐτοῦ πνεύματος τοῦ ἐνοικοῦντος ἐν ὑμῖν
a.gpm   adv   v.fai.3s   r.gp.2 a.apn d.apn n.apn p.g r.gsm.3 n.gsn   d.gsn pt.pa.gsn p.d r.dp.2
3738   2443 2779   7007 2570   3836 5393 1328 899   4460   3836 1940   1877 7007

¹²Therefore, brothers, we have an obligation – but it is not to the sinful nature, to live   according to it. ¹³For if
ˌἌρα οὖνˌ   ἀδελφοί → ἐσμὲν ὀφειλέται   οὐ τῇ σαρκὶ ←   → ˌτοῦ ζῆνˌ κατὰ   ←   σάρκα γὰρ εἰ
cj cj   n.vpm   v.pai.1p n.npm   pl d.dsf n.dsf   d.gsn n.pa p.a   n.asf cj cj
726 4036   81   1639   4050   4024 3836 4922   3836 2409 2848   4922 1142 1623

you live according to the sinful nature, you will   die;   but if by the Spirit you put to death   the
→ ζῆτε κατὰ   ←   σάρκα ←   → μέλλετε ἀποθνῄσκειν δὲ εἰ → πνεύματι → → θανατοῦτε τὰς
v.pai.2p p.a   n.asf   v.pai.2p f.pa   cj cj   n.dsn   v.pai.2p   d.apf
2409   2848   4922   3516   633   1254 1623   4460   2506   3836

misdeeds of the body, you will live, ¹⁴because those who are led   by the Spirit of God   are sons of God.
πράξεις → τοῦ σώματος → → ζήσεσθε γὰρ ὅσοι   → ἄγονται →   πνεύματι → θεοῦ οὗτοι εἰσιν υἱοὶ θεοῦ
n.apf   d.gsn n.gsn   v.fmi.2p cj r.npm   v.ppi.3p   n.dsn   n.gsm r.npm v.pai.3p n.npm n.gsm
4552   3836 5393   2409   1142 4012   72   4460   2536   4047 1639   5626 2536

¹⁵For you did not receive a spirit that makes you a slave   again to fear, but you received the Spirit of sonship.
γὰρ → → οὐ ἐλάβετε πνεῦμα →   →   →   δουλείας πάλιν εἰς φόβον ἀλλὰ → ἐλάβετε πνεῦμα υἱοθεσίας
cj   pl v.aai.2p n.asn   n.gsf   adv p.a n.asm cj   v.aai.2p n.asn n.gsf
1142 3284 3284 4024 3284 4460   1525   4099 1650 5832 247   3284   4460   5625

And by him we cry,   "Abba, Father." ¹⁶The Spirit himself testifies with our spirit   that we are God's
ἐν ᾧ → κράζομεν ἀββα ὁ πατήρ τὸ πνεῦμα αὐτὸ συμμαρτυρεῖ ← ἡμῶν ˌτῷ πνεύματιˌ ὅτι → ἐσμὲν θεοῦ
p.d r.dsn v.pai.1p n.vsm d.vsm n.vsm d.nsn n.nsn r.nsn v.pai.3s   r.gp.1 d.dsn n.dsn cj   v.pai.1p n.gsm
1877 4005 3189   5   3836 4252   3836 4460   899 5210   7005 3836 4460   4022   1639 2536

children. ¹⁷Now if we are children, then we are heirs –   heirs   of God and co-heirs   with Christ, if
τέκνα   δὲ εἰ   τέκνα   καὶ   κληρονόμοι μὲν κληρονόμοι → θεοῦ δὲ συγκληρονόμοι → Χριστοῦ εἴπερ
n.npn   cj cj   n.npn   adv   n.npm   pl n.npm   n.gsm cj n.npm   n.gsm   cj
5451   1254 1623 5451   2779   3101   3525 3101   2536 1254 5169   5986   1642

indeed we share in his sufferings in order that we may also share in his glory.
←   →   →   συμπάσχομεν ἵνα ←   →   →   καὶ → → συνδοξασθῶμεν
                v.pai.1p   cj   adv   v.aps.1p
               5224   2671   5280 5280 2779   5280

Future Glory

^{8:18} I consider that our present   sufferings are not worth comparing with the glory that will   be
γὰρ → Λογίζομαι ὅτι τὰ ˌτοῦ νῦν καιροῦˌ παθήματα οὐκ ἄξια   πρὸς τὴν δόξαν μέλλουσαν →
cj   v.pmi.1s   cj d.npn d.gsm adv n.gsm n.npn   pl a.npn   p.a d.asf n.asf pt.pa.asf
1142 3357   4022 3836 3836 3814 2789 4077   4024 545   4639 3836 1518 3516

σαρκὶ ὄντες θεῷ ἀρέσαι οὐ δύνανται. ¶ ⁹ ὑμεῖς δὲ οὐκ ἐστε ἐν σαρκὶ ἀλλὰ ἐν πνεύματι, εἴπερ πνεῦμα θεοῦ οἰκεῖ ἐν ὑμῖν. εἰ δέ τις πνεῦμα Χριστοῦ οὐκ ἔχει, οὗτος οὐκ ἔστιν αὐτοῦ. ¹⁰ εἰ δὲ Χριστὸς ἐν ὑμῖν, τὸ μὲν σῶμα νεκρὸν διὰ ἁμαρτίαν τὸ δὲ πνεῦμα ζωὴ διὰ δικαιοσύνην. ¹¹ εἰ δὲ τὸ πνεῦμα τοῦ ἐγείραντος τὸν Ἰησοῦν ἐκ νεκρῶν οἰκεῖ ἐν ὑμῖν, ὁ ἐγείρας Χριστὸν ἐκ νεκρῶν ζωοποιήσει καὶ τὰ θνητὰ σώματα ὑμῶν διὰ τοῦ ἐνοικοῦντος αὐτοῦ πνεύματος ἐν ὑμῖν. ¶ ¹² Ἄρα οὖν, ἀδελφοί, ὀφειλέται ἐσμὲν οὐ τῇ σαρκὶ τοῦ κατὰ σάρκα ζῆν, ¹³ εἰ γὰρ κατὰ σάρκα ζῆτε, μέλλετε ἀποθνῄσκειν· εἰ δὲ πνεύματι τὰς πράξεις τοῦ σώματος θανατοῦτε, ζήσεσθε. ¹⁴ ὅσοι γὰρ πνεύματι θεοῦ ἄγονται, οὗτοι υἱοὶ θεοῦ εἰσιν. ¹⁵ οὐ γὰρ ἐλάβετε πνεῦμα δουλείας πάλιν εἰς φόβον ἀλλὰ ἐλάβετε πνεῦμα υἱοθεσίας ἐν ᾧ κράζομεν, Αββα ὁ πατήρ. ¹⁶ αὐτὸ τὸ πνεῦμα συμμαρτυρεῖ τῷ πνεύματι ἡμῶν ὅτι ἐσμὲν τέκνα θεοῦ. ¹⁷ εἰ δὲ τέκνα, καὶ κληρονόμοι· κληρονόμοι μὲν θεοῦ, συγκληρονόμοι δὲ Χριστοῦ, εἴπερ συμπάσχομεν ἵνα καὶ συνδοξασθῶμεν.

revealed   in us. ¹⁹ The creation waits in eager expectation for the sons of God to be
ἀποκαλυφθῆναι εἰς ἡμᾶς γὰρ τῆς κτίσεως ἀπεκδέχεται ⌐ἡ ἀποκαραδοκία⌐ → τῶν υἱῶν → ⌐τοῦ θεοῦ⌐
f.ap p.a r.ap.1 cj d.gsf n.gsf v.pmi.3s d.nsf n.nsf d.gpm n.gpm d.gsm n.gsm
636 1650 7005 1142 d.gsf 3232 587 3836 638 3836 5626 3836 2536

revealed. ²⁰ For the creation was subjected to frustration, not by its own choice, but by the will of the one
⌐τὴν ἀποκάλυψιν⌐ γὰρ ἡ κτίσις → ὑπετάγη → ⌐τῇ ματαιότητι⌐ οὐχ → → ἑκοῦσα ἀλλὰ διὰ τὸν ←
d.asf n.asf cj d.nsf n.nsf v.api.3s d.dsf n.dsf pl a.nsf cj p.a d.asm
3836 637 1142 3836 3232 5718 3836 3470 4024 1776 247 1328 3836

who subjected it, in hope ²¹ that the creation itself will be liberated from its bondage to decay and
← ὑποτάξαντα ἐφ᾽ ἐλπίδι ὅτι καὶ ἡ κτίσις αὐτὴ → → ἐλευθερωθήσεται ἀπὸ τῆς δουλείας → ⌐τῆς φθορᾶς⌐
pt.aa.asm p.d n.dsf cj adv d.nsf n.nsf r.nsf v.fpi.3s p.g d.gsf n.gsf d.gsf n.gsf
5718 2093 1828 4022 2779 3836 3232 899 1802 608 3836 1525 3836 5785

brought into the glorious freedom of the children of God. ¶ ²² We know that the whole creation has
εἰς τὴν ⌐τῆς δόξης⌐ ἐλευθερίαν → τῶν τέκνων → ⌐τοῦ θεοῦ⌐ γὰρ → οἴδαμεν ὅτι ἡ πᾶσα κτίσις →
p.a d.asf 3836 d.gsf n.gsf d.gpn n.gpn d.gsm n.gsm cj v.rai.1p cj d.nsf a.nsf n.nsf
1650 3836 3836 1518 1800 3836 5451 3836 2536 1142 3857 4022 3836 4246 3232

been groaning as in the pains of childbirth right up to the present time. ²³ Not only so, but we
→ συστενάζει καὶ συνωδίνει ← ἄχρι → τοῦ νῦν δὲ οὐ μόνον ἀλλὰ καὶ ἡμεῖς
v.pai.3s cj v.pai.3s p.g d.gsm adv cj pl adv cj adv r.np.1
5367 2779 5349 948 3836 3814 1254 4024 3667 247 2779 7005

ourselves, who have the firstfruits of the Spirit, groan inwardly as we wait eagerly for our
αὐτοὶ → ἔχοντες τὴν ἀπαρχὴν → τοῦ πνεύματος καὶ στενάζομεν αὐτοὶ ἐν ἑαυτοῖς → → ἀπεκδεχόμενοι
r.npm pt.pa.npm d.asf n.asf d.gsn n.gsn adv v.pai.1p r.npm p.d r.dpm.1 pt.pm.npm
899 2400 3836 569 3836 4460 2779 5100 899 1877 1571 587

adoption as sons, the redemption of our bodies. ²⁴ For in this hope we were saved. But hope that is seen
υἱοθεσίαν ← τὴν ἀπολύτρωσιν → ἡμῶν ⌐τοῦ σώματος⌐ γὰρ → τῇ ἐλπίδι → ἐσώθημεν δὲ ἐλπὶς → βλεπομένη
n.asf d.asf n.asf r.gp.1 d.gsn n.gsn cj d.dsf n.dsf v.api.1p cj n.nsf pt.pp.nsf
5625 3836 667 5393 7005 3836 5393 1142 3836 1828 5392 1254 1828 1063

is no hope at all. Who hopes for what he already has? ²⁵ But if we hope for what we do not yet have,
ἔστιν οὐκ ἐλπὶς γὰρ τίς ἐλπίζει ὃ → βλέπει δὲ εἰ → ἐλπίζομεν ← ὃ → → οὐ βλέπομεν
v.pai.3s pl n.nsf cj r.nsm v.pai.3s r.asn v.pai.3s cj cj v.pai.1p r.asn pl v.pai.1p
1639 4024 1828 1142 5515 1827 4005 1063 1254 1623 1827 4005 1063 1063 4024 1063

we wait for it patiently. ¶ ²⁶ In the same way, the Spirit helps us in our
→ ἀπεκδεχόμεθα ⌐δι᾽ ὑπομονῆς⌐ δὲ → → Ὡσαύτως ← καὶ τὸ πνεῦμα συναντιλαμβάνεται ← ⌐ἡμῶν
v.pmi.1p p.g n.gsf cj adv adv d.nsn n.nsn v.pmi.3s r.gp.1
587 1328 5705 1254 6058 2779 3836 4460 5269 819 7005

weakness. We do not know what we ought to pray for, but the Spirit himself intercedes
⌐τῇ ἀσθενείᾳ⌐ γὰρ → τὸ → οὐκ οἴδαμεν τί → ⌐καθὸ δεῖ⌐ προσευξώμεθα ἀλλὰ τὸ πνεῦμα αὐτὸ ὑπερεντυγχάνει
d.dsf n.dsf cj d.asn pl v.rai.1p r.asn cj v.pai.3s v.ams.1p cj d.nsn n.nsn r.nsn v.pai.3s
3836 819 1142 3857 3836 3857 4024 3857 5515 4667 2771 1256 4667 247 3836 4460 899 5659

for us with groans that words cannot express. ²⁷ And he who searches our hearts knows the mind of the
← στεναγμοῖς → → → → ἀλαλήτοις δὲ ὁ ← ἐραυνῶν τὰς καρδίας οἶδεν τί τὸ φρόνημα → τοῦ
n.dpm a.dpm cj d.nsm pt.pa.nsm d.apf n.apf v.rai.3s r.nsn d.nsn n.nsn d.gsn
5099 227 1254 3836 2236 3836 2840 3857 5515 3836 5859 3836

Spirit, because the Spirit intercedes for the saints in accordance with God's will.
πνεύματος ὅτι ἐντυγχάνει ὑπὲρ ἁγίων κατὰ θεόν
n.gsn cj v.pai.3s p.g a.gpm p.a n.asm
4460 4022 1961 5642 41 2848 2536

More Than Conquerors

^{8:28} And we know that in all things God works for the good of those who love him, who have
δὲ → Οἴδαμεν ὅτι → πάντα ← συνεργεῖ εἰς ἀγαθόν → τοῖς ← ἀγαπῶσιν ⌐τὸν θεόν⌐ τοῖς →
cj v.rai.1p cj a.apn v.pai.3s p.a a.asn d.dpm pt.pa.dpm d.asm n.asm d.dpm
1254 3857 4022 4246 5300 1650 19 3836 26 3836 2536 3836

been called according to his purpose. ²⁹ For those God foreknew he also predestined to be conformed to the likeness
οὖσιν κλητοῖς κατὰ ← πρόθεσιν ὅτι οὓς προέγνω → καὶ προώρισεν συμμόρφους ← τῆς εἰκόνος
pt.pa.dpm a.dpm p.a n.asf cj r.apm v.aai.3s adv v.aai.3s a.apm d.gsf n.gsf
1639 3105 2848 4606 4022 4005 4589 4633 2779 4633 5215 3836 1635

^{8:18} Λογίζομαι γὰρ ὅτι οὐκ ἄξια τὰ παθήματα τοῦ νῦν καιροῦ πρὸς τὴν μέλλουσαν δόξαν ἀποκαλυφθῆναι εἰς ἡμᾶς. ¹⁹ ἡ γὰρ ἀποκαραδοκία τῆς κτίσεως τὴν ἀποκάλυψιν τῶν υἱῶν τοῦ θεοῦ ἀπεκδέχεται. ²⁰ τῇ γὰρ ματαιότητι ἡ κτίσις ὑπετάγη, οὐχ ἑκοῦσα ἀλλὰ διὰ τὸν ὑποτάξαντα, ἐφ᾽ ἐλπίδι ²¹ ὅτι καὶ αὐτὴ ἡ κτίσις ἐλευθερωθήσεται ἀπὸ τῆς δουλείας τῆς φθορᾶς εἰς τὴν ἐλευθερίαν τῆς δόξης τῶν τέκνων τοῦ θεοῦ. ¶ ²² οἴδαμεν γὰρ ὅτι πᾶσα ἡ κτίσις συστενάζει καὶ συνωδίνει ἄχρι τοῦ νῦν· ²³ οὐ μόνον δέ, ἀλλὰ καὶ αὐτοὶ τὴν ἀπαρχὴν τοῦ πνεύματος ἔχοντες, ἡμεῖς καὶ αὐτοὶ ἐν ἑαυτοῖς στενάζομεν υἱοθεσίαν ἀπεκδεχόμενοι, τὴν ἀπολύτρωσιν τοῦ σώματος ἡμῶν. ²⁴ τῇ γὰρ ἐλπίδι ἐσώθημεν· ἐλπὶς δὲ βλεπομένη οὐκ ἔστιν ἐλπίς· ὃ γὰρ βλέπει τίς ἐλπίζει; ²⁵ εἰ δὲ ὃ οὐ βλέπομεν ἐλπίζομεν, δι᾽ ὑπομονῆς ἀπεκδεχόμεθα. ¶ ²⁶ Ὡσαύτως δὲ καὶ τὸ πνεῦμα συναντιλαμβάνεται τῇ ἀσθενείᾳ ἡμῶν· τὸ γὰρ τί προσευξώμεθα καθὸ δεῖ οὐκ οἴδαμεν, ἀλλὰ αὐτὸ τὸ πνεῦμα ὑπερεντυγχάνει στεναγμοῖς ἀλαλήτοις· ²⁷ ὁ δὲ ἐραυνῶν τὰς καρδίας οἶδεν τί τὸ φρόνημα τοῦ πνεύματος, ὅτι κατὰ θεὸν ἐντυγχάνει ὑπὲρ ἁγίων.

^{8:28} οἴδαμεν δὲ ὅτι τοῖς ἀγαπῶσιν τὸν θεὸν πάντα συνεργεῖ εἰς ἀγαθόν, τοῖς κατὰ πρόθεσιν κλητοῖς οὖσιν. ²⁹ ὅτι οὓς προέγνω,

of his   Son,   that he   might be   the firstborn among many   brothers. **30** And those he predestined,
αὐτοῦ ⌐τοῦ υἱοῦ₎ εἰς αὐτόν →   ⌐τὸ εἶναι₎   πρωτότοκον ἐν   πολλοῖς ἀδελφοῖς   δὲ οὓς → προώρισεν   τούτους
r.gsm.3 d.gsm n.gsm p.a r.asm.3   d.asn f.pa   a.asm   p.d   a.dpm n.dpm   cj r.apm v.aai.3s   r.apm
5626 899 3836 5626 1650 899   3836 1639   4758   1877   4498 81   1254 4005 4633   4047

he also called;   those he called,   he also justified;   those he justified,   he also glorified. ¶
↱ καὶ ἐκάλεσεν καὶ οὓς → ἐκάλεσεν τούτους ↱ καὶ ἐδικαίωσεν δὲ οὓς → ἐδικαίωσεν τούτους ↱ καὶ ἐδόξασεν
adv v.aai.3s cj r.apm   v.aai.3s r.apm   adv v.aai.3s cj r.apm   v.aai.3s r.apm   adv v.aai.3s
2813 2779 2813 4005   2813 4047   2779 1467 1254 4005   1467 4047   1519 2779 1519

31 What, then, shall we say   in   response to this? If God   is for us,   who can be against us?   **32**   He who did
Τί οὖν →   → ἐροῦμεν πρὸς ←   ← ταῦτα εἰ ὁ θεός₎   ὑπὲρ ἡμῶν τίς   καθ᾽   ἡμῶν γε   ὅς
r.asn cj   v.fai.1p p.a   r.apn cj d.nsm n.nsm   p.g r.gp.1 r.nsm   p.g   r.gp.1 pl   r.nsm
5515 4036   3306 4639   4047 1623 3836 2536   5642 7005 5515   2848   7005 1145 4005 5767

not spare   his own Son, but   gave   him   up for us   all   – how will he not also, along with him, graciously
οὐκ ἐφείσατο τοῦ ἰδίου υἱοῦ ἀλλὰ παρέδωκεν αὐτόν ↰ ὑπὲρ ἡμῶν πάντων   πῶς ↱   οὐχὶ καὶ →   σὺν αὐτῷ χαρίσεται
pl v.ami.3s d.gsm a.gsm n.gsm cj v.aai.3s r.asm.3   p.g r.gp.1 a.gpm   pl   pl adv adv   p.d r.dsm.3 v.fmi.3s
4024 5767 3836 2625 5626 247 4140 899 4140 5642 7005 4246   4802   5919 5919 4049 2779   5250 899 5919

give us   all   things? **33** Who will bring any charge   against those whom God has chosen? It is God who justifies.
← ἡμῖν ⌐τὰ πάντα₎   ←   τίς → →   ἐγκαλέσει κατὰ   θεοῦ   ἐκλεκτῶν   θεὸς ὁ   δικαιῶν
r.dp.1 d.apn a.apn   r.nsm   v.fai.3s p.g   n.gsm   a.gpm   n.nsm d.nsm   pt.pa.nsm
7005 3836 4246   5515   1592 2848   2536   1723   2536 3836 1467

34 Who is he that condemns? Christ Jesus, who died   – more than that, who was raised to life –   is
τίς ὁ ←   κατακρινῶν Χριστὸς Ἰησοῦς ὁ   ἀποθανών δὲ μᾶλλον ←   ←   ἐγερθείς   ὃς καὶ ἐστιν
r.nsm d.nsm   pt.pa.nsm n.nsm n.nsm d.nsm   pt.aa.nsm cj adv.c   pt.ap.nsm   r.nsm adv v.pai.3s
5515 3836   2891 5986 2652 3836   633 1254 3437   1586   4005 2779 1639

at the right hand of God   and   is also interceding for us.   **35** Who shall separate us   from the love   of
ἐν δεξιᾷ ←   → ⌐τοῦ θεοῦ₎   ὃς ↱ καὶ ἐντυγχάνει ὑπὲρ ἡμῶν   τίς →   χωρίσει ἡμᾶς ἀπὸ τῆς ἀγάπης →
p.d a.dsf   d.gsm n.gsm   r.nsm adv v.pai.3s p.g r.gp.1   r.nsm   v.fai.3s r.ap.1 p.g d.gsf n.gsf
1877 1288   3836 2536   4005 1961 2779 1961 5642 7005   5515   6004 7005 608 3836 27

Christ?   Shall trouble or hardship or persecution or famine or nakedness or danger or sword? **36** As   it is
⌐τοῦ Χριστοῦ₎ θλῖψις ἢ στενοχωρία ἢ διωγμὸς ἢ λιμὸς ἢ γυμνότης ἢ κίνδυνος ἢ μάχαιρα καθὼς →   →
d.gsm n.gsm n.nsf cj n.nsf cj n.nsm cj n.nsm cj n.nsf cj n.nsm cj n.nsf
3836 5986 2568 2445 5103 2445 1501 2445 3350 2445 1219 2445 3074 2445 3479 ?777

written: "For your sake we face death   all   day   long; we are considered as sheep   to be
γέγραπται ὅτι ἕνεκεν σοῦ ↰   →   → θανατούμεθα ὅλην ⌐τὴν ἡμέραν₎   →   → ἐλογίσθημεν ὡς πρόβατα → →
v.rpi.3s cj p.g r.gs.2   v.ppi.1p a.asf d.asf n.asf   v.api.1p cj n.npn
1211 4022 1914 5148 1914   2506 3910 3836 2465 3910   3357 6055 4585

slaughtered." **37** No, in all   these   things we are more than conquerors through him who loved   us. **38** For I am
σφαγῆς ἀλλ᾽ ἐν πᾶσιν τούτοις ←   → ← → ὑπερνικῶμεν διὰ   τοῦ   ἀγαπήσαντος ἡμᾶς   γὰρ → →
n.gsf cj p.d a.dpn r.dpn   v.pai.1p p.g   d.gsm   pt.aa.gsm r.ap.1   cj
5375 247 1877 4246 4047   5664 1328   3836   26 7005   1142

convinced that neither death   nor life, neither angels nor demons, neither the present nor the future,   nor any
πέπεισμαι ὅτι οὔτε θάνατος οὔτε ζωὴ οὔτε ἄγγελοι οὔτε ἀρχαὶ οὔτε ἐνεστῶτα οὔτε μέλλοντα οὔτε
v.rpi.1s cj cj n.nsm cj n.nsf cj n.npm cj n.npf cj pt.ra.npn cj pt.pa.npn cj
4275 4022 4046 2505 4046 2437 4046 34 4046 794 4046 1931 4046 3516 4046

powers, **39** neither height nor depth, nor anything else in all creation, will be able   to separate us   from the love
δυνάμεις οὔτε   ὕψωμα οὔτε βάθος οὔτε τις   ἑτέρα   κτίσις →   → δυνήσεται → χωρίσαι ἡμᾶς ἀπὸ τῆς ἀγάπης
n.npf cj   n.nsn cj n.nsn cj r.nsn   r.nsf   n.nsf   v.fpi.3s   f.aa r.ap.1 p.g d.gsf n.gsf
1539 4046   5739 4046 958 4046 5516   2283   3232   1538   6004 7005 608 3836 27

of God   that is in Christ Jesus our Lord.
→ ⌐τοῦ θεοῦ₎ τῆς   ἐν Χριστῷ Ἰησοῦ ἡμῶν ⌐τῷ κυρίῳ₎
d.gsm n.gsm d.gsf p.d n.dsm n.dsm r.gp.1 d.dsm n.dsm
3836 2536 3836 1877 5986 2652 7005 3836 3261

God's Sovereign Choice

9:1 I speak the truth   in Christ – I   am not lying,   my conscience   confirms   it in the Holy
→ λέγω   Ἀλήθειαν ἐν Χριστῷ ↰   → οὐ ψεύδομαι μου ⌐τῆς συνειδήσεως₎ συμμαρτυρούσης μοι ἐν   ἁγίῳ
v.pai.1s n.asf p.d n.dsm   pl v.pmi.1s r.gs.1 d.gsf n.gsf pt.pa.gsf r.ds.1 p.d a.dsn
3306 237 1877 5986   6017 6017 4024 6017 1609 3836 5287 5210 1609 1877 41

καὶ προώρισεν συμμόρφους τῆς εἰκόνος τοῦ υἱοῦ αὐτοῦ, εἰς τὸ εἶναι αὐτὸν πρωτότοκον ἐν πολλοῖς ἀδελφοῖς· **30** οὓς δὲ προώρισεν, τούτους καὶ ἐκάλεσεν· καὶ οὓς ἐκάλεσεν, τούτους καὶ ἐδικαίωσεν· οὓς δὲ ἐδικαίωσεν, τούτους καὶ ἐδόξασεν. ¶ **31** Τί οὖν ἐροῦμεν πρὸς ταῦτα; εἰ ὁ θεὸς ὑπὲρ ἡμῶν, τίς καθ᾽ ἡμῶν; **32** ὅς γε τοῦ ἰδίου υἱοῦ οὐκ ἐφείσατο ἀλλὰ ὑπὲρ ἡμῶν πάντων παρέδωκεν αὐτόν, πῶς οὐχὶ καὶ σὺν αὐτῷ τὰ πάντα ἡμῖν χαρίσεται; **33** τίς ἐγκαλέσει κατὰ ἐκλεκτῶν θεοῦ; θεὸς ὁ δικαιῶν· **34** τίς ὁ κατακρινῶν; Χριστὸς [Ἰησοῦς] ὁ ἀποθανών, μᾶλλον δὲ ἐγερθείς, ὃς καί ἐστιν ἐν δεξιᾷ τοῦ θεοῦ, ὃς καὶ ἐντυγχάνει ὑπὲρ ἡμῶν. **35** τίς ἡμᾶς χωρίσει ἀπὸ τῆς ἀγάπης τοῦ Χριστοῦ; θλῖψις ἢ στενοχωρία ἢ διωγμὸς ἢ λιμὸς ἢ γυμνότης ἢ κίνδυνος ἢ μάχαιρα; **36** καθὼς γέγραπται ὅτι Ἕνεκεν σοῦ θανατούμεθα ὅλην τὴν ἡμέραν, ἐλογίσθημεν ὡς πρόβατα σφαγῆς. **37** ἀλλ᾽ ἐν τούτοις πᾶσιν ὑπερνικῶμεν διὰ τοῦ ἀγαπήσαντος ἡμᾶς. **38** πέπεισμαι γὰρ ὅτι οὔτε θάνατος οὔτε ζωὴ οὔτε ἄγγελοι οὔτε ἀρχαὶ οὔτε ἐνεστῶτα οὔτε μέλλοντα οὔτε δυνάμεις **39** οὔτε ὕψωμα οὔτε βάθος οὔτε τις κτίσις ἑτέρα δυνήσεται ἡμᾶς χωρίσαι ἀπὸ τῆς ἀγάπης τοῦ θεοῦ τῆς ἐν Χριστῷ Ἰησοῦ τῷ κυρίῳ ἡμῶν.

9:1 Ἀλήθειαν λέγω ἐν Χριστῷ, οὐ ψεύδομαι, συμμαρτυρούσης μοι τῆς συνειδήσεώς μου ἐν πνεύματι ἁγίῳ, **2** ὅτι λύπη μοί

Spirit — 2 I have great sorrow and unceasing anguish in my heart. 3 For I could wish that I myself
πνεύματι ὅτι μοί ἐστιν μεγάλη λύπη καὶ ἀδιάλειπτος ὀδύνη → μου τῇ καρδίᾳ. γὰρ → → ηὐχόμην ἐγὼ αὐτὸς
n.dsn cj r.ds.1 v.pai.3s a.nsf n.nsf cj a.nsf n.nsf r.gs.1 d.dsf n.dsf cj v.imi.1s r.ns.1 r.nsm
4460 4022 1609 1639 3489 3383 2779 89 3850 2840 1609 3836 2840 1142 2377 1609 899

were cursed and cut off from Christ for the sake of my brothers, those of my own race, 4
εἶναι ἀνάθεμα ← ← ← ἀπὸ τοῦ Χριστοῦ ὑπὲρ ← ← μου τῶν ἀδελφῶν τῶν → μου κατὰ σάρκα, συγγενῶν οἵτινες
f.pa n.nsn p.g d.gsm n.gsm p.g r.gs.1 d.gpm d.gpm r.gs.1 p.a n.asf n.gpm r.npm
1639 353 608 3836 5986 5642 1609 3836 81 3836 2848 1609 2848 4922 5150 4015

the people of Israel. Theirs is the adoption as sons; theirs the divine glory, the covenants, the
εἰσιν → Ἰσραηλῖται ὧν ἡ υἱοθεσία ← ← καὶ ἡ δόξα καὶ αἱ διαθῆκαι καὶ ἡ
v.pai.3p n.npm r.gpm d.nsf n.nsf cj d.nsf n.nsf cj d.npf n.npf cj d.nsf
1639 2703 4005 3836 5625 2779 3836 1518 2779 3836 1347 2779 3836

receiving of the law, the temple worship and the promises. 5 Theirs are the patriarchs, and from them is
→ → → νομοθεσία καὶ ἡ λατρεία καὶ αἱ ἐπαγγελίαι ὧν οἱ πατέρες καὶ ἐξ ὧν
n.nsf cj d.nsf n.nsf cj d.npf n.npf r.gpm d.npm n.npm cj p.g r.gpm
3792 2779 3836 3301 2779 3836 2039 4005 3836 4252 2779 1666 4005

traced the human ancestry of Christ, who is God over all, forever praised! Amen. ¶
τὸ κατὰ σάρκα, ← ὁ Χριστὸς ὁ ὢν θεὸς ἐπὶ πάντων εἰς τοὺς αἰῶνας, εὐλογητὸς ἀμήν.
d.asn p.a n.asf d.nsm n.nsm d.nsm n.nsm v.pt.pa.nsm n.nsm p.g a.gpm p.a d.apm n.apm a.nsm pl
3836 2848 4922 3836 5986 3836 1639 2536 2093 4246 1650 3836 172 2329 297

6 It is not as though God's word had failed. For not all who are descended from Israel are
δὲ Οὐχ οἷον ← ὅτι τοῦ θεοῦ ὁ λόγος, → ἐκπέπτωκεν γὰρ οὐ πάντες οἱ ἐξ Ἰσραὴλ οὗτοι
cj pl r.nsn cj d.gsm n.gsm d.nsm n.nsm v.rai.3s cj pl a.npm d.npm p.g n.nsm r.npm
1254 4024 3888 4022 3836 2536 3836 3364 1738 1142 4024 4246 3836 1666 2702 4047

Israel. 7 Nor because they are his descendants are they all Abraham's children. On the contrary, "It is through
Ἰσραήλ οὐδ ὅτι → εἰσιν σπέρμα πάντες Ἀβραὰμ τέκνα → → ἀλλ ἐν
n.nsm cj cj v.pai.3p n.nsn a.npm n.gsm n.npn cj p.d
2702 4028 4022 1639 5065 4246 11 5451 247 1877

Isaac that your offspring will be reckoned." 8 In other words, it is not the natural children who are God's
Ἰσαὰκ σοι σπέρμα → → κληθήσεται τοῦτ ἐστιν οὐ τὰ τῆς σαρκὸς τέκνα ταῦτα τοῦ θεοῦ,
n.dsm r.ds.2 n.nsn v.fpi.3s r.nsn v.pai.3s pl d.npn d.gsf n.gsf n.npn r.npn d.gsn n.gsn
2693 5148 5065 2813 4047 1639 4024 3836 3836 4922 5451 4047 3836 2536

children, but it is the children of the promise who are regarded as Abraham's offspring. 9 For this was how the
τέκνα ἀλλὰ τὰ τέκνα → τῆς ἐπαγγελίας → λογίζεται εἰς σπέρμα γὰρ οὗτος
n.npn cj d.npn n.npn d.gsf n.gsf v.ppi.3s p.a n.asn cj r.nsm
5451 247 3836 5451 3836 2039 3357 1650 5065 1142 4047

promise was stated: "At the appointed time I will return, and Sarah will have a son." ¶ 10 Not
ἐπαγγελίας ὁ λόγος, κατὰ τὸν τοῦτον καιρὸν → ἐλεύσομαι καὶ τῇ Σάρρᾳ → ἔσται υἱός. δὲ Οὐ
n.gsf d.nsm n.nsm p.a d.asm r.asm n.asm v.fmi.1s cj d.dsf n.dsf v.fmi.3s n.nsm cj pl
2039 3836 3364 2848 3836 4047 2789 2262 2779 3836 4925 1639 5626 1254 4024

only that, but Rebekah's children had one and the same father, our father Isaac. 11 Yet, before the
μόνον ἀλλὰ καὶ Ῥεβέκκα κοίτην ἔχουσα, ἐξ ἑνός ἡμῶν τοῦ πατρὸς, Ἰσαὰκ γὰρ μήπω
adv cj adv n.nsf n.asf pt.pa.nsf p.g a.gsm r.gp.1 d.gsm n.gsm n.gsm cj adv
3667 247 2779 4831 3130 2400 1666 1651 7005 3836 4252 2693 1142 3609

twins were born or had done anything good or bad — in order that God's purpose in
→ γεννηθέντων μηδὲ → πραξάντων τι ἀγαθὸν ἢ φαῦλον ἵνα ← ← τοῦ θεοῦ, ἡ πρόθεσις κατ
pt.ap.gpm cj pt.aa.gpm r.asn a.asn cj a.asn cj d.gsm n.gsm d.nsf n.nsf p.a
1164 3593 4556 5516 19 2445 5765 2671 3836 2536 3836 4606 2848

election might stand: 12 not by works but by him who calls — she was told, "The older will serve the
ἐκλογὴν → μένῃ οὐκ ἐξ ἔργων ἀλλ ἐκ τοῦ καλοῦντος αὐτῇ → ἐρρέθη ὅτι ὁ μείζων → δουλεύσει τῷ
n.asf v.pas.3s pl p.g n.gpn cj p.g d.gsm pt.pa.gsm r.dsf.3 v.api.3s cj d.nsm a.nsm.c v.fai.3s d.dsm
1724 3531 4024 1666 2240 247 1666 3836 2813 899 3306 4022 3836 3489 1526 3836

younger." 13 Just as it is written: "Jacob I loved, but Esau I hated." ¶ 14 What then shall we say?
ἐλάσσονι καθὼς ← → γέγραπται, τὸν Ἰακὼβ → ἠγάπησα δὲ τὸν Ἠσαῦ, ἐμίσησα Τί οὖν → → ἐροῦμεν μὴ
a.dsm.c cj v.rpi.3s d.asm n.asm v.aai.1s cj d.asm n.asm v.aai.1s r.asn cj v.fai.1p pl
1781 2777 1211 3836 2609 26 1254 3836 2481 3631 5515 4036 3306 3590

ἐστιν μεγάλη καὶ ἀδιάλειπτος ὀδύνη τῇ καρδίᾳ μου. 3 ηὐχόμην γὰρ ἀνάθεμα εἶναι αὐτὸς ἐγὼ ἀπὸ τοῦ Χριστοῦ ὑπὲρ τῶν ἀδελφῶν μου τῶν συγγενῶν μου κατὰ σάρκα, 4 οἵτινές εἰσιν Ἰσραηλῖται, ὧν ἡ υἱοθεσία καὶ ἡ δόξα καὶ αἱ διαθῆκαι καὶ ἡ νομοθεσία καὶ ἡ λατρεία καὶ αἱ ἐπαγγελίαι, 5 ὧν οἱ πατέρες καὶ ἐξ ὧν ὁ Χριστὸς τὸ κατὰ σάρκα, ὁ ὢν ἐπὶ πάντων θεὸς εὐλογητὸς εἰς τοὺς αἰῶνας, ἀμήν. ¶ 6 Οὐχ οἷον δὲ ὅτι ἐκπέπτωκεν ὁ λόγος τοῦ θεοῦ. οὐ γὰρ πάντες οἱ ἐξ Ἰσραὴλ οὗτοι Ἰσραήλ· 7 οὐδ ὅτι εἰσὶν σπέρμα Ἀβραὰμ πάντες τέκνα, ἀλλ, Ἐν Ἰσαὰκ κληθήσεταί σοι σπέρμα. 8 τοῦτ ἔστιν, οὐ τὰ τέκνα τῆς σαρκὸς ταῦτα τέκνα τοῦ θεοῦ ἀλλὰ τὰ τέκνα τῆς ἐπαγγελίας λογίζεται εἰς σπέρμα. 9 ἐπαγγελίας γὰρ ὁ λόγος οὗτος, Κατὰ τὸν καιρὸν τοῦτον ἐλεύσομαι καὶ ἔσται τῇ Σάρρᾳ υἱός. ¶ 10 οὐ μόνον δέ, ἀλλὰ καὶ Ῥεβέκκα ἐξ ἑνὸς κοίτην ἔχουσα, Ἰσαὰκ τοῦ πατρὸς ἡμῶν· 11 μήπω γὰρ γεννηθέντων μηδὲ πραξάντων τι ἀγαθὸν ἢ φαῦλον, ἵνα ἡ κατ ἐκλογὴν πρόθεσις τοῦ θεοῦ μένῃ, 12 οὐκ ἐξ ἔργων ἀλλ ἐκ τοῦ καλοῦντος, ἐρρέθη αὐτῇ ὅτι Ὁ μείζων δουλεύσει τῷ ἐλάσσονι, 13 καθὼς γέγραπται, Τὸν Ἰακὼβ ἠγάπησα, τὸν δὲ Ἠσαῦ ἐμίσησα ¶

Is God unjust? Not at all! **15** For he says to Moses, "I will have mercy on whom I have mercy,
παρὰ ⌐τῷ θεῷ⌐ ἀδικία ⌐μὴ γένοιτο⌐ ← γὰρ λέγει → ⌐τῷ Μωϋσεῖ⌐ ἐλεήσω ← ⌐ὃν ἂν⌐ → ἐλεῶ
p.d d.dsm n.dsm n.nsf pl v.amo.3s cj v.pai.3s d.dsm n.dsm v.fai.1s r.asm pl v.pas.1s
4123 3836 2536 94 3590 1181 1142 3306 3836 3707 1796 4005 323 1796

and I will have compassion on whom I have compassion." **16** It does not, therefore, depend on man's desire
καὶ → → οἰκτιρήσω ← ⌐ὃν ἂν⌐ → οἰκτίρω ⌐οὐ ⌐ἄρα οὖν⌐ → ⌐τοῦ θέλοντος⌐
cj v.fai.1s r.asm pl v.pas.1s pl cj cj d.gsm pt.pa.gsm
2779 3882 4005 323 3882 4024 726 4036 3836 2527

or effort, but on God's mercy. **17** For the Scripture says to Pharaoh: "I raised you up for this
οὐδὲ ⌐τοῦ τρέχοντος⌐ ἀλλὰ → θεοῦ ⌐τοῦ ἐλεῶντος⌐ γὰρ ἡ γραφὴ λέγει ⌐τῷ Φαραώ⌐ ὅτι → ἐξήγειρά σε ← εἰς τοῦτο
cj d.gsm pt.pa.gsm cj n.gsm d.gsm pt.pa.gsm cj d.nsf n.nsf v.pai.3s d.dsm n.dsm cj v.aai.1s r.as.2 p.a r.asn
4028 3836 5556 247 1796 2536 3836 1790 1142 3836 1210 3306 3836 5755 4022 1995 5148 1995 1650 4047

very purpose, that I might display my power in you and that my name might be proclaimed in all
αὐτὸ ← ὅπως → ἐνδείξωμαι μου ⌐τὴν δύναμίν⌐ ἐν σοὶ καὶ ὅπως μου ⌐τὸ ὄνομα⌐ → → διαγγελῇ ἐν πάσῃ
r.asn cj v.ams.1s r.gs.1 d.asf n.asf p.d r.ds.2 cj cj r.gs.1 d.asn n.asn v.aps.3s p.d a.dsf
899 4047 3968 1892 1609 3836 1539 1877 5148 2779 3968 1609 3836 3950 1334 1877 4246

the earth." **18** Therefore God has mercy on whom he wants to have mercy, and he hardens whom he wants to harden.
τῇ γῇ ⌐ἄρα οὖν⌐ → ἐλεεῖ ← ὃν → θέλει δὲ σκληρύνει ὃν → θέλει
d.dsf n.dsf cj cj v.pai.3s r.asm v.pai.3s cj v.pai.3s r.asm v.pai.3s
3836 1178 726 4036 1796 4005 2527 1254 5020 4005 2527

¶ **19** One of you will say to me: "Then why does God still blame us? For who resists his will?"
οὖν → → Ἐρεῖς μοι οὖν τί → ἔτι μέμφεται γὰρ τίς ἀνθέστηκεν αὐτοῦ ⌐τῷ βουλήματι⌐
cj v.fai.2s r.ds.1 cj r.asn adv v.pmi.3s cj r.nsm v.rai.3s r.gsm.3 d.dsn n.dsn
4036 3306 1609 4036 5515 2285 3522 1142 5515 468 899 3836 1088

20 But who are you, O man, to talk back to God? "Shall what is formed say to him who
μενοῦνγε τίς εἶ σὺ ὦ ἄνθρωπε → → ὁ ἀνταποκρινόμενος → ⌐τῷ θεῷ⌐ μὴ → τὸ πλάσμα ἐρεῖ → τῷ ←
pl r.nsm v.pai.2s r.ns.2 j n.vsm d.nsm pt.pm.nsm d.dsm n.dsm pl d.nsn n.nsn v.fai.3s d.dsm
3529 5515 1639 5148 6043 476 3836 503 3836 2536 3590 3836 4420 3306 3836

formed it, 'Why did you make me like this?'" **21** Does not the potter have the right to make out of the
πλάσαντι τί → ἐποίησας με οὕτως ἢ → οὐκ ὁ κεραμεὺς ἔχει ἐξουσίαν → ποιῆσαι ἐκ ← τοῦ
pt.aa.dsm r.asn v.aai.2s r.as.1 adv cj pl d.nsm n.nsm v.pai.3s n.asf f.aa p.g d.gsn
4421 5515 4472 1609 4048 2445 2400 4024 3836 3038 2400 2026 4472 1666 3836

same lump of clay some pottery for noble purposes and some for common use? ¶ **22** What if
αὐτοῦ φυράματος → ⌐τοῦ πηλοῦ⌐ μὲν ὃ σκεῦος εἰς τιμὴν ← δὲ ὃ εἰς ἀτιμίαν ← δὲ εἰ
r.gsn n.gsn d.gsm n.gsm cj r.asn n.asn p.a n.asf pl r.asn p.a n.asf cj cj
899 5878 3836 4384 3525 4005 5007 1650 5507 1254 4005 1650 871 1254 1623

God, choosing to show his wrath and make his power known, bore with great patience the
ὁ θεός θέλων → ἐνδείξασθαι τὴν ὀργὴν καὶ → αὐτοῦ ⌐τὸ δυνατόν⌐ γνωρίσαι ἤνεγκεν ἐν πολλῇ μακροθυμίᾳ
d.nsm n.nsm pt.pa.nsm f.am d.asf n.asf cj r.gsm.3 d.asn a.asn f.aa v.aai.3s p.d a.dsf n.dsf
3836 2536 2527 1892 3836 3973 2779 1192 899 3836 1543 1192 5770 1877 4498 3429

objects of his wrath – prepared for destruction? **23** What if he did this to make the riches of his glory
σκεύη → ὀργῆς κατηρτισμένα εἰς ἀπώλειαν καὶ ἵνα → τὸν πλοῦτον → αὐτοῦ ⌐τῆς δόξης⌐
n.apn n.gsf pt.rp.apn p.a n.asf cj cj d.asm n.asm r.gsm.3 d.gsf n.gsf
5007 3973 2936 1650 724 2779 2671 1192 3836 4458 1518 899 3836 1518

known to the objects of his mercy, whom he prepared in advance for glory – **24** even us, whom he also called,
γνωρίσῃ ἐπὶ σκεύη → ἐλέους ἃ → προητοίμασεν ← ← εἰς δόξαν ἡμᾶς Οὓς → καὶ ἐκάλεσεν
v.aas.3s p.a n.apn n.gsn r.apn v.aai.3s p.a n.asf r.ap.1 r.apm adv v.aai.3s
1192 2093 5007 1799 4005 4602 1650 1518 7005 4005 2813 2779 2813

not only from the Jews but also from the Gentiles? **25** As he says in Hosea: "I will call them 'my
οὐ μόνον ἐξ Ἰουδαίων ἀλλὰ καὶ ἐξ ἐθνῶν ὡς καὶ → λέγει ἐν ⌐τῷ Ὡσηὲ⌐ → καλέσω μου
pl adv p.g a.gpm cj adv p.g n.gpn cj adv v.pai.3s p.d d.dsm n.dsm v.fai.1s r.gs.1
4024 3667 1666 2681 247 2779 1666 1620 6055 2779 3306 1877 3836 6060 2813 1609

people' who are not my people; and I will call her 'my loved one' who is not my loved one," **26** and, "It will
λαόν τὸν οὐ μου λαόν καὶ ἠγαπημένην τὴν οὐκ ἠγαπημένην ← καὶ
n.asm d.asm pl r.gs.1 n.asm cj pt.rp.asf d.asf pl pt.rp.asf cj
3295 3836 4024 1609 3295 2779 26 3836 4024 26 2779

14 Τί οὖν ἐροῦμεν; μὴ ἀδικία παρὰ τῷ θεῷ; μὴ γένοιτο. **15** τῷ Μωϋσεῖ γὰρ λέγει, Ἐλεήσω ὃν ἂν ἐλεῶ καὶ οἰκτιρήσω ὃν ἂν οἰκτίρω. **16** ἄρα οὖν οὐ τοῦ θέλοντος οὐδὲ τοῦ τρέχοντος ἀλλὰ τοῦ ἐλεῶντος θεοῦ. **17** λέγει γὰρ ἡ γραφὴ τῷ Φαραὼ ὅτι Εἰς αὐτὸ τοῦτο ἐξήγειρά σε ὅπως ἐνδείξωμαι ἐν σοὶ τὴν δύναμίν μου καὶ ὅπως διαγγελῇ τὸ ὄνομά μου ἐν πάσῃ τῇ γῇ. **18** ἄρα οὖν ὃν θέλει ἐλεεῖ, ὃν δὲ θέλει σκληρύνει. ¶ **19** Ἐρεῖς μοι οὖν, Τί [οὖν] ἔτι μέμφεται; τῷ γὰρ βουλήματι αὐτοῦ τίς ἀνθέστηκεν; **20** ὦ ἄνθρωπε, μενοῦνγε σὺ τίς εἶ ὁ ἀνταποκρινόμενος τῷ θεῷ; μὴ ἐρεῖ τὸ πλάσμα τῷ πλάσαντι, Τί με ἐποίησας οὕτως; **21** ἢ οὐκ ἔχει ἐξουσίαν ὁ κεραμεὺς τοῦ πηλοῦ ἐκ τοῦ αὐτοῦ φυράματος ποιῆσαι ὃ μὲν εἰς τιμὴν σκεῦος ὃ δὲ εἰς ἀτιμίαν; ¶ **22** εἰ δὲ θέλων ὁ θεὸς ἐνδείξασθαι τὴν ὀργὴν καὶ γνωρίσαι τὸ δυνατὸν αὐτοῦ ἤνεγκεν ἐν πολλῇ μακροθυμίᾳ σκεύη ὀργῆς κατηρτισμένα εἰς ἀπώλειαν, **23** καὶ ἵνα γνωρίσῃ τὸν πλοῦτον τῆς δόξης αὐτοῦ ἐπὶ σκεύη ἐλέους ἃ προητοίμασεν εἰς δόξαν; **24** οὓς καὶ ἐκάλεσεν ἡμᾶς οὐ μόνον ἐξ Ἰουδαίων ἀλλὰ καὶ ἐξ ἐθνῶν, **25** ὡς καὶ ἐν τῷ Ὡσηὲ λέγει, Καλέσω τὸν οὐ λαόν μου λαόν μου καὶ τὴν οὐκ ἠγαπημένην ἠγαπημένην· **26** καὶ ἔσται ἐν τῷ τόπῳ οὗ ἐρρέθη αὐτοῖς, Οὐ λαός μου ὑμεῖς, ἐκεῖ κληθήσονται υἱοὶ

happen that in the very place where it was said to them, 'You are not my people,' they will be called
ἔσται ἐν τῷ τόπῳ οὗ → ἐρρέθη → αὐτοῖς ὑμεῖς οὐ μου λαός ἐκεῖ → → κληθήσονται
v.fmi.3s p.d d.dsm n.dsm adv v.api.3s r.dpm.3 r.np.2 pl r.gs.1 n.nsm adv v.fpi.3p
1639 1877 3836 5536 4023 3306 899 7007 4024 1609 3295 1695 2813

'sons of the living God.'" ¶ [27] Isaiah cries out concerning Israel: "Though the number of the
υἱοὶ → ζῶντος θεοῦ δὲ Ἠσαΐας κράζει ← ὑπὲρ ⌐τοῦ Ἰσραὴλ⌐ ἐὰν ὁ ἀριθμὸς → τῶν
n.npm pt.pa.gsm n.gsm cj n.nsm v.pai.3s p.g d.gsn n.gsm cj d.nsm n.nsm d.gpm
5626 2536 2409 2536 1254 2480 3189 5642 3836 2702 1569 3836 750 5626 3836

Israelites be like the sand by the sea, only the remnant will be saved. [28] For the Lord will carry out his
⌐υἱῶν Ἰσραὴλ⌐ ᾖ ὡς ἡ ἄμμος → τῆς θαλάσσης τὸ ὑπόλειμμα → σωθήσεται γὰρ κύριος → ποιήσει ←
n.gpm n.gsm v.pas.3s pl d.nsf n.nsf d.gsf n.gsf d.nsn n.nsn v.fpi.3s cj n.nsm v.fai.3s
5626 2702 1639 6055 3836 302 3836 2498 3836 5698 5392 1142 3261 4472

sentence on earth with speed and finality." ¶ [29] It is just as Isaiah said previously: "Unless the
λόγον ἐπὶ ⌐τῆς γῆς⌐ συντέμνων καὶ συντελῶν καὶ καθὼς ← Ἠσαΐας προείρηκεν ← ⌐εἰ μὴ⌐
n.asm p.g d.gsf n.gsf pt.pa.nsm cj pt.pa.nsm cj cj n.nsm v.rai.3s cj pl
3364 2093 3836 1178 5335 2779 5334 2779 2777 2480 4597 1623 3590

Lord Almighty had left us descendants, we would have become like Sodom, we would have been
κύριος σαβαὼθ → ἐγκατέλιπεν ἡμῖν σπέρμα ↱ ἂν → ἐγενήθημεν ὡς Σόδομα καὶ ↱ ἂν → →
n.nsm n.gpm v.aai.3s r.dp.1 n.asn pl v.api.1p pl n.npn cj pl
3261 4877 1593 7005 5065 1181 323 1181 6055 5047 2779 3929 323

like Gomorrah."
ὡμοιώθημεν ὡς Γόμορρα
v.api.1p pl n.nsf
3929 6055 1202

Israel's Unbelief

[9:30] What then shall we say? That the Gentiles, who did not pursue righteousness, have obtained it,
Τί οὖν → → ἐροῦμεν ὅτι ἔθνη τὰ μὴ διώκοντα δικαιοσύνην → κατέλαβεν δικαιοσύνην
r.asn cj v.fai.1p cj n.npn d.npn pl pt.pa.npn n.asf v.aai.3s n.asf
5515 4036 3306 4022 1620 3836 1503 3590 1503 1466 2898 1466

a righteousness that is by faith; [31] but Israel, who pursued a law of righteousness, has not attained it.
δὲ δικαιοσύνην τὴν ἐκ πίστεως δὲ Ἰσραὴλ → διώκων νόμον δικαιοσύνης ↱ οὐκ ἔφθασεν εἰς νόμον
cj n.asf d.asf p.g n.gsf cj n.nsm pt.pa.nsm n.asm n.gsf pl v.aai.3s p.a n.asm
1254 1466 3836 1666 4411 1254 2702 1503 3795 1466 5777 4024 5777 1650 3795

[32] Why not? Because they pursued it not by faith but as if it were by works. They stumbled over the
⌐διὰ τί⌐ ὅτι οὐκ ἐκ πίστεως ἀλλ' ὡς ← ἐξ ἔργων → προσέκοψαν ← τῷ
p.a r.asn cj pl p.g n.gsf cj pl p.g n.gpn v.aai.3p d.dsm
1328 5515 4022 4024 1666 4411 247 6055 1666 2240 4684 3836

"stumbling stone." [33] As it is written: "See, I lay in Zion a stone that causes men to stumble and a
⌐τοῦ προσκόμματος⌐ λίθῳ καθὼς → γέγραπται ἰδοὺ → τίθημι ἐν Σιὼν λίθον → → προσκόμματος καὶ
d.gsn n.gsn n.dsm cj v.rpi.3s j v.pai.1s p.d n.dsf n.asm n.gsn cj
3836 4682 3345 2777 1211 2627 5502 1877 4994 3345 4682 2779

rock that makes them fall, and the one who trusts in him will never be put to shame." ¶
πέτραν → → σκανδάλου καὶ ὁ ← πιστεύων ἐπ' αὐτῷ ↱ οὐ → → καταισχυνθήσεται
n.asf n.gsn cj d.nsm pt.pa.nsm p.d r.dsm.3 pl v.fpi.3s
4376 4998 2779 3836 4409 2093 899 2875 4024 2875

[10:1] Brothers, my heart's desire and prayer to God for the Israelites is that they may be saved.
Ἀδελφοί μὲν ἐμῆς ⌐τῆς καρδίας⌐ ἡ εὐδοκία καὶ ἡ δέησις πρὸς ⌐τὸν θεὸν⌐ ὑπὲρ r.gpm.3 εἰς σωτηρίαν
n.vpm n.gsf.1 d.gsf n.gsf d.nsf n.nsf cj d.nsf n.nsf p.a d.asm n.asm p.g p.a n.asf
81 3525 1847 3836 2840 3836 2306 2779 3836 1255 4639 3836 2536 5642 899 1650 5401

[2] For I can testify about them that they are zealous for God, but their zeal is not based on knowledge. [3] Since
γὰρ → μαρτυρῶ → αὐτοῖς ὅτι → ἔχουσιν ζῆλον → θεοῦ ἀλλ' οὐ κατ' ← ἐπίγνωσιν γὰρ
cj v.pai.1s r.dpm.3 cj v.pai.3p n.asm n.gsm cj pl p.a n.asf cj
1142 3455 899 4022 2400 2419 2536 247 4024 2848 2106 1142

they did not know the righteousness that comes from God and sought to establish their own,
→ ἀγνοοῦντες τὴν δικαιοσύνην → → ⌐τοῦ θεοῦ⌐ καὶ ζητοῦντες στῆσαι τὴν ἰδίαν
pt.pa.npm d.asf n.asf d.gsm n.gsm cj pt.pa.npm f.aa d.asf a.asf
51 3836 1466 3836 2536 2779 2426 2705 3836 2625

θεοῦ ζῶντος. ¶ [27] Ἠσαΐας δὲ κράζει ὑπὲρ τοῦ Ἰσραήλ, Ἐὰν ᾖ ὁ ἀριθμὸς τῶν υἱῶν Ἰσραὴλ ὡς ἡ ἄμμος τῆς θαλάσσης, τὸ ὑπόλειμμα σωθήσεται· [28] λόγον γὰρ συντελῶν καὶ συντέμνων ποιήσει κύριος ἐπὶ τῆς γῆς. ¶ [29] καὶ καθὼς προείρηκεν Ἠσαΐας, Εἰ μὴ κύριος Σαβαὼθ ἐγκατέλιπεν ἡμῖν σπέρμα, ὡς Σόδομα ἂν ἐγενήθημεν καὶ ὡς Γόμορρα ἂν ὡμοιώθημεν.

[9:30] Τί οὖν ἐροῦμεν; ὅτι ἔθνη τὰ μὴ διώκοντα δικαιοσύνην κατέλαβεν δικαιοσύνην, δικαιοσύνην δὲ τὴν ἐκ πίστεως, [31] Ἰσραὴλ δὲ διώκων νόμον δικαιοσύνης εἰς νόμον οὐκ ἔφθασεν. [32] διὰ τί; ὅτι οὐκ ἐκ πίστεως ἀλλ' ὡς ἐξ ἔργων· προσέκοψαν τῷ λίθῳ τοῦ προσκόμματος, [33] καθὼς γέγραπται, Ἰδοὺ τίθημι ἐν Σιὼν λίθον προσκόμματος καὶ πέτραν σκανδάλου, καὶ ὁ πιστεύων ἐπ' αὐτῷ οὐ καταισχυνθήσεται. [10:1] Ἀδελφοί, ἡ μὲν εὐδοκία τῆς ἐμῆς καρδίας καὶ ἡ δέησις πρὸς τὸν θεὸν ὑπὲρ αὐτῶν εἰς σωτηρίαν. [2] μαρτυρῶ γὰρ αὐτοῖς ὅτι ζῆλον θεοῦ ἔχουσιν ἀλλ' οὐ κατ' ἐπίγνωσιν· [3] ἀγνοοῦντες γὰρ τὴν τοῦ θεοῦ δικαιοσύνην καὶ τὴν ἰδίαν

they did not submit   to God's   righteousness. **4**   Christ is the end of the law   so that there
[δικαιοσύνην]   →   →   οὐχ ὑπετάγησαν →   ‚τοῦ θεοῦ‚ ‚τῇ δικαιοσύνῃ   γὰρ Χριστὸς   τέλος →   νόμου εἰς ←
n.asf   pl   v.api.3p   d.gsm n.gsm d.dsf n.dsf   cj   n.nsn   n.nsn   n.gsm p.a
1466   5718 5718 4024 5718   1466 3836 2536 3836 1466   1142 5986   5465   3795 1650

may be righteousness for everyone who believes. ¶ **5**   Moses describes in this way the righteousness that is
          δικαιοσύνην   →   παντὶ   τῷ   πιστεύοντι   γὰρ Μωϋσῆς γράφει   τὴν δικαιοσύνην   τὴν
          n.asf   a.dsm d.dsm pt.pa.dsm   cj   n.nsm   v.pai.3s   d.asf n.asf   d.asf
          1466   4246 3836 4409   1142 3707 1211   3836 1466   3836

by the law: "The man   who does   these things will live   by them." **6** But the righteousness that is by
ἐκ τοῦ νόμου ὅτι ὁ   ἄνθρωπος ← ποιήσας αὐτὰ ←   → ζήσεται ἐν αὐτοῖς   δὲ   ἡ   δικαιοσύνη   ἐκ
p.g d.gsm n.gsm cj d.nsm n.nsm   pt.aa.nsm r.apn.3   v.fmi.3s p.d r.dpn.3   cj   d.nsf n.nsf   p.g
1666 3836 3795 4022 3836 476   3836 4472 899   2409 1877 899   1254 3836 1466   1666

faith   says: "Do not say in your heart,   'Who will ascend   into heaven?'"   (that is, to bring Christ
πίστεως οὕτως λέγει →   μὴ εἴπῃς ἐν σου ‚τῇ καρδίᾳ τίς →   ἀναβήσεται εἰς ‚τὸν οὐρανόν‚ τοῦτ᾽ ἔστιν → →   Χριστὸν
n.gsf   adv   v.pai.3s   pl v.aas.2s p.d r.gs.2 d.dsf n.dsf r.nsm   v.fmi.3s p.a d.asm n.asm   r.nsn v.pai.3s   n.asm
4411   4048   3306 3306   3590 3306 1877 5148 3836 2840 5515   326   1650 3836 4041   4047 1639   2864 2864   5986

down) **7** "or 'Who will descend into the deep?'" (that is, to bring Christ up   from the dead). **8** But what
καταγαγεῖν   ἤ   τίς →   καταβήσεται εἰς τὴν ἄβυσσον τοῦτ᾽ ἔστιν →   Χριστὸν ἀναγαγεῖν ἐκ   νεκρῶν ἀλλὰ τί
f.aa   cj   r.nsm   v.fmi.3s p.a d.asf n.asf r.nsn v.pai.3s   n.asm f.aa p.g   a.gpm   cj   r.asn
2864   2445 5515   2849   1650 3836 12   4047 1639   343 343   5986 343 1666   3738   247 5515

does it say? "The word is   near you; it is in your mouth   and in your heart,"   that is,   the word of
→   → λέγει τὸ   ῥῆμα ἐστιν ἐγγύς σου   ἐν σου ‚τῷ στόματι‚ καὶ ἐν σου ‚τῇ καρδίᾳ‚ τοῦτ᾽ ἔστιν τὸ ῥῆμα →
      v.pai.3s d.nsn   n.nsn v.pai.3s adv r.gs.2   p.d r.gs.2 d.dsn n.dsn   cj p.d r.gs.2 d.dsf n.dsf   r.nsn v.pai.3s d.nsn n.nsn
      3306 3836   4839 1639 1584 5148   1877 5148 3836 5125   2779 1877 5148 3836 2840   4047 1639 3836 4839

faith   we are proclaiming: **9** That if you confess   with your mouth,   "Jesus is Lord," and believe in
‚τῆς πίστεως‚ ὃ   →   → κηρύσσομεν   ὅτι ἐὰν   ὁμολογήσῃς ἐν σου ‚τῷ στόματι‚ Ἰησοῦν   κύριον καὶ πιστεύσῃς ἐν
d.gsf n.gsf   r.asn   v.pai.1p   cj   cj   v.aas.2s p.d r.gs.2 d.dsn n.dsn n.asm   n.asm cj v.aas.2s p.d
3836 4411   4005   3062   4022 1569   3933 1877 5148 3836 5125 2652   3261 2779 4409 1877

your heart   that God   raised him from the dead, you will be saved. **10** For it is with your heart that you
σου ‚τῇ καρδίᾳ‚ ὅτι ὁ   θεὸς‚ ἤγειρεν αὐτὸν ἐκ   νεκρῶν →   → → σωθήσῃ   γὰρ   → →   καρδίᾳ   →
r.gs.2 d.dsf n.dsf cj d.nsm n.nsm v.aai.3s r.asm.3 p.g   a.gpm   v.fpi.2s   cj   n.dsf
5148 3836 2840 4022 3836 2536 1586 899 1666   3738   5392   1142   2840

believe *and are* justified,   and it is with your mouth that you confess *and are* saved. **11** As the Scripture says,
πιστεύεται   εἰς δικαιοσύνην δὲ   →   → στόματι → ὁμολογεῖται   εἰς σωτηρίαν   γὰρ ἡ γραφή   λέγει
v.ppi.3s   p.a n.asf   cj   n.dsn   v.ppi.3s   p.a n.asf   cj d.nsf n.nsf   v.pai.3s
4409   1650 1466   1254   5125   3933   1650 5401   1142 3836 1210   3306

"Anyone who trusts   in him will never be put to shame." **12** For there is   no difference between   Jew
πᾶς   ὁ   πιστεύων ἐπ᾽ αὐτῷ   οὐ →   → → καταισχυνθήσεται   γὰρ →   ἐστιν οὐ διαστολὴ →   τε Ἰουδαίου
a.nsm d.nsm pt.pa.nsm p.d r.dsm.3   pl   v.fpi.3s   cj   v.pai.3s pl n.nsf   cj a.gsm
4246 3836 4409 2093 899   2875 4024   2875   1142   1639 4024 1405   2681 5445 2681

and Gentile – the same Lord is Lord of all   and richly blesses   all   who call   on him, **13** for,
καὶ Ἕλληνος γὰρ ὁ αὐτὸς κύριος → πάντων   πλουτῶν ←   εἰς πάντας τοὺς ἐπικαλυμένους ← αὐτὸν γὰρ
cj n.gsm cj d.nsm r.nsm n.nsm   a.gpm   pt.pa.nsm   p.a a.apm d.apm pt.pm.apm   r.asm.3 cj
2779 1818 1142 3836 899 3261   4246   4456   1650 4246 3836 2126   899 1142

"Everyone who   calls   on the name of the Lord will be saved." ¶ **14** How, then, can they call
πᾶς   ‚ὃς ἂν‚ ἐπικαλέσηται ← τὸ ὄνομα → κυρίου → σωθήσεται   Πῶς οὖν   →   ἐπικαλέσωνται
a.nsm r.nsm pl v.ams.3s   d.asn n.asn   n.gsm   v.fpi.3s   adv cj   v.ams.3p
4246 4005 323 2126   3836 3950   3261   5392   4802 4036   2126

on the one they have not believed in? And how can they believe in the one of whom they have not heard? And
→ ὃν → → οὐκ ἐπίστευσαν εἰς δὲ   πῶς →   πιστεύσωσιν →   οὗ   →   οὐκ ἤκουσαν δὲ
r.asm   pl v.aai.3p p.a cj   cj   v.aas.3p   r.gsm   pl v.aai.3p cj
4005   4024 4409 1650 1254   4802   4409   4005   4024 201 1254

how can they hear   without someone preaching to them? **15** And how can they preach   unless   they are
πῶς →   ἀκούσωσιν χωρὶς →   κηρύσσοντος   δὲ πῶς   κηρύξωσιν ‚ἐὰν μὴ‚ → →
adv   v.aas.3p p.g   pt.pa.gsm   cj adv   v.aas.3p   cj pl
4802   201 6006   3062   1254 4802   3062   1569 3590

[δικαιοσύνην] ζητοῦντες στῆσαι, τῇ δικαιοσύνῃ τοῦ θεοῦ οὐχ ὑπετάγησαν· **4** τέλος γὰρ νόμου Χριστὸς εἰς δικαιοσύνην παντὶ τῷ πιστεύοντι ¶ **5** Μωϋσῆς γὰρ γράφει τὴν δικαιοσύνην τὴν ἐκ [τοῦ] νόμου ὅτι ὁ ποιήσας αὐτὰ ἄνθρωπος ζήσεται ἐν αὐτοῖς. **6** ἡ δὲ ἐκ πίστεως δικαιοσύνη οὕτως λέγει, Μὴ εἴπῃς ἐν τῇ καρδίᾳ σου, Τίς ἀναβήσεται εἰς τὸν οὐρανόν; τοῦτ᾽ ἔστιν Χριστὸν καταγαγεῖν· **7** ἤ, Τίς καταβήσεται εἰς τὴν ἄβυσσον; τοῦτ᾽ ἔστιν Χριστὸν ἐκ νεκρῶν ἀναγαγεῖν. **8** ἀλλὰ τί λέγει; Ἐγγύς σου τὸ ῥῆμά ἐστιν ἐν τῷ στόματί σου καὶ ἐν τῇ καρδίᾳ σου, τοῦτ᾽ ἔστιν τὸ ῥῆμα τῆς πίστεως ὃ κηρύσσομεν. **9** ὅτι ἐὰν ὁμολογήσῃς ἐν τῷ στόματί σου κύριον Ἰησοῦν καὶ πιστεύσῃς ἐν τῇ καρδίᾳ σου ὅτι ὁ θεὸς αὐτὸν ἤγειρεν ἐκ νεκρῶν, σωθήσῃ· **10** καρδίᾳ γὰρ πιστεύεται εἰς δικαιοσύνην, στόματι δὲ ὁμολογεῖται εἰς σωτηρίαν. **11** λέγει γὰρ ἡ γραφή, Πᾶς ὁ πιστεύων ἐπ᾽ αὐτῷ οὐ καταισχυνθήσεται. **12** οὐ γὰρ ἐστιν διαστολὴ Ἰουδαίου τε καὶ Ἕλληνος, ὁ γὰρ αὐτὸς κύριος πάντων, πλουτῶν εἰς πάντας τοὺς ἐπικαλουμένους αὐτόν· **13** Πᾶς γὰρ ὃς ἂν ἐπικαλέσηται τὸ ὄνομα κυρίου σωθήσεται. ¶ **14** Πῶς οὖν ἐπικαλέσωνται εἰς ὃν οὐκ ἐπίστευσαν; πῶς δὲ πιστεύσωσιν οὗ οὐκ ἤκουσαν; πῶς δὲ ἀκούσωσιν χωρὶς κηρύσσοντος; **15** πῶς δὲ κηρύξωσιν ἐὰν μὴ

sent?   As   it is written,   "How beautiful are the feet   of those who bring good   news!"   ¶
ἀποσταλῶσιν   καθὼς → → γέγραπται ὡς   ὡραῖοι   οἱ πόδες → τῶν ←   ⌐τὰ ἀγαθά⌐ εὐαγγελιζομένων
v.aps.3p   cj   v.rpi.3s   pl   a.npm   d.npm n.npm   d.gpn   d.apn a.apn   pt.pm.gpm
690   2777   1211   6055   6053   3836 4546   3836   2294   3836 19   2294

16 But not all   the Israelites accepted the good news.   For Isaiah   says, "Lord, who has believed our   message?"
Ἀλλ' οὐ πάντες   ὑπήκουσαν τῷ →   εὐαγγελίῳ γὰρ Ἠσαΐας λέγει κύριε   τίς → ἐπίστευσεν ἡμῶν ⌐τῇ ἀκοῇ⌐
cj   pl   a.npm   v.aai.3p   d.dsn →   n.dsn   cj   n.nsm   v.pai.3s   n.vsm   r.nsm → v.aai.3s   r.gp.1   d.dsf n.dsf
247   4024   4246   5634   3836   2295   1142   2480   3306   3261   5515   4409   7005   3836 198

17 Consequently, faith   comes from hearing the message, and the message is heard through the word   of Christ.
ἄρα   ⌐ἡ πίστις⌐   ἐξ ἀκοῆς   δὲ ἡ ἀκοὴ   διὰ   ῥήματος → Χριστοῦ
cj   d.nsf n.nsf   p.g n.gsf   cj d.nsf n.nsf   p.g   n.gsn   n.gsm
726   3836 4411   1666 198   1254 3836 198   1328   4839   5986

18 But I ask: Did they not hear?   Of   course they did: "Their voice   has gone out into all   the earth,
ἀλλὰ → λέγω μὴ →   οὐκ ἤκουσαν μενοῦνγε   αὐτῶν ὁ φθόγγος, → ἐξῆλθεν   εἰς πᾶσαν τὴν γῆν
cj   v.pai.1s pl →   pl v.aai.3p pl   r.gpm.3 d.nsm n.nsm → v.aai.3s   p.a a.asf d.asf n.asf
247   3306 3590 201   201 4024 201   3529   899 3836 5782   2002   1650 4246 3836 1178

their words   to the ends of the world."   **19** Again I ask: Did Israel not understand? First, Moses says,
καὶ αὐτῶν ⌐τὰ ῥήματα⌐ εἰς τὰ πέρατα → τῆς οἰκουμένης   ἀλλὰ → λέγω μὴ ⌐ Ἰσραὴλ οὐκ ἔγνω   πρῶτος Μωϋσῆς λέγει
cj   r.gpm.3 ⌐d.npn n.npn⌐ p.a d.apn n.apn → d.gsf n.gsf   cj → v.pai.1s pl ⌐ n.nsm pl v.aai.3s   a.nsm n.nsm v.pai.3s
2779   899 3836 4839   1650 3836 4306   3836 3876   247   3306 3590 1182   2702 4024 1182   4755 3707 3306

"I will make you envious   by those who are not a nation; I will make you angry   by a nation that has no
ἐγὼ ↱ → ὑμᾶς παραζηλώσω ἐπ'   οὐκ ἔθνει ↱ → ↱ ὑμᾶς παροργιῶ ἐπ'   ἔθνει → → →
r.ns.1   r.ap.2 v.fai.1s p.d   pl n.dsn   r.ap.2 v.fai.1s p.d   n.dsn
1609 4143 4143 7007 4143 2093   4024 1620   4239 4239 4239 7007 4239 2093   1620

understanding."   **20** And Isaiah boldly   says, "I was found by those who did not seek   me; I revealed myself to
ἀσυνέτῳ   δὲ Ἠσαΐας ἀποτολμᾷ καὶ λέγει   εὑρέθην ἐν τοῖς ←   μὴ ζητοῦσιν ἐμὲ → ἐγενόμην ἐμφανὴς →
a.dsn   cj n.nsm v.pai.3s cj v.pai.3s   v.api.1s p.d d.dpm   pl pt.pa.dpm r.as.1 v.ami.1s a.nsm
852   1254 2480 703 2779 3306   2351 1877 3836   2426 3590 2426 1609 1181 1871

those who did not ask   for me."   **21** But concerning Israel   he says, "All day   long I have held   out
τοῖς ←   μὴ ἐπερωτῶσιν ← ἐμὲ   δὲ πρὸς   τὸν Ἰσραὴλ → λέγει ὅλην ⌐τὴν ἡμέραν⌐ → → ἐξεπέτασα ←
d.dpm ←   pl pt.pa.dpm ← r.as.1   cj p.a   d.asm n.asm → v.pai.3s a.asf d.asf n.asf   v.aai.1s
3836   2089 3590 2089 1609   1254 4639   3836 2702   3306 3910 3836 2465   1736

my hands   to   a disobedient and obstinate people."
μου ⌐τὰς χεῖρας⌐ πρὸς ἀπειθοῦντα καὶ ἀντιλέγοντα λαόν
r.gs.1 d.apf n.apf p.a pt.pa.asm cj pt.pa.asm n.asm
1609 3836 5931 4639 578 2779 515 3295

The Remnant of Israel

11:1 I ask then: Did God   reject his   people? By no   means!   I am an Israelite
→ Λέγω οὖν μὴ ὁ θεὸς ἀπώσατο αὐτοῦ ⌐τὸν λαόν⌐ μὴ γένοιτο ← γὰρ καὶ → εἰμί Ἰσραηλίτης
v.pai.1s cj pl d.nsm n.nsm v.ami.3s r.gsm.3 d.asm n.asm pl v.amo.3s cj cj v.pai.1s n.nsm
3306 4036 3590 723 3836 2536 723 899 3836 3295 3590 1181 1142 2779 1639 2703

myself, a descendant   of Abraham, from the tribe of Benjamin. **2** God   did not reject his   people, whom he
ἐγὼ ἐκ σπέρματος → Ἀβραάμ → φυλῆς Βενιαμίν ⌐ὁ θεὸς⌐ → οὐκ ἀπώσατο αὐτοῦ ⌐τὸν λαόν⌐ ὃν →
r.ns.1 p.g n.gsn n.gsm n.gsf n.asf d.nsm n.nsm pl v.ami.3s r.gsm.3 d.asm n.asm r.asm
1609 1666 5065 11 5876 1021 3836 2536 723 4024 2536 899 3836 3295 4005

foreknew.   Don't you know what the Scripture says in the passage about Elijah – how he appealed to God
προέγνω ἢ οὐκ οἴδατε τί ἡ γραφή λέγει ἐν Ἠλίᾳ ὡς ἐντυγχάνει ⌐τῷ θεῷ⌐
v.aai.3s cj pl v.rai.2p r.asn d.nsf n.nsf v.pai.3s p.d n.dsm cj v.pai.3s d.dsm n.dsm
4589 2445 4024 3857 5515 3836 1210 3306 1877 2460 6055 1961 3836 2536

against Israel: **3** "Lord, they have killed   your prophets   and torn   down your altars;   I   am
κατὰ ⌐τοῦ Ἰσραήλ⌐ κύριε ἀπέκτειναν σου ⌐τοὺς προφήτας⌐ κατέσκαψαν ← σου ⌐τὰ θυσιαστήρια⌐ κἀγὼ →
p.g d.gsm n.gsm n.vsm v.aai.3p r.gs.2 d.apm n.apm v.aai.3p r.gs.2 d.apn n.apn crasis
2848 3836 2702 3261 650 5148 3836 4737 2940 5148 3836 2603 2743 5699

the only one left,   and they are trying to kill   me"? **4** And what was God's answer   to him? "I
μόνος ← ὑπελείφθην καὶ ζητοῦσιν ⌐τὴν ψυχήν μου⌐ ἀλλὰ τί λέγει → ὁ χρηματισμός → αὐτῷ →
a.nsm v.api.1s cj v.pai.3p d.asf n.asf r.gs.1 cj r.asn v.pai.3s d.nsm n.nsm r.dsm.3
3668 5699 2779 2426 3836 6034 1609 247 5515 3306 3836 5977 899

ἀποσταλῶσιν; καθὼς γέγραπται, Ὡς ὡραῖοι οἱ πόδες ⌐τῶν εὐαγγελιζομένων [τὰ] ἀγαθά. ¶ **16** Ἀλλ' οὐ πάντες ὑπήκουσαν τῷ εὐαγγελίῳ. Ἠσαΐας γὰρ λέγει, Κύριε, τίς ἐπίστευσεν τῇ ἀκοῇ ἡμῶν; **17** ἄρα ἡ πίστις ἐξ ἀκοῆς, ἡ δὲ ἀκοὴ διὰ ῥήματος Χριστοῦ. **18** ἀλλὰ λέγω, μὴ οὐκ ἤκουσαν; μενοῦνγε, Εἰς πᾶσαν τὴν γῆν ἐξῆλθεν ὁ φθόγγος αὐτῶν καὶ εἰς τὰ πέρατα τῆς οἰκουμένης τὰ ῥήματα αὐτῶν. **19** ἀλλὰ λέγω, μὴ Ἰσραὴλ οὐκ ἔγνω; πρῶτος Μωϋσῆς λέγει, Ἐγὼ παραζηλώσω ὑμᾶς ἐπ' οὐκ ἔθνει, ἐπ' ἔθνει ἀσυνέτῳ παροργιῶ ὑμᾶς. **20** Ἠσαΐας δὲ ἀποτολμᾷ καὶ λέγει, Εὑρέθην [ἐν] τοῖς ἐμὲ μὴ ζητοῦσιν, ἐμφανὴς ἐγενόμην τοῖς ἐμὲ μὴ ἐπερωτῶσιν. **21** πρὸς δὲ τὸν Ἰσραὴλ λέγει, Ὅλην τὴν ἡμέραν ἐξεπέτασα τὰς χεῖράς μου πρὸς λαὸν ἀπειθοῦντα καὶ ἀντιλέγοντα.

11:1 Λέγω οὖν, μὴ ἀπώσατο ὁ θεὸς τὸν λαὸν αὐτοῦ; μὴ γένοιτο· καὶ γὰρ ἐγὼ Ἰσραηλίτης εἰμί, ἐκ σπέρματος Ἀβραάμ, φυλῆς Βενιαμίν. **2** οὐκ ἀπώσατο ὁ θεὸς τὸν λαὸν αὐτοῦ ὃν προέγνω. ἢ οὐκ οἴδατε ἐν Ἠλίᾳ τί λέγει ἡ γραφή, ὡς ἐντυγχάνει τῷ θεῷ κατὰ τοῦ Ἰσραήλ; **3** Κύριε, τοὺς προφήτας σου ἀπέκτειναν, τὰ θυσιαστήρια σου κατέσκαψαν, κἀγὼ ὑπελείφθην μόνος καὶ ζητοῦσιν τὴν ψυχήν μου. **4** ἀλλὰ τί λέγει αὐτῷ ὁ χρηματισμός; Κατέλιπον ἐμαυτῷ ἑπτακισχιλίους ἄνδρας, οἵτινες οὐκ ἔκαμψαν

have reserved for myself seven   thousand   who have not bowed the knee to Baal."   **5** So too,
→ κατέλιπον → ἐμαυτῷ ἑπτακισχιλίους ←   ἄνδρας οἵτινες → οὐκ ἔκαμψαν γόνυ → ‚τῇ Βάαλ‚ οὖν οὕτως καὶ
v.aai.1s   r.dsm.1 a.apm   n.apm r.npm   pl v.aai.3p n.asn d.dsf n.dsm cj adv adv
2901   1831   2233   467   4015   2828 4024 2828 1205 3836 955 4036 4048 2779

at the present time there is   a remnant chosen   by grace. **6** And if by grace, then it is no   longer by
ἐν τῷ νῦν   καιρῷ → γέγονεν λεῖμμα ‚κατ᾽ ἐκλογὴν‚ → χάριτος δὲ εἰ → χάριτι   οὐκέτι ←   ἐξ
p.d d.dsm adv n.dsm v.rai.3s n.nsn p.a n.asf   n.gsf cj cj   n.dsf   adv   p.g
1877 3836 3814 2789 1181   3307 2848 1724   5921   1254 1623 5921   4033   1666

works; *if it were*, grace   would no   longer be   grace. ¶ **7** What then? What Israel sought so earnestly
ἔργων ἐπεὶ   ‚ἡ χάρις‚ →   οὐκέτι   γίνεται χάρις   Τί   οὖν ὁ   Ἰσραήλ ἐπιζητεῖ ←
n.gpn cj   d.nsf n.nsf   adv   v.pmi.3s n.nsf   r.nsn cj r.asn n.nsm v.pai.3s
2240 2075   3836 5921   4033   1181   5921   5515 4036 4005 2702 2118

it   did not obtain, but the elect did.   The others were hardened, **8** as   it is written: "God   gave
τοῦτο →   → οὐκ ἐπέτυχεν δὲ ἡ ἐκλογὴ ἐπέτυχεν δὲ οἱ λοιποὶ →   ἐπωρώθησαν καθὼς → γέγραπται ‚ὁ θεὸς‚ ἔδωκεν
r.asn   pl v.aai.3s cj d.nsf n.nsf v.aai.3s cj d.npm a.npm   v.api.3p   adv   v.rpi.3s d.nsm n.nsm v.aai.3s
4047   2209 2209 4024 2209 3836 1724 2209 1254 3836 3370   4800   2777   1211   3836 2536 1443

them a spirit of stupor,   eyes   *so that they could not see*   and ears *so that they could not hear,*
αὐτοῖς πνεῦμα → κατανύξεως ὀφθαλμοὺς →   μὴ ‚τοῦ βλέπειν‚ καὶ ὦτα →   μὴ ‚τοῦ ἀκούειν‚
r.dpm.3 n.asn   n.gsf   n.apm   pl d.gsn f.pa   cj n.apn   pl d.gsn f.pa
899   4460   2919   4057   1063 1063   3590 3836 1063 2779 4044 201 201 3590 3836 201

to this *very   day."* **9** And David says: "May their table   become   a snare and a trap,   a
ἕως τῆς σήμερον ἡμέρας καὶ Δαυὶδ λέγει "May αὐτῶν ἡ τράπεζα γενηθήτω εἰς παγίδα καὶ εἰς θήραν καὶ εἰς
p.g d.gsf adv   n.gsf cj n.nsm v.pai.3s   r.gpm.3 d.nsf n.nsf v.apm.3s p.a n.asf cj p.a n.asf cj p.a
2401 3836 4958 2465 2779 1253 3306   899 3836 5544 1181 1650 4075 2779 1650 2560 2779 1650

stumbling block and   a retribution for them. **10** May their eyes   be darkened   *so they cannot see,*
σκάνδαλον ←   καὶ εἰς ἀνταπόδομα → αὐτοῖς →   αὐτῶν οἱ ὀφθαλμοὶ → σκοτισθήτωσαν   μὴ ‚τοῦ βλέπειν‚
n.asn   cj p.a n.asn   r.dpm.3   r.gpm.3 d.npm n.npm v.apm.3p   pl d.gsn f.pa
4998   2779 1650 501   899 5029   899 3836 4057   5029   3590 3836 1063

and their backs   be bent   forever."
καὶ αὐτῶν ‚τὸν νῶτον‚ → σύγκαμψον ‚διὰ παντὸς‚
cj r.gpm.3 d.asm n.asm   v.aam.2s p.g a.gsm
2779 899 3836 3822   5159   1328 4246

Ingrafted Branches

11:11 Again I ask: Did they stumble so as to fall   beyond recovery? Not   at all! Rather, because of
οὖν → Λέγω μὴ →   → ἔπταισαν ἵνα ← πέσωσιν   μὴ γένοιτο ← ἀλλὰ → →
cj   v.pai.1s pl   v.aai.3p cj   v.aas.3p   pl v.amo.3s   cj
4036 3306 3590   4760 2671 4406   3590 1181   247   4183 4183

their transgression,   salvation has come to the Gentiles to make Israel envious. **12** But if their
αὐτῶν ‚τῷ παραπτώματι‚ ἡ σωτηρία →   τοῖς ἔθνεσιν εἰς → αὐτούς ‚τὸ παραζηλῶσαι‚ δὲ εἰ αὐτῶν
r.gpm.3 d.dsn n.dsn   d.nsf n.nsf   d.dpn n.dpn p.a r.apm.3 d.asn f.aa   cj cj r.gpm.3
899 3836 4183   3836 5401   3836 1620 1650 4143 899 3836 4143   1254 1623 899

transgression means riches for the world, and their loss   means riches for the Gentiles, how much greater
‚τὸ παράπτωμα‚   πλοῦτος →   κόσμου καὶ αὐτῶν ‚τὸ ἥττημα‚   πλοῦτος →   ἐθνῶν →   πόσῳ μᾶλλον
d.nsn n.nsn   n.nsm   n.gsm cj r.gpm.3 d.nsn n.nsn   n.nsm   n.gpn   r.dsn adv.c
3836 4183   4458   3180 2779 899 3836 2488   4458   1620   4531 3437

riches will their fullness   bring! ¶ **13** I am talking to you Gentiles.   Inasmuch as I am the
αὐτῶν ‚τὸ πλήρωμα‚ δὲ → λέγω →   ὑμῖν ‚τοῖς ἔθνεσιν‚ οὖν ‚ἐφ᾽ ὅσον‚ ← μὲν ἐγὼ εἰμι
r.gpm.3 d.nsn n.nsn cj   v.pai.1s r.dp.2 d.dpn n.dpn cj p.a r.asn   pl r.ns.1 v.pai.1s
899 3836 4445   1254   3306   7007 3836 1620 4036 2093 4012   3525 1609 1639

apostle to the Gentiles, I make much of my ministry   **14** *in the hope that* I may somehow arouse   my own
ἀπόστολος →   ἐθνῶν → δοξάζω ← μου ‚τὴν διακονίαν‚   εἴ →   πως παραζηλώσω μου τὴν
n.nsm   n.gpn   v.pai.1s   r.gs.1 d.asf n.asf   cj   pl v.fai.1s r.gs.1 d.asf
693   1620   1519   1609 3836 1355   1623 4143 4143 4803 4143 1609 3836

people to envy and save some of them. **15** For if their rejection   is the reconciliation of the world, what will their
σάρκα ← ← καὶ σώσω τινὰς ἐξ αὐτῶν   γὰρ εἰ αὐτῶν ἡ ἀποβολὴ‚   καταλλαγὴ →   κόσμου τίς   ἡ
n.asf   cj v.fai.1s r.apm p.g r.gpm.3 cj cj r.gpm.3 d.nsf n.nsf n.nsf   n.gsm r.nsf d.nsf
4922 4143 4143 2779 5392 5516 1666 899 1142 1623 899 3836 613   2903   3180 5515 3836

γόνυ τῇ Βάαλ. **5** οὕτως οὖν καὶ ἐν τῷ νῦν καιρῷ λεῖμμα κατ᾽ ἐκλογὴν χάριτος γέγονεν· **6** εἰ δὲ χάριτι, οὐκέτι ἐξ ἔργων, ἐπεὶ ἡ χάρις οὐκέτι γίνεται χάρις. ¶ **7** τί οὖν; ὃ ἐπιζητεῖ Ἰσραήλ, τοῦτο οὐκ ἐπέτυχεν, ἡ δὲ ἐκλογὴ ἐπέτυχεν· οἱ δὲ λοιποὶ ἐπωρώθησαν, **8** καθὼς γέγραπται, Ἔδωκεν αὐτοῖς ὁ θεὸς πνεῦμα κατανύξεως, ὀφθαλμοὺς τοῦ μὴ βλέπειν καὶ ὦτα τοῦ μὴ ἀκούειν, ἕως τῆς σήμερον ἡμέρας. **9** καὶ Δαυὶδ λέγει, Γενηθήτω ἡ τράπεζα αὐτῶν εἰς παγίδα καὶ εἰς θήραν καὶ εἰς σκάνδαλον καὶ εἰς ἀνταπόδομα αὐτοῖς, **10** σκοτισθήτωσαν οἱ ὀφθαλμοὶ αὐτῶν τοῦ μὴ βλέπειν καὶ τὸν νῶτον αὐτῶν διὰ παντὸς σύγκαμψον.

11:11 Λέγω οὖν, μὴ ἔπταισαν ἵνα πέσωσιν; μὴ γένοιτο· ἀλλὰ τῷ αὐτῶν παραπτώματι ἡ σωτηρία τοῖς ἔθνεσιν εἰς τὸ παραζηλῶσαι αὐτούς. **12** εἰ δὲ τὸ παράπτωμα αὐτῶν πλοῦτος κόσμου καὶ τὸ ἥττημα αὐτῶν πλοῦτος ἐθνῶν, πόσῳ μᾶλλον τὸ πλήρωμα αὐτῶν. ¶ **13** Ὑμῖν δὲ λέγω τοῖς ἔθνεσιν· ἐφ᾽ ὅσον μὲν οὖν εἰμι ἐγὼ ἐθνῶν ἀπόστολος, τὴν διακονίαν μου δοξάζω, **14** εἴ πως παραζηλώσω μου τὴν σάρκα καὶ σώσω τινὰς ἐξ αὐτῶν. **15** εἰ γὰρ ἡ ἀποβολὴ αὐτῶν καταλλαγὴ κόσμου, τίς ἡ πρόσλημψις

acceptance be but life from the dead? **16** If the part of the dough offered as firstfruits is holy, then the whole
πρόσλημψις εἰ μὴ ζωὴ ἐκ νεκρῶν δὲ εἰ ἡ ἀπαρχὴ ἁγία καὶ τὸ
n.nsf cj pl n.nsf p.g a.gpm cj cj d.nsf n.nsf a.nsf adv d.nsn
4691 1623 3590 2437 1666 3738 1254 1623 3836 569 41 2779 3836

batch is holy; if the root is holy, so are the branches. ¶ **17** If some of the branches have been
φύραμα καὶ εἰ ἡ ῥίζα ἁγία καὶ οἱ κλάδοι δὲ Εἰ τινες → τῶν κλάδων → →
n.nsn cj cj d.nsf n.nsf a.nsf cj d.npm n.npm cj Εἰ n.npm d.gpm n.gpm
5878 2779 1623 3836 4844 41 2779 3836 3080 1254 1623 5516 3836 3080

broken off, and you, though a wild olive shoot, have been grafted in among the others and now
ἐξεκλάσθησαν ← δὲ σὺ ὢν ἀγριέλαιος → ἐνεκεντρίσθης ← ἐν αὐτοῖς καὶ
v.api.3p cj r.ns.2 pt.pa.nsm n.nsf v.api.2s p.d r.dpm.3 cj
1709 1254 5148 1639 66 1596 1877 899 2779

share in the nourishing sap from the olive root, **18** do not boast over those branches. If
ἐγένου συγκοινωνὸς → τῆς → πιότητος → τῆς ⌐τῆς ἐλαίας⌐ ῥίζης → μὴ κατακαυχῶ ← τῶν κλάδων δὲ εἰ
v.ami.2s n.nsm d.gsf n.gsf d.gsf d.gsf n.gsf n.gsf pl v.pmm.2s d.gpm n.gpm cj cj
1181 5171 3836 4404 3836 3836 1777 4844 3590 2878 3836 3080 1254 1623

you do, consider this: You do not support the root, but the root supports you. **19** You will say then,
→ κατακαυχᾶσαι σὺ → οὐ βαστάζεις τὴν ῥίζαν ἀλλὰ ἡ ῥίζα σέ → ἐρεῖς οὖν
v.pmi.2s r.ns.2 pl v.pai.2s d.asf n.asf cj d.nsf n.nsf r.as.2 v.fai.2s cj
2878 5148 1002 4024 1002 3836 4844 247 3836 4844 5148 3306 4036

"Branches were broken off so that I could be grafted in." **20** Granted. But they were broken off because
κλάδοι → ἐξεκλάσθησαν ← ἵνα ← ἐγὼ → ἐγκεντρισθῶ καλῶς → ἐξεκλάσθησαν ←
n.npm v.api.3p cj r.ns.1 v.aps.1s adv v.api.3p
3080 1709 2671 1609 1596 2822 1709

of unbelief, and you stand by faith. Do not be arrogant, but be afraid. **21** For if God did not spare
→ ⌐τῇ ἀπιστίᾳ⌐ δὲ σὺ ἕστηκας → ⌐τῇ πίστει⌐ μὴ φρόνει ὑψηλὰ ἀλλὰ → φοβοῦ γὰρ εἰ ὁ θεὸς οὐκ ἐφείσατο
d.dsf n.dsf cj r.ns.2 v.rai.2s d.dsf n.dsf pl v.pam.2s a.apn cj v.ppm.2s cj cj d.nsm n.nsm pl v.ami.3s
3836 602 1254 5148 2705 3836 4411 3590 5858 5734 247 5828 1142 1623 3836 2536 5767 4024 5767

the natural branches, he will not spare you either. ¶ **22** Consider therefore the kindness and
τῶν ⌐κατὰ φύσιν⌐ κλάδων [μή πως] → → οὐδὲ φείσεται σοῦ ἴδε οὖν χρηστότητα καὶ
d.gpm p.a n.asf n.gpm cj pl adv v.fmi.3s r.gs.2 v.aam.2s cj n.asf cj
3836 2848 5882 3080 3590 4803 4028 5767 5148 2623 4036 5983 2779

sternness of God: sternness to those who fell, but kindness to you, provided that you continue in his
ἀποτομίαν → θεοῦ μὲν ἀποτομία ἐπὶ τοὺς ← πεσόντας δὲ χρηστότης θεοῦ ἐπὶ σὲ ἐὰν → → ἐπιμένῃς ← τῇ
n.asf n.gsm p.a n.nsf p.a d.apm pt.aa.apm cj n.nsf n.gsm p.a r.as.2 cj v.pas.2s d.dsf
704 2536 3525 704 2093 3836 4406 1254 5983 2536 2093 5148 1569 2152 3836

kindness. Otherwise, you also will be cut off. **23** And if they do not persist in unbelief, they will be
χρηστότητι ἐπεὶ σὺ καὶ → ἐκκοπήσῃ ← δὲ ἐὰν κἀκεῖνοι μὴ ἐπιμένωσιν ←τῇ ἀπιστίᾳ they will be
n.dsf cj r.ns.2 adv v.fpi.2s cj cj adv pl v.pas.3p d.dsf n.dsf
5983 2075 5148 2779 1716 1254 1569 2797 2152 3590 2152 3836 602

grafted in, for God is able to graft them in again. **24** After all, if you were cut out of an
ἐγκεντρισθήσονται ← γὰρ ὁ θεὸς ἐστιν δυνατὸς → ἐγκεντρίσαι αὐτοὺς πάλιν γὰρ ← εἰ σὺ → ἐξεκόπης ἐκ →
v.fpi.3p cj d.nsm n.nsm v.pai.3s a.nsm f.aa r.apm.3 adv cj cj r.ns.2 v.api.2s p.g
1596 1142 3836 2536 1639 1543 1596 899 4099 1142 1623 5148 1716 1666

olive tree that is wild by nature, and contrary to nature were grafted into a cultivated olive
→ ⌐τῆς ἀγριελαίου⌐ ← ← ⌐κατὰ φύσιν⌐ καὶ παρὰ ← φύσιν⌐ ἐνεκεντρίσθης εἰς
d.gsf n.gsf p.a n.asf cj p.a n.asf v.api.2s p.a
3836 66 2848 5882 2779 4123 5882 1596 1650

tree, how much more readily will these, the natural branches, be grafted into their own olive tree!
καλλιέλαιον → πόσῳ μᾶλλον → οὗτοι οἱ ⌐κατὰ φύσιν⌐ → ἐγκεντρισθήσονται ← τῇ ἰδίᾳ → ἐλαίᾳ
n.asf r.dsn adv.c r.npm d.npm p.a n.asf v.fpi.3p d.dsf a.dsf n.dsf
2814 4531 3437 1596 4047 3836 2848 5882 1596 3836 2625 1777

All Israel Will Be Saved
11:25 I do not want you to be ignorant of this mystery, brothers, so that you may not be
γὰρ → → Οὐ θέλω ὑμᾶς → → ἀγνοεῖν τοῦτο ⌐τὸ μυστήριον⌐ ἀδελφοί ἵνα ← → ἦτε μὴ ←
cj pl v.pai.1s r.ap.2 f.pa r.asn d.asn n.asn n.vpm cj v.pas.2p pl
1142 2527 2527 4024 2527 7007 51 4047 3836 3696 81 2671 1639 3590 1639

εἰ μὴ ζωὴ ἐκ νεκρῶν; **16** εἰ δὲ ἡ ἀπαρχὴ ἁγία, καὶ τὸ φύραμα· καὶ εἰ ἡ ῥίζα ἁγία, καὶ οἱ κλάδοι. ¶ **17** Εἰ δέ τινες τῶν κλάδων ἐξεκλάσθησαν, σὺ δὲ ἀγριέλαιος ὢν ἐνεκεντρίσθης ἐν αὐτοῖς καὶ συγκοινωνὸς τῆς ῥίζης τῆς πιότητος τῆς ἐλαίας ἐγένου, **18** μὴ κατακαυχῶ τῶν κλάδων· εἰ δὲ κατακαυχᾶσαι οὐ σὺ τὴν ῥίζαν βαστάζεις ἀλλὰ ἡ ῥίζα σέ. **19** ἐρεῖς οὖν, Ἐξεκλάσθησαν κλάδοι ἵνα ἐγὼ ἐγκεντρισθῶ. **20** καλῶς· τῇ ἀπιστίᾳ ἐξεκλάσθησαν, σὺ δὲ τῇ πίστει ἕστηκας. μὴ ὑψηλὰ φρόνει ἀλλὰ φοβοῦ· **21** εἰ γὰρ ὁ θεὸς τῶν κατὰ φύσιν κλάδων οὐκ ἐφείσατο, [μή πως] οὐδὲ σοῦ φείσεται. ¶ **22** ἴδε οὖν χρηστότητα καὶ ἀποτομίαν θεοῦ· ἐπὶ μὲν τοὺς πεσόντας ἀποτομία, ἐπὶ δὲ σὲ χρηστότης θεοῦ, ἐὰν ἐπιμένῃς τῇ χρηστότητι, ἐπεὶ καὶ σὺ ἐκκοπήσῃ. **23** κἀκεῖνοι δέ, ἐὰν μὴ ἐπιμένωσιν τῇ ἀπιστίᾳ, ἐγκεντρισθήσονται· δυνατὸς γάρ ἐστιν ὁ θεὸς πάλιν ἐγκεντρίσαι αὐτούς. **24** εἰ γὰρ σὺ ἐκ τῆς κατὰ φύσιν ἐξεκόπης ἀγριελαίου καὶ παρὰ φύσιν ἐνεκεντρίσθης εἰς καλλιέλαιον, πόσῳ μᾶλλον οὗτοι οἱ κατὰ φύσιν ἐγκεντρισθήσονται τῇ ἰδίᾳ ἐλαίᾳ.

11:25 Οὐ γὰρ θέλω ὑμᾶς ἀγνοεῖν, ἀδελφοί, τὸ μυστήριον τοῦτο, ἵνα μὴ ἦτε [παρ'] ἑαυτοῖς φρόνιμοι, ὅτι πώρωσις ἀπὸ μέρους

conceited: Israel has experienced a hardening in part until the full number of the
παρ᾽ ἑαυτοῖς φρόνιμοι ὅτι τῷ Ἰσραὴλ → γέγονεν πώρωσις ἀπὸ μέρους ἄχρι οὗ τὸ πλήρωμα ← → τῶν
p.d r.dpm.2 a.npm cj d.dsm n.dsm v.rai.3s n.nsf p.g n.gsn p.g r.gsm d.nsn n.nsn d.gpn
4123 1571 5861 4022 3836 2702 1181 4801 608 3538 948 4005 3836 4445 3836

Gentiles has come in. ²⁶ And so all Israel will be saved, as it is written: "The deliverer will come from
ἐθνῶν → εἰσέλθῃ καὶ οὕτως πᾶς Ἰσραὴλ → σωθήσεται καθὼς → → γέγραπται ὁ ῥυόμενος → ἥξει ἐκ
n.gpn v.aas.3s cj adv a.nsm n.nsm v.fpi.3s cj v.rpi.3s d.nsm pt.pm.nsm v.fai.3s p.g
1620 1656 2779 4048 4246 2702 5392 2777 1211 3836 4861 2457 1666

Zion; he will turn godlessness away from Jacob. ²⁷ And this is my covenant with them when I take
Σιὼν → → ἀποστρέψει ἀσεβείας ἀπὸ Ἰακώβ καὶ αὕτη παρ᾽ ἐμοῦ ἡ διαθήκη → αὐτοῖς ὅταν → ἀφέλωμαι
n.gsf v.fai.3s n.apf p.g n.gsm cj r.nsf p.g r.gs.1 d.nsf n.nsf r.dpm.3 cj v.ams.1s
4994 695 813 695 608 2609 2779 4047 4123 1609 3836 1347 899 4020 904

away their sins." ¶ ²⁸ As far as the gospel is concerned, they are enemies on your account; but
← αὐτῶν τὰς ἁμαρτίας μὲν κατὰ ← ← τὸ εὐαγγέλιον ← ← ἐχθροὶ δι᾽ ὑμᾶς ← δὲ
r.gpm.3 d.apf n.apf pl cj d.asn n.asn a.npm p.a r.ap.2 cj
899 3836 281 3525 2848 3836 2295 2848 2848 2398 1328 7007 1328 1254

as far as election is concerned, they are loved on account of the patriarchs, ²⁹ for God's gifts and
κατὰ ← τὴν ἐκλογὴν ἀγαπητοὶ διὰ ← τοὺς πατέρας γὰρ τοῦ θεοῦ τὰ χαρίσματα καὶ
p.a d.asf n.asf a.npm p.a d.apm n.apm cj d.gsm n.gsm d.npn n.npn cj
2848 3836 1724 2848 2848 28 1328 3836 4252 1142 3836 2536 3836 5922 2779

his call are irrevocable. ³⁰ Just as you who were at one time disobedient to God have now received
ἡ κλῆσις ἀμεταμέλητα γὰρ ὥσπερ ὑμεῖς → → ποτε ἠπειθήσατε τῷ θεῷ δὲ νῦν →
d.nsf n.nsf a.npn cj cj r.np.2 adv v.aai.2p d.dsm n.dsm cj adv
3836 3104 294 1142 6061 7007 578 4537 578 3836 2536 1254 1796 3814

mercy as a result of their disobedience, ³¹ so they too have now become disobedient in order that they too may
ἠλεήθητε → → τούτων τῇ ἀπειθείᾳ οὕτως οὗτοι καὶ → νῦν ἠπείθησαν ἵνα ← αὐτοὶ καὶ →
v.api.2p r.gpm d.dsf n.dsf adv r.npm cj adv v.aai.3p cj r.npm cj adv
1796 577 577 577 577 4047 3836 577 4048 4047 2779 578 3814 578 2671 899 2779 1796

now receive mercy as a result of God's mercy to you. ³² For God has bound all men over to
νῦν ἐλεηθῶσιν → → → ἐλέει τῷ ὑμετέρῳ γὰρ ὁ θεὸς → συνέκλεισεν τοὺς πάντας εἰς
adv v.aps.3p n.dsn d.dsn r.dsn.2 cj d.nsm n.nsm v.aai.3s d.apm a.apm p.a
3814 1796 1799 3836 5629 1142 3836 2536 5168 3836 4246 5168 1650

disobedience so that he may have mercy on them all.
ἀπείθειαν ἵνα ← → → ἐλεήσῃ ← → τοὺς πάντας
n.asf cj v.aas.3s d.apm a.apm
577 2671 1796 3836 4246

Doxology

11:33 Oh, the depth of the riches of the wisdom and knowledge of God! How unsearchable his judgments,
Ὦ βάθος → πλούτου καὶ σοφίας καὶ γνώσεως → θεοῦ ὡς ἀνεξεραύνητα αὐτοῦ τὰ κρίματα
j n.nsn n.gsm cj n.gsf cj n.gsf n.gsm pl a.npn r.gsm.3 d.npn n.npn
6043 958 4458 2779 5053 2779 1194 2536 6055 451 899 3836 3210

and his paths beyond tracing out! ³⁴ "Who has known the mind of the Lord? Or who has been his
καὶ αὐτοῦ αἱ ὁδοὶ ἀνεξιχνίαστοι ← γὰρ τίς → ἔγνω νοῦν → κυρίου ἢ τίς → ἐγένετο αὐτοῦ
cj r.gsm.3 d.npf n.npf n.npf cj r.nsm v.aai.3s n.asm n.gsm cj r.nsm v.ami.3s r.gsm.3
2779 899 3836 3847 453 1142 5515 1182 3808 3261 2445 5515 1181 899

counselor?" ³⁵ "Who has ever given to God, that God should repay him?" ³⁶ For from him and
σύμβουλος ἢ τίς → προέδωκεν αὐτῷ καὶ → ἀνταποδοθήσεται αὐτῷ ὅτι ἐξ αὐτοῦ καὶ
n.nsm cj r.nsm v.aai.3s r.dsm.3 cj v.fpi.3s r.dsm.3 cj r.gsm.3 cj
5207 2445 5515 4594 899 2779 500 899 4022 1666 899 2779

through him and to him are all things. To him be the glory forever! Amen.
δι᾽ αὐτοῦ καὶ εἰς αὐτὸν τὰ πάντα → αὐτῷ ἡ δόξα εἰς τοὺς αἰῶνας ἀμήν
p.g r.gsm.3 cj p.a r.asm.3 d.npn a.npn r.dsm.3 d.nsf n.nsf p.a d.apm n.apm pl
1328 899 2779 1650 899 3836 4246 899 3836 1518 1650 3836 172 297

Living Sacrifices

12:1 Therefore, I urge you, brothers, in view of God's mercy, to offer your bodies as
οὖν → Παρακαλῶ ὑμᾶς ἀδελφοί διὰ ← τοῦ θεοῦ τῶν οἰκτιρμῶν → παραστῆσαι ὑμῶν τὰ σώματα
cj v.pai.1s r.ap.2 n.vpm p.g d.gsm n.gsm d.gpm n.gpm f.aa r.gp.2 d.apn n.apn
4036 4151 7007 81 1328 3836 2536 3836 3880 4225 7007 3836 5393

τῷ Ἰσραὴλ γέγονεν ἄχρις οὗ τὸ πλήρωμα τῶν ἐθνῶν εἰσέλθῃ ²⁶ καὶ οὕτως πᾶς Ἰσραὴλ σωθήσεται, καθὼς γέγραπται, Ἥξει ἐκ Σιὼν ὁ ῥυόμενος, ἀποστρέψει ἀσεβείας ἀπὸ Ἰακώβ. ¶ ²⁷ καὶ αὕτη αὐτοῖς ἡ παρ᾽ ἐμοῦ διαθήκη, ὅταν ἀφέλωμαι τὰς ἁμαρτίας αὐτῶν. ¶ ²⁸ κατὰ μὲν τὸ εὐαγγέλιον ἐχθροὶ δι᾽ ὑμᾶς, κατὰ δὲ τὴν ἐκλογὴν ἀγαπητοὶ διὰ τοὺς πατέρας· ²⁹ ἀμεταμέλητα γὰρ τὰ χαρίσματα καὶ ἡ κλῆσις τοῦ θεοῦ. ³⁰ ὥσπερ γὰρ ὑμεῖς ποτε ἠπειθήσατε τῷ θεῷ, νῦν δὲ ἠλεήθητε τῇ τούτων ἀπειθείᾳ, ³¹ οὕτως καὶ οὗτοι νῦν ἠπείθησαν τῷ ὑμετέρῳ ἐλέει, ἵνα καὶ αὐτοὶ [νῦν] ἐλεηθῶσιν. ³² συνέκλεισεν γὰρ ὁ θεὸς τοὺς πάντας εἰς ἀπείθειαν, ἵνα τοὺς πάντας ἐλεήσῃ.

11:33 Ὦ βάθος πλούτου καὶ σοφίας καὶ γνώσεως θεοῦ· ὡς ἀνεξεραύνητα τὰ κρίματα αὐτοῦ καὶ ἀνεξιχνίαστοι αἱ ὁδοὶ αὐτοῦ. ³⁴ Τίς γὰρ ἔγνω νοῦν κυρίου; ἢ τίς σύμβουλος αὐτοῦ ἐγένετο; ³⁵ ἢ τίς προέδωκεν αὐτῷ, καὶ ἀνταποδοθήσεται αὐτῷ; ³⁶ ὅτι ἐξ αὐτοῦ καὶ δι᾽ αὐτοῦ καὶ εἰς αὐτὸν τὰ πάντα· αὐτῷ ἡ δόξα εἰς τοὺς αἰῶνας, ἀμήν.

12:1 Παρακαλῶ οὖν ὑμᾶς, ἀδελφοί, διὰ τῶν οἰκτιρμῶν τοῦ θεοῦ παραστῆσαι τὰ σώματα ὑμῶν θυσίαν ζῶσαν ἁγίαν

living sacrifices, holy and pleasing to God — this is your spiritual act of worship. **2** Do not conform any
ζῶσαν θυσίαν ἁγίαν εὐάρεστον → ⌐τῷ θεῷ⌐ ὑμῶν λογικὴν → → ⌐τὴν λατρείαν⌐ καὶ → μὴ συσχηματίζεσθε
pt.pa.asf n.asf a.asf a.asf d.dsm n.dsm r.gp.2 a.asf d.asf n.asf cj pl v.ppm.2p
2409 2602 41 2298 3836 2536 7007 3358 3836 3301 2779 5372 3590 5372

longer to the pattern of this world, but be transformed by the renewing of your mind. Then you will be
← ← ← ← τούτῳ τῷ αἰῶνι ἀλλὰ → μεταμορφοῦσθε → τῇ ἀνακαινώσει → τοῦ νοὸς ὑμᾶς
r.dsm d.dsm n.dsm cj v.ppm.2p d.dsf d.dsf n.dsf d.gsm n.gsm r.ap.2
4047 3836 172 247 3565 3836 364 3836 3808 7007

able to test and approve what God's will is — his good, pleasing and perfect will. ¶
εἰς ⌐τὸ δοκιμάζειν⌐ ← ← τί ⌐τοῦ θεοῦ⌐ ⌐τὸ θέλημα⌐ τὸ ἀγαθὸν καὶ εὐάρεστον καὶ τέλειον
p.a d.asn f.pa r.nsn d.gsm n.gsm d.nsn n.nsn d.nsn a.nsn cj a.nsn cj a.nsn
1650 3836 1507 5515 3836 2536 3836 2525 3836 19 2779 2298 2779 5455

3 For by the grace given me I say to every one of you: Do not think of yourself more highly
γὰρ διὰ τῆς χάριτος ⌐τῆς δοθείσης⌐ μοι → Λέγω παντὶ ← τῷ ὄντι ἐν ὑμῖν → μὴ ὑπερφρονεῖν ← ←
cj p.g d.gsf n.gsf d.gsf pt.ap.gsf r.ds.1 v.pai.1s a.dsm d.dsm pt.pa.dsm p.d r.dp.2 pl f.pa
1142 1328 3836 5921 3836 1443 1609 3306 4246 3836 1639 1877 7007 5672 3590 5672

than you ought, but rather think of yourself with sober judgment, in accordance with the
παρ᾽ ὃ ⌐δεῖ φρονεῖν⌐ ἀλλὰ φρονεῖν εἰς ⌐τὸ σωφρονεῖν⌐ ← ἑκάστῳ ὡς
p.a r.asn v.pai.3s f.pa cj f.pa p.a d.asn f.pa r.dsm cj
4123 4005 1256 5858 247 5858 1650 3836 5404 1667 6055

measure of faith God has given you. **4** Just as each of us has one body with many members, and
μέτρον → πίστεως ὁ θεὸς⌐ → ἐμέρισεν γὰρ καθάπερ ← ἔχομεν ἐν ἑνὶ σώματι πολλὰ μέλη δὲ
n.asn n.gsf d.nsm n.nsm v.aai.3s cj cj v.pai.1p p.d a.dsn n.dsn a.apn n.apn cj
3586 4411 3836 2536 3532 1142 2749 2400 1877 1651 5393 4498 3517 1254

these members do not all have the same function, **5** so in Christ we who are many form one body, and
τὰ μέλη → οὐ πάντα ἔχει τὴν αὐτὴν πρᾶξιν οὕτως ἐν Χριστῷ → οἱ πολλοὶ ἐσμεν ἓν σῶμα δὲ
d.npn n.npn pl a.npn v.pai.3s d.asf r.asf n.asf adv p.d n.dsm d.npm a.npm v.pai.1p a.nsn n.nsn cj
3836 3517 2400 4024 4246 2400 3836 899 4552 4048 1877 5986 1639 3836 4498 1639 1651 5393 1254

each member belongs to all the others. **6** We have different gifts, according to the grace given
⌐καθ᾽ εἷς ⌐τὸ μέλη⌐ ἀλλήλων δὲ ἔχοντες διάφορα χαρίσματα κατὰ ← τὴν χάριν ⌐τὴν δοθεῖσαν⌐
p.a a.nsm d.asn n.npn r.gpm cj pt.pa.npm a.apn n.apn p.a d.asf n.asf d.asf pt.ap.asf
2848 1651 3836 3517 253 1254 2400 1427 5922 2848 3836 5921 3836 1443

us. If a man's gift is prophesying, let him use it in proportion to his faith. **7** If it is serving, let him
ἡμῖν εἴτε προφητείαν κατὰ ⌐τὴν ἀναλογίαν⌐ → τῆς πίστεως εἴτε διακονίαν ἐν
r.dp.1 cj n.asf p.a d.asf n.asf d.gsf n.gsf cj n.asf p.d
7005 1664 4735 2848 3836 381 3836 4411 1664 1355 1877

serve; if it is teaching, let him teach; **8** if it is encouraging, let him encourage; if it is
⌐τῇ διακονίᾳ⌐ εἴτε ὁ διδάσκων⌐ ἐν ⌐τῇ διδασκαλίᾳ⌐ εἴτε ὁ παρακαλῶν⌐ ἐν ⌐τῇ παρακλήσει⌐
d.dsf n.dsf cj d.nsm pt.pa.nsm p.d d.dsf n.dsf cj d.nsm pt.pa.nsm p.d d.dsf n.dsf
3836 1355 1664 3836 1438 1877 3836 1436 1664 3836 4151 1877 3836 4155

contributing to the needs of others, let him give generously; if it is leadership, let him govern diligently; if it
⌐ὁ μεταδιδοὺς⌐ ἐν ἁπλότητι ὁ προϊστάμενος⌐ ⌐ἐν σπουδῇ⌐
d.nsm pt.pa.nsm p.d n.dsf d.nsm pt.pm.nsm p.d n.dsf
3836 3556 1877 605 3836 4613 1877 5082

is showing mercy, let him do it cheerfully.
→ ⌐ὁ ἐλεῶν⌐ ἐν ἱλαρότητι⌐
d.nsm pt.pa.nsm p.d n.dsf
3836 1790 1877 2660

Love

12:9 Love must be sincere. Hate what is evil; cling to what is good. **10** Be devoted to
Ἡ ἀγάπη⌐ ἀνυπόκριτος ἀποστυγοῦντες τὸ → πονηρόν κολλώμενοι → τῷ → ἀγαθῷ φιλόστοργοι εἰς
d.nsf n.nsf a.nsf pt.pa.npm d.asn a.asn pt.pp.npm d.dsn a.dsn a.npm p.a
3836 27 537 696 3836 4505 3140 3836 19 5816 1650

one another in brotherly love. Honor one another above yourselves. **11** Never be lacking in
ἀλλήλους ← → ⌐τῇ φιλαδελφίᾳ⌐ ← ⌐τῇ τιμῇ προηγούμενοι⌐ ἀλλήλους ← ← μὴ ὀκνηροί →
r.apm d.dsf n.dsf d.dsf n.dsf pt.pm.npm r.apm pl a.npm
253 3836 5789 3836 5507 4605 253 4605 3590 3891

εὐάρεστον τῷ θεῷ, τὴν λογικὴν λατρείαν ὑμῶν· ² καὶ μὴ συσχηματίζεσθε τῷ αἰῶνι τούτῳ, ἀλλὰ μεταμορφοῦσθε τῇ ἀνακαινώσει τοῦ νοὸς εἰς τὸ δοκιμάζειν ὑμᾶς τί τὸ θέλημα τοῦ θεοῦ, τὸ ἀγαθὸν καὶ εὐάρεστον καὶ τέλειον. ¶ ³ Λέγω γὰρ διὰ τῆς χάριτος τῆς δοθείσης μοι παντὶ τῷ ὄντι ἐν ὑμῖν μὴ ὑπερφρονεῖν παρ᾽ ὃ δεῖ φρονεῖν ἀλλὰ φρονεῖν εἰς τὸ σωφρονεῖν, ἑκάστῳ ὡς ὁ θεὸς ἐμέρισεν μέτρον πίστεως. ⁴ καθάπερ γὰρ ἐν ἑνὶ σώματι πολλὰ μέλη ἔχομεν, τὰ δὲ μέλη πάντα οὐ τὴν αὐτὴν ἔχει πρᾶξιν, ⁵ οὕτως οἱ πολλοὶ ἓν σῶμά ἐσμεν ἐν Χριστῷ, τὸ δὲ καθ᾽ εἷς ἀλλήλων μέλη. ⁶ ἔχοντες δὲ χαρίσματα κατὰ τὴν χάριν τὴν δοθεῖσαν ἡμῖν διάφορα, εἴτε προφητείαν κατὰ τὴν ἀναλογίαν τῆς πίστεως, ⁷ εἴτε διακονίαν ἐν τῇ διακονίᾳ, εἴτε ὁ διδάσκων ἐν τῇ διδασκαλίᾳ, ⁸ εἴτε ὁ παρακαλῶν ἐν τῇ παρακλήσει· ὁ μεταδιδοὺς ἐν ἁπλότητι, ὁ προϊστάμενος ἐν σπουδῇ, ὁ ἐλεῶν ἐν ἱλαρότητι.

¹²·⁹ Ἡ ἀγάπη ἀνυπόκριτος. ἀποστυγοῦντες τὸ πονηρόν, κολλώμενοι τῷ ἀγαθῷ, ¹⁰ τῇ φιλαδελφίᾳ εἰς ἀλλήλους φιλόστοργοι, τῇ τιμῇ ἀλλήλους προηγούμενοι, ¹¹ τῇ σπουδῇ μὴ ὀκνηροί, τῷ πνεύματι ζέοντες, τῷ κυρίῳ δουλεύοντες, ¹² τῇ ἐλπίδι χαίροντες,

zeal,	but keep	your	spiritual	fervor,	serving		the Lord.	**12** Be joyful		in hope,		patient		in affliction,
᾿τῇ σπουδῇ᾿	→	τῷ	πνεύματι	ζέοντες	δουλεύοντες	τῷ	κυρίῳ	χαίροντες	→	᾿τῇ ἐλπίδι᾿	ὑπομένοντες	→	᾿τῇ	θλίψει᾿
d.dsf n.dsf		d.dsn	n.dsn	pt.pa.npm	pt.pa.npm	d.dsm	n.dsm	pt.pa.npm		d.dsf n.dsf	pt.pa.npm		d.dsf	n.dsf
3836 5082		2417	3836 4460	2417	1526	3836	3261	5897		3836 1828	5702		3836	2568

faithful		in prayer.	**13** Share		with God's		people	who are in	need.	Practice	hospitality.	¶
προσκαρτεροῦντες	→	᾿τῇ προσευχῇ᾿	κοινωνοῦντες		᾿τῶν ἁγίων᾿	←	ταῖς		χρείαις	διώκοντες	᾿τὴν φιλοξενίαν᾿	
pt.pa.npm		d.dsf n.dsf	pt.pa.npm		d.gpm		d.dpf		n.dpf	pt.pa.npm	d.asf n.asf	
4674		3836 4666	3125		3836 41		3836		5970	1503	3836 5810	

14 Bless	those who	persecute	you;	bless	and	do	not	curse.	**15** Rejoice	with	those who rejoice;	mourn	with	those
εὐλογεῖτε	τοὺς ←	διώκοντας	ὑμᾶς	εὐλογεῖτε	καὶ	↑	μὴ	καταρᾶσθε	χαίρειν	μετὰ →	→ χαιρόντων	κλαίειν	μετὰ →	
v.pam.2p	d.apm	pt.pa.apm	r.ap.2	v.pam.2p	cj	pl		v.pmm.2p	f.pa	p.g	pt.pa.gpm	f.pa	p.g	
2328	3836	1503	7007	2328	2779	2933	3590	2933	5897	3552	5897	3081	3552	

who mourn.	**16** Live		in harmony	with	one	another.	Do	not be		proud,		but	be willing to
→ κλαιόντων	φρονοῦντες	→	᾿τὸ αὐτὸ	εἰς	ἀλλήλους ←		↑	μὴ	φρονοῦντες	᾿τὰ ὑψηλὰ᾿	ἀλλὰ		
pt.pa.gpm	pt.pa.npm		d.asn r.asn	p.a	r.apm				pt.pa.npm	d.apn a.apn	cj		
3081	5858		3836 899	1650	253			5858	3590 5858	3836 5734	247		

associate	with people		of low position.	Do	not be		conceited.	¶	**17** Do	not	repay
συναπαγόμενοι	᾿τοῖς ταπεινοῖς᾿	←	↑	μὴ	γίνεσθε	φρόνιμοι	παρ᾿	᾿ἑαυτοῖς᾿	→	μηδενὶ	ἀποδιδόντες
pt.pp.npm	a.dpm			pl	v.pmm.2p	a.npm	p.d	r.dpm.2		a.dsm	pt.pa.npm
5270	3836 5424			1181	3590 1181	5861	4123	1571		625 3594	625

anyone	evil	for	evil.	Be careful to do	→	what is right	in	the eyes	of everybody.	**18** If	it is possible,
	κακὸν	ἀντὶ	κακοῦ	προνοούμενοι	→	᾿καλὰ	ἐνώπιον	←	᾿πάντων ἀνθρώπων᾿	εἰ	δυνατὸν
	a.asn	p.g	a.gsn	pt.pm.npm		a.apn	p.g		a.gpm n.gpm	cj	a.nsn
	3594	2805	505 2805	4629		2819	1967		4246 476	1623	1543

as	far as it depends	on you,	live at peace		with	everyone.	**19** Do	not take revenge,		my friends,
᾿τὸ ἐξ᾿		ὑμῶν →	εἰρηνεύοντες	μετὰ	᾿πάντων ἀνθρώπων᾿	↑	μὴ →	ἐκδικοῦντες ἑαυτοὺς →		ἀγαπητοί
d.asn		r.gp.2	pt.pa.npm	p.g	a.gpm n.gpm		pl	pt.pa.npm r.apm.2		a.vpm
3836 1666		7007	1644	3552	4246 476		1688 3590	1688 1571		28

but	leave	room	for God's wrath,	for	it is written:	"It is mine	to avenge;	I	will repay,"	says	the Lord.	**20** On
ἀλλὰ	δότε	τόπον	᾿τῇ ὀργῇ᾿	γάρ →	γέγραπται	ἐμοὶ	ἐκδίκησις	ἐγὼ →	ἀνταποδώσω	λέγει	κύριος	→
cj	v.aam.2p	n.asm	d.dsf n.dsf	cj	v.rpi.3s	r.ds.1	n.nsf	r.ns.1	v.fai.1s	v.pai.3s	n.nsm	
247	1443	5536	3836 3973	1142	1211	1609	1689	1609	500	3306	3261	

the contrary:	"If	your	enemy	is hungry,	feed	him;	if	he is thirsty,	give	him	something to drink.		In doing
᾿ ἀλλὰ	ἐὰν	σου	᾿ὁ ἐχθρός᾿	→ πεινᾷ	ψώμιζε	αὐτόν	ἐὰν →	→ διψᾷ	↑	αὐτόν	→	ποτίζε γὰρ →	ποιῶν
cj	cj	r.gs.2	d.nsm n.nsm	v.pas.3s	v.pam.2s	r.asm.3	cj →	v.pas.3s		r.asm.3		v.pam.2s cj	pt.pa.nsm
247	1569	5148	3836 2398	4277	6039	899	1569	1498		4540 899		4540 1142	4472

this,	you will heap		burning	coals	on	his	head."	**21** Do	not be	overcome	by evil,		but	overcome
τοῦτο	→	σωρεύσεις	πυρὸς	ἄνθρακας	ἐπὶ	αὐτοῦ	᾿τὴν κεφαλὴν᾿	↑	μὴ →	νικῶ	ὑπὸ ᾿τοῦ κακοῦ᾿		ἀλλὰ	νίκα
r.asn		v.fai.2s	n.gsn	n.apm	p.a	r.gsm.3	d.asf n.asf		pl	v.ppm.2s	p.g d.gsn a.gsn		cj	v.pam.2s
4047		5397	4786	472	2093	899	3836 3051		3771 3590	3771	5679 3836 2805		247	3771

evil		with good.
᾿τὸ κακόν᾿	ἐν	᾿τῷ ἀγαθῷ᾿
d.asn a.asn	p.d	d.dsn a.dsn
3836 2805	1877	3836 19

Submission to the Authorities

13:1 Everyone		must submit		himself to	the	governing	authorities,	for	there	is	no	authority	except	that
᾿Πᾶσα ψυχὴ᾿	→	ὑποτασσέσθω	←	↑		ὑπερεχούσαις	ἐξουσίαις	γὰρ →		ἔστιν	οὐ	ἐξουσία	᾿εἰ μὴ᾿	ὑπὸ
a.nsf n.nsf		v.pmm.3s				pt.pa.dpf	n.dpf	cj		v.pai.3s	pl	n.nsf	cj pl	p.g
4246 6034		5718				5660	2026	1142		1639	4024	2026	1623 3590	5679

which	God	has established.		The	authorities	that	exist	have	been	established	by	God.	**2** Consequently,	he	who
←	θεοῦ		δὲ	αἱ			οὖσαι →		εἰσίν	τεταγμέναι	ὑπὸ	θεοῦ	ὥστε		ὁ
	n.gsm		cj	d.npf			pt.pa.npf		v.pai.3p	pt.rp.npf	p.g	n.gsm	cj		d.nsm
	2536	5679 5679	1254	3836			1639		1639	5435	5679	2536	6063		3836

rebels		against	the	authority	is rebelling	against	what	God		has instituted,	and	those	who do		so
ἀντιτασσόμενος	←	τῇ	ἐξουσίᾳ	ἀνθέστηκεν	←	→	᾿τοῦ θεοῦ᾿		τῇ διαταγῇ	δὲ	οἱ	←	ἀνθεστηκότες	←
pt.pm.nsm		d.dsf	n.dsf	v.rai.3s			d.gsm n.gsm		d.dsf n.dsf	cj	d.npm		pt.ra.npm	
530		3836	2026	468		1408	3836 2536		3836 1408	1254	3836		468	

τῇ θλίψει ὑπομένοντες, τῇ προσευχῇ προσκαρτεροῦντες. ¹³ ταῖς χρείαις τῶν ἁγίων κοινωνοῦντες, τὴν φιλοξενίαν διώκοντες. ¶
¹⁴ εὐλογεῖτε τοὺς διώκοντας [ὑμᾶς], εὐλογεῖτε καὶ μὴ καταρᾶσθε. ¹⁵ χαίρειν μετὰ χαιρόντων, κλαίειν μετὰ κλαιόντων. ¹⁶ τὸ
αὐτὸ εἰς ἀλλήλους φρονοῦντες, μὴ τὰ ὑψηλὰ φρονοῦντες ἀλλὰ τοῖς ταπεινοῖς συναπαγόμενοι. μὴ γίνεσθε φρόνιμοι παρ᾿
ἑαυτοῖς. ¶ ¹⁷ μηδενὶ κακὸν ἀντὶ κακοῦ ἀποδιδόντες, προνοούμενοι καλὰ ἐνώπιον πάντων ἀνθρώπων· ¹⁸ εἰ δυνατὸν τὸ ἐξ ὑμῶν,
μετὰ πάντων ἀνθρώπων εἰρηνεύοντες· ¹⁹ μὴ ἑαυτοὺς ἐκδικοῦντες, ἀγαπητοί, ἀλλὰ δότε τόπον τῇ ὀργῇ, γέγραπται γάρ, Ἐμοὶ
ἐκδίκησις, ἐγὼ ἀνταποδώσω, λέγει κύριος. ²⁰ ἀλλὰ ἐὰν πεινᾷ ὁ ἐχθρός σου, ψώμιζε αὐτόν· ἐὰν διψᾷ, πότιζε αὐτόν· τοῦτο γὰρ
ποιῶν ἄνθρακας πυρὸς σωρεύσεις ἐπὶ τὴν κεφαλὴν αὐτοῦ. ²¹ μὴ νικῶ ὑπὸ τοῦ κακοῦ ἀλλὰ νίκα ἐν τῷ ἀγαθῷ τὸ κακόν.
¹³:¹ Πᾶσα ψυχὴ ἐξουσίαις ὑπερεχούσαις ὑποτασσέσθω. οὐ γὰρ ἔστιν ἐξουσία εἰ μὴ ὑπὸ θεοῦ, αἱ δὲ οὖσαι ὑπὸ θεοῦ
τεταγμέναι εἰσίν. ² ὥστε ὁ ἀντιτασσόμενος τῇ ἐξουσίᾳ τῇ τοῦ θεοῦ διαταγῇ ἀνθέστηκεν, οἱ δὲ ἀνθεστηκότες ἑαυτοῖς κρίμα

will bring   judgment on themselves. **3** For rulers   hold no terror for those who do   right, but   for those who
→ λήμψονται κρίμα   → ἑαυτοῖς   γὰρ ιοἱ ἄρχοντες εἰσὶν οὐκ φόβος   → τῷ   ← ἔργῳ ἀγαθῷ ἀλλὰ   → τῷ ←
v.fmi.3p   n.asn   r.dpm.3   cj d.npm n.npm   v.pai.3p pl n.nsm   d.dsn   n.dsn a.dsn cj   d.dsn
3284   3210   1571   1142 3836 807   1639 4024 5832   3836   2240 19 247   3836

do wrong.   Do you want to be free from fear   of the one in authority? Then do   what is right and he will
κακῷ   δὲ → → θέλεις   μὴ   φοβεῖσθαι   τὴν   ← ἐξουσίαν   ποιεῖ τὸ → ἀγαθὸν καὶ   ἕξεις
a.dsn   cj   v.pai.2s   pl   f.pp   d.asf   n.asf   v.pam.2s d.asn   a.asn cj   v.fai.2s
2805   1254   2527   3590   5828   3836   2026   4472 3836   19 2779   2400

commend you.   **4** For he is   God's servant to do you good.   But if you do   wrong,   be afraid, for
ἔπαινον   ← ἐξ αὐτῆς γὰρ → ἐστιν θεοῦ διάκονος εἰς ← σοὶ ιτὸ ἀγαθόν, δὲ ἐὰν → ποιῇς ιτὸ κακόν, → φοβοῦ γὰρ
n.asm   p.g r.gsf.3 cj   v.pai.3s n.gsm n.nsm p.a r.ds.2 d.asn a.asn cj cj   v.pas.2s d.asn a.asn   v.ppm.2s cj
2047   2400 1666 899 1142   1639 2536 1356 1650 5148 3836 19 1254 1569   4472 3836 2805   5828 1142

he does not bear the sword   for nothing.   He is   God's servant, an agent of wrath to bring punishment   on
→ → οὐ φορεῖ τὴν μάχαιραν   εἰκῇ   γὰρ → ἐστιν θεοῦ διάκονος ἔκδικος εἰς ὀργὴν → → ιτῷ πράσσοντι, ←
pl v.pai.3s d.asf n.asf   adv   cj   v.pai.3s n.gsm n.nsm   n.nsm p.a n.asf   d.dsm pt.pa.dsm
5841 5841 4024 5841 3836 3479   1632   1142   1639 2536 1356   1690 1650 3973   3836 4556

the wrongdoer. **5** Therefore, it is necessary to submit   to the authorities, not only because of possible punishment
τὸ κακὸν   διὸ   ἀνάγκη → ὑποτάσσεσθαι ←   οὐ μόνον διὰ   ← ιτὴν ὀργὴν,
d.asn a.asn   cj   n.nsf   f.pp   pl adv p.a   d.asf n.asf
3836 2805   1475   340   5718   4024 3667 1328   3836 3973

but also because of conscience. ¶   **6** This   is also why you pay taxes, for the authorities are God's
ἀλλὰ καὶ διὰ   ← ιτὴν συνείδησιν,   γὰρ ιδιὰ τοῦτο, καὶ ← → τελεῖτε φόρους γὰρ   εἰσὶν θεοῦ
cj adv p.a   d.asf n.asf   cj p.a r.asn adv   v.pai.2p n.apm cj   v.pai.3p n.gsm
247 2779 1328   3836 5287   1142 1328 4047 2779 4047   5464 5843 1142   1639 2536

servants, who give their full time   to governing. **7** Give everyone what you owe him: If you owe
λειτουργοὶ → →   προσκαρτεροῦντες εἰς ιαὐτὸ τοῦτο, ἀπόδοτε πᾶσιν τὰς   ὀφειλάς   τῷ
n.npm   pt.pa.npm   p.a r.asn r.asn v.aam.2p a.dpm d.apf   n.apf   d.dsm
3313   4674   1650 899 4047 625 4246 3836   4051   3836

taxes,   pay taxes;   if revenue, then revenue;   if respect, then respect;   if honor, then honor.
ιτὸν φόρον,   ιτὸν φόρον, τῷ   ιτὸ τέλος,   ιτὸ τέλος, τῷ   ιτὸν φόβον,   ιτὸν φόβον, τῷ   ιτὴν τιμήν,   ιτὴν τιμήν.
d.asm n.asm   d.asm n.asm d.dsm   d.asn n.asn   d.asn n.asn d.dsm   d.asm n.asm   d.asm n.asm d.dsm   d.asf n.asf   d.asf n.asf
3836 5843   3836 5843 3836   3836 5465   3836 5465 3836   3836 5832   3836 5832 3836   3836 5507   3836 5507

Love, for the Day Is Near

13:8   Let no debt remain outstanding, except the continuing debt to love   one   another, for
Μηδενὶ → μηδὲν ὀφείλετε ←   ← ιεἰ μή,   → ιτὸ ἀγαπᾶν, ἀλλήλους ←   γὰρ
a.dsm   a.asn v.pam.2p   cj pl   d.asn f.pa   r.apm   cj
3594 4053 3594 4053   3594   1623 3590   3836 26   253   1142

he who loves his fellowman has fulfilled the law. **9** The commandments, "Do not commit adultery," "Do not
ὁ   ἀγαπῶν τὸν ἕτερον → πεπλήρωκεν νόμον γὰρ τὸ   οὐ → μοιχεύσεις → οὐ
d.nsm   pt.pa.nsm d.asm r.asm   v.rai.3s   n.asm cj d.nsn   pl   v.fai.2s   pl
3836   26 3836 2283   4444   3795 1142 3836   4024   3658   4024

murder," "Do not steal," "Do not covet,"   and whatever other commandment there may be, are summed
φονεύσεις → οὐ κλέψεις → οὐκ ἐπιθυμήσεις καὶ ιεἴ τις, ἑτέρα ἐντολὴ   → ἀνακεφαλαιοῦται
v.fai.2s   pl v.fai.2s   pl v.fai.2s   cj cj r.nsf r.nsf n.nsf   v.ppi.3s
5839   3096 4024 3096   2121 4024 2121   2779 1623 5516 2283 1953   368

up in this one rule: "Love   your neighbor as yourself." **10** Love   does   no harm to its
← ἐν τούτῳ ιτῷ λόγῳ, [ἐν τῷ] ἀγαπήσεις σου ιτὸν πλησίον, ὡς σεαυτόν ιἡ ἀγάπῃ, ἐργάζεται οὐκ κακὸν → τῷ
p.d r.dsn d.dsm n.dsm p.d d.dsm v.fai.2s r.gs.2 d.asm   cj r.asm.2 d.nsf n.nsf v.pmi.3s   pl a.asn   d.dsm
1877 4047 3836 3364 1877 3836 26 5148 3836   6055 4932 3836 27 2237   4024 2805   3836

neighbor. Therefore love   is the fulfillment of the law. ¶ **11** And do this, understanding the present time.
πλησίον οὖν   ιἡ ἀγάπη, πλήρωμα → νόμου   Καὶ τοῦτο εἰδότες   τὸν   καιρόν
adv cj   d.nsf n.nsf   n.nsn   n.gsm   cj r.asn pt.ra.npm   d.asm   n.asm
4446 4036   3836 27   4445   3795   2779 4047 3857   3836   2789

The hour has come for you to wake   up from your slumber, because our salvation   is nearer   now than
ὅτι ὥρα ἤδη ὑμᾶς → ἐγερθῆναι ←   ἐξ   ὕπνου γὰρ ἡμῶν ἡ σωτηρία   ἐγγύτερον νῦν ἢ
cj n.nsf adv r.ap.2 f.ap   p.g   n.gsm cj r.gp.1 d.nsf n.nsf   adv.c adv pl
4022 6052 2453 7007 1586   1666   5678 1142 7005 3836 5401   1584 3814 2445

λήμψονται. **3** οἱ γὰρ ἄρχοντες οὐκ εἰσὶν φόβος τῷ ἀγαθῷ ἔργῳ ἀλλὰ τῷ κακῷ. θέλεις δὲ μὴ φοβεῖσθαι τὴν ἐξουσίαν· τὸ ἀγαθὸν ποίει, καὶ ἕξεις ἔπαινον ἐξ αὐτῆς· **4** θεοῦ γὰρ διάκονός ἐστιν σοὶ εἰς τὸ ἀγαθόν. ἐὰν δὲ τὸ κακὸν ποιῇς, φοβοῦ· οὐ γὰρ εἰκῇ τὴν μάχαιραν φορεῖ· θεοῦ γὰρ διάκονός ἐστιν ἔκδικος εἰς ὀργὴν τῷ τὸ κακὸν πράσσοντι. **5** διὸ ἀνάγκη ὑποτάσσεσθαι, οὐ μόνον διὰ τὴν ὀργὴν ἀλλὰ καὶ διὰ τὴν συνείδησιν. ¶ **6** διὰ τοῦτο γὰρ καὶ φόρους τελεῖτε· λειτουργοὶ γὰρ θεοῦ εἰσιν εἰς αὐτὸ τοῦτο προσκαρτεροῦντες. **7** ἀπόδοτε πᾶσιν τὰς ὀφειλάς, τῷ τὸν φόρον τὸν φόρον, τῷ τὸ τέλος τὸ τέλος, τῷ τὸν φόβον τὸν φόβον, τῷ τὴν τιμὴν τὴν τιμήν.

13:8 Μηδενὶ μηδὲν ὀφείλετε εἰ μὴ τὸ ἀλλήλους ἀγαπᾶν· ὁ γὰρ ἀγαπῶν τὸν ἕτερον νόμον πεπλήρωκεν. **9** τὸ γὰρ Οὐ μοιχεύσεις, Οὐ φονεύσεις, Οὐ κλέψεις, Οὐκ ἐπιθυμήσεις, καὶ εἴ τις ἑτέρα ἐντολή, ἐν τῷ λόγῳ τούτῳ ἀνακεφαλαιοῦται [ἐν τῷ] Ἀγαπήσεις τὸν πλησίον σου ὡς σεαυτόν. **10** ἡ ἀγάπη τῷ πλησίον κακὸν οὐκ ἐργάζεται· πλήρωμα οὖν νόμου ἡ ἀγάπη. ¶ **11** Καὶ τοῦτο εἰδότες τὸν καιρόν, ὅτι ὥρα ἤδη ὑμᾶς ἐξ ὕπνου ἐγερθῆναι, νῦν γὰρ ἐγγύτερον ἡμῶν ἡ σωτηρία ἢ ὅτε ἐπιστεύσαμεν. **12** ἡ νὺξ προέκοψεν,

when	we	first	believed.	¹² The	night	is nearly	over;	the	day	is almost	here.	So	let us put		aside	the
ὅτε	→		ἐπιστεύσαμεν	ἡ	νὺξ	→	→	προέκοψεν	δὲ	ἡ	ἡμέρα	→	→	ἤγγικεν	οὖν	→	ἀποθώμεθα		τὰ
cj			v.aai.1p	d.nsf	n.nsf			v.aai.3s	cj	d.nsf	n.nsf			v.rai.3s	cj		v.ams.1p		d.apn
4021			4409	3836	3816			4621	1254	3836	2465			1581	4036		700		3836

deeds	of darkness	and	put		on	the armor	of light.	¹³ Let us behave		decently,	as	in	the daytime,	not
ἔργα	⌐τοῦ σκότους⌐	δὲ	ἐνδυσώμεθα	←	τὰ	ὅπλα	⌐τοῦ φωτός⌐	→	περιπατήσωμεν	εὐσχημόνως	ὡς	ἐν	ἡμέρα	μὴ
n.apn	d.gsn n.gsn	cj	v.ams.1p		d.apn	n.apn	d.gsn n.gsn		v.aas.1p	adv	cj	p.d	n.dsf	pl
2240	3836 5030	1254	1907		3836	3960	3836 5890		4344	2361	6055	1877	2465	3590

in	orgies	and	drunkenness,	not	in	sexual immorality	and	debauchery,	not	in	dissension	and	jealousy.	¹⁴ Rather,
→	κώμοις	καὶ	μέθαις	μὴ	→	κοίταις	καὶ	ἀσελγείαις	μὴ	→	ἔριδι	καὶ	ζήλω	ἀλλὰ
	n.dpm	cj	n.dpf	pl		n.dpf	cj	n.dpf	pl		n.dsf	cj	n.dsm	cj
	3269	2779	3494	3590		3130	2779	816	3590		2251	2779	2419	247

clothe	yourselves with	the	Lord	Jesus	Christ,	and	do	not	think		about	how to gratify	the	desires	of
ἐνδύσασθε	←		τὸν	κύριον	Ἰησοῦν	Χριστὸν	καὶ		μὴ	⌐ποιεῖσθε⌐	πρόνοιαν⌐	←	εἰς	←	ἐπιθυμίας	→
v.amm.2p			d.asm	n.asm	n.asm	n.asm	cj		4472	3590 4472	v.pmm.2p	n.asf		p.a		n.apf
1907			3836	3261	2652	5986	2779				4630			1650		2123

the	sinful	nature.
τῆς	σαρκὸς	
d.gsf	n.gsf	
3836	4922	

The Weak and the Strong

14:1	Accept		him whose	faith	is weak,		without	passing judgment	on	disputable	matters.	²
δὲ	προσλαμβάνεσθε	Τὸν		⌐τῇ	πίστει	→	ἀσθενοῦντα	μὴ	εἰς	διακρίσεις	διαλογισμῶν	←	μὲν
cj	v.pmm.2p	d.asm		d.dsf	n.dsf		pt.pa.asm	pl	p.a	n.apf	n.gpm		pl
1254	4689	3836		3836	4411		820	3590	1650	1360	1369		3525

One man's	faith	allows him to eat		everything,	but	another man,	whose faith is weak,		eats	only	vegetables.
ὃς	πιστεύει	→	φαγεῖν	πάντα	δὲ	ὁ	ἀσθενῶν	ἐσθίει		λάχανα
r.nsm	v.pai.3s		f.aa	a.apn	cj	d.nsm	pt.pa.nsm	v.pai.3s		n.apn
4005	4409		2266	4246	1254	3836	820	2266		3303

³ The	man	who eats	everything	must	not	look		down	on	him	who does	not,	and	the	man	who	does	not
ὁ		⌐ἐσθίων	→		μὴ	ἐξουθενείτω	←	←	τὸν	→	ἐσθίοντα	μὴ	δὲ	ὁ				μὴ
d.nsm		pt.pa.nsm			pl	v.pam.3s			d.asm		pt.pa.asm	pl	cj	d.nsm				pl
3836		2266			2024	7074			3836		2266	3590	1254	3836				3590

eat	everything	must	not	condemn	the	man	who does,	for	God	has	accepted	him.	⁴ Who	are	you	to
ἐσθίων	→	μὴ	κρινέτω	τὸν	←	←	ἐσθίοντα	γὰρ	⌐ὁ	θεός⌐	→	προσελάβετο	αὐτόν	τίς	εἶ	σὺ
pt.pa.nsm		pl	v.pam.3s	d.asm			pt.pa.asm	cj	d.nsm	n.nsm		v.ami.3s	r.asm.3	r.nsm	v.pai.2s	r.ns.2
2266		3590	3212	3836			2266	1142	3836	2536		4689	899	5515	1639	5148

judge	someone else's	servant?	To his	own	master	he stands	or	falls.	And	he will stand,		for	the	Lord	is
⌐ὁ	κρίνων	ἀλλότριον	←	οἰκέτην	→	τῷ	ἰδίῳ	κυρίῳ	→	στήκει	ἢ	πίπτει	δέ	→	→	σταθήσεται	γὰρ	ὁ	κύριος	→
d.nsm	pt.pa.nsm	a.asm		n.asm		d.dsm	a.dsm	n.dsm		v.pai.3s	cj	v.pai.3s	cj			v.fpi.3s	cj	d.nsm	n.nsm	
3836	3212	259		3860		3836	2625	3261		5112	2445	4406	1254			2705	1142	3836	3261	

able	to	make	him	stand.	¶	⁵		One	man	considers	one	day		more	sacred	than	*another;*
δυνατεῖ	→	→	αὐτὸν	στῆσαι			[γὰρ]	μὲν	Ὃς		κρίνει		ἡμέραν		παρ'	ἡμέραν	δὲ
v.pai.3s			r.asm.3	f.aa			cj	pl	r.nsm		v.pai.3s		n.asf		p.a	n.asf	pl
1542		2705	899	2705			1142	3525	4005		3212		2465		4123	2465	1254

another man	considers	every	day	alike.	Each	one	should be	fully	convinced	in	his	own	mind.	⁶ He	who
ὃς	κρίνει	πᾶσαν	ἡμέραν		ἕκαστος	←	←	→	πληροφορείσθω	ἐν	τῷ	ἰδίῳ	νοΐ	ὁ	
r.nsm	v.pai.3s	a.asf	n.asf		r.nsm				v.ppm.3s	p.d	d.dsm	a.dsm	n.dsm	d.nsm	
4005	3212	4246	2465		1667				4442	1877	3836	2625	3808	3836	

regards	one	day	as special,	does	so	to the	Lord.	He	who	eats	meat,	eats	to the	Lord,	for	he	gives
φρονῶν	⌐τὴν	ἡμέραν⌐		φρονεῖ	←	→	κυρίῳ	καὶ	ὁ	→	ἐσθίων	ἐσθίει	→	κυρίῳ	γὰρ	→	→
pt.pa.nsm	d.asf	n.asf		v.pai.3s			n.dsm	cj	d.nsm		pt.pa.nsm	v.pai.3s		n.dsm	cj
5858	3836	2465		5858			3261	2779	3836		2266	2266		3261	1142

thanks	to God;	and	he	who abstains,	does		so	to the	Lord	and	gives	thanks	to God.	⁷ For	none	of
εὐχαριστεῖ	⌐τῷ θεῷ⌐	καὶ	ὁ	←	⌐μὴ	ἐσθίων⌐	οὐκ	ἐσθίει⌐	←	κυρίῳ	καὶ	→	εὐχαριστεῖ	→	⌐τῷ θεῷ⌐	γὰρ	οὐδεὶς
v.pai.3s	d.dsm n.dsm	cj	d.nsm		pl	pt.pa.nsm	pl	v.pai.3s		n.dsm	cj		v.pai.3s		d.dsm n.dsm	cj	a.nsm
2373	3836 2536	2779	3836		3590	2266	4024	2266		3261	2779		2373		3836 2536	1142	4029

ἡ δὲ ἡμέρα ἤγγικεν. ἀποθώμεθα οὖν τὰ ἔργα τοῦ σκότους, ἐνδυσώμεθα [δὲ] τὰ ὅπλα τοῦ φωτός. ¹³ ὡς ἐν ἡμέρα εὐσχημόνως περιπατήσωμεν, μὴ κώμοις καὶ μέθαις, μὴ κοίταις καὶ ἀσελγείαις, μὴ ἔριδι καὶ ζήλω, ¹⁴ ἀλλὰ ἐνδύσασθε τὸν κύριον Ἰησοῦν Χριστὸν καὶ τῆς σαρκὸς πρόνοιαν μὴ ποιεῖσθε εἰς ἐπιθυμίας.

¹⁴:¹ Τὸν δὲ ἀσθενοῦντα τῇ πίστει προσλαμβάνεσθε, μὴ εἰς διακρίσεις διαλογισμῶν. ² ὃς μὲν πιστεύει φαγεῖν πάντα, ὁ δὲ ἀσθενῶν λάχανα ἐσθίει. ³ ὁ ἐσθίων τὸν μὴ ἐσθίοντα μὴ ἐξουθενείτω, ὁ δὲ μὴ ἐσθίων τὸν ἐσθίοντα μὴ κρινέτω, ὁ θεὸς γὰρ αὐτὸν προσελάβετο. ⁴ σὺ τίς εἶ ὁ κρίνων ἀλλότριον οἰκέτην; τῷ ἰδίῳ κυρίῳ στήκει ἢ πίπτει· σταθήσεται δέ, δυνατεῖ γὰρ ὁ κύριος στῆσαι αὐτόν. ¶ ⁵ ὃς μὲν [γὰρ] κρίνει ἡμέραν παρ' ἡμέραν, ὃς δὲ κρίνει πᾶσαν ἡμέραν· ἕκαστος ἐν τῷ ἰδίῳ νοΐ πληροφορείσθω. ⁶ ὁ φρονῶν τὴν ἡμέραν κυρίῳ φρονεῖ· καὶ ὁ ἐσθίων κυρίῳ ἐσθίει, εὐχαριστεῖ γὰρ τῷ θεῷ· καὶ ὁ μὴ ἐσθίων κυρίῳ οὐκ ἐσθίει καὶ εὐχαριστεῖ τῷ θεῷ. ⁷ οὐδεὶς γὰρ ἡμῶν ἑαυτῷ ζῇ καὶ οὐδεὶς ἑαυτῷ ἀποθνήσκει· ⁸ ἐάν τε γὰρ ζῶμεν, τῷ κυρίῳ ζῶμεν, ἐὰν

us lives to himself alone and none of us dies to himself alone. **8** If we live, we live to the Lord; and
ἡμῶν ζῇ → ἑαυτῷ καὶ οὐδεὶς ἀποθνῄσκει → ἑαυτῷ γὰρ τε ἐάν → ζῶμεν ζῶμεν → τῷ κυρίῳ τε
r.gp.1 v.pai.3s r.dsm.3 cj a.nsm v.pai.3s r.dsm.3 cj cj cj v.pas.1p v.pai.1p d.dsm n.dsm cj
7005 2409 1571 2779 4029 633 1571 1142 5445 1569 2409 2409 3836 3261 5445

if we die, we die to the Lord. So, whether we live or die, we belong to the Lord.
ἐάν → ἀποθνῄσκωμεν ἀποθνῄσκομεν → τῷ κυρίῳ οὖν ἐάν τε ζῶμεν ἐάν τε ἀποθνῄσκωμεν ἐσμὲν → τοῦ κυρίου
cj v.pas.1p v.pai.1p d.dsm n.dsm cj cj cj v.pas.1p cj cj v.pas.1p v.pai.1p d.gsm n.gsm
1569 633 633 3836 3261 4036 1569 5445 2409 1569 5445 633 1639 3836 3261

¶ **9** For this very reason, Christ died and returned to life so that he might be the Lord of both the
γὰρ εἰς τοῦτο ← ← Χριστὸς ἀπέθανεν καὶ → → ἔζησεν ἵνα ← → → → κυριεύσῃ → καὶ
cj p.a r.asn n.nsm v.aai.3s cj v.aai.3s cj v.aas.3s cj
1142 1650 4047 5986 633 2779 2409 2671 3259 3738 2779

dead and the living. **10** You, then, why do you judge your brother? Or why do you look down on your
νεκρῶν καὶ ζώντων Σὺ δὲ τί → κρίνεις σου ⌐τὸν ἀδελφόν⌐ ἢ καὶ τί → σὺ ἐξουθενεῖς → σου
a.gpm cj pt.pa.gpm r.ns.2 cj r.asn v.pai.2s r.gs.2 d.asm n.asm cj adv r.asn r.ns.2 v.pai.2s r.gs.2
3738 2779 2409 5148 1254 5515 3212 5148 3836 81 2445 2779 5515 2024 5148 2024 5148

brother? For we will all stand before God's judgment seat. **11** It is written: "'As surely as I live,'
⌐τὸν ἀδελφόν⌐ γὰρ → → πάντες παραστησόμεθα ← ⌐τοῦ θεοῦ⌐ ⌐τῷ βήματι⌐ γὰρ → γέγραπται ἐγὼ ζῶ
d.asm n.asm cj a.npm v.fmi.1p d.gsm n.gsm d.dsn n.dsn cj v.rpi.3s r.ns.1 v.pai.1s
3836 81 1142 4225 4225 4246 4225 3836 2536 3836 1037 1142 1211 1609 2409

says the Lord, 'every knee will bow before me; every tongue will confess to God.'" **12** So then, each
λέγει κύριος ὅτι πᾶν γόνυ → κάμψει → ἐμοὶ καὶ πᾶσα γλῶσσα → ἐξομολογήσεται → ⌐τῷ θεῷ⌐ οὖν ἄρα ἕκαστος
v.pai.3s n.nsm cj a.nsn n.nsn v.fai.3s r.ds.1 cj a.nsf n.nsf v.fmi.3s d.dsm n.dsm cj cj r.nsm
3306 3261 4022 4246 1205 2828 1609 2779 4246 1185 2018 3836 2536 4036 726 1667

of us will give an account of himself to God. ¶ **13** Therefore let us stop passing judgment on
→ ἡμῶν → δώσει λόγον περὶ ἑαυτοῦ → [τῷ θεῷ] οὖν → Μηκέτι → κρίνωμεν ←
r.gp.1 v.fai.3s n.asn p.g r.gsm.3 d.dsm n.dsm cj adv v.pas.1p
7005 1443 3364 4309 1571 3836 2536 4036 3212 3212 3600 3212

one another. Instead, *make up your mind* not to put any stumbling block or obstacle in your
ἀλλήλους ← ⌐ἀλλὰ μᾶλλον⌐ κρίνατε τοῦτο μὴ → ⌐τὸ τιθέναι⌐ πρόσκομμα ← ἢ σκάνδαλον → τῷ
r.apm cj adv.c v.aam.2p r.asn pl d.asn f.pa n.asn cj n.asn d.dsm
253 247 3437 3212 4047 3590 3836 5502 4682 2445 4998 3836

brother's way. **14** As one who is in the Lord Jesus, I am fully convinced that no food is unclean in itself.
ἀδελφῷ ἐν κυρίῳ Ἰησοῦ → → οἶδα καὶ πέπεισμαι ὅτι οὐδὲν → κοινὸν δι' ἑαυτοῦ
n.dsm p.d n.dsm n.dsm v.rai.1s cj v.rpi.1s cj a.nsn a.nsn p.g r.gsn.3
81 1877 3261 2652 3857 2779 4275 4022 4029 3123 1328 1571

But if anyone regards something as unclean, then for him it is unclean. **15** If your brother is
εἰ μὴ τῷ λογιζομένῳ τι εἶναι κοινὸν → ἐκείνῳ κοινόν γὰρ εἰ σου ὁ ἀδελφός →
cj pl d.dsm pt.pm.dsm r.asn f.pa a.asn r.dsm a.nsn cj cj r.gs.2 d.nsm n.nsm
1623 3590 3836 3357 5516 1639 3123 1697 3123 1142 1623 5148 3836 81

distressed because of what you eat, you are no longer acting in love. Do not by your eating destroy
λυπεῖται διὰ ← → → βρῶμα → οὐκέτι ← περιπατεῖς κατὰ ἀγάπην μὴ → σου ⌐τῷ βρώματι⌐ ἀπόλλυε
v.ppi.3s p.a n.asn adv v.pai.2s p.a n.asf pl r.gs.2 d.dsn n.dsn v.pam.2s
3382 1328 1109 4344 4344 4033 4344 2848 27 660 3590 5148 3836 1109 660

your brother for whom Christ died. **16** Do not allow what you consider good to be spoken of as evil.
ἐκεῖνον ὑπὲρ οὗ Χριστὸς ἀπέθανεν οὖν → μὴ → ὑμῶν ⌐τὸ ἀγαθόν⌐ → βλασφημείσθω ← ←
r.asn p.g r.gsn n.nsm v.aai.3s cj pl r.gp.2 d.nsn a.nsn v.ppm.3s
1697 5642 4005 5986 633 4036 1059 3590 1059 19 7007 3836 19 1059

17 For the kingdom of God is not a matter of eating and drinking, but of righteousness, peace and joy in
γὰρ ἡ βασιλεία → ⌐τοῦ θεοῦ⌐ ἐστιν οὐ βρῶσις καὶ πόσις ἀλλὰ δικαιοσύνη καὶ εἰρήνη καὶ χαρὰ ἐν
cj d.nsf n.nsf d.gsm n.gsm v.pai.3s pl n.nsf cj n.nsf cj n.nsf cj n.nsf cj n.nsf p.d
1142 3836 993 3836 2536 1639 4024 1111 2779 4530 247 1466 2779 1645 2779 5915 1877

the Holy Spirit, **18** because anyone who serves Christ in this way is pleasing to God and approved by
ἁγίῳ πνεύματι γὰρ ὁ δουλεύων ⌐τῷ Χριστῷ⌐ ἐν τούτῳ εὐάρεστος → ⌐τῷ θεῷ⌐ καὶ δόκιμος →
a.dsn n.dsn cj d.nsm pt.pa.nsm d.dsm n.dsm p.d r.dsn a.nsm d.dsm n.dsm cj a.nsm
41 4460 1142 3836 1526 3836 5986 1877 4047 2298 3836 2536 2779 1511

men. ¶ **19** Let us therefore make every effort to do what leads to peace and to
⌐τοῖς ἀνθρώποις⌐ → → ⌐Ἄρα οὖν⌐ → → διώκωμεν ← ← τὰ → ⌐τῆς εἰρήνης⌐ καὶ τὰ →
d.dpm n.dpm cj cj v.pas.1p d.apn d.gsf n.gsf cj d.apn
3836 476 1503 1503 726 4036 1503 3836 3836 1645 2779 3836 3869

τε ἀποθνῄσκωμεν, τῷ κυρίῳ ἀποθνῄσκομεν. ἐάν τε οὖν ζῶμεν ἐάν τε ἀποθνῄσκωμεν, τοῦ κυρίου ἐσμέν. ¶ **9** εἰς τοῦτο γὰρ Χριστὸς ἀπέθανεν καὶ ἔζησεν, ἵνα καὶ νεκρῶν καὶ ζώντων κυριεύσῃ. **10** σὺ δὲ τί κρίνεις τὸν ἀδελφόν σου; ἢ καὶ σὺ τί ἐξουθενεῖς τὸν ἀδελφόν σου; πάντες γὰρ παραστησόμεθα τῷ βήματι τοῦ θεοῦ, **11** γέγραπται γάρ, Ζῶ ἐγώ, λέγει κύριος, ὅτι ἐμοὶ κάμψει πᾶν γόνυ καὶ πᾶσα γλῶσσα ἐξομολογήσεται τῷ θεῷ. **12** ἄρα [οὖν] ἕκαστος ἡμῶν περὶ ἑαυτοῦ λόγον δώσει [τῷ θεῷ]. ¶ **13** Μηκέτι οὖν ἀλλήλους κρίνωμεν· ἀλλὰ τοῦτο κρίνατε μᾶλλον, τὸ μὴ τιθέναι πρόσκομμα τῷ ἀδελφῷ ἢ σκάνδαλον. **14** οἶδα καὶ πέπεισμαι ἐν κυρίῳ Ἰησοῦ ὅτι οὐδὲν κοινὸν δι' ἑαυτοῦ, εἰ μὴ τῷ λογιζομένῳ τι κοινὸν εἶναι, ἐκείνῳ κοινόν. **15** εἰ γὰρ διὰ βρῶμα ὁ ἀδελφός σου λυπεῖται, οὐκέτι κατὰ ἀγάπην περιπατεῖς· μὴ τῷ βρώματί σου ἐκεῖνον ἀπόλλυε ὑπὲρ οὗ Χριστὸς ἀπέθανεν. **16** μὴ βλασφημείσθω οὖν ὑμῶν τὸ ἀγαθόν. **17** οὐ γάρ ἐστιν ἡ βασιλεία τοῦ θεοῦ βρῶσις καὶ πόσις ἀλλὰ δικαιοσύνη καὶ εἰρήνη καὶ χαρὰ ἐν πνεύματι ἁγίῳ· **18** ὁ γὰρ ἐν τούτῳ δουλεύων τῷ Χριστῷ εὐάρεστος τῷ θεῷ καὶ δόκιμος τοῖς ἀνθρώποις. ¶ **19** ἄρα οὖν

mutual   edification. **20** Do not destroy the work of God   for   the sake of food.   All   food is
ⸯτῆς εἰς ἀλλήλουςⸯ ⸯτῆς οἰκοδομῆςⸯ   ⸯ   μὴ κατάλυε τὸ ἔργον → ⸯτοῦ θεοῦⸯ ἕνεκεν ←   ← βρώματος μὲν πάντα
d.gsf p.a r.apm   d.gsf n.gsf   pl v.pam.2s d.asn n.asn   d.gsm n.gsm p.g   n.gsn   pl   a.npn
3836 1650 253   3836 3869   2907 3590 2907 3836 2240   3836 2536   1914   1109   3525 4246

clean, but it is wrong for a man   to eat   anything that *causes someone else to stumble.*   **21** It is
καθαρὰ ἀλλὰ κακὸν → ⸯτῷ ἀνθρώπῳⸯ ⸯτῷ ἐσθίοντιⸯ   διὰ   προσκόμματος
a.npn   cj   a.asn   d.dsm n.dsm   d.dsm pt.pa.dsm   p.g   n.gsn
2754   247 2805   3836 476   3836 2266   1328   4682

better not to eat   meat or drink wine or   to do anything else that will cause your brother   to fall.
καλὸν μὴ ⸯτὸ φαγεῖνⸯ κρέα μηδὲ πιεῖν οἶνον μηδὲ   ἐν ᾧ ←   ←   ← σου ὁ ἀδελφόςⸯ προσκόπτει
a.nsn pl d.nsn f.aa   n.apn cj   f.aa   n.asn cj   p.d r.dsn   r.gs.2 d.nsm n.nsm   v.pai.3s
2819   3590 3836 2266   3200 3593 4403   3885   3593   1877 4005   5148 3836 81   4684

¶ **22** So whatever you believe   about these things   keep between   yourself and   God.
ⸯ ⸯπίστιν ἣν ἔχειςⸯ   σὺ ἔχε   κατὰ σεαυτὸν   ἐνώπιον ⸯτοῦ θεοῦⸯ
   n.asf r.asf v.pai.2s   r.ns.2 v.pam.2s   p.a r.asm.2   p.g   d.gsm n.gsm
   2400   4411 4005 2400   5148 2400   2848 4932   1967   3836 2536

Blessed is the man who does not condemn himself by what he approves. **23** But the man who has doubts   is
μακάριος ὁ   →   μὴ κρίνων ἑαυτὸν ἐν ᾧ → δοκιμάζει   δὲ ὁ   →   διακρινόμενος →
a.nsm   d.nsm   pl pt.pa.nsm r.asm.3 p.d r.dsn v.pai.3s cj d.nsm   pt.pm.nsm
3421   3836   3212 3590 3212 1571 1877 4005 1507   1254 3836   1359

condemned if he eats, because his eating is not from faith; and everything that does not come from faith is
κατακέκριται ἐὰν → φάγῃ ὅτι   οὐκ ἐκ πίστεως δὲ πᾶν ὃ   οὐκ   ἐκ πίστεως ἐστίν
v.rpi.3s   cj   v.aas.3s cj   pl p.g n.gsf cj a.nsn r.nsn pl   p.g n.gsf v.pai.3s
2891   1569 2266 4022   4024 1666 4411   1254 4246 4005 4024   1666 4411   1639

sin.   ¶ **15:1** We who are strong ought   to bear   with the failings   of the weak   and not to please
ἁμαρτία δὲ ἡμεῖς οἱ   δυνατοὶ Ὀφείλομεν → βαστάζειν   τὰ ἀσθενήματα → τῶν ἀδυνάτων καὶ μὴ → ἀρέσκειν
n.nsf   cj r.np.1 d.npm a.npm   v.pai.1p   f.pa   d.apn n.apn   d.gpm a.gpm   cj   pl   f.pa
281   1254 7005 3836   1543   4053   1002   3836 821   3836 105   2779 3590   743

ourselves. **2** Each of us   should please his neighbor for his good, to build   him up. **3** For even Christ   did
ἑαυτοῖς ἕκαστος → ἡμῶν →   ἀρεσκέτω τῷ πλησίον   εἰς τὸ ἀγαθὸν πρὸς οἰκοδομήν   ←   γὰρ καὶ ὁ Χριστὸςⸯ →
r.dpm.1 r.nsm   r.gp.1   v.pam.3s d.dsm adv   p.a d.asn a.asn p.a n.asf   cj adv d.nsm n.nsm
1571   1667   7005   743 3836 4446   1650 3836 19   4639 3869   1142 2779 3836 5986   743

not please himself but, as it is written: "The insults   of those who insult   you have fallen on me." **4** For
οὐχ ἤρεσεν ἑαυτῷ ἀλλὰ καθὼς γέγραπται οἱ ὀνειδισμοὶ → τῶν ← ὀνειδιζόντων σε → ἐπέπεσαν ἐπ' ἐμέ γὰρ
pl   v.aai.3s r.dsm.3 cj   cj   v.rpi.3s d.npm n.npm   d.gpm   pt.pa.gpm r.as.2   v.aai.3p p.a r.as.1 cj
4024 743   1571 247 2777 1211   3836 3944   3836   3943   5148   2158   2093 1609 1142

everything that was written   in the past was written to teach   us,   so that through endurance   and
ὅσα   ←   προεγράφη   ←   ←   ἐγράφη εἰς ⸯτὴν διδασκαλίανⸯ ἡμετέραν ἵνα ← διὰ ⸯτῆς ὑπομονῆςⸯ καὶ
r.npn   v.api.3s   v.api.3s p.a d.asf n.asf   r.asf.1 cj   p.g d.gsf n.gsf   cj
4012   4592   1211   1650 3836 1436   2466   2671   1328 3836 5705   2779

the encouragement of the Scriptures we might have hope.   ¶ **5**   May the God who gives endurance
διὰ τῆς παρακλήσεως → τῶν γραφῶν → → ἔχωμεν ⸯτὴν ἐλπίδαⸯ   δὲ → ὁ θεὸς → ⸯτῆς ὑπομονῆςⸯ
p.g d.gsf n.gsf   d.gpf n.gpf   v.pas.1p d.asf n.asf   cj   d.nsm n.nsm d.gsf n.gsf
1328 3836 4155   3836 1210   2400 3836 1828   1254 1443 3836 2536 3836 5705

and encouragement give you a *spirit of unity*   among yourselves *as   you follow* Christ Jesus, **6** so that
καὶ ⸯτῆς παρακλήσεωςⸯ δῴη ὑμῖν ⸯτὸ αὐτὸ φρονεῖνⸯ ἐν   ἀλλήλοις κατὰ   Χριστὸν Ἰησοῦν ἵνα ←
cj   d.gsf n.gsf   v.aao.3s r.dp.2 d.asn r.asn f.pa p.d r.dpm   p.a   n.asm   n.asm   cj
2779 3836 4155   1443 7007 3836 899 5858   1877 253   2848   5986   2652   2671

with one heart   and   mouth you may glorify the God and Father of our Lord   Jesus Christ. ¶
→   ὁμοθυμαδὸν ἐν ἑνὶ στόματι → → δοξάζητε τὸν θεὸν καὶ πατέρα → ἡμῶν ⸯτοῦ κυρίουⸯ Ἰησοῦ Χριστοῦ
    adv   p.d a.dsn n.dsn   v.pas.2p   d.asm n.asm cj n.asm   r.gp.1 d.gsm n.gsm   n.gsm n.gsm
    3924   1877 1651 5125   1519   3836 2536 2779 4252   3261 7005 3836 3261   2652 5986

7 Accept   one   another, then, just as   Christ   accepted you, in order to bring praise to God.
προσλαμβάνεσθε ἀλλήλους ←   Διὸ καθὼς καὶ ὁ Χριστὸςⸯ προσελάβετο ὑμᾶς εἰς ←   δόξαν ⸯτοῦ θεοῦⸯ
v.pmm.2p   r.apm   cj   cj   adv d.nsm n.nsm   v.ami.3s   r.ap.2 p.a   n.asf d.gsm n.gsm
4689   253   1475 2777 2779 3836 5986   4689   7007 1650   1518   3836 2536

τὰ τῆς εἰρήνης διώκωμεν καὶ τὰ τῆς οἰκοδομῆς τῆς εἰς ἀλλήλους. **20** μὴ ἕνεκεν βρώματος κατάλυε τὸ ἔργον τοῦ θεοῦ. πάντα μὲν καθαρά, ἀλλὰ κακὸν τῷ ἀνθρώπῳ τῷ διὰ προσκόμματος ἐσθίοντι. **21** καλὸν τὸ μὴ φαγεῖν κρέα μηδὲ πιεῖν οἶνον μηδὲ ἐν ᾧ ὁ ἀδελφός σου προσκόπτει. ¶ **22** σὺ πίστιν [ἣν] ἔχεις κατὰ σεαυτὸν ἔχε ἐνώπιον τοῦ θεοῦ. μακάριος ὁ μὴ κρίνων ἑαυτὸν ἐν ᾧ δοκιμάζει· **23** ὁ δὲ διακρινόμενος ἐὰν φάγῃ κατακέκριται, ὅτι οὐκ ἐκ πίστεως· πᾶν δὲ ὃ οὐκ ἐκ πίστεως ἁμαρτία ἐστίν.

15:1 Ὀφείλομεν δὲ ἡμεῖς οἱ δυνατοὶ τὰ ἀσθενήματα τῶν ἀδυνάτων βαστάζειν καὶ μὴ ἑαυτοῖς ἀρέσκειν. **2** ἕκαστος ἡμῶν τῷ πλησίον ἀρεσκέτω εἰς τὸ ἀγαθὸν πρὸς οἰκοδομήν· **3** καὶ γὰρ ὁ Χριστὸς οὐχ ἑαυτῷ ἤρεσεν· ἀλλὰ καθὼς γέγραπται, Οἱ ὀνειδισμοὶ τῶν ὀνειδιζόντων σε ἐπέπεσαν ἐπ' ἐμέ. **4** ὅσα γὰρ προεγράφη, εἰς τὴν ἡμετέραν διδασκαλίαν ἐγράφη, ἵνα διὰ τῆς ὑπομονῆς καὶ διὰ τῆς παρακλήσεως τῶν γραφῶν τὴν ἐλπίδα ἔχωμεν. ¶ **5** ὁ δὲ θεὸς τῆς ὑπομονῆς καὶ τῆς παρακλήσεως δῴη ὑμῖν τὸ αὐτὸ φρονεῖν ἐν ἀλλήλοις κατὰ Χριστὸν Ἰησοῦν, **6** ἵνα ὁμοθυμαδὸν ἐν ἑνὶ στόματι δοξάζητε τὸν θεὸν καὶ πατέρα τοῦ κυρίου ἡμῶν Ἰησοῦ Χριστοῦ. ¶ **7** Διὸ προσλαμβάνεσθε ἀλλήλους, καθὼς καὶ ὁ Χριστὸς προσελάβετο ὑμᾶς εἰς δόξαν τοῦ θεοῦ. **8** λέγω γὰρ

8 For I tell you that Christ has become a servant of the Jews on behalf of God's truth, to confirm
γὰρ → λέγω Χριστὸν → γεγενῆσθαι διάκονον → περιτομῆς ὑπὲρ ← θεοῦ ἀληθείας εἰς ᾽τὸ βεβαιῶσαι᾽
cj v.pai.1s n.asm f.rp n.asm n.gsf p.g n.gsm n.gsf p.a d.asn f.aa
1142 3306 5986 1181 1356 4364 5642 2536 237 1650 3836 1011

the promises made to the patriarchs **9** so that the Gentiles may glorify God for his mercy, as it is written:
τὰς ἐπαγγελίας → → τῶν πατέρων δὲ → τὰ ἔθνη → δοξάσαι ᾽τὸν θεόν᾽ ὑπὲρ ἐλέους καθὼς → γέγραπται
d.apf n.apf d.gpm n.gpm cj d.apn n.apn f.aa d.asm n.asm p.g n.gsf adv v.rpi.3s
3836 2039 3836 4252 1254 3836 1620 1519 3836 2536 5642 1799 2777 1211

"Therefore I will praise you among the Gentiles; I will sing hymns to your name." **10** Again, it
᾽διὰ τοῦτο᾽ → → ἐξομολογήσομαι σοι ἐν ἔθνεσιν καὶ → ψαλῶ → σου ᾽τῷ ὀνόματι᾽ καὶ πάλιν
p.a r.asn v.fmi.1s r.ds.2 p.d n.dpn cj v.fai.1s r.gs.2 d.dsn n.dsn cj adv
1328 4047 2018 5148 1877 1620 2779 6010 3950 5148 3836 3950 2779 4099

says, "Rejoice, O Gentiles, with his people." **11** And again, "Praise the Lord, all you Gentiles, and sing
λέγει εὐφράνθητε → ἔθνη μετὰ αὐτοῦ ᾽τοῦ λαοῦ᾽ καὶ πάλιν αἰνεῖτε τὸν κύριον πάντα → ᾽τὰ ἔθνη᾽ καὶ ἐπαινεσάτωσαν
v.pai.3s v.apm.2p n.vpn p.g r.gsm.3 d.gsm n.gsm cj adv v.pam.2p d.asm n.asm a.vpn d.vpn n.vpn cj v.aam.3p
3306 2370 1620 3552 899 3836 3295 2779 4099 140 3836 3261 4246 3836 1620 2779 2046

praises to him, all you peoples." **12** And again, Isaiah says, "The Root of Jesse will spring up, one who
← αὐτὸν πάντες → ᾽οἱ λαοί᾽ καὶ πάλιν Ἠσαΐας λέγει ἡ ῥίζα ᾽τοῦ Ἰεσσαί᾽ ἔσται → καὶ ὁ
r.asm.3 a.npm d.npm n.npm cj adv n.nsm v.pai.3s d.nsf n.nsf d.gsm n.gsm v.fmi.3s cj d.nsm
899 4246 3836 3295 2779 4099 2480 3306 3836 4844 3836 2649 1639 2779 3836

will arise to rule over the nations; the Gentiles will hope in him." ¶ **13** May the God of
→ ἀνιστάμενος → ἄρχειν ← ἐθνῶν ἔθνη → ἐλπιοῦσιν ἐπ᾽ αὐτῷ δὲ Ὁ θεὸς
pt.pm.nsm f.pa n.gpn n.npn v.fai.3p p.d r.dsm.3 cj d.nsm n.nsm
482 806 1620 1620 1827 2093 899 1254 4444 3836 2536

hope fill you with all joy and peace as you trust in him, so that you may overflow
᾽τῆς ἐλπίδος᾽ πληρώσαι ὑμᾶς → πάσης χαρᾶς καὶ εἰρήνης ἐν ᾽τῷ πιστεύειν᾽ εἰς ← ὑμᾶς → ᾽τὸ περισσεύειν᾽
d.gsf n.gsf v.aao.3s r.ap.2 a.gsf n.gsf cj n.gsf p.d d.dsn f.pa p.a r.ap.2 d.asn f.pa
3836 1828 4444 7007 5915 5915 2779 1645 1877 3836 4409 1650 7007 3836 4355

with hope by the power of the Holy Spirit.
ἐν ᾽τῇ ἐλπίδι᾽ ἐν δυνάμει → ἁγίου πνεύματος
p.d d.dsf n.dsf p.d n.dsf a.gsn n.gsn
1877 3836 1828 1877 1539 41 4460

Paul the Minister to the Gentiles

15:14 I myself am convinced, my brothers, that you yourselves are full of goodness,
δὲ ἐγὼ αὐτὸς καὶ → Πέπεισμαι μου ἀδελφοί περὶ ὅτι ὑμῶν → αὐτοὶ καὶ ἐστε μεστοί → ἀγαθωσύνης
cj r.ns.1 r.nsm adv v.rpi.1s r.gs.1 n.vpm p.g cj r.gp.2 r.npm adv v.pai.2p a.npm n.gsf
1254 1609 899 2779 4275 1609 81 4309 4022 7007 1639 899 2779 1639 3550 20

complete in knowledge and competent to instruct one another. **15** I have written you quite
πεπληρωμένοι → πάσης ᾽τῆς γνώσεως᾽ δυνάμενοι καὶ → νουθετεῖν ἀλλήλους ← δὲ → → ἔγραψα ὑμῖν
pt.rp.npm a.gsf d.gsf n.gsf pt.pp.npm cj f.pa r.apm cj v.aai.1s r.dp.2
4444 4246 3836 1194 1538 2779 3805 253 1254 1211 7007

boldly on some points, as if to remind you of them again, because of the grace God
τολμηρότερον ἀπὸ → μέρους ὡς ← ἐπαναμιμνῄσκων ὑμᾶς διὰ ← τὴν χάριν ὑπὸ ᾽τοῦ θεοῦ᾽
adv.c p.g n.gsn pl pt.pa.nsm r.ap.2 p.a d.asf n.asf p.g d.gsm n.gsm
5529 608 3538 6055 2057 7007 1328 3836 5921 5679 3836 2536

gave me **16** to be a minister of Christ Jesus to the Gentiles with the priestly duty of
᾽τὴν δοθεῖσαν᾽ μοι εἰς ᾽τὸ εἶναι᾽ λειτουργὸν → Χριστοῦ Ἰησοῦ εἰς ᾽τὰ ἔθνη᾽ → → ἱερουργοῦντα ←
d.asf pt.ap.asf r.ds.1 p.a r.as.1 d.asn f.pa n.asm n.gsm n.gsm p.a d.apn n.apn pt.pa.asm
3836 1443 1609 1650 1609 3836 1639 3313 5986 2652 1650 3836 1620 2646

proclaiming the gospel of God, so that the Gentiles might become an offering acceptable to God,
τὸ εὐαγγέλιον → ᾽τοῦ θεοῦ᾽ ἵνα → τῶν ἐθνῶν → γένηται ᾽ἡ προσφορά᾽ εὐπρόσδεκτος
d.asn n.asn d.gsm n.gsm cj d.gpn n.gpn v.ams.3s d.nsf n.nsf a.nsf
3836 2295 3836 2536 2671 3836 1620 1181 3836 4714 2347

sanctified by the Holy Spirit. ¶ **17** Therefore I glory in Christ Jesus in my service to God.
ἡγιασμένη ἐν ἁγίῳ πνεύματι οὖν → ᾽ἔχω τὴν καύχησιν᾽ ἐν Χριστῷ Ἰησοῦ → τὰ πρὸς ᾽τὸν θεόν᾽
pt.rp.nsf p.d a.dsn n.dsn cj v.pai.1s d.asf n.asf p.d n.dsm n.dsm d.apn p.a d.asm n.asm
39 1877 41 4460 4036 2400 3836 3018 1877 5986 2652 3836 4639 3836 2536

Χριστὸν διάκονον γεγενῆσθαι περιτομῆς ὑπὲρ ἀληθείας θεοῦ, εἰς τὸ βεβαιῶσαι τὰς ἐπαγγελίας τῶν πατέρων, **9** τὰ δὲ ἔθνη ὑπὲρ ἐλέους δοξάσαι τὸν θεόν, καθὼς γέγραπται, Διὰ τοῦτο ἐξομολογήσομαί σοι ἐν ἔθνεσιν καὶ τῷ ὀνόματί σου ψαλῶ. **10** καὶ πάλιν λέγει, Εὐφράνθητε, ἔθνη, μετὰ τοῦ λαοῦ αὐτοῦ. **11** καὶ πάλιν, Αἰνεῖτε, πάντα τὰ ἔθνη, τὸν κύριον καὶ ἐπαινεσάτωσαν αὐτὸν πάντες οἱ λαοί. **12** καὶ πάλιν Ἠσαΐας λέγει, Ἔσται ἡ ῥίζα τοῦ Ἰεσσαὶ καὶ ὁ ἀνιστάμενος ἄρχειν ἐθνῶν, ἐπ᾽ αὐτῷ ἔθνη ἐλπιοῦσιν. ¶ **13** ὁ δὲ θεὸς τῆς ἐλπίδος πληρώσαι ὑμᾶς πάσης χαρᾶς καὶ εἰρήνης ἐν τῷ πιστεύειν, εἰς τὸ περισσεύειν ὑμᾶς ἐν τῇ ἐλπίδι ἐν δυνάμει πνεύματος ἁγίου.

15:14 Πέπεισμαι δέ, ἀδελφοί μου, καὶ αὐτὸς ἐγὼ περὶ ὑμῶν ὅτι καὶ αὐτοὶ μεστοί ἐστε ἀγαθωσύνης, πεπληρωμένοι πάσης [τῆς] γνώσεως, δυνάμενοι καὶ ἀλλήλους νουθετεῖν. **15** τολμηρότερον δὲ ἔγραψα ὑμῖν ἀπὸ μέρους ὡς ἐπαναμιμνῄσκων ὑμᾶς διὰ τὴν χάριν τὴν δοθεῖσάν μοι ὑπὸ τοῦ θεοῦ **16** εἰς τὸ εἶναί με λειτουργὸν Χριστοῦ Ἰησοῦ εἰς τὰ ἔθνη, ἱερουργοῦντα τὸ εὐαγγέλιον τοῦ θεοῦ, ἵνα γένηται ἡ προσφορὰ τῶν ἐθνῶν εὐπρόσδεκτος, ἡγιασμένη ἐν πνεύματι ἁγίῳ. ¶ **17** ἔχω οὖν [τὴν] καύχησιν ἐν Χριστῷ

18 I will not venture to speak of anything except what   Christ has accomplished through me *in leading* the
γὰρ → → οὐ τολμήσω → λαλεῖν τι → ὧν οὐ Χριστὸς → κατειργάσατο δι᾽ ἐμοῦ εἰς
cj   pl v.fai.1s f.pa r.asn r.gpn pl n.nsm v.ami.3s p.g r.gs.1 p.a
1142 5528 5528 4024 5528 3281 5516 4024 4005 4024 5986 2981 1328 1609 1650

Gentiles to obey   God by what I have said and done – **19** by the power of signs and miracles, through the power
ἐθνῶν ὑπακοὴν → λόγῳ καὶ ἔργῳ ἐν δυνάμει → σημείων καὶ τεράτων ἐν δυνάμει
n.gpn n.asf   n.dsm cj n.dsn p.d n.dsf   n.gpn cj n.gpn p.d n.dsf
1620 5633   3364 2779 2240 1877 1539 4956 2779 5469 1877 1539

of the Spirit.   So from Jerusalem   all the way around to   Illyricum,   I have fully
→ πνεύματος [θεοῦ] ὥστε ἀπὸ Ἰερουσαλὴμ καὶ → → κύκλῳ μέχρι τοῦ Ἰλλυρικοῦ με πεπληρωκέναι
n.gsn n.gsm cj p.g n.gsf cj adv p.g d.gsn n.gsn r.as.1 f.ra
4460 2536 6063 608 2647 2779 3241 3588 3836 2665 1609 4444

proclaimed the gospel of Christ.   **20**   It has always been my ambition   to preach   the gospel
← τὸ εὐαγγέλιον → τοῦ Χριστοῦ δὲ οὕτως → → → φιλοτιμούμενον → εὐαγγελίζεσθαι ← ←
d.asn n.asn d.gsm n.gsm cj adv pt.pm.asm f.pm
3836 2295 3836 5986 1254 4048 5818 2294

where Christ was not known, so that I would not be building on someone else's foundation. **21** Rather, as   it is
ὅπου Χριστὸς → οὐχ ὠνομάσθη ἵνα → μὴ → οἰκοδομῶ ἐπ᾽ ἀλλότριον θεμέλιον ἀλλὰ καθὼς
cj n.nsm pl v.api.3s cj pl v.pas.1s p.a a.asm n.asm cj cj
3963 5986 3951 4024 3951 2671 3868 3868 3590 3868 2093 259 2529 247 2777

written: "Those who were not told   about him will see,   and those who have not heard   will understand."
γέγραπται οἷς ← → οὐκ ἀνηγγέλη περὶ αὐτοῦ → ὄψονται καὶ οἳ ← → οὐκ ἀκηκόασιν → συνήσουσιν
v.rpi.3s r.dpm pl v.api.3s p.g r.gsm.3 v.fmi.3p cj r.npm pl v.rai.3p v.fai.3p
1211 4005 334 4024 334 4309 899 3972 2779 4005 201 4024 201 5317

22 This is why   I have often been hindered from coming to you.
Διὸ ← καὶ → → τὰ πολλὰ ἐνεκοπτόμην τοῦ ἐλθεῖν πρὸς ὑμᾶς
adv cj d.apn a.apn v.ipi.1s d.gsn f.aa p.a r.ap.2
1475 2779 1601 1601 3836 4498 1601 3836 2262 4639 7007

Paul's Plan to Visit Rome

15:23 But now that there is   no more place for me to work in these regions,   and since I have been
δὲ νυνὶ ἔχων μηκέτι ← τόπον ἐν τούτοις τοῖς κλίμασι δὲ → → ἔχων ←
cj adv pt.pa.nsm adv n.asm p.d r.dpn d.dpn n.dpn cj pt.pa.nsm
1254 3815 2400 3600 5536 1877 4047 3836 3107 1254 2400

longing for many years to see   you, **24** I plan to do so when I go   to Spain.   I hope to
ἐπιποθίαν ἀπὸ πολλῶν ἐτῶν → τοῦ ἐλθεῖν πρὸς ὑμᾶς ὡς ἂν → πορεύωμαι εἰς τὴν Σπανίαν γὰρ → ἐλπίζω →
n.asf p.g a.gpn n.gpn d.gsn f.aa p.a r.ap.2 cj cj v.pms.1s p.a d.asf n.asf cj v.pai.1s
2163 608 4498 2291 3836 2262 4639 7007 6055 323 4513 1650 3836 5056 1142 1827

visit   you while passing   through and to have   you assist   me on my journey there,   after I
θεάσασθαι ὑμᾶς → διαπορευόμενος → καὶ → ὑφ᾽ ὑμῶν προπεμφθῆναι ← ἐκεῖ ἐὰν πρῶτον →
f.am r.ap.2 pt.pm.nsm cj p.g r.gp.2 f.ap adv cj adv
2517 7007 1388 2779 4636 4636 5679 7007 4636 1695 1569 4754

have enjoyed your company for a while. **25** Now, however, I am on my way   to Jerusalem in the service of the
→ ἐμπλησθῶ ὑμῶν → ἀπὸ μέρους Νυνὶ δὲ → → πορεύομαι εἰς Ἰερουσαλὴμ διακονῶν τοῖς
v.aps.1s r.gp.2 p.g n.gsn adv cj v.pmi.1s p.a n.asf pt.pa.nsm d.dpm
1858 7007 1858 608 3538 3815 1254 4513 1650 2647 1354 3836

saints there. **26** For Macedonia and Achaia were pleased to make   a contribution for the poor among the
ἁγίοις γὰρ Μακεδονία καὶ Ἀχαΐα → εὐδόκησαν → ποιήσασθαι τινὰ κοινωνίαν εἰς τοὺς πτωχοὺς → τῶν
a.dpm cj n.nsf cj n.nsf v.aai.3p f.am r.asf n.asf p.a d.apm a.apm d.gpm
41 1142 3423 2779 938 2305 4472 5516 3126 1650 3836 4777 3836

saints   in Jerusalem. **27** They were pleased to do it, and indeed they owe   it to them. For if the
ἁγίων τῶν ἐν Ἰερουσαλήμ γὰρ → εὐδόκησαν καὶ → ὀφειλέται εἰσὶν αὐτῶν γὰρ εἰ τὰ
a.gpm d.gpm p.d n.dsf cj v.aai.3p cj n.npm v.pai.3p r.gpm.3 cj cj d.npn
41 3836 1877 2647 1142 2305 2779 4050 1639 899 1142 1623 3836

Gentiles have shared   in the Jews' spiritual blessings, they owe   it to the Jews to share   with
ἔθνη → ἐκοινώνησαν ← τοῖς αὐτῶν πνευματικοῖς ← ὀφείλουσιν καὶ → λειτουργῆσαι →
n.npn v.aai.3p d.dpn r.gpm.3 a.dpn v.pai.3p adv f.aa
1620 3125 3836 899 4461 4053 2779 3310

Ἰησοῦ τὰ πρὸς τὸν θεόν· **18** οὐ γὰρ τολμήσω τι λαλεῖν ὧν οὐ κατειργάσατο Χριστὸς δι᾽ ἐμοῦ εἰς ὑπακοὴν ἐθνῶν, λόγῳ καὶ ἔργῳ, **19** ἐν δυνάμει σημείων καὶ τεράτων, ἐν δυνάμει πνεύματος [θεοῦ]· ὥστε με ἀπὸ Ἰερουσαλὴμ καὶ κύκλῳ μέχρι τοῦ Ἰλλυρικοῦ πεπληρωκέναι τὸ εὐαγγέλιον τοῦ Χριστοῦ, **20** οὕτως δὲ φιλοτιμούμενον εὐαγγελίζεσθαι οὐχ ὅπου ὠνομάσθη Χριστός, ἵνα μὴ ἐπ᾽ ἀλλότριον θεμέλιον οἰκοδομῶ, **21** ἀλλὰ καθὼς γέγραπται, Οἷς οὐκ ἀνηγγέλη περὶ αὐτοῦ ὄψονται, καὶ οἳ οὐκ ἀκηκόασιν συνήσουσιν. **22** Διὸ καὶ ἐνεκοπτόμην τὰ πολλὰ τοῦ ἐλθεῖν πρὸς ὑμᾶς· **15:23** νυνὶ δὲ μηκέτι τόπον ἔχων ἐν τοῖς κλίμασι τούτοις, ἐπιποθίαν δὲ ἔχων τοῦ ἐλθεῖν πρὸς ὑμᾶς ἀπὸ πολλῶν ἐτῶν, **24** ὡς ἂν πορεύωμαι εἰς τὴν Σπανίαν· ἐλπίζω γὰρ διαπορευόμενος θεάσασθαι ὑμᾶς καὶ ὑφ᾽ ὑμῶν προπεμφθῆναι ἐκεῖ ἐὰν ὑμῶν πρῶτον ἀπὸ μέρους ἐμπλησθῶ. **25** νυνὶ δὲ πορεύομαι εἰς Ἰερουσαλὴμ διακονῶν τοῖς ἁγίοις. **26** εὐδόκησαν γὰρ Μακεδονία καὶ Ἀχαΐα κοινωνίαν τινὰ ποιήσασθαι εἰς τοὺς πτωχοὺς τῶν ἁγίων τῶν ἐν Ἰερουσαλήμ. **27** εὐδόκησαν γὰρ καὶ ὀφειλέται εἰσὶν αὐτῶν· εἰ γὰρ τοῖς πνευματικοῖς αὐτῶν ἐκοινώνησαν τὰ ἔθνη, ὀφείλουσιν καὶ ἐν τοῖς σαρκικοῖς λειτουργῆσαι αὐτοῖς. **28** τοῦτο οὖν

them   their material blessings. **28** So after I have completed this   task and have made sure   that they have
αὐτοῖς ἐν τοῖς σαρκικοῖς ←   οὖν →   →   ἐπιτελέσας τοῦτο ←   καὶ →   σφραγισάμενος   αὐτοῖς
r.dpm.3 p.d d.dpn a.dpn   cj   pt.aa.nsm   r.asn cj   pt.am.nsm   r.dpm.3
899 1877 1877 4920   4036   2200   4047   2779   5381   899

received this fruit,   I will go   to   Spain and *visit   you on the way.* **29**   I know that when I
τοῦτον ⸤τὸν καρπὸν⸥ → → ἀπελεύσομαι εἰς Σπανίαν   δι' ὑμῶν   δὲ → οἶδα ὅτι   →
r.asm d.asm n.asm   v.fmi.1s   p.a n.asf   p.g r.gp.2   cj   v.rai.1s 4022
4047   3836 2843   599   1650 5056   1328 7007   1254   3857

come   to   you, I will come   in the full   measure of the blessing of Christ. ¶ **30** I urge   you,
ἐρχόμενος πρὸς ὑμᾶς → → ἐλεύσομαι ἐν   πληρώματι ←   →   εὐλογίας → Χριστοῦ   δὲ → Παρακαλῶ ὑμᾶς
pt.pm.nsm p.a r.ap.2   v.fmi.1s p.d n.dsn   n.gsf   n.gsm   cj   v.pai.1s r.ap.2
2262   4639 7007   2262   1877 4445   2330   5986   1254 4151   7007

brothers, by our Lord   Jesus Christ and by the love   of the Spirit, to join me in my struggle   by
ἀδελφοί διὰ ἡμῶν ⸤τοῦ κυρίου⸥ Ἰησοῦ Χριστοῦ καὶ διὰ τῆς ἀγάπης → τοῦ πνεύματος → ↑ μοι → συναγωνίσασθαι   ἐν
n.vpm   p.g r.gp.1 d.gsm n.gsm n.gsm n.gsm   cj p.g d.gsf n.gsf   d.gsn n.gsn   f.am   5253   f.am   p.d
81   1328 7005 3836 3261   2652 5986   2779 1328 3836 27   3836 4460   5253 5253 1609   5253   1877

praying   to God   for me. **31** Pray that I may be rescued from the unbelievers in Judea   and that my
⸤ταῖς προσευχαῖς⸥ πρὸς ⸤τὸν θεόν⸥ ὑπὲρ ἐμοῦ   ἵνα → → →   ῥυσθῶ ἀπὸ τῶν ἀπειθούντων ἐν τῇ Ἰουδαίᾳ καὶ   μου
d.dpf n.dpf   p.a d.asm n.asm p.g r.gs.1   cj   v.aps.1s p.g d.gpm pt.pa.gpm   p.d d.dsf n.dsf cj   r.gs.1
3836   4666   4639 3836 2536   5642 1609   2671   4861   608 3836 578   1877 3836 2677   2779   1609

service   in Jerusalem may be acceptable to the saints there, **32** so that by God's will   I may come
⸤ἡ διακονία⸥ ἡ εἰς Ἰερουσαλὴμ → γένηται εὐπρόσδεκτος → τοῖς ἁγίοις   ἵνα ← → διὰ θεοῦ θελήματος → → ἐλθὼν
d.nsf n.nsf   d.nsf p.a n.asf   v.ams.3s a.nsm   d.dpm a.dpm   cj   p.g n.gsm n.gsn   pt.aa.nsm
3836 1355   3836 1650 2647   1181   2347   3836 41   2671   1328 2536 2525   2262

to   you with joy and together with you be refreshed. **33**   The God of peace   be with you all.   Amen.
πρὸς ὑμᾶς ἐν χαρᾷ →   → ὑμῖν → συναναπαύσωμαι   δὲ Ὁ θεὸς → ⸤τῆς εἰρήνης⸥ μετὰ ὑμῶν πάντων ἀμήν
p.a r.ap.2 p.d n.dsf   r.dp.2   v.ams.1s   cj d.nsm n.nsm   d.gsf n.gsf   p.g r.gp.2 a.gpm   pl
4639 7007 1877 5915   5265   7007   5265   1254 3836 2536   3836 1645   3552 7007 4246   297

Personal Greetings

16:1   I commend to you our   sister   Phoebe,   a servant of the church   in Cenchrea. **2** I
δὲ → Συνίστημι → ὑμῖν ἡμῶν ⸤τὴν ἀδελφὴν⸥ Φοίβην   οὖσαν [καὶ] διάκονον → τῆς ἐκκλησίας τῆς ἐν Κεγχρεαῖς
cj   v.pai.1s   r.dp.2 r.gp.1 d.asf n.asf   n.asf   pt.pa.asf cj   n.asf   d.gsf n.gsf   d.gsf p.d n.dpf
1254 5319   7007 7005 3836 80   5833   1639   2779   1356   3836 1711   3836 1877 3020

ask   you to receive   her in the Lord in a way worthy of the saints and to give   her any   help
ἵνα → → προσδέξησθε αὐτὴν ἐν   κυρίῳ → → ἀξίως → τῶν ἁγίων καὶ → παραστῆτε αὐτῇ ⸤ἐν ᾧ ἂν⸥ πράγματι
cj   v.ams.2p   r.asf.3 p.d   n.dsm   adv   d.gpm a.gpm cj   v.aas.2p   r.dsf.3 p.d r.dsn pl   n.dsn
2671   4657   899   1877   3261   547   3836 41   2779   4225   899   1877 4005 323 4547

she may need from you, for   she has been a great help   to many people, including me. **3** Greet
→ → χρῄζῃ → ὑμῶν γὰρ καὶ αὐτὴ ἐγενήθη   προστάτις → πολλῶν   καὶ   ἐμοῦ αὐτοῦ Ἀσπάσασθε
v.pas.3s   r.gp.2 cj adv r.nsf v.api.3s   n.nsf   a.gpm   cj   r.gs.1 r.gsm v.amm.2p
5974   7007 1142 2779 899 1181   4706   4498   2779   1609 899   832

Priscilla and Aquila, my fellow workers   in Christ Jesus. **4** They risked their lives   for me.
Πρίσκαν καὶ Ἀκύλαν μου → ⸤τοὺς συνεργούς⸥ ἐν Χριστῷ Ἰησοῦ οἵτινες ὑπέθηκαν ἑαυτῶν ⸤τὸν τράχηλον⸥ ὑπὲρ ⸤τῆς ψυχῆς μου⸥
n.asf   cj n.asm r.gs.1   d.apm n.apm   p.d n.dsm n.dsm   r.npm   v.aai.3p r.gpm.3 d.asm n.asm   p.g d.gsf n.gsf r.gs.1
4571   2779 217   1609   3836 5301   1877 5986   2652   4015   5719   5549   3836 6034   5642 3836 6034 1609

Not only I but all   the churches of the Gentiles are grateful to them. **5** Greet also the church   that meets
οὐκ μόνος ἐγὼ ἀλλὰ καὶ πᾶσαι αἱ ἐκκλησίαι → τῶν ἐθνῶν εὐχαριστῶ → οἷς   καὶ τὴν ἐκκλησίαν
pl a.nsm r.ns.1 cj adv a.npf d.npf n.npf   d.gpn n.gpn v.pai.1s   r.dpm   cj d.asf n.asf
4024 3668 1609 247 2779 4246 3836 1711   3836 1620   2373   4005   2779 3836 1711

at their house.   Greet   my dear friend   Epenetus, who was the first   convert to Christ in the
αὐτῶν ⸤κατ' οἶκον⸥ ἀσπάσασθε μου ⸤τὸν ἀγαπητόν⸥ Ἐπαίνετον ὅς ἐστιν   ἀπαρχὴ   εἰς Χριστόν →
r.gpm.3 p.a n.asm   v.amm.2p   r.gs.1 d.asm a.asm   n.asm   r.nsm v.pai.3s n.nsf   p.a n.asm
899   2848 3875   832   1609 3836 28   2045   4005 1639   569   1650 5986

province of Asia.   ¶ **6** Greet   Mary,   who worked very hard for you. ¶ **7** Greet   Andronicus and
→   → ⸤τῆς Ἀσίας⸥   ἀσπάσασθε Μαρίαν ἥτις ἐκοπίασεν πολλὰ ← εἰς ὑμᾶς   ἀσπάσασθε Ἀνδρόνικον καὶ
d.gsf n.gsf   v.amm.2p   n.asf r.nsf v.aai.3s a.apn   p.a r.ap.2   v.amm.2p   n.asm   cj
3836 823   832   3451   4015 4015   3159   1650 7007   832   438   2779

ἐπιτελέσας καὶ σφραγισάμενος αὐτοῖς τὸν καρπὸν τοῦτον, ἀπελεύσομαι δι᾽ ὑμῶν εἰς Σπανίαν· ²⁹ οἶδα δὲ ὅτι ἐρχόμενος πρὸς ὑμᾶς ἐν πληρώματι εὐλογίας Χριστοῦ ἐλεύσομαι. ¶ ³⁰ Παρακαλῶ δὲ ὑμᾶ[ς ἀδελφοί,] διὰ τοῦ κυρίου ἡμῶν Ἰησοῦ Χριστοῦ καὶ διὰ τῆς ἀγάπης τοῦ πνεύματος συναγωνίσασθαί μοι ἐν ταῖς προσευχαῖς ὑπὲρ ἐμοῦ πρὸς τὸν θεόν, ³¹ ἵνα ῥυσθῶ ἀπὸ τῶν ἀπειθούντων ἐν τῇ Ἰουδαίᾳ καὶ ἡ διακονία μου ἡ εἰς Ἰερουσαλὴμ εὐπρόσδεκτος τοῖς ἁγίοις γένηται, ³² ἵνα ἐν χαρᾷ ἐλθὼν πρὸς ὑμᾶς διὰ θελήματος θεοῦ συναναπαύσωμαι ὑμῖν. ³³ ὁ δὲ θεὸς τῆς εἰρήνης μετὰ πάντων ὑμῶν, ἀμήν.

¹⁶:¹ Συνίστημι δὲ ὑμῖν Φοίβην τὴν ἀδελφὴν ἡμῶν, οὖσαν [καὶ] διάκονον τῆς ἐκκλησίας τῆς ἐν Κεγχρεαῖς, ² ἵνα αὐτὴν προσδέξησθε ἐν κυρίῳ ἀξίως τῶν ἁγίων καὶ παραστῆτε αὐτῇ ἐν ᾧ ἂν ὑμῶν χρῄζῃ πράγματι· καὶ γὰρ αὐτὴ προστάτις πολλῶν ἐγενήθη καὶ ἐμοῦ αὐτοῦ. ³ Ἀσπάσασθε Πρίσκαν καὶ Ἀκύλαν τοὺς συνεργούς μου ἐν Χριστῷ Ἰησοῦ, ⁴ οἵτινες ὑπὲρ τῆς ψυχῆς μου τὸν ἑαυτῶν τράχηλον ὑπέθηκαν, οἷς οὐκ ἐγὼ μόνος εὐχαριστῶ ἀλλὰ καὶ πᾶσαι αἱ ἐκκλησίαι τῶν ἐθνῶν, ⁵ καὶ τὴν κατ᾽ οἶκον αὐτῶν ἐκκλησίαν. ἀσπάσασθε Ἐπαίνετον τὸν ἀγαπητόν μου, ὅς ἐστιν ἀπαρχὴ τῆς Ἀσίας εἰς Χριστόν. ¶ ⁶ ἀσπάσασθε Μαρίαν, ἥτις πολλὰ ἐκοπίασεν εἰς ὑμᾶς. ¶ ⁷ ἀσπάσασθε Ἀνδρόνικον καὶ Ἰουνιᾶν τοὺς συγγενεῖς μου καὶ συναιχμαλώτους μου,

Junias, my relatives who have been in prison with me. They are outstanding among the
Ἰουνιᾶν μου ⸤τοὺς συγγενεῖς⸥ καὶ → → → → συναιχμαλώτους ← μου οἵτινες εἰσιν ἐπίσημοι ἐν τοῖς
n.asm r.gs.1 d.apm n.apm cj n.apm r.gs.1 r.npm v.pai.3p a.npm p.d d.dpm
2686 1609 3836 5150 2779 5257 1609 4015 1639 2168 1877 3836

apostles, and they were in Christ before I was. **8** Greet Ampliatus, whom I love in the Lord.
ἀποστόλοις καὶ οἳ γέγοναν ἐν Χριστῷ πρὸ ἐμοῦ ἀσπάσασθε Ἀμπλιᾶτον μου ⸤τὸν ἀγαπητόν⸥ ἐν κυρίῳ
n.dpm adv r.npm v.rai.3p p.d n.dsm p.g r.gs.1 v.amm.2p n.asm r.gs.1 d.asm a.asm p.d n.dsm
693 2779 4005 1181 1877 5986 4574 1609 832 309 1609 3836 28 1877 3261

9 Greet Urbanus, our fellow worker in Christ, and my dear friend Stachys. **10** Greet Apelles, tested
ἀσπάσασθε Οὐρβανὸν ἡμῶν → ⸤τὸν συνεργόν⸥ ἐν Χριστῷ καὶ μου ⸤τὸν ἀγαπητόν⸥ Στάχυν ἀσπάσασθε Ἀπελλῆν →
v.amm.2p n.asm r.gp.1 d.asm n.asm p.d n.dsm cj r.gs.1 d.asm a.asm n.asm v.amm.2p n.asm
832 4042 7005 3836 5301 1877 5986 2779 1609 3836 28 5093 832 593

and approved in Christ. Greet those who belong to the household of Aristobulus. **11** Greet Herodion, my
→ ⸤τὸν δόκιμον⸥ ἐν Χριστῷ ἀσπάσασθε τοὺς ← ἐκ ← τῶν → → Ἀριστοβούλου ἀσπάσασθε Ἡρωδίωνα μου
d.asm a.asm p.d n.dsm v.amm.2p d.apm p.g d.gpm n.gsm v.amm.2p n.asm r.gs.1
3836 1511 1877 5986 832 3836 1666 3836 755 832 2479 1609

relative. Greet those in the household of Narcissus who are in the Lord. **12** Greet Tryphena and
⸤τὸν συγγενῆ⸥ ἀσπάσασθε τοὺς ἐκ τῶν → Ναρκίσσου τοὺς ὄντας ἐν κυρίῳ ἀσπάσασθε Τρύφαιναν καὶ
d.asm n.asm v.amm.2p d.apm p.g d.gpm n.gsm d.apm pt.pa.apm p.d n.dsm v.amm.2p n.asf cj
3836 5150 832 3836 1666 3836 3727 3836 1639 1877 3261 832 5586 2779

Tryphosa, those women who work hard in the Lord. Greet my dear friend Persis, another woman who
Τρυφῶσαν τὰς ← ← κοπιώσας ← ἐν κυρίῳ ἀσπάσασθε τὴν ἀγαπητὴν Περσίδα ἥτις
n.asf d.apf pt.pa.apf p.d n.dsm v.amm.2p d.asf a.asf n.asf r.nsf
5589 3836 3159 1877 3261 832 3836 28 4372 4015

has worked very hard in the Lord. **13** Greet Rufus, chosen in the Lord, and his mother, who has been
→ ἐκοπίασεν πολλὰ ← ἐν κυρίῳ ἀσπάσασθε Ῥοῦφον ⸤τὸν ἐκλεκτὸν⸥ ἐν κυρίῳ καὶ αὐτοῦ ⸤τὴν μητέρα⸥
v.aai.3s a.apn p.d n.dsm v.amm.2p n.asm d.asm a.asm p.d n.dsm cj r.gsm.3 d.asf n.asf
3159 4498 1877 3261 832 4859 3836 1723 1877 3261 2779 899 3836 3613

a mother to me, too. **14** Greet Asyncritus, Phlegon, Hermes, Patrobas, Hermas and the brothers with them.
→ ἐμοῦ καὶ ἀσπάσασθε Ἀσύγκριτον Φλέγοντα Ἑρμῆν Πατροβᾶν Ἑρμᾶν καὶ τοὺς ἀδελφούς σὺν αὐτοῖς
r.gs.1 cj v.amm.2p n.asm n.asm n.asm n.asm n.asm cj d.apm n.apm p.d r.dpm.3
1609 2779 832 850 5823 2258 4259 2254 2779 3836 81 5250 899

15 Greet Philologus, Julia, Nereus and his sister, and Olympas and all the saints with them.
ἀσπάσασθε Φιλόλογον καὶ Ἰουλίαν Νηρέα καὶ αὐτοῦ ⸤τὴν ἀδελφὴν⸥ καὶ Ὀλυμπᾶν καὶ πάντας τοὺς ἁγίους σὺν αὐτοῖς
v.amm.2p n.asm cj n.asf n.asm cj r.gsm.3 d.asf n.asf cj n.asm cj a.apm d.apm a.apm p.d r.dpm.3
832 5807 2779 2684 3759 2779 899 3836 80 2779 3912 2779 4246 3836 41 5250 899

16 Greet one another with a holy kiss. All the churches of Christ send greetings. ¶ **17** I
ἀσπάσασθε ἀλλήλους ← ἐν ἁγίῳ φιλήματι πᾶσαι αἱ ἐκκλησίαι → τοῦ Χριστοῦ ἀσπάζονται ὑμᾶς δὲ →
v.amm.2p r.apm p.d a.dsn n.dsn a.npf d.npf n.npf d.gsm n.gsm v.pmi.3p r.ap.2 cj
832 253 1877 41 5799 4246 3836 1711 3836 5986 832 7007 1254

urge you, brothers, to watch out for those who cause divisions and put obstacles in your way that
Παρακαλῶ ὑμᾶς ἀδελφοί → σκοπεῖν ← ← τοὺς ← ποιοῦντας ⸤ιὰς διχοστασίας⸥ καὶ ← ⸤τὰ σκάνδαλα⸥
v.pai.1s r.ap.2 n.vpm f.pa d.apm pt.pa.apm d.apf n.apf cj d.apn n.apn
4151 7007 81 5023 3836 4472 3836 1496 2779 4472 3836 4998

are contrary to the teaching you have learned. Keep away from them. **18** For such people are not
παρὰ ← τὴν διδαχὴν ἣν ὑμεῖς → ἐμάθετε καὶ ἐκκλίνετε ← ἀπ᾽ αὐτῶν γὰρ οἱ τοιοῦτοι ← οὐ
p.a d.asf n.asf r.asf r.np.2 v.aai.2p cj v.pam.2p p.g r.gpm.3 cj d.npm r.npm pl
4123 3836 1439 4005 7007 3443 2779 1712 608 899 1142 3836 5525 1526 4024

serving our Lord Christ, but their own appetites. By smooth talk and flattery they
δουλεύουσιν ἡμῶν ⸤τῷ κυρίῳ⸥ Χριστῷ ἀλλὰ τῇ ἑαυτῶν κοιλίᾳ καὶ διὰ → ⸤τῆς χρηστολογίας⸥ καὶ εὐλογίας →
v.pai.3p r.gp.1 d.dsm n.dsm n.dsm cj d.dsf r.gpm.3 n.dsf cj p.g d.gsf n.gsf cj n.gsf
1526 7005 3836 3261 5986 247 3836 1571 3120 2779 1328 3836 5981 2779 2330

deceive the minds of naive people. **19** Everyone has heard about your obedience, so I am full of
ἐξαπατῶσιν τὰς καρδίας → ⸤τῶν ἀκάκων⸥ γὰρ εἰς πάντας → ἀφίκετο ὑμῶν ἡ ὑπακοὴ οὖν → → →
v.pai.3p d.apf n.apf d.gpm a.gpm cj p.a a.apm v.ami.3s r.gp.2 d.nsf n.nsf cj
1987 3836 2840 3836 179 1142 1650 4246 919 7007 3836 5633 4036

οἵτινές εἰσιν ἐπίσημοι ἐν τοῖς ἀποστόλοις, οἳ καὶ πρὸ ἐμοῦ γέγοναν ἐν Χριστῷ. **8** ἀσπάσασθε Ἀμπλιᾶτον τὸν ἀγαπητόν μου ἐν κυρίῳ. **9** ἀσπάσασθε Οὐρβανὸν τὸν συνεργὸν ἡμῶν ἐν Χριστῷ καὶ Στάχυν τὸν ἀγαπητόν μου. **10** ἀσπάσασθε Ἀπελλῆν τὸν δόκιμον ἐν Χριστῷ. ἀσπάσασθε τοὺς ἐκ τῶν Ἀριστοβούλου. **11** ἀσπάσασθε Ἡρῳδίωνα τὸν συγγενῆ μου. ἀσπάσασθε τοὺς ἐκ τῶν Ναρκίσσου τοὺς ὄντας ἐν κυρίῳ. **12** ἀσπάσασθε Τρύφαιναν καὶ Τρυφῶσαν τὰς κοπιώσας ἐν κυρίῳ. ἀσπάσασθε Περσίδα τὴν ἀγαπητήν, ἥτις πολλὰ ἐκοπίασεν ἐν κυρίῳ. **13** ἀσπάσασθε Ῥοῦφον τὸν ἐκλεκτὸν ἐν κυρίῳ καὶ τὴν μητέρα αὐτοῦ καὶ ἐμοῦ. **14** ἀσπάσασθε Ἀσύγκριτον, Φλέγοντα, Ἑρμῆν, Πατροβᾶν, Ἑρμᾶν καὶ τοὺς σὺν αὐτοῖς ἀδελφούς. **15** ἀσπάσασθε Φιλόλογον καὶ Ἰουλίαν, Νηρέα καὶ τὴν ἀδελφὴν αὐτοῦ, καὶ Ὀλυμπᾶν καὶ τοὺς σὺν αὐτοῖς πάντας ἁγίους. **16** Ἀσπάσασθε ἀλλήλους ἐν φιλήματι ἁγίῳ. Ἀσπάζονται ὑμᾶς αἱ ἐκκλησίαι πᾶσαι τοῦ Χριστοῦ. ¶ **17** Παρακαλῶ δὲ ὑμᾶς, ἀδελφοί, σκοπεῖν τοὺς τὰς διχοστασίας καὶ τὰ σκάνδαλα παρὰ τὴν διδαχὴν ἣν ὑμεῖς ἐμάθετε ποιοῦντας, καὶ ἐκκλίνετε ἀπ᾽ αὐτῶν· **18** οἱ γὰρ τοιοῦτοι τῷ κυρίῳ ἡμῶν Χριστῷ οὐ δουλεύουσιν ἀλλὰ τῇ ἑαυτῶν κοιλίᾳ, καὶ διὰ τῆς χρηστολογίας καὶ εὐλογίας ἐξαπατῶσιν τὰς καρδίας τῶν ἀκάκων. **19** ἡ γὰρ ὑμῶν ὑπακοὴ εἰς πάντας ἀφίκετο· ἐφ᾽ ὑμῖν οὖν χαίρω, θέλω δὲ ὑμᾶς σοφοὺς εἶναι εἰς τὸ ἀγαθόν,

joy | over | you; | but | I want | you | to be | wise | about | what | is good, | and | innocent | about | what | is evil. | ¶ | **20**
χαίρω | ἐφ᾽ | ὑμῖν | δὲ | θέλω | ὑμᾶς | εἶναι | σοφοὺς | εἰς | τὸ | ἀγαθὸν | δὲ | ἀκεραίους | εἰς | τὸ | κακόν | | δὲ
v.pai.1s | p.d | r.dp.2 | cj | v.pai.1s | r.ap.2 | f.pa | a.apm | p.a | d.asn | a.asn | cj | a.apm | p.a | d.asn | a.asn | | cj
5897 | 2093 | 7007 | 1254 | 2527 | 7007 | 1639 | 5055 | 1650 | 3836 | 19 | 1254 | 193 | 1650 | 3836 | 2805 | | 1254

The | God | of peace | | will soon | | crush | Satan | under | your | feet. | ¶ | The | grace of | | our
ὁ | θεὸς | τῆς εἰρήνης | ↱ | ἐν | τάχει | συντρίψει | τὸν σατανᾶν | ὑπὸ | ὑμῶν | τοὺς πόδας | | Ἡ | χάρις | ↱ | ἡμῶν
d.nsm | n.nsm | d.gsf n.gsf | | p.d | n.dsn | v.fai.3s | d.asm n.asm | p.g | r.gp.2 | d.apm n.apm | | d.nsf | n.nsf | | r.gp.1
3836 | 2536 | 3836 1645 | 5341 | 1877 | 5443 | 5341 | 3836 4928 | 5679 | 7007 | 3836 4546 | | 3836 | 5921 | 3261 | 7005

Lord | Jesus | be with | you. | ¶ | **21** Timothy, | my | | fellow worker, | | sends his | greetings | to you, | as | do Lucius,
τοῦ κυρίου | Ἰησοῦ | μεθ᾽ | ὑμῶν | | Τιμόθεος | μου | ὁ | συνεργός, | ↱ | Ἀσπάζεται | ὑμᾶς | καὶ | Λούκιος
d.gsm n.gsm | n.gsm | p.g | r.gp.2 | | n.nsm | r.gs.1 | d.nsm | n.nsm | | v.pmi.3s | r.ap.2 | cj | n.nsm
3836 3261 | 2652 | 3552 | 7007 | | 5510 | 1609 | 3836 | 5301 | | 832 | 7007 | 2779 | 3372

Jason | and | Sosipater, | my | relatives. | ¶ | **22** I, | Tertius, | who | wrote | down | this | letter, | greet | you | in | the
καὶ Ἰάσων | καὶ | Σωσίπατρος | μου | οἱ συγγενεῖς | | ἐγὼ | Τέρτιος | ὁ | γράψας | ← | τὴν | ἐπιστολὴν | ἀσπάζομαι | ὑμᾶς | ἐν
cj n.nsm | cj | n.nsm | r.gs.1 | d.npm n.npm | | r.ns.1 | n.nsm | d.nsm | n.nsm | | d.asf | n.asf | v.pmi.1s | r.ap.2 | p.d
2779 2619 | 2779 | 5399 | 1609 | 3836 5150 | | 1609 | 5470 | 3836 | 1211 | | 3836 | 2186 | 832 | 7007 | 1877

Lord. | ¶ | **23** Gaius, | whose | | hospitality | I | and | the | whole | church | here enjoy, | sends | you | his | greetings.
κυρίῳ | | Γάϊος | ὁ | ξένος | μου | καὶ | τῆς | ὅλης | ἐκκλησίας | ↱ | ὑμᾶς | ἀσπάζεται
n.dsm | | n.nsm | d.nsm | n.nsm | r.gs.1 | cj | d.gsf | a.gsf | n.gsf | | r.ap.2 | v.pmi.3s
3261 | | 1127 | 3836 | 3828 | 1609 | 2779 | 3836 | 3910 | 1711 | 832 | 7007 | 832

Erastus, | who | is the | city's | director | of public works, | and | our | brother | Quartus | send | you | their | greetings. | ¶
Ἔραστος | ὁ | τῆς πόλεως | οἰκονόμος | ← | ← | ← | καὶ ὁ | ἀδελφός | Κούαρτος | ↱ | ὑμᾶς | ἀσπάζεται
n.nsm | d.nsm | d.gsf n.gsf | n.nsm | | | | cj d.nsm | n.nsm | n.nsm | | r.ap.2 | v.pmi.3s
2235 | 3836 | 3836 4484 | 3874 | | | 2779 3836 | 81 | 3181 | | 832 | 7007 | 832

25 Now | to him who is able | to establish | you | by | my | gospel | and | the | proclamation | of Jesus | Christ, | according
δὲ | Τῷ | δυναμένῳ | στηρίξαι | ὑμᾶς | κατὰ | μου | τὸ εὐαγγέλιον | καὶ | τὸ | κήρυγμα | Ἰησοῦ | Χριστοῦ | κατὰ
cj | d.dsm | pt.pp.dsm | f.aa | r.ap.2 | p.a | r.gs.1 | d.asn n.asn | cj | d.asn | n.asn | n.gsm | n.gsm | p.a
1254 | 3836 | 1538 | 5114 | 7007 | 2848 | 1609 | 3836 2295 | 2779 | 3836 | 3060 | 2652 | 5986 | 2848

to | the revelation | of the mystery | hidden | for long | ages | past, | **26** but | now | revealed | and | made known
← | ἀποκάλυψιν | μυστηρίου | σεσιγημένου | χρόνοις | αἰωνίοις | | δὲ | νῦν | φανερωθέντος | τε | γνωρισθέντος
| n.asf | n.gsn | pt.rp.gsn | n.dpm | a.dpm | | cj | adv | pt.ap.gsn | cj | pt.ap.gsn
637 | 3696 | 4967 | 5989 | 173 | | 1254 | 3814 | 5746 | 5445 | 1192

through | the prophetic | writings | by | the | command | of the | eternal | God, | so that | all | nations | might believe | and
διὰ | προφητικῶν | γραφῶν | κατ᾽ | ἐπιταγὴν | τοῦ | αἰωνίου | θεοῦ | εἰς | πάντα | τὰ ἔθνη | πίστεως | εἰς
p.g | a.gpf | n.gpf | p.a | n.asf | d.gsm | a.gsm | n.gsm | p.a | a.apn | d.apn n.apn | n.gsf | p.a
1328 | 4738 | 1210 | 2848 | 2198 | 3836 | 173 | 2536 | 1650 | 4246 | 3836 1620 | 4411 | 1650

obey | him — | **27** to | the only | wise | God | be | glory | forever | through | Jesus | Christ! | Amen. | ¶
ὑπακοὴν | | μόνῳ | σοφῷ | θεῷ | ᾧ | ἡ δόξα | εἰς τοὺς αἰῶνας | διὰ | Ἰησοῦ | Χριστοῦ | ἀμήν
n.asf | | a.dsm | a.dsm | n.dsm | r.dsm | d.nsf n.nsf | p.a d.apm n.apm | p.g | n.gsm | n.gsm | pl
5633 | | 3668 | 5055 | 2536 | 4005 | 3836 1518 | 1650 3836 172 | 1328 | 2652 | 5986 | 297

ἀκεραίους δὲ εἰς τὸ κακόν. ¶ 20 ὁ δὲ θεὸς τῆς εἰρήνης συντρίψει τὸν Σατανᾶν ὑπὸ τοὺς πόδας ὑμῶν ἐν τάχει. ¶ ἡ χάρις τοῦ κυρίου ἡμῶν Ἰησοῦ μεθ᾽ ὑμῶν. ¶ 21 Ἀσπάζεται ὑμᾶς Τιμόθεος ὁ συνεργός μου, καὶ Λούκιος καὶ Ἰάσων καὶ Σωσίπατρος οἱ συγγενεῖς μου. ¶ 22 ἀσπάζομαι ὑμᾶς ἐγὼ Τέρτιος ὁ γράψας τὴν ἐπιστολὴν ἐν κυρίῳ. ¶ 23 ἀσπάζεται ὑμᾶς Γάϊος ὁ ξένος μου καὶ ὅλης τῆς ἐκκλησίας ¶ ἀσπάζεται ὑμᾶς Ἔραστος ὁ οἰκονόμος τῆς πόλεως καὶ Κούαρτος ὁ ἀδελφός. ¶ 25 [Τῷ δὲ δυναμένῳ ὑμᾶς στηρίξαι κατὰ τὸ εὐαγγέλιόν μου καὶ τὸ κήρυγμα Ἰησοῦ Χριστοῦ, κατὰ ἀποκάλυψιν μυστηρίου χρόνοις αἰωνίοις σεσιγημένου, 26 φανερωθέντος δὲ νῦν διά τε γραφῶν προφητικῶν κατ᾽ ἐπιταγὴν τοῦ αἰωνίου θεοῦ εἰς ὑπακοὴν πίστεως εἰς πάντα τὰ ἔθνη γνωρισθέντος, 27 μόνῳ σοφῷ θεῷ, διὰ Ἰησοῦ Χριστοῦ, ᾧ ἡ δόξα εἰς τοὺς αἰῶνας, ἀμήν.]

1 Corinthians

1:1 Paul, called to be an apostle of Christ Jesus by the will of God, and our brother Sosthenes, ¶
Παῦλος κλητὸς ἀπόστολος Χριστοῦ Ἰησοῦ διὰ θελήματος θεοῦ καὶ ὁ ἀδελφὸς Σωσθένης
n.nsm a.nsm n.nsm n.gsm n.gsm p.g n.gsn n.gsm cj d.nsm n.nsm n.nsm
4263 3105 693 5986 2652 1328 2525 2536 2779 3836 81 5398

2 To the church of God in Corinth, to those sanctified in Christ Jesus and called to be holy,
τῇ ἐκκλησίᾳ τοῦ θεοῦ τῇ οὔσῃ ἐν Κορίνθῳ ἡγιασμένοις ἐν Χριστῷ Ἰησοῦ κλητοῖς ἁγίοις
d.dsf n.dsf d.gsm n.gsm d.dsf pt.pa.dsf p.d n.dsf pt.rp.dpm p.d n.dsm n.dsm a.dpm a.dpm
3836 1711 3836 2536 3836 1639 1877 3172 39 1877 5986 2652 3105 41

together with all those everywhere who call on the name of our Lord Jesus Christ – their
σὺν πᾶσιν τοῖς ἐν παντὶ τόπῳ ἐπικαλουμένοις τὸ ὄνομα ἡμῶν τοῦ κυρίου Ἰησοῦ Χριστοῦ αὐτῶν
p.d a.dpm d.dpm p.d a.dsm n.dsm pt.pm.dpm d.asn n.asn r.gp.1 d.gsm n.gsm n.gsm n.gsm r.gpm.3
5250 4246 3836 1877 4246 5536 2126 3836 3950 3261 7005 3836 3261 2652 5986 899

Lord and ours: ¶ **3** Grace and peace to you from God our Father and the Lord Jesus Christ.
καὶ ἡμῶν χάρις καὶ εἰρήνη ὑμῖν ἀπὸ θεοῦ ἡμῶν πατρὸς καὶ κυρίου Ἰησοῦ Χριστοῦ
cj r.gp.1 n.nsf cj n.nsf r.dp.2 p.g n.gsm r.gp.1 n.gsm cj n.gsm n.gsm n.gsm
2779 7005 5921 2779 1645 7007 608 2536 7005 4252 2779 3261 2652 5986

Thanksgiving

1:4 I always thank God for you because of his grace given you in Christ Jesus. **5** For
πάντοτε Εὐχαριστῶ μου τῷ θεῷ περὶ ὑμῶν ἐπὶ τοῦ θεοῦ τῇ χάριτι τῇ δοθείσῃ ὑμῖν ἐν Χριστῷ Ἰησοῦ ὅτι
adv v.pai.1s r.gs.1 d.dsm n.dsm p.g r.gp.2 p.d d.gsm n.gsm d.dsf n.dsf d.dsf pt.ap.dsf r.dp.2 p.d n.dsm n.dsm cj
2373 4121 2373 3836 2536 4309 7007 2093 3836 2536 3836 5921 3836 1443 7007 1877 5986 2652 4022

in him you have been enriched in every way – in all your speaking and in all your knowledge – **6** because our
ἐν αὐτῷ ἐπλουτίσθητε ἐν παντὶ ἐν παντὶ λόγῳ καὶ πάσῃ γνώσει καθὼς τὸ
p.d r.dsm.3 v.api.2p p.d a.dsn p.d a.dsn n.dsm cj a.dsf n.dsf cj d.nsn
1877 899 4457 1877 4246 1877 4246 3364 2779 4246 1194 2777 3836

testimony about Christ was confirmed in you. **7** Therefore you do not lack any spiritual gift as
μαρτύριον τοῦ Χριστοῦ ἐβεβαιώθη ἐν ὑμῖν ὥστε ὑμᾶς μὴ ὑστερεῖσθαι ἐν μηδενὶ χαρίσματι
n.nsn d.gsm n.gsm v.api.3s p.d r.dp.2 cj r.ap.2 pl f.pp p.d a.dsn n.dsn
3457 3836 5986 1011 1877 7007 6063 7007 3590 5728 1877 3594 5922

you eagerly wait for our Lord Jesus Christ to be revealed. **8** He will keep you strong to
ἀπεκδεχομένους ἡμῶν τοῦ κυρίου Ἰησοῦ Χριστοῦ τὴν ἀποκάλυψιν καὶ ὃς ὑμᾶς βεβαιώσει ἕως
pt.pm.apm r.gp.1 d.gsm n.gsm n.gsm n.gsm d.asf n.asf adv r.nsm r.ap.2 v.fai.3s p.g
587 7005 3836 3261 2652 5986 3836 637 2779 4005 1011 1011 2401

the end, so that you will be blameless on the day of our Lord Jesus Christ. **9** God, who has called
τέλους ἀνεγκλήτους ἐν τῇ ἡμέρᾳ ἡμῶν τοῦ κυρίου Ἰησοῦ Χριστοῦ ὁ θεός δι᾽ οὗ ἐκλήθητε
n.gsn a.apm p.d d.dsf n.dsf r.gp.1 d.gsm n.gsm n.gsm n.gsm d.nsm n.nsm p.g r.gsm v.api.2p
5465 441 1877 3836 2465 7005 3836 3261 2652 5986 3836 2536 1328 4005 2813

you into fellowship with his Son Jesus Christ our Lord, is faithful.
εἰς κοινωνίαν αὐτοῦ τοῦ υἱοῦ Ἰησοῦ Χριστοῦ ἡμῶν τοῦ κυρίου πιστός
p.a n.asf r.gsm.3 d.gsm n.gsm n.gsm n.gsm r.gp.1 d.gsm n.gsm a.nsm
1650 3126 899 3836 5626 2652 5986 7005 3836 3261 4412

Divisions in the Church

1:10 I appeal to you, brothers, in the name of our Lord Jesus Christ, that all of you
δὲ Παρακαλῶ ὑμᾶς ἀδελφοί διὰ τοῦ ὀνόματος ἡμῶν τοῦ κυρίου Ἰησοῦ Χριστοῦ ἵνα πάντες
cj v.pai.1s r.ap.2 n.vpm p.g d.gsn n.gsn r.gp.1 d.gsm n.gsm n.gsm n.gsm cj a.npm
1254 4151 7007 81 1328 3836 3950 3261 7005 3836 3261 2652 5986 2671 4246

agree with one another so that there may be no divisions among you and that you may be perfectly
τὸ αὐτὸ λέγητε καὶ ᾖ μὴ σχίσματα ἐν ὑμῖν δὲ ἦτε
d.asn r.asn v.pas.2p cj v.pas.3s pl n.npn p.d r.dp.2 cj v.pas.2p
3836 899 3306 2779 1639 3590 5388 1877 7007 1254 1639

united in mind and thought. **11** My brothers, some from Chloe's household have
κατηρτισμένοι ἐν τῷ αὐτῷ νοΐ καὶ ἐν τῇ αὐτῇ γνώμῃ γάρ μου ἀδελφοί ὑπὸ τῶν Χλόης
pt.rp.npm p.d d.dsm r.dsm n.dsn cj p.d d.dsf r.dsf n.dsf cj r.gs.1 n.vpm p.g d.gpm n.gsf
2936 1877 3836 899 3808 2779 1877 3836 899 1191 1142 1609 81 5679 3836 5951

1:1 Παῦλος κλητὸς ἀπόστολος Χριστοῦ Ἰησοῦ διὰ θελήματος θεοῦ καὶ Σωσθένης ὁ ἀδελφὸς ¶ **2** τῇ ἐκκλησίᾳ τοῦ θεοῦ τῇ οὔσῃ ἐν Κορίνθῳ, ἡγιασμένοις ἐν Χριστῷ Ἰησοῦ, κλητοῖς ἁγίοις, σὺν πᾶσιν τοῖς ἐπικαλουμένοις τὸ ὄνομα τοῦ κυρίου ἡμῶν Ἰησοῦ Χριστοῦ ἐν παντὶ τόπῳ, αὐτῶν καὶ ἡμῶν· ¶ **3** χάρις ὑμῖν καὶ εἰρήνη ἀπὸ θεοῦ πατρὸς ἡμῶν καὶ κυρίου Ἰησοῦ Χριστοῦ.

1:4 Εὐχαριστῶ τῷ θεῷ μου πάντοτε περὶ ὑμῶν ἐπὶ τῇ χάριτι τοῦ θεοῦ τῇ δοθείσῃ ὑμῖν ἐν Χριστῷ Ἰησοῦ, **5** ὅτι ἐν παντὶ ἐπλουτίσθητε ἐν αὐτῷ, ἐν παντὶ λόγῳ καὶ πάσῃ γνώσει, **6** καθὼς τὸ μαρτύριον τοῦ Χριστοῦ ἐβεβαιώθη ἐν ὑμῖν, **7** ὥστε ὑμᾶς μὴ ὑστερεῖσθαι ἐν μηδενὶ χαρίσματι ἀπεκδεχομένους τὴν ἀποκάλυψιν τοῦ κυρίου ἡμῶν Ἰησοῦ Χριστοῦ· **8** ὃς καὶ βεβαιώσει ὑμᾶς ἕως τέλους ἀνεγκλήτους ἐν τῇ ἡμέρᾳ τοῦ κυρίου ἡμῶν Ἰησοῦ [Χριστοῦ]. **9** πιστὸς ὁ θεός, δι᾽ οὗ ἐκλήθητε εἰς κοινωνίαν τοῦ υἱοῦ αὐτοῦ Ἰησοῦ Χριστοῦ τοῦ κυρίου ἡμῶν.

1:10 Παρακαλῶ δὲ ὑμᾶς, ἀδελφοί, διὰ τοῦ ὀνόματος τοῦ κυρίου ἡμῶν Ἰησοῦ Χριστοῦ, ἵνα τὸ αὐτὸ λέγητε πάντες καὶ μὴ ᾖ ἐν ὑμῖν σχίσματα, ἦτε δὲ κατηρτισμένοι ἐν τῷ αὐτῷ νοΐ καὶ ἐν τῇ αὐτῇ γνώμῃ. **11** ἐδηλώθη γάρ μοι περὶ ὑμῶν, ἀδελφοί μου,

informed me　　　that there are　quarrels among you. **12**　What I mean is this:　One　of you says,　"I
ἐδηλώθη　μοι περὶ ὑμῶν ὅτι →　εἰσιν ἔριδες ἐν　ὑμῖν δὲ　→ λέγω τοῦτο ὅτι ἕκαστος → ὑμῶν λέγει μέν ἐγὼ
v.api.3s　v.ds.1 p.g r.gp.2 cj　v.pai.3p n.npf p.d　r.dp.2 cj　v.pai.1s r.asn cj r.nsm → r.gp.2 v.pai.3s pl r.ns.1
1317　1609 4309 7007 4022　1639 2251 1877　7007 1254　3306 4047 4022 1667　7007 3306 3525 1609

follow Paul"; another, "I follow Apollos"; another, "I follow Cephas"; still another, "I follow Christ." ¶
εἰμι Παύλου δὲ ἐγὼ Ἀπολλῶ δὲ ἐγὼ Κηφᾶ δὲ ἐγὼ Χριστοῦ
v.pai.1s n.gsm cj r.ns.1 n.gsm cj r.ns.1 n.gsm cj r.ns.1 n.gsm
1639 4263 1254 1609 663 1254 1609 3064 1254 1609 5986

13 Is Christ divided?　Was Paul crucified for you?　Were you baptized into the name of Paul?　**14** I am
→ ὁ Χριστός, μεμέρισται μὴ Παῦλος ἐσταυρώθη ὑπὲρ ὑμῶν ἢ → ἐβαπτίσθητε εἰς τὸ ὄνομα → Παύλου
d.nsm n.nsm v.rpi.3s pl n.nsm v.api.3s p.g r.gp.2 cj v.api.2p p.a d.asn n.asn n.gsm
3532 3836 5986 3532 3590 5090 4263 5090 5642 7007 2445 966 1650 3836 3950 4263

thankful　　　that I did not baptize any of you except Crispus and Gaius, **15** so no one can say that you
εὐχαριστῶ [τῷ θεῷ] ὅτι → → οὐδένα ἐβάπτισα ← → ὑμῶν εἰ μὴ Κρίσπον καὶ Γάϊον ἵνα μή τις → εἴπῃ ὅτι →
v.pai.1s d.dsm n.dsm cj a.asm v.aai.1s r.gp.2 cj pl n.asm cj n.asm cj pl r.nsm v.aas.3s cj
2373 3836 2536 4022 966 966 4029 966 4029 7007 1623 3590 3214 2779 1127 2671 3590 5516 3306 4022

were baptized into my name. **16** (Yes, I also baptized the household of Stephanas; beyond that, I don't
→ ἐβαπτίσθητε εἰς ἐμὸν τὸ ὄνομα δὲ → καὶ ἐβάπτισα τὸν οἶκον → Στεφανᾶ λοιπὸν ← → οὐκ
v.api.2p p.a r.asn.1 d.asn n.asn cj adv v.aai.1s d.asm n.asm n.gsm adv pl
966 1650 1847 3836 3950 1254 966 2779 966 3836 3875 5107 3370 3857 4024

remember if I baptized anyone else.) **17** For Christ did not send me to baptize, but to preach the gospel –
οἶδα εἰ → ἐβάπτισα τινα ἄλλον γὰρ Χριστὸς → οὐ ἀπέστειλεν με → βαπτίζειν ἀλλὰ → εὐαγγελίζεσθαι ←
v.rai.1s cj v.aai.1s r.asm r.asm cj n.nsm pl v.aai.3s r.as.1 f.pa cj f.pm
3857 1623 966 5516 257 1142 5986 690 4024 690 1609 966 247 2294

not with words of human wisdom, lest the cross of Christ be emptied of its power.
οὐκ ἐν λόγου → σοφία ἵνα μὴ ὁ σταυρὸς → τοῦ Χριστοῦ, → κενωθῇ
pl p.d n.dsf pl pl d.nsm n.nsm d.gsm n.gsm v.aps.3s
4024 1877 3364 5053 2671 3590 3836 5089 3836 5986 3033

Christ the Wisdom and Power of God

1:18 For the message of the cross is foolishness to those who are perishing, but to us who are
γὰρ μὲν Ὁ λόγος ὁ → τοῦ σταυροῦ ἐστίν μωρία → τοῖς ← → ἀπολλυμένοις δὲ → ἡμῖν τοῖς
cj pl d.nsm n.nsm d.nsm d.gsm n.gsm v.pai.3s n.nsf d.dpm pt.pm.dpm cj r.dp.1 d.dpm
1142 3525 3836 3364 3836 3836 5089 1639 3702 3836 660 1254 7005 3836

being saved it is the power of God. **19** For it is written: "I will destroy the wisdom of the wise; the
→ σῳζομένοις → ἐστιν δύναμις → θεοῦ γὰρ → γέγραπται → → ἀπολῶ τὴν σοφίαν → τῶν σοφῶν καὶ τὴν
pt.pp.dpm v.pai.3s n.nsf n.gsm cj v.rpi.3s v.fai.1s d.asf n.asf d.gpm a.gpm cj d.asf
5392 1639 1539 2536 1142 1211 660 3836 5053 3836 5055 2779 3836

intelligence of the intelligent I will frustrate." ¶ **20** Where is the wise man? Where is the scholar? Where is the
σύνεσιν → τῶν συνετῶν → ἀθετήσω ποῦ σοφός ← ποῦ γραμματεύς ποῦ
n.asf d.gpm a.gpm v.fai.1s adv a.nsm adv n.nsm adv
5304 3836 5305 119 4543 5055 4543 1208 4543

philosopher of this age? Has not God made foolish the wisdom of the world? **21** For since in the
συζητητής → τούτου τοῦ αἰῶνος, οὐχὶ ὁ θεός, → ἐμώρανεν τὴν σοφίαν → τοῦ κόσμου γὰρ ἐπειδὴ ἐν τῇ
n.nsm r.gsm d.gsm n.gsm pl d.nsm n.nsm v.aai.3s d.asf n.asf d.gsm n.gsm cj cj p.d d.dsf
5186 172 4047 3836 172 3701 4049 3836 2536 3701 3836 5053 3836 3180 1142 2076 1877 3836

wisdom of God the world through its wisdom did not know him, God was pleased through the
σοφία → τοῦ θεοῦ, ὁ κόσμος διὰ τῆς σοφίας → οὐκ ἔγνω τὸν θεόν, ὁ θεὸς, → εὐδόκησεν διὰ τῆς
n.dsf d.gsm n.gsm d.nsm n.nsm p.g d.gsf n.gsf pl v.aai.3s d.asm n.asm d.nsm n.nsm v.aai.3s p.g d.gsf
5053 3836 2536 3836 3180 1328 3836 5053 4024 1182 3836 2536 3836 2536 2305 1328 3836

foolishness of what was preached to save those who believe. **22** Jews demand miraculous signs and
μωρίας → τοῦ → κηρύγματος → σῶσαι τοὺς ← πιστεύοντας καὶ ἐπειδὴ Ἰουδαῖοι αἰτοῦσιν σημεῖα καὶ
n.gsf d.gsn n.gsn f.aa d.apm pt.pa.apm cj cj a.npm v.pai.3p n.apn cj
3702 3836 3060 5392 3836 4409 2779 2076 2681 160 4956 2779

Greeks look for wisdom, **23** but we preach Christ crucified: a stumbling block to Jews and foolishness
Ἕλληνες ζητοῦσιν ← σοφίαν δὲ ἡμεῖς κηρύσσομεν Χριστὸν ἐσταυρωμένον μὲν σκάνδαλον ← → Ἰουδαίοις δὲ μωρίαν
n.npm v.pai.3p n.asf cj r.np.1 v.pai.1p n.asm pt.rp.asm pl n.asn a.dpm cj n.asf
1818 2426 5053 1254 7005 3062 5986 5090 3525 4998 2681 1254 3702

ὑπὸ τῶν Χλόης ὅτι ἔριδες ἐν ὑμῖν εἰσιν. **12** λέγω δὲ τοῦτο ὅτι ἕκαστος ὑμῶν λέγει, Ἐγὼ μέν εἰμι Παύλου, Ἐγὼ δὲ Ἀπολλῶ, Ἐγὼ δὲ Κηφᾶ, Ἐγὼ δὲ Χριστοῦ. ¶ **13** μεμέρισται ὁ Χριστός; μὴ Παῦλος ἐσταυρώθη ὑπὲρ ὑμῶν, ἢ εἰς τὸ ὄνομα Παύλου ἐβαπτίσθητε; **14** εὐχαριστῶ [τῷ θεῷ] ὅτι οὐδένα ὑμῶν ἐβάπτισα εἰ μὴ Κρίσπον καὶ Γάϊον, **15** ἵνα μή τις εἴπῃ ὅτι εἰς τὸ ἐμὸν ὄνομα ἐβαπτίσθητε. **16** ἐβάπτισα δὲ καὶ τὸν Στεφανᾶ οἶκον, λοιπὸν οὐκ οἶδα εἴ τινα ἄλλον ἐβάπτισα. **17** οὐ γὰρ ἀπέστειλέν με Χριστὸς βαπτίζειν ἀλλὰ εὐαγγελίζεσθαι, οὐκ ἐν σοφίᾳ λόγου, ἵνα μὴ κενωθῇ ὁ σταυρὸς τοῦ Χριστοῦ.

1:18 Ὁ λόγος γὰρ ὁ τοῦ σταυροῦ τοῖς μὲν ἀπολλυμένοις μωρία ἐστίν, τοῖς δὲ σῳζομένοις ἡμῖν δύναμις θεοῦ ἐστιν. **19** γέγραπται γάρ, Ἀπολῶ τὴν σοφίαν τῶν σοφῶν καὶ τὴν σύνεσιν τῶν συνετῶν ἀθετήσω. ¶ **20** ποῦ σοφός; ποῦ γραμματεύς; ποῦ συζητητὴς τοῦ αἰῶνος τούτου; οὐχὶ ἐμώρανεν ὁ θεὸς τὴν σοφίαν τοῦ κόσμου; **21** ἐπειδὴ γὰρ ἐν τῇ σοφίᾳ τοῦ θεοῦ οὐκ ἔγνω ὁ κόσμος διὰ τῆς σοφίας τὸν θεόν, εὐδόκησεν ὁ θεὸς διὰ τῆς μωρίας τοῦ κηρύγματος σῶσαι τοὺς πιστεύοντας· **22** ἐπειδὴ καὶ Ἰουδαῖοι σημεῖα αἰτοῦσιν καὶ Ἕλληνες σοφίαν ζητοῦσιν, **23** ἡμεῖς δὲ κηρύσσομεν Χριστὸν ἐσταυρωμένον, Ἰουδαίοις μὲν σκάνδαλον, ἔθνεσιν δὲ

to Gentiles, 24 but to those whom God has called, both Jews and Greeks, Christ the power of God and the
→ ἔθνεσιν δὲ τοῖς αὐτοῖς ← κλητοῖς τε Ἰουδαίοις καὶ Ἕλλησιν Χριστὸν δύναμιν → θεοῦ καὶ
n.dpn cj d.dpm r.dpm.3 a.dpm cj a.dpm cj a.dpm n.asm n.asf n.gsm cj
1620 1254 3836 899 3105 5445 2681 2779 1818 5986 1539 2536 2779

wisdom of God. 25 For the foolishness of God is wiser than man's wisdom, and the weakness of
σοφίαν → θεοῦ ὅτι τὸ μωρὸν → τοῦ θεοῦ ἐστιν σοφώτερον ← τῶν ἀνθρώπων καὶ τὸ ἀσθενὲς →
n.asf n.gsm cj d.nsn a.nsn d.gsm n.gsm v.pai.3s a.nsn.c d.gpm n.gpm cj d.nsn a.nsn
5053 2536 4022 3836 3704 3836 2536 1639 5055 3836 476 2779 3836 822

God is stronger than man's strength. ¶ 26 Brothers, think of what you were when you were
→ τοῦ θεοῦ ἰσχυρότερον ← τῶν ἀνθρώπων γὰρ ἀδελφοί Βλέπετε ὑμῶν
d.gsm n.gsm a.nsn.c d.gpm n.gpm cj n.vpm v.pai.2p r.gp.2
3836 2536 2708 3836 476 1142 81 1063 7007

called. Not many of you were wise by human standards; not many were influential; not many were of
τὴν κλῆσιν ὅτι οὐ πολλοὶ σοφοὶ κατὰ σάρκα ← οὐ πολλοὶ δυνατοί οὐ πολλοὶ
d.asf n.asf cj pl a.npm a.npm p.a n.asf pl a.npm a.npm pl a.npm
3836 3104 4022 4024 4498 5055 2848 4922 4024 4498 1543 4024 4498

noble birth. 27 But God chose the foolish things of the world to shame the wise; God chose
εὐγενεῖς ← ἀλλὰ ὁ θεὸς ἐξελέξατο τὰ μωρὰ ← → τοῦ κόσμου ἵνα καταισχύνῃ τοὺς σοφοὺς καὶ ὁ θεὸς ἐξελέξατο
a.npm cj d.nsm n.nsm v.ami.3s d.apn a.apn d.gsm n.gsm cj v.pas.3s d.apm a.apm cj d.nsm n.nsm v.ami.3s
2302 247 3836 2536 1721 3836 3704 3836 3180 2671 2875 3836 5055 2779 3836 2536 1721

the weak things of the world to shame the strong. 28 He chose the lowly things of this world and the
τὰ ἀσθενῆ ← → τοῦ κόσμου ἵνα καταισχύνῃ τὰ ἰσχυρά καὶ ὁ θεός, ἐξελέξατο τὰ ἀγενῆ ← → τοῦ κόσμου καὶ τὰ
d.apn a.apn d.gsm n.gsm cj v.pas.3s d.apn a.apn cj d.nsm n.nsm v.ami.3s d.apn a.apn d.gsm n.gsm cj d.apn
3836 822 3836 3180 2671 2875 3836 2708 2779 3836 2536 1721 3836 38 3836 3180 2779 3836

despised things – and the things that are not – to nullify the things that are, 29 so that no one may
ἐξουθενημένα τὰ ← ὄντα μὴ ἵνα καταργήσῃ τὰ ← ← ὄντα ὅπως ← μὴ πᾶσα σάρξ →
pt.rp.apn d.apn pt.pa.apn pl cj v.aas.3s d.apn pt.pa.apn cj pl a.nsf n.nsf
2024 3836 1639 3590 2671 2934 3836 1639 3968 3590 4246 4922

boast before him. 30 It is because of him that you are in Christ Jesus, who has become for us wisdom
καυχήσηται ἐνώπιον τοῦ θεοῦ δὲ ἐξ → αὐτοῦ ὑμεῖς ἐστε ἐν Χριστῷ Ἰησοῦ ὃς → ἐγενήθη → ἡμῖν σοφία
v.ams.3s p.g d.gsm n.gsm cj p.g r.gsm.3 r.np.2 v.pai.2p p.d n.dsm n.dsm r.nsm v.api.3s r.dp.1 n.nsf
3016 1967 3836 2536 1254 1666 899 7007 1639 1877 5986 2652 4005 1181 7005 5053

from God – that is, our righteousness, holiness and redemption. 31 Therefore, as it is written: "Let him who
ἀπὸ θεοῦ τε ← δικαιοσύνη καὶ ἁγιασμὸς καὶ ἀπολύτρωσις ἵνα καθὼς → γέγραπται → ὁ ←
p.g n.gsm cj n.nsf cj n.nsm cj n.nsf cj cj v.rpi.3s d.nsm
608 2536 5445 1466 2779 40 2779 667 2671 2777 1211 3836

boasts boast in the Lord." ¶ 2:1 When I came to you, brothers, I did not come with eloquence
καυχώμενος καυχάσθω ἐν κυρίῳ Κἀγὼ ἐλθὼν πρὸς ὑμᾶς ἀδελφοί → οὐ ἦλθον καθ' ὑπεροχὴν
pt.pm.nsm v.pmm.3s p.d n.dsm crasis pt.aa.nsm p.a r.ap.2 n.vpm pl v.aai.1s p.a n.asf
3016 3016 1877 3261 2262 2743 2262 4639 7007 2262 2262 4024 2262 2848 5667

or superior wisdom as I proclaimed to you the testimony about God. 2 For I resolved to know nothing
λόγου ἢ σοφίας → → καταγγέλλων ὑμῖν ὺ μυστήριον → τοῦ θεοῦ γὰρ → ἔκρινα → εἰδέναι οὐ τι
n.gsm cj n.gsf pt.pa.nsm r.dp.2 d.asn n.asn d.gsm n.gsm cj v.aai.1s f.ra pl r.asn
3364 2445 5053 2859 7007 3836 3696 3836 2536 1142 3212 3857 4024 5516

while I was with you except Jesus Christ and him crucified. 3 I came to you in weakness and fear,
→ ἐν ὑμῖν εἰ μὴ Ἰησοῦν Χριστὸν καὶ τοῦτον ἐσταυρωμένον κἀγὼ ἐγενόμην πρὸς ὑμᾶς ἐν ἀσθενείᾳ καὶ ἐν φόβῳ
p.d r.dp.2 cj pl n.asm n.asm cj r.asm pt.rp.asm crasis v.ami.1s p.a r.ap.2 p.d n.dsf cj p.d n.dsm
1877 7007 1623 3590 2652 5986 2779 4047 5090 2743 1181 4639 7007 1877 819 2779 1877 5832

and with much trembling. 4 My message and my preaching were not with wise and persuasive words, but
καὶ ἐν πολλῷ τρόμῳ καὶ μου ὁ λόγος καὶ μου τὸ κήρυγμα οὐκ ἐν σοφίας πειθοῖς λόγοις ἀλλ'
cj p.d a.dsm n.dsm cj r.gs.1 d.nsm n.nsm cj r.gs.1 d.nsn n.nsn pl p.d n.gsf a.dpm n.dpm cj
2779 1877 4498 5571 2779 1609 3836 3364 2779 1609 3836 3060 4024 1877 5053 4273 3364 247

with a demonstration of the Spirit's power, 5 so that your faith might not rest on men's wisdom, but
ἐν ἀποδείξει → πνεύματος καὶ δυνάμεως ἵνα ← ὑμῶν ἡ πίστις → μὴ ᾖ ἐν ἀνθρώπων σοφίᾳ ἀλλ'
p.d n.dsf n.gsn cj n.gsf cj r.gp.2 d.nsf n.nsf pl v.pas.3s p.d n.gpm n.dsf cj
1877 618 4460 2779 1539 2671 7007 3836 4411 3590 1639 1877 476 5053 247

μωρίαν, 24 αὐτοῖς δὲ τοῖς κλητοῖς, Ἰουδαίοις τε καὶ Ἕλλησιν, Χριστὸν θεοῦ δύναμιν καὶ θεοῦ σοφίαν· 25 ὅτι τὸ μωρὸν τοῦ θεοῦ σοφώτερον τῶν ἀνθρώπων ἐστὶν καὶ τὸ ἀσθενὲς τοῦ θεοῦ ἰσχυρότερον τῶν ἀνθρώπων. ¶ 26 Βλέπετε γὰρ τὴν κλῆσιν ὑμῶν, ἀδελφοί, ὅτι οὐ πολλοὶ σοφοὶ κατὰ σάρκα, οὐ πολλοὶ δυνατοί, οὐ πολλοὶ εὐγενεῖς· 27 ἀλλὰ τὰ μωρὰ τοῦ κόσμου ἐξελέξατο ὁ θεός, ἵνα καταισχύνῃ τοὺς σοφούς, καὶ τὰ ἀσθενῆ τοῦ κόσμου ἐξελέξατο ὁ θεός, ἵνα καταισχύνῃ τὰ ἰσχυρά, 28 καὶ τὰ ἀγενῆ τοῦ κόσμου καὶ τὰ ἐξουθενημένα ἐξελέξατο ὁ θεός, τὰ μὴ ὄντα, ἵνα τὰ ὄντα καταργήσῃ, 29 ὅπως μὴ καυχήσηται πᾶσα σὰρξ ἐνώπιον τοῦ θεοῦ. 30 ἐξ αὐτοῦ δὲ ὑμεῖς ἐστε ἐν Χριστῷ Ἰησοῦ, ὃς ἐγενήθη σοφία ἡμῖν ἀπὸ θεοῦ, δικαιοσύνη τε καὶ ἁγιασμὸς καὶ ἀπολύτρωσις, 31 ἵνα καθὼς γέγραπται, Ὁ καυχώμενος ἐν κυρίῳ καυχάσθω. 2:1 Κἀγὼ ἐλθὼν πρὸς ὑμᾶς, ἀδελφοί, ἦλθον οὐ καθ' ὑπεροχὴν λόγου ἢ σοφίας καταγγέλλων ὑμῖν τὸ μαρτύριον «μυστήριον» τοῦ θεοῦ. 2 οὐ γὰρ ἔκρινά τι εἰδέναι ἐν ὑμῖν εἰ μὴ Ἰησοῦν Χριστὸν καὶ τοῦτον ἐσταυρωμένον. 3 κἀγὼ ἐν ἀσθενείᾳ καὶ ἐν φόβῳ καὶ ἐν τρόμῳ πολλῷ ἐγενόμην πρὸς ὑμᾶς, 4 καὶ ὁ λόγος μου καὶ τὸ κήρυγμά μου οὐκ ἐν πειθοῖ[ς] σοφίας [λόγοις] ἀλλ' ἐν ἀποδείξει πνεύματος καὶ δυνάμεως, 5 ἵνα ἡ πίστις ὑμῶν μὴ ᾖ ἐν σοφίᾳ ἀνθρώπων ἀλλ' ἐν δυνάμει θεοῦ.

on God's power.
ἐν θεοῦ δυνάμει
p.d n.gsm n.dsf
1877 2536 1539

Wisdom From the Spirit

2:6 We do, however, speak a message of wisdom among the mature, but not the wisdom of this age
↱ ↱ δὲ λαλοῦμεν Σοφίαν ἐν τοῖς τελείοις δὲ οὐ σοφίαν ↱ τούτου ᾽τοῦ αἰῶνος᾽
cj v.pai.1p n.asf p.d d.dpm a.dpm cj pl n.asf r.gsm d.gsm n.gsm
3281 3281 1254 3281 5053 1877 3836 5455 1254 4024 5053 172 4047 3836 172

or of the rulers of this age, who are coming to nothing. ⁷ No, we speak of God's secret
οὐδὲ → τῶν ἀρχόντων → τούτου ᾽τοῦ αἰῶνος᾽ τῶν → → καταργουμένων ἀλλὰ → λαλοῦμεν ← θεοῦ ἐν μυστηρίῳ᾽
cj d.gpm n.gpm r.gsm d.gsm n.gsm d.gpm pt.pp.gpm cj v.pai.1p n.gsm p.d n.dsn
4028 3836 807 172 4047 3836 172 3836 2934 247 3281 2536 1877 3696

wisdom, a wisdom that has been hidden and that God destined for our glory before time began.
σοφίαν τὴν → → ἀποκεκρυμμένην ἣν ὁ θεὸς᾽ προώρισεν εἰς ἡμῶν δόξαν πρὸ ᾽τῶν αἰώνων᾽ ←
n.asf d.asf pt.rp.asf r.asf d.nsm n.nsm v.aai.3s p.a r.gp.1 n.asf p.g d.gpm n.gpm
5053 3836 648 4005 3836 2536 4633 1650 7005 1518 4574 3836 172

⁸ None of the rulers of this age understood it; for if they had, they would not have crucified the
οὐδεὶς → τῶν ἀρχόντων → τούτου ᾽τοῦ αἰῶνος᾽ ἔγνωκεν ἦν γὰρ εἰ ἔγνωσαν → ἂν οὐκ ἐσταύρωσαν τὸν
a.nsm d.gpm n.gpm r.gsm d.gsm n.gsm v.rai.3s r.asf cj cj v.aai.3p pl pl v.aai.3p d.asm
4029 3836 807 172 4047 3836 172 1182 4005 1142 1623 1182 5090 323 4024 5090 3836

Lord of glory. ⁹ However, as it is written: "No eye has seen, no ear has heard, no mind
κύριον → ᾽τῆς δόξης᾽ ἀλλὰ καθὼς → γέγραπται ἃ οὐκ ὀφθαλμὸς → εἶδεν καὶ οὐκ οὖς → ἤκουσεν καὶ οὐκ ἐπὶ καρδίαν
n.asm d.gsf n.gsf cj cj v.rpi.3s r.apn pl n.nsm v.aai.3s cj pl n.nsn v.aai.3s cj pl p.a n.asf
3261 3836 1518 247 2777 1211 4005 4024 4057 1625 2779 4024 4044 201 2779 4024 2093 2840

has conceived what God has prepared for those who love him" – ¹⁰ but God has revealed it to
ἀνθρώπου → ἀνέβη ἃ ὁ θεὸς᾽ ἡτοίμασεν → τοῖς ← ἀγαπῶσιν αὐτόν δὲ ὁ θεὸς᾽ → ἀπεκάλυψεν →
n.gsm v.aai.3s r.apn d.nsm n.nsm v.aai.3s d.dpm pt.pa.dpm r.asm.3 cj d.nsm n.nsm v.aai.3s
476 326 4005 3836 2536 2286 3836 26 899 1254 3836 2536 636

us by his Spirit. ¶ The Spirit searches all things, even the deep things of God. ¹¹ For who among
ἡμῖν διὰ τοῦ πνεύματος γὰρ τὸ πνεῦμα ἐραυνᾷ πάντα ← καὶ τὰ βάθη ← → ᾽τοῦ θεοῦ᾽ γὰρ τίς →
r.dp.1 p.g d.gsn n.gsn cj d.nsn n.nsn v.pai.3s a.apn cj d.apn n.apn d.gsm n.gsm cj r.nsm
7005 1328 3836 4460 1142 3836 4460 2236 4246 2779 3836 958 3836 2536 1142 5515

men knows the thoughts of a man except the man's spirit within him? In the same way
ἀνθρώπων οἶδεν τὰ ← → ᾽τοῦ ἀνθρώπου᾽ εἰ μὴ τὸ ᾽τοῦ ἀνθρώπου᾽ πνεῦμα τὸ ἐν αὐτῷ οὕτως ← →
n.gpm v.rai.3s d.apn d.gsm n.gsm cj pl d.nsn d.gsm n.gsm n.nsn d.nsn p.d r.dsm.3 adv
476 3857 3836 3836 476 1623 3590 3836 3836 476 4460 3836 1877 899 4048

no one knows the thoughts of God except the Spirit of God. ¹² We have not received the spirit of
καὶ οὐδεὶς ← ἔγνωκεν τὰ ← → ᾽τοῦ θεοῦ᾽ εἰ μὴ τὸ πνεῦμα → ᾽τοῦ θεοῦ᾽ δὲ ἡμεῖς → οὐ ἐλάβομεν τὸ πνεῦμα
adv a.nsm v.rai.3s d.apn d.gsm n.gsm cj pl d.nsn n.nsn d.gsm n.gsm cj r.np.1 pl v.aai.1p d.asn n.asn
2779 4029 1182 3836 3836 2536 1623 3590 3836 4460 3836 2536 1254 7005 3284 4024 3284 3836 4460

the world but the Spirit who is from God, that we may understand what God has freely given us.
τοῦ κόσμου ἀλλὰ τὸ πνεῦμα τὸ ἐκ ᾽τοῦ θεοῦ᾽ ἵνα → → εἰδῶμεν τὰ ὑπὸ ᾽τοῦ θεοῦ᾽ → → χαρισθέντα ἡμῖν
d.gsm n.gsm cj d.asn n.asn d.asn p.g d.gsm n.gsm cj v.ras.1p d.apn p.g d.gsm n.gsm pt.ap.apn r.dp.1
3836 3180 247 3836 4460 3836 1666 3836 2536 2671 3857 3836 5679 3836 2536 5919 7005

¹³ This is what we speak, not in words taught us by human wisdom but in words taught by the Spirit,
ἃ καὶ → λαλοῦμεν οὐκ ἐν λόγοις διδακτοῖς → ἀνθρωπίνης σοφίας ἀλλ᾽ ἐν διδακτοῖς → πνεύματος
r.apn adv v.pai.1p pl p.d n.d a.dpm a.gsf n.gsf cj p.d a.dpm n.gsn
4005 2779 3281 4024 1877 3364 1435 474 5053 247 1877 1435 4460

expressing spiritual truths in spiritual words. ¹⁴ The man without the Spirit does not accept the things
συγκρίνοντες πνευματικὰ → πνευματικοῖς δὲ ἄνθρωπος → ψυχικὸς οὐ δέχεται τὰ ←
pt.pa.npm a.apn a.dpn cj n.nsm a.nsm pl v.pmi.3s d.apn
5173 4461 4461 1254 476 6035 1312 4024 1312 3836

that come from the Spirit of God, for they are foolishness to him, and he cannot understand them,
→ → → τοῦ πνεύματος → ᾽τοῦ θεοῦ᾽ γὰρ → ἐστιν μωρία → αὐτῷ καὶ → οὐ δύναται᾽ γνῶναι
d.gsn n.gsn d.gsm n.gsm cj v.pai.3s n.nsf r.dsm.3 cj pl v.ppi.3s f.aa
3836 4460 3836 2536 1142 1639 3702 899 2779 1538 4024 1538 1182

---

²·⁶ Σοφίαν δὲ λαλοῦμεν ἐν τοῖς τελείοις, σοφίαν δὲ οὐ τοῦ αἰῶνος τούτου οὐδὲ τῶν ἀρχόντων τοῦ αἰῶνος τούτου τῶν καταργουμένων· ⁷ ἀλλὰ λαλοῦμεν θεοῦ σοφίαν ἐν μυστηρίῳ τὴν ἀποκεκρυμμένην, ἣν προώρισεν ὁ θεὸς πρὸ τῶν αἰώνων εἰς δόξαν ἡμῶν, ⁸ ἣν οὐδεὶς τῶν ἀρχόντων τοῦ αἰῶνος τούτου ἔγνωκεν· εἰ γὰρ ἔγνωσαν, οὐκ ἂν τὸν κύριον τῆς δόξης ἐσταύρωσαν. ⁹ ἀλλὰ καθὼς γέγραπται, ῍Α ὀφθαλμὸς οὐκ εἶδεν καὶ οὖς οὐκ ἤκουσεν καὶ ἐπὶ καρδίαν ἀνθρώπου οὐκ ἀνέβη, ἃ ἡτοίμασεν ὁ θεὸς τοῖς ἀγαπῶσιν αὐτόν. ¹⁰ ἡμῖν δὲ ἀπεκάλυψεν ὁ θεὸς διὰ τοῦ πνεύματος· ¶ τὸ γὰρ πνεῦμα πάντα ἐραυνᾷ, καὶ τὰ βάθη τοῦ θεοῦ. ¹¹ τίς γὰρ οἶδεν ἀνθρώπων τὰ τοῦ ἀνθρώπου εἰ μὴ τὸ πνεῦμα τοῦ ἀνθρώπου τὸ ἐν αὐτῷ; οὕτως καὶ τὰ τοῦ θεοῦ οὐδεὶς ἔγνωκεν εἰ μὴ τὸ πνεῦμα τοῦ θεοῦ. ¹² ἡμεῖς δὲ οὐ τὸ πνεῦμα τοῦ κόσμου ἐλάβομεν ἀλλὰ τὸ πνεῦμα τὸ ἐκ τοῦ θεοῦ, ἵνα εἰδῶμεν τὰ ὑπὸ τοῦ θεοῦ χαρισθέντα ἡμῖν· ¹³ ἃ καὶ λαλοῦμεν οὐκ ἐν διδακτοῖς ἀνθρωπίνης σοφίας λόγοις ἀλλ᾽ ἐν διδακτοῖς πνεύματος, πνευματικοῖς πνευματικὰ συγκρίνοντες. ¹⁴ ψυχικὸς δὲ ἄνθρωπος οὐ δέχεται τὰ τοῦ πνεύματος τοῦ θεοῦ· μωρία γὰρ αὐτῷ ἐστιν

because they are spiritually discerned. **15** The spiritual man makes judgments about all things, but he
ὅτι   →   →   πνευματικῶς ἀνακρίνεται   δὲ   ὁ   πνευματικὸς ←   ἀνακρίνει   ⌊τὰ⌋ πάντα ←   δὲ
cj   adv   adv   v.ppi.3s   cj   d.nsm   a.nsm   v.pai.3s   d.apn   a.apn   cj
4022   373   373   4462   373   1254   3836   4461   373   3836   4246   1254   373

himself is not subject to any man's judgment: **16** "For who has known the mind of the Lord that he may
αὐτὸς → → ὑπ᾽ ← οὐδενὸς ←   ἀνακρίνεται γὰρ τίς → ἔγνω νοῦν → κυρίου ὃς →
r.nsm   p.g   a.gsm   v.ppi.3s   cj   r.nsm   v.aai.3s   n.asm   n.gsm   r.nsm
899   373 4029 5679   4029   373   1142 5515   1182   3808   3261   4005

instruct him?" But we have the mind of Christ.
συμβιβάσει αὐτόν δὲ ἡμεῖς ἔχομεν νοῦν → Χριστοῦ
v.fai.3s   r.asm.3   cj   r.np.1   v.pai.1p   n.asm   n.gsm
5204   899   1254   7005   2400   3808   5986

On Divisions in the Church

3:1 Brothers, I could not address you as spiritual but as worldly – mere infants in Christ. **2** I gave
ἀδελφοί Κἀγὼ ἠδυνήθην οὐκ λαλῆσαι ὑμῖν ὡς πνευματικοῖς ἀλλ᾽ ὡς σαρκίνοις ὡς νηπίοις ἐν Χριστῷ → ἐπότισα
n.vpm   crasis   v.api.1s   pl   f.aa   r.dp.2   pl   a.dpm   cj   pl   a.dpm   pl   a.dpm   p.d   n.dsm   v.aai.1s
81   2743   1538   4024   3281   7007   6055   4461   247   6055   4921   6055   3758   1877   5986   4540

you milk, not solid food, for you were not yet ready for it. Indeed, you are still not ready. **3** You are still
ὑμᾶς γάλα οὐ → βρῶμα γὰρ → → οὔπω ← ἐδύνασθε ἀλλ᾽ → → ἔτι νῦν οὐδὲ δύνασθε γὰρ → ἐστε ἔτι
r.ap.2   n.asn   pl   n.asn   cj   adv   v.ipi.2p   cj   adv   adv   adv   v.ppi.2p   cj   v.pai.2p   adv
7007   1128   4024   1109   1142   1538   1538   4037   1538   247   1538 1538 2285 3814 4028   1538   1142   1639   2285

worldly. For since there is jealousy and quarreling among you, are you not worldly? Are you not acting like
σαρκικοί γὰρ ὅπου ζῆλος καὶ ἔρις ἐν ὑμῖν ἐστε ← οὐχὶ σαρκικοί καὶ → → περιπατεῖτε κατὰ
a.npm   cj   cj   n.nsm   cj   n.nsf   p.d   r.dp.2   v.pai.2p   pl   a.npm   cj   v.pai.2p   p.a
4920   1142   3963   2419   2779   2251   1877   7007   1639   4049   4920   2779   4344   2848

mere men? **4** For when one says, "I follow Paul," and another, "I follow Apollos," are you not mere men?
ἄνθρωπον γὰρ ὅταν τις λέγῃ μέν ἐγὼ εἰμι Παύλου δὲ ἕτερος ἐγὼ Ἀπολλῶ ἐστε ← οὐκ ἄνθρωποι
n.asm   cj   cj   r.nsm   v.pas.3s   pl   r.ns.1   v.pai.1s   n.gsm   cj   r.nsm   r.ns.1   n.gsm   v.pai.2p   pl   n.npm
476   1142   4020   5516   3306   3525   1609   1639   4263   1254   2283   1609   663   1639   4024   476

¶ **5** What, after all, is Apollos? And what is Paul? Only servants, through whom you came to believe –
Τί οὖν ἐστιν Ἀπολλῶς δὲ τί ἐστιν Παῦλος διάκονοι δι᾽ ὧν → ἐπιστεύσατε καὶ
r.nsn   cj   v.pai.3s   n.nsm   cj   r.nsn   v.pai.3s   n.nsm   n.npm   p.g   r.gpm   v.aai.2p   cj
5515   4036   1639   663   1254   5515   1639   4263   1356   1328   4005   4409   2779

as the Lord has assigned to each his task. **6** I planted the seed, Apollos watered it, but God made it grow.
ὡς ὁ κύριος → ἔδωκεν → ἑκάστῳ ἐγὼ ἐφύτευσα Ἀπολλῶς ἐπότισεν ἀλλὰ ὁ θεός, → → ηὔξανεν
cj   d.nsm   n.nsm   v.aai.3s   r.dsm   r.ns.1   v.aai.1s   n.nsm   v.aai.3s   cj   d.nsm   n.nsm   v.iai.3s
6055   3836   3261   1443   1667   1609   5885   663   4540   247   3836   2536   889

7 So neither he who plants nor he who waters is anything, but only God, who makes things grow. **8** The
ὥστε οὔτε ὁ φυτεύων οὔτε ὁ ποτίζων ἐστίν τι ἀλλ᾽ θεός ὁ → αὐξάνων δὲ ὁ
cj   cj   d.nsm   pt.pa.nsm   cj   d.nsm   pt.pa.nsm   v.pai.3s   r.nsn   cj   n.nsm   d.nsm   pt.pa.nsm   cj   d.nsm
6063   4046   3836   5885   4046   3836   4540   1639   5516   247   2536   3836   889   1254   3836

man who plants and the man who waters have one purpose, and each will be rewarded according
φυτεύων καὶ ὁ ← ποτίζων εἰσίν ἕν δὲ ἕκαστος τὸν ἴδιον → λήμψεται μισθὸν κατὰ
pt.pa.nsm   cj   d.nsm   pt.pa.nsm   v.pai.3p   a.nsn   cj   r.nsm   d.asm   a.asm   v.fmi.3s   n.asm   p.a
5885   2779   3836   4540   1639   1651   1254   1667   3836   2625   3284   3635   2848

to his own labor. **9** For we are God's fellow workers; you are God's field, God's building. ¶ **10** By the grace
τὸν ἴδιον κόπον γὰρ → ἐσμεν θεοῦ συνεργοί → ἐστε θεοῦ γεώργιον θεοῦ οἰκοδομή Κατὰ τὴν χάριν
d.asm   a.asm   n.asm   cj   v.pai.1p   n.gsm   n.npm   v.pai.2p   n.gsm   n.nsn   n.gsm   n.nsf   p.a   d.asf   n.asf
3836   2625   3160   1142   1639   2536   5301   1639   2536   1176   2536   3869   2848   3836   5921

God has given me, I laid a foundation as an expert builder, and someone else is building on it. But
τοῦ θεοῦ → τὴν δοθεῖσαν μοι → ἔθηκα θεμέλιον ὡς σοφὸς ἀρχιτέκτων δὲ ἄλλος → ἐποικοδομεῖ ← δὲ
d.gsm   n.gsm   d.asf   pt.ap.asf   r.ds.1   v.aai.1s   n.asm   pl   n.nsm   n.nsm   cj   r.nsm   v.pai.3s   cj
3836   2536   3836   1443   1609   5502   2529   6055   5055   802   1254   257   2224   1254

each one should be careful how he builds. **11** For no one can lay any foundation other than the one
ἕκαστος ← → βλεπέτω πῶς → ἐποικοδομεῖ γὰρ οὐδεὶς ← δύναται θεῖναι θεμέλιον ἄλλον παρὰ τὸν ←
r.nsm   v.pam.3s   cj   v.pai.3s   cj   a.nsm   v.ppi.3s   f.aa   n.asm   r.asm   p.a   d.asm
1667   1063   4802   2224   1142   4029   1538   5502   2529   257   4123   3836

καὶ οὐ δύναται γνῶναι, ὅτι πνευματικῶς ἀνακρίνεται. **15** ὁ δὲ πνευματικὸς ἀνακρίνει [τὰ] πάντα, αὐτὸς δὲ ὑπ᾽ οὐδενὸς ἀνακρίνεται. **16** τίς γὰρ ἔγνω νοῦν κυρίου, ὃς συμβιβάσει αὐτόν; ἡμεῖς δὲ νοῦν Χριστοῦ ἔχομεν.

3:1 Κἀγώ, ἀδελφοί, οὐκ ἠδυνήθην λαλῆσαι ὑμῖν ὡς πνευματικοῖς ἀλλ᾽ ὡς σαρκίνοις, ὡς νηπίοις ἐν Χριστῷ. **2** γάλα ὑμᾶς ἐπότισα, οὐ βρῶμα· οὔπω γὰρ ἐδύνασθε. ἀλλ᾽ οὐδὲ ἔτι νῦν δύνασθε. **3** ἔτι γὰρ σαρκικοί ἐστε. ὅπου γὰρ ἐν ὑμῖν ζῆλος καὶ ἔρις, οὐχὶ σαρκικοί ἐστε καὶ κατὰ ἄνθρωπον περιπατεῖτε; **4** ὅταν γὰρ λέγῃ τις, Ἐγὼ μέν εἰμι Παύλου, ἕτερος δέ, Ἐγὼ Ἀπολλῶ, οὐκ ἄνθρωποί ἐστε; **5** τί οὖν ἐστιν Ἀπολλῶς; τί δέ ἐστιν Παῦλος; διάκονοι δι᾽ ὧν ἐπιστεύσατε, καὶ ἑκάστῳ ὡς ὁ κύριος ἔδωκεν. **6** ἐγὼ ἐφύτευσα, Ἀπολλῶς ἐπότισεν, ἀλλ᾽ ὁ θεὸς ηὔξανεν· **7** ὥστε οὔτε ὁ φυτεύων ἐστίν τι οὔτε ὁ ποτίζων ἀλλ᾽ ὁ αὐξάνων θεός. **8** ὁ φυτεύων δὲ καὶ ὁ ποτίζων ἕν εἰσιν, ἕκαστος δὲ τὸν ἴδιον μισθὸν λήμψεται κατὰ τὸν ἴδιον κόπον· **9** θεοῦ γάρ ἐσμεν συνεργοί, θεοῦ γεώργιον, θεοῦ οἰκοδομή ἐστε. ¶ **10** Κατὰ τὴν χάριν τοῦ θεοῦ τὴν δοθεῖσάν μοι ὡς σοφὸς ἀρχιτέκτων θεμέλιον ἔθηκα, ἄλλος δὲ ἐποικοδομεῖ. ἕκαστος δὲ βλεπέτω πῶς ἐποικοδομεῖ. **11** θεμέλιον γὰρ ἄλλον οὐδεὶς δύναται θεῖναι παρὰ τὸν

already laid,   which is   Jesus   Christ.   **12**   If   any man builds   on this foundation using gold,   silver,   costly
κείμενον   ὅς   ἐστιν   Ἰησοῦς   Χριστός   δέ εἰ   τις   ←   ἐποικοδομεῖ   ἐπὶ   τὸν   θεμέλιον   χρυσόν   ἄργυρον   τιμίους
pt.pm.asm   r.nsm   v.pai.3s   n.nsm   n.nsm   cj cj   r.nsm   v.pai.3s   p.a   d.asm   n.asm   n.asm   n.asm   a.apm
3023   4005   1639   2652   5986   1254 1623   5516   2224   2093   3836   2529   5996   738   5508

stones,   wood,   hay   or straw,   **13** his   work   will be   shown for what it is, because the Day will bring   it to
λίθους   ξύλα   χόρτον   καλάμην   ἑκάστου   τὸ ἔργον   γενήσεται   φανερὸν   γὰρ   ἡ   ἡμέρα   →   δηλώσει   ←
n.apm   n.apn   n.asm   n.asf   r.gsm   d.nsn n.nsn   v.fmi.3s   a.nsn   cj   d.nsf   n.nsf   v.fai.3s
3345   3833   5965   2811   1667   3836 2240   1181   5745   1142   3836   2465   1317

light.   It will be revealed   with fire, and the fire   will test   the quality   of each   man's
←   ὅτι → → →   ἀποκαλύπτεται ἐν   πυρὶ καὶ τὸ πῦρ   [αὐτό]   →   δοκιμάσει   ὁποῖον   ἐστιν   ἑκάστου
cj   v.ppi.3s   p.d   n.dsn cj d.nsn n.nsn   r.nsn   v.fai.3s   r.nsn   v.pai.3s   r.gsm
4022   636   1877   4786 2779 3836 4786   899   1507   3961   1639   1667

work.   **14** If   what   he has built   survives, he will receive   his reward.   **15** If   it   is
τὸ ἔργον   εἴ   τινος τὸ ἔργον   ὃ → →   ἐποικοδόμησεν   μενεῖ   →   λήμψεται   μισθὸν   εἴ   τινος τὸ ἔργον   →
d.asn n.asn   cj   r.gsm d.nsn n.nsn   r.asn   v.aai.3s   v.fai.3s   v.fmi.3s   n.asm   cj   r.gsm d.nsn n.nsn
3836 2240   1623   5516 3836 2240   4005   2224   3531   3284   3635   1623   5516 3836 2240

burned   up, he will suffer loss;   he himself will be saved,   but only as one escaping   through the
κατακαήσεται   ← → →   ζημιωθήσεται δὲ   αὐτὸς   →   →   σωθήσεται δὲ   οὕτως ὡς   ←   ←   διὰ
v.fpi.3s   v.fpi.3s   cj   r.nsm   v.fpi.3s cj   adv   pl   p.g
2876   2423   1254 5392   899   5392 1254   4048 6055   1328

flames.   ¶   **16** Don't you know that you yourselves are   God's temple and that God's   Spirit   lives in you?
πυρός   Οὐκ   →   οἴδατε ὅτι   →   ἐστε θεοῦ ναὸς καὶ   τοῦ θεοῦ   τὸ πνεῦμα   οἰκεῖ ἐν   ὑμῖν
n.gsn   pl   v.rai.2p   cj   v.pai.2p n.gsm n.nsm cj   d.gsm n.gsm   d.nsn n.nsn   v.pai.3s p.d   r.dp.2
4786   4024   3857   4022   1639 2536 3724 2779   3836 2536   3836 4460   3861 1877   7007

17 If   anyone destroys God's   temple,   God   will destroy him; for God's   temple   is   sacred, and you   are
εἴ   τις   φθείρει   τοῦ θεοῦ   τὸν ναὸν   ὁ θεὸς   →   φθερεῖ   τοῦτον γὰρ   τοῦ θεοῦ   ὁ ναὸς   ἐστιν ἅγιος   ὑμεῖς ἐστε
cj   r.nsm   v.pai.3s   d.gsm n.gsm   d.asm n.asm   d.nsm n.nsm   v.fai.3s   r.asm cj   d.gsm n.gsm   d.nsm n.nsm   v.pai.3s a.nsm   r.np.2 v.pai.2p
1623   5516   5780   3836 2536   3836 3724   3836 2536   5780   4047 1142   3836 2536   3836 3724   1639 41   7007 1639

that temple.   ¶   **18** Do not   deceive   yourselves.   If   any one of   you thinks he   is   wise   by the standards of
οἵτινες   ←   Μηδεὶς   ἐξαπατάτω ἑαυτὸν   εἴ   τις   ἐν ὑμῖν   δοκεῖ   εἶναι σοφὸς ἐν   →
r.npm   a.nsm   v.pam.3s r.asm.3   cj   r.nsm   p.d r.dp.2   v.pai.3s   f.pa a.nsm p.d
4015   1987   3594 1987   1571   1623   5516   1877 7007   1506   1639 5055 1877   172

this age,   he should become a "fool" so that he may become wise.   **19** For the wisdom of this   world   is
τούτῳ τῷ αἰῶνι   →   →   γενέσθω   μωρὸς ἵνα   ←   →   →   γένηται σοφός   γὰρ ἡ σοφία   →   τούτου τοῦ κόσμου   ἐστιν
r.dsm d.dsm n.dsm   v.amm.3s   a.nsm cj   v.ams.3s a.nsm   cj d.nsf n.nsf   r.gsm d.gsm n.gsm   v.pai.3s
4047 3836 172   1181   3704 2671   1181 5055   1142 3836 5053   4047 3836 3180   1639

foolishness in   God's   sight. As it is written: "He catches   the wise   in their craftiness";   **20** and again, "The
μωρία   παρὰ τῷ θεῷ   γὰρ   → γέγραπται ὁ   δρασσόμενος   τοὺς σοφοὺς ἐν αὐτῶν τῇ πανουργίᾳ   καὶ πάλιν
n.nsf   p.d d.dsm n.dsm   γὰρ   v.rpi.3s d.nsm   pt.pm.nsm   d.apm a.apm p.d r.gpm.3 d.dsf n.dsf   cj adv
3702   4123 3836 2536   4123   1142   1211   3836 1533   3836 5055 1877 899 3836 4111   2779 4099

Lord knows that the thoughts   of the wise   are futile."   **21** So then, no   more boasting about men!
κύριος γινώσκει   τοὺς διαλογισμοὺς   → τῶν σοφῶν ὅτι εἰσὶν μάταιοι   ὥστε   ←   μηδεὶς   ←   καυχάσθω ἐν   ἀνθρώποις γὰρ
n.nsm v.pai.3s   d.apm n.apm   d.gpm a.gpm cj v.pai.3p a.npm   cj   a.nsm   v.pmm.3s p.d   n.dpm   cj
3261 1182   3836 1369   3836 5055 4022 1639 3469   6063   3594   3016 1877   476   1142

All   things are   yours,   **22** whether Paul   or Apollos or Cephas or the world or life or death   or the present or
πάντα   ←   ἐστιν ὑμῶν   εἴτε   Παῦλος   εἴτε Ἀπολλῶς εἴτε Κηφᾶς   εἴτε   κόσμος εἴτε ζωὴ εἴτε θάνατος   εἴτε   ἐνεστῶτα εἴτε
a.npn   v.pai.3s r.gp.2   cj   n.nsm   cj n.nsm cj n.nsm   cj   n.nsm cj n.nsf cj n.nsm   cj   pt.ra.npn cj
4246   1639 7007   1664   4263   1664 663 1664 3064   1664   3180 1664 2437 1664 2505   1664   1931 1664

the future   – all   are yours,   **23** and you   are of Christ, and Christ is of God.
μέλλοντα   πάντα   ὑμῶν   δὲ ὑμεῖς   → Χριστοῦ δὲ   Χριστὸς   → θεοῦ
pt.pa.npn   a.npn   r.gp.2   cj r.np.2   n.gsm cj   n.nsm   n.gsn
3516   4246   7007   1254 7007   5986 1254   5986   2536

Apostles of Christ

4:1 So   then,   men   ought to regard   us   as servants of Christ and as those entrusted with the secret
οὕτως   ←   ἄνθρωπος   →   → λογιζέσθω ἡμᾶς   ὡς ὑπηρέτας   → Χριστοῦ καὶ   →   οἰκονόμους   ←   μυστηρίων
adv   n.nsm   v.pmm.3s r.ap.1   pl n.apm   n.gsm cj   n.apm   n.gpn
4048   476   3357 6055   5677 5986 2779   3874   3696

κείμενον, ὅς ἐστιν Ἰησοῦς Χριστός. ¹² εἰ δέ τις ἐποικοδομεῖ ἐπὶ τὸν θεμέλιον χρυσόν, ἄργυρον, λίθους τιμίους, ξύλα, χόρτον, καλάμην, ¹³ ἑκάστου τὸ ἔργον φανερὸν γενήσεται, ἡ γὰρ ἡμέρα δηλώσει, ὅτι ἐν πυρὶ ἀποκαλύπτεται· καὶ ἑκάστου τὸ ἔργον ὁποῖόν ἐστιν τὸ πῦρ [αὐτὸ] δοκιμάσει. ¹⁴ εἴ τινος τὸ ἔργον μενεῖ ὃ ἐποικοδόμησεν, μισθὸν λήμψεται· ¹⁵ εἴ τινος τὸ ἔργον κατακαήσεται, ζημιωθήσεται, αὐτὸς δὲ σωθήσεται, οὕτως δὲ ὡς διὰ πυρός. ¶ ¹⁶ οὐκ οἴδατε ὅτι ναὸς θεοῦ ἐστε καὶ τὸ πνεῦμα τοῦ θεοῦ οἰκεῖ ἐν ὑμῖν; ¹⁷ εἴ τις τὸν ναὸν τοῦ θεοῦ φθείρει, φθερεῖ τοῦτον ὁ θεός· ὁ γὰρ ναὸς τοῦ θεοῦ ἅγιός ἐστιν, οἵτινές ἐστε ὑμεῖς. ¶ ¹⁸ Μηδεὶς ἑαυτὸν ἐξαπατάτω· εἴ τις δοκεῖ σοφὸς εἶναι ἐν ὑμῖν ἐν τῷ αἰῶνι τούτῳ, μωρὸς γενέσθω, ἵνα γένηται σοφός. ¹⁹ ἡ γὰρ σοφία τοῦ κόσμου τούτου μωρία παρὰ τῷ θεῷ ἐστιν. γέγραπται γάρ, Ὁ δρασσόμενος τοὺς σοφοὺς ἐν τῇ πανουργίᾳ αὐτῶν· ²⁰ καὶ πάλιν, Κύριος γινώσκει τοὺς διαλογισμοὺς τῶν σοφῶν ὅτι εἰσὶν μάταιοι. ²¹ ὥστε μηδεὶς καυχάσθω ἐν ἀνθρώποις· πάντα γὰρ ὑμῶν ἐστιν, ²² εἴτε Παῦλος εἴτε Ἀπολλῶς εἴτε Κηφᾶς, εἴτε κόσμος εἴτε ζωὴ εἴτε θάνατος, εἴτε ἐνεστῶτα εἴτε μέλλοντα· πάντα ὑμῶν, ²³ ὑμεῖς δὲ Χριστοῦ, Χριστὸς δὲ θεοῦ.

⁴:¹ Οὕτως ἡμᾶς λογιζέσθω ἄνθρωπος ὡς ὑπηρέτας Χριστοῦ καὶ οἰκονόμους μυστηρίων θεοῦ. ² ὧδε λοιπὸν ζητεῖται ἐν τοῖς

things of God. **2** Now   it is required that   those who have been given a trust   must   prove faithful. **3**
← → θεοῦ ⌊ὧδε λοιπὸν⌋ → ζητεῖται ἵνα ἐν τοῖς ← → → → οἰκονόμοις ↗ τις εὑρεθῇ πιστός δὲ
n.gsm adv adv v.ppi.3s cj p.d d.dpm n.dpm r.nsm v.aps.3s a.nsm cj
2536 6045 3370 2426 2671 1877 3836 3874 4412 5516 2351 4412 1254

I care very little if I am judged by you or by any human court; indeed, I do not even judge
ἐμοὶ ἐστιν εἰς → ἐλάχιστον ἵνα I ἀνακριθῶ ὑφ' ὑμῶν ἢ ὑπὸ ἀνθρωπίνης ἡμέρας ἀλλ' ↗ οὐδὲ ἀνακρίνω
r.ds.1 v.pai.3s p.a a.asn.s cj v.aps.1s p.g r.gp.2 cj p.g a.gsf n.gsf cj adv v.pai.1s
1609 1639 1650 1788 2671 373 5679 7007 2445 5679 474 2465 247 373 373 4028 373

myself. **4** My conscience is clear, but that does not make me innocent. It is the Lord who
ἐμαυτόν γὰρ ἐμαυτῷ σύνοιδα οὐδὲν ἀλλ' ἐν τούτῳ ↗ οὐκ → → δεδικαίωμαι δὲ → ἐστιν κύριος ὁ
r.asm.1 cj r.dsm.1 v.rai.1s a.asn cj p.d r.dsn pl v.rpi.1s cj v.pai.3s n.nsm d.nsm
1831 1142 1831 5323 4029 247 1877 4047 1467 4024 1467 1254 1639 3261 3836

judges me. **5** Therefore judge nothing before the appointed time; wait till the Lord comes. He will bring
ἀνακρίνων με ὥστε κρίνετε μὴ τι πρὸ → καιροῦ ⌊ἕως ἂν⌋ ὁ κύριος ἔλθῃ καὶ ὃς → →
pt.pa.nsm r.as.1 cj v.pam.2p pl pl p.g n.gsm cj d.nsm n.nsm v.aas.3s cj r.nsm
373 1609 6063 3212 3590 5516 4574 2789 2401 323 3836 3261 2262 2779 4005

to light what is hidden in darkness and will expose the motives of men's hearts. At that time each
→ φωτίσει τὰ → κρυπτὰ → ⌊τοῦ σκότους⌋ καὶ → φανερώσει τὰς βουλὰς → ⌊τῶν καρδιῶν⌋ καὶ τότε → ἑκάστῳ
v.fai.3s d.apn a.apn d.gsn n.gsn cj v.fai.3s d.apf n.apf d.gpf n.gpf cj adv r.dsm
5894 3836 3220 3836 5030 2779 5746 3836 1087 3836 2840 2779 5538 1667

will receive his praise from God. ¶ **6** Now, brothers, I have applied these things to myself and
→ γενήσεται ὁ ἔπαινος ἀπὸ ⌊τοῦ θεοῦ⌋ δὲ ἀδελφοί → → μετεσχημάτισα Ταῦτα ← εἰς ἐμαυτὸν καὶ
v.fmi.3s d.nsm n.nsm p.g d.gsn n.gsn cj n.vpm v.aai.1s r.apn p.a r.asm.1 cj
1181 3836 2047 608 3836 2536 1254 81 3571 4047 1650 1831 2779

Apollos for your benefit, so that you may learn from us the meaning of the saying, "Do not go beyond what is
Ἀπολλῶν δι' ὑμᾶς → ἵνα → → μάθητε ἐν ἡμῖν τὸ → μὴ ὑπὲρ ἃ →
n.asm p.a r.ap.2 cj v.aas.2p p.d r.dp.1 d.asn pl p.a r.apn
663 1328 7007 1328 2671 3443 1877 7005 3836 3590 5642 4005

written." Then you will not take pride in one man over against another. **7** For who makes you different
γέγραπται ἵνα → → μὴ ↘ φυσιοῦσθε εἰς ὑπὲρ ⌊τοῦ ἑνὸς⌋ κατὰ ← ⌊τοῦ ἑτέρου⌋ γὰρ τίς ↗ σε διακρίνει
v.rpi.3s cj pl v.ppi.2p a.nsm p.g d.gsn a.gsm p.g d.gsm r.gsm cj r.nsm r.as.2 v.pai.3s
1211 2671 5881 5881 3590 5881 1651 5642 3836 1651 2848 3836 2283 1142 5515 1359 5148 1359

from anyone else? What do you have that you did not receive? And if you did receive it, why do you
δὲ τί → → ἔχεις ὃ → οὐκ ἔλαβες δὲ εἰ καὶ → ἔλαβες τί → →
cj r.asn v.pai.2s r.asn pl v.aai.2s cj cj cj v.aai.2s r.asn
1254 5515 2400 4005 3284 3784 4024 3284 1254 1623 2779 3284 5515

boast as though you did not? ¶ **8** Already you have all you want! Already you have
καυχᾶσαι ὡς ← → ↗ μὴ λαβών ἤδη → → → ⌊κεκορεσμένοι ἐστέ⌋ ἤδη → →
v.pmi.2s pl pl pt.aa.nsm adv pt.rp.npm v.pai.2p adv
3016 6055 3284 3284 3590 3284 2453 3170 1639 2453

become rich! You have become kings – and that without us! How I wish that you really had
→ ἐπλουτήσατε → → → ἐβασιλεύσατε χωρὶς ἡμῶν καὶ → → ὄφελον ↗ γε
v.aai.2p v.aai.2p p.g r.gp.1 cj pl pl
4456 996 6006 7005 2779 4054 996 1145

become kings so that we might be kings with you! **9** For it seems to me that God has put
→ ἐβασιλεύσατε ἵνα ← ἡμεῖς καὶ → συμβασιλεύσωμεν ὑμῖν γὰρ → δοκῶ ὁ θεός → →
v.aai.2p cj r.np.1 adv v.aas.1p r.dp.2 cj v.pai.1s d.nsm n.nsm
996 2671 7005 2779 5203 7007 1142 1506 3836 2536 617 617

us apostles on display at the end of the procession, like men condemned to die in the arena. We
ἡμᾶς ⌊τοὺς ἀποστόλους⌋ → ἀπέδειξεν → ἐσχάτους ὡς ἐπιθανατίους ← → ὅτι →
r.ap.1 d.apm n.apm v.aai.3s a.apm pl a.apm cj
7005 3836 693 2274 2274 6055 2119 4022

have been made a spectacle to the whole universe, to angels as well as to men. **10** We are fools for
→ ἐγενήθημεν θέατρον → τῷ κόσμῳ καὶ → ἀγγέλοις καὶ ← → ἀνθρώποις ἡμεῖς μωροὶ διὰ
v.api.1p n.nsn d.dsm n.dsm cj n.dpm cj n.dpm r.np.1 a.npm p.a
1181 2519 3836 3180 2779 34 2779 476 7005 3704 1328

Christ, but you are so wise in Christ! We are weak, but you are strong! You are honored, we are
Χριστόν δὲ ὑμεῖς φρόνιμοι ἐν Χριστῷ ἡμεῖς ἀσθενεῖς δὲ ὑμεῖς ἰσχυροί ὑμεῖς ἔνδοξοι δὲ ἡμεῖς
n.asm cj r.np.2 a.npm p.d n.dsm r.np.1 a.npm cj r.np.2 a.npm r.np.2 a.npm cj r.np.1
5986 1254 7007 5861 1877 5986 7005 822 1254 7007 2708 7007 1902 1254 7005

οἰκονόμοις, ἵνα πιστός τις εὑρεθῇ. ³ ἐμοὶ δὲ εἰς ἐλάχιστόν ἐστιν, ἵνα ὑφ' ὑμῶν ἀνακριθῶ ἢ ὑπὸ ἀνθρωπίνης ἡμέρας· ἀλλ' οὐδὲ ἐμαυτὸν ἀνακρίνω. ⁴ οὐδὲν γὰρ ἐμαυτῷ σύνοιδα, ἀλλ' οὐκ ἐν τούτῳ δεδικαίωμαι, ὁ δὲ ἀνακρίνων με κύριός ἐστιν. ⁵ ὥστε μὴ πρὸ καιροῦ τι κρίνετε ἕως ἂν ἔλθῃ ὁ κύριος, ὃς καὶ φωτίσει τὰ κρυπτὰ τοῦ σκότους καὶ φανερώσει τὰς βουλὰς τῶν καρδιῶν· καὶ τότε ὁ ἔπαινος γενήσεται ἑκάστῳ ἀπὸ τοῦ θεοῦ. ¶ ⁶ Ταῦτα δέ, ἀδελφοί, μετεσχημάτισα εἰς ἐμαυτὸν καὶ Ἀπολλῶν δι' ὑμᾶς, ἵνα ἐν ἡμῖν μάθητε τὸ Μὴ ὑπὲρ ἃ γέγραπται, ἵνα μὴ εἷς ὑπὲρ τοῦ ἑνὸς φυσιοῦσθε κατὰ τοῦ ἑτέρου. ⁷ τίς γάρ σε διακρίνει; τί δὲ ἔχεις ὃ οὐκ ἔλαβες; εἰ δὲ καὶ ἔλαβες, τί καυχᾶσαι ὡς μὴ λαβών; ¶ ⁸ ἤδη κεκορεσμένοι ἐστέ, ἤδη ἐπλουτήσατε, χωρὶς ἡμῶν ἐβασιλεύσατε· καὶ ὄφελόν γε ἐβασιλεύσατε, ἵνα καὶ ἡμεῖς ὑμῖν συμβασιλεύσωμεν. ⁹ δοκῶ γάρ, ὅτι ὁ θεὸς ἡμᾶς τοὺς ἀποστόλους ἐσχάτους ἀπέδειξεν ὡς ἐπιθανατίους, ὅτι θέατρον ἐγενήθημεν τῷ κόσμῳ καὶ ἀγγέλοις καὶ ἀνθρώποις. ¹⁰ ἡμεῖς μωροὶ διὰ Χριστόν, ὑμεῖς δὲ φρόνιμοι ἐν Χριστῷ· ἡμεῖς ἀσθενεῖς, ὑμεῖς δὲ ἰσχυροί· ὑμεῖς ἔνδοξοι, ἡμεῖς δὲ ἄτιμοι. ¹¹ ἄχρι τῆς ἄρτι ὥρας

dishonored! **11** To this very hour we go hungry and thirsty, we are in rags, we are brutally
ἄτιμοι ἄχρι τῆς ἄρτι ὥρας καὶ → πεινῶμεν καὶ διψῶμεν καὶ → γυμνιτεύομεν καὶ → κολαφιζόμεθα
a.npm p.g d.gsf adv n.gsf cj v.pai.1p cj v.pai.1p cj v.pai.1p cj v.ppi.1p
872 948 3836 785 6052 2779 4277 2779 1498 2779 1217 2779 3139

treated, we are homeless. **12** We work hard with our own hands. When we are cursed, we
← καὶ → ἀστατοῦμεν καὶ → κοπιῶμεν ἐργαζόμενοι ← → ταῖς ἰδίαις χερσίν → → → λοιδορούμενοι →
v.pai.1p cj v.pai.1p pt.pm.npm d.dpf a.dpf n.dpf pt.pp.npm
2779 841 2779 3159 2237 3836 2625 5931 3366

bless; when we are persecuted, we endure it; **13** when we are slandered, we answer kindly. Up to this
εὐλογοῦμεν → → → διωκόμενοι → ἀνεχόμεθα → → → δυσφημούμενοι → παρακαλοῦμεν ἕως ἄρτι
v.pai.1p pt.pp.npm v.pmi.1p pt.pp.npm v.pai.1p p.g adv
2328 1503 462 1555 4151 2401 785

moment we have become the scum of the earth, the refuse of the world. ¶ **14** I am not writing
← → → ἐγενήθημεν περίψημα → πάντων ὡς περικαθάρματα → τοῦ κόσμου → → Οὐκ γράφω
v.api.1p n.nsn a.gpn pl n.npn d.gsm n.gsm pl v.pai.1s
1181 4370 4246 6055 4326 3836 3180 1211 1211 4024 1211

this to shame you, but to warn you, as my dear children. **15** Even though you have ten thousand
ταῦτα → ἐντρέπων ὑμᾶς ἀλλ᾽ → νουθετῶν ← ὡς μου ἀγαπητά τέκνα γὰρ ἐὰν → ἔχητε μυρίους ←
r.apn pt.pa.nsm r.ap.2 cj pt.pa.nsm pl r.gs.1 a.apn n.apn cj cj v.pas.2p a.apm
4047 1956 7007 247 3805 6055 1609 28 5451 1142 1569 2400 3692

guardians in Christ, you do not have many fathers, for in Christ Jesus I became your father through
παιδαγωγοὺς ἐν Χριστῷ ἀλλ᾽ οὐ πολλοὺς πατέρας γὰρ ἐν Χριστῷ Ἰησοῦ ἐγὼ → ὑμᾶς ἐγέννησα διὰ
n.apm p.d n.dsm cj pl a.apm n.apm cj p.d n.dsm n.dsm r.ns.1 r.ap.2 v.aai.1s p.g
4080 1877 5986 247 4024 4498 4252 1142 1877 5986 2652 1609 1164 7007 1164 1328

the gospel. **16** Therefore I urge you to imitate me. **17** For this reason I am sending to you Timothy,
τοῦ εὐαγγελίου οὖν → Παρακαλῶ ὑμᾶς → μιμηταί γίνεσθε μου Διὰ τοῦτο ← ← → ἔπεμψα → ὑμῖν Τιμόθεον
d.gsn n.gsn cj v.pai.1s r.ap.2 n.npm v.pmm.2p r.gs.1 p.a r.asn v.aai.1s r.dp.2 n.asm
3836 2295 4036 4151 7007 1181 3629 1181 1609 1328 4047 4287 7007 5510

my son whom I love, who is faithful in the Lord. He will remind you of my way of life
ὅς ἐστίν μου τέκνον ἀγαπητὸν καὶ πιστὸν ἐν κυρίῳ ὅς → ἀναμνήσει ὑμᾶς ← μου τὰς ὁδούς ←
r.nsm v.pai.3s r.gs.1 n.nsn a.nsn cj a.nsn p.d n.dsm r.nsm v.fai.3s r.ap.2 r.gs.1 d.apf n.apf
4005 1639 1609 5451 28 2779 4412 1877 3261 4005 389 7007 389 1609 3836 3847

in Christ Jesus, which agrees with what I teach everywhere in every church. ¶ **18** Some of you have
τὰς ἐν Χριστῷ Ἰησοῦ → καθὼς ← → διδάσκω πανταχοῦ ἐν πάσῃ ἐκκλησίᾳ δέ τινες ← ← →
d.apf p.d n.dsm n.dsm cj v.pai.1s adv p.d a.dsf n.dsf cj r.npm
3836 1877 5986 2652 2777 1438 4116 1877 4246 1711 1254 5516

become arrogant, as if I were not coming to you. **19** But I will come to you very soon, if the Lord is
→ ἐφυσιώθησαν Ὡς ← μου → μὴ ἐρχομένου πρὸς ὑμᾶς δὲ → ἐλεύσομαι πρὸς ὑμᾶς ταχέως ἐὰν ὁ κύριος
v.api.3p pl r.gs.1 pl pt.pm.gsm p.a r.ap.2 cj v.fmi.1s p.a r.ap.2 adv cj d.nsm n.nsm
5881 6055 1609 2262 3590 2262 4639 7007 1254 2262 4639 7007 5441 1569 3836 3261

willing, and then I will find out not only how these arrogant people are talking, but what power they
θελήσῃ καὶ → → γνώσομαι οὐ → τῶν πεφυσιωμένων ← τὸν λόγον ἀλλὰ τὴν δύναμιν
v.aas.3s cj v.fmi.1s pl d.gpm pt.rp.gpm d.asm n.asm cj d.asf n.asf
2527 2779 1182 4024 3836 5881 3836 3364 247 3836 1539

have. **20** For the kingdom of God is not a matter of talk but of power. **21** What do you prefer? Shall I come to
γὰρ ἡ βασιλεία → τοῦ θεοῦ οὐ → λόγῳ ἀλλ᾽ ἐν δυνάμει τί → → θέλετε → ἔλθω πρὸς
cj d.nsf n.nsf d.gsm n.gsm pl p.d n.dsm cj p.d n.dsf r.asn v.pai.2p v.aas.1s p.a
1142 3836 993 3836 2536 4024 1877 3364 247 1877 1539 5515 2527 2262 4639

you with a whip, or in love and with a gentle spirit?
ὑμᾶς ἐν ῥάβδῳ ἢ ἐν ἀγάπῃ τε → πραΰτητος πνεύματι
r.ap.2 p.d n.dsf cj p.d n.dsf cj n.gsf n.dsn
7007 1877 4811 2445 1877 27 5445 4559 4460

Expel the Immoral Brother!

5:1 It is actually reported that there is sexual immorality among you, and of a kind that does not occur
→ → Ὅλως ἀκούεται → πορνεία ἐν ὑμῖν καὶ → τοιαύτη πορνεία ἥτις οὐδὲ
adv v.ppi.3s n.nsf p.d r.dp.2 cj r.nsf n.nsf r.nsf adv
201 201 3914 201 4518 1877 7007 2779 5525 4518 4015 4028

καὶ πεινῶμεν καὶ διψῶμεν καὶ γυμνιτεύομεν καὶ κολαφιζόμεθα καὶ ἀστατοῦμεν **12** καὶ κοπιῶμεν ἐργαζόμενοι ταῖς ἰδίαις χερσίν·
λοιδορούμενοι εὐλογοῦμεν, διωκόμενοι ἀνεχόμεθα, **13** δυσφημούμενοι παρακαλοῦμεν· ὡς περικαθάρματα τοῦ κόσμου ἐγενήθημεν,
πάντων περίψημα ἕως ἄρτι. ¶ **14** Οὐκ ἐντρέπων ὑμᾶς γράφω ταῦτα ἀλλ᾽ ὡς τέκνα μου ἀγαπητὰ νουθετῶ[ν]. **15** ἐὰν γὰρ μυρίους
παιδαγωγοὺς ἔχητε ἐν Χριστῷ ἀλλ᾽ οὐ πολλοὺς πατέρας· ἐν γὰρ Χριστῷ Ἰησοῦ διὰ τοῦ εὐαγγελίου ἐγὼ ὑμᾶς ἐγέννησα.
16 παρακαλῶ οὖν ὑμᾶς, μιμηταί μου γίνεσθε. **17** διὰ τοῦτο ἔπεμψα ὑμῖν Τιμόθεον, ὅς ἐστίν μου τέκνον ἀγαπητὸν καὶ πιστὸν ἐν
κυρίῳ, ὃς ὑμᾶς ἀναμνήσει τὰς ὁδούς μου τὰς ἐν Χριστῷ [Ἰησοῦ], καθὼς πανταχοῦ ἐν πάσῃ ἐκκλησίᾳ διδάσκω. ¶ **18** ὡς μὴ
ἐρχομένου δέ μου πρὸς ὑμᾶς ἐφυσιώθησάν τινες· **19** ἐλεύσομαι δὲ ταχέως πρὸς ὑμᾶς ἐὰν ὁ κύριος θελήσῃ, καὶ γνώσομαι οὐ τὸν
λόγον τῶν πεφυσιωμένων ἀλλὰ τὴν δύναμιν· **20** οὐ γὰρ ἐν λόγῳ ἡ βασιλεία τοῦ θεοῦ ἀλλ᾽ ἐν δυνάμει. **21** τί θέλετε; ἐν ῥάβδῳ
ἔλθω πρὸς ὑμᾶς ἢ ἐν ἀγάπῃ πνεύματί τε πραΰτητος;

5:1 Ὅλως ἀκούεται ἐν ὑμῖν πορνεία, καὶ τοιαύτη πορνεία ἥτις οὐδὲ ἐν τοῖς ἔθνεσιν, ὥστε γυναῖκά τινα τοῦ πατρὸς ἔχειν.

even among pagans: A man has his father's wife.   **2** And you are proud!   Shouldn't you rather
ἐν   ιτοῖς ἔθνεσιν ὥστε   τινα ἔχειν τοῦ πατρὸς γυναῖκα καὶ ὑμεῖς ἐστε πεφυσιωμένοι καὶ οὐχὶ   → μᾶλλον
p.d   d.dpn n.dpn   cj   r.asm f.pa d.gsm n.gsm   n.asf   cj r.np.2 v.pai.2p pt.rp.npm   cj   pl   adv.c
1877 3836   1620   6063   5516 2400 3836   4252   1222   2779 7007 1639   5881   2779 4049   4291 3437

have been filled with grief   and have put out of your fellowship the man who did   this? **3**
 →   →   →   →   ἐπενθήσατε ἵνα   →   ἀρθῇ ἐκ ὑμῶν μέσου ὁ   ←   ←   πράξας τὸ ἔργον τοῦτο γάρ μὲν
                          v.aai.2p cj   v.aps.3s p.g r.gp.2 r.gsm d.nsm   pt.aa.nsm d.asn n.asn r.asn cj cj
                          4291   2671   149   1666 7007 3545 3836   4556   3836 2240 4047 1142 3525

Even though I am not physically present,   I am with you in spirit. And I have already passed judgment
 →   →   ἐγὼ →   ιτῷ σώματι   ἀπὼν δὲ → παρὼν ←   τῷ πνεύματι   → ἤδη   κέκρικα
           r.ns.1   d.dsn n.dsn pt.pa.nsm cj pt.pa.nsm   d.dsn n.dsn   adv   v.rai.1s
583   583 1609 583 583 3836 5393 583   1254 4205   3836 4460   3212 3212 2453   3212

on the one who did   this, just as if I were present. **4** When you are assembled in the name of our
 ← τὸν ←   ←   κατεργασάμενον οὕτως τοῦτο ὡς ← ← → παρὼν   → ὑμῶν → συναχθέντων ἐν τῷ ὀνόματι → ἡμῶν
    d.asm   pt.am.asm   adv   r.asn pl   pt.pa.nsm   r.gp.2   pt.ap.gpm p.d d.dsn n.dsn   r.gp.1
    3836   2981   4048 4047 6055   4205   5251   5251   1877 3836 3950   3261 7005

Lord   Jesus and I am with you in spirit,   and the power of our Lord   Jesus is present,
ιτοῦ κυρίου Ἰησοῦ καὶ ἐμοῦ σὺν → ιτοῦ πνεύματος τῇ δυνάμει → ἡμῶν ιτοῦ κυρίου Ἰησοῦ
d.gsm n.gsm   n.gsm cj r.gs.1 p.d   d.gsn n.gsn   d.dsf n.dsf   r.gp.1 d.gsm n.gsm   n.gsm
3836 3261   2652 2779 1847 5250   3836 4460   3836 1539   3261 7005 3836 3261   2652

5 hand   this   man over to Satan,   so that the sinful nature may be destroyed and his spirit saved on
     παραδοῦναι ιτὸν τοιοῦτον ←   →   τῷ σατανᾷ εἰς ← τῆς σαρκός   → ὄλεθρον ἵνα τὸ πνεῦμα σωθῇ ἐν
     f.aa   d.asm r.asm   d.dsm n.dsm p.a   d.gsf n.gsf   n.asm   cj d.nsn n.nsn v.aps.3s p.d
     4140   3836 5525   4140 3836 4928 1650   3836 4922   3897   2671 3836 4460 5392   1877

the day of the Lord. ¶ **6** Your boasting   is not good. Don't you know that a little yeast works through the
τῇ ἡμέρᾳ τοῦ κυρίου   ὑμῶν ιτὸ καύχημα Οὐ καλὸν οὐκ →   οἴδατε ὅτι   μικρὰ ζύμη ζυμοῖ ←   τὸ
d.dsf n.dsf d.gsm n.gsm   r.gp.2 d.nsn n.nsn pl a.nsn pl   v.rai.2p cj   a.nsf n.nsf v.pai.3s   d.asn
3836 2465 3836 3261   7007 3836 3017   4024 2819 4024   3857 4022 3625 2434 2435   3836

whole batch of dough? **7** Get rid   of the old   yeast that you may be a new batch without yeast – as
ὅλον φύραμα ←   ἐκκαθάρατε ← τὴν παλαιὰν ζύμην ἵνα →   → ἦτε νέον φύραμα →   ἄζυμοι καθὼς
a.asn n.asn   v.aam.2p   d.asf a.asf   n.asf cj   v.pas.2p a.nsn n.nsn   a.npm cj
3910 5878   1705   3836 4094   2434 2671   1639 3742 5878   109   2777

you really are. For Christ,   our Passover lamb, has been sacrificed. **8** Therefore let us keep the Festival, not
 →   ἐστε γὰρ Χριστός καὶ ἡμῶν ιτὸ πάσχα   →   ἐτύθη   ὥστε   →   →   →   ἑορτάζωμεν μὴ
     v.pai.2p cj n.nsm   cj r.gp.1 d.nsn n.nsn   v.aps.3s   cj   v.pas.1p   pl
     1639 1142 5986 2779 7005 3836 4247   2604   6063   2037   3590

with the old   yeast,   the yeast of malice and wickedness, but with bread without yeast, the bread of
ἐν   παλαιᾷ ζύμῃ μηδὲ ἐν ζύμῃ → κακίας καὶ πονηρίας ἀλλ ἐν   →   ἀζύμοις
p.d   a.dsf n.dsf cj p.d n.dsf   n.gsf cj n.gsf   cj   p.d   a.dpn
1877 4094 2434 3593 1877 2434   2798 2779 4504   247 1877   109

sincerity and truth. ¶ **9** I have written you in my letter not to associate   with sexually immoral
ειλικρινείας καὶ ἀληθείας   →   Ἔγραψα ὑμῖν ἐν τῇ ἐπιστολῇ μὴ → συναναμίγνυσθαι ←   → πόρνοις
n.gsf   cj n.gsf   →   v.aai.1s r.dp.2 p.d d.dsf n.dsf pl   f.pm   n.dpm
1636   2779 237   1211 7007 1877 3836 2186 3590   5264   4521

people – **10** not at all   meaning the people of this world   who are immoral, or the greedy   and swindlers,
 ←   οὐ πάντως   → τούτου ιτοῦ κόσμου τοῖς → πόρνοις ἢ τοῖς πλεονέκταις καὶ ἅρπαξιν
           pl adv   r.gsm d.gsm n.gsm d.dpm   n.dpm cj d.dpm n.dpm   cj n.dpm
           4024 4122   3180 4047 3836 3180 3836   4521 2445 3836 4431   2779 774

or idolaters. *In that case* you would have to leave this world. **11** But now I am writing you that you
ἢ εἰδωλολάτραις ιἐπεὶ ἄρα   →   →   ὠφείλετε ἐξελθεῖν ἐκ τοῦ κόσμου δὲ νῦν → ἔγραψα ὑμῖν   →
cj n.dpm   cj pl   v.iai.2p f.aa   p.g d.gsm n.gsm cj adv   v.aai.1s r.dp.2
2445 1629   2075 726   4053   2002   1666 3836 3180 1254 3814   1211 7007   5264

must not associate   with   anyone who calls   himself a brother but is sexually immoral or
 →   μὴ συναναμίγνυσθαι ← ἐάν τις   ιὀνομαζόμενος ᾖ   ἀδελφὸς   → πόρνος ἢ
     pl f.pm   cj r.nsm   pt.pp.nsm   v.pas.3s n.nsm   n.nsm cj
5264 3590 5264   1569 5516   3951   1639   81   4521 2445

2 καὶ ὑμεῖς πεφυσιωμένοι ἐστὲ καὶ οὐχὶ μᾶλλον ἐπενθήσατε, ἵνα ἀρθῇ ἐκ μέσου ὑμῶν ὁ τὸ ἔργον τοῦτο πράξας; 3 ἐγὼ μὲν γὰρ ἀπὼν τῷ σώματι παρὼν δὲ τῷ πνεύματι, ἤδη κέκρικα ὡς παρὼν τὸν οὕτως τοῦτο κατεργασάμενον· 4 ἐν τῷ ὀνόματι τοῦ κυρίου [ἡμῶν] Ἰησοῦ συναχθέντων ὑμῶν καὶ τοῦ ἐμοῦ πνεύματος σὺν τῇ δυνάμει τοῦ κυρίου ἡμῶν Ἰησοῦ, 5 παραδοῦναι τὸν τοιοῦτον τῷ Σατανᾷ εἰς ὄλεθρον τῆς σαρκός, ἵνα τὸ πνεῦμα σωθῇ ἐν τῇ ἡμέρᾳ τοῦ κυρίου. ¶ 6 Οὐ καλὸν τὸ καύχημα ὑμῶν. οὐκ οἴδατε ὅτι μικρὰ ζύμη ὅλον τὸ φύραμα ζυμοῖ; 7 ἐκκαθάρατε τὴν παλαιὰν ζύμην, ἵνα ἦτε νέον φύραμα, καθὼς ἐστε ἄζυμοι· καὶ γὰρ τὸ πάσχα ἡμῶν ἐτύθη Χριστός. 8 ὥστε ἑορτάζωμεν μὴ ἐν ζύμῃ παλαιᾷ μηδὲ ἐν ζύμῃ κακίας καὶ πονηρίας ἀλλ᾽ ἐν ἀζύμοις εἰλικρινείας καὶ ἀληθείας. ¶ 9 Ἔγραψα ὑμῖν ἐν τῇ ἐπιστολῇ μὴ συναναμίγνυσθαι πόρνοις, 10 οὐ πάντως τοῖς πόρνοις τοῦ κόσμου τούτου ἢ τοῖς πλεονέκταις καὶ ἅρπαξιν ἢ εἰδωλολάτραις, ἐπεὶ ὠφείλετε ἄρα ἐκ τοῦ κόσμου ἐξελθεῖν. 11 νῦν δὲ ἔγραψα ὑμῖν μὴ συναναμίγνυσθαι ἐάν τις ἀδελφὸς ὀνομαζόμενος ἢ πόρνος ἢ πλεονέκτης ἢ εἰδωλολάτρης ἢ λοίδορος ἢ μέθυσος ἢ ἅρπαξ.

greedy, | an idolater | or | a slanderer, | | a drunkard | or | a swindler. | With such | | | a man do | not | even | eat.
πλεονέκτης | ἢ | εἰδωλολάτρης | ἢ | λοίδορος | ἢ | μέθυσος | ἢ | ἅρπαξ | τῷ | τοιούτῳ ← | → | μηδὲ ← | συνεσθίειν
n.nsm | cj | n.nsm | cj | n.nsm | cj | n.nsm | cj | a.nsm | d.dsm | r.dsm | | adv | f.pa
4431 | 2445 | 1629 | 2445 | 3368 | 2445 | 3500 | 2445 | 774 | 3836 | 5525 | 5303 | 3593 | 5303

¶ **12** What business is it of mine to judge those outside the church? Are you not to judge those inside? **13**
γὰρ τί | | μοι | → κρίνειν | τοὺς | ἔξω | | ὑμεῖς | οὐχὶ | → κρίνετε | τοὺς | ἔσω | δὲ
cj cj | | r.ds.1 | f.pa | d.apm | adv | | r.np.2 | pl | v.pai.2p | d.apm | adv | cj
1142 5515 | | 1609 | 3212 | 3836 | 2032 | | 3212 | 7007 | 4049 | 3212 | 3836 | 2276 | 1254

God will judge those outside. "Expel the wicked man from among you."
ὁ | θεὸς | κρινεῖ | τοὺς | ἔξω | ἐξάρατε | τὸν | πονηρὸν ← | ἐξ ← | ὑμῶν | αὐτῶν
d.nsm | n.nsm | v.fai.3s | d.apm | adv | v.aam.2p | d.asm | a.asm | p.g | r.gp.2 | r.gpm
3836 | 2536 | 3212 | 3836 | 2032 | 1976 | 3836 | 4505 | 1666 | 7007 | 899

Lawsuits Among Believers

6:1 If any of you has a dispute with another, dare he take it before the ungodly for judgment instead of
τις | → ὑμῶν | ἔχων | πρᾶγμα | πρὸς | τὸν ἕτερον | Τολμᾷ ← | → | ἐπὶ | τῶν ἀδίκων | → κρίνεσθαι | καὶ οὐχὶ ←
r.nsm | r.gp.2 | pt.pa.nsm | n.asn | p.a | d.asm r.asm | v.pai.3s | | p.g | d.gpm a.gpm | f.pm | cj pl
2400 | 5516 7007 | 2400 | 4547 | 4639 | 3836 2283 | 5528 | 3212 3212 | 2093 | 3836 96 | 3212 | 2779 4049

before the saints? **2** Do you not know that the saints will judge the world? And if you are to judge the
ἐπὶ | τῶν ἁγίων | ἢ | → οὐκ οἴδατε ὅτι | οἱ ἅγιοι | → κρινοῦσιν | τὸν κόσμον | καὶ εἰ | ἐν ὑμῖν | → κρίνεται ὁ
p.g | d.gpm a.gpm | cj | pl v.rai.2p cj | d.npm a.npm | v.fai.3p | d.asm n.asm | cj cj | p.d r.dp.2 | v.ppi.3s d.nsm
2093 | 3836 41 | 2445 | 3857 3857 4024 3857 | 4022 3836 41 | 3212 | 3836 3180 | 2779 1623 | 1877 7007 | 3212 3836

world, are you not competent to judge trivial cases? **3** Do you not know that we will judge angels? How
κόσμος | ἐστε ← | → ἀνάξιοι | κριτηρίων | ἐλαχίστων | → | οὐκ οἴδατε ὅτι | → | κρινοῦμεν | ἀγγέλους | μήτι γε
n.nsm | v.pai.2p | a.npm | n.gpn | a.gpn.s | | pl v.rai.2p cj | | v.fai.1p | n.apm | pl
3180 | 1639 | 396 | 3215 | 1788 | | 3857 3857 4024 3857 4022 | | 3212 | 34 | 3614 1145

much more the things of this life! **4** Therefore, if you have disputes about such matters, appoint as judges
← | ← | → | → | βιωτικά | οὖν | μὲν ἐάν | → ἔχητε | κριτήρια | → | → βιωτικά | καθίζετε ←
| | | | a.apn | cj | pl cj | v.pas.2p | n.apn | | a.apn | v.pam.2p
| | | | 1053 | 4036 | 3525 1569 | 2400 | 3215 | | 1053 | 2767

even men of little account in the church! **5** I say this to shame you. Is it possible that there
τούτους | τοὺς ἐξουθενημένους | ἐν | τῇ ἐκκλησίᾳ | λέγω | πρὸς | ἐντροπὴν | ὑμῖν | οὕτως ←
r.apm | d.apm pt.rp.apm | p.d | d.dsf n.dsf | v.pai.1s | p.a | n.asf | r.dp.2 | adv
4047 | 3836 2024 | 1877 | 3836 1711 | 3306 | 4639 | 1959 | 7007 | 4048

is nobody among you wise enough to judge a dispute between believers? **6** But
ἔνι | οὐκ οὐδεὶς | ἐν | ὑμῖν σοφός | ὃς | δυνήσεται | → διακρῖναι ← | ἀνὰ μέσον | τοῦ ἀδελφοῦ | αὐτοῦ | ἀλλὰ
v.pai.3s | pl a.nsm | p.d | r.dp.2 a.nsm | r.nsm | v.fpi.3s | f.aa | p.a n.asn | d.gsm n.gsm | r.gsm.3 | cj
1928 | 4024 4029 | 1877 | 7007 5055 | 4005 | 1538 | 1359 | 324 3545 | 3836 81 | 899 | 247

instead, one brother goes to law against another – and this in front of unbelievers! ¶ **7** The very
← | ἀδελφὸς | → κρίνεται μετὰ | ἀδελφοῦ | καὶ | τοῦτο ἐπὶ | ← | ἀπίστων | [οὖν] | μὲν
| n.nsm | v.pmi.3s p.g | n.gsm | cj | r.asn p.a | | a.gpm | cj | pl
| 81 | 3212 3552 | 81 | 2779 | 4047 2093 | | 603 | 4036 | 3525

fact that you have lawsuits among you means you have been completely defeated already. Why not rather be
ὅτι | → ἔχετε | κρίματα | μεθ' | ἑαυτῶν ἐστιν | ὑμῖν | ὅλως | ἥττημα | Ἤδη | διὰ τί | οὐχὶ μᾶλλον →
cj | v.pai.2p | n.apn | p.g | r.gpm.2 v.pai.3s | r.dp.2 | adv | n.nsn | adv | p.a r.asn | pl adv.c
4022 | 2400 | 3210 | 3552 | 1571 1639 | 7007 | 3914 | 2488 | 2453 | 1328 5515 | 4049 3437

wronged? Why not rather be cheated? **8** Instead, you yourselves cheat and do wrong, and you do this to
ἀδικεῖσθε | διὰ τί | οὐχὶ μᾶλλον | ἀποστερεῖσθε | ἀλλὰ | ὑμεῖς | ἀδικεῖτε καὶ | ἀποστερεῖτε καὶ | τοῦτο
v.pmi.2p | p.a r.asn | pl adv.c | v.pmi.2p | cj | r.np.2 | v.pai.2p cj | v.pai.2p cj | r.asn
92 | 1328 5515 | 4049 3437 | 691 | 247 | 7007 | 92 2779 | 691 2779 | 4047

your brothers. ¶ **9** Do you not know that the wicked will not inherit the kingdom of God? Do not
ἀδελφούς | Ἢ | → οὐκ οἴδατε ὅτι | ἄδικοι | οὐ κληρονομήσουσιν | βασιλείαν | → θεοῦ | μὴ
n.apm | cj | pl v.rai.2p cj | a.npm | pl v.fai.3p | n.asf | n.gsm | pl
81 | 2445 | 3857 3857 4024 3857 4022 | 96 | 3099 4024 3099 | 993 | 2536 4414 | 3590

be deceived: Neither the sexually immoral nor idolaters nor adulterers nor male prostitutes nor homosexual
→ πλανᾶσθε | οὔτε | πόρνοι | οὔτε εἰδωλολάτραι | οὔτε μοιχοὶ | οὔτε → | μαλακοὶ | οὔτε ἀρσενοκοῖται
v.ppm.2p | cj | n.npm | cj n.npm | cj n.npm | cj | a.npm | cj n.npm
4414 | 4046 | 4521 | 4046 1629 | 4046 3659 | 4046 | 3434 | 4046 780

τῷ τοιούτῳ μηδὲ συνεσθίειν. ¶ **12** τί γὰρ μοι τοὺς ἔξω κρίνειν; οὐχὶ τοὺς ἔσω ὑμεῖς κρίνετε; **13** τοὺς δὲ ἔξω ὁ θεὸς κρινεῖ. ἐξάρατε τὸν πονηρὸν ἐξ ὑμῶν αὐτῶν.

6:1 Τολμᾷ τις ὑμῶν πρᾶγμα ἔχων πρὸς τὸν ἕτερον κρίνεσθαι ἐπὶ τῶν ἀδίκων καὶ οὐχὶ ἐπὶ τῶν ἁγίων; **2** ἢ οὐκ οἴδατε ὅτι οἱ ἅγιοι τὸν κόσμον κρινοῦσιν; καὶ εἰ ἐν ὑμῖν κρίνεται ὁ κόσμος, ἀνάξιοί ἐστε κριτηρίων ἐλαχίστων; **3** οὐκ οἴδατε ὅτι ἀγγέλους κρινοῦμεν, μήτιγε βιωτικά; **4** βιωτικὰ μὲν οὖν κριτήρια ἐὰν ἔχητε, τοὺς ἐξουθενημένους ἐν τῇ ἐκκλησίᾳ, τούτους καθίζετε; **5** πρὸς ἐντροπὴν ὑμῖν λέγω. οὕτως οὐκ ἔνι ἐν ὑμῖν οὐδεὶς σοφός, ὃς δυνήσεται διακρῖναι ἀνὰ μέσον τοῦ ἀδελφοῦ αὐτοῦ; **6** ἀλλὰ ἀδελφὸς μετὰ ἀδελφοῦ κρίνεται καὶ τοῦτο ἐπὶ ἀπίστων; ¶ **7** ἤδη μὲν [οὖν] ὅλως ἥττημα ὑμῖν ἐστιν ὅτι κρίματα ἔχετε μεθ' ἑαυτῶν. διὰ τί οὐχὶ μᾶλλον ἀδικεῖσθε; διὰ τί οὐχὶ μᾶλλον ἀποστερεῖσθε; **8** ἀλλὰ ὑμεῖς ἀδικεῖτε καὶ ἀποστερεῖτε, καὶ τοῦτο ἀδελφούς. ¶ **9** ἢ οὐκ οἴδατε ὅτι ἄδικοι θεοῦ βασιλείαν οὐ κληρονομήσουσιν; μὴ πλανᾶσθε· οὔτε πόρνοι οὔτε εἰδωλολάτραι οὔτε μοιχοὶ οὔτε

offenders **10** nor thieves nor the greedy   nor drunkards nor slanderers nor swindlers will inherit   the kingdom
←   οὔτε κλέπται   οὔτε   πλεονέκται   οὐ   μέθυσοι   οὐ   λοίδοροι   οὐχ   ἅρπαγες   →   κληρονομήσουσιν   βασιλείαν
   cj   n.npm   cj   n.npm   pl   n.npm   pl   n.npm   pl   a.npm   v.fai.3p   n.asf
   4046   3095   4046   4431   4024   3500   4024   3368   4024   774   3099   993

of God. **11** And that   is what some of you were. But   you were washed,   you were sanctified,   you were
→ θεοῦ   καὶ   ταῦτα   ←   τινες   ἦτε   ἀλλὰ   →   ἀπελούσασθε ἀλλὰ   →   →   ἡγιάσθητε   ἀλλὰ   →
  n.gsn   cj   r.npn   r.npm   v.iai.2p   cj   v.ami.2p   cj   v.api.2p   cj
  2536   2779   4047   5516   1639   247   666   247   39   247

justified   in the name   of the Lord Jesus Christ and by the Spirit   of our   God.
ἐδικαιώθητε ἐν   τῷ   ὀνόματι   →   τοῦ   κυρίου   Ἰησοῦ   Χριστοῦ καὶ   ἐν   τῷ   πνεύματι ⌐   ἡμῶν ⌐τοῦ θεοῦ⌐
v.api.2p   p.d   d.dsn   n.dsn   d.gsm   n.gsm   n.gsm   n.gsm   cj   p.d   d.dsn   n.dsn   r.gp.1   d.gsm   n.gsm
1467   1877   3836   3950   3836   3261   2652   5986   2779   1877   3836   4460   2536   7005   3836   2536

Sexual Immorality

6:12"Everything is permissible for me" – but not everything is beneficial. "Everything is permissible for me" –
    Πάντα   →   ἔξεστιν   →   μοι   ἀλλ'   οὐ   πάντα   →   συμφέρει   πάντα   →   ἔξεστιν   →   μοι
    a.npn   v.pai.3s   r.ds.1   cj   pl   a.npn   v.pai.3s   a.npn   v.pai.3s   r.ds.1
    4246   1997   1609   247   4024   4246   5237   4246   1997   1609

but I   will not be mastered   by anything. **13** "Food   for the stomach and the stomach for food"   –   but
ἀλλ' ἐγώ ⌐   οὐκ   ἐξουσιασθήσομαι ὑπό τινος   ⌐τὰ βρώματα⌐   →   τῇ   κοιλίᾳ   καὶ   ἡ   κοιλία   ⌐τοῖς βρώμασιν⌐   δὲ
cj   r.ns.1   pl   v.fpi.1s   p.g   r.gsn   d.npn   n.npn   d.dsf   n.dsf   cj   d.nsf   n.nsf   d.dpn   n.dpn   cj
247   1609   2027   4024   2027   5679   5516   3836   1109   3836   3120   2779   3836   3120   3836   1109   1254

God   will destroy   them   both.   The body is not meant for sexual immorality, but   for the
ὁ   θεός⌐   →   καταργήσει ⌐καὶ ταύτην καὶ ταῦτα⌐   δὲ   τὸ   σῶμα   οὐ   ⌐τῇ πορνείᾳ⌐   ἀλλὰ   τῷ
d.nsm   n.nsm   v.fai.3s   cj   r.asf   cj   r.apn   cj   d.nsn   n.nsn   pl   d.dsf   n.dsf   247   d.dsm
3836   2536   2934   2779   4047   2779   4047   1254   3836   5393   4024   3836   4518   3836

Lord, and the Lord for the body. **14**   By his   power   God   raised the Lord from the dead, and he
κυρίῳ καὶ ὁ   κύριος   →   τῷ   σώματι   δὲ   διὰ   αὐτοῦ ⌐τῆς δυνάμεως⌐   ὁ   θεός   καὶ   ἤγειρεν   τὸν   κύριον   καὶ   →
n.dsm   cj   d.nsm   n.nsm   d.dsn   n.dsn   cj   p.g   r.gsm.3   d.gsf   n.gsf   d.nsm   n.nsm   cj   v.aai.3s   d.asm   n.asm   cj
3261   2779   3836   3261   3836   5393   1254   1328   899   3836   1539   3836   2536   2779   1586   3836   3261   2779

will raise   us   also. **15** Do you not know that your bodies   are members of Christ himself? Shall I   then take
→   ἐξεγερεῖ ἡμᾶς   οὐκ οἴδατε ὅτι   ὑμῶν ⌐τὰ σώματα⌐   ἐστιν μέλη   →   Χριστοῦ   οὖν   ἄρας
  v.fai.3s   r.ap.1   pl   v.rai.2p   cj   r.gp.2   d.npn   n.npn   v.pai.3s   n.npn   n.gsm   cj   pt.aa.nsm
  1995   7005   3857   3857   4024   3857   4022   7007   3836   5393   1639   3517   5986   149   149   4036   149

the members of Christ   and unite   them with a prostitute? Never!   **16**   Do you not know that he   who
τὰ   μέλη   → ⌐τοῦ Χριστοῦ⌐   ποιήσω μέλη   →   πόρνης   μὴ   γένοιτο⌐   [ἢ]   ⌐   →   οὐκ οἴδατε ὅτι   ὁ   ←
d.apn   n.apn   d.gsm   n.gsm   v.aas.1s   n.apn   n.gsf   pl   v.amo.3s   cj   pl   v.rai.2p   cj   d.nsm
3836   3517   3836   5986   4472   3517   4520   3590   1181   2445   3857   3857   4024   3857   4022   3836

unites   himself with a prostitute is   one with her in body? For it is said, "The two will become one   flesh."
κολλώμενος ←   →   ⌐τῇ πόρνῃ⌐   ἐστιν ἐν   →   σῶμα   γὰρ   →   φησίν οἱ   δύο   →   ἔσονται ⌐εἰς μίαν⌐   σάρκα
pt.pp.nsm   d.dsf   n.dsf   v.pai.3s   a.nsn   n.nsn   cj   v.pai.3s   d.npm   a.npm   v.fmi.3p   p.a   a.asf   n.asf
3140   3836   4520   1639   1651   5393   1142   5774   3836   1545   1639   1650   1651   4922

17 But he who unites   himself with the Lord is   one with him in spirit.   ¶   **18** Flee   from sexual immorality.
δὲ   ὁ   ←   κολλώμενος ←   →   τῷ   κυρίῳ ἐστιν ἐν   →   πνεῦμα   Φεύγετε ←   →   ⌐τὴν πορνείαν⌐
cj   d.nsm   pt.pp.nsm   d.dsm   n.dsm   v.pai.3s   a.nsn   n.nsn   v.pam.2p   d.asf   n.asf
1254   3836   3140   3836   3261   1639   1651   4460   5771   3836   4518

All other sins   a man   commits are   outside his body,   but he who sins sexually sins   against his
πᾶν →   ἁμάρτημα   ἄνθρωπος   ὃ   ἐὰν ποιήσῃ   ἐστιν ἐκτὸς   τοῦ σώματος   δὲ   ὁ   πορνεύων ἁμαρτάνει εἰς   τὸ
a.nsn   4005   n.nsn   n.nsm   r.asn   r.asn   v.aas.3s   v.pai.3s   p.g   d.gsn   n.gsn   cj   d.nsm   pt.pa.nsm   v.pai.3s   p.a   d.asn
4246   4005   280   476   4005   1569   4472   1639   1760   3836   5393   1254   3836   4519   279   1650   3836

own body. **19**   Do you not know that your body   is a temple of the Holy Spirit,   who is   in you, whom you
ἴδιον σῶμα   ἢ   οὐκ οἴδατε ὅτι   ὑμῶν ⌐τὸ σῶμα⌐   ναός   τοῦ   ἁγίου   πνεύματος   ἐστιν ἐν   ὑμῖν οὗ   →
a.asn   n.asn   cj   pl   v.rai.2p   cj   r.gp.2   d.nsn   n.nsn   n.nsm   d.gsn   a.gsn   n.gsn   v.pai.3s   p.d   r.dp.2   r.gsn
2625   5393   2445   3857   3857   4024   3857   4022   7007   3836   5393   3724   3836   41   4460   1639   1877   7007   4005

have received from God?   You are not your   own;   **20**   you were bought   at a price. Therefore honor
→   ἔχετε   ἀπὸ   θεοῦ   καὶ   →   ἐστὲ οὐκ ἑαυτῶν   ←   γὰρ   →   →   ἠγοράσθητε   τιμῆς   δὴ   δοξάσατε
  v.pai.2p   p.g   n.gsm   cj   v.pai.2p   pl   r.gpm.2   cj   v.api.2p   n.gsf   pl   v.aam.2p
  2400   608   2536   2779   1639   4024   1571   1142   60   5507   1314   1519

μαλακοὶ οὔτε ἀρσενοκοῖται   **10** οὔτε κλέπται οὔτε πλεονέκται, οὐ μέθυσοι, οὐ λοίδοροι, οὐχ ἅρπαγες βασιλείαν θεοῦ κληρονομήσουσιν.   **11** καὶ ταῦτα τινες ἦτε· ἀλλὰ ἀπελούσασθε, ἀλλὰ ἡγιάσθητε, ἀλλὰ ἐδικαιώθητε ἐν τῷ ὀνόματι τοῦ κυρίου Ἰησοῦ Χριστοῦ καὶ ἐν τῷ πνεύματι τοῦ θεοῦ ἡμῶν.

   6:12 Πάντα μοι ἔξεστιν ἀλλ' οὐ πάντα συμφέρει· πάντα μοι ἔξεστιν ἀλλ' οὐκ ἐγὼ ἐξουσιασθήσομαι ὑπό τινος.   **13** τὰ βρώματα τῇ κοιλίᾳ καὶ ἡ κοιλία τοῖς βρώμασιν, ὁ δὲ θεὸς καὶ ταύτην καὶ ταῦτα καταργήσει. τὸ δὲ σῶμα οὐ τῇ πορνείᾳ ἀλλὰ τῷ κυρίῳ, καὶ ὁ κύριος τῷ σώματι·   **14** ὁ δὲ θεὸς καὶ τὸν κύριον ἤγειρεν καὶ ἡμᾶς ἐξεγερεῖ διὰ τῆς δυνάμεως αὐτοῦ.   **15** οὐκ οἴδατε ὅτι τὰ σώματα ὑμῶν μέλη Χριστοῦ ἐστιν; ἄρας οὖν τὰ μέλη τοῦ Χριστοῦ ποιήσω πόρνης μέλη; μὴ γένοιτο.   **16** [ἢ] οὐκ οἴδατε ὅτι ὁ κολλώμενος τῇ πόρνῃ ἓν σῶμά ἐστιν; Ἔσονται γάρ, φησίν, οἱ δύο εἰς σάρκα μίαν.   **17** ὁ δὲ κολλώμενος τῷ κυρίῳ ἓν πνεῦμά ἐστιν. ¶ **18** φεύγετε τὴν πορνείαν. πᾶν ἁμάρτημα ὃ ἐὰν ποιήσῃ ἄνθρωπος ἐκτὸς τοῦ σώματός ἐστιν· ὁ δὲ πορνεύων εἰς τὸ ἴδιον σῶμα ἁμαρτάνει.   **19** ἢ οὐκ οἴδατε ὅτι τὸ σῶμα ὑμῶν ναὸς τοῦ ἐν ὑμῖν ἁγίου πνεύματός ἐστιν οὗ ἔχετε ἀπὸ θεοῦ, καὶ οὐκ ἐστὲ ἑαυτῶν;   **20** ἠγοράσθητε γὰρ τιμῆς· δοξάσατε δὴ τὸν θεὸν ἐν τῷ σώματι ὑμῶν.

God   with your body.
ⸯτὸν θεὸνⸯ ἐν   ὑμῶν ⸯτῷ σώματιⸯ
d.asm n.asm p.d r.gp.2 d.dsn n.dsn
3836 2536 1877 7007 3836 5393

Marriage

7:1 Now for the matters you wrote about: It is good for a man not to marry. **2** But since there is
δὲ Περὶ ὧν ←   → ἐγράψατε   καλὸν → ἀνθρώπῳ μὴ → ⸯἅπτεσθαι γυναικόςⸯ δὲ διὰ
cj p.g r.gpn   v.aai.2p   a.nsn   n.dsm pl   f.pm   n.gsf   cj p.a
1254 4309 4005   1211   2819   476 3590 721   1222   1254 1328

so much immorality, each man should have his own wife, and each woman her own husband. **3** The
ⸯτὰς πορνείαςⸯ ἕκαστος ←   → ἐχέτω τὴν ἑαυτοῦ γυναῖκα καὶ ἑκάστη ← ἐχέτω τὸν ἴδιον ἄνδρα ὁ
d.apf n.apf   r.nsm   v.pam.3s d.asf r.gsm.3 n.asf cj r.nsf   v.pam.3s d.asm a.asm n.asm d.nsm
3836 4518   1667   2400 3836 1571 1222   2779 1667   2400 3836 2625 467 3836

husband should fulfill his marital duty to his wife, and likewise the wife to her husband. **4** The wife's
ἀνήρ → ἀποδιδότω τὴν → ὀφειλὴν → τῇ γυναικὶ δὲ ὁμοίως καὶ ἡ γυνὴ → τῷ ἀνδρί ἡ γυνὴ
n.nsm v.pam.3s d.asf   n.asf   d.dsf n.dsf cj adv adv d.nsf n.nsf d.dsm n.dsm d.nsf n.nsf
467   625   3836   4051   3836 1222 3931 2779 3836 1222 3836 467 3836 1222

body does not belong to her alone but also to her husband. In the same way, the husband's body
σώματος → οὐκ ἐξουσιάζει τοῦ ἰδίου ἀλλὰ ὁ ἀνήρ δὲ → ὁμοίως καὶ ὁ ἀνὴρ σώματος
n.gsn   pl v.pai.3s   d.gsn a.gsn cj d.nsm n.nsm cj adv adv d.nsm n.nsm n.gsn
5393   2027 4024 2027 3836 2625 247 3836 467 1254 3931 2779 3836 467 5393

does not belong to him alone but also to his wife. **5** Do not deprive each other except by mutual
→ οὐκ ἐξουσιάζει τοῦ ἰδίου ἀλλὰ ἡ γυνή → μὴ ἀποστερεῖτε ἀλλήλους ← εἰ μήτι ἂν ἐκ συμφώνου
pl v.pai.3s   d.gsn a.gsn cj d.nsf n.nsf pl v.pam.2p   r.apm   cj cj cj p.g n.gsn
2027 4024 2027 3836 2625 247 3836 1222 691 3590 691   253   1623 3614 323 1666 5247

consent and for a time, so that you may devote yourselves to prayer. Then come together again so
← πρὸς καιρὸν ἵνα ← → σχολάσητε ← → ⸯτῇ προσευχῇⸯ καὶ ἦτε ἐπὶ τὸ αὐτὸ πάλιν ἵνα
   p.a n.asm cj   v.aas.2p   d.dsf n.dsf   cj v.pas.2p p.a d.asn r.asn adv cj
   4639 2789   2671   5390   3836 4666   2779 1639 2093 3836 899 4099 2671

that Satan will not tempt you because of your lack of self-control. **6** I say this as a concession,
← ὁ σατανᾶςⸯ μὴ πειράζῃ ὑμᾶς διὰ ὑμῶν ⸯτὴν ἀκρασίανⸯ ← δὲ → λέγω τοῦτο κατὰ συγγνώμην
   d.nsm n.nsm pl v.pas.3s r.ap.2 p.a r.gp.2 d.asf n.asf   cj v.pai.1s r.asn p.a n.asf
   3836 4928 4279 3590 4279 7007 1328 7007 3836 202   1254 3306 4047 2848 5152

not as a command. **7** I wish that all men were as I am. But each man has his own
οὐ κατ' ἐπιταγήν δὲ → θέλω πάντας ἀνθρώπους εἶναι ὡς καὶ ἐμαυτόν ἀλλὰ ἕκαστος ← ἔχει ἴδιον ←
pl p.a n.asf   cj v.pai.1s a.apm n.apm   f.pa pl pl r.asm.1 cj r.nsm   v.pai.3s a.asn
4024 2848 2198   1254 2527 4246 476   1639 6055 2779 1831 247 1667   2400 2625

gift from God; one *has this gift,* another *has that.* ¶ **8** Now to the unmarried and the widows I say:
χάρισμα ἐκ θεοῦ ὁ μὲν οὕτως ὁ δὲ οὕτως δὲ → τοῖς ἀγάμοις καὶ ταῖς χήραις → Λέγω
n.asn   p.g n.gsn d.nsm pl adv d.nsm cj adv cj d.dpm a.dpm   cj d.dpf n.dpf   v.pai.1s
5922   1666 2536 3836 3525 4048 3836 1254 4048 1254 3836 23   2779 3836 5939   3306

It is good for them to stay unmarried, as I am. **9** But if they cannot control themselves, they should
καλὸν → αὐτοῖς ἐὰν → μείνωσιν ὡς κἀγώ δὲ εἰ → οὐκ ἐγκρατεύονται ←
a.nsn   r.dpm.3 cj   v.aas.3p cj crasis cj cj pl v.pmi.3p
2819   899   1569   3531   6055 2743 1254 1623 1603 4024 1603

marry, for it is better to marry than to burn with passion. ¶ **10** To the married I give this
γαμησάτωσαν γὰρ → ἐστιν κρεῖττον γαμῆσαι ἢ → πυροῦσθαι ← δὲ → Τοῖς γεγαμηκόσιν → →
v.aam.3p   cj   v.pai.3s a.nsn.c f.aa   pl   f.pp   cj d.dpm pt.ra.dpm
1138   1142 1639 3202 1138   2445 4792   1254 3836 1138

command (not I, but the Lord): A wife must not separate from her husband. **11** But if she does, she
παραγγέλλω οὐκ ἐγώ ἀλλὰ ὁ κύριος γυναῖκα → μὴ χωρισθῆναι ἀπὸ ἀνδρός δὲ ἐὰν καὶ → χωρισθῇ →
v.pai.1s   pl r.ns.1 cj d.nsm n.nsm n.asf   pl f.ap   p.g n.gsm   cj cj adv   v.aps.3s
4133   4024 1609 247 3836 3261 1222   6004 3590 6004 608 467   1254 1569 2779 6004

must remain unmarried or else be reconciled to her husband. And a husband must not divorce his wife. ¶
→ μενέτω ἄγαμος ἢ → καταλλαγήτω τῷ ἀνδρί καὶ ἄνδρα μὴ ἀφιέναι γυναῖκα
  v.pam.3s a.nsf cj v.apm.3s   d.dsm n.dsm cj n.asm pl f.pa   n.asf
  3531   23   2445 2904   3836 467   2779 467 3590 918   1222

7:1 Περὶ δὲ ὧν ἐγράψατε, καλὸν ἀνθρώπῳ γυναικὸς μὴ ἅπτεσθαι· **2** διὰ δὲ τὰς πορνείας ἕκαστος τὴν ἑαυτοῦ γυναῖκα ἐχέτω καὶ ἑκάστη τὸν ἴδιον ἄνδρα ἐχέτω. **3** τῇ γυναικὶ ὁ ἀνὴρ τὴν ὀφειλὴν ἀποδιδότω, ὁμοίως δὲ καὶ ἡ γυνὴ τῷ ἀνδρί. **4** ἡ γυνὴ τοῦ ἰδίου σώματος οὐκ ἐξουσιάζει ἀλλὰ ὁ ἀνήρ, ὁμοίως δὲ καὶ ὁ ἀνὴρ τοῦ ἰδίου σώματος οὐκ ἐξουσιάζει ἀλλὰ ἡ γυνή. **5** μὴ ἀποστερεῖτε ἀλλήλους, εἰ μήτι ἂν ἐκ συμφώνου πρὸς καιρόν, ἵνα σχολάσητε τῇ προσευχῇ καὶ πάλιν ἐπὶ τὸ αὐτὸ ἦτε, ἵνα μὴ πειράζῃ ὑμᾶς ὁ Σατανᾶς διὰ τὴν ἀκρασίαν ὑμῶν. **6** τοῦτο δὲ λέγω κατὰ συγγνώμην οὐ κατ' ἐπιταγήν. **7** θέλω δὲ πάντας ἀνθρώπους εἶναι ὡς καὶ ἐμαυτόν· ἀλλὰ ἕκαστος ἴδιον ἔχει χάρισμα ἐκ θεοῦ, ὁ μὲν οὕτως, ὁ δὲ οὕτως. ¶ **8** Λέγω δὲ τοῖς ἀγάμοις καὶ ταῖς χήραις, καλὸν αὐτοῖς ἐὰν μείνωσιν ὡς κἀγώ· **9** εἰ δὲ οὐκ ἐγκρατεύονται, γαμησάτωσαν, κρεῖττον γάρ ἐστιν γαμῆσαι ἢ πυροῦσθαι. ¶ **10** τοῖς δὲ γεγαμηκόσιν παραγγέλλω, οὐκ ἐγὼ ἀλλὰ ὁ κύριος, γυναῖκα ἀπὸ ἀνδρὸς μὴ χωρισθῆναι, **11** —ἐὰν δὲ καὶ χωρισθῇ, μενέτω ἄγαμος ἢ τῷ ἀνδρὶ καταλλαγήτω,— καὶ ἄνδρα γυναῖκα μὴ ἀφιέναι. ¶ **12** Τοῖς δὲ λοιποῖς λέγω ἐγὼ οὐχ ὁ

12 To the rest I say this (I, not the Lord): If any brother has a wife who is not a believer and she is
δὲ Τοῖς λοιποῖς λέγω ἐγὼ οὐχ ὁ κύριος εἴ τις ἀδελφὸς ἔχει γυναῖκα ἄπιστον καὶ αὕτη
cj d.dpm a.dpm v.pai.1s r.ns.1 pl d.nsm n.nsm cj r.nsm n.nsm v.pai.3s n.asf a.asf cj r.nsf
1254 3836 3370 3306 1609 4024 3836 3261 1623 5516 81 2400 1222 603 2779 4047

willing to live with him, he must not divorce her. **13** And if a woman has a husband who is not a believer
συνευδοκεῖ οἰκεῖν μετ᾽ αὐτοῦ μὴ ἀφιέτω αὐτήν καὶ εἴ τις γυνὴ ἔχει ἄνδρα ἄπιστον
v.pai.3s f.pa p.g r.gsm.3 pl v.pam.3s r.asf.3 cj cj r.nsf n.nsf v.pai.3s n.asm a.asm
5306 3861 3552 899 3590 918 899 2779 1623 5516 1222 2400 467 603

and he is willing to live with her, she must not divorce him. **14** For the unbelieving husband has been
καὶ οὗτος συνευδοκεῖ οἰκεῖν μετ᾽ αὐτῆς μὴ ἀφιέτω τὸν ἄνδρα γὰρ ὁ ὁ ἄπιστος ἀνὴρ
cj r.nsm v.pai.3s f.pa p.g r.gsf.3 pl v.pam.3s d.asm n.asm cj d.nsm d.nsm a.nsm n.nsm
2779 4047 5306 3861 3552 899 3590 918 3836 467 1142 3836 3836 603 467

sanctified through his wife, and the unbelieving wife has been sanctified through her believing husband. Otherwise
ἡγίασται ἐν τῇ γυναικὶ καὶ ἡ ἡ ἄπιστος γυνὴ ἡγίασται ἐν τῷ ἀδελφῷ ἐπεὶ ἄρα
v.rpi.3s p.d d.dsf n.dsf cj d.nsf d.nsf a.nsf n.nsf v.rpi.3s p.d d.dsm n.dsm cj cj
39 1877 3836 1222 2779 3836 3836 603 1222 39 1877 3836 81 2075 726

your children would be unclean, but *as it is*, they are holy. ¶ **15** But if the unbeliever leaves, let him
ὑμῶν τὰ τέκνα ἐστιν ἀκάθαρτα δὲ νῦν ἐστιν ἅγια δὲ εἰ ὁ ἄπιστος χωρίζεται
r.gp.2 d.npn n.npn v.pai.3s a.npn cj adv v.pai.3s a.npn cj cj d.nsm a.nsm v.ppi.3s
7007 3836 5451 1639 176 1254 3814 1639 41 1254 1623 3836 603 6004

do so. A believing man or woman is not bound in such circumstances; God has called
χωριζέσθω ὁ ἀδελφὸς ἢ ἡ ἀδελφὴ οὐ δεδούλωται ἐν τοῖς τοιούτοις δὲ ὁ θεός κέκληκεν
v.ppm.3s d.nsm n.nsm cj d.nsf n.nsf pl v.rpi.3s p.d d.dpn r.dpn cj d.nsm n.nsm v.rai.3s
6004 3836 81 2445 3836 80 1530 4024 1530 1877 3836 5525 1254 3836 2536 2813

us to live in peace. **16** How do you know, wife, whether you will save your husband? Or, how do you know,
ὑμᾶς ἐν εἰρήνῃ γὰρ τί οἶδας γύναι εἰ σώσεις τὸν ἄνδρα ἢ τί οἶδας
r.ap.2 p.d n.dsf cj r.asn v.rai.2s n.vsf cj v.fai.2s d.asm n.asm cj r.asn v.rai.2s
7007 1877 1645 1142 5515 3857 1222 1623 5392 3836 467 2445 5515 3857

husband, whether you will save your wife? ¶ **17** Nevertheless, each one *should* *retain the place in*
ἄνερ εἰ σώσεις τὴν γυναῖκα Εἰ μὴ ἑκάστῳ οὕτως περιπατείτω
n.vsm cj v.fai.2s d.asf n.asf cj pl r.dsm adv v.pam.3s
467 1623 5392 3836 1222 1623 3590 1667 4048 4344

life that the Lord assigned to him and to which God has called him. This is the rule I lay
ὡς ὁ κύριος ἐμέρισεν ὡς ὁ θεός κέκληκεν ἕκαστον καὶ οὕτως διατάσσομαι
cj d.nsm n.nsm v.aai.3s cj d.nsm n.nsm v.rai.3s r.asm cj adv v.pmi.1s
6055 3836 3261 3532 6055 3836 2536 2813 1667 2779 4048 1411

down in all the churches. **18** Was a man already circumcised when he was called? He should not become
ἐν πάσαις ταῖς ἐκκλησίαις τις περιτετμημένος ἐκλήθη μὴ
p.d a.dpf d.dpf n.dpf r.nsm pt.rp.nsm v.api.3s pl
1877 4246 3836 1711 5516 4362 2813 2177 2177 3590

uncircumcised. Was a man uncircumcised when he was called? He should not be circumcised. **19** Circumcision is
ἐπισπάσθω τις ἐν ἀκροβυστίᾳ κέκληται μὴ περιτεμνέσθω ἡ περιτομὴ ἐστιν
v.ppm.3s r.nsm p.d n.dsf v.rpi.3s pl v.ppm.3s d.nsf n.nsf v.pai.3s
2177 5516 1877 213 2813 4362 4362 3590 4362 3836 4364 1639

nothing and uncircumcision is nothing. Keeping God's commands is what counts. **20** Each one should remain
οὐδέν καὶ ἡ ἀκροβυστία ἐστιν οὐδέν ἀλλὰ τήρησις θεοῦ ἐντολῶν ἕκαστος μενέτω
a.nsn cj d.nsf n.nsf v.pai.3s a.nsn cj n.nsf n.gsm n.gpf r.nsm v.pam.3s
4029 2779 3836 213 1639 4029 247 5499 2536 1953 1667 3531

in the situation which he was in when God called him. **21** Were you a slave when you were called? Don't let it
ἐν ταύτῃ ᾗ ἐκλήθη ἐν τῇ κλήσει δοῦλος ἐκλήθης μή
p.d r.dsf r.dsf v.api.3s p.d d.dsf n.dsf n.nsm v.api.2s pl
1877 4047 4005 2813 1877 3836 3104 1529 2813 3590

trouble you – although if you can gain your freedom, *do* *so.* **22** For he who was a slave when he
μελέτω σοι ἀλλ᾽ εἰ καὶ δύνασαι γενέσθαι ἐλεύθερος χρῆσαι μᾶλλον γὰρ ὁ δοῦλος
v.pam.3s r.ds.2 cj cj adv v.ppi.2s f.am a.nsm v.amm.2s adv.c cj d.nsm n.nsm
3508 5148 247 1623 2779 1538 1181 1801 5968 3437 1142 3836 1529

κύριος· εἴ τις ἀδελφὸς γυναῖκα ἔχει ἄπιστον καὶ αὕτη συνευδοκεῖ οἰκεῖν μετ᾽ αὐτοῦ, μὴ ἀφιέτω αὐτήν· ¹³ καὶ γυνὴ εἴ τις ἔχει ἄνδρα ἄπιστον καὶ οὗτος συνευδοκεῖ οἰκεῖν μετ᾽ αὐτῆς, μὴ ἀφιέτω τὸν ἄνδρα. ¹⁴ ἡγίασται γὰρ ὁ ἀνὴρ ὁ ἄπιστος ἐν τῇ γυναικὶ καὶ ἡγίασται ἡ γυνὴ ἡ ἄπιστος ἐν τῷ ἀδελφῷ· ἐπεὶ ἄρα τὰ τέκνα ὑμῶν ἀκάθαρτά ἐστιν, νῦν δὲ ἅγιά ἐστιν. ¶ ¹⁵ εἰ δὲ ὁ ἄπιστος χωρίζεται, χωριζέσθω· οὐ δεδούλωται ὁ ἀδελφὸς ἢ ἡ ἀδελφὴ ἐν τοῖς τοιούτοις· ἐν δὲ εἰρήνῃ κέκληκεν ἡμᾶς «ὑμᾶς» θεός. ¹⁶ τί γὰρ οἶδας, γύναι, εἰ τὸν ἄνδρα σώσεις; ἢ τί οἶδας, ἄνερ, εἰ τὴν γυναῖκα σώσεις; ¶ ¹⁷ Εἰ μὴ ἑκάστῳ ὡς ἐμέρισεν ὁ κύριος, ἕκαστον ὡς κέκληκεν ὁ θεός, οὕτως περιπατείτω. καὶ οὕτως ἐν ταῖς ἐκκλησίαις πάσαις διατάσσομαι. ¹⁸ περιτετμημένος τις ἐκλήθη, μὴ ἐπισπάσθω· ἐν ἀκροβυστίᾳ κέκληταί τις, μὴ περιτεμνέσθω. ¹⁹ ἡ περιτομὴ οὐδέν ἐστιν καὶ ἡ ἀκροβυστία οὐδέν ἐστιν, ἀλλὰ τήρησις ἐντολῶν θεοῦ. ²⁰ ἕκαστος ἐν τῇ κλήσει ᾗ ἐκλήθη, ἐν ταύτῃ μενέτω. ²¹ δοῦλος ἐκλήθης, μή σοι μελέτω· ἀλλ᾽ εἰ καὶ δύνασαι ἐλεύθερος γενέσθαι, μᾶλλον χρῆσαι. ²² ὁ γὰρ ἐν κυρίῳ κληθεὶς δοῦλος ἀπελεύθερος κυρίου ἐστίν, ὁμοίως ὁ

was called	by	the	Lord	is		the Lord's	freedman;	similarly,	he			who was a free		man when he was called	is
→ κληθεὶς	ἐν		κυρίῳ	ἐστίν		κυρίου	ἀπελεύθερος	ὁμοίως	ὁ	←	→	→ ἐλεύθερος	←	→ κληθεὶς	ἐστιν
pt.ap.nsm	p.d		n.dsm	v.pai.3s		n.gsm	n.nsm	adv	d.nsm			a.nsm		pt.ap.nsm	v.pai.3s
2813	1877		3261	1639		3261	592	3931	3836			1801		2813	1639

Christ's slave.	**23** You were	bought	at a price;	do	not become	slaves of men.	**24** Brothers,	each	man, as
Χριστοῦ δοῦλος	→	ἠγοράσθητε →	τιμῆς	μὴ	γίνεσθε	δοῦλοι → ἀνθρώπων	ἀδελφοί	ἕκαστος ←	παρὰ
n.gsm n.nsm		v.api.2p	n.gsf	pl	v.pmm.2p	n.npm n.gpm	n.vpm	a.nsm	
5986 1529		60	5507	1181	3590 1181	1529 476	81	1667	4123

responsible to God,	should remain	in	the situation		God called him to.	¶	**25** Now about virgins:	I
← ← θεῷ	μενέτω	ἐν	τούτῳ	ἐν ᾧ	ἐκλήθη ←		δὲ Περὶ ⌐τῶν παρθένων⌐	→
n.dsm	v.pam.3s	p.d	r.dsn	p.d r.dsn	v.api.3s		cj p.g d.gpf n.gpf	
2536	3531	1877	4047	1877 4005	2813		1254 4309 3836 4221	

have no command	from the Lord,	but I	give	a judgment	as	one who	by	the Lord's	mercy	is	trustworthy.
ἔχω οὐκ ἐπιταγὴν	→	κυρίου δὲ	→ δίδωμι	γνώμην	ὡς →	→	ὑπὸ	κυρίου	ἠλεημένος	εἶναι	πιστὸς
v.pai.1s pl n.asf		n.gsm cj	v.pai.1s	n.asf			p.g	n.gsm	pt.rp.nsm	f.pa	a.nsm
2400 4024 2198		3261 1254	1443	1191	6055 1796	1796	5679	3261	1796	1639	4412

26 Because of	the present crisis,	I think	that	it	is	good for you	to remain	*as*	*you are.*
οὖν διὰ	← τὴν ἐνεστῶσαν ἀνάγκην	καλὸν → Νομίζω	ὅτι	τοῦτο ὑπάρχειν	καλὸν	→ ἀνθρώπῳ	⌐τὸ εἶναι⌐	οὕτως	
cj p.a	d.asf pt.ra.asf n.asf	a.asn v.pai.1s	cj	r.asn f.pa	a.asn	n.dsm	d.nsn f.pa	adv	
4036 1328	3836 1931 340	2819 3787	4022	4047 5639	2819	476	3836 1639	4048	

27 *Are you married?*		Do not seek	a divorce.	*Are you unmarried?*		Do not look for a wife.	**28** But if
⌐δέδεσαι γυναικί⌐	→	μὴ ζήτει	λύσιν	⌐λέλυσαι ἀπὸ γυναικός⌐	→	μὴ ζήτει ← γυναῖκα	δὲ ἐὰν καὶ
v.rpi.2s n.dsf	pl	v.pam.2s	n.asf	v.rpi.2s p.g n.gsf		pl v.pam.2s n.asf	cj cj adv
1313 1222	2426	3590 2426	3386	3395 608 1222		2426 3590 2426 1222	1254 1569 2779

you do marry,	you have	not	sinned;	and if	a virgin		marries,	she has	not sinned.	But	*those*	*who*	*marry*	will
→ γαμήσῃς →	οὐχ	ἥμαρτες	καὶ ἐὰν	⌐ἡ παρθένος⌐		γήμῃ		οὐχ	ἥμαρτεν	δὲ	οἱ	←	τοιοῦτοι	
v.aas.2s	pl	v.aai.2s	cj cj	d.nsf n.nsf		v.aas.3s		pl	v.aai.3s	cj	d.npm		r.npm	
1138	4024	279	279 2779	3836 4221		1138		4024	279	1254	3836		5525	

face	many troubles	in this life,	and I	want to spare	you this.	¶	**29**	What I mean, brothers, is that	the
ἕξουσιν	θλῖψιν →	τῇ σαρκὶ δὲ	ἐγὼ →	→ φείδομαι	ὑμῶν		δὲ	Τοῦτο → φημι ἀδελφοί	ὁ
v.fai.3p	n.asf	d.dsf n.dsf cj	r.ns.1	v.pmi.1s	r.gp.2		cj	r.asn v.pai.1s n.vpm	d.nsm
2400	2568	3836 4922 1254	1609	5767	7007		1254	4047 5774 81	3836

time	is	short.	From	now on	those who have	wives	should live	as if they had	none;
καιρὸς	ἐστίν	συνεσταλμένος →	τὸ λοιπόν,	← ←	ἵνα καὶ οἱ	← ἔχοντες γυναῖκας	→ ὦσιν ὡς	← ἔχοντες	μὴ καὶ
n.nsm	v.pai.3s	pt.rp.nsm	d.asn adv		cj cj d.npm	pt.pa.npm n.apf	v.pas.3p pl	pt.pa.npm	pl cj
2789	1639	5366	3836 3370		2671 2779 3836	2400 1222	1639 6055	2400	3590 2779

30 those who mourn,	as if they did	not;	those who are happy,	as if they were	not;	those who
οἱ ← κλαίοντες ὡς	← κλαίοντες	μὴ καὶ οἱ	← χαίροντες ὡς	← χαίροντες	μὴ καὶ οἱ	←
d.npm pt.pa.npm pl	pt.pa.npm	pl cj d.npm	pt.pa.npm pl	pt.pa.npm	pl cj d.npm	
3836 3081 6055	3081	3590 2779 3836	5897 6055	5897	3590 2779 3836	

buy	something,	as if it	were not	theirs to keep;	**31**	those who use	the things of the world,	as if not
ἀγοράζοντες	ὡς	← ←	μὴ	→ κατέχοντες	καὶ οἱ	χρώμενοι	→ τὸν κόσμον	ὡς ← μὴ
pt.pa.npm	pl		pl	pt.pa.npm	cj d.npm	pt.pm.npm	d.asm n.asm	pl pl
60	6055	2988 2988	3590	2988	2779 3836	5968	3836 3180	6055 3590

engrossed	in them.	For this	world	in its present	form	is	passing away.	¶	**32**	I would like	you to
καταχρώμενοι	γὰρ τούτου	⌐τοῦ κόσμου⌐	τὸ	σχῆμα	→ παράγει		δὲ	→ Θέλω ὑμᾶς →
pt.pm.npm	cj r.gsm	d.gsm n.gsm	d.nsn	n.nsn	v.pai.3s		cj	v.pai.1s r.ap.2
2974	1142 4047	3836 3180	3836	5386	4135		1254	2527 7007

be	free from concern.	An unmarried	man	is concerned	about	the Lord's	affairs – how he can	please	the
εἶναι →	ἀμερίμνους	⌐ὁ ἄγαμος⌐	→ μεριμνᾷ	←	τὰ ⌐τοῦ κυρίου⌐	→ πῶς →	→ ἀρέσῃ	τῷ
f.pa	a.apm	d.nsm a.nsm	v.pai.3s		d.apn d.gsm n.gsm		adv	v.aas.3s	d.dsm
1639	291	3836 23	3534		3836 3836 3261	3836	4802	743	3836

Lord.	**33** But a married	man	is concerned	about the affairs	of this world	– how he can	please	his wife	– **34** and his
κυρίῳ	δὲ ⌐ὁ γαμήσας⌐	→ μεριμνᾷ	←	τὰ	τοῦ κόσμου	πῶς →	→ ἀρέσῃ	τῇ γυναικί	καὶ
n.dsm	cj d.nsm pt.aa.nsm	v.pai.3s		d.apn	d.gsm n.gsm	adv	v.aas.3s	d.dsf n.dsf	cj
3261	1254 3836 1138	3534		3836	3836 3180	4802	743	3836 1222	2779

interests are divided.	An unmarried	woman	or	virgin	is concerned	about	the Lord's	affairs:	Her aim
→ μεμέρισται καὶ	⌐ἡ ἄγαμος⌐	⌐ἡ γυνὴ	καὶ	ἡ παρθένος⌐	→ μεριμνᾷ	←	τὰ ⌐τοῦ κυρίου⌐		ἵνα
v.rpi.3s cj	d.nsf a.nsf	d.nsf n.nsf	cj	d.nsf n.nsf	v.pai.3s		d.apn d.gsm n.gsm		cj
3532 2779	3836 23	3836 1222	2779	3836 4221	3534		3836 3836 3261	3836	2671

ἐλεύθερος κληθεὶς δοῦλός ἐστιν Χριστοῦ. **23** τιμῆς ἠγοράσθητε· μὴ γίνεσθε δοῦλοι ἀνθρώπων. **24** ἕκαστος ἐν ᾧ ἐκλήθη, ἀδελφοί, ἐν τούτῳ μενέτω παρὰ θεῷ. ¶ **25** Περὶ δὲ τῶν παρθένων ἐπιταγὴν κυρίου οὐκ ἔχω, γνώμην δὲ δίδωμι ὡς ἠλεημένος ὑπὸ κυρίου πιστὸς εἶναι. **26** Νομίζω οὖν τοῦτο καλὸν ὑπάρχειν διὰ τὴν ἐνεστῶσαν ἀνάγκην, ὅτι καλὸν ἀνθρώπῳ τὸ οὕτως εἶναι. **27** δέδεσαι γυναικί, μὴ ζήτει λύσιν· λέλυσαι ἀπὸ γυναικός, μὴ ζήτει γυναῖκα. **28** ἐὰν δὲ καὶ γαμήσῃς, οὐχ ἥμαρτες, καὶ ἐὰν γήμῃ ἡ παρθένος, οὐχ ἥμαρτεν· θλῖψιν δὲ τῇ σαρκὶ ἕξουσιν οἱ τοιοῦτοι, ἐγὼ δὲ ὑμῶν φείδομαι. ¶ **29** τοῦτο δέ φημι, ἀδελφοί, ὁ καιρὸς συνεσταλμένος ἐστίν· τὸ λοιπόν, ἵνα καὶ οἱ ἔχοντες γυναῖκας ὡς μὴ ἔχοντες ὦσιν **30** καὶ οἱ κλαίοντες ὡς μὴ κλαίοντες καὶ οἱ χαίροντες ὡς μὴ χαίροντες καὶ οἱ ἀγοράζοντες ὡς μὴ κατέχοντες, **31** καὶ οἱ χρώμενοι τὸν κόσμον ὡς μὴ καταχρώμενοι· παράγει γὰρ τὸ σχῆμα τοῦ κόσμου τούτου. ¶ **32** θέλω δὲ ὑμᾶς ἀμερίμνους εἶναι. ὁ ἄγαμος μεριμνᾷ τὰ τοῦ κυρίου, πῶς ἀρέσῃ τῷ κυρίῳ· **33** ὁ δὲ γαμήσας μεριμνᾷ τὰ τοῦ κόσμου, πῶς ἀρέσῃ τῇ γυναικί, **34** καὶ μεμέρισται. καὶ ἡ γυνὴ ἡ ἄγαμος καὶ ἡ παρθένος μεριμνᾷ τὰ τοῦ κυρίου,

is to be   devoted to the Lord in both body   and spirit.   But a married   woman is concerned about
→   →   ἦ   ἁγία   ←   ←   ←   →   καὶ ⌐τῷ σώματι⌐ καὶ ⌐τῷ πνεύματι⌐ δὲ   ⌐ἡ γαμήσασα⌐ ←   → μεριμνᾷ   ←
v.pas.3s a.nsf   cj   d.dsn n.dsn cj   d.dsn n.dsn cj   d.nsf pt.aa.nsf   v.pai.3s
1639   41   5393 3836 5393   2779 3836 4460   1254 3836 1138   3534

the affairs of this world – how she can please her husband. 35 I am saying this for your own good,   not to
τὰ →   → τοῦ κόσμου πῶς → ἀρέσῃ τῷ ἀνδρί δὲ → λέγω τοῦτο πρὸς ὑμῶν αὐτῶν ⌐τὸ σύμφορον⌐ οὐχ ἵνα
d.apn   d.gsm n.gsm   cj   v.aas.3s τῷ dsm n.dsm cj   v.pai.1s r.asn p.a r.gpn r.gpm d.asn n.asn   pl cj
3836   3836 3180   4802   743   3836 467   1254   3306 4047 4639 7007 899   3836 5239   4024 2671

restrict   you, but that you may live in a right   way   in undivided   devotion to the Lord. ¶
⌐ἐπιβάλω βρόχον⌐ ὑμῖν ἀλλὰ πρὸς   ⌐τὸ εὔσχημον⌐ καὶ ἀπερισπάστως εὐπάρεδρον → τῷ κυρίῳ
v.aas.1s n.asm   r.dp.2 cj p.a   d.asn a.asn   cj   adv   n.asn   d.dsm n.dsm
2095   1105   7007 247 4639   3836 2363   2779 597   2339   3836 3261

36 If anyone thinks he is acting improperly toward the virgin he   is engaged to, and if she is   getting
δὲ Εἰ τις νομίζει → → → ἀσχημονεῖν ἐπὶ τὴν παρθένον αὐτοῦ   ἐὰν → ἦ   ὑπέρακμος
cj cj r.nsm v.pai.3s   f.pa   p.a d.asf n.asf r.gsm.3   cj   v.pas.3s
1254 1623 5516 3787   858   2093 3836 4221   899   1569   1639 5644

along in years and   he feels he ought to marry, he should do   as he wants. He is not sinning. They
καὶ οὕτως →   ὀφείλει → γίνεσθαι →   ποιείτω ὃ   θέλει   → οὐχ ἁμαρτάνει
cj   adv   v.pai.3s f.pm   v.pam.3s r.asn v.pai.3s   pl v.pai.3s
2779 4048   4053   1181   4472 4005 2527   279 279 4024 279

should get married. 37 But the man who has settled   the matter in his   own mind, who is under no
→ γαμείτωσαν δὲ → → ὃς → ⌐ἕστηκεν ἑδραῖος⌐ ἐν αὐτοῦ τῇ καρδίᾳ → → ἔχων μὴ
v.pam.3p   cj   r.nsm v.rai.3s a.nsm   p.d r.gsm.3 d.dsf n.dsf   pt.pa.nsm pl
1138   1254   4005 2705   1612   1877 899 3836 2840   2400 3590

compulsion but has control over his own will,   and who has made up   his mind,   not to marry
ἀνάγκην δὲ ἔχει ἐξουσίαν περὶ τοῦ ἰδίου θελήματος καὶ τοῦτο → → κέκρικεν ← ἐν ἰδίᾳ ⌐τῇ καρδίᾳ⌐ τηρεῖν
n.asf   cj   v.pai.3s n.asf p.g d.gsn a.gsn n.gsn   cj   r.asn   v.rai.3s   p.d a.dsf d.dsf n.dsf f.pa
340   1254 2400 2026   4309 3836 2625 2525   2779 4047   3212   1877 2625 3836 2840   5498

the virgin – this man also does the right thing. 38 So then, he who marries the   virgin does right,
ἑαυτοῦ τὴν παρθένον   → ποιήσει καλῶς ←   ὥστε καὶ ὁ ← γαμίζων τὴν ἑαυτοῦ παρθένον ποιεῖ καλῶς
r.gsm.3 d.asf n.asf   v.fai.3s adv   cj   cj d.nsm pt.pa.nsm d.asf r.gsm.3 n.asf v.pai.3s adv
1571   3836 4221   4472   2822   6063 2779 3836 1139   3836 1571 4221   4472 2822

but he who does not marry her does even better. ¶ 39 A woman is bound to her husband as   long as
καὶ ὁ ←   μὴ γαμίζων ποιήσει → κρεῖσσον   Γυνὴ → δέδεται ἐφ' αὐτῆς ὁ ἀνήρ⌐ ὅσον χρόνον
cj   d.nsm   pl pt.pa.nsm v.fai.3s adv.c   n.nsf   v.rpi.3s p.a r.gsf.3 d.nsm n.nsm r.asn n.asm
2779 3836   1139 3590   4472   3202   1222   1313   2093 899   3836 467   4012 5989

he lives. But if her husband dies, she is   free   to marry   anyone she wishes, but he must belong to the
→ ζῇ δὲ ἐὰν ὁ ἀνήρ κοιμηθῇ → ἐστιν ἐλευθέρα → γαμηθῆναι ᾧ → θέλει   μόνον ἐν
v.pai.3s cj cj d.nsm n.nsm v.aps.3s v.pai.3s a.nsf   f.ap   r.dsm v.pai.3s   adv   p.d
2409   1254 1569 3836 467 3121   1639 1801   1138   4005 2527   3667 1877

Lord. 40 In my judgment, she is   happier if she stays as she is – and I think that I   too have the
κυρίῳ δὲ κατὰ ἐμὴν ⌐τὴν γνώμην⌐ → ἐστιν μακαριωτέρα ἐὰν → μείνῃ οὕτως ← ← δὲ → δοκῶ κἀγὼ ← ἔχειν
n.dsm cj   p.a r.asf.1 d.asf n.asf   v.pai.3s a.nsf.c   cj   v.aas.3s adv   cj   v.pai.1s crasis f.pa
3261   1254 2848 1847 3836 1191   1639 3421   1569   3531 4048   1254 1506   2743   2400

Spirit of God.
πνεῦμα → θεοῦ
n.asn   n.gsm
4460   2536

Food Sacrificed to Idols

8:1 Now about food sacrificed to idols: We know that we all   possess knowledge. Knowledge puffs
δὲ Περὶ → → → → ⌐τῶν εἰδωλοθύτων⌐ οἴδαμεν ὅτι → πάντες ἔχομεν γνῶσιν ⌐ἡ γνῶσις⌐ φυσιοῖ
cj   p.g   d.gpn n.gpn   v.rai.1p cj   a.npm v.pai.1p n.asf   d.nsf n.nsf   v.pai.3s
1254 4309   3836 1628   3857   4022 4246 2400   1194   3836 1194   5881

up, but love   builds up. 2 The man who thinks he knows something does not yet know as   he ought
← δὲ ⌐ἡ ἀγάπη⌐ οἰκοδομεῖ εἰ τις ← δοκεῖ → ἐγνωκέναι τι → οὔπω ἔγνω καθὼς → δεῖ
cj   d.nsf n.nsf v.pai.3s   cj r.nsm   v.pai.3s f.ra   r.asn   adv   v.aai.3s cj   v.pai.3s
1254 3836 27   3868   1623 5516   1506   1182   5516 1182 4037 1182 2777   1256

ἵνα ᾖ ἁγία καὶ τῷ σώματι καὶ τῷ πνεύματι· ἡ δὲ γαμήσασα μεριμνᾷ τὰ τοῦ κόσμου, πῶς ἀρέσῃ τῷ ἀνδρί. 35 τοῦτο δὲ πρὸς τὸ
ὑμῶν αὐτῶν σύμφορον λέγω, οὐχ ἵνα βρόχον ὑμῖν ἐπιβάλω ἀλλὰ πρὸς τὸ εὔσχημον καὶ εὐπάρεδρον τῷ κυρίῳ ἀπερισπάστως. ¶
36 Εἰ δέ τις ἀσχημονεῖν ἐπὶ τὴν παρθένον αὐτοῦ νομίζει, ἐὰν ᾖ ὑπέρακμος καὶ οὕτως ὀφείλει γίνεσθαι, ὃ θέλει ποιείτω, οὐχ
ἁμαρτάνει, γαμείτωσαν. 37 ὃς δὲ ἕστηκεν ἐν τῇ καρδίᾳ αὐτοῦ ἑδραῖος μὴ ἔχων ἀνάγκην, ἐξουσίαν δὲ ἔχει περὶ τοῦ ἰδίου
θελήματος καὶ τοῦτο κέκρικεν ἐν τῇ ἰδίᾳ καρδίᾳ, τηρεῖν τὴν ἑαυτοῦ παρθένον, καλῶς ποιήσει. 38 ὥστε καὶ ὁ γαμίζων τὴν
ἑαυτοῦ παρθένον καλῶς ποιεῖ καὶ ὁ μὴ γαμίζων κρεῖσσον ποιήσει. ¶ 39 Γυνὴ δέδεται ἐφ' ὅσον χρόνον ζῇ ὁ ἀνὴρ αὐτῆς· ἐὰν
δὲ κοιμηθῇ ὁ ἀνήρ, ἐλευθέρα ἐστὶν ᾧ θέλει γαμηθῆναι, μόνον ἐν κυρίῳ. 40 μακαριωτέρα δέ ἐστιν ἐὰν οὕτως μείνῃ, κατὰ τὴν
ἐμὴν γνώμην· δοκῶ δὲ κἀγὼ πνεῦμα θεοῦ ἔχειν.
8:1 Περὶ δὲ τῶν εἰδωλοθύτων, οἴδαμεν ὅτι πάντες γνῶσιν ἔχομεν. ἡ γνῶσις φυσιοῖ, ἡ δὲ ἀγάπη οἰκοδομεῖ· 2 εἴ τις δοκεῖ

to know. **3** But　　the man who loves　God　　　is known　by God. ¶ **4** So then, about eating　　food
γνῶναι δέ εἰ τις ← ἀγαπᾷ ⸌τὸν θεόν⸍ οὗτος → ἔγνωσται ὑπ᾽ αὐτοῦ οὖν Περὶ ⸌τῆς βρώσεως⸍ →
f.aa cj r.nsm v.pai.3s d.asm n.asm r.nsm v.rpi.3s p.g r.gsm.3 cj p.g d.gsf n.gsf
1182 1254 1623 5516 26 3836 2536 4047 1182 5679 899 4036 4309 3836 1111

sacrificed to idols:　　　We know　that an idol　is nothing at all in the world and that there is no　God
⸌τῶν εἰδωλοθύτων⸍ → οἴδαμεν ὅτι εἴδωλον οὐδὲν ἐν κόσμῳ καὶ ὅτι οὐδεὶς θεὸς
d.gpn n.gpn v.rai.1p cj n.nsn a.nsn p.d n.dsm cj cj a.nsm n.nsm
3836 1628 3857 4022 1631 4029 1877 3180 2779 4022 4029 2536

but　one. **5** For　even if there are so-called gods, whether in heaven or on earth (as　indeed there are
⸌εἰ μὴ⸍ εἷς γὰρ καὶ εἴπερ ← → εἰσὶν λεγόμενοι θεοὶ εἴτε ἐν οὐρανῷ εἴτε ἐπὶ γῆς ὥσπερ → εἰσὶν
cj pl a.nsm cj adv cj v.pai.3p pt.pp.npm n.npm cj p.d n.dsm cj p.g n.gsf cj v.pai.3p
1623 3590 1651 1142 2779 1642 1639 3306 2536 1664 1877 4041 1664 2093 1178 6061 1639

many "gods" and many "lords"), **6** yet for us　there is but one God, the Father, from whom all　　things came
πολλοὶ θεοὶ καὶ πολλοὶ κύριοι ἀλλ᾽ → ἡμῖν εἷς θεὸς ὁ πατὴρ ἐξ οὗ ⸌τὰ πάντα⸍ ←
a.npm n.npm cj a.npm n.npm cj r.dp.1 a.nsm n.nsm d.nsm n.nsm p.g r.gsm d.npn a.npn
4498 2536 2779 4498 3261 247 7005 1651 2536 3836 4252 1666 4005 3836 4246

and for whom we　live; and there is but one Lord, Jesus　Christ, through whom all　　things came and
καὶ εἰς αὐτόν ἡμεῖς καὶ εἷς κύριος Ἰησοῦς Χριστὸς δι᾽ οὗ ⸌τὰ πάντα⸍ ← καὶ
cj p.a r.asm.3 r.np.1 cj a.nsm n.nsm n.nsm n.nsm p.g r.gsm d.npn a.npn cj
2779 1650 899 7005 2779 1651 3261 2652 5986 1328 4005 3836 4246 2779

through whom we　live. ¶ **7** But not everyone knows　this.　Some people are still　so accustomed
δι᾽ αὐτοῦ ἡμεῖς Ἀλλ᾽ οὐκ ἐν πᾶσιν ⸌ἡ γνῶσις⸍ δέ τινὲς ← ἕως ἄρτι ⸌τῇ συνηθείᾳ⸍
p.g r.gsm.3 r.np.1 cj pl p.d a.dpm d.nsf n.nsf cj r.npm p.g adv d.dsf n.dsf
1328 899 7005 247 4024 1877 4246 3836 1194 1254 5516 2401 785 3836 5311

to idols　that when they eat　such food they think of it as having been sacrificed to an idol,　and
⸌τοῦ εἰδώλου⸍ → ἐσθίουσιν ὡς → → εἰδωλόθυτον καὶ
d.gsn n.gsn v.pai.3p pl n.asn cj
3836 1631 2266 6055 1628 2779

since their conscience　is　weak, it is defiled. **8** But food does not bring　us　near to God;　we are no
αὐτῶν ⸌ἡ συνείδησις⸍ οὖσα ἀσθενὴς → μολύνεται δὲ βρῶμα → οὐ παραστήσει ἡμᾶς → ⸌τῷ θεῷ⸍ οὔτε
r.gpm.3 d.nsf n.nsf pt.pa.nsf a.nsf v.ppi.3s cj n.nsn pl v.fai.3s r.ap.1 d.dsm n.dsm cj
1639 899 3836 5287 1639 822 3662 1254 1109 4225 4024 4225 7005 4225 3836 2536 5728 5728 4046

worse　if　we do not eat,　and no better　if　we do. ¶ **9** Be careful, however,　that the exercise
ὑστερούμεθα ἐὰν → μὴ φάγωμεν οὔτε → περισσεύομεν ἐὰν → φάγωμεν βλέπετε δὲ πῶς ἡ →
v.ppi.1p cj pl v.aas.1p cj v.pai.1p cj v.aas.1p v.pam.2p cj d.nsf
5728 1569 2266 2266 3590 2266 4046 4355 1569 2266 1063 1254 4803 3836 2026

of your freedom　does not become a stumbling block to the weak. **10** For if　anyone with a weak
ὑμῶν ἐξουσία αὕτη → μὴ γένηται πρόσκομμα ← τοῖς ἀσθενέσιν γὰρ ἐὰν τις ⸌ἀσθενοῦς ὄντος⸍
r.gp.2 n.nsf r.nsf cj v.ams.3s n.nsn d.dpm a.dpm cj cj r.nsm a.gsm pt.pa.gsm
2026 7007 2026 4047 1181 3590 1181 4682 3836 822 1142 1569 5516 822 1639

conscience　sees you who have　this knowledge eating　in an idol's　temple, won't he be emboldened
ἡ συνείδησις αὐτοῦ ἴδῃ σὲ τὸν ἔχοντα γνῶσιν κατακείμενον ἐν εἰδωλείῳ ← οὐχὶ → οἰκοδομηθήσεται
d.nsf n.nsf r.gsm.3 v.aas.3s r.as.2 d.asm pt.pa.asm n.asf pt.pm.asm p.d n.dsn pl v.fpi.3s
3836 5287 899 1625 5148 3836 2400 1194 2879 1877 1627 4049 3868

to eat　what has been sacrificed to idols? **11** So this weak　brother,　for whom Christ died,　is
εἰς ⸌τὸ ἐσθίειν⸍ τὰ → → εἰδωλόθυτα γὰρ ὁ ἀσθενῶν ὁ ἀδελφός δι᾽ ὃν Χριστὸς ἀπέθανεν →
p.a d.asn f.pa d.apn n.apn cj d.nsm pt.pa.nsm d.nsm n.nsm p.a r.asm n.nsm v.aai.3s
1650 3836 2266 3836 1628 1142 3836 820 3836 81 1328 4005 5986 633

destroyed by your knowledge. **12** When you sin　against your brothers in　this way and wound　their
ἀπόλλυται ἐν σῇ ⸌τῇ γνώσει⸍ δὲ → → ἁμαρτάνοντες εἰς τοὺς ἀδελφοὺς οὕτως ← ← καὶ τύπτοντες αὐτῶν
v.pmi.3s p.d r.dsf.2 d.dsf n.dsf cj pt.pa.npm p.a d.apm n.apm adv cj pt.pa.npm r.gpm.3
660 1877 5050 3836 1194 1254 279 1650 3836 81 4048 2779 5597 899

weak　conscience,　you sin　against Christ. **13** Therefore, if　what I eat　causes my brother　to
ἀσθενοῦσαν ⸌τὴν συνείδησιν⸍ → ἁμαρτάνετε εἰς Χριστὸν διόπερ εἰ → βρῶμα μου ⸌τὸν ἀδελφόν⸍ →
pt.pa.asf d.asf n.asf v.pai.2p p.a n.asm cj cj n.nsn r.gs.1 d.asm n.asm
820 3836 5287 279 1650 5986 1478 1623 1109 4997 1609 3836 81

ἐγνωκέναι τι, οὔπω ἔγνω καθὼς δεῖ γνῶναι· **3** εἰ δέ τις ἀγαπᾷ τὸν θεόν, οὗτος ἔγνωσται ὑπ᾽ αὐτοῦ. ¶ **4** Περὶ τῆς βρώσεως οὖν τῶν εἰδωλοθύτων, οἴδαμεν ὅτι οὐδὲν εἴδωλον ἐν κόσμῳ καὶ ὅτι οὐδεὶς θεὸς εἰ μὴ εἷς. **5** καὶ γὰρ εἴπερ εἰσὶν λεγόμενοι θεοὶ εἴτε ἐν οὐρανῷ εἴτε ἐπὶ γῆς, ὥσπερ εἰσὶν θεοὶ πολλοὶ καὶ κύριοι πολλοί, **6** ἀλλ᾽ ἡμῖν εἷς θεὸς ὁ πατὴρ ἐξ οὗ τὰ πάντα καὶ ἡμεῖς εἰς αὐτόν, καὶ εἷς κύριος Ἰησοῦς Χριστὸς δι᾽ οὗ τὰ πάντα καὶ ἡμεῖς δι᾽ αὐτοῦ. ¶ **7** Ἀλλ᾽ οὐκ ἐν πᾶσιν ἡ γνῶσις· τινὲς δὲ τῇ συνηθείᾳ ἕως ἄρτι τοῦ εἰδώλου ὡς εἰδωλόθυτον ἐσθίουσιν, καὶ ἡ συνείδησις αὐτῶν ἀσθενὴς οὖσα μολύνεται. **8** βρῶμα δὲ ἡμᾶς οὐ παραστήσει τῷ θεῷ· οὔτε ἐὰν μὴ φάγωμεν ὑστερούμεθα, οὔτε ἐὰν φάγωμεν περισσεύομεν. ¶ **9** βλέπετε δὲ μή πως ἡ ἐξουσία ὑμῶν αὕτη πρόσκομμα γένηται τοῖς ἀσθενέσιν. **10** ἐὰν γάρ τις ἴδῃ σὲ τὸν ἔχοντα γνῶσιν ἐν εἰδωλείῳ κατακείμενον, οὐχὶ ἡ συνείδησις αὐτοῦ ἀσθενοῦς ὄντος οἰκοδομηθήσεται εἰς τὸ τὰ εἰδωλόθυτα ἐσθίειν; **11** ἀπόλλυται γὰρ ὁ ἀσθενῶν ἐν τῇ σῇ γνώσει, ὁ ἀδελφὸς δι᾽ ὃν Χριστὸς ἀπέθανεν. **12** οὕτως δὲ ἁμαρτάνοντες εἰς τοὺς ἀδελφοὺς καὶ τύπτοντες αὐτῶν τὴν συνείδησιν ἀσθενοῦσαν εἰς Χριστὸν ἁμαρτάνετε. **13** διόπερ εἰ βρῶμα σκανδαλίζει τὸν ἀδελφόν μου, οὐ μὴ φάγω κρέα εἰς τὸν αἰῶνα, ἵνα μὴ τὸν ἀδελφόν μου σκανδαλίσω.

fall   into sin, I   will never   eat   meat again,   so that I   will not cause him   to fall.
σκανδαλίζει ←   ‚οὐ μὴ‚   φάγω   κρέα ‚εἰς τὸν αἰῶνα‚ ἵνα →   μὴ   ‚τὸν ἀδελφόν μου‚ → σκανδαλίσω
v.pai.3s   pl pl   v.aas.1s n.apn p.a d.asm n.asm cj   pl   d.asm n.asm r.gs.1   v.aas.1s
4997   2266 2266 4024 3590 2266 3200 1650 3836 172 2671 4997 4997 3590 4997 3836 81 1609   4997

The Rights of an Apostle

9:1 Am I not free?   Am I not an apostle?   Have I not seen Jesus   our   Lord?   Are you not the result
      εἰμὶ ← Οὐκ ἐλεύθερος εἰμὶ ← οὐκ ἀπόστολος →   οὐχὶ ἑόρακα Ἰησοῦν ἡμῶν ‚τὸν κύριον‚ ἐστε ὑμεῖς οὐ
      v.pai.1s pl a.nsm   v.pai.1s pl n.nsm   pl v.rai.1s n.asm r.gp.1 d.asm n.asm v.pai.2p r.np.2 pl
      1639 4024 1801   1639 4024 693   3972 3972 4049 3972 2652 7005 3836 3261 1639 7007 4024

of my work   in the Lord? **2** Even though I   may not be   an apostle to others,   surely I am to you! For
μου ‚τὸ ἔργον‚ ἐν   κυρίῳ   εἰ   →   οὐκ εἰμὶ   ἀπόστολος → ἄλλοις ἀλλά γε   → εἰμὶ → ὑμῖν γὰρ
r.gs.1 d.nsn n.nsn p.d n.dsm   cj   pl v.pai.1s n.nsm   r.dpm   cj   cj   v.pai.1s r.dp.2 cj
1609 3836 2240 1877 3261   1623   1639 1639 4024 1639 693 257   247 1145   1639 7007 1142

you are the seal   of my apostleship   in the Lord. ¶ **3** This is   my defense   to those who sit in
ὑμεῖς ἐστε ἡ σφραγίς → μου ‚τῆς ἀποστολῆς‚ ἐν   κυρίῳ   αὕτη ἐστιν ἐμὴ ‚Ἡ ἀπολογία‚ → τοῖς ←
r.np.2 v.pai.2p d.nsf n.nsf r.gs.1 d.gsf n.gsf p.d n.dsm   r.nsf v.pai.3s r.nsf.1 d.nsf n.nsf   d.dpm
7007 1639 3836 5382   692 1609 3836 692 1877 3261   4047 1639 1847 3836 665   3836

judgment   on me. **4** Don't we have the right   to food and drink? **5** Don't we have the right   to take   a
ἀνακρίνουσιν ← ἐμὲ   μὴ οὐκ‚   ἔχομεν   ἐξουσίαν   φαγεῖν καὶ πεῖν   ‚μὴ οὐκ‚ → ἔχομεν   ἐξουσίαν   περιάγειν
pt.pa.dpm   r.as.1   pl pl   v.pai.1p n.asf   f.aa   cj f.aa   pl pl   v.pai.1p n.asf   f.pa
373   1609   3590 4024 2400   2026   2266 2779 4403   3590 4024 2400   2026   4310

believing wife   along with us, as do the other apostles and the Lord's   brothers and Cephas? **6** Or is it only
ἀδελφὴν γυναῖκα →   ← ὡς καὶ οἱ λοιποὶ ἀπόστολοι καὶ οἱ ‚τοῦ κυρίου‚ ἀδελφοὶ καὶ Κηφᾶς   ἢ   μόνος
n.asf   n.asf   adv cj d.npm a.npm n.npm   cj d.npm d.gsm n.gsm n.npm cj n.nsm   cj   a.nsm
80   1222   4310 4310 4310 6055 2779 3836 3370 693 2779 3836 3836 3261 81   2779 3064   2445   3668

I   and Barnabas who   must   work   for a living? ¶ **7** Who serves   as a soldier at his own
ἐγὼ καὶ Βαρναβᾶς οὐκ ἔχομεν ἐξουσίαν μὴ ἐργάζεσθαι   Τίς στρατεύεται ← ← → ἰδίοις
r.ns.1 cj n.nsm   pl v.pai.1p n.asf   pl f.pm   r.nsm v.pmi.3s   a.dpn
1609 2779 982   4024 2400 2026   3590 2237   5515 5129   2625

expense? Who plants a vineyard and does not eat of its   grapes? Who tends   a flock and does not
ὀψωνίοις ποτέ τίς φυτεύει ἀμπελῶνα καὶ   →   οὐκ ἐσθίει αὐτοῦ ‚τὸν καρπὸν‚ ἢ τίς ποιμαίνει ποίμνην καὶ   οὐκ
n.dpn   adv r.nsm v.pai.3s n.asm cj   pl v.pai.3s r.gsm.3 d.asm n.asm cj r.nsm v.pai.3s n.asf cj   pl
4077   4537 5515 5885   308   2779   4024 2266 899 3836 2843   2445 5515 4477 4479   2779   4024

drink of the milk?   **8**   Do I say   this merely *from a human point of view?* Doesn't   the Law
ἐσθίει ἐκ τοῦ γάλακτος τῆς ποίμνης Μὴ →   → λαλῶ ταῦτα   κατὰ ἄνθρωπον   ἢ οὐ   καὶ ὁ νόμος
v.pai.3s p.g d.gsn n.gsn d.gsf n.gsf pl   v.pai.1s r.apn p.a n.asm   cj pl   adv d.nsm n.nsm
2266 1666 3836 1128 3836 4479 3590   3281 4047   2848 476   2445 4024 2779 3836 3795

say the same thing? **9** For it is written in the Law of Moses: "Do not muzzle an ox while it is treading out the
λέγει ταῦτα → γὰρ → γέγραπται ἐν τῷ νόμῳ → Μωϋσέως → οὐ κημώσεις βοῦν →   ἀλοῶντα ← ←
v.pai.3s r.apn   cj   v.rpi.3s   p.d d.dsm n.dsm   n.gsm   pl v.fai.3s n.asm   pt.pa.asm
3306 4047   1142   1211   1877 3836 3795   3707   4024 3055 1091   262

grain." Is it about oxen   that God   is concerned? **10** Surely he says this for us, doesn't he? Yes, this was
       μὴ   ‚τῶν βοῶν‚ ‚τῷ θεῷ‚ → μέλει   ἢ πάντως → λέγει δι' ἡμᾶς   γὰρ
       pl   d.gpm n.gpm d.dsm n.dsm v.pai.3s   cj adv   v.pai.3s p.a r.ap.1   cj
       3590   3836 1091 3836 2536 3508   2445 4122 3306 1328 7005   1142

written for us, because   when the plowman plows   and the thresher threshes, they ought to do so in the
ἐγράφη δι' ἡμᾶς ὅτι   ἐπ' ἐλπίδι → ὁ ἀροτριᾶν ἀροτριᾶν καὶ ὁ ἀλοῶν   →   ὀφείλει   ἐπ'
v.api.3s p.a r.ap.1 cj p.d n.dsf   d.nsm f.pa   pt.pa.nsm cj d.nsm pt.pa.nsm   v.pai.3s   p.d
1211 1328 7005 4022 2093 1828   3836 769   769   2779 3836 262   4053   2093

hope of sharing in the harvest. **11** If we have sown   spiritual seed among you, is it too much if we
ἐλπίδι → ‚τοῦ μετέχειν‚   εἰ ἡμεῖς → ἐσπείραμεν ‚τὰ πνευματικὰ‚   ὑμῖν →   μέγα εἰ ἡμεῖς
n.dsf   d.gsn f.pa   cj r.np.1   v.aai.1p d.apn a.apn   r.dp.2   a.nsn cj r.np.1
1828   3836 3576   1623 7005   5062   3836 4461   5062 7007   3489 1623 7005

reap   a material harvest from you? **12** If others have   this right of support from you, shouldn't we have it
θερίσομεν ‚τὰ σαρκικὰ‚   ὑμῶν Εἰ ἄλλοι μετέχουσιν τῆς ἐξουσίας   →   ὑμῶν οὐ   ἡμεῖς
v.fai.1p d.apn a.apn   r.gp.2 cj r.npm v.pai.3p d.gsf n.gsf   r.gp.2 pl   r.np.1
2545   3836 4920   2545   7007 1623 257 3576   3836 2026   7007 4024   7005

9:1 Οὐκ εἰμὶ ἐλεύθερος; οὐκ εἰμὶ ἀπόστολος; οὐχὶ Ἰησοῦν τὸν κύριον ἡμῶν ἑόρακα; οὐ τὸ ἔργον μου ὑμεῖς ἐστε ἐν κυρίῳ;
2 εἰ ἄλλοις οὐκ εἰμὶ ἀπόστολος, ἀλλά γε ὑμῖν εἰμι· ἡ γὰρ σφραγίς μου τῆς ἀποστολῆς ὑμεῖς ἐστε ἐν κυρίῳ. ¶ **3** Ἡ ἐμὴ ἀπολογία
τοῖς ἐμὲ ἀνακρίνουσίν ἐστιν αὕτη. **4** μὴ οὐκ ἔχομεν ἐξουσίαν φαγεῖν καὶ πεῖν; **5** μὴ οὐκ ἔχομεν ἐξουσίαν ἀδελφὴν γυναῖκα
περιάγειν ὡς καὶ οἱ λοιποὶ ἀπόστολοι καὶ οἱ ἀδελφοὶ τοῦ κυρίου καὶ Κηφᾶς; **6** ἢ μόνος ἐγὼ καὶ Βαρναβᾶς οὐκ ἔχομεν ἐξουσίαν
μὴ ἐργάζεσθαι; ¶ **7** τίς στρατεύεται ἰδίοις ὀψωνίοις ποτέ; τίς φυτεύει ἀμπελῶνα καὶ τὸν καρπὸν αὐτοῦ οὐκ ἐσθίει; ἢ τίς
ποιμαίνει ποίμνην καὶ ἐκ τοῦ γάλακτος τῆς ποίμνης οὐκ ἐσθίει; **8** Μὴ κατὰ ἄνθρωπον ταῦτα λαλῶ ἢ καὶ ὁ νόμος ταῦτα οὐ
λέγει; **9** ἐν γὰρ τῷ Μωϋσέως νόμῳ γέγραπται, Οὐ κημώσεις βοῦν ἀλοῶντα. μὴ τῶν βοῶν μέλει τῷ θεῷ **10** ἢ δι' ἡμᾶς πάντως
λέγει; δι' ἡμᾶς γὰρ ἐγράφη ὅτι ὀφείλει ἐπ' ἐλπίδι ὁ ἀροτριῶν ἀροτριᾶν καὶ ὁ ἀλοῶν ἐπ' ἐλπίδι τοῦ μετέχειν. **11** εἰ ἡμεῖς ὑμῖν
τὰ πνευματικὰ ἐσπείραμεν, μέγα εἰ ἡμεῖς ὑμῶν τὰ σαρκικὰ θερίσομεν; **12** εἰ ἄλλοι τῆς ὑμῶν ἐξουσίας μετέχουσιν, οὐ μᾶλλον

all the more?	¶	But	we did	not	use		this	right.		On the contrary, we	put		up with	anything
μᾶλλον		ἀλλ᾽		οὐκ	ἐχρησάμεθα	ταύτῃ	τῇ	ἐξουσίᾳ·		ἀλλὰ	στέγομεν			πάντα
adv.c		cj		pl	v.ami.1p	r.dsf	d.dsf	n.dsf		cj	v.pai.1p			a.apn
3437		247	5968	5968	4024	5968	4047	3836	2026	247	5095			4246

rather	than	hinder		the	gospel	of Christ.	**13** Don't	you	know	that	those who	work		in	the
ἵνα μή		τινα	ἐγκοπὴν	δῶμεν	τῷ	εὐαγγελίῳ	τοῦ Χριστοῦ.	Οὐκ	οἴδατε	ὅτι	οἱ	ἐργαζόμενοι		τὰ
cj		r.asf	n.asf	v.aas.1p	d.dsn	n.dsn	d.gsm n.gsm	pl	v.rai.2p	cj	d.npm	pt.pm.npm		d.apn
2671	3590	5516	1600	1443	3836	3836	5986	4024	3857	4022	3836	2237		3836

temple			get their food		from	the	temple, and	those who	serve		at the	altar	share		in what
ἱερὰ	[τὰ]		ἐσθίουσιν	ἐκ	τοῦ	ἱεροῦ		οἱ		παρεδρεύοντες	τῷ	θυσιαστηρίῳ	συμμερίζονται
n.apn	d.apn		v.pai.3p	p.g	d.gsn	n.gsn		d.npm		pt.pa.npm	d.dsn	n.dsn	v.pmi.3p
2641	3836		2266	1666	3836	2639		3836		4204	3836	2603	5211

is offered	on the altar?	**14**	In the same way,	the	Lord	has	commanded	that	those who	preach		the
τῷ	θυσιαστηρίῳ	καὶ	οὕτως	ὁ	κύριος	διέταξεν		τοῖς	καταγγέλλουσιν	τὸ
d.dsn	n.dsn	cj	adv	d.nsm	n.nsm	v.aai.3s		d.dpm	pt.pa.dpm	d.asn
3836	2603	2779	4048	3836	3261	1411		2859		3836

gospel	should	receive	their	living	from	the	gospel.	¶	**15** But I		have	not	used	any	of these	rights.
εὐαγγέλιον			ζῆν	ἐκ	τοῦ	εὐαγγελίου		δὲ	Ἐγὼ	οὐ	κέχρημαι	οὐδενὶ	τούτων·
n.asn			f.pa	p.g	d.gsn	n.gsn		cj	r.ns1	pl	v.rmi.1s	a.dsn	r.gpn
2295			2409	1666	3836	2295		1254	1609	5968	4024	5968	4029	4047

And I	am not	writing	this	in the hope	that	you will do	such things	for me.	I	would	rather
δὲ	Οὐκ ἔγραψα	ταῦτα		ἵνα		γένηται	οὕτως	ἐν	ἐμοὶ γὰρ	μοι	καλὸν	μᾶλλον
cj	pl v.aai.1s	r.apn		cj		v.ams.3s	adv	p.d	r.ds.1 cj	r.ds.1	a.nsn	adv.c
1254	1211 1211 4024	1211	4047	2671		1181	4048	1877	1609 1142	1609	2819 633	3437

die	than	have	anyone	deprive	me	of	this	boast.	**16** Yet	when I	preach		the gospel, I	cannot	boast,	for
ἀποθανεῖν	ἢ		οὐδεὶς	κενώσει	μου	τὸ	καύχημα	γὰρ	ἐὰν	εὐαγγελίζωμαι		μοι	οὐκ ἔστιν	καύχημα γάρ
f.aa	pl		a.nsm	v.fai.3s	r.gs.1	d.asn	n.asn	cj	cj	v.pms.1s		r.ds.1	pl v.pai.3s	n.nsn cj
633	2445	3033	4029	3033	1609	3836	3017	1142	1569	2294		1609	4024 1639	3017 1142

I	am compelled		to preach.		Woe	to me	if	I	do	not	preach	the gospel!	**17**	If	I
μοι	ἐπίκειται ἀνάγκη·			γάρ	ἐστιν	οὐαὶ	μοί	ἐὰν		μὴ	εὐαγγελίσωμαι		γάρ	εἰ
r.ds.1	v.pmi.3s n.nsf			cj	v.pai.3s	j	r.ds.1	cj		pl	v.ams.1s		cj	cj
1609	2130 340			1142	1639	4026	1609	1569	2294	2294 3590	2294		1142	1623

preach		voluntarily,	I	have	a reward;		if	not	voluntarily,	*I*	*am*	*simply*	*discharging*	*the*	*trust*	*committed*
πράσσω	τοῦτο	ἑκών		ἔχω	μισθὸν	δὲ	εἰ		ἄκων					πεπίστευμαι	οἰκονομίαν
v.pai.1s	r.asn	a.nsm		v.pai.1s	n.asm	cj	cj		a.nsm					v.rpi.1s	n.asf
4556	4047	1776		2400	3635	1254	1623		220					4409	3873

to me.	**18** What	then	is	my	reward?	Just this:	that	in preaching		the gospel	I	may	offer	it	free
	τίς	οὖν	ἐστιν	μου ὁ	μισθός;		ἵνα	εὐαγγελιζόμενος				θήσω	τὸ	εὐαγγέλιον	ἀδάπανον
	r.nsm	cj	v.pai.3s	r.gs.1 d.nsm	n.nsm		cj	pt.pm.nsm				v.fai.1s	d.asn	n.asn	a.asn
	5515	4036	1639	1609 3836	3635		2671	2294				5502	3836	2295	78

of charge,	and so	not	make	use		of my	rights	in	preaching	it.	¶	**19**	Though	I	am
	εἰς	μὴ		τὸ καταχρήσασθαι		μου	τῇ ἐξουσίᾳ	ἐν	τῷ εὐαγγελίῳ			γὰρ		ὢν
	p.a	pl		d.asn f.am		r.gs.1	d.dsf n.dsf	p.d	d.dsn n.dsn			cj		pt.pa.nsm
	1650	3590		3836 2974		1609	3836 2026	1877	3836 2295			1142		1639

free	and	*belong*	*to*	*no*	*man,*	I	make	myself	a slave	to everyone,	to	win	as many		as
Ἐλεύθερος		ἐκ	πάντων				ἐμαυτὸν	ἐδούλωσα	πᾶσιν	ἵνα	κερδήσω	τοὺς πλείονας
a.nsm		p.g	a.gpm				r.asm.1	v.aai.1s	a.dpm	cj	v.aas.1s	d.apm a.apm.c
1801		1666	4246		1530 1530		1831	1530	4246	2671	3045	3836 4498

possible.	**20**	To the	Jews	I	became	like a	Jew,	to	win	the	Jews.	To those	under	the	law	I became
	καὶ	τοῖς	Ἰουδαίοις	ἐγενόμην	ὡς		Ἰουδαῖος	ἵνα	κερδήσω		Ἰουδαίους	τοῖς	ὑπὸ		νόμον
	cj	d.dpm	a.dpm	v.ami.1s	pl		a.nsm	cj	v.aas.1s		a.apm	d.dpm	p.a		n.asm
	2779	3836	2681	1181	6055		2681	2671	3045		2681	3836	5679		3795

like one	under	the	law	(though	I	myself	am	not	under	the law),	so	as to	win	those	under	the law.	**21** To
ὡς	ὑπὸ		νόμον			αὐτὸς	ὢν	μὴ	ὑπὸ		νόμον	ἵνα		κερδήσω	τοὺς	ὑπὸ	νόμον
pl	p.a		n.asm			r.nsm	pt.pa.nsm	pl	p.a		n.asm	cj		v.aas.1s	d.apm	p.a	n.asm
6055	5679		3795	1639	1639	899	1639	3590	5679		3795	2671		3045	3836	5679	3795

ἡμεῖς; ¶ Ἀλλ᾽ οὐκ ἐχρησάμεθα τῇ ἐξουσίᾳ ταύτῃ, ἀλλὰ πάντα στέγομεν, ἵνα μή τινα ἐγκοπὴν δῶμεν τῷ εὐαγγελίῳ τοῦ Χριστοῦ. **13** οὐκ οἴδατε ὅτι οἱ τὰ ἱερὰ ἐργαζόμενοι [τὰ] ἐκ τοῦ ἱεροῦ ἐσθίουσιν, οἱ τῷ θυσιαστηρίῳ παρεδρεύοντες τῷ θυσιαστηρίῳ συμμερίζονται; **14** οὕτως καὶ ὁ κύριος διέταξεν τοῖς τὸ εὐαγγέλιον καταγγέλλουσιν ἐκ τοῦ εὐαγγελίου ζῆν. ¶ **15** ἐγὼ δὲ οὐ κέχρημαι οὐδενὶ τούτων. οὐκ ἔγραψα δὲ ταῦτα, ἵνα οὕτως γένηται ἐν ἐμοί· καλὸν γάρ μοι μᾶλλον ἀποθανεῖν ἤ— τὸ καύχημά μου οὐδεὶς κενώσει. **16** ἐὰν γὰρ εὐαγγελίζωμαι, οὐκ ἔστιν μοι καύχημα· ἀνάγκη γάρ μοι ἐπίκειται· οὐαὶ γάρ μοί ἐστιν ἐὰν μὴ εὐαγγελίσωμαι. **17** εἰ γὰρ ἑκὼν τοῦτο πράσσω, μισθὸν ἔχω· εἰ δὲ ἄκων, οἰκονομίαν πεπίστευμαι· **18** τίς οὖν μού ἐστιν ὁ μισθός; ἵνα εὐαγγελιζόμενος ἀδάπανον θήσω τὸ εὐαγγέλιον εἰς τὸ μὴ καταχρήσασθαι τῇ ἐξουσίᾳ μου ἐν τῷ εὐαγγελίῳ. ¶ **19** Ἐλεύθερος γὰρ ὢν ἐκ πάντων πᾶσιν ἐμαυτὸν ἐδούλωσα, ἵνα τοὺς πλείονας κερδήσω· **20** καὶ ἐγενόμην τοῖς Ἰουδαίοις ὡς Ἰουδαῖος, ἵνα Ἰουδαίους κερδήσω· τοῖς ὑπὸ νόμον ὡς ὑπὸ νόμον, μὴ ὢν αὐτὸς ὑπὸ νόμον, ἵνα τοὺς ὑπὸ νόμον κερδήσω· **21** τοῖς ἀνόμοις ὡς

those not having the law | I became | like one not having the law | (though I am | not free from God's law | but
τοῖς → → → ἀνόμοις | ὡς → → → → ἄνομος → ὢν μὴ | θεοῦ ἄνομος ἀλλ'
d.dpm | a.dpm | pl | a.nsm | pt.pa.nsm pl pl | n.gsm a.nsm | cj
3836 | 491 | 6055 | 491 | 1639 3590 491 491 | 2536 491 | 247

am under Christ's law), | so as to win | those not having the law. | **22** To the weak | I became weak, to
→ Χριστοῦ ἔννομος ἵνα ← κερδάνω τοὺς → → → ἀνόμους → τοῖς ἀσθενέσιν ἐγενόμην ἀσθενής ἵνα
n.gsm a.nsm | cj | v.aas.1s d.apm d.apm | a.apm | d.dpm a.dpm | v.ami.1s a.nsm cj
1937 5986 1937 2671 | 3045 3836 | 491 | 3836 822 | 1181 822 2671

win the weak. | I have become all things to all men so that by all possible means I might save some.
κερδάνω τοὺς ἀσθενεῖς → → γέγονα πάντα → τοῖς πᾶσιν ← ἵνα ← → πάντως ← → → σώσω τινάς
v.aas.1s d.apm a.apm | v.rai.1s a.npn d.dpm a.dpm cj adv | v.aas.1s r.apm
3045 3836 822 | 1181 4246 3836 4246 2671 4122 | 5392 5516

23 I do all this for the sake of the gospel, that I may share in its blessings. ¶ **24** Do you not
δὲ → ποιῶ πάντα ← διὰ ← τὸ εὐαγγέλιον ἵνα → γένωμαι συγκοινωνὸς ← αὐτοῦ | Οὐκ
cj v.pai.1s a.apn p.a d.asn n.asn cj v.ams.1s n.nsm r.gsn.3 | pl
1254 4472 4246 1328 3836 2295 2671 1181 5171 899 | 3857 3857 4024

know that in a race all the runners run, but only one gets the prize? Run in such a way as
οἴδατε ὅτι ἐν σταδίῳ μὲν πάντες οἱ τρέχοντες τρέχουσιν δὲ εἰς λαμβάνει τὸ βραβεῖον τρέχετε οὕτως ← ← ἵνα
v.rai.2p cj p.d n.dsn pl a.npm d.npm pt.pa.npm v.pai.3p cj a.nsm v.pai.3s d.asn n.asn v.pam.2p adv cj
3857 4022 1877 5084 3525 4246 3836 5556 5556 1254 1651 3284 3836 1092 5556 4048 2671

to get the prize. **25** Everyone who competes in the games goes into strict training. They do it to
← καταλάβητε δὲ πᾶς ὁ ἀγωνιζόμενος ← ← ← πάντα ἐγκρατεύεται οὖν μὲν ἐκεῖνοι ἵνα
v.aas.2p cj a.nsm d.nsm pt.pm.nsm a.apn v.pmi.3s cj pl r.npm cj
2898 1254 4246 3836 76 1603 1603 4246 1603 4036 3525 1697 2671

get a crown that will not last; but we do it to get a crown that will last forever. **26** Therefore I do not run
λάβωσιν στέφανον → φθαρτὸν δὲ ἡμεῖς → ἄφθαρτον τοίνυν ἐγὼ → οὐκ τρέχω
v.aas.3p n.asm a.asm cj r.np.1 a.asm cj r.ns.1 pl v.pai.1s
3284 5109 5778 1254 7005 915 5523 1609 5556 4024 5556

like a man running aimlessly; I do not fight like a man beating the air. **27** No, I beat my body
ὡς → → οὕτως ἀδήλως; → → οὐκ πυκτεύω ὡς → οὕτως δέρων ἀέρα ἀλλὰ → ὑπωπιάζω μου τὸ σῶμα
pl adv adv pl v.pai.1s pl adv pt.pa.nsm n.asn cj v.pai.1s r.gs.1 d.asn n.asn
6055 4048 85 4782 4782 4024 4782 6055 1296 4048 1296 113 247 5724 1609 3836 5393

and make it my slave so that after I have preached to others, I myself will not be disqualified for the prize.
καὶ → → δουλαγωγῶ μή πως ← → → → κηρύξας → ἄλλοις αὐτὸς → → γένωμαι ἀδόκιμος
cj v.pai.1s cj pl pt.aa.nsm r.dpm r.nsm v.ams.1s a.nsm
2779 1524 3590 4803 3062 257 1181 899 1181 3590 1181 99

Warnings From Israel's History

10:1 For I do not want you to be ignorant of the fact, brothers, that our forefathers were all under the
γὰρ → → Οὐ θέλω ὑμᾶς → ἀγνοεῖν ἀδελφοί ὅτι ἡμῶν οἱ πατέρες ἦσαν πάντες ὑπὸ τὴν
cj pl v.pai.1s r.ap.2 f.pa n.vpm cj r.gp.1 d.npm n.npm v.iai.3p a.npm p.a d.asf
1142 2527 2527 4024 2527 7577 7007 51 81 4022 7005 3836 4252 1639 4246 5679 3836

cloud and that they all passed through the sea. **2** They were all baptized into Moses in the
νεφέλην καὶ → πάντες διῆλθον διὰ τῆς θαλάσσης καὶ → πάντες ἐβαπτίσθησαν εἰς τὸν Μωϋσῆν ἐν τῇ
n.asf cj a.npm v.aai.3p p.g d.gsf n.gsf cj a.npm v.api.3p p.a d.asm n.asm p.d d.dsf
3749 2779 4246 1451 1328 3836 2498 2779 966 966 4246 966 1650 3836 3707 1877 3836

cloud and in the sea. **3** They all ate the same spiritual food **4** and drank the same spiritual
νεφέλῃ καὶ ἐν τῇ θαλάσσῃ καὶ → πάντες ἔφαγον τὸ αὐτὸ πνευματικὸν βρῶμα καὶ πάντες ἔπιον τὸ αὐτὸ πνευματικὸν
n.dsf cj p.d d.dsf n.dsf cj a.npm v.aai.3p d.asn r.asn a.asn n.asn cj a.npm v.aai.3p d.asn r.asn a.asn
3749 2779 1877 3836 2498 2779 2266 4246 2266 3836 899 4461 1109 2779 4246 4403 3836 899 4461

drink; for they drank from the spiritual rock that accompanied them, and that rock was Christ.
πόμα γὰρ → ἔπινον ἐκ πνευματικῆς πέτρας ἀκολουθούσης δὲ ἡ πέτρα ἦν ὁ Χριστός.
n.asn cj v.iai.3p p.g a.gsf n.gsf pt.pa.gsf cj d.nsf n.nsf v.iai.3s d.nsm n.nsm
4503 1142 4403 1666 4461 4376 199 1254 3836 4376 1639 3836 5986

5 Nevertheless, God was not pleased with most of them; their bodies were scattered over the
Ἀλλ' ὁ θεός → οὐκ εὐδόκησεν ἐν τοῖς πλείοσιν → αὐτῶν γὰρ → κατεστρώθησαν ἐν τῇ
cj d.nsm n.nsm pl v.aai.3s p.d d.dpm a.dpm.c r.gpm.3 cj v.api.3p p.d d.dsf
247 3836 2536 4024 2305 1877 3836 4498 899 1142 2954 1877 3836

ἄνομος, μὴ ὢν ἄνομος θεοῦ ἀλλ' ἔννομος Χριστοῦ, ἵνα κερδάνω τοὺς ἀνόμους· **22** ἐγενόμην τοῖς ἀσθενέσιν ἀσθενής, ἵνα τοὺς ἀσθενεῖς κερδήσω· τοῖς πᾶσιν γέγονα πάντα, ἵνα πάντως τινὰς σώσω. **23** πάντα δὲ ποιῶ διὰ τὸ εὐαγγέλιον, ἵνα συγκοινωνὸς αὐτοῦ γένωμαι. ¶ **24** Οὐκ οἴδατε ὅτι οἱ ἐν σταδίῳ τρέχοντες πάντες μὲν τρέχουσιν, εἷς δὲ λαμβάνει τὸ βραβεῖον; οὕτως τρέχετε ἵνα καταλάβητε. **25** πᾶς δὲ ὁ ἀγωνιζόμενος πάντα ἐγκρατεύεται, ἐκεῖνοι μὲν οὖν ἵνα φθαρτὸν στέφανον λάβωσιν, ἡμεῖς δὲ ἄφθαρτον. **26** ἐγὼ τοίνυν οὕτως τρέχω ὡς οὐκ ἀδήλως, οὕτως πυκτεύω ὡς οὐκ ἀέρα δέρων· **27** ἀλλὰ ὑπωπιάζω μου τὸ σῶμα καὶ δουλαγωγῶ, μή πως ἄλλοις κηρύξας αὐτὸς ἀδόκιμος γένωμαι.

10:1 Οὐ θέλω γὰρ ὑμᾶς ἀγνοεῖν, ἀδελφοί, ὅτι οἱ πατέρες ἡμῶν πάντες ὑπὸ τὴν νεφέλην ἦσαν καὶ πάντες διὰ τῆς θαλάσσης διῆλθον **2** καὶ πάντες εἰς τὸν Μωϋσῆν ἐβαπτίσθησαν ἐν τῇ νεφέλῃ καὶ ἐν τῇ θαλάσσῃ **3** καὶ πάντες τὸ αὐτὸ πνευματικὸν βρῶμα ἔφαγον **4** καὶ πάντες τὸ αὐτὸ πνευματικὸν ἔπιον πόμα· ἔπινον γὰρ ἐκ πνευματικῆς ἀκολουθούσης πέτρας, ἡ πέτρα δὲ ἦν ὁ Χριστός. **5** ἀλλ' οὐκ ἐν τοῖς πλείοσιν αὐτῶν εὐδόκησεν ὁ θεός, κατεστρώθησαν γὰρ ἐν τῇ ἐρήμῳ. ¶ **6** ταῦτα δὲ τύποι ἡμῶν

desert. ¶ **6** Now these things occurred as examples *to keep us from setting our hearts on evil*
ἐρήμῳ   δὲ Ταῦτα ← ἐγενήθησαν τύποι ἡμῶν εἰς   ἡμᾶς ‚τὸ μὴ εἶναι‚ ἐπιθυμητὰς → κακῶν
n.dsf   cj r.npn   v.api.3p   n.npm r.gp.1 p.a   r.ap.1 d.asn pl f.pa n.apm   a.gpn
2245   1254 4047   1181   5596   7005 1650   7005 3836 3590 1639 2122   2805

things as they did. **7** Do not be idolaters, as some of them were; as it is written: "The people
← καθὼς κἀκεῖνοι ἐπεθύμησαν → μηδὲ γίνεσθε εἰδωλολάτραι καθώς τινες → αὐτῶν ὥσπερ → γέγραπται ὁ λαὸς
   cj   adv   v.aai.3p   cj   v.pmm.2p n.npm   cj   r.npm   r.gp.3 cj   v.rpi.3s d.nsm n.nsm
   2777 2797   2121   1181 3593 1181   1629   2777 5516   899   6061   1211   3836 3295

sat down to eat and drink and got up to indulge in pagan revelry." **8** We should not commit sexual
ἐκάθισεν ←   φαγεῖν καὶ πεῖν καὶ ἀνέστησαν ← → παίζειν ←   μηδὲ →
v.aai.3s   f.aa   cj f.aa cj v.aai.3p   f.pa   cj
2767   2266   2779 4403 2779 482   4089   4519 4519   3593

immorality, as some of them did – and in one day twenty-three thousand of them died. **9** We should not
πορνεύωμεν καθώς τινες → αὐτῶν ἐπόρνευσαν καὶ → μιᾷ ἡμέρα εἴκοσι τρεῖς χιλιάδες   ἔπεσαν → → μηδὲ
v.pas.1p   cj   r.npm   r.gpm.3 v.aai.3p   cj   a.dsf n.dsf a.npf a.npf n.npf   v.aai.3p   cj
4519   2777 5516   899   4519   2779   1651 2465 1633   5552 5942   4406 1733 1733 3593

test the Lord, as some of them did – and were killed by snakes. **10** And do not grumble,
ἐκπειράζωμεν τὸν Χριστόν καθώς τινες → αὐτῶν ἐπείρασαν καὶ → ἀπώλλυντο ὑπὸ ‚τῶν ὄφεων‚   → μηδὲ γογγύζετε
v.pas.1p   d.asm n.asm cj   r.npm   r.gp.3 v.aai.3p cj   v.imi.3p p.g d.gpm n.gpm   cj   v.pam.2p
1733   3836 5986   2777 5516   899   4279   2779   660   5679 3836 4058   3593 1197 3593 1197

as some of them did – and were killed by the destroying angel. ¶ **11** These things happened
καθάπερ τινὲς → αὐτῶν ἐγόγγυσαν καὶ → ἀπώλοντο ὑπὸ τοῦ   ὀλοθρευτοῦ   δὲ ταῦτα ← συνέβαινεν
cj   r.npm   r.gpm.3 v.aai.3p cj   v.ami.3p p.g d.gsm n.gsm   cj r.npn   v.iai.3s
2749   5516   899   1197   2779   660   5679 3836 3904   1254 4047   5201

to them as examples and were written down as warnings for us, on whom the fulfillment of the ages has
→ ἐκείνοις τυπικῶς δὲ → ἐγράφη ← πρὸς νουθεσίαν → ἡμῶν εἰς οὓς τὰ   τέλη → τῶν αἰώνων →
   r.dpm   adv   cj   v.api.3s   p.a n.asf   r.gp.1 p.a r.apm d.npn n.npn   d.gpm n.gpm
   1697   5595   1254   1211   4639 3804   7005 1650 4005 3836 5465   3836 172

come. **12** So, if you think you are standing firm, be careful that you don't fall! **13** No temptation has seized you
κατήντηκεν Ὥστε εἰ ‚ὁ δοκῶν‚ ἑστάναι ← → βλεπέτω → μὴ πέσῃ οὐκ πειρασμὸς → εἴληφεν ὑμᾶς
v.rai.3s   cj   d.nsm pt.pa.nsm f.ra   v.pam.3s   cj v.aas.3s pl n.nsm   v.rai.3s r.ap.2
2918   6063   3836 1506   2705   1063   3590 4406 4024 4280   3284   7007

except what is common to man. And God is faithful; he will not let you be tempted beyond what
‚εἰ μὴ‚ → → → → ἀνθρώπινος δὲ ‚ὁ θεός‚ πιστὸς ὃς → οὐκ ἐάσει ὑμᾶς → πειρασθῆναι ὑπὲρ ὃ
cj   a.nsn   cj d.nsm n.nsm a.nsm r.nsm   pl v.fai.3s r.ap.2 f.ap   p.a r.asn
1623 3590 474   1254 3836 2536 4412   4005   1572 1572   7007   4279   5642 4005

you can bear. But when you are tempted, he will also provide a way out so that you can
→ δύνασθε ἀλλὰ σὺν ‚τῷ πειρασμῷ‚ → καὶ ποιήσει ‚τὴν ἔκβασιν‚ ← → τοῦ δύνασθαι‚
   v.ppi.2p cj   p.d d.dsm n.dsm   adv v.fai.3s d.asf n.asf   d.gsn f.pp
   1538   247 5250 3836 4280   2779 4472   3836 1676   3836 1538

stand up under it.
ὑπενεγκεῖν ←
f.aa
5722

Idol Feasts and the Lord's Supper
10:14 Therefore, my dear friends, flee from idolatry. **15** I speak to sensible people; judge for
Διόπερ   μου → ἀγαπητοί φεύγετε ἀπὸ ‚τῆς εἰδωλολατρίας‚ → λέγω ὡς φρονίμοις ← κρίνατε
cj   r.gs.1   a.vpm   v.pam.2p p.g d.gsf n.gsf   v.pai.1s pl a.dpm   v.aam.2p
1478   1609   5771   5770   608 3836 1630   3306   6055 5861   3212

yourselves what I say. **16** Is not the cup of thanksgiving for which we give thanks a participation in the
ὑμεῖς   ὃ   → φημι   Τὸ ἐστιν οὐχὶ Τὸ ποτήριον ‚τῆς εὐλογίας‚ ὃ   → εὐλογοῦμεν κοινωνία → τοῦ
r.np.2   r.asn   v.pai.1s v.pai.3s pl d.nsn n.nsn d.gsf n.gsf   r.asn   v.pai.1p n.nsf   d.gsn
7007   4005   5774   1639 4049 3836 4539   3836 2330   4005   2328   3126   3836

blood of Christ? And is not the bread that we break a participation in the body of Christ?
αἵματος → ‚τοῦ Χριστοῦ‚ ἐστιν οὐχὶ τὸν ἄρτον ὃν → κλῶμεν κοινωνία → τοῦ σώματος → ‚τοῦ Χριστοῦ‚
n.gsn   d.gsm n.gsm   v.pai.3s pl d.asm n.asm r.asm v.pai.1p n.nsf   d.gsn n.gsn   d.gsm n.gsm
135   3836 5986   1639 4049 3836 788   4005   3089   3126   3836 5393   3836 5986

ἐγενήθησαν, εἰς τὸ μὴ εἶναι ἡμᾶς ἐπιθυμητὰς κακῶν, καθὼς κἀκεῖνοι ἐπεθύμησαν. ⁷ μηδὲ εἰδωλολάτραι γίνεσθε καθώς τινες αὐτῶν, ὥσπερ γέγραπται, Ἐκάθισεν ὁ λαὸς φαγεῖν καὶ πεῖν καὶ ἀνέστησαν παίζειν. ⁸ μηδὲ πορνεύωμεν, καθώς τινες αὐτῶν ἐπόρνευσαν καὶ ἔπεσαν μιᾷ ἡμέρα εἴκοσι τρεῖς χιλιάδες. ⁹ μηδὲ ἐκπειράζωμεν τὸν κύριον, «Χριστόν,» καθώς τινες αὐτῶν ἐπείρασαν καὶ ὑπὸ τῶν ὄφεων ἀπώλλυντο. ¹⁰ μηδὲ γογγύζετε, καθάπερ τινὲς αὐτῶν ἐγόγγυσαν καὶ ἀπώλοντο ὑπὸ τοῦ ὀλοθρευτοῦ. ¶ ¹¹ ταῦτα δὲ τυπικῶς συνέβαινεν ἐκείνοις, ἐγράφη δὲ πρὸς νουθεσίαν ἡμῶν, εἰς οὓς τὰ τέλη τῶν αἰώνων κατήντηκεν. ¹² ὥστε ὁ δοκῶν ἑστάναι βλεπέτω μὴ πέσῃ. ¹³ πειρασμὸς ὑμᾶς οὐκ εἴληφεν εἰ μὴ ἀνθρώπινος· πιστὸς δὲ ὁ θεός, ὃς οὐκ ἐάσει ὑμᾶς πειρασθῆναι ὑπὲρ ὃ δύνασθε ἀλλὰ ποιήσει σὺν τῷ πειρασμῷ καὶ τὴν ἔκβασιν τοῦ δύνασθαι ὑπενεγκεῖν.

¹⁰:¹⁴ Διόπερ, ἀγαπητοί μου, φεύγετε ἀπὸ τῆς εἰδωλολατρίας. ¹⁵ ὡς φρονίμοις λέγω· κρίνατε ὑμεῖς ὅ φημι. ¹⁶ τὸ ποτήριον τῆς εὐλογίας ὃ εὐλογοῦμεν, οὐχὶ κοινωνία ἐστὶν τοῦ αἵματος τοῦ Χριστοῦ; τὸν ἄρτον ὃν κλῶμεν, οὐχὶ κοινωνία τοῦ σώματος τοῦ

17 Because there is one loaf, we, who are many, are one body, for we all partake of the one loaf. ¶
ὅτι   εἷς   ἄρτος → οἱ   πολλοί   ἐσμεν   ἓν   σῶμα   γάρ → οἱ   πάντες   μετέχομεν   ἐκ   τοῦ   ἑνὸς   ἄρτου
cj   a.nsm   n.nsm   d.npm   a.npm   v.pai.1p   a.nsn   n.nsn   cj   d.npm   a.npm   v.pai.1p   p.g   d.gsm   a.gsn   n.gsm
4022   1651   788   1639   3836   4498   1639   1651   5393   1142   3576   3836   4246   3576   1666   3836   1651   788

18 Consider the people of Israel: Do not those who eat the sacrifices participate in the altar? **19**
βλέπετε   ⌐κατὰ σάρκα⌐   τὸν Ἰσραὴλ   εἰσίν   οὐχ   οἱ ← ἐσθίοντες   τὰς   θυσίας   κοινωνοὶ → τοῦ   θυσιαστηρίου   Τί
v.pam.2p   p.a   n.asf   d.asm   n.asm   v.pai.3p   pl   d.npm   pt.pa.npm   d.apf   n.apf   n.npm   d.gsn   n.gsn   r.asn
1063   2848   4922   3836   2702   1639   4024   3836   2266   3836   2602   3128   3836   2603   5515

Do I mean then that a sacrifice offered to an idol is anything, or that an idol is anything? **20** No, but
→ φημι   οὖν   ὅτι → εἰδωλόθυτον   ἐστιν   τί   ἢ   ὅτι   εἴδωλον   ἐστιν   τί   ἀλλ᾽
v.pai.1s   cj   cj   n.nsn   v.pai.3s   r.nsn   cj   cj   n.nsn   v.pai.3s   r.nsn   cj
5774   4036   4022   1628   1639   5516   2445   4022   1631   1639   5516   247

the sacrifices of pagans are offered to demons, not to God, and I do not want you to be
ὅτι   ἃ → θύουσιν   [θύουσιν] → δαιμονίοις   καὶ   οὐ → θεῷ   δὲ → οὐ   θέλω   ὑμᾶς → γίνεσθαι
cj   r.apn   v.pai.3p   v.pai.3p   n.dpn   cj   pl   n.dsm   cj   pl   v.pai.1s   r.ap.2   f.pm
4022   4005   2604   2604   1228   2779   4024   2536   1254   2527   2527   4024   2527   7007   1181

participants with demons. **21** You cannot drink the cup of the Lord and the cup of demons too; you
κοινωνοὺς   τῶν   δαιμονίων → ⌐οὐ δύνασθε⌐   πίνειν   ποτήριον → κυρίου   καὶ   ποτήριον   δαιμονίων →
n.apm   d.gpn   n.gpn   pl   v.ppi.2p   f.pa   n.asn   n.gsm   cj   n.asn   n.gpn
3128   3836   1228   4024   1538   4403   4539   3261   2779   4539   1228

cannot have a part in both the Lord's table and the table of demons. **22** Are we trying to arouse the
⌐οὐ δύνασθε⌐ → μετέχειν ← κυρίου   τραπέζης   καὶ   τραπέζης → δαιμονίων   ἢ   τὸν
pl   v.ppi.2p   f.pa   n.gsm   n.gsf   cj   n.gsf   n.gpn   cj   d.asm
4024   1538   3576   3261   5544   2779   5544   1228   2445   4143   4143   4143   4143   3836

Lord's jealousy? Are we stronger than he?
κύριον   παραζηλοῦμεν   μὴ → ἐσμεν   ἰσχυρότεροι → αὐτοῦ
n.asm   v.pai.1p   pl   v.pai.1p   a.npm.c   r.gsm.3
3261   4143   3590   1639   2708   899

The Believer's Freedom

10:23 "Everything is permissible" – but not everything is beneficial. "Everything is permissible" – but not
Πάντα → ἔξεστιν   ἀλλ᾽   οὐ   πάντα → συμφέρει   πάντα → ἔξεστιν   ἀλλ᾽   οὐ
a.npn   v.pai.3s   cj   pl   a.npn   v.pai.3s   a.npn   v.pai.3s   cj   pl
4246   1997   247   4024   4246   5237   4246   1997   247   4024

everything is constructive. **24** Nobody should seek his own good, but the good of others. ¶ **25** Eat
πάντα → οἰκοδομεῖ   μηδεὶς → ζητείτω   ἑαυτοῦ ← τὸ   ἀλλὰ   τὸ ← → ⌐τοῦ ἑτέρου⌐   ἐσθίετε
a.npn   v.pai.3s   a.nsm   v.pam.3s   r.gsm.3   d.asn   cj   d.asn   d.gsm   r.gsm   v.pam.2p
4246   3868   3594   2426   1571   3836   247   3836   3836   2283   2266

anything sold in the meat market without raising questions of conscience, **26** for, "The earth is the
Πᾶν   ⌐τὸ πωλούμενον⌐   ἐν   μακέλλῳ ← μηδὲν → ἀνακρίνοντες   διὰ   ⌐τὴν συνείδησιν⌐   γάρ   ἡ   γῆ   τοῦ
a.asn   d.asn pt.pp.asn   p.d   n.dsn   a.asn   pt.pa.npm   p.a   d.asf n.asf   cj   d.nsf   n.nsf   d.gsm
4246   3836 4797   1877   3425   3594   373   1328   3836 5287   1142   3836   1178   3836

Lord's, and everything in it." ¶ **27** If some unbeliever invites you to a meal and you want to go,
κυρίου   καὶ   ⌐τὸ πλήρωμα⌐ → αὐτῆς   εἴ   τις   ⌐τῶν ἀπίστων⌐   καλεῖ   ὑμᾶς   καὶ → θέλετε → πορεύεσθαι
n.gsm   cj   d.nsn n.nsn   r.gsf.3   cj   r.nsm   d.gpm a.gpm   v.pai.3s   r.ap.2   cj   v.pai.2p   f.pm
3261   2779   3836 4445   899   1623   5516   3836   603   2813   7007   2779   2527   4513

eat whatever is put before you without raising questions of conscience. **28** But if anyone says to
ἐσθίετε   πᾶν   ⌐τὸ παρατιθέμενον⌐ ← ὑμῖν   μηδὲν → ἀνακρίνοντες   διὰ   ⌐τὴν συνείδησιν⌐   δέ   ἐὰν   τις   εἴπῃ →
v.pam.2p   a.asn   d.asn pt.pp.asn   r.dp.2   a.asn   pt.pa.npm   p.a   d.asf n.asf   cj   cj   r.nsm   v.aas.3s
2266   4246   3836 4192   7007   3594   373   1328   3836 5287   1254   1569   5516   3306

you, "This has been offered in sacrifice," then do not eat it, both for the sake of the man who told you
ὑμῖν   τοῦτο → ἐστιν   ἱερόθυτον → μὴ   ἐσθίετε   δι᾽   ἐκεῖνον   τὸν   μηνύσαντα
r.dp.2   r.nsn   v.pai.3s   a.nsn   pl   v.pam.2p   p.a   r.asm   d.asm   pt.aa.asm
7007   4047   1639   2638   2266   3590   2266   1328   1697   3836   3606

and for conscience' sake — **29** the other man's conscience, I mean, not yours. For why should my
καὶ   ⌐τὴν συνείδησιν⌐   ἀλλὰ   τὴν   ⌐τοῦ ἑτέρου⌐   συνείδησιν → λέγω   δὲ   οὐχὶ   ⌐τὴν ἑαυτοῦ⌐   γάρ   ἱνατί → μου
cj   d.asf n.asf   cj   d.asf   d.gsm r.gsm   n.asf   v.pai.1s   cj   pl   d.asf r.gsm.3   cj   cj   r.gs.1
2779   3836 5287   247   3836   3836 2283   5287   3306   1254   4049   3836 1571   1142   2672   3212   1609

Χριστοῦ ἐστιν; ¹⁷ ὅτι εἷς ἄρτος, ἓν σῶμα οἱ πολλοὶ ἐσμεν, οἱ γὰρ πάντες ἐκ τοῦ ἑνὸς ἄρτου μετέχομεν. ¶ ¹⁸ βλέπετε τὸν Ἰσραὴλ κατὰ σάρκα· οὐχ οἱ ἐσθίοντες τὰς θυσίας κοινωνοὶ τοῦ θυσιαστηρίου εἰσίν; ¹⁹ τί οὖν φημι; ὅτι εἰδωλόθυτόν τί ἐστιν ἢ ὅτι εἴδωλόν τί ἐστιν; ²⁰ ἀλλ᾽ ὅτι ἃ θύουσιν «θύουσιν,» τὰ ἔθνη, δαιμονίοις καὶ οὐ θεῷ [θύουσιν]· οὐ θέλω δὲ ὑμᾶς κοινωνοὺς τῶν δαιμονίων γίνεσθαι. ²¹ οὐ δύνασθε ποτήριον κυρίου πίνειν καὶ ποτήριον δαιμονίων, οὐ δύνασθε τραπέζης κυρίου μετέχειν καὶ τραπέζης δαιμονίων. ²² ἢ παραζηλοῦμεν τὸν κύριον; μὴ ἰσχυρότεροι αὐτοῦ ἐσμεν;

^{10:23} Πάντα ἔξεστιν ἀλλ᾽ οὐ πάντα συμφέρει· πάντα ἔξεστιν ἀλλ᾽ οὐ πάντα οἰκοδομεῖ. ²⁴ μηδεὶς τὸ ἑαυτοῦ ζητείτω ἀλλὰ τὸ τοῦ ἑτέρου. ¶ ²⁵ Πᾶν τὸ ἐν μακέλλῳ πωλούμενον ἐσθίετε μηδὲν ἀνακρίνοντες διὰ τὴν συνείδησιν· ²⁶ τοῦ κυρίου γὰρ ἡ γῆ καὶ τὸ πλήρωμα αὐτῆς. ¶ ²⁷ εἴ τις καλεῖ ὑμᾶς τῶν ἀπίστων καὶ θέλετε πορεύεσθαι, πᾶν τὸ παρατιθέμενον ὑμῖν ἐσθίετε μηδὲν ἀνακρίνοντες διὰ τὴν συνείδησιν. ²⁸ ἐὰν δέ τις ὑμῖν εἴπῃ, Τοῦτο ἱερόθυτόν ἐστιν, μὴ ἐσθίετε δι᾽ ἐκεῖνον τὸν μηνύσαντα καὶ τὴν συνείδησιν· ²⁹ συνείδησιν δὲ λέγω οὐχὶ τὴν ἑαυτοῦ ἀλλὰ τὴν τοῦ ἑτέρου. ἱνατί γὰρ ἡ ἐλευθερία μου κρίνεται ὑπὸ ἄλλης

freedom	be judged	by	another's	conscience?	**30** If	I	take part		in the meal with	thankfulness,	why	am I
ἡ ἐλευθερία	κρίνεται	ὑπὸ	ἄλλης	συνειδήσεως	εἰ	ἐγὼ→	μετέχω		→	χάριτι	τί	τ.asn
d.nsf n.nsf	v.ppi.3s	p.g	r.gsf	n.gsf	cj	r.ns.1	v.pai.1s			n.dsf	r.asn	5515
3836 1800	3212	5679	257	5287	1623	1609	3576			5921	5515	

denounced	because of	something	I	thank	God for?	¶	**31** So	whether	you eat	or	drink	or	whatever	you
βλασφημοῦμαι	ὑπὲρ	οὗ	ἐγὼ	εὐχαριστῶ			οὖν Εἴτε		ἐσθίετε	εἴτε	πίνετε	εἴτε	τι	
v.ppi.1s	p.g	r.gsf	r.ns.1	v.pai.1s			cj cj		v.pai.2p	cj	v.pai.2p	cj	r.asn	
1059	5642	4005	1609	2373			4036 1664		2266	1664	4403	1664	5516	

do,	do	it all	for	the glory	of God.	**32**	Do	not cause	anyone	to stumble,	whether	Jews,		Greeks
ποιεῖτε	ποιεῖτε	πάντα εἰς		δόξαν →	θεοῦ	καὶ	γίνεσθε →		→	ἀπρόσκοποι		Ἰουδαίοις	καὶ	Ἕλλησιν
v.pai.2p	v.pam.2p	a.apn p.a		n.asf	n.gsm	cj	v.pmm.2p			a.npm		a.dpm	cj	n.dpm
4472	4472	4246 1650		1518	2536	2779	1181			718		2681	2779	1818

or	the church	of God	— **33**	even as	I	try to	please	everybody	in every way.	For I		am not	seeking	my
καὶ	τῇ ἐκκλησίᾳ →	τοῦ θεοῦ		καθὼς κἀγὼ		→	ἀρέσκω	πᾶσιν	→ πάντα			μὴ	ζητῶν	ἐμαυτοῦ
cj	d.dsf n.dsf	d.gsm n.gsm		cj crasis			v.pai.1s	a.dpm	a.apn			pl	pt.pa.nsm	r.gsm.1
2779	3836 1711	3836 2536		2743 2777			743	4246	2426	2426 2426		3590	3629	1831

own good	but	the good	of many,	so that	they may be saved.	**11:1** Follow	my	example,	as	I	follow
τὸ σύμφορον	ἀλλὰ	τὸ →	τῶν πολλῶν	ἵνα	σωθῶσιν	γίνεσθε	μου	μιμηταί	καθὼς	κἀγὼ	
d.asn n.asn	cj	d.asn	d.gpm a.gpm	cj	v.aps.3p	v.pmm.2p	r.gs.1	n.npm	cj	crasis	
3836 5239	247	3836	3836 4498	2671	5392	1181	1609	3629	2777	2743	

the example	of Christ.
→	Χριστοῦ
	n.gsm
	5986

Propriety in Worship

11:2	I praise	you	for	remembering	me	in	everything	and	for	holding to	the teachings,	just	as	I passed
δὲ	Ἐπαινῶ	ὑμᾶς	ὅτι	μέμνησθε	μου →		πάντα	καὶ		κατέχετε ←	τὰς παραδόσεις	καθὼς ←		→ παρέδωκα
cj	v.pai.1s	r.ap.2	cj	v.rpi.2p	r.gs.1		a.apn	cj		v.pai.2p	d.apf n.apf	cj		v.aai.1s
1254	2046	7007	4022	3630	1609		4246	2779		2988	3836 4142	2777		4140

them on to you.	¶	**3** Now	I want	you	to	realize	that	the	head	of every	man	is	Christ,	and	the head
ὑμῖν		δὲ	Θέλω	ὑμᾶς →		εἰδέναι	ὅτι	ἡ	κεφαλὴ →	παντὸς	ἀνδρὸς	ἐστιν	ὁ Χριστός,	δὲ	κεφαλὴ
r.dp.2		cj	v.pai.1s	r.ap.2		f.ra	cj	d.nsf	n.nsf	a.gsm	n.gsm	v.pai.3s	d.nsm n.nsm	cj	n.nsf
7007		1254	2527	7007		3857	4022	3836	3051	4246	467	1639	3836 5986	1254	3051

of the woman	is	man,	and	the head	of Christ	is	God.	**4** Every	man	who	prays		or	prophesies
→	γυναικὸς	ὁ ἀνήρ	δὲ	κεφαλὴ	τοῦ Χριστοῦ	ὁ	θεός	πᾶς	ἀνὴρ →		προσευχόμενος		ἢ	προφητεύων
	n.gsf	d.nsm n.nsm	cj	n.nsf	d.gsm n.gsm	d.nsm	n.nsm	a.nsm	n.nsm		pt.pm.nsm		cj	pt.pa.nsm
	1222	3836 467	1254	3051	3836 5986	3836	2536	4246	467		4667		2445	4736

with his head	*covered*	dishonors	his	head.	**5** And	every	woman	who	prays		or	prophesies	with	her
κατὰ	κεφαλῆς ἔχων	καταισχύνει	αὐτοῦ	τὴν κεφαλήν	δὲ	πᾶσα	γυνὴ	→	προσευχομένη		ἢ	προφητεύουσα →		τῇ
p.g	n.gsf pt.pa.nsm	v.pai.3s	r.gsf.3	d.asf n.asf	cj	a.nsf	n.nsf		pt.pm.nsf		cj	pt.pa.nsf		d.dsf
2848	3051 2400	2875	899	3836 3051	1254	4246	1222		4667		2445	4736		3836

head	uncovered	dishonors	her	head	—	it is	*just*		*as though*	her head	were shaved.
κεφαλῇ	ἀκατακαλύπτῳ	καταισχύνει	αὐτῆς	τὴν κεφαλήν	γὰρ →	ἐστιν	ἓν	καὶ τὸ	αὐτό	τῇ	ἐξυρημένῃ
n.dsf	a.dsf	v.pai.3s	r.gsf.3	d.asf n.asf	cj	v.pai.3s	a.nsn	cj d.nsn	r.nsn	d.dsf	pt.rp.dsf
3051	184	2875	899	3836 3051	1142	1639	1651	2779 3836	899	3836 3834

6	If	a woman	does	not	cover		her head,	she should have her	hair	cut	off;	and	if	it is	a disgrace
γὰρ	εἰ	γυνὴ	→	οὐ	κατακαλύπτεται		←	καὶ → →	→	κειράσθω	←	δὲ	εἰ		αἰσχρὸν
cj	cj	n.nsf		pl	v.pmi.3s			adv		v.amm.3s		cj	cj		a.nsn
1142	1623	1222		2877	4024			2779		3025		1254	1623		156

for	a woman	to have	her	hair	cut	or	shaved	off,	she should	cover		her head.	**7**	A man	ought
→	γυναικὶ	→	→	τὸ	κείρασθαι	ἢ	ξυρᾶσθαι		→	κατακαλυπτέσθω ←				Ἀνὴρ	ὀφείλει
	n.dsf			d.nsn	f.am	cj	f.pm			v.pmm.3s				n.nsm	v.pai.3s
	1222			3836	3025	2445	3834			2877			1142 3525	467	4053

not	to cover		his	head,	since	he is		the image	and	glory	of God;	but	the	woman	is	the glory of
οὐκ	→	κατακαλύπτεσθαι	τὴν	κεφαλὴν →	→	ὑπάρχων		εἰκὼν	καὶ	δόξα →	θεοῦ	δὲ	ἡ	γυνὴ	ἐστιν	δόξα →
pl		f.pm	d.asf	n.asf		pt.pa.nsm		n.nsf	cj	n.nsf	n.gsm	cj	d.nsf	n.nsf	v.pai.3s	n.nsf
4024		2877	3836	3051		5639		1635	2779	1518	2536	1254	3836	1222	1639	1518

συνειδήσεως; ³⁰ εἰ ἐγὼ χάριτι μετέχω, τί βλασφημοῦμαι ὑπὲρ οὗ ἐγὼ εὐχαριστῶ; ³¹ εἴτε οὖν ἐσθίετε εἴτε πίνετε εἴτε τι ποιεῖτε, πάντα εἰς δόξαν θεοῦ ποιεῖτε. ³² ἀπρόσκοποι καὶ Ἰουδαίοις γίνεσθε καὶ Ἕλλησιν καὶ τῇ ἐκκλησίᾳ τοῦ θεοῦ, ³³ καθὼς κἀγὼ πάντα πᾶσιν ἀρέσκω μὴ ζητῶν τὸ ἐμαυτοῦ σύμφορον ἀλλὰ τὸ τῶν πολλῶν, ἵνα σωθῶσιν. ¹¹·¹ μιμηταί μου γίνεσθε καθὼς κἀγὼ Χριστοῦ.

¹¹·² Ἐπαινῶ δὲ ὑμᾶς ὅτι πάντα μου μέμνησθε καί, καθὼς παρέδωκα ὑμῖν, τὰς παραδόσεις κατέχετε. ¶ ³ θέλω δὲ ὑμᾶς εἰδέναι ὅτι παντὸς ἀνδρὸς ἡ κεφαλὴ ὁ Χριστός ἐστιν, κεφαλὴ δὲ γυναικὸς ὁ ἀνήρ, κεφαλὴ δὲ τοῦ Χριστοῦ ὁ θεός. ⁴ πᾶς ἀνὴρ προσευχόμενος ἢ προφητεύων κατὰ κεφαλῆς ἔχων καταισχύνει τὴν κεφαλὴν αὐτοῦ. ⁵ πᾶσα δὲ γυνὴ προσευχομένη ἢ προφητεύουσα ἀκατακαλύπτῳ τῇ κεφαλῇ καταισχύνει τὴν κεφαλὴν αὐτῆς· ἓν γάρ ἐστιν καὶ τὸ αὐτὸ τῇ ἐξυρημένῃ. ⁶ εἰ γὰρ οὐ κατακαλύπτεται γυνή, καὶ κειράσθω· εἰ δὲ αἰσχρὸν γυναικὶ τὸ κείρασθαι ἢ ξυρᾶσθαι, κατακαλυπτέσθω. ⁷ ἀνὴρ μὲν γὰρ οὐκ ὀφείλει κατακαλύπτεσθαι τὴν κεφαλὴν εἰκὼν καὶ δόξα θεοῦ ὑπάρχων· ἡ γυνὴ δὲ δόξα ἀνδρός ἐστιν. ⁸ οὐ γάρ ἐστιν ἀνὴρ ἐκ γυναικὸς

man. **8** For man did not come from woman, but woman from man; **9** neither was man created for woman,
ἀνδρός γὰρ ἀνήρ ἐστιν οὐ ἐκ γυναικὸς ἀλλὰ γυνὴ ἐξ ἀνδρός γὰρ καὶ οὐκ ➚ ἀνὴρ ἐκτίσθη διὰ τὴν γυναῖκα
n.gsm cj n.nsm v.pai.3s pl p.g n.gsf cj n.nsf p.g n.gsm cj adv pl n.nsm v.api.3s p.a d.asf n.asf
467 1142 467 1639 4024 1666 1222 247 1222 1666 467 1142 2779 4024 3231 467 3231 1328 3836 1222

but woman for man. **10** For this reason, and because of the angels, the woman ought to have a sign of
ἀλλὰ γυνὴ διὰ τὸν ἄνδρα διὰ τοῦτο ← διὰ ← τοὺς ἀγγέλους ἡ γυνὴ ὀφείλει ➙ ἔχειν
cj n.nsf p.a d.asm n.asm p.a r.asn p.a d.apm n.apm d.nsf n.nsf v.pai.3s f.pa
247 1222 1328 3836 467 1328 4047 1328 3836 34 3836 1222 4053 2400

authority on her head. ¶ **11** In the Lord, however, woman is not independent of man, nor is man
ἐξουσίαν ἐπὶ τῆς κεφαλῆς ἐν κυρίῳ πλὴν γυνὴ οὔτε χωρὶς ← ἀνδρὸς οὔτε ἀνὴρ
n.asf p.g d.gsf n.gsf p.d n.dsm cj n.nsf cj p.g n.gsm cj n.nsm
2026 2093 3836 3051 1877 3261 4440 1222 4046 6006 467 4046 467

independent of woman. **12** For as woman came from man, so also man *is born* of woman. But
χωρὶς ← γυναικὸς γὰρ ὥσπερ ἡ γυνὴ ἐκ τοῦ ἀνδρός οὕτως καὶ ὁ ἀνὴρ διὰ τῆς γυναικός δὲ
p.g n.gsf cj d.nsf n.nsf p.g d.gsm n.gsm adv adv d.nsm n.nsm p.g d.gsf n.gsf cj
6006 1222 1142 6061 3836 1222 1666 3836 467 4048 2779 3836 467 1328 3836 1222 1254

everything comes from God. **13** Judge for yourselves: Is it proper for a woman to pray to God with
τὰ πάντα ἐκ τοῦ θεοῦ κρίνατε Ἐν ὑμῖν αὐτοῖς ἐστὶ πρέπον γυναῖκα προσεύχεσθαι τῷ θεῷ
d.npn a.npn p.g d.gsm n.gsm v.aam.2p p.d r.dp.2 r.dpm v.pai.3s pt.pa.nsn n.asf f.pm d.dsm n.dsm
3836 4246 1666 3836 2536 3212 1877 7007 899 1639 4560 1222 4667 3836 2536

her head uncovered? **14** Does not the very nature of things teach you that if a man has long hair, it is a
ἀκατακάλυπτον οὐδὲ ἡ αὐτὴ φύσις διδάσκει ὑμᾶς ὅτι μὲν ἐὰν ἀνὴρ ➙ ➙ κομᾷ ➙ ἐστιν
a.asf pl d.nsf r.nsf n.nsf v.pai.3s r.ap.2 cj pl cj n.nsm v.pas.3s v.pai.3s
184 1438 4028 3836 899 5882 1438 7007 4022 3525 1569 467 3150 1639

disgrace to him, **15** but that if a woman has long hair, it is her glory? For long hair is given to her as a
ἀτιμία αὐτῷ δὲ ἐὰν γυνὴ ➙ ➙ κομᾷ ➙ ἐστιν αὐτῇ δόξα ὅτι ➙ ἡ κόμη ➙ δέδοται αὐτῇ ἀντὶ
n.nsf r.dsm.3 cj cj n.nsf v.pas.3s v.pai.3s r.dsf.3 n.nsf cj d.nsf n.nsf v.rpi.3s r.dsf.3 p.g
871 899 1254 1569 1222 3150 1639 899 1518 4022 3836 3151 1443 899 505

covering. **16** If anyone wants to be contentious about this, we have no other practice nor do the
περιβολαίου δὲ Εἰ τις δοκεῖ εἶναι φιλόνεικος ἡμεῖς ἔχομεν οὐκ τοιαύτην συνήθειαν οὐδὲ αἱ
n.gsn cj cj r.nsm v.pai.3s f.pa a.nsm r.np.1 v.pai.1p pl r.asf n.asf cj d.npf
4316 1254 1623 5516 1506 1639 5809 7005 2400 4024 5525 5311 4028 3836

churches of God.
ἐκκλησίαι τοῦ θεοῦ
n.npf d.gsm n.gsm
1711 3836 2536

The Lord's Supper

11:17 In the following directives I have no praise for you, for your meetings do more harm than
δὲ Τοῦτο παραγγέλλων ➙ ➙ οὐκ ἐπαινῶ ὅτι ➙ συνέρχεσθε ➙ εἰς τὸ ἧσσον ἀλλὰ οὐκ
cj r.asn pt.pa.nsm pl v.pai.1s cj v.pmi.2p p.a d.asn a.asn.c cj pl
1254 4047 4133 2046 2046 4024 2046 4022 5302 1650 3836 2482 247 4024

good. **18** In the first place, I hear that when you come together as a church, there are
εἰς τὸ κρεῖσσον γὰρ μὲν ➙ πρῶτον ➙ ἀκούω ➙ ὑμῶν συνερχομένων ἐν ἐκκλησίᾳ ὑπάρχειν
p.a d.asn a.asn.c cj pl adv v.pai.1s r.gp.2 pt.pm.gpm p.d n.dsf f.pa
1650 3836 3202 1142 3525 4754 201 5302 7007 5302 1877 1711 5639

divisions among you, and to some extent I believe it. **19** *No doubt* *there have* to be differences among you
σχίσματα ἐν ὑμῖν καὶ ➙ τι μέρος ➙ πιστεύω γὰρ δεῖ καὶ ➙ εἶναι αἱρέσεις ἐν ὑμῖν
n.apn p.d r.dp.2 cj r.asn n.asn v.pai.1s cj v.pai.3s adv f.pa n.apf p.d r.dp.2
5388 1877 7007 2779 5516 3538 4409 1142 1256 2779 1639 146 1877 7007

to show which of you have God's approval. **20** When you come together, it is
[καὶ] ἵνα φανεροὶ ἐν ὑμῖν γένωνται οἱ δόκιμοι οὖν ὑμῶν Συνερχομένων ➙ ἐπὶ τὸ αὐτὸ ➙ ἐστιν
adv cj a.npm p.d r.dp.2 v.ams.3p d.npm a.npm cj r.gp.2 pt.pm.gpm p.a d.asn r.asn v.pai.3s
2779 2671 5745 1877 7007 1181 3836 1511 4036 5302 7007 5302 2093 3836 899 1639

not the Lord's Supper you eat, **21** for as you eat, each of you goes ahead without
οὐκ κυριακὸν δεῖπνον ➙ φαγεῖν γὰρ ἐν τῷ φαγεῖν ἕκαστος προλαμβάνει ← τὸ ἴδιον δεῖπνον
pl a.asn n.asn f.aa cj p.d d.dsn f.aa r.nsm v.pai.3s d.asn a.asn n.asn
4024 3258 1270 2266 1142 1877 3836 2266 1667 4624 3836 2625 1270

ἀλλὰ γυνὴ ἐξ ἀνδρός· **9** καὶ γὰρ οὐκ ἐκτίσθη ἀνὴρ διὰ τὴν γυναῖκα, ἀλλὰ γυνὴ διὰ τὸν ἄνδρα. **10** διὰ τοῦτο ὀφείλει ἡ γυνὴ ἐξουσίαν ἔχειν ἐπὶ τῆς κεφαλῆς διὰ τοὺς ἀγγέλους. ¶ **11** πλὴν οὔτε γυνὴ χωρὶς ἀνδρὸς οὔτε ἀνὴρ χωρὶς γυναικὸς ἐν κυρίῳ· **12** ὥσπερ γὰρ ἡ γυνὴ ἐκ τοῦ ἀνδρός, οὕτως καὶ ὁ ἀνὴρ διὰ τῆς γυναικός· τὰ δὲ πάντα ἐκ τοῦ θεοῦ. **13** ἐν ὑμῖν αὐτοῖς κρίνατε· πρέπον ἐστὶν γυναῖκα ἀκατακάλυπτον τῷ θεῷ προσεύχεσθαι; **14** οὐδὲ ἡ φύσις αὐτὴ διδάσκει ὑμᾶς ὅτι ἀνὴρ μὲν ἐὰν κομᾷ ἀτιμία αὐτῷ ἐστιν, **15** γυνὴ δὲ ἐὰν κομᾷ δόξα αὐτῇ ἐστιν; ὅτι ἡ κόμη ἀντὶ περιβολαίου δέδοται [αὐτῇ]. **16** Εἰ δέ τις δοκεῖ φιλόνεικος εἶναι, ἡμεῖς τοιαύτην συνήθειαν οὐκ ἔχομεν οὐδὲ αἱ ἐκκλησίαι τοῦ θεοῦ.

11:17 Τοῦτο δὲ παραγγέλλων οὐκ ἐπαινῶ ὅτι οὐκ εἰς τὸ κρεῖσσον ἀλλὰ εἰς τὸ ἧσσον συνέρχεσθε. **18** πρῶτον μὲν γὰρ συνερχομένων ὑμῶν ἐν ἐκκλησίᾳ ἀκούω σχίσματα ἐν ὑμῖν ὑπάρχειν καὶ μέρος τι πιστεύω· **19** δεῖ γὰρ καὶ αἱρέσεις ἐν ὑμῖν εἶναι, ἵνα [καὶ] οἱ δόκιμοι φανεροὶ γένωνται ἐν ὑμῖν. **20** Συνερχομένων οὖν ὑμῶν ἐπὶ τὸ αὐτὸ οὐκ ἔστιν κυριακὸν δεῖπνον φαγεῖν· **21** ἕκαστος γὰρ τὸ ἴδιον δεῖπνον προλαμβάνει ἐν τῷ φαγεῖν, καὶ ὃς μὲν πεινᾷ ὃς δὲ μεθύει. **22** μὴ γὰρ οἰκίας οὐκ ἔχετε

waiting for anybody else. | One remains hungry, | another gets drunk. **22** | Don't you have homes to
καὶ μὲν ὃς → | πεινᾷ δὲ ὃς → μεθύει | γὰρ μὴ οὐκ → ἔχετε οἰκίας εἰς
cj pl r.nsm | v.pai.3s pl r.nsm v.pai.3s | cj pl pl v.pai.2p n.apf p.a
2779 3525 4005 | 4277 1254 4005 3501 | 1142 3590 4024 2400 3864 1650

eat | and drink in? Or do you despise | the church | of God | and humiliate | those who have | nothing?
ⸯτὸ ἐσθίεινⸯ καὶ πίνειν ἢ → → καταφρονεῖτε τῆς ἐκκλησίας → ⸯτοῦ θεοῦⸯ καὶ καταισχύνετε τοὺς ← ἔχοντας μὴ
d.asn f.pa cj f.pa cj v.pai.2p d.gsf n.gsf d.gsm n.gsm cj v.pai.2p d.apm pt.pa.apm pl
3836 2266 2779 4403 2445 2969 3836 1711 3836 2536 2779 2875 3836 2400 3590

What shall I say to you? Shall I praise you for this? Certainly not! | ¶ | **23** For I | received from the
τί → → εἴπω → ὑμῖν → ἐπαινέσω ὑμᾶς ἐν τούτῳ οὐκ ἐπαινῶ | | γὰρ Ἐγω παρέλαβον ἀπὸ τοῦ
r.asn v.aas.1s r.dp.2 v.aas.1s r.ap.2 p.d r.dsn pl v.pai.1s | | cj r.ns.1 v.aai.1s p.g d.gsm
5515 3306 7007 2046 7007 1877 4047 4024 2046 | | 1142 1609 4161 608 3836

Lord what I also passed on to you: | The Lord Jesus, on the night | he was betrayed, took bread, **24** and
κυρίου ὃ → καὶ παρέδωκα ← → ὑμῖν ὅτι ὁ κύριος Ἰησοῦς ἐν τῇ νυκτὶ ᾗ → παρεδίδετο ἔλαβεν ἄρτον καὶ
n.gsm r.asn adv v.aai.1s r.dp.2 cj d.nsm n.nsm n.nsm p.d d.dsf n.dsf r.dsf v.imi.3s v.aai.3s n.asm cj
3261 4005 4140 2779 4140 7007 4022 3836 3261 2652 1877 3836 3816 4005 4140 3284 788 2779

when he had given thanks, | he broke it and said, "This is my body, | which is for you; do this in
→ → → εὐχαριστήσας → ἔκλασεν καὶ εἶπεν Τοῦτό ἐστιν τὸ σῶμα τὸ ὑπὲρ ὑμῶν ποιεῖτε τοῦτο εἰς
pt.aa.nsm v.aai.3s cj v.aai.3s r.nsn v.pai.3s r.gs.1 d.nsn n.nsn d.nsn p.g r.gp.2 v.pam.2p r.asn p.a
2373 3089 2779 3306 4047 1639 1609 3836 5393 3836 5642 7007 4472 4047 1650

remembrance of me." **25** In the same way, after supper | he took the cup, saying, "This cup is
ⸯτὴν ἀνάμνησινⸯ ἐμὴν καὶ → ὡσαύτως ← μετὰ ⸯτὸ δειπνῆσαιⸯ τὸ ποτήριον λέγων τοῦτο ⸯτὸ ποτήριονⸯ ἐστὶν
d.asf n.asf r.asf.1 adv adv p.a d.asn f.aa d.asn n.asn pt.pa.nsm r.nsn d.nsn n.nsn v.pai.3s
3836 390 1847 2779 6058 3552 3836 1268 3836 4539 3306 4047 3836 4539 1639

the new covenant in my blood; do this, whenever you drink it, in remembrance of me." **26** For whenever
ἡ καινὴ διαθήκη ἐν ἐμῷ ⸯτῷ αἵματιⸯ ποιεῖτε τοῦτο ⸯὁσάκιςⸯ ἐὰν → πίνητε εἰς ⸯτὴν ἀνάμνησινⸯ ἐμὴν γὰρ ⸯὁσάκιςⸯ ἐὰν
d.nsf a.nsf n.nsf p.d r.dsn.1 d.dsn n.dsn v.pam.2p r.asn adv pl v.pas.2p p.a d.asf n.asf r.asf.1 cj adv pl
3836 2785 1347 1877 1847 3836 135 4472 4047 4006 1569 4403 1650 3836 390 1847 1142 4006 1569

you eat this bread and drink this cup, you proclaim the Lord's death until he comes. ¶
→ ἐσθίητε τοῦτον ⸯτὸν ἄρτονⸯ καὶ πίνητε τὸ ποτήριον → καταγγέλλετε τὸν ⸯτοῦ κυρίουⸯ θάνατον ἄχρι οὗ → ἔλθη
v.pas.2p r.asm d.asm n.asm cj v.pas.2p d.asn n.asn v.pai.2p d.asm d.gsm n.gsm n.asm p.gs r.gsm v.aas.3s
2266 4047 3836 788 2779 4403 3836 4539 2859 3836 3836 3261 2505 948 4005 2262

27 Therefore, whoever eats the bread or drinks the cup of the Lord in an unworthy manner will be guilty of
Ὥστε ⸯὃς ἂνⸯ ἐσθίῃ τὸν ἄρτον ἢ πίνῃ τὸ ποτήριον → τοῦ κυρίου → ἀναξίως ← → ἔσται ἔνοχος
cj r.nsm pl v.pas.3s d.asm n.asm cj v.pas.3s d.asn n.asn d.gsm n.gsm adv v.fmi.3s a.nsm
6063 4005 323 2266 3836 788 2445 4403 3836 4539 3836 3261 397 1639 1944

sinning against the body and blood of the Lord. **28** A man ought to examine himself before he
← → τοῦ σώματος καὶ ⸯτοῦ αἵματοςⸯ → τοῦ κυρίου δὲ ἄνθρωπος → δοκιμαζέτω ἑαυτὸν καὶ οὕτως →
d.gsn n.gsn cj d.gsn n.gsn d.gsm n.gsm cj n.nsm v.pam.3s r.asm.3 cj adv
3836 5393 2779 3836 135 3836 3261 1254 476 1507 1571 2779 4048

eats of the bread and drinks of the cup. **29** For anyone who eats and drinks without recognizing the body of
ἐσθιέτω ἐκ τοῦ ἄρτου καὶ πινέτω ἐκ τοῦ ποτηρίου γὰρ ὁ ← ἐσθίων καὶ πίνων μὴ διακρίνων τὸ σῶμα
v.pam.3s p.g d.gsm n.gsm cj v.pam.3s p.g d.gsm n.gsn cj d.nsm pt.pa.nsm cj pt.pa.nsm pl pt.pa.nsm d.asn n.asn
2266 1666 3836 788 2779 4403 1666 3836 4539 1142 3836 2266 2779 4403 3590 1359 3836 5393

the Lord eats and drinks judgment on himself. **30** *That is why* many among you are weak and sick, and a
ἐσθίει καὶ πίνει κρίμα → ἑαυτῷ ⸯδιὰ τοῦτοⸯ πολλοὶ ἐν ὑμῖν ἀσθενεῖς καὶ ἄρρωστοι καὶ
v.pai.3s cj v.pai.3s n.asn r.dsm.3 p.a r.asn a.npm p.d r.dp.2 a.npm cj a.npm cj
2266 2779 4403 3210 1571 1328 4047 4498 1877 7007 822 2779 779 2779

number of you have fallen asleep. **31** But if we judged ourselves, we would not come under judgment. **32** When
ἱκανοί ← ← κοιμῶνται δὲ εἰ διεκρίνομεν ἑαυτοὺς → ἂν οὐκ → ἐκρινόμεθα δὲ →
a.npm v.ppi.3p cj cj v.iai.1p r.apm.2 pl pl v.ipi.1p cj
2653 3121 1254 1623 1359 1571 323 4024 3212 1254

we are judged by the Lord, we are being disciplined so that we will not be condemned with the world. ¶
→ → κρινόμενοι ὑπὸ τοῦ κυρίου → → παιδευόμεθα ἵνα ← → → μὴ → κατακριθῶμεν σὺν τῷ κόσμῳ
pt.pp.npm p.g d.gsm n.gsm v.ppi.1p cj pl v.aps.1p p.d d.dsm n.dsm
3212 5679 3836 3261 4084 2671 3590 2891 5250 3836 3180

εἰς τὸ ἐσθίειν καὶ πίνειν; ἢ τῆς ἐκκλησίας τοῦ θεοῦ καταφρονεῖτε, καὶ καταισχύνετε τοὺς μὴ ἔχοντας; τί εἴπω ὑμῖν; ἐπαινέσω ὑμᾶς; ἐν τούτῳ οὐκ ἐπαινῶ. ¶ ²³ Ἐγὼ γὰρ παρέλαβον ἀπὸ τοῦ κυρίου, ὃ καὶ παρέδωκα ὑμῖν, ὅτι ὁ κύριος Ἰησοῦς ἐν τῇ νυκτὶ ᾗ παρεδίδετο ἔλαβεν ἄρτον ²⁴ καὶ εὐχαριστήσας ἔκλασεν καὶ εἶπεν, Τοῦτό μού ἐστιν τὸ σῶμα τὸ ὑπὲρ ὑμῶν· τοῦτο ποιεῖτε εἰς τὴν ἐμὴν ἀνάμνησιν. ²⁵ ὡσαύτως καὶ τὸ ποτήριον μετὰ τὸ δειπνῆσαι λέγων, Τοῦτο τὸ ποτήριον ἡ καινὴ διαθήκη ἐστὶν ἐν τῷ ἐμῷ αἵματι· τοῦτο ποιεῖτε, ὁσάκις ἐὰν πίνητε, εἰς τὴν ἐμὴν ἀνάμνησιν. ²⁶ ὁσάκις γὰρ ἐὰν ἐσθίητε τὸν ἄρτον τοῦτον καὶ τὸ ποτήριον πίνητε, τὸν θάνατον τοῦ κυρίου καταγγέλλετε ἄχρις οὗ ἔλθη. ¶ ²⁷ Ὥστε ὃς ἂν ἐσθίῃ τὸν ἄρτον ἢ πίνῃ τὸ ποτήριον τοῦ κυρίου ἀναξίως, ἔνοχος ἔσται τοῦ σώματος καὶ τοῦ αἵματος τοῦ κυρίου. ²⁸ δοκιμαζέτω δὲ ἄνθρωπος ἑαυτὸν καὶ οὕτως ἐκ τοῦ ἄρτου ἐσθιέτω καὶ ἐκ τοῦ ποτηρίου πινέτω· ²⁹ ὁ γὰρ ἐσθίων καὶ πίνων κρίμα ἑαυτῷ ἐσθίει καὶ πίνει μὴ διακρίνων τὸ σῶμα «σῶμα.» τοῦ κυρίου ³⁰ διὰ τοῦτο ἐν ὑμῖν πολλοὶ ἀσθενεῖς καὶ ἄρρωστοι καὶ κοιμῶνται ἱκανοί. ³¹ εἰ δὲ ἑαυτοὺς διεκρίνομεν, οὐκ ἂν ἐκρινόμεθα· ³² κρινόμενοι δὲ ὑπὸ [τοῦ] κυρίου παιδευόμεθα, ἵνα μὴ σὺν τῷ κόσμῳ κατακριθῶμεν. ¶ ³³ ὥστε, ἀδελφοί μου,

33 So then, my brothers, when you come together to eat, wait for each other. **34** If anyone is
Ὥστε ← μου ἀδελφοί → → συνερχόμενοι ← εἰς τὸ φαγεῖν, ἐκδέχεσθε ἀλλήλους → εἴ τις →
cj   r.gs.1 n.vpm   pt.pm.npm   p.a d.asn f.aa v.pmm.2p   r.apm   cj r.nsm
6063   1609 81   5302   1650 3836 2266 1683   253   1623 5516

hungry, he should eat at home, so that when you meet together it may not result in judgment. ¶ And
πεινᾷ → → ἐσθιέτω ἐν οἴκῳ ἵνα → → συνέρχησθε → → μὴ εἰς κρίμα δὲ
v.pai.3s   v.pam.3s p.d n.dsm cj   v.pms.2p   pl p.a n.asn cj
4277   2266 1877 3875 2671   5302   3590 1650 3210 1254

when I come I will give further directions.
ὡς ἂν ἔλθω → → διατάξομαι τὰ λοιπὰ ←
cj pl v.aas.1s   v.fmi.1s d.apn a.apn
6055 323 2262   1411 3836 3370

Spiritual Gifts

12:1 Now about spiritual gifts, brothers, I do not want you to be ignorant. **2** You know that when you
δὲ Περὶ τῶν πνευματικῶν ← ἀδελφοί → οὐ θέλω ὑμᾶς → → ἀγνοεῖν → Οἴδατε ὅτι ὅτε →
cj p.g d.gpn   n.vpm   pl v.pai.1s r.ap.2   f.pa   v.rai.2p cj cj
1254 4309 3836 4461   81   2527 2527 4024 2527 7007   51   3857 4022 4021

were pagans, *somehow or other* you were influenced and led astray to mute idols. **3** Therefore I
ἦτε ἔθνη ὡς ἂν → → ἤγεσθε → ἀπαγόμενοι πρὸς τὰ ἄφωνα τὰ εἴδωλα διὸ
v.iai.2p n.npn cj pl   v.ipi.2p   pt.pp.npm p.a d.apn a.apn d.apn n.apn cj
1639 1620 6055 323   72   552 4639 3836 936 3836 1631 1475

tell you that no one who is speaking by the Spirit of God says, "Jesus be cursed," and no one can
γνωρίζω ὑμῖν ὅτι οὐδεὶς → → λαλῶν ἐν πνεύματι → θεοῦ λέγει Ἰησοῦς Ἀνάθεμα καὶ οὐδεὶς ← δύναται
v.pai.1s r.dp.2 cj a.nsm   pt.pa.nsm p.d   n.dsn   n.gsm v.pai.3s n.nsm n.nsn cj a.nsm v.ppi.3s
1192 7007 4022 4029   3281 1877   4460   2536 3306 2652 353 2779 4029 1538

say, "Jesus is Lord," except by the Holy Spirit. ¶ **4** There are different kinds of gifts, but the
εἰπεῖν Ἰησοῦς Κύριος εἰ μὴ ἐν ἁγίῳ πνεύματι δὲ → εἰσίν Διαιρέσεις ← χαρισμάτων δὲ τὸ
f.aa n.nsm n.nsm cj pl p.d a.dsn n.dsn   cj   v.pai.3p n.npf   n.gpn cj d.nsn
3306 2652 3261 1623 3590 1877 41 4460   1254   1639 1348   5922 1254 3836

same Spirit. **5** There are different kinds of service, but the same Lord. **6** There are different kinds of
αὐτὸ πνεῦμα καὶ → εἰσίν διαιρέσεις ← → διακονιῶν καὶ ὁ αὐτὸς κύριος καὶ → εἰσίν διαιρέσεις ← →
r.nsn n.nsn cj   v.pai.3p n.npf   n.gpf cj d.nsm r.nsm n.nsm cj   v.pai.3p n.npf
899 4460 2779   1639 1348   1355 2779 3836 899 3261 2779   1639 1348

working, but the same God works all of them in all men. ¶ **7** Now to each one the
ἐνεργημάτων δὲ ὁ αὐτὸς θεὸς ὁ ἐνεργῶν τὰ πάντα ← ἐν πᾶσιν ← δὲ → ἑκάστῳ ἡ
n.gpn cj d.nsm r.nsm n.nsm d.nsm pt.pa.nsm d.apn a.apn   p.d a.dpm   cj   r.dsm d.nsf
1920 1254 3836 899 2536 3836 1919 3836 4246   1877 4246   1254   1667 3836

manifestation of the Spirit is given for the common good. **8** To one there is given through the Spirit
φανέρωσις → τοῦ πνεύματος → δίδοται πρὸς τὸ συμφέρον ← γὰρ μὲν ᾧ → → δίδοται διὰ τοῦ πνεύματος
n.nsf d.gsn n.gsn   v.ppi.3s p.g d.asn pt.pa.asn   cj pl r.dsm   v.ppi.3s p.g d.gsn n.gsn
5748 3836 4460   1443 4639 3836 5237   1142 3525 4005   1443 1328 3836 4460

the message of wisdom, to another the message of knowledge by means of the same Spirit, **9** to another faith by
λόγος → σοφίας δὲ ἄλλῳ λόγος → γνώσεως κατὰ ← τὸ αὐτὸ πνεῦμα → ἑτέρῳ πίστις ἐν
n.nsm n.gsf pl r.dsm n.nsm   n.gsf p.a   d.asn r.asn n.asn   r.dsm n.nsf p.d
3364 5053 1254 257 3364   1194 2848   3836 899 4460   2283 4411 1877

the same Spirit, to another gifts of healing by that one Spirit, **10** to another miraculous powers,
τῷ αὐτῷ πνεύματι δὲ ἄλλῳ χάρισμα → ἰαμάτων ἐν τῷ ἑνὶ πνεύματι → ἄλλῳ ἐνεργήματα δυνάμεων [δὲ]
d.dsn r.dsn n.dsn pl r.dsm n.nsn   n.gpn p.d d.dsn a.dsn n.dsn   r.dsm n.npn n.gpf   pl
3836 899 4460 1254 257 5922   2611 1877 3836 1651 4460   257 1920 1539   1254

to another prophecy, to another distinguishing between spirits, to another speaking in different kinds of
→ ἄλλῳ προφητεία [δὲ] → ἄλλῳ διακρίσεις ← πνευμάτων ἑτέρῳ → → γένη →
r.dsm n.nsf   pl   r.dsm n.npf   n.gpn r.dsm   n.npn
257 4735   1254   257 1360   4460 2283   1169

tongues, and to still another the interpretation of tongues. **11** All these are the work of one and the same
γλωσσῶν δὲ → ἄλλῳ ἑρμηνεία → γλωσσῶν δὲ πάντα ταῦτα → → ἐνεργεῖ τὸ ἓν καὶ τὸ αὐτὸ
n.gpf pl   r.dsm n.nsf   n.gpf cj a.apn r.apn   v.pai.3s d.nsn a.nsn cj d.nsn r.nsn
1185 1254   257 2255   1185 1254 4246 4047   1919 3836 1651 2779 3836 899

συνερχόμενοι εἰς τὸ φαγεῖν ἀλλήλους ἐκδέχεσθε. ³⁴ εἴ τις πεινᾷ, ἐν οἴκῳ ἐσθιέτω, ἵνα μὴ εἰς κρίμα συνέρχησθε. ¶ Τὰ δὲ λοιπὰ ὡς ἂν ἔλθω διατάξομαι.

12:1 Περὶ δὲ τῶν πνευματικῶν, ἀδελφοί, οὐ θέλω ὑμᾶς ἀγνοεῖν. ² Οἴδατε ὅτι ὅτε ἔθνη ἦτε πρὸς τὰ εἴδωλα τὰ ἄφωνα ὡς ἂν ἤγεσθε ἀπαγόμενοι. ³ διὸ γνωρίζω ὑμῖν ὅτι οὐδεὶς ἐν πνεύματι θεοῦ λαλῶν λέγει, Ἀνάθεμα Ἰησοῦς, καὶ οὐδεὶς δύναται εἰπεῖν, Κύριος Ἰησοῦς, εἰ μὴ ἐν πνεύματι ἁγίῳ. ¶ ⁴ Διαιρέσεις δὲ χαρισμάτων εἰσίν, τὸ δὲ αὐτὸ πνεῦμα· ⁵ καὶ διαιρέσεις διακονιῶν εἰσιν, καὶ ὁ αὐτὸς κύριος· ⁶ καὶ διαιρέσεις ἐνεργημάτων εἰσίν, ὁ δὲ αὐτὸς θεὸς ὁ ἐνεργῶν τὰ πάντα ἐν πᾶσιν. ¶ ⁷ ἑκάστῳ δὲ δίδοται ἡ φανέρωσις τοῦ πνεύματος πρὸς τὸ συμφέρον. ⁸ ᾧ μὲν γὰρ διὰ τοῦ πνεύματος δίδοται λόγος σοφίας, ἄλλῳ δὲ λόγος γνώσεως κατὰ τὸ αὐτὸ πνεῦμα, ⁹ ἑτέρῳ πίστις ἐν τῷ αὐτῷ πνεύματι, ἄλλῳ δὲ χαρίσματα ἰαμάτων ἐν τῷ ἑνὶ πνεύματι, ¹⁰ ἄλλῳ δὲ ἐνεργήματα δυνάμεων, ἄλλῳ [δὲ] προφητεία, ἄλλῳ [δὲ] διακρίσεις πνευμάτων, ἑτέρῳ γένη γλωσσῶν, ἄλλῳ δὲ ἑρμηνεία γλωσσῶν· ¹¹ πάντα δὲ ταῦτα ἐνεργεῖ τὸ ἓν καὶ τὸ αὐτὸ πνεῦμα διαιροῦν ἰδίᾳ ἑκάστῳ καθὼς βούλεται.

Spirit, and he gives   them to each   one, just   as he determines.
πνεῦμα   →   διαιροῦν   → ἑκάστῳ ἰδίᾳ καθὼς ←   βούλεται
n.nsn   pt.pa.nsn   r.dsm   a.dsf cj   v.pmi.3s
4460   1349   1667   2625   2777   1089

One Body, Many Parts

12:12   The   body is   a unit, though it is made   up of many   parts; and though all   its
γὰρ τὸ Καθάπερ σῶμα ἔστιν ἕν   καὶ   →   ἔχει   ←   πολλὰ μέλη δὲ →   πάντα ⌜τοῦ σώματος⌝
cj   d.nsn   n.nsn v.pai.3s a.nsn cj   v.pai.3s   a.apn n.apn cj   a.npn d.gsn n.gsn
1142 3836 2749   5393 1639   1651 2779   2400   4498 3517 1254   4246   3836 5393

parts   are   many, they form one body. So   it is with Christ.   **13** For we   were all   baptized   by
⌜τὰ μέλη⌝ ὄντα πολλὰ →   ἐστιν ἕν σῶμα οὕτως καὶ   ὁ Χριστός· γὰρ ἡμεῖς καὶ → πάντες ἐβαπτίσθημεν ἐν
d.npn n.npn pt.pa.npn a.npn   v.pai.3s a.nsn n.nsn adv   adv   d.nsm n.nsm   cj r.np.1 adv   a.npm v.api.1p   p.d
3836 3517 1639 4498   1639   1651 5393 4048 2779   3836 5986   1142 7005 2779   4246   966   1877

one Spirit   into one body – whether Jews   or   Greeks,   slave or   free   – and we were all   given the one
ἑνὶ πνεύματι εἰς ἓν σῶμα   εἴτε   Ἰουδαῖοι εἴτε Ἕλληνες εἴτε δοῦλοι εἴτε ἐλεύθεροι καὶ → → πάντες   →   ἓν
a.dsn n.dsn p.a a.asn n.asn   cj   n.npm cj   n.npm   cj   n.npm cj   a.npm   cj   a.npm   a.asn
1651 4460   1650 1651 5393   1664   2681   1664 1818   1664 1529   1664 1801   2779   4540 4540 4246   4540   1651

Spirit to drink. ¶ **14** Now   the body is   not made up of one part but of many. **15** If   the foot should
πνεῦμα → ἐποτίσθημεν   γὰρ Καὶ τὸ σῶμα ἔστιν οὐκ   ἓν μέλος ἀλλὰ πολλά   ἐὰν ὁ πούς →
n.asn   v.api.1p   cj adv d.nsn n.nsn v.pai.3s pl   a.nsn n.nsn cj   a.npn   cj d.nsm n.nsm
4460   4540   1142 2779 3836 5393 1639 4024   1651 3517 247   4498   1569 3836 4546

say, "Because I am   not a hand, I   do not belong to the body," it would not for   that reason cease to be   part
εἴπη ὅτι → εἰμι οὐκ χείρ → → οὐκ εἰμι ἐκ τοῦ σώματος   οὐ παρὰ τοῦτο ←   οὐκ ἔστιν ἐκ
v.aas.3s cj   v.pai.1s pl n.nsf   pl v.pai.1s p.g d.gsn n.gsn   pl p.a r.asn   pl   v.pai.3s p.g
3306 4022   1639 4024 5931   1639 1639 4024 1639 1666 3836 5393   4024 4123 4047   4024 1639 1666

of the body. **16** And if   the ear should say, "Because I am   not an eye,   I   do not belong to the body," it
⌜ τοῦ σώματος⌝ καὶ ἐὰν τὸ οὖς →   εἴπη ὅτι → εἰμι οὐκ ὀφθαλμός → → οὐκ εἰμι ἐκ τοῦ σώματος
d.gsn n.gsn   cj cj d.nsn n.nsn   v.aas.3s cj   v.pai.1s pl n.nsm   pl v.pai.1s p.g d.gsn n.gsn
3836 5393   2779 1569 3836 4044   3306 4022   1639 4024 4057   1639 1639 4024 1639 1666 3836 5393

would not for   that reason cease to be   part of the body. **17** If the whole body were an eye,   where would the
οὐ παρὰ τοῦτο ←   οὐκ ἔστιν ἐκ ← τοῦ σώματος εἰ τὸ ὅλον σῶμα   ὀφθαλμός ποῦ   ἡ
pl p.a r.asn   pl   v.pai.3s p.g   d.gsn n.gsn cj d.nsn a.nsn n.nsn   n.nsm   cj   d.nsf
4024 4123 4047   4024 1639 1666 3836 5393   1623 3836 3910 5393   4057   4543   3836

sense of hearing be? If   the whole body were an ear, where would the sense of smell   be? **18** But in fact God
→ → ἀκοή   εἰ ὅλον   ἀκοή ποῦ   ἡ → ὄσφρησις   δὲ νυνὶ   ὁ θεὸς
n.nsf   cj   a.nsn   n.nsf adv   d.nsf   n.nsf   cj adv   d.nsm n.nsm
198   1623 3910   198 4543   3836   4018   1254 3815   3836 2536

has arranged the parts in the body, every one of them, just as he wanted them to be. **19** If they were
→ ἔθετο   τὰ μέλη ἐν τῷ σώματι ἕκαστον ἓν → αὐτῶν καθὼς ←   ἠθέλησεν   δὲ εἰ   ἦν
v.ami.3s   d.apn n.apn p.d d.dsn n.dsn r.asn a.asn   r.gpn.3 cj   v.aai.3s   cj cj v.iai.3s
5502   3836 3517 1877 3836 5393 1667 1651   899   2777   2527   1254 1623 1639

all   one part, where would the body be? **20** As it is, there are   many parts, but one body. ¶ **21** The
⌜τὰ πάντα⌝ ἓν μέλος ποῦ   τὸ σῶμα   δὲ νῦν ←   μὲν πολλὰ μέλη δὲ ἓν σῶμα   δὲ ὁ
d.npn a.npn a.nsn n.nsn adv   d.nsn n.nsn cj adv   pl a.npn n.npn cj a.nsn n.nsn   cj d.nsm
3836 4246 1651 3517 4543   3836 5393   1254 3814   3525 4498 3517 1254 1651 5393   1254 3836

eye   cannot   say   to the hand, "I don't need   you!" And   the head cannot say to the feet, "I
ὀφθαλμὸς οὐ δύναται εἰπεῖν τῇ χειρί ⌜ οὐ ⌝χρείαν ἔχω σου ἢ πάλιν ἡ κεφαλὴ   →   τοῖς ποσίν
n.nsm   pl v.ppi.3s f.aa   d.dsf n.dsf   pl n.asf v.pai.1s r.gs.2 cj adv   d.nsf n.nsf   d.dpm n.dpm
4057   4024 1538   3306   3836 5931   4024 5970 2400 5148 2445 4099 3836 3051   3836 4546 2400

don't need   you!" **22** On the contrary,   those parts of the body that seem to be   weaker
οὐκ ⌜χρείαν ἔχω⌝ ὑμῶν   ἀλλὰ πολλῷ μᾶλλον⌝ τὰ μέλη → τοῦ σώματος → δοκοῦντα → ὑπάρχειν ἀσθενέστερα
pl n.asf v.pai.1s r.gp.2   cj   a.dsn adv.c   d.npn n.npn   d.gsn n.gsn   pt.pa.npn   f.pa   a.npn.c
4024 5970 2400 7007   247 4498 3437   3836 3517   3836 5393   1506   5639   822

are indispensable, **23** and the parts   that we think are less honorable   we treat   with
ἐστιν ἀναγκαῖα   καὶ ἃ   → ⌜τοῦ σώματος⌝ → δοκοῦμεν εἶναι → ἀτιμότερα τούτοις → περιτίθεμεν ←
v.pai.3s a.npn   cj r.apn   d.gsn n.gsn   v.pai.1p f.pa   a.apn.c r.dpn   v.pai.1p
1639 338   2779 4005   3836 5393   1506   1639   872   4047   4363

12:12 Καθάπερ γὰρ τὸ σῶμα ἕν ἐστιν καὶ μέλη πολλὰ ἔχει, πάντα δὲ τὰ μέλη τοῦ σώματος πολλὰ ὄντα ἕν ἐστιν σῶμα, οὕτως καὶ ὁ Χριστός· 13 καὶ γὰρ ἐν ἑνὶ πνεύματι ἡμεῖς πάντες εἰς ἓν σῶμα ἐβαπτίσθημεν, εἴτε Ἰουδαῖοι εἴτε Ἕλληνες εἴτε δοῦλοι εἴτε ἐλεύθεροι, καὶ πάντες ἓν πνεῦμα ἐποτίσθημεν. ¶ 14 καὶ γὰρ τὸ σῶμα οὐκ ἔστιν ἓν μέλος ἀλλὰ πολλά. 15 ἐὰν εἴπῃ ὁ πούς, Ὅτι οὐκ εἰμι χείρ, οὐκ εἰμι ἐκ τοῦ σώματος, οὐ παρὰ τοῦτο οὐκ ἔστιν ἐκ τοῦ σώματος; 16 καὶ ἐὰν εἴπῃ τὸ οὖς, Ὅτι οὐκ εἰμι ὀφθαλμός, οὐκ εἰμι ἐκ τοῦ σώματος, οὐ παρὰ τοῦτο οὐκ ἔστιν ἐκ τοῦ σώματος; 17 εἰ ὅλον τὸ σῶμα ὀφθαλμός, ποῦ ἡ ἀκοή; εἰ ὅλον ἀκοή, ποῦ ἡ ὄσφρησις; 18 νυνὶ δὲ ὁ θεὸς ἔθετο τὰ μέλη, ἓν ἕκαστον αὐτῶν ἐν τῷ σώματι καθὼς ἠθέλησεν. 19 εἰ δὲ ἦν τὰ πάντα ἓν μέλος, ποῦ τὸ σῶμα; 20 νῦν δὲ πολλὰ μὲν μέλη, ἓν δὲ σῶμα. ¶ 21 οὐ δύναται δὲ ὁ ὀφθαλμὸς εἰπεῖν τῇ χειρί, Χρείαν σου οὐκ ἔχω, ἢ πάλιν ἡ κεφαλὴ τοῖς ποσίν, Χρείαν ὑμῶν οὐκ ἔχω· 22 ἀλλὰ πολλῷ μᾶλλον τὰ δοκοῦντα μέλη τοῦ σώματος ἀσθενέστερα ὑπάρχειν ἀναγκαῖά ἐστιν, 23 καὶ ἃ δοκοῦμεν ἀτιμότερα εἶναι τοῦ σώματος τούτοις τιμὴν περισσοτέραν περιτίθεμεν, καὶ τὰ

special   honor. And the parts that are unpresentable   are treated with special   modesty,   **24** while our
περισσοτέραν τιμήν   καὶ τὰ ←   ἀσχήμονα   ἡμῶν → ἔχει ←   περισσοτέραν εὐσχημοσύνην δὲ   ἡμῶν
a.asf.c   n.asf   cj   d.npn   a.npn   r.gp.1   v.pai.3s   a.asf.c   n.asf   cj   r.gp.1
4358   5507   2779 3836   860   7005   2400   4358   2362   1254 7005

presentable parts need   no special treatment. But God   has combined   the members of the body and has
ⸯτὰ εὐσχήμοναⸯ ←   ⸯχρείαν ἔχειⸯ οὐ   ἀλλὰ ⸯὁ θεὸςⸯ → συνεκέρασεν   τὸ σῶμα →
d.npn n.npn   n.asf v.pai.3s v   cj   d.nsm n.nsm   v.aai.3s   d.asn n.asn
3836 2363   2363 5970 2400 4024   247 3836 2536   5166   3836 5393

given greater   honor to the parts that lacked it, **25** so that there should be no division in the body, but   that
δοὺς περισσοτέραν τιμήν → τῷ ←   ὑστερουμένῳ   ἵνα   ᾖ   μὴ σχίσμα ἐν τῷ σώματι ἀλλὰ
pt.aa.nsm a.asf.c   n.asf   d.dsn   pt.pp.dsn   cj   v.pas.3s pl n.nsn p.d d.dsn n.dsn cj
1443 4358   5507   3836   5728   2671   1639 3590 5388   1877 3836 5393 247

its parts should have equal   concern   for each   other. **26** If one part suffers, every part   suffers with it;
τὰ μέλη   →   ⸯτὸ αὐτὸⸯ μεριμνῶσιν ὑπὲρ ἀλλήλων ←   καὶ εἴτε ἓν μέλος πάσχει   πάντα ⸯτὰ μέληⸯ συμπάσχει ←   ←
d.npn n.npn   d.asn r.asn v.pas.3p p.g r.gpn   cj cj a.nsn n.nsn v.pai.3s a.npn d.npn n.npn v.pai.3s
3836 3517   3534 3534   3836 899 3534 5642 253   2779 1664 1651 3517 4248   4246 3836 3517   5224

if one part is honored, every part   rejoices with it. ¶   **27** Now you are the body of Christ, and each one
εἴτε ἓν μέλος → δοξάζεται πάντα ⸯτὰ μέληⸯ συγχαίρει ←   ←   δὲ ὑμεῖς ἐστε   σῶμα → Χριστοῦ καὶ →   μέλη
cj a.nsn n.nsn   v.ppi.3s a.npn d.npn n.npn v.ppi.3s   cj r.np.2 v.pai.2p n.nsn   n.gsm   cj   n.npn
1664 1651 3517   1519   4246 3836 3517   5176   1254 7007 1639   5393   5986   2779   3517

of you is a part   of it. **28** And   in the church God   has appointed first of all apostles,   second
ⸯἐκ μέρουςⸯ ←   Καὶ μὲν οὓς ἐν τῇ ἐκκλησίᾳ ὁ θεὸς → ἔθετο   πρῶτον ←   ἀποστόλους δεύτερον
p.g n.gsn   cj   pl r.apm p.d d.dsf n.dsf d.nsm n.nsm v.ami.3s adv   n.apm   adv
1666 3538   2779 3525 4005 1877 3836 1711 3836 2536   5502   4754   693   1311

prophets, third teachers,   then workers of miracles, also those having gifts   of healing, those able to
προφήτας τρίτον διδασκάλους ἔπειτα →   → δυνάμεις ἔπειτα →   χαρίσματα → ἰαμάτων   →
n.apm   adv   n.apm   adv   n.apf   adv   n.apn   n.gpn
4737   5568   1437   2083   1539   2083   5922   2611

help   others, those with gifts of administration, and those speaking in different kinds of tongues. **29** Are all
ἀντιλήμψεις ←   →   →   →   κυβερνήσεις   →   →   →   γένη → γλωσσῶν   μὴ   πάντες
n.apf   n.apf   n.apn   n.gpf   pl   a.npm
516   3236   1185   1185   1185   1169   1185   3590 4246

apostles? Are all   prophets?   Are all teachers?   Do all   work miracles? **30** Do all have gifts
ἀπόστολοι μὴ   πάντες προφῆται   μὴ πάντες διδάσκαλοι μὴ πάντες → δυνάμεις μὴ → πάντες ἔχουσιν χαρίσματα
n.npm pl   a.npm n.npm   pl a.npm n.npm   pl a.npm   n.npf   pl   a.npm v.pai.3p n.apn
693 3590   4246   4737   3590 4246 1437   3590 4246   1539   3590 2400 4246 2400   5922

of healing? Do all   speak in tongues? Do all   interpret? **31** But eagerly desire the greater   gifts.
→ ἰαμάτων μὴ πάντες λαλοῦσιν γλώσσαις μὴ πάντες διερμηνεύουσιν δὲ   ζηλοῦτε τὰ ⸯτὰ μείζοναⸯ χαρίσματα
n.gpn   pl a.npm v.pai.3p n.dpf   pl a.npm v.pai.3p   cj   v.pam.2p d.apn d.apn a.apn.c n.apn
2611   3590 4246 3281   1185   3590 4246 1450   1254 2420   3836 3836 3489   5922

Love

12:31 And now I will show   you the most excellent   way. ¶ **13:1** If   I speak in the tongues of
Καὶ ἔτι → → δείκνυμι ὑμῖν   →   ⸯκαθ' ὑπερβολὴνⸯ ὁδὸν   Ἐὰν → λαλῶ → ταῖς γλώσσαις →
cj   adv   v.pai.1s r.dp.2   p.a n.asf   n.asf   cj   v.pas.1s   d.dpf n.dpf
2779 2285   1259   7007   2848 5651   3847   1569   3281   3836 1185

men   and of angels,   but have not love, I am   only a resounding gong   or a clanging cymbal. **2**
ⸯτῶν ἀνθρώπωνⸯ καὶ → ⸯτῶν ἀγγέλωνⸯ δὲ ἔχω μὴ ἀγάπην → γέγονα   ἠχῶν   χαλκὸς ἢ ἀλαλάζον κύμβαλον καὶ
d.gpm n.gpm   cj   d.gpm n.gpm   cj v.pai.1s pl n.asf   pt.ra.nsm n.nsm   n.nsm   pt.pa.nsn n.nsn   cj
3836 476   2779 3836 34   1254 2400 3590 27   1181   5910   2445 226 3247   2779

If I have the gift of prophecy and can fathom all   mysteries   and all   knowledge, and if I have   a
ἐὰν → ἔχω   προφητείαν καὶ →   εἰδῶ   πάντα ⸯτὰ μυστήριαⸯ καὶ πᾶσαν ⸯτὴν γνῶσινⸯ καὶ ἐὰν → ἔχω πᾶσαν
cj v.pas.1s   n.asf   cj   v.ras.1s a.apn d.apn n.apn   cj   a.asf d.asf n.asf   cj   cj v.pas.1s a.asf
1569 2400   4735   2779   3857   4246 3836 3696   2779 4246 3836 1194   2779 1569 2400 4246

faith   that can move   mountains, but have not love, I am nothing. **3** If I give all I possess   to
ⸯτὴν πίστινⸯ ὥστε → μεθιστάναι ὄρη   δὲ ἔχω μὴ ἀγάπην εἰμι οὐθέν   κἂν → ψωμίσω πάντα μου ⸯτὰ ὑπάρχονταⸯ
d.asf n.asf cj   f.pa   n.apn   cj v.pas.1s pl n.asf v.pai.1s a.nsn   crasis v.aas.1s a.apn r.gs.1 d.apn pt.pa.apn
3836 4411   6063   3496   4001   1254 2400 3590 27   1639 4032   2829 6039   4246 1609 3836 5639

ἀσχήμονα ἡμῶν εὐσχημοσύνην περισσοτέραν ἔχει, 24 τὰ δὲ εὐσχήμονα ἡμῶν οὐ χρείαν ἔχει «ἔχει.» τιμῆς. ἀλλὰ ὁ θεὸς συνεκέρασεν τὸ σῶμα τῷ ὑστερουμένῳ περισσοτέραν δοὺς τιμήν, 25 ἵνα μὴ ᾖ σχίσμα ἐν τῷ σώματι ἀλλὰ τὸ αὐτὸ ὑπὲρ ἀλλήλων μεριμνῶσιν τὰ μέλη. 26 καὶ εἴτε πάσχει ἓν μέλος, συμπάσχει πάντα τὰ μέλη· εἴτε δοξάζεται [ἓν] μέλος, συγχαίρει πάντα τὰ μέλη ¶ 27 Ὑμεῖς δέ ἐστε σῶμα Χριστοῦ καὶ μέλη ἐκ μέρους. 28 καὶ οὓς μὲν ἔθετο ὁ θεὸς ἐν τῇ ἐκκλησίᾳ πρῶτον ἀποστόλους, δεύτερον προφήτας, τρίτον διδασκάλους, ἔπειτα δυνάμεις, ἔπειτα χαρίσματα ἰαμάτων, ἀντιλήμψεις, κυβερνήσεις, γένη γλωσσῶν. 29 μὴ πάντες ἀπόστολοι; μὴ πάντες προφῆται; μὴ πάντες διδάσκαλοι; μὴ πάντες δυνάμεις; 30 μὴ πάντες χαρίσματα ἔχουσιν ἰαμάτων; μὴ πάντες γλώσσαις λαλοῦσιν; μὴ πάντες διερμηνεύουσιν;
12:31 ζηλοῦτε δὲ τὰ χαρίσματα τὰ μείζονα. Καὶ ἔτι καθ' ὑπερβολὴν ὁδὸν ὑμῖν δείκνυμι. 13:1 Ἐὰν ταῖς γλώσσαις τῶν ἀνθρώπων λαλῶ καὶ τῶν ἀγγέλων, ἀγάπην δὲ μὴ ἔχω, γέγονα χαλκὸς ἠχῶν ἢ κύμβαλον ἀλαλάζον. 2 καὶ ἐὰν ἔχω προφητείαν καὶ εἰδῶ τὰ μυστήρια πάντα καὶ πᾶσαν τὴν γνῶσιν καὶ ἐὰν ἔχω πᾶσαν τὴν πίστιν ὥστε ὄρη μεθιστάναι, ἀγάπην δὲ μὴ ἔχω, οὐθέν εἰμι. 3 κἂν ψωμίσω πάντα τὰ ὑπάρχοντά μου καὶ ἐὰν παραδῶ τὸ σῶμά μου ἵνα καυθήσωμαι, «καυχήσωμαι,» ἀγάπην

the poor and　　surrender my body　　　to the flames,　　but have not love, I gain　　nothing. ¶
καὶ ἐὰν παραδῶ　μου ⸆τὸ σῶμα⸆　ἵνα　καυχήσωμαι δὲ ἔχω μὴ ἀγάπην → ὠφελοῦμαι οὐδὲν
cj cj v.aas.1s　r.gs.1 d.asn n.asn cj　v.ams.1s cj v.pas.1s pl n.asf　v.ppi.1s a.asn
2779 1569 4140　1609 3836 5393 2671　3016 1254 2400 3590 27　6067 4029

4 Love　is patient,　love　is kind.　It　does not envy, it　does not boast,　it is not proud.
Ἡ ἀγάπη → μακροθυμεῖ ἡ ἀγάπη, → χρηστεύεται ⸆ → οὐ ζηλοῖ ἡ ἀγάπη, → οὐ περπερεύεται ⸆ → οὐ φυσιοῦται
d.nsf n.nsf v.pai.3s d.nsf n.nsf v.pmi.3s pl v.pai.3s d.nsf n.nsf pl v.pmi.3s pl v.ppi.3s
3836 27 3428 3836 27 5980 2420 2420 4024 2420 3836 27 4371 4024 4371 5881 5881 4024 5881

5 It is not rude,　it is not self-seeking,　it is not easily angered,　it keeps no record of wrongs.　**6** Love
→ → οὐκ ἀσχημονεῖ → → οὐ ⸆ζητεῖ τὰ ἑαυτῆς⸆ → → οὐ → παροξύνεται → οὐ λογίζεται ⸆τὸ κακόν⸆
pl v.pai.3s pl v.pai.3s d.apn r.gsf.3 pl v.ppi.3s pl v.pmi.3s d.asn a.asn
858 858 4024 858 2426 2426 4024 2426 3836 1571 4236 4236 4024 4236 3357 3357 4024 3357 3836 2805

does not delight in evil　but rejoices with the truth.　**7** It always protects, always trusts, always hopes, always
→ οὐ χαίρει ἐπὶ ⸆τῇ ἀδικίᾳ⸆ δὲ συγχαίρει ← τῇ ἀληθείᾳ → πάντα στέγει, πάντα πιστεύει, πάντα ἐλπίζει, πάντα
pl v.pai.3s p.d d.dsf n.dsf cj v.pai.3s d.dsf n.dsf a.apn v.pai.3s a.apn v.pai.3s a.apn v.pai.3s a.apn
5897 4024 5897 2093 3836 94 1254 5176 3836 237 5095 4246 5095 4246 4409 4246 1827 4246

perseveres. ¶　**8** Love　never　fails. But where there are prophecies,　they will cease;　where there are
ὑπομένει　Ἡ ἀγάπη, οὐδέποτε πίπτει δὲ εἴτε　προφητεῖαι →　καταργηθήσονται εἴτε
v.pai.3s d.nsf n.nsf adv v.pai.3s cj cj n.npf v.fpi.3p cj
5702 3836 27 4030 4406 1254 1664 4735 2934 1664

tongues, they will be stilled;　where there is knowledge, it will pass　away.　**9** For we know　in part and
γλῶσσαι → → → παύσονται εἴτε　γνῶσις → → καταργηθήσεται ←　γὰρ → γινώσκομεν ἐκ μέρους καὶ
n.npf v.fmi.3p cj n.nsf v.fpi.3s cj v.pai.1p p.g n.gsn cj
1185 4264 1664 1194 2934 1142 1182 1666 3538 2779

we prophesy　in part,　**10** but when perfection comes, the imperfect disappears.　**11** When I was a child, I talked
→ προφητεύομεν ἐκ μέρους δὲ ὅταν ⸆τὸ τέλειον⸆ ἔλθῃ τὸ ⸆ἐκ μέρους⸆ καταργηθήσεται ὅτε → ἤμην νήπιος → ἐλάλουν
v.pai.1p p.g n.gsn cj cj d.nsn a.nsn v.aas.3s d.nsn p.g n.gsn v.fpi.3s cj v.imi.1s a.nsm v.iai.1s
4736 1666 3538 1254 4020 3836 5455 2262 3836 1666 3538 2934 4021 1639 3758 3281

like a child, I thought like a child, I reasoned like a child. When I became a man, I put childish ways
ὡς νήπιος → ἐφρόνουν ὡς νήπιος → ἐλογιζόμην ὡς νήπιος ὅτε → γέγονα ἀνήρ → κατήργηκα ⸆τοῦ νηπίου⸆ τὰ
pl a.nsm v.iai.1s pl a.nsm v.imi.1s pl a.nsm cj v.rai.1s n.nsm v.rai.1s d.gsn a.gsn d.apn
6055 3758 5858 6055 3758 3357 6055 3758 4021 1181 467 2934 3836 3758 3836

behind me. **12** Now we see　but a poor reflection as in a mirror;　then we shall see face　to
↰ γὰρ ἄρτι → βλέπομεν ἐν → αἰνίγματι δι' ἐσόπτρου δὲ τότε → πρόσωπον πρὸς
cj adv v.pai.1p p.d n.dsn p.g n.gsn cj adv n.asn p.a
2934 1142 785 1063 1877 141 1328 2269 1254 5538 4725 4639

face.　Now I know in part;　then I shall know　fully, even as　I am fully known. ¶
πρόσωπον ἄρτι → γινώσκω ἐκ μέρους δὲ τότε → ἐπιγνώσομαι ← καθὼς καὶ → → ἐπεγνώσθην
n.asn adv v.pai.1s p.g n.gsn cj adv v.fmi.1s cj adv v.api.1s
4725 785 1182 1666 3538 1254 5538 2105 2777 2779 2105

13 And now these three　remain: faith, hope and love.　But the greatest of these is love.
δὲ Νυνὶ ταῦτα τὰ τρία μένει πίστις ἐλπίς ἀγάπη δὲ μείζων → τούτων ⸆ἡ ἀγάπη
cj adv r.npn d.npn a.npn v.pai.3s n.nsf n.nsf n.nsf cj a.nsf.c r.gpn d.nsf n.nsf
1254 3815 4047 3836 5552 3531 4411 1828 27 1254 3489 4047 3836 27

Gifts of Prophecy and Tongues

14:1 Follow the way of love　and eagerly desire spiritual　gifts,　especially　the gift of prophecy.
Διώκετε ⸆τὴν ἀγάπην, δὲ → ζηλοῦτε ⸆τὰ πνευματικά⸆ ← δὲ μᾶλλον ἵνα → προφητεύητε
v.pam.2p d.asf n.asf cj v.pam.2p d.apn a.apn cj adv.c cj v.pas.2p
1503 3836 27 1254 2420 3836 4461 1254 3437 2671 4736

2 For anyone who speaks in a tongue does not speak to men　but to God. Indeed, no　one understands him;
γὰρ ὁ ← λαλῶν → γλώσσῃ → οὐκ λαλεῖ → ἀνθρώποις ἀλλὰ → θεῷ γὰρ οὐδεὶς ← ἀκούει
cj d.nsm pt.pa.nsm n.dsf pl v.pai.3s n.dpm cj n.dsm cj a.nsm v.pai.3s
1142 3836 3281 1185 3281 4024 3281 476 247 2536 1142 4029 201

he utters mysteries with his spirit.　**3** But everyone who prophesies speaks to men　for their strengthening,
δὲ → λαλεῖ μυστήρια → πνεύματι δὲ ὁ ← προφητεύων λαλεῖ → ἀνθρώποις οἰκοδομὴν καὶ
cj v.pai.3s n.apn n.dsn cj d.nsm pt.pa.nsm v.pai.3s n.dpm n.asf cj
1254 3281 3696 4460 1254 3836 4736 3281 476 3869 2779

δὲ μὴ ἔχω, οὐδὲν ὠφελοῦμαι. ¶ **4** Ἡ ἀγάπη μακροθυμεῖ, χρηστεύεται ἡ ἀγάπη, οὐ ζηλοῖ, [ἡ ἀγάπη] οὐ περπερεύεται, οὐ φυσιοῦται, **5** οὐκ ἀσχημονεῖ, οὐ ζητεῖ τὰ ἑαυτῆς, οὐ παροξύνεται, οὐ λογίζεται τὸ κακόν, **6** οὐ χαίρει ἐπὶ τῇ ἀδικίᾳ, συγχαίρει δὲ τῇ ἀληθείᾳ· **7** πάντα στέγει, πάντα πιστεύει, πάντα ἐλπίζει, πάντα ὑπομένει. ¶ **8** Ἡ ἀγάπη οὐδέποτε πίπτει· εἴτε δὲ προφητεῖαι, καταργηθήσονται· εἴτε γλῶσσαι, παύσονται· εἴτε γνῶσις, καταργηθήσεται. **9** ἐκ μέρους γὰρ γινώσκομεν καὶ ἐκ μέρους προφητεύομεν· **10** ὅταν δὲ ἔλθῃ τὸ τέλειον, τὸ ἐκ μέρους καταργηθήσεται. **11** ὅτε ἤμην νήπιος, ἐλάλουν ὡς νήπιος, ἐφρόνουν ὡς νήπιος, ἐλογιζόμην ὡς νήπιος· ὅτε γέγονα ἀνήρ, κατήργηκα τὰ τοῦ νηπίου. **12** βλέπομεν γὰρ ἄρτι δι' ἐσόπτρου ἐν αἰνίγματι, τότε δὲ πρόσωπον πρὸς πρόσωπον· ἄρτι γινώσκω ἐκ μέρους, τότε δὲ ἐπιγνώσομαι καθὼς καὶ ἐπεγνώσθην. ¶ **13** νυνὶ δὲ μένει πίστις, ἐλπίς, ἀγάπη, τὰ τρία ταῦτα· μείζων δὲ τούτων ἡ ἀγάπη.

14:1 Διώκετε τὴν ἀγάπην, ζηλοῦτε δὲ τὰ πνευματικά, μᾶλλον δὲ ἵνα προφητεύητε. **2** ὁ γὰρ λαλῶν γλώσσῃ οὐκ ἀνθρώποις λαλεῖ ἀλλὰ θεῷ· οὐδεὶς γὰρ ἀκούει, πνεύματι δὲ λαλεῖ μυστήρια· **3** ὁ δὲ προφητεύων ἀνθρώποις λαλεῖ οἰκοδομὴν καὶ παράκλησιν

encouragement and comfort. **⁴** He who speaks in a tongue edifies himself, but he who prophesies edifies the
παράκλησιν   καὶ   παραμυθίαν   ὁ ←   λαλῶν →   γλώσσῃ   οἰκοδομεῖ   ἑαυτὸν   δὲ   ὁ ←   προφητεύων   οἰκοδομεῖ
n.asf   cj   n.asf   d.nsm   pt.pa.nsm   n.dsf   v.pai.3s   r.asm.3   cj   d.nsm   pt.pa.nsm   v.pai.3s
4155   2779   4171   3836   3281   1185   3868   1571   1254   3836   4736   3868

church. **⁵** I would like every one of you to speak in tongues, but I would rather have you prophesy. He
ἐκκλησίαν   δὲ → →   θέλω   πάντας   ὑμᾶς   λαλεῖν →   γλώσσαις   δὲ   μᾶλλον   ἵνα →   προφητεύητε   δὲ   ὁ
n.asf   cj   v.pai.1s   a.apm   r.ap.2   f.pa   n.dpf   cj   adv.c   cj   v.pas.2p   cj   d.nsm
1711   1254   2527   4246   7007   3281   1185   1254   3437   2671   4736   1254   3836

who prophesies is greater than one who speaks in tongues, unless he interprets, so that the church may be
← προφητεύων   μείζων   ἢ   ὁ ←   λαλῶν →   γλώσσαις   ἐκτὸς   εἰ   μὴ →   διερμηνεύῃ   ἵνα ←   ἡ   ἐκκλησία →   λάβῃ
pt.pa.nsm   a.nsm.c   pl   d.nsm   pt.pa.nsm   n.dpf   adv   cj   pl   v.pas.3s   cj   d.nsf   n.nsf   v.aas.3s
4736   3489   2445   3836   3281   1185   1760   1623   3590   1450   2671   3836   1711   3284

edified. ¶ **⁶** Now, brothers, if I come to you and speak in tongues, what good will I be to you,
οἰκοδομὴν   δέ   Νῦν   ἀδελφοί   ἐὰν →   ἔλθω   πρὸς   ὑμᾶς   λαλῶν →   γλώσσαις   τί   ὠφελήσω ← ← ←   ὑμᾶς
n.asf   cj   adv   n.vpm   cj   v.aas.1s   p   r.ap.2   pt.pa.nsm   n.dpf   r.asn   v.fai.1s   r.ap.2
3869   1254   3814   81   1569   2262   4639   7007   3281   1185   5515   6067   7007

unless I bring you some revelation or knowledge or prophecy or word of instruction? **⁷** Even in the
ἐὰν   μὴ →   λαλήσω   ὑμῖν   ἢ →   ἐν   ἀποκαλύψει   ἢ   ἐν   γνώσει   ἢ   ἐν   προφητείᾳ   ἢ → →   ἐν   διδαχῇ   ὅμως
cj   pl   v.aas.1s   r.dp.2   cj   p.d   n.dsf   cj   p.d   n.dsf   cj   p.d   n.dsf   cj   p.d   n.dsf   adv
1569   3590   3281   7007   2445   1877   637   2445   1877   1194   2445   1877   4735   2445   1877   1439   3940

case of lifeless things that make sounds, such as the flute or harp, how will anyone know what tune is
τὰ   ἄψυχα ←   διδόντα   φωνήν   εἴτε ←   αὐλὸς   εἴτε   κιθάρα   πῶς → →   γνωσθήσεται   τὸ ← ←
d.npn   a.npn   pt.pa.npn   n.asf   cj   n.nsm   cj   n.nsf   cj   v.fpi.3s   d.nsn
3836   953   1443   5889   1664   888   1664   3067   4802   1182   3836

being played unless there is a distinction in the notes? **⁸** Again, if the trumpet does
→   αὐλούμενον   ἢ   τὸ   κιθαριζόμενον   ἐὰν   μὴ →   δῷ   διαστολὴν →   τοῖς   φθόγγοις   γὰρ   καὶ   ἐὰν   σάλπιγξ →
pt.pp.nsn   cj   d.nsn   pt.pp.nsn   cj   pl   v.aas.3s   n.asf   d.dpm   n.dpm   cj   cj   cj   n.nsf
884   2445   3836   3068   1569   3590   1443   1405   3836   5782   1142   2779   1569   4894   1443

not sound a clear call, who will get ready for battle? **⁹** So it is with you. Unless you speak
→   δῷ   ἄδηλον   φωνήν   τίς →   παρασκευάσεται   εἰς   πόλεμον   καὶ   οὕτως ←   ὑμεῖς   ἐὰν   μὴ →   δῶτε
v.aas.3s   a.asf   n.asf   r.nsm   v.fmi.3s   p.a   n.asm   adv   adv   r.np.2   cj   pl   v.aas.2p
83   1443   83   5889   5515   4186   1650   4483   2779   4048   7007   1569   3590   1443

intelligible words with your tongue, how will anyone know what you are saying? You will just be
εὔσημον   λόγον   διὰ   τῆς   γλώσσης   πῶς → →   γνωσθήσεται   τὸ →   λαλούμενον   γάρ → →   ἔσεσθε
a.asm   n.asm   p.g   d.gsf   n.gsf   cj   v.fpi.3s   d.nsn   pt.pp.nsn   cj   v.fmi.2p
2358   3364   1328   3836   1185   4802   1182   3836   3281   1142   1639

speaking into the air. **¹⁰** Undoubtedly there are all sorts of languages in the world, yet none of them is without
λαλοῦντες   εἰς   ἀέρα   τοσαῦτα   εἰ   τύχοι   εἰσιν →   γένη →   φωνῶν   ἐν   κόσμῳ   καὶ   οὐδὲν →
pt.pa.npm   p.a   n.asm   r.npn   cj   v.aao.3s   v.pai.3p   n.npn   n.gpf   p.d   n.dsm   cj   a.nsn
3281   1650   113   5537   1623   5593   1639   1169   5889   1877   3180   2779   4029

meaning. **¹¹** If then I do not grasp the meaning of what someone is saying, I am a foreigner to the speaker, and
ἄφωνον   ἐὰν   οὖν →   μὴ   εἰδῶ   τὴν   δύναμιν →   τῆς   φωνῆς →   ἔσομαι   βάρβαρος →   τῷ   λαλοῦντι   καὶ
a.nsn   cj   cj   pl   v.ras.1s   d.asf   n.asf   d.gsf   n.gsf   v.fmi.1s   n.nsm   d.dsm   pt.pa.dsm   cj
936   1569   4036   3590   3857   3836   1539   3836   5889   1639   975   3836   3281   2779

he is a foreigner to me. **¹²** So it is with you. Since you are eager to have spiritual gifts, try to
ὁ   λαλῶν   βάρβαρος   ἐν   ἐμοί   καὶ   οὕτως ← ←   ὑμεῖς   ἐπεὶ →   ἐστε   ζηλωταί   πνευμάτων ←   ζητεῖτε   ἵνα
d.nsm   pt.pa.nsm   n.nsm   p.d   r.ds.1   adv   adv   r.np.2   cj   v.pai.2p   n.npm   n.gpn   v.pam.2p   cj
3836   3281   975   1877   1609   2779   4048   7007   2075   1639   2421   4460   2426   2671

excel in gifts that build up the church. ¶ **¹³** For this reason anyone who speaks in a tongue should
περισσεύητε   πρὸς   τὴν   οἰκοδομὴν ←   τῆς   ἐκκλησίας   Διὸ ← ←   ὁ ←   λαλῶν →   γλώσσῃ →
v.pas.2p   p.a   d.asf   n.asf   d.gsf   n.gsf   cj   d.nsm   pt.pa.nsm   n.dsf
4355   4639   3836   3869   3836   1711   1475   3836   3281   1185

pray that he may interpret what he says. **¹⁴** For if I pray in a tongue, my spirit prays, but my
προσευχέσθω   ἵνα → →   διερμηνεύῃ   γὰρ   ἐὰν →   προσεύχωμαι →   γλώσσῃ   μου   τὸ   πνεῦμα   προσεύχεται   δὲ   μου
v.pmm.3s   cj   v.pas.3s   cj   cj   v.pms.1s   n.dsf   r.gs.1   d.nsn   n.nsn   v.pmi.3s   cj   r.gs.1
4667   2671   1450   1142   1569   4667   1185   1609   3836   4460   4667   1254   1609

καὶ παραμυθίαν. ⁴ ὁ λαλῶν γλώσσῃ ἑαυτὸν οἰκοδομεῖ· ὁ δὲ προφητεύων ἐκκλησίαν οἰκοδομεῖ. ⁵ θέλω δὲ πάντας ὑμᾶς λαλεῖν γλώσσαις, μᾶλλον δὲ ἵνα προφητεύητε· μείζων δὲ ὁ προφητεύων ἢ ὁ λαλῶν γλώσσαις ἐκτὸς εἰ μὴ διερμηνεύῃ, ἵνα ἡ ἐκκλησία οἰκοδομὴν λάβῃ. ¶ ⁶ Νῦν δέ, ἀδελφοί, ἐὰν ἔλθω πρὸς ὑμᾶς γλώσσαις λαλῶν, τί ὑμᾶς ὠφελήσω ἐὰν μὴ ὑμῖν λαλήσω ἢ ἐν ἀποκαλύψει ἢ ἐν γνώσει ἢ ἐν προφητείᾳ ἢ [ἐν] διδαχῇ; ⁷ ὅμως τὰ ἄψυχα φωνὴν διδόντα, εἴτε αὐλὸς εἴτε κιθάρα, ἐὰν διαστολὴν τοῖς φθόγγοις μὴ δῷ, πῶς γνωσθήσεται τὸ αὐλούμενον ἢ τὸ κιθαριζόμενον; ⁸ καὶ γὰρ ἐὰν ἄδηλον σάλπιγξ φωνὴν δῷ, τίς παρασκευάσεται εἰς πόλεμον; ⁹ οὕτως καὶ ὑμεῖς διὰ τῆς γλώσσης ἐὰν μὴ εὔσημον λόγον δῶτε, πῶς γνωσθήσεται τὸ λαλούμενον; ἔσεσθε γὰρ εἰς ἀέρα λαλοῦντες. ¹⁰ τοσαῦτα εἰ τύχοι γένη φωνῶν εἰσιν ἐν κόσμῳ καὶ οὐδὲν ἄφωνον· ¹¹ ἐὰν οὖν μὴ εἰδῶ τὴν δύναμιν τῆς φωνῆς, ἔσομαι τῷ λαλοῦντι βάρβαρος καὶ ὁ λαλῶν ἐν ἐμοὶ βάρβαρος. ¹² οὕτως καὶ ὑμεῖς, ἐπεὶ ζηλωταί ἐστε πνευμάτων, πρὸς τὴν οἰκοδομὴν τῆς ἐκκλησίας ζητεῖτε ἵνα περισσεύητε. ¶ ¹³ διὸ ὁ λαλῶν γλώσσῃ προσευχέσθω ἵνα διερμηνεύῃ· ¹⁴ ἐὰν [γὰρ] προσεύχωμαι γλώσσῃ, τὸ πνεῦμά μου προσεύχεται, ὁ δὲ νοῦς μου ἄκαρπός ἐστιν. ¹⁵ τί οὖν ἐστιν; προσεύξομαι τῷ

mind   is   unfruitful.   **15** So what shall I do?   I will pray   with my spirit,   but I   will also pray   with my
ὁ   νοῦς, ἐστιν ἄκαρπος   οὖν τί   ἐστιν → προσεύξομαι →   τῷ πνεύματι δὲ   καὶ προσεύξομαι →   τῷ
d.nsm n.nsm v.pai.3s a.nsm   cj   r.nsn   v.pai.3s   v.fmi.1s   d.dsn n.dsn   cj   adv   v.fmi.1s   d.dsm
3836 3808 1639 182   4036 5515   1639   4667   3836 4460   1254 4667 4667 2779 4667   3836

mind; I will sing with my spirit,   but I   will also sing with my mind.   **16**   If you are praising God with your
νοΐ   →   ψαλῶ →   τῷ πνεύματι δὲ   →   καὶ ψαλῶ   τῷ νοΐ   ἐπεὶ ἐὰν   →   εὐλογῇς   ἐν
n.dsm   v.fai.1s   d.dsn n.dsn   cj   adv   v.fai.1s d.dsn n.dsn   cj   cj   v.pas.2s   p.d
3808   6010   3836 4460   1254 6010 6010 2779 6010   3836 3808   2075 1569   2328   1877

spirit,   how can one who finds   himself among   those who do not understand say "Amen" to your
πνεύματι πῶς → ὁ   ←   ἀναπληρῶν ←   ⌜τὸν τόπον⌝ τοῦ   ←   ἰδιώτου   ἐρεῖ ⌜τὸ ἀμήν⌝ ἐπὶ σῇ
n.dsn   cj   d.nsm   pt.pa.nsm   d.asm n.asm d.gsm   n.gsm   v.fai.3s d.asn pl   p.d r.dsf.2
4460   4802 3306 3836   405   3836 5536 3836   2626   3306 3836 297 2093 5050

thanksgiving, since he does not know what you are saying? **17**   You may be giving thanks   well enough, but
⌜τῇ εὐχαριστίᾳ⌝ ἐπειδὴ →   οὐκ οἶδεν τί   →   λέγεις   γὰρ μὲν σὺ   →   εὐχαριστεῖς καλῶς ←   ἀλλ᾽
d.dsf n.dsf   cj   pl v.rai.3s r.asn   v.pai.2s   cj pl r.ns.2   v.pai.2s   adv   cj
3836 2374   2076   3857 3857 4024 4857 5515   3306   1142 3525 5148   2373   2822   247

the other man is not edified.   ¶   **18** I thank   God   that I speak in tongues more   than all of you.
ὁ   ἕτερος ←   οὐκ οἰκοδομεῖται   → Εὐχαριστῶ ⌜τῷ θεῷ⌝   → λαλῶ   γλώσσαις μᾶλλον →   πάντων   ὑμῶν
d.nsm r.nsm   pl v.ppi.3s   v.pai.1s   d.dsm n.dsm   v.pai.1s   n.dpf   adv.c   a.gpm   r.gp.2
3836 2283   3868 4024 3868   2373   3836 2536   3281   1185   3437   4246   7007

19 But in the church I would rather speak five intelligible words to   instruct others than ten thousand words
ἀλλὰ ἐν   ἐκκλησίᾳ →   →   θέλω λαλῆσαι πέντε ⌜τῷ νοΐ μου⌝ λόγους ἵνα καὶ κατηχήσω ἄλλους ἢ   →   μυρίους λόγους
cj   p.d   n.dsf   v.pai.1s f.aa   a.apm d.dsm n.dsm r.gs.1 n.apm cj   adv v.aas.1s r.apm   pl   a.apm   n.apm
247 1877 1711   2527   3281   4297 3836 3808 1609 3364   2671 2779 2994   257   2445 3692   3364

in a tongue.   ¶ **20** Brothers, stop   thinking   like children.   In regard to evil   be infants, but in
ἐν γλώσσῃ   Ἀδελφοί   μὴ γίνεσθε ⌜ταῖς φρεσὶν⌝ παιδία   ἀλλὰ →   ⌜τῇ κακίᾳ⌝   νηπιάζετε δὲ   →
p.d n.dsf   n.vpm   pl v.pmm.2p d.dpf n.dpf   n.npn   cj   d.dsf n.dsf   v.pam.2p cj
1877 1185   81   3590 1181   3836 5856   4086   247   3836 2798   3757   1254

your thinking be   adults. **21** In the Law it is written: "Through men of strange tongues   and through the
ταῖς φρεσὶν   γίνεσθε τέλειοι ἐν τῷ νόμῳ → γέγραπται ὅτι ἐν   ἑτερογλώσσοις καὶ ἐν
d.dpf n.dpf   v.pmm.2p a.npm   p.d d.dsm n.dsm   v.rpi.3s   cj p.d   a.dpm   cj   p.d
3836 5856   1181   5455   1877 3836 3795   1211   4022 1877   2280   2779 1877

lips   of foreigners I will speak to this people,   but even then they will not listen   to me," says the Lord.
χείλεσιν → ἑτέρων   → λαλήσω → τούτῳ ⌜τῷ λαῷ⌝ καὶ οὕτως ←   →   οὐδ᾽ εἰσακούσονται ←   μου λέγει   κύριος
n.dpn   n.gpm   v.fai.1s   r.dsm d.dsm n.dsm cj   adv   adv   v.fmi.3p   r.gs.1 v.pai.3s n.nsm
5927   2283   3281   4047   3836 3295 2779 4048   1653 1653 4028 1653   1609 3306   3261

¶ **22** Tongues, then, are   a sign,   not for believers   but for unbelievers; prophecy,   however, is for
⌜αἱ γλῶσσαι⌝ ὥστε εἰσιν εἰς   σημεῖον οὐ   →   ⌜τοῖς πιστεύουσιν⌝ ἀλλὰ → ⌜τοῖς ἀπίστοις⌝ ἡ προφητεία⌝ δὲ
d.npf n.npf   cj   v.pai.3p p.a   n.asn   pl   d.dpm pt.pa.dpm   cj   d.dpm a.dpm   d.nsf n.nsf   cj
3836 1185   6063 1639   1650 4956   4024   3836 4409   247   3836 603   3836 4735   1254

believers,   not for unbelievers. **23** So if the whole church comes together   and everyone speaks in
⌜τοῖς πιστεύουσιν⌝ ἀλλὰ οὐ   → ⌜τοῖς ἀπίστοις⌝   οὖν Ἐὰν ἡ   ὅλη ἐκκλησία συνέλθῃ ⌜ἐπὶ τὸ αὐτὸ⌝ καὶ πάντες λαλῶσιν →
d.dpm pt.pa.dpm   cj   pl   d.dpm a.dpm   cj cj   d.nsf a.nsf n.nsf   v.aas.3s p.a d.asn r.asn   cj   a.npm   v.pas.3p
3836 4409   247   4024   3836 603   4036 1569 3836 3910 1711   5302   2093 3836 899   2779 4246   3281

tongues, and some who do not understand or some unbelievers come   in, will they not say   that you are out of
γλώσσαις δὲ   ἰδιῶται   ἢ   ἄπιστοι εἰσέλθωσιν ←   οὐκ ἐροῦσιν ὅτι   →   →   →
n.dpf   cj   n.npm   cj   a.npm   v.aas.3p   pl v.fai.3p cj
1185   1254   2626   2445 603   1656   3306 3306 4024 3306   4022

your mind? **24** But if an unbeliever or someone who does not understand comes in   while everybody is
→ μαίνεσθε   δὲ ἐὰν τις ἄπιστος   ἢ   →   →   ἰδιώτης εἰσέλθῃ ← δὲ →   πάντες
v.pmi.2p   cj   cj r.nsm a.nsm   cj   n.nsm   v.aas.3s   cj   a.npm
3419   1254 1569 5516 603   2445   2626   1656   1254 4736 4246

prophesying, he will be convinced by all   that he is a sinner and will be judged   by all,   **25** and the secrets of
προφητεύωσιν →   → ἐλέγχεται ὑπὸ πάντων   → ἀνακρίνεται ὑπὸ πάντων   τὰ κρυπτὰ   →
v.pas.3p   v.ppi.3s   p.g a.gpm   v.ppi.3s   p.g a.gpm   d.npn a.npn
4736   1794   5679 4246   373   5679 4246   3836 3220   2840

his   heart   will be   laid bare.   So he will fall down   and worship God, exclaiming,
αὐτοῦ ⌜τῆς καρδίας⌝ → γίνεται → φανερὰ καὶ οὕτως →   πεσὼν ⌜ἐπὶ πρόσωπον⌝ προσκυνήσει ⌜τῷ θεῷ⌝ ἀπαγγέλλων ὅτι
r.gsm.3 d.gsf n.gsf   v.pmi.3s   a.npn cj adv   pt.aa.nsm p.a n.asn   v.fai.3s   d.dsm n.dsm pt.pa.nsm   cj
899   3836 2840   1181   5745 2779 4048   4406   2093 4725   4686   3836 2536 550   4022

πνεύματι, προσεύξομαι δὲ καὶ τῷ νοΐ· ψαλῶ τῷ πνεύματι, ψαλῶ δὲ καὶ τῷ νοΐ. **16** ἐπεὶ ἐὰν εὐλογῇς [ἐν] πνεύματι, ὁ ἀναπληρῶν τὸν τόπον τοῦ ἰδιώτου πῶς ἐρεῖ τὸ Ἀμήν ἐπὶ τῇ σῇ εὐχαριστίᾳ; ἐπειδὴ τί λέγεις οὐκ οἶδεν· **17** σὺ μὲν γὰρ καλῶς εὐχαριστεῖς ἀλλ᾽ ὁ ἕτερος οὐκ οἰκοδομεῖται. ¶ **18** εὐχαριστῶ τῷ θεῷ, πάντων ὑμῶν μᾶλλον γλώσσαις λαλῶ· **19** ἀλλὰ ἐν ἐκκλησίᾳ θέλω πέντε λόγους τῷ νοΐ μου λαλῆσαι, ἵνα καὶ ἄλλους κατηχήσω, ἢ μυρίους λόγους ἐν γλώσσῃ. ¶ **20** Ἀδελφοί, μὴ παιδία γίνεσθε ταῖς φρεσὶν ἀλλὰ τῇ κακίᾳ νηπιάζετε, ταῖς δὲ φρεσὶν τέλειοι γίνεσθε. **21** ἐν τῷ νόμῳ γέγραπται ὅτι Ἐν ἑτερογλώσσοις καὶ ἐν χείλεσιν ἑτέρων λαλήσω τῷ λαῷ τούτῳ καὶ οὐδ᾽ οὕτως εἰσακούσονταί μου, λέγει κύριος. ¶ **22** ὥστε αἱ γλῶσσαι εἰς σημεῖόν εἰσιν οὐ τοῖς πιστεύουσιν ἀλλὰ τοῖς ἀπίστοις, ἡ δὲ προφητεία οὐ τοῖς ἀπίστοις ἀλλὰ τοῖς πιστεύουσιν. **23** Ἐὰν οὖν συνέλθῃ ἡ ἐκκλησία ὅλη ἐπὶ τὸ αὐτὸ καὶ πάντες λαλῶσιν γλώσσαις, εἰσέλθωσιν δὲ ἰδιῶται ἢ ἄπιστοι, οὐκ ἐροῦσιν ὅτι μαίνεσθε; **24** ἐὰν δὲ πάντες προφητεύωσιν, εἰσέλθῃ δέ τις ἄπιστος ἢ ἰδιώτης, ἐλέγχεται ὑπὸ πάντων, ἀνακρίνεται ὑπὸ πάντων, **25** τὰ κρυπτὰ τῆς καρδίας αὐτοῦ φανερὰ γίνεται, καὶ οὕτως πεσὼν ἐπὶ πρόσωπον προσκυνήσει τῷ θεῷ ἀπαγγέλλων ὅτι Ὄντως ὁ θεὸς ἐν ὑμῖν ἐστιν.

"God   is   really   among   you!"
ὁ θεὸς   ἐστιν   ὄντως   ἐν   ὑμῖν
d.nsm n.nsm   v.pai.3s   adv   p.d   r.dp.2
3836 2536   1639   3953   1877   7007

Orderly Worship

14:26 What   then   shall we say,   brothers?   When   you   come   together,   everyone   has   a hymn,   or   a word of
Τί   οὖν   →   →   ἐστιν   ἀδελφοί   ὅταν   →   συνέρχησθε ←   ἕκαστος   ἔχει   ψαλμὸν   ἔχει   →   →
r.nsn   cj   v.pai.3s n.vpm   cj   v.pms.2p   r.nsm   v.pai.3s n.asm   v.pai.3s
5515   4036   1639   81   4020   5302   1667   2400   6011   2400

instruction,   a revelation,   a tongue or   an interpretation.   All   of these must be   done for   the
διδαχὴν   ἔχει   ἀποκάλυψιν ἔχει   γλῶσσαν   ἔχει   ἑρμηνείαν   πάντα ←   →   γινέσθω   πρὸς
n.asf   v.pai.3s a.asf   v.pai.3s n.asf   v.pai.3s n.asf   a.npn   v.pmm.3s   p.a
1439   2400   637   2400   1185   2400   2255   4246   1181   4639

strengthening of the church.   **27** If   anyone   speaks in a tongue,   two – or at the most   three – should speak,
οἰκοδομὴν   εἴτε τις   λαλεῖ →   γλώσσῃ κατὰ δύο ἢ   τὸ πλεῖστον τρεῖς   καὶ
n.asf   cj   r.nsm v.pai.3s n.dsf p.a a.apm cj d.asn a.asn.s a.apm   cj
3869   1664 5516   3281   1185   2848 1545 2445 3836 4498 5552   2779

one   at a time, and   someone must interpret.   **28**   If there is   no interpreter,   the speaker should keep quiet
ἀνὰ μέρος ←   ←   καὶ εἷς   →   διερμηνευέτω   δὲ   ἐὰν →   ᾖ   μὴ διερμηνευτής   →   σιγάτω
p.a n.asn   cj a.nsm   v.pam.3s   cj   cj   v.pas.3s pl n.nsm   v.pam.3s
324 3538   2779 1651   1450   1254 1569   1639 3590 1449   4967

in   the church and speak   to himself and God.   ¶   **29**   Two or three prophets should speak,   and the
ἐν   ἐκκλησίᾳ δὲ λαλείτω ἑαυτῷ καὶ τῷ θεῷ   δὲ δύο ἢ τρεῖς προφῆται   →   λαλείτωσαν καὶ οἱ
p.d n.dsf   cj   v.pam.3s r.dsm.3 cj d.dsm n.dsm   cj a.npm cj a.npm n.npm   v.pam.3p cj d.npm
1877 1711   1254 1281   1571   2779 3836 2536   1254 1545 2445 5552 4737   3281   2779 3836

others should weigh   carefully what is said.   **30** And if   a revelation comes to someone who is sitting   down,   the
ἄλλοι →   διακρινέτωσαν ←   δὲ ἐὰν ἀποκαλυφθῇ ←   → ἄλλῳ   → καθημένῳ   ὁ
r.npm   v.pam.3p   cj cj v.aps.3s   r.dsm   pt.pm.dsm   d.nsm
257   1359   1254 1569 636   257   2764   3836

first   speaker should stop.   **31** For you can   all   prophesy   in   turn so that everyone may be   instructed and
πρῶτος   →   σιγάτω   γὰρ   → δύνασθε πάντες προφητεύειν καθ' ἕνα ἵνα → πάντες   → μανθάνωσιν καὶ
a.nsm   v.pam.3s   cj   v.ppi.2p a.npm f.pa   p.a a.asm cj   a.npm   v.pas.3p   cj
4755   4967   1142   1538   4246   4736   2848 1651 2671   4246   3443   2779

encouraged.   **32**   The spirits   of prophets are subject   to the control of prophets.   **33** For God   is   not a
πάντες παρακαλῶνται καὶ   πνεύματα → προφητῶν → ὑποτάσσεται ←   ←   προφήταις γὰρ ὁ θεὸς ἐστιν οὐ
a.npm v.pps.3p   cj   n.npn   n.gpm   v.ppi.3s   n.dpm   cj d.nsm n.nsm v.pai.3s pl
4246   4151   2779   4460   4737   5718   4737   1142 3836 2536 1639   4024

God of disorder   but   of peace.   ¶   As in   all   the congregations of the saints,   **34** women   should remain
→   ἀκαταστασίας ἀλλὰ → εἰρήνης   Ὡς ἐν πάσαις ταῖς ἐκκλησίαις τῶν ἁγίων   αἱ γυναῖκες   →
    n.gsf   cj   n.gsf   pl p.d a.dpf d.dpf n.dpf   d.gpm a.gpm   d.npf n.npf
    189   247   1645   6055 1877 4246 3836 1711   3836 41   3836 1222

silent   in   the churches.   They are not allowed   to speak, but   must be in submission,   as   the Law
σιγάτωσαν ἐν ταῖς ἐκκλησίαις γὰρ αὐταῖς → οὐ ἐπιτρέπεται → λαλεῖν ἀλλὰ →   → ὑποτασσέσθωσαν καθὼς καὶ ὁ νόμος
v.pam.3p p.d d.dpf n.dpf   cj r.dpf.3   pl v.ppi.3s   f.pa cj   v.ppm.3p   cj   adv d.nsm n.nsm
4967   1877 3836 1711   1142 899   2205 4024   3281 247   5718   2777 2779 3836 3795

says.   **35**   If   they want   to inquire about something, they should ask   their own   husbands at home; for it
λέγει   δὲ εἰ →   θέλουσιν μαθεῖν   τι   ἐπερωτάτωσαν τοὺς ἰδίους ἄνδρας ἐν οἴκῳ γὰρ
v.pai.3s cj cj   v.pai.3p f.aa   r.asn   v.pam.3p   d.apm a.apm n.apm   p.d n.dsm cj
3306   1254 1623   2527   3443   5516   2089   3836 2625   467   1877 3875 1142

is   disgraceful for a woman to speak in   the church.   ¶   **36**   Did the word of God   originate with you? Or
ἐστιν αἰσχρὸν   →   γυναικὶ → λαλεῖν ἐν ἐκκλησίᾳ   ἢ   ὁ λόγος τοῦ θεοῦ ἐξῆλθεν ἀφ' ὑμῶν ἢ
v.pai.3s a.nsn   n.dsf   f.pa p.d n.dsf   cj   d.nsm n.nsm d.gsm n.gsm v.aai.3s p.g r.gp.2 cj
1639   156   1222   3281 1877 1711   2445 2002 3836 3364 3836 2536 2002   608 7007 2445

are   you the only   people it has reached?   **37** If   anybody thinks he is   a prophet or spiritually gifted, let him
εἰς ὑμᾶς   μόνους ←   → κατήντησεν   Εἴ τις   δοκεῖ → εἶναι προφήτης ἢ πνευματικός ←   →
p.a r.ap.2 a.apm   v.aai.3s   cj r.nsm v.pai.3s f.pa n.nsm   cj a.nsm
1650 7007 3668   2918   1623 5516 1506   1639 4737   2445 4461

---

¹⁴:²⁶ Τί οὖν ἐστιν, ἀδελφοί; ὅταν συνέρχησθε, ἕκαστος ψαλμὸν ἔχει, διδαχὴν ἔχει, ἀποκάλυψιν ἔχει, γλῶσσαν ἔχει, ἑρμηνείαν ἔχει· πάντα πρὸς οἰκοδομὴν γινέσθω. ²⁷ εἴτε γλώσσῃ τις λαλεῖ, κατὰ δύο ἢ τὸ πλεῖστον τρεῖς καὶ ἀνὰ μέρος, καὶ εἷς διερμηνευέτω· ²⁸ ἐὰν δὲ μὴ ᾖ διερμηνευτής, σιγάτω ἐν ἐκκλησίᾳ, ἑαυτῷ δὲ λαλείτω καὶ τῷ θεῷ. ¶ ²⁹ προφῆται δὲ δύο ἢ τρεῖς λαλείτωσαν καὶ οἱ ἄλλοι διακρινέτωσαν· ³⁰ ἐὰν δὲ ἄλλῳ ἀποκαλυφθῇ καθημένῳ, ὁ πρῶτος σιγάτω. ³¹ δύνασθε γὰρ καθ' ἕνα πάντες προφητεύειν, ἵνα πάντες μανθάνωσιν καὶ πάντες παρακαλῶνται. ³² καὶ πνεύματα προφητῶν προφήταις ὑποτάσσεται, ³³ οὐ γάρ ἐστιν ἀκαταστασίας ὁ θεὸς ἀλλὰ εἰρήνης. ¶ Ὡς ἐν πάσαις ταῖς ἐκκλησίαις τῶν ἁγίων ³⁴ αἱ γυναῖκες ἐν ταῖς ἐκκλησίαις σιγάτωσαν· οὐ γὰρ ἐπιτρέπεται αὐταῖς λαλεῖν, ἀλλὰ ὑποτασσέσθωσαν, καθὼς καὶ ὁ νόμος λέγει. ³⁵ εἰ δέ τι μαθεῖν θέλουσιν, ἐν οἴκῳ τοὺς ἰδίους ἄνδρας ἐπερωτάτωσαν· αἰσχρὸν γάρ ἐστιν γυναικὶ λαλεῖν ἐν ἐκκλησίᾳ. ¶ ³⁶ ἢ ἀφ' ὑμῶν ὁ λόγος τοῦ θεοῦ ἐξῆλθεν, ἢ εἰς ὑμᾶς μόνους κατήντησεν; ³⁷ Εἴ τις δοκεῖ προφήτης εἶναι ἢ πνευματικός, ἐπιγινωσκέτω ἃ γράφω ὑμῖν

acknowledge that what I am writing to you is the Lord's command. **38** If he ignores this, he himself will be
ἐπιγινωσκέτω ἃ → γράφω ὑμῖν ὅτι ἐστὶν κυρίου ἐντολή δέ εἰ τις ἀγνοεῖ → →
v.pam.3s r.apn v.pai.1s r.dp.2 cj v.pai.3s n.gsm n.nsf cj cj r.nsm v.pai.3s
2105 4005 1211 7007 4022 1639 3261 1953 1254 1623 5516 51

ignored. ¶ **39** Therefore, my brothers, be eager to prophesy, and do not forbid speaking in tongues. **40** But
ἀγνοεῖται Ὥστε μου ἀδελφοί → ζηλοῦτε ⸤τὸ προφητεύειν⸥ καὶ μὴ κωλύετε ⸤τὸ λαλεῖν⸥ → γλώσσαις δέ
v.pmi.3s cj r.gs.1 n.vpm v.pam.2p d.asn f.pa cj pl v.pam.2p d.asn f.pa n.dpf cj
51 6063 1609 81 2420 3836 4736 2779 3266 3590 3266 3836 3281 1185 1254

everything should be done in a fitting and orderly way.
πάντα → γινέσθω ← εὐσχημόνως καὶ ⸤κατὰ τάξιν⸥ ←
a.npn v.pmm.3s adv cj p.a n.asf
4246 1181 2361 2779 2848 5423

The Resurrection of Christ

15:1 Now, brothers, I want to remind you of the gospel I preached to you, which you received and
δέ ἀδελφοί → Γνωρίζω ὑμῖν τὸ εὐαγγέλιον ὃ → εὐηγγελισάμην → ὑμῖν ὃ καὶ → παρελάβετε καὶ
cj n.vpm v.pai.1s r.dp.2 d.asn n.asn r.asn v.ami.1s r.dp.2 r.asn adv v.aai.2p adv
1254 81 1192 7007 3836 2295 4005 2294 7007 4005 2779 4161 2779

on which you have taken your stand. **2** By this gospel you are saved, if you hold firmly to the word I
ἐν ᾧ καὶ → ἑστήκατε δι᾽ οὗ καὶ → σῴζεσθε εἰ → κατέχετε ← τίνι λόγῳ →
p.d r.dsn adv v.rai.2p p.g r.gsn adv v.ppi.2p cj v.pai.2p r.dsm n.dsm
1877 4005 2779 2705 1328 4005 2779 5392 1623 2988 5515 3364

preached to you. Otherwise, you have believed in vain. ¶ **3** For what I received I passed on to
εὐηγγελισάμην → ὑμῖν ⸤ἐκτὸς εἰ μὴ⸥ → ἐπιστεύσατε εἰκῇ γὰρ ὃ καὶ → παρέλαβον → παρέδωκα ← →
v.ami.1s r.dp.2 adv cj pl v.aai.2p adv cj r.asn adv v.aai.1s v.aai.1s
2294 7007 1760 1623 3590 4409 1632 1142 4005 2779 4161 4140

you as of first importance: that Christ died for our sins according to the Scriptures, **4** that he
ὑμῖν ἐν ← πρώτοις ← ὅτι Χριστὸς ἀπέθανεν ὑπὲρ ἡμῶν ⸤τῶν ἁμαρτιῶν⸥ κατὰ ← τὰς γραφὰς καὶ ὅτι →
r.dp.2 p.d a.dpn cj n.nsm v.aai.3s p.g r.gp.1 d.gpf n.gpf p.a d.apf n.apf cj cj
7007 1877 4755 4022 5986 633 5642 7005 3836 281 2848 3836 1210 2779 4022

was buried, that he was raised on the third day according to the Scriptures, **5** and that he appeared to
→ ἐτάφη καὶ ὅτι → ἐγήγερται τῇ ⸤τῇ τρίτῃ⸥ ἡμέρᾳ κατὰ ← τὰς γραφὰς καὶ ὅτι → ὤφθη
v.api.3s cj cj v.rpi.3s d.dsf d.dsf a.dsf n.dsf p.a d.apf n.apf cj cj v.api.3s
2507 2779 4022 1586 3836 3836 5569 2465 2848 3836 1210 2779 4022 3972

Peter, and then to the Twelve. **6** After that, he appeared to more than five hundred of the brothers at the
Κηφᾷ εἶτα → τοῖς δώδεκα ἔπειτα ← → ὤφθη → ἐπάνω πεντακοσίοις ← → ἀδελφοῖς → ἐφάπαξ
n.dsm adv d.dpm a.dpm adv v.api.3s adv a.dpm n.dpm adv
3064 1663 3836 1557 2083 3972 2062 4296 81 2384

same time, most of whom are still living, though some have fallen asleep. **7** Then he appeared to
ἐφάπαξ ⸤οἱ πλείονες⸥ ἐξ ὧν → ⸤ἕως ἄρτι⸥ μένουσιν δέ → τινὲς → ἐκοιμήθησαν ἔπειτα → ὤφθη
adv d.npm a.npm.c p.g r.gpm p.g adv v.pai.3p cj r.npm v.api.3p adv v.api.3s
2384 3836 4498 1666 4005 3531 2401 3531 1254 5516 3121 2083 3972

James, then to all the apostles, **8** and last of all he appeared to me also, as to one abnormally born.
Ἰακώβῳ εἶτα → πᾶσιν τοῖς ἀποστόλοις δέ ἔσχατον → πάντων → ὤφθη → κἀμοί ← ὡσπερεὶ → τῷ ἐκτρώματι ←
n.dsm adv a.dpm d.dpm n.dpm cj adv a.gpm v.api.3s crasis pl d.dsn n.dsn
2610 1663 4246 3836 693 1254 2274 4246 3972 2743 6062 3836 1765

¶ **9** For I am the least of the apostles and do not even deserve to be called an apostle, because I
γὰρ Ἐγώ εἰμι ὁ ἐλάχιστος τῶν ἀποστόλων ὃς εἰμὶ οὐκ ἱκανὸς → καλεῖσθαι ἀπόστολος διότι
cj r.ns.1 v.pai.1s d.nsm a.nsm.s d.gpm n.gpm r.nsm v.pai.1s pl a.nsm f.pp n.nsm cj
1142 1609 1639 3836 1788 3836 693 4005 1639 4024 2653 2813 693 1484

persecuted the church of God. **10** But by the grace of God I am what I am, and his grace to me
ἐδίωξα τὴν ἐκκλησίαν ⸤τοῦ θεοῦ⸥ δέ χάριτι θεοῦ → εἰμι ὃ → εἰμι καὶ αὐτοῦ ⸤ἡ χάρις⸥ ἡ εἰς ἐμὲ
v.aai.1s d.asf n.asf d.gsm n.gsm cj n.dsf n.gsm v.pai.1s r.nsn v.pai.1s cj r.gsm.3 d.nsf n.nsf d.nsf p.a r.as.1
1503 3836 1711 3836 2536 1254 5921 2536 1639 4005 1639 2779 899 3836 5921 3836 1650 1609

was not without effect. No, I worked harder than all of them – yet not I, but the grace of God
ἐγενήθη οὐ → κενή ἀλλὰ → ἐκοπίασα περισσότερον → πάντων → αὐτῶν δέ οὐκ ἐγὼ ἀλλὰ ἡ χάρις → ⸤τοῦ θεοῦ⸥
v.api.3s pl a.nsf cj v.aai.1s adv.c a.gpm r.gpm.3 cj pl r.ns.1 cj d.nsf n.nsf d.gsm n.gsm
1181 4024 3031 247 3159 4358 4246 899 1254 4024 1609 247 3836 5921 3836 2536

ὅτι κυρίου ἐστὶν ἐντολή· **38** εἰ δέ τις ἀγνοεῖ, ἀγνοεῖται. ¶ **39** ὥστε, ἀδελφοί [μου], ζηλοῦτε τὸ προφητεύειν καὶ τὸ λαλεῖν μὴ κωλύετε γλώσσαις· **40** πάντα δὲ εὐσχημόνως καὶ κατὰ τάξιν γινέσθω.

15:1 Γνωρίζω δὲ ὑμῖν, ἀδελφοί, τὸ εὐαγγέλιον ὃ εὐηγγελισάμην ὑμῖν, ὃ καὶ παρελάβετε, ἐν ᾧ καὶ ἑστήκατε, **2** δι᾽ οὗ καὶ σῴζεσθε, τίνι λόγῳ εὐηγγελισάμην ὑμῖν εἰ κατέχετε, ἐκτὸς εἰ μὴ εἰκῇ ἐπιστεύσατε. ¶ **3** παρέδωκα γὰρ ὑμῖν ἐν πρώτοις, ὃ καὶ παρέλαβον, ὅτι Χριστὸς ἀπέθανεν ὑπὲρ τῶν ἁμαρτιῶν ἡμῶν κατὰ τὰς γραφὰς **4** καὶ ὅτι ἐτάφη καὶ ὅτι ἐγήγερται τῇ ἡμέρᾳ τῇ τρίτῃ κατὰ τὰς γραφὰς **5** καὶ ὅτι ὤφθη Κηφᾷ εἶτα τοῖς δώδεκα· **6** ἔπειτα ὤφθη ἐπάνω πεντακοσίοις ἀδελφοῖς ἐφάπαξ, ἐξ ὧν οἱ πλείονες μένουσιν ἕως ἄρτι, τινὲς δὲ ἐκοιμήθησαν· **7** ἔπειτα ὤφθη Ἰακώβῳ εἶτα τοῖς ἀποστόλοις πᾶσιν· **8** ἔσχατον δὲ πάντων ὡσπερεὶ τῷ ἐκτρώματι ὤφθη κἀμοί. ¶ **9** Ἐγὼ γάρ εἰμι ὁ ἐλάχιστος τῶν ἀποστόλων ὃς οὐκ εἰμὶ ἱκανὸς καλεῖσθαι ἀπόστολος, διότι ἐδίωξα τὴν ἐκκλησίαν τοῦ θεοῦ· **10** χάριτι δὲ θεοῦ εἰμι ὅ εἰμι, καὶ ἡ χάρις αὐτοῦ ἡ εἰς ἐμὲ οὐ κενὴ ἐγενήθη, ἀλλὰ περισσότερον αὐτῶν πάντων ἐκοπίασα, οὐκ ἐγὼ δὲ ἀλλὰ ἡ χάρις τοῦ θεοῦ [ἡ] σὺν ἐμοί. **11** εἴτε οὖν ἐγὼ εἴτε ἐκεῖνοι, οὕτως

that was with me. **11** Whether, then, it was I or they, this is what we preach, and this is what you believed.
ἡ σὺν ἐμοί εἴτε οὖν ἐγὼ εἴτε ἐκεῖνοι οὕτως ← ← → κηρύσσομεν καὶ οὕτως ← ← → ἐπιστεύσατε
d.nsf p.d r.ds.1 cj cj r.ns.1 cj r.npm adv v.pai.1p cj adv v.aai.2p
3836 5250 1609 1664 4036 1609 1664 1697 4048 3062 2779 4048 4409

The Resurrection of the Dead

15:12 But if it is preached that Christ has been raised from the dead, how can some of you say that
δὲ Εἰ → κηρύσσεται ὅτι Χριστὸς → → ἐγήγερται ἐκ νεκρῶν πῶς → τινες ἐν ὑμῖν λέγουσιν ὅτι
cj cj v.ppi.3s cj n.nsm v.rpi.3s p.g a.gpm cj r.npm p.d r.dp.2 v.pai.3p cj
1254 1623 3062 4022 5986 1586 1666 3738 4802 3306 5516 1877 7007 3306 4022

there is no resurrection of the dead? **13** If there is no resurrection of the dead, then not even Christ has
ἔστιν οὐκ ἀνάστασις → νεκρῶν δὲ εἰ → ἔστιν οὐκ ἀνάστασις → νεκρῶν οὐδὲ ← Χριστὸς →
v.pai.3s pl n.nsf a.gpm cj cj v.pai.3s pl n.nsf a.gpm adv n.nsm
1639 4024 414 3738 1254 1623 1639 4024 414 3738 4028 5986

been raised. **14** And if Christ has not been raised, our preaching is useless and so is your
ἐγήγερται δὲ εἰ Χριστὸς οὐκ ἐγήγερται ἄρα [καὶ] ἡμῶν ⌐τὸ κήρυγμα⌐ κενὸν καὶ κενὴ ὑμῶν
v.rpi.3s cj cj n.nsm pl v.rpi.3s cj adv r.gp.1 d.nsn n.nsn a.nsn cj a.nsf r.gp.2
1586 1254 1623 5986 1586 4024 726 2779 7005 3836 3060 3031 2779 3031 7007

faith. **15** More than that, we are then found to be false witnesses about God, for we have testified
⌐ἡ πίστις⌐ δὲ καὶ ← ← → εὑρισκόμεθα → ψευδομάρτυρες ⌐τοῦ θεοῦ⌐ ὅτι → ἐμαρτυρήσαμεν
d.nsf n.nsf cj adv v.ppi.1p n.npm d.gsm n.gsm cj v.aai.1p
3836 4411 1254 2779 2351 6020 3836 2536 4022 3455

about God that he raised Christ from the dead. But he did not raise him if in fact the dead are not
κατὰ ⌐τοῦ θεοῦ⌐ ὅτι → ἤγειρεν ⌐τὸν Χριστόν⌐ → οὐκ ἤγειρεν ὂν εἴπερ ἄρα ← νεκροὶ → οὐκ
p.g d.gsm n.gsm cj v.aai.3s d.asm n.asm pl v.aai.3s r.asm cj cj a.npm pl
2848 3836 2536 4022 1586 3836 5986 1586 1586 4024 1586 4005 1642 726 3738 1586 4024

raised. **16** For if the dead are not raised, then Christ has not been raised either. **17** And if Christ has not been
ἐγείρονται γὰρ εἰ νεκροὶ → οὐκ ἐγείρονται Χριστὸς → οὐδὲ → ἐγήγερται δὲ εἰ Χριστὸς → οὐκ
v.ppi.3s cj cj a.npm pl v.ppi.3s n.nsm adv v.rpi.3s cj cj n.nsm pl
1586 1142 1623 3738 1586 4024 1586 5986 1586 4028 1586 1254 1623 5986 1586 4074

raised, your faith is futile; you are still in your sins. **18** Then those also who have fallen asleep in
ἐγήγερται ὑμῶν ⌐ἡ πίστις⌐ ματαία → ἐστὲ ἔτι ἐν ὑμῶν ⌐ταῖς ἁμαρτίαις⌐ ἄρα οἱ καὶ ← → κοιμηθέντες ἐν
v.rpi.3s r.gp.2 d.nsf n.nsf a.nsf v.pai.2p adv p.d r.gp.2 d.dpf n.dpf cj d.npm adv pt.ap.npm p.d
1586 7007 3836 4411 3469 1639 2285 1877 7007 3836 281 726 3836 2779 3836 3121 1877

Christ are lost. **19** If only for this life we have hope in Christ, we are to be pitied more than all
Χριστῷ ἀπώλοντο εἰ μόνον ἐν ταύτῃ ⌐τῇ ζωῇ⌐ → ἐσμὲν ἠλπικότες ἐν Χριστῷ → ἐσμέν ἐλεεινότεροι ← → πάντων
n.dsm v.ami.3p cj adv p.d r.dsf d.dsf n.dsf v.pai.1p pt.ra.npm p.d n.dsm v.pai.1p a.npm.c a.gpm
5986 660 1623 3667 1877 4047 3836 2437 1639 1827 1877 5986 1639 1795 4246

men. ¶ **20** But Christ has indeed been raised from the dead, the firstfruits of those who have fallen
ἀνθρώπων δὲ Χριστὸς Νυνὶ → ἐγήγερται ἐκ νεκρῶν ἀπαρχὴ → τῶν →
n.gpm cj n.nsm adv v.rpi.3s p.g a.gpm n.nsf d.gpm
476 1254 5986 3815 1586 1666 3738 569 3836

asleep. **21** For since death came through a man, the resurrection of the dead comes also through a man.
κεκοιμημένων γὰρ ἐπειδὴ θάνατος δι᾽ ἀνθρώπου ἀνάστασις → νεκρῶν καὶ δι᾽ ἀνθρώπου
pt.rp.gpm cj cj n.nsm p.g n.gsm n.nsf a.gpm adv p.g n.gsm
3121 1142 2076 2505 1328 476 414 3738 2779 1328 476

22 For as in Adam all die, so in Christ all will be made alive. **23** But each
γὰρ ὥσπερ ἐν ⌐τῷ Ἀδὰμ⌐ πάντες ἀποθνῄσκουσιν οὕτως καὶ ἐν ⌐τῷ Χριστῷ⌐ πάντες → → → ζῳοποιηθήσονται δὲ Ἕκαστος
cj cj p.d d.dsm n.dsm a.npm v.pai.3p adv adv p.d d.dsm n.dsm a.npm v.fpi.3p cj n.nsm
1142 6061 1877 3836 77 4246 633 4048 2779 1877 3836 5986 4246 2443 1254 1667

in his own turn: Christ, the firstfruits; then, when he comes, those who belong to him. **24** Then the
ἐν τῷ ἰδίῳ τάγματι Χριστός ἀπαρχὴ ἔπειτα ἐν αὐτοῦ ⌐τῇ παρουσίᾳ⌐ οἱ ← → ⌐τοῦ Χριστοῦ⌐ εἶτα τὸ
p.d d.dsn a.dsn n.dsn n.nsm n.nsf adv p.d r.gsm.3 d.dsf n.dsf d.npm d.gsm n.gsm adv d.nsn
1877 3836 2625 5413 5986 569 2083 1877 899 3836 4242 3836 3836 5986 1663 3836

end will come, when he hands over the kingdom to God the Father after he has destroyed all
τέλος ὅταν → παραδιδῷ ← τὴν βασιλείαν → ⌐τῷ θεῷ⌐ καὶ πατρί ὅταν → → καταργήσῃ πᾶσαν
n.nsn cj v.pas.3s d.asf n.asf d.dsm n.dsm cj n.dsm cj v.aas.3s a.asf
5465 4020 4140 3836 993 3836 2536 2779 4252 4020 2934 4246

κηρύσσομεν καὶ οὕτως ἐπιστεύσατε.
15:12 Εἰ δὲ Χριστὸς κηρύσσεται ὅτι ἐκ νεκρῶν ἐγήγερται, πῶς λέγουσιν ἐν ὑμῖν τινες ὅτι ἀνάστασις νεκρῶν οὐκ ἔστιν; **13** εἰ δὲ ἀνάστασις νεκρῶν οὐκ ἔστιν, οὐδὲ Χριστὸς ἐγήγερται· **14** εἰ δὲ Χριστὸς οὐκ ἐγήγερται, κενὸν ἄρα [καὶ] τὸ κήρυγμα ἡμῶν, κενὴ καὶ ἡ πίστις ὑμῶν· **15** εὑρισκόμεθα δὲ καὶ ψευδομάρτυρες τοῦ θεοῦ, ὅτι ἐμαρτυρήσαμεν κατὰ τοῦ θεοῦ ὅτι ἤγειρεν τὸν Χριστόν, ὂν οὐκ ἤγειρεν εἴπερ ἄρα νεκροὶ οὐκ ἐγείρονται. **16** εἰ γὰρ νεκροὶ οὐκ ἐγείρονται, οὐδὲ Χριστὸς ἐγήγερται· **17** εἰ δὲ Χριστὸς οὐκ ἐγήγερται, ματαία ἡ πίστις ὑμῶν, ἔτι ἐστὲ ἐν ταῖς ἁμαρτίαις ὑμῶν, **18** ἄρα καὶ οἱ κοιμηθέντες ἐν Χριστῷ ἀπώλοντο. **19** εἰ ἐν τῇ ζωῇ ταύτῃ ἐν Χριστῷ ἠλπικότες ἐσμὲν μόνον, ἐλεεινότεροι πάντων ἀνθρώπων ἐσμέν. ¶ **20** Νυνὶ δὲ Χριστὸς ἐγήγερται ἐκ νεκρῶν ἀπαρχὴ τῶν κεκοιμημένων. **21** ἐπειδὴ γὰρ δι᾽ ἀνθρώπου θάνατος, καὶ δι᾽ ἀνθρώπου ἀνάστασις νεκρῶν. **22** ὥσπερ γὰρ ἐν τῷ Ἀδὰμ πάντες ἀποθνῄσκουσιν, οὕτως καὶ ἐν τῷ Χριστῷ πάντες ζῳοποιηθήσονται. **23** ἕκαστος δὲ ἐν τῷ ἰδίῳ τάγματι· ἀπαρχὴ Χριστός, ἔπειτα οἱ τοῦ Χριστοῦ ἐν τῇ παρουσίᾳ αὐτοῦ, **24** εἶτα τὸ τέλος, ὅταν παραδιδῷ τὴν βασιλείαν τῷ θεῷ καὶ

dominion,   authority and power. **25** For he   must reign   until   he has put all   his enemies under
ἀρχὴν   καὶ πᾶσαν ἐξουσίαν καὶ δύναμιν   γὰρ αὐτὸν δεῖ βασιλεύειν ἄχρι οὗ → → θῇ   πάντας τοὺς ἐχθροὺς ὑπὸ
n.asf   cj   a.asf   n.asf   cj   n.asf   cj   r.asm.3   v.pai.3s   f.pa   p.g   r.gsm   v.aas.3s   a.apm   d.apm a.apm   p.a
794   2779 4246   2026   2779 1539   1142 899   1256   948   4005   5502   4246   3836 2398   5679

his feet.   **26** The last   enemy to be destroyed is death.   **27** For he "has put   everything under his
αὐτοῦ ⌐τοὺς πόδας⌐   ἔσχατος ἐχθρὸς → → καταργεῖται ὁ θάνατος⌐   γὰρ → → ὑπέταξεν πάντα   ὑπὸ αὐτοῦ
r.gsm.3   d.apm n.apm   a.nsm   a.nsm   v.ppi.3s   d.nsm n.nsm   cj   v.aai.3s a.apn   p.a   r.gsm.3
899   3836 4546   2274   2398   2934   3836 2505   1142   5718   4246   5679   899

feet."   Now when it says that "everything" has been put   under him, it is clear that *this does*   *not include*
⌐τοὺς πόδας⌐ δὲ   ὅταν → εἴπῃ ὅτι πάντα → → ὑποτέτακται ←   δῆλον ὅτι   ἐκτὸς
d.apm n.apm   cj   cj   v.aas.3s cj   a.npn   v.rpi.3s   a.nsn cj   p.g
3836 4546   1254   4020   3306 4022 4246   5718   1316 4022   1760

God himself, who put everything under   Christ. **28** When he has done   this,   then   the Son
τοῦ → ⌐τὰ πάντα⌐ ὑποτάξαντος αὐτῷ   δὲ ὅταν → → ὑποταγῇ αὐτῷ ⌐τὰ πάντα⌐ τότε [καὶ] ὁ υἱὸς
d.gsm   d.apn a.apn   pt.aa.gsm   r.dsm.3   cj   cj   v.aps.3s   r.dsm.3 d.npn a.apn   adv   adv   d.nsm n.nsm
3836   3836 4246   5718   899   1254 4020   5718   899   3836 4246   5538   2779   3836 5626

himself will be made subject   to him who put everything under   him, so that God   may be   all
αὐτὸς → → ὑποταγήσεται → τῷ ← → ⌐τὰ πάντα⌐ ὑποτάξαντι αὐτῷ ἵνα ←   ὁ θεὸς → ᾖ   [τὰ] πάντα
r.nsm   v.fpi.3s   d.dsm   d.apn a.apn   pt.aa.dsm   r.dsm.3 cj   d.nsm n.nsm   v.pas.3s d.npn a.npn
899   5718   3836   5718 3836 4246   5718   899   2671   3836 2536   1639   3836 4246

in all.   ¶   **29** Now if there is no resurrection, what will those do   who are baptized   for the dead? If
ἐν πᾶσιν   Ἐπεὶ   τί → → ποιήσουσιν οἱ → βαπτιζόμενοι ὑπὲρ τῶν νεκρῶν εἰ
p.d a.dpn   cj   r.asn   v.fai.3p   d.npm   pt.pp.npm   p.g   d.gpm a.gpm   cj
1877 4246   2075   5515   4472   3836   5642   966   3836 3738   1623

the dead are not raised   at   all, why   are people baptized   for them? **30** And as for us, why do we   endanger
νεκροὶ → οὐκ ἐγείρονται ὅλως → τί καὶ → βαπτίζονται ὑπὲρ αὐτῶν   καὶ   Τί → ἡμεῖς κινδυνεύομεν
a.npm   pl   v.ppi.3p   adv   r.asn adv   v.ppi.3p   p.g   r.gpm.3   cj   r.asn   r.np.1   v.pai.1p
3738   1586 4024   1586   3914   5515 2779   966   5642   899   2779   5515   7005 3073

ourselves every hour? **31** I die   every day   – *I mean that,* brothers – just as surely as I glory   over
πᾶσαν ὥραν   → ἀποθνήσκω καθ᾽ ἡμέραν νὴ   [ἀδελφοί]   → ἔχω καύχησιν⌐
a.asf   n.asf   v.pai.1s   p.a   n.asf   pl   n.vpm   v.pai.1s n.asf
4246   6052   633   2848   2465   3755   81   2400   3018

you   in Christ Jesus our Lord. **32** If I fought   wild beasts in Ephesus for   merely human
⌐τὴν ὑμετέραν⌐ ἣν ἐν Χριστῷ Ἰησοῦ ἡμῶν τῷ κυρίῳ⌐ εἰ ἐθηριομάχησα ←   ἐν Ἐφέσῳ κατὰ ←   ἄνθρωπον
d.asf a.asf   r.asf p.d   n.dsm   n.dsm   r.gp.1 d.dsm n.dsm   cj   v.aai.1s   p.d n.dsf   p.a   n.asm
3836 5629   4005 1877   5986   2652   7005 3836 3261   1623   2562   1877 2387   2848   476

reasons, what have I   gained? If the dead are not raised, "Let us eat   and drink, for tomorrow we
→ τί μοι ⌐τὸ ὄφελος⌐ εἰ   νεκροὶ → οὐκ ἐγείρονται → φάγωμεν καὶ πίωμεν γὰρ αὔριον   →
r.nsn   r.ds.1 d.nsn n.nsn   cj   a.npm   pl   v.ppi.3p   v.aas.1p   cj   v.aas.1p cj   adv
5515   1609 3836 4055   1623   3738   1586 4024 1586   2266   2779 4403   1142 892

die."   **33** Do not be misled: "Bad company corrupts good   character." **34** Come back to your senses   *as you*
ἀποθνῄσκομεν   → μὴ → πλανᾶσθε κακαὶ ὁμιλίαι φθείρουσιν χρηστὰ ἤθη → → → → ἐκνήψατε
v.pai.1p   pl   v.ppm.2p n.npf   n.npf   v.pai.3p   a.apn   n.npn   v.aam.2p
633   4414 3590   4414   2805   3918   5780   5982 2456   1729

ought, and stop sinning; for there are some who are   ignorant of God – I say this to   your shame.
δικαίως καὶ μὴ ἁμαρτάνετε γὰρ   τινες ἔχουσιν ἀγνωσίαν → θεοῦ → λαλῶ   πρὸς ὑμῖν ἐντροπὴν
adv   cj   pl   v.pam.2p cj   r.npm   v.pai.3p   n.asf   n.gsm → v.pai.1s   p.a   r.dp.2 n.asf
1469   2779 3590   279   1142   5516   2400   57   2536   3281   4639   7007 1959

The Resurrection Body

15:35 But   someone may ask, "How are the dead raised?   With what kind of body will they come?" **36** How
Ἀλλὰ   τις   → ἐρεῖ πῶς → οἱ νεκροί ἐγείρονται δὲ → → ποίῳ → σώματι →   ἔρχονται
cj   r.nsm   v.fai.3s   r.dsn   d.npm a.npm   v.ppi.3p   cj   r.dsn   n.dsn   v.pmi.3p
247   5516   3306 4020   1586 3836 3738   1586   1254   4481   5393   2262

foolish! What you sow   does not come to life   unless   it dies. **37**   When you sow,   you do not
ἄφρων ὃ   σὺ σπείρεις → οὐ   → ζῳοποιεῖται ⌐ἐὰν μὴ⌐ → ἀποθάνῃ καὶ ὃ →   σπείρεις → οὐ
n.vsm   r.asn   r.ns.2 v.pai.2s   pl   v.ppi.3s   cj   pl   v.aas.3s   cj   r.asn   v.pai.2s   pl
933   4005   5148 5062   4024   2443   1569 3590   633   2779 4005   5062   5062 4024

πατρί, ὅταν καταργήσῃ πᾶσαν ἀρχὴν καὶ πᾶσαν ἐξουσίαν καὶ δύναμιν. **25** δεῖ γὰρ αὐτὸν βασιλεύειν ἄχρι οὗ θῇ πάντας τοὺς ἐχθροὺς ὑπὸ τοὺς πόδας αὐτοῦ. **26** ἔσχατος ἐχθρὸς καταργεῖται ὁ θάνατος· **27** πάντα γὰρ ὑπέταξεν ὑπὸ τοὺς πόδας αὐτοῦ. ὅταν δὲ εἴπῃ ὅτι πάντα ὑποτέτακται, δῆλον ὅτι ἐκτὸς τοῦ ὑποτάξαντος αὐτῷ τὰ πάντα. **28** ὅταν δὲ ὑποταγῇ αὐτῷ τὰ πάντα, τότε [καὶ] αὐτὸς ὁ υἱὸς ὑποταγήσεται τῷ ὑποτάξαντι αὐτῷ τὰ πάντα, ἵνα ᾖ ὁ θεὸς [τὰ] πάντα ἐν πᾶσιν. ¶ **29** Ἐπεὶ τί ποιήσουσιν οἱ βαπτιζόμενοι ὑπὲρ τῶν νεκρῶν; εἰ ὅλως νεκροὶ οὐκ ἐγείρονται, τί καὶ βαπτίζονται ὑπὲρ αὐτῶν; **30** τί καὶ ἡμεῖς κινδυνεύομεν πᾶσαν ὥραν; **31** καθ᾽ ἡμέραν ἀποθνήσκω, νὴ τὴν ὑμετέραν καύχησιν, [ἀδελφοί,] ἣν ἔχω ἐν Χριστῷ Ἰησοῦ τῷ κυρίῳ ἡμῶν. **32** εἰ κατὰ ἄνθρωπον ἐθηριομάχησα ἐν Ἐφέσῳ, τί μοι τὸ ὄφελος; εἰ νεκροὶ οὐκ ἐγείρονται, Φάγωμεν καὶ πίωμεν, αὔριον γὰρ ἀποθνή σκομεν. **33** μὴ πλανᾶσθε· Φθείρουσιν ἤθη χρηστὰ ὁμιλίαι κακαί. **34** ἐκνήψατε δικαίως καὶ μὴ ἁμαρτάνετε, ἀγνωσίαν γὰρ θεοῦ τινες ἔχουσιν, πρὸς ἐντροπὴν ὑμῖν λαλῶ.

15:35 Ἀλλὰ ἐρεῖ τις, Πῶς ἐγείρονται οἱ νεκροί; ποίῳ δὲ σώματι ἔρχονται; **36** ἄφρων, σὺ ὃ σπείρεις, οὐ ζῳοποιεῖται ἐὰν μὴ ἀποθάνῃ· **37** καὶ ὃ σπείρεις, οὐ τὸ σῶμα τὸ γενησόμενον σπείρεις ἀλλὰ γυμνὸν κόκκον εἰ τύχοι σίτου ἢ τινος τῶν λοιπῶν· **38** ὁ

plant   the   body that will be,   but   just   a seed, perhaps of wheat or of something else.   **38** But
σπείρεις   τὸ   σῶμα   τὸ   → γενησόμενον   ἀλλὰ γυμνὸν κόκκον εἰ τύχοι, → σίτου   ἤ   τινος   ⌐τῶν λοιπῶν⌐   δὲ
v.pai.2s d.asn n.asn d.asn   pt.fm.asn   cj   a.asm   n.asm   cj v.aao.3s   n.gsm cj   r.gsn   d.gpn a.gpn   cj
5062   3836 5393   3836   1181   247   1218   3133   1623 5593   4992 2445 5516   3836 3370   1254

God   gives it   a body as   he has   determined, and to each kind of seed   he gives its   own   body.
ὁ   θεὸς δίδωσιν αὐτῷ σῶμα καθὼς →   → ἠθέλησεν,   καὶ → ἑκάστῳ ←   → ⌐τῶν σπερμάτων⌐ ἴδιον ← σῶμα
d.nsm n.nsm v.pai.3s r.dsm.3 n.asn c.adv   v.aai.3s   cj   r.dsm   d.gpn n.gpn   a.asn   n.asn
3836 2536   1443   899   5393 2777   2527   2779   1667   3836 5065   2625   5393

39 All   flesh is not the same: Men   have one kind of flesh,   animals have another,   birds
πᾶσα σὰρξ   Οὐ ἡ αὐτὴ σὰρξ ἀλλὰ μὲν ἀνθρώπων   →   ἄλλη   δὲ κτηνῶν   ἄλλη   δὲ σὰρξ πτηνῶν
a.nsf n.nsf pl d.nsf r.nsf n.nsf   cj   pl   n.gpm   r.nsf   pl   n.gpn   r.nsf   pl n.nsf n.gpn
4246 4922   4024 3836 899   4922   247   3525   257   1254 3229   257   1254 4922 4764

another   and fish another.   **40** There are also heavenly bodies and there are earthly bodies; but   the splendor
ἄλλη   σὰρξ δὲ ἰχθύων ἄλλη.   καὶ ἐπουράνια σώματα καὶ   ἐπίγεια σώματα ἀλλὰ μὲν ἡ δόξα
r.nsf n.nsf cj n.gpm r.nsf   cj   a.npn   n.npn   cj   a.npn   n.npn   cj   pl d.nsf n.nsf
257   4922   1254 2716   257   2779 2230   5393   2779   2103   5393   247   3525 3836 1518

of the heavenly bodies is one kind, and the splendor of the earthly bodies is another. **41** The sun has one kind of
→ τῶν ἐπουρανίων ←   ἑτέρα   δὲ ἡ   → τῶν ἐπιγείων ←   ἑτέρα   ἡλίου →   ἄλλη
d.gpn a.gpn   r.nsf pl d.nsf   d.gpn a.gpn   r.nsf   n.gsm   r.nsf
3836 2230   2283 1254 3836   3836 2103   2283   2463   257

splendor,   the moon another   and the stars another;   and star differs from star   in splendor. ¶
δόξα   καὶ   σελήνης ἄλλη   δόξα καὶ   ἀστέρων ἄλλη   δόξα γὰρ ἀστὴρ διαφέρει ←   ἀστέρος ἐν δόξῃ
n.nsf cj   n.gsf   r.nsf n.nsf cj   n.gpm   r.nsf   n.nsf cj   n.nsm   v.pai.3s   n.gsm   p.d n.dsf
1518 2779   4943   257   1518 2779   843   257   1518 1142 843   1422   843   1877 1518

42 So   will it be   with the resurrection of the dead. The body that is sown   is   perishable, it is raised ἐν
οὕτως ← ← καὶ   ἡ ἀνάστασις → τῶν νεκρῶν   → σπείρεται ἐν φθορᾷ   → ἐγείρεται ἐν
adv   adv d.nsf n.nsf   d.gpm a.gpm   v.ppi.3s p.d n.dsf   v.ppi.3s   p.d
4048   2779 3836   414   3836 3738   5062   1877 5785   1586   1877

imperishable;   **43** it is sown   in dishonor, it is raised in glory; it is sown   in weakness, it is raised in power; **44** it is
ἀφθαρσίᾳ   → σπείρεται ἐν ἀτιμίᾳ   → ἐγείρεται ἐν δόξῃ → σπείρεται ἐν ἀσθενείᾳ → ἐγείρεται ἐν δυνάμει   →
n.dsf   v.ppi.3s p.d n.dsf   v.ppi.3s p.d n.dsf   v.ppi.3s p.d n.dsf   v.ppi.3s p.d n.dsf
914   5062   1877 871   1586   1877 1518   5062   1877 819   1586   1877 1539

sown   a natural body, it is raised a spiritual body.   ¶ If there is   a natural body, there is   also a
σπείρεται ψυχικὸν σῶμα → ἐγείρεται πνευματικὸν σῶμα.   Εἰ → ἔστιν ψυχικὸν σῶμα → ἔστιν καὶ
v.ppi.3s   a.nsn   n.nsn   v.ppi.3s   n.nsn   n.nsn   cj   v.pai.3s a.nsn   n.nsn   v.pai.3s adv
5062   6035   5393   1586   4461   5393   1623   1639 6035   5393   1639   2779

spiritual body. **45** So   it is written: "The first man   Adam became   a living being"; the last   Adam,
πνευματικόν ←   οὕτως καὶ → γέγραπται ὁ πρῶτος ἄνθρωπος Ἀδὰμ ἐγένετο εἰς ζῶσαν ψυχὴν ὁ ἔσχατος Ἀδὰμ
a.nsn   adv   adv   v.rpi.3s d.nsm a.nsm   n.nsm   n.nsm v.ami.3s p.a pt.pa.asf n.asf d.nsm a.nsm n.nsm
4461   4048   2779   1211   3836 4755   476   77   1181   1650 2409   6034 3836 2274   77

a life-giving spirit. **46**   The spiritual   did not come first, but the natural, and after that the spiritual.
εἰς ζωοποιοῦν πνεῦμα ἀλλ' τὸ πνευματικὸν οὐ   πρῶτον ἀλλὰ τὸ ψυχικόν   ἔπειτα ← τὸ πνευματικόν
p.a pt.pa.asn n.asn   cj   d.nsn a.nsn   pl   adv   cj   d.nsn a.nsn   adv   d.nsn a.nsn
1650 2443   4460   247 3836 4461   4024   4754   247 3836 6035   2083   3836 4461

47 The first   man   was of the dust of the earth, the second man   from heaven. **48** As   was the earthly man, so
ὁ πρῶτος ἄνθρωπος   ἐκ   χοϊκός → γῆς ὁ δεύτερος ἄνθρωπος ἐξ οὐρανοῦ   οἷος ὁ χοϊκός ← καὶ
d.nsm a.nsm n.nsm   p.g   a.nsn   n.gsf d.nsm a.nsm   n.nsm   p.g n.gsm   r.nsm d.nsm a.nsm   adv
3836 4755   476   1666 5954   1178 3836 1311   476   1666 4041   3888 3836 5954   2779

are those who are of the earth; and as   is the man from heaven,   so also   are those who are of heaven.
τοιοῦτοι οἱ → → χοϊκοί καὶ οἷος ὁ ← → ἐπουράνιος καὶ τοιοῦτοι → οἱ → → ἐπουράνιοι
r.npm   d.npm   a.npm cj   r.nsm d.nsm   a.nsm   adv r.npm   d.npm   a.npm
5525   3836   5954   2779 3888 3836   2230   2779 5525   3836   2230

49 And just   as we have borne   the likeness of the earthly man, so shall we bear   the likeness of the man from
καὶ καθὼς ← ← ἐφορέσαμεν τὴν εἰκόνα τοῦ χοϊκοῦ   → καὶ → → φορέσομεν τὴν εἰκόνα → τοῦ ← →
cj   cj   v.aai.1p   d.asf n.asf d.gsm a.gsm   adv   v.fai.1p   d.asf n.asf   d.gsm
2779 2777   5841   3836 1635 3836 5954   2779   5841   3836 1635   3836

δὲ θεὸς δίδωσιν αὐτῷ σῶμα καθὼς ἠθέλησεν, καὶ ἑκάστῳ τῶν σπερμάτων ἴδιον σῶμα. ³⁹ οὐ πᾶσα σὰρξ ἡ αὐτὴ σὰρξ ἀλλὰ
ἄλλη μὲν ἀνθρώπων, ἄλλη δὲ σὰρξ κτηνῶν, ἄλλη δὲ σὰρξ πτηνῶν, ἄλλη δὲ ἰχθύων. ⁴⁰ καὶ σώματα ἐπουράνια, καὶ σώματα
ἐπίγεια· ἀλλὰ ἑτέρα μὲν ἡ τῶν ἐπουρανίων δόξα, ἑτέρα δὲ ἡ τῶν ἐπιγείων. ⁴¹ ἄλλη δόξα ἡλίου, καὶ ἄλλη δόξα σελήνης, καὶ
ἄλλη δόξα ἀστέρων· ἀστὴρ γὰρ ἀστέρος διαφέρει ἐν δόξῃ. ¶ ⁴² Οὕτως καὶ ἡ ἀνάστασις τῶν νεκρῶν. σπείρεται ἐν φθορᾷ,
ἐγείρεται ἐν ἀφθαρσίᾳ· ⁴³ σπείρεται ἐν ἀτιμίᾳ, ἐγείρεται ἐν δόξῃ· σπείρεται ἐν ἀσθενείᾳ, ἐγείρεται ἐν δυνάμει· ⁴⁴ σπείρεται
σῶμα ψυχικόν, ἐγείρεται σῶμα πνευματικόν. ¶ εἰ ἔστιν σῶμα ψυχικόν, ἔστιν καὶ πνευματικόν. ⁴⁵ οὕτως καὶ γέγραπται,
Ἐγένετο ὁ πρῶτος ἄνθρωπος Ἀδὰμ εἰς ψυχὴν ζῶσαν, ὁ ἔσχατος Ἀδὰμ εἰς πνεῦμα ζωοποιοῦν. ⁴⁶ ἀλλ' οὐ πρῶτον τὸ πνευματικὸν
ἀλλὰ τὸ ψυχικόν, ἔπειτα τὸ πνευματικόν. ⁴⁷ ὁ πρῶτος ἄνθρωπος ἐκ γῆς χοϊκός, ὁ δεύτερος ἄνθρωπος ἐξ οὐρανοῦ. ⁴⁸ οἷος ὁ
χοϊκός, τοιοῦτοι καὶ οἱ χοϊκοί, καὶ οἷος ὁ ἐπουράνιος, τοιοῦτοι καὶ οἱ ἐπουράνιοι· ⁴⁹ καὶ καθὼς ἐφορέσαμεν τὴν εἰκόνα τοῦ

heaven. ¶ **50** I declare to you, brothers, that flesh and blood cannot inherit the kingdom of
ἐπουρανίου δέ → φημι Τοῦτο ἀδελφοί ὅτι σὰρξ καὶ αἷμα ‚οὐ δύναται‚ κληρονομῆσαι βασιλείαν →
a.gsm cj r.asn v.pai.1s n.vpm cj n.nsf cj n.nsn pl v.ppi.3s f.aa n.asf
2230 1254 5774 4047 81 4022 4922 2779 135 4024 1538 3099 993

God, nor does the perishable inherit the imperishable. **51** Listen, I tell you a mystery: We will not all
θεοῦ οὐδὲ → ἡ φθορὰ κληρονομεῖ τὴν ἀφθαρσίαν ἰδοὺ → λέγω ὑμῖν μυστήριον → → οὐ πάντες
n.gsm cj d.nsf n.nsf v.pai.3s d.asf n.asf v.pai.1s r.dp.2 n.asn pl a.npm
2536 4028 3836 5785 3099 3836 914 2627 3306 7007 3696 3121 3121 4024 4246

sleep, but we will all be changed — **52** in a flash, in the twinkling of an eye, at the last trumpet.
κοιμηθησόμεθα δὲ → → πάντες → ἀλλαγησόμεθα ἐν ἀτόμῳ ἐν ῥιπῇ ὀφθαλμοῦ ἐν τῇ ἐσχάτῃ σάλπιγγι
v.fpi.1p cj a.npm v.fpi.1p p.d a.dsn p.d n.dsf n.gsm p.d d.dsf a.dsf n.dsf
3121 1254 248 248 4246 248 1877 875 1877 4846 4057 1877 3836 2274 4894

For the trumpet will sound, the dead will be raised imperishable, and we will be changed. **53** For the
γὰρ → → σαλπίσει καὶ οἱ νεκροὶ → ἐγερθήσονται ἄφθαρτοι καὶ ἡμεῖς → → ἀλλαγησόμεθα γὰρ τὸ
cj v.fai.3s cj d.npm a.npm v.fpi.3p a.npm cj r.np.1 v.fpi.1p cj d.asn
1142 4895 2779 3836 3738 1586 915 2779 7005 248 1142 3836

perishable must clothe itself with the imperishable, and the mortal with immortality. **54**
φθαρτὸν τοῦτο Δεῖ ἐνδύσασθαι → → ἀφθαρσίαν καὶ τὸ θνητὸν τοῦτο ἐνδύσασθαι → ἀθανασίαν δὲ
a.asn r.asn v.pai.3s f.am n.asf cj d.asn a.asn r.asn f.am n.asf cj
5778 4047 1256 1907 914 2779 3836 2570 4047 1907 114 1254

When the perishable has been clothed with the imperishable, and the mortal with immortality,
ὅταν τὸ φθαρτὸν τοῦτο → ἐνδύσηται → ἀφθαρσίαν καὶ τὸ θνητὸν τοῦτο ἐνδύσηται → ἀθανασίαν
cj d.nsn a.nsn r.nsn v.ams.3s n.asf cj d.nsn a.nsn r.nsn v.ams.3s n.asf
4020 3836 5778 4047 1907 914 2779 3836 2570 4047 1907 114

then the saying that is written will come true: "Death has been swallowed up in victory." **55** "Where, O
τότε ὁ λόγος ὁ → γεγραμμένος → γενήσεται ὁ θάνατος, → → κατεπόθη εἰς νῖκος ποῦ →
adv d.nsm n.nsm d.nsm pt.rp.nsm v.fmi.3s d.nsm n.nsm v.api.3s p.a n.asn adv
5538 3836 3364 3836 1211 1181 3836 2505 2927 1650 3777 4543

death, is your victory? Where, O death, is your sting?" **56** The sting of death is sin, and the
θάνατε σου ‚τὸ νῖκος‚ ποῦ → θάνατε σου ‚τὸ κέντρον‚ δὲ τὸ κέντρον ‚τοῦ θανάτου‚ ἡ ἁμαρτία δὲ ἡ
n.vsm r.gs.2 d.nsn n.nsn cj n.vsm r.gs.2 d.nsn n.nsn cj d.nsn n.nsn d.gsm n.gsm d.nsf n.nsf cj d.nsf
2505 5148 3836 3777 4543 2505 5148 3836 3034 1254 3836 3034 3836 2505 3836 281 1254 3836

power of sin is the law. **57** But thanks be to God! He gives us the victory through our Lord
δύναμις → ‚τῆς ἁμαρτίας‚ ὁ νόμος δὲ χάρις → ‚τῷ θεῷ‚ τῷ διδόντι ἡμῖν τὸ νῖκος διὰ ἡμῶν ‚τοῦ κυρίου‚
n.nsf d.gsf n.gsf d.nsm n.nsm cj n.nsf d.dsm n.dsm d.dsm pt.pa.dsm r.dp.1 d.asn n.asn p.g r.gp.1 d.gsm n.gsm
1539 3836 281 3836 3795 1254 5921 3836 2536 3836 1443 7005 3836 3777 1328 7005 3836 3261

Jesus Christ. ¶ **58** Therefore, my dear brothers, stand firm. Let nothing move you. Always give
Ἰησοῦ Χριστοῦ Ὥστε μου ἀγαπητοί ἀδελφοί γίνεσθε ἑδραῖοι → ἀμετακίνητοι πάντοτε περισσεύοντες
n.gsm n.gsm cj r.gs.1 a.vpm n.vpm v.pmm.2p a.npm a.npm adv pt.pa.npm
2652 5986 6063 1609 28 81 1181 1612 293 4121 4355

yourselves fully to the work of the Lord, because you know that your labor in the Lord is not in vain.
← → → ἐν τῷ ἔργῳ → τοῦ κυρίου ὅτι → εἰδότες ὑμῶν ‚ὁ κόπος‚ ἐν κυρίῳ ἔστιν οὐκ → κενὸς
p.d d.dsn n.dsn d.gsm n.gsm cj pt.ra.npm r.gp.2 d.nsm n.nsm p.d n.dsm v.pai.3s pl a.nsm
1877 3836 2240 3836 3261 4022 3857 7007 3836 3160 1877 3261 1639 4024 3031

The Collection for God's People

16:1 Now about the collection for God's people: Do what I told the Galatian
δὲ Περὶ τῆς λογείας τῆς εἰς ‚τοὺς ἁγίους‚ ← ποιήσατε οὕτως καὶ ὑμεῖς ὥσπερ → διέταξα ταῖς ‚τῆς Γαλατίας‚
cj p.g d.gsf n.gsf d.gsf p.a d.apm a.apm v.aam.2p adv adv r.np.2 cj v.aai.1s d.dpf d.gsf n.gsf
1254 4309 3836 3356 3836 1650 3836 41 4472 4048 2779 7007 6061 1411 3836 3836 1130

churches to do. **2** On the first day of every week, each one of you should set aside a sum
ἐκκλησίαις κατὰ μίαν → σαββάτου ἕκαστος → ὑμῶν → τιθέτω παρ᾽ ἑαυτῷ ‚ὅ τι ἐὰν
n.dpf p.a a.asf n.gsn r.nsm r.gp.2 v.pam.3s p.d r.dsm.3 r.asn r.asn pl
1711 2848 1651 4879 1667 7007 5502 4123 1571 4005 5516 1569

of money in keeping with his income, saving it up, so that when I come no collections will have to be
→ → → εὐοδῶται θησαυρίζων ← ἵνα ← ὅταν → ἔλθω τότε μὴ λογείαι → → →
v.pps.3s pt.pa.nsm cj cj v.aas.1s adv pl n.npf
2338 2564 2671 4020 2262 5538 3590 3356

χοϊκοῦ, φορέσομεν καὶ τὴν εἰκόνα τοῦ ἐπουρανίου. ¶ **50** Τοῦτο δέ φημι, ἀδελφοί, ὅτι σὰρξ καὶ αἷμα βασιλείαν θεοῦ κληρονομῆσαι οὐ δύναται οὐδὲ ἡ φθορὰ τὴν ἀφθαρσίαν κληρονομεῖ. **51** ἰδοὺ μυστήριον ὑμῖν λέγω· πάντες οὐ κοιμηθησόμεθα, πάντες δὲ ἀλλαγησόμεθα, **52** ἐν ἀτόμῳ, ἐν ῥιπῇ ὀφθαλμοῦ, ἐν τῇ ἐσχάτῃ σάλπιγγι· σαλπίσει γὰρ καὶ οἱ νεκροὶ ἐγερθήσονται ἄφθαρτοι καὶ ἡμεῖς ἀλλαγησόμεθα. **53** δεῖ γὰρ τὸ φθαρτὸν τοῦτο ἐνδύσασθαι ἀφθαρσίαν καὶ τὸ θνητὸν τοῦτο ἐνδύσασθαι ἀθανασίαν. **54** ὅταν δὲ τὸ φθαρτὸν τοῦτο ἐνδύσηται ἀφθαρσίαν καὶ τὸ θνητὸν τοῦτο ἐνδύσηται ἀθανασίαν, τότε γενήσεται ὁ λόγος ὁ γεγραμμένος, Κατεπόθη ὁ θάνατος εἰς νῖκος. **55** ποῦ σου, θάνατε, τὸ νῖκος; ποῦ σου, θάνατε, τὸ κέντρον; **56** τὸ δὲ κέντρον τοῦ θανάτου ἡ ἁμαρτία, ἡ δὲ δύναμις τῆς ἁμαρτίας ὁ νόμος· **57** τῷ δὲ θεῷ χάρις τῷ διδόντι ἡμῖν τὸ νῖκος διὰ τοῦ κυρίου ἡμῶν Ἰησοῦ Χριστοῦ ¶ **58** Ὥστε, ἀδελφοί μου ἀγαπητοί, ἑδραῖοι γίνεσθε, ἀμετακίνητοι, περισσεύοντες ἐν τῷ ἔργῳ τοῦ κυρίου πάντοτε, εἰδότες ὅτι ὁ κόπος ὑμῶν οὐκ ἔστιν κενὸς ἐν κυρίῳ.

16:1 Περὶ δὲ τῆς λογείας τῆς εἰς τοὺς ἁγίους ὥσπερ διέταξα ταῖς ἐκκλησίαις τῆς Γαλατίας, οὕτως καὶ ὑμεῖς ποιήσατε. **2** κατὰ μίαν σαββάτου ἕκαστος ὑμῶν παρ᾽ ἑαυτῷ τιθέτω θησαυρίζων ὅ τι ἐὰν εὐοδῶται, ἵνα μὴ ὅταν ἔλθω τότε λογεῖαι γίνωνται. **3** ὅταν

made. **3** Then, when I arrive, I will give letters of introduction to the men you approve and send
γίνωνται δὲ ὅταν παραγένωμαι δι' ἐπιστολῶν οὓς ἐὰν δοκιμάσητε πέμψω
v.pms.3p cj cj v.ams.1s p.g n.gpf r.apm pl v.aas.2p v.fai.1s
1181 1254 4020 4134 1328 2186 4005 1569 1507 4287

them with your gift to Jerusalem. **4** If it seems advisable for me to go also, they will
τούτους ἀπενεγκεῖν ὑμῶν τὴν χάριν εἰς Ἰερουσαλήμ δὲ ἐὰν ᾖ ἄξιον καμὲ τοῦ πορεύεσθαι
r.apm f.aa r.gp.2 d.asf n.asf p.a n.asf cj cj v.pas.3s a.nsn crasis d.gsn f.pm
4047 708 7007 3836 5921 1650 2647 1254 1569 1639 545 4513 2743 3836 4513 2743

accompany me.
πορεύσονται σὺν ἐμοὶ
v.fmi.3p p.d r.ds.1
4513 5250 1609

Personal Requests

16:5 After I go through Macedonia, I will come to you – for I will be going through Macedonia.
δὲ ὅταν διέλθω Μακεδονίαν Ἐλεύσομαι πρὸς ὑμᾶς γὰρ διέρχομαι Μακεδονίαν
cj cj v.aas.1s n.asf v.fmi.1s p.a r.ap.2 cj v.pmi.1s n.asf
1254 4020 1451 3423 2262 4639 7007 1142 1451 3423

6 Perhaps I will stay with you awhile, or even spend the winter, so that you can help me on my
δὲ παραμενῶ πρὸς ὑμᾶς τυχὸν ἢ καὶ παραχειμάσω ἵνα ὑμεῖς προπέμψητε με
cj v.fai.1s p.a r.ap.2 pt.aa.asn cj adv v.fai.1s cj r.np.2 v.aas.2p r.as.1
1254 4169 4639 7007 5593 2445 2779 4199 2671 7007 4636 1609 4636 4636

journey, wherever I go. **7** I do not want to see you now and make only a passing visit; I hope to
οὗ ἐὰν πορεύωμαι γὰρ οὐ θέλω ἰδεῖν ὑμᾶς ἄρτι ἐν παρόδῳ γὰρ ἐλπίζω
adv pl v.pms.1s cj pl v.pai.1s f.aa r.ap.2 adv p.d n.dsf cj v.pai.1s
4636 4023 1569 4513 1142 2527 2527 4024 2527 1625 7007 785 1877 4227 1142 1827

spend some time with you, if the Lord permits. **8** But I will stay on at Ephesus until Pentecost, **9** because
ἐπιμεῖναι τινὰ χρόνον πρὸς ὑμᾶς ἐὰν ὁ κύριος ἐπιτρέψῃ δὲ ἐπιμενῶ ἐν Ἐφέσῳ ἕως τῆς πεντηκοστῆς γὰρ
f.aa r.asm n.asm p.a r.ap.2 cj d.nsm n.nsm v.aas.3s cj v.fai.1s p.d n.dsf p.g d.gsf n.gsf cj
2152 5516 5989 4639 7007 1569 3836 3261 2205 1254 2152 1877 2387 2401 3836 4300 1142

a great door for effective work has opened to me, and there are many who oppose me. ¶ **10** If
μεγάλη θύρα καὶ ἐνεργής ἀνέῳγεν μοι καὶ πολλοί ἀντικείμενοι δὲ Ἐὰν
a.nsf n.nsf cj a.nsf v.rai.3s r.ds.1 cj a.npm pt.pm.npm cj cj
3489 2598 2779 1921 487 1609 2779 512 512 4498 512 1254 1569

Timothy comes, see to it that he has nothing to fear while he is with you, for he is carrying on the work of
Τιμόθεος ἔλθῃ βλέπετε ἵνα γένηται ἀφόβως πρὸς ὑμᾶς γὰρ ἐργάζεται τὸ ἔργον
n.nsm v.aas.3s v.pam.2p cj v.ams.3s adv p.a r.ap.2 cj v.pmi.3s d.asn n.asn
5510 2262 1063 2671 1181 925 4639 7007 1142 2237 3836 2240

the Lord, just as I am. **11** No one, then, should refuse to accept him. Send him on his way in peace
κυρίου ὡς καγώ μή τις οὖν ἐξουθενήσῃ αὐτὸν δὲ προπέμψατε αὐτὸν ἐν εἰρήνῃ
n.gsm cj crasis pl r.nsm cj v.aas.3s r.asm.3 cj v.aam.2p r.asm.3 p.d n.dsf
3261 6055 2743 3590 5516 4036 2024 899 1254 4636 899 4636 4636 4636 1877 1645

so that he may return to me. I am expecting him along with the brothers. ¶ **12** Now about our brother
ἵνα ἔλθῃ πρός με γὰρ ἐκδέχομαι αὐτὸν μετὰ τῶν ἀδελφῶν δὲ Περὶ τοῦ ἀδελφοῦ
cj v.aas.3s p.a r.as.1 cj v.pmi.1s r.asm.3 p.g d.gpm n.gpm cj p.g d.gsm n.gsm
2671 2262 4639 1609 1142 1683 899 3552 3836 81 1254 4309 3836 81

Apollos: I strongly urged him to go to you with the brothers. He was quite unwilling to go
Ἀπολλῶ πολλὰ παρεκάλεσα αὐτὸν ἵνα ἔλθῃ πρὸς ὑμᾶς μετὰ τῶν ἀδελφῶν καὶ ἦν πάντως οὐκ θέλημα ἵνα ἔλθῃ
n.gsm a.apn v.aai.1s r.asm.3 cj v.aas.3s p.a r.ap.2 p.g d.gpm n.gpm cj v.iai.3s adv pl n.nsn cj v.aas.3s
663 4151 4498 4151 899 2671 2262 4639 7007 3552 3836 81 2779 1639 4122 4024 2525 2671 2262

now, but he will go when he has the opportunity. ¶ **13** Be on your guard; stand firm in the faith; be
νῦν δὲ ἐλεύσεται ὅταν εὐκαιρήσῃ Γρηγορεῖτε στήκετε ἐν τῇ πίστει
adv cj v.fmi.3s cj v.aas.3s v.pam.2p v.pam.2p p.d d.dsf n.dsf
3814 1254 2262 4020 2320 1213 5112 1877 3836 4411

men of courage; be strong. **14** Do everything in love. ¶ **15** You know that the household of Stephanas
ἀνδρίζεσθε κραταιοῦσθε γινέσθω πάντα ὑμῶν ἐν ἀγάπῃ οἴδατε ὅτι τὴν οἰκίαν Στεφανᾶ
v.pmm.2p v.ppm.2p v.pmm.3s a.npn r.gp.2 p.d n.dsf v.rai.2p cj d.asf n.asf n.gsm
437 3194 1181 4246 7007 1877 27 3857 4022 3836 3864 5107

δὲ παραγένωμαι, οὓς ἐὰν δοκιμάσητε, δι' ἐπιστολῶν τούτους πέμψω ἀπενεγκεῖν τὴν χάριν ὑμῶν εἰς Ἰερουσαλήμ· **4** ἐὰν δὲ ἄξιον ᾖ τοῦ καμὲ πορεύεσθαι, σὺν ἐμοὶ πορεύσονται.

16:5 Ἐλεύσομαι δὲ πρὸς ὑμᾶς ὅταν Μακεδονίαν διέλθω· Μακεδονίαν γὰρ διέρχομαι, **6** πρὸς ὑμᾶς δὲ τυχὸν παραμενῶ ἢ καὶ παραχειμάσω, ἵνα ὑμεῖς με προπέμψητε οὗ ἐὰν πορεύωμαι. **7** οὐ θέλω γὰρ ὑμᾶς ἄρτι ἐν παρόδῳ ἰδεῖν, ἐλπίζω γὰρ χρόνον τινὰ ἐπιμεῖναι πρὸς ὑμᾶς ἐὰν ὁ κύριος ἐπιτρέψῃ. **8** ἐπιμενῶ δὲ ἐν Ἐφέσῳ ἕως τῆς πεντηκοστῆς· **9** θύρα γάρ μοι ἀνέῳγεν μεγάλη καὶ ἐνεργής, καὶ ἀντικείμενοι πολλοί. ¶ **10** Ἐὰν δὲ ἔλθῃ Τιμόθεος, βλέπετε, ἵνα ἀφόβως γένηται πρὸς ὑμᾶς· τὸ γὰρ ἔργον κυρίου ἐργάζεται ὡς καγώ· **11** μή τις οὖν αὐτὸν ἐξουθενήσῃ. προπέμψατε δὲ αὐτὸν ἐν εἰρήνῃ, ἵνα ἔλθῃ πρός με· ἐκδέχομαι γὰρ αὐτὸν μετὰ τῶν ἀδελφῶν. ¶ **12** Περὶ δὲ Ἀπολλῶ τοῦ ἀδελφοῦ, πολλὰ παρεκάλεσα αὐτόν, ἵνα ἔλθῃ πρὸς ὑμᾶς μετὰ τῶν ἀδελφῶν· καὶ πάντως οὐκ ἦν θέλημα ἵνα νῦν ἔλθῃ· ἐλεύσεται δὲ ὅταν εὐκαιρήσῃ. ¶ **13** Γρηγορεῖτε, στήκετε ἐν τῇ πίστει, ἀνδρίζεσθε, κραταιοῦσθε. **14** πάντα ὑμῶν ἐν ἀγάπῃ γινέσθω. ¶ **15** Παρακαλῶ δὲ ὑμᾶς, ἀδελφοί· οἴδατε τὴν οἰκίαν Στεφανᾶ, ὅτι ἐστὶν

were the first   converts in Achaia,   and they have devoted themselves to the service   of the saints.   I
ἐστὶν   ἀπαρχὴ ←   → ⌐τῆς Ἀχαΐας⌐ καὶ →   ἔταξαν   ἑαυτούς   εἰς   διακονίαν →   τοῖς ἁγίοις   δὲ →
v.pai.3s   n.nsf   d.gsf n.gsf   cj   v.aai.3p   r.apm.3   p.a   n.asf   d.dpm a.dpm   cj
1639   569   3836 938   2779   5435   1571   1650   1355   3836 41   1254

urge   you, brothers, **16** to   submit   to such as these   and to everyone who joins in the work,
Παρακαλῶ ὑμᾶς ἀδελφοί   ἵνα καὶ ὑμεῖς ὑποτάσσησθε →   →   ⌐τοῖς τοιούτοις⌐ καὶ →   παντὶ   τῷ →   →   → συνεργοῦντι
v.pai.1s   r.ap.2   n.vpm   cj   adv 2779 r.np.2 v.pps.2p   d.dpm   r.dpm   cj   a.dsm   d.dsm   pt.pa.dsm
4151   7007   81   2671 adv 2779 7007 5718   3836   5525   2779   4246   3836   5300

and labors   at it. **17**   I was glad when Stephanas,   Fortunatus and Achaicus arrived,   because they have
καὶ κοπιῶντι   δὲ →   →   χαίρω ἐπὶ   Στεφανᾶ   καὶ Φορτουνάτου καὶ   Ἀχαϊκοῦ ⌐τῇ παρουσίᾳ⌐ ὅτι   οὗτοι →
cj   pt.pa.dsm   cj   v.pai.1s p.d   n.gsm   cj   n.gsm   cj   n.gsm   d.dsf n.dsf   cj   r.npm
2779 3159   1254   5897 2093   5107   2779 5847   2779   939   3836 4242   4022   4047

supplied   what was lacking from you.   **18** For they refreshed my   spirit   and yours   also.   Such
ἀνεπλήρωσαν τὸ   ὑστέρημα   ὑμέτερον   γὰρ →   ἀνέπαυσαν ἐμὸν ⌐τὸ πνεῦμα⌐ καὶ ⌐τὸ ὑμῶν⌐   οὖν ⌐τοὺς τοιούτους⌐
v.aai.3p   d.asn   n.asn   r.asn.2   cj   v.aai.3p   r.asn.1 d.asn n.asn   cj   d.asn r.gp.2   cj   d.apm r.apm
405   3836   5729   5629   1142   399   1847 3836 4460   2779 3836 7007   4036 3836 5525

men deserve recognition.
←   →   ἐπιγινώσκετε
          v.pam.2p
          2105

Final Greetings

16:19 The churches in the province of Asia   send you greetings. Aquila and Priscilla greet   you warmly
αἱ   ἐκκλησίαι   →   → ⌐τῆς Ἀσίας⌐   ὑμᾶς Ἀσπάζονται   Ἀκύλας καὶ   Πρίσκα   ἀσπάζεται ὑμᾶς πολλὰ
d.npf   n.npf   d.gsf n.gsf   r.ap.2 v.pmi.3p   n.nsm   cj   n.nsf   v.pmi.3s   r.ap.2 a.apn
3836   1711   3836 823   832   7007 832   217   2779   4571   832   7007 4498

in the Lord, and so does the church that meets at   their house. **20** All   the brothers here send you greetings.
ἐν   κυρίῳ   σὺν   τῇ   ἐκκλησίᾳ   κατ᾽ αὐτῶν οἶκον   πάντες οἱ   ἀδελφοὶ   ↱   ὑμᾶς ἀσπάζονται
p.d   n.dsm   p.d   d.dsf   n.dsf   p.a   r.gpm.3   n.asm   a.npm   d.npm n.npm   r.ap.2 v.pmi.3p
1877   3261   5250   3836   1711   2848   899   3875   4246   3836 81   832   7007 832

Greet   one   another with a holy kiss.   ¶   **21** I, Paul,   write this greeting in my own hand.   ¶   **22** If
Ἀσπάσασθε ἀλλήλους ←   ἐν   ἁγίῳ φιλήματι   ¶   Παύλου   Ὁ   ἀσπασμὸς → ἐμῇ τῇ   χειρὶ   ¶   εἴ
v.amm.2p   r.apm   p.d   a.dsn n.dsn   n.gsm   d.nsm n.nsm   r.dsf.1 d.dsf n.dsf   cj
832   253   1877   41   5799   4263   3836 833   1847 3836 5931   1623

anyone does not love the Lord — a curse   be   on him. Come, O Lord!   ¶   **23** The   grace of the Lord Jesus be
τις   ↱   οὐ   φιλεῖ τὸν   κύριον   ἀνάθεμα ἤτω ←   ←   θά   μαράνα   ἡ   χάρις   τοῦ κυρίου Ἰησοῦ
r.nsm   pl   v.pai.3s d.asm n.asm   n.nsn   v.pam.3s   j   j   d.nsf n.nsf   d.gsm n.gsm   n.gsm
5516   5797 4024 5797 3836 3261   353   1639   3448   3448   3836 5921   3836 3261 2652

with you.   ¶   **24** My love   to   all   of you in Christ Jesus. Amen.   ¶
μεθ᾽ ὑμῶν   μου   ἀγάπη   μετὰ πάντων →   ὑμῶν ἐν   Χριστῷ Ἰησοῦ
p.g   r.gp.2   r.gs.1 d.nsf n.nsf   p.g   a.gpm   r.gp.2 p.d   n.dsm   n.dsm
3552   7007   1609 3836 27   3552 4246   7007 1877 5986   2652

ἀπαρχὴ τῆς Ἀχαΐας καὶ εἰς διακονίαν τοῖς ἁγίοις ἔταξαν ἑαυτούς· ¹⁶ ἵνα καὶ ὑμεῖς ὑποτάσσησθε τοῖς τοιούτοις καὶ παντὶ τῷ συνεργοῦντι καὶ κοπιῶντι. ¹⁷ χαίρω δὲ ἐπὶ τῇ παρουσίᾳ Στεφανᾶ καὶ Φορτουνάτου καὶ Ἀχαϊκοῦ, ὅτι τὸ ὑμέτερον ὑστέρημα οὗτοι ἀνεπλήρωσαν· ¹⁸ ἀνέπαυσαν γὰρ τὸ ἐμὸν πνεῦμα καὶ τὸ ὑμῶν. ἐπιγινώσκετε οὖν τοὺς τοιούτους. ¹⁹ Ἀσπάζονται ὑμᾶς αἱ ἐκκλησίαι τῆς Ἀσίας. ἀσπάζεται ὑμᾶς ἐν κυρίῳ πολλὰ Ἀκύλας καὶ Πρίσκα σὺν τῇ κατ᾽ οἶκον αὐτῶν ἐκκλησίᾳ. ²⁰ ἀσπάζονται ὑμᾶς οἱ ἀδελφοὶ πάντες. Ἀσπάσασθε ἀλλήλους ἐν φιλήματι ἁγίῳ. ¶ ²¹ Ὁ ἀσπασμὸς τῇ ἐμῇ χειρὶ Παύλου. ¶ ²² εἴ τις οὐ φιλεῖ τὸν κύριον, ἤτω ἀνάθεμα. Μαρανα ¶ ²³ ἡ χάρις τοῦ κυρίου Ἰησοῦ μεθ᾽ ὑμῶν. ¶ ²⁴ ἡ ἀγάπη μου μετὰ πάντων ὑμῶν ἐν Χριστῷ Ἰησοῦ. ἀμήν. ¶

2 Corinthians

1:1 Paul, an apostle of Christ Jesus by the will of God, and Timothy our brother, ¶ To the
church of God in Corinth, together with all the saints throughout Achaia: ¶

2 Grace and peace to you from God our Father and the Lord Jesus Christ.

The God of All Comfort

1:3 Praise be to the God and Father of our Lord Jesus Christ, the Father of compassion and the God of all comfort, **4** who comforts us in all our troubles, so that we can comfort those in any trouble with the comfort we ourselves have received from God. **5** For just as the sufferings of Christ flow over into our lives, so also through Christ our comfort overflows. **6** If we are distressed, it is for your comfort and salvation; if we are comforted, it is for your comfort, which produces in you patient endurance of the same sufferings we suffer. **7** And our hope for you is firm, because we know that just as you share in our sufferings, so also you share in our comfort. ¶

8 We do not want you to be uninformed, brothers, about the hardships we suffered in the province of Asia. We were under great pressure, far beyond our ability to endure, so that we despaired even of life. **9** Indeed, in *our hearts* we felt the sentence of death. But this happened that we might not

---

1:1 Παῦλος ἀπόστολος Χριστοῦ Ἰησοῦ διὰ θελήματος θεοῦ καὶ Τιμόθεος ὁ ἀδελφὸς ¶ τῇ ἐκκλησίᾳ τοῦ θεοῦ τῇ οὔσῃ ἐν Κορίνθῳ σὺν τοῖς ἁγίοις πᾶσιν τοῖς οὖσιν ἐν ὅλῃ τῇ Ἀχαΐᾳ, ¶ **2** χάρις ὑμῖν καὶ εἰρήνη ἀπὸ θεοῦ πατρὸς ἡμῶν καὶ κυρίου Ἰησοῦ Χριστοῦ.

1:3 Εὐλογητὸς ὁ θεὸς καὶ πατὴρ τοῦ κυρίου ἡμῶν Ἰησοῦ Χριστοῦ, ὁ πατὴρ τῶν οἰκτιρμῶν καὶ θεὸς πάσης παρακλήσεως, **4** ὁ παρακαλῶν ἡμᾶς ἐπὶ πάσῃ τῇ θλίψει ἡμῶν εἰς τὸ δύνασθαι ἡμᾶς παρακαλεῖν τοὺς ἐν πάσῃ θλίψει διὰ τῆς παρακλήσεως ἧς παρακαλούμεθα αὐτοὶ ὑπὸ τοῦ θεοῦ. **5** ὅτι καθὼς περισσεύει τὰ παθήματα τοῦ Χριστοῦ εἰς ἡμᾶς, οὕτως διὰ τοῦ Χριστοῦ περισσεύει καὶ ἡ παράκλησις ἡμῶν. **6** εἴτε δὲ θλιβόμεθα, ὑπὲρ τῆς ὑμῶν παρακλήσεως καὶ σωτηρίας· εἴτε παρακαλούμεθα, ὑπὲρ τῆς ὑμῶν παρακλήσεως τῆς ἐνεργουμένης ἐν ὑπομονῇ τῶν αὐτῶν παθημάτων ὧν καὶ ἡμεῖς πάσχομεν. **7** καὶ ἡ ἐλπὶς ἡμῶν βεβαία ὑπὲρ ὑμῶν εἰδότες ὅτι ὡς κοινωνοί ἐστε τῶν παθημάτων, οὕτως καὶ τῆς παρακλήσεως. ¶ **8** Οὐ γὰρ θέλομεν ὑμᾶς ἀγνοεῖν, ἀδελφοί, ὑπὲρ τῆς θλίψεως ἡμῶν τῆς γενομένης ἐν τῇ Ἀσίᾳ, ὅτι καθ᾽ ὑπερβολὴν ὑπὲρ δύναμιν ἐβαρήθημεν ὥστε ἐξαπορηθῆναι ἡμᾶς καὶ τοῦ ζῆν· **9** ἀλλὰ αὐτοὶ ἐν ἑαυτοῖς τὸ ἀπόκριμα τοῦ θανάτου ἐσχήκαμεν, ἵνα μὴ πεποιθότες ὦμεν ἐφ᾽ ἑαυτοῖς ἀλλ᾽ ἐπὶ

rely	on ourselves	but	on	God,	who	raises	the dead.	[10] He has	delivered	us	from	such	a deadly	peril,
πεποιθότες	ἐφ᾽ ἑαυτοῖς	ἀλλ᾽	ἐπὶ	τῷ θεῷ	τῷ	ὃς →	ἐγείροντι	τοὺς νεκρούς	ἐρρύσατο	ἡμᾶς	ἐκ	τηλικούτου	θανάτου ←	
pt.ra.npm	p.d r.dpm.1	cj	p.d	d.dsm n.dsm	d.dsm	pt.pa.dsm	d.apm a.apm	r.nsm	v.ami.3s	r.ap.1	p.g	r.gsm	n.gsm	
4275	2093 1571	247	2093	3836 2536	3836	1586	3836 3738	4005	4861	7005	1666	5496	2505	

and	he will	deliver	us.	On	him	we have	set	our hope	that	he will	continue to	deliver us,	[11] as	you
καὶ →	→	ῥύσεται		εἰς	ὃν	→ →	→	ἠλπίκαμεν	καὶ ὅτι	→	ἔτι	ῥύσεται	→	ὑμῶν καὶ
cj		v.fmi.3s		p.a	r.asm			v.rai.1p	adv		adv	v.fmi.3s		r.gp.2 adv
2779		4861		1650	4005			1827	2779 4022	4861 4861	2285	4861		5348 7007 2779

help	us	by	your	prayers.	Then	many		will give	thanks	on	our	behalf	for	the	gracious
συνυπουργούντων	ἡμῶν	ὑπὲρ	τῇ	δεήσει	ἵνα	ἐκ πολλῶν	προσώπων	→	εὐχαριστηθῇ	ὑπὲρ	ἡμῶν	←		τὸ	χάρισμα
pt.pa.gpm	r.gp.1	p.g	d.dsf	n.dsf	cj	p.g a.gpn	n.gpn		v.aps.3s	p.g	r.gp.1			d.nsn	n.nsn
5348	7005	5642	3836	1255	2671	1666 4498	4725		2373	5642	7005	5642		3836	5922

favor	granted	us	in answer to the prayers of	many.
←	←	εἰς ἡμᾶς		διὰ πολλῶν
		p.a r.ap.1		p.g a.gpn
		1650 7005		1328 4498

Paul's Change of Plans

[1:12] Now	this	is	our	boast:		Our conscience	testifies		that	we have	conducted	ourselves	in the
γὰρ	αὕτη	ἐστίν	ἡμῶν	˻Ἡ καύχησις˼	ἡμῶν	˻τῆς συνειδήσεως˼	˻τὸ μαρτύριον˼	ὅτι	→	→	ἀνεστράφημεν ←		ἐν τῷ
cj	r.nsf	v.pai.3s	r.gp.1	d.nsf n.nsf	r.gp.1	d.gsf n.gsf	d.nsn n.nsn	cj			v.api.1p		p.d d.dsm
1142	4047	1639	7005	3836 3018	7005	3836 5287	3836 3457	4022			418		1877 3836

world,	and	especially	in our relations	with	you,	in the	holiness	and	sincerity	that are	from	God.		We
κόσμῳ	δὲ	περισσοτέρως		πρὸς	ὑμᾶς ἐν		ἁπλότητι	καὶ	εἰλικρινείᾳ	→		˻τοῦ θεοῦ˼	[καὶ]	
n.dsm	cj	adv.c		p.a	r.ap.2 p.d		n.dsf	cj	n.dsf			d.gsm n.gsm	cj	
3180	1254	4359		4639	7007 1877		605	2779	1636			3836 2536	2779	

have done so	not	according to	worldly	wisdom	but	according to	God's	grace.	[13] For	we do	not	write	you	anything
	οὐκ ἐν	←	σαρκικῇ	σοφίᾳ	ἀλλ᾽	ἐν	← θεοῦ	χάριτι	γὰρ →	→	οὐ	γράφομεν	ὑμῖν	ἄλλα
	pl pl		a.dsf	n.dsf	cj	p.d	n.gsm	n.dsf	cj		pl	v.pai.1p	r.dp.2	r.apn
	4024 1877		4920	5053	247	1877	2536	5921	1142 1211	1211	4024	1211	7007	257

			you	cannot	read		or	understand.	And	I hope	that,	[14] as		you		have	understood	us	in
ἀλλ᾽	ἢ	ἃ	→	ἀναγινώσκετε	ἢ	καὶ ἐπιγινώσκετε	δὲ	ἐλπίζω ὅτι	καθὼς →	καὶ →	ἐπέγνωτε	ἡμᾶς ἀπὸ
cj	pl	r.apn		v.pai.2p	cj	adv v.pai.2p	cj	v.pai.1s	adv	adv	v.aai.2p	r.ap.1 p.g
247	2445	4005		336	2445	2779 2105	1254	1827 4022	2777 2105	2779 2105	2105	7005 608

part,	you will come to	understand	fully		that	you		can boast	of us	just		as	we will	boast		of
μέρους →	→	→	ἐπιγνώσεσθε	ἕως τέλους,	ὅτι	ὑμεῖς	καὶ	→	ἡμῶν	καθάπερ	←	←	˻ἐσμεν	καύχημα˼	→
n.gsn			v.fmi.2p	p.g n.gsn	cj	r.np.2	adv		r.gp.1	adv			v.pai.1p	n.nsn	
3538			2105	2401 5465	4022	7007	2779		7005	2749			1639	3017	

you	in	the	day	of	the Lord		Jesus.	¶	[15]	Because	I was	confident		of this,	I	planned	to visit
ὑμῶν	ἐν	τῇ	ἡμέρᾳ →	τοῦ	κυρίου	[ἡμῶν]	Ἰησοῦ		Καὶ →		˻τῇ	πεποιθήσει˼	→	ταύτη	→	ἐβουλόμην	→ ἐλθεῖν
r.gp.2	p.d	d.dsf	n.dsf	d.gsm	n.gsm	r.gp.1	n.gsm		cj		d.dsf	n.dsf		r.dsf		v.imi.1s	f.aa
7007	1877	3836	2465	3836	3261	7005	2652		2779		3836	4301		4047		1089	2262

	you	first	so	that	you might	benefit	twice.	[16]	I planned	to visit		you on	my way	to	Macedonia	and
πρὸς	ὑμᾶς	πρότερον	ἵνα	←	→	σχῆτε	χάριν	δευτέραν	καὶ		→ διελθεῖν	δι᾽	ὑμῶν	εἰς	Μακεδονίαν	καὶ
p.a	r.ap.2	adv.c	cj			v.aas.2p	n.asf	a.asf	cj		f.aa	p.g	r.gp.2	p.a	n.asf	cj
4639	7007	4728	2671			2400	5921	1311	2779		1451	1328	7007	1650	3423	2779

to come	back	to	you	from	Macedonia,	and then	to have		you	send		me on my way	to	Judea.
→ ἐλθεῖν	πάλιν	πρὸς	ὑμᾶς	ἀπὸ	Μακεδονίας	καὶ		ὑφ᾽	ὑμῶν	προπεμφθῆναι			εἰς	˻τὴν Ἰουδαίαν˼
f.aa	adv	p.a	r.ap.2	p.g	n.gsf	cj		p.g	r.gp.2	f.ap			p.a	d.asf n.asf
2262	4099	4639	7007	608	3423	2779		4636	5679 7007	4636			1650	3836 2677

[17]	When	I	planned	this,		did I	do	it lightly?		Or			do I	make		my plans	in	a
οὖν		→ βουλόμενος	τοῦτο	ἄρα	μήτι		ἐχρησάμην	˻τῇ ἐλαφρίᾳ˼	ἢ	ἃ	βουλεύομαι	→	βουλεύομαι	←		κατὰ
cj		pt.pm.nsm	r.asn	adv	pl		v.ami.1s	d.dsf n.dsf	cj	r.apn	v.pmi.1s		v.pmi.1s			p.a
4036		1089	4047	726	3614		5968	3836 1786	2445	4005	1086		1086			2848

worldly	manner	so	that	*in*	*the same*	*breath*		I	*say,*	"Yes,	yes"	and	"No,	no"?	¶	[18] But	as	surely
σάρκα	←		ἵνα	→	ᾖ			παρ᾽	ἐμοὶ	τὸ ναὶ	ναὶ	καὶ	τὸ οὒ	οὔ		δὲ		
n.asf			cj		v.pas.3s			p.d	r.ds.1	d.nsn pl	pl	cj	d.nsn pl	pl		cj		
4922			2671		1639			4123	1609	3836 3721	3721	2779	3836 4024	4024		1254		

τῷ θεῷ τῷ ἐγείροντι τοὺς νεκρούς· [10] ὃς ἐκ τηλικούτου θανάτου ἐρρύσατο ἡμᾶς καὶ ῥύσεται, εἰς ὃν ἠλπίκαμεν [ὅτι] καὶ ἔτι ῥύσεται, [11] συνυπουργούντων καὶ ὑμῶν ὑπὲρ ἡμῶν τῇ δεήσει, ἵνα ἐκ πολλῶν προσώπων τὸ εἰς ἡμᾶς χάρισμα διὰ πολλῶν εὐχαριστηθῇ ὑπὲρ ἡμῶν.

[1:12] Ἡ γὰρ καύχησις ἡμῶν αὕτη ἐστίν, τὸ μαρτύριον τῆς συνειδήσεως ἡμῶν, ὅτι ἐν ἁγιότητι «ἁπλότητι» καὶ εἰλικρινείᾳ τοῦ θεοῦ, [καὶ] οὐκ ἐν σοφίᾳ σαρκικῇ ἀλλ᾽ ἐν χάριτι θεοῦ, ἀνεστράφημεν ἐν τῷ κόσμῳ, περισσοτέρως δὲ πρὸς ὑμᾶς. [13] οὐ γὰρ ἄλλα γράφομεν ὑμῖν ἀλλ᾽ ἢ ἃ ἀναγινώσκετε ἢ καὶ ἐπιγινώσκετε· ἐλπίζω δὲ ὅτι ἕως τέλους ἐπιγνώσεσθε, [14] καθὼς καὶ ἐπέγνωτε ἡμᾶς ἀπὸ μέρους, ὅτι καύχημα ὑμῶν ἐσμεν καθάπερ καὶ ὑμεῖς ἡμῶν ἐν τῇ ἡμέρᾳ τοῦ κυρίου [ἡμῶν] Ἰησοῦ. ¶ [15] Καὶ ταύτῃ τῇ πεποιθήσει ἐβουλόμην πρότερον πρὸς ὑμᾶς ἐλθεῖν, ἵνα δευτέραν χάριν σχῆτε, [16] καὶ δι᾽ ὑμῶν διελθεῖν εἰς Μακεδονίαν καὶ πάλιν ἀπὸ Μακεδονίας ἐλθεῖν πρὸς ὑμᾶς καὶ ὑφ᾽ ὑμῶν προπεμφθῆναι εἰς τὴν Ἰουδαίαν. [17] τοῦτο οὖν βουλόμενος μήτι ἄρα τῇ ἐλαφρίᾳ ἐχρησάμην; ἢ ἃ βουλεύομαι κατὰ σάρκα βουλεύομαι, ἵνα ᾖ παρ᾽ ἐμοὶ τὸ Ναὶ ναὶ καὶ τὸ Οὒ οὔ; ¶ [18] πιστὸς δὲ ὁ θεὸς ὅτι ὁ

as God   is faithful,   our message   to you is   not "Yes" and "No." **19** For the Son of God,   Jesus
ὁ θεός πιστὸς ὅτι ἡμῶν ὁ λόγος ὁ πρὸς ὑμᾶς ἔστιν οὐκ ναὶ καὶ οὔ γὰρ ὁ υἱὸς → τοῦ θεοῦ Ἰησοῦ
d.nsm n.nsm a.nsm cj r.gp.1 d.nsm n.nsm d.nsm p.a r.ap.2 v.pai.3s pl pl cj pl cj d.nsm n.nsm d.gsm n.gsm n.nsm
3836 2536 4412 4022 7005 3836 3364 3836 4639 7007 1639 4024 3721 2779 4024 1142 3836 5626 3836 2536 2652

Christ, who was preached among you   by me and Silas   and Timothy, was   not "Yes" and "No," but
Χριστὸς ὁ → κηρυχθεὶς ἐν ὑμῖν δι' ἡμῶν δι' ἐμοῦ καὶ Σιλουανοῦ καὶ Τιμοθέου ἐγένετο οὐκ ναὶ καὶ οὔ ἀλλὰ
n.nsm d.nsm pt.ap.nsm p.d r.dp.2 p.g r.gp.1 p.g r.gs.1 cj n.gsm cj n.gsm v.ami.3s pl pl cj pl cj
5986 3836 3062 1877 7007 1328 7005 1328 1609 2779 4977 2779 5510 1181 4024 3721 2779 4024 247

in him it has always been "Yes." **20** For no matter how many promises God has made, they are "Yes" in Christ.
ἐν αὐτῷ → → γέγονεν ναὶ γὰρ ὅσαι ← ἐπαγγελίαι θεοῦ τὸ ναὶ ἐν αὐτῷ
p.d r.dsm.3 v.rai.3s pl cj r.npf n.npf n.gsm d.nsn pl p.d r.dsm.3
1877 899 1181 3721 1142 4012 2039 2536 3836 3721 1877 899

And so through him the "Amen" is spoken by us to the glory of God. **21** Now it is God who makes both us
καὶ διὸ δι' αὐτοῦ τὸ ἀμὴν δι' ἡμῶν πρὸς δόξαν → τῷ θεῷ δὲ θεὸς ὁ ἡμᾶς
adv cj r.gsm.3 d.nsn pl p.g r.gp.1 p.a n.asf d.dsm n.dsm cj n.nsm d.nsm r.ap.1
2779 1475 1328 899 3836 297 1328 7005 4639 1518 3836 2536 1254 2536 3836 7005

and you stand firm in Christ. He anointed us, **22** set his seal of ownership on us, and
σὺν ὑμῖν βεβαιῶν ← εἰς Χριστὸν καὶ → χρίσας ἡμᾶς καὶ σφραγισάμενος ← ἡμᾶς καὶ
p.d r.dp.2 pt.pa.nsm p.a n.asm cj pt.aa.nsm r.ap.1 adv d.nsm pt.am.nsm r.ap.1 cj
5250 7007 1011 1650 5986 2779 5987 7005 2779 3836 5381 7005 2779

put his Spirit in our hearts as a deposit, guaranteeing what is to come. ¶ **23** I
δοὺς τοῦ πνεύματος ἐν ἡμῶν ταῖς καρδίαις τὸν ἀρραβῶνα δὲ Ἐγὼ
pt.aa.nsm d.gsn n.gsn p.d r.gp.1 d.dpf n.dpf d.asm n.asm cj r.ns.1
1443 3836 4460 1877 7005 3836 2840 3836 775 1254 1609

call God as my witness that it was in order to spare you that I did not return to
ἐπικαλοῦμαι τὸν θεὸν μάρτυρα τὴν ἐμὴν ψυχήν ὅτι → → φειδόμενος ὑμῶν → οὐκέτι ἦλθον εἰς
v.pmi.1s d.asm n.asm n.asm r.asf.1 n.asf cj pt.pm.nsm r.gp.2 adv v.aai.1s p.a
2126 3836 2536 3459 3836 1847 6034 4022 5767 7007 2262 2262 4033 2262 1650

Corinth. **24** Not that we lord it over your faith, but we work with you for your joy, because
Κόρινθον οὐχ ὅτι → κυριεύομεν ὑμῶν τῆς πίστεως ἀλλὰ → συνεργοί ἐσμεν ← → ὑμῶν τῆς χαρᾶς γὰρ
n.asf pl cj v.pai.1p r.gp.2 d.gsf n.gsf cj n.npm v.pai.1p r.gp.2 d.gsf n.gsf cj
3172 4024 4022 3259 7007 3836 4411 247 5301 1639 7007 3836 5915 1142

it is by faith you stand firm. **2:1** So I made up my mind that I would not make another painful
τῇ πίστει → ἑστήκατε ← γὰρ → Ἔκρινα ← ἐμαυτῷ τοῦτο → μὴ πάλιν ἐν λύπῃ
d.dsf n.dsf v.rai.2p cj v.aai.1s r.dsm.1 r.asn pl adv p.d n.dsf
3836 4411 2705 1142 3212 1831 4047 2262 2262 3590 2262 4099 1877 3383

visit to you. **2** For if I grieve you, who is left to make me glad but you whom I have
τὸ ἐλθεῖν πρὸς ὑμᾶς γὰρ εἰ ἐγὼ λυπῶ ὑμᾶς καὶ τίς → με ὁ εὐφραίνων εἰ μὴ ὁ ἐξ ἐμοῦ →
d.asn f.aa p.a r.ap.2 cj cj r.ns.1 v.pai.1s r.ap.2 cj r.nsm r.as.1 d.nsm pt.pa.nsm cj pl d.nsm p.g r.gs.1
3836 2262 4639 7007 1142 1623 1609 3382 7007 2779 5515 2370 1609 3836 2370 1623 3590 3836 1666 1609

grieved? **3** I wrote as I did so that when I came I should not be distressed by those who ought to
λυπούμενος καὶ →ἔγραψα τοῦτο αὐτό ἵνα → ἐλθὼν μὴ σχῶ λύπην ἀφ' ὧν ← ἔδει
pt.pp.nsm cj v.aai.1s r.asn r.asn cj pt.aa.nsm pl v.aas.1s n.asf p.g r.gpm v.iai.3s
3382 2779 1211 4047 899 2671 2262 2400 2400 3590 2400 3383 608 4005 1256 5897

make me rejoice. I had confidence in all of you, that you would all share my joy, **4** For I wrote you
→ με χαίρειν πεποιθὼς ἐπὶ πάντας ὑμᾶς ὅτι ὑμῶν πάντων ἐστιν ἐμὴ ἡ χαρὰ γὰρ → ἔγραψα ὑμῖν
r.as.1 f.pa pt.ra.nsm p.a a.apm r.ap.2 cj r.gp.2 a.gpm v.pai.3s r.nsf.1 d.nsf n.nsf cj v.aai.1s r.dp.2
5897 1609 5897 4275 2093 4246 7007 4022 7007 4246 1639 1847 3836 5915 1142 1211 7007

out of great distress and anguish of heart and with many tears, not to grieve you but to let you know the
ἐκ ← πολλῆς θλίψεως καὶ συνοχῆς → καρδίας διὰ πολλῶν δακρύων οὐχ ἵνα λυπηθῆτε ← ἀλλὰ ἵνα → γνῶτε
p.g a.gsf n.gsf cj n.gsf n.gsf p.g a.gpn n.gpn pl cj v.aps.2p cj cj v.aas.2p
1666 4498 2568 2779 5330 2840 1328 4498 1232 4024 2671 3382 247 2671 1182

depth of my love for you.
περισσοτέρως τὴν ἀγάπην ἣν ἔχω εἰς ὑμᾶς
adv.c d.asf n.asf r.asf v.pai.1s p.a r.ap.2
4359 3836 27 4005 2400 1650 7007

λόγος ἡμῶν ὁ πρὸς ὑμᾶς οὐκ ἔστιν Ναὶ καὶ Οὔ. **19** ὁ τοῦ θεοῦ γὰρ υἱὸς Ἰησοῦς Χριστὸς ὁ ἐν ὑμῖν δι' ἡμῶν κηρυχθείς, δι' ἐμοῦ καὶ Σιλουανοῦ καὶ Τιμοθέου, οὐκ ἐγένετο Ναὶ καὶ Οὔ ἀλλὰ Ναὶ ἐν αὐτῷ γέγονεν. **20** ὅσαι γὰρ ἐπαγγελίαι θεοῦ, ἐν αὐτῷ τὸ Ναί· διὸ καὶ δι' αὐτοῦ τὸ Ἀμὴν τῷ θεῷ πρὸς δόξαν δι' ἡμῶν. **21** ὁ δὲ βεβαιῶν ἡμᾶς σὺν ὑμῖν εἰς Χριστὸν καὶ χρίσας ἡμᾶς θεός, **22** ὁ καὶ σφραγισάμενος ἡμᾶς καὶ δοὺς τὸν ἀρραβῶνα τοῦ πνεύματος ἐν ταῖς καρδίαις ἡμῶν. ¶ **23** Ἐγὼ δὲ μάρτυρα τὸν θεὸν ἐπικαλοῦμαι ἐπὶ τὴν ἐμὴν ψυχήν, ὅτι φειδόμενος ὑμῶν οὐκέτι ἦλθον εἰς Κόρινθον. **24** οὐχ ὅτι κυριεύομεν ὑμῶν τῆς πίστεως ἀλλὰ συνεργοί ἐσμεν τῆς χαρᾶς ὑμῶν· τῇ γὰρ πίστει ἑστήκατε.

2:1 ἔκρινα γὰρ ἐμαυτῷ τοῦτο τὸ μὴ πάλιν ἐν λύπῃ πρὸς ὑμᾶς ἐλθεῖν. **2** εἰ γὰρ ἐγὼ λυπῶ ὑμᾶς, καὶ τίς ὁ εὐφραίνων με εἰ μὴ ὁ λυπούμενος ἐξ ἐμοῦ; **3** καὶ ἔγραψα τοῦτο αὐτό, ἵνα μὴ ἐλθὼν λύπην σχῶ ἀφ' ὧν ἔδει με χαίρειν, πεποιθὼς ἐπὶ πάντας ὑμᾶς ὅτι ἡ ἐμὴ χαρὰ πάντων ὑμῶν ἐστιν. **4** ἐκ γὰρ πολλῆς θλίψεως καὶ συνοχῆς καρδίας ἔγραψα ὑμῖν διὰ πολλῶν δακρύων, οὐχ ἵνα λυπηθῆτε ἀλλὰ τὴν ἀγάπην ἵνα γνῶτε ἣν ἔχω περισσοτέρως εἰς ὑμᾶς.

Forgiveness for the Sinner

2:5 If anyone has caused grief, he has not so much grieved me as he has grieved all of you, to
δέ Εἰ τις → → λελύπηκεν → → οὐκ λελύπηκεν ἐμὲ ἀλλὰ πάντας ὑμᾶς ἀπὸ
cj cj r.nsm v.rai.3s pl v.rai.3s r.as.1 cj a.apm r.ap.2 p.g
1254 1623 5516 3382 3382 3382 4024 3382 1609 247 4246 7007 608

some extent – not to put it too severely. **6** The punishment inflicted on him by the majority is sufficient for
μέρους ← ἵνα μὴ → → → ἐπιβαρῶ αὕτη ἡ ἐπιτιμία ἡ ὑπὸ τῶν πλειόνων ἱκανὸν →
n.gsn cj pl v.pas.1s r.nsf d.nsf n.nsf d.nsf p.g d.gpm a.gpm.c a.nsn
3538 2671 3590 2096 4047 3836 2204 3836 5679 3836 4498 2653

him. **7** *Now instead,* you ought to forgive and comfort him, so that he will not be
ᾳτῷ τοιούτῳᾳ ὥστε μᾶλλον τοὐναντίον ὑμᾶς → χαρίσασθαι καὶ παρακαλέσαι πως ← ὁ τοιοῦτος → μὴ
d.dsm r.dsm cj adv.c crasis r.ap.2 f.am cj f.aa pl d.nsm r.nsm cj
3836 5525 6063 3437 5539 7007 5919 2779 4151 4803 3836 5525 2927 3590

overwhelmed by excessive sorrow. **8** I urge you, therefore, to reaffirm your love for him. **9** The reason
καταποθῇ → περισσοτέρα ᾳτῇ λύπῃᾳ → παρακαλῶ ὑμᾶς διὸ → κυρῶσαι ἀγάπην εἰς αὐτὸν γὰρ → ᾳεἰς τοῦτοᾳ
v.aps.3s a.dsf.c d.dsf n.dsf v.pai.1s r.ap.2 cj f.aa n.asf p.a r.asm.3 cj p.a r.asn
2927 3383 4358 3836 3383 4151 7007 1475 3263 1650 899 1142 1650 4047

I wrote you was to see if you would stand the test and be obedient in everything. **10** If you
ᾳ καὶ ἔγραψαᾳ ἵνα γνῶ ὑμῶν τὴν δοκιμὴν εἰ ἐστε ὑπήκοοι εἰς πάντα δὲ →
adv v.aai.1s cj v.aas.1s r.gp.2 d.asf n.asf cj v.pai.2p a.npm p.a a.apn cj
1211 2779 1211 2671 1182 7007 3836 1509 1623 1639 5675 1650 4246 1254

forgive anyone, I also forgive him. And what I have forgiven – if there was anything to forgive – I
χαρίζεσθε ᾧ τι κἀγώ ← γὰρ καὶ ὃ κεχάρισμαι εἴ τι ἐγὼ
v.pmi.2p r.dsm r.asn crasis cj adv r.asn v.rmi.1s cj r.asn r.ns.1
5919 4005 5516 2743 1142 2779 4005 5919 1623 5516 1609

have forgiven in the sight of Christ for your sake, **11** in order that Satan might not outwit us. For
→ κεχάρισμαι ἐν προσώπῳ → Χριστοῦ δι' ὑμᾶς ← ἵνα → ὑπὸ ᾳτοῦ σατανᾶᾳ → μὴ πλεονεκτηθῶμεν ← γὰρ
v.rmi.1s p.d n.dsn n.gsm p.a r.ap.2 cj p.g d.gsm n.gsm pl v.aps.1p cj
5919 1877 4725 5986 1328 7007 1328 2671 5679 3836 4928 4430 3590 4430 1142

we are not unaware of his schemes.
→ → οὐ ἀγνοοῦμεν → αὐτοῦ ᾳτὰ νοήματαᾳ
pl v.pai.1p r.gsm.3 d.apn n.apn
51 51 4024 51 899 3836 3784

Ministers of the New Covenant

2:12 Now when I went to Troas to preach the gospel of Christ and found that the Lord
δε → → Ἐλθὼν εἰς ᾳτὴν Τρῳάδαᾳ εἰς ᾳτὸ εὐαγγέλιονᾳ ← → ᾳτοῦ Χριστοῦᾳ καὶ ἐν κυρίῳ
cj pt.aa.nsm p.a d.asf n.asf p.a d.asn n.asn d.gsm n.gsm cj p.d n.dsm
1254 2262 1650 3836 5590 1650 3836 2295 3836 5986 2779 1877 3261

had opened a door for me, **13** I still had no peace of mind, because I did not find my
→ ἀνεῳγμένης θύρας → μοι ἔσχηκα οὐκ ἄνεσιν → ᾳτῷ πνεύματι μουᾳ με → ᾳτῷ εὑρεῖνᾳ μου
pt.rp.gsf n.gsf r.ds.1 v.rai.1s pl n.asf d.dsn n.dsn r.gs.1 r.as.1 pl d.dsn f.aa r.gs.1
487 2598 1609 2400 4024 457 3836 4460 1609 1609 2351 3590 3836 2351 1609

brother Titus there. So I said good-by to them and went on to Macedonia. ¶ **14** But thanks be to
ᾳτὸν ἀδελφόνᾳ Τίτον ἀλλὰ → ἀποταξάμενος → αὐτοῖς ἐξῆλθον εἰς Μακεδονίαν δὲ χάρις →
d.asm n.asm n.asm cj pt.am.nsm r.dpm.3 v.aai.1s p.a n.asf cj n.nsf
3836 81 5519 247 698 899 2002 1650 3423 1254 5921

God, who always leads us in triumphal procession in Christ and through us spreads
ᾳΤῷ θεῷᾳ τῷ πάντοτε θριαμβεύοντι ἡμᾶς ← ← ἐν ᾳτῷ Χριστῷᾳ καὶ δι' ἡμῶν φανεροῦντι
d.dsm n.dsm d.dsm adv pt.pa.dsm r.ap.1 p.d d.dsm n.dsm cj p.g r.gp.1 pt.pa.dsm
3836 2536 3836 4121 2581 7005 1877 3836 5986 2779 1328 7005 5746

everywhere the fragrance of the knowledge of him. **15** For we are to God the aroma of Christ among those
ᾳἐν παντὶ τόπῳᾳ τὴν ὀσμὴν → τῆς γνώσεως → αὐτοῦ ὅτι → ἐσμὲν ᾳτῷ θεῷᾳ εὐωδία → Χριστοῦ ἐν τοῖς
p.d a.dsm n.dsm d.asf n.asf d.gsf n.gsf r.gsm.3 cj v.pai.1p d.dsm n.dsm n.nsf n.gsm p.d d.dpm
1877 4246 5536 3836 4011 3836 1194 899 4022 1639 3836 2536 2380 5986 1877 3836

who are being saved and those who are perishing. **16** To the one we are the smell of
← → σῳζομένοις καὶ ἐν τοῖς ← → ἀπολλυμένοις μὲν → οἷς ὀσμὴ →
pt.pp.dpm cj p.d d.dpm pt.pm.dpm pl r.dpm n.nsf
5392 2779 1877 3836 660 3525 4005 4011

2:5 Εἰ δέ τις λελύπηκεν, οὐκ ἐμὲ λελύπηκεν, ἀλλὰ ἀπὸ μέρους, ἵνα μὴ ἐπιβαρῶ, πάντας ὑμᾶς. **6** ἱκανὸν τῷ τοιούτῳ ἡ ἐπιτιμία αὕτη ἡ ὑπὸ τῶν πλειόνων, **7** ὥστε τοὐναντίον μᾶλλον ὑμᾶς χαρίσασθαι καὶ παρακαλέσαι, μή πως τῇ περισσοτέρᾳ λύπῃ καταποθῇ ὁ τοιοῦτος. **8** διὸ παρακαλῶ ὑμᾶς κυρῶσαι εἰς αὐτὸν ἀγάπην· **9** εἰς τοῦτο γὰρ καὶ ἔγραψα, ἵνα γνῶ τὴν δοκιμὴν ὑμῶν, εἰ εἰς πάντα ὑπήκοοί ἐστε. **10** ᾧ δέ τι χαρίζεσθε, κἀγώ· καὶ γὰρ ἐγὼ ὃ κεχάρισμαι, εἴ τι κεχάρισμαι, δι' ὑμᾶς ἐν προσώπῳ Χριστοῦ, **11** ἵνα μὴ πλεονεκτηθῶμεν ὑπὸ τοῦ Σατανᾶ· οὐ γὰρ αὐτοῦ τὰ νοήματα ἀγνοοῦμεν.

2:12 Ἐλθὼν δὲ εἰς τὴν Τρῳάδα εἰς τὸ εὐαγγέλιον τοῦ Χριστοῦ καὶ θύρας μοι ἀνεῳγμένης ἐν κυρίῳ, **13** οὐκ ἔσχηκα ἄνεσιν τῷ πνεύματί μου τῷ μὴ εὑρεῖν με Τίτον τὸν ἀδελφόν μου, ἀλλὰ ἀποταξάμενος αὐτοῖς ἐξῆλθον εἰς Μακεδονίαν. ¶ **14** Τῷ δὲ θεῷ χάρις τῷ πάντοτε θριαμβεύοντι ἡμᾶς ἐν τῷ Χριστῷ καὶ τὴν ὀσμὴν τῆς γνώσεως αὐτοῦ φανεροῦντι δι' ἡμῶν ἐν παντὶ τόπῳ· **15** ὅτι Χριστοῦ εὐωδία ἐσμὲν τῷ θεῷ ἐν τοῖς σῳζομένοις καὶ ἐν τοῖς ἀπολλυμένοις, **16** οἷς μὲν ὀσμὴ ἐκ θανάτου εἰς θάνατον, οἷς δὲ ὀσμὴ

death; | | to the other, the fragrance of life. | | And who is equal to such a task? 17
ἐκ θανάτου εἰς θάνατον, | δὲ → οἷς | ὀσμὴ → ἐκ ζωῆς εἰς ζωήν. | καὶ τίς ἱκανός πρὸς ταῦτα | γὰρ
p.g n.gsm p.a n.asm | pl r.dpm | n.nsf | p.g n.gsf p.a n.asf | cj r.nsm a.nsm p.a r.apn | cj
1666 2505 1650 2505 | 1254 4005 | 4011 | 1666 2437 1650 2437 | 2779 5515 2653 4639 4047 | 1142

Unlike so many, we do not peddle the word of God for profit. On the contrary, in Christ we
ὡς οἱ πολλοὶ → ἐσμεν οὐ καπηλεύοντες τὸν λόγον → τοῦ θεοῦ, ← ← → → ἀλλ᾽ ἐν Χριστῷ →
pl d.npm a.npm v.pai.1p pl pt.pa.npm d.asm n.asm d.gsm n.gsm cj p.d n.dsm
6055 3836 4498 1639 4024 2836 3836 3364 3836 2536 2836 2836 247 1877 5986

speak before God with sincerity, like men sent from God. ¶ 3:1 Are we beginning to commend
λαλοῦμεν κατέναντι θεοῦ ὡς ἐξ εἰλικρινείας ἀλλ᾽ ὡς ἐκ θεοῦ Ἀρχόμεθα → συνιστάνειν
v.pai.1p p.g n.gsm pl p.g n.gsf cj pl p.g n.gsm v.pmi.1p f.pa
3281 2978 2536 6055 1666 1636 247 6055 1666 2536 806 5319

ourselves again? Or do we need, like some people, letters of recommendation to you or from you? 2 You
ἑαυτοὺς πάλιν ἢ μὴ → χρῄζομεν ὥς τινες ← ἐπιστολῶν συστατικῶν πρὸς ὑμᾶς ἢ ἐξ ὑμῶν →
r.apm.1 adv cj pl v.pai.1p pl r.npm n.gpf a.gpf p.a r.ap.2 cj p.g r.gp.2
1571 4099 2445 3590 5974 6055 5516 2186 5364 4639 7007 2445 1666 7007 1639

yourselves are our letter, written on our hearts, known and read by
ὑμεῖς ἐστε ἡμῶν ἡ ἐπιστολὴ ἐγγεγραμμένη ἐν ἡμῶν ταῖς καρδίαις, γινωσκομένη καὶ ἀναγινωσκομένη ὑπὸ
r.np.2 v.pai.2p r.gp.1 d.nsf n.nsf pt.rp.nsf p.d r.gp.1 d.dpf n.dpf pt.pp.nsf cj pt.pp.nsf p.g
7007 1639 7005 3836 2186 1582 1877 7005 3836 2840 1182 2779 336 5679

everybody. 3 You show that you are a letter from Christ, the result of our ministry, written not
πάντων ἀνθρώπων. φανερούμενοι ὅτι → ἐστὲ ἐπιστολὴ → Χριστοῦ ὑφ᾽ ← ἡμῶν διακονηθεῖσα ἐγγεγραμμένη οὐ
a.gpm n.gpm pt.pp.npm cj v.pai.2p n.nsf n.gsm p.g r.gp.1 pt.ap.nsf pt.rp.nsf pl
4246 476 5746 4022 1639 2186 5986 5679 7005 1354 1582 4024

with ink but with the Spirit of the living God, not on tablets of stone but on tablets of human hearts.
→ μέλανι ἀλλὰ → πνεύματι → ζῶντος θεοῦ οὐκ ἐν πλαξὶν λιθίναις ἀλλ᾽ ἐν πλαξὶν σαρκίναις καρδίαις
a.dsn cj n.dsn pt.pa.gsm n.gsm pl p.d n.dpf a.dpf cj p.d n.dpf a.dpf n.dpf
3506 247 4460 2409 2536 4024 1877 4419 3343 247 1877 4419 4921 2840

¶ 4 Such confidence as this is ours through Christ before God. 5 Not that we are competent in
δὲ Πεποίθησιν τοιαύτην → ἔχομεν διὰ τοῦ Χριστοῦ πρὸς τὸν θεόν. οὐχ ὅτι → ἐσμεν ἱκανοί ἀφ᾽
cj n.asf r.asf v.pai.1p p.g d.gsm n.gsm p.a d.asm n.asm pl cj v.pai.1p a.npm p.g
1254 5525 4301 5525 2400 1328 3836 5986 4639 3836 2536 4024 4022 1639 2653 608

ourselves to claim anything for ourselves, but our competence comes from God. 6 He has made us
ἑαυτῶν → λογίσασθαί τι ὡς ἐξ ἑαυτῶν ἀλλ᾽ ἡμῶν ἡ ἱκανότης ἐκ τοῦ θεοῦ. ὃς καὶ → → ἡμᾶς
r.gpm.1 f.am r.asn pl p.g r.gpm.1 cj r.gp.1 d.nsf n.nsf p.g d.gsm n.gsm r.nsm adv r.ap.1
1571 3357 5516 6055 1666 1571 247 7005 3836 2654 1666 3836 2536 4005 2779 2655 2655 7005

competent as ministers of a new covenant – not of the letter but of the Spirit; for the letter kills, but
ἱκάνωσεν διακόνους → καινῆς διαθήκης οὐ → γράμματος ἀλλὰ πνεύματος γὰρ τὸ γράμμα ἀποκτέννει δὲ
v.aai.3s n.apm a.gsf n.gsf pl n.gsn cj n.gsn cj d.nsn n.nsn v.pai.3s cj
2655 1356 2785 1347 4024 1207 247 4460 1142 3836 1207 650 1254

the Spirit gives life.
τὸ πνεῦμα → ζῳοποιεῖ.
d.nsn n.nsn v.pai.3s
3836 4460 2443

The Glory of the New Covenant

3:7 Now if the ministry that brought death, which was engraved in letters on stone, came with
δὲ Εἰ ἡ διακονία → → τοῦ θανάτου → → ἐντετυπωμένη ἐν γράμμασιν → λίθοις ἐγενήθη ἐν
cj cj d.nsf n.nsf d.gsm n.gsm pt.rp.nsf p.d n.dpn n.dpm v.api.3s p.d
1254 1623 3836 1355 3836 2505 1963 1877 1207 3345 1181 1877

glory, so that the Israelites could not look steadily at the face of Moses because of
δόξῃ, ὥστε ← τοὺς υἱοὺς Ἰσραὴλ δύνασθαι μὴ ἀτενίσαι εἰς τὸ πρόσωπον → Μωϋσέως διὰ ←
n.dsf cj d.apm n.apm n.gsm f.pp pl f.aa p.a d.asn n.asn n.gsm p.a
1518 6063 3836 5626 2702 1538 3590 867 1650 3836 4725 3707 1328

its glory, fading though it was, 8 will not the ministry of the Spirit be even
τοῦ προσώπου αὐτοῦ τὴν δόξαν, τὴν καταργουμένην. πῶς οὐχὶ ἡ διακονία → τοῦ πνεύματος ἔσται →
d.gsn n.gsn r.gsm.3 d.asf n.asf d.asf pt.pp.asf pl pl d.nsf n.nsf d.gsn n.gsn v.fmi.3s
3836 4725 899 3836 1518 3836 2934 4802 4049 3836 1355 3836 4460 1639

ἐκ ζωῆς εἰς ζωήν. καὶ πρὸς ταῦτα τίς ἱκανός; 17 οὐ γὰρ ἐσμεν ὡς οἱ πολλοὶ καπηλεύοντες τὸν λόγον τοῦ θεοῦ, ἀλλ᾽ ὡς ἐξ εἰλικρινείας, ἀλλ᾽ ὡς ἐκ θεοῦ κατέναντι θεοῦ ἐν Χριστῷ λαλοῦμεν.

3:1 Ἀρχόμεθα πάλιν ἑαυτοὺς συνιστάνειν; ἢ μὴ χρῄζομεν ὥς τινες συστατικῶν ἐπιστολῶν πρὸς ὑμᾶς ἢ ἐξ ὑμῶν; 2 ἡ ἐπιστολὴ ἡμῶν ὑμεῖς ἐστε, ἐγγεγραμμένη ἐν ταῖς καρδίαις ἡμῶν, γινωσκομένη καὶ ἀναγινωσκομένη ὑπὸ πάντων ἀνθρώπων, 3 φανερούμενοι ὅτι ἐστὲ ἐπιστολὴ Χριστοῦ διακονηθεῖσα ὑφ᾽ ἡμῶν, ἐγγεγραμμένη οὐ μέλανι ἀλλὰ πνεύματι θεοῦ ζῶντος, οὐκ ἐν πλαξὶν λιθίναις ἀλλ᾽ ἐν πλαξὶν καρδίαις σαρκίναις. ¶ 4 Πεποίθησιν δὲ τοιαύτην ἔχομεν διὰ τοῦ Χριστοῦ πρὸς τὸν θεόν. 5 οὐχ ὅτι ἀφ᾽ ἑαυτῶν ἱκανοί ἐσμεν λογίσασθαί τι ὡς ἐξ ἑαυτῶν, ἀλλ᾽ ἡ ἱκανότης ἡμῶν ἐκ τοῦ θεοῦ, 6 ὃς καὶ ἱκάνωσεν ἡμᾶς διακόνους καινῆς διαθήκης, οὐ γράμματος ἀλλὰ πνεύματος· τὸ γὰρ γράμμα ἀποκτέννει, τὸ δὲ πνεῦμα ζῳοποιεῖ.

3:7 Εἰ δὲ ἡ διακονία τοῦ θανάτου ἐν γράμμασιν ἐντετυπωμένη λίθοις ἐγενήθη ἐν δόξῃ, ὥστε μὴ δύνασθαι ἀτενίσαι τοὺς υἱοὺς Ἰσραὴλ εἰς τὸ πρόσωπον Μωϋσέως διὰ τὴν δόξαν τοῦ προσώπου αὐτοῦ τὴν καταργουμένην, 8 πῶς οὐχὶ μᾶλλον ἡ

more glorious? **9** If the ministry that condemns men is glorious, how much more glorious is the
μᾶλλον ἐν δόξῃ γὰρ εἰ τῇ διακονίᾳ ⌜τῆς κατακρίσεως δόξα πολλῷ μᾶλλον περισσεύει δόξῃ ← ἡ
adv.c p.d n.dsf cj cj d.dsf n.dsf d.gsf n.gsf n.nsf a.dsn adv.c v.pai.3s n.dsf d.nsf
3437 1877 1518 1142 1623 3836 1355 3836 2892 1518 4498 3437 4355 1518 4355 3836

ministry that brings righteousness! **10** For what was glorious has no glory now in
διακονία → ⌜τῆς δικαιοσύνης⌝ γὰρ καὶ τὸ → δεδοξασμένον → οὐ δεδόξασται ἐν τούτῳ τῷ μέρει εἵνεκεν
n.nsf d.gsf n.gsf cj cj d.nsn pt.rp.nsn pl v.rpi.3s p.d d.dsn d.dsn n.dsn p.g
1355 3836 1466 1142 2779 3836 1519 1519 4024 1519 1877 4047 3836 3538 1641

comparison with the surpassing glory. **11** And if what was fading away came with glory, how much greater is
← ← τῆς ὑπερβαλλούσης δόξης γὰρ εἰ τὸ → καταργούμενον ← διὰ δόξης πολλῷ μᾶλλον
d.gsf pt.pa.gsf n.gsf cj cj d.nsn pt.pp.nsn p.g n.gsf a.dsn adv.c
3836 5650 1518 1142 1623 3836 2934 1328 1518 4498 3437

the glory of that which lasts! ¶ **12** Therefore, since we have such a hope, we are very bold. **13**
ἐν δόξῃ τὸ ← μένον οὖν → → Ἔχοντες τοιαύτην ἐλπίδα → χρώμεθα πολλῇ παρρησίᾳ καὶ
p.d n.dsf d.nsn pt.pa.nsn cj pt.pa.npm r.asf n.asf v.pmi.1p a.dsf n.dsf cj
1877 1518 3836 3531 4036 2400 5525 1828 5968 4498 4244 2779

We are not like Moses, who would put a veil over his face to keep the Israelites from
οὐ καθάπερ Μωϋσῆς → → ἐτίθει κάλυμμα ἐπὶ αὐτοῦ ⌜τὸ πρόσωπον⌝ πρὸς μὴ τοὺς υἱοὺς Ἰσραὴλ
pl cj n.nsm v.iai.3s n.asn p.a r.gsm.3 d.asn n.asn p.a pl d.apm n.apm n.gsm
4024 2749 3707 5502 2820 2093 899 3836 4725 4639 3590 3836 5626 2702

gazing at it while the radiance was fading away. **14** But their minds were made dull, for
⌜τὸ ἀτενίσαι at it while τοῦ καταργουμένου⌝ εἰς τὸ τέλος, ἀλλὰ αὐτῶν ⌜τὰ νοήματα⌝ → ἐπωρώθη γὰρ
d.asn f.aa d.gsn pt.pp.gsn p.a d.asn n.asn cj r.gpm.3 d.npn n.npn v.api.3s cj
3836 867 3836 2934 1650 3836 5465 247 899 3836 3784 4800 1142

to this day the same veil remains when the old covenant is read. It has not been
ἄχρι → ⌜τῆς σήμερον ἡμέρας⌝ τὸ αὐτὸ κάλυμμα μένει ἐπὶ τῆς παλαιᾶς διαθήκης → τῇ ἀναγνώσει ⌜ → μὴ →
p.g d.gsf adv n.gsf d.nsn r.nsn n.nsn v.pai.3s p.d d.gsf a.gsf n.gsf d.dsf n.dsf pl
948 3836 4958 2465 3836 899 2820 3531 2093 3836 4094 1347 3836 342 365 365 3590

removed, because only in Christ is it taken away. **15** Even to this day when Moses is
ἀνακαλυπτόμενον ὅτι only ἐν Χριστῷ → → καταργεῖται ← ἀλλ᾽ ἕως ← σήμερον ἡνίκα ἂν Μωϋσῆς →
pt.pp.nsn cj p.d n.dsm v.ppi.3s cj p.g adv cj pl n.nsm
365 4022 1877 5986 2934 247 2401 4958 2471 323 3707

read, a veil covers their hearts. **16** But whenever anyone turns to the Lord, the veil is
ἀναγινώσκηται κάλυμμα κεῖται ἐπὶ αὐτῶν ⌜τὴν καρδίαν⌝ δὲ ⌜ἡνίκα ἐὰν⌝ → ἐπιστρέψῃ πρὸς κύριον τὸ κάλυμμα →
v.pps.3s n.nsn v.pmi.3s p.a r.gpm.3 d.asf n.asf cj cj pl v.aas.3s p.a n.asm d.nsn n.nsn
336 2820 3023 2093 899 3836 2840 1254 2471 1569 2188 4639 3261 3836 2820

taken away. **17** Now the Lord is the Spirit, and where the Spirit of the Lord is, there is freedom. **18** And we,
περιαιρεῖται ← δὲ ὁ κύριος ἐστιν τὸ πνεῦμα δὲ οὗ τὸ πνεῦμα → κυρίου ἐλευθερία δὲ ἡμεῖς
v.ppi.3s cj d.nsm n.nsm v.pai.3s d.nsn n.nsn cj adv d.nsn n.nsn n.gsm n.nsf cj r.np.1
4311 1254 3836 3261 1639 3836 4460 1254 4023 3836 4460 3261 1800 1254 7005

who with unveiled faces all reflect the Lord's glory, are being transformed into his likeness
→ → ἀνακεκαλυμμένῳ προσώπῳ πάντες κατοπτριζόμενοι τὴν κυρίου δόξαν → μεταμορφούμεθα ← ⌜τὴν αὐτὴν εἰκόνα
pt.rp.dsn n.dsn a.npm pt.pm.npm d.asf n.gsm n.asf v.ppi.1p d.asf r.asf n.asf
365 4725 4246 3002 3836 3261 1518 3565 3836 899 1635

with ever-increasing glory, which comes from the Lord, who is the Spirit.
ἀπὸ ⌜εἰς δόξαν⌝ δόξης καθάπερ ἀπὸ κυρίου πνεύματος
p.g p.a n.asf n.gsf pl p.g n.gsm n.gsn
608 1650 1518 1518 2749 608 3261 4460

Treasures in Jars of Clay

4:1 Therefore, since through God's mercy we have this ministry, we do not lose heart. **2** Rather, we
⌜Διὰ τοῦτο⌝ → καθὼς ἠλεήθημεν → ἔχοντες ταύτην ⌜τὴν διακονίαν⌝ → οὐκ ἐγκακοῦμεν ← ἀλλὰ
p.a r.asn cj v.api.1p pt.pa.npm r.asf d.asf n.asf pl v.pai.1p cj
1328 4047 2400 2777 1796 2400 4047 3836 1355 1591 1591 4024 1591 247

have renounced secret and shameful ways; we do not use deception, nor do we distort the
→ ἀπειπάμεθα ⌜τὰ κρυπτὰ ⌜τῆς αἰσχύνης⌝ → → μὴ περιπατοῦντες ἐν πανουργίᾳ μηδὲ → → δολοῦντες τὸν
v.ami.1p d.apn a.apn d.gsf n.gsf pl pt.pa.npm p.d n.dsf cj pt.pa.npm d.asm
584 3836 3220 3836 158 4344 4344 3590 4344 1877 4111 3593 1516 3836

διακονία τοῦ πνεύματος ἔσται ἐν δόξῃ; ⁹ εἰ γὰρ τῇ διακονίᾳ τῆς κατακρίσεως δόξα, πολλῷ μᾶλλον περισσεύει ἡ διακονία τῆς δικαιοσύνης δόξῃ. ¹⁰ καὶ γὰρ οὐ δεδόξασται τὸ δεδοξασμένον ἐν τούτῳ τῷ μέρει εἵνεκεν τῆς ὑπερβαλλούσης δόξης. ¹¹ εἰ γὰρ τὸ καταργούμενον διὰ δόξης, πολλῷ μᾶλλον τὸ μένον ἐν δόξῃ. ¶ ¹² Ἔχοντες οὖν τοιαύτην ἐλπίδα πολλῇ παρρησίᾳ χρώμεθα ¹³ καὶ οὐ καθάπερ Μωϋσῆς ἐτίθει κάλυμμα ἐπὶ τὸ πρόσωπον αὐτοῦ πρὸς τὸ μὴ ἀτενίσαι τοὺς υἱοὺς Ἰσραὴλ εἰς τὸ τέλος τοῦ καταργουμένου. ¹⁴ ἀλλὰ ἐπωρώθη τὰ νοήματα αὐτῶν. ἄχρι γὰρ τῆς σήμερον ἡμέρας τὸ αὐτὸ κάλυμμα ἐπὶ τῇ ἀναγνώσει τῆς παλαιᾶς διαθήκης μένει, μὴ ἀνακαλυπτόμενον ὅτι ἐν Χριστῷ καταργεῖται· ¹⁵ ἀλλ᾽ ἕως σήμερον ἡνίκα ἂν ἀναγινώσκηται Μωϋσῆς, κάλυμμα ἐπὶ τὴν καρδίαν αὐτῶν κεῖται· ¹⁶ ἡνίκα δὲ ἐὰν ἐπιστρέψῃ πρὸς κύριον, περιαιρεῖται τὸ κάλυμμα. ¹⁷ ὁ δὲ κύριος τὸ πνεῦμά ἐστιν· οὗ δὲ τὸ πνεῦμα κυρίου, ἐλευθερία. ¹⁸ ἡμεῖς δὲ πάντες ἀνακεκαλυμμένῳ προσώπῳ τὴν δόξαν κυρίου κατοπτριζόμενοι τὴν αὐτὴν εἰκόνα μεταμορφούμεθα ἀπὸ δόξης εἰς δόξαν καθάπερ ἀπὸ κυρίου πνεύματος.
⁴:¹ Διὰ τοῦτο, ἔχοντες τὴν διακονίαν ταύτην καθὼς ἠλεήθημεν, οὐκ ἐγκακοῦμεν ² ἀλλὰ ἀπειπάμεθα τὰ κρυπτὰ τῆς αἰσχύνης, μὴ περιπατοῦντες ἐν πανουργίᾳ μηδὲ δολοῦντες τὸν λόγον τοῦ θεοῦ ἀλλὰ τῇ φανερώσει τῆς ἀληθείας συνιστάνοντες ἑαυτοὺς πρὸς

word of God.   On the contrary, by setting forth the truth   plainly   we commend   ourselves to   every
λόγον → ‿τοῦ θεοῦ‿ → →   ἀλλὰ   ↗   τῆς ἀληθείας ‿τῇ φανερώσει‿ → συνιστάνοντες ἑαυτοὺς πρὸς πᾶσαν
n.asm d.gsm n.gsm   cj   d.gsf n.gsf   d.dsf n.dsf   pt.pa.npm   r.apm.3 p.a a.asf
3364   3836 2536   247   5748   3836 237   3836 5748   5319   1571   4639 4246

man's   conscience in   the sight of God.   ³ And even if   our   gospel   is   veiled,   it is
ἀνθρώπων συνείδησιν ἐνώπιον ← ←   ‿τοῦ θεοῦ‿ δὲ καὶ εἰ ἡμῶν ‿τὸ εὐαγγέλιον‿ ἔστιν κεκαλυμμένον → ἐστιν
n.gpm   n.asf   p.g   d.gsm n.gsm cj   adv cj r.gp.1 d.nsn n.nsn v.pai.3s v.tr.rp.nsn   v.pai.3s
476   5287   1967   3836 2536 1254 2779 1623 7005 3836 2295 1639 2821   1639

veiled   to those who are perishing.   ⁴   The god of this   age   has blinded the minds of
κεκαλυμμένον ἐν τοῖς ←   → ἀπολλυμένοις ἐν οἷς ὁ θεὸς ↗ τούτου ‿τοῦ αἰῶνος‿ → ἐτύφλωσεν τὰ νοήματα →
pt.rp.nsn   p.d d.dpm   pt.pm.dpm   p.d r.dpm d.nsm n.nsm r.gsm d.gsm n.gsm   v.aai.3s d.apn n.apn
2821   1877 3836   660   1877 4005 3836 2536 172   4047 3836 172   5604 3836 3784

unbelievers, so that they cannot see   the light   of the gospel   of the glory of Christ,   who is the
‿τῶν ἀπίστων‿ εἰς ←   μὴ   ‿τὸ αὐγάσαι‿ τὸν φωτισμὸν → τοῦ εὐαγγελίου → τῆς δόξης → ‿τοῦ Χριστοῦ‿ ὅς ἐστιν
d.gpm a.gpm   p.a   pl   d.asn f.aa   d.asm n.asm   d.gsn n.gsn   d.gsf n.gsf d.gsm n.gsm   r.nsm v.pai.3s
3836 603   1650   3590   3836 878   3836 5895   3836 2295   3836 1518   3836 5986   4005 1639

image of God. ⁵ For we do not preach   ourselves, but Jesus   Christ as Lord, and ourselves as your servants for
εἰκὼν → ‿τοῦ θεοῦ‿ γὰρ → ↗ Οὐ κηρύσσομεν ἑαυτοὺς ἀλλὰ Ἰησοῦν Χριστὸν κύριον δὲ ἑαυτοὺς ὑμῶν δούλους διὰ
n.nsf   d.gsm n.gsm cj   pl v.pai.1p   r.apm.1   cj   n.asm n.asm   n.asm cj r.apm.1   r.gp.2 n.apm   p.a
1635   3836 2536   1142   4024 3062   1571   247 2652   5986   3261   1254 1571   7007   1529   1328

Jesus' sake. ⁶ For God,   who said, "Let light shine out of darkness,"   made his light shine   in our
Ἰησοῦν   ὅτι ‿ὁ θεὸς‿ ὁ εἰπών, ↗ φῶς λάμπει ἐκ ← σκότους ὃς → →   → ἔλαμψεν ἐν ἡμῶν
n.asm   cj d.nsm n.nsm d.nsm pt.aa.nsm n.nsn v.fai.3s p.g n.gsn   r.nsm   v.aai.3s p.d r.gp.1
2652   1328 4022 3836 2536 3290 3290   5890 3290   1666 5030   4005   3290   1877 7005

hearts   to   give us the light   of the knowledge of the glory of God   in the face   of
‿ταῖς καρδίαις‿ πρὸς ↗ → φωτισμὸν → τῆς γνώσεως → τῆς δόξης → ‿τοῦ θεοῦ‿ ἐν προσώπῳ → [Ἰησοῦ]
d.dpf n.dpf   p.a   n.asm   d.gsf n.gsf   d.gsf n.gsf d.gsm n.gsm p.d n.dsn   n.dsm
3836 2840   4639   5895   3836 1194   3836 1518   3836 2536 1877 4725   2652

Christ. ¶ ⁷ But we have   this   treasure   in jars   of clay   to show that this all-surpassing
Χριστοῦ   δὲ → Ἔχομεν τοῦτον ‿τὸν θησαυρὸν‿ ἐν σκεύεσιν ὀστρακίνοις → → ἵνα ἡ ὑπερβολὴ
n.gsm   cj   v.pai.1p r.asm d.asm n.asm   p.d n.dpn   a.dpn   cj d.nsf n.nsf
5986   1254 2400   4047   3836 2565   1877 5007   4017   2671 3836 5651

power   is   from God   and not from us. ⁸ We are hard pressed on every side, but not crushed;
‿τῆς δυνάμεως‿ ᾖ   → ‿τοῦ θεοῦ‿ καὶ μὴ ἐξ ἡμῶν → → θλιβόμενοι ἐν παντὶ ← ἀλλ᾽ οὐ στενοχωρούμενοι
d.gsf n.gsf   v.pas.3s d.gsm n.gsm cj pl p.g r.gp.1   pt.pp.npm p.d a.dsn   cj   pl pt.pp.npm
3836 1539   1639   3836 2536 2779 3590 1666 7005   2567   1877 4246   247 4024 5102

perplexed, but not in despair; ⁹ persecuted, but not abandoned;   struck   down, but not destroyed. ¹⁰ We
ἀπορούμενοι ἀλλ᾽ οὐκ → ἐξαπορούμενοι διωκόμενοι ἀλλ᾽ οὐκ ἐγκαταλειπόμενοι καταβαλλόμενοι ← ἀλλ᾽ οὐκ ἀπολλύμενοι
pt.pm.npm   cj pl   pt.pm.npm   pt.pp.npm   cj pl   pt.pp.npm   pt.pp.npm   cj pl pt.pm.npm
679   247 4024   1989   1503   247 4024 1593   2850   247 4024 660   4367

always carry   around in our body the death   of Jesus,   so that the life of Jesus   may also be revealed
πάντοτε περιφέροντες ← ἐν τῷ σώματι τὴν νέκρωσιν → ‿τοῦ Ἰησοῦ‿ ἵνα ← ἡ ζωὴ → ‿τοῦ Ἰησοῦ‿ → καὶ → φανερωθῇ
adv   pt.pa.npm   p.d d.dsn n.dsn d.asf n.asf   d.gsm n.gsm cj   d.nsf n.nsf d.gsm n.gsm adv   v.aps.3s
4121   4367   1877 3836 5393 3836 3740   3836 2652   2671 3836 2437 3836 2652   2779   5746

in our body. ¹¹ For we   who are alive are always being given   over to death for Jesus' sake, so that
ἐν ἡμῶν ‿τῷ σώματι‿ γὰρ ἡμεῖς οἱ → ζῶντες ↗ ἀεὶ   παραδιδόμεθα ← εἰς θάνατον διὰ Ἰησοῦν ↰ ἵνα ← καὶ
p.d r.gp.1 d.dsn n.dsn cj r.np.1 d.npm pt.pa.npm adv   v.ppi.1p   p.a n.asm   p.a n.asm   cj   adv
1877 7005 3836 5393   1142 7005 3836   2409   107   4140   1650 2505   1328 2652   2671   2779

his   life   may be revealed in our mortal body. ¹² So then, death   is at work   in us, but
‿τοῦ Ἰησοῦ‿ ‿ἡ ζωὴ‿ → → φανερωθῇ ἐν ἡμῶν θνητῇ ‿τῇ σαρκί‿ ὥστε ← ὁ θάνατος‿ → ἐνεργεῖται ἐν ἡμῖν δὲ
d.gsm n.gsm d.nsf n.nsf   v.aps.3s p.d r.gp.1 a.dsf d.dsf n.dsf cj   d.nsm n.nsm   v.pmi.3s p.d r.dp.1 cj
3836 2652 3836 2437   5746   1877 7005 2570 3836 4922   6063   3836 2505   1919   1877 1877 1254

life   is at work in you. ¶ ¹³   It is written: "I believed; therefore I have spoken." With that
‿ἡ ζωὴ‿ ἐν ὑμῖν‿   δὲ κατὰ → ‿τὸ γεγραμμένον‿ ἐπίστευσα διὸ → → ἐλάλησα Ἔχοντες τὸ
d.nsf n.nsf p.d r.dp.2   cj p.a   d.asn pt.rp.asn   v.aai.1s cj   v.aai.1s pt.pa.npm d.asn
3836 2437 1877 7007   1254 2848 3836 1211   4409   1475   3281   2400   3836

πᾶσαν συνείδησιν ἀνθρώπων ἐνώπιον τοῦ θεοῦ. ³ εἰ δὲ καὶ ἔστιν κεκαλυμμένον τὸ εὐαγγέλιον ἡμῶν, ἐν τοῖς ἀπολλυμένοις ἐστὶν κεκαλυμμένον, ⁴ ἐν οἷς ὁ θεὸς τοῦ αἰῶνος τούτου ἐτύφλωσεν τὰ νοήματα τῶν ἀπίστων εἰς τὸ μὴ αὐγάσαι τὸν φωτισμὸν τοῦ εὐαγγελίου τῆς δόξης τοῦ Χριστοῦ, ὅς ἐστιν εἰκὼν τοῦ θεοῦ. ⁵ οὐ γὰρ ἑαυτοὺς κηρύσσομεν ἀλλὰ Ἰησοῦν Χριστὸν κύριον, ἑαυτοὺς δὲ δούλους ὑμῶν διὰ Ἰησοῦν. ⁶ ὅτι ὁ θεὸς ὁ εἰπών, Ἐκ σκότους φῶς λάμψει, ὃς ἔλαμψεν ἐν ταῖς καρδίαις ἡμῶν πρὸς φωτισμὸν τῆς γνώσεως τῆς δόξης τοῦ θεοῦ ἐν προσώπῳ [Ἰησοῦ] Χριστοῦ. ¶ ⁷ Ἔχομεν δὲ τὸν θησαυρὸν τοῦτον ἐν ὀστρακίνοις σκεύεσιν, ἵνα ἡ ὑπερβολὴ τῆς δυνάμεως ᾖ τοῦ θεοῦ καὶ μὴ ἐξ ἡμῶν· ⁸ ἐν παντὶ θλιβόμενοι ἀλλ᾽ οὐ στενοχωρούμενοι, ἀπορούμενοι ἀλλ᾽ οὐκ ἐξαπορούμενοι, ⁹ διωκόμενοι ἀλλ᾽ οὐκ ἐγκαταλειπόμενοι, καταβαλλόμενοι ἀλλ᾽ οὐκ ἀπολλύμενοι, ¹⁰ πάντοτε τὴν νέκρωσιν τοῦ Ἰησοῦ ἐν τῷ σώματι περιφέροντες, ἵνα καὶ ἡ ζωὴ τοῦ Ἰησοῦ ἐν τῷ σώματι ἡμῶν φανερωθῇ. ¹¹ ἀεὶ γὰρ ἡμεῖς οἱ ζῶντες εἰς θάνατον παραδιδόμεθα διὰ Ἰησοῦν, ἵνα καὶ ἡ ζωὴ τοῦ Ἰησοῦ φανερωθῇ ἐν τῇ θνητῇ σαρκὶ ἡμῶν. ¹² ὥστε ὁ θάνατος ἐν ἡμῖν ἐνεργεῖται, ἡ δὲ ζωὴ ἐν ὑμῖν. ¶ ¹³ ἔχοντες δὲ τὸ αὐτὸ πνεῦμα τῆς πίστεως κατὰ τὸ γεγραμμένον, Ἐπίστευσα,

same	spirit	of faith		we	also	believe	and	therefore	speak,	[14] because	we know	that	the one	who	raised	the
αὐτὸ	πνεῦμα →	⸢τῆς πίστεως⸣		ἡμεῖς	καὶ	πιστεύομεν	καὶ	διὸ	λαλοῦμεν		→ εἰδότες	ὅτι	ὁ		ἐγείρας	τὸν
r.asn	n.asn	d.gsf n.gsf		r.np.1	cj	v.pai.1p	cj	adv	v.pai.1p		pt.ra.npm	cj	d.nsm		pt.aa.nsm	d.asm
899	4460	3836 4411		7005	2779	4409	2779	1475	3281		3857	4022	3836		1586	3836

Lord	Jesus	from the dead	will	also	raise	us	with	Jesus	and	present		us	with	you	in his presence.	[15]	All
κύριον	Ἰησοῦν			καὶ	ἐγερεῖ	ἡμᾶς	σὺν	Ἰησοῦ	καὶ	παραστήσει			σὺν	ὑμῖν			γὰρ ⸢τὰ πάντα
n.asm	n.asm			cj	v.fai.3s	r.ap.1	p.d	n.dsm	cj	v.fai.3s			p.d	r.dp.2			cj d.npn a.npn
3261	2652		1586	2779	1586	7005	5250	2652	2779	4225			5250	7007			1142 3836 4246

this	is	for	your	benefit,	so	that	the	grace	that	is reaching		more		and	more people	may cause
←	δι᾽	ὑμᾶς	↔		ἵνα	←	ἡ	χάρις	→	πλεονάσασα	⸤διὰ	τῶν	πλειόνων⸥			
	p.a	r.ap.2			cj		d.nsf	n.nsf		pt.aa.nsf	p.g	d.gpm	a.gpm.c			
	1328	7007			2671		3836	5921		4429	1328	3836	4498		4355	4355

thanksgiving		to overflow	to	the	glory	of God.	¶	[16]	Therefore	we do	not	lose	heart.	Though
⸢τὴν εὐχαριστίαν⸣	→	περισσεύσῃ	εἰς	τὴν	δόξαν →	⸤τοῦ θεοῦ⸥			Διὸ		οὐκ	ἐγκακοῦμεν	←	⸤ἀλλ᾽ εἰ καὶ⸥
d.asf n.asf		v.aas.3s	p.a	d.asf	n.asf	d.gsm n.gsm			cj		pl	v.pai.1p		cj cj adv
3836 2374		4355	1650	3836	1518	3836 2536			1475	1591	1591	4024	1591	247 1623 2779

outwardly		we	are wasting	away,	yet	inwardly	we	are being renewed		day	by	day.	[17] For	our
⸤ὁ	ἔξω ἄνθρωπος⸥	ἡμῶν →	διαφθείρεται	←	ἀλλ᾽	ὁ	ἔσω ἡμῶν →	→ ἀνακαινοῦται		ἡμέρᾳ	καὶ	ἡμέρᾳ	γὰρ	ἡμῶν
d.nsm	adv n.nsm	r.gp.1	v.ppi.3s		cj	d.nsm	adv r.gp.1	v.ppi.3s		n.dsf	cj	n.dsf	cj	r.gp.1
3836	2032 476	7005	1425		247	3836	2276 7005	363		2465	2779	2465	1142	7005

light		and	momentary	troubles		are	achieving	for us	an	eternal		glory	that
⸤τὸ	ἐλαφρὸν⸥		παραυτίκα	⸤τῆς θλίψεως⸥ →			κατεργάζεται	ἡμῖν	αἰώνιον	βάρος		δόξης	
d.nsn	a.nsn		adv	d.gsf n.gsf			v.pmi.3s	r.dp.1	a.asn	n.asn		n.gsf	
3836	1787		4194	3836 2568			2981	7005	173	983		1518	

far				outweighs	them	all.	[18] So	we fix	our	eyes		not on	what is seen,		but	on	what is
⸤καθ᾽	ὑπερβολὴν	εἰς	ὑπερβολὴν⸥					↔	ἡμῶν	σκοπούντων	μὴ		τὰ	→ βλεπόμενα	ἀλλὰ		τὰ →
p.a	n.asf	p.a	n.asf						r.gp.1	pt.pa.gpm	pl		d.apn	pt.pp.apn	cj		d.apn
2848	5651	1650	5651			983		5023 5023 5023	7005	5023	3590		3836	1063	247		3836

unseen.		For	what is seen		is temporary,	but	what is		unseen		is eternal.
μὴ	βλεπόμενα⸣	γὰρ	τὰ	→ βλεπόμενα	πρόσκαιρα	δὲ	τὰ	→	⸤μὴ βλεπόμενα⸥		αἰώνια
pl	pt.pp.apn	cj	d.npn	pt.pp.npn	a.npn	cj	d.npn		pl pt.pp.npn		a.npn
3590	1063	1142	3836	1063	4672	1254	3836		3590 1063		173

Our Heavenly Dwelling

5:1 Now	we know	that	if	the	earthly	tent		we	live	in	is destroyed,	we have	a building	from	God,	an
γὰρ	→ Οἴδαμεν	ὅτι	ἐὰν	ἡ	ἐπίγειος	⸤τοῦ σκήνους⸥		ἡμῶν	οἰκία	→	καταλυθῇ	→ ἔχομεν	οἰκοδομὴν	ἐκ	θεοῦ	
cj	v.rai.1p	cj	cj	d.nsf	a.nsf	d.gsn n.gsn		r.gp.1	n.nsf		v.aps.3s	v.pai.1p	n.asf	p.g	n.gsm	
1142	3857	4022	1569	3836	2103	3836 5011		7005	3864		2907	2400	3869	1666	2536	

eternal	house	in	heaven,		not built	by	human hands.		[2]	Meanwhile		we groan,	longing		to be
αἰώνιον	οἰκίαν	ἐν	⸤τοῖς οὐρανοῖς⸥	→	ἀχειροποίητον			γὰρ	⸤καὶ	ἐν	τούτῳ⸥	στενάζομεν	ἐπιποθοῦντες	→	→
a.asf	n.asf	p.d	d.dpm n.dpm		a.asf			cj	adv	p.d	r.dsn	v.pai.1p	pt.pa.npm		
173	3864	1877	3836 4041		942			1142	2779	1877	4047	5100	2160		

clothed		with	our	heavenly		dwelling,	[3] because		when we are clothed,		we will	not	be found
⸤τὸ ἐπενδύσασθαι⸥	←		ἡμῶν	⸤τὸ ἐξ	οὐρανοῦ⸥	⸤τὸ οἰκητήριον⸥	⸤εἴ	γε καὶ⸥	→ ἐκδυσάμενοι	↔	↔	οὐ →	εὑρεθησόμεθα
d.asn f.am			r.gp.1	d.asn p.g	n.gsn	d.asn n.asn	cj	pl adv	pt.am.npm			pl	v.fpi.1p
3836 2086			7005	3836 1666	4041	3836 3863	1623	1145 2779	1694		2351 2351	4024	2351

naked.	[4] For		while	we are		in	this tent,	we groan		and	are burdened,	because	we do	not	wish		to be
γυμνοὶ	γὰρ	καὶ	→	⸤οἱ ὄντες⸥		ἐν	⸤τῷ σκήνει⸥	στενάζομεν			βαρούμενοι	⸤ἐφ᾽ ᾧ⸥	→	οὐ	θέλομεν	→	→
a.npm	cj	adv		d.npm pt.pa.npm		p.d	d.dsn n.dsn	v.pai.1p			pt.pp.npm	p.d r.dsn		pl	v.pai.1p		
1218	1142	2779		3836 1639		1877	3836 5011	5100			976	2093 4005	2527 2527	4024	2527		

unclothed	but	to be	clothed		with	our	heavenly	dwelling,	so that	what is	mortal		may be	swallowed	up	by
ἐκδύσασθαι	ἀλλ᾽	→	ἐπενδύσασθαι						ἵνα	←	τὸ →	θνητὸν	→	καταποθῇ	←	ὑπὸ
f.am	cj		f.am						cj		d.nsn	a.nsn		v.aps.3s		p.g
1694	247		2086						2671		3836	2570		2927		5679

life.	[5] Now		it is	God	who	has	made		us	for	this	very	purpose	and has	given		us	the	Spirit		as a
⸤τῆς ζωῆς⸥	δὲ			θεὸς	ὁ	→	κατεργασάμενος		ἡμᾶς	εἰς	τοῦτο	αὐτὸ		→	⸤ὁ δοὺς⸥		ἡμῖν	τοῦ	πνεύματος		
d.gsf n.gsf	cj			n.nsm	d.nsm		pt.am.nsm		r.ap.1	p.a	r.asn	r.asn			d.nsm pt.aa.nsm		r.dp.1	d.gsn	n.gsn		
3836 2437	1254			2536	3836		2981		7005	1650	4047	899			3836 1443		7005	3836	4460		

διὸ ἐλάλησα, καὶ ἡμεῖς πιστεύομεν, διὸ καὶ λαλοῦμεν, [14] εἰδότες ὅτι ὁ ἐγείρας τὸν κύριον Ἰησοῦν καὶ ἡμᾶς σὺν Ἰησοῦ ἐγερεῖ καὶ παραστήσει σὺν ὑμῖν. [15] τὰ γὰρ πάντα δι᾽ ὑμᾶς, ἵνα ἡ χάρις πλεονάσασα διὰ τῶν πλειόνων τὴν εὐχαριστίαν περισσεύσῃ εἰς τὴν δόξαν τοῦ θεοῦ. ¶ [16] Διὸ οὐκ ἐγκακοῦμεν, ἀλλ᾽ εἰ καὶ ὁ ἔξω ἡμῶν ἄνθρωπος διαφθείρεται, ἀλλ᾽ ὁ ἔσω ἡμῶν ἀνακαινοῦται ἡμέρᾳ καὶ ἡμέρᾳ. [17] τὸ γὰρ παραυτίκα ἐλαφρὸν τῆς θλίψεως ἡμῶν καθ᾽ ὑπερβολὴν εἰς ὑπερβολὴν αἰώνιον βάρος δόξης κατεργάζεται ἡμῖν, [18] μὴ σκοπούντων ἡμῶν τὰ βλεπόμενα ἀλλὰ τὰ μὴ βλεπόμενα· τὰ γὰρ βλεπόμενα πρόσκαιρα, τὰ δὲ μὴ βλεπόμενα αἰώνια.

    5:1 Οἴδαμεν γὰρ ὅτι ἐὰν ἡ ἐπίγειος ἡμῶν οἰκία τοῦ σκήνους καταλυθῇ, οἰκοδομὴν ἐκ θεοῦ ἔχομεν, οἰκίαν ἀχειροποίητον αἰώνιον ἐν τοῖς οὐρανοῖς. [2] καὶ γὰρ ἐν τούτῳ στενάζομεν τὸ οἰκητήριον ἡμῶν τὸ ἐξ οὐρανοῦ ἐπενδύσασθαι ἐπιποθοῦντες, [3] εἴ γε καὶ ἐνδυσάμενοι «ἐκδυσάμενοι» οὐ γυμνοὶ εὑρεθησόμεθα. [4] καὶ γὰρ οἱ ὄντες ἐν τῷ σκήνει στενάζομεν βαρούμενοι, ἐφ᾽ ᾧ οὐ θέλομεν ἐκδύσασθαι ἀλλ᾽ ἐπενδύσασθαι, ἵνα καταποθῇ τὸ θνητὸν ὑπὸ τῆς ζωῆς. [5] ὁ δὲ κατεργασάμενος ἡμᾶς εἰς αὐτὸ τοῦτο

deposit,   guaranteeing what is to come. ¶ **6** Therefore we are always confident and know that as long as
ˌτὸν ἀρραβῶναˌ ←   ←   ←   οὖν → ← πάντοτε Θαρροῦντες καὶ εἰδότες ὅτι → →
d.asm n.asm   cj   adv pt.pa.npm cj pt.ra.npm cj
3836 775   4036   2509 2509 4121 2509 2779 3857 4022

we are at home   in the body we are away   from the Lord. **7**   We live   by faith, not by sight. **8** We
→ → → ἐνδημοῦντες ἐν τῷ σώματι → → ἐκδημοῦμεν ἀπὸ τοῦ κυρίου γὰρ → περιπατοῦμεν διὰ πίστεως οὐ διὰ εἴδους →
pt.pa.npm p.d n.dsn v.pai.1p p.g d.gsm n.gsm cj v.pai.1p p.g n.gsf pl p.g n.gsn
1897 1877 3836 5393 1685 608 3836 3261 1142 4344 1328 4411 4024 1328 1626

are confident, *I say,* and would prefer   to be away   from the body and at home   with the Lord.
→ θαρροῦμεν δὲ καὶ → ˌεὐδοκοῦμεν μᾶλλονˌ → ἐκδημῆσαι ἐκ τοῦ σώματος καὶ → ἐνδημῆσαι πρὸς τὸν κύριον
v.pai.1p cj cj v.pai.1p adv.c f.aa p.g d.gsn n.gsn cj f.aa p.a d.asm n.asm
2509 1254 2779 2305 3437 1685 1666 3836 5393 2779 1897 4639 3836 3261

9   So we   make it our goal   to please   him, whether we are at home   in the body or
καὶ διὸ → καὶ → → → φιλοτιμούμεθα → ˌεἶναι εὐάρεστοι αὐτῷ εἴτε → → ἐνδημοῦντες ← εἴτε
adv cj adv v.pmi.1p f.pa a.npm r.dsm.3 cj pt.pa.npm cj
2779 1475 5818 2779 5818 1639 2298 899 1664 1897 1664

away   from it. **10** For we   must all   appear   before   the judgment seat of Christ,   that each
ἐκδημοῦντες ← γὰρ ἡμᾶς δεῖ ˌτοὺς πάντας φανερωθῆναι ἔμπροσθεν τοῦ → βήματος → ˌτοῦ Χριστοῦˌ ἵνα ἕκαστος
pt.pa.npm cj r.ap.1 v.pai.3s d.apm a.apm f.ap p.g d.gsn n.gsn d.gsm n.gsm cj r.nsm
1685 1142 7005 1256 3836 4246 5746 1869 3836 1037 3836 5986 2671 1667

one may receive   what is due him for   the things done while   in the body, whether good or bad.
← κομίσηται ← ← ← πρὸς ἃ ← ἔπραξεν τὰ διὰ τοῦ σώματος εἴτε ← ἀγαθὸν εἴτε φαῦλον
v.ams.3s p.a r.apn v.aai.3s d.apn p.g d.gsn n.gsn cj a.asn cj a.asn
3152 4639 4005 4556 3836 1328 3836 5393 1664 19 1664 5765

The Ministry of Reconciliation

5:11 Since, then, we know   what it is to fear   the Lord, we try to persuade men.   What we are is
→ οὖν → Εἰδότες ˌτὸν φόβον τοῦ κυρίου → → πείθομεν ἀνθρώπους δὲ → →
cj pt.ra.npm d.asm n.asm d.gsm n.gsm v.pai.1p n.apm cj
3857 4036 3857 3836 5832 3836 3261 4275 476 1254

plain   to God, and I hope it is   also plain   to your conscience.   **12** We are not trying to commend
πεφανερώμεθα → θεῷ δὲ → ἐλπίζω → καὶ πεφανερῶσθαι ἐν ὑμῶν ˌταῖς συνειδήσεσιν → → οὐ → συνιστάνομεν
v.rpi.1p n.dsm cj v.pai.1s adv f.rp p.d r.gp.2 d.dpf n.dpf pl v.pai.1p
5746 2536 1254 1827 5746 5746 2779 5746 1877 7007 3836 5287 5319 5319 4024 5319 5319 5319

ourselves to you again, but   are giving   you an opportunity to take pride   in us, so that you can answer
ἑαυτοὺς → ὑμῖν πάλιν ἀλλὰ → διδόντες ὑμῖν ἀφορμὴν → καυχήματος ὑπὲρ ἡμῶν ἵνα ← → ἔχητε
r.apm.1 r.dp.2 adv cj pt.pa.npm r.dp.2 n.asf n.gsn p.g r.gp.1 cj v.pas.2p
1571 7007 4099 247 1443 7007 929 3017 5642 7005 2671 2400

those who take pride   in what is seen   rather   than in what is in the heart. **13** If we are out of
πρὸς τοὺς → καυχωμένους ἐν → → προσώπῳ ˌκαὶ μὴ → ← ἐν καρδίᾳ γὰρ εἴτε → ἐξέστημεν
p.a d.apm pt.pm.apm p.d n.dsn cj pl p.d n.dsf cj cj v.aai.1p
4639 3836 3016 1877 4725 2779 3590 1877 2840 1142 1664 2014

our mind, it is for the sake of God; if   we are in   our right mind, it is for you. **14** For Christ's   love
→ → → → θεῷ εἴτε → → σωφρονοῦμεν ← ← → ὑμῖν γὰρ ˌτοῦ Χριστοῦˌ ἡ ἀγάπη
n.dsm cj v.pai.1p r.dp.2 cj d.gsm n.gsm d.nsf n.nsf
2536 1664 5404 7007 1142 3836 5986 3836 27

compels us, because we are convinced   that one died   for all,   and therefore all   died. **15** And he
συνέχει ἡμᾶς → → → κρίναντας τοῦτο ὅτι εἷς ἀπέθανεν ὑπὲρ πάντων ἄρα ˌοἱ πάντεςˌ ἀπέθανον καὶ
v.pai.3s r.ap.1 pt.aa.apm r.asn cj a.nsm v.aai.3s p.g a.gpm cj d.npm a.npm v.aai.3p cj
5309 7005 3212 4047 4022 1651 633 5642 4246 726 3836 4246 633 2779

died   for all,   that those who live should no   longer live for themselves but   for him who died   for
ἀπέθανεν ὑπὲρ πάντων ἵνα οἱ → ζῶντες → μηκέτι → ζῶσιν → ἑαυτοῖς ἀλλὰ → τῷ → ἀποθανόντι ὑπὲρ
v.aai.3s p.g a.gpm cj d.npm pt.pa.npm adv v.pas.3p r.dpm.3 cj d.dsm pt.aa.dsm p.g
633 5642 4246 2671 3836 2409 2409 3600 2409 1571 247 3836 633 5642

them and was raised   again. ¶ **16** So   from now   on we   regard no   one from a worldly point of view.
αὐτῶν καὶ → ἐγερθέντι   Ὥστε ἀπὸ ˌτοῦ νῦνˌ ← ἡμεῖς οἴδαμεν οὐδένα ← κατὰ σάρκα ↑ ↑ ↑
r.gpm.3 cj pt.ap.dsm cj p.g d.gsn adv r.np.1 v.rai.1p a.asm p.a n.asf
899 2779 1586 6063 608 3836 3814 7005 3857 4029 2848 4922 2848 2848 2848

θεός, ὁ δοὺς ἡμῖν τὸν ἀρραβῶνα τοῦ πνεύματος. ¶ 6 Θαρροῦντες οὖν πάντοτε καὶ εἰδότες ὅτι ἐνδημοῦντες ἐν τῷ σώματι ἐκδημοῦμεν ἀπὸ τοῦ κυρίου· 7 διὰ πίστεως γὰρ περιπατοῦμεν, οὐ διὰ εἴδους· 8 θαρροῦμεν δὲ καὶ εὐδοκοῦμεν μᾶλλον ἐκδημῆσαι ἐκ τοῦ σώματος καὶ ἐνδημῆσαι πρὸς τὸν κύριον. 9 διὸ καὶ φιλοτιμούμεθα, εἴτε ἐνδημοῦντες εἴτε ἐκδημοῦντες, εὐάρεστοι αὐτῷ εἶναι. 10 τοὺς γὰρ πάντας ἡμᾶς φανερωθῆναι δεῖ ἔμπροσθεν τοῦ βήματος τοῦ Χριστοῦ, ἵνα κομίσηται ἕκαστος τὰ διὰ τοῦ σώματος πρὸς ἃ ἔπραξεν, εἴτε ἀγαθὸν εἴτε φαῦλον.

5:11 Εἰδότες οὖν τὸν φόβον τοῦ κυρίου ἀνθρώπους πείθομεν, θεῷ δὲ πεφανερώμεθα· ἐλπίζω δὲ καὶ ἐν ταῖς συνειδήσεσιν ὑμῶν πεφανερῶσθαι. 12 οὐ πάλιν ἑαυτοὺς συνιστάνομεν ὑμῖν ἀλλὰ ἀφορμὴν διδόντες ὑμῖν καυχήματος ὑπὲρ ἡμῶν, ἵνα ἔχητε πρὸς τοὺς ἐν προσώπῳ καυχωμένους καὶ μὴ ἐν καρδίᾳ. 13 εἴτε γὰρ ἐξέστημεν, θεῷ· εἴτε σωφρονοῦμεν, ὑμῖν. 14 ἡ γὰρ ἀγάπη τοῦ Χριστοῦ συνέχει ἡμᾶς, κρίναντας τοῦτο, ὅτι εἷς ὑπὲρ πάντων ἀπέθανον· ἄρα οἱ πάντες ἀπέθανον· 15 καὶ ὑπὲρ πάντων ἀπέθανεν, ἵνα οἱ ζῶντες μηκέτι ἑαυτοῖς ζῶσιν ἀλλὰ τῷ ὑπὲρ αὐτῶν ἀποθανόντι καὶ ἐγερθέντι. ¶ 16 Ὥστε ἡμεῖς ἀπὸ τοῦ νῦν οὐδένα

Though we once regarded Christ in this way, we do so no longer. **17** Therefore, if anyone is in
εἰ   καὶ ἐγνώκαμεν Χριστὸν κατὰ → σάρκα ἀλλὰ → γινώσκομεν νῦν οὐκέτι ←   ὥστε εἴ τις ἐν
cj   adv v.rai.1p n.asm p.a n.asf cj   v.pai.1p adv adv   cj cj r.nsm p.d
1623   1182 2779 5986 2848 4922 247   1182 3814 4033   6063 1623 5516 1877

Christ, he is a new creation; the old has gone, the new has come! **18** All this is from God,
Χριστῷ καινὴ κτίσις· τὰ ἀρχαῖα → παρῆλθεν ἰδοὺ καινά → γέγονεν δὲ τὰ πάντα· ἐκ τοῦ θεοῦ,
n.dsm a.nsf n.nsf d.npn a.npn v.aai.3s v.aai.3s a.npn v.rai.3s cj d.npn a.npn p.g d.gsm n.gsm
5986 2785 3232 3836 792 4216 2627 2785 1181 1254 3836 4246 1666 3836 2536

who reconciled us to himself through Christ and gave us the ministry of reconciliation: **19** that God was
τοῦ καταλλάξαντος ἡμᾶς → ἑαυτῷ διὰ Χριστοῦ καὶ δόντος ἡμῖν τὴν διακονίαν → τῆς καταλλαγῆς, ὡς ὅτι θεὸς ἦν
d.gsm pt.aa.gsm r.ap.1 r.dsm.3 p.g n.gsm cj pt.aa.gsm r.dp.1 d.asf n.asf d.gsf n.gsf pl cj n.nsm v.iai.3s
3836 2904 7005 1571 1328 5986 2779 1443 7005 3836 1355 3836 2903 6055 4022 2536 1639

reconciling the world to himself in Christ, not counting men's sins against them. And he has
καταλλάσσων κόσμον ἑαυτῷ ἐν Χριστῷ μὴ λογιζόμενος αὐτῶν τὰ παραπτώματα, αὐτοῖς καὶ → →
pt.pa.nsm n.asm r.dsm.3 p.d n.dsm pl pt.pm.nsm r.gpm.3 d.apn n.apn r.dpm.3 cj
2904 3180 1571 1877 5986 3590 3357 899 3836 4183 899 2779

committed to us the message of reconciliation. **20** We are therefore Christ's ambassadors, as though God
θέμενος ἐν ἡμῖν τὸν λόγον → τῆς καταλλαγῆς, οὖν Ὑπὲρ Χριστοῦ πρεσβεύομεν ὡς ← τοῦ θεοῦ,
pt.am.nsm p.d r.dp.1 d.asm n.asm d.gsf n.gsf cj p.g n.gsm v.pai.1p pl d.gsm n.gsm
5502 1877 7005 3836 3364 3836 2903 4563 4563 4036 5642 5986 4563 6055 3836 2536

were making his appeal through us. We implore you on Christ's behalf: Be reconciled to God. **21** God
→ → → παρακαλοῦντος δι' ἡμῶν → δεόμεθα ὑπὲρ Χριστοῦ ← → καταλλάγητε τῷ θεῷ
pt.pa.gsm p.g r.gp.1 v.pmi.1p p.g n.gsm v.apm.2p d.dsm n.dsm
4151 1328 7005 1289 5642 5986 2904 3836 2536

made him who had no sin to be sin for us, so that in him we might become the righteousness
ἐποίησεν τὸν γνόντα μὴ ἁμαρτίαν ἁμαρτίαν ὑπὲρ ἡμῶν ἵνα ἐν αὐτῷ ἡμεῖς → γενώμεθα δικαιοσύνη
v.aai.3s d.asm pt.aa.asm pl n.asf n.asf p.g r.gp.1 cj p.d r.dsm.3 r.np.1 v.ams.1p n.nsf
4472 3836 1182 3590 281 281 5642 7005 2671 1877 899 7005 1181 1466

of God. ¶ **6:1** As God's fellow workers we urge you not to receive God's grace in vain.
→ θεοῦ δὲ καὶ Συνεργοῦντες → καὶ παρακαλοῦμεν ὑμᾶς μὴ → δέξασθαι τοῦ θεοῦ, τὴν χάριν, εἰς κενὸν
n.gsm cj pt.pa.npm adv v.pai.1p r.ap.2 pl f.am d.gsm n.gsm d.asf n.asf p.a a.asn
2536 1254 5300 4151 2779 4151 7007 3590 1312 3836 2536 3836 5921 1650 3031

2 For he says, "In the time of my favor I heard you, and in the day of salvation I helped you." I *tell you,*
γάρ → λέγει → καιρῷ δεκτῷ ἐπήκουσά σου καὶ ἐν ἡμέρᾳ → σωτηρίας → ἐβοήθησά σοι ἰδοὺ
cj v.pai.3s n.dsm a.dsm v.aai.1s r.gs.2 cj p.d n.dsf n.gsf v.aai.1s r.ds.2 j
1142 3306 2789 1283 2052 5148 2779 1877 2465 5401 1070 5148 2627

now is the time of God's favor, now is the day of salvation.
νῦν καιρὸς εὐπρόσδεκτος ἰδοὺ νῦν ἡμέρα → σωτηρίας
adv n.nsm a.nsm j adv n.nsf n.gsf
3814 2789 2347 2627 3814 2465 5401

Paul's Hardships

6:3 We put no stumbling block in anyone's path, so that our ministry will not be discredited. **4** Rather,
→ διδόντες Μηδεμίαν προσκοπήν ← ἐν μηδενὶ ἵνα ← ἡ διακονία → μὴ → μωμηθῇ ἀλλ'
pt.pa.npm a.asf n.asf p.d a.dsn cj d.nsf n.nsf pl v.aps.3s cj
1443 3594 4683 1877 3594 2671 3836 1355 3699 3590 3699 247

as servants of God we commend ourselves in every way: in great endurance; in troubles, hardships and
ὡς διάκονοι → θεοῦ → συνίσταντες ἑαυτοὺς ἐν παντί → ἐν πολλῇ ὑπομονῇ ἐν θλίψεσιν ἐν ἀνάγκαις ἐν
pl n.npm n.gsm pt.pa.npm r.apm.1 p.d a.dsn p.d a.dsf n.dsf p.d n.dpf p.d n.dpf p.d
6055 1356 2536 5319 1571 1877 4246 1877 4498 5705 1877 2568 1877 340 1877

distresses; **5** in beatings, imprisonments and riots; in hard work, sleepless nights and hunger;
στενοχωρίαις ἐν πληγαῖς ἐν φυλακαῖς ἐν ἀκαταστασίαις ἐν → κόποις ἐν ἀγρυπνίαις ← ἐν νηστείαις
n.dpf p.d n.dpf p.d n.dpf p.d n.dpf p.d n.dpm p.d n.dpf p.d n.dpf
5103 1877 4435 1877 5871 1877 189 1877 3160 1877 71 1877 3763

6 in purity, understanding, patience and kindness; in the Holy Spirit and in sincere love; **7** in
ἐν ἁγνότητι ἐν γνώσει ἐν μακροθυμίᾳ ἐν χρηστότητι ἐν ἁγίῳ πνεύματι ἐν ἀνυποκρίτῳ ἀγάπῃ ἐν
p.d n.dsf p.d n.dsf p.d n.dsf p.d n.dsf p.d a.dsn n.dsn p.d a.dsf n.dsf p.d
1877 55 1877 1194 1877 3429 1877 5983 1877 41 4460 1877 537 27 1877

οἴδαμεν κατὰ σάρκα· εἰ καὶ ἐγνώκαμεν κατὰ σάρκα Χριστόν, ἀλλὰ νῦν οὐκέτι γινώσκομεν. **17** ὥστε εἴ τις ἐν Χριστῷ, καινὴ κτίσις· τὰ ἀρχαῖα παρῆλθεν, ἰδοὺ γέγονεν καινά· **18** τὰ δὲ πάντα ἐκ τοῦ θεοῦ τοῦ καταλλάξαντος ἡμᾶς ἑαυτῷ διὰ Χριστοῦ καὶ δόντος ἡμῖν τὴν διακονίαν τῆς καταλλαγῆς, **19** ὡς ὅτι θεὸς ἦν ἐν Χριστῷ κόσμον καταλλάσσων ἑαυτῷ, μὴ λογιζόμενος αὐτοῖς τὰ παραπτώματα αὐτῶν καὶ θέμενος ἐν ἡμῖν τὸν λόγον τῆς καταλλαγῆς. **20** ὑπὲρ Χριστοῦ οὖν πρεσβεύομεν ὡς τοῦ θεοῦ παρακαλοῦντος δι' ἡμῶν· δεόμεθα ὑπὲρ Χριστοῦ, καταλλάγητε τῷ θεῷ. **21** τὸν μὴ γνόντα ἁμαρτίαν ὑπὲρ ἡμῶν ἁμαρτίαν ἐποίησεν, ἵνα ἡμεῖς γενώμεθα δικαιοσύνη θεοῦ ἐν αὐτῷ.

6:1 Συνεργοῦντες δὲ καὶ παρακαλοῦμεν μὴ εἰς κενὸν τὴν χάριν τοῦ θεοῦ δέξασθαι ὑμᾶς· **2** λέγει γάρ, Καιρῷ δεκτῷ ἐπήκουσά σου καὶ ἐν ἡμέρᾳ σωτηρίας ἐβοήθησά σοι. ἰδοὺ νῦν καιρὸς εὐπρόσδεκτος, ἰδοὺ νῦν ἡμέρα σωτηρίας·

6:3 μηδεμίαν ἐν μηδενὶ διδόντες προσκοπήν, ἵνα μὴ μωμηθῇ ἡ διακονία, **4** ἀλλ' ἐν παντὶ συνιστάντες ἑαυτοὺς ὡς θεοῦ διάκονοι, ἐν ὑπομονῇ πολλῇ, ἐν θλίψεσιν, ἐν ἀνάγκαις, ἐν στενοχωρίαις, **5** ἐν πληγαῖς, ἐν φυλακαῖς, ἐν ἀκαταστασίαις, ἐν κόποις, ἐν ἀγρυπνίαις, ἐν νηστείαις, **6** ἐν ἁγνότητι, ἐν γνώσει, ἐν μακροθυμίᾳ, ἐν χρηστότητι, ἐν πνεύματι ἁγίῳ, ἐν ἀγάπῃ ἀνυποκρίτῳ,

truthful speech and in the power of God; with weapons of righteousness in the right hand and in the left;
ἀληθείας λόγῳ ἐν δυνάμει → θεοῦ διὰ ⸂τῶν ὅπλων⸃ ⸂τῆς δικαιοσύνης⸃ → τῶν δεξιῶν ← καὶ → ἀριστερῶν
n.gsf n.dsm p.d n.dsf n.gsm p.g d.gpn n.gpn d.gsf n.gsf d.gpf a.gpf cj a.gpf
237 3364 1877 1539 2536 1328 3836 3960 3836 1466 3836 1288 2779 754

8 through glory and dishonor, bad report and good report; genuine, yet regarded as impostors; **9** known,
διὰ δόξης καὶ ἀτιμίας, διὰ → δυσφημίας καὶ → εὐφημίας ἀληθεῖς καὶ → ὡς πλάνοι ἐπιγινωσκόμενοι
p.g n.gsf cj n.gsf p.g n.gsf cj n.gsf a.npm cj pl a.npm pt.pp.npm
1328 1518 2779 871 1328 1556 2779 2367 239 2779 6055 4418 2105

yet regarded as unknown; dying, and yet we live on; beaten, and yet not killed; **10**
καὶ → ὡς ἀγνοούμενοι ὡς ἀποθνῄσκοντες καὶ ἰδοὺ → ζῶμεν ← ὡς παιδευόμενοι καὶ μὴ θανατούμενοι ὡς
cj pl pt.pp.npm pl pt.pa.npm cj j v.pai.1p pl pt.pp.npm cj pl pt.pp.npm pl
2779 6055 51 6055 633 2779 2627 2409 6055 4084 2779 3590 2506 6055

sorrowful, yet always rejoicing; poor, yet making many rich; having nothing, and yet possessing
λυπούμενοι δὲ ἀεὶ χαίροντες ὡς πτωχοὶ δὲ → πολλοὺς πλουτίζοντες ὡς ἔχοντες μηδὲν καὶ κατέχοντες
pt.pp.npm cj adv pt.pa.npm pl a.npm cj a.apm pt.pa.npm pl pt.pa.npm a.asn cj pt.pa.npm
3382 1254 107 5897 6055 4777 1254 4457 4498 4457 6055 2400 3594 2779 2988

everything. ¶ **11** We have spoken freely to you, Corinthians, and opened wide our hearts to
πάντα ἡμῶν → ⸂Τὸ στόμα ἀνέῳγεν⸃ πρὸς ὑμᾶς Κορίνθιοι πεπλάτυνται ← ἡμῶν ἡ καρδία
a.apn r.gp.1 d.nsn n.nsn v.rai.3s p.a r.ap.2 n.vpm v.rpi.3s r.gp.1 d.nsf n.nsf
4246 7005 487 3836 5125 487 4639 7007 3171 4425 7005 3836 2840

you. **12** We are not withholding our affection from you, but you are withholding yours from us.
ἐν ἡμῖν → οὐ στενοχωρεῖσθε → δὲ → → στενοχωρεῖσθε ἐν τοῖς σπλάγχνοις ὑμῶν
p.d r.dp.1 pl v.ppi.2p cj v.ppi.2p p.d d.dpn n.dpn r.gp.2
1877 7005 5102 4024 5102 5073 1254 5102 1877 3836 5073 7007

13 As a fair exchange – I speak as to my children – open wide your hearts also.
δὲ αὐτὴν ⸂τὴν ἀντιμισθίαν⸃ → λέγω ὡς → τέκνοις ὑμεῖς πλατύνθητε ← καὶ
cj r.asf d.asf n.asf v.pai.1s pl n.dpn r.np.2 v.apm.2p cj
1254 899 3836 521 3306 6055 5451 7007 4425 2779

Do Not Be Yoked With Unbelievers

6:14 Do not be yoked together with unbelievers. For what do righteousness and wickedness have in
→ Μὴ γίνεσθε ἑτεροζυγοῦντες ← → ἀπίστοις γὰρ τίς δικαιοσύνη καὶ ἀνομία
pl v.pmm.2p pt.pa.npm a.dpm cj r.nsf n.dsf cj n.dsf
1181 3590 1181 2282 603 1142 5515 1466 2779 490

common? Or what fellowship can light have with darkness? **15** What harmony is there between Christ and
μετοχή ἢ τίς κοινωνία φωτὶ πρὸς σκότος δὲ τίς συμφώνησις Χριστοῦ πρὸς
n.nsf cj r.nsf n.nsf n.dsn p.a n.asn cj r.nsf n.nsf n.gsm p.a
3580 2445 5515 3126 5890 4639 5030 1254 5515 5245 5986 4639

Belial? What does a believer have in common with an unbeliever? **16** What agreement is there between the
Βελιὰρ ἢ τίς πιστῷ → μερὶς μετὰ ἀπίστου δὲ τίς συγκατάθεσις
n.asm cj r.nsf a.dsm n.nsf p.g a.gsm cj r.nsf n.nsf
1016 2445 5515 4412 3535 3552 603 1254 5515 5161

temple of God and idols? For we are the temple of the living God. As God has said: "I will
ναῷ → θεοῦ μετὰ εἰδώλων γὰρ ἡμεῖς ἐσμεν ναός → ζῶντος θεοῦ καθὼς ὁ θεός → εἶπεν ὅτι → →
n.dsm n.gsm p.g n.gpn cj r.np.1 v.pai.1p n.nsm pt.pa.gsm n.gsm cj d.nsm n.nsm v.aai.3s cj
3724 2536 3552 1631 1142 7005 1639 3724 2409 2536 2777 3836 2536 3306 4022

live with them and walk among them, and I will be their God, and they will be my people."
ἐνοικήσω ἐν αὐτοῖς καὶ ἐμπεριπατήσω ← καὶ → → ἔσομαι αὐτῶν θεός καὶ αὐτοὶ → ἔσονται μου λαός
v.fai.1s p.d r.dpm.3 cj v.fai.1s cj v.fmi.1s r.gpm.3 n.nsm cj r.npm v.fmi.3p r.gs.1 n.nsm
1940 1877 899 2779 1853 2779 1639 899 2536 2779 899 1639 1609 3295

17 "Therefore come out from them and be separate, says the Lord. Touch no unclean thing, and I will
διὸ ἐξέλθατε ἐκ μέσου αὐτῶν καὶ → ἀφορίσθητε λέγει κύριος καὶ ἅπτεσθε μὴ ἀκαθάρτου ← κἀγὼ
cj v.aam.2p p.g n.gsn r.gpm.3 cj v.apm.2p v.pai.3s n.nsm cj v.pmm.2p pl a.gsn crasis
1475 2002 1666 3545 899 2779 928 3306 3261 2779 721 3590 176 2743

receive you." **18** "I will be a Father to you, and you will be my sons and daughters, says the Lord
εἰσδέξομαι ὑμᾶς καὶ → ἔσομαι πατέρα εἰς ὑμῖν καὶ ὑμεῖς → ἔσεσθε μοι εἰς υἱοὺς καὶ θυγατέρας λέγει κύριος
v.fmi.1s r.ap.2 cj v.fmi.1s n.asm p.a r.dp.2 cj r.np.2 v.fmi.2p r.ds.1 p.a n.apm cj n.apf v.pai.3s n.nsm
1654 7007 2779 1639 4252 1650 7007 2779 7007 1639 1609 1650 5626 2779 2588 3306 3261

---

⁷ ἐν λόγῳ ἀληθείας, ἐν δυνάμει θεοῦ· διὰ τῶν ὅπλων τῆς δικαιοσύνης τῶν δεξιῶν καὶ ἀριστερῶν, ⁸ διὰ δόξης καὶ ἀτιμίας, διὰ δυσφημίας καὶ εὐφημίας· ὡς πλάνοι καὶ ἀληθεῖς, ⁹ ὡς ἀγνοούμενοι καὶ ἐπιγινωσκόμενοι, ὡς ἀποθνῄσκοντες καὶ ἰδοὺ ζῶμεν, ὡς παιδευόμενοι καὶ μὴ θανατούμενοι, ¹⁰ ὡς λυπούμενοι ἀεὶ δὲ χαίροντες, ὡς πτωχοὶ πολλοὺς δὲ πλουτίζοντες, ὡς μηδὲν ἔχοντες καὶ πάντα κατέχοντες. ¶ ¹¹ Τὸ στόμα ἡμῶν ἀνέῳγεν πρὸς ὑμᾶς, Κορίνθιοι, ἡ καρδία ἡμῶν πεπλάτυνται· ¹² οὐ στενοχωρεῖσθε ἐν ἡμῖν, στενοχωρεῖσθε δὲ ἐν τοῖς σπλάγχνοις ὑμῶν· ¹³ τὴν δὲ αὐτὴν ἀντιμισθίαν, ὡς τέκνοις λέγω, πλατύνθητε καὶ ὑμεῖς.

⁶·¹⁴ Μὴ γίνεσθε ἑτεροζυγοῦντες ἀπίστοις· τίς γὰρ μετοχὴ δικαιοσύνῃ καὶ ἀνομίᾳ ἢ τίς κοινωνία φωτὶ πρὸς σκότος; ¹⁵ τίς δὲ συμφώνησις Χριστοῦ πρὸς Βελιάρ, ἢ τίς μερὶς πιστῷ μετὰ ἀπίστου; ¹⁶ τίς δὲ συγκατάθεσις ναῷ θεοῦ μετὰ εἰδώλων; ἡμεῖς γὰρ ναὸς θεοῦ ἐσμεν ζῶντος, καθὼς εἶπεν ὁ θεὸς ὅτι Ἐνοικήσω ἐν αὐτοῖς καὶ ἐμπεριπατήσω καὶ ἔσομαι αὐτῶν θεὸς καὶ αὐτοὶ ἔσονταί μου λαός. ¹⁷ διὸ ἐξέλθατε ἐκ μέσου αὐτῶν καὶ ἀφορίσθητε, λέγει κύριος, καὶ ἀκαθάρτου μὴ ἅπτεσθε· κἀγὼ εἰσδέξομαι ὑμᾶς ¹⁸ καὶ ἔσομαι ὑμῖν εἰς πατέρα καὶ ὑμεῖς ἔσεσθέ μοι εἰς υἱοὺς καὶ θυγατέρας, λέγει κύριος παντοκράτωρ. ⁷·¹ ταύτας οὖν

Almighty." **7:1** Since we have these promises, dear friends, let us purify ourselves from everything that
παντοκράτωρ οὖν → → ἔχοντες ταύτας ⸤τὰς ἐπαγγελίας⸥ → ἀγαπητοί → καθαρίσωμεν ἑαυτοὺς ἀπὸ παντὸς
n.nsm cj pt.pa.npm r.apf d.apf n.apf a.vpm v.aas.1p r.apm.1 p.g a.gsm
4120 4036 2400 4047 3836 2039 28 2751 1571 608 4246

contaminates body and spirit, perfecting holiness out of reverence for God.
μολυσμοῦ σαρκὸς καὶ πνεύματος ἐπιτελοῦντες ἁγιωσύνην ἐν φόβῳ → θεοῦ
n.gsm n.gsf cj n.gsn pt.pa.npm n.asf p.d n.dsm n.gsm
3663 4922 2779 4460 2200 43 1877 5832 2536

Paul's Joy

7:2 Make room for us in your hearts. We have wronged no one, we have corrupted no one, we have
Χωρήσατε ← ἡμᾶς ἠδικήσαμεν οὐδένα ← → ἐφθείραμεν οὐδένα
v.aam.2p r.ap.1 v.aai.1p a.asm v.aai.1p a.asm
6003 7005 92 4029 5780 4029

exploited no one. **3** I do not say this to condemn you; I have said before that you have such a
ἐπλεονεκτήσαμεν οὐδένα ← → → οὐ λέγω πρὸς κατάκρισιν γὰρ → → προείρηκα ← ὅτι → ἐστε
v.aai.1p a.asm pl v.pai.1s p.a n.asf cj v.rai.1s cj v.pai.2p
4430 4029 3306 3306 4024 3306 4639 2892 1142 4597 4022 1639

place in our hearts that we would live or die with you. **4** I have great confidence in you;
ἐν ἡμῶν ⸤ταῖς καρδίαις⸥ εἰς → συζῆν καὶ ⸤τὸ συναποθανεῖν⸥ ← μοι πολλή παρρησία πρὸς ὑμᾶς
p.d r.gp.1 d.dpf n.dpf p.a f.pa cj d.asn f.aa r.ds.1 a.nsf n.nsf p.a r.ap.2
1877 7005 3836 2840 1650 5182 2779 3836 5271 1609 4498 4244 4639 7007

I take great pride in you. I am greatly encouraged; in all our troubles my joy knows no
μοι πολλή καύχησις ὑπὲρ ὑμῶν → → ⸤πεπλήρωμαι τῇ παρακλήσει⸥ ἐπὶ πάσῃ ἡμῶν ⸤τῇ θλίψει⸥ ⸤τῇ χαρᾷ⸥ →
r.ds.1 a.nsf n.nsf p.g r.gp.2 v.rpi.1s d.dsf n.dsf p.d a.dsf r.gp.1 d.dsf n.dsf d.dsf n.dsf
1609 4498 3018 5642 7007 4444 3836 4155 2093 4246 7005 3836 2568 3836 5915

bounds. ¶ **5** For when we came into Macedonia, this body of ours had no rest, but we
ὑπερπερισσεύομαι γὰρ → ἡμῶν Καὶ ἐλθόντων εἰς Μακεδονίαν ἡ σὰρξ → ἡμῶν ἔσχηκεν οὐδεμίαν ἄνεσιν ἀλλ᾽ →
v.pmi.1s cj r.gp.1 cj pt.aa.gpm p.a n.asf d.nsf n.nsf r.gp.1 v.rai.3s a.asf n.asf cj
5668 1142 2262 7005 2779 1650 3423 3836 4922 7005 2400 4029 457 247

were harassed at every turn – conflicts on the outside, fears within. **6** But God, who comforts the downcast,
→ θλιβόμενοι ἐν παντὶ → μάχαι → ἔξωθεν φόβοι ἔσωθεν ἀλλ᾽ ὁ θεός, ὁ παρακαλῶν τοὺς ταπεινοὺς
pt.pp.npm p.d a.dsn n.npf adv n.npm adv cj d.nsm n.nsm d.nsm pt.pa.nsm d.apm a.apm
2567 1877 4246 3480 2033 5832 2277 247 3836 2536 3836 4151 3836 5424

comforted us by the coming of Titus, **7** and not only by his coming but also by the comfort you
παρεκάλεσεν ἡμᾶς ἐν τῇ παρουσίᾳ → Τίτου δὲ οὐ μόνον ἐν αὐτοῦ ⸤τῇ παρουσίᾳ⸥ ἀλλὰ καὶ ἐν τῇ παρακλήσει ᾗ ἐφ᾽ ὑμῖν
v.aai.3s r.ap.1 p.d d.dsf n.dsf n.gsm cj pl adv p.d r.gsm.3 d.dsf n.dsf cj adv p.d d.dsf n.dsf r.dsf p.d r.dp.2
4151 7005 1877 3836 4242 5519 1254 4024 3667 1877 899 3836 4242 247 2779 1877 3836 4155 2093 2093 7007

had given him. He told us about your longing for me, your deep sorrow, your ardent concern
→ παρεκλήθη ← ἀναγγέλλων ἡμῖν ὑμῶν ⸤τὴν ἐπιπόθησιν⸥ ὑμῶν ⸤τὸν ὀδυρμόν⸥ ὑμῶν → ⸤τὸν ζῆλον⸥
v.api.3s pt.pa.nsm r.dp.1 r.gp.2 d.asf n.asf r.gp.2 d.asm n.asm r.gp.2 d.asm n.asm
4151 334 7005 334 7007 3836 2161 7007 3836 3851 7007 3836 2419

for me, so that my joy was greater than ever. ¶ **8** Even if I caused you sorrow by my letter, I
ὑπὲρ ἐμοῦ ὥστε ← με χαρῆναι μᾶλλον Ὅτι καὶ εἰ → → ὑμᾶς ἐλύπησα ἐν τῇ ἐπιστολῇ →
p.g r.gs.1 cj r.as.1 f.ap adv.c cj adv cj r.ap.2 v.aai.1s p.d d.dsf n.dsf
5642 1609 6063 1609 5897 3437 4022 2779 1623 3382 3382 7007 3382 1877 3836 2186 3564

do not regret it. Though I did regret it – I see that my letter hurt you, but only for
→ οὐ μεταμέλομαι ⸤εἰ καὶ⸥ → μετεμελόμην [γὰρ] βλέπω ὅτι ἐκείνη ἡ ἐπιστολὴ ἐλύπησεν ὑμᾶς εἰ καὶ πρὸς
pl v.ppi.1s cj adv v.ipi.1s cj v.pai.1s cj r.nsf d.nsf n.nsf v.aai.3s r.ap.2 cj adv p.a
3564 4024 3564 1623 2779 3564 1142 1063 4022 1697 3836 2186 3382 7007 1623 2779 4639

a little while – **9** yet now I am happy, not because you were made sorry, but because your sorrow led you to
ὥραν ← νῦν → χαίρω οὐχ ὅτι ἐλυπήθητε ἀλλ᾽ ὅτι → ἐλυπήθητε εἰς
n.asf adv v.pai.1s pl cj v.api.2p cj cj v.api.2p p.a
6052 3814 5897 4024 4022 3382 247 4022 3382 1650

repentance. For you became sorrowful as God intended and so were not harmed in any way by us. **10**
μετάνοιαν γὰρ → → ἐλυπήθητε κατὰ θεόν ← ἵνα → → ζημιωθῆτε ἐν μηδενὶ ← ἐξ ἡμῶν γὰρ
n.asf cj v.api.2p p.a n.asm cj v.aps.2p p.d a.dsn p.g r.gp.1 cj
3567 1142 3382 2848 2536 2848 2671 2423 3594 2423 1877 3594 1666 7005 1142

ἔχοντες τὰς ἐπαγγελίας, ἀγαπητοί, καθαρίσωμεν ἑαυτοὺς ἀπὸ παντὸς μολυσμοῦ σαρκὸς καὶ πνεύματος, ἐπιτελοῦντες ἁγιωσύνην ἐν φόβῳ θεοῦ.

7:2 Χωρήσατε ἡμᾶς· οὐδένα ἠδικήσαμεν, οὐδένα ἐφθείραμεν, οὐδένα ἐπλεονεκτήσαμεν. **3** πρὸς κατάκρισιν οὐ λέγω· προείρηκα γὰρ ὅτι ἐν ταῖς καρδίαις ἡμῶν ἐστε εἰς τὸ συναποθανεῖν καὶ συζῆν. **4** πολλή μοι παρρησία πρὸς ὑμᾶς, πολλή μοι καύχησις ὑπὲρ ὑμῶν· πεπλήρωμαι τῇ παρακλήσει, ὑπερπερισσεύομαι τῇ χαρᾷ ἐπὶ πάσῃ τῇ θλίψει ἡμῶν. ¶ **5** Καὶ γὰρ ἐλθόντων ἡμῶν εἰς Μακεδονίαν οὐδεμίαν ἔσχηκεν ἄνεσιν ἡ σὰρξ ἡμῶν ἀλλ᾽ ἐν παντὶ θλιβόμενοι· ἔξωθεν μάχαι, ἔσωθεν φόβοι. **6** ἀλλ᾽ ὁ παρακαλῶν τοὺς ταπεινοὺς παρεκάλεσεν ἡμᾶς ὁ θεὸς ἐν τῇ παρουσίᾳ Τίτου, **7** οὐ μόνον δὲ ἐν τῇ παρουσίᾳ αὐτοῦ ἀλλὰ καὶ ἐν τῇ παρακλήσει ᾗ παρεκλήθη ἐφ᾽ ὑμῖν, ἀναγγέλλων ἡμῖν τὴν ὑμῶν ἐπιπόθησιν, τὸν ὑμῶν ὀδυρμόν, τὸν ὑμῶν ζῆλον ὑπὲρ ἐμοῦ ὥστε με μᾶλλον χαρῆναι. ¶ **8** ὅτι εἰ καὶ ἐλύπησα ὑμᾶς ἐν τῇ ἐπιστολῇ, οὐ μεταμέλομαι· εἰ καὶ μετεμελόμην, βλέπω [γὰρ] ὅτι ἡ ἐπιστολὴ ἐκείνη εἰ καὶ πρὸς ὥραν ἐλύπησεν ὑμᾶς, **9** νῦν χαίρω, οὐχ ὅτι ἐλυπήθητε ἀλλ᾽ ὅτι ἐλυπήθητε εἰς μετάνοιαν· ἐλυπήθητε γὰρ κατὰ θεόν, ἵνα ἐν μηδενὶ ζημιωθῆτε ἐξ ἡμῶν. **10** ἡ γὰρ κατὰ θεὸν λύπη μετάνοιαν εἰς σωτηρίαν ἀμεταμέλητον ἐργάζεται· ἡ δὲ τοῦ κόσμου

Godly sorrow brings repentance that leads to salvation and leaves no regret, but worldly sorrow
ˌκατὰ θεὸνˌ ἡ λύπη μετάνοιαν → εἰς σωτηρίαν ἐργάζεται → ἀμεταμέλητον δὲ ˌτοῦ κόσμουˌ ἡ λύπη
p.a n.asm d.nsf n.nsf n.asf p.a n.asf v.pmi.3s a.asf cj d.gsm n.gsm d.nsf n.nsf
2848 2536 3836 3383 3567 1650 5401 2237 294 1254 3836 3180 3836 3383

brings death. **11** See what this godly sorrow has produced in you: what earnestness,
κατεργάζεται θάνατον γὰρ ἰδοὺ ˌαὐτὸ τοῦτοˌ ˌκατὰ θεὸνˌ ˌτὸ λυπηθῆναιˌ → κατειργάσατο πόσην → ὑμῖν σπουδήν
v.pmi.3s n.asm cj r.nsn r.nsn r.asn p.a n.asm d.npn f.ap v.ami.3s r.asf r.dp.2 n.asf
2981 2505 1142 2627 899 4047 2848 2536 3836 3382 2981 4531 7007 5082

what eagerness to clear yourselves, what indignation, what alarm, what longing, what concern, what readiness
ἀλλὰ → → ἀπολογίαν ← ἀλλὰ ἀγανάκτησιν ἀλλὰ φόβον ἀλλὰ ἐπιπόθησιν ἀλλὰ ζῆλον ἀλλὰ →
cj n.asf cj n.asf cj n.asm cj n.asf cj n.asm cj
247 665 247 25 247 5832 247 2161 247 2419 247

to see justice done. At every point you have proved yourselves to be innocent in this matter. **12** So *even*
→ → ἐκδίκησιν ← ἐν παντὶ → → συνεστήσατε ἑαυτοὺς → εἶναι ἀγνοὺς → τῷ πράγματι ἄρα εἰ
n.asf p.d a.dsn v.aai.2p r.apm.2 f.pa a.apm d.dsn n.dsn cj cj
1689 1877 4246 5319 1571 1639 54 3836 4547 726 1623

though I wrote to you, it was not on account of the one who did the wrong or of the injured party,
καὶ → ἔγραψα ὑμῖν οὐχ ἕνεκεν ← ← τοῦ → ← ἀδικήσαντος οὐδὲ ἕνεκεν τοῦ ἀδικηθέντος
adv v.aai.1s r.dp.2 pl p.g d.gsm pt.aa.gsm cj p.g d.gsm pt.ap.gsm
2779 1211 7007 4024 1914 3836 92 4028 1914 3836 92

but rather that before God you could see for yourselves how devoted to us you are.
ἀλλ᾽ ἕνεκεν → ἐνώπιον ˌτοῦ θεοῦˌ → ˌτοῦ φανερωθῆναιˌ πρὸς ὑμᾶς ˌτὴν σπουδὴνˌ τὴν ὑπὲρ ἡμῶν ὑμῶν
cj p.g p.g d.gsm n.gsm d.gsn f.ap p.a r.ap.2 d.asf n.asf d.asf p.g r.gp.1 r.gp.2
247 1914 5746 1967 3836 2536 3836 5746 4639 7007 3836 5082 3836 5642 7005 7007

13 By all this we are encouraged. ¶ In addition to our own encouragement, we were especially
διὰ τοῦτο → παρακεκλήμεθα δὲ Ἐπὶ ← ← ἡμῶν ˌτῇ παρακλήσειˌ → → ˌπερισσοτέρως μᾶλλονˌ
p.a r.asn v.rpi.1p cj p.d r.gp.1 d.dsf n.dsf adv.c adv.c
1328 4047 4151 1254 2093 7005 3836 4155 5897 5897 4359 3437

delighted to see how happy Titus was, because his spirit has been refreshed by all of you. **14**
ἐχάρημεν ἐπὶ ˌτῇ χαρᾷˌ Τίτου ὅτι αὐτοῦ ˌτὸ πνεῦμαˌ → ἀναπέπαυται ἀπὸ πάντων → ὑμῶν ὅτι εἴ
v.api.1p p.d d.dsf n.dsf n.gsm cj r.gsm.3 d.nsn n.nsn v.rpi.3s p.g a.gpm r.gp.2 cj cj
5897 2093 3836 5915 5519 4022 899 3836 4460 399 608 4246 7007 4022 1623

I had boasted to him about you, and you have not embarrassed me. But just as everything we said to
→ → κεκαύχημαι τι → αὐτῷ ὑπὲρ ὑμῶν → οὐ κατησχύνθην ← ἀλλ᾽ ὡς ← πάντα → ἐλαλήσαμεν →
v.rmi.1s r.asn r.dsm.3 p.g r.gp.2 pl v.api.1s cj cj a.apn v.aai.1p
3016 5516 899 5642 7007 2875 4024 2875 247 6055 4246 3281

you was true, so our boasting about you to Titus has proved to be true as well. **15** And his
ὑμῖν ˌἐν ἀληθείᾳˌ οὕτως ἡμῶν ἡ καύχησις ἐπὶ Τίτου → ἐγενήθη ἡ ἀλήθεια καὶ καὶ αὐτοῦ
r.dp.2 p.d n.dsf adv r.gp.1 d.nsf n.nsf p.g n.gsm v.api.3s d.nsf n.nsf adv cj r.gsm.3
7007 1877 237 4048 7005 3836 3018 2093 5519 1181 3836 237 2779 2779 899

affection for you is all the greater when he remembers that you were all obedient, receiving
ˌτὰ σπλάγχναˌ εἰς ὑμᾶς ἐστιν ᾽ περισσοτέρως → → ἀναμιμνῃσκομένου ὑμῶν πάντων ˌτὴν ὑπακοὴνˌ ἐδέξασθε
d.npn n.npn p.a r.ap.2 v.pai.3s adv.c pt.pp.gsm r.gp.2 a.gpm d.asf n.asf v.ami.2p
3836 5073 1650 7007 1639 4359 389 7007 4246 3836 5633 1312

him with fear and trembling. **16** I am glad I can have complete confidence in you.
αὐτόν ὡς μετὰ φόβου καὶ τρόμου → → χαίρω ὅτι → ˌἐν παντὶˌ θαρρῶ ἐν ὑμῖν
r.asm.3 cj p.g n.gsm cj n.gsm v.pai.1s cj p.d a.dsn v.pai.1s p.d r.dp.2
899 6055 3552 5832 2779 5571 5897 4022 2509 2509 2509 1877 4246 2509 1877 7007

Generosity Encouraged

8:1 And now, brothers, we want you to know about the grace that God has given the
δὲ ← ἀδελφοί → ὑμῖν Γνωρίζομεν ← τὴν χάριν ˌτοῦ θεοῦˌ ˌτὴν δεδομένηνˌ ἐν ταῖς
cj n.vpm r.dp.2 v.pai.1p d.asf n.asf d.gsm n.gsm d.asf pt.rp.asf p.d d.dpf
1254 81 1192 1192 7007 1192 3836 5921 3836 2536 3836 1443 1877 3836

Macedonian churches. **2** Out of the most severe trial, their overflowing joy and their
ˌτῆς Μακεδονίαςˌ ἐκκλησίαις ὅτι ἐν ← πολλῇ ˌδοκιμῇ θλίψεωςˌ αὐτῶν ἡ περισσεία ˌτῆς χαρᾶςˌ καὶ αὐτῶν
d.gsf n.gsf n.dpf cj p.d a.dsf n.dsf n.gsf r.gpm.3 d.nsf n.nsf d.gsf n.gsf cj r.gpm.3
3836 3423 1711 4022 1877 4498 1509 2568 899 3836 4353 3836 5915 2779 899

λύπη θάνατον κατεργάζεται. ¹¹ ἰδοὺ γὰρ αὐτὸ τοῦτο τὸ κατὰ θεὸν λυπηθῆναι πόσην κατειργάσατο ὑμῖν σπουδήν, ἀλλὰ ἀπολογίαν, ἀλλὰ ἀγανάκτησιν, ἀλλὰ φόβον, ἀλλὰ ἐπιπόθησιν, ἀλλὰ ζῆλον, ἀλλὰ ἐκδίκησιν. ἐν παντὶ συνεστήσατε ἑαυτοὺς ἁγνοὺς εἶναι τῷ πράγματι. ¹² ἄρα εἰ καὶ ἔγραψα ὑμῖν, οὐχ ἕνεκεν τοῦ ἀδικήσαντος οὐδὲ ἕνεκεν τοῦ ἀδικηθέντος ἀλλ᾽ ἕνεκεν τοῦ φανερωθῆναι τὴν σπουδὴν ὑμῶν τὴν ὑπὲρ ἡμῶν πρὸς ὑμᾶς ἐνώπιον τοῦ θεοῦ. ¹³ διὰ τοῦτο παρακεκλήμεθα. ¶ Ἐπὶ δὲ τῇ παρακλήσει ἡμῶν περισσοτέρως μᾶλλον ἐχάρημεν ἐπὶ τῇ χαρᾷ Τίτου, ὅτι ἀναπέπαυται τὸ πνεῦμα αὐτοῦ ἀπὸ πάντων ὑμῶν· ¹⁴ ὅτι εἴ τι αὐτῷ ὑπὲρ ὑμῶν κεκαύχημαι, οὐ κατῃσχύνθην, ἀλλ᾽ ὡς πάντα ἐν ἀληθείᾳ ἐλαλήσαμεν ὑμῖν, οὕτως καὶ ἡ καύχησις ἡμῶν ἡ ἐπὶ Τίτου ἀλήθεια ἐγενήθη. ¹⁵ καὶ τὰ σπλάγχνα αὐτοῦ περισσοτέρως εἰς ὑμᾶς ἐστιν ἀναμιμνῃσκομένου τὴν πάντων ὑμῶν ὑπακοήν, ὡς μετὰ φόβου καὶ τρόμου ἐδέξασθε αὐτόν. ¹⁶ χαίρω ὅτι ἐν παντὶ θαρρῶ ἐν ὑμῖν.

⁸:¹ Γνωρίζομεν δὲ ὑμῖν, ἀδελφοί, τὴν χάριν τοῦ θεοῦ τὴν δεδομένην ἐν ταῖς ἐκκλησίαις τῆς Μακεδονίας, ² ὅτι ἐν πολλῇ δοκιμῇ θλίψεως ἡ περισσεία τῆς χαρᾶς αὐτῶν καὶ ἡ κατὰ βάθους πτωχεία αὐτῶν ἐπερίσσευσεν εἰς τὸ πλοῦτος τῆς ἁπλότητος

extreme	poverty	welled	up in	rich	generosity.	[3] For I	testify	that	they gave as	much as
⸤κατὰ βάθους⸥	ἡ πτωχεία	ἐπερίσσευσεν ←	εἰς τὸ πλοῦτος	⸤τῆς ἁπλότητος⸥	αὐτῶν	ὅτι	μαρτυρῶ		κατὰ ←	←
p.g n.gsn	d.nsf n.nsf	v.aai.3s	p.a d.asn n.asn	d.gsf n.gsf	r.gpm.3	cj	v.pai.1s		p.a	
2848 958	3836 4775	4355	1650 3836 4458	3836 605	899	4022	3455		2848	

they were able,	and	even beyond their ability.	*Entirely on their own,*	[4] they urgently		pleaded
δύναμιν	καὶ	παρὰ δύναμιν	αὐθαίρετοι	⤍ μετὰ πολλῆς παρακλήσεως		δεόμενοι
n.asf	cj	p.a n.asf	a.npm		p.g a.gsf n.gsf	pt.pp.npm
1539	2779	4123 1539	882	1289 3552 4498 4155		1289

with us	for	the privilege	of sharing	in this service	to the saints.	[5] And	they did not do as	we
⤍ ἡμῶν	⤍ τὴν χάριν	καὶ	⸤τὴν κοινωνίαν⸥	⤍ τῆς διακονίας	τῆς εἰς τοὺς ἁγίους	καὶ	οὐ καθὼς ⤍	
r.gp.1	d.asf n.asf	cj	d.asf n.asf	d.gsf n.gsf	d.gsf p.a d.apm a.apm	cj	pl cj	
7005	3836 5921	2779	3836 3126	3836 1355	3836 1650 3836 41	2779	4024 2777	

expected,	but	they gave	themselves	first	to the Lord	and then	to us	in	keeping with	God's will.	[6] So we
ἠλπίσαμεν	ἀλλὰ ⤍	ἔδωκαν	ἑαυτοὺς	πρῶτον	τῷ κυρίῳ	καὶ	⤍ ἡμῖν	διὰ ←	←	θεοῦ θελήματος	εἰς ἡμᾶς
v.aai.1p	cj	v.aai.3p	r.apm.3	adv	d.dsm n.dsm	cj	r.dp.1	p.g		n.gsm n.gsn	p.a r.ap.1
1827	247	1443	1571	4754	3836 3261	2779	7005	1328		2536 2525	1650 7005

urged	Titus,	since	he had earlier made a beginning,	to bring	also	to completion	this	act of
⸤τὸ παρακαλέσαι⸥	Τίτον	ἵνα καθὼς ⤍	προενήρξατο οὕτως ⤍	καὶ ⤍		ἐπιτελέσῃ	καὶ ταύτην	r.asf
d.asn f.aa	n.asm	cj cj	v.ami.3s adv	cj		v.aas.3s	adv r.asf	
3836 4151	5519	2671 2777	4599 4048	2200 2200 2779		2200	2779 4047	

grace	on your part.	[7] But	just as	you excel	in everything	– in faith,	in speech,	in knowledge,	in
⸤τὴν χάριν⸥	εἰς ὑμᾶς ←	Ἀλλ᾽	ὥσπερ ←	περισσεύετε ἐν	παντὶ	⤍ πίστει	καὶ λόγῳ	καὶ γνώσει	καὶ ⤍
d.asf n.asf	p.a r.ap.2	cj	cj	v.pai.2p p.d	a.dsn	n.dsf	cj n.dsm	cj n.dsf	cj
3836 5921	1650 7007 1650	247	6061	4355 1877	4246	4411	2779 3364	2779 1194	2779

complete	earnestness	and	in your	love	for us	– see that	you also excel	in	this grace	of giving.
πάσῃ	σπουδῇ	καὶ	⤍ ἐν ὑμῖν	⸤τῇ ἀγάπῃ⸥	ἐξ ἡμῶν	ἵνα ←	καὶ περισσεύητε ἐν	ταύτῃ	⸤τῇ χάριτι⸥
a.dsf	n.dsf	cj	p.d r.dp.2	d.dsf n.dsf	p.g r.gp.1	cj	adv v.pas.2p p.d	r.dsf	d.dsf n.dsf
4246	5082	2779	27 1877 7007	3836 27	1666 7005	2671	4355 2779 4355 1877	4047	3836 5921

¶ [8]

I	am not commanding	you,	but	I want to test	the sincerity	of your	love	by comparing
	Οὐ ⸤κατ᾽ ἐπιταγὴν λέγω⸥		ἀλλὰ	δοκιμάζων τὸ γνήσιον	⤍ ὑμετέρας	⸤τῆς ἀγάπης⸥	καὶ διὰ ←
pl p.a n.asf v.pai.1s		cj	pt.pa.nsm d.asn a.asn	r.gsf.2	d.gsf n.gsf	cj p.g
3306 3306 4024 2848 2198 3306		247	1507 3836 1188 27	5629	3836 27	2779 1328

it with	the earnestness	of others.	[9] For	you know	the	grace of	our	Lord	Jesus Christ,	that though	he was
← ←	τῆς σπουδῆς	ἑτέρων	γὰρ ⤍	γινώσκετε	τὴν	χάριν	ἡμῶν	⸤τοῦ κυρίου⸥	Ἰησοῦ Χριστοῦ	ὅτι ⤍	⤍ ὢν
	d.gsf n.gsf	r.gpm	cj	v.pai.2p	d.asf	n.asf	r.gp.1	d.gsm n.gsm	n.gsm n.gsm	cj	pt.pa.nsm
	3836 5082	2283	1142	1182	3836	5921	3261 7005	3836 3261	2652 5986	4022	1639

rich,	yet	for your sakes	he became poor,	so that	you	through his	poverty	might become rich.	¶
πλούσιος	δι᾽ ὑμᾶς ←	⤍	ἐπτώχευσεν ἵνα	ὑμεῖς	⤍ ἐκείνου	τῇ πτωχείᾳ		πλουτήσητε	
a.nsm	p.a r.ap.2		v.aai.3s cj	r.np.2	r.gsm	d.dsf n.dsf		v.aas.2p	
4454	1328 7007 1328		4776 2671	7007 4775	1697	3836 4775		4456	

[10]

And here is	my advice	about	what is best	for you in	this matter:	Last	year	you were the
καὶ	δίδωμι	γνώμην γὰρ	τοῦτο ⤍ συμφέρει ⤍	ὑμῖν ἐν	τούτῳ ←	οἵτινες ⤍	ἀπὸ πέρυσι	
cj	v.pai.1s	n.asf cj	r.nsn v.pai.3s	r.dp.2 p.d	r.dsn	r.npm	p.g adv	
2779	1443	1191 1142	4047 5237	7007 1877	4047	4015	608 4373	

first	not only	to give	but	also	to have the desire	to do so.	[11] Now	finish	the work,
προενήρξασθε	οὐ μόνον ⤍	τὸ ποιῆσαι	ἀλλὰ καὶ ⤍		⤍ τὸ θέλειν		δὲ νυνὶ	καὶ ἐπιτελέσατε ⤍	τὸ ποιῆσαι
v.ami.2p	pl adv	d.asn f.aa	cj cj		d.asn f.pa		cj adv	adv v.aam.2p	d.asn f.aa
4599	4024 3667	3836 4472	247 2779		3836 2527		1254 3815	2779 2200	3836 4472

so that	your eager	willingness	to do it	*may be matched by*	your completion	of it, according to your
ὅπως ←	καθάπερ ἡ	προθυμία	⸤τοῦ θέλειν⸥	οὕτως	⸤τὸ ἐπιτελέσαι⸥	ἐκ ← τοῦ
cj	cj d.nsf	n.nsf	d.gsn f.pa	adv	d.nsn f.aa	p.g d.gsn
3968	2749 3836	4608	3836 2527	4048	3836 2200	1666 3836

means.	[12] For if	the willingness is there,	the gift is acceptable	according to what	one has,	not according to
ἔχειν	γὰρ εἰ ἡ	προθυμία ⤍ πρόκειται	εὐπρόσδεκτος καθὸ		ἐὰν ⤍	ἔχῃ οὐ καθὸ
f.pa	cj cj d.nsf	n.nsf v.pmi.3s	a.nsm cj		pl	v.pas.3s pl cj
2400	1142 1623 3836	4608 4618	2347 2771		1569	2400 4024 2771

what he does not have.	¶	[13]	Our desire is not that	others	might be relieved	while you	are hard pressed, but
⤍ ⤍ οὐκ ἔχει			γὰρ οὐ ἵνα	ἄλλοις	ἄνεσις	ὑμῖν ⤍	θλῖψις ἀλλ᾽
pl v.pai.3s			cj pl cj	r.dpm	n.nsf	r.dp.2	n.nsf cj
2400 2400 4024 2400			1142 4024 2671	257	457	7007	2568 247

αὐτῶν· [3] ὅτι κατὰ δύναμιν, μαρτυρῶ, καὶ παρὰ δύναμιν, αὐθαίρετοι [4] μετὰ πολλῆς παρακλήσεως δεόμενοι ἡμῶν τὴν χάριν καὶ τὴν κοινωνίαν τῆς διακονίας τῆς εἰς τοὺς ἁγίους· [5] καὶ οὐ καθὼς ἠλπίσαμεν ἀλλ᾽ ἑαυτοὺς ἔδωκαν πρῶτον τῷ κυρίῳ καὶ ἡμῖν διὰ θελήματος θεοῦ [6] εἰς τὸ παρακαλέσαι ἡμᾶς Τίτον, ἵνα καθὼς προενήρξατο οὕτως καὶ ἐπιτελέσῃ εἰς ὑμᾶς καὶ τὴν χάριν ταύτην. [7] ἀλλ᾽ ὥσπερ ἐν παντὶ περισσεύετε, πίστει καὶ λόγῳ καὶ γνώσει καὶ πάσῃ σπουδῇ καὶ τῇ ἐξ ὑμῶν «ἡμῶν» ἐν ὑμῖν «ὑμῖν» ἀγάπῃ, ἵνα καὶ ἐν ταύτῃ τῇ χάριτι περισσεύητε. ¶ [8] Οὐ κατ᾽ ἐπιταγὴν λέγω ἀλλὰ διὰ τῆς ἑτέρων σπουδῆς καὶ τὸ τῆς ὑμετέρας ἀγάπης γνήσιον δοκιμάζων· [9] γινώσκετε γὰρ τὴν χάριν τοῦ κυρίου ἡμῶν Ἰησοῦ Χριστοῦ, ὅτι δι᾽ ὑμᾶς ἐπτώχευσεν πλούσιος ὤν, ἵνα ὑμεῖς τῇ ἐκείνου πτωχείᾳ πλουτήσητε. ¶ [10] καὶ γνώμην ἐν τούτῳ δίδωμι· τοῦτο γὰρ ὑμῖν συμφέρει, οἵτινες οὐ μόνον τὸ ποιῆσαι ἀλλὰ καὶ τὸ θέλειν προενήρξασθε ἀπὸ πέρυσι· [11] νυνὶ δὲ καὶ τὸ ποιῆσαι ἐπιτελέσατε, ὅπως καθάπερ ἡ προθυμία τοῦ θέλειν, οὕτως καὶ τὸ ἐπιτελέσαι ἐκ τοῦ ἔχειν. [12] εἰ γὰρ ἡ προθυμία πρόκειται, καθὸ ἐὰν ἔχῃ εὐπρόσδεκτος, οὐ καθὸ οὐκ ἔχει ¶ [13] οὐ γὰρ ἵνα ἄλλοις ἄνεσις, ὑμῖν θλῖψις, ἀλλ᾽ ἐξ ἰσότητος· [14] ἐν τῷ νῦν καιρῷ τὸ ὑμῶν περίσσευμα εἰς τὸ ἐκείνων ὑστέρημα,

that there might be equality. **14** At the present time your plenty will supply what they need, so that
ἐξ ἰσότητος ἐν τῷ νῦν καιρῷ ὑμῶν ⸢τὸ περίσσευμα⸣ εἰς τὸ ἐκείνων ὑστέρημα ἵνα ←
p.g n.gsf p.d d.dsm adv n.dsm r.gp.2 d.nsn n.nsn p.a d.asn r.gpm n.asn cj
1666 2699 1877 3836 3814 2789 7007 3836 4354 1650 3836 1697 5729 2671

in turn their plenty will supply what you need. Then there will be equality, **15** as it is written:
καὶ ἐκείνων ⸢τὸ περίσσευμα⸣ γένηται εἰς τὸ ὑμῶν ὑστέρημα ὅπως → → γένηται ἰσότης καθὼς → γέγραπται
adv r.gpm d.nsn n.nsn v.ams.3s p.a d.asn r.gp.2 n.nsn cj v.ams.3s n.nsf cj v.rpi.3s
2779 1697 3836 4354 1181 1650 3836 7007 5729 3968 1181 2699 2777 1211

"He who gathered much did not have too much, and he who gathered little did not have too little."
ὁ ⸢τὸ πολὺ⸣ ↱ οὐκ → ἐπλεόνασεν καὶ ὁ ← ⸢τὸ ὀλίγον⸣ → οὐκ → ἠλαττόνησεν
d.nsm d.asn a.asn pl v.aai.3s cj d.nsm d.asn a.asn pl v.aai.3s
3836 3836 4498 4429 4024 4429 2779 3836 3836 3900 1782 4024 1782

Titus Sent to Corinth

8:16 I thank God, who put into the heart of Titus the same concern I have for you. **17** For Titus *not only*
δὲ Χάρις ⸢τῷ θεῷ⸣ τῷ δόντι ἐν τῇ καρδίᾳ → Τίτου τὴν αὐτὴν σπουδὴν ὑπὲρ ὑμῶν ὅτι μὲν
cj n.nsf d.dsm n.dsm d.dsm pt.aa.dsm p.d d.dsf n.dsf n.gsm d.asf r.asf n.asf p.g r.gp.2 cj pl
1254 5921 3836 2536 3836 1443 1877 3836 2840 5519 3836 899 5082 5642 7007 4022 3525

welcomed our appeal, but he is coming to you with much enthusiasm and on his own
ἐδέξατο τὴν παράκλησιν δὲ → ἐξῆλθεν πρὸς ὑμᾶς ὑπάρχων αὐθαίρετος → σπουδαιότερος → →
v.ami.3s d.asf n.asf cj v.aai.3s p.a r.ap.2 pt.pa.nsm a.nsm a.nsm.c
1312 3836 4155 1254 2002 4639 7007 5639 882 5080

initiative. **18** And we are sending along with him the brother who is praised by all the churches for his
αὐθαίρετος δὲ → → συνεπέμψαμεν ← μετ᾽ αὐτοῦ τὸν ἀδελφὸν οὗ ὁ ἔπαινος⸣ διὰ πασῶν τῶν ἐκκλησιῶν
a.nsm cj v.aai.1p p.g r.gsm.3 d.asm n.asm r.gsm d.nsm n.nsm p.g a.gpf d.gpf n.gpf
882 1254 5225 3552 899 3836 81 4005 3836 2047 1328 4246 3836 1711

service to the gospel. **19** *What is more,* he was chosen by the churches to accompany us as
ἐν τῷ εὐαγγελίῳ δὲ ⸢οὐ μόνον⸣ ἀλλὰ καὶ → → χειροτονηθεὶς ὑπὸ τῶν ἐκκλησιῶν συνέκδημος ἡμῶν
p.d d.dsn n.dsn cj pl adv cj adv pt.ap.nsm p.g d.gpf n.gpf n.nsm r.gp.1
1877 3836 2295 1254 4024 3667 247 2779 5936 5679 3836 1711 5292 7005

we carry the offering, which we administer in order to honor the Lord himself and to show
σὺν τῇ χάριτι ταύτῃ τῇ ὑφ᾽ ἡμῶν⸣ διακονουμένῃ → → πρὸς ⸢τὴν δόξαν⸣ τοῦ κυρίου αὐτοῦ καὶ
p.d d.dsf n.dsf r.dsf d.dsf p.g r.gp.1 pt.pp.dsf p.a d.asf n.asf d.gsm n.gsm r.gsm cj
5250 3836 5921 4047 3836 5679 7005 1354 4639 3836 1518 3836 3261 899 2779

our eagerness to help. **20** We want to avoid any criticism of the way we administer
ἡμῶν ⸢τὴν προθυμίαν⸣ στελλόμενοι τοῦτο τις μὴ μωμήσηται ἡμᾶς ὑφ᾽ ← ἡμῶν ⸢τῇ διακονουμένῃ⸣
r.gp.1 d.asf n.asf pt.pm.npm r.asn r.nsm cj v.ams.3s r.ap.1 p.g r.gp.1 d.dsf pt.pp.dsf
7005 3836 4608 5097 4047 5516 3590 3699 7005 5679 7005 3836 1354

this liberal gift. **21** For we are taking pains to do what is right, not only in the eyes of the Lord but
ἐν ταύτῃ ⸢τῇ ἁδρότητι⸣ ← γὰρ προνοοῦμεν → καλὰ οὐ μόνον → ἐνώπιον ← κυρίου ἀλλὰ
p.d r.dsf d.dsf n.dsf cj v.pai.1p a.apn pl adv p.g n.gsm cj
1877 4047 3836 103 1142 4629 2819 4024 3667 1967 3261 247

also in the eyes of men. ¶ **22** In addition, we are sending with them our brother who has often
καὶ → ἐνώπιον ← ἀνθρώπων δὲ → συνεπέμψαμεν αὐτοῖς ἡμῶν ⸢τὸν ἀδελφὸν⸣ ὃν → πολλάκις
adv p.g n.gpm cj v.aai.1p r.dpm.3 r.gp.1 d.asm n.asm r.asm adv
2779 1967 476 1254 5225 899 7005 3836 81 4005 4490

proved to us in many ways that he is zealous, and now even more so because of his great
ἐδοκιμάσαμεν ← ← ἐν πολλοῖς ← → ὄντα σπουδαῖον δὲ νυνὶ → πολὺ σπουδαιότερον → → πολλῇ
v.aai.1p p.d a.dpn pt.pa.asm a.asm cj adv adv a.asm.c a.dsf
1507 1877 4498 1639 5080 1254 3815 4498 5080 4498

confidence in you. **23** As for Titus, he is my partner and fellow worker among you; as for our brothers,
πεποιθήσει τῇ εἰς ὑμᾶς εἴτε ὑπὲρ Τίτου ἐμὸς κοινωνὸς καὶ συνεργός εἰς ὑμᾶς εἴτε ἡμῶν ἀδελφοὶ
n.dsf d.dsf p.a r.ap.2 cj p.g n.gsm r.nsm.1 n.nsm cj n.nsm p.a r.ap.2 cj r.gp.1 n.npm
4301 3836 1650 7007 1664 5642 5519 1847 3128 2779 5301 1650 7007 1664 7005 81

they are representatives of the churches and an honor to Christ. **24** Therefore show these men the proof of
ἀπόστολοι → ἐκκλησιῶν δόξα → Χριστοῦ οὖν ἐνδεικνύμενοι εἰς αὐτοὺς ← τὴν ἔνδειξιν →
n.npm n.gpf n.nsf n.gsm cj pt.pm.npm p.a r.apm.3 d.asf n.asf
693 1711 1518 5986 4036 1892 1650 899 3836 1893 27

ἵνα καὶ τὸ ἐκείνων περίσσευμα γένηται εἰς τὸ ὑμῶν ὑστέρημα, ὅπως γένηται ἰσότης, **15** καθὼς γέγραπται, Ὁ τὸ πολὺ οὐκ ἐπλεόνασεν, καὶ ὁ τὸ ὀλίγον οὐκ ἠλαττόνησεν.

8:16 Χάρις δὲ τῷ θεῷ τῷ δόντι τὴν αὐτὴν σπουδὴν ὑπὲρ ὑμῶν ἐν τῇ καρδίᾳ Τίτου, **17** ὅτι τὴν μὲν παράκλησιν ἐδέξατο, σπουδαιότερος δὲ ὑπάρχων αὐθαίρετος ἐξῆλθεν πρὸς ὑμᾶς. **18** συνεπέμψαμεν δὲ μετ᾽ αὐτοῦ τὸν ἀδελφὸν οὗ ὁ ἔπαινος ἐν τῷ εὐαγγελίῳ διὰ πασῶν τῶν ἐκκλησιῶν, **19** οὐ μόνον δέ, ἀλλὰ καὶ χειροτονηθεὶς ὑπὸ τῶν ἐκκλησιῶν συνέκδημος ἡμῶν σὺν τῇ χάριτι ταύτῃ τῇ διακονουμένῃ ὑφ᾽ ἡμῶν πρὸς τὴν [αὐτοῦ] τοῦ κυρίου δόξαν καὶ προθυμίαν ἡμῶν, **20** στελλόμενοι τοῦτο, μή τις ἡμᾶς μωμήσηται ἐν τῇ ἁδρότητι ταύτῃ τῇ διακονουμένῃ ὑφ᾽ ἡμῶν· **21** προνοοῦμεν γὰρ καλὰ οὐ μόνον ἐνώπιον κυρίου ἀλλὰ καὶ ἐνώπιον ἀνθρώπων. ¶ **22** συνεπέμψαμεν δὲ αὐτοῖς τὸν ἀδελφὸν ἡμῶν ὃν ἐδοκιμάσαμεν ἐν πολλοῖς πολλάκις σπουδαῖον ὄντα, νυνὶ δὲ πολὺ σπουδαιότερον πεποιθήσει πολλῇ τῇ εἰς ὑμᾶς. **23** εἴτε ὑπὲρ Τίτου, κοινωνὸς ἐμὸς καὶ εἰς ὑμᾶς συνεργός· εἴτε ἀδελφοὶ ἡμῶν, ἀπόστολοι ἐκκλησιῶν, δόξα Χριστοῦ. **24** τὴν οὖν ἔνδειξιν τῆς ἀγάπης ὑμῶν καὶ ἡμῶν καυχήσεως ὑπὲρ ὑμῶν

your love   and the reason for our pride   in   you, so that the churches *can see*   *it.* ¶   **9:1**
ὑμῶν ⸤τῆς ἀγάπης⸥ καὶ   ἡμῶν καυχήσεως ὑπὲρ ὑμῶν εἰς ←   τῶν ἐκκλησιῶν πρόσωπον   γὰρ μὲν
r.gp.2 d.gsf n.gsf cj   r.gp.1 n.gsf   p.g r.gp.2 p.a   d.gpf n.gpf   n.asn   cj pl
7007 3836 27   2779   7005 3018   5642 7007 1650   3836 1711   4725   1142 3525

There is   no   need   for me to write   to you about this service   to the saints. ² For I know your
→   ἐστιν περισσόν →   μοί → ⸤τὸ γράφειν⸥ → ὑμῖν Περὶ τῆς διακονίας τῆς εἰς τοὺς ἁγίους γὰρ → οἶδα ὑμῶν
→   v.pai.3s a.nsn   r.ds.1 d.nsn f.pa   r.dp.2 Περὶ d.gsf n.gsf d.gsf p.a d.apm a.apm cj   v.rai.1s r.gp.2
      1639   4356   1609   3836 1211   7007 4309 3836 1355   3836 1650 3836 41   1142 3857 7007

eagerness   to help, and I have been boasting about it   to the Macedonians, telling them that since last
⸤τὴν προθυμίαν⸥ →   →   καυχῶμαι   ἦν ὑπὲρ ὑμῶν →   Μακεδόσιν   ὅτι ἀπὸ →
d.asf n.asf   v.pmi.1s   r.asf p.g r.gp.2   n.dpm   cj p.g
3836 4608   3016   4005 5642 7007   3424   4022 608

year   you in Achaia were ready   to give; and your enthusiasm has stirred most   of them to action.
πέρυσι   Ἀχαΐα →   παρεσκεύασται   καὶ ὑμῶν ⸤τὸ ζῆλος⸥ →   ἠρέθισεν ⸤τοὺς πλείονας⸥ ←   ←   ←
adv   n.nsf   v.rmi.3s   cj r.gp.2 d.nsn 2419   v.aai.3s d.apm a.apm.c
4373   938   4186   2779 7007 3836   ἠρέθισεν 2241 3836 4498   2241 2241

³ But I am sending the brothers in order that our boasting   about you in this matter   should not prove
δὲ →   ἔπεμψα   τοὺς ἀδελφούς ἵνα ←   ἡμῶν ⸤τὸ καύχημα⸥ τὸ ὑπὲρ ὑμῶν ἐν τούτῳ ⸤τῷ μέρει⸥ → μὴ
cj   v.aai.1s   d.apm n.apm   cj   r.gp.1 d.nsn n.nsn d.nsn p.g r.gp.2 p.d r.dsn d.dsn n.dsn pl
1254   4287   3836 81   2671   7005 3836 3017 3836 5642 7007 1877 4047 3836 3538 3033   3590

hollow, but that you may be ready,   as   I said you would be. ⁴ For   if any Macedonians come with
κενωθῇ   ἵνα → ἦτε → παρεσκευασμένοι καθὼς → ἔλεγον   μή πως ἐὰν   Μακεδόνες ἔλθωσιν σὺν
v.aps.3s   cj   v.pas.2p pt.rm.npm   cj   v.iai.3p   cj pl cj   n.npm   v.aas.3p p.d
3033   2671   4186   4186   2777   3306   3590 4803 1569   3424   2262   5250

me and find   you unprepared,   we   – not to say anything about you – would be ashamed   of having
ἐμοὶ καὶ εὕρωσιν ὑμᾶς ἀπαρασκευάστους ἡμεῖς   ἵνα μὴ λέγω   ὑμεῖς   → καταισχυνθῶμεν
r.ds.1 cj v.aas.3p r.ap.2 a.apm   r.np.1   cj pl   v.pas.1s   r.np.2   v.aps.1p
1609 2779 2351   7007 564   7005   2671 3590 3306   7007   2875

been so   confident. ⁵ So I thought it necessary to urge   the brothers to visit   you in advance
ταύτῃ ἐν ⸤τῇ ὑποστάσει⸥ οὖν → ἡγησάμην ← ἀναγκαῖον → παρακαλέσαι τοὺς ἀδελφούς ἵνα προέλθωσιν εἰς ὑμᾶς ←
r.dsf p.d d.dsf n.dsf   cj   v.ami.1s a.nsn   f.aa   d.apm n.apm cj v.aas.3p   p.a r.ap.2
4047 1877 3836 5712   4036 2451   338   4151   3836 81   2671 4601   1650 7007 4601 4601

and finish   the arrangements for the generous gift   you had promised.   Then it   will be   ready
καὶ προκαταρτίσωσιν ← ←   τὴν →   εὐλογίαν ὑμῶν προεπηγγελμένην   ταύτην → εἶναι ἑτοίμην
cj v.aas.3p   d.asf   n.asf   r.gp.2 pt.rp.asf   r.asf   f.pa a.asf
2779 4616   3836   2330   7007 4600   4047   1639 2289

as a generous gift,   not as one grudgingly given.
οὕτως ὡς →   εὐλογίαν καὶ μὴ ὡς →   πλεονεξίαν ←
adv pl   n.asf   cj pl pl   n.asf
4048 6055   2330   2779 3590 6055 4432

Sowing Generously

9:6   Remember this: Whoever sows   sparingly will also reap sparingly, and whoever sows   generously will
δὲ   Τοῦτο ὁ   σπείρων φειδομένως →   καὶ θερίσει φειδομένως καὶ ὁ   σπείρων ⸤ἐπ᾽ εὐλογίαις⸥ →
cj   r.asn d.nsm   pt.pa.nsm adv   adv v.fai.3s adv   cj d.nsm pt.pa.nsm p.d n.dpf
1254   4047 3836   5062   5768   2545 2545   5768   2779 3836 5062   2093 2330   2545

also reap generously. ⁷ Each man should give what he has decided in his heart to give, not reluctantly or under
καὶ θερίσει ⸤ἐπ᾽ εὐλογίαις⸥ ἕκαστος   καθὼς → → προῄρηται → τῇ καρδίᾳ   μὴ ἐκ λύπης ἢ ἐξ
adv v.fai.3s p.d n.dpf   r.nsm   cj   v.rmi.3s   d.dsf n.dsf   pl p.g n.gsf cj p.g
2779 2545   2093 2330   1667   2777   4576   3836 2840   3590 1666 3383 2445 1666

compulsion, for God   loves a cheerful giver. ⁸ And God   is able   to make all grace abound   to you, so
ἀνάγκης   γὰρ ὁ θεός⸥ ἀγαπᾷ ἱλαρὸν δότην δὲ ὁ θεός⸥ → δυνατεῖ →   πᾶσαν χάριν περισσεῦσαι εἰς ὑμᾶς ἵνα
n.gsf   cj d.nsm n.nsm v.pai.3s a.asm n.asm cj d.nsm n.nsm v.pai.3s a.asf n.asf f.aa   p.a r.ap.2 cj
340   1142 3836 2536 26   2659   1522 1254 3836 2536 1542   4355 5921 4246 4355   1650 7007 2671

that in all   things at all   times, having all   that you need,   you will abound in every good work.
←   ἐν παντὶ ←   → πάντοτε ←   ἔχοντες πᾶσαν →   αὐτάρκειαν   → περισσεύητε εἰς πᾶν ἀγαθὸν ἔργον
p.d a.dsn   adv   pt.pa.npm a.asf   n.asf   v.pas.2p   p.a a.asn a.asn n.asn
1877 4246   4121   2400   4246   894   4355   1650 4246 19   2240

εἰς αὐτοὺς ἐνδεικνύμενοι εἰς πρόσωπον τῶν ἐκκλησιῶν. **9:1** Περὶ μὲν γὰρ τῆς διακονίας τῆς εἰς τοὺς ἁγίους περισσόν μοί ἐστιν τὸ γράφειν ὑμῖν· ² οἶδα γὰρ τὴν προθυμίαν ὑμῶν ἣν ὑπὲρ ὑμῶν καυχῶμαι Μακεδόσιν, ὅτι Ἀχαΐα παρεσκεύασται ἀπὸ πέρυσι, καὶ τὸ ὑμῶν ζῆλος ἠρέθισεν τοὺς πλείονας. ³ ἔπεμψα δὲ τοὺς ἀδελφούς, ἵνα μὴ τὸ καύχημα ἡμῶν τὸ ὑπὲρ ὑμῶν κενωθῇ ἐν τῷ μέρει τούτῳ, ἵνα καθὼς ἔλεγον παρεσκευασμένοι ἦτε, ⁴ μή πως ἐὰν ἔλθωσιν σὺν ἐμοὶ Μακεδόνες καὶ εὕρωσιν ὑμᾶς ἀπαρασκευάστους καταισχυνθῶμεν ἡμεῖς, ἵνα μὴ λέγω ὑμεῖς, ἐν τῇ ὑποστάσει ταύτῃ. ⁵ ἀναγκαῖον οὖν ἡγησάμην παρακαλέσαι τοὺς ἀδελφούς, ἵνα προέλθωσιν εἰς ὑμᾶς καὶ προκαταρτίσωσιν τὴν προεπηγγελμένην εὐλογίαν ὑμῶν, ταύτην ἑτοίμην εἶναι οὕτως ὡς εὐλογίαν καὶ μὴ ὡς πλεονεξίαν.

    9:6 Τοῦτο δέ, ὁ σπείρων φειδομένως φειδομένως καὶ θερίσει, καὶ ὁ σπείρων ἐπ᾽ εὐλογίαις ἐπ᾽ εὐλογίαις καὶ θερίσει. ⁷ ἕκαστος καθὼς προῄρηται τῇ καρδίᾳ, μὴ ἐκ λύπης ἢ ἐξ ἀνάγκης· ἱλαρὸν γὰρ δότην ἀγαπᾷ ὁ θεός. ⁸ δυνατεῖ δὲ ὁ θεὸς πᾶσαν χάριν περισσεῦσαι εἰς ὑμᾶς, ἵνα ἐν παντὶ πάντοτε πᾶσαν αὐτάρκειαν ἔχοντες περισσεύητε εἰς πᾶν ἔργον ἀγαθόν, ⁹ καθὼς γέγραπται,

9 As   it is written: "He has scattered abroad his gifts to the poor; his   righteousness endures forever."
καθὼς → γέγραπται →   →   ἐσκόρπισεν ←   →   ἔδωκεν   τοῖς πένησιν αὐτοῦ ἡ δικαιοσύνη   μένει   εἰς τὸν αἰῶνα
cj   v.rpi.3s   v.aai.3s   d.dpm n.dpm r.gsm.3 d.nsf n.nsf v.pai.3s p.a d.asm n.asm
2777   1211   5025   1443 4288   899   3836 1466   3531   1650 3836 172

10 Now he who supplies seed   to the sower   and bread for food will also supply   and increase your store of
δὲ   ὁ   ἐπιχορηγῶν σπόρον → τῷ σπείροντι καὶ ἄρτον εἰς βρῶσιν → χορηγήσει καὶ πληθυνεῖ   ὑμῶν
cj   d.nsm pt.pa.nsm n.asm   d.dsm pt.pa.dsm cj n.asm p.a n.asf   v.fai.3s adv v.fai.3s r.gp.2
1254 3836 2220   5078   3836 5062   2779 788 1650 1111   5961   2779 4437   7007

seed   and will enlarge the harvest of your righteousness. **11** You will be made rich   in every way so that
τὸν σπόρον καὶ → αὐξήσει τὰ γενήματα → ὑμῶν τῆς δικαιοσύνης.   →   →   →   πλουτιζόμενοι ἐν παντὶ ← εἰς ←
d.asm n.asm cj   v.fai.3s d.apn n.apn   r.gp.2 d.gsf n.gsf   pt.pp.npm   p.d a.dsn   p.a
3836 5078   2779 889   3836 1163   7007 3836 1466   4457   1877 4246   1650

you can be generous on every occasion, and through us your generosity will result   in thanksgiving to God.
ἁπλότητα → πᾶσαν ←   δι' ἡμῶν ἥτις ← → κατεργάζεται ← εὐχαριστίαν → τῷ θεῷ
n.asf   a.asf   p.g r.gp.1 r.nsf   v.pmi.3s   n.asf   d.dsm n.dsm
605   4246   1328 7005 4015   2981   2374   3836 2536

¶ **12** This service   that you perform is not only supplying the needs of God's   people but
ὅτι ταύτης ἡ διακονία τῆς → λειτουργίας ἐστὶν οὐ μόνον προσαναπληροῦσα τὰ ὑστερήματα τῶν ἁγίων ← ἀλλὰ
cj r.gsf d.nsf n.nsf d.gsf   n.gsf   v.pai.3s pl adv pt.pa.nsf   d.apn n.apn d.gpm a.gpm   cj
4022 4047 3836 1355 3836   3311   1639 4024 3667 4650   3836 5729   3836 41   247

is also overflowing in many expressions of thanks   to God. **13** Because of the service   by which you
→ καὶ περισσεύουσα διὰ πολλῶν ←   →   εὐχαριστιῶν → τῷ θεῷ διὰ ←   ταύτης τῆς διακονίας
adv pt.pa.nsf   p.g a.gpf   n.gpf   d.dsm n.dsm p.g   r.gsf d.gsf n.gsf
4355 2779 4355   1328 4498   2374   3836 2536 1328   4047 3836 1355

have proved   yourselves, men will praise   God   for the obedience that accompanies your confession of the
τῆς δοκιμῆς   δοξάζοντες τὸν θεόν ἐπὶ τῇ ὑποταγῇ τῆς ←   ὑμῶν ὁμολογίας εἰς τὸ
d.gsf n.gsf   pt.pa.npm d.asm n.asm p.d d.dsf n.dsf d.gsf   r.gp.2 n.gsf p.a d.asn
3836 1509   1519   3836 2536 2093 3836 5717 3836   7007 3934   1650 3836

gospel   of Christ,   and for your generosity in sharing   with them and with everyone else. **14** And in their
εὐαγγέλιον → τοῦ Χριστοῦ καὶ → ἁπλότητι → τῆς κοινωνίας εἰς αὐτοὺς καὶ εἰς πάντας ←   καὶ → αὐτῶν
n.asn   d.gsm n.gsm cj   n.dsf   d.gsf n.gsf p.a r.apm.3 cj p.a a.apm   cj   r.gpm.3
2295   3836 5986   2779   605   3836 3126   1650 899 2779 1650 4246   2779   899

prayers for you their hearts   will go out to you, because of the surpassing   grace God   has given you.
δεήσει ὑπὲρ ὑμῶν ἐπιποθούντων ← ← → ὑμᾶς διὰ ← τὴν ὑπερβάλλουσαν χάριν τοῦ θεοῦ → ἐφ' ὑμῖν
n.dsf p.g r.gp.2 pt.pa.gpm   r.ap.2 p.g d.asf pt.pa.asf   n.asf d.gsm n.gsm   p.d r.dp.2
1255 5642 7007 2160   7007 1328 3836 5650   5921 3836 2536   2093 7007

15 Thanks be to God for his indescribable gift!
Χάρις τῷ θεῷ ἐπὶ αὐτοῦ τῇ ἀνεκδιηγήτῳ δωρεᾷ
n.nsf d.dsm n.dsm p.d r.gsm.3 d.dsf a.dsf n.dsf
5921 3836 2536 2093 899 3836 442   1561

Paul's Defense of His Ministry

10:1 By the meekness and gentleness of Christ,   I appeal   to you – I,   Paul, who   am "timid"
δὲ διὰ τῆς πραΰτητος καὶ ἐπιεικείας → τοῦ Χριστοῦ → παρακαλῶ → ὑμᾶς ἐγὼ Αὐτὸς Παῦλος ὃς μὲν ταπεινὸς
cj p.g d.gsf n.gsf cj n.gsf   d.gsm n.gsm   v.pai.1s   r.ap.2 r.ns.1 r.nsm n.nsm r.nsm pl a.nsm
1254 1328 3836 4559 2779 2116   3836 5986   4151   7007 1609 899 4263   4005 3525 5424

when face   to face with you, but "bold" when away! **2** I beg   you that when I come I may not have
κατὰ πρόσωπον ἐν ὑμῖν δὲ θαρρῶ   ἀπὼν εἰς ὑμᾶς δὲ δέομαι → παρὼν μὴ
p.a n.asn   p.d r.dp.2 cj v.pai.1s pt.pa.nsm p.a r.ap.2 cj v.ppi.1s pt.pa.nsm pl
2848 4725   1877 7007 1254 2509 583 1650 7007 1254 1289   4205   3590

to be as bold   *as I expect*   to be   toward some people who think   that we
→ τὸ θαρρῆσαι τῇ πεποιθήσει ᾗ λογίζομαι τολμῆσαι ἐπί τινας ← τοὺς λογιζομένους ἡμᾶς
d.asn f.aa   d.dsf n.dsf   r.dsf v.pmi.1s f.aa p.a r.apm   d.apm pt.pm.apm r.ap.1
3836 2509   3836 4301   4005 3357   5528 2093 5516   3836 3357   7005

live   by the standards of this world. **3** For though we live in the world, we do not wage
περιπατοῦντας ὡς κατὰ ← ← σάρκα γὰρ → περιπατοῦντες Ἐν σαρκὶ → οὐ →
pt.pa.apm pl p.a   n.asf cj   pt.pa.npm   p.d n.dsf   pl
4344 6055 2848   4922 1142   4344   1877 4922   5129 5129 4024

Ἐσκόρπισεν, ἔδωκεν τοῖς πένησιν, ἡ δικαιοσύνη αὐτοῦ μένει εἰς τὸν αἰῶνα. **10** ὁ δὲ ἐπιχορηγῶν σπόρον τῷ σπείροντι καὶ ἄρτον εἰς βρῶσιν χορηγήσει καὶ πληθυνεῖ τὸν σπόρον ὑμῶν καὶ αὐξήσει τὰ γενήματα τῆς δικαιοσύνης ὑμῶν· **11** ἐν παντὶ πλουτιζόμενοι εἰς πᾶσαν ἁπλότητα, ἥτις κατεργάζεται δι' ἡμῶν εὐχαριστίαν τῷ θεῷ· ¶ **12** ὅτι ἡ διακονία τῆς λειτουργίας ταύτης οὐ μόνον ἐστὶν προσαναπληροῦσα τὰ ὑστερήματα τῶν ἁγίων, ἀλλὰ καὶ περισσεύουσα διὰ πολλῶν εὐχαριστιῶν τῷ θεῷ· **13** διὰ τῆς δοκιμῆς τῆς διακονίας ταύτης δοξάζοντες τὸν θεὸν ἐπὶ τῇ ὑποταγῇ τῆς ὁμολογίας ὑμῶν εἰς τὸ εὐαγγέλιον τοῦ Χριστοῦ καὶ ἁπλότητι τῆς κοινωνίας εἰς αὐτοὺς καὶ εἰς πάντας, **14** καὶ αὐτῶν δεήσει ὑπὲρ ὑμῶν ἐπιποθούντων ὑμᾶς διὰ τὴν ὑπερβάλλουσαν χάριν τοῦ θεοῦ ἐφ' ὑμῖν. **15** χάρις τῷ θεῷ ἐπὶ τῇ ἀνεκδιηγήτῳ αὐτοῦ δωρεᾷ.

10:1 Αὐτὸς δὲ ἐγὼ Παῦλος παρακαλῶ ὑμᾶς διὰ τῆς πραΰτητος καὶ ἐπιεικείας τοῦ Χριστοῦ, ὃς κατὰ πρόσωπον μὲν ταπεινὸς ἐν ὑμῖν, ἀπὼν δὲ θαρρῶ εἰς ὑμᾶς· **2** δέομαι δὲ τὸ μὴ παρὼν θαρρῆσαι τῇ πεποιθήσει ᾗ λογίζομαι τολμῆσαι ἐπί τινας τοὺς λογιζομένους ἡμᾶς ὡς κατὰ σάρκα περιπατοῦντας. **3** ἐν σαρκὶ γὰρ περιπατοῦντες οὐ κατὰ σάρκα στρατευόμεθα, **4** τὰ γὰρ

war   as   the world does.   **4** The weapons we   fight   with are not the weapons of the world.   On
στρατευόμεθα κατὰ   σάρκα ↩   γὰρ τὰ   ὅπλα   ἡμῶν ⌐τῆς στρατείας⌐ ←   οὐ   σαρκικὰ →
v.pmi.1p   p.a   n.asf   cj d.npn n.npn r.gp.1 d.gsf n.gsf   pl   a.npn
5129   2848   4922   2848 1142 3836 3960   7005 3836 5127   4024   4920

the contrary, they have divine   power to demolish strongholds.   **5** We demolish   arguments and every pretension
→ ἀλλὰ   ⌐τῷ θεῷ⌐ δυνατὰ πρὸς καθαίρεσιν ὀχυρωμάτων   → καθαιροῦντες λογισμοὺς καὶ πᾶν ὕψωμα
   cj   d.sm n.dsm a.npn p.a n.asf   n.gpn   pt.pa.npm   n.apm   cj a.asn n.asn
   247   3836 2536 1543 4639 2746   4065   2747   3361   2779 4246 5739

that sets itself up   against the knowledge of God,   and we take captive   every thought to make it
→ → → ἐπαιρόμενον κατὰ   τῆς γνώσεως ⌐τοῦ θεοῦ⌐ καὶ → αἰχμαλωτίζοντες πᾶν   νόημα   εἰς ←   ←
          pt.pp.asn   p.g   d.gsf n.gsf   d.gsm n.gsm cj   pt.pa.npm   a.asn n.asn p.a
          2048   2848   3836 1194   3836 2536 2779   170   4246 3784 1650

obedient   to Christ.   **6** And we will be   ready   to punish every act of disobedience,   once your obedience
⌐τὴν ὑπακοὴν⌐ → ⌐τοῦ Χριστοῦ⌐ καὶ → → ἔχοντες ἐν ἑτοίμῳ → ἐκδικῆσαι πᾶσαν → παρακοήν   ὅταν ὑμῶν ἡ ὑπακοή
d.asf n.asf   d.gsm n.gsm   cj   pt.pa.npm p.d a.dsn   f.aa   a.asf   n.asf   cj   r.gp.2 d.nsf n.nsf
3836 5633   3836 5986   2779   2400   1877 2289   1688   4246   4157   4020   7007 3836 5633

is complete.   ¶   **7** You are looking only on the surface of things. If anyone is confident   that he belongs to
→ πληρωθῇ   βλέπετε κατὰ ← Τὰ πρόσωπον ←   εἴ τις   ⌐πέποιθεν ἑαυτῷ⌐ →   εἶναι   ←
   v.aps.3s   v.pai.2p p.a   d.apn n.asn   cj r.nsm v.rai.3s r.dsm.3   f.pa
   4444   1063   2848   3836 4725   1623 5516 4275   1571   1639

Christ,   he   should consider again   that   we   belong to Christ just   as much as he.   **8** For even
Χριστοῦ ἐφ᾽ ἑαυτοῦ → λογιζέσθω πάλιν τοῦτο ὅτι   οὕτως καὶ ἡμεῖς → → Χριστοῦ καθὼς ←   αὐτὸς γὰρ τε
n.gsm p.g   r.gsm.3   v.pmm.3s adv   r.asn cj   adv   adv r.np.1   n.gsm   cj   r.nsm cj   cj
5986   2093 1571   3357   4099   4047 4022 4048 2779 7005   5986   2777   899   1142 5445

if I boast   *somewhat freely*   about the authority   the Lord gave us   for building you up *rather than*
ἐὰν → καυχήσωμαι τι   περισσότερον περὶ   τῆς ἐξουσίας ἧς ὁ   κύριος ἔδωκεν ἡμῶν εἰς οἰκοδομὴν ←   ←   καὶ   οὐκ
cj   v.ams.1s   r.asn   adv.c   p.g   d.gsf n.gsf   r.gsf d.nsm n.nsm v.aai.3s r.gp.1 p.a n.asf   cj   pl
1569   3016   5516   4358   4309   3836 2026   4005 3836 3261   1443   7005 1650 3869   2779 4024

pulling   you   down, I will not be ashamed   of it.   **9** I   do not want to seem *to*   *be trying* to frighten
εἰς καθαίρεσιν ὑμῶν ↩   → → οὐκ → αἰσχυνθήσομαι   ἵνα → → μὴ   → δόξω ὡς ἂν   → ἐκφοβεῖν
p.a   n.asf   r.gp.2   pl   v.fpi.1s   cj   pl   v.aas.1s pl pl   f.pa
1650 2746   7007   2746   159 159 4024 159   2671 1506 1506 3590   1506   6055 323   1768

you with my letters.   **10** For some say,   "His letters   are weighty and forceful, but in person
ὑμᾶς διὰ τῶν ἐπιστολῶν   → φησίν ὅτι αἱ ἐπιστολαὶ μὲν   βαρεῖαι καὶ ἰσχυραί δὲ → ⌐ἡ παρουσία τοῦ σώματος⌐
r.ap.2 p.g   d.gpf n.gpf   v.pai.3s cj d.npf n.npf   pl   a.npf   cj   a.npf   cj   d.nsf n.nsf d.gsn n.gsn
7007 1328 3836 2186   5774   4022 3836 2186   3525   987   2779 2708   1254   3836 4242 3836 5393

he is unimpressive and his speaking amounts to nothing."   **11** Such   people should realize   that what we
→ → ἀσθενὴς   καὶ ὁ λόγος → → ἐξουθενημένος ὁ   τοιοῦτος   λογιζέσθω τοῦτο ὅτι οἷοι
      a.nsf   cj d.nsm n.nsm   pt.rp.nsm   d.nsm r.nsm   v.pmm.3s r.asn cj   r.npm
      822   2779 3836 3364   2024   3836 5525   3357   4047 4022 3888

are   in our letters   when we are absent,   we will be in our actions when we are present.   ¶
ἐσμεν ⌐τῷ λόγῳ⌐ δι᾽ ἐπιστολῶν → → → ἀπόντες τοιοῦτοι καὶ   ⌐τῷ ἔργῳ⌐ ←   → → παρόντες
v.pai.1p d.dsm n.dsm p.g n.gpf   pt.pa.npm r.npm   adv   d.dsn n.dsn   pt.pa.npm
1639   3836 3364 1328 2186   583   5525   2779   3836 2240   4205

12   We do not dare   to classify or compare ourselves with some who commend   themselves.   When they
γὰρ → → Οὐ τολμῶμεν → ἐγκρῖναι ἢ   συγκρῖναι ἑαυτοὺς →   τισιν τῶν συνιστανόντων ἑαυτοὺς   ἀλλὰ → they
cj   pl   v.pai.1p   f.aa   cj   f.aa   r.apm.1   r.dpm d.gpm pt.pa.gpm   r.apm.3   cj
1142   5528 5528 4024 5528   1605   2445 5173   1571   5173 5516 3836 5319   1571   247 3582

measure themselves by themselves and compare   themselves with themselves, they are not wise.   **13** We, however,
μετροῦντες ἑαυτοὺς ἐν ἑαυτοῖς καὶ συγκρίνοντες ἑαυτοὺς → ἑαυτοῖς   αὐτοὶ οὐ συνιᾶσιν ἡμεῖς δὲ
pt.pa.npm r.apm.3   p.d r.dpm.3 cj pt.pa.npm   r.apm.3   r.dpm.3   r.npm pl v.pai.3p r.np.1 cj
3582   1571   1877 1571   2779 5173   1571   1571   899   5317 4024 5317   7005 1254

will not boast   beyond proper   limits, but will confine our boasting to   the field   God
→ οὐκ καυχησόμεθα εἰς ⌐τὰ ἄμετρα⌐   ἀλλὰ   κατὰ τὸ ⌐μέτρον τοῦ κανόνος⌐ οὗ ὁ   θεὸς
   pl v.fmi.1p   p.a d.apn a.apn   cj   p.a d.asn n.asn d.gsm n.gsm   r.gsm d.nsm n.nsm
   3016 4024   1650 3836 296   247   2848 3836 3586   3836 2834   4005 3836 2536

has assigned to us, a field   that reaches even to   you.   **14** We are not going   too far   in our boasting,
→ ἐμέρισεν   ἡμῖν μέτρου ἐφικέσθαι καὶ ἄχρι ὑμῶν   γὰρ → οὐ ὑπερεκτείνομεν ←   ←   ἑαυτούς
   v.aai.3s   r.dp.1 n.gsn   f.am   adv p.g   r.gp.2   cj   pl v.pai.1p   r.apm.1
   3532   7005 3586   2779   948 3836 7005   1142 1571 5657 4024 5657   1571

ὅπλα τῆς στρατείας ἡμῶν οὐ σαρκικὰ ἀλλὰ δυνατὰ τῷ θεῷ πρὸς καθαίρεσιν ὀχυρωμάτων, λογισμοὺς καθαιροῦντες ⁵ καὶ πᾶν ὕψωμα ἐπαιρόμενον κατὰ τῆς γνώσεως τοῦ θεοῦ, καὶ αἰχμαλωτίζοντες πᾶν νόημα εἰς τὴν ὑπακοὴν τοῦ Χριστοῦ, ⁶ καὶ ἐν ἑτοίμῳ ἔχοντες ἐκδικῆσαι πᾶσαν παρακοήν, ὅταν πληρωθῇ ὑμῶν ἡ ὑπακοή. ¶ ⁷ Τὰ κατὰ πρόσωπον βλέπετε. εἴ τις πέποιθεν ἑαυτῷ Χριστοῦ εἶναι, τοῦτο λογιζέσθω πάλιν ἐφ᾽ ἑαυτοῦ, ὅτι καθὼς αὐτὸς Χριστοῦ, οὕτως καὶ ἡμεῖς. ⁸ ἐὰν [τε] γὰρ περισσότερόν τι καυχήσωμαι περὶ τῆς ἐξουσίας ἡμῶν ἧς ἔδωκεν ὁ κύριος εἰς οἰκοδομὴν καὶ οὐκ εἰς καθαίρεσιν ὑμῶν, οὐκ αἰσχυνθήσομαι. ⁹ ἵνα μὴ δόξω ὡς ἂν ἐκφοβεῖν ὑμᾶς διὰ τῶν ἐπιστολῶν· ¹⁰ ὅτι, Αἱ ἐπιστολαὶ μέν, φησίν, βαρεῖαι καὶ ἰσχυραί, ἡ δὲ παρουσία τοῦ σώματος ἀσθενὴς καὶ ὁ λόγος ἐξουθενημένος. ¹¹ τοῦτο λογιζέσθω ὁ τοιοῦτος, ὅτι οἷοί ἐσμεν τῷ λόγῳ δι᾽ ἐπιστολῶν ἀπόντες, τοιοῦτοι καὶ παρόντες τῷ ἔργῳ. ¶ ¹² Οὐ γὰρ τολμῶμεν ἐγκρῖναι ἢ συγκρῖναι ἑαυτούς τισιν τῶν ἑαυτοὺς συνιστανόντων, ἀλλὰ αὐτοὶ ἐν ἑαυτοῖς ἑαυτοὺς μετροῦντες καὶ συγκρίνοντες ἑαυτοὺς ἑαυτοῖς οὐ συνιᾶσιν. ¹³ ἡμεῖς δὲ οὐκ εἰς τὰ ἄμετρα καυχησόμεθα ἀλλὰ κατὰ τὸ μέτρον τοῦ κανόνος οὗ ἐμέρισεν ἡμῖν ὁ θεὸς μέτρου, ἐφικέσθαι ἄχρι καὶ ὑμῶν. ¹⁴ οὐ γὰρ ὡς μὴ ἐφικνούμενοι εἰς

as would be the case if we had not come   to you, for we   did get   as   far as you with the gospel
ὡς ← ← ← ← ←   μὴ   ἐφικνούμενοι εἰς ὑμᾶς γὰρ → καὶ →   ἐφθάσαμεν ἄχρι ← ←   ὑμῶν ἐν   τῷ εὐαγγελίῳ
pl   pl   pt.pm.npm   p.a r.ap.2 cj   adv   v.aai.1p p.g   r.gp.2 p.d   d.dsn n.dsn
6055   2391 2391 3590 2391   1650 7007 1142 5777 2779   5777 948   7007 1877   3836 2295

of Christ.   [15] Neither do we go beyond our limits by boasting of work done by others.   Our hope is
→   ⌐τοῦ Χριστοῦ⌐ οὐκ   εἰς   τὰ   ἄμετρα καυχώμενοι κόποις   ἐν   ἀλλοτρίοις δὲ   →   ἐλπίδα ἔχοντες
   d.gsm n.gsm   pl   p.a   d.apn a.apn   pt.pm.npm   n.dpm   p.d   a.dpm   cj   n.asf pt.pa.npm
   3836 5986   4024   1650   3836 296   3016   3160   1877   259   1254 2400   1828 2400

that, as your faith   continues to grow,   our *area of activity* among you will greatly   expand,   [16] so
→   ὑμῶν ⌐τῆς πίστεως⌐ →   →   αὐξανομένης ἡμῶν κατὰ τὸν κανόνα ἐν   ὑμῖν   εἰς περισσείαν⌐ μεγαλυνθῆναι
   r.gp.2 d.gsf n.gsf   pt.pp.gsf   r.gp.1 p.a   d.asm n.asm   p.d   r.dp.2   p.a   n.asf   f.ap
   889 7007   3836 4411   889   7005 2848   3836 2834   1877   7007   3486 1650 4353   3486

that we can preach   the gospel in the regions beyond   you. For we do not want to boast   about work
→   →   →   εὐαγγελίσασθαι ← ←   εἰς τὰ   →   ὑπερέκεινα ὑμῶν   →   →   οὐκ   →   →   καυχήσασθαι εἰς   →
       f.am   p.a   d.apn   p.g   r.gp.2   pl   f.am   p.a
       2294   1650 3836   5654   7007   3016 3016 4024   3016   1650

already   done in another man's territory.   [17] But, "Let him who boasts   boast   in the Lord."   [18] For it is not the
⌐τὰ ἕτοιμα⌐ ←   ἐν   ἀλλοτρίῳ   κανόνι   δὲ   →   Ὁ ←   καυχώμενος καυχάσθω ἐν   κυρίῳ   γὰρ   οὐ ὁ
d.apn a.apn   p.d   a.dsm   n.dsm   cj   d.nsm   pt.pm.nsm   v.pmm.3s   p.d   n.dsm   cj   pl   d.nsm
3836 2289   1877 259   2834   1254   3016 3836   3016   3016   1877   3261   1142   4024 3836

one who commends himself who   is   approved, but the one whom the Lord commends.
←   ←   συνιστάνων ἑαυτὸν ἐκεῖνος ἐστιν δόκιμος   ἀλλὰ →   →   ὃν   ὁ   κύριος συνίστησιν
       pt.pa.nsm   r.asm.3   r.nsm   v.pai.3s a.nsm   cj   r.asm   d.nsm n.nsm   v.pai.3s
       5319   1571   1697   1639   1511   247   4005   3836 3261   5319

Paul and the False Apostles

[11:1] I hope   you will put   up with a little   of my foolishness; but   you are already doing   that.
→   Ὄφελον →   →   ἀνείχεσθε ←   μικρόν τι⌐   →   μου ἀφροσύνης ἀλλὰ →   καὶ   ἀνέχεσθε μου
pl   v.imi.2p   a.asn r.asn   r.gs.1 n.gsf   cj   adv   v.pmi.2p   r.gs.1
1051   462   3625 5516   932 1609   932   247   462   462   2779   462   1609

[2]   I am jealous for you with a godly jealousy.   I promised you to one husband, to Christ,   so that I might
γὰρ →   ζηλῶ   ὑμᾶς →   θεοῦ   ζήλῳ   γὰρ →   ἡρμοσάμην ὑμᾶς → ἑνὶ ἀνδρὶ   →   ⌐τῷ Χριστῷ⌐   →
cj   v.pai.1s   r.ap.2   n.gsm   n.dsm   cj   v.ami.1s   r.ap.2   a.dsm n.dsm   d.dsm n.dsm
1142   2420   7007   2536   2419   1142   764   7007   1651 467   3836 5986

present   you as a pure virgin   to him. [3] But I am afraid   that just as Eve   was deceived by the serpent's
παραστῆσαι   ἁγνὴν παρθένον   δὲ →   φοβοῦμαι μὴ ὡς ← Εὕαν   ἐξηπάτησεν ἐν ὁ   ὄφις   αὐτοῦ
f.aa   a.asf   n.asf   cj   v.ppi.1s   cj cj   n.asf   v.aai.3s   p.d d.nsm n.nsm   r.gsm.3
4225   54   4221   1254   5828   3590 6055   2293   1987   1877 3836 4058   899

cunning,   your minds   may somehow be led astray from your sincere   and pure   devotion   to
⌐τῇ πανουργίᾳ⌐ ὑμῶν ⌐τὰ νοήματα⌐ →   πως   →   φθαρῇ   ἀπὸ τῆς ἁπλότητος καὶ ⌐τῆς ἁγνότητος⌐   τῆς εἰς
d.dsf n.dsf   r.gp.2 d.npn n.npn   pl   v.aps.3s   p.g   d.gsf n.gsf   cj   d.gsf n.gsf   d.gsf p.a
3836 4111   7007 3836 3784   5780 4803   5780   608   3836 605   2779   3836 55   3836 1650

Christ.   [4] For if   someone comes   to you and preaches a Jesus   other than the Jesus we preached, or if you
⌐τὸν Χριστόν⌐ γὰρ εἰ   μὲν ὁ   ἐρχόμενος   κηρύσσει   Ἰησοῦν ἄλλον οὐκ   ὃν   →   ἐκηρύξαμεν ἢ   →
d.asm n.asm   cj   cj   pl   d.nsm   pt.pm.nsm   v.pai.3s   n.asm   r.asm   pl   r.asm   v.aai.1p   cj
3836 5986   1142 1623 3525 3836   2262   3062   2652   257   4024   4005   3062 3062   2445

receive   a different spirit from the one you   received, or a different gospel   from the one you   accepted,
λαμβάνετε ἕτερον πνεῦμα   ὃ ←   οὐκ ἐλάβετε   ἢ   ἕτερον   εὐαγγέλιον   ὃ   →   οὐκ ἐδέξασθε
v.pai.2p   r.asn   n.asn   r.asn   pl   v.aai.2p   cj   r.asn   n.asn   r.asn   pl   v.ami.2p
3284   2283   4460   4005   3284 4024 3284   2445 2283   2295   4005   1312 4024 1312

you put   up with it easily enough. [5] But I   do not think   I am in the least inferior   to those
→   ἀνέχεσθε ←   →   ← καλῶς ←   γὰρ →   →   Λογίζομαι   →   μηδὲν ὑστερηκέναι → τῶν
   v.pmi.2p   adv   cj   v.pmi.1s   a.asn   f.ra   d.gpm
   462   2822   1142 3357 3357 3594 3357   3594   5728   3836

"super-apostles."   [6]   I may not be a trained speaker, but I do have knowledge.   We have made this
⌐ὑπερλίαν ἀποστόλων⌐   δὲ καὶ εἰ   οὐ   ἰδιώτης ⌐τῷ λόγῳ⌐ ἀλλ'   ⌐τῇ γνώσει⌐ ἀλλ' →   →
adv   n.gpm   cj   adv cj   pl   n.nsm   d.dsm n.dsm   cj   d.dsf n.dsf   cj
5663   693   1254 2779 1623   4024   2626   3836 3364   247   3836 1194   247 5746 5746 5746

ὑμᾶς ὑπερεκτείνομεν ἑαυτούς, ἄχρι γὰρ καὶ ὑμῶν ἐφθάσαμεν ἐν τῷ εὐαγγελίῳ τοῦ Χριστοῦ. [15] οὐκ εἰς τὰ ἄμετρα καυχώμενοι ἐν ἀλλοτρίοις κόποις, ἐλπίδα δὲ ἔχοντες αὐξανομένης τῆς πίστεως ὑμῶν ἐν ὑμῖν μεγαλυνθῆναι κατὰ τὸν κανόνα ἡμῶν εἰς περισσείαν [16] εἰς τὰ ὑπερέκεινα ὑμῶν εὐαγγελίσασθαι, οὐκ ἐν ἀλλοτρίῳ κανόνι εἰς τὰ ἕτοιμα καυχήσασθαι. [17] Ὁ δὲ καυχώμενος ἐν κυρίῳ καυχάσθω· [18] οὐ γὰρ ὁ ἑαυτὸν συνιστάνων, ἐκεῖνός ἐστιν δόκιμος, ἀλλὰ ὃν ὁ κύριος συνίστησιν.

[11:1] Ὄφελον ἀνείχεσθέ μου μικρόν τι ἀφροσύνης· ἀλλὰ καὶ ἀνέχεσθέ μου. [2] ζηλῶ γὰρ ὑμᾶς θεοῦ ζήλῳ, ἡρμοσάμην γὰρ ὑμᾶς ἑνὶ ἀνδρὶ παρθένον ἁγνὴν παραστῆσαι τῷ Χριστῷ· [3] φοβοῦμαι δὲ μή πως, ὡς ὁ ὄφις ἐξηπάτησεν Εὕαν ἐν τῇ πανουργίᾳ αὐτοῦ, φθαρῇ τὰ νοήματα ὑμῶν ἀπὸ τῆς ἁπλότητος [καὶ τῆς ἁγνότητος] τῆς εἰς τὸν Χριστόν. [4] εἰ μὲν γὰρ ὁ ἐρχόμενος ἄλλον Ἰησοῦν κηρύσσει ὃν οὐκ ἐκηρύξαμεν, ἢ πνεῦμα ἕτερον λαμβάνετε ὃ οὐκ ἐλάβετε, ἢ εὐαγγέλιον ἕτερον ὃ οὐκ ἐδέξασθε, καλῶς ἀνέχεσθε. [5] λογίζομαι γὰρ μηδὲν ὑστερηκέναι τῶν ὑπερλίαν ἀποστόλων. [6] εἰ δὲ καὶ ἰδιώτης τῷ λόγῳ, ἀλλ' οὐ τῇ γνώσει, ἀλλ'

perfectly clear — to you in every way. ¶ [7] Was it a sin for me to lower myself in order to
ἐν παντὶ φανερώσαντες εἰς ὑμᾶς ἐν πᾶσιν ←   Ἦ ἐποίησα ἁμαρτίαν ← → ταπεινῶν ἐμαυτὸν ἵνα
p.d a.dsn pt.aa.npm p.a r.ap.2 p.d a.dpn   cj v.aai.1s n.asf   pt.pa.nsm r.asm.1 cj
1877 4246 5746 1650 7007 1877 4246   2445 4472 281   4472 4472 5427 1831 2671

elevate you by preaching the gospel of God to you free of charge? [8] I robbed other churches by
ὑψωθῆτε ὑμεῖς ὅτι εὐηγγελισάμην τὸ εὐαγγέλιον → τοῦ θεοῦ ὑμῖν δωρεὰν ← ← → ἐσύλησα ἄλλας ἐκκλησίας →
v.aps.2p r.np.2 cj v.ami.1s d.asn n.asn   d.gsn n.gsn r.dp.2 adv   v.aai.1s r.apf n.apf
5738 7007 4022 2294 3836 2295 3836 2536 7007 1562   5195 257 1711

receiving support from them so as to serve you. [9] And when I was with you and needed something, I
λαβὼν ὀψώνιον → → πρὸς τὴν διακονίαν ὑμῶν καὶ → → παρὼν πρὸς ὑμᾶς καὶ ὑστερηθεὶς ←
pt.aa.nsm n.asn   p.a d.asf n.asf r.gp.2 cj   pt.pa.nsm p.a r.ap.2 cj pt.ap.nsm
3284 4072 4639 3836 1355 7007 2779   4205 4639 7007 2779 5728   2915

was not a burden to anyone, for the brothers who came from Macedonia supplied what I needed.
↱ οὐ κατενάρκησα οὐθενός γὰρ οἱ ἀδελφοὶ → ἐλθόντες ἀπὸ Μακεδονίας προσανεπλήρωσαν τὸ μου ὑστέρημα καὶ
pl v.aai.1s a.gsm cj d.npm n.npm pt.aa.npm p.g n.gsf v.aai.3p d.asn r.gs.1 n.asn cj
2915 4024 2915 4032 1142 3836 81 2262 608 3423 4650 3836 1609 5729 2779

I have kept myself from being a burden to you in any way, and will continue to do so. [10] As surely as the truth
→ ἐτήρησα ἐμαυτὸν ἀβαρῆ → ὑμῖν ἐν παντὶ καὶ → τηρήσω ἀλήθεια
v.aai.1s r.asm.1 a.asm r.dp.2 p.d a.dsn cj v.fai.1s n.nsf
5498 1831 4 7007 1877 4246 2779 5498 237

of Christ is in me, nobody in the regions of Achaia will stop this boasting of mine. [11] Why?
→ Χριστοῦ ἔστιν ἐν ἐμοὶ ὅτι οὐ ἐν τοῖς κλίμασιν τῆς Ἀχαΐας → φραγήσεται αὐτη ἡ καύχησις, εἰς ἐμὲ διὰ τί
n.gsm v.pai.3s p.d r.ds.1 cj pl p.d d.dpn n.dpn d.gsf n.gsf v.fpi.3s r.nsf d.nsf n.nsf p.a r.as.1 p.a r.asn
5986 1639 1877 1609 4022 4024 1877 3836 3107 3836 938 5852 4047 3836 3018 1650 1609 1328 5515

Because I do not love you? God knows I do! [12] And I will keep on doing what I am doing in order to cut
ὅτι ↱ οὐκ ἀγαπῶ ὑμᾶς ὁ θεὸς οἶδεν δὲ → → καὶ → ποιήσω Ὃ → ποιῶ ἵνα ← ← ἐκκόψω
cj pl v.pai.1s r.ap.2 d.nsm n.nsm v.rai.3s cj adv v.fai.1s r.asn v.pai.1s cj v.aas.1s
4022 26 26 4024 26 7007 3836 2536 3857 1254 2779 4472 4005 4472 2671 1716

the ground from under those who want an opportunity to be considered *equal with* us in the things they
τὴν ἀφορμὴν τῶν ← θελόντων ἀφορμὴν ἵνα εὑρεθῶσιν καθὼς καὶ ἡμεῖς ἐν ᾧ
d.asf n.asf d.gpm pt.pa.gpm n.asf cj v.aps.3p cj adv r.np.1 p.d r.dsn
3836 929 3836 2527 929 2671 2351 2777 2779 7005 1877 4005

boast about. ¶ [13] For such men are false apostles, deceitful workmen, masquerading as
καυχῶνται γὰρ οἱ τοιοῦτοι → ψευδαπόστολοι δόλιοι ἐργάται μετασχηματιζόμενοι εἰς
v.pmi.3p cj d.npm r.npm n.npm a.npm n.npm pt.pm.npm p.a
3016 1142 3836 5525 6013 1513 2239 3571 1650

apostles of Christ. [14] And no wonder, for Satan himself masquerades as an angel of light. [15] It is not
ἀποστόλους → Χριστοῦ καὶ οὐ θαῦμα γὰρ ὁ σατανᾶς, αὐτὸς μετασχηματίζεται εἰς ἄγγελον → φωτός → οὐ
n.apm n.gsm cj pl n.nsn cj d.nsm n.nsm r.nsm v.pmi.3s p.a n.asm n.gsn pl
693 5986 2779 4024 2512 1142 3836 4928 899 3571 1650 34 5890 4024

surprising, then, if his servants masquerade as servants of righteousness. Their end will be
μέγα οὖν εἰ καὶ αὐτοῦ οἱ διάκονοι μετασχηματίζονται ὡς διάκονοι → δικαιοσύνης ὧν τὸ τέλος → ἔσται
a.nsn cj cj adv r.gsm.3 d.npm n.npm v.pmi.3p pl n.npm n.gsf r.gpm d.nsn n.nsn v.fmi.3s
3489 4036 1623 2779 899 3836 1356 3571 6055 1356 1466 4005 3836 5465 1639

what their actions deserve.
κατὰ τὰ αὐτῶν ἔργα ↰
p.a d.apn r.gpm.3 n.apn
2848 3836 899 2240 2848

Paul Boasts About His Sufferings

[11:16] I repeat: Let no one take me for a fool. But if you do, then receive me just as you would a
→ λέγω Πάλιν → μή τίς δόξη με εἶναι ἄφρονα δὲ εἰ μή γε κἂν δέξασθε με ὡς
v.pai.1s adv pl r.nsm v.aas.3s r.as.1 f.pa a.asm cj cj pl pl crasis v.amm.2p r.as.1 pl
3306 4099 1506 3590 5516 1506 1609 1639 933 1254 1623 3590 1145 2829 1312 1609 6055

fool, so that I may do a little boasting. [17] In this self-confident boasting I am not talking
ἄφρονα ἵνα ← κἀγὼ → → μικρόν τι καυχήσωμαι ὃ λαλῶ ἐν ταύτῃ τῇ ὑποστάσει τῆς καυχήσεως → → οὐ λαλῶ
a.asm cj crasis a.asn r.asn v.ams.1s r.asn v.pai.1s p.d r.dsf d.dsf n.dsf d.gsf n.gsf pl v.pai.1s
933 2671 2743 3016 3016 3625 5516 3016 4005 3281 1877 4047 3836 5712 3836 3018 3281 3281 4024 3281

ἐν παντὶ φανερώσαντες ἐν πᾶσιν εἰς ὑμᾶς. ¶ [7] Ἦ ἁμαρτίαν ἐποίησα ἐμαυτὸν ταπεινῶν ἵνα ὑμεῖς ὑψωθῆτε, ὅτι δωρεὰν τὸ τοῦ θεοῦ εὐαγγέλιον εὐηγγελισάμην ὑμῖν; [8] ἄλλας ἐκκλησίας ἐσύλησα λαβὼν ὀψώνιον πρὸς τὴν ὑμῶν διακονίαν, [9] καὶ παρὼν πρὸς ὑμᾶς καὶ ὑστερηθεὶς οὐ κατενάρκησα οὐθενός· τὸ γὰρ ὑστέρημά μου προσανεπλήρωσαν οἱ ἀδελφοὶ ἐλθόντες ἀπὸ Μακεδονίας. καὶ ἐν παντὶ ἀβαρῆ ἐμαυτὸν ὑμῖν ἐτήρησα καὶ τηρήσω. [10] ἔστιν ἀλήθεια Χριστοῦ ἐν ἐμοὶ ὅτι ἡ καύχησις αὕτη οὐ φραγήσεται εἰς ἐμὲ ἐν τοῖς κλίμασιν τῆς Ἀχαΐας. [11] διὰ τί; ὅτι οὐκ ἀγαπῶ ὑμᾶς; ὁ θεὸς οἶδεν. [12] Ὃ δὲ ποιῶ, καὶ ποιήσω, ἵνα ἐκκόψω τὴν ἀφορμὴν τῶν θελόντων ἀφορμήν, ἵνα ἐν ᾧ καυχῶνται εὑρεθῶσιν καθὼς καὶ ἡμεῖς. ¶ [13] οἱ γὰρ τοιοῦτοι ψευδαπόστολοι, ἐργάται δόλιοι, μετασχηματιζόμενοι εἰς ἀποστόλους Χριστοῦ. [14] καὶ οὐ θαῦμα· αὐτὸς γὰρ ὁ Σατανᾶς μετασχηματίζεται εἰς ἄγγελον φωτός. [15] οὐ μέγα οὖν εἰ καὶ οἱ διάκονοι αὐτοῦ μετασχηματίζονται ὡς διάκονοι δικαιοσύνης· ὧν τὸ τέλος ἔσται κατὰ τὰ ἔργα αὐτῶν.

[11:16] Πάλιν λέγω, μή τίς με δόξῃ ἄφρονα εἶναι· εἰ δὲ μή γε, κἂν ὡς ἄφρονα δέξασθέ με, ἵνα κἀγὼ μικρόν τι καυχήσωμαι. [17] ὃ λαλῶ, οὐ κατὰ κύριον λαλῶ ἀλλ᾽ ὡς ἐν ἀφροσύνῃ, ἐν ταύτῃ τῇ ὑποστάσει τῆς καυχήσεως. [18] ἐπεὶ πολλοὶ καυχῶνται κατὰ σάρκα,

as the Lord would, but as a fool.
κατὰ κύριον ἀλλ᾽ ὡς ἐν ἀφροσύνῃ
p.a n.asm cj pl p.d n.dsf
2848 3261 247 6055 1877 932

18 Since many are boasting in the way the world does, I too will
ἐπεὶ πολλοὶ → καυχῶνται κατὰ ← σάρκα κἀγὼ
cj a.npm v.pmi.3p p.a n.asf crasis
2075 4498 3016 2848 4922 2743

boast. **19** You gladly put up with fools since you are so wise!
καυχήσομαι γὰρ → ἡδέως ἀνέχεσθε ← ⸂τῶν ἀφρόνων⸃ → → ὄντες φρόνιμοι γὰρ
v.fmi.1s cj adv v.pmi.2p d.gpm a.gpm pt.pa.npm a.npm cj
3016 1142 462 2452 462 3836 933 1639 5861 1142

20 In fact, you even put up
→ ← ἀνέχεσθε ←
v.pmi.2p
462

with anyone who enslaves you or exploits you or takes advantage of you or pushes
← εἴ τις καταδουλοῖ ὑμᾶς τις εἴ κατεσθίει τις εἴ λαμβάνει τις εἴ ἐπαίρεται
cj r.nsm v.pai.3s r.ap.2 r.nsm cj v.pai.3s r.nsm cj v.pai.3s r.nsm cj v.pmi.3s
1623 5516 2871 7007 5516 1623 2983 5516 1623 3284 5516 1623 2048

himself forward or slaps you in the face. **21** To my shame I admit that we were too weak for
← ← τις εἴ δέρει ὑμᾶς εἰς πρόσωπον κατὰ ἀτιμίαν → λέγω ὡς ὅτι ἡμεῖς → ἠσθενήκαμεν
r.nsm cj v.pai.3s r.ap.2 p.a n.asn p.a n.asf v.pai.1s pl cj r.np.1 v.rai.1p
5516 1623 1296 7007 1650 4725 2848 871 3306 6055 4022 7005 820

that! ¶ What anyone else dares to boast about – I am speaking as a fool – I also dare to
δ᾽ ⸂Ἐν ᾧ⸃ τις ἄν τολμᾷ → → λέγω ἐν ἀφροσύνῃ κἀγὼ ← τολμῶ
cj p.d r.dsn r.nsm pl v.pas.3s v.pai.1s p.d n.dsf crasis v.pai.1s
1254 1877 4005 5516 323 5528 3306 1877 932 2743 5528

boast about. **22** Are they Hebrews? So am I. Are they Israelites? So am I. Are they Abraham's descendants? So
εἰσιν ← Ἑβραῖοί κἀγώ ← εἰσιν Ἰσραηλῖταί κἀγώ ← εἰσιν Ἀβραάμ σπέρμα κἀγώ
v.pai.3p n.npm crasis v.pai.3p n.npm adv v.pai.3p n.gsm n.nsn adv
1639 1578 2743 1639 2703 2743 1639 11 5065 2743

am I. **23** Are they servants of Christ? (I am out of my mind to talk like this.) I am more. I have worked
← ← εἰσιν διάκονοι Χριστοῦ → → → → → παραφρονῶν λαλῶ ἐγώ ὑπέρ ἐν κόποις
v.pai.3p n.npm n.gsm pt.pa.nsm v.pai.1s r.ns.1 adv p.d n.dpm
1639 1356 5986 3281 3281 4196 3281 1609 5642 1877 3160

much harder, been in prison more frequently, been flogged more severely, and been
περισσοτέρως ← ἐν φυλακαῖς περισσοτέρως ← ἐν πληγαῖς ὑπερβαλλόντως
adv.c p.d n.dpf adv.c p.d n.dpf adv
4359 1877 5871 4359 1877 4435 5649

exposed to death again and again. **24** Five times I received from the Jews the forty lashes minus
ἐν θανάτοις πολλάκις ← ← πεντάκις → ἔλαβον Ὑπὸ Ἰουδαίων τεσσεράκοντα παρὰ
p.d n.dpm adv adv v.aai.1s p.g a.gpm a.apf p.a
1877 2505 4490 4294 3284 5679 2681 5477 4123

one. **25** Three times I was beaten with rods, once I was stoned, three times I was shipwrecked, I spent a
μίαν τρὶς → ἐρραβδίσθην ← ἅπαξ → ἐλιθάσθην τρὶς ← ἐναυάγησα → πεποίηκα
a.asf adv v.api.1s adv v.api.1s adv v.aai.1s v.rai.1s
1651 5565 4810 562 3342 5565 3728 4472

night and a day in the open sea, **26** I have been constantly on the move. I have been in danger from
νυχθήμερον ← ← ἐν τῷ → βυθῷ πολλάκις → → ὁδοιπορίαις → κινδύνοις →
n.asn p.d d.dsm n.dsm adv n.dpf n.dpm
3819 1877 3836 1113 4490 3845 3074

rivers, in danger from bandits, in danger from my own countrymen, in danger from Gentiles; in danger in
ποταμῶν → κινδύνοις → λῃστῶν → κινδύνοις ἐκ → γένους → κινδύνοις ἐξ ἐθνῶν → κινδύνοις ἐν
n.gpm n.dpm n.gpm n.dpm p.g n.gsn n.dpm p.g n.gpn n.dpm p.d
4532 3074 3334 3074 1666 1169 3074 1666 1620 3074 1877

the city, in danger in the country, in danger at sea; and in danger from false brothers. **27** I have
πόλει → κινδύνοις ἐν ἐρημίᾳ → κινδύνοις ἐν θαλάσσῃ → κινδύνοις ἐν ψευδαδέλφοις ←
n.dsf n.dpm p.d n.dsf n.dpm p.d n.dsf n.dpm p.d n.dpm
4484 3074 1877 2244 3074 1877 2498 3074 1877 6012

labored and toiled and have often gone without sleep; I have known hunger and thirst and have
κόπῳ καὶ μόχθῳ πολλάκις ἐν → ἀγρυπνίαις ἐν λιμῷ καὶ δίψει
n.dsm cj n.dsm adv p.d n.dpf p.d n.dsm cj n.dsn
3160 2779 3677 4490 1877 71 1877 3350 2779 1499

often gone without food; I have been cold and naked. **28** Besides *everything else,* I face
πολλάκις ἐν → νηστείαις ἐν ψύχει καὶ γυμνότητι χωρὶς τῶν παρεκτὸς μοι
adv p.d n.dpf p.d n.dsn cj n.dsf p.g d.gpn adv r.ds.1
4490 1877 3763 1877 6036 2779 1219 6006 3836 4211 1609

κἀγὼ καυχήσομαι. **19** ἡδέως γὰρ ἀνέχεσθε τῶν ἀφρόνων φρόνιμοι ὄντες· **20** ἀνέχεσθε γὰρ εἴ τις ὑμᾶς καταδουλοῖ, εἴ τις κατεσθίει, εἴ τις λαμβάνει, εἴ τις ἐπαίρεται, εἴ τις εἰς πρόσωπον ὑμᾶς δέρει. **21** κατὰ ἀτιμίαν λέγω, ὡς ὅτι ἡμεῖς ἠσθενήκαμεν ¶ ἐν ᾧ δ᾽ ἄν τις τολμᾷ, ἐν ἀφροσύνῃ λέγω, τολμῶ κἀγώ. **22** Ἑβραῖοί εἰσιν; κἀγώ. Ἰσραηλῖταί εἰσιν; κἀγώ. σπέρμα Ἀβραάμ εἰσιν; κἀγώ. **23** διάκονοι Χριστοῦ εἰσιν; παραφρονῶν λαλῶ, ὑπὲρ ἐγώ· ἐν κόποις περισσοτέρως, ἐν φυλακαῖς περισσοτέρως, ἐν πληγαῖς ὑπερβαλλόντως, ἐν θανάτοις πολλάκις. **24** ὑπὸ Ἰουδαίων πεντάκις τεσσεράκοντα παρὰ μίαν ἔλαβον, **25** τρὶς ἐραβδίσθην, ἅπαξ ἐλιθάσθην, τρὶς ἐναυάγησα, νυχθήμερον ἐν τῷ βυθῷ πεποίηκα· **26** ὁδοιπορίαις πολλάκις, κινδύνοις ποταμῶν, κινδύνοις λῃστῶν, κινδύνοις ἐκ γένους, κινδύνοις ἐξ ἐθνῶν, κινδύνοις ἐν πόλει, κινδύνοις ἐν ἐρημίᾳ, κινδύνοις ἐν θαλάσσῃ, κινδύνοις ἐν ψευδαδέλφοις, **27** κόπῳ καὶ μόχθῳ, ἐν ἀγρυπνίαις πολλάκις, ἐν λιμῷ καὶ δίψει, ἐν νηστείαις πολλάκις, ἐν ψύχει καὶ γυμνότητι· **28** χωρὶς τῶν παρεκτὸς ἡ ἐπίστασίς μοι ἡ καθ᾽ ἡμέραν, ἡ μέριμνα πασῶν τῶν ἐκκλησιῶν. **29** τίς ἀσθενεῖ καὶ οὐκ ἀσθενῶ; τίς

daily | the | pressure | of my | concern | for all | | the | churches. | 29 Who | is weak, | and I | | | do not | | feel weak? | Who is
ἡ | καθ᾽ | ἡμέραν | ἡ | ἐπίστασις | ἡ | μέριμνα | → | πασῶν | τῶν | ἐκκλησιῶν | τίς | → ἀσθενεῖ | καὶ | → | ↑ | οὐκ | → | ἀσθενῶ | τίς | →
d.nsf | p.a | n.asf | d.nsf | n.nsf | d.nsf | n.nsf | | a.gpf | d.gpf | n.gpf | r.nsm | v.pai.3s | cj | | | pl | | v.pai.1s | r.nsm |
3836 | 2848 | 2465 | 3836 | 2180 | 3836 | 3533 | | 4246 | 3836 | 1711 | 5515 | 820 | 2779 | 820 | 820 | 4024 | | 820 | 5515 |

led | | into sin, | and | I | | do not | inwardly burn? | ¶ | 30 If | I | must boast, | | I will boast | | of the things
σκανδαλίζεται | ← | ← | καὶ | ἐγὼ | οὐκ | | πυροῦμαι | | | Εἰ | δεῖ | καυχᾶσθαι | → | → | καυχήσομαι | ← | τὰ | ←
v.ppi.3s | | | cj | r.ns.1 | pl | | v.ppi.1s | | | cj | v.pai.3s | f.pm | | | v.fmi.1s | | d.apn |
4997 | | | 2779 | 1609 | 4792 | 4024 | 4792 | | | 1623 | 1256 | 3016 | | | 3016 | | 3836 |

that | show | my | weakness. | 31 The | God | and | Father | of the | Lord | Jesus, | who | is to be | | praised | forever, | | knows
μου | τῆς ἀσθενείας | | | ὁ | θεὸς | καὶ | πατὴρ | → | τοῦ | κυρίου | Ἰησοῦ | ὁ | → | → | ὢν | εὐλογητὸς | εἰς | τοὺς | αἰῶνας, | οἶδεν
r.gs.1 | d.gsf | n.gsf | | d.nsm | n.nsm | cj | n.nsm | | d.gsm | n.gsm | n.gsm | d.nsm | | | pt.pa.nsm | a.nsm | p.a | d.apm | n.apm | v.rai.3s
1609 | 3836 | 819 | | 3836 | 2536 | 2779 | 4252 | | 3836 | 3261 | 2652 | 3836 | | | 1639 | 2329 | 1650 | 3836 | 172 | 3857

that | I | am not | lying. | 32 In | Damascus | the | governor | under | King | | Aretas | had | the | city | | of the | Damascenes
ὅτι | → | οὐ | ψεύδομαι | ἐν | Δαμασκῷ | ὁ | ἐθνάρχης | → | | τοῦ βασιλέως, | Ἀρέτα | → | τὴν | πόλιν | → | | Δαμασκηνῶν
cj | | pl | v.pmi.1s | p.d | n.dsf | d.nsm | n.nsm | | | d.gsm | n.gsm | n.gsm | | d.asf | n.asf | | | a.gpm
4022 | 6017 | 6017 | 4024 | 6017 | 1877 | 1242 | 3836 | 1617 | | 745 | 3836 | 995 | 745 | 5864 | 3836 | 4484 | | 1241

guarded | in order to | arrest | me. | 33 But | I | was | lowered | in | a basket | from | a window | in | the | wall | and | slipped through
ἐφρούρει | → | → | πιάσαι | με, | καὶ | → | → | ἐχαλάσθην | ἐν | σαργάνῃ | διὰ | θυρίδος | διὰ | τοῦ | τείχους | καὶ | ἐξέφυγον | ←
v.iai.3s | | | f.aa | r.as.1 | cj | | | v.api.1s | p.d | n.dsf | p.g | n.gsf | p.g | d.gsn | n.gsn | cj | v.aai.1s |
5864 | | | 4389 | 1609 | 2779 | | | 5899 | 1877 | 4914 | 1328 | 2600 | 1328 | 3836 | 5446 | 2779 | 1767 |

his | hands.
αὐτοῦ | τὰς χεῖρας
r.gsm.3 | d.apf | n.apf
899 | 3836 | 5931

Paul's Vision and His Thorn

12:1 I | must | go on boasting. | | Although | there is | | nothing | to be gained, | | I will go | | on to | visions | and
δεῖ | → | → | Καυχᾶσθαι | μὲν | → | ↑ | οὐ | → | συμφέρον | δὲ | → | ἐλεύσομαι | ← | εἰς | ὀπτασίας | καὶ
v.pai.3s | | | f.pm | pl | | | pl | | pt.pa.nsn | cj | | v.fmi.1s | | p.a | n.apf | cj
1256 | 3016 | 3525 | 5237 | | 5237 | 5237 | 4024 | | 5237 | 1254 | | 2262 | 1650 | 3965 | 2779

revelations | from | the Lord. | 2 I | know | a man | in | Christ | who | fourteen | | years | ago | | was | caught | up to
ἀποκαλύψεις | → | | κυρίου | οἶδα | ἄνθρωπον | ἐν | Χριστῷ | | δεκατεσσάρων | ἐτῶν | | πρὸ | τὸν τοιοῦτον | → | ἁρπαγέντα | ← | ἕως
n.apf | | | n.gsm | v.rai.1s | n.asm | p.d | n.dsm | | a.gpn | n.gpn | | p.g | d.asm | r.asm | | pt.ap.asm | | p.g
637 | | | 3261 | 3857 | 476 | 1877 | 5986 | | 1280 | 2291 | | 4574 | 3836 | 5525 | | 773 | | 2401

the third | heaven. | Whether | it was | in | the | body | | or | out | of the | body | I | do not know | – | God | | knows.
τρίτου | οὐρανοῦ | εἴτε | | ἐν | | σώματι | οὐκ | οἶδα | εἴτε | ἐκτὸς | ← | τοῦ | σώματος | → | οὐκ | οἶδα | ὁ | θεὸς | οἶδεν
a.gsn | n.gsm | cj | | p.d | | n.dsn | pl | v.rai.1s | cj | p.g | | d.gsn | n.gsn | | pl | v.rai.1s | d.nsm | n.nsm | v.rai.3s
5569 | 4041 | 1664 | | 1877 | | 5393 | 4024 | 3857 | 1664 | 1760 | | 3836 | 5393 | | 3857 | 3857 | 3836 | 2536 | 3857

3 And | I | know | that | this | man | | – whether | in | | the | body | or | apart from | the | body | I | do not know, | but
καὶ | → οἶδα | → | | τοιοῦτον | τὸν ἄνθρωπον | εἴτε | | ἐν | | | σώματι | εἴτε | χωρὶς | | τοῦ | σώματος | → | | οὐκ οἶδα
cj | v.rai.1s | | | r.asm | d.asm | n.asm | cj | | p.d | | | n.dsn | cj | p.g | | d.gsn | n.gsn | | | pl | v.rai.1s
2779 | 3857 | 4022 | 5525 | 3836 | 476 | 1664 | | 1877 | | 5393 | 1664 | 6006 | | 3836 | 5393 | 3857 | 3857 | 4024 | 3857

God | knows – | 4 | | was | caught up to | paradise. | | He heard | inexpressible | things, | things that | man | | is | not
ὁ | θεὸς | οἶδεν | ὅτι | → | ἡρπάγη | εἰς | τὸν παράδεισον, | καὶ | → | ἤκουσεν | ἄρρητα | ῥήματα | ἃ | ← | ἀνθρώπῳ | οὐκ
d.nsm | n.nsm | v.rai.3s | cj | | v.api.3s | p.a | d.asm | n.asm | cj | | v.aai.3s | a.apn | n.apn | r.apn | | n.dsm | pl
3836 | 2536 | 3857 | 4022 | | 773 | 1650 | 3836 | 4137 | 2779 | 201 | 777 | 4839 | 4005 | | 476 | 1997 | 4024

permitted | to tell. | 5 I | will boast | | about | a man | like | that, | | but I | will not boast | | about | myself, | except
ἐξὸν | → λαλῆσαι | → | καυχήσομαι | ὑπὲρ | → | τοῦ | τοιούτου, | δὲ | → | οὐ | καυχήσομαι | ὑπὲρ | ἐμαυτοῦ | εἰ | μὴ
pt.pa.nsn | f.aa | | v.fmi.1s | p.g | | d.gsm | r.gsm | cj | | pl | v.fmi.1s | p.g | r.gsm.1 | cj | pl
1997 | 3281 | | 3016 | 5642 | | 3836 | 5525 | 1254 | 3016 | 3016 | 4024 | 3016 | 5642 | 1831 | 1623 | 3590

about | my | weaknesses. | 6 Even if | I | should | choose to boast, | | I | would not be | | a fool, | because | I would be
ἐν | ταῖς ἀσθενείαις | γὰρ | Ἐὰν | → | → | θελήσω | καυχήσασθαι | → | → | οὐκ | ἔσομαι | ἄφρων | γὰρ | |
p.d | d.dpf | n.dpf | cj | cj | | v.aas.1s | f.am | | | pl | v.fmi.1s | a.nsm | cj |
1877 | 3836 | 819 | 1142 | 1569 | | 2527 | 3016 | 1639 | 1639 | 4024 | 1639 | 933 | 1142 |

speaking | the truth. | But I | refrain, | so | no one | will | think | | more | of | me | than | is | warranted | by what | I | do | or
ἐρῶ | ἀλήθειαν | δὲ | φείδομαι | → | μή | τις | λογίσηται | ὑπὲρ | εἰς | ἐμὲ | ← | | | ὃ | με | βλέπει | ἢ
v.fai.1s | n.asf | cj | v.pmi.1s | cj | r.nsm | | v.ams.3s | p.a | p.a | r.as.1 | | | | r.asn | r.as.1 | v.pai.3s | cj
3306 | 237 | 1254 | 5767 | 3590 | 5516 | | 3357 | 5642 | 1650 | 1609 | 5642 | 5642 | 5642 | 4005 | 1609 | 1063 | 2445

σκανδαλίζεται καὶ οὐκ ἐγὼ πυροῦμαι; ¶ 30 Εἰ καυχᾶσθαι δεῖ, τὰ τῆς ἀσθενείας μου καυχήσομαι. 31 ὁ θεὸς καὶ πατὴρ τοῦ κυρίου Ἰησοῦ οἶδεν, ὁ ὢν εὐλογητὸς εἰς τοὺς αἰῶνας, ὅτι οὐ ψεύδομαι. 32 ἐν Δαμασκῷ ὁ ἐθνάρχης Ἀρέτα τοῦ βασιλέως ἐφρούρει τὴν πόλιν Δαμασκηνῶν πιάσαι με, 33 καὶ διὰ θυρίδος ἐν σαργάνῃ ἐχαλάσθην διὰ τοῦ τείχους καὶ ἐξέφυγον τὰς χεῖρας αὐτοῦ.

12:1 Καυχᾶσθαι δεῖ, οὐ συμφέρον μέν, ἐλεύσομαι δὲ εἰς ὀπτασίας καὶ ἀποκαλύψεις κυρίου. 2 οἶδα ἄνθρωπον ἐν Χριστῷ πρὸ ἐτῶν δεκατεσσάρων, εἴτε ἐν σώματι οὐκ οἶδα, εἴτε ἐκτὸς τοῦ σώματος οὐκ οἶδα, ὁ θεὸς οἶδεν, ἁρπαγέντα τὸν τοιοῦτον ἕως τρίτου οὐρανοῦ. 3 καὶ οἶδα τὸν τοιοῦτον ἄνθρωπον, εἴτε ἐν σώματι εἴτε χωρὶς τοῦ σώματος οὐκ οἶδα, ὁ θεὸς οἶδεν, 4 ὅτι ἡρπάγη εἰς τὸν παράδεισον καὶ ἤκουσεν ἄρρητα ῥήματα ἃ οὐκ ἐξὸν ἀνθρώπῳ λαλῆσαι. 5 ὑπὲρ τοῦ τοιούτου καυχήσομαι, ὑπὲρ δὲ ἐμαυτοῦ οὐ καυχήσομαι εἰ μὴ ἐν ταῖς ἀσθενείαις. 6 ἐὰν γὰρ θελήσω καυχήσασθαι, οὐκ ἔσομαι ἄφρων, ἀλήθειαν γὰρ ἐρῶ· φείδομαι δέ, μή τις εἰς ἐμὲ λογίσηται ὑπὲρ ὃ βλέπει με ἢ ἀκούει [τι] ἐξ ἐμοῦ ¶ 7 καὶ τῇ ὑπερβολῇ τῶν ἀποκαλύψεων. διὸ ἵνα μὴ ὑπεραίρωμαι,

say.   ¶   **7**   To keep me from becoming conceited because of these surpassingly great revelations,
ἀκούει [τι]   καὶ διὸ ἵνα μὴ →   →   ὑπεραίρωμαι →   → τῶν ˌτῇ ὑπερβολῇˌ ← ἀποκαλύψεων
v.pai.3s   r.asn   cj cj cj pl   v.pps.1s   d.gpf d.dsf n.dsf   n.gpf
201   5516   2779 1475 2671 3590   5643   3836 3836 5651   637

there was given me a thorn in my flesh, a messenger of Satan, to torment me.   **8** Three times I
→   → ἐδόθη μοι σκόλοψ → τῇ σαρκί ἄγγελος → σατανᾶ ἵνα κολαφίζῃ με ἵνα μὴ ὑπεραίρωμαι τρίς ←   →
    v.api.3s   n.ds.1 n.nsm   d.dsf n.dsf n.nsm   n.gsm cj v.pai.3s r.as.1 cj cj v.pps.1s adv
    1443   1609 5022   3836 4922 34   4928 2671 3139 1609 2671 3590 5643 5565

pleaded with the Lord to take it away from me. **9** But he said to me, "My grace is sufficient for
παρεκάλεσα ← τὸν κύριον ὑπὲρ τούτου ἵνα ἀποστῇ ἀπ᾽ ἐμοῦ καὶ → εἴρηκεν → μοι μου ˌἡ χάρις˒ ἀρκεῖ →
v.aai.1s   d.asm n.asm p.g r.gsn cj v.aas.3s   p.g r.gs.1 cj   v.rai.3s   r.ds.1 r.gs.1 d.nsf n.nsf v.pai.3s
4151   3836 3261 5642 4047 2671 923   608 1609 2779   3306   1609 1609 3836 5921 758

you, for my power is made perfect in weakness." Therefore I will boast all the more gladly about my
σοι γὰρ ἡ δύναμις → → τελεῖται ἐν ἀσθενείᾳ οὖν → → καυχήσομαι → → μᾶλλον ἥδιστα ἐν μου
r.ds.2 cj d.nsf n.nsf   v.ppi.3s p.d n.dsf   cj   v.fmi.1s   adv.c adv.s p.d r.gs.1
5148 1142 3836 1539   5464 1877 819   4036   3016   3437 2452 1877 1609

weaknesses, so that Christ's power may rest on me. **10** That is why, for Christ's sake, I delight in
ˌταῖς ἀσθενείαιςˌ ἵνα ← ˌτοῦ Χριστοῦˌ ˌἡ δύναμις˒ → ἐπισκηνώσῃ ἐπ᾽ ἐμέ διὸ → ὑπὲρ Χριστοῦ ← εὐδοκῶ ἐν
d.dpf n.dpf   cj   d.gsm n.gsm   d.nsf n.nsf   v.aas.3s p.a r.as.1 cj   p.g n.gsm   v.pai.1s p.d
3836 819   2671   3836 5986   3836 1539   2172 2093 1609 1475   5642 5986   2305 1877

weaknesses, in insults, in hardships, in persecutions, in difficulties. For when I am weak, then I am strong.
ἀσθενείαις ἐν ὕβρεσιν ἐν ἀνάγκαις ἐν διωγμοῖς καὶ → στενοχωρίαις γὰρ ὅταν → → ἀσθενῶ τότε → εἰμι δυνατός
n.dpf p.d n.dpf p.d n.dpf p.d n.dpm   cj   n.dpf   cj cj   v.pas.1s adv   v.pai.1s a.nsm
819 1877 5615 1877 340 1877 1501   2779   5103   1142 4020   820 5538   1639 1543

Paul's Concern for the Corinthians

12:11 I have made a fool of myself, but you drove me to it. I ought to have been commended by
→ → Γέγονα ἄφρων ← ← ὑμεῖς ἠναγκάσατε με ← γὰρ ἐγὼ ὤφειλον → → συνίστασθαι ὑφ᾽
   v.rai.1s a.nsm   r.np.2 v.aai.2p r.as.1   cj r.ns.1 v.iai.1s   f.pp   p.g
   1181 933 1181 1181   7007 337 1609 337 337 1142 1609 4053   5319   5679

you, for I am not in the least inferior to the "super-apostles," even though I am nothing. **12**   The things that
ὑμῶν γὰρ → οὐδὲν ὑστέρησα → τῶν ˌὑπερλίαν ἀποστόλωνˌ καὶ εἰ → εἰμι οὐδέν μὲν τὰ
r.gp.2 cj   a.asn   v.aai.1s → d.gpm adv n.gpm adv cj   v.pai.1s a.nsn pl d.npn
7007 1142 5728 5728 4029   5728 3836 5663   693   2779 1623   1639 4029 3525 3836

mark an apostle — signs, wonders and miracles – were done among you with great
σημεῖα ˌτοῦ ἀποστόλουˌ τε σημείοις καὶ τέρασιν καὶ δυνάμεσιν → κατειργάσθη ἐν ὑμῖν ἐν πάσῃ
n.npn d.gsm n.gsm cj n.dpn cj n.dpn cj n.dpf   v.api.3s p.d r.dp.2 p.d a.dsf
4956 3836 693 5445 4956 2779 5469 2779 1539   2981 1877 7007 1877 4246

perseverance. **13** How were you inferior to the other churches, except that I was never a burden
ὑπομονῇ γὰρ τί ἐστιν ὃ ἡσσώθητε ὑπὲρ τὰς λοιπὰς ἐκκλησίας εἰ μὴ ὅτι ἐγὼ αὐτὸς → οὐ κατενάρκησα
n.dsf cj r.asn v.pai.3s r.asn v.api.2p p.a d.apf a.apf n.apf cj pl cj r.ns.1 r.nsm   pl v.aai.1s
5705 1142 5515 1639 4005 2273 5642 3836 3370 1711 1623 3590 4022 1609 899   4024 2915

to you? Forgive me this wrong! ¶ **14** Now I am ready to visit you for the third time, and I
→ ὑμῶν χαρίσασθε μοι ταύτην ˌτὴν ἀδικίανˌ   Ἰδοὺ → ἔχω ἑτοίμως → ἐλθεῖν πρὸς ὑμᾶς τοῦτο τρίτον ← καὶ →
r.gp.2 v.amm.2p r.ds.1 r.asf d.asf n.asf   j   v.pai.1s adv   f.aa p.a r.ap.2 r.asn adv   cj
7007 5919 1609 4047 3836 94   2627   2400 2290   2262 4639 7007 4047 5568   2779 2915

will not be a burden to you, because what I want is not your possessions but you. After all, children should
→ οὐ → καταναρκήσω γὰρ → ζητῶ οὐ ὑμῶν τὰ ἀλλὰ ὑμᾶς γὰρ ← ˌτὰ τέκναˌ ὀφείλει
pl pl   v.fai.1s cj   v.pai.1s pl r.gp.2 d.npn   cj r.ap.2 cj   d.npn n.npn v.pai.3s
2915 4024   2915 1142   2426 4024 7007 3836   247 7007 1142   3836 5451 4053

not have to save up for their parents, but parents for their children. **15** So I will very gladly spend for
οὐ → θησαυρίζειν → τοῖς γονεῦσιν ἀλλὰ ˌοἱ γονεῖςˌ → τοῖς τέκνοις δὲ ἐγὼ → → ἥδιστα δαπανήσω ὑπὲρ
pl   f.pa   d.dpm n.dpm cj d.npm n.npm   d.dpn n.dpn cj r.ns.1   adv.s v.fai.1s p.g
4024   2564   3836 1204 247 3836 1204   3836 5451 1254 1609 1251   2452 1251 5642

you everything I have and expend myself as well. If I love you more, will you love
ˌτῶν ψυχῶν ὑμῶνˌ καὶ ἐκδαπανηθήσομαι ← εἰ → ἀγαπῶν ὑμᾶς περισσοτέρως ἀγαπῶμαι
d.gpf n.gpf r.gp.2 cj v.fpi.1s   cj → pt.pa.nsm r.ap.2 adv.c   v.ppi.1s
3836 6034 7007 2779 1682   1623 26 7007 4359   26

ἐδόθη μοι σκόλοψ τῇ σαρκί, ἄγγελος Σατανᾶ, ἵνα με κολαφίζῃ, ἵνα μὴ ὑπεραίρωμαι. ⁸ ὑπὲρ τούτου τρὶς τὸν κύριον παρεκάλεσα ἵνα ἀποστῇ ἀπ᾽ ἐμοῦ. ⁹ καὶ εἴρηκέν μοι, Ἀρκεῖ σοι ἡ χάρις μου, ἡ γὰρ δύναμις ἐν ἀσθενείᾳ τελεῖται. ἥδιστα οὖν μᾶλλον καυχήσομαι ἐν ταῖς ἀσθενείαις μου, ἵνα ἐπισκηνώσῃ ἐπ᾽ ἐμὲ ἡ δύναμις τοῦ Χριστοῦ. ¹⁰ διὸ εὐδοκῶ ἐν ἀσθενείαις, ἐν ὕβρεσιν, ἐν ἀνάγκαις, ἐν διωγμοῖς καὶ στενοχωρίαις, ὑπὲρ Χριστοῦ· ὅταν γὰρ ἀσθενῶ, τότε δυνατός εἰμι.

¹²˸¹¹ Γέγονα ἄφρων, ὑμεῖς με ἠναγκάσατε. ἐγὼ γὰρ ὤφειλον ὑφ᾽ ὑμῶν συνίστασθαι· οὐδὲν γὰρ ὑστέρησα τῶν ὑπερλίαν ἀποστόλων εἰ καὶ οὐδέν εἰμι. ¹² τὰ μὲν σημεῖα τοῦ ἀποστόλου κατειργάσθη ἐν ὑμῖν ἐν πάσῃ ὑπομονῇ, σημείοις τε καὶ τέρασιν καὶ δυνάμεσιν. ¹³ τί γάρ ἐστιν ὃ ἡσσώθητε ὑπὲρ τὰς λοιπὰς ἐκκλησίας, εἰ μὴ ὅτι αὐτὸς ἐγὼ οὐ κατενάρκησα ὑμῶν; χαρίσασθέ μοι τὴν ἀδικίαν ταύτην. ¶ ¹⁴ Ἰδοὺ τρίτον τοῦτο ἑτοίμως ἔχω ἐλθεῖν πρὸς ὑμᾶς, καὶ οὐ καταναρκήσω· οὐ γὰρ ζητῶ τὰ ὑμῶν ἀλλὰ ὑμᾶς. οὐ γὰρ ὀφείλει τὰ τέκνα τοῖς γονεῦσιν θησαυρίζειν ἀλλὰ οἱ γονεῖς τοῖς τέκνοις. ¹⁵ ἐγὼ δὲ ἥδιστα δαπανήσω καὶ ἐκδαπανηθήσομαι ὑπὲρ τῶν ψυχῶν ὑμῶν. εἰ περισσοτέρως ὑμᾶς ἀγαπῶ[ν], ἧσσον ἀγαπῶμαι; ¹⁶ ἔστω δέ, ἐγὼ οὐ κατεβάρησα

me less? **16** Be that as it may, I have not been a burden to you. Yet, crafty fellow that I am, I
← ἧσσον δέ Ἔστω ← ← ← ἐγώ οὐ → → κατεβάρησα ὑμᾶς ἀλλά πανοῦργος ← → ὑπάρχων →
adv.c cj v.pam.3s r.ns.1 pl v.aai.1s r.ap.2 cj a.nsm pt.pa.nsm
2482 1254 1639 1609 2851 4024 2851 7007 247 4112 5639

caught you by trickery! **17** Did I exploit you through any of the men I sent you? **18** I urged
ἔλαβον ὑμᾶς → δόλῳ μή → → ἐπλεονέκτησα ὑμᾶς δι᾽ αὐτοῦ τινα ὧν → ἀπέσταλκα πρὸς ὑμᾶς → παρεκάλεσα
v.aai.1s r.ap.2 n.dsm pl v.aai.1s r.ap.2 p.g r.gsm.3 r.asm r.gpm v.rai.1s p.a r.ap.2 v.aai.1s
3284 7007 1515 3590 4430 7007 1328 899 5516 4005 690 4639 7007 4151

Titus to go to you and I sent our brother with him. Titus did not exploit you, did he? Did we not
Τίτον καί → συναπέστειλα τὸν ἀδελφόν ← ← Τίτος → μήτι ἐπλεονέκτησεν ὑμᾶς ← → οὐ
n.asm cj v.aai.1s d.asm n.asm n.nsm pl v.aai.3s r.ap.2 pl
5519 2779 5273 3836 81 5273 5273 5519 4430 3614 4430 7007 3614 3614 4344 4344 4024

act in the same spirit and follow the same course? ¶ **19** Have you been thinking all along that
περιεπατήσαμεν → τῷ αὐτῷ πνεύματι → οὐ τοῖς αὐτοῖς ἴχνεσιν → → → δοκεῖτε → Πάλαι ὅτι
v.aai.1p d.dsn r.dsn n.dsn pl d.dpn r.dpn n.dpn v.pai.2p adv cj
4344 3836 899 4460 4024 3836 899 2717 1506 4093 4022

we have been defending ourselves to you? We have been speaking in the sight of God as those in Christ; and
→ → → ἀπολογούμεθα → ὑμῖν λαλοῦμεν → κατέναντι → θεοῦ ἐν Χριστῷ δέ
v.pmi.1p r.dp.2 v.pai.1p p.g n.gsm p.d n.dsm cj
664 7007 3281 2978 2536 1877 5986 1254

everything we do, dear friends, is for your strengthening. **20** For I am afraid that when I come I may not find
ⸯτὰ πάνταⸯ → ἀγαπητοί ὑπὲρ ὑμῶν ⸯτῆς οἰκοδομῆςⸯ γάρ → φοβοῦμαι μή πως, → → ἐλθὼν → → οὐχ εὕρω
d.npn a.npn a.vpm p.g r.gp.2 d.gsf n.gsf cj v.ppi.1s cj pl pt.aa.nsm pl v.aas.1s
3836 4246 28 5642 7007 3836 3836 1142 5828 3590 4803 2262 2351 2351 4024 2351

you as I want you to be, and you may not find me as you want me to be. I fear that there may be
ὑμᾶς οἵους → θέλω κἀγὼ ὑμῖν → οὐ εὑρεθῶ οἷον → θέλετε μή πως
r.ap.2 r.apm v.pai.1s crasis r.dp.2 pl v.aps.1s r.asm v.pai.2p cj pl
7007 3888 2527 2743 7007 2351 4024 2351 3888 2527 3590 4803

quarreling, jealousy, outbursts of anger, factions, slander, gossip, arrogance and disorder. **21** I am afraid that
ἔρις ζῆλος → → θυμοί ἐριθεῖαι καταλαλιαί ψιθυρισμοί φυσιώσεις ἀκαταστασίαι μή
n.nsf n.nsm n.npm n.npf n.npf n.npm n.npf n.npf cj
2251 2419 2596 2249 2896 6030 5883 189 3590

when I come again my God will humble me before you, and I will be grieved over many who have
→ μου ἐλθόντος πάλιν μου ὁ θεός → ταπεινώσῃ με πρὸς ὑμᾶς καί → → → πενθήσω ← πολλοὺς τῶν →
r.gs.1 pt.aa.gsm adv r.gs.1 d.nsm n.nsm v.aas.3s r.as.1 p.a r.ap.2 cj v.aas.1s a.apm d.gpm
2262 1609 2262 4099 1609 3836 2536 5427 1609 4639 7007 2779 4291 4498 3836

sinned earlier and have not repented of the impurity, sexual sin and debauchery in which they have
προημαρτηκότων ← καί → μή μετανοησάντων ἐπὶ τῇ ἀκαθαρσίᾳ καί πορνείᾳ καί ἀσελγείᾳ ᾗ →
pt.ra.gpm cj pl pt.aa.gpm p.d d.dsf n.dsf cj n.dsf cj n.dsf r.dsf
4579 2779 3566 3590 3566 2093 3836 174 2779 4518 2779 816 4005

indulged.
ἔπραξαν
v.aai.3p
4556

Final Warnings

13:1 This will be my third visit to you. "Every matter must be established by the testimony of two or three
τοῦτο → → → Τρίτον ἔρχομαι πρὸς ὑμᾶς πᾶν ῥῆμα → σταθήσεται ἐπὶ στόματος → δύο καὶ τριῶν
r.asn adv v.pmi.1s p.a r.ap.2 a.nsn n.nsn v.fpi.3s p.g n.gsn a.gpm cj a.gpm
4047 2262 2262 2262 5568 2262 4639 7007 4246 4839 2705 2093 5125 1545 2779 5552

witnesses." **2** I already gave you a warning when I was with you the second time. I now repeat it
μαρτύρων ⸯπροείρηκα καὶ προλέγωⸯ ὡς → παρὼν ← τὸ δεύτερον ← καὶ νῦν
n.gpm v.rai.1s cj v.pai.1s pl pt.pa.nsm d.asn adv cj adv
3459 4597 2779 4625 6055 4205 3836 1311 2779 3814

while absent: On my return I will not spare those who sinned earlier or any of the
→ ἀπὼν ὅτι ἐὰν → ⸯἐλθω εἰς τὸ πάλινⸯ → → οὐ φείσομαι, τοῖς ← προημαρτηκόσιν ← καὶ πᾶσιν → τοῖς
pt.pa.nsm cj cj v.aas.1s p.a d.asn adv pl v.fmi.1s d.dpm pt.ra.dpm cj a.dpm d.dpm
583 4022 1569 2262 1650 3836 4099 5767 5767 4024 5767 3836 4579 2779 4246 3836

others, **3** since you are demanding proof that Christ is speaking through me. He is not weak in dealing with
λοιποῖς ἐπεὶ → → ζητεῖτε δοκιμὴν Χριστοῦ → ⸯτοῦ λαλοῦντοςⸯ ἐν ἐμοὶ ὃς → οὐκ ἀσθενεῖ εἰς ← ←
a.dpm cj v.pai.2p n.asf n.gsm d.gsm pt.pa.gsm p.d r.ds.1 r.nsm pl v.pai.3s p.a
3370 2075 2426 1509 5986 3836 3836 1877 1609 4005 820 4024 820 1650

ὑμᾶς· ἀλλὰ ὑπάρχων πανοῦργος δόλῳ ὑμᾶς ἔλαβον. ¹⁷ μή τινα ὧν ἀπέσταλκα πρὸς ὑμᾶς, δι᾽ αὐτοῦ ἐπλεονέκτησα ὑμᾶς; ¹⁸ παρεκάλεσα Τίτον καὶ συναπέστειλα τὸν ἀδελφόν· μήτι ἐπλεονέκτησεν ὑμᾶς Τίτος; οὐ τῷ αὐτῷ πνεύματι περιεπατήσαμεν; οὐ τοῖς αὐτοῖς ἴχνεσιν; ¶ ¹⁹ Πάλαι δοκεῖτε ὅτι ὑμῖν ἀπολογούμεθα. κατέναντι θεοῦ ἐν Χριστῷ λαλοῦμεν· τὰ δὲ πάντα, ἀγαπητοί, ὑπὲρ τῆς ὑμῶν οἰκοδομῆς. ²⁰ φοβοῦμαι γὰρ μή πως ἐλθὼν οὐχ οἵους θέλω εὕρω ὑμᾶς κἀγὼ εὑρεθῶ ὑμῖν οἷον οὐ θέλετε· μή πως ἔρις, ζῆλος, θυμοί, ἐριθεῖαι, καταλαλιαί, ψιθυρισμοί, φυσιώσεις, ἀκαταστασίαι· ²¹ μή πάλιν ἐλθόντος μου ταπεινώσῃ με ὁ θεός μου πρὸς ὑμᾶς καὶ πενθήσω πολλοὺς τῶν προημαρτηκότων καὶ μή μετανοησάντων ἐπὶ τῇ ἀκαθαρσίᾳ καὶ πορνείᾳ καὶ ἀσελγείᾳ ᾗ ἔπραξαν.

¹³:¹ Τρίτον τοῦτο ἔρχομαι πρὸς ὑμᾶς· ἐπὶ στόματος δύο μαρτύρων καὶ τριῶν σταθήσεται πᾶν ῥῆμα. ² προείρηκα καὶ προλέγω, ὡς παρὼν τὸ δεύτερον καὶ ἀπὼν νῦν, τοῖς προημαρτηκόσιν καὶ τοῖς λοιποῖς πᾶσιν, ὅτι ἐὰν ἔλθω εἰς τὸ πάλιν οὐ φείσομαι, ³ ἐπεὶ

you, but is powerful among you. **4** For *to be sure,* he was crucified in weakness, yet he lives by God's power.
ὑμᾶς ἀλλὰ → δυνατεῖ ἐν ὑμῖν γὰρ καὶ → ἐσταυρώθη ἐξ ἀσθενείας ἀλλὰ → ζῇ ἐκ θεοῦ δυνάμεως
r.ap.2 cj v.pai.3s p.d r.dp.2 cj adv v.api.3s p.g n.gsf cj v.pai.3s p.g n.gsm n.gsf
7007 247 1542 1877 7007 1142 2779 5090 1666 819 247 2409 1666 2536 1539

Likewise, we are weak in him, yet by God's power we will live with him to serve you. ¶
ᵧγὰρ καὶ ἡμεῖς → ἀσθενοῦμεν ἐν αὐτῷ ἀλλὰ ἐκ θεοῦ δυνάμεως → ζήσομεν σὺν αὐτῷ εἰς ὑμᾶς
cj adv r.np.1 v.pai.1p p.d r.dsm.3 cj p.g n.gsm n.gsf v.fai.1p p.d r.dsm.3 p.a r.ap.2
1142 2779 7005 820 1877 899 247 1666 2536 1539 2409 5250 899 1650 7007

5 Examine yourselves to see whether you are in the faith; test yourselves. Do you not realize that
πειράζετε Ἑαυτοὺς εἰ → ἐστὲ ἐν τῇ πίστει δοκιμάζετε ἑαυτοὺς ἢ ↱ ↱ ἑαυτοὺς οὐκ ἐπιγινώσκετε ὅτι
v.pam.2p r.apm.2 cj v.pai.2p p.d d.dsf n.dsf v.pam.2p r.apm.2 cj r.apm.2 pl v.pai.2p cj
4279 1571 1623 1639 1877 3836 4411 1507 1571 2445 2105 2105 1571 4024 2105 4022

Christ Jesus is in you – unless, of course, you fail the test? **6** And I trust that you will discover that
Χριστὸς Ἰησοῦς ἐν ὑμῖν ᵧεἰ μήτιᵧ → ᵧἀδόκιμοι ἐστεᵧ ← ← δὲ →ἐλπίζω ὅτι → → γνώσεσθε ὅτι
n.nsm n.nsm p.d r.dp.2 cj cj a.npm v.pai.2p cj v.pai.1s cj v.fmi.2p cj
5986 2652 1877 7007 1623 3614 99 1639 1254 1827 4022 1182 4022

we have not failed the test. **7** Now we pray to God that you will not do anything wrong. Not that
ἡμεῖς ἐσμεν οὐκ ἀδόκιμοι ← ← δὲ → εὐχόμεθα πρὸς ᵧτὸν θεόνᵧ ὑμᾶς → μὴ ποιῆσαι μηδέν κακὸν οὐχ ἵνα
r.np.1 v.pai.1p pl a.npm cj v.pmi.1p p.a d.asm n.asm r.ap.2 pl f.aa a.asn a.asn pl cj
7005 1639 4024 99 1254 2377 4639 3836 2536 7007 4472 3590 4472 3594 2805 4024 2671

people will see that we have stood the test but that you will do what is right even though we may seem
→ φανῶμεν ἡμεῖς δόκιμοι ← ← ἀλλ' ἵνα ὑμεῖς → ποιῆτε τὸ καλὸν δὲ ← ἡμεῖς → ὦμεν
v.aps.1p r.np.1 a.npm cj cj r.np.1 v.pas.2p d.asn a.asn cj r.np.1 v.pas.1p
5743 7005 1511 247 2671 7007 4472 3836 2819 1254 7005 1639

to have failed. **8** For we cannot do anything against the truth, but only for the truth. **9** We are glad
ὡς ἀδόκιμοι γὰρ ᵧοὐ δυνάμεθαᵧ → τι κατὰ τῆς ἀληθείας ἀλλὰ ὑπὲρ τῆς ἀληθείας γὰρ χαίρομεν
pl a.npm cj pl v.ppi.1p r.asn p.g d.gsf n.gsf cj p.g d.gsf n.gsf cj v.pai.1p
6055 99 1142 4024 1538 5516 2848 3836 237 247 5642 3836 237 1142 5897

whenever we are weak but you are strong; and our prayer is for your perfection. **10** This is why
ὅταν ἡμεῖς→ἀσθενῶμενδὲ ὑμεῖςἦτε δυνατοὶκαὶ → εὐχόμεθατοῦτο ← ὑμῶνᵧτὴν κατάρτισινᵧ ᵧΔιὰτοῦτοᵧ ←
cj r.np.1 v.pas.1p cj r.np.2 v.pas.2p a.npm adv v.pmi.1p r.asn r.gp.2 d.asf n.asf p.a r.asn
4020 7005 820 1254 7007 1639 1543 2779 2377 2377 7007 3836 2937 1328 4047

I write these things whenIam absent,that whenI comeI maynot havetobe harshinmy use of
→ γράφω ταῦτα ← → → ἀπὼνἵνα → παρὼν μὴ → ἀποτόμως→ χρήσωμαικατὰ
v.pai.1s r.apn pt.pa.nsmcj pt.pa.nsm pl adv v.ams.1s p.a
1211 4047 583 2671 4205 3590 705 5968 2848

authority – the authority the Lord gave me for building you up, not for tearing you down.
ᵧτὴνἐξουσίανᵧ ἣν → ὁ κύριος ἔδωκεν μοι εἰς οἰκοδομὴν ← καὶ οὐκ εἰς καθαίρεσιν ←
d.asf n.asf r.asf d.nsm n.nsm v.aai.3s r.ds.1 p.a n.asf cj pl p.a n.asf
3836 2026 4005 3836 3261 1443 1609 1650 3869 2779 4024 1650 2746

Final Greetings

13:11 Finally, brothers, good-by. Aim for perfection, listen to my appeal, be of one mind, live in
Λοιπόν ἀδελφοί χαίρετε → → καταρτίζεσθε → → παρακαλεῖσθε ↱ ← ᵧτὸ αὐτὸᵧ φρονεῖτε → →
adv n.vpm v.pam.2p v.ppm.2p v.ppm.2p d.asn r.asn v.pam.2p
3370 81 5897 2936 4151 5858 5858 3836 899 5858

peace. And the God of love and peace will be with you. ¶ **12** Greet one another with a holy
εἰρηνεύετε καὶ ὁ θεὸς → ᵧτῆς ἀγάπηςᵧ καὶ εἰρήνης → ἔσται μεθ' ὑμῶν Ἀσπάσασθε ἀλλήλους ← ἐν ἁγίῳ
v.pam.2p cj d.nsm n.nsm d.gsf n.gsf cj n.gsf v.fmi.3s p.g r.gp.2 v.amm.2p r.apm p.d a.dsn
1644 2779 3836 2536 3836 27 2779 1645 1639 3552 7007 832 253 1877 41

kiss. **13** All the saints send their greetings. ¶ **14** May the grace of the Lord Jesus Christ, and the love
φιλήματι πάντες οἱ ἅγιοι → Ἀσπάζονται ὑμᾶς Ἡ χάρις → τοῦ κυρίου Ἰησοῦ Χριστοῦ καὶ ἡ ἀγάπη
n.dsn a.npm d.npm a.npm v.pmi.3p r.ap.2 d.nsf n.nsf d.gsm n.gsm n.gsm n.gsm cj d.nsf n.nsf
5799 4246 3836 41 832 7007 3836 5921 3836 3261 2652 5986 2779 3836 27

of God, and the fellowship of the Holy Spirit be with you all.
→ ᵧτοῦ θεοῦᵧ καὶ ἡ κοινωνία → τοῦ ἁγίου πνεύματος μετὰ ὑμῶν πάντων
d.gsm n.gsm cj d.nsf n.nsf d.gsn a.gsn n.gsn p.g r.gp.2 a.gpm
3836 2536 2779 3836 3126 3836 41 4460 3552 7007 4246

δοκιμὴν ζητεῖτε τοῦ ἐν ἐμοὶ λαλοῦντος Χριστοῦ, ὃς εἰς ὑμᾶς οὐκ ἀσθενεῖ ἀλλὰ δυνατεῖ ἐν ὑμῖν. 4 καὶ γὰρ ἐσταυρώθη ἐξ ἀσθενείας, ἀλλὰ ζῇ ἐκ δυνάμεως θεοῦ. καὶ γὰρ ἡμεῖς ἀσθενοῦμεν ἐν αὐτῷ, ἀλλὰ ζήσομεν σὺν αὐτῷ ἐκ δυνάμεως θεοῦ εἰς ὑμᾶς ¶ 5 Ἑαυτοὺς πειράζετε εἰ ἐστὲ ἐν τῇ πίστει, ἑαυτοὺς δοκιμάζετε· ἢ οὐκ ἐπιγινώσκετε ἑαυτοὺς ὅτι Χριστὸς Ἰησοῦς ἐν ὑμῖν; εἰ μήτι ἀδόκιμοί ἐστε. 6 ἐλπίζω δὲ ὅτι γνώσεσθε ὅτι ἡμεῖς οὐκ ἐσμὲν ἀδόκιμοι. 7 εὐχόμεθα δὲ πρὸς τὸν θεὸν μὴ ποιῆσαι ὑμᾶς κακὸν μηδέν, οὐχ ἵνα ἡμεῖς δόκιμοι φανῶμεν, ἀλλ' ἵνα ὑμεῖς τὸ καλὸν ποιῆτε, ἡμεῖς δὲ ὡς ἀδόκιμοι ὦμεν. 8 οὐ γὰρ δυνάμεθά τι κατὰ τῆς ἀληθείας ἀλλὰ ὑπὲρ τῆς ἀληθείας. 9 χαίρομεν γὰρ ὅταν ἡμεῖς ἀσθενῶμεν, ὑμεῖς δὲ δυνατοὶ ἦτε· τοῦτο καὶ εὐχόμεθα, τὴν ὑμῶν κατάρτισιν. 10 διὰ τοῦτο ταῦτα ἀπὼν γράφω, ἵνα παρὼν μὴ ἀποτόμως χρήσωμαι κατὰ τὴν ἐξουσίαν ἣν ὁ κύριος ἔδωκέν μοι εἰς οἰκοδομὴν καὶ οὐκ εἰς καθαίρεσιν.

13:11 Λοιπόν, ἀδελφοί, χαίρετε, καταρτίζεσθε, παρακαλεῖσθε, τὸ αὐτὸ φρονεῖτε, εἰρηνεύετε, καὶ ὁ θεὸς τῆς ἀγάπης καὶ εἰρήνης ἔσται μεθ' ὑμῶν. ¶ 12 ἀσπάσασθε ἀλλήλους ἐν ἁγίῳ φιλήματι. 13 ἀσπάζονται ὑμᾶς οἱ ἅγιοι πάντες. ¶ 14 Ἡ χάρις τοῦ κυρίου Ἰησοῦ Χριστοῦ καὶ ἡ ἀγάπη τοῦ θεοῦ καὶ ἡ κοινωνία τοῦ ἁγίου πνεύματος μετὰ πάντων ὑμῶν.

Galatians

1:1 Paul, an apostle – sent not from men nor by man, but by Jesus Christ and God the Father, who
Παῦλος ἀπόστολος οὐκ ἀπ᾽ ἀνθρώπων οὐδὲ δι᾽ ἀνθρώπου ἀλλὰ διὰ Ἰησοῦ Χριστοῦ καὶ θεοῦ πατρὸς τοῦ
n.nsm n.nsm pl p.g n.gpm cj p.g n.gsm cj p.g n.gsm n.gsm cj n.gsm n.gsm d.gsm
4263 693 4024 608 476 4028 1328 476 247 1328 2652 5986 2779 2536 4252 3836

raised him from the dead – **2** and all the brothers with me, ¶ To the churches in Galatia: ¶
ἐγείραντος αὐτὸν ἐκ νεκρῶν καὶ πάντες οἱ ἀδελφοὶ σὺν ἐμοὶ ταῖς ἐκκλησίαις ⟶ ⌐τῆς Γαλατίας⌐
pt.aa.gsm r.asm.3 p.g a.gpm cj a.npm d.npm n.npm p.d r.ds.1 d.dpf n.dpf d.gsf n.gsf
1586 899 1666 3738 2779 4246 3836 81 5250 1609 3836 1711 3836 1130

3 Grace and peace to you from God our Father and the Lord Jesus Christ, **4** who gave himself for our
χάρις καὶ εἰρήνη ὑμῖν ἀπὸ θεοῦ ἡμῶν πατρὸς καὶ κυρίου Ἰησοῦ Χριστοῦ τοῦ δόντος ἑαυτὸν ὑπὲρ ἡμῶν
n.nsf cj n.nsf r.dp.2 p.g n.gsm r.gp.1 n.gsm cj n.gsm n.gsm n.gsm d.gsm pt.aa.gsm r.asm.3 p.g r.gp.1
5921 2779 1645 7007 608 2536 7005 4252 2779 3261 2652 5986 3836 1443 1571 5642 7005

sins to rescue us from the present evil age, according to the will of our God and
⌐τῶν ἁμαρτιῶν⌐ ὅπως ἐξέληται ἡμᾶς ἐκ τοῦ ⌐τοῦ ἐνεστῶτος⌐ πονηροῦ αἰῶνος κατὰ ⟵ τὸ θέλημα ⟶ ἡμῶν ⌐τοῦ θεοῦ⌐ καὶ
d.gpf n.gpf cj v.ams.3s rap.1 p.g d.gsm d.gsm pt.ra.gsm a.gsm n.gsm p.a d.asn n.asn r.gp.1 d.gsm n.gsm cj
3836 281 3968 1975 7005 1666 3836 3836 1931 4505 172 2848 3836 2525 2536 7005 3836 2536 2779

Father, **5** to whom be glory *for ever* *and ever.* Amen.
πατρὸς ᾧ ἡ δόξα εἰς ⌐τοὺς αἰῶνας⌐ ⌐τῶν αἰώνων⌐ ἀμήν
n.gsm r.dsm d.nsf n.nsf p.a d.apm n.apm d.gpm n.gpm pl
4252 4005 3836 1518 1650 3836 172 3836 172 297

No Other Gospel

1:6 I am astonished that you are so quickly deserting the one who called you by the grace of
⟶ ⟶ Θαυμάζω ὅτι οὕτως ⟶ ⟶ ταχέως μετατίθεσθε ἀπὸ τοῦ ⟵ ⟵ καλέσαντος ὑμᾶς ἐν χάριτι ⟶
v.pai.1s cj adv adv v.ppi.2p p.g d.gsm pt.aa.gsm r.ap.2 p.d n.dsf
2513 4022 4048 5441 3572 608 3836 2813 7007 1877 5921

Christ and are turning to a different gospel – **7** which is *really no gospel at all.* Evidently some people are
Χριστοῦ ⟶ εἰς ἕτερον εὐαγγέλιον ὃ ἔστιν οὐκ ἄλλο εἰ μὴ τινές ⟵ εἰσιν
n.gsm p.a r.asn n.asn r.nsn v.pai.3s pl r.nsn cj pl r.npm v.pai.3p
5986 1650 2283 2295 4005 1639 4024 257 1623 3590 5516 1639

throwing you into confusion and are trying to pervert the gospel of Christ. **8** But even if we or
⟶ ὑμᾶς ⟶ ⌐οἱ ταράσσοντες⌐ καὶ ⟶ θέλοντες μεταστρέψαι τὸ εὐαγγέλιον ⟶ ⌐τοῦ Χριστοῦ⌐ ἀλλὰ καὶ ἐὰν ἡμεῖς ἢ
r.ap.2 d.npm pt.pa.npm cj pt.pa.npm f.aa d.asn n.asn d.gsm n.gsm cj adv cj r.np.1 cj
5429 7007 3836 5429 2779 2527 3570 3836 2295 3836 5986 247 2779 1569 7005 2445

an angel from heaven should preach a gospel other than the one we preached to you, let him be
ἄγγελος ἐξ οὐρανοῦ ⟶ εὐαγγελίζηται ⟵ ⟵ ὑμῖν παρ᾽ ὃ εὐηγγελισάμεθα ⟶ ὑμῖν ⟶ ἔστω
n.nsm p.g n.gsm v.pms.3s r.dp.2 p.a r.asn v.ami.1p r.dp.2 v.pam.3s
34 1666 4041 2294 7007 4123 4005 2294 7007 1639

eternally condemned! **9** As we have already said, so now I say again: If anybody is preaching to you a
⟶ ἀνάθεμα ὡς ⟶ ⟶ ⟶ προειρήκαμεν καὶ ἄρτι ⟶ λέγω πάλιν εἴ τις ⟶ εὐαγγελίζεται ⟶ ὑμᾶς
n.nsn cj v.rai.1p cj adv v.pai.1s adv cj r.nsm v.pmi.3s r.ap.2
353 6055 4597 2779 785 3306 4099 1623 5516 2294 7007

gospel other than what you accepted, let him be eternally condemned! ¶ **10** Am I now trying to win the
⟵ παρ᾽ ⟵ ὃ ⟶ παρελάβετε ⟶ ἔστω ⟶ ἀνάθεμα γὰρ ⟶ ⟶ Ἄρτι πείθω ⟵ ⟵ ⟶
p.a r.asn v.aai.2p v.pam.3s n.nsn cj adv v.pai.1s
2294 4123 4005 4161 1639 353 1142 4275 4275 785 4275

approval of men, or of God? Or am I trying to please men? If I were still trying to please men,
⟵ ἀνθρώπους ἢ ⌐τὸν θεόν⌐ ἢ ⟶ ζητῶ ⟶ ἀρέσκειν ἀνθρώποις εἰ ⟶ ἔτι ⟶ ⟶ ἤρεσκον ἀνθρώποις
n.apm cj d.asm n.asm cj v.pai.1s f.pa n.dpm cj adv v.iai.1s n.dpm
476 2445 3836 2536 2445 2426 743 476 1623 743 743 2285 743 476

I would not be a servant of Christ.
⟶ ἂν οὐκ ἤμην δοῦλος ⟶ Χριστοῦ
pl pl v.imi.1s n.nsm n.gsm
1639 323 4024 1639 1529 5986

1:1 Παῦλος ἀπόστολος οὐκ ἀπ᾽ ἀνθρώπων οὐδὲ δι᾽ ἀνθρώπου ἀλλὰ διὰ Ἰησοῦ Χριστοῦ καὶ θεοῦ πατρὸς τοῦ ἐγείραντος αὐτὸν ἐκ νεκρῶν, **2** καὶ οἱ σὺν ἐμοὶ πάντες ἀδελφοὶ ¶ ταῖς ἐκκλησίαις τῆς Γαλατίας, ¶ **3** χάρις ὑμῖν καὶ εἰρήνη ἀπὸ θεοῦ πατρὸς ἡμῶν καὶ κυρίου Ἰησοῦ Χριστοῦ **4** τοῦ δόντος ἑαυτὸν ὑπὲρ τῶν ἁμαρτιῶν ἡμῶν, ὅπως ἐξέληται ἡμᾶς ἐκ τοῦ αἰῶνος τοῦ ἐνεστῶτος πονηροῦ κατὰ τὸ θέλημα τοῦ θεοῦ καὶ πατρὸς ἡμῶν, **5** ᾧ ἡ δόξα εἰς τοὺς αἰῶνας τῶν αἰώνων, ἀμήν.
1:6 Θαυμάζω ὅτι οὕτως ταχέως μετατίθεσθε ἀπὸ τοῦ καλέσαντος ὑμᾶς ἐν χάριτι [Χριστοῦ] εἰς ἕτερον εὐαγγέλιον, **7** ὃ οὐκ ἔστιν ἄλλο, εἰ μή τινές εἰσιν οἱ ταράσσοντες ὑμᾶς καὶ θέλοντες μεταστρέψαι τὸ εὐαγγέλιον τοῦ Χριστοῦ. **8** ἀλλὰ καὶ ἐὰν ἡμεῖς ἢ ἄγγελος ἐξ οὐρανοῦ εὐαγγελίζηται [ὑμῖν] παρ᾽ ὃ εὐηγγελισάμεθα ὑμῖν, ἀνάθεμα ἔστω. **9** ὡς προειρήκαμεν καὶ ἄρτι πάλιν λέγω, εἴ τις ὑμᾶς εὐαγγελίζεται παρ᾽ ὃ παρελάβετε, ἀνάθεμα ἔστω. ¶ **10** Ἄρτι γὰρ ἀνθρώπους πείθω ἢ τὸν θεόν; ἢ ζητῶ ἀνθρώποις ἀρέσκειν; εἰ ἔτι ἀνθρώποις ἤρεσκον, Χριστοῦ δοῦλος οὐκ ἂν ἤμην.

Paul Called by God

1:11 I want you to know, brothers, that the gospel I preached is not *something that*
γὰρ → → ὑμῖν → Γνωρίζω ἀδελφοί, τὸ εὐαγγέλιον ὑπ᾽ ἐμοῦ τὸ εὐαγγελισθὲν ὅτι ἔστιν οὐκ
cj r.dp.2 v.pai.1s n.vpm d.asn n.asn r.gs.1 d.asn pt.ap.asn cj v.pai.3s pl
1142 1192 1192 7007 1192 81 3836 2295 5679 1609 3836 2294 4022 1639 4024

man made up. **12** I did not receive it from any man, nor was I taught it; rather, I received it
κατὰ ἄνθρωπον· γὰρ ἐγὼ οὐδὲ παρέλαβον αὐτὸ παρὰ ἀνθρώπου οὔτε → → ἐδιδάχθην ἀλλὰ
p.a n.asm cj r.ns.1 cj v.aai.1s r.asn.3 p.g n.gsm cj v.api.1s cj
2848 476 1142 1609 4028 4161 899 4123 476 4046 1438 247

by revelation from Jesus Christ. ¶ **13** For you have heard of my previous way of life in
δι᾽ ἀποκαλύψεως → Ἰησοῦ Χριστοῦ. γὰρ → → Ἠκούσατε ← ἐμὴν ποτε → → τὴν ἀναστροφήν, ἐν
p.g n.gsf n.gsm n.gsm cj v.aai.2p r.asf.1 adv d.asf n.asf p.d
1328 637 2652 5986 1142 201 1847 4537 3836 419 1877

Judaism, how intensely I persecuted the church of God and tried to destroy it. **14** I was
τῷ Ἰουδαϊσμῷ ὅτι → καθ᾽ ὑπερβολὴν → ἐδίωκον τὴν ἐκκλησίαν → τοῦ θεοῦ καὶ → ἐπόρθουν αὐτήν καὶ →
d.dsm n.dsm cj p.a n.asf v.iai.1s d.asf n.asf d.gsm n.gsm cj v.iai.1s r.asf.3 cj
3836 2682 4022 2848 5651 1503 3836 1711 3836 2536 2779 4514 899 2779

advancing in Judaism beyond many Jews of my own age and was extremely zealous for the
προέκοπτον ἐν τῷ Ἰουδαϊσμῷ ὑπὲρ πολλοὺς συνηλικιώτας ἐν μου τῷ γένει ὑπάρχων περισσοτέρως ζηλωτὴς → τῶν
v.iai.1s p.d d.dsm n.dsm p.a a.apm n.apm p.d r.gs.1 d.dsn n.dsn pt.pa.nsm adv.c n.nsm d.gpf
4621 1877 3836 2682 5642 4498 5312 1877 1609 3836 1169 5639 4359 2421 3836

traditions of my fathers. **15** But when God, who set me apart from birth and called me by his
παραδόσεων → μου πατρικῶν δὲ Ὅτε ὁ θεὸς ὁ με ἀφορίσας ἐκ κοιλίας μητρός μου καὶ καλέσας διὰ αὐτοῦ
n.gpf r.gs.1 a.gpf cj cj d.nsm n.nsm d.nsm r.as.1 pt.aa.nsm p.g n.gsf n.gsf r.gs.1 cj pt.aa.nsm p.g r.gsm.3
4142 1609 4257 1254 4021 3836 2536 3836 928 1609 928 1666 3120 3613 1609 2779 2813 1328 899

grace, was pleased **16** to reveal his Son in me so that I might preach him among the Gentiles,
τῆς χάριτος, → εὐδόκησεν → ἀποκαλύψαι αὐτοῦ τὸν υἱὸν ἐν ἐμοί ἵνα ← → εὐαγγελίζωμαι αὐτὸν ἐν τοῖς ἔθνεσιν
d.gsf n.gsf v.aai.3s f.aa r.gsm.3 d.asm n.asm p.d r.ds.1 cj v.pms.1s r.asm.3 p.d d.dpn n.dpn
3836 5921 2305 636 899 3836 5626 1877 1609 2671 2294 899 1877 3836 1620

I did not consult any man, **17** nor did I go up to Jerusalem to see those who were apostles
→ οὐ προσανεθέμην → σαρκὶ καὶ αἵματι, οὐδὲ → ἀνῆλθον εἰς Ἱεροσόλυμα πρὸς τοὺς ← ἀποστόλους
pl pl v.ami.1s n.dsf cj n.dsn cj v.aai.1s p.a n.apn p.a d.apm n.apm
4651 4651 4024 4651 4922 2779 135 4028 456 1650 2642 4639 3836 693

before I was, but I went immediately into Arabia and later returned to Damascus. ¶ **18** Then after
πρὸ ἐμοῦ ἀλλὰ → ἀπῆλθον εὐθέως εἰς Ἀραβίαν καὶ πάλιν ὑπέστρεψα εἰς Δαμασκόν. Ἔπειτα μετὰ
p.g r.gs.1 cj v.aai.1s adv p.a n.asf cj adv v.aai.1s p.a n.asf adv p.a
4574 1609 247 599 2311 1650 728 2779 4099 5715 1650 1242 2083 3552

three years, I went up to Jerusalem to get acquainted with Peter and stayed with him fifteen days. **19** I
τρία ἔτη → ἀνῆλθον ← εἰς Ἱεροσόλυμα → → ἱστορῆσαι ← Κηφᾶν καὶ ἐπέμεινα πρὸς αὐτὸν δεκαπέντε ἡμέρας δὲ →
a.apn n.apn v.aai.1s p.a n.apn f.aa n.asm cj v.aai.1s p.a r.asm.3 a.apf n.apf cj
5552 2291 456 1650 2642 2707 3064 2779 2152 4639 899 1278 2465 1254

saw none of the other apostles – only James, the Lord's brother. **20** I assure you before God that
εἶδον οὐκ → τῶν ἕτερον ἀποστόλων εἰ μὴ Ἰάκωβον τὸν τοῦ κυρίου, ἀδελφὸν δὲ ἰδοὺ ἐνώπιον τοῦ θεοῦ ὅτι
v.aai.1s pl d.gpm r.asm n.gpm cj pl n.asm d.asm d.gsm n.gsm n.asm cj j p.g d.gsm n.gsm cj
1625 4024 3836 2283 693 1623 3590 2610 3836 3836 3261 81 1254 2627 1967 3836 2536 4022

what I am writing you is no lie. **21** Later I went to Syria and Cilicia. **22** I was
ἃ → → γράφω ὑμῖν οὐ ψεύδομαι. Ἔπειτα ἦλθον εἰς τὰ κλίματα τῆς Συρίας, καὶ τῆς Κιλικίας· δὲ → ἤμην
r.apn v.pai.1s r.dp.2 pl v.pmi.1s adv v.aai.1s p.a d.apn n.apn d.gsf n.gsf cj d.gsf n.gsf cj v.imi.1s
4005 1211 7007 6017 4024 6017 2083 2262 1650 3836 3107 3836 5353 2779 3836 3070 1254 1639

personally unknown to the churches of Judea that are in Christ. **23** They only heard the
τῷ προσώπῳ ἀγνοούμενος → ταῖς ἐκκλησίαις τῆς Ἰουδαίας, ταῖς ἐν Χριστῷ δὲ → μόνον ἀκούοντες ἦσαν
d.dsn n.dsn pt.pp.nsm d.dpf n.dpf d.gsf n.gsf d.dpf p.d n.dsm cj adv pt.pa.npm v.iai.3p
3836 4725 51 3836 1711 3836 2677 3836 1877 5986 1254 3667 201 1639

report: "The man who formerly persecuted us is now preaching the faith he once tried to destroy."
ὅτι ὁ ← ποτε διώκων ἡμᾶς → νῦν εὐαγγελίζεται τὴν πίστιν ἣν ποτε → ἐπόρθει
cj d.nsm adv pt.pa.nsm r.ap.1 adv v.pmi.3s d.asf n.asf r.asf adv v.iai.3s
4022 3836 4537 1503 7005 2294 3814 2294 3836 4411 4005 4514 4537 4514

1:11 Γνωρίζω γὰρ ὑμῖν, ἀδελφοί, τὸ εὐαγγέλιον τὸ εὐαγγελισθὲν ὑπ᾽ ἐμοῦ ὅτι οὐκ ἔστιν κατὰ ἄνθρωπον· **12** οὐδὲ γὰρ ἐγὼ παρὰ ἀνθρώπου παρέλαβον αὐτὸ οὔτε ἐδιδάχθην ἀλλὰ δι᾽ ἀποκαλύψεως Ἰησοῦ Χριστοῦ. ¶ **13** Ἠκούσατε γὰρ τὴν ἐμὴν ἀναστροφήν ποτε ἐν τῷ Ἰουδαϊσμῷ, ὅτι καθ᾽ ὑπερβολὴν ἐδίωκον τὴν ἐκκλησίαν τοῦ θεοῦ καὶ ἐπόρθουν αὐτήν, **14** καὶ προέκοπτον ἐν τῷ Ἰουδαϊσμῷ ὑπὲρ πολλοὺς συνηλικιώτας ἐν τῷ γένει μου, περισσοτέρως ζηλωτὴς ὑπάρχων τῶν πατρικῶν μου παραδόσεων. **15** ὅτε δὲ εὐδόκησεν [ὁ θεὸς] ὁ ἀφορίσας με ἐκ κοιλίας μητρός μου καὶ καλέσας διὰ τῆς χάριτος αὐτοῦ **16** ἀποκαλύψαι τὸν υἱὸν αὐτοῦ ἐν ἐμοί, ἵνα εὐαγγελίζωμαι αὐτὸν ἐν τοῖς ἔθνεσιν, εὐθέως οὐ προσανεθέμην σαρκὶ καὶ αἵματι **17** οὐδὲ ἀνῆλθον εἰς Ἱεροσόλυμα πρὸς τοὺς πρὸ ἐμοῦ ἀποστόλους, ἀλλὰ ἀπῆλθον εἰς Ἀραβίαν καὶ πάλιν ὑπέστρεψα εἰς Δαμασκόν. ¶ **18** Ἔπειτα μετὰ ἔτη τρία ἀνῆλθον εἰς Ἱεροσόλυμα ἱστορῆσαι Κηφᾶν καὶ ἐπέμεινα πρὸς αὐτὸν ἡμέρας δεκαπέντε, **19** ἕτερον δὲ τῶν ἀποστόλων οὐκ εἶδον εἰ μὴ Ἰάκωβον τὸν ἀδελφὸν τοῦ κυρίου. **20** ἃ δὲ γράφω ὑμῖν, ἰδοὺ ἐνώπιον τοῦ θεοῦ ὅτι οὐ ψεύδομαι. **21** ἔπειτα ἦλθον εἰς τὰ κλίματα τῆς Συρίας καὶ τῆς Κιλικίας· **22** ἤμην δὲ ἀγνοούμενος τῷ προσώπῳ ταῖς ἐκκλησίαις τῆς Ἰουδαίας ταῖς ἐν Χριστῷ. **23** μόνον δὲ ἀκούοντες ἦσαν ὅτι Ὁ διώκων ἡμᾶς ποτε νῦν εὐαγγελίζεται τὴν πίστιν ἥν ποτε ἐπόρθει, **24** καὶ ἐδόξαζον ἐν ἐμοὶ τὸν θεόν.

24 And they praised God because of me.
καὶ → ἐδόξαζον ⸢τὸν θεὸν⸣ ἐν ← ἐμοὶ
cj   v.iai.3p   d.asm n.asm   p.d   r.ds.1
2779   1519   3836 2536   1877   1609

Paul Accepted by the Apostles

2:1 Fourteen years later I went up again to Jerusalem, this time with Barnabas. I took
Ἔπειτα ⸢διὰ δεκατεσσάρων⸣ ἐτῶν → ἀνέβην ← πάλιν εἰς Ἱεροσόλυμα μετὰ Βαρναβᾶ → συμπαραλαβὼν
adv   p.g   a.gpn   n.gpn   v.aai.1s   adv   p.a   n.apn   p.g   n.gsm   pt.aa.nsm
2083   1328   1280   2291   326   4099   1650   2642   3552   982   5221

Titus along also. **2** I went in response to a revelation and set before them the gospel that I preach
Τίτον ↰ καὶ δὲ → ἀνέβην κατὰ ← ← ἀποκάλυψιν καὶ ἀνεθέμην ← αὐτοῖς τὸ εὐαγγέλιον ὃ → κηρύσσω
n.asm   adv   cj   v.aai.1s   p.a   n.asf   cj   v.ami.1s   r.dpm.3   d.asn n.asn   r.asn   v.pai.1s
5519   5221   2779   1254   326   2848   637   2779   423   899   3836 2295   4005   3062

among the Gentiles. But I did this privately to those who seemed to be leaders, for fear that I was running
ἐν τοῖς ἔθνεσιν δὲ → → ⸢κατ᾽ ἰδίαν⸣ τοῖς ← δοκοῦσιν μή πως → → τρέχω
p.d   d.dpn n.dpn   cj   p.a   a.asf   d.dpm   pt.pa.dpm   cj   pl   v.pas.1s
1877   3836 1620   1254   2848 2625   3836   1506   3590 4803   5556

or had run my race in vain. **3** Yet not even Titus, who was with me, was compelled to be circumcised, even
ἢ → ἔδραμον ← ← εἰς κενὸν ἀλλ᾽ οὐδὲ ← Τίτος ὁ σὺν ἐμοὶ ἠναγκάσθη → περιτμηθῆναι
cj   v.aai.1s   p.a a.asn   cj   adv   n.nsm n.nsm   p.d r.ds.1   v.api.3s   f.ap
2445   5556   1650 3031   247   4028   5519 3836   5250 337   337   4362

though he was a Greek. **4** This matter arose because some false brothers had infiltrated
→ ὢν Ἕλλην δὲ → → διὰ οἵτινες → ⸢τοὺς παρεισάκτους ψευδαδέλφους⸣ → παρεισῆλθον
pt.pa.nsm   n.nsm   cj   p.a   r.npm   d.apm a.apm   n.apm   v.aai.3p
1639   1818   1254   1328   4015   3836 4207   6012   4209

our ranks to spy on the freedom we have in Christ Jesus and to make us slaves. **5** We
← → κατασκοπῆσαι ← τὴν ἐλευθερίαν ἡμῶν ἣν → ἔχομεν ἐν Χριστῷ Ἰησοῦ ἵνα → ἡμᾶς καταδουλώσουσιν
f.aa   d.asf n.asf   r.gp.1 r.asf   v.pai.1p   p.d n.dsm   n.dsm   cj   r.ap.1   v.fai.3p
2945   3836 1800   7005 4005   2400   1877 5986   2652   2671   7005   2871   1634

did not give in to them for a moment, so that the truth of the gospel might remain with you. ¶
→ οὐδὲ ⸢εἴξαμεν τῇ ὑποταγῇ⸣ ← οἷς πρὸς ὥραν ἵνα → ἡ ἀλήθεια → τοῦ εὐαγγελίου → διαμείνῃ πρὸς ὑμᾶς
adv   v.aai.1p   d.dsf n.dsf   r.dpm   p.a   n.asf   cj   d.nsf n.nsf   d.gsn n.gsn   v.aas.3s   p.a r.ap.2
1634   4028   1634   3836 5717   4005   4639   6052   2671   3836 237   3836 2295   1373   4639 7007

6 *As for* those who seemed to be important – whatever they were makes no difference to me;
δὲ Ἀπὸ τῶν δοκούντων εἶναι τι ὁποῖοι ἦσαν ποτε → οὐδέν διαφέρει → μοι
cj   p.g   d.gpm   pt.pa.gpm   f.pa   r.asn   r.npm   v.iai.3p   pl   a.asn   v.pai.3s   r.ds.1
1254   608   3836   1506   1639   5516   3961   1639   4537 1422   4029 1422   1609

God does not judge by external appearance – those men added nothing to my message.
⸢ὁ θεὸς⸣ → οὐ λαμβάνει ← ⸢πρόσωπον ἀνθρώπου⸣ γὰρ οἱ δοκοῦντες προσανέθεντο οὐδὲν → ἐμοὶ
d.nsm n.nsm   pl   v.pai.3s   n.asn   n.gsm   cj   d.npm   pt.pa.npm   v.ami.3p   a.asn   r.ds.1
3836 2536   3284   4024 3284   4725   476   1142   3836   1506   4651   4029   1609

7 On the contrary, they saw that I had been entrusted with the task of preaching the gospel to the
ἀλλὰ → τοὐναντίον ἰδόντες ὅτι → → πεπίστευμαι ← τὸ εὐαγγέλιον → τῆς
cj   crasis   pt.aa.npm   cj   v.rpi.1s   d.asn n.asn   d.gsf
247   5539   1625   4022   4409   3836 2295   3836

Gentiles, just as Peter had been to the Jews. **8** For God, who was at work in the ministry of Peter as an
ἀκροβυστίας καθὼς ← Πέτρος → τῆς περιτομῆς γὰρ ὁ ← ← ἐνεργήσας ← Πέτρῳ εἰς
n.gsf   cj   n.nsm   d.gsf n.gsf   cj   d.nsm   pt.aa.nsm   n.dsm   p.a
213   2777   4377   3836 4364   1142 3836   1919   4377   1650

apostle to the Jews, was also at work in my ministry as an apostle to the Gentiles. **9** James, Peter
ἀποστολὴν → τῆς περιτομῆς → καὶ ἐνήργησεν ← ἐμοὶ εἰς τὰ ἔθνη καὶ Ἰάκωβος καὶ Κηφᾶς
n.asf   d.gsf n.gsf   adv   v.aai.3s   r.ds.1   p.a d.apn n.apn   cj   n.nsm   cj   n.nsm
692   3836 4364   1919   1919   1609   1650 3836 1620   2779 2610   2779 3064

and John, those reputed to be pillars, gave me and Barnabas the right hand of fellowship when they
καὶ Ἰωάννης οἱ δοκοῦντες → εἶναι στῦλοι ἔδωκαν ἐμοὶ καὶ Βαρναβᾷ δεξιὰς → κοινωνίας →
cj   n.nsm   d.npm   pt.pa.npm   f.pa   n.npm   v.aai.3p   r.ds.1 cj   n.dsm   a.apf   n.gsf
2779   2722   3836   1506   1639   5146   1443   1609 2779 982   1288   3126

2:1 Ἔπειτα διὰ δεκατεσσάρων ἐτῶν πάλιν ἀνέβην εἰς Ἱεροσόλυμα μετὰ Βαρναβᾶ συμπαραλαβὼν καὶ Τίτον· 2 ἀνέβην δὲ κατὰ ἀποκάλυψιν· καὶ ἀνεθέμην αὐτοῖς τὸ εὐαγγέλιον ὃ κηρύσσω ἐν τοῖς ἔθνεσιν, κατ᾽ ἰδίαν δὲ τοῖς δοκοῦσιν, μή πως εἰς κενὸν τρέχω ἢ ἔδραμον. 3 ἀλλ᾽ οὐδὲ Τίτος ὁ σὺν ἐμοί, Ἕλλην ὤν, ἠναγκάσθη περιτμηθῆναι· 4 διὰ δὲ τοὺς παρεισάκτους ψευδαδέλφους, οἵτινες παρεισῆλθον κατασκοπῆσαι τὴν ἐλευθερίαν ἡμῶν ἣν ἔχομεν ἐν Χριστῷ Ἰησοῦ, ἵνα ἡμᾶς καταδουλώσουσιν, 5 οἷς οὐδὲ πρὸς ὥραν εἴξαμεν τῇ ὑποταγῇ, ἵνα ἡ ἀλήθεια τοῦ εὐαγγελίου διαμείνῃ πρὸς ὑμᾶς. ¶ 6 ἀπὸ δὲ τῶν δοκούντων εἶναι τι,— ὁποῖοί ποτε ἦσαν οὐδέν μοι διαφέρει· πρόσωπον [ὁ] θεὸς ἀνθρώπου οὐ λαμβάνει— ἐμοὶ γὰρ οἱ δοκοῦντες οὐδὲν προσανέθεντο, 7 ἀλλὰ τοὐναντίον ἰδόντες ὅτι πεπίστευμαι τὸ εὐαγγέλιον τῆς ἀκροβυστίας καθὼς Πέτρος τῆς περιτομῆς, 8 ὁ γὰρ ἐνεργήσας Πέτρῳ εἰς ἀποστολὴν τῆς περιτομῆς ἐνήργησεν καὶ ἐμοὶ εἰς τὰ ἔθνη, 9 καὶ γνόντες τὴν χάριν τὴν δοθεῖσάν μοι, Ἰάκωβος καὶ Κηφᾶς καὶ Ἰωάννης, οἱ δοκοῦντες στῦλοι εἶναι, δεξιὰς ἔδωκαν ἐμοὶ καὶ Βαρναβᾷ κοινωνίας,

recognized the grace given to me. They agreed that we should go to the Gentiles, and they to the Jews.
γνόντες τὴν χάριν ⌐τὴν δοθεῖσαν⌐ → μοι ἵνα ἡμεῖς εἰς τὰ ἔθνη δὲ αὐτοὶ εἰς τὴν περιτομήν
pt.aa.npm d.asf n.asf d.asf pt.ap.asf r.ds.1 cj r.np.1 p.a d.apn n.apn cj r.npm p.a d.asf n.asf
1182 3836 5921 3836 1443 1609 2671 7005 1650 3836 1620 1254 899 1650 3836 4364

10 All they asked was that we should continue to remember the poor, the very thing I was eager to do.
μόνον ἵνα → → → μνημονεύωμεν τῶν πτωχῶν ὃ καὶ αὐτὸ τοῦτο → ἐσπούδασα → ποιῆσαι
adv cj v.pas.1p d.gpm a.gpm r.asn cj r.asn r.asn v.aai.1s f.aa
3667 2671 3648 3836 4777 4005 2779 899 4047 5079 4472

Paul Opposes Peter

2:11 When Peter came to Antioch, I opposed him to his face, because he was clearly in the
δὲ Ὅτε Κηφᾶς ἦλθεν εἰς Ἀντιόχειαν → ἀντέστην κατὰ αὐτῷ πρόσωπον ὅτι → ἦν
cj cj n.nsm v.aai.3s p.a n.asf v.aai.1s p.a r.dsm.3 n.asn cj v.iai.3s
1254 4021 3064 2262 1650 522 468 2848 899 4725 4022 1639

wrong. **12** Before certain men came from James, he used to eat with the Gentiles. But when they
κατεγνωσμένος γὰρ πρὸ τινας ⌐τοῦ ἐλθεῖν⌐ ἀπὸ Ἰακώβου → → → συνήσθιεν μετὰ τῶν ἐθνῶν δὲ ὅτε →
pt.rp.nsm cj p.g r.apm d.gsn f.aa p.g n.gsm v.iai.3s p.g d.gpn n.gpn cj cj
2861 1142 4574 5516 3836 2262 608 2610 5303 3552 3836 1620 1254 4021

arrived, he began to draw back and separate himself from the Gentiles because he was afraid of those who
ἦλθον → → → ὑπέστελλεν ← καὶ ἀφώριζεν ἑαυτόν → → φοβούμενος ← τοὺς
v.aai.3p v.iai.3s cj v.iai.3s r.asm.3 pt.pp.nsm d.apm
2262 5713 2779 928 1571 5828 3836

belonged to the circumcision group. **13** The other Jews joined him in his hypocrisy, so
ἐκ ← τοὺς περιτομῆς καὶ οἱ λοιποὶ Ἰουδαῖοι καὶ συνυπεκρίθησαν αὐτῷ ← [καὶ] ὥστε
p.g d.apm n.gsf cj d.npm a.npm a.npm cj v.api.3p r.dsm.3 cj cj
1666 3836 4364 2779 3836 3370 2681 2779 5347 899 5347 5347 5347 2779 6063

that by their hypocrisy even Barnabas was led astray. ¶ **14** When I saw that they were not
← → αὐτῶν ⌐τῇ ὑποκρίσει καὶ Βαρναβᾶς → → συναπήχθη ἀλλ᾽ ὅτε → εἶδον ὅτι → → οὐκ
r.gpm.3 d.dsf n.dsf adv n.nsm v.api.3s cj cj v.aai.1s cj pl
5694 899 3836 5694 2779 982 5270 247 4021 1625 4022 3980 3980 4024

acting in line with the truth of the gospel, I said to Peter in front of them all, "You
ὀρθοποδοῦσιν ← ← πρὸς τὴν ἀλήθειαν → τοῦ εὐαγγελίου → εἶπον → ⌐τῷ Κηφᾷ ἔμπροσθεν ← ← πάντων εἰ σὺ
v.pai.3p p.a d.asf n.asf d.gsn n.gsn v.aai.1s d.dsm n.dsm p.g a.gpm cj r.ns.2
3980 4639 3836 237 3836 2295 3306 3836 3064 1869 4246 1623 5148

are a Jew, yet you live like a Gentile and not like a Jew. How is it, then, that you force Gentiles
ὑπάρχων Ἰουδαῖος → ζῇς → ἐθνικῶς καὶ οὐχὶ → Ἰουδαϊκῶς πῶς → → → ἀναγκάζεις ⌐τὰ ἔθνη⌐
pt.pa.nsm a.nsm v.pai.2s adv cj pl adv cj v.pai.2s d.apn n.apn
5639 2681 2409 1619 2779 4049 2680 4802 337 3836 1620

to follow Jewish customs? ¶ **15** "We who are Jews by birth and not 'Gentile sinners' **16** know that a
→ → ἰουδαΐζειν ← ἡμεῖς Ἰουδαῖοι φύσει καὶ οὐκ ἐξ ἐθνῶν ἁμαρτωλοί [δὲ] εἰδότες ὅτι
f.pa r.np.1 a.npm n.dsf cj pl p.g n.gpn a.npm cj pt.ra.npm cj
2678 7005 2681 5882 2779 4024 1666 1620 283 1254 3857 4022

man is not justified *by observing* the law, but by faith in Jesus Christ. So we, too, have put our
ἄνθρωπος → οὐ δικαιοῦται ἐξ ἔργων νόμου ἐὰν μὴ διὰ πίστεως → Ἰησοῦ Χριστοῦ ἡμεῖς καὶ
n.nsm pl v.ppi.3s p.g n.gpn n.gsm cj pl p.g n.gsf n.gsm n.gsm r.np.1 cj
476 1467 4024 1467 1666 2240 3795 1569 3590 1328 4411 2652 5986 7005 2779

faith in Christ Jesus that we may be justified by faith in Christ and not *by observing* the law,
ἐπιστεύσαμεν εἰς Χριστὸν Ἰησοῦν ἵνα → → → δικαιωθῶμεν ἐκ πίστεως → Χριστοῦ καὶ οὐκ ἐξ ἔργων νόμου
v.aai.1p p.a n.asm n.asm cj v.aps.1p p.g n.gsf n.gsm cj pl p.g n.gpn n.gsm
4409 1650 5986 2652 2671 1467 1666 4411 5986 2779 4024 1666 2240 3795

because *by observing* the law no one will be justified. ¶ **17** "If, while we seek to be
ὅτι ἐξ ἔργων νόμου οὐ ⌐πᾶσα σάρξ⌐ → δικαιωθήσεται δὲ εἰ ζητοῦντες → →
cj p.g n.gpn n.gsm pl a.nsf n.nsf v.fpi.3s cj cj pt.pa.npm
4022 1666 2240 3795 4024 4246 4922 1467 1254 1623 2426

justified in Christ, it becomes evident that we ourselves are sinners, *does that mean that* Christ promotes
δικαιωθῆναι ἐν Χριστῷ → εὑρέθημεν ← καὶ αὐτοὶ ἁμαρτωλοί ἄρα Χριστὸς διάκονος
f.ap p.d n.dsm v.api.1p adv r.npm a.npm pl n.nsm n.nsm
1467 1877 5986 2351 2779 899 283 727 5986 1356

ἵνα ἡμεῖς εἰς τὰ ἔθνη, αὐτοὶ δὲ εἰς τὴν περιτομήν· 10 μόνον τῶν πτωχῶν ἵνα μνημονεύωμεν, ὃ καὶ ἐσπούδασα αὐτὸ τοῦτο ποιῆσαι. 2:11 Ὅτε δὲ ἦλθεν Κηφᾶς εἰς Ἀντιόχειαν, κατὰ πρόσωπον αὐτῷ ἀντέστην, ὅτι κατεγνωσμένος ἦν. 12 πρὸ τοῦ γὰρ ἐλθεῖν τινας ἀπὸ Ἰακώβου μετὰ τῶν ἐθνῶν συνήσθιεν· ὅτε δὲ ἦλθον, ὑπέστελλεν καὶ ἀφώριζεν ἑαυτὸν φοβούμενος τοὺς ἐκ περιτομῆς. 13 καὶ συνυπεκρίθησαν αὐτῷ [καὶ] οἱ λοιποὶ Ἰουδαῖοι, ὥστε καὶ Βαρναβᾶς συναπήχθη αὐτῶν τῇ ὑποκρίσει. ¶ 14 ἀλλ᾽ ὅτε εἶδον ὅτι οὐκ ὀρθοποδοῦσιν πρὸς τὴν ἀλήθειαν τοῦ εὐαγγελίου, εἶπον τῷ Κηφᾷ ἔμπροσθεν πάντων, Εἰ σὺ Ἰουδαῖος ὑπάρχων ἐθνικῶς καὶ οὐχὶ Ἰουδαϊκῶς ζῇς, πῶς τὰ ἔθνη ἀναγκάζεις Ἰουδαΐζειν; ¶ 15 Ἡμεῖς φύσει Ἰουδαῖοι καὶ οὐκ ἐξ ἐθνῶν ἁμαρτωλοί· 16 εἰδότες [δὲ] ὅτι οὐ δικαιοῦται ἄνθρωπος ἐξ ἔργων νόμου ἐὰν μὴ διὰ πίστεως Ἰησοῦ Χριστοῦ, καὶ ἡμεῖς εἰς Χριστὸν Ἰησοῦν ἐπιστεύσαμεν, ἵνα δικαιωθῶμεν ἐκ πίστεως Χριστοῦ καὶ οὐκ ἐξ ἔργων νόμου, ὅτι ἐξ ἔργων νόμου οὐ δικαιωθήσεται πᾶσα σάρξ. ¶ 17 εἰ δὲ ζητοῦντες δικαιωθῆναι ἐν Χριστῷ εὑρέθημεν καὶ αὐτοὶ ἁμαρτωλοί, ἄρα Χριστὸς ἁμαρτίας διάκονος; μὴ γένοιτο. 18 εἰ γὰρ ἃ

sin?   Absolutely not! **18**   If   I   rebuild   what   I   destroyed,   I   prove   that   I   am a
ἁμαρτίας →   μὴ γένοιτο.   γὰρ εἰ → ┌πάλιν οἰκοδομῶ┐ ταῦτα ἃ → κατέλυσα → συνιστάνω   ἐμαυτὸν
n.gsf   pl v.amo.3s   cj cj   adv v.pai.1s   r.apn r.apn   v.aai.1s   v.pai.1s   r.asm.1
281   3590 1181   1142 1623   4099 3868   4047 4005   2907   5319   1831

lawbreaker. **19** For through the law   I   died   to the law   so that   I   might live for God. **20** I have been   crucified
παραβάτην   γὰρ διὰ   νόμου ἐγὼ ἀπέθανον →   νόμῳ ἵνα ← → →   ζήσω → θεῷ → → →   συνεσταύρωμαι
n.asm   cj p.g   n.gsm r.ns.1 v.aai.1s   n.dsm cj   v.aas.1s → n.dsm   v.rpi.1s
4127   1142 1328   3795 1609 633   3795 2671   2409 2536   5365

with Christ and I   no   longer live, but Christ lives in me.   The life I live   in the body, I live by faith
← Χριστῷ δὲ ἐγὼ οὐκέτι ←   ζῶ δὲ Χριστός· ζῇ ἐν ἐμοὶ δὲ ὃ   ζῶ νῦν ἐν   σαρκί, ζῶ ἐν πίστει
  n.dsm cj r.ns.1 adv   v.pai.1s cj n.nsm v.pai.3s p.d r.ds.1 cj r.asn   v.pai.1s adv p.d   n.dsf v.pai.1s p.d n.dsf
  5986 1254 1609 4033   2409 1254 5986 2409 1877 1609 1254 4005   2409 3814 1877   4922 2409 1877 4411

  in the Son of God,   who loved   me and gave   himself for me. **21** I do not set   aside the grace of
τῇ → τοῦ υἱοῦ → ┌τοῦ θεοῦ┐ τοῦ ἀγαπήσαντός με καὶ παραδόντος ἑαυτὸν ὑπὲρ ἐμοῦ.   Οὐκ ἀθετῶ ←   τὴν χάριν →
d.dsf → d.gsm n.gsm d.gsm n.gsm d.gsm pt.aa.gsm r.as.1 cj pt.aa.gsm r.asm.3 p.g r.gs.1   pl v.pai.1s   d.asf n.asf
3836 3836 5626 3836 2536 3836 26 1609 2779 4140 1571 5642 1609   119 119 4024 119   3836 5921

God,   for if   righteousness could be gained   through the law,   Christ died   for nothing!"
┌τοῦ θεοῦ┐ γὰρ εἰ   δικαιοσύνη   διὰ   νόμου ἄρα Χριστὸς ἀπέθανεν →   δωρεάν·
d.gsm n.gsm cj cj   n.nsf   p.g   n.gsm r.nsm n.nsm v.aai.3s   adv
3836 2536 1142 1623   1466   1328   3795 726 5986 633   1562

Faith or Observance of the Law

3:1 You foolish Galatians! Who has bewitched you?   *Before your very eyes*   Jesus   Christ was clearly
Ὦ ἀνόητοι Γαλάται τίς → ἐβάσκανεν ὑμᾶς οἷς κατ' ←   ὀφθαλμοὺς Ἰησοῦς Χριστὸς → →
j a.vpm n.vpm r.nsm → v.aai.3s r.ap.2 r.dpm p.a ←   n.apm n.nsm n.nsm
6043 485 1129 5515 1001 7007 4005 2848 4005   4057 2652 5986

portrayed as crucified. **2** I would like to learn just one thing from you: Did you receive the Spirit *by observing*
προεγράφη ἐσταυρωμένος → →   θέλω → μαθεῖν → μόνον τοῦτο ἀφ' ὑμῶν → → ἐλάβετε τὸ πνεῦμα ἐξ ἔργων
v.api.3s pt.rp.nsm   v.pai.1s f.aa adv r.asn p.g r.gp.2   v.aai.2p d.asn n.asn p.g n.gpn
4592 5319   2527 3443 3667 4047 608 7007   3284 3836 4460 1666 2240

the law, or *by believing* what you heard? **3**   Are you so foolish? After beginning with the Spirit, are you now
νόμου ἢ ἐξ πίστεως → → ἀκοῆς οὕτως ἐστε ←   ἀνόητοι → ἐναρξάμενοι → πνεύματι → → νῦν
n.gsm cj p.g n.gsf → n.gsf adv v.pai.2p ←   a.npm → pt.am.npm n.dsii   adv
3795 2445 1666 4411 198 4048 1639   485 1887 4460 2200 2200 3814

trying to attain your goal   by human effort? **4** Have you suffered so   much for nothing – if it really   was
→ → → ἐπιτελεῖσθε → σαρκὶ →   → ἐπάθετε τοσαῦτα ←   εἰκῇ   εἴ γε καὶ
v.ppi.2p n.dsf   v.aai.2p r.apn   adv   cj pl adv
2200 4922   4248 5537   1632   1623 1145 2779

for nothing? **5**   Does God give   you his Spirit and work   miracles among you *because you observe* the law,
→ εἰκῇ οὖν ὁ ἐπιχορηγῶν ὑμῖν τὸ πνεῦμα καὶ ἐνεργῶν δυνάμεις ἐν ὑμῖν ἐξ   ἔργων   νόμου
adv cj d.nsm pt.pa.nsm r.dp.2 d.asn n.asn cj pt.pa.nsm n.apf p.d r.dp.2 p.g   n.gpn   n.gsm
1632 4036 2220 3836 2220 7007 3836 4460 2779 1919 1539 1877 7007 1666   2240   3795

or *because you believe* what you heard? ¶ **6** Consider Abraham: "He believed God,   and it was credited to
ἢ ἐξ πίστεως → ἀκοῆς →   Καθὼς Ἀβραὰμ ἐπίστευσεν τῷ θεῷ καὶ → ἐλογίσθη
cj p.g n.gsf n.gsf   cj n.nsm v.aai.3s d.dsm n.dsm cj v.api.3s
2445 1666 4411 198   2777 11 4409 3836 2536 2779 3357

him as righteousness." **7** Understand, then, that those who believe   are children of Abraham. **8**   The
αὐτῷ εἰς δικαιοσύνην   γινώσκετε ἄρα ὅτι οἱ → ἐκ πίστεως, οὗτοι εἰσιν υἱοί → Ἀβραάμ   δὲ ἡ
r.dsm.3 p.g n.asf   v.pam.2p cj cj d.npm → p.g n.gsf r.npm v.pai.3p n.npm n.gsm   cj d.nsf
899 1650 1466   1182 726 4022 3836 1666 4411 4047 5626 5626 11   1254 3836

Scripture foresaw that God   would justify the Gentiles by faith, and announced   the gospel in advance to
γραφὴ προϊδοῦσα ὅτι ┌ὁ θεὸς┐ → δικαιοῖ τὰ ἔθνη ἐκ πίστεως προευηγγελίσατο ← ← →
n.nsf pt.aa.nsf cj d.nsm n.nsm → v.pai.3s d.apn n.apn p.g n.gsf v.ami.3s
1210 4632 4022 3836 2536 1467 3836 1620 1666 4411 4603

Abraham: "All nations will be blessed   through you." **9** So those who have faith   are blessed
┌τῷ Ἀβραὰμ┐ ὅτι πάντα ┌τὰ ἔθνη┐ → ἐνευλογηθήσονται ἐν   σοὶ ὥστε οἱ ←   ┌ἐκ πίστεως┐ εὐλογοῦνται
d.dsm n.dsm cj a.npn d.npn n.npn → v.fpi.3p p.d   r.ds.2 cj d.npm   p.g n.gsf v.ppi.3p
3836 11 4022 4246 3836 1620 1922 1877   5148 6063 3836   1666 4411 2328

κατέλυσα ταῦτα πάλιν οἰκοδομῶ, παραβάτην ἐμαυτὸν συνιστάνω. ¹⁹ ἐγὼ γὰρ διὰ νόμου νόμῳ ἀπέθανον, ἵνα θεῷ ζήσω. Χριστῷ συνεσταύρωμαι· ²⁰ ζῶ δὲ οὐκέτι ἐγώ, ζῇ δὲ ἐν ἐμοὶ Χριστός· ὃ δὲ νῦν ζῶ ἐν σαρκί, ἐν πίστει ζῶ τῇ τοῦ υἱοῦ τοῦ θεοῦ τοῦ ἀγαπήσαντός με καὶ παραδόντος ἑαυτὸν ὑπὲρ ἐμοῦ. ²¹ οὐκ ἀθετῶ τὴν χάριν τοῦ θεοῦ· εἰ γὰρ διὰ νόμου δικαιοσύνη, ἄρα Χριστὸς δωρεὰν ἀπέθανεν.

³:¹ Ὦ ἀνόητοι Γαλάται, τίς ὑμᾶς ἐβάσκανεν, οἷς κατ' ὀφθαλμοὺς Ἰησοῦς Χριστὸς προεγράφη ἐσταυρωμένος; ² τοῦτο μόνον θέλω μαθεῖν ἀφ' ὑμῶν· ἐξ ἔργων νόμου τὸ πνεῦμα ἐλάβετε ἢ ἐξ ἀκοῆς πίστεως; ³ οὕτως ἀνόητοί ἐστε, ἐναρξάμενοι πνεύματι νῦν σαρκὶ ἐπιτελεῖσθε; ⁴ τοσαῦτα ἐπάθετε εἰκῇ; εἴ γε καὶ εἰκῇ. ⁵ ὁ οὖν ἐπιχορηγῶν ὑμῖν τὸ πνεῦμα καὶ ἐνεργῶν δυνάμεις ἐν ὑμῖν, ἐξ ἔργων νόμου ἢ ἐξ ἀκοῆς πίστεως; ¶ ⁶ καθὼς Ἀβραὰμ ἐπίστευσεν τῷ θεῷ, καὶ ἐλογίσθη αὐτῷ εἰς δικαιοσύνην.
⁷ Γινώσκετε ἄρα ὅτι οἱ ἐκ πίστεως, οὗτοι υἱοί εἰσιν Ἀβραάμ. ⁸ προϊδοῦσα δὲ ἡ γραφὴ ὅτι ἐκ πίστεως δικαιοῖ τὰ ἔθνη ὁ θεός, προευηγγελίσατο τῷ Ἀβραὰμ ὅτι Ἐνευλογηθήσονται ἐν σοὶ πάντα τὰ ἔθνη· ⁹ ὥστε οἱ ἐκ πίστεως εὐλογοῦνται σὺν τῷ πιστῷ

along with Abraham, the man of faith. ¶ **10** All who rely *on observing* the law are under a curse, for
→ σὺν Ἀβραάμ τῷ ← πιστῷ γὰρ Ὅσοι ← εἰσίν ἐξ ἔργων νόμου εἰσὶν ὑπὸ κατάραν γὰρ
p.d n.dsm d.dsm a.dsm cj r.npm v.pai.3p p.g n.gpn n.gsm v.pai.3p p.a n.asf cj
5250 11 3836 4412 1142 4012 1639 1666 2240 3795 1639 5679 2932 1142

it is written: "Cursed is everyone who does not continue to do everything written in
→ → γέγραπται ὅτι ἐπικατάρατος πᾶς ὃς → οὐκ ἐμμένει → τοῦ ποιῆσαι πᾶσιν αὐτά τοῖς γεγραμμένοις ἐν
v.rpi.3s cj a.nsm r.nsm pl v.pai.3s d.gsn f.aa a.dpn r.apn.3 d.dpn pt.rp.dpn p.d
1211 4022 2129 4246 4005 1844 4024 1844 3836 4472 4246 899 3836 1211 1877

the Book of the Law." **11** Clearly no one is justified before God by the law, because, "The righteous
τῷ βιβλίῳ → τοῦ νόμου δὲ ὅτι δῆλον οὐδεὶς → δικαιοῦται παρὰ τῷ θεῷ ἐν νόμῳ ὅτι ὁ δίκαιος
d.dsn n.dsn d.gsn n.gsn cj cj a.nsn a.nsm v.ppi.3s p.d d.dsm n.dsm p.d n.dsm cj d.nsm a.nsm
3836 1046 3836 3795 1254 4022 1316 4029 1467 4123 3836 2536 1877 3795 4022 3836 1465

will live by faith." **12** The law is not based on faith; on the contrary, "The man who does these things
→ ζήσεται ἐκ πίστεως δὲ ὁ νόμος ἔστιν οὐκ ἐκ πίστεως → → ἀλλ᾽ ὁ ← ← ποιήσας αὐτά ←
v.fmi.3s p.g n.gsf cj d.nsm n.nsm v.pai.3s pl p.g n.gsf d.nsm pt.aa.nsm r.apn.3
2409 1666 4411 1254 3836 3795 4024 1666 4411 247 3836 4472 899

will live by them." **13** Christ redeemed us from the curse of the law by becoming a curse for us, for it is
→ ζήσεται ἐν αὐτοῖς Χριστὸς ἐξηγόρασεν ἡμᾶς ἐκ τῆς κατάρας τοῦ νόμου γενόμενος κατάρα ὑπὲρ ἡμῶν ὅτι →
v.fmi.3s p.d r.dpn.3 n.nsm v.aai.3s r.ap.1 p.g d.gsf n.gsf d.gsm n.gsm pt.am.nsm n.nsf p.g r.gp.1 cj
2409 1877 899 5986 1973 7005 1666 3836 2932 3836 3795 1181 2932 5642 7005 4022

written: "Cursed is everyone who is hung on a tree." **14** He redeemed us in order that the blessing given to
γέγραπται ἐπικατάρατος πᾶς ὁ → κρεμάμενος ἐπὶ ξύλου ἵνα ← ← ἡ εὐλογία →
v.rpi.3s a.nsm a.nsm d.nsm pt.pm.nsm p.g n.gsn cj d.nsf n.nsf
1211 2129 4246 3836 3203 2093 3833 2671 3836 2330

Abraham might come to the Gentiles through Christ Jesus, so that by faith we might receive the
τοῦ Ἀβραάμ → γένηται εἰς τὰ ἔθνη ἐν Χριστῷ Ἰησοῦ ἵνα ← διὰ τῆς πίστεως → → λάβωμεν τὴν
d.gsn n.gsm v.ams.3s p.a d.apn n.apn p.d n.dsm n.dsm cj p.g d.gsf n.gsf v.aas.1p d.asf
3836 11 1181 1650 3836 1620 1877 5986 2652 2671 1328 3836 4411 3284 3836

promise of the Spirit.
ἐπαγγελίαν → τοῦ πνεύματος
n.asf d.gsn n.gsn
2039 3836 4460

The Law and the Promise

3:15 Brothers, *let me take an example from everyday life.* Just as no one can set aside or
Ἀδελφοί → → κατὰ ἄνθρωπον λέγω ὅμως ← οὐδεὶς ← → ἀθετεῖ ἤ
n.vpm p.a n.asm v.pai.1s adv a.nsm v.pai.3s cj
81 3306 3306 2848 476 3306 3940 4029 119 2445

add to a human covenant that has been duly established, so it is in this case. **16** The promises were
ἐπιδιατάσσεται ← ἀνθρώπου διαθήκην → → → κεκυρωμένην δὲ αἱ ἐπαγγελίαι →
v.pmi.3s n.gsm n.asf pt.rp.asf cj d.npf n.npf
2112 476 1347 3263 1254 3836 2039

spoken to Abraham and to his seed. The Scripture does not say "and to seeds," meaning
ἐρρέθησαν τῷ Ἀβραάμ καὶ → αὐτοῦ τῷ σπέρματι → οὐ λέγει καὶ → τοῖς σπέρμασιν ὡς ἐπὶ
v.api.3p d.dsm n.dsm cj r.gsm.3 d.dsn n.dsn pl v.pai.3s cj d.dpn n.dpn pl p.g
3306 3836 11 2779 899 3836 5065 3306 4024 3306 2779 3836 5065 6055 2093

many people, but "and to your seed," meaning one person, who is Christ. **17** What I mean is this:
πολλῶν ← ἀλλ᾽ καὶ → σου τῷ σπέρματι ὡς ← ἐφ᾽ ἑνός ← ὅς ἐστιν Χριστός δὲ → λέγω τοῦτο
a.gpn cj cj r.gs.2 d.dsn n.dsn pl p.g a.gsn r.nsm v.pai.3s n.nsm cj v.pai.1s r.asn
4498 247 2779 5065 5148 3836 5065 6055 2093 1651 4005 1639 5986 1254 3306 4047

The law, introduced 430 years later, does not set aside the covenant previously established
ὁ νόμος γεγονὼς τετρακόσια καὶ τριάκοντα ἔτη μετὰ → οὐκ ἀκυροῖ ← διαθήκην → προκεκυρωμένην
d.nsm n.nsm pt.ra.nsm a.apn cj a.apn n.apn p.a pl v.pai.3s n.asf pt.rp.asf
3836 3795 1181 5484 2779 5558 2291 3552 218 4024 218 1347 4623

by God and thus do away with the promise. **18** For if the inheritance depends on the law, then it
ὑπὸ τοῦ θεοῦ εἰς → τὸ καταργῆσαι ← τὴν ἐπαγγελίαν γὰρ εἰ ἡ κληρονομία ἐκ ← νόμου
p.g d.gsm n.gsm p.a d.asn f.aa d.asf n.asf cj cj d.nsf n.nsf p.g n.gsm
5679 3836 2536 1650 3836 2934 3836 2039 1142 1623 3836 3100 1666 3795

Ἀβραάμ. ¶ **10** ὅσοι γὰρ ἐξ ἔργων νόμου εἰσίν, ὑπὸ κατάραν εἰσίν· γέγραπται γὰρ ὅτι Ἐπικατάρατος πᾶς ὃς οὐκ ἐμμένει πᾶσιν τοῖς γεγραμμένοις ἐν τῷ βιβλίῳ τοῦ νόμου τοῦ ποιῆσαι αὐτά. **11** ὅτι δὲ ἐν νόμῳ οὐδεὶς δικαιοῦται παρὰ τῷ θεῷ δῆλον, ὅτι Ὁ δίκαιος ἐκ πίστεως ζήσεται· **12** ὁ δὲ νόμος οὐκ ἔστιν ἐκ πίστεως, ἀλλ᾽ Ὁ ποιήσας αὐτὰ ζήσεται ἐν αὐτοῖς. **13** Χριστὸς ἡμᾶς ἐξηγόρασεν ἐκ τῆς κατάρας τοῦ νόμου γενόμενος ὑπὲρ ἡμῶν κατάρα, ὅτι γέγραπται, Ἐπικατάρατος πᾶς ὁ κρεμάμενος ἐπὶ ξύλου, **14** ἵνα εἰς τὰ ἔθνη ἡ εὐλογία τοῦ Ἀβραὰμ γένηται ἐν Χριστῷ Ἰησοῦ, ἵνα τὴν ἐπαγγελίαν τοῦ πνεύματος λάβωμεν διὰ τῆς πίστεως.

3:15 Ἀδελφοί, κατὰ ἄνθρωπον λέγω· ὅμως ἀνθρώπου κεκυρωμένην διαθήκην οὐδεὶς ἀθετεῖ ἢ ἐπιδιατάσσεται. **16** τῷ δὲ Ἀβραὰμ ἐρρέθησαν αἱ ἐπαγγελίαι καὶ τῷ σπέρματι αὐτοῦ. οὐ λέγει, Καὶ τοῖς σπέρμασιν, ὡς ἐπὶ πολλῶν ἀλλ᾽ ὡς ἐφ᾽ ἑνός, Καὶ τῷ σπέρματί σου, ὅς ἐστιν Χριστός. **17** τοῦτο δὲ λέγω· διαθήκην προκεκυρωμένην ὑπὸ τοῦ θεοῦ ὁ μετὰ τετρακόσια καὶ τριάκοντα ἔτη γεγονὼς νόμος οὐκ ἀκυροῖ εἰς τὸ καταργῆσαι τὴν ἐπαγγελίαν. **18** εἰ γὰρ ἐκ νόμου ἡ κληρονομία, οὐκέτι ἐξ ἐπαγγελίας· τῷ δὲ Ἀβραὰμ δι᾽

no   longer depends on a promise; but God   in his grace gave   it to Abraham   through a promise. ¶
οὐκέτι ←   ἐξ   ← ἐπαγγελίας δὲ ὁ θεός˻   κεχάρισται → ˻τῷ Ἀβραὰμ δι’   ἐπαγγελίας
adv   p.g   n.gsf   cj d.nsm n.nsm   v.rmi.3s   d.dsm n.dsm p.g   n.gsf
4033   1666   2039   1254 3836 2536   5919   3836 11   1328   2039

19 What, then, was the purpose of the law? It was added because of transgressions until   the Seed to whom
Τί οὖν   ὁ νόμος → → προσετέθη χάριν ← ˻τῶν παραβάσεων ˻ἄχρις οὗ τὸ σπέρμα → ᾧ
r.asn cj   d.nsm n.nsm   v.api.3s p.g   d.gpf n.gpf   p.g r.gsm d.nsn n.nsn r.dsn
5515 4036   3836 3795   4707 5920   3836 4126   948 4005 3836 5065 4005

the promise referred had come. The law was put into effect   through angels by   a mediator. **20** A mediator,
ἐπήγγελται ← → ἔλθῃ   → διαταγεὶς δι’   ἀγγέλων ἐν χειρὶ μεσίτου   ὁ μεσίτης˻
v.rpi.3s   v.aas.3s   pt.ap.nsm p.g   n.gpm p.d n.dsf n.gsm   d.nsm n.nsm
2040   2262   1411 1328   34 1877 5931 3542   3836 3542

however, does not represent just one party; but God   is one. ¶   **21** Is the law, therefore, opposed to the
δὲ   → οὐκ ἔστιν   ἑνός ← δὲ ˻ὁ θεός˻ ἔστιν εἷς   ὁ νόμος οὖν   κατὰ ← τῶν
cj   pl v.pai.3s a.gsm cj d.nsm n.nsm v.pai.3s a.nsm   d.nsm n.nsm cj   p.g   d.gpf
1254 1639 4024 1639 1651 1254 3836 2536 1639 1651 3836 3795 4036 2848 3836

promises of God? Absolutely not!   For if a law had been given that could impart life,   then
ἐπαγγελιῶν → ˻τοῦ θεοῦ˻ μὴ γένοιτο, γὰρ εἰ νόμος ἐδόθη ὁ δυνάμενος → ζωοποιῆσαι
n.gpf   d.gsm n.gsm   pl v.amo.3s cj cj n.nsm   v.api.3s d.nsm pt.pp.nsm f.aa
2039   3836 2536   3590 1181 1142 1623 3795   1443 3836 1538   2443

righteousness would certainly have come by the law. **22** But the Scripture declares that the whole world is a
˻ἡ δικαιοσύνη˻ ἂν ὄντως → ἦν ἐκ νόμου ἀλλὰ ἡ γραφὴ   τὰ πάντα ←
d.nsf n.nsf   pl adv v.iai.3s p.g n.gsm cj d.nsf n.nsf   d.apn a.apn
3836 1466   323 3953   1639 1666 3795 247 3836 1210   5168   3836 4246

prisoner of sin,   so that what was promised, being given through faith in Jesus Christ, might be given to
συνέκλεισεν ὑπὸ ἁμαρτίαν ἵνα ← ἡ ἐπαγγελία   ἐκ πίστεως → Ἰησοῦ Χριστοῦ → → δοθῇ →
v.aai.3s p.a n.asf cj   d.nsf n.nsf   p.g n.gsf   n.gsm n.gsm   v.aps.3s
5168 5679 281 2671 3836 2039   1666 4411 2652 5986   1443

those who believe. ¶ **23** Before this faith came, we were held prisoners by the law, locked   up
τοῖς ← πιστεύουσιν δὲ Πρὸ τὴν πίστιν ˻τοῦ ἐλθεῖν˻ ἐφρουρούμεθα ὑπὸ νόμον συγκλειόμενοι ←
d.dpm pt.pa.dpm   cj p.g d.asf n.asf d.gsn f.aa   v.ipi.1p p.a n.asm pt.pp.npm
3836 4409   1254 4574 3836 4411 3836 2262   5864 5679 3795 5168

until faith   should be revealed. **24** So the law *was* *put in charge* *to lead us* *to* Christ
εἰς ˻τὴν μέλλουσαν πίστιν → ἀποκαλυφθῆναι ὥστε ὁ νόμος γέγονεν παιδαγωγὸς → → ἡμῶν εἰς Χριστόν
p.a d.asf pt.pa.asf n.asf   f.ap   cj d.nsm n.nsm v.rai.3s n.nsm   r.gp.1 p.a n.asm
1650 3836 3516 4411   636   6063 3836 3795 1181 4080   1650 1650 1650 5986

that we might be justified   by faith. **25** Now that faith has come, we are no longer under the
ἵνα → → δικαιωθῶμεν ἐκ πίστεως δὲ ˻τῆς πίστεως˻ → ἐλθούσης → ἐσμεν οὐκέτι   ὑπὸ
cj   v.aps.1p p.g n.gsf cj d.gsf n.gsf pt.aa.gsf v.pai.1p adv p.a
2671   1467 1666 4411 1254 2262 3836 4411 2262 1639 4033 5679

supervision of the law.
παιδαγωγόν
n.asm
4080

Sons of God

3:26 You are all sons of God through faith in Christ Jesus, **27** for all of you who were baptized
γὰρ → ἐστε Πάντες υἱοὶ → θεοῦ διὰ ˻τῆς πίστεως˻ ἐν Χριστῷ Ἰησοῦ γὰρ ὅσοι → ← → ἐβαπτίσθητε
cj   v.pai.2p n.npm n.npm n.gsm p.g d.gsf n.gsf p.d n.dsm n.dsm cj r.npm   v.api.2p
1142 1639 4246 5626 2536 1328 3836 4411 1877 5986 2652 1142 4012 966 4012 966

into Christ have clothed yourselves with Christ. **28** There is neither Jew nor Greek, slave nor
εἰς Χριστὸν → ἐνεδύσασθε ← ← Χριστόν → ἔνι οὐκ Ἰουδαῖος οὐδὲ Ἕλλην οὐκ ἔνι δοῦλος οὐδὲ
p.a n.asm   v.ami.2p n.asm   v.pai.3s pl a.nsm cj n.nsm pl v.pai.3s n.nsm cj
1650 5986 1907   5986   1928 4024 2681 4028 1818 4024 1928 1529 4028

free,   male nor female, for you are all one in Christ Jesus. **29** If you belong to Christ, then you
ἐλεύθερος οὐκ ἔνι ἄρσεν καὶ θῆλυ γὰρ ὑμεῖς ἐστε πάντες εἷς ἐν Χριστῷ Ἰησοῦ δὲ εἰ ὑμεῖς → → Χριστοῦ ἄρα →
a.nsm pl v.pai.3s a.nsn cj a.nsn cj r.np.2 v.pai.2p a.npm a.nsm p.d n.dsm n.dsm cj cj r.np.2 n.gsm cj
1801 4024 1928 781 2779 2559 1142 7007 1639 4246 1651 1877 5986 2652 1254 1623 7007 5986 726

ἐπαγγελίας κεχάρισται ὁ θεός. ¶ **19** Τί οὖν ὁ νόμος; τῶν παραβάσεων χάριν προσετέθη, ἄχρις οὗ ἔλθῃ τὸ σπέρμα ᾧ ἐπήγγελται, διαταγεὶς δι’ ἀγγέλων ἐν χειρὶ μεσίτου. **20** ὁ δὲ μεσίτης ἑνὸς οὐκ ἔστιν, ὁ δὲ θεὸς εἷς ἐστιν. ¶ **21** Ὁ οὖν νόμος κατὰ τῶν ἐπαγγελιῶν [τοῦ θεοῦ]; μὴ γένοιτο. εἰ γὰρ ἐδόθη νόμος ὁ δυνάμενος ζωοποιῆσαι, ὄντως ἐκ νόμου ἂν ἦν ἡ δικαιοσύνη· **22** ἀλλὰ συνέκλεισεν ἡ γραφὴ τὰ πάντα ὑπὸ ἁμαρτίαν, ἵνα ἡ ἐπαγγελία ἐκ πίστεως Ἰησοῦ Χριστοῦ δοθῇ τοῖς πιστεύουσιν. ¶ **23** Πρὸ τοῦ δὲ ἐλθεῖν τὴν πίστιν ὑπὸ νόμον ἐφρουρούμεθα συγκλειόμενοι εἰς τὴν μέλλουσαν πίστιν ἀποκαλυφθῆναι, **24** ὥστε ὁ νόμος παιδαγωγὸς ἡμῶν γέγονεν εἰς Χριστόν, ἵνα ἐκ πίστεως δικαιωθῶμεν· **25** ἐλθούσης δὲ τῆς πίστεως οὐκέτι ὑπὸ παιδαγωγόν ἐσμεν.

3:26 Πάντες γὰρ υἱοὶ θεοῦ ἐστε διὰ τῆς πίστεως ἐν Χριστῷ Ἰησοῦ· **27** ὅσοι γὰρ εἰς Χριστὸν ἐβαπτίσθητε, Χριστὸν ἐνεδύσασθε. **28** οὐκ ἔνι Ἰουδαῖος οὐδὲ Ἕλλην, οὐκ ἔνι δοῦλος οὐδὲ ἐλεύθερος, οὐκ ἔνι ἄρσεν καὶ θῆλυ· πάντες γὰρ ὑμεῖς εἷς ἐστε ἐν Χριστῷ Ἰησοῦ. **29** εἰ δὲ ὑμεῖς Χριστοῦ, ἄρα τοῦ Ἀβραὰμ σπέρμα ἐστέ, κατ’ ἐπαγγελίαν κληρονόμοι. **4:1** Λέγω δέ, ἐφ’

are Abraham's seed, and heirs according to the promise. ¶ **4:1** What I am saying is that
ἐστέ ⌐τοῦ Ἀβραάμ σπέρμα κληρονόμοι κατ᾿ ← ἐπαγγελίαν δὲ → → Λέγω
v.pai.2p d.gsm n.gsm n.nsn n.npm p.a n.asf cj v.pai.1s
1639 3836 11 5065 3101 2848 2039 1254 3306

as *long as* the heir is a child, he is no different from a slave, although he owns the
⌐ἐφ᾿ ὅσον χρόνον⌐ ὁ κληρονόμος ἐστιν νήπιος → → οὐδὲ διαφέρει ← δούλου → → ⌐ὢν κύριος⌐
p.a r.nsn n.asm d.nsm n.nsm v.pai.3s n.nsm adv v.pai.3s n.gsm pt.pa.nsm n.nsm
2093 4012 5989 3836 3101 1639 3758 1422 1422 4029 1422 1529 1639 3261

whole estate. **2** He is subject to guardians and trustees until the time set by his father. **3** So also, when
πάντων ἀλλὰ → ἐστιν ὑπὸ ← ἐπιτρόπους καὶ οἰκονόμους ἄχρι τῆς προθεσμίας ← → τοῦ πατρός οὕτως καὶ ὅτε
a.gpn cj v.pai.3s p.a n.apm cj n.apm p.g d.gsf n.gsf d.gsm n.gsm adv adv cj
4246 247 1639 5679 2207 2779 3874 948 3836 4607 3836 4252 4048 2779 4021

we were children, we were in slavery under the basic principles of the world. **4** But when the time had
ἡμεῖς ἦμεν νήπιοι → ἤμεθα → δεδουλωμένοι ὑπὸ τὰ στοιχεῖα ← → τοῦ κόσμου δὲ ὅτε τοῦ χρόνου →
r.np.1 v.iai.1p a.npm v.imi.1p pt.rp.npm p.a d.apn n.apn d.gsm n.gsm cj cj d.gsm n.gsm
7005 1639 3758 1639 1530 5679 3836 5122 3836 3180 1254 4021 3836 5989 2262

fully come, God sent his Son, born of a woman, born under law, **5** to redeem those
⌐τὸ πλήρωμα⌐ ἦλθεν ὁ θεός ἐξαπέστειλεν αὐτοῦ ⌐τὸν υἱόν⌐ γενόμενον ἐκ γυναικός γενόμενον ὑπὸ νόμον ἵνα ἐξαγοράσῃ τοὺς
d.nsn n.nsn v.aai.3s d.nsm n.nsm v.aai.3s r.gsm.3 d.asm n.asm pt.am.asm p.g n.gsf pt.am.asm p.a n.asm cj v.aas.3s d.apm
3836 4445 2262 3836 2536 1990 899 3836 5626 1181 1666 1222 1181 5679 3795 2671 1973 3836

under law, that we might receive the full rights of sons. **6** Because you are sons, God sent the
ὑπὸ νόμον ἵνα → → ἀπολάβωμεν τὴν → υἱοθεσίαν ← δὲ Ὅτι → ἐστε υἱοί ὁ θεός ἐξαπέστειλεν τὸ
p.a n.asm cj v.aas.1p d.asf n.asf cj cj v.pai.2p n.npm d.nsm n.nsm v.aai.3s d.asn
5679 3795 2671 655 3836 5625 1254 4022 1639 5626 3836 2536 1990 3836

Spirit of his Son into our hearts, the Spirit who calls out, "Abba, Father." **7** So you are no
πνεῦμα → αὐτοῦ ⌐τοῦ υἱοῦ⌐ εἰς ἡμῶν ⌐τὰς καρδίας⌐ κρᾶζον ← ἀββὰ ὁ πατήρ ὥστε → εἶ οὐκέτι
n.asn r.gsm.3 d.gsm n.gsm p.a r.gp.1 d.apf n.apf pt.pa.asn n.vsm d.vsm n.vsm cj v.pai.2s adv
4460 5626 899 3836 5626 1650 7005 3836 2840 3189 5 3836 4252 6063 1639 4033

longer a slave, but a son; and since you are a son, God has made you also an heir.
← δοῦλος ἀλλὰ υἱός δὲ εἰ → υἱός διὰ θεοῦ καὶ κληρονόμος
n.nsm cj n.nsm cj cj n.nsm p.g n.gsm adv n.nsm
1529 247 5626 1254 1623 5626 1328 2536 2779 3101

Paul's Concern for the Galatians

4:8 Formerly, when you did not know God, you were slaves to those who by nature are not gods.
Ἀλλὰ τότε μὲν → → οὐκ εἰδότες θεόν → → ἐδουλεύσατε τοῖς ← → φύσει οὖσιν μὴ θεοῖς
cj adv pl pl pt.ra.npm n.asm v.aai.2p d.dpm n.dsf pt.pa.dpm pl n.dpm
247 5538 3525 3857 3857 4024 3857 2536 1526 3836 5882 1639 3590 2536

9 But now that you know God – or rather are known by God – how is it that you are turning back to those
δὲ νῦν → γνόντες θεόν δὲ μᾶλλον → γνωσθέντες ὑπὸ θεοῦ πῶς ← ← → ἐπιστρέφετε πάλιν ἐπὶ τὰ
cj adv pt.aa.npm n.asm cj adv.c pt.ap.npm p.g n.gsm pl v.pai.2p adv p.a d.apn
1254 3814 1182 2536 1254 3437 1182 5679 2536 4802 2188 4099 2093 3836

weak and miserable principles? Do you wish to be enslaved by them all over again? **10** You are observing special
ἀσθενῆ καὶ πτωχὰ στοιχεῖα → → θέλετε → δουλεύειν οἷς πάλιν ← ἄνωθεν → παρατηρεῖσθε
a.apn cj a.apn n.apn v.pai.2p f.pa r.dpn adv adv v.pmi.2p
822 2779 4777 5122 2527 1526 4005 4099 540 4190

days and months and seasons and years! **11** I fear for you, that somehow *I have wasted my efforts* on you. ¶
ἡμέρας καὶ μῆνας καὶ καιροὺς καὶ ἐνιαυτούς → φοβοῦμαι → ὑμᾶς → ⌐μή πως⌐ κεκοπίακα εἰκῇ εἰς ὑμᾶς
n.apf cj n.apm cj n.apm cj n.apm v.pai.1s r.ap.2 cj pl v.rai.1s adv p.a r.ap.2
2465 2779 3604 2779 2789 2779 1929 5828 7007 3590 4803 3159 1632 1650 7007

12 I plead with you, brothers, become like me, for I became like you. You have done me no wrong. **13** As
δέομαι ὑμῶν ἀδελφοί Γίνεσθε ὡς ἐγὼ ὅτι κἀγὼ ὡς ὑμεῖς με οὐδέν ἠδικήσατε δὲ
v.ppi.1s r.gp.2 n.vpm v.pmm.2p cj r.ns.1 cj crasis cj r.np.2 r.as.1 a.asn v.aai.2p cj
1289 7007 81 1181 6055 1609 4022 2743 6055 7007 1609 92 92 1254

you know, it was because of an illness that I first preached the gospel to you. **14** Even
→ οἴδατε δι᾿ ← ⌐ἀσθένειαν τῆς σαρκός⌐ ὅτι → ⌐τὸ πρότερον⌐ εὐηγγελισάμην ← → ὑμῖν καὶ
v.rai.2p p.a n.asf d.gsf n.gsf cj d.asn adv.c v.ami.1s r.dp.2 cj
3857 1328 819 3836 4922 4022 3836 4728 2294 7007 2779

ὅσον χρόνον ὁ κληρονόμος νήπιός ἐστιν, οὐδὲν διαφέρει δούλου κύριος πάντων ὤν, ² ἀλλὰ ὑπὸ ἐπιτρόπους ἐστὶν καὶ οἰκονόμους ἄχρι τῆς προθεσμίας τοῦ πατρός. ³ οὕτως καὶ ἡμεῖς, ὅτε ἦμεν νήπιοι, ὑπὸ τὰ στοιχεῖα τοῦ κόσμου ἤμεθα δεδουλωμένοι· ⁴ ὅτε δὲ ἦλθεν τὸ πλήρωμα τοῦ χρόνου, ἐξαπέστειλεν ὁ θεὸς τὸν υἱὸν αὐτοῦ, γενόμενον ἐκ γυναικός, γενόμενον ὑπὸ νόμον, ⁵ ἵνα τοὺς ὑπὸ νόμον ἐξαγοράσῃ, ἵνα τὴν υἱοθεσίαν ἀπολάβωμεν. ⁶ Ὅτι δέ ἐστε υἱοί, ἐξαπέστειλεν ὁ θεὸς τὸ πνεῦμα τοῦ υἱοῦ αὐτοῦ εἰς τὰς καρδίας ἡμῶν κρᾶζον, Αββα ὁ πατήρ. ⁷ ὥστε οὐκέτι εἶ δοῦλος ἀλλὰ υἱός· εἰ δὲ υἱός, καὶ κληρονόμος διὰ θεοῦ.

4:8 Ἀλλὰ τότε μὲν οὐκ εἰδότες θεὸν ἐδουλεύσατε τοῖς φύσει μὴ οὖσιν θεοῖς· ⁹ νῦν δὲ γνόντες θεόν, μᾶλλον δὲ γνωσθέντες ὑπὸ θεοῦ, πῶς ἐπιστρέφετε πάλιν ἐπὶ τὰ ἀσθενῆ καὶ πτωχὰ στοιχεῖα οἷς πάλιν ἄνωθεν δουλεύειν θέλετε; ¹⁰ ἡμέρας παρατηρεῖσθε καὶ μῆνας καὶ καιροὺς καὶ ἐνιαυτούς, ¹¹ φοβοῦμαι ὑμᾶς μή πως εἰκῇ κεκοπίακα εἰς ὑμᾶς. ¶ ¹² Γίνεσθε ὡς ἐγώ, ὅτι κἀγὼ ὡς ὑμεῖς, ἀδελφοί, δέομαι ὑμῶν. οὐδέν με ἠδικήσατε· ¹³ οἴδατε δὲ ὅτι δι᾿ ἀσθένειαν τῆς σαρκὸς εὐηγγελισάμην ὑμῖν τὸ πρότερον,

though my illness was a trial to you, you did not treat me with contempt or scorn. Instead, you
← μου ἐν τῇ σαρκί ⌐τὸν πειρασμὸν⌐ ὑμῶν → οὐκ → → ἐξουθενήσατε οὐδὲ ἐξεπτύσατε ἀλλὰ →
r.gs.1 p.d d.dsf n.dsf d.asm n.asm r.gp.2 pl v.aai.2p cj v.aai.2p cj
1609 1877 3836 4922 3836 4280 7007 2024 2024 4024 2024 4028 1746 247

welcomed me as if I were an angel of God, as if I were Christ Jesus himself. 15 What has happened to all your
ἐδέξασθε με ὡς ἄγγελον → θεοῦ ὡς Χριστὸν Ἰησοῦν οὖν ποῦ ← ← ← ὑμῶν
v.ami.2p r.as.1 cj n.asm n.gsn cj n.asm n.asm cj cj r.gp.2
1312 1609 6055 34 2536 6055 5986 2652 4036 4543 7007

joy? I can testify that, if you could have done so, you would have torn out your
ὁ μακαρισμὸς γὰρ μαρτυρῶ ὑμῖν ὅτι εἰ → δυνατὸν ← → → → ἐξορύξαντες ← ὑμῶν
d.nsm n.nsm cj v.pai.1s r.dp.2 cj cj a.nsn pt.aa.npm r.gp.2
3836 3422 1142 3455 7007 4022 1623 1543 2021 7007

eyes and given them to me. 16 Have I now become your enemy by telling you the truth? ¶
⌐τοὺς ὀφθαλμοὺς⌐ ἐδώκατε → μοι → → ὥστε γέγονα ὑμῶν ἐχθρὸς →→ ὑμῖν ἀληθεύων
d.apm n.apm v.aai.2p r.ds.1 cj v.rai.1s r.gp.2 a.nsm r.dp.2 pt.pa.nsm
3836 4057 1443 1609 1181 1181 6063 1181 7007 2398 7007 238

17 Those people are zealous to win you over, but for no good. What they want is to alienate you from us, so
→ ζηλοῦσιν ὑμᾶς οὐ καλῶς ἀλλὰ → θέλουσιν ἐκκλεῖσαι ὑμᾶς ἵνα
v.pai.3p r.ap.2 pl adv cj v.pai.3p f.aa r.ap.2 cj
2420 7007 4024 2822 247 2527 1710 7007 2671

that you may be zealous for them. 18 It is fine to be zealous, provided the purpose is good, and to be so always
← → → ζηλοῦτε ← αὐτοὺς δὲ καλὸν → ζηλοῦσθαι ἐν καλῷ καὶ πάντοτε
v.pai.2p r.apm.3 cj a.nsn f.pp p.d a.dsn cj adv
2420 899 1254 2819 2420 1877 2819 2779 4121

and not just when I am with you. 19 My dear children, for whom I am again in the pains of childbirth
μὴ μόνον ἐν με ⌐τῷ παρεῖναι⌐ πρὸς ὑμᾶς μου → τέκνα → οὓς →→ πάλιν → ὠδίνω ← ←
pl adv p.d r.as.1 d.dsn f.pa p.a r.ap.2 r.gs.1 n.vpn r.apm adv v.pai.1s
3590 3667 1877 1609 3836 4205 4639 7007 1609 5451 4005 6048 6048 4099 6048

until Christ is formed in you, 20 how I wish I could be with you now and change my tone, because
⌐μέχρις οὖ⌐ Χριστὸς → μορφωθῇ ἐν ὑμῖν δὲ → ἤθελον →→ παρεῖναι πρὸς ὑμᾶς ἄρτι καὶ ἀλλάξαι μου ⌐τὴν φωνήν⌐ ὅτι
p.g r.gsm n.nsm v.aps.3s p.d r.dp.2 cj v.iai.1s f.pa p.a r.ap.2 adv cj f.aa r.gs.1 d.asf n.asf cj
3588 4005 5986 3672 1877 7007 1254 2527 4205 4639 7007 785 2779 248 1609 3836 5889 4022

I am perplexed about you!
→ → ἀποροῦμαι ἐν ὑμῖν
v.pmi.1s p.d r.dp.2
679 1877 7007

Hagar and Sarah

4:21 Tell me, you who want to be under the law, are you not aware of what the law says? 22 For it is
Λέγετέ μοι οἱ → θέλοντες εἶναι ὑπὸ νόμον →→ οὐκ ἀκούετε ← τὸν νόμον γὰρ →→
v.pam.2p r.ds.1 d.vpm pt.pa.vpm f.pa p.a n.asm pl v.pai.2p d.asm n.asm cj
3306 1609 3836 2527 1639 5679 3795 201 201 4024 201 3836 3795 1142

written that Abraham had two sons, one by the slave woman and the other by the free woman. 23
γέγραπται ὅτι Ἀβραὰμ ἔσχεν δύο υἱοὺς ἕνα ἐκ τῆς παιδίσκης ← καὶ ἕνα ἐκ τῆς ἐλευθέρας ← ἀλλ' μὲν
v.rpi.3s cj n.nsm v.aai.3s a.apm n.apm a.asm p.g d.gsf n.gsf cj a.asm p.g d.gsf a.gsf cj pl
1211 4022 11 2400 1545 5626 1651 1666 3836 4087 2779 1651 1666 3836 1801 247 3525

His son by the slave woman was born in the ordinary way; but his son by the free woman
ὁ ἐκ τῆς παιδίσκης ← → γεγέννηται ⌐κατὰ σάρκα⌐ δὲ ὁ ← ἐκ τῆς ἐλευθέρας ←
d.nsm p.g d.gsf n.gsf v.rpi.3s p.a n.asf cj d.nsm p.g d.gsf a.gsf
3836 1666 3836 4087 1164 2848 4922 1254 3836 1666 3836 1801

was born as the result of a promise. ¶ 24 These things may be taken figuratively, for the women represent
δι' ← ← ἐπαγγελίας ἅτινά ἐστιν ἀλληγορούμενα γάρ → αὗται εἰσιν
p.g n.gsf r.npn v.pai.3s pt.pp.npn cj r.npf v.pai.3p
1328 2039 4015 1639 251 1142 4047 1639

two covenants. One covenant is from Mount Sinai and bears children who are to be slaves: This is Hagar.
δύο διαθῆκαι μὲν μία ἀπὸ ὄρους Σινᾶ γεννῶσα ← εἰς δουλείαν ἥτις ἐστιν Ἀγάρ
a.npf n.npf pl a.nsf p.g n.gsn n.gsn pt.pa.nsf p.a n.asf r.nsf v.pai.3s n.nsf
1545 1347 3525 1651 608 4001 4982 1164 1650 1525 4015 1639 29

14 καὶ τὸν πειρασμὸν ὑμῶν ἐν τῇ σαρκί μου οὐκ ἐξουθενήσατε οὐδὲ ἐξεπτύσατε, ἀλλὰ ὡς ἄγγελον θεοῦ ἐδέξασθέ με, ὡς Χριστὸν Ἰησοῦν. 15 ποῦ οὖν ὁ μακαρισμὸς ὑμῶν; μαρτυρῶ γὰρ ὑμῖν ὅτι εἰ δυνατὸν τοὺς ὀφθαλμοὺς ὑμῶν ἐξορύξαντες ἐδώκατέ μοι. 16 ὥστε ἐχθρὸς ὑμῶν γέγονα ἀληθεύων ὑμῖν; ¶ 17 ζηλοῦσιν ὑμᾶς οὐ καλῶς, ἀλλὰ ἐκκλεῖσαι ὑμᾶς θέλουσιν, ἵνα αὐτοὺς ζηλοῦτε· 18 καλὸν δὲ ζηλοῦσθαι ἐν καλῷ πάντοτε καὶ μὴ μόνον ἐν τῷ παρεῖναί με πρὸς ὑμᾶς. 19 τέκνα μου, οὓς πάλιν ὠδίνω μέχρις οὗ μορφωθῇ Χριστὸς ἐν ὑμῖν· 20 ἤθελον δὲ παρεῖναι πρὸς ὑμᾶς ἄρτι καὶ ἀλλάξαι τὴν φωνήν μου, ὅτι ἀποροῦμαι ἐν ὑμῖν.

4:21 Λέγετέ μοι, οἱ ὑπὸ νόμον θέλοντες εἶναι, τὸν νόμον οὐκ ἀκούετε; 22 γέγραπται γὰρ ὅτι Ἀβραὰμ δύο υἱοὺς ἔσχεν, ἕνα ἐκ τῆς παιδίσκης καὶ ἕνα ἐκ τῆς ἐλευθέρας. 23 ἀλλ' ὁ μὲν ἐκ τῆς παιδίσκης κατὰ σάρκα γεγέννηται, ὁ δὲ ἐκ τῆς ἐλευθέρας δι' ἐπαγγελίας. ¶ 24 ἅτινά ἐστιν ἀλληγορούμενα· αὗται γάρ εἰσιν δύο διαθῆκαι, μία μὲν ἀπὸ ὄρους Σινᾶ εἰς δουλείαν γεννῶσα,

25 Now Hagar stands for Mount Sinai in Arabia and corresponds to the present city of Jerusalem, because she
δὲ ˻τὸ Ἁγάρ˼ ἐστὶν ← ὄρος Σινᾶ ἐν ˻τῇ Ἀραβίᾳ˼ δὲ συστοιχεῖ → τῇ νῦν Ἰερουσαλὴμ γὰρ →
pl d.nsn n.nsf v.pai.3s n.nsn n.nsn p.d d.dsf n.dsf cj v.pai.3s d.dsf adv n.dsf cj
1254 3836 29 1639 4001 4982 1877 3836 728 1254 5368 3836 3814 2647 1142

is in slavery with her children. **26** But the Jerusalem that is above is free, and she is our mother. **27** For it is
→ → δουλεύει μετὰ αὐτῆς ˻τῶν τέκνων˼ δὲ ἡ Ἰερουσαλὴμ ἄνω ἐστὶν ἐλευθέρα ἥτις ἐστὶν ἡμῶν μήτηρ γὰρ → →
v.pai.3s p.g r.gsf.3 d.gpn n.gpn pl d.nsf n.nsf adv v.pai.3s a.nsf r.nsf v.pai.3s r.gp.1 n.nsf cj
1526 3552 899 3836 5451 1254 3836 2647 539 1639 1801 4015 1639 7005 3613 1142

written: "Be glad, O barren woman, who bears no children; break forth and cry aloud, you who have no
γέγραπται → εὐφράνθητι → στεῖρα ← ἡ τίκτουσα οὐ → ῥῆξον καὶ βόησον → ἡ ↱ οὐκ
v.rpi.3s v.apm.2s n.vsf d.vsf pt.pa.vsf pl v.aam.2s cj v.aam.2s d.vsf pl
1211 2370 5096 3836 5503 4024 5503 4838 2779 1066 3836 6048 4024

labor pains; because more are the children of the desolate woman than of her who has a husband." ¶
→ ὠδίνουσα ὅτι πολλὰ τὰ τέκνα → τῆς ἐρήμου ← ˻μᾶλλον ἢ˼ → → τῆς ἐχούσης ˻τὸν ἄνδρα˼
pt.pa.vsf cj a.npn d.npn n.npn d.gsf a.gsf adv.c pl d.gsf pt.pa.gsf d.asm n.asm
6048 4022 4498 3836 5451 3836 2245 3437 2445 3836 2400 3836 467

28 Now you, brothers, like Isaac, are children of promise. **29** *At that time* the son born *in the*
δὲ ὑμεῖς ἀδελφοί κατὰ Ἰσαὰκ ἐστὲ τέκνα → ἐπαγγελίας ἀλλ᾽ ὥσπερ τότε ὁ γεννηθεὶς ˻κατὰ σάρκα˼
cj r.np.2 n.vpm p.a n.asm v.pai.2p n.npn n.gsf cj adv adv d.nsm pt.ap.nsm p.a n.asf
1254 7007 81 2848 2693 1639 5451 2039 247 6061 5538 3836 1164 2848 4922

ordinary way persecuted the son born by *the power of the* Spirit. It is the same now. **30** But what does the
ἐδίωκεν τὸν ← κατὰ πνεῦμα καὶ → → οὕτως νῦν ἀλλὰ τί → ἡ
v.iai.3s d.asm p.a n.asn adv adv adv cj r.asn d.nsf
1503 3836 2848 4460 2779 4048 3814 247 5515 3306 3836

Scripture say? "Get rid of the slave woman and her son, for the slave woman's son will never
γραφή λέγει → ἔκβαλε ← τὴν παιδίσκην ← καὶ αὐτῆς ˻τὸν υἱόν˼ γὰρ ὁ ˻τῆς παιδίσκης˼ ← υἱὸς → ˻οὐ μὴ˼
n.nsf v.pai.3s v.aam.2s d.asf n.asf cj r.gsf.3 d.asm n.asm cj d.nsm d.gsf n.gsf n.nsm pl pl
1210 3306 1675 3836 4087 2779 899 3836 5626 1142 3836 3836 4087 5626 3099 4024 3590

share in the inheritance with the free woman's son." **31** Therefore, brothers, we are not children of the
→ → κληρονομήσει μετὰ τοῦ ˻τῆς ἐλευθέρας˼ ← υἱοῦ διό ἀδελφοί → ἐσμὲν οὐκ τέκνα →
v.fai.3s p.g d.gsm d.gsf a.gsf n.gsm cj n.vpm v.pai.1p pl n.npn
3099 3552 3836 3836 1801 5626 1475 81 1639 4024 5451

slave woman, but of the free woman.
παιδίσκης ← ἀλλὰ τῆς ἐλευθέρας ←
n.gsf cj d.gsf a.gsf
4087 247 3836 1801

Freedom in Christ

5:1 It is for freedom that Christ has set us free. Stand firm, then, and do not let yourselves be
→ ˻Τῇ ἐλευθερίᾳ˼ Χριστὸς → ἡμᾶς ἠλευθέρωσεν στήκετε ← οὖν καὶ μὴ → →
d.dsf n.dsf n.nsm r.ap.1 v.aai.3s v.pam.2p cj cj pl
3836 1800 5986 1802 1802 7005 1802 5112 4036 2779 1923 3590

burdened again by a yoke of slavery. ¶ **2** *Mark my words!* I, Paul, tell you that if you let yourselves be
ἐνέχεσθε πάλιν → ζυγῷ → δουλείας Ἴδε ἐγὼ Παῦλος λέγω ὑμῖν ὅτι ἐὰν → →
v.ppm.2p adv n.dsm n.gsf pl r.ns.1 n.nsm v.pai.1s r.dp.2 cj cj
1923 4099 2433 1525 2623 1609 4263 3306 7007 4022 1569

circumcised, Christ will be of no value to you at all. **3** Again I declare to every man who lets himself
περιτέμνησθε Χριστὸς → → οὐδὲν ὠφελήσει ὑμᾶς ← ← δὲ πάλιν → μαρτύρομαι → παντὶ ἀνθρώπῳ → →
v.pps.2p n.nsm a.asn v.fai.3s r.ap.2 cj adv v.pmi.1s a.dsm n.dsm
4362 5986 6067 6067 6067 4029 6067 7007 4029 4029 1254 4099 3458 4246 476

be circumcised that he is obligated to obey the whole law. **4** You who are trying to be justified by law have
→ περιτεμνομένῳ ὅτι → ἐστὶν ὀφειλέτης → ποιῆσαι τὸν ὅλον νόμον οἵτινες → → → δικαιοῦσθε ἐν νόμῳ →
pt.pm.dsm cj v.pai.3s n.nsm f.aa d.asm a.asm n.asm r.npm v.ppi.2p p.d n.dsm
4362 4022 1639 4050 4472 3836 3910 3795 2934 4015 1467 1877 3795

been alienated from Christ; you have fallen away from grace. **5** But by faith we *eagerly await* through the
→ κατηργήθητε ἀπὸ Χριστοῦ → → ἐξεπέσατε ← ˻τῆς χάριτος˼ γὰρ ἐκ πίστεως ἡμεῖς ἐλπίδα →
v.api.2p p.g n.gsm v.aai.2p d.gsf n.gsf cj p.g n.gsf r.np.1 n.asf
2934 608 5986 1738 3836 5921 1142 1666 4411 7005 1828

ἥτις ἐστὶν Ἁγάρ. ²⁵ τὸ δὲ Ἁγὰρ Σινᾶ ὄρος ἐστὶν ἐν τῇ Ἀραβίᾳ· συστοιχεῖ δὲ τῇ νῦν Ἰερουσαλήμ, δουλεύει γὰρ μετὰ τῶν τέκνων αὐτῆς. ²⁶ ἡ δὲ ἄνω Ἰερουσαλὴμ ἐλευθέρα ἐστίν, ἥτις ἐστὶν μήτηρ ἡμῶν· ²⁷ γέγραπται γάρ, Εὐφράνθητι, στεῖρα ἡ οὐ τίκτουσα, ῥῆξον καὶ βόησον, ἡ οὐκ ὠδίνουσα· ὅτι πολλὰ τὰ τέκνα τῆς ἐρήμου μᾶλλον ἢ τῆς ἐχούσης τὸν ἄνδρα. ¶ ²⁸ ὑμεῖς δέ, ἀδελφοί, κατὰ Ἰσαὰκ ἐπαγγελίας τέκνα ἐστέ. ²⁹ ἀλλ᾽ ὥσπερ τότε ὁ κατὰ σάρκα γεννηθεὶς ἐδίωκεν τὸν κατὰ πνεῦμα, οὕτως καὶ νῦν. ³⁰ ἀλλὰ τί λέγει ἡ γραφή; Ἔκβαλε τὴν παιδίσκην καὶ τὸν υἱὸν αὐτῆς· οὐ γὰρ μὴ κληρονομήσει ὁ υἱὸς τῆς παιδίσκης μετὰ τοῦ υἱοῦ τῆς ἐλευθέρας. ³¹ διό, ἀδελφοί, οὐκ ἐσμὲν παιδίσκης τέκνα ἀλλὰ τῆς ἐλευθέρας.

⁵:¹ τῇ ἐλευθερίᾳ ἡμᾶς Χριστὸς ἠλευθέρωσεν· στήκετε οὖν καὶ μὴ πάλιν ζυγῷ δουλείας ἐνέχεσθε. ¶ ² Ἴδε ἐγὼ Παῦλος λέγω ὑμῖν ὅτι ἐὰν περιτέμνησθε, Χριστὸς ὑμᾶς οὐδὲν ὠφελήσει. ³ μαρτύρομαι δὲ πάλιν παντὶ ἀνθρώπῳ περιτεμνομένῳ ὅτι ὀφειλέτης ἐστὶν ὅλον τὸν νόμον ποιῆσαι. ⁴ κατηργήθητε ἀπὸ Χριστοῦ, οἵτινες ἐν νόμῳ δικαιοῦσθε, τῆς χάριτος ἐξεπέσατε. ⁵ ἡμεῖς γὰρ

Spirit   the   righteousness   for which   we hope.   **6** For in   Christ   Jesus   neither   circumcision   nor   uncircumcision   has
πνεύματι   δικαιοσύνης   →   ἀπεκδεχόμεθα   γὰρ   ἐν   Χριστῷ   Ἰησοῦ   οὔτε   περιτομή   οὔτε   ἀκροβυστία   →
n.dsn   n.gsf   v.pmi.1p   cj   p.d   n.dsm   n.dsm   cj   n.nsf   cj   n.nsf
4460   1466   587   1142   1877   5986   2652   4046   4364   4046   213   2710

any value.   The only thing that counts is   faith   expressing itself   through   love.   ¶   **7** You   were running a
τι   ἰσχύει   ἀλλὰ   πίστις   ἐνεργουμένη   ←   δι'   ἀγάπης   →   →   Ἐτρέχετε
r.asn   v.pai.3s   cj   n.nsf   pt.pm.nsf   p.g   n.gsf   v.iai.2p
5516   2710   247   4411   1919   1328   27   5556

good   race.   Who   cut   in on you   and kept   you from obeying the truth?   **8** That kind of persuasion   does not
καλῶς   ←   τίς   ἐνέκοψεν   ←   ὑμᾶς   μὴ   πείθεσθαι   →   τῇ   ἀληθείᾳ   ἡ   ←   πεισμονὴ   οὐκ
adv   r.nsm   v.aai.3s   r.ap.2   pl   f.pp   d.dsf   n.dsf   d.nsf   n.nsf   pl
2822   5556   5515   1601   7007   3590   4275   3836   237   3836   4282   4024

come   from   the one who calls   you.   **9** "A   little   yeast   works   through   the whole   batch   of dough."   **10** I   am confident
ἐκ   τοῦ   ←   ←   καλοῦντος   ὑμᾶς   μικρὰ   ζύμη   ζυμοῖ   ←   τὸ   ὅλον   φύραμα   ←   ←   ἐγὼ   πέποιθα
p.g   d.gsm   pt.pa.gsm   r.ap.2   a.nsf   n.nsf   v.pai.3s   d.asn   a.asn   n.asn   r.ns.1   v.rai.1s
1666   3836   2813   7007   3625   2434   2435   3836   3910   5878   1609   4275

in the Lord   that   you   will take   no   other   view.   The one who is   throwing you   into confusion   will
εἰς   ὑμᾶς   ἐν   κυρίῳ   ὅτι   →   →   οὐδὲν   ἄλλο   φρονήσετε   δὲ   ὁ   ←   ←   ←   ←   ὑμᾶς   →   ταράσσων
p.a   r.ap.2   p.d   n.dsm   cj   a.asn   r.asn   v.fai.2p   cj   d.nsm   r.ap.2   pt.pa.nsm
1650   7007   1877   3261   4022   5858   5858   5858   4029   257   5858   1254   3836   5429   5429   7007   5429

pay   the penalty,   whoever   he may be.   **11**   Brothers,   if   I   am still   preaching   circumcision,   why am I   still
βαστάσει   τὸ   κρίμα   ὅστις   ἐὰν   →   →   ᾖ   δὲ   ἀδελφοί   εἰ   Ἐγὼ   →   ἔτι   κηρύσσω   περιτομὴν   τί   →   ἔτι
v.fai.3s   d.asn   n.asn   r.nsm   pl   v.pas.3s   cj   n.vpm   cj   r.ns.1   adv   v.pai.1s   n.asf   r.asn   adv
1002   3836   3210   4015   1569   1639   1254   81   1623   1609   4364   2285   3062   4364   5515   1503   1503   2285

being persecuted?   In   that case   the offense   of the cross   has been abolished.   **12** As for those agitators,   I
→   διώκομαι   ἄρα   ←   ←   τὸ   σκάνδαλον   →   τοῦ   σταυροῦ   →   →   κατήργηται   οἱ   ἀναστατοῦντες   ὑμᾶς   →
v.ppi.1s   cj   d.nsn   n.nsn   d.gsm   n.gsm   v.rpi.3s   d.npm   pt.pa.npm   r.ap.2
1503   726   3836   4998   3836   5089   2934   3836   415   7007

wish   they would go the whole way and   emasculate   themselves!   ¶   **13**   You,   my brothers,   were   called   to
Ὄφελον   καὶ   →   →   ἀποκόψονται   ←   γὰρ   ὑμεῖς   ἀδελφοί   →   ἐκλήθητε   ἐπ'
pl   cj   v.fmi.3p   cj   r.np.2   n.vpm   v.api.2p   p.d
4054   2779   644   1142   7007   81   2813   2093

be   free.   But   do not   use   your   freedom   to   indulge   the sinful nature;   rather,   serve   one   another   in
←   ἐλευθερίᾳ   μόνον   μὴ   τὴν   ἐλευθερίαν   εἰς   ἀφορμὴν   τῇ   σαρκί   ←   ἀλλὰ   δουλεύετε   ἀλλήλοις   ←   διὰ
n.dsf   adv   pl   d.asf   n.asf   p.a   n.asf   d.dsf   n.dsf   cj   v.pam.2p   r.dpm   p.g
1800   3667   3590   3836   1800   1650   929   3836   4922   247   1526   253   1328

love.   **14**   The entire   law   is summed   up in   a single   command: "Love   your   neighbor   as
τῆς   ἀγάπης   γὰρ   ὁ   πᾶς   νόμος   πεπλήρωται   →   ἐν   ἑνὶ   λόγῳ   ἐν   τῷ   Ἀγαπήσεις   σου   τὸν   πλησίον   ὡς
d.gsf   n.gsf   cj   d.nsm   a.nsm   n.nsm   v.rpi.3s   p.d   a.dsm   n.dsm   p.d   d.dsn   v.fai.2s   r.gs.2   d.asm   adv
3836   27   1142   3836   4246   3795   4444   1877   1651   3364   1877   3836   26   5148   3836   4446   6055

yourself."   **15**   If   you   keep on   biting   and   devouring   each   other,   watch out   or   you will be destroyed by
σεαυτόν   δὲ   εἰ   →   →   →   δάκνετε   καὶ   κατεσθίετε   ἀλλήλους   ←   βλέπετε   μὴ   →   →   →   ἀναλωθῆτε   ὑπ'
r.asm.2   cj   cj   v.pai.2p   cj   v.pai.2p   r.apm   v.pam.2p   cj   v.aps.2p   p.g
4932   1254   1623   1231   2779   2983   253   1063   3590   384   5679

each   other.
ἀλλήλων   ←
r.gpm
253

Life by the Spirit

5:16 So   I   say,   live   by the Spirit,   and you   will not   gratify   the desires   of the sinful nature.   **17** For the
δὲ   Λέγω   περιπατεῖτε   →   πνεύματι   καὶ   →   οὐ   μὴ   τελέσητε   ἐπιθυμίαν   →   σαρκὸς   ←   γὰρ   ἡ
cj   v.pai.1s   v.pam.2p   n.dsn   cj   pl   pl   v.aas.2p   n.asf   n.gsf   cj   d.nsf
1254   3306   4344   4460   2779   5464   5464   4024   3590   5464   2123   4922   1142   3836

sinful nature   desires   what is contrary   to the Spirit,   and the   Spirit   what is contrary   to the sinful nature.   They
σὰρξ   ←   ἐπιθυμεῖ   κατὰ   ←   τοῦ   πνεύματος   δὲ   τὸ   πνεῦμα   κατὰ   ←   τῆς   σαρκός   ←   γὰρ   ταῦτα
n.nsf   v.pai.3s   p.g   d.gsn   n.gsn   cj   d.nsn   n.nsn   p.g   d.gsf   n.gsf   cj   r.npn
4922   2121   2848   3836   4460   1254   3836   4460   2848   3836   4922   1142   4047

πνεύματι ἐκ πίστεως ἐλπίδα δικαιοσύνης ἀπεκδεχόμεθα. **6** ἐν γὰρ Χριστῷ Ἰησοῦ οὔτε περιτομή τι ἰσχύει οὔτε ἀκροβυστία ἀλλὰ πίστις δι' ἀγάπης ἐνεργουμένη. ¶ **7** Ἐτρέχετε καλῶς· τίς ὑμᾶς ἐνέκοψεν [τῇ] ἀληθείᾳ μὴ πείθεσθαι; **8** ἡ πεισμονὴ οὐκ ἐκ τοῦ καλοῦντος ὑμᾶς. **9** μικρὰ ζύμη ὅλον τὸ φύραμα ζυμοῖ. **10** ἐγὼ πέποιθα εἰς ὑμᾶς ἐν κυρίῳ ὅτι οὐδὲν ἄλλο φρονήσετε· ὁ δὲ ταράσσων ὑμᾶς βαστάσει τὸ κρίμα, ὅστις ἐὰν ᾖ. **11** ἐγὼ δέ, ἀδελφοί, εἰ περιτομὴν ἔτι κηρύσσω, τί ἔτι διώκομαι; ἄρα κατήργηται τὸ σκάνδαλον τοῦ σταυροῦ. **12** ὄφελον καὶ ἀποκόψονται οἱ ἀναστατοῦντες ὑμᾶς. ¶ **13** Ὑμεῖς γὰρ ἐπ' ἐλευθερίᾳ ἐκλήθητε, ἀδελφοί· μόνον μὴ τὴν ἐλευθερίαν εἰς ἀφορμὴν τῇ σαρκί, ἀλλὰ διὰ τῆς ἀγάπης δουλεύετε ἀλλήλοις. **14** ὁ γὰρ πᾶς νόμος ἐν ἑνὶ λόγῳ πεπλήρωται, ἐν τῷ Ἀγαπήσεις τὸν πλησίον σου ὡς σεαυτόν. **15** εἰ δὲ ἀλλήλους δάκνετε καὶ κατεσθίετε, βλέπετε μὴ ὑπ' ἀλλήλων ἀναλωθῆτε.

5:16 Λέγω δέ, πνεύματι περιπατεῖτε καὶ ἐπιθυμίαν σαρκὸς οὐ μὴ τελέσητε. **17** ἡ γὰρ σὰρξ ἐπιθυμεῖ κατὰ τοῦ πνεύματος, τὸ δὲ πνεῦμα κατὰ τῆς σαρκός, ταῦτα γὰρ ἀλλήλοις ἀντίκειται, ἵνα μὴ ἃ ἐὰν θέλητε ταῦτα ποιῆτε. **18** εἰ δὲ πνεύματι ἄγεσθε, οὐκ

are in conflict   with each   other, so that you do not do   what   you want. **18** But if you are led   by
→ ἀντίκειται → ἀλλήλοις ← ἵνα ← τοῦτο → μὴ ποιῆτε ταῦτα ἃ ἐὰν → θέλητε δὲ εἰ → ἄγεσθε
v.pmi.3s   r.dpn   cj   pl v.pas.2p r.apn r.apn pl v.pas.2p cj cj   v.ppi.2p
512   253   2671   4472 4472 3590 4472 4047 4005 1569 2527 1254 1623   72

the Spirit,   you are not under law. ¶   **19**   The acts of the sinful nature are obvious: sexual
πνεύματι → ἐστὲ οὐκ ὑπὸ νόμον.   δὲ τὰ ἔργα τῆς σαρκός ← ἐστιν φανερὰ ἅτινά ἐστιν →
n.dsn   v.pai.2p p.a n.asn   cj d.npn n.npn d.gsf n.gsf   v.pai.3s a.npn r.npn v.pai.3s
4460   1639 4024 5679 3795   1254 3836 2240 3836 4922   1639 5745 4015 1639

immorality, impurity and debauchery; **20** idolatry   and witchcraft; hatred, discord, jealousy, fits of rage, selfish
πορνεία ἀκαθαρσία ἀσέλγεια   εἰδωλολατρία   φαρμακεία ἔχθραι ἔρις ζῆλος → θυμοί
n.nsf   n.nsf   n.nsf   n.nsf   n.nsf   n.npf   n.nsf n.nsm   n.npm
4518   174   816   1630   5758   2397   2251 2419   2596

ambition, dissensions, factions **21** and envy; drunkenness, orgies, and the like.   I warn   you, as   I did
ἐριθεῖαι διχοστασίαι αἱρέσεις   φθόνοι μέθαι   κῶμοι καὶ τὰ ὅμοια τούτοις ἃ → προλέγω ὑμῖν καθὼς →
n.npf   n.npf   n.npf   n.npm n.npf   n.npm cj d.npn a.npn r.dpn r.apn v.pai.1s r.dp.2 cj
2249   1496   146   5784   3494   3269 2779 3836 3927 4047 4005 4625 7007 2777

before, that those who live   like this   will not inherit   the kingdom of God. ¶ **22** But the
προεῖπον ὅτι οἱ ← πράσσοντες ← ⌜τὰ τοιαῦτα⌝ → οὐ κληρονομήσουσιν βασιλείαν → θεοῦ   δὲ ὁ
v.aai.1s ὅτι d.npm   pt.pa.npm   d.apn r.apn   pl v.fai.3p   n.asf   n.gsm   cj d.nsm
4597   4022 3836   4556   3836 5525   3099 4024 3099   993   2536   1254 3836

fruit of the Spirit   is   love, joy, peace, patience, kindness, goodness, faithfulness, **23** gentleness and self-control.
καρπὸς → τοῦ πνεύματος ἐστιν ἀγάπη χαρὰ εἰρήνη μακροθυμία χρηστότης ἀγαθωσύνη πίστις   πραΰτης   ἐγκράτεια
n.nsm   d.gsn n.gsn   v.pai.3s n.nsf n.nsf n.nsf   n.nsf   n.nsf   n.nsf   n.nsf   n.nsf   n.nsf
2843   3836 4460   1639   27   5915 1645   3429   5983   20   4411   4559   1602

Against such things   there is no law. **24** Those who belong to Christ   Jesus have crucified the sinful
κατὰ → ⌜τῶν τοιούτων⌝ → ἔστιν οὐκ νόμος δὲ οἱ   ⌜τοῦ Χριστοῦ⌝ Ἰησοῦ → ἐσταύρωσαν τὴν σάρκα
p.g   d.gpn r.gpn   v.pai.3s pl n.nsm cj d.npm   d.gsm n.gsm   n.gsm   v.aai.3p   d.asf n.asf
2848   3836 5525   1639   4024 3795 1254 3836   3836 5986   2652   5090   3836 4922

nature with its passions and desires. **25** Since we live by the Spirit,   let us keep   in step with the
← σὺν τοῖς παθήμασιν καὶ ⌜ταῖς ἐπιθυμίαις⌝ Εἰ → ζῶμεν πνεύματι καὶ → στοιχῶμεν
   p.d d.dpn n.dpn   cj d.dpf n.dpf   cj   v.pai.1p n.dsn   cj   v.pas.1p
   5250 3836 4077   2779 3836 2123   1623   2409   4460   2779   5123

Spirit. **26** Let us not become conceited, provoking   and envying   each   other.
πνεύματι → → μὴ γινώμεθα κενόδοξοι προκαλούμενοι ἀλλήλους φθονοῦντες ἀλλήλοις ←
n.dsn   pl v.pms.1p a.npm   pt.pm.npm   r.apm   pt.pa.npm   r.dpm
4460   1181 1181 3590 1181   3030   4614   253   5783   253

Doing Good to All

6:1 Brothers, if   someone is caught in a sin,   you who are spiritual   should restore
καὶ Ἀδελφοί ἐὰν ἄνθρωπος → προλημφθῇ ἔν τινι παραπτώματι ὑμεῖς οἱ πνευματικοὶ → καταρτίζετε
adv   n.vpm   cj   n.nsm   v.aps.3s   p.d r.dsn n.dsn   r.np.2 d.npm a.npm   v.pam.2p
2779   81   1569 476   4624   1877 5516 4183   7007 3836 4461   2936

him   gently.   But watch yourself, or you also may be tempted. **2** Carry   each   other's
⌜τὸν τοιοῦτον⌝ ⌜ἐν πνεύματι πραΰτητος⌝ σκοπῶν σεαυτὸν μὴ σὺ καὶ → πειρασθῇς βαστάζετε Ἀλλήλων ←
d.asm r.asm   p.d n.dsn   n.gsf   pt.pa.nsm r.asm.2 pl r.ns.2 adv   v.aps.2s   v.pam.2p   r.gpm
3836 5525   1877 4460   4559   5023   4932 3590 5148 2779   4279   1002   253

burdens, and in   this way you will fulfill   the law of Christ. **3**   If anyone thinks he is   something
⌜τὰ βάρη⌝ καὶ οὕτως ← ← → ἀναπληρώσετε τὸν νόμον ⌜τοῦ Χριστοῦ⌝ γὰρ εἰ τις δοκεῖ → εἶναι τι
d.apn n.apn   cj adv   v.fai.2p   d.asm n.asm d.gsm n.gsm   cj   cj   r.nsm v.pai.3s   f.pa r.nsn
3836 983   2779 4048   405   3836 3795   3836 5986   1142 1623 5516 1506   1639 5516

when he is   nothing, he deceives himself. **4** Each one should test   his own actions.   Then he can
→ ὢν μηδὲν → φρεναπατᾷ ἑαυτόν δὲ ἕκαστος → δοκιμαζέτω ἑαυτοῦ → ⌜τὸ ἔργον⌝ καὶ τότε →
  pt.pa.nsm a.nsn   v.pai.3s   r.asm.3 cj   r.nsm   v.pam.3s   r.gsm.3   d.asn n.asn cj adv
  1639 3594   5854   1571   1254 1667   1507   1571   3836 2240 2779 5538

take pride   in himself,   without comparing himself to somebody else, **5** for each   one should carry
ἕξει ⌜τὸ καύχημα⌝ εἰς ἑαυτὸν μόνον καὶ οὐκ   εἰς ⌜τὸν ἕτερον⌝ γὰρ ἕκαστος ← → βαστάσει
v.fai.3s d.asn n.asn   p.a r.asm.3 adv cj pl   p.a d.asm r.asm   cj   r.nsm   v.fai.3s
2400 3836 3017   1650 1571   3668 2779 4024   1650 3836 2283   1142 1667   1002

ἐστὲ ὑπὸ νόμον. ¶ ¹⁹ φανερὰ δέ ἐστιν τὰ ἔργα τῆς σαρκός, ἅτινά ἐστιν πορνεία, ἀκαθαρσία, ἀσέλγεια, ²⁰ εἰδωλολατρία, φαρμακεία, ἔχθραι, ἔρις, ζῆλος, θυμοί, ἐριθεῖαι, διχοστασίαι, αἱρέσεις, ²¹ φθόνοι, μέθαι, κῶμοι καὶ τὰ ὅμοια τούτοις, ἃ προλέγω ὑμῖν καθὼς προεῖπον ὅτι οἱ τὰ τοιαῦτα πράσσοντες βασιλείαν θεοῦ οὐ κληρονομήσουσιν. ¶ ²² Ὁ δὲ καρπὸς τοῦ πνεύματός ἐστιν ἀγάπη χαρὰ εἰρήνη, μακροθυμία χρηστότης ἀγαθωσύνη, πίστις ²³ πραΰτης ἐγκράτεια· κατὰ τῶν τοιούτων οὐκ ἔστιν νόμος. ²⁴ οἱ δὲ τοῦ Χριστοῦ [Ἰησοῦ] τὴν σάρκα ἐσταύρωσαν σὺν τοῖς παθήμασιν καὶ ταῖς ἐπιθυμίαις. ²⁵ εἰ ζῶμεν πνεύματι, πνεύματι καὶ στοιχῶμεν. ²⁶ μὴ γινώμεθα κενόδοξοι, ἀλλήλους προκαλούμενοι, ἀλλήλοις φθονοῦντες.

⁶:¹ Ἀδελφοί, ἐὰν καὶ προλημφθῇ ἄνθρωπος ἔν τινι παραπτώματι, ὑμεῖς οἱ πνευματικοὶ καταρτίζετε τὸν τοιοῦτον ἐν πνεύματι πραΰτητος, σκοπῶν σεαυτὸν μὴ καὶ σὺ πειρασθῇς. ² Ἀλλήλων τὰ βάρη βαστάζετε καὶ οὕτως ἀναπληρώσετε τὸν νόμον τοῦ Χριστοῦ. ³ εἰ γὰρ δοκεῖ τις εἶναί τι μηδὲν ὤν, φρεναπατᾷ ἑαυτόν. ⁴ τὸ δὲ ἔργον ἑαυτοῦ δοκιμαζέτω ἕκαστος, καὶ τότε εἰς ἑαυτὸν μόνον τὸ καύχημα ἕξει καὶ οὐκ εἰς τὸν ἕτερον· ⁵ ἕκαστος γὰρ τὸ ἴδιον φορτίον βαστάσει. ¶ ⁶ Κοινωνείτω δὲ ὁ κατηχούμενος

his own load. ¶ **6** Anyone who receives instruction in the word must share all good things
τὸ ἴδιον φορτίον δὲ ὁ   κατηχούμενος ← τὸν λόγον → Κοινωνείτω ἐν πᾶσιν ἀγαθοῖς ←
d.asn a.asn n.asn   cj d.nsm   pt.pp.nsm   d.asm n.asm   v.pam.3s   p.d a.dpn a.dpn
3836 2625 5845   1254 3836   2994   3836 3364   3125   1877 4246 19

with his instructor. ¶ **7** Do not be deceived: God cannot be mocked. A man reaps what
τῷ κατηχοῦντι   Μὴ πλανᾶσθε θεὸς οὐ   μυκτηρίζεται γὰρ ἄνθρωπος θερίσει τοῦτο καὶ ὃ ἐὰν
d.dsm pt.pa.dsm   pl v.ppm.2p n.nsm pl   v.ppi.3s   cj n.nsm v.fai.3s r.asn adv r.asn cj
3836 2994   4414 3590 2536 4024   3682   1142 476 2545 4047 2779 4005 1569

he sows. **8** The one who sows to please his sinful nature, from that nature will reap destruction; the
σπείρῃ ὅτι ὁ   σπείρων εἰς   ἑαυτοῦ τὴν σάρκα   ἐκ τῆς σαρκὸς → θερίσει φθοράν δὲ ὁ
v.pas.3s cj d.nsm   pt.pa.nsm p.a   r.gsm.3 d.asf n.asf   p.g d.gsf n.gsf   v.fai.3s n.asf cj d.nsm
5062 4022 3836   5062 1650   1571 3836 4922   1666 3836 4922   2545 5785 1254 3836

one who sows to please the Spirit, from the Spirit will reap eternal life. **9** Let us not become weary in
σπείρων εἰς   τὸ πνεῦμα ἐκ τοῦ πνεύματος → θερίσει αἰώνιον ζωήν δὲ μὴ → ἐγκακῶμεν ←
pt.pa.nsm p.a   d.asn n.asn p.g d.gsn n.gsn   v.fai.3s a.asf n.asf cj pl v.pas.1p
5062 1650   3836 4460 1666 3836 4460   2545 173 2437 1254 1591 1591 3590   1591

doing good, for at the proper time we will reap a harvest if we do not give up. **10** Therefore, as we
ποιοῦντες τὸ καλόν γὰρ → ἰδίῳ καιρῷ → θερίσομεν ← μὴ ἐκλυόμενοι Ἄρα οὖν ὡς
pt.pa.npm d.asn a.asn cj   a.dsm n.dsm   v.fai.1p   pl pt.pp.npm cj cj adv
4472 3836 2819 1142   2625 2789   2545   1725 1725 1725 3590 1725   726 4036 6055

have opportunity, let us do good to all people, especially to those who belong to the family
ἔχομεν καιρόν ἐργαζώμεθα τὸ ἀγαθόν πρὸς πάντας δὲ μάλιστα πρὸς τοὺς → οἰκείους
v.pai.1p n.asm v.pms.1p d.asn a.asn p.a a.apm cj adv.s p.a d.apm   n.apm
2400 2789 2237 3836 19 4639 4246 1254 3436 4639 3836   3858

of believers.
πίστεως
n.gsf
4411

Not Circumcision but a New Creation

6:11 See what large letters I use as I write to you with my own hand! ¶ **12** Those who want to
ἴδετε πηλίκοις γράμμασιν ἔγραψα ὑμῖν ἐμῇ τῇ χειρί Ὅσοι ← θέλουσιν →
v.aam.2p r.dpn n.dpn v.aai.1s r.dp.2 r.dsf.1 d.dsf n.dsf r.npm   v.pai.3p
1625 4383 1207 1211 700/ 5931 1847 3836 5931 4012   2527

make a good impression outwardly are trying to compel you to be circumcised. The only reason they do
εὐπροσωπῆσαι ἐν σαρκί οὗτοι → ἀναγκάζουσιν ὑμᾶς → περιτέμνεσθαι μόνον ἵνα
f.aa p.d n.dsf r.npm   v.pai.3p r.ap.2   f.pp adv cj
2349 1877 4922 4047   337 7007   4362 3667 2671

this is to avoid being persecuted for the cross of Christ. **13** Not even those who are circumcised
μὴ διώκωνται τῷ σταυρῷ τοῦ Χριστοῦ γὰρ οὐδὲ οἱ περιτεμνόμενοι αὐτοὶ
pl v.pps.3p d.dsm n.dsm d.gsm n.gsm cj adv d.npm pt.pp.npm r.npm
1503 1503 3590 1503 3836 5089 3836 5986 1142 4028 3836 4362 899

obey the law, yet they want you to be circumcised that they may boast about your flesh.
φυλάσσουσιν νόμον ἀλλὰ θέλουσιν ὑμᾶς → περιτέμνεσθαι ἵνα → καυχήσωνται ἐν ὑμετέρᾳ τῇ σαρκὶ
v.pai.3p n.asm cj v.pai.3p r.ap.2   f.pp cj   v.ams.3p p.d r.dsf.2 d.dsf n.dsf
5875 3795 247 2527 7007   4362 2671   3016 1877 5629 3836 4922

14 May I never boast except in the cross of our Lord Jesus Christ, through which the world
δὲ Ἐμοὶ μὴ γένοιτο καυχᾶσθαι εἰ μὴ ἐν τῷ σταυρῷ ἡμῶν τοῦ κυρίου Ἰησοῦ Χριστοῦ δι᾽ οὗ κόσμος
cj r.ds.1 pl v.amo.3s f.pm cj pl p.d d.dsm n.dsm r.gp.1 d.gsm n.gsm n.gsm n.gsm p.g r.gsm n.nsm
1254 1181 1609 3590 1181 3016 1623 3590 1877 3836 5089 3261 7005 3836 3261 2652 5986 1328 4005 3180

has been crucified to me, and I to the world. **15** Neither circumcision nor uncircumcision means anything; *what*
ἐσταύρωται ἐμοὶ κἀγὼ κόσμῳ γὰρ οὔτε περιτομή οὔτε ἀκροβυστία ἐστιν τί ἀλλὰ
v.rpi.3s r.ds.1 crasis n.dsm cj cj n.nsf cj n.nsf v.pai.3s r.nsn cj
5090 1609 2743 3180 1142 4046 4364 4046 213 1639 5516 247

counts is a new creation. **16** Peace and mercy to all who follow this rule, even to the Israel of
καινὴ κτίσις καὶ εἰρήνη καὶ ἔλεος ἐπ᾽ αὐτοὺς ὅσοι στοιχήσουσιν τούτῳ τῷ κανόνι καὶ ἐπὶ τὸν Ἰσραὴλ →
a.nsf n.nsf cj n.nsf cj n.nsn p.a r.apm.3 r.npm v.fai.3p r.dsm d.dsm n.dsm cj p.a d.asm n.asm
2785 3232 2779 1645 2779 1799 2093 899 4012 5123 4047 3836 2834 2779 2093 3836 2702

τὸν λόγον τῷ κατηχοῦντι ἐν πᾶσιν ἀγαθοῖς. ¶ ⁷ Μὴ πλανᾶσθε, θεὸς οὐ μυκτηρίζεται. ὃ γὰρ ἐὰν σπείρῃ ἄνθρωπος, τοῦτο καὶ θερίσει· ⁸ ὅτι ὁ σπείρων εἰς τὴν σάρκα ἑαυτοῦ ἐκ τῆς σαρκὸς θερίσει φθοράν, ὁ δὲ σπείρων εἰς τὸ πνεῦμα ἐκ τοῦ πνεύματος θερίσει ζωὴν αἰώνιον. ⁹ τὸ δὲ καλὸν ποιοῦντες μὴ ἐγκακῶμεν, καιρῷ γὰρ ἰδίῳ θερίσομεν μὴ ἐκλυόμενοι. ¹⁰ ἄρα οὖν ὡς καιρὸν ἔχομεν, ἐργαζώμεθα τὸ ἀγαθὸν πρὸς πάντας, μάλιστα δὲ πρὸς τοὺς οἰκείους τῆς πίστεως.

⁶:¹¹ Ἴδετε πηλίκοις ὑμῖν γράμμασιν ἔγραψα τῇ ἐμῇ χειρί. ¶ ¹² ὅσοι θέλουσιν εὐπροσωπῆσαι ἐν σαρκί, οὗτοι ἀναγκάζουσιν ὑμᾶς περιτέμνεσθαι, μόνον ἵνα τῷ σταυρῷ τοῦ Χριστοῦ μὴ διώκωνται. ¹³ οὐδὲ γὰρ οἱ περιτεμνόμενοι αὐτοὶ νόμον φυλάσσουσιν ἀλλὰ θέλουσιν ὑμᾶς περιτέμνεσθαι, ἵνα ἐν τῇ ὑμετέρᾳ σαρκὶ καυχήσωνται. ¹⁴ ἐμοὶ δὲ μὴ γένοιτο καυχᾶσθαι εἰ μὴ ἐν τῷ σταυρῷ τοῦ κυρίου ἡμῶν Ἰησοῦ Χριστοῦ, δι᾽ οὗ ἐμοὶ κόσμος ἐσταύρωται κἀγὼ κόσμῳ. ¹⁵ οὔτε γὰρ περιτομή τί ἐστιν οὔτε ἀκροβυστία ἀλλὰ καινὴ κτίσις. ¹⁶ καὶ ὅσοι τῷ κανόνι τούτῳ στοιχήσουσιν, εἰρήνη ἐπ᾽ αὐτοὺς καὶ ἔλεος καὶ ἐπὶ τὸν Ἰσραὴλ τοῦ θεοῦ. ¶

God. ¶ 17 Finally, let no one cause me trouble, for I bear on my body the marks of
ˌτοῦ θεοῦˌ ˌΤοῦ λοιποῦˌ μηδεὶς ← παρεχέτω μοι κόπους γὰρ ἐγὼ βαστάζω ἐν μου ˌτῷ σώματίˌ τὰ στίγματα →
d.gsm n.gsm d.gsn adv a.nsm v.pam.3s r.ds.1 n.apm cj r.ns.1 v.pai.1s p.d r.gs.1 d.dsn n.dsn d.apn n.apn
3836 2536 3836 3370 4218 3594 4218 1609 3160 1142 1609 1002 1877 1609 3836 5393 3836 5116

Jesus. ¶ 18 The grace of our Lord Jesus Christ be with your spirit, brothers. Amen.
ˌτοῦ Ἰησοῦˌ Ἡ χάρις → ἡμῶν ˌτοῦ κυρίουˌ Ἰησοῦ Χριστοῦ μετὰ ὑμῶν ˌτοῦ πνεύματοςˌ ἀδελφοί ἀμήν
d.gsm n.gsm d.nsf n.nsf r.gp.1 d.gsm n.gsm n.gsm n.gsm p.g r.gp.2 d.gsn n.gsn n.vpm pl
3836 2652 3836 5921 3261 7005 3836 3261 2652 5986 3552 7007 3836 4460 81 297

---

17 Τοῦ λοιποῦ κόπους μοι μηδεὶς παρεχέτω· ἐγὼ γὰρ τὰ στίγματα τοῦ Ἰησοῦ ἐν τῷ σώματί μου βαστάζω. ¶ 18 Ἡ χάρις τοῦ κυρίου ἡμῶν Ἰησοῦ Χριστοῦ μετὰ τοῦ πνεύματος ὑμῶν, ἀδελφοί· ἀμήν.

Ephesians

1:1 Paul, an apostle of Christ Jesus by the will of God, ¶ To the saints in Ephesus,
Παῦλος ἀπόστολος → Χριστοῦ Ἰησοῦ διὰ θελήματος θεοῦ τοῖς ἁγίοις τοῖς οὖσιν ἐν Ἐφέσῳ
n.nsm n.nsm n.gsm n.gsm p.g n.gsn n.gsm d.dpm a.dpm d.ddpm pt.pa.dpm p.d n.dsf
4263 693 5986 2652 1328 2525 2536 3836 41 3836 1639 1877 2387

the faithful in Christ Jesus: ¶ **2** Grace and peace to you from God our Father and the Lord Jesus Christ.
καὶ πιστοῖς ἐν Χριστῷ Ἰησοῦ χάρις καὶ εἰρήνη → ὑμῖν ἀπὸ θεοῦ ἡμῶν πατρὸς καὶ κυρίου Ἰησοῦ Χριστοῦ
cj a.dpm p.d n.dsm n.dsm n.nsf cj n.nsf r.dp.2 p.g n.gsm r.gp.1 n.gsm cj n.gsm n.gsm n.gsm
2779 4412 1877 5986 2652 5921 2779 1645 7007 608 2536 7005 4252 2779 3261 2652 5986

Spiritual Blessings in Christ

1:3 Praise be to the God and Father of our Lord Jesus Christ, who has blessed us in the heavenly
Εὐλογητὸς ὁ θεὸς καὶ πατὴρ → ἡμῶν τοῦ κυρίου Ἰησοῦ Χριστοῦ ὁ → εὐλογήσας ἡμᾶς ἐν τοῖς ἐπουρανίοις
a.nsm d.nsm n.nsm cj n.nsm r.gp.1 d.gsm n.gsm n.gsm n.gsm d.nsm pt.aa.nsm r.ap.1 p.d d.dpn a.dpn
2329 3836 2536 2779 4252 3261 7005 3836 3261 2652 5986 3836 2328 7005 1877 3836 2230

realms with every spiritual blessing in Christ. **4** For he chose us in him before the creation of the world
← ἐν πάσῃ πνευματικῇ εὐλογίᾳ ἐν Χριστῷ καθὼς → ἐξελέξατο ἡμᾶς ἐν αὐτῷ πρὸ καταβολῆς → κόσμου ἡμᾶς
p.d a.dsf a.dsf n.dsf p.d n.dsm cj v.ami.3s r.ap.1 p.d r.dsm.3 p.g n.gsf n.gsm r.ap.1
1877 4246 4461 2330 1877 5986 2777 1721 7005 1877 899 4574 2856 3180 7005

to be holy and blameless in his sight. In love **5** he predestined us to be adopted as his sons
→ εἶναι ἁγίους καὶ ἀμώμους αὐτοῦ κατενώπιον ἐν ἀγάπῃ → προορίσας ἡμᾶς εἰς ← υἱοθεσίαν ← εἰς αὐτόν →
f.pa a.apm cj a.apm r.gsm.3 p.g p.d n.dsf pt.aa.nsm r.ap.1 p.a n.asf p.a r.asm.3
1639 41 2779 320 2979 899 2979 1877 27 4633 7005 1650 5625 1650 899 5625

through Jesus Christ, in accordance with his pleasure and will — **6** to the praise of his glorious
διὰ Ἰησοῦ Χριστοῦ κατὰ ← ← αὐτοῦ τὴν εὐδοκίαν τοῦ θελήματος εἰς ← ἔπαινον → αὐτοῦ δόξης
p.g n.gsm n.gsm p.a r.gsm.3 d.asf n.asf d.gsn n.gsn p.a n.asm r.gsm.3 n.gsf
1328 2652 5986 2848 899 3836 2306 3836 2525 1650 2047 1518 899 1518

grace, which he has freely given us in the One he loves. **7** In him we have redemption through
τῆς χάριτος ἧς → → ἐχαρίτωσεν ἡμᾶς ἐν τῷ ← ἠγαπημένῳ Ἐν ᾧ → ἔχομεν τὴν ἀπολύτρωσιν διὰ
d.gsf n.gsf r.gsf v.aai.3s r.ap.1 p.d d.dsm pt.rp.dsm p.d r.dsm v.pai.1p d.asf n.asf p.g
3836 5921 4005 5923 7005 1877 3836 26 1877 4005 2400 3836 667 1328

his blood, the forgiveness of sins, in accordance with the riches of God's grace **8** that he
αὐτοῦ τοῦ αἵματος τὴν ἄφεσιν τῶν παραπτωμάτων κατὰ ← ← τὸ πλοῦτος → αὐτοῦ τῆς χάριτος ἧς →
r.gsm.3 d.gsn n.gsn d.asf n.asf d.gpn n.gpn p.a d.asn n.asn r.gsm.3 d.gsf n.gsf r.gsf
899 3836 135 3836 912 3836 4183 2848 3836 4458 5921 899 3836 5921 4005

lavished on us with all wisdom and understanding. **9** And he made known to us the mystery of his
ἐπερίσσευσεν εἰς ἡμᾶς ἐν πάσῃ σοφίᾳ καὶ φρονήσει → → γνωρίσας → ἡμῖν τὸ μυστήριον → αὐτοῦ
v.aai.3s p.a r.ap.1 p.d a.dsf n.dsf cj n.dsf pt.aa.nsm r.dp.1 d.asn n.asn r.gsm.3
4355 1650 7005 1877 4246 5053 2779 5860 1192 7005 3836 3696 2525 899

will according to his good pleasure, which he purposed in Christ, **10** to be put into effect when
τοῦ θελήματος κατὰ ← αὐτοῦ τὴν εὐδοκίαν ἣν → προέθετο ἐν αὐτῷ εἰς οἰκονομίαν
d.gsn n.gsn p.a r.gsm.3 d.asf n.asf r.asf v.ami.3s p.d r.dsm.3 p.a n.asf
3836 2525 2848 899 3836 2306 4005 4729 1877 899 1650 3873

the times will have reached their fulfillment — to bring all things in heaven and on
τῶν καιρῶν τοῦ πληρώματος → ἀνακεφαλαιώσασθαι τὰ πάντα τὰ ἐπὶ τοῖς οὐρανοῖς καὶ τὰ ἐπὶ
d.gpm n.gpm d.gsn n.gsn f.am d.apn a.apn d.apn p.d d.dpm n.dpm cj d.apn p.g
3836 2789 3836 4445 368 3836 4246 3836 2093 3836 4041 2779 3836 2093

earth together under one head, even Christ. ¶ **11** In him we were also chosen, having been
τῆς γῆς ← ← ← ἐν τῷ Χριστῷ ἐν αὐτῷ Ἐν ᾧ → καὶ ἐκληρώθημεν → →
d.gsf n.gsf p.d d.dsm n.dsm p.d r.dsm.3 p.d r.dsm adv v.api.1p
3836 1178 368 368 368 1877 3836 5986 1877 899 1877 4005 3103 3103 2779 3103

predestined according to the plan of him who works out everything in conformity with the purpose of
προορισθέντες κατὰ ← πρόθεσιν τοῦ ἐνεργοῦντος ← τὰ πάντα κατὰ ← τὴν βουλὴν
pt.ap.npm p.a n.asf d.gsm pt.pa.gsm d.apn a.apn p.a d.asf n.asf
4633 2848 4606 3836 1919 3836 4246 2848 3836 1087 2525

1:1 Παῦλος ἀπόστολος Χριστοῦ Ἰησοῦ διὰ θελήματος θεοῦ ¶ τοῖς ἁγίοις τοῖς οὖσιν [ἐν Ἐφέσῳ] καὶ πιστοῖς ἐν Χριστῷ Ἰησοῦ ¶ **2** χάρις ὑμῖν καὶ εἰρήνη ἀπὸ θεοῦ πατρὸς ἡμῶν καὶ κυρίου Ἰησοῦ Χριστοῦ.

1:3 Εὐλογητὸς ὁ θεὸς καὶ πατὴρ τοῦ κυρίου ἡμῶν Ἰησοῦ Χριστοῦ, ὁ εὐλογήσας ἡμᾶς ἐν πάσῃ εὐλογίᾳ πνευματικῇ ἐν τοῖς ἐπουρανίοις ἐν Χριστῷ, **4** καθὼς ἐξελέξατο ἡμᾶς ἐν αὐτῷ πρὸ καταβολῆς κόσμου εἶναι ἡμᾶς ἁγίους καὶ ἀμώμους κατενώπιον αὐτοῦ ἐν ἀγάπῃ, **5** προορίσας ἡμᾶς εἰς υἱοθεσίαν διὰ Ἰησοῦ Χριστοῦ εἰς αὐτόν, κατὰ τὴν εὐδοκίαν τοῦ θελήματος αὐτοῦ, **6** εἰς ἔπαινον δόξης τῆς χάριτος αὐτοῦ ἧς ἐχαρίτωσεν ἡμᾶς ἐν τῷ ἠγαπημένῳ. **7** ἐν ᾧ ἔχομεν τὴν ἀπολύτρωσιν διὰ τοῦ αἵματος αὐτοῦ, τὴν ἄφεσιν τῶν παραπτωμάτων, κατὰ τὸ πλοῦτος τῆς χάριτος αὐτοῦ **8** ἧς ἐπερίσσευσεν εἰς ἡμᾶς, ἐν πάσῃ σοφίᾳ καὶ φρονήσει, **9** γνωρίσας ἡμῖν τὸ μυστήριον τοῦ θελήματος αὐτοῦ, κατὰ τὴν εὐδοκίαν αὐτοῦ ἣν προέθετο ἐν αὐτῷ **10** εἰς οἰκονομίαν τοῦ πληρώματος τῶν καιρῶν, ἀνακεφαλαιώσασθαι τὰ πάντα ἐν τῷ Χριστῷ, τὰ ἐπὶ τοῖς οὐρανοῖς καὶ τὰ ἐπὶ τῆς γῆς ἐν αὐτῷ. ¶ **11** ἐν ᾧ καὶ ἐκληρώθημεν προορισθέντες κατὰ πρόθεσιν τοῦ τὰ πάντα ἐνεργοῦντος κατὰ τὴν βουλὴν τοῦ θελήματος αὐτοῦ

his will, **12** in order that we, who were the first to hope in Christ, might be for the praise
αὐτοῦ τοῦ θελήματος, εἰς ← ἡμᾶς τοὺς → → προηλπικότας ἐν τῷ Χριστῷ → τὸ εἶναι εἰς ἔπαινον
r.gsm.3 d.gsn n.gsn / p.a / r.ap.1 d.apm / pt.ra.apm / p.d d.dsm n.dsm / d.asn f.pa p.a n.asm
899 3836 2525 / 1650 / 7005 3836 / 4598 / 1877 3836 5986 / 3836 1639 1650 2047

of his glory. **13** And you also were included in Christ when you heard the word of truth, the gospel
αὐτοῦ δόξης καὶ ὑμεῖς Ἐν ᾧ → → ἀκούσαντες τὸν λόγον τῆς ἀληθείας τὸ εὐαγγέλιον
r.gsm.3 n.gsf / adv r.np.2 / p.d r.dsm / pt.aa.npm / d.asm n.asm / d.gsf n.gsf / d.asn n.asn
1518 899 / 1518 7007 / 1877 4005 / 201 / 3836 3364 / 3836 237 / 3836 2295

of your salvation. Having believed, you were marked in him with a seal, the promised Holy
ὑμῶν τῆς σωτηρίας, καὶ πιστεύσαντες → → ἐσφραγίσθητε ἐν ᾧ τῷ τῆς ἐπαγγελίας τῷ ἁγίῳ
r.gp.2 d.gsf n.gsf / adv pt.aa.npm / v.api.2p / p.d r.dsm / d.dsn d.gsf n.gsf / d.dsn a.dsn
5401 7007 3836 5401 / 2779 4409 / 5381 / 1877 4005 / 5381 5381 5381 / 3836 3836 2039 / 3836 41

Spirit, **14** who is a deposit guaranteeing our inheritance until the redemption of those who are God's
πνεύματι ὅ ἐστιν ἀρραβὼν ← ἡμῶν τῆς κληρονομίας, εἰς ἀπολύτρωσιν → τῆς ←
n.dsn r.nsn v.pai.3s n.nsm / r.gp.1 d.gsf n.gsf / p.a n.asf / d.gsf
4460 4005 1639 775 / 7005 3836 3100 / 1650 667 / 3836

possession – to the praise of his glory.
περιποιήσεως εἰς ἔπαινον → αὐτοῦ τῆς δόξης
n.gsf / p.a n.asm / r.gsm.3 d.gsf n.gsf
4348 / 1650 2047 / 1518 899 3836 1518

Thanksgiving and Prayer

1:15 For this reason, ever since I heard about your faith in the Lord Jesus and your love
Διὰ τοῦτο ← ← κἀγὼ ἀκούσας ← καθ᾽ ὑμᾶς τὴν πίστιν ἐν τῷ κυρίῳ Ἰησοῦ καὶ τὴν ἀγάπην
p.a r.asn / crasis pt.aa.nsm / p.a r.ap.2 d.asf n.asf / p.d d.dsm n.dsm n.dsm cj d.asf n.asf
1328 4047 / 2743 201 / 2848 7007 3836 4411 / 1877 3836 3261 2652 2779 3836 27

for all the saints, **16** I have not stopped giving thanks for you, remembering you in my prayers.
τὴν εἰς πάντας τοὺς ἁγίους → → οὐ παύομαι → εὐχαριστῶν ὑπὲρ ὑμῶν μνείαν ποιούμενος ἐπὶ μου τῶν προσευχῶν
d.asf p.a a.apm d.apm a.apm / pl v.pmi.1s / pt.pa.nsm p.g r.gp.2 n.asf pt.pm.nsm / p.g r.gs.1 d.gpf n.gpf
3836 1650 4246 3836 41 / 4024 4264 4264 / 2373 5642 7007 3644 4472 / 2093 1609 3836 4666

17 I keep asking that the God of our Lord Jesus Christ, the glorious Father, may give you the Spirit of
ἵνα ὁ θεὸς ἡμῶν τοῦ κυρίου Ἰησοῦ Χριστοῦ ὁ τῆς δόξης πατὴρ δῴη ὑμῖν πνεῦμα →
cj d.nsm n.nsm r.gp.1 d.gsm n.gsm n.gsm n.gsm d.nsm d.gsf n.gsf n.nsm / v.aas.3s r.dp.2 n.asn
2671 3836 2536 3261 7005 3836 3261 2652 5986 3836 3836 1518 4252 / 1443 7007 4460

wisdom and revelation, so that you may know him better. **18** I pray also that the eyes of your
σοφίας καὶ ἀποκαλύψεως ἐν ἐπιγνώσει αὐτοῦ ← τοὺς ὀφθαλμοὺς → ὑμῶν
n.gsf cj n.gsf / p.d n.dsf r.gsm.3 / d.apm n.apm r.gp.2
5053 2779 637 / 1877 2106 2106 / 3836 4057 2840 7007

heart may be enlightened in order that you may know the hope to which he has called
τῆς καρδίας → → πεφωτισμένους εἰς τὸ εἰδέναι ὑμᾶς τίς ἐστιν ἡ ἐλπὶς τῆς αὐτοῦ κλήσεως
d.gsf n.gsf / pt.rp.apm p.a d.asn f.ra r.ap.2 / r.nsf v.pai.3s d.nsf n.nsf / d.gsf r.gsm.3 n.gsf
3836 2840 / 5894 1650 3836 3857 7007 / 5515 1639 3836 1828 / 3836 899 3104

you, the riches of his glorious inheritance in the saints, **19** and his incomparably great
τίς ὁ πλοῦτος αὐτοῦ τῆς δόξης τῆς κληρονομίας ἐν τοῖς ἁγίοις καὶ τί αὐτοῦ ὑπερβάλλον τὸ μέγεθος
r.nsm d.nsm n.nsm / r.gsm.3 d.gsf n.gsf / d.gsf n.gsf / p.d d.dpm a.dpm / cj r.nsn r.gsm.3 pt.pa.nsn / d.nsn n.nsn
5515 3836 4458 / 1518 899 3836 1518 / 3836 3100 / 1877 3836 41 / 2779 5515 899 5650 / 3836 3490

power for us who believe. That power is like the working of his mighty strength, **20** which he
τῆς δυνάμεως εἰς ἡμᾶς τοὺς πιστεύοντας κατὰ τὴν ἐνέργειαν αὐτοῦ τοῦ κράτους τῆς ἰσχύος Ἣν →
d.gsf n.gsf / p.a r.ap.1 d.apm pt.pa.apm / p.a d.asf n.asf / r.gsm.3 d.gsn n.gsn / d.gsf n.gsf / r.asf
3836 1539 / 1650 7005 3836 4409 / 2848 3836 1918 / 3197 899 3836 3197 / 3836 2709 / 4005

exerted in Christ when he raised him from the dead and seated him at his right hand in the
ἐνήργησεν ἐν τῷ Χριστῷ → → ἐγείρας αὐτὸν ἐκ νεκρῶν καὶ καθίσας ἐν αὐτοῦ δεξιᾷ ← ἐν τοῖς
v.aai.3s p.d d.dsm n.dsm / pt.aa.nsm r.asm.3 p.g / a.gpm cj pt.aa.nsm / p.d r.gsm.3 a.dsf / p.d d.dpn
1919 1877 3836 5986 / 1586 899 1666 / 3738 2779 2767 / 1877 899 1288 / 1877 3836

heavenly realms, **21** far above all rule and authority, power and dominion, and every title that can be
ἐπουρανίοις ← → ὑπεράνω πάσης ἀρχῆς καὶ ἐξουσίας καὶ δυνάμεως καὶ κυριότητος καὶ παντὸς ὀνόματος → → →
a.dpn / p.g a.gsf n.gsf cj n.gsf / cj n.gsf cj n.gsf / cj a.gsn n.gsn
2230 / 5645 4246 794 2779 2026 / 2779 1539 2779 3262 / 2779 4246 3950

---

¹² εἰς τὸ εἶναι ἡμᾶς εἰς ἔπαινον δόξης αὐτοῦ τοὺς προηλπικότας ἐν τῷ Χριστῷ. ¹³ ἐν ᾧ καὶ ὑμεῖς ἀκούσαντες τὸν λόγον τῆς ἀληθείας, τὸ εὐαγγέλιον τῆς σωτηρίας ὑμῶν, ἐν ᾧ καὶ πιστεύσαντες ἐσφραγίσθητε τῷ πνεύματι τῆς ἐπαγγελίας τῷ ἁγίῳ, ¹⁴ ὅ ἐστιν ἀρραβὼν τῆς κληρονομίας ἡμῶν, εἰς ἀπολύτρωσιν τῆς περιποιήσεως, εἰς ἔπαινον τῆς δόξης αὐτοῦ.

¹·¹⁵ Διὰ τοῦτο κἀγὼ ἀκούσας τὴν καθ᾽ ὑμᾶς πίστιν ἐν τῷ κυρίῳ Ἰησοῦ καὶ τὴν ἀγάπην τὴν εἰς πάντας τοὺς ἁγίους ¹⁶ οὐ παύομαι εὐχαριστῶν ὑπὲρ ὑμῶν μνείαν ποιούμενος ἐπὶ τῶν προσευχῶν μου, ¹⁷ ἵνα ὁ θεὸς τοῦ κυρίου ἡμῶν Ἰησοῦ Χριστοῦ, ὁ πατὴρ τῆς δόξης, δῴη ὑμῖν πνεῦμα σοφίας καὶ ἀποκαλύψεως ἐν ἐπιγνώσει αὐτοῦ, ¹⁸ πεφωτισμένους τοὺς ὀφθαλμοὺς τῆς καρδίας [ὑμῶν] εἰς τὸ εἰδέναι ὑμᾶς τίς ἐστιν ἡ ἐλπὶς τῆς κλήσεως αὐτοῦ, τίς ὁ πλοῦτος τῆς δόξης τῆς κληρονομίας αὐτοῦ ἐν τοῖς ἁγίοις, ¹⁹ καὶ τί τὸ ὑπερβάλλον μέγεθος τῆς δυνάμεως αὐτοῦ εἰς ἡμᾶς τοὺς πιστεύοντας κατὰ τὴν ἐνέργειαν τοῦ κράτους τῆς ἰσχύος αὐτοῦ. ²⁰ ἣν ἐνήργησεν ἐν τῷ Χριστῷ ἐγείρας αὐτὸν ἐκ νεκρῶν καὶ καθίσας ἐν δεξιᾷ αὐτοῦ ἐν τοῖς ἐπουρανίοις ²¹ ὑπεράνω πάσης ἀρχῆς καὶ ἐξουσίας καὶ δυνάμεως καὶ κυριότητος καὶ παντὸς ὀνόματος ὀνομαζομένου, οὐ μόνον ἐν τῷ αἰῶνι τούτῳ ἀλλὰ

given,   not only in   the present age   but also in the one to come.   **22** And God placed   all   things under   his
ὀνομαζομένου οὐ μόνον ἐν τῷ τούτῳ αἰῶνι ἀλλὰ καὶ ἐν τῷ ←   → μέλλοντι   καὶ   ὑπέταξεν πάντα ←   ὑπὸ αὐτοῦ
pt.pp.gsn   pl adv   p.d d.dsm r.dsm n.dsm cj adv p.d d.dsm   pt.pa.dsm cj   v.aai.3s a.apn   p.a r.gsm.3
3951   4024 3667 1877 3836 4047 172   247 2779 1877 3836   3516   2779   5718   4246   5679 899

feet   and appointed him   to be head   over everything for the church, **23** which is   his   body,   the fullness
ιτοὺς πόδας_ καὶ ἔδωκεν   αὐτὸν   κεφαλὴν ὑπὲρ πάντα   → τῇ ἐκκλησίᾳ ἥτις   ἐστὶν αὐτοῦ ιτὸ σῶμα_ τὸ πλήρωμα
d.apm n.apm cj   v.aai.3s r.asm.3 n.asf   p.a a.apn   d.dsf n.dsf   r.nsf v.pai.3s r.gsm.3 d.nsn n.nsn d.nsn n.nsn
3836 4546   2779 1443   899   3051   5642 4246   3836 1711   4015   1639 899   3836 5393 3836 4445

of him who fills   everything in every way.
→ τοῦ ←   πληρουμένου ιτὰ πάντα_ ἐν πᾶσιν ←
d.gsm   pt.pp.gsm   d.apn a.apn p.d a.dpn
3836 4444   3836 4246   1877 4246

Made Alive in Christ

2:1 As for you, you   were dead in your transgressions   and sins,   **2** in which you used to
Καὶ ←   ὑμᾶς ὄντας νεκροὺς → ὑμῶν ιτοῖς παραπτώμασιν_ καὶ ιταῖς ἁμαρτίαις_ ἐν αἷς   → ποτε   →
cj   r.ap.2 pt.pa.apm a.apm   r.gp.2 d.dpn n.dpn   cj d.dpf n.dpf   p.d r.dpf   adv
2779   7007 1639 3738   7007 3836 4183   2779 3836 281   1877 4005   4344 4537

live   when you followed the ways of this world   and of   the ruler   of the kingdom of the air,
περιεπατήσατε →   κατὰ   τὸν αἰῶνα → τούτου ιτοῦ κόσμου_   κατὰ τὸν ἄρχοντα → τῆς ἐξουσίας → τοῦ ἀέρος
v.aai.2p   p.a   d.asm n.asm   d.gsm n.gsm   p.a d.asm n.asm   d.gsf n.gsf   d.gsm n.gsm
4344   2848   3836 172   4047 3836 3180   2848 3836 807   3836 2026   3836 113

the spirit   who is now at work   in those who are disobedient. **3** All   of us   also lived   among
τοῦ πνεύματος τοῦ → νῦν → ἐνεργοῦντος ἐν τοῖς   ←   ιυἱοῖς τῆς ἀπειθείας_ πάντες ἡμεῖς καὶ ἀνεστράφημεν ἐν
d.gsn n.gsn   d.gsn   adv   pt.pa.gsn p.d d.dpm   n.dpm d.gsf n.gsf   a.npm r.np.1 adv v.api.1p   p.d
3836 4460   3836   1919   1919   1877 3836   5626 3836 577   4246   7005 2779 418   1877

them at one time, gratifying the cravings of our sinful   nature and following its   desires   and
οἷς ποτε ←   ←   ἐν   ταῖς ἐπιθυμίαις → ἡμῶν ιτῆς σαρκὸς_   ποιοῦντες ιτῆς σαρκὸς_ ιτὰ θελήματα_ καὶ
r.dpm adv   p.d d.dpf n.dpf   r.gp.1 d.gsf n.gsf   pt.pa.npm d.gsf n.gsf   d.apn n.apn cj
4005 4537   1877 3836 2123   4922 3836 4922   4472   3836 4922   3836 2525   2779

thoughts.   Like   the rest, we were by nature objects of wrath. **4** But because of his great love
ιτῶν διανοιῶν_ καὶ ὡς   καὶ οἱ λοιποί → ἤμεθα φύσει τέκνα   → ὀργῆς δὲ διὰ   ←   αὐτοῦ πολλὴν ιτὴν ἀγάπην_ ἣν
d.gpf n.gpf   adv cj   cj d.npm a.npm   v.imi.1p n.dsf n.npn   n.gsf cj p.a   r.gsm.3 a.asf d.asf n.asf   r.asf
3836 1379   2779 6055 2779 3836 3370   1639 5882 5451   3973   1254 1328   899   4498 3836 27   4005

for us, God,   who is   rich in mercy, **5** made us alive   with Christ   even when we
ἠγάπησεν ἡμᾶς ὁ θεὸς   → ὢν πλούσιος ἐν ἐλέει καὶ   συνεζωοποίησεν ← ιτῷ Χριστῷ_   → ἡμᾶς
v.aai.3s r.ap.1 d.nsm n.nsm pt.pa.nsm a.nsm p.d n.dsn adv   v.aai.3s   d.dsm n.dsm   r.ap.1
26   7005 3836 2536   1639 4454   1877 1799 2779   5188   3836 5986   7005

were dead in   transgressions – it is   by grace you have been saved. **6** And God raised   us up with Christ and
ὄντας νεκροὺς τοῖς παραπτώμασιν → ἐστε → χάριτι →   σεσῳσμένοι καὶ   συνήγειρεν ← ←   ←   καὶ
pt.pa.apm a.apm d.dpn n.dpn   v.pai.2p n.dsf   pt.rp.npm cj   v.aai.3s   cj
1639 3738   3836 4183   1639   5921   5392   2779   5283   2779

seated   us with him in the heavenly realms in Christ Jesus, **7** in order that in the coming   ages   he
συνεκάθισεν ←   ←   ἐν τοῖς ἐπουρανίοις ἐν Χριστῷ Ἰησοῦ ἵνα   → ἐν τοῖς ιτοῖς ἐπερχομένοις_ αἰῶσιν →
v.aai.3s   p.d d.dpn a.dpn   p.d n.dsm n.dsm cj   p.d d.dpm d.dpm pt.pm.dpm   n.dpm
5154   1877 3836 2230   1877 5986 2652   2671   1877 3836 3836 2088   172

might show the incomparable riches of his grace,   expressed in his kindness to us in Christ Jesus.
→ ἐνδείξηται τὸ ὑπερβάλλον πλοῦτος → αὐτοῦ ιτῆς χάριτος_ ἐν χρηστότητι ἐφ’ ἡμᾶς ἐν Χριστῷ Ἰησοῦ
v.ams.3s   d.asn pt.pa.asn   n.asn   r.gsm.3 d.gsf n.gsf   p.d n.dsf   p.a r.ap.1 p.d n.dsm n.dsm
1892   3836 5650   4458   899   3836 5921   1877 5983   2093 7005 1877 5986 2652

8 For it is   by grace   you have been saved,   through faith – and this not from yourselves, it is the gift of
γὰρ → ἐστε → ιΤῇ χάριτι_ →   → σεσῳσμένοι διὰ πίστεως   καὶ τοῦτο οὐκ ἐξ ὑμῶν   τὸ δῶρον
cj v.pai.2p d.dsf n.dsf   pt.rp.npm p.g n.gsf   cj r.nsn pl p.g r.gp.2   d.nsn n.nsn
1142 1639   3836 5921   5392   1328 4411   2779 4047 4024 1666 7007   3836 1565

God – **9** not by works, so that no one can boast. **10** For we are God's workmanship, created   in Christ Jesus to
θεοῦ   οὐκ ἐξ ἔργων ἵνα   μή τις → καυχήσηται   γὰρ → ἐσμεν αὐτοῦ ποίημα   κτισθέντες ἐν Χριστῷ Ἰησοῦ ἐπὶ
n.gsm   pl p.g n.gpn cj   pl r.nsm   v.ams.3s   cj   v.pai.1p r.gsm.3 n.nsn   pt.ap.npm p.d n.dsm n.dsm p.d
2536   4024 1666 2240 2671 3590 5516   3016   1142 1639 899   4473   3231   1877 5986 2652 2093

καὶ ἐν τῷ μέλλοντι· ²² καὶ πάντα ὑπέταξεν ὑπὸ τοὺς πόδας αὐτοῦ καὶ αὐτὸν ἔδωκεν κεφαλὴν ὑπὲρ πάντα τῇ ἐκκλησίᾳ, ²³ ἥτις ἐστὶν τὸ σῶμα αὐτοῦ, τὸ πλήρωμα τοῦ τὰ πάντα ἐν πᾶσιν πληρουμένου. ²:¹ Καὶ ὑμᾶς ὄντας νεκροὺς τοῖς παραπτώμασιν καὶ ταῖς ἁμαρτίαις ὑμῶν, ² ἐν αἷς ποτε περιεπατήσατε κατὰ τὸν αἰῶνα τοῦ κόσμου τούτου, κατὰ τὸν ἄρχοντα τῆς ἐξουσίας τοῦ ἀέρος, τοῦ πνεύματος τοῦ νῦν ἐνεργοῦντος ἐν τοῖς υἱοῖς τῆς ἀπειθείας· ³ ἐν οἷς καὶ ἡμεῖς πάντες ἀνεστράφημέν ποτε ἐν ταῖς ἐπιθυμίαις τῆς σαρκὸς ἡμῶν ποιοῦντες τὰ θελήματα τῆς σαρκὸς καὶ τῶν διανοιῶν, καὶ ἤμεθα τέκνα φύσει ὀργῆς ὡς καὶ οἱ λοιποί· ⁴ ὁ δὲ θεὸς πλούσιος ὢν ἐν ἐλέει, διὰ τὴν πολλὴν ἀγάπην αὐτοῦ ἣν ἠγάπησεν ἡμᾶς, ⁵ καὶ ὄντας ἡμᾶς νεκροὺς τοῖς παραπτώμασιν συνεζωοποίησεν τῷ Χριστῷ,— χάριτί ἐστε σεσῳσμένοι— ⁶ καὶ συνήγειρεν καὶ συνεκάθισεν ἐν τοῖς ἐπουρανίοις ἐν Χριστῷ Ἰησοῦ, ⁷ ἵνα ἐνδείξηται ἐν τοῖς αἰῶσιν τοῖς ἐπερχομένοις τὸ ὑπερβάλλον πλοῦτος τῆς χάριτος αὐτοῦ ἐν χρηστότητι ἐφ᾽ ἡμᾶς ἐν Χριστῷ Ἰησοῦ. ⁸ τῇ γὰρ χάριτί ἐστε σεσῳσμένοι διὰ πίστεως· καὶ τοῦτο οὐκ ἐξ ὑμῶν, θεοῦ τὸ δῶρον· ⁹ οὐκ ἐξ ἔργων, ἵνα μή τις καυχήσηται. ¹⁰ αὐτοῦ γάρ ἐσμεν ποίημα, κτισθέντες ἐν

do good   works, which God   prepared   in advance for   us to do.
← ἀγαθοῖς ἔργοις οἷς ὁ θεὸς, προητοίμασεν ← ← ἵνα ἐν αὐτοῖς → → περιπατήσωμεν
a.dpn n.dpn r.dpn d.nsm n.nsm v.aai.3s cj p.d r.dpn.3 v.aas.1p
19 2240 4005 3836 2536 4602 2671 1877 899 4344

One in Christ

2:11 Therefore, remember that formerly you who are Gentiles by birth and called "uncircumcised" by
Διὸ μνημονεύετε ὅτι ποτὲ ὑμεῖς τὰ → ἔθνη ἐν σαρκί, οἱ λεγόμενοι ἀκροβυστία ὑπὸ
cj v.pam.2p cj adv r.np.2 d.npn n.npn p.d n.dsf d.npm pt.pp.npm n.nsf p.g
1475 3648 4022 4537 7007 3836 1620 1877 4922 3836 3306 213 5679

those who call   themselves "the circumcision" (that done in the body by the hands   of men) – **12** remember
τῆς → λεγομένης ← περιτομῆς ἐν σαρκί → χειροποιήτου
d.gsf pt.pp.gsf n.gsf p.d n.dsf a.gsf
3836 3306 4364 5935 1877 4922 5935

that at that time   you were separate from Christ, excluded   from citizenship   in Israel   and
ὅτι ἐκείνῳ τῷ καιρῷ → ἦτε χωρὶς → Χριστοῦ ἀπηλλοτριωμένοι → τῆς πολιτείας τοῦ Ἰσραὴλ καὶ
cj r.dsm d.dsm n.dsm v.iai.2p p.g n.gsm pt.rp.npm d.gsf n.gsf d.gsm n.gsm cj
4022 2789 3836 2789 1639 6006 5986 558 3836 4486 3836 2702 2779

foreigners to the covenants of the promise, without hope and without God in the world. **13** But now in Christ
ξένοι → τῶν διαθηκῶν → τῆς ἐπαγγελίας μὴ ἔχοντες, ἐλπίδα καὶ → ἄθεοι ἐν τῷ κόσμῳ δὲ νυνὶ ἐν Χριστῷ
n.npm d.gpf n.gpf d.gsf n.gsf pl pt.pa.npm n.asf cj a.npm p.d d.dsm n.dsm cj adv p.d n.dsm
3828 3836 1347 3836 2039 3590 2400 1828 2779 117 1877 3836 3180 1254 3815 1877 5986

Jesus you who once were far   away have been brought near through the blood of Christ.   ¶ **14** For he
Ἰησοῦ ὑμεῖς οἳ ποτὲ ὄντες μακρὰν ← → ἐγενήθητε ἐγγὺς ἐν τῷ αἵματι → τοῦ Χριστοῦ γὰρ →
n.dsm r.np.2 d.npm adv pt.pa.npm adv v.api.2p adv p.d d.dsn n.dsn d.gsm n.gsm cj
2652 7007 4005 4537 1639 3426 1181 1584 1877 3836 135 3836 5986 1142 1639

himself is   our peace,   who has made the two   one and has destroyed the barrier, the dividing wall   of
Αὐτὸς ἐστιν ἡμῶν ἡ εἰρήνη, ὁ → ποιήσας τὰ ἀμφότερα ἓν καὶ → λύσας τὸ μεσότοιχον τοῦ → φραγμοῦ
r.nsm v.pai.3s r.gp.1 d.nsf n.nsf d.nsm pt.aa.nsm d.apn a.asn a.asn cj pt.aa.nsm d.asn n.asn d.gsm n.gsm
899 1639 7005 3836 1645 3836 4472 3836 317 1651 2779 3395 3836 3546 3836 5850

hostility, **15** by abolishing in his   flesh   the law with its commandments and   regulations. His purpose was
τὴν ἔχθραν, καταργήσας ἐν αὐτοῦ τῇ σαρκὶ, τὸν νόμον → τῶν ἐντολῶν ἐν δόγμασιν
d.asf n.asf pt.aa.nsm p.d r.gsm.3 d.dsf n.dsf d.asm n.asm d.gpf n.gpf p.d n.dpn
3836 2397 2934 1877 899 3836 4922 3836 3795 3836 1953 1877 1504

to create in himself   one new   man   out of the two, thus making peace, **16** and in this one body to
ἵνα κτίσῃ ἐν αὐτῷ εἰς ἕνα καινὸν ἄνθρωπον τοὺς δύο → ποιῶν εἰρήνην καὶ ἐν ἑνὶ σώματι →
cj v.aas.3s p.d r.dsm.3 p.a a.asm a.asm n.asm d.apm a.apm pt.pa.nsm n.asf cj p.d a.dsn n.dsn
2671 3231 1877 899 1650 1651 2785 476 3836 1545 4472 1645 2779 1877 1651 5393

reconcile   both   of them to God   through the cross, by which he put to death   their hostility.
ἀποκαταλλάξῃ τοὺς ἀμφοτέρους → τῷ θεῷ, διὰ τοῦ σταυροῦ → → → ἀποκτείνας τὴν ἔχθραν ἐν
v.aas.3s d.apm a.apm d.dsm n.dsm p.g d.gsm n.gsm pt.aa.nsm d.asf n.asf p.d
639 3836 317 3836 2536 1328 3836 5089 650 3836 2397 1877

17 He came and preached   peace to you who were far   away and peace to those who were near. **18** For
αὐτῷ καὶ ἐλθὼν εὐηγγελίσατο εἰρήνην → ὑμῖν τοῖς → μακρὰν ← καὶ εἰρήνην → τοῖς ← → ἐγγὺς ὅτι
r.dsm.3 cj pt.aa.nsm v.ami.3s n.asf r.dp.2 d.dpm adv cj n.asf d.dpm adv cj
899 2779 2262 2294 1645 7007 3836 3426 2779 1645 3836 1584 4022

through him we both   have access   to the Father by one Spirit. ¶ **19** Consequently,   you are
δι' αὐτοῦ → οἱ ἀμφότεροι ἔχομεν τὴν προσαγωγὴν πρὸς τὸν πατέρα ἐν ἑνὶ πνεύματι Ἄρα οὖν → ἐστὲ
p.g r.gsm.3 d.npm a.npm v.pai.1p d.asf n.asf p.a d.asm n.asm p.d a.dsn n.dsn cj cj v.pai.2p
1328 899 2400 3836 317 2400 3836 4643 4639 3836 4252 1877 1651 4460 726 4036 1639

no   longer foreigners and aliens,   but   fellow citizens with God's   people and members of God's
οὐκέτι ← ξένοι καὶ πάροικοι ἀλλὰ ἐστὲ → συμπολῖται τῶν ἁγίων, καὶ οἰκεῖοι → τοῦ θεοῦ,
adv n.npm cj n.npm cj v.pai.2p n.npm d.gpm a.gpm cj n.npm d.gsm n.gsm
4033 3828 2779 4230 247 1639 5232 3836 41 2779 3858 3836 2536

household, **20** built   on the foundation of the apostles and prophets, with Christ Jesus himself as   the
← ἐποικοδομηθέντες ἐπὶ τῷ θεμελίῳ → τῶν ἀποστόλων καὶ προφητῶν → Χριστοῦ Ἰησοῦ αὐτοῦ ὄντος
pt.ap.npm p.d d.dsm n.dsm d.gpm n.gpm cj n.gpm n.gsm n.gsm r.gsm pt.pa.gsm
3858 2224 2093 3836 2529 3836 693 2779 4737 5986 2652 899 1639

Χριστῷ Ἰησοῦ ἐπὶ ἔργοις ἀγαθοῖς οἷς προητοίμασεν ὁ θεός, ἵνα ἐν αὐτοῖς περιπατήσωμεν.

2:11 Διὸ μνημονεύετε ὅτι ποτὲ ὑμεῖς τὰ ἔθνη ἐν σαρκί, οἱ λεγόμενοι ἀκροβυστία ὑπὸ τῆς λεγομένης περιτομῆς ἐν σαρκὶ χειροποιήτου, **12** ὅτι ἦτε τῷ καιρῷ ἐκείνῳ χωρὶς Χριστοῦ, ἀπηλλοτριωμένοι τῆς πολιτείας τοῦ Ἰσραὴλ καὶ ξένοι τῶν διαθηκῶν τῆς ἐπαγγελίας, ἐλπίδα μὴ ἔχοντες καὶ ἄθεοι ἐν τῷ κόσμῳ. **13** νυνὶ δὲ ἐν Χριστῷ Ἰησοῦ ὑμεῖς οἵ ποτε ὄντες μακρὰν ἐγενήθητε ἐγγὺς ἐν τῷ αἵματι τοῦ Χριστοῦ. ¶ **14** Αὐτὸς γάρ ἐστιν ἡ εἰρήνη ἡμῶν, ὁ ποιήσας τὰ ἀμφότερα ἓν καὶ τὸ μεσότοιχον τοῦ φραγμοῦ λύσας, τὴν ἔχθραν ἐν τῇ σαρκὶ αὐτοῦ, **15** τὸν νόμον τῶν ἐντολῶν ἐν δόγμασιν καταργήσας, ἵνα τοὺς δύο κτίσῃ ἐν ἑαυτῷ «αὐτῷ» εἰς ἕνα καινὸν ἄνθρωπον ποιῶν εἰρήνην **16** καὶ ἀποκαταλλάξῃ τοὺς ἀμφοτέρους ἐν ἑνὶ σώματι τῷ θεῷ διὰ τοῦ σταυροῦ, ἀποκτείνας τὴν ἔχθραν ἐν αὐτῷ. **17** καὶ ἐλθὼν εὐηγγελίσατο εἰρήνην ὑμῖν τοῖς μακρὰν καὶ εἰρήνην τοῖς ἐγγύς· **18** ὅτι δι' αὐτοῦ ἔχομεν τὴν προσαγωγὴν οἱ ἀμφότεροι ἐν ἑνὶ πνεύματι πρὸς τὸν πατέρα. ¶ **19** ἄρα οὖν οὐκέτι ἐστὲ ξένοι καὶ πάροικοι ἀλλὰ ἐστὲ συμπολῖται τῶν ἁγίων καὶ οἰκεῖοι τοῦ θεοῦ, **20** ἐποικοδομηθέντες ἐπὶ τῷ θεμελίῳ τῶν ἀποστόλων καὶ προφητῶν, ὄντος

chief cornerstone. **21** In him the whole building is joined   together and rises to become a holy temple in the
→ ἀκρογωνιαίου ἐν ᾧ πᾶσα οἰκοδομὴ → συναρμολογουμένη ←   αὔξει εἰς ←   ἅγιον ναὸν ἐν
a.gsm   p.d r.dsm a.nsf n.nsf   pt.pp.nsf   v.pai.3s p.a   a.asm n.asm p.d
214   1877 4005 4246 3869   5274   891 1650   41 3724 1877

Lord. **22** And in him you too are being built   together to become a dwelling   in which God   lives by
κυρίῳ ἐν ᾧ ὑμεῖς καὶ → → συνοικοδομεῖσθε ←   εἰς ← κατοικητήριον → → ⌐τοῦ θεοῦ⌐ ← ἐν
n.dsm   p.d r.dsm r.np.2 adv   v.ppi.2p   p.a   n.asn   d.gsm n.gsm   p.d
3261   1877 4005 7007 2779   5325   1650   2999   3836 2536   1877

his Spirit.
πνεύματι
n.dsn
4460

Paul the Preacher to the Gentiles

3:1 For   this reason I, Paul, the prisoner of Christ   Jesus for the sake of you Gentiles – ¶
⌐Τούτου χάριν⌐ ← ← ἐγὼ Παῦλος ὁ δέσμιος → ⌐τοῦ Χριστοῦ⌐ Ἰησοῦ ὑπὲρ ← ← ὑμῶν ⌐τῶν ἐθνῶν⌐
r.gsn   p.g   r.ns.1 n.nsm d.nsm n.nsm   d.gsm n.gsm n.gsm p.g   r.gp.2 d.gpn n.gpn
4047   5920   1609 4263 3836 1300   3836 5986 2652 5642   7007 3836 1620

2 Surely you have heard about the administration of God's grace   that was given to me for you, **3** that is,
⌐εἴ γε⌐ → → ἠκούσατε → τὴν οἰκονομίαν → ⌐τοῦ θεοῦ⌐ ⌐τῆς χάριτος⌐ τῆς → δοθείσης μοι εἰς ὑμᾶς ὅτι ←
cj pl   v.aai.2p   d.asf n.asf   d.gsm n.gsm d.gsf n.gsf d.gsf   pt.ap.gsf r.ds.1 p.a r.ap.2   cj
1623 1145   201   3836 3873   5921 3836 2536 3836 5921 3836   1443 1609 1650 7007   4022

the mystery made known to me by revelation, as I have already written briefly. **4** In reading this,
τὸ μυστήριον → ἐγνωρίσθη → μοι κατὰ ἀποκάλυψιν καθὼς → I have already προέγραψα ἐν ὀλίγῳ → ἀναγινώσκοντες this,
d.nsn n.nsn   v.api.3s   r.ds.1 p.a n.asf cj   v.aai.1s p.d a.dsn   pt.pa.npm
3836 3696   1192   1609 2848 637 2777   4592 1877 3900   336

then, you will be able to understand my insight into the mystery of Christ, **5** which was not made
⌐πρὸς ὅ⌐ → → δύνασθε νοῆσαι μου ⌐τὴν σύνεσιν⌐ ἐν τῷ μυστηρίῳ → ⌐τοῦ Χριστοῦ⌐ ὅ ↦ οὐκ →
p.a r.asn   v.ppi.2p f.aa r.gs.1 d.asf n.asf p.d d.dsn n.dsn   d.gsm n.gsm r.nsn   pl
4639 4005   1538 3783 1609 3836 5304 1877 3836 3696   3836 5986 4005   1192 4024

known to men in other generations as it has now been revealed by the Spirit to God's
ἐγνωρίσθη → τοῖς υἱοῖς ⌐τῶν ἀνθρώπων⌐ → ἑτέραις γενεαῖς ὡς → νῦν → ἀπεκαλύφθη ἐν πνεύματι ↦ αὐτοῦ
v.api.3s   d.dpm n.dpm d.gpm n.gpm   r.dpf n.dpf cj   adv   v.api.3s p.d n.dsn   r.gsm.3
1192   3836 5626 3836 476   2283 1155 6055   636 636 3814   636 1877 4460   41 899

holy apostles and prophets. **6** This mystery is that through the gospel the Gentiles are heirs
⌐τοῖς ἁγίοις⌐ ἀποστόλοις καὶ προφήταις εἶναι διὰ τοῦ εὐαγγελίου τὰ ἔθνη συγκληρονόμα
d.dpm a.dpm n.dpm cj n.dpm   f.pa p.g d.gsn n.gsn d.apn n.apn a.apn
3836 41 693 2779 4737   1639 1328 3836 2295 3836 1620 5169

together with Israel, members together of one body, and sharers together in the promise in Christ Jesus. ¶
← καὶ σύσσωμα ← ← ← ← καὶ συμμέτοχα → τῆς ἐπαγγελίας ἐν Χριστῷ Ἰησοῦ
cj a.apn   cj a.apn   d.gsf n.gsf p.d n.dsm n.dsm
2779 5362   2779 5212   3836 2039 1877 5986 2652

7 I became a servant of this gospel by the gift of God's grace given me through the working of
→ ἐγενήθην διάκονος → οὗ → κατὰ τὴν δωρεὰν ↦ ⌐τοῦ θεοῦ⌐ ⌐τῆς χάριτος⌐ ⌐τῆς δοθείσης⌐ μοι κατὰ τὴν ἐνέργειαν ↦
v.api.1s n.nsm   r.gsn   p.a d.asf n.asf   d.gsm n.gsm d.gsf n.gsf d.gsf pt.ap.gsf r.ds.1 p.a d.asf n.asf
1181 1356   4005   2848 3836 1561   5921 3836 2536 3836 5921 3836 1443 1609 2848 3836 1918   1539

his power. **8** Although I am less than the least of all God's people, this grace was given me: to
αὐτοῦ ⌐τῆς δυνάμεως⌐ Although τῷ ἐλαχιστοτέρῳ → πάντων ἁγίων ← αὕτη ἡ χάρις → ἐδόθη Ἐμοὶ →
r.gsm.3 d.gsf n.gsf   d.dsm a.dsm.c   a.gpm a.gpm   r.nsf d.nsf n.nsf   v.api.3s r.ds.1
899 3836 1539   3836 1788   4246 41   4047 3836 5921   1443 1609

preach to the Gentiles the unsearchable riches of Christ, **9** and to make plain to everyone the
εὐαγγελίσασθαι → τοῖς ἔθνεσιν τὸ ἀνεξιχνίαστον πλοῦτος → ⌐τοῦ Χριστοῦ⌐ καὶ → φωτίσαι πάντας τίς ἡ
f.am   d.dpn n.dpn d.asn a.asn n.asn   d.gsm n.gsm cj   f.aa a.apm r.nsf d.nsf
2294   3836 1620 3836 453 4458   3836 5986 2779   5894 4246 5515 3836

administration of this mystery, which for ages past was kept hidden in God, who created all
οἰκονομία → τοῦ μυστηρίου τοῦ ἀπὸ ⌐τῶν αἰώνων⌐ ← → ἀποκεκρυμμένου ἐν τῷ θεῷ τῷ κτίσαντι ⌐τὰ πάντα⌐
n.nsf   d.gsn n.gsn d.gsn p.g d.gpm n.gpm   pt.rp.gsn p.d d.dsm n.dsm d.dsm pt.aa.dsm d.apn a.apn
3873   3836 3696 3836 608 3836 172   648 1877 3836 2536 3836 3231 3836 4246

ἀκρογωνιαίου αὐτοῦ Χριστοῦ Ἰησοῦ, ²¹ ἐν ᾧ πᾶσα ἡ οἰκοδομὴ συναρμολογουμένη αὔξει εἰς ναὸν ἅγιον ἐν κυρίῳ, ²² ἐν ᾧ καὶ ὑμεῖς συνοικοδομεῖσθε εἰς κατοικητήριον τοῦ θεοῦ ἐν πνεύματι.

3:1 Τούτου χάριν ἐγὼ Παῦλος ὁ δέσμιος τοῦ Χριστοῦ [Ἰησοῦ] ὑπὲρ ὑμῶν τῶν ἐθνῶν— ¶ ² εἴ γε ἠκούσατε τὴν οἰκονομίαν τῆς χάριτος τοῦ θεοῦ τῆς δοθείσης μοι εἰς ὑμᾶς, ³ [ὅτι] κατὰ ἀποκάλυψιν ἐγνωρίσθη μοι τὸ μυστήριον, καθὼς προέγραψα ἐν ὀλίγῳ, ⁴ πρὸς ὃ δύνασθε ἀναγινώσκοντες νοῆσαι τὴν σύνεσίν μου ἐν τῷ μυστηρίῳ τοῦ Χριστοῦ, ⁵ ὃ ἑτέραις γενεαῖς οὐκ ἐγνωρίσθη τοῖς υἱοῖς τῶν ἀνθρώπων ὡς νῦν ἀπεκαλύφθη τοῖς ἁγίοις ἀποστόλοις αὐτοῦ καὶ προφήταις ἐν πνεύματι, ⁶ εἶναι τὰ ἔθνη συγκληρονόμα καὶ σύσσωμα καὶ συμμέτοχα τῆς ἐπαγγελίας ἐν Χριστῷ Ἰησοῦ διὰ τοῦ εὐαγγελίου, ¶ ⁷ οὗ ἐγενήθην διάκονος κατὰ τὴν δωρεὰν τῆς χάριτος τοῦ θεοῦ τῆς δοθείσης μοι κατὰ τὴν ἐνέργειαν τῆς δυνάμεως αὐτοῦ. ⁸ ἐμοὶ τῷ ἐλαχιστοτέρῳ πάντων ἁγίων ἐδόθη ἡ χάρις αὕτη, τοῖς ἔθνεσιν εὐαγγελίσασθαι τὸ ἀνεξιχνίαστον πλοῦτος τοῦ Χριστοῦ ⁹ καὶ φωτίσαι [πάντας] τίς ἡ οἰκονομία τοῦ μυστηρίου τοῦ ἀποκεκρυμμένου ἀπὸ τῶν αἰώνων ἐν τῷ θεῷ τῷ τὰ πάντα κτίσαντι, ¹⁰ ἵνα

things. **10** His intent was that now, through the church, the manifold wisdom of God should be made known
→ ἵνα νῦν διὰ τῆς ἐκκλησίας ἡ πολυποίκιλος σοφία → ˻τοῦ θεοῦ˼ → → γνωρισθῇ
cj adv p.g d.gsf n.gsf d.nsf a.nsf n.nsf d.gsm n.gsm v.aps.3s
2671 3814 1328 3836 1711 3836 4497 5053 3836 2536 1192

to the rulers and authorities in the heavenly realms, **11** according to his eternal purpose which he
→ ταῖς ἀρχαῖς καὶ ˻ταῖς ἐξουσίαις˼ ˻ἐν τοῖς ἐπουρανίοις˼ ← κατὰ ← ˻τῶν αἰώνων˼ πρόθεσιν ἣν →
d.dpf n.dpf cj d.dpf n.dpf p.d d.dpn n.dpn p.a d.gpm n.gpm n.asf r.asf
3836 794 2779 3836 2026 1877 3836 2230 2848 3836 172 4606 4005

accomplished in Christ Jesus our Lord. **12** In him and through faith in him we may approach God
ἐποίησεν ἐν ˻τῷ Χριστῷ˼ Ἰησοῦ ἡμῶν ˻τῷ κυρίῳ˼ ἐν ᾧ καὶ διὰ ˻τῆς πίστεως˼ → αὐτοῦ ἔχομεν προσαγωγὴν
v.aai.3s p.d d.dsm n.dsm n.dsm r.gp.1 d.dsm n.dsm p.d r.dsm cj p.g d.gsf n.gsf r.gsm.3 v.pai.1p n.asf
4472 1877 3836 5986 2652 7005 3836 3261 1877 4005 2779 1328 3836 4411 899 2400 4643

with freedom and confidence. **13** I ask you, therefore, not to be discouraged because of my sufferings
˻τὴν παρρησίαν˼ ἐν πεποιθήσει → αἰτοῦμαι διὸ μὴ → → ἐγκακεῖν ἐν ← μου ˻ταῖς θλίψεσιν˼
d.asf n.asf p.d n.dsf v.pmi.1s cj pl f.pa p.d r.gs.1 d.dpf n.dpf
3836 4244 1877 4301 160 1475 3590 1591 1877 1609 3836 2568

for you, which are your glory.
ὑπὲρ ὑμῶν ἥτις ἐστὶν ὑμῶν δόξα
p.g r.gp.2 r.nsf v.pai.3s r.gp.2 n.nsf
5642 7007 4015 1639 7007 1518

A Prayer for the Ephesians

3:14 For this reason I kneel before the Father, **15** from whom his whole family in heaven
˻Τούτου χάριν˼ ← ← → ˻κάμπτω τὰ γόνατά μου˼ πρὸς τὸν πατέρα ἐξ οὗ πᾶσα πατριὰ ἐν οὐρανοῖς
r.gsn p.g v.pai.1s d.apn n.apn r.gs.1 p.a d.asm n.asm p.g r.gsm a.nsf n.nsf p.d n.dpm
4047 5920 2828 3836 1205 1609 4639 3836 4252 1666 4005 4246 4255 1877 4041

and on earth derives its name. **16** I pray that out of his glorious riches he may strengthen you with
καὶ ἐπὶ γῆς → → ὀνομάζεται ἵνα κατὰ ← αὐτοῦ ˻τῆς δόξης˼ ˻τὸ πλοῦτος˼ → → δῷ κραταιωθῆναι ὑμῖν →
cj p.a n.gsf v.ppi.3s cj p.a r.gsm.3 d.gsf n.gsf d.asn n.asn v.aas.3s f.ap r.dp.2
2779 2093 1178 3951 2671 2848 899 3836 1518 3836 4458 1443 3194 7007

power through his Spirit in your inner being, **17** so that Christ may dwell in your hearts
δυνάμει διὰ αὐτοῦ ˻τοῦ πνεύματος˼ εἰς τὸν ἔσω ἄνθρωπον ˻τὸν Χριστὸν˼ → κατοικῆσαι ἐν ὑμῶν ˻ταῖς καρδίαις˼
n.dsf p.g r.gsm.3 d.gsn n.gsn p.a d.asm adv n.asm d.asm n.asm f.aa p.d r.gp.2 d.dpf n.dpf
1539 1328 899 3836 4460 1650 3836 2276 476 3836 5986 2997 1877 7007 3836 2840

through faith. And I pray that you, being rooted and established in love, **18** may have power, together
διὰ ˻τῆς πίστεως˼ ἐρριζωμένοι καὶ τεθεμελιωμένοι ἐν ἀγάπῃ ἵνα → → ἐξισχύσητε σὺν
p.g d.gsf n.gsf pt.rp.npm cj pt.rp.npm p.d n.dsf cj v.aas.2p p.d
1328 3836 4411 4845 2779 2530 1877 27 2671 2015 5250

with all the saints, to grasp how wide and long and high and deep is the love of Christ,
← πᾶσιν τοῖς ἁγίοις → καταλαβέσθαι τί ˻τὸ πλάτος˼ καὶ μῆκος καὶ ὕψος καὶ βάθος ἀγάπην ˻τοῦ Χριστοῦ˼
a.dpm d.dpm a.dpm f.am r.nsn d.nsn n.nsn cj n.nsn cj n.nsn cj n.nsn n.asf d.gsm n.gsm
4246 3836 41 2898 5515 3836 4424 2779 3601 2779 5737 2779 958 27 3836 5986

19 and to know this love that surpasses knowledge – that you may be filled to the measure of all the
τε → γνῶναι ← ˻τὴν ὑπερβάλλουσαν˼ ˻τῆς γνώσεως˼ ἵνα → → πληρωθῆτε εἰς ← ← ← πᾶν τὸ
cj f.aa d.asf pt.pa.asf d.gsf n.gsf cj v.aps.2p p.a a.asn d.asn
5445 1182 27 3836 5650 3836 1194 2671 4444 1650 4246 3836

fullness of God. ¶ **20** Now to him who is able to do immeasurably more than all we ask
πλήρωμα ˻τοῦ θεοῦ˼ δὲ → Τῷ → δυναμένῳ → ποιῆσαι ὑπερεκπερισσοῦ ὑπὲρ ← πάντα ὧν → αἰτούμεθα
n.asn d.gsm n.gsm cj d.dsm pt.pp.dsm f.aa adv p.a a.apn r.gpn v.pmi.1p
4445 3836 2536 1254 3836 1538 4472 5655 5642 4246 4005 160

or imagine, according to his power that is at work within us, **21** to him be glory in the church and in
ἢ νοοῦμεν κατὰ ← τὴν δύναμιν τὴν → ἐνεργουμένην ἐν ἡμῖν αὐτῷ ἡ δόξα ἐν τῇ ἐκκλησίᾳ καὶ ἐν
cj v.pai.1p p.a d.asf n.asf d.asf pt.pm.asf p.d r.dp.1 r.dsm.3 d.nsf n.nsf p.d d.dsf n.dsf cj p.d
2445 3783 2848 3836 1539 3836 1919 1877 7005 899 3836 1518 1877 3836 1711 2779 1877

Christ Jesus throughout all generations, *for ever and ever!* Amen.
Χριστῷ Ἰησοῦ εἰς πάσας ˻τὰς γενεὰς˼ ˻τοῦ αἰῶνος˼ ˻τῶν αἰώνων˼ ἀμήν
n.dsm n.dsm p.a a.apf d.apf n.apf d.gsm n.gsm d.gpm n.gpm pl
5986 2652 1650 4246 3836 1155 3836 172 3836 172 297

γνωρισθῇ νῦν ταῖς ἀρχαῖς καὶ ταῖς ἐξουσίαις ἐν τοῖς ἐπουρανίοις διὰ τῆς ἐκκλησίας ἡ πολυποίκιλος σοφία τοῦ θεοῦ, **11** κατὰ πρόθεσιν τῶν αἰώνων ἣν ἐποίησεν ἐν τῷ Χριστῷ Ἰησοῦ τῷ κυρίῳ ἡμῶν, **12** ἐν ᾧ ἔχομεν τὴν παρρησίαν καὶ προσαγωγὴν ἐν πεποιθήσει διὰ τῆς πίστεως αὐτοῦ. **13** διὸ αἰτοῦμαι μὴ ἐγκακεῖν ἐν ταῖς θλίψεσίν μου ὑπὲρ ὑμῶν, ἥτις ἐστὶν δόξα ὑμῶν.

3:14 Τούτου χάριν κάμπτω τὰ γόνατά μου πρὸς τὸν πατέρα, **15** ἐξ οὗ πᾶσα πατριὰ ἐν οὐρανοῖς καὶ ἐπὶ γῆς ὀνομάζεται, **16** ἵνα δῷ ὑμῖν κατὰ τὸ πλοῦτος τῆς δόξης αὐτοῦ δυνάμει κραταιωθῆναι διὰ τοῦ πνεύματος αὐτοῦ εἰς τὸν ἔσω ἄνθρωπον, **17** κατοικῆσαι τὸν Χριστὸν διὰ τῆς πίστεως ἐν ταῖς καρδίαις ὑμῶν, ἐν ἀγάπῃ ἐρριζωμένοι καὶ τεθεμελιωμένοι, **18** ἵνα ἐξισχύσητε καταλαβέσθαι σὺν πᾶσιν τοῖς ἁγίοις τί τὸ πλάτος καὶ μῆκος καὶ ὕψος καὶ βάθος, **19** γνῶναί τε τὴν ὑπερβάλλουσαν τῆς γνώσεως ἀγάπην τοῦ Χριστοῦ, ἵνα πληρωθῆτε εἰς πᾶν τὸ πλήρωμα τοῦ θεοῦ. ¶ **20** Τῷ δὲ δυναμένῳ ὑπὲρ πάντα ποιῆσαι ὑπερεκπερισσοῦ ὧν αἰτούμεθα ἢ νοοῦμεν κατὰ τὴν δύναμιν τὴν ἐνεργουμένην ἐν ἡμῖν, **21** αὐτῷ ἡ δόξα ἐν τῇ ἐκκλησίᾳ καὶ ἐν Χριστῷ Ἰησοῦ εἰς πάσας τὰς γενεὰς τοῦ αἰῶνος τῶν αἰώνων, ἀμήν.

Unity in the Body of Christ

4:1 As a   prisoner for the Lord, then, I   urge   you to live   a life worthy of the calling   you have
ὁ   δέσμιος   ἐν   κυρίῳ   οὖν   ἐγὼ Παρακαλῶ ὑμᾶς → περιπατῆσαι ← ἀξίως → τῆς κλήσεως ἧς →
d.nsm n.nsm   p.d   n.dsm   cj   r.ns.1 v.pai.1s r.ap.2   f.aa   adv   d.gsf n.gsf r.gsf
3836 1300   1877   3261   4036   1609 4151   7007   4344   547   3836 3104 4005

received. **2** Be completely humble   and gentle; be   patient,   bearing with one   another in love.
ἐκλήθητε μετὰ πάσης   ταπεινοφροσύνης καὶ πραΰτητος μετὰ μακροθυμίας ἀνεχόμενοι   ἀλλήλων ← ἐν ἀγάπῃ
v.api.2p μετὰ a.gsf   n.gsf   cj   n.gsf   p.g n.gsf   pt.pm.npm   r.gpm   p.d n.dsf
2813 3552 4246   5425   2779 4559   3552 3429   462   253   1877 27

3 Make every effort   to keep the unity of the Spirit   through the bond   of peace.   **4** There is one body
σπουδάζοντες → τηρεῖν τὴν ἑνότητα → τοῦ πνεύματος ἐν τῷ συνδέσμῳ ⌐τῆς εἰρήνης⌐ Ἓν σῶμα
pt.pa.npm   f.pa d.asf n.asf   d.gsn n.gsn p.d d.dsm n.dsm   d.gsf n.gsf   a.nsn n.nsn
5079   5498 3836 1942   3836 4460 1877 3836 5278   3836 1645   1651 5393

and one Spirit – just   as   you were called   to one hope when you were called   – **5** one Lord, one faith, one
καὶ ἓν πνεῦμα καθὼς ← καὶ → → ἐκλήθητε ἐν μιᾷ ἐλπίδι ὑμῶν ⌐τῆς κλήσεως⌐ εἰς κύριος μία πίστις ἐν
cj a.nsn n.nsn   cj   adv   v.api.2p p.d a.dsf n.dsf r.gp.2 d.gsf n.gsf   a.nsm n.nsm a.nsf n.nsf a.nsn
2779 1651 4460   2777   2779   2813 1877 1651 1828 7007 3836 3104   1651 3261 1651 4411 1651

baptism; **6** one God and Father of all,   who is over all   and through all   and in all. ¶ **7** But to each
βάπτισμα εἷς θεὸς καὶ πατὴρ πάντων ὁ ἐπὶ πάντων καὶ διὰ   πάντων καὶ ἐν πᾶσιν   δὲ ἑκάστῳ
n.nsn a.nsm n.nsm cj n.nsm a.gpm d.nsm p.g a.gpm cj p.g   a.gpm cj p.d a.dpm   cj r.dsm
967 1651 2536 2779 4252 4246 3836 2093 4246 2779 1328   4246 2779 1877 4246   1254 1667

one of us   grace   has been given as   Christ   apportioned it.   **8** This is why it says: "When he
Ἑνὶ ἡμῶν ἡ χάρις⌐ → → ἐδόθη κατὰ ⌐τοῦ Χριστοῦ⌐ ⌐τὸ μέτρον⌐ ⌐τῆς δωρεᾶς⌐ διὸ ← → λέγει →
a.dsm r.gp.1 d.nsf n.nsf   v.api.3s p.a d.gsm n.gsm   d.asn n.asn   d.gsf n.gsf   cj   v.pai.3s
1651 7005 3836 5921   1443 2848 3836 5986   3836 3586   3836 1561   1475   3306

ascended on high, he led   captives   in his train and gave gifts   to men."   **9** (What does   "he
ἀναβὰς εἰς ὕψος → ἠχμαλώτευσεν αἰχμαλωσίαν ← ← ← ἔδωκεν δόματα τοῖς ἀνθρώποις δὲ τί → → τὸ →
pt.aa.nsm p.a n.asn → v.aai.3s   n.asf   v.aai.3s n.apn d.dpm n.dpm   cj r.nsn   d.nsn
326 1650 5737   169   168   169 169 169   1443 1517 3836 476   1254 5515   1639 3836

ascended" mean except that he also descended to the lower,   earthly regions? **10** He   who descended is   the
ἀνέβη ἔστιν ⌐εἰ μὴ⌐ ὅτι → καὶ κατέβη εἰς τὰ κατώτερα ⌐τῆς γῆς⌐ μέρη   αὐτός ὁ καταβὰς ἔστιν καὶ ὁ
v.aai.3s v.pai.3s cj pl cj   adv v.aai.3s p.a d.apn a.apn.c d.gsf n.gsf n.apn   r.nsm d.nsm pt.aa.nsm v.pai.3s adv d.nsm
326 1639 1623 3590 4022 2849 2779 2849 1650 3836 3005 3836 1178 3538   899 3836 2849 1639 2779 3836

very one who ascended higher than all   the heavens, in order to fill   the whole universe.) **11**   It was he
← ← ἀναβὰς ὑπεράνω → πάντων τῶν οὐρανῶν ἵνα → ← πληρώσῃ τὰ πάντα ←   Καὶ   αὐτὸς
pt.aa.nsm p.g   a.gpm d.gpm n.gpm cj → v.aas.3s d.apn a.apn ←   cj   r.nsm
326 5645   4246 3836 4041 2671   4444 3836 4246   2779   899

who gave some   to be apostles, some   to be prophets, some   to be evangelists, and some   to be
ἔδωκεν ⌐τοὺς μὲν⌐ ἀποστόλους ⌐τοὺς δὲ⌐ προφήτας ⌐τοὺς δὲ⌐ εὐαγγελιστάς → ⌐τοὺς δὲ⌐
v.aai.3s d.apm pl   n.apm   d.apm pl   n.apm   d.apm pl   n.apm   d.apm pl
1443 3836 3525   693   3836 1254   4737   3836 1254   2296   1254 3836 1254

pastors and teachers, **12** to   prepare   God's   people for works of service,   so that the body   of
ποιμένας καὶ διδασκάλους πρὸς ⌐τὸν καταρτισμὸν⌐ ⌐τῶν ἁγίων⌐ ← εἰς ἔργον → διακονίας εἰς ← τοῦ σώματος
n.apm cj n.apm   p.a d.asm n.asm   d.gpm a.gpm   p.a n.asn → n.gsf p.a   d.gsn n.gsn
4478 2779 1437   4639 3836 2938   3836 41   1650 2240 1355 1650   3836 5393

Christ   may be built   up **13** until we all   reach   unity   in the faith   and in the knowledge
⌐τοῦ Χριστοῦ⌐ οἰκοδομὴν ← μέχρι ⌐οἱ πάντες⌐ καταντήσωμεν εἰς ⌐τὴν ἑνότητα⌐ → τῆς πίστεως καὶ → τῆς ἐπιγνώσεως
d.gsm n.gsm   n.asf   cj d.npm a.npm   v.aas.1p p.a d.asf n.asf   d.gsf n.gsf cj   d.gsf n.gsf
3836 5986   3869   3588 2918 3836 4246 2918 1650 3836 1942   3836 4411 2779   3836 2106

of the Son of God   and become mature,   attaining to the whole measure of the fullness   of Christ. ¶
→ τοῦ υἱοῦ → ⌐τοῦ θεοῦ⌐ εἰς τέλειον ἄνδρα εἰς ἡλικίας μέτρον → τοῦ πληρώματος → ⌐τοῦ Χριστοῦ⌐
d.gsm n.gsm d.gsm n.gsm   p.a a.asm n.asm p.a n.gsf n.asn   d.gsn n.gsn   d.gsm n.gsm
3836 5626 3836 2536   1650 5455 467 1650 2461 3586   3836 4445   3836 5986

14 Then we will no   longer be   infants, tossed   back and forth by the waves, and blown   here and
ἵνα → → μηκέτι   ὦμεν νήπιοι κλυδωνιζόμενοι ← ← ←   καὶ περιφερόμενοι ← ←
cj → → adv   v.pas.1p n.npm pt.pp.npm   cj pt.pp.npm
2671 1639 1639 3600   1639 3758 3115   2779 4367

4:1 Παρακαλῶ οὖν ὑμᾶς ἐγὼ ὁ δέσμιος ἐν κυρίῳ ἀξίως περιπατῆσαι τῆς κλήσεως ἧς ἐκλήθητε, **2** μετὰ πάσης ταπεινοφροσύνης καὶ πραΰτητος, μετὰ μακροθυμίας, ἀνεχόμενοι ἀλλήλων ἐν ἀγάπῃ, **3** σπουδάζοντες τηρεῖν τὴν ἑνότητα τοῦ πνεύματος ἐν τῷ συνδέσμῳ τῆς εἰρήνης· **4** ἓν σῶμα καὶ ἓν πνεῦμα, καθὼς καὶ ἐκλήθητε ἐν μιᾷ ἐλπίδι τῆς κλήσεως ὑμῶν· **5** εἷς κύριος, μία πίστις, ἓν βάπτισμα, **6** εἷς θεὸς καὶ πατὴρ πάντων, ὁ ἐπὶ πάντων καὶ διὰ πάντων καὶ ἐν πᾶσιν. ¶ **7** Ἑνὶ δὲ ἑκάστῳ ἡμῶν ἐδόθη ἡ χάρις κατὰ τὸ μέτρον τῆς δωρεᾶς τοῦ Χριστοῦ. **8** διὸ λέγει, Ἀναβὰς εἰς ὕψος ἠχμαλώτευσεν αἰχμαλωσίαν, ἔδωκεν δόματα τοῖς ἀνθρώποις. **9** τὸ δὲ Ἀνέβη τί ἐστιν, εἰ μὴ ὅτι καὶ κατέβη εἰς τὰ κατώτερα [μέρη] τῆς γῆς; **10** ὁ καταβὰς αὐτός ἐστιν καὶ ὁ ἀναβὰς ὑπεράνω πάντων τῶν οὐρανῶν, ἵνα πληρώσῃ τὰ πάντα. **11** καὶ αὐτὸς ἔδωκεν τοὺς μὲν ἀποστόλους, τοὺς δὲ προφήτας, τοὺς δὲ εὐαγγελιστάς, τοὺς δὲ ποιμένας καὶ διδασκάλους, **12** πρὸς τὸν καταρτισμὸν τῶν ἁγίων εἰς ἔργον διακονίας, εἰς οἰκοδομὴν τοῦ σώματος τοῦ Χριστοῦ, **13** μέχρι καταντήσωμεν οἱ πάντες εἰς τὴν ἑνότητα τῆς πίστεως καὶ τῆς ἐπιγνώσεως τοῦ υἱοῦ τοῦ θεοῦ, εἰς ἄνδρα τέλειον, εἰς μέτρον ἡλικίας τοῦ πληρώματος τοῦ Χριστοῦ, ¶ **14** ἵνα μηκέτι ὦμεν νήπιοι,

there by every wind of teaching and by the cunning and craftiness of men in their deceitful
← → παντὶ ἀνέμῳ → ⌐τῆς διδασκαλίας⌐ ἐν τῇ κυβείᾳ ἐν πανουργίᾳ → ⌐τῶν ἀνθρώπων⌐ πρὸς τὴν ⌐τῆς πλάνης⌐
a.dsm n.dsm d.gsf n.gsf p.d d.dsf n.dsf p.d n.dsf d.gpm n.gpm p.a d.asf d.gsf n.gsf
4246 449 3836 1436 1877 3836 3235 1877 4111 3836 476 4639 3836 3836 4415

scheming. **15** Instead, speaking the truth in love, we will in all things grow up into him who is the
μεθοδείαν δὲ ἀληθεύοντες ← ἐν ἀγάπῃ → ⌐τὰ πάντα⌐ ← αὐξήσωμεν ← εἰς αὐτὸν ὅς ἐστιν ἡ
n.asf cj pt.pa.npm p.d n.dsf d.apn a.apn v.aas.1p p.a r.asm.3 r.nsm v.pai.3s d.nsf
3497 1254 238 1877 27 889 889 3836 4246 889 1650 899 4005 1639 3836

Head, that is, Christ. **16** From him the whole body, joined and held together by every
κεφαλή Χριστός ἐξ οὗ τὸ πᾶν σῶμα συναρμολογούμενον καὶ συμβιβαζόμενον ← διὰ πάσης
n.nsf n.nsm p.g r.gsm d.nsn a.nsn n.nsn pt.pp.nsn cj pt.pp.nsn p.g a.gsf
3051 5986 1666 4005 3836 4246 5393 5274 2779 5204 1328 4246

supporting ligament, grows and builds itself up in love, as each part
⌐τῆς ἐπιχορηγίας⌐ ἁφῆς ⌐τὴν αὔξησιν τοῦ σώματος⌐ εἰς οἰκοδομὴν ἑαυτοῦ ↰ ἐν ἀγάπῃ ἐν μέτρῳ ⌐ἑνὸς ἑκάστου⌐ μέρους
d.gsf n.gsf n.gsf d.asf n.asf d.gsn n.gsn p.a n.asf r.gsn.3 p.d n.dsf p.d n.dsn a.gsn r.gsn n.gsn
3836 2221 913 3836 890 3836 5393 1650 3869 1571 3869 1877 27 1877 3586 1651 1667 3538

does its work.
ποιεῖται κατ᾽ ἐνέργειαν
v.pmi.3s p.a n.asf
4472 2848 1918

Living as Children of Light

4:17 So I tell you this, and insist on it in the Lord, that you must no longer live as the
οὖν → λέγω Τοῦτο καὶ μαρτύρομαι ἐν κυρίῳ ὑμᾶς → μηκέτι ← περιπατεῖν καθὼς καὶ τὰ
cj v.pai.1s r.asn cj v.pmi.1s p.d n.dsm r.ap.2 adv f.pa cj adv d.npn
4036 3306 4047 2779 3458 1877 3261 7007 4344 3600 4344 2777 2779 3836

Gentiles do, in the futility of their thinking. **18** They are darkened in their understanding and
ἔθνη περιπατεῖ ἐν ματαιότητι → αὐτῶν ⌐τοῦ νοὸς⌐ → ὄντες ἐσκοτωμένοι → τῇ διανοίᾳ
n.npn v.pai.3s p.d n.dsf r.gpn.3 d.gsn n.gsn pt.pa.npm pt.rp.npm d.dsf n.dsf
1620 4344 1877 3470 3808 899 3836 3808 1639 5031 3836 1379

separated from the life of God because of the ignorance that is in them due to the hardening of
ἀπηλλοτριωμένοι ← τῆς ζωῆς → ⌐τοῦ θεοῦ⌐ διὰ ← τὴν ἄγνοιαν τὴν οὖσαν ἐν αὐτοῖς διὰ ← τὴν πώρωσιν →
pt.rp.npm d.gsf n.gsf d.gsm n.gsm p.a d.asf n.asf d.asf pt.pa.asf p.d r.dpm.3 p.a d.asf n.asf
558 3836 2437 3836 2536 1328 3836 53 3836 1639 1877 899 1328 3836 4801 2840

their hearts. **19** Having lost all sensitivity, they have given themselves over to sensuality so as to indulge
αὐτῶν ⌐τῆς καρδίας⌐ → → → ἀπηλγηκότες οἵτινες → παρέδωκαν ἑαυτοὺς ← → ⌐τῇ ἀσελγείᾳ⌐ εἰς ← ← ἐργασίαν
r.gpm.3 d.gsf n.gsf pt.ra.npm r.npm v.aai.3p r.apm.3 d.dsf n.dsf p.a n.asf
899 3836 2840 556 4015 4140 1571 3836 816 1650 2238

in every kind of impurity, with a continual lust for more. ¶ **20** You, however, did not come to know
← πάσης ← ἀκαθαρσίας ἐν → πλεονεξίᾳ ὑμεῖς δὲ → οὐχ → → ἐμάθετε
a.gsf n.gsf p.d n.dsf r.np.2 cj pl pl v.aai.2p
4246 174 1877 4432 7007 1254 3443 4024 3443

Christ that way. **21** Surely you heard of him and were taught in him in accordance with the truth
⌐τὸν Χριστόν⌐ οὕτως → εἴ γε → ἠκούσατε ← αὐτὸν καὶ → ἐδιδάχθητε ἐν αὐτῷ καθὼς ← ← ἀλήθεια
d.asm n.asm adv cj pl v.aai.2p r.asm.3 cj v.api.2p p.d r.dsm.3 cj n.nsf
3836 5986 4048 1623 1145 201 899 2779 1438 1877 899 2777 237

that is in Jesus. **22** You were taught, with regard to your former way of life, to put off your old
→ ἐστιν ἐν ⌐τῷ Ἰησοῦ⌐ ὑμᾶς κατὰ ← τὴν προτέραν ἀναστροφὴν ← → ἀποθέσθαι τὸν παλαιὸν
v.pai.3s p.d d.dsm n.dsm r.ap.2 p.a d.asf a.asf.c n.asf f.am d.asm a.asm
1639 1877 3836 2652 7007 2848 3836 4728 419 700 3836 4094

self, which is being corrupted by its deceitful desires; **23** to be made new in the attitude of your
ἄνθρωπον τὸν → → φθειρόμενον κατὰ τὰς ⌐τῆς ἀπάτης⌐ ἐπιθυμίας δὲ → → ἀνανεοῦσθαι → τῷ πνεύματι ↱ ὑμῶν
n.asm d.asm pt.pp.asm p.a d.apf d.gsf n.gsf n.apf cj f.pp d.dsn n.dsn r.gp.2
476 3836 5780 2848 3836 3836 573 2123 1254 391 3836 4460 3808 7007

minds; **24** and to put on the new self, created to be like God in true righteousness and
⌐τοῦ νοὸς⌐ καὶ → ἐνδύσασθαι ← τὸν καινὸν ἄνθρωπον ⌐τὸν κτισθέντα⌐ κατὰ θεὸν ἐν ⌐τῆς ἀληθείας⌐ δικαιοσύνῃ καὶ
d.gsm n.gsm cj f.am d.asm a.asm n.asm d.asm pt.ap.asm p.a n.asm p.d d.gsf n.gsf n.dsf cj
3836 3808 2779 1907 3836 2785 476 3836 3231 2848 2536 1877 3836 237 1466 2779

κλυδωνιζόμενοι καὶ περιφερόμενοι παντὶ ἀνέμῳ τῆς διδασκαλίας ἐν τῇ κυβείᾳ τῶν ἀνθρώπων, ἐν πανουργίᾳ πρὸς τὴν μεθοδείαν τῆς πλάνης. ¹⁵ ἀληθεύοντες δὲ ἐν ἀγάπῃ αὐξήσωμεν εἰς αὐτὸν τὰ πάντα, ὅς ἐστιν ἡ κεφαλή, Χριστός, ¹⁶ ἐξ οὗ πᾶν τὸ σῶμα συναρμολογούμενον καὶ συμβιβαζόμενον διὰ πάσης ἁφῆς τῆς ἐπιχορηγίας κατ᾽ ἐνέργειαν ἐν μέτρῳ ἑνὸς ἑκάστου μέρους τὴν αὔξησιν τοῦ σώματος ποιεῖται εἰς οἰκοδομὴν ἑαυτοῦ ἐν ἀγάπῃ.

⁴:¹⁷ Τοῦτο οὖν λέγω καὶ μαρτύρομαι ἐν κυρίῳ, μηκέτι ὑμᾶς περιπατεῖν, καθὼς καὶ τὰ ἔθνη περιπατεῖ ἐν ματαιότητι τοῦ νοὸς αὐτῶν, ¹⁸ ἐσκοτωμένοι τῇ διανοίᾳ ὄντες, ἀπηλλοτριωμένοι τῆς ζωῆς τοῦ θεοῦ διὰ τὴν ἄγνοιαν τὴν οὖσαν ἐν αὐτοῖς, διὰ τὴν πώρωσιν τῆς καρδίας αὐτῶν, ¹⁹ οἵτινες ἀπηλγηκότες ἑαυτοὺς παρέδωκαν τῇ ἀσελγείᾳ εἰς ἐργασίαν ἀκαθαρσίας πάσης ἐν πλεονεξίᾳ. ¶ ²⁰ ὑμεῖς δὲ οὐχ οὕτως ἐμάθετε τὸν Χριστόν, ²¹ εἴ γε αὐτὸν ἠκούσατε καὶ ἐν αὐτῷ ἐδιδάχθητε, καθὼς ἐστιν ἀλήθεια ἐν τῷ Ἰησοῦ, ²² ἀποθέσθαι ὑμᾶς κατὰ τὴν προτέραν ἀναστροφὴν τὸν παλαιὸν ἄνθρωπον τὸν φθειρόμενον κατὰ τὰς ἐπιθυμίας τῆς ἀπάτης, ²³ ἀνανεοῦσθαι δὲ τῷ πνεύματι τοῦ νοὸς ὑμῶν ²⁴ καὶ ἐνδύσασθαι τὸν καινὸν ἄνθρωπον τὸν κατὰ θεὸν κτισθέντα

holiness. ¶ **25** Therefore each of you must put off falsehood and speak truthfully to his neighbor,
ὁσιότητι   Διὸ   ἕκαστος   ←   ἀποθέμενοι   ⌐τὸ ψεῦδος⌐   λαλεῖτε ἀλήθειαν   μετὰ αὐτοῦ   ⌐τοῦ πλησίον⌐
n.dsf   cj   r.nsm   pt.am.npm   d.asn n.asn   v.pam.2p n.asf   p.g r.gsm.3   d.gsm adv
4009   1475   1667   700   3836 6022   3281 237   3552 899   3836 4446

for we are all members of one body. **26** "In your anger do not sin": Do not let the sun go down
ὅτι → ἐσμὲν μέλη → ἀλλήλων ←   ὀργίζεσθε καὶ → μὴ ἁμαρτάνετε   μὴ → ὁ ἥλιος ἐπιδυέτω
cj   v.pai.1p n.npn   r.gpm   v.ppm.2p cj   pl v.pam.2p   pl   d.nsm n.nsm v.pam.3s
4022   1639 3517   253   3974 2779   3590 279   2115 3590 2115 3836 2463 2115

while you are still angry, **27** and do not give the devil a foothold. ¶ **28** He who has been stealing must
ἐπὶ ὑμῶν ⌐τῷ παροργισμῷ⌐ → μηδὲ δίδοτε τῷ διαβόλῳ τόπον   ὁ   κλέπτων →
p.d r.gp.2   d.dsm n.dsm   cj v.pam.2p d.dsm n.dsm n.asm   d.nsm   pt.pa.nsm
2093 7007   3836 4240   3593 1443 3593 1443 3836 1333 5536   3836   3096

steal no longer, but must work, doing something useful with his own hands, that he may have
κλεπτέτω μηκέτι ← δὲ μᾶλλον → κοπιάτω ἐργαζόμενος τὸ   ἀγαθόν → ταῖς ἰδίαις χερσὶν ἵνα → → ἔχῃ
v.pam.3s adv   cj adv.c   v.pam.3s pt.pm.nsm d.asn   a.asn   d.dpf a.dpf n.dpf cj   v.pas.3s
3096 3600   1254 3437   3159 2237 3836   19   3836 2625 5931 2671   2400

something to share with those in need. **29** Do not let any unwholesome talk come out of your
→ μεταδιδόναι → τῷ ἔχοντι χρείαν → μὴ → πᾶς σαπρὸς   λόγος ἐκπορευέσθω ἐκ → ὑμῶν
f.pa   d.dsm pt.pa.dsm n.asf   pl → a.nsm a.nsm   n.nsm v.pmm.3s   p.g r.gp.2
3556   3836 2400 5970   1744 3590 1744 4246 4911   3364 1744   1666 5125 7007

mouths, but only what is helpful for building others up according to their needs, that it may benefit those
⌐τοῦ στόματος⌐ ἀλλὰ εἴ τις ἀγαθὸς πρὸς οἰκοδομὴν ← ← → τῆς χρείας ἵνα → ⌐δῷ χάριν⌐ τοῖς
d.gsn n.gsn   cj cj r.nsm a.nsm p.a n.asf   d.gsf n.gsf cj   v.aas.3s n.asf d.dpm
3836 5125   247 1623 5516 19 4639 3869   3836 5970 2671   1443 5921 3836

who listen. **30** And do not grieve the Holy Spirit of God, with whom you were sealed for the day of
← ἀκούουσιν καὶ → μὴ λυπεῖτε τὸ ⌐τὸ ἅγιον⌐ πνεῦμα ⌐τοῦ θεοῦ⌐ ἐν ᾧ → ἐσφραγίσθητε εἰς ἡμέραν
pt.pa.dpm   cj → pl v.pam.2p d.asn d.asn a.asn n.asn   d.gsm n.gsm p.d r.dsn   v.api.2p p.a n.asf
201   2779   3382 3590 3382 3836 3836 41 4460   3836 2536 1877 4005   5381 1650 2465

redemption. **31** Get rid of all bitterness, rage and anger, brawling and slander, along with every
ἀπολυτρώσεως → ἀρθήτω ἀφ᾽ ὑμῶν πᾶσα πικρία καὶ θυμὸς καὶ ὀργὴ καὶ κραυγὴ καὶ βλασφημία → σὺν πάσῃ
n.gsf   v.apm.3s p.g r.gp.2 a.nsf n.nsf cj n.nsm cj n.nsf cj n.nsf cj n.nsf   p.d a.dsf
667   149 608 7007 4246 4394 2779 2596 2779 3973 2779 3199 2779 1060   5250 4246

form of malice. **32** Be kind and compassionate to one another, forgiving each other, just as in
← κακίᾳ [δὲ] γίνεσθε χρηστοί εὔσπλαγχνοι εἰς ἀλλήλους ← χαριζόμενοι ἑαυτοῖς καθὼς καὶ ἐν
n.dsf   cj v.pmm.2p a.npm a.npm p.a r.apm   pt.pm.npm r.dpm.2 cj   adv p.d
2798   1254 1181 5982 2359 1650 253   5919 1571 2777   2779 1877

Christ God forgave you. ¶ **5:1** Be imitators of God, therefore, as dearly loved children **2** and
Χριστῷ ὁ θεὸς ἐχαρίσατο ὑμῖν   Γίνεσθε μιμηταὶ → ⌐τοῦ θεοῦ⌐ οὖν ὡς → ἀγαπητὰ τέκνα καὶ
n.dsm d.nsm n.nsm v.ami.3s r.dp.2   v.pmm.2p n.npm   d.gsm n.gsm cj ← pl   a.npn n.npn cj
5986 3836 2536 5919 7007   1181 3629   3836 2536 4036 6055   28 5451 2779

live a life of love, just as Christ loved us and gave himself up for us as a
περιπατεῖτε ← ἐν ἀγάπῃ καθὼς → καὶ ὁ Χριστὸς ἠγάπησεν ἡμᾶς καὶ παρέδωκεν ἑαυτὸν ↱ ὑπὲρ ἡμῶν εἰς
v.pam.2p   p.d n.dsf cj   adv d.nsm n.nsm v.aai.3s r.ap.1 cj v.aai.3s r.asm.3   p.g r.gp.1 p.a
4344   1877 27 2777   2779 3836 5986 26 7005 2779 4140 1571   4140 7005 1650

fragrant offering and sacrifice to God. ¶ **3** But among you there must not be even a hint of
⌐ὀσμὴν εὐωδίας⌐ προσφορὰν καὶ θυσίαν → ⌐τῷ θεῷ⌐   δὲ ἐν ὑμῖν → μηδὲ ὀνομαζέσθω ← ←
n.asf n.gsf   n.asf cj n.asf   d.dsm n.dsm   cj p.d r.dp.2   adv v.ppm.3s
4011 2380   4714 2779 2602   3836 2536   1254 1877 7007   3593 3951
    3951 3951

sexual immorality, or of any kind of impurity, or of greed, because these are improper for God's holy people.
Πορνεία καὶ πᾶσα ← ἀκαθαρσία ἢ πλεονεξία καθὼς → → πρέπει → → ἁγίοις
n.nsf cj a.nsf   n.nsf cj n.nsf cj   v.pai.3s   a.dpm
4518 2779 4246   174 2445 4432 2777   4560   41

4 Nor should there be obscenity, foolish talk or coarse joking, which are out of place, but rather
καὶ αἰσχρότης καὶ μωρολογία ← ἢ εὐτραπελία ← ἃ → οὐκ ἀνῆκεν ἀλλὰ μᾶλλον
cj   n.nsf cj n.nsf   cj n.nsf   r.npn → οὐκ v.iai.3s cj adv.c
2779   157 2779 3703   2445 2365   4005 465 4024 465 247 3437

ἐν δικαιοσύνῃ καὶ ὁσιότητι τῆς ἀληθείας. ¶ ²⁵ Διὸ ἀποθέμενοι τὸ ψεῦδος λαλεῖτε ἀλήθειαν ἕκαστος μετὰ τοῦ πλησίον αὐτοῦ, ὅτι ἐσμὲν ἀλλήλων μέλη. ²⁶ ὀργίζεσθε καὶ μὴ ἁμαρτάνετε· ὁ ἥλιος μὴ ἐπιδυέτω ἐπὶ [τῷ] παροργισμῷ ὑμῶν, ²⁷ μηδὲ δίδοτε τόπον τῷ διαβόλῳ. ¶ ²⁸ ὁ κλέπτων μηκέτι κλεπτέτω, μᾶλλον δὲ κοπιάτω ἐργαζόμενος ταῖς [ἰδίαις] χερσὶν τὸ ἀγαθόν, ἵνα ἔχῃ μεταδιδόναι τῷ χρείαν ἔχοντι. ²⁹ πᾶς λόγος σαπρὸς ἐκ τοῦ στόματος ὑμῶν μὴ ἐκπορευέσθω, ἀλλὰ εἴ τις ἀγαθὸς πρὸς οἰκοδομὴν τῆς χρείας, ἵνα δῷ χάριν τοῖς ἀκούουσιν. ³⁰ καὶ μὴ λυπεῖτε τὸ πνεῦμα τὸ ἅγιον τοῦ θεοῦ, ἐν ᾧ ἐσφραγίσθητε εἰς ἡμέραν ἀπολυτρώσεως. ³¹ πᾶσα πικρία καὶ θυμὸς καὶ ὀργὴ καὶ κραυγὴ καὶ βλασφημία ἀρθήτω ἀφ᾽ ὑμῶν σὺν πάσῃ κακίᾳ. ³² γίνεσθε [δὲ] εἰς ἀλλήλους χρηστοί, εὔσπλαγχνοι, χαριζόμενοι ἑαυτοῖς, καθὼς καὶ ὁ θεὸς ἐν Χριστῷ ἐχαρίσατο ὑμῖν.

⁵:¹ γίνεσθε οὖν μιμηταὶ τοῦ θεοῦ ὡς τέκνα ἀγαπητά, ² καὶ περιπατεῖτε ἐν ἀγάπῃ, καθὼς καὶ ὁ Χριστὸς ἠγάπησεν ἡμᾶς καὶ παρέδωκεν ἑαυτὸν ὑπὲρ ἡμῶν προσφορὰν καὶ θυσίαν τῷ θεῷ εἰς ὀσμὴν εὐωδίας. ¶ ³ πορνεία δὲ καὶ ἀκαθαρσία πᾶσα ἢ πλεονεξία μηδὲ ὀνομαζέσθω ἐν ὑμῖν, καθὼς πρέπει ἁγίοις, ⁴ καὶ αἰσχρότης καὶ μωρολογία ἢ εὐτραπελία, ἃ οὐκ ἀνῆκεν, ἀλλὰ

thanksgiving. **5** For of this you can be sure: No immoral, impure or greedy person – such
εὐχαριστία γὰρ → τοῦτο → → ἴστε γινώσκοντες⸎ ὅτι ⸌πᾶς οὐκ πόρνος ἢ ἀκάθαρτος ἢ πλεονέκτης ← ὅ
n.nsf cj r.asn v.ram.2p pt.pa.npm cj a.nsm pl n.nsm cj a.nsm cj n.nsm r.nsn
2374 1142 4047 3857 1182 4022 4246 4521 2445 176 2445 4431 4005

a man is an idolater – has any inheritance in the kingdom of Christ and of God. **6** Let no one
ἔστιν εἰδωλολάτρης ἔχει κληρονομίαν ἐν τῇ βασιλείᾳ ← ⸌τοῦ Χριστοῦ⸎ καὶ → θεοῦ → Μηδεὶς ←
v.pai.3s n.nsm v.pai.3s n.asf p.d d.dsf n.dsf d.gsm n.gsm cj n.gsm a.nsm
1639 1629 2400 3100 1877 3836 993 3836 5986 2779 2536 572 3594

deceive you with empty words, for because of such things God's wrath comes on those who are
ἀπατάτω ὑμᾶς → κενοῖς λόγοις γὰρ διὰ ← ταῦτα ← ⸌τοῦ θεοῦ⸎ ἡ ὀργὴ ἔρχεται ἐπὶ τοὺς υἱοὺς → →
v.pam.3s r.ap.2 a.dpm n.dpm cj p.a r.apn d.gsm n.gsm d.nsf n.nsf v.pmi.3s p.a d.apm n.apm
572 7007 3031 3364 1142 1328 4047 3836 2536 3836 3973 2262 2093 3836 5626

disobedient. **7** Therefore do not be partners with them. ¶ **8** For you were once darkness, but now you are
⸌τῆς ἀπειθείας⸎ οὖν → μὴ γίνεσθε συμμέτοχοι ← αὐτῶν γὰρ → ἦτε ποτε σκότος δὲ νῦν
d.gsf n.gsf cj pl v.pdm.2p a.npm r.gpm.3 cj v.iai.2p pl n.nsn cj adv
3836 577 4036 3590 1181 5212 899 1142 1639 4537 5030 1254 3814

light in the Lord. Live as children of light **9** (for the fruit of the light consists in all goodness,
φῶς ἐν κυρίῳ περιπατεῖτε ὡς τέκνα → φωτὸς γὰρ ὁ καρπὸς → τοῦ φωτὸς ἐν πάσῃ ἀγαθωσύνῃ καὶ
n.nsn p.d n.dsm v.pam.2p pl n.npn n.gsn cj d.nsm n.nsm d.gsn n.gsn p.d a.dsf n.dsf cj
5890 1877 3261 4344 6055 5451 5890 1142 3836 2843 3836 5890 1877 4246 20 2779

righteousness and truth) **10** and find out what pleases the Lord. **11** Have nothing to do with
δικαιοσύνῃ καὶ ἀληθείᾳ δοκιμάζοντες ← τί ἐστιν εὐάρεστον τῷ κυρίῳ καὶ → μὴ → συγκοινωνεῖτε ←
n.dsf cj n.dsf pt.pa.npm r.nsn v.pai.3s a.nsn d.dsm n.dsm cj pl v.pam.2p
1466 2779 237 1507 5515 1639 2298 3836 3261 2779 5170 3590 5170

the fruitless deeds of darkness, but rather expose them. **12** For it is shameful even to mention what
τοῖς ⸌τοῖς ἀκάρποις⸎ ἔργοις → ⸌τοῦ σκότους⸎ δὲ μᾶλλον καὶ ἐλέγχετε γὰρ → ἐστιν αἰσχρόν καὶ → λέγειν τὰ ὑπ'
d.dpn d.dpn a.dpn n.dpn d.gsn n.gsn cj adv.c adv v.pam.2p cj v.pai.3s a.nsn adv f.pa d.apn p.g
3836 3836 182 2240 3836 5030 1254 3437 2779 1794 1142 1639 156 2779 3306 3836 5679

the disobedient do in secret. **13** But everything exposed by the light becomes visible, **14** for it is light that
αὐτῶν γινόμενα → κρυφῇ δὲ τὰ πάντα ἐλεγχόμενα ὑπὸ τοῦ φωτὸς → φανεροῦται γὰρ → ἐστιν ⸌τὸ φῶς⸎ →
r.gpm.3 pt.pm.apn adv cj d.npn a.npn pt.pp.npn p.g d.gsn n.gsn v.ppi.3s cj v.pai.3s d.nsn n.nsn
899 1181 3225 1254 3836 4246 1794 5679 3836 5890 5746 1142 1639 3836 5890 5746

makes everything visible. This is why it is said: "Wake up, O sleeper, rise from the dead, and
→ πᾶν φανερούμενον διὸ ← ← → λέγει Ἔγειρε ← ὁ καθεύδων καὶ ἀνάστα ἐκ τῶν νεκρῶν καὶ
a.nsn pt.pp.nsn cj v.pai.3s v.pam.2s d.vsm pt.pa.vsm cj v.aam.2s p.g d.gpm a.gpm cj
5746 4246 5746 3306 1586 3836 2761 2779 482 1666 3836 3738 2779

Christ will shine on you." ¶ **15** Be very careful, then, how you live – not as unwise but as
ὁ Χριστός⸎ ἐπιφαύσει ← σοι ἀκριβῶς Βλέπετε οὖν πῶς → περιπατεῖτε μὴ ὡς ἄσοφοι ἀλλ' ὡς
d.nsm n.nsm v.fai.3s r.ds.2 adv v.pam.2p cj cj v.pai.2p pl pl a.npm cj pl
3836 5986 2213 5148 1063 209 1063 4036 4802 4344 3590 6055 831 247 6055

wise, **16** making the most of every opportunity, because the days are evil. **17** Therefore do not be foolish,
σοφοί ἐξαγοραζόμενοι ← ← → ⸌τὸν καιρόν⸎ ὅτι αἱ ἡμέραι εἰσὶν πονηραί ⸌διὰ τοῦτο⸎ → μὴ γίνεσθε ἄφρονες
a.npm pt.pm.npm d.asm n.asm cj d.npf n.npf v.pai.3p a.npf p.a r.asn pl v.pmm.2p a.npm
5055 1973 3836 2789 4022 2465 1639 4505 1328 4047 3590 1181 933

but understand what the Lord's will is. **18** Do not get drunk on wine, which leads to debauchery.
ἀλλὰ συνίετε τί τὸ ⸌τοῦ κυρίου⸎ θέλημα καὶ → μὴ μεθύσκεσθε οἴνῳ ἐν ᾧ ἐστιν ← ἀσωτία
cj v.pam.2p r.nsn d.nsn d.gsm n.gsm n.nsn cj pl v.ppm.2p n.dsm p.d r.dsm v.pai.3s n.nsf
247 5317 5515 3836 3836 3261 2525 2779 3499 3590 3499 3885 1877 4005 1639 861

Instead, be filled with the Spirit. **19** Speak to one another with psalms, hymns and spiritual songs.
ἀλλὰ → πληροῦσθε ἐν πνεύματι λαλοῦντες → ἑαυτοῖς ← ἐν ψαλμοῖς καὶ ὕμνοις καὶ πνευματικαῖς ᾠδαῖς
cj v.ppm.2p p.d n.dsn pt.pa.npm r.dpm.2 p.d n.dpm cj n.dpm cj a.dpf n.dpf
247 4444 1877 4460 3281 1571 1877 6011 2779 5631 2779 4461 6046

Sing and make music in your heart to the Lord, **20** always giving thanks to God the Father
ᾄδοντες καὶ → ψάλλοντες → ὑμῶν ⸌τῇ καρδίᾳ⸎ → τῷ κυρίῳ πάντοτε → εὐχαριστοῦντες → ⸌τῷ θεῷ⸎ καὶ πατρί
pt.pa.npm cj pt.pa.npm r.gp.2 d.dsf n.dsf d.dsm n.dsm adv pt.pa.npm d.dsm n.dsm cj n.dsm
106 2779 6010 2840 7007 3836 2840 3836 3261 4121 2373 3836 2536 2779 4252

μᾶλλον εὐχαριστία. ⁵ τοῦτο γὰρ ἴστε γινώσκοντες, ὅτι πᾶς πόρνος ἢ ἀκάθαρτος ἢ πλεονέκτης, ὅ ἐστιν εἰδωλολάτρης, οὐκ ἔχει κληρονομίαν ἐν τῇ βασιλείᾳ τοῦ Χριστοῦ καὶ θεοῦ. ⁶ Μηδεὶς ὑμᾶς ἀπατάτω κενοῖς λόγοις· διὰ ταῦτα γὰρ ἔρχεται ἡ ὀργὴ τοῦ θεοῦ ἐπὶ τοὺς υἱοὺς τῆς ἀπειθείας. ⁷ μὴ οὖν γίνεσθε συμμέτοχοι αὐτῶν· ¶ ⁸ ἦτε γάρ ποτε σκότος, νῦν δὲ φῶς ἐν κυρίῳ· ὡς τέκνα φωτὸς περιπατεῖτε ⁹ —ὁ γὰρ καρπὸς τοῦ φωτὸς ἐν πάσῃ ἀγαθωσύνῃ καὶ δικαιοσύνῃ καὶ ἀληθείᾳ— ¹⁰ δοκιμάζοντες τί ἐστιν εὐάρεστον τῷ κυρίῳ, ¹¹ καὶ μὴ συγκοινωνεῖτε τοῖς ἔργοις τοῖς ἀκάρποις τοῦ σκότους, μᾶλλον δὲ καὶ ἐλέγχετε. ¹² τὰ γὰρ κρυφῇ γινόμενα ὑπ' αὐτῶν αἰσχρόν ἐστιν καὶ λέγειν, ¹³ τὰ δὲ πάντα ἐλεγχόμενα ὑπὸ τοῦ φωτὸς φανεροῦται, ¹⁴ πᾶν γὰρ τὸ φανερούμενον φῶς ἐστιν. διὸ λέγει, Ἔγειρε, ὁ καθεύδων, καὶ ἀνάστα ἐκ τῶν νεκρῶν, καὶ ἐπιφαύσει σοι ὁ Χριστός. ¶ ¹⁵ Βλέπετε οὖν ἀκριβῶς πῶς περιπατεῖτε μὴ ὡς ἄσοφοι ἀλλ' ὡς σοφοί, ¹⁶ ἐξαγοραζόμενοι τὸν καιρόν, ὅτι αἱ ἡμέραι πονηραί εἰσιν. ¹⁷ διὰ τοῦτο μὴ γίνεσθε ἄφρονες, ἀλλὰ συνίετε τί τὸ θέλημα τοῦ κυρίου. ¹⁸ καὶ μὴ μεθύσκεσθε οἴνῳ, ἐν ᾧ ἐστιν ἀσωτία, ἀλλὰ πληροῦσθε ἐν πνεύματι, ¹⁹ λαλοῦντες ἑαυτοῖς [ἐν] ψαλμοῖς καὶ ὕμνοις καὶ ᾠδαῖς πνευματικαῖς, ᾄδοντες καὶ ψάλλοντες τῇ καρδίᾳ ὑμῶν τῷ κυρίῳ, ²⁰ εὐχαριστοῦντες πάντοτε ὑπὲρ πάντων ἐν ὀνόματι τοῦ κυρίου ἡμῶν Ἰησοῦ Χριστοῦ τῷ θεῷ καὶ πατρί. ¶ ²¹ ὑποτασσόμενοι

for	everything,	in	the name	of	our	Lord	Jesus	Christ.	¶	²¹ Submit	to one	another	out of
ὑπὲρ	πάντων	ἐν	ὀνόματι →		ἡμῶν	⌐τοῦ κυρίου⌐	Ἰησοῦ	Χριστοῦ		Ὑποτασσόμενοι →	ἀλλήλοις ←		ἐν ←
p.g	a.gpn	p.d	n.dsn		r.gp.1	d.gsm n.gsm	n.gsm	n.gsm		pt.pp.npm	r.dpm		
5642	4246	1877	3950		7005	3836 3261	2652	5986		5718	253		1877

reverence	for Christ.
φόβῳ	→ Χριστοῦ
n.dsm	n.gsm
5832	5986

Wives and Husbands

^{5:22}Wives,		submit to	your	husbands		as		to the Lord.	²³ For	the husband	is	the head	of the wife
⌐αἱ γυναῖκες⌐		→ ἰδίοις	⌐τοῖς	ἀνδράσιν⌐		ὡς	→	τῷ κυρίῳ	ὅτι	ἀνήρ	ἐστιν	κεφαλὴ →	τῆς γυναικὸς
d.vpf n.vpf		a.dpm	d.dpm	n.dpm		pl		d.dsm n.dsm	cj	n.nsm	v.pai.3s	n.nsf	d.gsf n.gsf
3836 1222		467	2625	3836	467	6055		3836 3261	4022	467	1639	3051	3836 1222

as		Christ		is the head	of the church,		his body,	of which	he	is the Savior.	²⁴ Now	as	the church
ὡς	καὶ	ὁ	Χριστὸς⌐	κεφαλὴ	τῆς ἐκκλησίας	τοῦ σώματος			αὐτὸς	σωτήρ	ἀλλὰ	ὡς	ἡ ἐκκλησία
cj	cj	d.nsm	n.nsm	n.nsf	d.gsf n.gsf	d.gsn n.gsn			r.nsm	n.nsm	cj	cj	d.nsf n.nsf
6055	2779	3836	5986	3051	3836 1711	3836 5393			899	5400	247	6055	3836 1711

submits	to Christ,	so	also	wives		should submit	to their	husbands	in	everything.	¶
ὑποτάσσεται →	⌐τῷ Χριστῷ⌐	οὕτως καὶ		⌐αἱ γυναῖκες⌐		→	τοῖς	ἀνδράσιν	ἐν	παντί	
v.ppi.3s	d.dsm n.dsm	adv	adv	d.npf n.npf			d.dpm	n.dpm	p.d	a.dsn	
5718	3836 5986	4048	2779	3836 1222			3836	467	1877	4246	

²⁵ Husbands,	love	your	wives,	just	as		Christ	loved	the church	and	gave	himself	up	for	her
⌐Οἱ ἄνδρες⌐	ἀγαπᾶτε	τὰς	γυναῖκας	καθὼς ←	καὶ	ὁ	Χριστὸς⌐	ἠγάπησεν	τὴν ἐκκλησίαν	καὶ	παρέδωκεν	ἑαυτὸν	→	ὑπὲρ	αὐτῆς
d.vpm n.vpm	v.pam.2p	d.apf	n.apf	cj	adv	d.nsm	n.nsm	v.aai.3s	d.asf n.asf	cj	v.aai.3s	r.asm.3		p.g	r.gsf.3
3836 467	26	3836	1222	2777	2779	3836	5986	26	3836 1711	2779	4140	1571		5642	899

²⁶ to	make her	holy,	cleansing	her	by the	washing	with water		through	the word,	²⁷ and to		present	her	to
ἵνα →	αὐτὴν	ἁγιάσῃ	καθαρίσας	→	τῷ	λουτρῷ	⌐τοῦ ὕδατος⌐	ἐν		ῥήματι	ἵνα	αὐτὸς	παραστήσῃ		→
cj	r.asf.3	v.aas.3s	pt.aa.nsm		d.dsn	n.dsn	d.gsn n.gsn	p.d		n.dsn	cj	r.nsm	v.aas.3s		
2671	899	39	2751		3836	3373	3836 5623	1877		4839	2671	899	4225		

himself	as a radiant	church,		without	stain	or	wrinkle	or	any	other	blemish,	but		holy	and
ἑαυτῷ	ἔνδοξον	⌐τὴν ἐκκλησίαν⌐	μὴ	ἔχουσαν⌐	σπίλον	ἢ	ῥυτίδα	ἤ	τι		⌐τῶν τοιούτων⌐	ἀλλ’	ἵνα	ᾖ	ἁγία	καὶ
r.dsm.3	a.asf	d.asf n.asf	pl	pt.pa.asf	n.asm	cj	n.asf	cj	r.asn		d.gpn r.gpn	cj	cj	v.pas.3s	a.nsf	cj
1571	1902	3836 1711	3590	2400	5070	2445	4869	2445	5516		3836 5525	247	2671	1639	41	2779

blameless.	²⁸ In	this same way,		husbands		ought		to love	their	wives		as	their	own	bodies.
ἄμωμος	οὕτως ←		→ ←	⌐οἱ ἄνδρες⌐	[καὶ]	ὀφείλουσιν	→	ἀγαπᾶν	ἑαυτῶν	⌐τὰς γυναῖκας⌐	ὡς	τὰ	ἑαυτῶν	σώματα
a.nsf	adv			d.npm n.npm	cj	v.pai.3p		f.pa	r.gpm.3	d.apf n.apf	cj	d.apn	r.gpm.3	n.apn
320	4048			3836 467	2779	4053		26	1571	3836 1222	6055	3836	1571	5393

He	who loves	his	wife		loves	himself.	²⁹ After all,	no	one ever	hated	his own	body,	but	he feeds
ὁ	← ἀγαπῶν	ἑαυτοῦ	⌐τὴν γυναῖκα⌐		ἀγαπᾷ	ἑαυτὸν	γάρ ←	Οὐδεὶς ←	ποτε	ἐμίσησεν	τὴν ἑαυτοῦ	σάρκα	ἀλλὰ →	ἐκτρέφει
d.nsm	pt.pa.nsm	r.gsm.3	d.asf n.asf		v.pai.3s	r.asm.3	cj	a.nsm	adv	v.aai.3s	d.asf r.gsm.3	n.asf	cj	v.pai.3s
3836	26	1571	3836 1222		26	1571	1142	4029	4537	3631	3836 1571	4922	247	1763

and cares	for it,		just	as		Christ		does the	church	— ³⁰ for	we are	members	of	his	body.
καὶ θάλπει ←	αὐτήν	καθὼς ←		καὶ	ὁ	Χριστὸς⌐		τὴν	ἐκκλησίαν	ὅτι →	ἐσμὲν μέλη		→	αὐτοῦ	⌐τοῦ σώματος⌐
cj v.pai.3s	r.asf.3	cj		adv	d.nsm	n.nsm		d.asf	n.asf	cj	v.pai.1p	n.npn		r.gsm.3	d.gsn n.gsn
2779 2499	899	2777		2779	3836	5986		3836	1711	4022	1639 3517			899	3836 5393

³¹ “For		this reason	a man		will leave		his	father	and	mother		and be united		to	his	wife,
⌐ἀντὶ	τούτου⌐	→	ἄνθρωπος		καταλείψει		τὸν	πατέρα	καὶ	⌐τὴν μητέρα⌐		καὶ →	προσκολληθήσεται		πρὸς	αὐτοῦ	⌐τὴν γυναῖκα⌐
p.g	r.gsn		n.nsm		v.fai.3s		d.asm	n.asm	cj	d.asf n.asf		cj	v.fpi.3s		p.a	r.gsm.3	d.asf n.asf
505	4047		476		2901		3836	4252	2779	3836 3613		2779	4681		4639	899	3836 1222

and	the two	will become		one	flesh.”	³² This is		a profound	mystery		– but	I	am talking	about	Christ	and
καὶ	οἱ δύο	→ ἔσονται	εἰς	μίαν	σάρκα	τοῦτο ἐστίν	μέγα		⌐τὸ μυστήριον⌐	δὲ	ἐγὼ →	λέγω	εἰς	Χριστὸν	καὶ
cj	d.npm a.npm	v.fmi.3p	p.a	a.asf	n.asf	r.nsn v.pai.3s	a.nsn		d.nsn n.nsn	cj	r.ns.1	v.pai.1s	p.a	n.asm	cj
2779	3836 1545	1639	1650	1651	4922	4047 1639	3489		3836 3696	1254	1609	3306	1650	5986	2779

the church.	³³ However,		each	one		of you	also	must	love	his	wife		as	he loves
εἰς τὴν ἐκκλησίαν	πλὴν		οὕτως	ἕκαστος	⌐καθ’	ἕνα⌐	ὑμεῖς	καὶ	ἀγαπάτω	ἑαυτοῦ	⌐τὴν γυναῖκα⌐		ὡς
p.a d.asf n.asf	cj		adv	r.nsm	d.npm	a.asm	r.np.2	adv	v.pam.3s	r.gsm.3	d.asf n.asf		cj
1650 3836 1711	4440		4048	1667	3836	2848	7007	2779	26	1571	3836 1222		6055

ἀλλήλοις ἐν φόβῳ Χριστοῦ,

5:22 Αἱ γυναῖκες τοῖς ἰδίοις ἀνδράσιν ὡς τῷ κυρίῳ, **23** ὅτι ἀνήρ ἐστιν κεφαλὴ τῆς γυναικὸς ὡς καὶ ὁ Χριστὸς κεφαλὴ τῆς ἐκκλησίας, αὐτὸς σωτὴρ τοῦ σώματος· **24** ἀλλὰ ὡς ἡ ἐκκλησία ὑποτάσσεται τῷ Χριστῷ, οὕτως καὶ αἱ γυναῖκες τοῖς ἀνδράσιν ἐν παντί. ¶ **25** Οἱ ἄνδρες, ἀγαπᾶτε τὰς γυναῖκας, καθὼς καὶ ὁ Χριστὸς ἠγάπησεν τὴν ἐκκλησίαν καὶ ἑαυτὸν παρέδωκεν ὑπὲρ αὐτῆς, **26** ἵνα αὐτὴν ἁγιάσῃ καθαρίσας τῷ λουτρῷ τοῦ ὕδατος ἐν ῥήματι, **27** ἵνα παραστήσῃ αὐτὸς ἑαυτῷ ἔνδοξον τὴν ἐκκλησίαν, μὴ ἔχουσαν σπίλον ἢ ῥυτίδα ἤ τι τῶν τοιούτων, ἀλλ’ ἵνα ᾖ ἁγία καὶ ἄμωμος. **28** οὕτως ὀφείλουσιν [καὶ] οἱ ἄνδρες ἀγαπᾶν τὰς ἑαυτῶν γυναῖκας ὡς τὰ ἑαυτῶν σώματα. ὁ ἀγαπῶν τὴν ἑαυτοῦ γυναῖκα ἑαυτὸν ἀγαπᾷ. **29** οὐδεὶς γάρ ποτε τὴν ἑαυτοῦ σάρκα ἐμίσησεν ἀλλὰ ἐκτρέφει καὶ θάλπει αὐτήν, καθὼς καὶ ὁ Χριστὸς τὴν ἐκκλησίαν, **30** ὅτι μέλη ἐσμὲν τοῦ σώματος αὐτοῦ. **31** ἀντὶ τούτου καταλείψει ἄνθρωπος [τὸν] πατέρα καὶ [τὴν] μητέρα καὶ προσκολληθήσεται πρὸς τὴν γυναῖκα αὐτοῦ, καὶ ἔσονται οἱ δύο εἰς σάρκα μίαν. **32** τὸ μυστήριον τοῦτο μέγα ἐστίν· ἐγὼ δὲ λέγω εἰς Χριστὸν καὶ εἰς τὴν ἐκκλησίαν. **33** πλὴν

himself, and the wife   must respect her husband.
ἑαυτόν δὲ ἡ γυνὴ ἵνα   φοβῆται τὸν ἄνδρα
r.asm.3 cj d.nsf n.nsf cj v.pps.3s d.asm n.asm
1571 1254 3836 1222 2671 5828 3836 467

Children and Parents

6:1 Children, obey your parents in the Lord, for this is right. **2** "Honor your father and
⸆Τὰ τέκνα⸃ ὑπακούετε ὑμῶν ⸆τοῖς γονεῦσιν⸃ ἐν κυρίῳ γάρ τοῦτο ἐστιν δίκαιον τίμα σου ⸆τὸν πατέρα⸃ καὶ
d.vpn n.vpn v.pam.2p r.gp.2 d.dpm n.dpm p.d n.dsm cj r.nsn v.pai.3s a.nsn v.pam.2s r.gs.2 d.asm n.asm cj
3836 5451 5634 7007 3836 1204 1877 3261 1142 4047 1639 1465 5506 5148 3836 4252 2779

mother" – which is the first commandment with a promise – **3** "that it may go well with you and that you
⸆τὴν μητέρα⸃ ἥτις ἐστιν πρώτη ἐντολὴ ἐν ἐπαγγελίᾳ ἵνα → → γένηται εὖ → σοι καὶ →
d.asf n.asf r.nsf v.pai.3s a.nsf n.nsf p.d n.dsf cj v.ams.3s adv r.ds.2 cj
3836 3613 4015 1639 4755 1953 1877 2039 2671 1181 2292 5148 2779

may enjoy long life on the earth." ¶ **4** Fathers, do not exasperate your children; instead, bring
→ ἔσῃ μακροχρόνιος ← ἐπὶ τῆς γῆς Καὶ οἱ πατέρες, → μὴ παροργίζετε ὑμῶν ⸆τὰ τέκνα⸃ ἀλλὰ ἐκτρέφετε
v.fmi.2s a.nsm p.g d.gsf n.gsf d.vpm n.vpm pl v.pam.2p r.gp.2 d.apn n.apn cj v.pam.2p
1639 3432 2093 3836 1178 2779 3836 4252 4239 3590 4239 7007 3836 5451 247 1763

them up in the training and instruction of the Lord.
αὐτὰ ↰ ἐν παιδείᾳ καὶ νουθεσίᾳ → κυρίου
r.apn.3 p.d n.dsf cj n.dsf n.gsm
899 1763 1877 4082 2779 3804 3261

Slaves and Masters

6:5 Slaves, obey your earthly masters with respect and fear, and with sincerity of heart,
⸆Οἱ δοῦλοι⸃ ὑπακούετε τοῖς ⸆κατὰ σάρκα⸃ κυρίοις μετὰ φόβου καὶ τρόμου ἐν ἁπλότητι → ⸆τῆς καρδίας⸃ ὑμῶν
d.vpm n.vpm v.pam.2p d.dpm p.a n.asf n.dpm p.g n.gsm cj n.gsm p.d n.dsf d.gsf n.gsf r.gp.2
3836 1529 5634 3836 2848 4922 3261 3552 5832 2779 5571 1877 605 2840 3836 2840 7007

just as you would obey Christ. **6** Obey them not only to win their favor when their eye is on
ὡς ← ⸆τῷ Χριστῷ⸃ μὴ ὡς → → ἀνθρωπάρεσκοι κατ' ὀφθαλμοδουλίαν ← is on
cj d.dsm n.dsm pl pl a.npm p.a n.asf
6055 3836 5986 3590 6055 473 2848 4056

you, but like slaves of Christ, doing the will of God from your heart. **7** Serve wholeheartedly, as if
← ἀλλ' ὡς δοῦλοι → Χριστοῦ ποιοῦντες τὸ θέλημα → ⸆τοῦ θεοῦ⸃ ἐκ ψυχῆς δουλεύοντες μετ' εὐνοίας ὡς ←
cj pl n.npm n.gsm pt.pa.npm d.asn n.asn d.gsm n.gsm p.g n.gsf pt.pa.npm p.g n.gsf pl
247 6055 1529 5986 4472 3836 2525 3836 2536 1666 6034 1526 3552 2334 6055

you were serving the Lord, not men, **8** because you know that the Lord will reward everyone for
τῷ κυρίῳ καὶ οὐκ ἀνθρώποις, → → εἰδότες ὅτι παρὰ κυρίου → κομίσεται τοῦτο ἕκαστος
d.dsm n.dsm cj pl n.dpm pt.ra.npm cj p.g n.gsm v.fmi.3s r.asn r.nsm
3836 3261 2779 4024 476 3857 4022 4123 3261 3152 4047 1667

whatever good he does, whether he is slave or free. ¶ **9** And masters, treat your slaves in the
⸆ἐάν τι⸃ ἀγαθὸν → ποιήσῃ εἴτε δοῦλος εἴτε ἐλεύθερος Καὶ οἱ κύριοι, ποιεῖτε πρὸς αὐτούς τὰ
cj r.asn a.asn v.aas.3s cj n.nsm cj a.nsm cj d.vpm n.vpm v.pam.2p p.a r.apm.3 d.apn
1569 5516 19 4472 1664 1529 1664 1801 2779 3836 3261 4472 4639 899 3836

same way. Do not threaten them, since you know that he who is both their Master and yours is
αὐτὰ ← → ⸆ἀνιέντες τὴν ἀπειλήν⸃ → εἰδότες ὅτι → καὶ αὐτῶν ὁ κύριος καὶ ὑμῶν ἐστιν
r.apn pt.pa.npm d.asf n.asf pt.ra.npm cj cj r.gpm.3 d.nsm n.nsm cj r.gp.2 v.pai.3s
899 479 3836 581 3857 4022 1639 2779 899 3836 3261 2779 7007 1639

in heaven, and there is no favoritism with him.
ἐν οὐρανοῖς καὶ ἔστιν οὐκ προσωπολημψία παρ' αὐτῷ
p.d n.dpm cj v.pai.3s pl n.nsf p.d r.dsm.3
1877 4041 2779 1639 4024 4721 4123 899

The Armor of God

6:10 Finally, be strong in the Lord and in his mighty power. **11** Put on the full armor of
⸆Τοῦ λοιποῦ⸃ → ἐνδυναμοῦσθε ἐν κυρίῳ καὶ ἐν αὐτοῦ ⸆τῷ κράτει⸃ ⸆τῆς ἰσχύος⸃ ἐνδύσασθε ← τὴν → πανοπλίαν →
d.gsn adv v.ppm.2p p.d n.dsm cj p.d r.gsm.3 d.dsn n.dsn d.gsf n.gsf v.amm.2p d.asf n.asf
3836 3370 1904 1877 3261 2779 1877 899 3836 3197 3836 2709 1907 3836 4110

καὶ ὑμεῖς οἱ καθ' ἕνα, ἕκαστος τὴν ἑαυτοῦ γυναῖκα οὕτως ἀγαπάτω ὡς ἑαυτόν, ἡ δὲ γυνὴ ἵνα φοβῆται τὸν ἄνδρα.
   6:1 Τὰ τέκνα, ὑπακούετε τοῖς γονεῦσιν ὑμῶν [ἐν κυρίῳ]· τοῦτο γάρ ἐστιν δίκαιον. **2** τίμα τὸν πατέρα σου καὶ τὴν μητέρα, ἥτις ἐστὶν ἐντολὴ πρώτη ἐν ἐπαγγελίᾳ, **3** ἵνα εὖ σοι γένηται καὶ ἔσῃ μακροχρόνιος ἐπὶ τῆς γῆς. ¶ **4** Καὶ οἱ πατέρες, μὴ παροργίζετε τὰ τέκνα ὑμῶν ἀλλὰ ἐκτρέφετε αὐτὰ ἐν παιδείᾳ καὶ νουθεσίᾳ κυρίου.
   6:5 Οἱ δοῦλοι, ὑπακούετε τοῖς κατὰ σάρκα κυρίοις μετὰ φόβου καὶ τρόμου ἐν ἁπλότητι τῆς καρδίας ὑμῶν ὡς τῷ Χριστῷ, **6** μὴ κατ' ὀφθαλμοδουλίαν ὡς ἀνθρωπάρεσκοι ἀλλ' ὡς δοῦλοι Χριστοῦ ποιοῦντες τὸ θέλημα τοῦ θεοῦ ἐκ ψυχῆς, **7** μετ' εὐνοίας δουλεύοντες ὡς τῷ κυρίῳ καὶ οὐκ ἀνθρώποις, **8** εἰδότες ὅτι ἕκαστος ἐάν τι ποιήσῃ ἀγαθόν, τοῦτο κομίσεται παρὰ κυρίου εἴτε δοῦλος εἴτε ἐλεύθερος. ¶ **9** Καὶ οἱ κύριοι, τὰ αὐτὰ ποιεῖτε πρὸς αὐτούς, ἀνιέντες τὴν ἀπειλήν, εἰδότες ὅτι καὶ αὐτῶν καὶ ὑμῶν ὁ κύριός ἐστιν ἐν οὐρανοῖς καὶ προσωπολημψία οὐκ ἔστιν παρ' αὐτῷ.
   6:10 Τοῦ λοιποῦ, ἐνδυναμοῦσθε ἐν κυρίῳ καὶ ἐν τῷ κράτει τῆς ἰσχύος αὐτοῦ. **11** ἐνδύσασθε τὴν πανοπλίαν τοῦ θεοῦ πρὸς τὸ

God | so | that | you | can | | take | your | stand | against | the | devil's | | schemes. | **12** For | our | struggle | is | | not
ⸯτοῦ θεοῦ | πρός ← | | ὑμᾶς | ⸯτὸ δύνασθαι | → | → | στῆναι | πρὸς | τὰς | ⸯτοῦ διαβόλου | μεθοδείας | ὅτι | ἡμῖν | ⸯἡ πάλη | ἔστιν | οὐκ
d.gsm n.gsm | p.a | | r.ap.2 | ⸯτὸ f.pp | | | f.aa | p.a | d.apf | d.gsm n.gsm | n.apf | cj | r.dp.1 | d.nsf n.nsf | v.pai.3s | pl
3836 2536 | 4639 | | 7007 | 3836 1538 | | | 2705 | 4639 | 3836 | 3836 1333 | 3497 | 4022 | 7005 | 3836 4097 | 1639 | 4024

against | flesh | and | blood, | but | against | the | rulers, | against | the | authorities, | against | the | powers | | of this
πρὸς | σάρκα | καὶ | αἷμα | ἀλλὰ | πρὸς | τὰς | ἀρχάς | πρὸς | τὰς | ἐξουσίας | πρὸς | τοὺς | κοσμοκράτορας | ↱ | τούτου
p.a | n.asf | cj | n.asn | cj | p.a | d.apf | n.apf | p.a | d.apf | n.apf | p.a | d.apm | n.apm | | r.gsn
4639 | 4922 | 2779 | 135 | 247 | 4639 | 3836 | 794 | 4639 | 3836 | 2026 | 4639 | 3836 | 3179 | | 5030 4047

dark | world | and | against | the | spiritual | forces | of evil | | in | the | heavenly | realms. | **13** Therefore | | put | on
ⸯτοῦ σκότους | ↰ | | πρὸς | τὰ | πνευματικὰ | ← | ⸯτῆς πονηρίας | ἐν | τοῖς | ἐπουρανίοις | ← | | ⸯδιὰ τοῦτο | ἀναλάβετε | ←
d.gsn n.gsn | | | p.a | d.apn | a.apn | | d.gsf n.gsf | p.d | d.dpm | a.dpm | | | p.a r.asn | v.aam.2p
3836 5030 | 3179 | | 4639 | 3836 | 4461 | | 3836 4504 | 1877 | 3836 | 2230 | | | 1328 4047 | 377

the | full | armor | of God, | so | that | when | the | day | of evil | | comes, | you | may | be | able | | to | stand | | your
τὴν | → | πανοπλίαν | ⸯτοῦ θεοῦ | ἵνα | | ἐν | τῇ | ἡμέρᾳ | ⸯτῇ πονηρᾷ | → | | | | | δυνηθῆτε | → | → | ἀντιστῆναι | |
d.asf | | n.asf | d.gsm n.gsm | cj | | p.d | d.dsf | n.dsf | d.dsf a.dsf | | | | | | v.aps.2p | | | f.aa | |
3836 | 4110 | 3836 2536 | 2671 | | 1877 | 3836 | 2465 | 3836 4505 | | | | | | 1538 | | | 468 | |

ground, | and | after | you | have | done | | everything, | to | stand. | **14** Stand | firm | then, | with | the | belt | of | truth | buckled
| καὶ | → | → | κατεργασάμενοι | ἅπαντα | → | στῆναι | στῆτε | οὖν | ἐν | | | | ἀληθείᾳ | περιζωσάμενοι
| cj | | | pt.am.npm | a.apn | | f.aa | v.aam.2p | cj | p.d | | | | n.dsf | pt.am.npm
| 2779 | | | 2981 | 570 | | 2705 | 2705 | 4036 | 1877 | | | | 237 | 4322

around | your | waist, | | with | the | breastplate | of | righteousness | | in | place, | **15** and | with | your | feet | fitted | | with
← | ὑμῶν | ⸯτὴν ὀσφὺν | καὶ | | τὸν | θώρακα | → | ⸯτῆς δικαιοσύνης | ἐνδυσάμενοι | καὶ | | | τοὺς | πόδας | ὑποδησάμενοι | ἐν
| r.gp.2 | d.asf n.asf | cj | | d.asm | n.asm | | d.gsf n.gsf | pt.am.npm | cj | | | d.apm | n.apm | pt.am.npm | p.d
| 7007 | 3836 4019 | 2779 | | 3836 | 2606 | | 3836 1466 | 1907 | 2779 | | | 3836 | 4546 | 5686 | 1877

the | readiness | that | comes | from | the | gospel | | of peace. | **16** In | addition | to | all | | this, | take | | up | the | shield | of
| ἑτοιμασίᾳ | → | | → | τοῦ | εὐαγγελίου | ⸯτῆς εἰρήνης | ἐν | | → | ← | πᾶσιν | ← | ἀναλαβόντες | ← | | τὸν | θυρεὸν | →
| n.dsf | | | | d.gsn | n.gsn | d.gsf n.gsf | p.d | | | | a.dpn | | pt.aa.npm | | | d.asm | n.asm
| 2288 | | | | 3836 | 2295 | 3836 1645 | 1877 | | | | 4246 | | 377 | | | 3836 | 2599

faith, | | with | which | you | can | | extinguish | all | | the | flaming | | arrows | of the | evil | one. | **17** Take | the
ⸯτῆς πίστεως | ἐν | ᾧ | → | | δυνήσεσθε | σβέσαι | πάντα | τὰ | ⸯτὰ πεπυρωμένα | βέλη | → | τοῦ | πονηροῦ | | καὶ | δέξασθε | τὴν
d.gsf n.gsf | p.d | r.dsm | | | v.fmi.2p | f.aa | a.apn | d.apn | d.apn pt.rp.apn | n.apn | | d.gsm | a.gsm | | cj | v.amm.2p | d.asf
3836 4411 | 1877 | 4005 | | | 1538 | 4931 | 4246 | 3836 | 3836 4792 | 1018 | | 3836 | 4505 | | 2779 | 1312 | 3836

helmet | | of | salvation | and | the | sword | | of the | Spirit, | which | is | | the | word | of | God. | **18** And | pray | | in | the
περικεφαλαίαν | → | ⸯτοῦ σωτηρίου | καὶ | τὴν | μάχαιραν | → | τοῦ | πνεύματος | ὅ | ἐστιν | → | ῥῆμα | → | θεοῦ | | προσευχόμενοι | ἐν
n.asf | | d.gsn n.gsn | cj | d.asf | n.asf | | d.gsn | n.gsn | r.nsn | v.pai.3s | | n.nsn | | n.gsm | | pt.pm.npm | p.d
4330 | | 3836 5402 | 2779 | 3836 | 3479 | | 3836 | 4460 | 4005 | 1639 | | 4839 | | 2536 | | 4667 | 1877

Spirit | on | all | occasions | with | all | | kinds | of | prayers | and | requests. | | With | this | in | mind, | be | alert | | and
πνεύματι | ἐν | παντὶ | καιρῷ | Διὰ | πάσης | ← | → | προσευχῆς | καὶ | δεήσεως | καὶ | εἰς | αὐτὸ | ← | | → | ἀγρυπνοῦντες
n.dsn | p.d | a.dsm | n.dsm | p.g | a.gsf | | | n.gsf | cj | n.gsf | cj | p.a | r.asn.3 | | | | pt.pa.npm
4460 | 1877 | 4246 | 2789 | 1328 | 4246 | | | 4666 | 2779 | 1255 | 2779 | 1650 | 899 | | | | 70

always | keep | | on | | praying | for | all | | the | saints. | ¶ | **19** Pray | also | for | me, | that | whenever | I | open | my
ⸯἐν πάσῃ | προσκαρτερήσει | → | καὶ | δεήσει | περὶ | πάντων | τῶν | ἁγίων | | καὶ | ὑπὲρ | ἐμοῦ | ἵνα | ἐν | | ἀνοίξει | μου
p.d a.dsf | n.dsf | | cj | n.dsf | p.g | a.gpm | d.gpm | a.gpm | | cj | p.g | r.gs.1 | cj | p.d | | n.dsf | r.gs.1
1877 4246 | 4675 | | 2779 | 1255 | 4309 | 4246 | 3836 | 41 | | 2779 | 5642 | 1609 | 2671 | 1877 | | 489 | 1609

mouth, | words | may | be | given | me | so | that | I | | will | fearlessly | | make | known | the | mystery | of the | gospel, | **20** for
ⸯτοῦ στόματος | λόγος | → | → | δοθῇ | μοι | → | ↱ | → | ⸯἐν παρρησίᾳ | → | γνωρίσαι | τὸ | μυστήριον | → | τοῦ | εὐαγγελίου | ὑπὲρ
d.gsn n.gsn | n.nsm | | | v.aps.3s | r.ds.1 | | | | p.d n.dsf | | f.aa | d.asn | n.asn | | d.gsn | n.gsn | p.g
3836 5125 | 3364 | | | 1443 | 1609 | 1192 1192 | 1192 1192 | 1877 4244 | | 1192 | 3836 | 3696 | | 3836 | 2295 | 5642

which | I | am | an | ambassador | in | chains. | Pray | that | I | may | declare | | it | fearlessly, | as | I | should.
οὗ | → | → | | πρεσβεύω | ἐν | ἁλύσει | ἵνα | → | | παρρησιάσωμαι | ἐν | αὐτῷ | ↰ | | ὡς | με | δεῖ | λαλῆσαι
r.gsn | | | | v.pai.1s | p.d | n.dsf | cj | | | v.ams.1s | p.d | r.dsn.3 | | | cj | r.as.1 | v.pai.3s | f.aa
4005 | | | | 4563 | 1877 | 268 | 2671 | | | 4245 | 1877 | 899 | 4245 | | 6055 | 1609 | 1256 | 3281

Final Greetings

6:21 Tychicus, | the | dear | | brother | and | faithful | servant | in | the | Lord, | will | tell | | you | everything, | so | that
δὲ | Τύχικος | ὁ | ἀγαπητὸς | ἀδελφὸς | καὶ | πιστὸς | διάκονος | ἐν | | κυρίῳ | → | γνωρίσει | ὑμῖν | πάντα | Ἵνα | ←
cj | n.nsm | d.nsm | a.nsm | n.nsm | cj | a.nsm | n.nsm | p.d | | n.dsm | | v.fai.3s | r.dp.2 | a.apn | cj
1254 | 5608 | 3836 | 28 | 81 | 2779 | 4412 | 1356 | 1877 | | 3261 | | 1192 | 7007 | 4246 | 2671

δύνασθαι ὑμᾶς στῆναι πρὸς τὰς μεθοδείας τοῦ διαβόλου· ¹² ὅτι οὐκ ἔστιν ἡμῖν ἡ πάλη πρὸς αἷμα καὶ σάρκα, ἀλλὰ πρὸς τὰς ἀρχάς, πρὸς τὰς ἐξουσίας, πρὸς τοὺς κοσμοκράτορας τοῦ σκότους τούτου, πρὸς τὰ πνευματικὰ τῆς πονηρίας ἐν τοῖς ἐπουρανίοις. ¹³ διὰ τοῦτο ἀναλάβετε τὴν πανοπλίαν τοῦ θεοῦ, ἵνα δυνηθῆτε ἀντιστῆναι ἐν τῇ ἡμέρᾳ τῇ πονηρᾷ καὶ ἅπαντα κατεργασάμενοι στῆναι. ¹⁴ στῆτε οὖν περιζωσάμενοι τὴν ὀσφὺν ὑμῶν ἐν ἀληθείᾳ καὶ ἐνδυσάμενοι τὸν θώρακα τῆς δικαιοσύνης ¹⁵ καὶ ὑποδησάμενοι τοὺς πόδας ἐν ἑτοιμασίᾳ τοῦ εὐαγγελίου τῆς εἰρήνης, ¹⁶ ἐν πᾶσιν ἀναλαβόντες τὸν θυρεὸν τῆς πίστεως, ἐν ᾧ δυνήσεσθε πάντα τὰ βέλη τοῦ πονηροῦ [τὰ] πεπυρωμένα σβέσαι· ¹⁷ καὶ τὴν περικεφαλαίαν τοῦ σωτηρίου δέξασθε καὶ τὴν μάχαιραν τοῦ πνεύματος, ὅ ἐστιν ῥῆμα θεοῦ. ¹⁸ διὰ πάσης προσευχῆς καὶ δεήσεως προσευχόμενοι ἐν παντὶ καιρῷ ἐν πνεύματι, καὶ εἰς αὐτὸ ἀγρυπνοῦντες ἐν πάσῃ προσκαρτερήσει καὶ δεήσει περὶ πάντων τῶν ἁγίων ¶ ¹⁹ καὶ ὑπὲρ ἐμοῦ, ἵνα μοι δοθῇ λόγος ἐν ἀνοίξει τοῦ στόματός μου, ἐν παρρησίᾳ γνωρίσαι τὸ μυστήριον τοῦ εὐαγγελίου, ²⁰ ὑπὲρ οὗ πρεσβεύω ἐν ἁλύσει, ἵνα ἐν αὐτῷ παρρησιάσωμαι ὡς δεῖ με λαλῆσαι.

⁶·²¹ Ἵνα δὲ εἰδῆτε καὶ ὑμεῖς τὰ κατ᾽ ἐμέ, τί πράσσω, πάντα γνωρίσει ὑμῖν Τύχικος ὁ ἀγαπητὸς ἀδελφὸς καὶ πιστὸς διάκονος

you	also	may know	*how*			*I am*	and what	I am	doing.	²² I	am	sending	him	to	you	for	this	very	purpose,	that
ὑμεῖς	καὶ	→	εἰδῆτε	ˌτὰ	κατ᾽	ἐμέˌ			τί	→	→	πράσσω		→	→	ἔπεμψα	ὃν	πρὸς	ὑμᾶς	εἰς	τοῦτο	αὐτὸ	←	ἵνα
r.np.2	adv		v.ras.2p	d.apn	p.a	r.as.1			r.asn			v.pai.1s				v.aai.1s	r.asm	p.a	r.ap.2	p.a	r.asn	r.asn		cj
7007	2779		3857	3836	2848	1609			5515			4556				4287	4005	4639	7007	1650	4047	899		2671

you	may know	*how*		*we are,*	and that	he may	encourage	you.		¶	²³ Peace	to the	brothers,
→	→	γνῶτε	ˌτὰ	περὶ	ἡμῶνˌ		καὶ	→	→	παρακαλέσῃ	ˌτὰς	καρδίας	ὑμῶν			Εἰρήνη	→	τοῖς	ἀδελφοῖς
		v.aas.2p	d.apn	p.g	r.gp.1		cj			v.aas.3s	d.apf	n.apf	r.gp.2			n.nsf		d.dpm	n.dpm
		1182	3836	4309	7005		2779			4151	3836	2840	7007			1645		3836	81

and	love	with	faith	from	God	the	Father	and	the	Lord	Jesus	Christ.	²⁴ Grace	to	all	who	love	our
καὶ	ἀγάπη	μετὰ	πίστεως	ἀπὸ	θεοῦ		πατρὸς	καὶ		κυρίου	Ἰησοῦ	Χριστοῦ	ˌἡ χάριςˌ	μετὰ	πάντων	τῶν	ἀγαπώντων	ἡμῶν
cj	n.nsf	p.g	n.gsf	p.g	n.gsm		n.gsm	cj		n.gsm	n.gsm	n.gsm	d.nsf n.nsf	p.g	a.gpm	d.gpm	pt.pa.gpm	r.gp.1
2779	27	3552	4411	608	2536		4252	2779		3261	2652	5986	3836 5921	3552	4246	3836	26	7005

Lord	Jesus	Christ	with an	undying	love.
ˌτὸν κύριονˌ	Ἰησοῦν	Χριστὸν	ἐν	ἀφθαρσίᾳ	
d.asm n.asm	n.asm	n.asm	p.d	n.dsf	
3836 3261	2652	5986	1877	914	

ἐν κυρίῳ, ²² ὃν ἔπεμψα πρὸς ὑμᾶς εἰς αὐτὸ τοῦτο, ἵνα γνῶτε τὰ περὶ ἡμῶν καὶ παρακαλέσῃ τὰς καρδίας ὑμῶν. ¶ ²³ Εἰρήνη τοῖς ἀδελφοῖς καὶ ἀγάπη μετὰ πίστεως ἀπὸ θεοῦ πατρὸς καὶ κυρίου Ἰησοῦ Χριστοῦ. ²⁴ ἡ χάρις μετὰ πάντων τῶν ἀγαπώντων τὸν κύριον ἡμῶν Ἰησοῦν Χριστὸν ἐν ἀφθαρσίᾳ.

Philippians

1:1 Paul and Timothy, servants of Christ Jesus, ¶ To all the saints in Christ Jesus at
Παῦλος καὶ Τιμόθεος δοῦλοι → Χριστοῦ Ἰησοῦ → πᾶσιν τοῖς ἁγίοις ἐν Χριστῷ Ἰησοῦ τοῖς οὖσιν ἐν
n.nsm cj n.nsm n.npm n.gsm n.gsm a.dpm d.dpm a.dpm p.d n.dsm n.dsm d.dpm pt.pa.dpm p.d
4263 2779 5510 1529 5986 2652 4246 3836 41 1877 5986 2652 3836 1639 1877

Philippi, together with the overseers and deacons: ¶ **2** Grace and peace to you from God our Father and the
Φιλίπποις σὺν ← ἐπισκόποις καὶ διακόνοις χάρις καὶ εἰρήνη ὑμῖν ἀπὸ θεοῦ ἡμῶν πατρὸς καὶ
n.dpm p.d n.dpm cj n.dpm n.nsf cj n.nsf r.dp.2 p.g n.gsm r.gp.1 n.gsm cj
5804 5250 2176 2779 1356 5921 2779 1645 7007 608 2536 7005 4252 2779

Lord Jesus Christ.
κυρίου Ἰησοῦ Χριστοῦ
n.gsm n.gsm n.gsm
3261 2652 5986

Thanksgiving and Prayer

1:3 I thank my God every time I remember you. **4** In all my prayers for all of you, I always
→ Εὐχαριστῶ μου ⌐τῷ θεῷ ἐπὶ πάσῃ ⌐τῇ μνείᾳ ὑμῶν ἐν πάσῃ μου δεήσει ὑπὲρ πάντων → ὑμῶν πάντοτε
v.pai.1s r.gs.1 d.dsm n.dsm p.d a.dsf d.dsf n.dsf r.gp.2 p.d a.dsf r.gs.1 n.dsf p.g a.gpm r.gp.2 adv
2373 1609 3836 2536 2093 4246 3836 3644 7007 1877 4246 1609 1255 5642 4246 7007 4121

pray with joy **5** because of your partnership in the gospel from the first day until now,
⌐τὴν δέησιν ποιούμενος, μετὰ χαρᾶς ἐπὶ ← ὑμῶν τῇ κοινωνίᾳ εἰς τὸ εὐαγγέλιον ἀπὸ τῆς πρώτης ἡμέρας ἄχρι ⌐τοῦ νῦν
d.asf n.asf pt.pm.nsm p.g n.gsf p.d r.gp.2 d.dsf n.dsf p.a d.asn n.asn p.g d.gsf a.gsf n.gsf p.g d.gsm adv
3836 1255 4472 3552 5915 2093 7007 3836 3126 1650 3836 2295 608 3836 4755 2465 948 3836 3814

6 being confident of this, that he who began a good work in you will carry it on to completion until the
→ πεποιθὼς ← αὐτὸ τοῦτο ὅτι ὁ ← ἐναρξάμενος ἀγαθὸν ἔργον ἐν ὑμῖν → → → → ἐπιτελέσει ἄχρι
pt.ra.nsm r.asn r.asn cj d.nsm pt.am.nsm a.asn n.asn p.d r.dp.2 v.fai.3s p.g
4275 899 4047 4022 3836 1887 19 2240 1877 7007 2200 948

day of Christ Jesus. ¶ **7** It is right for me to feel this way about all of you, since I
ἡμέρας → Χριστοῦ Ἰησοῦ Καθώς → ἐστιν δίκαιον → ἐμοὶ → φρονεῖν τοῦτο ὑπὲρ πάντων → ὑμῶν διὰ με
n.gsf n.gsm n.gsm cj v.pai.3s a.nsn r.ds.1 f.pa r.asn p.g a.gpm r.gp.2 p.a r.as.1
2465 5986 2652 2777 1639 1465 1609 5858 4047 5642 4246 7007 1328 1609

have you in my heart; for whether I am in chains or defending and confirming the gospel,
⌐τὸ ἔχειν ὑμᾶς ἐν τῇ καρδίᾳ τε μου ἐν ⌐τοῖς δεσμοῖς καὶ ἐν ⌐τῇ ἀπολογίᾳ καὶ βεβαιώσει τοῦ εὐαγγελίου
d.asn f.pa r.ap.2 p.d d.dsf n.dsf cj r.gs.1 p.d d.dpm n.dpm cj p.d d.dsf n.dsf cj n.dsf d.gsn n.gsn
3836 2400 7007 1877 3836 2840 5445 1609 1877 3836 1301 2779 1877 3836 665 2779 1012 3836 2295

all of you share in God's grace with me. **8** God can testify how I long for all
πάντας ὑμᾶς ⌐συγκοινωνούς ὄντας, ⌐τῆς χάριτος, → μου γὰρ ὁ θεός μάρτυς μου ὡς → ἐπιποθῶ πάντας
a.apm r.ap.2 n.apm pt.pa.apm d.gsf n.gsf r.gs.1 cj d.nsm n.nsm n.nsm r.gs.1 cj v.pai.1s a.apm
4246 7007 5171 1639 3836 5921 1609 1142 3836 2536 3459 1609 6055 2160 4246

of you with the affection of Christ Jesus. ¶ **9** And this is my prayer: that your love may abound
ὑμᾶς ἐν σπλάγχνοις → Χριστοῦ Ἰησοῦ Καὶ τοῦτο → → προσεύχομαι ἵνα ὑμῶν ἡ ἀγάπη → περισσεύῃ ἔτι
r.ap.2 p.d n.dpn n.gsm n.gsm cj r.asn v.pmi.1s cj r.gp.2 d.nsf n.nsf v.pas.3s adv
7007 1877 5073 5986 2652 2779 4047 4667 2671 7007 3836 27 4355 2285

more and more in knowledge and depth of insight, **10** so that you may be able to discern what is best
μᾶλλον καὶ μᾶλλον ἐν ἐπιγνώσει καὶ πάσῃ αἰσθήσει εἰς ὑμᾶς → → → → ⌐τὸ δοκιμάζειν⌐ τὰ → διαφέροντα
adv.c cj adv.c p.d n.dsf cj a.dsf n.dsf p.a r.ap.2 d.asn f.pa d.apn pt.pa.apn
3437 2779 3437 1877 2106 2779 4246 151 1650 7007 3836 1507 3836 1422

and may be pure and blameless until the day of Christ, **11** filled with the fruit of righteousness
ἵνα → ἦτε εἰλικρινεῖς καὶ ἀπρόσκοποι εἰς ἡμέραν → Χριστοῦ πεπληρωμένοι ← καρπὸν → δικαιοσύνης
cj v.pas.2p a.npm cj a.npm p.a n.asf n.gsm pt.rp.npm n.asm n.gsf
2671 1639 1637 2779 718 1650 2465 5986 4444 2843 1466

that comes through Jesus Christ — to the glory and praise of God.
τὸν διὰ Ἰησοῦ Χριστοῦ εἰς δόξαν καὶ ἔπαινον → θεοῦ
d.asm p.g n.gsm n.gsm p.a n.asf cj n.asm n.gsm
3836 1328 2652 5986 1650 1518 2779 2047 2536

1:1 Παῦλος καὶ Τιμόθεος δοῦλοι Χριστοῦ Ἰησοῦ ¶ πᾶσιν τοῖς ἁγίοις ἐν Χριστῷ Ἰησοῦ τοῖς οὖσιν ἐν Φιλίπποις σὺν ἐπισκόποις καὶ διακόνοις, ¶ **2** χάρις ὑμῖν καὶ εἰρήνη ἀπὸ θεοῦ πατρὸς ἡμῶν καὶ κυρίου Ἰησοῦ Χριστοῦ.

1:3 Εὐχαριστῶ τῷ θεῷ μου ἐπὶ πάσῃ τῇ μνείᾳ ὑμῶν **4** πάντοτε ἐν πάσῃ δεήσει μου ὑπὲρ πάντων ὑμῶν, μετὰ χαρᾶς τὴν δέησιν ποιούμενος, **5** ἐπὶ τῇ κοινωνίᾳ ὑμῶν εἰς τὸ εὐαγγέλιον ἀπὸ τῆς πρώτης ἡμέρας ἄχρι τοῦ νῦν, **6** πεποιθὼς αὐτὸ τοῦτο, ὅτι ὁ ἐναρξάμενος ἐν ὑμῖν ἔργον ἀγαθὸν ἐπιτελέσει ἄχρι ἡμέρας Χριστοῦ Ἰησοῦ· ¶ **7** καθώς ἐστιν δίκαιον ἐμοὶ τοῦτο φρονεῖν ὑπὲρ πάντων ὑμῶν διὰ τὸ ἔχειν με ἐν τῇ καρδίᾳ ὑμᾶς, ἔν τε τοῖς δεσμοῖς μου καὶ ἐν τῇ ἀπολογίᾳ καὶ βεβαιώσει τοῦ εὐαγγελίου συγκοινωνούς μου τῆς χάριτος πάντας ὑμᾶς ὄντας. **8** μάρτυς γάρ μου ὁ θεὸς ὡς ἐπιποθῶ πάντας ὑμᾶς ἐν σπλάγχνοις Χριστοῦ Ἰησοῦ. ¶ **9** καὶ τοῦτο προσεύχομαι, ἵνα ἡ ἀγάπη ὑμῶν ἔτι μᾶλλον καὶ μᾶλλον περισσεύῃ ἐν ἐπιγνώσει καὶ πάσῃ αἰσθήσει **10** εἰς τὸ δοκιμάζειν ὑμᾶς τὰ διαφέροντα, ἵνα ἦτε εἰλικρινεῖς καὶ ἀπρόσκοποι εἰς ἡμέραν Χριστοῦ, **11** πεπληρωμένοι καρπὸν δικαιοσύνης τὸν διὰ Ἰησοῦ Χριστοῦ εἰς δόξαν καὶ ἔπαινον θεοῦ.

Paul's Chains Advance the Gospel

1:12 Now I want you to know, brothers, that *what has happened* *to* *me* has really served to advance the
δὲ   → βούλομαι ὑμᾶς → Γινώσκειν ἀδελφοί ὅτι τὰ   κατ᾽ ἐμὲ → μᾶλλον ἐλήλυθεν εἰς προκοπὴν τοῦ
cj   v.pmi.1s r.ap.2   f.pa   n.vpm   cj   d.npn   p.a r.as.1   adv.c v.rai.3s   p.a   n.asf   d.gsn
1254   1089   7007   1182   81   4022   3836   2848 1609   2262   3437   2262   1650   4620   3836

gospel. **13** As a result, it has become clear throughout the whole palace guard and to everyone else
εὐαγγελίου ὥστε ← ← → → γενέσθαι φανεροὺς ἐν   τῷ ὅλῳ → πραιτωρίῳ καὶ   πάσιν ⌐τοῖς λοιποῖς⌐
n.gsn   cj   f.am   a.apm   p.d   d.dsn a.dsn   n.dsn   cj   a.dpm   d.dpm a.dpm
2295   6063   1181   5745   1877   3836 3910   4550   2779   3370 4246   3836 3370

that I am in chains for Christ. **14** Because of my chains, most of the brothers in the Lord
μου ⌐τοὺς δεσμούς⌐ ἐν Χριστῷ καὶ → μου τοῖς δεσμοῖς ⌐τοὺς πλείονας⌐ → τῶν ἀδελφῶν ἐν   κυρίῳ
r.gs.1 d.apm n.apm   p.d n.dsm   cj   r.gs.1 d.dpm n.dpm   d.apm a.apm.c   d.gpm n.gpm   p.d   n.dsm
1609 3836 1301   1877 5986   1301   1301 1609 3836 1301   3836 4498   3836 81   1877   3261

have been encouraged to speak the word of God more courageously and fearlessly. ¶ **15** It is true that
→ → πεποιθότας → λαλεῖν τὸν λόγον   περισσοτέρως τολμᾶν   ἀφόβως   μὲν
   pt.ra.apm   f.pa   d.asm n.asm   adv   f.pa   adv   pl
   4275   3281   3836 3364   4359   5528   925   3525

some preach Christ out of envy and rivalry, but others out of goodwill. **16** The latter do so in
τινὲς κηρύσσουσιν ⌐τὸν Χριστόν⌐ καὶ διὰ ← φθόνον καὶ ἔριν   δὲ τινὲς καὶ δι᾽   εὐδοκίαν   μὲν οἱ   ἐξ
r.npm v.pai.3p   d.asm n.asm   adv διὰ   n.asm   cj n.asf   pl r.npm adv δι᾽   n.asf   pl d.npm   p.g
5516 3062   3836 5986   2779 1328   5784   2779 2251   1254 5516 2779 1328   2306   3525 3836   1666

love, knowing that I am put here for the defense of the gospel. **17** The former preach Christ out
ἀγάπης εἰδότες ὅτι → κεῖμαι εἰς   ἀπολογίαν → τοῦ εὐαγγελίου δὲ οἱ   καταγγέλλουσιν ⌐τὸν Χριστόν⌐ ἐξ
n.gsf pt.ra.npm cj   v.pmi.1s p.a   n.asf   d.gsn n.gsn   pl d.npm   v.pai.3p   d.asm n.asm   p.g
27   3857   4022   3023   1650   665   3836 2295   1254 3836   2859   3836 5986   1666

of selfish ambition, not sincerely, supposing that they can stir up trouble for me while I am in chains.
← ἐριθείας ←   οὐχ ἁγνῶς οἰόμενοι   ἐγείρειν ← θλῖψιν → μου → ⌐τοῖς δεσμοῖς⌐
  n.gsf   adv adv   pt.pm.npm   f.pa   n.asf   r.gs.1   d.dpm n.dpm
  2249   4024 56   3887   1586   2568   1301   1609   1301 3836 1301

18 But what does it matter? The important thing is that in every way, whether from false motives or true,
γὰρ Τί   πλὴν   ὅτι → παντὶ τρόπῳ εἴτε → προφάσει   εἴτε ἀληθείᾳ
cj   r.nsn   cj   cj   a.dsm n.dsm εἴτε   n.dsf   εἴτε n.dsf
1142 5515   4440   4022   4246 5573 1664   4733   1664 237

Christ is preached. And because of this I rejoice. ¶ Yes, and I will continue to rejoice, **19** for I know
Χριστὸς →καταγγέλλεται καὶ ἐν ← τούτῳ →χαίρω   Ἀλλὰ καὶ →→→ → χαρήσομαι   γὰρ →οἶδα
n.nsm   v.ppi.3s   cj p.d   r.dsn v.pai.1s   cj adv   v.fpi.1s   cj v.rai.1s
5986   2859   2779 1877   4047 5897   247 2779   5897   1142 3857

that through your prayers and the help given by the Spirit of Jesus Christ, *what has happened* *to* *me*
ὅτι διὰ ὑμῶν ⌐τῆς δεήσεως⌐ καὶ ἐπιχορηγίας → → τοῦ πνεύματος → Ἰησοῦ Χριστοῦ τοῦτο   μοι
cj   p.g r.gp.2 d.gsf n.gsf   cj n.gsf   d.gsn n.gsn   n.gsm n.gsm r.nsn   r.ds.1
4022 1328 7007 3836 1255   2779 2221   3836 4460   2652 5986 4047   1609

will turn out for my deliverance. **20** I eagerly expect and hope that I will in no way be
→ ἀποβήσεται ← εἰς σωτηρίαν κατὰ μου   ⌐τὴν ἀποκαραδοκίαν⌐ καὶ ἐλπίδα ὅτι →→ ἐν οὐδενὶ →
v.fmi.3s   p.a n.asf   p.a r.gs.1   d.asf n.asf   cj n.asf cj   p.d a.dsn
609   1650 5401   2848 1609   3836 638   2779 1828 4022   159 159   1877 4029

ashamed, but will have sufficient courage so that now as always Christ will be exalted in my
αἰσχυνθήσομαι ἀλλ᾽   ἐν πάσῃ παρρησίᾳ καὶ νῦν ὡς πάντοτε Χριστός →→ μεγαλυνθήσεται ἐν μου
v.fpi.1s   cj   p.d a.dsf n.dsf   adv adv pl adv   n.nsm   v.fpi.3s   p.d r.gs.1
159   247   1877 4246 4244   2779 3814 6055 4121   5986   3486   1877 1609

body, whether by life or by death. **21** For to me, to live is Christ and to die is gain. **22** If I
⌐τῷ σώματι⌐ εἴτε διὰ ζωῆς εἴτε διὰ θανάτου   γὰρ →Ἐμοὶ ⌐τὸ ζῆν⌐ Χριστὸς καὶ ⌐τὸ ἀποθανεῖν⌐ κέρδος   δὲ εἰ
d.dsn n.dsn   cj διὰ p.g n.gsf εἴτε διὰ p.g n.gsm   cj   r.ds.1 d.nsn f.pa   n.nsm cj   d.nsn f.aa   n.nsn   cj cj
3836 5393   1664 1328 2437 1664 1328 2505   1142   1609   3836 2409   5986 2779   3836 633   3046   1254 1623

am to go on living in the body, this will mean fruitful labor for me. Yet what shall I choose? I do not know!
→ → → ⌐τὸ ζῆν⌐ ἐν σαρκί τοῦτο   καρπὸς ἔργου → μοι καὶ τί → → αἱρήσομαι →→ οὐ γνωρίζω
d.nsn f.pa p.d   n.dsf r.nsn   n.nsm n.gsn   r.ds.1 cj r.asn   v.fmi.1s   pl v.pai.1s
3836 2409 1877   4922 4047   2843 2240   1609 2779 5515   145   1192 1192 4024 1192

1:12 Γινώσκειν δὲ ὑμᾶς βούλομαι, ἀδελφοί, ὅτι τὰ κατ᾽ ἐμὲ μᾶλλον εἰς προκοπὴν τοῦ εὐαγγελίου ἐλήλυθεν, **13** ὥστε τοὺς δεσμούς μου φανεροὺς ἐν Χριστῷ γενέσθαι ἐν ὅλῳ τῷ πραιτωρίῳ καὶ τοῖς λοιποῖς πᾶσιν, **14** καὶ τοὺς πλείονας τῶν ἀδελφῶν ἐν κυρίῳ πεποιθότας τοῖς δεσμοῖς μου περισσοτέρως τολμᾶν ἀφόβως τὸν λόγον τοῦ θεοῦ λαλεῖν. ¶ **15** Τινὲς μὲν καὶ διὰ φθόνον καὶ ἔριν, τινὲς δὲ καὶ δι᾽ εὐδοκίαν τὸν Χριστὸν κηρύσσουσιν· **16** οἱ μὲν ἐξ ἀγάπης, εἰδότες ὅτι εἰς ἀπολογίαν τοῦ εὐαγγελίου κεῖμαι, **17** οἱ δὲ ἐξ ἐριθείας τὸν Χριστὸν καταγγέλλουσιν, οὐχ ἁγνῶς, οἰόμενοι θλῖψιν ἐγείρειν τοῖς δεσμοῖς μου. **18** τί γάρ; πλὴν ὅτι παντὶ τρόπῳ, εἴτε προφάσει εἴτε ἀληθείᾳ, Χριστὸς καταγγέλλεται, καὶ ἐν τούτῳ χαίρω. ¶ ἀλλὰ καὶ χαρήσομαι, **19** οἶδα γὰρ ὅτι τοῦτό μοι ἀποβήσεται εἰς σωτηρίαν διὰ τῆς ὑμῶν δεήσεως καὶ ἐπιχορηγίας τοῦ πνεύματος Ἰησοῦ Χριστοῦ **20** κατὰ τὴν ἀποκαραδοκίαν καὶ ἐλπίδα μου, ὅτι ἐν οὐδενὶ αἰσχυνθήσομαι ἀλλ᾽ ἐν πάσῃ παρρησίᾳ ὡς πάντοτε καὶ νῦν μεγαλυνθήσεται Χριστὸς ἐν τῷ σώματί μου, εἴτε διὰ ζωῆς εἴτε διὰ θανάτου. **21** ἐμοὶ γὰρ τὸ ζῆν Χριστὸς καὶ τὸ ἀποθανεῖν κέρδος. **22** εἰ δὲ τὸ ζῆν ἐν σαρκί, τοῦτό μοι

23 I am torn   between the two: I desire   to depart   and be   with Christ,   which is
δὲ → → συνέχομαι ἐκ   τῶν δύο → ⸢τὴν ἐπιθυμίαν ἔχων⸣ εἰς ⸢τὸ ἀναλῦσαι⸣ καὶ εἶναι σὺν Χριστῷ   [γὰρ]
cj   v.ppi.1s   p.g   d.gpn a.gpn   d.asf   n.asf   p.a d.asn f.aa   cj   f.pa   p.d   n.dsm   cj
1254   5309   1666 3836 1545   3836   2123   2400 1650 3836 386   2779 1639 5250 5986   1142

better by far;   **24** but it is more   necessary   for you   that I remain   in the body. **25** Convinced of this,
κρεῖσσον → ⸢πολλῷ μᾶλλον⸣ δὲ   →   ἀναγκαιότερον δι᾽ ὑμᾶς   ⸢τὸ ἐπιμένειν⸣ ἐν τῇ σαρκί καὶ πεποιθὼς ← τοῦτο
a.nsn.c   a.dsn adv.c   cj   a.nsn.c   p.a r.ap.2   d.nsn f.pa   p.d d.dsf n.dsf   cj   pt.ra.nsm   r.asn
3202   4498   3437   1254   338   1328 7007   3836 2152   1877 3836 4922   2779 4275   4047

I know that I will remain, and I will continue with all of you for your progress   and joy   in the faith,
→ οἶδα ὅτι → → μενῶ   καὶ → → παραμενῶ → πᾶσιν ὑμῖν εἰς ὑμῶν ⸢τὴν προκοπὴν⸣ καὶ χαρὰν → τῆς πίστεως
v.rai.1s cj   v.fai.1s cj   v.fai.1s   a.dpm   r.dp.2 p.a r.gp.2   d.asf n.asf   cj   n.asf   d.gsf n.gsf
3857   4022   3531   2779   4169   4246   7007 1650 7007 3836 4620   2779 5915   3836 4411

26 so that through my being   with you again your joy   in Christ Jesus will overflow *on account of me.*
ἵνα ← διὰ ἐμῆς ⸢τῆς παρουσίας⸣ πρὸς ὑμᾶς πάλιν ὑμῶν ⸢τὸ καύχημα⸣ ἐν Χριστῷ Ἰησοῦ → περισσεύῃ ἐν ἐμοὶ
cj   p.g r.gsf.1 d.gsf n.gsf   p.a   r.ap.2 adv   r.gp.2 d.nsn n.nsn   p.d n.dsm   n.dsm   v.pas.3s   p.d r.ds.1
2671   1328 1847 3836 4242   4639 7007 4099 7007 3836 3017   1877 5986   2652   4355   1877 1609

¶   **27** Whatever happens, conduct yourselves in a manner worthy of the gospel   of Christ.   Then, whether I
Μόνον ←   πολιτεύεσθε ← → →   ἀξίως → τοῦ εὐαγγελίου → ⸢τοῦ Χριστοῦ⸣ ἵνα εἴτε
adv   v.pmm.2p   adv   d.gsn n.gsn   d.gsm n.gsm   cj   cj
3667   4488   547   3836 2295   3836 5986   2671 1664

come and see you or only hear   about you in my absence, I will know that you stand firm in one spirit,
ἐλθὼν καὶ ἰδὼν ὑμᾶς εἴτε ἀκούω τὰ περὶ ὑμῶν → → ἀπὼν   ὅτι → στήκετε ← ἐν ἑνὶ πνεύματι
pt.aa.nsm cj pt.aa.nsm r.ap.2 cj v.pas.1s d.apn p.g r.gp.2   pt.pa.nsm   cj   v.pai.2p   p.d a.dsn n.dsn
2262   2779 1625   7007 1664 201   3836 4309 7007   583   4022   5112   1877 1651 4460

contending as one man   for the faith of the gospel **28** without being frightened in any   way   by those who
συναθλοῦντες μιᾷ ψυχῇ ← τῇ πίστει → τοῦ εὐαγγελίου καὶ μὴ → πτυρόμενοι ἐν μηδενὶ ← ὑπὸ τῶν ←
pt.pa.npm   a.dsf n.dsf   d.dsf n.dsf   d.gsn n.gsn   cj   pl   pt.pp.npm   p.d a.dsn   p.g d.gpm
5254   1651 6034   3836 4411   3836 2295   2779 3590   4769   1877 3594   5679 3836

oppose   you. This is   a sign   to them that they will be destroyed, but that you will be saved   – and that
ἀντικειμένων ἥτις ἐστὶν ἔνδειξις → αὐτοῖς   ἀπωλείας δὲ ὑμῶν   σωτηρίας καὶ τοῦτο
pt.pm.gpm   r.nsf v.pai.3s n.nsf   r.dpm.3   n.gsf   cj   r.gp.2   n.gsf   cj   r.nsn
512   4015 1639   1893   899   724   1254 7007   5401   2779 4047

by God. **29** For it has been granted to you   on behalf of Christ not only to believe   on him, but also to
ἀπὸ θεοῦ ὅτι → → → ἐχαρίσθη ὑμῖν τὸ ὑπὲρ ← ← Χριστοῦ οὐ μόνον ⸢τὸ πιστεύειν⸣ εἰς αὐτὸν ἀλλὰ καὶ →
p.g n.gsm   cj   v.api.3s   r.dp.2 d.nsn p.g   n.gsm   pl   adv   d.nsn f.pa   p.a r.asm.3 cj   adv
608 2536   4022   5919   7007 3836 5642   5986   4024 3667   3836 4409   1650 899   247   2779

suffer   for him, **30** since you are going through the same struggle   you saw I   had, and now hear
⸢τὸ πάσχειν⸣ ὑπὲρ αὐτοῦ → → → ἔχοντες → τὸν αὐτὸν ἀγῶνα οἷον → εἴδετε ⸢ἐν ἐμοὶ⸣ καὶ νῦν ἀκούετε
d.nsn f.pa   p.g r.gsm.3   pt.pa.npm   d.asm r.asm n.asm   r.asm   v.aai.2p p.d r.ds.1 cj   adv v.pai.2p
3836 4248   5642 899   2400   3836 899   74   3888   1625 1877 1609 2779 3814 201

that I   still have.
⸢ἐν ἐμοί⸣
p.d r.ds.1
1877 1609

Imitating Christ's Humility

2:1 If you have any encouragement from *being united with* Christ, if any comfort   from his love, if any
Εἴ   τις παράκλησις   ἐν Χριστῷ εἴ τι παραμύθιον → ἀγάπης εἴ τις
cj   r.nsf n.nsf   p.d n.dsm   cj r.nsn n.nsn   n.gsf   cj r.nsf
1623   5516 4155   1877 5986   1623 5516 4172   27   1623 5516

fellowship with the Spirit, if any tenderness and compassion, **2** then make my joy   complete *by being*
κοινωνία → πνεύματος εἴ τις σπλάγχνα καὶ οἰκτιρμοί οὖν → μου ⸢τὴν χαρὰν⸣ πληρώσατε ἵνα φρονῆτε
n.nsf   n.gsn   cj r.nsm n.npn   cj   n.npm   cj   r.gs.1 d.asf n.asf   v.aam.2p   cj   v.pas.2p
3126   4460   1623 5516 5073   2779 3880   4036   1609 3836 5915   4444   2671 5858

like-minded, having the same love,   being one in spirit and purpose. **3** Do nothing out of selfish
⸢τὸ αὐτὸ⸣ ἔχοντες τὴν αὐτὴν ἀγάπην   τὸ σύμψυχοι ⸢τὸ ἓν⸣ φρονοῦντες μηδὲν κατ᾽ ← ἐριθείαν
d.asn r.asn   pt.pa.npm d.asf r.asf n.asf   d.asn a.npm   d.asn a.asn pt.pa.npm   a.asn   p.a   n.asf
3836 899   2400   3836 899   27   3836 5249   3836 1651 5858   3594   2848   2249

καρπὸς ἔργου, καὶ τί αἱρήσομαι οὐ γνωρίζω. ²³ συνέχομαι δὲ ἐκ τῶν δύο, τὴν ἐπιθυμίαν ἔχων εἰς τὸ ἀναλῦσαι καὶ σὺν Χριστῷ εἶναι, πολλῷ [γὰρ] μᾶλλον κρεῖσσον· ²⁴ τὸ δὲ ἐπιμένειν [ἐν] τῇ σαρκὶ ἀναγκαιότερον δι᾽ ὑμᾶς. ²⁵ καὶ τοῦτο πεποιθὼς οἶδα ὅτι μενῶ καὶ παραμενῶ πᾶσιν ὑμῖν εἰς τὴν ὑμῶν προκοπὴν καὶ χαρὰν τῆς πίστεως, ²⁶ ἵνα τὸ καύχημα ὑμῶν περισσεύῃ ἐν Χριστῷ Ἰησοῦ ἐν ἐμοὶ διὰ τῆς ἐμῆς παρουσίας πάλιν πρὸς ὑμᾶς. ¶ ²⁷ Μόνον ἀξίως τοῦ εὐαγγελίου τοῦ Χριστοῦ πολιτεύεσθε, ἵνα εἴτε ἐλθὼν καὶ ἰδὼν ὑμᾶς εἴτε ἀπὼν ἀκούω τὰ περὶ ὑμῶν, ὅτι στήκετε ἐν ἑνὶ πνεύματι, μιᾷ ψυχῇ συναθλοῦντες τῇ πίστει τοῦ εὐαγγελίου ²⁸ καὶ μὴ πτυρόμενοι ἐν μηδενὶ ὑπὸ τῶν ἀντικειμένων, ἥτις ἐστὶν αὐτοῖς ἔνδειξις ἀπωλείας, ὑμῶν δὲ σωτηρίας, καὶ τοῦτο ἀπὸ θεοῦ· ²⁹ ὅτι ὑμῖν ἐχαρίσθη τὸ ὑπὲρ Χριστοῦ, οὐ μόνον τὸ εἰς αὐτὸν πιστεύειν ἀλλὰ καὶ τὸ ὑπὲρ αὐτοῦ πάσχειν, ³⁰ τὸν αὐτὸν ἀγῶνα ἔχοντες, οἷον εἴδετε ἐν ἐμοὶ καὶ νῦν ἀκούετε ἐν ἐμοί.

²:¹ Εἴ τις οὖν παράκλησις ἐν Χριστῷ, εἴ τι παραμύθιον ἀγάπης, εἴ τις κοινωνία πνεύματος, εἴ τις σπλάγχνα καὶ οἰκτιρμοί, ² πληρώσατέ μου τὴν χαρὰν ἵνα τὸ αὐτὸ φρονῆτε, τὴν αὐτὴν ἀγάπην ἔχοντες, σύμψυχοι, τὸ ἓν φρονοῦντες, ³ μηδὲν κατ᾽ ἐριθείαν

ambition or   vain   conceit, but   in humility   consider others   better   than yourselves. **4** Each
← μηδὲ κατὰ κενοδοξίαν ← ἀλλὰ ᾿τῇ ταπεινοφροσύνῃ᾿ ἡγούμενοι ἀλλήλους ὑπερέχοντας → ἑαυτῶν ἕκαστος
cj / p.a / n.asf / cj / d.dsf / n.dsf / pt.pm.npm / r.apm / pt.pa.apm / r.gpm.2 / r.nsm
3593 / 2848 / 3029 / 247 / 3836 / 5425 / 2451 / 253 / 5660 / 1571 / 1667

of you should look   not only to your   own interests, but also   to the interests of others. ¶ **5** Your
← → → σκοποῦντες μὴ ἑαυτῶν ← τὰ ἀλλὰ καὶ ἕκαστοι τὰ → ἑτέρων ᾿ἐν ὑμῖν᾿
pt.pa.npm / pl / r.gpm.2 / d.apn / cj / cj / r.nsm / d.apn / r.gpm / p.d / r.dp.2
5023 / 3590 / 1571 / 3836 / 247 / 2779 / 1667 / 3836 / 2283 / 1877 / 7007

attitude   should be the same as that   of Christ Jesus: **6** Who, being   in   very nature God, did not consider
φρονεῖτε Τοῦτο ὃ καὶ ἐν Χριστῷ Ἰησοῦ ὃς ὑπάρχων ἐν → μορφῇ θεοῦ → οὐχ ἡγήσατο
v.pam.2p / r.asn / r.nsn / adv / p.d / n.dsm / n.dsm / r.nsm / pt.pa.nsm / p.d / n.dsf / n.gsm / pl / v.ami.3s
5858 / 4047 / 4005 / 2779 / 1877 / 5986 / 2652 / 4005 / 5639 / 1877 / 3671 / 2536 / 2451 4024 / 2451

equality   with God something to be grasped, **7** but made himself nothing, taking the very nature of a servant,
᾿τὸ εἶναι ἴσα᾿ → θεῷ ἁρπαγμὸν ἀλλὰ ↱ ἑαυτὸν ἐκένωσεν λαβών → μορφὴν δούλου
d.asn f.pa a.apn / n.dsm / n.asm / cj / r.asm.3 / v.aai.3s / pt.aa.nsm / n.asf / n.gsm
3836 1639 2698 / 2536 / 772 / 247 3033 / 1571 / 3033 / 3284 / 3671 / 1529

being made   in human likeness. **8** And being found in appearance as a man, he humbled himself and
→ γενόμενος ἐν ἀνθρώπων ὁμοιώματι καὶ → εὑρεθεὶς → σχήματι ὡς ἄνθρωπος → ἐταπείνωσεν ἑαυτὸν
pt.am.nsm / p.d / n.gpm / n.dsn / cj / pt.ap.nsm / n.dsn / pl / n.nsm / v.aai.3s / r.asm.3
1181 / 1877 / 476 / 3930 / 2779 / 2351 / 5386 / 6055 / 476 / 5427 / 1571

became obedient to   death – even death on a cross! **9** Therefore   God   exalted him to the highest
γενόμενος ὑπήκοος μέχρι θανάτου δὲ θανάτου → σταυροῦ διὸ καὶ ὁ θεὸς ὑπερύψωσεν αὐτὸν ← ←
pt.am.nsm / a.nsm / p.g / n.gsm / cj / n.gsm / n.gsm / cj / adv / d.nsm / n.nsm / v.aai.3s / r.asm.3
1181 / 5675 / 3588 / 2505 / 1254 / 2505 / 5089 / 1475 / 2779 / 3836 / 2536 / 5671 / 899 / 5671 5671 5671

place and gave   him the name that is above every name, **10** that at the name of Jesus every knee should bow, in
↰ καὶ ἐχαρίσατο αὐτῷ τὸ ὄνομα τὸ ὑπὲρ πᾶν ὄνομα ἵνα ἐν τῷ ὀνόματι → Ἰησοῦ πᾶν γόνυ → κάμψῃ
cj / v.ami.3s / r.dsm.3 / d.asn / n.asn / d.asn / p.a / a.asn / n.asn / cj / p.d / d.dsn / n.dsn / n.gsm / a.nsn / n.nsn / v.aas.3s
5671 / 2779 / 5919 / 899 / 3836 / 3950 / 3836 / 5642 / 4246 / 3950 / 2671 / 1877 / 3836 / 3950 / 2652 / 4246 / 1205 / 2828

heaven   and on earth   and under the earth, **11** and every tongue confess   that Jesus Christ is Lord, to
ἐπουρανίων καὶ → ἐπιγείων καὶ → καταχθονίων καὶ πᾶσα γλῶσσα ἐξομολογήσηται ὅτι Ἰησοῦς Χριστὸς κύριος εἰς
a.gpm / cj / a.gpm / cj / a.gpm / cj / a.nsf / n.nsf / v.ams.3s / cj / n.nsm / n.nsm / n.nsm / p.a
2230 / 2779 / 2103 / 2779 / 2973 / 2779 / 4246 / 1185 / 2018 / 4022 / 2652 / 5986 / 3261 / 1650

the glory of God the Father.
δόξαν → θεοῦ πατρός
n.asf / n.gsm / n.gsm
1518 / 2536 / 4252

Shining as Stars

2:12 Therefore, my dear friends, as   you have always obeyed – not   only in my presence, but now
Ὥστε μου ἀγαπητοί καθὼς → πάντοτε ὑπηκούσατε μὴ ὡς μόνον ἐν μου ᾿τῇ παρουσίᾳ᾿ ἀλλὰ νῦν
cj / r.gs.1 / a.vpm / cj / adv / v.aai.2p / pl / pl / adv / p.d / r.gs.1 / d.dsf / n.dsf / cj / adv
6063 / 1609 / 28 / 2777 / 5634 5634 / 4121 5634 / 3590 / 6055 / 3667 / 1877 / 1609 / 3836 / 4242 / 247 / 3814

much more in my absence   – continue to work   out your salvation   with fear and trembling, **13** for it
πολλῷ μᾶλλον ἐν μου ᾿τῇ ἀπουσίᾳ᾿ → → κατεργάζεσθε ← ἑαυτῶν ᾿τὴν σωτηρίαν᾿ μετὰ φόβου καὶ τρόμου γάρ →
a.dsn / adv.c / p.d / r.gs.1 / d.dsf / n.dsf / v.pmm.2p / r.gpm.2 / d.asf n.asf / p.g / n.gsm / cj / n.gsm / cj
4498 / 3437 / 1877 / 1609 / 3836 / 707 / 2981 / 1571 / 3836 5401 / 3552 / 5832 / 2779 / 5571 / 1142

is God who works in you to will   and to act   according to his good   purpose. ¶ **14** Do
ἐστιν θεὸς ὁ ἐνεργῶν ἐν ὑμῖν καὶ ᾿τὸ θέλειν᾿ καὶ → ᾿τὸ ἐνεργεῖν᾿ ὑπὲρ → τῆς εὐδοκίας ← ποιεῖτε
v.pai.3s / n.nsm / d.nsm / pt.pa.nsm / p.d / r.dp.2 / cj / d.asn f.pa / cj / d.asn f.pa / p.g / d.gsf / n.gsf / v.pam.2p
1639 / 2536 / 3836 / 1919 / 1877 / 7007 / 2779 / 3836 2527 / 2779 / 3836 1919 / 5642 / 3836 / 2306 / 4472

everything without complaining or arguing, **15** so that you may become blameless and pure, children of God
Πάντα χωρὶς γογγυσμῶν καὶ διαλογισμῶν ἵνα → → γένησθε ἄμεμπτοι καὶ ἀκέραιοι τέκνα → θεοῦ
a.apn / p.g / n.gpm / cj / n.gpm / cj / v.ams.2p / a.npm / cj / a.npm / n.npn / n.gsm
4246 / 6006 / 1198 / 2779 / 1369 / 2671 / 1181 / 289 / 2779 / 193 / 5451 / 2536

without fault in a crooked and depraved generation, in which you shine like stars in the universe **16** as
→ ἄμωμα μέσον σκολιᾶς καὶ διεστραμμένης γενεᾶς ἐν οἷς → φαίνεσθε ὡς φωστῆρες ἐν κόσμῳ →
a.npn / p.g / a.gsf / cj / pt.rp.gsf / n.gsf / p.d / r.dpm / v.pmi.2p / pl / n.npm / p.d / n.dsm
320 / 3545 / 5021 / 2779 / 1406 / 1155 / 1877 / 4005 / 5743 / 6055 / 5891 / 1877 / 3180

μηδὲ κατὰ κενοδοξίαν ἀλλὰ τῇ ταπεινοφροσύνῃ ἀλλήλους ἡγούμενοι ὑπερέχοντας ἑαυτῶν, 4 μὴ τὰ ἑαυτῶν ἕκαστος σκοποῦντες ἀλλὰ [καὶ] τὰ ἑτέρων ἕκαστοι. ¶ 5 τοῦτο φρονεῖτε ἐν ὑμῖν ὃ καὶ ἐν Χριστῷ Ἰησοῦ, 6 ὃς ἐν μορφῇ θεοῦ ὑπάρχων οὐχ ἁρπαγμὸν ἡγήσατο τὸ εἶναι ἴσα θεῷ, 7 ἀλλὰ ἑαυτὸν ἐκένωσεν μορφὴν δούλου λαβών, ἐν ὁμοιώματι ἀνθρώπων γενόμενος· καὶ σχήματι εὑρεθεὶς ὡς ἄνθρωπος 8 ἐταπείνωσεν ἑαυτὸν γενόμενος ὑπήκοος μέχρι θανάτου, θανάτου δὲ σταυροῦ. 9 διὸ καὶ ὁ θεὸς αὐτὸν ὑπερύψωσεν καὶ ἐχαρίσατο αὐτῷ τὸ ὄνομα τὸ ὑπὲρ πᾶν ὄνομα, 10 ἵνα ἐν τῷ ὀνόματι Ἰησοῦ πᾶν γόνυ κάμψῃ ἐπουρανίων καὶ ἐπιγείων καὶ καταχθονίων 11 καὶ πᾶσα γλῶσσα ἐξομολογήσηται ὅτι κύριος Ἰησοῦς Χριστὸς εἰς δόξαν θεοῦ πατρός.

2:12 Ὥστε, ἀγαπητοί μου, καθὼς πάντοτε ὑπηκούσατε, μὴ ὡς ἐν τῇ παρουσίᾳ μου μόνον ἀλλὰ νῦν πολλῷ μᾶλλον ἐν τῇ ἀπουσίᾳ μου, μετὰ φόβου καὶ τρόμου τὴν ἑαυτῶν σωτηρίαν κατεργάζεσθε· 13 θεὸς γάρ ἐστιν ὁ ἐνεργῶν ἐν ὑμῖν καὶ τὸ θέλειν καὶ τὸ ἐνεργεῖν ὑπὲρ τῆς εὐδοκίας. ¶ 14 πάντα ποιεῖτε χωρὶς γογγυσμῶν καὶ διαλογισμῶν, 15 ἵνα γένησθε ἄμεμπτοι καὶ ἀκέραιοι, τέκνα θεοῦ ἄμωμα μέσον γενεᾶς σκολιᾶς καὶ διεστραμμένης, ἐν οἷς φαίνεσθε ὡς φωστῆρες ἐν κόσμῳ, 16 λόγον ζωῆς ἐπέχοντες,

you hold   out the word of life – in order that I   may boast on the day of Christ that I   did not run
→ ἐπέχοντες ←   λόγον → ζωῆς εἰς →   ἐμοί   καύχημα εἰς   ἡμέραν → Χριστοῦ ὅτι →   οὐκ ἔδραμον
pt.pa.npm   n.asm   n.gsf p.a   r.ds.1 n.asn   p.a   n.asf   n.gsm   cj   pl v.aai.1s
2091   3364   2437 1650   1609   3017   1650   2465   5986   4022   4024 5556

          or   labor   for nothing. [17] But   even if I am being poured   out like a drink offering on the sacrifice and
εἰς κενὸν οὐδὲ ἐκοπίασα εἰς κενόν   Ἀλλὰ καὶ εἰ → → → σπένδομαι ←   ←   ←   ←   ←   ἐπὶ τῇ θυσίᾳ   καὶ
p.a a.asn v.aai.1s p.a a.asn   cj   adv cj   v.ppi.1s   p.d d.dsf n.dsf cj
1650 3031 4028 3159 1650 3031   247 2779 1623   5064   2093 3836 2602   2779

service coming from your faith,   I am glad and rejoice with all   of you. [18] So   you too should be
λειτουργίᾳ ←   → ὑμῶν ⌐τῆς πίστεως⌐ → χαίρω καὶ συγχαίρω ← πᾶσιν ὑμῖν δὲ ⌐τὸ αὐτὸ⌐ ὑμεῖς καὶ   →
n.dsf   r.gp.2 d.gsf n.gsf   v.pai.1s cj v.pai.1s   a.dpm r.dp.2 cj d.asn r.asn r.np.2 adv
3311   4411   3836 4411   5897   2779 5176   4246   7007   1254 3836 899 7007 2779

glad   and rejoice   with me.
χαίρετε καὶ συγχαίρετε ←   μοι
v.pam.2p cj v.pam.2p   r.ds.1
5897   2779 5176   1609

Timothy and Epaphroditus

2:19   I hope in the Lord Jesus to send Timothy to you soon, that I   also may be cheered when I
δὲ Ἐλπίζω ἐν   κυρίῳ Ἰησοῦ → πέμψαι Τιμόθεον → ὑμῖν ταχέως ἵνα καγὼ ←   →   → εὐψυχῶ →
cj v.pai.1s p.d n.dsm n.dsm f.aa   n.asm   r.dp.2 adv cj crasis   v.pas.1s
1254 1827   1877 3261 2652   4287   5510   7007 5441 2671 2743   2379

receive news about you. [20] I have no   one else like   him, who takes a genuine interest in   your
γνοὺς τὰ περὶ ὑμῶν γὰρ → ἔχω οὐδένα ←   ἰσόψυχον ←   ὅστις ⌐   γνησίως μεριμνήσει τὰ ⌐
pt.aa.nsm d.apn p.g r.gp.2 cj v.pai.1s a.asm   a.asm   r.nsm   adv   v.fai.3s   d.apn
1182   3836 4309 7007 1142 2400 4029   2701   4015 3534   1189   3534   3836 7007

welfare. [21] For everyone looks   out for his own interests, not those of Jesus Christ. [22] But you know   that
⌐περὶ ὑμῶν⌐ γὰρ οἱ πάντες⌐ ζητοῦσιν ← ← → ⌐τὰ ἑαυτῶν⌐ οὐ τὰ → Ἰησοῦ Χριστοῦ δὲ →   γινώσκετε
p.g r.gp.2 cj d.npm a.npm v.pai.3p   d.apn r.gpm.3 pl d.apn n.gsm n.gsm   cj   v.pai.2p
4309 7007   1142 3836 4246 2426   3836 1571   4024 3836 2652   5986   1254   1187

Timothy has proved   himself, because as a son with his father he has served   with me in the work of the
⌐τὴν δοκιμὴν⌐ αὐτοῦ ὅτι →   ὡς τέκνον →   πατρὶ → ἐδούλευσεν σὺν ἐμοὶ εἰς   →   τὸ
d.asf n.asf   r.gsm.3 cj   cj n.nsn   n.dsm   v.aai.3s p.d r.ds.1 p.a   d.asn
3836 1509   899   4022   6055 5451   4252   1526   5250 1609   1650   3836

gospel. [23] I hope, therefore, to send him   as   soon as I see how things go with me. [24] And I am
εὐαγγέλιον μὲν → ἐλπίζω οὖν   → πέμψαι τοῦτον ἐξαυτῆς ὡς ἂν ← → ἀφίδω τὰ   περὶ ἐμὲ δὲ → →
n.asn   pl v.pai.1s cj   f.aa   r.asm   adv   cj pl   v.aas.1s d.apn p.a r.as.1 cj
2295   3525 1827   4036   4287   4047   1994   6055 323   927   3836   4309 1609 1254

confident in the Lord that I   myself will come   soon. ¶ [25] But I think   it is necessary to send back
πέποιθα ἐν   κυρίῳ ὅτι καὶ → αὐτὸς → ἐλεύσομαι ταχέως   δὲ → ἡγησάμην   Ἀναγκαῖον → πέμψαι
v.rai.1s p.d n.dsm cj adv   r.nsm   v.fmi.1s   adv   cj v.ami.1s   a.nsn   f.aa
4275   1877 3261 4022 2779 899   2262   5441   1254 2451   338   4287

to   you Epaphroditus, my brother,   fellow worker and fellow   soldier,   who is also your messenger,
πρὸς ὑμᾶς Ἐπαφρόδιτον μου ⌐τὸν ἀδελφὸν⌐ καὶ συνεργὸν καὶ συστρατιώτην   δὲ   ὑμῶν ἀπόστολον
p.a r.ap.2 n.asm   r.gs.1 d.asm n.asm cj n.asm   cj n.asm   cj   r.gp.2 n.asm
4639 7007 2073   1609 3836 81   2779 5301   2779 5369   1254   7007 693

whom you sent to take care   of my needs. [26] For he longs   for all   of you and is distressed
καὶ   λειτουργὸν μου ⌐τῆς χρείας⌐ ἐπειδὴ → ἐπιποθῶν ἦν ← πάντας ὑμᾶς καὶ ἀδημονῶν
cj   n.asm   r.gs.1 d.gsf n.gsf cj   pt.pa.nsm v.iai.3s a.apm r.ap.2 cj pt.pa.nsm
2779   3313   5970 1609 3836 n.gsf 2076   2160   1639   4246 7007 2779 86

because you heard   he was ill. [27] Indeed he was ill,   and almost   died. But God   had
διότι → ἠκούσατε ὅτι → →   ἠσθένησεν γὰρ καὶ   ἠσθένησεν παραπλήσιον θανάτῳ ἀλλὰ ὁ θεὸς
cj   v.aai.2p cj   v.aai.3s cj adv   v.aai.3s adv   n.dsm cj d.nsm n.nsm
1484   201   4022   820   1142 2779   820   4180   2505   247 3836 2536

mercy on him, and not on him only but also on me, to spare   me sorrow upon sorrow. [28] Therefore I am all
ἠλέησεν ← αὐτὸν δὲ οὐκ αὐτὸν μόνον ἀλλὰ καὶ   ἐμέ ἵνα μὴ σχῶ   λύπην ἐπὶ λύπην   οὖν   →
v.aai.3s r.asm.3 cj pl r.asm.3 adv cj adv   r.as.1 cj pl v.aas.1s n.asf p.a n.asf cj
1796   899   1254 4024 899   3667 247 2779   1609 2671 3590 2400 3383 2093 3383   4036   4287 4287

εἰς καύχημα ἐμοὶ εἰς ἡμέραν Χριστοῦ, ὅτι οὐκ εἰς κενὸν ἔδραμον οὐδὲ εἰς κενὸν ἐκοπίασα. 17 ἀλλὰ εἰ καὶ σπένδομαι ἐπὶ τῇ θυσίᾳ καὶ λειτουργίᾳ τῆς πίστεως ὑμῶν, χαίρω καὶ συγχαίρω πᾶσιν ὑμῖν· 18 τὸ δὲ αὐτὸ καὶ ὑμεῖς χαίρετε καὶ συγχαίρετέ μοι. 2:19 Ἐλπίζω δὲ ἐν κυρίῳ Ἰησοῦ Τιμόθεον ταχέως πέμψαι ὑμῖν, ἵνα κἀγὼ εὐψυχῶ γνοὺς τὰ περὶ ὑμῶν. 20 οὐδένα γὰρ ἔχω ἰσόψυχον, ὅστις γνησίως τὰ περὶ ὑμῶν μεριμνήσει· 21 οἱ πάντες γὰρ τὰ ἑαυτῶν ζητοῦσιν, οὐ τὰ Ἰησοῦ Χριστοῦ. 22 τὴν δὲ δοκιμὴν αὐτοῦ γινώσκετε, ὅτι ὡς πατρὶ τέκνον σὺν ἐμοὶ ἐδούλευσεν εἰς τὸ εὐαγγέλιον. 23 τοῦτον μὲν οὖν ἐλπίζω πέμψαι ὡς ἂν ἀφίδω τὰ περὶ ἐμὲ ἐξαυτῆς· 24 πέποιθα δὲ ἐν κυρίῳ ὅτι καὶ αὐτὸς ταχέως ἐλεύσομαι. ¶ 25 Ἀναγκαῖον δὲ ἡγησάμην Ἐπαφρόδιτον τὸν ἀδελφὸν καὶ συνεργὸν καὶ συστρατιώτην μου, ὑμῶν δὲ ἀπόστολον καὶ λειτουργὸν τῆς χρείας μου, πέμψαι πρὸς ὑμᾶς, 26 ἐπειδὴ ἐπιποθῶν ἦν πάντας ὑμᾶς καὶ ἀδημονῶν, διότι ἠκούσατε ὅτι ἠσθένησεν. 27 καὶ γὰρ ἠσθένησεν παραπλήσιον θανάτῳ· ἀλλὰ ὁ θεὸς ἠλέησεν αὐτόν, οὐκ αὐτὸν δὲ μόνον ἀλλὰ καὶ ἐμέ, ἵνα μὴ λύπην ἐπὶ λύπην σχῶ. 28 σπουδαιοτέρως οὖν ἔπεμψα αὐτόν, ἵνα ἰδόντες αὐτὸν πάλιν χαρῆτε κἀγὼ ἀλυπότερος ὦ. 29 προσδέχεσθε οὖν αὐτὸν ἐν κυρίῳ

the more eager   to send him, so that when you see   him again you may be glad   and I may have less
→   σπουδαιοτέρως   ἔπεμψα αὐτὸν ἵνα   ἰδόντες αὐτὸν πάλιν →   χαρῆτε καγὼ   ὦ
   adv.c   v.aai.1s r.asm.3 cj   pt.aa.npm r.asm.3 adv   v.aps.2p crasis   v.pas.1s
   5081   4287   899   2671   1625   899   4099   5897   2743   1639

anxiety. **29**   Welcome him in the Lord with great joy,   and honor   men   like him, **30** because he
ἀλυπότερος   οὖν προσδέχεσθε αὐτὸν ἐν   κυρίῳ μετὰ πάσης χαρᾶς καὶ ἐντίμους ἔχετε τοὺς τοιούτους   ←   ὅτι
a.nsm.c   cj   v.pmm.2p   r.asm.3 p.d   n.dsm p.g   a.gsf   n.gsf cj   a.apm   v.pam.2p d.apm r.apm   cj
267   4036 4657   899   1877   3261   3552 4246 5915 2779 1952   2400   3836 5525   4022

almost died   for the work of Christ, risking   his life to make   up for the help
μέχρι θανάτου ἤγγισεν διὰ τὸ ἔργον → Χριστοῦ παραβολευσάμενος τῇ ψυχῇ ἵνα ἀναπληρώσῃ ←   τῆς λειτουργίας
p.g   n.gsm   v.aai.3s   p.a d.asn n.asn   n.gsm   pt.am.nsm   d.dsf n.dsf cj   v.aas.3s   d.gsf n.gsf
3588 2505   1581   1328 3836 2240   5986   4129   3836 6034 2671 405   3836 3311

you *could not give*   me.
ὑμῶν   τὸ ὑστέρημα πρός με
r.gp.2   d.asn n.asn   p.a r.as.1
7007   3836 5729   4639 1609

No Confidence in the Flesh

3:1 Finally,   my brothers, rejoice in the Lord! It is no trouble   for me to write   the same things to you
Τὸ λοιπόν,   μου ἀδελφοί χαίρετε ἐν κυρίῳ   οὐκ ὀκνηρόν μὲν → ἐμοὶ → γράφειν τὰ αὐτὰ ←   ὑμῖν
d.asn adv   r.gs.1 n.vpm v.pam.2p p.d n.dsm   pl   a.nsn   pl r.ds.1 f.pa   d.apn r.apn   r.dp.2
3836 3370   1609 81   5897   1877 3261   4024 3891 3525 1609 1211 3836 899   7007

again, and it is a safeguard for you. ¶   **2** Watch out for those dogs,   those men who do   evil,
δὲ   ἀσφαλές → ὑμῖν   Βλέπετε ← ← τοὺς κύνας βλέπετε τοὺς   ἐργάτας κακοὺς βλέπετε
cj   a.nsn   r.dp.2   v.pam.2p   d.apm n.apm v.pam.2p d.apm   n.apm   a.apm v.pam.2p
1254   855   7007   1063   3836 3264 1063   3836   2239   2805   1063

those mutilators of the flesh. **3** For it is we   who are the circumcision, we who worship   by the Spirit of God,
τὴν κατατομήν ← ← ← γάρ   ἡμεῖς ἐσμεν ἡ περιτομή   οἱ λατρεύοντες →   πνεύματι θεοῦ καὶ
d.asf n.asf   cj   r.np.1   v.pai.1p d.nsf n.nsf   d.npm pt.pa.npm   n.dsn   n.gsm cj
3836 2961   1142 1639   3836 4364   3836 3302   4460   2536 2779

who glory   in Christ Jesus, and who put no confidence in the flesh – **4** though I myself have reasons for such
καυχώμενοι ἐν Χριστῷ Ἰησοῦ καὶ   οὐκ πεποιθότες ἐν σαρκὶ καίπερ ἐγὼ   ἔχων
pt.pm.npm   p.d n.dsm n.dsm cj   pl   pt.ra.npm   p.d n.dsf   cj   r.ns.1   pt.pa.nsm
3016   1877 5986   2652   2779   4275 4024 4275   1877 4922 2788   1609   2400

confidence.   ¶   If anyone else thinks he has reasons to put confidence in the flesh, I   have
πεποίθησιν καὶ ἐν σαρκί   Εἴ τις   ἄλλος δοκεῖ   → → πεποιθέναι ἐν σαρκί ἐγὼ
n.asf   adv p.d n.dsf   cj   r.nsm r.nsm v.pai.3s   f.ra   p.d n.dsf r.ns.1
4301   2779 1877 4922   1623 5516 257   1506   4275   1877 4922 1609

more: **5** circumcised on the eighth   day, of the people of Israel, of the tribe of Benjamin, a Hebrew of Hebrews;
μᾶλλον περιτομῇ   → ὀκταήμερος ← ἐκ γένους Ἰσραήλ → φυλῆς → Βενιαμίν   Ἑβραῖος ἐξ Ἑβραίων
adv.c   n.dsf   a.nsm   p.g n.gsn   n.gsm   n.gsf   n.nsm   n.nsm   p.g n.gpm
3437   4364   3892   1666 1169   2702   5876   1021   1578   1666 1578

in regard to the law, a Pharisee; **6** as for zeal, persecuting the church; as for legalistic   righteousness,
κατὰ ← ← νόμον Φαρισαῖος   κατὰ ← ζῆλος διώκων   τὴν ἐκκλησίαν κατὰ ← τὴν ἐν νόμῳ δικαιοσύνην
p.a   n.asm n.nsm   p.a   n.asn pt.pa.nsm d.asf n.asf   p.a   d.asf p.d n.dsm n.asf
2848   3795 5757   2848   2419 1503   3836 1711   2848   3836 1877 3795 1466

    faultless. ¶   **7** But whatever was to my profit   I now consider loss   for the sake of Christ.
γενόμενος ἄμεμπτος   Ἀλλά ἅτινα   ἦν → μοι κέρδη ταῦτα → ἥγημαι ζημίαν διὰ ←   τὸν Χριστόν
pt.am.nsm a.nsm   cj   r.npn   v.iai.3s   r.ds.1 n.npn r.apn   v.rmi.1s n.asf   p.a   d.asm n.asm
1181   289   247 4015   1639   3046 4047   2451   2422   1328   3836 5986

8 *What is more,*   I consider everything   a loss compared to the surpassing greatness of knowing
ἀλλὰ μενοῦνγε   καὶ → ἡγοῦμαι πάντα   εἶναι ζημίαν διὰ ← τὸ ὑπερέχον   τῆς γνώσεως
cj   pl   adv → v.pmi.1s a.apn   f.pa n.asf   p.a   d.asn pt.pa.asn   d.gsf n.gsf
247   3529   2779 2451   4246   1639 2422   1328   3836 5660   3836 1194

Christ Jesus my Lord,   for whose sake I have lost   all   things. I consider them rubbish, that I
Χριστοῦ Ἰησοῦ μου τοῦ κυρίου δι᾽ ὃν ← → ἐζημιώθην τὰ πάντα   καὶ → ἡγοῦμαι σκύβαλα ἵνα →
n.gsm   n.gsm r.gs.1 d.gsm n.gsm   p.a r.asm   v.api.1s   d.apn a.apn   cj   v.pmi.1s   n.apn   cj
5986   2652   1609 3836 3261   1328 4005   1328 2423   3836 4246   2779 2451   5032   2671

may gain   Christ **9** and be found in him, not having a righteousness of my own that comes from the law, but
→ κερδήσω Χριστὸν καὶ   εὑρεθῶ ἐν αὐτῷ μὴ ἔχων   δικαιοσύνην ἐμὴν ← τὴν ἐκ ← νόμου ἀλλὰ
   v.aas.1s n.asm   cj   v.aps.1s p.d r.dsm.3 pl pt.pa.nsm n.asf   r.asf.1   d.asf p.g   n.gsm cj
   3045   5986   2779   2351   1877 899   3590 2400   1466   1847   3836 1666   3795 247

μετὰ πάσης χαρᾶς καὶ τοὺς τοιούτους ἐντίμους ἔχετε, 30 ὅτι διὰ τὸ ἔργον Χριστοῦ μέχρι θανάτου ἤγγισεν παραβολευσάμενος τῇ ψυχῇ, ἵνα ἀναπληρώσῃ τὸ ὑμῶν ὑστέρημα τῆς πρός με λειτουργίας.

     3:1 Τὸ λοιπόν, ἀδελφοί μου, χαίρετε ἐν κυρίῳ. τὰ αὐτὰ γράφειν ὑμῖν ἐμοὶ μὲν οὐκ ὀκνηρόν, ὑμῖν δὲ ἀσφαλές. ¶ 2 Βλέπετε τοὺς κύνας, βλέπετε τοὺς κακοὺς ἐργάτας, βλέπετε τὴν κατατομήν. 3 ἡμεῖς γάρ ἐσμεν ἡ περιτομή, οἱ πνεύματι θεοῦ λατρεύοντες καὶ καυχώμενοι ἐν Χριστῷ Ἰησοῦ καὶ οὐκ ἐν σαρκὶ πεποιθότες, 4 καίπερ ἐγὼ ἔχων πεποίθησιν καὶ ἐν σαρκί. ¶ εἴ τις δοκεῖ ἄλλος πεποιθέναι ἐν σαρκί, ἐγὼ μᾶλλον· 5 περιτομῇ ὀκταήμερος, ἐκ γένους Ἰσραήλ, φυλῆς Βενιαμίν, Ἑβραῖος ἐξ Ἑβραίων, κατὰ νόμον Φαρισαῖος, 6 κατὰ ζῆλος διώκων τὴν ἐκκλησίαν, κατὰ δικαιοσύνην τὴν ἐν νόμῳ γενόμενος ἄμεμπτος. ¶ 7 [ἀλλὰ] ἅτινα ἦν μοι κέρδη, ταῦτα ἥγημαι διὰ τὸν Χριστὸν ζημίαν. 8 ἀλλὰ μενοῦνγε καὶ ἡγοῦμαι πάντα ζημίαν εἶναι διὰ τὸ ὑπερέχον τῆς γνώσεως Χριστοῦ Ἰησοῦ τοῦ κυρίου μου, δι᾽ ὃν τὰ πάντα ἐζημιώθην, καὶ ἡγοῦμαι σκύβαλα, ἵνα Χριστὸν κερδήσω 9 καὶ εὑρεθῶ

that which is through faith in Christ — the righteousness that comes from God and is by faith. **10** I want to
τὴν ← διὰ πίστεως → Χριστοῦ τὴν δικαιοσύνην ← ← θεοῦ ἐπὶ τῇ πίστει
d.asf p.g n.gsf n.gsm d.asf n.asf p.g n.gsm p.d d.dsf n.dsf
3836 1328 4411 5986 3836 1466 1666 2536 2093 3836 4411

know Christ and the power of his resurrection and the fellowship of sharing in his sufferings,
τοῦ γνῶναι αὐτὸν καὶ τὴν δύναμιν αὐτοῦ τῆς ἀναστάσεως καὶ τὴν κοινωνίαν αὐτοῦ τῶν παθημάτων
d.gsn f.aa r.asm.3 cj d.asf n.asf r.gsm.3 d.gsf n.gsf cj d.asf n.asf r.gsm.3 d.gpn n.gpn
3836 1182 899 2779 3836 1539 414 899 3836 414 2779 3836 3126 4077 899 3836 4077

becoming like him in his death, **11** and so, somehow, to attain to the resurrection from the dead.
συμμορφιζόμενος αὐτοῦ τῷ θανάτῳ εἴ πως καταντήσω εἰς τὴν ἐξανάστασιν τὴν ἐκ νεκρῶν
pt.pp.nsm r.gsm.3 d.dsm n.dsm cj pl v.fai.1s p.a d.asf n.asf d.asf p.g a.gpm
5214 2505 899 3836 2505 1623 4803 2918 1650 3836 1983 3836 1666 3738

Pressing on Toward the Goal

3:12 Not that I have already obtained all this, or have already been made perfect, but I press on to
Οὐχ ὅτι ἤδη ἔλαβον ἢ ἤδη τετελείωμαι δὲ διώκω εἰ καὶ
pl cj adv v.aai.1s cj adv v.rpi.1s cj v.pai.1s cj adv
4024 4022 3284 3284 2453 3284 2445 5457 2453 5457 1254 1503 1623 2779

take hold of that *for which* Christ Jesus took hold of me. **13** Brothers, I do not consider myself yet
καταλάβω ἐφ' ᾧ καὶ ὑπὸ Χριστοῦ Ἰησοῦ κατελήμφθην ἀδελφοί ἐγώ οὐ λογίζομαι ἐμαυτὸν
v.aas.1s p.d r.dsn adv p.g n.gsm n.gsm v.api.1s n.vpm r.ns.1 pl v.pmi.1s r.asm.1
2898 2093 4005 2779 5679 5986 2652 2898 81 1609 3357 4024 3357 1831

to have taken hold of it. But one thing I do: Forgetting what is behind and straining toward what
κατειληφέναι δὲ ἓν μὲν ἐπιλανθανόμενος τὰ ὀπίσω δὲ ἐπεκτεινόμενος τοῖς
f.ra cj a.asn pl pt.pm.nsm d.apn adv cj pt.pm.nsm d.dpn
2898 1254 1651 3525 2140 3836 3958 1254 2085 3836

is ahead, **14** I press on toward the goal *to win* the prize for which God has called me heavenward in
ἔμπροσθεν διώκω κατὰ σκοπὸν εἰς τὸ βραβεῖον τοῦ θεοῦ τῆς κλήσεως ἄνω ἐν
adv v.pai.1s p.a n.asm p.a d.asn n.asn d.gsm n.gsm d.gsf n.gsf adv p.d
1869 1503 2848 5024 1650 3836 1092 3104 3836 2536 3836 3104 539 1877

Christ Jesus. ¶ **15** All of us who are mature should take such a view of things. And if *on some point*
Χριστῷ Ἰησοῦ οὖν Ὅσοι ← ← τέλειοι τοῦτο φρονῶμεν καὶ εἴ τι
n.dsm n.dsm cj r.npm a.npm r.asn v.pas.1p cj cj r.asn
5986 2652 4036 4012 5455 5858 5858 4047 5858 2779 1623 5516

you think differently, that too God will make clear to you. **16** Only let us live up to what we
φρονεῖτε ἑτέρως τοῦτο καὶ ὁ θεὸς ἀποκαλύψει ὑμῖν πλὴν στοιχεῖν τῷ αὐτῷ εἰς ὃ
v.pai.2p adv r.asn cj d.nsm n.nsm v.fai.3s r.dp.2 cj f.pa d.dsn r.dsn p.a r.asn
5858 2284 4047 2779 3836 2536 636 7007 4440 5123 3836 899 1650 4005

have already attained. ¶ **17** Join with others in following my example, brothers, and take note of those who
ἐφθάσαμεν γίνεσθε μου Συμμιμηταί ἀδελφοί καὶ σκοπεῖτε τοὺς
v.aai.1p v.pam.2p r.gs.1 n.npm n.vpm cj v.pam.2p d.apm
5777 1181 5213 5213 1609 5213 81 2779 5023 3836

live according to the pattern we gave you. **18** For, as I have often told you before and now say
οὕτω περιπατοῦντας καθὼς τύπον ἡμᾶς ἔχετε γὰρ πολλάκις ἔλεγον ὑμῖν δὲ νῦν λέγω
adv pt.pa.apm cj n.asm r.ap.1 v.pai.2p cj adv v.iai.1s r.dp.2 cj adv v.pai.1s
4048 4344 2777 5596 7005 2400 1142 3306 3306 4490 3306 7007 1254 3814 3306

again even with tears, many live as enemies of the cross of Christ. **19** Their destiny is
καὶ κλαίων πολλοὶ περιπατοῦσιν οὓς τοὺς ἐχθρούς τοῦ σταυροῦ τοῦ Χριστοῦ ὧν τὸ τέλος
adv pt.pa.nsm a.npm v.pai.3p r.apm d.apm a.apm d.gsm n.gsm d.gsm n.gsm r.gpm d.nsn n.nsn
2779 3081 4498 4344 4005 3836 2398 3836 5089 3836 5986 4005 3836 5465

destruction, their god is their stomach, and their glory is in their shame. Their mind is on earthly
ἀπώλεια ὧν ὁ θεὸς ἡ κοιλία καὶ ἡ δόξα ἐν αὐτῶν τῇ αἰσχύνῃ οἱ φρονοῦντες τὰ ἐπίγεια
n.nsf r.gpm d.nsm n.nsm d.nsf n.nsf cj d.nsf n.nsf p.d r.gpm.3 d.dsf n.dsf d.npm pt.pa.npm d.apn a.apn
724 4005 3836 2536 3836 3120 2779 3836 1518 1877 899 3836 158 3836 5858 3836 2103

things. **20** But our citizenship is in heaven. And we eagerly await a Savior from there, the Lord Jesus
γὰρ ἡμῶν τὸ πολίτευμα ὑπάρχει ἐν οὐρανοῖς καὶ ἀπεκδεχόμεθα σωτῆρα ἐξ οὗ κύριον Ἰησοῦν
cj r.gp.1 d.nsn n.nsn v.pai.3s p.d n.dpm adv v.pmi.1p n.asm p.g r.gsm n.asm n.asm
1142 7005 3836 4487 5639 1877 4041 2779 587 5400 1666 4005 3261 2652

ἐν αὐτῷ, μὴ ἔχων ἐμὴν δικαιοσύνην τὴν ἐκ νόμου ἀλλὰ τὴν διὰ πίστεως Χριστοῦ, τὴν ἐκ θεοῦ δικαιοσύνην ἐπὶ τῇ πίστει, **10** τοῦ γνῶναι αὐτὸν καὶ τὴν δύναμιν τῆς ἀναστάσεως αὐτοῦ καὶ [τὴν] κοινωνίαν [τῶν] παθημάτων αὐτοῦ, συμμορφιζόμενος τῷ θανάτῳ αὐτοῦ, **11** εἴ πως καταντήσω εἰς τὴν ἐξανάστασιν τὴν ἐκ νεκρῶν. **3:12** Οὐχ ὅτι ἤδη ἔλαβον ἢ ἤδη τετελείωμαι, διώκω δὲ εἰ καὶ καταλάβω, ἐφ' ᾧ καὶ κατελήμφθην ὑπὸ Χριστοῦ [Ἰησοῦ]. **13** ἀδελφοί, ἐγὼ ἐμαυτὸν οὔπω «οὐ» λογίζομαι κατειληφέναι· ἓν δέ, τὰ μὲν ὀπίσω ἐπιλανθανόμενος τοῖς δὲ ἔμπροσθεν ἐπεκτεινόμενος, **14** κατὰ σκοπὸν διώκω εἰς τὸ βραβεῖον τῆς ἄνω κλήσεως τοῦ θεοῦ ἐν Χριστῷ Ἰησοῦ. ¶ **15** Ὅσοι οὖν τέλειοι, τοῦτο φρονῶμεν· καὶ εἴ τι ἑτέρως φρονεῖτε, καὶ τοῦτο ὁ θεὸς ὑμῖν ἀποκαλύψει· **16** πλὴν εἰς ὃ ἐφθάσαμεν, τῷ αὐτῷ στοιχεῖν. ¶ **17** Συμμιμηταί μου γίνεσθε, ἀδελφοί, καὶ σκοπεῖτε τοὺς οὕτω περιπατοῦντας καθὼς ἔχετε τύπον ἡμᾶς. **18** πολλοὶ γὰρ περιπατοῦσιν οὓς πολλάκις ἔλεγον ὑμῖν, νῦν δὲ καὶ κλαίων λέγω, τοὺς ἐχθροὺς τοῦ σταυροῦ τοῦ Χριστοῦ, **19** ὧν τὸ τέλος ἀπώλεια, ὧν ὁ θεὸς ἡ κοιλία καὶ ἡ δόξα ἐν τῇ αἰσχύνῃ αὐτῶν, οἱ τὰ ἐπίγεια φρονοῦντες. **20** ἡμῶν γὰρ τὸ πολίτευμα ἐν οὐρανοῖς

Christus, **21** who, the power that enables him to bring everything under his control, will transform

Christ,	21 who,	by	the	power	that enables	him		to bring	everything	under	his	control,	will transform
Χριστόν	ὅς	κατὰ	τὴν	ἐνέργειαν →	⌐τοῦ δύνασθαι⌐	αὐτὸν	καὶ →		⌐τὰ πάντα⌐	→	αὐτῷ	ὑποτάξαι →	μετασχηματίσει
n.asm	r.nsm	p.a	d.asf	n.asf	d.gsn f.pp	r.asm.3	adv		d.apn a.apn		r.dsm.3	f.aa	v.fai.3s
5986	4005	2848	3836	1918	3836 1538	899	2779 5718 5718		3836 4246	5718	899	5718	3571

our	lowly		bodies	so that	they will be	like		his	glorious	body.	¶	**4:1** Therefore,	my
ἡμῶν	⌐τῆς ταπεινώσεως⌐		⌐τὸ σῶμα⌐			σύμμορφον	αὐτοῦ	⌐τῆς δόξης⌐	⌐τῷ σώματι⌐			῞Ωστε	μου
r.gp.1	d.gsf n.gsf		d.asn n.asn			a.asn	r.gsm.3	d.gsf n.gsf	d.dsn n.dsn			cj	r.gs.1
7005	3836 5428		3836 5393			5215	899	3836 1518	3836 5393			6063	1609

brothers,	you whom	I	love	and	long	for,	my	joy	and	crown,	that is how	you should	stand	firm	in	the
ἀδελφοί	→		→ ἀγαπητοὶ	καὶ	ἐπιπόθητοι	←	μου	χαρὰ	καὶ	στέφανος	οὕτως ←	→	στήκετε ←		ἐν	
n.vpm			a.vpm	cj	a.vpm		r.gs.1	n.vsf	cj	n.vsm	adv		v.pam.2p		p.d	
81			28	2779	2162		1609	5915	2779	5109	4048		5112		1877	

Lord,	dear friends!
κυρίῳ →	ἀγαπητοί
n.dsm	a.vpm
3261	28

Exhortations

4:2 I plead	with	Euodia	and	I plead	with	Syntyche	to	agree			with each	other	in	the Lord.	**3** Yes,
→ παρακαλῶ ←		Εὐοδίαν	καὶ	→ παρακαλῶ ←		Συντύχην	→	⌐τὸ αὐτὸ φρονεῖν⌐	←	←		←	ἐν	κυρίῳ	ναὶ
v.pai.1s		n.asf	cj	v.pai.1s		n.asf		d.asn r.asn f.pa					p.d	n.dsm	pl
4151		2337	2779	4151		5345		3836 899 5858					1877	3261	3721

and	I ask	you,	loyal	yokefellow,	help	these	women	who		have	contended	at	my	side	in	the	cause	of	the
καὶ	→ ἐρωτῶ	σέ	γνήσιε	σύζυγε	συλλαμβάνου	αὐταῖς ←		αἵτινες	→		συνήθλησαν	→	μοι		ἐν	←	←		τῷ
adv	v.pai.1s	r.as.2	a.vsm	n.vsm	v.pmm.2s	r.dpf.3		r.npf			v.aai.3p		r.ds.1		p.d				d.dsn
2779	2263	5148	1188	5187	5197	899		4015			5254		1609		1877				3836

gospel,	along	with		Clement	and	the	rest		of my	fellow	workers,	whose	names		are	in	the	book	of life.
εὐαγγελίῳ →	μετὰ	καὶ		Κλήμεντος	καὶ	τῶν	λοιπῶν	→	μου	συνεργῶν	←	ὧν	⌐τὰ ὀνόματα⌐		ἐν		βίβλῳ	→	ζωῆς
n.dsn	p.g	adv		n.gsm	cj	d.gpm	a.gpm		r.gs.1	n.gpm		r.gpm	d.npn n.npn		p.d		n.dsf		n.gsf
2295	3552	2779		3098	2779	3836	3370		1609	5301		4005	3836 3950		1877		1047		2437

¶	**4** Rejoice	in	the	Lord	always.	I will	say it	again:	Rejoice!	**5** Let	your	gentleness	be		evident	to all.
	Χαίρετε	ἐν		κυρίῳ	πάντοτε	→ ἐρῶ	πάλιν	χαίρετε		ὑμῶν	⌐τὸ ἐπιεικὲς⌐	γνωσθήτω		→ πᾶσιν	ἀνθρώποις
	v.pam.2p	p.d		n.dsm	adv	v.fai.1s	adv	v.pam.2p		r.gp.2	d.nsn a.nsn	v.apm.3s		a.dpm	n.dpm
	5897	1877		3261	4121	3306	4099	5897		1182	3836 2117	1182		4246	476

The	Lord	is	near.	**6** Do	not	be anxious	about	anything,	but	in	everything,	by	prayer		and	petition,	with
ὁ	κύριος	ἐγγύς		→	μηδὲν →	μεριμνᾶτε ←		←	ἀλλ᾽	ἐν	παντὶ	→	⌐τῇ προσευχῇ⌐		καὶ	⌐τῇ δεήσει⌐	μετὰ
d.nsm	n.nsm	adv			a.asn	v.pam.2p			cj	p.d	a.dsf		d.dsf n.dsf		cj	d.dsf n.dsf	p.g
3836	3261	1584			3534	3594		3534	247	1877	4246		3836 4666		2779	3836 1255	3552

thanksgiving,	present	your	requests		to	God.	**7** And	the	peace	of God,	which	transcends	all
εὐχαριστίας	γνωριζέσθω	ὑμῶν	⌐τὰ αἰτήματα⌐		πρὸς	⌐τὸν θεόν⌐	καὶ	ἡ	εἰρήνη	→ ⌐τοῦ θεοῦ⌐	ἡ	ὑπερέχουσα	πάντα
n.gsf	v.ppm.3s	r.gp.2	d.npn n.npn		p.a	d.asm n.asm	cj	d.nsf	n.nsf	d.gsm n.gsm	d.nsf	pt.pa.nsf	a.asm
2374	1192	7007	3836 161		4639	3836 2536	2779	3836	1645	3836 2536	3836	5660	4246

understanding,	will	guard	your	hearts		and	your	minds		in	Christ	Jesus.	¶	**8** Finally,		brothers,
νοῦν	→	φρουρήσει	ὑμῶν	⌐τὰς καρδίας⌐		καὶ	ὑμῶν	⌐τὰ νοήματα⌐		ἐν	Χριστῷ	Ἰησοῦ		⌐Τὸ λοιπόν⌐		ἀδελφοί
n.asm		v.fai.3s	r.gp.2	d.apf n.apf		cj	r.gp.2	d.apn n.apn		p.d	n.dsm	n.dsm		d.asn adv		n.vpm
3808		5864	7007	3836 2840		2779	7007	3836 3784		1877	5986	2652		3836 3370		81

whatever	is	true,	whatever	is	noble,	whatever	is	right,	whatever	is	pure,	whatever	is	lovely,		whatever	is
ὅσα	ἐστὶν	ἀληθῆ	ὅσα		σεμνά	ὅσα		δίκαια	ὅσα		ἁγνά	ὅσα		προσφιλῆ		ὅσα	
r.npn	v.pai.3s	a.npn	r.npn		a.npn	r.npn		a.npn	r.npn		a.npn	r.npn		a.npn		r.npn	
4012	1639	239	4012		4948	4012		1465	4012		54	4012		4713		4012	

admirable	– if	anything	is	excellent	or		praiseworthy	– think		about	such	things.	**9** Whatever		you	have
εὔφημα	εἴ	τις		ἀρετὴ	καὶ	εἴ	τις	ἔπαινος		λογίζεσθε ←		ταῦτα	ἃ		καὶ →	
a.npn	cj	r.nsf		n.nsf	cj	cj	r.nsm	n.nsm		v.pmm.2p		r.apn	r.apn		cj	
2368	1623	5516		746	2779	1623	5516	2047		3357		4047	4005		2779	

learned	or	received	or	heard	from	me,	or	seen	in	me	– put	it	into	practice.	And	the	God	of peace
ἐμάθετε	καὶ	παρελάβετε	καὶ	ἠκούσατε		καὶ	εἴδετε	ἐν	ἐμοί	→	ταῦτα		πράσσετε	καὶ	ὁ	θεὸς	⌐τῆς εἰρήνης⌐
v.aai.2p	cj	v.aai.2p	cj	v.aai.2p		cj	v.aai.2p	p.d	r.ds.1		r.apn		v.pam.2p	cj	d.nsm	n.nsm	d.gsf n.gsf
3443	2779	4161	2779	201		2779	1625	1877	1609		4556		4556	2779	3836	2536	3836 1645

ὑπάρχει, ἐξ οὗ καὶ σωτῆρα ἀπεκδεχόμεθα κύριον Ἰησοῦν Χριστόν, **21** ὃς μετασχηματίσει τὸ σῶμα τῆς ταπεινώσεως ἡμῶν σύμμορφον τῷ σώματι τῆς δόξης αὐτοῦ κατὰ τὴν ἐνέργειαν τοῦ δύνασθαι αὐτὸν καὶ ὑποτάξαι αὐτῷ τὰ πάντα. **4:1** ῞Ωστε, ἀδελφοί μου ἀγαπητοὶ καὶ ἐπιπόθητοι, χαρὰ καὶ στέφανός μου, οὕτως στήκετε ἐν κυρίῳ, ἀγαπητοί.
4:2 Εὐοδίαν παρακαλῶ καὶ Συντύχην παρακαλῶ τὸ αὐτὸ φρονεῖν ἐν κυρίῳ. **3** ναὶ ἐρωτῶ καὶ σέ, γνήσιε σύζυγε, συλλαμβάνου αὐταῖς, αἵτινες ἐν τῷ εὐαγγελίῳ συνήθλησάν μοι μετὰ καὶ Κλήμεντος καὶ τῶν λοιπῶν συνεργῶν μου, ὧν τὰ ὀνόματα ἐν βίβλῳ ζωῆς. ¶ **4** Χαίρετε ἐν κυρίῳ πάντοτε· πάλιν ἐρῶ, χαίρετε. **5** τὸ ἐπιεικὲς ὑμῶν γνωσθήτω πᾶσιν ἀνθρώποις. ὁ κύριος ἐγγύς. **6** μηδὲν μεριμνᾶτε, ἀλλ᾽ ἐν παντὶ τῇ προσευχῇ καὶ τῇ δεήσει μετὰ εὐχαριστίας τὰ αἰτήματα ὑμῶν γνωριζέσθω πρὸς τὸν θεόν. **7** καὶ ἡ εἰρήνη τοῦ θεοῦ ἡ ὑπερέχουσα πάντα νοῦν φρουρήσει τὰς καρδίας ὑμῶν καὶ τὰ νοήματα ὑμῶν ἐν Χριστῷ Ἰησοῦ. ¶ **8** Τὸ λοιπόν, ἀδελφοί, ὅσα ἐστὶν ἀληθῆ, ὅσα σεμνά, ὅσα δίκαια, ὅσα ἁγνά, ὅσα προσφιλῆ, ὅσα εὔφημα, εἴ τις ἀρετὴ καὶ εἴ τις ἔπαινος, ταῦτα λογίζεσθε· **9** ἃ καὶ ἐμάθετε καὶ παρελάβετε καὶ ἠκούσατε καὶ εἴδετε ἐν ἐμοί, ταῦτα πράσσετε· καὶ ὁ θεὸς τῆς εἰρήνης ἔσται μεθ᾽ ὑμῶν.

will be   with you.
→   ἔσται μεθ᾽ ὑμῶν
    v.fmi.3s p.g   r.gp.2
    1639   3552   7007

Thanks for Their Gifts

4:10   I rejoice greatly in the Lord that *at last* you have renewed your concern   for me.   Indeed,
    δὲ → Ἐχάρην μεγάλως ἐν   κυρίῳ ὅτι ἤδη ποτὲ →   →   ἀνεθάλετε → ⌐τὸ φρονεῖν⌐ ὑπὲρ ἐμοῦ ἐφ᾽ ᾧ καὶ
    cj   v.api.1s adv   p.d   n.dsm ὅτι adv ποτε   v.aai.2p   d.asn f.pa   p.g   r.gs.1 p.d r.dsn adv
    1254 5897   3487 1877 3261 4022 2453 4537   352   3836 5858   5642 1609 2093 4005 2779

you have been concerned, but you had no opportunity to show it. **11** I   am not   saying this because I am in
→   →   ἐφρονεῖτε   δὲ → →   ἠκαιρεῖσθε   →   ↑ οὐχ ὅτι λέγω
        v.iai.2p   cj   v.imi.2p   pl   ὅτι   v.pai.1s
        5858   1254   177   3306 3306 4024 4022 3306

need,   for I have learned to be   content *whatever*   *the circumstances.* **12** I know   what it is to be in
⌐καθ᾽ ὑστέρησιν⌐ γὰρ ἐγώ → ἔμαθον → εἶναι αὐτάρκης ἐν οἷς εἰμι⌐   →   οἶδα καὶ   → → → →
p.a   n.asf   1142 r.ns.1 v.aai.1s f.pa n.nsm p.d r.dpn v.pai.1s   v.rai.1s cj
2848 5730   1609   3443   1639 895 1877 4005 1639   3857 2779

need,   and I know   what it is to have plenty.   I have learned the secret of being content *in any and*
ταπεινοῦσθαι → οἶδα καὶ   → → → περισσεύειν → μεμύημαι ← ←   ἐν παντὶ καὶ →
f.pp   v.rai.1s cj   f.pa   v.rpi.1s   p.d p.dsn cj p.d
5427   3857 2779   4355   3679   1877 4246 2779 1877

every situation, whether well   fed or hungry, whether living in plenty   or in want. **13** I can do
πᾶσιν   καὶ   χορτάζεσθαι ← καὶ πεινᾶν καὶ   → περισσεύειν καὶ → ὑστερεῖσθαι   ἰσχύω
a.dpn   cj   f.pp   cj f.pa   cj   f.pa   cj   f.pp   v.pai.1s
4246   2779 5963   2779 4277 2779   4355   2779 5728   2710

everything through him who gives me strength.   ¶   **14** Yet it was   good of you to share   in my
πάντα ἐν   τῷ ← →   με ἐνδυναμοῦντι   πλὴν ἐποιήσατε καλῶς ↖ ←   συγκοινωνήσαντες ← μου
a.apn p.d d.dsm   r.as.1 pt.pa.dsm   cj   v.aai.2p adv   pt.aa.npm   r.gs.1
4246 1877 3836   1904 1904   4440 4472   2822 4472 4472 5170   1609

troubles. **15** Moreover,   as you Philippians know,   in the early days of your acquaintance with the gospel,   when
⌐τῇ θλίψει⌐ δὲ καὶ⌐   ὑμεῖς Φιλιππήσιοι οἴδατε ὅτι ἐν   ἀρχῇ   →   τοῦ εὐαγγελίου ὅτε
d.dsf n.dsf cj adv   r.np.2 n.vpm   v.rai.2p ὅτι p.d   n.dsf   d.gsn n.gsn   cj
3836 2568   1254 2779   7007 5803   3857 4022 1877 794   3836 2295   4021

I set   out from Macedonia, not   one church shared   with me in the matter of giving and receiving, except
→ ἐξῆλθον   ἀπὸ Μακεδονίας οὐδεμία ← ἐκκλησία ἐκοινώνησεν ←   μοι εἰς   λόγον   → δόσεως καὶ λήμψεως ⌐εἰ μὴ⌐
v.aai.1s   p.g n.gsf   a.nsf   n.nsf   v.aai.3s   r.ds.1 p.a n.asm   n.gsf cj n.gsf   cj pl
2002   608 3423   4029   1711   3125   1609 1650 3364   1521 2779 3331   1623 3590

you only; **16** for even when I was in Thessalonica, you sent   me aid   again and again when I was in need.
ὑμεῖς μόνοι   ὅτι καὶ   ἐν Θεσσαλονίκῃ →   ἐπέμψατε μοι   καὶ ἅπαξ καὶ δὶς   εἰς ⌐τὴν χρείαν⌐
r.np.2 a.npm   ὅτι adv   p.d n.dsf   v.aai.2p r.ds.1 cj adv cj adv   p.a d.asf n.asf
7007 3668   4022 2779   1877 2553   4287   1609 2779 562 2779 1489 1650 3836 5970

17 Not that I am looking for a gift,   but I am looking for   what may be credited   to your account.
οὐχ ὅτι → → ἐπιζητῶ ←   ⌐τὸ δόμα⌐ ἀλλὰ → → ἐπιζητῶ   τὸν καρπὸν τὸν   → πλεονάζοντα εἰς ὑμῶν λόγον
pl cj   v.pai.1s   d.asn n.asn cj   v.pai.1s   d.asm n.asm d.asm   pt.pa.asm   p.a r.gp.2 n.asm
4024 4022   2118   3836 1517 247   2118   3836 2843 3836   4429   1650 7007 3364

18   I have received full   payment and even   more; I am amply supplied,   now that I have received from
δὲ → → ἀπέχω   πάντα ←   καὶ περισσεύω →   → → πεπλήρωμαι   →   δεξάμενος παρὰ
1254   v.pai.1s πάντα   cj v.pai.1s   v.rpi.1s   pt.am.nsm p.g
        600   4246   2779 4355   4444   1312   4123

Epaphroditus the gifts you   sent. They are a fragrant offering, an acceptable sacrifice, pleasing to God.
Ἐπαφροδίτου τὰ ←   ⌐παρ᾽ ὑμῶν⌐ →   εὐωδίας ὀσμὴν   δεκτήν   θυσίαν   εὐάρεστον → ⌐τῷ θεῷ⌐
n.gsm   d.apn p.g   r.gp.2   n.gsf   n.asf   a.asf   n.asf   a.asf   d.dsm n.dsm
2073   3836   4123 7007   2380   4011   1283   2602   2298   3836 2536

19 And my God   will meet   all   your needs according to his   glorious riches   in Christ Jesus.   ¶
δὲ μου ὁ θεός⌐   →   πληρώσει πᾶσαν ὑμῶν χρείαν κατὰ   ← αὐτοῦ ⌐ἐν δόξῃ⌐ ⌐τὸ πλοῦτος⌐ ἐν Χριστῷ Ἰησοῦ
cj r.gs.1 d.nsm n.nsm   v.fai.3s a.asf r.gp.2 n.asf p.a   r.gsm.3 p.d n.dsf d.asn n.asn   p.d n.dsm n.dsm
1254 1609 3836 2536   4444   4246 7007 5970 2848   899   1877 1518 3836 4458   1877 5986   2652

4:10 Ἐχάρην δὲ ἐν κυρίῳ μεγάλως ὅτι ἤδη ποτὲ ἀνεθάλετε τὸ ὑπὲρ ἐμοῦ φρονεῖν, ἐφ᾽ ᾧ καὶ ἐφρονεῖτε, ἠκαιρεῖσθε δέ. **11** οὐχ ὅτι καθ᾽ ὑστέρησιν λέγω, ἐγὼ γὰρ ἔμαθον ἐν οἷς εἰμι αὐτάρκης εἶναι. **12** οἶδα καὶ ταπεινοῦσθαι, οἶδα καὶ περισσεύειν· ἐν παντὶ καὶ ἐν πᾶσιν μεμύημαι, καὶ χορτάζεσθαι καὶ πεινᾶν καὶ περισσεύειν καὶ ὑστερεῖσθαι· **13** πάντα ἰσχύω ἐν τῷ ἐνδυναμοῦντί με ¶ **14** πλὴν καλῶς ἐποιήσατε συγκοινωνήσαντές μου τῇ θλίψει. **15** Οἴδατε δὲ καὶ ὑμεῖς, Φιλιππήσιοι, ὅτι ἐν ἀρχῇ τοῦ εὐαγγελίου, ὅτε ἐξῆλθον ἀπὸ Μακεδονίας, οὐδεμία μοι ἐκκλησία ἐκοινώνησεν εἰς λόγον δόσεως καὶ λήμψεως εἰ μὴ ὑμεῖς μόνοι, **16** ὅτι καὶ ἐν Θεσσαλονίκῃ καὶ ἅπαξ καὶ δὶς εἰς τὴν χρείαν μοι ἐπέμψατε. **17** οὐχ ὅτι ἐπιζητῶ τὸ δόμα, ἀλλὰ ἐπιζητῶ τὸν καρπὸν τὸν πλεονάζοντα εἰς λόγον ὑμῶν. **18** ἀπέχω δὲ πάντα καὶ περισσεύω· πεπλήρωμαι δεξάμενος παρὰ Ἐπαφροδίτου τὰ παρ᾽ ὑμῶν, ὀσμὴν εὐωδίας, θυσίαν δεκτήν, εὐάρεστον τῷ θεῷ. **19** ὁ δὲ θεός μου πληρώσει πᾶσαν χρείαν ὑμῶν κατὰ τὸ πλοῦτος αὐτοῦ ἐν

20

To our	God	and	Father	be	glory	*for ever*	*and ever.*	Amen.
δὲ → ἡμῶν	‚τῷ‚ θεῷ‚	καὶ	πατρὶ	‚ἡ	δόξα	εἰς ‚τοὺς αἰῶνας‚	‚τῶν αἰώνων‚	ἀμήν
cj r.gp.1	d.dsm n.dsm	cj	n.dsm	d.nsf	n.nsf	p.a d.apm n.apm	d.gpm n.gpm	pl
1254 2536 7005	3836 2536	2779	4252	3836	1518	1650 3836 172	3836 172	297

Final Greetings

4:21

Greet	all	the	saints	in	Christ	Jesus.	The	brothers	who are	with	me	send greetings.	**22**	All	the
Ἀσπάσασθε	πάντα		ἅγιον	ἐν	Χριστῷ	Ἰησοῦ.	οἱ	ἀδελφοί		σὺν	ἐμοὶ →	ἀσπάζονται ὑμᾶς		πάντες	οἱ
v.amm.2p	a.asm		a.asm	p.d	n.dsm	n.dsm	d.npm	n.npm		p.d	r.ds.1	v.pmi.3p r.ap.2		a.npm	d.npm
832	4246		41	1877	5986	2652	3836	81		5250	1609	832 7007		4246	3836

saints	send you	greetings,		especially	those who	belong to	Caesar's	household.	¶	**23**	The	grace	of the	Lord
ἅγιοι	→ ὑμᾶς	ἀσπάζονται	δὲ	μάλιστα	οἱ	ἐκ ←	← Καίσαρος	‚τῆς οἰκίας‚			Ἡ	χάρις	→ τοῦ	κυρίου
a.npm	r.ap.2	v.pmi.3p	cj	adv.s	d.npm	p.g	n.gsm	d.gsf n.gsf			d.nsf	n.nsf	d.gsm	n.gsm
41	832	7007	1254	3436	3836	1666	2790	3836 3864			3836	5921	3836	3261

Jesus	Christ	be	with	your	spirit.	Amen.
Ἰησοῦ	Χριστοῦ	μετὰ	ὑμῶν	‚τοῦ πνεύματος‚		Ἀμήν.
n.gsm	n.gsm	p.g	r.gp.2	d.gsn n.gsn		
2652	5986	3552	7007	3836 4460		

δόξῃ ἐν Χριστῷ Ἰησοῦ. ¶ 20 τῷ δὲ θεῷ καὶ πατρὶ ἡμῶν ἡ δόξα εἰς τοὺς αἰῶνας τῶν αἰώνων, ἀμήν.
4:21 Ἀσπάσασθε πάντα ἅγιον ἐν Χριστῷ Ἰησοῦ. ἀσπάζονται ὑμᾶς οἱ σὺν ἐμοὶ ἀδελφοί. 22 ἀσπάζονται ὑμᾶς πάντες οἱ ἅγιοι, μάλιστα δὲ οἱ ἐκ τῆς Καίσαρος οἰκίας. ¶ 23 ἡ χάρις τοῦ κυρίου Ἰησοῦ Χριστοῦ μετὰ τοῦ πνεύματος ὑμῶν. ἀμήν.

Colossians

1:1 Paul, an apostle of Christ Jesus by the will of God, and Timothy our brother, ¶ **2** To the holy
Παῦλος ἀπόστολος → Χριστοῦ Ἰησοῦ διὰ θελήματος → θεοῦ καὶ Τιμόθεος ὁ ἀδελφὸς τοῖς ἁγίοις
n.nsm n.nsm n.gsm n.gsm p.g n.gsn n.gsm cj n.nsm d.nsm n.nsm d.dpm a.dpm
4263 693 5986 2652 1328 2525 2536 2779 5510 3836 81 3836 41

and faithful brothers in Christ at Colosse: ¶ Grace and peace to you from God our Father.
καὶ πιστοῖς ἀδελφοῖς ἐν Χριστῷ ἐν Κολοσσαῖς χάρις καὶ εἰρήνη → ὑμῖν ἀπὸ θεοῦ ἡμῶν πατρός
cj a.dpm n.dpm p.d n.dsm p.d n.dpf n.nsf cj n.nsf r.dp.2 p.g n.gsm r.gp.1 n.gsm
2779 4412 81 1877 5986 1877 3145 5921 2779 1645 7007 608 2536 7005 4252

Thanksgiving and Prayer

1:3 We always thank God, the Father of our Lord Jesus Christ, when we pray for you,
→ πάντοτε Εὐχαριστοῦμεν τῷ θεῷ πατρὶ → ἡμῶν τοῦ κυρίου Ἰησοῦ Χριστοῦ → προσευχόμενοι περὶ ὑμῶν
adv v.pai.1p d.dsm n.dsm n.dsm r.gp.1 d.gsm n.gsm n.gsm n.gsm pt.pm.npm p.g r.gp.2
2373 4121 2373 3836 2536 4252 3261 7005 3836 3261 2652 5986 4667 4309 7007

4 because we have heard of your faith in Christ Jesus and of the love you have for all the saints –
→ → → ἀκούσαντες ← ὑμῶν τὴν πίστιν ἐν Χριστῷ Ἰησοῦ καὶ τὴν ἀγάπην ἣν → ἔχετε εἰς πάντας τοὺς ἁγίους
pt.aa.npm r.gp.2 d.asf n.asf p.d n.dsm n.dsm cj d.asf n.asf r.asf v.pai.2p p.a a.apm d.apm a.apm
201 7007 3836 4411 1877 5986 2652 2779 3836 27 4005 2400 1650 4246 3836 41

5 the faith and love that spring from the hope that is stored up for you in heaven and that you have
διὰ τὴν ἐλπίδα τὴν → ἀποκειμένην ← → ὑμῖν ἐν τοῖς οὐρανοῖς ἣν → →
p.a d.asf n.asf d.asf pt.pm.asf r.dp.2 p.d d.dpm n.dpm r.asf
1328 3836 1828 3836 641 7007 1877 3836 4041 4005

already heard about in the word of truth, the gospel **6** that has come to you. All
προηκούσατε ← ἐν τῷ λόγῳ → τῆς ἀληθείας τοῦ εὐαγγελίου τοῦ → παρόντος εἰς ὑμᾶς καθὼς καὶ ἐν παντὶ
v.aai.2p p.d d.dsm n.dsm d.gsf n.gsf d.gsn n.gsn d.gsn pt.pa.gsn p.a r.ap.2 cj cj p.d a.dsm
4578 1877 3836 3364 3836 237 3836 2295 3836 4205 1650 7007 2777 2779 1877 4246

over the world this gospel is bearing fruit and growing, just as it has been doing among you since
← τῷ κόσμῳ ἐστὶν καρποφορούμενον ← καὶ αὐξανόμενον καθὼς ← καὶ ἐν ὑμῖν ἀφ'
d.dsm n.dsm v.pai.3s pt.pp.nsn cj pt.pp.nsn cj adv cj p.d r.dp.2 p.g
3836 3180 1639 2844 2779 889 2777 2779 1877 7007 608

the day you heard it and understood God's grace in all its truth. **7** You learned it from Epaphras,
ἧς ἡμέρας → ἠκούσατε καὶ ἐπέγνωτε τοῦ θεοῦ τὴν χάριν ἐν ἀληθείᾳ καθὼς → ἐμάθετε ἀπὸ Ἐπαφρᾶ
r.gsf n.gsf v.aai.2p cj v.aai.2p d.gsm n.gsm d.asf n.asf p.d n.dsf cj v.aai.2p p.g n.gsm
4005 2465 201 2779 2105 3836 2536 3836 5921 1877 237 2777 3443 608 2071

our dear fellow servant, who is a faithful minister of Christ on our behalf, **8** and who also told us
ἡμῶν ἀγαπητοῦ → συνδούλου ὅς ἐστιν πιστὸς διάκονος → τοῦ Χριστοῦ ὑπὲρ ὑμῶν ← ὁ καὶ δηλώσας ἡμῖν
r.gp.1 a.gsm n.gsm r.nsm v.pai.3s a.nsm n.nsm d.gsm n.gsm p.g r.gp.2 d.nsm adv pt.aa.nsm r.dp.1
7005 28 5281 4005 1639 4412 1356 3836 5986 5642 7007 3836 2779 1317 7005

of your love in the Spirit. ¶ **9** For this reason, since the day we heard about you, we
ὑμῶν τὴν ἀγάπην ἐν πνεύματι Διὰ τοῦτο ← ← καὶ ἀφ' ἧς ἡμέρας → ἠκούσαμεν ἡμεῖς
r.gp.2 d.asf n.asf p.d n.dsn p.a r.asn adv p.g r.gsf n.gsf v.aai.1p r.np.1
7007 3836 27 1877 4460 1328 4047 2779 608 4005 2465 201 7005

have not stopped praying for you and asking God to fill you with the knowledge of his
→ οὐ παυόμεθα προσευχόμενοι ὑπὲρ ὑμῶν καὶ αἰτούμενοι ἵνα πληρωθῆτε ← ← τὴν ἐπίγνωσιν → αὐτοῦ
pl v.pmi.1p pt.pm.npm p.g r.gp.2 cj pt.pm.npm cj v.aps.2p d.asf n.asf r.gsm.3
4264 4024 4264 4667 5642 7007 2779 160 2671 4444 3836 2106 2525 899

will through all spiritual wisdom and understanding. **10** And we pray this in order that you may live
τοῦ θελήματος ἐν πάσῃ πνευματικῇ σοφίᾳ καὶ συνέσει → → → → περιπατῆσαι
d.gsn n.gsn p.d a.dsf a.dsf n.dsf cj n.dsf f.aa
3836 2525 1877 4246 4461 5053 2779 5304 4344

a life worthy of the Lord and may please him in every way: bearing fruit in every good work,
← ἀξίως → τοῦ κυρίου ἀρεσκείαν εἰς πᾶσαν ← καρποφοροῦντες ἐν παντὶ ἀγαθῷ ἔργῳ καὶ
adv d.gsm n.gsm n.asf p.a a.asf pt.pa.npm p.d a.dsn a.dsn n.dsn cj
547 3836 3261 742 1650 4246 2844 1877 4246 19 2240 2779

1:1 Παῦλος ἀπόστολος Χριστοῦ Ἰησοῦ διὰ θελήματος θεοῦ καὶ Τιμόθεος ὁ ἀδελφὸς ¶ **2** τοῖς ἐν Κολοσσαῖς ἁγίοις καὶ πιστοῖς ἀδελφοῖς ἐν Χριστῷ, ¶ χάρις ὑμῖν καὶ εἰρήνη ἀπὸ θεοῦ πατρὸς ἡμῶν.

1:3 Εὐχαριστοῦμεν τῷ θεῷ πατρὶ τοῦ κυρίου ἡμῶν Ἰησοῦ Χριστοῦ πάντοτε περὶ ὑμῶν προσευχόμενοι, **4** ἀκούσαντες τὴν πίστιν ὑμῶν ἐν Χριστῷ Ἰησοῦ καὶ τὴν ἀγάπην ἣν ἔχετε εἰς πάντας τοὺς ἁγίους **5** διὰ τὴν ἐλπίδα τὴν ἀποκειμένην ὑμῖν ἐν τοῖς οὐρανοῖς, ἣν προηκούσατε ἐν τῷ λόγῳ τῆς ἀληθείας τοῦ εὐαγγελίου **6** τοῦ παρόντος εἰς ὑμᾶς, καθὼς καὶ ἐν παντὶ τῷ κόσμῳ ἐστὶν καρποφορούμενον καὶ αὐξανόμενον καθὼς καὶ ἐν ὑμῖν, ἀφ' ἧς ἡμέρας ἠκούσατε καὶ ἐπέγνωτε τὴν χάριν τοῦ θεοῦ ἐν ἀληθείᾳ· **7** καθὼς ἐμάθετε ἀπὸ Ἐπαφρᾶ τοῦ ἀγαπητοῦ συνδούλου ἡμῶν, ὅς ἐστιν πιστὸς ὑπὲρ ἡμῶν «ὑμῶν» διάκονος τοῦ Χριστοῦ, **8** ὁ καὶ δηλώσας ἡμῖν τὴν ὑμῶν ἀγάπην ἐν πνεύματι ¶ **9** Διὰ τοῦτο καὶ ἡμεῖς, ἀφ' ἧς ἡμέρας ἠκούσαμεν, οὐ παυόμεθα ὑπὲρ ὑμῶν προσευχόμενοι καὶ αἰτούμενοι, ἵνα πληρωθῆτε τὴν ἐπίγνωσιν τοῦ θελήματος αὐτοῦ ἐν πάσῃ σοφίᾳ καὶ συνέσει πνευματικῇ, **10** περιπατῆσαι ἀξίως τοῦ κυρίου εἰς πᾶσαν ἀρεσκείαν, ἐν παντὶ ἔργῳ ἀγαθῷ καρποφοροῦντες καὶ αὐξανόμενοι

growing in the knowledge of God, **11** being strengthened with all power according to his glorious might
αὐξανόμενοι → τῇ ἐπιγνώσει → ⌐τοῦ θεοῦ⌐ → δυναμούμενοι ἐν πάσῃ δυνάμει κατὰ ← αὐτοῦ ⌐τῆς δόξης⌐ ⌐τὸ κράτος⌐
pt.pp.npm   d.dsf n.dsf   d.gsm n.gsm   pt.pp.npm   p.d a.dsf n.dsf p.a   r.gsm.3 d.gsf n.gsf d.asn n.asn
889   3836 2106   3836 2536   1540   1877 4246 1539 2848   899 3836 1518 3836 3197

so that you may have great endurance and patience, and joyfully **12** giving thanks to the Father, who has
εἰς ← πάσαν ὑπομονὴν καὶ μακροθυμίαν Μετὰ χαρᾶς → εὐχαριστοῦντες → τῷ πατρὶ τῷ →
p.a ← a.asf n.asf cj n.asf p.g n.gsf   pt.pa.npm   d.dsm n.dsm d.dsm
1650 ← 4246 5705 2779 3429 3552 5915   2373   3836 4252 3836

qualified you to share in the inheritance of the saints in the kingdom of light. **13** For he has rescued us from
ἱκανώσαντι ὑμᾶς εἰς ⌐τὴν μερίδα⌐ → τοῦ κλήρου → τῶν ἁγίων ἐν τῷ φωτί· ὃς → ἐρρύσατο ἡμᾶς ἐκ
pt.aa.dsm r.ap.2 p.a d.asf n.asf   d.gsm n.gsm   d.gpm a.gpm p.d d.dsn   n.dsn r.nsm   v.ami.3s r.ap.1 p.g
2655 7007 1650 3836 3535   3836 3102   3836 41 1877 3836   5890 4005   4861 7005 1666

the dominion of darkness and brought us into the kingdom of the Son he loves, **14** in whom we have
τῆς ἐξουσίας → ⌐τοῦ σκότους⌐ καὶ μετέστησεν εἰς τὴν βασιλείαν → τοῦ υἱοῦ αὐτοῦ ⌐τῆς ἀγάπης⌐ ἐν ᾧ → ἔχομεν
d.gsf n.gsf   d.gsm n.gsm cj v.aai.3s p.a d.asf n.asf   d.gsm n.gsm r.gsm.3 d.gsf n.gsf p.d r.dsm → v.pai.1p
3836 2026   3836 5030 2779 3496 1650 3836 993   3836 5626 899 3836 27 1877 4005   2400

redemption, the forgiveness of sins.
⌐τὴν ἀπολύτρωσιν⌐ τὴν ἄφεσιν → ⌐τῶν ἁμαρτιῶν⌐
d.asf n.asf d.asf n.asf d.gpf n.gpf
3836 667 3836 912 3836 281

The Supremacy of Christ

1:15 He is the image of the invisible God, the firstborn over all creation. **16** For by him all things
ὅς ἐστιν εἰκὼν → τοῦ ⌐τοῦ ἀοράτου⌐ θεοῦ πρωτότοκος → πάσης κτίσεως ὅτι ἐν αὐτῷ ⌐τὰ πάντα⌐ ←
r.nsm v.pai.3s n.nsf   d.gsm d.gsm a.gsm n.gsm a.nsm   a.gsf n.gsf cj p.d r.dsm.3 d.npn a.npn
4005 1639 1635   3836 3836 548 2536 4758   4246 3232 4022 1877 899 3836 4246

were created: things in heaven and on earth, visible and invisible, whether thrones or powers or
→ ἐκτίσθη ἐν ⌐τοῖς οὐρανοῖς⌐ καὶ ἐπὶ ⌐τῆς γῆς⌐ ⌐τὰ ὁρατὰ⌐ καὶ ⌐τὰ ἀόρατα⌐ εἴτε θρόνοι εἴτε κυριότητες εἴτε
v.api.3s p.d d.dpm n.dpm cj p.g d.gsf n.gsf d.npn a.npn cj d.npn a.npn cj n.npm cj n.npf cj
3231 1877 3836 4041 2779 2093 3836 1178 3836 3971 2779 3836 548 1664 2585 1664 3262 1664

rulers or authorities; all things were created by him and for him. **17** He is before all things, and
ἀρχαὶ εἴτε ἐξουσίαι ⌐τὰ πάντα⌐ ← → ἔκτισται δι' αὐτοῦ καὶ εἰς αὐτὸν καὶ αὐτός ἐστιν πρὸ πάντων ← καὶ
n.npf cj n.npf d.npn a.npn   v.rpi.3s p.g r.gsm.3 cj p.a r.asm.3 cj r.nsm v.pai.3s p.g a.gpn ← cj
794 1664 2026 3836 4246   3231 1328 899 2779 1650 899 2779 899 1639 4574 4246 2779

in him all things hold together. **18** And he is the head of the body, the church; he is the
ἐν αὐτῷ ⌐τὰ πάντα⌐ ← συνέστηκεν ← καὶ αὐτός ἐστιν ἡ κεφαλὴ → τοῦ σώματος τῆς ἐκκλησίας ὅς ἐστιν
p.d r.dsm.3 d.npn a.npn ← v.rai.3s ← cj r.nsm v.pai.3s d.nsf n.nsf   d.gsn n.gsn d.gsf n.gsf r.nsm v.pai.3s
1877 899 3836 4246 ← 5319 ← 2779 899 1639 3836 3051   3836 5393 3836 1711 4005 1639

beginning and the firstborn from among the dead, so that in everything he might have the supremacy. **19** For
ἀρχή πρωτότοκος ἐκ ← τῶν νεκρῶν ἵνα ← ἐν πᾶσιν αὐτὸς → γένηται πρωτεύων ὅτι
n.nsf a.nsm p.g ← d.gpm a.gpm cj ← p.d a.dpn r.nsm → v.ams.3s pt.pa.nsm cj
794 4758 1666 ← 3836 3738 2671 ← 1877 4246 899   1181 4750 4022

God was pleased to have all his fullness dwell in him, **20** and through him to reconcile to himself
→ εὐδόκησεν → → πᾶν τὸ πλήρωμα κατοικῆσαι ἐν αὐτῷ καὶ δι' αὐτοῦ → ἀποκαταλλάξαι εἰς αὐτόν
v.aai.3s   a.asn d.asn n.asn f.aa p.d r.dsm.3 cj p.g r.gsm.3   f.aa p.a r.asm.3
2305 2997 2997 4246 3836 4445 2997 1877 899 2779 1328 899   639 1650 899

all things, whether things on earth or things in heaven, by making peace
⌐τὰ πάντα⌐ [δι' αὐτοῦ] εἴτε τὰ ἐπὶ ⌐τῆς γῆς⌐ εἴτε τὰ ἐν ⌐τοῖς οὐρανοῖς⌐ → εἰρηνοποιήσας
d.apn a.apn p.g r.gsm.3 cj d.apn p.g d.gsf n.gsf cj d.apn p.d d.dpm n.dpm   pt.aa.nsm
3836 4246 1328 899 1664 3836 2093 3836 1178 1664 3836 1877 3836 4041   1647

through his blood, shed on the cross. ¶ **21** Once you were alienated from God and were
διὰ αὐτοῦ ⌐τοῦ αἵματος⌐ → → τοῦ σταυροῦ Καὶ ποτε ὑμᾶς ὄντας ἀπηλλοτριωμένους καὶ
p.g r.gsm.3 d.gsn n.gsn   d.gsm n.gsm cj adv r.ap.2 pt.pa.apm pt.rp.apm   cj
1328 899 3836 135   3836 5089 2779 4537 7007 1639 558   2779

enemies in your minds because of your evil behavior. **22** But now he has reconciled you by Christ's
ἐχθροὺς → τῇ διανοίᾳ ἐν ← τοῖς ⌐τοῖς πονηροῖς⌐ ἔργοις δὲ νυνὶ → → ἀποκατήλλαξεν ἐν αὐτοῦ
a.apm   d.dsf n.dsf p.d ← d.dpn d.dpn a.dpn n.dpn cj adv   v.aai.3s p.d r.gsm.3
2398   3836 1379 1877 ← 3836 3836 4505 2240 1254 3815   639 1877 899

τῇ ἐπιγνώσει τοῦ θεοῦ, ¹¹ ἐν πάσῃ δυνάμει δυναμούμενοι κατὰ τὸ κράτος τῆς δόξης αὐτοῦ εἰς πᾶσαν ὑπομονὴν καὶ μακροθυμίαν. μετὰ χαρᾶς ¹² εὐχαριστοῦντες τῷ πατρὶ τῷ ἱκανώσαντι ὑμᾶς εἰς τὴν μερίδα τοῦ κλήρου τῶν ἁγίων ἐν τῷ φωτί· ¹³ ὃς ἐρρύσατο ἡμᾶς ἐκ τῆς ἐξουσίας τοῦ σκότους καὶ μετέστησεν εἰς τὴν βασιλείαν τοῦ υἱοῦ τῆς ἀγάπης αὐτοῦ, ¹⁴ ἐν ᾧ ἔχομεν τὴν ἀπολύτρωσιν, τὴν ἄφεσιν τῶν ἁμαρτιῶν·

¹:¹⁵ ὅς ἐστιν εἰκὼν τοῦ θεοῦ τοῦ ἀοράτου, πρωτότοκος πάσης κτίσεως, ¹⁶ ὅτι ἐν αὐτῷ ἐκτίσθη τὰ πάντα ἐν τοῖς οὐρανοῖς καὶ ἐπὶ τῆς γῆς, τὰ ὁρατὰ καὶ τὰ ἀόρατα, εἴτε θρόνοι εἴτε κυριότητες εἴτε ἀρχαὶ εἴτε ἐξουσίαι· τὰ πάντα δι' αὐτοῦ καὶ εἰς αὐτὸν ἔκτισται· ¹⁷ καὶ αὐτός ἐστιν πρὸ πάντων καὶ τὰ πάντα ἐν αὐτῷ συνέστηκεν, ¹⁸ καὶ αὐτός ἐστιν ἡ κεφαλὴ τοῦ σώματος τῆς ἐκκλησίας· ὅς ἐστιν ἀρχή, πρωτότοκος ἐκ τῶν νεκρῶν, ἵνα γένηται ἐν πᾶσιν αὐτὸς πρωτεύων. ¹⁹ ὅτι ἐν αὐτῷ εὐδόκησεν πᾶν τὸ πλήρωμα κατοικῆσαι ²⁰ καὶ δι' αὐτοῦ ἀποκαταλλάξαι τὰ πάντα εἰς αὐτόν, εἰρηνοποιήσας διὰ τοῦ αἵματος τοῦ σταυροῦ αὐτοῦ, [δι' αὐτοῦ] εἴτε τὰ ἐπὶ τῆς γῆς εἴτε τὰ ἐν τοῖς οὐρανοῖς. ¶ ²¹ Καὶ ὑμᾶς ποτε ὄντας ἀπηλλοτριωμένους καὶ ἐχθροὺς τῇ διανοίᾳ ἐν τοῖς ἔργοις τοῖς πονηροῖς, ²² νυνὶ δὲ ἀποκατήλλαξεν ἐν τῷ σώματι τῆς σαρκὸς αὐτοῦ διὰ τοῦ θανάτου παραστῆσαι ὑμᾶς

physical	body		through	death		to present	you	holy		in	his	sight,		without	blemish	and	free
⸏τῆς σαρκὸς⸐	⸏τῷ σώματι⸐	διὰ		⸏τοῦ θανάτου⸐	→	παραστῆσαι	ὑμᾶς	ἁγίους	→	αὐτοῦ	κατενώπιον	καὶ	→		ἀμώμους	καὶ	→
d.gsf n.gsf	d.dsn n.dsn	p.g		d.gsm n.gsm		f.aa	r.ap.2	a.apm		r.gsm.3	p.g	cj			a.apm	cj	
3836 4922	3836 5393	1328		3836 2505		4225	7007	41		899	2979	2779			320	2779	

from	accusation –	²³ if		you continue	in	your	faith,	established	and	firm,		not	moved		from	the	hope
→	ἀνεγκλήτους	εἴ	γε	→ ἐπιμένετε	→	τῇ	πίστει	τεθεμελιωμένοι	καὶ	ἑδραῖοι	καὶ	μὴ	μετακινούμενοι	ἀπὸ	τῆς	ἐλπίδος
→	a.apm	cj	pl	v.pai.2p		d.dsf	n.dsf	pt.rp.npm	cj	a.npm	cj	pl	pt.pp.npm	p.g	d.gsf	n.gsf
	441	1623	1145	2152		3836	4411	2530	2779	1612	2779	3590	3560	608	3836	1828

held	out	in	the gospel.	This is	the gospel	that	you heard		and	that has been	proclaimed	to	every	creature	
→	→	→	τοῦ εὐαγγελίου			οὗ	→ ἠκούσατε	τοῦ	→		κηρυχθέντος	ἐν	πάσῃ	κτίσει	τῇ
			d.gsn n.gsn			r.gsn	v.aai.2p	d.gsn			pt.ap.gsn	p.d	a.dsf	n.dsf	d.dsf
			3836 2295			4005	201	3836			3062	1877	4246	3232	3836

under heaven,		and of which	I,	Paul,		have become	a servant.		
ὑπὸ	⸏τὸν οὐρανόν⸐	→ οὗ	ἐγὼ	Παῦλος	→	ἐγενόμην	διάκονος		
p.a	d.asm n.asm	r.gsn	r.ns.1	n.nsm		v.ami.1s	n.nsm		
5679	3836 4041	4005	1609	4263		1181	1356		

Paul's Labor for the Church

^{1:24}Now	I rejoice	in	what	was suffered	for	you,	and	I fill up		in	my	flesh		what	is still	lacking
Νῦν	→ χαίρω	ἐν	τοῖς	→ παθήμασιν	ὑπὲρ	ὑμῶν	καὶ	→ ἀνταναπληρῶ	ἐν	⸏τῇ	μου	σαρκί⸐	τὰ	→	→	ὑστερήματα
adv	v.pai.1s	p.d	d.dpn	n.dpn	p.g	r.gp.2	cj	v.pai.1s	p.d	d.dsf	r.gs.1	n.dsf	d.apn			n.apn
3814	5897	1877	3836	4077	5642	7007	2779	499	1877	3836	1609	4922	3836			5729

in regard to	Christ's	afflictions,	for the sake of	his	body,	which is		the church.	²⁵	I	have become
→ →	⸏τοῦ Χριστοῦ⸐	⸏τῶν θλίψεων⸐	ὑπὲρ ←	← αὐτοῦ	⸏τοῦ σώματος⸐	ὅ	ἐστιν ἡ	ἐκκλησία	ἧς	ἐγὼ	→ ἐγενόμην
	d.gsm n.gsm	d.gpf n.gpf	p.g	r.gsm.3	d.gsn n.gsn	r.nsn	v.pai.3s d.nsf	n.nsf	r.gsf	r.ns.1	v.ami.1s
	3836 5986	3836 2568	5642	899	3836 5393	4005	1639 3836	1711	4005	1609	1181

its servant	by	the commission	God	gave		me to	present	to	you	the	word	of God		in its fullness –
διάκονος	κατὰ	τὴν οἰκονομίαν	⸏τοῦ θεοῦ⸐	⸏τὴν δοθεῖσαν⸐	μοι	→	→	εἰς	ὑμᾶς	τὸν	λόγον	⸏τοῦ θεοῦ⸐	→	πληρῶσαι
n.nsm	p.a	d.asf n.asf	d.gsm n.gsm	d.asf pt.ap.asf	r.ds.1			p.a	r.ap.2	d.asm	n.asm	d.gsm n.gsm		f.aa
1356	2848	3836 3873	3836 2536	3836 1443	1609	4444	4444	1650	7007	3836	3364	3836 2536		4444

²⁶ the	mystery	that	has been	kept	hidden		for	ages		and		generations,	but	is	now	disclosed	to the
τὸ	μυστήριον	τὸ	→	→	ἀποκεκρυμμένον	ἀπὸ	⸏τῶν αἰώνων⸐		καὶ	ἀπὸ	⸏τῶν γενεῶν⸐		δὲ	→	νῦν	ἐφανερώθη	→ τοῖς
d.asn	n.asn	d.asn			pt.rp.asn	p.g	d.gpm n.gpm		cj	p.g	d.gpf n.gpf		cj		adv	v.api.3s	d.dpm
3836	3696	3836			648	608	3836 172		2779	608	3836 1155		1254		5746	3814	5746	3836

saints.	²⁷ To them	God		has chosen	to make	known	among	the	Gentiles	the	glorious	riches	of	this
ἁγίοις	αὐτοῦ	→ οἷς	ὁ θεὸς	→	ἠθέλησεν →	→	γνωρίσαι	ἐν	τοῖς	ἔθνεσιν	τί	τὸ	⸏τῆς δόξης⸐	πλοῦτος ⸏	⸐τούτου
a.dpm	r.gsm.3	r.dpm	d.nsm n.nsm		v.aai.3s		f.aa	p.d	d.dpn	n.dpn	r.nsn	d.nsn	d.gsf n.gsf	n.nsm	r.gsn
41	899	4005	3836 2536		2527		1192	1877	3836	1620	5515	3836	3836 1518	4458	3696 4047

mystery,	which is		Christ	in	you,	the	hope	of glory.	¶	²⁸ We	proclaim		him,	admonishing	
⸏τοῦ μυστηρίου⸐	ὅ	ἐστιν	Χριστὸς	ἐν	ὑμῖν	ἡ	ἐλπὶς	→ ⸏τῆς δόξης⸐		ἡμεῖς	καταγγέλλομεν	ὃν		νουθετοῦντες	πάντα
d.gsn n.gsn	r.nsn	v.pai.3s	n.nsm	p.d	r.dp.2	d.nsf	n.nsf	d.gsf n.gsf		r.np.1	v.pai.1p	r.asm		pt.pa.npm	a.asm
3836 3696	4005	1639	5986	1877	7007	3836	1828	3836 1518		7005	2859	4005		3805	4246

	and	teaching	everyone		with	all	wisdom,	so that	we may	present		everyone		perfect	in
ἄνθρωπον	καὶ	διδάσκοντες	⸏πάντα ἄνθρωπον⸐	ἐν	πάσῃ	σοφίᾳ	ἵνα ←	→	παραστήσωμεν	⸏πάντα ἄνθρωπον⸐	τέλειον	ἐν		
n.asm	cj	pt.pa.npm	a.asm n.asm	p.d	a.dsf	n.dsf	cj		v.aas.1p	a.asm n.asm	a.asm	p.d		
476	2779	1438	4246 476	1877	4246	5053	2671		4225	4246 476	5455	1877		

Christ.	²⁹ To this end		I labor,	struggling	with	all	his	energy,		which	so powerfully	works		in	me. ¶
Χριστῷ	εἰς ὃ	→ καὶ	κοπιῶ	ἀγωνιζόμενος	κατὰ		αὐτοῦ	⸏τὴν ἐνέργειαν⸐	τὴν	→	ἐν δυνάμει	ἐνεργουμένην	ἐν	ἐμοὶ	
n.dsm	p.a r.asn	cj	v.pai.1s	pt.pm.nsm	p.a		r.gsm.3	d.asf n.asf	d.asf		p.d n.dsf	pt.pm.asf	p.d	r.ds.1	
5986	1650 4005	2779	3159	74	2848		899	3836 1918	3836		1877 1539	1919	1877	1609	

^{2:1}	I want	you	to know	how	much	I am	struggling	for	you	and for	those	at	Laodicea,	and	for all	who have
γὰρ	Θέλω	ὑμᾶς	→ εἰδέναι	ἡλίκον ←		→ ἔχω	ἀγῶνα	ὑπὲρ	ὑμῶν	καὶ	τῶν	ἐν	Λαοδικείᾳ	καὶ	ὅσοι ←	
cj	v.pai.1s	r.ap.2	f.ra	a.asm		v.pai.1s	n.asm	p.g	r.gp.2	cj	d.gpm	p.d	n.dsf	cj	r.npm	
1142	2527	7007	3857	2462		2400	74	5642	7007	2779	3836	1877	3293	2779	4012	3972

ἁγίους καὶ ἀμώμους καὶ ἀνεγκλήτους κατενώπιον αὐτοῦ, ²³ εἴ γε ἐπιμένετε τῇ πίστει τεθεμελιωμένοι καὶ ἑδραῖοι καὶ μὴ μετακινούμενοι ἀπὸ τῆς ἐλπίδος τοῦ εὐαγγελίου οὗ ἠκούσατε, τοῦ κηρυχθέντος ἐν πάσῃ κτίσει τῇ ὑπὸ τὸν οὐρανόν, οὗ ἐγενόμην ἐγὼ Παῦλος διάκονος.

^{1:24} Νῦν χαίρω ἐν τοῖς παθήμασιν ὑπὲρ ὑμῶν καὶ ἀνταναπληρῶ τὰ ὑστερήματα τῶν θλίψεων τοῦ Χριστοῦ ἐν τῇ σαρκί μου ὑπὲρ τοῦ σώματος αὐτοῦ, ὅ ἐστιν ἡ ἐκκλησία, ²⁵ ἧς ἐγενόμην ἐγὼ διάκονος κατὰ τὴν οἰκονομίαν τοῦ θεοῦ τὴν δοθεῖσάν μοι εἰς ὑμᾶς πληρῶσαι τὸν λόγον τοῦ θεοῦ, ²⁶ τὸ μυστήριον τὸ ἀποκεκρυμμένον ἀπὸ τῶν αἰώνων καὶ ἀπὸ τῶν γενεῶν— νῦν δὲ ἐφανερώθη τοῖς ἁγίοις αὐτοῦ, ²⁷ οἷς ἠθέλησεν ὁ θεὸς γνωρίσαι τί τὸ πλοῦτος τῆς δόξης τοῦ μυστηρίου τούτου ἐν τοῖς ἔθνεσιν, ὅ ἐστιν Χριστὸς ἐν ὑμῖν, ἡ ἐλπὶς τῆς δόξης· ¶ ²⁸ ὃν ἡμεῖς καταγγέλλομεν νουθετοῦντες πάντα ἄνθρωπον καὶ διδάσκοντες πάντα ἄνθρωπον ἐν πάσῃ σοφίᾳ, ἵνα παραστήσωμεν πάντα ἄνθρωπον τέλειον ἐν Χριστῷ· ²⁹ εἰς ὃ καὶ κοπιῶ ἀγωνιζόμενος κατὰ τὴν ἐνέργειαν αὐτοῦ τὴν ἐνεργουμένην ἐν ἐμοὶ ἐν δυνάμει. ^{2:1} Θέλω γὰρ ὑμᾶς εἰδέναι ἡλίκον ἀγῶνα ἔχω ὑπὲρ ὑμῶν καὶ τῶν ἐν Λαοδικείᾳ καὶ ὅσοι οὐχ ἑόρακαν τὸ πρόσωπόν μου ἐν σαρκί, ² ἵνα παρακληθῶσιν αἱ καρδίαι αὐτῶν συμβιβασθέντες ἐν ἀγάπῃ

not met   me personally.   **2** My purpose is that they may be encouraged in heart   and
οὐχ ἑόρακαν μου ‚τὸ πρόσωπον ἐν σαρκί‚   → → →   → παρακληθῶσιν ‚αἱ καρδίαι‚ αὐτῶν
pl v.rai.3p r.gs.1 d.asn n.asn p.d n.dsf   cj   v.aps.3p d.npf n.npf r.gpm.3
4024 3972 1609 3836 4725 1877 4922   2671   4151 3836 2840 899

united   in love,   so that they may have the full riches of complete   understanding, in order that
συμβιβασθέντες ἐν ἀγάπῃ καὶ εἰς ←   πᾶν πλοῦτος → ‚τῆς πληροφορίας‚ ‚τῆς συνέσεως‚ εἰς ← ←
pt.ap.npm p.d n.dsf cj p.a   a.asn n.asn d.gsf n.gsf d.gsf n.gsf p.a
5204 1877 27 2779 1650   4246 4458 3836 4443 3836 5304 1650

they may know   the mystery of God,   namely, Christ, **3** in whom are hidden all   the treasures of
→ ἐπίγνωσιν τοῦ μυστηρίου → τοῦ θεοῦ‚   Χριστοῦ ἐν ᾧ εἰσιν ἀπόκρυφοι πάντες οἱ θησαυροὶ →
n.asf d.gsn n.gsn d.gsm n.gsm   n.gsn p.d r.dsm v.pai.3p a.npm a.npm d.npm n.npm
2106 3836 3696 3836 2536   5986 1877 4005 1639 649 4246 3836 2565

wisdom   and knowledge. **4** I tell you this   so that no   one may deceive   you by fine-sounding arguments.
‚τῆς σοφίας‚ καὶ γνώσεως   → λέγω Τοῦτο ἵνα ←   μηδεὶς ←   → παραλογίζηται ὑμᾶς ἐν πιθανολογίᾳ
d.gsf n.gsf cj n.gsf   v.pai.1s r.asn cj   a.nsm   v.pms.3s r.ap.2 p.d n.dsf
3836 5053 2779 1194   3306 4047 2671   3594   4165 7007 1877 4391

5 For though   I am absent from you in body,   I am present with you in spirit   and delight   to
γὰρ εἰ   καὶ → → ἄπειμι   → ‚τῇ σαρκί‚ ἀλλὰ → εἰμι   σὺν ὑμῖν ‚τῷ πνεύματι‚ χαίρων καὶ →
cj cj   adv v.pai.1s   d.dsf n.dsf cj v.pai.1s   p.d r.dp.2 d.dsn n.dsn pt.pa.nsm cj
1142 1623   2779 583   3836 4922 247 1639   5250 7007 3836 4460 5897 2779

see   how orderly   you are and how firm   your faith   in Christ is.
βλέπων   ‚τὴν τάξιν‚ ὑμῶν καὶ   ‚τὸ στερέωμα‚ ὑμῶν ‚τῆς πίστεως‚ εἰς Χριστὸν
pt.pa.nsm   d.asf n.asf r.gp.2 cj   d.asn n.asn r.gp.2 d.gsf n.gsf p.a n.asm
1063   3836 5423 7007 2779   3836 5106 7007 3836 4411 1650 5986

Freedom From Human Regulations Through Life With Christ

2:6 So then, just as you received Christ   Jesus as Lord,   continue to live   in him, **7** rooted and
οὖν ← Ὡς ← → παρελάβετε ‚τὸν Χριστὸν‚ Ἰησοῦν ‚τὸν κύριον‚ →   → περιπατεῖτε ἐν αὐτῷ ἐρριζωμένοι καὶ
cj cj v.aai.2p d.asm n.asm n.asm d.asm n.asm   v.pam.2p p.d r.dsm.3 pt.rp.npm cj
4036 6055 4161 3836 5986 2652 3836 3261   4344 1877 899 4845 2779

built   up in him,   strengthened in the faith as   you were taught,   and overflowing with
ἐποικοδομούμενοι ← ἐν αὐτῷ καὶ βεβαιούμενοι → τῇ πίστει καθὼς → →   ἐδιδάχθητε   περισσεύοντες ἐν
pt.pp.npm p.d r.dsm.3 cj pt.pp.npm d.dsf n.dsf cj   v.api.2p   pt.pa.npm p.d
2224 1877 899 2779 1011 3836 4411 2777   1438   4355 1877

thankfulness. ¶ **8** See   to it that no one takes you captive   through hollow and deceptive
εὐχαριστίᾳ   Βλέπετε ← μή τις → ὑμᾶς ‚ἔσται ὁ συλαγωγῶν‚ διὰ   κενῆς καὶ ἀπάτης
n.dsf   v.pam.2p cj r.nsm r.ap.2 v.fmi.3s d.nsm pt.pa.nsm p.g   a.gsf cj n.gsf
2374   1063 3590 5516 5194 7007 1639 3836 5194 1328   3031 2779 573

philosophy,   which depends on human   tradition   and   the basic   principles of this world rather
‚τῆς φιλοσοφίας‚ κατὰ ← ← ‚τῶν ἀνθρώπων‚ ‚τὴν παράδοσιν‚   κατὰ τὰ στοιχεῖα ←   → τοῦ κόσμου ‚καὶ οὐ‚
d.gsf n.gsf p.a d.gpm n.gpm d.asf n.asf   p.a d.apn n.apn   d.gsm n.gsm cj pl
3836 5814 2848 3836 476 3836 4142   2848 3836 5122   3836 3180 2779 4024

than on Christ. ¶ **9** For in Christ all   the fullness of the Deity   lives in bodily   form, **10** and you have been
← κατὰ Χριστόν ὅτι ἐν αὐτῷ πᾶν τὸ πλήρωμα   τῆς θεότητος κατοικεῖ → σωματικῶς →   καὶ → →   ἐστὲ
p.a n.asm cj p.d r.dsm.3 a.nsn d.nsn n.nsn   d.gsf n.gsf v.pai.3s adv   cj   v.pai.2p
2848 5986 4022 1877 899 4246 3836 4445   3836 2540 2997 5395   2779   1639

given fullness   in Christ, who is   the head   over every power and authority. **11** In him you were also
→ πεπληρωμένοι ἐν αὐτῷ ὅς ἐστιν ἡ κεφαλὴ   πάσης ἀρχῆς καὶ ἐξουσίας Ἐν ᾧ → → καὶ
pt.rp.npm p.d r.dsm.3 r.nsm v.pai.3s d.nsf n.nsf   a.gsf n.gsf cj n.gsf p.d r.dsm   cj
4444 1877 899 4005 1639 3836 3051   4246 794 2779 2026 1877 4005 4362 4362   2779

circumcised,   in the putting off of the sinful   nature, not with a circumcision done by the hands   of
‚περιετμήθητε περιτομῇ‚ ἐν τῇ ἀπεκδύσει → τοῦ ‚τῆς σαρκός‚ σώματος   → → →   ἀχειροποιήτῳ
v.api.2p n.dsf p.d d.dsf n.dsf d.gsn d.gsf n.gsf n.gsn   a.dsf
4362 4364 1877 3836 589 3836 3836 4922 5393   942

men but with the circumcision done by Christ, **12** having been buried   with him in baptism   and
ἐν τῇ περιτομῇ → ‚τοῦ Χριστοῦ‚ →   συνταφέντες   αὐτῷ ἐν ‚τῷ βαπτισμῷ‚ καὶ
p.d d.dsf n.dsf d.gsm n.gsm   pt.ap.npm   r.dsm.3 p.d d.dsm n.dsm adv
1877 3836 4364 3836 5986   5313   899 1877 3836 968 2779

καὶ εἰς πᾶν πλοῦτος τῆς πληροφορίας τῆς συνέσεως, εἰς ἐπίγνωσιν τοῦ μυστηρίου τοῦ θεοῦ, Χριστοῦ, ³ ἐν ᾧ εἰσιν πάντες οἱ θησαυροὶ τῆς σοφίας καὶ γνώσεως ἀπόκρυφοι. ⁴ Τοῦτο λέγω, ἵνα μηδεὶς ὑμᾶς παραλογίζηται ἐν πιθανολογίᾳ. ⁵ εἰ γὰρ καὶ τῇ σαρκὶ ἄπειμι, ἀλλὰ τῷ πνεύματι σὺν ὑμῖν εἰμι, χαίρων καὶ βλέπων ὑμῶν τὴν τάξιν καὶ τὸ στερέωμα τῆς εἰς Χριστὸν πίστεως ὑμῶν.

²:⁶ Ὡς οὖν παρελάβετε τὸν Χριστὸν Ἰησοῦν τὸν κύριον, ἐν αὐτῷ περιπατεῖτε, ⁷ ἐρριζωμένοι καὶ ἐποικοδομούμενοι ἐν αὐτῷ καὶ βεβαιούμενοι τῇ πίστει καθὼς ἐδιδάχθητε, περισσεύοντες ἐν εὐχαριστίᾳ. ¶ ⁸ βλέπετε μή τις ὑμᾶς ἔσται ὁ συλαγωγῶν διὰ τῆς φιλοσοφίας καὶ κενῆς ἀπάτης κατὰ τὴν παράδοσιν τῶν ἀνθρώπων, κατὰ τὰ στοιχεῖα τοῦ κόσμου καὶ οὐ κατὰ Χριστόν· ¶ ⁹ ὅτι ἐν αὐτῷ κατοικεῖ πᾶν τὸ πλήρωμα τῆς θεότητος σωματικῶς, ¹⁰ καὶ ἐστὲ ἐν αὐτῷ πεπληρωμένοι, ὅς ἐστιν ἡ κεφαλὴ πάσης ἀρχῆς καὶ ἐξουσίας. ¹¹ ἐν ᾧ καὶ περιετμήθητε περιτομῇ ἀχειροποιήτῳ ἐν τῇ ἀπεκδύσει τοῦ σώματος τῆς σαρκός, ἐν τῇ περιτομῇ τοῦ Χριστοῦ, ¹² συνταφέντες αὐτῷ ἐν τῷ βαπτισμῷ, ἐν ᾧ καὶ συνηγέρθητε διὰ τῆς πίστεως τῆς ἐνεργείας τοῦ θεοῦ τοῦ ἐγείραντος

raised　with him　through　your　faith　in the　power　of God,　who raised　him　from the dead. ¶
συνηγέρθητε ἐν ᾧ διὰ τῆς πίστεως → τῆς ἐνεργείας ⌐τοῦ θεοῦ⌐ τοῦ ἐγείραντος αὐτὸν ἐκ νεκρῶν
v.api.2p　p.d　r.dsm　p.g　d.gsf　n.gsf　d.gsf　n.gsf　d.gsm　n.gsm　d.gsm　pt.aa.gsm　r.asm.3　p.g　a.gpm
5283　1877　4005　1328　3836　4411　3836　1918　3836　2536　3836　1586　899　1666　3738

13 When　you　were　dead　in　your　sins　and in the　uncircumcision　of　your　sinful　nature,　God made
καὶ → ὑμᾶς ὄντας νεκροὺς ἐν τοῖς παραπτώμασιν καὶ → τῇ ἀκροβυστίᾳ → ὑμῶν ⌐τῆς σαρκὸς⌐ ←　→
cj　r.ap.2　pt.pa.apm　a.apm　p.d　d.dpn　n.dpn　cj　d.dsf　n.dsf　r.gp.2　d.gsf　n.gsf
2779　1639　7007　1639　3738　1877　3836　4183　2779　3836　213　4922　7007　3836　4922　5188

you　alive　with　Christ.　He forgave　us　all　our　sins,　**14** having　canceled　the　written　code, with
ὑμᾶς συνεζωοποίησεν σὺν αὐτῷ χαρισάμενος ἡμῖν πάντα τὰ παραπτώματα → ἐξαλείψας τὸ χειρόγραφον ←　→
r.ap.2　v.aai.3s　p.d　r.dsm.3　pt.am.nsm　r.dp.1　a.apn　d.apn　n.apn　pt.aa.nsm　d.asn　n.asn
7007　5188　5250　899　5919　7005　4246　3836　4183　1981　3836　5934

its　regulations,　that　was　against　us　and that stood　opposed　to us;　he took　it　away,　nailing　it
τοῖς δόγμασιν ὃ ἦν καθ᾽ ἡμῶν → ὑπεναντίον → ἡμῖν καὶ → ἦρκεν αὐτὸ ἐκ τοῦ μέσου προσηλώσας αὐτὸ
d.dpn　n.dpn　r.nsn　v.iai.3s　p.g　r.gp.1　a.nsn　r.dp.1　cj　v.rai.3s　r.asn.3　p.g　d.gsn　n.gsn　pt.aa.nsm　r.asn.3
3836　1504　4005　1639　2848　7005　5641　7005　2779　149　899　1666　3836　3545　4669　899

to the cross.　**15** And having　disarmed　the　powers　and authorities,　he made a　public　spectacle　of them,
→ τῷ σταυρῷ → ἀπεκδυσάμενος τὰς ἀρχὰς καὶ ⌐τὰς ἐξουσίας⌐ → → ⌐ἐν παρρησίᾳ⌐ ἐδειγμάτισεν
d.dsm　n.dsm　pt.am.nsm　d.apf　n.apf　cj　d.apf　n.apf　p.d　n.dsf　v.aai.3s
3836　5089　588　3836　794　2779　3836　2026　1258　1258　1258　1877　4244　1258

triumphing　over them　by the cross. ¶　**16** Therefore	do	not let	anyone	judge	you	by	what you	eat	or
θριαμβεύσας ← αὐτοὺς ἐν αὐτῷ οὖν → Μὴ τις κρινέτω ὑμᾶς ἐν → βρώσει καὶ ἐν
pt.aa.nsm　r.apm.3　p.d　r.dsm.3　cj　pl　r.nsm　v.pam.3s　r.ap.2　p.d　n.dsf　cj　p.d
2581　899　1877　899　4036　3590　3212　5516　3212　7007　1877　1111　2779　1877

drink,　or　with	regard	to a	religious	festival,	a New	Moon	celebration	or a	Sabbath	day.	**17** These	are	a
πόσει ἢ ἐν μέρει ← → ἑορτῆς ἢ νεομηνίας ← ← ἢ σαββάτων ← ἅ ἐστιν
n.dsf　cj　p.d　n.dsf　n.gsf　cj　n.gsf　cj　n.gpn　r.npn　v.pai.3s
4530　2445　1877　3538　2038　2445　3741　2445　4879　4005　1639

shadow　of the	things	that	were	to	come;	the	reality,	however,	is	found in	Christ.	**18** Do	not	let
σκιὰ → τῶν → → → μελλόντων δὲ τὸ σῶμα ⌐τοῦ Χριστοῦ⌐ μηδεὶς ←
n.nsf　d.gpn　pt.pa.gpn　cj　d.nsn　n.nsn　d.gsm　n.gsm　a.nsm
5014　3836　3516　1254　3836　5393　3836　5986　2857　3594　2857

anyone	who	delights	in	false	humility	and the	worship	of angels	disqualify	you	for the prize.	Such a
← → θέλων ἐν ταπεινοφροσύνῃ καὶ θρησκείᾳ → ⌐τῶν ἀγγέλων⌐ καταβραβευέτω ὑμᾶς ← ← →
pt.pa.nsm　p.d　n.dsf　cj　n.dsf　d.gpm　n.gpm　v.pam.3s　r.ap.2
3594　2527　1877　5425　2779　2579　3836　34　7007　2857　2857　2857

person	goes	into	great	detail	about	what	he has	seen,	and	his	unspiritual	mind	puffs	him up with
→ → → → ἐμβατεύων ← ἃ → ἑόρακεν ὑπὸ αὐτοῦ ⌐τῆς σαρκὸς⌐ ⌐τοῦ νοὸς⌐ φυσιούμενος → →
pt.pa.nsm　r.apn　v.rai.3s　p.g　r.gsm.3　d.gsf　n.gsf　d.gsm　n.gsm　pt.pp.nsm
1836　4005　3972　5679　899　3836　4922　3836　3808　5881

idle	notions.	**19** He	has	lost	connection	with the	Head,	from	whom	the	whole	body,	supported	and
εἰκῇ καὶ → → οὐ κρατῶν ← τὴν κεφαλήν ἐξ οὗ τὸ πᾶν σῶμα ἐπιχορηγούμενον καὶ
adv　cj　pl　pt.pa.nsm　d.asf　n.asf　p.g　r.gsn　d.nsn　a.nsn　n.nsn　pt.pp.nsn　cj
1632　2779　3195　3195　4024　3195　3836　3051　1666　4005　3836　4246　5393　2220　2779

held	together	by	its	ligaments	and	sinews,	grows	as	God	causes	it to grow.	¶	**20** Since	you
συμβιβαζόμενον ← διὰ τῶν ἁφῶν καὶ συνδέσμων αὔξει ⌐τοῦ θεοῦ⌐ ⌐τὴν αὔξησιν⌐ Εἰ →
pt.pp.nsn　p.g　d.gpf　n.gpf　cj　n.gpm　v.pai.3s　d.gsm　n.gsm　d.asf　n.asf　cj
5204　1328　3836　913　2779　5278　891　3836　2536　3836　890　1623

died	with	Christ	to	the	basic	principles	of this	world,	why,	as	though	you	still	belonged	to it,	do you
ἀπεθάνετε σὺν Χριστῷ ἀπὸ τῶν στοιχείων → τοῦ κόσμου τί ὡς → → ζῶντες ἐν κόσμῳ
v.aai.2p　p.d　n.dsm　p.g　d.gpn　n.gpn　d.gsm　n.gsm　r.asn　pl　pt.pa.npm　p.d　n.dsm
633　5250　5986　608　3836　5122　3836　3180　5515　6055　2409　1877　3180

submit	to its rules:	**21** "Do	not	handle!	Do	not	taste!	Do	not	touch!"?	**22** These	are	all	destined	to	perish with
δογματίζεσθε ← → μὴ ἅψῃ → μηδὲ γεύσῃ → μηδὲ θίγῃς → ἅ ἐστιν πάντα → εἰς φθορὰν →
v.ppi.2p　pl　v.ams.2s　cj　v.ams.2s　cj　v.aas.2s　r.npn　v.pai.3s　a.npn　p.a　n.asf
1505　3590　721　1174　3593　1174　2566　3593　2566　4005　1639　4246　1650　5785

use,	because	they	are	based	on	human	commands	and	teachings.	**23** Such	regulations	indeed
⌐τῇ ἀποχρήσει⌐ κατὰ → ← ⌐τῶν ἀνθρώπων⌐ ⌐τὰ ἐντάλματα⌐ καὶ διδασκαλίας ἅτινα ← ἐστιν μέν
d.dsf　n.dsf　p.a　d.gpm　n.gpm　d.apn　n.apn　cj　n.apf　r.npn　v.pai.3s　pl
3836　712　2848　3836　476　3836　1945　2779　1436　4015　1639　3525

αὐτὸν ἐκ νεκρῶν· ¶ ¹³ καὶ ὑμᾶς νεκροὺς ὄντας [ἐν] τοῖς παραπτώμασιν καὶ τῇ ἀκροβυστίᾳ τῆς σαρκὸς ὑμῶν, συνεζωοποίησεν ὑμᾶς σὺν αὐτῷ, χαρισάμενος ἡμῖν πάντα τὰ παραπτώματα. ¹⁴ ἐξαλείψας τὸ καθ᾽ ἡμῶν χειρόγραφον τοῖς δόγμασιν ὃ ἦν ὑπεναντίον ἡμῖν, καὶ αὐτὸ ἦρκεν ἐκ τοῦ μέσου προσηλώσας αὐτὸ τῷ σταυρῷ· ¹⁵ ἀπεκδυσάμενος τὰς ἀρχὰς καὶ τὰς ἐξουσίας ἐδειγμάτισεν ἐν παρρησίᾳ, θριαμβεύσας αὐτοὺς ἐν αὐτῷ. ¹⁶ Μὴ οὖν τις ὑμᾶς κρινέτω ἐν βρώσει καὶ ἐν πόσει ἢ ἐν μέρει ἑορτῆς ἢ νεομηνίας ἢ σαββάτων· ¹⁷ ἅ ἐστιν σκιὰ τῶν μελλόντων, τὸ δὲ σῶμα τοῦ Χριστοῦ. ¹⁸ μηδεὶς ὑμᾶς καταβραβευέτω θέλων ἐν ταπεινοφροσύνῃ καὶ θρησκείᾳ τῶν ἀγγέλων, ἃ ἑόρακεν ἐμβατεύων, εἰκῇ φυσιούμενος ὑπὸ τοῦ νοὸς τῆς σαρκὸς αὐτοῦ, ¹⁹ καὶ οὐ κρατῶν τὴν κεφαλήν, ἐξ οὗ πᾶν τὸ σῶμα διὰ τῶν ἁφῶν καὶ συνδέσμων ἐπιχορηγούμενον καὶ συμβιβαζόμενον αὔξει τὴν αὔξησιν τοῦ θεοῦ. ¶ ²⁰ Εἰ ἀπεθάνετε σὺν Χριστῷ ἀπὸ τῶν στοιχείων τοῦ κόσμου, τί ὡς ζῶντες ἐν κόσμῳ δογματίζεσθε; ²¹ Μὴ ἅψῃ μηδὲ γεύσῃ μηδὲ θίγῃς, ²² ἅ ἐστιν πάντα εἰς φθορὰν τῇ ἀποχρήσει, κατὰ τὰ ἐντάλματα καὶ διδασκαλίας τῶν

have an appearance of wisdom, with their self-imposed worship, their false humility and their harsh
ἔχοντα λόγον → σοφίας ἐν ἐθελοθρησκίᾳ ← καὶ → ταπεινοφροσύνῃ καὶ ἀφειδίᾳ
pt.pa.npn n.asm n.gsf p.d n.dsf cj n.dsf cj n.dsf
2400 3364 5053 1877 1615 2779 5425 2779 910

treatment of the body, but they lack any value in restraining sensual indulgence.
← → σώματος οὐκ ἐν τινι τιμῇ πρὸς ⌐τῆς σαρκός⌐ πλησμονὴν
n.gsn pl p.d r.dsf n.dsf p.a d.gsf n.gsf n.asf
5393 4024 1877 5516 5507 4639 3836 4922 4447

Rules for Holy Living

3:1 Since, then, you have been raised with Christ, set your hearts on things above, where Christ
Εἰ οὖν → → → συνηγέρθητε ← ⌐τῷ Χριστῷ⌐ → ζητεῖτε τὰ ἄνω οὗ ὁ Χριστός⌐
cj cj v.api.2p d.dsm n.dsm v.pam.2p d.apn adv adv d.nsm n.nsm
1623 4036 5283 3836 5986 2426 3836 539 4023 3836 5986

is seated at the right hand of God. **2** Set your minds on things above, not on earthly things. **3** For you
ἐστιν καθήμενος ἐν δεξιᾷ → ⌐τοῦ θεοῦ⌐ φρονεῖτε ← τὰ ἄνω μὴ ⌐ἐπὶ τῆς γῆς⌐ τὰ γὰρ →
v.pai.3s pt.pm.nsm p.d a.dsf d.gsn n.gsn v.pam.2p d.apn adv pl p.d d.gsf n.gsf d.apn cj
1639 2764 1877 1288 3836 2536 5858 3836 539 3590 5858 2093 3836 1178 3836 1142

died, and your life is now hidden with Christ in God. **4** When Christ, who is your life,
ἀπεθάνετε καὶ ὑμῶν ἡ ζωὴ → κέκρυπται σὺν ⌐τῷ Χριστῷ⌐ ἐν ⌐τῷ θεῷ⌐ ὅταν ὁ Χριστός⌐ ⌐ὑμῶν ἡ ζωή⌐
v.aai.2p cj r.gp.2 d.nsf n.nsf v.rpi.3s p.d d.dsm n.dsm p.d d.dsm n.dsm cj d.nsm n.nsm r.gp.2 d.nsf n.nsf
633 2779 7007 3836 2437 3221 5250 3836 5986 1877 3836 2536 4020 3836 5986 7007 3836 2437

appears, then you also will appear with him in glory. ¶ **5** Put to death, therefore, whatever belongs
φανερωθῇ τότε ὑμεῖς καὶ → φανερωθήσεσθε σὺν αὐτῷ ἐν δόξῃ Νεκρώσατε οὖν ⌐τὰ μέλη⌐ τὰ ἐπὶ
v.aps.3s adv r.np.2 adv v.fpi.2p p.d r.dsm.3 p.d n.dsf v.aam.2p cj d.apn n.apn d.apn p.g
5746 5538 7007 2779 5746 5250 899 1877 1518 3739 4036 3836 3517 3836 2093

to your earthly nature: sexual immorality, impurity, lust, evil desires and greed, which is idolatry.
← ⌐τῆς γῆς⌐ ← πορνείαν ← ἀκαθαρσίαν πάθος κακήν ἐπιθυμίαν καὶ ⌐τὴν πλεονεξίαν⌐ ἥτις ἐστὶν εἰδωλολατρία
d.gsf n.gsf n.asf n.asf n.asn a.asf n.asf cj d.asf n.asf r.nsf v.pai.3s n.nsf
3836 1178 4518 174 4079 2805 2123 2779 3836 4432 4015 1639 1630

6 Because of these, the wrath of God is coming. **7** You usedto walkin
δι' ← ἃ ἡ ὀργὴ → ⌐τοῦ θεοῦ⌐ → ἔρχεται [ἐπὶ τοὺς υἱοὺς τῆς ἀπειθείας] ὑμεῖςκαὶποτε→ περιεπατήσατεἐν
p.a r.apn d.nsf n.nsf d.gsm n.gsm v.pmi.3s p.a d.apm n.apm d.gsf n.gsf r.np.2cj adv v.aai.2pp.d
1328 4005 3836 3973 3836 2536 2262 2093 3836 5626 3836 577 70072779 4537 4344 1877

these ways, in the life you once lived. **8** But now you must rid yourselves of all such things as
οἷς ← ὅτε ἐν τούτοις → ἐζῆτε δὲ νυνὶ ὑμεῖς καὶ → ἀπόθεσθε ← ← ⌐τὰ πάντα⌐ ←
r.dpn cj p.d r.dpn v.iai.2p cj adv r.np.2 adv v.amm.2p d.apn a.apn
4005 4021 1877 4047 2409 1254 3815 7007 2779 700 3836 4246

these: anger, rage, malice, slander, and filthy language from your lips. **9** Do not lie to each
ὀργήν θυμόν κακίαν βλασφημίαν αἰσχρολογίαν ← ἐκ ὑμῶν ⌐τοῦ στόματος⌐ μὴ ψεύδεσθε εἰς ἀλλήλους
n.asf n.asm n.asf n.asf n.asf p.g r.gp.2 d.gsn n.gsn pl v.pmm.2p p.a r.apm
3973 2596 2798 1060 155 1666 7007 3836 5125 6017 3590 6017 1650 253

other, since you have taken off your old self with its practices **10** and have put on the
← → → ἀπεκδυσάμενοι ← τὸν παλαιὸν ἄνθρωπον σὺν αὐτοῦ ⌐ταῖς πράξεσιν⌐ καὶ → ἐνδυσάμενοι ← τὸν
pt.am.npm d.asm a.asm n.asm p.d r.gsm.3 d.dpf n.dpf cj pt.am.npm d.asm
588 3836 4094 476 5250 899 3836 4552 2779 1907 3836

new self, which is being renewed in knowledge in the image of its Creator. **11** Here there is no
νέον τὸν → ἀνακαινούμενον εἰς ἐπίγνωσιν κατ' εἰκόνα → αὐτόν ⌐τοῦ κτίσαντος⌐ ὅπου → ἔνι οὐ
a.asm d.asm pt.pp.asm p.a n.asf p.a n.asf r.asm.3 d.gsm pt.aa.gsm adv v.pai.3s pl
3742 3836 363 1650 2106 2848 1635 3231 899 3836 3231 3963 1928 4024

Greek or Jew, circumcised or uncircumcised, barbarian, Scythian, slave or free, but Christ is all,
Ἕλλην καὶ Ἰουδαῖος περιτομὴ καὶ ἀκροβυστία βάρβαρος Σκύθης δοῦλος ἐλεύθερος ἀλλὰ Χριστός ⌐τὰ πάντα⌐
n.nsm cj a.nsm n.nsf cj n.nsf n.nsm n.nsm n.nsm a.nsm cj n.nsm d.npn a.npn
1818 2779 2681 4364 2779 213 975 5033 1529 1801 247 5986 3836 4246

and is in all. ¶ **12** Therefore, as God's chosen people, holy and dearly loved, clothe yourselves with
καὶ ἐν πᾶσιν οὖν ὡς ⌐τοῦ θεοῦ⌐ ἐκλεκτοὶ ← ἅγιοι καὶ → ἠγαπημένοι Ἐνδύσασθε ← ←
cj p.d a.dpn cj pl d.gsm n.gsm a.npm a.npm cj pt.rp.npm v.amm.2p
2779 1877 4246 4036 6055 3836 2536 1723 41 2779 26 1907

ἀνθρώπων, ²³ ἅτινά ἐστιν λόγον μὲν ἔχοντα σοφίας ἐν ἐθελοθρησκίᾳ καὶ ταπεινοφροσύνῃ [καὶ] ἀφειδίᾳ σώματος, οὐκ ἐν τιμῇ τινι πρὸς πλησμονὴν τῆς σαρκός.

³:¹ Εἰ οὖν συνηγέρθητε τῷ Χριστῷ, τὰ ἄνω ζητεῖτε, οὗ ὁ Χριστός ἐστιν ἐν δεξιᾷ τοῦ θεοῦ καθήμενος· ² τὰ ἄνω φρονεῖτε, μὴ τὰ ἐπὶ τῆς γῆς. ³ ἀπεθάνετε γὰρ καὶ ἡ ζωὴ ὑμῶν κέκρυπται σὺν τῷ Χριστῷ ἐν τῷ θεῷ· ⁴ ὅταν ὁ Χριστὸς φανερωθῇ, ἡ ζωὴ ὑμῶν, τότε καὶ ὑμεῖς σὺν αὐτῷ φανερωθήσεσθε ἐν δόξῃ. ¶ ⁵ Νεκρώσατε οὖν τὰ μέλη ὑμῶν τὰ ἐπὶ τῆς γῆς, πορνείαν ἀκαθαρσίαν πάθος ἐπιθυμίαν κακήν, καὶ τὴν πλεονεξίαν, ἥτις ἐστὶν εἰδωλολατρία, ⁶ δι' ἃ ἔρχεται ἡ ὀργὴ τοῦ θεοῦ [ἐπὶ τοὺς υἱοὺς τῆς ἀπειθείας]. ⁷ ἐν οἷς καὶ ὑμεῖς περιεπατήσατέ ποτε, ὅτε ἐζῆτε ἐν τούτοις· ⁸ νυνὶ δὲ ἀπόθεσθε καὶ ὑμεῖς τὰ πάντα, ὀργήν, θυμόν, κακίαν, βλασφημίαν, αἰσχρολογίαν ἐκ τοῦ στόματος ὑμῶν· ⁹ μὴ ψεύδεσθε εἰς ἀλλήλους, ἀπεκδυσάμενοι τὸν παλαιὸν ἄνθρωπον σὺν ταῖς πράξεσιν αὐτοῦ ¹⁰ καὶ ἐνδυσάμενοι τὸν νέον τὸν ἀνακαινούμενον εἰς ἐπίγνωσιν κατ' εἰκόνα τοῦ κτίσαντος αὐτόν, ¹¹ ὅπου οὐκ ἔνι Ἕλλην καὶ Ἰουδαῖος, περιτομὴ καὶ ἀκροβυστία, βάρβαρος, Σκύθης, δοῦλος, ἐλεύθερος, ἀλλὰ [τὰ] πάντα καὶ ἐν πᾶσιν Χριστός ¶ ¹² Ἐνδύσασθε οὖν, ὡς ἐκλεκτοὶ τοῦ θεοῦ ἅγιοι καὶ ἠγαπημένοι, σπλάγχνα οἰκτιρμοῦ χρηστότητα ταπεινοφροσύνην

compassion,	kindness,	humility,		gentleness	and patience.	**13** Bear	with each	other	and	forgive
⸤σπλάγχνα οἰκτιρμοῦ⸥	χρηστότητα	ταπεινοφροσύνην		πραΰτητα	μακροθυμίαν	ἀνεχόμενοι ←	ἀλλήλων ←		καὶ	χαριζόμενοι
n.apn	n.gsm	n.asf	n.asf		n.asf	n.asf	pt.pm.npm	r.gpm		cj	pt.pm.npm
5073	3880	5983	5425		4559	3429	462	253		2779	5919

	whatever	grievances	you may have		against	one another.	Forgive	as		the Lord	forgave	you.
ἐάν	τις	μομφήν →	→	ἔχῃ	πρός	τινα ἑαυτοῖς		καθὼς	καὶ ὁ	κύριος	ἐχαρίσατο	ὑμῖν οὕτως καὶ
cj	r.nsm	n.asf		v.pas.3s	p.a	r.asm r.dpm.2		adv	adv d.nsm	n.nsm	v.ami.3s	r.dp.2 adv adv
1569	5516	3664		2400	4639	5516 1571		2777	2779 3836	3261	5919	7007 4048 2779

14 And over	all	these	virtues put on love,		which	binds	them all together in	perfect	unity. ¶
ὑμεῖς δὲ ἐπὶ	πᾶσιν	τούτοις	⸤τὴν ἀγάπην⸥	ὅ	ἐστιν σύνδεσμος	← →	⸤τῆς τελειότητος⸥
r.np.2 cj p.d	a.dpn	r.dpn	d.asf n.asf	r.nsn	v.pai.3s n.nsm		d.gsf n.gsf
7007 1254 2093	4246	4047	3836 27	4005	1639 5278		3836 5456

15	Let	the	peace	of Christ	rule	in	your hearts,			since as members of	one	body		you were
καὶ →	ἡ	εἰρήνη →	⸤τοῦ Χριστοῦ⸥	βραβευέτω ἐν	ὑμῶν ⸤ταῖς καρδίαις⸥				ἐν ἑνὶ	σώματι καὶ →	→
cj	d.nsf	n.nsf	d.gsm d.gsm	v.pam.3s p.d	r.gp.2 d.dpf n.dpf				p.d a.dsn	n.dsn adv	
2779	3836	1645	3836 5986	1093 1877	7007 3836 2840				1877 1651	5393 2779	

called	to peace.	And be	thankful.	**16** Let	the word	of Christ		dwell	in	you	richly	as you teach		and
ἐκλήθητε	εἰς ἥν	καὶ	γίνεσθε εὐχάριστοι	→	Ὁ λόγος	⸤τοῦ Χριστοῦ⸥		ἐνοικείτω	ἐν	ὑμῖν	πλουσίως	→	→	διδάσκοντες καὶ
v.api.2p	p.a r.asf	cj	v.pmm.2p a.npm		d.nsm n.nsm	d.gsm d.gsm		v.pam.3s	p.d	r.dp.2	adv			pt.pa.npm cj
2813	1650 4005	2779	1181 2375		1940 3836 3364	3836 5986		1940	1877	7007	4455			1438 2779

admonish	one	another with	all	wisdom,	and as you sing	psalms,	hymns	and spiritual	songs	with
νουθετοῦντες	ἑαυτοὺς ←	ἐν	πάσῃ σοφίᾳ		→ →	ᾄδοντες ψαλμοῖς	ὕμνοις	πνευματικαῖς	ᾠδαῖς	ἐν
pt.pa.npm	r.apm.2	p.d	a.dsf n.dsf			pt.pa.npm n.dpm	n.dpm	a.dpf	n.dpf	p.d
3805	1571	1877	4246 5053			106 6011	5631	4461	6046	1877

gratitude	in	your hearts		to God.	**17** And whatever		you do,	whether in	word or		deed, do it
⸤τῇ χάριτι⸥	ἐν	ὑμῶν ⸤ταῖς καρδίαις⸥	→	⸤τῷ θεῷ⸥	καὶ ⸤πᾶν ὅ	τι	ἐὰν⸥ →	ποιῆτε	ἐν λόγῳ	ἢ	ἐν ἔργῳ
d.dsf n.dsf	p.d	r.gp.2 d.dpf n.dpf		d.dsm n.dsm	cj a.asn r.asn	r.asn	pl	v.pas.2p	p.d n.dsm	cj	p.d n.dsn
3836 5921	1877	7007 3836 2840		3836 2536	2779 4246 4005	5516	1569	4472	1877 3364	2445	1877 2240

all	in the name	of the Lord	Jesus,	giving thanks		to God		the Father	through him.
πάντα ἐν	ὀνόματι →	κυρίου	Ἰησοῦ	εὐχαριστοῦντες	→	⸤τῷ θεῷ⸥		πατρὶ	δι᾽ αὐτοῦ.
a.apn p.d	n.dsn	n.gsm	n.gsm	pt.pa.npm		d.dsm n.dsm		n.dsm	p.g r.gsm.3
4246 1877	3950	3261	2652	2373		3836 2536		4252	1328 899

Rules for Christian Households

3:18 Wives,		submit	to	your husbands,	as	is fitting	in	the Lord.	¶	**19** Husbands,		love	your	wives
⸤Αἱ γυναῖκες⸥		ὑποτάσσεσθε →	τοῖς	ἀνδράσιν	ὡς	→ ἀνῆκεν	ἐν	κυρίῳ		⸤Οἱ ἄνδρες⸥		ἀγαπᾶτε	τὰς	γυναῖκας
d.vpf n.vpf		v.ppm.2p	d.dpm	n.dpm	cj	v.iai.3s	p.d	n.dsm		d.vpm n.vpm		v.pam.2p	d.apf	n.apf
3836 1222		5718	3836	467	6055	465	1877	3261		3836 467		26	3836	1222

and	do not be harsh		with them.	¶	**20** Children,		obey	your parents	in	everything,	for this
καὶ →	μὴ → πικραίνεσθε	πρὸς	αὐτάς		⸤Τὰ τέκνα⸥		ὑπακούετε	τοῖς γονεῦσιν	κατὰ	πάντα	γὰρ τοῦτο
cj	pl v.ppm.2p	p.a	r.apf.3		d.vpn n.vpn		v.pam.2p	d.dpm n.dpm	p.a	a.apn	cj r.nsn
2779 4393	3590 4393	4639	899		3836 5451		5634	3836 1204	2848	4246	1142 4047

pleases	the Lord.	¶	**21** Fathers,		do not	embitter	your children,	or		they will become discouraged. ¶
⸤εὐάρεστον ἐστιν⸥	ἐν κυρίῳ		⸤Οἱ πατέρες⸥	→	μὴ	ἐρεθίζετε	ὑμῶν ⸤τὰ τέκνα⸥	ἵνα	μὴ	→ ἀθυμῶσιν
a.nsn v.pai.3s	p.d n.dsm		d.vpm n.vpm		pl	v.pam.2p	r.gp.2 d.apn n.apn	cj	pl	v.pas.3p
2298 1639	1877 3261		3836 4252		2241	3590 2241	7007 3836 5451	2671	3590	126

22 Slaves,		obey	your	earthly		masters	in	everything; and do it,	not	only when	their	eye		is on
⸤Οἱ δοῦλοι⸥		ὑπακούετε	τοῖς	⸤κατὰ σάρκα⸥		κυρίοις	κατὰ	πάντα	μὴ		ἐν	→	ὀφθαλμοδουλίᾳ ←	←
d.vpm n.vpm		v.pam.2p	d.dpm	p.a n.asf		n.dpm	p.a	a.apn	pl		p.d		n.dsf	
3836 1529		5634	3836	2848 4922		3261	2848	4246	3590		1877		4056	

you	and to win their favor,		but with	sincerity	of heart	and reverence	for the Lord.	**23** Whatever		you do,
←	ὡς → ἀνθρωπάρεσκοι	ἀλλ᾽	ἐν	ἁπλότητι	καρδίας	φοβούμενοι	τὸν κύριον	ὃ ἐὰν		→ ποιῆτε
pl	a.npm	a.npm	p.d	n.dsf	n.gsf	pt.pp.npm	d.asm n.asm	r.asn pl		v.pas.2p
6055	473	247	1877	605	2840	5828	3836 3261	4005 1569		4472

work	at it with all	your heart,	as	working	for the Lord,		not for men,	**24** since you know	that you will
ἐργάζεσθε	ἐκ	ψυχῆς ὡς		→	⸤τῷ κυρίῳ⸥	καὶ οὐκ	ἀνθρώποις	→	→ εἰδότες ὅτι →	→
v.pmm.2p	p.g	n.gsf pl			d.dsm n.dsm	cj pl	n.dpm		pt.ra.npm cj
2237	1666	6034 6055			3836 3261	2779 4024	476		3857 4022

πραΰτητα μακροθυμίαν, ¹³ ἀνεχόμενοι ἀλλήλων καὶ χαριζόμενοι ἑαυτοῖς ἐάν τις πρός τινα ἔχῃ μομφήν· καθὼς καὶ ὁ κύριος ἐχαρίσατο ὑμῖν, οὕτως καὶ ὑμεῖς· ¹⁴ ἐπὶ πᾶσιν δὲ τούτοις τὴν ἀγάπην, ὅ ἐστιν σύνδεσμος τῆς τελειότητος. ¶ ¹⁵ καὶ ἡ εἰρήνη τοῦ Χριστοῦ βραβευέτω ἐν ταῖς καρδίαις ὑμῶν, εἰς ἣν καὶ ἐκλήθητε ἐν ἑνὶ σώματι· καὶ εὐχάριστοι γίνεσθε. ¹⁶ ὁ λόγος τοῦ Χριστοῦ ἐνοικείτω ἐν ὑμῖν πλουσίως, ἐν πάσῃ σοφίᾳ διδάσκοντες καὶ νουθετοῦντες ἑαυτούς, ψαλμοῖς ὕμνοις ᾠδαῖς πνευματικαῖς ἐν [τῇ] χάριτι ᾄδοντες ἐν ταῖς καρδίαις ὑμῶν τῷ θεῷ· ¹⁷ καὶ πᾶν ὅ τι ἐὰν ποιῆτε ἐν λόγῳ ἢ ἐν ἔργῳ, πάντα ἐν ὀνόματι κυρίου Ἰησοῦ, εὐχαριστοῦντες τῷ θεῷ πατρὶ δι᾽ αὐτοῦ.

³:¹⁸ Αἱ γυναῖκες, ὑποτάσσεσθε τοῖς ἀνδράσιν ὡς ἀνῆκεν ἐν κυρίῳ. ¶ ¹⁹ Οἱ ἄνδρες, ἀγαπᾶτε τὰς γυναῖκας καὶ μὴ πικραίνεσθε πρὸς αὐτάς. ¶ ²⁰ Τὰ τέκνα, ὑπακούετε τοῖς γονεῦσιν κατὰ πάντα, τοῦτο γὰρ εὐάρεστόν ἐστιν ἐν κυρίῳ. ¶ ²¹ Οἱ πατέρες, μὴ ἐρεθίζετε τὰ τέκνα ὑμῶν, ἵνα μὴ ἀθυμῶσιν. ¶ ²² Οἱ δοῦλοι, ὑπακούετε κατὰ πάντα τοῖς κατὰ σάρκα κυρίοις, μὴ ἐν ὀφθαλμοδουλίᾳ ὡς ἀνθρωπάρεσκοι, ἀλλ᾽ ἐν ἁπλότητι καρδίας φοβούμενοι τὸν κύριον. ²³ ὃ ἐὰν ποιῆτε, ἐκ ψυχῆς ἐργάζεσθε ὡς τῷ κυρίῳ καὶ οὐκ ἀνθρώποις, ²⁴ εἰδότες ὅτι ἀπὸ κυρίου ἀπολήμψεσθε τὴν ἀνταπόδοσιν τῆς κληρονομίας. τῷ κυρίῳ Χριστῷ

receive	an inheritance		from the Lord			as a reward.			It is the Lord	Christ	you	are serving.	25	Anyone
ἀπολήμψεσθε	⌐τῆς κληρονομίας⌐	ἀπὸ	κυρίου			⌐τὴν ἀνταπόδοσιν⌐			τῷ	κυρίῳ	Χριστῷ →	→ δουλεύετε	γὰρ	ὁ
v.fmi.2p	d.gsf n.gsf	p.g	n.gsm			d.asf n.asf			d.dsm	n.dsm	n.dsm		cj	d.nsm
655	3836 3100	608	3261			3836 502			3836	3261	5986	1526	1142	3836

who does wrong	will be repaid		for his wrong,		and there is		no	favoritism.		4:1 Masters,	provide	your
← ἀδικῶν →	κομίσεται	ὃ	→ ἠδίκησεν	καὶ		ἔστιν	οὐκ	προσωπολημψία	¶	⌐Οἱ κύριοι⌐	παρέχεσθε	τοῖς
pt.pa.nsm	v.fmi.3s	r.asn	v.aai.3s	cj		v.pai.3s	pl	n.nsf		d.vpm n.vpm	v.pmm.2p	d.dpm
92	3152	4005	92	2779		1639	4024	4721		3836 3261	4218	3836

slaves	with	what is right		and fair,			because you know		that	you	also	have	a Master	in	heaven.
δούλοις	↩	τὸ	→ δίκαιον	καὶ	⌐τὴν ἰσότητα⌐	→	→ εἰδότες	ὅτι		ὑμεῖς	καὶ	ἔχετε	κύριον	ἐν	οὐρανῷ
n.dpm	d.asn		a.asn	cj	d.asf n.asf		pt.ra.npm	cj		r.np.2	adv	v.pai.2p	n.asm	p.d	n.dsm
1529	4218	3836	1465	2779	3836 2699		3857	4022		7007	2779	2400	3261	1877	4041

Further Instructions

4:2 Devote	yourselves to prayer,		being watchful			and thankful.		3 And pray		for
προσκαρτερεῖτε ←	→ ⌐Τῇ προσευχῇ⌐ →		γρηγοροῦντες	ἐν	αὐτῇ	⌐ἐν εὐχαριστίᾳ⌐		προσευχόμενοι	ἅμα	περὶ
v.pam.2p	d.dsf n.dsf		pt.pa.npm	p.d	r.dsf.3	p.d n.dsf		pt.pm.npm	adv	p.g
4674	3836 4666		1213	1877	899	1877 2374		4667	275	4309

us,	too,	that	God	may open		a door	for our	message,	so that	we may proclaim	the mystery	of Christ,
ἡμῶν	καὶ	ἵνα	ὁ θεὸς	ἀνοίξῃ	ἡμῖν	θύραν →	τοῦ λόγου		→	→ λαλῆσαι	τὸ μυστήριον	⌐τοῦ Χριστοῦ⌐
r.gp.1	adv	cj	d.nsm n.nsm	v.aas.3s	r.dp.1	n.asf	d.gsm n.gsm			f.aa	d.asn n.asn	d.gsm n.gsm
7005	2779	2671	3836 2536	487	7005	2598	3836 3364			3281	3836 3696	3836 5986

for which		I am in chains.	4 Pray that	I may proclaim	it	clearly,	as I	should.		5 Be	wise	in the way
δι' ὃ	καὶ	→ → δέδεμαι	ἵνα	→ φανερώσω	αὐτὸ	←	ὡς με	δεῖ	λαλῆσαι	Ἐν σοφίᾳ	→	→
p.a r.asn	adv	v.rpi.1s	cj	v.aas.1s	r.asn.3		cj r.as.1	v.pai.3s	f.aa	p.d n.dsf		
1328 4005	2779	1313	2671	5746	899	5746	6055 1609	1256	3281	1877 5053		

you act	toward	outsiders;	make		the most of	every opportunity.		6 Let your	conversation	be always	full of
→ περιπατεῖτε	πρὸς	⌐τοὺς ἔξω⌐	ἐξαγοραζόμενοι	←	←	τὸν	καιρὸν	⌐ὑμῶν ὁ λόγος⌐		πάντοτε ἐν	
v.pam.2p	p.a	d.apm adv	v.pm.npm			d.asm	n.asm	r.gp.2 d.nsm n.nsm		adv p.d	
4344	4639	3836 2032	1973			3836	2789	7007 3836 3364		4121 1877	

grace,	seasoned	with salt,	so that	you	may	know	how		to answer	everyone.
χάριτι	ἠρτυμένος →	ἅλατι →	→	→		εἰδέναι	πῶς	δεῖ ὑμᾶς	→ ἀποκρίνεσθαι	⌐ἑνὶ ἑκάστῳ⌐
n.dsf	pt.rp.nsm	n.dsn				f.ra	cj	v.pai.3s r.ap.2	f.pm	a.dsm a.dsm
5921	789	229				3857	4802	1256 7007	646	1651 1667

Final Greetings

4:7 Tychicus	will tell	you	all	the news	about	me.	He is	a dear	brother,	a faithful	minister	and	fellow
Τύχικος	→ γνωρίσει	ὑμῖν	πάντα	Τὰ ←	κατ'	ἐμὲ	ὁ	ἀγαπητὸς	ἀδελφὸς	πιστὸς	διάκονος	καὶ	→
n.nsm	v.fai.3s	r.dp.2	a.apn	d.apn	p.a	r.as.1	d.nsm	a.nsm	n.nsm	a.nsm	n.nsm	cj	
5608	1192	7007	4246	3836	2848	1609	3836	28	81	4412	1356	2779	

servant	in	the Lord.	8 I am sending	him	to	you	for the	express purpose	that	you may	know	about	our
σύνδουλος	ἐν	κυρίῳ	→ ἔπεμψα	ὃν	πρὸς	ὑμᾶς	εἰς	τοῦτο αὐτὸ	ἵνα	→ →	γνῶτε	περὶ	ἡμῶν
n.nsm	p.d	n.dsm	v.aai.1s	r.asm	p.a	r.ap.2	p.a	r.asn r.asn	cj		v.aas.2p	p.g	r.gp.1
5281	1877	3261	4287	4005	4639	7007	1650	4047 899	2671		1182	4309	7005

circumstances	and	that	he may encourage	your	hearts.		9 He is coming	with	Onesimus,	our	faithful	and	dear
τὰ	καὶ	→	παρακαλέσῃ	ὑμῶν	⌐τὰς καρδίας⌐			σὺν	Ὀνησίμῳ	τῷ	πιστῷ	καὶ	ἀγαπητῷ
d.apn	cj		v.aas.3s	r.gp.2	d.apf n.apf			p.d	n.dsm	d.dsm	a.dsm	cj	a.dsm
3836	2779		4151	7007	3836 2840			5250	3946	3836	4412	2779	28

brother,	who	is	one of you.		They will tell		you	everything	that is	happening	here.		10 My	fellow
ἀδελφῷ	ὅς	ἐστιν	ἐξ ὑμῶν →		→ γνωρίσουσιν		ὑμῖν	πάντα	τὰ ←	←	ὧδε	¶	μου	→
n.dsm	r.nsm	v.pai.3s	p.g r.gp.2		v.fai.3p		r.dp.2	a.apn	d.apn		adv		r.gs.1	
81	4005	1639	1666 7007		1192		7007	4246	3836		6045		1609	

prisoner	Aristarchus	sends	you	his greetings,	as	does	Mark,	the	cousin	of Barnabas.	(You have	received
⌐ὁ συναιχμάλωτος⌐	Ἀρίσταρχος →		ὑμᾶς →	Ἀσπάζεται	καὶ		Μᾶρκος	ὁ	ἀνεψιὸς	Βαρναβᾶ	→	ἐλάβετε
d.nsm n.nsm	n.nsm		r.ap.2	v.pmi.3s	cj		n.nsm	d.nsm	n.nsm	n.gsm		v.aai.2p
3836 5257	752		7007	832	2779		3453	3836	463	982		3284

instructions	about	him;	if	he comes	to	you,	welcome	him.)	11 Jesus,	who	is called	Justus,	also sends greetings.
ἐντολάς	περὶ	οὗ	ἐὰν →	ἔλθῃ	πρὸς	ὑμᾶς	δέξασθε	αὐτόν	Ἰησοῦς	ὁ	→ λεγόμενος	Ἰοῦστος	καὶ
n.apf	p.g	r.gsm	v.aas.3s		p.a	r.ap.2	v.amm.2p	r.asm.3	n.nsm	d.nsm	pt.pp.nsm	n.nsm	cj
1953	4309	4005	1569	2262	4639	7007	1312	899	2652	3836	3306	2688	2779

δουλεύετε· 25 ὁ γὰρ ἀδικῶν κομίσεται ὃ ἠδίκησεν, καὶ οὐκ ἔστιν προσωπολημψία. 4:1 Οἱ κύριοι, τὸ δίκαιον καὶ τὴν ἰσότητα τοῖς δούλοις παρέχεσθε, εἰδότες ὅτι καὶ ὑμεῖς ἔχετε κύριον ἐν οὐρανῷ.

4:2 Τῇ προσευχῇ προσκαρτερεῖτε, γρηγοροῦντες ἐν αὐτῇ ἐν εὐχαριστίᾳ, 3 προσευχόμενοι ἅμα καὶ περὶ ἡμῶν, ἵνα ὁ θεὸς ἀνοίξῃ ἡμῖν θύραν τοῦ λόγου λαλῆσαι τὸ μυστήριον τοῦ Χριστοῦ, δι' ὃ καὶ δέδεμαι, 4 ἵνα φανερώσω αὐτὸ ὡς δεῖ με λαλῆσαι. 5 Ἐν σοφίᾳ περιπατεῖτε πρὸς τοὺς ἔξω τὸν καιρὸν ἐξαγοραζόμενοι. 6 ὁ λόγος ὑμῶν πάντοτε ἐν χάριτι, ἅλατι ἠρτυμένος, εἰδέναι πῶς δεῖ ὑμᾶς ἑνὶ ἑκάστῳ ἀποκρίνεσθαι.

4:7 Τὰ κατ' ἐμὲ πάντα γνωρίσει ὑμῖν Τύχικος ὁ ἀγαπητὸς ἀδελφὸς καὶ πιστὸς διάκονος καὶ σύνδουλος ἐν κυρίῳ, 8 ὃν ἔπεμψα πρὸς ὑμᾶς εἰς αὐτὸ τοῦτο, ἵνα γνῶτε τὰ περὶ ἡμῶν καὶ παρακαλέσῃ τὰς καρδίας ὑμῶν, 9 σὺν Ὀνησίμῳ τῷ πιστῷ καὶ ἀγαπητῷ ἀδελφῷ, ὅς ἐστιν ἐξ ὑμῶν· πάντα ὑμῖν γνωρίσουσιν τὰ ὧδε. ¶ 10 Ἀσπάζεται ὑμᾶς Ἀρίσταρχος ὁ συναιχμάλωτός μου καὶ Μᾶρκος ὁ ἀνεψιὸς Βαρναβᾶ (περὶ οὗ ἐλάβετε ἐντολάς, ἐὰν ἔλθῃ πρὸς ὑμᾶς, δέξασθε αὐτὸν 11 καὶ Ἰησοῦς ὁ λεγόμενος Ἰοῦστος, οἱ ὄντες

These are the   only Jews   among my fellow   workers   for the kingdom of God,   and they have
οὗτοι   οἱ ὄντες μόνοι ἐκ περιτομῆς   συνεργοὶ ←   εἰς τὴν βασιλείαν → τοῦ θεοῦ   οἵτινες →
r.npm   d.npm pt.pa.npm a.npm p.g n.gsf   n.npm   p.a d.asf n.asf   d.gsm n.gsm   r.npm
4047   3836 1639 3668 1666 4364   5301   1650 3836 993   3836 2536   4015

proved   a comfort   to me. **12** Epaphras, who is one of   you   and a servant of Christ Jesus, sends greetings.   He is
ἐγενήθησαν παρηγορία → μοι   Ἐπαφρᾶς ὁ   ἐξ ὑμῶν   δοῦλος → Χριστοῦ Ἰησοῦ →   ἀσπάζεται ὑμᾶς   →
v.api.3p   n.nsf → r.ds.1   n.nsm   d.nsm   p.g ὑμῶν   n.nsm   n.gsm   n.gsm   v.pmi.3s   r.ap.2   →
1181   4219   1609   2071   3836   1666 7007   1529   5986   2652   832   7007   76   76

always wrestling   in   prayer   for you, that you may   stand firm in   all   the will   of God,   mature
πάντοτε ἀγωνιζόμενος ἐν ταῖς προσευχαῖς ὑπὲρ ὑμῶν ἵνα →   σταθῆτε ← ἐν παντὶ   θελήματι → τοῦ θεοῦ   τέλειοι
adv   pt.pm.nsm   p.d d.dpf n.dpf   p.g r.gp.2 cj   v.aps.2p   p.d a.dsn   n.dsn   d.gsm n.gsm   a.npm
4121   76   1877 3836 4666   5642 7007 2671   2705   1877 4246   2525   3836 2536   5455

and fully assured.   **13**   I vouch   for him that he is   working hard for   you   and for those at Laodicea and
καὶ → πεπληροφορημένοι   γὰρ → μαρτυρῶ → αὐτῷ ὅτι → ἔχει πόνον πολὺν ὑπὲρ ὑμῶν καὶ ↩ τῶν ἐν Λαοδικείᾳ καὶ
cj → pt.rp.npm   cj → v.pai.1s → r.dsm.3 cj → v.pai.3s n.asm a.asm p.g r.gp.2 cj   d.gpm p.d n.dsf   cj
2779   4442   1142   3455   899   4022   2400 4506 4498 5642 7007 2779 5642 3836 1877 3293   2779

      Hierapolis. **14** Our dear   friend   Luke, the doctor, and Demas send   greetings.   **15** Give my greetings   to the
τῶν ἐν Ἱεραπόλει   ὁ   ἀγαπητὸς Λουκᾶς ὁ ἰατρὸς καὶ Δημᾶς → ἀσπάζεται ὑμᾶς   Ἀσπάσασθε ← τοὺς
d.gpm p.d n.dsf   d.nsm   a.nsm   n.nsm d.nsm n.nsm cj n.nsm → v.pmi.3s   r.ap.2   v.amm.2p   d.apm
3836 1877 2631   3836   28   3371   3836 2620 2779 1318   832   7007   832   3836

brothers at Laodicea, and to Nympha and the church   in   her   house. ¶   **16**   After this letter   has been
ἀδελφοὺς ἐν Λαοδικείᾳ καὶ ↩ Νύμφαν καὶ τὴν ἐκκλησίαν κατ᾽ αὐτῆς οἶκον   καὶ ὅταν ἡ ἐπιστολὴ →   →
n.apm   p.d n.dsf   cj ↩ n.asf   cj d.asf n.asf   p.a r.gsf.3 n.asm   cj cj d.nsf n.nsf
81   1877 3293   2779 832 3809   2779 3836 1711   2848 899 3875   2779 4020 3836 2186

read   to   you, see   that it is also read   in the church   of the Laodiceans and that you in   turn
ἀναγνωσθῇ παρ᾽ ὑμῖν ποιήσατε ἵνα → ↩ καὶ ἀναγνωσθῇ ἐν τῇ ἐκκλησίᾳ → Λαοδικέων καὶ ἵνα ὑμεῖς καὶ ←
v.aps.3s   p.d r.dp.2 v.aam.2p ἵνα → 336 336 2779 v.aps.3s p.d d.dsf n.dsf → n.gpm   cj cj r.np.2 cj adv
336   4123 7007 4472   2671   336   1877 3836 1711   3294   2779 2671 7007 2779

read   the letter from Laodicea. ¶   **17**   Tell   Archippus: "See to it that you complete   the work
ἀναγνῶτε τὴν   ἐκ Λαοδικείας   καὶ εἴπατε Ἀρχίππῳ   Βλέπε ← ← ἵνα → πληροῖς αὐτὴν τὴν διακονίαν ἣν
v.aas.2p d.asf   p.g n.gsf   cj v.aam.2p n.dsm   v.pam.2s   cj → v.pas.2s r.asf.3 d.asf n.asf   r.asf
336   3836   1666 3293   2779 3306 800   1063   2671   4444   899 3836 1355   4005

you have received in the Lord." ¶   **18** I, Paul,   write this   greeting in   my own hand. Remember my chains.
→ → παρέλαβες ἐν κυρίῳ   Παύλου   Ὁ ἀσπασμὸς → ἐμῇ τῇ χειρὶ μνημονεύετε μου τῶν δεσμῶν
      v.aai.2s p.d n.dsm   n.gsm   d.nsm n.nsm → r.dsf.1 d.dsf n.dsf v.pam.2p   r.gs.1 d.gpm n.gpm
      4161   1877 3261   4263   3836 833   5931 1847 3836 5931 3648   1609 3836 1301

Grace   be with you.
ἡ χάρις   μεθ᾽ ὑμῶν
d.nsf n.nsf   p.g r.gp.2
3836 5921   3552 7007

ἐκ περιτομῆς, οὗτοι μόνοι συνεργοὶ εἰς τὴν βασιλείαν τοῦ θεοῦ, οἵτινες ἐγενήθησάν μοι παρηγορία. ¹² ἀσπάζεται ὑμᾶς Ἐπαφρᾶς ὁ ἐξ ὑμῶν, δοῦλος Χριστοῦ [Ἰησοῦ], πάντοτε ἀγωνιζόμενος ὑπὲρ ὑμῶν ἐν ταῖς προσευχαῖς, ἵνα σταθῆτε τέλειοι καὶ πεπληροφορημένοι ἐν παντὶ θελήματι τοῦ θεοῦ. ¹³ μαρτυρῶ γὰρ αὐτῷ ὅτι ἔχει πολὺν πόνον ὑπὲρ ὑμῶν καὶ τῶν ἐν Λαοδικείᾳ καὶ τῶν ἐν Ἱεραπόλει. ¹⁴ ἀσπάζεται ὑμᾶς Λουκᾶς ὁ ἰατρὸς ὁ ἀγαπητὸς καὶ Δημᾶς. ¹⁵ Ἀσπάσασθε τοὺς ἐν Λαοδικείᾳ ἀδελφοὺς καὶ Νύμφαν καὶ τὴν κατ᾽ οἶκον αὐτῆς ἐκκλησίαν. ¶ ¹⁶ καὶ ὅταν ἀναγνωσθῇ παρ᾽ ὑμῖν ἡ ἐπιστολή, ποιήσατε ἵνα καὶ ἐν τῇ Λαοδικέων ἐκκλησίᾳ ἀναγνωσθῇ, καὶ τὴν ἐκ Λαοδικείας ἵνα καὶ ὑμεῖς ἀναγνῶτε. ¶ ¹⁷ καὶ εἴπατε Ἀρχίππῳ, Βλέπε τὴν διακονίαν ἣν παρέλαβες ἐν κυρίῳ, ἵνα αὐτὴν πληροῖς. ¶ ¹⁸ Ὁ ἀσπασμὸς τῇ ἐμῇ χειρὶ Παύλου. μνημονεύετέ μου τῶν δεσμῶν. ἡ χάρις μεθ᾽ ὑμῶν.

1 Thessalonians

1:1 Paul, Silas and Timothy, ¶ To the church of the Thessalonians in God the Father and the
Παῦλος καὶ Σιλουανὸς καὶ Τιμόθεος   τῇ ἐκκλησίᾳ → Θεσσαλονικέων ἐν θεῷ πατρὶ καὶ
n.nsm cj n.nsm cj n.nsm   d.dsf n.dsf   n.gpm p.d n.dsm n.dsm cj
4263 2779 4977 2779 5510   3836 1711   2552 1877 2536 4252 2779

Lord Jesus Christ: ¶ Grace and peace to you.
κυρίῳ Ἰησοῦ Χριστῷ χάρις καὶ εἰρήνη → ὑμῖν
n.dsm n.dsm n.dsm n.nsf cj n.nsf r.dp.2
3261 2652 5986 5921 2779 1645 7007

Thanksgiving for the Thessalonians' Faith

1:2 We always thank God for all of you, mentioning you in our prayers. **3** We
→ πάντοτε Εὐχαριστοῦμεν τῷ θεῷ περὶ πάντων → ὑμῶν μνείαν ποιούμενοι ἐπὶ ἡμῶν τῶν προσευχῶν →
adv v.pai.1p d.dsm n.dsm p.g a.gpm r.gp.2 n.asf pt.pm.npm p.g r.gp.1 d.gpf n.gpf
2373 4121 2373 3836 2536 4309 4246 7007 3644 4472 2093 7005 3836 4666 3648

continually remember before our God and Father your work produced by faith, your labor
ἀδιαλείπτως μνημονεύοντες ἔμπροσθεν ἡμῶν τοῦ θεοῦ καὶ πατρὸς ὑμῶν τοῦ ἔργου → τῆς πίστεως καὶ τοῦ κόπου
adv pt.pa.npm p.g r.gp.1 d.gsm n.gsm cj n.gsm r.gp.2 d.gsn n.gsn d.gsf n.gsf cj d.gsm n.gsm
90 3648 1869 7005 3836 2536 2779 4252 7007 3836 2240 3836 4411 2779 3836 3160

prompted by love, and your endurance inspired by hope in our Lord Jesus Christ. ¶ **4** For
→ → τῆς ἀγάπης καὶ τῆς ὑπομονῆς → τῆς ἐλπίδος ἡμῶν τοῦ κυρίου Ἰησοῦ Χριστοῦ →
d.gsf n.gsf cj d.gsf n.gsf d.gsf n.gsf r.gp.1 d.gsm n.gsm n.gsm n.gsm
3836 27 2779 3836 5705 3836 1828 3261 7005 3836 3261 2652 5986

we know, brothers loved by God, that he has chosen you, **5** because our gospel came to you
→ εἰδότες ἀδελφοὶ ἠγαπημένοι ὑπὸ τοῦ θεοῦ τὴν ἐκλογὴν ὑμῶν ὅτι ἡμῶν τὸ εὐαγγέλιον ἐγενήθη εἰς ὑμᾶς
pt.ra.npm n.vpm pt.rp.vpm p.g d.gsm n.gsm d.asf n.asf r.gp.2 cj r.gp.1 d.nsn n.nsn v.api.3s p.a r.ap.2
3857 81 26 5679 3836 2536 3836 1724 7007 4022 7005 3836 2295 1181 1650 7007

not simply with words, but also with power, with the Holy Spirit and with deep conviction. You know
οὐκ μόνον ἐν λόγῳ ἀλλὰ καὶ ἐν δυνάμει καὶ ἐν ἁγίῳ πνεύματι καὶ ἐν πολλῇ πληροφορίᾳ καθὼς → οἴδατε
pl adv p.d n.dsm cj adv p.d n.dsf cj p.d a.dsn n.dsn cj p.d a.dsf n.dsf cj v.rai.2p
4024 3667 1877 3364 247 2779 1877 1539 2779 1877 41 4460 2779 1877 4498 4443 2777 3857

how we lived among you for your sake. **6** You became imitators of us and of the Lord; in spite of severe
οἷοι ἐγενήθημεν ἐν ὑμῖν δι᾽ ὑμᾶς ↰ Καὶ ὑμεῖς ἐγενήθητε μιμηταὶ → ἡμῶν καὶ → τοῦ κυρίου ἐν πολλῇ
r.npm v.api.1p p.d r.dp.2 p.a r.ap.2 cj r.np.2 v.api.2p n.npm r.gp.1 cj d.gsm n.gsm p.d a.dsf
3888 1181 1877 7007 1328 7007 1328 2779 7007 1181 3629 7005 2779 3836 3261 1877 4498

suffering, you welcomed the message with the joy given by the Holy Spirit. **7** And so you became a model to
θλίψει → δεξάμενοι τὸν λόγον μετὰ χαρᾶς → → ἁγίου πνεύματος ὥστε ὑμᾶς γενέσθαι τύπον →
n.dsf pt.am.npm d.asm n.asm p.g n.gsf a.gsn n.gsn cj r.ap.2 fam n.asm
2568 1312 3836 3364 3552 5915 41 4460 6063 7007 1181 5596

all the believers in Macedonia and Achaia. **8** The Lord's message rang out from you not only
πᾶσιν τοῖς πιστεύουσιν ἐν τῇ Μακεδονίᾳ καὶ ἐν τῇ Ἀχαΐᾳ γὰρ ὁ τοῦ κυρίου λόγος ἐξήχηται ← ἀφ᾽ ὑμῶν οὐ μόνον
a.dpm d.dpm pt.pa.dpm p.d d.dsf n.dsf cj p.d d.dsf n.dsf cj d.nsm d.gsm n.gsm n.nsm v.rpi.3s p.g r.gp.2 pl adv
4246 3836 3836 1877 3836 3423 2779 1877 3836 938 1142 3836 3836 3261 3364 2010 608 7007 4024 3667

in Macedonia and Achaia — your faith in God has become known everywhere.
ἐν τῇ Μακεδονίᾳ καὶ ἐν τῇ Ἀχαΐᾳ ἀλλ᾽ ὑμῶν ἡ πίστις ἡ πρὸς τὸν θεὸν → → ἐξελήλυθεν ἐν παντὶ τόπῳ
p.d d.dsf n.dsf cj p.d d.dsf n.dsf cj r.gp.2 d.nsf n.nsf d.nsf p.a d.asm n.asm v.rai.3s p.d a.dsm n.dsm
1877 3836 3423 2779 1877 3836 938 247 7007 3836 4411 3836 4639 3836 2536 2002 1877 4246 5536

Therefore we do not need to say anything about it, **9** for they themselves report what kind
ὥστε ἡμᾶς → μὴ χρείαν ἔχειν → λαλεῖν τι γὰρ → αὐτοὶ ἀπαγγέλλουσιν περὶ ἡμῶν ὁποίαν ←
cj r.ap.1 pl n.asf f.pa f.pa r.asn cj r.npm v.pai.3p p.g r.gp.1 r.asf
6063 7005 3590 5970 2400 3281 5516 1142 550 899 550 4309 7005 3961

of reception you gave us. They tell how you turned to God from idols to serve the
← εἴσοδον ἔσχομεν πρὸς ὑμᾶς καὶ πῶς → ἐπεστρέψατε πρὸς τὸν θεὸν ἀπὸ τῶν εἰδώλων → δουλεύειν
n.asf v.aai.1p p.a r.ap.2 cj cj v.aai.2p p.a d.asm n.asm p.g d.gpn n.gpn f.pa
1658 2400 4639 7007 2779 4802 2188 4639 3836 2536 608 3836 1631 1526

1:1 Παῦλος καὶ Σιλουανὸς καὶ Τιμόθεος ¶ τῇ ἐκκλησίᾳ Θεσσαλονικέων ἐν θεῷ πατρὶ καὶ κυρίῳ Ἰησοῦ Χριστῷ, ¶ χάρις ὑμῖν καὶ εἰρήνη.

1:2 Εὐχαριστοῦμεν τῷ θεῷ πάντοτε περὶ πάντων ὑμῶν μνείαν ποιούμενοι ἐπὶ τῶν προσευχῶν ἡμῶν, ἀδιαλείπτως **3** μνημονεύοντες ὑμῶν τοῦ ἔργου τῆς πίστεως καὶ τοῦ κόπου τῆς ἀγάπης καὶ τῆς ὑπομονῆς τῆς ἐλπίδος τοῦ κυρίου ἡμῶν Ἰησοῦ Χριστοῦ ἔμπροσθεν τοῦ θεοῦ καὶ πατρὸς ἡμῶν, ¶ **4** εἰδότες, ἀδελφοὶ ἠγαπημένοι ὑπὸ [τοῦ] θεοῦ, τὴν ἐκλογὴν ὑμῶν, **5** ὅτι τὸ εὐαγγέλιον ἡμῶν οὐκ ἐγενήθη εἰς ὑμᾶς ἐν λόγῳ μόνον ἀλλὰ καὶ ἐν δυνάμει καὶ ἐν πνεύματι ἁγίῳ καὶ [ἐν] πληροφορίᾳ πολλῇ, καθὼς οἴδατε οἷοι ἐγενήθημεν [ἐν] ὑμῖν δι᾽ ὑμᾶς. **6** καὶ ὑμεῖς μιμηταὶ ἡμῶν ἐγενήθητε καὶ τοῦ κυρίου, δεξάμενοι τὸν λόγον ἐν θλίψει πολλῇ μετὰ χαρᾶς πνεύματος ἁγίου, **7** ὥστε γενέσθαι ὑμᾶς τύπον πᾶσιν τοῖς πιστεύουσιν ἐν τῇ Μακεδονίᾳ καὶ ἐν τῇ Ἀχαΐᾳ. **8** ἀφ᾽ ὑμῶν γὰρ ἐξήχηται ὁ λόγος τοῦ κυρίου οὐ μόνον ἐν τῇ Μακεδονίᾳ καὶ [ἐν τῇ] Ἀχαΐᾳ, ἀλλ᾽ ἐν παντὶ τόπῳ ἡ πίστις ὑμῶν ἡ πρὸς τὸν θεὸν ἐξελήλυθεν, ὥστε μὴ χρείαν ἔχειν ἡμᾶς λαλεῖν τι. **9** αὐτοὶ γὰρ περὶ ἡμῶν ἀπαγγέλλουσιν ὁποίαν εἴσοδον ἔσχομεν πρὸς ὑμᾶς, καὶ πῶς ἐπεστρέψατε πρὸς τὸν θεὸν ἀπὸ τῶν εἰδώλων δουλεύειν θεῷ ζῶντι καὶ ἀληθινῷ **10** καὶ

living and true   God, **10** and to wait   for his Son   from heaven,   whom he raised from the dead —
ζῶντι καὶ ἀληθινῷ θεῷ   καὶ → ἀναμένειν ← αὐτοῦ τὸν υἱὸν ἐκ ⌐τῶν οὐρανῶν⌐ ὃν → ἤγειρεν ἐκ τῶν νεκρῶν
pt.pa.dsm cj a.dsm n.dsm   cj   f.pa   r.gsm.3 d.asm n.asm p.g d.gpm n.gpm r.asm   v.aai.3s p.g d.gpm a.gpm
2409 2779 240 2536   2779   388   899 3836 5626 1666 3836 4041 4005   1586 1666 3836 3738

Jesus, who rescues us   from the coming   wrath.
Ἰησοῦν τὸν ῥυόμενον ἡμᾶς ἐκ τῆς ⌐τῆς ἐρχομένης⌐ ὀργῆς
n.asm d.asm pt.pm.asm r.ap.1 p.g d.gsf d.gsf pt.pm.gsf n.gsf
2652 3836 4861 7005 1666 3836 3836 2262 3973

Paul's Ministry in Thessalonica

2:1   You know, brothers, that our visit   to you was   not a failure. **2**   We had previously
γὰρ Αὐτοὶ οἴδατε ἀδελφοί   ὅτι ἡμῶν ⌐τὴν εἴσοδον⌐ τὴν πρὸς ὑμᾶς γέγονεν οὐ κενὴ   ἀλλὰ → →
cj r.npm v.rai.2p n.vpm   cj r.gp.1 d.asf n.asf d.asf p.a r.ap.2 v.rai.3s pl a.nsf   cj
1142 899 3857 81   4022 7005 3836 1658 3836 4639 7007 1181 4024 3031   247

suffered and been insulted in Philippi, as you know, but *with the help of* our God   we dared
προπαθόντες καὶ → ὑβρισθέντες ἐν Φιλίπποις καθὼς → οἴδατε ἀλλʼ *ἐν* ἡμῶν τῷ θεῷ → ἐπαρρησιασάμεθα
pt.aa.npm cj   pt.ap.npm p.d n.dpm cj   v.rai.2p p.d r.gp.1 d.dsm n.dsm v.ami.1p
4634 2779   5614 1877 5804 2777   3857 1877 7005 3836 2536 4245

to tell you his   gospel   *in spite of* strong opposition. **3** For the appeal   we make does not
→ λαλῆσαι πρὸς ὑμᾶς ⌐τοῦ θεοῦ⌐ ⌐τὸ εὐαγγέλιον⌐ ἐν   πολλῷ ἀγῶνι   γὰρ ἡ παράκλησις ἡμῶν   οὐκ
f.aa p.a r.ap.2 d.gsm n.gsm d.asn n.asn p.d   n.dsm n.dsm   cj d.nsf n.nsf r.gp.1   pl
3281 4639 7007 3836 2536 3836 2295 1877   4498 74   1142 3836 4155 7005   4024

spring from error or   impure   motives, nor are we trying to trick you. **4** On the contrary,   we
→ ἐκ πλάνης οὐδὲ ἐξ ἀκαθαρσίας ←   οὐδὲ   ⌐ἐν δόλῳ⌐   ἀλλʼ ←   οὕτως →
p.g n.gsf cj p.g n.gsf   cj   p.d n.dsm   cj   adv
1666 4415 4028 1666 174   4028   1877 1515   247   4048

speak as   men approved by God   to be entrusted with the gospel.   We are not trying to please
λαλοῦμεν καθὼς   δεδοκιμάσμεθα ὑπὸ ⌐τοῦ θεοῦ⌐ → πιστευθῆναι ← τὸ εὐαγγέλιον ⸉ → οὐχ → ἀρέσκοντες ὡς
v.pai.1p cj   v.rpi.1p p.g d.gsm n.gsm   f.ap   d.asn n.asn pl 743 pl   pt.pa.npm pl
3281 2777   1507 5679 3836 2536   4409   3836 2295 4024 743 743   6055

men but God, who tests   our hearts. **5**   You know we never   used flattery,
ἀνθρώποις ἀλλὰ θεῷ τῷ δοκιμάζοντι ἡμῶν ⌐τὰς καρδίας⌐ γάρ καθὼς → οἴδατε ⸉ ⌐Οὔτε ποτε ἐγενήθημεν ἐν λόγῳ κολακείας⌐
n.dpm cj n.dsm d.dsm pt.pa.dsm r.gp.1 d.apf n.apf cj cj   v.rai.2p   adv v.api.1p p.d n.dsm n.gsf
476 247 2536 3836 1507 7005 3836 2840 1142 2777   3857 1181 4046 4537 1181 1877 3364 3135

nor did we put on a mask   to cover up greed   – God is our witness. **6** We were not looking for praise from
οὔτε   ⌐ἐν προφάσει⌐   → πλεονεξίας θεὸς   μάρτυς   οὔτε ζητοῦντες ← δόξαν ἐξ
cj   p.d n.dsf   n.gsf n.nsm   n.nsm   cj pt.pa.npm   n.asf p.g
4046   1877 4733   4432 2536   3459   2426 2426 4046 2426   1518 1666

men, not from you or   anyone else. ¶ As apostles of Christ we could   have been a burden   to
ἀνθρώπων οὔτε ἀφʼ ὑμῶν οὔτε ἀπʼ ἄλλων ←   ὡς ἀπόστολοι → Χριστοῦ δυνάμενοι →   εἶναι ⌐ἐν βάρει⌐
n.gpm cj p.g r.gp.2 cj p.g n.gpm   pl n.npm   n.gsn pt.pp.npm   f.pa p.d n.dsn
476 4046 608 7007 4046 608 257   6055 693   5986 1538   1639 1877 983

you, **7** but we were   gentle among you, like   a mother caring for her   little children. **8** We loved   you
ἀλλʼ → ἐγενήθημεν νήπιοι ἐν μέσῳ ὑμῶν ὡς ἐὰν   τροφὸς θάλπη ← ἑαυτῆς ⌐τὰ τέκνα⌐   ὁμειρόμενοι ὑμῶν
cj → v.api.1p a.npm p.d n.dsn r.gp.2 pl   n.nsf v.pas.3s r.gsf.3 d.apn n.apn   pt.pm.npm r.gp.2
247 1181 3758 1877 3545 7007 6055 1569   5577 2499 1571 3836 5451   3916 7007

so   much that we were delighted to share   with you not only the gospel   of God   but our   lives
οὕτως ←   → εὐδοκοῦμεν μεταδοῦναι ← ὑμῖν οὐ μόνον τὸ εὐαγγέλιον → ⌐τοῦ θεοῦ⌐ ἀλλὰ ἑαυτῶν ⌐τὰς ψυχάς⌐
adv ←   → v.iai.1p f.aa ← r.dp.2 adv adv d.asn n.asn   d.gsm n.gsm cj r.gpm.1 d.apf n.apf
4048   2305 3556 7007 4024 3667 3836 2295   3836 2536 247 1571 3836 6034

as well, because you had become so dear   to us. **9** Surely you remember, brothers, our toil   and hardship;
καὶ ← διότι → ἐγενήθητε ἀγαπητοὶ → ἡμῖν γάρ → Μνημονεύετε ἀδελφοί ἡμῶν ⌐τὸν κόπον⌐ καὶ ⌐τὸν μόχθον⌐
adv ← cj → v.api.2p a.npm → r.dp.1 cj → v.pai.2p n.vpm r.gp.1 d.asm n.asm cj d.asm n.asm
2779 1484 1181 28 7005 1142 3648 81 7005 3836 3160 2779 3836 3677

we worked night and day in order not to be a burden   to anyone   while we preached the
→ ἐργαζόμενοι νυκτὸς καὶ ἡμέρας πρὸς ← μὴ → → ⌐τὸ ἐπιβαρῆσαι⌐ τινα ὑμῶν   → ἐκηρύξαμεν τὸ
pt.pm.npm n.gsf cj n.gsf p.a ← pl → d.asn f.aa r.asm r.gp.2   v.aai.1p d.asn
2237 3816 2779 2465 4639 3590 3836 2096 5516 7007   3062 3836

ἀναμένειν τὸν υἱὸν αὐτοῦ ἐκ τῶν οὐρανῶν, ὃν ἤγειρεν ἐκ [τῶν] νεκρῶν, Ἰησοῦν τὸν ῥυόμενον ἡμᾶς ἐκ τῆς ὀργῆς τῆς ἐρχομένης.

2:1 Αὐτοὶ γὰρ οἴδατε, ἀδελφοί, τὴν εἴσοδον ἡμῶν τὴν πρὸς ὑμᾶς ὅτι οὐ κενὴ γέγονεν, **2** ἀλλὰ προπαθόντες καὶ ὑβρισθέντες, καθὼς οἴδατε, ἐν Φιλίπποις ἐπαρρησιασάμεθα ἐν τῷ θεῷ ἡμῶν λαλῆσαι πρὸς ὑμᾶς τὸ εὐαγγέλιον τοῦ θεοῦ ἐν πολλῷ ἀγῶνι. **3** ἡ γὰρ παράκλησις ἡμῶν οὐκ ἐκ πλάνης οὐδὲ ἐξ ἀκαθαρσίας οὐδὲ ἐν δόλῳ, **4** ἀλλὰ καθὼς δεδοκιμάσμεθα ὑπὸ τοῦ θεοῦ πιστευθῆναι τὸ εὐαγγέλιον, οὕτως λαλοῦμεν, οὐχ ὡς ἀνθρώποις ἀρέσκοντες ἀλλὰ θεῷ τῷ δοκιμάζοντι τὰς καρδίας ἡμῶν. **5** οὔτε γάρ ποτε ἐν λόγῳ κολακείας ἐγενήθημεν, καθὼς οἴδατε, οὔτε ἐν προφάσει πλεονεξίας, θεὸς μάρτυς, **6** οὔτε ζητοῦντες ἐξ ἀνθρώπων δόξαν οὔτε ἀφʼ ὑμῶν οὔτε ἀπʼ ἄλλων. ¶ **7** δυνάμενοι ἐν βάρει εἶναι ὡς Χριστοῦ ἀπόστολοι. ἀλλὰ ἐγενήθημεν ἤπιοι «νήπιοι» ἐν μέσῳ ὑμῶν, ὡς ἐὰν τροφὸς θάλπῃ τὰ ἑαυτῆς τέκνα, **8** οὕτως ὁμειρόμενοι ὑμῶν εὐδοκοῦμεν μεταδοῦναι ὑμῖν οὐ μόνον τὸ εὐαγγέλιον τοῦ θεοῦ ἀλλὰ καὶ τὰς ἑαυτῶν ψυχάς, διότι ἀγαπητοὶ ἡμῖν ἐγενήθητε. **9** μνημονεύετε γάρ, ἀδελφοί, τὸν κόπον ἡμῶν καὶ τὸν μόχθον· νυκτὸς

gospel	of God	→	to you. ¶	**10** You	are witnesses,	and so is	God,	of how	holy,	righteous	and
εὐαγγέλιον	⸤τοῦ θεοῦ⸥	→	εἰς ὑμᾶς	ὑμεῖς	μάρτυρες	καὶ	ὁ θεός	ὡς	ὁσίως	καὶ δικαίως	καὶ
n.asn	d.gsm n.gsm		p.a r.ap.2	r.np.2	n.npm	cj	d.nsm n.nsm	adv	adv	adv adv	adv
2295	3836 2536		1650 7007	7007	3459	2779	3836 2536	6055	4010	2779 1469	2779

blameless	we were	→	among	you who	believed.	**11** For	you	know	that	we dealt with	each		of you	as a
ἀμέμπτως	→ ἐγενήθημεν	→	ὑμῖν	τοῖς	πιστεύουσιν	καθάπερ	→	οἴδατε	ὡς		ἕκαστον	ἕνα	→ ὑμῶν	ὡς
adv	v.api.1p		r.dp.2	d.dpm	pt.pa.dpm	cj		v.rai.2p	cj		r.asm	a.asm	r.gp.2	cj
290	1181		7007	3836	4409	2749		3857	6055		1667	1651	7007	6055

father	deals with	his	own	children,	**12** encouraging,		comforting		and	urging		you	to	live		lives
πατὴρ	→	ἑαυτοῦ ←		τέκνα	παρακαλοῦντες	καὶ	παραμυθούμενοι	ὑμᾶς	καὶ	μαρτυρόμενοι	ὑμᾶς	εἰς	⸤τὸ	περιπατεῖν⸥ ←	
n.nsm		r.gsm.3		n.apn	pt.pa.npm	cj	pt.pm.npm	r.ap.2	cj	pt.pm.npm	r.ap.2	p.a	d.asn	f.pa	
4252		1571		5451	4151	2779	4170	7007	2779	3455	7007	1650	3836	4344	

worthy	of God,		who calls	you	into	his	kingdom	and	glory. ¶	**13** And			we	also
ἀξίως	→	⸤τοῦ θεοῦ⸥	τοῦ καλοῦντος	ὑμᾶς	εἰς	ἑαυτοῦ	⸤τὴν βασιλείαν⸥	καὶ	δόξαν	Καὶ	διὰ	τοῦτο	ἡμεῖς	καὶ
adv		d.gsm n.gsm	d.gsm pt.pa.gsm	r.ap.2	p.a	r.gsm.3	d.asf n.asf	cj	n.asf	cj	p.a	r.asn	r.np.1	adv
547		3836 2536	3836 2813	7007	1650	1571	3836 993	2779	1518	2779	1328	4047	7005	2779

thank	God	continually	because,	when you	received	the	word of God,		which you	heard	from us,
εὐχαριστοῦμεν	⸤τῷ θεῷ⸥	ἀδιαλείπτως	ὅτι	→	παραλαβόντες		λόγον	⸤τοῦ θεοῦ⸥	→	ἀκοῆς	παρ' ἡμῶν
v.pai.1p	d.dsm n.dsm	adv	cj		pt.aa.npm		n.asm	d.gsm n.gsm		n.gsf	p.g r.gp.1
2373	3836 2536	90	4022		4161		3364	3836 2536		198	4123 7005

you accepted	it	not	as	the	word	of men,	but	as	it	actually	is,	the	word	of God,	which		is at work
→ ἐδέξασθε		οὐ			λόγον	→ ἀνθρώπων	ἀλλὰ	καθὼς	↰	ἀληθῶς	ἐστιν		λόγον	→ θεοῦ	ὃς	καὶ	→ ἐνεργεῖται
v.ami.2p		pl			n.asm	n.gpm	cj	cj		adv	v.pai.3s		n.asm	n.gsm	r.nsm	cj	v.pmi.3s
1312		4024			3364	476	247	2777		1639	242		3364	2536	4005	2779	1919

in	you who	believe.	**14** For you,	brothers,	became	imitators	of	God's	churches	in	Judea,	which are
ἐν	ὑμῖν τοῖς	πιστεύουσιν	γὰρ ὑμεῖς	ἀδελφοί	ἐγενήθητε	μιμηταὶ	→	⸤τοῦ θεοῦ⸥	⸤τῶν ἐκκλησιῶν⸥	ἐν	⸤τῇ Ἰουδαίᾳ⸥	τῶν οὐσῶν
p.d	r.dp.2 d.dpm	pt.pa.dpm	cj r.np.2	n.vpm	v.api.2p	n.npm		d.gsm n.gsm	d.gpf n.gpf	p.d	d.dsf n.dsf	d.gpf pt.pa.gpf
1877	7007 3836	4409	1142 7007	81	1181	3629		1711 3836 2536	3836 1711	1877	3836 2677	3836 1639

in	Christ	Jesus:	You	suffered	from	your	own	countrymen	the	same	things		those	churches	suffered
ἐν	Χριστῷ	Ἰησοῦ	ὅτι ὑμεῖς	καὶ ἐπάθετε	ὑπὸ	τῶν	ἰδίων	συμφυλετῶν	τὰ	αὐτὰ		καθὼς	αὐτοὶ		καὶ
p.d	n.dsm	n.dsm	cj r.np.2	adv v.aai.2p	p.g	d.gpm	a.gpm	n.gpm	d.apn	r.apn		cj	r.npm		adv
1877	5986	2652	4022 7007	2779 4248	5679	3836	2625	5241	3836	899		2777	899		2779

from the Jews,		**15** who		killed		the Lord	Jesus	and the	prophets	and also	drove	us	out.		They
ὑπὸ τῶν Ἰουδαίων		τῶν	καὶ	ἀποκτεινάντων	τὸν	κύριον	Ἰησοῦν	καὶ τοὺς	προφήτας	καὶ	ἐκδιωξάντων	ἡμᾶς	←	καὶ	→
p.g d.gpm a.gpm		d.gpm	cj	pt.aa.gpm	d.asm	n.asm	n.asm	cj d.apm	n.apm	cj	pt.aa.gpm	r.ap.1		cj	
5679 3836 2681		3836	2779	650	3836	3261	2652	2779 3836	4737	2779	1691	7005	1691	2779	743

displease	God	and	are hostile	to all	men	**16** in their effort to keep		us	from speaking	to the	Gentiles
⸤μὴ ἀρεσκόντων⸥	θεῷ	καὶ	ἐναντίων	→ πᾶσιν	ἀνθρώποις	→	→ κωλυόντων	ἡμᾶς	λαλῆσαι	→ τοῖς	ἔθνεσιν
pl pt.pa.gpm	n.dsm	cj	a.gpm	a.dpm	n.dpm		pt.pa.gpm	r.ap.1	f.aa	d.dpn	n.dpn
3590 743	2536	2779	1885	4246	476		3266	7005	3281	3836	1620

so	that they may be saved.	In this way	they	always	heap		up their	sins		to the limit.	The
ἵνα	← → σωθῶσιν	εἰς	→	πάντοτε	⸤τὸ ἀναπληρῶσαι⸥	←	αὐτῶν	τὰς ἁμαρτίας	⸤↰ ←	δὲ	ἡ
cj	v.aps.3p p.a			adv	d.asn f.aa		r.gpm.3	d.apf n.apf		cj	d.nsf
2671	5392 1650			4121	3836 405		899	3836 281	405 405 405	1254	3836

wrath	of God	has come	upon	them	at	last.
ὀργὴ	→	ἔφθασεν	ἐπ'	αὐτοὺς	εἰς	τέλος
n.nsf		v.aai.3s	p.a	r.apm.3	p.a	n.asn
3973		5777	2093	899	1650	5465

Paul's Longing to See the Thessalonians

2:17 But,	brothers,	when we	were	torn	away	from	you	for	a	short	time	(in person,	not	in	thought),
δὲ	ἀδελφοί	→ ἡμεῖς	→	ἀπορφανισθέντες	←	ἀφ'	ὑμῶν	πρὸς	ὥρας	καιρὸν		προσώπῳ	οὐ	→	καρδίᾳ
cj	n.vpm	r.np.1		pt.ap.npm		p.g	r.gp.2	p.a	n.gsf	n.asm		n.dsn	pl		n.dsf
1254	81	682 7005		682		608	7007	4639	6052	2789		4725	4024		2840

out of	our	intense	longing	we made	every		effort	to see	you.	**18** For	we wanted	to come
ἐν ←	πολλῇ	ἐπιθυμίᾳ	→ →	περισσοτέρως	ἐσπουδάσαμεν	→	ἰδεῖν	⸤τὸ πρόσωπον	ὑμῶν⸥	διότι	→ ἠθελήσαμεν	→ ἐλθεῖν
p.d	a.dsf	n.dsf		adv.c	v.aai.1p		f.aa	d.asn n.asn	r.gp.2	cj	v.aai.1p	f.aa
1877	4498	2123	5079 5079	4359	5079		1625	3836 4725	7007	1484	2527	2262

καὶ ἡμέρας ἐργαζόμενοι πρὸς τὸ μὴ ἐπιβαρῆσαί τινα ὑμῶν ἐκηρύξαμεν εἰς ὑμᾶς τὸ εὐαγγέλιον τοῦ θεοῦ. ¶ **10** ὑμεῖς μάρτυρες καὶ ὁ θεός, ὡς ὁσίως καὶ δικαίως καὶ ἀμέμπτως ὑμῖν τοῖς πιστεύουσιν ἐγενήθημεν, **11** καθάπερ οἴδατε, ὡς ἕνα ἕκαστον ὑμῶν ὡς πατὴρ τέκνα ἑαυτοῦ **12** παρακαλοῦντες ὑμᾶς καὶ παραμυθούμενοι καὶ μαρτυρόμενοι εἰς τὸ περιπατεῖν ὑμᾶς ἀξίως τοῦ θεοῦ τοῦ καλοῦντος ὑμᾶς εἰς τὴν ἑαυτοῦ βασιλείαν καὶ δόξαν. ¶ **13** Καὶ διὰ τοῦτο καὶ ἡμεῖς εὐχαριστοῦμεν τῷ θεῷ ἀδιαλείπτως, ὅτι παραλαβόντες λόγον ἀκοῆς παρ' ἡμῶν τοῦ θεοῦ ἐδέξασθε οὐ λόγον ἀνθρώπων ἀλλὰ καθώς ἐστιν ἀληθῶς λόγον θεοῦ, ὃς καὶ ἐνεργεῖται ἐν ὑμῖν τοῖς πιστεύουσιν. **14** ὑμεῖς γὰρ μιμηταὶ ἐγενήθητε, ἀδελφοί, τῶν ἐκκλησιῶν τοῦ θεοῦ τῶν οὐσῶν ἐν τῇ Ἰουδαίᾳ ἐν Χριστῷ Ἰησοῦ, ὅτι τὰ αὐτὰ ἐπάθετε καὶ ὑμεῖς ὑπὸ τῶν ἰδίων συμφυλετῶν καθὼς καὶ αὐτοὶ ὑπὸ τῶν Ἰουδαίων, **15** τῶν καὶ τὸν κύριον ἀποκτεινάντων Ἰησοῦν καὶ τοὺς προφήτας καὶ ἡμᾶς ἐκδιωξάντων καὶ θεῷ μὴ ἀρεσκόντων καὶ πᾶσιν ἀνθρώποις ἐναντίων, **16** κωλυόντων ἡμᾶς τοῖς ἔθνεσιν λαλῆσαι ἵνα σωθῶσιν, εἰς τὸ ἀναπληρῶσαι αὐτῶν τὰς ἁμαρτίας πάντοτε. ἔφθασεν δὲ ἐπ' αὐτοὺς ἡ ὀργὴ τοῦ θεοῦ εἰς τέλος.

2:17 Ἡμεῖς δέ, ἀδελφοί, ἀπορφανισθέντες ἀφ' ὑμῶν πρὸς καιρὸν ὥρας, προσώπῳ οὐ καρδίᾳ, περισσοτέρως ἐσπουδάσαμεν τὸ

to	you	– certainly	I,	Paul,	did,	*again*		*and again*	– but	Satan		stopped us.	[19] For	what	is	our	hope,
πρὸς	ὑμᾶς	μὲν	ἐγώ	Παῦλος	‚καὶ	ἅπαξ‚	καὶ	δίς	καὶ	ὁ	σατανᾶς‚	ἐνέκοψεν ἡμᾶς	γὰρ	τίς		ἡμῶν	ἐλπὶς	ἤ
p.a	r.ap.2	pl	r.ns.1	n.nsm	cj	adv	cj	adv	cj	d.nsm	n.nsm	v.aai.3s r.ap.1	cj	r.nsf		r.gp.1	n.nsf	cj
4639	7007	3525	1609	4263	2779	562	2779	1489	2779	3836	4928	1601 7005	1142	5515		7005	1828	2445

our joy,	or	the	crown	in which	we will	glory		in the	presence	of	our	Lord		Jesus	when	he
χαρὰ	ἤ		στέφανος →	→	→	καυχήσεως	→	ἔμπροσθεν	‚	ἡμῶν‚	‚τοῦ κυρίου‚	Ἰησοῦ	ἐν	αὐτοῦ
n.nsf	cj		n.nsm			n.gsf		p.g		r.gp.1	d.gsm n.gsm	n.gsm	p.d	r.gsm.3
5915	2445		5109			3018		1869		3261 7005	3836 3261	2652	1877	899

comes?		Is it not		you? [20]	Indeed,	you	are	our	glory	and joy.	¶	[3:1] So	when	we could	stand	it
‚τῇ παρουσίᾳ‚	ἤ	οὐχὶ	καὶ	ὑμεῖς	γὰρ	ὑμεῖς	ἐστε	ἡμῶν	‚ἡ δόξα‚	καὶ ‚ἡ χαρά‚		Διὸ	→	→	→	στέγοντες ←
d.dsf n.dsf	cj	pl	cj	r.np.2	cj	r.np.2	v.pai.2p	r.gp.1	d.nsf n.nsf	cj d.nsf n.nsf		cj				pt.pa.npm
3836 4242	2445	4049	2779	7007	1142	7007	1639	7005	3836 1518	2779 3836 5915		1475				5095

no	longer,	we	thought		it best	to be	left		by	ourselves	in	Athens.	[2]	We	sent		Timothy,	who is
μηκέτι ←		εὐδοκήσαμεν ←	→	→	καταλειφθῆναι	→	μόνοι	ἐν	Ἀθήναις	καὶ	→	ἐπέμψαμεν	Τιμόθεον		
adv		v.aai.1p			f.ap		a.npm	p.d	n.dpf	cj		v.aai.1p	n.asm		
3600		2305			2901		3668	1877	121	2779		4287	5510		

our	brother	and	God's	fellow	worker	in	spreading	the	gospel	of	Christ,		to	strengthen	and
ἡμῶν	‚τὸν ἀδελφὸν‚	καὶ	‚τοῦ θεοῦ‚	συνεργὸν ←		ἐν		τῷ	εὐαγγελίῳ	→	‚τοῦ Χριστοῦ‚	εἰς	‚τὸ στηρίξαι‚	καὶ
r.gp.1	d.asm n.asm	cj	d.gsm n.gsm	n.asm		p.d		d.dsn	n.dsn		d.gsm n.gsm	p.a	d.asn f.aa	cj
7005	3836 81	2779	3836 2536	5301		1877		3836 2295			3836 5986	1650	3836 5114	2779

encourage	you	in	your	faith,	[3]	so that	no	one	would be	unsettled		by	these	trials.		You
παρακαλέσαι	ὑμᾶς	ὑπὲρ	ὑμῶν	‚τῆς πίστεως‚	→	→	μηδένα ←	→	→	‚τὸ σαίνεσθαι‚	ἐν	ταύταις	‚ταῖς θλίψεσιν‚	γὰρ	αὐτοὶ
f.aa	r.ap.2	p.g	r.gp.2	d.gsf n.gsf			a.asm			d.asn f.pp	p.d	r.dpf	d.dpf n.dpf	cj	r.npm
4151	7007	5642	7007	3836 4411			4883	4883	3594	3836 4883	1877	4047	3836 2568	1142	899

know	quite well	that	we were	destined	for	them.	[4]	In fact,	when	we were	with	you,	we kept	telling		you	that
οἴδατε		ὅτι	→	→	κείμεθα	εἰς	τοῦτο	γὰρ	καὶ ←		ὅτε	→	ἦμεν	πρὸς	ὑμᾶς →	→	προελέγομεν	ὑμῖν ὅτι
v.rai.2p		cj			v.pmi.1p	p.a	r.asn	cj	adv		cj		v.iai.1p	p.a	r.ap.2		v.iai.1p	r.dp.2 cj
3857		4022			3023	1650	4047	1142	2779		4021		1639	4639	7007		4625	7007 4022

we would	be	persecuted.	And	it turned	out	that	way,	as	you well	know.	[5] For		this reason,	when I		could
→	μέλλομεν	→	θλίβεσθαι	καὶ	→	ἐγένετο ←	καθὼς	←	καὶ →	οἴδατε	‚διὰ τοῦτο‚		→	καγὼ	
	v.pai.1p		f.pp	adv		v.ami.3s	cj		cj	v.rai.2p	p.a r.asn			crasis	
	3516		2567	2779		1181	2777		2779	3857	1328 4047			5095 2743	

stand	it	no	longer,	I	sent	to	find		out	about	your	faith.		I was	afraid	that	in some	way	the	tempter
στέγων ←		μηκέτι ←			ἔπεμψα	‚εἰς τὸ γνῶναι‚	←			ὑμῶν	‚τὴν πίστιν‚		μή	→	→	πως	ὁ	πειράζων
pt.pa.nsm		adv			v.aai.1s	p.a d.asn f.aa				r.gp.2	d.asf n.asf		cj			pl	d.nsm	pt.pa.nsm
5095		3600			4287	1650 3836 1182				7007	3836 4411		3590			4803	3836	4279

might have	tempted	you	and	our	efforts		might have	been	useless.
→	ἐπείρασεν	ὑμᾶς	καὶ	ἡμῶν	ὁ κόπος‚	→	→	γένηται	‚εἰς κενόν‚
	v.aai.3s	r.ap.2	cj	r.gp.1	d.nsm n.nsm			v.ams.3s	p.a a.asn
	4279	7007	2779	7005	3836 3160			1181	1650 3031

Timothy's Encouraging Report

[3:6] But	Timothy	has just	now	come	to	us	from	you	and	has	brought	good		news		about	your
δὲ	Τιμοθέου	→	Ἄρτι ←	ἐλθόντος	πρὸς	ἡμᾶς	ἀφ'	ὑμῶν	καὶ	→	→	εὐαγγελισαμένου		ἡμῖν			ὑμῶν
cj	n.gsm		adv	pt.aa.gsm	p.a	r.ap.1	p.g	r.gp.2	cj			pt.am.gsm		r.dp.1			r.gp.2
1254	5510		2262 785	2262	4639	7005	608	7007	2779			2294		7005			7007

faith	and	love.		He has	told	us	that	you	always	have	pleasant	memories	of us	and	that you
‚τὴν πίστιν‚	καὶ	‚τὴν ἀγάπην‚	καὶ				ὅτι	→	πάντοτε	ἔχετε	ἀγαθὴν	μνείαν	→ ἡμῶν	καὶ	
d.asf n.asf	cj	d.asf n.asf	cj				cj		adv	v.pai.2p	a.asf	n.asf	r.gp.1	cj	
3836 4411	2779	3836 27	2779				4022	2400	4121	2400	19	3644	7005		

long	to see	us,	just	as we	also	long	to see	you.	[7] Therefore,		brothers,	in	all	our	distress	and
ἐπιποθοῦντες	→ ἰδεῖν	ἡμᾶς	καθάπερ ←	ἡμεῖς	καὶ			ὑμᾶς	‚διὰ τοῦτο‚		ἀδελφοί	ἐπὶ	πάσῃ	ἡμῶν	‚τῇ ἀνάγκῃ‚	καὶ
pt.pa.npm	f.aa	r.ap.1	cj	r.np.1	adv			r.ap.2	p.a r.asn		n.vpm	p.d	a.dsf	r.gp.1	d.dsf n.dsf	cj
2160	1625	7005	2749	7005	2779			7007	1328 4047		81	2093	4246	7005	3836 340	2779

persecution	we were	encouraged	about	you	because	of	your	faith.	[8]	For	now	we	really	live,	since	you	are
θλίψει	→	→ παρεκλήθημεν	ἐφ'	ὑμῖν	διὰ	←	ὑμῶν	‚τῆς πίστεως‚	ὅτι		νῦν	→		ζῶμεν	ἐὰν	ὑμεῖς	→
n.dsf		v.api.1p	p.d	r.dp.2	p.g		r.gp.2	d.gsf n.gsf	cj		adv			v.pai.1p	cj	r.np.2	
2568		4151	2093	7007	1328		7007	3836 4411	4022		3814			2409	1569	7007	

πρόσωπον ὑμῶν ἰδεῖν ἐν πολλῇ ἐπιθυμίᾳ. [18] διότι ἠθελήσαμεν ἐλθεῖν πρὸς ὑμᾶς, ἐγὼ μὲν Παῦλος καὶ ἅπαξ καὶ δίς, καὶ ἐνέκοψεν ἡμᾶς ὁ Σατανᾶς. [19] τίς γὰρ ἡμῶν ἐλπὶς ἢ χαρὰ ἢ στέφανος καυχήσεως— ἢ οὐχὶ καὶ ὑμεῖς— ἔμπροσθεν τοῦ κυρίου ἡμῶν Ἰησοῦ ἐν τῇ αὐτοῦ παρουσίᾳ; [20] ὑμεῖς γὰρ ἐστε ἡ δόξα ἡμῶν καὶ ἡ χαρά.

[3:1] Διὸ μηκέτι στέγοντες εὐδοκήσαμεν καταλειφθῆναι ἐν Ἀθήναις μόνοι [2] καὶ ἐπέμψαμεν Τιμόθεον, τὸν ἀδελφὸν ἡμῶν καὶ συνεργὸν τοῦ θεοῦ ἐν τῷ εὐαγγελίῳ τοῦ Χριστοῦ, εἰς τὸ στηρίξαι ὑμᾶς καὶ παρακαλέσαι ὑπὲρ τῆς πίστεως ὑμῶν [3] τὸ μηδένα σαίνεσθαι ἐν ταῖς θλίψεσιν ταύταις. αὐτοὶ γὰρ οἴδατε ὅτι εἰς τοῦτο κείμεθα· [4] καὶ γὰρ ὅτε πρὸς ὑμᾶς ἦμεν, προελέγομεν ὑμῖν ὅτι μέλλομεν θλίβεσθαι, καθὼς καὶ ἐγένετο καὶ οἴδατε. [5] διὰ τοῦτο καγὼ μηκέτι στέγων ἔπεμψα εἰς τὸ γνῶναι τὴν πίστιν ὑμῶν, μή πως ἐπείρασεν ὑμᾶς ὁ πειράζων καὶ εἰς κενὸν γένηται ὁ κόπος ἡμῶν.

[3:6] Ἄρτι δὲ ἐλθόντος Τιμοθέου πρὸς ἡμᾶς ἀφ' ὑμῶν καὶ εὐαγγελισαμένου ἡμῖν τὴν πίστιν καὶ τὴν ἀγάπην ὑμῶν καὶ ὅτι ἔχετε μνείαν ἡμῶν ἀγαθὴν πάντοτε, ἐπιποθοῦντες ἡμᾶς ἰδεῖν καθάπερ καὶ ἡμεῖς ὑμᾶς, [7] διὰ τοῦτο παρεκλήθημεν, ἀδελφοί, ἐφ' ὑμῖν ἐπὶ πάσῃ τῇ ἀνάγκῃ καὶ θλίψει ἡμῶν διὰ τῆς ὑμῶν πίστεως, [8] ὅτι νῦν ζῶμεν ἐὰν ὑμεῖς στήκετε ἐν κυρίῳ. [9] τίνα γὰρ εὐχαριστίαν

standing firm in the Lord. **9** How can we thank God enough for you in return for all the
στήκετε ← ἐν κυρίῳ γὰρ τίνα δυνάμεθα ← εὐχαριστίαν τῷ θεῷ περὶ ὑμῶν → ἀνταποδοῦναι ἐπὶ πάσῃ τῇ
v.pai.2p p.d n.dsm cj r.asf v.ppi.1p n.asf d.dsm n.dsm p.g r.gp.2 f.aa p.d a.dsf d.dsf
5112 1877 3261 1142 5515 1538 2374 3836 2536 4309 7007 500 2093 4246 3836

joy we have in the presence of our God because of you? **10** Night and day we pray most
χαρᾷ ᾗ → χαίρομεν → ἔμπροσθεν → ἡμῶν τοῦ θεοῦ δι᾽ ← ὑμᾶς νυκτὸς καὶ ἡμέρας → δεόμενοι →
n.dsf r.dsf v.pai.1p p.g r.gp.1 d.gsm n.gsm p.a r.ap.2 n.gsf cj n.gsf pt.pp.npm
5915 4005 5897 1869 2536 3836 2536 1328 7007 3816 2779 2465 1289

earnestly that we may see you again and supply what is lacking in your faith. ¶
ὑπερεκπερισσοῦ εἰς → → τὸ ἰδεῖν ὑμῶν τὸ πρόσωπον καὶ καταρτίσαι τὰ ὑστερήματα → ὑμῶν τῆς πίστεως
adv p.a d.asn f.aa r.gp.2 d.asn n.asn cj f.aa d.apn n.apn r.gp.2 d.gsf n.gsf
5655 1650 3836 1625 7007 3836 4725 2779 2936 3836 5729 7007 3836 4411

11 Now may our God and Father himself and our Lord Jesus clear the way for us to come to you.
δὲ → ἡμῶν ὁ θεὸς καὶ πατὴρ Αὐτὸς καὶ ἡμῶν ὁ κύριος Ἰησοῦς κατευθύναι τὴν ὁδὸν → ἡμῶν πρὸς ὑμᾶς
cj r.gp.1 d.nsm n.nsm cj n.nsm r.nsm cj r.gp.1 d.nsm n.nsm n.nsm v.aao.3s d.asf n.asf r.gp.1 p.a r.ap.2
1254 2985 7005 3836 2536 2779 4252 899 2779 7005 3836 3261 2652 2985 3836 3847 7005 4639 7007

12 May the Lord make your love increase and overflow for each other and for everyone else, just as
δὲ → ὁ κύριος → ὑμᾶς τῇ ἀγάπῃ πλεονάσαι καὶ περισσεύσαι εἰς ἀλλήλους ← καὶ εἰς πάντας ← καθάπερ
cj d.nsm n.nsm r.ap.2 d.dsf n.dsf v.aao.3s cj v.aao.3s p.a r.apm cj p.a a.apm cj
1254 4429 3836 3261 4429 7007 3836 27 4355 2779 4355 1650 253 2779 1650 4246 2749

ours does for you. **13** May he strengthen your hearts so that you will be blameless and holy in
καὶ ἡμεῖς εἰς ὑμᾶς → εἰς τὸ στηρίξαι ὑμῶν τὰς καρδίας ← ← ἀμέμπτους ἐν ἁγιωσύνῃ →
adv r.np.1 p.a r.ap.2 p.a d.asn f.aa r.gp.2 d.apf n.apf a.apf p.d n.dsf
2779 7005 1650 7007 1650 3836 5114 7007 3836 2840 1650 1650 289 1877 43

the presence of our God and Father when our Lord Jesus comes with all his holy
→ ἔμπροσθεν → ἡμῶν τοῦ θεοῦ καὶ πατρὸς ἐν ἡμῶν τοῦ κυρίου Ἰησοῦ τῇ παρουσίᾳ μετὰ πάντων αὐτοῦ τῶν ἁγίων
p.g r.gp.1 d.gsm n.gsm cj n.gsm p.d r.gp.1 d.gsm n.gsm n.gsm d.dsf n.dsf p.g a.gpm r.gsm.3 d.gpm a.gpm
1869 2536 7005 3836 2536 2779 4252 1877 7005 3836 3261 2652 3836 4242 3552 4246 899 3836 41

ones.
← [ἀμήν]
pl
297

Living to Please God

4:1 Finally, brothers, we instructed you how to live in order to please
οὖν Λοιπὸν ἀδελφοί ἵνα καθὼς παρ᾽ ἡμῶν παρελάβετε ← πῶς δεῖ ὑμᾶς → τὸ περιπατεῖν καὶ → → ἀρέσκειν
cj adv n.vpm cj cj p.g r.gp.1 v.aai.2p cj v.pai.3s r.ap.2 d.asn f.aa cj f.pa
4036 3370 81 2671 2777 4123 7005 4161 4802 1256 7007 3836 4344 2779 743

God, as in fact you are living. Now we ask you and urge you in the Lord Jesus to do
θεῷ καθὼς καὶ ← → → περιπατεῖτε → ἐρωτῶμεν ὑμᾶς καὶ παρακαλοῦμεν ἐν κυρίῳ Ἰησοῦ ἵνα περισσεύητε
n.dsm cj adv v.pai.2p v.pai.1p r.ap.2 cj v.pai.1p p.d n.dsm n.dsm cj v.pas.2p
2536 2777 2779 4344 2263 7007 2779 4151 1877 3261 2652 2671 4355

this more and more. **2** For you know what instructions we gave you by the authority of the Lord Jesus. ¶
μᾶλλον ← → γὰρ → οἴδατε τίνας παραγγελίας → ἐδώκαμεν ὑμῖν διὰ ← → τοῦ κυρίου Ἰησοῦ
adv.c cj v.rai.2p r.apf n.apf v.aai.1p r.dp.2 p.g d.gsm n.gsm n.gsm
3437 1142 3857 5515 4132 1443 7007 1328 3836 3261 2652

3 It is God's will that you should be sanctified: that you should avoid sexual
γάρ Τοῦτο ἐστιν τοῦ θεοῦ θέλημα ὑμῶν ὁ ἁγιασμὸς ὑμᾶς → ἀπέχεσθαι ἀπὸ τῆς πορνείας
cj r.nsn v.pai.3s d.gsm n.gsm n.nsn r.gp.2 d.nsm n.nsm r.ap.2 f.pm p.g d.gsf n.gsf
1142 4047 1639 3836 2536 2525 7007 3836 40 7007 600 608 3836 4518

immorality; **4** that each of you should learn to control his own body in a way that is holy and honorable,
← ἕκαστον → ὑμῶν εἰδέναι κτᾶσθαι τὸ ἑαυτοῦ σκεῦος ἐν ἁγιασμῷ καὶ τιμῇ
r.asm r.gp.2 f.ra f.pm d.asn r.gsm.3 n.asn p.d n.dsm cj n.dsf
1667 7007 3857 3227 3836 1571 5007 1877 40 2779 5507

5 not in passionate lust like the heathen, who do not know God; **6** and that in this matter no one
μὴ ἐν πάθει ἐπιθυμίας καθάπερ καὶ τὰ ἔθνη τὰ → μὴ εἰδότα τὸν θεόν ἐν τῷ πράγματι μὴ ←
pl p.d n.dsn n.gsf pl adv d.npn n.npn d.npn pl pt.ra.npn d.asm n.asm p.d d.dsn n.dsn pl
3590 1877 4079 2123 2749 2779 3836 1620 3836 3857 3590 3857 3836 2536 1877 3836 4547 3590

δυνάμεθα τῷ θεῷ ἀνταποδοῦναι περὶ ὑμῶν ἐπὶ πάσῃ τῇ χαρᾷ ᾗ χαίρομεν δι᾽ ὑμᾶς ἔμπροσθεν τοῦ θεοῦ ἡμῶν, **10** νυκτὸς καὶ ἡμέρας ὑπερεκπερισσοῦ δεόμενοι εἰς τὸ ἰδεῖν ὑμῶν τὸ πρόσωπον καὶ καταρτίσαι τὰ ὑστερήματα τῆς πίστεως ὑμῶν; ¶ **11** Αὐτὸς δὲ ὁ θεὸς καὶ πατὴρ ἡμῶν καὶ ὁ κύριος ἡμῶν Ἰησοῦς κατευθύναι τὴν ὁδὸν ἡμῶν πρὸς ὑμᾶς· **12** ὑμᾶς δὲ ὁ κύριος πλεονάσαι καὶ περισσεύσαι τῇ ἀγάπῃ εἰς ἀλλήλους καὶ εἰς πάντας καθάπερ καὶ ἡμεῖς εἰς ὑμᾶς, **13** εἰς τὸ στηρίξαι ὑμῶν τὰς καρδίας ἀμέμπτους ἐν ἁγιωσύνῃ ἔμπροσθεν τοῦ θεοῦ καὶ πατρὸς ἡμῶν ἐν τῇ παρουσίᾳ τοῦ κυρίου ἡμῶν Ἰησοῦ μετὰ πάντων τῶν ἁγίων αὐτοῦ. «αὐτοῦ[.» ἀμήν].

4:1 Λοιπὸν οὖν, ἀδελφοί, ἐρωτῶμεν ὑμᾶς καὶ παρακαλοῦμεν ἐν κυρίῳ Ἰησοῦ, ἵνα καθὼς παρελάβετε παρ᾽ ἡμῶν τὸ πῶς δεῖ ὑμᾶς περιπατεῖν καὶ ἀρέσκειν θεῷ, καθὼς καὶ περιπατεῖτε, ἵνα περισσεύητε μᾶλλον. **2** οἴδατε γὰρ τίνας παραγγελίας ἐδώκαμεν ὑμῖν διὰ τοῦ κυρίου Ἰησοῦ. ¶ **3** τοῦτο γάρ ἐστιν θέλημα τοῦ θεοῦ, ὁ ἁγιασμὸς ὑμῶν, ἀπέχεσθαι ὑμᾶς ἀπὸ τῆς πορνείας, **4** εἰδέναι ἕκαστον ὑμῶν τὸ ἑαυτοῦ σκεῦος κτᾶσθαι ἐν ἁγιασμῷ καὶ τιμῇ, **5** μὴ ἐν πάθει ἐπιθυμίας καθάπερ καὶ τὰ ἔθνη τὰ μὴ εἰδότα τὸν θεόν, **6** τὸ μὴ ὑπερβαίνειν καὶ πλεονεκτεῖν ἐν τῷ πράγματι τὸν ἀδελφὸν αὐτοῦ, διότι ἔκδικος κύριος περὶ πάντων

should wrong   his   brother   or   take advantage of him.   The Lord will punish men for all   such
→   ⸤τὸ ὑπερβαίνειν⸥ αὐτοῦ τὸν ἀδελφὸν⸥ καὶ →   πλεονεκτεῖν   διότι   κύριος ἔκδικος περὶ πάντων τούτων
    d.asn f.pa   r.gsm.3 d.asn n.asm cj   f.pa   cj   n.nsm   n.nsm   p.g a.gpn r.gpn
    3836 5648   899   3836 81   2779   4430   1484   3261   1690   4309 4246   4047

sins, as   we have already told   you and warned   you. [7] For God   did not call   us   to be
καθὼς καὶ →   →   →   προείπαμεν ὑμῖν καὶ διεμαρτυράμεθα   γὰρ ὁ θεὸς →   οὐ ἐκάλεσεν ἡμᾶς ἐπὶ
cj   adv   v.aai.1p   r.dp.2 cj v.ami.1p   cj d.nsm n.nsm   pl v.aai.3s r.ap.1 p.d
2777 2779   4597   7007 2779 1371   1142 3836 2536   2813 4024   2813   7005 2093

impure, but to live a holy   life. [8] Therefore, he who rejects this instruction does not reject man   but
ἀκαθαρσίᾳ ἀλλ᾽   ἐν ἁγιασμῷ   τοιγαροῦν ὁ ← ἀθετῶν   οὐκ ἀθετεῖ ἄνθρωπον ἀλλὰ
n.dsf   cj   p.d n.dsm   cj   d.nsm pt.pa.nsm   pl v.pai.3s n.asm   cj
174   247   1877 40   5521   3836   119   119 4024   119 476   247

God,   who   gives   you his Holy   Spirit.   ¶   [9] Now about brotherly   love we do not
⸤τὸν θεὸν⸥ τὸν [καὶ] διδόντα εἰς ὑμᾶς αὐτοῦ ⸤τὸ ἅγιον⸥ ⸤τὸ πνεῦμα⸥ δὲ Περὶ ⸤τῆς φιλαδελφίας⸥ ← → οὐ
d.asn n.asm d.asn adv   pt.pa.asm p.a r.ap.2 r.gsm.3 d.asn a.asn d.asn n.asn cj p.g d.gsf n.gsf   pl
3836 2536 3836   1443   1650 7007 899   3836 41   3836 4460 1254 4309 3836 5789   2400 4024

need   to write to you, for you yourselves have been taught   by God to love   each   other.
⸤χρείαν ἔχετε⸥ γράφειν → ὑμῖν γὰρ ὑμεῖς αὐτοὶ   ἐστε θεοδίδακτοι   εἰς ⸤τὸ ἀγαπᾶν⸥ ἀλλήλους
n.asf v.pai.2p f.pa   r.dp.2 cj r.np.2 r.npm   v.pai.2p a.npm   p.a d.asn f.pa   r.apm
5970 2400   1211   7007 1142 7007 899   1639 2531   1650 3836 26   253

[10] And in fact, you do love   all   the brothers   throughout Macedonia. Yet we urge   you,
καὶ γὰρ   → ποιεῖτε αὐτὸ εἰς πάντας τοὺς ἀδελφοὺς τοὺς ⸤ἐν ὅλῃ⸥ ⸤τῇ Μακεδονίᾳ⸥ δὲ → Παρακαλοῦμεν ὑμᾶς
adv cj   v.pai.2p r.asn.3 p.a a.apm d.apm n.apm d.apm p.d a.dsf d.dsf n.dsf   cj   v.pai.1p   r.ap.2
2779 1142   4472   899 1650 4246 3836 81   3836 1877 3910 3836 3423   1254 4151   7007

brothers, to do   so more and more. ¶ [11]   Make it your ambition to lead a quiet   life,   to
ἀδελφοί → περισσεύειν μᾶλλον ←   καὶ → →   φιλοτιμεῖσθαι → ἡσυχάζειν ← καὶ
n.vpm   f.pa   adv.c   cj   f.pa   f.pa   cj
81   4355   3437   2779   5818   2483   2779

mind   your own business and to work   with your   hands,   just as we told   you, [12] so that your
πράσσειν → ἴδια τὰ   καὶ → ἐργάζεσθαι → ὑμῶν ἰδίαις ⸤ταῖς χερσὶν⸥ καθὼς → παρηγγείλαμεν ὑμῖν ἵνα → →
f.pa   a.apn d.apn cj   f.pm   r.gp.2 a.dpf d.dpf n.dpf   cj   v.aai.1p   r.dp.2 cj
4556   2625 3836 2779   2237   7007 2625 3836 5931   2777   4133   7007 2671

daily life   may win the respect of outsiders and so that you will not   be dependent on anybody.
→ περιπατῆτε → → εὐσχημόνως πρὸς ⸤τοὺς ἔξω⸥ καὶ   μηδενὸς ἔχητε χρείαν
   v.pas.2p   adv   p.a d.apm adv cj   a.gsn v.pas.2p n.asf
   4344   2361   4639 3836 2032 2779   2400 2400 3594   2400 5970   3594

The Coming of the Lord

[4:13] Brothers, we do not want you to be ignorant about those who fall asleep, or   to grieve
δὲ ἀδελφοί → → Οὐ θέλομεν ὑμᾶς → ἀγνοεῖν περὶ τῶν ←   κοιμωμένων ἵνα μὴ → λυπῆσθε
cj n.vpm   pl v.pai.1p r.ap.2   f.pa   p.g d.gpm   pt.pp.gpm cj pl v.pps.2p
1254 81   2527 2527 4024 2527   51   4309 3836   3121   2671 3590 3382

like   the rest of men, who have no hope. [14]   We believe that Jesus died   and rose   again and
⸤καθὼς καὶ⸥ οἱ λοιποὶ   οἱ ἔχοντες μὴ ἐλπίδα γὰρ εἰ → πιστεύομεν ὅτι Ἰησοῦς ἀπέθανεν καὶ ἀνέστη   καὶ
pl   adv d.npm a.npm d.npm pt.pa.npm pl n.asf cj cj   v.pai.1p   cj n.nsm   v.aai.3s cj v.aai.3s   adv
2777   2779 3836 3370   3836 2400   3590 1828 1142 1623   4409   4022 2652   633   2779 482   2779

so   we believe that God   will bring with Jesus those who have fallen asleep   in him.   [15]
οὕτως → →   ⸤ὁ θεὸς⸥ → ἄξει σὺν αὐτῷ τοὺς ←   ←   κοιμηθέντας διὰ ⸤τοῦ Ἰησοῦ⸥ γὰρ Τοῦτο
adv   d.nsm n.nsm   v.fai.3s p.d r.dsm.3 d.apm   pt.ap.apm p.g d.gsm n.gsm   cj r.asn
4048   3836 2536   72   5250 899 3836   3121   1328 3836 2652   1142 4047

According to the Lord's own word, we tell   you that we who are still alive, who are left   till the
ἐν   κυρίου λόγῳ   λέγομεν ὑμῖν ὅτι ἡμεῖς οἱ → still ζῶντες οἱ → περιλειπόμενοι εἰς τὴν
p.d   n.gsm n.dsm   v.pai.1p r.dp.2 cj r.np.1 d.npm   pt.pa.npm d.npm pt.pp.npm p.a d.asf
1877   3261 3364   3306   7007 4022 7005 3836   2409   3836   4335   1650 3836

coming of the Lord, will certainly not precede those who have fallen asleep. [16] For the Lord himself will
παρουσίαν → τοῦ κυρίου →   ⸤οὐ μὴ⸥ φθάσωμεν τοὺς ←   ←   κοιμηθέντας   ὅτι ὁ κύριος αὐτὸς →
n.asf   d.gsm n.gsm   pl pl v.aas.1p d.apm   pt.ap.apm   cj d.nsm n.nsm r.nsm
4242   3836 3261 5777   4024 3590 5777 3836   3121   4022 3836 3261 899

τούτων, καθὼς καὶ προείπαμεν ὑμῖν καὶ διεμαρτυράμεθα. [7] οὐ γὰρ ἐκάλεσεν ἡμᾶς ὁ θεὸς ἐπὶ ἀκαθαρσίᾳ ἀλλ᾽ ἐν ἁγιασμῷ.
[8] τοιγαροῦν ὁ ἀθετῶν οὐκ ἄνθρωπον ἀθετεῖ ἀλλὰ τὸν θεὸν τὸν [καὶ] διδόντα τὸ πνεῦμα αὐτοῦ τὸ ἅγιον εἰς ὑμᾶς. ¶ [9] Περὶ δὲ
τῆς φιλαδελφίας οὐ χρείαν ἔχετε γράφειν ὑμῖν, αὐτοὶ γὰρ ὑμεῖς θεοδίδακτοί ἐστε εἰς τὸ ἀγαπᾶν ἀλλήλους, [10] καὶ γὰρ ποιεῖτε
αὐτὸ εἰς πάντας τοὺς ἀδελφοὺς [τοὺς] ἐν ὅλῃ τῇ Μακεδονίᾳ. παρακαλοῦμεν δὲ ὑμᾶς, ἀδελφοί, περισσεύειν μᾶλλον ¶ [11] καὶ
φιλοτιμεῖσθαι ἡσυχάζειν καὶ πράσσειν τὰ ἴδια καὶ ἐργάζεσθαι ταῖς [ἰδίαις] χερσὶν ὑμῶν, καθὼς ὑμῖν παρηγγείλαμεν, [12] ἵνα
περιπατῆτε εὐσχημόνως πρὸς τοὺς ἔξω καὶ μηδενὸς χρείαν ἔχητε.

[4:13] Οὐ θέλομεν δὲ ὑμᾶς ἀγνοεῖν, ἀδελφοί, περὶ τῶν κοιμωμένων, ἵνα μὴ λυπῆσθε καθὼς καὶ οἱ λοιποὶ οἱ μὴ ἔχοντες ἐλπίδα.
[14] εἰ γὰρ πιστεύομεν ὅτι Ἰησοῦς ἀπέθανεν καὶ ἀνέστη, οὕτως καὶ ὁ θεὸς τοὺς κοιμηθέντας διὰ τοῦ Ἰησοῦ ἄξει σὺν αὐτῷ. [15] Τοῦτο
γὰρ ὑμῖν λέγομεν ἐν λόγῳ κυρίου, ὅτι ἡμεῖς οἱ ζῶντες οἱ περιλειπόμενοι εἰς τὴν παρουσίαν τοῦ κυρίου οὐ μὴ φθάσωμεν τοὺς
κοιμηθέντας· [16] ὅτι αὐτὸς ὁ κύριος ἐν κελεύσματι, ἐν φωνῇ ἀρχαγγέλου καὶ ἐν σάλπιγγι θεοῦ, καταβήσεται ἀπ᾽ οὐρανοῦ καὶ οἱ

come   down from heaven, with a loud command, with the voice of the archangel and with the trumpet call of
καταβήσεται ← ἀπ' οὐρανοῦ ἐν → κελεύσματι ἐν φωνῇ → ἀρχαγγέλου καὶ ἐν σάλπιγγι ←
v.fmi.3s   p.g   n.gsm   p.d   n.dsn   p.d   n.dsf   n.gsm   cj   p.d   n.dsf
2849   608   4041   1877   3026   1877   5889   791   2779   1877   4894

God, and the dead in Christ will rise   first. [17] After that, we who are still alive and are left
θεοῦ καὶ οἱ νεκροὶ ἐν Χριστῷ → ἀναστήσονται πρῶτον ἔπειτα ← ἡμεῖς οἱ → ζῶντες οἱ → περιλειπόμενοι
n.gsm   cj   d.npm   a.npm   p.d   n.dsm   v.fmi.3p   adv   adv   r.np.1   d.npm   pt.pa.npm   d.npm   pt.pp.npm
2536   2779   3836   3738   1877   5986   482   4754   2083   7005   3836   2409   3836   4335

will be caught   up together with them in the clouds to meet the Lord in the air. And so we will
→ → ἁρπαγησόμεθα ← ἅμα σὺν αὐτοῖς ἐν νεφέλαις εἰς ἀπάντησιν τοῦ κυρίου εἰς ἀέρα καὶ οὕτως →
v.fpi.1p   adv   p.d   r.dpm.3   p.d   n.dpf   p.a   n.asf   d.gsm   n.gsm   p.a   n.asm   cj   adv
773   275   5250   899   1877   3749   1650   561   3836   3261   1650   113   2779   4048

be with the Lord forever. [18] Therefore encourage each other with these words. ¶ [5:1] Now, brothers,
ἐσόμεθα σὺν κυρίῳ πάντοτε Ὥστε παρακαλεῖτε ἀλλήλους ← ἐν τούτοις τοῖς λόγοις δὲ ἀδελφοί
v.fmi.1p   p.d   n.dsm   adv   cj   v.pam.2p   r.apm   p.d   r.dpm   d.dpm   n.dpm   cj   n.vpm
1639   5250   3261   4121   6063   4151   253   1877   4047   3836   3364   1254   81

about times and dates we do not need to write to you, [2] for you know very well that the
Περὶ τῶν χρόνων καὶ τῶν καιρῶν → οὐ χρείαν ἔχετε → γράφεσθαι ὑμῖν γὰρ αὐτοὶ οἴδατε → ἀκριβῶς ὅτι
p.g   d.gpm   n.gpm   cj   d.gpm   n.gpm   pl   n.asf   v.pai.2p   v.ppp   r.dp.2   cj   r.npm   v.rai.2p   adv   cj
4309   3836   5989   2779   3836   2789   2400   2400   4024   5970   2400   1211   7007   1142   899   3857   209   4022

day of the Lord will come   like a thief in the night. [3] While people are saying, "Peace and safety,"
ἡμέρα κυρίου → ἔρχεται οὕτως ὡς κλέπτης ἐν νυκτί ὅταν → λέγωσιν εἰρήνη καὶ ἀσφάλεια τότε
n.nsf   n.gsm   v.pmi.3s   adv   pl   n.nsm   p.d   n.dsf   cj   v.pas.3p   n.nsf   cj   n.nsf   adv
2465   3261   2262   4048   6055   3095   1877   3816   4020   3306   1645   2779   854   5538

destruction will come on them suddenly, as labor pains on a pregnant woman, and they will
ὄλεθρος → ἐφίσταται αὐτοῖς αἰφνίδιος ὥσπερ ἡ ὠδίν ← τῇ ἐν γαστρὶ ἐχούσῃ ← καὶ → →
n.nsm   v.pmi.3s   r.dpm.3   a.nsm   cj   d.nsf   n.nsf   d.dsf   p.d   n.dsf   pt.pa.dsf   cj
3897   2392   899   167   6061   3836   6047   3836   1877   1143   2400   2779   1767   1767

not escape. ¶ [4] But you, brothers, are not in darkness so that this day should surprise you like a
οὐ μὴ ἐκφύγωσιν δὲ ὑμεῖς ἀδελφοί ἐστὲ οὐκ ἐν σκότει ἵνα ← ἡ ἡμέρα → καταλάβῃ ὑμᾶς ὡς
pl   pl   v.aas.3p   cj   r.np.2   n.vpm   v.pai.2p   pl   p.d   n.dsn   cj   d.nsf   n.nsf   v.aas.3s   r.ap.2   pl
4024   3590   1767   1254   7007   81   1639   4024   1877   5030   2671   3836   2465   2898   7007   6055

thief. [5] You are all sons of the light and sons of the day. We do not belong to the night or to the
κλέπτης γὰρ ὑμεῖς ἐστε πάντες υἱοὶ → φωτός καὶ υἱοὶ → ἡμέρας → Οὐκ ἐσμὲν → νυκτὸς οὐδὲ →
n.nsm   cj   r.np.2   v.pai.2p   a.npm   n.npm   n.gsn   cj   n.npm   n.gsf   pl   v.pai.1p   n.gsf   cj
3095   1142   7007   1639   4246   5626   5890   2779   5626   2465   1639   1639   4024   1639   3816   4028

darkness. [6] So then, let us not be like others, who are asleep, but let us be alert and self-controlled.
σκότους οὖν ἄρα → μὴ → ὡς οἱ λοιποί → καθεύδωμεν ἀλλὰ → → γρηγορῶμεν καὶ νήφωμεν
n.gsn   cj   cj   pl   cj   d.npm   a.npm   v.pas.1p   cj   v.pas.1p   cj   v.pas.1p
5030   4036   726   2761   2761   3590   2761   6055   3836   3370   2761   247   1213   2779   3768

[7] For those who sleep, sleep at night, and those who get drunk, get drunk at night. [8] But since we
γὰρ Οἱ ← καθεύδοντες καθεύδουσιν → νυκτὸς καὶ οἱ ← μεθυσκόμενοι → μεθύουσιν → νυκτὸς δὲ → ἡμεῖς
cj   d.npm   pt.pa.npm   v.pai.3p   n.gsf   cj   d.npm   pt.pp.npm   v.pai.3p   n.gsf   cj   r.np.1
1142   3836   2761   2761   3816   2779   3836   3499   3501   3816   1254   7005

belong to the day, let us be self-controlled, putting on faith and love as a breastplate, and the hope of
ὄντες ἡμέρας → νήφωμεν ἐνδυσάμενοι ← πίστεως καὶ ἀγάπης θώρακα καὶ ἐλπίδα →
pt.pa.npm   n.gsf   v.pas.1p   pt.am.npm   n.gsf   cj   n.gsf   n.asm   cj   n.asf
1639   2465   3768   1907   4411   2779   27   2606   2779   1828

salvation as a helmet. [9] For God did not appoint us to suffer wrath but to receive salvation through
σωτηρίας περικεφαλαίαν ὅτι ὁ θεός → οὐκ ἔθετο ἡμᾶς εἰς ὀργὴν ἀλλὰ εἰς περιποίησιν σωτηρίας διὰ
n.gsf   n.asf   cj   d.nsm   n.nsm   pl   v.ami.3s   r.ap.1   p.a   n.asf   cj   p.a   n.asf   n.gsf   p.g
5401   4330   4022   3836   2536   5502   4024   5502   7005   1650   3973   247   1650   4348   5401   1328

our Lord Jesus Christ. [10] He died for us so that, whether we are awake or asleep, we may
ἡμῶν τοῦ κυρίου Ἰησοῦ Χριστοῦ τοῦ ἀποθανόντος ὑπὲρ ἡμῶν ἵνα εἴτε → γρηγορῶμεν εἴτε καθεύδωμεν →
r.gp.1   d.gsm   n.gsm   n.gsm   n.gsm   d.gsm   pt.aa.gsm   p.g   r.gp.1   cj   cj   v.pas.1p   cj   v.pas.1p
7005   3836   3261   2652   5986   3836   633   5642   7005   2671   1664   1213   1664   2761

νεκροὶ ἐν Χριστῷ ἀναστήσονται πρῶτον, [17] ἔπειτα ἡμεῖς οἱ ζῶντες οἱ περιλειπόμενοι ἅμα σὺν αὐτοῖς ἁρπαγησόμεθα ἐν νεφέλαις εἰς ἀπάντησιν τοῦ κυρίου εἰς ἀέρα· καὶ οὕτως πάντοτε σὺν κυρίῳ ἐσόμεθα. [18] Ὥστε παρακαλεῖτε ἀλλήλους ἐν τοῖς λόγοις τούτοις. [5:1] Περὶ δὲ τῶν χρόνων καὶ τῶν καιρῶν, ἀδελφοί, οὐ χρείαν ἔχετε ὑμῖν γράφεσθαι, [2] αὐτοὶ γὰρ ἀκριβῶς οἴδατε ὅτι ἡμέρα κυρίου ὡς κλέπτης ἐν νυκτὶ οὕτως ἔρχεται. [3] ὅταν λέγωσιν, Εἰρήνη καὶ ἀσφάλεια, τότε αἰφνίδιος αὐτοῖς ἐφίσταται ὄλεθρος ὥσπερ ἡ ὠδὶν τῇ ἐν γαστρὶ ἐχούσῃ, καὶ οὐ μὴ ἐκφύγωσιν. ¶ [4] ὑμεῖς δέ, ἀδελφοί, οὐκ ἐστὲ ἐν σκότει, ἵνα ἡ ἡμέρα ὑμᾶς ὡς κλέπτης καταλάβῃ· [5] πάντες γὰρ ὑμεῖς υἱοὶ φωτός ἐστε καὶ υἱοὶ ἡμέρας. οὐκ ἐσμὲν νυκτὸς οὐδὲ σκότους· [6] ἄρα οὖν μὴ καθεύδωμεν ὡς οἱ λοιποὶ ἀλλὰ γρηγορῶμεν καὶ νήφωμεν. [7] οἱ γὰρ καθεύδοντες νυκτὸς καθεύδουσιν καὶ οἱ μεθυσκόμενοι νυκτὸς μεθύουσιν· [8] ἡμεῖς δὲ ἡμέρας ὄντες νήφωμεν ἐνδυσάμενοι θώρακα πίστεως καὶ ἀγάπης καὶ περικεφαλαίαν ἐλπίδα σωτηρίας· [9] ὅτι οὐκ ἔθετο ἡμᾶς ὁ θεὸς εἰς ὀργὴν ἀλλὰ εἰς περιποίησιν σωτηρίας διὰ τοῦ κυρίου ἡμῶν Ἰησοῦ Χριστοῦ [10] τοῦ ἀποθανόντος ὑπὲρ ἡμῶν, ἵνα εἴτε γρηγορῶμεν εἴτε καθεύδωμεν ἅμα σὺν αὐτῷ ζήσωμεν. [11] Διὸ παρακαλεῖτε ἀλλήλους καὶ οἰκοδομεῖτε εἰς

live   together with   him.   **11** Therefore encourage one   another and build   each   other up, just   as in
ζήσωμεν ἅμα   σὺν   αὐτῷ   Διὸ   παρακαλεῖτε ἀλλήλους ←   καὶ   οἰκοδομεῖτε εἰς τὸν ἕνα   ←   καθὼς ← καὶ
v.aas.1p adv   p.d   r.dsm.3 cj   v.pam.2p   r.apm   cj   v.pam.2p   a.nsm d.asm a.asm   cj   adv
2409   275   5250   899   1475   4151   253   2779 3868   1651 3836 1651 3868   2777 2779

fact you are doing. ¶ **12** Now we ask   you,   brothers, to respect those who work   hard among you,
←   →   ποιεῖτε   δὲ → Ἐρωτῶμεν ὑμᾶς ἀδελφοί → εἰδέναι τοὺς ← κοπιῶντας ← ἐν   ὑμῖν   καὶ
         v.pai.2p   cj   v.pai.1p r.ap.2 n.vpm   f.ra   d.apm   pt.pa.apm   p.d   r.dp.2 cj
         4472   1254   2263   7007   81   3857   3836   3159   1877 7007   2779

who are over   you   in the Lord and who admonish you.   **13**   Hold them   in the highest   regard   in
→   → προϊσταμένους ὑμῶν ἐν   κυρίῳ καὶ → νουθετοῦντας ὑμᾶς καὶ   → αὐτοὺς →   ὑπερεκπερισσοῦ ἡγεῖσθαι ἐν
       pt.pm.apm   r.gp.2 p.d n.dsm cj   pt.pa.apm   r.ap.2 cj   r.apm.3   adv   f.pm   p.d
       4613   7007 1877 3261 2779   3805   7007 2451 2451 899   5655   2451   1877

love because of their work.   Live in peace with each   other. **14** And we urge   you,   brothers, warn
ἀγάπῃ διὰ   ← αὐτῶν τὸ ἔργον → εἰρηνεύετε ἐν   ἑαυτοῖς   δὲ → Παρακαλοῦμεν ὑμᾶς ἀδελφοί νουθετεῖτε
n.dsf p.a   r.gpm.3 d.asn n.asn v.pam.2p p.d   r.dpm.2   cj   v.pai.1p   r.ap.2 n.vpm   v.pam.2p
27   1328   899   3836 2240   1644   1877 1571   1254 4151   7007   81   3805

those who are idle, encourage the timid, help   the weak, be patient   with everyone. **15** Make sure that
τοὺς ←   ἀτάκτους παραμυθεῖσθε τοὺς ὀλιγοψύχους ἀντέχεσθε τῶν ἀσθενῶν → μακροθυμεῖτε πρὸς πάντας   ὁρᾶτε
d.apm   a.apm   v.pmm.2p   d.apm a.apm   v.pmm.2p d.gpm a.gpm   v.pam.2p   p.a a.apm   v.pam.2p
3836   864   4170   3836 3901   504   3836 822   3428   4639 4246   3972

nobody pays back   wrong for wrong, but   always try   to be kind   to each   other and to
μή τις ἀποδῷ   τινι κακὸν ἀντὶ κακοῦ ἀλλὰ πάντοτε διώκετε ←   τὸ ἀγαθὸν [καὶ] εἰς ἀλλήλους ←   καὶ εἰς
cj r.nsm v.aas.3s r.dsm a.asn p.g a.gsn cj   adv   v.pam.2p   d.asn a.asn   p.a r.apm   cj p.a
3590 5516 625   5516 2805 505 2805 247 4121   1503   3836 19   2779 1650 253   2779 1650

everyone else. ¶ **16** Be joyful always; **17** pray   continually; **18** give thanks   in all circumstances, for this is
πάντας   → χαίρετε Πάντοτε   προσεύχεσθε ἀδιαλείπτως   → εὐχαριστεῖτε ἐν παντὶ   γὰρ τοῦτο
a.apm   v.pam.2p v.pam.2p v.pmm.2p   adv   v.pam.2p   p.d a.dsn   cj r.nsn
4246   5897   4121   4667   90   2373   1877 4246   1142 4047

God's will for you in Christ Jesus. ¶ **19** Do not put   out the Spirit's fire; **20** do not treat prophecies with
θεοῦ θέλημα εἰς ὑμᾶς ἐν Χριστῷ Ἰησοῦ   → μὴ σβέννυτε ← τὸ πνεῦμα   → μὴ → προφητείας →
n.gsm n.nsn p.a r.ap.2 p.d n.dsm n.dsm   pl v.pam.2p   d.asn n.asn   pl   n.apf
2536 2525   1650 7007 1877 5986 2652   4931 3590 4931 3836 4460 4931   2024 3590 2024 4735

contempt. **21** Test   everything. Hold on to the good. **22** Avoid   every kind of evil.   ¶ **23**   May
ἐξουθενεῖτε δὲ δοκιμάζετε πάντα   κατέχετε ← τὸ καλὸν   ἀπέχεσθε ἀπὸ παντὸς εἴδους → πονηροῦ   δὲ →
v.pam.2p   cj   v.pam.2p   a.apn   v.pam.2p   d.asn a.asn v.pmm.2p p.g a.gsn n.gsn a.gsn   cj
2024   1254 1507   4246   2988   3836 2819   600   608 4246 1626   4505   1254 39

God   himself, the God of peace, sanctify you through and through. May your whole   spirit,
ὁ θεὸς Αὐτὸς   τῆς εἰρήνης ἀγιάσαι ὑμᾶς ὁλοτελεῖς ←   καὶ → ὑμῶν ὁλόκληρον τὸ πνεῦμα καὶ
d.nsm n.nsm r.nsm   d.gsf n.gsf v.aao.3s r.ap.2 a.apm   cj   r.gp.2 a.nsn   d.nsn n.nsn cj
3836 2536 899   3836 1645   39   7007 3911   2779 5498 7007 3908   3836 4460 2779

soul   and body   be kept blameless at the coming of our Lord   Jesus Christ. **24** The one who calls
ἡ ψυχὴ καὶ τὸ σῶμα → τηρηθείη ἀμέμπτως ἐν τῇ παρουσίᾳ → ἡμῶν τοῦ κυρίου Ἰησοῦ Χριστοῦ ὁ ← καλῶν
d.nsf n.nsf cj d.nsn n.nsn v.apo.3s adv   p.d d.dsf n.dsf r.gp.1 d.gsm n.gsm n.gsm n.gsm d.nsm pt.pa.nsm
3836 6034 2779 3836 5393 5498   290   1877 3836 4242 3261 7005 3836 3261 2652 5986 3836   2813

you is faithful and he will do it. ¶ **25** Brothers, pray   for us. **26** Greet   all   the brothers
ὑμᾶς πιστὸς καὶ ὃς → ποιήσει   Ἀδελφοί προσεύχεσθε [καὶ] περὶ ἡμῶν Ἀσπάσασθε πάντας τοὺς ἀδελφοὺς
r.ap.2 a.nsm cj r.nsm v.fai.3s   n.vpm   v.pmm.2p   cj   p.g r.gp.1 v.amm.2p a.apm d.apm n.apm
7007 4412 2779 4005 4472   81   4667   2779 4309 7005 832   4246   3836 81

with a holy kiss. **27** I charge you before the Lord to have this letter read   to all the brothers. ¶
ἐν ἁγίῳ φιλήματι → Ἐνορκίζω ὑμᾶς   τὸν κύριον → τὴν ἐπιστολὴν ἀναγνωσθῆναι → πᾶσιν τοῖς ἀδελφοῖς
p.d a.dsn n.dsn   v.pai.1s r.ap.2 d.asm n.asm   d.asf n.asf f.ap   a.dpm d.dpm n.dpm
1877 41 5799   1941   7007   3836 3261 336 336 3836 2186 336   4246 3836 81

28 The grace of our Lord   Jesus Christ be with you.
Ἡ χάρις → ἡμῶν τοῦ κυρίου Ἰησοῦ Χριστοῦ μεθ' ὑμῶν
d.nsf n.nsf r.gp.1 d.gsm n.gsm n.gsm n.gsm p.g r.gp.2
3836 5921 3261 7005 3836 3261 2652 5986   3552 7007

τὸν ἕνα, καθὼς καὶ ποιεῖτε. ¶ **12** Ἐρωτῶμεν δὲ ὑμᾶς, ἀδελφοί, εἰδέναι τοὺς κοπιῶντας ἐν ὑμῖν καὶ προϊσταμένους ὑμῶν ἐν κυρίῳ καὶ νουθετοῦντας ὑμᾶς **13** καὶ ἡγεῖσθαι αὐτοὺς ὑπερεκπερισσοῦ ἐν ἀγάπῃ διὰ τὸ ἔργον αὐτῶν. εἰρηνεύετε ἐν ἑαυτοῖς. **14** παρακαλοῦμεν δὲ ὑμᾶς, ἀδελφοί, νουθετεῖτε τοὺς ἀτάκτους, παραμυθεῖσθε τοὺς ὀλιγοψύχους, ἀντέχεσθε τῶν ἀσθενῶν, μακροθυμεῖτε πρὸς πάντας. **15** ὁρᾶτε μή τις κακὸν ἀντὶ κακοῦ τινι ἀποδῷ, ἀλλὰ πάντοτε τὸ ἀγαθὸν διώκετε [καὶ] εἰς ἀλλήλους καὶ εἰς πάντας. ¶ **16** Πάντοτε χαίρετε, **17** ἀδιαλείπτως προσεύχεσθε, **18** ἐν παντὶ εὐχαριστεῖτε· τοῦτο γὰρ θέλημα θεοῦ ἐν Χριστῷ Ἰησοῦ εἰς ὑμᾶς. ¶ **19** τὸ πνεῦμα μὴ σβέννυτε, **20** προφητείας μὴ ἐξουθενεῖτε, **21** πάντα δὲ δοκιμάζετε, τὸ καλὸν κατέχετε, **22** ἀπὸ παντὸς εἴδους πονηροῦ ἀπέχεσθε. ¶ **23** Αὐτὸς δὲ ὁ θεὸς τῆς εἰρήνης ἀγιάσαι ὑμᾶς ὁλοτελεῖς, καὶ ὁλόκληρον ὑμῶν τὸ πνεῦμα καὶ ἡ ψυχὴ καὶ τὸ σῶμα ἀμέμπτως ἐν τῇ παρουσίᾳ τοῦ κυρίου ἡμῶν Ἰησοῦ Χριστοῦ τηρηθείη. **24** πιστὸς ὁ καλῶν ὑμᾶς, ὃς καὶ ποιήσει. ¶ **25** Ἀδελφοί, προσεύχεσθε [καὶ] περὶ ἡμῶν. **26** Ἀσπάσασθε τοὺς ἀδελφοὺς πάντας ἐν φιλήματι ἁγίῳ. **27** Ἐνορκίζω ὑμᾶς τὸν κύριον ἀναγνωσθῆναι τὴν ἐπιστολὴν πᾶσιν τοῖς ἀδελφοῖς. ¶ **28** Ἡ χάρις τοῦ κυρίου ἡμῶν Ἰησοῦ Χριστοῦ μεθ' ὑμῶν.

2 Thessalonians

1:1 Paul, Silas and Timothy, ¶ To the church of the Thessalonians in God our Father and the Lord Jesus Christ: ¶ **2** Grace and peace to you from God the Father and the Lord Jesus Christ.

Thanksgiving and Prayer

1:3 We ought always to thank God for you, brothers, and rightly so, because your faith is growing more and more, and the love every one of you has for each other is increasing. **4** Therefore, among God's churches we boast about your perseverance and faith in all the persecutions and trials you are enduring. ¶ **5** All this is evidence that God's judgment is right, and as a result you will be counted worthy of the kingdom of God, for which you are suffering. **6** God is just: He will pay back trouble to those who trouble you **7** and give relief to you who are troubled, and to us as well. This will happen when the Lord Jesus is revealed from heaven in blazing fire with his powerful angels. **8** He will punish those who do not know God and do not obey the gospel of our Lord Jesus. **9** They will be punished with everlasting destruction and shut out from the presence of the Lord and from the majesty of his power **10** on the day he comes to be glorified in his holy people and to be marveled at among all those who have

---

1:1 Παῦλος καὶ Σιλουανὸς καὶ Τιμόθεος ¶ τῇ ἐκκλησίᾳ Θεσσαλονικέων ἐν θεῷ πατρὶ ἡμῶν καὶ κυρίῳ Ἰησοῦ Χριστῷ, ¶ **2** χάρις ὑμῖν καὶ εἰρήνη ἀπὸ θεοῦ πατρὸς [ἡμῶν] καὶ κυρίου Ἰησοῦ Χριστοῦ.

1:3 Εὐχαριστεῖν ὀφείλομεν τῷ θεῷ πάντοτε περὶ ὑμῶν, ἀδελφοί, καθὼς ἄξιόν ἐστιν, ὅτι ὑπεραυξάνει ἡ πίστις ὑμῶν καὶ πλεονάζει ἡ ἀγάπη ἑνὸς ἑκάστου πάντων ὑμῶν εἰς ἀλλήλους, **4** ὥστε αὐτοὺς ἡμᾶς ἐν ὑμῖν ἐγκαυχᾶσθαι ἐν ταῖς ἐκκλησίαις τοῦ θεοῦ ὑπὲρ τῆς ὑπομονῆς ὑμῶν καὶ πίστεως ἐν πᾶσιν τοῖς διωγμοῖς ὑμῶν καὶ ταῖς θλίψεσιν αἷς ἀνέχεσθε, ¶ **5** ἔνδειγμα τῆς δικαίας κρίσεως τοῦ θεοῦ εἰς τὸ καταξιωθῆναι ὑμᾶς τῆς βασιλείας τοῦ θεοῦ, ὑπὲρ ἧς καὶ πάσχετε, **6** εἴπερ δίκαιον παρὰ θεῷ ἀνταποδοῦναι τοῖς θλίβουσιν ὑμᾶς θλῖψιν **7** καὶ ὑμῖν τοῖς θλιβομένοις ἄνεσιν μεθ᾽ ἡμῶν, ἐν τῇ ἀποκαλύψει τοῦ κυρίου Ἰησοῦ ἀπ᾽ οὐρανοῦ μετ᾽ ἀγγέλων δυνάμεως αὐτοῦ **8** ἐν πυρὶ φλογός, διδόντος ἐκδίκησιν τοῖς μὴ εἰδόσιν θεὸν καὶ τοῖς μὴ ὑπακούουσιν τῷ εὐαγγελίῳ τοῦ κυρίου ἡμῶν Ἰησοῦ, **9** οἵτινες δίκην τίσουσιν ὄλεθρον αἰώνιον ἀπὸ προσώπου τοῦ κυρίου καὶ ἀπὸ τῆς δόξης τῆς ἰσχύος αὐτοῦ, **10** ὅταν ἔλθῃ ἐνδοξασθῆναι ἐν τοῖς ἁγίοις αὐτοῦ καὶ θαυμασθῆναι ἐν πᾶσιν τοῖς πιστεύσασιν, ὅτι ἐπιστεύθη

believed. This includes you, because you believed our testimony to you. ¶ **11** With this in mind, we
πιστεύσασιν ὅτι → ἐπιστεύθη ἡμῶν τὸ μαρτύριον ἐφ᾽ ὑμᾶς Εἰς ὃ καὶ →
pt.aa.dpm cj v.api.3s n.gp.1 d.nsn n.nsn p.a r.ap.2 p.a r.asn adv
4409 4022 4409 7005 3836 3457 2093 7007 1650 4005 2779 4667

constantly pray for you, that our God may count you worthy of his calling, and that by his power he
πάντοτε προσευχόμεθα περὶ ὑμῶν ἵνα ἡμῶν ὁ θεός, → → ὑμᾶς ἀξιώση → τῆς κλήσεως καὶ ἐν δυνάμει →
adv v.pmi.1p p.g r.gp.2 cj r.gp.1 d.nsm ὁ n.nsm r.ap.2 v.aas.3s d.gsf n.gsf cj p.d n.dsf
4121 4667 4309 7007 2671 7005 3836 2536 546 546 7007 546 3836 3104 2779 1877 1539

may fulfill every good purpose of yours and every act prompted by your faith. **12** We pray this so that the
→ πληρώση πᾶσαν ἀγαθωσύνης εὐδοκίαν καὶ ἔργον → πίστεως ὅπως ← τὸ
v.aas.3s a.asf n.gsf n.asf cj n.asn n.gsf cj d.nsn
4444 4246 20 2306 2779 2240 4411 3968 3836

name of our Lord Jesus may be glorified in you, and you in him, according to the grace of our God
ὄνομα → ἡμῶν τοῦ κυρίου Ἰησοῦ → → ἐνδοξασθῆ ἐν ὑμῖν καὶ ὑμεῖς ἐν αὐτῷ κατὰ → τὴν χάριν → ἡμῶν τοῦ θεοῦ
n.nsn r.gp.1 d.gsf n.gsf n.gsf v.aps.3s p.d r.dp.2 cj r.np.2 p.d r.dsm.3 p.a d.asf n.asf r.gp.1 d.gsm n.gsm
3950 3261 7005 3836 3261 2652 1901 1877 7007 2779 7007 1877 899 2848 3836 5921 2536 7005 3836 2536

and the Lord Jesus Christ.
καὶ κυρίου Ἰησοῦ Χριστοῦ
cj n.gsm n.gsm n.gsm
2779 3261 2652 5986

The Man of Lawlessness

2:1 Concerning the coming of our Lord Jesus Christ and our being gathered to him, we
δὲ ὑπὲρ τῆς παρουσίας → ἡμῶν τοῦ κυρίου Ἰησοῦ Χριστοῦ καὶ ἡμῶν → ἐπισυναγωγῆς ἐπ᾽ αὐτὸν →
cj p.g d.gsf n.gsf r.gp.1 d.gsm n.gsm n.gsm n.gsm cj r.gp.1 n.gsf p.a r.asm.3
1254 5642 3836 4242 3261 7005 3836 3261 2652 5986 2779 7005 2191 2093 899

ask you, brothers, **2** not to become easily unsettled or alarmed by some prophecy,
Ἐρωτῶμεν ὑμᾶς ἀδελφοί ὑμᾶς μὴ εἰς ← ταχέως τὸ σαλευθῆναι μηδὲ θροεῖσθαι ἀπὸ τοῦ νοὸς μηδὲ διὰ πνεύματος
v.pai.1p r.ap.2 n.vpm r.ap.2 pl p.a adv d.asn f.ap cj f.pp p.g d.gsm n.gsm cj p.g n.gsn
2263 7007 81 7007 3590 1650 5441 3836 4888 3593 2583 608 3836 3808 3593 1328 4460

report or letter supposed to have come from us, saying that the day of the Lord has already
μήτε διὰ λόγου μήτε δι᾽ ἐπιστολῆς ὡς ← ← δι᾽ ἡμῶν ὡς ὅτι ἡ ἡμέρα → τοῦ κυρίου ←
cj p.g n.gsm cj p.g n.gsf pl p.g r.gp.1 pl cj d.nsf n.nsf d.gsm n.gsm
3612 1328 3364 3612 1328 2186 6055 1328 7005 6055 4022 3836 2465 3836 3261

come. **3** Don't let anyone deceive you in any way, for that day will not come until the rebellion occurs and
ἐνέστηκεν Μή → τις ἐξαπατήση ὑμᾶς κατὰ μηδένα τρόπον ὅτι → μὴ ἔλθη ἐὰν ἡ ἀποστασία πρῶτον καὶ
v.rai.3s pl r.nsm v.aas.3s r.ap.2 p.a a.asm n.asm cj pl v.aas.3s cj d.nsf n.nsf adv cj
1931 3590 1987 5516 1987 7007 2848 3594 5573 4022 2262 3590 2262 1569 3836 686 4754 2779

the man of lawlessness is revealed, the man doomed to destruction. **4** He will oppose and will exalt
ὁ ἄνθρωπος → τῆς ἀνομίας → ἀποκαλυφθῆ ὁ υἱὸς → τῆς ἀπωλείας ὁ → ἀντικείμενος καὶ → ὑπεραιρόμενος
d.nsm n.nsm d.gsf n.gsf v.aps.3s d.nsm n.nsm d.gsf n.gsf d.nsm pt.pm.nsm cj pt.pm.nsm
3836 476 3836 490 636 3836 5626 3836 724 3836 512 2779 5643

himself over everything that is called God or is worshiped, so that he sets himself up in God's temple,
← ἐπὶ πάντα → λεγόμενον θεὸν ἢ σέβασμα ὥστε ← → καθίσαι αὐτὸν ← εἰς τοῦ θεοῦ τὸν ναόν
p.a a.asm pt.pp.asm n.asm cj n.asn cj f.aa r.asm.3 p.a d.gsm n.gsm d.asm n.asm
2093 4246 3306 2536 2445 4934 6063 2767 899 2767 1650 3836 2536 3836 3724

proclaiming himself to be God. ¶ **5** Don't you remember that when I was with you I used to tell you
ἀποδεικνύντα ἑαυτὸν ὅτι → ἔστιν θεός Οὐ → μνημονεύετε ὅτι ἔτι → ὢν πρὸς ὑμᾶς → ἔλεγον ὑμῖν
pt.pa.asm r.asm.3 cj v.pai.3s n.nsm pl v.pai.2p cj adv pt.pa.nsm p.a r.ap.2 v.iai.1s r.dp.2
617 1571 4022 1639 2536 4024 3648 4022 2285 1639 4639 7007 3306 7007

these things? **6** And now you know what is holding him back, so that he may be revealed at the proper
ταῦτα ← καὶ νῦν → οἴδατε τὸ → κατέχον ← εἰς αὐτὸν → τὸ ἀποκαλυφθῆναι ἐν τῷ ἑαυτοῦ
r.apn cj adv v.rai.2p d.asn pt.pa.asn p.a r.asm.3 d.asn f.ap p.d d.dsm r.gsm.3
4047 2779 3814 3857 3836 2988 1650 899 3836 636 1877 3836 1571

time. **7** For the secret power of lawlessness is already at work; but the one who now holds it back will
καιρῷ γὰρ τὸ μυστήριον → τῆς ἀνομίας → ἤδη → ἐνεργεῖται μόνον ὁ ← ἄρτι κατέχων ← →
n.dsm cj d.nsn n.nsn d.gsf n.gsf adv v.pmi.3s adv d.nsm adv pt.pa.nsm
2789 1142 3836 3696 3836 490 1919 2453 1919 3667 3836 785 2988

τὸ μαρτύριον ἡμῶν ἐφ᾽ ὑμᾶς, ἐν τῇ ἡμέρᾳ ἐκείνῃ. ¶ **11** εἰς ὃ καὶ προσευχόμεθα πάντοτε περὶ ὑμῶν, ἵνα ὑμᾶς ἀξιώση τῆς κλήσεως ὁ θεὸς ἡμῶν καὶ πληρώση πᾶσαν εὐδοκίαν ἀγαθωσύνης καὶ ἔργον πίστεως ἐν δυνάμει, **12** ὅπως ἐνδοξασθῆ τὸ ὄνομα τοῦ κυρίου ἡμῶν Ἰησοῦ ἐν ὑμῖν, καὶ ὑμεῖς ἐν αὐτῷ, κατὰ τὴν χάριν τοῦ θεοῦ ἡμῶν καὶ κυρίου Ἰησοῦ Χριστοῦ.

2:1 Ἐρωτῶμεν δὲ ὑμᾶς, ἀδελφοί, ὑπὲρ τῆς παρουσίας τοῦ κυρίου ἡμῶν Ἰησοῦ Χριστοῦ καὶ ἡμῶν ἐπισυναγωγῆς ἐπ᾽ αὐτὸν **2** εἰς τὸ μὴ ταχέως σαλευθῆναι ὑμᾶς ἀπὸ τοῦ νοὸς μηδὲ θροεῖσθαι, μήτε διὰ πνεύματος μήτε διὰ λόγου μήτε δι᾽ ἐπιστολῆς ὡς δι᾽ ἡμῶν, ὡς ὅτι ἐνέστηκεν ἡ ἡμέρα τοῦ κυρίου· **3** μή τις ὑμᾶς ἐξαπατήση κατὰ μηδένα τρόπον. ὅτι ἐὰν μὴ ἔλθη ἡ ἀποστασία πρῶτον καὶ ἀποκαλυφθῆ ὁ ἄνθρωπος τῆς ἀνομίας, ὁ υἱὸς τῆς ἀπωλείας, **4** ὁ ἀντικείμενος καὶ ὑπεραιρόμενος ἐπὶ πάντα λεγόμενον θεὸν ἢ σέβασμα, ὥστε αὐτὸν εἰς τὸν ναὸν τοῦ θεοῦ καθίσαι ἀποδεικνύντα ἑαυτὸν ὅτι ἔστιν θεός. ¶ **5** Οὐ μνημονεύετε ὅτι ἔτι ὢν πρὸς ὑμᾶς ταῦτα ἔλεγον ὑμῖν; **6** καὶ νῦν τὸ κατέχον οἴδατε εἰς τὸ ἀποκαλυφθῆναι αὐτὸν ἐν τῷ ἑαυτοῦ καιρῷ. **7** τὸ γὰρ μυστήριον

continue to do   so till he is taken out of the way.   **8** And then the lawless one will be revealed,   whom the
→   → γένηται ← ἕως   ἐκ ← μέσου καὶ τότε ὁ ἄνομος ← → → ἀποκαλυφθήσεται ὃν   ὁ
v.ams.3s   cj   p.g   n.gsn cj adv d.nsm a.nsm   v.fpi.3s   r.asm d.nsm
1181   2401   1666   3545 2779 5538 3836 491   636   4005 3836

Lord Jesus   will overthrow with the breath of his   mouth   and destroy   by the splendor of his
κύριος Ἰησοῦς → ἀνελεῖ → τῷ πνεύματι → αὐτοῦ τοῦ στόματος καὶ καταργήσει → τῇ ἐπιφανείᾳ → αὐτοῦ
n.nsm   n.nsm   v.fai.3s   d.dsn n.dsn   r.gsm.3 d.gsn n.gsn   cj v.fai.3s   d.dsn n.dsf   r.gsm.3
3261   2652   359   3836 4460   5125   3836 5125   2779 2934   3836 2211   899

coming.   **9** The coming of the lawless one will be in accordance with the work   of Satan   displayed in
τῆς παρουσίας   ἡ   παρουσία →   οὗ → ἐστιν κατ' ←   ἐνέργειαν → τοῦ σατανᾶ   ἐν
d.gsf n.gsf   d.nsf n.nsf   r.gsm   v.pai.3s p.a   n.asf   d.gsm n.gsm   p.d
3836 4242   3836 4242   4005   1639   2848   1918   3836 4928   1877

all   kinds of counterfeit miracles,   signs and wonders, **10** in every sort of evil   that deceives those who are
πάσῃ ← → ψεύδους δυνάμει καὶ σημείοις καὶ τέρασιν   ἐν πάσῃ ← → ἀδικίας   ἀπάτῃ τοῖς ← →
a.dsf   n.gsn   n.dsf   cj   n.dpn   cj   n.dpn   p.d a.dsf   n.gsf   n.dsf   d.dpm
4246   6022   1539   2779 4956   2779 5469   1877 4246   94   573   3836

perishing.   They perish because they refused   to love   the truth   and so   be saved.   **11**   For
ἀπολλυμένοις ἀνθ' ὧν   οὐκ ἐδέξαντο   τὴν ἀγάπην τῆς ἀληθείας εἰς αὐτούς → τὸ σωθῆναι   καὶ διὰ
pt.pm.dpm   p.g r.gpn   pl   v.ami.3p   d.asf n.asf   d.gsf n.gsf   p.a r.apm.3   d.asn f.ap   cj   p.a
660   505 4005   1312 4024   3836 27   3836 237   1650 899   3836 5392   2779 1328

this reason God   sends them a powerful delusion so that they will believe   the lie   **12** and so that all
τοῦτο   ὁ θεὸς   πέμπει αὐτοῖς ἐνέργειαν πλάνης εἰς ← αὐτοὺς → τὸ πιστεῦσαι τῷ ψεύδει   ἵνα ← πάντες
r.asn   d.nsm n.nsm v.pai.3s r.dpm.3 n.asf   n.gsf   p.a   r.apm.3   d.asn f.aa   d.dsn n.dsn   cj   a.npm
4047   3836 2536   4287   899   1918   4415   1650   899   3836 4409   3836 6022   2671   4246

will be condemned who have not believed the truth   but have delighted   in wickedness.
→ → κριθῶσιν   οἱ → μὴ πιστεύσαντες τῇ ἀληθείᾳ ἀλλὰ → εὐδοκήσαντες → τῇ ἀδικίᾳ
v.aps.3p   d.npm   pl pt.aa.npm   d.dsf n.dsf   cj   pt.aa.npm   d.dsf n.dsf
3212   3836   3590 4409   3836 237   247   2305   3836 94

Stand Firm

2:13 But we   ought   always to thank   God   for you, brothers loved   by the Lord, because from the
δὲ ἡμεῖς ὀφείλομεν πάντοτε → εὐχαριστεῖν τῷ θεῷ περὶ ὑμῶν ἀδελφοὶ ἠγαπημένοι ὑπὸ κυρίου ὅτι   → →
cj   r.np.1 v.pai.1p   adv   f.pai   d.dsm n.dsm p.g   r.gp.2 n.vpm   pt.rp.vpm   p.g   n.gsm   cj
1254 7005   4053   4121   2373   3836 2536   4309 7007   81   26   5679 3261   4022

beginning God   chose you to be saved   through the sanctifying work of the Spirit   and through belief in the
ἀπαρχὴν ὁ θεὸς εἵλατο ὑμᾶς εἰς ← σωτηρίαν ἐν   ἁγιασμῷ   πνεύματος καὶ   πίστει
n.asf   d.nsm n.nsm v.ami.3s r.ap.2 p.a   n.asf   p.d   n.dsm   n.gsn   cj   n.dsf
569   3836 2536 145   7007   1650   5401   1877   40   4460   2779   4411

truth. **14** He called you to this   through our gospel,   that you might share   in the glory of our
ἀληθείας → ἐκάλεσεν ὑμᾶς εἰς ὃ [καὶ] διὰ ἡμῶν τοῦ εὐαγγελίου εἰς   περιποίησιν   δόξης → ἡμῶν
n.gsf   v.aai.3s r.ap.2 p.a r.asn adv   p.g   r.gp.1 d.gsn n.gsn   p.a   n.asf   n.gsf   r.gp.1
237   2813   7007   1650 4005 2779 1328 7005 3836 2295   1650   4348   1518   3261 7005

Lord   Jesus Christ. **15** So then, brothers, stand firm and hold   to the teachings   we passed   on to you,
τοῦ κυρίου Ἰησοῦ Χριστοῦ οὖν Ἄρα ἀδελφοί στήκετε ← καὶ κρατεῖτε τὰς παραδόσεις ἃς ἡμῶν ἐδιδάχθητε ← ←
d.gsm n.gsm n.gsm n.gsm   cj   cj   n.vpm   v.pam.2p   cj   v.pam.2p   d.apf n.apf   r.apf r.gp.1 v.api.2p
3836 3261   2652 5986   4036 726   81   5112   2779 3195   3836 4142   4005 7005 1438

whether by word of mouth or by letter.   ¶   **16**   May our Lord   Jesus Christ himself and God
εἴτε διὰ λόγου   εἴτε δι' ἐπιστολῆς δὲ   ἡμῶν ὁ κύριος Ἰησοῦς Χριστὸς Αὐτὸς καὶ ὁ θεὸς
cj   p.g n.gsn   cj   p.g n.gsf   cj   r.gp.1 d.nsm n.nsm n.nsm   n.nsm   r.nsm   cj d.nsm n.nsm
1664 1328 3364   1664 1328 2186   1254   7005 3836 3261   2652   5986   899   2779 3836 2536

our Father, who loved   us and by his grace gave us eternal encouragement and good hope, **17** encourage
ἡμῶν ὁ πατὴρ ὁ ἀγαπήσας ἡμᾶς καὶ ἐν χάριτι δοὺς   αἰωνίαν παράκλησιν καὶ ἀγαθὴν ἐλπίδα παρακαλέσαι
r.gp.1 d.nsm n.nsm d.nsm pt.aa.nsm r.ap.1 cj   p.d n.dsf   pt.aa.nsm a.asf   n.asf   cj   a.asf   n.asf   v.aao.3s
7005 3836 4252 3836 26   7005   2779 1877 5921 1443   173   4155   2779 19   1828   4151

your hearts   and strengthen you in every good deed and word.
ὑμῶν τὰς καρδίας καὶ στηρίξαι   ἐν παντὶ ἀγαθῷ ἔργῳ καὶ λόγῳ
r.gp.2 d.apf n.apf cj   v.aao.3s   p.d a.dsn a.dsm n.dsn cj   n.dsn
7007 3836 2840   2779 5114   1877 4246   19   2240   2779 3364

ἤδη ἐνεργεῖται τῆς ἀνομίας· μόνον ὁ κατέχων ἄρτι ἕως ἐκ μέσου γένηται. ⁸ καὶ τότε ἀποκαλυφθήσεται ὁ ἄνομος, ὃν ὁ κύριος
[Ἰησοῦς] ἀνελεῖ τῷ πνεύματι τοῦ στόματος αὐτοῦ καὶ καταργήσει τῇ ἐπιφανείᾳ τῆς παρουσίας αὐτοῦ, ⁹ οὗ ἐστιν ἡ παρουσία
κατ' ἐνέργειαν τοῦ Σατανᾶ ἐν πάσῃ δυνάμει καὶ σημείοις καὶ τέρασιν ψεύδους ¹⁰ καὶ ἐν πάσῃ ἀπάτῃ ἀδικίας τοῖς
ἀπολλυμένοις, ἀνθ' ὧν τὴν ἀγάπην τῆς ἀληθείας οὐκ ἐδέξαντο εἰς τὸ σωθῆναι αὐτούς. ¹¹ καὶ διὰ τοῦτο πέμπει αὐτοῖς ὁ θεὸς
ἐνέργειαν πλάνης εἰς τὸ πιστεῦσαι αὐτοὺς τῷ ψεύδει, ¹² ἵνα κριθῶσιν πάντες οἱ μὴ πιστεύσαντες τῇ ἀληθείᾳ ἀλλὰ
εὐδοκήσαντες τῇ ἀδικίᾳ.
²:¹³ Ἡμεῖς δὲ ὀφείλομεν εὐχαριστεῖν τῷ θεῷ πάντοτε περὶ ὑμῶν, ἀδελφοὶ ἠγαπημένοι ὑπὸ κυρίου, ὅτι εἵλατο ὑμᾶς ὁ θεὸς
ἀπ' ἀρχῆς «ἀπαρχὴν» εἰς σωτηρίαν ἐν ἁγιασμῷ πνεύματος καὶ πίστει ἀληθείας, ¹⁴ εἰς ὃ [καὶ] ἐκάλεσεν ὑμᾶς διὰ τοῦ εὐαγγελίου
ἡμῶν εἰς περιποίησιν δόξης τοῦ κυρίου ἡμῶν Ἰησοῦ Χριστοῦ. ¹⁵ ἄρα οὖν, ἀδελφοί, στήκετε, καὶ κρατεῖτε τὰς παραδόσεις ἃς
ἐδιδάχθητε εἴτε διὰ λόγου εἴτε δι' ἐπιστολῆς ἡμῶν. ¶ ¹⁶ Αὐτὸς δὲ ὁ κύριος ἡμῶν Ἰησοῦς Χριστὸς καὶ [ὁ] θεὸς ὁ πατὴρ ἡμῶν
ὁ ἀγαπήσας ἡμᾶς καὶ δοὺς παράκλησιν αἰωνίαν καὶ ἐλπίδα ἀγαθὴν ἐν χάριτι, ¹⁷ παρακαλέσαι ὑμῶν τὰς καρδίας καὶ στηρίξαι

Request for Prayer

3:1 Finally,   brothers,   pray   for us   that the message of the   Lord   may spread   rapidly   and be honored,
⌜Τὸ λοιπὸν⌝ ἀδελφοί   προσεύχεσθε περὶ ἡμῶν ἵνα   ὁ   λόγος   →   τοῦ κυρίου   τρέχῃ   ←   καὶ →   δοξάζηται
d.asn adv   n.vpm   v.pmm.2p   p.g r.gp.1 cj d.nsm n.nsm   d.gsm n.gsm   v.pas.3s   cj   v.pps.3s
3836 3370   81   4667   4309 7005   2671 3836 3364   3836 3261   5556   2779   1519

just as   it was with you. **2** And pray that we may be delivered from wicked and evil   men,   for not
καθὼς ← καὶ   πρὸς ὑμᾶς καὶ   ἵνα   →   →   →   ῥυσθῶμεν   ἀπὸ ἀτόπων καὶ πονηρῶν ⌜τῶν ἀνθρώπων⌝ γὰρ οὐ
cj   cj   p.a r.ap2 cj   cj   v.aps.1p   p.g a.gpm   cj   a.gpm   d.gpm n.gpm   cj   pl
2777   2779   4639 7007   2779   2671   4861   608 876   2779 4505   3836 476   1142 4024

everyone has faith.   **3** But the Lord   is   faithful, and he will strengthen and protect   you   from the evil   one.
πάντων   ⌜ἡ πίστις⌝ δέ   ὁ   κύριος ἐστιν Πιστός   ὃς → στηρίξει   καὶ φυλάξει ὑμᾶς ἀπὸ τοῦ πονηροῦ ←
a.gpm   d.nsf n.nsf cj   d.nsm n.nsm v.pai.3s a.nsm   r.nsm   v.fai.3s   cj   v.fai.3s r.ap.2 p.g d.gsm a.gsm
4246   3836 4411   1254 3836 3261   1639   4412   4005   5114   2779 5875   7007   608 3836 4505

4 We have confidence in the Lord   that   you are doing and will continue to do   the things we
δὲ →   πεποίθαμεν ἐν   κυρίῳ ἐφ᾽ ὑμᾶς ὅτι   [καὶ] →   →   ποιεῖτε καὶ →   →   →   ποιήσετε ἃ
cj   v.rai.1p   p.d   n.dsm p.a r.ap.2 cj   cj   v.pai.2p cj   v.fai.2p r.apn
1254   4275   1877 3261 2093 7007   4022 2779   4472   2779   4472   4005

command.   **5** May the Lord   direct   your hearts   into God's   love   and Christ's
παραγγέλλομεν δὲ   Ὁ   κύριος κατευθύναι ὑμῶν ⌜τὰς καρδίας⌝ εἰς ⌜τοῦ θεοῦ⌝ ⌜τὴν ἀγάπην⌝ καὶ εἰς ⌜τοῦ Χριστοῦ⌝
v.pai.1p   cj   d.nsm n.nsm v.aao.3s   r.gp.2 d.apf n.apf p.a d.gsm n.gsm d.asf n.asf   cj   p.a d.gsm n.gsm
4133   1254 3836 3261   2985   7007 3836 2840   1650 3836 2536   3836 27   2779 1650 3836 5986

perseverance.
⌜τὴν ὑπομονὴν⌝
d.asf n.asf
3836 5705

Warning Against Idleness

3:6   In the name   of the Lord   Jesus Christ, we command   you, brothers,   to keep   away
δὲ ἐν   ὀνόματι → τοῦ κυρίου [ἡμῶν] Ἰησοῦ Χριστοῦ → Παραγγέλλομεν ὑμῖν ἀδελφοί   ὑμᾶς στέλλεσθαι ←
cj p.d n.dsn   d.gsm n.gsm r.gp.1 n.gsm n.gsm   v.pai.1p   r.dp.2 n.vpm   r.ap.2 f.pm
1254 1877 3950   3836 3261   7005   2652 5986   4133   7007 81   7007 5097

from every brother who is idle   and does not live   according to the teaching   you received   from
ἀπὸ   παντὸς ἀδελφοῦ ἀτάκτως →   μὴ περιπατοῦντος καὶ κατὰ ← τὴν παράδοσιν ἣν → παρελάβοσαν παρ᾽
p.g   a.gsm n.gsm   adv   pl pt.pa.gsm   cj   p.a   d.asf n.asf   r.asf   v.aai.3p   p.g
608   4246   81   865   3590 4344   2779 2848   3836 4142   4005   4161   4123

us. **7** For you yourselves know how you ought to follow   our example.   We were not idle   when we were
ἡμῶν γὰρ → Αὐτοὶ οἴδατε πῶς → δεῖ   → μιμεῖσθαι ἡμᾶς   ὅτι → →   οὐκ ἠτακτήσαμεν ἐν ←
r.gp.1 cj   r.npm   v.rai.2p cj   v.pai.3s   f.pm   r.ap.1   cj   pl v.aai.1p   p.d
7005 1142   899   3857   3857   4802   3628   7005   4022   4024 863   1877

with you, **8** nor did we eat   anyone's food without paying for it. On the contrary, we worked   night and
← ὑμῖν οὐδὲ →   → ἐφάγομεν παρά τινος ἄρτον → δωρεὰν   → ἀλλ᾽ → ἐργαζόμενοι νυκτὸς καὶ
r.dp.2 r.dp.2 cj   v.aai.1p p.g r.gsm n.asm   adv   cj   pt.pm.npm   n.gsf cj
7007 4028   4028   2266   4123 5515   788   1562   247   2237   3816   2779

day,   laboring and toiling so   that we would not be a burden   to any of you. **9** We did this, not because we
ἡμέρας ἐν κόπῳ καὶ μόχθῳ πρὸς ←   →   →   μὴ → ⌜τὸ ἐπιβαρῆσαί⌝ τινα → ὑμῶν   οὐχ ὅτι
n.gsf   p.d n.dsm cj   n.dsm p.a   pl   d.asn f.aai   r.asm   r.gp.2   pl   cj
2465   1877 3160 2779 3677   4639   3590   3836 2096   5516   7007   4024 4022   2400

do not have the right   to such help, but in order to make ourselves a model for you to follow.   **10** For
→ οὐκ ἔχομεν ἐξουσίαν   ἀλλ᾽ ἵνα ←   ← δῶμεν ἑαυτοὺς τύπον → ὑμῖν εἰς ⌜τὸ μιμεῖσθαι⌝ ἡμᾶς γὰρ
   pl v.pai.1p n.asf   cj   cj   v.aas.1p r.apm.3 n.asm   r.dp.2 p.a d.asn f.pm   r.ap.1 cj
2400 4024 2400 2026   247 2671   1443   1571   5596   7007 1650 3836 3628   7005   1142

even when we were with you, we gave you this rule: "If a man will not work,   he shall not eat." ¶
καὶ ὅτε → ἦμεν πρὸς ὑμᾶς, ὑμῖν τοῦτο παρηγγέλλομεν ὅτι εἴ τις   θέλει οὐ ἐργάζεσθαι →   μηδὲ ἐσθιέτω
adv cj   v.iai.1p p.a r.ap.2 r.dp.2 r.asn v.iai.1p   cj cj r.nsm v.pai.3s pl f.pm   cj   v.pam.3s
2779 4021   1639   4639 7007   7007 4047 4133   4022 1623 5527 2527 4024 2237   3593 2266

11   We hear   that some among you are   idle.   They are not busy;   they are
γὰρ → Ἀκούομεν   τινας ἐν   ὑμῖν περιπατοῦντας ἀτάκτως → μηδὲν ἐργαζομένους ἀλλὰ → →
cj   v.pai.1p   r.apm p.d   r.dp.2 pt.pa.apm   adv   a.asn pt.pm.apm   cj
1142   201   5516   1877 7007 4344   865   2237 2237   247

ἐν παντὶ ἔργῳ καὶ λόγῳ ἀγαθῷ.

3:1 Τὸ λοιπὸν προσεύχεσθε, ἀδελφοί, περὶ ἡμῶν, ἵνα ὁ λόγος τοῦ κυρίου τρέχῃ καὶ δοξάζηται καθὼς καὶ πρὸς ὑμᾶς, **2** καὶ ἵνα ῥυσθῶμεν ἀπὸ τῶν ἀτόπων καὶ πονηρῶν ἀνθρώπων· οὐ γὰρ πάντων ἡ πίστις. **3** πιστὸς δέ ἐστιν ὁ κύριος, ὃς στηρίξει ὑμᾶς καὶ φυλάξει ἀπὸ τοῦ πονηροῦ. **4** πεποίθαμεν δὲ ἐν κυρίῳ ἐφ᾽ ὑμᾶς, ὅτι ἃ παραγγέλλομεν [καὶ] ποιεῖτε καὶ ποιήσετε. **5** Ὁ δὲ κύριος κατευθύναι ὑμῶν τὰς καρδίας εἰς τὴν ἀγάπην τοῦ θεοῦ καὶ εἰς τὴν ὑπομονὴν τοῦ Χριστοῦ.

3:6 Παραγγέλλομεν δὲ ὑμῖν, ἀδελφοί, ἐν ὀνόματι τοῦ κυρίου [ἡμῶν] Ἰησοῦ Χριστοῦ στέλλεσθαι ὑμᾶς ἀπὸ παντὸς ἀδελφοῦ ἀτάκτως περιπατοῦντος καὶ μὴ κατὰ τὴν παράδοσιν ἣν παρελάβετε «παρελάβοσαν» παρ᾽ ἡμῶν. **7** αὐτοὶ γὰρ οἴδατε πῶς δεῖ μιμεῖσθαι ἡμᾶς, ὅτι οὐκ ἠτακτήσαμεν ἐν ὑμῖν **8** οὐδὲ δωρεὰν ἄρτον ἐφάγομεν παρά τινος, ἀλλ᾽ ἐν κόπῳ καὶ μόχθῳ νυκτὸς καὶ ἡμέρας ἐργαζόμενοι πρὸς τὸ μὴ ἐπιβαρῆσαί τινα ὑμῶν· **9** οὐχ ὅτι οὐκ ἔχομεν ἐξουσίαν, ἀλλ᾽ ἵνα ἑαυτοὺς τύπον δῶμεν ὑμῖν εἰς τὸ μιμεῖσθαι ἡμᾶς. **10** καὶ γὰρ ὅτε ἦμεν πρὸς ὑμᾶς, τοῦτο παρηγγέλλομεν ὑμῖν, ὅτι εἴ τις οὐ θέλει ἐργάζεσθαι μηδὲ ἐσθιέτω ¶ **11** ἀκούομεν γάρ τινας περιπατοῦντας ἐν ὑμῖν ἀτάκτως μηδὲν ἐργαζομένους ἀλλὰ περιεργαζομένους· **12** τοῖς δὲ τοιούτοις

busybodies. **12** Such people we command and urge in the Lord Jesus Christ to settle
περιεργαζομένους δὲ ⌊τοῖς τοιούτοις⌋ ← → παραγγέλλομεν καὶ παρακαλοῦμεν ἐν κυρίῳ Ἰησοῦ Χριστῷ ἵνα ⌊μετὰ ἡσυχίας⌋
pt.pm.apm   cj   d.dpm r.dpm   v.pai.1p   cj   v.pai.1p   p.d   n.dsm n.dsm n.dsm cj   p.g   n.gsf
4318   1254 3836 5525   4133   2779 4151   1877   3261 2652 5986 2671 3552 2484

down and earn the bread they eat. **13** And as for you, brothers, never tire of doing what is
←   ἐργαζόμενοι ἑαυτῶν τὸν ἄρτον → ἐσθίωσιν δὲ   ὑμεῖς ἀδελφοί μὴ ἐγκακήσητε → →   →   →
    pt.pm.npm   r.gpm.3 d.asm n.asm   v.pas.3p   cj   r.np.2 n.vpm pl   v.aas.2p
    2237   1571 3836 788   2266   1254   7007 81   3590 1591

right. ¶ **14** If anyone does not obey our instruction in this letter, take special note of him.
καλοποιοῦντες δέ Εἰ τις   οὐχ ὑπακούει ἡμῶν τῷ λόγῳ διὰ τῆς ἐπιστολῆς →   σημειοῦσθε ← τοῦτον
pt.pa.npm   cj cj r.nsm   pl v.pai.3s r.gp.1 d.dsm n.dsm p.g d.gsf n.gsf   v.pmm.2p   r.asm
2818   1254 1623 5516   5634 4024 5634   7005 3836 3364 1328 3836 2186   4957   4047

Do not associate with him, in order that he may feel ashamed. **15** Yet do not regard him as an enemy, but
→ μὴ συναναμίγνυσθαι ← αὐτῷ ἵνα ←   ←   → → → ἐντραπῇ καὶ → μὴ ἡγεῖσθε ὡς ἐχθρὸν ἀλλὰ
pl   f.pm   r.dsm.3 cj   v.aps.3s   cj   pl v.pmm.2p pl   a.asm cj
5264 3590 5264   899 2671   1956   2779 2451 3590 2451   6055 2398 247

warn him as a brother.
νουθετεῖτε ὡς ἀδελφόν
v.pam.2p   pl   n.asm
3805   6055 81

Final Greetings

3:16 Now may the Lord of peace himself give you peace at all times and in every way. The Lord
δὲ → ὁ κύριος → ⌊τῆς εἰρήνης⌋ Αὐτὸς δῴη ὑμῖν ⌊τὴν εἰρήνην⌋ διὰ παντὸς ←   ἐν παντὶ τρόπῳ ὁ κύριος
cj   d.nsm n.nsm   d.gsf n.gsf   r.nsm   v.aao.3s r.dp.2 d.asf n.asf   p.g   a.gsn   p.d   a.dsn   n.dsm   d.nsm n.nsm
1254 1443 3836 3261   3836 1645   899   1443 7007 3836 1645   1328 4246   1877   4246 5573   3836 3261

be with all of you. ¶ **17** I, Paul, write this greeting in my own hand, which is the distinguishing mark
μετὰ πάντων → ὑμῶν   Παύλου   Ὁ ἀσπασμός → ἐμῇ ⌊τῇ χειρὶ⌋ ὅ ἐστιν σημεῖον ←
p.g   a.gpm   r.gp.2   n.gsm   d.nsm n.nsm   r.dsf.1 d.dsf n.dsf r.nsn v.pai.3s n.nsn
3552 4246   7007   4263   3836 833   5931 1847   3836 5931 4005 1639   4956

in all my letters. This is how I write. ¶ **18** The grace of our Lord Jesus Christ be with you all.
ἐν πάσῃ ἐπιστολῇ οὕτως ← ← → γράφω   Ἡ χάρις → ἡμῶν ⌊τοῦ κυρίου⌋ Ἰησοῦ Χριστοῦ μετὰ ὑμῶν πάντων
p.d a.dsf   n.dsf   adv   v.pai.1s   d.nsf n.nsf   r.gp.1 d.gsm n.gsm   n.gsm n.gsm   p.g r.gp.2 a.gpm
1877 4246   2186   4048   1211   3836 5921   3261 7005 3836 3261   2652 5986   3552 7007 4246

παραγγέλλομεν καὶ παρακαλοῦμεν ἐν κυρίῳ Ἰησοῦ Χριστῷ, ἵνα μετὰ ἡσυχίας ἐργαζόμενοι τὸν ἑαυτῶν ἄρτον ἐσθίωσιν. ¹³ Ὑμεῖς δέ, ἀδελφοί, μὴ ἐγκακήσητε καλοποιοῦντες. ¶ ¹⁴ εἰ δέ τις οὐχ ὑπακούει τῷ λόγῳ ἡμῶν διὰ τῆς ἐπιστολῆς, τοῦτον σημειοῦσθε μὴ συναναμίγνυσθαι αὐτῷ, ἵνα ἐντραπῇ· ¹⁵ καὶ μὴ ὡς ἐχθρὸν ἡγεῖσθε, ἀλλὰ νουθετεῖτε ὡς ἀδελφόν.

³:¹⁶ Αὐτὸς δὲ ὁ κύριος τῆς εἰρήνης δῴη ὑμῖν τὴν εἰρήνην διὰ παντὸς ἐν παντὶ τρόπῳ. ὁ κύριος μετὰ πάντων ὑμῶν. ¶ ¹⁷ Ὁ ἀσπασμὸς τῇ ἐμῇ χειρὶ Παύλου, ὅ ἐστιν σημεῖον ἐν πάσῃ ἐπιστολῇ· οὕτως γράφω. ¶ ¹⁸ ἡ χάρις τοῦ κυρίου ἡμῶν Ἰησοῦ Χριστοῦ μετὰ πάντων ὑμῶν.

1 Timothy

1:1 Paul, an apostle of Christ Jesus by the command of God our Savior and of Christ Jesus our hope, ¶ **2** To Timothy my true son in the faith: ¶ Grace, mercy and peace from God the Father and Christ Jesus our Lord.

Warning Against False Teachers of the Law

1:3 As I urged you when I went into Macedonia, stay there in Ephesus so that you may command certain men not to teach false doctrines any longer **4** nor to devote themselves to myths and endless genealogies. These promote controversies rather than God's work — which is by faith. **5** The goal of this command is love, which comes from a pure heart and a good conscience and a sincere faith. **6** Some have wandered away from these and turned to meaningless talk. **7** They want to be teachers of the law, but they do not know what they are talking about or what they so confidently affirm. ¶ **8** We know that the law is good if one uses it properly. **9** We also know that law is made not for the righteous but for lawbreakers and rebels, the ungodly and sinful, the unholy and irreligious; for those who kill their fathers or mothers, for murderers, **10** for adulterers and perverts, for slave traders and liars and perjurers — and for whatever else is contrary to the sound doctrine

---

1:1 Παῦλος ἀπόστολος Χριστοῦ Ἰησοῦ κατ᾽ ἐπιταγὴν θεοῦ σωτῆρος ἡμῶν καὶ Χριστοῦ Ἰησοῦ τῆς ἐλπίδος ἡμῶν ¶ **2** Τιμοθέῳ γνησίῳ τέκνῳ ἐν πίστει, ¶ χάρις ἔλεος εἰρήνη ἀπὸ θεοῦ πατρὸς καὶ Χριστοῦ Ἰησοῦ τοῦ κυρίου ἡμῶν.

1:3 Καθὼς παρεκάλεσά σε προσμεῖναι ἐν Ἐφέσῳ πορευόμενος εἰς Μακεδονίαν, ἵνα παραγγείλῃς τισὶν μὴ ἑτεροδιδασκαλεῖν **4** μηδὲ προσέχειν μύθοις καὶ γενεαλογίαις ἀπεράντοις, αἵτινες ἐκζητήσεις παρέχουσιν μᾶλλον ἢ οἰκονομίαν θεοῦ τὴν ἐν πίστει. **5** τὸ δὲ τέλος τῆς παραγγελίας ἐστὶν ἀγάπη ἐκ καθαρᾶς καρδίας καὶ συνειδήσεως ἀγαθῆς καὶ πίστεως ἀνυποκρίτου, **6** ὧν τινες ἀστοχήσαντες ἐξετράπησαν εἰς ματαιολογίαν **7** θέλοντες εἶναι νομοδιδάσκαλοι, μὴ νοοῦντες μήτε ἃ λέγουσιν μήτε περὶ τίνων διαβεβαιοῦνται. ¶ **8** Οἴδαμεν δὲ ὅτι καλὸς ὁ νόμος, ἐάν τις αὐτῷ νομίμως χρῆται, **9** εἰδὼς τοῦτο, ὅτι δικαίῳ νόμος οὐ κεῖται, ἀνόμοις δὲ καὶ ἀνυποτάκτοις, ἀσεβέσι καὶ ἁμαρτωλοῖς, ἀνοσίοις καὶ βεβήλοις, πατρολῴαις καὶ μητρολῴαις, ἀνδροφόνοις **10** πόρνοις ἀρσενοκοίταις ἀνδραποδισταῖς ψεύσταις ἐπιόρκοις, καὶ εἴ τι ἕτερον τῇ ὑγιαινούσῃ διδασκαλίᾳ ἀντίκειται **11** κατὰ

11 that conforms to the glorious gospel of the blessed God, which he entrusted to me.
κατὰ ← τὸ ⌐τῆς δόξης⌐ εὐαγγέλιον → τοῦ μακαρίου θεοῦ ὃ ἐπιστεύθην ← ἐγώ
p.a d.asn d.gsf n.gsf n.asn d.gsm a.gsm n.gsm r.asn v.api.1s r.ns.1
2848 3836 3836 1518 2295 3836 3421 2536 4005 4409 1609

The Lord's Grace to Paul

1:12I thank Christ Jesus our Lord, who has given me strength, that he considered me faithful,
→ ⌐Χάριν ἔχω⌐ Χριστῷ Ἰησοῦ ἡμῶν ⌐τῷ κυρίῳ⌐ τῷ → → με ἐνδυναμώσαντι ὅτι → ἡγήσατο με πιστόν
n.asf v.pai.1s n.dsm n.dsm r.gp.1 d.dsm n.dsm d.dsm r.as.1 pt.aa.dsm cj v.ami.3s r.as.1 a.asf
5921 2400 5986 2652 7005 3836 3261 3836 1904 1904 1609 1904 4022 2451 1609 4412

appointing me to his service. **13** Even though I was once a blasphemer and a persecutor and a violent man,
θέμενος εἰς διακονίαν → → → ⌐ὄντα ⌐τὸ πρότερον⌐ βλάσφημον καὶ διώκτην καὶ ὑβριστήν ←
pt.am.nsm p.a n.asf pt.pa.asm d.asn adv.c a.asm cj n.asm cj n.asm
5502 1650 1355 1639 3836 4728 1061 2779 1502 2779 5616

I was shown mercy because I acted in ignorance and unbelief. **14** The grace of our Lord was
ἀλλὰ → → → ἠλεήθην ὅτι → ἐποίησα ἐν ἀγνοῶν ἀπιστίᾳ δὲ ἡ χάρις ↱ ἡμῶν ⌐τοῦ κυρίου⌐ →
cj v.api.1s cj v.aai.1s p.d pt.pa.nsm n.dsf cj d.nsf n.nsf r.gp.1 d.gsm n.gsm
247 1796 4022 4472 1877 51 602 1254 3836 5921 3261 7005 3836 3261

poured out on me abundantly, along with the faith and love that are in Christ Jesus. ¶ **15** Here is a
→ → → ὑπερεπλεόνασεν → μετὰ πίστεως καὶ ἀγάπης τῆς ἐν Χριστῷ Ἰησοῦ
v.aai.3s p.g n.gsf cj n.gsf d.gsf p.d n.dsm n.dsm
5670 3552 4411 2779 27 3836 1877 5986 2652

trustworthy saying that deserves full acceptance: Christ Jesus came into the world to save sinners
πιστὸς ⌐ὁ λόγος⌐ καὶ ἄξιος πάσης ἀποδοχῆς ὅτι Χριστὸς Ἰησοῦς ἦλθεν εἰς τὸν κόσμον → σῶσαι ἁμαρτωλοὺς
a.nsm d.nsm n.nsm cj a.nsm a.gsf n.gsf cj n.nsm n.nsm v.aai.3s p.a d.asm n.asm f.aa a.apm
4412 3836 3364 2779 545 4246 628 4022 5986 2652 2262 1650 3836 3180 5392 283

– of whom I am the worst. **16** But for that very reason I was shown mercy so that in me, the worst of
→ ὧν ἐγώ εἰμι πρῶτος ἀλλὰ διὰ τοῦτο, ← ← → → ἠλεήθην ἵνα → ἐν ἐμοὶ πρώτῳ
r.gpm r.ns.1 v.pai.1s a.nsm cj p.a r.asn v.api.1s cj p.d r.ds.1 a.dsm
4005 1609 1639 4755 247 1328 4047 1796 2671 1877 1609 4755

sinners, Christ Jesus might display his unlimited patience as an example for those who would believe on
Χριστὸς Ἰησοῦς → ἐνδείξηται τὴν ἅπασαν μακροθυμίαν πρὸς ὑποτύπωσιν τῶν ← μελλόντων πιστεύειν ἐπ'
n.nsm n.nsm v.ams.3s d.asf a.asf n.asf p.a n.asf d.gpm pt.pa.gpm f.pa p.d
5986 2652 1892 3836 570 3429 4639 5721 3836 3516 4409 2093

him and receive eternal life. **17** Now to the King eternal, immortal, invisible, the only God, be honor and glory
αὐτῷ εἰς αἰώνιον ζωήν δὲ → Τῷ βασιλεῖ ⌐τῶν αἰώνων⌐ ἀφθάρτῳ ἀοράτῳ μόνῳ θεῷ τιμὴ καὶ δόξα
r.dsm.3 p.a a.asf n.asf cj d.dsm n.dsm d.gpm n.gpm a.dsm a.dsm a.dsm n.dsm n.nsf cj n.nsf
899 1650 173 2437 1254 3836 995 3836 172 915 548 3668 2536 5507 2779 1518

for ever and ever. Amen. ¶ **18** Timothy, my son, I give you this instruction in
εἰς ⌐τοὺς αἰῶνας⌐ ⌐τῶν αἰώνων⌐ ἀμήν Τιμόθεε τέκνον παρατίθεμαι σοι Ταύτην ⌐τὴν παραγγελίαν⌐ κατὰ
p.a d.apm n.apm d.gpm n.gpm pl n.vsm n.vsn v.pmi.1s r.ds.2 r.asf d.asf n.asf p.a
1650 3836 172 3836 172 297 5510 5451 4192 5148 4047 3836 4132 2848

keeping with the prophecies once made about you, so that by following them you may fight the good
← ← τὰς προφητείας → προαγούσας ἐπὶ σὲ ἵνα ἐν αὐταῖς → στρατεύῃ τὴν καλὴν
d.apf n.apf pt.pa.apf p.a r.as.2 cj p.d r.dpf.3 v.pms.2s d.asf a.asf
3836 4735 4575 2093 5148 2671 1877 899 5129 3836 2819

fight, **19** holding on to faith and a good conscience. Some have rejected these and so have shipwrecked
στρατείαν ἔχων ← πίστιν καὶ ἀγαθὴν συνείδησιν τινες ἀπωσάμενοι ἥν → ἐναυάγησαν περὶ
n.asf pt.pa.nsm n.asf cj a.asf n.asf r.npm pt.am.npm r.asf v.aai.3p p.a
5127 2400 4411 2779 19 5287 5516 723 4005 3728 4309

their faith. **20** Among them are Hymenaeus and Alexander, whom I have handed over to Satan to be
τὴν πίστιν ὧν ἐστιν Ὑμέναιος καὶ Ἀλέξανδρος οὓς → παρέδωκα ← → ⌐τῷ σατανᾷ⌐ ἵνα
d.asf n.asf r.gpm v.pai.3s n.nsm cj n.nsm r.apm v.aai.1s d.dsm n.dsm cj
3836 4411 4005 1639 5628 2779 235 4005 4140 3836 4928 2671

taught not to blaspheme.
παιδευθῶσιν μὴ → βλασφημεῖν
v.aps.3p pl f.pa
4084 3590 1059

τὸ εὐαγγέλιον τῆς δόξης τοῦ μακαρίου θεοῦ, ὃ ἐπιστεύθην ἐγώ. **1:12** Χάριν ἔχω τῷ ἐνδυναμώσαντί με Χριστῷ Ἰησοῦ τῷ κυρίῳ ἡμῶν, ὅτι πιστόν με ἡγήσατο θέμενος εἰς διακονίαν **13** τὸ πρότερον ὄντα βλάσφημον καὶ διώκτην καὶ ὑβριστήν, ἀλλὰ ἠλεήθην, ὅτι ἀγνοῶν ἐποίησα ἐν ἀπιστίᾳ· **14** ὑπερεπλεόνασεν δὲ ἡ χάρις τοῦ κυρίου ἡμῶν μετὰ πίστεως καὶ ἀγάπης τῆς ἐν Χριστῷ Ἰησου ¶ **15** πιστὸς ὁ λόγος καὶ πάσης ἀποδοχῆς ἄξιος, ὅτι Χριστὸς Ἰησοῦς ἦλθεν εἰς τὸν κόσμον ἁμαρτωλοὺς σῶσαι, ὧν πρῶτός εἰμι ἐγώ. **16** ἀλλὰ διὰ τοῦτο ἠλεήθην, ἵνα ἐν ἐμοὶ πρώτῳ ἐνδείξηται Χριστὸς Ἰησοῦς τὴν ἅπασαν μακροθυμίαν πρὸς ὑποτύπωσιν τῶν μελλόντων πιστεύειν ἐπ' αὐτῷ εἰς ζωὴν αἰώνιον. **17** τῷ δὲ βασιλεῖ τῶν αἰώνων, ἀφθάρτῳ ἀοράτῳ μόνῳ θεῷ, τιμὴ καὶ δόξα εἰς τοὺς αἰῶνας τῶν αἰώνων, ἀμήν. ¶ **18** Ταύτην τὴν παραγγελίαν παρατίθεμαί σοι, τέκνον Τιμόθεε, κατὰ τὰς προαγούσας ἐπὶ σὲ προφητείας, ἵνα στρατεύῃ ἐν αὐταῖς τὴν καλὴν στρατείαν **19** ἔχων πίστιν καὶ ἀγαθὴν συνείδησιν, ἥν τινες ἀπωσάμενοι περὶ τὴν πίστιν ἐναυάγησαν, **20** ὧν ἐστιν Ὑμέναιος καὶ Ἀλέξανδρος, οὓς παρέδωκα τῷ Σατανᾷ, ἵνα παιδευθῶσιν μὴ βλασφημεῖν.

Instructions on Worship

2:1 I urge, then, first of all, that requests, prayers, intercession and thanksgiving be made for
→ Παρακαλῶ οὖν πρῶτον → πάντων δεήσεις προσευχάς ἐντεύξεις εὐχαριστίας → ποιεῖσθαι ὑπὲρ
v.pai.1s cj adv a.gpn n.apf n.apf n.apf n.apf f.pp p.g
4151 4036 4754 4246 1255 4666 1950 2374 4472 5642

everyone — **2** for kings and all those in authority, that we may live peaceful and quiet lives
⌐πάντων ἀνθρώπων⌐ ὑπὲρ βασιλέων καὶ πάντων τῶν ὄντων ἐν ὑπεροχῇ ἵνα → → διάγωμεν ἤρεμον καὶ ἡσύχιον βίον
a.gpm n.gpm p.g n.gpm cj a.gpm d.gpm pt.pa.gpm p.d n.dsf cj v.pas.1p a.asm cj a.asm n.asm
4246 476 5642 995 2779 4246 3836 1639 1877 5667 2671 1341 2475 2779 2485 1050

in all godliness and holiness. **3** This is good, and pleases God our Savior, **4** who wants all men
ἐν πάσῃ εὐσεβείᾳ καὶ σεμνότητι τοῦτο καλὸν καὶ ἀπόδεκτον ἐνώπιον θεοῦ ἡμῶν ⌐τοῦ σωτῆρος⌐ ὃς θέλει πάντας ἀνθρώπους
p.d a.dsf n.dsf cj n.dsf r.nsn a.nsn cj a.nsn p.g n.gsm r.gp.1 d.gsm n.gsm r.nsm v.pai.3s a.apm n.apm
1877 4246 2354 2779 4949 4047 2819 2779 621 1967 2536 7005 3836 5400 4005 2527 4246 476

to be saved and to come to a knowledge of the truth. **5** For there is one God and one mediator between God
→ → σωθῆναι καὶ → ἐλθεῖν εἰς ἐπίγνωσιν → ἀληθείας γὰρ εἷς θεὸς καὶ εἷς μεσίτης → θεοῦ
f.ap cj f.aa p.a n.asf n.gsf cj a.nsm n.nsm cj a.nsm n.nsm n.gsm
5392 2779 2262 1650 2106 237 1142 1651 2536 2779 1651 3542 2536

and men, the man Christ Jesus, **6** who gave himself as a ransom for all men — the testimony given in
καὶ ἀνθρώπων ἄνθρωπος Χριστὸς Ἰησοῦς ὁ δοὺς ἑαυτὸν ἀντίλυτρον ὑπὲρ πάντων τὸ μαρτύριον →
cj n.gpm n.nsm n.nsm n.nsm d.nsm pt.aa.nsm r.asm.3 n.asn p.g a.gpm d.nsn n.nsn
2779 476 476 5986 2652 3836 1443 1571 519 5642 4246 3836 3457

its proper time. **7** And for this purpose I was appointed a herald and an apostle — I am telling the truth, I am
ἰδίοις καιροῖς εἰς ὃ ἐγὼ → ἐτέθην κῆρυξ καὶ ἀπόστολος → → λέγω ἀλήθειαν
a.dpm n.dpm p.a r.asn r.ns.1 v.api.1s n.nsm cj n.nsm v.pai.1s n.asf
2625 2789 1650 4005 1609 5502 3061 2779 693 3306 237

not lying — and a teacher of the true faith to the Gentiles. ¶ **8** I want men
οὐ ψεύδομαι διδάσκαλος ἐν ἀληθείᾳ καὶ πίστει → ἐθνῶν οὖν → Βούλομαι ⌐τοὺς ἄνδρας⌐
pl v.pmi.1s n.nsm p.d n.dsf cj n.dsf n.gpn cj v.pmi.1s n.apm
4024 6017 1437 1877 237 2779 4411 1620 4036 1089 3836 467

everywhere to lift up holy hands in prayer, without anger or disputing. ¶ **9** I also
ἐν παντὶ τόπῳ → ἐπαίροντας ὁσίους χεῖρας προσεύχεσθαι χωρὶς ὀργῆς καὶ διαλογισμοῦ Ὡσαύτως [καὶ]
p.d a.dsm n.dsm pt.pa.apm a.apf n.apf f.pm p.g n.gsf cj n.gsm adv adv
1877 4246 5536 2048 4008 5931 4667 6006 3973 2779 1369 6058 2779

want women to dress modestly, with decency and propriety, not with braided hair or gold or
γυναῖκας → κοσμεῖν ἑαυτὰς ⌐ἐν καταστολῇ κοσμίῳ μετὰ αἰδοῦς καὶ σωφροσύνης μὴ ἐν πλέγμασιν καὶ χρυσίῳ ἢ
n.apf f.pa r.apf.3 p.d n.dsf a.dsf p.g n.gsf cj n.gsf pl p.d n.dpn cj n.dsn cj
1222 3175 1571 1877 2950 3177 3552 133 2779 5408 3590 1877 4427 2779 5992 2445

pearls or expensive clothes, **10** but with good deeds, appropriate for women who profess to worship
μαργαρίταις ἢ πολυτελεῖ ἱματισμῷ ἀλλ᾽ δι᾽ ἀγαθῶν ἔργων ὃ πρέπει → γυναιξὶν ἐπαγγελλομέναις →
n.dpm cj a.dsm n.dsm cj p.g a.gpn n.gpn r.nsn v.pai.3s n.dpf pt.pm.dpf
3449 2445 4500 2669 247 1328 19 2240 4005 4560 1222 2040

God. ¶ **11** A woman should learn in quietness and full submission. **12** I do not permit a woman
θεοσέβειαν Γυνὴ → μανθανέτω ἐν ἡσυχίᾳ ἐν πάσῃ ὑποταγῇ δὲ → οὐκ ἐπιτρέπω γυναικὶ
n.asf n.nsf v.pam.3s p.d n.dsf p.d a.dsf n.dsf cj pl v.pai.1s n.dsf
2537 1222 3443 1877 2484 1877 4246 5717 1254 2205 2205 4024 2205 1222

to teach or to have authority over a man; she must be silent. **13** For Adam was formed first, then Eve.
→ διδάσκειν οὐδὲ → αὐθεντεῖν ἀνδρός ἀλλ᾽ → εἶναι ἐν ἡσυχίᾳ γὰρ Ἀδὰμ → ἐπλάσθη πρῶτος εἶτα Εὕα
f.pa cj f.pa n.gsm cj f.pa p.d n.dsf cj n.nsm v.api.3s adv adv n.nsf
1438 4028 883 467 247 1639 1877 2484 1142 77 4421 4755 1663 2293

14 And Adam was not the one deceived; it was the woman who was deceived and became a sinner. **15** But
καὶ Ἀδὰμ → οὐκ ἠπατήθη δὲ ἡ γυνὴ → → ἐξαπατηθεῖσα γέγονεν ἐν παραβάσει δὲ
cj n.nsm pl v.api.3s cj d.nsf n.nsf pt.ap.nsf v.rai.3s p.d n.dsf cj
2779 77 572 4024 572 1254 3836 1222 1987 1181 1877 4126 1254

women will be saved through childbearing — if they continue in faith, love and holiness with propriety.
→ → σωθήσεται διὰ ⌐τῆς τεκνογονίας⌐ ἐὰν → μείνωσιν ἐν πίστει καὶ ἀγάπῃ καὶ ἁγιασμῷ μετὰ σωφροσύνης
v.fpi.3s p.g d.gsf n.gsf cj v.aas.3p p.d n.dsf cj n.dsf cj n.dsm p.g n.gsf
5392 1328 3836 5450 1569 3531 1877 4411 2779 40 2779 3552 5408

2:1 Παρακαλῶ οὖν πρῶτον πάντων ποιεῖσθαι δεήσεις προσευχὰς ἐντεύξεις εὐχαριστίας ὑπὲρ πάντων ἀνθρώπων, **2** ὑπὲρ βασιλέων καὶ πάντων τῶν ἐν ὑπεροχῇ ὄντων, ἵνα ἤρεμον καὶ ἡσύχιον βίον διάγωμεν ἐν πάσῃ εὐσεβείᾳ καὶ σεμνότητι. **3** τοῦτο καλὸν καὶ ἀπόδεκτον ἐνώπιον τοῦ σωτῆρος ἡμῶν θεοῦ, **4** ὃς πάντας ἀνθρώπους θέλει σωθῆναι καὶ εἰς ἐπίγνωσιν ἀληθείας ἐλθεῖν. **5** εἷς γὰρ θεός, εἷς καὶ μεσίτης θεοῦ καὶ ἀνθρώπων, ἄνθρωπος Χριστὸς Ἰησοῦς, **6** ὁ δοὺς ἑαυτὸν ἀντίλυτρον ὑπὲρ πάντων, τὸ μαρτύριον καιροῖς ἰδίοις. **7** εἰς ὃ ἐτέθην ἐγὼ κῆρυξ καὶ ἀπόστολος, ἀλήθειαν λέγω οὐ ψεύδομαι, διδάσκαλος ἐθνῶν ἐν πίστει καὶ ἀληθείᾳ. ¶ **8** Βούλομαι οὖν προσεύχεσθαι τοὺς ἄνδρας ἐν παντὶ τόπῳ ἐπαίροντας ὁσίους χεῖρας χωρὶς ὀργῆς καὶ διαλογισμοῦ. ¶ **9** ὡσαύτως [καὶ] γυναῖκας ἐν καταστολῇ κοσμίῳ μετὰ αἰδοῦς καὶ σωφροσύνης κοσμεῖν ἑαυτάς, μὴ ἐν πλέγμασιν καὶ χρυσίῳ ἢ μαργαρίταις ἢ ἱματισμῷ πολυτελεῖ, **10** ἀλλ᾽ ὃ πρέπει γυναιξὶν ἐπαγγελλομέναις θεοσέβειαν, δι᾽ ἔργων ἀγαθῶν. ¶ **11** γυνὴ ἐν ἡσυχίᾳ μανθανέτω ἐν πάσῃ ὑποταγῇ· **12** διδάσκειν δὲ γυναικὶ οὐκ ἐπιτρέπω οὐδὲ αὐθεντεῖν ἀνδρός, ἀλλ᾽ εἶναι ἐν ἡσυχίᾳ. **13** Ἀδὰμ γὰρ πρῶτος ἐπλάσθη, εἶτα Εὕα. **14** καὶ Ἀδὰμ οὐκ ἠπατήθη, ἡ δὲ γυνὴ ἐξαπατηθεῖσα ἐν παραβάσει γέγονεν· **15** σωθήσεται δὲ διὰ τῆς τεκνογονίας, ἐὰν μείνωσιν ἐν πίστει καὶ ἀγάπῃ καὶ ἁγιασμῷ μετὰ σωφροσύνης. «σωφροσύνης·»

Overseers and Deacons

3:1 Here is a trustworthy saying: If anyone sets his heart on being an overseer, he desires a noble task.
Πιστὸς ⌐ὁ λόγος.⌐ Εἴ τις ὀρέγεται ἐπισκοπῆς → ἐπιθυμεῖ καλοῦ ἔργου
a.nsm d.nsm n.nsm cj r.nsm v.pmi.3s n.gsf v.pai.3s a.gsn n.gsn
4412 3836 3364 1623 5516 3977 2175 2121 2819 2240

2 Now the overseer must be above reproach, the husband of but one wife, temperate, self-controlled,
οὖν τὸν ἐπίσκοπον δεῖ εἶναι → ἀνεπίλημπτον ἄνδρα → μιᾶς γυναικὸς νηφάλιον σώφρονα
cj d.asm n.asm v.pai.3s f.pa a.asm n.asm a.gsf n.gsf a.asm a.asm
4036 3836 2176 1256 1639 455 467 1651 1222 3767 5409

respectable, hospitable, able to teach, **3** not given to drunkenness, not violent but gentle, not quarrelsome, not a
κόσμιον φιλόξενον → διδακτικόν μὴ → πάροινον μὴ πλήκτην ἀλλὰ ἐπιεικῆ → ἄμαχον
a.asm a.asm a.asm pl n.asm pl n.asm cj a.asm a.asm
3177 5811 1434 3590 4232 3590 4438 247 2117 285

lover of money. **4** He must manage his own family well and see that his children obey him with
ἀφιλάργυρον ← προϊστάμενον τοῦ ἰδίου οἴκου καλῶς ἔχοντα τέκνα ἐν ὑποταγῇ μετὰ
a.asm pt.pm.asm d.gsm a.gsm n.gsm adv pt.pa.asm n.apn p.d n.dsf p.g
921 4613 3836 2625 3875 2822 2400 5451 1877 5717 3552

proper respect. **5** (If anyone does not know how to manage his own family, how can he take care of
πάσης σεμνότητος δὲ εἰ τις οὐκ οἶδεν → προστῆναι τοῦ ἰδίου οἴκου πῶς → ἐπιμελήσεται ←
a.gsf n.gsf cj cj r.nsm pl v.rai.3s f.aa d.gsm a.gsm n.gsm adv v.fmi.3s
4246 4949 1254 1623 5516 3857 4024 3857 4613 3836 2625 3875 4802 2150

God's church?) **6** He must not be a recent convert, or he may become conceited and fall under the same
θεοῦ ἐκκλησίας μὴ νεόφυτον ἵνα μὴ → → τυφωθεὶς ἐμπέσῃ εἰς
n.gsm n.gsf pl a.asm cj pl pt.ap.nsm v.aas.3s p.a
2536 1711 3590 3745 2671 3590 5605 1860 1650

judgment as the devil. **7** He must also have a good reputation with outsiders, so that he will not fall into
κρίμα ⌐τοῦ διαβόλου⌐ δὲ → δεῖ καὶ ἔχειν καλὴν μαρτυρίαν ἀπὸ ⌐τῶν ἔξωθεν⌐ ἵνα ← → → μὴ ἐμπέσῃ εἰς
n.asn d.gsm n.gsm cj v.pai.3s adv f.pa a.asf n.asf p.g d.gpm adv cj pl v.aas.3s p.a
3210 1333 3836 1333 1254 1256 2779 2400 2819 3456 608 3836 2033 2671 1860 1860 3590 1860 1650

disgrace and into the devil's trap. ¶ **8** Deacons, likewise, are to be men worthy of respect, sincere,
ὀνειδισμὸν καὶ ⌐τοῦ διαβόλου⌐ παγίδα Διακόνους ὡσαύτως → → σεμνούς μὴ διλόγους
n.asm cj d.gsm n.gsm n.asf n.apm adv a.apm pl a.apm
3944 2779 3836 1333 4075 1356 6058 4948 3590 1474

not indulging in much wine, and not pursuing dishonest gain. **9** They must keep hold of the deep truths
μὴ προσέχοντας πολλῷ οἴνῳ μὴ → αἰσχροκερδεῖς → → ἔχοντας ← τὸ → μυστήριον
pl pt.pa.apm a.dsm n.dsm pl a.apm pt.pa.apm d.asn n.asn
3590 4668 4498 3885 3590 153 2400 3836 3696

of the faith with a clear conscience. **10** They must first be tested; and then if there is nothing
→ τῆς πίστεως ἐν καθαρᾷ συνειδήσει δὲ καὶ οὗτοι → πρῶτον → δοκιμαζέσθωσαν εἶτα → ὄντες ἀνέγκλητοι
d.gsf n.gsf p.d a.dsf n.dsf cj adv r.npm → v.ppm.3p adv pt.pa.npm a.npm
3836 4411 1877 2754 5287 1254 2779 4047 1507 4754 1507 1663 1639 441

against them, let them serve as deacons. ¶ **11** In the same way, their wives are to be women
→ → → διακονείτωσαν ὡσαύτως ← → → Γυναῖκας
v.pam.3p adv n.apf
1354 6058 1222

worthy of respect, not malicious talkers but temperate and trustworthy in everything. ¶ **12** A deacon must
→ σεμνάς μὴ διαβόλους ← νηφαλίους πιστάς ἐν πᾶσιν διάκονοι →
a.apf pl a.apf a.apf a.apf p.d a.dpn n.npm
4948 3590 1333 3767 4412 1877 4246 1356

be the husband of but one wife and must manage his children and his household well. **13** Those who
ἔστωσαν ἄνδρες μιᾶς γυναικὸς προϊστάμενοι τέκνων καὶ ἰδίων ⌐τῶν οἴκων⌐ καλῶς γὰρ οἱ
v.pam.3p n.npm a.gsf n.gsf pt.pm.npm n.gpn cj a.gpm d.gpm n.npm adv cj d.npm
1639 467 1651 1222 4613 5451 2779 2625 3836 3875 2822 1142 3836

have served well gain an excellent standing and great assurance in their faith in Christ
→ διακονήσαντες καλῶς περιποιοῦνται καλὸν βαθμὸν ἑαυτοῖς καὶ πολλὴν παρρησίαν ἐν πίστει τῇ ἐν Χριστῷ
pt.aa.npm adv v.pmi.3p a.asm n.asm r.dpm.3 cj a.asf n.asf p.d n.dsf d.dsf p.d n.dsm
1354 2822 4347 2819 957 1571 2779 4498 4244 1877 4411 3836 1877 5986

3:1 Πιστὸς «πιστὸς» ὁ λόγος· «λόγος.» εἴ «Εἴ» τις ἐπισκοπῆς ὀρέγεται, καλοῦ ἔργου ἐπιθυμεῖ. **2** δεῖ οὖν τὸν ἐπίσκοπον ἀνεπίλημπτον εἶναι, μιᾶς γυναικὸς ἄνδρα, νηφάλιον σώφρονα κόσμιον φιλόξενον διδακτικόν, **3** μὴ πάροινον μὴ πλήκτην, ἀλλὰ ἐπιεικῆ ἄμαχον ἀφιλάργυρον, **4** τοῦ ἰδίου οἴκου καλῶς προϊστάμενον, τέκνα ἔχοντα ἐν ὑποταγῇ, μετὰ πάσης σεμνότητος **5** (εἰ δὲ τις τοῦ ἰδίου οἴκου προστῆναι οὐκ οἶδεν, πῶς ἐκκλησίας θεοῦ ἐπιμελήσεται; . **6** μὴ νεόφυτον, ἵνα μὴ τυφωθεὶς εἰς κρίμα ἐμπέσῃ τοῦ διαβόλου. **7** δεῖ δὲ καὶ μαρτυρίαν καλὴν ἔχειν ἀπὸ τῶν ἔξωθεν, ἵνα μὴ εἰς ὀνειδισμὸν ἐμπέσῃ καὶ παγίδα τοῦ διαβόλου. ¶ **8** Διακόνους ὡσαύτως σεμνούς, μὴ διλόγους, μὴ οἴνῳ πολλῷ προσέχοντας, μὴ αἰσχροκερδεῖς, **9** ἔχοντας τὸ μυστήριον τῆς πίστεως ἐν καθαρᾷ συνειδήσει. **10** καὶ οὗτοι δὲ δοκιμαζέσθωσαν πρῶτον, εἶτα διακονείτωσαν ἀνέγκλητοι ὄντες. ¶ **11** γυναῖκας ὡσαύτως σεμνάς, μὴ διαβόλους, νηφαλίους, πιστὰς ἐν πᾶσιν. ¶ **12** διάκονοι ἔστωσαν μιᾶς γυναικὸς ἄνδρες, τέκνων καλῶς προϊστάμενοι καὶ τῶν ἰδίων οἴκων. **13** οἱ γὰρ καλῶς διακονήσαντες βαθμὸν ἑαυτοῖς καλὸν περιποιοῦνται καὶ πολλὴν παρρησίαν ἐν πίστει τῇ

Jesus. ¶ 14 Although I hope to come to you soon,   I am writing you these instructions so that, 15 if I
Ἰησοῦ   ἐλπίζων ἐλθεῖν πρὸς σὲ ἐν τάχει   γράφω σοι Ταῦτα   ἵνα   δὲ ἐὰν
n.dsm   pt.pa.nsm f.aa   p.a r.as.2 p.d n.dsn   v.pai.1s r.ds.2 r.apn   cj   cj cj
2652   1827   2262 4639 5148 1877 5443   1211   5148   4047   2671   1254 1569

am delayed, you will know how people ought to conduct   themselves in God's household, which is the
βραδύνω   εἰδῇς   πῶς δεῖ   ἀναστρέφεσθαι   ἐν θεοῦ οἴκῳ   ἥτις ἐστὶν
v.pas.1s   v.ras.2s cj   v.pai.3s f.pm   p.d n.gsm n.dsm   r.nsf v.pai.3s
1094   3857   4802 1256   418   1877 2536 3875   4015 1639

church of the living God, the pillar and foundation of the truth. 16 Beyond   all question, the mystery of
ἐκκλησία   ζῶντος θεοῦ στῦλος καὶ ἑδραίωμα   τῆς ἀληθείας καὶ ὁμολογουμένως   τὸ μυστήριον
n.nsf   pt.pa.gsm n.gsm n.nsm cj n.nsn   d.gsf n.gsf   cj adv   d.nsn n.nsn
1711   2409   2536   5146   2779 1613   3836 237   2779 3935   3836 3696

godliness is great: He appeared in a body, was vindicated by the Spirit,   was seen by angels, was preached
τῆς εὐσεβείας ἐστὶν μέγα ὃς ἐφανερώθη ἐν σαρκί   ἐδικαιώθη ἐν πνεύματι   ὤφθη ἀγγέλοις   ἐκηρύχθη
d.gsf n.gsf   v.pai.3s a.nsn r.nsm v.api.3s p.d n.dsf v.api.3s p.d n.dsn   v.api.3s n.dpm   v.api.3s
3836 2354   1639   3489 4005 5746   1877 4922   4922? ...

among the nations, was believed on in the world, was taken   up in glory.
ἐν ἔθνεσιν   ἐπιστεύθη ἐν κόσμῳ   ἀνελήμφθη ἐν δόξῃ
p.d n.dpn   v.api.3s p.d n.dsm   v.api.3s   p.d n.dsf
1877 1620   4409   1877 3180   377   1877 1518

Instructions to Timothy

4:1 The Spirit clearly says that in later times some will abandon   the faith and follow   deceiving
δὲ Τὸ πνεῦμα ῥητῶς λέγει ὅτι ἐν ὑστέροις καιροῖς τινες   ἀποστήσονται τῆς πίστεως προσέχοντες πλάνοις
cj d.nsn n.nsn adv   v.pai.3s cj p.d a.dpm n.dpm r.npm   v.fmi.3p d.gsf n.gsf   pt.pa.npm a.dpn
1254 3836 4460 4843 3306 4022 1877 5731 2789 5516   923   3836 4411   4668   4418

spirits and things taught   by demons. 2 Such teachings come through hypocritical liars,   whose
πνεύμασιν καὶ διδασκαλίαις δαιμονίων   ἐν ὑποκρίσει ψευδολόγων ἰδίαν
n.dpn cj   n.dpf   n.gpn   p.d n.dsf   n.gpm   a.asf
4460 2779   1436   1228   1877 5694   6016   2625

consciences have been seared   as with a hot iron. 3 They forbid people to marry and order them to
τὴν συνείδησιν   κεκαυστηριασμένων   κωλυόντων   γαμεῖν
d.asf n.asf   pt.rp.gpm   pt.pa.gpm   f.pa
3836 5287   3013   3266   1138

abstain from certain foods,   which God   created to be received with thanksgiving by those who believe and
ἀπέχεσθαι   βρωμάτων ἃ ὁ θεὸς   ἔκτισεν εἰς μετάλημψιν μετὰ εὐχαριστίας   τοῖς   πιστοῖς καὶ
f.pm   n.gpn   r.apn d.nsm n.nsm v.aai.3s p.a n.asf p.g n.gsf   d.dpm   a.dpm cj
600   1109   4005 3836 2536 3231   1650 3562   3552 2374   3836   4412   2779

who know   the truth. 4 For everything God created is good, and nothing is to be rejected if it is received
ἐπεγνωκόσι τὴν ἀλήθειαν ὅτι πᾶν   θεοῦ κτίσμα καλὸν καὶ οὐδὲν   ἀπόβλητον   λαμβανόμενον
pt.ra.dpm d.asf n.asf   cj a.nsn   n.gsm n.nsn a.nsn cj a.nsn   a.nsn   pt.pp.nsn
2105 3836 237   4022 4246 2536 3233 2819 2779 4029   612   3284

with thanksgiving, 5 because it is consecrated by the word of God and prayer. ¶ 6 If you point   these things
μετὰ εὐχαριστίας   γὰρ   ἁγιάζεται διὰ λόγου θεοῦ καὶ ἐντεύξεως   ὑποτιθέμενος Ταῦτα
p.g n.gsf   cj   v.ppi.3s p.g n.gsm n.gsm cj n.gsf   pt.pm.nsm r.apn
3552 2374   1142   39   1328 1364 2536 2779 1950   5719   4047

out to the brothers, you will be a good minister of Christ Jesus, brought   up in the truths of the faith and of
τοῖς ἀδελφοῖς   ἔσῃ   καλὸς διάκονος Χριστοῦ Ἰησοῦ ἐντρεφόμενος   τοῖς λόγοις   τῆς πίστεως καὶ
d.dpm n.dpm   v.fmi.2s a.nsm n.gsm n.gsm n.gsm pt.pm.nsm   d.dpm n.dpm   d.gsf n.gsf cj
5719 3836 81   1639   2819 1356 5986 2652 1957   3836 3364   3836 4411 2779

the good teaching   that you have followed. 7 Have   nothing to do with godless myths   and old
τῆς καλῆς διδασκαλίας ᾗ   παρηκολούθηκας δὲ παραιτοῦ   βεβήλους τοὺς μύθους καὶ
d.gsf a.gsf n.gsf   r.dsf v.rai.2s   cj v.pmm.2s   a.apm d.apm n.apm cj
3836 2819 1436   4005 4158   1254 4148   1013 3836 3680 2779

wives' tales;   rather, train yourself to be godly. 8 For physical training   is of some   value, but
γραώδεις δὲ   Γύμναζε σεαυτὸν πρὸς εὐσέβειαν γὰρ σωματικὴ ἡ γυμνασία ἐστὶν πρὸς ὀλίγον ὠφέλιμος δὲ
a.apm cj   v.pam.2s r.asm.2 p.a n.asf   cj n.nsf   d.nsf n.nsf v.pai.3s p.a a.asn a.nsf cj
1212 1254   1214   4639   4639 2354   1142 5394   3836 1215 1639 4639 3900 6068 1254

ἐν Χριστῷ Ἰησοῦ. ¶ 14 Ταῦτά σοι γράφω ἐλπίζων ἐλθεῖν πρὸς σὲ ἐν τάχει· 15 ἐὰν δὲ βραδύνω, ἵνα εἰδῇς πῶς δεῖ ἐν οἴκῳ θεοῦ ἀναστρέφεσθαι, ἥτις ἐστὶν ἐκκλησία θεοῦ ζῶντος, στῦλος καὶ ἑδραίωμα τῆς ἀληθείας. 16 καὶ ὁμολογουμένως μέγα ἐστὶν τὸ τῆς εὐσεβείας μυστήριον· Ὃς ἐφανερώθη ἐν σαρκί, ἐδικαιώθη ἐν πνεύματι, ὤφθη ἀγγέλοις, ἐκηρύχθη ἐν ἔθνεσιν, ἐπιστεύθη ἐν κόσμῳ, ἀνελήμφθη ἐν δόξῃ.

4:1 Τὸ δὲ πνεῦμα ῥητῶς λέγει ὅτι ἐν ὑστέροις καιροῖς ἀποστήσονταί τινες τῆς πίστεως προσέχοντες πνεύμασιν πλάνοις καὶ διδασκαλίαις δαιμονίων, 2 ἐν ὑποκρίσει ψευδολόγων, κεκαυστηριασμένων τὴν ἰδίαν συνείδησιν, 3 κωλυόντων γαμεῖν, ἀπέχεσθαι βρωμάτων, ἃ ὁ θεὸς ἔκτισεν εἰς μετάλημψιν μετὰ εὐχαριστίας τοῖς πιστοῖς καὶ ἐπεγνωκόσι τὴν ἀλήθειαν. 4 ὅτι πᾶν κτίσμα θεοῦ καλὸν καὶ οὐδὲν ἀπόβλητον μετὰ εὐχαριστίας λαμβανόμενον· 5 ἁγιάζεται γὰρ διὰ λόγου θεοῦ καὶ ἐντεύξεως. ¶ 6 Ταῦτα ὑποτιθέμενος τοῖς ἀδελφοῖς καλὸς ἔσῃ διάκονος Χριστοῦ Ἰησοῦ, ἐντρεφόμενος τοῖς λόγοις τῆς πίστεως καὶ τῆς καλῆς διδασκαλίας ᾗ παρηκολούθηκας· 7 τοὺς δὲ βεβήλους καὶ γραώδεις μύθους παραιτοῦ. γύμναζε δὲ σεαυτὸν πρὸς εὐσέβειαν· 8 ἡ

godliness has value for all things, holding promise for both the present life and the life to come. ¶
ἡ εὐσέβεια ἐστιν ὠφέλιμος πρὸς πάντα ← ἔχουσα ἐπαγγελίαν → τῆς νῦν ζωῆς καὶ τῆς → μελλούσης
d.nsf n.nsf v.pai.3s a.nsf p.a a.apn pt.pa.nsf n.asf d.gsf adv n.gsf cj d.gsf pt.pa.gsf
3836 2354 1639 6068 4639 4246 2400 2039 3836 3814 2437 2779 3836 3516

9 This is a trustworthy saying that deserves full acceptance **10** (and for this we labor and strive), that we →
πιστὸς ὁ λόγος καὶ ἄξιος πάσης ἀποδοχῆς γὰρ εἰς τοῦτο → κοπιῶμεν καὶ ἀγωνιζόμεθα ὅτι →
a.nsm d.nsm n.nsm cj a.nsm a.gsf n.gsf cj p.a r.asn v.pai.1p cj v.pmi.1p cj
4412 3836 3364 2779 545 4246 628 1142 1650 4047 3159 2779 76 4022

have put our hope in the living God, who is the Savior of all men, and especially of those who
ἠλπίκαμεν ἐπὶ ζῶντι θεῷ ὅς ἐστιν σωτὴρ πάντων ἀνθρώπων μάλιστα
v.rai.1p p.d pt.pa.dsm n.dsm r.nsm v.pai.3s n.nsm a.gpm n.gpm adv.s
1827 2093 2409 2536 4005 1639 5400 4246 476 3436

believe. ¶ **11** Command and teach these things. **12** Don't let anyone look down on you because you are
πιστῶν Παράγγελλε καὶ δίδασκε ταῦτα ← Μηδείς → καταφρονείτω ← σου
a.gpm v.pam.2s cj v.pam.2s r.apn a.nsm v.pam.3s r.gs.2
4412 4133 2779 1438 4047 3594 2969 5148

young, but set an example for the believers in speech, in life, in love, in faith and in purity.
τῆς νεότητος ἀλλὰ γίνου τύπος → τῶν πιστῶν ἐν λόγῳ ἐν ἀναστροφῇ ἐν ἀγάπῃ ἐν πίστει ἐν ἀγνείᾳ
d.gsf n.gsf cj v.pmm.2s n.nsm d.gpm a.gpm p.d n.dsm p.d n.dsf p.d n.dsf p.d n.dsf p.d n.dsf
3836 3744 247 1181 5596 3836 4412 1877 3364 1877 419 1877 27 1877 4411 1877 48

13 Until I come, devote yourself to the public reading of Scripture, to preaching and to teaching. **14** Do not
ἕως → ἔρχομαι πρόσεχε ← → τῇ → ἀναγνώσει → τῇ παρακλήσει → τῇ διδασκαλίᾳ → μὴ
cj v.pmi.1s v.pam.2s d.dsf n.dsf d.dsf n.dsf d.dsf n.dsf pl
2401 2262 4668 3836 342 3836 4155 3836 1436 288 3590

neglect your gift, which was given you through a prophetic message when the body of elders
ἀμέλει ἐν σοὶ τοῦ χαρίσματος ὅ → ἐδόθη σοι διὰ προφητείας ← μετὰ → τοῦ πρεσβυτερίου
v.pam.2s p.d r.ds.2 d.gsn n.gsn r.nsn v.api.3s r.ds.2 p.g n.gsf p.g d.gsn n.gsn
288 1877 5148 3836 5922 4005 1443 5148 1328 4735 3552 3836 4564

laid their hands on you. ¶ **15** Be diligent in these matters; give yourself wholly to them, so that everyone
ἐπιθέσεως τῶν χειρῶν → μελέτα ταῦτα ἴσθι → ἐν τούτοις ἵνα ← πᾶσιν
n.gsf d.gpf n.gpf v.pam.2s r.apn v.pam.2s p.d r.dpn cj a.dpm
2120 3836 5931 2120 3509 4047 1639 1877 4047 2671 4246

may see your progress. **16** Watch your life and doctrine closely. Persevere in them, because if you do,
ᾖ φανερὰ σου ἡ προκοπή ἔπεχε σεαυτῷ ← καὶ τῇ διδασκαλίᾳ ← ἐπίμενε αὐτοῖς γὰρ → → ποιῶν
v.pas.3s a.nsf r.gs.2 d.nsf n.nsf v.pam.2s r.dsm.2 cj d.dsf n.dsf v.pam.2s r.dpn.3 cj pt.pa.nsm
1639 5745 5148 3836 4620 2091 4932 2779 3836 1436 2091 2152 899 1142 4472

you will save both yourself and your hearers.
τοῦτο → → σώσεις καὶ σεαυτὸν καὶ σου τοὺς ἀκούοντας
r.asn v.fai.2s cj r.asm.2 cj r.gs.2 d.apm pt.pa.apm
4047 5392 2779 4932 2779 5148 3836 201

Advice About Widows, Elders and Slaves

5:1 Do not rebuke an older man harshly, but exhort him as if he were your father. Treat younger men
μὴ ἐπιπλήξῃς Πρεσβυτέρῳ ← ← ἀλλὰ παρακάλει ὡς ← πατέρα νεωτέρους ←
pl v.aas.2s a.dsm cj v.pam.2s pl n.asm a.apm.c
2159 3590 2159 4565 2159 247 4151 6055 4252 3742

as brothers, **2** older women as mothers, and younger women as sisters, with absolute purity. ¶ **3** Give
ὡς ἀδελφούς πρεσβυτέρας ← ὡς μητέρας νεωτέρας ← ὡς ἀδελφὰς ἐν πάσῃ ἁγνείᾳ →
pl n.apm a.apf pl n.apf a.apf.c pl n.apf p.d a.dsf n.dsf
6055 81 4565 6055 3613 3742 6055 80 1877 4246 48

proper recognition to those widows who are really *in need*. **4** But if a widow has children or grandchildren, these
→ τίμα ← Χήρας τὰς ὄντως χήρας δέ εἰ τις χήρα ἔχει τέκνα ἢ ἔκγονα
v.pam.2s n.apf d.apf adv n.apf cj cj r.nsf n.nsf v.pai.3s n.apn cj n.apn
5506 5939 3836 3953 5939 1254 1623 5516 5939 2400 5451 2445 1681

should learn first of all to put their religion into practice by caring for their own family and so
→ μανθανέτωσαν πρῶτον ← ← → εὐσεβεῖν → τὸν ἴδιον οἶκον καὶ
v.pam.3p adv f.pa d.asm a.asm n.asm cj
3443 4754 2355 3836 2625 3875 2779

γὰρ σωματικὴ γυμνασία πρὸς ὀλίγον ἐστιν ὠφέλιμος, ἡ δὲ εὐσέβεια πρὸς πάντα ὠφέλιμός ἐστιν ἐπαγγελίαν ἔχουσα ζωῆς τῆς νῦν καὶ τῆς μελλούσης. ¶ **9** πιστὸς ὁ λόγος καὶ πάσης ἀποδοχῆς ἄξιος· **10** εἰς τοῦτο γὰρ κοπιῶμεν καὶ ἀγωνιζόμεθα, ὅτι ἠλπίκαμεν ἐπὶ θεῷ ζῶντι, ὅς ἐστιν σωτὴρ πάντων ἀνθρώπων μάλιστα πιστῶν. ¶ **11** Παράγγελλε ταῦτα καὶ δίδασκε. **12** μηδείς σου τῆς νεότητος καταφρονείτω, ἀλλὰ τύπος γίνου τῶν πιστῶν ἐν λόγῳ, ἐν ἀναστροφῇ, ἐν ἀγάπῃ, ἐν πίστει, ἐν ἁγνείᾳ. **13** ἕως ἔρχομαι πρόσεχε τῇ ἀναγνώσει, τῇ παρακλήσει, τῇ διδασκαλίᾳ. **14** μὴ ἀμέλει τοῦ ἐν σοὶ χαρίσματος, ὃ ἐδόθη σοι διὰ προφητείας μετὰ ἐπιθέσεως τῶν χειρῶν τοῦ πρεσβυτερίου. ¶ **15** ταῦτα μελέτα, ἐν τούτοις ἴσθι, ἵνα σου ἡ προκοπὴ φανερὰ ᾖ πᾶσιν. **16** ἔπεχε σεαυτῷ καὶ τῇ διδασκαλίᾳ, ἐπίμενε αὐτοῖς· τοῦτο γὰρ ποιῶν καὶ σεαυτὸν σώσεις καὶ τοὺς ἀκούοντάς σου.

5:1 Πρεσβυτέρῳ μὴ ἐπιπλήξῃς ἀλλὰ παρακάλει ὡς πατέρα, νεωτέρους ὡς ἀδελφούς, **2** πρεσβυτέρας ὡς μητέρας, νεωτέρας ὡς ἀδελφὰς ἐν πάσῃ ἁγνείᾳ. ¶ **3** Χήρας τίμα τὰς ὄντως χήρας. **4** εἰ δέ τις χήρα τέκνα ἢ ἔκγονα ἔχει, μανθανέτωσαν πρῶτον τὸν ἴδιον οἶκον εὐσεβεῖν καὶ ἀμοιβὰς ἀποδιδόναι τοῖς προγόνοις· τοῦτο γάρ ἐστιν ἀπόδεκτον ἐνώπιον τοῦ θεοῦ. **5** ἡ δὲ ὄντως χήρα

repaying   their parents and grandparents, for this is   pleasing to   God.   5   The widow who is
ᾳἀμοιβὰς ἀποδιδόναι τοῖς προγόνοις ←   γὰρ τοῦτο ἐστιν ἀπόδεκτον ἐνώπιον ᾳτοῦ θεοῦ, δὲ ἡ   χήρα
n.apf   f.pa   d.dpm n.dpm   cj   r.nsn   v.pai.3s a.nsn   p.g   d.gsm n.gsm   cj   d.nsf n.nsf
304   625   3836   4591   1142   4047   1639   621   1967   3836 2536   1254 3836   5939

really in need and left all alone   puts her hope in   God and continues night and day   to pray   and
ὄντως   καὶ →   →   μεμονωμένη →   →   ἤλπικεν ἐπὶ θεὸν καὶ προσμένει νυκτὸς καὶ ἡμέρας ᾳταῖς προσευχαῖς καὶ
adv   cj   pt.rp.nsf   v.rai.3s   p.a   n.asm cj   v.pai.3s   n.gsf   cj   n.gsf   d.dpf n.dpf   cj
3953   2779   3670   1827   2093 2536   2779   4693   3816   2779   2465   3836   4666   2779

to ask   God for help. 6 But the widow who lives   for pleasure is dead   even while she lives. 7 Give
ᾳταῖς δεήσεσιν,   ←   →   δὲ ἡ   ←   σπαταλῶσα ←   →   τέθνηκεν   →   →   ζῶσα παράγγελλε
d.dpf   n.dpf   cj d.nsf   pt.pa.nsf   v.rai.3s   pt.pa.nsf v.pam.2s
3836   1255   1254 3836   5059   2569   2409   4133

the people these instructions, too, so that no one may be   open to blame.   8   If anyone does not provide for
                 ταῦτα ←   καὶ ἵνα → ᾳ→ →   ὦσιν →   →   ἀνεπίλημπτοι δέ εἰ τις   →   οὐ προνοεῖ ←
                 r.apn   cj   cj   ᾳ   v.pas.3p   a.npm   cj   r.nsm   pl   v.pai.3s
                 4047   2779 2671 455   1639   455   1254 1623 5516   4629 4024 4629

his relatives, and especially for his immediate family, he has denied the faith and is   worse than an unbeliever. ¶
τῶν ἰδίων   καὶ μάλιστα   οἰκείων →   ἤρνηται τὴν πίστιν καὶ ἔστιν χείρων →   ἀπίστου
d.gpm a.gpm   cj   adv.s   n.gpm   v.rmi.3s   d.asf n.asf   cj   v.pai.3s a.nsm.c   a.gsm
3836   2625   2779 3436   3858   766   3836   4411   2779 1639   5937   603

9 No widow may be put on the list   of widows unless she is   over sixty,   has been faithful to
   Χήρα →   →   →   →   καταλεγέσθω   →   μὴ   →   γεγονυῖα ἔλαττον ᾳἐτῶν ἑξήκοντα,   ἑνὸς
   n.nsf   v.ppm.3s   pl   pt.ra.nsf   adv.c   n.gpn   a.gpn   a.gsm
   5939   2899   3590   1181   1781   2291   2008   1651

her husband,   10 and is well known   for her good deeds, such as bringing up children,   showing hospitality,
γυνή ἀνδρὸς   →   →   μαρτυρουμένη ἐν καλοῖς ἔργοις εἰ →   ἐτεκνοτρόφησεν εἰ →   ἐξενοδόχησεν
n.nsf n.gsm   pt.pp.nsf   p.d   a.dpn   n.dpn   cj   v.aai.3s   cj   v.aai.3s
1222   467   3455   1877   2819   2240   1623   5452   1623   3827

   washing the feet of the saints,   helping those in trouble   and   devoting   herself to all   kinds of
εἰ ἔνιψεν   πόδας →   ἁγίων εἰ ἐπήρκεσεν →   →   θλιβομένοις   εἰ ἐπηκολούθησεν ←   →   παντὶ
cj   v.aai.3s   n.apm   a.gpm cj   v.aai.3s   pt.pp.dpm   cj   v.aai.3s   a.dsn
1623 3782   4546   41   1623 2064   2567   1623 2051   4246

good deeds. ¶   11 As for younger widows, do   not put them on such a list. For when their sensual desires
ἀγαθῷ ἔργῳ   δὲ ←   νεωτέρας χήρας   παραιτοῦ →   ←   ←   ←   γὰρ ὅταν →   →
a.dsn n.dsn   cj   a.apf.c   n.apf   v.pmm.2s   cj   cj
19   2240   1254   3742   5939   4148   1142 4020

overcome their dedication   to Christ,   they want   to marry. 12 Thus they bring   judgment on themselves,
→   →   →   καταστρηνιάσωσιν ᾳτοῦ Χριστοῦ, → θέλουσιν → γαμεῖν →   ἔχουσαι κρίμα
             v.aas.3p   d.gsm n.gsm   v.pai.3p   f.pa   pt.pa.npf   n.asn
             2952   3836 5986   2527   1138   2400   3210

because they have broken their first pledge. 13   Besides, they get into the habit   of being idle and
ὅτι   →   →   ἠθέτησαν τὴν πρώτην πίστιν δὲ ᾳἅμα καὶ, →   →   →   μανθάνουσιν   ἀργαὶ
cj   v.aai.3p   d.asf a.asf   n.asf   cj   adv   adv   v.pai.3p   a.npf
4022   119   3836   4755   4411   1254 275   2779   3443   734

going   about from house   to house. And not only do they become idlers, but   also gossips and busybodies,
περιερχόμεναι ←   → ᾳτὰς οἰκίας, ←   →   δὲ οὐ μόνον   ἀργαὶ ἀλλὰ καὶ φλύαροι καὶ περίεργοι
pt.pm.npf   d.apf n.apf   cj   pl   adv   a.npf   cj   adv   a.npf   cj   a.npf
4320   3836   3864   1254 4024 3667   734   247   2779 5827   2779 4319

saying   things they ought not to. 14 So I counsel younger widows to marry, to have children, to manage their
λαλοῦσαι τὰ   →   δέοντα μὴ   οὖν Βούλομαι νεωτέρας ←   →   γαμεῖν →   τεκνογονεῖν →   →
pt.pa.npf d.apn   pt.pa.apn pl   cj   v.pmi.1s   a.apf.c   f.pa   f.pa
3281   3836   1256   3590   4036   1089   3742   1138   5449

homes   and to give the enemy   no   opportunity for   slander. 15   Some have in fact already
οἰκοδεσποτεῖν → διδόναι τῷ ἀντικειμένῳ μηδεμίαν ἀφορμὴν χάριν λοιδορίας γὰρ τινες →   →   →   ἤδη
f.pa   f.pa   d.dsm pt.pm.dsm   a.asf   n.asf   n.gsf   n.gsf   cj   r.npf   adv
3866   1443   3836   512   3594   929   5920   3367   1142 5516   1762   2453

turned   away to follow Satan.   ¶   16 If any woman who is a believer has widows in her family, she
ἐξετράπησαν → ὀπίσω ᾳτοῦ σατανᾶ,   εἴ τις   →   →   πιστὴ ἔχει χήρας
v.api.3p   p.g   d.gsm n.gsm   cj   r.nsf   a.nsf   v.pai.3s n.apf
1762   3958   3836 4928   1623 5516   4412   2400   5939

καὶ μεμονωμένη ἤλπικεν ἐπὶ θεὸν καὶ προσμένει ταῖς δεήσεσιν καὶ ταῖς προσευχαῖς νυκτὸς καὶ ἡμέρας, 6 ἡ δὲ σπαταλῶσα ζῶσα τέθνηκεν. 7 καὶ ταῦτα παράγγελλε, ἵνα ἀνεπίλημπτοι ὦσιν. 8 εἰ δέ τις τῶν ἰδίων καὶ μάλιστα οἰκείων οὐ προνοεῖ, τὴν πίστιν ἤρνηται καὶ ἔστιν ἀπίστου χείρων. ¶ 9 Χήρα καταλεγέσθω μὴ ἔλαττον ἐτῶν ἑξήκοντα γεγονυῖα, ἑνὸς ἀνδρὸς γυνή, 10 ἐν ἔργοις καλοῖς μαρτυρουμένη, εἰ ἐτεκνοτρόφησεν, εἰ ἐξενοδόχησεν, εἰ ἁγίων πόδας ἔνιψεν, εἰ θλιβομένοις ἐπήρκεσεν, εἰ παντὶ ἔργῳ ἀγαθῷ ἐπηκολούθησεν. ¶ 11 νεωτέρας δὲ χήρας παραιτοῦ· ὅταν γὰρ καταστρηνιάσωσιν τοῦ Χριστοῦ, γαμεῖν θέλουσιν 12 ἔχουσαι κρίμα ὅτι τὴν πρώτην πίστιν ἠθέτησαν· 13 ἅμα δὲ καὶ ἀργαὶ μανθάνουσιν περιερχόμεναι τὰς οἰκίας, οὐ μόνον δὲ ἀργαὶ ἀλλὰ καὶ φλύαροι καὶ περίεργοι, λαλοῦσαι τὰ μὴ δέοντα. 14 βούλομαι οὖν νεωτέρας γαμεῖν, τεκνογονεῖν, οἰκοδεσποτεῖν, μηδεμίαν ἀφορμὴν διδόναι τῷ ἀντικειμένῳ λοιδορίας χάριν· 15 ἤδη γὰρ τινες ἐξετράπησαν ὀπίσω τοῦ Σατανᾶ. ¶ 16 εἴ τις πιστὴ

should help them and not let the church be burdened with them, so that the church can help those
→ ἐπαρκείτω αὐταῖς καὶ μὴ ἡ ἐκκλησία → βαρείσθω ἵνα ← ἐπαρκέσῃ ταῖς
v.pam.3s r.dpf.3 cj pl d.nsf n.nsf v.ppm.3s cj v.aas.3s d.dpf
2064 899 2779 3590 976 3836 1711 976 2671 2064 3836

widows who are really *in need.* ¶ ¹⁷ The elders who direct the affairs of the church well are worthy
← ὄντως χήραις Οἱ πρεσβύτεροι → προεστῶτες καλῶς → ἀξιούσθωσαν
adv n.dpf d.npm n.npm pt.ra.npm adv v.ppm.3p
3953 5939 3836 4565 4613 2822 546

of double honor, especially those whose work is preaching and teaching. ¹⁸ For the Scripture says, "Do not
→ διπλῆς τιμῆς μάλιστα οἱ ← κοπιῶντες ← ἐν λόγῳ καὶ διδασκαλίᾳ γὰρ ἡ γραφή λέγει οὐ
a.gsf n.gsf adv.s d.npm pt.pa.npm p.d n.dsm cj n.dsf cj d.nsf n.nsf v.pai.3s pl
1487 5507 3436 3836 3159 1877 3364 2779 1436 1142 3836 1210 3306 5821 4024

muzzle the ox while it is treading out the grain," and "The worker deserves his wages." ¹⁹ Do not entertain an
φιμώσεις βοῦν → → ἀλοῶντα καὶ ὁ ἐργάτης ἄξιος αὐτοῦ ⸤τοῦ μισθοῦ⸥ → μὴ παραδέχου
v.fai.2s n.asm pt.pa.asm cj d.nsm n.nsm a.nsm r.gsm.3 d.gsm n.gsm pl v.ppm.2s
5821 1091 262 2779 3836 2239 545 899 3836 3635 4138 3590 4138

accusation against an elder unless it is brought by two or three witnesses. ²⁰ Those who sin are
κατηγορίαν κατὰ πρεσβυτέρου ἐκτὸς εἰ μὴ ἐπὶ δύο ἢ τριῶν μαρτύρων Τοὺς ← ἁμαρτάνοντας →
n.asf p.g a.gsm adv.c cj pl p.g a.gpm cj a.gpm n.gpm d.apm pt.pa.apm
2990 2848 4565 1760 1623 3590 2093 1545 2445 5552 3459 3836 279

to be rebuked publicly, so that the others may take warning. ¶ ²¹ I charge you, in the sight
→ → ἔλεγχε ἐνώπιον πάντων ἵνα καὶ οἱ λοιποὶ → ἔχωσιν φόβον → Διαμαρτύρομαι → ἐνώπιον
v.pam.2s p.g a.gpm cj adv d.npm a.npm v.pas.3p n.asm v.pmi.1s p.g
1794 1967 4246 2671 2779 3836 3370 2400 5832 1371 1967

of God and Christ Jesus and the elect angels, to keep these instructions without partiality, and to do
→ ⸤τοῦ θεοῦ⸥ καὶ Χριστοῦ Ἰησοῦ καὶ τῶν ἐκλεκτῶν ἀγγέλων ἵνα φυλάξῃς ταῦτα ← χωρὶς προκρίματος → ποιῶν
d.gsm n.gsm cj n.gsm n.gsm cj d.gpm a.gpm n.gpm cj v.aas.2s r.apn p.g n.gsn pt.pa.nsm
3836 2536 2779 5986 2652 2779 3836 1723 34 2671 5875 4047 6006 4622 4472

nothing out of favoritism. ¶ ²² Do not be hasty in the laying on of hands, and do not share in the
μηδὲν κατὰ πρόσκλισιν → μηδενὶ ταχέως → ἐπιτίθει ← χεῖρας ← μηδὲ κοινώνει
a.asn p.a n.asf a.dsn adv v.pam.2s n.apf adv v.pam.2s
3594 2848 4680 2202 3594 5441 2202 5931 3593 3125 3593 3125

sins of others. Keep yourself pure. ¶ ²³ Stop drinking only water, and use a little wine because of
ἁμαρτίαις → ἀλλοτρίαις τήρει σεαυτὸν ἁγνὸν Μηκέτι ὑδροπότει ← ← ἀλλὰ χρῶ ὀλίγῳ οἴνῳ διὰ
n.dpf a.dpf v.pam.2s r.asm.2 a.asm adv v.pam.2s cj v.pmm.2s a.dsm n.dsm p.a
281 259 5498 4932 54 3600 5621 247 5968 3900 3885 1328

your stomach and your frequent illnesses. ¶ ²⁴ The sins of some men are obvious, reaching the
τὸν στόμαχον καὶ σου πυκνάς ⸤τὰς ἀσθενείας⸥ αἱ ἁμαρτίαι → Τινῶν ἀνθρώπων εἰσὶν πρόδηλοι προάγουσαι
d.asm n.asm cj r.gs.2 a.apf d.apf n.apf d.npf n.npf r.gpm n.gpm v.pai.3p a.npf pt.pa.npf
3836 5126 2779 5148 4781 3836 819 3836 281 5516 476 1639 4593 4575

place of judgment ahead of them; the sins of others trail behind them. ²⁵ In the same way,
εἰς κρίσιν ← → ← δὲ τισὶν καὶ ἐπακολουθοῦσιν ← καὶ ὡσαύτως ←
p.a n.asf cj r.dpm adv v.pai.3p adv adv
1650 3213 4575 4575 4575 1254 5516 2779 2051 2779 6058

good deeds are obvious, and even those that are not cannot be hidden. ¶ ⁶:¹ All who are
⸤τὰ καλὰ⸥ ⸤τὰ ἔργα⸥ πρόδηλα καὶ → τὰ ἔχοντα ἄλλως οὐ δύνανται κρυβῆναι Ὅσοι ← εἰσὶν
d.npn a.npn d.npn n.npn a.npn cj d.npn pt.pa.npn adv pl v.ppi.3p f.ap r.npm v.pai.3p
3836 2819 3836 2240 4593 2779 2400 3836 2400 261 4024 1538 3221 4012 1639

under the yoke of slavery should consider their masters worthy of full respect, so that God's name
ὑπὸ ζυγὸν δοῦλοι ἡγείσθωσαν τοὺς ἰδίους δεσπότας ἀξίους → πάσης τιμῆς ἵνα ← ⸤τοῦ θεοῦ⸥ ⸤τὸ ὄνομα⸥
p.a n.asm n.npm v.pmm.3p d.apm a.apm n.apm a.apm a.gsf n.gsf cj d.gsm n.gsm d.nsn n.nsn
5679 2433 1529 2451 3836 2625 1305 545 4246 5507 2671 3836 2536 3836 3950

and our teaching may not be slandered. ² Those who have believing masters are not to show less
καὶ ἡ διδασκαλία → μὴ βλασφημῆται δὲ οἱ ← ἔχοντες πιστοὺς δεσπότας → μὴ →
cj d.nsf n.nsf pl v.pps.3s cj d.npm pt.pa.npm a.apm n.apm pl
2779 3836 1436 1059 3590 1059 1254 3836 2400 4412 1305 2969 3590

ἔχει χήρας, ἐπαρκείτω αὐταῖς καὶ μὴ βαρείσθω ἡ ἐκκλησία, ἵνα ταῖς ὄντως χήραις ἐπαρκέσῃ. ¶ ¹⁷ Οἱ καλῶς προεστῶτες πρεσβύτεροι διπλῆς τιμῆς ἀξιούσθωσαν, μάλιστα οἱ κοπιῶντες ἐν λόγῳ καὶ διδασκαλίᾳ. ¹⁸ λέγει γὰρ ἡ γραφή, Βοῦν ἀλοῶντα οὐ φιμώσεις, καί, Ἄξιος ὁ ἐργάτης τοῦ μισθοῦ αὐτοῦ. ¹⁹ κατὰ πρεσβυτέρου κατηγορίαν μὴ παραδέχου, ἐκτὸς εἰ μὴ ἐπὶ δύο ἢ τριῶν μαρτύρων. ²⁰ τοὺς ἁμαρτάνοντας ἐνώπιον πάντων ἔλεγχε, ἵνα καὶ οἱ λοιποὶ φόβον ἔχωσιν. ¶ ²¹ Διαμαρτύρομαι ἐνώπιον τοῦ θεοῦ καὶ Χριστοῦ Ἰησοῦ καὶ τῶν ἐκλεκτῶν ἀγγέλων, ἵνα ταῦτα φυλάξῃς χωρὶς προκρίματος, μηδὲν ποιῶν κατὰ πρόσκλισιν. ¶ ²² Χεῖρας ταχέως μηδενὶ ἐπιτίθει μηδὲ κοινώνει ἁμαρτίαις ἀλλοτρίαις· σεαυτὸν ἁγνὸν τήρει. ¶ ²³ Μηκέτι ὑδροπότει, ἀλλὰ οἴνῳ ὀλίγῳ χρῶ διὰ τὸν στόμαχον καὶ τὰς πυκνάς σου ἀσθενείας. ¶ ²⁴ Τινῶν ἀνθρώπων αἱ ἁμαρτίαι πρόδηλοί εἰσιν προάγουσαι εἰς κρίσιν, τισὶν δὲ καὶ ἐπακολουθοῦσιν· ²⁵ ὡσαύτως καὶ τὰ ἔργα τὰ καλὰ πρόδηλα, καὶ τὰ ἄλλως ἔχοντα κρυβῆναι οὐ δύνανται. ⁶:¹ Ὅσοι εἰσὶν ὑπὸ ζυγὸν δοῦλοι, τοὺς ἰδίους δεσπότας πάσης τιμῆς ἀξίους ἡγείσθωσαν, ἵνα μὴ τὸ ὄνομα τοῦ θεοῦ καὶ ἡ διδασκαλία βλασφημῆται. ² οἱ δὲ πιστοὺς ἔχοντες δεσπότας μὴ καταφρονείτωσαν, ὅτι ἀδελφοί εἰσιν, ἀλλὰ μᾶλλον δουλευέτωσαν, ὅτι πιστοί εἰσιν καὶ ἀγαπητοὶ οἱ τῆς εὐεργεσίας ἀντιλαμβανόμενοι. Ταῦτα δίδασκε καὶ παρακάλει.

respect | for them | because | they are | brothers. | Instead, | they are to serve | them even | better, | because | those
καταφρονείτωσαν | | ὅτι | εἰσιν | ἀδελφοί | ἀλλὰ | δουλευέτωσαν | μᾶλλον | | ὅτι | οἱ
v.pam.3p | | cj | v.pai.3p | n.npm | cj | v.pam.3p | adv.c | | cj | d.npm
2969 | | 4022 | 1639 | 81 | 247 | 1526 | 3437 | | 4022 | 3836

who benefit | from their | service | are | believers, | and | dear | to them. | These | are the things you are to teach
ἀντιλαμβανόμενοι | τῆς | εὐεργεσίας | εἰσιν | πιστοί | καὶ | ἀγαπητοὶ | | Ταῦτα | δίδασκε
pt.pm.npm | d.gsf | n.gsf | v.pai.3p | a.npm | cj | a.npm | | r.apn | v.pam.2s
514 | 3836 | 2307 | 1639 | 4412 | 2779 | 28 | | 4047 | 1438

and | urge | on them.
καὶ | παρακάλει
cj | v.pam.2s
2779 | 4151

Love of Money

6:3 If | anyone | teaches | false doctrines | and | does | not | agree | to the | sound | instruction | of | our
εἰ | τις | ἑτεροδιδασκαλεῖ | | καὶ | | μὴ | προσέρχεται | | ὑγιαίνουσιν | λόγοις | τοῖς | ἡμῶν
cj | r.nsm | v.pai.3s | | cj | | pl | v.pmi.3s | | pt.pa.dpm | n.dpm | d.dpm | r.gp.1
1623 | 5516 | 2281 | | 2779 4665 | | 3590 | 4665 | | 5617 | 3364 | 3836 3261 | 7005

Lord | Jesus | Christ | and to | godly | teaching, | [4] he is conceited | and understands | nothing. | He has
τοῦ κυρίου | Ἰησοῦ | Χριστοῦ | καὶ | κατ' εὐσέβειαν | τῇ διδασκαλίᾳ | τετύφωται | ἐπιστάμενος | μηδὲν | ἀλλὰ
d.gsm n.gsm | n.gsm | n.gsm | cj | n.asf | d.dsf n.dsf | v.rpi.3s | pt.pp.nsm | a.asn | cj
3836 3261 | 2652 | 5986 | 2779 1436 | 2848 2354 | 3836 1436 | 5605 | 2179 | 3594 | 247

an unhealthy | interest | in | controversies | and | quarrels | about words | that | result in | envy, | strife, | malicious talk,
νοσῶν | | περὶ | ζητήσεις | καὶ | λογομαχίας | | ἐξ | ὧν | γίνεται | φθόνος | ἔρις | βλασφημίαι
pt.pa.nsm | | p.a | n.apf | cj | n.apf | | p.g | r.gpn | v.pmi.3s | n.nsm | n.nsf | n.npf
3796 | | 4309 | 2428 | 2779 | 3363 | | 1666 | 4005 | 1181 | 5784 | 2251 | 1060

evil | suspicions [5] | and constant | friction | between | men | of corrupt | mind, | who have been
πονηραί | ὑπόνοιαι | | διαπαρατριβαὶ | | ἀνθρώπων | διεφθαρμένων | τὸν νοῦν | καὶ
a.npf | n.npf | | n.npf | | n.gpm | pt.rp.gpm | d.asm | cj
4505 | 5707 | | 1384 | | 476 | 1425 | 3836 3808 | 2779

robbed | of the truth | and who | think | that godliness | is | a means to | financial | gain. | ¶ [6] But
ἀπεστερημένων | τῆς ἀληθείας | | νομιζόντων | τὴν εὐσέβειαν | εἶναι | | πορισμὸν | | δὲ
pt.rp.gpm | d.gsf n.gsf | | pt.pa.gpm | d.asf n.asf | f.pa | | n.asm | | cj
691 | 3836 237 | | 3787 | 3836 2354 | 1639 | | 4516 | | 1254

godliness | with | contentment | is | great | gain. | [7] For | we brought | nothing | into | the | world, and | we can
ἡ εὐσέβεια | μετὰ | αὐταρκείας | Ἔστιν | μέγας | πορισμὸς | γὰρ | εἰσηνέγκαμεν | οὐδὲν | εἰς | τὸν | κόσμον | ὅτι | δυνάμεθα
d.nsf n.nsf | p.g | n.gsf | v.pai.3s | a.nsm | n.nsm | cj | v.aai.1p | a.asn | p.a | d.asm | n.asm | cj | v.ppi.1p
3836 2354 | 3552 | 894 | 1639 | 3489 | 4516 | 1142 | 1662 | 4029 | 1650 | 3836 | 3180 | 4022 | 1538

take | nothing | out of it. | [8] But if | we have | food | and | clothing, | we will be content | with that. | [9] People
ἐξενεγκεῖν | οὐδέ τι | | δὲ | ἔχοντες | διατροφὰς | καὶ | σκεπάσματα | ἀρκεσθησόμεθα | τούτοις | οἱ
f.aa | a.asn | | cj | pt.pa.npm | n.apf | cj | n.apn | v.fpi.1p | r.dpn | d.npm
1766 | 4028 5516 | 1766 | 1254 | 2400 | 1418 | 2779 | 5004 | 758 | 4047 | 1254 3836

who want | to get rich | fall | into | temptation | and a | trap | and into | many | foolish | and | harmful | desires
βουλόμενοι | πλουτεῖν | ἐμπίπτουσιν | εἰς | πειρασμὸν | καὶ | παγίδα | καὶ | πολλὰς | ἀνοήτους | καὶ | βλαβερὰς | ἐπιθυμίας
pt.pm.npm | f.pa | v.pai.3p | p.a | n.asm | cj | n.asf | cj | a.apf | a.apf | cj | a.apf | n.apf
1089 | 4456 | 1860 | 1650 | 4280 | 2779 | 4075 | 2779 | 4498 | 485 | 2779 | 1054 | 2123

that | plunge | men | into | ruin | and | destruction. | [10] For the love | of money is | a root of all | kinds
αἵτινες | βυθίζουσιν | τοὺς ἀνθρώπους | εἰς | ὄλεθρον | καὶ | ἀπώλειαν | γὰρ ἡ | φιλαργυρία | ἐστιν ῥίζα | πάντων
r.npf | v.pai.3p | d.apm n.apm | p.a | n.asm | cj | n.asf | cj d.nsf | n.nsf | v.pai.3s n.nsf | a.gpn
4015 | 1112 | 3836 476 | 1650 | 3897 | 2779 | 724 | 1142 3836 | 5794 | 1639 4844 | 4246

of evil. | Some people, | eager | for money, | have wandered | from the | faith | and | pierced | themselves
τῶν κακῶν | ἧς τινες | ὀρεγόμενοι | | ἀπεπλανήθησαν | ἀπὸ τῆς | πίστεως | καὶ | περιέπειραν | ἑαυτοὺς
d.gpn a.gpn | r.gsf r.npm | pt.pm.npm | | v.api.3p | p.g d.gsf | n.gsf | cj | v.aai.3p | r.apm.3
3836 2805 | 4005 5516 | 3977 | | 675 | 608 3836 | 4411 | 2779 | 4345 | 1571

with many | griefs.
πολλαῖς | ὀδύναις
a.dpf | n.dpf
4498 | 3850

6:3 εἴ τις ἑτεροδιδασκαλεῖ καὶ μὴ προσέρχεται ὑγιαίνουσιν λόγοις τοῖς τοῦ κυρίου ἡμῶν Ἰησοῦ Χριστοῦ καὶ τῇ κατ' εὐσέβειαν διδασκαλίᾳ, [4] τετύφωται, μηδὲν ἐπιστάμενος, ἀλλὰ νοσῶν περὶ ζητήσεις καὶ λογομαχίας, ἐξ ὧν γίνεται φθόνος ἔρις βλασφημίαι, ὑπόνοιαι πονηραί, [5] διαπαρατριβαὶ διεφθαρμένων ἀνθρώπων τὸν νοῦν καὶ ἀπεστερημένων τῆς ἀληθείας, νομιζόντων πορισμὸν εἶναι τὴν εὐσέβειαν. ¶ [6] ἔστιν δὲ πορισμὸς μέγας ἡ εὐσέβεια μετὰ αὐταρκείας· [7] οὐδὲν γὰρ εἰσηνέγκαμεν εἰς τὸν κόσμον, ὅτι οὐδὲ ἐξενεγκεῖν τι δυνάμεθα· [8] ἔχοντες δὲ διατροφὰς καὶ σκεπάσματα, τούτοις ἀρκεσθησόμεθα. [9] οἱ δὲ βουλόμενοι πλουτεῖν ἐμπίπτουσιν εἰς πειρασμὸν καὶ παγίδα καὶ ἐπιθυμίας πολλὰς ἀνοήτους καὶ βλαβεράς, αἵτινες βυθίζουσιν τοὺς ἀνθρώπους εἰς ὄλεθρον καὶ ἀπώλειαν. [10] ῥίζα γὰρ πάντων τῶν κακῶν ἐστιν ἡ φιλαργυρία, ἧς τινες ὀρεγόμενοι ἀπεπλανήθησαν ἀπὸ τῆς πίστεως καὶ ἑαυτοὺς περιέπειραν ὀδύναις πολλαῖς.

Paul's Charge to Timothy

6:11 But you, man of God, flee from all this, and pursue righteousness, godliness, faith, love, endurance
δέ Σύ ὦ ἄνθρωπε → θεοῦ φεῦγε ταῦτα δὲ δίωκε δικαιοσύνην εὐσέβειαν πίστιν ἀγάπην ὑπομονὴν
cj r.ns.2 j n.vsm n.gsm v.pam.2s r.apn cj v.pam.2s n.asf n.asf n.asf n.asf n.asf
1254 5148 6043 476 2536 5771 4047 1254 1503 1466 2354 4411 27 5705

and gentleness. **12** Fight the good fight of the faith. Take hold of the eternal life to which you were called
πραϋπαθίαν ἀγωνίζου τὸν καλὸν ἀγῶνα → τῆς πίστεως ἐπιλαβοῦ ← → τῆς αἰωνίου ζωῆς εἰς ἣν → → ἐκλήθης
n.asf v.pmm.2s d.asm a.asm n.asm d.gsf n.gsf v.amm.2s d.gsf a.gsf n.gsf p.a r.asf v.api.2s
4557 76 3836 2819 74 3836 4411 2138 3836 173 2437 1650 4005 2813

when you made your good confession in the presence of many witnesses. **13** In the sight of God, who
καὶ → ὡμολόγησας τὴν καλὴν ὁμολογίαν → → ἐνώπιον → πολλῶν μαρτύρων ἐνώπιον ⸤τοῦ θεοῦ⸥ τοῦ
cj v.aai.2s d.asf a.asf n.asf p.g a.gpm n.gpm p.g d.gsm n.gsm d.gsm
2779 3933 3836 2819 3934 1967 4498 3459 1967 3836 2536 3836

gives life to everything, and of Christ Jesus, who while testifying before Pontius Pilate made the good
→ ζωογονοῦντος ← ⸤τὰ πάντα⸥ καὶ → Χριστοῦ Ἰησοῦ τοῦ μαρτυρήσαντος ἐπὶ Ποντίου Πιλάτου ⸤ τὴν καλὴν
pt.pa.gsm d.apn a.apn cj n.gsm n.gsm d.gsm pt.aa.gsm p.g n.gsm n.gsm d.asf a.asf
2441 3836 4246 2779 5986 2652 3836 3455 2093 4508 4397 3455 3836 2819

confession, I charge you **14** to keep this command without spot or blame until the appearing of our
ὁμολογίαν → παραγγέλλω σοι σε → τηρῆσαι τὴν ἐντολὴν → ἄσπιλον ἀνεπίλημπτον μέχρι τῆς ἐπιφανείας → ἡμῶν
n.asf v.pai.1s r.ds.2 r.as.2 f.aa d.asf n.asf a.asf a.asf p.g d.gsf n.gsf r.gp.1
3934 4133 5148 5148 5498 3836 1953 834 455 3588 3836 2211 3261 7005

Lord Jesus Christ, **15** which God will bring about in his own time – God, the blessed and only Ruler, the
⸤τοῦ κυρίου⸥ Ἰησοῦ Χριστοῦ ἣν → δείξει ← → ἰδίοις καιροῖς ὁ μακάριος καὶ μόνος δυνάστης ὁ
d.gsm n.gsm n.gsm n.gsm r.asf v.fai.3s a.dpm n.dpm d.nsm a.nsm cj a.nsm n.nsm d.nsm
3836 3261 2652 5986 4005 1259 2625 2789 3836 3421 2779 3668 1541 3836

King of kings and Lord of lords, **16** who alone is immortal and who lives in
βασιλεὺς → ⸤τῶν βασιλευόντων⸥ καὶ κύριος → ⸤τῶν κυριευόντων⸥ ὁ μόνος ἔχων ἀθανασίαν οἰκῶν
n.nsm d.gpm pt.pa.gpm cj n.nsm d.gpm pt.pa.gpm d.nsm a.nsm pt.pa.nsm n.asf pt.pa.nsm
995 3836 3259 2779 3261 3836 3259 3836 3668 2400 114 3861

unapproachable light, whom no one has seen or can see. To him be honor and might forever. Amen.¶
ἀπρόσιτον φῶς ὃν οὐδεὶς ἀνθρώπων → εἶδεν οὐδὲ δύναται ἰδεῖν ᾧ τιμὴ καὶ κράτος αἰώνιον ἀμήν
a.asn n.nsn r.asm a.nsm n.gpm v.aai.3s cj v.ppi.3s f.aa r.dsm n.nsf cj n.nsn a.nsn pl
717 5890 4005 4029 476 1625 4028 1538 1625 4005 5507 2779 3197 173 297

17 Command those who are rich in this present world not to be arrogant nor to put their hope in
παράγγελλε Τοῖς ← → πλουσίοις ἐν τῷ νῦν αἰῶνι μὴ → ὑψηλοφρονεῖν μηδὲ → → → ἠλπικέναι ἐπὶ
v.pam.2s d.dpm a.dpm p.d d.dsm adv n.dsm pl f.pa cj f.ra p.g
4133 3836 4454 1877 3836 3814 172 3590 5735 3593 1827 2093

wealth, which is so uncertain, but to put their hope in God, who richly provides us with everything for our
πλούτου → → → ἀδηλότητι ἀλλ' ἐπὶ θεῷ τῷ πλουσίως παρέχοντι ἡμῖν πάντα εἰς
n.gsm n.dsf cj p.d n.dsm d.dsm adv pt.pa.dsm r.dp.1 a.apn p.a
4458 84 247 2093 2536 3836 4455 4218 7005 4246 1650

enjoyment. **18** Command them to do good, to be rich in good deeds, and to be generous and willing to
ἀπόλαυσιν → ἀγαθοεργεῖν → πλουτεῖν ἐν καλοῖς ἔργοις → εἶναι εὐμεταδότους → →
n.asf f.pa f.pa p.d a.dpn n.dpn f.pa a.apm
656 14 4456 1877 2819 2240 1639 2331

share. **19** In this way they will lay up treasure for themselves as a firm foundation for the coming age, so
κοινωνικούς → → ἀποθησαυρίζοντας → ἑαυτοῖς καλὸν θεμέλιον εἰς τὸ μέλλον ← ἵνα
a.apm pt.pa.apm r.dpm.3 a.asm n.asm p.a d.asn pt.pa.asn cj
3127 631 1571 2819 2529 1650 3836 3516 2671

that they may take hold of the life that is truly life. ¶ **20** Timothy, guard what has been entrusted to
← → → ἐπιλάβωνται τῆς ζωῆς ὄντως Ὦ Τιμόθεε φύλαξον τὴν → → παραθήκην ←
v.ams.3p d.gsf n.gsf adv j n.vsm v.aam.2s d.asf n.asf
2138 3836 2437 3953 6043 5510 5875 3836 4146

your care. Turn away from godless chatter and the opposing ideas of what is falsely called
← ← ἐκτρεπόμενος ← ← βεβήλους ⸤τὰς κενοφωνίας⸥ καὶ ἀντιθέσεις → τῆς → ψευδωνύμου
pt.pm.nsm a.apf d.apf n.apf cj n.apf d.gsf a.gsf
1762 1013 3836 3032 2779 509 3836 6024

6:11 Σὺ δέ, ὦ ἄνθρωπε θεοῦ, ταῦτα φεῦγε· δίωκε δὲ δικαιοσύνην εὐσέβειαν πίστιν, ἀγάπην ὑπομονὴν πραϋπαθίαν. 12 ἀγωνίζου τὸν καλὸν ἀγῶνα τῆς πίστεως, ἐπιλαβοῦ τῆς αἰωνίου ζωῆς, εἰς ἣν ἐκλήθης καὶ ὡμολόγησας τὴν καλὴν ὁμολογίαν ἐνώπιον πολλῶν μαρτύρων. 13 παραγγέλλω [σοι] ἐνώπιον τοῦ θεοῦ τοῦ ζωογονοῦντος τὰ πάντα καὶ Χριστοῦ Ἰησοῦ τοῦ μαρτυρήσαντος ἐπὶ Ποντίου Πιλάτου τὴν καλὴν ὁμολογίαν, 14 τηρῆσαί σε τὴν ἐντολὴν ἄσπιλον ἀνεπίλημπτον μέχρι τῆς ἐπιφανείας τοῦ κυρίου ἡμῶν Ἰησοῦ Χριστοῦ, 15 ἣν καιροῖς ἰδίοις δείξει ὁ μακάριος καὶ μόνος δυνάστης, ὁ βασιλεὺς τῶν βασιλευόντων καὶ κύριος τῶν κυριευόντων, 16 ὁ μόνος ἔχων ἀθανασίαν, φῶς οἰκῶν ἀπρόσιτον, ὃν εἶδεν οὐδεὶς ἀνθρώπων οὐδὲ ἰδεῖν δύναται· ᾧ τιμὴ καὶ κράτος αἰώνιον, ἀμήν. ¶ 17 Τοῖς πλουσίοις ἐν τῷ νῦν αἰῶνι παράγγελλε μὴ ὑψηλοφρονεῖν μηδὲ ἠλπικέναι ἐπὶ πλούτου ἀδηλότητι ἀλλ' ἐπὶ θεῷ τῷ παρέχοντι ἡμῖν πάντα πλουσίως εἰς ἀπόλαυσιν. 18 ἀγαθοεργεῖν, πλουτεῖν ἐν ἔργοις καλοῖς, εὐμεταδότους εἶναι, κοινωνικούς, 19 ἀποθησαυρίζοντας ἑαυτοῖς θεμέλιον καλὸν εἰς τὸ μέλλον, ἵνα ἐπιλάβωνται τῆς ὄντως ζωῆς. ¶ 20 Ὦ Τιμόθεε, τὴν παραθήκην φύλαξον ἐκτρεπόμενος τὰς βεβήλους κενοφωνίας καὶ ἀντιθέσεις τῆς ψευδωνύμου γνώσεως, 21 ἥν τινες

knowledge,	**21** which	some	have	professed	and in so doing	have	wandered	from	the	faith.	¶	Grace	be	with
γνώσεως	ἥν	τινες	→	ἐπαγγελλόμενοι		→	ἠστόχησαν	περὶ	τὴν	πίστιν		⸤Ἡ	χάρις⸥	μεθ᾽
n.gsf	r.asf	r.npm		pt.pm.npm			v.aai.3p	p.a	d.asf	n.asf		d.nsf	n.nsf	p.g
1194	4005	5516		2040			846	4309	3836	4411		3836	5921	3552

you.
ὑμῶν
r.gp.2
7007

ἐπαγγελλόμενοι περὶ τὴν πίστιν ἠστόχησαν. ¶ Ἡ χάρις μεθ᾽ ὑμῶν.

2 Timothy

1:1 Paul, an apostle of Christ Jesus by the will of God, according to the promise of life that is in
Παῦλος ἀπόστολος → Χριστοῦ Ἰησοῦ διὰ θελήματος → θεοῦ κατ' ← ἐπαγγελίαν → ζωῆς τῆς ἐν
n.nsm n.nsm n.gsm n.gsm p.g n.gsn n.gsm p.a n.asf n.gsf d.gsf p.d
4263 693 5986 2652 1328 2525 2536 2848 2039 2437 3836 1877

Christ Jesus, ¶ **2** To Timothy, my dear son: ¶ Grace, mercy and peace from God the Father and
Χριστῷ Ἰησοῦ → Τιμοθέῳ ἀγαπητῷ τέκνῳ χάρις ἔλεος εἰρήνη ἀπὸ θεοῦ πατρὸς καὶ
n.dsm n.dsm n.dsm a.dsn n.dsn n.nsf n.nsn n.nsf p.g n.gsm n.gsm cj
5986 2652 5510 28 5451 5921 1799 1645 608 2536 4252 2779

Christ Jesus our Lord.
Χριστοῦ Ἰησοῦ ἡμῶν τοῦ κυρίου
n.gsm n.gsm r.gp.1 d.gsm n.gsm
5986 2652 7005 3836 3261

Encouragement to Be Faithful

1:3 I thank God, whom I serve, as my forefathers did, with a clear conscience, as night and day
→ Χάριν ἔχω τῷ θεῷ ᾧ → λατρεύω ἀπὸ προγόνων ἐν καθαρᾷ συνειδήσει ὡς νυκτὸς καὶ ἡμέρας
n.asf v.pai.1s d.dsm n.dsm r.dsm v.pai.1s p.g n.gpm p.d a.dsf n.dsf cj n.gsf cj n.gsf
5921 2400 3836 2536 4005 3302 608 4591 1877 2754 5287 6055 3816 2779 2465

I constantly remember you in my prayers. **4** Recalling your tears, I long to see you, so
→ ἀδιάλειπτον ἔχω τὴν μνείαν περὶ σοῦ ἐν μου ταῖς δεήσεσιν μεμνημένος σου τῶν δακρύων → ἐπιποθῶν → ἰδεῖν σε ἵνα
a.asf v.pai.1s d.asf n.asf p.g r.gs.2 p.d r.gs.1 d.dpf n.dpf pt.rp.nsm r.gs.2 d.gpn n.gpn pt.pa.nsm f.aa r.as.2 cj
2400 89 2400 3836 3644 4309 5148 1877 1609 3836 1255 3630 5148 3836 1232 2160 1625 5148 2671

that I may be filled with joy. **5** I have been reminded of your sincere faith, which first lived in
← → → πληρωθῶ → χαρᾶς → λαβὼν ὑπόμνησιν → ἐν σοὶ ἀνυποκρίτου τῆς πίστεως ἥτις πρῶτον ἐνῴκησεν ἐν
v.aps.1s n.gsf pt.aa.nsm n.asf p.d r.ds.2 a.gsf d.gsf n.gsf r.nsf adv v.aai.3s p.d
4444 5915 3284 5704 4411 1877 5148 537 3836 4411 4015 4754 1940 1877

your grandmother Lois and in your mother Eunice and, I am persuaded, now lives in you also. **6** For this
σου τῇ μάμμῃ Λωΐδι καὶ σου τῇ μητρί Εὐνίκῃ δὲ → → πέπεισμαι ὅτι ἐν σοὶ καὶ Δι' ἣν
r.gs.2 d.dsf n.dsf n.dsf cj r.gs.2 d.dsf n.dsf n.dsf cj v.rpi.1s cj p.d r.ds.2 adv p.a r.asf
5148 3836 3439 3396 2779 5148 3836 3613 2332 1254 4275 4022 1877 5148 2779 1328 4005

reason I remind you to fan into flame the gift of God, which is in you through the laying on
αἰτίαν → ἀναμιμνῄσκω σε → → → ἀναζωπυρεῖν τὸ χάρισμα → τοῦ θεοῦ ὅ ἐστιν ἐν σοὶ διὰ τῆς ἐπιθέσεως ←
n.asf v.pai.1s r.as.2 t.pa d.asn n.asn d.gsm n.gsm r.nsn v.pai.3s p.d r.ds.2 p.g d.gsf n.gsf
162 389 5148 351 3836 5922 3836 2536 4005 1639 1877 5148 1328 3836 2120

of my hands. **7** For God did not give us a spirit of timidity, but a spirit of power, of love and of
→ μου τῶν χειρῶν γὰρ ὁ θεός → οὐ ἔδωκεν ἡμῖν πνεῦμα → δειλίας ἀλλὰ → δυνάμεως καὶ → ἀγάπης καὶ →
r.gs.1 d.gpf n.gpf cj d.nsm n.nsm pl v.aai.3s r.dp.1 n.asn n.gsf cj n.gsf cj n.gsf cj
5931 1609 3836 5931 1142 3836 2536 4024 1443 7005 4460 1261 247 1539 2779 27 2779

self-discipline. ¶ **8** So do not be ashamed to testify about our Lord, or ashamed of me his
σωφρονισμοῦ οὖν → μὴ → ἐπαισχυνθῇς τὸ μαρτύριον → ἡμῶν τοῦ κυρίου μηδὲ ἐμὲ αὐτοῦ
n.gsm cj pl v.aps.2s d.asn n.asn r.gp.1 d.gsm n.gsm cj r.as.1 r.gsm.3
5406 4036 2049 3590 2049 3836 3457 3261 7005 3836 3261 3593 1609 899

prisoner. But join with me in suffering for the gospel, by the power of God, **9** who has saved us and
τὸν δέσμιον ἀλλὰ → → → συγκακοπάθησον τῷ εὐαγγελίῳ κατὰ δύναμιν → θεοῦ τοῦ → σώσαντος ἡμᾶς καὶ
d.asm n.asm cj v.aam.2s d.dsn n.dsn p.a n.asf n.gsm d.gsm pt.aa.gsm r.ap.1 cj
3836 1300 247 5155 3836 2295 2848 1539 2536 3836 5392 7005 2779

called us to a holy life — not because of anything we have done but because of his own purpose and
καλέσαντος → ἁγίᾳ κλήσει οὐ κατὰ → ← ἡμῶν → τὰ ἔργα ἀλλὰ κατὰ ἰδίαν ← πρόθεσιν καὶ
pt.aa.gsm a.dsf n.dsf pl p.a r.gp.1 d.apn n.apn cj p.a a.asf n.asf cj
2813 41 3104 4024 2848 2240 7005 3836 2240 247 2848 2625 4606 2779

grace. This grace was given us in Christ Jesus before the beginning of time, **10** but it has now been
χάριν τὴν δοθεῖσαν ἡμῖν ἐν Χριστῷ Ἰησοῦ πρὸ αἰωνίων → χρόνων δὲ → νῦν →
n.asf d.asf pt.ap.asf r.dp.1 p.d n.dsm n.dsm p.g a.gpm n.gpm cj adv
5921 3836 1443 7005 1877 5986 2652 4574 173 5989 1254 5746 5746 3814

1:1 Παῦλος ἀπόστολος Χριστοῦ Ἰησοῦ διὰ θελήματος θεοῦ κατ' ἐπαγγελίαν ζωῆς τῆς ἐν Χριστῷ Ἰησοῦ ¶ **2** Τιμοθέῳ ἀγαπητῷ τέκνῳ, ¶ χάρις ἔλεος εἰρήνη ἀπὸ θεοῦ πατρὸς καὶ Χριστοῦ Ἰησοῦ τοῦ κυρίου ἡμῶν.

1:3 Χάριν ἔχω τῷ θεῷ, ᾧ λατρεύω ἀπὸ προγόνων ἐν καθαρᾷ συνειδήσει, ὡς ἀδιάλειπτον ἔχω τὴν περὶ σοῦ μνείαν ἐν ταῖς δεήσεσίν μου νυκτὸς καὶ ἡμέρας, **4** ἐπιποθῶν σε ἰδεῖν, μεμνημένος σου τῶν δακρύων, ἵνα χαρᾶς πληρωθῶ, **5** ὑπόμνησιν λαβὼν τῆς ἐν σοὶ ἀνυποκρίτου πίστεως, ἥτις ἐνῴκησεν πρῶτον ἐν τῇ μάμμῃ σου Λωΐδι καὶ τῇ μητρί σου Εὐνίκῃ, πέπεισμαι δὲ ὅτι καὶ ἐν σοί. **6** δι' ἣν αἰτίαν ἀναμιμνῄσκω σε ἀναζωπυρεῖν τὸ χάρισμα τοῦ θεοῦ, ὅ ἐστιν ἐν σοὶ διὰ τῆς ἐπιθέσεως τῶν χειρῶν μου. **7** οὐ γὰρ ἔδωκεν ἡμῖν ὁ θεὸς πνεῦμα δειλίας ἀλλὰ δυνάμεως καὶ ἀγάπης καὶ σωφρονισμοῦ. ¶ **8** μὴ οὖν ἐπαισχυνθῇς τὸ μαρτύριον τοῦ κυρίου ἡμῶν μηδὲ ἐμὲ τὸν δέσμιον αὐτοῦ, ἀλλὰ συγκακοπάθησον τῷ εὐαγγελίῳ κατὰ δύναμιν θεοῦ, **9** τοῦ σώσαντος ἡμᾶς καὶ καλέσαντος κλήσει ἁγίᾳ, οὐ κατὰ τὰ ἔργα ἡμῶν ἀλλὰ κατὰ ἰδίαν πρόθεσιν καὶ χάριν, τὴν δοθεῖσαν ἡμῖν ἐν Χριστῷ Ἰησοῦ πρὸ χρόνων αἰωνίων, **10** φανερωθεῖσαν δὲ νῦν διὰ τῆς ἐπιφανείας τοῦ σωτῆρος ἡμῶν Χριστοῦ Ἰησοῦ,

revealed	through	the	appearing	of	our	Savior,		Christ	Jesus,	who	has		destroyed		death		and has
φανερωθεῖσαν	διὰ	τῆς	ἐπιφανείας	→	ἡμῶν	τοῦ σωτῆρος		Χριστοῦ	Ἰησοῦ		μὲν	→	καταργήσαντος		τὸν θάνατον		δὲ
pt.ap.asf	p.g	d.gsf	n.gsf		r.gp.1	d.gsm n.gsm		n.gsm	n.gsm		pl		pt.aa.gsm		d.asm n.asm		cj
5746	1328	3836	2211	5400	7005	3836 5400		5986	2652	2934	3525		2934		3836 2505		1254 5894

brought	life	and	immortality	to	light		through	the	gospel.	[11] And	of	this	gospel	I		was appointed	a	herald	and
→	ζωὴν	καὶ	ἀφθαρσίαν	→	φωτίσαντος		διὰ	τοῦ	εὐαγγελίου	εἰς	ὃ		ἐγὼ		→	ἐτέθην		κῆρυξ	καὶ
	n.asf	cj	n.asf		pt.aa.gsm		p.g	d.gsn	n.gsn	p.a	r.asn		r.ns.1			v.api.1s		n.nsm	cj
5894	2437	2779	914		5894		1328	3836	2295	1650	4005		1609			5502		3061	2779

an apostle	and	a teacher.	[12] That		is	why		I	am suffering	*as*	*I am.*	Yet	I		am	not	ashamed,	because	I
ἀπόστολος	καὶ	διδάσκαλος	δι'	ἣν	αἰτίαν	←	καὶ		πάσχω	ταῦτα		ἀλλ'	→		οὐκ		ἐπαισχύνομαι	γὰρ	→
n.nsm	cj	n.nsm	p.a	r.asf	n.asf		adv		v.pai.1s	r.apn		cj			pl		v.ppi.1s	cj	
693	2779	1437	1328	4005	162		2779		4248	4047		247	2049	2049	4024	2049		1142	

know	whom	I	have	believed,	and	am	convinced	that	he	is	able	to	guard	what	I	have	entrusted		to him
οἶδα	ᾧ	→	→	πεπίστευκα	καὶ	→	πέπεισμαι	ὅτι	→	ἐστιν	δυνατός	→	φυλάξαι		μου				τὴν παραθήκην
v.rai.1s	r.dsm			v.rai.1s	cj		v.rpi.1s	cj		v.pai.3s	a.nsm		f.aa		r.gs.1				d.asf n.asf
3857	4005			4409	2779		4275	4022		1639	1543		5875		1609				3836 4146

for	that	day.	¶	[13] What	you	heard		from	me,	keep	as	the	pattern	of	sound		teaching,	with	faith
εἰς	ἐκείνην	τὴν ἡμέραν		ὧν	→	ἤκουσας	παρ'		ἐμοῦ	ἔχε			Ὑποτύπωσιν	→	ὑγιαινόντων		λόγων	ἐν	πίστει
p.a	r.asf	d.asf n.asf		r.gpm		v.aai.2s	p.g		r.gs.1	v.pam.2s			n.asf		pt.pa.gpm		n.gpm	p.d	n.dsf
1650	1697	3836 2465		4005		201	4123		1609	2400			5721		5617		3364	1877	4411

and	love		in	Christ	Jesus.	[14] Guard	the	good	deposit		that	was entrusted	to you	–	guard	it	with	the	help	of	the
καὶ	ἀγάπῃ	τῇ	ἐν	Χριστῷ	Ἰησοῦ	φύλαξον	τὴν	καλὴν	παραθήκην								διὰ	←	←	←	
cj	n.dsf	d.dsf	p.d	n.dsm	n.dsm	v.aam.2s	d.asf	a.asf	n.asf								p.g				
2779	27	3836	1877	5986	2652	5875	3836	2819	4146								1328				

Holy	Spirit		who	lives		in	us.	¶	[15] You	know		that	everyone		in	the	province	of	Asia		has
ἁγίου	πνεύματος	τοῦ	ἐνοικοῦντος		ἐν	ἡμῖν			Οἶδας	τοῦτο	ὅτι	πάντες		οἱ		→	→	τῇ	Ἀσίᾳ		→
a.gsn	n.gsn	d.gsn	pt.pa.gsn		p.d	r.dp.1			v.rai.2s	r.asn	cj	a.npm		d.npm				d.dsf	n.dsf		
41	4460	3836	1940		1877	7005			3857	4047	4022	4246		3836		1877			3836 823		

deserted		me, including	Phygelus	and	Hermogenes.	¶	[16] May	the	Lord	show	mercy	to	the	household	of
ἀπεστράφησαν	με	ὧν ἐστιν,	Φύγελος	καὶ	Ἑρμογένης		δῴη	ὁ	κύριος	ἔλεος	→	τῷ	οἴκῳ		
v.api.3p	r.as.1	r.gpm v.pai.3s	n.nsm	cj	n.nsm			d.nsm	n.nsm	v.aao.3s	n.asn		d.dsm	n.dsm	
695	1609	4005 1639	5869	2779	2259			1443 3836	3261	1443	1799		3836	3875	

Onesiphorus,	because	he often		refreshed	me	and	was	not	ashamed	of	my chains.	[17] On	the contrary,	when	he
Ὀνησιφόρου	ὅτι	→	πολλάκις	ἀνέψυξεν	με	καὶ	→	οὐκ	ἐπαισχύνθη	←	μου τὴν ἅλυσιν,	→	→	ἀλλὰ	→
n.gsm	cj		adv	v.aai.3s	r.as.1	cj		pl	v.api.3s		r.gs.1 d.asf n.asf			cj	
3947	4022	434	4490	434	1609	2779	2049	4024	2049		1609 3836 268			247	

was		in	Rome,	he searched	hard		for	me	until	he	found	me.	[18] May	the	Lord	grant	that	he	will find	mercy
γενόμενος	ἐν	Ῥώμῃ		ἐζήτησεν	σπουδαίως	←	με	καὶ	→	εὗρεν			δῴη	ὁ	κύριος		αὐτῷ	→	εὑρεῖν	ἔλεος
pt.am.nsm	p.d	n.dsf		v.aai.3s	adv		r.as.1	cj		v.aai.3s				d.nsm	n.nsm	v.aao.3s	r.dsm.3		f.aa	n.asn
1181	1877	4873		2426	5081		2426 1609	2779		2351				1443 3836	3261	1443	899		2351	1799

from	the	Lord	on	that	day!		You	know	very	well		in	how many	ways	he	helped		me in	Ephesus.	¶
παρὰ		κυρίου	ἐν	ἐκείνῃ	τῇ	ἡμέρᾳ	καὶ	σὺ	γινώσκεις	→	βέλτιον	ὅσα	←		←	→	διηκόνησεν	ἐν	Ἐφέσῳ	
p.g		n.gsm	p.d	r.dsf	d.dsf	n.dsf	cj	r.ns.2	v.pai.2s		adv.c	r.apn					v.aai.3s	p.d	n.dsf	
4123		3261	1877	1697	3836	2465	2779	5148	1182		1019	4012					1354	1877	2387	

[2:1] You	then,	my	son,	be	strong	in	the	grace	that	is	in	Christ	Jesus.	[2] And	the	things	you have	heard		me	say
Σὺ	οὖν	μου	τέκνον	ἐνδυναμοῦ	ἐν		τῇ	χάριτι	τῇ		ἐν	Χριστῷ	Ἰησοῦ	καὶ	ἃ			ἤκουσας	παρ'	ἐμοῦ	→
r.ns.2	cj	r.gs.1	n.vsn	v.ppm.2s	p.d		d.dsf	n.dsf	d.dsf		p.d	n.dsm	n.dsm	cj	r.apn			v.aai.2s	p.g	r.gs.1	
5148	4036	1609	5451	1904		1877	3836	5921	3836		1877	5986	2652	2779	4005			201	4123	1609	

in	the	presence	of	many	witnesses	entrust		to	reliable	men		who	will	also	be	qualified	to	teach
διὰ	←	←	←	πολλῶν	μαρτύρων	παράθου	ταῦτα		πιστοῖς	ἀνθρώποις		οἵτινες	→	καὶ	ἔσονται	ἱκανοὶ	→	διδάξαι
p.g				a.gpm	n.gpm	v.amm.2s	r.apn		a.dpm	n.dpm		r.npm		adv	v.fmi.3p	a.npm		f.aa
1328				4498	3459	4192	4047		4412	476		4015	1639	2779	1639	2653		1438

others.	[3] Endure		hardship	with us	like	a	good	soldier		of	Christ	Jesus.	[4] No	one	serving		as	a	soldier
ἑτέρους	Συγκακοπάθησον	←		←	ὡς	καλὸς	στρατιώτης	→		Χριστοῦ	Ἰησοῦ	οὐδεὶς	←		στρατευόμενος	←	←		
r.apm	v.aam.2s				pl	a.nsm	n.nsm			n.gsm	n.gsm	a.nsm			pt.pm.nsm				
2283	5155				6055	2819	5132			5986	2652	4029			5129				

καταργήσαντος μὲν τὸν θάνατον φωτίσαντος δὲ ζωὴν καὶ ἀφθαρσίαν διὰ τοῦ εὐαγγελίου [11] εἰς ὃ ἐτέθην ἐγὼ κῆρυξ καὶ ἀπόστολος καὶ διδάσκαλος, [12] δι' ἣν αἰτίαν καὶ ταῦτα πάσχω· ἀλλ' οὐκ ἐπαισχύνομαι, οἶδα γὰρ ᾧ πεπίστευκα καὶ πέπεισμαι ὅτι δυνατός ἐστιν τὴν παραθήκην μου φυλάξαι εἰς ἐκείνην τὴν ἡμέραν. ¶ [13] ὑποτύπωσιν ἔχε ὑγιαινόντων λόγων ὧν παρ' ἐμοῦ ἤκουσας ἐν πίστει καὶ ἀγάπῃ τῇ ἐν Χριστῷ Ἰησοῦ. [14] τὴν καλὴν παραθήκην φύλαξον διὰ πνεύματος ἁγίου τοῦ ἐνοικοῦντος ἐν ἡμῖν. ¶ [15] Οἶδας τοῦτο, ὅτι ἀπεστράφησάν με πάντες οἱ ἐν τῇ Ἀσίᾳ, ὧν ἐστιν Φύγελος καὶ Ἑρμογένης. ¶ [16] δῴη ἔλεος ὁ κύριος τῷ Ὀνησιφόρου οἴκῳ, ὅτι πολλάκις με ἀνέψυξεν καὶ τὴν ἅλυσίν μου οὐκ ἐπαισχύνθη, [17] ἀλλὰ γενόμενος ἐν Ῥώμῃ σπουδαίως ἐζήτησέν με καὶ εὗρεν· [18] δῴη αὐτῷ ὁ κύριος εὑρεῖν ἔλεος παρὰ κυρίου ἐν ἐκείνῃ τῇ ἡμέρᾳ. καὶ ὅσα ἐν Ἐφέσῳ διηκόνησεν, βέλτιον σὺ γινώσκεις. [2:1] Σὺ οὖν, τέκνον μου, ἐνδυναμοῦ ἐν τῇ χάριτι τῇ ἐν Χριστῷ Ἰησοῦ, [2] καὶ ἃ ἤκουσας παρ' ἐμοῦ διὰ πολλῶν μαρτύρων, ταῦτα παράθου πιστοῖς ἀνθρώποις, οἵτινες ἱκανοὶ ἔσονται καὶ ἑτέρους διδάξαι. [3] συγκακοπάθησον ὡς καλὸς στρατιώτης Χριστοῦ Ἰησοῦ. [4] οὐδεὶς στρατευόμενος ἐμπλέκεται ταῖς τοῦ βίου πραγματείαις, ἵνα τῷ στρατολογήσαντι ἀρέσῃ.

gets involved in civilian affairs   — he wants to please his commanding officer.   **5** Similarly,
→ ἐμπλέκεται ← ⌐τοῦ βίου, ⌐ταῖς πραγματείαις⌐ ἵνα → → ἀρέσῃ τῷ → στρατολογήσαντι δὲ καὶ
v.ppi.3s   d.gsm n.gsm d.dpf n.dpf   cj   v.aas.3s d.dsm   pt.aa.dsm   cj adv
1861   3836 1050 3836 4548   2671   743 3836   5133   1254 2779

if anyone competes as an athlete, he does not receive the victor's crown   unless   he competes according to the
ἐὰν τις ἀθλῇ ← ← → οὐ → → στεφανοῦται ⌐ἐὰν μὴ, → ἀθλήσῃ → → →
cj r.nsm v.pas.3s   pl   v.ppi.3s ⌐cj pl,   v.aas.3s
1569 5516 123   5110 5110 4024   5110   1569 3590   123

rules. **6** The hardworking farmer should be the first to receive   a share of the crops. **7** Reflect on what I am
νομίμως τὸν κοπιῶντα γεωργὸν δεῖ ← πρῶτον → μεταλαμβάνειν → τῶν καρπῶν νόει ← ὃ
adv d.asm pt.pa.asm n.asm v.pai.3s   adv   f.pa   d.gpm n.gpm v.pam.2s   r.asn
3789 3836 3159 1177 1256   4754   3561   3836 2843 3783   4005

saying, for the Lord will give you insight into all this. ¶ **8** Remember Jesus Christ, raised   from the
λέγω γὰρ ὁ κύριος → δώσει σοι σύνεσιν ἐν πᾶσιν →   Μνημόνευε Ἰησοῦν Χριστὸν ἐγηγερμένον ἐκ
v.pai.1s cj d.nsm n.nsm   v.fai.3s r.ds.2 n.asf p.d a.dpn   v.pam.2s n.asm n.asm pt.rp.asm p.g
3306 1142 3836 3261   1443 5148 5304 1877 4246   3648 2652 5986 1586 1666

dead, descended from David. *This is* my gospel,   **9** for which I am suffering even to the point of being
νεκρῶν ἐκ σπέρματος → Δαυίδ κατὰ μου ⌐τὸ εὐαγγέλιον, ἐν ᾧ → κακοπαθῶ μέχρι ← ← ← ←
a.gpm p.g n.gsn   n.gsm p.a r.gs.1 d.asn n.asn   p.d r.dsn   v.pai.1s p.g
3738 1666 5065   1253 2848 1609 3836 2295   1877 4005   2802 3588

chained like a criminal. But God's   word   is not chained. **10** Therefore   I endure everything for the sake of the
δεσμῶν ὡς κακοῦργος ἀλλὰ ⌐τοῦ θεοῦ, ὁ λόγος, οὐ δέδεται ⌐διὰ τοῦτο, → ὑπομένω πάντα διὰ ← ← ← τοὺς
n.gpm pl n.nsm cj d.gsm n.gsm d.nsm n.nsm pl v.rpi.3s p.a r.asn   v.pai.1s a.apn p.a   d.apm
1301 6055 2806 247 3836 2536 3836 3364 4024 1313 1328 4047   5702 4246 1328   3836

elect,   that they too may obtain the salvation that is in Christ Jesus, with eternal glory. ¶ **11** Here is a
ἐκλεκτούς ἵνα αὐτοὶ καὶ → τύχωσιν σωτηρίας τῆς ἐν Χριστῷ Ἰησοῦ μετὰ αἰωνίου δόξης
a.apm cj r.npm cj   v.aas.3p n.gsf d.gsf p.d n.dsm n.dsm p.g a.gsf n.gsf
1723 2671 899 2779   5593 5401 3836 1877 5986 2652 3552 173 1518

trustworthy saying: If we died   with him, we will also live   with him; **12** if we endure,   we will also
πιστὸς ⌐ὁ λόγος, γὰρ εἰ → συναπεθάνομεν ← → ← καὶ συζήσομεν ← εἰ → ὑπομένομεν ⌐ καὶ
a.nsm d.nsm n.nsm cj cj   v.aai.1p   adv v.fai.1p   cj   v.pai.1p   adv
4412 3836 3364 1142 1623   5271   5182 5182 2779 5182   1623   5702 5203 5203 2779

reign   with him. If we disown   him, he   will also disown us; **13** if we are faithless, he   will
συμβασιλεύσομεν ← εἰ → ἀρνησόμεθα κἀκεῖνος ⌐ ← → ἀρνήσεται ἡμᾶς εἰ → → ἀπιστοῦμεν ἐκεῖνος →
v.fai.1p   cj   v.fmi.1p crasis   v.fmi.3s r.ap.1 cj   v.pai.1p r.nsm
5203   1623   766 2797   766 7005 1623   601 1697

remain faithful, for he cannot   disown   himself.
μένει πιστός γὰρ → ⌐οὐ δύναται, ἀρνήσασθαι ἑαυτὸν
v.pai.3s a.nsm cj   pl v.ppi.3s f.am   r.asm.3
3531 4412 1142   4024 1538 766   1571

A Workman Approved by God

2:14 Keep reminding them of these things. Warn   them before God   against quarreling about words; it
   ὑπομίμνῃσκε Ταῦτα ← διαμαρτυρόμενος ἐνώπιον ⌐τοῦ θεοῦ, μὴ λογομαχεῖν ← ←
   v.pam.2s r.apn pt.pm.nsm p.g d.gsm n.gsm pl f.pa
   5703 4047 1371 1967 3836 2536 3590 3362

is of no value, and only ruins   those who listen. **15** Do your best   to present   yourself to God
ἐπ᾽ οὐδὲν χρήσιμον ἐπὶ καταστροφῇ τῶν → ἀκουόντων σπούδασον → παραστῆσαι σεαυτὸν → ⌐τῷ θεῷ,
p.a a.asn a.asn p.d n.dsf d.gpm pt.pa.gpm v.aam.2s f.aa r.asm.2 d.dsm n.dsm
2093 4029 5978 2093 2953 3836 201 5079 4225 4932 3836 2536

as one approved, a workman who does not need to be ashamed   and who correctly handles   the word of
→ δόκιμον ἐργάτην → → → ἀνεπαίσχυντον → → ὀρθοτομοῦντα τὸν λόγον
a.asm n.asm a.asm   pt.pa.asm d.asm n.asm
1511 2239 454   3982 3836 3364

truth. **16** Avoid godless chatter,   because those who indulge   in it will become more   and
⌐τῆς ἀληθείας, δὲ περιΐστασο βεβήλους ⌐τὰς κενοφωνίας, γὰρ → → προκόψουσιν ⌐ἐπὶ πλεῖον, ←
d.gsf n.gsf cj v.pmm.2s a.apf d.apf n.apf cj   v.fai.3p p.a adv.c
3836 237 1254 4325 1013 3836 3032 1142   4621 2093 4498

⁵ ἐὰν δὲ καὶ ἀθλῇ τις, οὐ στεφανοῦται ἐὰν μὴ νομίμως ἀθλήσῃ. ⁶ τὸν κοπιῶντα γεωργὸν δεῖ πρῶτον τῶν καρπῶν μεταλαμβάνειν. ⁷ νόει ὃ λέγω· δώσει γάρ σοι ὁ κύριος σύνεσιν ἐν πᾶσιν. ¶ ⁸ Μνημόνευε Ἰησοῦν Χριστὸν ἐγηγερμένον ἐκ νεκρῶν, ἐκ σπέρματος Δαυίδ, κατὰ τὸ εὐαγγέλιόν μου, ⁹ ἐν ᾧ κακοπαθῶ μέχρι δεσμῶν ὡς κακοῦργος, ἀλλὰ ὁ λόγος τοῦ θεοῦ οὐ δέδεται· ¹⁰ διὰ τοῦτο πάντα ὑπομένω διὰ τοὺς ἐκλεκτούς, ἵνα καὶ αὐτοὶ σωτηρίας τύχωσιν τῆς ἐν Χριστῷ Ἰησοῦ μετὰ δόξης αἰωνίου. ¶ ¹¹ πιστὸς ὁ λόγος· εἰ γὰρ συναπεθάνομεν, καὶ συζήσομεν· ¹² εἰ ὑπομένομεν, καὶ συμβασιλεύσομεν· εἰ ἀρνησόμεθα, κἀκεῖνος ἀρνήσεται ἡμᾶς· ¹³ εἰ ἀπιστοῦμεν, ἐκεῖνος πιστὸς μένει, ἀρνήσασθαι γὰρ ἑαυτὸν οὐ δύναται.

²:¹⁴ Ταῦτα ὑπομίμνῃσκε διαμαρτυρόμενος ἐνώπιον τοῦ θεοῦ μὴ λογομαχεῖν, ἐπ᾽ οὐδὲν χρήσιμον, ἐπὶ καταστροφῇ τῶν ἀκουόντων. ¹⁵ σπούδασον σεαυτὸν δόκιμον παραστῆσαι τῷ θεῷ, ἐργάτην ἀνεπαίσχυντον, ὀρθοτομοῦντα τὸν λόγον τῆς ἀληθείας. ¹⁶ τὰς δὲ βεβήλους κενοφωνίας περιΐστασο· ἐπὶ πλεῖον γὰρ προκόψουσιν ἀσεβείας ¹⁷ καὶ ὁ λόγος αὐτῶν ὡς

more ungodly. **17** Their teaching will spread like gangrene. Among them are Hymenaeus and Philetus,
← ἀσεβείας | καὶ αὐτῶν ὁ λόγος‚ | → ‚νομὴν ἕξει‚ | ὡς γάγγραινα | → | ὧν ἐστιν Ὑμέναιος | καὶ Φίλητος,
n.gsf | cj r.gpm.3 d.nsm n.nsm | n.asf v.fai.3s | pl n.nsf | | r.gpm v.pai.3s n.nsm | cj n.nsm
813 | 2779 899 3836 3364 | 3786 2400 | 6055 1121 | | 4005 1639 5628 | 2779 5801

18 who have wandered away from the truth. They say that the resurrection has already taken place, and they
οἵτινες → ἠστόχησαν ← περὶ τὴν ἀλήθειαν → λέγοντες [τὴν] ἀνάστασιν → ἤδη → γεγονέναι καὶ
r.npm | v.aai.3p | p.a d.asf n.asf | pt.pa.npm | d.asf n.asf | adv | f.ra cj
4015 | 846 | 4309 3836 237 | 3306 | 3836 414 | 2453 | 1181 2779

destroy the faith of some. **19** Nevertheless, God's solid foundation stands firm, sealed with this inscription:
ἀνατρέπουσιν τὴν πίστιν → τινων | μέντοι | ‚τοῦ θεοῦ‚ στερεὸς ὁ θεμέλιος‚ ἕστηκεν ← ἔχων ← ταύτην ‚τὴν σφραγίδα‚
v.pai.3p d.asf n.asf r.gpm | cj | d.gsm n.gsm a.nsm d.nsm n.nsm v.rai.3s pt.pa.nsm r.asf d.asf n.asf
426 3836 4411 5516 | 3530 | 3836 2536 5104 3836 2529 2705 2400 4047 3836 5382

"The Lord knows those who are his," and, "Everyone who confesses the name of the Lord must turn away
κύριος ἔγνω τοὺς ← ὄντας αὐτοῦ καὶ | πᾶς ὁ ὀνομάζων τὸ ὄνομα → κυρίου → ἀποστήτω ←
n.nsm v.aai.3s d.apm | pt.pa.apm r.gsm.3 cj | a.nsm d.nsm pt.pa.nsm d.nsn n.nsn n.gsm v.aam.3s
3261 1182 3836 | 1639 899 2779 | 4246 3836 3951 3836 3950 3261 923

from wickedness." ¶ **20** In a large house there are articles not only of gold and silver, but also of wood
ἀπὸ ἀδικίας‚ | | δὲ Ἐν μεγάλῃ οἰκίᾳ → ἔστιν σκεύη οὐκ μόνον χρυσᾶ καὶ ἀργυρᾶ ἀλλὰ καὶ ξύλινα
p.g n.gsf | | cj p.d a.dsf n.dsf | v.pai.3s n.npn pl adv a.npn cj a.npn cj adv a.npn
608 94 | | 1254 1877 3489 3864 | 1639 5007 4024 3667 5997 2779 739 247 2779 3832

and clay; some are for noble purposes and some for ignoble. **21** If a man cleanses himself from the
καὶ ὀστράκινα καὶ μὲν ἃ εἰς τιμὴν δὲ ἃ εἰς ἀτιμίαν οὖν ἐὰν τις ἐκκαθάρῃ ἑαυτὸν ἀπὸ
cj a.npn cj pl r.npn p.a n.asf pl r.npn p.a n.asf cj cj r.nsm v.aas.3s r.asm.3 p.g
2779 4017 2779 3525 4005 1650 5507 1254 4005 1650 871 4036 1569 5516 1705 1571 608

latter, he will be an instrument for noble purposes, made holy, useful to the Master and prepared to do
τούτων → ἔσται σκεῦος εἰς τιμήν → → ἡγιασμένον εὔχρηστον → τῷ δεσπότῃ ἡτοιμασμένον εἰς →
r.gpn | v.fmi.3s n.nsn p.a n.asf | pt.rp.nsn a.nsn | d.dsm n.dsm pt.rp.nsn p.a
4047 | 1639 5007 1650 5507 | 39 2378 | 3836 1305 2286 1650 2240

any good work. ¶ **22** Flee the evil desires of youth, and pursue righteousness, faith, love and peace,
πᾶν ἀγαθὸν ἔργον | δὲ φεῦγε Τὰς → ἐπιθυμίας νεωτερικὰς δὲ δίωκε δικαιοσύνην πίστιν ἀγάπην εἰρήνην
a.asn a.asn n.asn | cj v.pam.2s d.apf n.apf a.apf cj v.pam.2s n.asf n.asf n.asf n.asf
4246 19 2240 | 1254 5771 3836 2123 3754 1254 1503 1466 4411 27 1645

along with those who call on the Lord out of a pure heart. **23** Don't have anything to do with
→ μετὰ τῶν ← ἐπικαλουμένων ← τὸν κύριον ἐκ → καθαρᾶς καρδίας δὲ παραιτοῦ ←
p.g d.gpm | pt.pm.gpm d.asm n.asm p.g a.gsf n.gsf cj v.pmm.2s
3552 3836 | 2126 3836 3261 1666 2754 2840 1254 4148

foolish and stupid arguments, because you know they produce quarrels. **24** And the Lord's servant must not
μωρὰς καὶ ἀπαιδεύτους ‚τὰς ζητήσεις‚ → → εἰδὼς ὅτι → γεννῶσιν μάχας δὲ κυρίου δοῦλον δεῖ οὐ
a.apf cj a.apf d.apf n.apf | pt.ra.nsm cj | v.pai.3p n.apf cj n.gsm n.asm v.pai.3s pl
3704 2779 553 3836 2428 | 3857 4022 | 1164 3480 1254 3261 1529 1256 4024

quarrel; instead, he must be kind to everyone, able to teach, not resentful. **25** Those who oppose him
μάχεσθαι ἀλλὰ → εἶναι ἤπιον πρὸς πάντας → διδακτικόν → ἀνεξίκακον τοὺς ← ἀντιδιατιθεμένους
f.pm cj | f.pa a.asm p.a a.apm | a.asm | a.asm d.apm pt.pm.apm
3481 247 | 1639 2473 4639 4246 | 1434 | 452 3836 507

he must gently instruct, in the hope that God will grant them repentance leading them to a
→ ἐν πραΰτητι παιδεύοντα μήποτε ← → ὁ θεὸς → δώῃ αὐτοῖς μετάνοιαν → → εἰς
| p.d n.dsf pt.pa.asm | | d.nsm n.nsm v.aas.3s r.dpm.3 n.asf | p.a
4084 4084 1877 4559 4084 | 3607 | 3836 2536 1443 899 3567 | 1650

knowledge of the truth, **26** and that they will come to their senses and escape from the trap of the devil,
ἐπίγνωσιν → ἀληθείας καὶ → → → → → ἀνανήψωσιν ἐκ τῆς παγίδος → τοῦ διαβόλου
n.asf | n.gsf cj | v.aas.3p p.g d.gsf n.gsf d.gsm n.gsm
2106 | 237 2779 | 392 1666 3836 4075 3836 1333

who has taken them captive *to do* his will.
ὑπ᾽ αὐτοῦ → → ἐζωγρημένοι εἰς ἐκείνου ‚τὸ θέλημα‚
p.g r.gsm.3 | pt.rp.npm p.a r.gsm d.asn n.asn
5679 899 | 2436 1650 1697 3836 2525

γάγγραινα νομὴν ἕξει. ὧν ἐστιν Ὑμέναιος καὶ Φίλητος, **18** οἵτινες περὶ τὴν ἀλήθειαν ἠστόχησαν, λέγοντες [τὴν] ἀνάστασιν ἤδη γεγονέναι, καὶ ἀνατρέπουσιν τὴν τινων πίστιν. **19** ὁ μέντοι στερεὸς θεμέλιος τοῦ θεοῦ ἕστηκεν, ἔχων τὴν σφραγίδα ταύτην· Ἔγνω κύριος τοὺς ὄντας αὐτοῦ, καί, Ἀποστήτω ἀπὸ ἀδικίας πᾶς ὁ ὀνομάζων τὸ ὄνομα κυρίου. ¶ **20** Ἐν μεγάλῃ δὲ οἰκίᾳ οὐκ ἔστιν μόνον σκεύη χρυσᾶ καὶ ἀργυρᾶ ἀλλὰ καὶ ξύλινα καὶ ὀστράκινα, καὶ ἃ μὲν εἰς τιμὴν ἃ δὲ εἰς ἀτιμίαν· **21** ἐὰν οὖν τις ἐκκαθάρῃ ἑαυτὸν ἀπὸ τούτων, ἔσται σκεῦος εἰς τιμήν, ἡγιασμένον, εὔχρηστον τῷ δεσπότῃ, εἰς πᾶν ἔργον ἀγαθὸν ἡτοιμασμένον. ¶ **22** τὰς δὲ νεωτερικὰς ἐπιθυμίας φεῦγε, δίωκε δὲ δικαιοσύνην πίστιν ἀγάπην εἰρήνην μετὰ τῶν ἐπικαλουμένων τὸν κύριον ἐκ καθαρᾶς καρδίας. **23** τὰς δὲ μωρὰς καὶ ἀπαιδεύτους ζητήσεις παραιτοῦ, εἰδὼς ὅτι γεννῶσιν μάχας· **24** δοῦλον δὲ κυρίου οὐ δεῖ μάχεσθαι ἀλλὰ ἤπιον εἶναι πρὸς πάντας, διδακτικόν, ἀνεξίκακον, **25** ἐν πραΰτητι παιδεύοντα τοὺς ἀντιδιατιθεμένους, μήποτε δώῃ αὐτοῖς ὁ θεὸς μετάνοιαν εἰς ἐπίγνωσιν ἀληθείας **26** καὶ ἀνανήψωσιν ἐκ τῆς τοῦ διαβόλου παγίδος, ἐζωγρημένοι ὑπ᾽ αὐτοῦ εἰς τὸ ἐκείνου θέλημα.

Godlessness in the Last Days

3:1 But mark this: There will be   terrible times in the last   days.   **2**   People   will be
δὲ γίνωσκε Τοῦτο ὅτι →   →   ἐνστήσονται χαλεποὶ καιροὶ ἐν   ἐσχάταις ἡμέραις γὰρ οἱ ἄνθρωποι →   ἔσονται
cj v.pam.2s r.asn cj   v.fmi.3p   a.npm n.npm p.d a.dpf   n.dpf   cj d.npm n.npm   v.fmi.3p
1254 1182 4047 4022   1931   5901   2789 1877 2274   2465   1142 3836 476   1639

lovers of themselves, lovers   of money, boastful, proud,   abusive,   disobedient to their parents, ungrateful,
φίλαυτοι ← ←   φιλάργυροι ← ←   ἀλαζόνες ὑπερήφανοι βλάσφημοι ἀπειθεῖς   →   γονεῦσιν ἀχάριστοι
a.npm   a.npm   n.npm   a.npm   a.npm   a.npm   n.dpm   a.npm
5796   5795   225   5662   1061   579   1204   940

unholy,   **3** without love,   unforgiving, slanderous, without self-control, brutal, not lovers   of the good,
ἀνόσιοι   ἄστοργοι ἄσπονδοι διάβολοι →   ἀκρατεῖς   ἀνήμεροι → ἀφιλάγαθοι ← ←
a.npm   a.npm   a.npm   a.npm   a.npm   a.npm   a.npm
495   845   836   1333   203   466   920

4 treacherous, rash,   conceited, lovers   of pleasure rather than lovers of God – **5** having a form   of godliness but
προδόται   προπετεῖς τετυφωμένοι φιλήδονοι ←   μᾶλλον ἢ φιλόθεοι ←   ἔχοντες   μόρφωσιν → εὐσεβείας δὲ
n.npm   a.npm   pt.rp.npm n.npm   adv.c pl a.npm   pt.pa.npm n.asf   n.gsf   cj
4595   4637   5605   5798   3437   2445 5806   2400   3673   2354   1254

denying its   power.   Have   nothing to do with them.   ¶   **6**   They are the kind who worm
ἠρνημένοι αὐτῆς τὴν δύναμιν καὶ ἀποτρέπου ← ← ←   τούτους   γὰρ ἐκ τούτων εἰσιν → → οἱ ἐνδύνοντες
pt.rp.npm r.gsf.3 d.asf n.asf adv v.pmm.2s   r.apm   cj p.g r.gpm v.pai.3p   d.npm pt.pa.npm
766   899   3836 1539 2779 706   4047   1142 1666 4047 1639   3836 1905

their way into homes   and gain control   over weak-willed women, who are loaded   down with sins
← εἰς τὰς οἰκίας καὶ → αἰχμαλωτίζοντες ← γυναικάρια   σεσωρευμένα → ἁμαρτίαις
p.a d.apf n.apf cj   pt.pa.npm   n.apn   pt.rp.apn   n.dpf
1650 3836 3864 2779   170   1220   5397   281

and are swayed by all kinds of evil desires, **7** always learning but never   able   to acknowledge the
→ ἀγόμενα → ποικίλαις ← ἐπιθυμίαις πάντοτε μανθάνοντα καὶ μηδέποτε δυνάμενα → εἰς ἐπίγνωσιν ἐλθεῖν
pt.pp.apn a.dpf   n.dpf   adv   pt.pa.npn cj adv   pt.pp.apn p.a n.asf   f.aa
72   4476   2123   4121   3443   2779 3595   1538   1650 2106   2262

truth. **8** Just   as Jannes and Jambres opposed   Moses, so   also these men oppose   the truth –
ἀληθείας δὲ ὃν τρόπον ᾽Ἰάννης καὶ ᾽Ἰαμβρῆς ἀντέστησαν Μωϋσεῖ οὕτως καὶ οὗτοι ← ἀνθίστανται τῇ ἀληθείᾳ
n.gsf   cj r.asm n.asm n.nsm cj n.nsm   v.aai.3p   n.dsm adv   adv r.npm   v.pmi.3p   d.dsf n.dsf
237   1254 4005 5573 2614   2779 2612   468   3707   4048 2779 4047   468   3836 237

men   of depraved minds,   who, as far as the faith is concerned, are rejected. **9** But they will not get
ἄνθρωποι κατεφθαρμένοι τὸν νοῦν περὶ ← τὴν πίστιν ← ←   ἀδόκιμοι ἀλλ᾽ → → οὐ προκόψουσιν
n.npm   pt.rp.npm   d.asm n.asm p.a   d.asf n.asf   a.npm   cj   pl v.fai.3p
476   2967   3836 3808 4309   3836 4411 4309 4309   99   247 4621 4621 4024 4621

very   far because, as in the case of those men, their folly   will be   clear   to everyone.
ἐπὶ πλεῖον ← γὰρ ὡς καὶ ἡ   ← ἐκείνων αὐτῶν ἡ ἄνοια ἔσται ἐγένετο ἔκδηλος → πᾶσιν
p.a adv.c   cj cj adv d.nsf r.gpm   r.gpm.3 d.nsf n.nsf v.fmi.3s v.ami.3s a.nsf a.dpm
2093 4498   1142 6055 2779 3836 1697 899   3836 486 1639   1181   1684   4246

Paul's Charge to Timothy

3:10 You, however, know   all about my teaching,   my way of life, my purpose, faith,
Σὺ δὲ παρηκολούθησας ←   μου τῇ διδασκαλίᾳ τῇ ἀγωγῇ ←   τῇ προθέσει τῇ πίστει
r.ns.2 cj v.aai.2s   r.gs.1 d.dsf n.dsf d.dsf n.dsf   d.dsf n.dsf d.dsf n.dsf
5148 1254 4158   1609 3836 1436 3836 73   3836 4606 3836 4411

patience,   love,   endurance, **11** persecutions, sufferings – what kinds of things happened to me in
τῇ μακροθυμίᾳ τῇ ἀγάπῃ τῇ ὑπομονῇ τοῖς διωγμοῖς τοῖς παθήμασιν οἷα ← ← ←   ἐγένετο → μοι ἐν
d.dsf n.dsf   d.dsf n.dsf d.dsf n.dsf d.dpm n.dpm d.dpn n.dpn r.npn   v.ami.3s r.ds.1 p.d
3836 3429   3836 27   3836 5705   3836 1501   3836 4077   3888   1181   1609 1877

Antioch, Iconium and   Lystra, the persecutions I endured. Yet the Lord rescued me from all   of
᾽Ἀντιοχείᾳ ἐν ᾽Ἰκονίῳ   ἐν Λύστροις οἵους διωγμοὺς → ὑπήνεγκα καὶ ὁ κύριος ἐρρύσατο με ἐκ πάντων ←
n.dsf   p.d n.dsn   p.d n.dpn   r.apm n.apm   v.aai.1s cj d.nsm n.nsm v.ami.3s r.as.1 p.g a.gpn
522   1877 2658   1877 3388   3888 1501   5722   2779 3836 3261 4861   1609 1666 4246

3:1 Τοῦτο δὲ γίνωσκε, ὅτι ἐν ἐσχάταις ἡμέραις ἐνστήσονται καιροὶ χαλεποί· **2** ἔσονται γὰρ οἱ ἄνθρωποι φίλαυτοι φιλάργυροι ἀλαζόνες ὑπερήφανοι βλάσφημοι, γονεῦσιν ἀπειθεῖς, ἀχάριστοι ἀνόσιοι **3** ἄστοργοι ἄσπονδοι διάβολοι ἀκρατεῖς ἀνήμεροι ἀφιλάγαθοι **4** προδόται προπετεῖς τετυφωμένοι, φιλήδονοι μᾶλλον ἢ φιλόθεοι, **5** ἔχοντες μόρφωσιν εὐσεβείας τὴν δὲ δύναμιν αὐτῆς ἠρνημένοι· καὶ τούτους ἀποτρέπου. ¶ **6** ἐκ τούτων γάρ εἰσιν οἱ ἐνδύνοντες εἰς τὰς οἰκίας καὶ αἰχμαλωτίζοντες γυναικάρια σεσωρευμένα ἁμαρτίαις, ἀγόμενα ἐπιθυμίαις ποικίλαις, **7** πάντοτε μανθάνοντα καὶ μηδέποτε εἰς ἐπίγνωσιν ἀληθείας ἐλθεῖν δυνάμενα. **8** ὃν τρόπον δὲ ᾽Ἰάννης καὶ ᾽Ἰαμβρῆς ἀντέστησαν Μωϋσεῖ, οὕτως καὶ οὗτοι ἀνθίστανται τῇ ἀληθείᾳ, ἄνθρωποι κατεφθαρμένοι τὸν νοῦν, ἀδόκιμοι περὶ τὴν πίστιν. **9** ἀλλ᾽ οὐ προκόψουσιν ἐπὶ πλεῖον· ἡ γὰρ ἄνοια αὐτῶν ἔκδηλος ἔσται πᾶσιν, ὡς καὶ ἡ ἐκείνων ἐγένετο.

3:10 Σὺ δὲ παρηκολούθησάς μου τῇ διδασκαλίᾳ, τῇ ἀγωγῇ, τῇ προθέσει, τῇ πίστει, τῇ μακροθυμίᾳ, τῇ ἀγάπῃ, τῇ ὑπομονῇ, **11** τοῖς διωγμοῖς, τοῖς παθήμασιν, οἷά μοι ἐγένετο ἐν ᾽Ἀντιοχείᾳ, ἐν ᾽Ἰκονίῳ, ἐν Λύστροις, οἵους διωγμοὺς ὑπήνεγκα καὶ ἐκ πάντων

them. **12** In fact, everyone who wants to live a godly life in Christ Jesus will be persecuted, **13** while evil men
← ˻δὲ καὶ ← πάντες οἱ θέλοντες → ζῆν εὐσεβῶς → ἐν Χριστῷ Ἰησοῦ → → διωχθήσονται δὲ πονηροὶ ἄνθρωποι
　 cj adv a.npm d.npm pt.pa.npm f.pa adv p.d n.dsm n.dsm v.fpi.3p cj a.npm n.npm
　 1254 2532 4246 3836 2527 2409 2357 1877 5986 2652 1503 1254 4505 476

and impostors will go *from bad to worse,* deceiving and being deceived. **14** But as for you, continue in
καὶ γόητες → προκόψουσιν ἐπὶ ˻τὸ χεῖρον˼ πλανῶντες καὶ → πλανώμενοι δὲ ← Σὺ μένε ἐν
cj n.npm v.fai.3p p.a d.asn a.asn.c pt.pa.npm cj pt.pp.npm cj r.ns.2 v.pam.2s p.d
2779 1200 4621 2093 3836 5937 4414 2779 4414 1254 5148 3531 1877

what you have learned and have become convinced of, because you know those from whom you learned it, **15** and
οἷς → → ἔμαθες καὶ → → ἐπιστώθης ← → εἰδὼς παρὰ τίνων → ἔμαθες καὶ
r.dpn v.aai.2s cj v.api.2s pt.ra.nsm p.g r.gpm v.aai.2s cj
4005 3443 2779 4413 3857 4123 5515 3443 2779

how from infancy you have known the holy Scriptures, which are able to make you wise for salvation
ὅτι ἀπὸ βρέφους → οἶδας τὰ ἱερὰ γράμματα τὰ → δυνάμενά → σε σοφίσαι εἰς σωτηρίαν
cj p.g n.gsn v.rai.2s d.apn a.apn n.apn d.apn pt.pp.apn r.as.2 f.aa p.a n.asf
4022 608 1100 3857 3836 2641 1207 3836 1538 5054 5054 5148 5054 1650 5401

through faith in Christ Jesus. **16** All Scripture is God-breathed and is useful for teaching, rebuking,
διὰ πίστεως τῆς ἐν Χριστῷ Ἰησοῦ πᾶσα γραφὴ θεόπνευστος καὶ ὠφέλιμος πρὸς διδασκαλίαν πρὸς ἐλεγμόν
p.g n.gsf d.gsf p.d n.dsm n.dsm a.nsf n.nsf a.nsf cj a.nsf p.a n.asf p.a n.asm
1328 4411 3836 1877 5986 2652 4246 1210 2535 2779 6068 4639 1436 4639 1791

correcting and training in righteousness, **17** so that the man of God may be thoroughly
πρὸς ἐπανόρθωσιν πρὸς παιδείαν τὴν ἐν δικαιοσύνῃ ἵνα ← ὁ ἄνθρωπος → ˻τοῦ θεοῦ˼ → ᾖ ἄρτιος
p.a n.asf p.a n.asf d.asf p.d n.dsf cj d.nsm n.nsm d.gsm n.gsm v.pas.3s a.nsm
4639 2061 4639 4082 3836 1877 1466 2671 3836 476 3836 2536 1639 787

equipped for every good work. ¶ **4:1** In the presence of God and of Christ Jesus, who will judge
ἐξηρτισμένος πρὸς πᾶν ἀγαθὸν ἔργον ἐνώπιον → ˻τοῦ θεοῦ˼ καὶ → Χριστοῦ Ἰησοῦ τοῦ μέλλοντος κρίνειν
pt.rp.nsm p.a a.asn a.asn n.asn p.g d.gsm n.gsm cj n.gsm n.gsm d.gsm pt.pa.gsm f.pa
1992 4639 4246 19 2240 1967 3836 2536 2779 5986 2652 3836 3516 3212

the living and the dead, and in view of his appearing and his kingdom, I give you this charge:
ζῶντας καὶ νεκρούς καὶ αὐτοῦ ˻τὴν ἐπιφάνειαν˼ καὶ αὐτοῦ ˻τὴν βασιλείαν˼ → → Διαμαρτύρομαι
pt.pa.apm cj a.apm cj r.gsm.3 d.asf n.asf cj r.gsm.3 d.asf n.asf v.pmi.1s
2409 2779 3738 2779 899 3836 2211 2779 899 3836 993 1371

2 Preach the Word; be prepared in season and out of season; correct, rebuke and encourage – with great
κήρυξον τὸν λόγον → ἐπίστηθι → εὐκαίρως → → ἀκαίρως ἔλεγξον ἐπιτίμησον παρακάλεσον ἐν πάσῃ
v.aam.2s d.asm n.asm v.aam.2s adv adv v.aam.2s v.aam.2s v.aam.2s p.d a.dsf
3062 3836 3364 2392 2323 178 1794 2203 4151 1877 4246

patience and careful instruction. **3** For the time will come when men will not put up with sound
μακροθυμία καὶ ← διδαχῇ γὰρ καιρὸς → Ἔσται ὅτε → οὐκ ἀνέξονται ← ← ὑγιαινούσης
n.dsf cj n.dsf cj n.nsm v.fmi.3s cj pl v.fmi.3p pt.pa.gsf
3429 2779 4246 1439 1142 2789 1639 4021 4024 462 5617

doctrine. Instead, *to suit* their own desires, they will gather around them a great number of
˻τῆς διδασκαλίας˼ ἀλλὰ κατὰ τὰς ἰδίας ἐπιθυμίας → → ἐπισωρεύσουσιν ← ἑαυτοῖς
d.gsf n.gsf cj p.a d.apf a.apf n.apf v.fai.3p r.dpm.3
3836 1436 247 2848 3836 2625 2123 2197 1571

teachers to say what their itching ears want to hear. **4** They will turn their ears away from the
διδασκάλους τὴν κνηθόμενοι ἀκοήν καὶ μὲν → ἀποστρέψουσιν τὴν ἀκοὴν ἀπὸ τῆς
n.apm d.asf pt.pp.npm n.asf cj pl v.fai.3p d.asf n.asf p.g d.gsf
1437 3836 3117 198 2779 3525 695 3836 198 695 3836

truth and turn aside to myths. **5** But you, keep your head in all situations, endure hardship,
ἀληθείας δὲ ἐκτραπήσονται ἐπὶ ˻τοὺς μύθους˼ δὲ Σὺ νῆφε ← ἐν πᾶσιν ← κακοπάθησον ←
n.gsf cj v.fpi.3p p.a d.apm n.apm cj r.ns.2 v.pam.2s p.d a.dpn v.aam.2s
237 1254 1762 2093 3836 3680 1254 5148 3768 1877 4246 2802

do the work of an evangelist, discharge all the duties of your ministry. ¶ **6** For I am already being
ποίησον ἔργον → εὐαγγελιστοῦ πληροφόρησον ← ← ← σου ˻τὴν διακονίαν˼ γὰρ Ἐγὼ → ἤδη →
v.aam.2s n.asn n.gsm v.aam.2s r.gs.2 d.asf n.asf cj r.ns.1 adv
4472 2240 2296 4442 5148 3836 1355 1142 1609 5064 2453

με ἐρρύσατο ὁ κύριος. **12** καὶ πάντες δὲ οἱ θέλοντες εὐσεβῶς ζῆν ἐν Χριστῷ Ἰησοῦ διωχθήσονται. **13** πονηροὶ δὲ ἄνθρωποι καὶ γόητες προκόψουσιν ἐπὶ τὸ χεῖρον πλανῶντες καὶ πλανώμενοι. **14** σὺ δὲ μένε ἐν οἷς ἔμαθες καὶ ἐπιστώθης, εἰδὼς παρὰ τίνων ἔμαθες, **15** καὶ ὅτι ἀπὸ βρέφους [τὰ] ἱερὰ γράμματα οἶδας, τὰ δυνάμενά σε σοφίσαι εἰς σωτηρίαν διὰ πίστεως τῆς ἐν Χριστῷ Ἰησοῦ. **16** πᾶσα γραφὴ θεόπνευστος καὶ ὠφέλιμος πρὸς διδασκαλίαν, πρὸς ἐλεγμόν, πρὸς ἐπανόρθωσιν, πρὸς παιδείαν τὴν ἐν δικαιοσύνῃ, **17** ἵνα ἄρτιος ᾖ ὁ τοῦ θεοῦ ἄνθρωπος, πρὸς πᾶν ἔργον ἀγαθὸν ἐξηρτισμένος. **4:1** Διαμαρτύρομαι ἐνώπιον τοῦ θεοῦ καὶ Χριστοῦ Ἰησοῦ τοῦ μέλλοντος κρίνειν ζῶντας καὶ νεκρούς, καὶ τὴν ἐπιφάνειαν αὐτοῦ καὶ τὴν βασιλείαν αὐτοῦ· **2** κήρυξον τὸν λόγον, ἐπίστηθι εὐκαίρως ἀκαίρως, ἔλεγξον, ἐπιτίμησον, παρακάλεσον, ἐν πάσῃ μακροθυμίᾳ καὶ διδαχῇ. **3** ἔσται γὰρ καιρὸς ὅτε τῆς ὑγιαινούσης διδασκαλίας οὐκ ἀνέξονται ἀλλὰ κατὰ τὰς ἰδίας ἐπιθυμίας ἑαυτοῖς ἐπισωρεύσουσιν διδασκάλους κνηθόμενοι τὴν ἀκοὴν **4** καὶ ἀπὸ μὲν τῆς ἀληθείας τὴν ἀκοὴν ἀποστρέψουσιν, ἐπὶ δὲ τοὺς μύθους ἐκτραπήσονται. **5** σὺ δὲ νῆφε ἐν πᾶσιν, κακοπάθησον, ἔργον ποίησον εὐαγγελιστοῦ, τὴν διακονίαν σου πληροφόρησον. ¶ **6** Ἐγὼ γὰρ ἤδη σπένδομαι, καὶ ὁ καιρὸς τῆς

poured out like a drink offering, and the time has come for my departure. **7** I have fought the good fight,
σπένδομαι ← ← ← καὶ ὁ καιρὸς ἐφέστηκεν μου ⌐τῆς ἀναλύσεως⌐ → → ἠγώνισμαι τὸν καλὸν ἀγῶνα
v.ppi.1s   cj d.nsm n.nsm v.rai.3s r.gs.1 d.gsf n.gsf   v.rmi.1s d.asm a.asm n.asm
5064   2779 3836 2789 2392 385 1609 3836 385   76 3836 2819 74

I have finished the race, I have kept the faith. **8** Now there is in store for me the crown of righteousness,
→ → τετέλεκα τὸν δρόμον → → τετήρηκα τὴν πίστιν λοιπὸν → → ἀπόκειται μοι ὁ στέφανος → ⌐τῆς δικαιοσύνης⌐
v.rai.1s d.asm n.asm v.rai.1s d.asf n.asf adv v.pmi.3s r.ds.1 d.nsm n.nsm d.gsf n.gsf
5464 3836 1536 5498 3836 4411 3370 641 1609 3836 5109 3836 1466

which the Lord, the righteous Judge, will award to me on that day — and not only to me, but also to all
ὃν ὁ κύριος ὁ δίκαιος κριτής → ἀποδώσει → μοι ἐν ἐκείνῃ ⌐τῇ ἡμέρᾳ⌐ δὲ οὐ μόνον → ἐμοὶ ἀλλὰ καὶ → πᾶσι
r.asm d.nsm n.nsm d.nsm a.nsm n.nsm v.fai.3s r.ds.1 p.d r.dsf d.dsf n.dsf cj pl adv r.ds.1 cj adv a.dpm
4005 3836 3261 3836 1465 3216 625 1609 1877 1697 3836 2465 1254 4024 3667 1609 247 2779 4246

who have longed for his appearing.
τοῖς → ἠγαπηκόσι ← αὐτοῦ ⌐τὴν ἐπιφάνειαν⌐
d.dpm pt.ra.dpm r.gsm.3 d.asf n.asf
3836 26 899 3836 2211

Personal Remarks

4:9 Do your best to come to me quickly, **10** for Demas, because he loved this world, has deserted me
Σπούδασον → ἐλθεῖν πρός με ταχέως γὰρ Δημᾶς → → ἀγαπήσας νῦν ⌐τὸν αἰῶνα⌐ ἐγκατέλιπεν με
v.aam.2s f.aa p.a r.as.1 adv cj n.nsm pt.aa.nsm adv d.asm n.asm v.aai.3s r.as.1
5079 2262 4639 1609 5441 1142 1318 26 3814 3836 172 1593 1609

and has gone to Thessalonica. Crescens has gone to Galatia, and Titus to Dalmatia. **11** Only Luke is with me.
καὶ → ἐπορεύθη εἰς Θεσσαλονίκην Κρήσκης → εἰς Γαλατίαν Τίτος εἰς Δαλματίαν μόνος Λουκᾶς ἐστιν μετ' ἐμοῦ
cj v.api.3s p.a n.asf n.nsm p.a n.asf n.nsm p.a n.asf a.nsm n.nsm v.pai.3s p.g r.gs.1
2779 4513 1650 2553 3206 1650 1130 5519 1650 1237 3668 3371 1639 3552 1609

Get Mark and bring him with you, because he is helpful to me in my ministry. **12** I sent Tychicus
ἀναλαβὼν Μᾶρκον ἄγε μετὰ σεαυτοῦ γὰρ → ἐστιν εὔχρηστος → μοι εἰς διακονίαν δὲ → ἀπέστειλα Τύχικον
pt.aa.nsm n.asm v.pam.2s p.g r.gsm.2 cj v.pai.3s a.nsm r.ds.1 p.a n.asf cj v.aai.1s n.asm
377 3453 72 3552 4932 1142 1639 2378 1609 1650 1355 1254 690 5608

to Ephesus. **13** When you come, bring the cloak that I left with Carpus at Troas, and my scrolls, especially
εἰς Ἔφεσον → → ἐρχόμενος φέρε τὸν φαιλόνην ὃν → ἀπέλιπον παρὰ Κάρπῳ ἐν Τρῳάδι καὶ τὰ βιβλία μάλιστα
p.a n.asf pt.pm.nsm v.pam.2s d.asm n.asm r.asm v.aai.1s p.d n.dsm p.d n.dsf cj d.apn n.apn adv.s
1650 2387 2262 5770 3836 5742 4005 657 4123 2842 1877 5590 2779 3836 1046 3436

the parchments. ¶ **14** Alexander the metalworker did me a great deal of harm. The Lord will repay him
τὰς μεμβράνας Ἀλέξανδρος ὁ χαλκεὺς ἐνεδείξατο μοι πολλά κακὰ ὁ κύριος → ἀποδώσει αὐτῷ
d.apf n.apf n.nsm d.nsm n.nsm v.ami.3s r.ds.1 a.apn a.apn d.nsm n.nsm v.fai.3s r.dsm.3
3836 3521 235 3836 5906 1892 1609 4498 2805 3836 3261 625 899

for what he has done. **15** You too should be on your guard against him, because he strongly opposed our
κατὰ → αὐτοῦ ⌐τὰ ἔργα⌐ σὺ καὶ → → → → φυλάσσου ← ὃν γὰρ → λίαν ἀντέστη ἡμετέροις
p.a r.gsm.3 d.apn n.apn r.ns.2 adv v.pmm.2s r.asm cj adv v.aai.3s r.dpm.1
2848 2240 899 3836 2240 5148 2779 5875 4005 1142 468 3336 468 2466

message. ¶ **16** At my first defense, no one came to my support, but everyone deserted me. May
⌐τοῖς λόγοις⌐ Ἐν μου πρώτῃ ⌐τῇ ἀπολογίᾳ⌐ οὐδείς ← παρεγένετο → μοι ἀλλὰ πάντες ἐγκατέλιπον με
d.dpm n.dpm p.d r.gs.1 a.dsf d.dsf n.dsf a.nsm v.ami.3s r.ds.1 cj a.npm v.aai.3p r.as.1
3836 3364 1877 1609 4755 3836 665 4029 4134 1609 247 4246 1593 1609 3357

it not be held against them. **17** But the Lord stood at my side and gave me strength, so that through me the
→ μὴ → λογισθείη αὐτοῖς δὲ ὁ κύριος παρέστη → μοι καὶ με ἐνεδυνάμωσεν ἵνα ← δι' ἐμοῦ τὸ
pl v.apo.3s r.dpm.3 cj d.nsm n.nsm v.aai.3s r.ds.1 cj r.as.1 v.aai.3s cj p.g r.gs.1 d.nsn
3357 3590 3357 899 1254 3836 3261 4225 1609 2779 1609 1904 2671 1328 1609 3836

message might be fully proclaimed and all the Gentiles might hear it. And I was delivered from the lion's
κήρυγμα → → → πληροφορηθῇ καὶ πάντα τὰ ἔθνη → ἀκούσωσιν καὶ → ἐρρύσθην ἐκ λέοντος
n.nsn v.aps.3s cj a.npn d.npn n.npn v.aas.3p cj v.api.1s p.g n.gsm
3060 4442 2779 4246 3836 1620 201 2779 4861 1666 3329

mouth. **18** The Lord will rescue me from every evil attack and will bring me safely to his heavenly
στόματος ὁ κύριος → ῥύσεται με ἀπὸ παντὸς πονηροῦ ἔργου καὶ → σώσει εἰς αὐτοῦ ⌐τὴν ἐπουράνιον⌐
n.gsn d.nsm n.nsm v.fmi.3s r.as.1 p.g a.gsn a.gsn n.gsn cj v.fai.3s p.a r.gsm.3 d.asf a.asf
5125 3836 3261 4861 1609 608 4246 4505 2240 2779 5392 1650 899 3836 2230

ἀναλύσεώς μου ἐφέστηκεν. **7** τὸν καλὸν ἀγῶνα ἠγώνισμαι, τὸν δρόμον τετέλεκα, τὴν πίστιν τετήρηκα· **8** λοιπὸν ἀπόκειταί μοι ὁ τῆς δικαιοσύνης στέφανος, ὃν ἀποδώσει μοι ὁ κύριος ἐν ἐκείνῃ τῇ ἡμέρᾳ, ὁ δίκαιος κριτής, οὐ μόνον δὲ ἐμοὶ ἀλλὰ καὶ πᾶσι τοῖς ἠγαπηκόσι τὴν ἐπιφάνειαν αὐτοῦ. **4:9** Σπούδασον ἐλθεῖν πρός με ταχέως· **10** Δημᾶς γάρ με ἐγκατέλιπεν ἀγαπήσας τὸν νῦν αἰῶνα καὶ ἐπορεύθη εἰς Θεσσαλονίκην, Κρήσκης εἰς Γαλατίαν, Τίτος εἰς Δαλματίαν· **11** Λουκᾶς ἐστιν μόνος μετ' ἐμοῦ. Μᾶρκον ἀναλαβὼν ἄγε μετὰ σεαυτοῦ, ἔστιν γάρ μοι εὔχρηστος εἰς διακονίαν. **12** Τυχικὸν δὲ ἀπέστειλα εἰς Ἔφεσον. **13** τὸν φαιλόνην ὃν ἀπέλιπον ἐν Τρῳάδι παρὰ Κάρπῳ ἐρχόμενος φέρε, καὶ τὰ βιβλία μάλιστα τὰς μεμβράνας. ¶ **14** Ἀλέξανδρος ὁ χαλκεὺς πολλά μοι κακὰ ἐνεδείξατο· ἀποδώσει αὐτῷ ὁ κύριος κατὰ τὰ ἔργα αὐτοῦ· **15** ὃν καὶ σὺ φυλάσσου, λίαν γὰρ ἀντέστη τοῖς ἡμετέροις λόγοις. ¶ **16** Ἐν τῇ πρώτῃ μου ἀπολογίᾳ οὐδείς μοι παρεγένετο, ἀλλὰ πάντες με ἐγκατέλιπον· μὴ αὐτοῖς λογισθείη· **17** ὁ δὲ κύριός μοι παρέστη καὶ ἐνεδυνάμωσέν με, ἵνα δι' ἐμοῦ τὸ κήρυγμα πληροφορηθῇ καὶ ἀκούσωσιν πάντα τὰ ἔθνη, καὶ ἐρρύσθην ἐκ στόματος λέοντος. **18** ῥύσεταί με ὁ κύριος ἀπὸ παντὸς ἔργου πονηροῦ καὶ σώσει εἰς τὴν βασιλείαν αὐτοῦ τὴν ἐπουράνιον· ᾧ ἡ δόξα εἰς τοὺς αἰῶνας

kingdom.   To him be glory   *for ever*   and *ever.*   Amen.
⌐τὴν βασιλείαν⌐ →   ᾧ   ⌐ἡ δόξα⌐ εἰς ⌐τοὺς αἰῶνας⌐   τῶν αἰώνων⌐ ἀμήν
d.asf n.asf   r.dsm   d.nsf n.nsf p.a d.apm n.apm   d.gpm n.gpm   pl
3836 993   4005   3836 1518 1650 3836 172   3836 172   297

Final Greetings

4:19 Greet   Priscilla and Aquila and the household of Onesiphorus. **20** Erastus stayed in Corinth, and I left
Ἄσπασαι   Πρίσκαν καὶ Ἀκύλαν καὶ τὸν οἶκον   → Ὀνησιφόρου   Ἔραστος ἔμεινεν ἐν Κορίνθῳ δὲ → ἀπέλιπον
v.amm.2s   n.asf   cj   n.asm   cj d.asm n.asm   n.gsm   n.nsm   v.aai.3s p.d n.dsf   cj   v.aai.1s
832   4571   2779 217   2779 3836 3875   3947   2235   3531   1877 3172   1254 657

Trophimus sick   in Miletus. **21** Do your best to get here before winter. Eubulus greets   you, and so do
Τρόφιμον ἀσθενοῦντα ἐν Μιλήτῳ   → → Σπούδασον ἐλθεῖν ← πρὸ χειμῶνος Εὔβουλος Ἀσπάζεται σε καὶ
n.asm   pt.pa.asm p.d n.dsf   v.aam.2s   f.aa   p.g   n.gsm   n.nsm   v.pmi.3s r.as.2 cj
5576   820   1877 3626   5079   2262   4574 5930   2300   832   5148   2779

Pudens,   Linus,   Claudia and all   the brothers. ¶ **22** The Lord be with your spirit.   Grace   be
Πούδης καὶ Λίνος καὶ Κλαυδία καὶ πάντες οἱ ἀδελφοὶ   Ὁ κύριος μετὰ σου ⌐τοῦ πνεύματός⌐ ⌐ἡ χάρις⌐
n.nsm   cj   n.nsm cj n.nsf   cj a.npm d.npm n.npm   d.nsm n.nsm p.g r.gs.2 d.gsn n.gsn   d.nsf n.nsf
4545   2779 3352   2779 3086   2779 4246   3836 81   3836 3261   3552 5148   3836 4460   3836 5921

with you.
μεθ' ὑμῶν
p.g   r.gp.2
3552 7007

τῶν αἰώνων, ἀμήν.
4:19 Ἄσπασαι Πρίσκαν καὶ Ἀκύλαν καὶ τὸν Ὀνησιφόρου οἶκον. **20** Ἔραστος ἔμεινεν ἐν Κορίνθῳ, Τρόφιμον δὲ ἀπέλιπον ἐν Μιλήτῳ ἀσθενοῦντα. **21** Σπούδασον πρὸ χειμῶνος ἐλθεῖν. Ἀσπάζεταί σε Εὔβουλος καὶ Πούδης καὶ Λίνος καὶ Κλαυδία καὶ οἱ ἀδελφοὶ πάντες. ¶ **22** Ὁ κύριος μετὰ τοῦ πνεύματός σου. ἡ χάρις μεθ' ὑμῶν.

Titus

1:1 Paul, a servant of God and an apostle of Jesus Christ for the faith of God's elect and the knowledge
Παῦλος δοῦλος → θεοῦ δὲ ἀπόστολος → Ἰησοῦ Χριστοῦ κατὰ πίστιν → θεοῦ ἐκλεκτῶν καὶ ἐπίγνωσιν
n.nsm n.nsm n.gsm cj n.nsm n.gsm n.gsm n.asf n.gsm a.gpm cj n.asf
4263 1529 2536 1254 693 2652 5986 2848 4411 1723 2536 1723 2779 2106

of the truth that leads to godliness — **2** a faith and knowledge resting on the hope of eternal life, which God,
→ ἀληθείας τῆς κατ᾽ ← εὐσέβειαν ἐπ᾽ ἐλπίδι → αἰωνίου ζωῆς ἣν ὁ θεός,
n.gsf d.gsf p.a n.asf p.d n.dsf a.gsf n.gsf r.asf d.nsm n.nsm
237 3836 2848 2354 2093 1828 2437 173 2437 4005 3836 2536

who does not lie, promised before the beginning of time, **3** and at his appointed season he brought his
→ → → ἀψευδὴς ἐπηγγείλατο πρὸ αἰωνίων χρόνων δὲ → ἰδίοις → καιροῖς → → αὐτοῦ
a.nsm v.ami.3s p.g a.gpm n.gpm cj a.dpm n.dpm r.gsm.3
950 2040 4574 173 5989 1254 2789 2625 2789 5746 5746 899

word to light through the preaching entrusted to me by the command of God our Savior, ¶
ˌτὸν λόγονˌ → ἐφανέρωσεν ἐν κηρύγματι ὃ ἐπιστεύθην ἐγὼ κατ᾽ ἐπιταγὴν → ˌτοῦ θεοῦˌ ἡμῶν σωτῆρος
d.asm n.asm v.aai.3s p.d n.dsn r.asn v.api.1s r.ns.1 p.a n.asf d.gsm n.gsm r.gp.1 n.gsm
3836 3364 5746 1877 3060 4005 4409 1609 2848 2198 3836 2536 7005 5400

4 To Titus, my true son in our common faith: ¶ Grace and peace from God the Father and Christ Jesus
→ Τίτῳ γνησίῳ τέκνῳ κατὰ κοινὴν πίστιν χάρις καὶ εἰρήνη ἀπὸ θεοῦ πατρὸς καὶ Χριστοῦ Ἰησοῦ
n.dsm a.dsn n.dsn p.a a.asf n.asf n.nsf cj n.nsf p.g n.gsm n.gsm cj n.gsm n.gsm
5519 1188 5451 2848 3123 4411 5921 2779 1645 608 2536 4252 2779 5986 2652

our Savior.
ἡμῶν ˌτοῦ σωτῆροςˌ
r.gp.1 d.gsm n.gsm
7005 3836 5400

Titus' Task on Crete

1:5 The reason I left you in Crete was that you might straighten out what was left unfinished and
Τούτου χάριν → ἀπέλιπον σε ἐν Κρήτῃ ἵνα → → ἐπιδιορθώσῃ ← τὰ → → λείποντα καὶ
r.gsn p.g v.aai.1s r.as.2 p.d n.dsf cj v.ams.2s d.apn pt.pa.apn cj
4047 5920 657 5148 1877 3207 2671 2114 3836 3309 2779

appoint elders in every town, as I directed you. **6** An elder must be blameless, the husband of but
καταστήσῃς πρεσβυτέρους → κατὰ πόλιν ὡς ἐγὼ διεταξάμην σοι εἴ τις → ἐστιν ἀνέγκλητος ἀνήρ
v.aas.2s a.apm p.a n.asf cj r.ns.1 v.ami.1s r.ds.2 cj r.nsm v.pai.3s a.nsm n.nsm
2770 4565 2848 4484 6055 1609 1411 5148 1623 5516 1639 441 467

one wife, a man whose children believe and are not open to the charge of being wild and
μιᾶς γυναικὸς τέκνα ἔχων πιστά, μὴ → ἐν κατηγορίᾳ → ἀσωτίας ἢ
a.gsf n.gsf n.apn pt.pa.nsm a.apn pl p.d n.dsf a.gsf cj
1651 1222 5451 2400 4412 3590 1877 2990 861 2445

disobedient. **7** Since an overseer is entrusted with God's work, he must be blameless — not
ἀνυπότακτα. γὰρ ˌτὸν ἐπίσκοπονˌ ὡς → → θεοῦ οἰκονόμον → δεῖ εἶναι ἀνέγκλητον μὴ
a.apn cj d.asm n.asm pl n.gsm n.asm v.pai.3s f.pa a.asm pl
538 1142 3836 2176 6055 3874 3874 2536 3874 1256 1639 441 3590

overbearing, not quick-tempered, not given to drunkenness, not violent, not pursuing dishonest gain. **8** Rather he
αὐθάδη μὴ ὀργίλον μὴ → πάροινον μὴ πλήκτην μὴ → αἰσχροκερδῆ ἀλλὰ
a.asm pl pl n.asm pl n.asm pl a.asm cj
881 3590 3975 3590 4232 3590 4438 3590 153 247

must be hospitable, one who loves what is good, who is self-controlled, upright, holy and disciplined. **9** He must
φιλόξενον → φιλάγαθον → σώφρονα δίκαιον ὅσιον ἐγκρατῆ
a.asm a.asm a.asm a.asm a.asm a.asm
5811 5787 5409 1465 4008 1604

hold firmly to the trustworthy message as it has been taught, so that he can encourage
→ ἀντεχόμενον → τοῦ πιστοῦ λόγου κατὰ ← ← ˌτὴν διδαχὴνˌ ἵνα → ˌδυνατὸς ᾖ καὶ παρακαλεῖν
pt.pm.asm d.gsm a.gsm n.gsm p.a d.asf n.asf cj a.nsm v.pas.3s cj f.pa
504 3836 4412 3364 2848 2671 3836 1439 2671 1639 1543 1639 2779 4151

1:1 Παῦλος δοῦλος θεοῦ, ἀπόστολος δὲ Ἰησοῦ Χριστοῦ κατὰ πίστιν ἐκλεκτῶν θεοῦ καὶ ἐπίγνωσιν ἀληθείας τῆς κατ᾽ εὐσέβειαν **2** ἐπ᾽ ἐλπίδι ζωῆς αἰωνίου, ἣν ἐπηγγείλατο ὁ ἀψευδὴς θεὸς πρὸ χρόνων αἰωνίων, **3** ἐφανέρωσεν δὲ καιροῖς ἰδίοις τὸν λόγον αὐτοῦ ἐν κηρύγματι, ὃ ἐπιστεύθην ἐγὼ κατ᾽ ἐπιταγὴν τοῦ σωτῆρος ἡμῶν θεοῦ, ¶ **4** Τίτῳ γνησίῳ τέκνῳ κατὰ κοινὴν πίστιν, ¶ χάρις καὶ εἰρήνη ἀπὸ θεοῦ πατρὸς καὶ Χριστοῦ Ἰησοῦ τοῦ σωτῆρος ἡμῶν.

1:5 Τούτου χάριν ἀπέλιπόν σε ἐν Κρήτῃ, ἵνα τὰ λείποντα ἐπιδιορθώσῃ καὶ καταστήσῃς κατὰ πόλιν πρεσβυτέρους, ὡς ἐγώ σοι διεταξάμην, **6** εἴ τίς ἐστιν ἀνέγκλητος, μιᾶς γυναικὸς ἀνήρ, τέκνα ἔχων πιστά, μὴ ἐν κατηγορίᾳ ἀσωτίας ἢ ἀνυπότακτα. **7** δεῖ γὰρ τὸν ἐπίσκοπον ἀνέγκλητον εἶναι ὡς θεοῦ οἰκονόμον, μὴ αὐθάδη, μὴ ὀργίλον, μὴ πάροινον, μὴ πλήκτην, μὴ αἰσχροκερδῆ, **8** ἀλλὰ φιλόξενον φιλάγαθον σώφρονα δίκαιον ὅσιον ἐγκρατῆ, **9** ἀντεχόμενον τοῦ κατὰ τὴν διδαχὴν πιστοῦ λόγου, ἵνα δυνατὸς

others by sound　　　doctrine　　　and refute those who oppose　　it. ¶　　[10] For there are　many
ἐν ‚τῇ ὑγιαινούσῃ ‚τῇ διδασκαλίᾳ καὶ ἐλέγχειν τοὺς ἀντιλέγοντας γὰρ → Εἰσὶν πολλοὶ [καὶ]
p.d d.dsf pt.pa.dsf d.dsf n.dsf cj f.pa d.apm pt.pa.apm cj v.pai.3p a.npm adv
1877 3836 5617 3836 1436 2779 1794 3836 515 1142 1639 4498 2779

rebellious people, mere talkers　and deceivers, especially those of the circumcision group. [11] They must be
ἀνυπότακτοι ←　　→ ματαιολόγοι καὶ φρεναπάται μάλιστα οἱ ἐκ τῆς περιτομῆς οὓς δεῖ →
a.npm n.npm cj n.npm adv.s d.npm p.g d.gsf n.gsf r.apm v.pai.3s
538 3468 2779 5855 3436 3836 1666 3836 4364 4005 1256

silenced, because they are ruining　whole households by teaching　things they ought not to teach – and that
ἐπιστομίζειν οἵτινες → ἀνατρέπουσιν ὅλους οἴκους → διδάσκοντες ἃ → δεῖ μὴ
f.pa r.npm v.pai.3p a.apm n.apm pt.pa.npm r.apn v.pai.3s pl
2187 4015 426 3910 3875 1438 4005 1256 3590

for　the sake of dishonest gain. [12] Even one of　their own prophets has said, "Cretans are always liars, evil
χάριν ← ← ← αἰσχροῦ κέρδους τις ἐξ αὐτῶν αὐτῶν ἴδιος προφήτης → εἶπεν Κρῆτες → ἀεὶ ψεῦσται κακὰ
p.g a.gsn n.gsn r.nsm p.g r.gpm.3 r.gpm.3 a.nsm n.nsm v.aai.3s n.npm adv n.npm a.npn
5920 156 3046 5516 1666 899 899 2625 4737 3306 3205 6026 107 6026 2805

brutes, lazy gluttons." [13] This testimony　is　true. Therefore,　rebuke them sharply, so that they will be
θηρία ἀργαί γαστέρες αὕτη ἡ μαρτυρία ἐστὶν ἀληθής δι' ἣν αἰτίαν ἔλεγχε αὐτοὺς ἀποτόμως ἵνα ←
n.npn n.npf n.npf r.nsf d.nsf n.nsf v.pai.3s a.nsf p.a r.asf n.asf v.pam.2s r.apm.3 adv cj
2563 734 1143 4047 3836 3456 1639 239 1328 4005 162 1794 899 705 2671

sound　in the faith [14] and will pay no attention to Jewish　myths or to the commands of those　who
ὑγιαίνωσιν ἐν τῇ πίστει → → μὴ προσέχοντες → Ἰουδαϊκοῖς μύθοις καὶ → ἐντολαῖς → ἀνθρώπων
v.pas.3p p.d d.dsf n.dsf pl pt.pa.npm a.dpm n.dpm cj n.dpf n.gpm
5617 1877 3836 4411 4668 4668 3590 4668 2679 3680 2779 1953 476

reject　the truth. [15] To the pure,　all　things are pure,　but to those who are corrupted　and do not
ἀποστρεφομένων τὴν ἀλήθειαν → τοῖς καθαροῖς πάντα ← καθαρὰ δὲ → τοῖς ← → μεμιαμμένοις καὶ →
pt.pm.gpm d.asf n.asf d.dpm a.dpm a.npn a.npn cj d.dpm pt.rp.dpm cj
695 3836 237 3836 2754 4246 2754 1254 3836 3620 2779

believe, nothing is pure. In　fact, both their minds　and consciences　are corrupted. [16] They claim　to know
ἀπίστοις οὐδὲν καθαρόν ἀλλὰ ← καὶ αὐτῶν ὁ νοῦς καὶ ἡ συνείδησις → μεμίανται ὁμολογοῦσιν → εἰδέναι
a.dpm a.nsn a.nsn cj cj r.gpm.3 d.nsm n.nsm cj d.nsf n.nsf v.rpi.3s v.pai.3p f.ra
603 4029 2754 247 2779 899 3836 3808 2779 3836 5287 3620 3933 3857

God, but by their actions they deny　him. They are　detestable,　disobedient and unfit　for　doing anything
θεὸν δὲ → τοῖς ἔργοις → ἀρνοῦνται → ὄντες βδελυκτοὶ καὶ ἀπειθεῖς καὶ ἀδόκιμοι πρὸς ἔργον πᾶν
n.asm cj d.dpn n.dpn v.pmi.3p pt.pa.npm a.npm cj a.npm cj a.npm p.a n.asn a.asn
2536 1254 3836 2240 766 1639 1008 2779 579 2779 99 4639 2240 4246

good.
ἀγαθόν
a.asn
19

What Must Be Taught to Various Groups

[2:1] You must teach what is in accord with sound　　doctrine. [2] Teach the older　　men to be
δὲ Σὺ → λάλει ἃ → → πρέπει ← ὑγιαινούσῃ ‚τῇ διδασκαλίᾳ Πρεσβύτας ← → εἶναι
cj r.ns.2 v.pam.2s r.npn v.pai.3s pt.pa.dsf d.dsf n.dsf n.apm f.pa
1254 5148 3281 4005 4560 5617 3836 1436 4566 1639

temperate, worthy of respect, self-controlled, and sound　in faith,　in love　and in endurance. [3] Likewise,
νηφαλίους → → σεμνούς σώφρονας ὑγιαίνοντας → ‚τῇ πίστει → ‚τῇ ἀγάπῃ → ‚τῇ ὑπομονῇ ὡσαύτως
a.apm a.apm a.apm pt.pa.apm d.dsf n.dsf d.dsf n.dsf d.dsf n.dsf adv
3767 4948 5409 5617 3836 4411 3836 27 3836 5705 6058

teach the older　women to be reverent in the way they live,　not to be slanderers or　addicted　to
Πρεσβύτιδας ← → ἱεροπρεπεῖς ἐν → → καταστήματι μὴ → διαβόλους μὴ δεδουλωμένας →
n.apf a.apf p.d n.dsn pl a.apf cj pt.rp.apf
4567 2640 1877 2949 3590 1333 3590 1530

much wine, but to teach　　what is good. [4] Then they can train　　the younger women to　love
πολλῷ οἴνῳ καλοδιδασκάλους ← ← ἵνα → → σωφρονίζωσιν τὰς νέας ← εἶναι φιλάνδρους
a.dsm n.dsm a.apf cj v.pas.3p d.apf a.apf f.pa a.apf
4498 3885 2815 2671 5405 3836 3742 1639 5791

ᾗ καὶ παρακαλεῖν ἐν τῇ διδασκαλίᾳ τῇ ὑγιαινούσῃ καὶ τοὺς ἀντιλέγοντας ἐλέγχειν. ¶ [10] Εἰσὶν γὰρ πολλοὶ [καὶ] ἀνυπότακτοι, ματαιολόγοι καὶ φρεναπάται, μάλιστα οἱ ἐκ τῆς περιτομῆς, [11] οὓς δεῖ ἐπιστομίζειν, οἵτινες ὅλους οἴκους ἀνατρέπουσιν διδάσκοντες ἃ μὴ δεῖ αἰσχροῦ κέρδους χάριν. [12] εἶπέν τις ἐξ αὐτῶν ἴδιος αὐτῶν προφήτης, Κρῆτες ἀεὶ ψεῦσται, κακὰ θηρία, γαστέρες ἀργαί. [13] ἡ μαρτυρία αὕτη ἐστὶν ἀληθής. δι' ἣν αἰτίαν ἔλεγχε αὐτοὺς ἀποτόμως, ἵνα ὑγιαίνωσιν ἐν τῇ πίστει, [14] μὴ προσέχοντες Ἰουδαϊκοῖς μύθοις καὶ ἐντολαῖς ἀνθρώπων ἀποστρεφομένων τὴν ἀλήθειαν. [15] πάντα καθαρὰ τοῖς καθαροῖς· τοῖς δὲ μεμιαμμένοις καὶ ἀπίστοις οὐδὲν καθαρόν, ἀλλὰ μεμίανται αὐτῶν καὶ ὁ νοῦς καὶ ἡ συνείδησις. [16] θεὸν ὁμολογοῦσιν εἰδέναι, τοῖς δὲ ἔργοις ἀρνοῦνται, βδελυκτοὶ ὄντες καὶ ἀπειθεῖς καὶ πρὸς πᾶν ἔργον ἀγαθὸν ἀδόκιμοι.

[2:1] Σὺ δὲ λάλει ἃ πρέπει τῇ ὑγιαινούσῃ διδασκαλίᾳ. [2] πρεσβύτας νηφαλίους εἶναι, σεμνούς, σώφρονας, ὑγιαίνοντας τῇ πίστει, τῇ ἀγάπῃ, τῇ ὑπομονῇ· [3] πρεσβύτιδας ὡσαύτως ἐν καταστήματι ἱεροπρεπεῖς, μὴ διαβόλους μηδὲ οἴνῳ πολλῷ δεδουλωμένας,

their husbands and children, **5** to be self-controlled and pure, to be busy at home,   to be kind, and to be
←   φιλοτέκνους   σώφρονας   ἁγνὰς →   → οἰκουργοὺς   ἀγαθάς
                 a.apf   a.apf   a.apf   a.apf   a.apf
                 5817   5409   54   3877   19

subject   to their husbands,   so that no one will malign   the word of God.   ¶   **6** Similarly,
ὑποτασσομένας → ἰδίοις ⌐τοῖς ἀνδράσιν⌐ ἵνα   μὴ   →   βλασφημῆται ὁ λόγος → ⌐τοῦ θεοῦ⌐   ὡσαύτως
pt.pp.apf   a.dpm d.dpm n.dpm   cj   pl   v.pps.3s d.nsm n.nsm d.gsm n.gsm   adv
5718   467   2625 3836   467   2671   3590   1059   3836 3364   3836 2536   6058

encourage the young men to be self-controlled. **7** In everything   set   them an example by doing
παρακάλει Τοὺς νεωτέρους ←   → σωφρονεῖν   περὶ πάντα   σεαυτὸν παρεχόμενος   τύπον   ἔργων
v.pam.2s d.apm a.apm.c   f.pa   p.a a.apn   r.asm.2 pt.pm.nsm   n.asm   n.gpn
4151   3836 3742   5404   4309 4246   4932   4218   5596   2240

what is good. In your teaching   show integrity, seriousness **8** and soundness of speech that cannot be condemned,
καλῶν ἐν τῇ διδασκαλίᾳ   ἀφθορίαν σεμνότητα   ὑγιῆ   λόγον   →   ἀκατάγνωστον
a.gpn p.d d.dsf n.dsf   n.asf   n.asf   a.asm   n.asm   a.asm
2819 1877 3836 1436   917   4949   5618   3364   183

so that those who oppose   you may be ashamed because they have nothing bad   to say about us.   ¶
ἵνα ←   ὁ ἐξ ἐναντίας⌐   →   ἐντραπῇ   →   ἔχων μηδὲν φαῦλον   λέγειν περὶ ἡμῶν
cj   d.nsm p.g a.gsf   v.aps.3s   pt.pa.nsm a.asn a.asn   f.pa   p.g   r.gp.1
2671   3836 1666 1885   1956   2400 3594   5765   3306   4309 7005

9 Teach slaves to be subject to their masters in everything, to try to please   them, not to talk   back
Δούλους → → ὑποτάσσεσθαι ἰδίοις δεσπόταις ἐν πᾶσιν   → εἶναι εὐαρέστους   μὴ → ἀντιλέγοντας ←
n.apm   f.pp   a.dpm n.dpm   p.d a.dpn   f.pa   a.apm   pl   pt.pa.apm
1529   5718   2625   1305   1877 4246   1639   2298   3590 515

to them, **10** and not to steal   from them, but to show   that they can be fully   trusted, so that
μὴ → νοσφιζομένους   ἀλλὰ → ἐνδεικνυμένους ←   ⌐πᾶσαν ἀγαθήν⌐ πίστιν ἵνα
pl   pt.pm.apm   cj   pt.pm.apm   a.asf a.asf   n.asf   cj
3590 3802   247   1892   4246   19   4411   2671

in every way they will make the teaching   about God our Savior   attractive.   ¶   **11** For the grace of
ἐν πᾶσιν → → → τὴν διδασκαλίαν τὴν →   θεοῦ ἡμῶν ⌐τοῦ σωτῆρος⌐ κοσμῶσιν   γὰρ ἡ χάρις →
p.d a.dpn   d.asf n.asf   d.asf   n.gsm r.gp.1 d.gsm n.gsm v.pas.3p   cj   d.nsf n.nsf
1877 4246 3175 3175 3175 3836 1436 3836   2536 7005 3836 5400 3175   1142 3836 5921

God   that brings salvation has appeared to all   men. **12** It teaches us   to say   "No" to ungodliness
⌐τοῦ θεοῦ⌐ → → σωτήριος → Ἐπεφάνη → πᾶσιν ἀνθρώποις → παιδεύουσα ἡμᾶς ἵνα ἀρνησάμενοι ← ← ⌐τὴν ἀσέβειαν⌐
d.gsm n.gsm   a.nsf   v.api.3s   a.dpm n.dpm   pt.pa.nsf r.ap.1 cj r.am.npm   d.asf n.asf
3836 2536   5402   2210   4246 476   4084   7005 2671 766   3836 813

and worldly passions,   and to live   self-controlled,   upright and godly lives in this present age, **13** while we
καὶ κοσμικὰς ⌐τὰς ἐπιθυμίας⌐ → ζήσωμεν σωφρόνως   καὶ δικαίως καὶ εὐσεβῶς ← ἐν τῷ νῦν αἰῶνι
cj a.apf   d.apf n.apf   v.aas.1p adv   cj adv   cj adv   p.d d.dsm adv n.dsm
2779 3176   3836 2123   2409   5407   2779 1469   2779 2357   1877 3836 3814 172

wait   for the blessed hope – the glorious appearing of our great   God   and Savior, Jesus Christ,
προσδεχόμενοι ← τὴν μακαρίαν ἐλπίδα καὶ ⌐τῆς δόξης⌐ ἐπιφάνειαν ┐ ἡμῶν μεγάλου ⌐τοῦ θεοῦ⌐ καὶ σωτῆρος Ἰησοῦ Χριστοῦ
pt.pm.npm   d.asf a.asf   n.asf cj   d.gsf n.gsf n.asf   r.gp.1 a.gsm d.gsm n.gsm cj n.gsm   n.gsm n.gsm
4657   3836 3421   1828   2779 3836 1518   2211   2536 3489   3836 2536   2779 5400   2652 5986

14 who gave himself for us to redeem   us from all wickedness and to purify for himself a people that are
ὃς ἔδωκεν ἑαυτὸν ὑπὲρ ἡμῶν ἵνα λυτρώσηται ἡμᾶς ἀπὸ πάσης ἀνομίας καὶ καθαρίσῃ → ἑαυτῷ λαὸν
r.nsm v.aai.3s r.asm.3 p.g r.gp.1 cj v.ams.3s r.ap.1 p.g a.gsf n.gsf cj   v.aas.3s   r.dsm.3 n.asm
4005 1443   1571   5642 7005 2671 3390   7005 608 4246 490   2779 2751   1571   3295

his   very own, eager to do   what is good. ¶   **15** These, then, are the things you should teach.
περιούσιον ←   ζηλωτὴν ἔργων   καλῶν   Ταῦτα   λάλει καὶ
a.asm   n.asm   n.gpn   a.gpn   r.apn   v.pam.2s cj
4342   2421   2240   2819   4047   3281 2779

Encourage and rebuke with all authority. Do not let anyone despise   you.
παρακάλει καὶ ἔλεγχε μετὰ πάσης ἐπιταγῆς → μηδείς → ←   περιφρονείτω σου
v.pam.2s cj   v.pam.2s p.g a.gsf n.gsf   a.nsm   v.pam.3s r.gs.2
4151   2779 1794   3552 4246 2198   4368 3594 4368 3594 4368   5148

καλοδιδασκάλους, **4** ἵνα σωφρονίζωσιν τὰς νέας φιλάνδρους εἶναι, φιλοτέκνους **5** σώφρονας ἁγνὰς οἰκουργοὺς ἀγαθάς,
ὑποτασσομένας τοῖς ἰδίοις ἀνδράσιν, ἵνα μὴ ὁ λόγος τοῦ θεοῦ βλασφημῆται. ¶ **6** τοὺς νεωτέρους ὡσαύτως παρακάλει σωφρονεῖν
7 περὶ πάντα, σεαυτὸν παρεχόμενος τύπον καλῶν ἔργων, ἐν τῇ διδασκαλίᾳ ἀφθορίαν, σεμνότητα, **8** λόγον ὑγιῆ ἀκατάγνωστον,
ἵνα ὁ ἐξ ἐναντίας ἐντραπῇ μηδὲν ἔχων λέγειν περὶ ἡμῶν φαῦλον. ¶ **9** δούλους ἰδίοις δεσπόταις ὑποτάσσεσθαι ἐν πᾶσιν,
εὐαρέστους εἶναι, μὴ ἀντιλέγοντας, **10** μὴ νοσφιζομένους, ἀλλὰ πᾶσαν πίστιν ἐνδεικνυμένους ἀγαθήν, ἵνα τὴν διδασκαλίαν τὴν
τοῦ σωτῆρος ἡμῶν θεοῦ κοσμῶσιν ἐν πᾶσιν. ¶ **11** Ἐπεφάνη γὰρ ἡ χάρις τοῦ θεοῦ σωτήριος πᾶσιν ἀνθρώποις **12** παιδεύουσα
ἡμᾶς, ἵνα ἀρνησάμενοι τὴν ἀσέβειαν καὶ τὰς κοσμικὰς ἐπιθυμίας σωφρόνως καὶ δικαίως καὶ εὐσεβῶς ζήσωμεν ἐν τῷ νῦν αἰῶνι,
13 προσδεχόμενοι τὴν μακαρίαν ἐλπίδα καὶ ἐπιφάνειαν τῆς δόξης τοῦ μεγάλου θεοῦ καὶ σωτῆρος ἡμῶν Ἰησοῦ Χριστοῦ, **14** ὃς
ἔδωκεν ἑαυτὸν ὑπὲρ ἡμῶν, ἵνα λυτρώσηται ἡμᾶς ἀπὸ πάσης ἀνομίας καὶ καθαρίσῃ ἑαυτῷ λαὸν περιούσιον, ζηλωτὴν καλῶν
ἔργων. ¶ **15** Ταῦτα λάλει καὶ παρακάλει καὶ ἔλεγχε μετὰ πάσης ἐπιταγῆς· μηδείς σου περιφρονείτω.

Doing What Is Good

3:1 Remind the people to be subject to rulers and authorities, to be obedient, to be ready to do
Ὑπομίμνησκε αὐτοὺς → → ὑποτάσσεσθαι → ἀρχαῖς ἐξουσίαις → πειθαρχεῖν → εἶναι ἑτοίμους πρὸς ἔργον
v.pam.2s r.apm.3 f.pp n.dpf n.dpf f.pa f.pa a.apm p.a n.asn
5703 899 5718 794 2026 4272 1639 2289 4639 2240

whatever is good, **2** to slander no one, to be peaceable and considerate, and to show true humility
πᾶν ἀγαθὸν → βλασφημεῖν μηδένα ← → εἶναι ἀμάχους ἐπιεικεῖς → ἐνδεικνυμένους πᾶσαν πραΰτητα
a.asn a.asn f.pa a.asm f.pa a.apm a.apm pt.pm.apm a.asf n.asf
4246 19 1059 3594 1639 285 2117 1892 4246 4559

toward all men. ¶ **3** At one time we too were foolish, disobedient, deceived and enslaved by all
πρὸς πάντας ἀνθρώπους γάρ ποτε ← ἡμεῖς καὶ ᾖμεν ἀνόητοι ἀπειθεῖς πλανώμενοι δουλεύοντες → →
p.a a.apm n.apm cj adv r.np.1 adv v.iai.1p a.npm a.npm pt.pp.npm pt.pa.npm
4639 4246 476 1142 4537 7005 2779 1639 485 579 4414 1526

kinds of passions and pleasures. We lived in malice and envy, being hated and hating one another.
ποικίλαις ← ἐπιθυμίαις καὶ ἡδοναῖς διάγοντες ἐν κακίᾳ καὶ φθόνῳ → στυγητοί μισοῦντες ἀλλήλους ←
a.dpf n.dpf cj n.dpf pt.pa.npm p n.dsf cj n.dsm a.npm pt.pa.npm r.apm
4476 2123 2779 2454 1341 1877 2798 2779 5784 5144 3631 253

4 But when the kindness and love of God our Savior appeared, **5** he saved us, not because of
δὲ ὅτε ἡ χρηστότης καὶ ἡ φιλανθρωπία → τοῦ θεοῦ ἡμῶν σωτῆρος ἐπεφάνη ἔσωσεν ἡμᾶς οὐκ ἐξ ←
cj cj d.nsf n.nsf cj d.nsf n.nsf d.gsm n.gsm r.gp.1 n.gsm v.api.3s v.aai.3s r.ap.1 pl p.g
1254 4021 3836 5983 2779 3836 5792 3836 2536 7005 5400 2210 5392 7005 4024 1666

righteous things we had done, but because of his mercy. He saved us through the washing of
⸀τῶν ἐν δικαιοσύνῃ ἔργων ἃ ἡμεῖς → ἐποιήσαμεν ἀλλὰ κατὰ ← αὐτοῦ ⸀τὸ ἔλεος⸀ διὰ λουτροῦ →
d.gpn p n.dsf n.gpn r.apn r.np.1 v.aai.1p cj p.a r.gsm.3 d.asn n.asn p.g n.gsn
3836 1877 1466 2240 4005 7005 4472 247 2848 899 3836 1799 1328 3373

rebirth and renewal by the Holy Spirit, **6** whom he poured out on us generously through Jesus Christ
παλιγγενεσίας καὶ ἀνακαινώσεως → ἁγίου πνεύματος οὗ → ἐξέχεεν ← ἐφ᾽ ἡμᾶς πλουσίως διὰ Ἰησοῦ Χριστοῦ
n.gsf cj n.gsf a.gsn n.gsn r.gsn v.aai.3s p r.ap.1 adv p.g n.gsm n.gsm
4098 2779 364 41 4460 4005 1772 2093 7005 4455 1328 2652 5986

our Savior, **7** so that, having been justified by his grace, we might become heirs having the
ἡμῶν ⸀τοῦ σωτῆρος⸀ ἵνα ← δικαιωθέντες → ἐκείνου ⸀τῇ χάριτι⸀ → → γενηθῶμεν κληρονόμοι κατ᾽
r.gp.1 d.gsm n.gsm cj pt.ap.npm r.gsn d.dsf n.dsf v.aps.1p n.npm p.a
7005 3836 5400 2671 1467 5921 1697 3836 5921 1181 3101 2848

hope of eternal life. **8** This is a trustworthy saying. And I want you to stress these things, so that
ἐλπίδα → αἰωνίου ζωῆς Πιστὸς ὁ λόγος⸀ καὶ → βούλομαι σε διαβεβαιοῦσθαι περὶ τούτων → ἵνα ←
n.asf a.gsf n.gsf a.nsm d.nsm n.nsm cj v.pmi.1s r.as.2 f.pm p r.gpn cj
1828 173 2437 4412 3836 3364 2779 1089 5148 1331 4309 4047 2671

those who have trusted in God may be careful to devote themselves to doing what is good. These things
οἱ ← πεπιστευκότες θεῷ → φροντίζωσιν προΐστασθαι ← → ἔργων → καλῶν ταῦτα
d.npm pt.ra.npm n.dsm v.pas.3p f.pm n.gpn a.gpn r.npn
3836 4409 2536 5863 4613 2240 2819 4047

are excellent and profitable for everyone. ¶ **9** But avoid foolish controversies and genealogies and
ἔστιν καλὰ καὶ ὠφέλιμα → ⸀τοῖς ἀνθρώποις⸀ δὲ περιΐστασο μωρὰς ζητήσεις καὶ γενεαλογίας καὶ
v.pai.3s a.npn cj a.npn d.dpm n.dpm cj v.pmm.2s a.apf n.apf cj n.apf cj
1639 2819 2779 6068 3836 476 1254 4325 3704 2428 2779 1157 2779

arguments and quarrels about the law, because these are unprofitable and useless. **10** Warn a divisive person
ἔρεις καὶ μάχας νομικὰς γὰρ εἰσὶν ἀνωφελεῖς καὶ μάταιοι νουθεσίαν αἱρετικὸν ἄνθρωπον
n.apf cj n.apf a.apf cj v.pai.3p a.npf cj a.npf n.asf a.asm n.asm
2251 2779 3480 3788 1142 1639 543 2779 3469 3804 148 476

once, and then warn him a second time. After that, have nothing to do with him. **11** You may be sure that
μίαν καὶ δευτέραν μετὰ παραιτοῦ ← → ← ← → εἰδὼς ὅτι
a.asf cj a.asf p.a v.pmm.2s pt.ra.nsm cj
1651 2779 1311 3552 4148 3857 4022

such a man is warped and sinful; he is self-condemned.
ὁ τοιοῦτος → ἐξέστραπται καὶ ἁμαρτάνει ὢν αὐτοκατάκριτος
d.nsm r.nsm v.rpi.3s cj v.pai.3s pt.pa.nsm a.nsm
3836 5525 1750 2779 279 1639 896

3:1 Ὑπομίμνησκε αὐτοὺς ἀρχαῖς ἐξουσίαις ὑποτάσσεσθαι, πειθαρχεῖν, πρὸς πᾶν ἔργον ἀγαθὸν ἑτοίμους εἶναι, **2** μηδένα βλασφημεῖν, ἀμάχους εἶναι, ἐπιεικεῖς, πᾶσαν ἐνδεικνυμένους πραΰτητα πρὸς πάντας ἀνθρώπους. ¶ **3** Ἦμεν γάρ ποτε καὶ ἡμεῖς ἀνόητοι, ἀπειθεῖς, πλανώμενοι, δουλεύοντες ἐπιθυμίαις καὶ ἡδοναῖς ποικίλαις, ἐν κακίᾳ καὶ φθόνῳ διάγοντες, στυγητοί, μισοῦντες ἀλλήλους. **4** ὅτε δὲ ἡ χρηστότης καὶ ἡ φιλανθρωπία ἐπεφάνη τοῦ σωτῆρος ἡμῶν θεοῦ, **5** οὐκ ἐξ ἔργων τῶν ἐν δικαιοσύνῃ ἃ ἐποιήσαμεν ἡμεῖς ἀλλὰ κατὰ τὸ αὐτοῦ ἔλεος ἔσωσεν ἡμᾶς διὰ λουτροῦ παλιγγενεσίας καὶ ἀνακαινώσεως πνεύματος ἁγίου, **6** οὗ ἐξέχεεν ἐφ᾽ ἡμᾶς πλουσίως διὰ Ἰησοῦ Χριστοῦ τοῦ σωτῆρος ἡμῶν, **7** ἵνα δικαιωθέντες τῇ ἐκείνου χάριτι κληρονόμοι γενηθῶμεν κατ᾽ ἐλπίδα ζωῆς αἰωνίου. **8** Πιστὸς ὁ λόγος· καὶ περὶ τούτων βούλομαί σε διαβεβαιοῦσθαι, ἵνα φροντίζωσιν καλῶν ἔργων προΐστασθαι οἱ πεπιστευκότες θεῷ· ταῦτά ἐστιν καλὰ καὶ ὠφέλιμα τοῖς ἀνθρώποις. ¶ **9** μωρὰς δὲ ζητήσεις καὶ γενεαλογίας καὶ ἔρεις καὶ μάχας νομικὰς περιΐστασο· εἰσὶν γὰρ ἀνωφελεῖς καὶ μάταιοι. **10** αἱρετικὸν ἄνθρωπον μετὰ μίαν καὶ δευτέραν νουθεσίαν παραιτοῦ, **11** εἰδὼς ὅτι ἐξέστραπται ὁ τοιοῦτος καὶ ἁμαρτάνει ὢν αὐτοκατάκριτος.

Final Remarks

3:12 As   soon as I send   Artemas or   Tychicus to   you, do your best   to come to   me at   Nicopolis,
Ὅταν ←   ← → πέμψω Ἀρτεμᾶν ἢ   Τύχικον πρὸς σὲ → →   σπούδασον → ἐλθεῖν πρός με εἰς Νικόπολιν
cj   v.aas.1s n.asm cj   n.asm   p.a r.as.2   v.aam.2s   f.aa   p.a r.as.1 p.a n.asf
4020   4287 782 2445 5608   4639 5148   5079   2262   4639 1609 1650 3776

because I have decided to winter   there. **13** Do everything you can to help   Zenas the lawyer and Apollos on
γὰρ → → κέκρικα → παραχειμάσαι ἐκεῖ   → σπουδαίως →   → πρόπεμψον Ζηνᾶν τὸν νομικὸν καὶ Ἀπολλῶν ←
cj   v.rai.1s   f.aa   adv   adv   v.aam.2s   n.asm d.asm n.asm cj   n.asm
1142   3212   4199   1695   4636 5081   4636   2424 3836 3788 2779 663   4636

their way and see that *they have everything*   *they need.* **14** Our   people   must learn   to
← ←   → ἵνα   μηδὲν αὐτοῖς λείπῃ   δὲ οἱ ἡμέτεροι ←   καὶ → μανθανέτωσαν →
           cj   a.nsn r.dpm.3 v.pas.3s   cj d.npm r.npm.1   adv   v.pam.3p
4636 4636   2671   3594 899   3309   1254 3836 2466   2779   3443

devote   themselves to doing what is good, in   order that they may provide for daily   necessities and not live
προΐστασθαι ←   → ἔργων → → καλῶν ἵνα ←   ←   εἰς ἀναγκαίας ⌊τὰς χρείας⌋ μὴ ὦσιν
f.pm   n.gpn   a.gpn   cj   p.a a.apf   d.apf n.apf pl v.pas.3p
4613   2240   2819   2671   1650 338   3836 5970 3590 1639

unproductive lives. ¶ **15** Everyone   with me sends you greetings. Greet   those who love   us   in the faith.
ἄκαρποι   ⌊οἱ πάντες⌋ μετ' ἐμοῦ →   σε   Ἀσπάζονται ἄσπασαι τοὺς ← φιλοῦντας ἡμᾶς ἐν πίστει
a.npm   d.npm a.npm   p.g r.gs.1   r.as.2 v.pmi.3p   v.amm.2s d.apm   pt.pa.apm r.ap.1 p.d n.dsf
182   3836 4246   3552 1609   832 5148   832   832 3836   5797   7005 1877 4411

Grace   be with you all.
⌊Ἡ χάρις⌋   μετὰ ὑμῶν πάντων
d.nsf n.nsf   p.g r.gp.2 a.gpm
3836 5921   3552 7007 4246

3:12 Ὅταν πέμψω Ἀρτεμᾶν πρὸς σὲ ἢ Τυχικόν, σπούδασον ἐλθεῖν πρός με εἰς Νικόπολιν, ἐκεῖ γὰρ κέκρικα παραχειμάσαι. 13 Ζηνᾶν τὸν νομικὸν καὶ Ἀπολλῶν σπουδαίως πρόπεμψον, ἵνα μηδὲν αὐτοῖς λείπῃ. 14 μανθανέτωσαν δὲ καὶ οἱ ἡμέτεροι καλῶν ἔργων προΐστασθαι εἰς τὰς ἀναγκαίας χρείας, ἵνα μὴ ὦσιν ἄκαρποι. ¶ 15 Ἀσπάζονταί σε οἱ μετ' ἐμοῦ πάντες. Ἄσπασαι τοὺς φιλοῦντας ἡμᾶς ἐν πίστει. ἡ χάρις μετὰ πάντων ὑμῶν.

Philemon

1:1 Paul, a prisoner of Christ Jesus, and Timothy our brother, ¶ To Philemon our dear friend and
Παῦλος δέσμιος → Χριστοῦ Ἰησοῦ καὶ Τιμόθεος ὁ ἀδελφός → Φιλήμονι ἡμῶν ⌐τῷ ἀγαπητῷ⌐ καὶ
n.nsm n.nsm n.gsm n.gsm cj n.nsm d.nsm n.nsm n.dsm r.gp.1 d.dsm a.dsm cj
4263 1300 5986 2652 2779 5510 3836 81 5800 7005 3836 28 2779

fellow worker, **2** to Apphia our sister, to Archippus our fellow soldier and to the church that meets
→ συνεργῷ καὶ → Ἀπφίᾳ τῇ ἀδελφῇ καὶ → Ἀρχίππῳ ἡμῶν ⌐τῷ συστρατιώτῃ⌐ καὶ → τῇ ἐκκλησίᾳ → →
n.dsm cj n.dsf d.dsf n.dsf cj n.dsm r.gp.1 d.dsm n.dsm cj d.dsf n.dsf
5301 2779 722 3836 80 2779 800 7005 3836 5369 2779 3836 1711

in your home: ¶ **3** Grace to you and peace from God our Father and the Lord Jesus Christ.
κατ᾽ σου οἶκον χάρις → ὑμῖν καὶ εἰρήνη ἀπὸ θεοῦ ἡμῶν πατρὸς καὶ κυρίου Ἰησοῦ Χριστοῦ
p.a r.gs.2 n.asm n.nsf r.dp.2 cj n.nsf p.g n.gsm r.gp.1 n.gsm cj n.gsm n.gsm n.gsm
2848 5148 3875 5921 7007 2779 1645 608 2536 7005 4252 2779 3261 2652 5986

Thanksgiving and Prayer

1:4 I always thank my God as I remember you in my prayers, **5** because I hear about your
→ πάντοτε Εὐχαριστῶ μου ⌐τῷ θεῷ⌐ → ⌐μνείαν ποιούμενος⌐ σου ἐπὶ μου ⌐τῶν προσευχῶν⌐ → → ἀκούων ←
adv v.pai.1s r.gs.1 d.dsm n.dsm n.asf pt.pm.nsm r.gs.2 p.g r.gs.1 d.gpf n.gpf pt.pa.nsm
2373 4121 1609 3836 2536 3644 4472 5148 2093 1609 3836 4666 201 2400

faith in the Lord Jesus and your love for all the saints. **6** I pray that you may be
⌐τὴν πίστιν⌐ ἣν ἔχεις πρὸς τὸν κύριον Ἰησοῦν καὶ σου ⌐τὴν ἀγάπην⌐ καὶ εἰς πάντας τοὺς ἁγίους ὅπως → γένηται
d.asf n.asf r.asf v.pai.2s p.a d.asm n.asm n.asm cj r.gs.2 d.asf n.asf cj p.a a.apm d.apm a.apm cj v.ams.3s
3836 4411 4005 2400 4639 3836 3261 2652 2779 5148 3836 27 2779 1650 4246 3836 41 3968 1181

active in sharing your faith, so that you will have a full understanding of every good thing
ἐνεργὴς ἡ κοινωνία σου ⌐τῆς πίστεως⌐ ἐν ἐπιγνώσει → παντὸς ἀγαθοῦ τοῦ ἐν
a.nsf d.nsf n.nsf r.gs.2 d.gsf n.gsf p.d n.dsf a.gsn a.gsn d.gsn p.d
1921 3836 3126 5148 3836 4411 1877 2106 4246 19 3836 1877

we have in Christ. **7** Your love has given me great joy and encouragement, because you, brother,
ἡμῖν εἰς Χριστόν γὰρ σου ἐπὶ τῇ ἀγάπῃ → ἔσχον ← πολλὴν χαρὰν καὶ παράκλησιν ὅτι διὰ σοῦ ἀδελφέ
r.dp.1 p.a n.asm cj r.gs.2 p.d d.dsf n.dsf v.aai.1s a.asf n.asf cj n.asf cj p.g r.gs.2 n.vsm
7005 1650 5986 1142 5148 2093 3836 27 2400 4498 5915 2779 4155 4022 1328 5148 81

have refreshed the hearts of the saints.
→ ἀναπέπαυται τὰ σπλάγχνα → τῶν ἁγίων
v.rpi.3s d.npn n.npn d.gpm a.gpm
399 3836 5073 3836 41

Paul's Plea for Onesimus

1:8 Therefore, although in Christ I could be bold and order you to do what you ought to do,
Διὸ ↱ πολλὴν ἐν Χριστῷ → ἔχων παρρησίαν ἐπιτάσσειν σοι τὸ → ἀνῆκον ←
cj a.asf p.d n.dsm pt.pa.nsm n.asf f.pa r.ds.2 d.asn pt.pa.asn
1475 2400 4498 1877 5986 2400 4244 2199 5148 3836 465

9 yet I appeal to you on the basis of love. I then, as Paul – an old man and now also a
μᾶλλον → παρακαλῶ διὰ ← ← ⌐τὴν ἀγάπην⌐ τοιοῦτος ὢν ὡς Παῦλος πρεσβύτης ← δὲ νυνὶ καὶ
adv.c v.pai.1s p.a d.asf n.asf r.nsm pt.pa.nsm pl n.nsm n.nsm cj adv adv
3437 4151 1328 3836 27 5525 1639 6055 4263 4566 1254 3815 2779

prisoner of Christ Jesus – **10** I appeal to you for my son Onesimus, who became my son while I was in
δέσμιος → Χριστοῦ Ἰησοῦ → παρακαλῶ σε περὶ ἐμοῦ ⌐τοῦ τέκνου⌐ Ὀνήσιμον ὃν → → ἐγέννησα → → ἐν
n.nsm n.gsm n.gsm v.pai.1s r.as.2 p.g r.gsn.1 d.gsn n.gsn n.asm r.asm v.aai.1s p.d
1300 5986 2652 4151 5148 4309 1847 3836 5451 3946 4005 1164 1877

chains. **11** Formerly he was useless to you, but now he has become useful both to you and to me. ¶
⌐τοῖς δεσμοῖς⌐ ποτὲ ⌐τόν ἄχρηστον⌐ σοι δὲ νυνὶ εὔχρηστον καὶ → σοι καὶ → ἐμοὶ
d.dpm n.dpm adv d.asm a.asm r.ds.2 cj adv a.asm cj r.ds.2 cj r.ds.1
3836 1301 4537 3836 947 5148 1254 3815 2378 2779 5148 2779 1609

12 I am sending him – who is my very heart – back to you. **13** I would have liked to keep him
ὃν → ἀνέπεμψα αὐτόν τοῦτ᾽ ἔστιν ἐμά ⌐τὰ σπλάγχνα⌐ ← σοι ἐγὼ → ἐβουλόμην → κατέχειν Ὃν
r.asm v.aai.1s r.asm.3 r.nsn v.pai.3s r.apn.1 d.apn n.apn r.ds.2 r.ns.1 v.imi.1s f.pa r.asm
4005 402 899 4047 1639 1847 3836 5073 402 5148 1609 1089 2988 4005

1:1 Παῦλος δέσμιος Χριστοῦ Ἰησοῦ καὶ Τιμόθεος ὁ ἀδελφὸς ¶ Φιλήμονι τῷ ἀγαπητῷ καὶ συνεργῷ ἡμῶν **2** καὶ Ἀπφίᾳ τῇ ἀδελφῇ καὶ Ἀρχίππῳ τῷ συστρατιώτῃ ἡμῶν καὶ τῇ κατ᾽ οἶκόν σου ἐκκλησίᾳ, ¶ **3** χάρις ὑμῖν καὶ εἰρήνη ἀπὸ θεοῦ πατρὸς ἡμῶν καὶ κυρίου Ἰησοῦ Χριστοῦ.

1:4 Εὐχαριστῶ τῷ θεῷ μου πάντοτε μνείαν σου ποιούμενος ἐπὶ τῶν προσευχῶν μου, **5** ἀκούων σου τὴν ἀγάπην καὶ τὴν πίστιν, ἣν ἔχεις πρὸς τὸν κύριον Ἰησοῦν καὶ εἰς πάντας τοὺς ἁγίους, **6** ὅπως ἡ κοινωνία τῆς πίστεώς σου ἐνεργὴς γένηται ἐν ἐπιγνώσει παντὸς ἀγαθοῦ τοῦ ἐν ἡμῖν εἰς Χριστόν. **7** χαρὰν γὰρ πολλὴν ἔσχον καὶ παράκλησιν ἐπὶ τῇ ἀγάπῃ σου, ὅτι τὰ σπλάγχνα τῶν ἁγίων ἀναπέπαυται διὰ σοῦ, ἀδελφέ.

1:8 Διὸ πολλὴν ἐν Χριστῷ παρρησίαν ἔχων ἐπιτάσσειν σοι τὸ ἀνῆκον **9** διὰ τὴν ἀγάπην μᾶλλον παρακαλῶ, τοιοῦτος ὢν ὡς Παῦλος πρεσβύτης νυνὶ δὲ καὶ δέσμιος Χριστοῦ Ἰησοῦ· **10** παρακαλῶ σε περὶ τοῦ ἐμοῦ τέκνου, ὃν ἐγέννησα ἐν τοῖς δεσμοῖς, Ὀνήσιμον, **11** τόν ποτέ σοι ἄχρηστον νυνὶ δὲ [καὶ] σοὶ καὶ ἐμοὶ εὔχρηστον, ¶ **12** ὃν ἀνέπεμψά σοι, αὐτόν, τοῦτ᾽ ἔστιν τὰ ἐμὰ

with me　　so　that *he*　　　*could take your place*　in helping me while　I am in　chains　　　for the gospel.
πρὸς ἐμαυτὸν ἵνα ←　ὑπὲρ σοῦ　　　→ διακονῇ μοι →　ἐν τοῖς δεσμοῖς, →　τοῦ εὐαγγελίου
p.a　r.asm.1　cj　　p.g　r.gs.2　　　v.pas.3s r.ds.1　　p.d d.dpm n.dpm　　　d.gsn n.gsn
4639　1831　2671　5642 5148　　　1354 1609　　1877 3836 1301　　　3836 2295

14 But I　did not want　to do　　anything without your consent,　so that any favor　you do will be
δὲ ↱ → → ἠθέλησα → ποιῆσαι οὐδὲν χωρὶς σῆς τῆς γνώμης, ἵνα ←　ὡτὸ ἀγαθόν, σου → ᾖ
cj v.aai.1s f.aa a.asn p.g r.gsf.2 d.gsf n.gsf cj　d.nsn a.nsn r.gs.2　v.pas.3s
1254 2527 2527 4029 2527 4472 4029 6006 5050 3836 1191 2671　3836 19 5148　1639

spontaneous　and not forced.　**15**　Perhaps the reason　he was separated from you for a little while
κατὰ ἑκούσιον. ἀλλὰ μὴ ὡς κατὰ ἀνάγκην, γὰρ Τάχα → διὰ τοῦτο, → ἐχωρίσθη　　πρὸς ὥραν ←
p.a a.asn cj pl pl p.a n.asf cj adv p.a r.asn v.api.3s　p.a n.asf
2848 1730 247 3590 6055 2848 340 1142 5440 1328 4047 6004　4639 6052

was that you might have　him　back *for good*　— **16** no　longer as a slave, but better than a slave, as a dear
ἵνα → → ἀπέχῃς αὐτὸν ←　αἰώνιον οὐκέτι ← ὡς δοῦλον ἀλλ᾽ ὑπὲρ ← δοῦλον ἀγαπητόν
cj v.pas.2s r.asm.3　a.asm adv pl a.asn cj p.a n.asm a.asm
2671 600 899 600　173 4033 6055 1529 247 5642 1529 28

brother. He is very dear　　to me but even dearer to you, both as a man and as a brother in the Lord. ¶
ἀδελφόν. μάλιστα → ἐμοὶ δὲ πόσῳ μᾶλλον → σοὶ καὶ ἐν σαρκὶ καὶ　　ἐν κυρίῳ
n.asm adv.s r.ds.1 cj r.dsn adv.c r.ds.2 cj p.d n.dsf cj　p.d n.dsm
81 3436 1609 1254 4531 3437 5148 2779 1877 4922 2779　1877 3261

17 So if　you consider me a partner, welcome him　as you would welcome me. **18**　If he has done you any wrong
οὖν εἰ → ἔχεις με κοινόν, προσλαβοῦ αὐτὸν ὡς　ἐμέ. δὲ εἰ → → σε τι ἠδίκησεν
cj cj v.pai.2s r.as.1 n.asm v.amm.2s r.asm.3 cj　r.as.1 cj cj r.as.2 r.asn v.aai.3s
4036 1623 2400 1609 3128 4689 899 6055　1609 1254 1623 92 92 5148 5516 92

or owes you anything, charge it　to me. **19** I, Paul,　am writing this with my own hand.　I will pay　it back
ἢ ὀφείλει ἐλλόγα τοῦτο → ἐμοί ἐγὼ Παῦλος → ἔγραψα　→ ἐμῇ τῇ χειρί, ἐγὼ → ἀποτίσω ←
cj v.pai.3s v.pam.2s r.asn r.ds.1 r.ns.1 n.nsm v.aai.1s r.dsf.1 d.dsf n.dsf r.ns.1 v.fai.1s
2445 4053 1824 4047 1609 1609 4263 1211 1847 3836 5931 1609 702

—　not to mention　that　you owe　me your　very self. **20** *I do wish*, brother, that I　may have some
ἵνα μὴ → λέγω σοι ὅτι καὶ → προσοφείλεις μοι σεαυτόν ←　ναί ἀδελφέ, ἐγὼ → → →
cj pl v.pas.1s r.ds.2 cj adv v.pai.2s r.ds.1 r.asm.2　pl n.vsm r.ns.1
2671 3590 3306 5148 4022 2779 4695 1609 4932　3721 81 1609

benefit from you in the Lord; refresh　my heart　in Christ. **21** Confident of your obedience, I write to you,
ὀναίμην → σου ἐν κυρίῳ ἀνάπαυσον μου τὰ σπλάγχνα, ἐν Χριστῷ Πεποιθὼς → σου τῇ ὑπακοῇ, → ἔγραψα σοι
v.amo.1s r.gs.2 p.d n.dsm v.aam.2s r.gs.1 d.apn n.apn p.d n.dsm pt.ra.nsm r.gs.2 d.dsf n.dsf v.aai.1s r.ds.2
3949 5148 1877 3261 399 1609 3836 5073 1877 5986 4275 5633 5148 5633 1211 5148

knowing that you will do　even more than　I ask. ¶　**22**　And　one thing more: Prepare a guest room
εἰδὼς ὅτι → → ποιήσεις καὶ ὑπὲρ ἃ → λέγω δὲ ἅμα καὶ, ἑτοίμαζε ξενίαν
pt.ra.nsm cj v.fai.2s adv p.a r.apn v.pai.1s cj adv adv v.pam.2s n.asf
3857 4022 4472 2779 5642 4005 3306 1254 275 2779 2286 3825

for me, because I hope　to be restored　to you in answer to your prayers. ¶　**23** Epaphras, my fellow
→ μοι γὰρ → ἐλπίζω ὅτι → χαρισθήσομαι → ὑμῖν διὰ ← ὑμῶν τῶν προσευχῶν, Ἐπαφρᾶς μου →
r.ds.1 cj v.pai.1s cj v.fpi.1s r.dp.2 p.g r.gp.2 d.gpf n.gpf n.nsm r.gs.1
1609 1142 1827 4022 5919 1328 7007 3836 4666 2071 1609

prisoner　in Christ Jesus, sends you greetings. **24** And so do Mark, Aristarchus, Demas and Luke, my fellow
ὁ συναιχμάλωτος, ἐν Χριστῷ Ἰησοῦ, → σε Ἀσπάζεται Μᾶρκος Ἀρίσταρχος Δημᾶς Λουκᾶς μου →
d.nsm n.nsm p.d n.dsm n.dsm r.as.2 v.pmi.3s n.nsm n.nsm n.nsm n.nsm r.gs.1
3836 5257 1877 5986 2652 832 5148 832 3453 752 1318 3371 1609

workers.　¶　**25** The grace of the Lord Jesus Christ be with your spirit.
οἱ συνεργοί, Ἡ χάρις → τοῦ κυρίου Ἰησοῦ Χριστοῦ μετὰ ὑμῶν τοῦ πνεύματος,
d.npm n.npm d.nsf n.nsf d.gsm n.gsm n.gsm n.gsm p.g r.gp.2 d.gsn n.gsn
3836 5301 3836 5921 3836 3261 2652 5986 3552 7007 3836 4460

σπλάγχνα· **13** ὃν ἐγὼ ἐβουλόμην πρὸς ἐμαυτὸν κατέχειν, ἵνα ὑπὲρ σοῦ μοι διακονῇ ἐν τοῖς δεσμοῖς τοῦ εὐαγγελίου, **14** χωρὶς δὲ τῆς σῆς γνώμης οὐδὲν ἠθέλησα ποιῆσαι, ἵνα μὴ ὡς κατὰ ἀνάγκην τὸ ἀγαθόν σου ᾖ ἀλλὰ κατὰ ἑκούσιον. **15** τάχα γὰρ διὰ τοῦτο ἐχωρίσθη πρὸς ὥραν, ἵνα αἰώνιον αὐτὸν ἀπέχῃς, **16** οὐκέτι ὡς δοῦλον ἀλλὰ ὑπὲρ δοῦλον, ἀδελφὸν ἀγαπητόν, μάλιστα ἐμοί, πόσῳ δὲ μᾶλλον σοὶ καὶ ἐν σαρκὶ καὶ ἐν κυρίῳ. ¶ **17** Εἰ οὖν με ἔχεις κοινωνόν, προσλαβοῦ αὐτὸν ὡς ἐμέ. **18** εἰ δέ τι ἠδίκησέν σε ἢ ὀφείλει, τοῦτο ἐμοὶ ἐλλόγα. **19** ἐγὼ Παῦλος ἔγραψα τῇ ἐμῇ χειρί, ἐγὼ ἀποτίσω· ἵνα μὴ λέγω σοι ὅτι καὶ σεαυτόν μοι προσοφείλεις. **20** ναὶ ἀδελφέ, ἐγώ σου ὀναίμην ἐν κυρίῳ· ἀνάπαυσόν μου τὰ σπλάγχνα ἐν Χριστῷ. **21** Πεποιθὼς τῇ ὑπακοῇ σου ἔγραψά σοι, εἰδὼς ὅτι καὶ ὑπὲρ ἃ λέγω ποιήσεις. ¶ **22** ἅμα δὲ καὶ ἑτοίμαζέ μοι ξενίαν· ἐλπίζω γὰρ ὅτι διὰ τῶν προσευχῶν ὑμῶν χαρισθήσομαι ὑμῖν. ¶ **23** Ἀσπάζεταί σε Ἐπαφρᾶς ὁ συναιχμάλωτός μου ἐν Χριστῷ Ἰησοῦ, **24** Μᾶρκος, Ἀρίσταρχος, Δημᾶς, Λουκᾶς, οἱ συνεργοί μου. ¶ **25** Ἡ χάρις τοῦ κυρίου Ἰησοῦ Χριστοῦ μετὰ τοῦ πνεύματος ὑμῶν.

Hebrews

The Son Superior to the Angels

1:1 In the past God spoke to our forefathers through the prophets at many times and in various
→ → πάλαι ‚ὁ θεὸς‚ λαλήσας → τοῖς πατράσιν ἐν τοῖς προφήταις → Πολυμερῶς καὶ → →
adv d.nsm n.nsm pt.aa.nsm d.dpm n.dpm p.d d.dpm n.dpm adv cj
4093 3836 2536 3281 3836 4252 1877 3836 4737 4495 2779

ways, **2** but in these last days he has spoken to us by his Son, whom he appointed heir of
πολυτρόπως ἐπ᾽ τούτων ἐσχάτου ‚τῶν ἡμερῶν‚ → → ἐλάλησεν → ἡμῖν ἐν υἱῷ ὃν → ἔθηκεν κληρονόμον
adv p.g r.gpf a.gsm d.gpf n.gpf v.aai.3s r.dp.1 p.d n.dsm r.asm v.aai.3s n.asm
4502 2093 4047 2274 3836 2465 3281 7005 1877 5502 4005 5502 3101

all things, and through whom he made the universe. **3** The Son is the radiance of God's glory and the
πάντων ← καὶ δι᾽ οὗ → ἐποίησεν τοὺς αἰῶνας ὃς ← ὢν ἀπαύγασμα → ‚τῆς δόξης‚ καὶ
a.gpn adv p.g r.gsm v.aai.3s d.apm n.apm r.nsm pt.pa.nsm n.nsm d.gsf n.gsf cj
4246 2779 1328 4005 4472 3836 172 4005 1639 575 3836 1518 2779

exact representation of his being, sustaining all things by his powerful word. After he
→ χαρακτὴρ → αὐτοῦ ‚τῆς ὑποστάσεως‚ τε φέρων ‚τὰ πάντα‚ → αὐτοῦ ‚τῆς δυνάμεως‚ ‚τῷ ῥήματι‚ →
n.nsm r.gsm.3 d.gsf n.gsf cj pt.pa.nsm d.apn a.apn r.gsm.3 d.gsf n.gsf d.dsn n.dsn
5917 5712 899 3836 5712 5445 5770 3836 4246 4839 899 3836 1539 3836 4839

had provided purification for sins, he sat down at the right hand of the Majesty in heaven. **4** So
→ ποιησάμενος καθαρισμὸν → ‚τῶν ἁμαρτιῶν‚ → ἐκάθισεν ← ἐν δεξιᾷ → τῆς μεγαλωσύνης ἐν ὑψηλοῖς
pt.am.nsm n.asm d.gpf n.gpf v.aai.3s p.d a.dsf d.gsf n.gsf p.d a.dpm
4472 2752 3836 281 2767 1877 1288 3836 3488 1877 5734

he became as much superior to the angels as the name he has inherited is superior to theirs. ¶
→ γενόμενος τοσούτῳ κρείττων ‚τῶν ἀγγέλων‚ ὅσῳ ὄνομα → → κεκληρονόμηκεν διαφορώτερον παρ᾽ αὐτούς
pt.am.nsm r.dsn a.nsm.c d.gpm n.gpm r.dsn n.asn v.rai.3s a.asn.c p.a r.apm.3
1181 5537 3202 3836 34 4012 3950 3099 1427 4123 899

5 For to which of the angels did God ever say, "You are my Son; today I have become your Father"? Or again,
γὰρ → Τίνι → ‚τῶν ἀγγέλων‚ ποτε εἶπεν σύ εἶ μου υἱός σήμερον ἐγώ → → σε γεγέννηκα καὶ πάλιν
cj r.dsm d.gpm n.gpm adv v.aai.3s r.ns.2 v.pai.2s r.gs.1 n.nsm adv r.ns.1 r.as.2 v.rai.1s cj adv
1142 5515 3836 34 4537 3306 5148 1639 1609 5626 4958 1609 5148 1164 2779 4099

"I will be his Father, and he will be my Son"? **6** And again, when God brings his firstborn into
ἐγὼ ἔσομαι αὐτῷ εἰς πατέρα καὶ αὐτὸς → ἔσται μοι εἰς υἱόν δὲ πάλιν ὅταν εἰσαγάγῃ τὸν πρωτότοκον εἰς
r.ns.1 v.fmi.1s r.dsm.3 p.a n.asm cj r.nsm v.fmi.3s r.ds.1 p.a n.asm cj adv cj v.aas.3s d.asm a.asm p.a
1609 1639 899 1650 4252 2779 899 1639 1609 1650 5626 1254 4099 4020 1652 3836 4758 1650

the world, he says, "Let all God's angels worship him." **7** In speaking of the angels he
τὴν οἰκουμένην → λέγει καὶ πάντες θεοῦ ἄγγελοι προσκυνησάτωσαν αὐτῷ καὶ μὲν → πρὸς τοὺς ἀγγέλους →
d.asf n.asf v.pai.3s cj a.npm n.gsm n.npm v.aam.3p r.dsm.3 cj pl p.a d.apm n.apm
3836 3876 3306 2779 4246 2536 34 4686 899 2779 3525 4639 3836 34

says, "He makes his angels winds, his servants flames of fire." **8** But about the Son he says,
λέγει ὁ ποιῶν αὐτοῦ ‚τοὺς ἀγγέλους‚ πνεύματα καὶ αὐτοῦ ‚τοὺς λειτουργοὺς‚ φλόγα → πυρὸς δὲ πρὸς τὸν υἱόν
v.pai.3s d.nsm pt.pa.nsm r.gsm.3 d.apm n.apm n.apn cj r.gsm.3 d.apm n.apm n.asf n.gsn cj p.a d.asm n.asm
3306 3836 4472 899 3836 34 4460 2779 899 3836 3313 5825 4786 1254 4639 3836 5626

"Your throne, O God, will last for ever and ever, and righteousness will be the scepter
σου ‚ὁ θρόνος‚ → ὁ θεός, → εἰς ‚τὸν αἰῶνα‚ ‚τοῦ αἰῶνος‚ καὶ ἡ ῥάβδος τῆς εὐθύτητος‚ ῥάβδος
r.gs.2 d.nsm n.nsm d.vsm n.vsm p.a d.asm n.asm d.gsm n.gsm cj d.nsf n.nsf d.gsf n.gsf n.nsf
5148 3836 2585 3836 2536 1650 3836 172 3836 172 2779 3836 4811 3836 2319 4811

of your kingdom. **9** You have loved righteousness and hated wickedness; therefore God, your God, has
→ σου ‚τῆς βασιλείας‚ → → ἠγάπησας δικαιοσύνην καὶ ἐμίσησας ἀνομίαν ‚διὰ τοῦτο‚ ὁ θεὸς σου ‚ὁ θεὸς‚
r.gs.2 d.gsf n.gsf v.aai.2s n.asf cj v.aai.2s n.asf p.a r.asn d.nsm n.nsm r.gs.2 d.nsm n.nsm
993 5148 3836 993 26 1466 2779 3631 490 1328 4047 3836 2536 5148 3836 2536

set you above your companions by anointing you with the oil of joy." **10** He also says, "In the beginning, O
παρά σου ‚τοὺς μετόχους‚ ἔχρισεν σε → ἔλαιον ἀγαλλιάσεως καὶ κατ᾽ ἀρχάς →
p.a r.gs.2 d.apm n.apm v.aai.3s r.as.2 n.asn n.gsf cj p.a n.apf
4123 5148 3836 3581 5987 5148 1778 21 2779 2848 794

1:1 Πολυμερῶς καὶ πολυτρόπως πάλαι ὁ θεὸς λαλήσας τοῖς πατράσιν ἐν τοῖς προφήταις **2** ἐπ᾽ ἐσχάτου τῶν ἡμερῶν τούτων ἐλάλησεν ἡμῖν ἐν υἱῷ, ὃν ἔθηκεν κληρονόμον πάντων, δι᾽ οὗ καὶ ἐποίησεν τοὺς αἰῶνας· **3** ὃς ὢν ἀπαύγασμα τῆς δόξης καὶ χαρακτὴρ τῆς ὑποστάσεως αὐτοῦ, φέρων τε τὰ πάντα τῷ ῥήματι τῆς δυνάμεως αὐτοῦ, καθαρισμὸν τῶν ἁμαρτιῶν ποιησάμενος ἐκάθισεν ἐν δεξιᾷ τῆς μεγαλωσύνης ἐν ὑψηλοῖς, **4** τοσούτῳ κρείττων γενόμενος τῶν ἀγγέλων ὅσῳ διαφορώτερον παρ᾽ αὐτοὺς κεκληρονόμηκεν ὄνομα. ¶ **5** Τίνι γὰρ εἶπέν ποτε τῶν ἀγγέλων, Υἱός μου εἶ σύ, ἐγὼ σήμερον γεγέννηκά σε; καὶ πάλιν, Ἐγὼ ἔσομαι αὐτῷ εἰς πατέρα, καὶ αὐτὸς ἔσται μοι εἰς υἱόν; **6** ὅταν δὲ πάλιν εἰσαγάγῃ τὸν πρωτότοκον εἰς τὴν οἰκουμένην, λέγει, Καὶ προσκυνησάτωσαν αὐτῷ πάντες ἄγγελοι θεοῦ. **7** καὶ πρὸς μὲν τοὺς ἀγγέλους λέγει, Ὁ ποιῶν τοὺς ἀγγέλους αὐτοῦ πνεύματα καὶ τοὺς λειτουργοὺς αὐτοῦ πυρὸς φλόγα, **8** πρὸς δὲ τὸν υἱόν, Ὁ θρόνος σου ὁ θεὸς εἰς τὸν αἰῶνα τοῦ αἰῶνος, καὶ ἡ ῥάβδος τῆς εὐθύτητος ῥάβδος τῆς βασιλείας σου. **9** ἠγάπησας δικαιοσύνην καὶ ἐμίσησας ἀνομίαν· διὰ τοῦτο ἔχρισέν σε ὁ θεὸς ὁ θεός σου ἔλαιον ἀγαλλιάσεως παρὰ τοὺς μετόχους σου. **10** καί, Σὺ κατ᾽ ἀρχάς, κύριε, τὴν γῆν ἐθεμελίωσας, καὶ ἔργα

Lord, you laid the foundations of the earth, and the heavens are the work of your hands. **11** They will perish,
κύριε σὺ → ἐθεμελίωσας τὴν γῆν καὶ οἱ οὐρανοί εἰσιν ἔργα σού ⸢τῶν χειρῶν⸥ αὐτοὶ ἀπολοῦνται
n.vsm r.ns.2   v.aai.2s d.asf n.asf cj d.npm n.npm v.pai.3p n.npn r.gs.2 d.gpf n.gpf r.npm v.fmi.3p
3261 5148   2530 3836 1178 2779 3836 4041 1639 2240 5931 5148 3836 5931 899 660

but you remain; they will all wear out like a garment. **12** You will roll them up like a robe;
δὲ σὺ διαμένεις καὶ → → πάντες παλαιωθήσονται ← ὡς ἱμάτιον καὶ → → ἑλίξεις αὐτούς ↰ ὡσεὶ περιβόλαιον
cj r.ns.2 v.pai.2s cj   a.npm v.fpi.3p   pl n.nsn cj   v.fai.2s r.apm.3   adv n.asn
1254 5148 1373 2779 4096 4096 4246 4096   6055 2668 2779   1813 899 1813 6059 4316

like a garment they will be changed. But you remain the same, and your years will never end." **13** To
ὡς ἱμάτιον καὶ → → ἀλλαγήσονται δὲ σὺ εἶ ὁ αὐτός καὶ σου ⸢τὰ ἔτη⸥ ↰ οὐκ ἐκλείψουσιν δὲ πρὸς
pl n.nsn adv   v.fpi.3p cj r.ns.2 v.pai.2s d.nsm r.nsm cj r.gs.2 d.npn n.npn   pl v.fai.3p cj p.a
6055 2668 2779   248 1254 5148 1639 3836 899 2779 5148 3836 2291 1722 4024 1722 1254 4639

which of the angels did God ever say, "Sit at my right hand until I make your enemies a footstool for
τίνα → τῶν ἀγγέλων → ποτε εἴρηκεν Κάθου ἐκ μου δεξιῶν ← ἕως ἄν → θῶ σου ⸢τοὺς ἐχθρούς⸥ ὑποπόδιον →
r.asm   d.gpm n.gpm   adv v.rai.3s v.pmm.2s p.g r.gs.1 a.gpf   cj pl   v.aas.1s r.gs.2 d.apm a.apm n.asn
5515   3836 34   4537 3306 2764 1666 1609 1288   2401 323   5502 5148 3836 2398 5711 4546

your feet"? **14** Are not all angels ministering spirits sent to serve those who will
σου ⸢τῶν ποδῶν⸥ εἰσιν οὐχὶ πάντες λειτουργικὰ πνεύματα ἀποστελλόμενα εἰς διακονίαν διὰ τοὺς μέλλοντας
r.gs.2 d.gpm n.gpm v.pai.3p pl a.npm a.npn n.npn pt.pp.npn p.a n.asf p.a d.apm pt.pa.apm
5148 3836 4546 1639 4049 4246 3312 4460 690 1650 1355 1328 3836 3516

inherit salvation?
κληρονομεῖν σωτηρίαν
f.pa n.asf
3099 5401

Warning to Pay Attention

2:1 We must pay more careful attention, therefore, to what we have heard, so that we do not
ἡμᾶς δεῖ → περισσοτέρως ← προσέχειν ⸢Διὰ τοῦτο⸥ τοῖς → ἀκουσθεῖσιν → → → → μήποτε
r.ap.1 v.pai.3s   adv.c   f.pa p.a r.asn d.dpn   pt.ap.dpn   pl
7005 1256 4668 4359   4668 1328 4047 3836   201 3607 3607 4184 4184 3607

drift away. **2** For if the message spoken by angels was binding, and every violation and disobedience
παραρυῶμεν ← γὰρ εἰ ὁ λόγος λαληθεὶς δι' ἀγγέλων ἐγένετο βέβαιος καὶ πᾶσα παράβασις καὶ παρακοὴ
v.aps.1p   cj cj d.nsm n.nsm pt.ap.nsm p.g n.gpm v.ami.3s a.nsm cj a.nsf n.nsf cj n.nsf
4184   1142 1623 3836 3364 3281 1328 34 1181 1010 2779 4246 4126 2779 4157

received its just punishment, **3** how shall we escape if we ignore such a great salvation? This salvation,
ἔλαβεν ἔνδικον μισθαποδοσίαν πῶς → ἡμεῖς ἐκφευξόμεθα → → ἀμελήσαντες → → τηλικαύτης σωτηρίας
v.aai.3s a.asf n.asf pl   r.np.1 v.fmi.1p   pt.aa.npm   r.gsf n.gsf
3284 1899 3632 4802 1767 1767 288 5496 5401

which was first announced by the Lord, was confirmed to us by those who heard him. **4** God also
ἥτις πρώτη ἀρχὴν λαβοῦσα λαλεῖσθαι διὰ τοῦ κυρίου → ἐβεβαιώθη εἰς ἡμᾶς ὑπὸ τῶν ← ἀκουσάντων ⸢τοῦ θεοῦ⸥ also
r.nsf n.asf n.asf pt.aa.nsf f.pp p.g d.gsm n.gsm   v.api.3s p.a r.ap.1 p.g d.gpm   pt.aa.gpm d.gsm n.gsm
4015 3281 794 3284 3281 1328 3836 3261 1011 1650 7005 5679 3836 201 3836 2536

testified to it by signs, wonders and various miracles, and gifts of the Holy Spirit distributed
συνεπιμαρτυροῦντος ← ← τε σημείοις καὶ τέρασιν καὶ ποικίλαις δυνάμεσιν καὶ → → ἁγίου πνεύματος μερισμοῖς
pt.pa.gsm   cj n.dpn cj n.dpn cj a.dpf n.dpf cj   a.gsn n.gsn n.dpm
5296   4956 5445 4956 2779 5469 2779 4476 1539 2779 3536 41 4460 3536

according to his will.
κατὰ ← αὐτοῦ ⸢τὴν θέλησιν⸥
p.a   r.gsm.3 d.asf n.asf
2848   899 3836 2526

Jesus Made Like His Brothers

2:5 It is not to angels that he has subjected the world to come, about which we are speaking.
γὰρ Οὐ → ἀγγέλοις ὑπέταξεν τὴν οἰκουμένην → ⸢τὴν μέλλουσαν⸥ περὶ ἧς → λαλοῦμεν
cj pl   n.dpm v.aai.3s d.asf n.asf   d.asf pt.pa.asf p.g r.gsf   v.pai.1p
1142 4024 34 5718 3836 3876 3836 3516 4309 4005 3281

6 But there is a place where someone has testified: "What is man that you are mindful of him, the
δέ → → ποὺ τις → διεμαρτύρατο λέγων τί ἐστιν ἄνθρωπος ὅτι → → μιμνήσκῃ → αὐτοῦ ἢ
cj   adv r.nsm   v.ami.3s pt.pa.nsm r.nsn v.pai.3s n.nsm cj   v.ppi.2s   r.gsm.3 cj
1254 4543 5516 1371 3306 5515 1639 476 4022 3630 899 2445

τῶν χειρῶν σού εἰσιν οἱ οὐρανοί· ¹¹ αὐτοὶ ἀπολοῦνται, σὺ δὲ διαμένεις, καὶ πάντες ὡς ἱμάτιον παλαιωθήσονται, ¹² καὶ ὡσεὶ περιβόλαιον ἑλίξεις αὐτούς, ὡς ἱμάτιον καὶ ἀλλαγήσονται· σὺ δὲ ὁ αὐτὸς εἶ καὶ τὰ ἔτη σου οὐκ ἐκλείψουσιν. ¹³ πρὸς τίνα δὲ τῶν ἀγγέλων εἴρηκέν ποτε, Κάθου ἐκ δεξιῶν μου, ἕως ἂν θῶ τοὺς ἐχθρούς σου ὑποπόδιον τῶν ποδῶν σου; ¹⁴ οὐχὶ πάντες εἰσὶν λειτουργικὰ πνεύματα εἰς διακονίαν ἀποστελλόμενα διὰ τοὺς μέλλοντας κληρονομεῖν σωτηρίαν;

²:¹ Διὰ τοῦτο δεῖ περισσοτέρως προσέχειν ἡμᾶς τοῖς ἀκουσθεῖσιν, μήποτε παραρυῶμεν. ² εἰ γὰρ ὁ δι' ἀγγέλων λαληθεὶς λόγος ἐγένετο βέβαιος καὶ πᾶσα παράβασις καὶ παρακοὴ ἔλαβεν ἔνδικον μισθαποδοσίαν, ³ πῶς ἡμεῖς ἐκφευξόμεθα τηλικαύτης ἀμελήσαντες σωτηρίας, ἥτις ἀρχὴν λαβοῦσα λαλεῖσθαι διὰ τοῦ κυρίου ὑπὸ τῶν ἀκουσάντων εἰς ἡμᾶς ἐβεβαιώθη, ⁴ συνεπιμαρτυροῦντος τοῦ θεοῦ σημείοις τε καὶ τέρασιν καὶ ποικίλαις δυνάμεσιν καὶ πνεύματος ἁγίου μερισμοῖς κατὰ τὴν αὐτοῦ θέλησιν;

²:⁵ Οὐ γὰρ ἀγγέλοις ὑπέταξεν τὴν οἰκουμένην τὴν μέλλουσαν, περὶ ἧς λαλοῦμεν. ⁶ διεμαρτύρατο δέ πού τις λέγων, Τί ἐστιν

son of man   that you care   for him? **7** You made him   a little   lower   than the angels; you crowned
υἱὸς → ἀνθρώπου ὅτι → ἐπισκέπτῃ ← αὐτὸν You made αὐτὸν βραχύ τι ἠλάττωσας παρ' ἀγγέλους → ἐστεφάνωσας
n.nsm n.gsm cj v.pmi.2s r.asm.3 r.asm.3 adv r.asn v.aai.2s p.a n.apm v.aai.2s
5626 476 4022 2170 899 1783 1783 899 1099 5516 1783 4123 34 5110

him   with glory and honor **8** and put   everything under his   feet."   In putting   everything under him,
αὐτὸν → δόξῃ καὶ τιμῇ ὑπέταξας πάντα ὑποκάτω αὐτοῦ τῶν ποδῶν γὰρ ἐν τῷ ὑποτάξαι τὰ πάντα ← αὐτὸν
r.asm.3 n.dsf cj n.dsf v.aai.2s a.apn p.g r.gsm.3 d.gpm n.gpm cj p.d d.dsn f.aa d.apn a.apn r.dsm.3
899 1518 2779 5507 5718 4246 5691 899 3836 4546 1142 1877 3836 5718 3836 4246 5718 899

God left   nothing that is not subject   to him. Yet at present we do not   see   everything subject   to him.
ἀφῆκεν οὐδὲν → ἀνυπότακτον → αὐτῷ δὲ → Νῦν → οὔπω ὁρῶμεν τὰ πάντα ὑποτεταγμένα → αὐτῷ
v.aai.3s a.asn a.asn r.dsm.3 cj adv adv v.pai.1p d.apn a.apn pt.rp.apn r.dsm.3
918 4029 538 899 1254 3814 3972 3972 4037 3972 3836 4246 5718 899

9 But we see   Jesus, who was made a little   lower   than the angels, now crowned   with glory and
δὲ → βλέπομεν Ἰησοῦν τὸν → → βραχύ τι ἠλαττωμένον παρ' ἀγγέλους ἐστεφανωμένον → δόξῃ καὶ
cj v.pai.1p n.asm d.asm adv r.asn pt.rp.asm p.a n.apm pt.rp.asm n.dsf cj
1254 1063 2652 3836 1783 1783 1099 5516 4123 34 5110 1518 2779

honor because he suffered   death,   so   that by the grace of God he might taste   death for everyone. ¶
τιμῇ διὰ τὸ πάθημα τοῦ θανάτου ὅπως ← → χάριτι → θεοῦ γεύσηται θανάτου ὑπὲρ παντός
n.dsf p.a d.asn n.asn d.gsm n.gsm cj n.dsf n.gsm v.ams.3s n.gsm p.g a.gsm
5507 1328 3836 4077 3836 2505 3968 5921 2536 1174 2505 5642 4246

10 In bringing many   sons to glory, it was fitting that God, for whom   and through whom everything
γὰρ → ἀγαγόντα πολλοὺς υἱοὺς εἰς δόξαν → → ἔπρεπεν αὐτῷ δι' ὃν τὰ πάντα καὶ δι' οὗ τὰ πάντα
cj pt.aa.asm a.apm n.apm p.a n.asf v.iai.3s r.dsm.3 p.a r.asm d.npn a.npn cj p.g r.gsm d.npn a.npn
1142 72 4498 5626 1650 1518 4560 899 1328 4005 3836 4246 2779 1328 4005 3836 4246

exists, should make the author   of their salvation   perfect through suffering. **11** Both the one who makes men
→ → τὸν ἀρχηγὸν αὐτῶν τῆς σωτηρίας τελειῶσαι διὰ παθημάτων γὰρ τε ὁ
d.asm n.asm r.gpm.3 d.gsf n.gsf f.aa p.g n.gpn cj cj d.nsm
5457 5457 3836 795 5401 899 3836 5401 5457 1328 4077 1142 5445 3836

holy   and those who are made holy   are of the same family. So   Jesus is not ashamed   to call
ἁγιάζων καὶ οἱ ← ἁγιαζόμενοι ἐξ ἑνὸς πάντες δι' ἣν αἰτίαν → οὐκ ἐπαισχύνεται → καλεῖν
pt.pa.nsm cj d.npm pt.pp.npm p.g a.gsm a.npm p.a r.asf n.asf pl v.ppi.3s f.pa
39 2779 3836 39 1666 1651 4246 1328 4005 162 2049 4024 2049 2813

them brothers. **12** He says, "I will declare   your name   to my brothers;   in the presence of the congregation I
αὐτοὺς ἀδελφοὺς → λέγων → → ἀπαγγελῶ σου τὸ ὄνομα μου τοῖς ἀδελφοῖς ἐν μέσῳ → ἐκκλησίας →
r.apm.3 n.apm pt.pa.nsm v.fai.1s r.gs.2 d.asn n.asn r.gs.1 d.dpm n.dpm p.d n.dsn n.gsf
899 81 3306 550 5148 3836 3950 81 1609 3836 18// 3545 1/11

will sing   your praises." **13** And again, "I   will put my trust   in him." And again he says, "Here am I,   and the
→ ὑμνήσω σε καὶ πάλιν ἐγὼ ἔσομαι πεποιθὼς ἐπ' αὐτῷ καὶ πάλιν ἰδοὺ ἐγὼ καὶ τὰ
v.fai.1s r.as.2 cj adv r.ns.1 v.fmi.1s pt.ra.nsm p.d r.dsm.3 cj adv j r.ns.1 cj d.npn
5630 5148 5630 2779 4099 1609 1639 4275 2093 899 2779 4099 2627 1609 2779 3836

children God   has given me." **14** Since the children have   flesh and blood, he   too shared in
παιδία ἃ ὁ θεός → ἔδωκεν μοι οὖν Ἐπεὶ τὰ παιδία κεκοινώνηκεν σαρκὸς καὶ αἵματος αὐτὸς καὶ μετέσχεν ←
n.npn r.apn d.nsm n.nsm v.aai.3s r.ds.1 cj cj d.npn n.npn v.rai.3s n.gsf cj n.gsn r.nsm adv v.aai.3s
4086 4005 3836 2536 1443 1609 4036 2075 3836 4086 3125 4922 2779 135 899 2779 3576

their   humanity so   that by his death he might destroy   him who holds the power of death   – that
τῶν αὐτῶν παραπλησίως ἵνα → διὰ τοῦ θανάτου καταργήσῃ τὸν ἔχοντα τὸ κράτος τοῦ θανάτου τοῦτ'
d.gpn r.gpn adv cj p.g d.gsm n.gsm v.aas.3s d.asm pt.pa.asm d.asn n.asn d.gsm n.gsm r.nsn
3836 899 4181 2671 1328 3836 2505 2934 3836 2400 3836 3197 3836 2505 4047

is,   the devil   – **15** and free   those who   all   their lives   were held in slavery by their fear of death.
ἔστιν τὸν διάβολον καὶ ἀπαλλάξῃ τούτους ὅσοι διὰ παντὸς → τοῦ ζῆν ἦσαν ἔνοχοι ← δουλείας → φόβῳ θανάτου
v.pai.3s d.asm n.asm cj v.aas.3s r.apm r.npm p.g a.gsn d.gsn f.pa v.iai.3p a.npm n.gsf n.dsm n.gsm
1639 3836 1333 2779 557 4047 4012 1328 4246 3836 2409 1639 1944 1525 5832 2505

16 For surely it is not angels he helps,   but   Abraham's descendants. **17** For this reason he had   to be
γὰρ δήπου οὐ ἀγγέλων ἐπιλαμβάνεται ἀλλὰ ἐπιλαμβάνεται Ἀβραὰμ σπέρματος ὅθεν ← → ὤφειλεν →
cj adv pl n.gpm v.pmi.3s cj v.pmi.3s n.gsm n.gsn cj v.iai.3s
1142 1327 4024 34 2138 247 2138 11 5065 3854 4053

ἄνθρωπος ὅτι μιμνῄσκῃ αὐτοῦ, ἢ υἱὸς ἀνθρώπου ὅτι ἐπισκέπτῃ αὐτόν; [7] ἠλάττωσας αὐτὸν βραχύ τι παρ' ἀγγέλους, δόξῃ καὶ τιμῇ ἐστεφάνωσας αὐτόν, [8] πάντα ὑπέταξας ὑποκάτω τῶν ποδῶν αὐτοῦ. ἐν τῷ γὰρ ὑποτάξαι [αὐτῷ] τὰ πάντα οὐδὲν ἀφῆκεν αὐτῷ ἀνυπότακτον. νῦν δὲ οὔπω ὁρῶμεν αὐτῷ τὰ πάντα ὑποτεταγμένα· [9] τὸν δὲ βραχύ τι παρ' ἀγγέλους ἠλαττωμένον βλέπομεν Ἰησοῦν διὰ τὸ πάθημα τοῦ θανάτου δόξῃ καὶ τιμῇ ἐστεφανωμένον, ὅπως χάριτι θεοῦ ὑπὲρ παντὸς γεύσηται θανάτου. ¶
[10] Ἔπρεπεν γὰρ αὐτῷ, δι' ὃν τὰ πάντα καὶ δι' οὗ τὰ πάντα, πολλοὺς υἱοὺς εἰς δόξαν ἀγαγόντα τὸν ἀρχηγὸν τῆς σωτηρίας αὐτῶν διὰ παθημάτων τελειῶσαι. [11] ὅ τε γὰρ ἁγιάζων καὶ οἱ ἁγιαζόμενοι ἐξ ἑνὸς πάντες· δι' ἣν αἰτίαν οὐκ ἐπαισχύνεται ἀδελφοὺς αὐτοὺς καλεῖν [12] λέγων, Ἀπαγγελῶ τὸ ὄνομά σου τοῖς ἀδελφοῖς μου, ἐν μέσῳ ἐκκλησίας ὑμνήσω σε, [13] καὶ πάλιν, Ἐγὼ ἔσομαι πεποιθὼς ἐπ' αὐτῷ, καὶ πάλιν, Ἰδοὺ ἐγὼ καὶ τὰ παιδία ἅ μοι ἔδωκεν ὁ θεός. [14] ἐπεὶ οὖν τὰ παιδία κεκοινώνηκεν αἵματος καὶ σαρκός, καὶ αὐτὸς παραπλησίως μετέσχεν τῶν αὐτῶν, ἵνα διὰ τοῦ θανάτου καταργήσῃ τὸν τὸ κράτος ἔχοντα τοῦ θανάτου, τοῦτ' ἔστιν τὸν διάβολον, [15] καὶ ἀπαλλάξῃ τούτους, ὅσοι φόβῳ θανάτου διὰ παντὸς τοῦ ζῆν ἔνοχοι ἦσαν δουλείας. [16] οὐ γὰρ δήπου ἀγγέλων ἐπιλαμβάνεται ἀλλὰ σπέρματος Ἀβραὰμ ἐπιλαμβάνεται. [17] ὅθεν ὤφειλεν κατὰ πάντα τοῖς ἀδελφοῖς

made like   his brothers in   every way, in order that he might become a merciful and faithful high   priest
→   ὁμοιωθῆναι τοῖς ἀδελφοῖς κατὰ πάντα ←   ἵνα   →   γένηται ἐλεήμων καὶ πιστὸς ἀρχιερεὺς ←
    f.ap   d.dpm n.dpm p.a a.apn   cj   v.ams.3s a.nsm   cj n.nsm n.nsm
    3929   3836 81   2848 4246   2671   1181   1798   2779 4412 797

in service to   God,   and that he might make atonement for the sins of the people. 18 Because he
τὰ   πρὸς ⌐τὸν θεόν⌐ εἰς →   →   ⌐τὸ ἱλάσκεσθαι⌐ τὰς ἁμαρτίας → τοῦ λαοῦ   γὰρ ⌐ἐν ᾧ⌐
d.apn p.a d.asm n.asm p.a   d.asn v.pap   d.apf n.apf   d.gsm n.gsm cj   p.d r.dsn
3836   4639 3836 2536   1650   3836 2661   3836 281   3836 3295   1142 1877 4005 4248

himself suffered when he was tempted, he is able   to help   those who are being tempted.
αὐτὸς πέπονθεν →   →   → πειρασθεὶς → δύναται → βοηθῆσαι τοῖς ← ←   πειραζομένοις
r.nsm v.rai.3s   pt.ap.nsm   v.ppi.3s f.aa   d.dpm   pt.pp.dpm
899   4248   4279   1538   1070   3836   4279

Jesus Greater Than Moses

3:1 Therefore, holy brothers, who share in the heavenly calling, fix your thoughts on Jesus, the apostle and
       Ὅθεν   ἅγιοι ἀδελφοὶ → μέτοχοι ← ἐπουρανίου κλήσεως → → κατανοήσατε ← Ἰησοῦν τὸν ἀπόστολον καὶ
       cj   a.vpm n.vpm   n.vpm   a.gsf   n.gsf   v.aam.2p   n.asm d.asm n.asm   cj
       3854   41   81   3581   2230   3104   2917   2652   3836 693   2779

high   priest whom we confess. 2 He was faithful to the one who appointed him, just as Moses was faithful in
ἀρχιερέα ←   τῆς ἡμῶν ὁμολογίας ὄντα πιστὸν → τῷ ← ποιήσαντι αὐτὸν καὶ ὡς Μωϋσῆς ἐν
n.asm   d.gsf r.gp.1 n.gsf   pt.pa.asm a.asm d.dsm   pt.aa.dsm r.asm.3 adv cj n.nsm p.d
797   3836 7005 3934   1639   4412   3836   4472   899   2779 6055 3707   1877

all God's house. 3   Jesus has been found worthy of greater honor than Moses, just as the builder   of
ὅλῳ αὐτοῦ ⌐τῷ οἴκῳ⌐ γὰρ οὗτος → → ἠξίωται → πλείονος δόξης παρὰ Μωϋσῆν⌐καθ᾽ ὅσον⌐ ὁ   κατασκευάσας ←
a.dsm r.gsm.3 d.dsm n.dsm cj r.nsm   v.rpi.3s   a.gsf.c n.gsf p.a n.asm p.a r.asn d.nsm pt.aa.nsm
3910 899   3836 3875 1142 4047   546   4498   1518 4123 3707   2848 4012 3836 2941

a house has greater honor than the house itself. 4 For every house is built   by someone, but God   is the
← ← ἔχει πλείονα τιμὴν τοῦ οἴκου αὐτοῦ γὰρ πᾶς οἶκος → κατασκευάζεται ὑπό τινος δὲ ⌐ὁ θεός⌐ → →
      v.pai.3s a.asf.c n.asf d.gsm n.gsm r.asm.3 cj a.nsm n.nsm   v.ppi.3s   p.g r.gsm cj d.nsm n.nsm
      2400 4498   5507   3836 3875 899   1142 4246 3875   2941   5679 5516   1254 3836 2536

builder   of everything. 5   Moses was faithful as a servant in all God's house,   testifying to what
κατασκευάσας πάντα   καὶ μὲν Μωϋσῆς πιστὸς ὡς θεράπων ἐν ὅλῳ αὐτοῦ ⌐τῷ οἴκῳ⌐ εἰς μαρτύριον → τῶν
pt.aa.nsm   a.apn   cj pl n.nsm   a.nsm   pl n.nsm   p.d a.dsm r.gsm.3 d.dsm n.dsm p.a n.asn   d.gpn
2941   4246   2779 3525 3707   4412   6055 2544 1877 3910 899   3836 3875 1650 3457   3836

would be said   in the future. 6 But Christ is faithful as a son over God's house. And we are his house,
→   → λαληθησομένων ← ← ← δὲ Χριστὸς ὡς υἱὸς ἐπὶ αὐτοῦ ⌐τὸν οἶκον⌐ ἡμεῖς ἐσμεν οὗ οἶκος
     pt.fp.gpn   cj n.nsm   pl n.nsm p.g r.gsm.3 d.asm n.asm r.np.1 v.pai.1p cj n.nsm
     3281   1254 5986   6055 5626 2093 899   3836 3875   7005 1639   4005 3875

if we hold   on to our courage and the hope of which we boast.
ἐάνπερ → κατάσχωμεν ← ← τὴν παρρησίαν καὶ τῆς ἐλπίδος → → ⌐τὸ καύχημα⌐
cj   v.aas.1p   d.asf n.asf   cj d.gsf n.gsf   d.asn n.asn
1570   2988   3836 4244   2779 3836 1828   3836 3017

Warning Against Unbelief

3:7 So, as   the Holy   Spirit says: "Today, if you hear   his   voice,   8 do not harden   your
       Διὸ καθὼς τὸ ⌐τὸ ἅγιον⌐ πνεῦμα λέγει σήμερον ἐὰν → ἀκούσητε αὐτοῦ ⌐τῆς φωνῆς⌐ μὴ σκληρύνητε ὑμῶν
       cj cj   d.nsn d.nsn a.nsn n.nsn   v.pai.3s adv   cj   v.aas.2p r.gsm.3 d.gsf n.gsf   pl v.aas.2p   r.gp.2
       1475 2777 3836 3836 41   4460   3306   4958   1569   899   3836 5889   5020 3590   5020 7007

hearts   as you did in the rebellion, during the time of testing   in the desert, 9 where your
⌐τὰς καρδίας⌐ ὡς   ἐν τῷ παραπικρασμῷ κατὰ τὴν ἡμέραν → ⌐τοῦ πειρασμοῦ⌐ ἐν τῇ ἐρήμῳ οὗ ὑμῶν
d.apf n.apf   pl   p.d d.dsm n.dsm   p.a d.asf n.asf   d.gsm n.gsm   p.d d.dsf n.dsf   r.gsm r.gp.2
3836 2840   6055   1877 3836 4177   2848 3836 2465   3836 4280   1877 3836 2245   4023 7007

fathers   tested   and   tried   me and for forty   years saw what I   did. 10 That is why I was angry
⌐οἱ πατέρες⌐ ἐπείρασαν ἐν δοκιμασίᾳ καὶ → τεσσεράκοντα ἔτη εἶδον τὰ μου ἔργα → → διὸ προσώχθισα
d.npm n.npm   v.aai.3p   p.d n.dsf   cj   a.apn   n.apn v.aai.3p d.apn r.gs.1 n.apn   cj   v.aai.1s
3836 4252   4279   1877 1508   2779   5477   2291 1625   3836 2240 1609   1475   4696

with that generation, and I said, 'Their hearts are always going astray, and they have not known my ways.'
→ ταύτῃ τῇ γενεᾷ⌐ καὶ → εἶπον τῇ καρδίᾳ → ἀεὶ → πλανῶνται δὲ αὐτοὶ → οὐκ ἔγνωσαν μου ⌐τὰς ὁδούς⌐
r.dsf d.dsf n.dsf   cj   v.aai.1s d.dsf n.dsf   adv   v.ppi.3p cj r.npm   pl v.aai.3p r.gs.1 d.apf n.apf
1155 4047 3836 1155   2779 4414 3836 2840   107   4414   1254 899   4024 1182   1609 3836 3847

ὁμοιωθῆναι, ἵνα ἐλεήμων γένηται καὶ πιστὸς ἀρχιερεὺς τὰ πρὸς τὸν θεὸν εἰς τὸ ἱλάσκεσθαι τὰς ἁμαρτίας τοῦ λαοῦ. 18 ἐν ᾧ γὰρ πέπονθεν αὐτὸς πειρασθείς, δύναται τοῖς πειραζομένοις βοηθῆσαι.
    3:1 Ὅθεν, ἀδελφοὶ ἅγιοι, κλήσεως ἐπουρανίου μέτοχοι, κατανοήσατε τὸν ἀπόστολον καὶ ἀρχιερέα τῆς ὁμολογίας ἡμῶν Ἰησοῦν,
2 πιστὸν ὄντα τῷ ποιήσαντι αὐτὸν ὡς καὶ Μωϋσῆς ἐν [ὅλῳ] τῷ οἴκῳ αὐτοῦ. 3 πλείονος γὰρ οὗτος δόξης παρὰ Μωϋσῆν ἠξίωται,
καθ᾽ ὅσον πλείονα τιμὴν ἔχει τοῦ οἴκου ὁ κατασκευάσας αὐτόν· 4 πᾶς γὰρ οἶκος κατασκευάζεται ὑπό τινος, ὁ δὲ πάντα
κατασκευάσας θεός. 5 καὶ Μωϋσῆς μὲν πιστὸς ἐν ὅλῳ τῷ οἴκῳ αὐτοῦ ὡς θεράπων εἰς μαρτύριον τῶν λαληθησομένων, 6 Χριστὸς
δὲ ὡς υἱὸς ἐπὶ τὸν οἶκον αὐτοῦ· οὗ οἶκός ἐσμεν ἡμεῖς, ἐάν[περ] τὴν παρρησίαν καὶ τὸ καύχημα τῆς ἐλπίδος κατάσχωμεν.
    3:7 Διό, καθὼς λέγει τὸ πνεῦμα τὸ ἅγιον, Σήμερον ἐὰν τῆς φωνῆς αὐτοῦ ἀκούσητε, 8 μὴ σκληρύνητε τὰς καρδίας ὑμῶν ὡς
ἐν τῷ παραπικρασμῷ κατὰ τὴν ἡμέραν τοῦ πειρασμοῦ ἐν τῇ ἐρήμῳ, 9 οὗ ἐπείρασαν οἱ πατέρες ὑμῶν ἐν δοκιμασίᾳ καὶ εἶδον τὰ
ἔργα μου 10 τεσσεράκοντα ἔτη· διὸ προσώχθισα τῇ γενεᾷ ταύτῃ καὶ εἶπον, Ἀεὶ πλανῶνται τῇ καρδίᾳ, αὐτοὶ δὲ οὐκ ἔγνωσαν τὰς

11 So I declared on oath in my anger, 'They shall never enter my rest.'" ¶ **12** See to it,
ὡς → → → ὤμοσα ἐν μου ‹τῇ ὀργῇ⸜ ↦ ↦ εἰ εἰσελεύσονται εἰς μου ‹τὴν κατάπαυσιν⸜   Βλέπετε ← ←
cj v.aai.1s p.d r.gs.1 d.dsf n.dsf cj v.fmi.3p p.a r.gs.1 d.asf n.asf v.pam.2p
6055 3923 1877 1609 3836 3973 1656 1656 1623 1656 1650 1609 3836 2923 1063

brothers, that none of you has a sinful, unbelieving heart that turns away from the living God.
ἀδελφοί ‹μήποτε τινι⸜ ἐν ὑμῶν ἔσται πονηρὰ ἀπιστίας καρδία ἐν τῷ ἀποστῆναι ← ἀπὸ ζῶντος θεοῦ
n.vpm cj r.dsm p.d r.gp.2 v.fmi.3s a.nsf n.gsf n.nsf p.d d.dsn f.aa p.g pt.pa.gsm n.gsm
81 3607 5516 1877 7007 1639 4505 602 2840 1877 3836 923 608 2409 2536

13 But encourage one another daily, as long as it is called Today, so that none of
ἀλλὰ παρακαλεῖτε ἑαυτοὺς ← ‹καθ᾽ ἑκάστην ἡμέραν⸜ ἄχρις οὗ ← ← καλεῖται τὸ σήμερον ἵνα ← ‹μή τις⸜ ἐξ
cj v.pam.2p r.apm2 p.a r.asf n.asf p.g r.gsm v.ppi.3s d.nsn adv cj pl r.nsm p.g
247 4151 1571 2848 1667 2465 948 4005 2813 3836 4958 2671 3590 5516 1666

you may be hardened by sin's deceitfulness. **14** We have come to share in Christ if we
ὑμῶν → → σκληρυνθῇ ↗ ‹τῆς ἁμαρτίας⸜ ἀπάτη γὰρ → → γεγόναμεν μέτοχοι → ‹τοῦ Χριστοῦ⸜ ἐάνπερ →
r.gp.2 v.aps.3s d.gsf n.gsf n.dsf cj v.rai.1p n.npm d.gsm n.gsm cj
7007 5020 573 3836 281 573 1142 1181 3581 3836 5986 1570

hold firmly till the end the confidence *we had at first.* **15** As has just been said: "Today, if you
κατάσχωμεν βεβαίαν μέχρι τέλους τῆς ὑποστάσεως ‹τὴν ἀρχὴν⸜ ἐν ‹τῷ λέγεσθαι⸜ σήμερον ἐὰν →
v.aas.1p a.asf p.g n.gsn d.gsf n.gsf d.asf n.asf p.d d.dsn f.pp adv cj
2988 1010 3588 5465 3836 5712 3836 794 1877 3836 3306 4958 1569

hear his voice, do not harden your hearts as you did in the rebellion." ¶ **16** Who were
ἀκούσητε αὐτοῦ ‹τῆς φωνῆς⸜ ↗ μὴ σκληρύνητε ὑμῶν ‹τὰς καρδίας⸜ ὡς ← ἐν ‹τῷ παραπικρασμῷ⸜ γὰρ τίνες ←
v.aas.2p r.gsm.3 d.gsf n.gsf pl v.aas.2p r.gp.2 d.apf n.apf cj p.d d.dsm n.dsm cj r.npm
201 899 3836 5889 5020 3590 5020 7007 3836 2840 6055 1877 3836 4177 1142 5515

they who heard and rebelled? Were they not all those Moses led out of Egypt? **17** And with
← ἀκούσαντες παρεπίκραναν ἀλλ᾽ ← οὐ πάντες οἱ διὰ Μωϋσέως ἐξελθόντες ἐξ ← Αἰγύπτου δὲ →
pt.aa.npm v.aai.3p cj pl a.npm d.npm p.g n.gsm pt.aa.npm p.g n.gsf cj
201 4176 247 4024 4246 3836 1328 3707 2002 1666 131 1254

whom was he angry for forty years? Was it not with those who sinned, whose bodies fell in the
τίσιν → → προσώχθισεν → τεσσεράκοντα ἔτη οὐχὶ → τοῖς ← ἁμαρτήσασιν ὧν ‹τὰ κῶλα⸜ ἔπεσεν ἐν τῇ
r.dpm v.aai.3s a.apn n.apn pl d.dpm pt.aa.dpm r.gpm d.npn n.npn v.aai.3s p.d d.dsf
5515 4696 5477 2291 4049 3836 279 4005 3836 3265 4406 1877 3836

desert? **18** And to whom did God swear that they would never enter his rest if not to those who
ἐρήμῳ δὲ → τίσιν → ὤμοσεν μὴ εἰσελεύσεσθαι εἰς αὐτοῦ ‹τὴν κατάπαυσιν⸜ εἰ μὴ → τοῖς ←
n.dsf cj r.dpm v.aai.3s pl f.fm p.a r.gsm.3 d.asf n.asf cj pl d.dpm
2245 1254 5515 3923 3590 1656 1650 899 3836 2923 1623 3590 3836

disobeyed? **19** So we see that they were not able to enter, because of their unbelief.
ἀπειθήσασιν καὶ → βλέπομεν ὅτι ↗ → οὐκ ἠδυνήθησαν → εἰσελθεῖν δι᾽ ← ἀπιστίαν
pt.aa.dpm cj v.pai.1p cj pl v.api.3p f.aa p.g n.asf
578 2779 1063 4022 1538 1538 4024 1538 1656 1328 602

A Sabbath-Rest for the People of God

4:1 Therefore, since the promise of entering his rest still stands, let us be careful that
οὖν ↗ ἐπαγγελίας → εἰσελθεῖν εἰς αὐτοῦ ‹τὴν κατάπαυσιν⸜ → καταλειπομένης → → φοβηθῶμεν μήποτε
cj n.gsf f.aa p.a r.gsm.3 d.asf n.asf pt.pp.gsf v.aps.1p cj
4036 2901 2039 1656 1650 899 3836 2923 2901 5828 3607

none of you be found to have fallen short of it. **2** For we also have had the gospel preached to us, just as
τις ἐξ ὑμῶν → δοκῇ → ὑστερηκέναι ← γὰρ καὶ → ἐσμεν εὐηγγελισμένοι καθάπερ
r.nsm p.g r.gp.2 v.pas.3s f.ra cj adv v.pai.1p pt.rp.npm cj
5516 1666 7007 1506 5728 1142 1639 2779 1639 2294 2749

they did; but the message they heard was of no value to them, because those who heard did not
κἀκεῖνοι ἀλλ᾽ ὁ λόγος ‹τῆς ἀκοῆς⸜ ↗ → οὐκ ὠφέλησεν ἐκείνους τοῖς ← ἀκούσασιν ↗ μὴ
adv cj d.nsm n.nsm d.gsf n.gsf pl v.aai.3s r.apm d.dpm pt.aa.dpm pl
2797 247 3836 3364 3836 198 6067 6067 4024 6067 1697 3836 201 5166 3590

combine it with faith. **3** Now we who have believed enter that rest, just as God has
συγκεκερασμένους ← ‹τῇ πίστει⸜ γὰρ → οἱ πιστεύσαντες Εἰσερχόμεθα εἰς τὴν κατάπαυσιν καθὼς ←
pt.rp.apm d.dsf n.dsf cj d.npm pt.aa.npm v.pmi.1p p.a d.asf n.asf cj
5166 3836 4411 1142 1656 3836 4409 1656 1650 3836 2923 2777

ὁδούς μου, **11** ὡς ὤμοσα ἐν τῇ ὀργῇ μου· Εἰ εἰσελεύσονται εἰς τὴν κατάπαυσίν μου. ¶ **12** Βλέπετε, ἀδελφοί, μήποτε ἔσται ἔν τινι ὑμῶν καρδία πονηρὰ ἀπιστίας ἐν τῷ ἀποστῆναι ἀπὸ θεοῦ ζῶντος, **13** ἀλλὰ παρακαλεῖτε ἑαυτοὺς καθ᾽ ἑκάστην ἡμέραν, ἄχρις οὗ τὸ Σήμερον καλεῖται, ἵνα μὴ σκληρυνθῇ τις ἐξ ὑμῶν ἀπάτῃ τῆς ἁμαρτίας— **14** μέτοχοι γὰρ τοῦ Χριστοῦ γεγόναμεν, ἐάνπερ τὴν ἀρχὴν τῆς ὑποστάσεως μέχρι τέλους βεβαίαν κατάσχωμεν— **15** ἐν τῷ λέγεσθαι, Σήμερον ἐὰν τῆς φωνῆς αὐτοῦ ἀκούσητε, Μὴ σκληρύνητε τὰς καρδίας ὑμῶν ὡς ἐν τῷ παραπικρασμῷ. ¶ **16** τίνες γὰρ ἀκούσαντες παρεπίκραναν; ἀλλ᾽ οὐ πάντες οἱ ἐξελθόντες ἐξ Αἰγύπτου διὰ Μωϋσέως; **17** τίσιν δὲ προσώχθισεν τεσσεράκοντα ἔτη; οὐχὶ τοῖς ἁμαρτήσασιν, ὧν τὰ κῶλα ἔπεσεν ἐν τῇ ἐρήμῳ; **18** τίσιν δὲ ὤμοσεν, μὴ εἰσελεύσεσθαι εἰς τὴν κατάπαυσιν αὐτοῦ εἰ μὴ τοῖς ἀπειθήσασιν; **19** καὶ βλέπομεν ὅτι οὐκ ἠδυνήθησαν εἰσελθεῖν δι᾽ ἀπιστίαν.

    4:1 Φοβηθῶμεν οὖν, μήποτε καταλειπομένης ἐπαγγελίας εἰσελθεῖν εἰς τὴν κατάπαυσιν αὐτοῦ δοκῇ τις ἐξ ὑμῶν ὑστερηκέναι. **2** καὶ γὰρ ἐσμεν εὐηγγελισμένοι καθάπερ κἀκεῖνοι· ἀλλ᾽ οὐκ ὠφέλησεν ὁ λόγος τῆς ἀκοῆς ἐκείνους μὴ συγκεκερασμένος «συγκεκερασμένους» τῇ πίστει τοῖς ἀκούσασιν. **3** εἰσερχόμεθα γὰρ εἰς [τὴν] κατάπαυσιν οἱ πιστεύσαντες, καθὼς εἴρηκεν, Ὡς

said,　"So I declared on oath　in　my　anger,　'They shall never enter　　my rest.'"　　And　yet his
εἴρηκεν ὡς →　→　ὤμοσα ἐν μου ⌊τῇ ὀργῇ⌋　→　εἰ　εἰσελεύσονται εἰς μου ⌊τὴν κατάπαυσιν⌋ καίτοι ←　τῶν
v.rai.3s cj　　　　　v.aai.1s p.d d.dsf n.dsf　　　cj　v.fmi.3p　　　p.a r.gs.1 d.asf n.asf　cj　　　d.gpn
3306 6055　　　　　3923　3923 1877 1609 3836 3973　1656　1656 1623　1656　　　1650 1609 3836 2923　2792　　　3836

work　has been finished　since the creation　of the world.　⁴ For somewhere he has spoken about the seventh day
ἔργων → been →　γενηθέντων ἀπὸ　καταβολῆς →　κόσμου　γὰρ που　→　→ εἴρηκεν περὶ τῆς ἑβδόμης ←
n.gpn　　　　　pt.ap.gpn p.g　n.gsf　　　n.gsm　cj adv　　　v.rai.3s p.g d.gsf a.gsf
2240　　　　　1181 608　2856　　　3180　1142 4543　　　3306 4309 3836 1575

in　these words: "And on the seventh　day　God　rested　from all　his　work."　⁵ And again in the
οὕτως　　καὶ ἐν τῇ ⌊τῇ ἑβδόμῃ⌋ ἡμέρᾳ ὁ θεὸς κατέπαυσεν ἀπὸ πάντων αὐτοῦ ⌊τῶν ἔργων⌋ καὶ πάλιν ἐν τούτῳ
adv　　　cj p.d d.dsf d.dsf a.dsf n.dsf d.nsm n.nsm v.aai.3s p.g a.gpn r.gsm.3 d.gpn n.gpn cj adv p.d r.dsn
4048　　　2779 1877 3836 3836 1575 2465 3836 2536 2924 608 4246 899 3836 2240 2779 4099 1877 4047

passage above he says, "They shall never enter　　my rest."　　¶　　⁶　It still remains　that
← ← →　εἰ　εἰσελεύσονται εἰς μου ⌊τὴν κατάπαυσιν⌋　　　οὖν ἐπεὶ → ἀπολείπεται
　　　cj　v.fmi.3p　　p.a r.gs.1 d.asf n.asf　　　　cj cj　　v.ppi.3s
　　　1656　1656 1623　1656　　1650 1609 3836 2923　　　4036 2075　　657

some will enter　　that rest, and those who formerly had the gospel preached　to them did not go　in,
τινὰς → εἰσελθεῖν εἰς αὐτήν ← καὶ οἱ ← πρότερον → → εὐαγγελισθέντες　οὐκ εἰσῆλθον
r.apm　　f.aa p.a r.asf.3　cj d.npm　adv.c　　pt.ap.npm　　　pl v.aai.3p
5516　　1656 1650 899　2779 3836　4728　　2294　　　　1656 4024 1656

because of their disobedience.　⁷ Therefore God again set　a certain day,　calling it Today, when a long　time
δι'　←　ἀπείθειαν　←　πάλιν ὁρίζει τινὰ ἡμέραν σήμερον μετὰ τοσοῦτον χρόνον
p.a　　n.asf　　　　adv v.pai.3s r.asf n.asf adv p.a r.asm n.asm
1328　　577　　4036　4099 3988 5516 2465 4958 3552 5537 5989

later he spoke through David, as　was said　before: "Today, if you hear　his　voice,　do not harden
← → λέγων ἐν Δαυὶδ καθὼς → προείρηται ← σήμερον ἐὰν → ἀκούσητε αὐτοῦ ⌊τῆς φωνῆς⌋ → μὴ σκληρύνητε
　　　pt.pa.nsm p.d n.dsm cj v.rpi.3s adv cj　v.aas.2p r.gsm.3 d.gsf n.gsf pl v.aas.2p
3552　3306 1877 1253 2777 4597 4958 1569　201 899 3836 5889 5020 3590 5020

your hearts."　⁸ For if Joshua had given them rest,　God would not have spoken later　about another
ὑμῶν ⌊τὰς καρδίας⌋ γὰρ εἰ Ἰησοῦς → → αὐτοὺς κατέπαυσεν ἂν οὐκ → ἐλάλει ⌊μετὰ ταῦτα⌋ περὶ ἄλλης
r.gp.2 d.apf n.apf cj cj n.nsm　　r.apm.3 v.aai.3s pl pl　v.iai.3s p.a r.apn p.g r.gsf
7007 3836 2840 1142 1623 2652　　899 2924 323 4024　3281 3552 4047 4309 257

day.　⁹ There remains,　then, a Sabbath-rest for the people of God;　¹⁰ for anyone who enters　God's
ἡμέρας → ἀπολείπεται ἄρα σαββατισμὸς → τῷ λαῷ → ⌊τοῦ θεοῦ⌋ γὰρ ὁ εἰσελθὼν εἰς αὐτοῦ
n.gsf　v.ppi.3s cj n.nsm　d.dsm n.dsm d.gsm n.gsm cj d.nsm pt.aa.nsm p.a r.gsm.3
2465　657 726 4878　3836 3295 3836 2536 1142 3836 1656 1650 899

rest　also　rests　from his own work, just as God　did from his.　¹¹ Let us, therefore,
⌊τὴν κατάπαυσιν⌋ καὶ αὐτὸς κατέπαυσεν ἀπὸ αὐτοῦ τῶν ἔργων ὥσπερ ← ὁ θεός ἀπὸ ⌊τῶν ἰδίων⌋ οὖν
d.asf n.asf adv r.nsm v.aai.3s p.g r.gsm.3 d.gpn n.gpn cj d.nsm n.nsm p.g d.gpn a.gpn cj
3836 2923 2779 899 2924 608 899 3836 2240 6061 3836 2536 608 3836 2625 5079 5079 4036

make every effort　to enter　　that rest,　so that no one will fall by following their
→ → Σπουδάσωμεν → εἰσελθεῖν εἰς ἐκείνην ⌊τὴν κατάπαυσιν⌋ ἵνα ← μὴ τις → πέσῃ → αὐτῷ
v.aas.1p f.aa p.a r.asf d.asf n.asf cj pl r.nsm v.aas.3s r.dsn
5079 1656 1650 1697 3836 2923 2671 3590 5516 4406 5682 899

example　of disobedience.　¶　¹² For the word of God　is living and active.　Sharper than any
⌊τῷ ὑποδείγματι⌋ → ⌊τῆς ἀπειθείας⌋ γὰρ ὁ λόγος → ⌊τοῦ θεοῦ⌋ Ζῶν καὶ ἐνεργὴς καὶ τομώτερος ὑπὲρ πᾶσαν
d.dsn n.dsn d.gsf n.gsf cj d.nsm n.nsm d.gsm n.gsm pt.pa.nsm cj a.nsm cj a.nsm.c p.a a.asf
3836 5682 3836 577 1142 3836 3364 3836 2536 2409 2779 1921 2779 5533 5642 4246

double-edged sword,　it penetrates　even to dividing soul and spirit,　joints and marrow;　it judges the
δίστομον μάχαιραν καὶ → διϊκνούμενος ἄχρι ← μερισμοῦ ψυχῆς καὶ πνεύματος τε ἁρμῶν καὶ μυελῶν καὶ κριτικὸς
a.asf n.asf cj pt.pm.nsm p.g n.gsm n.gsf cj n.gsn cj n.gpm cj n.gpm cj a.nsm
1492 3479 2779 1459 948 3536 6034 2779 4460 5445 765 2779 3678 2779 3217

thoughts and attitudes of the heart.　¹³ Nothing in all creation is　hidden from God's sight.　Everything is
ἐνθυμήσεων καὶ ἐννοιῶν → καρδίας καὶ οὐκ κτίσις ἔστιν ἀφανὴς ἐνώπιον αὐτοῦ ← δὲ πάντα
n.gpf cj n.gpf n.gsf cj pl n.nsf v.pai.3s a.nsf p.g r.gsm.3 cj a.npn
1927 2779 1936 2840 2779 4024 3232 1639 905 1967 899 1967 1254 4246

ὤμοσα ἐν τῇ ὀργῇ μου, Εἰ εἰσελεύσονται εἰς τὴν κατάπαυσίν μου, καίτοι τῶν ἔργων ἀπὸ καταβολῆς κόσμου γενηθέντων. ⁴ εἴρηκεν γάρ που περὶ τῆς ἑβδόμης οὕτως, Καὶ κατέπαυσεν ὁ θεὸς ἐν τῇ ἡμέρᾳ τῇ ἑβδόμῃ ἀπὸ πάντων τῶν ἔργων αὐτοῦ, ⁵ καὶ ἐν τούτῳ πάλιν, Εἰ εἰσελεύσονται εἰς τὴν κατάπαυσίν μου. ¶ ⁶ ἐπεὶ οὖν ἀπολείπεται τινὰς εἰσελθεῖν εἰς αὐτήν, καὶ οἱ πρότερον εὐαγγελισθέντες οὐκ εἰσῆλθον δι' ἀπείθειαν, ⁷ πάλιν τινὰ ὁρίζει ἡμέραν, Σήμερον, ἐν Δαυὶδ λέγων μετὰ τοσοῦτον χρόνον, καθὼς προείρηται, Σήμερον ἐὰν τῆς φωνῆς αὐτοῦ ἀκούσητε, μὴ σκληρύνητε τὰς καρδίας ὑμῶν. ⁸ εἰ γὰρ αὐτοὺς Ἰησοῦς κατέπαυσεν, οὐκ ἂν περὶ ἄλλης ἐλάλει μετὰ ταῦτα ἡμέρας. ⁹ ἄρα ἀπολείπεται σαββατισμὸς τῷ λαῷ τοῦ θεοῦ. ¹⁰ ὁ γὰρ εἰσελθὼν εἰς τὴν κατάπαυσιν αὐτοῦ καὶ αὐτὸς κατέπαυσεν ἀπὸ τῶν ἔργων αὐτοῦ ὥσπερ ἀπὸ τῶν ἰδίων ὁ θεός. ¹¹ σπουδάσωμεν οὖν εἰσελθεῖν εἰς ἐκείνην τὴν κατάπαυσιν, ἵνα μὴ ἐν τῷ αὐτῷ τις ὑποδείγματι πέσῃ τῆς ἀπειθείας. ¶ ¹² Ζῶν γὰρ ὁ λόγος τοῦ θεοῦ καὶ ἐνεργὴς καὶ τομώτερος ὑπὲρ πᾶσαν μάχαιραν δίστομον καὶ διϊκνούμενος ἄχρι μερισμοῦ ψυχῆς καὶ πνεύματος, ἁρμῶν τε καὶ μυελῶν, καὶ κριτικὸς ἐνθυμήσεων καὶ ἐννοιῶν καρδίας· ¹³ καὶ οὐκ ἔστιν κτίσις ἀφανὴς ἐνώπιον αὐτοῦ, πάντα δὲ γυμνὰ καὶ τετραχηλισμένα

uncovered and laid   bare before   the eyes   of him to   whom we   must give account.
γυμνὰ   καὶ τετραχηλισμένα ←   τοῖς ὀφθαλμοῖς →   αὐτοῦ πρὸς ὃν   ἡμῖν   ὁ λόγος
a.npn   cj   pt.rp.npn   d.dpm n.dpm   r.gsm.3 p.a r.asm r.dp.1   d.nsm n.nsm
1218   2779 5548   3836 4057   899   4639 4005 7005   3836 3364

Jesus the Great High Priest

4:14 Therefore, since we have   a great high   priest who has gone   through the heavens, Jesus the Son of
       οὖν   →   → Ἔχοντες μέγαν ἀρχιερέα ←   →   διεληλυθότα ←   τοὺς οὐρανούς Ἰησοῦν τὸν υἱὸν →
       cj   pt.pa.npm a.asm n.asm   pt.ra.asm   d.apm n.asm   n.asm d.asm n.asm
       4036   2400 3489 797   1451   3836 4041   2652   3836 5626

God,   let us hold   firmly to the faith we profess. 15 For we do not have a high   priest who is unable   to
˻τοῦ θεοῦ˼ → κρατῶμεν ←   τῆς ὁμολογίας   γὰρ → → οὐ ἔχομεν ἀρχιερέα   ˻μὴ δυνάμενον˼
d.gsm n.gsm   v.pas.1p   d.gsf n.gsf   cj   pl v.pai.1p n.asm   pl pt.pp.asm
3836 2536   3195   3836 3934   1142 2400 2400 4024 2400 797   3590 1538

sympathize with our weaknesses,   but we have one who has been tempted   in   every way, just as we
συμπαθῆσαι → ἡμῶν ˻ταῖς ἀσθενείαις˼ δὲ → →   → → πεπειρασμένον κατὰ πάντα ←   καθ' ←
f.aa   r.gp.1 d.dpf n.dpf   cj   pt.rp.asm   p.a a.apn   p.a
5217   819   7005 819   1254   4279   2848 4246   4246

are   – yet was without sin.   16 Let us then approach   the throne of grace   with confidence, so that we
ὁμοιότητα   χωρὶς ἁμαρτίας   ⸓ ⸓ οὖν προσερχώμεθα τῷ θρόνῳ ˻τῆς χάριτος˼ μετὰ παρρησίας ἵνα ←   →
n.asf   p.g   n.gsf   ⸓ cj v.pms.1p   d.dsm n.dsm d.gsf n.gsf p.g n.gsf   cj
3928   6006 281   4665 4665 4036 4665   3836 2585 3836 5921 3552 4244   2671

may receive mercy and find   grace to help   us in our time   of need. ¶ 5:1   Every high   priest is
→ λάβωμεν ἔλεος καὶ εὕρωμεν χάριν εἰς βοήθειαν →   →   εὔκαιρον ←   γὰρ Πᾶς ἀρχιερεὺς
v.aas.1p   n.asn cj v.aas.1p n.asf p.a n.asf   a.asf   cj a.nsm n.nsm
3284   1799 2779 2351   5921 1650 1069   2322   1142 4246 797

selected   from among men   and is appointed to   represent them in matters related to   God,   to
λαμβανόμενος ἐξ ←   ἀνθρώπων → καθίσταται ὑπὲρ → ἀνθρώπων → τὰ →   πρὸς ˻τὸν θεόν˼ ἵνα
pt.pp.nsm   p.g   n.gpm   v.ppi.3s p.g   n.gpm   d.apn   p.a d.asm n.asm cj
3284   1666   476   2770   5642   476   3836   4639 3836 2536 2671

offer   gifts and sacrifices for sins. 2 He is able   to deal   gently with those who are ignorant and are
προσφέρῃ τε δῶρα καὶ θυσίας ὑπὲρ ἁμαρτιῶν δυνάμενος → μετριοπαθεῖν ←   τοῖς ←   →   ἀγνοοῦσιν καὶ →
v.pas.3s cj n.apn cj n.apf p.g n.gpf   pt.pp.nsm   f.pa   d.dpm   pt.pa.dpm cj
4712   5445 1565 2779 2602 5642 281   1538   3584   3836   51   2779

going astray,   since he himself is subject to weakness. 3 This   is why he has   to offer   sacrifices
→ πλανωμένοις ἐπεὶ καὶ ⸓ αὐτὸς → περίκειται ἀσθένειαν καὶ ˻δι' αὐτὴν˼   → ὀφείλει → προσφέρειν ←
pt.pp.dpm   cj   adv   r.nsm   v.pmi.3s   n.asf   cj p.a r.asf.3   v.pai.3s f.pa
4414   2075 2779 4329 899   4329   819   2779 1328 899   4053   4712

for his own   sins,   as   well as for the sins of the people. ¶ 4   No one takes   this
καὶ περὶ αὐτοῦ περὶ ἁμαρτιῶν ˻καθὼς οὕτως˼ περὶ   τοῦ λαοῦ   καὶ οὐχ τις λαμβάνει τὴν
adv p.g r.gsm.3 p.g n.gpf   pl   adv   p.g   d.gsm n.gsm   cj pl r.nsm v.pai.3s d.asf
2779 4309 899   4309 281   2777 4048   4309   3836 3295   2779 4024 5516 3284   3836

honor upon himself;   he must be called   by God,   just   as   Aaron was. 5 So   Christ   also did
τιμὴν →   ἑαυτῷ ἀλλὰ →   καλούμενος ὑπὸ ˻τοῦ θεοῦ˼ καθώσπερ ← καὶ Ἀαρών   οὕτως ὁ Χριστὸς καὶ →
n.asf   r.dsm.3 cj   pt.pp.nsm p.g d.gsm n.gsm p.g   adv n.nsm   adv d.nsm n.nsm adv
5507   1571   247   2813   5679 3836 2536 2778   2779 2   4048 3836 5986 2779 1519

not take upon himself the glory of becoming a high   priest. But God said   to him, "You are my Son;
οὐχ →   →   ἑαυτὸν ἐδόξασεν γενηθῆναι   ἀρχιερέα ← ἀλλ' ὁ λαλήσας πρὸς αὐτόν σὺ   εἶ μου υἱός
pl   r.asm.3 v.aai.3s f.ap   n.asm   cj   d.nsm pt.aa.nsm p.a r.asm.3 r.ns.2 v.pai.2s r.gs.1 n.nsm
4024 1519   1571   1519   1181   797   247 3836 3281   4639 899   5148 1639 1609 5626

today I have become your Father." 6   And he says in another place, "You are a priest forever, in
σήμερον ἐγώ → γεγέννηκα σε   καθὼς καὶ → λέγει ἐν ἑτέρῳ   σὺ   ἱερεὺς ˻εἰς τὸν αἰῶνα˼ κατὰ
adv   r.ns.1 v.rai.1s r.as.2   cj   adv   v.pai.3s p.d r.dsm   r.ns.2 n.nsm p.a d.asm n.asm   p.a
4958   1609 1164   5148 1164   2777 2779   3306 1877 2283   5148 2636 1650 3836 172   2848

the order of Melchizedek." ¶ 7 During the days   of Jesus' life   on earth, he offered   up   prayers
τὴν τάξιν →   Μελχισέδεκ   ἐν ταῖς ἡμέραις → αὐτοῦ ˻τῆς σαρκὸς˼ ←   ὃς προσενέγκας ← τε δεήσεις
d.asf n.asf   n.gsm   p.d d.dpf n.dpf   r.gsm.3 d.gsf n.gsf   r.nsm pt.aa.asm   cj n.apf
3836 5423   3519   1877 3836 2465   4922 899 3836 4922   4005 4712   5445 1255

τοῖς ὀφθαλμοῖς αὐτοῦ, πρὸς ὃν ἡμῖν ὁ λόγος.

⁴:¹⁴ Ἔχοντες οὖν ἀρχιερέα μέγαν διεληλυθότα τοὺς οὐρανούς, Ἰησοῦν τὸν υἱὸν τοῦ θεοῦ, κρατῶμεν τῆς ὁμολογίας. ¹⁵ οὐ γὰρ ἔχομεν ἀρχιερέα μὴ δυνάμενον συμπαθῆσαι ταῖς ἀσθενείαις ἡμῶν, πεπειρασμένον δὲ κατὰ πάντα καθ' ὁμοιότητα χωρὶς ἁμαρτίας. ¹⁶ προσερχώμεθα οὖν μετὰ παρρησίας τῷ θρόνῳ τῆς χάριτος, ἵνα λάβωμεν ἔλεος καὶ χάριν εὕρωμεν εἰς εὔκαιρον βοήθειαν. ⁵:¹ Πᾶς γὰρ ἀρχιερεὺς ἐξ ἀνθρώπων λαμβανόμενος ὑπὲρ ἀνθρώπων καθίσταται τὰ πρὸς τὸν θεόν, ἵνα προσφέρῃ δῶρά τε καὶ θυσίας ὑπὲρ ἁμαρτιῶν, ² μετριοπαθεῖν δυνάμενος τοῖς ἀγνοοῦσιν καὶ πλανωμένοις, ἐπεὶ καὶ αὐτὸς περίκειται ἀσθένειαν ³ καὶ δι' αὐτὴν ὀφείλει, καθὼς περὶ τοῦ λαοῦ, οὕτως καὶ περὶ αὐτοῦ προσφέρειν περὶ ἁμαρτιῶν. ¶ ⁴ καὶ οὐχ ἑαυτῷ τις λαμβάνει τὴν τιμὴν ἀλλὰ καλούμενος ὑπὸ τοῦ θεοῦ καθώσπερ καὶ Ἀαρών. ⁵ Οὕτως καὶ ὁ Χριστὸς οὐχ ἑαυτὸν ἐδόξασεν γενηθῆναι ἀρχιερέα ἀλλ' ὁ λαλήσας πρὸς αὐτόν, Υἱός μου εἶ σύ, ἐγὼ σήμερον γεγέννηκά σε· ⁶ καθὼς καὶ ἐν ἑτέρῳ λέγει, Σὺ ἱερεὺς εἰς τὸν αἰῶνα κατὰ τὴν τάξιν Μελχισέδεκ, ¶ ⁷ ὃς ἐν ταῖς ἡμέραις τῆς σαρκὸς αὐτοῦ δεήσεις τε καὶ ἱκετηρίας πρὸς τὸν δυνάμενον σῴζειν αὐτὸν ἐκ θανάτου μετὰ κραυγῆς ἰσχυρᾶς καὶ δακρύων προσενέγκας καὶ εἰσακουσθεὶς ἀπὸ τῆς εὐλαβείας, ⁸ καίπερ ὢν

and petitions with loud cries and tears to the one who could save him from death, and he was
καὶ ἱκετηρίας μετὰ ἰσχυρᾶς κραυγῆς καὶ δακρύων πρὸς τὸν δυνάμενον σῴζειν αὐτὸν ἐκ θανάτου καὶ →
cj n.apf p.g a.gsf n.gsf cj n.gpn p.a d.asm pt.pp.asm f.pa r.asm.3 p.g n.gsm cj
2779 2656 3552 2708 3199 2779 1232 4639 3836 1538 5392 899 1666 2505 2779

heard because of his reverent submission. **8** Although he was a son, he learned obedience from what he
εἰσακουσθεὶς ἀπὸ ← τῆς εὐλαβείας ← καίπερ → ὢν υἱός → ἔμαθεν ⸤τὴν ὑπακοὴν⸥ ἀφ᾽ ὧν →
pt.ap.nsm p.g d.gsf n.gsf cj pt.pa.nsm n.nsm v.aai.3s d.asf n.asf p.g r.gpn
1653 608 3836 2325 2788 1639 5626 3443 3836 5633 608 4005

suffered **9** and, once made perfect, he became the source of eternal salvation for all who obey him **10** and was
ἔπαθεν καὶ → τελειωθεὶς → ἐγένετο αἴτιος → αἰωνίου σωτηρίας → πᾶσιν τοῖς ὑπακούουσιν αὐτῷ →
v.aai.3s cj pt.ap.nsm v.ami.3s n.nsm a.gsf n.gsf a.dpm d.dpm pt.pa.dpm r.dsm.3
4248 2779 5457 1181 165 173 5401 4246 3836 5634 899

designated by God to be high priest in the order of Melchizedek.
προσαγορευθεὶς ὑπὸ ⸤τοῦ θεοῦ⸥ ← ← ἀρχιερεὺς ← κατὰ τὴν τάξιν → Μελχισέδεκ
pt.ap.nsm p.g d.gsm n.gsm n.nsm p.a d.asf n.asf n.gsm
4641 5679 3836 2536 4641 4641 797 2848 3836 5423 3519

Warning Against Falling Away

5:11 We have much to say about this, but it is hard to explain because you are slow to
ἡμῖν πολὺς ὁ λόγος⸥ Περὶ οὗ καὶ δυσερμήνευτος → λέγειν ἐπεὶ → γεγόνατε νωθροὶ
r.dp.1 a.nsm d.nsm n.nsm p.g r.gsn cj a.nsm f.pa cj v.rai.2p a.npm
7005 4498 3836 3364 4309 4005 2779 1549 3306 2075 1181 3821

learn. **12** In fact, though by this time you ought to be teachers, you need someone to
⸤ταῖς ἀκοαῖς⸥ γὰρ ← καὶ διὰ τὸν χρόνον → ὀφείλοντες εἶναι διδάσκαλοι → χρείαν ἔχετε τινὰ
d.dpf n.dpf cj adv p.a d.asm n.asm pt.pa.npm f.pa n.npm n.asf v.pai.2p r.asm
3836 198 1142 2779 1328 3836 5989 4053 1639 1437 5970 2400 5516

teach you the elementary truths of God's word all over again. You need
⸤τοῦ διδάσκειν⸥ ὑμᾶς τὰ ⸤τῆς ἀρχῆς⸥ στοιχεῖα → ⸤τοῦ θεοῦ⸥ ⸤τῶν λογίων⸥ → → πάλιν καὶ → γεγόνατε ⸤χρείαν ἔχοντες⸥
d.gsn f.pa r.ap.2 d.apn d.gsf n.gsf n.apn d.gsm n.gsm d.gpn n.gpn adv cj v.rai.2p n.asf pt.pa.npm
3836 1438 7007 3836 794 5122 3359 3836 2536 3836 3359 4099 2779 1181 5970 2400

milk, not solid food! **13** Anyone who lives on milk, being still an infant, is not acquainted
γάλακτος [καὶ] οὐ στερεᾶς τροφῆς γὰρ πᾶς ὁ μετέχων ← γάλακτος γὰρ ἐστιν νήπιος ἄπειρος
n.gsn pl a.gsf n.gsf cj a.nsm d.nsm pt.pa.nsm n.gsn cj v.pai.3s n.nsm a.nsm
1128 2779 4024 5104 5575 1142 4246 3836 3576 1128 1142 1639 3758 586

with the teaching about righteousness. **14** But solid food is for the mature, who by constant use have
← λόγου → δικαιοσύνης δὲ στερεὰ ἡ τροφή ἐστιν → τελείων τῶν διὰ ⸤τὴν ἕξιν⸥ ← ἐχόντων
n.gsm n.gsf cj a.nsf d.nsf n.nsf v.pai.3s a.gpm d.gpm p.a d.asf n.asf pt.pa.gpm
3364 1466 1254 5104 3836 5575 1639 5455 3836 1328 3836 2011 2400

trained themselves to distinguish good *from* evil. ¶ **6:1** Therefore let us leave the elementary
γεγυμνασμένα ⸤τὰ αἰσθητήρια⸥ πρὸς διάκρισιν τε καλοῦ καὶ κακοῦ Διὸ → → ἀφέντες τὸν ⸤τῆς ἀρχῆς⸥
pt.rp.apn d.apn n.apn p.a n.asf cj a.gsn cj a.gsn cj pt.aa.npm d.asn d.gsf n.gsf
1214 3836 152 4639 1360 5445 2819 2779 2805 1475 5770 5770 3836 3836 794

teachings about Christ and go on to maturity, not laying again the foundation of repentance
λόγον → ⸤τοῦ Χριστοῦ⸥ φερώμεθα ← ἐπὶ ⸤τὴν τελειότητα⸥ μὴ καταβαλλόμενοι πάλιν θεμέλιον → μετανοίας
n.asm d.gsm n.gsm v.pps.1p p.a d.asf n.asf pl pt.pm.npm adv n.asm n.gsf
3364 3836 5986 5770 2093 3836 5456 3590 2850 4099 2529 3567

from acts that lead to death, and of faith in God, **2** instruction about baptisms, the laying on of hands,
ἀπὸ ἔργων → → → νεκρῶν καὶ → πίστεως ἐπὶ θεόν διδαχῆς → βαπτισμῶν τε ἐπιθέσεως ← ← χειρῶν τε
p.g n.gpn a.gpn cj n.gsf p.a n.asm n.gsf n.gpm cj n.gsf n.gpf cj
608 2240 3738 2779 4411 2093 2536 1439 968 5445 2120 5931 5445

the resurrection of the dead, and eternal judgment. **3** And God permitting, we will do so. ¶
ἀναστάσεως → νεκρῶν καὶ αἰωνίου κρίματος καὶ ἐάνπερ ὁ θεός ἐπιτρέπῃ → ποιήσομεν τοῦτο
n.gsf a.gpm cj a.gsn n.gsn cj cj d.nsm n.nsm v.pas.3s v.fai.1p r.asn
414 3738 2779 173 3210 2779 1570 3836 2536 2205 4472 4047

4 It is impossible for those who have once been enlightened, who have tasted the heavenly gift,
γὰρ Ἀδύνατον τοὺς ← → ἅπαξ → φωτισθέντας τε → → γευσαμένους τῆς ⸤τῆς ἐπουρανίου⸥ δωρεᾶς καὶ
cj a.nsn d.apm adv pt.ap.apm cj pt.am.apm d.gsf d.gsf a.gsf n.gsf cj
1142 105 3836 5894 562 5894 5445 1174 3836 3836 2230 1561 2779

υἱός, ἔμαθεν ἀφ᾽ ὧν ἔπαθεν τὴν ὑπακοήν, ⁹ καὶ τελειωθεὶς ἐγένετο πᾶσιν τοῖς ὑπακούουσιν αὐτῷ αἴτιος σωτηρίας αἰωνίου, ¹⁰ προσαγορευθεὶς ὑπὸ τοῦ θεοῦ ἀρχιερεὺς κατὰ τὴν τάξιν Μελχισέδεκ.
⁵·¹¹ Περὶ οὗ πολὺς ἡμῖν ὁ λόγος καὶ δυσερμήνευτος λέγειν, ἐπεὶ νωθροὶ γεγόνατε ταῖς ἀκοαῖς. ¹² καὶ γὰρ ὀφείλοντες εἶναι διδάσκαλοι διὰ τὸν χρόνον, πάλιν χρείαν ἔχετε τοῦ διδάσκειν ὑμᾶς τινὰ τὰ στοιχεῖα τῆς ἀρχῆς τῶν λογίων τοῦ θεοῦ καὶ γεγόνατε χρείαν ἔχοντες γάλακτος [καὶ] οὐ στερεᾶς τροφῆς. ¹³ πᾶς γὰρ ὁ μετέχων γάλακτος ἄπειρος λόγου δικαιοσύνης, νήπιος γάρ ἐστιν· ¹⁴ τελείων δέ ἐστιν ἡ στερεὰ τροφή, τῶν διὰ τὴν ἕξιν τὰ αἰσθητήρια γεγυμνασμένα ἐχόντων πρὸς διάκρισιν καλοῦ τε καὶ κακοῦ.
⁶·¹ Διὸ ἀφέντες τὸν τῆς ἀρχῆς τοῦ Χριστοῦ λόγον ἐπὶ τὴν τελειότητα φερώμεθα, μὴ πάλιν θεμέλιον καταβαλλόμενοι μετανοίας ἀπὸ νεκρῶν ἔργων καὶ πίστεως ἐπὶ θεόν, ² βαπτισμῶν διδαχῆς ἐπιθέσεώς τε χειρῶν, ἀναστάσεώς τε νεκρῶν καὶ κρίματος αἰωνίου. ³ καὶ τοῦτο ποιήσομεν, ἐάνπερ ἐπιτρέπῃ ὁ θεός. ¶ ⁴ Ἀδύνατον γὰρ τοὺς ἅπαξ φωτισθέντας, γευσαμένους τε τῆς δωρεᾶς τῆς ἐπουρανίου καὶ μετόχους γενηθέντας πνεύματος ἁγίου ⁵ καὶ καλὸν γευσαμένους θεοῦ ῥῆμα δυνάμεις τε μέλλοντος αἰῶνος ⁶ καὶ

who have | shared | in the Holy | Spirit, | 5 | who have tasted | the goodness of the word of God and the
→ γενηθέντας | μετόχους → | ἁγίου | πνεύματος | καὶ | → γευσαμένους | καλὸν | ῥῆμα → θεοῦ τε
pt.ap.apm | n.apm | a.gsn | n.gsn | cj | pt.am.apm | a.asn | n.asn n.gsm cj
1181 | 3581 | 41 | 4460 | 2779 | 1174 | 2819 | 4839 2536 5445

powers of the coming age, | 6 if they fall | away, to be brought | back to repentance, because to
δυνάμεις → μέλλοντος αἰῶνος καὶ | → → παραπεσόντας ← | → ἀνακαινίζειν πάλιν εἰς μετάνοιαν | →
n.apf n.gsm n.gsm cj | pt.aa.apm | f.pa adv p.a n.asf
1539 3516 172 2779 | 4178 | 362 4099 1650 3567 | 416

their loss they are crucifying | the Son of God | all over again and subjecting him to public disgrace. | ¶
ἑαυτοῖς → → ἀνασταυροῦντας | τὸν υἱὸν τοῦ θεοῦ | → καὶ → παραδειγματίζοντας
r.dpm.3 | pt.pa.apm | d.asm n.asm d.gsm n.gsm | cj | pt.pa.apm
1571 | 416 | 3836 5626 3836 2536 416 416 416 | 2779 | 4136

7 Land that drinks in the rain often falling on it and that produces a crop useful to those for
γὰρ γῆ ἡ πιοῦσα ← τὸν ὑετὸν πολλάκις ἐρχόμενον ἐπ᾽ αὐτῆς καὶ → τίκτουσα βοτάνην εὔθετον → ἐκείνοις δι᾽
cj n.nsf d.nsf pt.aa.nsf d.asm n.asm adv pt.pm.asm p.g r.gsf.3 cj pt.pa.nsf n.asf a.asn r.dpm p.a
1142 1178 3836 4403 3836 5624 4490 2262 2093 899 2779 5503 1083 2310 1697 1328

whom it is farmed receives the blessing of God. | 8 But land that produces thorns and thistles is
οὓς καὶ → γεωργεῖται μεταλαμβάνει εὐλογίας ἀπὸ τοῦ θεοῦ | δὲ → ἐκφέρουσα ἀκάνθας καὶ τριβόλους
r.apm cj v.ppi.3s v.pai.3s n.gsf p.g d.gsm n.gsm | cj pt.pa.nsf n.apf cj n.apm
4005 2779 1175 3561 2330 608 3836 2536 | 1254 1766 180 2779 5560

worthless and is in danger of being cursed. In the end it will be burned. | ¶ | 9 Even though we
ἀδόκιμος καὶ → ἐγγύς ← κατάρας τὸ τέλος ἧς εἰς καῦσιν | δὲ εἰ καὶ
a.nsf cj p.g n.gsf d.nsn n.nsn r.gsf p.a n.asf | cj cj adv
99 2779 1584 2932 3836 5465 4005 1650 3011 | 1254 1623 2779

speak like this, dear friends, we are confident of better things in your case – things that accompany
λαλοῦμεν οὕτως ← → ἀγαπητοί → Πεπείσμεθα τὰ κρείσσονα ← περὶ ὑμῶν ← καὶ → ἐχόμενα
v.pai.1p adv a.vpm v.rpi.1p d.apn a.apn.c p.g r.gp.2 cj pt.pm.apn
3281 4048 28 4275 3836 3202 4309 7007 2779 2400

salvation. 10 God is not unjust; he will not forget your work and the love you have shown in
σωτηρίας γὰρ ὁ θεός, οὐ ἄδικος ἐπιλαθέσθαι ὑμῶν τοῦ ἔργου καὶ τῆς ἀγάπης ἧς ἐνεδείξασθε εἰς
n.gsf cj d.nsm n.nsm pl a.nsm f.am r.gp.2 d.gsn n.gsn cj d.gsf n.gsf r.gsf v.ami.2p p.a
5401 1142 3836 2536 4024 96 2140 2140 4024 2140 7007 3836 2240 2779 3836 27 4005 1892 1650

him as you have helped his people and continue to help them. 11 We want each of
τὸ ὄνομα αὐτοῦ, → → διακονήσαντες τοῖς ἁγίοις καὶ → διακονοῦντες δὲ → ἐπιθυμοῦμεν ἕκαστον →
d.asn n.asn r.gsm.3 pt.aa.npm d.dpm a.dpm cj pt.pa.npm cj v.pai.1p r.asm
3836 3950 899 1354 3836 41 2779 1354 1254 2121 1667

you to show this same diligence to the very end, in order to make your hope sure. 12 We do
ὑμῶν ἐνδείκνυσθαι τὴν αὐτὴν σπουδὴν ἄχρι ← → τέλους πρὸς ← → → τῆς ἐλπίδος πληροφορίαν ἵνα
r.gp.2 f.pm d.asf r.asf n.asf n.gsn p.g d.asf d.gsf n.gsf n.asf cj
7007 1892 3836 899 5082 948 5465 4639 4443 3836 3836 1828 4443 2671

not want you to become lazy, but to imitate those who through faith and patience inherit what has
μὴ → → γένησθε νωθροί δὲ μιμηταὶ τῶν ← διὰ πίστεως καὶ μακροθυμίας κληρονομούντων τὰς →
pl v.ams.2p a.npm cj n.npm d.gpm p.g n.gsf cj n.gsf pt.pa.gpm d.apf
3590 1181 3821 1254 3629 3836 1328 4411 2779 3429 3099 3836

been promised.
→ ἐπαγγελίας
n.apf
2039

The Certainty of God's Promise

6:13 When God made his promise to Abraham, since there was no one greater for him to
γὰρ ὁ θεός, ἐπαγγειλάμενος → Τῷ Ἀβραάμ, ἐπεὶ εἶχεν κατ᾽ οὐδενὸς ← μείζονος →
cj d.nsm n.nsm pt.am.nsm d.dsm n.dsm cj v.iai.3s p.g a.gsm a.gsm.c
1142 2040 3836 2536 2040 3836 11 2075 2400 2848 4029 3489

swear by, he swore by himself, 14 saying, "I will surely bless you and give you many
ὀμόσαι ← → ὤμοσεν καθ᾽ ἑαυτοῦ λέγων, εἰ μὴν εὐλογῶν, εὐλογήσω σε καὶ πληθύνων πληθυνῶ σε →
f.aa v.aai.3s p.g r.gsm.3 pt.pa.nsm cj pl pt.pa.nsm v.fai.1s r.as.2 cj pt.pa.nsm v.fai.1s r.as.2
3923 2848 3923 2848 1571 3306 2328 2328 1623 3605 2328 2328 5148 2779 4437 4437 5148 4437

παραπεσόντας, πάλιν ἀνακαινίζειν εἰς μετάνοιαν, ἀνασταυροῦντας ἑαυτοῖς τὸν υἱὸν τοῦ θεοῦ καὶ παραδειγματίζοντας ¶ 7 γῆ γὰρ ἡ πιοῦσα τὸν ἐπ᾽ αὐτῆς ἐρχόμενον πολλάκις ὑετὸν καὶ τίκτουσα βοτάνην εὔθετον ἐκείνοις δι᾽ οὓς καὶ γεωργεῖται, μεταλαμβάνει εὐλογίας ἀπὸ τοῦ θεοῦ· 8 ἐκφέρουσα δὲ ἀκάνθας καὶ τριβόλους, ἀδόκιμος καὶ κατάρας ἐγγύς, ἧς τὸ τέλος εἰς καῦσιν. ¶ 9 Πεπείσμεθα δὲ περὶ ὑμῶν, ἀγαπητοί, τὰ κρείσσονα καὶ ἐχόμενα σωτηρίας, εἰ καὶ οὕτως λαλοῦμεν. 10 οὐ γὰρ ἄδικος ὁ θεὸς ἐπιλαθέσθαι τοῦ ἔργου ὑμῶν καὶ τῆς ἀγάπης ἧς ἐνεδείξασθε εἰς τὸ ὄνομα αὐτοῦ, διακονήσαντες τοῖς ἁγίοις καὶ διακονοῦντες. 11 ἐπιθυμοῦμεν δὲ ἕκαστον ὑμῶν τὴν αὐτὴν ἐνδείκνυσθαι σπουδὴν πρὸς τὴν πληροφορίαν τῆς ἐλπίδος ἄχρι τέλους, 12 ἵνα μὴ νωθροὶ γένησθε, μιμηταὶ δὲ τῶν διὰ πίστεως καὶ μακροθυμίας κληρονομούντων τὰς ἐπαγγελίας.

6:13 Τῷ γὰρ Ἀβραὰμ ἐπαγγειλάμενος ὁ θεός, ἐπεὶ κατ᾽ οὐδενὸς εἶχεν μείζονος ὀμόσαι, ὤμοσεν καθ᾽ ἑαυτοῦ 14 λέγων, Εἰ μὴν εὐλογῶν εὐλογήσω σε καὶ πληθύνων πληθυνῶ σε· 15 καὶ οὕτως μακροθυμήσας ἐπέτυχεν τῆς ἐπαγγελίας. ¶ 16 ἄνθρωποι γὰρ

descendants." **15** And so   after waiting patiently,   Abraham received what was promised. ¶ **16** Men
↤   καὶ   οὕτως   μακροθυμήσας   ἐπέτυχεν   τῆς   ἐπαγγελίας   γὰρ ἄνθρωποι
      cj   adv   pt.aa.nsm   v.aai.3s   d.gsf   n.gsf   cj   n.npm
4437   2779   4048   3428   2209   3836   2039   1142   476

swear   by   someone greater   than themselves, and the oath   confirms what is said   and puts an end
ὀμνύουσιν κατά → ⌜τοῦ μείζονος⌝   καὶ ὁ   ὅρκος   εἰς   βεβαίωσιν   αὐτοῖς   πέρας
v.pai.3p   p.g   d.gsm a.gsm.c   cj   d.nsm n.nsm   p.a   n.asf   r.dpm.3   n.nsn
3923   2848   3836   3489   2779 3836   3992   1650   1012   899   4306

to all   argument. **17** Because   God   wanted   to make the unchanging nature of his   purpose   very
→ πάσης ἀντιλογίας   ἐν ᾧ⌝   ⌜ὁ θεός, βουλόμενος →   τὸ ἀμετάθετον ←   αὐτοῦ ⌜τῆς βουλῆς⌝ περισσότερον
   a.gsf   n.gsf   p.d r.dsn   d.nsm n.nsm pt.pm.nsm   d.asn a.asn   r.gsm.3 d.gsf n.gsf   adv.c
   4246   517   1877 4005   3836 2536   1089   2109 2109   3836 292   1087 899   3836 1087   4358

clear   to the heirs   of what was promised, he confirmed it with an oath. **18** God did this so that, by two
ἐπιδεῖξαι → τοῖς κληρονόμοις → τῆς → ἐπαγγελίας → ἐμεσίτευσεν →   ὅρκῳ   ἵνα ←   διὰ δύο
f.aa   d.dpm n.dpm   d.gsf   n.gsf   v.aai.3s   n.dsm   cj   p.g   a.gpn
2109   3836 3101   3836   2039   3541   3992   2671   1328 1545

unchangeable things   in which it is impossible for God   to lie,   we who have fled   to take hold
ἀμεταθέτων πραγμάτων ἐν οἷς   ἀδύνατον   ⌜τὸν θεόν, → ψεύσασθαι → οἱ   καταφυγόντες →   κρατῆσαι
a.gpn   n.gpn   p.d r.dpn   a.nsn   d.asm n.asm   f.am   d.npm   pt.aa.npm   f.aa
292   4547   1877 4005   105   3836 2536   6017   2400 3836   2966   3195

of the hope   offered   to us may be   greatly encouraged. **19** We have this hope as an anchor for the soul,
→ τῆς ἐλπίδος προκειμένης   ἔχωμεν ἰσχυρὰν παράκλησιν   ἣν → ἔχωμεν   ὡς   ἄγκυραν → τῆς ψυχῆς τε
   d.gsf n.gsf   pt.pm.gsf   v.pas.1p a.asf   n.asf   r.asf → v.pai.1p   pl   n.asf   d.gsf n.gsf   cj
   3836 1828   4618   2400   2708   4155   4005   2400   6055   46   3836 6034   5445

firm   and secure.   It enters   the inner   sanctuary behind the curtain,   **20** where Jesus, who went
ἀσφαλῆ καὶ   βεβαίαν καὶ → εἰσερχομένην εἰς τὸ   ἐσώτερον   τοῦ καταπετάσματος ὅπου   Ἰησοῦς   →
a.asf   2779   a.asf   cj   pt.pm.asf   p.a d.asn p.g   d.gsn n.gsn   cj   n.nsm
855   2779   1010   2779   1656   1650 3836 2278   3836 2925   3963   2652

before   us, has entered on   our behalf. He has become a high   priest forever,   in   the order of Melchizedek.
πρόδρομος   → εἰσῆλθεν ὑπὲρ ἡμῶν →   γενόμενος ἀρχιερεὺς ←   ⌜εἰς τὸν αἰῶνα⌝ κατὰ τὴν τάξιν → Μελχισέδεκ
n.nsm   v.aai.3s   p.g r.gp.1   pt.am.nsm   n.nsm   p.a d.asm n.asm   p.a d.asf n.asf → n.gsm
4596   1656   5642 7005 5642   1181   797   1650 3836 172   2848 3836 5423   3519

Melchizedek the Priest

7:1 This Melchizedek   was king   of Salem and priest of God   Most High.   He met
γὰρ Οὗτος ὁ   Μελχισέδεκ⌝   βασιλεὺς → Σαλήμ   ἱερεὺς → ⌜τοῦ θεοῦ, →   ⌜τοῦ ὑψίστου, ὁ   συναντήσας
cj   r.nsm   d.nsm n.nsm   n.nsm   n.gsf   n.nsm   d.gsm n.gsm   d.gsm a.gsm.s   d.nsm pt.aa.nsm
1142   4047   3836 3519   995   4889   2636   3836 2536   3836 5736   3836 5267

Abraham returning   from the defeat of the kings   and blessed   him, **2** and Abraham gave   him a tenth of
Ἀβραὰμ ὑποστρέφοντι ἀπὸ τῆς κοπῆς → τῶν βασιλέων καὶ εὐλογήσας αὐτόν, καὶ Ἀβραάμ ἐμέρισεν ᾧ → δεκάτην ἀπὸ
n.dsm   pt.pa.dsm   p.g d.gsf n.gsf   d.gpm n.gpm   cj   pt.aa.nsm   r.asm.3 adv   n.dsm   v.aai.3s   r.dsm   n.asf   p.g
11   5715   608 3836 3158   3836 995   2779 2328   899   2779 11   3532   4005 1281   608

everything.   First, his name means   "king   of righteousness";   then also, "king   of Salem" means
πάντων   μὲν πρῶτον   ἑρμηνευόμενος βασιλεὺς → δικαιοσύνης   δὲ ἔπειτα καὶ βασιλεὺς → Σαλήμ   ὅ ἐστιν⌝
a.gpn   pl   adv   pt.pp.nsm   n.nsm   n.gsf   cj   adv   adv   n.nsm   n.gsf   r.nsn v.pai.3s
4246   3525 4754   2257   995   1466   1254 2083   2779 995   4889   4005 1639

"king   of peace." **3** Without father or mother, without genealogy,   without beginning of days   or end of
βασιλεὺς → εἰρήνης   ἀπάτωρ ἀμήτωρ →   ἀγενεαλόγητος ἔχων μήτε   ἀρχὴν   → ἡμερῶν μήτε τέλος →
n.nsm   n.gsf   n.nsm   n.nsm   a.nsn   pt.pa.nsm cj   n.asf   n.gpn   cj   n.gsn
995   1645   574   298   37   2400   3612   794   2465   3612 5465

life,   like   the Son of God   he remains a priest forever. ¶ **4** Just think   how   great he
ζωῆς δὲ   ἀφωμοιωμένος τῷ υἱῷ → ⌜τοῦ θεοῦ, → μένει   ἱερεὺς ⌜εἰς τὸ διηνεκές⌝   δὲ Θεωρεῖτε πηλίκος ← οὗτος
n.gsf cj   pt.rp.nsm   d.dsm n.dsm → d.gsm n.gsm → v.pai.3s   n.nsm   p.a d.asn a.asn   cj   v.pam.2p   r.nsm   r.nsm
2437 1254   926   3836 5626   3836 2536   3531   2636   1650 3836 1457   1254 2555   4383   4047

was: Even the patriarch Abraham gave   him a tenth   of the plunder! **5** Now   the law requires
καὶ ὁ   πατριάρχης Ἀβραάμ ἔδωκεν ᾧ   δεκάτην ἐκ τῶν ἀκροθινίων   καὶ μὲν κατὰ τὸν νόμον ⌜ἐντολὴν ἔχουσιν⌝ ἐκ
adv d.nsm n.nsm   n.nsm   v.aai.3s r.dsm   n.asf   p.g d.gpn n.gpn   cj   pl   p.a   d.asm n.asm   n.asf   v.pai.3p   p.g
2779 3836 4256   4005   1443   1281   1281   1666 3836 215   2779 3525 2848   3836 3795   1953   2400   1666

κατὰ τοῦ μείζονος ὀμνύουσιν, καὶ πάσης αὐτοῖς ἀντιλογίας πέρας εἰς βεβαίωσιν ὁ ὅρκος· **17** ἐν ᾧ περισσότερον βουλόμενος ὁ θεὸς ἐπιδεῖξαι τοῖς κληρονόμοις τῆς ἐπαγγελίας τὸ ἀμετάθετον τῆς βουλῆς αὐτοῦ ἐμεσίτευσεν ὅρκῳ, **18** ἵνα διὰ δύο πραγμάτων ἀμεταθέτων, ἐν οἷς ἀδύνατον ψεύσασθαι [τὸν] θεόν, ἰσχυρὰν παράκλησιν ἔχωμεν οἱ καταφυγόντες κρατῆσαι τῆς προκειμένης ἐλπίδος· **19** ἣν ὡς ἄγκυραν ἔχομεν τῆς ψυχῆς ἀσφαλῆ τε καὶ βεβαίαν καὶ εἰσερχομένην εἰς τὸ ἐσώτερον τοῦ καταπετάσματος, **20** ὅπου πρόδρομος ὑπὲρ ἡμῶν εἰσῆλθεν Ἰησοῦς, κατὰ τὴν τάξιν Μελχισέδεκ ἀρχιερεὺς γενόμενος εἰς τὸν αἰῶνα.

     7:1 Οὗτος γὰρ ὁ Μελχισέδεκ, βασιλεὺς Σαλήμ, ἱερεὺς τοῦ θεοῦ τοῦ ὑψίστου, ὁ συναντήσας Ἀβραὰμ ὑποστρέφοντι ἀπὸ τῆς κοπῆς τῶν βασιλέων καὶ εὐλογήσας αὐτόν, **2** ᾧ καὶ δεκάτην ἀπὸ πάντων ἐμέρισεν Ἀβραάμ, πρῶτον μὲν ἑρμηνευόμενος βασιλεὺς δικαιοσύνης ἔπειτα δὲ καὶ βασιλεὺς Σαλήμ, ὅ ἐστιν βασιλεὺς εἰρήνης, **3** ἀπάτωρ ἀμήτωρ ἀγενεαλόγητος, μήτε ἀρχὴν ἡμερῶν μήτε ζωῆς τέλος ἔχων, ἀφωμοιωμένος δὲ τῷ υἱῷ τοῦ θεοῦ, μένει ἱερεὺς εἰς τὸ διηνεκές. ¶ **4** Θεωρεῖτε δὲ πηλίκος οὗτος, ᾧ [καὶ] δεκάτην Ἀβραὰμ ἔδωκεν ἐκ τῶν ἀκροθινίων ὁ πατριάρχης. **5** καὶ οἱ μὲν ἐκ τῶν υἱῶν Λευὶ τὴν ἱερατείαν λαμβάνοντες ἐντολὴν ἔχουσιν ἀποδεκατοῦν τὸν λαὸν κατὰ τὸν νόμον, τοῦτ᾽ ἔστιν τοὺς ἀδελφοὺς αὐτῶν, καίπερ ἐξεληλυθότας ἐκ τῆς ὀσφύος Ἀβραάμ· **6** ὁ δὲ

the descendants of Levi who become   priests   to collect   a tenth from the people – that is,   their
τῶν   υἱῶν → Λευὶ   οἱ   λαμβάνοντες   ιτὴν ἱερατείαν, →ἀποδεκατοῦν←   τὸν λαὸν   τοῦτ᾽ ἔστιν   αὐτῶν
d.gpm n.gpm   n.gsm d.npm pt.pa.npm   d.asf n.asf   f.pa   d.asm n.asm r.nsn v.pai.3s r.gpm.3
3836 5626   3322 3836 3284   3836 2632   620   3836 3295 4047 1639 899

brothers   – even though their brothers are descended   from Abraham. **6** This man, however, did not
ιτοὺς ἀδελφούς,   καίπερ← → ἐξεληλυθότας τῆς ὀσφύος ἐκ   Ἀβραάμ   ὁ ←   δὲ → μὴ
d.apm n.apm   cj   pt.ra.apm d.gsf n.gsf p.g   n.gsm   d.nsm   cj   pl
3836 81   2788   2002 3836 4019 1666   11   3836   1254   1156 3590

trace his descent   from Levi, yet he collected   a tenth from Abraham and blessed   him who had   the
→ → γενεαλογούμενος ἐξ   αὐτῶν   δεδεκάτωκεν ← ←   Ἀβραάμ   καὶ εὐλόγηκεν τὸν   ἔχοντα τὰς
pt.pp.nsm   p.g   r.gpm.3   v.rai.3s   n.gsm   cj v.rai.3s d.asm pt.pa.asm d.apf
1156   1666 899   1282   11   2779 2328 3836 2400 3836

promises. **7** And without   doubt   the lesser person is blessed   by the greater. **8**   In the one case, the
ἐπαγγελίας δὲ   χωρὶς   πάσης ἀντιλογίας τὸ   ἔλαττον ←   → εὐλογεῖται ὑπὸ τοῦ κρείττονος   καὶ μὲν ὧδε ←
n.apf   cj   p.g   a.gsf n.gsf   d.nsn a.nsn.c   v.ppi.3s p.g d.gsm a.gsm.c   cj pl adv
2039   1254   6006   4246 517   3836 1781   2328 5679 3836 3202   2779 3525 6045

tenth   is collected   by men   who die;   but in the other case, by him who is declared   to be
δεκάτας → λαμβάνουσιν ←   ἄνθρωποι →   ἀποθνῄσκοντες δὲ   ἐκεῖ ← ← ← → μαρτυρούμενος ὅτι → →
n.apf   v.pai.3p   n.npm →   pt.pa.npm   cj   adv   pt.pp.nsm   cj
1281   3284   476   633   1254 1695   3455   4022

living. **9**   *One   might even say that*   Levi, who collects the tenth, paid   the tenth through
ζῇ   καὶ ὡς ἔπος εἰπεῖν,   καὶ Λευὶ ὁ   λαμβάνων   δεκάτας δεδεκάτωται ←   δι᾽
v.pai.3s   cj cj n.asn f.aa   cj n.nsm d.nsm pt.pa.nsm   n.apf v.rpi.3s   p.g
2409   2779 6055 2229 3306   2779 3322 3836 3284   1281 1282   1328

Abraham, **10** because when Melchizedek met   Abraham, Levi was still in the body of his ancestor.
Ἀβραάμ   γὰρ   ὅτε   Μελχισέδεκ   συνήντησεν αὐτῷ   ἦν ἔτι ἐν τῇ ὀσφύϊ → τοῦ πατρὸς
n.gsm   cj   cj   n.nsm   v.aai.3s   r.dsm.3   v.iai.3s adv p.d d.dsf n.dsf   d.gsm n.gsm
11   1142   4021   3519   5267   899   1639 2285 1877 3836 4019   3836 4252

Jesus Like Melchizedek

7:11   If perfection could have been attained through the Levitical priesthood (for on the basis of it   the
οὖν μὲν Εἰ τελείωσις   → ἦν ←   διὰ   τῆς Λευιτικῆς ἱερωσύνης γὰρ ἐπ᾽ ←   → αὐτῆς,
cj pl cj n.nsf   v.iai.3s   p.g   d.gsf a.gsf   n.gsf   cj p.g   r.gsf.3
4036 3525 1623 5459   1639   1328   3836 3325   2648   1142 2093   899

law was given   to the people), why was there still need   for another priest to come   – one in   the
→ → νενομοθέτηται ← ὁ λαὸς τίς   ἔτι χρεία λέγεσθαι → ἕτερον ἱερέα → ἀνίστασθαι   κατὰ τὴν
v.rpi.3s   d.nsm n.nsm r.nsf   adv n.nsf f.pp   r.asm n.asm f.pm   p.a d.asf
3793   3836 3295 5515   2285 5970 3306   2283 2636 482   2848 3836

order of Melchizedek,   not in the order of Aaron? **12** For when there is a change   of the priesthood, there
τάξιν → Μελχισέδεκ   καὶ οὐ κατὰ τὴν τάξιν → Ἀαρὼν γὰρ →   → → μετατιθεμένης → τῆς ἱερωσύνης   →
n.asf   n.gsm   cj pl p.a d.asf n.asf n.gsm   cj   pt.pp.gsf   d.gsf n.gsf
5423   3519   2779 4024 2848 3836 5423 2   1142   3572   3836 2648   1181

must   also be   a change of the law. **13**   He of whom these things are said   belonged to a different tribe,
ιἐξ ἀνάγκης, καὶ γίνεται μετάθεσις → νόμου γὰρ → ἐφ᾽ ὃν ταῦτα ←   → λέγεται μετέσχηκεν ← ἑτέρας   φυλῆς
p.g n.gsf   adv v.pmi.3s n.nsf → n.gsm cj p.a r.asm r.npn   v.ppi.3s v.rai.3s   r.gsf   n.gsf
1666 340   2779 1181 3557 3795 1142 3576 2093 4005 4047   3306 3576   2283   5876

and no   one from that tribe has ever served   at the altar. **14** For it is clear   that our Lord   descended
οὐδεὶς ← ἀφ᾽ ἧς   προσέσχηκεν → τῷ θυσιαστηρίῳ γὰρ → πρόδηλον ὅτι ἡμῶν ὁ κύριος, ἀνατέταλκεν
a.nsm   p.g r.gsf   v.rai.3s   d.dsn n.dsn   cj → a.nsn cj r.gp.1 d.nsm n.nsm v.rai.3s
4029   608 4005   4668   3836 2603   1142 4593 4022 7005 3836 3261   422

from Judah, and in regard to that tribe Moses said   nothing about priests. **15** And what we have said is   even
ἐξ Ἰούδα εἰς → ἦν φυλὴν Μωϋσῆς ἐλάλησεν οὐδὲν περὶ ἱερέων καὶ   ἐστιν ἔτι
p.g n.gsm p.a   r.asf n.asf n.nsm v.aai.3s a.asn p.g n.gpm cj   v.pai.3s adv
1666 2683 1650   4005 5876 3707 3281 4029 4309 2636 2779   1639 2285

more   clear   if another priest   like   Melchizedek appears, **16** one who has become a priest not
περισσότερον κατάδηλον εἰ ἕτερος ἱερεὺς κατὰ ιτὴν ὁμοιότητα, Μελχισέδεκ ἀνίσταται → ὃς → γέγονεν   οὐ
adv.c   a.nsn   cj r.nsm n.nsm p.a d.asf n.asf   n.gsm   v.pmi.3s   r.nsm   v.rai.3s   pl
4358   2867   1623 2283 2636 2848 3836 3928   3519   482   4005   1181   4024

μὴ γενεαλογούμενος ἐξ αὐτῶν δεδεκάτωκεν Ἀβραὰμ καὶ τὸν ἔχοντα τὰς ἐπαγγελίας εὐλόγηκεν. **7** χωρὶς δὲ πάσης ἀντιλογίας τὸ ἔλαττον ὑπὸ τοῦ κρείττονος εὐλογεῖται. **8** καὶ ὧδε μὲν δεκάτας ἀποθνῄσκοντες ἄνθρωποι λαμβάνουσιν, ἐκεῖ δὲ μαρτυρούμενος ὅτι ζῇ. **9** καὶ ὡς ἔπος εἰπεῖν, δι᾽ Ἀβραὰμ καὶ Λευὶ ὁ δεκάτας λαμβάνων δεδεκάτωται· **10** ἔτι γὰρ ἐν τῇ ὀσφύϊ τοῦ πατρὸς ἦν ὅτε συνήντησεν αὐτῷ Μελχισέδεκ.

7:11 Εἰ μὲν οὖν τελείωσις διὰ τῆς Λευιτικῆς ἱερωσύνης ἦν, ὁ λαὸς γὰρ ἐπ᾽ αὐτῆς νενομοθέτηται, τίς ἔτι χρεία κατὰ τὴν τάξιν Μελχισέδεκ ἕτερον ἀνίστασθαι ἱερέα καὶ οὐ κατὰ τὴν τάξιν Ἀαρὼν λέγεσθαι; **12** μετατιθεμένης γὰρ τῆς ἱερωσύνης ἐξ ἀνάγκης καὶ νόμου μετάθεσις γίνεται. **13** ἐφ᾽ ὃν γὰρ λέγεται ταῦτα, φυλῆς ἑτέρας μετέσχηκεν, ἀφ᾽ ἧς οὐδεὶς προσέσχηκεν τῷ θυσιαστηρίῳ· **14** πρόδηλον γὰρ ὅτι ἐξ Ἰούδα ἀνατέταλκεν ὁ κύριος ἡμῶν, εἰς ἣν φυλὴν περὶ ἱερέων οὐδὲν Μωϋσῆς ἐλάλησεν. **15** καὶ περισσότερον ἔτι κατάδηλόν ἐστιν, εἰ κατὰ τὴν ὁμοιότητα Μελχισέδεκ ἀνίσταται ἱερεὺς ἕτερος, **16** ὃς οὐ κατὰ νόμον ἐντολῆς

on the basis of a regulation   as to his ancestry but   on   the basis of the power   of an indestructible life. ¹⁷ For it
κατά← νόμον ἐντολῆς → → σαρκίνης ἀλλὰ κατά← → δύναμιν ⌐ ἀκαταλύτου ζωῆς γὰρ
p.a   n.asm n.gsf   a.gsf   cj   p.a   n.asf   a.gsf   n.gsf cj
2848   3795   1953   4921   247   2848   1539   2437   186   2437   1142

is declared: "You are a priest forever,   in   the order of Melchizedek." ¶   ¹⁸   The former
→ μαρτυρεῖται ὅτι σὺ   ἱερεὺς εἰς τὸν αἰῶνα κατὰ τὴν τάξιν → Μελχισέδεκ   γὰρ μὲν   προαγούσης
v.ppi.3s cj r.ns.2 n.nsm n.asm d.asm n.asm p.a d.asf n.asf n.gsm   cj pl   pt.pa.gsf
3455 4022 5148 2636 1650 3836 172 2848 3836 5423 3519   1142 3525 4575

regulation is   set   aside because it   was weak   and useless ¹⁹ (for the law   made nothing perfect), and
ἐντολῆς γίνεται ἀθέτησις ← διὰ αὐτῆς ⌐τὸ ἀσθενὲς⌐ καὶ ἀνωφελές γὰρ ὁ νόμος → οὐδὲν ἐτελείωσεν δὲ
n.gsf v.pmi.3s n.nsf p.a r.gsf.3 d.asn a.asn cj a.asn cj d.nsm n.nsm a.asn v.aai.3s cj
1953 1181 120 1328 899 3836 822 2779 543 1142 3836 3795 5457 4029 5457 1254

a better   hope   is introduced, by which we draw near   to God.   ¶   ²⁰ And   it was not without an
κρείττονος ἐλπίδος ἐπεισαγωγὴ δι' ἧς → → ἐγγίζομεν → τῷ θεῷ   Καὶ καθ' ὅσον   οὐ χωρὶς
a.gsf.c n.gsf n.nsf p.g r.gsf v.pai.1p d.dsm n.dsm   cj p.a r.asn   pl p.g
3202 1828 2081 1328 4005 1581 3836 2536   2779 2848 4012   4024 6006

oath!   Others became   priests without any oath,   ²¹but   he became a priest with an oath
ὁρκωμοσίας γὰρ μὲν οἱ ⌐εἰσὶν γεγονότες⌐ ἱερεῖς χωρὶς ὁρκωμοσίας δὲ ὁ   μετὰ ὁρκωμοσίας
n.gsf cj pl d.npm v.pai.3p pt.ra.npm n.npm p.g n.gsf cj d.nsm   p.g n.gsf
3993 1142 3525 3836 1639 1181 2636 6006 3993 1254 3836   3552 3993

when God said   to   him: "The Lord has sworn and will not change   his mind: 'You are a priest
διὰ ⌐τοῦ λέγοντος⌐ πρὸς αὐτόν κύριος → ὤμοσεν καὶ ⌐ οὐ μεταμεληθήσεται ← σὺ ἱερεὺς
p.g d.gsm pt.pa.gsm p.a r.asm.3 n.nsm v.aai.3s cj pl v.fpi.3s r.ns.2 n.nsm
1328 3836 3306 4639 899 3261 3923 2779 3564 4024 3564 5148 2636

forever.'"   ²² Because of this   oath,   Jesus has become the guarantee of a better   covenant. ¶
εἰς τὸν αἰῶνα κατὰ → τοσοῦτο [καὶ] Ἰησοῦς → γέγονεν ἔγγυος → κρείττονος διαθήκης
p.a d.asm n.asm p.a r.asn adv n.nsm v.rai.3s n.nsm a.gsf.c n.gsf
1650 3836 172 2848 5537 2779 2652 1181 1583 3202 1347

²³ Now   there have been   many   of those priests, since death prevented   them from continuing in
Καὶ μὲν → → ⌐εἰσὶν γεγονότες⌐ ⌐οἱ πλείονες⌐ ἱερεῖς διὰ θανάτῳ ⌐τὸ κωλύεσθαι⌐ παραμένειν
cj pl v.pai.3p pt.ra.npm d.npm a.npm.c n.npm p.a n.dsm d.asn f.pp f.pa
2779 3525 1639 1181 3836 4498 2636 1328 2505 3836 3266 4169

office; ²⁴ but because Jesus lives   forever,   he has a permanent priesthood. ²⁵ Therefore   he is able   to
δὲ διὰ   αὐτὸν ⌐τὸ μένειν⌐ ⌐εἰς τὸν αἰῶνα⌐ ὁ ἔχει ἀπαράβατον ⌐τὴν ἱερωσύνην⌐ ὅθεν καὶ → δύναται
cj p.a r.asm.3 d.asn f.pa p.a d.asm n.asm d.nsm v.pai.3s a.asf d.asf n.asf cj adv v.ppi.3s
1254 1328 899 3836 3531 1650 3836 172 3836 2648 563 3836 2648 3854 2779 1538

save completely those who come   to God   through him, because he always lives to intercede
σῴζειν εἰς τὸ παντελὲς τοὺς ← προσερχομένους ← ⌐τῷ θεῷ⌐ δι' αὐτοῦ → πάντοτε ζῶν εἰς ⌐τὸ ἐντυγχάνειν⌐
f.pa p.a d.asn a.asn d.apm pt.pm.apm d.dsm n.dsm p.g r.gsm.3 adv pt.pa.nsm p.a d.asn f.pa
5392 1650 3836 4117 3836 4665 3836 2536 1328 899 2409 2409 4121 2409 4121 1650 3836 1961

for them. ¶ ²⁶ Such   a high   priest   meets our need – one who is holy, blameless, pure,   set
ὑπὲρ αὐτῶν   γὰρ Τοιοῦτος ἀρχιερεύς ← καὶ ⌐ ἡμῖν ἔπρεπεν   ὅσιος ἄκακος ἀμίαντος →
p.g r.gpm.3 cj r.nsm n.nsm adv r.dp.1 v.iai.3s a.nsm a.nsm a.nsm
5642 899 1142 5525 797 2779 4560 7005 4560 4008 179 299

apart   from sinners,   exalted   above the heavens. ²⁷ Unlike the other high   priests, he does
κεχωρισμένος ἀπὸ ⌐τῶν ἁμαρτωλῶν⌐ καὶ γενόμενος ὑψηλότερος ← τῶν οὐρανῶν ὥσπερ οἱ   ἀρχιερεῖς ← ὃς
pt.rp.nsm p.g d.gpm a.gpm cj pt.am.nsm a.nsm.c d.gpm n.gpm adv d.npm n.npm r.nsm
6004 608 3836 283 2779 1181 5734 3836 4041 6061 3836 797 4005 2400

not need   to offer   sacrifices day   after day, first   for his own sins,   and then for the sins of
οὐκ ἔχει ἀνάγκην → ἀναφέρειν θυσίας ⌐καθ' ἡμέραν⌐ ← πρότερον ὑπὲρ τῶν ἰδίων ἁμαρτιῶν ἔπειτα → τῶν
pl v.pai.3s n.asf f.pa n.apf p.a n.asf adv.c p.g d.gpf a.gpf n.gpf adv d.gpf
4024 2400 340 429 2602 2848 2465 4728 5642 3836 2625 281 2083 3836

the people.   He sacrificed for their sins once for all when he offered   himself. ²⁸ For the law   appoints as
τοῦ λαοῦ   γὰρ τοῦτο ἐποίησεν   ἐφάπαξ → ἀνενέγκας ἑαυτὸν γὰρ ὁ νόμος καθίστησιν
d.gsm n.gsm cj r.asn v.aai.3s adv pt.aa.nsm r.asm.3 cj d.nsm n.nsm v.pai.3s
3836 3295 1142 4047 4472 2384 429 1571 1142 3836 3795 2770

σαρκίνης γέγονεν ἀλλὰ κατὰ δύναμιν ζωῆς ἀκαταλύτου. ¹⁷ μαρτυρεῖται γὰρ ὅτι Σὺ ἱερεὺς εἰς τὸν αἰῶνα κατὰ τὴν τάξιν Μελχισέδεκ. ¶ ¹⁸ ἀθέτησις μὲν γὰρ γίνεται προαγούσης ἐντολῆς διὰ τὸ αὐτῆς ἀσθενὲς καὶ ἀνωφελές— ¹⁹ οὐδὲν γὰρ ἐτελείωσεν ὁ νόμος— ἐπεισαγωγὴ δὲ κρείττονος ἐλπίδος δι' ἧς ἐγγίζομεν τῷ θεῷ. ¶ ²⁰ Καὶ καθ' ὅσον οὐ χωρὶς ὁρκωμοσίας· οἱ μὲν γὰρ χωρὶς ὁρκωμοσίας εἰσὶν ἱερεῖς γεγονότες, ²¹ ὁ δὲ μετὰ ὁρκωμοσίας διὰ τοῦ λέγοντος πρὸς αὐτόν, Ὤμοσεν κύριος καὶ οὐ μεταμεληθήσεται, Σὺ ἱερεὺς εἰς τὸν αἰῶνα. ²² κατὰ τοσοῦτο [καὶ] κρείττονος διαθήκης γέγονεν ἔγγυος Ἰησοῦς. ¶ ²³ καὶ οἱ μὲν πλείονές εἰσιν γεγονότες ἱερεῖς διὰ τὸ θανάτῳ κωλύεσθαι παραμένειν· ²⁴ ὁ δὲ διὰ τὸ μένειν αὐτὸν εἰς τὸν αἰῶνα ἀπαράβατον ἔχει τὴν ἱερωσύνην· ²⁵ ὅθεν καὶ σῴζειν εἰς τὸ παντελὲς δύναται τοὺς προσερχομένους δι' αὐτοῦ τῷ θεῷ, πάντοτε ζῶν εἰς τὸ ἐντυγχάνειν ὑπὲρ αὐτῶν. ¶ ²⁶ Τοιοῦτος γὰρ ἡμῖν καὶ ἔπρεπεν ἀρχιερεύς, ὅσιος ἄκακος ἀμίαντος, κεχωρισμένος ἀπὸ τῶν ἁμαρτωλῶν καὶ ὑψηλότερος τῶν οὐρανῶν γενόμενος, ²⁷ ὃς οὐκ ἔχει καθ' ἡμέραν ἀνάγκην, ὥσπερ οἱ ἀρχιερεῖς, πρότερον ὑπὲρ τῶν ἰδίων ἁμαρτιῶν θυσίας ἀναφέρειν ἔπειτα τῶν τοῦ λαοῦ· τοῦτο γὰρ ἐποίησεν ἐφάπαξ ἑαυτὸν ἀνενέγκας. ²⁸ ὁ νόμος γὰρ ἀνθρώπους

high	priests	men	who	are	weak;	but	the	oath,		which	came	after	the	law,	appointed
ἀρχιερεῖς ←		ἀνθρώπους →	ἔχοντας		ἀσθένειαν	δὲ	ὁ	‚λόγος	τῆς ὁρκωμοσίας	τῆς		μετὰ	τὸν	νόμον	
n.apm		n.apm	pt.pa.apm		n.asf	cj	d.nsm	n.nsm	d.gsf n.gsf	d.gsf		p.a	d.asm	n.asm	
797		476	2400		819	1254	3836	3364	3836 3993	3836		3552	3836	3795	

the	Son,	who	has	been	made	perfect		forever.
υἱὸν →		→	→	→	τετελειωμένον	‚εἰς τὸν αἰῶνα‚
n.asm					pt.rp.asm	p.a d.asm n.asm
5626					5457	1650 3836 172

The High Priest of a New Covenant

8:1 The point   of what we are saying   is this: We do have   such   a high   priest, who sat   down

δὲ	Κεφάλαιον	ἐπὶ τοῖς →	λεγομένοις		ἔχομεν	τοιοῦτον	ἀρχιερέα	ὃς	ἐκάθισεν ←
cj	n.nsn	p.d d.dpn	pt.pp.dpn		v.pai.1p	r.asm	n.asm	r.nsm	v.aai.3s
1254	3049	2093 3836	3306		2400	5525	797	4005	2767

at   the right hand of the throne of the Majesty   in   heaven,   **2** and who serves   in the sanctuary,   the

ἐν	δεξιᾷ ←	→ τοῦ	θρόνου →	τῆς	μεγαλωσύνης	ἐν	‚τοῖς οὐρανοῖς‚		λειτουργὸς →	τῶν ἁγίων	καὶ	τῆς
p.d	a.dsf	d.gsm	n.gsm	d.gsf	n.gsf	p.d	d.dpm n.dpm		n.nsm	d.gpn a.gpn	cj	d.gsf
1877	1288	3836	2585	3836	3488	1877	3836 4041		3313	3836 41	2779	3836

true   tabernacle   set   up by the Lord, not by man.   ¶   **3**   Every high   priest is appointed to

‚τῆς ἀληθινῆς‚	σκηνῆς	ἣν	ἔπηξεν ←	ὁ	κύριος	οὐκ	ἄνθρωπος	γὰρ	Πᾶς	ἀρχιερεὺς ←	→ καθίσταται	εἰς
d.gsf a.gsf	n.gsf	r.asf	v.aai.3s	d.nsm	n.nsm	adv	n.nsm	cj	a.nsm	n.nsm	v.ppi.3s	p.a
3836 240	5008	4005	4381	3836	3261	4024	476	1142	4246	797	2770	1650

offer   both gifts and sacrifices, and so   it was necessary for this   one also to have something   to

‚τὸ προσφέρειν‚	τε	δῶρα καὶ	θυσίας		ὅθεν →	→ ἀναγκαῖον	→	τοῦτον	καὶ	→ ἔχειν	τι	ὃ →
d.asn f.pa	cj	n.apn cj	n.apf		cj	a.nsn		r.asm	adv	f.pa	r.asn	r.asn
3836 4712	5445	1565 2779	2602		3854	338		4047	2779	2400	5516	4005

offer.   **4**   If he were on earth, he would not be   a priest, for there are   already men who offer   the

προσενέγκῃ	οὖν μὲν εἰ →	ἦν	ἐπὶ γῆς	→ ἂν	οὐδ᾽ ἦν	ἱερεύς	→	ὄντων ←		τῶν	προσφερόντων	τὰ
v.aas.3s	cj cj cj	v.iai.3s	p.d n.gsf	pl	adv v.iai.3s	n.nsm		pt.pa.gpm		d.gpm	pt.pa.gpm	d.apn
4712	4036 3525 1623	1639	2093 1178	1639 323	4028 1639	2636		1639		3836	4712	3836

gifts prescribed by the law.   **5** They serve   at a sanctuary that   is a copy   and shadow of what is in

δῶρα κατὰ	← νόμον ←	λατρεύουσιν ← ←	οἵτινες	‚ὑποδείγματι‚	καὶ	σκιᾷ	→ τῶν →
n.apn p.a	n.asm	v.pai.3p	r.npm	n.dsn	cj	n.dsf	d.gpn
1565 2848	3795	3302	4015	5682	2779	5014	3836

heaven.   This is why Moses was warned   when he was about to build   the tabernacle: "See to it

ἐπουρανίων	καθὼς ← ←	Μωϋσῆς →	κεχρημάτισται →	→ →	μέλλων →	ἐπιτελεῖν τὴν	σκηνήν	γὰρ ὅρα	← φησιν
a.gpn	cj	n.nsm	v.rpi.3s		pt.pa.nsm	f.pa	d.asf n.asf	cj	v.pam.2s	v.pai.3s
2230	2777	3707	5976		3516	2200	3836	5008	1142 3972	5774

that you make everything according to the pattern shown   you on the mountain."   **6** But   the ministry

ποιήσεις πάντα	κατὰ	→ τὸν τύπον	‚τὸν δειχθέντα‚	σοι ἐν	τῷ ὄρει		δὲ	Νυνὶ	λειτουργίας
v.fai.2s a.apn	p.a	d.asm n.asm	d.asm pt.ap.asm	r.ds.2 p.d	d.dsn n.dsn		cj	adv	n.gsf
4472 4246	2848	3836 5596	3836 1259	5148 1877	3836 4001		1254	3815	3311

Jesus has received is as superior   to theirs as   the covenant of which he is mediator is   superior to the old

→ τέτυχεν	→ διαφορωτέρας	ὅσῳ καὶ	διαθήκης →		μεσίτης	ἔστιν κρείττονος
v.rai.3s	a.gsf.c	r.dsn adv	n.gsf		n.nsm	v.pai.3s a.gsf.c
5593	4012 1427	4012 2779	1347		3542	1639 3202

one, and it   is founded   on better   promises.   ¶   **7** For if   there had been nothing wrong   with that

ἥτις →	νενομοθέτηται ἐπὶ	κρείττοσιν ἐπαγγελίαις		γὰρ Εἰ	→ ἦν →	ἄμεμπτος	ἐκείνη
r.nsf	v.rpi.3s p.d	a.dpf.c n.dpf		cj cj	v.iai.3s	a.nsf	r.nsf
4015	3793 2093	3202 2039		1142 1623	1639	289	1697

first   covenant, no place would have been sought for another.   **8** But God found fault   with the people

‚ἡ πρώτη‚	οὐκ τόπος ἂν	→ →	ἐζητεῖτο →	δευτέρας	γὰρ		μεμφόμενος ←	αὐτοὺς
d.nsf a.nsf	pl n.nsm pl		v.ipi.3s	a.gsf	cj		pt.pm.nsm	r.apm.3
3836 4755	4024 5536 323		2426	1311	1142		3522	899

and said: "The time   is coming, declares the Lord,   when I will make   a new   covenant with the house

λέγει ἰδοὺ	ἡμέραι → ἔρχονται	λέγει	κύριος καὶ	→ συντελέσω	καινήν διαθήκην	ἐπὶ	τὸν οἶκον
v.pai.3s j	n.npf v.pmi.3p	v.pai.3s	n.nsm cj	v.fai.1s	a.asf n.asf	p.a	d.asm n.asm
3306 2627	2465 2262	3306	3261 2779	5334	2785 1347	2093	3836 3875

καθίστησιν ἀρχιερεῖς ἔχοντας ἀσθένειαν, ὁ λόγος δὲ τῆς ὁρκωμοσίας τῆς μετὰ τὸν νόμον υἱὸν εἰς τὸν αἰῶνα τετελειωμένον.

⁸·¹ Κεφάλαιον δὲ ἐπὶ τοῖς λεγομένοις, τοιοῦτον ἔχομεν ἀρχιερέα, ὃς ἐκάθισεν ἐν δεξιᾷ τοῦ θρόνου τῆς μεγαλωσύνης ἐν τοῖς οὐρανοῖς, ² τῶν ἁγίων λειτουργὸς καὶ τῆς σκηνῆς τῆς ἀληθινῆς, ἣν ἔπηξεν ὁ κύριος, οὐκ ἄνθρωπος. ¶ ³ πᾶς γὰρ ἀρχιερεὺς εἰς τὸ προσφέρειν δῶρά τε καὶ θυσίας καθίσταται· ὅθεν ἀναγκαῖον ἔχειν τι καὶ τοῦτον ὃ προσενέγκῃ. ⁴ εἰ μὲν οὖν ἦν ἐπὶ γῆς, οὐδ᾽ ἂν ἦν ἱερεύς, ὄντων τῶν προσφερόντων κατὰ νόμον τὰ δῶρα· ⁵ οἵτινες ὑποδείγματι καὶ σκιᾷ λατρεύουσιν τῶν ἐπουρανίων, καθὼς κεχρημάτισται Μωϋσῆς μέλλων ἐπιτελεῖν τὴν σκηνήν, Ὅρα γάρ φησιν, ποιήσεις πάντα κατὰ τὸν τύπον τὸν δειχθέντα σοι ἐν τῷ ὄρει· ⁶ νυν[ὶ] δὲ διαφορωτέρας τέτυχεν λειτουργίας, ὅσῳ καὶ κρείττονός ἐστιν διαθήκης μεσίτης, ἥτις ἐπὶ κρείττοσιν ἐπαγγελίαις νενομοθέτηται. ¶ ⁷ Εἰ γὰρ ἡ πρώτη ἐκείνη ἦν ἄμεμπτος, οὐκ ἂν δευτέρας ἐζητεῖτο τόπος. ⁸ μεμφόμενος γὰρ αὐτοὺς λέγει, Ἰδοὺ ἡμέραι ἔρχονται, λέγει κύριος, καὶ συντελέσω ἐπὶ τὸν οἶκον Ἰσραὴλ καὶ ἐπὶ τὸν οἶκον Ἰούδα διαθήκην καινήν,

of Israel and with the house of Judah. **9** It will not be like the covenant I made with their forefathers
→ Ἰσραὴλ καὶ ἐπὶ τὸν οἶκον → Ἰούδα οὐ κατὰ τὴν διαθήκην ἣν ἐποίησα → αὐτῶν ⌐τοῖς πατράσιν⌐
n.gsm cj p.a d.asm n.asm n.gsm pl p.a d.asf n.asf r.asf v.aai.1s r.gpm.3 d.dpm n.dpm
2702 2779 2093 3836 3875 2683 4024 2848 3836 1347 4005 4472 4252 899 3836 4252

when I took them by the hand to lead them out of Egypt, because they did not remain
ἐν ἡμέρᾳ μου ἐπιλαβομένου αὐτῶν → τῆς χειρὸς → ἐξαγαγεῖν αὐτοὺς ἐκ ← γῆς Αἰγύπτου ὅτι αὐτοὶ ⌐ οὐκ ἐνέμειναν
p.d n.dsf r.gs.1 pt.am.gsm r.gpm.3 d.gsf n.gsf f.aa r.apm.3 p.g n.gsf n.gsm cj r.npm pl v.aai.3p
1877 2465 1609 2138 899 3836 5931 1974 899 1666 1178 131 4022 899 1844 4024 1844

faithful to my covenant, and I turned away from them, declares the Lord. **10** This is the covenant I will
ἐν μου ⌐τῇ διαθήκῃ⌐ καγὼ ← ἠμέλησα ← → αὐτῶν λέγει κύριος ὅτι αὕτη ἡ διαθήκη ἣν → →
p.d r.gs.1 d.dsf n.dsf crasis v.aai.1s r.gpm.3 v.pai.3s n.nsm cj r.nsf d.nsf n.nsf r.asf
1877 1609 3836 1347 2743 288 899 3306 3261 4022 4047 3836 1347 4005

make with the house of Israel after that time, declares the Lord. I will put my laws in their
διαθήσομαι → τῷ οἴκῳ → Ἰσραὴλ μετὰ ἐκείνας τὰς ἡμέρας, λέγει κύριος → → διδοὺς μου νόμους εἰς αὐτῶν
v.fmi.1s d.dsm n.dsm n.gsm p.a r.apf d.apf n.apf v.pai.3s n.nsm pt.pa.nsm r.gs.1 n.apm p.a r.gpm.3
1416 3836 3875 2702 3552 1697 3836 2465 3306 3261 1443 1609 3795 1650 899

minds and write them on their hearts. I will be their God, and they will be my
⌐τὴν διάνοιαν⌐ καὶ ἐπιγράψω αὐτοὺς ἐπὶ αὐτῶν καρδίας καὶ → → ἔσομαι αὐτοῖς εἰς θεόν, καὶ αὐτοὶ → ἔσονται μοι εἰς
d.asf n.asf cj v.fai.1s r.apm.3 p.a r.gpm.3 n.apf cj v.fmi.1s r.dpm.3 p.a n.asm cj r.npm v.fmi.3p r.ds.1 p.a
3836 1379 2779 2108 899 2093 899 2840 2779 1639 899 1650 2536 2779 899 1639 1609 1650

people. **11** No longer will a man teach his neighbor, or a man his brother, saying, 'Know the
λαόν καὶ ⌐οὐ μὴ⌐ → ἕκαστος διδάξωσιν αὐτοῦ ⌐τὸν πολίτην⌐ καὶ ἕκαστος αὐτοῦ ⌐τὸν ἀδελφόν⌐ λέγων γνῶθι τὸν
n.asm cj pl pl r.nsm v.aas.3p r.gsm.3 d.asm n.asm cj r.nsm r.gsm.3 d.asm n.asm pt.pa.nsm v.aam.2s d.asm
3295 2779 4024 3590 1438 1667 1438 899 3836 4489 2779 1667 899 3836 81 3306 1182 3836

Lord,' because they will all know me, from the least of them to the greatest. **12** For I will forgive their
κύριον ὅτι → → πάντες εἰδήσουσιν με ἀπὸ μικροῦ → αὐτῶν ἕως μεγάλου ὅτι → ἔσομαι ἵλεως αὐτῶν
n.asm cj a.npm v.fai.3p r.as.1 p.g a.gsm r.gpm.3 p.g a.gsm cj v.fmi.1s r.gpm.3
3261 4022 3857 3857 4246 3857 1609 608 3625 899 2401 3489 4022 1639 2664 899

wickedness and will remember their sins no more." ¶ **13** By calling this covenant "new," he
⌐ταῖς ἀδικίαις⌐ καὶ → μνησθῶ αὐτῶν ⌐τῶν ἁμαρτιῶν⌐ οὐ μὴ ἔτι ἐν ⌐τῷ λέγειν⌐ καινὴν
d.dpf n.dpf cj v.aps.1s r.gpm.3 d.gpf n.gpf pl pl adv p.d d.dsn f.pa a.asf
3836 94 2779 3630 899 3836 281 4024 3590 2285 1877 3836 3306 2785 4096

has made the first one obsolete; and what is obsolete and aging will soon disappear.
↱ ↱ τὴν πρώτην ← πεπαλαίωκεν δὲ τὸ → παλαιούμενον καὶ γηράσκον ἐγγὺς ἀφανισμοῦ.
d.asf a.asf v.rai.3s cj d.nsn pt.pp.nsn cj pt.pa.nsn p.g n.gsm
4096 4096 3836 4755 1254 3836 4096 2779 1180 1584 907

Worship in the Earthly Tabernacle

9:1 Now the first covenant had regulations for worship and also an earthly sanctuary. **2**
οὖν μὲν [καὶ] ἡ πρώτη Εἶχε δικαιώματα → λατρείας τε ⌐ἅγιον ⌐τὸ κοσμικόν⌐ ← γὰρ
cj pl adv d.nsf a.nsf v.iai.3s n.apn n.gsf cj a.asn d.asn a.asn cj
4036 3525 2779 3836 4755 2400 1468 3301 5445 41 3836 3176 1142

A tabernacle was set up. In its first room were the lampstand, the table and the consecrated
σκηνὴ → κατεσκευάσθη ← ἐν ᾗ ἡ πρώτη τε ᾗ λυχνία καὶ ἡ τράπεζα καὶ ἡ πρόθεσις
n.nsf v.api.3s p.d r.dsf d.nsf a.nsf cj d.nsf n.nsf cj d.nsf n.nsf cj d.nsf n.nsf
5008 2941 1877 4005 3836 4755 5445 3836 3393 2779 3836 5544 2779 3836 4606

bread; this was called the Holy Place. **3** Behind the second curtain was a room called the Most
⌐τῶν ἄρτων⌐ ἥτις λέγεται Ἅγια ← δὲ μετὰ τὸ δεύτερον καταπέτασμα σκηνὴ ⌐ἡ λεγομένη⌐ →
d.gpm n.gpm r.nsf v.ppi.3s a.npn cj p.a d.asn a.asn n.asn n.nsf d.nsf pt.pp.nsf
3836 788 4015 3306 41 1254 3552 3836 1311 2925 5008 3836 3306

Holy Place, **4** which had the golden altar of incense and the gold-covered ark of
Ἅγια Ἁγίων ← ἔχουσα χρυσοῦν θυμιατήριον ← καὶ τὴν περικεκαλυμμένην πάντοθεν χρυσίῳ κιβωτὸν →
a.npn a.gpn pt.pa.nsf a.asn n.asn cj d.asf pt.rp.asf adv n.dsn n.asf
41 41 2400 5997 2593 2779 3836 4328 4119 5992 3066

the covenant. This ark contained the gold jar of manna, Aaron's staff that had budded,
τῆς διαθήκης ἐν ᾗ ← χρυσῆ στάμνος ἔχουσα ⌐τὸ μάννα⌐ καὶ Ἀαρὼν ἡ ῥάβδος ἡ → βλαστήσασα
d.gsf n.gsf p.d r.dsf a.nsf n.nsf pt.pa.nsf d.asn n.asn cj n.gsm d.nsf n.nsf d.nsf pt.aa.nsf
3836 1347 1877 4005 1877 5997 5085 2400 3836 3445 2779 2 3836 4811 3836 1056

---

9 οὐ κατὰ τὴν διαθήκην, ἣν ἐποίησα τοῖς πατράσιν αὐτῶν ἐν ἡμέρᾳ ἐπιλαβομένου μου τῆς χειρὸς αὐτῶν ἐξαγαγεῖν αὐτοὺς ἐκ γῆς Αἰγύπτου, ὅτι αὐτοὶ οὐκ ἐνέμειναν ἐν τῇ διαθήκῃ μου, κἀγὼ ἠμέλησα αὐτῶν, λέγει κύριος· **10** ὅτι αὕτη ἡ διαθήκη, ἣν διαθήσομαι τῷ οἴκῳ Ἰσραὴλ μετὰ τὰς ἡμέρας ἐκείνας, λέγει κύριος· διδοὺς νόμους μου εἰς τὴν διάνοιαν αὐτῶν καὶ ἐπὶ καρδίας αὐτῶν ἐπιγράψω αὐτούς, καὶ ἔσομαι αὐτοῖς εἰς θεόν, καὶ αὐτοὶ ἔσονταί μοι εἰς λαόν· **11** καὶ οὐ μὴ διδάξωσιν ἕκαστος τὸν πολίτην αὐτοῦ καὶ ἕκαστος τὸν ἀδελφὸν αὐτοῦ λέγων, Γνῶθι τὸν κύριον, ὅτι πάντες εἰδήσουσίν με ἀπὸ μικροῦ ἕως μεγάλου αὐτῶν, **12** ὅτι ἵλεως ἔσομαι ταῖς ἀδικίαις αὐτῶν καὶ τῶν ἁμαρτιῶν αὐτῶν οὐ μὴ μνησθῶ ἔτι. ¶ **13** ἐν τῷ λέγειν Καινὴν πεπαλαίωκεν τὴν πρώτην· τὸ δὲ παλαιούμενον καὶ γηράσκον ἐγγὺς ἀφανισμοῦ.

9:1 Εἶχε μὲν οὖν [καὶ] ἡ πρώτη δικαιώματα λατρείας τό τε ἅγιον κοσμικόν. **2** σκηνὴ γὰρ κατεσκευάσθη ἡ πρώτη ἐν ᾗ ἥ τε λυχνία καὶ ἡ τράπεζα καὶ ἡ πρόθεσις τῶν ἄρτων, ἥτις λέγεται Ἅγια· **3** μετὰ δὲ τὸ δεύτερον καταπέτασμα σκηνὴ ἡ λεγομένη Ἅγια Ἁγίων, **4** χρυσοῦν ἔχουσα θυμιατήριον καὶ τὴν κιβωτὸν τῆς διαθήκης περικεκαλυμμένην πάντοθεν χρυσίῳ, ἐν ᾗ στάμνος

and the stone tablets of the covenant. **5** Above the ark were the cherubim of the Glory, overshadowing the
καὶ αἱ πλάκες → τῆς διαθήκης δὲ ὑπεράνω αὐτῆς Χερουβιν → δόξης κατασκιάζοντα τὸ
cj d.npf n.npf d.gsf n.gsf cj p.g r.gsf.3 n.npn n.gsf pt.pa.npn d.asn
2779 3836 4419 3836 1347 1254 5645 899 5938 1518 2944 3836

atonement cover. But we cannot discuss these things in detail now. ¶ **6** When everything had been
ἱλαστήριον ← ⸂οὐκ ἔστιν⸃ λέγειν περὶ ὧν ← κατὰ μέρος νῦν δὲ → Τούτων →
n.asn pl v.pai.3s f.pa p.g r.gpn p.a n.gsn adv cj r.gpn
2663 4024 1639 3306 4309 4005 2848 3538 3814 1254 2941 4047

arranged like this, the priests entered regularly into the outer room to carry on their ministry.
κατεσκευασμένων οὕτως ← μὲν οἱ ἱερεῖς εἰσίασιν ⸤διὰ παντός⸥ εἰς τὴν πρώτην σκηνὴν → ἐπιτελοῦντες ← τὰς λατρείας
pt.rp.gpn adv pl d.npm n.npm v.pai.3p p.g a.gsm p.a d.asf a.asf n.asf pt.pa.npm d.apf n.apf
2941 4048 3525 3836 2636 1655 1328 4246 1650 3836 4755 5008 2200 3836 3301

7 But only the high priest entered the inner room, and that only once a year, and never without
δὲ μόνος ὁ ἀρχιερεύς ← εἰς τὴν δευτέραν ἅπαξ ⸤τοῦ ἐνιαυτοῦ⸥ οὐ χωρὶς
cj a.nsm d.nsm n.nsm p.a d.asf a.asf adv d.gsm n.gsm pl p.g
1254 3668 3836 797 1650 3836 1311 562 3836 1929 4024 6006

blood, which he offered for himself and for the sins the people had committed in ignorance. **8** The Holy
αἵματος ὃ → προσφέρει ὑπὲρ ἑαυτοῦ καὶ → τῶν τοῦ λαοῦ → ἀγνοημάτων τοῦ ⸤τοῦ ἁγίου⸥
n.gsn r.asn v.pai.3s p.g r.gsm.3 cj d.gpn d.gsm n.gsm n.gpn d.gsn d.gsn a.gsn
135 4005 4712 5642 1571 2779 3836 52 3836 3295 52 3836 3836 41

Spirit was showing by this that the way into the Most Holy Place had not yet been disclosed as long as the
πνεύματος → δηλοῦντος → τοῦτο τὴν ὁδὸν → τῶν ἁγίων ⸀ μήπω πεφανερῶσθαι ἔτι ← τῆς
n.gsn pt.pa.gsn r.asn d.asf n.asf d.gpn a.gpn adv f.rp adv d.gsf
4460 1317 4047 3836 3847 3836 41 5746 3609 5746 2285 3836

first tabernacle was still standing. **9** This is an illustration for the present time, indicating that the
πρώτης σκηνῆς → ⸤ἐχούσης στάσιν⸥ ἥτις παραβολὴ εἰς τὸν ⸤τὸν ἐνεστηκότα⸥ καιρὸν καθ᾽ ἣν τε
a.gsf n.gsf pt.pa.gsf n.asf r.nsf n.nsf p.a d.asm d.asm pt.ra.asm n.asm p.a r.asf cj
4755 5008 2400 5087 4015 4130 1650 3836 3836 1931 2789 2848 4005 5445

gifts and sacrifices being offered were not able to clear the conscience of the worshiper. **10** They are
δῶρα καὶ θυσίαι → προσφέρονται ⸀ μὴ δυνάμεναι → τελειῶσαι κατὰ συνείδησιν τὸν λατρεύοντα
n.npn cj n.npf v.ppi.3p pl pt.pp.npf f.aa p.a n.asf d.asm pt.pa.asm
1565 2779 2602 4712 1538 3590 1538 5457 2848 5287 3836 3302

only a matter of food and drink and various ceremonial washings – external regulations applying until the
μόνον ἐπὶ ← βρώμασιν καὶ πόμασιν καὶ διαφόροις → βαπτισμοῖς σαρκὸς δικαιώματα ἐπικείμενα μέχρι
adv p.d n.dpn cj n.dpn cj a.dpm n.dpm n.gsf n.npn pt.pm.npn p.g
3667 2093 1109 2779 4503 2779 1427 968 4922 1468 2130 3588

time of the new order.
καιροῦ → διορθώσεως
n.gsn n.gsf
2789 1481

The Blood of Christ

9:11 When Christ came as high priest of the good things that are already here, he went
δὲ ⸀ Χριστὸς παραγενόμενος → ἀρχιερεὺς → τῶν ἀγαθῶν ← → γενομένων ← ←
cj n.nsm pt.am.nsm n.nsm d.gpn a.gpn pt.am.gpn
1254 4134 5986 4134 797 3836 19 1181

through the greater and more perfect tabernacle that is not man-made, that is to say, not a part of this
διὰ τῆς μείζονος καὶ → τελειοτέρας σκηνῆς οὐ χειροποιήτου τοῦτ᾽ ἔστιν οὐ ⸀ ταύτης
p.g d.gsf a.gsf.c cj a.gsf.c n.gsf pl a.gsf.c r.nsn v.pai.3s pl r.gsf
1328 3836 3489 2779 5455 5008 4024 5935 4047 1639 4024 3232 4047

creation. **12** He did not enter by means of the blood of goats and calves; but he entered the Most Holy Place
⸤τῆς κτίσεως⸥ οὐδὲ δι᾽ αἵματος → τράγων καὶ μόσχων δὲ → εἰσῆλθεν εἰς τὰ ἅγια
d.gsf n.gsf cj p.g n.gsn n.gpm cj n.gpm cj v.aai.3s p.a d.apn a.apn
3836 3232 4028 1328 135 5543 2779 3675 1254 1656 1650 3836 41

once for all by his own blood, having obtained eternal redemption. **13** The blood of goats and bulls and
ἐφάπαξ ← ← διὰ τοῦ ἰδίου αἵματος → εὑράμενος αἰωνίαν λύτρωσιν γὰρ εἰ τὸ αἷμα → τράγων καὶ ταύρων καὶ
adv p.g d.gsn a.gsn n.gsn pt.am.nsm a.asf n.asf cj cj d.nsn n.nsn n.gpm cj n.gpm cj
2384 1328 3836 2625 135 2351 173 3391 1142 1623 3836 135 5543 5436 2779

χρυσῆ ἔχουσα τὸ μάννα καὶ ἡ ῥάβδος Ἀαρὼν ἡ βλαστήσασα καὶ αἱ πλάκες τῆς διαθήκης, ⁵ ὑπεράνω δὲ αὐτῆς Χερουβιν δόξης κατασκιάζοντα τὸ ἱλαστήριον· περὶ ὧν οὐκ ἔστιν νῦν λέγειν κατὰ μέρος. ¶ ⁶ Τούτων δὲ οὕτως κατεσκευασμένων εἰς μὲν τὴν πρώτην σκηνὴν διὰ παντὸς εἰσίασιν οἱ ἱερεῖς τὰς λατρείας ἐπιτελοῦντες, ⁷ εἰς δὲ τὴν δευτέραν ἅπαξ τοῦ ἐνιαυτοῦ μόνος ὁ ἀρχιερεύς, οὐ χωρὶς αἵματος ὃ προσφέρει ὑπὲρ ἑαυτοῦ καὶ τῶν τοῦ λαοῦ ἀγνοημάτων, ⁸ τοῦτο δηλοῦντος τοῦ πνεύματος τοῦ ἁγίου, μήπω πεφανερῶσθαι τὴν τῶν ἁγίων ὁδὸν ἔτι τῆς πρώτης σκηνῆς ἐχούσης στάσιν, ⁹ ἥτις παραβολὴ εἰς τὸν καιρὸν τὸν ἐνεστηκότα, καθ᾽ ἣν δῶρά τε καὶ θυσίαι προσφέρονται μὴ δυνάμεναι κατὰ συνείδησιν τελειῶσαι τὸν λατρεύοντα, ¹⁰ μόνον ἐπὶ βρώμασιν καὶ πόμασιν καὶ διαφόροις βαπτισμοῖς, δικαιώματα σαρκὸς μέχρι καιροῦ διορθώσεως ἐπικείμενα.

⁹:¹¹ Χριστὸς δὲ παραγενόμενος ἀρχιερεὺς τῶν γενομένων ἀγαθῶν διὰ τῆς μείζονος καὶ τελειοτέρας σκηνῆς οὐ χειροποιήτου, τοῦτ᾽ ἔστιν οὐ ταύτης τῆς κτίσεως, ¹² οὐδὲ δι᾽ αἵματος τράγων καὶ μόσχων διὰ δὲ τοῦ ἰδίου αἵματος εἰσῆλθεν ἐφάπαξ εἰς τὰ ἅγια αἰωνίαν λύτρωσιν εὑράμενος. ¹³ εἰ γὰρ τὸ αἷμα τράγων καὶ ταύρων καὶ σποδὸς δαμάλεως ῥαντίζουσα τοὺς κεκοινωμένους

the ashes of a heifer   sprinkled on those who are ceremonially unclean   sanctify them so   that they are
σποδὸς →   δαμάλεως ῥαντίζουσα ← τοὺς ←   →   →   κεκοινωμένους ἁγιάζει   πρὸς
n.nsf   n.gsf   pt.pa.nsf   d.apm   pt.rp.apm   v.pai.3s   p.a
5075   1239   4822   3836   3124   39   4639

outwardly clean.   ¹⁴How much more, then, will the blood of Christ,   who through the eternal Spirit
⸤τῆς σαρκὸς⸥ ⸤τὴν καθαρότητα⸥ →   πόσῳ   μᾶλλον   ⸤τὸ αἷμα⸥ → ⸤τοῦ Χριστοῦ⸥ ὃς διὰ   αἰωνίου πνεύματος
d.gsf n.gsf d.asf n.asf   r.dsn   adv.c   d.nsn n.nsn   d.gsm n.gsm   r.nsm p.g   a.gsn   n.gsn
3836 4922   3836 2755   4531   3437   2751 3836 135   3836 5986   4005 1328   173   4460

offered   himself unblemished to God,   cleanse our consciences   from acts that lead to death, so that we may
προσήνεγκεν ἑαυτὸν ἄμωμον   → ⸤τῷ θεῷ⸥ καθαριεῖ ἡμῶν ⸤τὴν συνείδησιν⸥ ἀπὸ ἔργων →   →   →   νεκρῶν εἰς ←
v.aai.3s   r.asm.3 a.asm   d.dsm n.dsm v.fai.3s r.gp.1 d.asf n.asf   p.g n.gpn   a.gpn p.a
4712   1571   320   3836 2536   2751   7005 3836 5287   608 2240   3738   1650

serve   the living God!   ¶ ¹⁵   For   this reason Christ is   the mediator of a new   covenant, that
⸤τὸ λατρεύειν⸥ ζῶντι θεῷ   Καὶ ⸤διὰ τοῦτο⸥ ←   ←   ἐστίν μεσίτης →   καινῆς διαθήκης ὅπως
d.asn f.pai   pt.pa.dsm n.dsm   cj   p.g   r.asn   v.pai.3s n.nsm   n.gsf n.gsf   cj
3836 3302   2409 2536   2779 1328   4047   1639   3542   2785 1347   3968

those who are called   may receive the promised eternal inheritance   → now that he has   died   as a
οἱ ←   κεκλημένοι   λάβωσιν τὴν ἐπαγγελίαν αἰωνίου ⸤τῆς κληρονομίας⸥   →   →   γενομένου θανάτου εἰς
d.npm   pt.rp.npm   v.aas.3p d.asf n.asf   a.gsf d.gsf n.gsf   pt.am.gsm n.gsm   p.a
3836   2813   3284 2039   173   3836 3100   1181   2505   1650

ransom   to set them free from the sins   committed under the first covenant. ¶ ¹⁶   In   the case of
ἀπολύτρωσιν   →   τῶν παραβάσεων   ἐπὶ   τῇ πρώτῃ διαθήκῃ   γὰρ Ὅπου ← ←   ←
n.asf   d.gpf n.gpf   p.d   d.dsf a.dsf n.dsf   cj   cj
667   3836 4126   2093 3836 4755 1347   1142 3963

a will,   it is necessary to prove   the death of the one who made   it, ¹⁷ because a will   is in force only when
διαθήκη   ἀνάγκη   → φέρεσθαι   θάνατον → τοῦ → ← διαθεμένου   γὰρ   διαθήκη → βεβαία   ἐπὶ
n.nsf   n.nsf   f.pp   n.asm   d.gsm   pt.am.gsm   cj   n.nsf   a.nsf   p.d
1347   340   5770   2505   3836   1416   1142   1347   1010   2093

somebody has died;   it never takes effect while the one who made   it is living. ¹⁸ This is why even the first
νεκροῖς ἐπεὶ → μήποτε → ἰσχύει ὅτε ὁ →   ←   διαθέμενος   → ζῇ   ὅθεν ←   →   → ἡ   πρώτη
a.dpm   cj   pl   v.pai.3s cj d.nsm   pt.am.nsm   v.pai.3s cj   d.nsf a.nsf
3738   2075   2710 3607   2710   4021 3836   1416   2409   3854   3836 4755

covenant was not put into effect   without blood. ¹⁹ When   Moses   had proclaimed every commandment
→   οὐδὲ →   → ἐγκεκαίνισται χωρὶς αἵματος γὰρ →   ὑπὸ Μωϋσέως →   λαληθείσης   πάσης ἐντολῆς
      adv   v.rpi.3s   p.g   n.gsn   cj   p.g n.gsm   pt.ap.gsf   a.gsf n.gsf
1590 4028   1590   6006   135   1142   5679 3707   3281   4246   1953

of the law   to all the people, he took the blood of calves,   together with water,
κατὰ τὸν νόμον → παντὶ τῷ λαῷ → λαβὼν τὸ αἷμα → ⸤τῶν μόσχων⸥ [καὶ τῶν τράγων] →   μετὰ ὕδατος καὶ
p.a d.asm n.asm   a.dsm d.dsm n.dsm   pt.aa.nsm d.asn n.asn d.gpm n.gpm cj   d.gpm n.gpm   p.g   n.gsn cj
2848 3836 3795   4246 3836 3295   3284 3836 135   3836 3675   2779 3836 5543   3552 5623   2779

scarlet wool and branches of hyssop, and sprinkled   the scroll and all   the people. ²⁰ He said, "This is the
κοκκίνου ἐρίου καὶ   ὑσσώπου   ἐρράντισεν τε αὐτό τὸ βιβλίον καὶ πάντα τὸν λαὸν   λέγων τοῦτο   τὸ
a.gsn   n.gsn cj   n.gsf   v.aai.3s cj r.asn d.asn n.asn cj   a.asm d.asm n.asm   pt.pa.nsm r.nsn   d.nsn
3132   2250 2779   5727   4822   5445 899 3836 1046 2779 4246 3836 3295   3306 4047   3836

blood of the covenant, which God   has commanded   you to keep." ²¹   In the same way, he sprinkled with
αἷμα → τῆς διαθήκης ἧς ὁ θεός⸥ ἐνετείλατο   πρὸς ὑμᾶς   δὲ   →   → ὁμοίως →   ἐρράντισεν →
n.nsn   d.gsf n.gsf   r.gsf d.nsm n.nsm v.ami.3s   p.a r.ap.2   cj   adv   v.aai.3s
135   3836 1347   4005 3836 2536   1948   4639 7007   1254   3931   4822

the blood both the tabernacle and everything   used in its ceremonies. ²² In fact, the law   requires that nearly
τῷ αἵματι καὶ τὴν σκηνὴν   καὶ ⸤πάντα τὰ σκεύη⸥ →   → τῆς λειτουργίας καὶ ←   τὸν νόμον κατὰ   σχεδὸν
d.dsn n.dsn cj d.asf n.asf   cj   a.apn d.apn n.apn   d.gsf n.gsf   cj   d.asm n.asm p.a   adv
3836 135   2779 3836 5008   2779 4246 3836 5007   3311   2779   3836 3795 2848   5385

everything be cleansed with blood, and without the shedding   of blood there is   no forgiveness. ¶ ²³ It
πάντα   → καθαρίζεται ἐν αἵματι καὶ χωρὶς   αἱματεκχυσίας ← ←   → γίνεται οὐ ἄφεσις   →
a.npn   v.ppi.3s   p.d n.dsn cj p.d   n.gsf   v.pmi.3s ou n.nsf
4246   2751   1877 135 2779 6006   136   1181 4024 912

ἁγιάζει πρὸς τὴν τῆς σαρκὸς καθαρότητα, ¹⁴ πόσῳ μᾶλλον τὸ αἷμα τοῦ Χριστοῦ, ὃς διὰ πνεύματος αἰωνίου ἑαυτὸν προσήνεγκεν ἄμωμον τῷ θεῷ, καθαριεῖ τὴν συνείδησιν ἡμῶν ἀπὸ νεκρῶν ἔργων εἰς τὸ λατρεύειν θεῷ ζῶντι. ¶ ¹⁵ Καὶ διὰ τοῦτο διαθήκης καινῆς μεσίτης ἐστίν, ὅπως θανάτου γενομένου εἰς ἀπολύτρωσιν τῶν ἐπὶ τῇ πρώτῃ διαθήκῃ παραβάσεων τὴν ἐπαγγελίαν λάβωσιν οἱ κεκλημένοι τῆς αἰωνίου κληρονομίας. ¶ ¹⁶ ὅπου γὰρ διαθήκη, θάνατον ἀνάγκη φέρεσθαι τοῦ διαθεμένου· ¹⁷ διαθήκη γὰρ ἐπὶ νεκροῖς βεβαία, ἐπεὶ μήποτε ἰσχύει ὅτε ζῇ ὁ διαθέμενος. ¹⁸ ὅθεν οὐδὲ ἡ πρώτη χωρὶς αἵματος ἐγκεκαίνισται· ¹⁹ λαληθείσης γὰρ πάσης ἐντολῆς κατὰ τὸν νόμον ὑπὸ Μωϋσέως παντὶ τῷ λαῷ, λαβὼν τὸ αἷμα τῶν μόσχων [καὶ τῶν τράγων] μετὰ ὕδατος καὶ ἐρίου κοκκίνου καὶ ὑσσώπου αὐτό τε τὸ βιβλίον καὶ πάντα τὸν λαὸν ἐρράντισεν ²⁰ λέγων, Τοῦτο τὸ αἷμα τῆς διαθήκης ἧς ἐνετείλατο πρὸς ὑμᾶς ὁ θεός. ²¹ καὶ τὴν σκηνὴν δὲ καὶ πάντα τὰ σκεύη τῆς λειτουργίας τῷ αἵματι ὁμοίως ἐρράντισεν. ²² καὶ σχεδὸν ἐν αἵματι πάντα καθαρίζεται κατὰ τὸν νόμον καὶ χωρὶς αἱματεκχυσίας οὐ γίνεται ἄφεσις. ¶ ²³ Ἀνάγκη οὖν τὰ μὲν ὑποδείγματα

was necessary, then, | for the copies | of the heavenly | things to be purified | with these sacrifices,
→ Ἀνάγκη οὖν μὲν | τὰ ὑποδείγματα | → τῶν ἐν τοῖς οὐρανοῖς, ← | → → καθαρίζεσθαι → | τούτοις
n.nsf cj cj | d.apn n.apn | d.gpn d.p d.dpm n.dpm | f.pp | r.dpn
340 4036 3525 | 3836 5682 | 3836 1877 3836 4041 | 2751 | 4047

but the heavenly things themselves with better | sacrifices than these. | [24] For Christ | did not enter | a man-made
δὲ τὰ ἐπουράνια αὐτὰ κρείττοσιν | θυσίαις παρὰ ταύτας. | γὰρ Χριστός | → οὐ εἰσῆλθεν εἰς | χειροποίητα
cj d.apn a.apn r.apn a.dpf.c | n.dpf p.a r.apf | cj n.nsm | pl v.aai.3s p.a | a.apn
1254 3836 2230 899 3202 | 2602 4123 4047 | 1142 5986 | 1656 4024 1656 1650 | 5935

sanctuary that was only a copy | of the true | one; | he entered | heaven | itself, now to appear | for
ἅγια ἀντίτυπα | τῶν ἀληθινῶν ← | ἀλλ᾽ | εἰς τὸν οὐρανόν, | αὐτὸν νῦν → ἐμφανισθῆναι | ὑπὲρ
a.apn n.apn | d.gpn a.gpn | cj | p.a d.asm n.asm | r.asm adv f.ap | p.g
41 531 | 3836 240 | 247 | 1650 3836 4041 | 899 3814 1872 | 5642

us | in God's | presence. | [25] Nor | did he enter heaven to offer | himself again | and again, the way the high
ἡμῶν → τοῦ θεοῦ, τῷ προσώπῳ, | οὐδ᾽ | ἵνα προσφέρῃ | ἑαυτόν πολλάκις ← | ← ← ὥσπερ ὁ ἀρχιερεὺς
r.gp.1 d.gsm n.gsm d.dsn n.dsn | cj | cj v.pas.3s | r.asm.3 adv | cj d.nsm n.nsm
7005 4725 3836 2536 3836 4725 | 4028 | 2671 4712 | 1571 4490 | 6061 3836 797

priest enters | the Most Holy Place | every year | with blood that is not | his own. | [26] Then Christ would have
εἰσέρχεται εἰς τὰ | ἅγια | κατ᾽ ἐνιαυτὸν ἐν | αἵματι → → ἀλλοτρίῳ | ← | ἐπεὶ αὐτὸν →
v.ppi.3s p.a d.apn | a.apn | p.a n.asm p.d | n.dsn a.dsn | | cj r.asm.3
1656 1650 3836 | 41 | 2848 1929 1877 | 135 259 | | 2075 899

had to suffer many times since the creation | of the world. But now he has appeared | once for all at the end
ἔδει παθεῖν πολλάκις ← ἀπὸ καταβολῆς → | κόσμου δὲ νυνὶ → → πεφανέρωται ἅπαξ ← | ← ἐπὶ συντελείᾳ
v.iai.3s f.aa adv p.g n.gsf | n.gsm cj adv v.rpi.3s adv | p.d n.dsf
1256 4248 4490 608 2856 | 3180 1254 3815 5746 562 | 2093 5333

of the ages | to do away | with sin | by the sacrifice of himself. | [27] Just as | man | is destined to
→ τῶν αἰώνων εἰς | → ἀθέτησιν → | τῆς ἁμαρτίας, | διὰ τῆς θυσίας → αὐτοῦ. | καὶ καθ᾽ ὅσον | τοῖς ἀνθρώποις, | ἀπόκειται →
d.gpm n.gpm p.a | n.asf | d.gsf n.gsf | p.g d.gsf n.gsf r.gsm.3 | cj p.a r.asn | d.dpm n.dpm | v.pmi.3s
3836 172 1650 | 120 | 3836 281 | 1328 3836 2602 899 | 2779 2848 4012 | 3836 476 | 641

die | once, and after that | to face judgment, | [28] so | Christ | was sacrificed | once to take | away
ἀποθανεῖν ἅπαξ | δὲ μετὰ τοῦτο | κρίσις | οὕτως καὶ ὁ | Χριστός, → | προσενεχθεὶς ἅπαξ | εἰς τὸ ἀνενεγκεῖν, ←
f.aa adv | cj p.a r.asn | n.nsf | adv adv d.nsm n.nsm | pt.ap.nsm adv | p.a d.asn f.aa
633 562 | 1254 3552 4047 | 3213 | 4048 2779 3836 5986 | 4712 562 | 1650 3836 429

the sins | of many people; and he will appear | a second | time, not | to bear sin, | but to bring salvation
ἁμαρτίας → πολλῶν ← | → ὀφθήσεται | ἐκ δευτέρου, | χωρὶς | ἁμαρτίας | εἰς σωτηρίαν
n.apf a.gpm | v.fpi.3s | p.g a.gsn | p.g | n.gsf | p.a n.asf
281 4498 | 3972 | 1666 1311 | 6006 | 281 | 1650 5401

to those who are waiting | for him.
→ τοῖς ← | ἀπεκδεχομένοις ← | αὐτόν.
d.dpm | pt.pm.dpm | r.asm.3
3836 | 587 | 899

Christ's Sacrifice Once for All

10:1 The law | is | only a shadow of the good | things that are coming | – not the realities
γὰρ ὁ νόμος ἔχων | Σκιὰν → τῶν ἀγαθῶν ← | → → μελλόντων | οὐκ τὴν εἰκόνα τῶν πραγμάτων,
cj d.nsm n.nsm pt.pa.nsm | n.asf d.gpn a.gpn | pt.pa.gpn | pl d.asf n.asf d.gpn n.gpn
1142 3836 3795 2400 | 5014 3836 19 | 3516 | 4024 3836 1635 3836 4547

themselves. For this reason it can | never, | by the same sacrifices | repeated | endlessly | year
αὐτὴν ← ← → | δύναται οὐδέποτε | ταῖς αὐταῖς θυσίαις | ἃς προσφέρουσιν | εἰς τὸ διηνεκὲς, | κατ᾽ ἐνιαυτὸν
r.asf | v.ppi.3s adv | d.dpf r.dpf n.dpf | r.apf v.pai.3p | p.a d.asn a.asn | p.a n.asm
899 1142 1142 1142 | 1538 4030 | 3836 899 2602 | 4005 4712 | 1650 3836 1457 | 2848 1929

after year, make perfect | those who draw | near to worship. | [2] If | it could, | would they not have stopped | being
→ → τελειῶσαι τοὺς ← | προσερχομένους ← | → → | ἐπεὶ | ἂν → | οὐκ → ἐπαύσαντο →
f.aa d.apm | pt.pm.apm | | cj | pl | pl pl v.ami.3p
5457 3836 | 4665 | | 2075 | 323 | 4264 4024 4264

offered? | For the worshipers | would have been | cleansed | once for all, and would no | longer have
προσφερόμεναι διὰ | τοὺς λατρεύοντας → | → → → | κεκαθαρισμένους | ἅπαξ ← | μηδεμίαν ἔτι
pt.pp.npf p.a | d.apm pt.pa.apm | | pt.rp.apm | adv | a.asf adv
4712 1328 | 3836 3302 | | 2751 | 562 | 3594 2285

τῶν ἐν τοῖς οὐρανοῖς τούτοις καθαρίζεσθαι, αὐτὰ δὲ τὰ ἐπουράνια κρείττοσιν θυσίαις παρὰ ταύτας. [24] οὐ γὰρ εἰς χειροποίητα εἰσῆλθεν ἅγια Χριστός, ἀντίτυπα τῶν ἀληθινῶν, ἀλλ᾽ εἰς αὐτὸν τὸν οὐρανόν, νῦν ἐμφανισθῆναι τῷ προσώπῳ τοῦ θεοῦ ὑπὲρ ἡμῶν· [25] οὐδ᾽ ἵνα πολλάκις προσφέρῃ ἑαυτόν, ὥσπερ ὁ ἀρχιερεὺς εἰσέρχεται εἰς τὰ ἅγια κατ᾽ ἐνιαυτὸν ἐν αἵματι ἀλλοτρίῳ, [26] ἐπεὶ ἔδει αὐτὸν πολλάκις παθεῖν ἀπὸ καταβολῆς κόσμου· νυνὶ δὲ ἅπαξ ἐπὶ συντελείᾳ τῶν αἰώνων εἰς ἀθέτησιν [τῆς] ἁμαρτίας διὰ τῆς θυσίας αὐτοῦ πεφανέρωται. [27] καὶ καθ᾽ ὅσον ἀπόκειται τοῖς ἀνθρώποις ἅπαξ ἀποθανεῖν, μετὰ δὲ τοῦτο κρίσις, [28] οὕτως καὶ ὁ Χριστὸς ἅπαξ προσενεχθεὶς εἰς τὸ πολλῶν ἀνενεγκεῖν ἁμαρτίας, ἐκ δευτέρου χωρὶς ἁμαρτίας ὀφθήσεται τοῖς αὐτὸν ἀπεκδεχομένοις εἰς σωτηρίαν.

10:1 Σκιὰν γὰρ ἔχων ὁ νόμος τῶν μελλόντων ἀγαθῶν, οὐκ αὐτὴν τὴν εἰκόνα τῶν πραγμάτων, κατ᾽ ἐνιαυτὸν ταῖς αὐταῖς θυσίαις ἃς προσφέρουσιν εἰς τὸ διηνεκὲς οὐδέποτε δύναται τοὺς προσερχομένους τελειῶσαι· [2] ἐπεὶ οὐκ ἂν ἐπαύσαντο προσφερόμεναι διὰ τὸ μηδεμίαν ἔχειν ἔτι συνείδησιν ἁμαρτιῶν τοὺς λατρεύοντας ἅπαξ κεκαθαρισμένους; [3] ἀλλ᾽ ἐν αὐταῖς

felt guilty for their sins. 3 But those sacrifices are an annual reminder of sins, 4 because it is
⌞τὸ ἔχειν⌟ συνείδησιν → ἁμαρτιῶν ἀλλ᾽ ἐν αὐταῖς ← ⌞κατ᾽ ἐνιαυτόν⌟ ἀνάμνησις → ἁμαρτιῶν γὰρ
d.asn f.pa n.asf n.gpf cj p.d r.dpf.3 p.a n.asm n.nsf n.gpf cj
3836 2400 5287 281 247 1877 899 2848 1929 390 281 1142

impossible for the blood of bulls and goats to take away sins. ¶ 5 Therefore, when Christ came
ἀδύνατον αἷμα → ταύρων καὶ τράγων → ἀφαιρεῖν ← ἁμαρτίας Διὸ → εἰσερχόμενος
a.nsn n.asn n.gpm cj n.gpm f.pa n.apf cj pt.pm.nsm
105 135 5436 2779 5543 904 281 1475 1656

into the world, he said: "Sacrifice and offering you did not desire, but a body you prepared for me; 6 with
εἰς τὸν κόσμον → λέγει θυσίαν καὶ προσφορὰν ↱ ↱ οὐκ ἠθέλησας δὲ σῶμα → κατηρτίσω → μοι ↱
p.a d.asm n.asm v.pai.3s n.asf cj n.asf pl v.aai.2s cj n.asn v.ami.2s r.ds.1
1650 3836 3180 3306 2602 2779 4714 2527 2527 4024 2527 1254 5393 2936 1609 2305

burnt offerings and sin offerings you were not pleased. 7 Then I said, 'Here I am – it is written
ὁλοκαυτώματα ← καὶ περὶ ἁμαρτίας ↱ ↱ οὐκ εὐδόκησας τότε → εἶπον ἰδοὺ → ἥκω → → γέγραπται
n.apn cj p.g n.gsf pl v.aai.2s adv v.aai.1s j v.rai.1s v.rpi.3s
3906 2779 4309 281 2305 2305 4024 2305 5538 3306 2627 2457 1211

about me in the scroll – I have come to do your will, O God.'" 8 First he said,
περὶ ἐμοῦ ἐν ⌞κεφαλίδι βιβλίου⌟ → ⌞τοῦ ποιῆσαι⌟ σου ⌞τὸ θέλημα⌟ → ⌞ὁ θεός⌟ ἀνώτερον → λέγων ὅτι
p.g r.gs.1 p.d n.dsf n.gsn d.gsn f.aa r.gs.2 d.asn n.asn d.vsm n.vsm adv.c pt.pa.nsm cj
4309 1609 1877 3053 1046 3836 4472 5148 3836 2525 3836 2536 542 3306 4022

"Sacrifices and offerings, burnt offerings and sin offerings you did not desire, nor were you
θυσίας καὶ προσφορὰς καὶ ὁλοκαυτώματα ← καὶ περὶ ἁμαρτίας ↱ ↱ οὐκ ἠθέλησας οὐδὲ → →
n.apf cj n.apf cj n.apn cj p.g n.gsf pl v.aai.2s cj
2602 2779 4714 2779 3906 2779 4309 281 2527 2527 4024 2527 4028

pleased with them" (although the law required them to be made). 9 Then he said, "Here I am, I have
εὐδόκησας ← νόμον κατὰ αἵτινες → → προσφέρονται τότε → εἴρηκεν ἰδοὺ → ἥκω
v.aai.2s n.asm p.a r.npf v.ppi.3p adv v.rai.3s j v.rai.1s
2305 3795 2848 4015 4712 5538 3306 2627 2457

come to do your will." He sets aside the first to establish the second. 10 And by that will, we
→ ⌞τοῦ ποιῆσαι⌟ σου ⌞τὸ θέλημα⌟ → ἀναιρεῖ ← τὸ πρῶτον ἵνα στήσῃ τὸ δεύτερον ἐν ᾧ θελήματι →
d.gsn f.aa r.gs.2 d.asn n.asn v.pai.3s d.asn a.asn cj v.aas.3s d.asn a.asn p.d r.dsn n.dsn
3836 4472 5148 3836 2525 359 3836 4755 2671 2705 3836 1311 1877 4005 2525

have been made holy through the sacrifice of the body of Jesus Christ once for all. ¶ 11
→ ἐσμὲν → ἡγιασμένοι διὰ τῆς προσφορᾶς → τοῦ σώματος → Ἰησοῦ Χριστοῦ ἐφάπαξ ← ← Καὶ μὲν
v.pai.1p pt.rp.npm p.g d.gsf n.gsf d.gsn n.gsn n.gsm n.gsm adv cj pl
1639 39 1328 3836 4714 3836 5393 2652 5986 2384 2779 3525

Day after day every priest stands and performs his religious duties; again and again he offers the
⌞καθ᾽ ἡμέραν⌟ ← ← πᾶς ἱερεὺς ἕστηκεν λειτουργῶν ← ← ← καὶ πολλάκις ← ← → προσφέρων τὰς
p.a n.asf a.nsm n.nsm v.rai.3s pt.pa.nsm cj adv pt.pa.nsm d.apf
2848 2465 4246 2636 2705 3310 2779 4490 4712 3836

same sacrifices, which can never take away sins. 12 But when this priest had offered for all
αὐτὰς θυσίας αἵτινες δύνανται οὐδέποτε περιελεῖν ← ἁμαρτίας δὲ ↱ οὗτος → προσενέγκας εἰς ⌞τὸ διηνεκὲς⌟
r.apf n.apf r.npf v.ppi.3p adv f.aa n.apf cj r.nsm pt.aa.nsm p.a d.asn a.asn
899 2602 4015 1538 4030 4311 281 1254 4712 4047 4712 1650 3836 1457

time one sacrifice for sins, he sat down at the right hand of God. 13 Since that time he waits for
← μίαν θυσίαν ὑπὲρ ἁμαρτιῶν → ἐκάθισεν ← ἐν δεξιᾷ ⌞τοῦ θεοῦ⌟ ⌞τὸ λοιπὸν⌟ ἐκδεχόμενος ἕως
a.asf n.asf p.g n.gpf v.aai.3s p.d a.dsf d.gsm n.gsm d.asn adv pt.pm.nsm cj
1651 2602 5642 281 2767 1877 1288 3836 2536 3836 3370 1683 2401

his enemies to be made his footstool, 14 because by one sacrifice he has made perfect
αὐτοῦ ⌞οἱ ἐχθροὶ⌟ → → τεθῶσιν αὐτοῦ ⌞ὑποπόδιον τῶν ποδῶν⌟ γὰρ μιᾷ προσφορᾷ → → → τετελείωκεν
r.gsm.3 d.npm a.npm v.aps.3p r.gsm.3 n.asn d.gpm n.gpm cj a.dsf n.dsf v.rai.3s
899 3836 2398 5502 899 5711 3836 4546 1142 1651 4714 5457

forever those who are being made holy. ¶ 15 The Holy Spirit also testifies to us about
⌞εἰς τὸ διηνεκὲς⌟ τοὺς ← → → → ἁγιαζομένους δὲ ⌞τὸ ἅγιον⌟ πνεῦμα καὶ Μαρτυρεῖ → ἡμῖν
p.a d.asn a.asn d.apm pt.pp.apm cj d.nsn d.nsn a.nsn n.nsn adv v.pai.3s r.dp.1
1650 3836 1457 3836 39 1254 3836 3836 41 4460 2779 3455 7005

ἀνάμνησις ἁμαρτιῶν κατ᾽ ἐνιαυτόν· 4 ἀδύνατον γὰρ αἷμα ταύρων καὶ τράγων ἀφαιρεῖν ἁμαρτίας. ¶ 5 Διὸ εἰσερχόμενος εἰς τὸν
κόσμον λέγει, Θυσίαν καὶ προσφορὰν οὐκ ἠθέλησας, σῶμα δὲ κατηρτίσω μοι· 6 ὁλοκαυτώματα καὶ περὶ ἁμαρτίας οὐκ εὐδόκησας.
7 τότε εἶπον, Ἰδοὺ ἥκω, ἐν κεφαλίδι βιβλίου γέγραπται περὶ ἐμοῦ, τοῦ ποιῆσαι ὁ θεὸς τὸ θέλημά σου. 8 ἀνώτερον λέγων ὅτι
Θυσίας καὶ προσφορὰς καὶ ὁλοκαυτώματα καὶ περὶ ἁμαρτίας οὐκ ἠθέλησας οὐδὲ εὐδόκησας, αἵτινες κατὰ νόμον προσφέρονται,
9 τότε εἴρηκεν, Ἰδοὺ ἥκω τοῦ ποιῆσαι τὸ θέλημά σου. ἀναιρεῖ τὸ πρῶτον ἵνα τὸ δεύτερον στήσῃ, 10 ἐν ᾧ θελήματι ἡγιασμένοι
ἐσμὲν διὰ τῆς προσφορᾶς τοῦ σώματος Ἰησοῦ Χριστοῦ ἐφάπαξ. ¶ 11 Καὶ πᾶς μὲν ἱερεὺς ἕστηκεν καθ᾽ ἡμέραν λειτουργῶν καὶ
τὰς αὐτὰς πολλάκις προσφέρων θυσίας, αἵτινες οὐδέποτε δύνανται περιελεῖν ἁμαρτίας, 12 οὗτος δὲ μίαν ὑπὲρ ἁμαρτιῶν
προσενέγκας θυσίαν εἰς τὸ διηνεκὲς ἐκάθισεν ἐν δεξιᾷ τοῦ θεοῦ, 13 τὸ λοιπὸν ἐκδεχόμενος ἕως τεθῶσιν οἱ ἐχθροὶ αὐτοῦ ὑποπόδιον
τῶν ποδῶν αὐτοῦ. 14 μιᾷ γὰρ προσφορᾷ τετελείωκεν εἰς τὸ διηνεκὲς τοὺς ἁγιαζομένους. ¶ 15 Μαρτυρεῖ δὲ ἡμῖν καὶ τὸ πνεῦμα

this.   First he says: 16 "This   is   the   covenant   I will make   with   them   after   that   time,   says the
γὰρ   μετὰ →   ⌐τὸ εἰρηκέναι⌐   αὕτη   ἡ   διαθήκη   ἣν →   →   διαθήσομαι   πρὸς   αὐτοὺς   μετὰ   ἐκείνας   ⌐τὰς ἡμέρας⌐   λέγει
cj   p.a   d.asn f.ra   r.nsf   d.nsf   n.nsf   r.asf   v.fmi.1s   p.a   r.apm.3   p.a   r.apf   d.apf n.apf   v.pai.3s
1142   3552   3836 3306   4047   3836   1347   4005   1416   4639   899   3552   1697   3836 2465   3306

Lord. I will put   my   laws   in   their   hearts, and I will write   them   on   their   minds."   17 Then he adds: "Their
κύριος →   →   διδοὺς   μου   νόμους   ἐπὶ   αὐτῶν   καρδίας   καὶ →   →   ἐπιγράψω   αὐτούς   ἐπὶ   αὐτῶν   ⌐τὴν διάνοιαν⌐   καὶ ←   ←   αὐτῶν
n.nsm   pt.pa.nsm   r.gs.1   n.apm   p.a   r.gpm.3   n.apf   cj   v.fai.1s   r.apm.3   p.a   r.gpm.3   d.asf n.asf   cj   r.gpm.3
3261   1443   1609   3795   2093   899   2840   2779   2108   899   2093   899   3836 1379   2779   899

sins   and   lawless   acts I will remember   no   more."   18 And   where   these   have been   forgiven,
⌐τῶν ἁμαρτιῶν⌐   καὶ   αὐτῶν   ⌐τῶν ἀνομιῶν⌐ ←   ←   μνησθήσομαι   ⌐οὐ μὴ⌐   ἔτι   δὲ   ὅπου   τούτων   ἄφεσις
d.gpf n.gpf   cj   r.gpm.3   d.gpf n.gpf   v.fpi.1s   pl pl   adv   cj   cj   r.gpf   n.nsf
3836 281   2779   899   3836 490   3630   4024 3590   2285   1254   3963   4047   912

there is no   longer any sacrifice for sin.
οὐκέτι ←   προσφορὰ περὶ ἁμαρτίας
adv   n.nsf   p.g   n.gsf
4033   4714   4309   281

A Call to Persevere

10:19 Therefore, brothers, since we have   confidence to enter   the Most Holy Place by the blood of Jesus,
οὖν   ἀδελφοί →   →   Ἔχοντες   παρρησίαν   εἰς   ⌐τὴν εἴσοδον⌐   τῶν   ἁγίων ←   ἐν   τῷ   αἵματι →   Ἰησοῦ
cj   n.vpm   pt.pa.npm   n.asf   p.a   d.asf n.asf   d.gpn   a.gpn   p.d   d.dsn   n.dsn   n.gsm
4036   81   2400   4244   1650 3836   1658   3836   41   1877   3836   135   2652

20   by a new   and living way opened   for us   through the curtain,   that is,   his   body,   21 and since
ἣν   πρόσφατον   καὶ   ζῶσαν   ὁδὸν   ἐνεκαίνισεν →   ἡμῖν   διὰ   τοῦ   καταπετάσματος   τοῦτ' ἔστιν   αὐτοῦ   ⌐τῆς σαρκὸς⌐   καὶ
r.asf   a.asf   cj   pt.pa.asf   n.asf   v.aai.3s   r.dp.1   p.g   d.gsn   n.gsn   r.nsn v.pai.3s   r.gsm.3   d.gsf n.gsf   cj
4005   4710   2779   2409   3847   1590   7005   1328   3836   2925   4047 1639   899   3836 4922   2779

we have a great priest over the house of God,   22 let us draw   near to God with a sincere   heart   in
μέγαν   ἱερέα   ἐπὶ   τὸν   οἶκον   ⌐τοῦ θεοῦ⌐ →   →   προσερχώμεθα ←   μετὰ   ἀληθινῆς καρδίας   ἐν
a.asm   n.asm   p.a   d.asm   n.asm   d.gsm n.gsm   v.pms.1p   p.a   a.gsf   n.gsf   p.d
3489   2636   2093   3836   3875   3836 2536   4665   3552   240   2840   1877

full   assurance of faith,   having our   hearts   sprinkled   to cleanse us from a guilty   conscience and having
πληροφορίᾳ ←   →   πίστεως →   τὰς   καρδίας   ῥεραντισμένοι ←   ἀπὸ   πονηρᾶς   συνειδήσεως καὶ →
n.dsf   n.gsf   d.apf   n.apf   pt.rp.npm   p.g   a.gsf   n.gsf   cj
4443   4411   4822   3836   2840   4822   608   4505   5287   2779 3374

our bodies washed   with pure   water.   23 Let us hold   unswervingly to the hope   we profess,   for he who
τὸ   σῶμα   λελουσμένοι →   καθαρῷ   ὕδατι →   →   κατέχωμεν ἀκλινῆ   ←   τῆς   ἐλπίδος   ⌐τὴν ὁμολογίαν⌐   γὰρ ὁ ←
d.asn   n.asn   pt.rp.npm   a.dsn   n.dsn   v.pas.1p   a.asf   d.gsf   n.gsf   d.asf n.asf   cj   d.nsm
3836   5393   3374   2754   5623   2988   195   2988 3836   1828   3836 3934   1142 3836

promised   is faithful.   24 And let us consider   how we may spur   one   another on toward love   and good
ἐπαγγειλάμενος   πιστὸς   καὶ   →   κατανοῶμεν εἰς   παροξυσμὸν ἀλλήλους ←   →   ←   ἀγάπης καὶ καλῶν
pt.am.nsm   a.nsm   cj   v.pas.1p   p.a   n.asm   r.apm   n.gsf   cj   a.gpn
2040   4412   2779   2917   1650   4237   253   4237 4237   27   2779   2819

deeds.   25 Let us not give   up meeting   together, as   some are in the habit of doing, but let us
ἔργων →   →   μὴ   ἐγκαταλείποντες ←   ⌐τὴν ἐπισυναγωγὴν⌐   ἑαυτῶν   καθὼς τισίν   ἔθος   ἀλλὰ → →
n.gpn   pl   pt.pa.npm   d.asf n.asf   r.gpm.1   cj   r.dpm   n.nsn   cj
2240   1593 1593 3590 1593   3836 2191   1571   2777   5516   1621   247

encourage   one another – and all   the more as you see   the Day approaching.   ¶   26 If we
παρακαλοῦντες   καὶ τοσούτῳ   μᾶλλον ὅσῳ →   βλέπετε τὴν   ἡμέραν   ἐγγίζουσαν   γὰρ → ἡμῶν
pt.pa.npm   cj   r.dsn   adv.c r.dsn   v.pai.2p d.asf   n.asf   pt.pa.asf   cj   r.gp.1
4151   2779 5537   3437 4012   1063 3836   2465   1581   1142 279 7005

deliberately keep on sinning   after we have received   the knowledge of the truth,   no   sacrifice for sins
Ἑκουσίως →   →   ἁμαρτανόντων μετὰ   ⌐τὸ λαβεῖν⌐   τὴν ἐπίγνωσιν →   τῆς   ἀληθείας   οὐκέτι θυσία   περὶ ἁμαρτιῶν
adv   pt.pa.gpm   p.a   d.asn f.aa   d.asf n.asf   d.gsf   n.gsf   adv   n.nsf   p.g   n.gpf
1731   279   3552   3836 3284   3836 2106   3836   237   4033   2602   4309 281

is left,   27 but only a   fearful expectation of judgment and of raging fire   that will   consume the enemies
→ ἀπολείπεται   δὲ ←   τις   φοβερὰ ἐκδοχὴ   →   κρίσεως   καὶ   ζῆλος   πυρός →   μέλλοντος ἐσθίειν   τοὺς ὑπεναντίους
v.ppi.3s   cj   r.nsf   a.nsf   n.nsf   n.gsf   cj   n.nsm   n.gsn   pt.pa.gsn   f.pa   d.apm a.apm
657   1254   5516   5829   1693   3213   2779   2419   4786   3516   2266   3836 5641

τὸ ἅγιον· μετὰ γὰρ τὸ εἰρηκέναι,   16 Αὕτη ἡ διαθήκη ἣν διαθήσομαι πρὸς αὐτοὺς μετὰ τὰς ἡμέρας ἐκείνας, λέγει κύριος· διδοὺς νόμους μου ἐπὶ καρδίας αὐτῶν καὶ ἐπὶ τὴν διάνοιαν αὐτῶν ἐπιγράψω αὐτούς,   17 ὕστερον λέγει καὶ τῶν ἁμαρτιῶν αὐτῶν καὶ τῶν ἀνομιῶν αὐτῶν οὐ μὴ μνησθήσομαι ἔτι.   18 ὅπου δὲ ἄφεσις τούτων, οὐκέτι προσφορὰ περὶ ἁμαρτίας.

10:19 Ἔχοντες οὖν, ἀδελφοί, παρρησίαν εἰς τὴν εἴσοδον τῶν ἁγίων ἐν τῷ αἵματι Ἰησοῦ,   20 ἣν ἐνεκαίνισεν ἡμῖν ὁδὸν πρόσφατον καὶ ζῶσαν διὰ τοῦ καταπετάσματος, τοῦτ' ἔστιν τῆς σαρκὸς αὐτοῦ,   21 καὶ ἱερέα μέγαν ἐπὶ τὸν οἶκον τοῦ θεοῦ,   22 προσερχώμεθα μετὰ ἀληθινῆς καρδίας ἐν πληροφορίᾳ πίστεως ῥεραντισμένοι τὰς καρδίας ἀπὸ συνειδήσεως πονηρᾶς καὶ λελουσμένοι τὸ σῶμα ὕδατι καθαρῷ·   23 κατέχωμεν τὴν ὁμολογίαν τῆς ἐλπίδος ἀκλινῆ, πιστὸς γὰρ ὁ ἐπαγγειλάμενος,   24 καὶ κατανοῶμεν ἀλλήλους εἰς παροξυσμὸν ἀγάπης καὶ καλῶν ἔργων,   25 μὴ ἐγκαταλείποντες τὴν ἐπισυναγωγὴν ἑαυτῶν, καθὼς ἔθος τισίν, ἀλλὰ παρακαλοῦντες, καὶ τοσούτῳ μᾶλλον ὅσῳ βλέπετε ἐγγίζουσαν τὴν ἡμέραν.   ¶ 26 Ἑκουσίως γὰρ ἁμαρτανόντων ἡμῶν μετὰ τὸ λαβεῖν τὴν ἐπίγνωσιν τῆς ἀληθείας, οὐκέτι περὶ ἁμαρτιῶν ἀπολείπεται θυσία,   27 φοβερὰ δέ τις ἐκδοχὴ κρίσεως καὶ

of God. **28** Anyone who rejected the law of Moses died without mercy on the testimony of two or three
τις → ἀθετήσας νόμον → Μωϋσέως ἀποθνήσκει χωρὶς οἰκτιρμῶν ἐπὶ ← δυσὶν ἢ τρισὶν
r.nsm pt.aa.nsm n.asm n.gsm v.pai.3s p.g n.gpm p.d a.dpm cj a.dpm
5516 119 3795 3707 633 6006 3880 2093 1545 2445 5552

witnesses. **29** How much more severely do you think a man deserves to be punished who has trampled the Son of
μάρτυσιν πόσῳ ← ← χείρονος → → δοκεῖτε ἀξιωθήσεται τιμωρίας ὁ → καταπατήσας τὸν υἱὸν →
n.dpn r.dsn a.gsf.c v.pai.2p v.fpi.3s n.gsf d.nsm pt.aa.nsm d.asm n.asm
3459 4531 5937 1506 546 5513 3836 2922 3836 5626

God under foot, who has treated as an unholy thing the blood of the covenant that sanctified him,
┌τοῦ θεοῦ┐ ← καὶ → → ἡγησάμενος κοινὸν → τὸ αἷμα → τῆς διαθήκης ἐν ᾧ ἡγιάσθη ←
d.gsm n.gsm cj pt.am.nsm a.asn d.asn n.asn d.gsf n.gsf p.d r.dsn v.api.3s
3836 2536 2922 2922 2779 2451 3123 3836 135 3836 1347 1877 4005 39

and who has insulted the Spirit of grace? **30** For we know him who said, "It is mine to avenge; I will
καὶ → → ἐνυβρίσας τὸ πνεῦμα ┌τῆς χάριτος┐ γὰρ → οἴδαμεν τὸν ← εἰπόντα ἐμοὶ ἐκδίκησις ἐγὼ
cj pt.aa.nsm d.asn n.asn d.gsf n.gsf cj v.rai.1p d.asm pt.aa.asm r.ds.1 n.nsf r.ns.1
2779 1964 3836 4460 3836 5921 1142 3857 3836 3306 1609 1689 1609

repay," and again, "The Lord will judge his people." **31** It is a dreadful thing to fall into the hands of
ἀνταποδώσω καὶ πάλιν κύριος → κρινεῖ αὐτοῦ ┌τὸν λαόν┐ φοβερὸν → ┌τὸ ἐμπεσεῖν┐ εἰς χεῖρας →
v.fai.1s cj adv n.nsm v.fai.3s r.gsm.3 d.asm n.asm a.nsn d.nsn f.aa p.a n.apf
500 2779 4099 3261 3212 899 3836 3295 5829 3836 1860 1650 5931

the living God. ¶ **32** Remember those earlier days after you had received the light, when you
ζῶντος θεοῦ δὲ Ἀναμιμνήσκεσθε τὰς πρότερον ἡμέρας → → → φωτισθέντες ┌ἐν αἷς┐ →
pt.pa.gsm n.gsm cj v.ppm.2p d.apf adv.c n.apf pt.ap.npm p.d r.dpf
2409 2536 1254 389 3836 4728 2465 5894 1877 4005

stood your ground in a great contest in the face of suffering. **33** Sometimes you were publicly exposed to
ὑπεμείνατε ← ← πολλὴν ἄθλησιν → → → παθημάτων μὲν τοῦτο θεατριζόμενοι →
v.aai.2p a.asf n.asf n.gpn pl r.asn pt.pp.npm
5702 4498 124 4077 3525 4047 2518 3944

insult and persecution; at other times you stood side by side with those who were so
τε ὀνειδισμοῖς καὶ θλίψεσιν δὲ τοῦτο ┌κοινωνοὶ γενηθέντες┐ → τῶν ← οὕτως
cj n.dpm cj n.dpf pl r.asn n.npm pt.ap.npm d.gpm adv
5445 3944 2779 2568 1254 4047 3128 1181 3836 418 4048

treated. **34** You sympathized with those in prison and joyfully accepted the confiscation of your
ἀναστρεφομένων γὰρ καὶ συνεπαθήσατε → τοῖς → δεσμίοις καὶ ┌μετὰ χαρᾶς┐ προσεδέξασθε τὴν ἁρπαγὴν ┌ ὑμῶν
pt.pp.gpm cj adv v.aai.2p d.dpm n.dpm cj p.g n.gsf v.ami.2p d.asf n.asf r.gp.2
418 1142 2779 5217 3836 1300 2779 3552 5915 4657 3836 771 5639 7007

property, because you knew that you yourselves had better and lasting possessions. ¶ **35** So do not
┌τῶν ὑπαρχόντων┐ → → γινώσκοντες ἑαυτοὺς ἔχειν κρείττονα καὶ μένουσαν ὕπαρξιν οὖν ┌ Μὴ
d.gpn pt.pa.gpn pt.pa.npm r.apm.2 f.pa a.apf.c cj pt.pa.asf n.asf cj
3836 5639 1182 1571 2400 3202 2779 3531 5638 4036 610 3590

throw away your confidence; it will be richly rewarded. **36** You need to persevere so that when
ἀποβάλητε ← ὑμῶν τὴν παρρησίαν, ἥτις → ἔχει μεγάλην μισθαποδοσίαν γὰρ → ┌ἔχετε χρείαν┐ ← ὑπομονῆς ἵνα ←
v.aas.2p r.gp.2 d.asf n.asf r.nsf v.pai.3s a.asf n.asf cj v.pai.2s n.asf n.gsf cj
610 7007 3836 4244 4015 2400 3489 3632 1142 2400 5970 5705 2671

you have done the will of God, you will receive what he has promised. **37** For in just a
→ ποιήσαντες τὸ θέλημα ┌τοῦ θεοῦ┐ → κομίσησθε τὴν → ἐπαγγελίαν γὰρ ἔτι μικρὸν ὅσον ὅσον┐
pt.aa.npm d.asn n.asn d.gsm n.gsm v.ams.2p d.asf n.asf cj adv a.asm r.asm r.asm
4472 3836 2525 3836 2536 3152 3836 2039 1142 2285 3625 4012 4012

very little while, "He who is coming will come and will not delay. **38** But my righteous one will live by faith.
ὁ ← → ἐρχόμενος → ἥξει καὶ → οὐ χρονίσει δὲ μου ┌ὁ δίκαιος┐ → ζήσεται ἐκ πίστεως
d.nsm pt.pm.nsm v.fai.3s cj pl v.fai.3s cj r.gs.1 d.nsm a.nsm v.fmi.3s p.g n.gsf
3836 2262 2457 2779 4024 5988 1254 1609 3836 1465 2409 1666 4411

And if he shrinks back, I will not be pleased with him." **39** But we are not of those who shrink
καὶ ἐὰν → ὑποστείληται ← ┌ἡ ψυχή μου┐ οὐκ → εὐδοκεῖ ἐν αὐτῷ δὲ ἡμεῖς ἐσμεν οὐκ → → ὑποστολῆς
cj cj v.ams.3s d.nsf n.nsf r.gs.1 pl v.pai.3s p.d r.dsm.3 cj r.np.1 v.pai.1p pl n.gsf
2779 1569 5713 3836 6034 1609 2305 4024 2305 1877 899 1254 7005 1639 4024 5714

πυρὸς ζῆλος ἐσθίειν μέλλοντος τοὺς ὑπεναντίους. ²⁸ ἀθετήσας τις νόμον Μωϋσέως χωρὶς οἰκτιρμῶν ἐπὶ δυσὶν ἢ τρισὶν μάρτυσιν
ἀποθνήσκει· ²⁹ πόσῳ δοκεῖτε χείρονος ἀξιωθήσεται τιμωρίας ὁ τὸν υἱὸν τοῦ θεοῦ καταπατήσας καὶ τὸ αἷμα τῆς διαθήκης κοινὸν
ἡγησάμενος, ἐν ᾧ ἡγιάσθη, καὶ τὸ πνεῦμα τῆς χάριτος ἐνυβρίσας; ³⁰ οἴδαμεν γὰρ τὸν εἰπόντα, Ἐμοὶ ἐκδίκησις, ἐγὼ ἀνταποδώσω.
καὶ πάλιν, Κρινεῖ κύριος τὸν λαὸν αὐτοῦ. ³¹ φοβερὸν τὸ ἐμπεσεῖν εἰς χεῖρας θεοῦ ζῶντος. ¶ ³² Ἀναμιμνήσκεσθε δὲ τὰς πρότερον
ἡμέρας, ἐν αἷς φωτισθέντες πολλὴν ἄθλησιν ὑπεμείνατε παθημάτων, ³³ τοῦτο μὲν ὀνειδισμοῖς τε καὶ θλίψεσιν θεατριζόμενοι, τοῦτο
δὲ κοινωνοὶ τῶν οὕτως ἀναστρεφομένων γενηθέντες. ³⁴ καὶ γὰρ τοῖς δεσμίοις συνεπαθήσατε καὶ τὴν ἁρπαγὴν τῶν ὑπαρχόντων
ὑμῶν μετὰ χαρᾶς προσεδέξασθε γινώσκοντες ἔχειν ἑαυτοὺς κρείττονα ὕπαρξιν καὶ μένουσαν. ¶ ³⁵ μὴ ἀποβάλητε οὖν τὴν
παρρησίαν ὑμῶν, ἥτις ἔχει μεγάλην μισθαποδοσίαν. ³⁶ ὑπομονῆς γὰρ ἔχετε χρείαν ἵνα τὸ θέλημα τοῦ θεοῦ ποιήσαντες κομίσησθε
τὴν ἐπαγγελίαν. ³⁷ ἔτι γὰρ μικρὸν ὅσον ὅσον, ὁ ἐρχόμενος ἥξει καὶ οὐ χρονίσει· ³⁸ ὁ δὲ δίκαιός μου ἐκ πίστεως ζήσεται, καὶ ἐὰν
ὑποστείληται, οὐκ εὐδοκεῖ ἡ ψυχή μου ἐν αὐτῷ. ³⁹ ἡμεῖς δὲ οὐκ ἐσμὲν ὑποστολῆς εἰς ἀπώλειαν ἀλλὰ πίστεως εἰς περιποίησιν
ψυχῆς.

back and are   destroyed, but   of those who believe and are   saved.
←   εἰς ⸤ἀπώλειαν⸥ ἀλλὰ →   →   πίστεως   εἰς ⸤περιποίησιν ψυχῆς⸥
       p.a   n.asf   cj   n.gsf   p.a   n.asf   n.gsf
       1650   724   247   4411   1650   4348   6034

By Faith

11:1 Now faith is   being sure   of what we hope   for and certain of what   we do not see.   **2**
δὲ   πίστις Ἔστιν →   ὑπόστασις →   →   → ἐλπιζομένων ←   ἔλεγχος → πραγμάτων   →   οὐ βλεπομένων   γὰρ
cj   n.nsf   v.pai.3s   n.nsf   pt.pp.gpn   n.nsm   n.gpn   pl   pt.pp.gpn   cj
1254   4411   1639   5712   1827   1793   4547   1063 1063   4024   1063   1142

This   is what the ancients   were commended for.   ¶   **3** By faith we understand that the universe was
⸤ἐν ταύτῃ⸥ ←   οἱ πρεσβύτεροι →   ἐμαρτυρήθησαν ←   Πίστει → νοοῦμεν   τοὺς αἰῶνας   →
p.d   r.dsf   d.npm a.npm   v.api.3p   n.dsf   v.pai.1p   d.apm   n.apm
1877   4047   3836   4565   3455   4411   3783   3836   172

formed   at God's command, so that what is seen   was not made   out of what was visible.   ¶
κατηρτίσθαι →   θεοῦ ῥήματι   εἰς ←   τὸ   → βλεπόμενον →   μὴ ⸤τὸ γεγονέναι⸥ ἐκ ←   →   φαινομένων
f.rp   n.gsm   n.dsn   p.a   d.asn   pt.pp.asn   pl   d.asn f.ra   p.g   pt.pm.gpn
2936   4839   2536   4839   1650   3836   1063   3590   3836 3836 1181   1666   5743

4 By faith Abel offered   God   a better   sacrifice than Cain did. By faith he was   commended as   a righteous
→   Πίστει Ἄβελ προσήνεγκεν ⸤τῷ θεῷ⸥   πλείονα θυσίαν   παρὰ Κάϊν   δι᾿ ἧς   →   ἐμαρτυρήθη   εἶναι   δίκαιος
    n.dsf   n.nsm   v.aai.3s   d.dsm n.dsm   a.asf.c   n.asf   p.a   n.asm   p.g   r.gsf   v.api.3s   f.pa   a.nsm
    4411   6   4712   3836   2536   4498   2602   4123   2782   1328 4005   3455   1639   1465

man, when God   spoke   well of his   offerings.   And by faith he still speaks, even though he is dead.   ¶
 →   ⸤τοῦ θεοῦ⸥ μαρτυροῦντος ←   ἐπὶ αὐτοῦ ⸤τοῖς δώροις⸥   καὶ   δι᾿ αὐτῆς   ἔτι λαλεῖ   →   →   ἀποθανὼν
        d.gsm n.gsm   pt.pa.gsm   p.d   r.gsm.3   d.dpn n.dpn   cj   p.g   r.gsf.3   adv   v.pai.3s   pt.aa.nsm
        3455   3836   2536   3455   2093   899   3836   1565   2779   1328 899   3281 2285   3281   633

5 By faith Enoch was taken   from this life, so that he did not experience death;   he could not be found,
→   Πίστει Ἑνὼχ →   μετετέθη   μὴ ⸤τοῦ ἰδεῖν⸥ θάνατον καὶ →   οὐχ   ηὑρίσκετο
    n.dsf   n.nsm   v.api.3s   pl   d.gsn f.aa   n.asm   cj   pl   v.ipi.3s
    4411   1970   3572   1625 1625   1625 1625   3590   3836 1625   2505   2779 2351 2351   4024   2351

because God   had taken   him   away. For before he was taken,   he was commended as one who
διότι   ὁ θεός⸥ →   μετέθηκεν αὐτὸν ←   γὰρ πρὸ   ⸤τῆς μεταθέσεως⸥   μεμαρτύρηται
cj   d.nsm n.nsm   v.aai.3s   r.asm.3   cj   p.g   d.gsf   n.gsf   v.rpi.3s
1484   3836   2536   3572   899   3572   1142   4574   3836   3557   3455

pleased   God.   **6** And without faith   it is impossible to please   God, because anyone who comes   to
εὐαρεστηκέναι ⸤τῷ θεῷ⸥   δὲ χωρὶς   πίστεως →   ἀδύνατον → εὐαρεστῆσαι   γὰρ   τὸν ←   προσερχόμενον ←
f.ra   d.dsm n.dsm   cj   p.g   n.gsf   a.nsn   f.ad   cj   d.asm   pt.pm.asm
2297   3836   2536   1254   6006   4411   105   2297   1142   3836   4665

him   must believe that he exists and that he rewards   those who earnestly seek   him.   ¶
⸤τῷ θεῷ⸥ δεῖ   πιστεῦσαι ὅτι → ἔστιν καὶ   → μισθαποδότης γίνεται⸥ τοῖς ←   ἐκζητοῦσιν αὐτὸν
d.dsm n.dsm v.pai.3s   f.aa   cj   v.pai.3s   cj   n.nsm   v.pmi.3s   d.dpm   pt.pa.dpm   r.asm.3
3836   2536   1256   4409   4022   1639   2779   3633   1181   3836   1699   899

7 By faith Noah, when warned   about things not   yet seen,   in holy fear   built   an ark to
→ Πίστει Νῶε →   χρηματισθεὶς περὶ τῶν   μηδέπω ← βλεπομένων →   εὐλαβηθεὶς κατεσκεύασεν   κιβωτὸν εἰς
   n.dsf   n.nsm   pt.ap.nsm   p.g   d.gpn   adv   pt.pp.gpn   pt.ap.nsm   v.aai.3s   n.asf   p.a
   4411   3820   5976   4309   3836   3596   1063   2326   2941   3066   1650

save   his family.   By his faith he condemned the world and became heir   of the righteousness that comes
σωτηρίαν αὐτοῦ ⸤τοῦ οἴκου⸥ δι᾿   ἧς   → κατέκρινεν τὸν κόσμον καὶ ἐγένετο κληρονόμος → τῆς δικαιοσύνης →   →
n.asf   r.gsm.3 d.gsm n.gsm   p.g   r.gsf   v.aai.3s   d.asm n.asm   cj   v.ami.3s   n.nsm   d.gsf   n.gsf
5401   899   3836   3875   1328   4005   2891   3836   3180   2779   1181   3101   3836   1466

by faith.   ¶   **8** By faith Abraham, when called   to go   to a place   he would later   receive   as his
κατὰ πίστιν   Πίστει Ἀβραὰμ   καλούμενος → ἐξελθεῖν εἰς   τόπον ὃν   ἤμελλεν λαμβάνειν εἰς
p.a   n.asf   n.dsf   n.nsm   pt.pp.nsm   f.aa   p.a   n.asm r.asm   v.iai.3s   f.pa   p.a
2848   4411   4411   11   2813   2002   1650   5536   4005   3516   3284   1650

inheritance, obeyed   and went, even though he did not know   where he was going. **9** By faith he made his
κληρονομίαν ὑπήκουσεν καὶ   ἐξῆλθεν →   →   μὴ ἐπιστάμενος ποῦ →   ἔρχεται → Πίστει →   →
n.asf   v.aai.3s   cj   v.aai.3s   pl   pt.pp.nsm   adv   v.pmi.3s   n.dsf
3100   5634   2779 2002   2179 2179   2179 2179   3590 2179   4543   2262   4411

11:1 Ἔστιν δὲ πίστις ἐλπιζομένων ὑπόστασις, πραγμάτων ἔλεγχος οὐ βλεπομένων. **2** ἐν ταύτῃ γὰρ ἐμαρτυρήθησαν οἱ πρεσβύτεροι. ¶ **3** Πίστει νοοῦμεν κατηρτίσθαι τοὺς αἰῶνας ῥήματι θεοῦ, εἰς τὸ μὴ ἐκ φαινομένων τὸ βλεπόμενον γεγονέναι. ¶ **4** Πίστει πλείονα θυσίαν Ἄβελ παρὰ Κάϊν προσήνεγκεν τῷ θεῷ, δι᾿ ἧς ἐμαρτυρήθη εἶναι δίκαιος, μαρτυροῦντος ἐπὶ τοῖς δώροις αὐτοῦ τοῦ θεοῦ, καὶ δι᾿ αὐτῆς ἀποθανὼν ἔτι λαλεῖ. ¶ **5** Πίστει Ἑνὼχ μετετέθη τοῦ μὴ ἰδεῖν θάνατον, καὶ οὐχ ηὑρίσκετο διότι μετέθηκεν αὐτὸν ὁ θεός. πρὸ γὰρ τῆς μεταθέσεως μεμαρτύρηται εὐαρεστηκέναι τῷ θεῷ· **6** χωρὶς δὲ πίστεως ἀδύνατον εὐαρεστῆσαι· πιστεῦσαι γὰρ δεῖ τὸν προσερχόμενον τῷ θεῷ ὅτι ἔστιν καὶ τοῖς ἐκζητοῦσιν αὐτὸν μισθαποδότης γίνεται. ¶ **7** Πίστει χρηματισθεὶς Νῶε περὶ τῶν μηδέπω βλεπομένων, εὐλαβηθεὶς κατεσκεύασεν κιβωτὸν εἰς σωτηρίαν τοῦ οἴκου αὐτοῦ δι᾿ ἧς κατέκρινεν τὸν κόσμον, καὶ τῆς κατὰ πίστιν δικαιοσύνης ἐγένετο κληρονόμος. ¶ **8** Πίστει καλούμενος Ἀβραὰμ ὑπήκουσεν ἐξελθεῖν εἰς τόπον ὃν ἤμελλεν λαμβάνειν εἰς κληρονομίαν, καὶ ἐξῆλθεν μὴ ἐπιστάμενος ποῦ ἔρχεται. **9** Πίστει παρῴκησεν εἰς γῆν τῆς ἐπαγγελίας ὡς ἀλλοτρίαν ἐν σκηναῖς κατοικήσας μετὰ Ἰσαὰκ καὶ Ἰακὼβ τῶν συγκληρονόμων τῆς ἐπαγγελίας τῆς αὐτῆς·

home in the promised land like a stranger in a foreign country; he lived in tents, as did Isaac and
παρῴκησεν εἰς ⌐τῆς ἐπαγγελίας⌐ γῆν ὡς ἀλλοτρίαν ← κατοικήσας ἐν σκηναῖς μετὰ Ἰσαὰκ καὶ
v.aai.3s p.a d.gsf n.gsf n.asf pl a.asf pt.aa.nsm p.d n.dpf p.g n.gsm cj
4228 1650 3836 2039 1178 6055 259 2997 1877 5008 3552 2693 2779

Jacob, who were heirs with him of the same promise. 10 For he was looking forward to the city with
Ἰακὼβ τῶν → συγκληρονόμων ← τῆς ⌐τῆς αὐτῆς⌐ ἐπαγγελίας γὰρ → ἐξεδέχετο ← τὴν πόλιν ἔχουσαν
n.gsf d.gpm n.gpm d.gsf d.gsf n.gsf n.gsf cj v.imi.3s d.asf n.asf pt.pa.asf
2609 3836 5169 3836 3836 899 2039 1142 1683 3836 4484 2400

foundations, whose architect and builder is God. ¶ 11 By faith Abraham, even though he was past
⌐τοὺς θεμελίους⌐ ἧς τεχνίτης καὶ δημιουργὸς ὁ θεός⌐ Πίστει καὶ ← παρὰ
d.apm n.apm r.gsf n.nsm cj n.nsm d.nsm n.nsm n.dsf adv p.a
3836 2529 4005 5493 2779 1321 3836 2536 4411 2779 4123

age – and Sarah herself was barren – was enabled to become a father because he considered him
⌐καιρὸν ἡλικίας⌐ καὶ Σάρρα αὐτὴ στεῖρα ἔλαβεν δύναμιν εἰς καταβολὴν σπέρματος ἐπεὶ → ἡγήσατο
n.asm n.gsf adv n.nsf r.nsf a.nsf v.aai.3s n.asf p.a n.asf n.gsn cj v.ami.3s
2789 2461 2779 4925 899 5096 3284 1539 1650 2856 5065 2075 2451

faithful who had made the promise. 12 And so from this one man, and he as good as dead, came
πιστὸν τὸν → ἐπαγγειλάμενον καὶ διὸ ἀφ' ἑνὸς ← καὶ ταῦτα νενεκρωμένου →
a.asm d.asm pt.am.asm adv cj p.g a.gsm cj r.apn pt.rp.gsm
4412 3836 2040 2779 1475 608 1651 2779 4047 3739

descendants as numerous as the stars in the sky and as countless as the sand on the
ἐγεννήθησαν καθὼς τῷ πλήθει ← τὰ ἄστρα τοῦ οὐρανοῦ καὶ ὡς ἡ ἀναρίθμητος ← ἡ ἄμμος ἡ παρὰ τὸ
v.api.3p pl d.dsn n.dsn d.npn n.npn d.gsm n.gsm cj pl d.nsf a.nsf d.nsf n.nsf d.nsf p.a d.asn
1164 2777 3836 4436 2777 3836 849 3836 4041 2779 6055 3836 410 6055 3836 302 3836 4123 3836

seashore. ¶ 13 All these people were still living by faith when they died. They did not receive
⌐χεῖλος τῆς θαλάσσης⌐ πάντες οὗτοι ← Κατὰ πίστιν → ἀπέθανον ⌐ μὴ λαβόντες
n.asn d.gsf n.gsf a.npm r.npm p.a n.asf v.aai.3p pl pt.aa.npm
5927 3836 2498 4246 4047 2848 4411 633 3284 3590 3284

the things promised; they only saw them and welcomed them from a distance. And they admitted that they
τὰς → ἐπαγγελίας → ἀλλὰ ἰδόντες καὶ ἀσπασάμενοι αὐτὰς → πόρρωθεν καὶ → ὁμολογήσαντες ὅτι →
d.apf n.apf cj pt.aa.npm cj pt.am.npm r.apf.3 adv cj pt.aa.npm cj
3836 2039 1625 247 1625 2779 832 899 4523 2779 3933 4022

were aliens and strangers on earth. 14 People who say such things show that they are looking for a
εἰσὶν ξένοι καὶ παρεπίδημοι ἐπὶ ⌐τῆς γῆς⌐ γὰρ οἱ ← λέγοντες τοιαῦτα ← ἐμφανίζουσιν ὅτι → → ἐπιζητοῦσιν
v.pai.3p n.npm cj n.npm p.g d.gsf n.gsf cj d.npm pt.pa.npm r.apn v.pai.3p cj v.pai.3p
1639 3828 2779 4215 2093 3836 1178 1142 3836 3306 5525 1872 4022 2118

country of their own. 15 If they had been thinking of the country they had left, they would have
πατρίδα ← καὶ μὲν εἰ → ἐμνημόνευον → ἐκείνης ἀφ' ἧς → ἐξέβησαν → ἂν
n.asf cj pl cj v.iai.3p r.gsf p.g r.gsf v.aai.3p pl
4258 2779 3525 1623 3648 1697 608 4005 2400 1674 2400 323

had opportunity to return. 16 Instead, they were longing for a better country – a heavenly one.
εἶχον καιρὸν → ἀνακάμψαι ⌐δὲ νῦν⌐ → ὀρέγονται ← κρείττονος ⌐τοῦτ' ἔστιν⌐ ἐπουρανίου
v.iai.3p n.asm f.aa cj adv v.pmi.3p a.gsf.c r.nsn v.pai.3s a.gsf
2400 2789 366 1254 3814 3977 3202 4047 1639 2230

Therefore God is not ashamed to be called their God, for he has prepared a city for them. ¶
διὸ ⌐ὁ θεὸς⌐ → οὐκ ἐπαισχύνεται αὐτοὺς → → ἐπικαλεῖσθαι αὐτῶν θεὸς γὰρ → → ἡτοίμασεν πόλιν → αὐτοῖς
cj d.nsm n.nsm pl v.ppi.3s r.apm.3 f.pp r.gpm.3 n.nsm cj v.aai.3s n.asf r.dpm.3
1475 3836 2536 2049 4024 2049 899 2126 899 2536 1142 2286 4484 899

17 By faith Abraham, when God tested him, offered Isaac as a sacrifice. He who had received
→ Πίστει Ἀβραὰμ → πειραζόμενος ← προσενήνοχεν ⌐τὸν Ἰσαὰκ⌐ ← καὶ ὁ → ἀναδεξάμενος
n.dsf n.nsm pt.pp.nsm v.rai.3s d.asm n.asm cj d.nsm pt.am.nsm
4411 11 4279 4712 3836 2693 4712 4712 4712 2779 3836 346

the promises was about to sacrifice his one and only son, 18 even though God had said to him, "It is
τὰς ἐπαγγελίας προσέφερεν τὸν μονογενῆ ← ← → ἐλαλήθη πρὸς ὃν ὅτι
d.apf n.apf v.iai.3s d.asm a.asm v.api.3s p.a r.asm cj
3836 2039 4712 3836 3666 3281 4639 4005 4022

through Isaac that your offspring will be reckoned." 19 Abraham reasoned that God could raise the
ἐν Ἰσαὰκ σοι σπέρμα → κληθήσεται λογισάμενος ὅτι ⌐ὁ θεὸς⌐ δυνατὸς ἐγείρειν καὶ ἐκ
p.d n.dsm r.ds.2 n.nsn v.fpi.3s pt.am.nsm cj d.nsm n.nsm a.nsm f.pa adv p.g
1877 2693 5148 5065 2813 3357 4022 3836 2536 1543 1586 2779 1666

¹⁰ ἐξεδέχετο γὰρ τὴν τοὺς θεμελίους ἔχουσαν πόλιν ἧς τεχνίτης καὶ δημιουργὸς ὁ θεός. ¶ ¹¹ Πίστει καὶ αὐτὴ Σάρρα στεῖρα δύναμιν εἰς καταβολὴν σπέρματος ἔλαβεν καὶ παρὰ καιρὸν ἡλικίας, ἐπεὶ πιστὸν ἡγήσατο τὸν ἐπαγγειλάμενον. ¹² διὸ καὶ ἀφ' ἑνὸς ἐγεννήθησαν, καὶ ταῦτα νενεκρωμένου, καθὼς τὰ ἄστρα τοῦ οὐρανοῦ τῷ πλήθει καὶ ὡς ἡ ἄμμος ἡ παρὰ τὸ χεῖλος τῆς θαλάσσης ἡ ἀναρίθμητος. ¶ ¹³ Κατὰ πίστιν ἀπέθανον οὗτοι πάντες, μὴ λαβόντες τὰς ἐπαγγελίας ἀλλὰ πόρρωθεν αὐτὰς ἰδόντες καὶ ἀσπασάμενοι καὶ ὁμολογήσαντες ὅτι ξένοι καὶ παρεπίδημοί εἰσιν ἐπὶ τῆς γῆς. ¹⁴ οἱ γὰρ τοιαῦτα λέγοντες ἐμφανίζουσιν ὅτι πατρίδα ἐπιζητοῦσιν. ¹⁵ καὶ εἰ μὲν ἐκείνης ἐμνημόνευον ἀφ' ἧς ἐξέβησαν, εἶχον ἂν καιρὸν ἀνακάμψαι· ¹⁶ νῦν δὲ κρείττονος ὀρέγονται, τοῦτ' ἔστιν ἐπουρανίου. διὸ οὐκ ἐπαισχύνεται αὐτοὺς ὁ θεὸς θεὸς ἐπικαλεῖσθαι αὐτῶν· ἡτοίμασεν γὰρ αὐτοῖς πόλιν. ¶ ¹⁷ Πίστει προσενήνοχεν Ἀβραὰμ τὸν Ἰσαὰκ πειραζόμενος καὶ τὸν μονογενῆ προσέφερεν, ὁ τὰς ἐπαγγελίας ἀναδεξάμενος, ¹⁸ πρὸς ὃν ἐλαλήθη ὅτι Ἐν Ἰσαὰκ κληθήσεταί σοι σπέρμα, ¹⁹ λογισάμενος ὅτι καὶ ἐκ νεκρῶν ἐγείρειν δυνατὸς ὁ θεός, ὅθεν αὐτὸν καὶ ἐν παραβολῇ

dead, and figuratively speaking, he did receive Isaac back from death. ¶ **20** By faith Isaac blessed
νεκρῶν καὶ ἐν παραβολῇ ← → ἐκομίσατο αὐτὸν ὅθεν → Πίστει καὶ Ἰσαὰκ εὐλόγησεν
a.gpm adv p.d n.dsf v.ami.3s r.asn.3 n.dsf cj n.nsm v.aai.3s
3738 2779 1877 4130 3152 899 3854 4411 2779 2693 2328

Jacob and Esau in regard to their future. ¶ **21** By faith Jacob, when he was dying, blessed
τὸν Ἰακὼβ καὶ τὸν Ἡσαῦ περὶ ← → μελλόντων Πίστει Ἰακὼβ → ἀποθνήσκων εὐλόγησεν
d.asm n.asm cj d.asm n.asm p.g pt.pa.gpn n.dsf n.nsm pt.pa.nsm v.aai.3s
3836 2609 2779 3836 2481 4309 3516 4411 2609 633 2328

each of Joseph's sons, and worshiped as he leaned on the top of his staff. ¶ **22** By faith
ἕκαστον ↱ Ἰωσὴφ τῶν υἱῶν καὶ προσεκύνησεν ἐπὶ τὸ ἄκρον ↱ αὐτοῦ τῆς ῥάβδου → Πίστει
r.asm n.gsm d.gpm n.gpm cj v.aai.3s p.a d.asn n.asn r.gsm.3 d.gsf n.gsf n.dsf
1667 5626 2737 3836 5626 2779 4686 2093 3836 216 4811 899 3836 4811 4411

Joseph, when his end was near, spoke about the exodus of the Israelites from Egypt and gave
Ἰωσὴφ → → τελευτῶν ← ἐμνημόνευσεν περὶ τῆς ἐξόδου τῶν υἱῶν Ἰσραὴλ καὶ ἐνετείλατο
n.nsm pt.pa.nsm v.aai.3s p.g d.gsf n.gsf d.gpm n.gpm n.gsm cj v.ami.3s
2737 5462 3648 4309 3836 2016 3836 5626 2702 2779 1948

instructions about his bones. ¶ **23** By faith Moses' parents hid him for three months
← περὶ αὐτοῦ τῶν ὀστέων Πίστει Μωϋσῆς ὑπὸ τῶν πατέρων αὐτοῦ ἐκρύβη ← τρίμηνον
p.g r.gsm.3 d.gpn n.gpn n.dsf n.nsm p.g d.gpm n.gpm r.gsm.3 v.api.3s n.asn
4309 899 3836 4014 4411 3707 5679 3836 4252 899 3221 5564

after he was born, because they saw he was no ordinary child, and they were not afraid of the
→ → γεννηθεὶς διότι → εἶδον → ἀστεῖον τὸ παιδίον καὶ ↱ → οὐκ ἐφοβήθησαν → τὸ
pt.ap.nsm cj v.aai.3p a.asn d.asn n.asn cj pl v.api.3p d.asn
1164 1484 1625 842 3836 4086 2779 5828 5828 4024 5828 3836

king's edict. ¶ **24** By faith Moses, when he had grown up, refused to be known as the son
τοῦ βασιλέως διάταγμα Πίστει Μωϋσῆς → → μέγας γενόμενος ← ἠρνήσατο → λέγεσθαι ← υἱὸς
d.gsm n.gsm n.asn n.dsf n.nsm a.nsm pt.am.nsm v.ami.3s f.pp n.nsm
3836 995 1409 4411 3707 3489 1181 766 3306 5626

of Pharaoh's daughter. **25** He chose to be mistreated along with the people of God rather than to enjoy the
↱ Φαραὼ θυγατρὸς → ἑλόμενος → συγκακουχεῖσθαι ← τῷ λαῷ → τοῦ θεοῦ μᾶλλον ἢ → ἔχειν
n.gsm n.gsf pt.am.nsm f.pm d.dsm n.dsm d.gsm n.gsm adv.c pl f.pa
2588 5755 2588 145 5156 3836 3295 3836 2536 3437 2445 2400

pleasures of sin for a short time. **26** He regarded disgrace for the sake of Christ as of greater
ἀπόλαυσιν ἁμαρτίας → πρόσκαιρον ← → ἡγησάμενος τὸν ὀνειδισμὸν → → τοῦ Χριστοῦ μείζονα
n.asf n.gsf a.asf pt.am.nsm d.asn n.asm d.gsm n.gsm a.asm.c
656 281 4672 2451 3836 3944 3836 5986 3489

value than the treasures of Egypt, because he was looking ahead to his reward. **27** By faith he left
πλοῦτον → τῶν θησαυρῶν → Αἰγύπτου γὰρ → → ἀπέβλεπεν ← εἰς τὴν μισθαποδοσίαν → Πίστει κατέλιπεν
n.asm d.gpm n.gpm n.gsf cj v.iai.3s p.a d.asf n.asf n.dsf v.aai.3s
4458 3836 2565 131 1142 611 1650 3836 3632 4411 2901

Egypt, not fearing the king's anger; he persevered because he saw him who is invisible. **28** By faith he
Αἴγυπτον μὴ φοβηθεὶς τὸν τοῦ βασιλέως θυμὸν γὰρ → ἐκαρτέρησεν ὡς → ὁρῶν τὸν ← → ἀόρατον → Πίστει →
n.asf pl pt.ap.nsm d.asm d.gsm n.gsm n.asm cj v.aai.3s pl pt.pa.nsm d.asm a.asm n.dsf
131 3590 5828 3836 3836 995 2596 1142 2846 6055 3972 3836 548 4411

kept the Passover and the sprinkling of blood, so that the destroyer of the firstborn would not touch the
πεποίηκεν τὸ πάσχα καὶ τὴν πρόσχυσιν → τοῦ αἵματος ἵνα ← ὁ ὀλοθρεύων → μὴ θίγῃ τὰ
v.rai.3s d.asn n.asn cj d.asf n.asf d.gsn n.gsn cj d.nsm pt.pa.nsm pl v.aas.3s d.apn
4472 3836 4247 2779 3836 4/17 3836 135 2671 3836 3905 2566 3590 2566 3836

firstborn of Israel. ¶ **29** By faith the people passed through the Red Sea as on dry land; but
πρωτότοκα αὐτῶν → Πίστει → διέβησαν ← τὴν ἐρυθρὰν θάλασσαν ὡς διὰ ξηρᾶς γῆς ἧς
a.apn r.gpm.3 n.dsf v.aai.3p d.asf a.asf n.asf pl p.g a.gsf n.gsf r.gsf
4758 899 4411 1329 3836 2261 2498 6055 1328 3831 1178 4005

when the Egyptians tried to do so, they were drowned. ¶ **30** By faith the walls of Jericho fell, after
↱ οἱ Αἰγύπτιοι πεῖραν λαβόντες → κατεπόθησαν → Πίστει τὰ τείχη → Ἰεριχὼ ἔπεσαν →
d.npm n.npm n.asf pt.aa.npm v.api.3p n.dsf d.npn n.npn n.gsf v.aai.3p
3284 3836 130 4278 3284 2927 4411 3836 5446 2637 4406

ἐκομίσατο. ¶ **20** Πίστει καὶ περὶ μελλόντων εὐλόγησεν Ἰσαὰκ τὸν Ἰακὼβ καὶ τὸν Ἡσαῦ. ¶ **21** Πίστει Ἰακὼβ ἀποθνήσκων ἕκαστον τῶν υἱῶν Ἰωσὴφ εὐλόγησεν καὶ προσεκύνησεν ἐπὶ τὸ ἄκρον τῆς ῥάβδου αὐτοῦ. ¶ **22** Πίστει Ἰωσὴφ τελευτῶν περὶ τῆς ἐξόδου τῶν υἱῶν Ἰσραὴλ ἐμνημόνευσεν καὶ περὶ τῶν ὀστέων αὐτοῦ ἐνετείλατο. ¶ **23** Πίστει Μωϋσῆς γεννηθεὶς ἐκρύβη τρίμηνον ὑπὸ τῶν πατέρων αὐτοῦ, διότι εἶδον ἀστεῖον τὸ παιδίον καὶ οὐκ ἐφοβήθησαν τὸ διάταγμα τοῦ βασιλέως. ¶ **24** Πίστει Μωϋσῆς μέγας γενόμενος ἠρνήσατο λέγεσθαι υἱὸς θυγατρὸς Φαραώ, **25** μᾶλλον ἑλόμενος συγκακουχεῖσθαι τῷ λαῷ τοῦ θεοῦ ἢ πρόσκαιρον ἔχειν ἁμαρτίας ἀπόλαυσιν, **26** μείζονα πλοῦτον ἡγησάμενος τῶν Αἰγύπτου θησαυρῶν τὸν ὀνειδισμὸν τοῦ Χριστοῦ· ἀπέβλεπεν γὰρ εἰς τὴν μισθαποδοσίαν. **27** Πίστει κατέλιπεν Αἴγυπτον μὴ φοβηθεὶς τὸν θυμὸν τοῦ βασιλέως· τὸν γὰρ ἀόρατον ὡς ὁρῶν ἐκαρτέρησεν. **28** Πίστει πεποίηκεν τὸ πάσχα καὶ τὴν πρόσχυσιν τοῦ αἵματος, ἵνα μὴ ὁ ὀλοθρεύων τὰ πρωτότοκα θίγῃ αὐτῶν. ¶ **29** Πίστει διέβησαν τὴν Ἐρυθρὰν Θάλασσαν ὡς διὰ ξηρᾶς γῆς, ἧς πεῖραν λαβόντες οἱ Αἰγύπτιοι κατεπόθησαν. ¶ **30** Πίστει τὰ τείχη Ἰεριχὼ ἔπεσαν κυκλωθέντα ἐπὶ ἑπτὰ ἡμέρας. ¶ **31** Πίστει Ῥαὰβ ἡ πόρνη οὐ συναπώλετο τοῖς ἀπειθήσασιν

the people had marched around them for seven days. ¶ **31** By faith the prostitute Rahab, because she
→   →   → κυκλωθέντα ←   ἐπὶ ἑπτὰ ἡμέρας   → Πίστει ἡ πόρνη   Ῥαὰβ   →   →   →
pt.ap.npn   p.a a.apf n.apf   n.dsf d.nsf n.nsf n.nsf
3240   2093 2231 2465   4411   3836 4520   4805

welcomed   the spies,   was not killed   with those who were disobedient.   ¶   **32** And what more
ɿδεξαμένη μετ' εἰρήνηςɹ ɿτοὺς κατασκόπουςɹ οὐ συναπώλετο ←   τοῖς ←   ←   ἀπειθήσασιν   Καὶ τί   ἔτι
pt.am.nsf p.g n.gsf   d.apm n.apm   pl v.ami.3s   d.dpm   pt.aa.dpm   cj r.asn adv
1312   3552 1645   3836   2946   4024 5272   3836   578   2779 5515 2285

shall I say?   I do not have   time   to tell   about Gideon, Barak, Samson, Jephthah,   David,
→   → λέγω γὰρ με → → ἐπιλείψει ὁ χρόνος → διηγούμενον περὶ Γεδεὼν Βαρὰκ Σαμψὼν Ἰεφθάε   τε Δαυίδ καὶ
v.pas.1s cj r.as.1   v.fai.3s d.nsm n.nsm pt.pm.asm   p.g n.gsm n.gsm n.gsm n.gsm   cj n.gsm cj
3306   1142 1609   2142 3836 5989   1455   4309 1146 973   4907   2650   5445 1253 2779

Samuel and the prophets, **33** who through faith conquered   kingdoms, administered justice, and gained what was
Σαμουὴλ καὶ τῶν προφητῶν,   οἳ διὰ πίστεως κατηγωνίσαντο βασιλείας, εἰργάσαντο δικαιοσύνην   ἐπέτυχον →
n.gsm   cj d.gpm n.gpm   d.npm p.g n.gsf v.ami.3p   n.apf   v.ami.3p   n.asf   v.aai.3p
4905   2779 3836 4737   4005 1328 4411   2865   993   2237   1466   2209

promised; who shut the mouths of lions, **34** quenched the fury of the flames, and escaped the edge of the
ἐπαγγελιῶν → ἔφραξαν στόματα → λεόντων   ἔσβεσαν   δύναμιν →   πυρός   ἔφυγον   στόματα →
n.gpf   v.aai.3p n.apn   n.gpm   v.aai.3p n.asf   n.gsn   v.aai.3p n.apn
2039   5852   5125   3329   4931   1539   4786   5771   5125

sword;   whose weakness was turned to strength; and who became powerful in battle and routed foreign
μαχαίρης ἀπὸ   ἀσθενείας → → → ἐδυναμώθησαν → ἐγενήθησαν ἰσχυροὶ ἐν πολέμῳ ἔκλιναν ἀλλοτρίων
n.gsf   p.g   n.gsf   v.api.3p   v.api.3p a.npm   p.d n.dsm v.aai.3p a.gpm
3479   608   819   1540   1181   2708   1877 4483 3111   259

armies. **35** Women received back their dead,   raised   to life again.   Others were tortured   and
παρεμβολὰς γυναῖκες Ἔλαβον αὐτῶν ɿτοὺς νεκροὺςɹ ɿἐξ ἀναστάσεωςɹ ← δὲ ἄλλοι → ἐτυμπανίσθησαν
n.apf   n.npf   v.aai.3p r.gpf.3 d.apm a.apm   p.g n.gsf   pl a.npm   v.api.3p
4213   1222   3284   899   3836 3738   1666 414   1254 257   5594

refused   to be released,   so that they might gain a better resurrection. **36** Some faced
ɿοὐ προσδεξάμενοιɹ ɿτὴν ἀπολύτρωσινɹ ἵνα ← → → τύχωσιν κρείττονος ἀναστάσεως δὲ ἕτεροι ἔλαβον πεῖρανɹ
pl pt.am.npm   d.asf n.asf   cj   v.aas.3p a.gsf.c   n.gsf   pl r.npm v.aai.3p n.asf
4024 4657   3836 667   2671   5593   3202   414   1254 2283 3284   4278

jeers   and flogging, while still others were chained and put in prison. **37** They were stoned;   they were sawed
ἐμπαιγμῶν καὶ μαστίγων δὲ ἔτι   δεσμῶν καὶ φυλακῆς   ἐλιθάσθησαν   ἐπρίσθησαν
n.gpm   cj n.gpf   cj adv   n.gpm cj   n.gsf   v.api.3p   v.api.3p
1849   2779 3465   1254 2285   1301   2779 5871   3342   4569

in two; they were put to death by the   sword. They went about in sheepskins and goatskins,
←   ←   →   → ἀπέθανον ἐν φόνῳ μαχαίρης → περιῆλθον ← ἐν μηλωταῖς ἐν ɿαἰγείοις δέρμασινɹ
v.aai.3p   p.d n.dsm n.gsf   v.aai.3p   p.d n.dpf   p.d a.dpn   n.dpn
633   1877 5840 3479   4320   1877 3603   1877 128   1293

destitute, persecuted and mistreated – **38** the world was not worthy of them. They wandered in deserts and
ὑστερούμενοι θλιβόμενοι κακουχούμενοι ὁ κόσμος ἦν οὐκ ἄξιος → ων → πλανώμενοι ἐν ἐρημίαις καὶ
pt.pp.npm   pt.pp.npm pt.pp.npm   d.nsm n.nsm v.iai.3s pl a.nsm r.gpm pt.pp.npm p.d n.dpf cj
5728   2567   2807   3836 3180 1639 4024 545   4005   4414   2093 2244 2779

mountains, and in caves and holes   in the ground. ¶ **39** These were all   commended for their
ὄρεσιν καὶ → σπηλαίοις καὶ ɿταῖς ὀπαῖςɹ → τῆς γῆς   Καὶ οὗτοι → πάντες μαρτυρηθέντες διὰ τῆς
n.dpn   cj   n.dpn   cj d.dpf n.dpf   d.gsf n.gsf   cj r.npm   a.npm pt.ap.npm   p.g d.gsf
4001   2779 5068   2779 3836 3956   3836 1178   2779 4047   4246 3455   1328 3836

faith, yet none of them received what had been promised. **40** God   had planned something better for us so
πίστεως οὐκ ἐκομίσαντο τὴν → → ἐπαγγελίαν ɿτοῦ θεοῦɹ → προβλεψαμένου τι   κρεῖττον περὶ ἡμῶν ἵνα
n.gsf   pl   v.ami.3p   d.asf   n.asf   d.gsm n.gsm pt.am.gsm   r.asn a.asn.c p.g r.gp.1 cj
4411   4024 3152   3836   2039   3836 2536   4587   5516   3202   4309 7005 2671

that only together with us would they be made perfect.
← only μὴ χωρὶς → ἡμῶν → → → τελειωθῶσιν
pl   p.g   r.gp.1   v.aps.3p
3590 6006   7005   5457

δεξαμένη τοὺς κατασκόπους μετ' εἰρήνης. ¶ **32** Καὶ τί ἔτι λέγω; ἐπιλείψει με γὰρ διηγούμενον ὁ χρόνος περὶ Γεδεών, Βαράκ, Σαμψών, Ἰεφθάε, Δαυίδ τε καὶ Σαμουὴλ καὶ τῶν προφητῶν, **33** οἳ διὰ πίστεως κατηγωνίσαντο βασιλείας, εἰργάσαντο δικαιοσύνην, ἐπέτυχον ἐπαγγελιῶν, ἔφραξαν στόματα λεόντων, **34** ἔσβεσαν δύναμιν πυρός, ἔφυγον στόματα μαχαίρης, ἐδυναμώθησαν ἀπὸ ἀσθενείας, ἐγενήθησαν ἰσχυροὶ ἐν πολέμῳ, παρεμβολὰς ἔκλιναν ἀλλοτρίων. **35** ἔλαβον γυναῖκες ἐξ ἀναστάσεως τοὺς νεκροὺς αὐτῶν· ἄλλοι δὲ ἐτυμπανίσθησαν οὐ προσδεξάμενοι τὴν ἀπολύτρωσιν, ἵνα κρείττονος ἀναστάσεως τύχωσιν· **36** ἕτεροι δὲ ἐμπαιγμῶν καὶ μαστίγων πεῖραν ἔλαβον, ἔτι δὲ δεσμῶν καὶ φυλακῆς· **37** ἐλιθάσθησαν, ἐπρίσθησαν, ἐν φόνῳ μαχαίρης ἀπέθανον, περιῆλθον ἐν μηλωταῖς, ἐν αἰγείοις δέρμασιν, ὑστερούμενοι, θλιβόμενοι, κακουχούμενοι, **38** ὧν οὐκ ἦν ἄξιος ὁ κόσμος, ἐπὶ ἐρημίαις πλανώμενοι καὶ ὄρεσιν καὶ σπηλαίοις καὶ ταῖς ὀπαῖς τῆς γῆς. ¶ **39** Καὶ οὗτοι πάντες μαρτυρηθέντες διὰ τῆς πίστεως οὐκ ἐκομίσαντο τὴν ἐπαγγελίαν, **40** τοῦ θεοῦ περὶ ἡμῶν κρεῖττόν τι προβλεψαμένου, ἵνα μὴ χωρὶς ἡμῶν τελειωθῶσιν.

God Disciplines His Sons

12:1 Therefore,   since   we   are   surrounded   by such   a great   cloud of witnesses,   let us throw   off
Τοιγαροῦν   καὶ →   ἡμεῖς   ἔχοντες   περικείμενον   ἡμῖν   τοσοῦτον ←   νέφος →   μαρτύρων → →   ἀποθέμενοι
cj   cj   r.np.1   pt.pa.npm   pt.pm.asn   r.dp.1   r.asn   n.asn   n.gpm   pt.am.npm
5521   2779   2400   7005   2400   4329   7005   5537   3751   3459   700

everything   that   hinders   and   the   sin   that so easily   entangles,   and let us run   with   perseverance   the race
πάντα   ὄγκον   καὶ   τὴν   ἁμαρτίαν → →   εὐπερίστατον → →   τρέχωμεν   δι᾿   ὑπομονῆς   ἀγῶνα
a.asm   n.asm   cj   d.asf   n.asf   a.asf   v.pas.1p   p.g   n.gsf   n.asm
4246   3839   2779   3836   281   2342   5556   1328   5705   74

marked   out for us.   **2** Let us fix   our eyes on Jesus,   the author   and   perfecter of our faith,   who for
τὸν προκείμενον ← → ἡμῖν →   ἀφορῶντες   εἰς   τὸν Ἰησοῦν,   ἀρχηγὸν   καὶ   τελειωτὴν →   τῆς   πίστεως   ὃς   ἀντὶ
d.asm   pt.pm.asm   r.dp.1   pt.pa.npm   p.a   d.asm   n.asm   n.asm   cj   n.asm   d.gsf   n.gsf   r.nsm   p.g
3836   4618   7005   927   1650   3836   2652   795   2779   5460   3836   4411   4005   505

the joy   set   before him   endured   the cross,   scorning   its shame,   and sat   down at   the right hand
τῆς χαρᾶς   προκειμένης ←   αὐτῷ   ὑπέμεινεν   σταυρὸν   καταφρονήσας   αἰσχύνης   τε   κεκάθικεν ←   ἐν   δεξιᾷ ←
d.gsf   pt.pm.gsf   r.dsm.3   v.aai.3s   n.asm   pt.aa.nsm   n.gsf   cj   v.rai.3s   p.d   a.dsf
3836   5915   4618   899   5702   5089   2969   158   5445   2767   1877   1288

of the throne of God.   **3**   Consider   him who   endured   such   opposition   from sinful
→ τοῦ θρόνου → τοῦ θεοῦ, →   γὰρ   ἀναλογίσασθε   τὸν ←   ὑπομεμενηκότα   τοιαύτην   ἀντιλογίαν   εἰς   ἑαυτὸν   ὑπὸ   τῶν ἁμαρτωλῶν,
d.gsm   n.gsm →   d.gsm   n.gsm   cj   v.amm.2p   d.asm   pt.ra.asm   r.asf   n.asf   p.a   r.asm.3   p.g   d.gpm   a.gpm
3836   2585   3836   2536   1142   382   3836   5702   5525   517   1650   1571   5679   3836   283

men,   so that   you will not   grow weary   and lose   heart.   ¶   **4** In   your   struggle   against
ἵνα ← → →   μὴ →   κάμπτε   ἐκλυόμενοι   ταῖς ψυχαῖς   ὑμῶν   πρὸς →   ἀνταγωνιζόμενοι
cj   pl →   v.aas.2p   pt.pp.npm   d.dpf   n.dpf   r.gp.2   p.a →   pt.pm.npm
2671   2827   2827   3590   2827   1725   3836   6034   7007   4639   497

sin,   you have not   yet   resisted   to   the point of shedding your blood.   **5** And you have   forgotten that
τὴν ἁμαρτίαν, → →   Οὔπω ←   ἀντικατέστητε   μέχρις ← ← →   αἵματος   καὶ → →   ἐκλέλησθε   τῆς
d.asf   n.asf → →   adv   v.aai.2p   p.g   n.gsn   cj   v.rmi.2p   d.gsf
3836   281   510   510   4037   510   3588   135   2779   1720   3836

word of encouragement   that addresses you as sons: "My son,   do not   make light   of the Lord's   discipline,   and do
παρακλήσεως   ἥτις   διαλέγεται   ὑμῖν   ὡς   υἱοῖς   μου   υἱέ   μὴ →   ὀλιγώρει →   κυρίου   παιδείας → →
n.gsf   r.nsf   v.pmi.3s   r.dp.2   pl   n.dpm   r.gs.1   n.vsm   pl   v.pam.2s   n.gsm   n.gsf
4155   4015   1363   7007   6055   5626   1609   5626   3902   3590   3902   4082   3261   4082   3593   1725

not lose   heart when   he   rebukes   you,   **6** because   the Lord   disciplines   those   he loves,   and   he punishes
μηδὲ ἐκλύου ← →   ὑπ᾿   αὐτοῦ   ἐλεγχόμενος ←   γὰρ   κύριος   παιδεύει   ὃν →   ἀγαπᾷ   δὲ →   μαστιγοῖ
cj   v.ppm.2s   p.g   r.gsm.3   pt.pp.nsm   cj   n.nsm   v.pai.3s   r.asm →   v.pai.3s   cj   v.pai.3s
3593   1725   1794   5679   1794   1142   3261   4084   4005   26   1254   3463

everyone   he accepts   as a son."   ¶   **7** Endure   hardship   as discipline;   God   is treating   you as sons.   For
πάντα   ὃν   παραδέχεται   υἱόν   ὑπομένετε   εἰς   παιδείαν   ὁ   θεός   προσφέρεται   ὑμῖν   ὡς   υἱοῖς   γὰρ
a.asm   r.asm   v.pmi.3s   n.asm   v.pai.2p   p.a   n.asf   d.nsm   n.nsm   v.ppi.3s   r.dp.2   pl   n.dpm   cj
4246   4005   4138   5626   5702   1650   4082   3836   2536   4712   7007   6055   5626   1142

what   son   is not   disciplined   by his father?   **8** If   you are   not   disciplined   (and everyone   undergoes
τίς   υἱὸς   ὃν   οὐ   παιδεύει   πατήρ   δὲ   εἰ →   ἐστε   χωρίς   παιδείας   πάντες   μέτοχοι   γεγόνασιν
r.nsm   n.nsm   r.asm   pl   v.pai.3s   n.nsm   cj   cj   v.pai.2p   p.g   n.gsf   a.npm   n.npm   v.rai.3p
5515   5626   4005   4084   4024   4084   4252   1254   1623   1639   6006   4082   4246   3581   1181

discipline),   then   you are   illegitimate   children   and   not   true sons.   **9** Moreover,   we have   all had   human
ἧς   ἄρα →   ἐστε   νόθοι ←   καὶ   οὐχ   υἱοὶ   εἶτα   μὲν → →   εἴχομεν   τῆς σαρκὸς   ἡμῶν,
r.gsf   cj →   v.pai.2p   a.npm   cj   pl   n.npm   adv   pl →   v.iai.1p   d.gsf   n.gsf   r.gp.1
4005   726   1639   3785   2779   4024   5626   1663   3525   2400   3836   4922   7005

fathers   who disciplined   us   and we respected   them for it.   How   much   more   should we
τοὺς πατέρας,   παιδευτὰς   καὶ →   ἐνετρεπόμεθα   [δὲ]   οὐ →   πολὺ   μᾶλλον → →
d.apm   n.apm   n.apm   cj   v.ipi.1p   cj   pl   adv   adv.c
3836   4252   4083   2779   1956   1254   4024   4498   3437

submit   to the Father   of our spirits   and live!   **10**   Our fathers   disciplined us   for   a little   while   as
ὑποταγησόμεθα →   τῷ πατρὶ →   τῶν πνευμάτων   καὶ   ζήσομεν   γὰρ   μὲν →   οἱ   ἐπαίδευον   πρὸς   ὀλίγας   ἡμέρας   κατὰ
v.fpi.1p →   d.dsm   n.dsm →   d.gpn   n.gpn   cj   v.fai.1p   cj   pl →   d.npm   v.iai.3p   p.a   a.apf   n.apf   p.a
5718   3836   4252   3836   4460   2779   2409   1142   3525   3836   4084   4639   3900   2465   2848

12:1 Τοιγαροῦν καὶ ἡμεῖς τοσοῦτον ἔχοντες περικείμενον ἡμῖν νέφος μαρτύρων, ὄγκον ἀποθέμενοι πάντα καὶ τὴν εὐπερίστατον ἁμαρτίαν, δι᾿ ὑπομονῆς τρέχωμεν τὸν προκείμενον ἡμῖν ἀγῶνα ² ἀφορῶντες εἰς τὸν τῆς πίστεως ἀρχηγὸν καὶ τελειωτὴν Ἰησοῦν, ὃς ἀντὶ τῆς προκειμένης αὐτῷ χαρᾶς ὑπέμεινεν σταυρὸν αἰσχύνης καταφρονήσας ἐν δεξιᾷ τε τοῦ θρόνου τοῦ θεοῦ κεκάθικεν. ³ ἀναλογίσασθε γὰρ τὸν τοιαύτην ὑπομεμενηκότα ὑπὸ τῶν ἁμαρτωλῶν εἰς ἑαυτὸν ἀντιλογίαν, ἵνα μὴ κάμπτε ταῖς ψυχαῖς ὑμῶν ἐκλυόμενοι. ¶ ⁴ Οὔπω μέχρις αἵματος ἀντικατέστητε πρὸς τὴν ἁμαρτίαν ἀνταγωνιζόμενοι. ⁵ καὶ ἐκλέλησθε τῆς παρακλήσεως, ἥτις ὑμῖν ὡς υἱοῖς διαλέγεται, Υἱέ μου, μὴ ὀλιγώρει παιδείας κυρίου μηδὲ ἐκλύου ὑπ᾿ αὐτοῦ ἐλεγχόμενος· ⁶ ὃν γὰρ ἀγαπᾷ κύριος παιδεύει, μαστιγοῖ δὲ πάντα υἱὸν ὃν παραδέχεται. ¶ ⁷ εἰς παιδείαν ὑπομένετε, ὡς υἱοῖς ὑμῖν προσφέρεται ὁ θεός. τίς γὰρ υἱὸς ὃν οὐ παιδεύει πατήρ; ⁸ εἰ δὲ χωρίς ἐστε παιδείας ἧς μέτοχοι γεγόνασιν πάντες, ἄρα νόθοι καὶ οὐχ υἱοί ἐστε. ⁹ εἶτα τοὺς μὲν τῆς σαρκὸς ἡμῶν πατέρας εἴχομεν παιδευτὰς καὶ ἐνετρεπόμεθα· οὐ πολὺ [δὲ] μᾶλλον ὑποταγησόμεθα τῷ πατρὶ τῶν πνευμάτων καὶ ζήσομεν; ¹⁰ οἱ μὲν γὰρ πρὸς ὀλίγας ἡμέρας κατὰ τὸ δοκοῦν αὐτοῖς ἐπαίδευον, ὁ δὲ ἐπὶ τὸ συμφέρον

they thought best; but God disciplines us for our good, that we may share in his holiness.
αὐτοῖς ‚τὸ δοκοῦν‚ ← δὲ ὁ ἐπὶ τὸ συμφέρον εἰς → → ‚τὸ μεταλαβεῖν‚ ← αὐτοῦ ‚τῆς ἁγιότητος‚ δὲ
r.dpm.3 d.asn pt.pa.asn cj d.nsm p.a d.asn pt.pa.asn p.a d.asn f.aa r.gsm.3 d.gsf n.gsf cj
899 3836 1506 1254 3836 2093 3836 5237 1650 3836 3561 899 3836 42 1254

No discipline seems pleasant at the time, but painful. Later on, however, it produces a harvest of
‚οὐ πᾶσα παιδεία μὲν δοκεῖ εἶναι χαρᾶς πρὸς τὸ παρὸν ἀλλὰ λύπης ὕστερον ← δὲ → ἀποδίδωσιν καρπὸν
pl a.nsf n.nsf pl v.pai.3s f.pa n.gsf p.a d.asn pt.pa.asn cj n.gsf adv.c cj v.pai.3s n.asm
4024 4246 4082 3525 1506 1639 5915 4639 3836 4205 247 3383 5731 1254 625 2843

righteousness and peace for those who have been trained by it. ¶ [12] Therefore, strengthen your
δικαιοσύνης εἰρηνικὸν → τοῖς ← → γεγυμνασμένοις δι᾽ αὐτῆς Διὸ ἀνορθώσατε τὰς
n.gsf a.asm d.dpm pt.rp.dpm p.g r.gsf.3 cj v.aam.2p d.apf
1466 1646 3836 1214 1328 899 1475 494 3836

feeble arms and weak knees. [13] "Make level paths for your feet," so that the lame may not
παρειμένας χεῖρας καὶ παραλελυμένα ‚τὰ γόνατα‚ καὶ ποιεῖτε ὀρθὰς τροχιὰς → ὑμῶν ‚τοῖς ποσὶν‚ ἵνα ← τὸ χωλὸν → μὴ
pt.rp.apf n.apf cj pt.rp.apn d.apn n.apn cj v.pam.2p a.apf n.apf r.gp.2 d.dpm n.dpm cj d.nsn a.nsn pl
4223 5931 2779 4168 3836 1205 2779 4472 3981 5579 7007 3836 4546 2671 3836 6000 1762 3590

be disabled, but rather healed.
→ ἐκτραπῇ δὲ μᾶλλον ἰαθῇ
v.aps.3s cj adv.c v.aps.3s
1762 1254 3437 2615

Warning Against Refusing God

[12:14] Make every effort to live in peace with all men and to be holy; without holiness no one will
διώκετε ← → ← Εἰρήνην μετὰ πάντων καὶ ‚τὸν ἁγιασμόν‚ χωρὶς οὗ οὐδεὶς ← →
v.pam.2p n.asf p.g a.gpm cj d.asm n.asm p.g r.gsm a.nsm
1503 1645 3552 4246 2779 3836 40 6006 4005 4029

see the Lord. [15] See to it that no one misses the grace of God and that no bitter root grows
ὄψεται τὸν κύριον ἐπισκοποῦντες ← ← μή τις ὑστερῶν ἀπὸ τῆς χάριτος → ‚τοῦ θεοῦ‚ → ‚μή τις‚ πικρίας ῥίζα φύουσα
v.fmi.3s d.asm n.asm pt.pa.npm cj r.nsm pt.pa.nsm p.g d.gsf n.gsf d.gsm n.gsf cj r.nsm n.gsf n.nsf pt.pa.nsf
3972 3836 3261 2174 3590 5516 5728 608 3836 5921 3836 2536 3590 5516 4394 4844 5886

up to cause trouble and defile many. [16] See that no one is sexually immoral, or is godless like Esau, who
ἄνω → ἐνοχλῇ καὶ δι᾽ αὐτῆς μιανθῶσιν πολλοί μή τις πόρνος ἢ βέβηλος ὡς Ἠσαῦ ὃς
adv v.pas.3s cj p.g r.gsf.3 v.aps.3p a.npm cj r.nsm n.nsm cj a.nsm pl n.nsm r.nsm
539 1943 2779 1328 899 3620 4498 3590 5516 4521 2445 1013 6055 2481 4005

for a single meal sold his inheritance rights as the oldest son. [17] Afterward, as you know, when
ἀντὶ μιᾶς βρώσεως ἀπέδετο ἑαυτοῦ ‚τὰ πρωτοτόκια‚ ← ← ← γὰρ μετέπειτα → → ἴστε ὅτι καὶ
p.g a.gsf n.gsf v.ami.3s r.gsm.3 d.apn n.apn cj adv v.rai.2p cj cj
505 1651 1111 625 1571 3836 4757 1142 3575 3857 4022 2779

he wanted to inherit this blessing, he was rejected. He could bring about no change of mind, though
→ θέλων → κληρονομῆσαι τὴν εὐλογίαν → ἀπεδοκιμάσθη γὰρ εὗρεν ← οὐχ μετανοίας τόπον καίπερ
pt.pa.nsm f.aa d.asf n.asf v.api.3s cj v.aai.3s pl n.gsf n.asm cj
2527 3099 3836 2330 627 1142 2351 4024 3567 5536 2788

he sought the blessing with tears. ¶ [18] You have not come to a mountain that can be touched
→ ἐκζητήσας αὐτὴν μετὰ δακρύων γὰρ → → Οὐ προσεληλύθατε ← → → → ψηλαφωμένῳ
pt.aa.nsm r.asf.3 p.g n.gpn cj pl v.rai.2p pt.pp.dsn
1699 899 3552 1232 1142 4665 4024 4665 6027

and that is burning with fire; to darkness, gloom and storm; [19] to a trumpet blast or to such a voice
καὶ → → κεκαυμένῳ → πυρὶ καὶ ← γνόφῳ καὶ ζόφῳ καὶ θυέλλῃ καὶ ← σάλπιγγος ἤχῳ καὶ ← φωνῇ
cj pt.rp.dsn n.dsn cj n.dsm cj n.dsm cj n.dsf cj n.gsf n.dsm cj n.dsf
2779 2794 4786 2779 1190 2779 2432 2779 2590 2779 4894 2491 2779 5889

speaking words that those who heard it begged that no further word be spoken to them, [20] because they
→ ῥημάτων ἧς οἱ ← ἀκούσαντες παρῃτήσαντο → μὴ λόγον προστεθῆναι → αὐτοῖς γὰρ
n.gpn r.gsf d.npm pt.aa.npm v.ami.3p pl n.asm f.ap r.dpm.3 cj
4839 4005 3836 201 4148 3590 3364 4707 899 1142 5770

could not bear what was commanded: "If even an animal touches the mountain, it must be stoned." [21] The
↱ οὐκ ἔφερον τὸ → διαστελλόμενον κἂν ← θηρίον θίγῃ τοῦ ὄρους → → λιθοβοληθήσεται καὶ τὸ
pl v.iai.3p d.asn pt.pp.asn crasis n.nsn v.aas.3s d.gsn n.gsn v.fpi.3s cj d.nsn
5770 4024 5770 3836 1403 2829 2563 2566 3836 4001 3344 2779 3836

εἰς τὸ μεταλαβεῖν τῆς ἁγιότητος αὐτοῦ. [11] πᾶσα δὲ παιδεία πρὸς μὲν τὸ παρὸν οὐ δοκεῖ χαρᾶς εἶναι ἀλλὰ λύπης, ὕστερον δὲ καρπὸν εἰρηνικὸν τοῖς δι᾽ αὐτῆς γεγυμνασμένοις ἀποδίδωσιν δικαιοσύνης. ¶ [12] Διὸ τὰς παρειμένας χεῖρας καὶ τὰ παραλελυμένα γόνατα ἀνορθώσατε, [13] καὶ τροχιὰς ὀρθὰς ποιεῖτε τοῖς ποσὶν ὑμῶν, ἵνα μὴ τὸ χωλὸν ἐκτραπῇ, ἰαθῇ δὲ μᾶλλον.

[12:14] Εἰρήνην διώκετε μετὰ πάντων καὶ τὸν ἁγιασμόν, οὗ χωρὶς οὐδεὶς ὄψεται τὸν κύριον, [15] ἐπισκοποῦντες μή τις ὑστερῶν ἀπὸ τῆς χάριτος τοῦ θεοῦ, μή τις ῥίζα πικρίας ἄνω φύουσα ἐνοχλῇ καὶ δι᾽ αὐτῆς μιανθῶσιν πολλοί, [16] μή τις πόρνος ἢ βέβηλος ὡς Ἠσαῦ, ὃς ἀντὶ βρώσεως μιᾶς ἀπέδετο τὰ πρωτοτόκια ἑαυτοῦ. [17] ἴστε γὰρ ὅτι καὶ μετέπειτα θέλων κληρονομῆσαι τὴν εὐλογίαν ἀπεδοκιμάσθη, μετανοίας γὰρ τόπον οὐχ εὗρεν καίπερ μετὰ δακρύων ἐκζητήσας αὐτήν. ¶ [18] Οὐ γὰρ προσεληλύθατε ψηλαφωμένῳ ὄρει καὶ κεκαυμένῳ πυρὶ καὶ γνόφῳ καὶ ζόφῳ καὶ θυέλλῃ [19] καὶ σάλπιγγος ἤχῳ καὶ φωνῇ ῥημάτων, ἧς οἱ ἀκούσαντες παρῃ τήσαντο μὴ προστεθῆναι αὐτοῖς λόγον, [20] οὐκ ἔφερον γὰρ τὸ διαστελλόμενον, Κἂν θηρίον θίγῃ τοῦ ὄρους, λιθοβοληθήσεται·

sight	was	so	terrifying	that	Moses	said,	"I am	trembling		with fear."	¶	22 But	you	have
φανταζόμενον	ἦν	οὕτω	φοβερὸν		Μωϋσῆς	εἶπεν →	εἰμι	ἔντρομος	καὶ	ἔκφοβος		ἀλλὰ →	→	
pt.pp.nsn	v.iai.3s	adv	a.nsn		n.nsm	v.aai.3s	v.pai.1s	a.nsm	cj	a.nsm		cj		
5751	1639	4048	5829		3707	3306	1639	1958	2779	1769		247		

come		to Mount	Zion,		to	the heavenly	Jerusalem,	the city	of the living	God.		You	have come	to
προσεληλύθατε ←	ὄρει	Σιὼν	καὶ	←		ἐπουρανίῳ	Ἰερουσαλὴμ	πόλει →	ζῶντος	θεοῦ	καὶ			←
v.rai.2p		n.dsf	cj			a.dsf		n.dsf	pt.pa.gsm	n.gsm	cj			
4665	4001	4994	2779	4665		2230	2647	4484	2409	2536	2779			4665

thousands	upon	thousands	of	angels	in	joyful	assembly,	23		to	the church	of the	firstborn,	whose	names	are
μυριάσιν	←		→	ἀγγέλων	→		πανηγύρει	καὶ	←		ἐκκλησίᾳ →		πρωτοτόκων			
n.dpf				n.gpm			n.dsf	cj			n.dsf		a.gpm			
3689				34			4108	2779	4665		1711		4758			

written		in	heaven.		You	have come	to	God,	the judge	of all		men,		to	the spirits	of righteous
ἀπογεγραμμένων	ἐν	οὐρανοῖς	καὶ				←	θεῷ	κριτῇ →	πάντων	καὶ	←		πνεύμασι →	δικαίων	
pt.rp.gpm	p.d	n.dpm	cj					n.dsm	n.dsm	a.gpm	cj			n.dpn	a.gpm	
616	1877	4041	2779				4665	2536	3216	4246	2779	4665		4460	1465	

men made	perfect,		24		to Jesus	the mediator	of a new covenant,	and	to	the sprinkled	blood	that speaks	a
→	τετελειωμένων	καὶ		→	Ἰησοῦ	μεσίτῃ →	νέας διαθήκης	καὶ	→	ῥαντισμοῦ	αἵματι →	λαλοῦντι	
	pt.rp.gpm	cj			n.dsm	n.dsm	a.gsf n.gsf	cj		n.gsm	n.dsn	pt.pa.dsn	
	5457	2779	4665		2652	3542	3742 1347	2779	4665	4823	135	3281	

better	word	than	the blood	of Abel.	¶	25 See		to it that you	do not	refuse		him who speaks.		If
κρεῖττον ←	παρὰ		ιτὸν Ἀβελι			Βλέπετε ←	←	→	μὴ	παραιτήσησθε	τὸν	←	λαλοῦντα	γὰρ εἰ
a.asn.c	p.a		d.asm n.asm			v.pam.2p			cj	v.ams.2p	d.asn		pt.pa.asm	cj cj
3202	3281	4123	3836 6			1063		4148	4148	3590 4148	3836		3281	1142 1623

they	did	not	escape	when	they	refused		him who	warned		them	on earth,	how	much	less		will we,	if
ἐκεῖνοι	→	οὐκ	ἐξέφυγον →		→	παραιτησάμενοι	τὸν	←	χρηματίζοντα		ἐπὶ	γῆς	→	πολὺ	μᾶλλον	ἡμεῖς →		
r.npm		pl	v.aai.3p			pt.am.npm	d.asm		pt.pa.asm		p.g	n.gsf		adv	adv.c	r.np.1		
1697		1767	4024 1767			4148	3836		5976		2093	1178		4498	3437	7005		695

we	turn		away	from	him who	warns	us	from heaven?	26 At	that time	his	voice		shook	the	earth,	but	now
οἱ	ἀποστρεφόμενοι	←	→		τὸν	←	ἀπ᾽	οὐρανῶν	τοτε	→	οὗ	ἡ φωνὴ		ἐσάλευσεν	τὴν	γῆν	δὲ	νῦν
d.npm	pt.pm.npm				d.asm		p.g	n.gpm	adv		r.gsm	d.nsf n.nsf		v.aai.3s	d.asf	n.asf	cj	adv
3836	695				3836		608	4041	5538		4005	3836 5889		4888	3836	1178	1254	3814

he	has	promised,		"Once	more	I	will	shake	not	only	the	earth	but	also	the heavens."	27	The	words	"once
→	→	ἐπήγγελται	λέγων	ἄπαξ	ἔτι	ἐγὼ		σείσω	οὐ	μόνον	τὴν	γῆν	ἀλλὰ	καὶ	τὸν οὐρανόν		δὲ	τὸ	←	ἄπαξ
		v.rmi.3s	pt.pa.nsm	adv	adv	r.ns.1		v.fai.1s	pl	adv	d.asf	n.asf	cj	adv	d.asm n.asm		cj	d.nsn		adv
		2040	3306	562	2285	1609		4940	4024	3667	3836	1178	247	2779	3836 4041		1254	3836		562

more"	indicate	the	removing	of	what	can be	shaken		—	that is,	created		things	— so	that	what	cannot	be
ἔτι	δηλοῖ	τὴν	μετάθεσιν	→	τῶν	→	σαλευομένων	ὡς	←	πεποιημένων			→	ἵνα	τὰ	μὴ		
adv	v.pai.3s	d.asf	n.asf		d.gpn		pt.pp.gpn	pl		pt.rp.gpn				cj	d.npn	pl		
2285	1317	3836	3557		3836		4888	6055		4472			2671	3836	3590		

shaken		may remain.	¶	28 Therefore,	since	we	are	receiving		a kingdom	that	cannot	be shaken,		let us
σαλευόμενα	→	μείνῃ		Διὸ	→	→	→	παραλαμβάνοντες		βασιλείαν	›	→	→	ἀσάλευτον	→
pt.pp.npn		v.dds.3s		cj				pt.pa.npm		n.asf				a.asf	
4888		3531		1475				4161		993				810	

be	thankful,	and so		worship	God	acceptably	with	reverence	and	awe,	29	for		our	"God		is a
ἔχωμεν	χάριν		ιδι᾽ ἧς	λατρεύωμεν	ιτῷ θεῷι	εὐαρέστως	μετὰ	εὐλαβείας	καὶ	δέους		γὰρ	καὶ	ἡμῶν	ὁ θεὸς		
v.pas.1p	n.asf		p.g r.gsf	v.pas.1p	d.dsm n.dsm	adv	p.g	n.gsf	cj	n.gsn		cj	adv	r.gp.1	d.nsm n.nsm		
2400	5921		1328 4005	3302	3836 2536	2299	3552	2325	2779	1290		1142	2779	7005	3836 2536		

consuming	fire."
καταναλίσκον	πῦρ
pt.pa.nsn	n.nsn
2914	4786

Concluding Exhortations

13:1 Keep on	loving		each other	as brothers.	2 Do	not	forget		to entertain	strangers,		for	by	so
μενέτω ←	Ἡ φιλαδελφία	←	←	←	→	μὴ	ἐπιλανθάνεσθε	→		ιτῆς φιλοξενίαςι		γὰρ	διὰ	ταύτης
v.pam.3s	d.nsf n.nsf					pl	v.pmm.2p			d.gsf n.gsf		cj	p.g	r.gsf
3531	3836 5789					2140 3590	2140			3836 5810		1142	1328	4047

21 καί, οὕτω φοβερὸν ἦν τὸ φανταζόμενον, Μωϋσῆς εἶπεν, Ἔκφοβός εἰμι καὶ ἔντρομος. ¶ 22 ἀλλὰ προσεληλύθατε Σιὼν ὄρει καὶ πόλει θεοῦ ζῶντος, Ἰερουσαλὴμ ἐπουρανίῳ, καὶ μυριάσιν ἀγγέλων, πανηγύρει 23 καὶ ἐκκλησίᾳ πρωτοτόκων ἀπογεγραμμένων ἐν οὐρανοῖς καὶ κριτῇ θεῷ πάντων καὶ πνεύμασι δικαίων τετελειωμένων 24 καὶ διαθήκης νέας μεσίτῃ Ἰησοῦ καὶ αἵματι ῥαντισμοῦ κρεῖττον λαλοῦντι παρὰ τὸν Ἀβελ. ¶ 25 Βλέπετε μὴ παραιτήσησθε τὸν λαλοῦντα· εἰ γὰρ ἐκεῖνοι οὐκ ἐξέφυγον ἐπὶ γῆς παραιτησάμενοι τὸν χρηματίζοντα, πολὺ μᾶλλον ἡμεῖς οἱ τὸν ἀπ᾽ οὐρανῶν ἀποστρεφόμενοι, 26 οὗ ἡ φωνὴ τὴν γῆν ἐσάλευσεν τότε, νῦν δὲ ἐπήγγελται λέγων, Ἔτι ἅπαξ ἐγὼ σείσω οὐ μόνον τὴν γῆν ἀλλὰ καὶ τὸν οὐρανόν. 27 τὸ δὲ Ἔτι ἅπαξ δηλοῖ [τὴν] τῶν σαλευομένων μετάθεσιν ὡς πεποιημένων, ἵνα μείνῃ τὰ μὴ σαλευόμενα. ¶ 28 Διὸ βασιλείαν ἀσάλευτον παραλαμβάνοντες ἔχωμεν χάριν, δι᾽ ἧς λατρεύωμεν εὐαρέστως τῷ θεῷ μετὰ εὐλαβείας καὶ δέους· 29 καὶ γὰρ ὁ θεὸς ἡμῶν πῦρ καταναλίσκον.

13:1 Ἡ φιλαδελφία μενέτω. 2 τῆς φιλοξενίας μὴ ἐπιλανθάνεσθε, διὰ ταύτης γὰρ ἔλαθόν τινες ξενίσαντες ἀγγέλους. 3 μιμνῄ

doing some people have entertained angels   without knowing it. **3** Remember those in prison as if you were their
← τινες ← → ξενίσαντες ἀγγέλους → ἔλαθον μιμνῄσκεσθε τῶν → δεσμίων ὡς
r.npm   pt.aa.npm   n.apm   v.aai.3p   v.ppm.2p   d.gpm → n.gpm   pl
5516   34   3291   3630   3836   1300   6055

fellow prisoners, and those who are mistreated as if you yourselves were suffering. ¶ **4** Marriage should
→ συνδεδεμένοι καὶ τῶν → κακουχουμένων ὡς → → αὐτοὶ ὄντες ἐν σώματι. ὁ γάμος
pt.rp.npm   adv   d.gpm   pt.pp.gpm   pl   r.npm   pt.pa.npm   p.d   n.dsn   d.nsm   n.nsm
5279   2779   3836   2807   6055 1639 1639   899   1639   1877   5393   3836   1141

be honored by all, and the marriage bed kept pure, for God   will judge the adulterer and all the sexually
Τίμιος ἐν πᾶσιν καὶ ἡ → κοίτη ἀμίαντος γὰρ ὁ θεός, → κρινεῖ μοιχοὺς καὶ πόρνους
a.nsm   p.d   a.dpn   cj   d.nsf   n.nsf   a.nsf   cj   d.nsm n.nsm   v.fai.3s   n.apm   cj   n.apm
5508   1877   4246   2779 3836   3130   299   1142 3836 2536   3212   3659   2779   4521

immoral. **5** Keep your lives free from the love of money   and be content with what you have, because God
←   ὁ τρόπος → → → → Ἀφιλάργυρος → ἀρκούμενοι → τοῖς → παροῦσιν γὰρ αὐτὸς
   d.nsm n.nsm   a.nsm   pt.pp.npm → d.dpn   pt.pa.dpn γὰρ r.nsm
   3836 5573   921   758   3836   4205   1142 899

has said, "Never will I leave you; never will I forsake you." **6** So we say with confidence, "The Lord
→ εἴρηκεν οὐ μή → ἀνῶ σε οὐδ' οὐ μή → → ἐγκαταλίπω σε ὥστε ἡμᾶς λέγειν → θαρροῦντας κύριος
v.rai.3s pl pl → v.aas.1s r.as.2 cj pl pl → v.aas.1s r.as.2 cj r.ap.1 f.pa pt.pa.apm n.nsm
3306 4024 3590   479 5148 4028 4024 3590   1593 5148 6063 7005 3306 2509 3261

is my helper; I will not be afraid. What can man do to me?" ¶ **7** Remember your
ἐμοὶ βοηθός [καὶ] → → οὐ → φοβηθήσομαι τί → ἄνθρωπος ποιήσει → μοι Μνημονεύετε ὑμῶν
r.ds.1 n.nsm cj → → pl → v.fpi.1s r.asn r.nsm v.fai.3s r.ds.1 v.pam.2p r.gp.2
1609 1071 2779 5828 5828 4024 5828 5515 4472 476 4472 1609 3648 7007

leaders, who spoke the word of God to you. Consider the outcome of their way of life
⌜τῶν ἡγουμένων⌝ οἵτινες ἐλάλησαν τὸν λόγον → τοῦ θεοῦ → ὑμῖν ὧν ἀναθεωροῦντες τὴν ἔκβασιν → τῆς ἀναστροφῆς ←
d.gpm pt.pm.gpm r.npm v.aai.3p d.asm n.asm d.gsm n.gsm r.dp.2 r.gpm pt.pa.npm d.asf n.asf d.gsf n.gsf
3836 2451 4015 3281 3836 3364 3836 2536 7007 4005 355 3836 1676 3836 419

and imitate their faith. **8** Jesus Christ is the same yesterday and today and forever. ¶ **9** Do not be
μιμεῖσθε τὴν πίστιν Ἰησοῦς Χριστὸς ὁ αὐτὸς ἐχθὲς καὶ σήμερον καὶ ⌜εἰς τοὺς αἰῶνας⌝ μὴ →
v.pmm.2p d.asf n.asf n.nsm n.nsm d.nsm r.nsm adv cj adv cj p.a d.apm n.apm pl
3628 3836 4411 2652 5986 3836 899 2396 2779 4958 2779 1650 3836 172 4195 3590

carried away by all kinds of strange teachings. It is good for our hearts to be strengthened by
παραφέρεσθε ← → ποικίλαις ← καὶ ξέναις Διδαχαῖς γὰρ καλὸν τὴν καρδίαν → βεβαιοῦσθαι
v.ppm.2p a.dpf cj a.dpf n.dpf γὰρ a.nsn d.asf n.asf f.pp
4195 4476 2779 3828 1439 1142 2819 3836 2840 1011

grace, not by ceremonial foods, which are of no value to those who eat them. **10** We have an
χάριτι οὐ → → βρώμασιν ἐν οἷς → → οὐκ ὠφελήθησαν οἱ ← περιπατοῦντες ἔχομεν
n.dsf pl n.dpn p.d r.dpn pl v.api.3p d.npm pt.pa.npm v.pai.1p
5921 4024 1109 1877 4005 6067 6067 4024 6067 3836 4344 2400

altar from which those who minister at the tabernacle have no right to eat. ¶ **11** The
θυσιαστήριον ἐξ οὗ οἱ ← λατρεύοντες τῇ σκηνῇ ἔχουσιν οὐκ ἐξουσίαν → φαγεῖν γὰρ ὧν διὰ τοῦ
n.asn p.g r.gsn d.npm pt.pa.npm d.dsf n.dsf v.pai.3p pl n.asf f.aa cj r.gpn p.g d.gsm
2603 1666 4005 3836 3302 3836 5008 2400 4024 2026 2266 1142 4005 1328 3836

high priest carries the blood of animals into the Most Holy Place as a sin offering, but the
ἀρχιερέως ← εἰσφέρεται τὸ αἷμα → ζῴων εἰς τὰ ἅγια περὶ ἁμαρτίας τούτων τὰ
n.gsm v.ppi.3s d.nsn n.nsn n.gpn p.a d.apn a.apn p.g n.gsf r.gpn d.npn
797 1662 3836 135 2442 1650 3836 41 4309 281 4047 3836

bodies are burned outside the camp. **12** And so Jesus also suffered outside the city gate to make the people
σώματα → κατακαίεται ἔξω τῆς παρεμβολῆς καὶ Διὸ Ἰησοῦς ἔπαθεν ἔξω τῆς πύλης ἵνα → τὸν λαόν
n.npn v.ppi.3s p.g d.gsf n.gsf adv cj n.nsm v.aai.3s p.g d.gsf n.gsf cj d.asm n.asm
5393 2876 2032 3836 4213 2779 1475 2652 4248 2032 3836 4783 2671 39 3836 3295

holy through his own blood. **13** Let us, then, go to him outside the camp, bearing the disgrace he
ἁγιάσῃ διὰ τοῦ ἰδίου αἵματος → τοίνυν ἐξερχώμεθα πρὸς αὐτὸν ἔξω τῆς παρεμβολῆς φέροντες τὸν ὀνειδισμὸν αὐτοῦ
v.aas.3s p.g d.gsn a.gsn n.gsn cj v.pms.1p p.a r.asm.3 p.g d.gsf n.gsf pt.pa.npm d.asm n.asm r.gsm.3
39 1328 3836 2625 135 2002 2002 5523 2002 4639 899 2032 3836 4213 5770 3836 3944 899

σκεσθε τῶν δεσμίων ὡς συνδεδεμένοι, τῶν κακουχουμένων ὡς καὶ αὐτοὶ ὄντες ἐν σώματι. ¶ **4** Τίμιος ὁ γάμος ἐν πᾶσιν καὶ ἡ κοίτη ἀμίαντος, πόρνους γὰρ καὶ μοιχοὺς κρινεῖ ὁ θεός. **5** Ἀφιλάργυρος ὁ τρόπος, ἀρκούμενοι τοῖς παροῦσιν. αὐτὸς γὰρ εἴρηκεν, Οὐ μή σε ἀνῶ οὐδ' οὐ μή σε ἐγκαταλίπω, **6** ὥστε θαρροῦντας ἡμᾶς λέγειν, Κύριος ἐμοὶ βοηθός, [καὶ] οὐ φοβηθήσομαι, τί ποιήσει μοι ἄνθρωπος; ¶ **7** Μνημονεύετε τῶν ἡγουμένων ὑμῶν, οἵτινες ἐλάλησαν ὑμῖν τὸν λόγον τοῦ θεοῦ, ὧν ἀναθεωροῦντες τὴν ἔκβασιν τῆς ἀναστροφῆς μιμεῖσθε τὴν πίστιν. **8** Ἰησοῦς Χριστὸς ἐχθὲς καὶ σήμερον ὁ αὐτὸς καὶ εἰς τοὺς αἰῶνας. ¶ **9** διδαχαῖς ποικίλαις καὶ ξέναις μὴ παραφέρεσθε· καλὸν γὰρ χάριτι βεβαιοῦσθαι τὴν καρδίαν, οὐ βρώμασιν ἐν οἷς οὐκ ὠφελήθησαν οἱ περιπατοῦντες. ¶ **10** ἔχομεν θυσιαστήριον ἐξ οὗ φαγεῖν οὐκ ἔχουσιν ἐξουσίαν οἱ τῇ σκηνῇ λατρεύοντες. ¶ **11** ὧν γὰρ εἰσφέρεται ζῴων τὸ αἷμα περὶ ἁμαρτίας εἰς τὰ ἅγια διὰ τοῦ ἀρχιερέως, τούτων τὰ σώματα κατακαίεται ἔξω τῆς παρεμβολῆς. **12** διὸ καὶ Ἰησοῦς, ἵνα ἁγιάσῃ διὰ τοῦ ἰδίου αἵματος τὸν λαόν, ἔξω τῆς πύλης ἔπαθεν. **13** τοίνυν ἐξερχώμεθα πρὸς αὐτὸν ἔξω τῆς παρεμβολῆς τὸν ὀνειδισμὸν

bore. **14** For here we do not have an enduring city, but we are looking for the city that is to come. ¶
γὰρ ὧδε   οὐ ἔχομεν μένουσαν πόλιν ἀλλὰ ἐπιζητοῦμεν τὴν μέλλουσαν
cj adv pl v.pai.1p pt.pa.asf n.asf cj v.pai.1p d.asf pt.pa.asf
1142 6045 2400 2400 4024 2400 3531 4484 247 2118 3836 3516

15 Through Jesus, therefore, let us continually offer to God a sacrifice of praise – the fruit of
Δι᾽ αὐτοῦ οὖν διὰ παντὸς ἀναφέρωμεν τῷ θεῷ θυσίαν αἰνέσεως τοῦτ᾽ ἔστιν καρπὸν
p.g r.gsm.3 cj p.g a.gsm v.pas.1p d.dsn n.dsm n.asf n.gsf r.nsn v.pai.3s n.asm
1328 899 4036 429 429 1328 4246 429 3836 2536 2602 139 4047 1639 2843

lips that confess his name. **16** And do not forget to do good and to share with others,
χειλέων ὁμολογούντων αὐτοῦ τῷ ὀνόματι δὲ μὴ ἐπιλανθάνεσθε τῆς εὐποιΐας καὶ κοινωνίας
n.gpn pt.pa.gpn r.gsm.3 d.dsn n.dsn cj pl v.pmm.2p d.gsf n.gsf cj n.gsf
5927 3933 899 3836 3950 1254 2140 3590 2140 3836 2343 2779 3126

for with such sacrifices God is pleased. ¶ **17** Obey your leaders and submit to their authority.
γὰρ τοιαύταις θυσίαις ὁ θεός εὐαρεστεῖται Πείθεσθε ὑμῶν τοῖς ἡγουμένοις καὶ ὑπείκετε
cj r.dpf n.dpf d.nsm n.nsm v.ppi.3s v.pmm.2p r.gp.2 d.dpm pt.pm.dpm cj v.pam.2p
1142 5525 2602 3836 2536 2297 4275 7007 3836 2451 2779 5640

They keep watch over you as men who must give an account. Obey them so that their
γὰρ αὐτοὶ ἀγρυπνοῦσιν ὑπὲρ τῶν ψυχῶν ὑμῶν ὡς ἀποδώσοντες λόγον ἵνα τοῦτο
cj r.npm v.pai.3p p.g d.gpf n.gpf r.gp.2 cj pt.fa.npm n.asm cj r.asn
1142 899 70 5642 3836 6034 7007 6055 625 3364 2671 4047

work will be a joy, not a burden, for that would be of no advantage to you. ¶ **18** Pray for
ποιῶσιν μετὰ χαρᾶς καὶ μὴ στενάζοντες γὰρ τοῦτο ἀλυσιτελὲς ὑμῖν Προσεύχεσθε περὶ
v.pas.3p p.g n.gsf cj pl pt.pa.npm cj r.nsn a.nsn r.dp.2 v.pmm.2p p.g
4472 3552 5915 2779 3590 5100 1142 4047 269 7007 4667 4309

us. We are sure that we have a clear conscience and desire to live honorably in every way.
ἡμῶν γὰρ πειθόμεθα ὅτι ἔχομεν καλὴν συνείδησιν θέλοντες ἀναστρέφεσθαι καλῶς ἐν πᾶσιν
r.gp.1 cj v.ppi.1p cj v.pai.1p a.asf n.asf pt.pa.npm f.pp adv p.d a.dpn
7005 1142 4275 4022 2400 2819 5287 2527 418 2822 1877 4246

19 I particularly urge you to pray so that I may be restored to you soon. ¶ **20** May the
δὲ περισσοτέρως παρακαλῶ τοῦτο ποιῆσαι ἵνα ἀποκατασταθῶ ὑμῖν τάχιον δὲ Ὁ
cj adv.c v.pai.1s r.asn f.aa cj v.aps.1s r.dp.2 adv.c cj d.nsm
1254 4151 4359 4151 4047 4472 2671 635 7007 5441 1254 2936 3836

God of peace, who through the blood of the eternal covenant brought back from the dead our
θεὸς τῆς εἰρήνης ἐν αἵματι αἰωνίου διαθήκης ὁ ἀναγαγὼν ἐκ νεκρῶν ἡμῶν
n.nsm d.gsf n.gsf p.d n.dsn a.gsf n.gsf d.nsm pt.aa.nsm p.g a.gpm r.gp.1
2536 3836 1645 1877 135 173 1347 3836 343 1666 3738 7005

Lord Jesus, that great Shepherd of the sheep, **21** equip you with everything good for doing his
τὸν κύριον Ἰησοῦν τὸν τὸν μέγαν ποιμένα τῶν προβάτων καταρτίσαι ὑμᾶς ἐν παντὶ ἀγαθῷ εἰς τὸ ποιῆσαι αὐτοῦ
d.asm n.asm n.asm d.asm d.asm a.asm n.asm d.gpn n.gpn v.aao.3s r.ap.2 p.d a.dsn a.dsn p.a d.asn f.aa r.gsm.3
3836 3261 2652 3836 3836 3489 4478 3836 4585 2936 7007 1877 4246 19 1650 3836 4472 899

will, and may he work in us what is pleasing to him, through Jesus Christ, to whom be glory for
τὸ θέλημα ποιῶν ἐν ἡμῖν τὸ εὐάρεστον ἐνώπιον αὐτοῦ διὰ Ἰησοῦ Χριστοῦ ᾧ ἡ δόξα εἰς
d.asn n.asn pt.pa.nsm p.d r.dp.1 d.asn a.asn p.g r.gsm.3 p.g n.gsm n.gsm r.dsm d.nsf n.nsf p.a
3836 2525 4472 1877 7005 3836 2298 1967 899 1328 2652 5986 4005 3836 1518 1650

ever and ever. Amen. ¶ **22** Brothers, I urge you to bear with my word of
τοὺς αἰῶνας τῶν αἰώνων ἀμήν δὲ ἀδελφοί Παρακαλῶ ὑμᾶς ἀνέχεσθε τοῦ λόγου
d.apm n.apm d.gpm n.gpm pl cj n.vpm v.pai.1s r.ap.2 v.pmm.2p d.gsm n.gsm
3836 172 3836 172 297 1254 81 4151 7007 462 3836 3364

exhortation, for I have written you only a short letter. ¶ **23** I want you to know that our
τῆς παρακλήσεως γὰρ καὶ ἐπέστειλα ὑμῖν διὰ βραχέων Γινώσκετε ἡμῶν
d.gsf n.gsf cj adv v.aai.1s r.dp.2 p.g a.gpm v.pai.2p r.gp.1
3836 4155 1142 2779 2182 7007 1328 1099 1182 7005

brother Timothy has been released. If he arrives soon, I will come with him to see you. ¶
τὸν ἀδελφὸν Τιμόθεον ἀπολελυμένον ἐὰν ἔρχηται τάχιον μεθ᾽ οὗ ὄψομαι ὑμᾶς
d.asm n.asm n.asm pt.rp.asm cj v.pms.3s adv.c p.g r.gsm v.fmi.1s r.ap.2
3836 81 5510 668 1569 2262 5441 3972 3972 3552 4005 3972 7007

αὐτοῦ φέροντες· **14** οὐ γὰρ ἔχομεν ὧδε μένουσαν πόλιν ἀλλὰ τὴν μέλλουσαν ἐπιζητοῦμεν. ¶ **15** δι᾽ αὐτοῦ [οὖν] ἀναφέρωμεν θυσίαν αἰνέσεως διὰ παντὸς τῷ θεῷ, τοῦτ᾽ ἔστιν καρπὸν χειλέων ὁμολογούντων τῷ ὀνόματι αὐτοῦ. **16** τῆς δὲ εὐποιΐας καὶ κοινωνίας μὴ ἐπιλανθάνεσθε· τοιαύταις γὰρ θυσίαις εὐαρεστεῖται ὁ θεός. ¶ **17** Πείθεσθε τοῖς ἡγουμένοις ὑμῶν καὶ ὑπείκετε, αὐτοὶ γὰρ ἀγρυπνοῦσιν ὑπὲρ τῶν ψυχῶν ὑμῶν ὡς λόγον ἀποδώσοντες, ἵνα μετὰ χαρᾶς τοῦτο ποιῶσιν καὶ μὴ στενάζοντες· ἀλυσιτελὲς γὰρ ὑμῖν τοῦτο. ¶ **18** Προσεύχεσθε περὶ ἡμῶν· πειθόμεθα γὰρ ὅτι καλὴν συνείδησιν ἔχομεν, ἐν πᾶσιν καλῶς θέλοντες ἀναστρέφεσθαι. **19** περισσοτέρως δὲ παρακαλῶ τοῦτο ποιῆσαι, ἵνα τάχιον ἀποκατασταθῶ ὑμῖν. ¶ **20** Ὁ δὲ θεὸς τῆς εἰρήνης, ὁ ἀναγαγὼν ἐκ νεκρῶν τὸν ποιμένα τῶν προβάτων τὸν μέγαν ἐν αἵματι διαθήκης αἰωνίου, τὸν κύριον ἡμῶν Ἰησοῦν, **21** καταρτίσαι ὑμᾶς ἐν παντὶ ἀγαθῷ εἰς τὸ ποιῆσαι τὸ θέλημα αὐτοῦ, ποιῶν ἐν ἡμῖν τὸ εὐάρεστον ἐνώπιον αὐτοῦ διὰ Ἰησοῦ Χριστοῦ, ᾧ ἡ δόξα εἰς τοὺς αἰῶνας [τῶν αἰώνων], ἀμήν. ¶ **22** Παρακαλῶ δὲ ὑμᾶς, ἀδελφοί, ἀνέχεσθε τοῦ λόγου τῆς παρακλήσεως, καὶ γὰρ διὰ βραχέων ἐπέστειλα ὑμῖν. ¶ **23** Γινώσκετε τὸν ἀδελφὸν ἡμῶν Τιμόθεον ἀπολελυμένον, μεθ᾽ οὗ ἐὰν τάχιον ἔρχηται ὄψομαι

24 Greet | all | your | leaders | and | all | God's | people. | Those | from | Italy | send | you | their
Ἀσπάσασθε | πάντας | ὑμῶν | ⌐τοὺς ἡγουμένους⌐ | καὶ | πάντας | ⌐τοὺς ἁγίους⌐ | οἱ | ἀπὸ | ⌐τῆς Ἰταλίας⌐ | ὑμᾶς
v.amm.2p | a.apm | r.gp.2 | d.apm pt.pm.apm | cj | a.apm | d.apm a.apm | d.npm | p.g | d.gsf n.gsf | r.ap.2
832 | 4246 | 7007 | 3836 2451 | 2779 | 4246 | 3836 41 | 3836 | 608 | 3836 2712 | 832 7007

greetings. ¶ | **25** Grace | be | with | you | all.
Ἀσπάζονται | Ἡ χάρις | μετὰ | ὑμῶν | πάντων
v.pmi.3p | d.nsf n.nsf | p.g | r.gp.2 | a.gpm
832 | 3836 5921 | 3552 | 7007 | 4246

ὑμᾶς. ¶ 24 Ἀσπάσασθε πάντας τοὺς ἡγουμένους ὑμῶν καὶ πάντας τοὺς ἁγίους. ἀσπάζονται ὑμᾶς οἱ ἀπὸ τῆς Ἰταλίας. ¶ 25 ἡ χάρις μετὰ πάντων ὑμῶν.

James

1:1 James, a servant of God and of the Lord Jesus Christ, ¶ To the twelve tribes *scattered* *among*
Ἰάκωβος δοῦλος → θεοῦ καὶ → κυρίου Ἰησοῦ Χριστοῦ → ταῖς δώδεκα φυλαῖς διασπορᾷ ταῖς ἐν
n.nsm n.nsm n.gsm cj n.gsm n.gsm n.gsm d.dpf a.dpf n.dpf n.dsf d.dpf p.d
2610 1529 2536 2779 3261 2652 5986 3836 1557 5876 1402 3836 1877

the nations: ¶ Greetings.
τῇ ↰ χαίρειν
d.dsf f.pa
3836 1402 5897

Trials and Temptations

1:2 Consider it pure joy, my brothers, whenever you face trials of many kinds, 3 because you
ἡγήσασθε Πᾶσαν χαρὰν μου ἀδελφοί ὅταν → περιπέσητε πειρασμοῖς → ποικίλοις ← → →
v.amm.2p a.asf n.asf r.gs.1 n.vpm cj v.aas.2p n.dpm a.dpm
2451 4246 5915 1609 81 4020 4346 4280 4476

know that the testing of your faith develops perseverance. 4 Perseverance must finish its work
γινώσκοντες ὅτι τὸ δοκίμιον ↱ ὑμῶν ⌞τῆς πίστεως⌟ κατεργάζεται ὑπομονήν δὲ ⌞ἡ ὑπομονή⌟ → ⌞ἐχέτω τέλειον⌟ ἔργον
pt.pa.npm cj d.nsn n.nsn r.gp.2 d.gsf n.gsf v.pmi.3s n.asf cj d.nsf n.nsf v.pam.3s a.asn n.asn
1182 4022 3836 1510 4411 7007 3836 4411 2981 5705 1254 3836 5705 2400 5455 2240

so that you may be mature and complete, not lacking anything. 5 If any of you lacks wisdom, he
ἵνα ← → → ἦτε τέλειοι καὶ ὁλόκληροι ἐν μηδενὶ λειπόμενοι ↰ δέ Εἰ τις → ὑμῶν λείπεται σοφίας →
cj v.pas.2p a.npm cj a.npm p.d a.dsn pt.pp.npm cj cj r.nsm r.gp.2 v.ppi.3s n.gsf
2671 1639 5455 2779 3908 1877 3594 3309 3594 1254 1623 5516 7007 3309 5053

should ask God, who gives generously to all without finding fault, and it will be given to
→ αἰτείτω παρὰ θεοῦ τοῦ διδόντος ἁπλῶς → πᾶσιν καὶ μὴ → ὀνειδίζοντος καὶ → → → δοθήσεται →
v.pam.3s p.g n.gsm d.gsm pt.pa.gsm adv a.dpm cj pl pt.pa.gsm cj v.fpi.3s
160 4123 2536 3836 1443 607 4246 2779 3590 3943 2779 1443

him. 6 when he asks, he must believe and not doubt, because he who doubts is like a wave of
αὐτῷ δὲ → → αἰτείτω ⌞ἐν πίστει⌟ μηδὲν διακρινόμενος γὰρ ὁ ← διακρινόμενος → ἔοικεν κλύδωνι →
r.dsm.3 cj v.pam.3s p.d n.dsf a.asn pt.pm.nsm cj d.nsm pt.pm.nsm v.rai.3s n.dsm
899 1254 160 1877 4411 3594 1359 1142 3836 1359 2036 3114

the sea, blown and tossed by the wind. 7 That man should not think he will receive
θαλάσσης ἀνεμιζομένῳ καὶ ῥιπιζομένῳ ↰ ↰ ↰ γὰρ ἐκεῖνος ⌞ὁ ἄνθρωπος⌟ ↱ μὴ οἰέσθω ὅτι → → λήμψεται
n.gsf pt.pp.dsm cj pt.pp.dsm cj r.nsm d.nsm n.nsm pl v.pmm.3s cj v.fmi.3s
2498 448 2779 484/ 448 448 448 1142 1697 3836 476 3887 3590 3887 4022 3284

anything from the Lord; 8 he is a double-minded man, unstable in all he does. ¶ 9 The brother
τι παρὰ τοῦ κυρίου δίψυχος ἀνὴρ ἀκατάστατος ἐν πάσαις αὐτοῦ ⌞ταῖς ὁδοῖς⌟ δὲ ὁ ἀδελφὸς
r.asn p.g d.gsm n.gsm a.nsm n.nsm a.nsm p.d a.dpf r.gsm.3 d.dpf n.dpf cj d.nsm n.nsm
5516 4123 3836 3261 1500 467 190 1877 4246 899 3836 3847 1254 3836 81

in humble circumstances ought to take pride in his high position. 10 But the one who is rich should
⌞ὁ ταπεινὸς⌟ ← → → → Καυχάσθω ἐν αὐτοῦ ⌞τῷ ὕψει⌟ ← δὲ ὁ ← ← → πλούσιος
d.nsm a.nsm v.pmm.3s p.d r.gsm.3 d.dsn n.dsn cj d.nsm a.nsm
3836 5424 3016 1877 899 3836 5737 1254 3836 4454

take pride in his low position, because he will pass away like a wild flower. 11 For the sun
ἐν αὐτοῦ ⌞τῇ ταπεινώσει⌟ ← ὅτι → → παρελεύσεται ← ὡς χόρτου ἄνθος γὰρ ὁ ἥλιος
p.d r.gsm.3 d.dsf n.dsf cj v.fmi.3s pl n.gsm n.nsn cj d.nsm n.nsm
1877 899 3836 5428 4022 4216 6055 5965 470 1142 3836 2463

rises with scorching heat and withers the plant; its blossom falls and its
ἀνέτειλεν σὺν → ⌞τῷ καύσωνι⌟ καὶ ἐξήρανεν τὸν χόρτον καὶ αὐτοῦ ⌞τὸ ἄνθος⌟ ἐξέπεσεν καὶ αὐτοῦ
v.aai.3s p.d d.dsm n.dsm cj v.aai.3s d.asm n.asm cj r.gsm.3 d.nsn n.nsn v.aai.3s cj r.gsm.3
422 5250 3836 3014 2779 3830 3836 5965 2779 899 3836 470 1738 2779 899

beauty is destroyed. In the same way, the rich man will fade away even while
⌞ἡ εὐπρέπεια τοῦ προσώπου⌟ → ἀπώλετο οὕτως ← ← καὶ ὁ πλούσιος → μαρανθήσεται ← ἐν
d.nsf n.nsf d.gsn n.gsn v.ami.3s adv adv d.nsm a.nsm v.fpi.3s p.d
3836 2346 3836 4725 660 4048 2779 3836 4454 3447 1877

1:1 Ἰάκωβος θεοῦ καὶ κυρίου Ἰησοῦ Χριστοῦ δοῦλος ¶ ταῖς δώδεκα φυλαῖς ταῖς ἐν τῇ διασπορᾷ ¶ χαίρειν.
1:2 Πᾶσαν χαρὰν ἡγήσασθε, ἀδελφοί μου, ὅταν πειρασμοῖς περιπέσητε ποικίλοις, 3 γινώσκοντες ὅτι τὸ δοκίμιον ὑμῶν τῆς
πίστεως κατεργάζεται ὑπομονήν. 4 ἡ δὲ ὑπομονὴ ἔργον τέλειον ἐχέτω, ἵνα ἦτε τέλειοι καὶ ὁλόκληροι ἐν μηδενὶ λειπόμενοι. 5 Εἰ
δέ τις ὑμῶν λείπεται σοφίας, αἰτείτω παρὰ τοῦ διδόντος θεοῦ πᾶσιν ἁπλῶς καὶ μὴ ὀνειδίζοντος καὶ δοθήσεται αὐτῷ. 6 αἰτείτω
δὲ ἐν πίστει μηδὲν διακρινόμενος· ὁ γὰρ διακρινόμενος ἔοικεν κλύδωνι θαλάσσης ἀνεμιζομένῳ καὶ ῥιπιζομένῳ. 7 μὴ γὰρ οἰέσθω
ὁ ἄνθρωπος ἐκεῖνος ὅτι λήμψεταί τι παρὰ τοῦ κυρίου, 8 ἀνὴρ δίψυχος, ἀκατάστατος ἐν πάσαις ταῖς ὁδοῖς αὐτοῦ. ¶
9 Καυχάσθω δὲ ὁ ἀδελφὸς ὁ ταπεινὸς ἐν τῷ ὕψει αὐτοῦ, 10 ὁ δὲ πλούσιος ἐν τῇ ταπεινώσει αὐτοῦ, ὅτι ὡς ἄνθος χόρτου
παρελεύσεται. 11 ἀνέτειλεν γὰρ ὁ ἥλιος σὺν τῷ καύσωνι καὶ ἐξήρανεν τὸν χόρτον καὶ τὸ ἄνθος αὐτοῦ ἐξέπεσεν καὶ ἡ εὐπρέπεια

he goes about his business. ¶ **12** Blessed is the man who perseveres under trial, because when he has
← ← ← αὐτοῦ ⌐ταῖς πορείαις⌐ Μακάριος ἀνήρ ὅς ὑπομένει ← πειρασμόν ὅτι → → → →
r.gsm.3 d.dpf n.dpf a.nsm n.nsm r.nsm v.pai.3s n.asm cj
899 3836 4512 3421 467 4005 5702 4280 4022

stood the test, he will receive the crown of life that God has promised to those who love him. ¶
γενόμενος δόκιμος → λήμψεται τὸν στέφανον ⌐τῆς ζωῆς⌐ ὅν ἐπηγγείλατο τοῖς → ἀγαπῶσιν αὐτόν
pt.am.nsm a.nsm v.fmi.3s d.asm n.asm d.gsf n.gsf r.asm v.ami.3s d.dpm pt.pa.dpm r.asm.3
1181 1511 3284 3836 5109 3836 2437 4005 2040 3836 26 899

13 When tempted, no one should say, "God is tempting me." For God cannot be tempted by
→ πειραζόμενος Μηδεὶς ← → λεγέτω ὅτι ἀπὸ θεοῦ → πειράζομαι γὰρ ὁ θεός → ἐστιν ἀπείραστος →
pt.pp.nsm a.nsm v.pam.3s cj p.g n.gsm v.ppi.1s cj d.nsm n.nsm v.pai.3s a.nsm
4279 3594 3306 4022 608 2536 4279 1142 3836 2536 585 1639 585

evil, nor does he tempt anyone; **14** but each one is tempted when, by his own evil desire, he is dragged
κακῶν δὲ → αὐτός πειράζει οὐδένα δὲ ἕκαστος ← → πειράζεται ὑπὸ τῆς ἰδίας ἐπιθυμίας ← → ἐξελκόμενος
a.gpn cj r.nsm v.pai.3s a.asm cj a.nsm v.ppi.3s p.g d.gsf a.gsf n.gsf pt.pp.nsm
2805 1254 4279 899 4279 4029 1254 1667 4279 5679 3836 2625 2123 1999

away and enticed. **15** Then, after desire has conceived, it gives birth to sin; and sin, when it is
καὶ δελεαζόμενος εἶτα → ἡ ἐπιθυμία → συλλαβοῦσα → → τίκτει ἁμαρτίαν δὲ ἡ ἁμαρτία → →
cj pt.pp.nsm adv d.nsf n.nsf pt.aa.nsf v.pai.3s n.asf cj d.nsf n.nsf
2779 1284 1663 3836 2123 5197 5503 281 1254 3836 281

full-grown, gives birth to death. ¶ **16** Don't be deceived, my dear brothers. **17** Every good and
ἀποτελεσθεῖσα → ἀποκύει θάνατον Μὴ → πλανᾶσθε μου ἀγαπητοί ἀδελφοί πᾶσα ἀγαθὴ δόσις καὶ πᾶν
pt.ap.nsf v.pai.3s n.asm pl v.ppm.2p r.gs.1 a.vpm n.vpm a.nsf a.nsf n.nsf cj a.nsn
699 652 2505 3590 4414 1609 28 81 4246 19 1521 2779 4246

perfect gift is from above, coming down from the Father of the heavenly lights, who does not
τέλειον δώρημα ἐστιν ἄνωθεν ← καταβαῖνον ← ἀπὸ τοῦ πατρὸς τῶν φώτων παρ᾽ ᾧ ἔνι οὐκ
a.nsn n.nsn v.pai.3s adv pt.pa.nsn p.g d.gsm n.gsm d.gpn n.gpn p.d r.dsm v.pai.3s pl
5455 1564 1639 540 2849 608 3836 4252 3836 5890 4123 4005 1928 4024

change like shifting shadows. **18** He chose to give us birth through the word of truth, that we might
παραλλαγή ἢ τροπῆς ἀποσκίασμα βουληθεὶς → ἀπεκύησεν ἡμᾶς ← → λόγῳ → ἀληθείας εἰς ἡμᾶς →
n.nsf cj n.gsf n.nsn pt.ap.nsm v.aai.3s r.ap.1 n.dsm n.gsf p.a r.ap.1
4164 2445 5572 684 1089 652 7005 652 3364 237 1650 7005

be a kind of firstfruits of all he created.
⌐τὸ εἶναι⌐ τινα ← ἀπαρχήν → αὐτοῦ ⌐τῶν κτισμάτων⌐
d.asn f.pa r.asf n.asf r.gsm.3 d.gpn n.gpn
3836 1639 5516 569 3233 899 3836 3233

Listening and Doing

1:19 My dear brothers, take note of this: Everyone should be quick to listen, slow to
μου ἀγαπητοί ἀδελφοί Ἴστε δὲ ⌐πᾶς ἄνθρωπος⌐ ἔστω ταχὺς εἰς ⌐τὸ ἀκοῦσαι⌐ βραδὺς εἰς
r.gs.1 a.vpm n.vpm v.ram.2p cj a.nsm n.nsm v.pam.3s a.nsm p.a d.asn f.aa a.nsm p.a
1609 28 81 3857 1254 4246 476 1639 5444 1650 3836 201 1096 1650

speak and slow to become angry, **20** for man's anger does not bring about the righteous life that God
⌐τὸ λαλῆσαι⌐ βραδὺς εἰς → ὀργήν γὰρ ἀνδρὸς ὀργὴ → οὐκ ἐργάζεται ← δικαιοσύνην θεοῦ
d.asn f.aa a.nsm p.a n.asf cj n.gsm n.nsf pl v.pmi.3s n.asf n.gsm
3836 3281 1096 1650 3973 1142 467 3973 4024 2237 1466 2536

desires. **21** Therefore, get rid of all moral filth and the evil that is so prevalent and humbly accept
← διὸ → ἀποθέμενοι ← πᾶσαν → ῥυπαρίαν καὶ κακίας → περισσείαν ἐν πραΰτητι δέξασθε
cj pt.am.npm a.asf n.asf cj n.gsf n.asf p.d n.dsf v.amm.2p
1475 700 4246 4864 2779 2798 4353 1877 4559 1312

the word planted in you, which can save you. ¶ **22** Do not merely listen to the word,
τὸν λόγον ἔμφυτον τὸν δυνάμενον σῶσαι ⌐τὰς ψυχὰς ὑμῶν⌐ δὲ μὴ μόνον ἀκροαταὶ ← λόγου
d.asm n.asm a.asm d.asm pt.pp.asm f.aa d.apf n.apf r.gp.2 cj pl adv n.npm n.gsm
3836 3364 1875 3836 1538 5392 3836 6034 7007 1254 212 3590 212 3364

and so deceive yourselves. Do what it says. **23** Anyone who listens to the word but does not
καὶ παραλογιζόμενοι ἑαυτούς ⌐Γίνεσθε ποιηταὶ⌐ ὅτι εἴ τις → ἀκροατὴς ← λόγου καὶ → οὐ
cj pt.pm.npm r.apm.2 v.pmm.2p n.npm cj cj r.nsm n.nsm n.gsm cj pl
2779 4165 1571 1181 4475 4022 1623 5516 212 3364 2779 1639 4024

τοῦ προσώπου αὐτοῦ ἀπώλετο· οὕτως καὶ ὁ πλούσιος ἐν ταῖς πορείαις αὐτοῦ μαρανθήσεται. ¶ **12** Μακάριος ἀνὴρ ὃς ὑπομένει πειρασμόν, ὅτι δόκιμος γενόμενος λήμψεται τὸν στέφανον τῆς ζωῆς ὃν ἐπηγγείλατο τοῖς ἀγαπῶσιν αὐτόν. ¶ **13** μηδεὶς πειραζόμενος λεγέτω ὅτι Ἀπὸ θεοῦ πειράζομαι· ὁ γὰρ θεὸς ἀπείραστός ἐστιν κακῶν, πειράζει δὲ αὐτὸς οὐδένα. **14** ἕκαστος δὲ πειράζεται ὑπὸ τῆς ἰδίας ἐπιθυμίας ἐξελκόμενος καὶ δελεαζόμενος· **15** εἶτα ἡ ἐπιθυμία συλλαβοῦσα τίκτει ἁμαρτίαν, ἡ δὲ ἁμαρτία ἀποτελεσθεῖσα ἀποκύει θάνατον. ¶ **16** Μὴ πλανᾶσθε, ἀδελφοί μου ἀγαπητοί. **17** πᾶσα δόσις ἀγαθὴ καὶ πᾶν δώρημα τέλειον ἄνωθέν ἐστιν καταβαῖνον ἀπὸ τοῦ πατρὸς τῶν φώτων, παρ᾽ ᾧ οὐκ ἔνι παραλλαγὴ ἢ τροπῆς ἀποσκίασμα. **18** βουληθεὶς ἀπεκύησεν ἡμᾶς λόγῳ ἀληθείας εἰς τὸ εἶναι ἡμᾶς ἀπαρχήν τινα τῶν αὐτοῦ κτισμάτων.

1:19 Ἴστε, ἀδελφοί μου ἀγαπητοί· ἔστω δὲ πᾶς ἄνθρωπος ταχὺς εἰς τὸ ἀκοῦσαι, βραδὺς εἰς τὸ λαλῆσαι, βραδὺς εἰς ὀργήν· **20** ὀργὴ γὰρ ἀνδρὸς δικαιοσύνην θεοῦ οὐκ ἐργάζεται. **21** διὸ ἀποθέμενοι πᾶσαν ῥυπαρίαν καὶ περισσείαν κακίας ἐν πραΰτητι, δέξασθε τὸν ἔμφυτον λόγον τὸν δυνάμενον σῶσαι τὰς ψυχὰς ὑμῶν. ¶ **22** Γίνεσθε δὲ ποιηταὶ λόγου καὶ μὴ μόνον ἀκροαταὶ παραλογιζόμενοι ἑαυτούς. **23** ὅτι εἴ τις ἀκροατὴς λόγου ἐστὶν καὶ οὐ ποιητής, οὗτος ἔοικεν ἀνδρὶ κατανοοῦντι τὸ πρόσωπον τῆς

do   what it says   is like   a man who looks   at his   face   in a mirror ²⁴ and,
ἐστὶν ποιητής·   οὗτος → ἔοικεν ἀνδρὶ → κατανοοῦντι ← ⸤τῆς γενέσεως αὐτοῦ⸥ ⸤τὸ πρόσωπον⸥ ἐν ἐσόπτρῳ γὰρ
v.pai.3s n.nsm   r.nsm v.rai.3s n.dsm pt.pa.dsm d.gsf n.gsf r.gsm.3 d.asn n.asn p.d n.dsn cj
1639 4475   4047 2036 467 2917 3836 1161 899 3836 4725 1877 2269 1142

after looking   at himself,   goes   away and immediately forgets   what he looks like. ²⁵ But the man who
κατενόησεν ← ἑαυτὸν καὶ ἀπελήλυθεν καὶ εὐθέως ἐπελάθετο ὁποῖος → ἦν ← δὲ ὁ ←
v.aai.3s r.asm.3 cj v.rai.3s cj adv v.ami.3s r.nsm v.iai.3s cj d.nsm
2917 1571 2779 599 2779 2311 2140 3961 1639 1254 3836

looks   intently into the perfect law   that gives freedom,   and continues to do this, not forgetting
παρακύψας ← εἰς τέλειον νόμον τὸν ⸤τῆς ἐλευθερίας⸥ καὶ παραμείνας   οὐκ ⸤ἐπιλησμονῆς γενόμενος⸥
pt.aa.nsm p.a a.asm n.asm d.asm d.gsf n.gsf cj pt.aa.nsm pl n.gsf pt.am.nsm
4160 1650 5455 3795 3836 3836 1800 2779 4169 4024 2144 1181

what he has heard,   but   doing it   – he   will be   blessed   in   what he   does. ¶ ²⁶ If   anyone considers
→ → ἀκροατὴς ἀλλὰ ποιητὴς ἔργου οὗτος → ἔσται μακάριος ἐν τῇ αὐτοῦ ποιήσει   Εἴ τις   δοκεῖ
n.nsm cj n.nsm n.gsn r.nsm v.fmi.3s a.nsm p.d d.dsf r.gsm.3 n.dsf cj cj v.pai.3s
212 247 4475 2240 4047 1639 3421 1877 3836 899 4474 1623 5516 1506

himself   religious and yet does not keep   a tight rein on his   tongue,   he deceives himself   and
εἶναι θρησκὸς → → μὴ χαλιναγωγῶν   αὐτοῦ γλῶσσαν ἀλλὰ → ἀπατῶν ⸤καρδίαν αὐτοῦ⸥
f.pa a.nsm pl pt.pa.nsm r.gsm.3 n.asf cj pt.pa.nsm n.asf r.gsm.3
1639 2580 5902 5902 3590 5902 899 1185 247 572 2840 899

his   religion   is worthless. ²⁷ Religion that God   our Father *accepts* *as* pure   and faultless is this: to
τούτου ⸤ἡ θρησκεία⸥ μάταιος   θρησκεία ⸤τῷ θεῷ⸥ καὶ πατρὶ παρὰ   καθαρὰ καὶ ἀμίαντος ἐστίν αὕτη →
r.gsm d.nsf n.nsf a.nsf n.nsf d.dsm n.dsm cj n.dsm p.d a.nsf cj a.nsf v.pai.3s r.nsf
4047 3836 2579 3469 2579 3836 2536 2779 4252 4123 2754 2779 299 1639 4047

look   after orphans and widows in their distress   and to keep oneself from being polluted by the world.
ἐπισκέπτεσθαι ← ὀρφανοὺς καὶ χήρας ἐν αὐτῶν ⸤τῇ θλίψει⸥ → τηρεῖν ἑαυτὸν → → ἄσπιλον ἀπὸ τοῦ κόσμου
f.pm a.apm cj n.apf p.d r.gpm.3 d.dsf n.dsf f.pa r.asm a.asm p.g d.gsm n.gsm
2170 4003 2779 5939 1877 899 3836 2568 5498 1571 834 608 3836 3180

Favoritism Forbidden

^{2:1} My brothers, as believers in   our glorious Lord   Jesus Christ, don't show   favoritism.   ²
μου Ἀδελφοί   ⸤τὴν πίστιν⸥ → ἡμῶν ⸤τῆς δόξης⸥ ⸤τοῦ κυρίου⸥ Ἰησοῦ Χριστοῦ μὴ ἔχετε ἐν προσωπολημψίαις   γὰρ
r.gs.1 n.vpm d.asf n.asf r.gp.1 d.gsf n.gsf d.gsm n.gsm n.gsm n.gsm pl v.pam.2p p.d n.dpf cj
1609 81 3836 4411 3261 7005 3836 1518 3836 3261 2652 5986 3590 2400 1877 4721 1142

Suppose a man comes into your meeting   wearing   a gold ring and   fine   clothes, and a poor   man in
ἐὰν   ἀνὴρ εἰσέλθῃ εἰς ὑμῶν συναγωγὴν χρυσοδακτύλιος ← ← ← ἐν λαμπρᾷ ἐσθῆτι δὲ πτωχὸς ← ἐν
cj n.nsm v.aas.3s p.a r.gp.2 n.asf a.nsm p.d a.dsf n.dsf cj a.nsm p.d
1569 467 1656 1650 7007 5252 5993 1877 3287 2264 1254 4777 1877

shabby clothes also comes in. ³   If you show   special attention to the man wearing fine   clothes and
ῥυπαρᾷ ἐσθῆτι καὶ εἰσέλθῃ ← δὲ εἰ ἐπιβλέψητε ← ἐπὶ τὸν   φοροῦντα ⸤τὴν λαμπρὰν⸥ ⸤τὴν ἐσθῆτα⸥ καὶ
a.dsf n.dsf adv v.aas.3s cj v.aas.2p p.a d.asm pt.pa.asm d.asf a.asf d.asf n.asf cj
4865 2264 2779 1656 1254 2098 2093 3836 5841 3836 3287 3836 2264 2779

say, "Here's a good seat for you," but say   to the poor man, "You stand there" or "Sit on the floor by my
εἴπητε ὧδε   καλῶς κάθου σὺ καὶ εἴπητε τῷ πτωχῷ ← σὺ στῆθι ἐκεῖ ἢ κάθου   ὑπὸ μου
v.aas.2p adv adv v.pmm.2s r.ns.2 cj v.aas.2p d.dsm a.dsm r.ns.2 v.aam.2s adv cj v.pmm.2s p.a r.gs.1
3306 6045 2822 2764 5148 2779 3306 3836 4777 5148 2705 1695 2445 2764 5679 1609

feet,"   ⁴ have you not discriminated among yourselves and become judges with evil   thoughts? ¶
⸤τὸ ὑποπόδιον⸥ → → οὐ διεκρίθητε ἐν ἑαυτοῖς καὶ ἐγένεσθε κριταὶ → πονηρῶν διαλογισμῶν
d.asn n.asn pl v.api.2p p.d r.dpm.2 cj v.ami.2p n.npm a.gpm n.gpm
3836 5711 1359 1359 4024 1359 1877 1571 2779 1181 3216 4505 1369

⁵ Listen,   my dear   brothers: Has not God   chosen those who are poor   in the eyes of the world to be
Ἀκούσατε μου ἀγαπητοί ἀδελφοί   οὐχ ὁ θεὸς ἐξελέξατο τοὺς ← → πτωχοὺς   → τῷ κόσμῳ
v.aam.2p r.gs.1 a.vpm n.vpm pl d.nsm n.nsm v.ami.3s d.apm a.apm d.dsm n.dsm
201 1609 28 81 1721 4024 3836 2536 1721 3836 4777 3836 3180

rich   in faith and to inherit   the kingdom   he promised those who love   him? ⁶ But you have insulted
πλουσίους ἐν πίστει καὶ κληρονόμους τῆς βασιλείας ἧς → ἐπηγγείλατο τοῖς ← ἀγαπῶσιν αὐτόν δὲ ὑμεῖς → ἠτιμάσατε
a.apm p.d n.dsf cj n.apm d.gsf n.gsf r.gsf v.ami.3s d.dpm pt.pa.dpm r.asm.3 cj r.np.2 v.aai.2p
4454 1877 4411 2779 3101 3836 993 4005 2040 3836 26 899 1254 7007 869

γενέσεως αὐτοῦ ἐν ἐσόπτρῳ· ²⁴ κατενόησεν γὰρ ἑαυτὸν καὶ ἀπελήλυθεν καὶ εὐθέως ἐπελάθετο ὁποῖος ἦν. ²⁵ ὁ δὲ παρακύψας εἰς νόμον τέλειον τὸν τῆς ἐλευθερίας καὶ παραμείνας, οὐκ ἀκροατὴς ἐπιλησμονῆς γενόμενος ἀλλὰ ποιητὴς ἔργου, οὗτος μακάριος ἐν τῇ ποιήσει αὐτοῦ ἔσται. ¶ ²⁶ Εἴ τις δοκεῖ θρησκὸς εἶναι μὴ χαλιναγωγῶν γλῶσσαν αὐτοῦ ἀλλὰ ἀπατῶν καρδίαν αὐτοῦ, τούτου μάταιος ἡ θρησκεία. ²⁷ θρησκεία καθαρὰ καὶ ἀμίαντος παρὰ τῷ θεῷ καὶ πατρὶ αὕτη ἐστίν, ἐπισκέπτεσθαι ὀρφανοὺς καὶ χήρας ἐν τῇ θλίψει αὐτῶν, ἄσπιλον ἑαυτὸν τηρεῖν ἀπὸ τοῦ κόσμου.

²:¹ Ἀδελφοί μου, μὴ ἐν προσωπολημψίαις ἔχετε τὴν πίστιν τοῦ κυρίου ἡμῶν Ἰησοῦ Χριστοῦ τῆς δόξης. ² ἐὰν γὰρ εἰσέλθῃ εἰς συναγωγὴν ὑμῶν ἀνὴρ χρυσοδακτύλιος ἐν ἐσθῆτι λαμπρᾷ, εἰσέλθῃ δὲ καὶ πτωχὸς ἐν ῥυπαρᾷ ἐσθῆτι, ³ ἐπιβλέψητε δὲ ἐπὶ τὸν φοροῦντα τὴν ἐσθῆτα τὴν λαμπρὰν καὶ εἴπητε, Σὺ κάθου ὧδε καλῶς, καὶ τῷ πτωχῷ εἴπητε, Σὺ στῆθι ἐκεῖ ἢ κάθου ὑπὸ τὸ ὑποπόδιόν μου, ⁴ οὐ διεκρίθητε ἐν ἑαυτοῖς καὶ ἐγένεσθε κριταὶ διαλογισμῶν πονηρῶν; ¶ ⁵ Ἀκούσατε, ἀδελφοί μου ἀγαπητοί· οὐχ ὁ θεὸς ἐξελέξατο τοὺς πτωχοὺς τῷ κόσμῳ πλουσίους ἐν πίστει καὶ κληρονόμους τῆς βασιλείας ἧς ἐπηγγείλατο τοῖς ἀγαπῶσιν αὐτόν; ⁶ ὑμεῖς δὲ ἠτιμάσατε τὸν πτωχόν. οὐχ οἱ πλούσιοι καταδυναστεύουσιν ὑμῶν καὶ αὐτοὶ ἕλκουσιν ὑμᾶς εἰς κριτήρια;

the poor. Is it not the rich who are exploiting you? Are they not the ones who are dragging you into
τὸν πτωχόν. οὐχ οἱ πλούσιοι → → καταδυναστεύουσιν ὑμῶν καὶ αὐτοὶ → ἕλκουσιν ὑμᾶς εἰς
d.asm a.asm   pl d.npm a.npm   v.pai.3p r.gp.2 cj r.npm   v.pai.3p r.ap.2 p.a
3836 4777   4024 3836 4454   2872 7007 2779 899   1816 7007 1650

court? **7** Are they not the ones who are slandering the noble name of him to whom you belong? ¶ **8** If
κριτήρια; αὐτοὶ οὐκ → βλασφημοῦσιν τὸ καλὸν ὄνομα → ἐφ᾽ ὑμᾶς ⌜τὸ ἐπικληθὲν⌝ Εἰ
n.apn r.npm pl   v.pai.3p d.asn a.asn n.asn   p.a r.ap.2 d.asn pt.ap.asn
3215 899 4024   1059 3836 2819 3950   2093 7007 3836 2126   1623

you really keep the royal law found in Scripture, "Love your neighbor as yourself," you are doing right.
→ μέντοι τελεῖτε βασιλικὸν νόμον κατὰ ⌜τὴν γραφήν⌝ ἀγαπήσεις σου ⌜τὸν πλησίον⌝ ὡς σεαυτόν → → ποιεῖτε καλῶς
cj v.pai.2p a.asm n.asm p.a d.asf n.asf v.fai.2s r.gs.2 d.asm adv cj r.asm.2 v.pai.2p adv
5464 3530 5464 997 3795 2848 3836 1210 26 5148 3836 4446 6055 4932 4472 2822

9 But if you show favoritism, you sin and are convicted by the law as lawbreakers. **10** For
δὲ εἰ → → προσωπολημπτεῖτε → ἐργάζεσθε ἁμαρτίαν⌋ → ἐλεγχόμενοι ὑπὸ τοῦ νόμου ὡς παραβάται γὰρ
cj cj v.pai.2p v.pmi.2p n.asf pt.pp.npm p.g d.gsm n.gsm pl n.npm cj
1254 1623 4719 2237 281 1794 5679 3836 3795 6055 4127 1142

whoever keeps the whole law and yet stumbles at just one point is guilty of breaking all of it. **11** For he
ὅστις τηρήσῃ τὸν ὅλον νόμον δὲ ← πταίσῃ ἐν ἑνὶ → γέγονεν ἔνοχος → πάντων γὰρ ὁ
r.nsm v.aas.3s d.asm a.asm n.asm cj v.aas.3s p.d a.dsn v.rai.3s a.nsm a.gpn cj d.nsm
4015 5498 3836 3910 3795 1254 4760 1877 1651 1181 1944 4246 1142 3836

who said, "Do not commit adultery," also said, "Do not murder." If you do not commit adultery but do
← εἰπών → μὴ → μοιχεύσῃς καὶ εἶπεν → μὴ φονεύσῃς δὲ εἰ → → οὐ → μοιχεύεις δὲ →
pt.aa.nsm pl v.aas.2s adv v.aai.3s pl v.aas.2s cj cj pl v.pai.2s cj
3306 3590 3658 2779 3306 3590 5839 1254 1623 3658 4024 3658 1254

commit murder, you have become a lawbreaker. ¶ **12** Speak and act as those who are
→ φονεύεις → → γέγονας ⌜παραβάτης νόμου⌝ οὕτως λαλεῖτε καὶ οὕτως ποιεῖτε ὡς → →
v.pai.2s v.rai.2s n.nsm n.gsm adv v.pam.2p cj adv v.pam.2p cj
5839 1181 4127 3795 4048 3281 2779 4048 4472 6055

going to be judged by the law that gives freedom, **13** because judgment without mercy will be shown to anyone
μέλλοντες → → κρίνεσθαι διὰ νόμου → ἐλευθερίας γὰρ ⌜ἡ κρίσις⌝ → ἀνέλεος → → τῷ
pt.pa.npm f.pp p.g n.gsm n.gsf cj d.nsf n.nsf a.nsf d.dsm
3516 3212 1328 3795 1800 1142 3836 3213 447 3836

who has not been merciful. Mercy triumphs over judgment!
← → μὴ ποιήσαντι ἔλεος ἔλεος κατακαυχᾶται ← κρίσεως
pl pt.aa.dsm n.asn n.nsn v.pmi.3s n.gsf
4472 3590 4472 1799 1799 2878 3213

Faith and Deeds

2:14 What good is it, my brothers, if a man claims to have faith but has no deeds? Can such faith
Τί ⌜τὸ ὄφελος⌋ μου ἀδελφοί ἐὰν τις λέγῃ → ἔχειν πίστιν δὲ ἔχῃ μὴ ἔργα μὴ δύναται ἡ πίστις
r.nsn d.nsn n.nsn r.gs.1 n.vpm cj r.nsm v.pas.3s f.pa n.asf cj v.pas.3s pl n.apn pl v.ppi.3s d.nsf n.nsf
5515 3836 4055 1609 81 1569 5516 3306 2400 4411 1254 2400 3590 2240 3590 1538 3836 4411

save him? **15** Suppose a brother or sister is without clothes and daily food. **16** If one of you
σῶσαι αὐτόν; ἐὰν ἀδελφὸς ἢ ἀδελφὴ ὑπάρχωσιν → γυμνοὶ καὶ λειπόμενοι ἐφημέρου ⌜τῆς τροφῆς⌝ δὲ τις ἐξ ὑμῶν
f.aa r.asm.3 cj n.nsm cj n.nsf v.pas.3p a.npm cj pt.pp.npm n.gsf d.gsf n.gsf cj r.nsm p.g r.gp.2
5392 899 1569 81 2445 80 5639 1218 2779 3309 2390 3836 5575 1254 5516 1666 7007

says to him, "Go, I wish you well; keep warm and well fed," but does nothing about his
εἴπῃ αὐτοῖς ὑπάγετε ἐν εἰρήνῃ → θερμαίνεσθε καὶ χορτάζεσθε δὲ δῶτε μὴ → αὐτοῖς
v.aas.3s r.dpm.3 v.pam.2p p.d n.dsf v.pmm.2p cj v.ppm.2p cj v.aas.2p pl r.dpm.3
3306 899 5632 1877 1645 2548 2779 5963 1254 1443 3590 899

physical needs, what good is it? **17** In the same way, faith by itself, if it is not accompanied
⌜τοῦ σώματος⌝ ⌜τὰ ἐπιτήδεια⌝ τί ⌜τὸ ὄφελος⌝ → οὕτως καὶ ἡ πίστις καθ᾽ ἑαυτήν ἐὰν → → μὴ ἔχῃ
d.gsn n.gsn d.apn a.apn r.nsn d.nsn n.nsn adv adv d.nsf n.nsf p.a r.asf.3 cj pl v.pas.3s
3836 5393 3836 2201 5515 3836 4055 4048 2779 3836 4411 2848 1571 1569 2400 2400 3590 2400

by action, is dead. ¶ **18** But someone will say, "You have faith; I have deeds." Show me your faith
← ἔργα ἐστιν νεκρά ᾽Αλλ᾽ τις → ἐρεῖ σὺ ἔχεις πίστιν κἀγὼ ἔχω ἔργα δεῖξόν μοι σου ⌜τὴν πίστιν⌝
n.apn v.pai.3s a.nsf cj r.nsm v.fai.3s r.ns.2 v.pai.2s n.asf crasis v.pai.1s n.apn v.aam.2s r.ds.1 r.gs.2 d.asf n.asf
2240 1639 3738 247 5516 3306 5148 2400 4411 2743 2400 2240 1259 1609 5148 3836 4411

[7] οὐκ αὐτοὶ βλασφημοῦσιν τὸ καλὸν ὄνομα τὸ ἐπικληθὲν ἐφ᾽ ὑμᾶς; ¶ [8] εἰ μέντοι νόμον τελεῖτε βασιλικὸν κατὰ τὴν γραφήν, ᾽Αγαπήσεις τὸν πλησίον σου ὡς σεαυτόν, καλῶς ποιεῖτε· [9] εἰ δὲ προσωπολημπτεῖτε, ἁμαρτίαν ἐργάζεσθε ἐλεγχόμενοι ὑπὸ τοῦ νόμου ὡς παραβάται. [10] ὅστις γὰρ ὅλον τὸν νόμον τηρήσῃ πταίσῃ δὲ ἐν ἑνί, γέγονεν πάντων ἔνοχος. [11] ὁ γὰρ εἰπών, Μὴ μοιχεύσῃς, εἶπεν καί, Μὴ φονεύσῃς· εἰ δὲ οὐ μοιχεύεις φονεύεις δέ, γέγονας παραβάτης νόμου. ¶ [12] οὕτως λαλεῖτε καὶ οὕτως ποιεῖτε ὡς διὰ νόμου ἐλευθερίας μέλλοντες κρίνεσθαι. [13] ἡ γὰρ κρίσις ἀνέλεος τῷ μὴ ποιήσαντι ἔλεος· κατακαυχᾶται ἔλεος κρίσεως.

[2:14] Τί τὸ ὄφελος, ἀδελφοί μου, ἐὰν πίστιν λέγῃ τις ἔχειν ἔργα δὲ μὴ ἔχῃ; μὴ δύναται ἡ πίστις σῶσαι αὐτόν; [15] ἐὰν ἀδελφὸς ἢ ἀδελφὴ γυμνοὶ ὑπάρχωσιν καὶ λειπόμενοι τῆς ἐφημέρου τροφῆς [16] εἴπῃ δέ τις αὐτοῖς ἐξ ὑμῶν, ῾Υπάγετε ἐν εἰρήνῃ, θερμαίνεσθε καὶ χορτάζεσθε, μὴ δῶτε δὲ αὐτοῖς τὰ ἐπιτήδεια τοῦ σώματος, τί τὸ ὄφελος; [17] οὕτως καὶ ἡ πίστις, ἐὰν μὴ ἔχῃ ἔργα, νεκρά ἐστιν καθ᾽ ἑαυτήν. ¶ [18] ᾽Αλλ᾽ ἐρεῖ τις, Σὺ πίστιν ἔχεις, κἀγὼ ἔργα ἔχω· δεῖξόν μοι τὴν πίστιν σου χωρὶς τῶν ἔργων, κἀγώ σοι δείξω

without deeds,　and I　　will show you　my　faith　　　by　what I do.　¹⁹You believe that there is　one
χωρὶς　ᴛῶν ἔργωνᴖ　→　καγώ　→　δείξω　σοι　μου　ᴛτὴν πίστινᴖ　ἐκ　→　→ ᴛῶν ἔργωνᴖ　σὺ　πιστεύεις ὅτι　→　　ἔστιν　εἷς
p.g　d.gpn n.gpn　　cj　　v.fai.1s　r.ds.2　r.gs.1　d.asf n.asf　p.g　　　d.gpn n.gpn　r.ns.2　v.pai.2s　cj　　v.pai.3s a.nsm
6006　3836 2240　　2743　　1259　5148　1609　3836 4411　1666　　3836 2240　5148　4409　4022　　1639　1651

God.　　Good!　Even the demons believe　　that – and shudder.　¶　²⁰　　You foolish man,　do you
ὁ　θεός,　ποιεῖς καλῶς καὶ　τὰ　δαιμόνια πιστεύουσιν　καὶ　φρίσσουσιν　　δὲ　ὦ　κενέ　ἄνθρωπε　→　→
d.nsm　n.nsm　v.pai.2s　adv　adv　d.npn　n.npn　v.pai.3p　　cj　v.pai.3p　　　　cj　　a.vsm　n.vsm
3836　2536　4472　2822　2779　3836 1228　4409　　2779　5857　　　1254　6043　3031　476

want evidence that faith　　without deeds　is useless?　²¹Was not our　ancestor Abraham considered righteous
Θέλεις γνῶναι　ὅτι ἡ πίστις ᴛχωρὶς　ᴛῶν ἔργωνᴖ　ἐστιν ἀργή　　οὐκ ἡμῶν ὁ πατήρᴖ Ἀβραὰμ　→　ἐδικαιώθη
v.pai.2s　f.aa　　cj　d.nsf n.nsf　p.g　　d.gpn n.gpn　v.pai.3s a.nsf　　pl　r.gp.1　d.nsm n.nsm　n.nsm　　v.api.3s
2527　1182　　4022　3836 4411　6006　3836 2240　1639　734　　1467　4024 7005 3836 4252　11　　　　1467

for what he did　when he offered　his　son　Isaac on the altar?　²²You see　　that his faith and his
ἐξ　→　→ ἔργων　→　→ ἀνενέγκας αὐτοῦ τὸν υἱὸν　Ἰσαὰκ ἐπὶ τὸ θυσιαστήριον　→　βλέπεις ὅτι ἡ πίστις καὶ αὐτοῦ
p.g　　n.gpn　　　pt.aa.nsm r.gsm.3 d.asm n.asm　n.asm　p.a d.asn n.asn　　v.pai.2s　cj　d.nsf n.nsf cj r.gsm.3
1666　2240　　　　899　899　3836 5626　2693　2093 3836 2603　　　1063　4022 3836 4411 2779 899

actions　　were working together, and his faith　was made complete by what he did.　²³And the scripture was
ᴛτοῖς ἔργοιςᴖ　→ συνήργει ←　　ἡ πίστις　ἐτελειώθη ἐκ　→ → ᴛῶν ἔργωνᴖ　καὶ ἡ γραφὴ
d.dpn n.dpn　　v.iai.3s　　　　d.nsf n.nsf　v.api.3s　p.g　　　d.gpn n.gpn　cj d.nsf n.nsf
3836 2240　　5300　　　　　3836 4411　5457　1666　　　3836 2240　2779 3836 1210

fulfilled that says,　　"Abraham believed God,　　and it was credited to him as righteousness," and he was
ἐπληρώθη ἡ λέγουσα δὲ Ἀβραὰμ　ἐπίστευσεν ᴛτῷ θεῷᴖ καὶ → → ἐλογίσθη → αὐτῷ εἰς δικαιοσύνην　καὶ → →
v.api.3s d.nsf pt.pa.nsf cj n.nsm　v.aai.3s d.dsm n.dsm cj　v.api.3s　r.dsm.3 p.a n.asf　cj
4444 3836 3306 1254 11　4409 3836 2536 2779　3357　899 1650 1466　2779

called God's friend.　²⁴You see　that a person　is justified by what he does and not by faith　alone.　¶　²⁵　In
ἐκλήθη θεοῦ φίλος　→ ὁρᾶτε ὅτι　ἄνθρωπος → δικαιοῦται ἐξ → → ἔργων καὶ οὐκ ἐκ πίστεως μόνον　δὲ →
v.api.3s n.gsm a.nsm　v.pai.2p cj　n.nsm　v.ppi.3s p.g　　n.gpn cj pl p.g n.gsf adv　cj
2813 2536 5813　3972 4022　476　1467　1666　　2240 2779 4024 1666 4411 3667　1254

the same way, was not even Rahab the prostitute considered righteous for what she did　when she gave lodging
→ ὁμοίως ←　οὐκ καὶ Ῥαὰβ ἡ πόρνη　→ ἐδικαιώθη ἐξ → → ἔργων　→ ὑποδεξαμένη
adv　　pl adv n.nsf d.nsf n.nsf　　v.api.3s p.g　　n.gpn　　pt.am.nsf
3931　1467 2779 4805 3836 4520　1467　1666　　2240　　5685

to the spies　and sent　them off in a different direction?　²⁶　As the body without the spirit is dead,
← τοὺς ἀγγέλους καὶ ἐκβαλοῦσα ←　ἑτέρᾳ ὁδῷ　γὰρ ὥσπερ τὸ σῶμα χωρὶς　πνεύματος ἐστιν νεκρόν
d.apm n.apm cj pt.aa.nsf　　r.dsf n.dsf　cj cj d.nsn n.nsn p.g　n.gsn v.pai.3s a.nsn
3836 34 2779 1675　　2283 3847　1142 6061 3836 5393 6006　4460 1639 3738

so　faith　without deeds is dead.
οὕτως καὶ ἡ πίστις χωρὶς ἔργων ἐστιν νεκρά
adv adv d.nsf n.nsf p.g n.gpn v.pai.3s a.nsf
4048 2779 3836 4411 6006 2240 1639 3738

Taming the Tongue

³:¹Not many of you should presume to be　teachers, my brothers, because you know that we who teach will
Μὴ πολλοὶ　→ γίνεσθε διδάσκαλοι μου ἀδελφοί → → εἰδότες ὅτι →
pl a.npm　v.pmm.2p n.npm r.gs.1 n.vpm　　pt.ra.npm cj
3590 4498　1181 1437 1609 81　　3857 4022

be　judged more strictly.　²We all　stumble in many ways. If anyone is　never at fault in what he says,
λημψόμεθα κρίμα μεῖζον ←　γὰρ → ἅπαντες πταίομεν → πολλὰ　εἴ τις　→ οὐ → πταίει ἐν → λόγῳ
v.fmi.1p n.asn a.asn.c　cj　　a.npm v.pai.1p　a.apn　cj r.nsm　pl　v.pai.3s p.a　n.dsm
3284 3210 3489　1142　570 4760　4498　1623 5516　4024　1877　n.dsm 3364

he is a perfect man, able　to keep　his whole body in check.　¶　³　When we put
οὗτος τέλειος ἀνὴρ δυνατὸς → χαλιναγωγῆσαι καὶ τὸ ὅλον σῶμα ←　δὲ εἰ → βάλλομεν
r.nsm a.nsm n.nsm a.nsm　f.aa　adv d.asn a.asn n.asn　　cj cj　v.pai.1p
4047 5455 467 1543　5902　2779 3836 3910 5393 5902 5902　1254 1623　965

bits　into the mouths of horses　to make them obey　us,　we can turn　the whole
ᴛτοὺς χαλινοὺςᴖ εἰς τὰ στόματα → ᴛῶν ἵππωνᴖ εἰς →　αὐτοὺς ᴛτὸ πείθεσθαιᴖ ἡμῖν καὶ →　μετάγομεν τὸ ὅλον
d.apm n.apm p.a d.apn n.apn　d.gpm n.gpn p.a　r.apm.3 d.asn f.pp r.dp.1 adv　v.pai.1p d.asn a.asn
3836 5903 1650 3836 5125　3836 2691 1650 4275　899 3836 4275 7005 2779　3555 3836 3910

ἐκ τῶν ἔργων μου τὴν πίστιν. ¹⁹ σὺ πιστεύεις ὅτι εἷς ἐστιν ὁ θεός, καλῶς ποιεῖς· καὶ τὰ δαιμόνια πιστεύουσιν καὶ φρίσσουσιν ¶ ²⁰ θέλεις δὲ γνῶναι, ὦ ἄνθρωπε κενέ, ὅτι ἡ πίστις χωρὶς τῶν ἔργων ἀργή ἐστιν; ²¹ Ἀβραὰμ ὁ πατὴρ ἡμῶν οὐκ ἐξ ἔργων ἐδικαιώθη ἀνενέγκας Ἰσαὰκ τὸν υἱὸν αὐτοῦ ἐπὶ τὸ θυσιαστήριον; ²² βλέπεις ὅτι ἡ πίστις συνήργει τοῖς ἔργοις αὐτοῦ καὶ ἐκ τῶν ἔργων ἡ πίστις ἐτελειώθη, ²³ καὶ ἐπληρώθη ἡ γραφὴ ἡ λέγουσα, Ἐπίστευσεν δὲ Ἀβραὰμ τῷ θεῷ, καὶ ἐλογίσθη αὐτῷ εἰς δικαιοσύνην καὶ φίλος θεοῦ ἐκλήθη. ²⁴ ὁρᾶτε ὅτι ἐξ ἔργων δικαιοῦται ἄνθρωπος καὶ οὐκ ἐκ πίστεως μόνον. ¶ ²⁵ ὁμοίως δὲ καὶ Ῥαὰβ ἡ πόρνη οὐκ ἐξ ἔργων ἐδικαιώθη ὑποδεξαμένη τοὺς ἀγγέλους καὶ ἑτέρᾳ ὁδῷ ἐκβαλοῦσα; ²⁶ ὥσπερ γὰρ τὸ σῶμα χωρὶς πνεύματος νεκρόν ἐστιν, οὕτως καὶ ἡ πίστις χωρὶς ἔργων νεκρά ἐστιν.

³:¹ Μὴ πολλοὶ διδάσκαλοι γίνεσθε, ἀδελφοί μου, εἰδότες ὅτι μεῖζον κρίμα λημψόμεθα. ² πολλὰ γὰρ πταίομεν ἅπαντες. εἴ τις ἐν λόγῳ οὐ πταίει, οὗτος τέλειος ἀνὴρ δυνατὸς χαλιναγωγῆσαι καὶ ὅλον τὸ σῶμα. ¶ ³ εἰ δὲ τῶν ἵππων τοὺς χαλινοὺς εἰς τὰ στόματα βάλλομεν εἰς τὸ πείθεσθαι αὐτοὺς ἡμῖν, καὶ ὅλον τὸ σῶμα αὐτῶν μετάγομεν. ⁴ ἰδοὺ καὶ τὰ πλοῖα τηλικαῦτα ὄντα

animal. **4** Or take ships as an example. Although they are so large and are driven by strong

σῶμα	αὐτῶν	ἰδοὺ	καὶ	τὰ	πλοῖα				ὄντα		τηλικαῦτα	καὶ		ἐλαυνόμενα	ὑπὸ	σκληρῶν
n.asn	r.gpm.3	j	adv	d.npn	n.npn				pt.pa.npn		r.npn	cj		pt.pp.npn	p.g	a.gpm
5393	899	2627	2779	3836	4450				1639		5496	2779		1785	5679	5017

winds, they are steered by a very small rudder wherever the pilot wants to go. **5** Likewise

ἀνέμων			μετάγεται	ὑπὸ		ἐλαχίστου	πηδαλίου	ὅπου		ἡ	ὁρμὴ	τοῦ	εὐθύνοντος	βούλεται		οὕτως	καὶ
n.gpm			v.ppi.3s	p.g		a.gsn.s	n.gsn	cj		d.nsf	n.nsf	d.gsn	pt.pa.gsm	v.pmi.3s		adv	adv
449			3555	5679		1788	4382	3963		3836	3995	3836	2316	1089		4048	2779

the tongue is a small part of the body, but it makes great boasts. Consider what a great forest is set on

ἡ	γλῶσσα	ἐστὶν	μικρὸν	μέλος		καὶ			μεγάλα	αὐχεῖ	ἰδοὺ		ἡλίκην	ὕλην		ἀνάπτει
d.nsf	n.nsf	v.pai.3s	a.nsn	n.nsn		cj			a.apn	v.pai.3s	j		a.asf	n.asf		v.pai.3s
3836	1185	1639	3625	3517		2779	902 902		3489	902	2627		2462	5627		409

fire by a small spark. **6** The tongue also is a fire, a world of evil among the *parts* of

	ἡλίκον	πῦρ	ἡ	γλῶσσα	καὶ		πῦρ	ὁ	κόσμος	τῆς ἀδικίας		ἡ	γλῶσσα	καθίσταται	ἐν	τοῖς	μέλεσιν
	a.nsn	n.nsn	d.nsf	n.nsf	cj		n.nsn	d.nsm	n.nsm	d.gsf n.gsf		d.nsf	n.nsf	v.pmi.3s	p.d	d.dpn	n.dpn
	2462	4786	3836	1185	2779		4786	3836	3180	3836 94		3836	1185	2770	1877	3836	3517

the body. It corrupts the whole person, sets the whole course of his life on fire, and is itself set

ἡμῶν	ἡ	σπιλοῦσα	τὸ	ὅλον	σῶμα	καὶ		τὸν τρόχον		τῆς	γενέσεως		φλογίζουσα	καὶ	
r.gp.1	d.nsf	pt.pa.nsf	d.asn	a.asn	n.asn	cj		d.asm n.asm		d.gsf	n.gsf		pt.pa.nsf	cj	
7005	3836	5071	3836	3910	5393	2779	5824	3836 5580		3836	1161		5824	2779	

on fire by hell. ¶ **7** All kinds of animals, birds, reptiles and creatures of the sea

	φλογιζομένη	ὑπὸ	τῆς γεέννης		γὰρ	πᾶσα	φύσις	τε	θηρίων	καὶ	πετεινῶν	τε	ἐρπετῶν	καὶ	ἐναλίων
	pt.pp.nsf	p.g	d.gsf n.gsf		cj	a.nsf	n.nsf	cj	n.gpn	cj	n.gpn	cj	n.gpn	cj	n.gpn
	5824	5679	3836 1147		1142	4246	5882	2563	5445	2563	2779	4374	5445	2260	2779	1879

are being tamed and have been tamed by man, **8** but no man can tame the

		δαμάζεται	καὶ		δεδάμασται	τῇ	φύσει	τῇ ἀνθρωπίνη	δὲ	οὐδεὶς	ἀνθρώπων	δύναται	δαμάσαι	τὴν
		v.ppi.3s	cj		v.rpi.3s	d.dsf	n.dsf	d.dsf a.dsf	cj	a.nsm	n.gpm	v.ppi.3s	f.aa	d.asf
		1238	2779		1238	3836	5882	3836 474	1254	4029	476	1538	1238	3836

tongue. It is a restless evil, full of deadly poison. ¶ **9** With the tongue we praise our Lord and

γλῶσσαν	ἀκατάστατον	κακόν	μεστὴ		θανατηφόρου	ἰοῦ		ἐν	αὐτῇ		εὐλογοῦμεν	τὸν	κύριον	καὶ
n.asf	a.nsn	a.nsn	a.nsf		a.gsn	n.gsm		p.d	r.dsf.3		v.pai.1p	d.asm	n.asm	cj
1185	190	2805	3550		2504	2675		1877	899		2328	3836	3261	2779

Father, and with it we curse men, who have been made in God's likeness. **10** Out of the same

πατέρα	καὶ	ἐν	αὐτῇ	καταρώμεθα	τοὺς ἀνθρώπους	τοὺς			γεγονότας	καθ᾽	θεοῦ	ὁμοίωσιν	ἐκ		τοῦ αὐτοῦ
n.asm	cj	p.d	r.dsf.3	v.pmi.1p	d.apm n.apm	d.apm			pt.ra.apm	p.a	n.gsm	n.asf	p.g		d.gsn r.gsn
4252	2779	1877	899	2933	3836 476	3836			1181	2848	2536	3932	1666		3836 899

mouth come praise and cursing. My brothers, this should not be. **11** Can both fresh water and

στόματος	ἐξέρχεται	εὐλογία	καὶ	κατάρα	μου	ἀδελφοί	ταῦτα	χρὴ	οὐ	οὕτως	γίνεσθαι	μήτι		τὸ γλυκὺ		καὶ
n.gsn	v.pmi.3s	n.nsf	cj	n.nsf	r.gs.1	n.vpm	r.npn	v.pai.3s	pl	adv	f.pm	pl		d.asn a.asn		cj
5125	2002	2330	2779	2932	1609	81	4047	5973	4024	4048	1181	3614		3836 1184		2779

salt water flow from the same spring? **12** My brothers, can a fig tree bear olives, or a grapevine

τὸ πικρὸν		βρύει	ἐκ	τῆς	αὐτῆς	ὀπῆς	ἡ	πηγή	μου	ἀδελφοί	μὴ	δύναται	συκῆ		ποιῆσαι	ἐλαίας	ἢ	ἄμπελος
d.asn a.asn		v.pai.3s	p.g	d.gsf	r.gsf	n.gsf	d.nsf	n.nsf	r.gs.1	n.vpm	pl	v.ppi.3s	n.nsf		f.aa	n.apf	cj	n.nsf
3836 4395		1108	1666	3836	899	4380	3836	4380	1609	81	3590	1538	5190		4472	1777	2445	306

bear figs? Neither can a salt spring produce fresh water.

σῦκα	οὔτε		ἁλυκὸν		ποιῆσαι	γλυκὺ	ὕδωρ
n.apn	adv		a.nsn		f.aa	a.asn	n.asn
5192	4046		266		4472	1184	5623

Two Kinds of Wisdom

3:13 Who is wise and understanding among you? Let him show it by his good life, by deeds done

Τίς	σοφὸς	καὶ	ἐπιστήμων	ἐν	ὑμῖν		δειξάτω	ἐκ	τῆς	καλῆς	ἀναστροφῆς	τὰ ἔργα	αὐτοῦ
r.nsm	a.nsm	cj	a.nsm	p.d	r.dp.2		v.aam.3s	p.g	d.gsf	a.gsf	n.gsf	d.apn n.apn	r.gsm.3
5515	5055	2779	2184	1877	7007		1259	1666	3836	2819	419	3836 2240	899

in the humility that comes from wisdom. **14** But if you harbor bitter envy and selfish ambition in your hearts,

ἐν	πραΰτητι			σοφίας	δὲ	εἰ		ἔχετε	πικρὸν	ζῆλον	καὶ	ἐριθείαν		ἐν	ὑμῶν	τῇ καρδίᾳ
p.d	n.dsf			n.gsf	cj	cj		v.pai.2p	a.asm	n.asm	cj	n.asm		p.d	r.gp.2	d.dsf n.dsf
1877	4559			5053	1254	1623		2400	4395	2419	2779	2249		1877	7007	3836 2840

καὶ ὑπὸ ἀνέμων σκληρῶν ἐλαυνόμενα, μετάγεται ὑπὸ ἐλαχίστου πηδαλίου ὅπου ἡ ὁρμὴ τοῦ εὐθύνοντος βούλεται, ⁵ οὕτως καὶ ἡ γλῶσσα μικρὸν μέλος ἐστὶν καὶ μεγάλα αὐχεῖ. Ἰδοὺ ἡλίκον πῦρ ἡλίκην ὕλην ἀνάπτει· ⁶ καὶ ἡ γλῶσσα πῦρ· ὁ κόσμος τῆς ἀδικίας ἡ γλῶσσα καθίσταται ἐν τοῖς μέλεσιν ἡμῶν, ἡ σπιλοῦσα ὅλον τὸ σῶμα καὶ φλογίζουσα τὸν τροχὸν τῆς γενέσεως καὶ φλογιζομένη ὑπὸ τῆς γεέννης. ¶ ⁷ πᾶσα γὰρ φύσις θηρίων τε καὶ πετεινῶν, ἑρπετῶν τε καὶ ἐναλίων δαμάζεται καὶ δεδάμασται τῇ φύσει τῇ ἀνθρωπίνῃ, ⁸ τὴν δὲ γλῶσσαν οὐδεὶς δαμάσαι δύναται ἀνθρώπων, ἀκατάστατον κακόν, μεστὴ ἰοῦ θανατηφόρου. ¶ ⁹ ἐν αὐτῇ εὐλογοῦμεν τὸν κύριον καὶ πατέρα καὶ ἐν αὐτῇ καταρώμεθα τοὺς ἀνθρώπους τοὺς καθ᾽ ὁμοίωσιν θεοῦ γεγονότας, ¹⁰ ἐκ τοῦ αὐτοῦ στόματος ἐξέρχεται εὐλογία καὶ κατάρα. οὐ χρή, ἀδελφοί μου, ταῦτα οὕτως γίνεσθαι. ¹¹ μήτι ἡ πηγὴ ἐκ τῆς αὐτῆς ὀπῆς βρύει τὸ γλυκὺ καὶ τὸ πικρόν; ¹² μὴ δύναται, ἀδελφοί μου, συκῆ ἐλαίας ποιῆσαι ἢ ἄμπελος σῦκα; οὔτε ἁλυκὸν γλυκὺ ποιῆσαι ὕδωρ.

³·¹³ Τίς σοφὸς καὶ ἐπιστήμων ἐν ὑμῖν; δειξάτω ἐκ τῆς καλῆς ἀναστροφῆς τὰ ἔργα αὐτοῦ ἐν πραΰτητι σοφίας. ¹⁴ εἰ δὲ ζῆλον

do not boast about it or deny the truth. 15 Such "wisdom" does not come down from heaven
↱ μὴ κατακαυχᾶσθε καὶ ψεύδεσθε κατὰ τῆς ἀληθείας αὕτη ⌊ἡ σοφία⌋ ἔστιν οὐκ κατερχομένη ← ← ἄνωθεν
pl v.pmm.2p cj v.pmm.2p p.g d.gsf n.gsf r.nsf d.nsf n.nsf v.pai.3s pl pt.pm.nsf adv
2878 3590 2878 2779 6017 2848 3836 237 4047 3836 5053 1639 4024 2982 540

but is earthly, unspiritual, of the devil. 16 For where you have envy and selfish ambition, there you find
ἀλλὰ ἐπίγειος ψυχική → δαιμονιώδης γὰρ ὅπου ζῆλος καὶ ἐριθεία ← ἐκεῖ
cj a.nsf a.nsf a.nsf cj cj n.nsm cj n.nsf adv
247 2103 6035 1229 1142 3963 2419 2779 2249 1695

disorder and every evil practice. ¶ 17 But the wisdom that comes from heaven is first of all pure;
ἀκαταστασία καὶ πᾶν φαῦλον πρᾶγμα δὲ ἡ σοφία → → ἄνωθεν ἐστιν μὲν πρῶτον ← ← ἁγνή
n.nsf cj a.nsn a.nsn n.nsn cj d.nsf n.nsf adv v.pai.3s pl adv a.nsf
189 2779 4246 5765 4547 1254 3836 5053 540 1639 3525 4754 54

then peace-loving, considerate, submissive, full of mercy and good fruit, impartial and sincere. 18
ἔπειτα εἰρηνική ἐπιεικής εὐπειθής μεστὴ → ἐλέους καὶ ἀγαθῶν καρπῶν ἀδιάκριτος ἀνυπόκριτος δὲ
adv a.nsf a.nsf a.nsf a.nsf n.gsn cj a.gpm n.gpm a.nsf a.nsf cj
2083 1646 2117 2340 3550 1799 2779 19 2843 88 537 1254

Peacemakers who sow in peace raise a harvest of righteousness.
⌊τοῖς ποιοῦσιν εἰρήνην⌋ ← σπείρεται ἐν εἰρήνῃ καρπὸς → δικαιοσύνης
d.dpm pt.pa.dpm n.asf v.ppi.3s p.d n.dsf n.nsm n.gsf
3836 4472 1645 5062 1877 1645 2843 1466

Submit Yourselves to God

4:1 What causes fights and quarrels among you? Don't they come from your desires that
Πόθεν ← πόλεμοι καὶ πόθεν μάχαι ἐν ὑμῖν οὐκ ἐντεῦθεν ἐκ ὑμῶν ⌊τῶν ἡδονῶν⌋ τῶν
cj n.npm cj cj n.npf p.d r.dp.2 pl adv p.g r.gp.2 d.gpf n.gpf d.gpf
4470 4483 2779 4470 3480 1877 7007 4024 1949 1666 7007 3836 2454 3836

battle within you? 2 You want something but don't get it. You kill and covet, but you
στρατευομένων ἐν ⌊τοῖς μέλεσιν ὑμῶν⌋ → ἐπιθυμεῖτε καὶ οὐκ ἔχετε → φονεύετε καὶ ζηλοῦτε καὶ ↱
pt.pm.gpf p.d d.dpn n.dpn r.gp.2 v.pai.2p cj pl v.pai.2p v.pai.2p cj v.pai.2p cj
5129 1877 3836 3517 7007 2121 2779 4024 2400 5839 2779 2420 2779 1538

cannot have what you want. You quarrel and fight. You do not have, because you do not ask
⌊οὐ δύνασθε⌋ → → ἐπιτυχεῖν → μάχεσθε καὶ πολεμεῖτε ↱ ↱ οὐκ ἔχετε διὰ ὑμᾶς ↱ μὴ ⌊τὸ αἰτεῖσθαι⌋
pl v.ppi.2p f.aa v.pmi.2p cj v.pai.2p pl v.pai.2p p.a r.ap.2 pl d.asn f.pm
4024 1538 2209 3481 2779 4482 2400 160 4024 2400 1328 7007 160 3590 3836 160

God. 3 When you ask, you do not receive, because you ask with wrong motives, that you may spend
→ αἰτεῖτε καὶ ↱ ↱ οὐ λαμβάνετε διότι → αἰτεῖσθε → κακῶς ← ἵνα → → δαπανήσητε
v.pai.2p cj pl v.pai.2p cj v.pmi.2p adv cj v.aas.2p
160 2779 3284 3284 4024 3284 1484 160 2809 2671 1251

what you get on your pleasures. ¶ 4 You adulterous people, don't you know that friendship with the world
ἐν ὑμῶν ⌊ταῖς ἡδοναῖς⌋ → μοιχαλίδες ← οὐκ → οἴδατε ὅτι ⌊ἡ φιλία⌋ → τοῦ κόσμου
p.d r.gp.2 d.dpf n.dpf n.vpf pl v.rai.2p cj d.nsf n.nsf d.gsm n.gsm
1877 7007 3836 2454 3655 4024 3857 4022 3836 5802 3836 3180

is hatred toward God? Anyone who chooses to be a friend of the world becomes an enemy of God.
ἐστιν ἔχθρα → ⌊τοῦ θεοῦ⌋ οὖν ⌊ὃς ἐὰν⌋ ← βουληθῇ → εἶναι φίλος → τοῦ κόσμου καθίσταται ἐχθρὸς → ⌊τοῦ θεοῦ⌋
v.pai.3s n.nsf d.gsm n.gsm cj r.nsm pl v.aps.3s f.pa a.nsm d.gsm n.gsm v.ppi.3s a.nsm d.gsm n.gsm
1639 2397 3836 2536 4036 4005 1569 1089 1639 5813 3836 3180 2770 2398 3836 2536

5 Or do you think Scripture says without reason that the spirit he caused to live in us *envies*
ἢ → → δοκεῖτε ὅτι ⌊ἡ γραφὴ⌋ λέγει κενῶς τὸ πνεῦμα ὃ → → → κατῴκισεν ἐν ἡμῖν ἐπιποθεῖ
cj v.pai.2p cj d.nsf n.nsf v.pai.3s adv v.aai.3s p.d r.dp.1 v.pai.3s
2445 1506 4022 3836 1210 3306 3036 3836 4460 4005 3001 1877 7005 2160

intensely? 6 But he gives us more grace. That is why Scripture says: "God opposes the proud but
⌊πρὸς φθόνον⌋ δὲ → δίδωσιν μείζονα χάριν διὸ ← ← λέγει ⌊ὁ θεὸς⌋ ἀντιτάσσεται ὑπερηφάνοις δὲ
p.a n.asm cj v.pai.3s a.asf.c n.asf cj v.pai.3s d.nsm n.nsm v.pmi.3s a.dpm cj
4639 5784 1254 1443 3489 5921 1475 3306 3836 2536 530 5662 1254

gives grace to the humble." ¶ 7 Submit yourselves, then, to God. Resist the devil, and he will
δίδωσιν χάριν → ταπεινοῖς ὑποτάγητε ← οὖν → ⌊τῷ θεῷ⌋ δὲ ἀντίστητε τῷ διαβόλῳ καὶ → →
v.pai.3s n.asf a.dpm v.apm.2p cj d.dsm n.dsm cj v.aam.2p d.dsm n.dsm cj
1443 5921 5424 5718 4036 3836 2536 1254 468 3836 1333 2779

πικρὸν ἔχετε καὶ ἐριθείαν ἐν τῇ καρδίᾳ ὑμῶν, μὴ κατακαυχᾶσθε καὶ ψεύδεσθε κατὰ τῆς ἀληθείας. 15 οὐκ ἔστιν αὕτη ἡ σοφία
ἄνωθεν κατερχομένη ἀλλὰ ἐπίγειος, ψυχική, δαιμονιώδης. 16 ὅπου γὰρ ζῆλος καὶ ἐριθεία, ἐκεῖ ἀκαταστασία καὶ πᾶν φαῦλον
πρᾶγμα. ¶ 17 ἡ δὲ ἄνωθεν σοφία πρῶτον μὲν ἁγνή ἐστιν, ἔπειτα εἰρηνική, ἐπιεικής, εὐπειθής, μεστὴ ἐλέους καὶ καρπῶν ἀγαθῶν,
ἀδιάκριτος, ἀνυπόκριτος. 18 καρπὸς δὲ δικαιοσύνης ἐν εἰρήνῃ σπείρεται τοῖς ποιοῦσιν εἰρήνην.
4:1 Πόθεν πόλεμοι καὶ πόθεν μάχαι ἐν ὑμῖν; οὐκ ἐντεῦθεν, ἐκ τῶν ἡδονῶν ὑμῶν τῶν στρατευομένων ἐν τοῖς μέλεσιν ὑμῶν;
2 ἐπιθυμεῖτε καὶ οὐκ ἔχετε, φονεύετε καὶ ζηλοῦτε καὶ οὐ δύνασθε ἐπιτυχεῖν, μάχεσθε καὶ πολεμεῖτε, οὐκ ἔχετε διὰ τὸ μὴ αἰτεῖσθαι
ὑμᾶς, 3 αἰτεῖτε καὶ οὐ λαμβάνετε διότι κακῶς αἰτεῖσθε, ἵνα ἐν ταῖς ἡδοναῖς ὑμῶν δαπανήσητε. ¶ 4 μοιχαλίδες, οὐκ οἴδατε
ὅτι ἡ φιλία τοῦ κόσμου ἔχθρα τοῦ θεοῦ ἐστιν; ὃς ἐὰν οὖν βουληθῇ φίλος εἶναι τοῦ κόσμου, ἐχθρὸς τοῦ θεοῦ καθίσταται. 5 ἢ
δοκεῖτε ὅτι κενῶς ἡ γραφὴ λέγει, Πρὸς φθόνον ἐπιποθεῖ τὸ πνεῦμα ὃ κατῴκισεν ἐν ἡμῖν, 6 μείζονα δὲ δίδωσιν χάριν; διὸ λέγει,
Ὁ θεὸς ὑπερηφάνοις ἀντιτάσσεται, ταπεινοῖς δὲ δίδωσιν χάριν. ¶ 7 ὑποτάγητε οὖν τῷ θεῷ, ἀντίστητε δὲ τῷ διαβόλῳ καὶ

flee from you. **8** Come near to God and he will come near to you. Wash your hands, you sinners, and
φεύξεται ἀφ᾽ ὑμῶν ἐγγίσατε ← → ˻τῷ θεῷ˼ καὶ → ἐγγιεῖ → ὑμῖν καθαρίσατε χεῖρας → ἁμαρτωλοί καὶ
v.fmi.3s p.g r.gp.2 v.aam.2p d.dsm n.dsm cj v.fai.3s r.dp.2 v.aam.2p n.apf a.vpm cj
5771 608 7007 1581 3836 2536 2779 1581 7007 2751 5931 283 2779

purify your hearts, you double-minded. **9** Grieve, mourn and wail. Change your laughter to
ἁγνίσατε καρδίας → δίψυχοι ταλαιπωρήσατε καὶ πενθήσατε καὶ κλαύσατε μετατραπήτω ὑμῶν ὁ γέλως εἰς
v.aam.2p n.apf a.vpm v.aam.2p cj v.aam.2p cj v.aam.2p v.apm.3s r.gp.2 d.nsm n.nsm p.a
49 2840 1500 5415 2779 4291 2779 3081 3573 7007 3836 1152 1650

mourning and your joy to gloom. **10** Humble yourselves before the Lord, and he will lift you up. ¶
πένθος καὶ ἡ χαρὰ εἰς κατήφειαν ταπεινώθητε ← ἐνώπιον κυρίου καὶ → ὑψώσει ὑμᾶς
n.asn cj d.nsf n.nsf p.a n.asf v.apm.2p p.g n.gsm cj v.fai.3s r.ap.2
4292 2779 3836 5915 1650 2993 5427 1967 3261 2779 5738 7007 5738

11 Brothers, do not slander one another. Anyone who speaks against his brother or judges him
ἀδελφοί → Μὴ καταλαλεῖτε ἀλλήλων ← ὁ → καταλαλῶν ← αὐτοῦ ἀδελφοῦ ἢ κρίνων ˻τὸν ἀδελφὸν˼
n.vpm pl v.pam.2p r.gpm d.nsm pt.pa.nsm r.gsm.3 n.gsm cj pt.pa.nsm d.asm n.asm
81 3590 2895 253 3836 2895 899 81 2445 3212 3836 81

speaks against the law and judges it. When you judge the law, you are not keeping it, but sitting in
καταλαλεῖ ← νόμου καὶ κρίνει νόμον δὲ εἰ → κρίνεις νόμον → εἰ οὐκ ποιητὴς νόμου ἀλλὰ →
v.pai.3s n.gsm cj v.pai.3s n.asm cj cj v.pai.2s n.asm v.pai.2s pl n.nsm n.gsm cj
2895 3795 2779 3212 3795 1254 1623 3212 3795 1639 4024 4475 3795 247

judgment on it. **12** There is only one Lawgiver and Judge, the one who is able to save and destroy. But
κριτής → ἐστιν εἷς ˻ὁ νομοθέτης˼ καὶ κριτής ὁ ← ← δυνάμενος σῶσαι καὶ ἀπολέσαι δὲ
n.nsm v.pai.3s a.nsm d.nsm n.nsm cj n.nsm d.nsm pt.pp.nsm f.aa cj f.aa cj
3216 1639 1651 3836 3794 2779 3216 3836 1538 5392 2779 660 1254

you – who are you to judge your neighbor?
σὺ τίς εἶ ← ὁ κρίνων τὸν πλησίον
r.ns.2 r.nsm v.pai.2s d.vsm pt.pa.vsm d.asm adv
5148 5515 1639 3836 3212 3836 4446

Boasting About Tomorrow

4:13 Now listen, you who say, "Today or tomorrow we will go to this or that city, spend
νῦν Ἄγε οἱ λέγοντες σήμερον ἢ αὔριον → πορευσόμεθα εἰς τήνδε ← ← ˻τὴν πόλιν˼ καὶ ποιήσομεν
adv v.pam.2s d.vpm pt.pa.vpm adv cj adv v.fmi.1p p.a r.asf d.asf n.asf cj v.fai.1p
3814 72 3836 3306 4958 2445 892 4513 1650 3840 3836 4484 2779 4472

a year there, carry on business and make money." **14** Why, you do not even know what will
ἐνιαυτὸν ἐκεῖ καὶ → ἐμπορευσόμεθα καὶ → κερδήσομεν οἵτινες → → οὐκ ἐπίστασθε τὸ
n.asm adv cj v.fmi.1p cj v.fai.1p r.npm pl v.ppi.2p d.asn
1929 1695 2779 1864 2779 3045 4015 2179 2179 4024 2179 3836

happen tomorrow. What is your life? You are a mist that appears for a little while and then vanishes.
← ˻τῆς αὔριον˼ ποία ὑμῶν ἡ ζωὴ γάρ → ἐστε ἀτμὶς ἡ φαινομένη πρὸς ὀλίγον ← καὶ ἔπειτα ἀφανιζομένη
d.gsf adv r.nsf r.gp.2 d.nsf n.nsf cj v.pai.2p n.nsf d.nsf pt.pp.nsf p.a a.asn cj adv pt.pp.nsf
3836 892 4481 7007 3836 2437 1142 1639 874 3836 5743 4639 3900 2779 2083 906

15 Instead, you ought to say, "If it is the Lord's will, we will live and do this or that." **16** As it
ἀντὶ ὑμᾶς → → ˻τοῦ λέγειν˼ ἐὰν → → ὁ κύριος θελήσῃ καὶ → ζήσομεν καὶ ποιήσομεν τοῦτο ἢ ἐκεῖνο δὲ νῦν ←
p.g r.ap.2 d.gsn f.pa cj d.nsm n.nsm v.aas.3s cj v.fai.1p cj v.fai.1p r.asn cj r.asn cj adv
505 7007 3836 3306 1569 2527 2527 3836 3261 2527 2779 2409 2779 4472 4047 2445 1697 1254 3814

is, you boast and brag. All such boasting is evil. **17** Anyone, then, who knows the good
← καυχᾶσθε ˻ἐν ταῖς ἀλαζονείαις˼ ὑμῶν. πᾶσα τοιαύτη καύχησις ἐστιν πονηρά → οὖν → εἰδότι καλὸν
v.pmi.2p p.d d.dpf n.dpf r.gp.2 a.nsf r.nsf n.nsf v.pai.3s a.nsf cj pt.ra.dsm a.asn
3016 1877 3836 224 7007 4246 5525 3018 1639 4505 3857 4036 3857 2819

he ought to do and doesn't do it, sins.
→ → ποιεῖν καὶ μὴ ποιοῦντι ˻ἁμαρτία αὐτῷ ἐστιν˼
 f.pa cj pl pt.pa.dsm n.nsf r.dsm.3 v.pai.3s
 4472 2779 3590 4472 281 899 1639

φεύξεται ἀφ᾽ ὑμῶν, **8** ἐγγίσατε τῷ θεῷ καὶ ἐγγιεῖ ὑμῖν. καθαρίσατε χεῖρας, ἁμαρτωλοί, καὶ ἁγνίσατε καρδίας, δίψυχοι. **9** ταλαιπωρήσατε καὶ πενθήσατε καὶ κλαύσατε. ὁ γέλως ὑμῶν εἰς πένθος μετατραπήτω καὶ ἡ χαρὰ εἰς κατήφειαν. **10** ταπεινώθητε ἐνώπιον κυρίου καὶ ὑψώσει ὑμᾶς. ¶ **11** Μὴ καταλαλεῖτε ἀλλήλων, ἀδελφοί. ὁ καταλαλῶν ἀδελφοῦ ἢ κρίνων τὸν ἀδελφὸν αὐτοῦ καταλαλεῖ νόμου καὶ κρίνει νόμον· εἰ δὲ νόμον κρίνεις, οὐκ εἶ ποιητὴς νόμου ἀλλὰ κριτής. **12** εἷς ἐστιν [ὁ] νομοθέτης καὶ κριτὴς ὁ δυνάμενος σῶσαι καὶ ἀπολέσαι· σὺ δὲ τίς εἶ ὁ κρίνων τὸν πλησίον;

4:13 Ἄγε νῦν οἱ λέγοντες, Σήμερον ἢ αὔριον πορευσόμεθα εἰς τήνδε τὴν πόλιν καὶ ποιήσομεν ἐκεῖ ἐνιαυτὸν καὶ ἐμπορευσόμεθα καὶ κερδήσομεν· **14** οἵτινες οὐκ ἐπίστασθε τὸ τῆς αὔριον ποία ἡ ζωὴ ὑμῶν· ἀτμὶς γάρ ἐστε ἡ πρὸς ὀλίγον φαινομένη, ἔπειτα καὶ ἀφανιζομένη. **15** ἀντὶ τοῦ λέγειν ὑμᾶς, Ἐὰν ὁ κύριος θελήσῃ καὶ ζήσομεν καὶ ποιήσομεν τοῦτο ἢ ἐκεῖνο. **16** νῦν δὲ καυχᾶσθε ἐν ταῖς ἀλαζονείαις ὑμῶν· πᾶσα καύχησις τοιαύτη πονηρά ἐστιν. **17** εἰδότι οὖν καλὸν ποιεῖν καὶ μὴ ποιοῦντι, ἁμαρτία αὐτῷ ἐστιν.

Warning to Rich Oppressors

5:1 Now listen, you rich people, weep and wail because of the misery that is coming
νῦν Ἄγε → οἱ πλούσιοι. κλαύσατε ὀλολύζοντες ἐπὶ ← ταῖς ταλαιπωρίαις ταῖς → ἐπερχομέναις
adv v.pam.2s d.vpm a.vpm v.aam.2p pt.pa.npm p.d d.dpf n.dpf d.dpf pt.pm.dpf
3814 72 3836 4454 3081 3909 2093 3836 5416 3836 2088

upon you. **2** Your wealth has rotted, and moths have eaten your clothes. **3** Your gold and
← ὑμῶν ὑμῶν ὁ πλοῦτος. → σέσηπεν καὶ ͺσητόβρωτα γέγονεν. ← ὑμῶν ͺτὰ ἱμάτια. ὑμῶν ὁ χρυσὸς καὶ
r.gp.2 r.gp.2 d.nsm n.nsm v.rai.3s cj n.npn v.rai.3s r.gp.2 d.npn n.npn r.gp.2 d.nsm n.nsm cj
7007 7007 3836 4458 4960 2779 4963 1181 7007 3836 2668 7007 3836 5996 2779

silver are corroded. Their corrosion will testify against you and eat your flesh like fire.
ὁ ἄργυρος. → κατίωται καὶ αὐτῶν ὁ ἰὸς ἔσται εἰς μαρτύριον. → ὑμῖν καὶ φάγεται ὑμῶν ͺτὰς σάρκας. ὡς πῦρ
d.nsm n.nsm v.rpi.3s cj r.gpm.3 d.nsm n.nsm v.fmi.3s p.a n.asn r.dp.2 cj v.fmi.3s r.gp.2 d.apf n.apf pl n.nsn
3836 738 2995 2779 899 3836 2675 1639 1650 3457 7007 2779 2266 7007 3836 4922 6055 4786

You have hoarded wealth in the last days. **4** Look! The wages you failed to pay the workmen
→ → ἐθησαυρίσατε ← ἐν ἐσχάταις ἡμέραις ἰδοὺ ὁ μισθὸς ἀφ᾽ ὑμῶν ὁ ἀπεστερημένος. ← ← τῶν ἐργατῶν
v.aai.2p p.d a.dpf n.dpf j d.nsm n.nsm p.g r.gp.2 d.nsm pt.rp.nsm d.gpm n.gpm
2564 1877 2274 2465 2627 3836 3635 608 7007 3836 691 3836 2239

who mowed your fields are crying out against you. The cries of the harvesters have reached the
τῶν ἀμησάντων ὑμῶν ͺτὰς χώρας. → κράζει ← καὶ αἱ βοαὶ τῶν θερισάντων → εἰσεληλύθασιν εἰς ͺτὰ
d.gpm pt.aa.gpm r.gp.2 d.apf n.apf v.pai.3s cj d.npf n.npf d.gpm pt.aa.gpm v.rai.3p p.a d.apn
3836 286 7007 3836 6001 3189 2779 3836 1068 3836 2545 1656 1650 3836

ears of the Lord Almighty. **5** You have lived on earth in luxury and self-indulgence. You have fattened
ὦτα → κυρίου σαβαὼθ → ἐτρυφήσατε ἐπὶ ͺτῆς γῆς. καὶ ἐσπαταλήσατε → → ἐθρέψατε
n.apn n.gsm n.gpm v.aai.2p p.g d.gsf n.gsf cj v.aai.2p v.aai.2p
4044 3261 4877 5587 2093 3836 1178 5587 5587 2779 5059 5555

yourselves in the day of slaughter. **6** You have condemned and murdered innocent men, who were not
ͺτὰς καρδίας ὑμῶν. ἐν ἡμέρᾳ → σφαγῆς. → → κατεδικάσατε ἐφονεύσατε ͺτὸν δίκαιον. → → οὐκ
d.apf n.apf r.gp.2 p.d n.dsf n.gsf v.aai.2p v.aai.2p d.asm a.asm pl
3836 2840 7007 1877 2465 5375 2868 5839 3836 1465 530 530 4024

opposing you.
ἀντιτάσσεται ὑμῖν
v.pmi.3s r.dp.2
530 7007

Patience in Suffering

5:7 Be patient, then, brothers, until the Lord's coming. See how the farmer waits for the land to
→ Μακροθυμήσατε οὖν ἀδελφοί ἕως τῆς ͺτοῦ κυρίου. παρουσίας ἰδοὺ ὁ γεωργὸς ἐκδέχεται τῆς γῆς
v.aam.2p cj n.vpm p.g d.gsf d.gsm n.gsm n.gsf j d.nsm n.nsm v.pmi.3s d.gsf n.gsf
3428 4036 81 2401 3836 3836 3261 4242 2627 3836 1177 1683 3836 1178

yield its valuable crop and how patient he is for the autumn and spring rains. **8** You too, be
τὸν τίμιον καρπὸν μακροθυμῶν ἐπ᾽ αὐτῷ ἕως → λάβῃ πρόϊμον καὶ ὄψιμον ← ὑμεῖς καὶ →
d.asm n.asm n.asm pt.pa.nsm p.d r.dsm.3 cj v.aas.3s n.asm cj n.asm r.np.2 adv
3836 5508 2843 3428 2093 899 2401 3284 4611 2779 4069 7007 2779

patient and stand firm, because the Lord's coming is near. **9** Don't grumble against
μακροθυμήσατε ͺστηρίξατε τὰς καρδίας ὑμῶν. ← ὅτι ἡ ͺτοῦ κυρίου. παρουσία → ἤγγικεν μὴ στενάζετε κατ᾽
v.aam.2p v.aam.2p d.apf n.apf r.gp.2 cj d.nsf d.gsm n.gsm n.nsf v.rai.3s pl v.pam.2p p.g
3428 5114 3836 2840 7007 4022 3836 3836 3261 4242 1581 3590 5100 2848

each other, brothers, or you will be judged. The Judge is standing at the door! ¶ **10** Brothers, as an
→ ἀλλήλων ἀδελφοί ͺἵνα μὴ. → → κριθῆτε ἰδοὺ ὁ κριτὴς ἕστηκεν πρὸ τῶν θυρῶν ἀδελφοί
r.gpm n.vpm cj pl v.aps.2p j d.nsm n.nsm v.rai.3s p.g d.gpf n.gpf n.vpm
253 81 2671 3590 3212 2627 3836 3216 2705 4574 3836 2598 81

example of patience in the face of suffering, take the prophets who spoke in the name of the
ὑπόδειγμα → ͺτῆς κακοπαθίας. καὶ ͺτῆς μακροθυμίας. λάβετε τοὺς προφήτας οἳ ἐλάλησαν ἐν τῷ ὀνόματι →
n.asn d.gsf n.gsf cj d.gsf n.gsf v.aam.2p d.apm n.apm r.npm v.aai.3p p.d d.dsn n.dsn
5682 3836 2801 2779 3836 3429 3284 3836 4737 4005 3281 1877 3836 3950

Lord. **11** As you know, we consider blessed those who have persevered. You have heard of Job's perseverance
κυρίου ἰδοὺ ← → → μακαρίζομεν τοὺς → → ὑπομείναντας → ἠκούσατε Ἰὼβ ͺτὴν ὑπομονὴν.
n.gsm j v.pai.1p d.apm pt.aa.apm v.aai.2p n.gsm d.asf n.asf
3261 2627 3420 3836 5702 201 2724 3836 5705

5:1 Ἄγε νῦν οἱ πλούσιοι, κλαύσατε ὀλολύζοντες ἐπὶ ταῖς ταλαιπωρίαις ὑμῶν ταῖς ἐπερχομέναις. **2** ὁ πλοῦτος ὑμῶν σέσηπεν καὶ τὰ ἱμάτια ὑμῶν σητόβρωτα γέγονεν, **3** ὁ χρυσὸς ὑμῶν καὶ ὁ ἄργυρος κατίωται καὶ ὁ ἰὸς αὐτῶν εἰς μαρτύριον ὑμῖν ἔσται καὶ φάγεται τὰς σάρκας ὑμῶν ὡς πῦρ. ἐθησαυρίσατε ἐν ἐσχάταις ἡμέραις. **4** ἰδοὺ ὁ μισθὸς τῶν ἐργατῶν τῶν ἀμησάντων τὰς χώρας ὑμῶν ὁ ἀπεστερημένος ἀφ᾽ ὑμῶν κράζει, καὶ αἱ βοαὶ τῶν θερισάντων εἰς τὰ ὦτα κυρίου Σαβαὼθ εἰσεληλύθασιν. **5** ἐτρυφήσατε ἐπὶ τῆς γῆς καὶ ἐσπαταλήσατε, ἐθρέψατε τὰς καρδίας ὑμῶν ἐν ἡμέρᾳ σφαγῆς, **6** κατεδικάσατε, ἐφονεύσατε τὸν δίκαιον, οὐκ ἀντιτάσσεται ὑμῖν.

5:7 Μακροθυμήσατε οὖν, ἀδελφοί, ἕως τῆς παρουσίας τοῦ κυρίου. ἰδοὺ ὁ γεωργὸς ἐκδέχεται τὸν τίμιον καρπὸν τῆς γῆς μακροθυμῶν ἐπ᾽ αὐτῷ ἕως λάβῃ πρόϊμον καὶ ὄψιμον. **8** μακροθυμήσατε καὶ ὑμεῖς, στηρίξατε τὰς καρδίας ὑμῶν, ὅτι ἡ παρουσία τοῦ κυρίου ἤγγικεν. **9** μὴ στενάζετε, ἀδελφοί, κατ᾽ ἀλλήλων ἵνα μὴ κριθῆτε· ἰδοὺ ὁ κριτὴς πρὸ τῶν θυρῶν ἕστηκεν. ¶ **10** ὑπόδειγμα λάβετε, ἀδελφοί, τῆς κακοπαθείας καὶ τῆς μακροθυμίας τοὺς προφήτας οἳ ἐλάλησαν ἐν τῷ ὀνόματι κυρίου. **11** ἰδοὺ μακαρίζομεν τοὺς ὑπομείναντας· τὴν ὑπομονὴν Ἰὼβ ἠκούσατε καὶ τὸ τέλος κυρίου εἴδετε, ὅτι πολύσπλαγχνός ἐστιν ὁ κύριος

and	have	seen	what		the Lord	finally	brought about.		The Lord	is		full of	compassion	and	mercy.	¶
καὶ	→	εἴδετε	τὸ τέλος		κυρίου	→	→	←	ὅτι ὁ	κύριος	ἐστιν	→	→ πολύσπλαγχνος	καὶ	οἰκτίρμων	
cj		v.aai.2p	d.asn n.asn		n.gsm				cj d.nsm	n.nsm	v.pai.3s		a.nsm	cj	a.nsm	
2779		1625	3836 5465		3261	5465	5465	5465	4022 3836	3261	1639		4499	2779	3881	

12 Above all, my brothers, do not swear – not by heaven or by earth or by anything else. Let

δέ	Πρὸ	πάντων	μου	ἀδελφοί	→	μὴ	ὀμνύετε	μήτε	→	⌜τὸν οὐρανὸν⌝	μήτε	→	⌜τὴν γῆν⌝	μήτε	→	τινὰ	ἄλλον	ὅρκον	→
cj	p.g	a.gpn	r.gs.1	n.vpm		pl	v.pam.2p	cj		d.asm n.asm	cj		d.asf n.asf	cj		r.asm	r.asm	n.asm	
1254	4574	4246	1609	81		3923	3590	3923		3836 4041	3612		3836 1178	3612		5516	257	3992	1639

your "Yes"	be	yes, and	your "No,"	no,	or		you will be	condemned.
δὲ ὑμῶν ⌜τὸ ναὶ⌝	ἤτω	ναὶ καὶ	⌜τὸ οὔ⌝	οὔ	ἵνα μὴ	→	πέσητε	⌜ὑπὸ κρίσιν⌝
cj r.gp.2 d.nsn pl	v.pam.3s	pl cj	d.nsn pl	pl	cj pl		v.aas.2p	p.a n.asf
1254 7007 3836 3721	1639	3721 2779	3836 4024	4024	2671 3590		4406	5679 3213

The Prayer of Faith

5:13 Is any one of you in trouble? He should pray. Is anyone happy? Let him sing songs of praise.

→	τις	ἐν	ὑμῖν	Κακοπαθεῖ	→	→	προσευχέσθω	→	τις	εὐθυμεῖ	→	→	ψαλλέτω
	r.nsm	p.d	r.dp.2	v.pai.3s			v.pmm.3s		r.nsm	v.pai.3s			v.pam.3s
2802	5516	1877	7007	2802			4667		2313	2313			6010

14 Is any one of you sick? He should call the elders of the church to pray over him

→	τις	ἐν	ὑμῖν	ἀσθενεῖ	→	προσκαλεσάσθω	τοὺς	πρεσβυτέρους	→	τῆς	ἐκκλησίας	καὶ	προσευξάσθωσαν	ἐπ'	αὐτὸν
	r.nsm	p.d	r.dp.2	v.pai.3s		v.amm.3s	d.apm	n.apm		d.gsf	n.gsf	cj	v.amm.3p	p.a	r.asm.3
820	5516	1877	7007	820		4673	3836	4565		3836	1711	2779	4667	2093	899

and	anoint	him	with	oil	in	the	name	of the Lord.	**15** And	the	prayer	offered	in	faith		will make	the
	ἀλείψαντες	αὐτὸν	→	ἐλαίῳ	ἐν	τῷ	ὀνόματι	→ τοῦ κυρίου	καὶ	ἡ	εὐχὴ	→	⌜τῆς	πίστεως⌝	→	→	τὸν
	pt.aa.npm	r.asm.3		n.dsn	p.d	d.dsn	n.dsn	d.gsm n.gsm	cj	d.nsf	n.nsf		d.gsf	n.gsf			d.asm
230	230	899		1778	1877	3836	3950	3836 3261	2779	3836	2376		3836	4411	5392	5392	3836

sick	person well;	the Lord	will raise	him	up. If	he has		sinned,	he	will be	forgiven.
κάμνοντα	← σώσει καὶ	ὁ κύριος	→ ἐγερεῖ	αὐτόν	← κἂν	ᾖ	πεποιηκώς	ἁμαρτίας	αὐτῷ	→	ἀφεθήσεται
pt.pa.asm	v.fai.3s cj	d.nsm n.nsm	v.fai.3s	r.asm.3	crasis	v.pas.3s	pt.ra.nsm	n.apf	r.dsm.3		v.fpi.3s
2827	5392 2779	3836 3261	1586	899	1586 2829	1639	4472	281	899		918

16 Therefore confess your sins to each other and pray for each other so that you may be healed.

οὖν	ἐξομολογεῖσθε	τὰς	ἁμαρτίας	→ ἀλλήλοις	←	καὶ	εὔχεσθε	ὑπὲρ	ἀλλήλων	←	ὅπως	←	→	→	ἰαθῆτε
cj	v.pmm.2p	d.apf	n.apf	r.dpm		cj	v.pmm.2p	p.g	r.gpm		cj				v.aps.2p
4036	2018	3836	281	253		2779	2377	5642	253		3968				2615

The	prayer	of a righteous	man	is	powerful		and	effective.	¶	**17** Elijah	was	a man		just like	us.
	δέησις	→	δικαίου	→	⌜Πολὺ	ἰσχύει⌝		ἐνεργουμένη		Ἡλίας	ἦν	ἄνθρωπος	→	ὁμοιοπαθὴς	ἡμῖν καὶ
	n.nsf		a.gsm		adv	v.pai.3s		pt.pm.nsf		n.nsm	v.iai.3s	n.nsm		a.nsm	r.dp.1 cj
	1255		1465		4498	2710		1919		2460	1639	476		3926	2779

He	prayed	earnestly	that it	would	not		rain,	and it	did	not	rain	on the land	for	three	and	a half
→	προσηύξατο	προσευχῇ			μὴ	βρέξαι	βρέξαι	καὶ		οὐκ	ἔβρεξεν	ἐπὶ τῆς γῆς	→	τρεῖς	καὶ	μῆνας ἕξ
	v.ami.3s	n.dsf			pl	f.aa	f.aa	cj		pl	v.aai.3s	p.g d.gsf n.gsf		a.apm	cj	n.apm a.apm
4667	4667	4666	1101	1101	1101	3590 1101	1101	2779	1101 1101	4024 1101	2093 3836 1178		5552	2779	3604 1971

years.	**18** Again	he prayed,	and	the heavens	gave	rain,	and	the earth	produced	its	crops.	¶	**19** My
ἐνιαυτοὺς	καὶ πάλιν	→ προσηύξατο	καὶ	ὁ οὐρανὸς	ἔδωκεν	ὑετὸν	καὶ	ἡ γῆ	ἐβλάστησεν	αὐτῆς	⌜τὸν καρπὸν⌝		μου
n.apm	cj adv	v.ami.3s	cj	d.nsm n.nsm	v.aai.3s	n.asm	cj	d.nsf n.nsf	v.aai.3s	r.gsf.3	d.asm n.asm		r.gs.1
1929	2779 4099	4667	2779	3836 4041	1443	5624	2779	3836 1178	1056	899	3836 2843		1609

brothers,	if	one	of	you should	wander	from	the	truth	and	someone	should bring	him	back,	**20** remember	this:
Ἀδελφοί	ἐάν	τις	ἐν	ὑμῖν →	πλανηθῇ	ἀπὸ	τῆς	ἀληθείας	καὶ	τις	→ ἐπιστρέψῃ	αὐτόν	→	γινωσκέτω	ὅτι
n.vpm	cj	r.nsm	p.d	r.dp.2	v.aps.3s	p.g	d.gsf	n.gsf	cj	r.nsm	v.aas.3s	r.asm.3		v.pam.3s	cj
81	1569	5516	1877	7007	4414	608	3836	237	2779	5516	2188	899	2188	1182	4022

Whoever	turns	a sinner	from the	error	of	his	way	will save	him		from	death	and	cover	over a
ὁ	ἐπιστρέψας	ἁμαρτωλὸν	ἐκ	πλάνης	→	αὐτοῦ	ὁδοῦ	→ σώσει	⌜ψυχὴν	αὐτοῦ⌝	ἐκ	θανάτου	καὶ	καλύψει	←
d.nsm	pt.aa.nsm	a.asm	p.g	n.gsf		r.gsm.3	n.gsf	v.fai.3s	n.asf	r.gsm.3	p.g	n.gsm	cj	v.fai.3s	
3836	2188	283	1666	4415		899	3847	5392	6034	899	1666	2505	2779	2821	

multitude	of sins.
πλῆθος	→ ἁμαρτιῶν
n.asn	n.gpf
4436	281

καὶ οἰκτίρμων. ¶ **12** Πρὸ πάντων δέ, ἀδελφοί μου, μὴ ὀμνύετε μήτε τὸν οὐρανὸν μήτε τὴν γῆν μήτε ἄλλον τινὰ ὅρκον· ἤτω δὲ ὑμῶν τὸ Ναὶ ναὶ καὶ τὸ Οὒ οὔ, ἵνα μὴ ὑπὸ κρίσιν πέσητε.

5:13 Κακοπαθεῖ τις ἐν ὑμῖν, προσευχέσθω· εὐθυμεῖ τις, ψαλλέτω· **14** ἀσθενεῖ τις ἐν ὑμῖν, προσκαλεσάσθω τοὺς πρεσβυτέρους τῆς ἐκκλησίας καὶ προσευξάσθωσαν ἐπ' αὐτὸν ἀλείψαντες [αὐτὸν] ἐλαίῳ ἐν τῷ ὀνόματι τοῦ κυρίου· **15** καὶ ἡ εὐχὴ τῆς πίστεως σώσει τὸν κάμνοντα καὶ ἐγερεῖ αὐτὸν ὁ κύριος· κἂν ἁμαρτίας ᾖ πεποιηκώς, ἀφεθήσεται αὐτῷ. **16** ἐξομολογεῖσθε οὖν ἀλλήλοις τὰς ἁμαρτίας καὶ εὔχεσθε ὑπὲρ ἀλλήλων ὅπως ἰαθῆτε. πολὺ ἰσχύει δέησις δικαίου ἐνεργουμένη. ¶ **17** Ἡλίας ἄνθρωπος ἦν ὁμοιοπαθὴς ἡμῖν, καὶ προσευχῇ προσηύξατο τοῦ μὴ βρέξαι, καὶ οὐκ ἔβρεξεν ἐπὶ τῆς γῆς ἐνιαυτοὺς τρεῖς καὶ μῆνας ἕξ· **18** καὶ πάλιν προσηύξατο, καὶ ὁ οὐρανὸς ὑετὸν ἔδωκεν καὶ ἡ γῆ ἐβλάστησεν τὸν καρπὸν αὐτῆς ¶ **19** Ἀδελφοί μου, ἐάν τις ἐν ὑμῖν πλανηθῇ ἀπὸ τῆς ἀληθείας καὶ ἐπιστρέψῃ τις αὐτόν, **20** γινωσκέτω ὅτι ὁ ἐπιστρέψας ἁμαρτωλὸν ἐκ πλάνης ὁδοῦ αὐτοῦ σώσει ψυχὴν αὐτοῦ ἐκ θανάτου καὶ καλύψει πλῆθος ἁμαρτιῶν.

1 Peter

1:1 Peter, an apostle   of Jesus Christ,   ¶   To God's elect,   strangers   in the world, scattered throughout
Πέτρος   ἀπόστολος → Ἰησοῦ Χριστοῦ   ἐκλεκτοῖς παρεπιδήμοις ← ←   διασπορᾶς ←
n.nsm   n.nsm   n.gsm   n.gsm   a.dpm   n.dpm   n.gsf
4377   693   2652   5986   1723   4215   1402

Pontus, Galatia, Cappadocia, Asia   and Bithynia, **2** who have been chosen according to the foreknowledge of God
Πόντου Γαλατίας Καππαδοκίας Ἀσίας καὶ Βιθυνίας   κατὰ ←   πρόγνωσιν → θεοῦ
n.gsm   n.gsf   n.gsf   n.gsf cj n.gsf   p.a   n.asf   n.gsm
4509   1130   2838   823   2779 1049   2848   4590   2536

the Father, through the sanctifying work of the Spirit,   for obedience to Jesus Christ and sprinkling by his blood: ¶
πατρὸς ἐν   ἁγιασμῷ ← →   πνεύματος εἰς ὑπακοὴν → Ἰησοῦ Χριστοῦ καὶ ῥαντισμὸν → αἵματος
n.gsm   p.d   n.dsm   n.gsn   p.a n.asf   n.gsm n.gsm   cj n.asm   n.gsn
4252   1877   40   4460   1650 5633   2652 5986   2779 4823   135

Grace and peace be yours in abundance.
χάρις   καὶ εἰρήνη → ὑμῖν → πληθυνθείη
n.nsf   cj n.nsf   r.dp.2   v.apo.3s
5921   2779 1645   4437 7007 4437

Praise to God for a Living Hope

1:3 Praise   be to the God and Father of our Lord   Jesus Christ! In his   great mercy he has given
Εὐλογητὸς   ὁ   θεὸς καὶ πατὴρ → ἡμῶν ┌τοῦ κυρίου┐ Ἰησοῦ Χριστοῦ κατὰ αὐτοῦ πολὺ ┌τὸ ἔλεος┐ ὁ → →
a.nsm   d.nsm n.nsm cj n.nsm r.gp.1 d.gsm n.gsm n.gsm n.gsm   p.a r.gsm.3 a.asn d.asn n.asn d.nsm
2329   3836 2536 2779 4252   3261 3836 3261   2652 5986   2848 899   4498 3836 1799 3836 335 335

us new   birth into a living hope through the resurrection of Jesus Christ from the dead, **4** and into an
ἡμᾶς ἀναγεννήσας ← εἰς ζῶσαν ἐλπίδα δι'   ἀναστάσεως → Ἰησοῦ Χριστοῦ ἐκ   νεκρῶν   εἰς
r.ap.1 pt.aa.nsm   p.a pt.pa.asf n.asf p.g   n.gsf   n.gsm n.gsm   p.g a.gpm   p.a
7005 335   1650 2409 1828 1328   414   2652 5986   1666 3738   1650

inheritance that can never perish,   spoil or fade   – kept   in heaven for you, **5** who through faith
κληρονομίαν → →   ἄφθαρτον καὶ ἀμίαντον καὶ ἀμάραντον τετηρημένην ἐν οὐρανοῖς εἰς ὑμᾶς τοὺς διὰ   πίστεως
n.asf   a.asf   cj a.asf   cj a.asf   pt.rp.asf   p.d n.dpm   p.a r.ap.2 d.apm p.g   n.gsf
3100   915   2779 299   2779 278   5498   1877 4041   1650 7007 3836 1328 4411

are shielded   by God's power until the coming of the salvation that is ready to be revealed   in the last
→ φρουρουμένους ἐν θεοῦ δυνάμει εἰς   σωτηρίαν   ἑτοίμην → ἀποκαλυφθῆναι ἐν ἐσχάτῳ
pt.pp.apm   p.d n.dsf   p.a   n.asf   a.asf   f.ap   p.d a.dsm
5864   1877 2536 1539 1650   5401   2289   636   1877 2274

time. **6** In this you greatly rejoice,   though now for a little while you may have had   to suffer grief in
καιρῷ ἐν ᾧ →   ἀγαλλιᾶσθε εἰ   ἄρτι → ὀλίγον   ┌δέον ἐστὶν┐ → λυπηθέντες   ἐν
n.dsm p.d r.dsm   v.pmi.2p   cj   adv   adv   pt.pa.nsn v.pai.3s pt.ap.npm   p.d
2789 1877 4005   22   1623 785   3900   1256 1639   3382   1877

all   kinds of trials. **7** These have come so that your faith   – of greater worth   than gold, which
ποικίλοις ←   πειρασμοῖς   ἵνα ← ὑμῶν ┌τῆς πίστεως┐ →   πολυτιμότερον → χρυσίου τοῦ
a.dpm   n.dpm   cj   r.gp.2 d.gsf n.gsf   a.nsn.c   n.gsn   d.gsn
4476   4280   2671 7007 3836 4411   4501   5992   3836

perishes   even though refined   by fire – may be proved genuine   and may result in praise,   glory and
ἀπολλυμένου δὲ ←   δοκιμαζομένου διὰ πυρὸς   ┌τὸ δοκίμιον┐ →   εὑρεθῇ εἰς ἔπαινον καὶ δόξαν καὶ
pt.pm.gsn cj   pt.pp.gsn   p.g n.gsn   d.nsn n.nsn   v.aps.3s p.a n.asm   cj n.asf cj
660   1254   1507   1328 4786   3836 1510   2351   1650 2047   2779 1518 2779

honor when Jesus Christ is revealed. **8** Though you have not seen him, you love   him; and even though you do
τιμὴν ἐν Ἰησοῦ Χριστοῦ ἀποκαλύψει   οὐκ ἰδόντες ὃν → ἀγαπᾶτε
n.asf p.d n.gsm n.gsm   n.dsf   pl pt.aa.npm r.asm → v.pai.2p
5507 1877 2652 5986   637   1625 1625 1625 4024 1625 4005   26   3972 3972   3972 3972

not see   him now,   you believe   in him and are filled   with an inexpressible and glorious joy, **9** for you
μὴ ὁρῶντες ἄρτι δὲ → πιστεύοντες εἰς ὃν   →   ἀγαλλιᾶσθε ←   ἀνεκλαλήτῳ καὶ δεδοξασμένῃ χαρᾷ →
pl pt.pa.npm adv cj   pt.pa.npm   p.a r.asm   v.pmi.2p   a.dsf   cj pt.rp.dsf   n.dsf
3590 3972   785 1254   4409   1650 4005   22   443   2779 1519   5915

1:1 Πέτρος ἀπόστολος Ἰησοῦ Χριστοῦ ¶ ἐκλεκτοῖς παρεπιδήμοις διασπορᾶς Πόντου, Γαλατίας, Καππαδοκίας, Ἀσίας καὶ Βιθυνίας, **2** κατὰ πρόγνωσιν θεοῦ πατρὸς ἐν ἁγιασμῷ πνεύματος εἰς ὑπακοὴν καὶ ῥαντισμὸν αἵματος Ἰησοῦ Χριστοῦ, ¶ χάρις ὑμῖν καὶ εἰρήνη πληθυνθείη.

1:3 Εὐλογητὸς ὁ θεὸς καὶ πατὴρ τοῦ κυρίου ἡμῶν Ἰησοῦ Χριστοῦ, ὁ κατὰ τὸ πολὺ αὐτοῦ ἔλεος ἀναγεννήσας ἡμᾶς εἰς ἐλπίδα ζῶσαν δι' ἀναστάσεως Ἰησοῦ Χριστοῦ ἐκ νεκρῶν, **4** εἰς κληρονομίαν ἄφθαρτον καὶ ἀμίαντον καὶ ἀμάραντον, τετηρημένην ἐν οὐρανοῖς εἰς ὑμᾶς **5** τοὺς ἐν δυνάμει θεοῦ φρουρουμένους διὰ πίστεως εἰς σωτηρίαν ἑτοίμην ἀποκαλυφθῆναι ἐν καιρῷ ἐσχάτῳ. **6** ἐν ᾧ ἀγαλλιᾶσθε, ὀλίγον ἄρτι εἰ δέον [ἐστὶν] λυπηθέντες ἐν ποικίλοις πειρασμοῖς, **7** ἵνα τὸ δοκίμιον ὑμῶν τῆς πίστεως πολυτιμότερον χρυσίου τοῦ ἀπολλυμένου διὰ πυρὸς δὲ δοκιμαζομένου, εὑρεθῇ εἰς ἔπαινον καὶ δόξαν καὶ τιμὴν ἐν ἀποκαλύψει Ἰησοῦ Χριστοῦ· **8** ὃν οὐκ ἰδόντες ἀγαπᾶτε, εἰς ὃν ἄρτι μὴ ὁρῶντες πιστεύοντες δὲ ἀγαλλιᾶσθε χαρᾷ ἀνεκλαλήτῳ καὶ δεδοξασμένῃ **9** κομιζόμενοι τὸ τέλος τῆς πίστεως [ὑμῶν] σωτηρίαν ψυχῶν. ¶ **10** Περὶ ἧς σωτηρίας ἐξεζήτησαν καὶ

are receiving   the goal of   your   faith,   the salvation of your souls.   ¶   **10** Concerning this salvation, the
→   κομιζόμενοι   τὸ   τέλος   →   ὑμῶν   ⸢τῆς πίστεως⸣   σωτηρίαν   →   ψυχῶν   περὶ   ἧς   σωτηρίας
pt.pm.npm   d.asn   n.asn   r.gp.2   d.gsf   n.gsf   n.asf   n.gpf   p.g   r.gsf   n.gsf
3152   3836   5465   4411   7007   3836   4411   5401   6034   4309   4005   5401

prophets, who   spoke   of   the grace   that was to come to   you, searched intently and with the greatest
προφῆται   οἱ   προφητεύσαντες   περὶ   τῆς   χάριτος   →   →   →   εἰς   ὑμᾶς   ἐξεζήτησαν   ←   καὶ   →   →   →
n.npm   d.npm   pt.aa.npm   p.g   d.gsf   n.gsf   p.a   r.ap.2   v.aai.3p   cj
4737   3836   4736   4309   3836   5921   1650   7007   1699   2779

care,   **11** trying to find   out the   time   and circumstances to which the Spirit of Christ in them
ἐξηραύνησαν   →   →   ἐραυνῶντες   ←   εἰς   ποῖον   καιρὸν   ἢ   τίνα   τὸ   πνεῦμα   →   Χριστοῦ ἐν   αὐτοῖς
v.aai.3p   pt.pa.npm   p.a   r.asm   n.asm   cj   r.asm   d.nsn   n.nsn   n.gsm   p.d   r.dpm.3
2001   2236   1650   4481   2789   2445   5515   3836   4460   5986   1877   899

was pointing when he predicted   the sufferings of Christ and the glories *that*   *would follow.* **12** It was
→   ἐδήλου   →   →   προμαρτυρόμενον   τὰ   παθήματα   εἰς Χριστὸν καὶ   τὰς   δόξας   ⸢μετὰ ταῦτα⸣
v.iai.3s   pt.pm.nsn   d.apn   n.apn   p.a   n.asm   cj   d.apf   n.apf   p.a   r.apn
1317   4626   3836   4077   1650   5986   2779   3836   1518   3552   4047

revealed   to them that they were not serving   themselves but you, when they spoke of the things that have
ἀπεκαλύφθη   →   οἷς   ὅτι   →   ←   οὐχ   διηκόνουν   αὐτά   ἑαυτοῖς   δὲ   ὑμῖν   ὰ   ←   ←
v.api.3s   r.dpm   cj   pl   v.iai.3p   r.apn.3   r.dpm.3   cj   r.dp.2   r.npn
636   4005   4022   1354   1354   4024   1354   899   1571   1254   7007   4005   334

now been told   you by those who have preached   the gospel to you by the Holy Spirit   sent   from
νῦν   →   ἀνηγγέλη   ὑμῖν διὰ   τῶν   ←   →   εὐαγγελισαμένων   ←   ←   ὑμᾶς ἐν   ἁγίῳ   πνεύματι ἀποσταλέντι ἀπ᾽
adv   v.api.3s   r.dp.2   p.g   d.gpm   pt.am.gpm   r.ap.2   p.d   a.dsn   n.dsn   pt.ap.dsn   p.g
3814   7007   1328   3836   2294   7007   1877   41   4460   690   608

heaven. Even angels long   to look   into these things.
οὐρανοῦ   ἄγγελοι ἐπιθυμοῦσιν →   παρακύψαι εἰς   ἃ   ←
n.gsm   n.npm   v.pai.3p   f.aa   p.a   r.apn
4041   34   2121   4160   1650   4005

Be Holy

1:13 Therefore, prepare   your minds   for action; be self-controlled; set your hope   fully   on
Διὸ   ⸢ἀναζωσάμενοι τὰς   ὀσφύας⸣ ὑμῶν ⸤τῆς διανοίας⸥   ←   →   νήφοντες   →   →   ἐλπίσατε τελείως ἐπὶ
cj   pt.am.npm   d.apf   n.apf   r.gp.2   d.gsf   n.gsf   pt.pa.npm   v.aam.2p   adv   p.a
1475   350   3836   4019   7007   3836   1379   350   350   3768   1827   5458   2093

the grace to be given   you when Jesus Christ is revealed.   **14** As obedient children,   do not conform   to the
τὴν   χάριν   →   φερομένην   ὑμῖν ἐν   Ἰησοῦ   Χριστοῦ   →   ἀποκαλύψει   ὡς   ὑπακοῆς   τέκνα   →   μὴ   συσχηματιζόμενοι →   ταῖς
d.asf   n.asf   pt.pp.asf   r.dp.2   p.d   n.gsm   n.gsm   n.dsf   pl   n.gsf   n.npn   pl   pt.pp.npm   d.dpf
3836   5921   5770   7007   1877   2652   5986   637   6055   5633   5451   3590   5372   3836

evil   desires you had   when you lived in ignorance.   **15** But just as he who called   you is holy, so
ἐπιθυμίαις   ←   πρότερον   ←   ὑμῶν   ἐν   ⸤τῇ   ἀγνοίᾳ⸥   ἀλλὰ κατὰ   ←   τὸν   →   καλέσαντα ὑμᾶς   ἅγιον καὶ   αὐτοὶ
n.dpf   adv.c   r.gp.2   p.d   d.dsf   n.dsf   cj   p.a   d.asm   pt.aa.asm   r.ap.2   a.asm   adv   r.npm
2123   4728   7007   1877   3836   53   247   2848   3836   2813   7007   41   2779   899

be   holy in all   you do;   **16** for   it is written: "Be   holy, because I   am holy."   ¶   **17** Since you
γενήθητε ἅγιοι ἐν   πάσῃ   →   ἀναστροφῇ   διότι   →   γέγραπται ὅτι   ἔσεσθε   ἅγιοι   ὅτι   ἐγὼ   εἰμι   ἅγιος   καὶ εἰ   →
v.apm.2p   a.npm   p.d   a.dsf   n.dsf   cj   v.rpi.3s   cj   v.fmi.2p   a.npm   cj   r.ns.1   v.pai.1s   a.nsm   cj   cj
1181   41   1877   4246   419   1484   1211   4022   1639   41   4022   1609   1639   41   2779   1623

call   on a Father who judges   each   man's work   impartially,   live   your lives   as
ἐπικαλεῖσθε   ←   πατέρα   τὸν   κρίνοντα κατὰ   ἑκάστου   ⸤τὸ   ἔργον⸥   ἀπροσωπολήμπτως ἀναστράφητε ὑμῶν ⸤τὸν χρόνον⸥
v.pmi.2p   n.asm   d.asm   pt.pa.asm   p.a   r.gsm   d.asn   n.asn   adv   v.apm.2p   r.gp.2   d.asm   n.asm
2126   4252   3836   3212   2848   1667   3836   2240   719   418   7007   3836   5989

strangers   here in   reverent fear.   **18** For you know   that it was not with perishable things such as silver   or   gold
⸤τῆς παροικίας⸥   ἐν   φόβῳ   →   εἰδότες ὅτι   →   οὐ   →   φθαρτοῖς   ←   ←   ἀργυρίῳ ἢ   χρυσίῳ
d.gsf   n.gsf   p.d   n.dsm   pt.ra.npm   cj   pl   a.dpn   n.dsn   cj   n.dsn
3836   4229   1877   5832   3857   4022   4024   5778   736   2445   5992

that you were redeemed from the empty   way of life   *handed*   *down to you from your forefathers,*
→   →   →   ἐλυτρώθητε ἐκ   τῆς   ματαίας   →   →   ἀναστροφῆς   ὑμῶν πατροπαραδότου
v.api.2p   p.g   d.gsf   a.gsf   n.gsf   r.gp.2   a.gsf
3390   1666   3836   3469   419   7007   4261

ἐξηραύνησαν προφῆται οἱ περὶ τῆς εἰς ὑμᾶς χάριτος προφητεύσαντες, **11** ἐραυνῶντες εἰς τίνα ἢ ποῖον καιρὸν ἐδήλου τὸ ἐν αὐτοῖς πνεῦμα Χριστοῦ προμαρτυρόμενον τὰ εἰς Χριστὸν παθήματα καὶ τὰς μετὰ ταῦτα δόξας. **12** οἷς ἀπεκαλύφθη ὅτι οὐχ ἑαυτοῖς ὑμῖν δὲ διηκόνουν αὐτά, ἃ νῦν ἀνηγγέλη ὑμῖν διὰ τῶν εὐαγγελισαμένων ὑμᾶς [ἐν] πνεύματι ἁγίῳ ἀποσταλέντι ἀπ᾽ οὐρανοῦ, εἰς ἃ ἐπιθυμοῦσιν ἄγγελοι παρακύψαι.

1:13 Διὸ ἀναζωσάμενοι τὰς ὀσφύας τῆς διανοίας ὑμῶν νήφοντες τελείως ἐλπίσατε ἐπὶ τὴν φερομένην ὑμῖν χάριν ἐν ἀποκαλύψει Ἰησοῦ Χριστοῦ. **14** ὡς τέκνα ὑπακοῆς μὴ συσχηματιζόμενοι ταῖς πρότερον ἐν τῇ ἀγνοίᾳ ὑμῶν ἐπιθυμίαις **15** ἀλλὰ κατὰ τὸν καλέσαντα ὑμᾶς ἅγιον καὶ αὐτοὶ ἅγιοι ἐν πάσῃ ἀναστροφῇ γενήθητε, **16** διότι γέγραπται [ὅτι] Ἅγιοι ἔσεσθε, ὅτι ἐγὼ ἅγιος [εἰμι] ¶ **17** Καὶ εἰ πατέρα ἐπικαλεῖσθε τὸν ἀπροσωπολήμπτως κρίνοντα κατὰ τὸ ἑκάστου ἔργον, ἐν φόβῳ τὸν τῆς παροικίας ὑμῶν χρόνον ἀναστράφητε, **18** εἰδότες ὅτι οὐ φθαρτοῖς, ἀργυρίῳ ἢ χρυσίῳ, ἐλυτρώθητε ἐκ τῆς ματαίας ὑμῶν ἀναστροφῆς

19 but | with | the precious | blood | of Christ, | | a lamb | without blemish | or | defect. | **20** | He was chosen | | before | the
ἀλλὰ → | τιμίῳ | αἵματι | Χριστοῦ | ὡς | ἀμνοῦ | | ἀμώμου | καὶ | ἀσπίλου | μὲν → | → | προεγνωσμένου | πρὸ
cj | a.dsn | n.dsn | n.gsn | pl | n.gsm | | a.gsn | cj | a.gsn | pl | | pt.rp.gsm | p.g
247 | 5508 | 135 | 5986 | 6055 | 303 | | 320 | 2779 | 834 | 3525 | | 4589 | 4574

creation | of the | world, | but | was | revealed | | in | these | last | times | for your sake. | **21** Through | him | you believe
καταβολῆς → | κόσμου | δὲ | → | φανερωθέντος | ἐπ᾽ | τῶν | ἐσχάτου | χρόνων | δι᾽ | ὑμᾶς | δι᾽ | αὐτοῦ → | ⸤τοὺς πιστοὺς⸥
n.gsf | n.gsm | cj | | pt.ap.gsm | p.g | d.gpm | a.gsm | n.gpm | p.a | r.ap.2 | p.g | r.gsm.3 | d.apm a.apm
2856 | 3180 | 1254 | | 5746 | 2093 | 3836 | 2274 | 5989 | 1328 | 7007 | 1328 | 899 | 3836 4412

in | God, | who | raised | him | from | the dead | and | glorified | | him, | and so | your | faith | | and | hope | are | in | God. ¶
εἰς | θεὸν | τὸν | ἐγείραντα | αὐτὸν | ἐκ | νεκρῶν | καὶ | ⸤δόξαν | δόντα⸥ | αὐτῷ | ὥστε | ὑμῶν | ⸤τὴν πίστιν⸥ | καὶ | ἐλπίδα | εἶναι | εἰς | θεόν
p.a | n.asm | d.asm | pt.aa.asm | r.asm.3 | p.g | a.gpm | cj | n.asf | pt.aa.asm | r.dsm.3 | cj | r.gp.2 | d.asf n.asf | cj | n.asf | f.pa | p.a | n.asm
1650 | 2536 | 3836 | 1586 | 899 | 1666 | 3738 | 2779 | 1518 | 1443 | 899 | 6063 | 7007 | 3836 4411 | 2779 | 1828 | 1639 | 1650 | 2536

22 Now that | you | have | purified | yourselves | | by | obeying | the | truth | so that | you | have | sincere | love
→ | → | → | ἡγνικότες | ⸤Τὰς | ψυχὰς | ὑμῶν⸥ | ἐν | ⸤τῇ | ὑπακοῇ | τῆς | ἀληθείας | εἰς ← | ← | ← | ἀνυπόκριτον | φιλαδελφίαν
| | | pt.ra.npm | d.apf | n.apf | r.gp.2 | p.d | d.dsf | n.dsf | d.gsf | n.gsf | p.a | | | a.asf | n.asf
| | | 49 | 3836 | 6034 | 7007 | 1877 | 3836 | 5633 | 3836 | 237 | 1650 | | | 537 | 5789

for | your brothers, | love | one | another | deeply, | from the | [| heart. | **23** For you have been | born
| → | ἀγαπήσατε | ἀλλήλους | ← | ἐκτενῶς | ἐκ | [καθαρᾶς] | καρδίας | | ἀναγεγεννημένοι
| | v.aam.2p | r.apm | | adv | p.g | a.gsf | n.gsf | | pt.rp.npm
| | 26 | 253 | | 1757 | 1666 | 2754 | 2840 | | 335

again, | not | of | perishable | seed, | but | of | imperishable, | through | the living | and | enduring | word | of God. | **24** For, | "All | men
← | οὐκ | ἐκ | φθαρτῆς | σπορᾶς | ἀλλὰ | | ἀφθάρτου | διὰ | ζῶντος | καὶ | μένοντος | λόγου | → | θεοῦ | διότι | πᾶσα | σὰρξ
| pl | p.g | a.gsf | n.gsf | cj | | a.gsf | p.g | pt.pa.gsm | cj | pt.pa.gsm | n.gsm | | n.gsm | cj | a.nsf | n.nsf
| 4024 | 1666 | 5778 | 5076 | 247 | | 915 | 1328 | 2409 | 2779 | 3531 | 3364 | | 2536 | 1484 | 4246 | 4922

are like | grass, | and | all | their | glory | is like | the | flowers | of the | field; | the | grass | withers | and | the | flowers | fall, | **25** but | the
ὡς | χόρτος | καὶ | πᾶσα | αὐτῆς | δόξα | ὡς | | ἄνθος | → | χόρτου | ὁ | χόρτος | ἐξηράνθη | καὶ | τὸ | ἄνθος | ἐξέπεσεν | δὲ | τὸ
pl | n.nsm | cj | a.nsf | r.gsf.3 | n.nsf | pl | | n.nsn | | n.gsm | d.nsm | n.nsm | v.api.3s | cj | d.nsn | n.nsn | v.aai.3s | cj | d.nsn
6055 | 5965 | 2779 | 4246 | 899 | 1518 | 6055 | | 470 | | 5965 | 3836 | 5965 | 3830 | 2779 | 3836 | 470 | 1738 | 1254 | 3836

word | of the Lord | stands | forever." | And | this | is | the | word | that | was preached | to | you. | ¶ | **2:1** Therefore,
ῥῆμα → | κυρίου | μένει | εἰς τὸν | αἰῶνα⸥ | δὲ | τοῦτό | ἐστιν | τὸ | ῥῆμα | τὸ → | εὐαγγελισθὲν | εἰς | ὑμᾶς | | οὖν
n.nsn | n.gsm | v.pai.3s | p.a d.asm | n.asm | cj | r.nsn | v.pai.3s | d.nsn | n.nsn | d.nsn | pt.ap.nsn | p.a | r.ap.2 | | cj
4839 | 3261 | 3531 | 1650 3836 | 172 | 1254 | 4047 | 1639 | 3836 | 4839 | 3836 | 2294 | 1650 | 7007 | | 4036

rid | | yourselves | of all | malice | and all | deceit, | | hypocrisy, | | envy, | and | slander | of every kind. | **2** Like
Ἀποθέμενοι ← | | ← | πᾶσαν | κακίαν | καὶ | πάντα | δόλον | καὶ | ὑποκρίσεις | καὶ | φθόνους | καὶ | καταλαλιάς | → πάσας ← | ὡς
pt.am.npm | | | a.asf | n.asf | cj | a.asn | n.asm | cj | n.apf | cj | n.apm | cj | n.apf | a.apf | pl
700 | | | 4246 | 2798 | 2779 | 4246 | 1515 | 2779 | 5694 | 2779 | 5784 | 2779 | 2896 | 4246 | 6055

newborn | babies, | crave | pure | spiritual | milk, | so | that | by | it | you may | grow | up | in | your salvation, | **3** now
ἀρτιγέννητα | βρέφη | ἐπιποθήσατε | ἄδολον | λογικὸν | ⸤τὸ | γάλα⸥ | ἵνα | ← | ἐν | αὐτῷ | αὐξηθῆτε | ← | εἰς | σωτηρίαν | εἰ
a.npn | n.npn | v.aam.2p | a.asn | a.asn | d.asn | n.asn | cj | | p.d | r.dsn.3 | v.aps.2p | | p.a | n.asf | cj
786 | 1100 | 2160 | 100 | 3358 | 3836 | 1128 | 2671 | | 1877 | 899 | 889 | | 1650 | 5401 | 1623

that | you | have | tasted | that | the | Lord | is good.
← | → | → | ἐγεύσασθε | ὅτι | ὁ | κύριος | χρηστός
| | | v.ami.2p | cj | d.nsm | n.nsm | a.nsm
| | | 1174 | 4022 | 3836 | 3261 | 5982

The Living Stone and a Chosen People

2:4 As | you | come | | to | him, | the living | Stone – | | rejected | | by | men | but | chosen | by | God | and
→ | → | προσερχόμενοι | πρὸς | ὃν | ζῶντα | λίθον | μὲν | ἀποδεδοκιμασμένον | ὑπὸ | ἀνθρώπων | δὲ | ἐκλεκτὸν | παρὰ | θεῷ
pt.pm.npm | p.a | r.asm | pt.pa.asm | n.asm | pl | pt.rp.asm | p.g | n.gpm | cj | a.asm | p.d | n.dsm
4665 | 4639 | 4005 | 2409 | 3345 | 3525 | 627 | 5679 | 476 | 1254 | 1723 | 4123 | 2536

precious | to him – | **5** you | also, | like | living | stones, | are | being built | | into | a spiritual | house | to be | a holy
ἔντιμον | αὐτῷ | αὐτοὶ | καὶ | ὡς | ζῶντες | λίθοι | → | οἰκοδομεῖσθε | ← | πνευματικὸς | οἶκος | εἰς ← | ἅγιον
a.asm | r.npm | cj | pl | pt.pa.npm | n.npm | | v.ppi.2p | | a.nsm | n.nsm | p.a | a.asn
1952 | 899 | 2779 | 6055 | 2409 | 3345 | | 3868 | | 4461 | 3875 | 1650 | 41

priesthood, | offering | spiritual | sacrifices | acceptable | to God | | through | Jesus | Christ. | **6** For | in | Scripture | it says:
ἱεράτευμα | ἀνενέγκαι | πνευματικὰς | θυσίας | εὐπροσδέκτους | → | ⸤τῷ | θεῷ⸥ | διὰ | Ἰησοῦ | Χριστοῦ | διότι | ἐν | γραφῇ | → περιέχει
n.asn | f.aa | a.apf | n.apf | a.apf | | d.dsm | n.dsm | p.g | n.gsm | n.gsm | cj | p.d | n.dsf | v.pai.3s
2633 | 429 | 4461 | 2602 | 2347 | | 3836 | 2536 | 1328 | 2652 | 5986 | 1484 | 1877 | 1210 | 4321

πατροπαραδότου. ¹⁹ ἀλλὰ τιμίῳ αἵματι ὡς ἀμνοῦ ἀμώμου καὶ ἀσπίλου Χριστοῦ, ²⁰ προεγνωσμένου μὲν πρὸ καταβολῆς κόσμου φανερωθέντος δὲ ἐπ᾽ ἐσχάτου τῶν χρόνων δι᾽ ὑμᾶς ²¹ τοὺς δι᾽ αὐτοῦ πιστοὺς εἰς θεὸν τὸν ἐγείραντα αὐτὸν ἐκ νεκρῶν καὶ δόξαν αὐτῷ δόντα, ὥστε τὴν πίστιν ὑμῶν καὶ ἐλπίδα εἶναι εἰς θεόν. ¶ ²² Τὰς ψυχὰς ὑμῶν ἡγνικότες ἐν τῇ ὑπακοῇ τῆς ἀληθείας εἰς φιλαδελφίαν ἀνυπόκριτον, ἐκ [καθαρᾶς] καρδίας ἀλλήλους ἀγαπήσατε ἐκτενῶς ²³ ἀναγεγεννημένοι οὐκ ἐκ σπορᾶς φθαρτῆς ἀλλὰ ἀφθάρτου διὰ λόγου ζῶντος θεοῦ καὶ μένοντος. ²⁴ διότι πᾶσα σὰρξ ὡς χόρτος καὶ πᾶσα δόξα αὐτῆς ὡς ἄνθος χόρτου· ἐξηράνθη ὁ χόρτος καὶ τὸ ἄνθος ἐξέπεσεν· ²⁵ τὸ δὲ ῥῆμα κυρίου μένει εἰς τὸν αἰῶνα. τοῦτο δέ ἐστιν τὸ ῥῆμα τὸ εὐαγγελισθὲν εἰς ὑμᾶς. ²:¹ Ἀποθέμενοι οὖν πᾶσαν κακίαν καὶ πάντα δόλον καὶ ὑποκρίσεις καὶ φθόνους καὶ πάσας καταλαλιάς, ² ὡς ἀρτιγέννητα βρέφη τὸ λογικὸν ἄδολον γάλα ἐπιποθήσατε, ἵνα ἐν αὐτῷ αὐξηθῆτε εἰς σωτηρίαν, ³ εἰ ἐγεύσασθε ὅτι χρηστὸς ὁ κύριος.

²:⁴ πρὸς ὃν προσερχόμενοι λίθον ζῶντα ὑπὸ ἀνθρώπων μὲν ἀποδεδοκιμασμένον παρὰ δὲ θεῷ ἐκλεκτὸν ἔντιμον, ⁵ καὶ αὐτοὶ ὡς λίθοι ζῶντες οἰκοδομεῖσθε οἶκος πνευματικὸς εἰς ἱεράτευμα ἅγιον ἀνενέγκαι πνευματικὰς θυσίας εὐπροσδέκτους [τῷ] θεῷ

"See, I lay a stone in Zion, a chosen and precious cornerstone, and the one who trusts in him will never be
ἰδοὺ → τίθημι λίθον ἐν Σιὼν ἐκλεκτὸν ἔντιμον ἀκρογωνιαῖον καὶ ὁ ← ← πιστεύων ἐπ᾽ αὐτῷ οὐ μὴ →
j v.pai.1s n.asm p.d n.dsf a.asm a.asm a.asm cj d.nsm pt.pa.nsm p.d r.dsm.3 pl pl
2627 5502 3345 1877 4994 1723 1952 214 2779 3836 4409 2093 899 2875 4024 3590

put to shame." ⁷Now to you who believe, this stone is precious. But to those who do not believe, "The stone
→ καταισχυνθῇ οὖν → ὑμῖν τοῖς πιστεύουσιν ιὴ τιμή, δὲ → → → → → ἀπιστοῦσιν λίθος
v.aps.3s cj r.dp.2 d.dpm pt.pa.dpm d.nsf n.nsf cj pt.pa.dpm n.nsm
2875 4036 7007 3836 4409 3836 5507 1254 601 3345

the builders rejected has become the capstone," ⁸and, "A stone that causes men to
ὃν οἱ οἰκοδομοῦντες ἀπεδοκίμασαν οὗτος → ἐγενήθη εἰς ̣κεφαλὴν γωνίας, καὶ → λίθος
r.asm d.npm pt.pa.npm v.aai.3p r.nsm v.api.3s p.a n.asf n.gsf cj n.nsm
4005 3836 3868 627 4047 1181 1650 3051 1224 2779 3345

stumble and a rock that makes them fall." They stumble because they disobey the message – which is
προσκόμματος καὶ πέτρα → σκανδάλου οἱ προσκόπτουσιν → → ἀπειθοῦντες τῷ λόγῳ
n.gsn cj n.nsf n.gsn r.npm v.pai.3p pt.pa.npm d.dsm n.dsm
4682 2779 4376 4998 4005 4684 578 3836 3364

also what they were destined for. ¶ ⁹But you are a chosen people, a royal priesthood, a holy nation, a
καὶ εἰς ὃ → ἐτέθησαν δὲ ὑμεῖς → ἐκλεκτὸν γένος βασίλειον ἱεράτευμα ἅγιον ἔθνος
adv p.a r.asn v.api.3p cj r.np.2 a.nsn n.nsn a.nsn n.nsn a.nsn n.nsn
2779 1650 4005 5502 1254 7007 1723 1169 994 2633 41 1620

people belonging to God, that you may declare the praises of him who called you out of darkness into
λαὸς εἰς περιποίησιν ὅπως → → ἐξαγγείλητε τὰς ἀρετὰς τοῦ ← καλέσαντος ὑμᾶς ἐκ ← σκότους εἰς
n.nsm p.a n.asf cj v.aas.2p d.apf n.apf d.gsm pt.aa.gsm r.ap.2 p.g n.gsn p.a
3295 1650 4348 3968 1972 3836 746 3836 2813 1666 1666 5030 1650

his wonderful light. ¹⁰Once you were not a people, but now you are the people of God; once you had not
αὐτοῦ θαυμαστὸν ̣τὸ φῶς, ποτε οἵ οὐ λαὸς δὲ νῦν λαὸς → θεοῦ οἱ → οὐκ
r.gsm.3 a.asn d.asn n.asn adv r.npm pl n.nsm cj adv n.nsm n.gsm d.npm pl
899 2515 3836 5890 4537 4005 4024 3295 1254 3814 3295 2536 3836 1796 4024

received mercy, but now you have received mercy. ¶ ¹¹Dear friends, I urge you, as aliens and
→ ἠλεημένοι δὲ νῦν → → ἐλεηθέντες ᾽Αγαπητοί → παρακαλῶ ὡς παροίκους καὶ
pt.rp.npm cj adv pt.ap.npm a.vpm v.pai.1s pl n.apm cj
1796 1254 3814 1796 28 4151 6055 4230 2779

strangers in the world, to abstain from sinful desires, which war against your soul. ¹²Live such
παρεπιδήμους ← ← → ἀπέχεσθαι σαρκικῶν ̣τῶν ἐπιθυμιῶν, αἵτινες στρατεύονται κατὰ τῆς ψυχῆς ἔχοντες
n.apm f.pm a.gpf d.gpf n.gpf r.npf v.pmi.3p p.g d.gsf n.gsf pt.pa.npm
4215 600 4920 3836 2123 4015 5129 2848 3836 6034 2400

good lives among the pagans that, though they accuse you of doing wrong, they may
καλὴν ̣τὴν ἀναστροφὴν ὑμῶν, ἐν τοῖς ἔθνεσιν ἵνα ἐν ᾧ καταλαλοῦσιν ὑμῶν ὡς κακοποιῶν
a.asf d.asf n.asf r.gp.2 p.d d.dpn n.dpn cj p.d r.dsn v.pai.3p r.gp.2 pl n.gpm
2819 3836 419 7007 1877 3836 1620 2671 1877 4005 2895 7007 6055 2804

see your good deeds and glorify God on the day he visits us.
ἐποπτεύοντες ἐκ τῶν καλῶν ἔργων δοξάσωσιν ̣τὸν θεὸν, ἐν ἡμέρᾳ → ἐπισκοπῆς
pt.pa.npm p.g d.gpn a.gpn n.gpn v.aas.3p d.asm n.asm p.d n.dsf n.gsf
2227 1666 3836 2819 2240 1519 3836 2536 1877 2465 2175

Submission to Rulers and Masters

²:¹³Submit yourselves for the Lord's sake to every authority instituted among men: whether to the king,
Ὑποτάγητε ← διὰ τὸν κύριον ↰ → πάσῃ κτίσει → ἀνθρωπίνῃ εἴτε → βασιλεῖ
v.apm.2p p.a d.asm n.asm a.dsf n.dsf a.dsf cj n.dsm
5718 1328 3836 3261 1328 4246 3232 474 1664 995

as the supreme authority, ¹⁴or to governors, who are sent by him to punish those who do wrong and
ὡς ὑπερέχοντι ← εἴτε → ἡγεμόσιν ὡς → πεμπομένοις δι᾽ αὐτοῦ εἰς ἐκδίκησιν → → κακοποιῶν δὲ
pl pt.pa.dsm cj n.dpm pl pt.pp.dpm p.g r.gsm.3 p.a n.asf n.gpm cj
6055 5660 1664 2450 6055 4287 1328 899 1650 1689 2804 1254

to commend those who do right. ¹⁵For it is God's will that by doing good you should
ἔπαινον → → → ἀγαθοποιῶν ὅτι οὕτως → ἐστιν ̣τοῦ θεοῦ, ̣τὸ θέλημα, → ἀγαθοποιοῦντας → →
n.asm n.gpm cj adv v.pai.3s d.gsm n.gsm d.nsn n.nsn pt.pa.apm
2047 18 4022 4048 1639 3836 2536 3836 2525 16

διὰ ᾽Ιησοῦ Χριστοῦ. ⁶διότι περιέχει ἐν γραφῇ, ᾽Ιδοὺ τίθημι ἐν Σιὼν λίθον ἀκρογωνιαῖον ἐκλεκτὸν ἔντιμον καὶ ὁ πιστεύων ἐπ᾽ αὐτῷ οὐ μὴ καταισχυνθῇ. ⁷ὑμῖν οὖν ἡ τιμὴ τοῖς πιστεύουσιν, ἀπιστοῦσιν δὲ λίθος ὃν ἀπεδοκίμασαν οἱ οἰκοδομοῦντες, οὗτος ἐγενήθη εἰς κεφαλὴν γωνίας ⁸καὶ λίθος προσκόμματος καὶ πέτρα σκανδάλου· οἳ προσκόπτουσιν τῷ λόγῳ ἀπειθοῦντες εἰς ὃ καὶ ἐτέθησαν. ¶ ⁹Ὑμεῖς δὲ γένος ἐκλεκτόν, βασίλειον ἱεράτευμα, ἔθνος ἅγιον, λαὸς εἰς περιποίησιν, ὅπως τὰς ἀρετὰς ἐξαγγείλητε τοῦ ἐκ σκότους ὑμᾶς καλέσαντος εἰς τὸ θαυμαστὸν αὐτοῦ φῶς· ¹⁰οἵ ποτε οὐ λαὸς νῦν δὲ λαὸς θεοῦ, οἱ οὐκ ἠλεημένοι νῦν δὲ ἐλεηθέντες. ¶ ¹¹Ἀγαπητοί, παρακαλῶ ὡς παροίκους καὶ παρεπιδήμους ἀπέχεσθαι τῶν σαρκικῶν ἐπιθυμιῶν αἵτινες στρατεύονται κατὰ τῆς ψυχῆς· ¹²τὴν ἀναστροφὴν ὑμῶν ἐν τοῖς ἔθνεσιν ἔχοντες καλήν, ἵνα, ἐν ᾧ καταλαλοῦσιν ὑμῶν ὡς κακοποιῶν ἐκ τῶν καλῶν ἔργων ἐποπτεύοντες δοξάσωσιν τὸν θεὸν ἐν ἡμέρᾳ ἐπισκοπῆς.

²:¹³Ὑποτάγητε πάσῃ ἀνθρωπίνῃ κτίσει διὰ τὸν κύριον, εἴτε βασιλεῖ ὡς ὑπερέχοντι, ¹⁴εἴτε ἡγεμόσιν ὡς δι᾽ αὐτοῦ πεμπομένοις εἰς ἐκδίκησιν κακοποιῶν ἔπαινον δὲ ἀγαθοποιῶν· ¹⁵ὅτι οὕτως ἐστὶν τὸ θέλημα τοῦ θεοῦ ἀγαθοποιοῦντας φιμοῦν τὴν τῶν ἀφρόνων

silence the ignorant talk of foolish men. ¹⁶ Live as free men, but do not use your freedom as a
φιμοῦν τὴν ἀγνωσίαν ← ↱ ἀφρόνων ⌐τῶν ἀνθρώπων⌐ ὡς ἐλεύθεροι καὶ ↗ μὴ ἔχοντες τὴν ἐλευθερίαν ὡς
f.pa d.asf n.asf 　 476 a.gpm d.gpm n.gpm pl n.npm cj 　 μη pt.pa.npm d.asf n.asf pl
5821 3836 57 　 933 3836 476 6055 1801 2779 2400 3590 2400 3836 1800 6055

cover-up for evil; live as servants of God. ¹⁷ Show proper respect to everyone: Love the brotherhood of
ἐπικάλυμμα → ⌐τῆς κακίας⌐ ἀλλ᾽ ὡς δοῦλοι → θεοῦ τιμήσατε ← πάντας ἀγαπᾶτε τὴν ἀδελφότητα
n.asn d.gsf n.gsf cj pl n.npm n.gsm v.aam.2p a.apm v.pam.2p d.asf n.asf
2127 3836 2798 247 6055 1529 2536 5506 4246 26 3836 82

believers, fear God, honor the king. ¶ ¹⁸ Slaves, submit yourselves to your masters with all
← φοβεῖσθε τὸν θεὸν τιμᾶτε τὸν βασιλέα ⌐Οἱ οἰκέται⌐ ὑποτασσόμενοι ← → τοῖς δεσπόταις ἐν παντὶ
v.ppm.2p d.asm n.asm v.pam.2p d.asm n.asm d.npm n.npm pt.pp.npm d.dpm n.dpm p.d a.dsm
5828 3836 2536 5506 3836 995 3836 3860 5718 3836 1305 1877 4246

respect, not only to those who are good and considerate, but also to those who are harsh. ¹⁹ For it is
φόβῳ οὐ μόνον → τοῖς ← → ἀγαθοῖς καὶ ἐπιεικέσιν ἀλλὰ καὶ → τοῖς ← → σκολιοῖς γὰρ τοῦτο
n.dsm adv d.dpm a.dpm cj a.dpm cj adv d.dpm a.dpm cj r.nsn
5832 4024 3667 3836 19 2779 2117 247 2779 3836 5021 1142 4047

commendable if a man bears up under the pain of unjust suffering because he is conscious of God. ²⁰ But how is
χάρις εἰ τις ὑποφέρει ← → λύπας → ἀδίκως πάσχων διὰ συνείδησιν θεοῦ γὰρ ποῖον
n.nsf cj r.nsm v.pai.3s n.apf adv pt.pa.nsm p.a n.asf n.gsm cj r.nsn
5921 1623 5516 5722 3383 97 4248 1328 5287 2536 1142 4481

it to your credit if you receive a beating for doing wrong and endure it? But if you suffer
κλέος εἰ καὶ → → κολαφιζόμενοι → → ἁμαρτάνοντες ὑπομενεῖτε ἀλλ᾽ εἰ → πάσχοντες καὶ
n.nsn cj cj pt.pp.npm pt.pa.npm v.fai.2p cj cj pt.pa.npm cj
3094 1623 2779 3139 279 5702 247 1623 4248 2779

for doing good and you endure it, this is commendable before God. ²¹ To this you were called,
→ ← ἀγαθοποιοῦντες καὶ ὑπομενεῖτε τοῦτο χάρις παρὰ θεῷ γὰρ εἰς τοῦτο ἐκλήθητε
pt.pa.npm v.fai.2p r.nsn n.nsf p.d n.dsm cj p.a r.asn v.api.2p
16 5702 4047 5921 4123 2536 1142 1650 4047 2813

because Christ suffered for you, leaving you an example, that you should follow in his
ὅτι καὶ Χριστὸς ἔπαθεν ὑπὲρ ὑμῶν ὑπολιμπάνων ὑμῖν ὑπογραμμὸν ἵνα → → ἐπακολουθήσητε ↗ αὐτοῦ
cj adv n.nsm v.aai.3s p.g r.gp.2 pt.pa.nsm r.dp.2 n.asm cj v.aas.2p r.gsm.3
4022 2779 5986 4248 5642 7007 5701 7007 5681 2671 2051 2717 899

steps. ²² "He committed no sin, and no deceit was found in his mouth." ²³ When they hurled their
⌐τοῖς ἴχνεσιν⌐ ὃς ἐποίησεν οὐκ ἁμαρτίαν οὐδὲ ← δόλος → εὑρέθη ἐν αὐτοῦ ⌐τῷ στόματι⌐ → → →
d.dpn n.dpn r.nsm v.aai.3s pl cj n.nsm v.api.3s p.d r.gsm.3 d.dsn n.dsn
3836 2717 4005 4472 4024 281 4028 1515 2351 1877 899 3836 5125

insults at him, he did not retaliate; when he suffered, he made no threats. Instead, he entrusted himself to
λοιδορούμενος ὃς → → οὐκ ἀντελοιδόρει → πάσχων ↗ → οὐκ ἠπείλει δὲ → παρεδίδου ←
pt.pp.nsm r.nsm pl v.iai.3s pt.pa.nsm pl v.iai.3s cj v.iai.3s
3366 4005 518 518 4024 518 4248 580 580 4024 580 1254 4140

him who judges justly. ²⁴ He himself bore our sins in his body on the tree, so that we might
τῷ κρίνοντι δικαίως ὃς αὐτὸς ἀνήνεγκεν ἡμῶν ⌐τὰς ἁμαρτίας⌐ ἐν αὐτοῦ ⌐τῷ σώματι⌐ ἐπὶ τὸ ξύλον ἵνα ← →
d.dsm pt.pa.dsm adv r.nsm r.nsm v.aai.3s r.gp.1 d.apf n.apf p.d r.gsm.3 d.dsn n.dsn p.a d.asn n.asn cj
3836 3212 1469 4005 899 429 7005 3836 281 1877 899 3836 5393 2093 3836 3833 2671

die to sins and live for righteousness; by his wounds you have been healed. ²⁵ For you were
ἀπογενόμενοι → ⌐ταῖς ἁμαρτίαις⌐ ζήσωμεν → τῇ δικαιοσύνῃ οὗ τῷ μώλωπι → → → ἰάθητε γὰρ ἦτε
pt.am.npm d.dpf n.dpf v.aas.1p d.dsf n.dsf r.gsm d.dsm n.dsm v.api.2p cj v.iai.2p
614 3836 281 2409 3836 1466 3698 4005 3836 3698 2615 1142 1639

like sheep going astray, but now you have returned to the Shepherd and Overseer of your souls.
ὡς πρόβατα → πλανώμενοι ἀλλὰ νῦν → → ἐπεστράφητε ἐπὶ τὸν ποιμένα καὶ ἐπίσκοπον ↗ ὑμῶν ⌐τῶν ψυχῶν⌐
pl n.npn pt.pp.npm cj adv v.api.2p p.a d.asm n.asm cj n.asm r.gp.2 d.gpf n.gpf
6055 4585 4414 247 3814 2188 2093 3836 4478 2779 2176 6034 7007 3836 6034

Wives and Husbands

3:1 Wives, in the same way be submissive to your husbands so that, if any of them do not
⌐αἱ γυναῖκες⌐ → → Ὁμοίως ← → ὑποτασσόμεναι → ἰδίοις ⌐τοῖς ἀνδράσιν⌐ ἵνα ← καὶ εἴ τινες → →
d.npf n.npf adv pt.pp.npf a.dpm d.dpm n.dpm cj cj cj r.npm
3836 1222 3931 5718 467 2625 3836 467 2671 2779 1623 5516

ἀνθρώπων ἀγνωσίαν. ¹⁶ ὡς ἐλεύθεροι καὶ μὴ ὡς ἐπικάλυμμα ἔχοντες τῆς κακίας τὴν ἐλευθερίαν ἀλλ᾽ ὡς θεοῦ δοῦλοι. ¹⁷ πάντας
τιμήσατε, τὴν ἀδελφότητα ἀγαπᾶτε, τὸν θεὸν φοβεῖσθε, τὸν βασιλέα τιμᾶτε. ¶ ¹⁸ Οἱ οἰκέται ὑποτασσόμενοι ἐν παντὶ φόβῳ τοῖς
δεσπόταις, οὐ μόνον τοῖς ἀγαθοῖς καὶ ἐπιεικέσιν ἀλλὰ καὶ τοῖς σκολιοῖς. ¹⁹ τοῦτο γὰρ χάρις εἰ διὰ συνείδησιν θεοῦ ὑποφέρει
τις λύπας πάσχων ἀδίκως. ²⁰ ποῖον γὰρ κλέος εἰ ἁμαρτάνοντες καὶ κολαφιζόμενοι ὑπομενεῖτε; ἀλλ᾽ εἰ ἀγαθοποιοῦντες καὶ
πάσχοντες ὑπομενεῖτε, τοῦτο χάρις παρὰ θεῷ. ²¹ εἰς τοῦτο γὰρ ἐκλήθητε, ὅτι καὶ Χριστὸς ἔπαθεν ὑπὲρ ὑμῶν ὑμῖν ὑπολιμπάνων
ὑπογραμμὸν ἵνα ἐπακολουθήσητε τοῖς ἴχνεσιν αὐτοῦ, ²² ὃς ἁμαρτίαν οὐκ ἐποίησεν οὐδὲ εὑρέθη δόλος ἐν τῷ στόματι αὐτοῦ,
²³ ὃς λοιδορούμενος οὐκ ἀντελοιδόρει πάσχων οὐκ ἠπείλει, παρεδίδου δὲ τῷ κρίνοντι δικαίως· ²⁴ ὃς τὰς ἁμαρτίας ἡμῶν αὐτὸς
ἀνήνεγκεν ἐν τῷ σώματι αὐτοῦ ἐπὶ τὸ ξύλον, ἵνα ταῖς ἁμαρτίαις ἀπογενόμενοι τῇ δικαιοσύνῃ ζήσωμεν, οὗ τῷ μώλωπι ἰάθητε.
²⁵ ἦτε γὰρ ὡς πρόβατα πλανώμενοι, ἀλλὰ ἐπεστράφητε νῦν ἐπὶ τὸν ποιμένα καὶ ἐπίσκοπον τῶν ψυχῶν ὑμῶν.
　³:¹ Ὁμοίως [αἱ] γυναῖκες, ὑποτασσόμεναι τοῖς ἰδίοις ἀνδράσιν, ἵνα καὶ εἴ τινες ἀπειθοῦσιν τῷ λόγῳ, διὰ τῆς τῶν γυναικῶν

believe   the word, they may be won   over without words by the behavior   of their wives, ² when they
ἀπειθοῦσιν τῷ λόγῳ →   → κερδηθήσονται ← ἄνευ λόγου διὰ τῆς ἀναστροφῆς → τῶν γυναικῶν →
v.pai.3p   d.dsm n.dsm   v.fpi.3p   p.g   n.gsm p.g d.gsf n.gsf   d.gpf n.gpf
578   3836 3364   3045   459   3364 1328 3836 419   3836 1222

see   the purity and reverence of your lives. ³ Your beauty should not come from outward adornment,
ἐποπτεύσαντες τὴν ἀγνὴν ἐν φόβῳ ὑμῶν ἀναστροφὴν ὧν   → οὐχ ἔστω   ἔξωθεν ὁ κόσμος
pt.aa.npm   d.asf a.asf p.d n.dsm r.gp.2 n.asf   r.gpf   pl v.pam.3s   pl   p.g   d.nsm n.nsm
2227   3836 54   1877 5832   7007 419   4005   1639 4024 1639   2033   3836 3180

such as braided hair   and the wearing of gold jewelry and   fine clothes. ⁴ Instead, it should be that of
ἐμπλοκῆς τριχῶν καὶ   περιθέσεως → χρυσίων   ἢ ἐνδύσεως → ἱματίων ἀλλ'   →
n.gsf   n.gpf cj   n.gsf   n.gpn   cj n.gsf   n.gpn   cj
1862   2582   2779 4324   5992   2445 1906   2668   247

your inner   self,   the unfading beauty of a gentle and quiet spirit,   which is of
ὁ κρυπτὸς τῆς καρδίας ἄνθρωπος ἐν τῷ ἀφθάρτῳ   → πραέως καὶ ἡσυχίου τοῦ πνεύματος ὅ   ἐστιν
d.nsm a.nsm d.gsf n.gsf   n.nsm p.d d.dsm n.dsn   a.gsn cj   a.gsn d.gsn n.gsn r.nsn v.pai.3s
3836 3220 3836 2840   476   1877 3836 915   4460   4558 2779 2485 3836 4460   4005 1639

great   worth in   God's   sight. ⁵ For this is the way   the holy women of the past who put their hope
πολυτελές ←   ἐνώπιον τοῦ θεοῦ   γὰρ οὕτως ← ← καὶ αἱ ἅγιαι γυναῖκες → ποτε αἱ   ἐλπίζουσαι
a.nsn   p.g   d.gsm n.gsm   cj adv   adv d.npf a.npf n.npf   adv d.npf   pt.pa.npf
4500   1967   3836 2536   1142 4048   2779 3836 41   1222   4537 3836   1827

in God used to make themselves beautiful. They were submissive to their own husbands, ⁶ like Sarah, who
εἰς θεὸν → → → ἑαυτὰς   ἐκόσμουν → ὑποτασσόμεναι → τοῖς ἰδίοις ἀνδράσιν ὡς Σάρρα →
p.a n.asm   rapf.3   v.iai.3p   pt.pp.npf   d.dpm a.dpm n.dpm cj n.nsf
1650 2536 3175 3175 3175 1571   3175   5718   3836 2625 467   6055 4925

obeyed Abraham   and called him her master. You are   her daughters if you do what is right   and
ὑπήκουσεν τῷ Ἀβραὰμ καλοῦσα αὐτὸν κύριον →   ἐγενήθητε ἧς τέκνα   →   → ἀγαθοποιοῦσαι καὶ
v.aai.3s d.dsm n.dsm pt.pa.nsf r.asm.3 n.asm   v.api.2p r.gsf n.npn   pt.pa.npf   cj
5634   3836 11   2813   899   3261   1181   4005 5451   16   2779

do not give   way to fear. ¶ ⁷ Husbands,   in the same way be considerate as you
→ μὴ φοβούμεναι μηδεμίαν πτόησιν ← ← Οἱ ἄνδρες,   ὁμοίως ←   κατὰ γνώσιν   ὡς
pl pt.pp.npf a.asf   n.asf   d.npm n.npm   adv   p.a   n.asf
5828 3590 5828 3594   4766   3836 467   3931   2848   1194

live   with your wives,   and treat them with respect as the weaker partner and as heirs
συνοικοῦντες ← τῷ γυναικείῳ ἀπονέμοντες ← τιμὴν ὡς   ἀσθενεστέρῳ σκεύει ὡς καὶ συγκληρονόμοις
pt.pa.npm   d.dsn n.dsn   pt.pa.npm   n.asf n.asf   a.dsn.c   n.dsn   pl adv 2779 n.dpf
5324   3836 1221   671   5507 6055   822   5007   6055 2779 5169

with you of the gracious gift of life, so that nothing will hinder your prayers.
← ← → χάριτος   → ζωῆς εἰς → μὴ   → τὸ ἐγκόπτεσθαι ὑμῶν τὰς προσευχὰς
          n.gsf   n.gsf p.a   pl   d.asn f.pp   r.gp.2 d.apf n.apf
          5921   2437 1650   3590   3836 1601   7007 3836 4666

Suffering for Doing Good

³·⁸ Finally, all of you, live in harmony with one another; be sympathetic, love   as brothers, be
δὲ Τὸ τέλος πάντες ← ←   ὁμόφρονες ← ←   συμπαθεῖς φιλάδελφοι ←
cj d.asn n.asn a.npm   a.npm   a.npm   a.npm
1254 3836 5465 4246   3939   5218   5790

compassionate and humble. ⁹ Do not repay   evil   with evil or insult   with insult, but   with
εὔσπλαγχνοι   ταπεινόφρονες → μὴ ἀποδιδόντες κακὸν ἀντὶ κακοῦ ἢ λοιδορίαν ἀντὶ λοιδορίας δὲ τοὐναντίον
a.npm   a.npm   pl pt.pa.npm   a.asn p.g a.gsn cj n.asf   p.g n.gsf   cj crasis
2359   5426   625 625   2805 505 2805 2445 3367   505 3367   1254 5539

blessing, because to this you were called so that you may inherit   a blessing. ¹⁰ For, "Whoever would love
εὐλογοῦντες ὅτι   εἰς τοῦτο → → ἐκλήθητε ἵνα ← → κληρονομήσητε εὐλογίαν   γὰρ ὁ   θέλων ἀγαπᾶν
pt.pa.npm cj   p.a r.asn   v.api.2p cj   v.aas.2p   n.asf   cj d.nsm pt.pa.nsm f.pa
2328   4022 1650 4047   2813   2671   3099   2330   1142 3836   2527   26

life and see good   days must keep his tongue from evil and his lips from deceitful speech. ¹¹ He must
ζωὴν καὶ ἰδεῖν ἀγαθὰς ἡμέρας παυσάτω τὴν γλῶσσαν ἀπὸ κακοῦ καὶ χείλη μὴ δόλον   τοῦ λαλῆσαι δὲ → →
n.asf cj f.aa a.apf n.apf   v.aam.3s d.asf n.asf p.g a.gsn cj   n.apn pl n.asm   d.gsn f.aa   cj
2437 2779 1625 19   2465   4264   3836 1185   608 2805 2779 5927 3590 1515   3836 3281   1254

ἀναστροφῆς ἄνευ λόγου κερδηθήσονται, ² ἐποπτεύσαντες τὴν ἐν φόβῳ ἁγνὴν ἀναστροφὴν ὑμῶν. ³ ὧν ἔστω οὐχ ὁ ἔξωθεν ἐμπλοκῆς τριχῶν καὶ περιθέσεως χρυσίων ἢ ἐνδύσεως ἱματίων κόσμος ⁴ ἀλλ' ὁ κρυπτὸς τῆς καρδίας ἄνθρωπος ἐν τῷ ἀφθάρτῳ τοῦ πραέως καὶ ἡσυχίου πνεύματος, ὅ ἐστιν ἐνώπιον τοῦ θεοῦ πολυτελές. ⁵ οὕτως γάρ ποτε καὶ αἱ ἅγιαι γυναῖκες αἱ ἐλπίζουσαι εἰς θεὸν ἐκόσμουν ἑαυτὰς ὑποτασσόμεναι τοῖς ἰδίοις ἀνδράσιν. ⁶ ὡς Σάρρα ὑπήκουσεν τῷ Ἀβραὰμ κύριον αὐτὸν καλοῦσα, ἧς ἐγενήθητε τέκνα ἀγαθοποιοῦσαι καὶ μὴ φοβούμεναι μηδεμίαν πτόησιν. ¶ ⁷ Οἱ ἄνδρες ὁμοίως, συνοικοῦντες κατὰ γνῶσιν ὡς ἀσθενεστέρῳ σκεύει τῷ γυναικείῳ, ἀπονέμοντες τιμὴν ὡς καὶ συγκληρονόμοις χάριτος ζωῆς εἰς τὸ μὴ ἐγκόπτεσθαι τὰς προσευχὰς ὑμῶν.

³·⁸ Τὸ δὲ τέλος πάντες ὁμόφρονες, συμπαθεῖς, φιλάδελφοι, εὔσπλαγχνοι, ταπεινόφρονες, ⁹ μὴ ἀποδιδόντες κακὸν ἀντὶ κακοῦ ἢ λοιδορίαν ἀντὶ λοιδορίας, τοὐναντίον δὲ εὐλογοῦντες ὅτι εἰς τοῦτο ἐκλήθητε ἵνα εὐλογίαν κληρονομήσητε. ¹⁰ ὁ γὰρ θέλων ζωὴν ἀγαπᾶν καὶ ἰδεῖν ἡμέρας ἀγαθὰς παυσάτω τὴν γλῶσσαν ἀπὸ κακοῦ καὶ χείλη τοῦ μὴ λαλῆσαι δόλον, ¹¹ ἐκκλινάτω δὲ

turn	from	evil	and	do		good;	he must seek		peace	and	pursue	it.	**12** For	the	eyes		of the	Lord	are
ἐκκλινάτω	ἀπὸ	κακοῦ	καὶ	ποιησάτω		ἀγαθόν	ζητησάτω	εἰρήνην		καὶ	διωξάτω	αὐτήν	ὅτι		ὀφθαλμοὶ	→		κυρίου	
v.aam.3s	p.g	a.gsn	cj	v.aam.3s		a.asn	v.aam.3s	n.asf		cj	v.aam.3s	r.asf.3	cj		n.npm			n.gsm	
1712	608	2805	2779	4472		19	2426	1645		2779	1503	899	4022		4057			3261	

on the	righteous	and	his	ears	are attentive	to	their	prayer,	but	the	face		of the	Lord	is against	those who
ἐπὶ	δικαίους	καὶ	αὐτοῦ	ὦτα	→	εἰς	αὐτῶν	δέησιν	δὲ		πρόσωπον	→		κυρίου	ἐπὶ	→ →
p.a	a.apm	cj	r.gsm.3	n.npn		p.a	r.gpm.3	n.asf	cj		n.nsn			n.gsm	p.a	
2093	1465	2779	899	4044		1650	899	1255	1254		4725			3261	2093	

do	evil."	¶	**13**	Who	is going to harm			you	if	you are		eager	to do good?		**14** But	even	if
ποιοῦντας	κακά			Καὶ	τίς	→ →	ὁ	κακώσων	ὑμᾶς	ἐὰν	→	γένησθε	ζηλωταὶ		τοῦ ἀγαθοῦ	ἀλλ᾽	καὶ	εἰ
pt.pa.apm	a.apn			cj	r.nsm		d.nsm	pt.fa.nsm	r.ap.2	cj		v.ams.2p	n.npm		d.gsn a.gsn	adv	adv	cj
4472	2805			2779	5515		3836	2808	7007	1569		1181	2421		3836 19	247	2779	1623

you	should suffer	for what	is right,		you are blessed.		"Do not	fear	what they	fear;	do not be
→ →	πάσχοιτε	διὰ →	→ δικαιοσύνην		μακάριοι	δὲ	μὴ	φοβηθῆτε	αὐτῶν	τὸν φόβον	μηδὲ →
	v.pao.2p	p.a	n.asf		a.npm	cj	pl	v.aps.2p	r.gpm.3	d.asm n.asm	cj
	4248	1328	1466		3421	1254	5828	3590 5828	899	3836 5832	5429 3593

frightened."	**15** But	in	your	hearts	set apart	Christ		as Lord.	Always	be	prepared	to	give an answer
ταραχθῆτε	δὲ	ἐν	ὑμῶν	ταῖς καρδίαις	ἁγιάσατε	τὸν Χριστὸν		κύριον	ἀεὶ		ἕτοιμοι	πρὸς ←	ἀπολογίαν
v.aps.2p	cj	p.d	r.gp.2	d.dpf n.dpf	v.aam.2p	d.asm n.asm		n.asm	adv		a.npm	p.a	n.asf
5429	1254	1877	7007	3836 2840	39	3836 5986		3261	107		2289	4639	665

to	everyone	who asks		you	to give	the reason	for	the	hope	that	you have.	But	do this with	gentleness	and
→	παντὶ	τῷ αἰτοῦντι		ὑμᾶς		λόγον	περὶ	τῆς	ἐλπίδος	ὑμῖν	ἐν	ἀλλὰ	μετὰ	πραΰτητος	καὶ
	a.dsm	d.dsm pt.pa.dsm		r.ap.2		n.asm	p.g	d.gsf	n.gsf	r.dp.2	p.d	cj	p.g	n.gsf	cj
	4246	3836 160		7007		3364	4309	3836	1828	7007	1877	247	3552	4559	2779

respect,	**16** keeping	a clear	conscience,	so that		those who speak	maliciously against	your	good
φόβου	ἔχοντες	ἀγαθὴν	συνείδησιν	ἵνα ←	ἐν ᾧ →		καταλαλεῖσθε ←	←	ὑμῶν ἀγαθὴν
n.gsm	pt.pa.npm	a.asf	n.asf	cj	p.d r.dsn		v.ppi.2p		r.gp.2 a.asf
5832	2400	19	5287	2671	1877 4005	2875	2895		7007 19

behavior	in	Christ	may be ashamed		of their	slander.	**17**	It is better,	if	it is	God's		will,		to
τὴν ἀναστροφήν	ἐν	Χριστῷ	→ κατaισχυνθῶσιν ←	οἱ	ἐπηρεάζοντες		γὰρ	κρεῖττον	εἰ	→ θέλοι	τοῦ θεοῦ		τὸ θέλημα	→
d.asf n.asf	p.d	n.dsm	v.aps.3p	d.npm	pt.pa.npm		cj	a.nsn	cj	v.pao.3s	d.gsn n.gsm		d.nsn n.nsn	
3836 419	1877	5986	2875	3836	2092		1142	3202	1623	2527	3836 2536		3836 2525	

suffer	for doing good		than	for doing evil.		**18** For		Christ	died	for	sins	once for all,	the
πάσχειν	→ → ἀγαθοποιοῦντας	ἢ	→	κακοποιοῦντας		ὅτι	καὶ	Χριστὸς	ἔπαθεν	περὶ	ἁμαρτιῶν	ἅπαξ ← ←
f.pa	pt.pa.apm	pl		pt.pa.apm		cj	adv	n.nsm	v.aai.3s	p.g	n.gpf	adv
4248	16	2445		2803		4022	2779	5986	4248	4309	281	562

righteous	for	the unrighteous,	to	bring	you	to God.		He was put to death		in the	body	but	made
δίκαιος	ὑπὲρ	ἀδίκων	ἵνα	προσαγάγῃ	ὑμᾶς	τῷ θεῷ	μὲν	→ → θανατωθεὶς	→		σαρκὶ	δὲ	
a.nsm	p.g	a.gpm	cj	v.aas.3s	r.ap.2	d.dsm n.dsm	pl	pt.ap.nsm			n.dsf	cj	
1465	5642	96	2671	4642	7007	3836 2536	3525	2506			4922	1254	

alive	by	the	Spirit,	**19** through	whom	also	he went	and	preached	to the	spirits	in	prison	**20** who disobeyed
ζωοποιηθεὶς	→		πνεύματι	ἐν	ᾧ	καὶ	→ πορευθεὶς	ἐκήρυξεν		τοῖς πνεύμασιν	ἐν	φυλακῇ	→	ἀπειθήσασιν
pt.ap.nsm			n.dsn	p.d	r.dsn	adv	pt.ap.nsm	v.aai.3s		d.dpn n.dpn	p.d	n.dsf		pt.aa.dpm
2443			4460	1877	4005	2779	4513	3062		3836 4460	1877	5871		578

long ago	when	God	waited	patiently	in	the days	of Noah	while	the ark		was being built.
ποτε	ὅτε	τοῦ θεοῦ	ἀπεξεδέχετο	ἡ μακροθυμία	ἐν	ἡμέραις	Νῶε		κιβωτοῦ	→	κατασκευαζομένης
adv	cj	d.gsm n.gsm	v.imi.3s	d.nsf n.nsf	p.d	n.dpf	n.gsm		n.gsf		pt.pp.gsf
4537	4021	3836 2536	587	3836 3429	1877	2465	3820 2941		3066		2941

In	it	only a few	people,		eight in all,	were saved		through	water,	**21** and	this		water symbolizes
εἰς	ἣν	ὀλίγοι	ψυχαί	τοῦτ᾽ ἔστιν ὀκτὼ		→	διεσώθησαν	δι᾽	ὕδατος	ὃ	καὶ		ἀντίτυπον
p.a	r.asf	a.npm	n.npf	r.nsn v.pai.3s a.npf			v.api.3p	p.g	n.gsn	r.nsn	adv		a.nsn
1650	4005	3900	6034	4047 1639 3893			1407	1328	5623	4005	2779		531

baptism	that	now	saves	you	also	—	not the	removal	of dirt	from the	body	but	the	pledge	of a	good	conscience
βάπτισμα		νῦν	σῴζει	ὑμᾶς			οὐ	ἀπόθεσις	→	ῥύπου	→	σαρκὸς	ἀλλὰ	ἐπερώτημα	→	ἀγαθῆς	συνειδήσεως
n.nsn		adv	v.pai.3s	r.ap.2			pl	n.nsf		n.gsm		n.gsf	cj	n.nsn		a.gsf	n.gsf
967		3814	5392	7007			4024	629		4866		4922	247	2090		19	5287

ἀπὸ κακοῦ καὶ ποιησάτω ἀγαθόν, ζητησάτω εἰρήνην καὶ διωξάτω αὐτήν· **12** ὅτι ὀφθαλμοὶ κυρίου ἐπὶ δικαίους καὶ ὦτα αὐτοῦ εἰς δέησιν αὐτῶν, πρόσωπον δὲ κυρίου ἐπὶ ποιοῦντας κακά. ¶ **13** Καὶ τίς ὁ κακώσων ὑμᾶς ἐὰν τοῦ ἀγαθοῦ ζηλωταὶ γένησθε; **14** ἀλλ᾽ εἰ καὶ πάσχοιτε διὰ δικαιοσύνην, μακάριοι. τὸν δὲ φόβον αὐτῶν μὴ φοβηθῆτε μηδὲ ταραχθῆτε, **15** κύριον δὲ τὸν Χριστὸν ἁγιάσατε ἐν ταῖς καρδίαις ὑμῶν, ἕτοιμοι ἀεὶ πρὸς ἀπολογίαν παντὶ τῷ αἰτοῦντι ὑμᾶς λόγον περὶ τῆς ἐν ὑμῖν ἐλπίδος, **16** ἀλλὰ μετὰ πραΰτητος καὶ φόβου, συνείδησιν ἔχοντες ἀγαθήν, ἵνα ἐν ᾧ καταλαλεῖσθε καταισχυνθῶσιν οἱ ἐπηρεάζοντες ὑμῶν τὴν ἀγαθὴν ἐν Χριστῷ ἀναστροφήν. **17** κρεῖττον γὰρ ἀγαθοποιοῦντας, εἰ θέλοι τὸ θέλημα τοῦ θεοῦ, πάσχειν ἢ κακοποιοῦντας. **18** ὅτι καὶ Χριστὸς ἅπαξ περὶ ἁμαρτιῶν ἀπέθανεν, «ἔπαθεν,» δίκαιος ὑπὲρ ἀδίκων, ἵνα ὑμᾶς προσαγάγῃ τῷ θεῷ θανατωθεὶς μὲν σαρκὶ ζωοποιηθεὶς δὲ πνεύματι· **19** ἐν ᾧ καὶ τοῖς ἐν φυλακῇ πνεύμασιν πορευθεὶς ἐκήρυξεν, **20** ἀπειθήσασίν ποτε ὅτε ἀπεξεδέχετο ἡ τοῦ θεοῦ μακροθυμία ἐν ἡμέραις Νῶε κατασκευαζομένης κιβωτοῦ εἰς ἣν ὀλίγοι, τοῦτ᾽ ἔστιν ὀκτὼ ψυχαί, διεσώθησαν δι᾽ ὕδατος. **21** ὃ καὶ ὑμᾶς ἀντίτυπον νῦν σῴζει βάπτισμα, οὐ σαρκὸς ἀπόθεσις ῥύπου ἀλλὰ συνειδήσεως ἀγαθῆς ἐπερώτημα εἰς

toward God. It saves you by the resurrection of Jesus Christ, [22] who has gone into heaven and is at God's
εἰς   θεόν   δι᾽   ἀναστάσεως   →   Ἰησοῦ Χριστοῦ   ὅς   →   πορευθεὶς εἰς   οὐρανόν   ἐστιν ἐν   τοῦ θεοῦ
p.a   n.asm   p.g   n.gsf   n.gsm n.gsm   r.nsm   pt.ap.nsm p.a   n.asm   v.pai.3s p.d d.gsm n.gsm
1650   2536   1328 414   2652 5986   4005   4513   1650 4041   1639 1877 3836 2536

right hand – with angels,   authorities and powers   in submission to him.
δεξιᾷ ←   ἀγγέλων   καὶ   ἐξουσιῶν   καὶ   δυνάμεων   →   ὑποταγέντων   →   αὐτῷ
a.dsf   n.gpm   cj   n.gpf   cj   n.gpf   pt.ap.gpm   r.dsm.3
1288   34   2779 2026   2779 1539   5718   899

Living for God

[4:1] Therefore, since Christ suffered in his body,   arm   yourselves also with the same attitude, because he
οὖν   Χριστοῦ παθόντος   →   σαρκὶ   ὑμεῖς   ὁπλίσασθε   ←   καὶ   →   τὴν   αὐτὴν   ἔννοιαν   ὅτι   ὁ
cj   n.gsm   pt.aa.gsm   n.dsf   r.np.2 v.amm.2p   adv   d.asf r.asf   n.asf   cj   d.nsm
4036   4248   5986   4922   7007   3959   2779   3836   899   1936   4022 3836

who has suffered in his body is done   with sin.   [2] As a result, he does not live   the rest   of his
←   →   παθὼν   →   σαρκὶ   →   πέπαυται   →   ἁμαρτίας   εἰς   ←   →   μηκέτι   τὸ   βιῶσαι   τὸν   ἐπίλοιπον χρόνον
    pt.aa.nsm   n.dsf   v.rmi.3s   n.gsf   p.a   adv   d.asn f.aa   d.asm a.asm   n.asm
    4248   4922   4264   281   1650   3600   3836 1051   3836   2145   5989

earthly life for evil human desires,   but rather for the will   of God.   [3] For you have spent   enough
ἐν   σαρκὶ   ←   ἀνθρώπων ἐπιθυμίαις ἀλλὰ   ←   θελήματι   θεοῦ   γὰρ   παρεληλυθὼς ἀρκετός
p.d n.dsf   n.gpm   n.dpf   cj   n.dsn   n.gsm cj   pt.ra.nsm   a.nsm
1877 4922   476   2123   247   2525   2536   1142   4216   757

time   in the past doing   what pagans choose   to do – living   in debauchery, lust,
ὁ   χρόνος   ←   →   κατειργάσθαι   τῶν ἐθνῶν   τὸ βούλημα   πεπορευμένους ἐν   ἀσελγείαις   ἐπιθυμίαις
d.nsm n.nsm   f.rm   d.gpn n.gpn d.asn n.asn   pt.rm.apm   p.d   n.dpf   n.dpf
3836 5989   4216 4216 4216 2981   3836 1620   3836 1088   4513   1877 816   2123

drunkenness, orgies, carousing and detestable idolatry.   [4]   They think it strange   that you do not
οἰνοφλυγίαις κώμοις πότοις   καὶ   ἀθεμίτοις   εἰδωλολατρίαις   ἐν   ᾧ   →   →   →   ξενίζονται   ὑμῶν   μὴ
n.dpf   n.dpm n.dpm   cj   a.dpf   n.dpf   p.d r.dsn   v.ppi.3p   r.gp.2   pl
3886   3269   4542   2779 116   1630   1877 4005   3826   7007   5340 3590

plunge   with them into the same flood   of dissipation, and they heap abuse   on you.   [5] But they will have
συντρεχόντων ←   εἰς   τὴν   αὐτὴν   ἀνάχυσιν   →   τῆς ἀσωτίας   βλασφημοῦντες   οἳ   →
pt.pa.gpm   p.a   d.asf r.asf   n.asf   d.gsf n.gsf   pt.pa.npm   r.npm
5340   1650 3836   899   431   3836 861   1059   4005

to give   account to him who is   ready to judge the living and the dead.   [6] For this   is the reason the
ἀποδώσουσιν λόγον   →   τῷ   ←   ἔχοντι   ἑτοίμως   →   κρῖναι   ζῶντας καὶ   νεκρούς   γὰρ   εἰς τοῦτο   ←   ←
v.fai.3p   n.asm   d.dsm   pt.pa.dsm adv   f.aa   pt.pa.apm cj   a.apm   cj   p.a r.asn
625   3364   3836   2400   2290   3212   2409   2779   3738   1142 1650 4047

gospel was preached   even to those who are now dead,   so that   they might be judged according to men   in
εὐηγγελίσθη καὶ   →   →   νεκροῖς ἵνα   ←   μὲν   ←   →   κριθῶσι κατὰ   ←   ἀνθρώπους   →
v.api.3s   adv   a.dpm cj   pl   v.aps.3p p.a   n.apm
2294   2779   3738   2671   3525   3212   2848   476

regard to the body, but live according to God in regard to the spirit.   ¶   [7]   The end of all   things is
→   →   σαρκὶ   δὲ   ζῶσι   κατὰ   ←   θεὸν   →   πνεύματι   δὲ   τὸ   τέλος   Πάντων ←   →
    n.dsf   cj   v.pas.3p p.a   n.asm   n.dsn   cj   d.nsn n.nsn   a.gpn
    4922   1254 2409   2848   2536   4460   1254 3836 5465   4246

near. Therefore be clear minded   and self-controlled so that you can pray.   [8] Above all,   love
ἤγγικεν οὖν   →   →   σωφρονήσατε καὶ   νήψατε   εἰς   ←   →   προσευχάς   πρὸ   πάντων   τὴν ἀγάπην   ἔχοντες
v.rai.3s n.dsf   v.aam.2p   cj   v.aam.2p p.a   n.apf   p.g   a.gpn   d.asf n.asf   pt.pa.npm
1581   4036   5404   2779 3768   1650   4666   4574 4246   3836 27   2400

each other deeply, because love   covers   over a multitude of sins.   [9] Offer hospitality to one   another
εἰς ἑαυτοὺς ←   ἐκτενῆ   ὅτι   ἀγάπη καλύπτει   ←   πλῆθος   →   ἁμαρτιῶν   φιλόξενοι   εἰς ἀλλήλους   →
p.a r.apm.2   a.asf   cj   n.nsf v.pai.3s   n.asn   n.gpf   a.npm   p.a r.apm
1650 1571   1756   4022 27   2821   4436   281   5811   1650 253

without grumbling. [10] Each   one should use whatever gift   he has received to serve   others,   faithfully
ἄνευ   γογγυσμοῦ   ἕκαστος ←   καθὼς   χάρισμα   →   ἔλαβεν   εἰς διακονοῦντες αὐτὸ ἑαυτοὺς ὡς   καλοὶ
p.g   n.gsm   r.nsm   cj   n.asn   v.aai.3s p.a pt.pa.npm   r.asn.3 r.apm.3 pl   a.npm
459   1198   1667   2777   5922   3284   1650 1354   899   1571   6055 2819

θεόν, δι᾽ ἀναστάσεως Ἰησοῦ Χριστοῦ, [22] ὅς ἐστιν ἐν δεξιᾷ [τοῦ] θεοῦ πορευθεὶς εἰς οὐρανὸν ὑποταγέντων αὐτῷ ἀγγέλων καὶ ἐξουσιῶν καὶ δυνάμεων.

[4:1] Χριστοῦ οὖν παθόντος σαρκὶ καὶ ὑμεῖς τὴν αὐτὴν ἔννοιαν ὁπλίσασθε, ὅτι ὁ παθὼν σαρκὶ πέπαυται ἁμαρτίας [2] εἰς τὸ μηκέτι ἀνθρώπων ἐπιθυμίαις ἀλλὰ θελήματι θεοῦ τὸν ἐπίλοιπον ἐν σαρκὶ βιῶσαι χρόνον. [3] ἀρκετὸς γὰρ ὁ παρεληλυθὼς χρόνος τὸ βούλημα τῶν ἐθνῶν κατειργάσθαι πεπορευμένους ἐν ἀσελγείαις, ἐπιθυμίαις, οἰνοφλυγίαις, κώμοις, πότοις καὶ ἀθεμίτοις εἰδωλολατρίαις. [4] ἐν ᾧ ξενίζονται μὴ συντρεχόντων ὑμῶν εἰς τὴν αὐτὴν τῆς ἀσωτίας ἀνάχυσιν βλασφημοῦντες, [5] οἳ ἀποδώσουσιν λόγον τῷ ἑτοίμως ἔχοντι κρῖναι ζῶντας καὶ νεκρούς. [6] εἰς τοῦτο γὰρ καὶ νεκροῖς εὐηγγελίσθη, ἵνα κριθῶσι μὲν κατὰ ἀνθρώπους σαρκὶ ζῶσι δὲ κατὰ θεὸν πνεύματι. ¶ [7] Πάντων δὲ τὸ τέλος ἤγγικεν. σωφρονήσατε οὖν καὶ νήψατε εἰς προσευχάς· [8] πρὸ πάντων τὴν εἰς ἑαυτοὺς ἀγάπην ἐκτενῆ ἔχοντες, ὅτι ἀγάπη καλύπτει πλῆθος ἁμαρτιῶν. [9] φιλόξενοι εἰς ἀλλήλους ἄνευ γογγυσμοῦ· [10] ἕκαστος καθὼς ἔλαβεν χάρισμα εἰς ἑαυτοὺς αὐτὸ διακονοῦντες ὡς καλοὶ οἰκονόμοι ποικίλης χάριτος θεοῦ. [11] εἴ τις λαλεῖ, ὡς

administering God's grace   in its various forms. **11** If   anyone speaks, he should do it as one speaking the very words
οἰκονόμοι   θεοῦ   χάριτος   ποικίλης ←   εἴ τις   λαλεῖ   ὡς   λόγια
n.npm   n.gsm n.gsf   a.gsf   cj r.nsm v.pai.3s   pl   n.npn
3874   2536   5921   4476   1623 5516 3281   6055   3359

of God. If anyone serves, he should do it   with the strength   God   provides, so that in all   things
→ θεοῦ εἴ τις   διακονεῖ   ὡς ἐξ   ἰσχύος   ἧς ὁ θεὸς χορηγεῖ   ἵνα ←   ἐν πᾶσιν ←
n.gsm cj r.nsm v.pai.3s   pl p.g n.gsf   r.gsf d.nsm n.nsm v.pai.3s cj   p.d a.dpn
2536   1623 5516 1354   6055 1666 2709   4005 3836 2536 5961   2671   1877 4246

God   may be praised through Jesus Christ. To him be   the glory and the power for ever   and
ὁ θεός   δοξάζηται   διὰ   Ἰησοῦ Χριστοῦ → ᾧ ἐστιν ἡ δόξα καὶ τὸ κράτος εἰς τοὺς αἰῶνας
d.nsm n.nsm   v.pps.3s   p.g   n.gsm n.gsm   r.dsm v.pai.3s d.nsf n.nsf cj d.nsn n.nsn p.a d.apm n.apm
3836 2536   1519   1328 2652 5986   4005 1639 3836 1518 2779 3836 3197 1650 3836 172

ever.   Amen.
τῶν αἰώνων ἀμήν
d.gpm n.gpm pl
3836 172   297

Suffering for Being a Christian

4:12 Dear friends, do not be surprised at the   painful trial you are   suffering, as though
→ Ἀγαπητοί   μὴ → ξενίζεσθε τῇ ἐν ὑμῖν πυρώσει ← ὑμῖν γινομένη πρὸς πειρασμὸν ὡς ←
a.vpm   pl   v.ppm.2p d.dsf p.d r.dp.2 n.dsf r.dp.2 pt.pm.dsf p.a n.asm pl
28   3826 3590   3826 1877 7007 4796   7007 1181 4639 4280 6055

something strange were happening to you. **13** But rejoice that you participate in the sufferings of Christ,   so that
→ ξένου   συμβαίνοντος → ὑμῖν   ἀλλὰ χαίρετε καθὸ   κοινωνεῖτε → τοῖς παθήμασιν τοῦ Χριστοῦ ἵνα ←
a.gsn   pt.pa.gsn   r.dp.2 cj   v.pam.2p cj   v.pai.2p   d.dpn n.ddpn   d.gsn n.gsm   cj
3828   5201   7007   247 5897   2771   3125   3836 4077   3836 5986   2671

you may be overjoyed   when his glory   is revealed.   **14** If you are insulted because of the
καὶ → →   χαρῆτε ἀγαλλιώμενοι ἐν αὐτοῦ τῆς δόξης   τῇ ἀποκαλύψει εἰ → ὀνειδίζεσθε ἐν
adv   v.aps.2p pt.pm.npm   p.d r.gsm.3 d.gsf n.gsf d.dsf n.dsf cj   v.ppi.2p   p.d
2779   5897   58   1877 899   3836 1518 3836 637   1623   3943   1877

name of Christ, you are blessed, for the Spirit of glory   and of God   rests on you. **15** If   you
ὀνόματι → Χριστοῦ   μακάριοι ὅτι τὸ πνεῦμα → τῆς δόξης καὶ τὸ τοῦ θεοῦ ἀναπαύεται ἐφ᾽ ὑμᾶς γάρ τις ὑμῶν
n.dsn   n.gsm   a.npm   cj d.nsn n.nsn   d.gsf n.gsf cj d.nsn d.gsm n.gsm v.pmi.3s p.a r.ap.2 cj r.nsm r.gp.2
3950   5986   3421   4022 3836 4460   3836 1518 2779 3836 3836 2536 399   2093 7007 1142 5516 7007

suffer, it should not be as a murderer or thief or any other kind of criminal, or even as a meddler.
πασχέτω   μὴ ὡς φονεὺς ἢ κλέπτης ἢ   κακοποιὸς ἢ   ὡς ἀλλοτριεπίσκοπος
v.pam.3s   pl pl n.nsm   cj n.nsm   cj   n.nsm   cj   pl n.nsm
4248   3590 6055 5838   2445 3095 2445   2804   2445   6055 258

16 However, if you suffer as a Christian, do not be ashamed, but praise God   that you bear that name.
δὲ   εἰ ὡς Χριστιανός → μὴ αἰσχυνέσθω δὲ δοξαζέτω τὸν θεὸν ἐν τούτῳ τῷ ὀνόματι
cj   cj pl n.nsm   pl v.pmm.3s   cj v.pam.3s d.asm n.asm p.d r.dsn d.dsn n.dsn
1254   1623 6055 5985   3590 159   1254 1519   3836 2536 1877 4047 3836 3950

17 For it is time   for judgment to begin   with the family of God;   and if it begins with us, what will
ὅτι ὁ καιρὸς → τὸ κρίμα → τοῦ ἄρξασθαι ἀπὸ τοῦ οἴκου → τοῦ θεοῦ δὲ εἰ πρῶτον ἀφ᾽ ἡμῶν τί
cj   d.nsm n.nsm d.asn n.asn d.gsn f.am   p.g d.gsm n.gsm d.gsm n.gsm cj cj adv   p.g r.gp.1 r.nsn
4022 3836 2789 3836 3210 3836 806   608 3836 3875 3836 2536 1254 1623 4754   608 7005 5515

the outcome be for those who do not obey   the gospel of God? **18** And, "If it is hard for the righteous to be
τὸ τέλος   → τῶν   → ἀπειθούντων τῷ εὐαγγελίῳ → τοῦ θεοῦ καὶ εἰ μόλις ὁ δίκαιος → →
d.nsn n.nsn   d.gpm   pt.pa.gpm   d.dsn n.dsn   d.gsn n.gsm cj cj adv   d.nsm a.nsm
3836 5465   3836   578   3836 2295   3836 2536 2779 1623 3660   3836 1465

saved, what will become of the ungodly and the sinner?" ¶ **19** So then, those who suffer   according to
σῴζεται ποῦ → φανεῖται ← ὁ ἀσεβὴς καὶ ἁμαρτωλός   ὥστε καὶ οἱ ←   πάσχοντες κατὰ
v.ppi.3s adv v.fmi.3s d.nsm a.nsm cj a.nsm   cj adv d.npm   pt.pa.npm p.a
5392   4543 5743   3836 815   2779 283   6063 2779 3836   4248   2848

God's   will   should commit   themselves to their faithful Creator and continue to do good.
τοῦ θεοῦ τὸ θέλημα   → παρατιθέσθωσαν τὰς ψυχὰς αὐτῶν → πιστῷ κτίστῃ ἐν   ἀγαθοποιίᾳ
d.gsm n.gsm d.asn n.asn v.pmm.3p   d.apf n.apf r.gpm.3 a.dsm n.dsm p.d   n.dsf
3836 2536 3836 2525 4192   3836 6034 899   4412 3234 1877   17

λόγια θεοῦ· εἴ τις διακονεῖ, ὡς ἐξ ἰσχύος ἧς χορηγεῖ ὁ θεός, ἵνα ἐν πᾶσιν δοξάζηται ὁ θεὸς διὰ Ἰησοῦ Χριστοῦ, ᾧ ἐστιν ἡ δόξα καὶ τὸ κράτος εἰς τοὺς αἰῶνας τῶν αἰώνων, ἀμήν.
4:12 Ἀγαπητοί, μὴ ξενίζεσθε τῇ ἐν ὑμῖν πυρώσει πρὸς πειρασμὸν ὑμῖν γινομένῃ ὡς ξένου ὑμῖν συμβαίνοντος, **13** ἀλλὰ καθὸ κοινωνεῖτε τοῖς τοῦ Χριστοῦ παθήμασιν χαίρετε, ἵνα καὶ ἐν τῇ ἀποκαλύψει τῆς δόξης αὐτοῦ χαρῆτε ἀγαλλιώμενοι. **14** εἰ ὀνειδίζεσθε ἐν ὀνόματι Χριστοῦ, μακάριοι, ὅτι τὸ τῆς δόξης καὶ τὸ τοῦ θεοῦ πνεῦμα ἐφ᾽ ὑμᾶς ἀναπαύεται. **15** μὴ γάρ τις ὑμῶν πασχέτω ὡς φονεὺς ἢ κλέπτης ἢ κακοποιὸς ἢ ὡς ἀλλοτριεπίσκοπος· **16** εἰ δὲ ὡς Χριστιανός, μὴ αἰσχυνέσθω, δοξαζέτω δὲ τὸν θεὸν ἐν τῷ ὀνόματι τούτῳ. **17** ὅτι [ὁ] καιρὸς τοῦ ἄρξασθαι τὸ κρίμα ἀπὸ τοῦ οἴκου τοῦ θεοῦ· εἰ δὲ πρῶτον ἀφ᾽ ἡμῶν, τί τὸ τέλος τῶν ἀπειθούντων τῷ τοῦ θεοῦ εὐαγγελίῳ; **18** καὶ εἰ ὁ δίκαιος μόλις σῴζεται, ὁ ἀσεβὴς καὶ ἁμαρτωλὸς ποῦ φανεῖται; ¶ **19** ὥστε καὶ οἱ πάσχοντες κατὰ τὸ θέλημα τοῦ θεοῦ πιστῷ κτίστῃ παρατιθέσθωσαν τὰς ψυχὰς αὐτῶν ἐν ἀγαθοποιίᾳ.

To Elders and Young Men

5:1 | To the elders | | among you, | I appeal | | as a fellow elder, | | | a witness of | Christ's
οὖν | Πρεσβυτέρους | ἐν | ὑμῖν → | παρακαλῶ → | | ὁ | συμπρεσβύτερος | καὶ | μάρτυς → | τοῦ Χριστοῦ
cj | a.apm | p.d | r.dp.2 | v.pai.1s | | d.nsm n.nsm | | cj | n.nsm | d.gsm n.gsm
4036 | 4565 | 1877 | 7007 | 4151 | | 3836 5236 | | 2779 | 3459 | 4077 3836 5986

sufferings | and | one who | also | will | | share | in the glory | to be revealed: | **2** Be shepherds | of | God's
τῶν παθημάτων | ὁ | | καὶ | τῆς μελλούσης | κοινωνός ← | | δόξης → | → ἀποκαλύπτεσθαι | → ποιμάνατε | | τοῦ θεοῦ
d.gpn n.gpn | d.nsm | | adv | d.gsf pt.pa.gsf | n.nsm | | n.gsf | f.pp | v.aam.2p | | d.gsm n.gsm
3836 4077 | 3836 | | 2779 | 3836 3516 | 3128 | | 1518 | 636 | 4477 | | 4480 3836 2536

flock | that is under | your care, | serving as overseers | – not | because you must, | but | because you are
τὸ ποίμνιον | ἐν | ὑμῖν | → ἐπισκοποῦντες | μὴ → | → ἀναγκαστῶς | ἀλλὰ |
d.asn n.asn | p.d | r.dp.2 | pt.pa.npm | pl | adv | cj |
3836 4480 | 1877 | 7007 | 2174 | 3590 | 339 | 247 |

willing, | as | God | wants you to be; | not | greedy | for money, | but | eager | to serve; | **3** not | lording | it over
ἑκουσίως | κατὰ | θεόν ← | ← ← ← | μηδὲ | αἰσχροκερδῶς ← | ← | ἀλλὰ | προθύμως ← | ← | μηδ᾽ ὡς | κατακυριεύοντες ← | ← →
adv | p.a | n.asm | | | adv | | cj | adv | | cj pl | pt.pa.npm |
1731 | 2848 | 2536 | 2848 2848 2848 | 3593 | 154 | | 247 | 4610 | | 3593 6055 | 2894 |

those entrusted | to you, | but | being | examples | to the flock. | **4** And | when | the | Chief Shepherd | appears, | you will
τῶν | κλήρων | ἀλλὰ | γινόμενοι | τύποι | τοῦ ποιμνίου | καὶ | → | τοῦ | ἀρχιποίμενος | φανερωθέντος → | →
d.gpm | n.gpm | cj | pt.pm.npm | n.npm | d.gsn n.gsn | cj | | d.gsm | n.gsm | pt.ap.gsm |
3836 | 3102 | 247 | 1181 | 5596 | 3836 4480 | 2779 | 5746 | 3836 | 799 | 5746 |

receive | the crown | of glory | that will never fade | away. | ¶ | **5** Young | men, | in the same | way be
κομιεῖσθε | τὸν στέφανον | τῆς δόξης → | → → ἀμαράντινον | → | | νεώτεροι | | | Ὁμοίως →
v.fmi.2p | d.asm n.asm | d.gsf n.gsf | a.asn | | | a.vpm.c | | | adv
3152 | 3836 5109 | 3836 1518 | 277 | | | 3742 | | | 3931

submissive | to those who are older. | All | of you, | clothe | yourselves with humility | toward
ὑποτάγητε → | → → πρεσβυτέροις δὲ | πάντες ← | ἐγκομβώσασθε ← | | τὴν ταπεινοφροσύνην |
v.apm.2p | a.dpm cj | a.vpm | v.amm.2p | | d.asf n.asf |
5718 | 4565 1254 | 4246 | 1599 | | 3836 5425 |

one | another, | because, | "God | opposes | the proud | but | gives | grace | to the humble." | **6** Humble
ἀλλήλοις ← | ὅτι | ὁ θεὸς | ἀντιτάσσεται | ὑπερηφάνοις | δὲ | δίδωσιν | χάριν → | ταπεινοῖς | Ταπεινώθητε
r.dpm | cj | d.nsm n.nsm | v.pmi.3s | a.dpm | cj | v.pai.3s | n.asf | a.dpm | v.apm.2p
253 | 4022 | 3836 2536 | 530 | 5662 | 1254 | 1443 | 5921 | 5424 | 5427

yourselves, | therefore, | under | God's | mighty | hand, | that | he may lift | you | up | in | due time. | **7** Cast | all
← | οὖν | ὑπὸ | τοῦ θεοῦ | κραταιὰν | τὴν χεῖρα | ἵνα → | → ὑψώσῃ | ὑμᾶς | ← | ἐν → | καιρῷ | ἐπιρίψαντες | πᾶσαν
| cj | p.a | d.gsm n.gsm | a.asf | d.asf n.asf | cj | v.aas.3s | r.ap.2 | | p.d | n.dsm | pt.aa.npm | a.asf
| 4036 | 5679 | 3836 2536 | 3193 | 3836 5931 | 2671 | 5738 | 5738 | 1877 | 2789 | 2166 | 4246

your anxiety | on | him | because | he | cares | for you. | ¶ | **8** Be self-controlled | and alert. | Your | enemy | the
ὑμῶν τὴν μέριμναν | ἐπ᾽ | αὐτόν | ὅτι | αὐτῷ | μέλει | περὶ ὑμῶν | | Νήψατε | γρηγορήσατε | ὑμῶν | ἀντίδικος | ὁ
r.gp.2 d.asf n.asf | p.a | r.asm.3 | cj | r.dsm.3 | v.pai.3s | p.g r.gp.2 | | v.aam.2p | v.aam.2p | r.gp.2 | n.nsm | d.nsm
7007 3836 3533 | 2093 | 899 | 4022 | 899 | 3508 | 4309 7007 | | 3768 | 1213 | 7007 | 508 | 3836

devil | prowls | around | like a | roaring | lion | looking for | someone | to devour. | **9** Resist | him, | standing firm | in the
διάβολος | περιπατεῖ ← | ὡς | ὠρυόμενος | λέων | ζητῶν ← | τινα | → καταπιεῖν | ἀντίστητε | ᾧ → | στερεοὶ → | τῇ
n.nsm | v.pai.3s | pl | pt.pm.nsm | n.nsm | pt.pa.nsm | r.asm | f.aa | v.aam.2p | r.dsm | a.npm | d.dsf
1333 | 4344 | 6055 | 6054 | 3329 | 2426 | 5516 | 2927 | 468 | 4005 | 5104 | 3836

faith, | because | you know | that | your | brothers | throughout | the world | are | undergoing | the same | kind of
πίστει → | → | εἰδότες | ὑμῶν | τῇ ἀδελφότητι | ἐν | τῷ κόσμῳ | → | ἐπιτελεῖσθαι | τὰ | αὐτὰ ←
n.dsf | | pt.ra.npm | r.gp.2 | d.dsf n.dsf | p.d | d.dsm n.dsm | | f.pp | d.apn | r.apn
4411 | | 3857 | 7007 | 3836 82 | 1877 | 3836 3180 | | 2200 | 3836 | 899

sufferings. | ¶ | **10** And | the | God | of all | grace, | who | called | you | to | his | eternal | glory | in | Christ,
τῶν παθημάτων | | δὲ | Ὁ | θεὸς | πάσης | χάριτος | ὁ | καλέσας | ὑμᾶς | εἰς | αὐτοῦ | αἰώνιον | τὴν δόξαν | ἐν | Χριστῷ Ἰησοῦ
d.gpn n.gpn | | cj | d.nsm | n.nsm | a.gsf | n.gsf | d.nsm | pt.aa.nsm | r.ap.2 | p.a | r.gsm.3 | a.asf | d.asf n.asf | p.d | n.dsm n.dsm
3836 4077 | | 1254 | 3836 | 2536 | 4246 | 5921 | 3836 | 2813 | 7007 | 1650 | 899 | 173 | 3836 1518 | 1877 | 5986 2652

after you have | suffered | a little | while, | will himself | restore | you | and make | you | strong, | firm | and steadfast. | **11** To
→ → | παθόντας | ὀλίγον ← | → | αὐτὸς | καταρτίσει | → | στηρίξει | σθενώσει | θεμελιώσει → |
| pt.aa.apm | adv | | r.nsm | v.fai.3s | | v.fai.3s | v.fai.3s | v.fai.3s |
| 4248 | 3900 | | 2936 899 | 2936 | | 5114 | 4964 | 2530 |

5:1 Πρεσβυτέρους οὖν ἐν ὑμῖν παρακαλῶ ὁ συμπρεσβύτερος καὶ μάρτυς τῶν τοῦ Χριστοῦ παθημάτων, ὁ καὶ τῆς μελλούσης ἀποκαλύπτεσθαι δόξης κοινωνός· **2** ποιμάνατε τὸ ἐν ὑμῖν ποίμνιον τοῦ θεοῦ [ἐπισκοποῦντες] μὴ ἀναγκαστῶς ἀλλὰ ἑκουσίως κατὰ θεόν, μηδὲ αἰσχροκερδῶς ἀλλὰ προθύμως. **3** μηδ᾽ ὡς κατακυριεύοντες τῶν κλήρων ἀλλὰ τύποι γινόμενοι τοῦ ποιμνίου· **4** καὶ φανερωθέντος τοῦ ἀρχιποίμενος κομιεῖσθε τὸν ἀμαράντινον τῆς δόξης στέφανον. ¶ **5** Ὁμοίως, νεώτεροι, ὑποτάγητε πρεσβυτέροις· πάντες δὲ ἀλλήλοις τὴν ταπεινοφροσύνην ἐγκομβώσασθε, ὅτι [Ὁ] θεὸς ὑπερηφάνοις ἀντιτάσσεται, ταπεινοῖς δὲ δίδωσιν χάριν. **6** Ταπεινώθητε οὖν ὑπὸ τὴν κραταιὰν χεῖρα τοῦ θεοῦ, ἵνα ὑμᾶς ὑψώσῃ ἐν καιρῷ, **7** πᾶσαν τὴν μέριμναν ὑμῶν ἐπιρίψαντες ἐπ᾽ αὐτόν, ὅτι αὐτῷ μέλει περὶ ὑμῶν. ¶ **8** Νήψατε, γρηγορήσατε. ὁ ἀντίδικος ὑμῶν διάβολος ὡς λέων ὠρυόμενος περιπατεῖ ζητῶν [τινα] καταπιεῖν· **9** ᾧ ἀντίστητε στερεοὶ τῇ πίστει εἰδότες τὰ αὐτὰ τῶν παθημάτων τῇ ἐν [τῷ] κόσμῳ ὑμῶν ἀδελφότητι ἐπιτελεῖσθαι. ¶ **10** Ὁ δὲ θεὸς πάσης χάριτος, ὁ καλέσας ὑμᾶς εἰς τὴν αἰώνιον αὐτοῦ δόξαν ἐν Χριστῷ, «Χριστῷ» [Ἰησοῦ], ὀλίγον παθόντας αὐτὸς καταρτίσει, στηρίξει, σθενώσει, θεμελιώσει. **11** αὐτῷ τὸ κράτος εἰς τοὺς αἰῶνας «αἰώνας,» τῶν

him   be   the   power   *for   ever*   *and ever.*   Amen.
αὐτῷ   τὸ   κράτος   εἰς   ⌊τοὺς   αἰῶνας⌋   ἀμήν
r.dsm.3   d.nsn   n.nsn   p.a   d.apm   n.apm   pl
899   3836   3197   1650   3836   172   297

Final Greetings

5:12 With   the   help   of   Silas,   whom   I   regard   as   a   faithful   brother,   I   have   written   to   you   briefly,
Διὰ   ←   ←   ←   Σιλουανοῦ   ὡς   →   λογίζομαι   πιστοῦ   ⌊τοῦ   ἀδελφοῦ⌋   →   →   ἔγραψα   →   ὑμῖν   ⌊δι᾽   ὀλίγων⌋
p.g   n.gsm   cj   v.pmi.1s   a.gsm   d.gsm   n.gsm   v.aai.1s   r.dp.2   p.g   a.gpn
1328   4977   6055   3357   4412   3836   81   1211   7007   1328   3900

encouraging   you   and   testifying   that   this   is   the   true   grace   of   God.   Stand   fast   in   it.   ¶   **13** She   who   is
παρακαλῶν   καὶ   ἐπιμαρτυρῶν   ταύτην   εἶναι   ἀληθῆ   χάριν   →   ⌊τοῦ   θεοῦ⌋   στῆτε   ←   εἰς   ἣν   ἡ
pt.pa.nsm   cj   pt.pa.nsm   r.asf   f.pa   a.asf   n.asf   d.gsm   n.gsm   v.aam.2p   p.a   r.asf   d.nsf
4151   2779   2148   4047   1639   239   5921   3836   2536   2705   1650   4005   3836

in   Babylon,   chosen   together   with   you,   sends   you   her   greetings,   and   so   does   my   son   Mark.   **14** Greet
ἐν   Βαβυλῶνι   συνεκλεκτὴ ←   →   ὑμᾶς   →   Ἀσπάζεται   καὶ   μου   ὁ   υἱός   Μᾶρκος   ἀσπάσασθε
p.d   n.dsf   a.nsf   r.ap.2   v.pmi.3s   cj   r.gs.1   d.nsm   n.nsm   n.nsm   v.amm.2p
1877   956   5293   832   7007   832   2779   1609   3836   5626   3453   832

one   another   with   a   kiss   of   love.   ¶   Peace   to   all   of   you   who   are   in   Christ.
ἀλλήλους   ←   ἐν   φιλήματι   →   ἀγάπης   Εἰρήνη   →   πᾶσιν   ὑμῖν   τοῖς   ἐν   Χριστῷ
r.apm   p.d   n.dsn   n.gsf   n.nsf   a.dpm   r.dp.2   d.dpm   p.d   n.dsm
253   1877   5799   27   1645   4246   7007   3836   1877   5986

αἰώνων, ἀμήν.
5:12 Διὰ Σιλουανοῦ ὑμῖν τοῦ πιστοῦ ἀδελφοῦ, ὡς λογίζομαι, δι᾽ ὀλίγων ἔγραψα παρακαλῶν καὶ ἐπιμαρτυρῶν ταύτην εἶναι ἀληθῆ χάριν τοῦ θεοῦ εἰς ἣν στῆτε. ¶ **13** Ἀσπάζεται ὑμᾶς ἡ ἐν Βαβυλῶνι συνεκλεκτὴ καὶ Μᾶρκος ὁ υἱός μου. **14** ἀσπάσασθε ἀλλήλους ἐν φιλήματι ἀγάπης. ¶ εἰρήνη ὑμῖν πᾶσιν τοῖς ἐν Χριστῷ.

2 Peter

1:1 Simon Peter, a servant and apostle of Jesus Christ, ¶ To those who through the righteousness of our
Συμεὼν Πέτρος δοῦλος καὶ ἀπόστολος → Ἰησοῦ Χριστοῦ τοῖς ← ἐν δικαιοσύνῃ → ἡμῶν
n.nsm n.nsm n.nsm cj n.nsm n.gsm n.gsm d.dpm p.d n.dsf r.gp.1
5208 4377 1529 2779 693 2652 5986 3836 1877 1466 7005

God and Savior Jesus Christ have received a faith as precious as ours: ¶ **2** Grace and peace be yours in
ⸯτοῦ θεοῦⸯ καὶ σωτῆρος Ἰησοῦ Χριστοῦ → λαχοῦσιν πίστιν → ἰσότιμον ← ἡμῖν χάρις καὶ εἰρήνη → ὑμῖν →
d.gsm n.gsm cj n.gsm n.gsm n.gsm pt.aa.dpm n.asf a.asf r.dp.1 n.nsf cj n.nsf r.dp.2
3836 2536 2779 5400 2652 5986 3275 4411 2700 7005 5921 2779 1645 4437 7007

abundance through the knowledge of God and of Jesus our Lord.
πληθυνθείη ἐν ἐπιγνώσει → ⸯτοῦ θεοῦⸯ καὶ → Ἰησοῦ ἡμῶν ⸯτοῦ κυρίουⸯ
v.apo.3s p.d n.dsf d.gsm n.gsm cj n.gsm r.gp.1 d.gsm n.gsm
4437 1877 2106 3836 2536 2779 2652 7005 3836 3261

Making One's Calling and Election Sure

1:3 His divine power has given us everything *we need* for life and godliness through our
Ὡς αὐτοῦ θείας ⸯτῆς δυνάμεωςⸯ → δεδωρημένης ἡμῖν πάντα τὰ πρὸς ζωὴν καὶ εὐσέβειαν διὰ τῆς
pl r.gsm.3 a.gsf d.gsf n.gsf pt.rm.gsf r.dp.1 a.apn d.apn p.a n.asf cj n.asf p.g d.gsf
6055 899 2521 3836 1539 1563 7005 4246 3836 4639 2437 2779 2354 1328 3836

knowledge of him who called us by his own glory and goodness. **4** Through these he has given us his very
ἐπιγνώσεως → τοῦ ← καλέσαντος ἡμᾶς → → ἰδίᾳ δόξῃ καὶ ἀρετῇ δι' ὧν → → δεδώρηται ἡμῖν τὰ →
n.gsf d.gsm pt.aa.gsm r.ap.1 a.dsf n.dsf cj n.dsf p.g r.gpn v.rmi.3s r.dp.1 d.apn
2106 3836 2813 7005 2625 1518 2779 746 1328 4005 1563 7005 3836

great and precious promises, so that through them you may participate in the divine nature and escape
μέγιστα καὶ τίμια ἐπαγγέλματα ἵνα ← διὰ τούτων → γένησθε κοινωνοὶ → θείας φύσεως ἀποφυγόντες
a.apn.s cj a.apn n.apn cj p.g r.gpn v.ams.2p n.npm a.gsf n.gsf pt.aa.npm
3492 2779 5508 2041 2671 1328 4047 1181 3128 2521 5882 709

the corruption in the world caused by evil desires. ¶ **5** For this very reason, make every
τῆς φθορᾶς ἐν τῷ κόσμῳ → ἐν ἐπιθυμίᾳ δὲ → τοῦτο ⸯΚαὶ αὐτὸⸯ παρεισενέγκαντες πᾶσαν
d.gsf n.gsf p.d d.dsn n.dsn p.d n.dsf cj r.asn r.asn pt.aa.npm a.asf
3836 5785 1877 3836 3180 1877 2123 1254 4047 2779 4047 4210 4246

effort to add to your faith goodness; and to goodness, knowledge; **6** and to knowledge, self-control;
σπουδὴν → ἐπιχορηγήσατε ἐν ὑμῶν ⸯτῇ πίστειⸯ ⸯτὴν ἀρετήνⸯ δὲ ἐν ⸯτῇ ἀρετῇⸯ ⸯτὴν γνῶσινⸯ δὲ ἐν ⸯτῇ γνώσειⸯ ⸯτὴν ἐγκράτειανⸯ
n.asf v.aam.2p p.d r.gp.2 d.dsf n.dsf d.asf n.asf cj p.d d.dsf n.dsf d.asf n.asf cj p.d d.dsf n.dsf d.asf n.asf
5082 2220 1877 7005 3836 4411 3836 746 1254 1877 3836 746 3836 1194 1254 1877 3836 1194 3836 1602

and to self-control, perseverance; and to perseverance, godliness; **7** and to godliness, brotherly kindness;
δὲ ἐν ⸯτῇ ἐγκρατείᾳⸯ ⸯτὴν ὑπομονήνⸯ δὲ ἐν ⸯτῇ ὑπομονῇⸯ ⸯτὴν εὐσέβειανⸯ δὲ ἐν ⸯτῇ εὐσεβείᾳⸯ → ⸯτὴν φιλαδελφίανⸯ
cj p.d d.dsf n.dsf d.asf n.asf cj p.d d.dsf n.dsf d.asf n.asf cj p.d d.dsf n.dsf d.asf n.asf
1254 1877 3836 1602 3836 5705 1254 1877 3836 5705 3836 2354 1254 1877 3836 2354 3836 5789

and to brotherly kindness, love. **8** For if you possess these qualities in increasing measure, they will
δὲ ἐν ⸯτῇ φιλαδελφίᾳⸯ ⸯτὴν ἀγάπηνⸯ γὰρ → ὑμῖν ὑπάρχοντα ταῦτα καὶ πλεονάζοντα ← → →
cj p.d d.dsf n.dsf d.asf n.asf cj r.dp.2 pt.pa.npn r.npn cj pt.pa.npn
1254 1877 3836 5789 3836 27 1142 5639 5639 4047 2779 4429 2770 2770

keep you from being ineffective and unproductive in your knowledge of our Lord Jesus Christ. **9** But if
οὐκ καθίστησιν ἀργοὺς οὐδὲ ἀκάρπους εἰς τὴν ἐπίγνωσιν → ἡμῶν ⸯτοῦ κυρίουⸯ Ἰησοῦ Χριστοῦ γὰρ
pl v.pai.3s a.apm cj a.apm p.a d.asf n.asf r.gp.1 d.gsm n.gsm n.gsm n.gsm cj
4024 2770 734 4028 182 1650 3836 2106 3261 7005 3836 3261 2652 5986 1142

anyone does not have them, he is nearsighted and blind, and has forgotten that he has been cleansed
ᾧ → μὴ πάρεστιν ταῦτα → ἐστιν μυωπάζων τυφλός → λήθην λαβὼν → → → ⸯτοῦ καθαρισμοῦⸯ
r.dsm pl v.pai.3s r.npn v.pai.3s pt.pa.nsm a.nsm n.asf pt.aa.nsm d.gsm n.gsm
4005 4205 3590 4205 4047 1639 3697 5603 3330 3284 3836 2752

from his past sins. ¶ **10** Therefore, my brothers, be all the more eager to make your
→ αὐτοῦ πάλαι ⸯτῶν ἁμαρτιῶνⸯ διὸ ἀδελφοί μᾶλλον σπουδάσατε → ποιεῖσθαι ὑμῶν
r.gsm.3 adv d.gpf n.gpf cj n.vpm adv.c v.aam.2p f.pm r.gp.2
281 899 4093 3836 281 1475 81 5079 3437 5079 4472 7007

1:1 Συμεὼν Πέτρος δοῦλος καὶ ἀπόστολος Ἰησοῦ Χριστοῦ ¶ τοῖς ἰσότιμον ἡμῖν λαχοῦσιν πίστιν ἐν δικαιοσύνῃ τοῦ θεοῦ ἡμῶν καὶ σωτῆρος Ἰησοῦ Χριστοῦ, ¶ **2** χάρις ὑμῖν καὶ εἰρήνη πληθυνθείη ἐν ἐπιγνώσει τοῦ θεοῦ καὶ Ἰησοῦ τοῦ κυρίου ἡμῶν.

1:3 Ὡς πάντα ἡμῖν τῆς θείας δυνάμεως αὐτοῦ τὰ πρὸς ζωὴν καὶ εὐσέβειαν δεδωρημένης διὰ τῆς ἐπιγνώσεως τοῦ καλέσαντος ἡμᾶς ἰδίᾳ δόξῃ καὶ ἀρετῇ, **4** δι' ὧν τὰ τίμια καὶ μέγιστα ἡμῖν ἐπαγγέλματα δεδώρηται, ἵνα διὰ τούτων γένησθε θείας κοινωνοὶ φύσεως ἀποφυγόντες τῆς ἐν τῷ κόσμῳ ἐν ἐπιθυμίᾳ φθορᾶς. ¶ **5** καὶ αὐτὸ τοῦτο δὲ σπουδὴν πᾶσαν παρεισενέγκαντες ἐπιχορηγήσατε ἐν τῇ πίστει ὑμῶν τὴν ἀρετήν, ἐν δὲ τῇ ἀρετῇ τὴν γνῶσιν, **6** ἐν δὲ τῇ γνώσει τὴν ἐγκράτειαν, ἐν δὲ τῇ ἐγκρατείᾳ τὴν ὑπομονήν, ἐν δὲ τῇ ὑπομονῇ τὴν εὐσέβειαν, **7** ἐν δὲ τῇ εὐσεβείᾳ τὴν φιλαδελφίαν, ἐν δὲ τῇ φιλαδελφίᾳ τὴν ἀγάπην. **8** ταῦτα γὰρ ὑμῖν ὑπάρχοντα καὶ πλεονάζοντα οὐκ ἀργοὺς οὐδὲ ἀκάρπους καθίστησιν εἰς τὴν τοῦ κυρίου ἡμῶν Ἰησοῦ Χριστοῦ ἐπίγνωσιν· **9** ᾧ γὰρ μὴ πάρεστιν ταῦτα, τυφλός ἐστιν μυωπάζων, λήθην λαβὼν τοῦ καθαρισμοῦ τῶν πάλαι αὐτοῦ ἁμαρτιῶν. ¶ **10** διὸ μᾶλλον, ἀδελφοί, σπουδάσατε βεβαίαν ὑμῶν τὴν κλῆσιν καὶ ἐκλογὴν ποιεῖσθαι· ταῦτα γὰρ ποιοῦντες οὐ μὴ πταίσητέ

calling and election sure. For if you do these things, you will never fall, **11** and you will
⸤τὴν κλῆσιν⸥ καὶ ἐκλογὴν βεβαίαν γὰρ → ποιοῦντες ταῦτα ← → → ⸤οὐ μὴ ποτε⸥ πταίσητε γὰρ οὕτως ὑμῖν →
d.asf n.asf cj n.asf a.asf cj pt.pa.npm r.apn pl pl adv v.aas.2p cj adv r.dp.2
3836 3104 2779 1724 1010 1142 4472 4047 4760 4760 4024 3590 4537 4760 1142 4048 7007

receive a rich welcome into the eternal kingdom of our Lord and Savior Jesus Christ.
ἐπιχορηγηθήσεται πλουσίως ⸤ἡ εἴσοδος⸥ εἰς τὴν αἰώνιον βασιλείαν → ἡμῶν ⸤τοῦ κυρίου⸥ καὶ σωτῆρος Ἰησοῦ Χριστοῦ.
v.fpi.3s adv d.nsf n.nsf p.a d.asf a.asf n.asf r.gp.1 d.gsm n.gsm cj n.gsm n.gsm n.gsm
2220 4455 3836 1658 1650 3836 173 993 3261 7005 3836 3261 2779 5400 2652 5986

Prophecy of Scripture

1:12 So I will always remind you of these things, even though you know them and are firmly
Διὸ → μελλήσω ἀεὶ ὑπομιμνῄσκειν ὑμᾶς περὶ τούτων ← καίπερ → εἰδότας καὶ →
cj v.fai.1s adv f.pa r.ap.2 p.g r.gpn cj pt.ra.apm cj
1475 3516 107 5703 7007 4309 4047 2788 3857 2779

established in the truth you now have. **13** I think it is right to refresh your memory as long as I
ἐστηριγμένους ἐν τῇ ἀληθείᾳ → → παρούσῃ δὲ ἡγοῦμαι δίκαιον → διεγείρειν ὑμᾶς ἐν ὑπομνήσει ἐφ᾽ ὅσον ← → ←
pt.rp.apm p.d d.dsf n.dsf pt.pa.dsf cj v.pmi.1s a.asn f.pa r.ap.2 p.d n.dsf p.a r.asn
5114 1877 3836 237 4205 1254 2451 1465 1444 7007 1877 5704 2093 4012

live in the tent of this body, **14** because I know that I will soon put it aside, as
εἰμὶ ἐν τῷ σκηνώματι τούτῳ → εἰδὼς ὅτι → ἐστιν ταχινή ἡ ἀπόθεσις ⸤τοῦ σκηνώματος μου⸥ → καθὼς
v.pai.1s p.d d.dsn n.dsn r.dsn pt.ra.nsm cj v.pai.3s a.nsf d.nsf n.nsf d.gsn n.gsn r.gs.1 cj
1639 1877 3836 5013 4047 3857 4022 1639 5442 3836 629 3836 5013 1609 629 2777

our Lord Jesus Christ has made clear to me. **15** And I will make every effort to see that after
καὶ ἡμῶν ὁ κύριος Ἰησοῦς Χριστὸς → → ἐδήλωσεν μοι δὲ → → → σπουδάσω καὶ → ἔχειν ← μετὰ
adv r.gp.1 d.nsm n.nsm n.nsm n.nsm v.aai.3s r.ds.1 cj v.fai.1s adv f.pa p.a
2779 7005 3836 3261 2652 5986 1317 1609 1254 5079 2779 2400 3552

my departure you will always be able to remember these things. ¶ **16** We did not follow
ἐμὴν ⸤τὴν ἔξοδον⸥ ὑμᾶς → ἑκάστοτε → ποιεῖσθαι ← ⸤τὴν μνήμην⸥ τούτων ← γὰρ → Οὐ ἐξακολουθήσαντες
r.asf.1 d.asf n.asf r.ap.2 adv f.pm d.asf n.asf r.gpn cj pl v.aa.npm
1847 3836 2016 7007 4472 1668 4472 3836 3647 4047 1142 1979 1979 4024 1979

cleverly invented stories when we told you about the power and coming of our Lord Jesus Christ,
→ σεσοφισμένοις μύθοις → ἐγνωρίσαμεν ὑμῖν τὴν δύναμιν καὶ παρουσίαν → ἡμῶν ⸤τοῦ κυρίου⸥ Ἰησοῦ Χριστοῦ
pt.rp.dpm n.dpm v.aai.1p r.dp.2 d.asf n.asf cj n.asf r.gp.1 d.gsm n.gsm n.gsm n.gsm
5054 3680 1192 7007 3836 1539 2779 4242 3261 7005 3836 3261 2652 5986

but we were eyewitnesses of his majesty. **17** For he received honor and glory from God the Father
ἀλλ᾽ γενηθέντες ἐπόπται → ἐκείνου ⸤τῆς μεγαλειότητος⸥ γὰρ → λαβὼν τιμὴν καὶ δόξαν παρὰ θεοῦ πατρὸς
cj pt.ap.npm n.npm r.gsf d.gsf n.gsf cj pt.aa.nsm n.asf cj n.asf p.g n.gsm n.gsm
247 1181 2228 3484 1697 3836 3484 1142 3284 5507 2779 1518 4123 2536 4252

when the voice came to him from the Majestic Glory, saying, "This is my Son, whom I
→ φωνῆς ἐνεχθείσης → αὐτῷ τοιᾶσδε ὑπὸ τῆς μεγαλοπρεποῦς δόξης οὗτος ἐστιν μου ὁ υἱός, ὁ μου
n.gsf pt.ap.gsf r.dsm.3 r.gsf p.g d.gsf a.gsf n.gsf r.nsm v.pai.3s r.gs.1 d.nsm n.nsm d.nsm r.gs.1
5770 5889 5770 899 5524 5679 3836 3485 1518 4047 1639 1609 3836 5626 3836 1609

love; with him I am well pleased." **18** We ourselves heard this voice that came from heaven
ἀγαπητός εἰς ὃν ἐγὼ → → εὐδόκησα καὶ ἡμεῖς → ἠκούσαμεν ταύτην ⸤τὴν φωνὴν⸥ → ἐνεχθεῖσαν ἐξ οὐρανοῦ
a.nsm p.a r.asm r.ns.1 v.aai.1s cj r.np.1 v.aai.1p r.asf d.asf n.asf pt.ap.asf p.g n.gsm
28 1650 4005 1609 2305 2779 7005 201 4047 3836 5889 5770 1666 4041

when we were with him on the sacred mountain. ¶ **19** And we have the word of the prophets made more
→ ὄντες σὺν αὐτῷ ἐν τῷ ἁγίῳ ὄρει καὶ ἔχομεν τὸν λόγον προφητικὸν →
pt.pa.npm p.d r.dsm.3 p.d d.dsn a.dsn n.dsn cj v.pai.1p d.asm n.asm a.asm
1639 5250 899 1877 3836 41 4001 2779 2400 3836 3364 4738

certain, and you will do well to pay attention to it, as to a light shining in a dark place, until the
βεβαιότερον → → ποιεῖτε καλῶς → προσέχοντες → ᾧ ὡς → λύχνῳ φαίνοντι ἐν αὐχμηρῷ τόπῳ ⸤ἕως οὗ⸥ →
a.asm.c v.pai.2p adv pt.pa.npm r.dsm pl n.dsm pt.pa.dsm p.d a.dsm n.dsm p.g r.gsm
1010 4472 2822 4668 4005 6055 3394 5743 1877 903 5536 2401 4005

day dawns and the morning star rises in your hearts. **20** Above all, you must understand that
ἡμέρα διαυγάσῃ καὶ → φωσφόρος ἀνατείλῃ ἐν ὑμῶν ⸤ταῖς καρδίαις⸥ πρῶτον τοῦτο → → γινώσκοντες ὅτι
n.nsf v.aas.3s cj n.nsm v.aas.3s p.d r.gp.2 d.dpf n.dpf adv r.asn pt.pa.npm cj
2465 1419 2779 5892 1877 7007 3836 2840 4754 4047 1182 4022

ποτε. ¹¹ οὕτως γὰρ πλουσίως ἐπιχορηγηθήσεται ὑμῖν ἡ εἴσοδος εἰς τὴν αἰώνιον βασιλείαν τοῦ κυρίου ἡμῶν καὶ σωτῆρος Ἰησοῦ Χριστοῦ. ¹:¹² Διὸ μελλήσω ἀεὶ ὑμᾶς ὑπομιμνῄσκειν περὶ τούτων καίπερ εἰδότας καὶ ἐστηριγμένους ἐν τῇ παρούσῃ ἀληθείᾳ. ¹³ δίκαιον δὲ ἡγοῦμαι, ἐφ᾽ ὅσον εἰμὶ ἐν τούτῳ τῷ σκηνώματι, διεγείρειν ὑμᾶς ἐν ὑπομνήσει, ¹⁴ εἰδὼς ὅτι ταχινή ἐστιν ἡ ἀπόθεσις τοῦ σκηνώματός μου καθὼς καὶ ὁ κύριος ἡμῶν Ἰησοῦς Χριστὸς ἐδήλωσέν μοι, ¹⁵ σπουδάσω δὲ καὶ ἑκάστοτε ἔχειν ὑμᾶς μετὰ τὴν ἐμὴν ἔξοδον τὴν τούτων μνήμην ποιεῖσθαι. ¶ ¹⁶ Οὐ γὰρ σεσοφισμένοις μύθοις ἐξακολουθήσαντες ἐγνωρίσαμεν ὑμῖν τὴν τοῦ κυρίου ἡμῶν Ἰησοῦ Χριστοῦ δύναμιν καὶ παρουσίαν ἀλλ᾽ ἐπόπται γενηθέντες τῆς ἐκείνου μεγαλειότητος. ¹⁷ λαβὼν γὰρ παρὰ θεοῦ πατρὸς τιμὴν καὶ δόξαν φωνῆς ἐνεχθείσης αὐτῷ τοιᾶσδε ὑπὸ τῆς μεγαλοπρεποῦς δόξης, Ὁ υἱός μου ὁ ἀγαπητός μου οὗτος ἐστιν εἰς ὃν ἐγὼ εὐδόκησα, ¹⁸ καὶ ταύτην τὴν φωνὴν ἡμεῖς ἠκούσαμεν ἐξ οὐρανοῦ ἐνεχθεῖσαν σὺν αὐτῷ ὄντες ἐν τῷ ἁγίῳ ὄρει ¶ ¹⁹ καὶ ἔχομεν βεβαιότερον τὸν προφητικὸν λόγον, ᾧ καλῶς ποιεῖτε προσέχοντες ὡς λύχνῳ φαίνοντι ἐν αὐχμηρῷ τόπῳ, ἕως οὗ ἡμέρα διαυγάσῃ καὶ φωσφόρος ἀνατείλῃ ἐν ταῖς καρδίαις ὑμῶν, ²⁰ τοῦτο πρῶτον γινώσκοντες ὅτι πᾶσα προφητεία γραφῆς ἰδίας

no	prophecy	of Scripture	came	about	by	the prophet's	own	interpretation.	[21] For	prophecy	never	had its
₍οὐ	πᾶσα	προφητεία	→	γραφῆς	γίνεται ←	→	ἰδίας	ἐπιλύσεως	γὰρ	προφητεία	₍οὐ ποτέᵧ	
pl	a.nsf	n.nsf		n.gsf	v.pmi.3s		a.gsf	n.gsf	cj	n.nsf	pl adv	
4024	4246	4735		1210	1181		2625	2146	1142	4735	4024 4537	

origin in the	will	of man,	but	men	spoke	from	God	as	they	were	carried	along	by	the	Holy	Spirit.
ἠνέχθη →	θελήματι	→ ἀνθρώπου	ἀλλὰ	ἄνθρωποι	ἐλάλησαν	ἀπὸ	θεοῦ	→	→	→	φερόμενοι ←		ὑπὸ		ἁγίου	πνεύματος
v.api.3s	n.dsn	n.gsn	cj	n.npm	v.aai.3p	p.g	n.gsm				pt.pp.npm		p.g		a.gsn	n.gsn
5770	2525	476	247	476	3281	608	2536				5770		5679		41	4460

False Teachers and Their Destruction

[2:1] But	there	were	also	false prophets	among	the	people,	just as	there	will	be	false	teachers
δὲ	there	Ἐγένοντο	καὶ →	ψευδοπροφῆται	ἐν	τῷ	λαῷ	καὶ ὡς →	→	ἔσονται	→		ψευδοδιδάσκαλοι
cj		v.ami.3p	adv	n.npm	p.d	d.dsm	n.dsm	adv cj		v.fmi.3p			n.npm
1254		1181	2779	6021	1877	3836	3295	2779 6055		1639			6015

among	you.	They	will	secretly introduce	destructive	heresies,	even	denying	the	sovereign	Lord	who	bought
ἐν	ὑμῖν	οἵτινες →	→	παρεισάξουσιν	ἀπωλείας	αἱρέσεις	καὶ	ἀρνούμενοι	τὸν	δεσπότην	Lord	who	ἀγοράσαντα
p.d	r.dp.2	r.npm		v.fai.3p	n.gsf	n.apf	adv	pt.pm.npm	d.asm	n.asm			pt.aa.asm
1877	7007	4015		4206	724	146	2779	766	3836	1305			60

them	– bringing	swift	destruction	on themselves.	[2]	Many	will follow		their	shameful		ways	and
αὐτοὺς	ἐπάγοντες	ταχινὴν	ἀπώλειαν	→ ἑαυτοῖς	καὶ	πολλοὶ	→ ἐξακολουθήσουσιν	αὐτῶν	₍ταῖς ἀσελγείαιςᵧ ←		δι᾽	
r.apm.3	pt.pa.npm	a.asf	n.asf	r.dpm.3	cj	a.npm	v.fai.3p	r.gpm.3	d.dpf n.dpf		p.a	
899	2042	5442	724	1571	2779	4498	1979	899	3836 816		1328	

will bring	the	way	of truth		into	disrepute.	[3]	In their	greed		these teachers	will exploit		you
οὓς →	→	ἡ	ὁδὸς	₍τῆς ἀληθείαςᵧ	→	βλασφημηθήσεται	καὶ ἐν		πλεονεξίᾳ			ἐμπορεύσονται	ὑμᾶς	
r.apm		d.nsf	n.nsf	d.gsf n.gsf		v.fpi.3s	cj p.d		n.dsf			v.fmi.3p	r.ap.2	
4005	1059	1059	3836	3847 3836 237		1059	2779 1877		4432			1864	7007	

with	stories	they	have	made up.	Their	condemnation	has long		been	hanging over	them,	and	their
→	λόγοις	→	πλαστοῖς	οἷς	₍τὸ κρίμαᵧ	→	ἔκπαλαι	οὐκ →	ἀργεῖ			καὶ	αὐτῶν
	n.dpm		a.dpm	r.dpm	d.nsn n.nsn		adv	pl	v.pai.3s			cj	r.gpm.3
	3364		4422	4005	3836 3210		733 1732	4024	733			2779	899

destruction	has	not	been	sleeping.	¶	[4] For	if	God	did	not	spare	angels	when	they	sinned,	but
₍ἡ ἀπώλειαᵧ	→	οὐ		νυστάζει		γὰρ	Εἰ	ὁ θεὸς	→	οὐκ	ἐφείσατο	ἀγγέλων	→	→	ἁμαρτησάντων	ἀλλὰ
d.nsf n.nsf		pl		v.pai.3s		cj	cj	d.nsm n.nsm		pl	v.ami.3s	n.gpm			pt.aa.gpm	cj
3836 724		3818	4024	3818		1142	1623	3836 2536		5767 4024	5/67	34			279	247

sent		them	to hell,	putting		them	into	gloomy	dungeons	to be	held		for judgment;	[5]	if	he	did	not
ταρταρώσας	←	←		παρέδωκεν	→	ζόφου	σειραῖς	→		τηρουμένους	εἰς	κρίσιν		καὶ	ᛁ →		οὐκ	
pt.aa.nsm				v.aai.3s		n.gsm	n.dpf			pt.pp.apm	p.a	n.asf		cj			pl	
5434				4140	4937	2432	4937			5498	1650	3213		2779	5767 5767		4024	

spare	the	ancient	world	when	he	brought	the	flood		on its	ungodly people,	but	protected	Noah,	a
ἐφείσατο	ἀρχαίου	κόσμου	→	→		ἐπάξας	κατακλυσμὸν	→	κόσμῳ	ἀσεβῶν ←		ἀλλὰ	ἐφύλαξεν	Νῶε	
v.ami.3s	a.gsm	n.gsm				pt.aa.nsm	n.asm		n.dsm	a.gpm		cj	v.aai.3s	n.asm	
5767	792	3180				2042	2886		3180	815		247	5875	3820	

preacher	of righteousness,	and seven others;	[6]	if	he condemned		the	cities	of Sodom	and	Gomorrah
κήρυκα	→ δικαιοσύνης	ὄγδοον	καὶ		κατέκρινεν	[καταστροφῇ]	πόλεις	→	Σοδόμων	καὶ	Γομόρρας
n.asm	n.gsf	a.asm	cj		v.aai.3s	n.dsf	n.apf		n.gpn	cj	n.gsf
3061	1466	3838	2779		2891	2953	4484		5047	2779	1202

by	burning	them	to ashes,	and made	them	an	example	of what is going		to	happen	to the	ungodly;	[7] and	if	he
→	→	→	τεφρώσας				ὑπόδειγμα	→	μελλόντων	τεθεικώς			ἀσεβέσιν	καὶ		
			pt.aa.nsm				n.asn		pt.pa.gpn	pt.ra.nsm			a.dpm	cj		
			5491				5682		3516	5502			814	2779		

rescued	Lot,	a righteous	man,	who	was	distressed		by	the	filthy	lives	of	lawless		men	[8] (for that
ἐρρύσατο	Λώτ	δίκαιον				καταπονούμενον	ὑπὸ	τῆς	ἐν	ἀσελγείᾳ	ἀναστροφῆς	→	₍τῶν ἀθέσμωνᵧ		γὰρ	ὁ
v.ami.3s	n.asm	a.asm				pt.pp.asm	p.g	d.gsf	p.d	n.dsf	n.gsf		d.gpm a.gpm		cj	d.nsm
4861	3397	1465				2930	5679	3836	1877	816	419		3836 118		1142	3836

righteous	man,	living	among	them	day	after	day,	was	tormented	in his	righteous	soul	by the	lawless	deeds
δίκαιος	←	ἐγκατοικῶν	ἐν	αὐτοῖς	ἡμέραν	ἐξ	ἡμέρας	→	ἐβασάνιζεν		δικαίαν	ψυχὴν	→	ἀνόμοις	ἔργοις
a.nsm		pt.pa.nsm	p.d	r.dpm.3	n.asf	p.g	n.gsf		v.iai.3s		a.asf	n.asf		a.dpn	n.dpn
1465		1594	1877	899	2465	1666	2465		989		1465	6034		491	2240

ἐπιλύσεως οὐ γίνεται· [21] οὐ γὰρ θελήματι ἀνθρώπου ἠνέχθη προφητεία ποτέ, ἀλλὰ ὑπὸ πνεύματος ἁγίου φερόμενοι ἐλάλησαν ἀπὸ θεοῦ ἄνθρωποι.

[2:1] Ἐγένοντο δὲ καὶ ψευδοπροφῆται ἐν τῷ λαῷ, ὡς καὶ ἐν ὑμῖν ἔσονται ψευδοδιδάσκαλοι, οἵτινες παρεισάξουσιν αἱρέσεις ἀπωλείας καὶ τὸν ἀγοράσαντα αὐτοὺς δεσπότην ἀρνούμενοι. ἐπάγοντες ἑαυτοῖς ταχινὴν ἀπώλειαν, [2] καὶ πολλοὶ ἐξακολουθήσουσιν αὐτῶν ταῖς ἀσελγείαις δι᾽ οὓς ἡ ὁδὸς τῆς ἀληθείας βλασφημηθήσεται, [3] καὶ ἐν πλεονεξίᾳ πλαστοῖς λόγοις ὑμᾶς ἐμπορεύσονται, οἷς τὸ κρίμα ἔκπαλαι οὐκ ἀργεῖ καὶ ἡ ἀπώλεια αὐτῶν οὐ νυστάζει. ¶ [4] Εἰ γὰρ ὁ θεὸς ἀγγέλων ἁμαρτησάντων οὐκ ἐφείσατο ἀλλὰ σιροῖς «σειραῖς» ζόφου ταρταρώσας παρέδωκεν εἰς κρίσιν τηρουμένους, [5] καὶ ἀρχαίου κόσμου οὐκ ἐφείσατο ἀλλὰ ὄγδοον Νῶε δικαιοσύνης κήρυκα ἐφύλαξεν κατακλυσμὸν κόσμῳ ἀσεβῶν ἐπάξας, [6] καὶ πόλεις Σοδόμων καὶ Γομόρρας τεφρώσας [καταστροφῇ] κατέκρινεν ὑπόδειγμα μελλόντων ἀσεβέ[σ]ιν τεθεικώς, [7] καὶ δίκαιον Λώτ καταπονούμενον ὑπὸ τῆς τῶν ἀθέσμων ἐν ἀσελγείᾳ ἀναστροφῆς ἐρρύσατο· [8] βλέμματι γὰρ καὶ ἀκοῇ ὁ δίκαιος ἐγκατοικῶν ἐν

he saw   and heard) – **9** if this is so, then the Lord knows how to rescue godly men from trials   and to hold
βλέμματι καὶ ἀκοῇ   κύριος οἶδεν → ῥύεσθαι εὐσεβεῖς ἐκ πειρασμοῦ δὲ → τηρεῖν
n.dsn cj n.dsf   n.nsm v.rai.3s   f.pm a.apm p.g n.gsm cj f.pa
1062 2779 198   3261 3857   4861 2356 1666 4280 1254 5498

the unrighteous for the day   of judgment, while continuing their punishment. **10** This is especially true of those
ἀδίκους εἰς ἡμέραν κρίσεως → → → κολαζομένους δὲ → μάλιστα ← τοὺς
a.apm p.a n.asf n.gsf   pt.pp.apm cj adv.s d.apm
96 1650 2465 3213   3134 1254 3436 3836

who follow   the corrupt   desire of the sinful nature and despise   authority. ¶ Bold
→ πορευομένους ὀπίσω   μιασμοῦ ἐν ἐπιθυμίᾳ → σαρκὸς ← καὶ καταφρονοῦντας κυριότητος τολμηταὶ
pt.pm.apm p.g n.gsm p.d n.dsf n.gsf cj pt.pa.apm n.gsf n.npm
4513 3958 3622 1877 2123 4922 2779 2969 3262 5532

and arrogant, these men are not afraid   to slander   celestial beings; **11** yet even angels, although they are
αὐθάδεις → → οὐ τρέμουσιν → βλασφημοῦντες δόξας ← ὅπου ἄγγελοι ὄντες
a.npm pl v.pai.3p pt.pa.npm n.apf cj n.npm pt.pa.npm
881 5554 5554 4024 5554 1059 1518 3963 34 1639

stronger and more powerful, do not bring slanderous accusations against such beings in   the presence of the
ἰσχύϊ καὶ μείζονες δυνάμει → οὐ φέρουσιν βλάσφημον κρίσιν κατʼ αὐτῶν παρὰ ←
n.dsf cj a.npm.c n.dsf pl v.pai.3p a.asf n.asf p.g r.gpm.3 p.a
2709 2779 3489 1539 5770 5770 1061 3213 2848 899 4123

Lord. **12** But these men blaspheme   in matters they do not understand. They are like brute beasts, creatures of
κυρίου δὲ Οὗτοι βλασφημοῦντες ἐν οἷς → → → ἀγνοοῦσιν ὡς ἄλογα ζῷα →
n.gsm cj r.npm pt.pa.npm p.d r.dpn v.pai.3p pl a.npn n.npn
3261 1254 4047 1059 1877 4005 51 6055 263 2442

instinct, born   only to be caught and destroyed, and like beasts   they too will perish. ¶
φυσικὰ γεγεννημένα εἰς ← ἅλωσιν καὶ φθορὰν → ἐν τῇ φθορᾷ αὐτῶν → καὶ → φθαρήσονται
a.npn pt.rp.npn p.a n.asf cj n.asf p.d d.dsf n.dsf r.gpm.3 adv v.fpi.3p
5879 1164 1650 274 2779 5785 1877 3836 5785 5780 2779 5780

13 They will be paid back with harm   for the harm they have done. Their idea   of pleasure is to carouse
μισθὸν ← ἀδικούμενοι → ἀδικίας → ἡγούμενοι ἡδονὴν τὴν τρυφὴν
n.asm ← ← n.gsf pt.pm.npm n.asf d.asf n.asf
3635 92 94 2451 2454 3836 5588

in broad daylight. They are blots and blemishes, reveling   in their pleasures   while they feast   with
ἐν → ἡμέρᾳ σπίλοι καὶ μῶμοι ἐντρυφῶντες ἐν αὐτῶν ταῖς ἀπάταις → → συνευωχούμενοι ←
p.d n.dsf n.npm cj n.npm pt.pa.npm p.d r.gpm.3 d.dpf n.dpf pt.pp.npm
1877 2465 5070 2779 3700 1960 1877 899 3836 573 5307

you. **14** With eyes   full of adultery,   they never stop   sinning; they seduce   the unstable;
ὑμῖν ἔχοντες ὀφθαλμοὺς μεστοὺς → μοιχαλίδος καὶ → → ἀκαταπαύστους ἁμαρτίας → δελεάζοντες ψυχὰς ἀστηρίκτους
r.dp.2 pt.pa.npm n.apm a.apm n.gsf cj a.apm n.gsf pt.pa.npm n.apf a.apf
7007 2400 4057 3550 3655 2779 188 281 1284 6034 844

they are   experts   in greed   – an accursed brood! **15** They have left   the straight way and
→ → καρδίαν γεγυμνασμένην → πλεονεξίας κατάρας τέκνα → → καταλείποντες εὐθεῖαν ὁδὸν
n.asf pt.rp.asf n.gsf n.gsf n.npn pt.pa.npm a.asf n.asf
1214 1214 2840 1214 4432 2932 5451 2901 2318 3847

wandered   off to follow   the way of Balaam   son of Beor,   who loved   the wages of wickedness.
ἐπλανήθησαν ← → ἐξακολουθήσαντες τῇ ὁδῷ τοῦ Βαλαὰμ → τοῦ Βοσόρ ὃς ἠγάπησεν μισθὸν → ἀδικίας
v.api.3p pt.aa.npm d.dsf n.dsf d.gsm n.gsm d.gsm n.gsm r.nsm v.aai.3s n.asm n.gsf
4414 1979 3836 3847 3836 1082 3836 1082 4005 26 3635 94

16 But he was rebuked for his   wrongdoing by a donkey   – a beast without speech – who spoke   with a man's
δὲ → ἔσχεν ἔλεγξιν → ἰδίας παρανομίας ὑποζύγιον → ἄφωνον → φθεγξάμενον ἐν ἀνθρώπου
cj v.aai.3s n.asf a.gsf n.gsf n.nsn a.nsn pt.am.nsn p.d n.gsm
1254 2400 1792 2625 4175 5689 936 5779 1877 476

voice and restrained the prophet's   madness. ¶ **17** These men are   springs without water   and mists
φωνῇ ἐκώλυσεν τὴν τοῦ προφήτου παραφρονίαν οὗτοι εἰσιν πηγαὶ → ἄνυδροι καὶ ὁμίχλαι
n.dsf v.aai.3s d.asf d.gsm n.gsm n.asf r.npm v.pai.3p n.npf a.npf cj n.npf
5889 3266 3836 3836 4737 4197 4047 1639 4380 536 2779 3920

αὐτοῖς ἡμέραν ἐξ ἡμέρας ψυχὴν δικαίαν ἀνόμοις ἔργοις ἐβασάνιζεν· ⁹ οἶδεν κύριος εὐσεβεῖς ἐκ πειρασμοῦ ῥύεσθαι, ἀδίκους δὲ εἰς ἡμέραν κρίσεως κολαζομένους τηρεῖν, ¹⁰ μάλιστα δὲ τοὺς ὀπίσω σαρκὸς ἐν ἐπιθυμίᾳ μιασμοῦ πορευομένους καὶ κυριότητος καταφρονοῦντας. ¶ Τολμηταὶ αὐθάδεις, δόξας οὐ τρέμουσιν βλασφημοῦντες, ¹¹ ὅπου ἄγγελοι ἰσχύϊ καὶ δυνάμει μείζονες ὄντες οὐ φέρουσιν κατʼ αὐτῶν παρὰ κυρίου βλάσφημον κρίσιν. ¹² οὗτοι δὲ ὡς ἄλογα ζῷα γεγεννημένα φυσικὰ εἰς ἅλωσιν καὶ φθορὰν ἐν οἷς ἀγνοοῦσιν βλασφημοῦντες, ἐν τῇ φθορᾷ αὐτῶν καὶ φθαρήσονται ¶ ¹³ ἀδικούμενοι μισθὸν ἀδικίας, ἡδονὴν ἡγούμενοι τὴν ἐν ἡμέρᾳ τρυφήν, σπίλοι καὶ μῶμοι ἐντρυφῶντες ἐν ταῖς ἀπάταις αὐτῶν συνευωχούμενοι ὑμῖν, ¹⁴ ὀφθαλμοὺς ἔχοντες μεστοὺς μοιχαλίδος καὶ ἀκαταπαύστους ἁμαρτίας, δελεάζοντες ψυχὰς ἀστηρίκτους, καρδίαν γεγυμνασμένην πλεονεξίας ἔχοντες, κατάρας τέκνα· ¹⁵ καταλείποντες εὐθεῖαν ὁδὸν ἐπλανήθησαν, ἐξακολουθήσαντες τῇ ὁδῷ τοῦ Βαλαὰμ τοῦ Βεώρ, «Βοσόρ,» ὃς μισθὸν ἀδικίας ἠγάπησεν ¹⁶ ἔλεγξιν δὲ ἔσχεν ἰδίας παρανομίας· ὑποζύγιον ἄφωνον ἐν ἀνθρώπου φωνῇ φθεγξάμενον ἐκώλυσεν τὴν τοῦ προφήτου παραφρονίαν. ¶ ¹⁷ Οὗτοί εἰσιν πηγαὶ ἄνυδροι καὶ ὁμίχλαι ὑπὸ λαίλαπος ἐλαυνόμεναι, οἷς ὁ ζόφος τοῦ σκότους

driven | by a storm. | Blackest | darkness | is reserved for them. | [18] For they | mouth | empty, | boastful words
ἐλαυνόμεναι | ὑπὸ | λαίλαπος | ὁ ζόφος, | ⌐τοῦ σκότους⌐ → | τετήρηται → | οἷς | γὰρ | φθεγγόμενοι | ματαιότητος | ὑπέρογκα ←
pt.pp.npf | p.g | n.gsf | d.nsm n.nsm | d.gsn n.gsn | v.rpi.3s | r.dpm | cj | pt.pm.npm | n.gsf | a.apn
1785 | 5679 | 3278 | 3836 2432 | 3836 5030 | 5498 | 4005 | 1142 | 5779 | 3470 | 5665

and, by appealing | to | the lustful | desires | of sinful | human nature, | they entice | people who are | just
| | ἐν | ἀσελγείαις | ἐπιθυμίαις → | σαρκὸς ← | → | δελεάζουσιν | τοὺς ← | → ὀλίγως
| | p.d | n.dpf | n.dpf | n.gsf | | v.pai.3p | d.apm | adv
| | 1877 | 816 | 2123 | 4922 | | 1284 | 3836 | 709 3903

escaping | from those who live | in error. | [19] They promise | them | freedom, | while they themselves
ἀποφεύγοντας ← | τοὺς ← ἀναστρεφομένους | ἐν πλάνη | → ἐπαγγελλόμενοι | αὐτοῖς | ἐλευθερίαν → | → | αὐτοὶ
pt.pa.apm | d.apm pt.pp.apm | p.d n.dsf | pt.pm.npm | r.dpm.3 | n.asf | | r.npm
709 | 3836 418 | 1877 4415 | 2040 | 899 | 1800 | 5639 5639 | 899

are | slaves of depravity | – for a | man is a slave | to whatever has mastered him. | [20] | If they have
ὑπάρχοντες | δοῦλοι | ⌐τῆς φθορᾶς⌐ | γὰρ τις ← | → δεδούλωται | ᾧ | ← ἥττηται | τούτῳ | γὰρ εἰ
pt.pa.npm | n.npm | d.gsf n.gsf | cj r.nsm | v.rpi.3s | r.dsn | v.rpi.3s | r.dsn | cj cj
5639 | 1529 | 3836 5785 | 1142 5516 | 1530 | 4005 | 2487 | 4047 | 1142 1623

escaped | the corruption | of the world | by knowing | our | Lord | and | Savior | Jesus Christ | and are | again
ἀποφυγόντες | τὰ μιάσματα | → τοῦ κόσμου | ἐν ἐπιγνώσει | ἡμῶν | ⌐τοῦ κυρίου⌐ | καὶ | σωτῆρος | Ἰησοῦ Χριστοῦ | δὲ → | πάλιν
pt.aa.npm | d.apn n.apn | d.gsm n.gsm | p.d n.dsf | r.gp.1 | d.gsm n.gsm | cj | n.gsm | n.gsm n.gsm | cj | adv
709 | 3836 3621 | 3836 3180 | 1877 2106 | 7005 | 3836 3261 | 2779 | 5400 | 2652 5986 | 1254 1861 | 4099

entangled | in it | and overcome, | they | are | worse off | at the end | than they were | at the beginning. | [21] | It
ἐμπλακέντες → | τούτοις | ἡττῶνται | αὐτοῖς | γέγονεν | χείρονα ← | τὰ ἔσχατα → | → | τῶν πρώτων | | γὰρ →
pt.ap.npm | r.dpn | v.ppi.3p | r.dpm.3 | v.rai.3s | a.npn.c | d.npn a.npn | | d.gpn a.gpn | | cj
1861 | 4047 | 2487 | 899 | 1181 | 5937 | 3836 2274 | | 3836 4755 | | 1142

would have been | better | for them | not to have known | the | way | of righteousness, | than to have known | it and
→ → ἦν | κρεῖττον → | αὐτοῖς | μὴ → | → ἐπεγνωκέναι | τὴν ὁδὸν | ⌐τῆς δικαιοσύνης⌐ | ἢ → | → ἐπιγνοῦσιν
v.iai.3s | a.nsn.c | r.dpm.3 | pl | f.ra | d.asf n.asf | d.gsf n.gsf | pl | pt.aa.dpm
1639 | 3202 | 899 | 3590 | 2105 | 3836 3847 | 3836 1466 | 2445 | 2105

then to turn | their backs on the | sacred | command | that was passed | on to them. | [22] Of them | the proverbs
→ ὑποστρέψαι ← | ← ἐκ τῆς | ἁγίας | ἐντολῆς | → παραδοθείσης ← | αὐτοῖς | → αὐτοῖς τὸ | παροιμίας
f.aa | p.g d.gsf | a.gsf | n.gsf | pt.ap.gsf | r.dpm.3 | r.dpm.3 d.asn | n.apsf
5715 | 1666 3836 | 41 | 1953 | 4140 | 899 | 899 3836 | 4231

are | true: | "A | dog | returns | to | its | vomit," | and, | "A sow | that is washed | goes back | to her
συμβέβηκεν | ⌐τῆς ἀληθοῦς⌐ | | κύων ἐπιστρέψας | ἐπὶ | ἴδιον | ⌐τὸ ἐξέραμα⌐ | καὶ | Ὗς | → λουσαμένη | → | εἰς
v.rai.3s | d.gsf a.gsf | | n.nsm pt.aa.nsm | p.a | a.asn | d.asn n.asn | cj | n.nsf | pt.am.nsf | | p.a
5201 | 3836 239 | | 3264 2188 | 2093 | 2625 | 3836 2000 | 2779 | 5725 | 3374 | | 1650

wallowing | in the mud."
κυλισμὸν → | βορβόρου
n.asm | n.gsm
3243 | 1079

The Day of the Lord

[3:1] Dear friends, | this | is now | my second | letter | to you. | I have written | both of them | as | reminders to
ἀγαπητοί | Ταύτην | ἤδη | δευτέραν | ἐπιστολήν | ὑμῖν | γράφω | ἐν | αἷς | ἐν ὑπομνήσει
a.vpm | r.asf | adv | a.asf | n.asf | r.dp.2 | v.pai.1s | p.d | r.dpf | p.d n.dsf
28 | 4047 | 2453 | 1311 | 2186 | 7007 | 1211 | 1877 | 4005 | 1877 5704

stimulate you | to wholesome | thinking. | [2] I | want you to recall | the words | spoken | in the past | by the holy
διεγείρω | ὑμῶν | εἰλικρινῆ | ⌐τὴν διάνοιαν⌐ ← | → μνησθῆναι | τῶν ῥημάτων | προειρημένων ← | ← | ὑπὸ τῶν ἁγίων
v.pai.1s | r.gp.2 | a.asf | d.asf n.asf | f.ap | d.gpn n.gpn | pt.rp.gpn | | p.g d.gpm a.gpm
1444 | 7007 | 1637 | 3836 1379 | 3630 | 3836 4839 | 4597 | | 5679 3836 41

prophets | and the | command | given | by our | Lord | and | Savior | through | your | apostles. | ¶ | [3] First | of all, | you
προφητῶν | καὶ τῆς | ἐντολῆς | → | τοῦ κυρίου | καὶ | σωτῆρος → | ὑμῶν | ⌐τῶν ἀποστόλων⌐ | | πρῶτον | τοῦτο →
n.gpm | cj d.gsf | n.gsf | | d.gsm n.gsm | cj | n.gsm | r.gp.2 | d.gpm n.gpm | | adv | r.asn
4737 | 2779 3836 | 1953 | | 3836 3261 | 2779 | 5400 | 7007 | 3836 693 | | 4754 | 4047

must understand | that | in | the last | days | scoffers | will come, | scoffing | and following | their | own
→ γινώσκοντες | ὅτι | ἐπ᾽ | τῶν ἐσχάτων | ἡμερῶν | ἐμπαῖκται → | ἐλεύσονται | [ἐν] | ἐμπαιγμονῇ | πορευόμενοι | κατὰ αὐτῶν | ἰδίας
pt.pa.npm | cj | p.g | d.gpf a.gpf | n.gpf | n.npm | v.fmi.3p | p.d | n.dsf | pt.pm.npm | p.a r.gpm.3 | a.apf
1182 | 4022 | 2093 | 3836 2274 | 2465 | 1851 | 2262 | 1877 | 1848 | 4513 | 2848 899 | 2625

τετήρηται. [18] ὑπέρογκα γὰρ ματαιότητος φθεγγόμενοι δελεάζουσιν ἐν ἐπιθυμίαις σαρκὸς ἀσελγείαις τοὺς ὀλίγως ἀποφεύγοντας τοὺς ἐν πλάνῃ ἀναστρεφομένους, [19] ἐλευθερίαν αὐτοῖς ἐπαγγελλόμενοι, αὐτοὶ δοῦλοι ὑπάρχοντες τῆς φθορᾶς· ᾧ γάρ τις ἥττηται, τούτῳ δεδούλωται. [20] εἰ γὰρ ἀποφυγόντες τὰ μιάσματα τοῦ κόσμου ἐν ἐπιγνώσει τοῦ κυρίου [ἡμῶν] καὶ σωτῆρος Ἰησοῦ Χριστοῦ, τούτοις δὲ πάλιν ἐμπλακέντες ἡττῶνται, γέγονεν αὐτοῖς τὰ ἔσχατα χείρονα τῶν πρώτων. [21] κρεῖττον γὰρ ἦν αὐτοῖς μὴ ἐπεγνωκέναι τὴν ὁδὸν τῆς δικαιοσύνης ἢ ἐπιγνοῦσιν ὑποστρέψαι ἐκ τῆς παραδοθείσης αὐτοῖς ἁγίας ἐντολῆς. [22] συμβέβηκεν αὐτοῖς τὸ τῆς ἀληθοῦς παροιμίας, Κύων ἐπιστρέψας ἐπὶ τὸ ἴδιον ἐξέραμα, καί, Ὗς λουσαμένη εἰς κυλισμὸν βορβόρου.

[3:1] Ταύτην ἤδη, ἀγαπητοί, δευτέραν ὑμῖν γράφω ἐπιστολὴν ἐν αἷς διεγείρω ὑμῶν ἐν ὑπομνήσει τὴν εἰλικρινῆ διάνοιαν [2] μνησθῆναι τῶν προειρημένων ῥημάτων ὑπὸ τῶν ἁγίων προφητῶν καὶ τῆς τῶν ἀποστόλων ὑμῶν ἐντολῆς τοῦ κυρίου καὶ σωτῆρος. ¶ [3] τοῦτο πρῶτον γινώσκοντες ὅτι ἐλεύσονται ἐπ᾽ ἐσχάτων τῶν ἡμερῶν [ἐν] ἐμπαιγμονῇ ἐμπαῖκται κατὰ τὰς ἰδίας

evil desires. **4** They will say, "Where is this 'coming' he promised? *Ever since* our fathers
→ ⸉τὰς ἐπιθυμίας⸊ καὶ → λέγοντες ποῦ ἐστιν τῆς παρουσίας αὐτοῦ ἡ ἐπαγγελία γὰρ ἀφ᾽ ἧς οἱ πατέρες
d.apf n.apf cj pt.pa.npm adv v.pai.3s d.gsf n.gsf r.gsm.3 d.nsf n.nsf cj p.g r.gsf d.npm n.npm
3836 2123 2779 3306 4543 1639 3836 4242 899 3836 2039 1142 608 4005 3836 4252

died, everything goes on as it has since the beginning of creation." **5** But they deliberately forget
ἐκοιμήθησαν πάντα διαμένει ← οὕτως ← ἀπ᾽ ἀρχῆς → κτίσεως γὰρ αὐτοὺς θέλοντας Λανθάνει τοῦτο
v.api.3p a.npn v.pai.3s adv p.g n.gsf n.gsf cj r.apm.3 pt.pa.apm v.pai.3s r.asn
3121 4246 1373 4048 608 794 3232 1142 899 2527 3291 4047

that long ago by God's word the heavens existed and the earth was formed out of water and by water.
ὅτι ἔκπαλαι ← → ⸉τοῦ θεοῦ⸊ ⸉τῷ λόγῳ⸊ οὐρανοὶ ἦσαν καὶ → γῆ → συνεστῶσα ἐξ ← ὕδατος καὶ δι᾽ ὕδατος
cj adv d.gsm n.gsm d.dsm n.dsm n.npm v.iai.3p cj n.nsf pt.ra.nsf p.g n.gsn cj p.g n.gsn
4022 1732 3836 2536 3836 3364 4041 1639 2779 1178 5319 1666 5623 2779 1328 5623

6 By these waters also the world of that time was deluged and destroyed. **7** By the same word the present
δι᾽ ὧν ὕδατι ὁ κόσμος → → τότε → κατακλυσθεὶς ἀπώλετο δὲ → τῷ αὐτῷ λόγῳ οἱ νῦν
p.g r.gpn n.dsn d.nsm n.nsm adv pt.ap.nsm v.ami.3s cj d.dsm r.dsm n.dsm d.npm adv
1328 4005 5623 3836 3180 5538 2885 660 1254 3836 899 3364 3836 3814

heavens and earth are reserved for fire, being kept for the day of judgment and destruction of
οὐρανοὶ καὶ ἡ γῆ εἰσὶν τεθησαυρισμένοι → πυρὶ → τηρούμενοι εἰς → ἡμέραν → κρίσεως καὶ ἀπωλείας →
n.npm cj d.nsf n.nsf v.pai.3p pt.rp.npm n.dsn pt.pp.npm p.a n.asf n.gsf cj n.gsf
4041 2779 3836 1178 1639 2564 4786 5498 1650 2465 3213 2779 724 476

ungodly men. ¶ **8** But do not forget this one thing, dear friends: With the Lord a day
ἀσεβῶν ⸉τῶν ἀνθρώπων⸊ δὲ ὑμᾶς → μὴ λανθανέτω τοῦτο Ἓν ← ἀγαπητοί ὅτι παρὰ κυρίῳ μία ἡμέρα
a.gpn d.gpm n.gpm cj r.ap.2 pl v.pam.3s r.nsn a.nsn a.vpm cj p.d n.dsm a.nsf n.nsf
815 3836 476 1254 7007 3291 3590 3291 4047 1651 28 4022 4123 3261 1651 2465

is like a thousand years, and a thousand years are like a day. **9** The Lord is not slow in keeping his promise,
ὡς χίλια ἔτη καὶ χίλια ἔτη ὡς μία ἡμέρα κύριος → οὐ βραδύνει τῆς ἐπαγγελίας
pl a.npn n.npn cj a.npn n.npn pl a.nsf n.nsf n.nsm pl v.pai.3s d.gsf n.gsf
6055 5943 2291 2779 5943 2291 6055 1651 2465 3261 4024 1094 3836 2039

as some understand slowness. He is patient with you, not wanting anyone to perish, but everyone to
ὡς τινες ἡγοῦνται βραδύτητα ἀλλὰ → μακροθυμεῖ εἰς ὑμᾶς μὴ βουλόμενος τινας → ἀπολέσθαι ἀλλὰ πάντας →
cj r.npm v.pmi.3p n.asf cj v.pai.3s p.a r.ap.2 pl pt.pp.nsm r.apm f.am cj a.apm
6055 5516 2451 1097 247 3428 1650 7007 3590 1089 5516 660 247 4246

come to repentance. ¶ **10** But the day of the Lord will come like a thief. The heavens will
χωρῆσαι εἰς μετάνοιαν δὲ ἡμέρα → κυρίου → Ἥξει ὡς κλέπτης ἐν ᾗ οἱ οὐρανοὶ →
f.aa p.a n.asf cj n.nsf n.gsn v.fai.3s pl n.nsm p.d r.dsf d.npm n.npm
6003 1650 3567 1254 2465 3261 2457 6055 3095 1877 4005 3836 4041

disappear with a roar; the elements will be destroyed by fire, and the earth and everything in it
παρελεύσονται → ῥοιζηδὸν δὲ στοιχεῖα → λυθήσεται καυσούμενα καὶ γῆ καὶ ⸉τὰ ἔργα⸊ ἐν αὐτῇ
v.fmi.3p adv cj n.npn v.fpi.3s pt.pp.npn cj n.nsf cj d.npn n.npn p.d r.dsf.3
4216 4853 1254 5122 3395 3012 2779 1178 2779 3836 2240 1877 899

will be laid bare. ¶ **11** Since everything will be destroyed in this way, what kind of people ought
→ → εὑρεθήσεται ← ⸉Τούτων πάντων⸊ → λυομένων → οὕτως ποταποὺς ← ← δεῖ
v.fpi.3s r.gpn a.gpn pt.pp.gpn adv r.apm v.pai.3s
2351 3395 4047 4246 3395 4048 4534 1256

you to be? You ought to live holy and godly lives **12** as you look forward to the day of
ὑμᾶς ὑπάρχειν ἐν ἀναστροφαῖς ἁγίαις καὶ εὐσεβείαις ← προσδοκῶντας → τῆς ἡμέρας →
r.ap.2 f.pa p.d n.dpf a.dpf cj n.dpf pt.pa.apm d.gsf n.gsf
7007 5639 1877 419 41 2779 2354 4659 3836 2465

God and speed its coming. That day will bring about the destruction of the heavens by fire, and
⸉τοῦ θεοῦ⸊ καὶ σπεύδοντας τὴν παρουσίαν δι᾽ ἣν ← ← → λυθήσονται ← οὐρανοὶ → πυρούμενοι καὶ
d.gsm n.gsm cj pt.pa.apm d.asf n.asf p.a r.asf v.fpi.3p n.npm pt.pp.npm cj
3836 2536 2779 5067 3836 4242 1328 4005 3395 4041 4792 2779

the elements will melt in the heat. **13** But in keeping with his promise we are looking forward to a
στοιχεῖα → τήκεται → καυσούμενα δὲ κατὰ ← ← αὐτοῦ ⸉τὸ ἐπάγγελμα⸊ → προσδοκῶμεν ←
n.npn v.ppi.3s pt.pp.npn cj p.a r.gsm.3 d.asn n.asn v.pai.1p
5122 5494 3012 1254 2848 899 3836 2041 4659

ἐπιθυμίας αὐτῶν πορευόμενοι **4** καὶ λέγοντες, Ποῦ ἐστιν ἡ ἐπαγγελία τῆς παρουσίας αὐτοῦ; ἀφ᾽ ἧς γὰρ οἱ πατέρες ἐκοιμήθησαν, πάντα οὕτως διαμένει ἀπ᾽ ἀρχῆς κτίσεως. **5** λανθάνει γὰρ αὐτοὺς τοῦτο θέλοντας ὅτι οὐρανοὶ ἦσαν ἔκπαλαι καὶ γῆ ἐξ ὕδατος καὶ δι᾽ ὕδατος συνεστῶσα τῷ τοῦ θεοῦ λόγῳ, **6** δι᾽ ὧν ὁ τότε κόσμος ὕδατι κατακλυσθεὶς ἀπώλετο· **7** οἱ δὲ νῦν οὐρανοὶ καὶ ἡ γῆ τῷ αὐτῷ λόγῳ τεθησαυρισμένοι εἰσὶν πυρὶ τηρούμενοι εἰς ἡμέραν κρίσεως καὶ ἀπωλείας τῶν ἀσεβῶν ἀνθρώπων. ¶ **8** Ἓν δὲ τοῦτο μὴ λανθανέτω ὑμᾶς, ἀγαπητοί, ὅτι μία ἡμέρα παρὰ κυρίῳ ὡς χίλια ἔτη καὶ χίλια ἔτη ὡς ἡμέρα μία. **9** οὐ βραδύνει κύριος τῆς ἐπαγγελίας, ὥς τινες βραδύτητα ἡγοῦνται, ἀλλὰ μακροθυμεῖ εἰς ὑμᾶς, μὴ βουλόμενός τινας ἀπολέσθαι ἀλλὰ πάντας εἰς μετάνοιαν χωρῆσαι. ¶ **10** Ἥξει δὲ ἡμέρα κυρίου ὡς κλέπτης, ἐν ᾗ οἱ οὐρανοὶ ῥοιζηδὸν παρελεύσονται στοιχεῖα δὲ καυσούμενα λυθήσεται καὶ γῆ καὶ τὰ ἐν αὐτῇ ἔργα εὑρεθήσεται. ¶ **11** τούτων οὕτως πάντων λυομένων ποταποὺς δεῖ ὑπάρχειν [ὑμᾶς] ἐν ἁγίαις ἀναστροφαῖς καὶ εὐσεβείαις, **12** προσδοκῶντας καὶ σπεύδοντας τὴν παρουσίαν τῆς τοῦ θεοῦ ἡμέρας δι᾽ ἣν οὐρανοὶ πυρούμενοι λυθήσονται καὶ στοιχεῖα καυσούμενα τήκεται. **13** καινοὺς δὲ οὐρανοὺς καὶ γῆν καινὴν κατὰ τὸ ἐπάγγελμα αὐτοῦ

new   heaven   and a   new   earth,   the home   of righteousness. ¶   **14** So then, dear friends, since you are
καινοὺς   οὐρανοὺς   καὶ   καινὴν   γῆν   ἐν   οἷς   κατοικεῖ   δικαιοσύνη   Διό ←   ἀγαπητοί →   →   →
a.apm   n.apm   cj   a.asf   n.asf   p.d r.dpm v.pai.3s   n.nsf   cj   a.vpm
2785   4041   2779   2785   1178   1877 4005 2997   1466   1475   28

looking   forward   to this,   make   every   effort   to be   found   spotless,   blameless   and at   peace with him.
προσδοκῶντες ←   ← ταῦτα → →   →   σπουδάσατε → → εὑρεθῆναι ἄσπιλοι   καὶ ἀμώμητοι ἐν   εἰρήνῃ αὐτῷ
pt.pa.npm   r.apn   v.aam.2p   f.ap   a.npm   cj   a.npm   p.d   n.dsf   r.dsm.3
4659   4047   5079   2351   834   2779 318   1877   1645   899

15   Bear in mind   that our   Lord's   patience   means salvation, just as our   dear   brother   Paul
καὶ   →   ἡγεῖσθε   ἡμῶν τοῦ κυρίου τὴν μακροθυμίαν   σωτηρίαν   καθὼς ← ἡμῶν ἀγαπητὸς ὁ ἀδελφὸς Παῦλος
cj   v.pmm.2p   r.gp.1 d.gsm n.gsm d.asf n.asf   n.asf   cj   r.gp.1 a.nsm   d.nsm n.nsm n.nsm
2779   2451   7005 3836 3261   3836 3429   5401   2777   7005 28   3836 81   4263

also wrote you with the wisdom that God gave   him. **16** He writes   the same way   in all   his   letters,
καὶ ἔγραψεν ὑμῖν κατὰ τὴν σοφίαν   δοθεῖσαν αὐτῷ   ὡς ←   ←   καὶ ἐν πάσαις   ἐπιστολαῖς
adv v.aai.3s r.dp.2 p.a d.asf   pt.ap.asf r.dsm.3   cj   2779 1877 a.dpf   n.dpf
2779 1211   7007 2848 3836 5053   1443   899   6055   2779 1877 4246   2186

speaking in them of these matters. His letters contain some things that are hard   to understand, which
λαλῶν   ἐν αὐταῖς περὶ τούτων ←   αἷς ←   ἐν   τινα   ἐστιν δυσνόητα ←   ←   ἃ
pt.pa.nsm p.d r.dpf.3 p.g r.gpn   r.dpf   p.d   r.npn   v.pai.3s a.npn   r.apn
3281   1877 899   4309 4047   4005   1877   5516   1639 1554   4005

ignorant   and unstable people distort,   as   they do the other Scriptures, to   their own   destruction. ¶
οἱ ἀμαθεῖς καὶ ἀστήρικτοι ←   στρεβλοῦσιν ὡς καὶ   τὰς λοιπὰς γραφὰς   πρὸς αὐτῶν ἰδίαν τὴν ἀπώλειαν
d.npm a.npm cj a.npm   v.pai.3p   cj adv   d.apf a.apf n.apf   p.a r.gpm.3 a.asf d.asf n.asf
3836 276   2779 844   5137   6055 2779   3836 3370 1210   4639 899   2625   3836 724

17 Therefore,   dear friends, since you already know   this, be on your guard   so that you may not be
οὖν   ὑμεῖς →   ἀγαπητοί → →   →   προγινώσκοντες   → →   φυλάσσεσθε ἵνα ←   ←   ↗   μὴ →
cj   r.np.2   a.vpm   pt.pa.npm   v.pmm.2p   cj   5270   3590
4036   7007   28   4589   5875   2671   5270   5270

carried   away by the error of lawless   men and fall   from your secure   position **18** But grow   in the
συναπαχθέντες ←   τῇ πλάνῃ τῶν ἀθέσμων   ἐκπέσητε ← ἰδίου τοῦ στηριγμοῦ,   δὲ αὐξάνετε ἐν
pt.ap.npm   d.dsf n.dsf d.gpm a.gpm   v.aas.2p   a.gsm d.gsm n.gsm   cj v.pam.2p p.d
5270   3836 4415 3836 118   1738   2625 3836 5113   1254 889   1877

grace and knowledge of our   Lord   and Savior Jesus Christ. To him be glory   both now and
χάριτι καὶ γνώσει   → ἡμῶν τοῦ κυρίου καὶ σωτῆρος Ἰησοῦ Χριστοῦ → αὐτῷ ἡ δόξα   καὶ νῦν καὶ
n.dsf cj n.dsf   r.gp.1 d.gsm n.gsm cj n.gsm n.gsm n.gsm   r.dsm.3 d.nsf n.nsf cj adv cj
5921 2779 1194   3261 3836 3261   2779 5400   2652 5986   899   3836 1518 2779 3814 2779

forever!   Amen.
εἰς ἡμέραν αἰῶνος, ἀμήν
p.a n.asf n.gsm   pl
1650 2465 172   297

προσδοκῶμεν, ἐν οἷς δικαιοσύνη κατοικεῖ. ¶ **14** Διό, ἀγαπητοί, ταῦτα προσδοκῶντες σπουδάσατε ἄσπιλοι καὶ ἀμώμητοι αὐτῷ εὑρεθῆναι ἐν εἰρήνῃ **15** καὶ τὴν τοῦ κυρίου ἡμῶν μακροθυμίαν σωτηρίαν ἡγεῖσθε, καθὼς καὶ ὁ ἀγαπητὸς ἡμῶν ἀδελφὸς Παῦλος κατὰ τὴν δοθεῖσαν αὐτῷ σοφίαν ἔγραψεν ὑμῖν, **16** ὡς καὶ ἐν πάσαις ἐπιστολαῖς λαλῶν ἐν αὐταῖς περὶ τούτων, ἐν αἷς ἐστιν δυσνόητά τινα, ἃ οἱ ἀμαθεῖς καὶ ἀστήρικτοι στρεβλοῦσιν ὡς καὶ τὰς λοιπὰς γραφὰς πρὸς τὴν ἰδίαν αὐτῶν ἀπώλειαν. ¶ **17** Ὑμεῖς οὖν, ἀγαπητοί, προγινώσκοντες φυλάσσεσθε, ἵνα μὴ τῇ τῶν ἀθέσμων πλάνῃ συναπαχθέντες ἐκπέσητε τοῦ ἰδίου στηριγμοῦ, **18** αὐξάνετε δὲ ἐν χάριτι καὶ γνώσει τοῦ κυρίου ἡμῶν καὶ σωτῆρος Ἰησοῦ Χριστοῦ. αὐτῷ ἡ δόξα καὶ νῦν καὶ εἰς ἡμέραν αἰῶνος. [ἀμήν.]

1 John

The Word of Life

1:1 That which was from the beginning, which we have heard, which we have seen with our
Ὃ ἦν ἀπ᾽ ἀρχῆς ὃ ἀκηκόαμεν ὃ ἑωράκαμεν ἡμῶν
r.nsn v.iai.3s p.g n.gsf r.asn v.rai.1p r.asn v.rai.1p r.gp.1
4005 1639 608 794 4005 201 4005 3972 4057 7005

eyes, which we have looked at and our hands have touched – this we proclaim concerning the
τοῖς ὀφθαλμοῖς ὃ ἐθεασάμεθα καὶ ἡμῶν αἱ χεῖρες ἐψηλάφησαν περὶ τοῦ
d.dpm n.dpm r.asn v.ami.1p cj r.gp.1 d.npf n.npf v.aai.3p p.g d.gsm
3836 4057 4005 2517 2779 7005 3836 5931 6027 4309 3836

Word of life. **2** The life appeared; we have seen it and testify to it, and we proclaim to you
λόγου τῆς ζωῆς καὶ ἡ ζωὴ ἐφανερώθη καὶ ἑωράκαμεν καὶ μαρτυροῦμεν καὶ ἀπαγγέλλομεν ὑμῖν
n.gsm d.gsf n.gsf cj d.nsf n.nsf v.api.3s cj v.rai.1p cj v.pai.1p cj v.pai.1p r.dp.2
3364 3836 2437 2779 3836 2437 5746 2779 3972 2779 3455 2779 550 7007

the eternal life, which was with the Father and has appeared to us. **3** We proclaim to you what we have
τὴν τὴν αἰώνιον ζωὴ ἥτις ἦν πρὸς τὸν πατέρα καὶ ἐφανερώθη ἡμῖν ἀπαγγέλλομεν καὶ ὑμῖν ὃ
d.asf d.asf a.asf n.asf r.nsf v.iai.3s p.a d.asm n.asm cj v.api.3s r.dp.1 v.pai.1p adv r.dp.2 r.asn
3836 3836 173 2437 4015 1639 4639 3836 4252 2779 5746 7005 550 2779 7007 4005

seen and heard, so that you also may have fellowship with us. And our fellowship is with the
ἑωράκαμεν καὶ ἀκηκόαμεν ἵνα ὑμεῖς καὶ ἔχητε κοινωνίαν μεθ᾽ ἡμῶν δὲ καὶ ἡ ἡμετέρα ἡ κοινωνία μετὰ τοῦ
v.rai.1p cj v.rai.1p cj r.np.2 cj v.pas.2p n.asf p.g r.gp.1 cj adv d.nsf r.nsf.1 d.nsf n.nsf p.g d.gsm
3972 2779 201 2671 7007 2779 2400 3126 3552 7005 1254 2779 3836 2466 3836 3126 3552 3836

Father and with his Son, Jesus Christ. **4** We write this to make our joy complete.
πατρὸς καὶ μετὰ αὐτοῦ τοῦ υἱοῦ Ἰησοῦ Χριστοῦ καὶ ἡμεῖς γράφομεν ταῦτα ἵνα ἡμῶν ἡ χαρὰ ᾖ πεπληρωμένη
n.gsm cj p.g r.gsm.3 d.gsm n.gsm n.gsm n.gsm cj r.np.1 v.pai.1p r.apn cj r.gp.1 d.nsf n.nsf v.pas.3s pt.rp.nsf
4252 2779 3552 899 3836 5626 2652 5986 2779 7005 1211 4047 2671 4444 7005 3836 5915 1639 4444

Walking in the Light

1:5 This is the message we have heard from him and declare to you: God is light;
Καὶ αὕτη ἔστιν ἡ ἀγγελία ἣν ἀκηκόαμεν ἀπ᾽ αὐτοῦ καὶ ἀναγγέλλομεν ὑμῖν ὅτι ὁ θεὸς ἔστιν φῶς
cj r.nsf v.pai.3s d.nsf n.nsf r.asf v.rai.1p p.g r.gsm.3 cj v.pal.1p r.dp.2 cj d.nsm n.nsm v.pai.3s n.nsn
2779 4047 1639 3836 32 4005 201 608 899 2779 334 7007 4022 3836 2536 1639 5890

in him there is no darkness at all. **6** If we claim to have fellowship with him yet walk in
καὶ ἐν αὐτῷ ἔστιν οὐκ σκοτία οὐδεμία Ἐὰν εἴπωμεν ὅτι ἔχομεν κοινωνίαν μετ᾽ αὐτοῦ καὶ περιπατῶμεν ἐν
cj p.d r.dsm.3 v.pai.3s pl n.nsf a.nsf cj v.aas.1p cj v.pai.1p n.asf p.g r.gsm.3 cj v.pas.1p p.d
2779 1877 899 1639 4024 5028 4029 1569 3306 4022 2400 3126 3552 899 2779 4344 1877

the darkness, we lie and do not live by the truth. **7** But if we walk in the light, as he is in
τῷ σκότει ψευδόμεθα καὶ οὐ ποιοῦμεν τὴν ἀλήθειαν δὲ ἐὰν περιπατῶμεν ἐν τῷ φωτὶ ὡς αὐτός ἐστιν ἐν
d.dsn n.dsn v.pmi.1p cj pl v.pai.1p d.asf n.asf cj cj v.pas.1p p.d d.dsn n.dsn cj r.nsm v.pai.3s p.d
3836 5030 6017 2779 4472 4024 4472 3836 237 1254 1569 4344 1877 3836 5890 6055 899 1639 1877

the light, we have fellowship with one another, and the blood of Jesus, his Son, purifies us from all
τῷ φωτὶ ἔχομεν κοινωνίαν μετ᾽ ἀλλήλων καὶ τὸ αἷμα Ἰησοῦ αὐτοῦ τοῦ υἱοῦ καθαρίζει ἡμᾶς ἀπὸ πάσης
d.dsn n.dsn v.pai.1p n.asf p.g r.gpm cj d.nsn n.nsn n.gsm r.gsm.3 d.gsm n.gsm v.pai.3s r.ap.1 p.g a.gsf
3836 5890 2400 3126 3552 253 2779 3836 135 2652 899 3836 5626 2751 7005 608 4246

sin. ¶ **8** If we claim to be without sin, we deceive ourselves and the truth is not in us.
ἁμαρτίας ἐὰν εἴπωμεν ὅτι ἔχομεν οὐκ ἁμαρτίαν πλανῶμεν ἑαυτοὺς καὶ ἡ ἀλήθεια ἔστιν οὐκ ἐν ἡμῖν
n.gsf cj v.aas.1p cj v.pai.1p pl n.asf v.pai.1p r.apm.1 cj d.nsf n.nsf v.pai.3s pl p.d r.dp.1
281 1569 3306 4022 2400 4024 281 4414 1571 2779 3836 237 1639 4024 1877 7005

9 If we confess our sins, he is faithful and just and will forgive us our sins and purify us
ἐὰν ὁμολογῶμεν ἡμῶν τὰς ἁμαρτίας ἐστιν πιστός καὶ δίκαιος ἵνα ἀφῇ ἡμῖν τὰς ἁμαρτίας καὶ καθαρίσῃ ἡμᾶς
cj v.pas.1p r.gp.1 d.apf n.apf v.pai.3s a.nsm cj a.nsm cj v.aas.3s r.dp.1 d.apf n.apf cj v.aas.3s r.ap.1
1569 3933 7005 3836 281 1639 4412 2779 1465 2671 918 7005 3836 281 2779 2751 7005

1:1 Ὃ ἦν ἀπ᾽ ἀρχῆς, ὃ ἀκηκόαμεν, ὃ ἑωράκαμεν τοῖς ὀφθαλμοῖς ἡμῶν, ὃ ἐθεασάμεθα καὶ αἱ χεῖρες ἡμῶν ἐψηλάφησαν περὶ τοῦ λόγου τῆς ζωῆς— **2** καὶ ἡ ζωὴ ἐφανερώθη, καὶ ἑωράκαμεν καὶ μαρτυροῦμεν καὶ ἀπαγγέλλομεν ὑμῖν τὴν ζωὴν τὴν αἰώνιον ἥτις ἦν πρὸς τὸν πατέρα καὶ ἐφανερώθη ἡμῖν— **3** ὃ ἑωράκαμεν καὶ ἀκηκόαμεν, ἀπαγγέλλομεν καὶ ὑμῖν, ἵνα καὶ ὑμεῖς κοινωνίαν ἔχητε μεθ᾽ ἡμῶν. καὶ ἡ κοινωνία δὲ ἡ ἡμετέρα μετὰ τοῦ πατρὸς καὶ μετὰ τοῦ υἱοῦ αὐτοῦ Ἰησοῦ Χριστοῦ. **4** καὶ ταῦτα γράφομεν ἡμεῖς, ἵνα ἡ χαρὰ ἡμῶν ᾖ πεπληρωμένη.

1:5 Καὶ ἔστιν αὕτη ἡ ἀγγελία ἣν ἀκηκόαμεν ἀπ᾽ αὐτοῦ καὶ ἀναγγέλλομεν ὑμῖν, ὅτι ὁ θεὸς φῶς ἔστιν καὶ σκοτία ἐν αὐτῷ οὐκ ἔστιν οὐδεμία. **6** Ἐὰν εἴπωμεν ὅτι κοινωνίαν ἔχομεν μετ᾽ αὐτοῦ καὶ ἐν τῷ σκότει περιπατῶμεν, ψευδόμεθα καὶ οὐ ποιοῦμεν τὴν ἀλήθειαν· **7** ἐὰν δὲ ἐν τῷ φωτὶ περιπατῶμεν ὡς αὐτός ἐστιν ἐν τῷ φωτί, κοινωνίαν ἔχομεν μετ᾽ ἀλλήλων καὶ τὸ αἷμα Ἰησοῦ τοῦ υἱοῦ αὐτοῦ καθαρίζει ἡμᾶς ἀπὸ πάσης ἁμαρτίας. ¶ **8** ἐὰν εἴπωμεν ὅτι ἁμαρτίαν οὐκ ἔχομεν, ἑαυτοὺς πλανῶμεν καὶ ἡ ἀλήθεια οὐκ ἔστιν ἐν ἡμῖν. **9** ἐὰν ὁμολογῶμεν τὰς ἁμαρτίας ἡμῶν, πιστός ἐστιν καὶ δίκαιος, ἵνα ἀφῇ ἡμῖν τὰς ἁμαρτίας καὶ

from	all	unrighteousness.	**10** If	we	claim		we have	not	sinned,		we make	him			out to be a liar		and his
ἀπὸ	πάσης	ἀδικίας	ἐὰν →	εἴπωμεν	ὅτι →	→	οὐχ	ἡμαρτήκαμεν		→	ποιοῦμεν	αὐτὸν			ψεύστην καὶ		αὐτοῦ
p.g	a.gsf	n.gsf	cj	v.aas.1p	cj		pl	v.rai.1p			v.pai.1p	r.asm.3			n.asm	cj	r.gsm.3
608	4246	94	1569	3306	4022	279	279	4024	279		4472	899			6026	2779	899

word		has	no	place	in	our lives.	¶	**2:1** My dear	children,	I	write	this	to you	so	that	you	will	not	sin.
ὁ	λόγος	ἔστιν	οὐκ ←		ἐν	ἡμῖν ←		μου →	Τεκνία	→	γράφω	ταῦτα	ὑμῖν ἵνα	←	→	→	→	μὴ	ἁμάρτητε
d.nsm	n.nsm	v.pai.3s	pl		p.d	r.dp.1		r.gs.1	n.vpn		v.pai.1s	r.apn	r.dp.2					pl	v.aas.2p
3836	3364	1639	4024		1877	7005		1609	5448		1211	4047	7007 2671	279	279	279	279	3590	279

But if	anybody	does sin,		we have	one		who speaks to		the	Father in	our defense	– Jesus		Christ, the
καὶ ἐὰν	τις	→	ἁμάρτῃ	ἔχομεν	παράκλητον	←	πρὸς	τὸν		πατέρα	←	Ἰησοῦν		Χριστὸν
cj cj	r.nsm		v.aas.3s	v.pai.1p	n.asm		p.a	d.asm		n.asm		n.asm		n.asm
2779 1569	5516		279	2400	4156		4639	3836	4252	4156 4156	4156	2652		5986

Righteous One.	**2**	He	is	the	atoning	sacrifice	for	our	sins,		and	not	only	for	ours		but	also
δίκαιον	←	καὶ αὐτὸς	ἔστιν		ἱλασμός	←	περὶ	ἡμῶν	⌐τῶν ἁμαρτιῶν⌐	δὲ	οὐ	μόνον		περὶ	⌐τῶν ἡμετέρων⌐	ἀλλὰ καὶ
a.asm		cj r.nsm	v.pai.3s		n.nsm		p.g	r.gp.1	d.gpf n.gpf	cj	pl	adv		p.g	d.gpf r.gpf.1	cj adv
1465		2779 899	1639		2662		4309	7005	3836 281	1254	4024	3667		4309	3836 2466	247 2779

for	the sins		of the	whole	world.	¶	**3**		We	know	that	we have	come	to know	him	if	we
περὶ	←		τοῦ	ὅλου	κόσμου			Καὶ ἐν	τούτῳ →	γινώσκομεν ὅτι	→	→	→	ἐγνώκαμεν	αὐτὸν ἐὰν		
p.g			d.gsm	a.gsm	n.gsm			cj p.d	r.dsn	v.pai.1p	cj			v.rai.1p	r.asm.3	cj	
4309			3180	3836	3910	3180		2779 1877	4047	1182	4022			1182	899	1569	

obey	his	commands.	**4** The	man who	says,		"I	know	him,"	but	does	not do		what	he	commands	is	a
τηρῶμεν	αὐτοῦ	⌐τὰς ἐντολὰς⌐	ὁ		→	λέγων ὅτι →		ἔγνωκα	αὐτὸν	καὶ	→		μὴ	τηρῶν		αὐτοῦ ⌐τὰς ἐντολὰς⌐	ἔστιν
v.pas.1p	r.gsm.3	d.apf n.apf	d.nsm			pt.pa.nsm		v.rai.1s	r.asm.3	cj			pl	pt.pa.nsm		r.gsm.3 d.apf n.apf	v.pai.3s
5498	899	3836 1953	3836		3306	4022 1182	899			2779	5498		3590	5498		899 3836 1953	1639

liar,	and	the	truth	is	not	in	him.	**5** But if	anyone	obeys	his	word,		God's	love	is	truly	made
ψεύστης	καὶ	ἡ	ἀλήθεια	ἔστιν	οὐκ	ἐν	τούτῳ	δ	→ ὃς ἂν	τηρῇ	αὐτοῦ	⌐τὸν λόγον⌐	⌐τοῦ θεοῦ⌐		ἡ ἀγάπη	→	ἀληθῶς →
n.nsm	cj	d.nsf	n.nsf	v.pai.3s	pl	p.d	r.dsn	cj	r.nsm pl	v.pas.3s	r.gsm.3	d.asm n.asm	d.gsm n.gsm		d.nsf n.nsf		adv
6026	2779	3836	237	1639	4024	1877	4047	1254	4005 323	5498	899	3836 3364	3836 2536	3836 27		5457	242

complete	in	him.	This		is how	we	know		we are	in	him:	**6** Whoever	claims	to	live	in	him
τετελείωται	ἐν	τούτῳ	⌐ἐν τούτῳ⌐	←	→	γινώσκομεν	ὅτι	→	ἐσμεν	ἐν	αὐτῷ	ὁ	λέγων	→	μένειν	ἐν	αὐτῷ καὶ αὐτὸς
v.rpi.3s	p.d	r.dsm	p.d r.dsn			v.pai.1p	cj		v.pai.1p	p.d	r.dsm.3	d.nsm	pt.pa.nsm		f.pa	p.d	r.dsm.3 adv r.nsm
5457	1877	4047	1877 4047			1182	4022		1639	1877	899	3836	3306		3531	1877	899 2779 899

	must	walk	as	Jesus	did.	¶	**7** Dear friends,	I	am	not	writing	you	a	new	command
[οὕτως]	ὀφείλει	περιπατεῖν	καθὼς	ἐκεῖνος	περιεπάτησεν		Ἀγαπητοί →	→		οὐκ	γράφω	ὑμῖν		καινὴν	ἐντολήν
adv	v.pai.3s	f.pa	cj	r.nsm	v.aai.3s		a.vpm			pl	v.pai.1s	r.dp.2		a.asf	n.asf
4048	4053	4344	2777	1697	4344		28	1211 1211	4024	1211		7007		2785	1953

but an	old	one,	which	you have	had	since	the beginning.	This	old		command	is	the	message
ἀλλ'	παλαιὰν	ἐντολὴν	ἣν →	→ εἴχετε	ἀπ'		ἀρχῆς	ἡ	⌐ἡ παλαιά⌐		ἐντολὴ	ἔστιν ὁ	λόγος	ὃν
cj	a.asf	n.asf	r.asf	v.iai.2p	p.g		n.gsf	d.nsf	d.nsf a.nsf		n.nsf	v.pai.3s d.nsm	n.nsm	r.asm
247	4094	1953	4005	2400	608		794	3836	3836 4094	1953		1639 3836	3364	4005

you have heard.	**8** Yet	I	am writing	you	a	new	command;	its	truth	is		seen	in	him	and		you, because	the
→ →	ἠκούσατε	πάλιν	→ γράφω	ὑμῖν		καινὴν	ἐντολήν	ὅ	ἀληθές	ἔστιν			ἐν	αὐτῷ καὶ	ἐν	ὑμῖν ὅτι		ἡ
	v.aai.2p	adv	v.pai.1s	r.dp.2		a.asf	n.asf	r.nsn	a.nsn	v.pai.3s			p.d	r.dsm.3 cj	p.d	r.dp.2 cj		d.nsf
	201	4099	1211	7007		2785	1953	239	4005	1639			1877	899 2779	1877	7007 4022		3836

darkness	is	passing	and	the	true		light	is	already	shining.	¶	**9** Anyone	who	claims	to	be	in	the light
σκοτία	→	παράγεται	καὶ	τὸ	⌐τὸ ἀληθινὸν⌐		φῶς	→	ἤδη	φαίνει		Ὁ		λέγων	→	εἶναι	ἐν	τῷ φωτὶ
n.nsf		v.ppi.3s	cj	d.nsn	d.nsn a.nsn		n.nsn		adv	v.pai.3s		d.nsm		pt.pa.nsm		f.pa	p.d	d.dsn n.dsn
5028		4135	2779	3836	3836 240		5890		2453	5743		3836		3306		1639	1877	3836 5890

but	hates	his	brother	is	still		in the	darkness.	**10** Whoever	loves	his	brother	lives	in	the	light, and
καὶ	μισῶν	αὐτοῦ	⌐τὸν ἀδελφὸν⌐	ἔστιν	⌐ἕως ἄρτι⌐		ἐν τῇ	σκοτίᾳ	ὁ		ἀγαπῶν	αὐτοῦ ⌐τὸν ἀδελφὸν⌐	μένει	ἐν	τῷ	φωτὶ καὶ
cj	pt.pa.nsm	r.gsm.3	d.asm n.asm	v.pai.3s	p.g adv		p.d d.dsf	n.dsf	d.nsm		pt.pa.nsm	r.gsm.3 d.asm n.asm	v.pai.3s	p.d	d.dsn	n.dsn cj
2779	3631	899	3836 81	1639	2401 785		1877 3836	5028	3836		26	899 3836 81	3531	1877	3836	5890 2779

there is		nothing	in	him	to make	him	stumble.	**11** But	whoever	hates	his	brother	is	in	the	darkness	and
→	ἔστιν	οὐκ	ἐν	αὐτῷ →	→	→	σκάνδαλον	δὲ	ὁ	μισῶν	αὐτοῦ	⌐τὸν ἀδελφὸν⌐	ἔστιν	ἐν	τῇ	σκοτίᾳ	καὶ
	v.pai.3s	pl	p.d	r.dsm.3			n.nsn	cj	d.nsm	pt.pa.nsm	r.gsm.3	d.asm n.asm	v.pai.3s	p.d	d.dsf	n.dsf	cj
	1639	4024	1877	899			4998	1254	3836	3631	899	3836 81	1639	1877	3836	5028	2779

καθαρίσῃ ἡμᾶς ἀπὸ πάσης ἀδικίας. 10 ἐὰν εἴπωμεν ὅτι οὐχ ἡμαρτήκαμεν, ψεύστην ποιοῦμεν αὐτὸν καὶ ὁ λόγος αὐτοῦ οὐκ ἔστιν ἐν ἡμῖν. 2:1 Τεκνία μου, ταῦτα γράφω ὑμῖν ἵνα μὴ ἁμάρτητε. καὶ ἐάν τις ἁμάρτῃ, παράκλητον ἔχομεν πρὸς τὸν πατέρα Ἰησοῦν Χριστὸν δίκαιον· 2 καὶ αὐτὸς ἱλασμός ἐστιν περὶ τῶν ἁμαρτιῶν ἡμῶν, οὐ περὶ τῶν ἡμετέρων δὲ μόνον ἀλλὰ καὶ περὶ ὅλου τοῦ κόσμου ¶ 3 Καὶ ἐν τούτῳ γινώσκομεν ὅτι ἐγνώκαμεν αὐτόν, ἐὰν τὰς ἐντολὰς αὐτοῦ τηρῶμεν. 4 ὁ λέγων ὅτι Ἔγνωκα αὐτὸν καὶ τὰς ἐντολὰς αὐτοῦ μὴ τηρῶν, ψεύστης ἐστὶν καὶ ἐν τούτῳ ἡ ἀλήθεια οὐκ ἔστιν· 5 ὃς δ' ἂν τηρῇ αὐτοῦ τὸν λόγον, ἀληθῶς ἐν τούτῳ ἡ ἀγάπη τοῦ θεοῦ τετελείωται, ἐν τούτῳ γινώσκομεν ὅτι ἐν αὐτῷ ἐσμεν. 6 ὁ λέγων ἐν αὐτῷ μένειν ὀφείλει καθὼς ἐκεῖνος περιεπάτησεν καὶ αὐτὸς [οὕτως] περιπατεῖν. ¶ 7 Ἀγαπητοί, οὐκ ἐντολὴν καινὴν γράφω ὑμῖν ἀλλ' ἐντολὴν παλαιὰν ἣν εἴχετε ἀπ' ἀρχῆς· ἡ ἐντολὴ ἡ παλαιά ἐστιν ὁ λόγος ὃν ἠκούσατε. 8 πάλιν ἐντολὴν καινὴν γράφω ὑμῖν, ὅ ἐστιν ἀληθὲς ἐν αὐτῷ καὶ ἐν ὑμῖν, ὅτι ἡ σκοτία παράγεται καὶ τὸ φῶς τὸ ἀληθινὸν ἤδη φαίνει. ¶ 9 ὁ λέγων ἐν τῷ φωτὶ εἶναι καὶ τὸν ἀδελφὸν αὐτοῦ μισῶν ἐν τῇ σκοτίᾳ ἐστὶν ἕως ἄρτι. 10 ὁ ἀγαπῶν τὸν ἀδελφὸν αὐτοῦ ἐν τῷ φωτὶ μένει καὶ σκάνδαλον ἐν αὐτῷ οὐκ ἔστιν· 11 ὁ δὲ μισῶν τὸν ἀδελφὸν αὐτοῦ ἐν τῇ σκοτίᾳ ἐστὶν καὶ ἐν τῇ σκοτίᾳ περιπατεῖ καὶ οὐκ οἶδεν ποῦ ὑπάγει, ὅτι ἡ σκοτία ἐτύφλωσεν τοὺς ὀφθαλμοὺς

walks | around | in | the | darkness; | | he | does | not | know | where | he | is | going, | because | the | darkness | | has | blinded
περιπατεῖ ← | | ἐν | τῇ | σκοτίᾳ | καὶ | | | οὐκ | οἶδεν | ποῦ | | → | → ὑπάγει | ὅτι | ἡ | σκοτία | → | ἐτύφλωσεν | τοὺς
v.pai.3s | | p.d | d.dsf | n.dsf | cj | | | pl | v.rai.3s | adv | | | v.pai.3s | cj | d.nsf | n.nsf | | v.aai.3s | d.apm
4344 | | 1877 | 3836 | 5028 | 2779 | 3857 | 3857 | 4024 | 3857 | 4543 | | | 5632 | 4022 | 3836 | 5028 | | 5604 | 3836

him. | ¶ | **¹²** I | write | to you, | dear | children, | because | your | sins | | | have | been | forgiven | on | account of
ὀφθαλμοὺς | αὐτοῦ | | → Γράφω | → ὑμῖν | → | τεκνία | ὅτι | ὑμῖν | αἱ ἁμαρτίαι | → | → | ἀφέωνται | διὰ | ←
n.apm | r.gsm.3 | | v.pai.1s | r.dp.2 | | n.vpn | cj | r.dp.2 | d.npf n.npf | | | v.rpi.3p | p.a
4057 | 899 | | 1211 | 7007 | | 5448 | 4022 | 7007 | 3836 281 | | | 918 | 1328

his | name. | ¶ | **¹³** I | write | to you, | fathers, | because | you | have | known | him | who is | from | the | beginning. | ¶
αὐτοῦ | ‚τὸ ὄνομα‚ | | → γράφω | → ὑμῖν | πατέρες | ὅτι | → | → | ἐγνώκατε | τὸν | ← | ἀπ' | ἀρχῆς
r.gsm.3 | d.asn n.asn | | v.pai.1s | r.dp.2 | n.vpm | cj | | | v.rai.2p | d.asm | | p.g | n.gsf
899 | 3836 3950 | | 1211 | 7007 | 4252 | 4022 | | | 1182 | 3836 | | 608 | 794

I | write | to you, | young | men, | because | you | have | overcome | the | evil | one. | ¶ | I | write | to you, | dear | children,
→ γράφω | → ὑμῖν | νεανίσκοι | ← | ὅτι | → | → | νενικήκατε | τὸν | πονηρόν | ← | | → ἔγραψα | → ὑμῖν | → | παιδία
v.pai.1s | r.dp.2 | n.vpm | | cj | | | v.rai.2p | d.asm | a.asm | | | v.aai.1s | r.dp.2 | | n.vpn
1211 | 7007 | 3734 | | 4022 | | | 3771 | 3836 | 4505 | | | 1211 | 7007 | | 4086

because | you | have | known | the | Father. | ¶ | **¹⁴** I | write | to you, | fathers, | because | you | have | known | him | who is | from
ὅτι | → | → | ἐγνώκατε | τὸν | πατέρα | | → ἔγραψα | → ὑμῖν | πατέρες | ὅτι | → | → | ἐγνώκατε | τὸν | ← | ἀπ'
cj | | | v.rai.2p | d.asm | n.asm | | v.aai.1s | r.dp.2 | n.vpm | cj | | | v.rai.2p | d.asm | | p.g
4022 | | | 1182 | 3836 | 4252 | | 1211 | 7007 | 4252 | 4022 | | | 1182 | 3836 | | 608

the | beginning. | ¶ | I | write | to you, | young | men, | because | you | are | strong, | and | the | word | of God | | lives | in
ἀρχῆς | | | → ἔγραψα | → ὑμῖν | νεανίσκοι | ← | ὅτι | → | → | ἐστε | ἰσχυροὶ | καὶ | ὁ | λόγος | → | ‚τοῦ θεοῦ‚ | μένει | ἐν
n.gsf | | | v.aai.1s | r.dp.2 | n.vpm | | cj | | | v.pai.2p | a.npm | cj | d.nsm | n.nsm | | d.gsm n.gsm | v.pai.3s | p.d
794 | | | 1211 | 7007 | 3734 | | 4022 | | | 1639 | 2708 | 2779 | 3836 | 3364 | | 3836 2536 | 3531 | 1877

you, | and | you | have | overcome | the | evil | | one.
ὑμῖν | καὶ | → | → | νενικήκατε | τὸν | πονηρόν | ←
r.dp.2 | cj | | | v.rai.2p | d.asm | a.asm
7007 | 2779 | | | 3771 | 3836 | 4505

Do Not Love the World

2:15 Do | not | love | the | world | or | anything | in | the | world. | If | anyone | loves | the | world, | the | love | | of | the | Father
→ | Μὴ | ἀγαπᾶτε | τὸν | κόσμον | μηδὲ | τὰ | ἐν | τῷ | κόσμῳ | ἐάν | τις | ἀγαπᾷ | τὸν | κόσμον | ἡ | ἀγάπη | → | τοῦ | πατρὸς
| pl | v.pam.2p | d.asm | n.asm | cj | d.apn | p.d | d.dsm | n.dsm | cj | r.nsm | v.pas.3s | d.asm | n.asm | d.nsf | n.nsf | | d.gsm | n.gsm
26 | 3590 | 26 | 3836 | 3180 | 3593 | 3836 | 1877 | 3836 | 3180 | 1569 | 5516 | 26 | 3836 | 3180 | 3836 | 27 | | 3836 | 4252

is | not | in | him. | **¹⁶** For | everything | | in | the | world | – | the | cravings | of | sinful | | man, | | the | lust | | of | his | eyes
ἔστιν | οὐκ | ἐν | αὐτῷ | ὅτι | πᾶν | τὸ | ἐν | τῷ | κόσμῳ | ἡ | ἐπιθυμία | ‚τῆς σαρκὸς‚ | | καὶ | ἡ | ἐπιθυμία | → | τῶν | ὀφθαλμῶν
v.pai.3s | pl | p.d | r.dsm.3 | cj | a.nsn | d.nsn | p.d | d.dsm | n.dsm | d.nsf | n.nsf | d.gsf n.gsf | | cj | d.nsf | n.nsf | | d.gpm | n.gpm
1639 | 4024 | 1877 | 899 | 4022 | 4246 | 3836 | 1877 | 3836 | 3180 | 3836 | 2123 | 3836 4922 | | 2779 | 3836 | 2123 | | 3836 | 4057

and | the | boasting | of | what | he | has | | and | does | – | comes | not | from | the | Father | but | from | the | world. | **¹⁷** | The | world
καὶ | ἡ | ἀλαζονεία | → | ‚τοῦ βίου‚ | ← | | | ἐστιν | οὐκ | ἐκ | τοῦ | πατρὸς | ἀλλὰ | ἐκ | τοῦ | κόσμου | καὶ | ὁ | κόσμος
cj | d.nsf | n.nsf | | d.gsm | n.gsm | | | v.pai.3s | pl | p.g | d.gsm | n.gsm | cj | p.g | d.gsm | n.gsm | cj | d.nsm | n.nsm
2779 | 3836 | 224 | | 3836 | 1050 | | | 1639 | 4024 | 1666 | 3836 | 4252 | 247 | 1666 | 3836 | 3180 | 2779 | 3836 | 3180

and | its | desires | pass | away, | but | the | man | who | does | the | will | of | God | | lives | forever.
καὶ | αὐτοῦ | ἡ | ἐπιθυμία | παράγεται | ← | δὲ | ὁ | | ← | ποιῶν | τὸ | θέλημα | → | ‚τοῦ θεοῦ‚ | μένει | εἰς τὸν αἰῶνα‚
cj | r.gsm.3 | d.nsf | n.nsf | v.ppi.3s | | cj | d.nsm | | | pt.pa.nsm | d.asn | n.asn | | d.gsm n.gsm | v.pai.3s | p.a d.asm n.asm
2779 | 899 | 3836 | 2123 | 4135 | | 1254 | 3836 | | | 4472 | 3836 | 2525 | | 3836 2536 | 3531 | 1650 3836 172

Warning Against Antichrists

2:18 Dear children, | this | is | the | last | hour; | and | as | | you | have | heard | that | the | antichrist | is | coming, | even | now
→ | Παιδία | → | ἐστίν | ἐσχάτη | ὥρα | καὶ | καθὼς | → | → | ἠκούσατε | ὅτι | | ἀντίχριστος | → | ἔρχεται | καὶ | νῦν
n.vpn | | v.pai.3s | a.nsf | n.nsf | cj | cj | | | v.aai.2p | cj | | n.nsm | | v.pmi.3s | adv | adv
4086 | | 1639 | 2274 | 6052 | 2779 | 2777 | | | 201 | 4022 | | 532 | | 2262 | 2779 | 3814

many | antichrists | have | come. | | This is how | we | know | | it | is | the | last | hour. | **¹⁹** They | went | out | from | us, | but
πολλοὶ | ἀντίχριστοι | → | γεγόνασιν | → | ὅθεν | γινώσκομεν | ὅτι | → | ἐστίν | ἐσχάτη | ὥρα | | ἐξῆλθαν | ἐξ | ← | ἡμῶν | ἀλλ'
a.npm | n.npm | | v.rai.3p | | cj | v.pai.1p | cj | | v.pai.3s | a.nsf | n.nsf | | v.aai.3p | p.g | | r.gp.1 | cj
4498 | 532 | | 1181 | | 3854 | 1182 | 4022 | | 1639 | 2274 | 6052 | | 2002 | 1666 | | 7005 | 247

αὐτοῦ. ¶ **¹²** Γράφω ὑμῖν, τεκνία, ὅτι ἀφέωνται ὑμῖν αἱ ἁμαρτίαι διὰ τὸ ὄνομα αὐτοῦ. ¶ **¹³** γράφω ὑμῖν, πατέρες, ὅτι ἐγνώκατε τὸν ἀπ' ἀρχῆς. ¶ γράφω ὑμῖν, νεανίσκοι, ὅτι νενικήκατε τὸν πονηρόν. ¶ **¹⁴** ἔγραψα ὑμῖν, παιδία, ὅτι ἐγνώκατε τὸν πατέρα ¶ ἔγραψα ὑμῖν, πατέρες, ὅτι ἐγνώκατε τὸν ἀπ' ἀρχῆς. ¶ ἔγραψα ὑμῖν, νεανίσκοι, ὅτι ἰσχυροί ἐστε καὶ ὁ λόγος τοῦ θεοῦ ἐν ὑμῖν μένει καὶ νενικήκατε τὸν πονηρόν.

2:15 Μὴ ἀγαπᾶτε τὸν κόσμον μηδὲ τὰ ἐν τῷ κόσμῳ. ἐάν τις ἀγαπᾷ τὸν κόσμον, οὐκ ἔστιν ἡ ἀγάπη τοῦ πατρὸς ἐν αὐτῷ· **¹⁶** ὅτι πᾶν τὸ ἐν τῷ κόσμῳ, ἡ ἐπιθυμία τῆς σαρκὸς καὶ ἡ ἐπιθυμία τῶν ὀφθαλμῶν καὶ ἡ ἀλαζονεία τοῦ βίου, οὐκ ἔστιν ἐκ τοῦ πατρὸς ἀλλ' ἐκ τοῦ κόσμου ἐστίν. **¹⁷** καὶ ὁ κόσμος παράγεται καὶ ἡ ἐπιθυμία αὐτοῦ, ὁ δὲ ποιῶν τὸ θέλημα τοῦ θεοῦ μένει εἰς τὸν αἰῶνα.

2:18 Παιδία, ἐσχάτη ὥρα ἐστίν, καὶ καθὼς ἠκούσατε ὅτι ἀντίχριστος ἔρχεται, καὶ νῦν ἀντίχριστοι πολλοὶ γεγόνασιν, ὅθεν γινώσκομεν ὅτι ἐσχάτη ὥρα ἐστίν. **¹⁹** ἐξ ἡμῶν ἐξῆλθαν ἀλλ' οὐκ ἦσαν ἐξ ἡμῶν· εἰ γὰρ ἐξ ἡμῶν ἦσαν, μεμενήκεισαν ἂν μεθ'

they did not really belong to us. For if they had belonged to us, they would have remained with us; but
→   →   οὐκ   ἦσαν   ἐξ   ἡμῶν   γὰρ   εἰ   →   ἦσαν   ἐξ   ἡμῶν   ἂν   →   μεμενήκεισαν   μεθ᾽   ἡμῶν   ἀλλ᾽   ἵνα
pl   v.iai.3p   p.g   r.gp.1   cj   cj   v.iai.3p   p.g   r.gp.1   pl   v.lai.3p   p.g   r.gp.1   cj   cj
1639   1639   4024   1666   7005   1142   1623   1639   1666   7005   3531   323   3531   3552   7005   247   2671

their going showed   that none of them belonged to us.   ¶   **20** But you have an anointing from the Holy
φανερωθῶσιν   ὅτι   οὐκ   πάντες   εἰσὶν   ἐξ   ἡμῶν   καὶ   ὑμεῖς   ἔχετε   χρῖσμα   ἀπὸ   τοῦ   ἁγίου
v.aps.3p   cj   pl   a.npm   v.pai.3p   p.g   r.gp.1   cj   r.np.2   v.pai.2p   n.asn   p.g   d.gsm   a.gsm
5746   4022   4024   4246   1639   1666   7005   2779   7007   2400   5984   608   3836   41

One, and all   of you know the truth. **21** I do not write to you because you do not know the truth, but because
←   καὶ   πάντες   →   οἴδατε   →   οὐκ   ἔγραψα   →   ὑμῖν   ὅτι   →   →   οὐκ   οἴδατε   τὴν   ἀλήθειαν   ἀλλ᾽   ὅτι
cj   a.npm   v.rai.2p   pl   v.aai.1s   r.dp.2   cj   pl   v.rai.2p   d.asf   n.asf   cj   cj
2779   4246   3857   1211   1211   4024   1211   7007   4022   3857   3857   4024   3857   3836   237   247   4022

you do know it   and because no   lie   comes from the truth. **22** Who is   the liar?   It is the man
→   →   οἴδατε   αὐτὴν   καὶ   ὅτι   ᵗοὐκ   πᾶν   ψεῦδος   ἔστιν   ἐκ   τῆς   ἀληθείας   Τίς   ἐστιν   ὁ   ψεύστης   εἰ   μὴ   ὁ
v.rai.2p   r.asf.3   cj   cj   pl   a.nsn   n.nsn   v.pai.3s   p.g   d.gsf   n.gsf   r.nsm   v.pai.3s   d.nsm   n.nsm   cj   pl   d.nsm
3857   899   2779   4022   4024   4246   6022   1639   1666   3836   237   5515   1639   3836   6026   1623   3590   3836

who denies   that Jesus is   the Christ. Such a man is   the antichrist – he denies   the Father and the
ᵗἀρνούμενος   οὐκ   ὅτι   Ἰησοῦς   ἔστιν   ὁ   Χριστός   οὗτός   ἐστιν   ὁ   ἀντίχριστος   ὁ   ἀρνούμενος   τὸν   πατέρα   καὶ   τὸν
pt.pm.nsm   pl   cj   n.nsm   v.pai.3s   d.nsm   n.nsm   r.nsm   v.pai.3s   d.nsm   n.nsm   d.nsm   pt.pm.nsm   d.asm   n.asm   cj   d.asm
766   4024   4022   2652   1639   3836   5986   4047   1639   3836   532   3836   766   3836   4252   2779   3836

Son. **23** No one who denies   the Son has the Father; whoever acknowledges the Son has the Father also. ¶
υἱόν   οὐδὲ   πᾶς   ὁ   ἀρνούμενος   τὸν   υἱὸν   ἔχει   τὸν   πατέρα   ὁ   ὁμολογῶν   τὸν   υἱὸν   ἔχει   τὸν   πατέρα   καὶ
n.asm   cj   a.nsm   d.nsm   pt.pm.nsm   d.asm   n.asm   v.pai.3s   d.asm   n.asm   d.nsm   pt.pa.nsm   d.asm   n.asm   v.pai.3s   d.asm   n.asm   adv
5626   4028   4246   3836   766   3836   5626   2400   3836   4252   3836   3933   3836   5626   2400   3836   4252   2779

24 See that what you have heard   from the beginning remains in you. If it   does,   you
→   →   ὃ   ὑμεῖς   →   ἠκούσατε   ἀπ᾽   ἀρχῆς   μενέτω   ἐν   ὑμῖν   ἐὰν   →   ἀπ᾽   ἀρχῆς   ἠκούσατε   ἐν   ὑμῖν   μείνῃ   ὑμεῖς
r.asn   r.np.2   v.aai.2p   p.g   n.gsf   v.pam.3s   p.d   r.dp.2   cj   r.asn   p.g   n.gsf   v.aai.2p   p.d   r.dp.2   v.aas.3s   r.np.2
3531   3531   4005   7007   201   608   794   3531   1877   7007   1569   4005   608   794   201   1877   7007   3531   7007

also will remain in   the Son and in   the Father. **25** And this is   what   he promised us – even
καὶ   →   μενεῖτε   ἐν   τῷ   υἱῷ   καὶ   ἐν   τῷ   πατρὶ   καὶ   αὕτη   ἐστὶν   ἡ   ἐπαγγελία   ἣν   αὐτὸς   ἐπηγγείλατο   ἡμῖν
adv   v.fai.2p   p.d   d.dsm   n.dsm   cj   p.d   d.dsm   n.dsm   cj   r.nsf   v.pai.3s   d.nsf   n.nsf   r.asf   r.nsm   v.ami.3s   r.dp.1
2779   3531   1877   3836   5626   2779   1877   3836   4252   2779   4047   1639   3836   2039   4005   899   2040   7005

eternal   life.   ¶   **26** I am writing these things to you about those who are trying to lead you astray.
ᵗτὴν αἰώνιον᾽   ᵗτὴν ζωὴν᾽   →   →   ἔγραψα   Ταῦτα   ←   →   ὑμῖν   περὶ   τῶν   ←   →   →   ὑμᾶς   πλανώντων
d.asf   a.asf   d.asf   n.asf   v.aai.1s   r.apn   r.dp.2   p.g   d.gpm   r.ap.2   pt.pa.gpm
3836   173   3836   2437   1211   4047   7007   4309   3836   4414   4414   4414   4414   7007   4414

27 As for you, the anointing   you received from him remains in   you, and you do not need   anyone to
καὶ   ←   ὑμεῖς   τὸ   χρῖσμα   ὃ   →   ἐλάβετε   ἀπ᾽   αὐτοῦ   μένει   ἐν   ὑμῖν   καὶ   →   →   οὐ   ἔχετεχρείαν   ἵνα   τις   →
cj   r.np.2   d.nsn   n.nsn   r.asn   v.aai.2p   p.g   r.gsm.3   v.pai.3s   p.d   r.dp.2   cj   pl   v.pai.2p   n.asf   cj   r.nsm
2779   7007   3836   5984   4005   3284   608   899   3531   1877   7007   2779   2400   4024   2400   5970   2671   5516

teach   you. But as his   anointing   teaches you about all   things and as that anointing is   real,   not
διδάσκῃ   ὑμᾶς   ἀλλ᾽   ὡς   αὐτοῦ   ᵗτὸ χρῖσμα᾽   διδάσκει   ὑμᾶς   περὶ   πάντων   ←   καὶ   ἐστιν   ἀληθές   καὶ   ἔστιν   οὐκ
v.pas.3s   r.ap.2   cj   cj   r.gsm.3   d.nsn   n.nsn   v.pai.3s   r.ap.2   p.g   a.gpn   cj   v.pai.3s   a.nsn   cj   v.pai.3s   pl
1438   7007   247   6055   899   3836   5984   1438   7007   4309   4246   2779   1639   239   2779   1639   4024

counterfeit –   just   as it has taught   you, remain in   him.
ψεῦδος   καὶ   καθὼς   ←   →   ἐδίδαξεν   ὑμᾶς   μένετε   ἐν   αὐτῷ
n.nsn   cj   cj   v.aai.3s   r.ap.2   v.pai.2p   p.d   r.dsm.3
6022   2779   2777   1438   7007   3531   1877   899

Children of God

2:28 And now, dear children, continue in him, so that when he appears we may be   confident and
Καὶ   νῦν   →   τεκνία   μένετε   ἐν   αὐτῷ   ἵνα   ←   ἐὰν   →   φανερωθῇ   →   σχῶμεν   παρρησίαν   καὶ
cj   adv   n.vpn   v.pam.2p   p.d   r.dsm.3   cj   cj   v.aps.3s   v.aas.1p   n.asf   cj
2779   3814   5448   3531   1877   899   2671   1569   5746   2400   4244   2779

unashamed   before him at his   coming.   ¶   **29** If you know that he is   righteous, you know   that
ᵗμὴ αἰσχυνθῶμεν᾽   ἀπ᾽   αὐτοῦ   ἐν   αὐτοῦ   ᵗτῇ παρουσίᾳ᾽   ἐὰν   →   εἰδῆτε   ὅτι   →   ἐστιν   δίκαιος   →   γινώσκετε   ὅτι
pl   v.aps.1p   p.g   r.gsm.3   p.d   r.gsm.3   d.dsf   n.dsf   cj   v.ras.2p   cj   v.pai.3s   a.nsm   v.pai.2p   cj
3590   159   608   899   1877   899   3836   4242   1569   3857   4022   1639   1465   1182   4022

ἡμῶν· ἀλλ᾽ ἵνα φανερωθῶσιν ὅτι οὐκ εἰσὶν πάντες ἐξ ἡμῶν. ¶ **20** καὶ ὑμεῖς χρῖσμα ἔχετε ἀπὸ τοῦ ἁγίου καὶ οἴδατε πάντες. **21** οὐκ ἔγραψα ὑμῖν ὅτι οὐκ οἴδατε τὴν ἀλήθειαν ἀλλ᾽ ὅτι οἴδατε αὐτὴν καὶ ὅτι πᾶν ψεῦδος ἐκ τῆς ἀληθείας οὐκ ἔστιν. **22** Τίς ἐστιν ὁ ψεύστης εἰ μὴ ὁ ἀρνούμενος ὅτι Ἰησοῦς οὐκ ἔστιν ὁ Χριστός; οὗτός ἐστιν ὁ ἀντίχριστος, ὁ ἀρνούμενος τὸν πατέρα καὶ τὸν υἱόν. **23** πᾶς ὁ ἀρνούμενος τὸν υἱὸν οὐδὲ τὸν πατέρα ἔχει, ὁ ὁμολογῶν τὸν υἱὸν καὶ τὸν πατέρα ἔχει. ¶ **24** ὑμεῖς ὃ ἠκούσατε ἀπ᾽ ἀρχῆς, ἐν ὑμῖν μενέτω. ἐὰν ἐν ὑμῖν μείνῃ ὃ ἀπ᾽ ἀρχῆς ἠκούσατε, καὶ ὑμεῖς ἐν τῷ υἱῷ καὶ ἐν τῷ πατρὶ μενεῖτε. **25** καὶ αὕτη ἐστὶν ἡ ἐπαγγελία ἣν αὐτὸς ἐπηγγείλατο ἡμῖν, τὴν ζωὴν τὴν αἰώνιον. ¶ **26** Ταῦτα ἔγραψα ὑμῖν περὶ τῶν πλανώντων ὑμᾶς. **27** καὶ ὑμεῖς τὸ χρῖσμα ὃ ἐλάβετε ἀπ᾽ αὐτοῦ, μένει ἐν ὑμῖν καὶ οὐ χρείαν ἔχετε ἵνα τις διδάσκῃ ὑμᾶς, ἀλλ᾽ ὡς τὸ αὐτοῦ χρῖσμα διδάσκει ὑμᾶς περὶ πάντων καὶ ἀληθές ἐστιν καὶ οὐκ ἔστιν ψεῦδος, καὶ καθὼς ἐδίδαξεν ὑμᾶς, μένετε ἐν αὐτῷ.

2:28 Καὶ νῦν, τεκνία, μένετε ἐν αὐτῷ, ἵνα ἐὰν φανερωθῇ σχῶμεν παρρησίαν καὶ μὴ αἰσχυνθῶμεν ἀπ᾽ αὐτοῦ ἐν τῇ παρουσίᾳ

everyone who does what is right has been born of him. ¶ **3:1** How great is the love the
καὶ πᾶς ὁ ποιῶν τὴν → δικαιοσύνην → → γεγέννηται ἐξ αὐτοῦ ἴδετε ποταπὴν ← ἀγάπην ὁ
adv a.nsm d.nsm pt.pa.nsm d.asf n.asf v.rpi.3s p.g r.gsm.3 v.aam.2p r.asf n.asf d.nsm
2779 4246 3836 4472 3836 1466 1164 1666 899 1625 4534 27 3836

Father has lavished on us, that we should be called children of God! And that is what we are! The reason
πατὴρ → δέδωκεν ἡμῖν ἵνα → → → κληθῶμεν τέκνα → θεοῦ καὶ → ἐσμέν ͺδιὰ τοῦτο͵
n.nsm v.rai.3s r.dp.1 cj v.aps.1p n.npn n.gsm cj v.pai.1p p.a r.asn
4252 1443 7005 2671 2813 5451 2536 2779 1639 1328 4047

the world does not know us is that it did not know him. ² Dear friends, now we are children of God, and
ὁ κόσμος ↱ οὐ γινώσκει ἡμᾶς ὅτι ↱ οὐκ ἔγνω αὐτόν ἀγαπητοί νῦν → ἐσμεν τέκνα → θεοῦ καὶ
d.nsm n.nsm pl v.pai.3s r.ap.1 cj pl v.aai.3s r.asm.3 a.vpm adv v.pai.1p n.npn n.gsm cj
3836 3180 1182 1182 7005 4022 1182 1182 4024 1182 899 28 3814 1639 5451 2536 2779

what we will be has not yet been made known. But we know that when he appears, we shall be like
τί → → ἐσόμεθα ↱ οὔπω ← → ἐφανερώθη → οἴδαμεν ὅτι ἐὰν → φανερωθῇ → → ἐσόμεθα ὅμοιοι
r.nsn v.fmi.1p adv v.api.3s v.rai.1p cj cj v.aps.3s v.fmi.1p a.npm
5515 1639 5746 4037 5746 3857 4022 1569 5746 1639 3927

him, for we shall see him as he is. ¶ ³ Everyone who has this hope in him purifies
αὐτῷ ὅτι → → ὀψόμεθα αὐτὸν καθὼς → ἐστιν καὶ πᾶς ὁ ἔχων ταύτην ͺτὴν ἐλπίδα͵ ἐπ᾽ αὐτῷ ἁγνίζει
r.dsm.3 cj v.fmi.1p r.asm.3 cj v.pai.3s cj a.nsm d.nsm pt.pa.nsm r.asf d.asf n.asf p.d r.dsm.3 v.pai.3s
899 4022 3972 899 2777 1639 2779 4246 3836 2400 4047 3836 1828 2093 899 49

himself, just as he is pure. ⁴ Everyone who sins breaks the law; *in fact*, sin is
ἑαυτὸν καθὼς ← ἐκεῖνος ἐστιν ἁγνός Πᾶς ὁ ͺποιῶν τὴν ἁμαρτίαν͵ καὶ ποιεῖ τὴν ἀνομίαν καὶ ͺἡ ἁμαρτία͵ ἐστὶν
r.asm.3 cj r.nsm v.pai.3s a.nsm a.nsm d.nsm pt.pa.nsm d.asf n.asf adv v.pai.3s d.asf n.asf cj d.nsf n.nsf v.pai.3s
1571 2777 1697 1639 54 4246 3836 4472 3836 281 2779 4472 3836 490 2779 3836 281 1639

lawlessness. ⁵ But you know that he appeared so that he might take away our sins. And in him is no
ͺἡ ἀνομία͵ καὶ → οἴδατε ὅτι ἐκεῖνος ἐφανερώθη ἵνα ← → → ἄρῃ ← τὰς ἁμαρτίας καὶ ἐν αὐτῷ ἔστιν οὐκ
d.nsf n.nsf cj v.rai.2p cj r.nsm v.api.3s cj v.aas.3s d.apf n.apf cj p.d r.dsm.3 v.pai.3s pl
3836 490 2779 3857 4022 1697 5746 2671 149 3836 281 2779 1877 899 1639 4024

sin. ⁶ No one who lives in him keeps on sinning. No one who continues to sin has either seen him
ἁμαρτία οὐχ πᾶς ὁ μένων ἐν αὐτῷ → ἁμαρτάνει οὐχ πᾶς ὁ → ἁμαρτάνων ↱ ἑώρακεν αὐτὸν
n.nsf pl a.nsm d.nsm pt.pa.nsm p.d r.dsm.3 v.pai.3s pl a.nsm d.nsm pt.pa.nsm v.rai.3s r.asm.3
281 4024 4246 3836 3531 1877 899 279 4024 4246 3836 279 3972 3972 899

or known him. ¶ ⁷ Dear children, do not let anyone lead you astray. He who does what is right
οὐδὲ ἔγνωκεν αὐτόν → Τεκνία → μηδεὶς ↱ → → ὑμᾶς πλανάτω ὁ ← ποιῶν τὴν δικαιοσύνην
cj v.rai.3s r.asm.3 n.vpn a.nsm r.ap.2 v.pam.3s d.nsm pt.pa.nsm d.asf n.asf
4028 1182 899 5448 4414 3594 4414 3594 4414 7007 4414 3836 4472 3836 1466

is righteous, just as he is righteous. ⁸ He who does what is sinful is of the devil, because the
ἐστιν δίκαιος καθὼς ← ἐκεῖνος ἐστιν δίκαιος ὁ → ποιῶν τὴν → ἁμαρτίαν ἐστίν ἐκ τοῦ διαβόλου ὅτι ὁ
v.pai.3s a.nsm cj r.nsm v.pai.3s a.nsm d.nsm pt.pa.nsm d.asf n.asf v.pai.3s p.g d.gsm n.gsm cj d.nsm
1639 1465 2777 1697 1639 1465 3836 4472 3836 281 1639 1666 3836 1333 4022 3836

devil has been sinning from the beginning. The reason the Son of God appeared was to destroy the
διάβολος → → ἁμαρτάνει ἀπ᾽ ἀρχῆς ͺεἰς τοῦτο͵ ὁ υἱὸς ͺτοῦ θεοῦ͵ ἐφανερώθη ἵνα λύσῃ τὰ
n.nsm v.pai.3s p.g n.gsf p.a r.asn d.nsm n.nsm d.gsm n.gsm v.api.3s cj v.aas.3s d.apn
1333 279 608 794 1650 4047 3836 5626 3836 2536 5746 2671 3395 3836

devil's work. ⁹ No one who is born of God will continue to sin, because God's seed remains
ͺτοῦ διαβόλου͵ ἔργα οὐ Πᾶς ὁ γεγεννημένος ἐκ ͺτοῦ θεοῦ͵ → ποιεῖ ← ἁμαρτίαν ὅτι αὐτοῦ σπέρμα μένει
d.gsm n.gsm n.apn pl a.nsm d.nsm pt.rp.nsm p.g d.gsm n.gsm v.pai.3s n.asf cj r.gsm.3 n.nsn v.pai.3s
3836 1333 2240 4024 4246 3836 1164 1666 3836 2536 4472 281 4022 899 5065 3531

in him; he cannot go on sinning, because he has been born of God. ¹⁰ This is how we know
ἐν αὐτῷ καὶ ͺοὐ δύναται͵ → ἁμαρτάνειν ὅτι → → γεγέννηται ἐκ ͺτοῦ θεοῦ͵ ἐν τούτῳ ἐστιν φανερά
p.d r.dsm.3 cj pl v.ppi.3s f.pa cj v.rpi.3s p.g d.gsm n.gsm p.d r.dsn v.pai.3s a.npn
1877 899 2779 1538 4024 1538 279 4022 1164 1666 3836 2536 1877 4047 1639 5745

who the children of God are and who the children of the devil are: Anyone who does not do what is
τὰ τέκνα ͺτοῦ θεοῦ͵ καὶ τὰ τέκνα → τοῦ διαβόλου πᾶς ὁ ↱ μὴ ποιῶν →
d.npn n.npn d.gsm n.gsm cj d.npn n.npn d.gsm n.gsm a.nsm d.nsm pl pt.pa.nsm
3836 5451 3836 2536 2779 3836 5451 3836 1333 4246 3836 3590 4472

αὐτοῦ. ¶ ²⁹ ἐὰν εἰδῆτε ὅτι δίκαιός ἐστιν, γινώσκετε ὅτι καὶ πᾶς ὁ ποιῶν τὴν δικαιοσύνην ἐξ αὐτοῦ γεγέννηται. ³·¹ ἴδετε ποταπὴν ἀγάπην δέδωκεν ἡμῖν ὁ πατήρ, ἵνα τέκνα θεοῦ κληθῶμεν, καὶ ἐσμέν. διὰ τοῦτο ὁ κόσμος οὐ γινώσκει ἡμᾶς, ὅτι οὐκ ἔγνω αὐτόν. ² Ἀγαπητοί, νῦν τέκνα θεοῦ ἐσμεν, καὶ οὔπω ἐφανερώθη τί ἐσόμεθα. οἴδαμεν ὅτι ἐὰν φανερωθῇ, ὅμοιοι αὐτῷ ἐσόμεθα, ὅτι ὀψόμεθα αὐτὸν καθώς ἐστιν. ¶ ³ καὶ πᾶς ὁ ἔχων τὴν ἐλπίδα ταύτην ἐπ᾽ αὐτῷ ἁγνίζει ἑαυτόν, καθὼς ἐκεῖνος ἁγνός ἐστιν. ⁴ Πᾶς ὁ ποιῶν τὴν ἁμαρτίαν καὶ τὴν ἀνομίαν ποιεῖ, καὶ ἡ ἁμαρτία ἐστὶν ἡ ἀνομία. ⁵ καὶ οἴδατε ὅτι ἐκεῖνος ἐφανερώθη, ἵνα τὰς ἁμαρτίας ἄρῃ, καὶ ἁμαρτία ἐν αὐτῷ οὐκ ἔστιν. ⁶ πᾶς ὁ ἐν αὐτῷ μένων οὐχ ἁμαρτάνει· πᾶς ὁ ἁμαρτάνων οὐχ ἑώρακεν αὐτὸν οὐδὲ ἔγνωκεν αὐτόν. ¶ ⁷ Τεκνία, μηδεὶς πλανάτω ὑμᾶς· ὁ ποιῶν τὴν δικαιοσύνην δίκαιός ἐστιν, καθὼς ἐκεῖνος δίκαιός ἐστιν· ⁸ ὁ ποιῶν τὴν ἁμαρτίαν ἐκ τοῦ διαβόλου ἐστίν, ὅτι ἀπ᾽ ἀρχῆς ὁ διάβολος ἁμαρτάνει. εἰς τοῦτο ἐφανερώθη ὁ υἱὸς τοῦ θεοῦ, ἵνα λύσῃ τὰ ἔργα τοῦ διαβόλου. ⁹ Πᾶς ὁ γεγεννημένος ἐκ τοῦ θεοῦ ἁμαρτίαν οὐ ποιεῖ, ὅτι σπέρμα αὐτοῦ ἐν αὐτῷ μένει, καὶ οὐ δύναται ἁμαρτάνειν, ὅτι ἐκ τοῦ θεοῦ γεγέννηται. ¹⁰ ἐν τούτῳ φανερά ἐστιν τὰ τέκνα τοῦ θεοῦ καὶ τὰ τέκνα

right	is	not	a child	of	God;	nor is	anyone	who	does not	love	his	brother.
δικαιοσύνην	ἐστιν	οὐκ	ἐκ	τοῦ θεοῦ		καὶ	ὁ →		μὴ	ἀγαπῶν	αὐτοῦ	τὸν ἀδελφὸν
n.asf	v.pai.3s	pl	p.g	d.gsm d.nsm		adv	d.nsm		pl	pt.pa.nsm	r.gsm.3	d.asm n.asm
1466	1639	4024	1666	3836 2536		2779	3836	26	3590	26	899	3836 81

Love One Another

3:11

This	is	the	message	you heard	from	the beginning:	We should	love	one	another.
Ὅτι αὕτη	ἐστιν	ἡ	ἀγγελία	ἣν → ἠκούσατε	ἀπ᾽	ἀρχῆς	ἵνα → →	ἀγαπῶμεν		ἀλλήλους ←
cj r.nsf	v.pai.3s	d.nsf	n.nsf	r.asf v.aai.2p	p.g	n.gsf	cj	v.pas.1p	26	r.apm
4022 4047	1639	3836	32	4005 201	608	794	2671			253

12

Do not be like	Cain,	who	belonged	to	the evil	one	and	murdered	his	brother.	And	why	did he
οὐ καθὼς	Κάϊν	ἦν		ἐκ	τοῦ πονηροῦ	←	καὶ	ἔσφαξεν	αὐτοῦ	τὸν ἀδελφὸν	καὶ	χάριν	τίνος ┐ → →
pl	n.nsm	v.iai.3s		p.g	d.gsm a.gsm		cj	v.aai.3s	r.gsm.3	d.asm n.asm	cj	p.g	r.gsn
4024 2777	2782	1639		1666	3836 4505		2779	5377	899	3836 81	2779	5920	5515

murder him?	Because	his	own actions	were	evil	and his	brother's	were righteous.	**13**	Do not be
ἔσφαξεν αὐτόν	ὅτι	αὐτοῦ τὰ	ἔργα	ἦν	πονηρὰ	δὲ αὐτοῦ	τοῦ ἀδελφοῦ	τὰ δίκαια	[Καὶ] →	μὴ →
v.aai.3s r.asm.3	cj	r.gsm.3 d.npn	n.npn	v.iai.3s	a.npn	cj r.gsm.3	d.gsm n.gsm	d.npn a.npn	cj	pl
5377 899	4022	899 3836	2240	1639	4505	1254 899	3836 81	3836 1465	2779	2513 3590

surprised,	my brothers,	if	the world	hates	you.	**14** We	know	that	we have	passed	from	death	to	life,
θαυμάζετε →	ἀδελφοί	εἰ	ὁ κόσμος	μισεῖ	ὑμᾶς	ἡμεῖς	οἴδαμεν	ὅτι	→ →	μεταβεβήκαμεν	ἐκ	τοῦ θανάτου	εἰς	τὴν ζωήν,
v.pam.2p	n.vpm	cj	d.nsm n.nsm	v.pai.3s	r.ap.2	r.np.1	v.rai.1p	cj		v.rai.1p	p.g	d.gsm n.gsm	p.a	d.asf n.asf
2513	81	1623	3836 3180	3631	7007	7005	3857	4022		3553	1666	3836 2505	1650	3836 2437

because	we love	our brothers.	Anyone	who	does not	love	remains	in	death.	**15** Anyone	who	hates	his
ὅτι	→ ἀγαπῶμεν	τοὺς ἀδελφούς	ὁ →		μὴ	ἀγαπῶν	μένει	ἐν	τῷ θανάτῳ	πᾶς	ὁ	μισῶν	αὐτοῦ
cj	v.pai.1p	d.apm n.apm	d.nsm		pl	pt.pa.nsm	v.pai.3s	p.d	d.dsm n.dsm	a.nsm	d.nsm	pt.pa.nsm	r.gsm.3
4022	26	3836 81	3836	26	3590	26	3531	1877	3836 2505	4246	3836	3631	899

brother	is	a murderer,	and you	know	that	no	murderer	has	eternal	life	in	him.	¶
τὸν ἀδελφὸν	ἐστίν	ἀνθρωποκτόνος	καὶ →	οἴδατε	ὅτι	πᾶς οὐκ	ἀνθρωποκτόνος	ἔχει	αἰώνιον	ζωὴν	μένουσαν ἐν	αὐτῷ	
d.asm n.asm	v.pai.3s	n.nsm	cj	v.rai.2p	cj	a.nsm pl	n.nsm	v.pai.3s	a.asf	n.asf	pt.pa.asf p.d	r.dsm.3	
3836 81	1639	475	2779	3857	4022	4246 4024	475	2400	173	2437	3531 1877	899	

16

This	is	how we	know	what	love	is:	Jesus Christ	laid	down	his	life	for	us.	And	we
ἐν τούτῳ	← ←	ἐγνώκαμεν		τὴν ἀγάπην		ὅτι	ἐκεῖνος	ἔθηκεν →		αὐτοῦ	τὴν ψυχὴν	ὑπὲρ	ἡμῶν	καὶ	ἡμεῖς
p.d r.dsn		v.rai.1p		d.asf n.asf		cj	r.nsm	v.aai.3s		r.gsm.3	d.asf n.asf	p.g	r.gp.1	cj	r.np.1
1877 4047		1182		3836 27		4022	1697	5502		899	3836 6034	5642	7005	2779	7005

ought	to lay	down	our lives	for	our brothers.	**17**	If anyone	has	material	possessions	and	sees	his
ὀφείλομεν	→ θεῖναι ←		τὰς ψυχὰς	ὑπὲρ	τῶν ἀδελφῶν	δ᾽	ὃς ἂν	ἔχῃ	τοῦ κόσμου	τὸν βίον	καὶ	θεωρῇ	αὐτοῦ
v.pai.1p	f.aa		d.apf n.apf	p.g	d.gpm n.gpm	cj	r.nsm pl	v.pas.3s	d.gsm n.gsm	d.asm n.asm	cj	v.pas.3s	r.gsm.3
4053	5502		3836 6034	5642	3836 81	1254	4005 323	2400	3836 3180	3836 1050	2779	2555	899

brother	in	need	but	*has no*	*pity*	on	him,	how	can	the	love	of	God	be	in	him?
τὸν ἀδελφὸν	ἔχοντα	χρείαν	καὶ	κλείσῃ	τὰ σπλάγχνα	αὐτοῦ	ἀπ᾽ αὐτοῦ	πῶς	→	ἡ	ἀγάπη	τοῦ θεοῦ	μένει	ἐν	αὐτῷ
d.asm n.asm	pt.pa.asm	n.asf	cj	v.aas.3s	d.apn n.apn	r.gsm.3	p.g r.gsm.3	adv		d.nsf	n.nsf	d.gsm n.gsm	v.pai.3s	p.d	r.dsm.3
3836 81	2400	5970	2779	3091	3836 5073	899	608 899	4802	3531	3836	27	3836 2536	3531	1877	899

18

Dear children,	let us not	love	with words	or	tongue	but	with	actions	and in	truth.	**19** This	then is	how we
Τεκνία	→ μὴ ἀγαπῶμεν →		λόγῳ	μηδὲ	τῇ γλώσσῃ	ἀλλὰ	ἐν	ἔργῳ	καὶ →	ἀληθείᾳ	ἐν τούτῳ	Καὶ	→
n.vpn	pl v.pas.1p		n.dsm	cj	d.dsf n.dsf	cj	p.d	n.dsn	cj	n.dsf	p.d r.dsn	cj	
5448	26 26 3590 26		3364	3593	3836 1185	247	1877	2240	2779	237	1877 4047	2779	

know	that	we belong	to	the truth,	and	how	we set	our hearts	at rest	in	his	presence	**20**		that
γνωσόμεθα	ὅτι	→ ἐσμέν	ἐκ	τῆς ἀληθείας	καὶ	→ →		ἡμῶν τὴν καρδίαν	→ πείσομεν	ἔμπροσθεν	αὐτοῦ				ὅτι
v.fmi.1p	cj	v.pai.1p	p.g	d.gsf n.gsf	cj			r.gp.1 d.asf n.asf	v.fai.1p	p.g	r.gsm.3				cj
1182	4022	1639	1666	3836 237	2779		4275 4275	7005 3836 2840	4275	1869	899	1869			4022

whenever	our	hearts	condemn	us.	For	God	is	greater	than	our hearts,	and	he knows	everything.	¶
ἐὰν	ἡμῶν	ἡ καρδία	καταγινώσκῃ		ὅτι	ὁ θεὸς	ἐστὶν	μείζων →		ἡμῶν τῆς καρδίας	καὶ	→ γινώσκει	πάντα	
cj	r.gp.1	d.nsf n.nsf	v.pas.3s		cj	d.nsm n.nsm	v.pai.3s	a.nsm.c		r.gp.1 d.gsf n.gsf	cj	v.pai.3s	a.apn	
1569	7005	3836 2840	2861		4022	3836 2536	1639	3489	2840	7005 3836 2840	2779	1182	4246	

21

Dear friends,	if	our	hearts	do not	condemn	us,	we have	confidence	before	God	**22** and	receive
→ Ἀγαπητοί	ἐὰν	ἡμῶν	ἡ καρδία	→ μὴ	καταγινώσκῃ	→	ἔχομεν	παρρησίαν	πρὸς	τὸν θεόν	καὶ	λαμβάνομεν
a.vpm	cj	r.gp.1	d.nsf n.nsf	pl	v.pas.3s		v.pai.1p	n.asf	p.a	d.asm n.asm	cj	v.pai.1p
28	1569	7005	3836 2840	2861 3590	2861		2400	4244	4639	3836 2536	2779	3284

τοῦ διαβόλου· πᾶς ὁ μὴ ποιῶν δικαιοσύνην οὐκ ἔστιν ἐκ τοῦ θεοῦ, καὶ ὁ μὴ ἀγαπῶν τὸν ἀδελφὸν αὐτοῦ.

3:11 Ὅτι αὕτη ἐστὶν ἡ ἀγγελία ἣν ἠκούσατε ἀπ᾽ ἀρχῆς, ἵνα ἀγαπῶμεν ἀλλήλους, **12** οὐ καθὼς Κάϊν ἐκ τοῦ πονηροῦ ἦν καὶ ἔσφαξεν τὸν ἀδελφὸν αὐτοῦ· καὶ χάριν τίνος ἔσφαξεν αὐτόν; ὅτι τὰ ἔργα αὐτοῦ πονηρὰ ἦν τὰ δὲ τοῦ ἀδελφοῦ αὐτοῦ δίκαια. **13** [καὶ] μὴ θαυμάζετε, ἀδελφοί, εἰ μισεῖ ὑμᾶς ὁ κόσμος. **14** ἡμεῖς οἴδαμεν ὅτι μεταβεβήκαμεν ἐκ τοῦ θανάτου εἰς τὴν ζωήν, ὅτι ἀγαπῶμεν τοὺς ἀδελφούς· ὁ μὴ ἀγαπῶν μένει ἐν τῷ θανάτῳ. **15** πᾶς ὁ μισῶν τὸν ἀδελφὸν αὐτοῦ ἀνθρωποκτόνος ἐστίν, καὶ οἴδατε ὅτι πᾶς ἀνθρωποκτόνος οὐκ ἔχει ζωὴν αἰώνιον ἐν αὐτῷ μένουσαν. ¶ **16** ἐν τούτῳ ἐγνώκαμεν τὴν ἀγάπην, ὅτι ἐκεῖνος ὑπὲρ ἡμῶν τὴν ψυχὴν αὐτοῦ ἔθηκεν· καὶ ἡμεῖς ὀφείλομεν ὑπὲρ τῶν ἀδελφῶν τὰς ψυχὰς θεῖναι. **17** ὃς δ᾽ ἂν ἔχῃ τὸν βίον τοῦ κόσμου καὶ θεωρῇ τὸν ἀδελφὸν αὐτοῦ χρείαν ἔχοντα καὶ κλείσῃ τὰ σπλάγχνα αὐτοῦ ἀπ᾽ αὐτοῦ, πῶς ἡ ἀγάπη τοῦ θεοῦ μένει ἐν αὐτῷ; **18** Τεκνία, μὴ ἀγαπῶμεν λόγῳ μηδὲ τῇ γλώσσῃ ἀλλὰ ἐν ἔργῳ καὶ ἀληθείᾳ. **19** [Καὶ] ἐν τούτῳ γνωσόμεθα ὅτι ἐκ τῆς ἀληθείας ἐσμέν, καὶ ἔμπροσθεν αὐτοῦ πείσομεν τὴν καρδίαν ἡμῶν, **20** ὅτι ἐὰν καταγινώσκῃ ἡμῶν ἡ καρδία, ὅτι μείζων ἐστὶν ὁ θεὸς τῆς καρδίας ἡμῶν καὶ γινώσκει πάντα. ¶ **21** Ἀγαπητοί, ἐὰν ἡ καρδία [ἡμῶν] μὴ καταγινώσκῃ, παρρησίαν ἔχομεν πρὸς τὸν θεὸν

from him anything we ask, because we obey his commands and do what pleases him. **23** And this
ἀπ' αὐτοῦ ὃ ἐάν → αἰτῶμεν ὅτι → τηροῦμεν αὐτοῦ τὰς ἐντολὰς καὶ ποιοῦμεν τὰ ἀρεστὰ ἐνώπιον αὐτοῦ Καὶ αὕτη
p.g r.gsm.3 r.asn pl v.pas.1p cj v.pai.1p r.gsm.3 d.apf n.apf cj v.pai.1p d.apn a.apn p.g r.gsm.3 cj r.nsf
608 899 4005 1569 160 4022 5498 899 3836 1953 2779 4472 3836 744 1967 899 2779 4047

is his command: to believe in the name of his Son, Jesus Christ, and to love one another
ἐστιν αὐτοῦ ἡ ἐντολὴ ἵνα πιστεύσωμεν → τῷ ὀνόματι → αὐτοῦ τοῦ υἱοῦ Ἰησοῦ Χριστοῦ καὶ ἀγαπῶμεν ἀλλήλους ←
v.pai.3s r.gsm.3 d.nsf n.nsf cj v.aas.1p d.dsn n.dsn r.gsm.3 d.gsm n.gsm n.gsm n.gsm cj v.pas.1p r.apm
1639 899 3836 1953 2671 4409 3836 3950 5626 899 3836 5626 2652 5986 2779 26 253

as he commanded us. **24** Those who obey his commands live in him, and he in them. And this
καθὼς → ἔδωκεν ἐντολὴν ἡμῖν καὶ ὁ → τηρῶν αὐτοῦ τὰς ἐντολάς μένει ἐν αὐτῷ καὶ αὐτὸς ἐν αὐτῷ καὶ ἐν τούτῳ
cj v.aai.3s n.asf r.dp.1 cj d.nsm pt.pa.nsm r.gsm.3 d.apf n.apf v.pai.3s p.d r.dsm.3 cj r.nsm p.d r.dsm.3 cj p.d r.dsn
2777 1443 1953 7005 2779 3836 5498 899 3836 1953 3531 1877 899 2779 899 1877 899 2779 1877 4047

is how we know that he lives in us: We know it by the Spirit he gave us.
← ← → γινώσκομεν ὅτι → μένει ἐν ἡμῖν ἐκ τοῦ πνεύματος οὗ → ἔδωκεν ἡμῖν
v.pai.1p cj v.pai.3s p.d r.dp.1 p.g d.gsn n.gsn r.gsn v.aai.3s r.dp.1
1182 4022 3531 1877 7005 1666 3836 4460 4005 1443 7005

Test the Spirits

4:1 Dear friends, do not believe every spirit, but test the spirits to see whether they are from God,
→ Ἀγαπητοί → μὴ πιστεύετε παντὶ πνεύματι ἀλλὰ δοκιμάζετε τὰ πνεύματα εἰ → ἔστιν ἐκ τοῦ θεοῦ
a.vpm pl v.pam.2p a.dsn n.dsn cj v.pam.2p d.apn n.apn cj v.pai.3s p.g d.gsm n.gsm
28 4409 3590 4409 4246 4460 247 1507 3836 4460 1623 1639 1666 3836 2536

because many false prophets have gone out into the world. **2** This is how you can recognize the Spirit of
ὅτι πολλοὶ → ψευδοπροφῆται → ἐξεληλύθασιν εἰς τὸν κόσμον ἐν τούτῳ → γινώσκετε τὸ πνεῦμα
cj a.npm n.npm v.rai.3p p.a d.asm n.asm p.d r.dsn v.pai.2p d.asn n.asn
4022 4498 6021 2002 1650 3836 3180 1877 4047 1182 3836 4460

God: Every spirit that acknowledges that Jesus Christ has come in the flesh is from God, **3** but every
τοῦ θεοῦ πᾶν πνεῦμα ὃ ὁμολογεῖ Ἰησοῦν Χριστὸν → ἐληλυθότα ἐν σαρκὶ ἐστιν ἐκ τοῦ θεοῦ καὶ πᾶν
d.gsm n.gsm a.nsn n.nsn r.nsn v.pai.3s n.asm n.asm pt.ra.asm p.d n.dsf v.pai.3s p.g d.gsm n.gsm cj a.nsn
3836 2536 4246 4460 4005 3933 2652 5986 2262 1877 4922 1639 1666 3836 2536 2779 4246

spirit that does not acknowledge Jesus is not from God. This is the spirit of the antichrist, which
πνεῦμα ὃ → μὴ ὁμολογεῖ τὸν Ἰησοῦν ἔστιν οὐκ ἐκ τοῦ θεοῦ καὶ τοῦτό ἐστιν τὸ τοῦ ἀντιχρίστου ὃ
n.nsn r.nsn pl v.pai.3s d.asm n.asm v.pai.3s pl p.g d.gsn n.gsn cj r.nsn v.pai.3s d.nsn d.gsm n.gsm r.asn
4460 4005 3590 3933 3836 2652 1639 4024 1666 3836 2536 2779 4047 1639 3836 3836 532 4005

you have heard is coming and even now is already in the world. ¶ **4** You, dear children, are from
→ → ἀκηκόατε ὅτι → ἔρχεται καὶ → νῦν ἐστιν ἤδη ἐν τῷ κόσμῳ ὑμεῖς τεκνία ἐστε ἐκ
v.rai.2p cj v.pmi.3s cj adv v.pai.3s adv p.d d.dsm n.dsm r.np.2 n.vpn v.pai.2p p.g
201 4022 2262 2779 3814 1639 2453 1877 3836 3180 7007 5448 1639 1666

God and have overcome them, because the one who is in you is greater than the one who is in the world.
τοῦ θεοῦ καὶ → νενικήκατε αὐτοὺς ὅτι ὁ → ἐν ὑμῖν ἐστιν μείζων ἢ ὁ → ἐν τῷ κόσμῳ
d.gsm n.gsm cj v.rai.2p r.apm.3 cj d.nsm p.d r.dp.2 v.pai.3s a.nsm.c cj d.nsm p.d d.dsm n.dsm
3836 2536 2779 3771 899 4022 3836 1877 7007 1639 3489 2445 3836 1877 3836 3180

5 They are from the world and therefore speak from the viewpoint of the world, and the world listens to them.
αὐτοὶ εἰσίν ἐκ τοῦ κόσμου διὰ τοῦτο λαλοῦσιν ἐκ ← τοῦ κόσμου καὶ ὁ κόσμος ἀκούει ← αὐτῶν
r.npm v.pai.3p p.g d.gsm n.gsm p.a r.asn v.pai.3p p.g d.gsm n.gsm cj d.nsm n.nsm v.pai.3s r.gpm.3
899 1639 1666 3836 3180 1328 4047 3281 1666 3836 3180 2779 3836 3180 201 899

6 We are from God, and whoever knows God listens to us; but whoever is not from God does not
ἡμεῖς ἐσμεν ἐκ τοῦ θεοῦ ὁ γινώσκων τὸν θεὸν ἀκούει ← ἡμῶν ὃς ἔστιν οὐκ ἐκ τοῦ θεοῦ → οὐκ
r.np.1 v.pai.1p p.g d.gsm n.gsm d.nsm pt.pa.nsm d.asm n.asm v.pai.3s r.gp.1 r.nsm v.pai.3s pl p.g d.gsm n.gsm pl
7005 1639 1666 3836 2536 3836 1182 3836 2536 201 7005 4005 1639 4024 1666 3836 2536 201 4024

listen to us. This is how we recognize the Spirit of truth and the spirit of falsehood.
ἀκούει ἡμῶν ἐκ τούτου → ← γινώσκομεν τὸ πνεῦμα τῆς ἀληθείας καὶ τὸ πνεῦμα τῆς πλάνης
v.pai.3s r.gp.1 p.g r.gsn v.pai.1p d.asn n.asn d.gsf n.gsf cj d.asn n.asn d.gsf n.gsf
201 7005 1666 4047 1182 3836 4460 3836 237 2779 3836 4460 3836 4415

[22] καὶ ὃ ἐὰν αἰτῶμεν λαμβάνομεν ἀπ' αὐτοῦ, ὅτι τὰς ἐντολὰς αὐτοῦ τηροῦμεν καὶ τὰ ἀρεστὰ ἐνώπιον αὐτοῦ ποιοῦμεν. [23] καὶ αὕτη ἐστὶν ἡ ἐντολὴ αὐτοῦ, ἵνα πιστεύσωμεν τῷ ὀνόματι τοῦ υἱοῦ αὐτοῦ Ἰησοῦ Χριστοῦ καὶ ἀγαπῶμεν ἀλλήλους, καθὼς ἔδωκεν ἐντολὴν ἡμῖν. [24] καὶ ὁ τηρῶν τὰς ἐντολὰς αὐτοῦ ἐν αὐτῷ μένει καὶ αὐτὸς ἐν αὐτῷ· καὶ ἐν τούτῳ γινώσκομεν ὅτι μένει ἐν ἡμῖν, ἐκ τοῦ πνεύματος οὗ ἡμῖν ἔδωκεν.

[4:1] Ἀγαπητοί, μὴ παντὶ πνεύματι πιστεύετε ἀλλὰ δοκιμάζετε τὰ πνεύματα εἰ ἐκ τοῦ θεοῦ ἐστιν, ὅτι πολλοὶ ψευδοπροφῆται ἐξεληλύθασιν εἰς τὸν κόσμον. [2] ἐν τούτῳ γινώσκετε τὸ πνεῦμα τοῦ θεοῦ· πᾶν πνεῦμα ὃ ὁμολογεῖ Ἰησοῦν Χριστὸν ἐν σαρκὶ ἐληλυθότα ἐκ τοῦ θεοῦ ἐστιν, [3] καὶ πᾶν πνεῦμα ὃ μὴ ὁμολογεῖ τὸν Ἰησοῦν ἐκ τοῦ θεοῦ οὐκ ἔστιν· καὶ τοῦτό ἐστιν τὸ τοῦ ἀντιχρίστου, ὃ ἀκηκόατε ὅτι ἔρχεται, καὶ νῦν ἐν τῷ κόσμῳ ἐστὶν ἤδη. ¶ [4] ὑμεῖς ἐκ τοῦ θεοῦ ἐστε, τεκνία, καὶ νενικήκατε αὐτούς, ὅτι μείζων ἐστὶν ὁ ἐν ὑμῖν ἢ ὁ ἐν τῷ κόσμῳ. [5] αὐτοὶ ἐκ τοῦ κόσμου εἰσίν, διὰ τοῦτο ἐκ τοῦ κόσμου λαλοῦσιν καὶ ὁ κόσμος αὐτῶν ἀκούει. [6] ἡμεῖς ἐκ τοῦ θεοῦ ἐσμεν, ὁ γινώσκων τὸν θεὸν ἀκούει ἡμῶν, ὃς οὐκ ἔστιν ἐκ τοῦ θεοῦ οὐκ ἀκούει

God's Love and Ours

4:7 Dear friends,   let us love   one   another,   for love   comes from God.   Everyone who loves
→   Ἀγαπητοί →   →   ἀγαπῶμεν ἀλλήλους ←   ὅτι ἡ ἀγάπη ἐστὶν ἐκ   τοῦ θεοῦ καὶ πᾶς ὁ   ἀγαπῶν
a.vpm   v.pas.1p   r.apm   cj d.nsf n.nsf   v.pai.3s   p.g d.gsm n.gsm cj a.nsm   d.nsm pt.pa.nsm
28   26   253   4022 3836 27   1639   1666 3836 2536 2779 4246   3836 26

has been born   of God   and knows God.   **8** Whoever does not love   does not know God,   because
→   →   γεγέννηται ἐκ   τοῦ θεοῦ καὶ γινώσκει τὸν θεόν ὁ   μὴ ἀγαπῶν   οὐκ ἔγνω τὸν θεόν ὅτι
v.rpi.3s   p.g d.gsm n.gsm cj v.pai.3s d.asm n.asm   d.nsm   pl pt.pa.nsm   pl v.aai.3s d.asm n.asm cj
1164   1666 3836 2536 2779 1182 3836 2536   3836   26 3590 26   4024 1182 3836 2536 4022

God   is   love.   **9** This   is how God showed   his   love   among us: He   sent   his
ὁ   θεὸς   ἐστὶν ἀγάπη ἐν τούτῳ ← ← →   ἐφανερώθη   τοῦ θεοῦ ἡ   ἀγάπη ἐν   ἡμῖν ὅτι ὁ   θεὸς   ἀπέσταλκεν αὐτοῦ
d.nsm n.nsm   v.pai.3s n.nsf   p.d r.dsn   v.api.3s   d.gsm n.gsm d.nsf n.nsf   p.d   r.dp.1 cj d.nsm n.nsm   v.rai.3s   r.gsm.3
3836 2536   1639 27   1877 4047   2536 5746   3836 2536 3836 27   1877   7005 4022 3836 2536   690   899

one   and only Son   into the world that we might live   through him.   **10** This   is   love: not that
τὸν μονογενῆ ←   τὸν υἱὸν εἰς τὸν κόσμον ἵνα →   ζήσωμεν δι'   αὐτοῦ ἐν τούτῳ ἐστὶν ἡ   ἀγάπη οὐχ ὅτι
d.asm a.asm   d.asm n.asm p.a d.asm n.asm cj   v.aas.1p p.g   r.gsm.3 p.d r.dsn v.pai.3s d.nsf n.nsf pl cj
3836 3666   3836 5626 1650 3836 3180 2671   2409 1328   899   1877 4047 1639 3836 27   4024 4022

we   loved   God,   but that he   loved   us   and sent   his   Son   as an atoning sacrifice for our
ἡμεῖς ἠγαπήκαμεν τὸν θεόν ἀλλ' ὅτι αὐτὸς ἠγάπησεν ἡμᾶς καὶ ἀπέστειλεν αὐτοῦ τὸν υἱὸν   ἱλασμὸν ←   περὶ ἡμῶν
r.np.1 v.rai.1p   d.asm n.asm cj cj r.nsm v.aai.3s r.ap.1 cj v.aai.3s r.gsm.3 d.asm n.asm   n.asm   p.g r.gp.1
7005 26   3836 2536 247 4022 899 26 7005 2779 690 899 3836 5626   2662   4309 7005

sins.   **11** Dear friends, since God   so   loved   us, we also ought   to love   one   another.   **12** No
τῶν ἁμαρτιῶν Ἀγαπητοί εἰ ὁ   θεὸς οὕτως ἠγάπησεν ἡμᾶς ἡμεῖς καὶ ὀφείλομεν →   ἀγαπᾶν ἀλλήλους ←   οὐδεὶς
d.gpf n.gpf   a.vpm cj d.nsm n.nsm adv v.aai.3s r.ap.1 r.np.1 adv v.pai.1p   f.pa   r.apm   a.nsm
3836 281   28 1623 3836 2536 4048 26 7005 7005 2779 4053   26   253   4029

one has ever seen   God; but if we love   one   another, God   lives in us and his   love   is
← → πώποτε τεθέαται θεὸν   ἐὰν → ἀγαπῶμεν ἀλλήλους ←   ὁ   θεὸς   μένει ἐν ἡμῖν καὶ αὐτοῦ ἡ ἀγάπη ἐστὶν
adv v.rmi.3s n.asm   cj v.pas.1p r.apm   d.nsm n.nsm v.pai.3s p.d r.dp.1 cj r.gsm.3 d.nsf n.nsf v.pai.3s
2517 4799 2517 2536   1569 26 253   3836 2536 3531 1877 7005 2779 899 3836 27 1639

made complete in us. ¶   **13**   We know   that we live   in him and he   in us, because he has
→ τετελειωμένη ἐν ἡμῖν   Ἐν τούτῳ γινώσκομεν ὅτι → μένομεν ἐν αὐτῷ καὶ αὐτὸς ἐν ἡμῖν ὅτι   →
pt.rp.nsf p.d r.dp.1   p.d r.dsn   v.pai.1p   cj   v.pai.1p p.d r.dsm.3 cj r.nsm p.d r.dp.1 cj
5457 1877 7005   1877 4047   1182   4022   3531 1877 899 2779 899 1877 7005 4022

given   us of his   Spirit.   **14** And we   have seen   and testify   that the Father has sent   his Son to
δέδωκεν ἡμῖν ἐκ αὐτοῦ τοῦ πνεύματος καὶ ἡμεῖς → τεθεάμεθα καὶ μαρτυροῦμεν ὅτι ὁ   πατὴρ → ἀπέσταλκεν τὸν υἱὸν
v.rai.3s r.dp.1 p.g r.gsm.3 d.gsn n.gsn   cj r.np.1   v.rmi.1p cj v.pai.1p cj d.nsm n.nsm   v.rai.3s d.asm n.asm
1443 7005 1666 899 3836 4460   2779 7005   2517 2779 3455 4022 3836 4252   690 3836 5626

be the Savior of the world.   **15** If anyone   acknowledges that Jesus   is   the Son of God,   God   lives in him
σωτῆρα → τοῦ κόσμου   → Ὃς ἐὰν ὁμολογήσῃ   ὅτι Ἰησοῦς ἐστιν ὁ   υἱὸς → τοῦ θεοῦ ὁ   θεὸς   μένει ἐν αὐτῷ
n.asm d.gsm n.gsm   r.nsm pl v.aas.3s   cj n.nsm v.pai.3s d.nsm n.nsm   d.gsm n.gsm d.nsm n.nsm   v.pai.3s p.d r.dsm.3
5400 3836 3180   4005 1569 3933   4022 2652 1639 3836 5626   3836 2536 3836 2536   3531 1877 899

and he   in God.   **16** And so we   know   and rely   on the love   God   has for us. ¶
καὶ αὐτὸς ἐν τῷ θεῷ   καὶ   ἡμεῖς ἐγνώκαμεν καὶ πεπιστεύκαμεν ← τὴν ἀγάπην ἣν ὁ   θεὸς ἔχει ἐν ἡμῖν
cj r.nsm p.d d.dsm n.dsm   cj   r.np.1 v.rai.1p cj v.rai.1p   d.asf n.asf r.asf d.nsm n.nsm v.pai.3s p.d r.dp.1
2779 899 1877 3836 2536   2779   7005 1182 2779 4409   3836 27 4005 3836 2536 2400 1877 7005

God   is   love.   Whoever lives in love   lives in God,   and God   in him.   **17** In this   way,
Ὁ   θεὸς   ἐστὶν ἀγάπη καὶ ὁ   μένων ἐν τῇ ἀγάπῃ μένει ἐν τῷ θεῷ καὶ ὁ   θεὸς   μένει ἐν αὐτῷ Ἐν τούτῳ ←
d.nsm n.nsm   v.pai.3s n.nsf cj d.nsm   pt.pa.nsm p.d d.dsf n.dsf   v.pai.3s p.d d.dsm n.dsm   cj d.nsm n.nsm   v.pai.3s p.d r.dsm.3   p.d r.dsn
3836 2536   1639 27 2779 3836   3531 1877 3836 27   3531 1877 3836 2536   2779 3836 2536   3531 1877 899   1877 4047

love   is made complete among us   so that we will have confidence on the day   of judgment, because in
ἡ   ἀγάπη → τετελείωται μεθ' ἡμῶν ἵνα →   ἔχωμεν παρρησίαν ἐν τῇ ἡμέρᾳ τῆς κρίσεως ὅτι   →
d.nsf n.nsf   v.rpi.3s r.gp.1 cj   v.pas.1p n.asf p.d d.dsf n.dsf   d.gsf n.gsf cj   p.d
3836 27   5457 3552 7005 2671   2400 4244 1877 3836 2465   3836 3213 4022   1877

this world   we   are like him.   **18** There is   no fear in love.   But perfect love   drives out
τούτῳ τῷ   κόσμῳ καὶ ἡμεῖς ἐσμεν καθὼς ἐκεῖνός ἐστιν →   ἔστιν οὐκ φόβος ἐν τῇ ἀγάπῃ ἀλλ' τελεία ἡ ἀγάπη βάλλει ἔξω
r.dsn d.dsm n.dsm adv r.np.1 v.pai.1p adv r.nsm   v.pai.3s   v.pai.3s pl n.nsm p.d d.dsf n.dsf   cj a.nsf d.nsf n.nsf v.pai.3s adv
4047 3836 3180 2779 7005 1639 2777 1697   1639   1639 4024 5832 1877 3836 27   247 5455 3836 27 965 2032

ἡμῶν. ἐκ τούτου γινώσκομεν τὸ πνεῦμα τῆς ἀληθείας καὶ τὸ πνεῦμα τῆς πλάνης.

4:7 Ἀγαπητοί, ἀγαπῶμεν ἀλλήλους, ὅτι ἡ ἀγάπη ἐκ τοῦ θεοῦ ἐστιν, καὶ πᾶς ὁ ἀγαπῶν ἐκ τοῦ θεοῦ γεγέννηται καὶ γινώσκει τὸν θεόν. **8** ὁ μὴ ἀγαπῶν οὐκ ἔγνω τὸν θεόν, ὅτι ὁ θεὸς ἀγάπη ἐστίν. **9** ἐν τούτῳ ἐφανερώθη ἡ ἀγάπη τοῦ θεοῦ ἐν ἡμῖν, ὅτι τὸν υἱὸν αὐτοῦ τὸν μονογενῆ ἀπέσταλκεν ὁ θεὸς εἰς τὸν κόσμον ἵνα ζήσωμεν δι' αὐτοῦ. **10** ἐν τούτῳ ἐστὶν ἡ ἀγάπη, οὐχ ὅτι ἡμεῖς ἠγαπήκαμεν τὸν θεὸν ἀλλ' ὅτι αὐτὸς ἠγάπησεν ἡμᾶς καὶ ἀπέστειλεν τὸν υἱὸν αὐτοῦ ἱλασμὸν περὶ τῶν ἁμαρτιῶν ἡμῶν. **11** Ἀγαπητοί, εἰ οὕτως ὁ θεὸς ἠγάπησεν ἡμᾶς, καὶ ἡμεῖς ὀφείλομεν ἀλλήλους ἀγαπᾶν. **12** θεὸν οὐδεὶς πώποτε τεθέαται. ἐὰν ἀγαπῶμεν ἀλλήλους, ὁ θεὸς ἐν ἡμῖν μένει καὶ ἡ ἀγάπη αὐτοῦ ἐν ἡμῖν τετελειωμένη ἐστιν. ¶ **13** Ἐν τούτῳ γινώσκομεν ὅτι ἐν αὐτῷ μένομεν καὶ αὐτὸς ἐν ἡμῖν, ὅτι ἐκ τοῦ πνεύματος αὐτοῦ δέδωκεν ἡμῖν. **14** καὶ ἡμεῖς τεθεάμεθα καὶ μαρτυροῦμεν ὅτι ὁ πατὴρ ἀπέσταλκεν τὸν υἱὸν σωτῆρα τοῦ κόσμου. **15** ὃς ἐὰν ὁμολογήσῃ ὅτι Ἰησοῦς ἐστιν ὁ υἱὸς τοῦ θεοῦ, ὁ θεὸς ἐν αὐτῷ μένει καὶ αὐτὸς ἐν τῷ θεῷ. **16** καὶ ἡμεῖς ἐγνώκαμεν καὶ πεπιστεύκαμεν τὴν ἀγάπην ἣν ἔχει ὁ θεὸς ἐν ἡμῖν. ¶ Ὁ θεὸς ἀγάπη ἐστίν, καὶ ὁ μένων ἐν τῇ ἀγάπῃ ἐν τῷ θεῷ μένει καὶ ὁ θεὸς ἐν αὐτῷ μένει. **17** ἐν τούτῳ τετελείωται ἡ ἀγάπη μεθ' ἡμῶν, ἵνα παρρησίαν ἔχωμεν ἐν τῇ ἡμέρᾳ τῆς κρίσεως, ὅτι καθὼς ἐκεῖνός ἐστιν καὶ ἡμεῖς ἐσμεν ἐν τῷ κόσμῳ τούτῳ. **18** φόβος οὐκ ἔστιν ἐν τῇ ἀγάπῃ ἀλλ' ἡ

fear,		because	fear		has	to do with	punishment.		The one who fears		is	not	made perfect	in
τὸν φόβον		ὅτι	ὁ	φόβος	ἔχει ← ← ←		κόλασιν	δὲ ὁ		φοβούμενος →	οὐ →		τετελείωται ἐν
d.asm n.asm		cj	d.nsm	n.nsm	v.pai.3s		n.asf	cj d.nsm		pt.pp.nsm	pl		v.rpi.3s p.d
3836 5832		4022	3836	5832	2400		3136	1254 3836		5828	5457 4024		5457 1877

love.	¶	[19] We	love	because he	first	loved	us.	[20] If	anyone	says,	"I love	God,"	yet hates
τῇ ἀγάπῃ		ἡμεῖς	ἀγαπῶμεν ὅτι	αὐτὸς	πρῶτος	ἠγάπησεν	ἡμᾶς	ἐάν	τις	εἴπῃ ὅτι →	ἀγαπῶ	τὸν θεὸν	καὶ μισῇ
d.dsf n.dsf		r.np.1	v.pai.1p	r.nsm.a	a.nsm	v.aai.3s	r.ap.1	cj	r.nsm	v.aas.3s cj	v.pai.1s	d.asm n.asm	cj v.pas.3s
3836 27		7005 26	4022	899	4755	26	7005	1569	5516	3306 4022	26	3836 2536	2779 3631

his	brother,	he is	a liar.	For	anyone who	does not	love	his	brother,	whom	he has seen,
αὐτοῦ	τὸν ἀδελφὸν	→ ἐστίν	ψεύστης γὰρ		ὁ	μὴ	ἀγαπῶν	αὐτοῦ	τὸν ἀδελφὸν	ὃν →	ἑώρακεν
r.gsm.3	d.asm n.asm	v.pai.3s	n.nsm cj		d.nsm	pl	pt.pa.nsm	r.gsm.3	d.asm n.asm	r.asm	v.rai.3s
899	3836 81	1639	6026 1142		3836 26	3590	26	899	3836 81	4005	3972

cannot	love	God,	whom	he has not seen.	[21] And	he	has given	us	this	command:	Whoever
οὐ δύναται	ἀγαπᾶν	τὸν θεὸν	ὃν →	→ οὐχ ἑώρακεν	καὶ	ἀπ' αὐτοῦ →	ἔχομεν ←		ταύτην	τὴν ἐντολὴν	ἵνα ὁ
pl v.ppi.3s	f.pa	d.asm n.asm	r.asm	pl v.rai.3s	cj	p.g r.gsm.3	v.pai.1p		r.asf	d.asf n.asf	cj d.nsm
4024 1538	26	3836 2536	4005	3972 3972 4024 3972	2779	608 899	2400		4047	3836 1953	2671 3836

loves	God	must also	love	his	brother.
ἀγαπῶν	τὸν θεὸν	καὶ ἀγαπᾷ		αὐτοῦ	τὸν ἀδελφὸν
pt.pa.nsm	d.asm n.asm	cj adv	v.pas.3s	r.gsm.3	d.asm n.asm
26	3836 2536	26 2779	26	899	3836 81

Faith in the Son of God

[5:1] Everyone	who believes	that	Jesus	is	the	Christ	is born	of	God,	and	everyone	who	loves	the
Πᾶς	ὁ πιστεύων	ὅτι	Ἰησοῦς	ἐστιν ὁ		Χριστός	→ γεγέννηται	ἐκ	τοῦ θεοῦ	καὶ	πᾶς	ὁ	ἀγαπῶν	τὸν
a.nsm	d.nsm pt.pa.nsm	cj	n.nsm	v.pai.3s d.nsm		n.nsm	v.rpi.3s	p.g	d.gsm n.gsm	cj	a.nsm	d.nsm	pt.pa.nsm	d.asm
4246	3836 4409	4022	2652	1639 3836		5986	1164	1666	3836 2536	2779	4246	3836	26	3836

father	loves	his	child	as well.	[2] This		is how	we know	that	we	love	the children	of
γεννήσαντα	ἀγαπᾷ	ἐξ αὐτοῦ	τὸν γεγεννημένον	καὶ ←		ἐν τούτῳ ←		γινώσκομεν ὅτι		→	ἀγαπῶμεν	τὰ τέκνα	→
pt.aa.asm	v.pai.3s	p.g r.gsm.3	d.asm pt.rp.asm	adv		p.d r.dsn		v.pai.1p	cj		v.pai.1p	d.apn n.apn	
1164	26	1666 899	3836 1164	2779		1877 4047		1182	4022		26	3836 5451	

God:	by	loving	God	and	carrying out	his	commands.	[3] This	is	love	for God:	to obey
τοῦ θεοῦ	ὅταν	ἀγαπῶμεν	τὸν θεὸν	καὶ	ποιῶμεν ←	αὐτοῦ	τὰς ἐντολὰς	γὰρ αὕτη	ἐστιν	ἡ ἀγάπη	τοῦ θεοῦ	ἵνα τηρῶμεν
d.gsm n.gsm	cj	v.pas.1p	d.asm n.asm	cj	v.pas.1p	r.gsm.3	d.apf n.apf	cj r.nsf	v.pai.3s	d.nsf n.nsf	d.gsm n.gsm	cj v.pas.1p
3836 2536	4020	26	3836 2536	2779	4472	899	3836 1953	1142 4047	1639	3836 27	3836 2536	2671 5498

his	commands.	And	his	commands	are	not	burdensome,	[4] for	everyone	born		of	God	overcomes
αὐτοῦ	τὰς ἐντολὰς	καὶ	αὐτοῦ	αἱ ἐντολαὶ	εἰσίν	οὐκ	βαρεῖαι	ὅτι	πᾶν	τὸ γεγεννημένον		ἐκ	τοῦ θεοῦ	νικᾷ
r.gsm.3	d.apf n.apf	cj	r.gsm.3	d.npf n.npf	v.pai.3p	pl	a.npf	cj	a.nsn	d.nsn pt.rp.nsn		p.g	d.gsm n.gsm	v.pai.3s
899	3836 1953	2779	899	3836 1953	1639	4024	987	4022	4246	3836 1164		1666	3836 2536	3771

the world.		This is		the victory	that has	overcome	the world,	even	our	faith.	[5]	Who is	it	that
τὸν κόσμον	καὶ	αὕτη ἐστιν	ἡ	νίκη	ἡ →	νικήσασα	τὸν κόσμον		ἡμῶν	ἡ πίστις	[δέ]	Τίς	ἐστιν ὁ	←
d.asm n.asm	cj	r.nsf v.pai.3s	d.nsf	n.nsf	d.nsf	pt.aa.nsf	d.asm n.asm		r.gp.1	d.nsf n.nsf	cj	r.nsm	v.pai.3s d.nsm
3836 3180	2779	4047 1639	3836	3772	3836	3771	3836 3180		7005	3836 4411	1254	5515	1639 3836

overcomes	the world?	Only	he who	believes	that	Jesus	is	the	Son	of God.	¶	[6] This is		the one who
νικῶν	τὸν κόσμον	εἰ μὴ	ὁ	πιστεύων	ὅτι	Ἰησοῦς	ἐστιν ὁ		υἱὸς	τοῦ θεοῦ		οὗτός	ἐστιν ὁ	←
pt.pa.nsm	d.asm n.asm	cj pl	d.nsm	pt.pa.nsm	cj	n.nsm	v.pai.3s d.nsm		n.nsm	d.gsm n.gsm		r.nsm	v.pai.3s d.nsm
3771	3836 3180	1623 3590	3836	4409	4022	2652	1639 3836		5626	3836 2536		4047	1639 3836

came by	water	and	blood	– Jesus	Christ.	He did	not	come	by	water	only,	but	by	water	and		blood.
ἐλθὼν	δι' ὕδατος	καὶ	αἵματος	Ἰησοῦς	Χριστός		οὐκ		ἐν	τῷ ὕδατι	μόνον	ἀλλ'	ἐν	τῷ ὕδατι	καὶ	ἐν	τῷ αἵματι
pt.aa.nsm	p.g n.gsn	cj	n.gsn	n.nsm	n.nsm		pl		p.d	d.dsn n.dsn	adv	cj	p.d	d.dsn n.dsn	cj	p.d	d.dsn n.dsn
2262	1328 5623	2779	135	2652	5986		4024		1877	3836 5623	3667	247	1877	3836 5623	2779	1877	3836 135

And	it is	the	Spirit	who	testifies,	because	the	Spirit	is	the	truth.	[7] For	there are	three	that	testify:	[8] the
καὶ	→ ἐστιν	τὸ	πνεῦμα	τὸ	μαρτυροῦν	ὅτι	τὸ	πνεῦμα	ἐστιν	ἡ	ἀλήθεια	ὅτι		εἰσιν	τρεῖς	οἱ μαρτυροῦντες	τὸ
cj	v.pai.3s	d.nsn	n.nsn	d.nsn	pt.pa.nsn	cj	d.nsn	n.nsn	v.pai.3s	d.nsf	n.nsf	cj		v.pai.3p	a.npm	d.npm pt.pa.npm	d.nsn
2779	1639	3836	4460	3836	3455	4022	3836	4460	1639	3836	237	4022		1639	5552	3836 3455	3836

Spirit,	the water	and the	blood;	and the	three	are	in	agreement.	[9]	We accept	man's		testimony,
πνεῦμα	καὶ τὸ ὕδωρ	καὶ τὸ	αἷμα	καὶ οἱ	τρεῖς	εἰσιν	→ εἰς τὸ ἕν		εἰ	→ λαμβάνομεν	τῶν ἀνθρώπων		τὴν μαρτυρίαν
n.nsn	cj d.nsn n.nsn	cj d.nsn	n.nsn	cj d.npm	a.npm	v.pai.3p	p.a d.asn a.asn		cj	v.pai.1p	d.gpm n.gpm		d.asf n.asf
4460	2779 3836 5623	2779 3836	135	2779 3836	5552	1639	1650 3836 1651		1623	3284	3836 476		3836 3456

τελεία ἀγάπη ἔξω βάλλει τὸν φόβον, ὅτι ὁ φόβος κόλασιν ἔχει, ὁ δὲ φοβούμενος οὐ τετελείωται ἐν τῇ ἀγάπῃ. ¶ [19] ἡμεῖς ἀγαπῶμεν, ὅτι αὐτὸς πρῶτος ἠγάπησεν ἡμᾶς. [20] ἐάν τις εἴπῃ ὅτι Ἀγαπῶ τὸν θεὸν καὶ τὸν ἀδελφὸν αὐτοῦ μισῇ, ψεύστης ἐστίν· ὁ γὰρ μὴ ἀγαπῶν τὸν ἀδελφὸν αὐτοῦ ὃν ἑώρακεν, τὸν θεὸν ὃν οὐχ ἑώρακεν οὐ δύναται ἀγαπᾶν. [21] καὶ ταύτην τὴν ἐντολὴν ἔχομεν ἀπ' αὐτοῦ, ἵνα ὁ ἀγαπῶν τὸν θεὸν ἀγαπᾷ καὶ τὸν ἀδελφὸν αὐτοῦ.

[5:1] Πᾶς ὁ πιστεύων ὅτι Ἰησοῦς ἐστιν ὁ Χριστός, ἐκ τοῦ θεοῦ γεγέννηται, καὶ πᾶς ὁ ἀγαπῶν τὸν γεννήσαντα ἀγαπᾷ [καὶ] τὸν γεγεννημένον ἐξ αὐτοῦ. [2] ἐν τούτῳ γινώσκομεν ὅτι ἀγαπῶμεν τὰ τέκνα τοῦ θεοῦ, ὅταν τὸν θεὸν ἀγαπῶμεν καὶ τὰς ἐντολὰς αὐτοῦ ποιῶμεν. [3] αὕτη γάρ ἐστιν ἡ ἀγάπη τοῦ θεοῦ, ἵνα τὰς ἐντολὰς αὐτοῦ τηρῶμεν, καὶ αἱ ἐντολαὶ αὐτοῦ βαρεῖαι οὐκ εἰσίν. [4] ὅτι πᾶν τὸ γεγεννημένον ἐκ τοῦ θεοῦ νικᾷ τὸν κόσμον· καὶ αὕτη ἐστὶν ἡ νίκη ἡ νικήσασα τὸν κόσμον, ἡ πίστις ἡμῶν. [5] τίς [δέ] ἐστιν ὁ νικῶν τὸν κόσμον εἰ μὴ ὁ πιστεύων ὅτι Ἰησοῦς ἐστιν ὁ υἱὸς τοῦ θεοῦ; ¶ [6] Οὗτός ἐστιν ὁ ἐλθὼν δι' ὕδατος καὶ αἵματος, Ἰησοῦς Χριστός, οὐκ ἐν τῷ ὕδατι μόνον ἀλλ' ἐν τῷ ὕδατι καὶ ἐν τῷ αἵματι· καὶ τὸ πνεῦμά ἐστιν τὸ μαρτυροῦν, ὅτι τὸ πνεῦμά ἐστιν ἡ ἀλήθεια. [7] ὅτι τρεῖς εἰσιν οἱ μαρτυροῦντες, [8] τὸ πνεῦμα καὶ τὸ ὕδωρ καὶ τὸ αἷμα, καὶ οἱ τρεῖς εἰς τὸ ἕν

but	God's	testimony	is	greater	because	it	is	the	testimony	of God,	which	he has given	about
	⸤τοῦ θεοῦ⸥	ἡ μαρτυρία	ἐστίν	μείζων	ὅτι	αὕτη	ἐστὶν	ἡ	μαρτυρία	→ ⸤τοῦ θεοῦ⸥	ὅτι	→ μεμαρτύρηκεν	περὶ
	d.gsm n.gsm	d.nsf n.nsf	v.pai.3s	a.nsf.c	cj	r.nsf	v.pai.3s	d.nsf	n.nsf	d.gsm n.gsm	cj	v.rai.3s	p.g
	3836 2536	3836 3456	1639	3489	4022	4047	1639	3836	3456	3836 2536	4022	3455	4309

his	Son.	**10** Anyone who	believes	in	the	Son	of God	has	this	testimony	in	his	heart.	Anyone	who	does	not
αὐτοῦ	⸤τοῦ υἱοῦ⸥	→ ὁ	πιστεύων	εἰς	τὸν	υἱὸν	⸤τοῦ θεοῦ⸥	ἔχει	τὴν	μαρτυρίαν	ἐν	ἑαυτῷ←	→	→ ὁ	→	μὴ
r.gsm.3	d.gsm n.gsm	d.nsm	pt.pa.nsm	p.a	d.asm	n.asm	d.gsm n.gsm	v.pai.3s	d.asf	n.asf	p.d	r.dsm.3		d.nsm		pl
899	3836 5626	3836	4409	1650	3836	5626	3836 2536	2400	3836	3456	1877	1571		3836	4409	3590

believe	God	has made	him	out to be	a liar,	because	he has	not	believed	the	testimony	God
πιστεύων	⸤τῷ θεῷ⸥	→ πεποίηκεν	αὐτόν	←	ψεύστην	ὅτι	→ →	οὐ	πεπίστευκεν	εἰς τὴν	μαρτυρίαν	ἣν ὁ θεὸς
pt.pa.nsm	d.dsm n.dsm	v.rai.3s	r.asm.3		n.asm	cj		pl	v.rai.3s	p.a d.asf	n.asf	r.asf d.nsm n.nsm
4409	3836 2536	4472	899	4472 4472 4472	6026	4022	4409 4409	4024	4409	1650 3836	3456	4005 3836 2536

has given	about	his	Son.	**11** And	this	is	the	testimony:	God	has given	us	eternal	life,	and	this
→ μεμαρτύρηκεν	περὶ	αὐτοῦ	⸤τοῦ υἱοῦ⸥	Καὶ	αὕτη	ἐστιν	ἡ	μαρτυρία	ὅτι	⸤ὁ θεός⸥	→ ἔδωκεν	ἡμῖν	αἰώνιον	ζωὴν	καὶ	αὕτη
v.rai.3s	p.g	r.gsm.3	d.gsm n.gsm	cj	r.nsf	v.pai.3s	d.nsf	n.nsf	cj	d.nsm n.nsm	v.aai.3s	r.dp.1	a.asf	n.asf	cj	r.nsf
3455	4309	899	3836 5626	2779	4047	1639	3836	3456	4022	3836 2536	1443	7005	173	2437	2779	4047

life	is	in	his	Son.	**12** He who	has	the	Son	has	life;	he	who	does	not	have	the	Son	of God	does
⸤ἡ ζωὴ⸥	ἐστὶν	ἐν	αὐτῷ	⸤τῷ υἱῷ⸥	→ ὁ	ἔχων	τὸν	υἱὸν	ἔχει	⸤τὴν ζωήν⸥	ὁ		→	μὴ	ἔχων	τὸν	υἱὸν	⸤τοῦ θεοῦ⸥	→
d.nsf n.nsf	v.pai.3s	p.d	r.gsm.3	d.dsm n.dsm	d.nsm	pt.pa.nsm	d.asm	n.asm	v.pai.3s	d.asf n.asf	d.nsm			pl	pt.pa.nsm	d.asm	n.asm	d.gsm n.gsm	
3836 2437	1639	1877	899	3836 5626	3836	2400	3836	5626	2400	3836 2437	3836		2400	3590	2400	3836	5626	3836 2536	2400

not	have	life.
οὐκ	ἔχει	⸤τὴν ζωήν⸥
pl	v.pai.3s	d.asf n.asf
4024	2400	3836 2437

Concluding Remarks

5:13 I	write	these things	to you	who	believe	in	the	name	of the	Son	of God	so that	you may	know	that
→ ἔγραψα		Ταῦτα←	→ ὑμῖν	τοῖς	πιστεύουσιν	εἰς	τὸ	ὄνομα	→ τοῦ	υἱοῦ	→ ⸤τοῦ θεοῦ⸥	ἵνα ←	→	εἰδῆτε	ὅτι
v.aai.1s		r.apn	r.dp.2	d.dpm	pt.pa.dpm	p.a	d.asn	n.asn	d.gsm	n.gsm	d.gsm n.gsm	cj		v.ras.2p	cj
1211		4047	7007	3836	4409	1650	3836	3950	3836	5626	3836 2536	2671		3857	4022

you have	eternal	life.	**14**	This	is	the	confidence	we have	in	approaching	God:	that	if	we	ask
→ ἔχετε	αἰώνιον	ζωήν		Καὶ	αὕτη	ἐστὶν	ἡ	παρρησία	ἣν	→ ἔχομεν	πρὸς	αὐτὸν	ὅτι	ἐὰν	αἰτώμεθα
v.pai.2p	a.asf	n.asf		cj	r.nsf	v.pai.3s	d.nsf	n.nsf	r.asf	v.pai.1p	p.a	r.asm.3	cj	cj	v.pms.1p
2400	173	2437		2779	4047	1639	3836	4244	4005	2400	4639	899	4022	1569	160

anything	according to	his	will,	he hears	us.	¶	**15** And	if	we know	that	he hears	us	— whatever	we
τι	κατὰ	← αὐτοῦ	⸤τὸ θέλημα⸥	→ ἀκούει	ἡμῶν		καὶ	ἐὰν	→ οἴδαμεν	ὅτι	→ ἀκούει	ἡμῶν	⸤ὃ ἐὰν⸥	→
r.asn	p.a	r.gsm.3	d.asn n.asn	v.pai.3s	r.gp.1		cj	cj	v.rai.1p	cj	v.pai.3s	r.gp.1	r.asn pl	
5516	2848	899	3836 2525	201	7005		2779	1569	3857	4022	201	7005	4005 1569	

ask	— we	know	that	we have	what	we	asked	of him.	**16** If	anyone	sees	his	brother
αἰτώμεθα	→	οἴδαμεν	ὅτι	→ ἔχομεν	τὰ	αἰτήματα	ἃ	ἠτήκαμεν ἀπʼ	αὐτοῦ	Ἐάν	τις	ἴδῃ	αὐτοῦ ⸤τὸν ἀδελφὸν⸥
v.pms.1p		v.rai.1p	cj	v.pai.1p	d.apn	n.apn	r.apn	v.rai.1p	p.g r.gsm.3	cj	r.nsm	v.aas.3s	r.gsm.3 d.asm n.asm
160		3857	4022	2400	3836	161	4005	160	608 899	1569	5516	1625	899 3836 81

commit	a sin	that does	not	lead	to	death,	he should pray	and	God will	give	him	life.	I refer	to those
ἁμαρτάνοντα	ἁμαρτίαν	→	μὴ	→ πρὸς	θάνατον	→ →	αἰτήσει	καὶ	→	δώσει	αὐτῷ	ζωήν	→	τοῖς
pt.pa.asm	n.asf		pl	p.a	n.asm		v.fai.3s	cj		v.fai.3s	r.dsm.3	n.asf		d.dpm
279	281		3590	4639	2505		160	2779		1443	899	2437		3836

whose	sin	does	not	lead	to	death.	There is	a	sin	that leads	to	death.	I	am	not	saying	that	he
←	ἁμαρτάνουσιν	μὴ	→ πρὸς	θάνατον	→	ἔστιν	ἁμαρτία	→	πρὸς	θάνατον	← →	→	οὐ	λέγω	ἵνα	→
pt.pa.dpm	pl		p.a	n.asm		v.pai.3s	n.nsf		p.a	n.asm			pl	v.pai.1s	cj	
279	3590		4639	2505		1639	281		4639	2505	3306 3306	4024	3306	2671

should pray	about	that.	**17** All	wrongdoing	is	sin,	and	there is	sin	that does	not	lead	to	death.	¶
→ ἐρωτήσῃ	περὶ	ἐκείνης	πᾶσα	ἀδικία	ἐστὶν	ἁμαρτία	καὶ	→ ἔστιν	ἁμαρτία	→	οὐ	→ πρὸς	θάνατον
v.aas.3s	p.g	r.gsf	a.nsf	n.nsf	v.pai.3s	n.nsf	cj	v.pai.3s	n.nsf		pl	p.a	n.asm
2263	4309	1697	4246	94	1639	281	2779	1639	281		4024	4639	2505

18 We	know	that	anyone	born	of	God	does	not	continue to sin;	the one who	was born
→ Οἴδαμεν	ὅτι	πᾶς	ὁ	γεγεννημένος	ἐκ	⸤τοῦ θεοῦ⸥	→	οὐχ	→ ἁμαρτάνει	ἀλλʼ ὁ	← → → γεννηθεὶς
v.rai.1p	cj	a.nsm	d.nsm	pt.rp.nsm	p.g	d.gsm n.gsm		pl	v.pai.3s	cj d.nsm	pt.ap.nsm
3857	4022	4246	3836	1164	1666	3836 2536	279	4024	279	247 3836	1164

εἰσίν. **9** εἰ τὴν μαρτυρίαν τῶν ἀνθρώπων λαμβάνομεν, ἡ μαρτυρία τοῦ θεοῦ μείζων ἐστίν· ὅτι αὕτη ἐστὶν ἡ μαρτυρία τοῦ θεοῦ ὅτι μεμαρτύρηκεν περὶ τοῦ υἱοῦ αὐτοῦ. **10** ὁ πιστεύων εἰς τὸν υἱὸν τοῦ θεοῦ ἔχει τὴν μαρτυρίαν ἐν ἑαυτῷ, ὁ μὴ πιστεύων τῷ θεῷ ψεύστην πεποίηκεν αὐτόν, ὅτι οὐ πεπίστευκεν εἰς τὴν μαρτυρίαν ἣν μεμαρτύρηκεν ὁ θεὸς περὶ τοῦ υἱοῦ αὐτοῦ. **11** καὶ αὕτη ἐστὶν ἡ μαρτυρία, ὅτι ζωὴν αἰώνιον ἔδωκεν ἡμῖν ὁ θεός, καὶ αὕτη ἡ ζωὴ ἐν τῷ υἱῷ αὐτοῦ ἐστιν. **12** ὁ ἔχων τὸν υἱὸν ἔχει τὴν ζωήν· ὁ μὴ ἔχων τὸν υἱὸν τοῦ θεοῦ τὴν ζωὴν οὐκ ἔχει.

5:13 Ταῦτα ἔγραψα ὑμῖν ἵνα εἰδῆτε ὅτι ζωὴν ἔχετε αἰώνιον, τοῖς πιστεύουσιν εἰς τὸ ὄνομα τοῦ υἱοῦ τοῦ θεοῦ. **14** καὶ αὕτη ἐστὶν ἡ παρρησία ἣν ἔχομεν πρὸς αὐτὸν ὅτι ἐάν τι αἰτώμεθα κατὰ τὸ θέλημα αὐτοῦ ἀκούει ἡμῶν. ¶ **15** καὶ ἐὰν οἴδαμεν ὅτι ἀκούει ἡμῶν ὃ ἐὰν αἰτώμεθα, οἴδαμεν ὅτι ἔχομεν τὰ αἰτήματα ἃ ᾐτήκαμεν ἀπʼ αὐτοῦ. **16** Ἐάν τις ἴδῃ τὸν ἀδελφὸν αὐτοῦ ἁμαρτάνοντα ἁμαρτίαν μὴ πρὸς θάνατον, αἰτήσει καὶ δώσει αὐτῷ ζωήν, τοῖς ἁμαρτάνουσιν μὴ πρὸς θάνατον. ἔστιν ἁμαρτία πρὸς θάνατον· οὐ περὶ ἐκείνης λέγω ἵνα ἐρωτήσῃ. **17** πᾶσα ἀδικία ἁμαρτία ἐστίν, καὶ ἔστιν ἁμαρτία οὐ πρὸς θάνατον. ¶ **18** Οἴδαμεν ὅτι πᾶς ὁ γεγεννημένος ἐκ τοῦ θεοῦ οὐχ ἁμαρτάνει, ἀλλʼ ὁ γεννηθεὶς ἐκ τοῦ θεοῦ τηρεῖ αὐτὸν καὶ ὁ πονηρὸς οὐχ ἅπτεται αὐτοῦ.

of God   keeps him safe, and the evil   one cannot harm   him. **19** We know that we are children of God,
ἐκ ⸤τοῦ θεοῦ⸥ τηρεῖ αὐτόν ←   καὶ ὁ   πονηρὸς ←   οὐχ ἅπτεται αὐτοῦ   →   οἴδαμεν ὅτι → ἐσμεν   ἐκ ⸤τοῦ θεοῦ⸥
p.g d.gsm n.gsm v.pai.3s r.asm.3   cj   d.nsm a.nsm   pl   v.pmi.3s r.gsm.3   v.rai.1p cj   v.pai.1p   p.g d.gsm n.gsm
1666 3836 2536   5498   899   5498 2779 3836 4505   4024 721   899   3857   4022   1639   1666 3836 2536

and that the whole world is under the control of the evil   one. **20** We know also that the Son of God   has
καὶ   ὁ   ὅλος κόσμος → κεῖται ←   ←   ἐν τῷ πονηρῷ ←   οἴδαμεν δὲ ὅτι ὁ υἱὸς → ⸤τοῦ θεοῦ⸥ →
cj   d.nsm a.nsm n.nsm   v.pmi.3s   p.d d.dsm a.dsm   v.rai.1p 1254 cj   d.nsm n.nsm   d.gsm n.gsm
2779   3836 3910   3180   3023   1877 3836 4505   3857 1254 4022 3836 5626   3836 2536

come and has given us understanding, so that we may know   him who is true.   And we are in him who
ἥκει καὶ → δέδωκεν ἡμῖν διάνοιαν   ἵνα ←   → γινώσκωμεν τὸν   →   ἀληθινόν καὶ → ἐσμὲν ἐν τῷ   ←
v.rai.3s cj   v.rai.3s r.dp.1 n.asf   cj   v.pas.1p   d.asm   a.asm   cj   v.pai.1p p.d d.dsm
2457 2779 1443   7005 1379   2671   1182   3836   240   2779   1639 1877 3836

is true — even in his Son   Jesus Christ. He is the true   God and eternal life. **21** Dear children, keep
→ ἀληθινῷ   ἐν αὐτοῦ ⸤τῷ υἱῷ⸥ Ἰησοῦ Χριστῷ οὗτος ἐστιν ὁ ἀληθινὸς θεὸς καὶ αἰώνιος ζωὴ   →   Τεκνία   φυλάξατε
→ a.dsm   p.d r.gsm.3 d.dsm n.dsm n.dsm n.dsm   r.nsm v.pai.3s d.nsm a.nsm   n.nsm cj   a.nsf n.nsf   n.vpn   v.aam.2p
240   1877 899   3836 5626 2652   5986   4047 1639 3836 240   2536 2779 173   2437   5448   5875

yourselves from idols.
ἑαυτὰ   ἀπὸ ⸤τῶν εἰδώλων⸥
r.apn.2   p.g d.gpn n.gpn
1571   608 3836 1631

2 John

1:1 The elder, ¶ To the chosen lady and her children, whom I love in the truth – and not
Ὁ πρεσβύτερος ἐκλεκτῇ κυρίᾳ καὶ αὐτῆς τοῖς τέκνοις, οὓς ἐγὼ ἀγαπῶ ἐν ἀληθείᾳ καὶ οὐκ
d.nsm a.nsm / a.dsf n.dsf cj r.gsf.3 d.dpn n.dpn / r.apm r.ns.1 v.pai.1s p.d n.dsf cj pl
3836 4565 / 1723 3257 2779 899 3836 5451 / 4005 1609 26 1877 237 2779 4024

I only, but also all who know the truth – **2** because of the truth, which lives in us and will be
ἐγὼ μόνος ἀλλὰ καὶ πάντες οἱ ἐγνωκότες τὴν ἀλήθειαν διὰ τὴν ἀλήθειαν τὴν μένουσαν ἐν ἡμῖν καὶ ἔσται
r.ns.1 a.nsm cj adv a.npm d.npm pt.ra.npm d.asf n.asf p.a d.asf n.asf d.asf pt.pa.asf p.d r.dp.1 cj v.fmi.3s
1609 3668 247 2779 4246 3836 1182 3836 237 1328 3836 237 3836 3531 1877 7005 2779 1639

with us forever: ¶ **3** Grace, mercy and peace from God the Father and from Jesus Christ, the
μεθ' ἡμῶν εἰς τὸν αἰῶνα χάρις ἔλεος εἰρήνη παρὰ θεοῦ πατρὸς καὶ παρὰ Ἰησοῦ Χριστοῦ τοῦ
p.g r.gp.1 p.a d.asm n.asm n.nsf n.nsn n.nsf p.a n.gsm n.gsm cj p.a n.gsm n.gsm d.gsm
3552 7005 1650 3836 172 5921 1799 1645 4123 2536 4252 2779 4123 2652 5986 3836

Father's Son, will be with us in truth and love. ¶ **4** It has given me great joy to find some
τοῦ πατρὸς υἱοῦ ἔσται μεθ' ἡμῶν ἐν ἀληθείᾳ καὶ ἀγάπῃ λίαν Ἐχάρην ὅτι εὕρηκα
d.gsm n.gsm n.gsm v.fmi.3s p.g r.gp.1 p.d n.dsf cj n.dsf adv v.api.1s cj v.rai.1s
3836 4252 5626 1639 3552 7005 1877 237 2779 27 5897 5897 5897 5897 3336 5897 4022 2351

of your children walking in the truth, just as the Father commanded us. **5** And now, dear lady,
ἐκ σου τῶν τέκνων περιπατοῦντας ἐν ἀληθείᾳ καθὼς παρὰ τοῦ πατρὸς ἐντολὴν ἐλάβομεν καὶ νῦν κυρία
p.g r.gs.2 d.gpn n.gpn pt.pa.apm p.d n.dsf cj p.g d.gsm n.gsm n.asf v.aai.1p cj adv n.vsf
1666 5148 3836 5451 4344 1877 237 2777 4123 3836 4252 1953 3284 2779 3814 3257

I am not writing you a new command but one we have had from the beginning. I ask that we
οὐχ γράφων σοι ὡς καινὴν ἐντολὴν ἀλλὰ ἣν εἴχομεν ἀπ' ἀρχῆς ἐρωτῶ σε ἵνα
pl pt.pa.nsm r.ds.2 pl a.asf n.asf cj r.asf v.iai.1p p.g n.gsf v.pai.1s r.as.2 cj
1211 1211 4024 1211 5148 6055 2785 1953 247 4005 2400 608 794 2263 5148 2671

love one another. **6** And this is love: that we walk in obedience to his commands.
ἀγαπῶμεν ἀλλήλους καὶ αὕτη ἐστὶν ἡ ἀγάπη ἵνα περιπατῶμεν κατὰ αὐτοῦ τὰς ἐντολὰς αὕτη ἡ
v.pas.1p r.apm cj r.nsf v.pai.3s d.nsf n.nsf cj v.pas.1p p.a r.gsm.3 d.apf n.apf r.nsf d.nsf
26 253 2779 4047 1639 3836 27 2671 4344 2848 899 3836 1953 4047 3836

As you have heard from the beginning, his command is that you walk in love. ¶ **7**
ἐντολή ἐστιν καθὼς ἠκούσατε ἀπ' ἀρχῆς ἵνα περιπατῆτε ἐν αὐτῇ Ὅτι
n.nsf v.pai.3s cj v.aai.2p p.g n.gsf cj v.pas.2p p.d r.dsf.3 cj
1953 1639 2777 201 608 794 2671 4344 1877 899 4022

Many deceivers, who do not acknowledge Jesus Christ as coming in the flesh, have gone out into the world.
πολλοὶ πλάνοι οἱ μὴ ὁμολογοῦντες Ἰησοῦν Χριστὸν ἐρχόμενον ἐν σαρκί ἐξῆλθον εἰς τὸν κόσμον
a.npm n.npm d.npm pl pt.pa.npm n.asm n.asm pt.pm.asm p.d n.dsf v.aai.3p p.a d.asm n.asm
4498 4418 3836 3933 3590 3933 2652 5986 2262 1877 4922 2002 1650 3836 3180

Any such person is the deceiver and the antichrist. **8** Watch out that you do not lose what you have
οὗτος ἐστιν ὁ πλάνος καὶ ὁ ἀντίχριστος βλέπετε ἑαυτοὺς ἵνα μὴ ἀπολέσητε ἃ
r.nsm v.pai.3s d.nsm n.nsm cj d.nsm n.nsm v.pam.2p r.apm.2 cj pl v.aas.2p r.apn
4047 1639 3836 4418 2779 3836 532 1063 1571 2671 660 660 3590 660 4005

worked for, but that you may be rewarded fully. **9** Anyone who runs ahead and does not continue in
εἰργασάμεθα ἀλλὰ ἀπολάβητε μισθὸν πλήρη Πᾶς ὁ προάγων καὶ μὴ μένων ἐν
v.ami.1p cj v.aas.2p n.asm a.asm a.nsm d.nsm pt.pa.nsm cj pl pt.pa.nsm p.d
2237 247 655 3635 4441 4246 3836 4575 2779 3531 3590 3531 1877

the teaching of Christ does not have God; whoever continues in the teaching has both the Father and
τῇ διδαχῇ τοῦ Χριστοῦ οὐκ ἔχει θεὸν ὁ μένων ἐν τῇ διδαχῇ οὗτος ἔχει καὶ τὸν πατέρα καὶ
d.dsf n.dsf d.gsm n.gsm pl v.pai.3s n.asm d.nsm pt.pa.nsm p.d d.dsf n.dsf r.nsm v.pai.3s cj d.asm n.asm cj
3836 1439 3836 5986 4024 2400 2536 3836 3531 1877 3836 1439 4047 2400 2779 3836 4252 2779

the Son. **10** If anyone comes to you and does not bring this teaching, do not take him into your house or
τὸν υἱὸν εἰ τις ἔρχεται πρὸς ὑμᾶς καὶ οὐ φέρει ταύτην τὴν διδαχὴν μὴ λαμβάνετε αὐτὸν εἰς οἰκίαν καὶ
d.asm n.asm cj r.nsm v.pmi.3s p.a r.ap.2 cj pl v.pai.3s r.asf d.asf n.asf pl v.pam.2p r.asm.3 p.a n.asf cj
3836 5626 1623 5516 2262 4639 7007 2779 4024 5770 4047 3836 1439 3590 3284 899 1650 3864 2779

1:1 Ὁ πρεσβύτερος ¶ ἐκλεκτῇ κυρίᾳ καὶ τοῖς τέκνοις αὐτῆς, οὓς ἐγὼ ἀγαπῶ ἐν ἀληθείᾳ, καὶ οὐκ ἐγὼ μόνος ἀλλὰ καὶ πάντες οἱ ἐγνωκότες τὴν ἀλήθειαν, **2** διὰ τὴν ἀλήθειαν τὴν μένουσαν ἐν ἡμῖν καὶ μεθ' ἡμῶν ἔσται εἰς τὸν αἰῶνα. ¶ **3** ἔσται μεθ' ἡμῶν χάρις ἔλεος εἰρήνη παρὰ θεοῦ πατρὸς καὶ παρὰ Ἰησοῦ Χριστοῦ τοῦ υἱοῦ τοῦ πατρὸς ἐν ἀληθείᾳ καὶ ἀγάπῃ. ¶ **4** Ἐχάρην λίαν ὅτι εὕρηκα ἐκ τῶν τέκνων σου περιπατοῦντας ἐν ἀληθείᾳ, καθὼς ἐντολὴν ἐλάβομεν παρὰ τοῦ πατρός. **5** καὶ νῦν ἐρωτῶ σε, κυρία, οὐχ ὡς ἐντολὴν καινὴν γράφων σοι ἀλλὰ ἣν εἴχομεν ἀπ' ἀρχῆς, ἵνα ἀγαπῶμεν ἀλλήλους. **6** καὶ αὕτη ἐστὶν ἡ ἀγάπη, ἵνα περιπατῶμεν κατὰ τὰς ἐντολὰς αὐτοῦ· αὕτη ἡ ἐντολή ἐστιν, καθὼς ἠκούσατε ἀπ' ἀρχῆς, ἵνα ἐν αὐτῇ περιπατῆτε. ¶ **7** ὅτι πολλοὶ πλάνοι ἐξῆλθον εἰς τὸν κόσμον, οἱ μὴ ὁμολογοῦντες Ἰησοῦν Χριστὸν ἐρχόμενον ἐν σαρκί· οὗτός ἐστιν ὁ πλάνος καὶ ὁ ἀντίχριστος. **8** βλέπετε ἑαυτούς, ἵνα μὴ ἀπολέσητε ἃ εἰργάσασθε «εἰργασάμεθα» ἀλλὰ μισθὸν πλήρη ἀπολάβητε. **9** πᾶς ὁ προάγων καὶ μὴ μένων ἐν τῇ διδαχῇ τοῦ Χριστοῦ θεὸν οὐκ ἔχει· ὁ μένων ἐν τῇ διδαχῇ, οὗτος καὶ τὸν πατέρα καὶ τὸν υἱὸν ἔχει. **10** εἴ τις ἔρχεται πρὸς ὑμᾶς καὶ ταύτην τὴν διδαχὴν οὐ φέρει, μὴ λαμβάνετε αὐτὸν εἰς οἰκίαν καὶ

welcome			him.	**11**	Anyone	who	welcomes			him	shares	in	his		wicked		work.	¶	**12** I	have
μὴ	χαίρειν	λέγετε	αὐτῷ	γὰρ	ὁ	←	λέγων χαίρειν			αὐτῷ	κοινωνεῖ	→	αὐτοῦ	τοῖς	πονηροῖς	τοῖς ἔργοις			→ ἔχων
pl	f.pa	v.pam.2p	r.dsm.3	cj	d.nsm		pt.pa.nsm f.pa			r.dsm.3	v.pai.3s		r.gsm.3	d.dpn	a.dpn	d.dpn n.dpn			pt.pa.nsm
3590	5897	899	899	1142	3836		3306 5897			899	3125		899	3836	4505	3836 2240			2400

much	to write		to you,	but	I	do	not	want		to use	paper	and	ink.	Instead,	I hope	to visit		you	and
Πολλὰ	→ γράφειν	→	ὑμῖν	→	→	οὐκ	ἐβουλήθην	διὰ	←	χάρτου	καὶ	μέλανος	ἀλλὰ	→ ἐλπίζω	γενέσθαι	πρὸς	ὑμᾶς	καὶ
a.apn	f.pa		r.dp.2			pl	v.api.1s	p.g		n.gsm	cj	a.gsn	cj	v.pai.1s	f.am	p.a	r.ap.2	cj
4498	1211		7007	1089	1089	4024	1089	1328		5925	2779	3506	247	1827	1181	4639	7007	2779

talk		with you	face	to	face,	so that		our	joy		may be complete.		¶	**13** The	children	of	your
λαλῆσαι		στόμα	πρὸς	στόμα	ἵνα	←	ἡμῶν	ἡ	χαρὰ		→ πεπληρωμένη ᾖ			τὰ	τέκνα	→	σου
f.aa		n.asn	p.a	n.asn	cj		r.gp.1	d.nsf	n.nsf		pt.rp.nsf	v.pas.3s		d.npn	n.npn		r.gs.2
3281		5125	4639	5125	2671		7005	3836	5915		4444	1639		3836	5451	80	5148

chosen	sister		send their greetings.		
τῆς ἐκλεκτῆς	τῆς ἀδελφῆς	→	Ἀσπάζεται σε		
d.gsf a.gsf	d.gsf n.gsf		v.pmi.3s	r.as.2	
3836 1723	3836 80	832	832	5148	

χαίρειν αὐτῷ μὴ λέγετε· ¹¹ ὁ λέγων γὰρ αὐτῷ χαίρειν κοινωνεῖ τοῖς ἔργοις αὐτοῦ τοῖς πονηροῖς. ¶ ¹² Πολλὰ ἔχων ὑμῖν γράφειν οὐκ ἐβουλήθην διὰ χάρτου καὶ μέλανος, ἀλλὰ ἐλπίζω γενέσθαι πρὸς ὑμᾶς καὶ στόμα πρὸς στόμα λαλῆσαι, ἵνα ἡ χαρὰ ἡμῶν πεπληρωμένη ᾖ. ¶ ¹³ Ἀσπάζεταί σε τὰ τέκνα τῆς ἀδελφῆς σου τῆς ἐκλεκτῆς.

3 John

1:1 The elder, ¶ To my dear friend Gaius, whom I love in the truth. ¶ **2** Dear friend, I pray that you may enjoy good health and that all may go well with you, even as your soul is getting along well. **3** It gave me great joy to have some brothers come and tell about your faithfulness to the truth and how you continue to walk in the truth. **4** I have no greater joy than to hear that my children are walking in the truth. ¶ **5** Dear friend, you are faithful in what you are doing for the brothers, even though they are strangers to you. **6** They have told the church about your love. You will do well to send them on their way in a manner worthy of God. **7** It was for the sake of the Name that they went out, receiving no help from the pagans. **8** We ought therefore to show hospitality to such men so that we may work together for the truth. ¶ **9** I wrote to the church, but Diotrephes, who loves to be first, will have nothing to do with us. **10** So if I come, I will call attention to what he is doing, gossiping maliciously about us. Not satisfied with that, he refuses to welcome the brothers. He also stops those who want to do so and puts them out of the church. ¶ **11** Dear friend, do not imitate what is evil but what is good. Anyone

---

1:1 Ὁ πρεσβύτερος ¶ Γαΐῳ τῷ ἀγαπητῷ, ὃν ἐγὼ ἀγαπῶ ἐν ἀληθείᾳ. ¶ **2** Ἀγαπητέ, περὶ πάντων εὔχομαί σε εὐοδοῦσθαι καὶ ὑγιαίνειν, καθὼς εὐοδοῦταί σου ἡ ψυχή. **3** ἐχάρην γὰρ λίαν ἐρχομένων ἀδελφῶν καὶ μαρτυρούντων σου τῇ ἀληθείᾳ, καθὼς σὺ ἐν ἀληθείᾳ περιπατεῖς. **4** μειζοτέραν τούτων οὐκ ἔχω χαράν, ἵνα ἀκούω τὰ ἐμὰ τέκνα ἐν τῇ ἀληθείᾳ περιπατοῦντα. ¶ **5** Ἀγαπητέ, πιστὸν ποιεῖς ὃ ἐὰν ἐργάσῃ εἰς τοὺς ἀδελφοὺς καὶ τοῦτο ξένους, **6** οἳ ἐμαρτύρησάν σου τῇ ἀγάπῃ ἐνώπιον ἐκκλησίας, οὓς καλῶς ποιήσεις προπέμψας ἀξίως τοῦ θεοῦ· **7** ὑπὲρ γὰρ τοῦ ὀνόματος ἐξῆλθον μηδὲν λαμβάνοντες ἀπὸ τῶν ἐθνικῶν. **8** ἡμεῖς οὖν ὀφείλομεν ὑπολαμβάνειν τοὺς τοιούτους, ἵνα συνεργοὶ γινώμεθα τῇ ἀληθείᾳ. ¶ **9** Ἔγραψά τι τῇ ἐκκλησίᾳ· ἀλλ' ὁ φιλοπρωτεύων αὐτῶν Διοτρέφης οὐκ ἐπιδέχεται ἡμᾶς. **10** διὰ τοῦτο, ἐὰν ἔλθω, ὑπομνήσω αὐτοῦ τὰ ἔργα ἃ ποιεῖ λόγοις πονηροῖς φλυαρῶν ἡμᾶς, καὶ μὴ ἀρκούμενος ἐπὶ τούτοις οὔτε αὐτὸς ἐπιδέχεται τοὺς ἀδελφοὺς καὶ τοὺς βουλομένους κωλύει καὶ ἐκ τῆς ἐκκλησίας ἐκβάλλει. ¶ **11** Ἀγαπητέ, μὴ μιμοῦ τὸ κακὸν ἀλλὰ τὸ ἀγαθόν. ὁ ἀγαθοποιῶν ἐκ τοῦ θεοῦ ἐστιν· ὁ κακοποιῶν οὐχ

who does what is good   is   from God.   Anyone who does what is evil   has not seen   God.
←   →   →   → ἀγαθοποιῶν ἐστιν ἐκ ⸤τοῦ θεοῦ⸥ ὁ   ←   →   →   → κακοποιῶν →   οὐχ ἑώρακεν ⸤τὸν θεόν⸥
pt.pa.nsm v.pai.3s p.g d.gsm n.gsm d.nsm   pt.pa.nsm   pl v.rai.3s d.asm n.asm
16   1639 1666 3836 2536 3836   2803   3972 4024 3972 3836 2536

12 Demetrius is well spoken   of by everyone – and even by the truth   itself.   We also speak   well of him,
   Δημητρίῳ →   μεμαρτύρηται ← ὑπὸ πάντων καὶ ←   ὑπὸ τῆς ἀληθείας αὐτῆς δὲ ἡμεῖς καὶ μαρτυροῦμεν ←
   n.dsm   v.rpi.3s   p.g a.gpm   cj   p.g d.gsf n.gsf r.gsf cj r.np.1 adv v.pai.1p
   1320   3455   5679 4246   2779   5679 3836 237   899   1254 7005 2779 3455

and you know that our testimony is   true.   ¶   **13** I have much to write   you, but I   do not want to do
καὶ →   οἶδας ὅτι ἡμῶν ἡ μαρτυρία ἐστιν ἀληθής   → εἶχον Πολλὰ γράψαι σοι ἀλλ᾽   οὐ θέλω → γράφειν
cj   v.rai.2s cj r.gp.1 d.nsf n.nsf v.pai.3s a.nsf   v.iai.1s a.apn f.aa   r.ds.2 cj   pl v.pai.1s f.pa
2779   3857 4022 7005 3836 3456 1639   239   2400 4498   1211   5148 247   2527 2527   4024 2527   1211

so   with pen   and ink.   **14** I hope to see you soon, and we will talk   face to face.   ¶ **15** Peace   to
← σοι διὰ καλάμου καὶ μέλανος δὲ → ἐλπίζω ἰδεῖν σε εὐθέως καὶ →   → λαλήσομεν στόμα πρὸς στόμα   εἰρήνη →
r.ds.2 p.g n.gsm cj n.gsn   cj   v.pai.1s f.aa r.ds.2 adv cj   v.fai.1p n.asn p.a n.asn   n.nsf
5148 1328 2812   2779 3506   1254   1827   1625 5148 2311 2779   3281   5125 4639 5125   1645

you. The friends here send their greetings. Greet the friends there by name.
σοι οἱ φίλοι   →   ἀσπάζονται σε ἀσπάζου τοὺς φίλους   κατ᾽ ὄνομα
r.ds.2 d.npm a.npm   v.pmi.3p r.as.2 v.pmm.2s d.apm n.apm   p.a n.asn
5148 3836 5813   832   5148 832   3836 5813   2848 3950

ἑώρακεν τὸν θεόν. ¹² Δημητρίῳ μεμαρτύρηται ὑπὸ πάντων καὶ ὑπὸ αὐτῆς τῆς ἀληθείας· καὶ ἡμεῖς δὲ μαρτυροῦμεν, καὶ οἶδας ὅτι ἡ μαρτυρία ἡμῶν ἀληθής ἐστιν. ¶ ¹³ Πολλὰ εἶχον γράψαι σοι ἀλλ᾽ οὐ θέλω διὰ μέλανος καὶ καλάμου σοι γράφειν· ¹⁴ ἐλπίζω δὲ εὐθέως σε ἰδεῖν, καὶ στόμα πρὸς στόμα λαλήσομεν. ¶ ¹⁵ εἰρήνη σοι. ἀσπάζονταί σε οἱ φίλοι. ἀσπάζου τοὺς φίλους κατ᾽ ὄνομα.

Jude

1:1 Jude, a servant of Jesus Christ and a brother of James, ¶ To those who have been called, who are
Ἰούδας δοῦλος → Ἰησοῦ Χριστοῦ δὲ ἀδελφὸς → Ἰακώβου τοῖς ← κλητοῖς → →
n.nsm n.nsm n.gsm n.gsm cj n.nsm n.gsm d.dpm a.dpm
2683 1529 2652 5986 1254 81 2610 3836 3105

loved by God the Father and kept by Jesus Christ: ¶ **2** Mercy, peace and love be yours in
ἠγαπημένοις ἐν θεῷ πατρὶ καὶ τετηρημένοις → Ἰησοῦ Χριστῷ καὶ ἔλεος εἰρήνη καὶ ἀγάπη ↗ ὑμῖν →
pt.rp.dpm p.d n.dsm n.dsm cj pt.rp.dpm n.dsm n.dsm cj n.nsn n.nsf cj n.nsf r.dp.2
26 1877 2536 4252 2779 5498 2652 5986 2779 1799 1645 2779 27 4437 7007

abundance.
πληθυνθείη
v.apo.3s
4437

The Sin and Doom of Godless Men

1:3 Dear friends, although I was very eager to write to you about the salvation we share, I felt I
→ Ἀγαπητοί → → ποιούμενος πᾶσαν σπουδὴν γράφειν ὑμῖν περὶ ⌜τῆς σωτηρίας⌝ ἡμῶν κοινῆς → ἔσχον
a.vpm pt.pm.nsm a.asf n.asf f.pa r.dp.2 p.g d.gsf n.gsf r.gp.1 a.gsf v.aai.1s
28 4472 4246 5082 1211 7007 4309 3836 5401 7005 3123 2400

had to write and urge you to contend for the faith that was once for all entrusted to the saints.
ἀνάγκην → γράψαι παρακαλῶν ὑμῖν ἐπαγωνίζεσθαι → τῇ πίστει ↗ ἅπαξ ← ← παραδοθείσῃ → τοῖς ἁγίοις
n.asf f.aa pt.pa.nsm r.dp.2 f.pm d.dsf n.dsf adv pt.ap.dsf d.dpm a.dpm
340 1211 4151 7007 2043 3836 4411 4140 562 4140 3836 41

4 For certain men whose condemnation was written about long ago have secretly slipped in
γὰρ τινες ἄνθρωποι οἱ εἰς τοῦτο τὸ κρίμα, → προγεγραμμένοι → πάλαι ← ← παρεισέδυσαν ←
cj r.npm n.npm d.npm p.a r.asn d.asn n.asn pt.rp.npm adv v.aai.3p
1142 5516 476 3836 1650 4047 3836 3210 4592 4093 4208

among you. They are godless men, who change the grace of our God into a license for immorality and
→ → ἀσεβεῖς → μετατιθέντες τὴν χάριτα ↗ ἡμῶν ⌜τοῦ θεοῦ⌝ εἰς ἀσέλγειαν ← ← καὶ
a.npm pt.pa.npm d.asf n.asf r.gp.1 d.gsm n.gsm p.a n.asf cj
815 3572 3836 5921 7005 3836 2536 1650 816 2779

deny Jesus Christ our only Sovereign and Lord. ¶ **5** Though you already know all this, I
ἀρνούμενοι Ἰησοῦν Χριστὸν ἡμῶν μόνον ⌜τὸν δεσπότην⌝ καὶ κύριον δὲ ὑμᾶς εἰδότας πάντα ← →
pt.pm.npm n.asm n.asm r.gp.1 adv d.asm n.asm cj n.asm cj r.ap.2 pt.ra.apm a.apn
766 2652 5986 7005 3668 3836 1305 2779 3261 1254 3857 7007 3857 4246

want to remind you that the Lord delivered his people out of Egypt, but later destroyed
βούλομαι → Ὑπομνῆσαι ὑμᾶς ὅτι ὁ κύριος ἅπαξ σώσας λαὸν ἐκ ← γῆς Αἰγύπτου ⌜τὸ δεύτερον⌝ ἀπώλεσεν
v.pmi.1s f.aa r.ap.2 cj d.nsm n.nsm adv pt.aa.nsm n.asm p.g n.gsf n.gsf d.asn a.asn v.aai.3s
1089 5703 7007 4022 3836 3261 562 5392 3295 1666 1178 131 3836 1311 660

those who did not believe. **6** And the angels who did not keep their positions of authority but abandoned
τοὺς ← μὴ πιστεύσαντας τε ἀγγέλους τοὺς ↗ μὴ τηρήσαντας ἑαυτῶν → → ⌜τὴν ἀρχὴν⌝ ἀλλὰ ἀπολιπόντας
d.apm pl pt.aa.apm cj n.apm d.apm pl pt.aa.apm r.gpm.3 d.asf n.asf cj pt.aa.apm
3836 4409 3590 4409 5445 34 3836 5498 3590 5498 1571 3836 794 247 657

their own home – these he has kept in darkness, bound with everlasting chains for judgment on the great
τὸ ἴδιον οἰκητήριον → τετήρηκεν ὑπὸ ζόφον ἀϊδίοις δεσμοῖς εἰς κρίσιν μεγάλης
d.asn a.asn n.asn v.rai.3s p.a n.asm a.dpm n.dpm p.a n.asf a.gsf
3836 2625 3863 5498 5679 2432 132 1301 1650 3213 3489

Day. **7** In a similar way, Sodom and Gomorrah and the surrounding towns gave
ἡμέρας ὡς ὅμοιον ⌜τὸν τρόπον⌝ τούτοις Σόδομα καὶ Γόμορρα καὶ αἱ περὶ αὐτὰς πόλεις ἐκπορνεύσασαι
n.gsf cj a.asm d.asm n.asm r.dpm n.npn cj n.nsf cj d.npf p.a r.apf.3 n.npf pt.aa.npf
2465 6055 3927 3836 5573 4047 5047 2779 1202 2779 3836 4309 899 4484 1745

themselves up to sexual immorality and perversion. They serve as an example of those who
← ← ← καὶ ἀπελθοῦσαι ὀπίσω σαρκὸς ἑτέρας⌝ → πρόκεινται δεῖγμα → → →
cj pt.aa.npf p.g n.gsf a.gsf v.pmi.3p n.asn
2779 599 3958 4922 2283 4618 1257

1:1 Ἰούδας Ἰησοῦ Χριστοῦ δοῦλος, ἀδελφὸς δὲ Ἰακώβου, ¶ τοῖς ἐν θεῷ πατρὶ ἠγαπημένοις καὶ Ἰησοῦ Χριστῷ τετηρημένοις κλητοῖς· ¶ **2** ἔλεος ὑμῖν καὶ εἰρήνη καὶ ἀγάπη πληθυνθείη.

1:3 Ἀγαπητοί, πᾶσαν σπουδὴν ποιούμενος γράφειν ὑμῖν περὶ τῆς κοινῆς ἡμῶν σωτηρίας ἀνάγκην ἔσχον γράψαι ὑμῖν παρακαλῶν ἐπαγωνίζεσθαι τῇ ἅπαξ παραδοθείσῃ τοῖς ἁγίοις πίστει. **4** παρεισέδυσαν γάρ τινες ἄνθρωποι, οἱ πάλαι προγεγραμμένοι εἰς τοῦτο τὸ κρίμα, ἀσεβεῖς, τὴν τοῦ θεοῦ ἡμῶν χάριτα μετατιθέντες εἰς ἀσέλγειαν καὶ τὸν μόνον δεσπότην καὶ κύριον ἡμῶν Ἰησοῦν Χριστὸν ἀρνούμενοι. ¶ **5** Ὑπομνῆσαι δὲ ὑμᾶς βούλομαι, εἰδότας ἅπαξ [ὑμᾶς] πάντα ὅτι [ὁ] κύριος λαὸν ἐκ γῆς Αἰγύπτου σώσας τὸ δεύτερον τοὺς μὴ πιστεύσαντας ἀπώλεσεν, **6** ἀγγέλους τε τοὺς μὴ τηρήσαντας τὴν ἑαυτῶν ἀρχὴν ἀλλὰ ἀπολιπόντας τὸ ἴδιον οἰκητήριον εἰς κρίσιν μεγάλης ἡμέρας δεσμοῖς ἀϊδίοις ὑπὸ ζόφον τετήρηκεν, **7** ὡς Σόδομα καὶ Γόμορρα καὶ αἱ περὶ αὐτὰς πόλεις τὸν ὅμοιον τρόπον τούτοις ἐκπορνεύσασαι καὶ ἀπελθοῦσαι ὀπίσω σαρκὸς ἑτέρας, πρόκεινται

suffer the punishment of eternal fire. ¶ **8** In the very same way, these dreamers pollute
ὑπέχουσαι δίκην → αἰωνίου πυρός μέντοι → → → Ὁμοίως ← καὶ οὗτοι ἐνυπνιαζόμενοι μὲν μιαίνουσιν
pt.pa.npf | n.asf | a.gsn | n.gsn | cj | adv | adv | r.npm | pt.pp.npm | pl | v.pai.3p
5674 1472 173 4786 3530 3931 2779 4047 1965 3525 3620

their own bodies, reject authority and slander celestial beings. **9** But even the archangel Michael, when
σάρκα δὲ ἀθετοῦσιν κυριότητα δὲ βλασφημοῦσιν δόξας ← δὲ ὁ ἀρχάγγελος Ὁ Μιχαὴλ ὅτε
n.asf | cj | v.pai.3p | n.asf | cj | v.pai.3p | n.apf | cj | d.nsm | n.nsm | d.nsm | n.nsm | cj
4922 1254 119 3262 1254 1059 1518 1254 3836 791 3836 3640 4021

he was disputing with the devil about the body of Moses, did not dare to bring a
διακρινόμενος διελέγετο → τῷ διαβόλῳ περὶ σώματος τοῦ Μωϋσέως οὐκ ἐτόλμησεν ἐπενεγκεῖν
pt.pm.nsm | v.imi.3s | d.dsm | n.dsm | p.g | n.gsn | d.gsn | n.gsm | pl | v.aai.3s | f.aa
1359 1363 3836 1333 4309 5393 3836 3707 5528 4024 5528 2214

slanderous accusation against him, but said, "The Lord rebuke you!" **10** Yet these men speak abusively
βλασφημίας κρίσιν ← ἀλλὰ εἶπεν κύριος ἐπιτιμήσαι σοι δὲ Οὗτοι βλασφημοῦσιν ←
n.gsf | n.asf | cj | v.aai.3s | n.nsm | v.aao.3s | r.ds.2 | cj | r.npm | v.pai.3p
1060 3213 2214 247 3306 3261 2203 5148 1254 4047 1059

against whatever they do not understand; and what things they do understand by instinct, like unreasoning
μὲν ὅσα → οὐκ οἴδασιν δὲ ὅσα ← → ἐπίστανται → φυσικῶς ὡς ἄλογα
pl | r.apn | pl | v.rai.3p | cj | r.apn | v.ppi.3p | adv | pl | a.npn
3525 4012 3857 3857 4024 3857 1254 4012 2179 5880 6055 263

animals – these are the very things that destroy them. ¶ **11** Woe to them! They have taken the way
τὰ ζῷα ἐν τούτοις φθείρονται οὐαὶ αὐτοῖς ὅτι → → ἐπορεύθησαν τῇ ὁδῷ
d.npn | n.npn | p.d | r.dpn | v.ppi.3p | j | r.dpm.3 | cj | v.api.3p | d.dsf | n.dsf
3836 2442 1877 4047 4026 899 4022 4513 3836 3847

of Cain; they have rushed for profit into Balaam's error; they have been destroyed in Korah's
τοῦ Κάϊν καὶ ἐξεχύθησαν μισθοῦ τοῦ Βαλαὰμ τῇ πλάνῃ καὶ ἀπώλοντο τοῦ Κόρε
d.gsm | n.gsm | cj | v.api.3p | n.gsm | d.gsm | n.gsm | d.dsf | n.dsf | cj | v.ami.3p | d.gsm | n.gsm
3836 2782 2779 1773 3635 4415 3836 962 3836 4415 2779 660 517 3836 3169

rebellion. ¶ **12** These men are blemishes at your love feasts, eating with you without
τῇ ἀντιλογίᾳ Οὗτοι εἰσιν οἱ σπιλάδες ἐν ὑμῶν ταῖς ἀγάπαις συνευωχούμενοι ←
d.dsf | n.dsf | r.npm | v.pai.3p | d.npm | n.npf | p.d | r.gp.2 | d.dpf | n.dpf | pt.pp.npm
3836 517 4047 1639 3836 5069 1877 7007 3836 27 5307

the slightest qualm – shepherds who feed only themselves. They are clouds without rain, blown along by
ἀφόβως ποιμαίνοντες ← ἑαυτοὺς νεφέλαι → ἄνυδροι παραφερόμεναι ← ὑπὸ
adv | pt.pa.npm | r.apm.3 | n.npf | a.npf | pt.pp.npf | p.g
925 4477 1571 3749 536 4195 5679

the wind; autumn trees, without fruit and uprooted – twice dead. **13** They are wild waves of the sea,
ἀνέμων φθινοπωρινὰ δένδρα → ἄκαρπα ἐκριζωθέντα δὶς ἀποθανόντα ἄγρια κύματα → θαλάσσης
n.gpm | a.npn | n.npn | a.npn | pt.ap.npn | adv | pt.aa.npn | a.npn | n.npn | n.gsf
449 5781 1285 182 1748 1489 633 67 3246 2498

foaming up their shame; wandering stars, for whom blackest darkness has been reserved forever. ¶
ἐπαφρίζοντα ← ἑαυτῶν τὰς αἰσχύνας, πλανῆται ἀστέρες → οἷς ὁ ζόφος τοῦ σκότους → τετήρηται εἰς αἰῶνα
pt.pa.npn | r.gpn.3 | d.apf | n.apf | n.npm | n.npm | r.dpm | d.nsm | n.nsm | d.gsn | n.gsn | v.rpi.3s | p.a | n.asm
2072 1571 3836 158 4417 843 4005 3836 2432 3836 5030 5498 1650 172

14 Enoch, the seventh from Adam, prophesied about these men: "See, the Lord is coming with
δὲ Ἐνὼχ ἕβδομος ἀπὸ Ἀδὰμ Προεφήτευσεν καὶ τούτοις λέγων ἰδοὺ κύριος ἦλθεν ἐν
cj | n.nsm | a.nsm | p.g | n.gsm | v.aai.3s | adv | r.dpm | pt.pa.nsm | j | n.nsm | v.aai.3s | p.d
1254 1970 1575 608 77 4736 2779 4047 3306 2627 3261 2262 1877

thousands upon thousands of his holy ones **15** to judge everyone, and to convict all the ungodly
μυριάσιν ← αὐτοῦ ἁγίαις ← ποιῆσαι κρίσιν κατὰ πάντων καὶ → ἐλέγξαι πᾶσαν ψυχὴν
n.dpf | r.gsm.3 | a.dpf | f.aa | n.asf | p.g | a.gpm | cj | f.aa | a.asf | n.asf
3689 41 899 41 4472 3213 2848 4246 2779 1794 4246 6034

of all the ungodly acts they have done in the ungodly way, and of all the harsh words
περὶ πάντων τῶν ἀσεβείας αὐτῶν ἔργων ὧν → → ἠσέβησαν καὶ περὶ πάντων τῶν σκληρῶν ← ὧν
p.g | a.gpn | d.gpn | n.gsf | r.gpm.3 | n.gpn | r.gpn | v.aai.3p | cj | p.g | a.gpn | d.gpn | a.gpn | r.gpn
4309 4246 3836 813 899 2240 4005 814 2779 4309 4246 3836 5017 4005

δεῖγμα πυρὸς αἰωνίου δίκην ὑπέχουσαι. ¶ **8** Ὁμοίως μέντοι καὶ οὗτοι ἐνυπνιαζόμενοι σάρκα μὲν μιαίνουσιν κυριότητα δὲ ἀθετοῦσιν δόξας δὲ βλασφημοῦσιν. **9** ὁ δὲ Μιχαὴλ ὁ ἀρχάγγελος, ὅτε τῷ διαβόλῳ διακρινόμενος διελέγετο περὶ τοῦ Μωϋσέως σώματος, οὐκ ἐτόλμησεν κρίσιν ἐπενεγκεῖν βλασφημίας ἀλλὰ εἶπεν, Ἐπιτιμήσαι σοι κύριος. **10** οὗτοι δὲ ὅσα μὲν οὐκ οἴδασιν βλασφημοῦσιν, ὅσα δὲ φυσικῶς ὡς τὰ ἄλογα ζῷα ἐπίστανται, ἐν τούτοις φθείρονται. ¶ **11** οὐαὶ αὐτοῖς, ὅτι τῇ ὁδῷ τοῦ Κάϊν ἐπορεύθησαν καὶ τῇ πλάνῃ τοῦ Βαλαὰμ μισθοῦ ἐξεχύθησαν καὶ τῇ ἀντιλογίᾳ τοῦ Κόρε ἀπώλοντο. ¶ **12** οὗτοί εἰσιν οἱ ἐν ταῖς ἀγάπαις ὑμῶν σπιλάδες συνευωχούμενοι ἀφόβως, ἑαυτοὺς ποιμαίνοντες, νεφέλαι ἄνυδροι ὑπὸ ἀνέμων παραφερόμεναι, δένδρα φθινοπωρινὰ ἄκαρπα δὶς ἀποθανόντα ἐκριζωθέντα, **13** κύματα ἄγρια θαλάσσης ἐπαφρίζοντα τὰς ἑαυτῶν αἰσχύνας, ἀστέρες πλανῆται οἷς ὁ ζόφος τοῦ σκότους εἰς αἰῶνα τετήρηται. ¶ **14** Προεφήτευσεν δὲ καὶ τούτοις ἕβδομος ἀπὸ Ἀδὰμ Ἐνὼχ λέγων, Ἰδοὺ ἦλθεν κύριος ἐν ἁγίαις μυριάσιν αὐτοῦ **15** ποιῆσαι κρίσιν κατὰ πάντων καὶ ἐλέγξαι πάντας «πᾶσαν» τοὺς ἀσεβεῖς ψυχὴν περὶ πάντων τῶν ἔργων ἀσεβείας αὐτῶν ὧν ἠσέβησαν καὶ περὶ πάντων τῶν σκληρῶν ὧν ἐλάλησαν κατ' αὐτοῦ ἁμαρτωλοὶ ἀσεβεῖς.

ungodly	sinners	have	spoken	against	him."	**16** These	men	are	grumblers	and	faultfinders;	they	follow
ἀσεβεῖς	ἁμαρτωλοὶ	→	ἐλάλησαν	κατ᾽	αὐτοῦ	Οὗτοι		εἰσιν	γογγυσταὶ	μεμψίμοιροι	→	πορευόμενοι	κατὰ
a.npm	a.npm		v.aai.3p	p.g	r.gsm.3	r.npm		v.pai.3p	n.npm	a.npm		pt.pm.npm	p.a
815	283		3281	2848	899	4047		1639	1199	3523		4513	2848

their	own	evil	desires;		they		boast		about	themselves	and	flatter		others	for	their	own
ἑαυτῶν	←	→	τὰς	ἐπιθυμίας	καὶ	τὸ	στόμα	λαλεῖ	ὑπέρογκα	→		αὐτῶν		θαυμάζοντες	πρόσωπα	χάριν	←
r.gpm.3			d.apf	n.apf	cj	d.nsn	n.nsn	v.pai.3s	a.apn			r.gpm.3		pt.pa.npm	n.apn	p.g
1571			3836	2123	2779	3836	5125	3281	5665			899		2513	4725	5920

advantage.
ὠφελείας
n.gsf
6066

A Call to Persevere

1:17	But,	dear	friends,	remember	what		the	apostles	of	our	Lord		Jesus	Christ
δὲ	ὑμεῖς	→	ἀγαπητοὶ	μνήσθητε	⌜τῶν ῥημάτων⌝	ὑπὸ	τῶν	ἀποστόλων		ἡμῶν	⌜τοῦ κυρίου⌝	Ἰησοῦ	Χριστοῦ
cj	r.np.2		a.vpm	v.apm.2p	d.gpn n.gpn	p.g	d.gpm	n.gpm		r.gp.1	d.gsm n.gsm	n.gsm	n.gsm
1254	7007		28	3630	3836 4839	5679	3836	693		3261	7005 3261	2652	5986

foretold.		**18**		They	said	to you,		"In	the last	times		there	will be		scoffers	who	will
⌜τῶν προειρημένων⌝			ὅτι	→	ἔλεγον	→	ὑμῖν	[ὅτι]	ἐπ᾽		ἐσχάτου	⌜τοῦ χρόνου⌝		→	ἔσονται	ἐμπαῖκται	→
d.gpn	pt.rp.gpn			cj		v.iai.3p		r.dp.2	cj	p.g		a.gsm	d.gsm n.gsm			v.fmi.3p	n.npm
3836	4597			4022		3306		7007	4022	2093		2274	3836 5989			1639	1851

follow		their	own	ungodly		desires."	**19** These	are	the	men	who	divide		you,	who	follow	mere
πορευόμενοι	κατὰ	τὰς	ἑαυτῶν	⌜τῶν ἀσεβειῶν⌝	ἐπιθυμίας		Οὗτοι	εἰσιν	οἱ			ἀποδιορίζοντες				
pt.pm.npm	p.a	d.apf	r.gpm.3	d.gpf n.gpf	n.apf		r.npm	v.pai.3p	d.npm			pt.pa.npm				
4513	2848	3836	1571	3836 813	2123		4047	1639	3836			626				

natural	instincts	and	do	not	have	the	Spirit.	¶	**20** But	you,	dear	friends,	build		yourselves	up	in	your
ψυχικοί	←		→	μὴ	ἔχοντες		πνεῦμα		δὲ	ὑμεῖς	→	ἀγαπητοὶ	ἐποικοδομοῦντες	ἑαυτοὺς	←	←	→	ὑμῶν
a.npm				pl	pt.pa.npm		n.asn		cj	r.np.2		a.vpm	pt.pa.npm	r.apm.2				r.gp.2
6035				3590	2400		4460		1254	7007		28	2224	1571		2224 4411		7007

most	holy	faith		and	pray		in	the Holy	Spirit.	**21** Keep	yourselves	in	God's	love	as	you	wait
→	ἁγιωτάτῃ	⌜τῇ πίστει⌝		προσευχόμενοι	ἐν	ἁγίῳ	πνεύματι	τηρήσατε	ἑαυτοὺς	ἐν	θεοῦ	ἀγάπῃ	→	→	προσδεχόμενοι
a.dsf.s	d.dsf n.dsf			pt.pm.npm	p.d	a.dsn	n.dsn	v.aam.2p	r.apm.2	p.d	n.gsm	n.dsf			pt.pm.npm
41	3836 4411			4667	1877	41	4460	5498	1571	1877	2536	27			4657

for	the	mercy	of	our	Lord		Jesus	Christ	to	bring	you	to	eternal	life.	¶	**22**		Be	merciful	to	those
←	τὸ	ἔλεος	→	ἡμῶν	⌜τοῦ κυρίου⌝	Ἰησοῦ	Χριστοῦ	εἰς	←	←	←	αἰώνιον	ζωὴν			Καὶ	μὲν	→	ἐλεᾶτε	←	οὓς
d.asn	n.asn		r.gp.1	d.gsm n.gsm	n.gsm	n.gsm	p.a					a.asf	n.asf			cj	pl		v.pam.2p		r.apm
3836	1799		3261	7005 3261	2652	5986	1650				173	2437			2779	3525		1790		4005

who	doubt;	**23**		snatch		others	from	the	fire	and	save	them;		to	others	show	mercy,	mixed	with	fear	—
→	διακρινομένους		δὲ	ἁρπάζοντες	οὓς	ἐκ		πυρὸς		σῴζετε		δὲ	→	οὓς	→	ἐλεᾶτε			ἐν	φόβῳ
pt.pm.apm			pl	pt.pa.npm	r.apm	p.g		n.gsn		v.pam.2p		pl		r.apm		v.pam.2p			p.d	n.dsm
1359			1254	773	4005	1666		4786		5392		1254	1790	4005		1790			1877	5832

hating	even	the	clothing	stained		by	corrupted	flesh.
μισοῦντες	καὶ	τὸν	χιτῶνα	ἐσπιλωμένον	ἀπὸ		⌜τῆς σαρκὸς⌝
pt.pa.npm	adv	d.asm	n.asm	pt.rp.asm	p.g		d.gsf n.gsf
3631	2779	3836	5945	5071	608		3836 4922

Doxology

1:24 | To | him | who | is | able | | to | keep | you | from | falling | | and | to | present | you | before | | his | glorious
--- | --- | --- | --- | --- | --- | --- | --- | --- | --- | --- | --- | --- | --- | --- | --- | --- | --- | --- | ---
| δὲ | Τῷ | ← | ← | → | δυναμένῳ | φυλάξαι | ὑμᾶς | ← | ἀπταίστους | καὶ | → | στῆσαι | | κατενώπιον | αὐτοῦ | ⌜τῆς δόξης⌝
| cj | d.dsm | | | | pt.pp.dsm | f.aa | r.ap.2 | | a.apm | cj | | f.aa | | p.g | r.gsm.3 | d.gsf n.gsf
| 1254 | 3836 | | | | 1538 | 5875 | 7007 | | 720 | 2779 | | 2705 | | 2979 | 899 | 3836 1518

presence	without	fault		and	with	great	joy		— **25**	to	the only	God	our	Savior	be	glory,	majesty,		power	and
←	←	ἀμώμους		ἐν		ἀγαλλιάσει				μόνῳ	θεῷ	ἡμῶν	σωτῆρι		δόξα	μεγαλωσύνη		κράτος	καὶ
	a.apm		p.d		n.dsf				a.dsm	n.dsm	r.gp.1	n.dsm		n.nsf	n.nsf		n.nsn	cj
	320		1877		21				3668	2536	7005	5400		1518	3488		3197	2779

16 Οὗτοί εἰσιν γογγυσταὶ μεμψίμοιροι κατὰ τὰς ἐπιθυμίας ἑαυτῶν πορευόμενοι, καὶ τὸ στόμα αὐτῶν λαλεῖ ὑπέρογκα, θαυμάζοντες πρόσωπα ὠφελείας χάριν.

1:17 Ὑμεῖς δέ, ἀγαπητοί, μνήσθητε τῶν ῥημάτων τῶν προειρημένων ὑπὸ τῶν ἀποστόλων τοῦ κυρίου ἡμῶν Ἰησοῦ Χριστοῦ **18** ὅτι ἔλεγον ὑμῖν [ὅτι] Ἐπ᾽ ἐσχάτου [τοῦ] χρόνου ἔσονται ἐμπαῖκται κατὰ τὰς ἑαυτῶν ἐπιθυμίας πορευόμενοι τῶν ἀσεβειῶν. **19** Οὗτοί εἰσιν οἱ ἀποδιορίζοντες, ψυχικοί, πνεῦμα μὴ ἔχοντες. ¶ **20** ὑμεῖς δέ, ἀγαπητοί, ἐποικοδομοῦντες ἑαυτοὺς τῇ ἁγιωτάτῃ ὑμῶν πίστει, ἐν πνεύματι ἁγίῳ προσευχόμενοι, **21** ἑαυτοὺς ἐν ἀγάπῃ θεοῦ τηρήσατε προσδεχόμενοι τὸ ἔλεος τοῦ κυρίου ἡμῶν Ἰησοῦ Χριστοῦ εἰς ζωὴν αἰώνιον. ¶ **22** καὶ οὓς μὲν ἐλεᾶτε διακρινομένους, **23** οὓς δὲ σῴζετε ἐκ πυρὸς ἁρπάζοντες, οὓς δὲ ἐλεᾶτε ἐν φόβῳ μισοῦντες καὶ τὸν ἀπὸ τῆς σαρκὸς ἐσπιλωμένον χιτῶνα.

1:24 Τῷ δὲ δυναμένῳ φυλάξαι ὑμᾶς ἀπταίστους καὶ στῆσαι κατενώπιον τῆς δόξης αὐτοῦ ἀμώμους ἐν ἀγαλλιάσει, **25** μόνῳ θεῷ σωτῆρι ἡμῶν διὰ Ἰησοῦ Χριστοῦ τοῦ κυρίου ἡμῶν δόξα μεγαλωσύνη κράτος καὶ ἐξουσία πρὸ παντὸς τοῦ αἰῶνος καὶ νῦν

authority,	through	Jesus	Christ	our	Lord,		before	all	ages,		now	and	forevermore!				Amen.
ἐξουσία	διά	Ἰησοῦ	Χριστοῦ	ἡμῶν	⌐τοῦ	κυρίου⌐	πρὸ	παντὸς	⌐τοῦ	αἰῶνος⌐	καὶ νῦν	καὶ	⌐εἰς	πάντας	τοὺς	αἰῶνας⌐	ἀμήν
n.nsf	p.g	n.gsm	n.gsm	r.gp.1	d.gsm	n.gsm	p.g	a.gsm	d.gsm	n.gsm	cj adv	cj	p.a	a.apm	d.apm	n.apm	pl
2026	1328	2652	5986	7005	3836	3261	4574	4246	3836	172	2779 3814	2779	1650	4246	3836	172	297

καὶ εἰς πάντας τοὺς αἰῶνας, ἀμήν.

Revelation

Prologue

1:1 The revelation of Jesus Christ, which God gave him to show his servants what must soon
Ἀποκάλυψις → Ἰησοῦ Χριστοῦ ἦν ὁ θεός, ἔδωκεν αὐτῷ → δεῖξαι αὐτοῦ τοῖς δούλοις, ἃ δεῖ ἐν τάχει
n.nsf · n.gsm n.gsm r.asf d.nsm n.nsm v.aai.3s r.dsm.3 f.aa r.gsm.3 d.dpm n.dpm r.apn v.pai.3s p.d n.dsn
637 · 2652 5986 4005 3836 2536 1443 899 1259 899 3836 1529 4005 1256 1877 5443

take place. He made it known by sending his angel to his servant John, **2** who testifies
γενέσθαι ← καὶ → → ἐσήμανεν → ἀποστείλας διὰ αὐτοῦ τοῦ ἀγγέλου ↱ αὐτοῦ τῷ δούλῳ Ἰωάννῃ ὃς ἐμαρτύρησεν
f.am · cj · · v.aai.3s · pt.aa.nsm p.g r.gsm.3 d.gsm n.gsm r.gsm.3 d.dsm n.dsm n.dsm r.nsm v.aai.3s
1181 · 2779 · · 4955 · 690 1328 899 3836 34 1529 899 3836 1529 2722 4005 3455

to everything he saw – that is, the word of God and the testimony of Jesus Christ. **3** Blessed is the one who
← ὅσα εἶδεν τὸν λόγον → τοῦ θεοῦ καὶ τὴν μαρτυρίαν → Ἰησοῦ Χριστοῦ Μακάριος ὁ ← ←
r.apn v.aai.3s d.asm n.asm d.gsm n.gsm cj d.asf n.asf n.gsm n.gsm a.nsm d.nsm
4012 1625 3836 3364 3836 2536 2779 3836 3456 2652 5986 3421 3836

reads the words of this prophecy, and blessed are those who hear it and take to heart what is
ἀναγινώσκων τοὺς λόγους → τῆς προφητείας καὶ οἱ ← ἀκούοντες καὶ τηροῦντες ← τὰ
pt.pa.nsm d.apm n.apm d.gsf n.gsf cj d.npm pt.pa.npm cj pt.pa.npm d.apn
336 3836 3364 3836 4735 2779 3836 201 2779 5498 3836

written in it, because the time is near.
γεγραμμένα ἐν αὐτῇ γὰρ ὁ καιρὸς ἐγγύς
pt.rp.apn p.d r.dsf.3 cj d.nsm n.nsm adv
1211 1877 899 1142 3836 2789 1584

Greetings and Doxology

1:4 John, To the seven churches in the province of Asia: Grace and peace to you from him who
Ἰωάννης → ταῖς ἑπτὰ ἐκκλησίαις ταῖς ἐν → → τῇ Ἀσίᾳ χάρις καὶ εἰρήνη → ὑμῖν ἀπὸ → ὁ
n.nsm d.dpf a.dpf n.dpf d.dpf p.d d.dsf n.dsf n.nsf cj n.nsf r.dp.2 p.g d.nsm
2722 3036 2231 1711 3836 1877 3836 823 5921 2779 1645 7007 608 3836

is, and who was, and who is to come, and from the seven spirits before his throne, **5** and from Jesus
ὢν καὶ ὁ ἦν καὶ ὁ → ἐρχόμενος καὶ ἀπὸ τῶν ἑπτὰ πνευμάτων ἃ ἐνώπιον αὐτοῦ τοῦ θρόνου, καὶ ἀπὸ Ἰησοῦ
pt.pa.nsm cj d.nsm v.iai.3s cj d.nsm pt.pm.nsm cj p.g d.gpn a.gpn n.gpn r.npn p.g r.gsm.3 d.gsm n.gsm cj p.g n.gsm
1639 2779 3836 1639 2779 3836 2262 2779 608 3836 2231 4460 4005 1967 899 3836 2585 2779 608 2652

Christ, who is the faithful witness, the firstborn from the dead, and the ruler of the kings of the earth. ¶
Χριστοῦ ὁ ὁ πιστός, μάρτυς ὁ πρωτότοκος → τῶν νεκρῶν καὶ ὁ ἄρχων → τῶν βασιλέων → τῆς γῆς. ¶
n.gsm d.nsm d.nsm a.nsm n.nsm d.nsm a.nsm d.gpm a.gpm cj d.nsm n.nsm d.gpm n.gpm d.gsf n.gsf
5986 3836 3836 4412 3459 3836 4758 3836 3738 2779 3836 807 3836 995 3836 1178

To him who loves us and has freed us from our sins by his blood, **6** and has made us to
→ Τῷ ← ἀγαπῶντι ἡμᾶς καὶ → λύσαντι ἡμᾶς ἐκ ἡμῶν τῶν ἁμαρτιῶν, ἐν αὐτοῦ τῷ αἵματι, καὶ → ἐποίησεν ἡμᾶς
d.dsm pt.pa.dsm r.ap.1 cj pt.aa.dsm r.ap.1 p.g r.gp.1 d.gpf n.gpf p.d r.gsm.3 d.dsn n.dsn cj v.aai.3s r.ap.1
3836 26 7005 2779 3395 7005 1666 7005 3836 281 1877 899 3836 135 2779 4472 7005

be a kingdom and priests to serve his God and Father – to him be glory and power *for ever*
βασιλείαν ἱερεῖς ↱ → αὐτοῦ τῷ θεῷ καὶ πατρί → αὐτῷ ἡ δόξα καὶ τὸ κράτος, εἰς τοὺς αἰῶνας
n.asf n.apm r.gsm.3 d.dsm n.dsm cj n.dsm r.dsm.3 d.nsf n.nsf cj d.nsn n.nsn p.a d.apm n.apm
993 2636 2536 2536 899 3836 2536 2779 4252 899 3836 1518 2779 3836 3197 1650 3836 172

and ever! Amen. ¶ **7** Look, he is coming with the clouds, and every eye will see him, even those
τῶν αἰώνων ἀμήν. ¶ Ἰδοὺ → ἔρχεται μετὰ τῶν νεφελῶν καὶ πᾶς ὀφθαλμὸς → ὄψεται αὐτὸν καὶ οἵτινες
d.gpm n.gpm pl Ἰδού v.pmi.3s p.g d.gpf n.gpf cj a.nsm n.nsm v.fmi.3s r.asm.3 cj r.npm
3836 172 297 2627 2262 3552 3836 3749 2779 4246 4057 3972 899 2779 4015

who pierced him; and all the peoples of the earth will mourn because of him. So shall it be! Amen. ¶
← ἐξεκέντησαν αὐτὸν καὶ πᾶσαι αἱ φυλαὶ → τῆς γῆς → κόψονται ἐπʼ ← αὐτόν ναί, ← ἀμήν
v.aai.3p r.asm.3 cj a.npf d.npf n.npf d.gsf n.gsf v.fmi.3p p.a r.asm.3 pl pl
1708 899 2779 4246 3836 5876 3836 1178 3164 2093 899 3721 297

8 "I am the Alpha and the Omega," says the Lord God, "who is, and who was, and who is to come,
Ἐγώ εἰμι τὸ ἄλφα καὶ τὸ ὦ λέγει ὁ κύριος θεός ὁ ὢν καὶ ὁ ἦν καὶ ὁ → ἐρχόμενος
r.ns.1 v.pai.1s d.nsn n.nsn cj d.nsn n.nsn v.pai.3s d.nsm n.nsm n.nsm d.nsm pt.pa.nsm cj d.nsm v.iai.3s cj d.nsm pt.pm.nsm
1609 1639 3836 270 2779 3836 6042 3306 3836 3261 2536 3836 1639 2779 3836 1639 2779 3836 2262

1:1 Ἀποκάλυψις Ἰησοῦ Χριστοῦ ἣν ἔδωκεν αὐτῷ ὁ θεὸς δεῖξαι τοῖς δούλοις αὐτοῦ ἃ δεῖ γενέσθαι ἐν τάχει, καὶ ἐσήμανεν ἀποστείλας διὰ τοῦ ἀγγέλου αὐτοῦ τῷ δούλῳ αὐτοῦ Ἰωάννῃ, **2** ὃς ἐμαρτύρησεν τὸν λόγον τοῦ θεοῦ καὶ τὴν μαρτυρίαν Ἰησοῦ Χριστοῦ ὅσα εἶδεν. **3** μακάριος ὁ ἀναγινώσκων καὶ οἱ ἀκούοντες τοὺς λόγους τῆς προφητείας καὶ τηροῦντες τὰ ἐν αὐτῇ γεγραμμένα, ὁ γὰρ καιρὸς ἐγγύς.

1:4 Ἰωάννης ταῖς ἑπτὰ ἐκκλησίαις ταῖς ἐν τῇ Ἀσίᾳ· χάρις ὑμῖν καὶ εἰρήνη ἀπὸ ὁ ὢν καὶ ὁ ἦν καὶ ὁ ἐρχόμενος καὶ ἀπὸ τῶν ἑπτὰ πνευμάτων ἃ ἐνώπιον τοῦ θρόνου αὐτοῦ **5** καὶ ἀπὸ Ἰησοῦ Χριστοῦ, ὁ μάρτυς, ὁ πιστός, ὁ πρωτότοκος τῶν νεκρῶν καὶ ὁ ἄρχων τῶν βασιλέων τῆς γῆς. ¶ Τῷ ἀγαπῶντι ἡμᾶς καὶ λύσαντι ἡμᾶς ἐκ τῶν ἁμαρτιῶν ἡμῶν ἐν τῷ αἵματι αὐτοῦ, **6** καὶ ἐποίησεν ἡμᾶς βασιλείαν, ἱερεῖς τῷ θεῷ καὶ πατρὶ αὐτοῦ, αὐτῷ ἡ δόξα καὶ τὸ κράτος εἰς τοὺς αἰῶνας [τῶν αἰώνων]· ἀμήν. ¶ **7** Ἰδοὺ ἔρχεται μετὰ τῶν νεφελῶν, καὶ ὄψεται αὐτὸν πᾶς ὀφθαλμὸς καὶ οἵτινες αὐτὸν ἐξεκέντησαν, καὶ κόψονται ἐπʼ αὐτὸν πᾶσαι αἱ φυλαὶ τῆς γῆς. ναί, ἀμήν. ¶ **8** Ἐγώ εἰμι τὸ Ἄλφα καὶ τὸ Ὦ, λέγει κύριος ὁ θεός, ὁ ὢν καὶ ὁ ἦν καὶ ὁ ἐρχόμενος,

the Almighty."
ο παντοκράτωρ
d.nsm n.nsm
3836 4120

One Like a Son of Man

1:9 I, John, your brother and companion in the suffering and kingdom and patient endurance that are
Ἐγώ Ἰωάννης ὑμῶν ὁ ἀδελφός καὶ συγκοινωνὸς ἐν τῇ θλίψει καὶ βασιλείᾳ καὶ → ὑπομονῇ
r.ns.1 n.nsm r.gp.2 d.nsm n.nsm cj n.nsm p.d d.dsf n.dsf cj n.dsf cj n.dsf
1609 2722 7007 3836 81 2779 5171 1877 3836 2568 2779 993 2779 5705

ours in Jesus, was on the island of Patmos because of the word of God and the testimony of
ἐν Ἰησοῦ ἐγενόμην ἐν τῇ νήσῳ τῇ καλουμένῃ Πάτμῳ διὰ ← τὸν λόγον ⸤τοῦ θεοῦ⸥ καὶ τὴν μαρτυρίαν →
p.d n.dsm v.ami.1s p.d d.dsf n.dsf d.dsf pt.pp.dsf n.dsm p.a d.asm n.asm d.gsm n.gsm cj d.asf n.asf
1877 2652 1181 1877 3836 3762 3836 2813 4253 1328 3836 3364 3836 2536 2779 3836 3456

Jesus. **10** On the Lord's Day I was in the Spirit, and I heard behind me a loud voice like a trumpet,
Ἰησοῦ ἐν τῇ κυριακῇ ἡμέρᾳ → ἐγενόμην ἐν πνεύματι καὶ → ἤκουσα ὀπίσω μου μεγάλην φωνὴν ὡς σάλπιγγος
n.gsm p.d d.dsf a.dsf n.dsf v.ami.1s p.d n.dsn cj v.aai.1s p.g r.gs.1 a.asf n.asf pl n.gsf
2652 1877 3836 3258 2465 1181 1877 4460 2779 201 3958 1609 3489 5889 6055 4894

11 which said: "Write on a scroll what you see and send it to the seven churches: to Ephesus,
→ λεγούσης γράψον εἰς βιβλίον ὃ → βλέπεις καὶ πέμψον ταῖς ἑπτὰ ἐκκλησίαις εἰς Ἔφεσον καὶ εἰς
pt.pa.gsf v.aam.2s p.a n.asn r.asn v.pai.2s cj v.aam.2s d.dpf a.dpf n.dpf p.a n.asf cj p.a
3306 1211 1650 1046 4005 1063 2779 4287 3836 2231 1711 1650 2387 2779 1650

Smyrna, Pergamum, Thyatira, Sardis, Philadelphia and Laodicea." ¶ **12** I
Σμύρναν καὶ εἰς Πέργαμον καὶ εἰς Θυάτειρα καὶ εἰς Σάρδεις καὶ εἰς Φιλαδέλφειαν καὶ εἰς Λαοδίκειαν Καὶ →
n.asf cj p.a n.asf cj p.a n.apn cj p.a n.apf cj p.a n.asf cj p.a n.asf cj
5044 2779 1650 4307 2779 1650 2587 2779 1650 4915 2779 1650 5788 2779 1650 3293 2779

turned around to see the voice that was speaking to me. And when I turned I saw seven golden
ἐπέστρεψα ← → βλέπειν τὴν φωνὴν ἥτις → ἐλάλει μετ᾽ ἐμοῦ καὶ → ἐπιστρέψας εἶδον ἑπτὰ χρυσᾶς
v.aai.1s f.pa d.asf n.asf r.nsf v.iai.3s p.g r.gs.1 cj pt.aa.nsm v.aai.1s a.apf a.apf
2188 1063 3836 5889 4015 3281 3552 1609 2779 2188 1625 2231 5997

lampstands, **13** and among the lampstands was someone "like a son of man," dressed in a robe reaching down
λυχνίας καὶ ἐν μέσῳ τῶν λυχνιῶν ὅμοιον υἱὸν → ἀνθρώπου ἐνδεδυμένον ← ← ←
n.apf cj p.d n.dsn d.gpf n.gpf a.asm n.asm n.gsm pt.rp.asm
3393 2779 1877 3545 3836 3393 3927 5626 476 1907

to his feet and with a golden sash around his chest. **14** His head and hair were white like
→ → ποδήρη καὶ πρὸς χρυσᾶν ζώνην περιεζωσμένον τοῖς μαστοῖς δὲ αὐτοῦ ἡ κεφαλὴ καὶ αἱ τρίχες λευκαὶ ὡς
n.asm cj p.a a.asf n.asf pt.rp.asm d.dpm n.dpm cj r.gsm.3 d.nsf n.nsf cj d.npf n.npf a.npf pl
4468 2779 4639 5997 2438 4322 3836 3466 1254 899 3836 3051 2779 3836 2582 3328 6055

wool, as white as snow, and his eyes were like blazing fire. **15** His feet were like bronze
ἔριον λευκόν ὡς χιὼν καὶ αὐτοῦ οἱ ὀφθαλμοὶ ὡς φλὸξ πυρός καὶ αὐτοῦ οἱ πόδες ὅμοιοι χαλκολιβάνῳ
n.nsn a.nsn pl n.nsf cj r.gsm.3 d.npm n.npm pl n.nsf n.gsn cj r.gsm.3 d.npm n.npm a.npm n.dsn
2250 3328 6055 5946 2779 899 3836 4057 6055 5825 4786 2779 899 3836 4546 3927 5909

glowing in a furnace, and his voice was like the sound of rushing waters. **16** In his right hand he
πεπυρωμένης ὡς ἐν καμίνῳ καὶ αὐτοῦ ἡ φωνὴ ὡς φωνὴ → πολλῶν ὑδάτων καὶ ἐν αὐτοῦ δεξιᾷ ⸤τῇ χειρὶ⸥ →
pt.rp.gsf pl p.d n.dsf cj r.gsm.3 d.nsf n.nsf pl n.nsf a.gpn n.gpn cj p.d r.gsm.3 a.dsf d.dsf n.dsf
4792 6055 1877 2825 2779 899 3836 5889 6055 5889 4498 5623 2779 1877 899 1288 3836 5931

held seven stars, and out of his mouth came a sharp double-edged sword. His face was like
ἔχων ἑπτὰ ἀστέρας καὶ ἐκ ← αὐτοῦ ⸤τοῦ στόματος⸥ ἐκπορευομένη ὀξεῖα δίστομος ρομφαία καὶ αὐτοῦ ἡ ὄψις ὡς
pt.pa.nsm a.apm n.apm cj p.g r.gsm.3 d.gsn n.gsn pt.pm.nsf a.nsf a.nsf n.nsf cj r.gsm.3 d.nsf n.nsf pl
2400 2231 843 2779 1666 899 3836 5125 1744 3955 1492 4855 2779 899 3836 4071 6055

the sun shining in all its brilliance. ¶ **17** When I saw him, I fell at his feet as though
ὁ ἥλιος φαίνει ἐν αὐτοῦ ⸤τῇ δυνάμει⸥ Καὶ ὅτε → εἶδον αὐτόν → ἔπεσα πρὸς αὐτοῦ ⸤τοὺς πόδας⸥ ὡς ←
d.nsm n.nsm v.pai.3s p.d r.gsm.3 d.dsf n.dsf cj cj v.aai.1s r.asm.3 v.aai.1s p.a r.gsm.3 d.apm n.apm pl
3836 2463 5743 1877 899 3836 1539 2779 4021 1625 899 4406 4639 899 3836 4546 6055

dead. Then he placed his right hand on me and said: "Do not be afraid. I am the First and the Last.
νεκρός καὶ → ἔθηκεν αὐτοῦ ⸤τὴν δεξιάν⸥ ← ἐπ᾽ ἐμὲ λέγων → μὴ → φοβοῦ ἐγώ εἰμι ὁ πρῶτος καὶ ὁ ἔσχατος
a.nsm cj v.aai.3s r.gsm.3 d.asf a.asf p.a r.as.1 pt.pa.nsm pl v.ppm.2s r.ns.1 v.pai.1s d.nsm a.nsm cj d.nsm a.nsm
3738 2779 5502 899 3836 1288 2093 1609 3306 3590 5828 1609 1639 3836 4755 2779 3836 2274

ὁ παντοκράτωρ.

1:9 Ἐγὼ Ἰωάννης, ὁ ἀδελφὸς ὑμῶν καὶ συγκοινωνὸς ἐν τῇ θλίψει καὶ βασιλείᾳ καὶ ὑπομονῇ ἐν Ἰησοῦ, ἐγενόμην ἐν τῇ νήσῳ τῇ καλουμένῃ Πάτμῳ διὰ τὸν λόγον τοῦ θεοῦ καὶ τὴν μαρτυρίαν Ἰησοῦ. **10** ἐγενόμην ἐν πνεύματι ἐν τῇ κυριακῇ ἡμέρᾳ καὶ ἤκουσα ὀπίσω μου φωνὴν μεγάλην ὡς σάλπιγγος **11** λεγούσης, Ὃ βλέπεις γράψον εἰς βιβλίον καὶ πέμψον ταῖς ἑπτὰ ἐκκλησίαις, εἰς Ἔφεσον καὶ εἰς Σμύρναν καὶ εἰς Πέργαμον καὶ εἰς Θυάτειρα καὶ εἰς Σάρδεις καὶ εἰς Φιλαδέλφειαν καὶ εἰς Λαοδίκειαν. ¶ **12** Καὶ ἐπέστρεψα βλέπειν τὴν φωνὴν ἥτις ἐλάλει μετ᾽ ἐμοῦ, καὶ ἐπιστρέψας εἶδον ἑπτὰ λυχνίας χρυσᾶς **13** καὶ ἐν μέσῳ τῶν λυχνιῶν ὅμοιον υἱὸν ἀνθρώπου ἐνδεδυμένον ποδήρη καὶ περιεζωσμένον πρὸς τοῖς μαστοῖς ζώνην χρυσᾶν. **14** ἡ δὲ κεφαλὴ αὐτοῦ καὶ αἱ τρίχες λευκαὶ ὡς ἔριον λευκὸν ὡς χιὼν καὶ οἱ ὀφθαλμοὶ αὐτοῦ ὡς φλὸξ πυρός **15** καὶ οἱ πόδες αὐτοῦ ὅμοιοι χαλκολιβάνῳ ὡς ἐν καμίνῳ πεπυρωμένης καὶ ἡ φωνὴ αὐτοῦ ὡς φωνὴ ὑδάτων πολλῶν, **16** καὶ ἔχων ἐν τῇ δεξιᾷ χειρὶ αὐτοῦ ἀστέρας ἑπτὰ καὶ ἐκ τοῦ στόματος αὐτοῦ ρομφαία δίστομος ὀξεῖα ἐκπορευομένη καὶ ἡ ὄψις αὐτοῦ ὡς ὁ ἥλιος φαίνει ἐν τῇ δυνάμει αὐτοῦ. ¶ **17** Καὶ ὅτε εἶδον αὐτόν, ἔπεσα πρὸς τοὺς πόδας αὐτοῦ ὡς νεκρός, καὶ ἔθηκεν τὴν δεξιὰν αὐτοῦ ἐπ᾽ ἐμὲ λέγων, Μὴ φοβοῦ· ἐγώ εἰμι ὁ πρῶτος

18 I am the Living One; I was dead, and behold I am alive *for ever* *and ever!* And I hold
καὶ ὁ ζῶν ← καὶ → ἐγενόμην νεκρὸς καὶ ἰδοὺ → εἰμι ζῶν εἰς τοὺς αἰῶνας τῶν αἰώνων καὶ → ἔχω
cj d.nsm pt.pa.nsm cj v.ami.1s a.nsm cj j v.pai.1s pt.pa.nsm p.a d.apm n.apm d.gpm n.gpm cj v.pai.1s
2779 3836 2409 2779 1181 3738 2779 2627 1639 2409 1650 3836 172 3836 172 2779 2400

the keys of death and Hades. ¶ **19** "Write, therefore, what you have seen, what is now and what
τὰς κλεῖς → τοῦ θανάτου καὶ τοῦ ἅδου γράψον οὖν ἃ → εἶδες καὶ ἃ εἰσιν καὶ ἃ
d.apf n.apf d.gsm n.gsm cj d.gsm n.gsm v.aam.2s cj r.apn v.aai.2s cj r.npn v.pai.3p cj r.npn
3836 3090 3836 2505 2779 3836 87 1211 4036 4005 1625 2779 4005 1639 2779 4005

will take place later. **20** The mystery of the seven stars that you saw in my right hand and of
→ μέλλει γενέσθαι ← μετὰ ταῦτα τὸ μυστήριον → τῶν ἑπτὰ ἀστέρων οὓς → εἶδες ἐπὶ μου τῆς δεξιᾶς ← καὶ →
v.pai.3s f.am p.a r.apn d.nsn n.nsn d.gpm a.gpm n.gpm r.apm v.aai.2s p.g r.gs.1 d.gsf a.gsf cj
3516 1181 3552 4047 3836 3696 3836 2231 843 4005 1625 2093 1609 3836 1288 2779

the seven golden lampstands is this: The seven stars are the angels of the seven churches, and the seven
τὰς ἑπτὰ τὰς χρυσᾶς λυχνίας οἱ ἑπτὰ ἀστέρες εἰσιν ἄγγελοι → τῶν ἑπτὰ ἐκκλησιῶν καὶ αἱ αἱ ἑπτὰ
d.apf a.apf d.apf a.apf n.apf d.npm a.npm n.npm v.pai.3p n.npm d.gpf a.gpf n.gpf cj d.npf d.npf a.npf
3836 2231 3836 5997 3393 3836 2231 843 1639 34 3836 2231 1711 2779 3836 3836 2231

lampstands are the seven churches.
λυχνίαι εἰσίν ἑπτὰ ἐκκλησίαι
n.npf v.pai.3p a.npf n.npf
3393 1639 2231 1711

To the Church in Ephesus

2:1 "To the angel of the church in Ephesus write: ¶ These are the words of him who holds the seven
→ Τῷ ἀγγέλῳ → τῆς ἐκκλησίας ἐν Ἐφέσῳ γράψον Τάδε λέγει ὁ ← κρατῶν τοὺς ἑπτὰ
d.dsm n.dsm d.gsf n.gsf p.d n.dsf v.aam.2s r.apn v.pai.3s d.nsm pt.pa.nsm d.apm a.apm
3836 34 3836 1711 1877 2387 1211 3840 3306 3836 3195 3836 2231

stars in his right hand and walks among the seven golden lampstands: **2** I know your deeds,
ἀστέρας ἐν αὐτοῦ τῇ δεξιᾷ ← ὁ περιπατῶν ἐν μέσῳ τῶν ἑπτὰ τῶν χρυσῶν λυχνιῶν → οἶδα σου τὰ ἔργα
n.apm p.d r.gsm.3 d.dsf n.dsf d.nsm pt.pa.nsm p.d n.dsn d.gpf a.gpf d.gpf a.gpf n.gpf v.rai.1s r.gs.2 d.apn n.apn
843 1877 899 3836 1288 3836 4344 1877 3545 3836 2231 3836 5997 3393 3857 5148 3836 2240

your hard work and your perseverance. I know that you cannot tolerate wicked men, that you have
καὶ τὸν κόπον καὶ σου τὴν ὑπομονὴν καὶ ὅτι → οὐ δύνῃ βαστάσαι κακούς καὶ
cj d.asm n.asm cj r.gs.2 d.asf n.asf cj cj pl v.ppi.2s f.aa a.apm cj
2779 3836 3160 2779 5148 3836 5705 2779 4022 4024 1538 1002 2805 2779

tested those who claim to be apostles but are not, and have found them false. **3** You have
ἐπείρασας τοὺς ← λέγοντας ἑαυτοὺς ἀποστόλους καὶ εἰσιν οὐκ καὶ → εὗρες αὐτοὺς ψευδεῖς καὶ → ἔχεις
v.aai.2s d.apm pt.pa.apm r.apm.3 n.apm cj v.pai.3p pl cj v.aai.2s r.apm.3 a.apm cj v.pai.2s
4279 3836 3306 1571 693 2779 1639 4024 2779 2351 899 6014 2779 2400

persevered and have endured hardships for my name, and have not grown weary. ¶ **4** Yet I hold this
ὑπομονὴν καὶ → ἐβάστασας διὰ μου τὸ ὄνομα καὶ → οὐ κεκοπίακες ἀλλὰ → ἔχω
n.asf cj v.aai.2s p.a r.gs.1 d.asn n.asn cj pl v.rai.2s cj v.pai.1s
5705 2779 1002 1328 1609 3836 3950 2779 3159 4024 3159 247 2400

against you: You have forsaken your first love. **5** Remember the height from which you have
κατὰ σοῦ ὅτι → ἀφῆκες σου τὴν πρώτην τὴν ἀγάπην οὖν μνημόνευε πόθεν ← →
p.g r.gs.2 cj v.aai.2s r.gs.2 d.asf a.asf d.asf n.asf cj v.pam.2s cj
2848 5148 4022 918 5148 3836 4755 3836 27 4036 3648 4470

fallen! Repent and do the things you did at first. If you do not repent, I will come to
πέπτωκας καὶ μετανόησον καὶ ποίησον τὰ ἔργα → πρῶτα δὲ εἰ μὴ ἐὰν → μὴ μετανοήσῃς → ἔρχομαι →
v.rai.2s cj v.aam.2s cj v.aam.2s d.apn n.apn a.apn cj cj pl cj pl v.aas.2s v.pmi.1s
4406 2779 3566 2779 4472 3836 2240 4755 1254 1623 3590 1569 3566 3590 3566 2262

you and remove your lampstand from its place. **6** But you have this in your favor: You hate the practices
σοι καὶ κινήσω σου τὴν λυχνίαν ἐκ αὐτῆς τοῦ τόπου ἀλλὰ → ἔχεις τοῦτο ὅτι → μισεῖς τὰ ἔργα
r.ds.2 cj v.fai.1s r.gs.2 d.asf n.asf p.g r.gsf.3 d.gsm n.gsm cj v.pai.2s r.asn cj v.pai.2s d.apn n.apn
5148 2779 3075 5148 3836 3393 1666 899 3836 5536 247 2400 4047 4022 3631 3836 2240

of the Nicolaitans, which I also hate. ¶ **7** He who has an ear, let him hear what the Spirit says to the
→ τῶν Νικολαϊτῶν ἃ καγὼ ← μισῶ Ὁ ← ἔχων οὓς → ἀκουσάτω τί τὸ πνεῦμα λέγει → ταῖς
d.gpm n.gpm r.apn crasis v.pai.1s d.nsm pt.pa.nsm n.asn v.aam.3s r.asn d.nsn n.nsn v.pai.3s d.dpf
3836 3774 4005 2743 3631 3836 2400 4044 201 5515 3836 4460 3306 3836

καὶ ὁ ἔσχατος ¹⁸ καὶ ὁ ζῶν, καὶ ἐγενόμην νεκρὸς καὶ ἰδοὺ ζῶν εἰμι εἰς τοὺς αἰῶνας τῶν αἰώνων καὶ ἔχω τὰς κλεῖς τοῦ θανάτου καὶ τοῦ ἅδου. ¶ ¹⁹ γράψον οὖν ἃ εἶδες καὶ ἃ εἰσιν καὶ ἃ μέλλει γενέσθαι μετὰ ταῦτα. ²⁰ τὸ μυστήριον τῶν ἑπτὰ ἀστέρων οὓς εἶδες ἐπὶ τῆς δεξιᾶς μου καὶ τὰς ἑπτὰ λυχνίας τὰς χρυσᾶς· οἱ ἑπτὰ ἀστέρες ἄγγελοι τῶν ἑπτὰ ἐκκλησιῶν εἰσιν καὶ αἱ λυχνίαι αἱ ἑπτὰ ἑπτὰ ἐκκλησίαι εἰσίν.

²·¹ Τῷ ἀγγέλῳ τῆς ἐν Ἐφέσῳ ἐκκλησίας γράψον· ¶ Τάδε λέγει ὁ κρατῶν τοὺς ἑπτὰ ἀστέρας ἐν τῇ δεξιᾷ αὐτοῦ, ὁ περιπατῶν ἐν μέσῳ τῶν ἑπτὰ λυχνιῶν τῶν χρυσῶν· ² Οἶδα τὰ ἔργα σου καὶ τὸν κόπον καὶ τὴν ὑπομονήν σου καὶ ὅτι οὐ δύνῃ βαστάσαι κακούς, καὶ ἐπείρασας τοὺς λέγοντας ἑαυτοὺς ἀποστόλους καὶ οὐκ εἰσιν καὶ εὗρες αὐτοὺς ψευδεῖς, ³ καὶ ὑπομονὴν ἔχεις καὶ ἐβάστασας διὰ τὸ ὄνομά μου καὶ οὐ κεκοπίακες. ¶ ⁴ ἀλλὰ ἔχω κατὰ σοῦ ὅτι τὴν ἀγάπην σου τὴν πρώτην ἀφῆκες. ⁵ μνημόνευε οὖν πόθεν πέπτωκας καὶ μετανόησον καὶ τὰ πρῶτα ἔργα ποίησον· εἰ δὲ μή, ἔρχομαί σοι καὶ κινήσω τὴν λυχνίαν σου ἐκ τοῦ τόπου αὐτῆς, ἐὰν μὴ μετανοήσῃς. ⁶ ἀλλὰ τοῦτο ἔχεις, ὅτι μισεῖς τὰ ἔργα τῶν Νικολαϊτῶν ἃ καγὼ μισῶ. ¶ ⁷ ὁ ἔχων οὓς

churches. To him who overcomes, I will give the right to eat　from the tree of life,　which is　in the
ἐκκλησίαις → Τῷ ← νικῶντι → → δώσω　→ φαγεῖν ἐκ τοῦ ξύλου ⌐τῆς ζωῆς⌐ ὅ ἐστιν ἐν τῷ
n.dpf　　　d.dsm　pt.pa.dsm　　　v.fai.1s　　f.aa　p.g　d.gsn n.gsn　d.gsf n.gsf　r.nsn v.pai.3s p.d d.dsm
1711　　　3836　3771　　　　　　1443　　　2266　1666　3836　3833　3836 2437　4005　1639　1877 3836

paradise of God.
παραδείσῳ → ⌐τοῦ θεοῦ⌐
n.dsm　　　d.gsm n.gsm
4137　　　3836　2536

To the Church in Smyrna

2:8　"To the angel of the church　in Smyrna write:　¶　These are the words of him who is the First
Καὶ → τῷ ἀγγέλῳ → τῆς ἐκκλησίας ἐν Σμύρνῃ γράψον　Τάδε　λέγει　ὁ πρῶτος
cj　　　d.dsm n.dsm　d.gsf n.gsf　p.d n.dsf　v.aam.2s　　r.apn　　v.pai.3s　d.nsm a.nsm
2779　　3836 34　　3836 1711　1877 5044　1211　　　3840　　3306　　3836 4755

and the Last, who died　and came to life　again.　**9** I know your afflictions and your poverty – yet you
καὶ ὁ ἔσχατος ὃς ⌐ἐγένετο νεκρὸς⌐ καὶ → → ἔζησεν　οἶδα σου ⌐τὴν θλῖψιν⌐ καὶ τὴν πτωχείαν ἀλλὰ →
cj d.nsm a.nsm r.nsm v.ami.3s a.nsm cj　　v.aai.3s　v.rai.1s r.gs.2 d.asf n.asf cj d.asf n.asf　cj
2779 3836 2274 4005 1181　3738 2779　　　2409　　3857 5148 3836 2568　2779 3836 4775　247

are rich!　I know the slander　of those who say　they　are Jews　and are not, but are a
εἶ πλούσιος καὶ　τὴν βλασφημίαν ἐκ τῶν ← λεγόντων ἑαυτοὺς εἶναι Ἰουδαίους καὶ εἰσὶν οὐ ἀλλὰ
v.pai.2s a.nsm cj　d.asf n.asf p.g d.gpm　pt.pa.gpm r.apm.3 f.pa n.apm　cj v.pai.3p pl cj
1639 4454 2779　3836 1060 1666 3836　3306 1571 1639 2681　2779 1639 4024 247

synagogue of Satan.　**10** Do not be afraid of what you are about to suffer. *I tell you,* the devil　will put
συναγωγὴ → ⌐τοῦ σατανᾶ⌐　→ μηδὲν → φοβοῦ ← ἃ → → μέλλεις → πάσχειν ἰδοὺ ὁ διάβολος μέλλει βάλλειν
n.nsf　　d.gsm n.gsm　　a.asn　v.ppm.2s r.apn　　v.pai.2s　f.pa　j　d.nsm n.nsm v.pai.3s f.pa
5252　　3836 4928　　5828 3594　5828　　3516　4248 2627 3836 1333 3516 965

some of you in prison to test　you, and you will suffer persecution for ten days. Be　faithful, even to the
ἐξ ὑμῶν εἰς φυλακὴν ἵνα πειρασθῆτε ← καὶ → → ἕξετε θλῖψιν → δέκα ἡμερῶν γίνου πιστὸς → → → the
p.g r.gp.2 p.a n.asf cj v.aps.2p　　cj　　v.fai.2p n.asf　a.gpf n.gpf v.pmm.2s a.nsm
1666 7007 1650 5871 2671 4279　2779　　2400 2568　1274 2465 1181 4412

point of death, and I will give you the crown　of life.　¶　**11** He who has　an ear, let him hear　what
ἄχρι → θανάτου καὶ → → δώσω σοι τὸν στέφανον → ⌐τῆς ζωῆς⌐　Ὁ ← ἔχων οὖς → ἀκουσάτω τί
p.g　n.gsm cj　　v.fai.1s r.ds.2 d.asm n.asm　d.gsf n.gsf　d.nsm　pt.pa.nsm n.asn　v.aam.3s r.asn
948　2505 2779　　1443 5148 3836 5109　3836 2437　3836　2400 4044　201 5515

the Spirit says to the churches. He who overcomes will not　be hurt　at all by the second　death.
τὸ πνεῦμα λέγει ταῖς ἐκκλησίαις Ὁ ← νικῶν → οὐ μὴ → ἀδικηθῇ ← ἐκ τοῦ ⌐τοῦ δευτέρου⌐ θανάτου
d.nsn n.nsn v.pai.3s d.dpf n.dpf d.nsm pt.pa.nsm pl pl v.aps.3s　p.g d.gsm d.gsm a.gsm n.gsm
3836 4460 3306 3836 1711 3836 3771 4024 3590 92 92　1666 3836 3836 1311 2505

To the Church in Pergamum

2:12　"To the angel of the church　in Pergamum write:　¶　These are the words of him who has　the
Καὶ → τῷ ἀγγέλῳ → τῆς ἐκκλησίας ἐν Περγάμῳ γράψον　Τάδε λέγει ὁ ἔχων τὴν
cj　　d.dsm n.dsm　d.gsf n.gsf　p.d n.dsf　v.aam.2s　　r.apn v.pai.3s d.nsm pt.pa.nsm d.asf
2779　　3836 34　　3836 1711　1877 4307　1211　　　3840 3306 3836 2400 3836

sharp,　double-edged sword.　**13** I know where you live　– where Satan　has his throne. Yet you remain
⌐τὴν ὀξεῖαν⌐ ⌐τὴν δίστομον⌐ ῥομφαίαν → οἶδα ποῦ → κατοικεῖς ὅπου ⌐τοῦ σατανᾶ⌐ ὁ θρόνος καὶ →
d.asf a.asf　d.asf a.asf　n.asf　　v.rai.1s adv　v.pai.2s cj　d.gsm n.gsm　d.nsm n.nsm cj
3836 3955　3836 1492　3836　　4855 4543　2997 3963　3836 4928　3836 2585 2779

true　to my name.　You did not renounce your faith in me, even in the days　of Antipas, my faithful
κρατεῖς ← μου ⌐τὸ ὄνομα⌐ καὶ → → οὐκ ἠρνήσω τὴν πίστιν → μου καὶ ἐν ταῖς ἡμέραις Ἀντιπᾶς μου ⌐ὁ πιστός⌐
v.pai.2s r.gs.1 d.asn n.asn cj　pl v.ami.2s d.asf n.asf r.gs.1 cj p.d d.dpf n.dpf n.nsm r.gs.1 d.nsm a.nsm
3195　1609 3836 3950 2779 766 766 4024 2779 3836 4411 1609 2779 1877 3836 2465 525 1609 3836 4412

witness,　who was put to death　in　your city – where Satan　lives.　¶　**14** Nevertheless, I have a
μου ὁ μάρτυς ὃς → → ἀπεκτάνθη παρ' ὑμῖν ὅπου ὁ σατανᾶς κατοικεῖ　ἀλλ' → ἔχω
r.gs.1 d.nsm n.nsm r.nsm　　v.api.3s p.d r.dp.2 cj d.nsm n.nsm v.pai.3s　cj　v.pai.1s
1609 3836 3459 4005　　650 4123 7007 3963 3836 4928 2997　247　2400

few　things against you:　You have people there who hold　to the teaching of Balaam, who taught
ὀλίγα ← κατὰ σοῦ ὅτι → ἔχεις ἐκεῖ → κρατοῦντας ← τὴν διδαχὴν → Βαλαάμ ὃς ἐδίδασκεν
a.apn　p.g r.gs.2 cj　v.pai.2s adv　pt.pa.apm　d.asf n.asf　n.gsm r.nsm v.iai.3s
3900　2848 5148 4022　2400 1695　3195　3836 1439　525 4005 1438

ἀκουσάτω τί τὸ πνεῦμα λέγει ταῖς ἐκκλησίαις. τῷ νικῶντι δώσω αὐτῷ φαγεῖν ἐκ τοῦ ξύλου τῆς ζωῆς, ὅ ἐστιν ἐν τῷ παραδείσῳ
τοῦ θεοῦ.

²:⁸ Καὶ τῷ ἀγγέλῳ τῆς ἐν Σμύρνῃ ἐκκλησίας γράψον· ¶ Τάδε λέγει ὁ πρῶτος καὶ ὁ ἔσχατος, ὃς ἐγένετο νεκρὸς καὶ ἔζησεν·
⁹ Οἶδά σου τὴν θλῖψιν καὶ τὴν πτωχείαν, ἀλλὰ πλούσιος εἶ, καὶ τὴν βλασφημίαν ἐκ τῶν λεγόντων Ἰουδαίους εἶναι ἑαυτοὺς καὶ
οὐκ εἰσὶν ἀλλὰ συναγωγὴ τοῦ Σατανᾶ. ¹⁰ μηδὲν φοβοῦ ἃ μέλλεις πάσχειν. ἰδοὺ μέλλει βάλλειν ὁ διάβολος ἐξ ὑμῶν εἰς φυλακὴν
ἵνα πειρασθῆτε καὶ ἕξετε θλῖψιν ἡμερῶν δέκα. γίνου πιστὸς ἄχρι θανάτου, καὶ δώσω σοι τὸν στέφανον τῆς ζωῆς. ¶ ¹¹ ὁ ἔχων
οὖς ἀκουσάτω τί τὸ πνεῦμα λέγει ταῖς ἐκκλησίαις. ὁ νικῶν οὐ μὴ ἀδικηθῇ ἐκ τοῦ θανάτου τοῦ δευτέρου.

²:¹² Καὶ τῷ ἀγγέλῳ τῆς ἐν Περγάμῳ ἐκκλησίας γράψον· ¶ Τάδε λέγει ὁ ἔχων τὴν ῥομφαίαν τὴν δίστομον τὴν ὀξεῖαν· ¹³ Οἶδα
ποῦ κατοικεῖς, ὅπου ὁ θρόνος τοῦ Σατανᾶ, καὶ κρατεῖς τὸ ὄνομά μου καὶ οὐκ ἠρνήσω τὴν πίστιν μου καὶ ἐν ταῖς ἡμέραις Ἀντιπᾶς
ὁ μάρτυς μου ὁ πιστός μου, ὃς ἀπεκτάνθη παρ' ὑμῖν, ὅπου ὁ Σατανᾶς κατοικεῖ. ¶ ¹⁴ ἀλλ' ἔχω κατὰ σοῦ ὀλίγα ὅτι ἔχεις ἐκεῖ
κρατοῦντας τὴν διδαχὴν Βαλαάμ, ὃς ἐδίδασκεν τῷ Βαλὰκ βαλεῖν σκάνδαλον ἐνώπιον τῶν υἱῶν Ἰσραὴλ φαγεῖν εἰδωλόθυτα καὶ

Balak to entice the Israelites to sin by eating food sacrificed to idols and by committing
⌐τῷ Βαλὰκ⌐ → βαλεῖν ἐνώπιον τῶν ⌐υἱῶν Ἰσραὴλ⌐ σκάνδαλον φαγεῖν → → εἰδωλόθυτα καὶ →
d.dsm n.dsm   f.aa p.g d.gpm n.gpm n.gsm   n.asn   f.aa   n.apn cj
3836 963   965 1967 3836 5626 2702   4998   2266   1628 2779

sexual immorality. **15** Likewise you also have those who hold to the teaching of the Nicolaitans. **16** Repent
→ πορνεῦσαι ⌐οὕτως ὁμοίως⌐ σὺ καὶ ἔχεις → → κρατοῦντας ← τὴν διδαχὴν → τῶν Νικολαϊτῶν μετανόησον
f.aa adv adv r.ns.2 adv adv v.pai.2s   pt.pa.apm   d.asf n.asf   d.gpm n.gpm v.aam.2s
4519 4048 3931 5148 2779 2400   3195   3836 1439   3836 3774 3566

therefore! Otherwise, I will soon come to you and will fight against them with the sword of my
οὖν δὲ εἰ μὴ⌐ → ταχὺ ἔρχομαι → σοι καὶ → πολεμήσω μετ᾽ αὐτῶν ἐν τῇ ῥομφαίᾳ → μου
cj cj cj pl → adv v.pmi.1s r.ds.2 cj   v.fai.1s p.g r.gpm.3 p.d d.dsf n.dsf   r.gs.1
4036 1254 1623 3590   2262 2262 5444 2262 5148 2779   4482 3552 899 1877 3836 4855   5125 1609

mouth. ¶ **17** He who has an ear, let him hear what the Spirit says to the churches. To him who
⌐τοῦ στόματος⌐ Ὁ ← ἔχων οὖς → ἀκουσάτω τί τὸ πνεῦμα λέγει → ταῖς ἐκκλησίαις Τῷ αὐτῷ ←
d.gsn n.gsn   d.nsm pt.pa.nsm n.asn → v.aam.3s r.asn d.nsn n.nsn v.pai.3s   d.dpf n.dpf d.dsm r.dsm.3
3836 5125   3836 2400 4044   201 5515 3836 4460 3306   3836 1711 3836 899

overcomes, I will give some of the hidden manna. I will also give him a white stone with a new
νικῶντι → → δώσω → τοῦ ⌐τοῦ κεκρυμμένου⌐ μάννα → → καὶ δώσω αὐτῷ λευκὴν ψῆφον καὶ → καινὸν
pt.pa.dsm → → v.fai.1s → d.gsn d.gsn pt.rp.gsn n.gsn → → cj v.fai.1s r.dsm.3 a.asf n.asf cj → a.asn
3771   1443   3836 3836 3221 3445   1443 1443 2779 1443 899 3328 6029 2779   2785

name written on it, known only to him who receives it.
ὄνομα γεγραμμένον ἐπὶ ⌐τὴν ψῆφον⌐ ὃ οὐδεὶς οἶδεν εἰ μὴ ὁ ← λαμβάνων
n.asn pt.rp.asn p.a d.asf n.asf r.asn a.nsm v.rai.3s cj pl d.nsm   pt.pa.nsm
3950 1211 2093 3836 6029 4005 4029 3857 1623 3590 3836   3284

To the Church in Thyatira

2:18 "To the angel of the church in Thyatira write: ¶ These are the words of the Son of God,
Καὶ → τῷ ἀγγέλῳ → τῆς ἐκκλησίας ἐν Θυατείροις γράψον Τάδε λέγει ὁ υἱὸς → ⌐τοῦ θεοῦ⌐
cj → d.dsm n.dsm → d.gsf n.gsf p.d n.dpn v.aam.2s r.apn v.pai.3s d.nsm n.nsm → d.gsm n.gsm
2779   3836 34   3836 1711 1877 2587 1211 3840 3306 3836 5626   3836 2536

whose eyes are like blazing fire and whose feet are like burnished bronze. **19** I know your
αὐτοῦ ⌐τοὺς ὀφθαλμοὺς⌐ ὁ ἔχων ὡς φλόγα πυρὸς καὶ αὐτοῦ ⌐οἱ πόδες⌐ ὅμοιοι χαλκολιβάνῳ → οἶδα σου
r.gsm.3 d.apm n.apm d.nsm pt.pa.nsm pl n.asf n.gsn cj r.gsm.3 d.npm n.npm a.npm   n.dsn → v.rai.1s r.gs.2
899 3836 4057 3836 2400 6055 5825 4786 2779 899 3836 4546 3927   5909   3857 5148

deeds, your love and faith, your service and perseverance, and that you are now doing
⌐τὰ ἔργα⌐ καὶ τὴν ἀγάπην καὶ ⌐τὴν πίστιν⌐ καὶ σου ⌐τὴν διακονίαν⌐ καὶ ⌐τὴν ὑπομονὴν⌐ καὶ σου ⌐τὰ ἔσχατα⌐ ⌐τὰ ἔργα⌐
d.apn n.apn cj d.asf n.asf cj d.asf n.asf cj r.gs.2 d.asf n.asf cj d.asf n.asf cj r.gs.2 d.apn a.apn d.apn n.apn
3836 2240 2779 3836 27 2779 3836 4411 2779 5148 3836 1355 2779 3836 5705 2779 5148 3836 2274 3836 2240

more than you did at first. ¶ **20** Nevertheless, I have this against you: You tolerate that woman
πλείονα → ⌐τῶν πρώτων⌐ ἀλλὰ → ἔχω κατὰ σοῦ ὅτι → ἀφεῖς τὴν γυναῖκα
a.apn.c → d.gpn a.gpn cj → v.pai.1s p.g r.gs.2 cj → v.pai.2s d.asf n.asf
4498   3836 4755 247   2400 2848 5148 4022   918 3836 1222

Jezebel, who calls herself a prophetess. By her teaching she misleads my servants into sexual
Ἰεζάβελ ἡ λέγουσα ἑαυτὴν προφῆτιν καὶ → διδάσκει καὶ → πλανᾷ ἐμοὺς ⌐τοὺς δούλους⌐ → →
n.asf d.nsf pt.pa.nsf r.asf.3 n.asf cj → v.pai.3s cj → v.pai.3s r.apm.1 d.apm n.apm
2630 3836 3306 1571 4739 2779   1438 2779   4414 1847 3836 1529

immorality and the eating of food sacrificed to idols. **21** I have given her time to repent of her
πορνεῦσαι καὶ → φαγεῖν → → εἰδωλόθυτα καὶ → ⌐ἔδωκα αὐτῇ χρόνον ἵνα μετανοήσῃ ἐκ αὐτῆς
f.aa cj f.aa → → n.apn cj → v.aai.1s r.dsf.3 n.asm cj v.aas.3s p.g r.gsf.3
4519 2779 2266   1628 2779   1443 899 5989 2671 3566 1666 899

immorality, but she is unwilling. **22** So I will cast her on a bed of suffering, and I will make those
⌐τῆς πορνείας⌐ καὶ → ⌐οὐ θέλει⌐ μετανοῆσαι ἰδοὺ → → βάλλω αὐτὴν εἰς κλίνην καὶ τοὺς
d.gsf n.gsf cj pl v.pai.3s f.aa j → → v.pai.1s r.asf.3 p.a n.asf cj d.apm
3836 4518 2779 4024 2527 3566 2627   965 899 1650 3109 2779 3836

who commit adultery with her suffer intensely, unless they repent of her ways. **23** I will
← → μοιχεύοντας μετ᾽ αὐτῆς εἰς θλῖψιν μεγάλην ⌐ἐὰν μὴ⌐ → μετανοήσωσιν ἐκ αὐτῆς ⌐τῶν ἔργων⌐ καὶ → →
pt.pa.apm p.g r.gsf.3 p.a n.asf a.asf cj pl → v.aas.3p p.g r.gsf.3 d.gpn n.gpn cj
3658 3552 899 1650 2568 3489 1569 3590   3566 1666 899 3836 2240 2779

πορνεῦσαι. **15** οὕτως ἔχεις καὶ σὺ κρατοῦντας τὴν διδαχὴν [τῶν] Νικολαϊτῶν ὁμοίως. **16** μετανόησον οὖν· εἰ δὲ μή, ἔρχομαί σοι ταχὺ καὶ πολεμήσω μετ᾽ αὐτῶν ἐν τῇ ῥομφαίᾳ τοῦ στόματός μου. ¶ **17** ὁ ἔχων οὖς ἀκουσάτω τί τὸ πνεῦμα λέγει ταῖς ἐκκλησίαις. τῷ νικῶντι δώσω αὐτῷ τοῦ μάννα τοῦ κεκρυμμένου καὶ δώσω αὐτῷ ψῆφον λευκήν, καὶ ἐπὶ τὴν ψῆφον ὄνομα καινὸν γεγραμμένον ὃ οὐδεὶς οἶδεν εἰ μὴ ὁ λαμβάνων.

2:18 Καὶ τῷ ἀγγέλῳ τῆς ἐν Θυατείροις ἐκκλησίας γράψον· ¶ Τάδε λέγει ὁ υἱὸς τοῦ θεοῦ, ὁ ἔχων τοὺς ὀφθαλμοὺς αὐτοῦ ὡς φλόγα πυρὸς καὶ οἱ πόδες αὐτοῦ ὅμοιοι χαλκολιβάνῳ· **19** Οἶδά σου τὰ ἔργα καὶ τὴν ἀγάπην καὶ τὴν πίστιν καὶ τὴν διακονίαν καὶ τὴν ὑπομονήν σου, καὶ τὰ ἔργα σου τὰ ἔσχατα πλείονα τῶν πρώτων. ¶ **20** ἀλλὰ ἔχω κατὰ σοῦ ὅτι ἀφεῖς τὴν γυναῖκα Ἰεζάβελ, ἡ λέγουσα ἑαυτὴν προφῆτιν καὶ διδάσκει καὶ πλανᾷ τοὺς ἐμοὺς δούλους πορνεῦσαι καὶ φαγεῖν εἰδωλόθυτα. **21** καὶ ἔδωκα αὐτῇ χρόνον ἵνα μετανοήσῃ, καὶ οὐ θέλει μετανοῆσαι ἐκ τῆς πορνείας αὐτῆς. **22** ἰδοὺ βάλλω αὐτὴν εἰς κλίνην καὶ τοὺς μοιχεύοντας μετ᾽ αὐτῆς εἰς θλῖψιν μεγάλην, ἐὰν μὴ μετανοήσωσιν ἐκ τῶν ἔργων αὐτῆς, **23** καὶ τὰ τέκνα αὐτῆς ἀποκτενῶ

strike her children dead. Then all the churches will know that I am he who searches hearts and
ἀποκτενῶ αὐτῆς τὰ τέκνα ἐν θανάτῳ καὶ πᾶσαι αἱ ἐκκλησίαι → γνώσονται ὅτι ἐγώ εἰμι ὁ ← ἐραυνῶν νεφροὺς καὶ
v.fai.1s r.gsf.3 d.apn n.apn p.d n.dsm cj a.npf d.npf n.npf v.fmi.3p cj r.ns.1 v.pai.1s d.nsm pt.pa.nsm n.apm cj
650 899 3836 5451 1877 2505 2779 4246 3836 1711 1182 4022 1609 1639 3836 2236 3752 2779

minds, and I will repay each of you according to your deeds. ²⁴ Now I say to the rest of you in Thyatira,
καρδίας καὶ → δώσω ἑκάστῳ ὑμῖν κατὰ ← ὑμῶν τὰ ἔργα δὲ → λέγω τοῖς λοιποῖς ὑμῖν τοῖς ἐν Θυατείροις
n.apf cj v.fai.1s r.dsm r.dp.2 p.a r.gp.2 d.apn n.apn cj v.pai.1s d.dpm d.dpm r.dp.2 d.dpm p.d n.dpn
2840 2779 1443 1667 7007 2848 7007 3836 2240 1254 3306 3836 3370 7007 3836 1877 2587

to you who do not hold to her teaching and have not learned Satan's so-called deep secrets
ὅσοι → οὐκ ἔχουσιν ← ταύτην τὴν διδαχὴν οἵτινες → οὐκ ἔγνωσαν τοῦ σατανᾶ ὡς λέγουσιν τὰ βαθέα ←
r.npm pl v.pai.3p r.asf d.asf n.asf r.npm pl v.aai.3p d.gsm n.gsm cj v.pai.3p d.apn a.apn
4012 2400 4024 2400 4047 3836 1439 4015 1182 4024 1182 3836 4928 6055 3306 3836 960

(I will not impose any other burden on you): ²⁵ Only hold on to what you have until I come. ¶
οὐ βάλλω → ἄλλο βάρος ἐφ᾽ ὑμᾶς πλὴν κρατήσατε ← ← ὃ → ἔχετε ἄχρις οὗ ἂν → ἥξω
pl v.pai.1s r.asn n.asn p.a r.ap.2 cj v.aam.2p r.asn v.pai.2p r.gsm.pl r.gsm pl v.aas.1s
965 965 4024 965 257 983 2093 7007 4440 3195 4005 2400 948 4005 323 2457

²⁶ To him who overcomes and does my will to the end, I will give authority over the nations — ²⁷
Καὶ → αὐτῷ ὁ νικῶν καὶ ὁ τηρῶν μου τὰ ἔργα ἄχρι τέλους → δώσω ἐξουσίαν ἐπὶ τῶν ἐθνῶν καὶ
cj r.dsm.3 d.nsm pt.pa.nsm cj d.nsm pt.pa.nsm r.gs.1 d.apn n.apn p.g n.gsn v.fai.1s n.asf p.g d.gpn n.gpn cj
2779 899 3836 3771 2779 3836 5498 1609 3836 2240 948 5465 1443 2026 2093 3836 1620 2779

'He will rule them with an iron scepter; he will dash them to pieces like pottery' — ¶
→ → ποιμανεῖ αὐτοὺς ἐν σιδηρᾷ ῥάβδῳ → συντρίβεται ← ὡς τὰ σκεύη τὰ κεραμικὰ
v.fai.3s r.apm.3 p.d a.dsf n.dsf v.ppi.3s cj d.npn n.npn d.npn a.npn
4477 899 1877 4971 4811 5341 6055 3836 5007 3836 3039

just as I have received authority from my Father. ²⁸ I will also give him the morning star. ²⁹ He who has
ὡς κἀγὼ εἴληφα παρὰ μου τοῦ πατρός → καὶ δώσω αὐτῷ τὸν τὸν πρωϊνόν ἀστέρα Ὁ ← ἔχων
cj crasis v.rai.1s p.g r.gs.1 d.gsm n.gsm cj v.fai.1s r.dsm.3 d.asm d.asm a.asm n.asm d.nsm pt.pa.nsm
6055 2779 3284 4123 1609 3836 4252 1443 1443 2779 1443 899 3836 3836 4748 843 3836 2400

an ear, let him hear what the Spirit says to the churches.
οὖς → → ἀκουσάτω τί τὸ πνεῦμα λέγει → ταῖς ἐκκλησίαις
n.asn v.aam.3s r.asn d.nsn n.nsn v.pai.3s d.dpf n.dpf
4044 201 5515 3836 4460 3306 3836 1711

To the Church in Sardis

³:¹ "To the angel of the church in Sardis write: ¶ These are the words of him who holds the
Καὶ → τῷ ἀγγέλῳ → τῆς ἐκκλησίας ἐν Σάρδεσιν γράψον Τάδε λέγει ὁ ← ἔχων τὰ
cj d.dsm n.dsm d.gsf n.gsf p.d n.dpf v.aam.2s r.apn v.pai.3s d.nsm pt.pa.nsm d.apn
2779 3836 34 3836 1711 1877 4915 1211 3840 3306 3836 2400 3836

seven spirits of God and the seven stars. I know your deeds; you have a reputation of being alive,
ἑπτὰ πνεύματα τοῦ θεοῦ καὶ τοὺς ἑπτὰ ἀστέρας οἶδα σου τὰ ἔργα ὅτι → ἔχεις ὄνομα ὅτι ζῇς
a.apn n.apn d.gsm n.gsm cj d.apm a.apm n.apm v.rai.1s r.gs.2 d.apn n.apn cj v.pai.2s n.asn cj v.pai.2s
2231 4460 3836 2536 2779 3836 2231 843 3857 5148 3836 2240 4022 2400 3950 4022 2409

but you are dead. ² Wake up! Strengthen what remains and is about to die, for I have not
καὶ → εἶ νεκρός γίνου γρηγορῶν καὶ στήρισον τὰ λοιπὰ ἃ → ἔμελλον ἀποθανεῖν γὰρ → → οὐ
cj v.pai.2s a.nsm v.pmm.2s pt.pa.nsm cj v.aam.2s d.apn a.apn r.npn v.iai.3p f.aa cj pl
2779 1639 3738 1181 1213 2779 5114 3836 3370 4005 3516 633 1142 2351 2351 4024

found your deeds complete in the sight of my God. ³ Remember, therefore, what you have received and
εὕρηκα σου τὰ ἔργα πεπληρωμένα → ἐνώπιον μου τοῦ θεοῦ μνημόνευε οὖν πῶς → εἴληφας καὶ
v.rai.1s r.gs.2 d.apn n.apn pt.rp.apn p.g r.gs.1 d.gsm n.gsm v.pam.2s cj cj v.rai.2s cj
2351 5148 3836 2240 4444 1967 1609 3836 2536 3648 4036 4802 3284 2779

heard; obey it, and repent. But if you do not wake up, I will come like a thief, and you will not
ἤκουσας καὶ τήρει καὶ μετανόησον οὖν ἐὰν → μὴ γρηγορήσῃς ← → ἥξω ὡς κλέπτης καὶ → → οὐ μὴ
v.aai.2s cj v.pam.2s cj v.aam.2s cj cj pl v.aas.2s v.fai.1s pl n.nsm cj pl pl
201 2779 5498 2779 3566 4036 1569 1213 3590 1213 2457 6055 3095 2779 1182 1182 4024 3590

know at what time I will come to you. ¶ ⁴ Yet you have a few people in Sardis who have not soiled
γνῷς → ποίαν ὥραν → ἥξω ἐπὶ σέ ἀλλὰ → ἔχεις ὀλίγα ὀνόματα ἐν Σάρδεσιν ἃ → οὐκ ἐμόλυναν
v.aas.2s r.asf n.asf v.fai.1s p.a r.as.2 cj v.pai.2s a.apn n.apn p.d n.dpf r.npn pl v.aai.3p
1182 4481 6052 2457 2093 5148 247 2400 3900 3950 1877 4915 4005 4024 3662

ἐν θανάτῳ. καὶ γνώσονται πᾶσαι αἱ ἐκκλησίαι ὅτι ἐγώ εἰμι ὁ ἐραυνῶν νεφροὺς καὶ καρδίας, καὶ δώσω ὑμῖν ἑκάστῳ κατὰ τὰ ἔργα ὑμῶν. ²⁴ ὑμῖν δὲ λέγω τοῖς λοιποῖς τοῖς ἐν Θυατείροις, ὅσοι οὐκ ἔχουσιν τὴν διδαχὴν ταύτην, οἵτινες οὐκ ἔγνωσαν τὰ βαθέα τοῦ Σατανᾶ ὡς λέγουσιν· οὐ βάλλω ἐφ᾽ ὑμᾶς ἄλλο βάρος, ²⁵ πλὴν ὃ ἔχετε κρατήσατε ἄχρι[ς] οὗ ἂν ἥξω. ¶ ²⁶ καὶ ὁ νικῶν καὶ ὁ τηρῶν ἄχρι τέλους τὰ ἔργα μου, δώσω αὐτῷ ἐξουσίαν ἐπὶ τῶν ἐθνῶν ²⁷ καὶ ποιμανεῖ αὐτοὺς ἐν ῥάβδῳ σιδηρᾷ ¶ ὡς τὰ σκεύη τὰ κεραμικὰ συντρίβεται, ²⁸ ὡς κἀγὼ εἴληφα παρὰ τοῦ πατρός μου, καὶ δώσω αὐτῷ τὸν ἀστέρα τὸν πρωϊνόν. ²⁹ ὁ ἔχων οὖς ἀκουσάτω τί τὸ πνεῦμα λέγει ταῖς ἐκκλησίαις.

³:¹ Καὶ τῷ ἀγγέλῳ τῆς ἐν Σάρδεσιν ἐκκλησίας γράψον· ¶ Τάδε λέγει ὁ ἔχων τὰ ἑπτὰ πνεύματα τοῦ θεοῦ καὶ τοὺς ἑπτὰ ἀστέρας· Οἶδά σου τὰ ἔργα ὅτι ὄνομα ἔχεις ὅτι ζῇς, καὶ νεκρὸς εἶ. ² γίνου γρηγορῶν καὶ στήρισον τὰ λοιπὰ ἃ ἔμελλον ἀποθανεῖν, οὐ γὰρ εὕρηκά σου τὰ ἔργα πεπληρωμένα ἐνώπιον τοῦ θεοῦ μου. ³ μνημόνευε οὖν πῶς εἴληφας καὶ ἤκουσας καὶ τήρει καὶ μετανόησον. ἐὰν οὖν μὴ γρηγορήσῃς, ἥξω ὡς κλέπτης, καὶ οὐ μὴ γνῷς ποίαν ὥραν ἥξω ἐπὶ σέ. ¶ ⁴ ἀλλὰ ἔχεις ὀλίγα ὀνόματα ἐν

their clothes.   They will walk   with me, dressed in white, for they are   worthy. **[5]** He who overcomes
αὐτῶν ⸆τὰ ἱμάτια καὶ → → περιπατήσουσιν μετ᾽ ἐμοῦ ἐν λευκοῖς ὅτι → εἰσιν ἄξιοι Ὁ ← νικῶν
r.gpm.3   d.apn n.apn   cj   v.fai.3p   p.g   r.gs.1   p.d a.dpn   cj   v.pai.3p a.npm   d.nsm   pt.pa.nsm
899   3836 2668   2779   4344   3552 1609   1877 3328   4022   1639 545   3836   3771

will, like them, be dressed   in white.   I   will never   blot   out his   name   from the book of
⸆ οὕτως ← → περιβαλεῖται ἐν λευκοῖς ἱματίοις καὶ ⸆ → ⸉οὐ μὴ⸊ ἐξαλείψω ← αὐτοῦ ⸃τὸ ὄνομα⸄ ἐκ τῆς βίβλου
adv   v.fmi.3s   p.d a.dpn   n.dpn   cj   pl pl   v.aas.1s   r.gsm.3 d.asn n.asn   p.g d.gsf n.gsf
4314 4048   4314   1877 3328   2668   2779 1981 1981 4024 3590   1981   899   3836 3950   1666 3836 1047

life,   but will acknowledge his   name   before my Father   and   his   angels. **[6]** He who has   an
⸃τῆς ζωῆς⸄ καὶ → ὁμολογήσω αὐτοῦ ⸃τὸ ὄνομα⸄ ἐνώπιον μου ⸃τοῦ πατρός⸄ καὶ ἐνώπιον αὐτοῦ ⸃τῶν ἀγγέλων⸄ Ὁ ← ἔχων
d.gsf n.gsf   cj → v.fai.1s   r.gsm.3 d.asn n.asn   p.g   r.gs.1 d.gsm n.gsm   cj   p.g   r.gsm.3 d.gpm n.gpm   d.nsm   pt.pa.nsm
3836 2437   2779   3933   899   3836 3950   1967   1609 3836 4252   2779   1967   899   3836 34   3836   2400

ear, let him hear   what the Spirit says to the churches.
οὖς → → ἀκουσάτω τί τὸ πνεῦμα λέγει → ταῖς ἐκκλησίαις
n.asn   v.aam.3s   r.asn d.nsn n.nsn v.pai.3s   d.dpf n.dpf
4044   201   5515 3836 4460   3306   3836 1711

To the Church in Philadelphia

3:7 "To the angel of the church in   Philadelphia write: ¶   These are the words of him who is holy
Καὶ → τῷ ἀγγέλῳ → τῆς ἐκκλησίας ἐν Φιλαδελφείᾳ γράφον·   Τάδε   λέγει   ὁ ←   ἅγιος
cj   d.dsm n.dsm   d.gsf n.gsf   p.d n.dsf   v.aam.2s   r.apn   v.pai.3s   d.nsm   a.nsm
2779   3836 34   3836 1711   1877 5788   1211   3840   3306   3836   41

and true,   who holds the key of David. What he opens   no   one can shut, and what he shuts
⸃ὁ ἀληθινός⸄ ὁ ἔχων τὴν κλεῖν → Δαυίδ ὁ → ← ἀνοίγων καὶ οὐδεὶς ←   κλείσει καὶ → → κλείων καὶ
d.nsm a.nsm   d.nsm pt.pa.nsm d.asf n.asf   n.gsm   d.nsm   pt.pa.nsm cj a.nsm   v.fai.3s cj   pt.pa.nsm cj
3836 240   3836 2400   3836 3090   1253   3836   487   2779 4029   3091   2779   3091   2779

no   one can open. **[8]** I know your deeds.   See, I have placed before you an open   door that no   one
οὐδεὶς ← → ἀνοίγει → οἶδα σου ⸃τὰ ἔργα⸄ ἰδοὺ → → δέδωκα ἐνώπιον σου ἠνεῳγμένην θύραν ἣν οὐδεὶς ←
a.nsm   v.pai.3s   v.rai.1s r.gs.2 d.apn n.apn   j   v.rai.1s   p.g   r.gs.2   pt.rp.asf   n.asf r.asf a.nsm
4029   487   3857   5148 3836 2240   2627   1443   1967   5148   487   2598   4005 4029

can   shut.   I know that you have little   strength, yet you have kept   my word   and have not denied
δύναται κλεῖσαι αὐτήν → ⸆ ὅτι → ἔχεις μικρὰν δύναμιν καὶ → → ἐτήρησας μου ⸃τὸν λόγον⸄ καὶ → → οὐκ ἠρνήσω
v.ppi.3s   f.aa   r.asf.3   cj   v.pai.2s a.asf   n.asf   cj   v.aai.2s   r.gs.1 d.asm n.asm   cj   pl   v.ami.2s
1538   3091   899   4022   2400 3625   1539   2779   5498   1609 3836 3364   2779 766 4024 766

my name.   **[9]**   I will make those who are of the synagogue of Satan,   who claim   to be
μου ⸃τὸ ὄνομα⸄ ἰδοὺ → → διδῶ   ἐκ τῆς συναγωγῆς → ⸃τοῦ σατανᾶ⸄ τῶν ⸃λεγόντων ἑαυτοὺς⸄ → εἶναι
r.gs.1 d.asn n.asn   j   v.pai.1s   p.g d.gsf n.gsf   d.gsm n.gsm   d.gpm pt.pa.gpm   r.apm.3   f.pa
1609 3836 3950   2627   1443   1666 3836 5252   3836 4928   3836 3306   1571   1639

Jews   though they are not, but   are liars   —   I will make them   come and fall   down
Ἰουδαίους καὶ → εἰσιν οὐκ ἀλλὰ → ψεύδονται ἰδοὺ → → ποιήσω αὐτοὺς ἵνα ἥξουσιν καὶ προσκυνήσουσιν ←
a.apm   cj   v.pai.3p pl cj   v.pmi.3p   j   v.fai.1s   r.apm.3 cj   v.fai.3p   cj   v.fai.3p
2681   2779   1639 4024 247   6017   2627   4472   899   2671 2457   2779 4686

at   your feet   and acknowledge that I   have loved   you. **[10]** Since you have kept   my command to
ἐνώπιον σου ⸃τῶν ποδῶν⸄ καὶ γνῶσιν ὅτι ἐγὼ → ἠγάπησα σε   ὅτι → → ἐτήρησας μου ⸃τὸν λόγον⸄
p.g   r.gs.2 d.gpm n.gpm   cj   v.aas.3p cj r.ns.1   v.aai.1s   r.as.2   cj   v.aai.2s   r.gs.1 d.asm n.asm
1967   5148 3836 4546   2779 1182   4022 1609   26   5148   4022   5498   1609 3836 3364

endure   patiently, I   will also keep   you from the hour of trial   that is going   to come   upon the
⸃τῆς ὑπομονῆς⸄ ← καγὼ → ← τηρήσω σε ἐκ τῆς ὥρας → ⸃τοῦ πειρασμοῦ⸄ τῆς → μελλούσης → ἔρχεσθαι ἐπὶ τῆς
d.gsf n.gsf   crasis   v.fai.1s r.as.2 p.g d.gsf n.gsf   ⸃τοῦ   n.gsm   d.gsf   pt.pa.gsf   f.pm   p.g   d.gsf
3836 5705   2743   5498 2743   5498 5148 1666 3836 6052   3836 4280   3836   3516   2262   2093 3836

whole world   to test   those who live   on the earth. ¶   **[11]** I am coming soon. Hold on to what you
ὅλης οἰκουμένης → πειράσαι τοὺς ← κατοικοῦντας ἐπὶ τῆς γῆς   → ἔρχομαι ταχύ κράτει ← ← ὃ
a.gsf   n.gsf   f.aa   d.apm ← pt.pa.apm   p.g d.gsf n.gsf   v.pmi.1s   adv   v.pam.2s   r.asn
3910   3876   4279   3836   2997   2093 3836 1178   2262   5444   3195   4005

have, so that no   one will take your crown.   **[12]** Him who overcomes I will make   a pillar in the temple
ἔχεις ἵνα ← μηδεὶς ← λάβῃ σου ⸃τὸν στέφανον⸄ Ὁ ← νικῶν → ποιήσω αὐτὸν στῦλον ἐν τῷ ναῷ
v.pai.2s cj   a.nsm   v.aas.3s r.gs.2 d.asm n.asm   d.nsm ← pt.pa.nsm   v.fai.1s r.asm.3   n.asm   p.d d.dsm n.dsm
2400   2671   3594   3284 5148 3836 5109   3836   3771   4472   899   5146   1877 3836 3724

Σάρδεσιν ἃ οὐκ ἐμόλυναν τὰ ἱμάτια αὐτῶν, καὶ περιπατήσουσιν μετ᾽ ἐμοῦ ἐν λευκοῖς, ὅτι ἄξιοί εἰσιν. **5** ὁ νικῶν οὕτως περιβαλεῖται ἐν ἱματίοις λευκοῖς καὶ οὐ μὴ ἐξαλείψω τὸ ὄνομα αὐτοῦ ἐκ τῆς βίβλου τῆς ζωῆς καὶ ὁμολογήσω τὸ ὄνομα αὐτοῦ ἐνώπιον τοῦ πατρός μου καὶ ἐνώπιον τῶν ἀγγέλων αὐτοῦ. **6** ὁ ἔχων οὖς ἀκουσάτω τί τὸ πνεῦμα λέγει ταῖς ἐκκλησίαις.

3:7 Καὶ τῷ ἀγγέλῳ τῆς ἐν Φιλαδελφείᾳ ἐκκλησίας γράφον· ¶ Τάδε λέγει ὁ ἅγιος, ὁ ἀληθινός, ὁ ἔχων τὴν κλεῖν Δαυίδ, ὁ ἀνοίγων καὶ οὐδεὶς κλείσει καὶ κλείων καὶ οὐδεὶς ἀνοίγει· **8** Οἶδά σου τὰ ἔργα, ἰδοὺ δέδωκα ἐνώπιόν σου θύραν ἠνεῳγμένην, ἣν οὐδεὶς δύναται κλεῖσαι αὐτήν, ὅτι μικρὰν ἔχεις δύναμιν καὶ ἐτήρησάς μου τὸν λόγον καὶ οὐκ ἠρνήσω τὸ ὄνομά μου. **9** ἰδοὺ διδῶ ἐκ τῆς συναγωγῆς τοῦ Σατανᾶ τῶν λεγόντων ἑαυτοὺς Ἰουδαίους εἶναι, καὶ οὐκ εἰσὶν ἀλλὰ ψεύδονται. ἰδοὺ ποιήσω αὐτοὺς ἵνα ἥξουσιν καὶ προσκυνήσουσιν ἐνώπιον τῶν ποδῶν σου καὶ γνῶσιν ὅτι ἐγὼ ἠγάπησά σε. **10** ὅτι ἐτήρησας τὸν λόγον τῆς ὑπομονῆς μου, καγὼ σε τηρήσω ἐκ τῆς ὥρας τοῦ πειρασμοῦ τῆς μελλούσης ἔρχεσθαι ἐπὶ τῆς οἰκουμένης ὅλης πειράσαι τοὺς κατοικοῦντας ἐπὶ τῆς γῆς. ¶ **11** ἔρχομαι ταχύ· κράτει ὃ ἔχεις, ἵνα μηδεὶς λάβῃ τὸν στέφανόν σου. **12** ὁ νικῶν ποιήσω αὐτὸν

of my God.   Never again will he leave   it.   I will write on him the name of my God   and the
→ μου ⌜τοῦ θεοῦ⌝ καὶ ⌜οὐ μὴ⌝ ἔτι → → ⌜ἐξωθέξέλθῃ⌝ καὶ → γράψω ἐπ' αὐτὸν τὸ ὄνομα ⌜μου ⌜τοῦ θεοῦ⌝ καὶ τὸ
r.gs.1 d.gsm n.gsm cj pl pl adv   adv v.aas.3s cj   v.fai.1s p.a r.asm.3 d.asn n.asn r.gs.1 d.gsm n.gsm cj d.asn
2536 1609 3836 2536 2779 4024 3590 2285   2032 2002 2779   1211 2093 899 3836 3950 2536 1609 3836 2536 2779 3836

name of the city of my God, the new Jerusalem, which is coming   down out of heaven   from my
ὄνομα → τῆς πόλεως → μου ⌜τοῦ θεοῦ⌝ τῆς καινῆς Ἰερουσαλὴμ ἡ → καταβαίνουσα ← ἐκ ← ⌜τοῦ οὐρανοῦ⌝ ἀπὸ μου
n.asn d.gsf n.gsf r.gs.1 d.gsm n.gsm d.gsf a.gsf n.gsf d.nsf → pt.pa.nsf p.g d.gsm n.gsm p.g r.gs.1
3950 3836 4484 2536 1609 3836 2536 3836 2785 2647 3836 2849 1666 3836 4041 608 1609

God;   and I will also write on him my new   name.   **13** He who has   an ear, let him hear   what the
⌜τοῦ θεοῦ⌝ καὶ → → → → → μου ⌜τὸ καινόν⌝ ⌜τὸ ὄνομα⌝ Ὁ → ἔχων οὖς → → ἀκουσάτω τί τὸ
d.gsm n.gsm cj   r.gs.1 d.asn a.asn d.asn n.asn d.nsm pt.pa.nsm n.asn v.aam.3s r.asn d.nsn
3836 2536 2779   1609 3836 2785 3836 3950 3836 2400 4044 201 5515 3836

Spirit says to the churches.
πνεῦμα λέγει → ταῖς ἐκκλησίαις
n.nsn v.pai.3s d.dpf n.dpf
4460 3306 3836 1711

To the Church in Laodicea

3:14 "To the angel of the church in Laodicea write: ¶ These are the words of the Amen, the
Καὶ → τῷ ἀγγέλῳ → τῆς ἐκκλησίας ἐν Λαοδικείᾳ γράψον· Τάδε λέγει ὁ ἀμὴν ὁ
cj d.dsm n.dsm d.gsf n.gsf p.d n.dsf v.aam.2s r.apn v.pai.3s d.nsm d.nsm d.nsm
2779 3836 34 3836 1711 1877 3293 1211 3840 3306 3836 297 3836

faithful and true   witness, the ruler of God's   creation.   **15** I know your deeds, that you are neither cold
⌜ὁ πιστὸς⌝ καὶ ἀληθινός μάρτυς ἡ ἀρχὴ → ⌜τοῦ θεοῦ⌝ ⌜τῆς κτίσεως⌝ οἶδα σου ⌜τὰ ἔργα⌝ ὅτι → εἶ οὔτε ψυχρὸς
d.nsm a.nsm cj a.nsm n.nsm d.nsf n.nsf d.gsm n.gsm d.gsf n.gsf v.rai.1s r.gs.2 d.apn n.apn cj v.pai.2s cj a.nsm
3836 4412 2779 240 3459 3836 794 3232 3836 2536 3836 3232 3857 5148 3836 2240 4022 1639 4046 6037

nor hot. I wish you were either one   or the other! **16** So, because you are lukewarm – neither hot nor
οὔτε ζεστός → ὄφελον → ἦς ψυχρὸς ἢ ζεστός οὕτως ὅτι → εἶ χλιαρὸς καὶ οὔτε ζεστὸς οὔτε
cj a.nsm pl v.iai.2s a.nsm cj a.nsm adv cj v.pai.2s a.nsm cj cj a.nsm cj
4046 2412 4054 1639 6037 2445 2412 4048 4022 1639 5950 2779 4046 2412 4046

cold – I am about to spit   you out of my mouth.   **17** You say, 'I am rich;   I have acquired
ψυχρός → μέλλω ἐμέσαι σε ἐκ ← μου ⌜τοῦ στόματος⌝ ὅτι → λέγεις ὅτι → εἰμι πλούσιος καὶ
a.nsm v.pai.1s f.aa r.as.2 p.g r.gs.1 d.gsn n.gsn cj v.pai.2s cj v.pai.1s a.nsm cj
6037 3516 1840 5148 1666 1609 3836 5125 4022 3306 4022 1639 4454 2779

wealth and do not need   a thing.' But you do not realize that you are wretched,   pitiful,
πεπλούτηκα καὶ → οὐδὲν ⌜χρείαν ἔχω⌝ καὶ → → οὐκ οἶδας ὅτι σὺ εἶ ὁ ταλαίπωρος καὶ ἐλεεινὸς καὶ
v.rai.1s cj a.asn n.asf v.pai.1s cj pl v.rai.2s cj r.ns.2 v.pai.2s d.nsm a.nsm cj a.nsm cj
4456 2779 2400 4029 5970 2400 4029 4029 2779 3857 3857 4024 3857 4022 5148 1639 3836 5417 2779 1795 2779

poor, blind and naked. **18** I counsel you to buy from me gold refined in the fire, so you can
πτωχὸς καὶ τυφλὸς καὶ γυμνός → συμβουλεύω σοι ἀγοράσαι παρ' ἐμοῦ χρυσίον πεπυρωμένον ἐκ πυρὸς ἵνα → →
a.nsm cj a.nsm cj a.nsm v.pai.1s r.ds.2 f.aa p.g r.gs.1 n.asn pt.rp.asn p.g n.gsn cj
4777 2779 5603 2779 1218 5205 5148 60 4123 1609 5992 4792 1666 4786 2671

become rich; and white clothes to wear, so you can cover   your shameful nakedness; and
→ πλουτήσῃς καὶ λευκὰ ἱμάτια ἵνα περιβάλῃ καὶ → μὴ φανερωθῇ σου ἡ αἰσχύνη ⌜τῆς γυμνότητος⌝ καὶ
v.aas.2s cj a.apn n.apn cj v.ams.2s cj pl v.aps.3s r.gs.2 d.nsf n.nsf d.gsf n.gsf cj
4456 2779 3328 2668 2671 4314 2779 3590 5746 5148 3836 158 3836 1219 2779

salve to put on your eyes,   so you can see. ¶ **19** Those whom I love I rebuke and
κολλούριον → ἐγχρῖσαι σου ⌜τοὺς ὀφθαλμούς⌝ ἵνα → → βλέπῃς ⌜ὅσους ἐὰν⌝ ← → φιλῶ ἐγὼ ἐλέγχω καὶ
n.asn f.aa r.gs.2 d.apm n.apm cj v.pas.2s r.apm pl v.pas.1s r.ns.1 v.pai.1s cj
3141 1608 5148 3836 4057 2671 1063 4012 1569 5797 1609 1794 2779

discipline. So be earnest, and repent. **20** Here I am! I stand at the door and knock. If anyone hears my
παιδεύω οὖν → ζήλευε καὶ μετανόησον Ἰδοὺ → ← ἕστηκα ἐπὶ τὴν θύραν καὶ κρούω ἐάν τις ἀκούσῃ μου
v.pai.1s cj v.pam.2s cj v.aam.2s v.rai.1s p.a d.asf n.asf cj v.pai.1s cj r.nsm v.aas.3s r.gs.1
4084 4036 2418 2779 3566 2627 2705 2093 3836 2598 2779 3218 1569 5516 201 1609

voice and opens the door,   I will come   in   and eat   with him, and he with me. ¶
⌜τῆς φωνῆς⌝ καὶ ἀνοίξῃ τὴν θύραν [καὶ] → → εἰσελεύσομαι ← πρὸς αὐτὸν καὶ δειπνήσω μετ' αὐτοῦ καὶ αὐτὸς μετ' ἐμοῦ
d.gsf n.gsf cj v.aas.3s d.asf n.asf adv v.fmi.1s p.a r.asm.3 cj v.fai.1s p.g r.gsm.3 cj r.nsm p.g r.gs.1
3836 5889 2779 487 3836 2598 2779 1656 4639 899 2779 1268 3552 899 2779 899 3552 1609

στύλον ἐν τῷ ναῷ τοῦ θεοῦ μου καὶ ἔξω οὐ μὴ ἐξέλθῃ ἔτι καὶ γράψω ἐπ' αὐτὸν τὸ ὄνομα τοῦ θεοῦ μου καὶ τὸ ὄνομα τῆς πόλεως τοῦ θεοῦ μου, τῆς καινῆς Ἰερουσαλὴμ ἡ καταβαίνουσα ἐκ τοῦ οὐρανοῦ ἀπὸ τοῦ θεοῦ μου, καὶ τὸ ὄνομά μου τὸ καινόν. **13** ὁ ἔχων οὖς ἀκουσάτω τί τὸ πνεῦμα λέγει ταῖς ἐκκλησίαις.

3:14 Καὶ τῷ ἀγγέλῳ τῆς ἐν Λαοδικείᾳ ἐκκλησίας γράψον· ¶ Τάδε λέγει ὁ Ἀμήν, ὁ μάρτυς ὁ πιστὸς καὶ ἀληθινός, ἡ ἀρχὴ τῆς κτίσεως τοῦ θεοῦ· **15** Οἶδά σου τὰ ἔργα ὅτι οὔτε ψυχρὸς εἶ οὔτε ζεστός. ὄφελον ψυχρὸς ἦς ἢ ζεστός. **16** οὕτως ὅτι χλιαρὸς εἶ καὶ οὔτε ζεστὸς οὔτε ψυχρός, μέλλω σε ἐμέσαι ἐκ τοῦ στόματός μου. **17** ὅτι λέγεις ὅτι Πλούσιός εἰμι καὶ πεπλούτηκα καὶ οὐδὲν χρείαν ἔχω, καὶ οὐκ οἶδας ὅτι σὺ εἶ ὁ ταλαίπωρος καὶ ἐλεεινὸς καὶ πτωχὸς καὶ τυφλὸς καὶ γυμνός, **18** συμβουλεύω σοι ἀγοράσαι παρ' ἐμοῦ χρυσίον πεπυρωμένον ἐκ πυρὸς ἵνα πλουτήσῃς, καὶ ἱμάτια λευκὰ ἵνα περιβάλῃ καὶ μὴ φανερωθῇ ἡ αἰσχύνη τῆς γυμνότητός σου, καὶ κολλ[ο]ύριον ἐγχρῖσαι τοὺς ὀφθαλμούς σου ἵνα βλέπῃς. ¶ **19** ἐγὼ ὅσους ἐὰν φιλῶ ἐλέγχω καὶ παιδεύω· ζήλευε οὖν καὶ μετανόησον. **20** ἰδοὺ ἕστηκα ἐπὶ τὴν θύραν καὶ κρούω· ἐάν τις ἀκούσῃ τῆς φωνῆς μου καὶ ἀνοίξῃ τὴν θύραν, [καὶ] εἰσελεύσομαι πρὸς αὐτὸν καὶ δειπνήσω μετ' αὐτοῦ καὶ αὐτὸς μετ' ἐμοῦ. ¶ **21** ὁ νικῶν δώσω αὐτῷ καθίσαι μετ' ἐμοῦ ἐν τῷ

21 To him who overcomes, I will give the right to sit with me on my throne, just as I overcame and
→ αὐτῷ Ὁ νικῶν → δώσω → καθίσαι μετ᾽ ἐμοῦ ἐν μου ⸤τῷ θρόνῳ⸥ ὡς κἀγὼ ἐνίκησα καί
r.dsm.3 d.nsm pt.pa.nsm v.fai.1s f.aa p.g r.gs.1 p.d r.gs.1 d.dsm n.dsm cj crasis v.aai.1s cj
899 3836 3771 1443 2767 3552 1609 1877 1609 3836 2585 6055 2743 3771 2779

sat down with my Father on his throne. **22** He who has an ear, let him hear what the Spirit says to
ἐκάθισα ← μετά μου ⸤τοῦ πατρός⸥ ἐν αὐτοῦ ⸤τῷ θρόνῳ⸥ Ὁ ← ἔχων οὖς → → ἀκουσάτω τί τό πνεῦμα λέγει →
v.aai.1s p.g r.gs.1 d.gsm n.gsm p.d r.gsm.3 d.dsm n.dsm d.nsm pt.pa.nsm n.asn v.aam.3s r.asn d.nsn n.nsn v.pai.3s
2767 3552 1609 3836 4252 1877 899 3836 2585 3836 2400 4044 201 5515 3836 4460 3306

the churches."
ταῖς ἐκκλησίαις
d.dpf n.dpf
3836 1711

The Throne in Heaven

4:1 After this I looked, and there before me was a door standing open in heaven. And the voice I
Μετὰ ταῦτα → εἶδον καὶ ἰδοὺ θύρα → ἠνεῳγμένη ἐν ⸤τῷ οὐρανῷ⸥ καὶ ἡ φωνὴ ἣν ↱
p.a r.apn v.aai.1s cj j n.nsf pt.rp.nsf p.d d.dsm n.dsm cj d.nsf n.nsf r.asf
3552 4047 1625 2779 2627 2598 487 1877 3836 4041 2779 3836 5889 4005 201

had first heard speaking to me like a trumpet said, "Come up here, and I will show you what must take
↱ ⸤ἡ πρώτη⸥ ἤκουσα λαλούσης μετ᾽ ἐμοῦ ὡς σάλπιγγος λέγων Ἀνάβα ← ὧδε καὶ → δείξω σοι ἃ δεῖ γενέσθαι
d.nsf a.nsf v.aai.1s pt.pa.gsf p.g r.gs.1 pl n.gsf pt.pa.nsm v.aam.2s adv cj v.fai.1s r.ds.2 r.apn v.pai.3s f.am
201 3836 4755 201 3281 3552 1609 6055 4894 3306 326 6045 2779 1259 5148 4005 1256 1181

place after this." **2** At once I was in the Spirit, and there before me was a throne in heaven and
← μετά ταῦτα Εὐθέως ← → ἐγενόμην ἐν πνεύματι καὶ ἰδοὺ → ἔκειτο θρόνος ἐν ⸤τῷ οὐρανῷ⸥ καί
p.a r.apn adv v.ami.1s p.d n.dsn cj j v.imi.3s n.nsm p.d d.dsm n.dsm cj
3552 4047 2311 1181 1877 4460 2779 2627 3023 2585 1877 3836 4041 2779

with someone sitting on it. **3** And the one who sat there had the appearance of jasper and
→ καθήμενος ἐπὶ τὸν θρόνον καὶ ὁ ← καθήμενος ὅμοιος ὁράσει λίθῳ ἰάσπιδι καί
pt.pm.nsm p.a d.asm n.asm cj d.nsm pt.pm.nsm a.nsm n.dsf n.dsm n.dsf cj
2764 2093 3836 2585 2779 3836 2764 3927 3970 3345 2618 2779

carnelian. A rainbow, resembling an emerald, encircled the throne. **4** Surrounding the throne were
σαρδίῳ καὶ ἶρις ὅμοιος ὁράσει σμαραγδίνῳ κυκλόθεν τοῦ θρόνου Καὶ κυκλόθεν τοῦ θρόνου
n.dsn cj n.nsf a.nsm n.dsf a.dsm p.g d.gsm n.gsm cj p.g d.gsm n.gsm
4917 2779 2692 3927 3970 5039 3239 3836 2585 2779 3239 3836 2585

twenty-four other thrones, and seated on them were twenty-four elders. They were
⸤εἴκοσι τέσσαρες⸥ θρόνους καὶ καθημένους ἐπὶ ⸤τοὺς θρόνους⸥ ⸤εἴκοσι τέσσαρας⸥ πρεσβυτέρους → →
a.apm a.apm n.apm cj pt.pm.apm p.a d.apm n.apm a.apm a.apm a.apm
1633 5475 2585 2779 2764 2093 3836 2585 1633 5475 4565

dressed in white and had crowns of gold on their heads. **5** From the throne came
περιβεβλημένους ἐν λευκοῖς ἱματίοις καὶ στεφάνους → χρυσοῦς ἐπὶ αὐτῶν ⸤τὰς κεφαλὰς⸥ Καὶ ἐκ τοῦ θρόνου ἐκπορεύονται
pt.rp.apm p.d a.dpn n.dpn cj n.apm a.apm p.a r.gpm.3 d.apf n.apf cj p.g d.gsm n.gsm v.pmi.3p
4314 1877 3328 2668 2779 5109 5997 2093 899 3836 3051 2779 1666 3836 2585 1744

flashes of lightning, rumblings and peals of thunder. Before the throne, seven lamps were blazing.
→ ἀστραπαὶ καὶ φωναὶ καὶ → βρονταί καὶ ἐνώπιον τοῦ θρόνου ἑπτὰ λαμπάδες πυρὸς → καιόμεναι
n.npf cj n.npf cj n.npf cj p.g d.gsm n.gsm a.npf n.npf n.gsn pt.pp.npf
847 2779 5889 2779 1103 2779 1967 3836 2585 2231 3286 4786 2794

These are the seven spirits of God. **6** Also before the throne there was what looked like a sea of glass,
ἅ εἰσιν τὰ ἑπτὰ πνεύματα → ⸤τοῦ θεοῦ⸥ καὶ ἐνώπιον τοῦ θρόνου ὡς θάλασσα ὑαλίνη
r.npn v.pai.3p d.npn a.npn n.npn d.gsm n.gsm cj p.g d.gsm n.gsm pl n.nsf a.nsf
4005 1639 3836 2231 4460 3836 2536 2779 1967 3836 2585 6055 2498 5612

clear as crystal. ¶ In the center, around the throne, were four living creatures, and
ὁμοία ← κρυστάλλῳ Καὶ ἐν μέσῳ τοῦ θρόνου καὶ κύκλῳ τοῦ θρόνου τέσσαρα ζῷα
a.nsf n.dsm cj p.d n.dsn d.gsm n.gsm cj p.g d.gsm n.gsm a.npn n.npn
3927 3223 2779 1877 3545 3836 2585 2779 3241 3836 2585 5475 2442

they were covered with eyes, in front and in back. **7** The first living creature was like a lion,
→ → γέμοντα ← ὀφθαλμῶν ἔμπροσθεν καὶ ὄπισθεν καὶ τὸ ⸤τὸ πρῶτον⸥ ζῷον ← ὅμοιον λέοντι καί
pt.pa.npn n.gpm adv cj adv cj d.nsn d.nsn a.nsn n.nsn a.nsn n.dsm cj
1154 4057 1869 2779 3957 2779 3836 3836 4755 2442 3927 3329 2779

θρόνου μου, ὡς κἀγὼ ἐνίκησα καὶ ἐκάθισα μετὰ τοῦ πατρός μου ἐν τῷ θρόνῳ αὐτοῦ. **22** ὁ ἔχων οὖς ἀκουσάτω τί τὸ πνεῦμα λέγει ταῖς ἐκκλησίαις. **4:1** Μετὰ ταῦτα εἶδον, καὶ ἰδοὺ θύρα ἠνεῳγμένη ἐν τῷ οὐρανῷ, καὶ ἡ φωνὴ ἡ πρώτη ἣν ἤκουσα ὡς σάλπιγγος λαλούσης μετ᾽ ἐμοῦ λέγων, Ἀνάβα ὧδε, καὶ δείξω σοι ἃ δεῖ γενέσθαι μετὰ ταῦτα. **2** εὐθέως ἐγενόμην ἐν πνεύματι, καὶ ἰδοὺ θρόνος ἔκειτο ἐν τῷ οὐρανῷ, καὶ ἐπὶ τὸν θρόνον καθήμενος, **3** καὶ ὁ καθήμενος ὅμοιος ὁράσει λίθῳ ἰάσπιδι καὶ σαρδίῳ, καὶ ἶρις κυκλόθεν τοῦ θρόνου ὅμοιος ὁράσει σμαραγδίνῳ. **4** καὶ κυκλόθεν τοῦ θρόνου θρόνους εἴκοσι τέσσαρες, καὶ ἐπὶ τοὺς θρόνους εἴκοσι τέσσαρας πρεσβυτέρους καθημένους περιβεβλημένους ἐν ἱματίοις λευκοῖς καὶ ἐπὶ τὰς κεφαλὰς αὐτῶν στεφάνους χρυσοῦς. **5** καὶ ἐκ τοῦ θρόνου ἐκπορεύονται ἀστραπαι καὶ φωναὶ καὶ βρονταί, καὶ ἑπτὰ λαμπάδες πυρὸς καιόμεναι ἐνώπιον τοῦ θρόνου, ἅ εἰσιν τὰ ἑπτὰ πνεύματα τοῦ θεοῦ, **6** καὶ ἐνώπιον τοῦ θρόνου ὡς θάλασσα ὑαλίνη ὁμοία κρυστάλλῳ. ¶ Καὶ ἐν μέσῳ τοῦ θρόνου καὶ κύκλῳ τοῦ θρόνου τέσσαρα ζῷα γέμοντα ὀφθαλμῶν ἔμπροσθεν καὶ ὄπισθεν. **7** καὶ τὸ ζῷον τὸ πρῶτον ὅμοιον λέοντι

the second   was like   an ox,   the third   had a face   like a man,   the fourth   was
τὸ δεύτερον ζῷον   ὅμοιον   μόσχῳ καὶ τὸ τρίτον ζῷον ἔχων ⸌τὸ πρόσωπον⸍ ὡς   ἀνθρώπου καὶ τὸ τέταρτον ζῷον
d.nsn a.nsn n.nsn   a.nsn   n.dsn cj d.nsn a.nsn n.nsn pt.pa.nsm d.asn n.asn   pl   n.gsm cj d.nsn a.nsn n.nsn
3836 1311 2442   3927   3675 2779 3836 5569 2442 2400 3836 4725   6055   476 2779 3836 5480 2442

like a flying eagle. **8** Each   of the four   living creatures had   six wings   and was covered
ὅμοιον πετομένῳ ἀετῷ   καὶ ⸌ἓν καθ᾽ ἓν αὐτῶν⸍ τὰ τέσσαρα ζῷα ←   ἔχων ἀνὰ ἓξ πτέρυγας → γέμουσιν
a.nsn pt.pm.dsm n.dsm   cj a.nsn p.a a.asn r.gpn.3 d.npn a.npn n.npn   pt.pa.nsm p.a a.apf n.apf   v.pai.3p
3927 4375 108   2779 1651 2848 1651 899 3836 5475 2442   2400 324 1971 4763   1154

with eyes   all around, even under his wings.   Day   and night they never stop   saying: Holy,
← ὀφθαλμῶν → κυκλόθεν καὶ ἔσωθεν   καὶ ἡμέρας καὶ νυκτὸς → οὐκ ⸌ἀνάπαυσιν ἔχουσιν⸍ λέγοντες ἅγιος
   n.gpm → adv   cj adv   cj n.gsf cj n.gsf   pl n.asf v.pai.3p pt.pa.npm a.nsm
   4057   3239   2779 2277   2779 2465 2779 3816   2400 4024 398 2400 3306 41

holy, holy is the Lord God Almighty,   who was, and   is,   and   is to come.” **9** Whenever the living
ἅγιος ἅγιος ὁ κύριος θεὸς ὁ παντοκράτωρ ὁ ἦν καὶ ὁ ὢν καὶ ὁ → ἐρχόμενος Καὶ ὅταν   τὰ ζῷα
a.nsm a.nsm d.nsm n.nsm n.nsm d.nsm n.nsm d.nsm v.iai.3s cj d.nsm pt.pa.nsm cj d.nsm   pt.pm.nsm cj cj   d.npn n.npn
41 41 3836 3261 2536 3836 4120   3836 1639 2779 3836 1639 2779 3836   2262 2779 4020   3836 2442

creatures give   glory,   honor and thanks   to him who sits   on the throne and who lives *for ever*
← δώσουσιν δόξαν καὶ τιμὴν καὶ εὐχαριστίαν → τῷ ← καθημένῳ ἐπὶ τῷ θρόνῳ τῷ ζῶντι εἰς ⸌τοὺς αἰῶνας⸍
  v.fai.3p n.asf cj n.asf cj n.asf → d.dsm ← pt.pm.dsm p.d d.dsm n.dsm d.dsm pt.pa.dsm p.a d.apm n.apm
  1443 1518 2779 5507 2779 2374   3836   2764 2093 3836 2585   3836 2409 1650 3836 172

and ever, **10** the twenty-four   elders   fall   down before him who sits   on the throne, and
⸌τῶν αἰώνων⸍ οἱ ⸌εἴκοσι τέσσαρες⸍ πρεσβύτεροι πεσοῦνται ← ἐνώπιον τοῦ ← καθημένου ἐπὶ τοῦ θρόνου καὶ
d.gpm n.gpm d.npm a.npm a.npm v.fmi.3p p.g d.gsm pt.pm.gsm p.g d.gsm n.gsm cj
3836 172 3836 1633 5475 4565 4406 1967 3836 2764 2093 3836 2585 2779

worship   him who lives *for ever*   *and ever.*   They lay   their crowns   before the
προσκυνήσουσιν τῷ ζῶντι εἰς ⸌τοὺς αἰῶνας⸍ ⸌τῶν αἰώνων⸍ καὶ → βαλοῦσιν αὐτῶν ⸌τοὺς στεφάνους⸍ ἐνώπιον τοῦ
v.fai.3p d.dsm pt.pa.dsm p.a d.apm n.apm d.gpm n.gpm cj v.fai.3p r.gpm.3 d.apm n.apm p.g d.gsm
4686 3836 2409 1650 3836 172 3836 172 2779 965 899 3836 5109 1967 3836

throne and say: **11** “You are worthy, our Lord   and God,   to receive glory   and honor   and
θρόνου λέγοντες εἶ ἄξιος ἡμῶν ὁ κύριος, καὶ ὁ θεός, λαβεῖν ⸌τὴν δόξαν⸍ καὶ ⸌τὴν τιμὴν⸍ καὶ
n.gsm pt.pa.npm v.pai.2s a.nsm r.gp.1 d.vsm n.vsm cj d.vsm n.vsm f.aa d.asf n.asf cj d.asf n.asf cj
2585 3306 1639 545 7005 3836 3261 2779 3836 2536 3284 3836 1518 2779 3836 5507 2779

power,   for you created all   things, and by your will   they were created   and have their being.”
⸌τὴν δύναμιν⸍ ὅτι σὺ ἔκτισας ⸌τὰ πάντα⸍ ← καὶ διὰ σου ⸌τὸ θέλημα⸍ → → ἐκτίσθησαν καὶ → → ἦσαν
d.asf n.asf cj r.ns.2 v.aai.2s d.apn a.apn   cj p.a r.gs.2 d.asn n.asn   v.api.3p cj v.iai.3p
3836 1539 4022 5148 3231 3836 4246   2779 1328 5148 3836 2525   3231 2779 1639

The Scroll and the Lamb

5:1 Then I saw in the right hand of him who sat   on the throne a scroll with writing   on
Καὶ → εἶδον ἐπὶ τὴν δεξιὰν ← → τοῦ ← καθημένου ἐπὶ τοῦ θρόνου βιβλίον → γεγραμμένον
cj v.aai.1s p.a d.asf a.asf d.gsm pt.pm.gsm p.g d.gsm n.gsm n.asn pt.rp.asn
2779 1625 2093 3836 1288 3836 2764 2093 3836 2585 1046 1211

both   sides and sealed   with seven seals. **2** And I saw a mighty angel proclaiming in a
⸌ἔσωθεν καὶ ὄπισθεν⸍ ← κατεσφραγισμένον → ἑπτὰ σφραγῖσιν καὶ → εἶδον ἰσχυρὸν ἄγγελον κηρύσσοντα ἐν
adv cj adv   pt.rp.asn → a.dpf n.dpf cj v.aai.1s a.asm n.asm pt.pa.asm p.d
2277 2779 3957   2958   2231 5382 2779 1625 2708 34 3062 1877

loud voice, “Who is worthy to break the seals   and open   the scroll?” **3** But no   one in heaven   or
μεγάλῃ φωνῇ τίς ἄξιος → λῦσαι τὰς σφραγῖδας αὐτοῦ καὶ ἀνοῖξαι τὸ βιβλίον καὶ οὐδεὶς ← ἐν ⸌τῷ οὐρανῷ⸍ οὐδὲ
a.dsf n.dsf r.nsm a.nsm f.aa d.apf n.apf r.gsn.3 cj f.aa d.asn n.asn cj a.nsm p.d d.dsm n.dsm cj
3489 5889 5515 545 3395 3836 5382 899 2779 487 3836 1046 2779 4029 1877 3836 4041 4028

on earth or under the earth could open the scroll or even look inside   **4** I wept *and wept*
ἐπὶ τῆς γῆς οὐδὲ ὑποκάτω τῆς γῆς ἐδύνατο ἀνοῖξαι τὸ βιβλίον οὔτε βλέπειν αὐτό καὶ → ἔκλαιον πολύ
p.g d.gsf n.gsf cj p.g d.gsf n.gsf v.ipi.3s f.aa d.asn n.asn cj f.pa r.asn.3 cj v.iai.1s adv
2093 3836 1178 4028 5691 3836 1178 1538 487 3836 1046 4046 1063 899 2779 3081 4498

because no   one was found who was worthy to open the scroll or look inside. **5** Then one of the
ὅτι οὐδεὶς ← → εὑρέθη ἄξιος → ἀνοῖξαι τὸ βιβλίον οὔτε βλέπειν αὐτό καὶ εἷς ἐκ τῶν
cj a.nsm v.api.3s a.nsm f.aa d.asn n.asn cj f.pa r.asn.3 cj a.nsm p.g d.gpm
4022 4029 2351 545 487 3836 1046 4046 1063 899 2779 1651 1666 3836

καὶ τὸ δεύτερον ζῷον ὅμοιον μόσχῳ καὶ τὸ τρίτον ζῷον ἔχων τὸ πρόσωπον ὡς ἀνθρώπου καὶ τὸ τέταρτον ζῷον ὅμοιον ἀετῷ πετομένῳ. ⁸ καὶ τὰ τέσσαρα ζῷα, ἓν καθ᾽ ἓν αὐτῶν ἔχων ἀνὰ πτέρυγας ἕξ, κυκλόθεν καὶ ἔσωθεν γέμουσιν ὀφθαλμῶν, καὶ ἀνάπαυσιν οὐκ ἔχουσιν ἡμέρας καὶ νυκτὸς λέγοντες, Ἅγιος ἅγιος ἅγιος κύριος ὁ θεὸς ὁ παντοκράτωρ, ὁ ἦν καὶ ὁ ὢν καὶ ὁ ἐρχόμενος. ⁹ καὶ ὅταν δώσουσιν τὰ ζῷα δόξαν καὶ τιμὴν καὶ εὐχαριστίαν τῷ καθημένῳ ἐπὶ τῷ θρόνῳ τῷ ζῶντι εἰς τοὺς αἰῶνας τῶν αἰώνων, ¹⁰ πεσοῦνται οἱ εἴκοσι τέσσαρες πρεσβύτεροι ἐνώπιον τοῦ καθημένου ἐπὶ τοῦ θρόνου καὶ προσκυνήσουσιν τῷ ζῶντι εἰς τοὺς αἰῶνας τῶν αἰώνων καὶ βαλοῦσιν τοὺς στεφάνους αὐτῶν ἐνώπιον τοῦ θρόνου λέγοντες, ¹¹ Ἄξιος εἶ, ὁ κύριος καὶ ὁ θεὸς ἡμῶν, λαβεῖν τὴν δόξαν καὶ τὴν τιμὴν καὶ τὴν δύναμιν, ὅτι σὺ ἔκτισας τὰ πάντα καὶ διὰ τὸ θέλημά σου ἦσαν καὶ ἐκτίσθησαν.

⁵:¹ Καὶ εἶδον ἐπὶ τὴν δεξιὰν τοῦ καθημένου ἐπὶ τοῦ θρόνου βιβλίον γεγραμμένον ἔσωθεν καὶ ὄπισθεν κατεσφραγισμένον σφραγῖσιν ἑπτά. ² καὶ εἶδον ἄγγελον ἰσχυρὸν κηρύσσοντα ἐν φωνῇ μεγάλῃ, Τίς ἄξιος ἀνοῖξαι τὸ βιβλίον καὶ λῦσαι τὰς σφραγῖδας αὐτοῦ; ³ καὶ οὐδεὶς ἐδύνατο ἐν τῷ οὐρανῷ οὐδὲ ἐπὶ τῆς γῆς οὐδὲ ὑποκάτω τῆς γῆς ἀνοῖξαι τὸ βιβλίον οὔτε βλέπειν αὐτό. ⁴ καὶ ἔκλαιον πολύ, ὅτι οὐδεὶς ἄξιος εὑρέθη ἀνοῖξαι τὸ βιβλίον οὔτε βλέπειν αὐτό. ⁵ καὶ εἷς ἐκ τῶν πρεσβυτέρων λέγει μοι, Μὴ κλαῖε,

elders | said | to me, | "Do not | weep! | See, | the Lion | | of | the | tribe | of Judah, | the | Root | of David, | has triumphed.
πρεσβυτέρων | λέγει → | μοι → | μὴ | κλαῖε | ἰδοὺ | ὁ λέων | ὁ | ἐκ | τῆς | φυλῆς → | Ἰούδα | ἡ | ῥίζα → | Δαυίδ → | ἐνίκησεν
a.gpm | v.pai.3s | v.rds.1 | pl | v.pam.2s | j | d.nsm n.nsm | d.nsm | p.g | d.gsf | n.gsf | n.gsm | d.nsf | n.nsf | n.gsm | v.aai.3s
4565 | 3306 | 1609 | 3081 | 3590 | 3081 | 2627 3836 3329 | 3836 | 1666 | 3836 | 5876 | 2683 | 3836 4844 | 1253 | 3771

He is able | to open | the | scroll | and | its | seven | seals." | ¶ | 6 Then | I saw | a Lamb, | looking | as | if it had
→ | ἀνοῖξαι | τὸ | βιβλίον | καὶ | αὐτοῦ | ἑπτὰ | ⌐τὰς σφραγῖδας⌐ | | Καὶ | εἶδον | ἀρνίον | | ὡς ←→
 | f.aa | d.asn | n.asn | cj | r.gsn.3 | a.apf | d.apf a.apf | | cj | v.aai.1s | n.asn | | pl
 | 487 | 3836 | 1046 | 2779 | 899 | 2231 | 3836 5382 | | 2779 | 1625 | 768 | | 6055

been slain, | standing | in | the | center | of the | throne, | | encircled | by the | four | living creatures | and | the
→ | ἐσφαγμένον | ἑστηκὸς | ἐν | | μέσῳ → | τοῦ | θρόνου | καὶ | ⌐ἐν μέσῳ⌐ | → | τῶν | τεσσάρων | ζῴων | | καὶ | τῶν
 | pt.rp.asn | pt.ra.asn | p.d | | n.dsn | d.gsm | n.gsm | cj | p.d n.dsn | | d.gpn | a.gpn | n.gpn | | cj | d.gpm
 | 5377 | 2705 | 1877 | | 3545 | 3836 | 2585 | 2779 | 1877 3545 | | 3836 | 5475 | 2442 | | 2779 | 3836

elders. | He had | seven | horns | and | seven | eyes, | | which | are | the | seven | spirits | of God | | sent | | out | into
πρεσβυτέρων | → ἔχων | ἑπτὰ | κέρατα | καὶ | ἑπτὰ | ὀφθαλμοὺς | | οἳ | εἰσιν | τὰ | ἑπτὰ | πνεύματα → | ⌐τοῦ θεοῦ⌐ | | ἀπεσταλμένοι ← | | εἰς
a.gpm | pt.pa.nsm | a.apn | n.apn | cj | a.apn | n.apm | | r.npm | v.pai.3p | d.npn | a.npn | n.npn | d.gsm n.gsm | | pt.rp.npm | | p.a
4565 | 2400 | 2231 | 3043 | 2779 | 2231 | 4057 | | 4005 | 1639 | 3836 | 2231 | 4460 | 3836 2536 | | 690 | | 1650

all | the | earth. | 7 | He came | and | took | the scroll | from | the | right | hand | of him who | sat | | on | the | throne. | 8 And
πᾶσαν | τὴν | γῆν | καὶ | → ἦλθεν | καὶ | εἴληφεν | | ἐκ | τῆς | δεξιᾶς | → | τοῦ | καθημένου | ἐπὶ | τοῦ | θρόνου | Καὶ
a.asf | d.asf | n.asf | cj | v.aai.3s | cj | v.rai.3s | | p.g | d.gsf | a.gsf | | d.gsm | pt.pm.gsm | p.g | d.gsm | n.gsm | cj
4246 | 3836 | 1178 | 2779 | 2262 | 2779 | 3284 | | 1666 | 3836 | 1288 | | 3836 | 2764 | 2093 | 3836 | 2585 | 2779

when | he had | taken it, | | the | four | living creatures | and the | twenty-four | | elders | fell | down | before | the
ὅτε | → → | ἔλαβεν | τὸ | βιβλίον | τὰ | τέσσαρα | ζῷα ← | | καὶ | οἱ | ⌐εἴκοσι τέσσαρες⌐ | πρεσβύτεροι | ἔπεσαν ← | | ἐνώπιον | τοῦ
cj | | v.aai.3s | d.asn | n.asn | d.npn | a.npn | n.npn | | cj | d.npm | a.npm a.npm | a.npm | v.aai.3p | | p.g | d.gsn
4021 | | 3284 | 3836 | 1046 | 3836 | 5475 | 2442 | | 2779 | 3836 | 1633 5475 | 4565 | 4406 | | 1967 | 3836

Lamb. | Each | one had | | a harp | and | they were | holding | golden | bowls | full | | of incense, | which | are | the
ἀρνίου | ἕκαστος ← | ἔχοντες | κιθάραν | καὶ | | | | χρυσᾶς | φιάλας | γεμούσας ← | θυμιαμάτων | αἳ | εἰσιν | αἳ
n.gsn | r.nsm | pt.pa.npm | n.asf | cj | | | | a.apf | n.apf | pt.pa.apf | n.gpn | r.npf | v.pai.3p | d.npf
768 | 1667 | 2400 | 3067 | 2779 | | | | 5997 | 5786 | 1154 | 2592 | 4005 | 1639 | 3836

prayers | of the saints. | 9 And | they sang | a new | song: | | "You | are | worthy | to take | the | scroll | and | to open
προσευχαὶ → | τῶν ἁγίων | καὶ | → ᾄδουσιν | καινὴν | ᾠδὴν | λέγοντες | | εἶ | ἄξιος | → λαβεῖν | τὸ | βιβλίον | καὶ | → ἀνοῖξαι
n.npf | d.gpn a.gpm | cj | v.pai.3p | a.asf | n.asf | pt.pa.npm | | v.pai.2s | a.nsm | f.aa | d.asn | n.asn | cj | f.aa
4666 | 3836 41 | 2779 | 2785 | 106 | 6046 | 3306 | | 1639 | 545 | 3284 | 3836 | 1046 | 2779 | 487

its | seals, | | because you | were | slain, | and with | your | blood | | you purchased | men | for God | | from | every
αὐτοῦ | ⌐τὰς σφραγῖδας⌐ | ὅτι | → | → | ἐσφάγης | καὶ | ἐν | σου | ⌐τῷ αἵματι⌐ | → | ἠγόρασας | → | ⌐τῷ θεῷ⌐ | ἐκ | πάσης
r.gsn.3 | d.apf n.apf | cj | | | v.api.2s | cj | p.d | r.gs.2 | d.dsn n.dsn | | v.aai.2s | | d.dsm n.dsm | p.g | a.gsf
899 | 3836 5382 | 4022 | | | 5377 | 2779 | 1877 | 5148 | 3836 135 | | 60 | | 3836 2536 | 1666 | 4246

tribe | and | language | and | people | and | nation. | 10 | You have | made | | them | to be | a kingdom | and | priests | to serve | our
φυλῆς | καὶ | γλώσσης | καὶ | λαοῦ | καὶ | ἔθνους | καὶ | → | ἐποίησας | αὐτοὺς | | βασιλείαν | καὶ | ἱερεῖς | → → | ἡμῶν
n.gsf | cj | n.gsf | cj | n.gsm | cj | n.gsn | cj | | v.aai.2s | r.apm.3 | | n.asf | cj | n.apm | | r.gp.1
5876 | 2779 | 1185 | 2779 | 3295 | 2779 | 1620 | 2779 | | 4472 | 899 | | 993 | 2779 | 2636 | 2536 2536 | 7005

God, | and | they will | reign | | on | the earth." | ¶ | 11 Then | I looked | and | heard | the | voice | of many | angels,
⌐τῷ θεῷ⌐ | καὶ | → | βασιλεύσουσιν | ἐπὶ | τῆς | γῆς | | Καὶ | → εἶδον | καὶ | ἤκουσα | | φωνὴν → | πολλῶν | ἀγγέλων | καὶ
d.dsm n.dsm | cj | | v.fai.3p | p.g | d.gsf | n.gsf | | cj | v.aai.1s | cj | v.aai.1s | | n.asf | a.gpm | n.gpm | cj
3836 2536 | 2779 | | 996 | 2093 | 3836 | 1178 | | 2779 | 1625 | 2779 | 201 | | 5889 | 4498 | 34 | 2779

numbering | | thousands | upon | thousands, | and | ten | | thousand | times | ten | | thousand. | They | encircled | the
ὁ | ἀριθμὸς | αὐτῶν ἦν | μυριάδες | → | μυριάδων | καὶ | χιλιάδες | | χιλιάδων | | | κύκλῳ | τοῦ
d.nsm | n.nsm | r.gpm.3 v.iai.3s | n.npf | | n.gpf | cj | n.npf | | n.gpf | | | | n.dsm | d.gsn
3836 | 750 | 899 1639 | 3689 | | 3689 | 2779 | 5942 | | 5942 | | | 3241 | 3836

throne | and | the | living creatures | and | the | elders. | 12 In a | loud | voice | they sang: | "Worthy | is | the | Lamb, | who was
θρόνου | καὶ | τῶν | ζῴων ← | καὶ | τῶν | πρεσβυτέρων | μεγάλῃ | φωνῇ | → | λέγοντες | ἄξιόν | ἐστιν | τὸ | ἀρνίον | τὸ →
n.gsm | cj | d.gpn | n.gpn | cj | d.gpm | a.gpm | a.dsf | n.dsf | | pt.pa.npm | a.nsn | v.pai.3s | d.nsn | n.nsn | d.nsn
2585 | 2779 | 3836 | 2442 | 2779 | 3836 | 4565 | 3489 | 5889 | | 3306 | 545 | 1639 | 3836 | 768 | 3836

slain, | | to receive | power | | and | wealth | and | wisdom | and | strength | and | honor | and | glory | and | praise!" | ¶
ἐσφαγμένον | → | λαβεῖν | ⌐τὴν δύναμιν⌐ | καὶ | πλοῦτον | καὶ | σοφίαν | καὶ | ἰσχὺν | καὶ | τιμὴν | καὶ | δόξαν | καὶ | εὐλογίαν
pt.rp.nsn | | f.aa | d.asf n.asf | cj | n.asm | cj | n.asf | cj | n.asf | cj | n.asf | cj | n.asf | cj | n.asf
5377 | | 3284 | 3836 1539 | 2779 | 4458 | 2779 | 5053 | 2779 | 2709 | 2779 | 5507 | 2779 | 1518 | 2779 | 2330

ἰδοὺ ἐνίκησεν ὁ λέων ὁ ἐκ τῆς φυλῆς Ἰούδα, ἡ ῥίζα Δαυίδ, ἀνοῖξαι τὸ βιβλίον καὶ τὰς ἑπτὰ σφραγῖδας αὐτοῦ. ¶ 6 Καὶ εἶδον ἐν μέσῳ τοῦ θρόνου καὶ τῶν τεσσάρων ζῴων καὶ ἐν μέσῳ τῶν πρεσβυτέρων ἀρνίον ἑστηκὸς ὡς ἐσφαγμένον ἔχων κέρατα ἑπτὰ καὶ ὀφθαλμοὺς ἑπτὰ οἵ εἰσιν τὰ [ἑπτὰ] πνεύματα τοῦ θεοῦ ἀπεσταλμένοι εἰς πᾶσαν τὴν γῆν. 7 καὶ ἦλθεν καὶ εἴληφεν ἐκ τῆς δεξιᾶς τοῦ καθημένου ἐπὶ τοῦ θρόνου. 8 καὶ ὅτε ἔλαβεν τὸ βιβλίον, τὰ τέσσαρα ζῷα καὶ οἱ εἴκοσι τέσσαρες πρεσβύτεροι ἔπεσαν ἐνώπιον τοῦ ἀρνίου ἔχοντες ἕκαστος κιθάραν καὶ φιάλας χρυσᾶς γεμούσας θυμιαμάτων, αἵ εἰσιν αἱ προσευχαὶ τῶν ἁγίων, 9 καὶ ᾄδουσιν ᾠδὴν καινὴν λέγοντες, Ἄξιος εἶ λαβεῖν τὸ βιβλίον καὶ ἀνοῖξαι τὰς σφραγῖδας αὐτοῦ, ὅτι ἐσφάγης καὶ ἠγόρασας τῷ θεῷ ἐν τῷ αἵματί σου ἐκ πάσης φυλῆς καὶ γλώσσης καὶ λαοῦ καὶ ἔθνους 10 καὶ ἐποίησας αὐτοὺς τῷ θεῷ ἡμῶν βασιλείαν καὶ ἱερεῖς, καὶ βασιλεύσουσιν ἐπὶ τῆς γῆς. ¶ 11 Καὶ εἶδον, καὶ ἤκουσα φωνὴν ἀγγέλων πολλῶν κύκλῳ τοῦ θρόνου καὶ τῶν ζῴων καὶ τῶν πρεσβυτέρων, καὶ ἦν ὁ ἀριθμὸς αὐτῶν μυριάδες μυριάδων καὶ χιλιάδες χιλιάδων 12 λέγοντες φωνῇ μεγάλῃ, Ἄξιόν ἐστιν τὸ ἀρνίον τὸ ἐσφαγμένον λαβεῖν τὴν δύναμιν καὶ πλοῦτον καὶ σοφίαν καὶ ἰσχὺν καὶ τιμὴν καὶ δόξαν καὶ εὐλογίαν. ¶

13 Then I heard every creature in heaven and on earth and under the earth and on the sea, and
καὶ → ἤκουσα πᾶν κτίσμα ὃ ἐν ⸤τῷ οὐρανῷ⸥ καὶ ἐπὶ ⸤τῆς γῆς⸥ καὶ ὑποκάτω τῆς γῆς καὶ ἐπὶ τῆς θαλάσσης καὶ
cj v.aai.1s a.asn n.asn r.nsn ⸤d.dsm n.dsm⸥ cj p.d ⸤d.gsf n.gsf⸥ cj p.g d.gsf n.gsf cj p.g d.gsf n.gsf cj
2779 201 4246 3233 4005 ⸤3836 4041⸥ 2779 1877 ⸤3836 1178⸥ 2779 5691 3836 1178 2779 2093 3836 2498 2779

all that is in them, singing: "To him who sits on the throne and to the Lamb be praise and honor
πάντα τὰ ἐν αὐτοῖς λέγοντας → τῷ καθημένῳ ἐπὶ τῷ θρόνῳ καὶ → τῷ ἀρνίῳ ἡ εὐλογία καὶ ἡ τιμὴ
a.apn d.apn p.d r.dpm.3 pt.pa.apm d.dsm pt.pm.dsm p.g d.dsm n.dsm cj d.dsn n.dsn d.nsf n.nsf cj d.nsf n.nsf
4246 3836 1877 899 3306 3836 2764 2093 3836 2585 2779 3836 768 3836 2330 2779 3836 5507

and glory and power, *for ever and ever!*" **14** The four living creatures said, "Amen," and the
καὶ ἡ δόξα καὶ ⸤τὸ κράτος⸥ εἰς τοὺς αἰῶνας ⸤τῶν αἰώνων⸥ καὶ τὰ τέσσαρα ζῷα ← ἔλεγον ἀμήν καὶ οἱ
cj d.nsf n.nsf cj ⸤d.nsn n.nsn⸥ p.a d.apm n.apm ⸤d.gpm n.gpm⸥ cj d.npn a.npn n.npn v.iai.3p pl cj d.npm
2779 3836 1518 2779 ⸤3836 3197⸥ 1650 3836 172 ⸤3836 172⸥ 2779 3836 5475 2442 3306 297 2779 3836

elders fell down and worshiped.
πρεσβύτεροι ἔπεσαν ← καὶ προσεκύνησαν
a.npm v.aai.3p cj v.aai.3p
4565 4406 2779 4686

The Seals

6:1 I watched as the Lamb opened the first of the seven seals. Then I heard one of the four living
Καὶ → εἶδον ὅτε τὸ ἀρνίον ἤνοιξεν μίαν ἐκ τῶν ἑπτὰ σφραγίδων καὶ → ἤκουσα ἑνὸς ἐκ τῶν τεσσάρων ζώων
cj v.aai.1s cj d.nsn n.nsn v.aai.3s a.asf p.g d.gpf a.gpf n.gpf cj v.aai.1s a.gsn p.g d.gpn a.gpn n.gpn
2779 1625 4021 3836 768 487 1651 1666 3836 2231 5382 2779 201 1651 1666 3836 5475 2442

creatures say in a voice like thunder, "Come!" **2** I looked, and there before me was a white horse!
← λέγοντος φωνὴ ὡς βροντῆς ἔρχου καὶ → εἶδον καὶ ἰδοὺ λευκός ἵππος καὶ ἐπ'
pt.pa.gsn n.dsf pl n.gsf v.pmm.2s cj v.aai.1s cj j a.nsm n.nsm cj p.a
3306 5889 6055 1103 2262 2779 1625 2779 2627 3328 2691 2779 2093

Its rider held a bow, and he was given a crown, and he rode out as a conqueror *bent on*
αὐτὸν ὁ καθήμενος, ἔχων τόξον καὶ αὐτῷ → ἐδόθη στέφανος καὶ → ἐξῆλθεν ← νικῶν καὶ ἵνα
r.asm.3 d.nsm pt.pm.nsm pt.pa.nsm n.asn cj r.dsm.3 v.api.3s n.nsm cj v.aai.3s pt.pa.nsm cj cj
899 3836 2764 2400 5534 2779 899 1443 5109 2779 2002 3771 2779 2671

conquest. ¶ **3** When the Lamb opened the second seal, I heard the second living creature say,
νικήσῃ Καὶ ὅτε ἤνοιξεν τὴν ⸤τὴν δευτέραν⸥ σφραγῖδα → ἤκουσα τοῦ δευτέρου ζῴου ← λέγοντος
v.aas.3s cj cj v.aai.3s d.asf d.asf a.asf n.asf v.aai.1s d.gsn a.gsn n.gsn pt.pa.gsn
3771 2779 4021 487 3836 3836 1311 5382 201 3836 1311 2442 3306

"Come!" **4** Then another horse came out, a fiery red one. Its rider was given power to
ἔρχου καὶ ἄλλος ἵππος ἐξῆλθεν ← → πυρρός ← καὶ ἐπ' αὐτὸν ⸤τῷ καθημένῳ⸥ → ἐδόθη αὐτῷ →
v.pmm.2s cj r.nsm n.nsm v.aai.3s a.nsm cj p.a r.asm.3 ⸤d.dsm pt.pm.dsm⸥ v.api.3s r.dsm.3
2262 2779 257 2691 2002 4794 2779 2093 899 ⸤3836 2764⸥ 1443 899

take peace from the earth and to make men slay each other. To him was given a large sword. ¶
λαβεῖν ⸤τὴν εἰρήνην⸥ ἐκ τῆς γῆς καὶ ἵνα σφάξουσιν ἀλλήλους ← καὶ αὐτῷ → ἐδόθη μεγάλη μάχαιρα
f.aa d.asf n.asf p.g d.gsf n.gsf cj cj v.fai.3p r.apm cj r.dsm.3 v.api.3s a.nsf n.nsf
3284 3836 1645 1666 3836 1178 2779 2671 5377 253 2779 899 1443 3489 3479

5 When the Lamb opened the third seal, I heard the third living creature say, "Come!" I
Καὶ ὅτε ἤνοιξεν τὴν ⸤τὴν τρίτην⸥ σφραγῖδα → ἤκουσα τοῦ τρίτου ζῴου ← λέγοντος ἔρχου καὶ →
cj cj v.aai.3s d.asf d.asf a.asf n.asf v.aai.1s d.gsn a.gsn n.gsn pt.pa.gsn v.pmm.2s cj
2779 4021 487 3836 3836 5569 5382 201 3836 5569 2442 3306 2262 2779

looked, and there before me was a black horse! Its rider was holding a pair of scales in his
εἶδον καὶ ἰδοὺ μέλας ἵππος καὶ ἐπ' αὐτὸν ὁ καθήμενος, → ἔχων → ζυγὸν ἐν τῇ χειρὶ αὐτοῦ
v.aai.1s cj j a.nsm n.nsm cj p.a r.asm.3 d.nsm pt.pm.nsm pt.pa.nsm n.asm p.d r.gsm.3
1625 2779 2627 3506 2691 2779 2093 899 3836 2764 2400 2433 1877 899

hand. **6** Then I heard what sounded like a voice among the four living creatures, saying, "A quart of wheat
⸤τῇ χειρὶ⸥ καὶ → ἤκουσα ὡς φωνὴν ἐν μέσῳ τῶν τεσσάρων ζώων ← λέγουσαν χοῖνιξ → σίτου
d.dsf n.dsf cj v.aai.1s pl n.asf p.d n.dsn d.gpn a.gpn n.gpn pt.pa.asf n.nsf n.gsm
3836 5931 2779 201 6055 5889 1877 3545 3836 5475 2442 3306 5955 4992

for a day's wages, and three quarts of barley for a day's wages, and do not damage the oil and the wine!" ¶
→ → δηναρίου καὶ τρεῖς χοίνικες κριθῶν → δηναρίου καὶ → μὴ ἀδικήσῃς τὸ ἔλαιον καὶ τὸν οἶνον
n.gsn cj a.npf n.npf n.gpf n.gsn cj pl v.aas.2s d.asn n.asn cj d.asm n.asm
1324 2779 5552 5955 3208 1324 2779 92 3590 92 3836 1778 2779 3836 3885

---

13 καὶ πᾶν κτίσμα ὃ ἐν τῷ οὐρανῷ καὶ ἐπὶ τῆς γῆς καὶ ὑποκάτω τῆς γῆς καὶ ἐπὶ τῆς θαλάσσης καὶ τὰ ἐν αὐτοῖς πάντα ἤκουσα λέγοντας, Τῷ καθημένῳ ἐπὶ τῷ θρόνῳ καὶ τῷ ἀρνίῳ ἡ εὐλογία καὶ ἡ τιμὴ καὶ ἡ δόξα καὶ τὸ κράτος εἰς τοὺς αἰῶνας τῶν αἰώνων. **14** καὶ τὰ τέσσαρα ζῷα ἔλεγον, Ἀμήν. καὶ οἱ πρεσβύτεροι ἔπεσαν καὶ προσεκύνησαν.

6:1 Καὶ εἶδον ὅτε ἤνοιξεν τὸ ἀρνίον μίαν ἐκ τῶν ἑπτὰ σφραγίδων, καὶ ἤκουσα ἑνὸς ἐκ τῶν τεσσάρων ζῴων λέγοντος ὡς φωνῇ βροντῆς, Ἔρχου. **2** καὶ εἶδον, καὶ ἰδοὺ ἵππος λευκός, καὶ ὁ καθήμενος ἐπ' αὐτὸν ἔχων τόξον καὶ ἐδόθη αὐτῷ στέφανος καὶ ἐξῆλθεν νικῶν καὶ ἵνα νικήσῃ. ¶ **3** Καὶ ὅτε ἤνοιξεν τὴν σφραγῖδα τὴν δευτέραν, ἤκουσα τοῦ δευτέρου ζῴου λέγοντος, Ἔρχου. **4** καὶ ἐξῆλθεν ἄλλος ἵππος πυρρός, καὶ τῷ καθημένῳ ἐπ' αὐτὸν ἐδόθη αὐτῷ λαβεῖν τὴν εἰρήνην ἐκ τῆς γῆς καὶ ἵνα ἀλλήλους σφάξουσιν καὶ ἐδόθη αὐτῷ μάχαιρα μεγάλη. ¶ **5** Καὶ ὅτε ἤνοιξεν τὴν σφραγῖδα τὴν τρίτην, ἤκουσα τοῦ τρίτου ζῴου λέγοντος, Ἔρχου. καὶ εἶδον, καὶ ἰδοὺ ἵππος μέλας, καὶ ὁ καθήμενος ἐπ' αὐτὸν ἔχων ζυγὸν ἐν τῇ χειρὶ αὐτοῦ. **6** καὶ ἤκουσα ὡς φωνὴν ἐν μέσῳ τῶν τεσσάρων ζῴων λέγουσαν, Χοῖνιξ σίτου δηναρίου καὶ τρεῖς χοίνικες κριθῶν δηναρίου, καὶ τὸ ἔλαιον καὶ τὸν οἶνον μὴ ἀδικήσῃς ¶

7 When the Lamb opened the fourth seal, I heard the voice of the fourth living creature say,
Καὶ ὅτε ἤνοιξεν τὴν ⌐τὴν τετάρτην σφραγῖδα → ἤκουσα φωνὴν → τοῦ τετάρτου ζῴου ← λέγοντος
cj cj v.aai.3s d.asf d.asf a.asf n.asf v.aai.1s n.asf d.gsn a.gsn n.gsn pt.pa.gsn
2779 4021 487 3836 3836 5480 5382 201 5889 3836 5480 2442 3306

"Come!" **8** I looked, and there before me was a pale horse! Its rider was named
ἔρχου καὶ → εἶδον καὶ ἰδοὺ χλωρός ἵππος καὶ ἐπάνω αὐτοῦ ⌐ὁ καθήμενος⌐ ὄνομα αὐτῷ
v.pmm.2s cj v.aai.1s cj idou a.nsm n.nsm cj p.g r.gsm.3 d.nsm pt.pm.nsm n.nsn r.dsm.3
2262 2779 1625 2779 2627 5952 2691 2779 2062 899 3836 2764 3950 899

Death, and Hades was following close behind him. They were given power over a fourth of the
⌐ὁ θάνατος⌐ καὶ ὁ ἅδης⌐ → ἠκολούθει μετ᾽ αὐτοῦ καὶ αὐτοῖς → ἐδόθη ἐξουσία ἐπὶ ⌐τὸ τέταρτον⌐ → τῆς
d.nsm n.nsm cj d.nsm n.nsm v.iai.3s p.g r.gsm.3 cj r.dpm.3 v.api.3s n.nsf p.a d.asn a.asn d.gsf
3836 2505 2779 3836 87 199 3552 899 2779 899 1443 2026 2093 3836 5480 3836

earth to kill by sword, famine and plague, and by the wild beasts of the earth. ¶ **9**
γῆς → ἀποκτεῖναι ἐν ῥομφαίᾳ καὶ ἐν λιμῷ καὶ ἐν θανάτῳ καὶ ὑπὸ τῶν θηρίων ← → τῆς γῆς Καὶ
n.gsf f.aa p.d n.dsf cj p.d n.dsm cj p.d n.dsm cj p.g d.gpn n.gpn d.gsf n.gsf cj
1178 650 1877 4855 2779 1877 3350 2779 1877 2505 2779 5679 3836 2563 3836 1178 2779

When he opened the fifth seal, I saw under the altar the souls of those who had been slain
ὅτε → ἤνοιξεν τὴν πέμπτην σφραγῖδα → εἶδον ὑποκάτω τοῦ θυσιαστηρίου τὰς ψυχὰς → τῶν ← → ἐσφαγμένων
cj v.aai.3s d.asf a.asf n.asf v.aai.1s p.g d.gsn n.gsn d.apf n.apf d.gpm pt.rp.gpm
4021 487 3836 4286 5382 1625 5691 3836 2603 3836 6034 3836 5377

because of the word of God and the testimony they had maintained. **10** They called out in a loud
διὰ ← τὸν λόγον → ⌐τοῦ θεοῦ⌐ καὶ διὰ τὴν μαρτυρίαν ἣν → → εἶχον καὶ → ἔκραξαν ← → μεγάλῃ
p.a d.asm n.asm d.gsm n.gsm cj p.a d.asf n.asf r.asf v.iai.3p cj v.aai.3p a.dsf
1328 3836 3364 3836 2536 2779 1328 3836 3456 4005 2400 2779 3189 3489

voice, "How long, Sovereign Lord, holy and true, until you judge the inhabitants of the
φωνῇ λέγοντες πότε ← ⌐ὁ δεσπότης⌐ ← ὁ ἅγιος⌐ καὶ ἀληθινός ἕως οὐ → κρίνεις ἐκ τῶν κατοικούντων ἐπὶ τῆς
n.dsf pt.pa.npm adv d.vsm n.vsm d.vsm a.vsm cj a.vsm p.g pl v.pai.2s p.g d.gpm pt.pa.gpm p.g d.gsf
5889 3306 4537 3836 1305 3836 41 2779 240 2401 4024 3212 1666 3836 2997 2093 3836

earth and avenge our blood?" **11** Then each of them was given a white robe, and they were told to wait
γῆς καὶ ἐκδικεῖς ἡμῶν ⌐τὸ αἷμα⌐ καὶ ἑκάστῳ αὐτοῖς → ἐδόθη λευκὴ στολὴ καὶ αὐτοῖς → ἐρρέθη ἵνα ἀναπαύσονται
n.gsf cj v.pai.2s r.gp.1 d.asn n.asn cj r.dsm r.dpm.3 v.api.3s a.nsf n.nsf cj r.dpm.3 v.api.3s cj v.fmi.3p
1178 2779 1688 7005 3836 135 2779 1667 899 1443 3328 5124 2779 899 3306 2671 399

a little longer, until the number of their fellow servants and brothers who were to be
ἔτι μικρὸν χρόνον ἕως καὶ αὐτῶν οἱ σύνδουλοι⌐ ← καὶ αὐτῶν οἱ ἀδελφοὶ οἱ μέλλοντες → →
adv a.asm n.asm cj adv r.gpm.3 d.npm n.npm cj r.gpm.3 d.npm n.npm d.npm pt.pa.npm
2285 3625 5989 2401 2779 899 3836 5281 2779 899 3836 81 3836 3516

killed as they had been was completed. ¶ **12** I watched as he opened the sixth seal.
ἀποκτέννεσθαι καὶ ὡς αὐτοί → πληρωθῶσιν Καὶ → εἶδον ὅτε → ἤνοιξεν τὴν ⌐τὴν ἕκτην σφραγῖδα καὶ
f.pp adv cj r.npm v.aps.3p cj v.aai.1s cj v.aai.3s d.asf d.asf a.asf n.asf cj
650 2779 6055 899 4444 2779 1625 4021 487 3836 3836 1761 5382 2779

There was a great earthquake. The sun turned black like sackcloth made of goat hair, the whole moon
→ ἐγένετο μέγας σεισμός καὶ ὁ ἥλιος ἐγένετο μέλας ὡς σάκκος τρίχινος καὶ ἡ ὅλη σελήνη
v.ami.3s a.nsm n.nsm cj d.nsm n.nsm v.ami.3s a.nsm cj n.nsm a.nsm cj d.nsf a.nsf n.nsf
1181 3489 4939 2779 3836 2463 1181 3506 6055 4884 5570 2779 3836 3910 4943

turned blood red, **13** and the stars in the sky fell to earth, as late figs drop from a fig
ἐγένετο ὡς αἷμα καὶ οἱ ἀστέρες → τοῦ οὐρανοῦ ἔπεσαν εἰς ⌐τὴν γῆν⌐ ὡς ⌐τοὺς ὀλύνθους⌐ αὐτῆς βάλλει ←
v.ami.3s pl n.nsn cj d.npm n.npm d.gsm n.gsm v.aai.3p p.a d.asf n.asf cj d.apm n.apm r.gsf.3 v.pai.3s
1181 6055 135 2779 3836 843 3836 4041 4406 1650 3836 1178 6055 3836 3913 899 965

tree when shaken by a strong wind. **14** The sky receded like a scroll, rolling up, and every mountain
συκῆ → σειομένη ὑπὸ μεγάλου ἀνέμου καὶ ὁ οὐρανὸς ἀπεχωρίσθη ὡς βιβλίον ἑλισσόμενον ← καὶ πᾶν ὄρος
n.nsf pt.pp.nsf p.g a.gsm n.gsm cj d.nsm n.nsm v.api.3s pl n.nsn pt.pp.nsn cj a.nsn n.nsn
5190 4940 5679 3489 449 2779 3836 4041 714 6055 1046 1813 2779 4246 4001

and island was removed from its place. ¶ **15** Then the kings of the earth, the princes, the
καὶ νῆσος → ἐκινήθησαν ἐκ αὐτῶν ⌐τόπων⌐ Καὶ οἱ βασιλεῖς → τῆς γῆς καὶ οἱ μεγιστᾶνες καὶ οἱ
cj n.nsf v.api.3p p.g r.gpn.3 d.gpm n.gpm cj d.npm n.npm d.gsf n.gsf cj d.npm n.npm cj d.npm
2779 3762 3075 1666 899 3836 5536 2779 3836 995 3836 1178 2779 3836 3491 2779 3836

---

7 Καὶ ὅτε ἤνοιξεν τὴν σφραγῖδα τὴν τετάρτην, ἤκουσα φωνὴν τοῦ τετάρτου ζῴου λέγοντος, Ἔρχου. **8** καὶ εἶδον, καὶ ἰδοὺ ἵππος χλωρός, καὶ ὁ καθήμενος ἐπάνω αὐτοῦ ὄνομα αὐτῷ [ὁ] Θάνατος, καὶ ὁ ᾅδης ἠκολούθει μετ᾽ αὐτοῦ καὶ ἐδόθη αὐτοῖς ἐξουσία ἐπὶ τὸ τέταρτον τῆς γῆς ἀποκτεῖναι ἐν ῥομφαίᾳ καὶ ἐν λιμῷ καὶ ἐν θανάτῳ καὶ ὑπὸ τῶν θηρίων τῆς γῆς. ¶ **9** Καὶ ὅτε ἤνοιξεν τὴν πέμπτην σφραγῖδα, εἶδον ὑποκάτω τοῦ θυσιαστηρίου τὰς ψυχὰς τῶν ἐσφαγμένων διὰ τὸν λόγον τοῦ θεοῦ καὶ διὰ τὴν μαρτυρίαν ἣν εἶχον. **10** καὶ ἔκραξαν φωνῇ μεγάλῃ λέγοντες, Ἕως πότε, ὁ δεσπότης ὁ ἅγιος καὶ ἀληθινός, οὐ κρίνεις καὶ ἐκδικεῖς τὸ αἷμα ἡμῶν ἐκ τῶν κατοικούντων ἐπὶ τῆς γῆς; **11** καὶ ἐδόθη αὐτοῖς ἑκάστῳ στολὴ λευκὴ καὶ ἐρρέθη αὐτοῖς ἵνα ἀναπαύσονται ἔτι χρόνον μικρόν, ἕως πληρωθῶσιν καὶ οἱ σύνδουλοι αὐτῶν καὶ οἱ ἀδελφοὶ αὐτῶν οἱ μέλλοντες ἀποκτέννεσθαι ὡς καὶ αὐτοί ¶ **12** Καὶ εἶδον ὅτε ἤνοιξεν τὴν σφραγῖδα τὴν ἕκτην, καὶ σεισμὸς μέγας ἐγένετο καὶ ὁ ἥλιος ἐγένετο μέλας ὡς σάκκος τρίχινος καὶ ἡ σελήνη ὅλη ἐγένετο ὡς αἷμα **13** καὶ οἱ ἀστέρες τοῦ οὐρανοῦ ἔπεσαν εἰς τὴν γῆν, ὡς συκῆ βάλλει τοὺς ὀλύνθους αὐτῆς ὑπὸ ἀνέμου μεγάλου σειομένη, **14** καὶ ὁ οὐρανὸς ἀπεχωρίσθη ὡς βιβλίον ἑλισσόμενον καὶ πᾶν ὄρος καὶ νῆσος ἐκ τῶν τόπων αὐτῶν ἐκινήθησαν. ¶ **15** καὶ οἱ βασιλεῖς τῆς γῆς καὶ οἱ μεγιστᾶνες καὶ οἱ χιλίαρχοι καὶ οἱ πλούσιοι καὶ οἱ ἰσχυροὶ καὶ πᾶς δοῦλος

generals, the rich, the mighty, and every slave and every free man hid in caves and
χιλίαρχοι καὶ οἱ πλούσιοι καὶ οἱ ἰσχυροὶ καὶ πᾶς δοῦλος καὶ ἐλεύθερος ἔκρυψαν ἑαυτοὺς εἰς ⌊τὰ σπήλαια⌋ καὶ
n.npm cj d.npm a.npm cj d.npm a.npm cj a.nsm n.nsm cj a.nsm v.aai.3p r.apm.3 p.a d.apn n.apn cj
5941 2779 3836 4454 2779 3836 2708 2779 4246 1529 2779 1801 3221 1571 1650 3836 5068 2779

among the rocks of the mountains. ¹⁶ They called to the mountains and the rocks, "Fall on us and hide
εἰς τὰς πέτρας → τῶν ὀρέων καὶ → λέγουσιν → τοῖς ὄρεσιν καὶ ταῖς πέτραις πέσετε ἐφ᾽ ἡμᾶς καὶ κρύψατε
p.a d.apf n.apf d.gpn n.gpn cj v.pai.3p d.dpn d.dpn cj d.dpf n.dpf v.aam.2p r.ap.1 cj v.aam.2p
1650 3836 4376 3836 4001 2779 3306 3836 4001 2779 3836 4376 4406 2093 7005 2779 3221

us from the face of him who sits on the throne and from the wrath of the Lamb! ¹⁷ For the great
ἡμᾶς ἀπὸ προσώπου → τοῦ ← καθημένου ἐπὶ τοῦ θρόνου καὶ ἀπὸ τῆς ὀργῆς → τοῦ ἀρνίου ὅτι ἡ ἡ μεγάλη
r.ap.1 p.g n.gsn d.gsm pt.pm.gsm p.g d.gsm n.gsm cj p.g d.gsf n.gsf d.gsn n.gsn cj d.nsf d.nsf a.nsf
7005 608 4725 3836 2764 2093 3836 2585 2779 608 3836 3973 3836 768 4022 3836 3836 3489

day of their wrath has come, and who can stand?"
ἡμέρα → αὐτῶν ⌊τῆς ὀργῆς⌋ → ἦλθεν καὶ τίς δύναται σταθῆναι
n.nsf r.gpm.3 d.gsf n.gsf v.aai.3s cj r.nsm v.ppi.3s f.ap
2465 3973 899 3836 3973 2262 2779 5515 1538 2705

144,000 Sealed

⁷:¹ After this I saw four angels standing at the four corners of the earth, holding back the four
Μετὰ τοῦτο εἶδον τέσσαρας ἀγγέλους ἑστῶτας ἐπὶ τὰς τέσσαρας γωνίας → τῆς γῆς κρατοῦντας ← τοὺς τέσσαρας
p.a r.asn v.aai.1s a.apm n.apm pt.ra.apm p.a d.apf a.apf n.apf d.gsf n.gsf pt.pa.apm d.apm a.apm
3552 4047 1625 5475 34 2705 2093 3836 5475 1224 3836 1178 3195 3836 5475

winds of the earth to prevent any wind from blowing on the land or on the sea or on any tree. ² Then
ἀνέμους → τῆς γῆς ἵνα μὴ ἄνεμος πνέῃ ἐπὶ τῆς γῆς μήτε ἐπὶ τῆς θαλάσσης μήτε ἐπὶ πᾶν δένδρον Καὶ
n.apm d.gsf n.gsf cj pl n.nsm v.pas.3s p.g d.gsf n.gsf cj p.g d.gsf n.gsf cj p.a a.asn n.asn cj
449 3836 1178 2671 3590 449 4463 2093 3836 1178 3612 2093 3836 2498 3612 2093 4246 1285 2779

I saw another angel coming up from the east, having the seal of the living God. He called
→ εἶδον ἄλλον ἄγγελον ἀναβαίνοντα ← ἀπὸ ⌊ἀνατολῆς ἡλίου⌋ ἔχοντα σφραγῖδα → ζῶντος θεοῦ καὶ → ἔκραξεν
v.aai.1s a.asm n.asm pt.pa.asm p.g n.gsf n.gsm pt.pa.asm n.asf pt.pa.gsm n.gsm cj v.aai.3s
1625 257 34 326 608 424 2463 2400 5382 2409 2536 2779 3189

out in a loud voice to the four angels who had been given power to harm the land and the sea:
← → μεγάλῃ φωνῇ → τοῖς τέσσαρσιν ἀγγέλοις οἷς → ἐδόθη αὐτοῖς → ἀδικῆσαι τὴν γῆν καὶ τὴν θάλασσαν
a.dsf n.dsf d.dpm a.dpm n.dpm r.dpm v.api.3s r.dpm.3 f.aa d.asf n.asf cj d.asf n.asf
3489 5889 3836 5475 34 4005 1443 899 92 3836 1178 2779 3836 2498

³ "Do not harm the land or the sea or the trees until we put a seal on the foreheads
λέγων ↱ μὴ ἀδικήσητε τὴν γῆν μήτε τὴν θάλασσαν μήτε τὰ δένδρα ἄχρι → → σφραγίσωμεν ἐπὶ τῶν μετώπων αὐτῶν
pt.pa.nsm pl v.aas.2p d.asf n.asf cj d.asf n.asf cj d.apn n.apn cj v.aas.1p p.g d.gpn n.gpn r.gpm.3
3306 92 3590 3836 1178 3612 3836 2498 3612 3836 1285 948 5381 2093 3836 3587 899

of the servants of our God." ⁴ Then I heard the number of those who were sealed:
τοὺς δούλους → ἡμῶν ⌊τοῦ θεοῦ⌋ Καὶ → ἤκουσα τὸν ἀριθμὸν → τῶν ← ἐσφραγισμένων
d.apm n.apm r.gp.1 d.gsm n.gsm cj v.aai.1s d.asm n.asm d.gpm pt.rp.gpm
3836 1529 2536 7005 3836 2536 2779 201 3836 750 3836 5381

144,000 from all the tribes of Israel. ⁵ From the tribe of Judah
⌊ἑκατὸν τεσσεράκοντα τέσσαρες χιλιάδες⌋ ἐσφραγισμένοι ἐκ πάσης φυλῆς → υἱῶν Ἰσραήλ ἐκ φυλῆς → Ἰούδα
a.npf a.npf a.npf n.npf pt.rp.npm p.g a.gsf n.gsf n.gpm n.gsm p.g n.gsf n.gsm
1669 5477 5475 5942 5381 1666 4246 5876 5626 2702 1666 5876 2683

12,000 were sealed, from the tribe of Reuben 12,000, from the tribe of Gad 12,000,
⌊δώδεκα χιλιάδες⌋ → ἐσφραγισμένοι ἐκ φυλῆς → Ῥουβὴν ⌊δώδεκα χιλιάδες⌋ ἐκ φυλῆς → Γὰδ ⌊δώδεκα χιλιάδες⌋
a.npf n.npf pt.rp.npm p.g n.gsf n.gsm a.npf n.npf p.g n.gsf n.gsm a.npf n.npf
1557 5942 5381 1666 5876 4857 1557 5942 1666 5876 1122 1557 5942

⁶ from the tribe of Asher 12,000, from the tribe of Naphtali 12,000, from the tribe of Manasseh
ἐκ φυλῆς → Ἀσὴρ ⌊δώδεκα χιλιάδες⌋ ἐκ φυλῆς → Νεφθαλὶμ ⌊δώδεκα χιλιάδες⌋ ἐκ φυλῆς → Μανασσῆ
p.g n.gsf n.gsm a.npf n.npf p.g n.gsf n.gsm a.npf n.npf p.g n.gsf n.gsm
1666 5876 818 1557 5942 1666 5876 3750 1557 5942 1666 5876 3442

12,000, ⁷ from the tribe of Simeon 12,000, from the tribe of Levi 12,000, from the tribe of
⌊δώδεκα χιλιάδες⌋ ἐκ φυλῆς → Συμεὼν ⌊δώδεκα χιλιάδες⌋ ἐκ φυλῆς → Λευὶ ⌊δώδεκα χιλιάδες⌋ ἐκ φυλῆς
a.npf n.npf p.g n.gsf n.gsm a.npf n.npf p.g n.gsf n.gsm a.npf n.npf p.g n.gsf
1557 5942 1666 5876 5208 1557 5942 1666 5876 3322 1557 5942 1666 5876

καὶ ἐλεύθερος ἔκρυψαν ἑαυτοὺς εἰς τὰ σπήλαια καὶ εἰς τὰς πέτρας τῶν ὀρέων ¹⁶ καὶ λέγουσιν τοῖς ὄρεσιν καὶ ταῖς πέτραις, Πέσετε ἐφ᾽ ἡμᾶς καὶ κρύψατε ἡμᾶς ἀπὸ προσώπου τοῦ καθημένου ἐπὶ τοῦ θρόνου καὶ ἀπὸ τῆς ὀργῆς τοῦ ἀρνίου, ¹⁷ ὅτι ἦλθεν ἡ ἡμέρα ἡ μεγάλη τῆς ὀργῆς αὐτῶν, καὶ τίς δύναται σταθῆναι;

⁷:¹ Μετὰ τοῦτο εἶδον τέσσαρας ἀγγέλους ἑστῶτας ἐπὶ τὰς τέσσαρας γωνίας τῆς γῆς, κρατοῦντας τοὺς τέσσαρας ἀνέμους τῆς γῆς ἵνα μὴ πνέῃ ἄνεμος ἐπὶ τῆς γῆς μήτε ἐπὶ τῆς θαλάσσης μήτε ἐπὶ πᾶν δένδρον. ² καὶ εἶδον ἄλλον ἄγγελον ἀναβαίνοντα ἀπὸ ἀνατολῆς ἡλίου ἔχοντα σφραγῖδα θεοῦ ζῶντος, καὶ ἔκραξεν φωνῇ μεγάλῃ τοῖς τέσσαρσιν ἀγγέλοις οἷς ἐδόθη αὐτοῖς ἀδικῆσαι τὴν γῆν καὶ τὴν θάλασσαν ³ λέγων, Μὴ ἀδικήσητε τὴν γῆν μήτε τὴν θάλασσαν μήτε τὰ δένδρα, ἄχρι σφραγίσωμεν τοὺς δούλους τοῦ θεοῦ ἡμῶν ἐπὶ τῶν μετώπων αὐτῶν. ⁴ καὶ ἤκουσα τὸν ἀριθμὸν τῶν ἐσφραγισμένων, ἑκατὸν τεσσεράκοντα τέσσαρες χιλιάδες, ἐσφραγισμένοι ἐκ πάσης φυλῆς υἱῶν Ἰσραήλ· ⁵ ἐκ φυλῆς Ἰούδα δώδεκα χιλιάδες ἐσφραγισμένοι, ἐκ φυλῆς Ῥουβὴν δώδεκα χιλιάδες, ἐκ φυλῆς Γὰδ δώδεκα χιλιάδες, ⁶ ἐκ φυλῆς Ἀσὴρ δώδεκα χιλιάδες, ἐκ φυλῆς Νεφθαλὶμ δώδεκα χιλιάδες, ἐκ φυλῆς Μανασσῆ δώδεκα χιλιάδες, ⁷ ἐκ φυλῆς Συμεὼν δώδεκα χιλιάδες, ἐκ φυλῆς Λευὶ δώδεκα χιλιάδες, ἐκ φυλῆς Ἰσσαχὰρ δώδεκα

Issachar 12,000,   **8** from the tribe of Zebulun 12,000,   from the tribe of Joseph 12,000,   from
Ἰσσαχὰρ δώδεκα χιλιάδες ἐκ φυλῆς → Ζαβουλῶν δώδεκα χιλιάδες ἐκ φυλῆς → Ἰωσὴφ δώδεκα χιλιάδες ἐκ
n.gsm   a.npf   n.npf   p.g n.gsf   n.gsm   a.npf   n.npf   p.g n.gsf   n.gsm   a.npf   n.npf   p.g
2704   1557   5942   1666 5876   2404   1557   5942   1666 5876   2737   1557   5942   1666

the tribe of Benjamin 12,000.
φυλῆς → Βενιαμὶν δώδεκα χιλιάδες ἐσφραγισμένοι
n.gsf   n.gsm   a.npf   n.npf   pt.rp.npm
5876   1021   1557   5942   5381

The Great Multitude in White Robes

7:9 After this I looked and there before me was a great multitude that no one could count, from
Μετὰ ταῦτα → εἶδον καὶ ἰδοὺ   πολὺς ὄχλος ὃν οὐδεὶς ← ἐδύνατο ἀριθμῆσαι αὐτὸν ἐκ
p.a r.apn   v.aai.1s cj j   a.nsm n.nsm r.asm a.nsm v.ipi.3s f.aa   r.asm.3 p.g
3552 4047   1625   2779 2627   4498 4063   4005 4029   1538   749   899   1666

every nation, tribe, people and language, standing before the throne and in front of the Lamb. They
παντὸς ἔθνους καὶ φυλῶν καὶ λαῶν καὶ γλωσσῶν ἑστῶτες ἐνώπιον τοῦ θρόνου καὶ ἐνώπιον ← ← τοῦ ἀρνίου →
a.gsn n.gsn cj n.gpf cj n.gpm cj n.gpf pt.ra.npm p.g d.gsm n.gsm cj p.g   d.gsn n.gsn
4246 1620   2779 5876 2779 3295 2779 1185 2705   1967 3836 2585 2779 1967   3836 768

were wearing white robes and were holding palm branches in their hands.   **10** And they cried out in a
περιβεβλημένους λευκὰς στολὰς καὶ   φοίνικες ← ἐν αὐτῶν ταῖς χερσίν καὶ → κράζουσιν
pt.rp.apm   a.apf n.apf cj   n.npm   p.d r.gpm.3 d.dpf n.dpf cj v.pai.3p
4314   3328   5124   2779   5836   1877 899   3836 5931 2779 3189

loud voice: "Salvation belongs to our God, who sits on the throne, and to the Lamb." **11** All
μεγάλη φωνῇ λέγοντες Ἡ σωτηρία → ἡμῶν τῷ θεῷ τῷ καθημένῳ ἐπὶ τῷ θρόνῳ καὶ → τῷ ἀρνίῳ Καὶ πάντες
a.dsf n.dsf pt.pa.npm d.nsf n.nsf r.gp.1 d.dsm n.dsm d.dsm pt.pm.dsm p.d d.dsm n.dsm cj d.dsn n.dsn cj a.npm
3489   5889 3306   3836 5401   2536 7005 3836 2536 3836 2764   2093 3836 2585 2779 3836 768   2779 4246

the angels were standing around the throne and around the elders and the four living creatures. They
οἱ ἄγγελοι → εἱστήκεισαν κύκλῳ τοῦ θρόνου καὶ τῶν πρεσβυτέρων καὶ τῶν τεσσάρων ζῴων ← καὶ →
d.npm n.npm v.lai.3p n.dsn d.gsm n.gsm cj d.gpm a.gpm cj d.gpn a.gpn n.gpn   cj
3836 34   2705   3241 3836 2585 2779 3836 4565 2779 3836 5475 2442   2779

fell down on their faces before the throne and worshiped God, **12** saying: "Amen! Praise and
ἔπεσαν ← ἐπὶ αὐτῶν τὰ πρόσωπα ἐνώπιον τοῦ θρόνου καὶ προσεκύνησαν τῷ θεῷ λέγοντες ἀμήν ἡ εὐλογία καὶ
v.aai.3p p.a r.gpm.3 d.apn n.apn ἐνώπιον d.gsm n.gsm cj v.aai.3p d.dsm n.dsm pt.pa.npm pl d.nsf n.nsf cj
4406   2093 899 3836 4725 1967 3836 2585 2779 4686   3836 2536 3306   297 3836 2330 2779

glory and wisdom and thanks and honor and power and strength be to our God *for*
ἡ δόξα καὶ ἡ σοφία καὶ ἡ εὐχαριστία καὶ ἡ τιμὴ καὶ ἡ δύναμις καὶ ἡ ἰσχὺς → ἡμῶν τῷ θεῷ εἰς
d.nsf n.nsf cj d.nsf n.nsf cj d.nsf n.nsf cj d.nsf n.nsf cj d.nsf n.nsf cj d.nsf n.nsf r.gp.1 d.dsm n.dsm p.a
3836 1518 2779 3836 5053 2779 3836 2374   2779 3836 5507 2779 3836 1539 2779 3836 2709 2536 7005 3836 2536 1650

ever and ever. Amen!" ¶ **13** Then one of the elders asked me, "These
τοὺς αἰῶνας τῶν αἰώνων ἀμήν   Καὶ εἷς ἐκ τῶν πρεσβυτέρων ἀπεκρίθη μοι λέγων οὗτοι
d.apm n.apm d.gpm n.gpm pl   cj a.nsm p.g d.gpm a.gpm v.api.3s r.ds.1 pt.pa.nsm r.npm
3836 172   3836 172   297   2779 1651 1666 3836 4565   646   1609 3306   4047

in white robes – who are they, and where did they come from?" **14** I answered,
οἱ περιβεβλημένοι τὰς λευκὰς τὰς στολὰς τίνες εἰσὶν ← καὶ πόθεν → → ἦλθον ← καὶ → εἴρηκα αὐτῷ
d.npm pt.rp.npm d.apf a.apf d.apf n.apf r.npm v.pai.3p cj cj v.aai.3p   cj v.rai.1s r.dsm.3
3836 4314   3836 3328 3836 5124 5515 1639   2779 4470   2262 4470 2779 3306 899

"Sir, you know." ¶ And he said, "These are they who have come out of the great
κύριε μου σὺ οἶδας   καὶ εἶπέν μοι εἰσὶν οἱ → → ἐρχόμενοι ἐκ ← τῆς τῆς μεγάλης
n.vsm r.gs.1 r.ns.2 v.rai.2s cj v.aai.3s r.ds.1 v.pai.3p d.npm pt.pm.npm p.g d.gsf d.gsf a.gsf
3261 1609 5148 3857   2779 3306 1609 4047 1639 3836   2262 1666 3836 3836 3489

tribulation; they have washed their robes and made them white in the blood of the Lamb.
θλίψεως καὶ → ἔπλυναν αὐτῶν τὰς στολὰς καὶ → αὐτὰς ἐλεύκαναν ἐν τῷ αἵματι → τοῦ ἀρνίου
n.gsf cj   v.aai.3p r.gpm.3 d.apf n.apf cj r.apf.3 v.aai.3p p.d d.dsn n.dsn d.gsn n.gsn
2568 2779   4459   899 3836 5124 2779 3326   899 3326   1877 3836 135   3836 768

15 Therefore, "they are before the throne of God and serve him day and night in his temple; and he
διὰ τοῦτο → εἰσιν ἐνώπιον τοῦ θρόνου → τοῦ θεοῦ καὶ λατρεύουσιν αὐτῷ ἡμέρας καὶ νυκτὸς ἐν αὐτῷ τῷ ναῷ καὶ ὁ
p.a r.asn v.pai.3p p.g d.gsm n.gsm d.gsm n.gsm cj v.pai.3p r.dsm.3 n.gsf cj n.gsf p.d r.dsm.3 d.dsm n.dsm cj d.nsm
1328 4047 1639 1967 3836 2585 3836 2536 2779 3302   899 2465 2779 3816 1877 899 3836 3724 2779 3836

χιλιάδες, **8** ἐκ φυλῆς Ζαβουλῶν δώδεκα χιλιάδες, ἐκ φυλῆς Ἰωσὴφ δώδεκα χιλιάδες, ἐκ φυλῆς Βενιαμὶν δώδεκα χιλιάδες ἐσφραγισμένοι.
7:9 Μετὰ ταῦτα εἶδον, καὶ ἰδοὺ ὄχλος πολύς, ὃν ἀριθμῆσαι αὐτὸν οὐδεὶς ἐδύνατο, ἐκ παντὸς ἔθνους καὶ φυλῶν καὶ λαῶν καὶ γλωσσῶν ἑστῶτες ἐνώπιον τοῦ θρόνου καὶ ἐνώπιον τοῦ ἀρνίου περιβεβλημένους στολὰς λευκὰς καὶ φοίνικες ἐν ταῖς χερσὶν αὐτῶν, **10** καὶ κράζουσιν φωνῇ μεγάλῃ λέγοντες, Ἡ σωτηρία τῷ θεῷ ἡμῶν τῷ καθημένῳ ἐπὶ τῷ θρόνῳ καὶ τῷ ἀρνίῳ. **11** καὶ πάντες οἱ ἄγγελοι εἱστήκεισαν κύκλῳ τοῦ θρόνου καὶ τῶν πρεσβυτέρων καὶ τῶν τεσσάρων ζῴων καὶ ἔπεσαν ἐνώπιον τοῦ θρόνου ἐπὶ τὰ πρόσωπα αὐτῶν καὶ προσεκύνησαν τῷ θεῷ **12** λέγοντες, Ἀμήν, ἡ εὐλογία καὶ ἡ δόξα καὶ ἡ σοφία καὶ ἡ εὐχαριστία καὶ ἡ τιμὴ καὶ ἡ δύναμις καὶ ἡ ἰσχὺς τῷ θεῷ ἡμῶν εἰς τοὺς αἰῶνας τῶν αἰώνων· ἀμήν. ¶ **13** Καὶ ἀπεκρίθη εἷς ἐκ τῶν πρεσβυτέρων λέγων μοι, Οὗτοι οἱ περιβεβλημένοι τὰς στολὰς τὰς λευκὰς τίνες εἰσὶν καὶ πόθεν ἦλθον; **14** καὶ εἴρηκα αὐτῷ, Κύριέ μου, σὺ οἶδας. ¶ καὶ εἶπέν μοι, Οὗτοί εἰσιν οἱ ἐρχόμενοι ἐκ τῆς θλίψεως τῆς μεγάλης καὶ ἔπλυναν τὰς στολὰς αὐτῶν καὶ ἐλεύκαναν αὐτὰς ἐν τῷ αἵματι τοῦ ἀρνίου. **15** διὰ τοῦτό εἰσιν ἐνώπιον τοῦ θρόνου τοῦ θεοῦ καὶ λατρεύουσιν αὐτῷ ἡμέρας καὶ νυκτὸς

who sits		on	the	throne	will spread	his	tent		over them.	[16] Never	again	will they hunger;		never	again	will
← καθήμενος	ἐπὶ	τοῦ	θρόνου	→	→ σκηνώσει	ἐπ'	αὐτούς		οὐ	ἔτι	→	→ πεινάσουσιν	οὐδὲ	ἔτι	→
pt.pm.nsm	p.g	d.gsm	n.gsm		v.fai.3s	p.a	r.apm.3		pl	adv		v.fai.3p	cj	adv	
2764	2093	3836	2585		5012	2093	899		4024	2285		4277	4028	2285	

they thirst.		The	sun	will not	beat	upon	them,	nor	any	scorching	heat.	[17] For	the	Lamb	at the center
→ διψήσουσιν	οὐδὲ	ὁ	ἥλιος	→ μὴ	πέσῃ	ἐπ'	αὐτοὺς	οὐδὲ	πᾶν	καῦμα		← ὅτι	τὸ	ἀρνίον	⌐τὸ ἀνὰ μέσον⌐
v.fai.3p	cj	d.nsm	n.nsm	pl	v.aas.3s	p.a	r.apm.3	cj	a.asn	n.nsn		cj	d.nsn	n.nsn	d.nsn p.a n.asn
1498	4028	3836	2463	4406	3590	4406	2093	899	4028	4246	3008	4022	3836	768	3836 324 3545

of the throne		will be	their	shepherd;		he will lead		them	to	springs	of living	water.	And	God		will
→ τοῦ	θρόνου	↗ ←	αὐτοὺς	ποιμανεῖ	καὶ	→	ὁδηγήσει	αὐτοὺς	ἐπὶ	πηγὰς	→ ζωῆς	ὑδάτων	καὶ	⌐ὁ θεὸς⌐		→
d.gsm	n.gsm		r.apm.3	v.fai.3s	cj		v.fai.3s	r.apm.3	p.a	n.apf	n.gsf	n.gpn	cj	d.nsm n.nsm		
3836	2585		4477 4477	899 4477	2779		3842	899	2093	4380	2437	5623	2779	3836 2536		

wipe	away	every	tear		from	their	eyes."
ἐξαλείψει ←		πᾶν	δάκρυον	ἐκ	αὐτῶν	⌐τῶν ὀφθαλμῶν⌐
v.fai.3s		a.asn	n.asn	p.g	r.gpm.3	d.gpm n.gpm
1981		4246	1232	1666	899	3836 4057

The Seventh Seal and the Golden Censer

8:1	When	he opened	the	seventh		seal,	there was		silence	in	heaven		for about	half	an hour. ¶
	Καὶ ὅταν	→ ἤνοιξεν	τὴν	⌐τὴν ἑβδόμην⌐	σφραγῖδα	→	ἐγένετο σιγὴ	ἐν	⌐τῷ οὐρανῷ⌐	→	ὡς	ἡμιώριον ← ←
	cj cj	v.aai.3s	d.asf	d.asf a.asf	n.asf		v.ami.3s n.nsf	p.d	d.dsm n.dsm		cj	n.asn
	2779 4020	487	3836	3836 1575	5382		1181 4968	1877	3836 4041		2469	6055 2469

[2] And	I	saw	the	seven	angels	who	stand	before	God,		and	to	them	were	given	seven	trumpets. ¶
Καὶ	→	εἶδον	τοὺς	ἑπτὰ	ἀγγέλους	οἳ	ἑστήκασιν	ἐνώπιον	⌐τοῦ θεοῦ⌐	καὶ	→	αὐτοῖς	→	ἐδόθησαν	ἑπτὰ	σάλπιγγες
cj		v.aai.1s	d.apm	a.apm	n.apm	r.npm	v.rai.3p	p.g	d.gsm n.gsm	cj		r.dpm.3		v.api.3p	a.npf	n.npf
2779		1625	3836	2231	34	4005	2705	1967	3836 2536	2779		899		1443	2231	4894

[3]	Another	angel,	who had	a golden	censer,	came	and	stood	at	the	altar.		He	was	given	much
Καὶ	ἄλλος	ἄγγελος	→ ἔχων	χρυσοῦν	λιβανωτὸν	ἦλθεν	καὶ	ἐστάθη	ἐπὶ	τοῦ	θυσιαστηρίου	καὶ	αὐτῷ	→	ἐδόθη	πολλὰ
cj	r.nsm	n.nsm	pt.pa.nsm	a.asm	n.asm	v.aai.3s	cj	v.api.3s	p.g	d.gsn	n.gsn	cj	r.dsm.3		v.api.3s	a.apn
2779	257	34	2400	5997	3338	2262	2779	2603	2093	3836	2603	2779	899		1443	4498

incense	to offer,	with	the	prayers	of	all	the	saints,	on	the	golden		altar		before	the throne.
θυμιάματα	ἵνα δώσει	→	ταῖς	προσευχαῖς	→	πάντων	τῶν	ἁγίων	ἐπὶ	τὸ	⌐τὸ χρυσοῦν⌐	θυσιαστήριον		τὸ	ἐνώπιον	τοῦ θρόνου
n.npn	cj v.fai.3s		d.dpf	n.dpf		a.gpm	d.gpm	a.gpm	p.a	d.asn	d.asn a.asn	n.asn		d.asn	p.g	d.gsm n.gsm
2592	2671 1443		3836	4666		4246	3836	41	2093	3836	3836 5997	2603		3836	1967	3836 2585

[4]	The	smoke	of the incense,		together with	the	prayers	of	the saints,	went up	before	God		from the
καὶ	ὁ	καπνὸς	→ τῶν θυμιαμάτων	→	→	ταῖς	προσευχαῖς	→	τῶν ἁγίων	ἀνέβη	ἐνώπιον	⌐τοῦ θεοῦ⌐	ἐκ	
cj	d.nsm	n.nsm	d.gpn n.gpn			d.dpf	n.dpf		d.gpm a.gpm	v.aai.3s	p.g	d.gsm n.gsm	p.g	
2779	3836	2837	3836 2592			3836	4666		3836 41	326	1967	3836 2536	1666	

angel's	hand.	[5] Then	the	angel	took	the	censer,		filled	it		with	fire		from the	altar,	and
⌐τοῦ ἀγγέλου⌐	χειρὸς	καὶ	ὁ	ἄγγελος	εἴληφεν	τὸν	λιβανωτὸν	καὶ	ἐγέμισεν	αὐτὸν	ἐκ	⌐τοῦ πυρός⌐	→	τοῦ	θυσιαστηρίου	καὶ
d.gsm n.gsm	n.gsf	cj	d.nsm	n.nsm	v.rai.3s	d.asm	n.asm	cj	v.aai.3s	r.asm.3	p.g	d.gsn n.gsn		d.gsn	n.gsn	cj
3836 34	5931	2779	3836	34	3284	3836	3338	2779	1153	899	1666	3836 4786		3836	2603	2779

hurled	it	on	the	earth;	and	there	came	peals	of thunder,		rumblings,		flashes	of lightning	and	an earthquake.
ἔβαλεν	εἰς	τὴν	γῆν	καὶ	→	ἐγένοντο	→	→	βρονταὶ	καὶ	φωναὶ	καὶ	→	→ ἀστραπαὶ	καὶ	σεισμός
v.aai.3s	p.a	d.asf	n.asf	cj		v.ami.3p			n.npf	cj	n.npf	cj		n.npf	cj	n.nsm
965	1650	3836	1178	2779		1181			1103	2779	5889	2779		847	2779	4939

The Trumpets

8:6 Then	the	seven	angels	who	had	the	seven	trumpets	prepared	to	sound	them.	¶	[7]	The	first
Καὶ	οἱ	ἑπτὰ	ἄγγελοι	οἱ	ἔχοντες	τὰς	ἑπτὰ	σάλπιγγας	ἡτοίμασαν	ἵνα	σαλπίσωσιν	αὐτούς		Καὶ	ὁ	πρῶτος
cj	d.npm	a.npm	n.npm	d.npm	pt.pa.npm	d.apf	a.apf	n.apf	v.aas.3p	cj	v.aas.3p	r.apm.3		cj	d.nsm	a.nsm
2779	3836	2231	34	3836	2400	3836	2231	4894	2286	2671	4895	899		2779	3836	4755

angel sounded	his trumpet,	and there		came	hail	and	fire	mixed		with	blood,	and	it was	hurled	down	upon	the
ἐσάλπισεν		καὶ		ἐγένετο	χάλαζα	καὶ	πῦρ	μεμιγμένα	ἐν		αἵματι	καὶ	→	ἐβλήθη		εἰς	τὴν
v.aai.3s		cj		v.ami.3s	n.nsf	cj	n.nsn	pt.rp.npn	p.d		n.dsn	cj		v.api.3s		p.a	d.asf
4895		2779		1181	5898	2779	4786	3624	1877		135	2779		965		1650	3836

ἐν τῷ ναῷ αὐτοῦ, καὶ ὁ καθήμενος ἐπὶ τοῦ θρόνου σκηνώσει ἐπ' αὐτούς. [16] οὐ πεινάσουσιν ἔτι οὐδὲ διψήσουσιν ἔτι οὐδὲ μὴ πέσῃ ἐπ' αὐτοὺς ὁ ἥλιος οὐδὲ πᾶν καῦμα, [17] ὅτι τὸ ἀρνίον τὸ ἀνὰ μέσον τοῦ θρόνου ποιμανεῖ αὐτοὺς καὶ ὁδηγήσει αὐτοὺς ἐπὶ ζωῆς πηγὰς ὑδάτων, καὶ ἐξαλείψει ὁ θεὸς πᾶν δάκρυον ἐκ τῶν ὀφθαλμῶν αὐτῶν.

[8:1] Καὶ ὅταν ἤνοιξεν τὴν σφραγῖδα τὴν ἑβδόμην, ἐγένετο σιγὴ ἐν τῷ οὐρανῷ ὡς ἡμιώριον. ¶ [2] καὶ εἶδον τοὺς ἑπτὰ ἀγγέλους οἳ ἐνώπιον τοῦ θεοῦ ἑστήκασιν, καὶ ἐδόθησαν αὐτοῖς ἑπτὰ σάλπιγγες. ¶ [3] Καὶ ἄλλος ἄγγελος ἦλθεν καὶ ἐστάθη ἐπὶ τοῦ θυσιαστηρίου ἔχων λιβανωτὸν χρυσοῦν, καὶ ἐδόθη αὐτῷ θυμιάματα πολλά, ἵνα δώσει ταῖς προσευχαῖς τῶν ἁγίων πάντων ἐπὶ τὸ θυσιαστήριον τὸ χρυσοῦν τὸ ἐνώπιον τοῦ θρόνου. [4] καὶ ἀνέβη ὁ καπνὸς τῶν θυμιαμάτων ταῖς προσευχαῖς τῶν ἁγίων ἐκ χειρὸς τοῦ ἀγγέλου ἐνώπιον τοῦ θεοῦ. [5] καὶ εἴληφεν ὁ ἄγγελος τὸν λιβανωτὸν καὶ ἐγέμισεν αὐτὸν ἐκ τοῦ πυρὸς τοῦ θυσιαστηρίου καὶ ἔβαλεν εἰς τὴν γῆν, καὶ ἐγένοντο βρονταὶ καὶ φωναὶ καὶ ἀστραπαὶ καὶ σεισμός.

[8:6] Καὶ οἱ ἑπτὰ ἄγγελοι οἱ ἔχοντες τὰς ἑπτὰ σάλπιγγας ἡτοίμασαν αὐτοὺς ἵνα σαλπίσωσιν. ¶ [7] Καὶ ὁ πρῶτος ἐσάλπισεν· καὶ ἐγένετο χάλαζα καὶ πῦρ μεμιγμένα ἐν αἵματι καὶ ἐβλήθη εἰς τὴν γῆν, καὶ τὸ τρίτον τῆς γῆς κατεκάη καὶ τὸ τρίτον τῶν δένδρων

earth. A third of the earth was burned up, a third of the trees were burned up, and all the
γῆν καὶ ⸤τὸ τρίτον⸥ → τῆς γῆς → κατεκάη ← καὶ ⸤τὸ τρίτον⸥ → τῶν δένδρων → κατεκάη ← καὶ πᾶς
n.asf cj d.nsn a.nsn d.gsf n.gsf v.api.3s cj d.nsn a.nsn d.gpn n.gpn v.api.3s cj a.nsm
1178 2779 3836 5569 3836 1178 2876 2779 3836 5569 3836 1285 2876 2779 4246

green grass was burned up. ¶ **8** The second angel sounded his trumpet, and something like a huge
χλωρὸς χόρτος → κατεκάη ← Καὶ ὁ δεύτερος ἄγγελος ἐσάλπισεν ← καὶ ὡς μέγα
a.nsm n.nsm v.api.3s cj d.nsm a.nsm n.nsm v.aai.3s cj pl a.nsn
5952 5965 2876 2779 3836 1311 34 4895 2779 6055 3489

mountain, all ablaze, was thrown into the sea. A third of the sea turned into blood, **9** a
ὄρος → ⸤πυρὶ καιόμενον⸥ ἐβλήθη εἰς τὴν θάλασσαν καὶ ⸤τὸ τρίτον⸥ → τῆς θαλάσσης ἐγένετο ← αἷμα καὶ
n.nsn n.dsn pt.pp.nsn v.api.3s p.a d.asf n.asf cj d.nsn a.nsn d.gsf n.gsf v.ami.3s n.nsn cj
4001 4786 2794 965 1650 3836 2498 2779 3836 5569 3836 2498 1181 135 2779

third of the living creatures in the sea died, and a third of the ships were
⸤τὸ τρίτον⸥ τῶν ⸤τὰ ἔχοντα ψυχὰς⸥ κτισμάτων τῶν ἐν τῇ θαλάσσῃ ἀπέθανεν καὶ ⸤τὸ τρίτον⸥ → τῶν πλοίων →
d.nsn a.nsn d.gpn pt.pa.npn n.apf n.gpn d.gpn p.d d.dsf n.dsf v.aai.3s cj d.nsn a.nsn d.gpn n.gpn
3836 5569 3836 3836 2400 6034 3233 3836 1877 3836 2498 633 2779 3836 5569 3836 4450

destroyed. ¶ **10** The third angel sounded his trumpet, and a great star, blazing like a torch, fell from
διεφθάρησαν Καὶ ὁ τρίτος ἄγγελος ἐσάλπισεν ← καὶ μέγας ἀστὴρ καιόμενος ὡς λαμπὰς ἔπεσεν ἐκ
v.api.3p cj d.nsm a.nsm n.nsm v.aai.3s cj a.nsm n.nsm pt.pp.nsm pl n.nsf v.aai.3s p.g
1425 2779 3836 5569 34 4895 2779 3489 843 2794 6055 3286 4406 1666

the sky on a third of the rivers and on the springs of water **11** the name of the star
τοῦ οὐρανοῦ καὶ ἔπεσεν ἐπὶ ⸤τὸ τρίτον⸥ → τῶν ποταμῶν καὶ ἐπὶ τὰς πηγὰς → ⸤τῶν ὑδάτων⸥ καὶ τὸ ὄνομα → τοῦ ἀστέρος
d.gsm n.gsm cj v.aai.3s p.a d.asn a.asn d.gpm n.gpm cj p.a d.apf n.apf d.gpn n.gpn cj d.nsn n.nsn d.gsm n.gsm
3836 4041 2779 4406 2093 3836 5569 3836 4532 2779 2093 3836 4380 3836 5623 2779 3836 3950 3836 843

is Wormwood. A third of the waters turned bitter, and many people died from the waters
λέγεται ὁ Ἄψινθος, καὶ τὸ τρίτον → τῶν ὑδάτων ἐγένετο εἰς ἄψινθον καὶ πολλοὶ ⸤τῶν ἀνθρώπων⸥ ἀπέθανον ἐκ τῶν ὑδάτων
v.ppi.3s d.nsm n.nsm cj d.nsn a.nsn d.gpn n.gpn v.ami.3s p.a n.asm cj a.npm d.gpm n.gpm v.aai.3p p.g d.gpn n.gpn
3306 3836 952 2779 3836 5569 3836 5623 1181 1650 952 2779 4498 3836 476 633 1666 3836 5623

that had become bitter. ¶ **12** The fourth angel sounded his trumpet, and a third of the sun
ὅτι → ἐπικράνθησαν Καὶ ὁ τέταρτος ἄγγελος ἐσάλπισεν ← καὶ ⸤τὸ τρίτον⸥ → τοῦ ἡλίου
cj v.api.3p cj d.nsm a.nsm n.nsm v.aai.3s cj d.nsn a.nsn d.gsm n.gsm
4022 4393 2779 3836 5480 34 4895 2779 3836 5569 3836 2463

was struck, a third of the moon, and a third of the stars, so that a third of them turned dark.
→ ἐπλήγη καὶ ⸤τὸ τρίτον⸥ → τῆς σελήνης καὶ ⸤τὸ τρίτον⸥ → τῶν ἀστέρων ἵνα ⸤τὸ τρίτον⸥ → αὐτῶν → σκοτισθῇ
v.api.3s cj d.nsn a.nsn d.gsf n.gsf cj d.nsn a.nsn d.gpm n.gpm cj d.nsn a.nsn r.gpm.3 v.aps.3s
4448 2779 3836 5569 3836 4943 2779 3836 5569 3836 843 2671 3836 5569 899 5029

A third of the day was without light, and also a third of the night. ¶ **13** As I watched, I
καὶ ⸤τὸ τρίτον⸥ αὐτῆς ἡ ἡμέρα → μὴ φάνῃ καὶ ὁμοίως ἡ νὺξ Καὶ → εἶδον καὶ
cj d.asn a.asn r.gsf.3 d.nsf n.nsf pl v.aas.3s cj adv d.nsf n.nsf cj v.aai.1s cj
2779 3836 5569 899 3836 2465 5743 3590 5743 2779 3931 3836 3816 2779 1625 2779

heard an eagle that was flying in midair call out in a loud voice: "Woe! Woe! Woe to the
ἤκουσα ἑνὸς ἀετοῦ → → πετομένου ἐν μεσουρανήματι λέγοντος ← → μεγάλῃ φωνῇ οὐαὶ οὐαὶ οὐαὶ ⸤τοὺς⸥
v.aai.1s a.gsm n.gsm pt.pm.gsm p.d n.dsn pt.pa.gsm a.dsf n.dsf j j j d.apm
201 1651 108 4375 1877 3547 3306 3489 5889 4026 4026 4026 3836

inhabitants of the earth, because of the trumpet blasts about to be sounded by the other three
κατοικοῦντας ἐπὶ τῆς γῆς ἐκ ← τῶν λοιπῶν ⸤τῆς σάλπιγγος⸥ φωνῶν ⸤τῶν μελλόντων⸥ σαλπίζειν → τῶν τριῶν
pt.pa.apm p.g d.gsf n.gsf p.g d.gpf a.gpf d.gsf n.gsf n.gpf d.gpm pt.pa.gpm f.pa d.gpf a.gpm
2997 2093 3836 1178 1666 3836 3370 3836 4894 5889 3836 3516 4895 34 3836 5552

angels!" ¶ **9:1** The fifth angel sounded his trumpet, and I saw a star that had fallen from the
ἀγγέλων Καὶ ὁ πέμπτος ἄγγελος ἐσάλπισεν ← καὶ εἶδον ἀστέρα → πεπτωκότα ἐκ τοῦ
n.gpm cj d.nsm a.nsm n.nsm v.aai.3s cj v.aai.1s n.asm pt.ra.asm p.g d.gsm
34 2779 3836 4286 34 4895 2779 1625 843 4406 1666 3836

sky to the earth. The star was given the key to the shaft of the Abyss. **2** When he opened the
οὐρανοῦ εἰς τὴν γῆν καὶ αὐτῷ → ἐδόθη ἡ κλεὶς → τοῦ φρέατος → τῆς ἀβύσσου καὶ → ἤνοιξεν τῆς τὸ φρέαρ
n.gsm p.a d.asf n.asf cj r.dsm.3 v.api.3s d.nsf n.nsf d.gsn n.gsn d.gsf n.gsf cj v.aai.3s d.gsf d.asn n.asn
4041 1650 3836 1178 2779 899 1443 3836 3090 3836 5853 3836 12 2779 487 3836 3836 5853

κατεκάη καὶ πᾶς χόρτος χλωρὸς κατεκάη. ¶ **8** Καὶ ὁ δεύτερος ἄγγελος ἐσάλπισεν· καὶ ὡς ὄρος μέγα πυρὶ καιόμενον ἐβλήθη εἰς τὴν θάλασσαν, καὶ ἐγένετο τὸ τρίτον τῆς θαλάσσης αἷμα **9** καὶ ἀπέθανεν τὸ τρίτον τῶν κτισμάτων τῶν ἐν τῇ θαλάσσῃ τὰ ἔχοντα ψυχὰς καὶ τὸ τρίτον τῶν πλοίων διεφθάρησαν. ¶ **10** Καὶ ὁ τρίτος ἄγγελος ἐσάλπισεν· καὶ ἔπεσεν ἐκ τοῦ οὐρανοῦ ἀστὴρ μέγας καιόμενος ὡς λαμπὰς καὶ ἔπεσεν ἐπὶ τὸ τρίτον τῶν ποταμῶν καὶ ἐπὶ τὰς πηγὰς τῶν ὑδάτων, **11** καὶ τὸ ὄνομα τοῦ ἀστέρος λέγεται ὁ Ἄψινθος, καὶ ἐγένετο τὸ τρίτον τῶν ὑδάτων εἰς ἄψινθον καὶ πολλοὶ τῶν ἀνθρώπων ἀπέθανον ἐκ τῶν ὑδάτων ὅτι ἐπικράνθησαν. ¶ **12** Καὶ ὁ τέταρτος ἄγγελος ἐσάλπισεν· καὶ ἐπλήγη τὸ τρίτον τοῦ ἡλίου καὶ τὸ τρίτον τῆς σελήνης καὶ τὸ τρίτον τῶν ἀστέρων, ἵνα σκοτισθῇ τὸ τρίτον αὐτῶν καὶ ἡ ἡμέρα μὴ φάνῃ τὸ τρίτον αὐτῆς καὶ ἡ νὺξ ὁμοίως. ¶ **13** Καὶ εἶδον, καὶ ἤκουσα ἑνὸς ἀετοῦ πετομένου ἐν μεσουρανήματι λέγοντος φωνῇ μεγάλῃ, Οὐαὶ οὐαὶ οὐαὶ τοὺς κατοικοῦντας ἐπὶ τῆς γῆς ἐκ τῶν λοιπῶν φωνῶν τῆς σάλπιγγος τῶν τριῶν ἀγγέλων τῶν μελλόντων σαλπίζειν. **9:1** Καὶ ὁ πέμπτος ἄγγελος ἐσάλπισεν· καὶ εἶδον ἀστέρα ἐκ τοῦ οὐρανοῦ πεπτωκότα εἰς τὴν γῆν, καὶ ἐδόθη αὐτῷ ἡ κλεὶς τοῦ φρέατος τῆς ἀβύσσου **2** καὶ ἤνοιξεν τὸ φρέαρ τῆς ἀβύσσου, καὶ ἀνέβη καπνὸς ἐκ τοῦ φρέατος ὡς καπνὸς καμίνου μεγάλης, καὶ ἐσκοτώθη ὁ ἥλιος καὶ ὁ ἀὴρ ἐκ τοῦ καπνοῦ

Abyss,   smoke rose from it   like the smoke from a gigantic furnace.   The sun   and sky   were
ἀβύσσου καὶ   καπνὸς ἀνέβη ἐκ   ⌐τοῦ φρέατος⌐   ὡς   καπνὸς →   μεγάλης καμίνου   καὶ ὁ   ἥλιος καὶ ⌐ὁ   ἀήρ⌐ →
n.gsf   cj   n.nsm v.aai.3s p.g d.gsn n.gsn   pl   n.nsm   a.gsf   n.gsf   cj d.nsm n.nsm cj d.nsm n.nsm
12   2779 2837   326   1666   6055 2837   3489   2825   2779 3836 2463 2779 3836 113

darkened by the smoke from the Abyss.   3 And out of the smoke locusts came   down upon the earth and were given
ἐσκοτώθη ἐκ τοῦ καπνοῦ →   τοῦ φρέατος   καὶ ἐκ ← τοῦ καπνοῦ ἀκρίδες ἐξῆλθον ←   εἰς τὴν γῆν καὶ →   ἐδόθη
v.api.3s p.g d.gsm n.gsm   d.gsn n.gsn   cj p.g   d.gsm n.gsm n.npf v.aai.3p   p.a d.asf n.asf cj   v.api.3s
5031   1666 3836 2837   3836 5853   2779 1666   3836 2837   210   2002   1650 3836 1178 2779   1443

          power like   that of scorpions   of the earth. 4   They were told   not to harm   the
αὐταῖς ἐξουσία ὡς   ἔχουσιν ἐξουσίαν   ⌐οἱ σκορπίοι⌐ → τῆς γῆς καὶ αὐταῖς →   ἐρρέθη ἵνα μὴ   ἀδικήσουσιν τὸν
r.dpf.3 n.nsf cj   v.pai.3p n.asf   d.npm n.npm   d.gsf n.gsf cj r.dpf.3   v.api.3s cj pl v.fai.3p   d.asm
899   2026   6055 2400   2026   3836 5026   3836 1178 2779 899   3306 2671 3590 92   3836

grass of the earth or any plant or   tree,   but   only those people   who did not have the seal   of
χόρτον → τῆς γῆς οὐδὲ πᾶν χλωρὸν οὐδὲ πᾶν δένδρον ⌐εἰ μὴ⌐   τοὺς ἀνθρώπους οἵτινες → οὐκ ἔχουσι τὴν σφραγῖδα →
n.asm   d.gsf n.gsf cj a.asn a.asn cj a.asn n.asn   cj pl   d.apm n.apm   r.npm   pl v.pai.3p d.asf n.asf
5965   3836 1178 4028 4246 5952 4028 4246 1285   1623 3590 3836 476   4015   4024 2400   3836 5382

God   on their foreheads. 5   They were not given power to kill   them, but only to torture   them
⌐τοῦ θεοῦ⌐ ἐπὶ τῶν μετώπων   καὶ αὐτοῖς → μὴ ἐδόθη   ἵνα ἀποκτείνωσιν αὐτούς ἀλλ' ←   ἵνα βασανισθήσονται ←
d.gsm n.gsm p.g d.gpn n.gpn   cj r.dpm.3   pl v.api.3s   cj v.aas.3p   r.apm.3 cj   cj v.fpi.3p
3836 2536   2093 3836 3587   2779 899   3590 1443   2671 650   899   247   2671 989

for five   months. And the agony   they suffered was like that of the sting   of a scorpion when it strikes a
→ πέντε μῆνας   καὶ ὁ βασανισμὸς αὐτῶν →   ὡς   βασανισμὸς → σκορπίου ὅταν → παίσῃ
a.apm n.apm   cj d.nsm n.nsm   r.gpf.3   pl   n.nsm   n.gsm   cj   v.aas.3s
4297 3604   2779 3836 990   899   6055   990   5026   4020   4091

man. 6   During those days   men   will seek   death,   but will not   find   it;
ἄνθρωπον καὶ ἐν ἐκείναις ⌐ταῖς ἡμέραις⌐ ⌐οἱ ἄνθρωποι⌐ → ζητήσουσιν τὸν θάνατον καὶ ⌐ οὐ μὴ εὑρήσουσιν αὐτόν καὶ
n.asm   cj p.d d.dpf   d.dpf n.dpf   d.npm n.npm   v.fai.3p d.asm n.asm   cj   pl pl v.fai.3p r.asm.3 cj
476   2779 1877 1697 3836 2465   3836 476   2426 3836 2505   2779   2351 4024 3590 2351   899   2779

they will long   to die, but death   will elude them. ¶   7   The locusts looked
→ →   ἐπιθυμήσουσιν → ἀποθανεῖν καὶ ⌐ὁ θάνατος⌐ → φεύγει ἀπ' αὐτῶν   Καὶ τὰ ὁμοιώματα τῶν ἀκρίδων ←
v.fai.3p   f.aa   cj d.nsm n.nsm   v.pai.3s p.g r.gpm.3   cj d.npn n.npn d.gpf n.gpf
2121   633   2779 3836 2505   5771   608 899   2779 3836 3930 3836 210 3930

like horses prepared   for battle.   On their heads   they wore something like crowns   of gold, and
ὅμοια ἵπποις ἡτοιμασμένοις εἰς πόλεμον καὶ → ⌐ἐπ' αὐτῶν ⌐τὰς κεφαλὰς⌐   ὡς   στέφανοι ὅμοιοι → χρυσῷ καὶ
a.npn n.dpm v.rp.dpm   p.a n.asm   cj   p.a r.gpm.3 d.apf n.apf   pl   n.npm   a.npm   n.dsm cj
3927   2691 2286   1650 4483   2779   2093 899   3836 3051   6055 5109   3927   5996 2779

their faces   resembled human faces. 8   Their   hair   was like women's hair, and their teeth
αὐτῶν ⌐τὰ πρόσωπα⌐ ὡς   ἀνθρώπων πρόσωπα καὶ → εἶχον τρίχας ὡς   γυναικῶν τρίχας καὶ αὐτῶν ⌐οἱ ὀδόντες⌐
r.gpm.3 d.npn n.npn pl   n.gpm   n.npn   cj   v.iai.3p n.apf pl   n.gpf   n.apf cj r.gpf.3 d.npm n.npm
899   3836 4725   6055 476   4725   2779   2400 2582   6055 1222   2582 2779 899   3836 3848

were like lions' teeth. 9   They had breastplates like breastplates of iron, and the sound of their wings
ἦσαν ὡς λεόντων καὶ → εἶχον θώρακας ὡς θώρακας → σιδηροῦς καὶ ἡ φωνὴ → αὐτῶν ⌐τῶν πτερύγων⌐
v.iai.3p pl n.gpm cj   v.iai.3p n.apm pl n.apm   a.apm   cj d.nsf n.nsf   r.gpf.3 d.gpf n.gpf
1639   6055 3329 2779   2400 2606   6055 2606   4971   2779 3836 5889   899   3836 4763

was like the thundering of many horses and chariots rushing into battle. 10   They had   tails and stings like
ὡς   φωνὴ → πολλῶν ἵππων   ἁρμάτων τρεχόντων εἰς πόλεμον καὶ → ἔχουσιν οὐρὰς καὶ κέντρα ὁμοίας
pl   n.nsf   a.gpm n.gpm   n.gpn pt.pa.gpm p.a n.asm cj   v.pai.3p n.apf cj n.apn a.apf
6055 5889   4498 2691   761   5556   1650 4483 2779   2400   4038 2779 3034 3927

scorpions, and in their tails   they had power   to torment people   for five   months. 11 They had
σκορπίοις καὶ ἐν αὐτῶν ⌐ταῖς οὐραῖς⌐ αὐτῶν → ⌐ἡ ἐξουσία⌐ → ἀδικῆσαι ⌐τοὺς ἀνθρώπους⌐ → πέντε μῆνας   ἔχουσιν
n.dpm   cj p.d r.gpf.3 d.dpf n.dpf r.gpf.3   d.nsf n.nsf   f.aa   d.apm n.apm   a.apm n.apm   v.pai.3p
5026   2779 1877 899 3836 4038   899   3836 2026   92   3836 476   4297 3604   2400

as king   over them the angel   of the Abyss, whose name in Hebrew is Abaddon, and in Greek,
βασιλέα ἐπ' αὐτῶν τὸν ἄγγελον → τῆς ἀβύσσου αὐτῷ ὄνομα → Ἑβραϊστὶ Ἀβαδδών καὶ → ⌐τῇ Ἑλληνικῇ⌐ ὄνομα ἔχει
n.asm   p.g r.gpf.3 d.asm n.asm   d.gsf n.gsf r.dsm.3 n.nsn   adv   n.nsn   cj   d.dsf   n.asn v.pai.3s
995   2093 899   3836 34   3836 12   899   3950   1580   3   2779   1877 3836 1819 3950 2400

τοῦ φρέατος. ³ καὶ ἐκ τοῦ καπνοῦ ἐξῆλθον ἀκρίδες εἰς τὴν γῆν, καὶ ἐδόθη αὐταῖς ἐξουσία ὡς ἔχουσιν ἐξουσίαν οἱ σκορπίοι τῆς γῆς. ⁴ καὶ ἐρρέθη αὐταῖς ἵνα μὴ ἀδικήσουσιν τὸν χόρτον τῆς γῆς οὐδὲ πᾶν χλωρὸν οὐδὲ πᾶν δένδρον, εἰ μὴ τοὺς ἀνθρώπους οἵτινες οὐκ ἔχουσι τὴν σφραγῖδα τοῦ θεοῦ ἐπὶ τῶν μετώπων. ⁵ καὶ ἐδόθη αὐτοῖς ἵνα μὴ ἀποκτείνωσιν αὐτούς, ἀλλ' ἵνα βασανισθήσονται μῆνας πέντε, καὶ ὁ βασανισμὸς αὐτῶν ὡς βασανισμὸς σκορπίου ὅταν παίσῃ ἄνθρωπον. ⁶ καὶ ἐν ταῖς ἡμέραις ἐκείναις ζητήσουσιν οἱ ἄνθρωποι τὸν θάνατον καὶ οὐ μὴ εὑρήσουσιν αὐτόν, καὶ ἐπιθυμήσουσιν ἀποθανεῖν καὶ φεύγει ὁ θάνατος ἀπ' αὐτῶν. ¶ ⁷ Καὶ τὰ ὁμοιώματα τῶν ἀκρίδων ὅμοια ἵπποις ἡτοιμασμένοις εἰς πόλεμον, καὶ ἐπὶ τὰς κεφαλὰς αὐτῶν ὡς στέφανοι ὅμοιοι χρυσῷ, καὶ τὰ πρόσωπα αὐτῶν ὡς πρόσωπα ἀνθρώπων, ⁸ καὶ εἶχον τρίχας ὡς τρίχας γυναικῶν, καὶ οἱ ὀδόντες αὐτῶν ὡς λεόντων ἦσαν, ⁹ καὶ εἶχον θώρακας ὡς θώρακας σιδηροῦς, καὶ ἡ φωνὴ τῶν πτερύγων αὐτῶν ὡς φωνὴ ἁρμάτων ἵππων πολλῶν τρεχόντων εἰς πόλεμον, ¹⁰ καὶ ἔχουσιν οὐρὰς ὁμοίας σκορπίοις καὶ κέντρα, καὶ ἐν ταῖς οὐραῖς αὐτῶν ἡ ἐξουσία αὐτῶν ἀδικῆσαι τοὺς ἀνθρώπους μῆνας πέντε, ¹¹ ἔχουσιν ἐπ' αὐτῶν βασιλέα τὸν ἄγγελον τῆς ἀβύσσου, ὄνομα αὐτῷ Ἑβραϊστὶ Ἀβαδδών, καὶ ἐν

Apollyon. ¶ **12** The first woe is past; two other woes are yet to come. ¶ **13** The sixth
Ἀπολλύων. Ἡ ἡ μία οὐαὶ → ἀπῆλθεν ἰδοὺ δύο οὐαὶ ἔτι → ἔρχεται μετὰ ταῦτα Καὶ ὁ ἕκτος
n.nsm   d.nsf d.nsf a.nsf   v.aai.3s j a.npf j adv v.pmi.3s p.a r.apn cj d.nsm a.nsm
661   3836 3836 1651 4026   599 2627 1545 4026 2285 2262 3552 4047 2779 3836 1761

angel sounded his trumpet, and I heard a voice coming from the horns of the golden
ἄγγελος ἐσάλπισεν ← κ αὶ → ἤκουσα μίαν φωνὴν → ἐκ τῶν [τεσσάρων] κεράτων τοῦ τοῦ χρυσοῦ
n.nsm v.aai.3s cj v.aai.1s a.asf n.asf p.g d.gpn a.gpn n.gpn d.gsn d.gsn a.gsn
34 4895 2779 201 1651 5889 1666 3836 5475 3043 3836 3836 5997

altar that is before God. **14** It said to the sixth angel who had the trumpet, "Release the four
θυσιαστηρίου τοῦ ἐνώπιον τοῦ θεοῦ. → λέγοντα → τῷ ἕκτῳ ἀγγέλῳ ὁ ἔχων τὴν σάλπιγγα λῦσον τοὺς τέσσαρας
n.gsn d.gsn p.g d.gsn n.gsm pt.pa.asm d.dsm a.dsm n.dsm d.nsm pt.pa.nsm d.asf n.asf v.aam.2s d.apm a.apm
2603 3836 1967 3836 2536 3306 3836 1761 34 3836 2400 3836 4894 3395 3836 5475

angels who are bound at the great river Euphrates." **15** And the four angels who had been kept
ἀγγέλους τοὺς → δεδεμένους ἐπὶ τῷ τῷ μεγάλῳ ποταμῷ Εὐφράτῃ καὶ οἱ τέσσαρες ἄγγελοι οἱ → → →
n.apm d.apm pt.rp.apm p.d d.dsm d.dsm a.dsm n.dsm n.dsm cj d.npm a.npm n.npm d.npm
34 3836 1313 2093 3836 3836 3489 4532 2371 2779 3836 5475 34 3836

ready for this very hour and day and month and year were released to kill a third of
ἡτοιμασμένοι εἰς τὴν ὥραν καὶ ἡμέραν καὶ μῆνα καὶ ἐνιαυτόν → ἐλύθησαν ἵνα ἀποκτείνωσιν τὸ τρίτον →
pt.rp.npm p.a d.asf n.asf cj n.asf cj n.asm cj n.asm v.api.3p cj v.aas.3p d.asn a.asn
2286 1650 3836 6052 2779 2465 2779 3604 2779 1929 3395 2671 650 3836 5569

mankind. **16** The number of the mounted troops was two hundred million. I heard their
τῶν ἀνθρώπων καὶ ὁ ἀριθμὸς → τῶν τοῦ ἱππικοῦ στρατευμάτων δισμυριάδες ← μυριάδων → ἤκουσα αὐτῶν
d.gpm n.gpm cj d.nsm n.nsm d.gpn d.gsn n.gsn n.gpn n.npf n.gpf v.aai.1s r.gpn.3
3836 476 2779 3836 750 3836 3836 2690 5128 1490 3689 201 899

number. ¶ **17** The horses and riders I saw in my vision looked like this:
τὸν ἀριθμὸν Καὶ τοὺς ἵππους καὶ τοὺς καθημένους ἐπ᾽ αὐτῶν → εἶδον ἐν τῇ ὁράσει → → οὕτως ἔχοντας
d.asm n.asm cj d.apm n.apm cj d.apm pt.pm.apm p.g r.gpm.3 v.aai.1s p.d d.dsf n.dsf adv pt.pa.apm
3836 750 2779 3836 2691 2779 3836 2764 2093 899 1625 1877 3836 3970 4048 2400

Their breastplates were fiery red, dark blue, and yellow as sulfur. The heads of the horses
θώρακας πυρίνους ← καὶ ὑακινθίνους καὶ → θειώδεις καὶ αἱ κεφαλαὶ → τῶν ἵππων
n.apm a.apm cj a.apm cj a.apm cj d.npf n.npf d.gpm n.gpm
2606 4791 2779 5610 2779 2523 2779 3836 3051 3836 2691

resembled the heads of lions, and out of their mouths came fire, smoke and sulfur. **18** A third of
ὡς κεφαλαὶ → λεόντων καὶ ἐκ ← αὐτῶν τῶν στομάτων ἐκπορεύεται πῦρ καὶ καπνὸς καὶ θεῖον τὸ τρίτον →
pl n.npf n.gpm cj p.g r.gpm.3 d.gpn n.gpn v.pmi.3s n.nsn cj n.nsm cj n.nsn d.nsn a.nsn
6055 3051 3329 2779 1666 899 3836 5125 1744 4786 2779 2837 2779 2520 3836 5569

mankind was killed by the three plagues of fire, smoke and sulfur that
τῶν ἀνθρώπων ἀπεκτάνθησαν ἀπὸ τῶν τριῶν πληγῶν τούτων ἐκ τοῦ πυρὸς καὶ τοῦ καπνοῦ καὶ τοῦ θείου τοῦ
d.gpm n.gpm v.api.3p p.g d.gpf a.gpf n.gpf r.gpf p.g d.gsn n.gsn cj d.gsm n.gsm cj d.gsn n.gsn d.gsn
3836 476 650 608 3836 5552 4435 4047 1666 3836 4786 2779 3836 2837 2779 3836 2520 3836

came out of their mouths. **19** The power of the horses was in their mouths and in their
ἐκπορευομένου ἐκ ← αὐτῶν τῶν στομάτων γὰρ ἡ ἐξουσία → τῶν ἵππων ἐστιν ἐν αὐτῶν τῷ στόματι καὶ ἐν αὐτῶν
pt.pm.gsn p.g r.gpm.3 d.gpn n.gpn cj d.nsf n.nsf d.gpm n.gpm v.pai.3s p.d r.gpm.3 d.dsn n.dsn cj p.d r.gpm.3
1744 1666 899 3836 5125 1142 3836 2026 3836 2691 1639 1877 899 3836 5125 2779 1877 899

tails; for their tails were like snakes, having heads with which they inflict injury. ¶
ταῖς οὐραῖς γὰρ αὐτῶν αἱ οὐραὶ ὅμοιαι ὄφεσιν ἔχουσαι κεφαλὰς καὶ ἐν αὐταῖς → → ἀδικοῦσιν
d.dpf n.dpf cj r.gpm.3 d.npf n.npf a.npf n.dpf pt.pa.npf n.apf cj p.d r.dpf.3 v.pai.3p
3836 4038 1142 899 3836 4038 3927 4058 2400 3051 2779 1877 899 92

20 The rest of mankind that were not killed by these plagues still did not repent of the
Καὶ οἱ λοιποὶ → τῶν ἀνθρώπων οἳ → οὐκ ἀπεκτάνθησαν ἐν ταύταις ταῖς πληγαῖς → οὐδὲ μετενόησαν ἐκ τῶν
cj d.npm a.npm d.gpm n.gpm r.npm pl v.api.3p p.d r.dpf d.dpf n.dpf adv v.aai.3p p.g d.gpn
2779 3836 3370 3836 476 4005 650 4024 650 1877 4047 3836 4435 3566 4028 3566 1666 3836

work of their hands; they did not stop worshiping demons, and idols of gold,
ἔργων → αὐτῶν τῶν χειρῶν ἵνα → → μὴ προσκυνήσουσιν τὰ δαιμόνια καὶ τὰ εἴδωλα τὰ χρυσᾶ καὶ
n.gpn r.gpm.3 d.gpf n.gpf cj pl v.fai.3p d.apn n.apn cj d.apn n.apn d.apn a.apn cj
2240 5931 3836 5931 2671 4686 4686 3590 4686 3836 1228 2779 3836 1631 3836 5997 2779

τῇ Ἑλληνικῇ ὄνομα ἔχει Ἀπολλύων. ¶ **12** Ἡ οὐαὶ ἡ μία ἀπῆλθεν· ἰδοὺ ἔρχεται ἔτι δύο οὐαὶ μετὰ ταῦτα. ¶ **13** Καὶ ὁ ἕκτος ἄγγελος ἐσάλπισεν· καὶ ἤκουσα φωνὴν μίαν ἐκ τῶν [τεσσάρων] κεράτων τοῦ θυσιαστηρίου τοῦ χρυσοῦ τοῦ ἐνώπιον τοῦ θεοῦ, **14** λέγοντα τῷ ἕκτῳ ἀγγέλῳ, ὁ ἔχων τὴν σάλπιγγα, Λῦσον τοὺς τέσσαρας ἀγγέλους τοὺς δεδεμένους ἐπὶ τῷ ποταμῷ τῷ μεγάλῳ Εὐφράτῃ. **15** καὶ ἐλύθησαν οἱ τέσσαρες ἄγγελοι οἱ ἡτοιμασμένοι εἰς τὴν ὥραν καὶ ἡμέραν καὶ μῆνα καὶ ἐνιαυτόν, ἵνα ἀποκτείνωσιν τὸ τρίτον τῶν ἀνθρώπων. **16** καὶ ὁ ἀριθμὸς τῶν στρατευμάτων τοῦ ἱππικοῦ δισμυριάδες μυριάδων, ἤκουσα τὸν ἀριθμὸν αὐτῶν. ¶ **17** καὶ οὕτως εἶδον τοὺς ἵππους ἐν τῇ ὁράσει καὶ τοὺς καθημένους ἐπ᾽ αὐτῶν, ἔχοντας θώρακας πυρίνους καὶ ὑακινθίνους καὶ θειώδεις, καὶ αἱ κεφαλαὶ τῶν ἵππων ὡς κεφαλαὶ λεόντων, καὶ ἐκ τῶν στομάτων αὐτῶν ἐκπορεύεται πῦρ καὶ καπνὸς καὶ θεῖον. **18** ἀπὸ τῶν τριῶν πληγῶν τούτων ἀπεκτάνθησαν τὸ τρίτον τῶν ἀνθρώπων, ἐκ τοῦ πυρὸς καὶ τοῦ καπνοῦ καὶ τοῦ θείου τοῦ ἐκπορευομένου ἐκ τῶν στομάτων αὐτῶν. **19** ἡ γὰρ ἐξουσία τῶν ἵππων ἐν τῷ στόματι αὐτῶν ἐστιν καὶ ἐν ταῖς οὐραῖς αὐτῶν, αἱ γὰρ οὐραὶ αὐτῶν ὅμοιαι ὄφεσιν, ἔχουσαι κεφαλὰς καὶ ἐν αὐταῖς ἀδικοῦσιν. ¶ **20** Καὶ οἱ λοιποὶ τῶν ἀνθρώπων, οἳ οὐκ ἀπεκτάνθησαν ἐν ταῖς πληγαῖς ταύταις, οὐδὲ μετενόησαν ἐκ τῶν ἔργων τῶν χειρῶν αὐτῶν, ἵνα μὴ

silver,   bronze,   stone   and wood   – idols that cannot   see   or hear   or walk.
ⸯτὰ ἀργυρᾶⸯ καὶ ⸯτὰ χαλκᾶⸯ καὶ ⸯτὰ λίθιναⸯ καὶ ⸯτὰ ξύλιναⸯ   ἃ ⸯοὔτε δύνανταιⸯ βλέπειν οὔτε ἀκούειν οὔτε περιπατεῖν
d.apn a.apn   cj   d.apn a.apn   cj   d.apn a.apn   cj   d.apn a.apn   r.npn cj   v.ppi.3p f.pa   cj   f.pa   cj   f.pa
3836 739   2779 3836 5911   2779 3836 3343   2779 3836 3832   4005 4046 1538   1063 4046 201   4046 4344

21 Nor   did they repent   of their murders,   their magic arts,   their sexual immorality
ⸯκαὶ οὐⸯ → → μετενόησαν ἐκ αὐτῶν ⸯτῶν φόνωνⸯ οὔτε ἐκ αὐτῶν ⸯτῶν φαρμάκωνⸯ ← οὔτε ἐκ αὐτῶν ⸯτῆς πορνείαςⸯ ←
cj pl   v.aai.3p   p.g r.gpm.3 d.gpm n.gpm   cj p.g r.gpm.3 d.gpm n.gpm   cj p.g r.gpm.3 d.gsf n.gsf
2779 4024   3566   1666 899 3836 5840   4046 1666 899 3836 5760   4046 1666 899 3836 4518

or   their thefts.
οὔτε ἐκ αὐτῶν ⸯτῶν κλεμμάτωνⸯ
cj p.g r.gpm.3 d.gpn n.gpn
4046 1666 899 3836 3092

The Angel and the Little Scroll

10:1 Then I saw another mighty angel coming   down from heaven.   He was robed   in a cloud,
Καὶ → εἶδον ἄλλον ἰσχυρὸν ἄγγελον καταβαίνοντα ← ἐκ ⸯτοῦ οὐρανοῦⸯ → → περιβεβλημένον ← νεφέλην
cj   v.aai.1s r.asm a.asm n.asm pt.pa.asm   p.g d.gsm n.gsm   pt.rp.asm ← n.asf
2779   1625 257 2708 34 2849   1666 3836 4041   4314   3749

with a rainbow above his   head;   his   face   was like the sun, and his   legs   were like fiery
καὶ ⸯἡ ἶριςⸯ ἐπὶ αὐτοῦ ⸯτῆς κεφαλῆςⸯ καὶ αὐτοῦ ⸯτὸ πρόσωπονⸯ ὡς ὁ ἥλιος καὶ αὐτοῦ ⸯοἱ πόδεςⸯ ὡς πυρός
cj d.nsf n.nsf p.g r.gsm.3 d.gsf n.gsf cj r.gsm.3 d.nsn n.nsn pl d.nsm n.nsm cj r.gsm.3 d.npm n.npm pl n.gsn
2779 3836 2692 2093 899 3836 3051 2779 899 3836 4725 6055 3836 2463 2779 899 3836 4546 6055 4786

pillars. **2** He was holding a little scroll,   which lay open   in his   hand.   He planted his   right
στῦλοι καὶ → → ἔχων βιβλαρίδιον → ἠνεῳγμένον ἐν αὐτοῦ ⸯτῇ χειρὶⸯ καὶ → ἔθηκεν αὐτοῦ ⸯτὸν δεξιὸνⸯ
n.npm cj   pt.pa.nsm n.asn   pt.rp.asn p.d r.gsm.3 d.dsf n.dsf cj   v.aai.3s r.gsm.3 d.asm a.asm
5146 2779   2400 1044   487 1877 899 3836 5931 2779   5502 899 3836 1288

foot   on the sea   and his left   foot on the land, **3** and he gave a loud shout like the roar   of a lion.
ⸯτὸν πόδαⸯ ἐπὶ τῆς θαλάσσης δὲ τὸν εὐώνυμον ἐπὶ τῆς γῆς καὶ → ἔκραξεν μεγάλῃ φωνῇ ὥσπερ μυκᾶται λέων
d.asm n.asm p.g d.gsf n.gsf cj d.asm a.asm p.g d.gsf n.gsf cj   v.aai.3s a.dsf n.dsf pl v.pmi.3s n.nsm
3836 4546 2093 3836 2498 1254 3836 2381 2093 3836 1178 2779   3189 3489 5889 6061 3681 3329

When he shouted, the   voices of the seven thunders spoke. **4** And when the seven thunders spoke, I was
καὶ ὅτε → ἔκραξεν τὰς ἑαυτῶν φωνάς αἱ ἑπτὰ βρονταὶ ἐλάλησαν καὶ ὅτε αἱ ἑπτὰ βρονταὶ ἐλάλησαν → →
cj cj   v.aai.3s d.apf r.gpf.3 n.apf d.npf a.npf n.npf v.aai.3p cj cj d.npf a.npf n.npf v.aai.3p
2779 4021   3189 3836 1571 5889 3836 2231 1103 3281 2779 4021 3836 2231 1103 3281

about to write; but I heard a voice from heaven   say,   "Seal   up what the seven thunders have said
ἤμελλον → γράφειν καὶ → ἤκουσα φωνὴν ἐκ ⸯτοῦ οὐρανοῦⸯ λέγουσαν σφράγισον ← ἃ αἱ ἑπτὰ βρονταί → ἐλάλησαν
v.iai.1s f.pa cj   v.aai.1s n.asf p.g d.gsm n.gsm pt.pa.asf v.aam.2s r.apn d.npf a.npf n.npf v.aai.3p
3516 1211 2779   201 5889 1666 3836 4041 3306 5381 4005 3836 2231 1103 3281

and do not write it   down." ¶ **5** Then the angel   I had seen standing on the sea   and on the land
καὶ → μὴ γράψῃς αὐτά ← Καὶ ὁ ἄγγελος ὃν → → εἶδον ἑστῶτα ἐπὶ τῆς θαλάσσης καὶ ἐπὶ τῆς γῆς
cj pl v.aas.2s r.apn.3   cj d.nsm n.nsm r.asm   v.aai.1s pt.ra.asm p.g d.gsf n.gsf cj p.g d.gsf n.gsf
2779 1211 3590 1211 899 1211   2779 3836 34 4005   1625 2705 2093 3836 2498 2779 2093 3836 1178

raised his   right   hand   to heaven. **6** And he swore by him who lives *for ever*   *and ever,*
ἦρεν αὐτοῦ ⸯτὴν δεξιὰνⸯ ⸯτὴν χεῖραⸯ εἰς ⸯτὸν οὐρανὸνⸯ καὶ → ὤμοσεν ἐν τῷ ← ζῶντι εἰς ⸯτοὺς αἰῶναςⸯ ⸯτῶν αἰώνωνⸯ
v.aai.3s r.gsm.3 d.asf a.asf d.asf n.asf p.a d.asm n.asm cj   v.aai.3s p.d d.dsm pt.pa.dsm p.a d.apm n.apm d.gpm n.gpm
149 899 3836 1288 3836 5931 1650 3836 4041 2779   3923 1877 3836 2409 1650 3836 172 3836 172

who created the heavens and all that is in them,   the earth and all that is in it,   and the sea   and all that
ὃς ἔκτισεν τὸν οὐρανὸν καὶ τὰ ἐν αὐτῷ καὶ τὴν γῆν καὶ τὰ ἐν αὐτῇ καὶ τὴν θάλασσαν καὶ τὰ
r.nsm v.aai.3s d.asm n.asm cj d.apn p.d r.dsm.3 cj d.asf n.asf cj d.apn p.d r.dsf.3 cj d.asf n.asf cj d.apn
4005 3231 3836 4041 2779 3836 1877 899 2779 3836 1178 2779 3836 1877 899 2779 3836 2498 2779 3836

is in it,   and said,   "There will be   no   more delay! **7** But in the days   when   the seventh angel is
ἐν αὐτῇ ὅτι → → ἔσται οὐκέτι χρόνος ἀλλ᾽ ἐν ταῖς ἡμέραις ὅταν τῆς φωνῆς τοῦ ἑβδόμου ἀγγέλου →
p.d r.dsf.3 cj   v.fmi.3s adv n.nsm p.d d.dpf n.dpf cj d.gsf n.gsf d.gsm a.gsm n.gsm
1877 899 4022   1639 4033 5989 247 1877 3836 2465 4020 3836 5889 3836 1575 34

about to sound   his trumpet,   the mystery of God   will be accomplished, just as he announced to his
μέλλῃ → σαλπίζειν ← καὶ τὸ μυστήριον → ⸯτοῦ θεοῦⸯ → ἐτελέσθη → ὡς → εὐηγγέλισεν ← ἑαυτοῦ
v.pas.3s f.pa   adv d.nsn n.nsn d.gsm n.gsm v.api.3s   cj   v.aai.3s r.gsm.3
3516 4895   2779 3836 3696 3836 2536 5464   6055   2294 1571

προσκυνήσουσιν τὰ δαιμόνια καὶ τὰ εἴδωλα τὰ χρυσᾶ καὶ τὰ ἀργυρᾶ καὶ τὰ χαλκᾶ καὶ τὰ λίθινα καὶ τὰ ξύλινα, ἃ οὔτε βλέπειν δύνανται οὔτε ἀκούειν οὔτε περιπατεῖν. **21** καὶ οὐ μετενόησαν ἐκ τῶν φόνων αὐτῶν οὔτε ἐκ τῶν φαρμάκων αὐτῶν οὔτε ἐκ τῆς πορνείας αὐτῶν οὔτε ἐκ τῶν κλεμμάτων αὐτῶν.
10:1 Καὶ εἶδον ἄλλον ἄγγελον ἰσχυρὸν καταβαίνοντα ἐκ τοῦ οὐρανοῦ περιβεβλημένον νεφέλην, καὶ ἡ ἶρις ἐπὶ τῆς κεφαλῆς αὐτοῦ καὶ τὸ πρόσωπον αὐτοῦ ὡς ὁ ἥλιος καὶ οἱ πόδες αὐτοῦ ὡς στῦλοι πυρός, **2** καὶ ἔχων ἐν τῇ χειρὶ αὐτοῦ βιβλαρίδιον ἠνεῳγμένον. καὶ ἔθηκεν τὸν πόδα αὐτοῦ τὸν δεξιὸν ἐπὶ τῆς θαλάσσης, τὸν δὲ εὐώνυμον ἐπὶ τῆς γῆς, **3** καὶ ἔκραξεν φωνῇ μεγάλῃ ὥσπερ λέων μυκᾶται. καὶ ὅτε ἔκραξεν, ἐλάλησαν αἱ ἑπτὰ βρονταὶ τὰς ἑαυτῶν φωνάς. **4** καὶ ὅτε ἐλάλησαν αἱ ἑπτὰ βρονταί, ἤμελλον γράφειν, καὶ ἤκουσα φωνὴν ἐκ τοῦ οὐρανοῦ λέγουσαν, Σφράγισον ἃ ἐλάλησαν αἱ ἑπτὰ βρονταί, καὶ μὴ αὐτὰ γράψῃς.⟨ ¶ **5** Καὶ ὁ ἄγγελος, ὃν εἶδον ἑστῶτα ἐπὶ τῆς θαλάσσης καὶ ἐπὶ τῆς γῆς, ἦρεν τὴν χεῖρα αὐτοῦ τὴν δεξιὰν εἰς τὸν οὐρανὸν **6** καὶ ὤμοσεν ἐν τῷ ζῶντι εἰς τοὺς αἰῶνας τῶν αἰώνων, ὃς ἔκτισεν τὸν οὐρανὸν καὶ τὰ ἐν αὐτῷ καὶ τὴν γῆν καὶ τὰ ἐν αὐτῇ καὶ τὴν θάλασσαν καὶ τὰ ἐν αὐτῇ, ὅτι χρόνος οὐκέτι ἔσται, **7** ἀλλ᾽ ἐν ταῖς ἡμέραις τῆς φωνῆς τοῦ ἑβδόμου ἀγγέλου, ὅταν μέλλῃ σαλπίζειν,

servants   the prophets."   ¶   **8** Then the voice that I had heard from heaven   spoke   to me once
ˌτοὺς δούλουςˌ τοὺς προφήτας   Καὶ   ἡ   φωνὴ ἦν →   →   ἤκουσα ἐκ ˌτοῦ οὐρανοῦˌ λαλοῦσαν μετ᾿ ἐμοῦ πάλιν
d.apm n.apm   d.apm n.apm   cj   d.nsf n.nsf r.asf   v.aai.1s p.g d.gsm n.gsm   pt.pa.asf p.g r.gs.1 adv
3836 1529   3836 4737   2779 3836 5889 4005   201 1666 3836 4041   3281   3552 1609 4099

more: "Go,   take   the scroll   that lies open   in the hand of the angel   who is standing on the
←   καὶ λέγουσαν ὕπαγε λάβε τὸ βιβλίον τὸ → ἠνεωγμένον ἐν τῇ χειρὶ → τοῦ ἀγγέλου τοῦ → ἑστῶτος ἐπὶ τῆς
     cj   pt.pa.asf v.pam.2s v.aam.2s d.asn n.asn d.asn v.rp.asn   p.d d.dsf n.dsf d.gsm n.gsm d.gsm pt.ra.gsm p.g d.gsf
     2779 3306   5632   3284   3836 1046 3836 487   1877 3836 5931 3836 34   3836 2705   2093 3836

sea   and on the land."   ¶ **9** So I went   to   the angel   and asked him to give   me the little scroll.
θαλάσσης καὶ ἐπὶ τῆς γῆς   καὶ ἀπῆλθα πρὸς τὸν ἄγγελον   λέγων αὐτῷ → δοῦναι μοι τὸ → βιβλαρίδιον
n.gsf   cj p.g d.gsf n.gsf   cj v.aai.1s p.a d.asm n.asm   pt.pa.nsm r.dsm.3 f.aa r.ds.1 d.asn n.asn
2498   2779 2093 3836 1178   2779 599   4639 3836 34   3306 899   1443 1609 3836   1044

       He said to me, "Take it and eat   it.   It   will turn your stomach   sour,   but in your mouth   it
καὶ → λέγει μοι λάβε καὶ κατάφαγε αὐτό καὶ ↱ ↱ → σου ˌτὴν κοιλίανˌ πικρανεῖ ἀλλ᾿ ἐν σου ˌτῷ στόματιˌ →
cj   v.pai.3s r.ds.1 v.aam.2s cj v.aam.2s r.asn.3 cj   r.gs.2 d.asf n.asf v.fai.3s cj p.d r.gs.2 d.dsn n.dsn
2779 3306   1609 3284 2779 2983   899   2779   5148 3836 3120   4393 247 1877 5148 3836 5125

will be   as sweet as honey." **10** I took   the little scroll   from the angel's   hand and ate   it.   It
→   ἔσται γλυκὺ ὡς μέλι   Καὶ → ἔλαβον τὸ → βιβλαρίδιον ἐκ τῆς ˌτοῦ ἀγγέλουˌ χειρὸς καὶ κατέφαγον αὐτό καὶ →
     v.fmi.3s a.nsn pl n.nsn   cj v.aai.1s d.asn   n.asn   p.g d.gsf d.gsm n.gsm n.gsf cj v.aai.1s r.asn.3 cj
     1639 1184 6055 3510   2779 3284 3836   1044   1666 3836 3836 34   5931 2779 2983   899 2779

tasted as sweet as honey in my mouth,   but when I had eaten it,   my stomach   turned sour.   **11** Then I was
ἦν   ὡς γλυκὺ μέλι ἐν μου ˌτῷ στόματιˌ καὶ ὅτε → → ἔφαγον αὐτό μου ἡ κοιλία → ἐπικράνθη   καὶ μοι →
v.iai.3s pl a.nsn n.nsn p.d r.gs.1 d.dsn n.dsn cj cj   v.aai.1s r.asn.3 r.gs.1 d.nsf n.nsf v.api.3s   cj r.ds.1
1639 6055 1184 3510 1877 1609 3836 5125 2779 4021   2266   899 1609 3836 3120   4393   2779 1609

told,   "You must prophesy again about many peoples,   nations,   languages and kings."
λέγουσιν σε δεῖ προφητεῦσαι πάλιν ἐπὶ πολλοῖς λαοῖς καὶ ἔθνεσιν καὶ γλώσσαις καὶ βασιλεῦσιν
v.pai.3p r.as.2 v.pai.3s f.aa adv p.d a.dpm n.dpm   cj n.dpn   cj n.dpf   cj n.dpm
3306   5148 1256 4736   4099 2093 4498 3295   2779 1620   2779 1185   2779 995

The Two Witnesses

11:1 I   was given a reed   like   a measuring rod   and was told, "Go and measure the temple of God
Καὶ μοι → ἐδόθη κάλαμος ὅμοιος   ῥάβδῳ   → λέγων ἔγειρε καὶ μέτρησον τὸν ναὸν → ˌτοῦ θεοῦˌ
cj   r.ds.1 v.api.3s n.nsm a.nsm   n.dsf   pt.pa.nsm v.pam.2s cj v.aam.2s d.asm n.asm d.gsm n.gsm
2779 1609 1443   2812   3927   4811   3306   1586 2779 3582   3836 3724   3836 2536

and the altar,   and count the worshipers there. **2** But exclude   the outer   court;   do not
καὶ τὸ θυσιαστήριον καὶ   τοὺς προσκυνοῦντας ˌἐν αὐτῷˌ καὶ ἔκβαλε ἔξωθεν, τὴν ˌτὴν ἔξωθενˌ αὐλὴν τοῦ ναοῦ καὶ → μὴ
cj d.asn n.asn   cj   d.apm pt.pa.apm p.d r.dsn.3 cj v.aam.2s ἔξωθεν d.asf d.asf adv n.asf d.gsm n.gsm cj pl
2779 3836 2603   2779   3836 4686   1877 899 2779 1675 2033   3836 3836 2033   885 3836 3724 2779 3582 3590

measure it,   because it has been given to the Gentiles. They will trample   on the holy   city for
μετρήσης αὐτὴν ὅτι → → → → ἐδόθη → τοῖς ἔθνεσιν καὶ → πατήσουσιν τὴν ˌτὴν ἁγίανˌ πόλιν
v.aas.2s r.asf.3 cj   v.api.3s d.dpn n.dpn cj   v.fai.3p   d.asf d.asf a.asf n.asf
3582   899   4022   1443   3836 1620 2779   4251   3836 3836 41   4484

42   months. **3** And I will give power to my two   witnesses,   and they will prophesy   for
ˌτεσσεράκοντα καὶ δύοˌ μῆνας Καὶ → → δώσω   → μου δυσὶν ˌτοῖς μάρτυσινˌ καὶ → → προφητεύσουσιν →
a.apm   cj a.apm n.apm cj   v.fai.1s   r.gs.1 a.dpm d.dpm n.dpm   cj   v.fai.3p
5477   2779 1545 3604   2779   1443   3459 1609 1545 3836 3459   2779   4736

1,260   days, clothed   in sackcloth." **4** These are   the two olive trees and the two lampstands
ˌχιλίας διακοσίας ἑξήκονταˌ ἡμέρας περιβεβλημένοι ← σάκκους   οὗτοί εἰσιν αἱ δύο ἐλαῖαι   καὶ αἱ δύο λυχνίαι
a.apf a.apf   a.apf   n.apf pt.rp.npm   n.apm   r.npm v.pai.3p d.npf a.npf n.npf cj d.npf a.npf n.npf
5943   1357   2008   2465   4314   4884   4047 1639 3836 1545 1777   2779 3836 1545 3393

that stand before the Lord of the earth. **5** If anyone tries to harm them, fire comes   from their
αἱ ἑστῶτες ἐνώπιον τοῦ κυρίου → τῆς γῆς   καὶ εἴ τις θέλει → ἀδικῆσαι αὐτούς πῦρ ἐκπορεύεται ἐκ αὐτῶν
d.npf pt.ra.npm p.g d.gsm n.gsm   d.gsf n.gsf cj cj r.nsm v.pai.3s f.aa r.apm.3 n.nsn v.pmi.3s p.g r.gpm.3
3836 2705   1967   3836 3261   3836 1178 2779 1623 5516 2527 92   4786   899   4484 1744   1666 899

καὶ ἐτελέσθη τὸ μυστήριον τοῦ θεοῦ, ὡς εὐηγγέλισεν τοὺς ἑαυτοῦ δούλους τοὺς προφήτας. ¶ **8** Καὶ ἡ φωνὴ ἣν ἤκουσα ἐκ τοῦ οὐρανοῦ πάλιν λαλοῦσαν μετ᾿ ἐμοῦ καὶ λέγουσαν, Ὕπαγε λάβε τὸ βιβλίον τὸ ἠνεῳγμένον ἐν τῇ χειρὶ τοῦ ἀγγέλου τοῦ ἑστῶτος ἐπὶ τῆς θαλάσσης καὶ ἐπὶ τῆς γῆς. ¶ **9** καὶ ἀπῆλθα πρὸς τὸν ἄγγελον λέγων αὐτῷ δοῦναί μοι τὸ βιβλαρίδιον. καὶ λέγει μοι, Λάβε καὶ κατάφαγε αὐτό, καὶ πικρανεῖ σου τὴν κοιλίαν, ἀλλ᾿ ἐν τῷ στόματί σου ἔσται γλυκὺ ὡς μέλι. **10** καὶ ἔλαβον τὸ βιβλαρίδιον ἐκ τῆς χειρὸς τοῦ ἀγγέλου καὶ κατέφαγον αὐτό, καὶ ἦν ἐν τῷ στόματί μου ὡς μέλι γλυκὺ καὶ ὅτε ἔφαγον αὐτό, ἐπικράνθη ἡ κοιλία μου. **11** καὶ λέγουσίν μοι, Δεῖ σε πάλιν προφητεῦσαι ἐπὶ λαοῖς καὶ ἔθνεσιν καὶ γλώσσαις καὶ βασιλεῦσιν πολλοῖς.

11:1 Καὶ ἐδόθη μοι κάλαμος ὅμοιος ῥάβδῳ, λέγων, Ἔγειρε καὶ μέτρησον τὸν ναὸν τοῦ θεοῦ καὶ τὸ θυσιαστήριον καὶ τοὺς προσκυνοῦντας ἐν αὐτῷ. **2** καὶ τὴν αὐλὴν τὴν ἔξωθεν τοῦ ναοῦ ἔκβαλε ἔξωθεν καὶ μὴ αὐτὴν μετρήσῃς, ὅτι ἐδόθη τοῖς ἔθνεσιν, καὶ τὴν πόλιν τὴν ἁγίαν πατήσουσιν μῆνας τεσσεράκοντα [καὶ] δύο. **3** καὶ δώσω τοῖς δυσὶν μάρτυσίν μου καὶ προφητεύσουσιν ἡμέρας χιλίας διακοσίας ἑξήκοντα περιβεβλημένοι σάκκους. **4** οὗτοί εἰσιν αἱ δύο ἐλαῖαι καὶ αἱ δύο λυχνίαι αἱ ἐνώπιον τοῦ κυρίου τῆς γῆς ἑστῶτες. **5** καὶ εἴ τις αὐτοὺς θέλει ἀδικῆσαι πῦρ ἐκπορεύεται ἐκ τοῦ στόματος αὐτῶν καὶ κατεσθίει τοὺς ἐχθροὺς

mouths	and	devours	their	enemies.		This is how	anyone	who wants	to harm	them	must
⸤τοῦ στόματος⸣	καὶ	κατεσθίει	αὐτῶν	⸤τοὺς ἐχθροὺς⸣	καὶ εἴ	οὕτως ←	τις	θελήσῃ →	ἀδικῆσαι	αὐτοὺς	δεῖ αὐτὸν
d.gsn n.gsn	cj	v.pai.3s	r.gpm.3	d.apm a.apm	cj cj	adv	r.nsm	v.aas.3s	f.aa	r.apm.3	v.pai.3s r.asm.3
3836 5125	2779	2983	899	3836 2398	2779 1623	4048	5516	2527	92	899	1256 899

die.	**6** These	men	have	power	to shut	up the sky	so that	it will not	rain	during the
ἀποκτανθῆναι	οὗτοι		ἔχουσιν	⸤τὴν ἐξουσίαν⸣	κλεῖσαι	τὸν οὐρανόν	ἵνα ← →	μὴ	⸤ὑετὸς βρέχῃ⸣ →	τὰς
f.ap	r.npm		v.pai.3p	d.asf n.asf	f.aa	d.asm n.asm	cj	pl	n.nsm v.pas.3s	d.apf
650	4047		2400	3836 2026	3091	3836 4041	2671 1101 1101	3590	5624 1101	3836

time	they	are prophesying;	and	they have	power	to turn	the waters	into	blood	and	to strike	the
ἡμέρας	αὐτῶν	⸤τῆς προφητείας⸣	καὶ →	ἔχουσιν	ἐξουσίαν →	στρέφειν ἐπὶ	τῶν ὑδάτων	αὐτὰ εἰς	αἷμα	καὶ →	πατάξαι	τὴν
n.apf	r.gpm.3	d.gsf n.gsf	cj	v.pai.3p	n.asf	f.pa p.g	d.gpn n.gpn	r.apn.3 p.a	n.asn	cj	f.aa	d.asf
2465	899	3836 4735	2779	2400	2026	5138 2093	3836 5623	899 1650	135	2779	4250	3836

earth	with	every	kind of	plague	as	often as		they want.	¶	**7** Now	when	they have	finished	their
γῆν	ἐν	πάσῃ →	←	πληγῇ	ὁσάκις ←	← ἐὰν		θελήσωσιν		Καὶ	ὅταν →	→	τελέσωσιν	αὐτῶν
n.asf	p.d	a.dsf		n.dsf	adv	pl		v.aas.3p		cj	cj		v.aas.3p	r.gpm.3
1178	1877	4246		4435	4006	1569		2527		2779	4020		5464	899

testimony,	the beast	that	comes	up from the	Abyss	will attack		them,	and	overpower		and
⸤τὴν μαρτυρίαν⸣	τὸ	θηρίον	τὸ ἀναβαῖνον	← ἐκ	τῆς ἀβύσσου →	⸤ποιήσει πόλεμον⸣	μετ'	αὐτῶν	καὶ	νικήσει	αὐτοὺς	καὶ
d.asf n.asf	d.nsn	n.nsn	d.nsn pt.pa.nsn	p.g	d.gsf n.gsf	v.fai.3s n.asm	p.g	r.gpm.3	cj	v.fai.3s	r.apm.3	cj
3836 3456	3836	2563	3836 326	1666	3836 12	4472 4483	3552	899	2779	3771	899	2779

kill	them.	**8** Their	bodies	will lie	in	the street	of the	great	city,	which	is	figuratively	called
ἀποκτενεῖ	αὐτούς	καὶ	αὐτῶν	⸤τὸ πτῶμα⸣	ἐπὶ	τῆς πλατείας →	τῆς	⸤τῆς μεγάλης⸣	πόλεως	ἥτις	→	πνευματικῶς	καλεῖται
v.fai.3s	r.apm.3	cj	r.gpm.3	d.nsn n.nsn	p.g	d.gsf n.gsf	d.gsf	d.gsf a.gsf	n.gsf	r.nsf		adv	v.ppi.3s
650	899	2779	899	3836 4773	2093	3836 4426	3836	3836 3489	4484	4015		2813	2813

Sodom	and	Egypt,	where	also	their	Lord		was crucified.	**9**	For three	and a	half	days	men	from every
Σόδομα	καὶ	Αἴγυπτος	ὅπου	καὶ	αὐτῶν	⸤ὁ κύριος⸣	→	ἐσταυρώθη	καὶ →	τρεῖς	καὶ	ἥμισυ	ἡμέρας		ἐκ
n.npn	cj	n.nsf	cj	adv	r.gpm.3	d.nsm n.nsm		v.api.3s	cj	a.apf	cj	n.asn	n.apf		p.g
5047	2779	131	3963	2779	899	3836 3261		5090	2779	5552	2779	2468	2465		1666

people,	tribe,	language	and	nation	will gaze	on their	bodies	and	refuse		them
⸤τῶν λαῶν⸣	καὶ	φυλῶν	καὶ	γλωσσῶν	καὶ	ἐθνῶν →	βλέπουσιν ←	αὐτῶν	⸤τὸ πτῶμα⸣	καὶ	⸤οὐκ ἀφίουσιν⸣	⸤τὰ πτῶματα⸣ αὐτῶν
d.gpm n.gpm	cj	n.gpf	cj	n.gpf	cj	n.gpn	v.pai.3p	r.gpm.3	d.asn n.asn	cj	pl v.pai.3p	d.apn n.apn r.gpm.3
3836 3295	2779	5876	2779	1185	2779	1620	1063	899	3836 4773	2779	4024 918	3836 4773 899

burial.	**10**	The inhabitants	of	the earth	will gloat	over	them	and	will celebrate	by sending
⸤τεθῆναι εἰς μνῆμα⸣	καὶ	οἱ κατοικοῦντες	ἐπὶ	τῆς γῆς →	χαίρουσιν	ἐπ'	αὐτοῖς	καὶ →	εὐφραίνονται	καὶ	πέμψουσιν
f.ap p.a n.asn	cj	d.npm pt.pa.npm	p.g	d.gsf n.gsf	v.pai.3p	p.d	r.dpm.3	cj	v.ppi.3p	cj	v.fai.3p
5502 1650 3645	2779	3836 2997	2093	3836 1178	5897	2093	899	2779	2370	2779	4287

each	other	gifts,	because	these	two	prophets	had	tormented	those	who	live	on the earth.	¶
ἀλλήλοις ←		δῶρα	ὅτι	οὗτοι	δύο	⸤οἱ προφῆται⸣		ἐβασάνισαν	τοὺς ←		κατοικοῦντας	ἐπὶ τῆς γῆς	
r.dpm		n.apn	cj	r.npm	a.npm	d.npm n.npm		v.aai.3p	d.apm		pt.pa.apm	p.g d.gsf n.gsf	
253		1565	4022	4047	1545	3836 4737		989	3836		2997	2093 3836 1178	

11 But	after	the three	and a	half	days	a breath	of life	from	God	entered	them,	and	they stood	on their
Καὶ	μετὰ	τὰς τρεῖς	καὶ	ἥμισυ	ἡμέρας	πνεῦμα →	ζωῆς ἐκ		⸤τοῦ θεοῦ⸣	εἰσῆλθεν	ἐν αὐτοῖς	καὶ →	ἔστησαν	ἐπὶ αὐτῶν
cj	p.a	d.apf a.apf	cj	n.asn	n.apf	n.nsn	n.gsf p.g		d.gsm n.gsm	v.aai.3s	p.d r.dpm.3	cj	v.aai.3p	p.a r.gpm.3
2779	3552	3836 5552	2779	2468	2465	4460	2437 1666		3836 2536	1656	1877 899	2779	2705	2093 899

feet,	and	terror	struck	those	who saw	them.	**12** Then	they heard	a loud	voice	from
⸤τοὺς πόδας⸣	καὶ	⸤φόβος μέγας⸣	ἐπέπεσεν	ἐπὶ τοὺς ←	θεωροῦντας	αὐτούς	καὶ →	ἤκουσαν	μεγάλης	φωνῆς ἐκ
d.apm n.apm	cj	n.nsm a.nsm	v.aai.3s	p.a d.apm	pt.pa.apm	r.apm.3	cj	v.aai.3p	a.gsf	n.gsf p.g
3836 4546	2779	5832 3489	2158	2093 3836	2555	899	2779	201	3489	5889 1666

heaven	saying	to them,	"Come	up here."	And	they went	up to	heaven	in a cloud,	while	their
⸤τοῦ οὐρανοῦ⸣	λεγούσης →	αὐτοῖς	ἀνάβατε ←	ὧδε	καὶ →	ἀνέβησαν	εἰς	⸤τὸν οὐρανὸν⸣	ἐν ⸤τῇ νεφέλῃ⸣	καὶ	αὐτῶν
d.gsm n.gsm	pt.pa.gsf	r.dpm.3	v.aam.2p	adv	cj	v.aai.3p	p.a	d.asm n.asm	p.d d.dsf n.dsf	cj	r.gpm.3
3836 4041	3306	899	326	6045	2779	326	1650	3836 4041	1877 3836 3749	2779	899

enemies	looked	on.	¶	**13**	At	that	very	hour	there was	a severe	earthquake	and a	tenth	of
⸤οἱ ἐχθροὶ⸣	ἐθεώρησαν ←	αὐτούς		Καὶ	ἐν	ἐκείνῃ	⸤τῇ ὥρᾳ⸣ →		ἐγένετο	μέγας	σεισμός	καὶ	τὸ δέκατον →	
d.npm a.npm	v.aai.3p	r.apm.3		cj	p.d	r.dsf	d.dsf n.dsf		v.ami.3s	a.nsm	n.nsm	cj	d.nsn a.nsn	
3836 2398	2555	899		2779	1877	1697	3836 6052		1181	3489	4939	2779	3836 1281	

αὐτῶν· καὶ εἴ τις θελήσῃ αὐτοὺς ἀδικῆσαι, οὕτως δεῖ αὐτὸν ἀποκτανθῆναι. ⁶ οὗτοι ἔχουσιν τὴν ἐξουσίαν κλεῖσαι τὸν οὐρανόν, ἵνα μὴ ὑετὸς βρέχῃ τὰς ἡμέρας τῆς προφητείας αὐτῶν, καὶ ἐξουσίαν ἔχουσιν ἐπὶ τῶν ὑδάτων στρέφειν αὐτὰ εἰς αἷμα καὶ πατάξαι τὴν γῆν ἐν πάσῃ πληγῇ ὁσάκις ἐὰν θελήσωσιν. ¶ ⁷ καὶ ὅταν τελέσωσιν τὴν μαρτυρίαν αὐτῶν, τὸ θηρίον τὸ ἀναβαῖνον ἐκ τῆς ἀβύσσου ποιήσει μετ' αὐτῶν πόλεμον καὶ νικήσει αὐτοὺς καὶ ἀποκτενεῖ αὐτούς. ⁸ καὶ τὸ πτῶμα αὐτῶν ἐπὶ τῆς πλατείας τῆς πόλεως τῆς μεγάλης, ἥτις καλεῖται πνευματικῶς Σόδομα καὶ Αἴγυπτος, ὅπου καὶ ὁ κύριος αὐτῶν ἐσταυρώθη. ⁹ καὶ βλέπουσιν ἐκ τῶν λαῶν καὶ φυλῶν καὶ γλωσσῶν καὶ ἐθνῶν τὸ πτῶμα αὐτῶν ἡμέρας τρεῖς καὶ ἥμισυ καὶ τὰ πτῶματα αὐτῶν οὐκ ἀφίουσιν τεθῆναι εἰς μνῆμα. ¹⁰ καὶ οἱ κατοικοῦντες ἐπὶ τῆς γῆς χαίρουσιν ἐπ' αὐτοῖς καὶ εὐφραίνονται καὶ δῶρα πέμψουσιν ἀλλήλοις, ὅτι οὗτοι οἱ δύο προφῆται ἐβασάνισαν τοὺς κατοικοῦντας ἐπὶ τῆς γῆς. ¶ ¹¹ καὶ μετὰ τὰς τρεῖς ἡμέρας καὶ ἥμισυ πνεῦμα ζωῆς ἐκ τοῦ θεοῦ εἰσῆλθεν ἐν αὐτοῖς, καὶ ἔστησαν ἐπὶ τοὺς πόδας αὐτῶν, καὶ φόβος μέγας ἐπέπεσεν ἐπὶ τοὺς θεωροῦντας αὐτούς. ¹² καὶ ἤκουσαν φωνῆς μεγάλης ἐκ τοῦ οὐρανοῦ λεγούσης αὐτοῖς, Ἀνάβατε ὧδε. καὶ ἀνέβησαν εἰς τὸν οὐρανὸν ἐν τῇ νεφέλῃ, καὶ

the city   collapsed.   Seven thousand people   were killed   in the earthquake, and the survivors
τῆς πόλεως ἔπεσεν   καὶ ἑπτὰ χιλιάδες ὀνόματα ἀνθρώπων → ἀπεκτάνθησαν ἐν τῷ σεισμῷ καὶ οἱ λοιποὶ
d.gsf n.gsf v.aai.3s   cj a.npf n.npf   n.npn   n.gpm   v.api.3p   p.d d.dsm n.dsm cj d.npm a.npm
3836 4484 4406   2779 2231 5942   3950   476   650   1877 3836 4939 2779 3836 3370

were   terrified and gave   glory to the God of heaven.   ¶   [14] The second   woe has passed;   the
ἐγένοντο ἔμφοβοι καὶ ἔδωκαν δόξαν → τῷ θεῷ → τοῦ οὐρανοῦ   Ἡ ἡ δευτέρα οὐαὶ → ἀπῆλθεν ἰδοὺ ἡ
v.ami.3p a.npm cj v.aai.3p n.asf   d.dsm n.dsm   d.gsm n.gsm   d.nsf d.nsf a.nsf j   v.aai.3s j   d.nsf
1181   1873 2779 1443 1518   3836 2536   3836 4041   3836 3836 1311 4026   599   2627 3836

third   woe is coming soon.
ἡ τρίτη οὐαὶ → ἔρχεται ταχύ
d.nsf a.nsf j   v.pmi.3s adv
3836 5569 4026   2262   5444

The Seventh Trumpet

[11:15]   The seventh angel   sounded his trumpet, and there were   loud   voices in heaven,   which said:
Καὶ ὁ ἕβδομος ἄγγελος ἐσάλπισεν ←   καὶ → ἐγένοντο μεγάλαι φωναὶ ἐν τῷ οὐρανῷ → λέγοντες
cj d.nsm a.nsm n.nsm v.aai.3s   cj   v.ami.3p a.npf n.npf p.d d.dsm n.dsm   pt.pa.npm
2779 3836 1575 34   4895   2779   1181   3489   5889 1877 3836 4041   3306

"The kingdom of the world has become the kingdom of our Lord   and of his Christ,   and he will
ἡ βασιλεία → τοῦ κόσμου → ἐγένετο   → ἡμῶν τοῦ κυρίου καὶ → αὐτοῦ τοῦ χριστοῦ καὶ →
d.nsf n.nsf   d.gsm n.gsm   v.ami.3s   r.gp.1 d.gsm n.gsm cj   r.gsm.3 d.gsm n.gsm cj
3836 993   3836 3180   1181   7005 3836 3261 2779   899 3836 5986 2779

reign   *for ever   and ever.*   [16] And the twenty-four   elders,   who were seated   on their
βασιλεύσει εἰς τοὺς αἰῶνας   τῶν αἰώνων   Καὶ οἱ εἴκοσι τέσσαρες πρεσβύτεροι οἱ → καθήμενοι ἐπὶ αὐτῶν
v.fai.3s p.a d.apm n.apm   d.gpm n.gpm   cj d.npm a.npm a.npm n.npm d.npm   pt.pm.npm p.a r.gpm.3
996   1650 3836 172   3836 172   2779 3836 1633 5475 4565 3836   2764 2093 899

thrones   before God,   fell on their faces   and worshiped God,   [17] saying: "We give thanks   to
τοὺς θρόνους ἐνώπιον τοῦ θεοῦ ἔπεσαν ἐπὶ αὐτῶν τὰ πρόσωπα καὶ προσεκύνησαν τῷ θεῷ   λέγοντες → εὐχαριστοῦμεν →
d.apm n.apm p.g d.gsm n.gsm v.aai.3p p.a r.gpm.3 d.apn n.apn cj v.aai.3p   d.dsm n.dsm   pt.pa.npm   v.pai.1p
3836 2585 1967 3836 2536 4406 2093 899 3836 4725 2779 4686   3836 2536   3306   2373

you, Lord God   Almighty,   the One who is   and who was, because you have taken your great
σοι κύριε ὁ θεὸς ὁ παντοκράτωρ ὁ ← ← ὢν καὶ ὁ ἦν ὅτι → εἴληφας σου τὴν μεγάλην
r.ds.2 n.vsm d.vsm n.vsm d.vsm n.vsm d.vsm   pt.pa.vsm cj d.vsm v.iai.3s cj   v.rai.2s r.gs.2 d.asf a.asf
5148 3261 3836 2536 3836 4120 3836   1639 2779 3836 1639 4022   3284 5148 3836 3489

power   and have begun to reign.   [18]   The nations were angry;   and your wrath   has come.   The
τὴν δύναμιν καὶ → → ἐβασίλευσας   καὶ τὰ ἔθνη → ὠργίσθησαν καὶ σου ἡ ὀργή → ἦλθεν καὶ ὁ
d.asf n.asf cj   v.aai.2s   cj d.npn n.npn   v.api.3p cj r.gs.2 d.nsf n.nsf   v.aai.3s cj d.nsm
3836 1539 2779   996   2779 3836 1620   3974 2779 5148 3836 3973   2262 2779 3836

time has come for judging the dead, and for rewarding   your servants   the prophets and your saints and
καιρὸς → κριθῆναι τῶν νεκρῶν καὶ → δοῦναι τὸν μισθὸν σου τοῖς δούλοις τοῖς προφήταις καὶ τοῖς ἁγίοις καὶ
n.nsm   f.ap d.gpm a.gpm cj   f.aa d.asm n.asm r.gs.2 d.dpm n.dpm d.dpm n.dpm cj d.dpm a.dpm cj
2789   3212 3836 3738 2779   1443 3836 3635 5148 3836 1529 3836 4737 2779 3836 41 2779

those who reverence your name,   both small   and great   — and for destroying those who
τοῖς ← φοβουμένοις σου τὸ ὄνομα   τοὺς μικροὺς καὶ τοὺς μεγάλους καὶ → διαφθεῖραι τοὺς ←
d.dpm   pt.pp.dpm r.gs.2 d.asn n.asn   d.apm a.apm cj d.apm a.apm cj   f.aa   d.apm
3836   5828 5148 3836 3950   3836 3625 2779 3836 3489 2779   1425   3836

destroy   the earth." ¶ [19] Then God's   temple   in heaven   was opened, and within his   temple
διαφθείροντας τὴν γῆν   Καὶ τοῦ θεοῦ ὁ ναός ὁ ἐν τῷ οὐρανῷ → ἠνοίγη καὶ ἐν αὐτοῦ τῷ ναῷ
pt.pa.apm d.asf n.asf   cj d.gsm n.gsm d.nsm n.nsm d.nsm p.d d.dsm n.dsm   v.api.3s cj p.d r.gsm.3 d.dsm n.dsm
1425 3836 1178   2779 3836 2536 3836 3724 3836 1877 3836 4041   487 2779 1877 899 3836 3724

was seen the ark   of his covenant.   And there came   flashes of lightning,   rumblings,   peals of thunder,
→ ὤφθη ἡ κιβωτὸς αὐτοῦ τῆς διαθήκης καὶ → ἐγένοντο → ἀστραπαὶ καὶ φωναὶ καὶ → βρονταὶ
v.api.3s d.nsf n.nsf r.gsm.3 d.gsf n.gsf cj   v.ami.3p   n.npf cj n.npf cj   n.npf
3972 3836 3066 1347 899 3836 1347 2779   1181   847 2779 5889 2779   1103

an earthquake and a great hailstorm.
καὶ σεισμὸς καὶ μεγάλη χάλαζα
cj n.nsm cj a.nsf n.nsf
2779 4939 2779 3489 5898

ἐθεώρησαν αὐτοὺς οἱ ἐχθροὶ αὐτῶν. ¶ [13] Καὶ ἐν ἐκείνῃ τῇ ὥρᾳ ἐγένετο σεισμὸς μέγας καὶ τὸ δέκατον τῆς πόλεως ἔπεσεν καὶ ἀπεκτάνθησαν ἐν τῷ σεισμῷ ὀνόματα ἀνθρώπων χιλιάδες ἑπτὰ καὶ οἱ λοιποὶ ἔμφοβοι ἐγένοντο καὶ ἔδωκαν δόξαν τῷ θεῷ τοῦ οὐρανοῦ. ¶ [14] Ἡ οὐαὶ ἡ δευτέρα ἀπῆλθεν· ἰδοὺ ἡ οὐαὶ ἡ τρίτη ἔρχεται ταχύ.

[11:15] Καὶ ὁ ἕβδομος ἄγγελος ἐσάλπισεν· καὶ ἐγένοντο φωναὶ μεγάλαι ἐν τῷ οὐρανῷ λέγοντες, Ἐγένετο ἡ βασιλεία τοῦ κόσμου τοῦ κυρίου ἡμῶν καὶ τοῦ Χριστοῦ αὐτοῦ, καὶ βασιλεύσει εἰς τοὺς αἰῶνας τῶν αἰώνων. [16] καὶ οἱ εἴκοσι τέσσαρες πρεσβύτεροι [οἱ] ἐνώπιον τοῦ θεοῦ καθήμενοι ἐπὶ τοὺς θρόνους αὐτῶν ἔπεσαν ἐπὶ τὰ πρόσωπα αὐτῶν καὶ προσεκύνησαν τῷ θεῷ [17] λέγοντες, Εὐχαριστοῦμέν σοι, κύριε ὁ θεὸς ὁ παντοκράτωρ, ὁ ὢν καὶ ὁ ἦν, ὅτι εἴληφας τὴν δύναμίν σου τὴν μεγάλην καὶ ἐβασίλευσας. [18] καὶ τὰ ἔθνη ὠργίσθησαν, καὶ ἦλθεν ἡ ὀργή σου καὶ ὁ καιρὸς τῶν νεκρῶν κριθῆναι καὶ δοῦναι τὸν μισθὸν τοῖς δούλοις σου τοῖς προφήταις καὶ τοῖς ἁγίοις καὶ τοῖς φοβουμένοις τὸ ὄνομά σου, τοὺς μικροὺς καὶ τοὺς μεγάλους, καὶ διαφθεῖραι τοὺς διαφθείροντας τὴν γῆν. ¶ [19] καὶ ἠνοίγη ὁ ναὸς τοῦ θεοῦ ὁ ἐν τῷ οὐρανῷ καὶ ὤφθη ἡ κιβωτὸς τῆς διαθήκης αὐτοῦ ἐν τῷ ναῷ αὐτοῦ, καὶ ἐγένοντο ἀστραπαὶ καὶ φωναὶ καὶ βρονταὶ καὶ σεισμὸς καὶ χάλαζα μεγάλη.

The Woman and the Dragon

12:1

A great and wondrous sign appeared in heaven: a woman clothed with the sun, with the
Καὶ μέγα σημεῖον ὤφθη ἐν τῷ οὐρανῷ γυνὴ περιβεβλημένη ← τὸν ἥλιον καὶ ἡ
cj a.nsn n.nsn v.api.3s p.d d.dsm n.dsm n.nsf pt.rp.nsf d.asm n.asm cj d.nsf
2779 3489 4956 3972 1877 3836 4041 1222 4314 3836 2463 2779 3836

moon under her feet and a crown of twelve stars on her head. **2** She was pregnant and
σελήνη ὑποκάτω αὐτῆς τῶν ποδῶν καὶ στέφανος → δώδεκα ἀστέρων ἐπὶ αὐτῆς τῆς κεφαλῆς καὶ → ἔχουσα ἐν γαστρὶ καὶ
n.nsf p.g r.gsf.3 d.gpm n.gpm cj n.nsm a.gpm n.gpm p.g r.gsf.3 d.gsf n.gsf cj pt.pa.nsf p.d n.dsf cj
4943 5691 899 3836 4546 2779 5109 1557 843 2093 899 3836 3051 2779 2400 1877 1143 2779

cried out in pain as she was about to give birth. **3** Then another sign appeared in heaven:
κράζει ← ὠδίνουσα καὶ → βασανιζομένη τεκεῖν καὶ ἄλλο σημεῖον ὤφθη ἐν τῷ οὐρανῷ
v.pai.3s pt.pa.nsf cj pt.pp.nsf f.aa cj r.nsn n.nsn v.api.3s p.d d.dsm n.dsm
3189 6048 2779 989 5503 2779 257 4956 3972 1877 3836 4041

an enormous red dragon with seven heads and ten horns and seven crowns on his heads.
καὶ ἰδοὺ μέγας πυρρὸς δράκων ἔχων ἑπτὰ κεφαλὰς καὶ δέκα κέρατα καὶ ἑπτὰ διαδήματα ἐπὶ αὐτοῦ τὰς κεφαλὰς
cj j a.nsm a.nsm n.nsm pt.pa.nsm a.apf n.apf cj a.apn n.apn cj a.apn n.apn p.a r.gsm.3 d.apf n.apf
2779 2627 3489 4794 1532 2400 2231 3051 2779 1274 3043 2779 2231 1343 2093 899 3836 3051

4 His tail swept a third of the stars out of the sky and flung them to the earth. The
καὶ αὐτοῦ ἡ οὐρὰ σύρει τὸ τρίτον τῶν ἀστέρων τοῦ οὐρανοῦ καὶ ἔβαλεν αὐτοὺς εἰς τὴν γῆν Καὶ ὁ
cj r.gsm.3 d.nsf n.nsf v.pai.3s d.asn a.asn d.gpm n.gpm d.gsm n.gsm cj v.aai.3s r.apm.3 p.a d.asf n.asf cj d.nsm
2779 899 3836 4038 5359 3836 5569 3836 843 5359 3836 4041 2779 965 899 1650 3836 1178 2779 3836

dragon stood in front of the woman who was about to give birth, so that he might devour her
δράκων ἔστηκεν ἐνώπιον ← τῆς γυναικὸς τῆς → μελλούσης → τεκεῖν ἵνα καταφάγῃ αὐτῆς
n.nsm v.rai.3s p.g d.gsf n.gsf d.gsf pt.pa.gsf f.aa cj v.aas.3s r.gsf.3
1532 2705 1967 3836 1222 3836 3516 5503 2671 2983 899

child the moment it was born. **5** She gave birth to a son, a male child, who will rule all the nations
τὸ τέκνον ὅταν τέκῃ καὶ → ἔτεκεν ← υἱὸν ἄρσεν ← ὃς μέλλει ποιμαίνειν πάντα τὰ ἔθνη
d.asn n.asn cj v.aas.3s cj v.aai.3s n.asm a.asn r.nsm v.pai.3s f.pa a.apn d.apn n.apn
3836 5451 4020 5503 2779 5503 5626 781 4005 3516 4477 4246 3836 1620

with an iron scepter. And her child was snatched up to God and to his throne. **6** The
ἐν σιδηρᾷ ῥάβδῳ καὶ αὐτῆς τὸ τέκνον → ἡρπάσθη πρὸς τὸν θεὸν καὶ πρὸς αὐτοῦ τὸν θρόνον καὶ ἡ
p.d a.dsf n.dsf cj r.gsf.3 d.nsn n.nsn v.api.3s p.a d.asm n.asm cj p.a r.gsm.3 d.asm n.asm cj d.nsf
1877 4971 4811 2779 899 3836 5451 773 4639 3836 2536 2779 4639 899 3836 2585 2779 3836

woman fled into the desert to a place prepared for her by God, where she might be
γυνὴ ἔφυγεν εἰς τὴν ἔρημον ὅπου ἔχει ἐκεῖ τόπον ἡτοιμασμένον ἀπὸ τοῦ θεοῦ ἐκεῖ ἵνα αὐτὴν →
n.nsf v.aai.3s p.a d.asf n.asf cj v.pai.3s adv n.asm pt.rp.asm p.g d.gsm n.gsm adv cj r.asf.3
1222 5771 1650 3836 2245 3963 2400 1695 5536 2286 608 3836 2536 1695 2671 899

taken care of for 1,260 days. ¶ **7** And there was war in heaven. Michael and
→ τρέφωσιν ← χιλίας διακοσίας ἑξήκοντα ἡμέρας Καὶ → ἐγένετο πόλεμος ἐν τῷ οὐρανῷ ὁ Μιχαὴλ καὶ
v.pas.3p a.apf a.apf a.apf n.apf cj v.ami.3s n.nsm p.d d.dsm n.dsm d.nsm n.nsm cj
5555 5943 1357 2008 2465 2779 1181 4483 1877 3836 4041 3836 3640 2779

his angels fought against the dragon, and the dragon and his angels fought back. **8** But he
αὐτοῦ οἱ ἄγγελοι τοῦ πολεμῆσαι μετὰ τοῦ δράκοντος καὶ ὁ δράκων καὶ αὐτοῦ οἱ ἄγγελοι ἐπολέμησεν καὶ →
r.gsm.3 d.npm n.npm d.gsn f.aa p.g d.gsm n.gsm cj d.nsm n.nsm cj r.gsm.3 d.npm n.npm v.aai.3s cj
899 3836 34 3836 4482 3552 3836 1532 2779 3836 1532 2779 899 3836 34 4482 2779 2710

was not strong enough, and they lost their place in heaven. **9** The great dragon was hurled
→ οὐκ ἴσχυσεν ← οὐδὲ εὑρέθη αὐτῶν τόπος ἔτι ἐν τῷ οὐρανῷ καὶ ὁ ὁ μέγας δράκων → ἐβλήθη
pl v.aai.3s cj v.api.3s r.gpm.3 n.nsm adv p.d d.dsm n.dsm cj d.nsm d.nsm a.nsm n.nsm v.api.3s
2710 4024 2710 4028 2351 4028 2351 899 5536 2285 1877 3836 4041 2779 3836 3836 3489 1532 965

down – that ancient serpent called the devil, or Satan, who leads the whole world astray. He
← ὁ ὁ ἀρχαῖος ὄφις καλούμενος ὁ Διάβολος καὶ ὁ Σατανᾶς ὁ → τὴν ὅλην οἰκουμένην πλανῶν →
d.nsm d.nsm a.nsm n.nsm pt.pp.nsm d.nsm n.nsm cj d.nsm n.nsm d.nsm d.asf a.asf n.asf pt.pa.nsm
3836 3836 792 4058 2813 3836 1333 2779 3836 4928 3836 4414 3836 3910 3876 4414

was hurled to the earth, and his angels with him. ¶ **10** Then I heard a loud voice in
→ ἐβλήθη εἰς τὴν γῆν καὶ αὐτοῦ οἱ ἄγγελοι ἐβλήθησαν μετ᾽ αὐτοῦ καὶ → ἤκουσα μεγάλην φωνὴν ἐν
v.api.3s p.a d.asf n.asf cj r.gsm.3 d.npm n.npm v.api.3p p.g r.gsm.3 cj v.aai.1s a.asf n.asf p.d
965 1650 3836 1178 2779 899 3836 34 965 3552 899 2779 201 3489 5889 1877

12:1 Καὶ σημεῖον μέγα ὤφθη ἐν τῷ οὐρανῷ, γυνὴ περιβεβλημένη τὸν ἥλιον, καὶ ἡ σελήνη ὑποκάτω τῶν ποδῶν αὐτῆς καὶ ἐπὶ τῆς κεφαλῆς αὐτῆς στέφανος ἀστέρων δώδεκα, ² καὶ ἐν γαστρὶ ἔχουσα, καὶ κράζει ὠδίνουσα καὶ βασανιζομένη τεκεῖν. ³ καὶ ὤφθη ἄλλο σημεῖον ἐν τῷ οὐρανῷ, καὶ ἰδοὺ δράκων μέγας πυρρὸς ἔχων κεφαλὰς ἑπτὰ καὶ κέρατα δέκα καὶ ἐπὶ τὰς κεφαλὰς αὐτοῦ ἑπτὰ διαδήματα, ⁴ καὶ ἡ οὐρὰ αὐτοῦ σύρει τὸ τρίτον τῶν ἀστέρων τοῦ οὐρανοῦ καὶ ἔβαλεν αὐτοὺς εἰς τὴν γῆν. καὶ ὁ δράκων ἔστηκεν ἐνώπιον τῆς γυναικὸς τῆς μελλούσης τεκεῖν, ἵνα ὅταν τέκῃ τὸ τέκνον αὐτῆς καταφάγῃ. ⁵ καὶ ἔτεκεν υἱὸν ἄρσεν, ὃς μέλλει ποιμαίνειν πάντα τὰ ἔθνη ἐν ῥάβδῳ σιδηρᾷ. καὶ ἡρπάσθη τὸ τέκνον αὐτῆς πρὸς τὸν θεὸν καὶ πρὸς τὸν θρόνον αὐτοῦ. ⁶ καὶ ἡ γυνὴ ἔφυγεν εἰς τὴν ἔρημον, ὅπου ἔχει ἐκεῖ τόπον ἡτοιμασμένον ἀπὸ τοῦ θεοῦ, ἵνα ἐκεῖ τρέφωσιν αὐτὴν ἡμέρας χιλίας διακοσίας ἑξήκοντα. ¶ ⁷ Καὶ ἐγένετο πόλεμος ἐν τῷ οὐρανῷ, ὁ Μιχαὴλ καὶ οἱ ἄγγελοι αὐτοῦ τοῦ πολεμῆσαι μετὰ τοῦ δράκοντος. καὶ ὁ δράκων ἐπολέμησεν καὶ οἱ ἄγγελοι αὐτοῦ, ⁸ καὶ οὐκ ἴσχυσεν οὐδὲ τόπος εὑρέθη αὐτῶν ἔτι ἐν τῷ οὐρανῷ. ⁹ καὶ ἐβλήθη ὁ δράκων ὁ μέγας, ὁ ὄφις ὁ ἀρχαῖος, ὁ καλούμενος Διάβολος καὶ ὁ Σατανᾶς, ὁ πλανῶν τὴν οἰκουμένην ὅλην, ἐβλήθη εἰς τὴν γῆν, καὶ οἱ ἄγγελοι αὐτοῦ μετ᾽ αὐτοῦ ἐβλήθησαν. ¶ ¹⁰ καὶ ἤκουσα φωνὴν μεγάλην ἐν τῷ οὐρανῷ λέγουσαν, Ἄρτι ἐγένετο ἡ σωτηρία

heaven say: "Now have come the salvation and the power and the kingdom of our God, and the
ᾳτῷ οὐρανῷᾳ λέγουσαν ἄρτι → ἐγένετο ἡ σωτηρία καὶ ἡ δύναμις καὶ ἡ βασιλεία → ἡμῶν ᾳτοῦ θεοῦᾳ καὶ ἡ
d.dsm n.dsm pt.pa.asf adv   v.ami.3s d.nsf n.nsf cj d.nsf n.nsf cj d.nsf n.nsf   r.gp.1 d.gsm n.gsm cj d.nsf
3836 4041 3306 785   1181 3836 5401 2779 3836 1539 2779 3836 993   2536 7005 3836 2536 2779 3836

authority of his Christ. For the accuser of our brothers, who accuses them before our God day
ἐξουσία → αὐτοῦ ᾳτοῦ χριστοῦᾳ ὅτι ὁ κατήγωρ ἡμῶν τῶν ἀδελφῶν ὁ κατηγορῶν αὐτοὺς ἐνώπιον ἡμῶν ᾳτοῦ θεοῦᾳ ἡμέρας
n.nsf   r.gsm.3 d.gsm n.gsm cj d.nsm n.nsm r.gp.1 d.gpm n.gpm d.nsm pt.pa.nsm r.apm.3 p.g r.gp.1 d.gsm n.gsm n.gsf
2026   5986 899 3836 5986 4022 3836 2992 81 7005 3836 81 3836 2989 899 1967 7005 3836 2536 2465

and night, has been hurled down. ¹¹ They overcame him by the blood of the Lamb and by the word of their
καὶ νυκτός → ἐβλήθη καὶ αὐτοὶ ἐνίκησαν αὐτὸν διὰ τὸ αἷμα → τοῦ ἀρνίου καὶ διὰ τὸν λόγον αὐτῶν
cj n.gsf v.api.3s cj r.npm v.aai.3p r.asm.3 p.a d.asn n.asn d.gsn n.gsn cj p.a d.asm n.asm r.gpm.3
2779 3816 965 2779 899 3771 899 1328 3836 135 3836 768 2779 1328 3836 3364 3456 899

testimony; they did not love their lives so much as to shrink from death. ¹² Therefore rejoice, you
ᾳτῆς μαρτυρίαςᾳ καὶ → οὐκ ἠγάπησαν αὐτῶν ᾳτὴν ψυχὴνᾳ ἄχρι θανάτου ᾳδιὰ τοῦτοᾳ εὐφραίνεσθε οἱ
d.gsf n.gsf cj pl v.aai.3p r.gpm.3 d.asf n.asf p.g n.gsm p.a r.asn v.ppm.2p d.vpm
3836 3456 2779 26 4024 26 899 3836 6034 948 2505 1328 4047 2370 3836

heavens and you who dwell in them! But woe to the earth and the sea, because the devil has gone
οὐρανοὶ καὶ οἱ ← σκηνοῦντες ἐν αὐτοῖς οὐαὶ τὴν γῆν καὶ τὴν θάλασσαν ὅτι ὁ διάβολος → κατέβη
n.vpm cj d.vpm pt.pa.vpm p.d r.dpm.3 j d.asf n.asf cj d.asf n.asf cj d.nsm n.nsm v.aai.3s
4041 2779 3836 5012 1877 899 4026 3836 1178 2779 3836 2498 4022 3836 1333 2849

down to you! He is filled with fury, because he knows that his time is short." ¶ ¹³ When the
← πρὸς ὑμᾶς → ἔχων ᾳθυμὸν μέγανᾳ εἰδὼς ὅτι → καιρὸν ἔχει ὀλίγον Καὶ ὅτε ὁ
p.a r.ap.2 pt.pa.nsm n.asm a.asm pt.ra.nsm cj n.asm v.pai.3s a.asm cj cj d.nsm
4639 7007 2400 2596 3489 3857 4022 2400 2789 2400 3900 2779 4021 3836

dragon saw that he had been hurled to the earth, he pursued the woman who had given birth to the male child.
δράκων εἶδεν ὅτι → → ἐβλήθη εἰς τὴν γῆν → ἐδίωξεν τὴν γυναῖκα ἥτις → → ἔτεκεν τὸν ἄρσενα ←
n.nsm v.aai.3s cj v.api.3s p.a d.asf n.asf v.aai.3s d.asf n.asf r.nsf v.aai.3s d.asm a.asm
1532 1625 4022 965 1650 3836 1178 1503 3836 1222 4015 5503 3836 781

¹⁴ The woman was given the two wings of a great eagle, so that she might fly to the place
καὶ τῇ γυναικὶ → ἐδόθησαν αἱ δύο πτέρυγες → ᾳτοῦ μεγάλουᾳ τοῦ ἀετοῦ ἵνα ← → → πέτηται εἰς τὸν τόπον
cj d.dsf n.dsf v.api.3p d.npf a.npf n.npf d.gsm a.gsm d.gsm n.gsm cj v.pms.3s p.a d.asm n.asm
2779 3836 1222 1443 3836 1545 4763 3836 3489 3836 108 2671 4375 1650 3836 5536

prepared for her in the desert, where she would be taken care of for a time, times and half a time,
αὐτῆς εἰς τὴν ἔρημον ὅπου → → → τρέφεται ← ἐκεῖ → καιρὸν καὶ καιροὺς καὶ ἥμισυ καιροῦ
r.gsf.3 p.a d.asf n.asf cj v.ppi.3s adv n.asm cj n.apm cj a.asn n.gsm
899 1650 3836 2245 3963 5555 1695 2789 2779 2789 2779 2468 2789

out of the serpent's reach. ¹⁵ Then from his mouth the serpent spewed water like a river, to overtake the
ἀπὸ ← τοῦ ὄφεως προσώπου καὶ ἐκ αὐτοῦ ᾳτοῦ στόματοςᾳ ὁ ὄφις ἔβαλεν ὕδωρ ὡς ποταμόν ἵνα ὀπίσω τῆς
p.g d.gsm n.gsm n.gsn cj p.g r.gsn.3 d.gsn n.gsn d.nsm n.nsm v.aai.3s n.asn pl n.asm cj p.g d.gsf
608 3836 4058 4725 2779 1666 899 3836 5125 3836 4058 965 5623 6055 4532 2671 3958 3836

woman and sweep her away with the torrent. ¹⁶ But the earth helped the woman by opening its
γυναικὸς ποιήσῃ αὐτὴν → → → ποταμοφόρητον καὶ ἡ γῆ ἐβοήθησεν τῇ γυναικὶ καὶ ἡ γῆ ἤνοιξεν αὐτῆς
n.gsf v.aas.3s r.ast.3 a.asf cj d.nsf n.nsf v.aai.3s d.dsf n.dsf cj d.nsf n.nsf v.aai.3s r.gsf.3
1222 4472 899 4533 2779 3836 1178 1070 3836 1222 2779 3836 1178 487 899

mouth and swallowing the river that the dragon had spewed out of his mouth. ¹⁷ Then the dragon was
ᾳτὸ στόμαᾳ καὶ κατέπιεν τὸν ποταμὸν ὃν ὁ δράκων → ἔβαλεν ἐκ ← αὐτοῦ ᾳτοῦ στόματοςᾳ καὶ ὁ δράκων →
d.asn n.asn cj v.aai.3s d.asm n.asm r.asm d.nsm n.nsm v.aai.3s p.g r.gsm.3 d.gsn n.gsn cj d.nsm n.nsm
3836 5125 2779 2927 3836 4532 4005 3836 1532 965 1666 899 3836 5125 2779 3836 1532

enraged at the woman and went off to make war against the rest of her offspring – those who
ὠργίσθη ἐπὶ τῇ γυναικὶ καὶ ἀπῆλθεν → ποιῆσαι πόλεμον μετὰ τῶν λοιπῶν → αὐτῆς ᾳτοῦ σπέρματοςᾳ τῶν ←
v.api.3s p.d d.dsf n.dsf cj v.aai.3s f.aa n.asm p.g d.gpn a.gpn r.gsf.3 d.gsn n.gsn d.gpm
3974 2093 3836 1222 2779 599 4472 4483 3552 3836 3370 5065 899 3836 5065 3836

obey God's commandments and hold to the testimony of Jesus. ¹³:¹And the dragon stood on the shore of the
τηρούντων ᾳτοῦ θεοῦᾳ ᾳτὰς ἐντολάςᾳ καὶ ἐχόντων ← τὴν μαρτυρίαν → Ἰησοῦ Καὶ ἐστάθη ἐπὶ τὴν ἄμμον → τῆς
pt.pa.gpm d.gsm n.gsm d.apf n.apf cj pt.pa.gpm d.asf n.asf n.gsm cj v.api.3s p.a d.asf n.asf d.gsf
5498 3836 2536 3836 1953 2779 2400 3836 3456 2652 2779 2705 2093 3836 302 3836

καὶ ἡ δύναμις καὶ ἡ βασιλεία τοῦ θεοῦ ἡμῶν καὶ ἡ ἐξουσία τοῦ Χριστοῦ αὐτοῦ, ὅτι ἐβλήθη ὁ κατήγωρ τῶν ἀδελφῶν ἡμῶν, ὁ κατηγορῶν αὐτοὺς ἐνώπιον τοῦ θεοῦ ἡμῶν ἡμέρας καὶ νυκτός. ¹¹ καὶ αὐτοὶ ἐνίκησαν αὐτὸν διὰ τὸ αἷμα τοῦ ἀρνίου καὶ διὰ τὸν λόγον τῆς μαρτυρίας αὐτῶν καὶ οὐκ ἠγάπησαν τὴν ψυχὴν αὐτῶν ἄχρι θανάτου. ¹² διὰ τοῦτο εὐφραίνεσθε, [οἱ] οὐρανοὶ καὶ οἱ ἐν αὐτοῖς σκηνοῦντες. οὐαὶ τὴν γῆν καὶ τὴν θάλασσαν, ὅτι κατέβη ὁ διάβολος πρὸς ὑμᾶς ἔχων θυμὸν μέγαν, εἰδὼς ὅτι ὀλίγον καιρὸν ἔχει. ¶ ¹³ Καὶ ὅτε εἶδεν ὁ δράκων ὅτι ἐβλήθη εἰς τὴν γῆν, ἐδίωξεν τὴν γυναῖκα ἥτις ἔτεκεν τὸν ἄρσενα. ¹⁴ καὶ ἐδόθησαν τῇ γυναικὶ αἱ δύο πτέρυγες τοῦ ἀετοῦ τοῦ μεγάλου, ἵνα πέτηται εἰς τὴν ἔρημον εἰς τὸν τόπον αὐτῆς, ὅπου τρέφεται ἐκεῖ καιρὸν καὶ καιροὺς καὶ ἥμισυ καιροῦ ἀπὸ προσώπου τοῦ ὄφεως. ¹⁵ καὶ ἔβαλεν ὁ ὄφις ἐκ τοῦ στόματος αὐτοῦ ὀπίσω τῆς γυναικὸς ὕδωρ ὡς ποταμόν, ἵνα αὐτὴν ποταμοφόρητον ποιήσῃ. ¹⁶ καὶ ἐβοήθησεν ἡ γῆ τῇ γυναικὶ καὶ ἤνοιξεν ἡ γῆ τὸ στόμα αὐτῆς καὶ κατέπιεν τὸν ποταμὸν ὃν ἔβαλεν ὁ δράκων ἐκ τοῦ στόματος αὐτοῦ. ¹⁷ καὶ ὠργίσθη ὁ δράκων ἐπὶ τῇ γυναικὶ καὶ ἀπῆλθεν ποιῆσαι πόλεμον μετὰ τῶν λοιπῶν τοῦ σπέρματος αὐτῆς τῶν τηρούντων τὰς ἐντολὰς τοῦ θεοῦ καὶ ἐχόντων τὴν

sea.
θαλάσσης
n.gsf
2498

The Beast out of the Sea

And I saw a beast coming out of the sea. He had ten horns and seven heads, with ten crowns
Καὶ → εἶδον θηρίον ἀναβαῖνον ἐκ ← τῆς θαλάσσης → ἔχον δέκα κέρατα καὶ ἑπτὰ κεφαλὰς καὶ δέκα διαδήματα
cj v.aai.1s n.asn pt.pa.asn p.g d.gsf n.gsf pt.pa.asn a.apn n.apn cj a.apf n.apf cj a.apn n.apn
2779 1625 2563 326 1666 3836 2498 2400 1274 3043 2779 2231 3051 2779 1274 1343

on his horns, and on each head a blasphemous name. 2 The beast I saw resembled a
ἐπὶ αὐτοῦ ⸤τῶν κεράτων⸥ καὶ ἐπὶ αὐτοῦ ⸤τὰς κεφαλὰς⸥ βλασφημίας ὀνόματα καὶ τὸ θηρίον ὃ → εἶδον ἦν ὅμοιον
p.g r.gsn.3 d.gpn n.gpn cj p.a r.gsn.3 d.apf n.apf n.gsf n.apn cj d.nsn n.nsn r.asn v.aai.1s v.iai.3s a.nsn
2093 899 3836 3043 2779 2093 899 3836 3051 1060 3950 2779 3836 2563 4005 1625 1639 3927

leopard, but had feet like those of a bear and a mouth like that of a lion. The dragon
παρδάλει καὶ ⸤οἱ πόδες⸥ αὐτοῦ ὡς → ἄρκου καὶ ⸤τὸ στόμα⸥ αὐτοῦ ὡς στόμα → λέοντος καὶ ὁ δράκων
n.dsf cj d.npm n.npm r.gsn.3 pl n.gsm cj d.nsn n.nsn r.gsn.3 pl n.nsn n.gsm cj d.nsm n.nsm
4203 2779 3836 4546 899 6055 759 2779 3836 5125 899 6055 5125 3329 2779 3836 1532

gave the beast his power and his throne and great authority. 3 One of the heads of the beast
ἔδωκεν αὐτῷ αὐτοῦ ⸤τὴν δύναμιν⸥ καὶ αὐτοῦ ⸤τὸν θρόνον⸥ καὶ μεγάλην ἐξουσίαν καὶ μίαν ἐκ τῶν κεφαλῶν → αὐτοῦ
v.aai.3s r.dsn.3 r.gsm.3 d.asf n.asf cj r.gsm.3 d.asm n.asm cj a.asf n.asf cj a.asf p.g d.gpf n.gpf r.gsn.3
1443 899 899 3836 1539 2779 899 3836 2585 2779 3489 2026 2779 1651 1666 3836 3051 899

seemed to have had a fatal wound, but the fatal wound had been healed. The whole
ὡς → → → ⸤εἰς θάνατον⸥ ἐσφαγμένην καὶ ἡ ⸤τοῦ θανάτου⸥ πληγὴ αὐτοῦ → → ἐθεραπεύθη Καὶ ἡ ὅλη
pl p.a n.asm pt.rp.asf cj d.nsf d.gsm n.gsm n.nsf r.gsn.3 v.api.3s cj d.nsf a.nsf
6055 5377 5377 5377 1650 2505 5377 2779 3836 3836 2505 4435 899 2543 2779 3836 3910

world was astonished and followed the beast. 4 Men worshiped the dragon because he had given authority to
γῆ → ἐθαυμάσθη ὀπίσω τοῦ θηρίου καὶ προσεκύνησαν τῷ δράκοντι ὅτι → → ἔδωκεν ⸤τὴν ἐξουσίαν⸥ →
n.nsf v.api.3s p.g d.gsn n.gsn cj v.aai.3p d.dsm n.dsm cj v.aai.3s d.asf n.asf
1178 2513 3958 3836 2563 2779 4686 3836 1532 4022 1443 3836 2026

the beast, and they also worshiped the beast and asked, "Who is like the beast? Who can make war
τῷ θηρίῳ καὶ → προσεκύνησαν τῷ θηρίῳ λέγοντες τίς ὅμοιος τῷ θηρίῳ καὶ τίς δύναται → πολεμῆσαι
d.dsn n.dsn cj v.aai.3p d.dsn n.dsn pt.pa.npm r.nsm a.nsm d.dsn n.dsn cj r.nsm v.ppi.3s f.aa
3836 2563 2779 4686 3836 2563 3306 5515 3927 3836 2563 2779 5515 1538 4482

against him?" ¶ 5 The beast was given a mouth to utter proud words and blasphemies and to
μετ᾽ αὐτοῦ Καὶ αὐτῷ → ἐδόθη στόμα → λαλοῦν μεγάλα καὶ βλασφημίας καὶ ἐδόθη αὐτῷ →
p.g r.gsn.3 cj r.dsn.3 v.api.3s n.nsn pt.pa.nsn a.apn cj n.apf cj v.api.3s r.dsn.3
3552 899 2779 899 1443 5125 3281 3489 2779 1060 2779 1443 899

exercise his authority for forty-two months. 6 He opened his mouth to blaspheme God,
ποιῆσαι ἐξουσία ⸤τεσσεράκοντα καὶ δύο⸥ μῆνας καὶ → ἤνοιξεν αὐτοῦ ⸤τὸ στόμα⸥ εἰς βλασφημίας πρὸς ⸤τὸν θεὸν⸥
f.aa n.nsf a.apm cj a.apm n.apm cj v.aai.3s r.gsn.3 d.asn n.asn p.a n.apf p.a d.asm n.asm
4472 2026 5477 2779 1545 3604 2779 487 899 3836 5125 1650 1060 4639 3836 2536

and to slander his name and his dwelling place and those who live in heaven. 7 He was
→ βλασφημῆσαι αὐτοῦ ⸤τὸ ὄνομα⸥ καὶ αὐτοῦ ⸤τὴν σκηνήν⸥ ← τοὺς ← σκηνοῦντας ἐν ⸤τῷ οὐρανῷ⸥ καὶ αὐτῷ →
f.aa r.gsm.3 d.asn n.asn cj r.gsm.3 d.asf n.asf d.apm pt.pa.apm p.d d.dsm n.dsm cj r.dsn.3
1059 899 3836 3950 2779 899 3836 5008 3836 5012 1877 3836 4041 2779 899

given power to make war against the saints and to conquer them. And he was given authority over every tribe,
ἐδόθη → ποιῆσαι πόλεμον μετὰ τῶν ἁγίων καὶ → νικῆσαι αὐτούς καὶ αὐτῷ → ἐδόθη ἐξουσία ἐπὶ πᾶσαν φυλὴν
v.api.3s f.aa n.asm p.g d.gpm a.gpm cj f.aa r.apm.3 cj r.dsn.3 v.api.3s n.nsf p.a a.asf n.asf
1443 4472 4483 3552 3836 41 2779 3771 899 2779 899 1443 2026 2093 4246 5876

people, language and nation. 8 All inhabitants of the earth will worship the beast – all whose
καὶ λαὸν καὶ γλῶσσαν καὶ ἔθνος καὶ πάντες ⸤οἱ κατοικοῦντες⸥ ἐπὶ τῆς γῆς → προσκυνήσουσιν αὐτὸν οὗ
cj n.asm cj n.asf cj n.asn cj a.npm d.npm pt.pa.npm p.g d.gsf n.gsf v.fai.3p r.asm.3 r.gsm
2779 3295 2779 1185 2779 1620 2779 4246 3836 2997 2093 3836 1178 4686 899 4005

names have not been written in the book of life belonging to the Lamb that was slain from
⸤τὸ ὄνομα⸥ αὐτοῦ οὐ → γέγραπται ἐν τῷ βιβλίῳ ⸤τῆς ζωῆς⸥ → → τοῦ ἀρνίου τοῦ → ἐσφαγμένου ἀπὸ
d.nsn n.nsn r.gsm.3 pl v.rpi.3s p.d d.dsn n.dsn d.gsf n.gsf d.gsn n.gsn d.gsn pt.rp.gsn p.g
3836 3950 899 1211 4005 1211 1877 3836 1046 3836 2437 3836 768 3836 5377 608

μαρτυρίαν Ἰησοῦ. ¹³:¹ καὶ ἐστάθη ἐπὶ τὴν ἄμμον τῆς θαλάσσης.

Καὶ εἶδον ἐκ τῆς θαλάσσης θηρίον ἀναβαῖνον, ἔχον κέρατα δέκα καὶ κεφαλὰς ἑπτὰ καὶ ἐπὶ τῶν κεράτων αὐτοῦ δέκα διαδήματα καὶ ἐπὶ τὰς κεφαλὰς αὐτοῦ ὄνομα «ὀνόμα[τα]» βλασφημίας. ² καὶ τὸ θηρίον ὃ εἶδον ἦν ὅμοιον παρδάλει καὶ οἱ πόδες αὐτοῦ ὡς ἄρκου καὶ τὸ στόμα αὐτοῦ ὡς στόμα λέοντος. καὶ ἔδωκεν αὐτῷ ὁ δράκων τὴν δύναμιν αὐτοῦ καὶ τὸν θρόνον αὐτοῦ καὶ ἐξουσίαν μεγάλην. ³ καὶ μίαν ἐκ τῶν κεφαλῶν αὐτοῦ ὡς ἐσφαγμένην εἰς θάνατον, καὶ ἡ πληγὴ τοῦ θανάτου αὐτοῦ ἐθεραπεύθη. καὶ ἐθαυμάσθη ὅλη ἡ γῆ ὀπίσω τοῦ θηρίου ⁴ καὶ προσεκύνησαν τῷ δράκοντι, ὅτι ἔδωκεν τὴν ἐξουσίαν τῷ θηρίῳ, καὶ προσεκύνησαν τῷ θηρίῳ λέγοντες, Τίς ὅμοιος τῷ θηρίῳ καὶ τίς δύναται πολεμῆσαι μετ᾽ αὐτοῦ; ¶ ⁵ Καὶ ἐδόθη αὐτῷ στόμα λαλοῦν μεγάλα καὶ βλασφημίας καὶ ἐδόθη αὐτῷ ἐξουσία ποιῆσαι μῆνας τεσσεράκοντα [καὶ] δύο. ⁶ καὶ ἤνοιξεν τὸ στόμα αὐτοῦ εἰς βλασφημίας πρὸς τὸν θεὸν βλασφημῆσαι τὸ ὄνομα αὐτοῦ καὶ τὴν σκηνὴν αὐτοῦ, τοὺς ἐν τῷ οὐρανῷ σκηνοῦντας. ⁷ καὶ ἐδόθη αὐτῷ ποιῆσαι πόλεμον μετὰ τῶν ἁγίων καὶ νικῆσαι αὐτούς, καὶ ἐδόθη αὐτῷ ἐξουσία ἐπὶ πᾶσαν φυλὴν καὶ λαὸν καὶ γλῶσσαν καὶ ἔθνος. ⁸ καὶ προσκυνήσουσιν αὐτὸν πάντες οἱ κατοικοῦντες ἐπὶ τῆς γῆς, οὗ οὐ γέγραπται τὸ ὄνομα αὐτοῦ ἐν τῷ βιβλίῳ τῆς

the creation   of the world. ¶ **9** He who has an ear, let him hear. **10** If anyone is to go into captivity,
καταβολῆς →   κόσμου   Εἴ → τις ἔχει οὖς → ἀκουσάτω   εἴ τις   εἰς αἰχμαλωσίαν
n.gsf   n.gsm   cj   r.nsm v.pai.3s n.asn → v.aam.3s   cj r.nsm   p.a n.asf
2856   3180   1623 2400 5516 2400 4044   201   1623 5516   1650 168

into captivity   he will go.   If anyone is to be killed   with the sword, with the sword he   will be
εἰς αἰχμαλωσίαν → → ὑπάγει εἴ τις   → → → ἀποκτανθῆναι ἐν   μαχαίρῃ ἐν   μαχαίρῃ αὐτὸν → →
p.a n.asf   v.pai.3s cj r.nsm   f.ap   p.d   n.dsf   p.d   n.dsf   r.asm.3
1650 168   5632   1623 5516   650   1877   3479   1877   3479   899

killed.   This calls for patient   endurance and faithfulness on the part of the saints.
ἀποκτανθῆναι Ὧδέ ἐστιν ← ἡ ὑπομονὴ   καὶ ἡ πίστις → → → → τῶν ἁγίων
f.ap   adv v.pai.3s   d.nsf n.nsf   cj d.nsf n.nsf   d.gpm a.gpm
650   6045 1639   3836 5705   2779 3836 4411   3836 41

The Beast out of the Earth

13:11 Then I saw another beast, coming   out of the earth.   He had two horns like a lamb, but he spoke
Καὶ → εἶδον ἄλλο θηρίον ἀναβαῖνον ἐκ ← τῆς γῆς καὶ → εἶχεν δύο κέρατα ὅμοια ἀρνίῳ καὶ → ἐλάλει
cj   v.aai.1s r.asn n.asn pt.pa.asn   p.g   d.gsf n.gsf cj   v.iai.3s a.apn n.apn a.apn n.dsn cj   v.iai.3s
2779   1625 257 2563 326   1666   3836 1178 2779   2400 1545 3043 3927 768 2779   3281

like a dragon. **12**   He exercised all   the authority of the first   beast on   his   behalf, and made the earth and
ὡς   δράκων καὶ → ποιεῖ   πᾶσαν τὴν ἐξουσίαν → τοῦ πρώτου θηρίου ἐνώπιον αὐτοῦ ←   καὶ ποιεῖ τὴν γῆν καὶ
pl   n.nsm cj   v.pai.3s   a.asf d.asf n.asf   d.gsn a.gsn n.gsn r.gsn.3   cj v.pai.3s d.asf n.asf cj
6055   1532 2779   4472   4246 3836 2026   3836 4755 2563 1967   899   1967   2779 4472 3836 1178 2779

its   inhabitants   worship   the first   beast, whose fatal   wound   had been
ἐν αὐτῇ τοὺς κατοικοῦντας ἵνα προσκυνήσουσιν τὸ τὸ πρῶτον θηρίον οὗ τοῦ θανάτου αὐτοῦ ἡ πληγὴ
p.d r.dsf.3 d.apm pt.pa.apm cj v.fai.3p d.asn d.asn a.asn n.asn r.gsn d.gsn n.gsm r.gsn.3 d.nsf n.nsf
1877 899 3836 2997 2671 4686 3836 3836 4755 2563 4005 3836 2505 899 3836 4435

healed. **13** And he performed great   and miraculous signs,   even causing fire to come   down from heaven
ἐθεραπεύθη καὶ → ποιεῖ   μεγάλα   σημεῖα ἵνα καὶ ποιῇ πῦρ καταβαίνειν ← ἐκ τοῦ οὐρανοῦ
v.api.3s cj   v.pai.3s a.apn   n.apn cj adv v.pas.3s n.asn f.pa   p.g d.gsm n.gsm
2543 2779   4472   4472   4956 2671 2779 4472 4786 2849   1666 3836 4041

to earth   in full view   of men.   **14**   Because of the signs   he   was given power to do   on behalf of
εἰς τὴν γῆν ἐνώπιον ← τῶν ἀνθρώπων   καὶ διὰ ← τὰ σημεῖα ἃ αὐτῷ ἐδόθη → ποιῆσαι → ἐνώπιον
p.a d.asf n.asf p.g   d.gpm n.gpm   cj p.a   d.apn n.apn r.npn r.dsn.3 v.api.3s   f.aa   p.g
1650 3836 1178 1967   3836 476   2779 1328   3836 4956 4005 899 1443   4472   1967

the first beast, he deceived the inhabitants of the earth. He ordered them   to set   up an
τοῦ θηρίου → πλανᾷ τοὺς κατοικοῦντας ἐπὶ τῆς γῆς → λέγων τοῖς κατοικοῦσιν ἐπὶ τῆς γῆς → ποιῆσαι ←
d.gsn n.gsn   v.pai.3s d.apm pt.pa.apm p.g d.gsf n.gsf   pt.pa.nsm d.dpm pt.pa.dpm p.g d.gsf n.gsf f.aa
3836 2563   4414   3836 2997   2093 3836 1178   3306   3836 2997   2093 3836 1178 4472

image in honor of the beast who was wounded   by the sword   and yet lived. **15**   He   was given power to give
εἰκόνα → → → τῷ θηρίῳ ὃς ἔχει τὴν πληγὴν → τῆς μαχαίρης καὶ   ἔζησεν Καὶ αὐτῷ → ἐδόθη → δοῦναι
n.asf   d.dsn n.dsn r.nsm v.pai.3s d.asf n.asf   d.gsf n.gsf cj   v.aai.3s cj r.dsn.3   v.api.3s   f.aa
1635   3836 2563 4005 2400 3836 4435   3836 3479 2779   2409   2779 899   1443   1443

breath to the image of the first beast, so that   it   could speak and cause   all   who
πνεῦμα → τῇ εἰκόνι → τοῦ θηρίου ἵνα   καὶ ἡ εἰκὼν τοῦ θηρίου   λαλήσῃ   ποιήσῃ [ἵνα] ὅσοι ἐὰν ←
n.asn   d.dsf n.dsf d.gsn   n.gsn cj   cj d.nsf n.nsf d.gsn n.gsn   v.aas.3s   v.aas.3s   r.npm pl
4460   3836 1635 3836   2563 2671   2779 3836 1635 3836 2563   3281   4472   2671   4012 1569

refused to worship   the image   to be killed. **16** He also forced everyone, small   and
μὴ → προσκυνήσωσιν τῇ εἰκόνι τοῦ θηρίου → ἀποκτανθῶσιν → καὶ ποιεῖ πάντας τοὺς μικροὺς καὶ
pl   v.aas.3p   d.dsf n.dsf d.gsn n.gsn   v.aps.3p   cj v.pai.3s a.apm d.apm a.apm cj
3590 4686   3836 1635 3836 2563   650   4472 2779 4472 4246 3836 3625 2779

great,   rich   and poor,   free   and slave,   to receive   a mark
τοὺς μεγάλους καὶ τοὺς πλουσίους καὶ τοὺς πτωχοὺς καὶ τοὺς ἐλευθέρους καὶ τοὺς δούλους ἵνα δῶσιν αὐτοῖς χάραγμα
d.apm a.apm cj d.apm a.apm cj d.apm a.apm cj d.apm a.apm cj d.apm n.apm cj v.aas.3p r.dpm.3 n.asn
3836 3489 2779 3836 4454 2779 3836 4777 2779 3836 1801 2779 3836 1529 2671 1443 899 5916

on his   right   hand   or on his   forehead, **17**   so that no one could buy   or sell   unless he
ἐπὶ αὐτῶν τῆς δεξιᾶς τῆς χειρὸς ἢ ἐπὶ αὐτῶν τὸ μέτωπον   καὶ ἵνα ← μή τις δύνηται ἀγοράσαι ἢ πωλῆσαι εἰ μὴ ὁ
p.g r.gpm.3 d.gsf a.gsf d.gsf n.gsf cj p.a r.gpm.3 d.asn n.asn   cj cj   pl r.nsm v.pps.3s f.aa   cj f.aa   cj pl d.nsm
2093 899 3836 1288 3836 5931 2445 2093 899 3836 3587   2779 2671   3590 5516 1538 60   2445 4797   1623 3590 3836

ζωῆς τοῦ ἀρνίου τοῦ ἐσφαγμένου ἀπὸ καταβολῆς κόσμου. ¶ **9** Εἴ τις ἔχει οὖς ἀκουσάτω. **10** εἴ τις εἰς αἰχμαλωσίαν, εἰς αἰχμαλωσίαν ὑπάγει· εἴ τις ἐν μαχαίρῃ ἀποκτανθῆναι αὐτὸν ἐν μαχαίρῃ ἀποκτανθῆναι. Ὧδέ ἐστιν ἡ ὑπομονὴ καὶ ἡ πίστις τῶν ἁγίων.

13:11 Καὶ εἶδον ἄλλο θηρίον ἀναβαῖνον ἐκ τῆς γῆς, καὶ εἶχεν κέρατα δύο ὅμοια ἀρνίῳ καὶ ἐλάλει ὡς δράκων. **12** καὶ τὴν ἐξουσίαν τοῦ πρώτου θηρίου πᾶσαν ποιεῖ ἐνώπιον αὐτοῦ, καὶ ποιεῖ τὴν γῆν καὶ τοὺς ἐν αὐτῇ κατοικοῦντας ἵνα προσκυνήσουσιν τὸ θηρίον τὸ πρῶτον, οὗ ἐθεραπεύθη ἡ πληγὴ τοῦ θανάτου αὐτοῦ. **13** καὶ ποιεῖ σημεῖα μεγάλα, ἵνα καὶ πῦρ ποιῇ ἐκ τοῦ οὐρανοῦ καταβαίνειν εἰς τὴν γῆν ἐνώπιον τῶν ἀνθρώπων, **14** καὶ πλανᾷ τοὺς κατοικοῦντας ἐπὶ τῆς γῆς διὰ τὰ σημεῖα ἃ ἐδόθη αὐτῷ ποιῆσαι ἐνώπιον τοῦ θηρίου, λέγων τοῖς κατοικοῦσιν ἐπὶ τῆς γῆς ποιῆσαι εἰκόνα τῷ θηρίῳ, ὃς ἔχει τὴν πληγὴν τῆς μαχαίρης καὶ ἔζησεν. **15** καὶ ἐδόθη αὐτῷ δοῦναι πνεῦμα τῇ εἰκόνι τοῦ θηρίου, ἵνα καὶ λαλήσῃ ἡ εἰκὼν τοῦ θηρίου καὶ ποιήσῃ [ἵνα] ὅσοι ἐὰν μὴ προσκυνήσωσιν τῇ εἰκόνι τοῦ θηρίου ἀποκτανθῶσιν. **16** καὶ ποιεῖ πάντας, τοὺς μικροὺς καὶ τοὺς μεγάλους, καὶ τοὺς πλουσίους καὶ τοὺς πτωχούς, καὶ τοὺς ἐλευθέρους καὶ τοὺς δούλους, ἵνα δῶσιν αὐτοῖς χάραγμα ἐπὶ τῆς χειρὸς αὐτῶν τῆς

had the mark, which is the name of the beast or the number of his name. ¶ ¹⁸ This calls for
ἔχων τὸ χάραγμα   τὸ ὄνομα → τοῦ θηρίου ἢ τὸν ἀριθμὸν → αὐτοῦ ⸤τοῦ ὀνόματος⸥   ῏Ωδε ἐστίν ←
pt.pa.nsm d.asn n.asn   d.asn n.asn   d.gsn n.gsn cj d.asn n.asn   r.gsn.3 d.gsn n.gsn   adv v.pai.3s
2400 3836 5916   3836 3950   3836 2563 2445 3836 750   3950 899 3836 3950   6045 1639

wisdom. If anyone has insight, let him calculate the number of the beast, for it is man's number. His
⸤ἡ σοφία⸥ ὁ   ἔχων νοῦν → → ψηφισάτω τὸν ἀριθμὸν → τοῦ θηρίου γὰρ → ἐστίν ἀνθρώπου ἀριθμός καὶ αὐτοῦ
d.nsf n.nsf d.nsm   pt.pa.nsm n.asm   v.aam.3s d.asn n.asm   d.gsn n.gsn cj v.pai.3s n.gsm n.nsm cj r.gsn.3
3836 5053 3836   2400 3808   6028 3836 750   3836 2563 1142 1639 476 750 2779 899

number is 666.
ὁ ἀριθμὸς⸥   ⸤ἑξακόσιοι ἑξήκοντα ἕξ⸥
d.nsm n.nsm   a.npm a.npm a.npm
3836 750   1980 2008 1971

The Lamb and the 144,000

¹⁴ˑ¹Then I looked, and there before me was the Lamb, standing on Mount Zion, and with him
Καὶ → εἶδον καὶ ἰδοὺ   τὸ ἀρνίον ἑστὸς ἐπὶ ⸤τὸ ὄρος⸥ Σιὼν καὶ μετ᾽ αὐτοῦ
cj   v.aai.1s cj j   d.nsn n.nsn pt.ra.nsn p.a d.asn n.asn n.asf cj p.g r.gsm.3
2779   1625 2779 2627   3836 768 2705 2093 3836 4001 4994 2779 3552 899

144,000 who had his name and his Father's name written on their
⸤ἑκατὸν τεσσεράκοντα τέσσαρες χιλιάδες⸥ → ἔχουσαι αὐτοῦ ⸤τὸ ὄνομα⸥ καὶ αὐτοῦ ⸤τοῦ πατρὸς⸥ ⸤τὸ ὄνομα⸥ γεγραμμένον ἐπὶ αὐτῶν
a.npf a.npf a.npf n.npf → pt.pa.npf r.gsm.3 d.asn n.asn cj r.gsm.3 d.gsn n.gsn d.asn n.asn pt.rp.asn p.g r.gpm.3
1669 5477 5475 5942 2400 899 3836 3950 2779 899 3836 4252 3836 3950 1211 2093 899

foreheads. ² And I heard a sound from heaven like the roar of rushing waters and like a loud peal of
⸤τῶν μετώπων⸥ καὶ → ἤκουσα φωνὴν ἐκ ⸤τοῦ οὐρανοῦ⸥ ὡς φωνὴν → πολλῶν ὑδάτων καὶ ὡς μεγάλης φωνὴ →
d.gpn n.gpn cj → v.aai.1s n.asf p.g d.gsm n.gsn pl n.asf → a.gpn n.gpn cj pl a.gsf n.asf
3836 3587 2779 201 5889 1666 3836 4041 6055 5889 4498 5623 2779 6055 3489 5889

thunder. The sound I heard was like that of harpists playing their harps. ³ And they sang
βροντῆς καὶ ἡ φωνὴ ἦν → ἤκουσα ὡς → κιθαρῳδῶν κιθαριζόντων ἐν αὐτῶν ⸤ταῖς κιθάραις⸥ καὶ → ᾄδουσιν
n.gsf cj d.nsf n.nsf r.asf v.aai.1s pl → n.gpm pt.pa.gpm p.d r.gpm.3 d.dpf n.dpf cj → v.pai.3p
1103 2779 3836 5889 4005 201 6055 3069 3068 1877 899 3836 3067 2779 106

a new song before the throne and before the four living creatures and the elders. No one
[ὡς] καινὴν ᾠδὴν ἐνώπιον τοῦ θρόνου καὶ ἐνώπιον τῶν τεσσάρων ζῴων ← καὶ τῶν πρεσβυτέρων καὶ οὐδεὶς
pl a.asf n.asf p.g d.gsm n.gsm cj p.g d.gpn a.gpn n.gpn cj d.gpm a.gpm cj a.nsm
6055 2785 6046 1967 3836 2585 2779 1967 3836 5475 2442 2779 3836 4565 2779 4029

could learn the song except the 144,000 who had been redeemed from the earth.
ἐδύνατο μαθεῖν τὴν ᾠδὴν ⸤εἰ μὴ⸥ αἱ ⸤ἑκατὸν τεσσεράκοντα τέσσαρες χιλιάδες⸥ οἱ → → ἠγορασμένοι ἀπὸ τῆς γῆς
v.ipi.3s f.aa d.asf n.asf cj pl d.npf a.npf a.npf a.npf n.npf d.npm → → pt.rp.npm p.g d.gsf n.gsf
1538 3443 3836 6046 1623 3590 3836 1669 5477 5475 5942 3836 60 608 3836 1178

⁴ These are those who did not defile themselves with women, for they kept themselves pure. They
οὗτοι εἰσιν οἱ ← → οὐκ ἐμολύνθησαν μετὰ γυναικῶν γὰρ → εἰσιν παρθένοι οὗτοι
r.npm v.pai.3p d.npm ← → pl v.api.3p p.g n.gpf cj → v.pai.3p n.npm r.npm
4047 1639 4005 3662 4024 3662 3552 1222 1142 1639 4221 4047

follow the Lamb wherever he goes. They were purchased from among men and offered as
⸤οἱ ἀκολουθοῦντες⸥ τῷ ἀρνίῳ ὅπου ἂν → ὑπάγῃ οὗτοι → ἠγοράσθησαν ἀπὸ ← ⸤τῶν ἀνθρώπων⸥
d.npm pt.pa.npm d.dsn n.dsn cj pl → v.pas.3s r.npm → v.api.3p p.g d.gpm n.gpm
3836 199 3836 768 3963 323 5632 4047 60 608 3836 476

firstfruits to God and the Lamb. ⁵ No lie was found in their mouths; they are blameless.
ἀπαρχὴ → ⸤τῷ θεῷ⸥ καὶ τῷ ἀρνίῳ καὶ οὐχ ψεῦδος → εὑρέθη ἐν αὐτῶν ⸤τῷ στόματι⸥ → εἰσιν ἄμωμοι
n.nsf → d.dsm n.dsm cj d.dsn n.dsn cj pl n.nsn → v.api.3s p.d r.gsm.3 d.dsn n.dsn → v.pai.3p a.npm
569 3836 2536 2779 3836 768 2779 4024 6022 2351 1877 899 3836 5125 1639 320

The Three Angels

¹⁴ˑ⁶Then I saw another angel flying in midair, and he had the eternal gospel to proclaim to
Καὶ → εἶδον ἄλλον ἄγγελον πετόμενον ἐν μεσουρανήματι → ἔχοντα αἰώνιον εὐαγγέλιον → εὐαγγελίσαι ἐπὶ
cj → v.aai.1s r.asm n.asm pt.pm.asm p.d n.dsn → pt.pa.asm a.asn n.asn → f.aa p.a
2779 1625 257 34 4375 1877 3547 2400 173 2295 2294 2093

δεξιᾶς ἢ ἐπὶ τὸ μέτωπον αὐτῶν ¹⁷ καὶ ἵνα μή τις δύνηται ἀγοράσαι ἢ πωλῆσαι εἰ μὴ ὁ ἔχων τὸ χάραγμα τὸ ὄνομα τοῦ θηρίου
ἢ τὸν ἀριθμὸν τοῦ ὀνόματος αὐτοῦ. ¶ ¹⁸ ῏Ωδε ἡ σοφία ἐστίν. ὁ ἔχων νοῦν ψηφισάτω τὸν ἀριθμὸν τοῦ θηρίου, ἀριθμὸς γὰρ
ἀνθρώπου ἐστίν, καὶ ὁ ἀριθμὸς αὐτοῦ ἑξακόσιοι ἑξήκοντα ἕξ.
    ¹⁴ˑ¹ Καὶ εἶδον, καὶ ἰδοὺ τὸ ἀρνίον ἑστὸς ἐπὶ τὸ ὄρος Σιὼν καὶ μετ᾽ αὐτοῦ ἑκατὸν τεσσεράκοντα τέσσαρες χιλιάδες ἔχουσαι
τὸ ὄνομα αὐτοῦ καὶ τὸ ὄνομα τοῦ πατρὸς αὐτοῦ γεγραμμένον ἐπὶ τῶν μετώπων αὐτῶν. ² καὶ ἤκουσα φωνὴν ἐκ τοῦ οὐρανοῦ ὡς
φωνὴν ὑδάτων πολλῶν καὶ ὡς φωνὴν βροντῆς μεγάλης, καὶ ἡ φωνὴ ἣν ἤκουσα ὡς κιθαρῳδῶν κιθαριζόντων ἐν ταῖς κιθάραις
αὐτῶν. ³ καὶ ᾄδουσιν [ὡς] ᾠδὴν καινὴν ἐνώπιον τοῦ θρόνου καὶ ἐνώπιον τῶν τεσσάρων ζῴων καὶ τῶν πρεσβυτέρων, καὶ οὐδεὶς
ἐδύνατο μαθεῖν τὴν ᾠδὴν εἰ μὴ αἱ ἑκατὸν τεσσεράκοντα τέσσαρες χιλιάδες, οἱ ἠγορασμένοι ἀπὸ τῆς γῆς. ⁴ οὗτοί εἰσιν οἱ μετὰ
γυναικῶν οὐκ ἐμολύνθησαν, παρθένοι γάρ εἰσιν, οὗτοι οἱ ἀκολουθοῦντες τῷ ἀρνίῳ ὅπου ἂν ὑπάγῃ. οὗτοι ἠγοράσθησαν ἀπὸ τῶν
ἀνθρώπων ἀπαρχὴ τῷ θεῷ καὶ τῷ ἀρνίῳ, ⁵ καὶ ἐν τῷ στόματι αὐτῶν οὐχ εὑρέθη ψεῦδος, ἄμωμοί εἰσιν.
    ¹⁴ˑ⁶ Καὶ εἶδον ἄλλον ἄγγελον πετόμενον ἐν μεσουρανήματι, ἔχοντα εὐαγγέλιον αἰώνιον εὐαγγελίσαι ἐπὶ τοὺς καθημένους ἐπὶ

those who live   on the earth –   to every nation,   tribe,   language and people. ⁷ He said   in a loud
τοὺς ← καθημένους ἐπὶ τῆς γῆς   καὶ ἐπὶ πᾶν ἔθνος   καὶ φυλὴν καὶ γλῶσσαν καὶ λαόν   → λέγων ἐν μεγάλῃ
d.apm   pt.pm.apm   p.g d.gsf n.gsf   cj   p.a a.asn n.asn   cj n.asf cj n.asf   cj n.asm   pt.pa.nsm p.d a.dsf
3836   2764   2093 3836 1178   2779 2093 4246 1620   2779 5876 2779 1185   2779 3295   3306 1877 3489

voice, "Fear   God   and give him glory, because the hour of his   judgment has come.   Worship   him
φωνῇ φοβήθητε τὸν θεὸν καὶ δότε αὐτῷ δόξαν ὅτι   ἡ ὥρα → αὐτοῦ τῆς κρίσεως → ἦλθεν καὶ προσκυνήσατε τῷ
n.dsf v.apm.2p d.asn n.asm cj   v.aam.2p r.dsm.3 n.asf cj   d.nsf n.nsf   r.gsm.3 d.gsf n.gsf   v.aai.3s cj   v.aam.2p   d.dsm
5889 5828   3836 2536 2779 1443 899 1518 4022 3836 6052   899 3836 3213   2262 2779 4686   3836

who made   the heavens,   the earth,   the sea   and the springs of water."   ¶   ⁸   A second
← ποιήσαντι τὸν οὐρανὸν καὶ τὴν γῆν καὶ θάλασσαν καὶ πηγὰς → ὑδάτων   Καὶ ἄλλος δεύτερος
pt.aa.dsm d.asm n.asm   cj   d.asf n.asf cj   n.asf   cj   n.apf   n.gpn   cj   r.nsm a.nsm
4472   3836 4041   2779 3836 1178 2779 2498   2779 4380   5623   2779 257 1311

angel followed   and said, "Fallen! Fallen is Babylon the Great, which made all   the nations drink   the
ἄγγελος ἠκολούθησεν λέγων ἔπεσεν ἔπεσεν ← Βαβυλὼν ἡ μεγάλη ἣ ↗   πάντα τὰ ἔθνη πεπότικεν ἐκ τοῦ
n.nsm v.aai.3s   pt.pa.nsm v.aai.3s v.aai.3s   n.nsf   d.nsf a.nsf r.nsf   a.apn d.apn n.apn v.rai.3s   p.g d.gsm
34   199   3306   4406   4406   956   3836 3489   4005   4540 3836 1620 4540   1666 3836

maddening wine of her adulteries."   ¶   ⁹   A third angel followed   them and said in a loud
τοῦ θυμοῦ οἴνου → αὐτῆς τῆς πορνείας   Καὶ ἄλλος τρίτος ἄγγελος ἠκολούθησεν αὐτοῖς λέγων ἐν μεγάλῃ
d.gsm n.gsm n.gsm   r.gsf.3 d.gsf n.gsf   cj   r.nsm a.nsm n.nsm v.aai.3s   r.dpm.3 pt.pa.nsm p.d a.dsf
3836 2596 3885   4518 899 3836 4518   2779 257 5569 34   199   899   3306 1877 3489

voice: "If anyone worships the beast and his   image   and receives his   mark   on the forehead or on the
φωνῇ εἴ τις   προσκυνεῖ τὸ θηρίον καὶ αὐτοῦ τὴν εἰκόνα καὶ λαμβάνει αὐτοῦ χάραγμα ἐπὶ τοῦ μετώπου ἢ ἐπὶ τὴν
n.dsf cj r.nsm v.pai.3s   d.asn n.asn cj   r.gsn.3 d.asf n.asf cj   v.pai.3s r.gsm.3 n.asn   p.g d.gsn n.gsn   cj p.a d.asf
5889 1623 5516 4686   3836 2563 2779 899 3836 1635 2779 5916   899 3284   2093 3836 3587   2445 2093 3836

hand, he,   too, will drink of the wine of God's   fury,   which has been poured   full   strength
χεῖρα αὐτοῦ αὐτός καὶ → πίεται ἐκ τοῦ οἴνου → τοῦ θεοῦ τοῦ θυμοῦ τοῦ   →   κεκερασμένου ἀκράτου ←
n.asf r.gsm.3 r.nsm adv   v.fmi.3s p.g d.gsm n.gsm   d.gsm n.gsm d.gsm n.gsm d.gsm   pt.rp.gsm   a.gsm
5931 899   899 2779   4403 1666 3836 3885   2596 3836 2536 3836 2596 3836   3042   204

into the cup of his wrath.   He will be tormented   with burning   sulfur in the presence of the holy
ἐν τῷ ποτηρίῳ αὐτοῦ τῆς ὀργῆς καὶ →   → βασανισθήσεται ἐν πυρὶ καὶ θείῳ →   → ἐνώπιον ← ἁγίων
p.d d.dsn n.dsn   r.gsm.3 d.gsf n.gsf cj   v.fpi.3s   p.d n.dsn cj n.dsn   p.g   a.gpm
1877 3836 4539   3973 3836 3973 2779   989   1877 4786 2779 2520   1967   41

angels and   of the Lamb. ¹¹ And the smoke of their torment   rises   for ever   and ever.   There
ἀγγέλων καὶ ἐνώπιον ← τοῦ ἀρνίου καὶ ὁ καπνὸς ↗ αὐτῶν τοῦ βασανισμοῦ ἀναβαίνει εἰς αἰῶνας αἰώνων καὶ →
n.gpm cj   p.g   d.gsm n.gsn cj   d.nsm n.nsm   r.gpn.3 d.gsm n.gsm   v.pai.3s p.a n.apm   n.gpm cj
34   2779 1967   3836 768   2779 3836 2837   990 899 3836 990   326   1650 172   172   2779

is   no rest   day   or night for those who worship   the beast and his   image,   or   for anyone
ἔχουσιν οὐκ ἀνάπαυσιν ἡμέρας καὶ νυκτὸς οἱ ← προσκυνοῦντες τὸ θηρίον καὶ αὐτοῦ τὴν εἰκόνα καὶ εἴ   τις
v.pai.3p pl n.asf   n.gsf cj   n.gsf d.npm   pt.pa.npm   d.asn n.asn cj   r.gsn.3 d.asf n.asf cj cj   r.nsm
2400   4024 398   2465 2779 3816 3836   4686   3836 2563 2779 899 3836 1635 2779 1623 5516

who receives the mark   of his name."   ¹² This calls for patient   endurance on the part of the saints who
λαμβάνει τὸ χάραγμα → αὐτοῦ τοῦ ὀνόματος Ὧδε ἐστίν ἡ ὑπομονὴ   → → → → τῶν ἁγίων οἱ
v.pai.3s d.asn n.asn   r.gsn.3 d.gsn n.gsn   adv v.pai.3s d.nsf n.nsf   d.gpm a.gpm d.npm
3284   3836 5916   3950 899 3836 3950   6045 1639   3836 5705   3836 41   3836

obey   God's   commandments and remain faithful to Jesus. ¶ ¹³ Then I heard a voice from heaven
τηροῦντες τοῦ θεοῦ τὰς ἐντολὰς καὶ τὴν πίστιν → Ἰησοῦ   Καὶ → ἤκουσα φωνῆς ἐκ τοῦ οὐρανοῦ
pt.pa.npm d.gsm n.gsm d.apf n.apf cj   d.asf n.asf   n.gsm   cj   v.aai.1s φωνῆς φωνῆς ἐκ d.gsm n.gsf
5498   3836 2536 3836 1953 2779 3836 4411   2652   2779   201   5889 1666 3836 4041

say,   "Write: Blessed are the dead who die   in the Lord from now on." ¶   "Yes," says the Spirit,
λεγούσης γράψον μακάριοι οἱ νεκροὶ οἱ ἀποθνῄσκοντες ἐν κυρίῳ ἀπ' ἄρτι ←   ναί λέγει τὸ πνεῦμα
pt.pa.gsf v.aam.2s a.npm   d.npm a.npm d.npm pt.pa.npm   p.d n.dsm p.g adv   pl   v.pai.3s d.nsn n.nsn
3306   1211   3421   3836 3738 3836 633   1877 3261 608 785   3721 3306 3836 4460

"they will rest   from their labor, for their deeds   will follow   them."
ἵνα →   → ἀναπαήσονται ἐκ αὐτῶν τῶν κόπων γὰρ αὐτῶν τὰ ἔργα   → ἀκολουθεῖ μετ' αὐτῶν
cj   v.fpi.3p   p.g r.gpm.3 d.gpm n.gpm cj   r.gpm.3 d.npn n.npn   v.pai.3s p.g r.gpm.3
2671   399   1666 899 3836 3160 1142 899 3836 2240   199   3552 899

τῆς γῆς καὶ ἐπὶ πᾶν ἔθνος καὶ φυλὴν καὶ γλῶσσαν καὶ λαόν, ⁷ λέγων ἐν φωνῇ μεγάλῃ, Φοβήθητε τὸν θεὸν καὶ δότε αὐτῷ δόξαν, ὅτι ἦλθεν ἡ ὥρα τῆς κρίσεως αὐτοῦ, καὶ προσκυνήσατε τῷ ποιήσαντι τὸν οὐρανὸν καὶ τὴν γῆν καὶ θάλασσαν καὶ πηγὰς ὑδάτων. ¶ ⁸ Καὶ ἄλλος ἄγγελος δεύτερος ἠκολούθησεν λέγων, Ἔπεσεν ἔπεσεν Βαβυλὼν ἡ μεγάλη ἣ ἐκ τοῦ οἴνου τοῦ θυμοῦ τῆς πορνείας αὐτῆς πεπότικεν πάντα τὰ ἔθνη. ¶ ⁹ Καὶ ἄλλος ἄγγελος τρίτος ἠκολούθησεν αὐτοῖς λέγων ἐν φωνῇ μεγάλῃ, Εἴ τις προσκυνεῖ τὸ θηρίον καὶ τὴν εἰκόνα αὐτοῦ καὶ λαμβάνει χάραγμα ἐπὶ τοῦ μετώπου αὐτοῦ ἢ ἐπὶ τὴν χεῖρα αὐτοῦ, ¹⁰ καὶ αὐτὸς πίεται ἐκ τοῦ οἴνου τοῦ θυμοῦ τοῦ θεοῦ τοῦ κεκερασμένου ἀκράτου ἐν τῷ ποτηρίῳ τῆς ὀργῆς αὐτοῦ καὶ βασανισθήσεται ἐν πυρὶ καὶ θείῳ ἐνώπιον ἀγγέλων ἁγίων καὶ ἐνώπιον τοῦ ἀρνίου. ¹¹ καὶ ὁ καπνὸς τοῦ βασανισμοῦ αὐτῶν εἰς αἰῶνας αἰώνων ἀναβαίνει, καὶ οὐκ ἔχουσιν ἀνάπαυσιν ἡμέρας καὶ νυκτὸς οἱ προσκυνοῦντες τὸ θηρίον καὶ τὴν εἰκόνα αὐτοῦ καὶ εἴ τις λαμβάνει τὸ χάραγμα τοῦ ὀνόματος αὐτοῦ. ¹² Ὧδε ἡ ὑπομονὴ τῶν ἁγίων ἐστίν, οἱ τηροῦντες τὰς ἐντολὰς τοῦ θεοῦ καὶ τὴν πίστιν Ἰησοῦ. ¶ ¹³ Καὶ ἤκουσα φωνῆς ἐκ τοῦ οὐρανοῦ λεγούσης, Γράψον· Μακάριοι οἱ νεκροὶ οἱ ἐν κυρίῳ ἀποθνῄσκοντες ἀπ' ἄρτι. ¶ ναί, λέγει τὸ πνεῦμα, ἵνα ἀναπαήσονται ἐκ τῶν κόπων αὐτῶν, τὰ γὰρ ἔργα αὐτῶν ἀκολουθεῖ μετ' αὐτῶν.

The Harvest of the Earth

14:14

I looked,	and	there before me was	a white	cloud,	and	seated	on	the	cloud	was one	"like	a son of
Καὶ → εἶδον	καὶ	ἰδοὺ	λευκή	νεφέλη	καὶ	καθήμενον	ἐπὶ	τὴν	νεφέλην		ὅμοιον	υἱὸν →
cj v.aai.1s	cj	j	a.nsf	n.nsf	cj	pt.pm.asm	p.a	d.asf	n.asf		a.asm	n.asm
2779 1625	2779	2627	3328	3749	2779	2764	2093	3836	3749		3927	5626

man"	with	a crown	of gold	on	his	head	and	a sharp	sickle	in	his	hand.	**15** Then	another	angel
ἀνθρώπου	ἔχων	στέφανον →	χρυσοῦν	ἐπὶ	αὐτοῦ	⸤τῆς κεφαλῆς⸥	καὶ	ὀξύ	δρέπανον	ἐν	αὐτοῦ	⸤τῇ χειρὶ⸥	καὶ	ἄλλος	ἄγγελος
n.gsm	pt.pa.nsm	a.asm	a.asm	p.g	r.gsm.3	d.gsf n.gsf	cj	a.asn	n.asn	p.d	r.gsm.3	d.dsf n.dsf	cj	r.nsm	n.nsm
476	2400	5109	5997	2093	899	3836 3051	2779	3955	1535	1877	899	3836 5931	2779	257	34

came	out of	the	temple	and called	in	a loud	voice	to him	who was sitting	on	the	cloud,	"Take	your
ἐξῆλθεν	ἐκ ←	τοῦ	ναοῦ	κράζων	ἐν	μεγάλη	φωνῇ	τῷ →	→ καθημένῳ	ἐπὶ	τῆς	νεφέλης	πέμψον	σου
v.aai.3s	p.g	d.gsm	n.gsm	pt.pa.nsm	p.d	a.dsf	n.dsf	d.dsm	pt.pm.dsm	p.a	d.gsf	n.gsf	v.aam.2s	r.gs.2
2002	1666	3836	3724	3189	1877	3489	5889	3836	2764	2093	3836	3749	4287	5148

sickle	and reap,	because	the	time	to reap	has come,	for	the	harvest	of the earth	is ripe."	**16** So	he	who
⸤τὸ δρέπανον⸥	καὶ θέρισον	ὅτι	ἡ	ὥρα →	θερίσαι →	ἦλθεν	ὅτι	ὁ	θερισμὸς →	τῆς γῆς →	ἐξηράνθη	καὶ	ὁ ←	
d.asn n.asn	cj v.aam.2s	cj	d.nsf	n.nsf	f.aa	v.aai.3s	cj	d.nsm	n.nsm	d.gsf n.gsf	v.api.3s	cj	d.nsm	
3836 1535	2779 2545	4022	3836	6052	2545	2262	4022	3836	2546	3836 1178	3830	2779	3836	

was seated	on	the	cloud	swung	his	sickle	over	the	earth,	and	the	earth	was harvested.	¶	**17**
→ καθήμενος	ἐπὶ	τῆς	νεφέλης	ἔβαλεν	αὐτοῦ	⸤τὸ δρέπανον⸥	ἐπὶ	τὴν	γῆν	καὶ	ἡ	γῆ	→ ἐθερίσθη		Καὶ
pt.pm.nsm	p.g	d.gsf	n.gsf	v.aai.3s	r.gsm.3	d.asn n.asn	p.a	d.asf	n.asf	cj	d.nsf	n.nsf	v.api.3s		cj
2764	2093	3836	3749	965	899	3836 1535	2093	3836	1178	2779	3836	1178	2545		2779

Another	angel	came	out of	the	temple	in	heaven,	and	he	too	had	a sharp	sickle.	**18** Still	another	angel,
ἄλλος	ἄγγελος	ἐξῆλθεν	ἐκ ←	τοῦ	ναοῦ	τοῦ ἐν	⸤τῷ οὐρανῷ⸥		αὐτὸς	καὶ	ἔχων	ὀξύ	δρέπανον	καὶ	ἄλλος	ἄγγελος
r.nsm	n.nsm	v.aai.3s	p.g	d.gsm	n.gsm	d.gsm p.d	d.dsm n.dsm		r.nsm	adv	pt.pa.nsm	a.asn	n.asn	cj	r.nsm	n.nsm
257	34	2002	1666	3836	3724	3836 1877	3836 4041		899	2779	2400	3955	1535	2779	257	34

who	had	charge	of	the	fire,	came	from	the	altar	and called	in	a loud	voice	to him	who had	the
ὁ	ἔχων	ἐξουσίαν	ἐπὶ	τοῦ	πυρός,	ἐξῆλθεν	ἐκ	τοῦ	θυσιαστηρίου	καὶ ἐφώνησεν →		μεγάλη	φωνῇ	τῷ →	→ ἔχοντι	τὸ
d.nsm	pt.pa.nsm	n.asf	p.g	d.gsn	n.gsn	v.aai.3s	p.g	d.gsn	n.gsn	cj v.aai.3s		a.dsf	n.dsf	d.dsm	pt.pa.dsm	d.asn
3836	2400	2026	2093	3836	4786	2002	1666	3836	2603	2779 5888		3489	5889	3836	2400	3836

sharp	sickle,	"Take	your	sharp	sickle	and gather	the	clusters	of grapes	from	the	earth's	vine,
⸤τὸ ὀξὺ⸥	δρέπανον	λέγων	πέμψον	σου	⸤τὸ ὀξὺ⸥	⸤τὸ δρέπανον⸥	καὶ τρύγησον	τοὺς	βότρυας ←	→	τῆς	⸤τῆς γῆς⸥	ἀμπέλου
d.asn a.asn	n.asn	pt.pa.nsm	v.aam.2s	r.gs.2	d.asn a.asn	d.asn n.asn	cj v.aam.2s	d.apm	n.apm		d.gsf	d.gsf n.gsf	n.gsf
3836 3955	1535	3306	4287	5148	3836 3955	3836 1535	2779 5582	3836	1084		3836	3836 1178	306

because	its	grapes	are ripe."	**19**	The	angel	swung	his	sickle	on	the	earth,	gathered	its
ὅτι	αὐτῆς	⸤αἱ σταφυλαὶ⸥ →	ἤκμασαν	καὶ	ὁ	ἄγγελος	ἔβαλεν	αὐτοῦ	⸤τὸ δρέπανον⸥	εἰς	τὴν	γῆν	καὶ ἐτρύγησεν	⸤τῆς γῆς⸥
cj	r.gsf.3	d.npf n.npf	v.aai.3p	cj	d.nsm	n.nsm	v.aai.3s	r.gsm.3	d.asn n.asn	p.a	d.asf	n.asf	cj v.aai.3s	d.gsf n.gsf
4022	899	3836 5091	196	2779	3836	34	965	899	3836 1535	1650	3836	1178	2779 5582	3836 1178

grapes	and threw	them	into	the	great	winepress	of	God's	wrath.	**20**	They were trampled	in	the
⸤τὴν ἄμπελον⸥	καὶ ἔβαλεν	εἰς	τὴν	⸤τὸν μέγαν⸥	ληνὸν	→	⸤τοῦ θεοῦ⸥	⸤τοῦ θυμοῦ⸥	καὶ	→ ἐπατήθη	ἡ
d.asf n.asf	cj v.aai.3s	p.a	d.asf	d.asm a.asm	n.asf		d.gsm n.gsm	d.gsm n.gsm	cj	v.api.3s	d.nsf
3836 306	2779 965	1650	3836	3836 3489	3332		2596 3836 2536	3836 2596	2779	4251	3836

winepress	outside	the	city,	and	blood	flowed	out of	the	press,	rising	as	high	as	the	horses'	bridles	for a
ληνὸς	ἔξωθεν	τῆς	πόλεως	καὶ	αἷμα	ἐξῆλθεν	ἐκ ←	τῆς	ληνοῦ		ἄχρι ←		→	τῶν	⸤τῶν ἵππων⸥	χαλινῶν	ἀπὸ ←
n.nsf	p.g	d.gsf	n.gsf	cj	n.nsn	v.aai.3s	p.g	d.gsf	n.gsf		p.g			d.gpm	d.gpm n.gpm	n.gpm	p.g
3332	2033	3836	4484	2779	135	2002	1666	3836	3332		948			3836	3836 2691	5903	608

distance	of 1,600		stadia.
←	← ⸤χιλίων	ἑξακοσίων⸥	σταδίων
	a.gpm	a.gpm	n.gpm
	5943	1980	5084

Seven Angels With Seven Plagues

15:1

I saw	in	heaven	another	great	and	marvelous	sign:	seven	angels	with	the	seven	last
Καὶ → εἶδον	ἐν	⸤τῷ οὐρανῷ⸥	ἄλλο	μέγα	καὶ	θαυμαστόν	σημεῖον	ἑπτὰ	ἀγγέλους	ἔχοντας		ἑπτὰ	⸤τὰς ἐσχάτας⸥
cj v.aai.1s	p.d	d.dsm n.dsm	r.asn	a.asn	cj	a.asn	n.asn	a.apm	n.apm	pt.pa.apm		a.apf	d.apf a.apf
2779 1625	1877	3836 4041	257	3489	2779	2515	4956	2231	34	2400		2231	3836 2274

14:14 Καὶ εἶδον, καὶ ἰδοὺ νεφέλη λευκή, καὶ ἐπὶ τὴν νεφέλην καθήμενον ὅμοιον υἱὸν ἀνθρώπου, ἔχων ἐπὶ τῆς κεφαλῆς αὐτοῦ στέφανον χρυσοῦν καὶ ἐν τῇ χειρὶ αὐτοῦ δρέπανον ὀξύ. **15** καὶ ἄλλος ἄγγελος ἐξῆλθεν ἐκ τοῦ ναοῦ κράζων ἐν φωνῇ μεγάλῃ τῷ καθημένῳ ἐπὶ τῆς νεφέλης, Πέμψον τὸ δρέπανόν σου καὶ θέρισον, ὅτι ἦλθεν ἡ ὥρα θερίσαι, ὅτι ἐξηράνθη ὁ θερισμὸς τῆς γῆς. **16** καὶ ἔβαλεν ὁ καθήμενος ἐπὶ τῆς νεφέλης τὸ δρέπανον αὐτοῦ ἐπὶ τὴν γῆν καὶ ἐθερίσθη ἡ γῆ. ¶ **17** Καὶ ἄλλος ἄγγελος ἐξῆλθεν ἐκ τοῦ ναοῦ τοῦ ἐν τῷ οὐρανῷ ἔχων καὶ αὐτὸς δρέπανον ὀξύ. **18** Καὶ ἄλλος ἄγγελος [ἐξῆλθεν] ἐκ τοῦ θυσιαστηρίου [ὁ] ἔχων ἐξουσίαν ἐπὶ τοῦ πυρός, καὶ ἐφώνησεν φωνῇ μεγάλῃ τῷ ἔχοντι τὸ δρέπανον τὸ ὀξὺ λέγων, Πέμψον σου τὸ δρέπανον τὸ ὀξὺ καὶ τρύγησον τοὺς βότρυας τῆς ἀμπέλου τῆς γῆς, ὅτι ἤκμασαν αἱ σταφυλαὶ αὐτῆς. **19** καὶ ἔβαλεν ὁ ἄγγελος τὸ δρέπανον αὐτοῦ εἰς τὴν γῆν καὶ ἐτρύγησεν τὴν ἄμπελον τῆς γῆς καὶ ἔβαλεν εἰς τὴν ληνὸν τοῦ θυμοῦ τοῦ θεοῦ τὸν μέγαν. **20** καὶ ἐπατήθη ἡ ληνὸς ἔξωθεν τῆς πόλεως καὶ ἐξῆλθεν αἷμα ἐκ τῆς ληνοῦ ἄχρι τῶν χαλινῶν τῶν ἵππων ἀπὸ σταδίων χιλίων ἑξακοσίων.

15:1 Καὶ εἶδον ἄλλο σημεῖον ἐν τῷ οὐρανῷ μέγα καὶ θαυμαστόν, ἀγγέλους ἑπτὰ ἔχοντας πληγὰς ἑπτὰ τὰς ἐσχάτας, ὅτι ἐν

plagues – last, because with them God's wrath is completed. ² And I saw what looked like a sea of
πληγὰς ὅτι ἐν αὐταῖς τοῦ θεοῦ ὁ θυμὸς → ἐτελέσθη Καὶ εἶδον ὡς θάλασσαν →
n.apf cj p.d r.dpf.3 d.gsm n.gsm d.nsm n.nsm v.api.3s cj v.aai.1s pl n.asf
4435 4022 1877 899 2536 3836 2596 5464 2779 1625 6055 2498

glass mixed with fire and, standing beside the sea, those who had been victorious over the
ὑαλίνην μεμιγμένην → πυρὶ καὶ ἑστῶτας ἐπὶ τὴν θάλασσαν ⸢τὴν ὑαλίνην⸣ τοὺς ← → → νικῶντας ἐκ τοῦ
a.asf pt.rp.asf n.dsn cj pt.ra.apm p.a d.asf n.asf d.asf a.asf d.apm pt.pa.apm p.g d.gsn
5612 3624 4786 2779 2705 2093 3836 2498 3836 5612 3836 3771 1666 3836

beast and his image and over the number of his name. They held harps given them by
θηρίου καὶ ἐκ αὐτοῦ τῆς εἰκόνος καὶ ἐκ τοῦ ἀριθμοῦ ⸢ αὐτοῦ ⸢τοῦ ὀνόματος⸣ ἔχοντας κιθάρας →
n.gsn cj p.g r.gsn.3 d.gsf n.gsf cj p.g d.gsm n.gsm r.gsn.3 d.gsn n.gsn pt.pa.apm n.apf
2563 2779 1666 899 3836 1635 2779 1666 3836 750 3950 899 3836 3950 2400 3067

God ³ and sang the song of Moses the servant of God and the song of the Lamb: "Great and
⸢τοῦ θεοῦ⸣ καὶ ᾄδουσιν τὴν ᾠδὴν → Μωϋσέως τοῦ δούλου → ⸢τοῦ θεοῦ⸣ καὶ τὴν ᾠδὴν → τοῦ ἀρνίου λέγοντες μεγάλα καὶ
d.gsm n.gsm cj v.pai.3p d.asf n.asf n.gsm d.gsm n.gsm d.gsm n.gsm cj d.asf n.asf d.gsm n.gsn pt.pa.npm a.npn cj
3836 2536 2779 106 3836 6046 3707 3836 1529 3836 2536 2779 3836 6046 3836 768 3306 3489 2779

marvelous are your deeds, Lord God Almighty. Just and true are your ways, King of the
θαυμαστὰ ⸢ σου ⸢τὰ ἔργα⸣ κύριε ὁ θεὸς ⸢ὁ παντοκράτωρ⸣ δίκαιαι καὶ ἀληθιναὶ ⸢ σου ⸢αἱ ὁδοί⸣ ὁ βασιλεὺς → τῶν
a.npn r.gs.2 d.npn n.npn n.vsm d.vsm n.vsm d.vsm n.vsm a.npf cj a.npf r.gs.2 d.npf n.npf d.vsm n.vsm d.gpn
2515 5148 3836 2240 3261 3836 2536 3836 4120 1465 2779 240 5148 3836 3847 3836 995 3836

ages. ⁴ Who will not fear you, O Lord, and bring glory to your name? For you alone are holy. All
ἐθνῶν τίς → ⸢οὐ μὴ⸣ φοβηθῇ → κύριε καὶ δοξάσει ← σου ⸢τὸ ὄνομα⸣ ὅτι μόνος ὅσιος ὅτι πάντα
n.gpn r.nsm pl pl v.aps.3s n.vsm cj v.fai.3s r.gs.2 d.asn n.asn cj a.nsm a.nsm cj a.npn
1620 5515 5828 4024 3590 5828 3261 2779 1519 5148 3836 3950 4022 3668 4008 4022 4246

nations will come and worship before you, for your righteous acts have been revealed." ¶ ⁵ And
⸢τὰ ἔθνη⸣ → ἥξουσιν καὶ προσκυνήσουσιν ἐνώπιον σου ὅτι σου ⸢τὰ δικαιώματα⸣ ← → ἐφανερώθησαν Καὶ
d.npn n.npn v.fai.3p cj v.fai.3p p.g r.gs.2 cj r.gs.2 d.npn n.npn v.api.3p cj
3836 1620 2457 2779 4686 1967 5148 4022 5148 3836 1468 5746 2779

After this I looked and in heaven the temple, that is, the tabernacle of the Testimony, was opened. ⁶ Out
μετὰ ταῦτα → εἶδον καὶ ἐν ⸢τῷ οὐρανῷ⸣ ὁ ναὸς τῆς σκηνῆς → τοῦ μαρτυρίου → ἠνοίγη καὶ ἐκ
p.a r.apn v.aai.1s cj p.d d.dsm n.dsm d.nsm n.nsm d.gsf n.gsf d.gsn n.gsn v.api.3s cj p.g
3552 4047 1625 2779 1877 3836 4041 3836 3724 3836 5008 3836 3457 487 2779 1666

of the temple came the seven angels with the seven plagues. They were dressed in clean, shining linen
← τοῦ ναοῦ ἐξῆλθον οἱ ἑπτὰ ἄγγελοι ⸢οἱ ἔχοντες⸣ τὰς ἑπτὰ πληγὰς → → ἐνδεδυμένοι ← καθαρὸν λαμπρὸν λίνον
d.gsm n.gsm v.aai.3p d.npm a.npm n.npm d.npm pt.pa.npm d.apf a.apf n.apf pt.rp.npm a.asn a.asn n.asn
3836 3724 2002 3836 2231 34 3836 2400 3836 2231 4435 1907 2754 3287 3351

and wore golden sashes around their chests. ⁷ Then one of the four living creatures gave to the seven
καὶ περιεζωσμένοι χρυσᾶς ζώνας περὶ τὰ στήθη καὶ ἓν ἐκ τῶν τεσσάρων ζῴων → ἔδωκεν → τοῖς ἑπτὰ
cj pt.rp.npm a.apf n.apf p.a d.apn n.apn cj a.nsn p.g d.gpn a.gpn n.gpn v.aai.3s d.dpm a.dpm
2779 4322 5997 2438 4309 3836 5111 2779 1651 1666 3836 5475 2442 1443 3836 2231

angels seven golden bowls filled with the wrath of God, who lives for ever and ever. ⁸ And the
ἀγγέλοις ἑπτὰ χρυσᾶς φιάλας γεμούσας ← τοῦ θυμοῦ → ⸢τοῦ θεοῦ⸣ τοῦ ζῶντος εἰς ⸢τοὺς αἰῶνας⸣ ⸢τῶν αἰώνων⸣ καὶ ὁ
n.dpm a.apf a.apf n.apf pt.pa.apf d.gsm n.gsm d.gsm n.gsm d.gsm pt.pa.gsm p.a d.apm n.apm d.gpm n.gpm cj d.nsm
34 2231 5997 5786 1154 3836 2596 3836 2536 3836 2409 1650 3836 172 3836 172 2779 3836

temple was filled with smoke from the glory of God and from his power, and no one could
ναὸς → ἐγεμίσθη → καπνοῦ ἐκ τῆς δόξης → ⸢τοῦ θεοῦ⸣ καὶ ἐκ αὐτοῦ ⸢τῆς δυνάμεως⸣ καὶ οὐδεὶς ← ἐδύνατο
n.nsm v.api.3s n.gsm p.g d.gsf n.gsf d.gsm n.gsm cj p.g r.gsm.3 d.gsf n.gsf cj a.nsm v.ipi.3s
3724 1153 2837 1666 3836 1518 3836 2536 2779 1666 899 3836 1539 2779 4029 1538

enter the temple until the seven plagues of the seven angels were completed.
εἰσελθεῖν εἰς τὸν ναὸν ἄχρι αἱ ἑπτὰ πληγαὶ → τῶν ἑπτὰ ἀγγέλων → τελεσθῶσιν
f.aa p.a d.asm n.asm cj d.npf a.npf n.npf d.gpm a.gpm n.gpm v.aps.3p
1656 1650 3836 3724 948 3836 2231 4435 3836 2231 34 5464

The Seven Bowls of God's Wrath

¹⁶:¹ Then I heard a loud voice from the temple saying to the seven angels, "Go, pour out the seven
Καὶ → ἤκουσα μεγάλης φωνῆς ἐκ τοῦ ναοῦ λεγούσης → τοῖς ἑπτὰ ἀγγέλοις ὑπάγετε καὶ ἐκχέετε ← τὰς ἑπτὰ
cj v.aai.1s a.gsf n.gsf p.g d.gsm n.gsm pt.pa.gsf d.dpm a.dpm n.dpm v.pam.2p cj v.pam.2p d.apf a.apf
2779 201 3489 5889 1666 3836 3724 3306 3836 2231 34 5632 2779 1772 3836 2231

αὐταῖς ἐτελέσθη ὁ θυμὸς τοῦ θεοῦ. ² Καὶ εἶδον ὡς θάλασσαν ὑαλίνην μεμιγμένην πυρὶ καὶ τοὺς νικῶντας ἐκ τοῦ θηρίου καὶ ἐκ τῆς εἰκόνος αὐτοῦ καὶ ἐκ τοῦ ἀριθμοῦ τοῦ ὀνόματος αὐτοῦ ἑστῶτας ἐπὶ τὴν θάλασσαν τὴν ὑαλίνην ἔχοντας κιθάρας τοῦ θεοῦ. ³ καὶ ᾄδουσιν τὴν ᾠδὴν Μωϋσέως τοῦ δούλου τοῦ θεοῦ καὶ τὴν ᾠδὴν τοῦ ἀρνίου λέγοντες, Μεγάλα καὶ θαυμαστὰ τὰ ἔργα σου, κύριε ὁ θεὸς ὁ παντοκράτωρ· δίκαιαι καὶ ἀληθιναὶ αἱ ὁδοί σου, ὁ βασιλεὺς τῶν αἰώνων· «ἐθνῶν·» ⁴ τίς οὐ μὴ φοβηθῇ, κύριε, καὶ δοξάσει τὸ ὄνομά σου; ὅτι μόνος ὅσιος, ὅτι πάντα τὰ ἔθνη ἥξουσιν καὶ προσκυνήσουσιν ἐνώπιόν σου, ὅτι τὰ δικαιώματά σου ἐφανερώθησαν. ¶ ⁵ Καὶ μετὰ ταῦτα εἶδον, καὶ ἠνοίγη ὁ ναὸς τῆς σκηνῆς τοῦ μαρτυρίου ἐν τῷ οὐρανῷ, ⁶ καὶ ἐξῆλθον οἱ ἑπτὰ ἄγγελοι [οἱ] ἔχοντες τὰς ἑπτὰ πληγὰς ἐκ τοῦ ναοῦ ἐνδεδυμένοι λίνον καθαρὸν λαμπρὸν καὶ περιεζωσμένοι περὶ τὰ στήθη ζώνας χρυσᾶς. ⁷ καὶ ἓν ἐκ τῶν τεσσάρων ζῴων ἔδωκεν τοῖς ἑπτὰ ἀγγέλοις ἑπτὰ φιάλας χρυσᾶς γεμούσας τοῦ θυμοῦ τοῦ θεοῦ τοῦ ζῶντος εἰς τοὺς αἰῶνας τῶν αἰώνων. ⁸ καὶ ἐγεμίσθη ὁ ναὸς καπνοῦ ἐκ τῆς δόξης τοῦ θεοῦ καὶ ἐκ τῆς δυνάμεως αὐτοῦ, καὶ οὐδεὶς ἐδύνατο εἰσελθεῖν εἰς τὸν ναὸν ἄχρι τελεσθῶσιν αἱ ἑπτὰ πληγαὶ τῶν ἑπτὰ ἀγγέλων.

¹⁶:¹ Καὶ ἤκουσα μεγάλης φωνῆς ἐκ τοῦ ναοῦ λεγούσης τοῖς ἑπτὰ ἀγγέλοις, Ὑπάγετε καὶ ἐκχέετε τὰς ἑπτὰ φιάλας τοῦ θυμοῦ

bowls of God's wrath on the earth." ¶ ² The first angel went and poured out his bowl
φιάλας ↱ τοῦ θεοῦ τοῦ θυμοῦ εἰς τὴν γῆν Καὶ ὁ πρῶτος ἀπῆλθεν καὶ ἐξέχεεν ← αὐτοῦ τὴν φιάλην
n.apf d.gsm n.gsm d.gsm n.gsm p.a d.asf n.asf cj d.nsm a.nsm v.aai.3s cj v.aai.3s r.gsm.3 d.asf n.asf
5786 2596 3836 2536 3836 2596 1650 3836 1178 2779 3836 4755 599 2779 1772 899 3836 5786

on the land, and ugly and painful sores broke out on the people who had the mark of the beast and
εἰς τὴν γῆν καὶ κακὸν καὶ πονηρὸν ἕλκος ἐγένετο ἐπὶ τοὺς ἀνθρώπους τοὺς ἔχοντας τὸ χάραγμα τοῦ θηρίου καὶ
p.a d.asf n.asf cj a.nsn cj a.nsn n.nsn v.ami.3s p.a d.apm n.apm d.apm pt.pa.apm d.asn n.asn d.gsn n.gsn cj
1650 3836 1178 2779 2805 2779 4505 1814 1181 2093 3836 476 3836 2400 3836 5916 3836 2563 2779

worshiped his image. ¶ ³ The second angel poured out his bowl on the sea, and it
τοὺς προσκυνοῦντας αὐτοῦ τῇ εἰκόνι Καὶ ὁ δεύτερος ἐξέχεεν ← αὐτοῦ τὴν φιάλην εἰς τὴν θάλασσαν καὶ →
d.apm pt.pa.apm r.gsm.3 d.dsf n.dsf cj d.nsm a.nsm v.aai.3s r.gsm.3 d.asf n.asf p.a d.asf n.asf cj
3836 4686 899 3836 1635 2779 3836 1311 1772 899 3836 5786 1650 3836 2498 2779

turned into blood like that of a dead man, and every living thing in the sea died. ¶ ⁴ The third
ἐγένετο ← αἷμα ὡς → νεκροῦ καὶ πᾶσα ζωῆς ψυχὴ τὰ ἐν τῇ θαλάσσῃ ἀπέθανεν Καὶ ὁ τρίτος
v.ami.3s n.nsn pl a.gsm cj a.nsf n.gsf n.nsf d.npn p.d d.dsf n.dsf v.aai.3s cj d.nsm a.nsm
1181 135 6055 3738 2779 4246 2437 6034 3836 1877 3836 2498 633 2779 3836 5569

angel poured out his bowl on the rivers and springs of water, and they became blood. ⁵ Then I
ἐξέχεεν ← αὐτοῦ τὴν φιάλην εἰς τοὺς ποταμοὺς καὶ τὰς πηγὰς → τῶν ὑδάτων καὶ → ἐγένετο αἷμα Καὶ →
v.aai.3s r.gsm.3 d.asf n.asf p.a d.apm n.apm cj d.apf n.apf d.gpn n.gpn cj v.ami.3s n.nsn cj
1772 899 3836 5786 1650 3836 4532 2779 3836 4380 3836 5623 2779 1181 135 2779

heard the angel in charge of the waters say: "You are just in these judgments, you who are and who
ἤκουσα τοῦ ἀγγέλου → τῶν ὑδάτων λέγοντος εἶ δίκαιος ὁ ὢν καὶ ὁ
v.aai.1s d.gsm n.gsm d.gpn n.gpn pt.pa.gsm v.pai.2s a.nsm d.vsm pt.pa.vsm cj d.vsm
201 3836 34 3836 5623 3306 1639 1465 3836 1639 2779 3836

were, the Holy One, because you have so judged; ⁶ for they have shed the blood of your saints and prophets, and
ἦν ὁ ὅσιος ← ὅτι → → ταῦτα ἔκρινας ὅτι → → ἐξέχεαν αἷμα → ἁγίων καὶ προφητῶν καὶ
v.iai.3s d.vsm a.vsm cj r.apn v.aai.2s cj v.aai.3p n.asn a.gpm cj n.gpm cj
1639 3836 4008 4022 4047 3212 4022 1772 135 41 2779 4737 2779

you have given them blood to drink as they deserve." ⁷ And I heard the altar respond: "Yes, Lord
→ → δέδωκας αὐτοῖς αἷμα → πιεῖν → ἄξιοί εἰσιν Καὶ → ἤκουσα τοῦ θυσιαστηρίου λέγοντος ναὶ κύριε
v.rai.2s r.dpm.3 n.asn f.aa a.npm v.pai.3p cj v.aai.1s d.gsn n.gsn pt.pa.gsn pl n.vsm
1443 899 135 4403 1639 545 1639 2779 201 3836 2603 3306 3721 3261

God Almighty, true and just are your judgments." ¶ ⁸ The fourth angel poured out his
ὁ θεὸς ὁ παντοκράτωρ ἀληθιναὶ καὶ δίκαιαι σου αἱ κρίσεις Καὶ ὁ τέταρτος ἐξέχεεν ← αὐτοῦ
d.vsm n.vsm d.vsm n.vsm a.npf cj a.npf r.gs.2 d.npf n.npf cj d.nsm a.nsm v.aai.3s r.gsm.3
3836 2536 3836 4120 240 2779 1465 5148 3836 3213 2779 3836 5480 1772 899

bowl on the sun, and the sun was given power to scorch people with fire. ⁹ They were
τὴν φιάλην ἐπὶ τὸν ἥλιον καὶ αὐτῷ ἐδόθη → καυματίσαι τοὺς ἀνθρώπους ἐν πυρὶ καὶ οἱ ἄνθρωποι →
d.asf n.asf p.a d.asm n.asm cj r.dsm.3 v.api.3s f.aa d.apm n.apm p.d n.dsn cj d.npm n.npm
3836 5786 2093 3836 2463 2779 899 1443 3009 3836 476 1877 4786 2779 3836 476

seared by the intense heat and they cursed the name of God, who had control over these
ἐκαυματίσθησαν → μέγα καῦμα καὶ → ἐβλασφήμησαν τὸ ὄνομα → τοῦ θεοῦ τοῦ ἔχοντος τὴν ἐξουσίαν ἐπὶ ταύτας
v.api.3p a.asn n.asn cj v.aai.3p d.asn n.asn d.gsm n.gsm d.gsm pt.pa.gsm d.asf n.asf p.a r.apf
3009 3489 3008 2779 1059 3836 3950 3836 2536 3836 2400 3836 2026 2093 4047

plagues, but they refused to repent and glorify him. ¶ ¹⁰ The fifth angel poured out his
τὰς πληγὰς καὶ → οὐ → μετενόησαν δοῦναι δόξαν αὐτῷ Καὶ ὁ πέμπτος ἐξέχεεν ← αὐτοῦ
d.apf n.apf cj pl v.aai.3p f.aa n.asf r.dsm.3 cj d.nsm a.nsm v.aai.3s r.gsn.3
3836 4435 2779 3566 4024 3566 1443 1518 899 2779 3836 4286 1772 899

bowl on the throne of the beast, and his kingdom was plunged into darkness. Men gnawed their
τὴν φιάλην ἐπὶ τὸν θρόνον → τοῦ θηρίου καὶ αὐτοῦ ἡ βασιλεία ἐγένετο → → ἐσκοτωμένη καὶ ἐμασῶντο αὐτῶν
d.asf n.asf p.a d.asm n.asm d.gsn n.gsn cj r.gsm.3 d.nsf n.nsf v.ami.3s pt.rp.nsf cj v.imi.3p r.gpm.3
3836 5786 2093 3836 2585 3836 2563 2779 899 3836 993 1181 5031 2779 3460 899

tongues in agony ¹¹ and cursed the God of heaven because of their pains and their
τὰς γλώσσας ἐκ τοῦ πόνου καὶ ἐβλασφήμησαν τὸν θεὸν τοῦ οὐρανοῦ ἐκ ← αὐτῶν τῶν πόνων καὶ ἐκ αὐτῶν
d.apf n.apf p.g d.gsm n.gsm cj v.aai.3p d.asm n.asm d.gsm n.gsm p.g r.gpm.3 d.gpm n.gpm cj p.g r.gpm.3
3836 1185 1666 3836 4506 2779 1059 3836 2536 3836 4041 1666 3836 4506 2779 1666 899

τοῦ θεοῦ εἰς τὴν γῆν. ¶ ² Καὶ ἀπῆλθεν ὁ πρῶτος καὶ ἐξέχεεν τὴν φιάλην αὐτοῦ εἰς τὴν γῆν, καὶ ἐγένετο ἕλκος κακὸν καὶ πονηρὸν ἐπὶ τοὺς ἀνθρώπους τοὺς ἔχοντας τὸ χάραγμα τοῦ θηρίου καὶ τοὺς προσκυνοῦντας τῇ εἰκόνι αὐτοῦ. ¶ ³ Καὶ ὁ δεύτερος ἐξέχεεν τὴν φιάλην αὐτοῦ εἰς τὴν θάλασσαν, καὶ ἐγένετο αἷμα ὡς νεκροῦ, καὶ πᾶσα ψυχὴ ζωῆς ἀπέθανεν τὰ ἐν τῇ θαλάσσῃ. ¶ ⁴ Καὶ ὁ τρίτος ἐξέχεεν τὴν φιάλην αὐτοῦ εἰς τοὺς ποταμοὺς καὶ τὰς πηγὰς τῶν ὑδάτων, καὶ ἐγένετο αἷμα. ⁵ καὶ ἤκουσα τοῦ ἀγγέλου τῶν ὑδάτων λέγοντος, Δίκαιος εἶ, ὁ ὢν καὶ ὁ ἦν, ὁ ὅσιος, ὅτι ταῦτα ἔκρινας, ⁶ ὅτι αἷμα ἁγίων καὶ προφητῶν ἐξέχεαν καὶ αἷμα αὐτοῖς [δ]έδωκας πιεῖν, ἄξιοί εἰσιν. ⁷ καὶ ἤκουσα τοῦ θυσιαστηρίου λέγοντος, Ναὶ κύριε ὁ θεὸς ὁ παντοκράτωρ, ἀληθιναὶ καὶ δίκαιαι αἱ κρίσεις σου. ¶ ⁸ Καὶ ὁ τέταρτος ἐξέχεεν τὴν φιάλην αὐτοῦ ἐπὶ τὸν ἥλιον, καὶ ἐδόθη αὐτῷ καυματίσαι τοὺς ἀνθρώπους ἐν πυρί. ⁹ καὶ ἐκαυματίσθησαν οἱ ἄνθρωποι καῦμα μέγα καὶ ἐβλασφήμησαν τὸ ὄνομα τοῦ θεοῦ τοῦ ἔχοντος τὴν ἐξουσίαν ἐπὶ τὰς πληγὰς ταύτας καὶ οὐ μετενόησαν δοῦναι αὐτῷ δόξαν. ¶ ¹⁰ Καὶ ὁ πέμπτος ἐξέχεεν τὴν φιάλην αὐτοῦ ἐπὶ τὸν θρόνον τοῦ θηρίου, καὶ ἐγένετο ἡ βασιλεία αὐτοῦ ἐσκοτωμένη, καὶ ἐμασῶντο τὰς γλώσσας αὐτῶν ἐκ τοῦ πόνου, ¹¹ καὶ ἐβλασφήμησαν τὸν

sores,	but	they refused	to repent	of	what		they had done.	¶	**12**	The sixth angel poured out his
⸤τῶν ἑλκῶν⸥	καὶ	→	οὐ → μετενόησαν	ἐκ	⸤τῶν ἔργων⸥	αὐτῶν ← ←				Καὶ ὁ ἕκτος ἐξέχεεν ← αὐτοῦ
d.gpn n.gpn	cj		pl v.aai.3p	p.g	d.gpn n.gpn	r.gpm.3				cj d.nsm a.nsm v.aai.3s r.gsm.3
3836 1814	2779	3566	4024 3566	1666	3836 2240	899 2240 2240				2779 3836 1761 1772 899

bowl	on	the great	river	Euphrates,	and	its	water	was	dried	up to	prepare	the	way	for the
⸤τὴν φιάλην⸥	ἐπὶ	τὸν μέγαν	ποταμὸν	⸤τὸν Εὐφράτην⸥	καὶ	αὐτοῦ	τὸ ὕδωρ	→	ἐξηράνθη	ἵνα	ἑτοιμασθῇ	ἡ	ὁδὸς	τῶν
d.asf n.asf	p.a	d.asm a.asm	n.asm	d.asm n.asm	cj	r.gsm.3	d.nsn n.nsn		v.api.3s	cj	v.aps.3s	d.nsf	n.nsf	d.gpm
3836 5786	2093	3836 3489	4532	3836 2371	2779	899	3836 5623		3830	2671	2286	3836	3847	3836

kings		from	the East.		**13** Then	I saw	three	evil		spirits	that looked	like	frogs;		they came	out of
βασιλέων	τῶν	ἀπὸ	⸤ἀνατολῆς ἡλίου⸥		Καὶ →	εἶδον	τρία	ἀκάθαρτα	πνεύματα			ὡς	βάτραχοι			ἐκ ←
n.gpm	d.gpm	p.g	n.gsf n.gsm		cj	v.aai.1s	a.apn	a.apn	n.apn			pl	n.npm			p.g
995	3836	608	424 2463		2779	1625	5552	176	4460			6055	1005			1666

the mouth	of the dragon,		out of the mouth	of the beast	and out of the mouth	of the false prophet.
τοῦ στόματος	τοῦ δράκοντος	καὶ ἐκ ←	τοῦ στόματος →	τοῦ θηρίου	καὶ ἐκ ← τοῦ στόματος →	τοῦ → ψευδοπροφήτου
d.gsn n.gsn	d.gsm n.gsm	cj p.g	d.gsn n.gsn	d.gsn n.gsn	cj p.g d.gsn n.gsn	d.gsm n.gsm
3836 5125	3836 1532	2779 1666	3836 5125	3836 2563	2779 1666 3836 5125	3836 6021

14	They are	spirits	of demons	performing	miraculous signs, and		they go		out to	the kings	of the
γὰρ →	εἰσὶν	πνεύματα →	δαιμονίων	ποιοῦντα	σημεῖα	ἃ	ἐκπορεύεται ←		ἐπὶ	τοὺς βασιλεῖς →	τῆς
cj	v.pai.3p	n.npn	n.gpn	pt.pa.npn	n.apn	r.npn	v.pmi.3s		p.a	d.apm n.apm	d.gsf
1142	1639	4460	1228	4472	4956	4005	1744		2093	3836 995	3836

whole	world,		to gather		them	for the battle	on	the great		day	of God	Almighty.	¶
ὅλης	οἰκουμένης	→	συναγαγεῖν	αὐτοὺς	εἰς	τὸν πόλεμον →	τῆς	⸤τῆς μεγάλης⸥	ἡμέρας →	⸤τοῦ θεοῦ⸥	τοῦ παντοκράτορος⸥		
a.gsf	n.gsf		f.aa	r.apm.3	p.a	d.asm n.asm	d.gsf	d.gsf a.gsf	n.gsf	d.gsm n.gsm	d.gsm n.gsm		
3910	3876		5251	1650	1650	3836 4483	3836	3836 3489	2465	3836 2536	3836 4120		

15 "Behold,	I come	like	a thief!	Blessed	is he	who		stays awake	and keeps	his	clothes	with him,	so that he
Ἰδοὺ	→ ἔρχομαι	ὡς	κλέπτης	μακάριος	ὁ	→		γρηγορῶν	καὶ τηρῶν	αὐτοῦ	⸤τὰ ἱμάτια⸥		ἵνα ← →
j	v.pmi.1s	pl	n.nsm	a.nsm	d.nsm			pt.pa.nsm	cj pt.pa.nsm	r.gsm.3	d.apn n.apn		cj
2627	2262	6055	3095	3421	3836			1213	2779 5498	899	3836 2668		2671 4344

may not go	naked	and be shamefully		exposed."	¶	**16** Then	they gathered	the kings	together	to
μὴ περιπατῇ	γυμνὸς	καὶ → ⸤τὴν ἀσχημοσύνην⸥	αὐτοῦ	βλέπωσιν		Καὶ →	συνήγαγεν	αὐτοὺς ←		εἰς
pl v.pas.3s	a.nsm	cj d.asf n.asf	r.gsm.3	v.pas.3p		cj	v.aai.3s	r.apm.3		p.a
4344 3590	4344 1218	2779 1063 3836 859	899	1063		2779	5251	899 5251		1650

the place	that	in Hebrew	is called	Armageddon.	¶	**17**	The seventh angel poured out his	bowl	into
τὸν τόπον	τὸν →	Ἑβραϊστὶ →	καλούμενον	Ἁρμαγεδών			Καὶ ὁ ἕβδομος ἐξέχεεν ← αὐτοῦ	⸤τὴν φιάλην⸥	ἐπὶ
d.asm n.asm	d.asm	adv	pt.pp.asm	n.asn			cj d.nsm a.nsm v.aai.3s r.gsm.3	d.asf n.asf	p.a
3836 5536	3836	1580	2813	762			2779 3836 1575 1772 899	3836 5786	2093

the air,	and out of	the temple	came	a loud	voice	from	the throne,	saying,	"It is done!"	**18** Then	there	came
τὸν ἀέρα	καὶ ἐκ ←	τοῦ ναοῦ	ἐξῆλθεν	μεγάλη	φωνὴ	ἀπὸ	τοῦ θρόνου	λέγουσα	→ γέγονεν	καὶ	→	ἐγένοντο
d.asm n.asm	cj p.g	d.gsm n.gsm	v.aai.3s	a.nsf	n.nsf	p.g	d.gsm n.gsm	pt.pa.nsf	v.rai.3s	cj		v.ami.3p
3836 113	2779 1666	3836 3724	2002	3489	5889	608	3836 2585	3306	1181	2779		1181

flashes of lightning,		rumblings,		peals of thunder	and		a severe	earthquake.	No	earthquake	like it	has
→	→ ἀστραπαὶ	καὶ	φωναὶ	καὶ	→ →	βρονταὶ	καὶ ἐγένετο	μέγας	σεισμὸς	οὐκ		οἷος ← →
	n.npf	cj	n.npf	cj		n.npf	cj v.ami.3s	a.nsm	n.nsm	pl		r.nsm
	847	2779	5889	2779		1103	2779 1181	3489	4939	4024		3888

ever occurred	since	man		has been	on earth,	so	tremendous		was the quake.	**19**	The great
ἐγένετο	⸤ἀφ᾽ οὗ⸥	ἄνθρωπος →	ἐγένετο	ἐπὶ ⸤τῆς γῆς⸥	→ τηλικοῦτος	οὕτω μέγας⸥		σεισμὸς	καὶ ἡ	⸤ἡ μεγάλη⸥	
v.ami.3s	r.gsm	n.nsm	v.ami.3s	p.g d.gsf n.gsf	r.nsm	adv a.nsm		n.nsm	cj d.nsf	d.nsf a.nsf	
1181	608	4005 476	1181	2093 3836 1178	5496	4048 3489		4939	2779 3836	3836 3489	

city	split	into	three	parts,	and	the	cities	of the nations	collapsed.		God	remembered	Babylon	the
πόλις	ἐγένετο	εἰς	τρία	μέρη	καὶ	αἱ	πόλεις →	τῶν ἐθνῶν	ἔπεσαν	καὶ ἐνώπιον	⸤τοῦ θεοῦ⸥	ἐμνήσθη	Βαβυλὼν	ἡ
n.nsf	v.ami.3s	p.a	a.apn	n.apn	cj	d.npf	n.npf	d.gpn n.gpn	v.aai.3p	cj p.g	d.gsm n.gsm	v.api.3s	n.nsf	d.nsf
4484	1181	1650	5552	3538	2779	3836	4484	3836 1620	4406	2779 1967	3836 2536	3630	956	3836

Great	and gave	her	the cup	filled	with	the wine	of the fury	of his	wrath.	**20**	Every	island	fled	away
μεγάλη	δοῦναι	αὐτῇ	τὸ ποτήριον →	→		τοῦ οἴνου →	τοῦ θυμοῦ →	αὐτοῦ	⸤τῆς ὀργῆς⸥		καὶ πᾶσα	νῆσος	ἔφυγεν ←
a.nsf	f.aa	r.dsf.3	d.asn n.asn			d.gsm n.gsm	d.gsm n.gsm	r.gsm.3	d.gsf n.gsf		cj a.nsf	n.nsf	v.aai.3s
3489	1443	899	3836 4539			3836 3885	3836 2596	899	3973 3973		2779 4246	3762	5771

θεὸν τοῦ οὐρανοῦ ἐκ τῶν πόνων αὐτῶν καὶ ἐκ τῶν ἑλκῶν αὐτῶν καὶ οὐ μετενόησαν ἐκ τῶν ἔργων αὐτῶν. ¶ **12** Καὶ ὁ ἕκτος ἐξέχεεν τὴν φιάλην αὐτοῦ ἐπὶ τὸν ποταμὸν τὸν μέγαν τὸν Εὐφράτην, καὶ ἐξηράνθη τὸ ὕδωρ αὐτοῦ, ἵνα ἑτοιμασθῇ ἡ ὁδὸς τῶν βασιλέων τῶν ἀπὸ ἀνατολῆς ἡλίου. **13** Καὶ εἶδον ἐκ τοῦ στόματος τοῦ δράκοντος καὶ ἐκ τοῦ στόματος τοῦ θηρίου καὶ ἐκ τοῦ στόματος τοῦ ψευδοπροφήτου πνεύματα τρία ἀκάθαρτα ὡς βάτραχοι· **14** εἰσὶν γὰρ πνεύματα δαιμονίων ποιοῦντα σημεῖα, ἃ ἐκπορεύεται ἐπὶ τοὺς βασιλεῖς τῆς οἰκουμένης ὅλης συναγαγεῖν αὐτοὺς εἰς τὸν πόλεμον τῆς ἡμέρας τῆς μεγάλης τοῦ θεοῦ τοῦ παντοκράτορος. ¶ **15** Ἰδοὺ ἔρχομαι ὡς κλέπτης. μακάριος ὁ γρηγορῶν καὶ τηρῶν τὰ ἱμάτια αὐτοῦ, ἵνα μὴ γυμνὸς περιπατῇ καὶ βλέπωσιν τὴν ἀσχημοσύνην αὐτοῦ. ¶ **16** καὶ συνήγαγεν αὐτοὺς εἰς τὸν τόπον τὸν καλούμενον Ἑβραϊστὶ Ἁρμαγεδών. ¶ **17** Καὶ ὁ ἕβδομος ἐξέχεεν τὴν φιάλην αὐτοῦ ἐπὶ τὸν ἀέρα, καὶ ἐξῆλθεν φωνὴ μεγάλη ἐκ τοῦ ναοῦ ἀπὸ τοῦ θρόνου λέγουσα, Γέγονεν. **18** καὶ ἐγένοντο ἀστραπαὶ καὶ φωναὶ καὶ βρονταὶ καὶ σεισμὸς ἐγένετο μέγας, οἷος οὐκ ἐγένετο ἀφ᾽ οὗ ἄνθρωπος ἐγένετο ἐπὶ τῆς γῆς τηλικοῦτος σεισμὸς οὕτω μέγας. **19** καὶ ἐγένετο ἡ πόλις ἡ μεγάλη εἰς τρία μέρη καὶ αἱ πόλεις τῶν ἐθνῶν ἔπεσαν. καὶ Βαβυλὼν ἡ μεγάλη ἐμνήσθη ἐνώπιον τοῦ θεοῦ δοῦναι αὐτῇ τὸ ποτήριον τοῦ οἴνου τοῦ θυμοῦ τῆς ὀργῆς αὐτοῦ. **20** καὶ πᾶσα

and the mountains could not be found. **21** From the sky huge hailstones of about a hundred pounds each
καὶ   ὄρη   οὐχ   εὑρέθησαν καὶ ἐκ   τοῦ οὐρανοῦ μεγάλη χάλαζα   ὡς   ταλαντιαία ←
cj   n.npn   pl   v.api.3p   cj   p.g d.gsm n.gsm   a.nsf   n.nsf   pl   a.nsf
2779   4001   2351   4024   2351   2779 1666 3836 4041   3489   5898   6055 5418

fell   upon men.   And they   cursed   God   on account of the plague of hail,
καταβαίνει ἐπὶ τοὺς ἀνθρώπους. καὶ οἱ ἄνθρωποι ἐβλασφήμησαν τὸν θεὸν ἐκ ←   ← τῆς πληγῆς ⌐τῆς χαλάζης⌐
v.pai.3s p.a d.apm n.apm   cj   d.npm n.npm   v.aai.3p   d.asn n.asm p.g   d.gsf n.gsf d.gsf n.gsf
2849   2093 3836 476   2779 3836 476   1059   3836 2536 1666   3836 4435   3836 5898

because the plague   was so   terrible.
ὅτι   ἡ   πληγὴ αὐτῆς ἐστὶν σφόδρα μεγάλη
cj   d.nsf n.nsf n.gsf.3 v.pai.3s adv   a.nsf
4022   3836 4435 899   1639   5379   3489

The Woman on the Beast

17:1 One of the seven angels who had   the seven bowls came and said   to me,   "Come, I will
Καὶ εἷς   ἐκ   τῶν ἑπτὰ ἀγγέλων τῶν ἐχόντων τὰς ἑπτὰ φιάλας ἦλθεν καὶ ἐλάλησεν μετ᾽ ἐμοῦ λέγων δεῦρο → →
cj   a.nsm p.g d.gpm a.gpm n.gpm   d.gpm pt.pa.gpm d.apf a.apf n.apf   v.aai.3s cj   v.aai.3s p.g r.gs.1 pt.pa.nsm j
2779 1651   1666 3836 2231 34   3836 2400   2231 2231 5786   2262   2779 3281   3552 1609 3306   1306

show you the punishment of the great   prostitute, who sits   on many waters. **2** With her the kings   of the
δείξω σοι τὸ κρίμα → τῆς ⌐τῆς μεγάλης⌐ πόρνης τῆς καθημένης ἐπὶ πολλῶν ὑδάτων μεθ᾽ ἧς   οἱ βασιλεῖς → τῆς
v.fai.1s r.ds.2 d.asn n.asn d.gsf d.gsf a.gsf   n.gsf   d.gsf pt.pm.gsf p.g a.gpn n.gpn p.g r.gsf d.npm n.npm   d.gsf
1259 5148 3836 3210   3836 3836 3489   4520   3836 2764   2093 4498 5623   3552 899 4005 995   3836

earth committed adultery and the inhabitants of the earth were intoxicated with the wine of her adulteries."   ¶
γῆς   →   ἐπόρνευσαν καὶ οἱ κατοικοῦντες τὴν γῆν → ἐμεθύσθησαν ἐκ τοῦ οἴνου → αὐτῆς ⌐τῆς πορνείας⌐
n.gsf   v.aai.3p   cj   d.npm pt.pa.npm   d.asf n.asf   v.api.3p   p.g d.gsm n.gsm   r.gsf.3 d.gsf n.gsf
1178   4519   2779 3836 2997   3836 1178   3499   1666 3836 3885   899   3836 4518

3 Then the angel carried   me away in the Spirit   into a desert.   There I saw a woman sitting   on a scarlet
καὶ   ἀπήνεγκέν με   ←   ἐν πνεύματι εἰς ἔρημον Καὶ   → εἶδον γυναῖκα καθημένην ἐπὶ κόκκινον
cj   v.aai.3s r.as.1   p.d n.dsn   p.a n.asf   cj   v.aai.1s n.asf   pt.pm.asf p.g a.asn
2779   708   1609 708   1877 4460   1650 2245   2779   1625   1222   2764   2093 3132

beast that was covered with blasphemous names and had seven heads and ten horns. **4** The woman was
θηρίον → → γέμοντα ←   βλασφημίας ὀνόματα ἔχων ἑπτὰ κεφαλὰς καὶ δέκα κέρατα καὶ ἡ   γυνὴ ἦν
n.asn   pt.pa.asn   n.gsf   n.apn   pt.pa.nsm a.apf n.apf cj   a.apn n.apn   cj   d.nsf n.nsf v.iai.3s
2563   1154   1060   3950   2400 2231 3051   2779 1274 3043   2779 3836 1222 1639

dressed   in purple   and scarlet, and was glittering with gold,   precious stones and pearls. She held a
περιβεβλημένη ← πορφυροῦν καὶ κόκκινον καὶ → κεχρυσωμένη χρυσίῳ καὶ τιμίῳ λίθῳ καὶ μαργαρίταις → ἔχουσα
pt.rp.nsf   a.asn   cj   a.asn   cj   pt.rp.nsf   n.dsn cj   a.dsm n.dsm cj   n.dpm   pt.pa.nsf
4314   4528   2779 3132   2779   5998   5992   2779 5508   3345 2779 3449   2400

golden cup   in her hand,   filled with abominable things and the filth   of her adulteries. **5** This title
χρυσοῦν ποτήριον ἐν αὐτῆς ⌐τῇ χειρὶ⌐ γέμον ← βδελυγμάτων   καὶ τὰ ἀκάθαρτα → αὐτῆς ⌐τῆς πορνείας⌐ καὶ ὄνομα
a.asn   n.asn   p.d r.gsf.3 d.dsf n.dsf pt.pa.asn n.gpn   cj   d.apn a.apn   r.gsf.3 d.gsf n.gsf   cj   n.nsn
5997   4539   1877 899   3836 5931 1154 1007   2779 3836 176   4518 899 3836 4518   2779 3950

was written   on her forehead: MYSTERY BABYLON THE GREAT THE MOTHER OF PROSTITUTES
→ γεγραμμένον ἐπὶ αὐτῆς ⌐τὸ μέτωπον⌐ μυστήριον Βαβυλὼν ἡ   μεγάλη ἡ   μήτηρ → ⌐τῶν πορνῶν⌐
pt.rp.nsn   p.a r.gsf.3 d.asn n.asn n.nsn   n.nsf   d.nsf a.nsf d.nsf n.nsf   d.gpf n.gpf
1211   2093 899   3836 3587   3696   956   3836 3489 3836 3613   3836 4520

AND OF THE ABOMINATIONS   OF THE EARTH. **6** I saw that the woman was drunk   with the blood of
καὶ → τῶν βδελυγμάτων   → τῆς γῆς   καὶ → εἶδον τὴν γυναῖκα → μεθύουσαν ἐκ τοῦ αἵματος →
cj   d.gpn n.gpn   d.gsf n.gsf cj   v.aai.1s d.asf n.asf   pt.pa.asf p.g d.gsn n.gsn
2779   3836 1007   3836 1178   2779 1625   3836 1222   3501   1666 3836 135

the saints,   the blood of those who bore testimony to Jesus. ¶   When I saw her, I was
τῶν ἁγίων καὶ ἐκ τοῦ αἵματος → τῶν ←   μαρτύρων → Ἰησοῦ   Καὶ   → ἰδὼν αὐτὴν →
d.gpm a.gpm cj p.g d.gsn n.gsn   d.gpm   n.gpm   n.gsm   cj   pt.aa.nsm r.asf.3
3836 41   2779 1666 3836 135   3836   3459   2652   2779   1625   899   2513 2513

greatly   astonished. **7** Then the angel said to me: "Why are you astonished? I will explain to you the
⌐θαῦμα μέγα⌐ ἐθαύμασα Καὶ ὁ   ἄγγελος εἶπεν → μοι ⌐διὰ τί⌐ → ἐθαύμασας ἐγὼ → ἐρῶ → σοι τὸ
n.asn a.asn v.aai.1s   cj d.nsm n.nsm v.aai.3s r.ds.1 p.a r.asn   v.aai.2s r.ns.1 v.fai.1s r.ds.2 d.asn
2512 3489   2513   2779 34   3306   1609   1328 5515   2513   1609   3306   5148 3836

νῆσος ἔφυγεν καὶ ὄρη οὐχ εὑρέθησαν. ²¹ καὶ χάλαζα μεγάλη ὡς ταλαντιαία καταβαίνει ἐκ τοῦ οὐρανοῦ ἐπὶ τοὺς ἀνθρώπους, καὶ ἐβλασφήμησαν οἱ ἄνθρωποι τὸν θεὸν ἐκ τῆς πληγῆς τῆς χαλάζης, ὅτι μεγάλη ἐστὶν ἡ πληγὴ αὐτῆς σφόδρα.
17:1 Καὶ ἦλθεν εἷς ἐκ τῶν ἑπτὰ ἀγγέλων τῶν ἐχόντων τὰς ἑπτὰ φιάλας καὶ ἐλάλησεν μετ᾽ ἐμοῦ λέγων, Δεῦρο, δείξω σοι τὸ κρίμα τῆς πόρνης τῆς μεγάλης τῆς καθημένης ἐπὶ ὑδάτων πολλῶν, ² μεθ᾽ ἧς ἐπόρνευσαν οἱ βασιλεῖς τῆς γῆς καὶ ἐμεθύσθησαν οἱ κατοικοῦντες τὴν γῆν ἐκ τοῦ οἴνου τῆς πορνείας αὐτῆς ¶ ³ καὶ ἀπήνεγκέν με εἰς ἔρημον ἐν πνεύματι. καὶ εἶδον γυναῖκα καθημένην ἐπὶ θηρίον κόκκινον, γέμον[τα] ὀνόματα βλασφημίας, ἔχων κεφαλὰς ἑπτὰ καὶ κέρατα δέκα. ⁴ καὶ ἡ γυνὴ ἦν περιβεβλημένη πορφυροῦν καὶ κόκκινον καὶ κεχρυσωμένη χρυσίῳ καὶ λίθῳ τιμίῳ καὶ μαργαρίταις, ἔχουσα ποτήριον χρυσοῦν ἐν τῇ χειρὶ αὐτῆς γέμον βδελυγμάτων καὶ τὰ ἀκάθαρτα τῆς πορνείας αὐτῆς ⁵ καὶ ἐπὶ τὸ μέτωπον αὐτῆς ὄνομα γεγραμμένον, μυστήριον, Βαβυλὼν ἡ μεγάλη, ἡ μήτηρ τῶν πορνῶν καὶ τῶν βδελυγμάτων τῆς γῆς. ⁶ καὶ εἶδον τὴν γυναῖκα μεθύουσαν ἐκ τοῦ αἵματος τῶν ἁγίων καὶ ἐκ τοῦ αἵματος τῶν μαρτύρων Ἰησοῦ. ¶ Καὶ ἐθαύμασα ἰδὼν αὐτὴν θαῦμα μέγα. ⁷ καὶ εἶπέν μοι ὁ ἄγγελος, Διὰ τί ἐθαύμασας; ἐγὼ ἐρῶ σοι τὸ μυστήριον τῆς γυναικὸς καὶ τοῦ θηρίου τοῦ βαστάζοντος αὐτὴν τοῦ ἔχοντος τὰς ἑπτὰ

mystery | of the | woman | and | of the | beast | she | rides, | | which has | | the | seven | heads | and | ten | horns.
μυστήριον → | τῆς | γυναικὸς | καὶ → | τοῦ | θηρίου | αὐτὴν | τοῦ βαστάζοντος | τοῦ | ἔχοντος | τὰς | ἑπτὰ | κεφαλὰς | καὶ | δέκα | τὰ κέρατα
n.asn | d.gsf | n.gsf | cj | d.gsn | n.gsn | r.asf.3 | d.gsn pt.pa.gsn | d.gsn | pt.pa.gsn | d.apf | a.apf | n.apf | cj | a.apn | d.apn n.apn
3696 | 3836 | 1222 | 2779 | 3836 | 2563 | 899 | 3836 1002 | 3836 | 2400 | 3836 | 2231 | 3051 | 2779 | 1274 | 3836 3043

8 The | beast, | which | you saw, | once was, | now is | not, | and will | come | | up out of | the | Abyss | and | go | to | his
Τὸ | θηρίον | ὃ | εἶδες, | ἦν | καὶ | ἔστιν | οὐκ | καὶ | μέλλει | ἀναβαίνειν | ἐκ ← | τῆς | ἀβύσσου | καὶ | ὑπάγει | εἰς
d.nsn | n.nsn | r.asn | v.aai.2s | v.iai.3s | v.pai.3s | pl | cj | v.pai.3s | f.pa | p.g | d.gsf | n.gsf | cj | v.pai.3s | p.a
3836 | 2563 | 4005 | 1625 | 1639 | 1639 | 4024 | 2779 | 3516 | 326 | 1666 | 3836 | 12 | 2779 | 5632 | 1650

destruction. | The inhabitants | of | the | earth | whose | names | | have | not | been | written | in | the | book | of life
ἀπώλειαν | καὶ οἱ | κατοικοῦντες | ἐπὶ | τῆς | γῆς | ὧν | τὸ ὄνομα | | οὐ → | | γέγραπται | ἐπὶ | τὸ | βιβλίον | τῆς ζωῆς
n.asf | cj d.npm | pt.pa.npm | p.g | d.gsf | n.gsf | r.gpm | d.nsn n.nsn | | pl | | v.rpi.3s | p.a | d.asn | n.asn | d.gsf n.gsf
724 | 2779 3836 | 2997 | 2093 | 3836 | 1178 | 4005 | 3836 3950 | 1211 | 4024 | 1211 | | 2093 | 3836 | 1046 | 3836 2437

from | the creation | of the world | | will be astonished | | | when they see | the | beast, | because | he | once was, | now is
ἀπὸ | καταβολῆς → | κόσμου → | | θαυμασθήσονται → | | | βλεπόντων τὸ | θηρίον | ὅτι | → | ἦν | καὶ | ἔστιν
p.g | n.gsf | n.gsm | | v.fpi.3p | | | pt.pa.gpm d.asn | n.asn | cj | | v.iai.3s | cj | v.pai.3s
608 | 2856 | 3180 | | 2513 | | | 1063 3836 | 2563 | 4022 | | 1639 | 2779 | 1639

not, | and yet will come. | ¶ | **9** "This calls for a | mind | with | wisdom. | The | seven | heads | are | seven | hills
οὐκ | καὶ | παρέσται | | ὧδε | ὁ | νοῦς | ὁ ἔχων | σοφίαν | Αἱ | ἑπτὰ | κεφαλαὶ | εἰσιν | ἑπτὰ | ὄρη | ὅπου
pl | cj | v.fmi.3s | | adv | d.nsm | n.nsm | d.nsm pt.pa.nsm | n.asf | d.npf | a.npf | n.npf | v.pai.3p | a.npn | n.npn | cj
4024 | 2779 | 4205 | | 6045 | 3836 | 3808 | 3836 2400 | 5053 | 3836 | 2231 | 3051 | 1639 | 2231 | 4001 | 3963

on | which | the | woman | sits. | **10** They | are | also | seven | kings. | Five | | have fallen, | one | is, | the | other | has | not | yet
ἐπ᾽ | αὐτῶν | ἡ | γυνὴ | κάθηται | | εἰσιν | καὶ | ἑπτὰ | βασιλεῖς | οἱ πέντε | | ἔπεσαν | ὁ | εἷς | ἔστιν | ὁ | ἄλλος | → | οὔπω ←
p.g | r.gpn.3 | d.nsf | n.nsf | v.pmi.3s | | v.pai.3p | cj | a.npm | n.npm | d.npm a.npm | | v.aai.3p | d.nsm | a.nsm | v.pai.3s | d.nsm | n.nsm | | adv
2093 | 899 | 3836 | 1222 | 2764 | | 1639 | 2779 | 2231 | 995 | 3836 4297 | | 4406 | 3836 | 1651 | 1639 | 3836 | 257 | 2262 | 4037

come; | but when | he does | come, | he | must | remain | for a little | while. | **11** | The | beast | who | once was, | and | now is
ἦλθεν | καὶ ὅταν | → | ἔλθῃ | αὐτὸν | δεῖ | μεῖναι | ὀλίγον ← | | | καὶ | τὸ | θηρίον | ὃ | ἦν | καὶ ← | ἔστιν
v.aai.3s | cj v.aas.3s | | v.aas.3s | r.asm.3 | v.pai.3s | f.aa | adv | | | cj | d.nsn | n.nsn | r.nsn | v.iai.3s | cj | v.pai.3s
2262 | 2779 4020 | | 2262 | 899 | 1256 | 3531 | 3900 | | | 2779 | 3836 | 2563 | 4005 | 1639 | 2779 | 1639

not, | | is | an eighth | king. | | He belongs | to | the | seven | and | is going | to | his destruction. | ¶ | **12** | "The
οὐκ | καὶ | αὐτὸς | ἐστιν | ὄγδοός | καὶ → | ἐστιν ἐκ | ← | τῶν | ἑπτὰ | καὶ | ὑπάγει εἰς | | ἀπώλειαν | | Καὶ | τὰ
pl | adv | r.nsm | v.pai.3s | a.nsm | cj | v.pai.3s p.g | | d.gpm | a.gpm | cj | v.pai.3s p.a | | n.asf | | cj | d.npn
4024 | 2779 | 899 | 1639 | 3838 | 2779 | 1639 1666 | | 3836 | 2231 | 2779 | 5632 1650 | | 724 | | 2779 | 3836

ten | horns | you saw | are | ten | kings | who | | have | not | yet | received | a kingdom, | but | who | for | one | hour | will
δέκα | κέρατα | ἃ → | εἶδες | εἰσιν | δέκα | βασιλεῖς | οἵτινες → | | οὔπω ← | | ἔλαβον | βασιλείαν | ἀλλὰ | | | μίαν | ὥραν →
a.npn | n.npn | r.apn | v.aai.2s | v.pai.3p | a.npm | n.npm | r.npm | | adv | | v.aai.3p | n.asf | cj | | | a.asf | n.asf
1274 | 3043 | 4005 | 1625 | 1639 | 1274 | 995 | 4015 | 3284 | 4037 | | 3284 | 993 | 247 | | | 1651 | 6052

receive | authority | as | kings | along with | | the beast. | **13** They | have | one | purpose | and | will give | | their | power
λαμβάνουσιν | ἐξουσίαν | ὡς | βασιλεῖς → | μετὰ | τοῦ | θηρίου | οὗτοι | ἔχουσιν | μίαν | γνώμην | καὶ → | διδόασιν | αὐτῶν | τὴν δύναμιν
v.pai.3p | n.asf | pl | n.npm | p.g | d.gsn | n.gsn | r.npm | v.pai.3p | a.asf | n.asf | cj | v.pai.3p | r.gpm.3 | d.asf n.asf
3284 | 2026 | 6055 | 995 | 3552 | 3836 | 2563 | 4047 | 2400 | 1651 | 1191 | 2779 | 1443 | 899 | 3836 1539

and | authority | to the | beast. | **14** They | will make | war | | against | the | Lamb, | but | the | Lamb | will | overcome | them
καὶ | ἐξουσίαν | τῷ | θηρίῳ | οὗτοι → | → | πολεμήσουσιν | μετὰ | | τοῦ | ἀρνίου | καὶ | τὸ | ἀρνίον → | | νικήσει | αὐτούς
cj | n.asf | d.dsn | n.dsn | r.npm | | v.fai.3p | p.g | | d.gsn | n.gsn | cj | d.nsn | n.nsn | | v.fai.3s | r.apm.3
2779 | 2026 | 3836 | 2563 | 4047 | | 4482 | 3552 | | 3836 | 768 | 2779 | 3836 | 768 | | 3771 | 899

because | he is | Lord | of lords | and | King | | of kings | – and | | with | him | will be | his | called, | chosen | and
ὅτι | ἐστιν | κύριος | κυρίων | καὶ | βασιλεὺς | βασιλέων | καὶ | οἱ | μετ᾽ | αὐτοῦ | | κλητοὶ | καὶ | ἐκλεκτοὶ | καὶ
cj | v.pai.3s | n.nsm | n.gpm | cj | n.nsm | n.gpm | cj | d.npm | p.g | r.gsm.3 | | a.npm | cj | a.npm | cj
4022 | 1639 | 3261 | 3261 | 2779 | 995 | 995 | 2779 | 3836 | 3552 | 899 | | 3105 | 2779 | 1723 | 2779

faithful | followers." | ¶ | **15** Then | the angel | said | to me, | "The | waters | | you saw, | where | the | prostitute | sits, | are
πιστοί | | | Καὶ | | λέγει | μοι | τὰ | ὕδατα | ἃ → | εἶδες | οὗ | ἡ | πόρνη | κάθηται | εἰσιν
a.npm | | | cj | | v.pai.3s | r.ds.1 | d.npn | n.npn | r.apn | v.aai.2s | adv | d.nsf | n.nsf | v.pmi.3s | v.pai.3p
4412 | | | 2779 | | 3306 | 1609 | 3836 | 5623 | 4005 | 1625 | 4023 | 3836 | 4520 | 2764 | 1639

peoples, | | multitudes, | | nations | and | languages. | **16** | The | beast | and | the | ten | horns | | you saw | will
λαοὶ | καὶ ὄχλοι | | καὶ ἔθνη | καὶ | γλῶσσαι | | καὶ | τὸ | θηρίον | καὶ | τὰ | δέκα | κέρατα | ἃ → | εἶδες | οὗτοι →
n.npm | cj n.npm | | cj n.npn | cj | n.npf | | cj | d.nsn | n.nsn | cj | d.npn | a.npn | n.npn | r.apn | v.aai.2s | r.npm
3295 | 2779 4063 | | 2779 1620 | 2779 | 1185 | | 2779 | 3836 | 2563 | 2779 | 3836 | 1274 | 3043 | 4005 | 1625 | 4047

κεφαλὰς καὶ τὰ δέκα κέρατα. **8** τὸ θηρίον ὃ εἶδες ἦν καὶ οὐκ ἔστιν καὶ μέλλει ἀναβαίνειν ἐκ τῆς ἀβύσσου καὶ εἰς ἀπώλειαν ὑπάγει, καὶ θαυμασθήσονται οἱ κατοικοῦντες ἐπὶ τῆς γῆς, ὧν οὐ γέγραπται τὸ ὄνομα ἐπὶ τὸ βιβλίον τῆς ζωῆς ἀπὸ καταβολῆς κόσμου, βλεπόντων τὸ θηρίον ὅτι ἦν καὶ οὐκ ἔστιν καὶ παρέσται ¶ **9** ὧδε ὁ νοῦς ὁ ἔχων σοφίαν. αἱ ἑπτὰ κεφαλαὶ ἑπτὰ ὄρη εἰσίν, ὅπου ἡ γυνὴ κάθηται ἐπ᾽ αὐτῶν. καὶ βασιλεῖς ἑπτά εἰσιν· **10** οἱ πέντε ἔπεσαν, ὁ εἷς ἔστιν, ὁ ἄλλος οὔπω ἦλθεν, καὶ ὅταν ἔλθῃ ὀλίγον αὐτὸν δεῖ μεῖναι. **11** καὶ τὸ θηρίον ὃ ἦν καὶ οὐκ ἔστιν καὶ αὐτὸς ὄγδοός ἐστιν καὶ ἐκ τῶν ἑπτά ἐστιν, καὶ εἰς ἀπώλειαν ὑπάγει. ¶ **12** καὶ τὰ δέκα κέρατα ἃ εἶδες δέκα βασιλεῖς εἰσιν, οἵτινες βασιλείαν οὔπω ἔλαβον, ἀλλὰ ἐξουσίαν ὡς βασιλεῖς μίαν ὥραν λαμβάνουσιν μετὰ τοῦ θηρίου. **13** οὗτοι μίαν γνώμην ἔχουσιν καὶ τὴν δύναμιν καὶ ἐξουσίαν αὐτῶν τῷ θηρίῳ διδόασιν. **14** οὗτοι μετὰ τοῦ ἀρνίου πολεμήσουσιν καὶ τὸ ἀρνίον νικήσει αὐτούς, ὅτι κύριος κυρίων ἐστὶν καὶ βασιλεὺς βασιλέων καὶ οἱ μετ᾽ αὐτοῦ κλητοὶ καὶ ἐκλεκτοὶ καὶ πιστοί. ¶ **15** Καὶ λέγει μοι, Τὰ ὕδατα ἃ εἶδες οὗ ἡ πόρνη κάθηται, λαοὶ καὶ ὄχλοι εἰσὶν καὶ ἔθνη καὶ γλῶσσαι. **16** καὶ τὰ δέκα κέρατα ἃ εἶδες καὶ τὸ θηρίον οὗτοι μισήσουσιν τὴν πόρνην καὶ

hate | the prostitute. | They will bring | | → | her | to ruin | and | leave | her | naked; | | they will eat | her
μισήσουσιν | τὴν πόρνην | καὶ | | → | ποιήσουσιν | αὐτὴν | ἠρημωμένην | καὶ | | γυμνὴν | καὶ | → | φάγονται | αὐτῆς
v.fai.3p | d.asf n.asf | cj | | | v.fai.3p | r.asf.3 | pt.rp.asf | cj | | a.asf | cj | | v.fmi.3p | r.gsf.3
3631 | 3836 4520 | 2779 | | | 4472 | 899 | 2246 | 2779 | | 1218 | 2779 | | 2266 | 899

flesh | and | burn | her | with | fire. | **17** For | God | | has put | it into | their | hearts | | to accomplish | his
ⸯτὰς σάρκαςⸯ | καὶ | κατακαύσουσιν | αὐτὴν | ἐν | πυρί | γὰρ | ὁ θεός | → | ἔδωκεν | εἰς | αὐτῶν | ⸯτὰς καρδίαςⸯ | | ποιῆσαι | αὐτοῦ
d.apf n.apf | cj | v.fai.3p | r.asf.3 | p.d | n.dsn | cj | d.nsm n.nsm | | v.aai.3s | p.a | r.gpm.3 | d.apf n.apf | | f.aa | r.gsm.3
3836 4922 | 2779 | 2876 | 899 | 1877 | 4786 | 1142 | 3836 2536 | | 1443 | 1650 | 899 | 3836 2840 | | 4472 | 899

purpose | | by agreeing | | | to give | the beast | their | power | to rule, | | until | God's | words
ⸯτὴν γνώμηνⸯ | καὶ | → ⸯποιῆσαι | μίαν | γνώμηνⸯ | καὶ | → δοῦναι | τῷ θηρίῳ | αὐτῶν | → | → | ⸯτὴν βασιλείανⸯ | ἄχρι | ⸯτοῦ θεοῦⸯ | οἱ λόγοι
d.asf n.asf | cj | f.aa | a.asf | n.asf | cj | f.aa | d.dsn n.dsn | r.gpm.3 | | | d.asf n.asf | c.g | d.gsm n.gsm | d.npm n.npm
3836 1191 | 2779 | 4472 | 1651 | 1191 | 2779 | 1443 | 3836 2563 | 899 | | | 3836 993 | 948 | 3836 2536 | 3836 3364

are fulfilled. | **18** | The | woman | | you saw | is | | the | great | city | that | rules | | over | the kings | of the
→ τελεσθήσονται | καὶ | ἡ | γυνὴ | ἣν | → εἶδες | ἔστιν | ἡ | ἡ μεγάλη | πόλις | ἡ | ⸯἔχουσα | βασιλείανⸯ | ἐπὶ | τῶν βασιλέων | → τῆς
v.fpi.3p | cj | d.nsf | n.nsf | r.asf | v.aai.2s | v.pai.3s | d.nsf | d.nsf a.nsf | n.nsf | d.nsf | pt.pa.nsf | n.asf | p.g | d.gpm n.gpm | d.gsf
5464 | 2779 | 3836 | 1222 | 4005 | 1625 | 1639 | 3836 | 3836 3489 | 4484 | 3836 | 2400 | 993 | 2093 | 3836 995 | 3836

earth."
γῆς
n.gsf
1178

The Fall of Babylon

18:1 After this | | I saw | another | angel | coming | | down | from | heaven. | | He had | | great | authority, | and | the
Μετὰ ταῦτα | → | εἶδον | ἄλλον | ἄγγελον | καταβαίνοντα | ← | ἐκ | | τοῦ οὐρανοῦ | | ἔχοντα | μεγάλην | ἐξουσίαν | καὶ | ἡ
p.a r.apn | | v.aai.1s | r.asm | n.asm | pt.pa.asm | | p.g | | d.gsm n.gsm | | pt.pa.asm | a.asf | n.asf | cj | d.nsf
3552 4047 | | 1625 | 257 | 34 | 2849 | | 1666 | | 3836 4041 | | 2400 | 3489 | 2026 | 2779 | 3836

earth | was | illuminated | by | his | splendor. | **2** | With | a mighty | voice | he shouted: | | "Fallen! | Fallen is | Babylon | the
γῆ | → | ἐφωτίσθη | ἐκ | αὐτοῦ | ⸯτῆς δόξηςⸯ | καὶ | ἐν | ἰσχυρᾷ | φωνῇ | → ἔκραξεν | λέγων | ἔπεσεν | ἔπεσεν | Βαβυλὼν | ἡ
n.nsf | | v.api.3s | p.g | r.gsm.3 | d.gsf n.gsf | cj | p.d | a.dsf | n.dsf | v.aai.3s | pt.pa.nsm | v.aai.3s | v.aai.3s | n.nsf | d.nsf
1178 | | 5894 | 1666 | 899 | 3836 1518 | 2779 | 1877 | 2708 | 5889 | 3189 | 3306 | 4406 | 4406 | 956 | 3836

Great! | She has | → | become | a home | | for demons | and | a haunt | for | every | evil | spirit, | | a haunt | for
μεγάλη | καὶ | → | ἐγένετο | κατοικητήριον | | δαιμονίων | καὶ | φυλακὴ | → | παντὸς | ἀκαθάρτου | πνεύματος | καὶ | φυλακὴ |
a.nsf | cj | | v.ami.3s | n.nsn | | n.gpn | cj | n.nsf | | a.gsn | a.gsn | n.gsn | cj | n.nsf |
3489 | 2779 | | 1181 | 2999 | | 1228 | 2779 | 5871 | | 4246 | 176 | 4460 | 2779 | 5871 |

every | unclean | | | | | and | detestable | bird. | **3** For | all | | the nations | have drunk
παντὸς | ἀκαθάρτου | [καὶ | φυλακὴ | παντὸς | θηρίου | ἀκαθάρτου] | καὶ | μεμισημένου | ὀρνέου | ὅτι | πάντα | τὰ ἔθνη | → | πέπωκαν ἐκ
a.gsn | a.gsn | cj | n.nsf | a.gsn | n.gsn | a.gsn | cj | pt.rp.gsn | n.gsn | cj | a.npn | d.npn n.npn | | v.rai.3p | p.g
4246 | 176 | 2779 | 5871 | 4246 | 2563 | 176 | 2779 | 3631 | 3997 | 4022 | 4246 | 3836 1620 | | 4403 | 1666

the maddening | wine | of | her | adulteries. | | The kings | of the earth | committed | | adultery | with | her, | and | the
τοῦ ⸯτοῦ θυμοῦⸯ | οἴνουⸯ | → | αὐτῆς | ⸯτῆς πορνείαςⸯ | καὶ | οἱ | βασιλεῖς | → τῆς γῆς | → | | ἐπόρνευσαν | μετ᾽ | αὐτῆς | καὶ | οἱ
d.gsm d.gsm n.gsm | n.gsm | | r.gsf.3 | d.gsf n.gsf | cj | d.npm | n.npm | d.gsf n.gsf | | | v.aai.3p | p.g | r.gsf.3 | cj | d.npm
3836 3836 2596 | 3885 | | 4518 899 | 3836 4518 | 2779 | 3836 | 995 | 3836 1178 | | | 4519 | 3552 | 899 | 2779 | 3836

merchants | of the earth | grew rich | | from | her | excessive | luxuries." | ¶ | **4** Then | I heard | another | voice
ἔμποροι | → τῆς γῆς | → ἐπλούτησαν ἐκ | | | αὐτῆς | ⸯτῆς δυνάμεωςⸯ | ⸯτοῦ στρήνουςⸯ | | Καὶ | → ἤκουσα | ἄλλην | φωνὴν
n.npm | d.gsf n.gsf | v.aai.3p | p.g | | r.gsf.3 | d.gsf n.gsf | d.gsn n.gsn | | cj | v.aai.1s | r.asf | n.asf
1867 | 3836 1178 | 4456 | 1666 | | 899 | 3836 1539 | 3836 5140 | | 2779 | 201 | 257 | 5889

from | heaven | say: | "Come out of | her, | my | people, | so that | | you will | not | share | | in her
ἐκ | ⸯτοῦ οὐρανοῦⸯ | λέγουσαν | ἐξέλθατε | ← ἐξ | αὐτῆς | μου | ⸯὁ λαόςⸯ | ἵνα | → | | μὴ | συγκοινωνήσητε | → | αὐτῆς
p.g | d.gsm n.gsm | pt.pa.asf | v.aam.2p | p.g r.gsf.3 | | r.gs.1 | d.vsm n.vsm | cj | | | pl | v.aas.2p | | r.gsf.3
1666 | 3836 4041 | 3306 | 2002 | 1666 899 | | 1609 | 3836 3295 | 2671 | | | 3590 | 5170 | | 899

sins, | so that | | you | will | not | receive | any of | her | plagues; | **5** for | her | sins | | are | piled | up
ⸯταῖς ἁμαρτίαιςⸯ | καὶ | ἵνα | ← | | → μὴ | λάβητε | ἐκ | αὐτῆς | ⸯτῶν πληγῶνⸯ | ὅτι | αὐτῆς | ⸯαἱ ἁμαρτίαιⸯ | → | | ἐκολλήθησαν | ←
d.dpf n.dpf | cj | cj | | | pl | v.aas.2p | p.g | r.gsf.3 | d.gpf n.gpf | cj | r.gsf.3 | d.npf n.npf | | | v.api.3p |
3836 281 | 2779 | 2671 | | | 3590 | 3284 | 1666 | 899 | 3836 4435 | 4022 | 899 | 3836 281 | | | 3140 |

to | heaven, | and | God | | has remembered | her | crimes. | **6** Give | back | to her | as | | she | has given;
ἄχρι | ⸯτοῦ οὐρανοῦⸯ | καὶ | ⸯὁ θεόςⸯ | → | ἐμνημόνευσεν | αὐτῆς | ⸯτὰ ἀδικήματαⸯ | ἀπόδοτε | ← | → αὐτῇ | ὡς | καὶ | αὐτὴ | → | ἀπέδωκεν καὶ
p.g | d.gsm n.gsm | cj | d.nsm n.nsm | | v.aai.3s | r.gsf.3 | d.apn n.apn | v.aam.2p | | r.dsf.3 | cj | adv | r.nsf | | v.aai.3s cj
948 | 3836 4041 | 2779 | 3836 2536 | | 3648 | 899 | 3836 93 | 625 | | 899 | 6055 | 2779 | 899 | | 625 2779

ἠρημωμένην ποιήσουσιν αὐτὴν καὶ γυμνὴν καὶ τὰς σάρκας αὐτῆς φάγονται καὶ αὐτὴν κατακαύσουσιν ἐν πυρί. **17** ὁ γὰρ θεὸς ἔδωκεν εἰς τὰς καρδίας αὐτῶν ποιῆσαι τὴν γνώμην αὐτοῦ καὶ ποιῆσαι μίαν γνώμην καὶ δοῦναι τὴν βασιλείαν αὐτῶν τῷ θηρίῳ ἄχρι τελεσθήσονται οἱ λόγοι τοῦ θεοῦ. **18** καὶ ἡ γυνὴ ἣν εἶδες ἔστιν ἡ πόλις ἡ μεγάλη ἡ ἔχουσα βασιλείαν ἐπὶ τῶν βασιλέων τῆς γῆς.

18:1 Μετὰ ταῦτα εἶδον ἄλλον ἄγγελον καταβαίνοντα ἐκ τοῦ οὐρανοῦ ἔχοντα ἐξουσίαν μεγάλην, καὶ ἡ γῆ ἐφωτίσθη ἐκ τῆς δόξης αὐτοῦ. **2** καὶ ἔκραξεν ἐν ἰσχυρᾷ φωνῇ λέγων, Ἔπεσεν ἔπεσεν Βαβυλὼν ἡ μεγάλη, καὶ ἐγένετο κατοικητήριον δαιμονίων καὶ φυλακὴ παντὸς πνεύματος ἀκαθάρτου καὶ φυλακὴ παντὸς ὀρνέου ἀκαθάρτου [καὶ φυλακὴ παντὸς θηρίου ἀκαθάρτου] καὶ μεμισημένου, **3** ὅτι ἐκ τοῦ οἴνου τοῦ θυμοῦ τῆς πορνείας αὐτῆς πέπωκαν πάντα τὰ ἔθνη καὶ οἱ βασιλεῖς τῆς γῆς μετ᾽ αὐτῆς ἐπόρνευσαν καὶ οἱ ἔμποροι τῆς γῆς ἐκ τῆς δυνάμεως τοῦ στρήνους αὐτῆς ἐπλούτησαν. ¶ **4** Καὶ ἤκουσα ἄλλην φωνὴν ἐκ τοῦ οὐρανοῦ λέγουσαν, Ἐξέλθατε ὁ λαός μου ἐξ αὐτῆς ἵνα μὴ συγκοινωνήσητε ταῖς ἁμαρτίαις αὐτῆς, καὶ ἐκ τῶν πληγῶν αὐτῆς ἵνα μὴ λάβητε, **5** ὅτι ἐκολλήθησαν αὐτῆς αἱ ἁμαρτίαι ἄχρι τοῦ οὐρανοῦ καὶ ἐμνημόνευσεν ὁ θεὸς τὰ ἀδικήματα αὐτῆς. **6** ἀπόδοτε

pay   her back double   for what   she has done. Mix   her a double portion from her own cup.
διπλώσατε ←   τὰ διπλᾶ   κατὰ τὰ ἔργα αὐτῆς   ←   κεράσατε αὐτῇ διπλοῦν   ἐν τῷ   ποτηρίῳ ᾧ
v.aam.2p   d.apn a.apn   p.a d.apn n.apn r.gsf.3   v.aam.2p r.dsf.3 a.asn   p.d d.dsn   n.dsn r.dsn
1488   3836 1487   2848 3836 2240 899   2240   3042 899 1487   1877 3836   4539 4005

7 Give her as   much torture   and grief as the glory   and luxury   she gave herself.   In her
ἐκέρασεν δότε αὐτῇ τοσοῦτον ←   βασανισμὸν καὶ πένθος ὅσα   ἐδόξασεν καὶ ἐστρηνίασεν ←   αὐτὴν ὅτι ἐν αὐτῆς
v.aai.3s v.aam.2p r.dsf.3 r.asm   n.asm   cj n.asn r.apn   v.aai.3s cj v.aai.3s   r.asf.3 cj p.d r.gsf.3
3042 1443 899 5537   990   2779 4292 4012   1519 2779 5139   899 4022 1877 899

heart   she boasts,   'I sit   as queen;   I am not a widow, and I   will never mourn.'   **8** Therefore
τῇ καρδίᾳ → λέγει ὅτι → κάθημαι βασίλισσα καὶ → εἰμι οὐκ χήρα καὶ → → οὐ μὴ ἴδω πένθος   διὰ τοῦτο
d.dsf n.dsf   v.pai.3s cj v.pmi.1s n.nsf   cj v.pai.1s pl n.nsf cj   pl pl v.aas.1s n.asn   p.a r.asn
3836 2840   3306 4022 2764 999   2779 1639 4024 5939 2779   1625 1625 4024 3590 1625 4292   1328 4047

in one day her plagues   will overtake her: death,   mourning and famine.   She will be consumed   by
ἐν μιᾷ ἡμέρᾳ αὐτῆς αἱ πληγαὶ → ἥξουσιν   θάνατος καὶ πένθος   καὶ λιμός   καὶ →   → κατακαυθήσεται ἐν
p.d a.dsf n.dsf r.gsf.3 d.npf n.npf   v.fai.3p   n.nsm   cj n.nsn   cj n.nsm   cj   v.fpi.3s   p.d
1877 1651 2465 899 3836 4435   2457   2505   2779 4292   2779 3350   2779   2876   1877

fire, for mighty is the Lord God   who judges her. ¶   **9**   "When the kings   of the earth who committed
πυρὶ ὅτι ἰσχυρὸς   κύριος ὁ θεὸς ὁ   κρίνας αὐτήν   Καὶ ὅταν οἱ   βασιλεῖς → τῆς γῆς οἱ
n.dsf cj a.nsm   n.nsm d.nsm n.nsm d.nsm   pt.aa.nsm r.asf.3   cj cj d.npm   n.npm   d.gsf n.gsf d.npm
4786 4022 2708   3261 3836 2536 3836   3212 899   2779 4020 3836   995   3836 1178 3836

adultery with her   and shared her luxury   see   the smoke of her burning,   they will weep   and
πορνεύσαντες μετ᾽ αὐτῆς καὶ   →   στρηνιάσαντες βλέπωσιν τὸν καπνὸν → αὐτῆς τῆς πυρώσεως →   → κλαύσουσιν καὶ
pt.aa.npm p.g r.gsf.3 cj   pt.aa.npm   v.pas.3p d.asm n.asm   r.gsf.3 d.gsf n.gsf   v.fai.3p cj
4519 3552 899 2779   5139   1063 3836 2837   4796 899 3836 4796   3081 2779

mourn   over her.   **10**   Terrified at her   torment,   they will stand   far   off and cry: "Woe! Woe,
κόψονται ἐπ᾽ αὐτὴν διὰ τὸν φόβον → αὐτῆς τοῦ βασανισμοῦ → → ἑστηκότες ἀπὸ μακρόθεν ← λέγοντες οὐαὶ οὐαί
v.fmi.3p p.a r.asf.3   p.a d.asm n.asm   r.gsf.3 d.gsm n.gsm   pt.ra.npm p.g adv   pt.pa.npm j j
3164 2093 899   1328 3836 5832   990 899 990   2705 608 3427   3306 4026 4026

O great   city,   O Babylon, city   of power!   In one hour your doom   has come!' ¶   **11**
→ ἡ μεγάλη ἡ πόλις   Βαβυλὼν ἡ πόλις   ἡ ἰσχυρά ὅτι → μιᾷ ὥρᾳ σου ἡ κρίσις   ἦλθεν   Καὶ
d.vsf a.vsf d.vsf n.vsf   n.vsf   d.vsf n.vsf   d.vsf a.vsf cj   a.dsf n.dsf r.gs.2 d.nsf n.nsf   v.aai.3s   cj
3836 3489 3836 4484   956   3836 4484   3836 2708 4022   1651 6052 5148 3836 3213   2262   2779

"The merchants of the earth will weep   and mourn   over her because no   one buys   their cargoes   any
οἱ ἔμποροι → τῆς γῆς → κλαίουσιν καὶ πενθοῦσιν ἐπ᾽ αὐτήν ὅτι   οὐδεὶς → ἀγοράζει αὐτῶν τὸν γόμον οὐκέτι
d.npm n.npm   d.gsf n.gsf   v.pai.3p cj v.pai.3p p.a r.asf.3 cj   a.nsm   v.pai.3s r.gpm.3 d.asm n.asm adv
3836 1867   3836 1178   3081 2779 4291 2093 899 4022   4029   60 899 3836 1203 4033

more – **12** cargoes of gold,   silver,   precious stones and pearls;   fine linen,   purple,   silk   and
← γόμον   χρυσοῦ καὶ ἀργύρου καὶ τιμίου   λίθου   καὶ μαργαριτῶν καὶ   βυσσίνου καὶ πορφύρας καὶ σιρικοῦ καὶ
n.asm   n.gsm cj n.gsm cj a.gsm   n.gsm   cj n.gpm   cj   a.gsn cj n.gsf   cj n.gsf cj
1203   5996 2779 738 2779 5508   3345   2779 3449   2779   1115 2779 4525   2779 4986 2779

scarlet cloth;   every sort of citron wood, and articles of every kind made of ivory,   costly
κοκκίνου ←   καὶ πᾶν ←   ← θύϊνον ξύλον καὶ σκεῦος   πᾶν ←   →   ᾽ ἐλεφάντινον καὶ πᾶν σκεῦος ἐκ τιμιωτάτου
a.gsn   cj a.asn   a.asn n.asn cj n.asn   a.asn   a.asn   cj a.asn n.asn p.g a.gsn.s
3132   2779 4246   2591 3833 2779 5007   4246   1804   2779 4246 5007 1666 5508

wood,   bronze,   iron   and marble;   **13**   cargoes of cinnamon and spice,   of incense,   myrrh and
ξύλου   καὶ χαλκοῦ   καὶ σιδήρου καὶ μαρμάρου   καὶ   κιννάμωμον καὶ ἄμωμον καὶ   θυμιάματα καὶ μύρον καὶ
n.gsn   cj n.gsm   cj n.gsm cj n.gsn   cj   n.asn   cj n.asn   cj   n.apn   cj n.asn cj
3833   2779 5910   2779 4970 2779 3454   2779   3077   2779 319   2779   2592   2779 3693 2779

frankincense,   of wine and olive oil,   of fine flour   and wheat;   cattle and sheep;   horses and
λίβανον   καὶ οἶνον καὶ ἔλαιον   καὶ   σεμίδαλιν καὶ σῖτον   καὶ κτήνη καὶ πρόβατα καὶ ἵππων καὶ
n.asm   cj n.asm cj n.asn   cj   n.asf   cj n.asm   cj n.apn   cj n.apn   cj n.gpm   cj
3337   2779 3885 2779 1778   2779   4947   2779 4992   2779 3229   2779 4585   2779 2691 2779

carriages; and bodies and souls of men.   ¶   **14**   "They will say, 'The fruit you longed   for is
ῥεδῶν   καὶ σωμάτων καὶ ψυχὰς → ἀνθρώπων   καὶ   ἡ   ὀπώρα σου τῆς ἐπιθυμίας τῆς ψυχῆς ← →
n.gpf   cj n.gpn   cj n.apf   n.gpm   cj   d.nsf   n.nsf r.gs.2 d.gsf n.gsf   d.gsf n.gsf
4832   2779 5393   2779 6034   476   2779   3836   3967 5148 3836 2123   3836 6034   2123

αὐτῇ ὡς καὶ αὐτὴ ἀπέδωκεν καὶ διπλώσατε τὰ διπλᾶ κατὰ τὰ ἔργα αὐτῆς, ἐν τῷ ποτηρίῳ ᾧ ἐκέρασεν κεράσατε αὐτῇ διπλοῦν, ⁷ ὅσα ἐδόξασεν αὐτὴν καὶ ἐστρηνίασεν, τοσοῦτον δότε αὐτῇ βασανισμὸν καὶ πένθος. ὅτι ἐν τῇ καρδίᾳ αὐτῆς λέγει ὅτι Κάθημαι βασίλισσα καὶ χήρα οὐκ εἰμι καὶ πένθος οὐ μὴ ἴδω. ⁸ διὰ τοῦτο ἐν μιᾷ ἡμέρᾳ ἥξουσιν αἱ πληγαὶ αὐτῆς, θάνατος καὶ πένθος καὶ λιμός, καὶ ἐν πυρὶ κατακαυθήσεται, ὅτι ἰσχυρὸς κύριος ὁ θεὸς ὁ κρίνας αὐτήν. ¶ ⁹ Καὶ κλαύσουσιν καὶ κόψονται ἐπ᾽ αὐτὴν οἱ βασιλεῖς τῆς γῆς οἱ μετ᾽ αὐτῆς πορνεύσαντες καὶ στρηνιάσαντες, ὅταν βλέπωσιν τὸν καπνὸν τῆς πυρώσεως αὐτῆς, ¹⁰ ἀπὸ μακρόθεν ἑστηκότες διὰ τὸν φόβον τοῦ βασανισμοῦ αὐτῆς λέγοντες, Οὐαὶ οὐαί, ἡ πόλις ἡ μεγάλη, Βαβυλὼν ἡ πόλις ἡ ἰσχυρά, ὅτι μιᾷ ὥρᾳ ἦλθεν ἡ κρίσις σου. ¶ ¹¹ Καὶ οἱ ἔμποροι τῆς γῆς κλαίουσιν καὶ πενθοῦσιν ἐπ᾽ αὐτήν, ὅτι τὸν γόμον αὐτῶν οὐδεὶς ἀγοράζει οὐκέτι ¹² γόμον χρυσοῦ καὶ ἀργύρου καὶ λίθου τιμίου καὶ μαργαριτῶν καὶ βυσσίνου καὶ πορφύρας καὶ σιρικοῦ καὶ κοκκίνου, καὶ πᾶν ξύλον θύϊνον καὶ πᾶν σκεῦος ἐλεφάντινον καὶ πᾶν σκεῦος ἐκ ξύλου τιμιωτάτου καὶ χαλκοῦ καὶ σιδήρου καὶ μαρμάρου, ¹³ καὶ κιννάμωμον καὶ ἄμωμον καὶ θυμιάματα καὶ μύρον καὶ λίβανον καὶ οἶνον καὶ ἔλαιον καὶ σεμίδαλιν καὶ σῖτον καὶ κτήνη καὶ πρόβατα, καὶ ἵππων καὶ ῥεδῶν καὶ σωμάτων, καὶ ψυχὰς ἀνθρώπων. ¶ ¹⁴ καὶ ἡ ὀπώρα σου τῆς ἐπιθυμίας

gone | from you. | All | your | riches | and | splendor | | have vanished, | | | never | | to be recovered.'
ἀπῆλθεν | ἀπὸ | σοῦ | καὶ | πάντα τὰ | λιπαρὰ | καὶ | τὰ λαμπρὰ → | ἀπώλετο | ἀπὸ | σοῦ καὶ | οὐκέτι | οὐ | μὴ → → | εὑρήσουσιν
v.aai.3s | p.g | r.gs.2 | cj | a.npn d.npn | n.npn | cj | d.npn a.npn | v.ami.3s | p.g | r.gs.2 cj | adv | pl | pl | v.fai.3p
599 | 608 | 5148 | 2779 | 4246 3836 | 3353 | 2779 | 3836 3287 | 660 | 608 | 5148 2779 | 4033 | 4024 | 3590 | 2351

15 The | merchants | who | sold | these | things | and | gained | their | wealth | | from | her | will | stand | far
αὐτὰ | Οἱ | ἔμποροι | | τούτων ← | → | → | οἱ | πλουτήσαντες | ἀπ' | αὐτῆς → | στήσονται | ἀπὸ μακρόθεν
r.apn.3 | | n.npm | | r.gpn | | | d.npm | a.aa.npm | p.g | r.gsf.3 | v.fmi.3p | p.g adv
899 | 3836 | 1867 | | 4047 | | | 3836 | 4456 | 608 | 899 | 2705 | 608 3427

off, | terrified | at her | torment. | | They will weep | and | mourn | **16** and | cry | | out: "'Woe! | Woe, O
← | διὰ τὸν φόβον | αὐτῆς | τοῦ βασανισμοῦ | → | → κλαίοντες | καὶ | πενθοῦντες | | λέγοντες ← | | οὐαὶ | οὐαί
| p.a d.asm n.asm | r.gsf.3 | d.gsm n.gsm | | pt.pa.npm | cj | pt.pa.npm | | pt.pa.npm | | j | j
| 1328 3836 5832 | 899 | 3836 990 | | 3081 | 2779 | 4291 | | 3306 | | 4026 | 4026

great | city, | dressed | | in fine linen, | | purple | and scarlet, | and | glittering | with | gold,
ἡ μεγάλη | ἡ πόλις | ἡ περιβεβλημένη ← | → | βύσσινον | καὶ | πορφυροῦν | καὶ | κόκκινον | καὶ | κεχρυσωμένη | ἐν | χρυσίῳ | καὶ
d.vsf a.vsf | d.vsf n.vsf | d.vsf pt.rp.vsf | | a.asn | cj | a.asn | cj | a.asn | cj | pt.rp.vsf | p.d | n.dsn | cj
3836 3489 | 3836 4484 | 3836 4314 | | 1115 | 2779 | 4528 | 2779 | 3132 | 2779 | 5998 | 1877 | 5992 | 2779

precious | stones | and pearls! | **17** | In | one | hour | such | | great | wealth | | has been brought to ruin!' | | ¶
τιμίῳ | λίθῳ | καὶ μαργαρίτῃ | ὅτι → | μιᾷ | ὥρᾳ | τοσοῦτος | | ὁ πλοῦτος | → | → | → ἠρημώθη | | Καὶ
a.dsm | n.dsm | cj n.dsm | cj | a.dsf | n.dsf | r.nsm | | d.nsm n.nsm | | | v.api.3s | | cj
5508 | 3345 | 2779 3449 | 4022 | 1651 | 6052 | 5537 | | 3836 4458 | | | 2246 | | 2779

"Every | sea captain, | and | all | who travel | | by ship, | | the sailors, and | all | who | earn | | their living from
πᾶς | → κυβερνήτης | καὶ | πᾶς ὁ | ἐπὶ τόπον πλέων ← | → | καὶ | ναῦται | καὶ | ὅσοι | → | ἐργάζονται ←
a.nsm | n.nsm | cj | a.nsm d.nsm | p.a n.asm pt.pa.nsm | | cj | n.npm | cj | r.npm | | v.pmi.3p
4246 | 3237 | 2779 | 4246 3836 | 2093 5536 4434 | | 2779 | 3731 | 2779 | 4012 | | 2237

the sea, | | will stand | far | | off. **18** | When | they see | | the | smoke | of her | burning, | | they will
τὴν θάλασσαν | → | ἔστησαν | ἀπὸ μακρόθεν | ← | καὶ → | → | βλέποντες | τὸν | καπνὸν | αὐτῆς | τῆς πυρώσεως | →
d.asf n.asf | | v.aai.3p | p.g adv | | cj | | pt.pa.npm | d.asm | n.asm | r.gsf.3 | d.gsf n.gsf
3836 2498 | | 2705 | 608 3427 | | 2779 | | 1063 | 3836 | 2837 | 4796 | 899 3836 4796

exclaim, | | 'Was there | ever | a city | like | this great | | city?' **19** | They will | throw | dust | on | their | heads, | | and
ἔκραζον | λέγοντες | τίς | | ὁμοία | τῇ | τῇ μεγάλῃ | πόλει | καὶ | → | ἔβαλον | χοῦν | ἐπὶ | αὐτῶν | τὰς κεφαλὰς | καὶ
v.iai.3p | pt.pa.npm | r.nsf | | a.nsf | d.dsf | d.dsf a.dsf | n.dsf | cj | | v.aai.3p | n.asm | p.a | r.gpm.3 | d.apf n.apf | cj
3189 | 3306 | 5515 | | 3927 | 3836 | 3836 3489 | 4484 | 2779 | | 965 | 5967 | 2093 | 899 | 3836 3051 | 2779

with | weeping | and | mourning | cry | out: | | "'Woe! | Woe, O | great | | city, | | where | all | | who had
→ | κλαίοντες | καὶ | πενθοῦντες | ἔκραζον ← | λέγοντες | οὐαὶ | | οὐαί | → ἡ μεγάλη | ἡ πόλις | | ἐν ᾗ | πάντες | οἱ | ἔχοντες
| pt.pa.npm | cj | pt.pa.npm | v.iai.3p | pt.pa.npm | j | | j | d.vsf a.vsf | d.vsf n.vsf | | p.d r.dsf | a.npm | d.npm | pt.pa.npm
| 3081 | 2779 | 4291 | 3306 | 3306 | 4026 | | 4026 | 3836 3489 | 3836 4484 | | 1877 4005 | 4246 | 3836 | 2400

ships | on the sea | | became rich | | through her | wealth! | | In one | hour | she has been brought to
τὰ πλοῖα | ἐν τῇ θαλάσσῃ | → | ἐπλούτησαν | ἐκ | αὐτῆς | τῆς τιμιότητος | ὅτι → | μιᾷ | ὥρᾳ | → | →
d.apn n.apn | p.d d.dsf n.dsf | | v.aai.3p | p.g | r.gsf.3 | d.gsf n.gsf | cj | a.dsf | n.dsf
3836 4450 | 1877 3836 2498 | | 4456 | 1666 | 899 | 3836 5509 | 4022 | 1651 | 6052

ruin! | **20** Rejoice | over her, | O heaven! | Rejoice, | | saints | and | apostles | and | prophets! | | God | has
ἠρημώθη | Εὐφραίνου | ἐπ' | αὐτῇ | οὐρανὲ | καὶ | οἱ ἅγιοι | καὶ | οἱ ἀπόστολοι | καὶ | οἱ προφῆται | ὅτι | ὁ θεὸς | →
v.api.3s | v.ppm.2s | p.d | r.dsf.3 | n.vsm | cj | d.vpm a.vpm | cj | d.vpm n.vpm | cj | d.vpm n.vpm | cj | d.nsm n.nsm
2246 | 2370 | 2093 | 899 | 4041 | 2779 | 3836 41 | 2779 | 3836 693 | 2779 | 3836 4737 | 4022 | 3836 2536

judged | her | for the way | she | treated | you.'" | ¶ | **21** Then | a | mighty | angel | picked up | a boulder | the size | of a
ἔκρινεν | ἐξ | → | αὐτῆς | τὸ κρίμα | ὑμῶν | | Καὶ | εἷς | ἰσχυρὸς | ἄγγελος | ἦρεν | → | λίθον | → | ὡς →
v.aai.3s | p.g | | r.gsf.3 | d.asn n.asn | r.gp.2 | | cj | a.nsm | a.nsm | n.nsm | v.aai.3s | | n.asm | | pl
3212 | 1666 3210 | 3210 | 899 | 3836 3210 | 7007 | | 2779 | 1651 | 2708 | 34 | 149 | | 3345 | | 6055

large | millstone | and | threw | it | into | the | sea, | | and said: | "With such | violence | the | great | city | of Babylon | will be
μέγαν | μύλινον | καὶ | ἔβαλεν | εἰς | τὴν | θάλασσαν | λέγων | | οὕτως | ὁρμήματι | ἡ | μεγάλη | πόλις | → Βαβυλὼν | →
a.asm | a.asm | cj | v.aai.3s | p.a | d.asf | n.asf | pt.pa.nsm | | adv | n.dsn | d.nsf | a.nsf | n.nsf | n.nsf
3489 | 3684 | 2779 | 965 | 1650 | 3836 | 2498 | 3306 | | 4048 | 3996 | 3836 | 3489 | 4484 | 956

thrown | down, | | never | to be | found | again. **22** | | The music | of | harpists | and | musicians, | | flute | players | and
βληθήσεται ← | καὶ | οὐ μὴ | → | εὑρεθῇ | ἔτι | καὶ | | φωνὴ | → | κιθαρῳδῶν | καὶ | μουσικῶν | καὶ | αὐλητῶν | καὶ
v.fpi.3s | cj | pl pl | → | v.aps.3s | adv | cj | | n.nsf | | n.gpm | cj | n.gpm | cj | n.gpm | cj
965 | 2779 | 4024 3590 | | 2351 | 2285 | 2779 | | 5889 | | 3069 | 2779 | 3676 | 2779 | 886 | 2779

τῆς ψυχῆς ἀπῆλθεν ἀπὸ σοῦ, καὶ πάντα τὰ λιπαρὰ καὶ τὰ λαμπρὰ ἀπώλετο ἀπὸ σοῦ καὶ οὐκέτι οὐ μὴ αὐτὰ εὑρήσουσιν. ¹⁵ οἱ ἔμποροι τούτων οἱ πλουτήσαντες ἀπ' αὐτῆς ἀπὸ μακρόθεν στήσονται διὰ τὸν φόβον τοῦ βασανισμοῦ αὐτῆς κλαίοντες καὶ πενθοῦντες ¹⁶ λέγοντες, Οὐαὶ οὐαί, ἡ πόλις ἡ μεγάλη, ἡ περιβεβλημένη βύσσινον καὶ πορφυροῦν καὶ κόκκινον καὶ κεχρυσωμένη [ἐν] χρυσίῳ καὶ λίθῳ τιμίῳ καὶ μαργαρίτῃ, ¹⁷ ὅτι μιᾷ ὥρᾳ ἠρημώθη ὁ τοσοῦτος πλοῦτος. ¶ Καὶ πᾶς κυβερνήτης καὶ πᾶς ὁ ἐπὶ τόπον πλέων καὶ ναῦται καὶ ὅσοι τὴν θάλασσαν ἐργάζονται, ἀπὸ μακρόθεν ἔστησαν ¹⁸ καὶ ἔκραζον βλέποντες τὸν καπνὸν τῆς πυρώσεως αὐτῆς λέγοντες, Τίς ὁμοία τῇ πόλει τῇ μεγάλῃ; ¹⁹ καὶ ἔβαλον χοῦν ἐπὶ τὰς κεφαλὰς αὐτῶν καὶ ἔκραζον κλαίοντες καὶ πενθοῦντες λέγοντες, Οὐαὶ οὐαί, ἡ πόλις ἡ μεγάλη, ἐν ᾗ ἐπλούτησαν πάντες οἱ ἔχοντες τὰ πλοῖα ἐν τῇ θαλάσσῃ ἐκ τῆς τιμιότητος αὐτῆς, ὅτι μιᾷ ὥρᾳ ἠρημώθη. ²⁰ Εὐφραίνου ἐπ' αὐτῇ, οὐρανὲ καὶ οἱ ἅγιοι καὶ οἱ ἀπόστολοι καὶ οἱ προφῆται, ὅτι ἔκρινεν ὁ θεὸς τὸ κρίμα ὑμῶν ἐξ αὐτῆς. ¶ ²¹ Καὶ ἦρεν εἷς ἄγγελος ἰσχυρὸς λίθον ὡς μύλινον μέγαν καὶ ἔβαλεν εἰς τὴν θάλασσαν λέγων, Οὕτως ὁρμήματι βληθήσεται Βαβυλὼν ἡ μεγάλη πόλις καὶ οὐ μὴ εὑρεθῇ ἔτι. ²² καὶ φωνὴ κιθαρῳδῶν καὶ μουσικῶν καὶ αὐλητῶν καὶ

trumpeters, will never   be heard   in you again.   No workman of any   trade will ever   be found in you
σαλπιστῶν ↱   ⸤οὐ μὴ → ἀκουσθῇ   ἐν σοὶ ἔτι   καὶ πᾶς τεχνίτης →   πάσης τέχνης ↱   ⸤οὐ μὴ → εὑρεθῇ ἐν σοὶ
n.gpm   pl pl   v.aps.3s p.d r.ds.2 adv   cj a.nsm n.nsm   a.gsf n.gsf   pl pl   v.aps.3s p.d r.ds.2
4896   201 4024 3590   201 5148 1877   2779 4246 5493   4246   5492   2351 4024 3590   2351 1877 5148

again.   The sound of a millstone will never   be heard   in you again. 23 The light of a lamp will never shine
ἔτι   καὶ   φωνὴ → μύλου   ↱   ⸤οὐ μὴ → ἀκουσθῇ ἐν σοὶ ἔτι   καὶ   φῶς → λύχνου   ↱   ⸤οὐ μὴ φάνῃ
adv   cj   n.nsf   n.gsm   pl pl   v.aps.3s p.d r.ds.2 adv   cj   n.nsn   n.gsm   pl pl   v.aas.3s
2285 2779   5889   3685   201 4024 3590   201 5148 1877   2779   5890   3394   4024 3590   5743

in you again.   The voice of bridegroom and bride will never   be heard   in you again.   Your merchants
ἐν σοὶ ἔτι   καὶ   φωνὴ → νυμφίου   καὶ νύμφης ↱   ⸤οὐ μὴ → ἀκουσθῇ ἐν σοὶ ἔτι   ὅτι σου ⸤οἱ ἔμποροι
p.d r.ds.2 adv cj   n.nsf   n.gsm   cj n.gsf   pl pl   v.aps.3s p.d r.ds.2 adv cj r.gs.2 d.npm n.npm
1877 5148 2285 2779   5889   3812   2779 3811   201 4024 3590   201 1877 5148 2285 4022 5148 3836 1867

were the world's great   men.   By your magic   spell all   the nations were led astray.   24   In
ἦσαν τῆς γῆς ⸤οἱ μεγιστᾶνες⸥   ὅτι ἐν σου ⸤τῇ φαρμακείᾳ ←   πάντα τὰ ἔθνη   →   → ἐπλανήθησαν καὶ ἐν
v.iai.3p d.gsf n.gsf d.npm n.npm   cj p.d r.gs.2 d.dsf n.dsf   a.npn d.npn n.npn   v.api.3p   cj p.d
1639   3836 1178 3836 3491   4022 1877 5148 3836 5758   4246 3836 1620   4414   2779 1877

her was found the blood of prophets and   of the saints, and of all   who have been killed   on the earth."
αὐτῇ → εὑρέθη αἷμα → προφητῶν καὶ →   ἁγίων καὶ → πάντων τῶν   →   ἐσφαγμένων ἐπὶ τῆς γῆς.
r.dsf.3 v.api.3s n.nsn   n.gpm   cj   a.gpm cj   a.gpm   d.gpm   pt.rp.gpm   p.g d.gsf n.gsf
899   2351   135   4737   2779   41   2779 4246   3836   5377   2093 3836 1178

Hallelujah!

19:1 After this I heard what sounded like the roar   of a great multitude in heaven   shouting:
Μετὰ ταῦτα → ἤκουσα →   →   ὡς   φωνὴν μεγάλην → πολλοῦ ὄχλου   ἐν ⸤τῷ οὐρανῷ⸥ λεγόντων
p.a   r.apn v.aai.1s   pl   n.asf a.asf   a.gsm n.gsm   p.d d.dsm n.dsm   pt.pa.gpm
3552 4047   201   6055 5889 3489   4498   4063   1877 3836 4041   3306

"Hallelujah! Salvation and glory   and power   belong to our God,   2 for true   and just   are his
ἀλληλουϊά ⸤ἡ σωτηρία καὶ ⸤ἡ δόξα⸥ καὶ ⸤ἡ δύναμις⸥ →   ἡμῶν ⸤τοῦ θεοῦ⸥ ὅτι ἀληθιναὶ καὶ δίκαιαι αὐτοῦ
j   d.nsf n.nsf   cj d.nsf n.nsf cj d.nsf n.nsf   r.gp.1 d.gsm n.gsm cj a.npf   cj a.npf   r.gsm.3
252   3836 5401   2779 3836 1518   2779 3836 1539   7005 3836 2536   4022 1465   2779 1465   899

judgments.   He has condemned the great   prostitute who corrupted the earth by her   adulteries.   He
⸤αἱ κρίσεις⸥ ὅτι →   → ἔκρινεν τὴν ⸤τὴν μεγάλην⸥ πόρνην   ἥτις ἔφθειρεν τὴν γῆν ἐν αὐτῆς ⸤τῇ πορνείᾳ⸥ καὶ →
d.npf n.npf cj   v.aai.3s d.asf d.asf a.asf n.asf   r.nsf v.aai.3s d.asf n.asf p.d r.gsf.3 d.dsf n.dsf cj
3836 3213   4022   3212   3836 3836 3489   4520   4015 5780   3836 1178 1877 899   3836 4518   2779

has avenged on   her the blood of his servants."   ¶ 3 And again   they shouted: ¶   "Hallelujah!
→ ἐξεδίκησεν ἐκ χειρὸς αὐτῆς τὸ αἷμα → αὐτοῦ ⸤τῶν δούλων⸥   καὶ δεύτερον → εἴρηκαν   ἀλληλουϊά
   v.aai.3s   p.g n.gsf r.gsf.3 d.asn n.asn   r.gsm.3 d.gpm n.gpm   cj adv   v.rai.3p   j
   1688   1666 5931 899   3836 135   1529 899   3836 1529   2779 1311   3306   252

The smoke from her goes   up for ever   and ever."   ¶   4 The twenty-four
καὶ ὁ   καπνὸς → αὐτῆς ἀναβαίνει ← εἰς ⸤τοὺς αἰῶνας⸥ ⸤τῶν αἰώνων⸥   καὶ οἱ εἴκοσι τέσσαρες⸥
cj d.nsm n.nsm   r.gsf.3 v.pai.3s   p.a d.apm n.apm   d.gpm n.gpm   cj d.npm a.npm a.npm a.npm
2779 3836 2837   899   326   1650 3836 172   3836 172   2779 3836 3836 1633 5475

elders   and the four   living creatures fell down and worshiped God, who was seated   on the throne.
πρεσβύτεροι καὶ τὰ τέσσαρα ζῷα   → ἔπεσαν   καὶ προσεκύνησαν ⸤τῷ θεῷ⸥ τῷ → καθημένῳ ἐπὶ τῷ θρόνῳ
a.npm   cj d.npn a.npn n.npn   v.aai.3p   cj v.aai.3p   d.dsm n.dsm d.dsm   pt.pm.dsm p.d d.dsm n.dsm
4565   2779 3836 5475 2442   4406   2779 4686   3836 2536 3836   2764   2093 3836 2585

And they cried: "Amen, Hallelujah!" ¶   5 Then a voice came from the throne, saying: "Praise our God,
→ λέγοντες ἀμὴν ἀλληλουϊά   Καὶ   φωνὴ ἐξῆλθεν ἀπὸ τοῦ θρόνου λέγουσα αἰνεῖτε ἡμῶν ⸤τῷ θεῷ⸥
   pt.pa.npm pl   j   cj   n.nsf v.aai.3s p.g d.gsm n.gsm pt.pa.nsf v.pam.2p r.gp.1 d.dsm n.dsm
   3306   297   252   2779   5889 2002   608 3836 2585   3306   140   7005 3836 2536

all   you his servants,   you who fear   him, both small   and great!"   ¶   6 Then I heard
πάντες ← αὐτοῦ οἱ δοῦλοι, [καὶ] → οἱ φοβούμενοι αὐτόν ⸤οἱ μικροὶ⸥ καὶ ⸤οἱ μεγάλοι⸥   Καὶ → ἤκουσα
a.vpm   r.gsm.3 d.vpm n.vpm   d.vpm pt.pp.vpm r.asm.3 d.vpm a.vpm cj d.vpm a.vpm   cj   v.aai.1s
4246   899   3836 1529 2779   3836 5828   899   3836 3625 2779 3836 3489   2779 201

what sounded like a great multitude,   like the roar of rushing waters and like loud   peals of thunder,
φωνὴν ὡς πολλοῦ ὄχλου   καὶ ὡς   φωνὴν → πολλῶν ὑδάτων καὶ ὡς ἰσχυρῶν φωνὴν → βροντῶν
n.asf pl a.gsm n.gsm   cj pl   n.asf   a.gpn n.gpn   cj pl a.gpf   n.asf   n.gpf
5889   6055 4498 4063   2779 6055   5889   4498   5623   2779 6055 2708   5889   1103

σαλπιστῶν οὐ μὴ ἀκουσθῇ ἐν σοὶ ἔτι, καὶ πᾶς τεχνίτης πάσης τέχνης οὐ μὴ εὑρεθῇ ἐν σοὶ ἔτι, καὶ φωνὴ μύλου οὐ μὴ ἀκουσθῇ
ἐν σοὶ ἔτι. 23 καὶ φῶς λύχνου οὐ μὴ φάνῃ ἐν σοὶ ἔτι, καὶ φωνὴ νυμφίου καὶ νύμφης οὐ μὴ ἀκουσθῇ ἐν σοὶ ἔτι· ὅτι οἱ ἔμποροί
σου ἦσαν οἱ μεγιστᾶνες τῆς γῆς, ὅτι ἐν τῇ φαρμακείᾳ σου ἐπλανήθησαν πάντα τὰ ἔθνη, 24 καὶ ἐν αὐτῇ αἷμα προφητῶν καὶ
ἁγίων εὑρέθη καὶ πάντων τῶν ἐσφαγμένων ἐπὶ τῆς γῆς.
19:1 Μετὰ ταῦτα ἤκουσα ὡς φωνὴν μεγάλην ὄχλου πολλοῦ ἐν τῷ οὐρανῷ λεγόντων, Ἀλληλουϊά· ἡ σωτηρία καὶ ἡ δόξα καὶ
ἡ δύναμις τοῦ θεοῦ ἡμῶν, 2 ὅτι ἀληθιναὶ καὶ δίκαιαι αἱ κρίσεις αὐτοῦ· ὅτι ἔκρινεν τὴν πόρνην τὴν μεγάλην ἥτις ἔφθειρεν τὴν
γῆν ἐν τῇ πορνείᾳ αὐτῆς, καὶ ἐξεδίκησεν τὸ αἷμα τῶν δούλων αὐτοῦ ἐκ χειρὸς αὐτῆς. ¶ 3 καὶ δεύτερον εἴρηκαν, ¶ Ἀλληλουϊά·
καὶ ὁ καπνὸς αὐτῆς ἀναβαίνει εἰς τοὺς αἰῶνας τῶν αἰώνων. ¶ 4 καὶ ἔπεσαν οἱ πρεσβύτεροι οἱ εἴκοσι τέσσαρες καὶ τὰ τέσσαρα
ζῷα καὶ προσεκύνησαν τῷ θεῷ τῷ καθημένῳ ἐπὶ τῷ θρόνῳ λέγοντες, Ἀμὴν Ἀλληλουϊά, ¶ 5 Καὶ φωνὴ ἀπὸ τοῦ θρόνου ἐξῆλθεν
λέγουσα, Αἰνεῖτε τῷ θεῷ ἡμῶν πάντες οἱ δοῦλοι αὐτοῦ [καὶ] οἱ φοβούμενοι αὐτόν, οἱ μικροὶ καὶ οἱ μεγάλοι. ¶ 6 καὶ ἤκουσα
ὡς φωνὴν ὄχλου πολλοῦ καὶ ὡς φωνὴν ὑδάτων πολλῶν καὶ ὡς φωνὴν βροντῶν ἰσχυρῶν λεγόντων, Ἀλληλουϊά, ὅτι ἐβασίλευσεν

shouting: "Hallelujah! For our Lord God Almighty reigns. **7** Let us rejoice and be glad and
λεγόντων ἀλληλουϊά ὅτι ἡμῶν κύριος ὁ θεὸς ὁ παντοκράτωρ, ἐβασίλευσεν → → χαίρωμεν καὶ → ἀγαλλιῶμεν καὶ
pt.pa.gpm j cj n.gp.1 n.nsm d.nsm n.nsm d.nsm n.nsm v.aai.3s v.pas.1p cj v.pas.1p cj
3306 252 4022 7005 3261 3836 2536 3836 4120 996 5897 2779 22 2779

give him glory! For the wedding of the Lamb has come, and his bride has made herself ready. **8**
δώσωμεν αὐτῷ τὴν δόξαν ὅτι ὁ γάμος → τοῦ ἀρνίου → ἦλθεν καὶ αὐτοῦ ἡ γυνὴ ↱ ↱ ἑαυτὴν ἡτοίμασεν καὶ
v.aas.1p r.dsm.3 d.asf n.asf cj d.nsm n.nsm d.gsn n.gsn v.aai.3s cj r.gsm.3 d.nsf n.nsf r.asf.3 v.aai.3s cj
1443 899 3836 1518 4022 3836 1141 3836 768 2262 2779 899 3836 1222 2286 2286 1571 2286 2779

Fine linen, bright and clean, was given her to wear." (Fine linen stands for the righteous acts
→ βύσσινον λαμπρὸν καθαρόν → ἐδόθη αὐτῇ ἵνα περιβάληται γὰρ ↱ τὸ βύσσινον ἐστίν ← τὰ δικαιώματα ←
a.asn a.asn a.asn v.api.3s r.dsf.3 cj v.ams.3s cj d.nsn n.nsn v.pai.3s d.npn n.npn
1115 3287 2754 1443 899 2671 4314 1142 3836 1115 1639 3836 1468

of the saints.) ¶ **9** Then the angel said to me, "Write: 'Blessed are those who are invited to the wedding
→ τῶν ἁγίων Καὶ λέγει → μοι γράψον μακάριοι οἱ → ← κεκλημένοι εἰς τὸ τοῦ γάμου
d.gpm a.gpm cj v.pai.3s r.ds.1 v.aam.2s a.npm d.npm pt.rp.npm p.a d.asn d.gsm n.gsm
3836 41 2779 3306 1609 1211 3421 3836 2813 1650 3836 3836 1141

supper of the Lamb!'" And he added, "These are the true words of God." ¶ **10** At this I fell
δεῖπνον → τοῦ ἀρνίου καὶ → λέγει μοι οὗτοι εἰσιν οἱ ἀληθινοὶ λόγοι τοῦ θεοῦ. καὶ ← → ἔπεσα
n.asn d.gsn n.gsn cj v.pai.3s r.ds.1 r.npm v.pai.3p d.npm a.npm n.npm d.gsm n.gsm cj v.aai.1s
1270 3836 768 2779 3306 1609 4047 1639 3836 240 3364 3836 2536 2779 4406

at his feet to worship him. But he said to me, "Do not do it! I am a fellow servant with you
ἔμπροσθεν αὐτοῦ τῶν ποδῶν προσκυνῆσαι αὐτῷ καὶ → λέγει → μοι μὴ ὅρα → εἰμι σύνδουλος → σού
p.g r.gsm.3 d.gpm n.gpm f.aa r.dsm.3 cj v.pai.3s r.ds.1 pl v.pam.2s v.pai.1s n.nsm r.gs.2
1869 899 3836 4546 4686 899 2779 3306 1609 3972 3590 3972 1639 5281 5148

and with your brothers who hold to the testimony of Jesus. Worship God! For the testimony of Jesus is
καὶ ↱ σου τῶν ἀδελφῶν τῶν ἐχόντων ← τὴν μαρτυρίαν → Ἰησοῦ προσκύνησον τῷ θεῷ. γὰρ ἡ μαρτυρία → Ἰησοῦ ἐστιν
cj r.gs.2 d.gpm n.gpm d.gpm pt.pa.gpm d.asf n.asf n.gsm v.aam.2s d.dsm n.dsm cj d.nsf n.nsf n.gsm v.pai.3s
2779 81 5148 3836 81 3836 2400 3836 3456 2652 4686 3836 2536 1142 3836 3456 2652 1639

the spirit of prophecy."
τὸ πνεῦμα → τῆς προφητείας.
d.nsn n.nsn d.gsf n.gsf
3836 4460 3836 4735

The Rider on the White Horse

19:11 I saw heaven standing open and there before me was a white horse, whose
Καὶ → εἶδον τὸν οὐρανὸν → ἠνεῳγμένον καὶ ἰδοὺ λευκὸς ἵππος καὶ ὁ
cj v.aai.1s d.asm n.asm pt.rp.asm cj j a.nsm n.nsm cj d.nsm
2779 1625 3836 4041 487 2779 2627 3328 2691 2779 3836

rider is called Faithful and True. With justice he judges and makes war. **12** His
καθήμενος ἐπ᾽ αὐτὸν → καλούμενος πιστὸς καὶ ἀληθινός καὶ ἐν δικαιοσύνῃ → κρίνει καὶ → πολεμεῖ δὲ αὐτοῦ
pt.pm.nsm p.a r.asm.3 pt.pp.nsm a.nsm cj a.nsm cj p.d n.dsf v.pai.3s cj v.pai.3s cj r.gsm.3
2764 2093 899 2813 4412 2779 240 2779 1877 1466 3212 2779 4482 1254 899

eyes are like blazing fire, and on his head are many crowns. He has a name written on him
οἱ ὀφθαλμοὶ ὡς φλὸξ πυρός καὶ ἐπὶ αὐτοῦ τὴν κεφαλὴν πολλὰ διαδήματα → ἔχων ὄνομα γεγραμμένον
d.npm n.npm pl n.nsf n.gsn cj p.a r.gsm.3 d.asf n.asf a.npn n.npn pt.pa.nsm n.asn pt.rp.asn
3836 4057 6055 5825 4786 2779 2093 899 3836 3051 4498 1343 2400 3950 1211

that no one knows but he himself. **13** He is dressed in a robe dipped in blood, and his
ὃ οὐδεὶς ← οἶδεν εἰ μὴ αὐτός. καὶ → περιβεβλημένος ← ἱμάτιον βεβαμμένον → αἵματι καὶ αὐτοῦ
r.asn a.nsm v.rai.3s cj pl r.nsm cj pt.rp.nsm n.asn pt.rp.asn n.dsn cj r.gsm.3
4005 4029 3857 1623 3590 899 2779 4314 2668 970 135 2779 899

name is the Word of God. **14** The armies of heaven were following him, riding on
τὸ ὄνομα κέκληται ὁ λόγος → τοῦ θεοῦ. Καὶ τὰ στρατεύματα [τὰ] ἐν τῷ οὐρανῷ → ἠκολούθει αὐτῷ ἐφ᾽
d.nsn n.nsn v.rpi.3s d.nsm n.nsm d.gsm n.gsm cj d.npn n.npn d.npn p.d d.dsm n.dsm v.iai.3s r.dsm.3 p.d
3836 3950 2813 3836 3364 3836 2536 2779 3836 5128 3836 1877 3836 4041 199 899 2093

white horses and dressed in fine linen, white and clean. **15** Out of his mouth comes a sharp
λευκοῖς ἵπποις ἐνδεδυμένοι ← → βύσσινον λευκὸν καθαρόν καὶ ἐκ ← αὐτοῦ τοῦ στόματος ἐκπορεύεται ὀξεῖα
a.dpm n.dpm pt.rp.npm a.asn a.asn a.asn cj p.g r.gsm.3 d.gsn n.gsn v.pmi.3s a.nsf
3328 2691 1907 1115 3328 2754 2779 1666 899 3836 5125 1744 3955

κύριος ὁ θεὸς [ἡμῶν] ὁ παντοκράτωρ. **7** χαίρωμεν καὶ ἀγαλλιῶμεν καὶ δώσωμεν τὴν δόξαν αὐτῷ, ὅτι ἦλθεν ὁ γάμος τοῦ ἀρνίου καὶ ἡ γυνὴ αὐτοῦ ἡτοίμασεν ἑαυτήν **8** καὶ ἐδόθη αὐτῇ ἵνα περιβάληται βύσσινον λαμπρὸν καθαρόν· τὸ γὰρ βύσσινον τὰ δικαιώματα τῶν ἁγίων ἐστίν. ¶ **9** Καὶ λέγει μοι, Γράψον· Μακάριοι οἱ εἰς τὸ δεῖπνον τοῦ γάμου τοῦ ἀρνίου κεκλημένοι. καὶ λέγει μοι, Οὗτοι οἱ λόγοι ἀληθινοὶ τοῦ θεοῦ εἰσιν. ¶ **10** καὶ ἔπεσα ἔμπροσθεν τῶν ποδῶν αὐτοῦ προσκυνῆσαι αὐτῷ. καὶ λέγει μοι, Ὅρα μή· σύνδουλός σού εἰμι καὶ τῶν ἀδελφῶν σου τῶν ἐχόντων τὴν μαρτυρίαν Ἰησοῦ· τῷ θεῷ προσκύνησον. ἡ γὰρ μαρτυρία Ἰησοῦ ἐστιν τὸ πνεῦμα τῆς προφητείας.

19:11 Καὶ εἶδον τὸν οὐρανὸν ἠνεῳγμένον, καὶ ἰδοὺ ἵππος λευκὸς καὶ ὁ καθήμενος ἐπ᾽ αὐτὸν [καλούμενος] πιστὸς καὶ ἀληθινός, καὶ ἐν δικαιοσύνῃ κρίνει καὶ πολεμεῖ. **12** οἱ δὲ ὀφθαλμοὶ αὐτοῦ [ὡς] φλὸξ πυρός, καὶ ἐπὶ τὴν κεφαλὴν αὐτοῦ διαδήματα πολλά, ἔχων ὄνομα γεγραμμένον ὃ οὐδεὶς οἶδεν εἰ μὴ αὐτός, **13** καὶ περιβεβλημένος ἱμάτιον βεβαμμένον αἵματι, καὶ κέκληται τὸ ὄνομα αὐτοῦ ὁ λόγος τοῦ θεοῦ. **14** καὶ τὰ στρατεύματα [τὰ] ἐν τῷ οὐρανῷ ἠκολούθει αὐτῷ ἐφ᾽ ἵπποις λευκοῖς, ἐνδεδυμένοι βύσσινον λευκὸν καθαρόν. **15** καὶ ἐκ τοῦ στόματος αὐτοῦ ἐκπορεύεται ῥομφαία ὀξεῖα, ἵνα ἐν αὐτῇ πατάξῃ τὰ ἔθνη, καὶ αὐτὸς ποιμανεῖ

sword	with	which	to	strike	down	the	nations.	"He	will	rule		them	with	an iron	scepter."		He	treads
ῥομφαία	ἐν	αὐτῇ	ἵνα	πατάξῃ		τὰ	ἔθνη	καὶ	αὐτὸς	ποιμανεῖ	αὐτοὺς	ἐν		σιδηρᾷ	ῥάβδῳ	καὶ	αὐτὸς	πατεῖ
n.nsf	p.d	r.dsf.3	cj	v.aas.3s		d.apn	n.apn	cj	r.nsm	v.fai.3s	r.apm.3	p.d		a.dsf	n.dsf	cj	r.nsm	v.pai.3s
4855	1877	899	2671	4250		3836	1620	2779	899	4477	899	1877		4971	4811	2779	899	4251

the	winepress		of the	fury	of the	wrath	of	God	Almighty.	**16**	On	his	robe	and	on	his
τὴν	ληνὸν	τοῦ οἴνου	→	τοῦ θυμοῦ	→	τῆς ὀργῆς		τοῦ θεοῦ	τοῦ παντοκράτορος		καὶ	ἐπὶ	τὸ ἱμάτιον	καὶ	ἐπὶ	αὐτοῦ
d.asf	n.asf	d.gsm n.gsm		d.gsm n.gsm		d.gsf n.gsf		d.gsm n.gsm	d.gsm n.gsm		cj	p.a	d.asn n.asn	cj	p.a	r.gsm.3
3836	3332	3836 3885		3836 2596		3836 3973		3836 2536	3836 4120		2779	2093	3836 2668	2779	2093	899

thigh		he has	this	name	written:	KING	OF	KINGS	AND	LORD	OF	LORDS.	¶	**17**	And	I	saw	an
τὸν μηρὸν	→	ἔχει	ὄνομα	γεγραμμένον	Βασιλεὺς		βασιλέων	καὶ	κύριος	→	κυρίων			Καὶ	→	εἶδον	ἕνα
d.asm n.asm		v.pai.3s	n.asn	pt.rp.asn	n.nsm		n.gpm	cj	n.nsm		n.gpm			cj		v.aai.1s	a.asm
3836 3611		2400	3950	1211	995		995	2779	3261		3261			2779		1625	1651

angel	standing	in	the	sun,		who	cried	in	a	loud	voice		to all	the	birds	flying		in
ἄγγελον	ἑστῶτα	ἐν	τῷ	ἡλίῳ	καὶ	→	ἔκραξεν	ἐν		μεγάλῃ	φωνῇ	λέγων	πᾶσιν	τοῖς	ὀρνέοις	τοῖς πετομένοις		ἐν
n.asm	pt.ra.asm	p.d	d.dsm	n.dsm	cj		v.aai.3s	p.d		a.dsf	n.dsf	pt.pa.nsm	a.dpn	d.dpn	n.dpn	d.dpn pt.pm.dpn		p.d
34	2705	1877	3836	2463	2779		3189	1877		3489	5889	3306	4246	3836	3997	3836 4375		1877

midair,	"Come,	gather	together	for	the	great	supper	of God,	**18**	so that	you may	eat	the	flesh	of
μεσουρανήματι	Δεῦτε	συνάχθητε ←		εἰς	τὸ	τὸ μέγα	δεῖπνον	→ τοῦ θεοῦ		ἵνα ←		φάγητε		σάρκας	→
n.dsn	adv	v.apm.2p		p.a	d.asn	d.asn a.asn	n.asn	d.gsm n.gsm		cj		v.aas.2p		n.apf	
3547	1307	5251		1650	3836	3836 3489	1270	3836 2536		2671		2266		4922	

kings,		generals,	and		mighty men,		of horses	and	their	riders,		and	the
βασιλέων	καὶ	σάρκας	χιλιάρχων	καὶ	σάρκας	ἰσχυρῶν	καὶ	σάρκας	→ ἵππων	καὶ	τῶν	καθημένων	ἐπ᾽ αὐτῶν	καὶ
n.gpm	cj	n.apf	n.gpm	cj	n.apf	a.gpm	cj	n.apf	n.gpm	cj	d.gpm	pt.pm.gpm	r.gpm.3	cj
995	2779	4922	5941	2779	4922	2708	2779	4922	2691	2779	3836	2764	2093 899	2779

flesh	of all	people,		free	and	slave,		small	and	great."	¶	**19**	Then	I	saw	the	beast	and	the
σάρκας	→ πάντων ←		τε	ἐλευθέρων	καὶ	δούλων	καὶ	μικρῶν	καὶ	μεγάλων			Καὶ	→	εἶδον	τὸ	θηρίον	καὶ	τοὺς
n.apf	a.gpm		cj	a.gpm	cj	a.gpm	cj	a.gpm	cj	a.gpm			cj		v.aai.1s	d.asn	n.asn	cj	d.apm
4922	4246		5445	1801	2779	1529	2779	3625	2779	3489			2779		1625	3836	2563	2779	3836

kings	of the earth	and	their	armies		gathered	together	to make	war		against	the	rider		on the
βασιλεῖς	→ τῆς γῆς	καὶ	αὐτῶν	τὰ στρατεύματα		συνηγμένα ←		ποιῆσαι	τὸν πόλεμον		μετὰ	τοῦ	καθημένου	ἐπὶ	τοῦ
n.apm	d.gsf n.gsf	cj	r.gpm.3	d.apn n.apn		pt.rp.apn		f.aa	d.asm n.asm		p.g	d.gsm	pt.pm.gsm	p.g	d.gsm
995	3836 1178	2779	899	3836 5128		5251		4472	3836 4483		3552	3836	2764	2093	3836

horse	and		his	army.	**20**	But	the	beast	was	captured,	and	with	him	the	false	prophet		who	had
ἵππου	καὶ	μετὰ	αὐτοῦ	τοῦ στρατεύματος		καὶ	τὸ	θηρίον	→	ἐπιάσθη	καὶ	μετ᾽	αὐτοῦ ὁ	→		ψευδοπροφήτης	ὁ	→	
n.gsm	cj	p.g	r.gsm.3	d.gsn n.gsn		cj	d.nsn	n.nsn		v.api.3s	cj	p.g	r.gsm.3 d.nsm			n.nsm	d.nsm		
2691	2779	3552	899	3836 5128		2779	3836	2563		4389	2779	3552	899 3836			6021	3836		

performed	the	miraculous	signs	on		his	behalf.	With	these	signs	he had	deluded	those	who	had	received	the
ποιήσας	τὰ		σημεῖα	ἐνώπιον	αὐτοῦ ←			ἐν	οἷς			ἐπλάνησεν	τοὺς	→		λαβόντας	τὸ
pt.aa.nsm	d.apn		n.apn	p.g	r.gsn.3			p.d	r.dpn			v.aai.3s	d.apm			pt.aa.apm	d.asn
4472	3836		4956	1967	899	1967		1877	4005			4414	3836			3284	3836

mark	of	the	beast	and	worshiped		his	image.	The	two	of them	were	thrown	alive	into	the
χάραγμα	→	τοῦ	θηρίου	καὶ	τοὺς προσκυνοῦντας		αὐτοῦ	τῇ εἰκόνι	οἱ	δύο		→	ἐβλήθησαν	ζῶντες	εἰς	τὴν
n.asn		d.gsn	n.gsn	cj	d.apm pt.pa.apm		r.gsn.3	d.dsf n.dsf	d.npm	a.npm			v.api.3p	pt.pa.npm	p.a	d.asf
5916		3836	2563	2779	3836 4686		899	3836 1635	3836	1545			965	2409	1650	3836

fiery	lake	of burning		sulfur.	**21**	The	rest	of them	were	killed		with	the	sword	that	came
τοῦ πυρὸς	λίμνην	τῆς καιομένης	ἐν	θείῳ		καὶ	οἱ	λοιποὶ ←		ἀπεκτάνθησαν	ἐν		τῇ	ῥομφαίᾳ	τῇ	ἐξελθούσῃ
d.gsn n.gsn	n.asf	d.gsf pt.pp.gsf	p.d	n.dsn		cj	d.npm	a.npm		v.api.3p	p.d		d.dsf	n.dsf	d.dsf	pt.aa.dsf
3836 4786	3349	3836 2794	1877	2520		2779	3836	3370		650	1877		3836	4855	3836	2002

out	of the	mouth		of the	rider		on	the horse,	and	all	the	birds	gorged		themselves	on	their
ἐκ	τοῦ	στόματος	αὐτοῦ	→	τοῦ καθημένου	ἐπὶ	τοῦ ἵππου		καὶ	πάντα	τὰ	ὄρνεα	ἐχορτάσθησαν	←		ἐκ	αὐτῶν
p.g	d.gsn	n.gsn	r.gsm.3		d.gsm pt.pm.gsm	p.g	d.gsm n.gsm		cj	a.npn	d.npn	n.npn	v.api.3p			p.g	r.gpm.3
1666	3836	5125	899		3836 2764	2093	3836 2691		2779	4246	3836	3997	5963			1666	899

flesh.
τῶν σαρκῶν
d.gpf n.gpf
3836 4922

αὐτοὺς ἐν ῥάβδῳ σιδηρᾷ, καὶ αὐτὸς πατεῖ τὴν ληνὸν τοῦ οἴνου τοῦ θυμοῦ τῆς ὀργῆς τοῦ θεοῦ τοῦ παντοκράτορος. **16** καὶ ἔχει ἐπὶ τὸ ἱμάτιον καὶ ἐπὶ τὸν μηρὸν αὐτοῦ ὄνομα γεγραμμένον· Βασιλεὺς βασιλέων καὶ κύριος κυρίων. ¶ **17** Καὶ εἶδον ἕνα ἄγγελον ἑστῶτα ἐν τῷ ἡλίῳ καὶ ἔκραξεν [ἐν] φωνῇ μεγάλῃ λέγων πᾶσιν τοῖς ὀρνέοις τοῖς πετομένοις ἐν μεσουρανήματι, Δεῦτε συνάχθητε εἰς τὸ δεῖπνον τὸ μέγα τοῦ θεοῦ **18** ἵνα φάγητε σάρκας βασιλέων καὶ σάρκας χιλιάρχων καὶ σάρκας ἰσχυρῶν καὶ σάρκας ἵππων καὶ τῶν καθημένων ἐπ᾽ αὐτῶν καὶ σάρκας πάντων ἐλευθέρων τε καὶ δούλων καὶ μικρῶν καὶ μεγάλων. ¶ **19** Καὶ εἶδον τὸ θηρίον καὶ τοὺς βασιλεῖς τῆς γῆς καὶ τὰ στρατεύματα αὐτῶν συνηγμένα ποιῆσαι τὸν πόλεμον μετὰ τοῦ καθημένου ἐπὶ τοῦ ἵππου καὶ μετὰ τοῦ στρατεύματος αὐτοῦ. **20** καὶ ἐπιάσθη τὸ θηρίον καὶ μετ᾽ αὐτοῦ ὁ ψευδοπροφήτης ὁ ποιήσας τὰ σημεῖα ἐνώπιον αὐτοῦ, ἐν οἷς ἐπλάνησεν τοὺς λαβόντας τὸ χάραγμα τοῦ θηρίου καὶ τοὺς προσκυνοῦντας τῇ εἰκόνι αὐτοῦ· ζῶντες ἐβλήθησαν οἱ δύο εἰς τὴν λίμνην τοῦ πυρὸς τῆς καιομένης ἐν θείῳ. **21** καὶ οἱ λοιποὶ ἀπεκτάνθησαν ἐν τῇ ῥομφαίᾳ τοῦ καθημένου ἐπὶ τοῦ ἵππου τῇ ἐξελθούσῃ ἐκ τοῦ στόματος αὐτοῦ, καὶ πάντα τὰ ὄρνεα ἐχορτάσθησαν ἐκ τῶν σαρκῶν αὐτῶν.

The Thousand Years

20:1 And I saw an angel coming down out of heaven, having the key to the Abyss and holding in
Καὶ → εἶδον ἄγγελον καταβαίνοντα ← ἐκ ⌐τοῦ οὐρανοῦ⌐ ἔχοντα τὴν κλεῖν → τῆς ἀβύσσου καὶ ἐπὶ
cj v.aai.1s n.asm pt.pa.asm p.g d.gsm n.gsm pt.pa.asm d.asf n.asf d.gsf n.gsf cj p.a
2779 1625 34 2849 1666 3836 4041 2400 3836 3090 3836 12 2779 2093

his hand a great chain. **2** He seized the dragon, that ancient serpent, who is the devil, or
αὐτοῦ ⌐τὴν χεῖρα⌐ μεγάλην ἄλυσιν καὶ → ἐκράτησεν τὸν δράκοντα ὁ ⌐ὁ ἀρχαῖος⌐ ὄφις ὃς ἐστιν Διάβολος καὶ
r.gsm.3 d.asf n.asf a.asf n.asf cj v.aai.3s d.asm n.asm d.nsm d.nsm a.nsm n.nsm r.nsm v.pai.3s n.nsm cj
899 3836 5931 3489 268 2779 3195 3836 1532 3836 3836 792 4058 4005 1639 1333 2779

Satan, and bound him for a thousand years. **3** He threw him into the Abyss, and locked and sealed it
⌐ὁ Σατανᾶς⌐ καὶ ἔδησεν αὐτὸν → χίλια ἔτη καὶ → ἔβαλεν αὐτὸν εἰς τὴν ἄβυσσον καὶ ἔκλεισεν καὶ ἐσφράγισεν
d.nsm n.nsm cj v.aai.3s r.asm.3 a.apn n.apn cj v.aai.3s r.asm.3 p.a d.asf n.asf cj v.aai.3s cj v.aai.3s
3836 4928 2779 1313 899 5943 2291 2779 965 899 1650 3836 12 2779 3091 2779 5381

over him, to keep him from deceiving the nations anymore until the thousand years were ended. After that,
ἐπάνω αὐτοῦ ἵνα → → μὴ πλανήσῃ τὰ ἔθνη ἔτι ἄχρι τὰ χίλια ἔτη → τελεσθῇ μετὰ ταῦτα
p.g r.gsm.3 cj pl v.aas.3s d.apn n.apn adv d.npn a.npn n.npn v.aps.3s p.a r.apn
2062 899 2671 3590 4414 3836 1620 2285 948 3836 5943 2291 5464 3552 4047

he must be set free for a short time. ¶ **4** I saw thrones on which were seated those who
αὐτὸν δεῖ λυθῆναι ← → μικρὸν χρόνον Καὶ → εἶδον θρόνους καὶ ἐπ᾽ αὐτοὺς → ἐκάθισαν καὶ αὐτοῖς ←
r.asm.3 v.pai.3s f.ap a.asm n.asm cj v.aai.1s n.apm cj p.a r.apm.3 v.aai.3p cj r.dpm.3
899 1256 3395 3625 5989 2779 1625 2585 2779 2093 899 2767 2779 899

had been given authority to judge. And I saw the souls of those who had been beheaded because of their
→ ἐδόθη κρίμα καὶ ⌐τὰς ψυχὰς⌐ → τῶν → πεπελεκισμένων διὰ ← τὴν
v.api.3s n.nsn cj d.apf n.apf d.gpm pt.rp.gpm p.a d.asf
1443 3210 2779 3836 6034 3836 4284 1328 3836

testimony for Jesus and because of the word of God. They had not worshiped the beast or his
μαρτυρίαν → Ἰησοῦ καὶ διὰ ← τὸν λόγον ⌐τοῦ θεοῦ⌐ καὶ οἵτινες → οὐ προσεκύνησαν τὸ θηρίον οὐδὲ αὐτοῦ
n.asf n.gsm cj p.a d.asm n.asm d.gsm n.gsm cj r.npm pl v.aai.3p d.asn n.asn cj r.gsn.3
3456 2652 2779 1328 3836 3364 3836 2536 2779 4015 4686 4024 4686 3836 2563 4028 899

image and had not received his mark on their foreheads or their hands. They came to life and
⌐τὴν εἰκόνα⌐ καὶ → οὐκ ἔλαβον τὸ χάραγμα ἐπὶ τὸ μέτωπον καὶ ἐπὶ αὐτῶν ⌐τὴν χεῖρα⌐ καὶ → → ἔζησαν καὶ
d.asf n.asf cj pl v.aai.3p d.asn n.asn p.a d.asn n.asn cj p.a r.gpm.3 d.asf n.asf cj v.aai.3p cj
3836 1635 2779 4024 3284 3836 5916 2093 3836 3587 2779 2093 899 3836 5931 2779 2409 2779

reigned with Christ a thousand years. **5** (The rest of the dead did not come to life until the thousand
ἐβασίλευσαν μετὰ ⌐τοῦ Χριστοῦ⌐ χίλια ἔτη οἱ λοιποὶ τῶν νεκρῶν → οὐκ → → ἔζησαν ἄχρι τὰ χίλια
v.aai.3p p.g d.gsm n.gsm a.apn n.apn d.npm a.npm d.gpm a.gpm pl v.aai.3p cj d.npn a.npn
996 3552 3836 5986 5943 2291 3836 3370 3836 3738 2409 4024 2409 948 3836 5943

years were ended.) This is the first resurrection. **6** Blessed and holy are those who have part in the first
ἔτη → τελεσθῇ Αὕτη ἡ ⌐ἡ πρώτη⌐ ἀνάστασις μακάριος καὶ ἅγιος ὁ → ἔχων μέρος ἐν τῇ ⌐τῇ πρώτῃ⌐
n.npn v.aps.3s r.nsf d.nsf d.nsf a.nsf n.nsf a.nsm cj a.nsm d.nsm pt.pa.nsm n.asn p.d d.dsf d.dsf a.dsf
2291 5464 4047 3836 3836 4755 414 3421 2779 41 3836 2400 3538 1877 3836 3836 4755

resurrection. The second death has no power over them, but they will be priests of God and of
ἀναστάσει ὁ δεύτερος θάνατος ἔχει οὐκ ἐξουσίαν ἐπὶ τούτων ἀλλ᾽ → → ἔσονται ἱερεῖς → ⌐τοῦ θεοῦ⌐ καὶ →
n.dsf d.nsm a.nsm n.nsm v.pai.3s pl n.asf p.g r.gpm pl v.fmi.3p n.npm d.gsm n.gsm cj
414 3836 1311 2505 2400 4024 2026 2093 4047 247 1639 2636 3836 2536 2779

Christ and will reign with him for a thousand years.
⌐τοῦ Χριστοῦ⌐ καὶ → βασιλεύσουσιν μετ᾽ αὐτοῦ → χίλια ⌐τὰ ἔτη⌐
d.gsm n.gsm cj v.fai.3p p.g r.gsm.3 a.apn d.apn n.apn
3836 5986 2779 996 3552 899 5943 3836 2291

Satan's Doom

20:7 When the thousand years are over, Satan will be released from his prison **8** and will
Καὶ ὅταν τὰ χίλια ἔτη → τελεσθῇ ⌐ὁ σατανᾶς⌐ → → λυθήσεται ἐκ αὐτοῦ ⌐τῆς φυλακῆς⌐ καὶ →
cj cj d.npn a.npn n.npn v.aps.3s d.nsm n.nsm v.fpi.3s p.g r.gsm.3 d.gsf n.gsf cj
2779 4020 3836 5943 2291 5464 3836 4928 3395 1666 899 3836 5871 2779

go out to deceive the nations in the four corners of the earth – Gog and Magog – to gather
ἐξελεύσεται ← πλανῆσαι τὰ ἔθνη τὰ ἐν ταῖς τέσσαρσιν γωνίαις → τῆς γῆς ⌐τὸν Γὼγ⌐ καὶ Μαγώγ → συναγαγεῖν
v.fmi.3s f.aa d.apn n.apn d.apn p.d d.dpf a.dpf n.dpf d.gsf n.gsf d.asm n.asm cj n.asm f.aa
2002 4414 3836 1620 3836 1877 3836 5475 1224 3836 1178 3836 1223 2779 3408 5251

²⁰:¹ Καὶ εἶδον ἄγγελον καταβαίνοντα ἐκ τοῦ οὐρανοῦ ἔχοντα τὴν κλεῖν τῆς ἀβύσσου καὶ ἄλυσιν μεγάλην ἐπὶ τὴν χεῖρα αὐτοῦ. ² καὶ ἐκράτησεν τὸν δράκοντα, ὁ ὄφις ὁ ἀρχαῖος, ὅς ἐστιν Διάβολος καὶ ὁ Σατανᾶς, καὶ ἔδησεν αὐτὸν χίλια ἔτη ³ καὶ ἔβαλεν αὐτὸν εἰς τὴν ἄβυσσον καὶ ἔκλεισεν καὶ ἐσφράγισεν ἐπάνω αὐτοῦ, ἵνα μὴ πλανήσῃ ἔτι τὰ ἔθνη ἄχρι τελεσθῇ τὰ χίλια ἔτη. μετὰ ταῦτα δεῖ λυθῆναι αὐτὸν μικρὸν χρόνον. ¶ ⁴ Καὶ εἶδον θρόνους καὶ ἐκάθισαν ἐπ᾽ αὐτοὺς καὶ κρίμα ἐδόθη αὐτοῖς, καὶ τὰς ψυχὰς τῶν πεπελεκισμένων διὰ τὴν μαρτυρίαν Ἰησοῦ καὶ διὰ τὸν λόγον τοῦ θεοῦ καὶ οἵτινες οὐ προσεκύνησαν τὸ θηρίον οὐδὲ τὴν εἰκόνα αὐτοῦ καὶ οὐκ ἔλαβον τὸ χάραγμα ἐπὶ τὸ μέτωπον καὶ ἐπὶ τὴν χεῖρα αὐτῶν. καὶ ἔζησαν καὶ ἐβασίλευσαν μετὰ τοῦ Χριστοῦ χίλια ἔτη. ⁵ οἱ λοιποὶ τῶν νεκρῶν οὐκ ἔζησαν ἄχρι τελεσθῇ τὰ χίλια ἔτη. αὕτη ἡ ἀνάστασις ἡ πρώτη. ⁶ μακάριος καὶ ἅγιος ὁ ἔχων μέρος ἐν τῇ ἀναστάσει τῇ πρώτῃ· ἐπὶ τούτων ὁ δεύτερος θάνατος οὐκ ἔχει ἐξουσίαν, ἀλλ᾽ ἔσονται ἱερεῖς τοῦ θεοῦ καὶ τοῦ Χριστοῦ καὶ βασιλεύσουσιν μετ᾽ αὐτοῦ [τὰ] χίλια ἔτη.

²⁰:⁷ Καὶ ὅταν τελεσθῇ τὰ χίλια ἔτη, λυθήσεται ὁ Σατανᾶς ἐκ τῆς φυλακῆς αὐτοῦ ⁸ καὶ ἐξελεύσεται πλανῆσαι τὰ ἔθνη τὰ ἐν

them for battle.   In number   they are like the sand on the seashore. **9** They marched across the
αὐτοὺς εἰς ⌐τὸν πόλεμον⌐ ὧν ὁ ἀριθμὸς αὐτῶν ὡς ἡ ἄμμος → τῆς θαλάσσης καὶ → ἀνέβησαν ἐπὶ τὸ
r.apm.3 p.a d.asm n.asm r.gpm d.nsm n.nsm r.gpm.3 pl d.nsf n.nsf d.gsf n.gsf cj v.aai.3p p.a d.asn
899 1650 3836 4483 4005 3836 750 899 6055 3836 302 3836 2498 2779 326 2093 3836

breadth of the earth and surrounded the camp   of God's   people,   the city he loves.   But fire
πλάτος → τῆς γῆς καὶ ἐκύκλευσαν τὴν παρεμβολὴν → ⌐τῶν ἁγίων⌐ ←   καὶ τὴν πόλιν ⌐τὴν ἠγαπημένην⌐ καὶ πῦρ
n.asn d.gsf n.gsf cj v.aai.3p d.asf n.asf d.gpm a.gpm cj d.asf n.asf d.asf pt.rp.asf cj n.nsn
4424 3836 1178 2779 3238 3836 4213 3836 41 2779 3836 4484 3836 26 2779 4786

came down from heaven   and devoured them. **10** And the devil,   who deceived them, was thrown into the lake
κατέβη ← ἐκ ⌐τοῦ οὐρανοῦ⌐ καὶ κατέφαγεν αὐτούς καὶ ὁ διάβολος ὁ πλανῶν αὐτοὺς → ἐβλήθη εἰς τὴν λίμνην
v.aai.3s p.g d.gsm n.gsm cj v.aai.3s r.apm.3 cj d.nsm n.nsm d.nsm pt.pa.nsm r.apm.3 v.api.3s p.a d.asf n.asf
2849 1666 3836 4041 2779 2983 899 2779 3836 1333 3836 4414 899 965 1650 3836 3349

of burning   sulfur, where   the beast and the false prophet   had been thrown.   They will be
→ ⌐τοῦ πυρὸς⌐ καὶ ⌐θείου⌐ ὅπου καὶ τὸ θηρίον καὶ ὁ → ψευδοπροφήτης   καὶ → →
d.gsn n.gsn cj n.gsn adv cj d.nsn n.nsn cj d.nsm n.nsm cj
3836 4786 2779 2520 3963 2779 3836 2563 2779 3836 6021 2779

tormented   day   and night *for ever*   *and ever.*
βασανισθήσονται ἡμέρας καὶ νυκτὸς εἰς ⌐τοὺς αἰῶνας⌐   ⌐τῶν αἰώνων⌐
v.fpi.3p n.gsf cj n.gsf p.a d.apm n.apm d.gpm n.gpm
989 2465 2779 3816 1650 3836 172 3836 172

The Dead Are Judged

20:11 Then I saw a great white throne and him who was seated   on it.   Earth and sky   fled
Καὶ → εἶδον μέγαν λευκὸν θρόνον καὶ τὸν ← → καθήμενον ἐπ' αὐτόν οὗ ἡ γῆ καὶ ὁ οὐρανὸς ἔφυγεν
cj v.aai.1s a.asm a.asm n.asm cj d.asm pt.pm.asm p.a r.asm.3 r.gsm d.nsf n.nsf cj d.nsm n.nsm v.aai.3s
2779 1625 3489 3328 2585 2779 3836 2764 2093 899 4005 3836 1178 2779 3836 4041 5771

from his presence, and there was   no place for them. **12** And I saw the dead, great   and small,
ἀπὸ τοῦ προσώπου καὶ → εὑρέθη οὐχ τόπος → αὐτοῖς καὶ → εἶδον τοὺς νεκρούς ⌐τοὺς μεγάλους⌐ καὶ ⌐τοὺς μικρούς⌐
p.g d.gsn n.gsn cj v.api.3s pl n.nsm r.dpm.3 cj v.aai.1s d.apm a.apm d.apm a.apm cj d.apm a.apm
608 3836 4725 2779 2351 4024 5536 899 2779 1625 3836 3738 3836 3489 2779 3836 3625

standing before the throne, and books were opened.   Another book was opened, which is   the book of
ἑστῶτας ἐνώπιον τοῦ θρόνου καὶ βιβλία → ἠνοίχθησαν καὶ ἄλλο βιβλίον → ἠνοίχθη ὅ ἐστιν →
pt.ra.apm p.g d.gsm n.gsm cj n.npn v.api.3p cj r.nsn n.nsn v.api.3s r.nsn v.pai.3s
2705 1967 3836 2585 2779 1046 487 2779 257 1046 487 4005 1639

life.   The dead were judged   according to what   they had done as recorded   in the books. **13**
⌐τῆς ζωῆς⌐ καὶ οἱ νεκροὶ → ἐκρίθησαν κατὰ ← ⌐τὰ ἔργα⌐ αὐτῶν ← ἐκ ⌐τῶν γεγραμμένων⌐ ἐν τοῖς βιβλίοις καὶ
d.gsf n.gsf cj d.npm a.npm v.api.3p p.a d.apn n.apn r.gpm.3 p.g d.gpn pt.rp.gpn p.d d.dpn n.dpn cj
3836 2437 2779 3836 3738 3212 2848 3836 2240 899 2240 1666 3836 1211 1877 3836 1046 2779

The sea   gave up the dead that were in it,   and death   and Hades   gave up the dead that were
ἡ θάλασσα ἔδωκεν ← τοὺς νεκροὺς τοὺς → ἐν αὐτῇ καὶ ⌐ὁ θάνατος⌐ καὶ ⌐ὁ ᾅδης⌐ ἔδωκαν ← τοὺς νεκροὺς τοὺς
d.nsf n.nsf v.aai.3s d.apm a.apm d.apm p.d r.dsf.3 cj d.nsm n.nsm cj d.nsm n.nsm v.aai.3p d.apm a.apm d.apm
3836 2498 1443 3836 3738 3836 1877 899 2779 3836 2505 2779 3836 87 1443 3836 3738 3836

in them, and each   person was judged   according to what   he had done. **14** Then death   and Hades
ἐν αὐτοῖς καὶ ἕκαστος → → ἐκρίθησαν κατὰ ← ⌐τὰ ἔργα⌐ αὐτῶν ← καὶ ⌐ὁ θάνατος⌐ καὶ ⌐ὁ ᾅδης⌐
p.d r.dpm.3 cj r.nsm v.api.3p p.a d.apn n.apn r.gpm.3 cj d.nsm n.nsm cj d.nsm n.nsm
1877 899 2779 1667 3212 2848 3836 2240 899 2240 2779 3836 2505 2779 3836 87

were thrown into the lake of fire.   The lake of fire   is the second   death. **15** If anyone's
→ ἐβλήθησαν εἰς τὴν λίμνην → ⌐τοῦ πυρός⌐ ἡ λίμνη → ⌐τοῦ πυρός⌐ οὗτος ἐστιν ὁ ὁ δεύτερος θάνατος καὶ εἴ τις
v.api.3p p.a d.asf n.asf d.gsn n.gsn d.nsf n.nsf d.gsn n.gsn r.nsm v.pai.3s d.nsm d.nsm a.nsm n.nsm cj cj r.nsm
965 1650 3836 3349 3836 4786 3836 3349 3836 4786 4047 1639 3836 3836 1311 2505 2779 1623 5516

name was not found written   in the book of life,   he was thrown into the lake of fire.
→ οὐχ εὑρέθη γεγραμμένος ἐν τῇ βίβλῳ ⌐τῆς ζωῆς⌐ → ἐβλήθη εἰς τὴν λίμνην ⌐τοῦ πυρός⌐
pl v.api.3s pt.rp.nsm p.d d.dsf n.dsf d.gsf n.gsf v.api.3s p.a d.asf n.asf d.gsn n.gsn
2351 4024 2351 1211 1877 3836 1047 3836 2437 965 1650 3836 3349 3836 4786

ταῖς τέσσαρσιν γωνίαις τῆς γῆς, τὸν Γὼγ καὶ Μαγώγ, συναγαγεῖν αὐτοὺς εἰς τὸν πόλεμον, ὧν ὁ ἀριθμὸς αὐτῶν ὡς ἡ ἄμμος τῆς θαλάσσης. 9 καὶ ἀνέβησαν ἐπὶ τὸ πλάτος τῆς γῆς καὶ ἐκύκλευσαν τὴν παρεμβολὴν τῶν ἁγίων καὶ τὴν πόλιν τὴν ἠγαπημένην. καὶ κατέβη πῦρ ἐκ τοῦ οὐρανοῦ καὶ κατέφαγεν αὐτούς. 10 καὶ ὁ διάβολος ὁ πλανῶν αὐτοὺς ἐβλήθη εἰς τὴν λίμνην τοῦ πυρὸς καὶ θείου ὅπου καὶ τὸ θηρίον καὶ ὁ ψευδοπροφήτης, καὶ βασανισθήσονται ἡμέρας καὶ νυκτὸς εἰς τοὺς αἰῶνας τῶν αἰώνων.

20:11 Καὶ εἶδον θρόνον μέγαν λευκὸν καὶ τὸν καθήμενον ἐπ' αὐτόν, οὗ ἀπὸ τοῦ προσώπου ἔφυγεν ἡ γῆ καὶ ὁ οὐρανὸς καὶ τόπος οὐχ εὑρέθη αὐτοῖς. 12 καὶ εἶδον τοὺς νεκρούς, τοὺς μεγάλους καὶ τοὺς μικρούς, ἑστῶτας ἐνώπιον τοῦ θρόνου. καὶ βιβλία ἠνοίχθησαν, καὶ ἄλλο βιβλίον ἠνοίχθη, ὅ ἐστιν τῆς ζωῆς, καὶ ἐκρίθησαν οἱ νεκροὶ ἐκ τῶν γεγραμμένων ἐν τοῖς βιβλίοις κατὰ τὰ ἔργα αὐτῶν. 13 καὶ ἔδωκεν ἡ θάλασσα τοὺς νεκροὺς τοὺς ἐν αὐτῇ καὶ ὁ θάνατος καὶ ὁ ᾅδης ἔδωκαν τοὺς νεκροὺς τοὺς ἐν αὐτοῖς, καὶ ἐκρίθησαν ἕκαστος κατὰ τὰ ἔργα αὐτῶν. 14 καὶ ὁ θάνατος καὶ ὁ ᾅδης ἐβλήθησαν εἰς τὴν λίμνην τοῦ πυρός. οὗτος ὁ θάνατος ὁ δεύτερός ἐστιν, ἡ λίμνη τοῦ πυρός. 15 καὶ εἴ τις οὐχ εὑρέθη ἐν τῇ βίβλῳ τῆς ζωῆς γεγραμμένος, ἐβλήθη εἰς τὴν λίμνην τοῦ πυρός.

The New Jerusalem

21:1 Then I saw a new heaven and a new earth, for the first heaven and the first earth had passed away,
Καὶ → εἶδον καινὸν οὐρανὸν καὶ καινήν γῆν γὰρ ὁ πρῶτος οὐρανὸς καὶ ἡ πρώτη γῆ → ἀπῆλθαν ←
cj v.aai.1s a.asm n.asm cj a.asf n.asf cj d.nsm a.nsm n.nsm cj d.nsf a.nsf n.nsf v.aai.3p
2779 1625 2785 4041 2779 2785 1178 1142 3836 4755 4041 2779 3836 4755 1178 599

and there was no longer any sea. **2** I saw the Holy City, the new Jerusalem, coming down
καὶ → ἔστιν οὐκ ἔτι ἡ θάλασσα καὶ → εἶδον τὴν ⌐τὴν ἁγίαν⌐ πόλιν καινὴν Ἰερουσαλὴμ καταβαίνουσαν ←
cj v.pai.3s pl adv d.nsf n.nsf cj v.aai.1s d.asf d.asf a.asf n.asf a.asf n.asf pt.pa.asf
2779 1639 4024 2285 3836 2498 2779 1625 3836 3836 41 4484 2785 2647 2849

out of heaven from God, prepared as a bride beautifully dressed for her husband. **3** And I heard a
ἐκ ← ⌐τοῦ οὐρανοῦ⌐ ἀπὸ ⌐τοῦ θεοῦ⌐ ἡτοιμασμένην ὡς νύμφην → κεκοσμημένην ⌐→ αὐτῆς⌐ ⌐τῷ ἀνδρὶ⌐ καὶ → ἤκουσα
p.g d.gsm n.gsm p.g d.gsm n.gsm pt.rp.asf pl n.asf pt.rp.asf r.gsf.3 d.dsm n.dsm cj v.aai.1s
1666 3836 4041 608 3836 2536 2286 6055 3811 3175 467 899 3836 467 2779 201

loud voice from the throne saying, "Now the dwelling of God is with men, and he will live with
μεγάλης φωνῆς ἐκ τοῦ θρόνου λεγούσης ἰδοὺ ἡ σκηνὴ → ⌐τοῦ θεοῦ⌐ μετὰ ⌐τῶν ἀνθρώπων⌐ καὶ → → σκηνώσει μετ'
a.gsf n.gsf p.g d.gsm n.gsm pt.pa.gsf j d.nsf n.nsf d.gsm n.gsm p.g d.gpm n.gpm cj v.fai.3s p.g
3489 5889 1666 3836 2585 3306 2627 3836 5008 3836 2536 3552 3836 476 2779 5012 3552

them. They will be his people, and God himself will be with them and be their God. **4** He will
αὐτῶν καὶ αὐτοὶ → ἔσονται αὐτοῦ λαοὶ καὶ ὁ θεὸς αὐτὸς → ἔσται μετ' αὐτῶν αὐτῶν θεός καὶ → →
r.gpm.3 cj r.npm v.fmi.3p r.gsm.3 n.npm cj d.nsm n.nsm r.nsm v.fmi.3s p.g r.gpm.3 r.gpm.3 n.nsm cj
899 2779 899 1639 899 3295 2779 3836 2536 899 1639 3552 899 899 2536 2779

wipe every tear from their eyes. There will be no more death or mourning or crying
ἐξαλείψει πᾶν δάκρυον ἐκ αὐτῶν ⌐τῶν ὀφθαλμῶν⌐ καὶ → → ἔσται οὐκ ἔτι ὁ θάνατος οὔτε πένθος οὔτε κραυγὴ
v.fai.3s a.asn n.asn p.g r.gpm.3 d.gpm n.gpm cj v.fmi.3s pl adv d.nsm n.nsm cj n.nsn cj n.nsf
1981 4246 1232 1666 899 3836 4057 2779 1639 4024 2285 3836 2505 4046 4292 4046 3199

or pain, for the old order of things has passed away." ¶ **5** He who was seated on the
οὔτε πόνος οὐκ ἔσται ἔτι ὅτι τὰ πρῶτα ← ← → ἀπῆλθαν ← Καὶ ὁ ← → καθήμενος ἐπὶ τῷ
cj n.nsm pl v.fmi.3s adv cj d.npn a.npn v.aai.3p cj d.nsm pt.pm.nsm p.d d.dsm
4046 4506 4024 1639 2285 4022 3836 4755 599 2779 3836 2764 2093 3836

throne said, "I am making everything new!" Then he said, "Write this down, for these words are
θρόνῳ εἶπεν ἰδοὺ → ποιῶ πάντα καινά καὶ → λέγει γράψον ὅτι οὗτοι ⌐οἱ λόγοι⌐ εἰσιν
n.dsm v.aai.3s j v.pai.1s a.apn a.apn cj v.pai.3s v.aam.2s cj r.npm d.npm n.npm v.pai.3p
2585 3306 2627 4472 4246 2785 2779 3306 1211 4022 4047 3836 3364 1639

trustworthy and true." ¶ **6** He said to me: "It is done. I am the Alpha and the Omega, the Beginning
πιστοὶ καὶ ἀληθινοί καὶ → εἶπεν μοι → γέγοναν ἐγώ εἰμι τὸ ἄλφα καὶ τὸ ὦ ἡ ἀρχὴ
a.npm cj a.npm cj v.aai.3s r.ds.1 v.rai.3p r.ns.1 v.pai.1s d.nsn n.nsn cj d.nsn n.nsn d.nsf n.nsf
4412 2779 240 2779 3306 1609 1181 1609 1639 3836 270 2779 3836 6042 3836 794

and the End. To him who is thirsty I will give to drink without cost from the spring of the water of life.
καὶ τὸ τέλος τῷ → διψῶντι ἐγώ → δώσω δωρεάν ἐκ τῆς πηγῆς τοῦ ὕδατος → ⌐τῆς ζωῆς⌐
cj d.nsn n.nsn d.dsm pt.pa.dsm r.ns.1 v.fai.1s adv p.g d.gsf n.gsf d.gsn n.gsn d.gsf n.gsf
2779 3836 5465 3836 1498 1609 1443 1562 1666 3836 4380 3836 5623 3836 2437

7 He who overcomes will inherit all this, and I will be his God and he will be my son. **8** But the
ὁ ← νικῶν → κληρονομήσει ταῦτα καὶ → ἔσομαι αὐτῷ θεὸς καὶ αὐτὸς → ἔσται μοι υἱός δὲ τοῖς
d.nsm pt.pa.nsm v.fai.3s r.apn cj v.fmi.1s r.dsm.3 n.nsm cj r.nsm v.fmi.3s r.ds.1 n.nsm cj d.dpm
3836 3771 3099 4047 2779 1639 899 2536 2779 899 1639 1609 5626 1254 3836

cowardly, the unbelieving, the vile, the murderers, the sexually immoral, those who
δειλοῖς καὶ ἀπίστοις καὶ ἐβδελυγμένοις καὶ φονεῦσιν καὶ πόρνοις ← καὶ →
a.dpm cj a.dpm cj pt.rp.dpm cj n.dpm cj n.dpm cj
1264 2779 603 2779 1009 2779 5838 2779 4521 2779

practice magic arts, the idolaters and all liars — their place will be in the fiery lake of
φαρμάκοις ← καὶ εἰδωλολάτραις καὶ πᾶσιν ⌐τοῖς ψευδέσιν⌐ αὐτῶν ⌐τὸ μέρος⌐ ἐν τῇ πυρὶ λίμνῃ
n.dpm cj n.dpm cj a.dpm d.dpm a.dpm r.gpm.3 d.nsn n.nsn p.d d.dsf d.nsn n.dsf
5761 2779 1629 2779 4246 3836 6014 899 3836 3538 1877 3836 4786 3349

burning sulfur. This is the second death." ¶ **9** One of the seven angels who had the
⌐τῇ καιομένῃ⌐ καὶ θείῳ ὅ ἐστιν ὁ ⌐ὁ δεύτερος⌐ θάνατος Καὶ εἷς ἐκ τῶν ἑπτὰ ἀγγέλων τῶν ἐχόντων τὰς
d.dsf pt.pp.dsf cj n.dsn r.nsn v.pai.3s d.nsm d.nsm a.nsm n.nsm cj a.nsm p.g d.gpm a.gpm n.gpm d.gpm pt.pa.gpm d.apf
3836 2794 2779 2520 4005 1639 3836 3836 1311 2505 2779 1651 1666 3836 2231 34 3836 2400 3836

21:1 Καὶ εἶδον οὐρανὸν καινὸν καὶ γῆν καινήν. ὁ γὰρ πρῶτος οὐρανὸς καὶ ἡ πρώτη γῆ ἀπῆλθαν καὶ ἡ θάλασσα οὐκ ἔστιν ἔτι. **2** καὶ τὴν πόλιν τὴν ἁγίαν Ἰερουσαλὴμ καινὴν εἶδον καταβαίνουσαν ἐκ τοῦ οὐρανοῦ ἀπὸ τοῦ θεοῦ ἡτοιμασμένην ὡς νύμφην κεκοσμημένην τῷ ἀνδρὶ αὐτῆς. **3** καὶ ἤκουσα φωνῆς μεγάλης ἐκ τοῦ θρόνου λεγούσης, Ἰδοὺ ἡ σκηνὴ τοῦ θεοῦ μετὰ τῶν ἀνθρώπων, καὶ σκηνώσει μετ' αὐτῶν, καὶ αὐτοὶ λαοὶ αὐτοῦ ἔσονται, καὶ αὐτὸς ὁ θεὸς μετ' αὐτῶν ἔσται [αὐτῶν θεός], **4** καὶ ἐξαλείψει πᾶν δάκρυον ἐκ τῶν ὀφθαλμῶν αὐτῶν, καὶ ὁ θάνατος οὐκ ἔσται ἔτι οὔτε πένθος οὔτε κραυγὴ οὔτε πόνος οὐκ ἔσται ἔτι, [ὅτι] τὰ πρῶτα ἀπῆλθαν. ¶ **5** Καὶ εἶπεν ὁ καθήμενος ἐπὶ τῷ θρόνῳ, Ἰδοὺ καινὰ ποιῶ πάντα, καὶ λέγει, Γράψον, ὅτι οὗτοι οἱ λόγοι πιστοὶ καὶ ἀληθινοί εἰσιν. ¶ **6** καὶ εἶπέν μοι, Γέγοναν. ἐγώ [εἰμι] τὸ Ἄλφα καὶ τὸ Ὦ, ἡ ἀρχὴ καὶ τὸ τέλος. ἐγὼ τῷ διψῶντι δώσω ἐκ τῆς πηγῆς τοῦ ὕδατος τῆς ζωῆς δωρεάν. **7** ὁ νικῶν κληρονομήσει ταῦτα καὶ ἔσομαι αὐτῷ θεὸς καὶ αὐτὸς ἔσται μοι υἱός. **8** τοῖς δὲ δειλοῖς καὶ ἀπίστοις καὶ ἐβδελυγμένοις καὶ φονεῦσιν καὶ πόρνοις καὶ φαρμάκοις καὶ εἰδωλολάτραις καὶ πᾶσιν τοῖς ψευδέσιν τὸ μέρος αὐτῶν ἐν τῇ λίμνῃ τῇ καιομένῃ πυρὶ καὶ θείῳ, ὅ ἐστιν ὁ θάνατος ὁ δεύτερος. ¶ **9** Καὶ ἦλθεν εἷς ἐκ τῶν ἑπτὰ ἀγγέλων τῶν

seven bowls full | of the seven last | plagues came and said | to me, | "Come, I will show you
ἑπτὰ φιάλας ⌐τῶν γεμόντων⌐ ← ⌐τῶν ἑπτὰ ⌐τῶν ἐσχάτων, πληγῶν ἦλθεν καὶ ἐλάλησεν μετ' ἐμοῦ λέγων δεῦρο → → δείξω σοι
a.apf n.apf d.gpm pt.pa.gpf d.gpf a.gpf d.gpf a.gpf n.gpf v.aai.3s cj v.aai.3s p.g r.gs.1 pt.pa.nsm j v.fai.1s r.ds.2
2231 5786 3836 1154 3836 2231 3836 2274 4435 2262 2779 3281 3552 1609 3306 1306 1259 5148

the bride, the wife | of the Lamb." **10** And he carried | me away in | the Spirit | to a mountain great and high, and
τὴν νύμφην τὴν γυναῖκα ⌐τοῦ ἀρνίου καὶ → ἀπήνεγκέν με ↰ ἐν πνεύματι ἐπὶ ὄρος μέγα καὶ ὑψηλόν καὶ
d.asf n.asf d.asf n.asf d.gsn n.gsn cj v.aai.3s r.as.1 p.d n.dsn p.a n.asn a.asn cj a.asn cj
3836 3811 3836 1222 3836 768 2779 708 1609 708 1877 4460 2093 4001 3489 2779 5734 2779

showed me the Holy | City, Jerusalem, coming | down out of heaven | from God. **11** It shone with the
ἔδειξεν μοι τὴν ⌐τὴν ἁγίαν, πόλιν Ἰερουσαλὴμ καταβαίνουσαν ← ἐκ ← ⌐τοῦ οὐρανοῦ ἀπὸ ⌐τοῦ θεοῦ ἔχουσαν ← τὴν
v.aai.3s r.ds.1 d.asf d.asf a.asf n.asf n.asf pt.pa.asf p.g d.gsm n.gsm p.g d.gsm n.gsm pt.pa.asf d.asf
1259 1609 3836 3836 41 4484 2647 2849 1666 3836 4041 608 3836 2536 2400 3836

glory of God, | and its | brilliance was like | that of a very precious jewel, like a jasper, | clear as
δόξαν → ⌐τοῦ θεοῦ, αὐτῆς ὁ φωστήρ, ὅμοιος ← → τιμιωτάτῳ λίθῳ ὡς ⌐λίθῳ ἰάσπιδι → →
n.asf d.gsm n.gsm r.gsf.3 d.nsm n.nsm a.nsm a.dsm.s n.dsm pl n.dsm n.dsf
1518 3836 2536 899 3836 5891 3927 5508 3345 6055 3345 2618

crystal. **12** It had | a great, | high wall with twelve gates, and with twelve angels at the gates. | On
κρυσταλλίζοντι → ἔχουσα μέγα καὶ ὑψηλόν τεῖχος ἔχουσα δώδεκα πυλῶνας καὶ δώδεκα ἀγγέλους ἐπὶ τοῖς πυλῶσιν καὶ
pt.pa.dsm pt.pa.nsf a.asn cj a.asn n.asn pt.pa.nsf a.apm n.apm cj a.apm n.apm p.d d.dpm n.dpm cj
3222 2400 3489 2779 5734 5446 2400 1557 4784 2779 1557 34 2093 3836 4784 2779

the gates were written | the names | of the twelve tribes of | Israel. **13** There were
→ ἐπιγεγραμμένα ὀνόματα ἅ ἐστιν [τὰ ὀνόματα] → τῶν δώδεκα φυλῶν → υἱῶν Ἰσραήλ
pt.rp.apn n.apn r.npn v.pai.3s d.npn n.npn d.gpf a.gpf n.gpf n.gpm n.gsm
2108 3950 4005 1639 3836 3950 3836 1557 5876 5626 2702

three gates | on the east, | three | on the north, | three | on the south and three | on
τρεῖς πυλῶνες ἀπὸ ἀνατολῆς καὶ τρεῖς πυλῶνες ἀπὸ βορρᾶ καὶ τρεῖς πυλῶνες ἀπὸ νότου καὶ τρεῖς πυλῶνες ἀπὸ
a.npm n.npm p.g n.gsf cj a.npm n.npm p.g n.gsm cj a.npm n.npm p.g n.gsm cj a.npm n.npm p.g
5552 4784 608 424 2779 5552 4784 608 1080 2779 5552 4784 608 3803 2779 5552 4784 608

the west. **14** The wall of the city | had twelve foundations, and on them were the | names of the twelve
δυσμῶν καὶ ⌐ὸ ⌐τεῖχος → τῆς πόλεως ἔχων δώδεκα θεμελίους καὶ ἐπ' αὐτῶν δώδεκα ὀνόματα → τῶν δώδεκα
n.gpf cj d.nsn n.nsn d.gsf n.gsf pt.pa.nsm a.apm n.apm cj p.g r.gpm.3 a.npn n.npn d.gpm a.gpm
1553 2779 3836 5446 3836 4484 2400 1557 2529 2779 2093 899 1557 3950 3836 1557

apostles of the Lamb. ¶ **15** The angel who talked with me had a measuring rod | of gold to measure
ἀποστόλων → τοῦ ἀρνίου Καὶ ὁ ← λαλῶν μετ' ἐμοῦ εἶχεν μέτρον κάλαμον → χρυσοῦν ἵνα μετρήσῃ
n.gpm d.gsn n.gsn cj d.nsm pt.pa.nsm p.g r.gs.1 v.iai.3s n.asn n.asm a.asm cj v.aas.3s
693 3836 768 2779 3836 3281 3552 1609 2400 3586 2812 5997 2671 3582

the city, | its | gates | and its | walls. **16** The city was laid out like a square, | as long
τὴν πόλιν καὶ αὐτῆς τοὺς πυλῶνας καὶ αὐτῆς ⌐τὸ τεῖχος καὶ ἡ πόλις → κεῖται ← τετράγωνος καὶ ⌐τὸ μῆκος
d.asf n.asf cj r.gsf.3 d.apm n.apm cj r.gsf.3 d.asn n.asn cj d.nsf n.nsf v.pmi.3s a.nsf cj d.nsn n.nsn
3836 4484 2779 899 3836 4784 2779 899 3836 5446 2779 3836 4484 3023 5481 2779 3836 3601

as | it was wide. | He measured the city | with the rod | and found it to be | 12,000
αὐτῆς ὅσον καὶ ⌐τὸ πλάτος καὶ → ἐμέτρησεν τὴν πόλιν → τῷ καλάμῳ ἐπὶ δώδεκα χιλιάδων
r.gsf.3 r.nsn adv d.nsn n.nsn cj v.aai.3s d.asf n.asf d.dsm n.dsm p.g a.gpf n.gpf
899 4012 2779 3836 4424 2779 3582 3836 4484 3836 2812 2093 1557 5942

stadia in length, | and as wide | and high | as it is long. **17** He measured its | wall | and it
σταδίων ⌐τὸ μῆκος καὶ ⌐τὸ πλάτος καὶ ⌐τὸ ὕψος αὐτῆς ἐστίν ἴσα καὶ → ἐμέτρησεν αὐτῆς ⌐τὸ τεῖχος
n.gpn d.nsn n.nsn cj d.nsn n.nsn cj d.nsn n.nsn r.gsf.3 v.pai.3s a.npn cj v.aai.3s r.gsf.3 d.asn n.asn
5084 3836 3601 2779 3836 4424 2779 3836 5737 899 2698 2698 1639 2698 2779 3582 899 3836 5446

was 144 | cubits thick, by man's | measurement, which the angel | was using. **18** The wall
ἑκατὸν τεσσεράκοντα τεσσάρων πηχῶν → ἀνθρώπου μέτρον ὅ ἀγγέλου ἐστιν καὶ τοῦ τείχους
a.gpm a.gpm a.gpm n.gpm n.gsm n.asn r.nsn n.gsm v.pai.3s cj d.gsn n.gsn
1669 5477 5475 4388 3586 476 3586 4005 34 1639 2779 3836 5446

was made | of jasper, and the city of pure | gold, as | pure as glass. **19** The foundations of the
αὐτῆς ⌐ἡ ἐνδώμησις, ἴασπις καὶ ἡ πόλις καθαρὸν χρυσίον ὅμοιον καθαρῷ ὑάλῳ οἱ θεμέλιοι → τοῦ
r.gsf.3 d.nsf n.nsf n.nsf cj d.nsf n.nsf a.nsn n.nsn a.nsn a.dsm n.dsm d.npm n.npm d.gsn
899 3836 1908 2618 2779 3836 4484 2754 5992 3927 2754 5613 3836 2529 3836

ἐχόντων τὰς ἑπτὰ φιάλας τῶν γεμόντων τῶν ἑπτὰ πληγῶν τῶν ἐσχάτων καὶ ἐλάλησεν μετ' ἐμοῦ λέγων, Δεῦρο, δείξω σοι τὴν νύμφην τὴν γυναῖκα τοῦ ἀρνίου. **10** καὶ ἀπήνεγκέν με ἐν πνεύματι ἐπὶ ὄρος μέγα καὶ ὑψηλόν, καὶ ἔδειξέν μοι τὴν πόλιν τὴν ἁγίαν Ἰερουσαλὴμ καταβαίνουσαν ἐκ τοῦ οὐρανοῦ ἀπὸ τοῦ θεοῦ **11** ἔχουσαν τὴν δόξαν τοῦ θεοῦ, ὁ φωστὴρ αὐτῆς ὅμοιος λίθῳ τιμιωτάτῳ ὡς λίθῳ ἰάσπιδι κρυσταλλίζοντι. **12** ἔχουσα τεῖχος μέγα καὶ ὑψηλόν, ἔχουσα πυλῶνας δώδεκα καὶ ἐπὶ τοῖς πυλῶσιν ἀγγέλους δώδεκα καὶ ὀνόματα ἐπιγεγραμμένα, ἅ ἐστιν [τὰ ὀνόματα] τῶν δώδεκα φυλῶν υἱῶν Ἰσραήλ· **13** ἀπὸ ἀνατολῆς πυλῶνες τρεῖς καὶ ἀπὸ βορρᾶ πυλῶνες τρεῖς καὶ ἀπὸ νότου πυλῶνες τρεῖς καὶ ἀπὸ δυσμῶν πυλῶνες τρεῖς. **14** καὶ τὸ τεῖχος τῆς πόλεως ἔχων θεμελίους δώδεκα καὶ ἐπ' αὐτῶν δώδεκα ὀνόματα τῶν δώδεκα ἀποστόλων τοῦ ἀρνίου. ¶ **15** Καὶ ὁ λαλῶν μετ' ἐμοῦ εἶχεν μέτρον κάλαμον χρυσοῦν, ἵνα μετρήσῃ τὴν πόλιν καὶ τοὺς πυλῶνας αὐτῆς καὶ τὸ τεῖχος αὐτῆς. **16** καὶ ἡ πόλις τετράγωνος κεῖται καὶ τὸ μῆκος αὐτῆς ὅσον [καὶ] τὸ πλάτος. καὶ ἐμέτρησεν τὴν πόλιν τῷ καλάμῳ ἐπὶ σταδίων δώδεκα χιλιάδων, τὸ μῆκος καὶ τὸ πλάτος καὶ τὸ ὕψος αὐτῆς ἴσα ἐστίν. **17** καὶ ἐμέτρησεν τὸ τεῖχος αὐτῆς ἑκατὸν τεσσεράκοντα τεσσάρων πηχῶν μέτρον ἀνθρώπου, ὅ ἐστιν ἀγγέλου. **18** καὶ ἡ ἐνδώμησις τοῦ τείχους αὐτῆς ἴασπις καὶ ἡ πόλις χρυσίον καθαρὸν ὅμοιον ὑάλῳ καθαρῷ.

city | walls | were | decorated | with | every | kind of | precious | stone. | The | first | | foundation | was | jasper, | the
ιτῆς πόλεωςͺ | τείχους → | | κεκοσμημένοι ← | παντὶ ← | | ← τιμίῳ | λίθῳ | ὁ | ιὁ πρῶτοςͺ | θεμέλιος | | ἴασπις | ὁ
d.gsf n.gsf | n.gsn | | pt.rp.npm | a.dsm | | a.dsm | n.dsm | d.nsm | d.nsm a.nsm | n.nsm | | n.nsf | d.nsm
3836 4484 | 5446 | | 3175 | 4246 | | 5508 | 3345 | 3836 | 3836 4755 | 2529 | | 2618 | 3836

second | sapphire, | the | third | chalcedony, | the | fourth | emerald, | 20 | the | fifth | sardonyx, | the | sixth | carnelian, | the | seventh
δεύτερος | σάπφιρος | ὁ | τρίτος | χαλκηδών | ὁ | τέταρτος | σμάραγδος | | ὁ | πέμπτος | σαρδόνυξ | ὁ | ἕκτος | σάρδιον | ὁ | ἕβδομος
a.nsm | n.nsf | d.nsm | a.nsm | n.nsf | d.nsm | a.nsm | n.nsm | | d.nsm | a.nsm | n.nsm | d.nsm | a.nsm | n.nsn | d.nsm | a.nsm
1311 | 4913 | 3836 | 5569 | 5907 | 3836 | 5480 | 5040 | | 3836 | 4286 | 4918 | 3836 | 1761 | 4917 | 3836 | 1575

chrysolite, | the | eighth | beryl, | the | ninth | topaz, | the | tenth | chrysoprase, | the | eleventh | jacinth, | and the | twelfth
χρυσόλιθος | ὁ | ὄγδοος | βήρυλλος | ὁ | ἔνατος | τοπάζιον | ὁ | δέκατος | χρυσόπρασος | ὁ | ἐνδέκατος | ὑάκινθος | | ὁ | δωδέκατος
n.nsm | d.nsm | a.nsm | n.nsm | d.nsm | a.nsm | n.nsn | d.nsm | a.nsm | n.nsm | d.nsm | a.nsm | n.nsm | | d.nsm | a.nsm
5994 | 3836 | 3838 | 1039 | 3836 | 1888 | 5535 | 3836 | 1281 | 5995 | 3836 | 1895 | 5611 | | 3836 | 1558

amethyst. | 21 | The | twelve | gates | were | twelve | pearls, | | each | gate | | made of | a single | pearl.
ἀμέθυστος | | καὶ οἱ | δώδεκα | πυλῶνες | | δώδεκα | μαργαρῖται | ἀνὰ | εἷς | ἕκαστος | ιτῶν πυλώνωνͺ | ἦν | ἐξ | ἑνὸς | μαργαρίτου καὶ
n.nsf | | cj | a.npm | n.npm | | a.npm | n.npm | p.a | a.nsm | a.nsm | d.gpm | v.iai.3s | p | a.gsm | n.gsm | cj
287 | | 2779 3836 | 1557 | 4784 | | 1557 | 3449 | 324 | 1651 | 1667 | 3836 4784 | 1639 | 1666 | 1651 | 3449 | 2779

The | great | street | of the | city | was of | pure | gold, | like | transparent | glass. | ¶ | 22 | I | did not see | a | temple
ἡ | → | πλατεῖα | → τῆς | πόλεως | | καθαρὸν | χρυσίον | ὡς | διαυγής | ὕαλος | | | Καὶ | | οὐκ εἶδον | | ναὸν
d.nsf | | n.nsf | d.gsf | n.gsf | | a.nsn | n.nsn | pl | a.nsf | n.nsf | | | cj | | pl v.aai.1s | | n.asm
3836 | | 4426 | 3836 | 4484 | | 2754 | 5992 | 6055 | 1420 | 5613 | | | 2779 | 1625 | 1625 4024 | 1625 | 3724

in | the city, | because | the | Lord | God | Almighty | | and the | Lamb | are | its | temple. | 23 | The | city | does | not
ἐν | αὐτῇ | γὰρ | ὁ | κύριος | ὁ θεὸς | ὁ παντοκράτωρ | | καὶ τὸ | ἀρνίον | ἐστιν | αὐτῆς | ναὸς | | καὶ ἡ | πόλις | → | οὐ
p.d | r.dsf.3 | cj | d.nsm | n.nsm | d.nsm n.nsm | d.nsm n.nsm | | cj d.nsn | n.nsn | v.pai.3s | r.gsf.3 | n.nsm | | cj d.nsf | n.nsf | | pl
1877 | 899 | 1142 | 3836 | 3261 | 3836 2536 | 3836 4120 | | 2779 3836 | 768 | 1639 | 899 | 3724 | | 2779 3836 | 4484 | 2400 | 4024

need | the | sun | or | the | moon | to | shine | on it, | for | the | glory | of God | | gives it | light, | and the | Lamb
ιχρείανͺ | ἔχει | τοῦ | ἡλίου | οὐδὲ | τῆς | σελήνης | ἵνα | φαίνωσιν | → αὐτῇ | γὰρ ἡ | δόξα | → ιτοῦ θεοῦͺ | → | αὐτὴν | ἐφώτισεν | καὶ τὸ | ἀρνίον
n.asf | v.pai.3s | d.gsm | n.gsm | cj | d.gsf | n.gsf | cj | v.pas.3p | r.dsf.3 | cj d.nsf | n.nsf | d.gsm n.gsm | | r.asf.3 | v.aai.3s | cj d.nsn | n.nsn
5970 | 2400 | 3836 | 2463 | 4028 | 3836 | 4943 | 2671 | 5743 | 899 | 1142 3836 | 1518 | 3836 2536 | | 899 | 5894 | 2779 3836 | 768

is | its | lamp. | 24 | The | nations | will | walk | | by | its | light, | and | the | kings | of | the | earth | will | bring
αὐτῆς | ὁ | λύχνος | | καὶ τὰ | ἔθνη | → | περιπατήσουσιν | διὰ | αὐτῆς | ιτοῦ φωτὸςͺ | καὶ | οἱ | βασιλεῖς | → τῆς | γῆς | → | φέρουσιν
r.gsf.3 | d.nsm | n.nsm | | cj d.npn | n.npn | | v.fai.3p | p.g | r.gsf.3 | d.gsn n.gsn | cj | d.npm | n.npm | d.gsf | n.gsf | | v.pai.3p
899 | 3836 | 3394 | | 2779 3836 | 1620 | | 4344 | 1328 | 899 | 3836 5890 | 2779 | 3836 | 995 | 3836 | 1178 | | 5770

their | splendor | into | it. | 25 | On | no | day | will | its | gates | | ever be | shut, | for | there will be | | no | night
αὐτῶν | ιτὴν δόξανͺ | εἰς | αὐτήν | καὶ | ιοὐ μὴͺ | ἡμέρας | → | αὐτῆς | οἱ | πυλῶνεςͺ | → | κλεισθῶσιν | γὰρ | → | ἔσται | οὐκ | νὺξ
r.gpm.3 | d.asf n.asf | p.a | r.asf.3 | cj | pl pl | n.gsf | | r.gsf.3 | d.npm | n.npm | | v.aps.3p | cj | | v.fmi.3s | pl | n.nsf
899 | 3836 1518 | 1650 | 899 | 2779 | 4024 3590 | 2465 | 3091 | 899 | 3836 | 4784 | | 3091 | 1142 | | 1639 | 4024 | 3816

there. | 26 | The | glory | and | honor | | of the | nations | will be | brought | into | it. | 27 | Nothing | impure | will ever | | enter
ἐκεῖ | | καὶ | τὴν | δόξαν | καὶ | ιτὴν τιμὴνͺ | → | τῶν | ἐθνῶν | → | οἴσουσιν | εἰς | αὐτήν | | καὶ | πᾶν | κοινὸν | ιοὐ μὴͺ | εἰσέλθη
adv | | cj | d.asf | n.asf | cj | d.asf n.asf | | d.gpn | n.gpn | | v.fai.3p | p.a | r.asf.3 | | cj | a.nsn | a.nsn | pl pl | v.aas.3s
1695 | | 2779 | 3836 | 1518 | 2779 | 3836 5507 | | 3836 | 1620 | | 5770 | 1650 | 899 | | 2779 | 4246 | 3123 | 1656 4024 3590 | 1656

it, | nor will | anyone | who | does | what is | shameful | or | deceitful, | but | only | those | whose | names | are | written
εἰς | αὐτὴν | καὶ | | ὁ | ποιῶν | βδέλυγμα | καὶ | ψεῦδος | εἰ | μὴ ← | οἱ | | → | γεγραμμένοι
p.a | r.asf.3 | cj | | d.nsm | pt.pa.nsm | n.asn | cj | n.asn | cj | pl | d.npm | | | pt.rp.npm
1650 | 899 | 2779 | | 3836 | 4472 | 1007 | 2779 | 6022 | 1623 | 3590 | 3836 | | | 1211

in | the | Lamb's | book | of life.
ἐν | τῷ | ιτοῦ ἀρνίουͺ | βιβλίῳ | → ιτῆς ζωῆςͺ
p.d | d.dsn | d.gsn n.gsn | n.dsn | d.gsf n.gsf
1877 | 3836 | 3836 768 | 1046 | 3836 2437

The River of Life

22:1 Then | the | angel | showed | me | the | river | | of the | water | of | life, | as | clear | as | crystal, | flowing | | from | the
Καὶ | | | ἔδειξεν | μοι | | ποταμὸν | → | ὕδατος | → | ζωῆς | λαμπρὸν | ὡς | | κρύσταλλον | ἐκπορευόμενον | ἐκ | τοῦ
cj | | | v.aai.3s | r.ds.1 | | n.asm | | n.gsn | | n.gsf | a.asm | pl | | n.asm | pt.pm.asm | p.g | d.gsm
2779 | | | 1259 | 1609 | | 4532 | | 5623 | | 2437 | 3287 | 6055 | | 3223 | 1744 | 1666 | 3836

throne | of God | | and | of the | Lamb | 2 | down | the | middle | of the | great | street | of the | city. | On | each | side | of
θρόνου | → ιτοῦ θεοῦͺ | καὶ | → | τοῦ | ἀρνίου | ἐν | | μέσῳ | → τῆς | → | πλατείας | → | αὐτῆς | καὶ | ἐντεῦθεν | καὶ | ἐκεῖθεν →
n.gsm | d.gsm n.gsm | cj | | d.gsn | n.gsn | p.d | | n.dsn | d.gsf | | n.gsf | | r.gsf.3 | cj | adv | cj | adv
2585 | 3836 2536 | 2779 | | 3836 | 768 | 1877 | | 3545 | 3836 | | 4426 | | 899 | 2779 | 1949 | 2779 | 1696

¹⁹ οἱ θεμέλιοι τοῦ τείχους τῆς πόλεως παντὶ λίθῳ τιμίῳ κεκοσμημένοι· ὁ θεμέλιος ὁ πρῶτος ἴασπις, ὁ δεύτερος σάπφιρος, ὁ τρίτος χαλκηδών, ὁ τέταρτος σμάραγδος, ²⁰ ὁ πέμπτος σαρδόνυξ, ὁ ἕκτος σάρδιον, ὁ ἕβδομος χρυσόλιθος, ὁ ὄγδοος βήρυλλος, ὁ ἔνατος τοπάζιον, ὁ δέκατος χρυσόπρασος, ὁ ἐνδέκατος ὑάκινθος, ὁ δωδέκατος ἀμέθυστος. ²¹ καὶ οἱ δώδεκα πυλῶνες δώδεκα μαργαρῖται, ἀνὰ εἷς ἕκαστος τῶν πυλώνων ἦν ἐξ ἑνὸς μαργαρίτου. καὶ ἡ πλατεῖα τῆς πόλεως χρυσίον καθαρὸν ὡς ὕαλος διαυγής. ¶ ²² Καὶ ναὸν οὐκ εἶδον ἐν αὐτῇ, ὁ γὰρ κύριος ὁ θεὸς ὁ παντοκράτωρ ναὸς αὐτῆς ἐστιν καὶ τὸ ἀρνίον. ²³ καὶ ἡ πόλις οὐ χρείαν ἔχει τοῦ ἡλίου οὐδὲ τῆς σελήνης ἵνα φαίνωσιν αὐτῇ, ἡ γὰρ δόξα τοῦ θεοῦ ἐφώτισεν αὐτήν, καὶ ὁ λύχνος αὐτῆς τὸ ἀρνίον. ²⁴ καὶ περιπατήσουσιν τὰ ἔθνη διὰ τοῦ φωτὸς αὐτῆς, καὶ οἱ βασιλεῖς τῆς γῆς φέρουσιν τὴν δόξαν αὐτῶν εἰς αὐτήν, ²⁵ καὶ οἱ πυλῶνες αὐτῆς οὐ μὴ κλεισθῶσιν ἡμέρας, νὺξ γὰρ οὐκ ἔσται ἐκεῖ, ²⁶ καὶ οἴσουσιν τὴν δόξαν καὶ τὴν τιμὴν τῶν ἐθνῶν εἰς αὐτήν. ²⁷ καὶ οὐ μὴ εἰσέλθη εἰς αὐτὴν πᾶν κοινὸν καὶ [ὁ] ποιῶν βδέλυγμα καὶ ψεῦδος εἰ μὴ οἱ γεγραμμένοι ἐν τῷ βιβλίῳ τῆς ζωῆς τοῦ ἀρνίου.

²²:¹ Καὶ ἔδειξέν μοι ποταμὸν ὕδατος ζωῆς λαμπρὸν ὡς κρύσταλλον, ἐκπορευόμενον ἐκ τοῦ θρόνου τοῦ θεοῦ καὶ τοῦ ἀρνίου.

the river   stood the tree of life, bearing twelve crops of fruit,   yielding   its   fruit   every   month.
τοῦ ποταμοῦ   ξύλον → ζωῆς ποιοῦν δώδεκα   καρποὺς ἀποδιδοῦν αὐτοῦ τὸν καρπὸν ⌐κατὰ ἕκαστον⌐ μῆνα
d.gsm n.gsm   n.nsn   n.gsf pt.pa.nsn a.apm   n.apm   pt.pa.nsn r.gsn.3 d.asm n.asm p.a r.asm   n.asm
3836 4532   3833   2437 4472   1557   2843   625   899   3836 2843 2848 1667   3604

And the leaves of the tree are for the healing of the nations. ³ No longer will there be any curse.   The
καὶ τὰ φύλλα → τοῦ ξύλου εἰς   θεραπείαν → τῶν ἐθνῶν   καὶ οὐκ ἔτι   →   →   ἔσται πᾶν κατάθεμα καὶ ὁ
cj   d.npn n.npn d.gsn n.gsn p.a   n.asf   d.gpn n.gpn   cj pl adv   v.fmi.3s a.nsn n.nsn   cj   d.nsm
2779 3836 5877 3836 3833 1650 2542   3836 1620   2779 4024 2285   1639 4246 2873   2779 3836

throne of God   and of the Lamb will be   in the city, and his   servants   will serve   him.   They will
θρόνος → τοῦ θεοῦ καὶ → τοῦ ἀρνίου → ἔσται ἐν αὐτῇ καὶ αὐτοῦ οἱ δοῦλοι → λατρεύσουσιν αὐτῷ   καὶ →
n.nsm   d.gsm n.gsm cj   d.gsn n.gsn   v.fmi.3s p.d r.dsf.3 cj r.gsm.3 d.npm n.npm   v.fai.3p   r.dsm.3 cj
2585   3836 2536   2779 3836 768   1639   1877 899   2779 899   3836 1529   3302   899   2779

see his   face,   and his   name   will be on their foreheads. ⁵ There will be   no more night.
ὄψονται αὐτοῦ ⌐τὸ πρόσωπον⌐ καὶ αὐτοῦ ⌐τὸ ὄνομα⌐   ἐπὶ αὐτῶν ⌐τῶν μετώπων⌐ καὶ →   →   ἔσται οὐκ ἔτι νὺξ   καὶ
v.fmi.3p r.gsn.3 d.asn n.asn   cj r.gsm.3 d.nsn n.nsn   p.g r.gpn.3 d.gpn n.gpn   cj   v.fmi.3s pl adv n.nsf cj
3972   899   3836 4725   2779 899   3836 3950   2093 899   3836 3587   2779   1639 4024 2285 3816 2779

They will not need   the light of a lamp or the light of the sun, for the Lord God   will give   them
→   →   οὐκ ἔχουσιν χρείαν   φωτὸς → λύχνου καὶ   φωτὸς →   ἡλίου ὅτι   κύριος ὁ θεὸς   →   →   ἐπ' αὐτοὺς
        pl v.pai.3p n.asf   n.gsn   n.gsn cj   n.gsn   n.gsn ⌐cj   n.nsm d.nsm n.nsm   p.a r.apm.3
2400 2400 4024 2400 5970   5890   3394   2779   5890   2463 4022   3261   3836 2536   2093 899

light. And they will reign for ever   and ever.   ¶ ⁶ The angel said to me, "These
φωτίσει καὶ → → βασιλεύσουσιν εἰς ⌐τοὺς αἰῶνας⌐ ⌐τῶν αἰώνων⌐ Καὶ   εἶπεν → μοι οὗτοι
v.fai.3s cj   v.fai.3p   p.a d.apm n.apm   d.gpm n.gpm   cj   v.aai.3s r.ds.1 r.npm
5894   2779   996   1650 3836 172   3836 172   2779   3306   1609 4047

words   are trustworthy and true.   The Lord, the God of the spirits   of the prophets, sent   his
⌐οἱ λόγοι⌐   πιστοὶ   καὶ ἀληθινοί καὶ ὁ κύριος ὁ θεὸς → τῶν πνευμάτων τῶν προφητῶν ἀπέστειλεν αὐτοῦ
d.npm n.npm   a.npm   cj a.npm   cj d.nsm n.nsm d.nsm n.nsm d.gpn n.gpn d.gpm n.gpm   v.aai.3s   r.gsm.3
3836 3364   4412   2779 240   2779 3836 3261 3836 2536 3836 4460   3836 4737   690   899

angel   to show his servants   the things that must soon   take place."
⌐τὸν ἄγγελον⌐ → δεῖξαι αὐτοῦ ⌐τοῖς δούλοις⌐ ἃ →   ←   δεῖ ἐν τάχει γενέσθαι
d.asm n.asm   f.aa r.gsm.3 d.dpm n.dpm   r.apn   v.pai.3s p.d n.dsn f.am
3836 34   1259 899   3836 1529   4005   1256 1877 5443   1181

Jesus Is Coming

22:7 "Behold, I am coming soon! Blessed is he who keeps the words of the prophecy in this   book." ¶
καὶ ἰδοὺ → → ἔρχομαι ταχύ μακάριος ὁ ← τηρῶν τοὺς λόγους → τῆς προφητείας → τούτου ⌐τοῦ βιβλίου⌐
cj   j   v.pmi.1s adv a.nsm   d.nsm pt.pa.nsm d.apm n.apm d.gsf n.gsf   r.gsn d.gsn n.gsn
2779 2627   2262   5444 3421   3836   4498   3836 3364 3836 4735   1046   4047 3836 1046

⁸ I,   John,   am the one who heard and saw these things. And when I had heard and seen   them, I fell
Κἀγὼ   Ἰωάννης   ὁ   ← ἀκούων καὶ βλέπων ταῦτα ←   καὶ ὅτε → ἤκουσα καὶ ἔβλεψα → ἔπεσα
crasis   n.nsm   d.nsm pt.pa.nsm cj pt.pa.nsm r.apn   cj cj   v.aai.1s cj v.aai.1s   v.aai.1s
2743   2722   3836   201   2779 1063   4047   2779 4021   201   2779 1063   4406

down to worship   at   the feet of the angel who had been showing   them to me. ⁹ But he said to me, "Do
→   → προσκυνῆσαι ἔμπροσθεν τῶν ποδῶν → τοῦ ἀγγέλου τοῦ → → δεικνύοντος ταῦτα → μοι   καὶ → λέγει → μοι   →
         f.aa   p.g   d.gpm n.gpm d.gsm n.gsm   d.gsm   pt.pa.gsm r.apn   r.ds.1 cj   v.pai.3s   r.ds.1
         4686   1869   3836 4546   3836 34   3836   1260   4047   1609 2779 3306   1609 3972

not do it! I am a fellow servant   with you and with your brothers   the prophets and of all who keep   the
μὴ ὅρα   → εἰμι → σύνδουλος → σού καὶ → σου ⌐τῶν ἀδελφῶν⌐ τῶν προφητῶν καὶ → τῶν τηρούντων τοὺς
pl v.pam.2s v.pai.1s n.nsm   r.gs.2 cj   r.gs.2 d.gpm n.gpm   d.gpm n.gpm   cj   d.gpm pt.pa.gpm d.apm
3590 3972   1639   5281   5148 2779 5148 3836 81   3836 4737   2779   3836 5498   3836

words of this book.   Worship God!"   ¶ ¹⁰ Then he told me, "Do not seal   up the words of the
λόγους → τούτου ⌐τοῦ βιβλίου⌐ προσκύνησον ⌐τῷ θεῷ⌐   Καὶ →   λέγει μοι μὴ σφραγίσῃς ← τοὺς λόγους τῆς
n.apm   r.gsn d.gsn n.gsn   v.aam.2s   d.dsm n.dsm   cj   v.pai.3s r.ds.1 pl v.aas.2s   d.apm n.apm d.gsf
3364   1046   4047 1046   4686   3836 2536   2779   3306   1609 3590 5381   3836 3364   4735 3836

---

² ἐν μέσῳ τῆς πλατείας αὐτῆς καὶ τοῦ ποταμοῦ ἐντεῦθεν καὶ ἐκεῖθεν ξύλον ζωῆς ποιοῦν καρποὺς δώδεκα, κατὰ μῆνα ἕκαστον ἀποδιδοῦν τὸν καρπὸν αὐτοῦ, καὶ τὰ φύλλα τοῦ ξύλου εἰς θεραπείαν τῶν ἐθνῶν. ³ καὶ πᾶν κατάθεμα οὐκ ἔσται ἔτι. καὶ ὁ θρόνος τοῦ θεοῦ καὶ τοῦ ἀρνίου ἐν αὐτῇ ἔσται, καὶ οἱ δοῦλοι αὐτοῦ λατρεύσουσιν αὐτῷ ⁴ καὶ ὄψονται τὸ πρόσωπον αὐτοῦ, καὶ τὸ ὄνομα αὐτοῦ ἐπὶ τῶν μετώπων αὐτῶν. ⁵ καὶ νὺξ οὐκ ἔσται ἔτι καὶ οὐκ ἔχουσιν χρείαν φωτὸς λύχνου καὶ φωτὸς ἡλίου, ὅτι κύριος ὁ θεὸς φωτίσει ἐπ' αὐτούς, καὶ βασιλεύσουσιν εἰς τοὺς αἰῶνας τῶν αἰώνων. ¶ ⁶ Καὶ εἶπέν μοι, Οὗτοι οἱ λόγοι πιστοὶ καὶ ἀληθινοί, καὶ ὁ κύριος ὁ θεὸς τῶν πνευμάτων τῶν προφητῶν ἀπέστειλεν τὸν ἄγγελον αὐτοῦ δεῖξαι τοῖς δούλοις αὐτοῦ ἃ δεῖ γενέσθαι ἐν τάχει.

22:7 καὶ ἰδοὺ ἔρχομαι ταχύ. μακάριος ὁ τηρῶν τοὺς λόγους τῆς προφητείας τοῦ βιβλίου τούτου. ¶ ⁸ Κἀγὼ Ἰωάννης ὁ ἀκούων καὶ βλέπων ταῦτα. καὶ ὅτε ἤκουσα καὶ ἔβλεψα, ἔπεσα προσκυνῆσαι ἔμπροσθεν τῶν ποδῶν τοῦ ἀγγέλου τοῦ δεικνύοντός μοι ταῦτα. ⁹ καὶ λέγει μοι, Ὅρα μή· σύνδουλός σού εἰμι καὶ τῶν ἀδελφῶν σου τῶν προφητῶν καὶ τῶν τηρούντων τοὺς λόγους τοῦ βιβλίου τούτου· τῷ θεῷ προσκύνησον. ¶ ¹⁰ καὶ λέγει μοι, Μὴ σφραγίσῃς τοὺς λόγους τῆς προφητείας τοῦ βιβλίου τούτου,

prophecy　　of this　book,　because　the time　is　near.　**11** Let him who does wrong continue to do wrong;
ˌτῆς προφητείαςˌ　τοῦ τούτου βιβλίου　γὰρ　ὁ καιρὸς ἐστιν ἐγγύς　　ὁ　　ἀδικῶν ἔτι　　ἀδικησάτω καὶ
d.gsf n.gsf　d.gsn r.gsn n.gsn　cj　d.nsm n.nsm v.pai.3s adv　　d.nsm　pt.pa.nsm adv　　v.aam.3s cj
3836 4735　3836 4047 1046　1142　3836 2789 1639 1584　92　3836　92　2285　92　2285　92 2779

let him who is vile　continue to be vile;　　let him who does right　continue to do　right;　and let
ὁ　　ῥυπαρὸς ἔτι　　ῥυπανθήτω καὶ　ὁ　　δίκαιος ἔτι　　ποιησάτω δικαιοσύνην καὶ
d.nsm　a.nsm adv　　v.apm.3s cj　d.nsm　a.nsm adv　　v.aam.3s n.asf　cj
4472 3836　4865 2285　　4862　2779 4472 3836　1465 2285　　4472　1466　2779 39

him who is holy continue to be holy.”　¶　**12** “Behold, I am coming soon!　My reward　is with me, and
ὁ　　ἅγιος ἔτι　　ἁγιασθήτω　Ἰδοὺ　ἔρχομαι ταχύ καὶ μου ὁ μισθός,　μετ’ ἐμοῦ
d.nsm　a.nsm adv　　v.apm.3s　j　v.pmi.1s adv cj r.gs.1 d.nsm n.nsm　p.g r.gs.1
3836　41 2285　　39　2627　2262 5444 2779 1609 3836 3635　3552 1609

I will give　to everyone according to what　he has done.　**13** I　am the Alpha and the Omega, the First
ἀποδοῦναι ἑκάστῳ ὡς　ˌτὸ ἔργον,ˌ αὐτοῦ ἐστιν　ἐγώ　τὸ ἄλφα καὶ τὸ ὦ　ὁ πρῶτος
f.aa r.dsm cj　d.nsn n.nsn r.gsm.3 v.pai.3s　r.ns.1　d.nsn n.nsn cj d.nsn　d.nsm a.nsm
625 1667 6055　3836 2240 899 1639　1609　3836 270 2779 3836 6042　3836 4755

and the Last,　the Beginning and the End.　¶　**14** “Blessed are those who wash　their robes,　that they
καὶ ὁ ἔσχατος ἡ ἀρχή　καὶ τὸ τέλος　Μακάριοι　οἱ　πλύνοντες αὐτῶν ˌτὰς στολάς,ˌ ἵνα αὐτῶν
cj d.nsm a.nsm d.nsf n.nsf　cj d.nsn n.nsn　a.npm　d.npm　pt.pa.npm r.gpm.3 d.apf n.apf　cj r.gpm.3
2779 3836 2274 3836 794　2779 3836 5465　3421　3836　4459 899 3836 5124　2671 899

may have the right　to the tree of life　and may go　through the gates　into the city.　**15** Outside are the
ἔσται ἡ ἐξουσία ἐπὶ τὸ ξύλον ˌτῆς ζωῆς,ˌ καὶ　εἰσέλθωσιν　τοῖς πυλῶσιν εἰς τὴν πόλιν　ἔξω　οἱ
v.fmi.3s d.nsf n.nsf p.a d.asn n.asn d.gsf n.gsf cj　v.aas.3p　d.dpm n.dpm p.a d.asf n.asf　adv　d.npm
1639 3836 2026 2093 3836 3833 3836 2437 2779　1656　3836 4784 1650 3836 4484　2032　3836

dogs,　those who practice magic　arts,　the sexually immoral,　the murderers,　the idolaters　and
κύνες καὶ οἱ　φάρμακοι　καὶ οἱ πόρνοι　καὶ οἱ φονεῖς　καὶ οἱ εἰδωλολάτραι καὶ
n.npm cj d.npm　n.npm　cj d.npm n.npm　cj d.npm n.npm　cj d.npm n.npm cj
3264 2779 3836　5761　2779 3836 4521　2779 3836 5838　2779 3836 1629　2779

everyone who loves and practices falsehood.　¶　**16** “I,　Jesus,　have sent　my angel　to give you this
πᾶς　φιλῶν καὶ ποιῶν ψεῦδος　Ἐγὼ Ἰησοῦς　ἔπεμψα μου ˌτὸν ἄγγελον,ˌ　ὑμῖν ταῦτα
a.nsm　pt.pa.nsm cj pt.pa.nsm n.asn　r.ns.1 n.nsm　v.aai.1s r.gs.1 d.asn n.asn　r.dp.2 r.apn
4246　5797 2779 4472 6022　1609 2652　4287 1609 3836 34　3455 3455 7007 4047

testimony for the churches. I　am　the Root and the Offspring of David, and the bright　Morning Star.” ¶
μαρτυρῆσαι ἐπὶ ταῖς ἐκκλησίαις ἐγώ εἰμι ἡ ῥίζα καὶ τὸ γένος　Δαυίδ　ὁ ὁ λαμπρός, ὁ πρωΐνός, ἀστήρ
f.aa p.d d.dpf n.dpf r.ns.1 v.pai.1s d.nsf n.nsf cj d.nsn n.nsn　n.gsm　d.nsm d.nsm a.nsm d.nsm a.nsm n.nsm
3455 2093 3836 1711 1609 1639 3836 4844 2779 3836 1169　1253　3836 3836 3287 3836 4748 843

17　The Spirit　and the bride say,　“Come!” And let him who hears say,　“Come!”　Whoever is thirsty,
Καὶ τὸ πνεῦμα καὶ ἡ νύμφη λέγουσιν ἔρχου　καὶ ὁ ἀκούων εἰπάτω ἔρχου　καὶ ὁ διψῶν
cj d.nsn n.nsn cj d.nsf n.nsf v.pai.3p v.pmm.2s　cj d.nsm pt.pa.nsm v.aam.3s v.pmm.2s　cj d.nsm pt.pa.nsm
2779 3836 4460 2779 3836 3811 3306 2262　2779 3306 3836 201 3306 2262　2779 3836 1498

let him come; and whoever wishes, let him take　the free　gift of the water of life.　¶　**18** I　warn　everyone
ἐρχέσθω ὁ θέλων　λαβέτω δωρεάν　ὕδωρ ζωῆς　ἐγώ Μαρτυρῶ παντὶ
v.pmm.3s d.nsm pt.pa.nsm　v.aam.3s adv　n.asn n.gsf　r.ns.1 v.pai.1s a.dsm
2262 3836 2527　3284 1562　5623 2437　1609 3455 4246

who hears　the words of the prophecy of this　book:　If anyone adds anything to them, God　will
τῷ ἀκούοντι τοὺς λόγους ˌτῆς προφετείαςˌ τούτου ˌτοῦ βιβλίου,ˌ ἐάν τις ἐπιθῇ　ἐπ’ αὐτὰ ὁ θεὸς
d.dsm pt.pa.dsm d.apm n.apm d.gsf n.gsf r.gsn d.gsn n.gsn cj r.nsm v.aas.3s　p.a r.apn.3 d.nsm n.nsm
3836 201 3836 3364 3836 4735 4047 3836 1046 1569 5516 2202　2093 899 3836 2536

add　to him the plagues described　in this book.　**19** And if anyone takes words　away from this
ἐπιθήσει ἐπ’ αὐτὸν τὰς πληγὰς ˌτὰς γεγραμμένας,ˌ ἐν τούτῳ τῷ βιβλίῳ　καὶ ἐάν τις ἀφέλῃ ˌτῶν λόγων,ˌ ἀπὸ ταύτης
v.fai.3s p.a r.asm.3 d.apf n.apf d.apf pt.rp.apf p.d r.dsn d.dsn n.dsn　cj cj r.nsm v.aas.3s d.gpm n.gpm p.g r.gsf
2202 2093 899 3836 4435 3836 1211 1877 4047 3836 1046　2779 1569 5516 904 3836 3364 904 608 4047

book　of prophecy,　God　will take away from him his　share　in the tree of life　and in the
ˌτοῦ βιβλίου,ˌ ˌτῆς προφητείας,ˌ ὁ θεὸς　ἀφελεῖ　αὐτοῦ ˌτὸ μέρος,ˌ ἀπὸ τοῦ ξύλου ˌτῆς ζωῆς,ˌ καὶ ἐκ τῆς
d.gsn n.gsn d.gsf n.gsf d.nsm n.nsm　v.fai.3s　r.gsm.3 d.asn n.asn p.g d.gsn n.gsn d.gsf n.gsf cj p.g d.gsf
3836 1046 3836 4735 3836 2536　904　899 3836 3538 608 3836 3833 3836 2437 2779 1666 3836

ὁ καιρὸς γὰρ ἐγγύς ἐστιν. **11** ὁ ἀδικῶν ἀδικησάτω ἔτι καὶ ὁ ῥυπαρὸς ῥυπανθήτω ἔτι, καὶ ὁ δίκαιος δικαιοσύνην ποιησάτω ἔτι καὶ ὁ ἅγιος ἁγιασθήτω ἔτι. ¶ **12** Ἰδοὺ ἔρχομαι ταχύ, καὶ ὁ μισθός μου μετ’ ἐμοῦ ἀποδοῦναι ἑκάστῳ ὡς τὸ ἔργον ἐστὶν αὐτοῦ. **13** ἐγὼ τὸ Ἄλφα καὶ τὸ Ὦ, ὁ πρῶτος καὶ ὁ ἔσχατος, ἡ ἀρχὴ καὶ τὸ τέλος. ¶ **14** Μακάριοι οἱ πλύνοντες τὰς στολὰς αὐτῶν, ἵνα ἔσται ἡ ἐξουσία αὐτῶν ἐπὶ τὸ ξύλον τῆς ζωῆς καὶ τοῖς πυλῶσιν εἰσέλθωσιν εἰς τὴν πόλιν. **15** ἔξω οἱ κύνες καὶ οἱ φάρμακοι καὶ οἱ πόρνοι καὶ οἱ φονεῖς καὶ οἱ εἰδωλολάτραι καὶ πᾶς φιλῶν καὶ ποιῶν ψεῦδος. ¶ **16** Ἐγὼ Ἰησοῦς ἔπεμψα τὸν ἄγγελόν μου μαρτυρῆσαι ὑμῖν ταῦτα ἐπὶ ταῖς ἐκκλησίαις. ἐγώ εἰμι ἡ ῥίζα καὶ τὸ γένος Δαυίδ, ὁ ἀστὴρ ὁ λαμπρὸς ὁ πρωϊνός. ¶ **17** Καὶ τὸ πνεῦμα καὶ ἡ νύμφη λέγουσιν, Ἔρχου. καὶ ὁ ἀκούων εἰπάτω, Ἔρχου. καὶ ὁ διψῶν ἐρχέσθω, ὁ θέλων λαβέτω ὕδωρ ζωῆς δωρεάν. ¶ **18** Μαρτυρῶ ἐγὼ παντὶ τῷ ἀκούοντι τοὺς λόγους τῆς προφητείας τοῦ βιβλίου τούτου· ἐάν τις ἐπιθῇ ἐπ’ αὐτά, ἐπιθήσει ὁ θεὸς ἐπ’ αὐτὸν τὰς πληγὰς τὰς γεγραμμένας ἐν τῷ βιβλίῳ τούτῳ, **19** καὶ ἐάν τις ἀφέλῃ ἀπὸ τῶν λόγων τοῦ βιβλίου τῆς προφητείας ταύτης, ἀφελεῖ ὁ θεὸς τὸ μέρος αὐτοῦ ἀπὸ τοῦ ξύλου τῆς ζωῆς καὶ ἐκ τῆς πόλεως τῆς ἁγίας τῶν γεγραμμένων ἐν τῷ βιβλίῳ τούτῳ.

holy	city,	which	are	described	in	this	book.	¶	[20] He	who	testifies	to	these	things	says,	"Yes,	I am
⌞τῆς ἁγίας⌟	πόλεως	τῶν	→	γεγραμμένων	ἐν	τούτῳ	⌞τῷ βιβλίῳ⌟		ὁ	←	μαρτυρῶν	←	ταῦτα	←	Λέγει	ναί	→ →
d.gsf a.gsf	n.gsf	d.gpm		pt.rp.gpm	p.d	r.dsn	d.dsn n.dsn		d.nsm		pt.pa.nsm		r.apn		v.pai.3s	pl	
3836 41	4484	3836		1211	1877	4047	3836 1046		3836		3455		4047		3306	3721	

coming	soon."	Amen.	¶	Come,	Lord	Jesus.	[21] The	¶	grace	of the	Lord	Jesus	be with	God's	people.
ἔρχομαι	ταχύ	Ἀμήν.		ἔρχου	κύριε	Ἰησοῦ.	Ἡ		χάρις	τοῦ	κυρίου	Ἰησοῦ	μετὰ	→	πάντων
v.pmi.1s	adv	pl		v.pmm.2s	n.vsm	n.vsm	d.nsf		n.nsf	d.gsm	n.gsm	n.gsm	p.g		a.gpm
2262	5444	297		2262	3261	2652	3836		5921	3836	3261	2652	3552		4246

Amen.
ἀμήν*
pl
297

¶ [20] Λέγει ὁ μαρτυρῶν ταῦτα, Ναί, ἔρχομαι ταχύ. ¶ Ἀμήν, ἔρχου κύριε Ἰησοῦ. ¶ [21] Ἡ χάρις τοῦ κυρίου Ἰησοῦ μετὰ τῶν ἁγίων. «πάντων.» ἀμήν.

Appendix A

Detailed Guidelines

The following guidelines are intended for those who know some Greek.

General

1. **Languages are not codes.** Please do not misunderstand the format of this text. There is almost never a one–for–one correlation between words of different languages, and meaning is conveyed more by groups of words.

   For example, in the following passage ὁ is placed under "who" and ἔχων is under "had." But as anyone who knows Greek will tell you, ὁ doesn't necessarily mean "who" and ἔχων does not mean "had." However, together ὁ ἔχων in this context does mean "who had."

Still	another	angel,	**who**	**had**	charge	of	the	fire,	came
καὶ	ἄλλος	ἄγγελος	ὁ	ἔχων	ἐξουσίαν	ἐπὶ	τοῦ	πυρός	ἐξῆλθεν
cj	r.nsm	n.nsm	d.nsm	pt.pa.nsm	n.asf	p.g	d.gsn	n.gsn	v.aai.3s
2779	257	34	3836	2400	2026	2093	3836	4786	2002

   If this sounds like gibberish, you probably do not know enough about Greek and should stop reading this section. If you want to learn more, I would recommend my *Greek for the Rest of Us*.

2. **Dynamic equivalence.** The dynamic theory of translation does not require grammatical equivalence. Nouns can be translated as verbs, verbs as prepositions, adjectives as nouns, etc. The point of a dynamic translation is to say the same thing, to get the same meaning across into the target language. Of course, the more dynamic a translation, the more interpretive it necessarily becomes, and the less useful it is for serious exegesis.

   Many participles are translated as finite verbs.

	He	**said**	in	a	loud	voice,	"Fear	God	and	give	him	glory,
→		λέγων	ἐν		μεγάλῃ	φωνῇ	φοβήθητε	⌐τὸν θεὸν⌐	καὶ	δότε	αὐτῷ	δόξαν
		pt.pa.nsm	p.d		a.dsf	n.dsf	v.apm.2p	d.asm n.asm	cj	v.aam.2p	r.dsm.3	n.asf
		3306	1877		3489	5889	5828	3836	2536	2779	1443	899	1518

   Indicative verbal forms can be changed to nonindicative, and vice versa.

If	we	claim		**to**	**have**	fellowship	with	him
Ἐὰν	→	εἴπωμεν	ὅτι	→	ἔχομεν	κοινωνίαν	μετ᾽	αὐτοῦ
cj		v.aas.1p	cj		v.pai.1p	n.asf	p.g	r.gsm.3
1569		3306	4022		2400	3126	3552	899

   Participle to preposition.

	It	had	a	great,		high	wall	**with**	twelve	gates,
→		ἔχουσα	μέγα	καὶ	ὑψηλόν	τεῖχος	ἔχουσα	δώδεκα	πυλῶνας
		pt.pa.nsf	a.asn	cj	a.asn	n.asn	pt.pa.nsf	a.apm	n.apm
		2400	3489	2779	5734	5446	2400	1557	4784

   Prepositional phrase to adjective.

And	we	will	be	**ready**		to	punish	every	act	of	disobedience
καὶ	→	→	ἔχοντες	⌐ἐν ἑτοίμῳ⌐	→	ἐκδικῆσαι	πᾶσαν	→	→	παρακοήν
cj			pt.pa.npm	p.d a.dsn		f.aa	a.asf			n.asf
2779			2400	1877 2289		1688	4246			4157

Verb to noun.

And	this	is	my	**prayer**:	that	your	love		may	abound
Καὶ	τοῦτο	→	→	προσεύχομαι	ἵνα	ὑμῶν	ἡ	ἀγάπη	→	περισσεύῃ
cj	r.asn			v.pmi.1s	cj	r.gp.2	d.nsf	n.nsf		v.pas.3s
2779	4047			4667	2671	7007	3836	27		4355

Noun to verb.

Be	clear	minded		and	self-controlled	so	that	you	can	**pray**.
→	→	σωφρονήσατε		καὶ	νήψατε	εἰς				προσευχάς
		v.aam.2p		cj	v.aam.2p	p.a				n.apf
		5404		2779	3768	1650				4666

Noun to pronoun.

saw	Simon	and	**his**		brother	Andrew	casting	a	net
εἶδεν	Σίμωνα	καὶ	Σίμωνος	⸤τὸν	ἀδελφὸν	Ἀνδρέαν	ἀμφιβάλλοντας	←	←
v.aai.3s	n.asm	cj	n.gsm	d.asm	n.asm	n.asm	pt.pa.apm		
1625	4981	2779	4981	3836	81	436	311		

Verb to adverb.

"Be	quiet!"	said	Jesus		**sternly**.		"Come	out	of	him!"
→	φιμώθητι	λέγων	ὁ	Ἰησοῦς⸥	αὐτῷ	ἐπετίμησεν	καὶ	ἔξελθε	←	ἐξ	αὐτοῦ
	v.apm.2s	pt.pa.nsm	d.nsm	n.nsm	r.dsm.3	v.aai.3s	cj	v.aam.2s		p.g	r.gsm.3
	5821	3306	3836	2652	899	2203	2779	2002		1666	899

The list could go on for pages.

3. **Meaning and function**. There are times when the translation translates a Greek word not so much with an English word that has the same meaning but with an English word that performs the same function in the sentence. The purist in me rebels against these situations, but the purpose of this text is to show how the NIV translated the passage.

The	words	I	say	to	you	**are**	not	just	my	own.
τὰ	ῥήματα	ἃ	ἐγὼ	λέγω	→	ὑμῖν	λαλῶ	οὐ	ἀπ'	ἐμαυτοῦ	←
d.apn	n.apn	r.apn	r.ns.1	v.pai.1s		r.dp.2	v.pai.1s	pl	p.g	r.gsm.1	
3836	4839	4005	1609	3306		7007	3281	4024	608	1831	

"I am of Paul" becomes "I follow Paul."

For	when	one	says,	"**I**	**follow**	**Paul**,"	and	another,	"I	follow	Apollos"
γὰρ	ὅταν	τις	λέγῃ	μέν	ἐγὼ	εἰμι	Παύλου	δέ	ἕτερος	ἐγὼ	Ἀπολλῶ
cj	cj	r.nsm	v.pas.3s	pl	r.ns.1	v.pai.1s	n.gsm	pl	r.nsm	r.ns.1	n.gsm
1142	4020	5516	3306	3525	1609	1639	4263	1254	2283	1609	663

ἵνα is often translated "to," although ἵνα is not a verb and the "to" is often part of an English infinitive.

It	is	better	for	you	**to**	lose	one	part		of	your	body
→	→	συμφέρει		σοι	ἵνα	ἀπόληται	ἓν	⸤τῶν	μελῶν⸥	→	σου
		v.pai.3s		r.ds.2	cj	v.ams.3s	a.nsn	d.gpn	n.gpn		r.gs.2
		5237		5148	2671	660	1651	3836	3517		5148

Much of the following will make sense only if you know some Greek.

you	received	your	good	...	Lazarus	**received**	bad
→	ἀπέλαβες	σου	⸤τὰ	ἀγαθά⸥	Λάζαρος	ὁμοίως	⸤τὰ	κακά⸥
	v.aai.2s	r.gs.2	d.apn	a.apn	n.nsm	adv	d.apn	a.apn
	655	5148	3836	19	3276	3931	3836	2805

For,	"Whoever	**would**	love	life	and	see	good	days
γὰρ	ὁ	θέλων	ἀγαπᾶν	ζωὴν	καὶ	ἰδεῖν	ἀγαθὰς	ἡμέρας
cj	d.nsm	pt.pa.nsm	f.pa	n.asf	cj	f.aa	a.apf	n.apf
1142	3836	2527	26	2437	2779	1625	19	2465

would	be	ashamed		of	having	been	**so**			confident.
→	→	καταισχυνθῶμεν					ταύτῃ	ἐν	⌐τῇ	ὑποστάσει⌐
		v.aps.1p					r.dsf	p.d	d.dsf	n.dsf
		2875					4047	1877	3836	5712

Was	**there**	ever	a	city	like		this	great		city?
→	τίς				ὁμοία	τῇ	⌐τῇ	μεγάλῃ⌐		πόλει
	r.nsf				a.nsf	d.dsf	d.dsf	a.dsf		n.dsf
	5515				3927	3836	3836	3489		4484

place	prepared		for	her	by	God,		**where**		she	might	be	taken	care	of
τόπον	ἡτοιμασμένον			ἀπὸ	⌐τοῦ	θεοῦ⌐	ἐκεῖ		ἵνα	αὐτὴν	→	→	→	τρέφωσιν ←	
n.asm	pt.rp.asm			p.g	d.gsm	n.gsm	adv		cj	r.asf.3				v.pas.3p	
5536	2286			608	3836	2536	1695		2671	899			5555	

On	that	of	**observing**		the	law?	No,	but	on	that	of	faith.
			⌐τῶν	ἔργων⌐			οὐχί	ἀλλὰ	διὰ	νόμου	→	πίστεως
			d.gpn	n.gpn			pl	cj	p.g	n.gsm		n.gsf
			3836	2240			4049	247	1328	3795		4411

But	I	am	afraid	**that**	**just**	as	Eve	was	deceived	by	the	serpent's	cunning
δὲ	→	→	φοβοῦμαι	μή	ὡς	←	Εὕαν		ἐξηπάτησεν	ἐν	ὁ	ὄφις	⌐τῆς πανουργία⌐
cj			v.ppi.1s	cj	cj		n.asf		v.aai.3s	p.d	d.nsm	n.nsm	d.dsf n.dsf
1254			5828	3590	6055		2293		1987	1877	3836	4058	3836 4111

	I	care	very	little	if	I	am	judged	by	you
δὲ	ἐμοὶ	ἐστιν	εἰς	→	ἐλάχιστον	ἵνα	→	→	ἀνακριθῶ	ὑφ᾽	ὑμῶν
cj	r.ds.1	v.pai.3s	p.a		a.asn.s	cj			v.aps.1s	p.g	r.gp.2
1254	1609	1639	1650		1788	2671			373	5679	7007

Be careful,	however,	that	the	exercise	of	your	freedom
→ βλέπετε	δὲ	πως	ἡ	→	→	ὑμῶν	ἐξουσία
v.pam.2p	cj	pl	d.nsf			r.gp.2	n.nsf
1063	1254	4803	3836	2026	2026	7007	2026

Without warning,	a	furious	storm	came	up	on	the	lake,
ἰδοὺ		μέγας	σεισμὸς	ἐγένετο	←	ἐν	τῇ	θαλάσσῃ
j		a.nsm	n.nsm	v.ami.3s		p.d	d.dsf	n.dsf
2627		3489	4939	1181		1877	3836	2498

4. **Rearrangement of sentences**. The dynamic theory of translation also allows for the rearrangement of sentence structure. Because Greek can attach meaning to word order, this often results in a loss of meaning and can make Bible study more difficult.

The Greek order of the following example is: ἀπεκρίθησαν οὖν οἱ γονεῖς αὐτοῦ καὶ εἶπαν· οἴδαμεν ὅτι οὗτός ἐστιν ὁ υἱὸς ἡμῶν καὶ ὅτι τυφλὸς ἐγεννήθη.

	"We	know		he	is		our	son,"	the		parents
οὖν	→	οἴδαμεν	ὅτι	οὗτος	ἐστιν	ἡμῶν	ὁ	υἱὸς⌐	οἱ	γονεῖς	αὐτοῦ
cj		v.rai.1p	cj	r.nsm	v.pai.3s	r.gp.1	d.nsm	n.nsm	d.npm	n.npm	r.gsm.3
4036		3857	4022	4047	1639	7005	3836	5626	3836	1204	899

answered,			"and	we	know		he	was	born	blind.
ἀπεκρίθησαν	καὶ	εἶπαν	καὶ			ὅτι	→	→	ἐγεννήθη	τυφλὸς
v.api.3p	cj	v.aai.3p	cj			cj			v.api.3s	a.nsm
646	2779	3306	2779			4022			1164	5603

When a translation alters sentence order, and this results in a conjunction that actually starts the Greek sentence being buried in the middle of the translation, I try to keep the conjunction at the beginning. For example, Greek often starts a sentence with a conjunction, the subject, and then a verb of speaking (e.g., "And Jesus said, 'I will be there and will comfort you.' "). The NIV almost always alters this construction to, " 'I will be there,' Jesus said, 'and I will comfort you.' " In this situation, I have kept the conjunction that starts the Greek sentence (e.g., δέ) at the beginning of the tagging for the sake of exegesis.

	"How	will	this	be,"	Mary	asked		the	angel,
δὲ	πῶς	↱	τοῦτο	ἔσται	Μαριὰμ	εἶπεν	πρὸς	τὸν	ἄγγελον
cj	cj		r.nsn	v.fmi.3s	n.nsf	v.aai.3s	p.a	d.asm	n.asm
1254	4802	1639	4047	1639	3452	3306	4639	3836	34

The NIV often moves words from one clause into another, especially from the main clause into a subordinate clause. In this example, the translator moved τοῦ ἑβδόμου ἀγγέλου from the main clause to the subordinate ὅταν clause.

But	in	the	days	when			the	seventh	angel	is	about	to	sound		his	trumpet
ἀλλ'	ἐν	ταῖς	ἡμέραις	ὅταν	τῆς	φωνῆς	τοῦ	ἑβδόμου	ἀγγέλου	→	μέλλῃ	→	σαλπίζειν	←		
cj	p.d	d.dpf	n.dpf	cj	d.gsf	n.gsf	d.gsm	a.gsm	n.gsm		v.pas.3s		f.pa			
247	1877	3836	2465	4020	3836	5889	3836	1575	34		3515		4895			

In Acts 8:6, the subject ("the crowds," οἱ ὄχλοι) is moved into the temporal clause.

When	**the**	**crowds**	heard		Philip	and	saw		the	miraculous
ἐν		αὐτοὺς	⌞τῷ	ἀκούειν⌟		καὶ	βλέπειν		τὰ	→
p.d		r.apm.3	d.dsn	f.pa		cj	f.pa		d.apn	
1877		899	3836	201		2779	1063		3836	

signs		he	did,	**they**		all		paid	close	attention
σημεῖα	ἃ	→	ἐποίει	⌞οἱ	ὄχλοι⌟	ὁμοθυμαδὸν	→			προσεῖχον
n.apn	r.apn		v.iai.3s	d.npm	n.npm	adv				v.iai.3p
4956	4005		4472	3836	4063	3924				4668

In Rev 19:15, ἐν αὐτῇ is actually inside the ἵνα clause.

	Out of	his		mouth	comes		a	sharp	sword	**with**
καὶ	ἐκ	←	αὐτοῦ	⌞τοῦ	στόματος⌟	ἐκπορεύεται		ὀξεῖα	ῥομφαία	ἐν
cj	p.g		r.gsm.3	d.gsn	n.gsn	v.pmi.3s		a.nsf	n.nsf	p.d
2779	1666		899	3836	5125	1744		3955	4855	1877

which	**to**	strike	down	the	nations.		"He	will	rule
αὐτῇ	ἵνα	πατάξῃ	←	τὰ	ἔθνη	καὶ	αὐτὸς	→	ποιμανεῖ
r.dsf.3	cj	v.aas.3s		d.apn	n.apn	cj	r.nsm		v.fai.3s
899	2671	4250		3836	1620	2779	899		4477

See the placement of ὑμεῖς in Mark 8:29 (καὶ αὐτὸς ἐπηρώτα αὐτούς· ὑμεῖς δὲ τίνα με λέγετε εἶναι;).

	"But	what	about	**you**?"	he		asked.		"Who	do	you
καὶ	δὲ			ὑμεῖς	αὐτὸς	ἐπηρώτα	αὐτούς	τίνα	→	→	
cj	cj			r.np.2	r.nsm	v.iai.3s	r.apm.3	r.asm			
2779	1254			7007	899	2089	899	5515			

say	I	am?"	Peter		answered,		"You	are
λέγετε	με	εἶναι	⌞ὁ	Πέτρος⌟	ἀποκριθεὶς	λέγει	αὐτῷ	σὺ	εἶ
v.pai.2p	r.as.1	f.pa	d.nsm	n.nsm	pt.ap.nsm	v.pai.3s	r.dsm.3	r.ns.2	v.pai.2s
3306	1609	1639	3836	4377	646	3306	899	5148	1639

See the placement of οἵτινες in Mark 9:1 (τινες ὧδε τῶν ἑστηκότων οἵτινες οὐ μὴ γεύσωνται θανάτου).

some	**who**	are	standing		here	will	not		taste	death
τινες	οἵτινες	εἰσίν	⌞τῶν	ἑστηκότων⌟	ὧδε	→	οὐ	μὴ	γεύσωνται	θανάτου
r.npm	r.npm	v.pai.3p	d.gpm	pt.ra.gpm	adv		pl	pl	v.ams.3p	n.gsm
5516	4015	1639	3836	2705	6045	1174	4024	3590	1174	2505

Sometimes this rearrangement is so complex that tagging the text is almost impossible (e.g., 1 Cor 4:13).

5. Weights, measures, and time designations. These are highly idiomatic. The NIV generally substitutes modern equivalents.

mixture of	myrrh	and	aloes,	about	***seventy-five pounds***.	
μίγμα →	σμύρνης	καὶ	ἀλόης	ὡς	ἑκατόν	λίτρας
n.asn	n.gsf	cj	n.gsf	pl	a.apf	n.apf
3623	5043	2779	264	6055	1669	3354

In	**a**	**little**	**while**	you	will	**see**	me	no	more,	
→	→	Μικρὸν ←		καὶ	→	→ θεωρεῖτέ	με	οὐκέτι ←		
		a.asn		cj		v.pai.2p	r.as.1	adv		
		3625		2779		2555	1609	4033		

A	*few*	*days*	*later,*	when	Jesus	again	entered		Capernaum,	
δι᾽	ἡμερῶν		→			πάλιν	εἰσελθὼν	εἰς	Καφαρναοὺμ	
p.g	n.gpf					adv	pt.aa.nsm	p.a	n.asf	
1328	2465		1656			4099	1656	1650	3019	

A	woman	is bound	to	her	husband	*as*	*long*	*as*	he	lives.
Γυνὴ	→ δέδεται ←		αὐτῆς	ὁ	ἀνὴρ,	ἐφ᾽	ὅσον	χρόνον,	→	ζῇ
n.nsf	v.rpi.3s		r.gsf.3	d.nsm	n.nsm	p.a	r.asm	n.asm		v.pai.3s
1222	1313		899	3836	467	2093	4012	5989		2409

6. Parallels. Greek, like any language, can omit words that the hearer would automatically understand. Often the translator will insert those words.

	If	you	forgive	anyone,		I	also	**forgive**	**him**.
δέ	→		χαρίζεσθε	ᾧ		τι	καγώ	←	
cj			v.pmi.2p	r.dsm		r.asn	crasis		
1254			5919	4005		5516	2743		

7. Long sentences. Because Greek uses longer sentences than modern English, the translations often break one sentence into two or more. When they do this, words must be added, usually to the beginning of the second sentence.

This matter arose	because	some	false	brothers		
διὰ	οἵτινες →		₍τοὺς	παρεισάκτους	ψευδαδέλφους₎	
p.a	r.npm		d.apm	a.apm	n.apm	
1328	4015		3836	4207	6012	

8. Helpful. The NIV often tries to be helpful by adding words that are not in the Greek but can be assumed from the context.

He	was	delivered	over	**to death**	for	our	sins	
ὅς	→	παρεδόθη	←		διὰ	ἡμῶν	₍τὰ παραπτώματα₎	
r.nsm		v.api.3s			p.a	r.gp.1	d.apn n.apn	
4005		4140			1328	7005	3836 4183	

	"This	is	**the meaning of**	the	parable:	The	seed	is	the	word of	God
δὲ	αὕτη	Ἔστιν		ἡ	παραβολή	ὁ	σπόρος	ἐστὶν ὁ	λόγος →	₍τοῦ	θεοῦ₎
cj	r.nsf	v.pai.3s		d.nsf	n.nsf	d.nsm	n.nsm	v.pai.3s d.nsm	n.nsm	d.gsm	n.gsm
1254	4047	1639		3836	4130	3836	5078	1639		3836	2536

Spirit	...	as	a	deposit,	**guaranteeing what is to come**
πνεύματος			₍τὸν	ἀρραβῶνα₎	
n.gsn			d.asm	n.asm	
4460			3836	775	

the	figurehead	of	the	twin	gods	**Castor and Pollux**.
→	παρασήμῳ	→	→		Διοσκούροις ←	
	a.dsn				n.dpm	
	4185				1483	

lest	the	cross	of	Christ		be	emptied	**of its power**.
₍ἵνα	μὴ	ὁ	σταυρὸς	→	₍τοῦ	Χριστοῦ₎	→	κενωθῇ
cj	pl	d.nsm	n.nsm		d.gsm	n.gsm		v.aps.3s
2671	3590	3836	5089		3836	5986		3033

9. **Greek text**. Where it is clear that the NIV followed a Greek variant reading not in the UBS Greek text, the variant is listed with an asterisk (Matt 1:8; the UBS reads, Ἀσάφ, word #811).

	Asa	the	father	of	Jehoshaphat,		Jehoshaphat
δὲ	Ἀσά *	ἐγέννησεν	ᵧτὸν	Ἰωσαφάτᵧ	δὲ	Ἰωσαφάτ
cj	n.nsm	v.aai.3s	d.asm	n.asm	cj	n.nsm
1254	809	1164	3836	2734	1254	2734

Where the critical texts are in doubt, I have listed the Greek word in brackets.

So	Jesus		said,		"When	you	have	lifted	up
οὖν	ὁ	Ἰησοῦς	εἶπεν	[αὐτοῖς]	ὅταν	→	→	ὑψώσητε	←
cj	d.nsm	n.nsm	v.aai.3s	r.dpm.3	cj			v.aas.2p	
4036	3836	2652	3306	899	4020			5738	

Beyond these two situations, it is often difficult to know for sure what Greek text the NIV is following because it is so dynamic in its translation.

The NIV also does not always follow the same versification as the Greek text. For example, 2 Cor 10:5 reads, "We demolish arguments and every pretension," but "we demolish arguments" comes from λογισμοὺς καθαιροῦντες in v 4.

Verbs

10. **Tenses**. In order to bring out the nuances of a tense, words sometimes must be added.

No	one	who	lives	in	him		**keeps**	**on**	sinning.
οὐχ	πᾶς	ὁ	μένων	ἐν	αὐτῷ	→		→	ἁμαρτάνει
pl	a.nsm	d.nsm	pt.pa.nsm	p.d	r.dsm.3				v.pai.3s
4024	4246	3836	3531	1877	899				279

You	who	are	**trying**	to	be	justified	by	law	have	been	alienated	from	Christ
↱	οἵτινες	→	→	→	→	δικαιοῦσθε	ἐν	νόμῳ	→	→	κατηργήθητε	ἀπὸ	Χριστοῦ
	r.npm					v.ppi.2p	p.d	n.dsm			v.api.2p	p.g	n.gsm
	2934	4015				1467	1877	3795			2934	608	5986

he	**kept**	**making**	signs		to	them
αὐτὸς	→	→	ᵧἦν	διανεύων,	→	αὐτοῖς
r.nsm			v.iai.3s	pt.pa.nsm		r.dpm.3
899			1639	1377		899

11. **Voice**. Actives can be changed to passives, but more often passives are changed to actives (because English prefers active constructions).

Then	I		**was**	**told**,	"You	must	prophesy	again	about
καὶ	μοι	→	λέγουσιν	σε	δεῖ	προφητεῦσαι	πάλιν	ἐπὶ	
cj	r.ds.1		v.pai.3p	r.as.2	v.pai.3s	f.aa	adv	p.d	
2779	1609		3306	5148	1256	4736	4099	2093	

that	deceiver		said,	'After	three	days	I	**will**	**rise**	again.'
ἐκεῖνος	ὁ	πλάνος,	εἶπεν	μετὰ	τρεῖς	ἡμέρας	→	→	ἐγείρομαι	
r.nsm	d.nsm	n.nsm	v.aai.3s	p.a	a.apf	n.apf			v.ppi.1s	
1697	3836	4418	3306	3552	5552	2465			1586	

This type of change can often affect the grammatical person in the translation. φανῶμεν is first person and "people" is third.

Not	that	**people**	will	see		that	we	have	stood
οὐχ	ἵνα		→	φανῶμεν			ἡμεῖς		δόκιμοι
pl	cj			v.aps.1p			r.np.1		a.npm
4024	2671			5743			7005		1511

12. Verbs and cases. There are many cases in which an English preposition following a verb could come from the verb or from the case of the following noun. I generally point back to the verb, especially if it is a compound verb.

The		tempter	came	**to**	him	and	said,	"If	you	are	the	Son	of	God
καὶ	ὁ	πειράζων	προσελθὼν	←	αὐτῷ		εἶπεν	εἰ	→	εἶ		υἱὸς	→	⌐υἱ⌐	θεοῦ
cj	d.nsm	pt.pa.nsm	pt.aa.nsm		r.dsm.3		v.aai.3s	cj		v.pai.2s		n.nsm		d.gsm	n.gsm
2779	3836	4279	4665		899		3306	1623		1639		5626		3836	2536

13. Compound verbs. When a compound verb is followed by the same preposition that forms the verb, I do not bracket the two words.

Then		Jesus	left		the	vicinity	of	Tyre	and	went
⌐Καὶ	πάλιν⌐		ἐξελθὼν	**ἐκ**	τῶν	ὁρίων	→	Τύρου		ἦλθεν
cj	adv		pt.aa.nsm	p.g	d.gpn	n.gpn		n.gsf		v.aai.3s
2779	4099		2002	1666	3836	3990		5602		22622

They	came	out	**of**	the	tombs,	and	after	Jesus'
καὶ	→	ἐξελθόντες	←	ἐκ	τῶν	μνημείων	μετὰ	αὐτοῦ
cj		pt.aa.npm		p.g	d.gpn	n.gpn	p.a	r.gsm.3
2779		2002		1666	3836	3646	3552	899

14. Periphrastic constructions. If a periphrastic construction is translated with a helping verb, the form of εἰμί is placed under that helping verb. If not, both parts are placed under the verb.

because	they	**were**	**harassed**	and	helpless,	like	sheep
ὅτι	→	ἦσαν	ἐσκυλμένοι	καὶ	ἐρριμμένοι	ὡσεὶ	πρόβατα
cj		v.iai.3p	pt.rp.npm	cj	pt.rp.npm	pl	n.npn
4022		1639	5035	2779	4849	6059	4585

We	write	this	to	make	our	joy	**complete**.
καὶ	ἡμεῖς	γράφομεν	ταῦτα	ἵνα	↱	ἡμῶν	ἡ	χαρὰ	ᾖ	πεπληρωμένη
cj	r.np.1	v.pai.1p	r.apn	cj		r.gp.1	d.nsf	n.nsf	v.pas.3s	pt.rp.nsf
2779	7005	1211	4047	2671	4444	7005	3836	5915	1639	4444

15. Adverbial participles generally require a helping word to bring out their full significance.

But	they	laughed	at	him.	¶	**After**	he	put	them
καὶ	→	κατεγέλων	←	αὐτοῦ	δὲ	→	→	ἐκβαλὼν
cj		v.iai.3p		r.gsm.3	cj			pt.aa.nsm
2779		2860		899	1254			1675

When	Jesus	got	out	of	the	boat,		a	man
καὶ	↱	αὐτοῦ	ἐξελθόντος	←	ἐκ	τοῦ	πλοίου	εὐθὺς	ἄνθρωπος
cj		r.gsm.3	pt.aa.gsm		p.g	d.gsn	n.gsn	adv	n.nsm
2779	2002	899	2002		1666	3836	4450	2318	476

since	you	are	going	through	the	same	struggle		you	saw
→	→	→	ἔχοντες	←	τὸν	αὐτὸν	ἀγῶνα	οἷον	→	εἴδετε
			pt.pa.npm		d.asm	r.asm	n.asm	r.asm		v.aai.2p
			2400		3836	899	74	3888		1625

For	**although**	they	knew	God,		they	neither	glorified	him
διότι	→	→	γνόντες	⌐τὸν	θεὸν⌐	↱	οὐχ	ἐδόξασαν
cj			pt.aa.npm	d.asm	n.asm		pl	v.aai.3p
1484			1182	3836	2536		1519	4024		1519

He	said	this	**to**	show	the	kind	of	death	he	was	going	to	die
δὲ	→	ἔλεγεν	τοῦτο	→	σημαίνων		ποίῳ	←	θανάτῳ	→	→	ἤμελλεν	→	ἀποθνῄσκειν
cj		v.iai.3s	r.asn		pt.pa.nsm		r.dsm		n.dsm			v.iai.3s		f.pa
1254		3306	4047		4955		4481		2505			3516		633

You	are	her	daughters	**if**	you	do	what	is	right
→	ἐγενήθητε	ἧς	τέκνα	→	→	→	→	→	ἀγαθοποιοῦσαι
	v.api.2p	r.gsf	n.npn						pt.pa.npf
	1181	4005	5451						16

Resist	him,	standing	firm	in	the	faith,	**because**	you	know
ἀντίστητε	ᾧ	→	στερεοὶ	→	τῇ	πίστει	→	→	εἰδότες
v.aam.2p	r.dsm		a.npm		d.dsf	n.dsf			pt.ra.npm
468	4005		5104		3836	4411			3857

16. Any substantival element of an articular participle is pointed toward the article, and the verbal parts toward the participle. If the participle is anarthrous, all elements are pointed toward the participle.

Then	I	heard	the	number	of	**those**	**who**	**were**	sealed:
Καὶ	→	ἤκουσα	τὸν	ἀριθμὸν	→	τῶν	←		ἐσφραγισμένων
cj		v.aai.1s	d.asm	n.asm		d.gpm			pt.rp.gpm
2779		201	3836	750		3836			5381

	Another	angel,	**who**	had	a	golden	censer,	came
Καὶ	ἄλλος	ἄγγελος	→	ἔχων		χρυσοῦν	λιβανωτὸν	ἦλθεν
cj	r.nsm	n.nsm		pt.pa.nsm		a.asm	n.asm	v.aai.3s
2779	257	34		2400		5997	3338	2262

17. Implied subjects are pointed toward the participle. If the subject is too specific and might confuse you when doing a word study, there is no arrow.

For	although	**they**	knew	God,		they	neither	glorified	him
διότι	→	→	γνόντες	τὸν	θεὸν	→	οὐχ	ἐδόξασαν	
cj			pt.aa.npm	d.asm	n.asm		pl	v.aai.3p	
1484			1182	3836	2536	1519	4024	1519	

This	is	**the**	**one**	**who**	came	by	water	and	blood
οὗτος	ἐστιν	ὁ	←	←	ἐλθὼν	δι᾽	ὕδατος	καὶ	αἵματος
r.nsm	v.pai.3s	d.nsm			pt.aa.nsm	p.g	n.gsn	cj	n.gsn
4047	1639	3836			2262	1328	5623	2779	135

	When	**Jesus**	landed	and	saw	a	large	crowd,		he	had	compassion
Καὶ	→		ἐξελθὼν		εἶδεν		πολὺν	ὄχλον	καὶ	→	→	ἐσπλαγχνίσθην
cj			pt.aa.nsm		v.aai.3s		a.asm	n.asm	cj			v.api.3s
2779			2002		1625		4498	4063	2779			5072

18. Articular infinitives usually have the article bracketed with the infinitive.

I	want	**to**	**know**	Christ	and	the	power	of	his	resurrection
	→	⌐τοῦ	γνῶναι⌐	αὐτὸν	καὶ	τὴν	δύναμιν	→	αὐτοῦ	⌐τῆς ἀναστάσεως⌐
		d.gsn	f.aa	r.asm.3	cj	d.asf	n.asf		r.gsm.3	d.gsf n.gsf
		3836	1182	899	2779	3836	1539	414	899	3836 414

eyes	**so**	**that**	**they**	**could**	**not**	**see**
ὀφθαλμοὺς	→	→			μὴ	⌐τοῦ	βλέπειν⌐
n.apm					pl	d.gsn	f.pa
4057	1063	1063			3590	3836	1063

	Before	certain	men	**came**		from	James,	he	used	to	eat
γὰρ	πρὸ	τινας	←	⌐τοῦ	ἐλθεῖν⌐	ἀπὸ	Ἰακώβου	→	→	→	συνήσθιεν
cj	p.g	r.apm		d.gsn	f.aa	p.g	n.gsm				v.iai.3s
1142	4574	5516		3836	2262	608	2610				5303

	When	the	crowds	**heard**		Philip	and	saw	the	miraculous	signs
δὲ	ἐν	αὐτοὺς	⌐τῷ	ἀκούειν⌐		Philip	καὶ	βλέπειν	τὰ	→	σημεῖα
cj	p.d	r.apm.3	d.dsn	f.pa			cj	f.pa	d.apn		n.apn
1254	1877	899	3836	201			2779	1063	3836		4956

	After	John		**was**	**put**		in	prison,
δὲ	Μετὰ	⌐τὸν	Ἰωάννην⌐	→	⌐τὸ	παραδοθῆναι⌐		
cj	p.a	d.asm	n.asm		d.asn	f.ap		
1254	3552	3836	2722		3836	4140		

won't	he	be	emboldened	**to**	**eat**	what	has	been	sacrificed	to	idols
οὐχὶ	→	→	οἰκοδομηθήσεται	εἰς	⌐τὸ	ἐσθίειν⌐	τὰ	→	→	→	εἰδωλόθυτα
pl			v.fpi.3s	p.a	d.asn	f.pa	d.apn				n.apn
4049			3868	1650	3836	2266	3836				1628

anyone	who	looks	at	a	woman			lustfully	
πᾶς	ὁ	βλέπων	←		γυναῖκα	πρὸς	τὸ	ἐπιθυμῆσαι	αὐτὴν
a.nsm	d.nsm	pt.pa.nsm			n.asf	p.a	d.asn	f.aa	r.asf.3
4246	3836	1063			1222	4639	3836	2121	899

Substantives

19. Definite article. The article can indicate the first attributive position for an adjective.

Jesus	said	to	the	man	with		the	shriveled	hand,
καὶ	λέγει	→	τῷ	ἀνθρώπῳ	τῷ	ἔχοντι	τὴν	ξηρὰν	χεῖρα
cj	v.pai.3s		d.dsm	n.dsm	d.dsm	pt.pa.dsm	d.asf	a.asf	n.asf
2779	3306		3836	476	3836	2400	3836	3831	5931

Modifiers in the second attributive position are tagged with their article.

Still	other	seed	fell	on	good		soil,	
δὲ	ἄλλα		ἔπεσεν	ἐπὶ	τὴν	καλὴν	τὴν	γῆν
pl	r.npn		v.aai.3s	p.a	d.asf	a.asf	d.asf	n.asf
1254	257		4406	2093	3836	2819	3836	1178

The article in the third attributive position is kept with the modifier.

seven	angels	with	the	seven	last		plagues
ἑπτὰ	ἀγγέλους	ἔχοντας		ἑπτὰ	τὰς	ἐσχάτας	πληγὰς
a.apm	n.apm	pt.pa.apm		a.apf	d.apf	a.apf	n.apf
2231	34	2400		2231	3836	2274	4435

Greek also uses the article when English does not, such as with proper names.

After	Jesus		was	born	in	Bethlehem
δὲ	→	Τοῦ	Ἰησοῦ	→	γεννηθέντος	ἐν	Βηθλέεμ
cj		d.gsm	n.gsm		pt.ap.gsm	p.d	n.dsf
1254	1164	3836	2652	1164	1877	1033

I usually keep the article with the word it is modifying.

in	preaching	the	gospel	of	his		Son,
ἐν	→	τῷ	εὐαγγελίῳ	→	αὐτοῦ	τοῦ	υἱοῦ
p.d		d.dsn	n.dsn		r.gsm.3	d.gsm	n.gsm
1877	2295	3836	2295		5626	899	3836	5626

The definite article (#3836) can function as many different English words, such as a personal or possessive pronoun.

They	said	to	him,	"John's	disciples		often	fast
δὲ	Οἱ	εἶπαν	πρὸς	αὐτόν	Ἰωάννου	οἱ	μαθηταὶ	πυκνὰ	νηστεύουσιν
cj	d.npm	v.aai.3p	p.a	r.asm.3	n.gsm	d.npm	n.npm	adv	v.pai.3p
1254	3836	3306	4639	899	2722	3836	3412	4781	3764

Husbands,	love	your	wives,	just	as		Christ	loved	the	church
Οἱ	ἄνδρες	ἀγαπᾶτε	τὰς	γυναῖκας	καθὼς	←	καὶ	ὁ	Χριστὸς	ἠγάπησεν	τὴν	ἐκκλησίαν
d.vpm	n.vpm	v.pam.2p	d.apf	n.apf	cj		adv	d.nsm	n.nsm	v.aai.3s	d.asf	n.asf
3836	467	26	3836	1222	2777		2779	3836	5986	26	3836	1711

20. The English indefinite article "a" is often left without a tag, unless it is translating an indefinite word like τις.

James,	a	servant	of	God	and	of	the	Lord	Jesus	Christ,
Ἰάκωβος	δοῦλος	→		θεοῦ	καὶ	→		κυρίου	Ἰησοῦ	Χριστοῦ
n.nsm	n.nsm			n.gsm	cj			n.gsm	n.gsm	n.gsm
2610	1529			2536	2779			3261	2652	5986

And	if	a	woman	has	a	husband	who	is	not	a	believer
καὶ	εἰ	τις	γυνὴ	ἔχει		ἄνδρα	→	→	→	→	ἄπιστον
cj	cj	r.nsf	n.nsf	v.pai.3s		n.asm					a.asm
2779	1623	5516	1222	2400		467					603

21. Adjectives. Here is the basic pattern I follow depending on how the NIV translated the construction.

of God
→ θεοῦ

of God
→ ⌐τοῦ θεοῦ⌐

of the God
→ τοῦ θεοῦ

of my God
→ τοῦ θεοῦ

of my God
_ μου ⌐τοῦ θεοῦ⌐

When adjectives function substantivally, English generally requires the insertion of a noun or pronoun.

But	you	have	an	anointing	from	the	Holy	**One**,
καὶ	ὑμεῖς	ἔχετε		χρῖσμα	ἀπὸ	τοῦ		ἁγίου ←
cj	r.np.2	v.pai.2p		n.asn	p.g	d.gsm		a.gsm
2779	7007	2400		5984	608	3836		41

I	tell	you,	on	that	night		two	**people**	will	be		in	one	bed;
λέγω	ὑμῖν	→	ταύτῃ	⌐τῇ	νυκτὶ⌐		δύο			ἔσονται	ἐπὶ	μιᾶς	κλίνης
v.pai.1s	r.dp.2		r.dsf	d.dsf	n.dsf		a.npm			v.fmi.3p	p.g	a.gsf	n.gsf
3306	7007		3816	4047	3836		3816	1545		1639	2093	1651	3109

I	write	to	you,	young	**men**,	because	you	are		strong
→	ἔγραψα	→	ὑμῖν	νεανίσκοι ←		ὅτι	→	ἐστε		ἰσχυροί
	v.aai.1s		r.dp.2	n.vpm		cj		v.pai.2p		a.npm
	1211		7007	3734		4022		1639		2708

Do	not	be	like	Cain,	who	belonged	to	the	evil	**one**
οὐ		καθὼς	Κάϊν		ἦν		ἐκ	τοῦ	πονηροῦ ←	
pl		cj	n.nsm		v.iai.3s		p.g	d.gsm	a.gsm	
4024		2777	2782		1639		1666	3836	4505	

Sometimes a verb is also added. I usually point the arrow under the verb toward the noun, recognizing that the verb is not derived merely from the noun but from the full construction.

For	we	are	taking	pains		to	do	**what**	is	**right**,
γὰρ	→	→	→	προνοοῦμεν		→	→	καλὰ		
cj				v.pai.1p				a.apn		
1142				4629				2819		

"But	woe	to	you	**who**	**are**	**rich**,
Πλὴν	οὐαὶ	→	ὑμῖν	τοῖς	→	πλουσίοις
cj	j		r.dp.2	d.dpm		a.dpm
4440	4026		7007	3836		4454

22. "Man." When "man" is inferred from the grammar and is functioning generically, I do not include an arrow under "man" out of sensitivity to the direction the English language appears to be going. But if context demands that the word refers to a male, I do use an arrow. If the English word is more generic, I am freer at including arrows.

"I	tell	you	the	truth,		the	**man**	who	does	not	enter
→	λέγω	ὑμῖν		⌐Ἀμὴν	ἀμὴν⌐	ὁ				μὴ	εἰσερχόμενος
	v.pai.1s	r.dp.2		pl	pl	d.nsm	←	→		pl	pt.pm.nsm
	3306	7007		297	297	3836		1656	3590	1656	

Watch	out	for	those	dogs,		those	**men**	who	do		evil,
Βλέπετε	←	←	τοὺς	κύνας	βλέπετε	τοὺς		←	ἐργάτας	κακοὺς
v.pam.2p			d.apm	n.apm	v.pam.2p	d.apm			n.apm	a.apm
1063			3836	3264	1063	3836			2239	2805

	Some	**men**	came		down	from	Judea		to	Antioch
Καί	τινες	←	κατελθόντε	←	ἀπὸ	⌐τῆς	Ἰουδαίας⌐			
cj	r.npm		pt.aa.npm		p.g	d.gsf	n.gsf			
2779	5516		2982		608	3836	2677			

I	will	boast		about	a	**man**	like	that,	
→	→	καυχήσομαι	ὑπὲρ	→	→	⌐τοῦ	τοιούτου⌐	
		v.fmi.1s	p.g			d.gsm	r.gsm	
		3016	5642			3836	5525	

"Why	does	this	**fellow**	talk	like	that?	He's	blaspheming!
τί	→	οὗτος	←	λαλεῖ	οὕτως	←	→	βλασφημεῖ
r.asn		r.nsm		v.pai.3s	adv			v.pai.3s
5515	3281	4047	3281	4048				1059

23. Antecedents. When the translation supplies the antecedent for a pronoun, I generally list the pronoun under the supplied antecedent.

The	**death**	he	died,	he	died	to	sin
γὰρ	ὃ	→	ἀπέθανεν	→	ἀπέθανεν	→	⌐τῇ	ἁμαρτίᾳ⌐
cj	r.asn		v.aai.3s		v.aai.3s		d.dsf	n.dsf
1142	4005		633		633		3836	281

24. Relative pronouns are generally linked with a word in the English relative clause. Often, however, the NIV often ignores a relative pronoun or changes a Greek relative clause into some other construction, in which case the Greek relative pronoun is often not translated.

"What	shall	**I**	do,	then,	with the	**one**	you	call	the	king	of	the	Jews"
τί	→	[θέλετε]	→	ποιήσω	οὖν		ὃν	→	λέγετε	τὸν	βασιλέα	→	τῶν	Ἰουδαίων
r.asn		v.pai.2p		v.aas.1s	cj		r.asm		v.pai.2p	d.asm	n.asm		d.gpm	a.gpm
5515	4472	2527		4472	4036		4005		3306	3836	995		3836	2681

and		the	star		they	had	seen	in	the	east	went	ahead	of	them
καὶ	ἰδοὺ	ὁ	ἀστὴρ	ὃν	→	→	εἶδον	ἐν	τῇ	ἀνατολῇ	προῆγεν	←	←	αὐτούς
cj	j	d.nsm	n.nsm	r.asm			v.aai.3p	p.d	d.dsf	n.dsf	v.iai.3s			r.apm.3
2779	2627	3836	843	4005			1625	1877	3836	424	4575			899

25. Accusative of Reference. When a word is in the accusative because it is an accusative of reference and the NIV uses a helping word, I do not include an arrow under that word lest it makes doing word studies too difficult.

he	might	make	atonement	**for**	the	sins	of	the	people.
→	→	→	⌐τὸ	ἱλάσκεσθαι⌐	τὰς	ἁμαρτίας	→	τοῦ	λαοῦ
			d.asn	f.pm	d.apf	n.apf		d.gsm	n.gsm
			3836	2661	3836	281		3836	3295

26. Double accusative. I do not include an arrow under the English words required to translate a double accusative.

and	has	made	us	**to be a**	kingdom	and	priests	to	serve	his	God
καὶ	→	ἐποίησεν	ἡμᾶς		βασιλείαν		ἱερεῖς	→	→	αὐτοῦ	⌐τῷ	θεῷ⌐
cj		v.aai.3s	r.ap.1		n.asf		n.apm			r.gsm.3	d.dsm	n.dsm
2779	4472	7005		993		2536	2536		899	3836	2536

I	will	not	leave	you	**as**	orphans;	I	will	come	to	you.
→	→	Οὐκ	ἀφήσω	ὑμᾶς		ὀρφανούς	→	→	ἔρχομαι	πρὸς	ὑμᾶς
		pl	v.fai.1s	r.ap.2		a.apm			v.pmi.1s	p.a	r.ap.2
918	918	4024	918	7007		4003			2262	4639	7007

27. Vocative. Often words are added to make the vocative more pronounced. I put arrows under these words.

Dear	children,	this	is	the	last	hour;	and	as	you	have	heard
→	Παιδία	→	ἐστίν		ἐσχάτη	ὥρα	καὶ	καθὼς	→	→	ἠκούσατε
	n.vpn		v.pai.3s		a.nsf	n.nsf	cj	cj			v.aai.2p
	4086		1639		2274	6052	2779	2777			201

	Do	not	be	surprised,	**my**	brothers,	if	the	world	hates	you.
Καὶ	↱	μὴ	→	θαυμάζετε	→	ἀδελφοί	εἰ	ὁ	κόσμος	μισεῖ	ὑμᾶς
cj		pl		v.pam.2p		n.vpm	cj	d.nsm	n.nsm	v.pai.3s	r.ap.2
2779	2513	3590		2513		81	1623	3836	3180	3631	7007

You	brood	of	vipers,	how	can	you	who	are		evil
→	γεννήματα	→	ἐχιδνῶν	πῶς	δύνασθε	←	→	ὄντες		πονηροὶ
	n.vpn		n.gpf	cj	v.ppi.2p			pt.pa.npm		a.npm
	1165		2399	4802	1538			1639		4505

28. Partitive Genitives are tagged as follows. The difference is whether the "some" idea is explicit in Greek.

Then	**some**	of	the	Pharisees	and	teachers	of	the	law
Τότε	τινες	→	τῶν	Φαρισαίων	καὶ	γραμματέων	←	←	←
adv	r.npm		d.gpm	n.gpm	cj	n.gpm			
5538	5516		3836	5757	2779	1208			

	Some	of	his	disciples		said	to	one	another,
οὖν		ἐκ	αὐτοῦ	⸤τῶν	μαθητῶν	εἶπαν	πρὸς	ἀλλήλους	←
cj		p.g	r.gsm.3	d.gpm	n.gpm	v.aai.3p	p.a	r.apm	
4036		1666	899	3836	3412	3306	4639	253	

Et cetera

29. Negations. More often than not, Greek negations negate the verb. The NIV tends to move the negation to a substantive. Matt 6:1 reads literally: "you will not have a reward" (μισθὸν οὐκ ἔχετε); but the NIV reads:

you	will	have	**no**	reward	from	your		Father
→	→	ἔχετε	οὐκ	μισθὸν	παρὰ	ὑμῶν	⸤τῷ	πατρὶ
		v.pai.2p	adv	n.asm	p.d	r.gp.2	d.dsm	n.dsm
		2400	4024	3635	4123	7007	3836	4252

30. Prepositions

I try to keep prepositions with their objects, although this isn't always possible.

	"Nazareth!	Can	anything	good	come	**from**	there?"
καὶ	↱	δύναται	τι	ἀγαθὸν	εἶναι	ἐκ	Ναζαρὲτ
cj		v.ppi.3s	r.asn	a.asn	f.pa	p.g	n.gsf
2779	3715	1538	5516	19	1639	1666	3715

For		God		does	not	show	favoritism.
γὰρ	**παρὰ**	⸤τῷ	θεῷ⸥	ἐστιν	οὐ		προσωπολημψία
cj	p.d	d.dsm	n.dsm	v.pai.3s	pl		n.nsf
1142	4123	3836	2536	1639	4024		4721

The αὐτοῦ is really the object of μετ᾽ (οἱ μετ᾽ αὐτοῦ) in the following example. There will be variety in how I tagged this type of construction.

	Simon	and	**his**	companions	went	to	look		for	him,
καὶ	Σίμων	καὶ	αὐτοῦ	⸤οἱ	μετ᾽⸥	→	→	κατεδίωξεν	←	αὐτὸν
cj	n.nsm	cj	r.gsm.3	d.npm	p.g			v.aai.3s		r.asm.3
2779	4981	2779	899	3836	3552			2870		899

In 2 Cor 6:16, the "between" comes from the later μετά (τίς ... συγκατάθεσις ναῷ θεοῦ μετὰ εἰδώλων). I have kept it, however, with its object.

What	agreement	is there	**between**	the	temple	of	God	and		idols?
τίς	συγκατάθεσις				ναῷ	→	θεοῦ		μετὰ	εἰδώλων
r.nsf	n.nsf				n.dsm		n.gsm		p.g	n.gpn
5515	5161				3724		2536		3552	1631

Often the definite article will turn a Greek prepositional phrase into a modifier in the attributive position, and this article is often not translated in English.

To	the	seven	churches		in	the	province	of	Asia:
→	ταῖς	ἑπτὰ	ἐκκλησίαις	ταῖς	ἐν		→	→	⌐τῇ ᾽Ασίᾳ⌐
	d.dpf	a.dpf	n.dpf	d.dpf	p.d				d.dsf n.dsf
	3836	2231	1711	3836	1877				3836 823

31. Often the first correlative is not translated.

	rejected		by	men	**but**	chosen	by	God
μὲν	ἀποδεδοκιμασμένον		ὑπὸ	ἀνθρώπων	δὲ	ἐκλεκτὸν	παρὰ	θεῷ
pl	pt.rp.asm		p.g	n.gpm	cj	a.asm	p.d	n.dsm
3525	627		5679	476	1254	1723	4123	2536

	the	captain	of	the	temple	guard	**and**	the	chief	priests
τε	ὅ	στρατηγὸς	→	τοῦ	ἱεροῦ	↰	καὶ	οἱ	→	ἀρχιερεῖς
cj	d.nsm	n.nsm		d.gsn	n.gsn		cj	d.npm		n.npm
5445	3836	5130		3836	2639	5130	2779	3836		797

I	have	declared	to	**both**	Jews	**and**	Greeks
→	→	διαμαρτυρόμενος		τε	᾽Ιουδαίοις	καὶ	῞Ελλησιν
		pt.pm.nsm		cj	a.dpm	cj	n.dpm
		1371		5445	2681	2779	1818

Sometimes the significance of the correlatives are carried by different words in the sentence (e.g., "some ... others"), but I tend to isolate the correlatives to make their presence clear.

	some	of	them	they	beat,		**others**	they	killed.
μὲν	οὓς			→	δέροντες	δὲ	οὓς	→	ἀποκτέννοντες
pl	r.apm				pt.pa.npm	pl	r.apm		pt.pa.npm
3525	4005				1296	1254	4005		650

32. Greek can start a sentence with a conjunction, which is often dropped out by the NIV because of English style.

	The	whole	town	gathered		at	the	door
καὶ	ἡ	ὅλη	πόλις	⌐ἦν	ἐπισυνηγμένη⌐	πρὸς	τὴν	θύραν
cj	d.nsf	a.nsf	n.nsf	v.iai.3s	pt.rp.nsf	p.a	d.asf	n.asf
2779	3836	3910	4484	1639	2190	4639	3836	2598

33. ὅτι can be translated with a word like "that," with quotation marks, or left untranslated.

When	Herod	realized	**that**	he	had	been	outwitted	by	the	Magi,
Τότε	῾Ηρῴδης	ἰδὼν	ὅτι	→	→	→	ἐνεπαίχθη	ὑπὸ	τῶν	μάγων,
adv	n.nsm	pt.aa.nsm	cj				v.api.3s	p.g	d.gpm	n.gpm
5538	2476	1625	4022				1850	5679	3836	3407

If	anyone	says,		"I	love	God,"	yet	hates	his	brother,
ἐάν	τις	εἴπῃ	ὅτι	→	ἀγαπῶ	⌐τὸν θεὸν⌐	καὶ	μισῇ	αὐτοῦ	⌐τὸν ἀδελφόν⌐
cj	r.nsm	v.aas.3s	cj		v.pai.1s	d.asm n.asm	cj	v.pas.3s	r.gsm.3	d.asm n.asm
1569	5516	3306	4022	26		3836 2536	2779	3631	899	3836 81

And	this	is	the	testimony:		God	has	given	us	eternal	life
Καὶ	αὕτη	ἐστὶν	ἡ	μαρτυρία	ὅτι	ὁ	θεός	→	ἔδωκεν	ἡμῖν	αἰώνιον ζωήν
cj	r.nsf	v.pai.3s	d.nsf	n.nsf	cj	d.nsm	n.nsm		v.aai.3s	r.dp.1	a.asf n.asf
2779	4047	1639	3836	3456	4022	3836	2536		1443	7005	173 2437

34. ἄν is placed under any word that implies contingency.

	"It	has	been	said,	**'Anyone**	who	divorces	his	wife
δὲ	→	→	→	Ἐρρέθη	⌐ὃς	ἄν⌐	←	ἀπολύσῃ	αὐτοῦ	⌐τὴν	γυναῖκα⌐
cj				v.api.3s	r.nsm	pl		v.aas.3s	r.gsm.3	d.asf	n.asf
1254				3306	4005	323		668	899	3836	1222

	If	you	believed	Moses,	you	**would**	believe	me,
γὰρ	εἰ	→	ἐπιστεύετε	Μωϋσεῖ	↱	ἄν	ἐπιστεύετε	ἐμοί
cj	cj		v.iai.2p	n.dsm		pl	v.iai.2p	r.ds.1
1142	1623		4409	3707	4409	323	4409	1609

35. "He answered and said to them." Biblical Greek is quite pleonastic (from an English point of view) on how it says, for example, "Jesus answered (ἀπεκρίθη) and (καὶ) said (εἶπεν) to them (αὐτοῖς)." The NIV does not reproduce the idiom. I merely put the first Greek verb under the English verb and do not try to associate the English verb with a particular word in the Greek idiom.

	They	**replied,**		"Some	say	John	the	Baptist;
δὲ	οἱ	ἀποκριθέντες	εἶπαν	"Some	say	Ἰωάννην	τὸν	βαπτιστήν
cj	d.npm	pt.ap.npm	v.aai.3p			n.asm	d.asm	n.asm
1254	3836	646	3306			2722	3836	969

	He	**replied,**				"I	will	also	ask	you	one	question.
δὲ	→	ἀποκριθεὶς	εἶπεν	πρὸς	αὐτούς	κἀγὼ	↱	↰	ἐρωτήσω	ὑμᾶς	ἕνα	λόγον
cj		pt.ap.nsm	v.aai.3s	p.a	r.apm.3	cj			v.fai.1s	r.ap.2	a.asm	n.asm
1254		646	3306	4639	899	2743	2263	2743	2263	7007	1651	3364

Jesus	**answered**			**them,**	"Destroy	this	temple,
Ἰησοῦς	ἀπεκρίθη	καὶ	εἶπεν	αὐτοῖς	λύσατε	τοῦτον	⌐τὸν	ναὸν⌐
n.nsm	v.api.3s	cj	v.aai.3s	r.dpm.3	v.aam.2p	r.asm	d.asm	n.asm
2652	646	2779	3306	899	3395	4047	3836	3724

36. Often Greek words that perform a single function must be separated. μή πῶς means "lest," but they are translated here as "so that ... not."

so	**that**	he		will	**not**	be	overwhelmed	by	excessive	sorrow
πως	←	⌐ὁ	τοιοῦτος⌐	↱	μὴ	→	καταποθῇ	↱	περισσοτέρᾳ	⌐τῇ	λύπῃ⌐
pl		d.nsmr.nsm			cj		v.aps.3s		a.dsf.c	d.dsf	n.dsf
4803		3836	5525	2927	3590	2927		3383	4358	3836	3383

Appendix B

Greek-English Dictionary

The first number in bold brackets is the Goodrick-Kohlenbgerger number, which corresponds to the numbers in the fourth line of each staff in *IRU*. Following it is the Greek word, its transliteration, frequency (i.e., the number of times it occurs in the New Testament) followed by an "x," and then its definition. If the entry ends with an asterisk, then all uses of the word in the New Testament have been noted. The final smaller number in brackets is the corresponding Strong's number (e.g., [2]); if there is no corresponding Strong's number, then there are double asterisks ([**]).

This dictionary is not designed to replace a full dictionary (such as *A Greek-English Lexicon of the New Testament* by Frederick William Danker) or word study (such as *New International Dictionary of New Testament Theology: Abridged Edition* by Verlyn D. Verbrugge), but it will help for quick reference.

Greek word

Transliteration

Frequency

Goodrick-Kohlenberger number

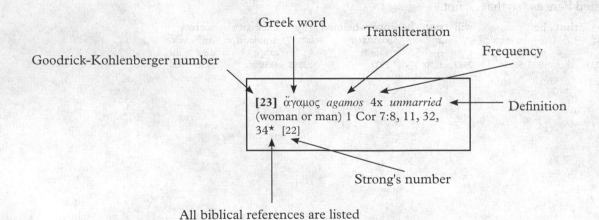

[23] ἄγαμος *agamos* 4x *unmarried* (woman or man) 1 Cor 7:8, 11, 32, 34* [22]

Definition

Strong's number

All biblical references are listed

[2] Ἀαρών *Aarōn* 5x *Aaron*, pr. name, in decl, the brother of Moses (Ex 4:14), Lk 1:15; Ac 7:40; Heb 5:4; 7:11; 9:4* [2]

[3] Ἀβαδδών *Abaddōn* 1x *Abaddon*, pr. name, indecl, alternate spelling: Ἀββαδών, the angel who rules in hell, Rev 9:11* [3]

[4] ἀβαρής *abarēs* 1x literally: *weightless*; figuratively: *not burdensome*, 2 Co 11:9* [4]

[5] ἀββά *abba* 3x *father*, Mk 14:36; Ro 8:15; Gal 4:6* [5]

[6] Ἅβελ *Habel* 4x *Abel*, pr. name, indecl, Mt 23:35; Lk 11:51; Heb 11:4; 12:24 [6]

[7] Ἀβιά *Abia* 3x *Abiajah*, pr. name, indecl. Hebrew is *Abijah*. (1) the son of Rehoboam (1 Chron 3:10) Mt 1:7; (2) the division of priests to which Zechariah belonged (1 Chron 24:10) Lk 1:5* [7]

[8] Ἀβιαθάρ *Abiathar* 1x *Abiathar*, pr. name, indecl, Mk 2:26* [8]

[9] Ἀβιληνή *Abilēnē* 1x *Abilene*, a district of the Syrian Decapolis; from *Abila*, the chief town, Lk 3:1* [9]

[10] Ἀβιούδ *Abioud* 2x *Abihud*, pr. name, indecl [10]

[11] Ἀβραάμ *Abraam* 73x *Abraham*, pr. name indecl [11]

[12] ἄβυσσος *abyssos* 9x *bottomless; place of the dead*, Lk 8:31; Ro 10:7 [12]

[13] Ἅγαβος *Hagabos* 2x *Agabus*, pr. name, Ac 11:28; 21:10* [13]

[14] ἀγαθοεργέω *agathoergeō* 2x *to do good, confer benefits*, Ac 14:17; 1 Ti 6:18* [14]

[16] ἀγαθοποιέω *agathopoieō* 9x *to do good, do well; to do what is morally correct* (1 Pet 2:15, 20) [15]

[17] ἀγαθοποιΐα *agathopoiia* 1x *well-doing*, 1 Pe 4:19* [16]

[18] ἀγαθοποιός *agathopoios* 1x *doing good* or *right*; subst., *a well-doer*, 1 Pet 2:14* [17]

[19] ἀγαθός *agathos* 102x *good, profitable, generous, upright, virtuous* [18]

[20] ἀγαθωσύνη *agathōsynē* 4x *goodness, virtue, beneficence*, Ro 5:14; Eph 5:9; 2 Th 1:11; *generosity*, Gal 5:22* [19]

[21] ἀγαλλίασις *agalliasis* 5x *exultation, extreme joy* [20]

[22] ἀγαλλιάω *agalliaō* 11x *to celebrate, praise;* usually in the middle in the N.T.

(ἀγαλλιάομαι) *to exult, rejoice exceedingly; to desire ardently*, Jn 8:56 [21]

[23] ἄγαμος *agamos* 4x *unmarried* (woman or man) 1 Cor 7:8, 11, 32, 34* [22]

[24] ἀγανακτέω *aganakteō* 7x *to be pained; to be angry, vexed, indignant; to manifest indignation*, Mk 14:4; Lk 13:14 [23]

[25] ἀγανάκτησις *aganaktēsis* 1x *indignation*, 2 Co 7:11* [24]

[26] ἀγαπάω *agapaō* 143x *to love, value, esteem, feel or manifest generous concern for, be faithful towards; to delight in, to set store upon*, Rev. 12:11 [25]

[27] ἀγάπη *agapē* 116x *love, generosity, kindly concern, devotedness;* pl. *love-feasts*, Jude 12 [26]

[28] ἀγαπητός *agapētos* 61x *beloved, dear; worthy of love* [27]

[29] Ἀγάρ *Hagar* 2x pr. name, indecl, *Hagar* (Gen 16), Gal 4:24, 25* [28]

[30] ἀγγαρεύω *angareuō* 3x *to press*, or *compel* another to go somewhere, or carry some burden, Mt 5:41; 27:32; Mk 15:21* [29]

[31] ἀγγεῖον *angeion* 1x *a vessel, flask*, Mt 25:4* [30]

[32] ἀγγελία *angelia* 2x *a messsage, doctrine*, or *precept*, delivered in the name of any one; *command*, 1 Jn 1:5; 3:11* [31]

[33] ἀγγέλλω *angellō* 1x *to tell, to announce*, Jn 20:18* [518]

[34] ἄγγελος *angelos* 175x *one sent, a messenger, angel* [32]

[35] ἄγγος *angos* 1x *vessel, container, basket*, Mt 13:48* [30]

[36] ἀγέλη *agelē* 7x *flock, herd* [34]

[37] ἀγενεαλόγητος *agenealogētos* 1x *not included in a genealogy; independent of genealogy*, Heb 7:3* [35]

[38] ἀγενής *agenēs* 1x lit., *without kin*; fig., *base, low, insignificant*, 1 Co 1:28* [36]

[39] ἁγιάζω *hagiazō* 28x *to separate, consecrate; cleanse, purify, sanctify; regard* or *reverence as holy* [37]

[40] ἁγιασμός *hagiasmos* 10x *sanctification, moral purity, sanctity* [38]

[41] ἅγιος *hagios* 233x *separate from common condition and use; dedicated.* Lk 2:23; *hallowed;* used of things, τὰ ἅγια, *the sanctuary;* and of persons, *saints*, e.g., members of the first Christian communi-

ties; *pure, righteous*, ceremonially or morally; *holy* [39, 40]

[42] ἁγιότης *hagiotēs* 1x *holiness, sanctity*, Heb 12:10* [41]

[43] ἁγιωσύνη *hagiōsynē* 3x *sanctification, sanctity, holiness*, Ro 1:4; 2 Co 7:1; 1 Th 3:13* [42]

[44] ἀγκάλη *ankalē* 1x *the arm*, Lk 2:28* [43]

[45] ἄγκιστρον *ankistron* 1x *a hook, fish-hook*, Mt 17:27* [44]

[46] ἄγκυρα *ankyra* 4x *an anchor*, Ac 27:29, 30, 40; Heb 6:19* [45]

[47] ἄγναφος *agnaphos* 2x *unshrunken; new*, Mt 9:16; Mk 2:21* [46]

[48] ἁγνεία *hagneia* 2x *purity, chastity*, 1 Ti 4:12; 5:2* [47]

[49] ἁγνίζω *hagnizō* 7x *to purify; to purify morally, reform, to live like one under a vow of abstinence*, as the Nazarites [48]

[50] ἁγνισμός *hagnismos* 1x *purification, abstinence*, Ac 21:26* [49]

[51] ἀγνοέω *agnoeō* 22x *to be ignorant; not to understand; sin through ignorance* [50]

[52] ἀγνόημα *agnoēma* 1x *error, sin of ignorance*, Heb 9:7* [51]

[53] ἄγνοια *agnoia* 4x *ignorance, willfulness*, Ac 3:17; 17:30; Eph 4:18; 1 Pet 1:14* [52]

[54] ἁγνός *hagnos* 8x *pure, chaste, modest, innocent, blameless* [53]

[55] ἁγνότης *hagnotēs* 2x *purity, life of purity*, 2 Co 6:6; 11:3* [54]

[56] ἁγνῶς *hagnōs* 1x *purely, with sincerity*, Phil 1:17* [55]

[57] ἀγνωσία *agnōsia* 2x *ignorance*, 1 Co 15:34; 1 Pe 2:15* [56]

[58] ἄγνωστος *agnōstos* 1x *unknown*, Ac 17:23* [57]

[59] ἀγορά *agora* 11x *a place of public concourse, forum, market-place; things said in the market, provision* [58]

[60] ἀγοράζω *agorazō* 30x *to buy; redeem, acquire* by a ransom or price paid [59]

[61] ἀγοραῖος *agoraios* 2x *one who visits the forum; a lounger, one who idles away his time in public places, a low fellow*, Ac 17:5; *pertaining to the forum, judicial;* ἀγόραιοι, *court days*, Ac 19:38* [60]

[62] ἄγρα *agra* 2x *a catching, thing taken, draught* of fishes, Lk 5:4, 9* [61]

[63] ἀγράμματος *agrammatos* 1x *illiterate, unlearned,* Ac 4:13* [62]

[64] ἀγραυλέω *agrauleō* 1x *to remain in the open air, to live outside,* especially *by night,* Lk 2:8* [63]

[65] ἀγρεύω *agreuō* 1x *to take in hunting, catch,* Mk 12:13* [64]

[66] ἀγριέλαιος *agrielaios* 2x *a wild olive-tree, oleaster,* Ro 11:17, 24* [65]

[67] ἄγριος *agrios* 3x *belonging to the field, wild; fierce, raging,* Mt 3:4; Mk 1:6; Jude 13* [66]

[68] Ἀγρίππας *Agrippas* 11x *Agrippa,* pr. name [67]

[69] ἀγρός *agros* 36x *a field,* especially *a cultivated field;* pl. *the country; lands, farms, villages* [68]

[70] ἀγρυπνέω *agrypneō* 4x *to be awake, watch; to be watchful, vigilant* [69]

[71] ἀγρυπνία *agrypnia* 2x *want of sleep, watching,* 2 Co 6:5; 11:27* [70]

[72] ἄγω *agō* 67x *to lead. bring; lead away, drive off,* as a booty of cattle; *conduct, accompany; lead out, produce; conduct with force, drag, hurry away; guide, incite, entice; convey one's self, go, go away; pass* or *spend* as time; *celebrate* [33, 71]

[73] ἀγωγή *agōgē* 1x *guidance, mode of instruction, discipline, course of life,* 2 Ti 3:10* [72]

[74] ἀγών *agōn* 6x *place of contest, race-course, stadium; a contest, strife, contention; peril, toil* [73]

[75] ἀγωνία *agōnia* 1x *contest, violent struggle; agony, anguish,* Lk 22:44* [74]

[76] ἀγωνίζομαι *agōnizomai* 8x *to be a combatant in the public games; to contend, fight, strive earnestly* [75]

[77] Ἀδάμ *Adam* 9x *Adam,* pr. name, indecl [76]

[78] ἀδάπανος *adapanos* 1x *without expense, gratuitous,* 1 Co 9:18* [77]

[79] Ἀδδί *Addi* 1x *Addi,* pr. name, indecl Lk 3:28* [78]

[80] ἀδελφή *adelphē* 26x *a sister; near kinswoman,* or *female relative, a female member of the Christian community* [79]

[81] ἀδελφός *adelphos* 343x *a brother, near kinsman* or *relative; one of the same nation* or *nature; one of equal rank and dignity; an associate, a member of the Christian community* [80]

[82] ἀδελφότης *adelphotēs* 2x *brotherhood, the body of the Christian brotherhood,* 1 Pe 2:17; 5:9* [81]

[83] ἄδηλος *adēlos* 2x *not apparent* or *obvious; uncertain, not distinct,* Lk 11:44; 1 Co 14:8* [82]

[84] ἀδηλότης *adēlotēs* 1x *uncertainty,* 1 Ti 6:17* [83]

[85] ἀδήλως *adēlōs* 1x *not manifestly, uncertainly, dubiously,* 1 Co 9:26* [84]

[86] ἀδημονέω *adēmoneō* 3x *to be depressed* or *dejected, full of anguish* or *sorrow,* Mt 26:37; Mk 14:33; Phil 2:26* [85]

[87] ᾅδης *hadēs* 10x *the invisible abode* or *mansion of the dead; the place of punishment, hell; the lowest place* or *condition,* Mt 11:23; Lk 10:15 [86]

[88] ἀδιάκριτος *adiakritos* 1x *undistinguishing, impartial,* Jas 3:17* [87]

[89] ἀδιάλειπτος *adialeiptos* 2x *unceasing, constant, settled,* Ro 9:2; 2 Ti 1:3* [88]

[90] ἀδιαλείπτως *adialeiptōs* 4x *unceasingly, by an unvarying practice,* Ro 1:9; 1 Th 1:2; 2:13; 5:17* [89]

[92] ἀδικέω *adikeō* 28x *to act unjustly; wrong; injure; violate a law* [91]

[93] ἀδίκημα *adikēma* 3x *an act of injustice, crime,* Ac 18:14; 24:20; Rev 18:5* [92]

[94] ἀδικία *adikia* 25x *injustice, wrong; iniquity, falsehood, deceitfulness* [93]

[96] ἄδικος *adikos* 12x *unjust, unrighteous, iniquitous, vicious; deceitful, fallacious* [94]

[97] ἀδίκως *adikōs* 1x *unjustly, undeservedly,* 1 Pe 2:19* [95]

[98] Ἀδμίν *Admin* 1x *Admin,* pr. name, indecl, Lk 3:33* [689]

[99] ἀδόκιμος *adokimos* 8x *unable to stand test, rejected, refuse, worthless* [96]

[100] ἄδολος *adolos* 1x *without deceit, sincere,* 1 Pe 2:2* [97]

[101] Ἀδραμυττηνός *Adramyttēnos* 1x *of Adramyttium,* a Greek city on the coast of Aeolia, in Asia Minor, Ac 27:2* [98]

[102] Ἀδρίας *Adrias* 1x *the Adriatic sea,* Ac 27:27* [99]

[103] ἁδρότης *hadrotēs* 1x *abundance,* 2 Co 8:20* [100]

[104] ἀδυνατέω *adynateō* 2x *not to be able; to be impossible,* Mt 17:20; Lk 1:37* [101]

[105] ἀδύνατος *adynatos* 10x *impotent, weak; impossible* [102]

[106] ᾄδω *adō* 5x *to sing,* Eph 5:19; Col 3:16; Rev 5:9; 14:3; 15:3* [103]

[107] ἀεί *aei* 7x *always, for ever, constantly* [104]

[108] ἀετός *aetos* 5x *an eagle,* Rev 12:14; or *vulture,* Lk 17:37 [105]

[109] ἄζυμος *azymos* 9x *unleavened;* τὰ ἄζυμα, *the feast of unleavened bread;* met. *pure from foreign matter, unadulterated, genuine;* τὸ ἄζυμον, *genuineness,* 1 Co 5:7, 8 [106]

[110] Ἀζώρ *Azōr* 2x *Azor,* pr. name, indecl, Mt 1:13f.* [107]

[111] Ἄζωτος *Azōtos* 1x *Azotus, Ashdod,* a seaport in Palestine, Ac 8:40* [108]

[113] ἀήρ *aēr* 7x *air, atmosphere* [109]

[114] ἀθανασία *athanasia* 3x *immortality,* 1 Co 15:53, 54; 1 Ti 6:16* [110]

[116] ἀθέμιτος *athemitos* 2x *unlawful, criminal, wicked,* Ac 10:28; 1 Pe 4:3* [111]

[117] ἄθεος *atheos* 1x *an atheist; godless, estranged from the knowledge and worship of the true God,* Eph 2:12* [112]

[118] ἄθεσμος *athesmos* 2x *lawless, unrestrained, licentious,* 2 Pe 2:7; 3:17* [113]

[119] ἀθετέω *atheteō* 16x pr. *to displace, set aside; to abrogate, annul, violate, swerve from; reject, condemn* [114]

[120] ἀθέτησις *athetēsis* 2x *abrogation, annulling,* Heb 7:18; 9:26* [115]

[122] Ἀθηναῖος *Athēnaios* 2x *Athenian, inhabiting* or *belonging to Athens,* Ac 17:21, 22* [117]

[123] ἀθλέω *athleō* 2x *to strive, contend, be a champion in the public games,* 2 Ti 2:5* [118]

[124] ἄθλησις *athlēsis* 1x *contest, combat, struggle, conflict,* Heb 10:32* [119]

[125] ἀθροίζω *athroizō* 1x *to collect, gather,* Lk 24:33* [4867]

[126] ἀθυμέω *athumeō* 1x *to be discouraged, lose heart,* Col 3:21* [120]

[127] ἀθῷος *athōos* 2x *unpunished;* metaph. *innocent,* Mt 27:4, 24* [121]

[128] αἴγειος *aigeios* 1x *belonging to a goat,* Heb 11:37* [122]

[129] αἰγιαλός *aigialos* 6x *seashore, beach,* Mt 13:2, 48; Jn 21:4; Ac 21:5; 27:39f.* [123]

[130] Αἰγύπτιος *Aigyptios* 5x *Egyptian* [124]

[131] Αἴγυπτος *Aigyptos* 25x *Egypt* [125]

[132] ἀΐδιος *aidios* 2x *always existing, eternal*, Ro 1:20; Jude 6 [126]

[133] αἰδώς *aidōs* 1x *modesty, reverence*, 1 Ti 2:9* [127]

[134] Αἰθίοψ *Aithiops* 2x *an Ethiopian*, Ac 8:27* [128]

[135] αἷμα *haima* 97x *blood; of the color of blood; bloodshed; blood-guiltiness; natural descent* [129]

[136] αἱματεκχυσία *haimatekchusia* 1x *an effusion* or *shedding of blood*, Heb 9:22* [130]

[137] αἱμορροέω *haimorroeō* 1x *to have a flow of blood*, Mt 9:20* [131]

[138] Αἰνέας *Aineas* 2x *Aeneas*, pr. name, Ac 9:33f.* [132]

[139] αἴνεσις *ainesis* 1x *praise*, Heb 13:15* [133]

[140] αἰνέω *aineō* 8x *to praise, celebrate* [134]

[141] αἴνιγμα *ainigma* 1x *an enigma, riddle, any thing obscurely expressed* or *intimated*, 1 Co 13:12* [135]

[142] αἶνος *ainos* 2x *praise*, Mt 21:16; Lk 18:43* [136]

[143] Αἰνών *Ainōn* 1x *Enon*, pr. name, indecl, where Jn was baptizing, Jn 3:23* [137]

[145] αἱρέω *haireō* 3x *some list as deponent* αἱρέομαι, *to take*; mid. *to choose* [138]

[146] αἵρεσις *hairesis* 9x *strictly, a choice* or *option*; hence, *a religious sect, faction*; by implication, *discord, contention* [139]

[147] αἱρετίζω *hairetizō* 1x *to choose, choose with delight* or *love*, Mt 12:18* [140]

[148] αἱρετικός *hairetikos* 1x *one who creates* or *fosters factions*, Tit 3:10* [141]

[149] αἴρω *airō* 101x *to take up, lift, raise; bear, carry; take away, remove; destroy, kill* [142]

[150] αἰσθάνομαι *aisthanomai* 1x *to perceive, understand*, Lk 9:45* [143]

[151] αἴσθησις *aisthēsis* 1x *perception, understanding*, Phil 1:9* [144]

[152] αἰσθητήριον *aisthētērion* 1x *an organ of perception; internal sense*, Heb 5:14* [145]

[153] αἰσχροκερδής *aischrokerdēs* 2x *eager for dishonorable gain, greedy*, 1 Ti 3:8; Tit 1:7* [146]

[154] αἰσχροκερδῶς *aischrokerdōs* 1x *for the sake of base gain, greedily*, 1 Pe 5:2* [147]

[155] αἰσχρολογία *aischrologia* 1x *vile* or *obscene language, foul talk*, Col 3:8* [148]

[156] αἰσχρός *aischros* 4x *strictly, deformed*, opposed to καλός; metaph. *shameful, indecent, dishonorable, vile*, 1 Co 11:6; 14:35; Eph 5:12; Tit 1:11* [149, 150]

[157] αἰσχρότης *aischrotēs* 1x *obscenity, indecency*, Eph 5:4* [151]

[158] αἰσχύνη *aischunē* 6x *shame, disgrace; cause of shame, dishonorable conduct* [152]

[160] αἰτέω *aiteō* 70x *to ask, request; demand; desire*, Ac 7:46 [154]

[161] αἴτημα *aitēma* 3x *a thing asked* or *sought for; petition, request*, Lk 23:24; Phil 4:6; 1 Jn 5:15* [155]

[162] αἰτία *aitia* 20x *cause, motive, incitement; accusation, crime, case* [156]

[165] αἴτιος *aitios* 5x *causative*; αἴτιος, *an author* or *causer*, Heb 5:9; τὸ αἴτιον, *equivalent to* aijtiva [158, 159]

[166] αἰτίωμα *aitiōma* 1x *charge, accusation*, Ac 25:7* [157]

[167] αἰφνίδιος *aiphnidios* 2x *unforeseen, unexpected, sudden*, Lk 21:34; 1 Th 5:3* [160]

[168] αἰχμαλωσία *aichmalōsia* 3x *captivity, state of captivity; captive multitude*, Eph 4:8; Rev 13:10* [161]

[169] αἰχμαλωτεύω *aichmalōteuō* 1x *to lead captive*; met. *to captivate*, Eph 4:8* [162]

[170] αἰχμαλωτίζω *aichmalōtizō* 4x *to lead captive*; by impl. *to subject*, Lk 21:24; Ro 7:23; 2 Co 10:5; 2 Ti 3:6* [163]

[171] αἰχμάλωτος *aichmalōtos* 1x *a captive*, Lk 4:18* [164]

[172] αἰών *aiōn* 122x pr. *a period of time of significant character; life; an era; an age*: hence, *a state of things marking an age* or *era; the present order of nature; the natural condition of man, the world*; ὁ αἰών, *illimitable duration, eternity*; as also, οἱ αἰῶνες, ὁ αἰὼν τῶν αἰώνων, οἱ αἰῶνες τῶν αἰώνων; by an Aramaism οἱ αἰῶνες, *the material universe*, Heb 1:2 [165]

[173] αἰώνιος *aiōnios* 71x *indeterminate as to duration, eternal, everlasting* [166]

[174] ἀκαθαρσία *akatharsia* 10x *uncleanness; lewdness; impurity* of motive, 1 Th 2:3 [167]

[176] ἀκάθαρτος *akathartos* 32x *impure, unclean; lewd; foul* [169]

[177] ἀκαιρέομαι *akaireomai* 1x *to be without opportunity* or *occasion*, Phil 4:10* [170]

[178] ἀκαίρως *akairōs* 1x *unseasonably*, 2 Ti 4:2* [171]

[179] ἄκακος *akakos* 2x *free from evil, innocent, blameless; simple*, Ro 16:18; Heb 7:26* [172]

[180] ἄκανθα *akantha* 14x *a thorn, thornbush*, Mt 7:16; 13:7; 27:29 [173]

[181] ἀκάνθινος *akanthinos* 2x *thorny, made of thorns*, Mk 15:17; Jn 19:5* [174]

[182] ἄκαρπος *akarpos* 7x *without fruit, unfruitful, barren*; by impl. *noxious* [175]

[183] ἀκατάγνωστος *akatagnōstos* 1x pr. *not worthy of condemnation* by a judge; hence, *irreprehensible*, Tit 2:8* [176]

[184] ἀκατακάλυπτος *akatakalyptos* 2x *uncovered, unveiled*, 1 Co 11:5, 13* [177]

[185] ἀκατάκριτος *akatakritos* 2x *uncondemned* in a public trial, Ac 16:37; 22:25* [178]

[186] ἀκατάλυτος *akatalytos* 1x *incapable of dissolution, indissoluble*; hence, *enduring, everlasting*, Heb 7:16* [179]

[188] ἀκατάπαυστος *akatapaustos* 1x *also spelled* ἀκατάπαστος, *which cannot be restrained* from a thing, *unceasing*, 2 Pet 2:14* [180]

[189] ἀκαταστασία *akatastasia* 5x pr. *instability*; hence, *an unsettled state; disorder, commotion, tumult, sedition*, Lk 21:9; 1 Co 14:33; 2 Co 6:5; 12:20; Jas 3:16* [181]

[190] ἀκατάστατος *akatastatos* 2x *unstable, inconstant; unquiet, turbulent*, Jas 1:8; 3:8* [182]

[193] ἀκέραιος *akeraios* 3x pr. *unmixed*: hence, *without mixture of vice* or *deceit, sincere, blameless*, Mt 10:16; Ro 16:19; Phil 2:15* [185]

[195] ἀκλινής *aklinēs* 1x *not declining, unwavering, steady*, Heb 10:23* [186]

[196] ἀκμάζω *akmazō* 1x *to flourish, ripen, be in one's prime,* Rev 14:18★ [187]

[197] ἀκμήν *akmēn* 1x pr. *the point of a weapon; point of time:* ἀκμήν, for κατἀκμήν, adv., *yet, still, even now,* Mt 15:16★ [188]

[198] ἀκοή *akoē* 24x *hearing; the act* or *sense of hearing,* 1 Co 12:17; 2 Pe 2:8; *the instrument of hearing, the ear,* Mk 7:35; *a thing heard;* announcement, *instruction, doctrine,* Jn 12:38; Ro 10:16; *report,* Mt 4:24, et al [189]

[199] ἀκολουθέω *akoloutheō* 90x *to follow; follow* as a disciple; *imitate* [190]

[201] ἀκούω *akouō* 428x some list the future active as a middle deponent, ἀκούσομαι, *to hear; to hearken, listen to,* Mk 4:3; Lk 19:48; *to heed, obey,* Mt 18:15; Ac 4:19; *to understand,* 1 Co 14:2; *to take in* or *admit* to mental acceptance, Mk 4:33; Jn 8:43, 47 [191]

[202] ἀκρασία *akrasia* 2x *intemperance, self-indulgence,* Mt 23:25; *unruly appetite, lustfulness,* 1 Co 7:5★ [192]

[203] ἀκρατής *akratēs* 1x *without self-control, intemperate,* 2 Ti 3:3 [193]

[204] ἄκρατος *akratos* 1x *unmixed, unmingled* wine, Rev 14:10★ [194]

[205] ἀκρίβεια *akribeia* 1x *accuracy, exactness; preciseness,* or *rigor, severe discipline,* Ac 22:3★ [195]

[207] ἀκριβής *akribēs* 1x *exact, strict,* Ac 26:5★ [★★]

[208] ἀκριβόω *akriboō* 2x *to inquire accurately* or *diligently,* Mt 2:7, 16 (see v. 8)★ [198]

[209] ἀκριβῶς *akribōs* 9x *accurately, diligently,* Mt 2:8; Lk 1:3; Ac 18:25; *circumspectly, strictly,* Eph 5:15; *precisely, distinctly,* 1 Th 5:2 [199, 197]

[210] ἀκρίς *akris* 4x *a locust,* Mt 3:4; Mk 1:6; Rev 9:3, 7★ [200]

[211] ἀκροατήριον *akroatērion* 1x *a place of audience,* Ac 25:23★ [201]

[212] ἀκροατής *akroatēs* 4x *a hearer,* Ro 2:13; Jas 1:22, 23, 25★ [202]

[213] ἀκροβυστία *akrobystia* 20x *foreskin; uncircumcision, the state of being uncircumcised,* Ro 4:10; *the abstract being put for the concrete, uncircumcised men,* i.e., *Gentiles,* Ro 4:9, et al [203]

[214] ἀκρογωνιαῖος *akrogōniaios* 2x literally: *lying at the extreme corner;* with λίθος, *corner* or *foundation stone,* Eph 2:20; 1 Pe 2:6★ [204]

[215] ἀκροθίνιον *akrothinion* 1x *the first-fruits* of the produce of the ground, which were taken from the top of the heap and offered to the gods; *the best and choicest of the spoils* of war, usually collected in a heap, Heb 7:4★ [205]

[216] ἄκρον *akron* 6x *the top, tip, end, extremity,* Mk 13:27; Lk 16:24; Heb 11:21 [206]

[217] Ἀκύλας *Akylas* 6x *Aquila,* pr. name, Paul's friend and Priscilla's husband, Ac 18:2, 18, 26; Ro 16:3; 1 Co 16:19; 2 Ti 4:19★ [207]

[218] ἀκυρόω *akyroō* 3x *to deprive of authority, annul, cancel,* Mt 15:6; Mk 7:13; Gal 3:17★ [208]

[219] ἀκωλύτως *akōlytōs* 1x *without hindrance, freely,* Ac 28:31★ [209]

[220] ἄκων *akōn* 1x *unwilling,* 1 Co 9:17★ [210]

[223] ἀλάβαστρος *alabastros* 4x can be masculine, feminine (2x), or neuter (ἀλάβαστρον, 2x), *an alabaster vase,* Mk 14:3 (2x); 26:7; Lk 7:37★ [211]

[224] ἀλαζονεία *alazoneia* 2x *arrogance; presumptuous speech,* Jas 4:16; *haughtiness,* 1 Jn 2:16★ [212]

[225] ἀλαζών *alazōn* 2x *prideful, arrogant, boasting,* Ro 1:30; 2 Ti 3:2★ [213]

[226] ἀλαλάζω *alalazō* 2x pr. *to raise the war-cry,* ἀλαλά: hence, *to utter* other *loud sounds; to wail,* Mk 5:38; *to tinkle, ring,* 1 Co 13:1★ [214]

[227] ἀλάλητος *alalētos* 1x *unutterable,* or, *unexpressed,* Ro 8:26★ [215]

[228] ἄλαλος *alalos* 3x *unable to speak* or *articulate,* Mk 7:37; 9:17, 25★ [216]

[229] ἅλας *halas* 8x variant spellings of ἅλα and ἁλός, *salt,* Mt 5:13; Mk 9:50; met. *the salt* of wisdom and prudence, Col 4:6 [217]

[230] ἀλείφω *aleiphō* 9x *to anoint* with oil or ointment [218]

[231] ἀλεκτοροφωνία *alektorophōnia* 1x *the cock-crowing, the third watch of the night,* intermediate to mid-night and daybreak, and termed *cock-crow,* Mk 13:35★ [219]

[232] ἀλέκτωρ *alektōr* 12x *a cock, rooster,* Mt 26:34; Mk 14:30; Lk 22:34; Jn 13:38 [220]

[233] Ἀλεξανδρεύς *Alexandreus* 2x *a native of Alexandria, an Alexandrine,* Ac 6:9; 18:24 [221]

[234] Ἀλεξανδρῖνος *Alexandrinos* 2x *Alexandrian,* Ac 27:6; 28:11★ [222]

[235] Ἀλέξανδρος *Alexandros* 6x *Alexander,* pr. name. (1) *The High Priest's kinsman,* Ac 4:6. (2) *A Jew of Ephesus,* Ac 19:33. (3) *The coppersmith,* 1 Ti 1:20; 2 Ti 4:14. (4) *Son of Simon of Cyrene,* Mk 15:21★ [223]

[236] ἄλευρον *aleuron* 2x *meal, flour,* Mt 13:33; Lk 13:21★ [224]

[237] ἀλήθεια *alētheia* 109x *truth,* Mk 5:33; *love of truth, sincerity,* 1 Co 5:8; divine *truth* revealed to man, Jn 1:17; *practice in accordance with* Gospel *truth,* Jn 3:21; 2 Jn 4 [225]

[238] ἀληθεύω *alētheuō* 2x *to speak* or *maintain the truth; to act truly* or *sincerely,* Gal 4:16; Eph 4:15★ [226]

[239] ἀληθής *alēthēs* 26x *true,* Jn 4:18; *worthy of credit,* Jn 5:31; *truthful,* Jn 7:18 [227]

[240] ἀληθινός *alēthinos* 28x *sterling,* Lk 16:11; *real,* Jn 6:32; 1 Th 1:9; *unfeigned, trustworthy, true,* Jn 19:35 [228]

[241] ἀλήθω *alēthō* 2x *to grind,* Mt 24:41; Lk 17:35★ [229]

[242] ἀληθῶς *alēthōs* 18x *truly, really,* Mt 14:33; *certainly, of a truth,* Jn 17:8; Ac 12:11: *truly, actually,* Jn 4:18 [230]

[243] ἁλιεύς *halieus* 5x *a fisherman,* Mt 4:18, 19; Mk 1:16, 17; Lk 5:2 [231]

[244] ἁλιεύω *halieuō* 1x *to fish,* Jn 21:3★ [232]

[245] ἁλίζω *halizō* 2x *to salt, season with salt, preserve by salting,* Mt 5:13; Mk 9:49★ [233]

[246] ἀλίσγημα *alisgēma* 1x *pollution, defilement,* Ac 15:20★ [234]

[247] ἀλλά *alla* 638x *but; however; but still more;* ἀλλάγε, *at all events;* ἀλλή, *unless, except.* Ἀλλά also serves to introduce a sentence with keenness and emphasis, Ro 6:5; 7:7; Phil 3:8; Jn 16:2 [235]

[248] ἀλλάσσω *allassō* 6x *to change, alter, transform,* Ac 6:14; Ro 1:23; 1 Co 15:51, 52; Gal 4:20; Heb 1:12 [236]

[249] ἀλλαχόθεν *allachothen* 1x *from another place* or *elsewhere,* Jn 10:1★ [237]

[250] ἀλλαχοῦ *allachou* 1x *elsewhere,* Mk 1:38★ [★★]

[251] ἀλληγορέω *allēgoreō* 1x *to say what is either designed* or *fitted to convey a meaning other than the literal one, to allegorize;* ἀλληγορούμενος, *adapted to another* *meaning, otherwise significant,* Gal 4:24★ [238]

[252] ἀλληλουϊά *hallēlouia* 4x (Hebrew) *hallelujah, praise Yahweh* or *the Lord,* Rev 19:1, 3, 4, 6★ [239]

[253] ἀλλήλων *allēlōn* 100x *one another, each other* [240]

[254] ἀλλογενής *allogenēs* 1x *of another race* or *nation,* i.e., not a Jew; *a stranger, foreigner,* Lk 17:18★ [241]

[256] ἅλλομαι *hallomai* 3x *to leap, jump, leap up,* Ac 3:8; 14:10; *to spring,* as water, Jn 4:14★ [242]

[257] ἄλλος *allos* 155x *another, some other;* ὁ ἄλλος, *the other;* οἱ ἄλλοι, *the others, the rest* [243]

[258] ἀλλοτριεπίσκοπος *allotriepiskopos* 1x pr. *one who meddles with the affairs of others, a busybody in other men's matters; factious,* 1 Pe 4:15★ [244]

[259] ἀλλότριος *allotrios* 14x *belonging to another,* Lk 16:12; *foreign,* Ac 7:6; Heb 11:9; *a foreigner, alien,* Mt 17:25 [245]

[260] ἀλλόφυλος *allophylos* 1x *of another race* or *nation,* i.e., not a Jew, *a foreigner,* Ac 10:28★ [246]

[261] ἄλλως *allōs* 1x *otherwise,* 1 Ti 5:25★ [247]

[262] ἀλοάω *aloaō* 3x *to thresh; to tread,* 1 Co 9:9, 10; 1 Ti 5:18★ [248]

[263] ἄλογος *alogos* 3x *without speech* or *reason, irrational, brute,* 2 Pe 2:12; Jude 10; *unreasonable, absurd,* Ac 25:27★ [249]

[264] ἀλόη *aloē* 1x *aloe, lign-aloe,* a tree which grows in India and Cochin-China, the wood of which is soft and bitter, though highly aromatic. It is used by the Orientals as a perfume; and employed for the purposes of embalming, Jn 19:39★ [250]

[266] ἁλυκός *halykos* 1x *brackish, bitter, salt,* Jas 3:12★ [252]

[267] ἄλυπος *alypos* 1x *free from grief* or *sorrow,* Phil 2:28★ [253]

[268] ἅλυσις *halysis* 11x *a chain,* Mk 5:3, 4 [254]

[269] ἀλυσιτελής *alysitelēs* 1x pr. *bringing in no revenue* or *profit;* hence, *unprofitable, useless; detrimental; ruinous, disastrous,* Heb 13:17★ [255]

[270] ἄλφα *alpha* 3x first letter of Greek alphabet, *Alpha,* Rev 1:8.; 21:6; 22:13★ [1]

[271] Ἀλφαῖος *Halphaios* 5x *Alphaeus,* pr. name (1) *Father of Jas the less,* Mt 10:3; Mk 3:18; Lk 6:15; Ac 1:13. (2) *Father of Levi,* (or Matthew) Mk 2:14★ [256]

[272] ἅλων *halōn* 2x *a threshing-floor, a place where corn is trodden out;* meton. *the corn which is trodden out,* Mt 3:12; Lk 3:17★ [257]

[273] ἀλώπηξ *alōpēx* 3x *a fox,* Mt 8:20; Lk 9:58; met. *a fox-like, crafty man,* Lk 13:32★ [258]

[274] ἅλωσις *halōsis* 1x *a taking, catching, capture,* 2 Pe 2:12★ [259]

[275] ἅμα *hama* 10x *also functions as an improper preposition with the genitive* (2t), *with, together with; at the same time* [260]

[276] ἀμαθής *amathēs* 1x *unlearned, uninstructed, rude,* 2 Pe 3:16★ [261]

[277] ἀμαράντινος *amarantinos* 1x *unfading;* hence, *enduring,* 1 Pe 5:4★ [262]

[278] ἀμάραντος *amarantos* 1x *unfading;* hence, *enduring,* 1 Pe 1:4★ [263]

[279] ἁμαρτάνω *hamartanō* 43x pr. *to miss a mark; to be in error,* 1 Co 15:34; Tit 3:11; *to sin,* Jn 5:14; *to be guilty of wrong,* Mt 18:15 [264]

[280] ἁμάρτημα *hamartēma* 4x *an error; sin, offence,* Mk 3:28; 4:12; Ro 3:25; 1 Co 6:18 [265]

[281] ἁμαρτία *hamartia* 173x *error; offence, sin,* Mt 1:21; *a principle* or *cause of sin,* Ro 7:7; *proneness to sin, sinful propensity,* Ro 7:17, 20; *guilt* or *imputation of sin,* Jn 9:41; Heb 9:26; *a guilty subject, sin-offering, expiatory victim,* 2 Co 5:21 [266]

[282] ἀμάρτυρος *amartyros* 1x *without testimony* or *witness, without evidence,* Ac 14:17★ [267]

[283] ἁμαρτωλός *hamartōlos* 47x *one who deviates from the path of virtue, a sinner,* Mk 2:17; *depraved,* Mk 8:38; *sinful, detestable,* Ro 7:13 [268]

[285] ἄμαχος *amachos* 2x *not disposed to fight; not quarrelsome* or *contentious,* 1 Ti 3:3; Tit 3:2★ [269]

[286] ἀμάω *amaō* 1x *to collect; to reap, mow* or *cut down,* Jas 5:4★ [270]

[287] ἀμέθυστος *amethustos* 1x *an amethyst,* a gem of a deep purple or violet color, so called from its supposed efficacy in keeping off drunkenness, Rev 21:20★ [271]

[288] ἀμελέω *ameleō* 4x *not to care for, to neglect, disregard,* Mt 22:5; 1 Ti 4:14; Heb 2:3; 8:9★ [272]

[289] ἄμεμπτος *amemptos* 5x *blameless, irreprehensible, without defect,* Lk 1:6; Phil 2:15; 3:6; 1 Th 3:13; Heb 8:7★ [273]

[290] ἀμέμπτως *amemptōs* 2x *blamelessly, unblamably, unexceptionably,* 1 Th 2:10; 5:23★ [274]

[291] ἀμέριμνος *amerimnos* 2x *free from care* or *solicitude,* Mt 28:14; 1 Co 7:32★ [275]

[292] ἀμετάθετος *ametathetos* 2x *unchangeable,* Heb 6:17, 18★ [276]

[293] ἀμετακίνητος *ametakinētos* 1x *immovable, firm,* 1 Co 15:58★ [277]

[294] ἀμεταμέλητος *ametamelētos* 2x *not to be repented of;* by impl. *irrevocable, enduring,* Ro 11:29; 2 Co 7:10★ [278]

[296] ἄμετρος *ametros* 2x *without* or *beyond measure, regardless of measure,* 2 Co 10:13, 15★ [280]

[297] ἀμήν *amēn* 129x *in truth, most certainly; so be it;* ὁ ἀμήν, *the faithful and true one,* Rev 3:14 [281]

[298] ἀμήτωρ *amētōr* 1x pr. *without mother; independent of maternal descent,* Heb 7:3★ [282]

[299] ἀμίαντος *amiantos* 4x pr. *unstained, unsoiled;* mct. *undefiled, chaste,* Heb 7:26; 13:4; *pure, sincere,* Jas 1:27; *undefiled, unimpaired,* 1 Pe 1:4★ [283]

[300] Ἀμιναδάβ *Aminadab* 3x *Aminadab,* pr. name, indecl, Mt 1:4; Lk 3:33★ [284]

[302] ἄμμος *ammos* 5x *sand,* Mt 7:26; Ro 9:27; Heb 11:12; Rev 12:18, 20★ [285]

[303] ἀμνός *amnos* 4x *a lamb,* Jn 1:29, 36; Ac 8:32; 1 Pe 1:19★ [286]

[304] ἀμοιβή *amoibē* 1x *(adequate) return, recompense,* 1 Ti 5:4★ [287]

[306] ἄμπελος *ampelos* 9x *a vine, grape-vine* [288]

[307] ἀμπελουργός *ampelourgos* 1x *a vine-dresser, gardner,* Lk 13:7★ [289]

[308] ἀμπελών *ampelōn* 23x *a vineyard* [290]

[309] Ἀμπλιᾶτος *Ampliatos* 1x *Ampliatus,* pr. name, Ro 16:8★ [291]

[310] ἀμύνομαι *amynomai* 1x *to ward off; to help, assist; to repel from oneself, resist, make a defence; to assume the office of protector and avenger,* Ac 7:24★ [292]

[311] ἀμφιβάλλω *amphiballō* 1x *to throw around; to cast* a net, Mk 1:16★ [906 + 293]

[312] ἀμφίβληστρον *amphiblēstron* 1x pr. *what is thrown around,* e.g., a garment; *a large kind of fish-net,* Mt 4:18* [293]

[313] ἀμφιέζω *amphiezō* 1x *to clothe,* Lk 12:28* [294]

[314] ἀμφιέννυμι *amphiennymi* 3x also spelled ἀμφιέζω and ἀμφιέννυμι, *to clothe, invest,* Mt 6:30; 11:8; Lk 7:25* [294]

[315] Ἀμφίπολις *Amphipolis* 1x *Amphipolis,* a city of Thrace, on the river Strymon, Ac 17:1* [295]

[316] ἄμφοδον *amphodon* 1x pr. *a road leading round a town* or *village; the street of a village,* Mk 11:4* [296]

[317] ἀμφότεροι *amphoteroi* 14x *both.* Only plural in the N.T. [297]

[318] ἀμώμητος *amōmētos* 1x *blameless, unblemished,* 2 Pe 3:14* [298]

[319] ἄμωμον *amōmon* 1x *amomum,* an odoriferous shrub, from which a precious ointment was prepared, Rev 18:13* [**]

[322] Ἀμώς *Amōs* 3x *Amos,* pr. name, indecl, Mt 1:10; Lk 3:25* [301]

[323] ἄν *an* 166x For the various constructions of this particle, and their significance, consult a grammar. At the beginning of a clause, it is another form of ἐάν, *if,* Jn 20:23 [302]

[324] ἀνά *ana* 13x prep. used in the N.T. only in certain forms. ἀνὰ μέρος, *in turn;* ἀνὰ μέσον, *through the midst, between;* ἀνὰ δηνάριον, *at the rate of a denarius;* with numerals, ἀνὰ ἑκατόν, *in parties of a hundred.* In composition, *step by step, up, back, again* [303]

[325] ἀναβαθμός *anabathmos* 2x *the act of ascending; means of ascent, steps, stairs,* Ac 21:35, 40* [304]

[326] ἀναβαίνω *anabainō* 82x *to go up, ascend,* Mt 5:1; *to climb,* Lk 19:4; *to go on board,* Mk 6:51; *to rise, mount upwards,* as smoke, Rev 8:4; *to grow* or *spring up,* as plants, Mt 13:7; *to spring up, arise,* as thoughts, Lk 24:38 [305]

[327] ἀναβάλλω *anaballō* 1x *to throw back;* mid. *to put off, defer, adjourn,* Ac 24:22* [306]

[328] ἀναβιβάζω *anabibazō* 1x *to cause to come up* or *ascend, draw* or *bring up,* Mt 13:48* [307]

[329] ἀναβλέπω *anablepō* 25x *to look upwards,* Mt 14:19; *to see again, recover sight,* Mt 11:5 [308]

[330] ἀνάβλεψις *anablepsis* 1x *recovery of sight,* Lk 4:18* [309]

[331] ἀναβοάω *anaboaō* 1x *to cry out* or *aloud, exclaim,* Mt 27:46* [310]

[332] ἀναβολή *anabolē* 1x *delay,* Ac 25:17* [311]

[333] ἀνάγαιον *anagaion* 2x *an upper room,* Mk 14:15; Lk 22:12* [508]

[334] ἀναγγέλλω *anangellō* 14x *to bring back word, announce, report,* Mk 5:14; *to declare, set forth, teach,* Jn 5:24 [312]

[335] ἀναγεννάω *anagennaō* 2x *to beget* or *bring forth again; to regenerate,* 1 Pe 1:3, 23* [313]

[336] ἀναγινώσκω *anaginōskō* 32x *to gather exact knowledge of, recognize, discern;* especially, *to read* [314]

[337] ἀναγκάζω *anankazō* 9x *to force, compel,* Ac 28:19; *to constrain, urge,* Lk 14:23 [315]

[338] ἀναγκαῖος *anankaios* 8x *necessary, indispensable,* 1 Co 12:22; *necessary, needful, right, proper,* Ac 13:46; 2 Co 9:5; Phil 1:24; 2:25; Heb 8:3; *near, intimate, closely connected,* as friends, Ac 10:24 [316]

[339] ἀναγκαστῶς *anankastōs* 1x *by constraint* or *compulsion, unwillingly,* opposite to ἑκουσίως, 1 Pe 5:2* [317]

[340] ἀνάγκη *anankē* 17x *necessity,* Mt 18:7; *constraint, compulsion,* 2 Co 9:7; *obligation of duty,* moral or spiritual *necessity,* Ro 13:5; *distress, trial, affliction,* Lk 21:23; 1 Co 7:26; 2 Co 6:4; 12:10; 1 Th 3:7 [318]

[341] ἀναγνωρίζω *anagnōrizō* 1x *to recognize;* pass. *to be made known,* or *to cause one's self to be recognized,* Ac 7:13* [319]

[342] ἀνάγνωσις *anagnōsis* 3x *reading,* Ac 13:15; 2 Co 3:14; 1 Ti 4:13* [320]

[343] ἀνάγω *anagō* 23x *to conduct; to lead* or *convey* up from a lower place to a higher, Lk 4:5; *to offer up,* as a sacrifice, Ac 7:41; *to lead out, produce,* Ac 12:4; as a nautical term (in the middle or passive), *to set sail, put to sea,* Lk 8:22 [321]

[344] ἀναδείκνυμι *anadeiknymi* 2x pr. *to show anything by raising it aloft,* as a torch; *to display, manifest, show plainly* or *openly,* Ac 1:24; *to mark out, constitute, appoint* by some outward sign, Lk 10:1* [322]

[345] ἀνάδειξις *anadeixis* 1x *a showing forth, manifestation; public entrance upon the duty* or *office to which one is consecrated,* Lk 1:80* [323]

[346] ἀναδέχομαι *anadechomai* 2x *to receive,* as opposed to shunning or refusing; *to receive* with hospitality, Ac 28:7; *to*

embrace a proffer or promise, Heb 11:17* [324]

[347] ἀναδίδωμι *anadidōmi* 1x *to give forth, up,* or *back; to deliver, present,* Ac 23:33* [325]

[348] ἀναζάω *anazaō* 3x *to live again, recover life, revive,* Ro 7:9; met. *to live a new and reformed life,* Lk 15:24, 32* [326]

[349] ἀναζητέω *anazēteō* 3x *to track; to seek diligently, inquire after, search for,* Lk 2:44, 45; Ac 11:25* [327]

[350] ἀναζώννυμι *anazōnnymi* 1x *to gird* with a belt or girdle; *to gird one's self,* 1 Pe 1:13* [328]

[351] ἀναζωπυρέω *anazōpyreō* 1x pr. *to kindle up a dormant fire;* met. *to revive, excite; to stir up, quicken* one's powers, 2 Ti 1:6* [329]

[352] ἀναθάλλω *anathallō* 1x *to grow* or *bloom again; to renew,* Phil 4:10* [330]

[353] ἀνάθεμα *anathema* 6x *a devoted thing,* ordinarily in a bad sense, *a person* or *thing accursed,* Ro 9:3; 1 Co 12:3; 16:22; Gal 1:8, 9; *a curse, execration, anathema,* Ac 23:14* [331]

[354] ἀναθεματίζω *anathematizō* 4x *to declare* any one *to be* ἀνάθεμα; *to curse, bind by a curse,* Mk 14:71; Ac 23:12, 14, 21* [332]

[355] ἀναθεωρέω *anatheōreō* 2x *to view, behold attentively, contemplate,* Ac 17:23; Heb 13:7* [333]

[356] ἀνάθημα *anathēma* 1x *a gift* or *offering consecrated to God,* Lk 21:5* [334]

[357] ἀναίδεια *anaideia* 1x pr. *shamelessness;* hence, *persistence,* without regard to time, place, or person, Lk 11:8* [335]

[358] ἀναίρεσις *anairesis* 1x *a taking up* or *away; a putting to death, murder,* Ac 8:1* [336]

[359] ἀναιρέω *anaireō* 24x pr. *to take up, lift,* as from the ground; *to take off, put to death, kill, murder,* Mt 2:16; *to take away, abolish, abrogate,* Heb 10:9; mid. *to take up* infants in order to bring them up, Ac 7:21 [337]

[360] ἀναίτιος *anaitios* 2x *guiltless, innocent,* Mt 12:5, 7* [338]

[361] ἀνακαθίζω *anakathizō* 2x *to set up;* intrans. *to sit up,* Lk 7:15; Ac 9:40* [339]

[362] ἀνακαινίζω *anakainizō* 1x *to renovate, renew,* Heb 6:6* [340]

[363] ἀνακαινόω *anakainoō* 2x *to invigorate, renew,* 2 Co 4:16; Col 3:10★ [341]

[364] ἀνακαίνωσις *anakainōsis* 2x *renovation, renewal,* Ro 12:2; Tit 3:5★ [342]

[365] ἀνακαλύπτω *anakalyptō* 2x *to unveil, uncover;* pass. *to be unveiled,* 2 Co 3:18; met. *to be disclosed* in true character and condition, 2 Co 3:14★ [343]

[366] ἀνακάμπτω *anakamptō* 4x pr. *to reflect, bend back;* hence, *to bend back* one's course, *return,* Mt 2:12; Lk 10:6; Ac 18:21; Heb 11:15★ [344]

[367] ἀνάκειμαι *anakeimai* 14x *to be laid up,* as offerings; later, *to lie, recline* at table, Mt 9:10 [345]

[368] ἀνακεφαλαιόω *anakephalaioō* 2x *to bring together several things under one, reduce under one head; to comprise,* Ro 13:9; Eph 1:10★ [346]

[369] ἀνακλίνω *anaklinō* 6x *to lay down,* Lk 2:7; *to cause to recline* at table, etc. Mk 6:39; Lk 9:15; 12:37; *to recline at table,* Mt 8:11 [347]

[371] ἀνακράζω *anakrazō* 5x *to cry aloud, exclaim, shout,* Mk 1:23; 6:49; Lk 4:33; 8:28; 23:18★ [349]

[373] ἀνακρίνω *anakrinō* 16x *to sift; to examine closely,* Ac 17:11; *to scrutinize, scan,* 1 Co 2:14, 15; 9:3; *to try* judicially, Lk 23:14; *to judge, give judgment upon,* 1 Co 4:3, 4; *to put questions, be inquisitive,* 1 Co 10:25, 27; Ac 11:12 v.l [350]

[374] ἀνάκρισις *anakrisis* 1x *investigation, judicial examination, hearing of a cause,* Ac 25:26★ [351]

[376] ἀνακύπτω *anakyptō* 4x pr. *to raise up one's self, look up,* Lk 13:11; Jn 8:7, 10; met. *to look up* cheerily, *to be cheered,* Lk 21:28★ [352]

[377] ἀναλαμβάνω *analambanō* 13x *to take up, receive up,* Mk 16:19; *to take up, carry,* Ac 7:43; *to take on board,* Ac 20:13, 14; *to take* in company, Ac 23:31; 2 Ti 4:11 [353]

[378] ἀνάλημψις *analēmpsis* 1x *a taking up, receiving up,* Lk 9:51★ [354]

[381] ἀναλογία *analogia* 1x *analogy, ratio, proportion,* Ro 12:6★ [356]

[382] ἀναλογίζομαι *analogizomai* 1x *to consider attentively,* Heb 12:3★ [357]

[383] ἄναλος *analos* 1x *without saltness, without the taste and pungency of salt, insipid,* Mk 9:50 [358]

[384] ἀναλόω *analoō* 2x see ἀναλίσκω [355]

[385] ἀνάλυσις *analysis* 1x pr. *dissolution;* met. *departure, death,* 2 Ti 4:6★ [359]

[386] ἀναλύω *analyō* 2x pr. *to loose, dissolve;* intrans. *to loose* in order to departure; *to depart,* Lk 12:36; *to depart* from life, Phil 1:23★ [360]

[387] ἀναμάρτητος *anamartētos* 1x *without sin, guiltless,* Jn 8:7★ [361]

[388] ἀναμένω *anamenō* 1x *to await, wait for, expect,* 1 Th 1:10★ [362]

[389] ἀναμιμνήσκω *anamimnēskō* 6x *to remind, cause to remember,* 1 Co 4:17; *to exhort,* 2 Ti 1:6; *to call to mind, recollect, remember,* Mk 11:21; 14:72; 2 Co 7:15; Heb 10:32★ [363]

[390] ἀνάμνησις *anamnēsis* 4x *remembrance; a commemoration, memorial,* Lk 22:19; 1 Co 11:24, 25; Heb 10:3★ [364]

[391] ἀνανεόω *ananeoō* 1x also spelled ἀνανεόομαι, *to renew;* pass. *to be renewed, be renovated,* by inward reformation, Eph 4:23★ [365]

[392] ἀνανήφω *ananēphō* 1x *to become sober;* met. *to recover sobriety* of mind, 2 Ti 2:26★ [366]

[393] Ἁνανίας *Hananias* 11x *Ananias,* pr. name I. *A Christian of Jerusalem,* Ac 5:1, etc. II. *A Christian of Damascus,* Ac 9:12, etc. III. *High Priest,* Ac 23:2; 24:1 [367]

[394] ἀναντίρρητος *anantirrētos* 1x *not to be contradicted, indisputable,* Ac 19:36★ [368]

[395] ἀναντιρρήτως *anantirrētōs* 1x pr. *without contradiction* or *gainsaying; without hesitation, promptly,* Ac 10:29★ [369]

[396] ἀνάξιος *anaxios* 1x *inadequate, unworthy,* 1 Co 6:2★ [370]

[397] ἀναξίως *anaxiōs* 1x *unworthily, in an improper manner,* 1 Co 11:27★ [371]

[398] ἀνάπαυσις *anapausis* 5x *rest, intermission,* Mt 11:29; Rev 4:8; 14:11; meton. *place of rest, fixed habitation,* Mt 12:43; Lk 11:24★ [372]

[399] ἀναπαύω *anapauō* 12x *to cause to rest, to soothe, refresh,* Mt 11:28; mid. *to take rest, repose, refreshment,* Mt 26:45; *to have a fixed place of rest, abide, dwell,* 1 Pe 4:14 [373]

[400] ἀναπείθω *anapeithō* 1x *to persuade* to a different opinion, *to seduce,* Ac 18:13★ [374]

[401] ἀνάπειρος *anapeiros* 2x also spelled ἀνάπηρος, *maimed, deprived of some member of the body,* or *at least of its use,* Lk 14:13, 21 [376]

[402] ἀναπέμπω *anapempō* 5x *to send back,* Phlm 12; *to send up, remit* to a tribunal, Lk 23:7, 11, 15; Ac 25:21★ [375]

[403] ἀναπηδάω *anapēdaō* 1x *to leap up, stand up,* Mk 10:50★ [450]

[404] ἀναπίπτω *anapiptō* 12x *to fall or recline backwards; to recline* at table, etc., Lk 11:37; *to throw one's self back,* Jn 21:20 [377]

[405] ἀναπληρόω *anaplēroō* 6x *to fill up, complete,* 1 Th 2:16; *to fulfil, confirm,* as a prophecy by the event, Mt 13:14; *to fill* the place of any one, 1 Co 14:16; *to supply, make good,* 1 Co 16:17; Phil 2:30; *to observe fully, keep* the law, Gal 6:2★ [378]

[406] ἀναπολόγητος *anapologētos* 2x *inexcusable,* Ro 1:20; 2:1★ [379]

[408] ἀναπτύσσω *anaptyssō* 1x *to roll back, unroll, unfold,* Lk 4:17★ [380]

[409] ἀνάπτω *anaptō* 2x *to light, kindle, set on fire,* Lk 12:49; Jas 3:5★ [381]

[410] ἀναρίθμητος *anarithmētos* 1x *innumerable,* Heb 11:12★ [382]

[411] ἀνασείω *anaseiō* 2x pr. *to shake up;* met. *to stir up, instigate,* Mk 15:11; Lk 23:5★ [383]

[412] ἀνασκευάζω *anaskeuazō* 1x pr. *to collect one's effects* or *baggage* (skeuvh) in order to remove; *to lay waste by carrying off* or *destroying* every thing; met. *to unsettle, pervert, subvert,* Ac 15:24★ [384]

[413] ἀνασπάω *anaspaō* 2x *to draw up, to draw out,* Lk 14:5; Ac 11:10★ [385]

[414] ἀνάστασις *anastasis* 42x *a raising* or *rising up; resurrection,* Mt 22:23; meton. *the author of resurrection,* Jn 11:25; met. *an uprising* into a state of higher advancement and blessedness, Lk 2:34 [386]

[415] ἀναστατόω *anastatoō* 3x *to lay waste, destroy; to disturb, throw into commotion,* Ac 17:6; *to excite to sedition and tumult,* Ac 21:38; *to disturb* the mind of any one by doubts, etc.; *to subvert, unsettle,* Gal 5:12★ [387]

[416] ἀνασταυρόω *anastauroō* 1x *to crucify again,* Heb 6:6★ [388]

[417] ἀναστενάζω *anastenazō* 1x *to sigh, groan deeply,* Mk 8:12★ [389]

[418] ἀναστρέφω *anastrephō* 9x *to overturn, throw down, to turn back, return,* Ac 5:22; 15:16; *to live, to conduct one's self,* 2 Co 1:12; Eph 2:3; 1 Ti 3:15; Heb 13:18; 1 Pe 1:17; 2 Pe 2:18; *to gaze,* Heb 10:33★ [390]

[419] ἀναστροφή *anastrophē* 13x *conversation, mode of life, conduct, deportment,* Gal 1:13 [391]

[421] ἀνατάσσομαι *anatassomai* 1x pr. *to arrange;* hence, *to compose,* Lk 1:1* [392]

[422] ἀνατέλλω *anatellō* 9x *to cause to rise,* Mt 5:45; intrans. *to rise,* as the sun, stars, etc., Mt 4:16; *to spring* by birth, Heb 7:14 [393]

[423] ἀνατίθημι *anatithēmi* 2x in N.T. only mid., *to submit to* a person's *consideration, statement,* or *report* of matters, Ac 25:14; Gal 2:2* [394]

[424] ἀνατολή *anatolē* 11x pr. *a rising* of the sun, etc.; *the place of rising, the east,* as also pl. ἀνατολαί, Mt 2:1, 2; met. *the dawn* or *day-spring,* Lk 1:78 [395]

[426] ἀνατρέπω *anatrepō* 3x pr. *to overturn, overthrow;* met. *to subvert, corrupt,* 2 Ti 2:18; Tit 1:11; Jn 2:15* [396]

[427] ἀνατρέφω *anatrephō* 3x *to nurse,* as an infant, Ac 7:20; *to bring up, educate,* Ac 7:21; 22:3* [397]

[428] ἀναφαίνω *anaphainō* 2x *to bring to light, display;* mid. and pass. *to appear,* Lk 19:11; a nautical term, *to come in sight of,* Ac 21:3* [398]

[429] ἀναφέρω *anapherō* 10x *to bear* or *carry upwards, lead up,* Mt 17:1; *to offer* sacrifices, Heb 7:27; *to bear aloft* or *sustain* a burden, as sins, 1 Pe 2:24; Heb 9:28 [399]

[430] ἀναφωνέω *anaphōneō* 1x *to exclaim, cry out,* Lk 1:42* [400]

[431] ἀνάχυσις *anachusis* 1x *a pouring out;* met. *excess, stream, flood,* 1 Pe 4:4* [401]

[432] ἀναχωρέω *anachōreō* 14x *to go backward; to depart, go away,* Mt 2:12; *to withdraw, retire,* Mt 9:24; Ac 23:19; 26:31 [402]

[433] ἀνάψυξις *anapsyxis* 1x pr. *a refreshing coolness* after heat; met. *refreshing, recreation, rest,* Ac 3:20* [403]

[434] ἀναψύχω *anapsychō* 1x *to recreate by fresh air; to refresh, cheer,* 2 Ti 1:16* [404]

[435] ἀνδραποδιστής *andrapodistēs* 1x *a man-stealer, kidnapper,* 1 Ti 1:10* [405]

[436] Ἀνδρέας *Andreas* 13x *Andrew,* pr. name [406]

[437] ἀνδρίζομαι *andrizomai* 1x *to render brave* or *manly;* mid. *to show* or *behave one's self like a man,* 1 Co 16:13* [407]

[438] Ἀνδρόνικος *Andronikos* 1x *Andronicus,* pr. name, Ro 16:7* [408]

[439] ἀνδροφόνος *androphonos* 1x *a homicide, man-slayer, murderer,* 1 Ti 1:9* [409]

[441] ἀνέγκλητος *anenklētos* 5x *unblamable, irreproachable,* 1 Co 1:8; Col 1:22; 1 Ti 3:10; Tit 1:6, 7* [410]

[442] ἀνεκδιήγητος *anekdiēgētos* 1x *which cannot be related, inexpressible, unutterable, indescribable,* 2 Co 9:15* [411]

[443] ἀνεκλάλητος *aneklalētos* 1x *unspeakable, ineffable,* 1 Pe 1:8* [412]

[444] ἀνέκλειπτος *anekleiptos* 1x *unfailing, exhaustless,* Lk 12:33* [413]

[445] ἀνεκτός *anektos* 5x *tolerable, supportable,* Mt 10:15; 11:22, 24; Lk 10:12, 14* [414]

[446] ἀνελεήμων *aneleēmōn* 1x *unmerciful, uncompassionate, cruel,* Ro 1:31* [415]

[447] ἀνέλεος *aneleos* 1x *merciless,* Jas 2:13* [448]

[448] ἀνεμίζω *anemizō* 1x *to agitate with the wind;* pass. *to be agitated* or *driven by the wind,* Jas 1:6* [416]

[449] ἄνεμος *anemos* 31x *the wind;* met. *a wind* of shifting doctrine, Eph 4:14 [417]

[450] ἀνένδεκτος *anendektos* 1x *impossible, what cannot be,* Lk 17:1* [418]

[451] ἀνεξεραύνητος *anexeraunētos* 1x also spelled ἀνεξερεύνητος, *unfathomable, incapable of human explanation,* Ro 11:33* [419]

[452] ἀνεξίκακος *anexikakos* 1x *enduring* or *patient under evils and injuries,* 2 Ti 2:24* [420]

[453] ἀνεξιχνίαστος *anexichniastos* 2x *to track out,* ἴχνος, *a track which cannot be explored, inscrutable, incomprehensible,* Ro 11:33; Eph 3:8* [421]

[454] ἀνεπαίσχυντος *anepaischuntos* 1x *without cause of shame, irreproachable,* 2 Ti 2:15* [422]

[455] ἀνεπίλημπτος *anepilēmptos* 3x also spelled ἀνεπίληπρος. pr. *not to be laid hold of;* met. *beyond reproach, unblamable,* 1 Ti 3:2; 5:7; 6:14* [423]

[456] ἀνέρχομαι *anerchomai* 3x *to ascend, go up,* Jn 6:3; Gal 1:17, 18* [424]

[457] ἄνεσις *anesis* 5x pr. *the relaxing* of a state of constraint; *relaxation* of rigor of confinement, Ac 24:23; met. *ease, rest, peace, tranquility,* 2 Co 2:13; 7:5; 8:13; 2 Th 1:7* [425]

[458] ἀνετάζω *anetazō* 2x *to examine thoroughly; to examine* by torture, Ac 22:24, 29* [426]

[459] ἄνευ *aneu* 3x some classify as an improper preposition, *without,* Mt 10:29; 1 Pe 3:1; 4:9* [427]

[460] ἀνεύθετος *aneuthetos* 1x *unfavorable situated, inconvenient,* Ac 27:12* [428]

[461] ἀνευρίσκω *aneuriskō* 2x *to find by diligent search,* Lk 2:16; Ac 21:4* [429]

[462] ἀνέχομαι *anechōmai* 15x also listed as ἀνέχω, but it is always in the middle in our literature, *to endure patiently,* 1 Cor 4:12; 2 Cor 11:20; 2 Thess 1:4; *to bear with,* Matt 17:7; *to suffer, admit, permit,* Acts 18:14; 2 Cor 11:4; 2 Tim 4:3; Heb 13:22 [430]

[463] ἀνεψιός *anepsios* 1x *a nephew, cousin,* Col 4:10* [431]

[464] ἄνηθον *anēthon* 1x *dill,* an aromatic plant, Mt 23:23* [432]

[465] ἀνήκω *anēkō* 3x *to come up to, to pertain to;* ἀνήκει, impers. *it is fit, proper, becoming,* Col 3:18; Eph 5:4; Phlm 8* [433]

[466] ἀνήμερος *anēmeros* 1x *savage, fierce, ferocious,* 2 Ti 3:3* [434]

[467] ἀνήρ *anēr* 216x *a male person of full age and stature,* as opposed to a child or female, 1 Co 13:11; *a husband,* Mt 1:16; *a man, human being, individual,* Lk 11:31; used also pleonastically with other nouns and adjectives, Lk 5:8; Ac 1:16 [435]

[468] ἀνθίστημι *anthistēmi* 14x *to oppose, resist, stand out against* [436]

[469] ἀνθομολογέομαι *anthomologeomai* 1x pr. *to come to an agreement;* hence, *to confess openly what is due; to confess, give thanks, render praise,* Lk 2:38* [437]

[470] ἄνθος *anthos* 4x *a flower,* Jas 1:10, 11; 1 Pe 1:24 (2t)* [438]

[471] ἀνθρακιά *anthrakia* 2x *a mass* or *heap of live coals,* Jn 18:18; 21:9 [439]

[472] ἄνθραξ *anthrax* 1x *a coal, burning coal,* Ro 12:20* [440]

[473] ἀνθρωπάρεσκος *anthrōpareskos* 2x *desirous of pleasing men,* Eph 6:6; Col 3:22* [441]

[474] ἀνθρώπινος *anthrōpinos* 7x *human, belonging to man,* 1 Co 2:4, 13; 4:3; 10:13; Jas 3:7; 1 Pe 2:13; *suited to man,* Ro 6:19* [442]

[475] ἀνθρωποκτόνος *anthrōpoktonos* 3x *a homicide, murderer,* Jn 8:44; 1 Jn 3:15* [443]

[476] ἄνθρωπος *anthrōpos* 550x *a human being,* Jn 16:21; Phil 2:7; *an individual,* Ro 3:28, et al. freq.; used also pleonastically with other words, Mt 11:19; et al.; met. *the* spiritual frame of the inner *man,* Ro 7:22; Eph 3:16; 1 Pe 3:4 [444]

[478] ἀνθύπατος *anthupatos* 5x *a proconsul,* Ac 13:7, 8, 12; 19:38 [446]

[479] ἀνίημι *aniēmi* 4x (1) *to loose, slacken,* Ac 27:40; *to unbind, unfasten,* Ac 16:26; (2) *to omit, dispense with,* Eph 6:9; (3) *to leave* or *neglect,* Heb 13:5* [447]

[481] ἄνιπτος *aniptos* 2x literally: *unwashed*; figuratively: *ceremonially unclean* Mt 15:20; Mk 7:2* [449]

[482] ἀνίστημι *anistēmi* 108x trans. *to cause to stand up* or *rise,* Ac 9:41; *to raise up,* as the dead, Jn 6:39; *to raise up* into existence, Mt 22:24; intrans. and mid., *to rise up,* Mt 9:9, *to rise up* into existence, Ac 7:18; 20:30 [450]

[483] Ἅννα *Hanna* 1x *Anna,* pr. name, Lk 2:26* [451]

[484] Ἅννας *Hannas* 4x *Annas,* pr. name, short version of Ἅνανος, Lk 3:2; Jn 18:13, 24; Ac 4:6* [452]

[485] ἀνόητος *anoētos* 6x *inconsiderate, unintelligent, unwise*; Lk 24:25; Ro 1:14; Gal 3:1, 3; Tit 3:3; *brutish,* 1 Ti 6:9 [453]

[486] ἄνοια *anoia* 2x *want of understanding; folly, rashness, madness,* Lk 6:11; 2 Ti 3:9* [454]

[487] ἀνοίγω *anoigō* 77x trans. *to open,* Mt 2:11; intrans. *to be opened, to be open,* Mt 3:16; Jn 1:52 [455]

[488] ἀνοικοδομέω *anoikodomeō* 2x *to rebuild,* Ac 15:16 (2t)* [456]

[489] ἄνοιξις *anoixis* 1x *an opening, act of opening,* Eph 6:19* [457]

[490] ἀνομία *anomia* 15x *lawlessness; violation of law,* 1 Jn 3:4; *iniquity, sin,* Mt 7:23 [458]

[491] ἄνομος *anomos* 9x *lawless, without law, not subject to law,* 1 Co 9:21; *lawless, violating law, wicked, impious,* Ac 2:23; *a transgressor,* Mk 15:28; Lk 22:37 [459]

[492] ἀνόμως *anomōs* 2x *without* the intervention of *law,* Ro 2:12 (2t) [460]

[494] ἀνορθόω *anorthoō* 3x *to restore to straightness* or *erectness,* Lk 13:13; *to re-invigorate,* Heb 12:12; *to re-erect,* Ac 15:16* [461]

[495] ἀνόσιος *anosios* 2x *impious, unholy,* 1 Ti 1:9; 2 Ti 3:2* [462]

[496] ἀνοχή *anochē* 2x *forbearance, patience,* Ro 2:4; 3:26* [463]

[497] ἀνταγωνίζομαι *antagōnizomai* 1x *to contend, strive against,* Heb 12:4* [464]

[498] ἀντάλλαγμα *antallagma* 2x *a price paid in exchange* for a thing; *compensation, equivalent ransom,* Mt 16:26; Mk 8:37* [465]

[499] ἀνταναπληρόω *antanaplēroō* 1x *to fill up, complete, supply,* Col 1:24* [466]

[500] ἀνταποδίδωμι *antapodidōmi* 7x *to repay, give back, return, recompense,* Lk 14:14 (2t); Ro 11:35; 12:19; 1 Th 3:9; 2 Th 1:6; Heb 10:30 [467]

[501] ἀνταπόδομα *antapodoma* 2x *repayment, recompense, retribution,* Lk 14:12; Ro 11:9* [468]

[502] ἀνταπόδοσις *antapodosis* 1x *recompense, reward,* Col 3:24* [469]

[503] ἀνταποκρίνομαι *antapokrinomai* 2x occurs in the N.T. only in the middle, *to answer, speak in answer,* Lk 14:6; *to reply against, contradict, dispute,* Ro 9:20* [470]

[504] ἀντέχω *antechō* 4x *to hold firmly, cling* or *adhere to; to be devoted to* any one, Lk 16:13; Tit 1:9; *to exercise a zealous care for* any one, 1 Th 5:14; Mk 6:24* [472]

[505] ἀντί *anti* 22x *over against*; hence, *in correspondence to, answering to,* Jn 1:16; *in place of,* Mt 2:22; *in retribution* or *return for,* Mt 5:38; *in consideration of,* Heb 12:2, 16; *on account of,* Mt 17:27; ἀνθ᾽ ὧν, *because,* Lk 1:20 [473]

[506] ἀντιβάλλω *antiballō* 1x pr. *to throw* or *toss from one to another;* met. *to agitate, to converse* or *discourse about,* Lk 24:17* [474]

[507] ἀντιδιατίθημι *antidiatithēmi* 1x *to set opposite*; mid. (only in the N.T.) *to be of an opposite opinion, to be adverse; opponent,* 2 Ti 2:25* [475]

[508] ἀντίδικος *antidikos* 5x *an opponent in a lawsuit,* Mt 5:25 (2t); Lk 12:58; 18:3; *an adversary,* 1 Pe 5:8* [476]

[509] ἀντίθεσις *antithesis* 1x pr. *opposition*; hence, *a question proposed for dispute, disputation,* 1 Ti 6:20* [477]

[510] ἀντικαθίστημι *antikathistēmi* 1x trans. *to set in opposition*; intrans. *to withstand, resist,* Heb 12:4* [478]

[511] ἀντικαλέω *antikaleō* 1x *to invite in return,* Lk 14:12* [479]

[512] ἀντίκειμαι *antikeimai* 8x pr. *occupy an opposite position*; met. *to oppose, be adverse to,* Gal 5:17; 1 Ti 1:10; *opponent, hostile,* Lk 13:7 [480]

[513] ἄντικρυς *antikrys* 1x can function as an improper preposition with the gen., also spelled ἀντικρύ, *opposite to, over against,* Ac 20:15* [481]

[514] ἀντιλαμβάνω *antilambanō* 3x *to aid, assist, help,* Lk 1:54; Ac 20:35; *to be a recipient,* 1 Ti 6:2* [482]

[515] ἀντιλέγω *antilegō* 11x *to speak against, contradict; to gainsay, deny,* Lk 20:27; *to oppose,* Jn 19:12; Ac 13:45; 28:19; Ro 10:21; Tit 1:9; 2:9; pass. *to be spoken against, decried,* Lk 2:34; Ac 28:22* [471, 483]

[516] ἀντίλημψις *antilēmpsis* 1x *aid, assistance;* meton, *one who aids* or *assists, a help,* 1 Co 12:28* [484]

[517] ἀντιλογία *antilogia* 4x *contradiction, question,* Heb 6:16; 7:7; *opposition, rebellion,* Jude 11; *hostility,* Heb 12:3* [485]

[518] ἀντιλοιδορέω *antiloidoreō* 1x *to reproach* or *revile again* or *in return,* 1 Pe 2:23* [486]

[519] ἀντίλυτρον *antilytron* 1x *a ransom,* 1 Ti 2:6* [487]

[520] ἀντιμετρέω *antimetreō* 1x *to measure in return,* Lk 6:38* [488]

[521] ἀντιμισθία *antimisthia* 2x *a retribution, recompense,* Ro 1:27; 2 Co 6:13* [489]

[522] Ἀντιόχεια *Antiocheia* 18x *Antioch,* pr. name I. *Antioch,* the metropolis of Syria, where the disciples first received the name of Christians II. *Antioch,* a city of Pisidia, Ac 13:14; 14:19; 2 Ti 3:11 [490]

[523] Ἀντιοχεύς *Antiocheus* 1x *an inhabitant of Antioch,* Ac 6:5* [491]

[524] ἀντιπαρέρχομαι *antiparerchomai* 2x *to pass over against, to pass along* without noticing, Lk 10:31, 32* [492]

[525] Ἀντιπᾶς *Antipas* 1x *Antipas,* pr. name, Rev 2:13* [493]

[526] Ἀντιπατρίς *Antipatris* 1x *Antipatris,* pr. name, Ac 23:31* [494]

[527] ἀντιπέρα *antipera* 1x can function as an improper preposition with the gen., *opposite,* Lk 8:26* [495]

[528] ἀντιπίπτω *antipiptō* 1x pr. *to fall upon, rush upon* any one; hence, *to resist by force, oppose, strive against,* Ac 7:51* [496]

[529] ἀντιστρατεύομαι *antistrateuomai* 1x *to war against; to contravene, oppose,* Ro 7:23★ [497]

[530] ἀντιτάσσω *antitassō* 5x *to post in adverse array,* as an army; mid. *to set oneself in opposition, resist,* Ac 18:6; Ro 13:2; Jas 5:6; *to be averse,* Jas 4:6; 1 Pe 5:5★ [498]

[531] ἀντίτυπος *antitypos* 2x *of correspondent stamp* or *form; corresponding, in correspondent fashion,* 1 Pe 3:21; τὸ ἀντίτυπον, *a copy, representation,* Heb 9:24★ [499]

[532] ἀντίχριστος *antichristos* 5x *antichrist, an opposer of Christ,* 1 Jn 2:18, 22; 4:3; 2 Jn 7; plural in 1 Jn 2:18★ [500]

[533] ἀντλέω *antleō* 4x *to draw,* e.g., wine, water, etc.; Jn 2:8, 9; 4:7, 15★ [501]

[534] ἄντλημα *antlēma* 1x pr. *that which is drawn; a bucket, vessel for drawing water,* Jn 4:11★ [502]

[535] ἀντοφθαλμέω *antophthalmeō* 1x pr. *to look in the face,* met. a nautical term, *to bear up against* the wind, Ac 27:15★ [503]

[536] ἄνυδρος *anydros* 4x *without water, dry,* 2 Pe 2:17; Jude 12; τόποι ἄνυδροι, *dry places,* and therefore, in the East, *barren, desert,* Mt 12:43; Lk 11:24★ [504]

[537] ἀνυπόκριτος *anypokritos* 6x *unfeigned, real, sincere,* Ro 12:9 [505]

[538] ἀνυπότακτος *anypotaktos* 4x *not subjected, not made subordinate,* Heb 2:8; *insubordinate, refractory, disorderly, contumacious, lawless,* 1 Ti 1:9; Tit 1:6, 10 [506]

[539] ἄνω *anō* 9x *above,* Ac 2:19; Gal 4:26; Col 3:1; *up, upwards,* Jn 11:41; ὁ, ἡ, τό, ἄνω, *that which is above,* Jn 8:23; ἕως ἄνω, *to the top* [507]

[540] ἄνωθεν *anōthen* 13x *from above, from a higher place,* Jn 3:31; of time, *from the first* or *beginning,* Ac 26:5; *from the source,* Lk 1:33; *again, anew,* Jn 3:3, 7; Gal 4:9; with a prep., *the top* or *upper part,* Mt 27:51 [509]

[541] ἀνωτερικός *anōterikos* 1x *upper, higher, inland,* Ac 19:1★ [510]

[543] ἀνωφελής *anōphelēs* 2x *useless, unprofitable,* Tit 3:9; Heb 7:18★ [512]

[544] ἀξίνη *axinē* 2x *an axe,* Mt 3:10; Lk 3:9★ [513]

[545] ἄξιος *axios* 41x pr. *of equal value; worthy, estimable,* Mt 10:11, 13; *worthy of, deserving,* either good or evil, Mt 10:10; *correspondent to,* Mt 3:8; Lk 3:8; Ac 26:20;

comparable, countervailing, Ro 8:18; *suitable, due,* Lk 23:41 [514]

[546] ἀξιόω *axioō* 7x *to judge* or *esteem worthy* or *deserving; to deem fitting, to require,* Ac 15:38; 28:22 [515]

[547] ἀξίως *axiōs* 6x *worthily,* Col 1:10; *suitably, in a manner becoming,* Ro 16:2 [516]

[548] ἀόρατος *aoratos* 5x *invisible,* Ro 1:20; Col 1:15, 16; 1 Ti 1:17; Heb 11:27 [517]

[550] ἀπαγγέλλω *apangellō* 45x *to announce that with which a person is charged,* or *which is called for by circumstances; to carry back word,* Mt 2:8; *to report,* Mt 8:33; *to declare plainly,* Heb 2:12; *to announce formally,* 1 Jn 1:2, 3 [518]

[551] ἀπάγχω *apanchō* 1x *to strangle;* mid. *to choke* or *strangle one's self, hang one's self,* Mt 27:5★ [519]

[552] ἀπάγω *apagō* 15x *to lead away,* Mt 26:57; *to conduct,* Mt 7:13, 14; pass. *to be led off* to execution, Ac 12:19; met. *to be led astray, seduced,* 1 Co 12:1 [520]

[553] ἀπαίδευτος *apaideutos* 1x *uninstructed, ignorant; silly, unprofitable,* 2 Ti 2:23★ [521]

[554] ἀπαίρω *apairō* 3x *to take away;* pass. *to be taken away; to be withdrawn,* Mt 9:15; Mk 2:20; Lk 5:35★ [522]

[555] ἀπαιτέω *apaiteō* 2x *to demand, require,* Lk 12:20; *to demand back,* Lk 6:30★ [523]

[556] ἀπαλγέω *apalgeō* 1x pr. *to desist from grief;* hence, *to become insensible* or *callous,* Eph 4:19★ [524]

[557] ἀπαλλάσσω *apallassō* 3x *to set free, deliver, set at liberty,* Heb 2:15; *to rid* judicially, Lk 12:58; mid. *to depart, remove,* Ac 19:12★ [525]

[558] ἀπαλλοτριόω *apallotrioō* 3x pass. *to be alienated from, be a stranger to; alien,* Eph 2:12; 4:18; Col 1:21★ [526]

[559] ἁπαλός *hapalos* 2x *soft, tender,* Mt 24:32; Mk 13:28★ [527]

[560] ἀπαντάω *apantaō* 2x *to meet, encounter,* Mk 14:13; Lk 17:12★ [528]

[561] ἀπάντησις *apantēsis* 3x *a meeting, encounter;* εἰς ἀπάντησιν, *to meet,* Mt 25:6; Ac 28:15; 1 Th 4:17★ [529]

[562] ἅπαξ *hapax* 14x *once,* 2 Co 11:25; *once for all,* Heb 6:4; 9:26, 28; 10:2; 1 Pe 3:18, 20; Jude 3; εἰδὼς ἅπαξ, *knowing once for ever, unfailingly, constantly,* Jude 5 [530]

[563] ἀπαράβατος *aparabatos* 1x *not transient; not to be superseded, unchangeable,* Heb 7:24★ [531]

[564] ἀπαρασκεύαστος *aparaskeuastos* 1x *unprepared,* 2 Co 9:4★ [532]

[565] ἀπαρνέομαι *aparneomai* 11x *to deny, disown,* Mt 26:34; *to renounce, disregard,* Mt 16:24 [533]

[568] ἀπαρτισμός *apartismos* 1x *completion, perfection,* Lk 14:28★ [535]

[569] ἀπαρχή *aparchē* 9x pr. *the first act of a sacrifice;* hence, *the firstfruits, first portion, firstling,* Ro 8:23 [536]

[570] ἅπας *hapas* 34x *all, the whole* [537]

[571] ἀπασπάζομαι *apaspazomai* 1x *to take leave of, say farwell to,* Ac 21:6★ [782]

[572] ἀπατάω *apataō* 3x *to deceive, seduce into error,* Eph 5:6; 1 Ti 2:14; Jas 1:26★ [538]

[573] ἀπάτη *apatē* 7x *deceit, deception, delusion* [539]

[574] ἀπάτωρ *apatōr* 1x pr. *without a father, fatherless;* hence, *independent of paternal descent,* Heb 7:3★ [540]

[575] ἀπαύγασμα *apaugasma* 1x *a radiance,* Heb 1:3★ [541]

[577] ἀπείθεια *apeitheia* 7x *an uncompliant disposition; obstinacy, disobedience, unbelief,* Ro 11:30, 32; Eph 2:2; 5:6; Heb 4:6, 11; Col. 3:6★ [543]

[578] ἀπειθέω *apeitheō* 14x *to be uncompliant; to refuse belief, disbelieve,* Jn 3:36; *to refuse belief and obedience,* Ro 10:21; 1 Pe 3:20; *to refuse conformity,* Ro 2:8 [544]

[579] ἀπειθής *apeithēs* 6x *who will not be persuaded, uncompliant; disobedient,* Lk 1:17; Ac 26:19; Ro 1:30; 2 Ti 3:2; Tit 1:16; 3:3 [545]

[580] ἀπειλέω *apeileō* 2x *to threaten, menace, rebuke,* Ac 4:17; 1 Pe 2:23★ [546]

[581] ἀπειλή *apeilē* 3x *threat, commination,* Ac 4:29; 9:1; *harshness of language,* Eph 6:9★ [547]

[582] ἄπειμι *apeimi* 7x *to be absent, away* 1 Co 5:3; 2 Cor 10:1, 11; 13:2, 10; Phil 1:27; Col 2:5★ [548]

[583] ἄπειμι *apeimi* 1x *to go away, depart, come* Ac 17:10★ [549]

[584] ἀπεῖπον *apeipon* 1x *to refuse, forbid, to renounce, disclaim,* 2 Co 4:2★ [550, 561]

[585] ἀπείραστος *apeirastos* 1x *inexperienced, untempted, incapable of being tempted*, Jas 1:13* [551]

[586] ἄπειρος *apeiros* 1x *inexperienced, unskillful, ignorant*, Heb 5:13* [552]

[587] ἀπεκδέχομαι *apekdechomai* 8x *to expect, wait* or *look for*, Ro 8:19, 23, 25; 1 Co 1:7; Gal 5:5; Phil 3:20; Heb 9:28 [553]

[588] ἀπεκδύομαι *apekdyomai* 2x *to put off, renounce*, Col 3:9; *to despoil* a rival, Col 2:15* [554]

[589] ἀπέκδυσις *apekdysis* 1x *a putting* or *stripping off, renunciation*, Col 2:11* [555]

[590] ἀπελαύνω *apelaunō* 1x *to drive away*, Ac 18:16* [556]

[591] ἀπελεγμός *apelegmos* 1x pr. *refutation;* by impl. *disrepute. contempt*, Ac 19:27* [557]

[592] ἀπελεύθερος *apeleutheros* 1x *a freed-man*, 1 Co 7:22* [558]

[593] Ἀπελλῆς *Apellēs* 1x *Apelles*, proper name, Ro 16:10* [559]

[594] ἀπελπίζω *apelpizo* 1x *to lay aside hope, despond, despair;* also, *to hope for* something *in return*, Lk 6:35* [560]

[595] ἀπέναντι *apenanti* 5x some classify as an improper preposition, *opposite to, over against*, Mt 27:61; *contrary to, in oppositition to, against*, Ac 17:7; *before, in the presence of*, Mt 27:24; Ro 3:18; Ac 3:16* [561]

[596] ἀπέραντος *aperantos* 1x *unlimited, interminable, endless*, 1 Ti 1:4* [562]

[597] ἀπερισπάστως *aperispastōs* 1x *without distraction, without care* or *solicitude*, 1 Co 7:35* [563]

[598] ἀπερίτμητος *aperitmētos* 1x pr. *uncircumcised;* met. *uncircumcised* in respect of untowardness and obduracy, Ac 7:51* [564]

[599] ἀπέρχομαι *aperchomai* 117x *to go away, depart*, Mt 8:18; *to go forth, pervade*, as a rumor, Mt 4:24; *to arrive* at a destination, Lk 23:33; *to pass away, disappear*, Rev 21:4; ἀπέρχομαι ὀπίσω, *to follow*, Mk 1:20 [565]

[600] ἀπέχω *apechō* 19x trans. *to have in full* what is due or is sought, Mt 6:2, 5, 16; Lk 6:24; Phil 4:18; *to have altogether*, Phlm 15; hence, *it is enough*, Mk 14:41; intrans. *to be distant*, Lk 7:6; *to be estranged*, Mt 15:8; Mk 7:6, mid. *to abstain from*, Ac 14:20 [566, 567, 568]

[601] ἀπιστέω *apisteō* 8x *to refuse belief, be incredulous, disbelieve*, Mk 16:11, 16; Lk 24:11, 41; Ac 28:24; *to prove false, violate one's faith, be unfaithful*, 2 Ti 2:13; Ro 3:3 [569]

[602] ἀπιστία *apistia* 11x *unbelief, want of trust and confidence; a state of unbelief*, 1 Ti 1:13; *violation of faith, faithlessness*, Ro 3:3; Heb 3:12, 19 [570]

[603] ἄπιστος *apistos* 23x *unbelieving, without confidence* in any one, Mt 17:17; *violating one's faith, unfaithful, false, treacherous*, Lk 12:46; *an unbeliever, infidel, pagan*, 1 Co 6:6; pass. *incredible*, Ac 26:8 [571]

[605] ἁπλότης *haplotēs* 8x *simplicity, sincerity, purity* of mind, Ro 12:8; 11:3; Eph 6:5; Col 3:22; *liberality*, as arising from simplicity and frankness of character, 2 Co 8:2; 9:11, 13; 11:3* [572]

[606] ἁπλοῦς *haplous* 2x pr. *single;* hence, *simple, uncompounded; sound, perfect*, Mt 6:22; Lk 11:34* [573]

[607] ἁπλῶς *haplōs* 1x *in simplicity; sincerely, really*, or, *liberally, bountifully*, Jas 1:5* [574]

[608] ἀπό *apo* 646x pr. *forth, from, away from;* hence, it variously signifies *departure; distance of time* or *place; avoidance; riddance; derivation from a quarter, source*, or *material; origination from agency* or *instrumentality* [575]

[609] ἀποβαίνω *apobainō* 4x *to step off; to disembark* from a ship, Lk 5:2; Jn 21:9; *to become, result, happen*, Lk 21:13; Phil 1:19* [576]

[610] ἀποβάλλω *apoballō* 2x *to cast* or *throw off, cast aside*, Mk 10:50; Heb 10:35* [577]

[611] ἀποβλέπω *apoblepō* 1x pr. *to look off from all other objects and at a single one;* hence, *to turn a steady gaze, to look with fixed and earnest attention*, Heb 11:26* [578]

[612] ἀπόβλητος *apoblētos* 1x pr. *to be cast away;* met. *to be condemned, regarded as vile*, 1 Ti 4:4* [579]

[613] ἀποβολή *apobolē* 2x *a casting off; rejection, reprobation*, Ro 11:15; *loss, deprivation*, of life, etc., Ac 27:22* [580]

[614] ἀπογίνομαι *apoginomai* 1x *to be away from, unconnected with; to die;* met. *to die* to a thing by renouncing it, 1 Pe 2:24* [581]

[615] ἀπογραφή *apographē* 2x *a register, inventory; registration, enrollment*, Lk 2:2; Ac 5:37* [582]

[616] ἀπογράφω *apographō* 4x pr. *to copy;* hence, *to register, enrol*, Lk 2:1; Heb 12:23; mid. *to procure the registration of one's name, to give in one's name for registration*, Lk 2:3, 5* [583]

[617] ἀποδείκνυμι *apodeiknymi* 4x *to point out, display; to prove, evince, demonstrate*, Ac 25:7; *to designate, proclaim, hold forth*, 2 Th 2:4; *to constitute, appoint*, Ac 2:22; 1 Co 4:9* [584]

[618] ἀπόδειξις *apodeixis* 1x *manifestation, demonstration, indubitable proof*, 1 Co 2:4* [585]

[620] ἀποδεκατόω *apodekatoō* 4x *to pay* or *give tithes of*, Mt 23:23; Lk 11:42; 18:12; *to tithe, levy tithes upon*, Heb 7:5* [586]

[621] ἀπόδεκτος *apodektos* 2x *acceptable, pleasant*, 1 Ti 2:3; 5:4* [587]

[622] ἀποδέχομαι *apodechomai* 7x *to receive* kindly or heartily, *welcome*, Lk 8:40; 9:11; Ac 18:27; 28:30; *to receive* with hearty assent, *embrace*, Ac 2:41; *to accept* with satisfaction, Ac 24:3* [588]

[623] ἀποδημέω *apodēmeō* 6x *to be absent from one's home* or *country; to go on travel*, Mt 21:33; 25:14, 15; Mk 12:1; Lk 15:13; 20:9* [589]

[624] ἀπόδημος *apodēmos* 1x *absent* in foreign countries, Mk 13:34* [590]

[625] ἀποδίδωμι *apodidōmi* 48x *to give in answer to a claim* or *expectation; to render* a due, Mt 12:36; 16:27; 21:41; 22:21; *to recompense*, Mt 6:4, 6, 18; *to discharge* an obligation, Mt 5:33; *to pay* a debt, Mt 5:26; *to render back, requite*, Ro 12:17; *to give back, restore*, Lk 4:20; 9:42; *to refund*, Lk 10:35; 19:8; mid., *to sell*, Ac 5:8; 7:9; Heb 12:16; pass., *to be sold*, Mt 18:25; *to be given up* at a request, Mt 27:58 [591]

[626] ἀποδιορίζω *apodiorizō* 1x pr. *to separate by intervening boundaries; to separate* or *divide*, Jude 19* [592]

[627] ἀποδοκιμάζω *apodokimazō* 9x *to reject upon trial; to reject*, Mt 21:42; Mk 12:10; Lk 20:17; 1 Pe 2:4, 7; pass., *to be disallowed* a claim, *declared useless*, Lk 9:22; 17:25; Heb 12:17 [593]

[628] ἀποδοχή *apodochē* 2x pr. *reception, welcome;* met. *reception* of hearty assent, 1 Ti 1:15; 4:9* [594]

[629] ἀπόθεσις *apothesis* 2x *a putting off* or *away, laying aside*, a euphemism for death, 1 Pe 3:21; 2 Pe 1:14* [595]

[630] ἀποθήκη *apothēkē* 6x *a place where anything is laid up for preservation, repository, granary, storehouse, barn*, Mt

3:12; 6:26; 13:30; Lk 3:17; 12:18, 24 [596]

[631] ἀποθησαυρίζω *apothēsaurizō* 1x pr. *to lay up in store, hoard;* met. *to treasure up, secure,* 1 Ti 6:19* [597]

[632] ἀποθλίβω *apothlibō* 1x pr. *to press out; to press close, press upon, crowd,* Lk 8:45* [598]

[633] ἀποθνήσκω *apothnēskō* 112x *to die,* Mt 8:32; *to decay, rot,* as seeds, Jn 12:24; 1 Co 15:36; *to wither, become dry,* as a tree, Jude 12; met. *to die* the death of final condemnation and misery, Jn 6:50; 8:21, 24; *to die* to a thing by renunciation or utter separation, Ro 6:2; Gal 2;19; Col 3:3; 1 Co 15:31 [599]

[635] ἀποκαθίστημι *apokathistēmi* 8x also spelled ἀποκαθιστάνω, *to restore* a thing to its former place or state, Mt 12:13; 17:11; Mk 3:5; 8:25 [600]

[636] ἀποκαλύπτω *apokalyptō* 26x pr. *uncover; to reveal,* Mt 11:25; pass. *to be disclosed,* Lk 2:35; Eph 3:5; *to be plainly signified, distinctly declared,* Ro 1:17, 18; *to be set forth, announced,* Gal 3:23; *to be discovered* in true character, 1 Co 3:13; *to be manifested, appear,* Jn 12:38;Ro 8:18; 2 Th 2:3, 6, 8; 1 Pe 1:5; 5:1 [601]

[637] ἀποκάλυψις *apokalypsis* 18x *a disclosure, revelation,* Ro 2:5; *manifestation, appearance,* Ro 8:19; 1 Co 1:7; 2 Th 1:7; 1 Pe 1:7, 13; 4:13; met. spiritual *enlightenment,* Lk 2:32 [602]

[638] ἀποκαραδοκία *apokaradokia* 2x *earnest expectation, eager hope,* Ro 8:19; Phil 1:20* [603]

[639] ἀποκαταλλάσσω *apokatallassō* 3x *to transfer from a certain state to another which is quite different;* hence, *to reconcile, restore to favor,* Eph 2:16; Col 1:20, 22* [604]

[640] ἀποκατάστασις *apokatastasis* 1x pr. *a restitution* or *restoration of* a thing to its former state; hence, *the renovation* of a new and better era, Ac 3:21* [605]

[641] ἀπόκειμαι *apokeimai* 4x *to be laid up, preserved,* Lk 19:20; *to be in store, be reserved, await* any one, Col 1:5; 2 Ti 4:8; Heb 9:27* [606]

[642] ἀποκεφαλίζω *apokephalizō* 4x *to behead,* Mt 14:10; Mk 6:16, 28; Lk 9:9 [607]

[643] ἀποκλείω *apokleiō* 1x *to close, shut up,* Lk 13:25* [608]

[644] ἀποκόπτω *apokoptō* 6x *to cut off,* Mk 9:43, 45; Jn 18:10, 26; Ac 27:32; *to castrate, make a eunich,* Gal 5:12* [609]

[645] ἀπόκριμα *apokrima* 1x *a judicial sentence,* 2 Co 1:9* [610]

[646] ἀποκρίνομαι *apokrinomai* 231x *to answer,* Mt 3:15; in N.T. *to respond to certain present circumstances, to avow,* Mt 11:25 [611]

[647] ἀπόκρισις *apokrisis* 4x *an answer, reply,* Lk 2:47; 20:26; Jn 1:22; 19:9 [612]

[648] ἀποκρύπτω *apokryptō* 4x *to hide away; to conceal, withhold from sight* or *knowledge,* Lk 10:21; 1 Co 2:7; Eph 3:9; Col 1:26* [613]

[649] ἀπόκρυφος *apokryphos* 3x *hidden away; concealed,* Mk 4:22; Lk 8:17; *stored up,* Col 2:3* [614]

[650] ἀποκτείνω *apokteinō* 74x also spelled ἀποκτέννω or ἀποκτένω, *to kill,* Mt 14:5; *to destroy, annihilate,* Mt 10:28; *to destroy* a hostile principle, Eph 2:16; met. *to kill* by spiritual condemnation, Ro 7:11; 2 Co 3:6 [615]

[652] ἀποκυέω *apokyeō* 2x pr. *to bring forth,* as women; met. *to generate, produce,* Jas 1:15; *to generate* by spiritual birth, Jas 1:18* [616]

[653] ἀποκυλίω *apokyliō* 3x *to roll away,* Mt 28:2; Mk 16:3, 4; Lk 24:2* [617]

[655] ἀπολαμβάνω *apolambanō* 10x *to receive* what is due, sought, or needed, Lk 23:41; Ro 1:27; Gal 4:5; Col 3:24; 2 Jn 8; *to receive in full,* Lk 16:25; *to receive back, recover,* Lk 6:34; 15:27; 18:30; mid. *to take aside, lead away,* Mk 7:33 [618]

[656] ἀπόλαυσις *apolausis* 2x *beneficial participation,* 1 Ti 6:17; *enjoyment, pleasure,* Heb 11:25* [619]

[657] ἀπολείπω *apoleipō* 7x *to leave, leave behind;* pass. *to be left, remain,* 2 Ti 4:13, 20; Heb 4:6, 9; 10:26; *to relinquish, forsake, desert,* Tit 1:5; Jude 6* [620]

[660] ἀπόλλυμι *apollymi* 90x *to destroy utterly; to kill,* Mt 2:13; *to bring to nought, make void,* 1 Co 1:19; *to lose, be deprived of,* Mt 10:42; *to be destroyed, perish,* Mt 9:17; *to be put to death, to die,* Mt 26:52; *to be lost, to stray,* Mt 10:6 [622]

[661] Ἀπολλύων *Apollyōn* 1x *Apollyon, Destroyer,* i.q. Ἀβαδδών, Rev 9:11* [623]

[662] Ἀπολλωνία *Apollōnia* 1x *Apollonia,* a city of Macedonia, Ac 17:1* [624]

[663] Ἀπολλῶς *Apollōs* 10x *Apollos,* pr. name, Ac 18:24; 19:1; 1 Co 1:12; 3:4-6, 22; 4:6; 16:12; Tit 3:13* [625]

[664] ἀπολογέομαι *apologeomai* 10x *to defend one's self against a charge, to make a defence,* Lk 12:11; 21:14 [626]

[665] ἀπολογία *apologia* 8x *a verbal defence,* Ac 22:1; 25:16 [627]

[666] ἀπολούω *apolouō* 2x *to cleanse by bathing;* mid. *to cleanse one's self; to procure one's self to be cleansed;* met., of sin, Ac 22:16; 1 Co 6:11* [628]

[667] ἀπολύτρωσις *apolytrōsis* 10x *redemption, a deliverance, procured by the payment of a ransom;* meton. the author of *redemption,* 1 Co 1:30; *deliverance,* simply, the idea of a ransom being excluded, Lk 21:28; Heb 11:35 [629]

[668] ἀπολύω *apolyō* 66x pr. *to loose; to release* from a tie or burden, Mt 18:27; *to divorce,* Mt 1:19; *to remit, forgive,* Lk 6:37; *to liberate, discharge,* Mt 27:15; *to dismiss,* Mt 15:23; Ac 19:40; *to allow to depart, to send away,* Mt 14:15; *to permit,* or, *signal departure* from life, Lk 2:29; mid. *depart,* Ac 28:25; pass. *to be rid,* Lk 13:12 [630]

[669] ἀπομάσσω *apomassō* 1x *to wipe off;* mid. *to wipe off one's self,* Lk 10:11* [631]

[671] ἀπονέμω *aponemō* 1x *to portion off; to assign, bestow,* 1 Pe 3:7* [632]

[672] ἀπονίπτω *aponiptō* 1x *to cleanse* a part of the body *by washing;* mid., of one's self, Mt 27:24* [633]

[674] ἀποπίπτω *apopiptō* 1x *to fall off* or *from,* Ac 9:18* [634]

[675] ἀποπλανάω *apoplanaō* 2x *to cause to wander;* met. *to deceive, pervert, seduce,* Mk 13:22; pass. *to wander;* met. *to swerve from, apostatize,* 1 Ti 6:10* [635]

[676] ἀποπλέω *apopleō* 4x *to depart by ship, sail away,* Ac 13:4; 14:26; 20:15; 27:1* [636]

[678] ἀποπνίγω *apopnigō* 2x *to choke, suffocate,* Lk 8:7; *to drown,* Lk 8:33* [638]

[679] ἀπορέω *aporeō* 6x also spelled ἀπορρίπτω, pr. *to be without means;* met. *to hesitate, be at a stand, be in doubt and perplexity,* Jn 13:22; Ac 25:20; 2 Co 4:8; Gal 4:20 [639]

[680] ἀπορία *aporia* 1x *doubt, uncertainty, perplexity,* Lk 21:25* [640]

[681] ἀπορίπτω *aporiptō* 1x *to throw off, throw down,* Ac 27:43* [641]

[682] ἀπορφανίζω *aporphanizō* 1x lit., *to make an orphan;* fig., *to deprive, bereave,* 1 Th 2:17* [642]

[684] ἀποσκίασμα *aposkiasma* 1x *a shadow cast;* met. *a shade, the slightest trace,* Jas 1:17★ [644]

[685] ἀποσπάω *apospaō* 4x *to draw away from; to draw out* or *forth,* Mt 26:51; *to draw away, seduce,* Ac 20:30; *to separate one's self, to part,* Lk 22:41; Ac 21:1★ [645]

[686] ἀποστασία *apostasia* 2x *a falling away, a rebellion, apostasy,* Ac 21:21; 2 Th 2:3★ [646]

[687] ἀποστάσιον *apostasion* 3x *defection, desertion,* as of a freedman from a patron; in N.T. *the act of putting away a wife, repudiation, divorce,* Mt 19:7; Mk 10:4; meton. *a bill of repudiation, deed of divorce,* Mt 5:31★ [647]

[689] ἀποστεγάζω *apostegazō* 1x *to remove* or *break through a covering* or *roof of a place,* Mk 2:4★ [648]

[690] ἀποστέλλω *apostellō* 132x *to send forth* a messenger, agent, message, or command, Mt 2:16; 10:5; *to put forth into action,* Mk 4:29; *to liberate, rid,* Lk 4:19; *to dismiss, send away,* Mk 12:3 [649]

[691] ἀποστερέω *apostereō* 6x *to deprive, detach; to debar,* 1 Co 7:5; *to deprive* in a bad sense, *defraud,* Mk 10:19; 1 Co 6:7; mid. *to suffer one's self to be deprived* or *defrauded,* 1 Co 6:8; pass. *to be destitute* or *devoid of,* 1 Ti 6:5; *to be unjustly withheld,* Jas 5:4★ [650]

[692] ἀποστολή *apostolē* 4x *a sending, expedition; office* or *duty of one sent as a messenger* or *agent; office of an apostle, apostleship,* Ac 1:25; Ro 1:5; 1 Co 9:2; Gal 2:8★ [651]

[693] ἀπόστολος *apostolos* 80x *one sent as a messenger* or *agent, the bearer of a commission, messenger,* Jn 13:16; *an apostle,* Mt 10:2 [652]

[694] ἀποστοματίζω *apostomatizō* 1x pr. *to speak* or *repeat offhand;* also, *to require* or *lead others to speak without premeditation,* as by questions calculated to elicit unpremeditated answers, *to endeavor to entrap into unguarded language,* Lk 11:53★ [653]

[695] ἀποστρέφω *apostrephō* 9x *to turn away; to remove,* Ac 3:26; Ro 11:26; 2 Ti 4:4; *to turn* a people from their allegiance, to their sovereign, *pervert, incite to revolt,* Lk 23:14; *to replace, restore,* Mt 26:52; *to turn away from* any one, *to slight, reject, repulse,* Mt 5:42; Tit 1:14; Heb 12:25; *to desert,* 2 Ti 1:15 [654]

[696] ἀποστυγέω *apostygeō* 1x *to shrink from with abhorrence, detest,* Ro 12:9★ [655]

[697] ἀποσυνάγωγος *aposynagōgos* 3x *expelled* or *excluded from the synagogue, excommunicated, cut off from the rights and privileges of a Jew, excluded from society,* Jn 9:22; 12:42; 16:2★ [656]

[698] ἀποτάσσω *apotassō* 6x middle: *to take leave of, bid farewell to,* Lk 9:61; Ac 18:18, 21; 2 Co 2:13; *to dismiss, send away,* Mk 6:46; fig: *to renounce, forsake,* Lk 14:33 [657]

[699] ἀποτελέω *apoteleō* 2x *to complete;* pass. *to be perfected, to arrive at full stature* or *measure,* Lk 13:32; Jas 1:15★ [658]

[700] ἀποτίθημι *apotithēmi* 9x mid: *to lay off, lay down* or *aside,* as garments, Ac 7:58; me [659]

[701] ἀποτινάσσω *apotinassō* 2x *to shake off,* Lk 9:5; Ac 28:5★ [660]

[702] ἀποτίνω *apotinō* 1x *to pay off* what is claimed or due; *to repay, refund, make good,* Phlm 19★ [661]

[703] ἀποτολμάω *apotolmaō* 1x *to dare* or *risk outright; to speak outright, without reserve* or *restraint,* Ro 10:20 [662]

[704] ἀποτομία *apotomia* 2x pr. *abruptness;* met. *severity, rigor,* Ro 11:22 (2t)★ [663]

[705] ἀποτόμως *apotomōs* 2x *sharply, severely,* 2 Co 13:10; Tit 1:13★ [664]

[706] ἀποτρέπω *apotrepō* 1x mid: *to turn* any one *away* from a thing; mid. *to turn one's self away* from any one, *to avoid, shun,* 2 Ti 3:5★ [665]

[707] ἀπουσία *apousia* 1x *absence,* Phil 2:12★ [666]

[708] ἀποφέρω *apopherō* 6x *to bear* or *carry away, conduct away,* Mk 15:1; Lk 16:22; Ac 19:12; 1 Co 16:3; Rev 17:3; 21:10★ [667]

[709] ἀποφεύγω *apopheugō* 3x *to flee from, escape;* met. *to be rid, be freed from,* 2 Pe 1:4; 2:18, 20★ [668]

[710] ἀποφθέγγομαι *apophthengomai* 3x *to speak out, declare,* particularly solemn, weighty, or pithy sayings, Ac 2:4, 14; 26:25★ [669]

[711] ἀποφορτίζομαι *apophortizomai* 1x *to unload,* Ac 21:3★ [670]

[712] ἀπόχρησις *apochrēsis* 1x *a using up,* or, *a discharge of an intended use,* Col 2:22★ [671]

[713] ἀποχωρέω *apochōreō* 3x *to go from* or *away, depart,* Mt 7:23; Lk 9:39; Ac 13:13★ [672]

[714] ἀποχωρίζω *apochōrizō* 2x *to separate;* pass. *to be swept aside,* Rev 6:14; mid. *to part,* Ac 15:39★ [673]

[715] ἀποψύχω *apopsychō* 1x pr. *to breathe out, faint away, die;* met. *to faint at heart, be dismayed,* Lk 21:26★ [674]

[716] Ἄππιος *Appios* 1x *the forum* or *marketplace, of Appius;* a village on the Appian road, near Rome, Ac 28:15★ [675]

[717] ἀπρόσιτος *aprositos* 1x *unapproached, unapproachable,* 1 Ti 6:16★ [676]

[718] ἀπρόσκοπος *aproskopos* 3x *not stumbling* or *jarring;* met. *not stumbling* or *jarring* against moral rule, *unblamable, clear,* Ac 24:16; Phil 1:10; *free from offensiveness,* 1 Co 10:32★ [677]

[719] ἀπροσωπολήμπτως *aprosōpolēmptōs* 1x *without respect of persons, impartially,* 1 Pe 1:17★ [678]

[720] ἄπταιστος *aptaistos* 1x *free from stumbling;* met. *free from* moral *stumbling, offence; irreprehensible,* Jude 24★ [679]

[721] ἅπτω *haptō* 39x pr. *to bring in contact, fit, fasten; to light, kindle,* Mk 4:21; Lk 8:16; *to touch,* Mt 8:3; *to meddle, venture to partake,* Col 2:21; *to have intercourse with, to know carnally,* 1 Co 7:1; by impl. *to harm,* 1 Jn 5:18 [680, 681]

[722] Ἀπφία *Apphia* 1x *Apphia,* pr. name, Phlm 2★ [682]

[723] ἀπωθέω *apōtheō* 6x *to thrust away, repel from one's self, repulse,* Ac 7:27; *to refuse, reject, cast off,* Ac 7:39; 13:46; Ro 11:1, 2; 1 Ti 1:19★ [683]

[724] ἀπώλεια *apōleia* 18x *consumption, destruction; waste, profusion,* Mt 26:8; Mk 14:4; *destruction, state of being destroyed,* Ac 25:6; *eternal ruin, perdition,* Mt 7:13; Ac 8:20 [684]

[725] ἀρά *ara* 1x pr. *a prayer;* more commonly *a prayer for evil; curse, cursing, imprecation,* Ro 3:14★ [685]

[726] ἄρα *ara* 49x a particle which denotes, first, transition from one thing to another by natural sequence; secondly, logical inference; in which case the premises are either expressed, Mt 12:28, or to be variously supplied, *therefore, then, consequently; as a result,* Ac 17:27 [686]

[727] ἆρα *ara* 3x inferential particle, used mainly in interrogations, Lk 18:8; Ac 8:30; Gal 2:17★ [687]

[728] Ἀραβία *Arabia* 2x *Arabia*, Gal 1:17; 4:25★ [688]

[730] Ἀράμ *Aram* 2x *Aram*, pr. name, indecl, Mt 1:3-4★ [689]

[731] ἄραφος *araphos* 1x *not sewed, seamless*, Jn 19:23★ [729]

[732] Ἄραψ *Araps* 1x *an Arabian*, Ac 2:11★ [690]

[733] ἀργέω *argeō* 1x pr. *to be unemployed; to be inoperative, to linger*, 2 Pe 2:3★ [691]

[734] ἀργός *argos* 8x pr. *inactive, unemployed*, Mt 20:3, 6; *idle, averse from labor*, 1 Ti 5:13; Tit 1:12; met. 2 Pe 1:8; *unprofitable, hollow*, or by impl., *injurious*, Mt 12:36; Jas 2:20★ [692]

[736] ἀργύριον *argyrion* 20x *silver*; meton. *money*, Mt 25:18, 27 [694]

[737] ἀργυροκόπος *argyrokopos* 1x *a forger of silver, silversmith*, Ac 19:24★ [695]

[738] ἄργυρος *argyros* 5x *silver*; meton. *anything made of silver; money*, Jas 5:3 [696]

[739] ἀργυροῦς *argyrous* 3x *made of silver*, Ac 19:24; 2 Ti 2:20; Rev 9:20★ [693]

[741] Ἀρεοπαγίτης *Areopagitēs* 1x *a judge of the court of Areopagus*, Ac 17:34★ [698]

[742] ἀρεσκεία *areskeia* 1x *a pleasing, desire of pleasing*, Col 1:10★ [699]

[743] ἀρέσκω *areskō* 17x *to please*, Mt 14:6; *to be pleasing, acceptable*, Ac 6:5; *to consult the pleasure of* any one, Ro 15:1, 2, 3; 1 Co 10:33; *to seek favor with*, Gal 1:10; 1 Th 2:4 [700]

[744] ἀρεστός *arestos* 4x *pleasing, acceptable*, Ac 12:3; 1 Jn 3:22; 8:29, *deemed proper*, Ac 6:2 [701]

[745] Ἀρέτας *Haretas* 1x *Aretas*, pr. name, 2 Co 11:32★ [702]

[746] ἀρετή *aretē* 5x *goodness, good quality* of any kind; *a gracious act* of God, 1 Pe 2:9; 2 Pe 1:3; *virtue, uprightness*, Phil 4:8; 2 Pe 1:5★ [703]

[748] ἀρήν *arēn* 1x *a sheep, lamb*, Lk 10:3★ [704]

[749] ἀριθμέω *arithmeō* 3x *to count*, Mt 10:30; Lk 12:7; Rev 7:9★ [705]

[750] ἀριθμός *arithmos* 18x *a number*, Lk 22:3; Jn 6:10; Ac 4:4; Rev 20:8; 13:18 [706]

[751] Ἀριμαθαία *Harimathaia* 4x *Arimathea*, a town of Palestine, Mt 27:57; Mk 15:43; Lk 23:51; Jn 19:38★ [707]

[752] Ἀρίσταρχος *Aristarchos* 5x *Aristarchus*, pr. name, Ac 19:29; 20:4; 27:2; Col 4:10; Phlm 24★ [708]

[753] ἀριστάω *aristaō* 3x *to take the first meal, breakfast*, Jn 21:12, 15; also, *to take a mid-day meal*, Lk 11:37★ [709]

[754] ἀριστερός *aristeros* 4x *the left hand*, Mt 6:3; so ἐξ ἀριστερῶν, sc. μερῶν, Lk 23:33; 2 Co 6:7; Mk 10:37★ [710]

[755] Ἀριστόβουλος *Aristoboulos* 1x *Aristobulus*, pr. name, Ro 16:10★ [711]

[756] ἄριστον *ariston* 3x pr. *the first meal, breakfast*; afterwards extended to signify also *a slight mid-day meal, luncheon*, Mt 22:4; Lk 11:38; 14:12★ [712]

[757] ἀρκετός *arketos* 3x *sufficient, enough*, Mt 6:34; 10:25; 1 Pe 4:3★ [713]

[758] ἀρκέω *arkeō* 8x pr. *to ward off*; thence; *to be of service, avail; to suffice, be enough*, Mt 25:9; pass. *to be contented, satisfied*, Lk 3:14; 1 Ti 6:8; Heb 13:5; 3 Jn 10 [714]

[759] ἄρκος *arkos* 1x also spelled ἄρκτος, *a bear*, Rev 13:2★ [715]

[761] ἅρμα *harma* 4x *a chariot, vehicle*, Ac 8:28, 29, 38; Rev 9:9★ [716]

[762] Ἁρμαγεδών *Harmagedōn* 1x *Armageddon*, Rev 16:16★ [717]

[764] ἁρμόζω *harmozō* 1x *to fit together; to join, unite*, in marriage, *espouse, betroth*, 2 Co 11:2★ [718]

[765] ἁρμός *harmos* 1x *a joint* or *articulation* of the bones, Heb 4:12★ [719]

[766] ἀρνέομαι *arneomai* 33x *to deny, disclaim, disown*, Mt 10:33; *to renounce*, Tit 2:12; *to decline, refuse*, Heb 11:24; absol. *to deny, contradict*, Lk 8:15 [720]

[767] Ἀρνί *Arni* 1x *Arni*, proper name, Lk 3:33★ [★★]

[768] ἀρνίον *arnion* 30x *a young lamb, lamb*, Jn 21:15; Rev 5:6, 8 [721]

[769] ἀροτριάω *arotriaō* 3x *to plow*, Lk 17:7; 1 Co 9:10★ [722]

[770] ἄροτρον *arotron* 1x *a plow*, Lk 9:62★ [723]

[771] ἁρπαγή *harpagē* 3x *plunder, pillage; the act of plundering*, Heb 10:34; *prey, spoil*, Mt 23:25; Lk 11:39★ [724]

[772] ἁρπαγμός *harpagmos* 1x *eager seizure*; in N.T., *a thing retained with an eager grasp*, or *eagerly claimed and conspicuously exercised*, Phil 2:6★ [725]

[773] ἁρπάζω *harpazō* 14x *to seize*, as a wild beast, Jn 10:12; *take away by force, snatch away*, Mt 13:19; Jn 10:28, 29; Ac 23:10; Jude 23; met. *to seize on with avidity, eagerly, appropriate*, Mt 11:12; *to convey away suddenly, transport hastily*, Jn 6:15 [726]

[774] ἅρπαξ *harpax* 5x pr. *raveneous, ravening*, as a wild beast, Mt 7:15; met. *rapacious, given to extortion and robbery, an extortioner*, Lk 18:11; 1 Co 5:10, 11; 6:10★ [727]

[775] ἀρραβών *arrabōn* 3x *a pledge, earnest*, 2 Co 1:22; 5:5; Eph 1:14★ [728]

[777] ἄρρητος *arrētos* 1x pr. *not spoken; what ought not to be spoken, secret; which cannot be spoken* or *uttered*, 2 Co 12:4★ [731]

[779] ἄρρωστος *arrōstos* 5x *ill, sick, an invalid*, Mt 14:14; Mk 6:5, 13; 16:18; 1 Co 11:30 [732]

[780] ἀρσενοκοίτης *arsenokoitēs* 2x *a male engaging in same-gender sexual activity, a sodomite, pedarest*, 1 Co 6:9; 1 Ti 1:10★ [733]

[781] ἄρσην *arsēn* 9x *male, of the male sex*, Mt 19:4; Mk 10:6; Lk 2:23; Ro 1:27; Gal 3:28; Rev 12:5, 13★ [730]

[782] Ἀρτεμᾶς *Artemas* 1x *Artemas*, pr. name, Tit 3:12★ [734]

[783] Ἄρτεμις *Artemis* 5x *Artemis* or *Diana*, Ac 19:24, 27, 28, 34, 35★ [735]

[784] ἀρτέμων *artemōn* 1x *a topsail, foresail*; or, according to others, *the dolon* of Pliny and Pollux, a small sail near the prow of the ship, which was hoisted when the wind was too strong to use the larger sails, Ac 27:40★ [736]

[785] ἄρτι *arti* 36x pr. *at the present moment, close upon it* either before of after; *now, at the present juncture*, Mt 3:15; *forthwith, presently; just now, recently*, 1 Th 3:6; ἕως ἄρτι, *until now, hitherto*, Mt 11:12; Jn 2:10; ἀπ᾽ ἄρτι, or ἀπάρτι, *from this time, henceforth*, Mt 23:39 [737]

[786] ἀρτιγέννητος *artigennētos* 1x *just born, new-born*, 1 Pe 2:2★ [738]

[787] ἄρτιος *artios* 1x *entirely suited; complete* in accomplishment, *ready*, 2 Ti 3:17★ [739]

[788] ἄρτος *artos* 97x *bread; a loaf* or *thin cake of bread*, Mt 26:26; *food*, Mt 15:2; Mk 3:20; *bread, maintenance, living, necessaries of life*, Mt 6:11; Lk 11:3; 2 Th 3:8 [740]

[789] ἀρτύω *artyō* 3x pr. *to fit, prepare; to season, make savoury*, Mk 9:50; Lk 14:34; Col 4:6★ [741]

[790] Ἀρφαξάδ *Arphaxad* 1x *Arphaxad*, pr. name, indecl, Lk 3:36* [742]

[791] ἀρχάγγελος *archangelos* 2x *an archangel, chief angel*, 1 Th 4:16; Jude 9* [743]

[792] ἀρχαῖος *archaios* 11x *old, ancient, of former age*, Mt 5:21, 33; *of long standing, old, veteran*, Ac 21:16; ἀφήμερῶν ἀρχαίων, *from early days, from an early period*, of the Gospel, Ac 15:7 [744]

[793] Ἀρχέλαος *Archelaos* 1x *Archelaus*, pr. name, Mt 2:22* [745]

[794] ἀρχή *archē* 55x *a beginning*, Mt 24:8; *an extremity, corner*, or, *an attached cord*, Ac 10:11; 11:5; *first place, headship; high estate, eminence*, Jude 6; *authority*, Lk 20:20; *an authority, magistrate*, Lk 12:11; *a principality, prince*, of spiritual existence, Eph 3:10; 6:12; ἀπ᾿ ἀρχῆς, ἐξ ἀρχῆς, *from the first, originally*, Mt 19:4, 8; Lk 1:2; Jn 6:64; 2 Th 2:13; 1 Jn 1:1; 2:7; ἐν ἀρχῇ, κατ᾿ ἀρχάς, *in the beginning* of things, Jn 1:1, 2; Heb 1.10, ἐν ἀρχῇ, *at the first*, Ac 11:15; τὴν ἀρχήν, used adverbially, *wholly, altogether*, Jn 8:25 [746]

[795] ἀρχηγός *archēgos* 4x *a chief, leader, prince*, Ac 5:31; *a prime author*, Ac 3:15; Heb 2:10; 12:2* [747]

[796] ἀρχιερατικός *archieratikos* 1x *belonging to* or *connected with the high-priest* or *his office*, Ac 4:6* [748]

[797] ἀρχιερεύς *archiereus* 122x *a high-priest, chief-priest* [749]

[799] ἀρχιποίμην *archipoimēn* 1x *chief shepherd*, 1 Pe 5:4* [750]

[800] Ἄρχιππος *Archippos* 2x *Archippus*, pr. name, Col 4:17; Phlm 2, inscr. and subsc.* [751]

[801] ἀρχισυνάγωγος *archisynagōgos* 9x *a president* or *moderating elder of a synagogue*, Mk 5:22, 35, 36, 38; Lk 8:49 [752]

[802] ἀρχιτέκτων *architektōn* 1x *architect, head* or *master-builder*, 1 Co 3:10* [753]

[803] ἀρχιτελώνης *architelōnēs* 1x *a chief publican, chief collector of the customs* or *taxes*, Lk 19:2* [754]

[804] ἀρχιτρίκλινος *architriklinos* 3x *director of a feast*, Jn 2:8, 9* [755]

[806] ἄρχω *archō* 86x (1) pr. (act.) *to be first; to rule*, Mk 10:42; Ro 15:12 (2) mid. *to begin*, Mt 4:17; *to take commencement*, Lk 24:27; 1 Pe 4:17 [756, 757]

[807] ἄρχων *archōn* 37x *one invested with power and dignity, chief, ruler, prince, magistrate*, Mt 9:23; 20:25 [758]

[808] ἄρωμα *arōma* 4x *an aromatic substance, spice*, etc., Mk 16:1; Lk 23:56; 24:1; Jn 19:40* [759]

[810] ἀσάλευτος *asaleutos* 2x *unshaken, immovable*, Ac 27:41; met. *firm, stable, enduring*, Heb 12:28* [761]

[811] Ἀσάφ *Asaph* 2x *Asaph*, pr. name, indecl, Mt 1:7, 8* [760]

[812] ἄσβεστος *asbestos* 3x *unquenched; inextinguishable, unquenchable*, Mt 3:12; Mk 9:43; Lk 3:17* [762]

[813] ἀσέβεια *asebeia* 6x *impiety, ungodliness; dishonesty, wickedness*, Ro 1:18; 11:26; 2 Ti 2:16; Tit 2:12; Jude 15, 18* [763]

[814] ἀσεβέω *asebeō* 1x *to be impious, to act impiously* or *wickedly, live an impious life*, 2 Pe 2:6; Jude 15* [764]

[815] ἀσεβής *asebēs* 9x *impious, ungodly; wicked, sinful*, Ro 4:5; 5:6 [765]

[816] ἀσέλγεια *aselgeia* 10x *intemperance; licentiousness, lasciviousness*, Ro 13:13; *insolence, outrageous behavior*, Mk 7:22 [766]

[817] ἄσημος *asēmos* 1x pr. *not marked*; met. *not noted, not remarkable, unknown to fame, ignoble, mean, inconsiderable*, Ac 21:39* [767]

[818] Ἀσήρ *Asēr* 2x *Asher*, pr. name, indecl (Gen 30:13; 49:20; 2 Chron 30:11) Lk 2:36; Rev 7:6* [768]

[819] ἀσθένεια *astheneia* 24x *want of strength, weakness, feebleness*, 1 Co 15:43; bodily *infirmity, state of ill health, sickness*, Mt 8:17; Lk 5:15; met. *infirmity, frailty, imperfection*, intellectual and moral, Ro 6:19; 1 Co 2:3; Heb 5:2; 7:28; *suffering, affliction, distress, calamity*, Ro 8:26 [769]

[820] ἀσθενέω *astheneō* 33x *to be weak, infirm, deficient in strength; to be inefficient*, Ro 8:3; 2 Co 13:3; *to be sick*, Mt 25:36; met. *to be weak* in faith, *to doubt, hesitate, be unsettled, timid*, Ro 14:1; 1 Co 8:9, 11, 12; 2 Co 11:29; *to be deficient in authority, dignity*, or *power, be contemptible*, 2 Co 11:21; 13:3, 9; *to be afflicted, distressed, needy*, Ac 20:35; 2 Co 12:10; 13:4, 9 [770]

[821] ἀσθένημα *asthenēma* 1x pr. *weakness, infirmity*, met. *doubt, hesitation*, Ro 15:1* [771]

[822] ἀσθενής *asthenēs* 26x *without strength, weak, infirm*, Mt 26:41; Mk 14:38; 1 Pe 3:7; *helpless*, Ro 5:6; *imperfect,*

inefficient, Gal 4:9; *feeble, without energy*, 2 Co 10:10; *infirm* in body, *sick, sickly*, Mt 25:39, 43, 44; *weak*, mentally or spiritually, *dubious, hesitating*, 1 Co 8:7, 10; 9:22; 1 Th 5:14; *afflicted, distressed, oppressed with calamities*, 1 Co 4:10 [772]

[823] Ἀσία *Asia* 18x *Asia*, the Roman province, Ac 19:27 [773]

[824] Ἀσιανός *Asianos* 1x *belonging to the Roman province of Asia*, Ac 20:4* [774]

[825] Ἀσιάρχης *Asiarchēs* 1x *an Asiarch*, an officer in the province of Asia, as in other eastern provinces of the Roman empire, selected, with others, from the more opulent citizens, to preside over the things pertaining to religious worship, and to exhibit annual public games at their own expense in honor of the gods, in the manner of the aediles at Rome, Ac 19:31* [775]

[826] ἀσιτία *asitia* 1x *abstinence from food, fasting*, Ac 27:21* [776]

[827] ἄσιτος *asitos* 1x *abstaining from food, fasting*, Ac 27:33* [777]

[828] ἀσκέω *askeō* 1x pr. *to work* materials; absol. *to train* or *exert one's self, make endeavor*, Ac 24:16* [778]

[829] ἀσκός *askos* 12x *a leathern bag* or *bottle, bottle of skin*, Mt 9:17; Mk 2:22; Lk 5:37, 38 [779]

[830] ἀσμένως *asmenōs* 1x *gladly, joyfully*, Ac 21:17* [780]

[831] ἄσοφος *asophos* 1x *unwise; destitute of* Christian *wisdom*, Eph 5:15* [781]

[832] ἀσπάζομαι *aspazomai* 59x *to salute, greet, welcome, express good wishes, pay respects*, Mt 10:12; Mk 9:15, et al. freq.; *to bid farewell*, Ac 20:1; 21:6; *to treat with affection*, Mt 5:47; met. *to embrace* mentally, *welcome* to the heart of understanding, Heb 11:13 [782]

[833] ἀσπασμός *aspasmos* 10x *salutation, greeting*, Mt 23:7; Mk 12:38 [783]

[834] ἄσπιλος *aspilos* 4x *spotless, unblemished, pure*, 1 Ti 6:14; Jas 1:27; 1 Pe 1:19; 2 Pe 3:14* [784]

[835] ἀσπίς *aspis* 1x *an asp*, a species of serpent of the most deadly venom, Ro 3:13* [785]

[836] ἄσπονδος *aspondos* 1x pr. *unwilling to make a treaty;* hence, *implacable, irreconcilable*, 2 Ti 3:3* [786]

[837] ἀσσάριον *assarion* 2x dimin. of the Latin, *as*, a Roman brass coin of the value of one-tenth of a denarius, or δραχμή, used to convey the idea of a trifle or very small sum, like the term *a mil* (equals one-tenth of a cent), Mt 10:29; Lk 12:6* [787]

[839] ἆσσον *asson* 1x *nearer; very nigh, close;* used as the compar. of ἄγχι, Ac 27:13* [788]

[840] Ἄσσος *Assos* 2x *Assos*, a maritime city of Mysia, in Asia Minor, Ac 20:13-14* [789]

[841] ἀστατέω *astateō* 1x *to be unsettled, to be a wanderer, be homeless,* 1 Co 4:11* [790]

[842] ἀστεῖος *asteios* 2x pr. *belonging to a city; well bred, polite, polished;* hence, *elegant, fair, comely, beautiful,* Ac 7:20; Heb 11:23* [791]

[843] ἀστήρ *astēr* 24x *a star, luminous body like a star, luminary,* Mt 2:2, 7, 9, 10; Rev 1:16 [792]

[844] ἀστήρικτος *astēriktos* 2x *not made firm; unsettled, unstable, unsteady,* 2 Pe 2:14; 3:16* [793]

[845] ἄστοργος *astorgos* 2x *devoid of natural* or *instinctive affection, without affection to kindred,* Ro 1:31; 2 Ti 3:3* [794]

[846] ἀστοχέω *astocheō* 3x pr. *to miss the mark;* met. *to err, deviate, swerve from,* 1 Ti 1:6; 6:21; 2 Ti 2:18* [795]

[847] ἀστραπή *astrapē* 9x *lightning,* Mt 24:27; *brightness, lustre,* Lk 11:36 [796]

[848] ἀστράπτω *astraptō* 2x *to lighten, flash as lightning,* Lk 17:24; *to be bright, shining,* Lk 24:4* [797]

[849] ἄστρον *astron* 4x *a constellation; a star,* Lk 21:25; Ac 7:43; 27:20; Heb 11:12* [798]

[850] Ἀσύγκριτος *Asynkritos* 1x *Asyncritus,* pr. name, Ro 16:14* [799]

[851] ἀσύμφωνος *asymphōnos* 1x *discordant in sound;* met. *discordant, at difference,* Ac 28:25* [800]

[852] ἀσύνετος *asynetos* 5x *unintelligent, dull,* Mt 15:16; Mk 7:18; *reckless, perverse,* Ro 1:21, 31; *unenlightened, heathenish,* Ro 10:19 [801]

[853] ἀσύνθετος *asynthetos* 1x *unable to be trusted, undutiful,* Ro 1:31* [802]

[854] ἀσφάλεια *asphaleia* 3x pr. *state of security from falling, firmness; safety, security,* 1 Th 5:3; *certainty, truth,* Lk 1:4; *means of security,* Ac 5:23* [803]

[855] ἀσφαλής *asphalēs* 5x pr. *firm, secure from falling; firm, sure, steady, immovable,* Heb 6:19; met. *certain, sure,* Ac

21:34; 22:30; 25:26; *safe, making secure,* Phil 3:1* [804]

[856] ἀσφαλίζω *asphalizō* 4x mid: *to make fast, safe,* or *secure,* Mt 27:64, 65, 66; Ac 16:24* [805]

[857] ἀσφαλῶς *asphalōs* 3x *securely, safely; without fail, safely,* Mk 14:44; Ac 16:23; *certainly, assuredly,* Ac 2:36* [806]

[858] ἀσχημονέω *aschēmoneō* 2x *to behave in an unbecoming manner* or *indecorously,* 1 Co 13:5; *to behave in a manner open to censure,* 1 Co 7:36* [807]

[859] ἀσχημοσύνη *aschēmosynē* 2x pr. *external indecorum; nakedness, shame, pudenda,* Rev 16:15; *indecency, infamous lust* or *lewdness,* Ro 1:27* [808]

[860] ἀσχήμων *aschēmōn* 1x *indecorous, uncomely, indecent,* 1 Co 12:23* [809]

[861] ἀσωτία *asōtia* 3x *dissoluteness, debauchery,* Eph 5:18; Tit 1:6; 1 Pe 4:4* [810]

[862] ἀσώτως *asōtōs* 1x *dissolutely, loosely,* Lk 15:13* [811]

[863] ἀτακτέω *atakteō* 1x pr. *to infringe military order;* met. *to be irregular, behave disorderly, to be lazy,* 2 Th 3:7* [812]

[864] ἄτακτος *ataktos* 1x pr. used of soldiers, *disorderly;* met. *irregular* in conduct, *disorderly, lazy,* 1 Th 5:14* [813]

[865] ἀτάκτως *ataktōs* 2x *disorderly, irresponsible,* 2 Th 3:6, 11* [814]

[866] ἄτεκνος *ateknos* 2x *childless,* Lk 20:28, 29* [815]

[867] ἀτενίζω *atenizō* 14x *to fix one's eyes upon, look steadily, gaze intently,* Lk 4:20 [816]

[868] ἄτερ *ater* 2x improper prep with the gen., *without,* Lk 22:6, 35* [817]

[869] ἀτιμάζω *atimazō* 7x also spelled ἀτιμάω and ἀντιμόω, *to dishonor, slight,* Jn 8:49; Ro 2:23; Jas 2:6; *to treat with indignity,* Mk 12:4; Lk 20:11; Ac 5:41; *to abuse, debase,* Ro 1:24* [818]

[871] ἀτιμία *atimia* 7x *dishonor, infamy,* Ro 1:26; *shame,* 1 Co 11:14; *meanness, vileness,* 1 Co 15:43; 2 Co 6:8; *a dishonorable use,* Ro 9:21; 2 Ti 2:20; κατὰ ἀτιμίαν, *slightingly, disparagingly,* 2 Co 11:21 [819]

[872] ἄτιμος *atimos* 4x *unhonored, without honor,* Mt 13:57; Mk 6:4; *despised,* 1 Co 4:10; 12:23* [820]

[874] ἀτμίς *atmis* 2x *an exhalation, vapor, smoke,* Ac 2:19; Jas 4:14* [822]

[875] ἄτομος *atomos* 1x *indivisible,* and by impl. *exceedingly minute;* ἐν ἀτόμῳ, sc. χρόνῳ, *in an indivisible point of time, in an instant* or *moment,* 1 Co 15:52* [823]

[876] ἄτοπος *atopos* 4x pr. *out of place; inopportune, unsuitable, absurd; new, unusual, strange;* in N.T. *improper, amiss, wicked,* Lk 23:41; Ac 25:5; 2 Th 3:2; *noxious, harmful,* Ac 28:6* [824]

[877] Ἀττάλεια *Attaleia* 1x *Attalia,* a city of Pamphylia, Ac 14:25* [825]

[878] αὐγάζω *augazō* 1x *to see distinctly, discern,* or possibly *to shine, give light* at 2 Co 4:4* [826]

[879] αὐγή *augē* 1x *radiance; daybreak, dawn,* Ac 20:11* [827]

[881] αὐθάδης *authadēs* 2x *one who pleases himself, willful, obstinate; arrogant, stubborn,* Tit 1:7; 2 Pe 2:10* [829]

[882] αὐθαίρετος *authairetos* 2x pr. *one who chooses his own course of action; acting spontaneously, of one's own accord,* 2 Co 8:3, 17* [830]

[883] αὐθεντέω *authenteō* 1x *to have authority over, domineer,* 1 Ti 2:12* [831]

[884] αὐλέω *auleō* 3x *to play on a pipe* or *flute, pipe,* Mt 11:17; Lk 7:32; 1 Co 14:7* [832]

[885] αὐλή *aulē* 12x pr. *an unroofed enclosure; court-yard; sheepfold,* Jn 10:1, 16; *an exterior court,* i.q. προαύλιον, *an enclosed place between the door and the street,* Rev 11:2; *an interior court, quadrangle,* the open court in the middle of Oriental houses, which are commonly built in the form of a square enclosing this court, Mt 26:58, 69; by synec. *a house, mansion, palace,* Mt 26:3; Lk 11:21 [833]

[886] αὐλητής *aulētēs* 2x *a player on a pipe* or *flute,* Mt 9:23; Rev 18:22* [834]

[887] αὐλίζομαι *aulizomai* 2x pr. *to pass the time in a court-yard; to lodge;* hence, *to pass the night* in any place, *to lodge at night, pass* or *remain through the night,* Mt 21:17; Lk 21:37* [835]

[888] αὐλός *aulos* 1x *a pipe* or *flute,* 1 Co 14:7* [836]

[889] αὐξάνω *auxanō* 21x also spelled αὔξω, trans. *to cause to grow* or *increase;* pass. *to be increased, enlarged,* Mt 13:32; 1 Co 3:6, 7; intrans. *to increase, grow,* Mt 6:28; Mk 4:8 [837]

[890] αὔξησις *auxēsis* 2x *increase, growth,* Eph 4:16; Col 2:19* [838]

[891] αὔξω *auxō* 2x see αὐξάνω, Eph 2:21; Col 2:19★ [837]

[892] αὔριον *aurion* 14x *tomorrow*, Mt 6:30; ἡ αὔριον, sc. ἡμέρα, *the next day*, Mt 6:34 [839]

[893] αὐστηρός *austēros* 2x pr. *harsh, sour in flavor;* met. *harsh, rigid, ungenerous,* Lk 19:21, 22★ [840]

[894] αὐτάρκεια *autarkeia* 2x *a competence of the necessaries of life,* 2 Co 9:8; *a frame of mind viewing one's lot as sufficient, contentedness,* 1 Ti 6:6★ [841]

[895] αὐτάρκης *autarkēs* 1x pr. *sufficient* or *adequate in one's self; contented with one's lot,* Phil 4:11★ [842]

[896] αὐτοκατάκριτος *autokatakritos* 1x *self-condemned,* Tit 3:11★ [843]

[897] αὐτόματος *automatos* 2x *self-excited, acting spontaneously, spontaneous, of his own accord,* Mk 4:8; Ac 12:10★ [844]

[898] αὐτόπτης *autoptēs* 1x *an eye-witness,* Lk 1:2★ [845]

[899] αὐτός *autos* 5,597x *self, very, alone,* Mk 6:31; 2 Co 12:13; *of one's self, of one's own motion,* Jn 16:27; used also in the oblique cases independently as a personal pron. of the third person; ὁ αὐτός, *the same; unchangeable,* Heb 1:12; κατὰ τὸ αὐτό, *at the same time, together,* Ac 14:1; ἐπὶ τὸ αὐτό, *in one and the same place,* Mt 22:34; *at the same time, together,* Ac 3:1 [846, 847, 848]

[7000] αὐτοῦ *autou* 4x *here,* Mt 26:36; Lk 9:27; *there,* Ac 18:19; 21:4★

[900] αὐτόφωρος *autophōros* 1x pr. *caught in the act of theft,* Jn 8:4★ [1888]

[901] αὐτόχειρ *autocheir* 1x *acting* or *doing anything with one's own hands,* Ac 27:19★ [849]

[902] αὐχέω *aucheō* 1x *to boast,* Jas 3:5★ [3166]

[903] αὐχμηρός *auchmēros* 1x *squalid, filthy;* by impl. *dark, obscure, murky,* 2 Pe 1:19★ [850]

[904] ἀφαιρέω *aphaireō* 10x *to take away, remove,* Lk 1:25; 10:42; *to take off, cut off, remove by cutting off,* Mt 26:15; Mk 14:47; Lk 22:50 [851]

[905] ἀφανής *aphanēs* 1x *out of sight; not manifest, hidden, concealed,* Heb 4:13★ [852]

[906] ἀφανίζω *aphanizō* 5x *to remove out of sight, cause to disappear;* pass. *to disappear, vanish,* Jas 4:14; by impl. *to destroy, consume,* so that nothing shall be left visible, Mt 6:19, 20; met. *to spoil,*

deform, disfigure, Mt 6:16; *to perish,* Ac 13:41★ [853]

[907] ἀφανισμός *aphanismos* 1x *a disappearing, vanishing away;* met. *destruction, abolition, abrogation,* Heb 8:13★ [854]

[908] ἄφαντος *aphantos* 1x *not appearing, not seen, invisible;* hence, ἄφαντος γενέσθαι, *to disappear, vanish,* Lk 24:31★ [855]

[909] ἀφεδρών *aphedrōn* 2x *a latrine,* Mt 15:17; Mk 7:19★ [856]

[910] ἀφειδία *apheidia* 1x pr. *the disposition of one who is* ἀφειδής, *unsparing;* hence, in N.T. *unsparingness* in the way of rigorous treatment, *non-indulgence,* Col 2:23★ [857]

[911] ἀφελότης *aphelotēs* 1x *sincerity, simplicity,* Ac 2:46 [858]

[912] ἄφεσις *aphesis* 17x *dismission, deliverance,* from captivity, Lk 4:18 (2t); *remission, forgiveness, pardon,* Mt 26:28 [859]

[913] ἀφή *haphē* 2x *a fastening; a ligament,* by which the different members are connected, *commissure, joint,* Eph 4:16; Col 2:19★ [860]

[914] ἀφθαρσία *aphtharsia* 7x *incorruptibility,* 1 Co 15:42, 53, 54; *immortality,* Ro 2:7; 2 Ti 1:10; *soundness, purity;* ἐν ἀφθαρσίᾳ, *purely, sincerely* or *constantly, unfailingly,* Eph 6:24 [861]

[915] ἄφθαρτος *aphthartos* 8x *incorruptible, immortal, imperishable, undying, enduring,* Ro 1:23; 1 Co 9:25; 15:52 [862]

[917] ἀφθορία *aphthoria* 1x pr. *incapability of decay;* met. *incorruptness, integrity, genuineness, purity,* Tit 2:7★ [90]

[918] ἀφίημι *aphiēmi* 143x *to send away, dismiss, suffer to depart; to emit, send forth;* τὴν φωνήν, *the voice, to cry out, utter an exclamation,* Mk 15:37; τὸ πνεῦμα, *the spirit, to expire,* Mt 27:50; *to omit, pass over* or *by; to let alone, care not for,* Mt 15:14; 23:23; Heb 6:1; *to permit, suffer, let, forbid not; to give up, yield, resign,* Mt 5:40; *to remit, forgive, pardon; to relax, suffer to become less intense,* Rev 2:4; *to leave, depart from; to desert, forsake; to leave remaining* or *alone; to leave behind,* sc. at one's death, Mk 12:19, 20, 21, 22; Jn 14:27 [863]

[919] ἀφικνέομαι *aphikneomai* 1x *to come, arrive at; to reach* as a report, Ro 16:19★ [864]

[920] ἀφιλάγαθος *aphilagathos* 1x *not a lover of good* and *good men,* 2 Ti 3:3★ [865]

[921] ἀφιλάργυρος *aphilargyros* 2x *not fond of money, not covetous, generous,* 1 Ti 3:3; Heb 13:5★ [866]

[922] ἄφιξις *aphixis* 1x *arrival; departure,* Ac 20:29★ [867]

[923] ἀφίστημι *aphistēmi* 14x trans. *to put away, separate; to draw off* or *away, withdraw, induce to revolt,* Ac 5:37; intrans., and mid., *to depart, go away from,* Lk 2:37; met. *to desist* or *refrain from, let alone,* Ac 5:38; 22:29; 2 Co 12:8; *to make defection, fall away, apostatize,* Lk 8:13; 1 Ti 4:1; Heb 3:12; *to withdraw from, have no intercourse with,* 1 Ti 6:5; *to abstain from,* 2 Ti 2:19 [868]

[924] ἄφνω *aphnō* 3x *suddenly, unexpectedly,* Ac 2:2; 16:26; 28:6★ [869]

[925] ἀφόβως *aphobōs* 4x *fearlessly, boldly, intrepidly,* Phil 1:14; *securely, peacefully, tranquilly,* Lk 1:74; 1 Co 16:10; *boldly, shamelessly,* Jude 12★ [870]

[926] ἀφομοιόω *aphomoioō* 1x *to assimilate, cause to resemble,* Heb 7:3★ [871]

[927] ἀφοράω *aphoraō* 2x *to view with undivided attention* by looking away from every other object; *to regard fixedly and earnestly,* Heb 12:2; *to see distinctly,* Phil 2:23★ [542, 872]

[928] ἀφορίζω *aphorizō* 10x *to limit off; to separate, sever* from the rest, Mt 13:49; *to separate* from society, *cut off from all intercourse, excommunicate,* Lk 6:22; *to set apart, select,* Ac 13:2; Ro 1:1; Gal 1:15 [873]

[929] ἀφορμή *aphormē* 7x pr. *a starting point; means* to accomplish an object; *occasion, opportunity,* Ro 7:8, 11 [874]

[930] ἀφρίζω *aphrizō* 2x *to froth, foam,* Mk 9:18, 20★ [875]

[931] ἀφρός *aphros* 1x *froth, foam,* Lk 9:39★ [876]

[932] ἀφροσύνη *aphrosynē* 4x *inconsiderateness, folly;* boastful *folly,* 2 Co 11:1, 17, 21; in N.T. *foolishness, levity, wickedness, impiety,* Mk 7:22★ [877]

[933] ἄφρων *aphrōn* 11x *unwise, inconsiderate, simple, foolish,* Lk 11:40; 12:20; 1 Co 15:36; *ignorant,* religiously *unenlightened,* Ro 2:20; Eph 5:17; 1 Pe 2:15; boastfully *foolish, vain,* 2 Co 11:16, 19 [878]

[934] ἀφυπνόω *aphypnoō* 1x *to awake from sleep;* in N.T. *to go off into sleep, fall asleep,* Lk 8:23★ [879]

[936] ἄφωνος *aphōnos* 4x *dumb, destitute of the power of speech,* 1 Co 12:2; 2 Pe

2:16; *silent, mute, uttering no voice,* Ac 8:32; *inarticulate, consisting of inarticulate sounds, unmeaning,* 1 Co 14:10* [880]

[937] Ἀχάζ *Achaz* 2x *Ahaz,* pr. name, indecl, Mt 1:9* [881]

[938] Ἀχαΐα *Achaia* 10x *Achaia,* the Roman province, comprehending all Greece to the south of Thessaly [882]

[939] Ἀχαϊκός *Achaikos* 1x *Achaicus,* pr. name, 1 Co 16:17* [883]

[940] ἀχάριστος *acharistos* 2x *unthankful, ungrateful,* Lk 6:35; 2 Ti 3:2* [884]

[942] ἀχειροποίητος *acheiropoiētos* 3x *not made with hands,* Mk 14:58; 2 Co 5:1; Col 2:11* [886]

[943] Ἀχίμ *Achim* 2x *Achim,* pr. name, indecl, Mt 1:14* [885]

[944] ἀχλύς *achlys* 1x *a mist; darkening, dimness,* of the sight, Ac 13:11* [887]

[945] ἀχρεῖος *achreios* 2x *useless, unprofitable, worthless,* Mt 25:30; *unmeritorious,* Lk 17:10* [888]

[946] ἀχρειόω *achreioō* 1x also ἀχρεόω, pas., *to render useless;* met., *to become corrupt, depraved,* Ro 3:12* [889]

[947] ἄχρηστος *achrēstos* 1x *unuseful, useless, unprofitable,* and by impl. *detrimental, causing loss,* Phlm 11* [890]

[948] ἄχρι *achri* 49x improper prep with the gen., also functioning as a conj, also spelled ἄχρις (Gal 3:19; Heb 3:13; Rev 2:25), with respect to place, *as far as;* to time, *until, during;* as a conj., *until* [891]

[949] ἄχυρον *achuron* 2x *chaff, straw* broken up by treading out the grain, Mt 3:12; Lk 3:17* [892]

[950] ἀψευδής *apseudēs* 1x *free from falsehood; incapable of falsehood,* Tit 1:2* [893]

[952] ἄψινθος *apsinthos* 2x see ἀψίνθιον [894]

[953] ἄψυχος *apsychos* 1x *void of life* or *sense, inanimate,* 1 Co 14:7* [895]

[955] Βάαλ *Baal* 1x *Baal,* (Hebrew for *Master*) pr. name, indecl., Ro 11:4* [896]

[956] Βαβυλών *Babylōn* 12x *Babylon,* 1 Pe 5:13 [897]

[957] βαθμός *bathmos* 1x pr. *a step, stair;* met. *grade* of dignity, *degree, rank, standing,* 1 Ti 3:13* [898]

[958] βάθος *bathos* 8x *depth;* τὸ βάθος, *deep water,* Lk 5:4; Mt 13:5; met. *fullness, abundance, immensity,* Ro 11:33; *an*

extreme degree, 2 Co 8:2; pl. *profundities, deep-laid plans,* 1 Co 2:10; Rev 2:24 [899]

[959] βαθύνω *bathunō* 1x *to deepen, excavate,* Lk 6:48* [900]

[960] βαθύς *bathus* 4x *deep,* Jn 4:11; met. *deep, profound,* Ac 20:9; Rev 2:24; ὄρθρου βαθέος, lit. *at deep morning twilight, at the earliest dawn,* Lk 24:1* [901]

[961] βάϊον *baion* 1x *a palm branch,* Jn 12:13* [902]

[962] Βαλαάμ *Balaam* 3x *Balaam,* pr. name, indecl. [903]

[963] Βαλάκ *Balak* 1x *Balak,* pr. name, indecl., Rev 2:14* [904]

[964] βαλλάντιον *ballantion* 4x also spelled βαλάντιον, *a bag, purse,* Lk 10:4; 12:33; 22:35, 36* [905]

[965] βάλλω *ballō* 122x pluperfect, ἐβεβλήμην, *to throw, cast; to lay,* Rev 2:22; Mt 8:6, 14; *to put, place,* Jas 3:3; *to place, deposit,* Mt 27:6; Mk 12:41-44; Lk 21:1-4; Jn 12:6; *to pour,* Jn 13:5; *to thrust,* Jn 18:11; 20:27; Mk 7:33; Rev 14:19; *to send forth,* Mt 10:34; *to assault, strike,* Mk 14:65; met. *to suggest,* Jn 13:2; intrans. *to rush, beat,* as the wind, Ac 27:14 [906]

[966] βαπτίζω *baptizō* 77x pr. *to dip, immerse; to cleanse* or *purify by washing; to administer the rite of baptism, to baptize;* met. with various reference to the ideas associated with Christian baptism as an act of dedication, e.g. marked designation, devotion, trial, etc.; mid. *to procure baptism for one's self, to undergo baptism,* Ac 22:16 [907]

[967] βάπτισμα *baptisma* 19x pr. *immersion; baptism, ordinance of baptism,* Mt 3:7; Ro 6:4; met. *baptism* in the trial of suffering, Mt 20:22, 23; Mk 10:38, 39 [908]

[968] βαπτισμός *baptismos* 4x pr. *an act of dipping* or *immersion: a baptism,* Col 2:12; Heb 6:2; *an ablution,* Mk 7:4; Heb 9:10* [909]

[969] βαπτιστής *baptistēs* 12x *one who baptizes, a baptist,* Mt 3:1; 11:11, 12 [910]

[970] βάπτω *baptō* 4x *to dip,* Jn 13:26; Lk 16:24; *to dye,* Rev 19:13* [911]

[972] Βαραββᾶς *Barabbas* 11x *Barabbas,* pr. name [912]

[973] Βαράκ *Barak* 1x *Barak,* pr. name, indecl., Heb 11:32* [913]

[974] Βαραχίας *Barachias* 1x *Barachias,* pr. name, Mt 23:35 [914]

[975] βάρβαρος *barbaros* 6x pr. *one to whom a pure Greek dialect is not native;*

one who is not a proper Greek, a barbarian, Ro 1:14; Col 3:11; Ac 28:2, 4; *a foreigner speaking a strange language,* 1 Co 14:11* [915]

[976] βαρέω *bareō* 6x *to be heavy upon, weigh down, burden, oppress,* as sleep, Mt 26:43; Mk 14:40; Lk 9:32; *calamities,* 2 Co 1:8; 5:4; or, *trouble, care, expense,* etc. 1 Ti 5:16* [916]

[977] βαρέως *bareōs* 2x *heavily;* met. *with difficulty, dully, stupidly,* Mt 13:15; Ac 28:27* [917]

[978] Βαρθολομαῖος *Bartholomaios* 4x *Bartholomew,* pr. name [918]

[979] Βαριησοῦς *Bariēsous* 1x *Bar-jesus,* pr. name, Ac 13:6* [919]

[980] Βαριωνᾶ *Bariōna* 1x also Βὰρ Ἰωνᾶ or Βαριωνᾶς, *Bar-jona,* pr. name, Mt 16:17* [920]

[982] Βαρναβᾶς *Barnabas* 28x *Barnabas,* pr. name, Ac 4:36; 13:1f.; 14:12; 15:2f.; 1 Co 9:6; Gal 2:1, 9, 13; Col 4:10 [921]

[983] βάρος *baros* 6x *weight, heaviness; a burden, anything grievous and hard to be borne,* Mt 20:12; Ac 15:28; Gal 6:2; Rev 2:24; *burden, charge* or *weight, influence, dignity, honor,* 1 Th 2:7; with another noun in government, *fulness, abundance, excellence,* 2 Co 4:17* [922]

[984] Βαρσαββᾶς *Barsabbas* 2x *Bar-sabas,* pr. name (1) *Joseph, surnamed Justus,* Ac 1:23 (2) *Judas,* Ac 15:22* [923]

[985] Βαρτιμαῖος *Bartimaios* 1x *Bartimaeus,* pr. name, Mk 10:46* [924]

[987] βαρύς *barys* 6x *heavy;* met. *burdensome, oppressive* or *difficult of observance,* as precepts, Mt 23:4; 1 Jn 5:3; *weighty, important, momentous,* Mt 23:23; Ac 25:7; *grievous, oppressive, afflictive, violent,* Ac 20:29; *authoritative, strict, stern, severe,* 2 Co 10:10* [926]

[988] βαρύτιμος *barytimos* 1x *of great price, precious,* Mt 26:7* [927]

[989] βασανίζω *basanizō* 12x pr. *to apply the lapis Lydius* or *touchstone;* met. *to examine, scrutinize, try,* either by words or torture; in N.T. *to afflict, torment;* pass. *to be afflicted, tormented, pained,* by diseases, Mt 8:6, 29, 35; *to be tossed, agitated,* as by the waves, Mt 14:24 [928]

[990] βασανισμός *basanismos* 6x pr. *examination by torture; torment, torture,* Rev 9:5; 14:11; 18:7, 10, 15* [929]

[991] βασανιστής *basanistēs* 1x pr. *an inquisitor, tormentor;* in N.T. *a keeper of a prison, jailer,* Mt 18:34* [930]

[992] βάσανος *basanos* 3x pr. *lapis Lydius*, a species of stone from Lydia, which being applied to metals was thought to indicate any alloy which might be mixed with them, and therefore used in the trial of metals; hence, *examination* of a person, especially by torture; in N.T. *torture, torment, severe pain,* Mt 4:24; Lk 16:23, 28* [931]

[993] βασιλεία *basileia* 162x *a kingdom, realm,* the region or country governed by a king; *kingly power, authority, dominion, reign; royal dignity,* the title and honor of king; ἡ βασιλεία, Mt 9:35, ἡ βασιλεία τοῦ θεοῦ or τοῦ Χριστου or τοῦ οὐρανοῦ or τῶν οὐρανῶν, *the reign* or *kingdom of the Messiah,* both in a false and true conception of it; used also with various limitation, of its administration and coming history, as in the parables; its distinctive nature, Ro 14:17; its requirements, privileges, rewards, consummation [932]

[994] βασίλειος *basileios* 2x *royal, regal;* met. *possessed of high prerogatives and distinction,* 1 Pe 2:9; τὰ βασίλεια, sc. δώματα, *regal mansion, palaces,* Lk 7:25* [933, 934]

[995] βασιλεύς *basileus* 115x *a king, monarch, one possessing regal authority* [935]

[996] βασιλεύω *basileuō* 21x *to possess regal authority, be a king, reign; to rule, govern,* Mt 2:22; met. *to be in force, predominate, prevail,* Ro 5:14, 17, 21; met. *to be in kingly case, fare royally,* 1 Co 4:8 [936]

[997] βασιλικός *basilikos* 5x *royal, regal,* Ac 12:20, 21; βασιλικός, used as a subst. *a person attached to the king, courtier,* Jn 4:46, 49; met. *royal, of the highest excellence,* Jas 2:8* [937]

[999] βασίλισσα *basilissa* 4x *a queen,* Mt 12:42; Lk 11:31; Ac 8:27; Rev 18:7* [938]

[1000] βάσις *basis* 1x pr. *a step; the foot,* Ac 3:7* [939]

[1001] βασκαίνω *baskainō* 1x pr. *to slander;* thence, *to bewitch* by spells, or by any other means; *to delude,* Gal 3:1* [940]

[1002] βαστάζω *bastazō* 27x pr. *to lift, raise, bear aloft; to bear, carry* in the hands or about the person; *carry* as a message, Ac 9:15; *to take away, remove,* Mt 8:17; Jn 20:15; *to take up,* Jn 10:31; Lk 14:27; *to bear* as a burden *endure, suffer; to sustain,* Ro 11:18; *to bear with, tolerate; to sustain* mentally, *comprehend,* Jn 16:12 [941]

[1003] βάτος *batos* 5x *a thorn-bush,* Mk 12:26; Lk 6:44; 20:37; Ac 7:30, 35* [942]

[1004] βάτος *batos* 1x *a bath,* a measure for liquids, which is stated by Josephus (*Ant.* 8.57) to contain seventy-two sextarii, or about thirteen and one half gallons. Others estimate it to be nine gallons; and others, seven and one half gallons, Lk 16:6* [943]

[1005] βάτραχος *batrachos* 1x *a frog,* Rev 16:13 [944]

[1006] βατταλογέω *battalogeō* 1x also spelled βαττολογέω, pr. *to stammer;* hence, *to babble; to use vain repetitions,* Mt 6:7* [945]

[1007] βδέλυγμα *bdelygma* 6x *an abomination, an abominable thing,* Mt 24:15; Mk 13:14; *idolatry with all its pollution,* Lk 16:15; Rev 17:4, 5; 21:27* [946]

[1008] βδελυκτός *bdelyktos* 1x *abominable, detestable,* Tit 1:16* [947]

[1009] βδελύσσομαι *bdelyssomai* 2x *to abominate, loathe, detest, abhor,* Ro 2:22; pass. *to be abominable, detestable,* Rev 21:8* [948]

[1010] βέβαιος *bebaios* 8x *firm, stable, steadfast,* Heb 3:14; 6:19; *sure, certain, established,* Ro 4:16 [949]

[1011] βεβαιόω *bebaioō* 8x *to confirm, establish; to render constant and unwavering,* 1 Co 1:8; *to strengthen* or *establish* by arguments or proofs, *ratify,* Mk 16:20; *to verify,* as promises, Ro 15:8 [950]

[1012] βεβαίωσις *bebaiōsis* 2x *confirmation, firm establishment,* Phil 1:7; Heb 6:16* [951]

[1013] βέβηλος *bebēlos* 5x pr. *what is open and accessible to all;* hence, *profane, not religious, not connected with religion; unholy; a despiser, scorner,* 1 Ti 1:9; 4:7 [952]

[1014] βεβηλόω *bebēloō* 2x *to profane, pollute, violate,* Mt 12:5; Ac 24:6* [953]

[1015] Βεελζεβούλ *Beelzeboul* 7x variant spellings of Βεελζεβούβ and βεελζεβούλ, *Beelzeboul,* pr. name, indecl., Mt 10:25 [954]

[1016] Βελιάρ *Beliar* 1x *Belial,* pr. name, indecl., 2 Co 6:15* [955]

[1017] βελόνη *belonē* 1x pr. *the point of a spear; a needle,* Lk 18:25* [4476]

[1018] βέλος *belos* 1x *a missile weapon, dart, arrow,* Eph 6:16* [956]

[1019] βελτίων *beltiōn* 1x *better;* βέλτιον, as an adv., *very well, too well to need informing,* 2 Ti 1:18* [957]

[1021] Βενιαμίν *Beniamin* 4x *Benjamin,* pr. name, indecl. Ac 13:21; Ro 11:1; Phil 3:5; Rev 7:8* [958]

[1022] Βερνίκη *Bernikē* 3x *Bernice,* pr. name, Ac 25:13, 23; 26:30* [959]

[1023] Βέροια *Beroia* 2x *Berea,* a town of Macedonia, Ac 17:10, 13* [960]

[1024] Βεροιαῖος *Beroiaios* 1x *belonging to Berea,* Ac 20:4* [961]

[1029] Βηθανία *Bēthania* 12x *Bethany* (1) A village near Jerusalem, at the Mount of Olives, Mt 21:17; Mk 11:1. (2) A village beyond the Jordan, Jn 1:28 [963]

[1031] Βηθεσδά *Bēthesda* 1x *Bethesda,* indecl., Jn 5:2* [964]

[1033] Βηθλέεμ *Bēthleem* 8x *Bethlehem,* indecl., a town in Palestine [965]

[1034] Βηθσαϊδά *Bēthsaida* 7x also spelled Βηθσαϊδάν (1035) *Bethsaida,* indecl. (1) A city of Galilee, Mt 11:21; Mk 6:45,. (2) A city of Lower Gaulanitis, near the Lake of Gennesareth, Lk 9:10 [966]

[1036] Βηθφαγή *Bēthphagē* 3x *Bethphage,* indecl., a part of the Mount of Olives, Mt 21:1; Mk 11:1; Lk 19:29* [967]

[1037] βῆμα *bēma* 12x *a step, footstep, foot-breadth, space to set the foot on,* Ac 7:5; *an elevated place ascended by steps, tribunal, throne,* Mt 27:19; Ac 12:21 [968]

[1039] βήρυλλος *bēryllos* 1x *a beryl,* a precious stone of a sea-green color, found chiefly in India, Rev 21:20* [969]

[1040] βία *bia* 3x *force, impetus, violence,* Ac 5:26; 21:35; 27:41* [970]

[1041] βιάζω *biazō* 2x also written as a middle deponent, βιάζομαι, *to urge, constrain, overpower by force; to press earnestly forward, to rush,* Lk 16:16; pass. *to be an object of a forceful movement,* Mt 11:12* [971]

[1042] βίαιος *biaios* 1x *violent, strong,* Ac 2:2* [972]

[1043] βιαστής *biastēs* 1x *one who uses violence,* or *is impetuous; one who is forceful in eager pursuit,* Mt 11:12* [973]

[1044] βιβλαρίδιον *biblaridion* 3x *a small volume* or *scroll, a little book,* Rev 10:2, 9, 10* [974]

[1046] βιβλίον *biblion* 34x *a written volume* or *roll, book,* Lk 4:17, 20; *a scroll, bill, billet,* Mt 19:7; Mk 10:4 [975]

[1047] βίβλος *biblos* 10x pr. *the inner bark* or *rind of the papyrus,* which was anciently used instead of paper; hence, *a written volume* or *roll, book, catalogue, account*, Mt 1:1; Mk 12:26 [976]

[1048] βιβρώσκω *bibrōskō* 1x *to eat*, Jn 6:13* [977]

[1049] Βιθυνία *Bithunia* 2x *Bithynia*, a province of Asia Minor, Ac 16:7; 1 Pe 1:1* [978]

[1050] βίος *bios* 10x *life; means of living; sustenance, maintenance, substance, goods*, Mk 12:44; Lk 8:14, 43; 15:12, 30; 21:4; 1 Ti 2:2; 2 Ti 2:4; 1 Jn 2:16; 3:17* [979]

[1051] βιόω *bioō* 1x *to live*, 1 Pe 4:2* [980]

[1052] βίωσις *biōsis* 1x *manner of life*, Ac 26:4* [981]

[1053] βιωτικός *biōtikos* 3x *pertaining to this life* or *the things of this life*, Lk 21:34; 1 Co 6:3, 4* [982]

[1054] βλαβερός *blaberos* 1x *hurtful*, 1 Ti 6:9* [983]

[1055] βλάπτω *blaptō* 2x pr. *to weaken, hinder, disable; to hurt, harm, injure*, Mk 16:18; Lk 4:35* [984]

[1056] βλαστάνω *blastanō* 4x also spelled βλαστάω, intrans. *to germinate, bud, sprout, spring up*, Mt 13:26; Mk 4:27; Heb 9:4; trans. and causative, *to cause to shoot, to produce, yield*, Jas 5:18* [985]

[1058] Βλάστος *Blastos* 1x *Blastus*, pr. name, Ac 12:20* [986]

[1059] βλασφημέω *blasphēmeō* 34x *to defame, revile, slander*, Mt 27:39; *to speak of God* or *divine things in terms of impious irreverence, to blaspheme*, Mt 9:3; 26:65 [987]

[1060] βλασφημία *blasphēmia* 18x *slander, railing, reproach*, Mt 15:19; Mk 7:22; *blasphemy*, Mt 12:31; 26:65 [988]

[1061] βλάσφημος *blasphēmos* 4x *slanderous, railing, reproachful*, 2 Ti 3:2; 2 Pe 2:11; *blasphemous*, Ac 6:11, 13; 1 Ti 1:13 [989]

[1062] βλέμμα *blemma* 1x *a look; the act of seeing, sight*, 2 Pe 2:8* [990]

[1063] βλέπω *blepō* 133x *to have the faculty of sight, to see*, Mt 12:22; *to exercise sight, to see*, Mt 6:4; *to look towards or at*, Mt 22:16; *to face*, Ac 27:12; *to take heed*, Mt 24:4; in N.T., βλέπειν ἀπό, *to beware of, shun*, Mk 8:15; trans., *to cast a look on*, Mt 5:28; *to see, behold*, Mt 13:17; *to observe*, Mt 7:3; *to have an eye to, see to*, Mk 13:9; Col 4:17; 2 Jn 8; *to discern* mentally, *perceive*, Ro 7:23; 2 Co 7:8; Jas 2:22;

to guard against, Phil 3:2; pass., *to be an object of sight, be visible*, Ro 8:24 [991]

[1064] βλητέος *blēteos* 1x *requiring to be cast or put*, Lk 5:38* [992]

[1065] Βοανηργές *Boanērges* 1x *Boanerges*, pr. name, indecl., Mk 3:17* [993]

[1066] βοάω *boaō* 12x *to cry out; to exclaim, proclaim*, Mt 3:3; 15:34; Ac 8:7; πρός τινα, *to invoke, implore the aid of any one*, Lk 18:7 [994]

[1067] Βόες *Boes* 2x *Boaz*, pr. name, indecl., Mt 1:5* [1003]

[1068] βοή *boē* 1x *a cry, outcry, exclamation*, Jas 5:4* [995]

[1069] βοήθεια *boētheia* 2x *help, succor*, Heb 4:16; meton. pl. *helps, contrivances for relief and safety*, Ac 27:17* [996]

[1070] βοηθέω *boētheō* 8x *to run to the aid of those who cry for help; to advance to the assistance of any one, help, aid, succor*, Mt 15:25; Mk 9:22, 24 [997]

[1071] βοηθός *boēthos* 1x *a helper*, Heb 13:6* [998]

[1073] βόθυνος *bothunos* 3x *a pit, well* or *cistern*, Mt 12:11; 15:14; Lk 6:39* [999]

[1074] βολή *bolē* 1x *a cast, a throw; the distance to which a thing can be thrown*, Lk 22:41* [1000]

[1075] βολίζω *bolizō* 2x *to take soundings, sound* Ac 27:28* [1001]

[1078] Βόος *Boos* 1x also spelled Βόοζ, *Boaz*, pr. name, indecl., Lk 3:32* [1003]

[1079] βόρβορος *borboros* 1x *mud, mire, dung, filth*, 2 Pe 2:22* [1004]

[1080] βορρᾶς *borras* 2x pr. *the north* or *N.N.E. wind*; meton. *the north*, Lk 13:29; Rev 21:13* [1005]

[1081] βόσκω *boskō* 9x *to feed, pasture, tend while grazing*; βόσκομαι, *to feed, be feeding*, Mt 8:30, 33; Lk 8:32, 34 [1006]

[1082] Βοσόρ *Bosor* 1x *Bosor*, pr. name, indecl., 2 Pe 2:15* [1007]

[1083] βοτάνη *botanē* 1x *herb, herbage, produce of the earth*, Heb 6:7* [1008]

[1084] βότρυς *botrys* 1x *a bunch or cluster of grapes*, Rev 14:18* [1009]

[1085] βουλευτής *bouleutēs* 2x *a counsellor, senator; member of the Sanhedrin*, Mk 15:43; Lk 23:50* [1010]

[1086] βουλεύω *bouleuō* 6x mid., *to give counsel; to deliberate*, Lk 14:31; Jn 12:10; 11:53; *to purpose, determine*, Ac 27:39; 2 Co 1:17 (2t)* [1011]

[1087] βουλή *boulē* 12x *counsel, purpose, design, determination, decree*, Lk 7:30; 23:51, et al. freq.; by impl. *secret thoughts, cogitations* of the mind, 1 Co 4:5 [1012]

[1088] βούλημα *boulēma* 3x *purpose, will, determination*, Ac 27:43; Ro 9:19; 1 Pe 4:3* [1013]

[1089] βούλομαι *boulomai* 37x *to be willing, disposed*, Mk 15:15; Ac 25:20; 28:18; *to intend*, Mt 1:19; Ac 5:28; 12:4; 2 Co 1:15; *to desire*, 1 Ti 6:9; *to choose, be pleased*, Jn 18:39; Ac 18:15; Jas 3:4; *to will, decree, appoint*, Lk 22:42; Jas 1:18; 1 Co 12:11; 1 Ti 2:8; 5:14; ἐβουλόμην, *I could wish*, Ac 25:22 [1014]

[1090] βουνός *bounos* 2x *a hill, rising ground*, Lk 3:5; 23:30* [1015]

[1091] βοῦς *bous* 8x *an ox, a bull or cow*, an animal of the ox kind, Lk 13:15 [1016]

[1092] βραβεῖον *brabeion* 2x *a prize* bestowed on victors in the public games, such as a crown, wreath, chaplet, garland, etc., 1 Co 9:24; Phil 3:14* [1017]

[1093] βραβεύω *brabeuō* 1x pr. *to be a director* or *arbiter in the public games;* in N.T. *to preside, direct, rule, govern, be predominate*, Col 3:15* [1018]

[1094] βραδύνω *bradynō* 2x *to be slow, to delay*, 1 Ti 3:15; 2 Pe 3:9* [1019]

[1095] βραδυπλοέω *bradyploeō* 1x *to sail slowly*, Ac 27:7* [1020]

[1096] βραδύς *bradys* 3x *slow, not hasty*, Jas 1:19; *slow* of understanding, *heavy, stupid*, Lk 24:25* [1021]

[1097] βραδύτης *bradytēs* 1x *slowness, tardiness, delay*, 2 Pe 3:9* [1022]

[1098] βραχίων *brachiōn* 3x *the arm; the arm* as a symbol of power, Lk 1:51; Jn 12:38; Ac 13:17* [1023]

[1099] βραχύς *brachus* 7x *short, brief; few, small*, Lk 22:58; Jn 6:7; Ac 5:34; 27:28; Heb 2:7, 9; 13:22* [1024]

[1100] βρέφος *brephos* 8x *a child; whether unborn, an embryo, fetus*, Lk 1:41, 44; *or just born, an infant*, Lk 2:12, 16; Ac 7:19; *or partly grown*, Lk 18:15; 2 Ti 3:15; met. *a babe in simplicity of faith*, 1 Pe 2:2* [1025]

[1101] βρέχω *brechō* 7x *to wet, moisten*, Lk 7:38; *to rain, cause or send rain*, Mt 5:45; Lk 17:29 [1026]

[1103] βροντή *brontē* 12x *thunder*, Mk 3:17; Jn 12:29 [1027]

[1104] βροχή *brochē* 2x *rain*, Mt 7:25, 27* [1028]

[1105] βρόχος *brochos* 1x *a cord, noose,* 1 Co 7:35* [1029]

[1106] βρυγμός *brygmos* 7x *gnashing of teeth together,* Mt 8:12, 13, 42, 50; 22:13; 24:51; 25:30; Lk 13:28* [1030]

[1107] βρύχω *brychō* 1x *to grate* or *gnash* the teeth, Ac 7:54* [1031]

[1108] βρύω *bryō* 1x pr. *to be full, to swell* with anything; *to emit, send forth,* Jas 3:11* [1032]

[1109] βρῶμα *brōma* 17x *food,* Mt 14:15; Mk 7:19; *solid food,* 1 Co 3:2 [1033]

[1110] βρώσιμος *brōsimos* 1x *eatable, that may be eaten,* Lk 24:41* [1034]

[1111] βρῶσις *brōsis* 11x *eating, the act of eating,* Ro 14:17; 1 Co 8:4; *meat, food,* Jn 6:27; Heb 12:16; *a canker* or *rust,* Mt 6:19, 20 [1035]

[1112] βυθίζω *bythizō* 2x *to immerse, submerge, cause to sink,* Lk 5:7; *to plunge deep, drown,* 1 Ti 6:9* [1036]

[1113] βυθός *bythos* 1x *the bottom, lowest part; the deep, sea,* 2 Co 11:25* [1037]

[1114] βυρσεύς *byrseus* 3x *a tanner, leather-dresser,* Ac 9:43; 10:6, 32* [1038]

[1115] βύσσινος *byssinos* 5x *made of fine linen* or *fine cotton,* Rev 18:16; 18:8 (2t), 14* [1039]

[1116] βύσσος *byssos* 1x *byssus,* a species of fine cotton highly prized by the ancients, Lk 16:19* [1040]

[1117] βωμός *bōmos* 1x pr. *a slightly-elevated spot, base, pedestal;* hence, *an altar,* Ac 17:23* [1041]

[1119] Γαββαθα *Gabbatha* 1x *Gabbatha,* pr. name, indecl., Jn 19:13* [1042]

[1120] Γαβριήλ *Gabriēl* 2x *Gabriel,* pr. name, indecl., Lk 1:19, 26* [1043]

[1121] γάγγραινα *gangraina* 1x *gangrene, mortification,* 2 Ti 2:17* [1044]

[1122] Γάδ *Gad* 1x *Gad,* pr. name, indecl., Rev 7:5* [1045]

[1123] Γαδαρηνός *Gadarēnos* 1x *an inhabitant of Gadara,* the chief city of Perea, Mt 8:28* [1046]

[1124] Γάζα *Gaza* 1x *Gaza,* a strong city of Palestine, Ac 8:26* [1048]

[1125] γάζα *gaza* 1x *treasure, treasury,* Ac 8:27* [1047]

[1126] γαζοφυλάκιον *gazophylakion* 5x also spelled γαζοφυλακεῖον, *a treasury; the sacred treasure,* Mk 12:41, 43; Lk 21:1; Jn 8:20* [1049]

[1127] Γάϊος *Gaios* 5x *Gaius,* pr. name. (1) Of Macedonia, Ac 19:29. (2) Of Corinth, 1 Co 1:14. (3) Of Derbe, Ac 20:4. (4) A Christian to whom Jn addressed his third Epistle, 3 Jn 1; Ro 16:23* [1050]

[1128] γάλα *gala* 5x *milk,* 1 Co 9:7; met. spiritual *milk,* consisting in the elements of Christian instruction, 1 Co 3:2; Heb 5:12, 13; spiritual *nutriment,* 1 Pe 2:2* [1051]

[1129] Γαλάτης *Galatēs* 1x *a Galatian, inhabitant of Galatia,* Gal 3:1* [1052]

[1130] Γαλατία *Galatia* 4x *Galatia* or *Gallo-Graecia,* a province of Asia Minor, 1 Co 6:1; Gal 1:2; 2 Ti 4:10; 1 Pe 1:1* [1053]

[1131] Γαλατικός *Galatikos* 2x *Galatian,* Ac 16:6; 18:23* [1054]

[1132] γαλήνη *galēnē* 3x *tranquillity of the sea, a calm,* Mt 8:26; Mk 4:39; Lk 8:24* [1055]

[1133] Γαλιλαία *Galilaia* 61x *Galilee,* a district of Palestine north of Samaria, Mt 4:15 [1056]

[1134] Γαλιλαῖος *Galilaios* 11x *a native of Galilee,* Mt 26:69; Mk 14:70; Lk 13:1; Jn 4:45; Ac 1:11 [1057]

[1136] Γαλλίων *Galliōn* 3x *Gallio,* pr. name, Ac 18:12, 14, 17* [1058]

[1137] Γαμαλιήλ *Gamaliēl* 2x *Gamaliel,* pr. name, indecl. [1059]

[1138] γαμέω *gameō* 28x *to marry,* Mt 5:32, et al.; absol. *to marry, enter the marriage state,* Mt 19:10, et al.; mid. *to marry, be married,* Mk 10:12; 1 Co 7:39 [1060]

[1139] γαμίζω *gamizō* 7x also spelled γαμίσκω, *to give in marriage, permit to marry,* 1 Co 7:38 [1061]

[1140] γαμίσκω *gamiskō* 1x see γαμίζω [1061]

[1141] γάμος *gamos* 16x *a wedding; nuptial festivities, a marriage festival,* Mt 22:2; 25:10; Jn 2:1, 2; Rev 19:7, 9; any *feast* or *banquet,* Lk 12:36; 14:8; *the marriage state,* Heb 13:4 [1062]

[1142] γάρ *gar* 1,041x *for;* it is, however, frequently used with an ellipsis of the clause to which it has reference, and its force must then be variously expressed: Mt 15:27; 27:23, et al.; it is also sometimes epexegetic, or introductory of an intimated detail of circumstances, *now, then, to wit,* Mt 1:18 [1063]

[1143] γαστήρ *gastēr* 9x *the belly, stomach; the womb,* Lk 1:31; ἐν γαστρὶ ἔχειν, *to be with child,* Mt 1:18, 23; 24:19, et al.; γαστέρες, *gluttons,* Tit 1:12 [1064]

[1145] γε *ge* 24x an enclitic particle imparting emphasis; indicating that a particular regard is to be had to the term to which it is attached. Its force is to be conveyed, when this is possible, by various expression; *at least, indeed, even* [1065]

[1146] Γεδεών *Gedeōn* 1x *Gideon* (Judges 6-8), pr. name, indecl., Heb 11:32* [1066]

[1147] γέεννα *geenna* 12x *Gehenna,* pr. *the valley of Hinnom,* south of Jerusalem, once celebrated for the horrid worship of Moloch, and afterwards polluted with every species of filth, as well as the carcasses of animals, and dead bodies of malefactors; to consume which, in order to avert the pestilence which such a mass of corruption would occasion, constant fires were kept burning; hence, *hell, the fires of Tartarus, the place of punishment in Hades,* Mt 5:22, 29, 30; 10:28; 18:9, et al. [1067]

[1149] Γεθσημανί *Gethsēmani* 2x *Gethsemane,* pr. name, indecl., Mt 26:36; Mk 14:32* [1068]

[1150] γείτων *geitōn* 4x *a neighbor,* Lk 14:12; 15:6, 9; Jn 9:8* [1069]

[1151] γελάω *gelaō* 2x *to laugh, smile;* by impl. *to be merry, happy, to rejoice,* Lk 6:21, 25* [1070]

[1152] γέλως *gelōs* 1x *laughter;* by impl. *mirth, joy, rejoicing,* Jas 4:9* [1071]

[1153] γεμίζω *gemizō* 8x *to fill,* Mt 4:37; 15:36, et al. [1072]

[1154] γέμω *gemō* 11x *to be full,* Mt 23:27; Lk 11:39, et al. [1073]

[1155] γενεά *genea* 43x pr. *birth;* hence, *progeny; a generation* of mankind, Mt 11:16; 23:36, et al.; *a generation,* a step in a genealogy, Mt 1:17; *a generation,* an interval of time, *an age;* in N.T. *course of life,* in respect of its events, interests, or character, Lk 16:8; Ac 13:36 [1074]

[1156] γενεαλογέω *genealogeō* 1x *to reckon one's descent, derive one's origin,* Heb 7:6* [1075]

[1157] γενεαλογία *genealogia* 2x *genealogy, catalogue of ancestors, history of descent,* 1 Ti 1:4; Tit 3:9* [1076]

[1160] γενέσια *genesia* 2x pr. *a day observed in memory of the dead;* in N.T. equivalent to γενέθλια, *celebration of one's birthday, birthday-festival,* Mt 14:6; Mk 6:21* [1077]

[1161] γένεσις *genesis* 5x *birth, nativity,* Mt 1:18; Lk 1:14; Jas 1:23; *successive generation, descent, lineage,* Mt 1:1; meton. *life,* Jas 3:6; Mt 1:18* [1078]

[1162] γενετή *genetē* 1x *birth,* Jn 9:1* [1079]

[1163] γένημα *genēma* 4x *natural produce, fruit, increase,* Mt 26:29; Mk 14:25; Lk 12:18; 22:18; 2 Co 9:10* [1081]

[1164] γεννάω *gennaō* 97x *to beget, generate,* Mt 1:2-16, et al.; *of women, to bring forth, bear, give birth to,* Lk 1:13, 57, et al.; pass. *to be born, produced,* Mt 2:1, 4, et al.; met. *to produce, excite, give occasion to, effect,* 2 Ti 2:23; from the Hebrew, *to constitute as son, to constitute as king,* or *as the representative* or *viceregent of God,* Ac 13:33; Heb 1:5; 5:5; by impl. *to be a parent to* any one; pass. *to be a son* or *child to* any one, Jn 1:13; 1 Co 4:15, et al. [1080]

[1165] γέννημα *gennēma* 4x *what is born* or *produced, offspring, progeny, brood,* Mt 3:7; 12:34, et al.; *fruit, produce,* Mt 26:29; Mk 14:25, et al.; *fruit, increase,* Lk 12:18; 2 Co 9:10 [1081]

[1166] Γεννησαρέτ *Gennēsaret* 3x *Gennesaret,* a lake of Palestine, called also the *Sea of Tiberias,* Mt 14:34; Mk 6:53; Lk 5:1* [1082]

[1168] γεννητός *gennētos* 2x *born* or *produced of,* Mt 11:11; Lk 7:28* [1084]

[1169] γένος *genos* 20x *offspring, progeny,* Ac 17:28, 29; *family, kindred, lineage,* Ac 7:13, et al.; *race, nation, people,* Mk 7:26; Ac 4:36, et al.; *kind, sort, species,* Mt 13:47, et al. [1085]

[1170] Γερασηνός *Gerasēnos* 3x also spelled Γεργεσηνός, *from Gerasene,* belonging to the city of Gerasa, Mk 5:1; Lk 8:26, 37* [1086]

[1172] γερουσία *gerousia* 1x *a senate, assembly of elders; the elders* of Israel collectively, Ac 5:21* [1087]

[1173] γέρων *gerōn* 1x *an old man,* Jn 3:4* [1088]

[1174] γεύομαι *geuomai* 15x *to taste,* Mt 27:34; Jn 2:9; absol. *to take food,* Ac 10:10, et al.; met. *to have perception of, experience,* Heb 6:4, 5; 1 Pe 2:3; θανάτου γεύεσθαι, *to experience death, to die,* Mt 16:28, et al. [1089]

[1175] γεωργέω *geōrgeō* 1x *to cultivate, till the earth,* Heb 6:7* [1090]

[1176] γεώργιον *geōrgion* 1x *cultivated field* or *ground, a farm,* 1 Co 3:9* [1091]

[1177] γεωργός *geōrgos* 19x *a farmer, one who tills the earth,* 2 Ti 2:6; Jas 5:7; in N.T. spc. *a vine-dresser, keeper of a vineyard,* i.q. ajmpelourgov", Mt 21:33, 34, et al. [1092]

[1178] γῆ *gē* 250x *earth, soil,* Mt 13:5; Mk 4:8, et al.; *the ground, surface of the earth,* Mt 10:29; Lk 6:49, et al.; *the land, as opposed to the sea or a lake,* Lk 5:11; Jn 21:8, 9, 11; *the earth, world,* Mt 5:18, 35, et al.; by synec. *the inhabitants of the earth,* Mt 5:13; 6:10; 10:34; *a land, region, tract, country, territory,* Mt 2:20; 14:34; by way of eminence, *the* chosen *land,* Mt 5:5; 24:30; 27:45; Eph 6:3; *the inhabitants of a region* or *country,* Mt 10:15; 11:24, et al. [1093]

[1179] γῆρας *gēras* 1x gen. also in ρους, *old age,* Lk 1:36* [1094]

[1180] γηράσκω *gēraskō* 2x *to be* or *become old,* Jn 21:18; Heb 8:13* [1095]

[1181] γίνομαι *ginomai* 669x pluperfect, ἐγενόει (3rd sg), *to come into existence; to be created, exist by creation,* Jn 1:3, 10; Heb 11:3; Jas 3:9; *to be born, produced, grow,* Mt 21:19; Jn 8:58, et al.; *to arise, come on, occur,* as the phenomena of nature, etc.; Mt 8:24, 26; 9:16, et al.; *to come, approach,* as morning or evening, Mt 8:16; 14:15, 23; *to be appointed, constituted, established,* Mk 2:27; Gal 3:17, et al.; *to take place, come to pass, happen, occur,* Mt 1:22; 24:6, 20, 21, 34, et al. freq.; *to be done, performed, effected,* Mt 21:42, et al.; *to be fulfilled, satisfied,* Mt 6:10; 26:42, et al.; *to come into a particular state* or *condition; to become, assume the character and appearance* of anything, Mt 5:45, et al.; *to become* or *be made* anything, *be changed* or *converted,* Mt 4:3; 21:42; Mk 1:17, et al.; *to be,* Mt 11:26; 19:8; γίνεσθαι ὑπό τινα, *to be subject to,* Gal 4:4; γίνεσθαι ἐν ἑαυτῷ, *to come to one's self, to recover from a trance* or *surprise,* Ac 12:11; μὴ γένοιτο, *let it not be, far be it from, God forbid,* Lk 20:16; Ro 3:4, 31, et al.; *to be kept, celebrated, solemnized,* as festivals, Mt 26:2, et al.; *to be finished, completed,* Heb 4:3 [1096]

[1182] γινώσκω *ginōskō* 222x *to know,* whether the action be inceptive or complete and settled; *to perceive,* Mt 22:18; Mk 5:29; 8:17; 12:12; Lk 8:46; *to mark, discern,* Mt 25:24; Lk 19:44; *to ascertain by examination,* Mk 6:38; Jn 7:51; Ac 23:28; *to understand,* Mk 4:13; Lk 18:34; Jn 12:16; 13:7; Ac 8:30; 1 Co 14:7, 9; *to acknowledge,* Mt 7:23; 2 Co 3:2; *to resolve, conclude,* Lk 16:4; Jn 7:26; 17:8; *to be assured,* Lk 21:20; Jn 6:69; 8:52; 2 Pe 1:20; *to be skilled, to be master of* a thing, Mt 16:3; Ac 21:37; *to know carnally,* Mt 1:25; Lk 1:34; from the Hebrew, *to view with favor,* 1 Co 8:3; Gal 4:9 [1097]

[1183] γλεῦκος *gleukos* 1x pr. *the unfermented juice of grapes;* hence, *sweet new wine,* Ac 2:13* [1098]

[1184] γλυκύς *glykys* 4x *sweet,* Jas 3:11-12; Rev 10:9, 10* [1099]

[1185] γλῶσσα *glōssa* 50x *the tongue,* Mk 7:33, 35, et al.; meton. *speech, talk,* 1 Jn 3:18; *a tongue, language,* Ac 2:11; 1 Co 13:1, et al.; meton. *a language not proper to a speaker, a gift* or *faculty of such language,* Mk 16:17; 1 Co 14:13, 14, 26, et al.; from Hebrew, *a nation,* as defined by its language, Rev 5:9, et al.; let. *a tongue-shaped flale,* Ac 2:3 [1100]

[1186] γλωσσόκομον *glōssokomon* 2x pr. *a box for keeping the tongues, mouthpieces,* or *reeds* of musical instruments; hence, genr. *any box* or *receptacle;* in N.T. *a purse, money-bag,* Jn 12:6; 13:29* [1101]

[1187] γναφεύς *gnapheus* 1x *a fuller, a bleacher,* Mk 9:3* [1102]

[1188] γνήσιος *gnēsios* 4x *lawful, legitimate,* as children; *genuine,* in faith, etc.; 1 Ti 1:2; Tit 1:4; *true, sincere,* 2 Co 8:8; Phil 4:3* [1103]

[1189] γνησίως *gnēsiōs* 1x *genuinely, sincerely,* Phil 2:20* [1104]

[1190] γνόφος *gnophos* 1x *a thick cloud, darkness,* Heb 12:18* [1105]

[1191] γνώμη *gnōmē* 9x *the mind,* as the means of knowing and judging; *assent,* Phlm 14; *purpose, resolution,* Ac 20:3; *opinion, judgment,* 1 Co 1:10; 7:40; *suggestion, suggested advice,* as distinguished from positive injunction, 1 Co 7:25; 2 Co 8:10; Ac 20:3 [1106]

[1192] γνωρίζω *gnōrizō* 25x *to make known, reveal, declare,* Jn 15:15; 17:26, et al.; *to know,* Phil 1:22 [1107]

[1194] γνῶσις *gnōsis* 29x *knowledge,* Lk 1:77; *knowledge* of an especial kind and relatively high character, Lk 11:52; Ro 2:20; 1 Ti 6:20; more particularly in respect of Christian enlightenment, Ro 15:14; 1 Co 8:10; 12:8; 2 Co 11:6, et al. [1108]

[1195] γνώστης *gnōstēs* 1x *one acquainted with* a thing, *knowing, skilful,* Ac 26:3* [1109]

[1196] γνωστός *gnōstos* 15x *known,* Jn 18:15, 16, et al.; *certain, incontrovertible,* Ac 4:16; τὸ γνωστόν, *that which is known* or *is cognizable, the unquestionable* *attributes,* Ro 1:19; subst. *an acquaintance,* Lk 2:44; 23:49 [1110]

[1197] γογγύζω *gongyzō* 8x *to speak privately and in a low voice, mutter,* Jn 7:32; *to utter secret and sullen discontent, express indignant complaint, murmur, grumble,* Mt 20:11; Lk 5:30; Jn 6:41, 43, 61; 1 Co 10:10★ [1111]

[1198] γογγυσμός *gongysmos* 4x *a muttering, murmuring, low and suppressed discourse,* Jn 7:12; *the expression of secret and sullen discontent, murmuring, complaint,* Ac 6:1; Phil 2:14; 1 Pe 4:9★ [1112]

[1199] γογγυστής *gongystēs* 1x *a murmurer, grumbler,* Jude 16★ [1113]

[1200] γόης *goēs* 1x *a juggler, diviner;* hence, by impl. *an impostor, cheat,* 2 Ti 3:13★ [1114]

[1201] Γολγοθᾶ *Golgotha* 3x *Golgotha,* pr. name, Mt 27:33; Mk 15:22; Jn 19:17★ [1115]

[1202] Γόμορρα *Gomorra* 4x *Gomorrha* (Genesis 19), pr. name, Mt 10:15; Ro 9:29; 2 Pe 2:6; Jude 7★ [1116]

[1203] γόμος *gomos* 3x *the cargo* of a ship, Ac 21:3; by impl. *merchandise,* Rev 18:11, 12★ [1117]

[1204] γονεύς *goneus* 20x *a father;* pl. in N.T. *parents,* Mt 10:21; Lk 2:27, 41; 2 Co 12:14 [1118]

[1205] γόνυ *gony* 12x *the knee,* Lk 22:41; Heb 12:12, et al. [1119]

[1206] γονυπετέω *gonypeteō* 4x *to fall upon one's knees, to kneel before,* Mt 17:14; 27:29; Mk 1:40; 10:17★ [1120]

[1207] γράμμα *gramma* 14x pr. *that which is written* or *drawn; a letter, character of the alphabet, a writing, book,* Jn 5:47; *an acknowledgment of debt, an account, a bill, note,* Lk 16:6, 7; *an epistle, letter,* Ac 28:21; Gal 6:11; ἱερὰ γράμματα, *the sacred books of the Old Testament, the Jewish Scriptures,* 2 Ti 3:15; spc. *the letter* of the law of Moses, *the bare literal sense,* Ro 2:27, 29; 7:6; 2 Co 3:6, 7; pl. *letters, learning,* Jn 7:15; Ac 26:24★ [1121]

[1208] γραμματεύς *grammateus* 63x *a scribe; a clerk, town-clerk, registrar, recorder,* Ac 19:35; *one skilled in the Jewish law, a teacher* or *interpreter of the law,* Mt 2:4; 5:20, et al. freq.; genr. *a religious teacher,* Mt 13:52; by synec. *any one distinguished for learning* or *wisdom,* 1 Co 1:20 [1122]

[1209] γραπτός *graptos* 1x *written,* Ro 2:15★ [1123]

[1210] γραφή *graphē* 50x *a writing;* in N.T. *the Holy Scriptures, the Jewish Scrip-tures,* or *Books of the Old Testament,* Mt 21:42; Jn 5:39, et al.; by synec. *doctrines, declarations, oracles,* or *promises* contained in the sacred books, Mt 22:29; Mk 12:24, et al.; spc. *a prophecy,* Mt 26:54; Mk 14:49; Lk 4:21; 24:27, 32; with the addition of προφητική, Ro 16:26; of τῶν προφητῶν, Mt 26:56 [1124]

[1211] γράφω *graphō* 191x *to engrave, write,* according to the ancient method of writing on plates of metal, waxes tables, etc., Jn 8:6, 8; *to write* on parchment, paper, etc., generally, Mt 27:37, et al.; *to write letters to another,* Ac 23:25; 2 Co 2:9; 13:10, et al.; *to describe in writing,* Jn 1:46; Ro 10:5; *to inscribe* in a catalogue, etc., Lk 10:20; Rev 13:8; 17:8, et al.; *to write a law, command,* or *enact in writing,* Mk 10:5; 12:19; Lk 2:23, et al. [1125]

[1212] γραώδης *graōdēs* 1x *old-woman-ish;* by impl. *silly, absurd,* 1 Ti 4:7★ [1126]

[1213] γρηγορέω *grēgoreō* 22x *to be awake, to watch,* Mt 26:38, 40, 41; Mk 14:34; 37, 38; *to be alive,* 1 Th 5:10; met. *to be watchful, attentive, vigilant, circumspect,* Mt 25:13; Mk 13:35, et al. [1127]

[1214] γυμνάζω *gymnazō* 4x pr. *to train in gymnastic discipline;* hence, *to exercise* in anything, *train to use, discipline,* 1 Ti 4:7; Heb 5:14; 12:11; 2 Pe 2:14★ [1128]

[1215] γυμνασία *gymnasia* 1x pr. *gymnastic exercise;* hence, *bodily discipline* of any kind, 1 Ti 4:8★ [1129]

[1217] γυμνιτεύω *gymniteuō* 1x *to be poorly clad,* 1 Co 4:11★ [1130]

[1218] γυμνός *gymnos* 15x *naked, without clothing,* Mk 14:51, 52; *without the upper garment, and clad only with an inner garment* or *tunic,* Jn 21:7; *poorly* or *meanly clad, destitute of proper and sufficient clothing,* Mt 25:36, 38, 43, 44; Ac 19:16; Jas 2:15; met. *unclothed* with a body, 2 Co 5:3; *not covered, uncovered, open, manifest,* Heb 4:13; *bare, mere,* 1 Co 15:37; *naked* of spiritual *clothing,* Rev 3:17; 16:15; 17:16 [1131]

[1219] γυμνότης *gymnotēs* 3x *nakedness; want of proper and sufficient clothing,* Ro 8:35; 2 Co 11:27; spiritual *nakedness, being destitute of* spiritual *clothing,* Rev 3:18★ [1132]

[1220] γυναικάριον *gynaikarion* 1x *a little woman; a trifling, weak, silly woman,* 2 Ti 3:6★ [1133]

[1221] γυναικεῖος *gynaikeios* 1x *pertaining to women, female,* 1 Pe 3:7★ [1134]

[1222] γυνή *gynē* 215x *a woman,* Mt 5:28, et al.; *a married woman, wife,* Mt 5:31, 32; 14:3, et al.; in the voc. ὦ γύναι, *O woman!* an ordinary mode of addressing females under every circumstance; met. used of the Church, as united to Christ, Rev 19:7; 21:9 [1135]

[1223] Γώγ *Gōg* 1x *Gog,* pr. name of a nation, indecl., Rev 20:8★ [1136]

[1224] γωνία *gōnia* 9x *an* exterior *angle, projecting corner,* Mt 6:5; 21:42; *an* interior *angle;* by impl. *a dark corner, obscure place,* Ac 26:26; *corner, extremity,* or *quarter* of the earth, Rev 7:1; 20:8 [1137]

[1227] δαιμονίζομαι *daimonizomai* 13x in N.T. *to be possessed, afflicted, vexed,* by a *demon* or *evil spirit,* i.q. δαιμόνιον ἔχειν, Mt 4:24; 8:16, 28, 33 [1139]

[1228] δαιμόνιον *daimonion* 63x *a* heathen *god, deity,* Ac 17:18; 1 Co 10:20, 21; Rev 9:20; in N.T., *a demon, evil spirit,* Mt 7:22; 9:33, 34; 10:8; 12:24 [1140]

[1229] δαιμονιώδης *daimoniōdēs* 1x *pertaining to* or *proceeding from demons; demonic, devilish,* Jas 3:15★ [1141]

[1230] δαίμων *daimōn* 1x *a god, a superior power;* in N.T. *a malignant demon, evil angel,* Mt 8:31★ [1142]

[1231] δάκνω *daknō* 1x *to bite, sting;* met. *to molest, vex, injure,* Gal 5:15★ [1143]

[1232] δάκρυον *dakryon* 10x also spelled δάκρυ, *a tear* [1144]

[1233] δακρύω *dakryō* 1x *to shed tears, weep,* Jn 11:35★ [1145]

[1234] δακτύλιος *daktylios* 1x *a ring for the finger,* Lk 15:22★ [1146]

[1235] δάκτυλος *daktylos* 8x *a finger,* Mt 23:4; Mk 7:33; from Hebrew, *power,* Lk 11:20 [1147]

[1236] Δαλμανουθά *Dalmanoutha* 1x *Dalmanutha,* indecl., a small town on the shore of the Sea of Tiberias, Mk 8:10★ [1148]

[1237] Δαλματία *Dalmatia* 1x *Dalmatia,* 2 Ti 4:10★ [1149]

[1238] δαμάζω *damazō* 4x also spelled δανείζω, *to subdue, tame,* Mk 5:4; Jas 3:7; met. *to restrain within proper limits,* Jas 3:8★ [1150]

[1239] δάμαλις *damalis* 1x *a heifer, young cow,* Heb 9:13★ [1151]

[1240] Δάμαρις *Damaris* 1x *Damaris,* pr. name, Ac 17:34★ [1152]

[1241] Δαμασκηνός *Damaskēnos* 1x *A Damascene, a native of Damascus,* 2 Co 11:32★ [1153]

[1242] Δαμασκός *Damaskos* 15x *Damascus*, the capital city of Syria [1154]

[1244] δανείζω *daneizō* 4x see δανίζω [1155]

[1245] δάνειον *daneion* 1x *a loan, debt*, Mt 18:27* [1156]

[1248] Δανιήλ *Daniēl* 1x *Daniel*, pr. name, indecl., Mt 24:15* [1158]

[1250] δανιστής *danistēs* 1x *a money-lender, creditor*, Lk 7:41* [1157]

[1251] δαπανάω *dapanaō* 5x *to expend, be at expense*, Mk 5:26; Ac 21:24; 2 Co 12:15; *to spend, waste, consume by extravagance*, Lk 15:14; Jas 4:3* [1159]

[1252] δαπάνη *dapanē* 1x *expense, cost*, Lk 14:28* [1160]

[1253] Δαυίδ *Dauid* 59x also spelled Δανείδ and Δαβίδ, *David*, pr. name, indecl., Mt 1:6; Lk 1:27; Ac 2:29; Ro 1:3; 2 Ti 2:28 [1138]

[1254] δέ *de* 2,792x a conjunctive particle, marking the superaddition of a clause, whether in opposition or in continuation, to what has preceded, and it may be variously rendered *but, on the other hand, and, also, now*, etc.; καὶ δέ, when there is a special superaddition in continuation, *too, yea*, etc. It sometimes is found at the commencement of the apodosis of a sentence, Ac 11:17. It serves also to mark the resumption of an interrupted discourse, 2 Co 2:10; Gal 2:6 [1161]

[1255] δέησις *deēsis* 18x *entreaty; prayer, supplication*, Lk 1:13; 2:37; 5:33 [1162]

[1256] δεῖ *dei* 101x *it is binding, it is necessary, it is proper; it is inevitable*, Ac 21:22 [1163]

[1257] δεῖγμα *deigma* 1x pr. *that which is shown, a specimen, sample;* met. *an example* by way of warning, Jude 7* [1164]

[1258] δειγματίζω *deigmatizō* 2x *to make a public show* or *spectacle of*, Mt 1:19; Col 2:15* [1165]

[1259] δείκνυμι *deiknymi* 30x also formed δεικνύω 3x, *to show, point out, present to the sight*, Mt 4:8; 8:4; *to exhibit, permit to see, cause to be seen*, Jn 2:18; 10:32; 1 Ti 6:15; *to demonstrate, prove*, Jas 2:18; 3:13; met. *to teach, make known, declare, announce*, Mt 16:21; Jn 5:20; Ac 10:28 [1166]

[1260] δεικνύω *deiknyō* 3x see δείκνυμι, Mt 16:21; Jn 2:18; Rev 22:8* [**]

[1261] δειλία *deilia* 1x *timidity*, 2 Ti 1:7* [1167]

[1262] δειλιάω *deiliaō* 1x *to be timid, be in fear*, Jn 14:27* [1168]

[1264] δειλός *deilos* 3x *timid, fearful, cowardly*, Mt 8:26; Mk 4:40; Rev 21:8* [1169]

[1265] δεῖνα *deina* 1x *such a one, a certain one*, Mt 26:18* [1170]

[1267] δεινῶς *deinōs* 2x *dreadfully, grievously, greatly, terribly*, Mt 8:6; Lk 11:53* [1171]

[1268] δειπνέω *deipneō* 4x *to eat* or *dine*, Lk 17:8; 22:20; 1 Co 11:25; Rev 3:20 [1172]

[1270] δεῖπνον *deipnon* 16x pr. *a meal; supper, the principal meal taken in the evening*, Lk 14:12; Jn 13:2, 4; meton. *food*, 1 Co 11:21; *a feast, banquet*, Mt 23:6; Mk 6:21; 12:39 [1173]

[1272] δεισιδαιμονία *deisidaimonia* 1x *fear of the gods;* in a bad sense, *superstition; a form of religious belief*, Ac 25:19* [1175]

[1273] δεισιδαίμων *deisidaimōn* 1x *reverencing the gods and divine things, religious;* in a bad sense, *superstitious;* in N.T. *careful and precise in the discharge of religious services*, Ac 17:22* [1174]

[1274] δέκα *deka* 25x *ten*, Mt 20:24; 25:1; ἡμερῶν δέκα, *ten days, a few days, a short time*, Rev 2:10 [1176]

[1277] δεκαοκτώ *dekaoktō* 2x *eighteen*, Lk 13:4, 11* [1176 + 2532 + 3638]

[1278] δεκαπέντε *dekapente* 3x *fifteen*, indecl., Jn 11:18; Ac 27:28; Gal 1:18* [1178]

[1279] Δεκάπολις *Dekapolis* 3x *Decapolis*, a district of Palestine beyond Jordan, Mk 5:20; 7:31; Mt 4:25* [1179]

[1280] δεκατέσσαρες *dekatessares* 5x *fourteen*, Mt 1:17; 2 Co 12:2; Gal 2:1* [1180]

[1281] δέκατος *dekatos* 7x *tenth*, Jn 1:39; Rev 11:13; 21:20; δεκάτη, sc. μερίς, *a tenth part, tithe*, Heb 7:2, 4, 8, 9* [1181, 1182]

[1282] δεκατόω *dekatoō* 2x *to cause to pay tithes;* pass. *to be tithed, pay tithes*, Heb 7:6, 9* [1183]

[1283] δεκτός *dektos* 5x *accepted, acceptable, agreeable, approved*, Lk 4:24; Ac 10:35; Phil 4:18; by impl. when used of a certain time, *marked by* divine *acceptance, propitious*, Lk 4:19; 2 Co 6:2* [1184]

[1284] δελεάζω *deleazō* 3x pr. *to entrap, take* or *catch* with a bait; met. *allure, entice*, Jas 1:14; 2 Pe 2:14, 18* [1185]

[1285] δένδρον *dendron* 25x *a tree*, Mt 3:10; 7:17; 13:32 [1186]

[1287] δεξιολάβος *dexiolabos* 1x *one posted on the right hand; a flank guard; a light armed spearman*, Ac 23:23* [1187]

[1288] δεξιός *dexios* 54x *right*, as opposed to left, Mt 5:29, 30; Lk 6:6; ἡ δεξιά, sc. χείρ, *the right hand*, Mt 6:3; 27:29; τὰ δεξιά, sc. μέρη, *the parts towards the right hand, the right hand side;* καθίζειν, or, καθῆσθαι, or, ἑστάναι, ἐκ δεξιῶν [μερῶν] τινος, *to sit* or *stand at the right hand of any one*, as a mark of the highest honor and dignity which he can bestow, Mt 20:20; 26:64; εἶνι ἐκ δεξιῶν [μερῶν] τινος, *to be at one's right hand*, as a helper, Ac 2:25; δεξιὰς (χεῖρας) διδόναι, *to give the right hand* to any one, as a pledge of sincerity in one's promises, Gal 2:9 [1188]

[1289] δέομαι *deomai* 22x *to be in want, to need; to ask, request*, Mt 9:38; Lk 5:12; 8:28, 38; in N.T. absol. *to pray, offer prayer, beseech, supplicate*, Lk 21:36; 22:32; Ac 4:31; 8:22, 24 [1189]

[1290] δέος *deos* 1x *fear*, Heb 12:28* [127]

[1291] Δερβαῖος *Derbaios* 1x *an inhabitant of Derbe*, Ac 20:4* [1190]

[1292] Δέρβη *Derbē* 3x *Derbe*, a city of Lycaonia, Ac 14:6, 20; 16:0* [1191]

[1293] δέρμα *derma* 1x *the skin* of an animal, Heb 11:37* [1192]

[1294] δερμάτινος *dermatinos* 2x *made of skin, leathern*, Mt 3:4; Mk 1:6* [1193]

[1296] δέρω *derō* 15x *to skin, flay;* hence, *to eat, scourge, beat*, Mt 21:35; Mk 12:3, 5; 13:9 [1194]

[1297] δεσμεύω *desmeuō* 3x *to bind, bind up*, as a bundle, Mt 23:4; *to bind, confine*, Lk 8:29; Ac 22:4* [1195]

[1299] δέσμη *desmē* 1x *a bundle*, as of tares, Mt 13:30* [1197]

[1300] δέσμιος *desmios* 16x *one bound, a prisoner*, Mt 27:15, 16; Mk 15:6 [1198]

[1301] δεσμός *desmos* 18x *a bond, anything by which one is bound, a cord, chain, fetters*, etc.; and by meton. *imprisonment*, Lk 8:29; Ac 16:26; 20:23; *a string* or *ligament*, as of the tongue, Mk 7:35; met. *an impediment, infirmity*, Lk 13:16 [1199]

[1302] δεσμοφύλαξ *desmophylax* 3x *a keeper of a prison, jailer,* Ac 16:23, 27, 36* [1200]

[1303] δεσμωτήριον *desmōtērion* 4x *a prison,* Mt 11:2; Ac 5:21, 23; 16:26* [1201]

[1304] δεσμώτης *desmōtēs* 2x *a prisoner,* i.q. δέσμιος, Ac 27:1, 42* [1202]

[1305] δεσπότης *despotēs* 10x *a lord, master,* especially of slaves, 1 Ti 6:1, 2; 2 Ti 2:21; Tit 2:9; 1 Pet 2:18; by impl. as denoting the possession of supreme authority, *Lord, sovereign,* used of God, Lk 2:29; Ac 4:24; Rev 6:10; and of Christ, 2 Pe 2:1; Jude 4 [1203]

[1306] δεῦρο *deuro* 9x *here;* used also as a sort of imperative, *come, Come here!* Mt 19:21; Mk 10:21; used of time, ἄχρι τοῦ δεῦρο, sc. χρόνου, *to the present time,* Ro 1:13 [1204]

[1307] δεῦτε *deute* 12x *come,* Mt 4:19; 01:28; as a particle of exhortation, incitement, etc., and followed by an imperative, *come now,* etc., Mt 21.38, 28:6 [1205]

[1308] δευτεραῖος *deuteraios* 1x *on the second day* of a certain state or process, and used as an epithet of the subject or agent, Ac 28:13* [1206]

[1311] δεύτερος *deuteros* 43x *second,* Mt 22:26; τὸ δεύτερον, *again, the second time, another time,* Jude 5; so ἐκ δευτέρου, Mt 26:42; and ἐν τῷ δευτέρῳ, Ac 7:13 [1208]

[1312] δέχομαι *dechomai* 56x *to take into one's hands,* etc., Lk 2:28; 16:6, 7; *to receive,* Ac 22:5; 28:21; Phil 4:18; *to receive into and retain, contain,* Ac 3:21; met. *to receive* by the hearing, *learn, acquire a knowledge of,* 2 Co 11:4; Jas 1:21; *to receive, admit, grant access to, receive kindly, welcome,* Mt 10:40, 41; 18:5; *to receive* in hospitality, *entertain,* Lk 9:53; Heb 11:31; *to bear with, bear patiently,* 2 Co 11:16; met. *to receive, approve, assent to,* Mt 11:14; Lk 8:13; Ac 8:14; 11:1; *to admit,* and by impl. *to embrace, follow,* 1 Co 2:14; 2 Co 8:17 [1209]

[1313] δέω *deō* 43x *to bind, tie,* Mt 13:30; 21:2; *to bind, confine,* Mt 27:2; 14:3; *to impede, hinder,* 2 Ti 2:9; *to bind* with infirmity, Lk 13:16; *to bind* by a legal or moral tie, as marriage, Ro 7:2; 1 Co 7:27, 39; by impl. *to impel, compel,* Ac 20:22; in N.T. *to pronounce* or *declare to be binding* or *obligatory,* or, *to declare to be prohibited and unlawful,* Mt 16:19; 18:18 [1210]

[1314] δή *dē* 5x a particle that adds an intensity of expression to a term or clause. Its simplest and most ordinary uses are when it gives impressiveness to an affirmation, *indeed, really, doubtless,* Mt 13:23; or earnestness to a call, injunction, or entreaty, Lk 2:15; Ac 13:2; 15:36; 1 Co 16:20* [1211]

[1316] δῆλος *dēlos* 3x pr. *clearly visible; plain, manifest, evident,* Mt 26:73; 1 Co 15:27; Gal 3:11* [1212]

[1317] δηλόω *dēloō* 7x *to render manifest* or *evident; to make known, to tell, relate, declare,* 1 Co 1:11; Col 1:8; *to show, point out, bring to light,* 1 Co 3:13; *to indicate, signify,* Heb 9:8; 12:27; 1 Pe 1:11 [1213]

[1318] Δημᾶς *Dēmas* 3x *Demas,* pr. name, Col 4:14; 2 Ti 4:10; Phlm 24* [1214]

[1319] δημηγορέω *dēmēgoreō* 1x *to address a public assembly, to deliver a public oration,* Ac 12:21* [1215]

[1320] Δημήτριος *Dēmētrios* 3x *Demetrius,* pr. name (1) *The Ephesian silversmith,* Ac 19:24, 38 (2) *A certain Christian,* 3 Jn 12* [1216]

[1321] δημιουργός *dēmiourgos* 1x pr. *one who labors for the public,* or, *exercises some public calling; an architect,* especially, the Divine *Architect* of the universe, Heb 11:10 [1217]

[1322] δῆμος *dēmos* 4x *the people,* Ac 12:22; 17:5; 19:30, 33* [1218]

[1323] δημόσιος *dēmosios* 4x *public, belonging to the public,* Ac 5:18; δημοσίᾳ, *publicly,* Ac 16:37; 18:28; 20:20* [1219]

[1324] δηνάριον *dēnarion* 16x Latin *denarius,* a Roman silver coin; the name originally meant *ten asses,* Mt 18:28; Mk 6:37; Rev 6:6 [1220]

[1327] δήπου *dēpou* 1x *now in some way, surely,* Heb 2:16* [1222]

[1328] διά *dia* 667x (1) gen., *through,* used of place or medium, Mt 7:13; Lk 6:1; 2 Co 11:33; *through,* of time, *during, in the course of,* Heb 2:15; Ac 5:19; *through,* of immediate agency, causation, instrumentality, *by means of, by,* Jn 1:3; Ac 3:18; of means or manner, *through, by, with,* Lk 8:4; 2 Co 5:7; 8:8; of state or condition, *in a state of,* Ro 4:11; (2) acc., used of causation which is not direct and immediate in the production of a result, *on account of, because of, for the sake of, with a view to,* Mk 2:27; Jn 1:31; rarely, *through, while subject to* a state of untoward circumstances, Gal 4:13 [1223]

[1329] διαβαίνω *diabainō* 3x *to pass through* or *over,* Lk 16:26; Ac 16:9; Heb 11:29* [1224]

[1330] διαβάλλω *diaballō* 1x *to throw* or *convey through* or *over; to thrust through; to defame, inform against,* Lk 16:1* [1225]

[1331] διαβεβαιόομαι *diabebaioomai* 2x *to assert strongly, insist,* 1 Ti 1:7; Tit 3:8* [1226]

[1332] διαβλέπω *diablepō* 3x *to look through; to view steadily,* Mk 8:25; *to see clearly* or *steadily,* Mt 7:5; Lk 6:42* [1227]

[1333] διάβολος *diabolos* 37x *slanderer,* 1 Ti 3:11; 2 Ti 3:3; Tit 2:3; *a treacherous informer, traitor,* Jn 6:70; ὁ διάβολος, *the devil* [1228]

[1334] διαγγέλλω *diangellō* 3x *to publish abroad,* Lk 9:60; Ro 9:17; *to certify* to the public, Ac 21:26* [1229]

[1335] διαγίνομαι *diaginomai* 3x pas., *to continue through; to intervene, elapse* of time, Mk 16:1; Ac 25:13; 27:9* [1230]

[1336] διαγινώσκω *diaginōskō* 2x pr. *to distinguish; to resolve determinately; to examine, inquire into,* judicially, Ac 23:15; 24:22* [1231]

[1338] διάγνωσις *diagnōsis* 1x pr. *an act of distinguishing* or *discernment; a determination; examination* judicially, *hearing, trial,* Ac 25:21* [1233]

[1339] διαγογγύζω *diagongyzō* 2x *to murmur, mutter,* Lk 15:2; 19:7* [1234]

[1340] διαγρηγορέω *diagrēgoreō* 1x *to remain awake; to wake thoroughly,* Lk 9:32* [1235]

[1341] διάγω *diagō* 2x *to conduct* or *carry through* or *over; to pass* or *spend* time, *live,* 1 Ti 2:2; Tit 3:3* [1236]

[1342] διαδέχομαι *diadechomai* 1x *to receive by transmission; to receive in return,* Ac 7:45* [1237]

[1343] διάδημα *diadēma* 3x pr. *a band* or *fillet; a diadem,* the badge of a sovereign, Rev 12:3; 13:1; 19:12* [1238]

[1344] διαδίδωμι *diadidōmi* 4x *to deliver from hand to hand; to distribute, divide,* Lk 11:22; 18:22; Jn 6:11; Ac 4:35* [1239]

[1345] διάδοχος *diadochos* 1x *a successor,* Ac 24:27* [1240]

[1346] διαζώννυμι *diazōnnymi* 3x *to gird firmly round,* Jn 13:4, 5; mid. *to gird round one's self,* Jn 21:7* [1241]

[1347] διαθήκη *diathēkē* 33x *a testamentary disposition, will; a covenant,* Heb 9:16, 17; Gal 3:15; in N.T., *a covenant of God with men,* Gal 3:17; 4:24; Heb 9:4; Mt 26:28; *the writings of the old covenant,* 2 Co 3:14 [1242]

[1348] διαίρεσις *diairesis* 3x *a division; a distinction, difference, diversity,* 1 Co 12:4, 5, 6* [1243]

[1349] διαιρέω *diaireō* 2x *to divide, to divide out, distribute,* Lk 15:12; 1 Co 12:11* [1244]

[1350] διακαθαίρω *diakathairō* 1x *to cleanse thoroughly,* Lk 3:17* [1245]

[1351] διακαθαρίζω *diakatharizō* 1x *to cleanse thoroughly,* Mt 3:12 [1245]

[1352] διακατελέγχομαι *diakatelenchomai* 1x *to maintain discussion strenuously and thoroughly, to totally refute,* Ac 18:28* [1246]

[1354] διακονέω *diakoneō* 37x *to wait, attend upon, serve,* Mt 8:15; Mk 1:31; Lk 4:39; *to be an attendant* or *assistant,* Ac 19:22; *to minister to, relieve, assist,* or *supply with the necessaries of life, provide the means of living,* Mt 4:11; 27:55; Mk 1:13; 15:41; Lk 8:3; *to fill the office of* διάκονος, *deacon, perform the duties of deacon,* 1 Ti 3:10, 13; 1 Pe 4:11; *to convey in charge, administer,* 2 Co 3:3; 8:19, 20; 1 Pe 1:12; 4:10; pass. *to receive service,* Mt 20:28; Mk 10:45 [1247]

[1355] διακονία *diakonia* 34x *serving, service, waiting, attendance, the act of rendering friendly offices,* Lk 10:40; 2 Ti 4:11; Heb 1:14; *relief, aid,* Ac 6:1; 11:29; 2 Co 8:4; 9:1, 12, 13; *a commission,* Ac 12:25; Ro 15:31; *a commission* or *ministry* in the service of the Gospel, Ac 1:17, 25; 20:24; Ro 11:13; 2 Co 4:1; 5:18; 1 Ti 1:12; *service* in the Gospel, Ac 6:4; 21:19; 1 Co 16:15; 2 Co 6:3; 11:8; Eph 4:12; Rev 2:19; *a function, ministry,* or *office* in the Church, Ro 12:7; 1 Co 12:5; Col 4:17; 2 Ti 4:5; *a ministering in the conveyance of a revelation from God,* 2 Co 3:7, 8, 9 [1248]

[1356] διάκονος *diakonos* 29x *one who renders service* to another; *an attendant, servant,* Mt 20:26; 22:13; Jn 2:5, 9; *one who executes a commission, a deputy,* Ro 13:4; Χριστοῦ, Θεοῦ, ἐν κυρίῳ, etc. *a* commissioned *minister* or *preacher* of the Gospel, 1 Co 3:5; 2 Co 6:4; *a minister* charged with an announcement or sentence, 2 Co 3:6; Gal 2:17; Col 1:23; *a minister* charged with a significant characteristic, Ro 15:8; *a servitor, devoted follower,* Jn 12:26; *a deacon* or *deaconess,*
whose official duty was to superintend the alms of the Church, with other kindred services, Ro 16:1; Phil 1:1; 1 Ti 3:8, 12 [1249]

[1357] διακόσιοι *diakosioi* 8x *two hundred,* Mk 6:37; Jn 6:7; 21:8; Ac 23:23f.* [1250]

[1358] διακούω *diakouō* 1x *to hear* a thing *through; to hear* judicially, Ac 23:35* [1251]

[1359] διακρίνω *diakrinō* 19x *to separate, sever; to make a distinction* or *difference,* Ac 15:9; 1 Co 11:29; *to make to differ, distinguish, prefer, confer a superiority,* 1 Co 4:7; *to examine, scrutinize, estimate,* 1 Co 11:31; 14:29; *to discern, discriminate,* Mt 16:3; *to judge, to decide a cause,* 1 Co 6:5; *to dispute, contend,* Ac 11:2; Jude 9; *to make a distinction* mentally, Jas 2:4; Jude 22; in N.T. *to hesitate, be in doubt, doubt,* Mt 21:21; Mk 11:23 [1252]

[1360] διάκρισις *diakrisis* 3x *a separation; a distinction,* or, *doubt,* Ro 14:1; *a discerning, the act of discerning* or *distinguishing,* Heb 5:14; *the faculty of distinguishing and estimating,* 1 Co 12:10* [1253]

[1361] διακωλύω *diakōlyō* 1x *to hinder, restrain, prohibit,* Mt 3:14* [1254]

[1362] διαλαλέω *dialaleō* 2x *to talk with;* by impl. *to consult, deliberate,* Lk 6:11; *to divulge, publish, spread by rumor,* Lk 1:65* [1255]

[1363] διαλέγομαι *dialegomai* 13x *to discourse, argue, reason,* Ac 17:2, 17; 24:12; *to address, speak to,* Heb 12:5; *to contend, dispute,* Mk 9:34; Jude 9 [1256]

[1364] διαλείπω *dialeipō* 1x *to leave an interval; to intermit, cease,* Lk 7:45* [1257]

[1365] διάλεκτος *dialektos* 6x *speech; manner of speaking; peculiar language* of a nation, *dialect, vernacular idiom,* Ac 1:19; 2:6, 8; 21:40; 22:2; 26:14 [1258]

[1367] διαλλάσσομαι *diallassomai* 1x *to be reconciled* to another, Mt 5:24* [1259]

[1368] διαλογίζομαι *dialogizomai* 16x pr. *to make a settlement of accounts; to reason, deliberate, ponder, consider,* Mt 16:7, 8; Mk 2:6, 8; Jn 11:50; *to dispute, contend,* Mk 9:33 [1260]

[1369] διαλογισμός *dialogismos* 14x *reasoning, thought, cogitation, purpose,* Mt 15:19; Mk 7:21; *discourse, dispute, disputation, contention,* Lk 9:46; *doubt, hesitation, scruple,* Lk 24:38 [1261]

[1370] διαλύω *dialyō* 1x *to dissolve, dissipate, disperse,* Ac 5:36* [1262]

[1371] διαμαρτύρομαι *diamartyromai* 15x *to make solemn affirmation, protest; to make a solemn and earnest charge,* Lk 16:28; Ac 2:40; *to declare solemnly and earnestly,* Ac 8:25; 18:5 [1263]

[1372] διαμάχομαι *diamachomai* 1x *to fight out, to fight resolutely;* met. *to contend vehemently, insist,* Ac 23:9* [1264]

[1373] διαμένω *diamenō* 5x *to continue throughout; to continue, be permanent* or *unchanged,* Lk 1:22; Gal 2:5; Heb 1:11; 2 Pe 3:4; *to continue, remain constant,* Lk 22:28 [1265]

[1374] διαμερίζω *diamerizō* 11x *to divide into parts and distribute,* Mt 27:35; Mk 15:24; Ac 2:3; pass. in N.T. *to be in a state of dissension,* Lk 11:17, 18; 12:52, 53 [1266]

[1375] διαμερισμός *diamerismos* 1x *division;* met. in N.T. *disunion, dissension,* Lk 12:51* [1267]

[1376] διανέμω *dianemō* 1x *to distribute; to divulge, spread abroad,* Ac 4:17* [1268]

[1377] διανεύω *dianeuō* 1x *to signify by a nod, beckon, make signs,* Lk 1:22* [1269]

[1378] διανόημα *dianoēma* 1x *thought,* Lk 11:17* [1270]

[1379] διάνοια *dianoia* 12x pr. *thought, intention; the mind, intellect, understanding,* Mt 22:37; Mk 12:30; Lk 10:27; *an operation of the understanding, thought, imagination,* Lk 1:51; *insight, comprehension,* 1 Jn 5:20; *mode of thinking and feeling, disposition of mind and heart, the affection,* Eph 2:3; Col 1:21 [1271]

[1380] διανοίγω *dianoigō* 8x *to open,* Mk 7:34, 35; Lk 2:23; 24:31; Ac 7:56; met. *to open* the sense of a thing, *explain, expound,* Lk 24:32; Ac 17:3; διανοίγειν τὸν νοῦν, τὴν καρδίαν, *to open the mind, the heart,* so as to understand and receive, Lk 24:45; Ac 16:14* [1272]

[1381] διανυκτερεύω *dianyktereuō* 1x *to pass the night, spend the whole night,* Lk 6:12* [1273]

[1382] διανύω *dianyō* 1x *to complete, finish,* Ac 21:7* [1274]

[1384] διαπαρατριβή *diaparatribē* 1x *constant disputation,* 1 Ti 6:5* [3859]

[1385] διαπεράω *diaperaō* 6x *to pass through* or *over,* Mt 9:1; 14:34; Mk 5:21; 6:53; Lk 16:26; Ac 21:2* [1276]

[1386] διαπλέω *diapleō* 1x *to sail through* or *over,* Ac 27:5* [1277]

[1387] διαπονέομαι *diaponeomai* 2x pr. *to be thoroughly exercised with labor; to be wearied; to be vexed*, Ac 4:2; 16:18* [1278]

[1388] διαπορεύομαι *diaporeuomai* 5x *to go* or *pass through*, Lk 6:1; 13:22; Ac 16:4; *to pass by*, Lk 18:36 [1279]

[1389] διαπορέω *diaporeō* 4x *to be utterly at a loss; to be in doubt and perplexity*, Lk 9:7; Ac 2:12; 5:24; 10:17 [1280]

[1390] διαπραγματεύομαι *diapragmateuomai* 1x *to despatch a matter thoroughly; to make profit in business, gain in trade*, Lk 19:15* [1281]

[1391] διαπρίω *diapriō* 2x *to divide with a saw, saw asunder; to grate* the teeth in a rage; pass. met. *to be cut* to the heart, *to be enraged*, Ac 5:33; 7:54* [1282]

[1395] διαρπάζω *diarpazō* 3x *to plunder, spoil, pillage*, Mt 12:29; Mk 3:27 (2t)* [1283]

[1397] διασαφέω *diasapheō* 2x *to make known, declare, tell plainly*, or *fully*, Mt 13:36; 18:31* [1285]

[1398] διασείω *diaseiō* 1x pr. *to shake thoroughly* or *violently; to harass, intimidate, extort from*, Lk 3:14* [1286]

[1399] διασκορπίζω *diaskorpizō* 9x *to disperse, scatter*, Mt 26:31; Mk 14:27; *to dissipate, waste*, Lk 15:13; 16:1; *to winnow*, or, *to strew*, Mt 25:24, 26 [1287]

[1400] διασπάω *diaspaō* 2x *to pull* or *tear asunder* or *in pieces, burst*, Mk 5:4; Ac 23:10* [1288]

[1401] διασπείρω *diaspeirō* 3x *to scatter abroad* or *in every direction*, as seen; *to disperse*, Ac 8:1, 4; 11:19* [1289]

[1402] διασπορά *diaspora* 3x pr. *a scattering*, as of seed; *dispersion*; in N.T. meton. *the dispersed portion* of the Jews, specially termed *the dispersion*, Jn 7:35; Jas 1:1; 1 Pe 1:1* [1290]

[1403] διαστέλλω *diastellō* 8x *to determine, issue a decision; to state* or *explain distinctly and accurately*; hence, *to admonish, direct, charge, command*, Ac 15:24; Heb 12:20; when followed by a negative clause, *to interdict, prohibit*, Mt 16:30; Mk 5:43 [1291]

[1404] διάστημα *diastēma* 1x *interval, space, distance*, Ac 5:7 [1292]

[1405] διαστολή *diastolē* 3x *distinction, difference*, Ro 3:22; 10:12; 1 Co 14:7* [1293]

[1406] διαστρέφω *diastrephō* 7x *to distort, turn away*; met. *to pervert, corrupt*, Mt 17:17; Lk 9:41; *to turn out of the way*,

cause to make defection, Lk 23:2; Ac 13:8; διεστραμμένος, *perverse, corrupt, erroneous* [1294]

[1407] διασώζω *diasōzō* 8x *to bring safely through; to convey in safety*, Ac 23:24; pass. *to reach a place* or *state of safety*, Ac 27:43, 44; 28:1, 4; 1 Pe 3:20; *to heal, to restore to health*, Mt 14:36; Lk 7:3* [1295]

[1408] διαταγή *diatagē* 2x *an injunction, institute, ordinance*, Ro 13:2; Ac 7:53* [1296]

[1409] διάταγμα *diatagma* 1x *a mandate, commandment, ordinance*, Heb 11:23* [1297]

[1410] διαταράσσω *diatarassō* 1x *to throw into a state of perturbation, to move* or *trouble greatly*, Lk 1:29* [1298]

[1411] διατάσσω *diatassō* 16x pr. *to arrange, make a precise arrangement; to prescribe*, 1 Co 11:34; 16:1; Tit 1:5; *to direct*, Lk 8:55; Ac 20:13; *to charge*, Mt 11:1; *to command*, Ac 18:2; *to ordain*, Gal 3:19 [1299]

[1412] διατελέω *diateleō* 1x *to complete, finish*; intrans. *to continue, persevere*, in a certain state or course of action, Ac 27:33* [1300]

[1413] διατηρέω *diatēreō* 2x *to watch carefully, guard with vigilance; to treasure up*, Lk 2:51; ἑαυτὸν ἐκ, *to keep one's self from, to abstain wholly from*, Ac 15:29* [1301]

[1416] διατίθημι *diatithēmi* 7x in N.T. only mid., so some list as διατίθεμαι, *to arrange; to arrange according to one's own mind; to make a disposition, to make a will; to settle the terms of a covenant, to ratify*, Ac 3:25; Heb 8:10; 10:16; *to assign*, Lk 22:29 [1303]

[1417] διατρίβω *diatribō* 9x pr. *to rub, wear away by friction*; met. *to pass* or *spend* time, *to remain, stay, tarry, continue*, Jn 3:22; 11:54; Ac 12:19; 14:3, 28 [1304]

[1418] διατροφή *diatrophē* 1x *food, sustenance*, 1 Ti 6:8* [1305]

[1419] διαυγάζω *diaugazō* 1x *to shine through, shine out, dawn*, 2 Pet 1:19* [1306]

[1420] διαυγής *diaugēs* 1x *translucent, transparent*, Rev 21:21* [1307]

[1422] διαφέρω *diapherō* 13x *to convey through, across*, Mk 11:16; *to carry different ways* or *into different parts, separate*; pass. *to be borne, driven*, or *tossed hither and thither*, Ac 27:27; *to be proclaimed, published*, Ac 13:49; intrans. met. *to differ*,

1 Co 15:41; *to excel, be better* or *of greater value, be superior*, Mt 6:26; 10:31; impers. διαφέρει, *it makes a difference, it is of consequence*; with οὐδέν, *it makes no difference, it is nothing*, Gal 2:6 [1308]

[1423] διαφεύγω *diapheugō* 1x *to flee through, escape by flight*, Ac 27:42* [1309]

[1424] διαφημίζω *diaphēmizō* 3x *to report, proclaim, publish, spread abroad*, Mt 9:31; 28:15; Mk 1:45* [1310]

[1425] διαφθείρω *diaphtheirō* 6x *to corrupt* or *destroy utterly; to waste, bring to decay*, Lk 12:33; 2 Co 4:16; *to destroy*, Rev 8:9; 11:18 (2t); met. *to corrupt, pervert utterly*, 1 Ti 6:5* [1311]

[1426] διαφθορά *diaphthora* 6x *corruption, dissolution*, Ac 2:27, 31; 13:34, 35, 36, 37* [1312]

[1427] διάφορος *diaphoros* 4x *different, diverse, of different kinds*, Ro 12:6; Heb 9:10; *excellent, superior*, Heb 1:4; 8:6* [1313]

[1428] διαφυλάσσω *diaphylassō* 1x *to keep* or *guard carefully* or *with vigilance; to guard, protect*, Lk 4:10* [1314]

[1429] διαχειρίζω *diacheirizō* 2x pr. *to have in the hands, to manage*; mid. later, *to kill*, Ac 5:30; 26:21* [1315]

[1430] διαχλευάζω *diachleuazō* 1x *to jeer outright, deride*, Ac 2:13* [5512]

[1431] διαχωρίζω *diachōrizō* 1x *to depart, go away*, Lk 9:33* [1316]

[1434] διδακτικός *didaktikos* 2x *apt* or *qualified to teach*, 1 Ti 3:2; 2 Ti 2:24* [1317]

[1435] διδακτός *didaktos* 3x pr. *taught, teachable*, of things; in N.T. *taught*, of person, Jn 6:45; 1 Co 2:13* [1318]

[1436] διδασκαλία *didaskalia* 21x *the act* or *occupation of teaching*, Ro 12:7; 1 Ti 4:13; *information, instruction*, Ro 15:4; 2 Ti 3:16; *matter taught, precept, doctrine*, Mt 15:9; 1 Ti 1:10 [1319]

[1437] διδάσκαλος *didaskalos* 59x *a teacher, master*, Ro 2:20; in N.T. as an equivalent, to ῥαββί, Jn 1:39 [1320]

[1438] διδάσκω *didaskō* 97x *to teach*, Mt 4:23; 22:16; *to teach* or *speak in a public assembly*, 1 Ti 2:12; *to direct, admonish*, Mt 28:15; Ro 2:21 [1321]

[1439] διδαχή *didachē* 30x *instruction, the giving of instruction, teaching*, Mk 4:2; 12:38; *instruction, what is taught, doctrine*, Mt 16:12; Jn 7:16, 17; meton. *mode of teaching and kind of doctrine taught*, Mt 7:28; Mk 1:27 [1322]

[1440] δίδραχμον *didrachmon* 2x *a didrachmon* or *double drachma*, a silver coin equal to the drachma of Alexandria, to two Attic drachmas, to two Roman denarii, and to the half-shekel of the Jews, Mt 17:24 (2t)★ [1323]

[1441] Δίδυμος *Didymos* 3x *a twin; Didymus*, the Greek equivalent to the name Thomas, Jn 11:16; 20:24; 21:2★ [1324]

[1443] δίδωμι *didōmi* 415x pluperfect, ἐδεδώκειν, *to give, bestow, present,* Mt 4:9; 6:11; Jn 3:16; 17:2, et al. freq.; *to give, cast, throw,* Mt 7:6; *to supply, suggest,* Mt 10:19; Mk 13:11; *to distribute* alms, Mt 19:21; Lk 11:41; *to pay* tribute, etc., Mt 22:17; Mk 12:14; Lk 20:22; *to be the author* or *source* of a thing, Lk 12:51; Ro 11:8; *to grant, permit, allow,* Ac 2:27; 13:35; Mt 13:11; 19:11; *to deliver to, entrust, commit to the charge* of anyone, Mt 25:15; Mk 12:9; *to give* or *deliver up,* Lk 22:19; Jn 6:51; *to reveal, teach,* Ac 7:38; *to appoint, constitute,* Eph 1:22; 4:11; *to consecrate, devote, offer in sacrifice,* 2 Co 8:5; Gal 1:4; Rev 8:3; *to present, expose* one's self in a place, Ac 19:31; *to recompense,* Rev 2:23; *to attribute, ascribe,* Jn 9:24; Rev 11:13; from the Hebrew, *to place, put, fix, inscribe,* Heb 8:10; 10:16; *to infix, impress,* 2 Co 12:7; Rev 13:16; *to inflict,* Jn 18:22; 19:3; 2 Th 1:8; *to give in charge, assign,* Jn 5:36; 17:4; Rev 9:5; *to exhibit, put forth,* Mt 24:24; Ac 2:19; *to yield, bear fruit,* Mt 13:8; διδόναι ἐργασίαν, *to endeavor, strive,* Lk 12:58; διδόναι ἀπόκρισιν, *to answer, reply,* Jn 1:22; διδόναι τόπον, *to give place, yield,* Lk 14:9; Ro 12:19 [1325]

[1444] διεγείρω *diegeirō* 6x *to arouse* or *awake thoroughly,* Mt 1:24; Mk 4:38, 39; Lk 8:24; pass. *to be raised, excited, agitated,* as a sea, Jn 6:18; met. *to stir up, arouse, animate,* 2 Pe 1:13; 3:1 [1326]

[1445] διενθυμέομαι *dienthumeomai* 1x *to revolve thoroughly in the mind, consider carefully, ponder, reflect,* Ac 10:19★ [1760]

[1447] διέξοδος *diexodos* 1x *a passage throughout; a line of road, a thoroughfare,* Mt 22:9★ [1327]

[1449] διερμηνευτής *diermēneutēs* 1x *an interpreter,* 1 Co 14:28★ [1328]

[1450] διερμηνεύω *diermēneuō* 6x *to explain, interpret, translate,* Lk 24:27; Ac 9:36; 1 Co 14:5, 13, 27; *to be able to interpret,* 1 Co 12:30★ [1329]

[1451] διέρχομαι *dierchomai* 43x *to pass through,* Mk 10:25; Lk 4:30; *to pass over, cross,* Mk 4:35; Lk 8:22; *to pass along,* Lk 19:4; *to proceed,* Lk 2:15; Ac 9:38; *to travel through* or *over* a country, *wander about,* Mt 12:43; Lk 9:6; *to transfix, pierce,* Lk 2:35; *to spread abroad, be prevalent,* as a rumor, Lk 5:15; met. *to extend to,* Ro 5:12 [1330]

[1452] διερωτάω *dierōtaō* 1x *to sift by questioning,* of persons; in N.T., of things, *to ascertain by inquiry,* Ac 10:17★ [1331]

[1453] διετής *dietēs* 1x *of two years; of the age of two years,* Mt 2:16★ [1332]

[1454] διετία *dietia* 2x *the space of two years,* Ac 24:27; 28:30★ [1333]

[1455] διηγέομαι *diēgeomai* 8x pr. *to lead throughout; to declare thoroughly, detail, recount, relate, tell,* Mk 5:16; 9:9; Lk 8:39; Ac 8:33; Heb 11:32 [1334]

[1456] διήγησις *diēgēsis* 1x *a narration, relation, history,* Lk 1:1★ [1335]

[1457] διηνεκής *diēnekēs* 4x *continuous, uninterrupted;* εἰς τὸ διηνεκές, *perpetually,* Heb 7:3; 10:1, 12, 14★ [1336]

[1458] διθάλασσος *dithalassos* 1x *surrounded on both sides by the sea;* τόπος διθάλασσος, *a shoal* or *sand-bank formed by the confluence of opposite currents,* Ac 27:41★ [1337]

[1459] διϊκνέομαι *diikneomai* 1x *to go* or *pass through; to penetrate,* Heb 4:12★ [1338]

[1460] διΐστημι *diistēmi* 3x *to set at an interval, apart; to station at an interval* from a former position, Ac 27:28; intrans. *to stand apart; to depart, be parted,* Lk 24:51; of time, *to intervene, be interposed,* Lk 22:59★ [1339]

[1462] διϊσχυρίζομαι *diischurizomai* 2x *to feel* or *express reliance; to affirm confidently, insist,* Lk 22:59; Ac 12:15★ [1340]

[1464] δικαιοκρισία *dikaiokrisia* 1x *just* or *righteous judgment,* Ro 2:5★ [1341]

[1465] δίκαιος *dikaios* 79x *just, equitable, fair,* Mt 20:4; Lk 12:57; Jn 5:30; Col 4:1; of persons, *just, righteous,* absolutely, Jn 17:25; Ro 3:10, 26; 2 Ti 4:8; 1 Pet 3:18; 1 Jn 1:9; 2:1, 29; Rev 16:5; *righteous* by account and acceptance, Ro 2:13; 5:19; in ordinary usage, *just, upright, innocent, pious,* Mt 5:45; 9:13, et al. freq.; ὁ δίκαιος, *the Just One,* one of the distinctive titles of the Messiah, Ac 3:14; 7:52; 22:14 [1342]

[1466] δικαιοσύνη *dikaiosynē* 92x *fair and equitable dealing, justice,* Ac 17:31; Heb 11:33; Ro 9:28; *integrity, virtue,* Lk 1:75; Eph 5:9; in N.T. *generosity, alms,* 2 Co 9:10, v.r.; Mt 6:1; *piety, godliness,* Ro 6:13; *investiture with the attribute of righteousness, acceptance as righteous, justification,* Ro 4:11; 10:4, et al. freq.; *a provision* or *mean for justification,* Ro 1:17; 2 Co 3:9; *an instance of justification,* 2 Co 5:21 [1343]

[1467] δικαιόω *dikaioō* 39x pr. *to make* or *render right* or *just;* mid. *to act with justice,* Rev 22:11; *to avouch to be good and true, to vindicate,* Mt 11:19; Lk 7:29; *to set forth as good and just,* Lk 10:29; 16:15; in N.T. *to hold as guiltless, to accept as righteous, to justify,* Ro 3:26, 30; 4:5; 8:30, 33; pass. *to be held acquitted, to be cleared,* Ac 13:39; Ro 3:24; 6:7; *to be approved, to stand approved, to stand accepted,* Ro 2:13; 3:20, 28 [1344]

[1468] δικαίωμα *dikaiōma* 10x pr. *a rightful act, act of justice, equity; a sentence,* of condemnation, Rev 15:4; in N.T., of acquittal, *justification,* Ro 5:16; *a decree, law, ordinance,* Lk 1:6; Ro 1:32; 2:26; 8:4; Heb 9:1, 10; *a meritorious act, an instance of perfect righteousness,* Ro 5:18; Rev 19:8★ [1345]

[1469] δικαίως *dikaiōs* 5x *justly, with strict justice,* 1 Pe 2:23; *deservedly,* Lk 23:41; *as it is right, fit* or *proper,* 1 Co 15:34; *uprightly, honestly, piously, religiously,* 1 Th 2:10; Tit 2:12★ [1346]

[1470] δικαίωσις *dikaiōsis* 2x pr. *a making right* or *just; a declaration of right* or *justice; a judicial sentence;* in N.T., *acquittal, acceptance, justification,* Ro 4:25; 5:18★ [1347]

[1471] δικαστής *dikastēs* 2x *a judge,* Ac 7:27, 35★ [1348]

[1472] δίκη *dikē* 3x *right, justice;* in N.T. *judicial punishment, vengeance,* 2 Th 1:9; Jude 7; *sentence of punishment, judgment,* Ac 25:15; personified, *the goddess of justice* or *vengeance, Nemesis, Paena,* Ac 28:4 [1349]

[1473] δίκτυον *diktyon* 12x *a net, fishing-net,* Mt 4:20, 21 [1350]

[1474] δίλογος *dilogos* 1x pr. *saying the same thing twice;* in N.T. *double-tongued, speaking one thing and meaning another, deceitful in words,* 1 Ti 3:8★ [1351]

[1475] διό *dio* 53x inferential conj., *on which account, wherefore, therefore,* Mt 27:8; 1 Co 12:3 [1352]

[1476] διοδεύω *diodeuō* 2x *to travel through* a place, *traverse,* Lk 8:1; Ac 17:1 [1353]

[1477] Διονύσιος *Dionysios* 1x *Dionysius,* pr. name, Ac 17:34★ [1354]

[1478] διόπερ *dioper* 2x inferential conj., *on this very account, for this very reason, wherefore,* 1 Co 8:13; 10:14★ [1355]

[1479] διοπετής *diopetes* 1x *which fell from Jupiter,* or *heaven;* τοῦ διοπετοῦς, sc. ἀγάλματος, *image* or *statue;* for discussion of ellipsis see grammars, Ac 19:35★ [1356]

[1480] διόρθωμα *diorthōma* 1x *correction, emendation, reformation,* Ac 24:2★ [2735]

[1481] διόρθωσις *diorthōsis* 1x *a complete rectification, reformation,* Heb 9:10 [1357]

[1482] διορύσσω *dioryssō* 4x *to dig* or *break through,* Mt 6:19, 20; 24:43; Lk 12:39★ [1358]

[1483] Διόσκουροι *Dioskouroi* 1x *the Dioscuri, Castor and Pollux,* sons of Jupiter by Leda, and patrons of sailors, Ac 28:11★ [1359]

[1484] διότι *dioti* 23x *on the account that, because,* Lk 2:7; 21:28; *in as much as,* Lk 1:13; Ac 18:10 [1360]

[1485] Διοτρέφης *Diotrephēs* 1x *Diotrephes,* pr. name, 3 Jn 9★ [1361]

[1487] διπλοῦς *diplous* 4x *double,* Mt 23:15; 1 Ti 5:17; Rev 18:6 [1362]

[1488] διπλόω *diploō* 1x *to double; to render back double,* Rev 18:6★ [1363]

[1489] δίς *dis* 6x *twice,* Mk 14:30, 72; in the sense of *entirely, utterly,* Jude 12; ἄπαξ καὶ δίς, *once and again, repeatedly,* Phil 4:16 [1364]

[1490] δισμυριάς *dismyrias* 1x *twice ten thousand, two myriads,* Rev 9:16★ [1417 + 3461]

[1491] διστάζω *distazō* 2x *to doubt, waver, hesitate,* Mt 14:31; 28:17★ [1365]

[1492] δίστομος *distomos* 3x pr. *having two mouths; two-edged,* Heb 4:12; Rev 1:16; 2:12★ [1366]

[1493] δισχίλιοι *dischilioi* 1x *two thousand,* Mk 5:13★ [1367]

[1494] διϋλίζω *diylizō* 1x *to strain, filter thoroughly; to strain out* or *off,* Mt 23:24★ [1368]

[1495] διχάζω *dichazō* 1x *to cut asunder, disunite;* met. *to cause to disagree, set at variance,* Mt 10:35★ [1369]

[1496] διχοστασία *dichostasia* 2x *a standing apart; a division, dissension,* Ro 16:17; Gal 5:20★ [1370]

[1497] διχοτομέω *dichotomeō* 2x pr. *to cut into two parts, cut asunder;* in N.T. *to*

inflict a punishment of extreme severity, Mt 24:51; Lk 12:46★ [1371]

[1498] διψάω *dipsaō* 16x *to thirst, be thirsty,* Mt 25:35, 37, 42, 44; met. *to thirst after* in spirit, *to desire* or *long for ardently,* Mt 5:6; Jn 4:14; 6:35 [1372]

[1499] δίψος *dipsos* 1x *thirst,* 2 Co 11:27★ [1373]

[1500] δίψυχος *dipsychos* 2x *double-minded, inconstant, fickle,* Jas 1:8; 4:8★ [1374]

[1501] διωγμός *diōgmos* 10x pr. *chase, pursuit; persecution* (specifically for religious reasons), Mt 13:21; Mk 4:17; 10:30 [1375]

[1502] διώκτης *diōktēs* 1x *a persecutor,* 1 Ti 1:13★ [1376]

[1503] διώκω *diōkō* 45x *to put in rapid motion; to pursue; to follow, pursue the direction of,* Lk 17:23; *to follow eagerly, endeavor earnestly to acquire,* Ro 9:30, 31; 12:13; *to press forwards,* Phil 3:12, 14; *to pursue with malignity, persecute,* Mt 5:10, 11, 12, 44 [1377]

[1504] δόγμα *dogma* 5x *a decree, statute, ordinance,* Lk 2:1; Ac 16:4; 17:7; Eph 2:15; Col 2:14★ [1378]

[1505] δογματίζω *dogmatizō* 1x *to decree, prescribe an ordinance;* mid. *to suffer laws to be imposed on one's self, to submit to, bind one's self by, ordinances,* Col 2:20★ [1379]

[1506] δοκέω *dokeō* 62x *to think, imagine, suppose, presume,* Mt 3:9; 6:7; *to seem, appear,* Lk 10:36; Ac 17:18; *it seems; it seems good, best,* or *right, it pleases,* Lk 1:3; Ac 15:22, 25 [1380]

[1507] δοκιμάζω *dokimazō* 22x *to test, assay* metals, 1 Pe 1:7; *to prove, try, examine, scrutinize,* Lk 14:19; Ro 12:2; *to put to the proof, tempt,* Heb 3:9; *to approve after trial, judge worthy, choose,* Ro 14:22; 1 Co 16:3; 2 Co 8:22; *to decide upon* after examination, *judge of, distinguish, discern,* Lk 12:56; Ro 2:18; Phil 1:10 [1381]

[1508] δοκιμασία *dokimasia* 1x *proof, probation, testing, examination,* Heb 3:9★ [1381]

[1509] δοκιμή *dokimē* 7x *trial, proof by trial,* 2 Co 8:2; *the state* or *disposition of that which has been tried and approved, approved character* or *temper,* Ro 5:4; 2 Co 2:9; Phil 2:22; *proof, document, evidence,* 2 Co 8:2; 13:3★ [1382]

[1510] δοκίμιον *dokimion* 2x *that by means of which anything is tried, proof, criterion, test; trial, the act of trying* or *putting*

to proof, Jas 1:3; *approved character,* 1 Pe 1:7★ [1383]

[1511] δόκιμος *dokimos* 7x *proved, tried; approved* after examination and trial, Ro 16:10; Jas 1:12; by impl. *acceptable,* Ro 14:18 [1384]

[1512] δοκός *dokos* 6x *a beam* or *spar* of timber, Mt 7:3, 4, 5; Lk 6:41, 42★ [1385]

[1513] δόλιος *dolios* 1x *fraudulent, deceitful,* 2 Co 11:13★ [1386]

[1514] δολιόω *dolioō* 1x *to deceive, use fraud* or *deceit,* Ro 3:13★ [1387]

[1515] δόλος *dolos* 11x pr. *a bait* or *contrivance for entrapping, fraud, deceit, cunning, guile,* Mt 26:4; Mk 7:22; 14:1 [1388]

[1516] δολόω *doloō* 1x pr. *to entrap, beguile; to adulterate, corrupt, falsify,* 2 Co 4:2★ [1389]

[1517] δόμα *doma* 4x *a gift, present,* Mt 7:11; Lk 11:13; Eph 4:8; Phil 4:17★ [1390]

[1518] δόξα *doxa* 166x pr. *a seeming; appearance; a notion, imagination, opinion; the opinion which obtains respecting one; reputation, credit, honor, glory;* in N.T. *honorable consideration,* Lk 14:10; *praise, glorification, honor,* Jn 5:41, 44; Ro 4:20; 15:7; *dignity, majesty,* Ro 1:23; 2 Co 3:7; *a glorious manifestation, glorious working,* Jn 11:40; 2 Pe 1:3; pl. *dignitaries,* 2 Pe 2:10; Jude 8; *glorification in a future state of bliss,* 2 Co 4:17; 2 Ti 2:10; *pride, ornament,* 1 Co 11:15; 1 Th 2:20; *splendid array, pomp, magnificence,* Mt 6:29; 19:28; *radiance, dazzling lustre,* Lk 2:9; Ac 22:11 [1391]

[1519] δοξάζω *doxazō* 61x *to think, suppose, judge; to extol, magnify,* Mt 6:2; Lk 4:15; in N.T. *to adore, worship,* Ro 1:21; *to invest with dignity* or *majesty,* 2 Co 3:10; Heb 5:5; *to signalize with a manifestation of dignity, excellence,* or *majesty,* Jn 12:28; 13:32; *to glorify* by admission to a state of bliss, *to beatify,* Ro 8:30 [1392]

[1520] Δορκάς *Dorkas* 2x *Dorcas,* pr. name, signifying a *gazelle* or *antelope,* Ac 9:36, 39★ [1393]

[1521] δόσις *dosis* 2x pr. *giving, outlay;* Phil 4:15; *a donation, gift,* Jas 1:17★ [1394]

[1522] δότης *dotēs* 1x *a giver,* 2 Co 9:7★ [1395]

[1524] δουλαγωγέω *doulagōgeō* 1x pr. *to bring into slavery; to treat as a slave;*

to discipline into subjection, 1 Co 9:27★ [1396]

[1525] δουλεία *douleia* 5x *slavery, bondage, servile condition;* in N.T. met. with reference to degradation and unhappiness, Ro 8:15, 21; Gal 4:24; 5:1; Heb 2:15★ [1397]

[1526] δουλεύω *douleuō* 25x *to be a slave* or *servant; to be in slavery* or *subjection,* Jn 8:33; Ac 7:7; Ro 9:12; *to discharge the duties of a slave* or *servant,* Eph 6:7; 1 Ti 6:2; *to serve, be occupied in the service of, be devoted, subservient,* Mt 6:24; Lk 15:29; Ac 20:19; Ro 14:18; 16:18; met. *to be enthralled, involved in a slavish service,* spiritually or morally, Gal 4:9, 25; Tit 3:3 [1398]

[1527] δούλη *doulē* 3x *female slave, bondmaid,* Lk 1:38, 48; Ac 2:18★ [1399]

[1528] δοῦλος *doulos* 126x *a male slave,* or *servant,* of various degrees, Mt 8:9, et al. freq.; *a servitor, person of mean condition,* Phil 2:7; fem. δούλη, *a female slave; a handmaiden,* Lk 1:38, 48; Ac 2:18; δοῦλος, used figuratively, in a bad sense, *one involved in* moral or spiritual *thraldom,* Jn 8:34; Ro 6:17, 20; 1 Co 7:23; 2 Pe 2:19; in a good sense, *a* devoted *servant* or *minister,* Ac 16:17; Ro 1:1; *one pledged* or *bound to serve,* 1 Co 7:22; 2 Co 4:5 [1400, 1401]

[1530] δουλόω *douloō* 8x *to reduce to servitude, enslave, oppress by retaining in servitude,* Ac 7:6; 2 Pe 2:19; met. *to render subservient,* 1 Co 9:19; pass. *to be under restraint,* 1 Co 7:15; *to be in bondage,* spiritually or morally, Gal 4:3; Tit 2:3; *to become devoted to the service of,* Ro 6:18, 22★ [1402]

[1531] δοχή *dochē* 2x pr. *reception of* guests; in N.T. *a banquet, feast,* Lk 5:29; 14:13 [1403]

[1532] δράκων *drakōn* 13x *a dragon* or *large serpent;* met. *the devil* or *Satan,* Rev 12:3, 4, 7, 9, 13, 16, 17; 13:2, 4, 11; 16:13; 20:2 [1404]

[1533] δράσσομαι *drassomai* 1x pr. *to grasp with the hand, clutch; to lay hold of, seize, take, catch,* 1 Co 3:19★ [1405]

[1534] δραχμή *drachmē* 3x *a drachma,* an Attic silver coin of nearly the same value as the Roman *denarius,* Lk 15:8, 9★ [1406]

[1535] δρέπανον *drepanon* 8x *an instrument with a curved blade,* as *a sickle,* Mk 4:29; Rev 14:14, 15, 16, 17, 18, 19★ [1407]

[1536] δρόμος *dromos* 3x *a course, race, race-course;* met. *course* of life or ministry, *career,* Ac 13:25; 20:24; 2 Ti 4:7★ [1408]

[1537] Δρούσιλλα *Drousilla* 1x *Drusilla,* pr. name, Ac 24:24★ [1409]

[1538] δύναμαι *dynamai* 210x *to be able,* either intrinsically and absolutely, which is the ordinary signification; or, for specific reasons, Mt 9:15; Lk 16:2 [1410]

[1539] δύναμις *dynamis* 119x *power; strength, ability,* Mt 25:15; Heb 11:11; *efficacy,* 1 Co 4:19, 20; Phil 3:10; 1 Th 1:5; 2 Ti 3:5; *energy,* Col 1:29; 2 Ti 1:7; *meaning, purport* of language, 1 Co 14:11; *authority,* Lk 4:36; 9:1; *might, power, majesty,* Mt 22:29; 24:30; Ac 3:12; Ro 9:17; 2 Th 1:7; 2 Pe 1:16; in N.T. *a manifestation* or *instance of power, mighty means,* Ac 8:10; Ro 1:16; 1 Co 1:18, 24; ἡ δύναμις, *omnipotence,* Mt 26:64; Lk 22:69; Mt 14:62; pl. *authorities,* Ro 8:38; Eph 1:21; 1 Pe 3:22; *miraculous power,* Mk 5:30; Lk 1:35; 5:17; 6:19; 8:46; 24:49; 1 Co 2:4; *a miracle,* Mt 11:20, 21, et al. freq.; *a worker of miracles,* 1 Co 12:28, 29; from the Hebrew αἱ δυνάμεις τῶν οὐρανῶν, *the heavenly luminaries,* Mt 24:29; Mk 13:25; Lk 21:26; αἱ δυνάμεις, *the spiritual powers,* Mt 14:2; Mk 6:14 [1411]

[1540] δυναμόω *dynamoō* 2x *to strengthen, confirm,* Col 1:11; Heb 11:34★ [1412]

[1541] δυνάστης *dynastēs* 3x *a potentate, sovereign; prince,* Lk 1:52; 1 Ti 6:15; *a person of rank and authority,* Ac 8:27★ [1413]

[1542] δυνατέω *dynateō* 3x *to be powerful, mighty, to show one's self powerful,* 2 Co 9:8; 13:3; Ro 14:4★ [1414]

[1543] δυνατός *dynatos* 32x *able, having power, powerful, mighty;* δυνατὸς εἶναι, *to be able,* i.q. δύνασθαι, Lk 14:31; Ac 11:17; ὁ δυνατός, *the Mighty One, God,* Lk 1:49; τὸ δυνατόν, *power,* i.q. δύναμις, Ro 9:22; *valid, powerful, efficacious,* 2 Co 10:4; *distinguished for rank, authority,* or *influence,* Ac 25:5; 1 Co 1:26; *distinguished for skill* or *excellence,* Lk 24:19; Ac 7:22; Ro 15:1; δυνατόν and δυνατά, *possible, capable of being done,* Mt 19:26; 24:24 [1415]

[1544] δύνω *dynō* 2x *to sink, go down, set* as the sun, Mk 1:32; Lk 4:40★ [1416]

[1545] δύο *dyo* 135x *two,* Mt 6:24; 21:38, 31, et al. freq.; οἱ δύο, *both,* Jn 20:4; δύο ἢ τρεῖς, *two or three, some, a few,* Mt 18:20; from the Hebrew, δύο δύο, *two and two,* Mk 6:7, i.q. ἀνὰ δύο, Lk 10:1, and κατὰ δύο, 1 Co 14:27 [1417]

[1546] δυσβάστακτος *dysbastaktos* 1x *difficult* or *grievous to be borne, oppressive,* Lk 11:46 [1419]

[1548] δυσεντέριον *dysenterion* 1x *dysentery,* Ac 28:8★ [1420]

[1549] δυσερμήνευτος *dysermēneutos* 1x *difficult to be explained, hard to be understood,* Heb 5:11★ [1421]

[1550] δύσις *dysis* 1x *west,* Mk 16:8 (shorter ending) [★★]

[1551] δύσκολος *dyskolos* 1x pr. *peevish about food; hard to please, disagreeable;* in N.T., *difficult,* Mk 10:24★ [1422]

[1552] δυσκόλως *dyskolōs* 3x *with difficulty, hardly,* Mt 19:23; Mk 10:23; Lk 18:24★ [1423]

[1553] δυσμή *dysmē* 5x *a sinking* or *setting;* pl. δυσμαί, *the setting of the sun;* hence, *the west,* Mt 8:11; 24:27 [1424]

[1554] δυσνόητος *dysnoētos* 1x *hard to be understood,* 2 Pe 3:16★ [1425]

[1555] δυσφημέω *dysphēmeō* 1x pr. *to use ill words; to reproach, revile,* 1 Co 4:13★ [987]

[1556] δυσφημία *dysphēmia* 1x *ill words; words of ill omen; reproach, contumely,* 2 Co 6:8★ [1426]

[1557] δώδεκα *dōdeka* 75x *twelve,* Mt 9:20; 10:1; οἱ δώδεκα, *the twelve* apostles, Mt 26:14, 20 [1427]

[1558] δωδέκατος *dōdekatos* 1x *the twelfth,* Rev 21:20★ [1428]

[1559] δωδεκάφυλον *dōdekaphylon* 1x *twelve tribes,* Ac 26:7★ [1429]

[1560] δῶμα *dōma* 7x pr. *a house;* synec. *a roof,* Mt 10:27; 24:17 [1430]

[1561] δωρεά *dōrea* 11x *a gift, free gift, benefit,* Jn 4:10; Ac 2:38 [1431]

[1562] δωρεάν *dōrean* 9x *gratis, gratuitously, freely,* Mt 10:8; Ro 3:24; in N.T. *undeservedly, without cause,* Jn 15:25; *in vain,* Gal 2:21 [1432]

[1563] δωρέομαι *dōreomai* 3x *to give freely, grant,* Mk 15:45; 2 Pe 1:3, 4★ [1433]

[1564] δώρημα *dōrēma* 2x *a gift, free gift,* Ro 5:16; Jas 1:17★ [1434]

[1565] δῶρον *dōron* 19x *a gift, present,* Mt 2:11; Eph 2:8; Rev 11:10; *an offering, sacrifice,* Mt 5:23, 24; 8:4; δῶρον, σχ. ἐστι[ν], *it is consecrated to God,* Mt 15:5; Mk 7:11; *contribution* to the temple, Lk 21:1, 4 [1435]

[1568] ἔα *ea* 1x *Ha!* an expression of surprise or displeasure, Lk 4:34* [1436]

[1569] ἐάν *ean* 350x *if,* ἐὰν μή, *except, unless;* also equivalent to ἀλλά, Gal 2:16. Ἐάν, in N.T. as in the later Greek, is substituted for ἄν after relative words, Mt 5:19. Tends to be an indicator for the subjunctive mood. [1437]

[1570] ἐάνπερ *eanper* 3x *if it be that, if indeed, if at all events,* Heb 3:6, 14; 6:3 [1437 + 4007]

[1571] ἑαυτοῦ *heautou* 319x *himself, herself, itself,* Mt 8:22; 12:26; 9:21; also used for the first and second persons, Ro 8:23; Mt 23:31; also equivalent to ἀλλήλων, Mk 10:26; Jn 12:19; ἀφ᾽ ἑαυτοῦ, ἀφ᾽ ἑαυτῶν, *of himself, themselves, voluntarily, spontaneously,* Lk 12:57; 21:30; *of one's own will merely,* Jn 5:19; δι᾽ ἑαυτοῦ, *of itself, in its own nature,* Ro 14:14; ἐξ ἑαυτῶν, *of one's own self,* 2 Co 3:5; καθ᾽ ἑαυτόν, *by one's self, alone,* Ac 28:16; Jas 2:17; παρ᾽ ἑαυτῷ, *with one's self, at home,* 1 Co 16:2; πρὸς ἑαυτόν, *to one's self, to one's home,* Lk 24:12; Jn 20:10; or, *with one's self,* Lk 18:11 [1438]

[1572] ἐάω *eaō* 11x *to let, allow, permit, suffer to be done,* Mt 24:43; Lk 4:41; *to let be, let alone, desist from, stop,* Lk 22:51; *to commit* a ship to the sea, *let her drive,* Ac 27:40 [1439]

[1573] ἑβδομήκοντα *hebdomēkonta* 5x *seventy,* indecl., Ac 7:14; οἱ ἑβδομήκοντα, *the seventy* disciples, Lk 10:1, 17; Ac 23:23* [1440]

[1574] ἑβδομηκοντάκις *hebdomēkontakis* 1x indecl, *seventy times,* Mt 18:22* [1441]

[1575] ἕβδομος *hebdomos* 9x *seventh,* Jn 4:52; Heb 4:4; Jude 14; Rev 8:1 [1442]

[1576] Ἕβερ *Eber* 1x *Heber,* pr. name, indecl., Lk 3:35* [1443]

[1578] Ἑβραῖος *Hebraios* 4x *a Hebrew, one descended from Abraham the Hebrew,* 2 Co 11:22; Phil 3:5; in N.T., *a Jew of Palestine, one speaking Aramaic,* opp. to Ἑλληνιστής, Ac 6:1* [1445]

[1579] Ἑβραΐς *Hebrais* 3x *the Hebrew* dialect, i.e., the Hebrew-Aramaic dialect of Palestine, Ac 21:40; 22:2; 26:14* [1446]

[1580] Ἑβραϊστί *Hebraisti* 7x *in Hebrew* or *Aramaic,* Jn 5:2; 19:13, 17, 20; 20:16; Rev 9:11; 16:16* [1447]

[1581] ἐγγίζω *engizō* 42x pr. *to cause to approach;* in N.T. intrans. *to approach, draw near,* Mt 21:1; Lk 18:35;

met. *to be at hand,* Mt 3:2; 4:17; μέχρι θανάτου ἐγγίζειν, *to be at the point of death,* Phil 2:30; from Hebrew *to draw near* to God, *to offer* Him *reverence and worship,* Mt 15:8; Heb 7:19; Jas 4:8; used of God, *to draw near* to men, *assist* them, *bestow favors* on them, Jas 4:8 [1448]

[1582] ἐγγράφω *engraphō* 3x *to engrave, inscribe,* Lk 10:20; met. ἐγγεγραμμένος, *imprinted,* 2 Co 3:2, 3* [1449]

[1583] ἔγγυος *engyos* 1x *a guarantee, sponsor,* Heb 7:22* [1450]

[1584] ἐγγύς *engys* 31x some view as an improper prep., followed by gen. or dat., *near,* as to place, Lk 19:11; *close at hand,* Ro 10:8; *near,* in respect of ready interposition, Phil 4:5; *near,* as to time, Mt 24:32, 33; *near to God,* as being in covenant with him, Eph 2:13; οἱ ἐγγύς, *the people near* to God, the Jews, Eph 2:17 [1451]

[1586] ἐγείρω *egeirō* 144x *to excite, arouse, awaken,* Mt 8:25; mid. *to awake,* Mt 2:13, 20, 21; met. mid. *to rouse one's self* to a better course of conduct, Ro 13:11; Eph 5:14; *to raise* from the dead, Jn 12:1; and mid. *to rise* from the dead, Mt 27:52; Jn 5:21; met. *to raise* as it were from the dead, 2 Co 4:14; *to raise up, cause to rise up* from a prone posture, Ac 3:7; and mid. *to rise up,* Mt 17:7; *to restore to health,* Jas 5:15; met. et seq. ἐπή, *to excite* to war; mid. *to rise up against,* Mt 24:7; *to raise up again, rebuild,* Jn 2:19, 20; *to raise up* from a lower place, *to draw up* or *out* of a ditch, Mt 12:10; from Hebrew, *to raise up, to cause to arise* or *exist,* Ac 13:22, 23; mid. *to arise, exist, appear,* Mt 3:9; 11:11 [1453]

[1587] ἔγερσις *egersis* 1x pr. *the act of waking* or *rising up; resurrection resuscitation,* Mt 27:53* [1454]

[1589] ἐγκαίνια *enkainia* 1x *initiation, consecration;* in N.T. *the feast of rededication,* an annual festival of eight days in the month Kislev, Jn 10:22* [1456]

[1590] ἐγκαινίζω *enkainizō* 2x *to initiate, consecrate, dedicate, renovate; to institute,* Heb 9:18; 10:20* [1457]

[1592] ἐγκαλέω *enkaleō* 7x can be followed by a dative, *to bring a charge against, accuse; to institute judicial proceedings,* Ac 19:38, 40; 23:28, 29; 26:2, 7; Ro 8:33 [1458]

[1593] ἐγκαταλείπω *enkataleipō* 10x *to leave, leave behind; to forsake, abandon,* Mt 27:46; Mk 15:34; Ac 2:27, 30; Ro 9:29; 2 Co 4:9; 2 Ti 4:10, 16; Heb 10:25; 13:5* [1459]

[1594] ἐγκατοικέω *enkatoikeō* 1x *to dwell in,* or *among,* 2 Pe 2:8* [1460]

[1595] ἐγκαυχάομαι *enkauchaomai* 1x *to boast in,* or *of,* 2 Th 1:4* [2620]

[1596] ἐγκεντρίζω *enkentrizō* 6x *to ingraft;* met. Ro 11:17, 19, 23, 24* [1461]

[1598] ἔγκλημα *enklēma* 2x *an accusation, charge, crimination,* Ac 23:29; 25:16* [1462]

[1599] ἐγκομβόομαι *enkomboomai* 1x pr. *to put on a garment which is to be tied;* in N.T. *to put on, clothe one's self with;* met. 1 Pe 5:5* [1463]

[1600] ἐγκοπή *enkopē* 1x alsn spelled ἐκκοπή, pr. *an incision,* e.g. a trench, etc., cut in the way of an enemy; *an impediment, hindrance,* 1 Co 9:12* [1464]

[1601] ἐγκόπτω *enkoptō* 5x pr. *to cut* or *strike in;* hence, *to impede, interrupt, hinder,* Ro 15:22; 1 Th 2:18; 1 Pe 3:7; Gal 5:7; Ac 24:4* [1465]

[1602] ἐγκράτεια *enkrateia* 4x *self-control, continence, temperance,* Ac 24:25; Gal 4:23; 2 Pe 1:6* [1466]

[1603] ἐγκρατεύομαι *enkrateuomai* 2x *to possess the power of self-control* or *continence,* 1 Co 7:9; *to practise abstinence,* 1 Co 9:25* [1467]

[1604] ἐγκρατής *enkratēs* 1x *strong, stout; possessed of mastery; master of self,* Tit 1:8* [1468]

[1605] ἐγκρίνω *enkrinō* 1x *to judge* or *reckon among, consider as belonging to, adjudge to the number of; class with, place in the same rank,* 2 Co 10:12* [1469]

[1606] ἐγκρύπτω *enkryptō* 2x *to conceal in* anything; *to mix, intermix,* Mt 13:33; Lk 13:21* [1470]

[1608] ἐγχρίω *enchriō* 1x *to rub in, anoint,* Rev 3:18* [1472]

[1609] ἐγώ *egō* 2,666x *I,* gen., ἐμοῦ [μου], dat., ἐμοί [μοι], acc., ἐμέ [με] [1473, 1691, 1698, 1700, 2248, 2249, 2254, 2257, 3165, 3427, 3450]

[1610] ἐδαφίζω *edaphizō* 1x pr. *to form a level and firm surface; to level with the ground, overthrow, raze, destroy,* Lk 19:44* [1474]

[1611] ἔδαφος *edaphos* 1x pr. *a bottom, base;* hence, *the ground,* Ac 22:7* [1475]

[1612] ἑδραῖος *hedraios* 3x *sedentary;* met. *settled, steady, firm, steadfast, constant,* 1 Co 7:37; 15:58; Col 1:23* [1476]

[1613] ἑδραίωμα *hedraiōma* 1x *a basis, foundation,* 1 Ti 3:15* [1477]

[1614] Ἑζεκίας *Hezekias* 2x *Hezekiah*, pr. name, Mt 1:9f.* [1478]

[1615] ἐθελοθρησκία *ethelothrēskia* 1x also spelled ἐθελοθρησκεία, *self-made religion*, Col 2:23* [1479]

[1616] ἐθίζω *ethizō* 1x *to accustom*; pass. *to be customary*, Lk 2:27* [1480]

[1617] ἐθνάρχης *ethnarchēs* 1x *a governor, chief* of any tribe or nation, 2 Co 11:32* [1481]

[1618] ἐθνικός *ethnikos* 4x *national*; in N.T. *Gentile, heathen, not Israelites*, Mt 5:47; 6:7; 18:17; 3 Jn 7* [1482]

[1619] ἐθνικῶς *ethnikōs* 1x *like a Gentile*, Gal 2:14* [1483]

[1620] ἔθνος *ethnos* 162x *a multitude, company*, Ac 17:26; 1 Pe 2:9; Rev 21:24; *a nation, people*, Mt 20:25; 21:43; pl. ἔθνη, from the Hebrew, *nations* or *people* as distinguished from the Jews, *the heathen, Gentiles*, Mt 4:15; 10:5; Lk 2:32 [1484]

[1621] ἔθος *ethos* 12x *a custom, usage, habit*, Lk 2:42; 22:39; *an institute, rite*, Lk 1:9; Ac 6:14; 15:1 [1485]

[1623] εἰ *ei* 502x *if*, Mt 4:3, 6; 12:7; Ac 27:39, freq.; *since*, Ac 4:9; *whether*, Mk 9:23; Ac 17:11; *that*, in certain expressions, Ac 26:8, 23; Heb 7:15; by a suppression of the apodosis of a sentence, eij serves to express a wish; *O if! O that!* Lk 19:42; 22:42; also a strong negation, Mk 8:12; Heb 3:11; 4:3; εἰ καί, *if even, though, although*, Lk 18:4; εἰ μή, *unless, except*, Mt 11:27; also equivalent to ἀλλά, *but*, Mt 12:4; Mk 13:32; Lk 4:26, 27; εἰ μήτι, *unless perhaps, unless it be*, Lk 9:13; εἴ τις, εἴ τι, pr. *if any one; whosoever, whatsoever*, Mt 18:28. The syntax of this particle must be learned from the grammars. As an interrogative particle, *whether*, Ac 17:11; in N.T. as a mere note of interrogation, Lk 22:49 [1487]

[1624] εἰδέα *eidea* 1x *appearance, face*, Mt 28:3* [2397]

[1626] εἶδος *eidos* 5x *form, external appearance*, Lk 3:22; 9:29; Jn 5:37; *kind, species*, 1 Th 5:22; *sight, perception*, 2 Co 5:7* [1491]

[1627] εἰδωλεῖον *eidōleion* 1x *a heathen temple*, 1 Co 8:10* [1493]

[1628] εἰδωλόθυτος *eidōlothutos* 9x as a noun *meat offered to an idol*, Ac 15:29; 21:25; 1 Co 8:1, 4, 7, 10; 10:19; Rev 2:14, 20* [1494]

[1629] εἰδωλολάτρης *eidōlolatrēs* 7x *an idolater, worshipper of idols*, 1 Co 5:10,

11; 6:9; 10:7; Eph 5:5; Rev 21:8; 22:15* [1496]

[1630] εἰδωλολατρία *eidōlolatria* 4x *idolatry, worship of idols*, 1 Co 10:14; Gal 5:20; Col 3:5; 1 Pe 4:3* [1495]

[1631] εἴδωλον *eidōlon* 11x pr. *a form, shape, figure; image* or *statue*; hence, *an idol, image of a god*, Ac 7:41; *a heathen god*, 1 Co 8:4, 7; for εἰδωλόθυτον, *the flesh of victims sacrificed to idols*, Ac 15:20; Ro 2:22; 1 Co 10:19; 12:12; 2 Co 6:16; 1 Th 1:9; 1 Jn 5:21; Rev 9:20* [1497]

[1632] εἰκῆ *eikē* 6x *without plan* or *system; without cause, rashly*, Col 2:18; *to no purpose, in vain*, Ro 13:4; 1 Co 15:2; Gal 3:4 (2t); 4:11* [1500]

[1633] εἴκοσι *eikosi* 11x *twenty*, Lk 14:31; Ac 27:28 [1501]

[1634] εἴκω *eikō* 1x (1) *to yield, give place, submit*, Gal 2:5. (2) the perfect form ἔοικα (2036) is from this same root and functions as a present, Jm 1:6, 23 (ἔοικεν, 3 sg). Some list it as a separate word, but see the discussion in Liddell and Scott* [1502]

[1635] εἰκών *eikōn* 23x *a material image, likeness, effigy*, Mt 22:20; Mk 12:16; *a representation, exact image*, 1 Co 11:7; 15:49; Rev 13:14f.; *resemblance*, Ro 1:23; 8:29; Col 3:10; Heb 10:1 [1504]

[1636] εἰλικρίνεια *eilikrineia* 3x *clearness, purity*; met. *sincerity, integrity, ingenuousness*, 1 Co 5:8; 2 Co 1:12; 2:17* [1505]

[1637] εἰλικρινής *eilikrinēs* 2x pr. *that which being viewed in the sunshine is found clear and pure*; met. *spotless, sincere, ingenuous*, Phil 1:10; 2 Pe 3:1* [1506]

[1639] εἰμί *eimi* 2,462x *to be, to exist*, Jn 1:1; 17:5; Mt 6:30; Lk 4:25, freq.; ἐστί[ν], *it is possible, proper*, Heb 9:5; a simple linking verb ("copula") to the subject and predicate, and therefore in itself affecting the force of the sentence only by its tense, mood, etc., Jn 1:1; 15:1, freq.; it also forms a frequent circumlocution with the participles of the present and perfect of other verbs, Mt 19:22; Mk 2:6 [1488, 1498, 1510, 1511, 1526, 2070, 2071, 2252, 2258, 2277, 2468, 5600, 5607]

[1641] ἕνεκεν *heineken* 2x see ἕνεκα, *on account of*, Lk 4:18; Ac 28:20; 2 Co 3:10* [1752]

[1642] εἴπερ *eiper* 6x *if indeed, if it be so that, granted*, Ro 8:9; 1 Co 15:15; *since indeed, since*, 2 Th 1:6; 1 Pe 2:3; *although indeed*, 1 Co 8:5 [1512]

[1644] εἰρηνεύω *eirēneuō* 4x *to be at peace; to cultivate peace, concord*, or *harmony*, Mt 9:50; Ro 12:18; 2 Co 13:11; 1 Th 5:13* [1514]

[1645] εἰρήνη *eirēnē* 92x *peace*, Lk 14:32; Ac 12:20; *tranquillity*, Lk 11:21; Jn 16:33; 1 Th 5:3; *concord, unity, love of peace*, Mt 10:34; Lk 12:51; meton. *the author of peace*, Eph 2:14; from the Hebrew *every kind of blessing and good*, Lk 1:79; 2:14, 29; meton. *a salutation expressive of good wishes, a benediction, blessing*, Mt 10:13 [1515]

[1646] εἰρηνικός *eirēnikos* 2x *pertaining to peace; peaceable, disposed to peace*, Jas 3:17; from the Hebrew, *profitable, blissful*, Heb 12:11* [1516]

[1647] εἰρηνοποιέω *eirēnopoieō* 1x *to make peace*, Col 1:20* [1517]

[1648] εἰρηνοποιός *eirēnopoios* 1x *a peace-maker, one who cultivates peace and concord*, Mt 5:9* [1518]

[1650] εἰς *eis* 1,767x *to, as far as, to the extent of*, Mt 2:23; 4:24; *until*, Jn 13:1; *against*, Mt 18:15; Lk 12:10; *before, in the presence of*, Ac 22:30; *in order to, for, with a view to*, Mk 1:38; *for the use* or *service of*, Jn 6:9; Lk 9:13; 1 Co 16:1; *with reference to*, 2 Co 10:13, 16; *in accordance with*, Mt 12:41; Lk 11:32; 2 Ti 2:26; also equivalent to ejn, Jn 1:18; *by*, in forms of swearing, Mt 5:35; from the Hebrew, εἶναι, γίνεσθαι εἰς, *to become, result in, amount to*, Mt 19:5; 1 Co 4:3; εἰς τί, *why, wherefore*, Mt 26:8 [1519]

[1651] εἷς *heis* 345x numeral *one*, Mt 10:29, freq.; *only*, Mk 12:6; *one virtually by union*, Mt 19:5, 6; Jn 10:30; *one and the same*, Lk 12:52; Ro 3:30; *one in respect of office and standing*, 1 Co 3:8; equivalent to τις, *a certain one*, Mt 8:19; 16:14; *a, an*, Mt 21:19; Jas 4:13; εἷς ἕκαστος, *each one, every one*, Lk 4:40; Ac 2:3; εἷς τὸν ἕνα, *one another*, 1 Th 5:11; εἷς καὶ εἷς, *the one- and the other*, Mt 20:21; εἷς καθ᾽ εἷς and ὁδὲ καθ᾽ εἷς, *one by one, one after another, in succession*, Mk 14:19; Jn 8:9; as an ordinal, *first*, Mt 28:1 [1520, 3391]

[1652] εἰσάγω *eisagō* 11x *to lead* or *bring in, introduce, conduct* or *usher in* or *to a place or person*, Lk 2:27; 14:21; 22:54; Jn 18:16; Ac 9:8; 21:28f., 37; Heb 1:6 [1521]

[1653] εἰσακούω *eisakouō* 5x *to hear* or *hearken to, to heed*, 1 Co 14:21; *to listen to the prayers of any one, accept one's petition*, Mt 6:7; Lk 1:13; Ac 10:31; Heb 5:7* [1522]

[1654] εἰσδέχομαι *eisdechomai* 1x *to admit; to receive into favor, receive kindly, accept with favor*, 2 Co 6:17★ [1523]

[1655] εἴσειμι *eiseimi* 4x *to go in, enter*, Ac 3:3; 21:18, 26; Heb 9:6★ [1524]

[1656] εἰσέρχομαι *eiserchomai* 194x *to go or come in, enter*, Mt 7:13; 8:5, 8; spc. *to enter* by force, *break in*, Mk 3:27; Ac 20:29; met. with εἰς κόσμον, *to begin to exist, come into existence*, Ro 5:12; 2 Jn 7; or, *to make one's appearance on earth*, Heb 10:5; *to enter into* or *take possession of*, Lk 22:3; Jn 13:27; *to enter into, enjoy, partake of*, Mt 19:23, 24; *to enter into* any one's labor, *be his successor*, Jn 4:38; *to fall into, be placed in* certain circumstances, Mt 26:41; *to be put into*, Mt 15:11; Ac 11:8; *to present one's self before*, Ac 19:30; met. *to arise, spring up*, Lk 9:46; from the Hebrew, εἰσέρχεσθαι καὶ ἐξέρχεσθαι, *to go in and out, to live, discharge the ordinary functions of life*, Ac 1:21 [1525]

[1657] εἰσκαλέομαι *eiskaleomai* 1x *to call in; to invite in*, Ac 10:23★ [1528]

[1658] εἴσοδος *eisodos* 5x *a place of entrance; the act of entrance*, Heb 10:19; *admission, reception*, 1 Th 1:9; 2 Pe 1:11; *a coming, approach, access*, 1 Th 2:1; *entrance* upon office, *commencement* or *beginning* of ministry, Ac 13:24★ [1529]

[1659] εἰσπηδάω *eispēdaō* 1x *to leap* or *spring in, rush in eagerly*, Ac 16:29★ [1530]

[1660] εἰσπορεύομαι *eisporeuomai* 18x *to go* or *come in, enter*, Mk 1:21; 5:40; *to come to, visit*, Ac 28:30; *to be put in*, Mt 15:17; Mk 7:15, 18, 19; *to intervene*, Mk 4:19 [1531]

[1661] εἰστρέχω *eistrechō* 1x *to run in*, Ac 12:14★ [1532]

[1662] εἰσφέρω *eispherō* 8x *to bring in* or *into*, Lk 5:18, 19; 1 Ti 6:7; Heb 13:11; *to bring to* the ears of any one, *to announce*, Ac 17:20; *to lead into*, Mt 6:13; Lk 11:4; *drag in*, Lk 12:11★ [1533]

[1663] εἶτα *eita* 15x *then, afterwards*, Mk 4:17, 28; Lk 8:12; *in the next place*, 1 Co 12:28; *besides, furthermore*, Heb 12:9 [1534]

[1664] εἴτε *eite* 65x *whether*, Ro 12:6, 7, 8; 1 Co 3:22; 2 Co 1:6; 1 Th 5:10 [1535]

[1665] εἴωθα *eiōtha* 4x perfect of an obsolete present ἔθω, pluperfect is εἰώθειν, *to be accustomed, to be usual*, Mt 27:15; Mk 10:1; Lk 4:16; Ac 17:2★ [1486]

[1666] ἐκ *ek* 915x ἐξ before vowels, with genitive, *from, out of*, a place, Mt

2:15; 3:17; *of, from, out of*, denoting origin or source, Mt 1:3; 21:19; *of, from* some material, Mt 3:9; Ro 9:21; *of, from, among*, partitively, Mt 6:27; 21:31; Mk 9:17; *from*, denoting cause, Rev 8:11; 17:6; means or instrument, Mt 12:33, 37; *by, through*, denoting the author or efficient cause, Mt 1:18; Jn 10:32; *of*, denoting the distinguishing mark of a class, Ro 2:8; Gal 3:7; of time, *after*, 2 Co 4:6; Rev 17:11; *from, after, since*, Mt 19:12; Lk 8:27; *for, with*, denoting a rate of payment, price, Mt 20:2; 27:7; *at*, denoting position, Mt 20:21, 23; after passive verbs, *by, of, from*, marking the agent, Mt 15:5; Mk 7:11; forming with certain words a periphrasis for an adverb, Mt 26:42, 44; Mk 6:51; Lk 23:8; put after words of freeing, Ro 7:24; 2 Co 1:10; used partitively after verbs of eating, drinking, etc., Jn 6:26; 1 Co 9:7 [1537]

[1667] ἕκαστος *hekastos* 82x *each (one), every (one) separately*, Mt 16:27; Lk 13:15 [1538]

[1668] ἑκάστοτε *hekastote* 1x *always*, 2 Pe 1:15★ [1539]

[1669] ἑκατόν *hekaton* 17x *one hundred*, Mt 13:8; Mk 4:8 [1540]

[1670] ἑκατονταετής *hekatontaetēs* 1x *a hundred years old*, Ro 4:19★ [1541]

[1671] ἑκατονταπλασίων *hekatontaplasiōn* 3x *a hundredfold*, Mt 19:29; Mk 10:30; Lk 8:8★ [1542]

[1672] ἑκατοντάρχης *hekatontarches* 20x the text varies between this form and ἑκατόνταρχος, *commander of a hundred men, a centurion*, Lk 23:47; Ac 10:1; 27:1ff. [1543]

[1674] ἐκβαίνω *ekbainō* 1x *to go forth, go out of*, Heb 11:15★ [1831]

[1675] ἐκβάλλω *ekballō* 81x pluperfect, ἐκβεβλήκειν, *to cast out, eject by force*, Mt 15:17; Ac 27:38; *to expel, force away*, Lk 4:29; Ac 7:58; *to refuse*, Jn 6:37; *to extract*, Mt 7:4; *to reject with contempt, despise, contemn*, Lk 6:22; in N.T. *to send forth, send out*, Mt 9:38; Lk 10:2; *to send away, dismiss*, Mt 9:25; Mk 1:12; met. *to spread abroad*, Mt 12:20; *to bring out, produce*, Mt 12:35; 13:52 [1544]

[1676] ἔκβασις *ekbasis* 2x *a way out, egress*; hence, *result, issue*, Heb 13:7; *means of clearance* or *successful endurance*, 1 Co 10:13★ [1545]

[1678] ἐκβολή *ekbolē* 1x *a casting out*; especially, *a throwing overboard* of a cargo, Ac 27:18★ [1546]

[1681] ἔκγονος *ekgonos* 1x *born of, descended from*; as a noun ἔκγονα, *descendants, grandchildren*, 1 Ti 5:4★ [1549]

[1682] ἐκδαπανάω *ekdapanaō* 1x *to expend, consume, exhaust*, 2 Co 12:15★ [1550]

[1683] ἐκδέχομαι *ekdechomai* 6x pr. *to receive from* another; *to expect, look for*, Ac 17:16; *to wait for, to wait*, 1 Co 11:33; 16:11; Heb 11:10; 10:13; Jas 5:7★ [1551]

[1684] ἔκδηλος *ekdēlos* 1x *clearly manifest, evident*, 2 Ti 3:9★ [1552]

[1685] ἐκδημέω *ekdēmeō* 3x pr. *to be absent from home, go abroad, travel*; hence, *to be absent from* any place or person, 2 Co 5:6, 8, 9★ [1553]

[1686] ἐκδίδωμι *ekdidōmi* 4x middle, *to give out, to give up; to put out* at interest; in N.T. *to let out* to tenants, Mt 21:33, 41; Lark 12:1; Lk 20:9★ [1554]

[1687] ἐκδιηγέομαι *ekdiēgeomai* 2x *to narrate fully, detail*, Ac 13:14; 15:3★ [1555]

[1688] ἐκδικέω *ekdikeō* 6x pr. *to execute right and justice; to punish*, 2 Co 10:6; Rev 6:10; 19:2; in N.T. *to right, avenge* a person, Lk 18:3, 5; Ro 12:9★ [1556]

[1689] ἐκδίκησις *ekdikēsis* 9x *vengeance, punishment, retributive justice*, Lk 21:22; Ro 12:19; 2 Co 7:11; 1 Pe 2:14; ἐκδίκησιν ποιεῖν, *to vindicate, avenge*, Lk 18:7, 8; διδόναι ἐκδίκησιν, *to inflict vengeance*, Ac 7:24; 2 Th 1:8; Heb 10:30★ [1557]

[1690] ἔκδικος *ekdikos* 2x *an avenger, one who inflicts punishment*, Ro 13:4; 1 Th 4:6★ [1558]

[1691] ἐκδιώκω *ekdiōkō* 1x pr. *to chase away, drive out*; in N.T. *to persecute, vex, harass*, 1 Th 2:15★ [1559]

[1692] ἔκδοτος *ekdotos* 1x *delivered up*, Ac 2:23★ [1560]

[1693] ἐκδοχή *ekdochē* 1x *a looking for, expectation*, Heb 10:27★ [1561]

[1694] ἐκδύω *ekdyō* 6x pr. *to go out from; to take off, strip, unclothe*, Mt 27:28, 31; mid. *to lay aside, to put off*, Mk 15:20; Lk 10:30; 2 Co 5:3f.★ [1562]

[1695] ἐκεῖ *ekei* 105x *there, in that place*, Mt 2:13, 15; *to that place*, Mt 2:22; 17:20 [1563]

[1696] ἐκεῖθεν *ekeithen* 37x *from there*, Mt 4:21; 5:26 [1564]

[1697] ἐκεῖνος *ekeinos* 265x demonstrative adjective or noun, *that, this, he*, etc., Mt 17:27; 10:14; 2 Ti 4:8; in contrast with οὗτος, referring to the former of two things previously mentioned, Lk 18:14 [1565]

[1698] ἐκεῖσε *ekeise* 2x *there, at that place,* Ac 21:3; 22:5* [1566]

[1699] ἐκζητέω *ekzēteō* 7x *to seek out, investigate diligently, scrutinize,* 1 Pe 1:10; *to ask for, beseech earnestly,* Heb 12:17; *to seek diligently* or *earnestly after,* Ac 15:17; Ro 3:11; Heb 10:6; from the Hebrew, *to require, exact, demand,* Lk 11:50, 51; Heb 12:07* [1567]

[1700] ἐκζήτησις *ekzētēsis* 1x *useless speculation,* 1 Ti 1:4* [2214]

[1701] ἐκθαμβέω *ekthambeō* 4x pas., *to be amazed, astonished, awe-struck,* Mk 9:15; 14:33; 16:5, 6* [1568]

[1703] ἐκθαυμάζω *ekthaumazō* 1x *to wonder at, wonder greatly,* Mk 12:17* [2296]

[1704] ἔκθετος *ekthetos* 1x *exposed, cast out, abandoned,* Ac 7:18* [1570]

[1705] ἐκκαθαίρω *ekkathairō* 2x *to cleanse thoroughly, purify,* 2 Ti 2:21; *to purge out, eliminate,* 1 Co 5:7* [1571]

[1706] ἐκκαίω *ekkaiō* 1x pas., *to blaze out, to be inflamed,* Ro 1:27* [1572]

[1708] ἐκκεντέω *ekkenteō* 2x *to stab, pierce deeply,* Jn 19:37; Rev 1:7* [1574]

[1709] ἐκκλάω *ekklaō* 3x *to break off,* pas., *be broken,* Ro 11:17, 19, 20* [1575]

[1710] ἐκκλείω *ekkleiō* 2x *to shut out, exclude; to shut of, separate, insulate;* Gal 4:17; *to leave no place for, eliminate,* Ro 3:27* [1576]

[1711] ἐκκλησία *ekklēsia* 114x *a popular assembly,* Ac 19:32, 39, 41; in N.T. *the congregation* of the children of Israel, Ac 7:38; transferred to the Christian body, of which the congregation of Israel was a figure, *the Church,* 1 Co 12:28; Col 1:18; a local portion of the *Church,* a local *church,* Ro 16:1; *a* Christian *congregation,* 1 Co 14:4 [1577]

[1712] ἐκκλίνω *ekklinō* 3x *to deflect, deviate,* Ro 3:12; *to decline* or *turn away from, avoid,* Ro 16:17; 1 Pe 3:11 [1578]

[1713] ἐκκολυμβάω *ekkolymbaō* 1x *to swim out* to land, Ac 27:42* [1579]

[1714] ἐκκομίζω *ekkomizō* 1x *to carry out, bring out;* especially, *to carry out* a corpse for burial, Lk 7:12* [1580]

[1716] ἐκκόπτω *ekkoptō* 10x *to cut out; to cut off,* Mt 3:10; 5:30; met. *to cut off* an occasion, *remove, prevent,* 2 Co 11:12; *to*

render ineffectual, Mt 7:19; 18:8; Lk 3:9; 12:7, 9; Ro 11:22, 24; 1 Pe 3:7* [1581]

[1717] ἐκκρεμάννυμι *ekkremannymi* 1x mid., *to hang upon* a speaker, *fondly listen to, be earnestly attentive,* Lk 19:48* [1582]

[1718] ἐκλαλέω *eklaleō* 1x *to speak out; to tell, utter, divulge,* Ac 23:22* [1583]

[1719] ἐκλάμπω *eklampō* 1x *to shine out* or *forth,* Mt 13:43* [1584]

[1720] ἐκλανθάνομαι *eklanthanomai* 1x *to make to forget; to forget entirely,* Heb 12:5* [1585]

[1721] ἐκλέγομαι *eklegomai* 22x *to pick out;* in N.T. *to choose, select,* Lk 6:13; 10:42; in N.T. *to choose out* as the recipients of special favor and privilege, Ac 13:17; 1 Co 1:27 [1586]

[1722] ἐκλείπω *ekleipō* 4x *to fail, die out,* Lk 22:32; *to come to an end,* Heb 1:12; *to be defunct,* Lk 16:9; 23:45* [1587]

[1723] ἐκλεκτός *eklektos* 22x *chosen out, selected;* in N.T. *chosen* as a recipient of special privilege, *elect,* Col 3:12; *specially beloved,* Lk 23:35; *possessed of prime excellence, exalted,* 1 Ti 5:21; *choice, precious,* 1 Pe 2:4, 6 [1588]

[1724] ἐκλογή *eklogē* 7x *the act of choosing out, election;* in N.T. *election* to privilege by divine grace, Ro 9:11; 11:5, 28; 1 Th 1:4; 2 Pe 1:10; ἡ ἐκλογή, *the elect,* Ro 11:7; ἐκλογῆς, equivalent to ἐκλεκτόν, by Hebraism, Ac 9:15* [1589]

[1725] ἐκλύω *eklyō* 5x *to be weary, exhausted, faint,* Mt 15:32; Mk 8:3; Gal 6:9; *to lose courage, to faint,* Heb 12:3, 5* [1590]

[1726] ἐκμάσσω *ekmassō* 5x *to wipe off; to wipe dry,* Lk 7:38, 44; Jn 11:2; 12:3; 13:5* [1591]

[1727] ἐκμυκτηρίζω *ekmyktērizō* 2x *to mock, deride, scoff at,* Lk 16:14; 23:35* [1592]

[1728] ἐκνεύω *ekneuō* 1x pr. *to swim out, to escape by swimming;* hence, generally, *to escape, get clear of* a place, Jn 5:13; though ἐκνεύσας, in this place, may be referred to ἐκνεύω, *to deviate, withdraw* * [1593]

[1729] ἐκνήφω *eknēphō* 1x pr. *to awake sober after intoxication;* met. *to shake off mental bewilderment, to wake up* from delusion and folly, 1 Co 15:34* [1594]

[1730] ἑκούσιος *hekousios* 1x *voluntary, spontaneous,* Phlm 14* [1595]

[1731] ἑκουσίως *hekousiōs* 2x *voluntarily, spontaneously,* Heb 10:26; 1 Pe 5:2* [1596]

[1732] ἔκπαλαι *ekpalai* 2x *of old, long since,* 2 Pe 2:3; 3:5* [1597]

[1733] ἐκπειράζω *ekpeirazō* 4x *to tempt, put to the test,* Mt 4:7; Lk 4:12; 1 Co 10:9; *to try, sound,* Lk 10:25* [1598]

[1734] ἐκπέμπω *ekpempō* 2x *to send out,* or *away,* Ac 13:4; 17:10* [1599]

[1735] ἐκπερισσῶς *ekperissōs* 1x *exceedingly, vehemently,* Mk 14:31* [1537 + 4053]

[1736] ἐκπετάννυμι *ekpetannymi* 1x pluperfect, ἐκπεπετάκειν, *to stretch forth, expand, extend,* Ro 10:21* [1600]

[1737] ἐκπηδάω *ekpēdaō* 1x *to leap forth, rush out,* Ac 14:14* [1530]

[1738] ἐκπίπτω *ekpiptō* 10x *to fall off* or *from,* Ac 12:7; 27:32; met. *to fall from, forfeit, lose,* Gal 5:4; 2 Pe 3:17; *to be cast ashore,* Ac 27:17, 26, 29; *to fall to the ground, be fruitless, ineffectual,* Ro 9:6; *to cease, come to an end,* Jas 1:11; 1 Pe 1:24* [1601]

[1739] ἐκπλέω *ekpleō* 3x *to sail out of* or *from a place,* Ac 15:39; 18:18; 20:6* [1602]

[1740] ἐκπληρόω *ekplēroō* 1x *to fill out, complete, fill up;* met. *to fulfil, perform, accomplish,* Ac 13:33* [1603]

[1741] ἐκπλήρωσις *ekplērōsis* 1x pr. *a filling up, completion;* hence, *a fulfilling, accomplishment,* Ac 21:26* [1604]

[1742] ἐκπλήσσω *ekplēssō* 13x pr. *to strike out of;* hence, *to strike out of* one's *wits, to astound, amaze;* pass., *overwhelmed,* Mt 7:28; 13:54 [1605]

[1743] ἐκπνέω *ekpneō* 3x *to breathe out; to expire, die,* Mk 15:37, 39; Lk 23:46* [1606]

[1744] ἐκπορεύομαι *ekporeuomai* 33x *to go from* or *out of* a place, *depart from,* Mk 11:19; 13:1; *to be voided,* Mk 7:19; *to be cast out,* Mt 17:21; *to proceed from, be spoken,* Mt 4:4; 15:11; *to burst forth,* Rev 4:5; *to be spread abroad,* Lk 4:37; *to flow out,* Rev 22:1; from the Hebrew, ἐκπορεύομαι καὶ εἰσπορεύομαι. see εἰσέρχομαι, Ac 9:28 [1607]

[1745] ἐκπορνεύω *ekporneuō* 1x *to be given to fornication, indulge in immorality,* Jude 7* [1608]

[1746] ἐκπτύω *ekptyō* 1x lit., *to spit out;* met. *to reject,* Gal 4:14* [1609]

[1748] ἐκριζόω *ekrizoō* 4x *to root up, eradicate, pull out by the roots*, Mt 13:29; 15:13; Lk 17:6; Jude 12* [1610]

[1749] ἔκστασις *ekstasis* 7x pr. *a displacement*; hence, *a displacement of the mind from its ordinary state and self-possession; amazement, astonishment*, Mk 5:42; *excess of fear; fear, terror*, Mk 16:8; Lk 5:26; Ac 3:10; in N.T. *an ecstasy, a trance*, Ac 10:10; 11:5; 22:17* [1611]

[1750] ἐκστρέφω *ekstrephō* 1x pr. *to turn out of, to turn inside out*; hence, *to change entirely*; in N.T. pass. *to be perverted*, Tit 3:11* [1612]

[1752] ἐκταράσσω *ektarassō* 1x *to disturb, disquiet, throw into confusion*, Ac 16:20* [1613]

[1753] ἐκτείνω *ekteinō* 16x *to stretch out*, Mt 8:3; 12:13; *to lay* hands on any one, Lk 22:53; *to exert* power and energy, Ac 4:30; *to cast out, let down* an anchor, Ac 27:30 [1614]

[1754] ἐκτελέω *ekteleō* 2x *to bring to an end, to finish, complete*, Lk 14:29, 30* [1615]

[1755] ἐκτένεια *ekteneia* 1x pr. *extension*; in N.T. *intenseness, intentness*; ἐν ἐκτενείᾳ, *intently, perseverance, earnestness*, Ac 26:7* [1616]

[1756] ἐκτενής *ektenēs* 1x pr. *extended*; met. *intense, earnest, fervent, eager*, 1 Pe 4:8* [1618]

[1757] ἐκτενῶς *ektenos* 3x *intensely, fervently, earnestly*, Lk 22:44; Ac 12:5; 1 Pe 1:22* [1617, 1619]

[1758] ἐκτίθημι *ektithēmi* 4x pr. *to place outside, put forth; to expose* an infant, Ac 7:21; met. *to set forth, declare, explain*, Ac 11:4; 18:26; 28:23* [1620]

[1759] ἐκτινάσσω *ektinassō* 4x *to shake out, shake off*, Mt 10:14; Mk 6:11; Ac 13:51; 18:6* [1621]

[1760] ἐκτός *ektos* 8x also functions as an improper prep. (4t), *without, on the outside*; τὸ ἐκτός, *the exterior, outside*, Mt 23:26; met. *besides*, Ac 26:22; 1 Co 15:27; ἐκτὸς εἰ μή, *unless, except*, 1 Co 14:5 [1622]

[1761] ἕκτος *hektos* 14x *sixth*, Mt 20:5; 27:45 [1623]

[1762] ἐκτρέπω *ektrepō* 5x mid. and pas., *to turn out* or *aside*, Heb 12:13; *to turn aside* or *away, swerve*, 1 Ti 1:6; 5:15; 2 Ti 4:4; *to turn from, avoid*, 1 Ti 6:20* [1624]

[1763] ἐκτρέφω *ektrephō* 2x *to nourish, promote health and strength*, Eph 5:29; *to bring up, educate*, Eph 6:4* [1625]

[1765] ἔκτρωμα *ektrōma* 1x *an abortion, baby prematurely born*, 1 Co 15:8* [1626]

[1766] ἐκφέρω *ekpherō* 8x *to bring forth, carry out*, Lk 15:22; Ac 5:15; 1 Ti 6:7; *to carry out* for burial, Ac 5:6, 9, 10; *to produce, yield*, Mk 8:23; Heb 6:8* [1627]

[1767] ἐκφεύγω *ekpheugō* 8x intrans. *to flee out, to make an escape*, Ac 16:27; 19:16; trans. *to escape, avoid*, Lk 21:36; Ro 2:3 [1628]

[1768] ἐκφοβέω *ekphobeō* 1x *to terrify*, 2 Co 10:9* [1629]

[1769] ἔκφοβος *ekphobos* 2x *frightened, horrified*, Mk 9:6; Heb 12:21* [1630]

[1770] ἐκφύω *ekphyō* 2x lit. *to cause to grow, to generate; to put forth, shoot*, Mt 24:32; Mk 13:28* [1631]

[1772] ἐκχέω *ekcheō* 16x also formed as ἐκχύννομαι (11x), *to pour out*, Rev 16:1, 2, 3; *to shed* blood, Mt 26:28; Mk 14:24; pass. *to gush out*, Ac 1:18; *to spill, scatter*, Mt 9:17; Jn 2:15; met. *to give largely, bestow liberally*, Ac 2:17, 18, 33; 10:45; pass. *to rush headlong* into anything, *be abandoned to*, Jude 11 [1632]

[1773] ἐκχύννομαι *ekchunnomai* 11x see ἐκχέω [1632]

[1774] ἐκχωρέω *ekchōreō* 1x *to go out, depart from, flee*, Lk 21:21* [1633]

[1775] ἐκψύχω *ekpsychō* 3x *to expire, give up one's spirit*, Ac 5:5, 10; 12:23* [1634]

[1776] ἑκών *hekōn* 2x *willing, voluntary*, Ro 8:20; 1 Co 9:17* [1635]

[1777] ἐλαία *elaia* 15x *an olive tree*, Mt 21:1; 24:3; *an olive, fruit of the olive tree*, Jas 3:12, ὄρος τῶν ἐλαιῶν, *the Mount of Olives*, Mt 21:1 [1636]

[1778] ἔλαιον *elaion* 11x *olive oil, oil*, Mt 25:3, 4, 8; Mk 6:13 [1637]

[1779] ἐλαιών *elaiōn* 1x *an olive garden*; in N.T. the mount *Olivet*, Lk 19:29; 21:37; Ac 1:12* [1638]

[1780] Ἐλαμίτης *Elamitēs* 1x *an Elamite; an inhabitant of Elam*, a province of Persia, Ac 2:9* [1639]

[1781] ἐλάσσων *elassōn* 4x ἐλάττων (1784) is the Attic form of this word. Twice it is used with σσ (Jn 2:10; Ro 9:12) and twice with ττ (1 Ti 5:9; Heb 7:7). It is used as the comparative of μικρός, *less; less* in age, *younger*, Ro 9:12; *less* in dignity, *inferior*, Heb 7:7; *less* in

quality, *inferior, worse*, Jn 2:10; 1 Ti 5:9* [1640]

[1782] ἐλαττονέω *elattoneō* 1x trans. *to make less*; intrans. *to be less, inferior; to have too little, want, lack*, 2 Co 8:15* [1641]

[1783] ἐλαττόω *elattoō* 3x *to make less or inferior*, Heb 2:7; pass. *to be made less or inferior*, Heb 2:9; *to decline* in importance, Jn 3:30* [1642]

[1785] ἐλαύνω *elaunō* 5x *to drive, urge forward, spur on*, Lk 8:29; Jas 3:4; 2 Pe 2:17; *to impel* a vessel by oars, *to row*, Mk 6:48; Jn 6:19* [1643]

[1786] ἐλαφρία *elaphria* 1x *lightness in weight*; hence, *lightness of mind, levity*, 2 Co 1:17* [1644]

[1787] ἐλαφρός *elaphros* 2x *light, not heavy*, Mt 11:30; 2 Co 4:17* [1645]

[1788] ἐλάχιστος *elachistos* 14x used as the superlative of μικρός, *smallest, least*, Mt 2:6; 5:19 [1646, 1647]

[1789] Ἐλεάζαρ *Eleazar* 2x *Eleazar*, pr. name, indecl., Mt 1:15* [1648]

[1790] ἐλεάω *eleaō* 4x see ἐλεέω, *have mercy on*, Ro 9:16; 12:8; Jude 22, 23* [1653]

[1791] ἐλεγμός *elegmos* 1x *reproof*, 2 Ti 3:16, a later equivalent to ἔλεγχος* [1650]

[1792] ἔλεγξις *elenxis* 1x *reproof, rebuke*, 2 Pe 2:16* [1649]

[1793] ἔλεγχος *elenchos* 1x pr. *a trial in order to proof, a proof*; meton. *a certain persuasion*, Heb 11:1* [1650]

[1794] ἐλέγχω *elenchō* 17x *to put to proof, to test; to convict*, Jn 8:46; Jas 2:9; *to refute, confute*, 1 Co 14:24; Tit 1:9; *to detect, lay bare, expose*, Jn 3:20; Eph 5:11, 13; *to reprove, rebuke*, Mt 18:15; Lk 3:19; 1 Ti 5:20; *to discipline, chastise*, Heb 12:5; Rev 3:19; pass. *to experience conviction*, Jn 3:20; 1 Co 14:24 [1651]

[1795] ἐλεεινός *eleeinos* 2x *pitiable, wretched, miserable*, 1 Co 15:19; Rev 3:17* [1652]

[1796] ἐλεέω *eleeō* 28x also formed as ἐλεάω 4x, *to pity, have compassion on*; pass. *to receive pity, experience compassion*, Mt 5:7; 9:27; 15:22; *to be gracious to* any one, *show gracious favor and saving mercy towards*; pass. *to be an object of gracious favor and saving mercy*, Ro 11:30, 31; spc. *to obtain pardon and forgiveness*, 1 Ti 1:13, 16 [1653]

[1797] ἐλεημοσύνη *eleēmosynē* 13x *pity, compassion*; in N.T. *an act of kindness,* *alms, almsgiving,* Mt 6:2, 3, 4; Lk 11:41 [1654]

[1798] ἐλεήμων *eleēmōn* 2x *merciful, pitiful, compassionate,* Mt 5:7; Heb 2:17* [1655]

[1799] ἔλεος *eleos* 27x *pity, mercy, compassion,* Mt 9:13; 12:7; Lk 1:50, 78; meton. *benefit which results from compassion, kindness, mercies, blessing,* Lk 1:54, 58, 72; 10:37; Ro 9:23 [1656]

[1800] ἐλευθερία *eleutheria* 11x *liberty, freedom,* 1 Co 10:29; Gal 2:4 [1657]

[1801] ἐλεύθερος *eleutheros* 23x *free, in a state of freedom* as opposed to slavery, 1 Co 12:13; Gal 3:28; *free, exempt,* Mt 17:26; 1 Co 7:39; *unrestricted, unfettered,* 1 Co 9:1; *free* from the dominion of sin, etc., Jn 8:36; Ro 6:20; *free in the possession of Gospel privileges,* 1 Pe 2:16 [1658]

[1802] ἐλευθερόω *eleutheroō* 7x *to free, set free,* Jn 8:32, 36; Ro 6:18, 22; 8:2, 21; Gal 5:1* [1659]

[1803] ἔλευσις *eleusis* 1x *a coming, advent,* Ac 7:52* [1660]

[1804] ἐλεφάντινος *elephantinos* 1x *ivory, made of ivory,* Rev 18:12* [1661]

[1806] Ἐλιακίμ *Eliakim* 3x also spelled Ἐλιακείμ, *Eliakim,* pr. name, indecl., Mt 1:13; Lk 3:30* [1662]

[1808] Ἐλιέζερ *Eliezer* 1x *Eliezer,* pr. name, indecl., Lk 3:29* [1663]

[1809] Ἐλιούδ *Elioud* 2x *Eliud,* the father of Eleazar, Mt 1:14, 15* [1664]

[1810] Ἐλισάβετ *Elisabet* 9x *Elizabeth,* the wife of Zechariah and mother of John the Baptist, Lk 1:5, 13, 24, 36, 57 [1665]

[1811] Ἐλισαῖος *Elisaios* 1x also spelled Ἐλισσαῖος, *Elisha,* pr. name, Lk 4:27* [1666]

[1813] ἑλίσσω *helissō* 2x *to roll, fold up,* as garments, Heb 1:12; Rev 6:14* [1507, 1667]

[1814] ἕλκος *helkos* 3x pr. *a wound;* hence, *an ulcer, sore,* Lk 16:21; Rev 16:2, 11* [1668]

[1815] ἑλκόω *helkoō* 1x pass. *to be afflicted with ulcers,* Lk 16:20* [1669]

[1817] Ἑλλάς *Hellas* 1x *Hellas, Greece;* in N.T. *the southern portion of Greece* as distinguished from Macedonia, Ac 20:2* [1671]

[1818] Ἕλλην *Hellēn* 25x *a Greek,* Ac 18:17; Ro 1:14; *one not a Jew, a Gentile,* Ac 14:1; 16:1, 3 [1672]

[1819] Ἑλληνικός *Hellēnikos* 1x *Greek, Grecian,* Rev 9:11* [1673]

[1820] Ἑλληνίς *Hellēnis* 2x *a female Greek,* Mk 7:26; Ac 17:12* [1674]

[1821] Ἑλληνιστής *Hellēnistēs* 3x pr. *one who uses the language and follows the customs of the Greeks;* in N.T. *a Jew by blood, but a native of a Greek-speaking country, Hellenist,* Ac 6:1; 9:29; 11:20* [1675]

[1822] Ἑλληνιστί *Hellēnisti* 2x *in the Greek language,* Jn 19:20; Ac 21:37* [1676]

[1824] ἐλλογέω *ellogeō* 2x *to enter in an account, to put* or *charge to one's account,* Phlm 18; in N.T. *to impute,* Ro 5:13* [1677]

[1825] Ἐλμαδάμ *Elmadam* 1x also spelled Ἐλμωδάμ, *Elmadam,* pr. name, indecl., Lk 3:28* [1678]

[1827] ἐλπίζω *elpizō* 31x *to hope, expect,* Lk 23:8; 24:21; *to repose hope and confidence in, trust, confide,* Mt 12:21; Jn 5:45 [1679]

[1828] ἐλπίς *elpis* 53x pr. *expectation; hope,* Ac 24:15; Ro 5:4; meton. *the object of hope, thing hoped for,* Ro 8:24; Gal 5:5; *the author* or *source of hope,* Col 1:27; 1 Ti 1:1; *trust, confidence,* 1 Pe 1:21; ἐπ᾽ ἐλπίδι, *in security, with a guarantee,* Ac 2:26; Ro 8:20 [1680]

[1829] Ἐλύμας *Elymas* 1x *Elymas,* pr. name, Ac 13:8* [1681]

[1830] ἐλωΐ *elōi* 2x Aramaic for, *my God,* Mk 15:34* [1682]

[1831] ἐμαυτοῦ *emautou* 37x *myself, my own,* Lk 7:7; Jn 5:31 [1683]

[1832] ἐμβαίνω *embainō* 16x *to step in; to go on board* a ship, *embark,* Mt 8:23; 9:1; 13:2 [1684]

[1833] ἐμβάλλω *emballō* 1x *to cast into,* Lk 12:5* [1685]

[1835] ἐμβάπτω *embaptō* 2x *to dip in,* Mt 26:23; *to dip* for food in a dish, Mk 14:20* [1686]

[1836] ἐμβατεύω *embateuō* 1x pr. *to step into* or *upon;* met. *to search into, investigate; to pry into intrusively,* Col 2:18* [1687]

[1837] ἐμβιβάζω *embibazō* 1x *to cause to step into* or *upon; to set in* or *upon;* especially, *to put on board,* Ac 27:6* [1688]

[1838] ἐμβλέπω *emblepō* 11x *to look attentively, gaze earnestly,* at an object, followed by εἰς, Mk 6:26; Ac 1:11; *to direct a glance, to look searchingly* or *significantly,* at a person, followed by the dat., Mk 10:21; 14:67; Lk 22:61; absol. *to see clearly,* Mk 8:25; Ac 22:11 [1689]

[1839] ἐμβριμάομαι *embrimaomai* 5x Attic spelling, ejmbrimovomai, *to be greatly agitated,* Jn 11:33, 38; *to charge* or *forbid sternly* or *vehemently,* Mt 9:30; Mk 1:43; *to express indignation, to censure,* Mk 14:5* [1690]

[1840] ἐμέω *emeō* 1x *to vomit,* Rev 3:16* [1692]

[1841] ἐμμαίνομαι *emmainomai* 1x *to be mad against, be furious toward,* Ac 26:11* [1693]

[1842] Ἐμμανουήλ *Emmanouēl* 1x *Emmanuel,* pr. name, indecl., Mt 1:23* [1694]

[1843] Ἐμμαοῦς *Emmaous* 1x *Emmaus,* pr. name, indecl., of a village near Jerusalem, Lk 24:13* [1695]

[1844] ἐμμένω *emmenō* 4x pr. *to remain in* a place; met. *to abide by, to continue firm in, persevere in,* Ac 14:22; 28:30; Gal 3:10; Heb 8:9* [1696]

[1846] Ἐμμώρ *Hemmōr* 1x also spelled Ἐμμόρ, *Hamor,* pr. name, indecl., Ac 7:16 [1697]

[1847] ἐμός *emos* 76x *my, mine,* Jn 7:16; 8:37 [1699]

[1848] ἐμπαιγμονή *empaigmonē* 1x *mocking, scoffing, derision,* 2 Pe 3:3* [**]

[1849] ἐμπαιγμός *empaigmos* 1x *mocking, scoffing, scorn,* Heb 11:36* [1701]

[1850] ἐμπαίζω *empaizō* 13x *to play upon, deride, mock, treat with scorn, ridicule,* Mt 20:19; 27:29; by impl. *to delude, deceive,* Mt 2:16 [1702]

[1851] ἐμπαίκτης *empaiktēs* 2x *a mocker, derider, scoffer,* 2 Pe 3:3; Jude 18* [1703]

[1853] ἐμπεριπατέω *emperipateō* 1x pr. *to walk about in* a place; met. in N.T. *to live among, be conversant with,* 2 Co 6:16* [1704]

[1858] ἐμπίπλημι *empiplēmi* 5x also spelled ἐμπίμπλημι (1855) and ἐμπιμπλάω (1857), *to fill,* Ac 14:17; pass. *to be satisfied, satiated, full,* Lk 1:53; 6:25; Jn 6:12; met. *to have the full enjoyment of,* Ro 15:24* [1705]

[1859] ἐμπίμπρημι *empimprēmi* 1x also spelled ἐμπίπρημι and ἐμπρήθω, *to set on fire, burn down,* Mt 22:7* [1714]

[1860] ἐμπίπτω *empiptō* 7x *to fall into,* Mt 12:11; Lk 14:5; *to encounter,* Lk 10:36; *to be involved in,* 1 Ti 3:6, 7; 6:9;

εἰς χεῖρας, *to fall under the chastisement of,* Heb 10:31 [1706]

[1861] ἐμπλέκω *emplekō* 2x pr. *to intertwine;* met. *to implicate, entangle, involve;* pass. *to be implicated, involved,* or *to entangle one's self in,* 2 Ti 2:4; 2 Pe 2:20★ [1707]

[1862] ἐμπλοκή *emplokē* 1x *braiding* or *plaiting* of hair, 1 Pe 3:3★ [1708]

[1863] ἐμπνέω *empneō* 1x gen., *to breathe into* or *upon; to respire, breathe;* met. *to breathe of, be animated with the spirit of,* Ac 9:1★ [1709]

[1864] ἐμπορεύομαι *emporeuomai* 2x *to travel; to travel for business' sake; to trade, traffic,* Jas 4:13; by impl., trans., *to make a gain of, deceive for one's own advantage,* 2 Pe 2:3★ [1710]

[1865] ἐμπορία *emporia* 1x *business, trade,* Mt 22:5★ [1711]

[1866] ἐμπόριον *emporion* 1x *a mart, marketplace, emporium;* met. *traffic,* Jn 2:16★ [1712]

[1867] ἔμπορος *emporos* 5x pr. *a passenger by sea; a traveller; one who travels about for traffic, a merchant,* Mt 13:45; Rev 18:3, 11, 15, 23★ [1713]

[1869] ἔμπροσθεν *emprosthen* 48x also an improper prep., *before, in front of,* Lk 19:4; Phil 3:14; *before, in the presence of, in the face of,* Mt 5:24; 23:14; *before, previous to,* Jn 1:15, 27, 30; from the Hebrew, *in the sight* or *estimation of,* Mt 11:26; 18:14 [1715]

[1870] ἐμπτύω *emptyō* 6x followed by the dat., or εἰς and the acc., *to spit upon,* Mt 26:67; 27:30 [1716]

[1871] ἐμφανής *emphanēs* 2x *apparent, conspicuous, obvious to the sight,* Ac 10:40; met. *manifest, known, comprehended,* Ro 10:20★ [1717]

[1872] ἐμφανίζω *emphanizō* 10x *to cause to appear clearly; to communicate, report,* Ac 23:15, 22; *to bring charges against,* Ac 24:1; 25:2, 15, *to manifest, intimate plainly,* Heb 11:14; *to reveal, make known,* Jn 14:21, 22; pass. *to appear, be visible,* Mt 27:53; *to present one's self,* Heb 9:24★ [1718]

[1873] ἔμφοβος *emphobos* 5x *terrible;* in N.T. *terrified,* Lk 24:5, 37; Ac 10:4; 24:25; Rev 11:13★ [1719]

[1874] ἐμφυσάω *emphysaō* 1x *to blow* or *breathe into, inflate;* in N.T. *to breathe upon,* Jn 20:22★ [1720]

[1875] ἔμφυτος *emphytos* 1x *implanted, ingrafted, infixed,* Jas 1:21★ [1721]

[1877] ἐν *en* 2,752x followed by the dat., *in,* Mt 8:6; Mk 12:26; Rev 6:6,; *upon,* Lk 8:32; *among,* Mt 11:11; *before, in the presence of,* Mk 8:38; *in the sight, estimation of,* 1 Co 14:11; *before,* judicially, 1 Co 6:2; *in,* of state, occupation, habit, Mt 21:22; Lk 7:25; Ro 4:10; *in the case of,* Mt 17:12; *in respect of,* Lk 1:7; 1 Co 1:7; *on occasion of, on the ground of,* Mt 6:7; Lk 1:21; used of the thing by which an oath is made, Mt 5:34; of the instrument, means, efficient cause, Ro 12:21; Ac 4:12; *equipped with, furnished with,* 1 Co 4:21; Heb 9:25; *arrayed with, accompanied by,* Lk 14:31; Jude 14; of time, *during, in the course of,* Mt 2:1; in N.T. of demoniacal possession, *possessed by,* Mk 5:2 [1722]

[1878] ἐναγκαλίζομαι *enankalizomai* 2x *to take into* or *embrace in one's arms,* Mk 9:36; 10:16★ [1723]

[1879] ἐνάλιος *enalios* 1x *marine, living in the sea,* Jas 3:7★ [1724]

[1882] ἔναντι *enanti* 2x also an improper prep., *over against, in the presence of,* Lk 1:8; Ac 8:21★ [1725]

[1883] ἐναντίον *enantion* 8x acc sg neut of ἐναντίος used adverbially; the adj. does not appear in the N.T., improper prep., *before, in the presence of,* Lk 1:6; 20:26; Ac 8:32; 2 Co 2:7; Gal 2:7; 1 Pe 3:9; from the Hebrew, *in the sight* or *estimation of,* Ac 7:10; with τοῦ θεοῦ, an intensive expression, Lk 24:19★ [1726]

[1885] ἐναντίος *enantios* 8x *opposite to, over against,* Mk 15:39; *contrary,* as the wind, Mt 14:24; Ac 26:9; 28:17; ὁ ἐξ ἐναντίας, *an adverse party, enemy,* Tit 2:8; *adverse, hostile, counter,* 1 Th 2:15 [1727]

[1887] ἐνάρχομαι *enarchomai* 2x *to begin, commence,* Gal 3:3; Phil 1:6★ [1728]

[1888] ἔνατος *enatos* 10x *the ninth,* Mt 20:5; 27:45f.; Mk 15:33f.; Lk 23:44; Ac 3:1; 10:3, 30; Rev 21:20★ [1766]

[1890] ἐνδεής *endeēs* 1x *indigent, poor, needy,* Ac 4:34★ [1729]

[1891] ἔνδειγμα *endeigma* 1x *a token, evidence, proof,* 2 Th 1:5★ [1730]

[1892] ἐνδείκνυμι *endeiknymi* 11x *to manifest, display,* Ro 9:17, 22; Heb 6:10; *to give outward proof of,* Ro 2:15; *to display a certain bearing towards a person; hence, to perpetrate openly,* 2 Ti 4:14★ [1731]

[1893] ἔνδειξις *endeixis* 4x *a pointing out;* met. *manifestation, public declaration,* Ro 3:25, 26; *a token, sign, proof,* i.q. ἔνδειγμα, 2 Co 8:24; Phil 1:28★ [1732]

[1894] ἔνδεκα *hendeka* 6x *eleven,* indecl. numeral, Mt 28:16; Mk 16:14; Lk 24:9, 33; Ac 1:26; 2:14★ [1733]

[1895] ἑνδέκατος *hendekatos* 3x *eleventh,* Mt 20:6, 9; Rev 21:20★ [1734]

[1896] ἐνδέχομαι *endechomai* 1x *to admit, approve; to be possible,* impersonal, *it is possible,* Lk 13:33★ [1735]

[1897] ἐνδημέω *endēmeō* 3x *to dwell in* a place, *be at home,* 2 Co 5:6, 8, 9★ [1736]

[1898] ἐνδιδύσκω *endidyskō* 2x a later form, equivalent to ἐνδύω, *to dress (oneself),* Mark 15:17; 16:19★ [1737]

[1899] ἔνδικος *endikos* 2x *fair, just,* Ro 3:8; Heb 2:2★ [1738]

[1901] ἐνδοξάζομαι *endoxazomai* 2x *to invest with glory;* pass. *to be glorified, to be made a subject of glorification,* 2 Th 1:10, 12★ [1740]

[1902] ἔνδοξος *endoxos* 4x *honored,* 1 Co 4:10; *notable, memorable,* Lk 13:17; *splendid, gorgeous,* Lk 7:25; *in unsullied array,* Eph 5:27★ [1741]

[1903] ἔνδυμα *endyma* 8x *clothing, a garment,* Mt 6:25, 28; 22:11, 12; in particular, *an outer garment, cloak, mantle,* Mt 3:4; 7:15; 28:3; Lk 12:23★ [1742]

[1904] ἐνδυναμόω *endynamoō* 7x *to empower, invigorate,* Phil 4:13; 1 Ti 1:12; 2 Ti 4:17; mid. *to summon up vigor, put forth energy,* Eph 6:10; 2 Ti 2:1; pass. *to acquire strength, be invigorated, be strong,* Ac 9:22; Ro 4:20★ [1743]

[1905] ἐνδύνω *endynō* 1x *enter, creep in,* 2 Ti 3:6★ [1744]

[1906] ἔνδυσις *endysis* 1x *a putting on,* or *wearing* of clothes, 1 Pe 3:3★ [1745]

[1907] ἐνδύω *endyō* 27x *to enter,* 2 Ti 3:6; *to put on, clothe, invest, array,* Mt 27:31; Mk 15:17, 20; mid. *clothe one's self, be clothed,* Mt 22:11, 27, 31; trop. *to be clothed* with spiritual gifts, graces, or character, Lk 24:49; Ro 13:14 [1746]

[1908] ἐνδώμησις *endōmēsis* 1x *construction, material,* Rev 21:18★ [1739]

[1909] ἐνέδρα *enedra* 2x pr. *a sitting in* or *on a spot; an ambush,* or *lying in wait,* Ac 23:16; 25:3★ [1747]

[1910] ἐνεδρεύω *enedreuō* 2x *to lie in wait* or *ambush for,* Ac 23:21; *to endeavor to entrap,* Lk 11:54★ [1748]

[1912] ἐνειλέω *eneileō* 1x *to envelope,* Mk 15:46★ [1750]

[1913] ἔνειμι *eneimi* 7x *to be in* or *within;* τὰ ἐνόντα, *those things which are within,* Lk 11:41* [1751]

[1915] ἕνεκεν *heneken* 24x *also spelled* ἕνεκα, *with the genitive, on account of, for the sake of, by reason of.* Our text has ἕνεκεν 20x, ἕνεκα 4x (Mt 19:5; Lk 6:2; Ac 19:32; 26:21)* [1752]

[1916] ἐνενήκοντα *enenēkonta* 4x indecl, *ninety,* Mt 18:12, 13; Lk 15:4, 7* [1768]

[1917] ἐνεός *eneos* 1x *dumb, speechless,* Ac 9:7* [1769]

[1918] ἐνέργεια *energeia* 8x *energy, efficacy, power,* Phil 3:21; Col 2:12; *active energy, operation,* Eph 1:19; 3:7; 4:16; Col 1:29; 2 Th 2:9, 11* [1753]

[1919] ἐνεργέω *energeō* 21x *to effect,* 1 Co 12:6, 11; Gal 3:5; Eph 1:11; Phil 2:13; *to put into operation,* Eph 1:20; absol. *to be active,* Mt 14:2; Mk 6:14; Eph 2:2; in N.T. *to communicate energy and efficiency,* Gal 2:8; pass. or mid. *to come into activity, be actively developed; to be active, be in operation,* towards a result, 2 Co 4:12; 2 Th 2:7; *to be an active power* or *principle,* Ro 7:5; 1 Th 2:12; *instinct with activity; in action, operative,* 2 Co 1:6; Gal 5:6; Eph 3:20; Col 1:29; *earnest,* Jas 5:16 [1754]

[1920] ἐνέργημα *energēma* 2x *an effect, thing effected, activity,* 1 Co 12:6; *operation, working,* 1 Co 12:10* [1755]

[1921] ἐνεργής *energēs* 3x *active,* Phlm 6; *efficient, energetic,* Heb 4:12; *adapted to accomplish* a thing, *effectual,* 1 Co 16:9* [1756]

[1922] ἐνευλογέω *eneulogeō* 2x *to bless in respect of,* or *by means of,* Ac 3:25; Gal 3:8* [1757]

[1923] ἐνέχω *enechō* 3x *to hold within; to fix upon;* in N.T. intrans. (sc. χόλον) *to entertain a grudge against,* Mk 6:19; *to be exasperated against,* Lk 11:53; pass. *to be entangled, held fast in,* Gal 5:1* [1758]

[1924] ἐνθάδε *enthade* 8x pr. *to this place,* Jn 4:15, 16; also, *here, in this place,* Lk 24:41; Ac 10:8; 16:28; 17:6; 25:17, 24* [1759]

[1925] ἔνθεν *enthen* 2x *from this place,* Mt 17:20; Lk 16:26* [1782]

[1926] ἐνθυμέομαι *enthumeomai* 2x *to ponder in one's mind, think of, meditate on,* Mt 1:20; 9:4* [1760]

[1927] ἐνθύμησις *enthumēsis* 4x *the act of thought, reflection,* Mt 9:4; 12:25; Heb 4:12; *the result of thought, invention, device,* Ac 17:29* [1761]

[1929] ἐνιαυτός *eniautos* 14x *a year,* more particularly as being a cycle of seasons, and in respect of its revolution, Jn 11:49, 51; 18:13; in N.T. *an era,* Lk 4:19 [1763]

[1931] ἐνίστημι *enistēmi* 7x *to place in* or *upon;* intrans., *to stand close upon; to be at hand, impend, to be present,* Ro 8:38; 2 Th 2:2; Heb 9:9 [1764]

[1932] ἐνισχύω *enischuō* 2x *to strengthen, impart strength and vigor,* Lk 22:43; intrans. *to gain, acquire,* or *recover strength and vigor, be strengthened,* Ac 9:19* [1765]

[1933] ἐννέα *ennea* 5x indecl, *nine,* Mt 18:12f.; Lk 15:4, 7; 17:17* [1767]

[1935] ἐννεύω *enneuō* 1x *to nod at, signify by a nod; to make signs; to intimate by signs,* Lk 1:62* [1770]

[1936] ἔννοια *ennoia* 2x *notion, idea; thought, purpose, intention,* Heb 4:12; 1 Pe 4:1* [1771]

[1937] ἔννομος *ennomos* 2x *within law; lawful, legal,* Ac 19:39; in N.T. *subject* or *under a law, obedient to a law,* 1 Co 9:21* [1772]

[1939] ἔννυχος *ennychos* 1x *nocturnal, while still dark,* Mk 1:35* [1773]

[1940] ἐνοικέω *enoikeō* 5x *to dwell in, inhabit;* in N.T. met. *to be indwelling* spiritually, Ro 8:11; Col 3:16; 2 Ti 1:14; *to be infixed* mentally, 2 Ti 1:5; *of the Deity, to indwell,* by special presence, 2 Co 6:16* [1774]

[1941] ἐνορκίζω *enorkizō* 1x *to adjure,* 1 Th 5:27* [3726]

[1942] ἑνότης *henotēs* 2x *oneness, unity,* Eph 4:3, 13* [1775]

[1943] ἐνοχλέω *enochleō* 2x *to trouble, annoy; to be a trouble,* Lk 6:18; Heb 12:15* [1776]

[1944] ἔνοχος *enochos* 10x *held in* or *by; subjected to,* Heb 2:15; *subject to, liable to, guilty, deserving,* Mt 5:21, 22; 26:66; Mk 3:29; 14:64; *an offender against,* 1 Co 11:27; Jas 2:10* [1777]

[1945] ἔνταλμα *entalma* 3x *a precept, commandment, ordinance,* Mt 15:9; Mk 7:7; Col 2:22* [1778]

[1946] ἐνταφιάζω *entaphiazō* 2x *to prepare* a body *for burial,* Mt 26:12; absol. *to make the ordinary preparations for burial,* Jn 19:40* [1779]

[1947] ἐνταφιασμός *entaphiasmos* 2x *preparation* of a corpse *for burial, burial* itself, Mk 14:8; Jn 12:7* [1780]

[1948] ἐντέλλω *entellō* 15x some list as ἐντέλλομαι, mid., *to enjoin, charge, command,* Mt 4:6; 15:4; 17:9; *to direct,* Mt 19:7; Mk 10:3 [1781]

[1949] ἐντεῦθεν *enteuthen* 10x *hence, from this place,* Mt 17:20; Lk 4:9; ἐντεῦθεν καὶ ἐντεῦθεν, *on each side,* Rev 22:2; *hence, from this cause,* Jas 4:1 [1782]

[1950] ἔντευξις *enteuxis* 2x pr. *a meeting with;* hence *address; prayer, supplication, intercession,* 1 Ti 2:1; 4:5* [1783]

[1952] ἔντιμος *entimos* 5x *honored, estimable, dear,* Lk 7:2; 14:8; Phil 2:29; *highly-valued, precious, costly,* 1 Pe 2:4, 6* [1784]

[1953] ἐντολή *entolē* 67x *an injunction; a precept, commandment, law,* Mt 5:19; 15:3, 6; *an order, direction,* Ac 17:15; *an edict,* Jn 11:57; *a direction,* Mk 10:5; *a commission,* Jn 10:18, *a charge* of matters to be proclaimed or received, Jn 12:49, 50; 1 Ti 6:14; 2 Pe 2:21 [1785]

[1954] ἐντόπιος *entopios* 1x *in* or *of a place; an inhabitant, citizen,* Ac 21:12* [1786]

[1955] ἐντός *entos* 2x improper prep., gen., *inside, within,* Lk 17:21; τὸ ἐντός, *the interior, inside,* Mt 23:26* [1787]

[1956] ἐντρέπω *entrepō* 9x mid., *to revere, reverence, regard,* Mt 21:37; Mk 12:6; absol. *to feel shame, be put to shame,* 2 Th 3:14; Tit 2:8; pass., *be put to shame,* 2 Th 3:14; Tit 3:8 [1788]

[1957] ἐντρέφω *entrephō* 1x *to nourish in, bring up* or *educate in,* 1 Ti 4:6* [1789]

[1958] ἔντρομος *entromos* 3x *trembling, terrified,* Ac 7:32; 16:29; Heb 12:21* [1790]

[1959] ἐντροπή *entropē* 2x *humiliation;* in N.T. *shame,* 1 Co 6:5; 15:34* [1791]

[1960] ἐντρυφάω *entruphaō* 1x *to live luxuriously, riot, revel,* 2 Pe 2:13* [1792]

[1961] ἐντυγχάνω *entynchanō* 5x *to fill in with, meet; to have conversation with, address; to address* or *apply to* any one, Ac 25:24; ὑπέρ τινος, *to intercede for any one, plead the cause of,* Ro 8:27, 34; Heb 7:25; κατά τινος, *to address a representation* or *suit against any one, to accuse, complain of,* Ro 11:2* [1793]

[1962] ἐντυλίσσω *entylissō* 3x *to wrap up in, inwrap, envelope,* Mt 27:59; Lk 23:53; *to wrap up, roll* or *fold together,* Jn 20:7* [1794]

[1963] ἐντυπόω *entypoō* 1x *to impress a figure, instamp, engrave,* 2 Co 3:7* [1795]

[1964] ἐνυβρίζω *enybrizō* 1x *to insult, outrage,* Heb 10:29* [1796]

[1965] ἐνυπνιάζομαι *enypniazomai* 2x *to dream,* in N.T. *to dream* under supernatural impression, Ac 2:17; *to dream* delusion, *have visions,* Jude 8* [1797]

[1966] ἐνύπνιον *enypnion* 1x *a dream;* in N.T. *a supernatural suggestion* or *impression received during sleep, a sleep-vision,* Ac 2:17* [1798]

[1967] ἐνώπιον *enōpion* 94x gen., *before, in the presence of,* Lk 5:25; 8:47; *in front of,* Rev 4:5, 6; *immediately preceding as a forerunner,* Lk 1:17; Rev 16:19; from the Hebrew, *in the presence of,* metaphysically, *i.e.* in the sphere of sensation or thought, Lk 12:9; 15:10; Ac 10:31; *in the eyes of, in the judgment of,* Lk 16:15; 24:11; Ac 4:19 [1799]

[1968] Ἐνώς *Enōs* 1x *Enos,* pr. name, indecl., Lk 3:38* [1800]

[1969] ἐνωτίζομαι *enōtizomai* 1x *to give ear, listen, pay attention to,* Ac 2:14* [1801]

[1970] Ἐνώχ *Henōch* 3x *Enoch,* pr. name, indecl., Lk 3:37; Heb 11:5; 1 Pe 3:19; Jude 14* [1802]

[1971] ἕξ *hex* 13x *six,* indecl., Mt 17:1; Mk 9:2 [1803]

[1972] ἐξαγγέλλω *exangellō* 2x *to tell forth, divulge, publish; to declare abroad, celebrate,* 1 Pe 2:9, shorter ending of Mark* [1804]

[1973] ἐξαγοράζω *exagorazō* 4x *to buy out* of the hands of a person; *to redeem, set free,* Gal 3:13; 4:5; mid. *to redeem, buy off, to secure for one's self* or *one's own use; to rescue* from loss or misapplication, Eph 5:16; Col 4:5* [1805]

[1974] ἐξάγω *exagō* 12x *to bring* or *lead out, conduct out of,* Mk 8:23; 15:20; Lk 24:50 [1806]

[1975] ἐξαιρέω *exaireō* 8x *to take out of; to pluck out, tear out,* Mt 5:29; 18:9; mid. *to take out of, select, choose,* Ac 26:17; *to rescue, deliver,* Ac 7:10, 34; 12:11; 23:27; Gal 1:4* [1807]

[1976] ἐξαίρω *exairō* 1x pr. *to lift up out of;* in N.T. *to remove, eject,* 1 Co 5:13* [1808]

[1977] ἐξαιτέω *exaiteō* 1x *to ask for; to demand;* mid. *to demand for one's self,* Lk 22:31; also, *to obtain by asking** [1809]

[1978] ἐξαίφνης *exaiphnēs* 5x *suddenly, unexpectedly,* Mk 13:36; Lk 2:13; 9:39; Ac 9:3; 22:6* [1810]

[1979] ἐξακολουθέω *exakoloutheō* 3x *to follow out; to imitate,* 2 Pe 2:2, 15; *to observe as a guide,* 2 Pe 1:16* [1811]

[1980] ἐξακόσιοι *hexakosioi* 2x *six hundred,* Rev 13:18; 14:20* [1812]

[1981] ἐξαλείφω *exaleiphō* 5x pr. *to anoint* or *smear over;* hence, *to wipe off* or *away,* Rev 7:17; 21:4; *to blot out, obliterate,* Col 2:14; Rev 3:5; met. *to wipe out* guilt, Ac 3:19* [1813]

[1982] ἐξάλλομαι *exallomai* 1x *to leap* or *spring up* or *forth,* Ac 3:8* [1814]

[1983] ἐξανάστασις *exanastasis* 1x *a raising up; a dislodgment; a rising up; a resurrection from* the dead, Phil 3:11* [1815]

[1984] ἐξανατέλλω *exanatellō* 2x *to raise up, make to spring up;* intrans. *to rise up, sprout, spring up* or *forth,* Mt 13:5; Mk 4:5* [1816]

[1985] ἐξανίστημι *exanistēmi* 3x *to cause to rise up, raise up;* from the Hebrew, *to raise up* into existence, Mk 12:19; Lk 20:28; intrans. *to rise up from, stand forth,* Ac 15:5* [1817]

[1987] ἐξαπατάω *exapataō* 6x pr. *to deceive thoroughly; to deceive, delude,* Ro 7:11; 16:18; 1 2 Co 3:18; 11:3; 2 Th 2:3; 1 Ti 2:14* [1818]

[1988] ἐξάπινα *exapina* 1x *suddenly, immediately, unexpectedly,* Mk 9:8* [1819]

[1989] ἐξαπορέω *exaporeō* 2x some list as a deponent ἐξαπορέομαι, pas., *to be in the utmost perplexity* or *despair,* 2 Co 1:8; 4:8* [1820]

[1990] ἐξαποστέλλω *exapostellō* 13x *to send out* or *forth; to send away, dismiss,* Lk 1:53; *to dispatch* on a service or agency, Ac 7:12; *to send forth* as a pervading influence, Gal 4:6 [1821]

[1992] ἐξαρτίζω *exartizō* 2x *to equip* or *furnish completely,* 2 Ti 3:17; *to complete* time, Ac 21:5* [1822]

[1993] ἐξαστράπτω *exastraptō* 1x pr. *to flash forth;* hence, *to glisten as lightning,* Lk 9:29* [1823]

[1994] ἐξαυτῆς *exautēs* 6x *at the very time; presently, instantly, immediately,* Mk 6:25; Ac 10:33; 11:11 [1824]

[1995] ἐξεγείρω *exegeirō* 2x *to raise up* from the dead, 1 Co 6:14; *to raise up into* existence, or *into a certain condition,* Ro 9:17* [1825]

[1996] ἔξειμι *exeimi* 4x *to go out* or *forth,* Ac 13:42; *to depart,* Ac 17:15; 20:7; ἐπὶ τὴν γῆν, *to get to land,* from the water, Ac 27:43 [1826]

[1999] ἐξέλκω *exelkō* 1x *to draw* or *drag out;* met. *to withdraw, allure, hurry away,* Jas 1:14* [1828]

[2000] ἐξέραμα *exerama* 1x *vomit,* 2 Pe 2:22* [1829]

[2001] ἐξεραυνάω *exeraunaō* 1x *to search out, to examine closely,* 1 Pe 1:10* [1830]

[2002] ἐξέρχομαι *exerchomai* 218x *to go* or *come out of; to come out,* Mt 5:26; 8:34; *to proceed, emanate, take rise from,* Mt 2:6; 15:18; 1 Co 14:36; *to come abroad,* 1 Jn 4:1; *to go forth, go away, depart,* Mt 9:31; Lk 5:8; *to escape,* Jn 10:39; *to pass away, come to an end,* Ac 16:19 [1831]

[2003] ἔξεστιν *exestin* 31x 3rd person sing of the unused ἔξειμι (#1997) used impersonally, *it is possible; it is permitted, it is lawful,* Mt 12:2, 4; Mk 3:4; Lk 6:9; Ac 22:25; 1 Co 6:12 [1832]

[2004] ἐξετάζω *exetazō* 3x *to search out; to inquire by interrogation, examine strictly,* Mt 2:8; 10:11; *to interrogate,* Jn 21:12* [1833]

[2007] ἐξηγέομαι *exēgeomai* 6x *to be a leader; to detail, to set forth in language; to tell, narrate, recount,* Lk 24:35; Ac 10:8; *to make known, reveal,* Jn 1:18; Ac 15:12, 14; 21:19* [1834]

[2008] ἑξήκοντα *hexēkonta* 9x indecl, *sixty,* Mt 13:8, 23 [1835]

[2009] ἑξῆς *hexēs* 5x *successively, in order;* in N.T. with the article ὁ, ἡ, τό, ἑξῆς, *next,* Lk 7:11; 9:37; Ac 21:1; 25:17; 27:18* [1836]

[2010] ἐξηχέω *exēcheō* 1x act., *to make to sound forth;* pas., *to sound forth,* 1 Th 1:8* [1837]

[2011] ἕξις *hexis* 1x *a condition of body* or *mind,* strictly, as resulting from practice; *habit,* Heb 5:14* [1838]

[2014] ἐξίστημι *existēmi* 17x pr. *to put out of its place; to astonish, amaze,* Lk 24:22; Ac 8:9, 11; intrans. *to be astonished,* Mt 12:23; *to be beside one's self,* Mk 3:21; 2 Co 5:13 [1839]

[2015] ἐξισχύω *exischuō* 1x *to be fully able, be strong,* Eph 3:18* [1840]

[2016] ἔξοδος *exodos* 3x *a way out, a going out; a going out, departure, the exodus,* Heb 11:22; met. *a departure* from life, *decease, death,* Lk 9:31; 2 Pe 1:15* [1841]

[2017] ἐξολεθρεύω *exolethreuō* 1x *to destroy utterly, root out,* Ac 3:23* [1842]

[2018] ἐξομολογέομαι *exomologeomai* 10x *to agree, bind one's self, promise,* Lk

22:6; mid. *to confess*, Mt 3:6; *to profess openly*, Phil 2:11; Rev 3:5; *to make open avowal* of benefits; *to praise, celebrate*, Mt 11:25; Lk 10:21 [1843]

[2019] ἐξορκίζω *exorkizō* 1x *to put an oath* to a person, *to adjure*, Mt 26:63* [1844]

[2020] ἐξορκιστής *exorkistēs* 1x pr. *one who puts an oath;* in N.T. *an exorcist, one who by various kinds of incantations,* etc., *pretended to expel demons*, Ac 19:13* [1845]

[2021] ἐξορύσσω *exoryssō* 2x *to dig out* or *through, force up*, Mk 2:4; *to pluck out* the eyes, Gal 4:15* [1846]

[2022] ἐξουδενέω *exoudeneō* 1x also spelled ἐξουδενόω, *to treat with contempt,* Mk 9:12* [1847]

[2024] ἐξουθενέω *exoutheneō* 11x also spelled ἐξουθενόω, *to make light of, set at naught, despise, treat with contempt and scorn*, Lk 18:9; *to neglect, disregard*, 1 Th 5:20; ἐξουθενημένος, *contemptible*, 2 Co 10:10; *of small account*, 1 Co 1:28; 6:4; by impl. *to reject with contempt*, Ac 4:11 [1848]

[2026] ἐξουσία *exousia* 102x *power, ability, faculty*, Mt 9:8; 10:1; *efficiency, energy*, Lk 4:32; *liberty, licence*, Jn 10:18; Ac 5:4; *authority, rule, dominion, jurisdiction*, Mt 8:9; 28:18; meton. pl. *authorities, potentates, powers*, Lk 12:11; 1 Co 15:24; Eph 1:21; *right, authority, full power*, Mt 9:6; 21:23; *privilege, prerogative*, Jn 1:12; perhaps, *a veil*, 1 Co 11:10 [1849]

[2027] ἐξουσιάζω *exousiazō* 4x *to have* or *exercise power* or *authority over* anyone, Lk 22:25; *to possess independent control over*, 1 Co 7:4 (2t); pass. *to be subject to, under the power* or *influence of*, 1 Co 6:12* [1850]

[2029] ἐξοχή *exochē* 1x pr. *prominence, anything prominent;* in N.T. *eminence, distinction*, Ac 25:23* [1851]

[2030] ἐξυπνίζω *exypnizō* 1x *to awake, arouse* from sleep, Jn 11:11* [1852]

[2031] ἔξυπνος *exypnos* 1x *awake, aroused from sleep*, Ac 16:27* [1853]

[2032] ἔξω *exō* 63x can function as an improper prep., *without, out of doors;* Mt 12:46, 47; ὁ, ἡ, τὸ ἔξω, *outer, external, foreign*, Ac 26:11; 2 Co 4:16; met. *not belonging to one's community*, Mk 4:11; 1 Co 5:12, 13; *out, away,* from a place or person, Mt 5:13; 13:48; as a prep., *out of,* Mk 5:10 [1854]

[2033] ἔξωθεν *exōthen* 13x can function as an improper prep., *out-*wardly, externally*, Mt 23:27, 28; Mk 7:15; ὁ, ἡ, τὸ ἔξωθεν, *outer, external*, Mt 23:25; Lk 11:39; τὸ ἔξωθεν, *the exterior*, Lk 11:40; οἱ ἔξωθεν, *those who are without* the Christian community, 1 Ti 3:7 [1855]

[2034] ἐξωθέω *exōtheō* 2x *to expel, drive out*, Ac 7:45; *to propel, urge forward*, Ac 27:39* [1856]

[2035] ἐξώτερος *exōteros* 3x comparative in form but used as a superlative, *outer, exterior, external*, Mt 8:12; 22:13; 25:30* [1857]

[2036] ἔοικα *eoika* 2x see εἴκω (1634a), dat., *to be like*, Jas 1:6, 23* [1503]

[2037] ἑορτάζω *heortazō* 1x *to keep a feast, celebrate a festival*, 1 Co 5:8* [1858]

[2038] ἑορτή *heortē* 25x *a solemn feast, public festival*, Lk 2:41; 22:1; Jn 13:1; spc. used of *the passover*, Mt 26:5; 27:15 [1859]

[2039] ἐπαγγελία *epangelia* 52x *annunciation*, 2 Ti 1:1; *a promise, act of promising*, Ac 13:23, 32; 23:21; meton. *the thing promised, promised favor and blessing*, Lk 24:49; Ac 1:4 [1860]

[2040] ἐπαγγέλλομαι *epangellomai* 15x *to declare, to promise, undertake*, Mk 14:11; Ro 4:21; *to profess*, 1 Ti 2:10 [1861]

[2041] ἐπάγγελμα *epangelma* 2x *a promise*, 2 Pe 3:13; meton. *promised favor* or *blessing*, 2 Pe 1:4* [1862]

[2042] ἐπάγω *epagō* 3x *to bring upon, cause to come upon*, 2 Pe 2:1, 5; met. *to cause to be imputed* or *attributed to, to bring guilt upon*, Ac 5:28* [1863]

[2043] ἐπαγωνίζομαι *epagōnizomai* 1x *to contend strenuously in defence of*, Jude 3* [1864]

[2044] ἐπαθροίζω *epathroizō* 1x act., *to gather together, to collect close upon,* or *beside;* pas., *to crowd upon*, Lk 11:29* [1865]

[2045] Ἐπαίνετος *Epainetos* 1x *Epaenetus*, pr. name, Ro 16:5* [1866]

[2046] ἐπαινέω *epaineō* 6x *to praise, commend, applaud*, Lk 16:8; Ro 15:11; 1 Co 11:2, 17, 22 (2t)* [1867]

[2047] ἔπαινος *epainos* 11x *praise, applause, honor paid*, Ro 2:29; 2 Co 8:18; meton. *ground* or *reason of praise* or *commendation*, Phil 4:8; *approval*, Ro 13:3; 1 Pe 2:14; 1 Co 4:5 [1868]

[2048] ἐπαίρω *epairō* 19x *to lift up, raise, elevate; to hoist*, Ac 27:40; τὴν φωνήν, *to lift up the voice, to speak in* a loud voice, Lk 11:27; τὰς χεῖρας, *to lift up the hands* in prayer, Lk 24:50; 1 Ti 2:8; τοὺς ὀφθαλμούς, *to lift up the eyes, to look*, Mt 17:8; τὴν κεφαλήν, *to lift up the head, to be encouraged, animated*, Lk 21:28; τὴν πτέρναν, *to lift up the heel, to attack, assault;* or, *to seek one's overthrow* or *destruction*, Jn 13:18; pass. *to be borne upwards*, Ac 1:9; met. mid. *to exalt one's self, assume consequence, be elated*, 2 Co 10:5 [1869]

[2049] ἐπαισχύνομαι *epaischunomai* 11x *to be ashamed of*, Mk 8:38; Lk 9:26; Ro 1:16; 6:21; 2 Ti 1:8, 12, 16; Heb 2:11; 11:16* [1870]

[2050] ἐπαιτέω *epaiteō* 2x *to prefer a suit* or *request in respect of certain circumstances; to ask alms, beg*, Lk 16:3; 18:35* [1871]

[2051] ἐπακολουθέω *epakoloutheō* 4x *to follow upon; to accompany, be attendant*, Mk 16:20; *to appear later*, 1 Ti 5:24; met. *to follow* one's steps, *to imitate*, 1 Pe 2:21; *to follow* a work, *pursue, prosecute, be studious of, devoted to*, 1 Ti 5:10* [1872]

[2052] ἐπακούω *epakouō* 1x gen., *to listen* or *hearken to; to hear with favor*, 2 Co 6:2* [1873]

[2053] ἐπακροάομαι *epakroaomai* 1x gen., *to hear, hearken, listen to*, Ac 16:25* [1874]

[2054] ἐπάν *epan* 3x with subj., *whenever, as soon as*, Mt 2:8; Lk 11:22, 34* [1875]

[2055] ἐπάναγκες *epanankes* 1x *of necessity, necessarily;* τὰ ἐπάναγκες, *necessary things*, Ac 15:28* [1876]

[2056] ἐπανάγω *epanagō* 3x *to bring up* or *back;* intrans. *to return*, Mt 21:18; a nautical term, *to put off from shore*, Lk 5:3, 4* [1877]

[2057] ἐπαναμιμνῄσκω *epanamimnēskō* 1x *to remind, put in remembrance*, Ro 15:15* [1878]

[2058] ἐπαναπαύομαι *epanapauomai* 2x pr. *to make to rest upon;* mid. *to rest upon; to abide with*, Lk 10:6; *to rely on, confide in, abide by confidingly*, Ro 2:17* [1879]

[2059] ἐπανέρχομαι *epanerchomai* 2x *to come back, return*, Lk 10:35; 19:15* [1880]

[2060] ἐπανίστημι *epanistēmi* 2x *to raise up against;* mid. *to rise up against in rebellion*, Mt 10:21; Mk 13:12* [1881]

[2061] ἐπανόρθωσις *epanorthōsis* 1x *correction, reformation, improvement*, 2 Ti 3:16* [1882]

[2062] ἐπάνω *epanō* 19x *can function as an improper prep., above, over, upon, of place,* Mt 2:9; 5:14; *over, of authority,* Lk 19:17, 19; *above, more than,* Mk 14:5 [1883]

[2063] ἐπάρατος *eparatos* 1x *accursed,* Jn 7:49* [1944]

[2064] ἐπαρκέω *eparkeō* 3x dat., pr. *to ward off; to assist, relieve, succor;* 1 Ti 5:10, 16 (2t)* [1884]

[2065] ἐπαρχεία *eparcheia* 2x *province,* Ac 23:34; 25:1* [1885]

[2068] ἔπαυλις *epaulis* 1x pr. *a place to pass the night in; cottage, farm;* in N.T. *a dwelling, habitation, farm,* Ac 1:20* [1886]

[2069] ἐπαύριον *epaurion* 17x *tomorrow;* ἡ ἐπαύριον, sc. ἡμέρα, *the next* or *following day,* Mt 27:62; Mk 11:12 [1887]

[2071] Ἐπαφρᾶς *Epaphras* 3x *Epaphras,* pr. name, Col 1:7; 4:12; Phlm 23* [1889]

[2072] ἐπαφρίζω *epaphrizō* 1x *to foam out; to pour out like foam, vomit forth,* Jude 13* [1890]

[2073] Ἐπαφρόδιτος *Epaphroditos* 2x *Epaphroditus,* pr. name, Phil 2:25; 4:18* [1891]

[2074] ἐπεγείρω *epegeirō* 2x *to raise* or *stir up against, excite* or *instigate against,* Ac 13:50; 14:2* [1892]

[2075] ἐπεί *epei* 26x *when, after, since, because, in as much as,* Mt 18:32; 27:6; *for, for then, for else, since in that case,* Ro 3:6; 11:6 [1893]

[2076] ἐπειδή *epeidē* 10x *since, because, in as much as,* Mt 21:46; Lk 11:6; Ac 13:46 [1894]

[2077] ἐπειδήπερ *epeidēper* 1x *since now, since indeed, considering that,* Lk 1:1* [1895]

[2079] ἔπειμι *epeimi* 5x *to come upon; to come after; to succeed immediately,* Ac 7:26; 16:11; 20:15; 21:18; 23:11* [1966]

[2081] ἐπεισαγωγή *epeisagōgē* 1x *a superinduction, a further introduction, whether by way of addition or substitution,* Heb 7:19* [1898]

[2082] ἐπεισέρχομαι *epeiserchomai* 1x *to come in upon, invade, surprise,* Lk 21:35* [1904]

[2083] ἔπειτα *epeita* 16x *thereupon, then, after that, in the next place, afterwards,* Mk 7:5; Lk 16:7 [1899]

[2084] ἐπέκεινα *epekeina* 1x *BAGD* say it is an adverb with the gen.; others

classify it as an improper prep., gen., *on yonder side, beyond,* Ac 7:43* [1900]

[2085] ἐπεκτείνομαι *epekteinomai* 1x pr. *to stretch out farther;* in N.T. mid. *to reach out towards, strain for,* Phil 3:13* [1901]

[2086] ἐπενδύομαι *ependyomai* 2x *to put on over* or *in addition to;* mid. *to put on one's self in addition; to be further invested,* 2 Co 5:2, 4* [1902]

[2087] ἐπενδύτης *ependytēs* 1x *the outer* or *upper tunic,* worn between the inner tunic and the external garments, Jn 21:7* [1903]

[2088] ἐπέρχομαι *eperchomai* 9x *to come to,* Ac 14:19; *to come upon,* Lk 1:35; 21:26; Ac 1:8; Jas 5:1; *to be coming on, to succeed,* Eph 2:7; *to occur, happen to,* Ac 8:24; 13:40; *to come against, attack,* Lk 11:22* [1904]

[2089] ἐπερωτάω *eperōtaō* 56x *to interrogate, question, ask,* Mt 12:10; 17:10; in N.T. *to request, require,* Mt 16:1; from the Hebrew, ἐπερωτᾶν τὸν Θεόν, *to seek after, desire an acquaintance with God,* Ro 10:20 [1905]

[2090] ἐπερώτημα *eperōtēma* 1x pr. *an interrogation, question;* in N.T. *profession, pledge,* 1 Pe 3:21* [1906]

[2091] ἐπέχω *epechō* 5x trans. *to hold out, present, exhibit, display,* Phil 2:16; intrans. *to observe, take heed to, attend to,* Lk 14:7; Ac 3:5; 1 Ti 4:16; *to stay, delay,* Ac 19:22* [1907]

[2092] ἐπηρεάζω *epēreazō* 2x *to harass, insult,* Lk 6:28; *to mistreat, abuse,* 1 Pe 3:16* [1908]

[2093] ἐπί *epi* 890x (1) *with the gen., upon, on,* Mt 4:6; 9:2; 27:19; *in, of locality,* Mk 8:4; *near upon, by, at,* Mt 21:19; Jn 21:1; *upon, over, of authority,* Mt 2:22; Ac 8:27; *in the presence of,* especially in a judicial sense, 2 Co 7:14; Ac 25:9; *in the case of, in respect of,* Jn 6:2; Gal 3:16; *in the time of, at the time of,* Ac 11:28; Ro 1:10; ἐπ᾽ ἀληθείας, *really, bona fide,* Mk 12:32; (2) *with the dat., upon, on,* Mt 14:8; Mk 2:21; Lk 12:44; *close upon, by,* Mt 24:33; Jn 4:6; *in the neighborhood* or *society of,* Ac 28:14; *over, of authority,* Mt 24:47; *to, of addition, besides,* Mt 25:20; Eph 6:16; Col 3:14; *supervening upon, after,* 2 Co 1:4; 7:4; *immediately upon,* Jn 4:27; *upon, of the object of an act, towards, to,* Mk 5:33; Lk 18:7; Ac 5:35; *against, of hostile posture or disposition,* Lk 12:52; *in dependence upon,* Mt 4:4; Lk 5:5; Ac 14:3; *upon the ground of,* Mt 19:9; Lk 1:59; Phil 1:3; Heb 7:11; 8:6; 9:17; *with a view*

to, Gal 5:13; 1 Th 4:7; (3) *with the acc., upon,* with the idea of previous or present motion, Mt 4:5; 14:19, 26; *towards, of place, to,* Mt 3:13; 22:34; *towards, of the object of an action,* Lk 6:35; 9:38; *against, of hostile movement,* Mt 10:21; *over, of authority,* Lk 1:33; *to the extent of,* both of place and time, Rev 21:16; Ro 7:1; *near, by,* Mt 9:9; *about, at, of time,* Ac 3:1; *in order to, with a view to, for the purpose of,* Mt 3:7; Lk 7:44 [1909]

[2094] ἐπιβαίνω *epibainō* 6x pr. *to step upon; to mount,* Mt 21:5; *to go on board,* Ac 21:2; 27:2, *to enter,* Ac 20:18; *to enter upon,* Ac 21:4; 25:1* [1910]

[2095] ἐπιβάλλω *epiballō* 18x *to cast* or *throw upon,* Mk 11:7; 1 Co 7:35; *to lay on, apply to,* Lk 9:62; *to put on, sew on,* Mt 9:16; Lk 5:36; τὰς χεῖρας, *to lay hands on, offer violence to, seize,* Mt 26:50; also, *to lay hand to, undertake, commence,* Ac 12:1; intrans. *to rush, dash, beat into,* Mk 4:37; *to ponder, reflect on,* Mk 14:72; *to fall to one's share, pertain to,* Lk 15:12 [1911]

[2096] ἐπιβαρέω *epibareō* 3x *to burden;* met. *to be burdensome, chargeable to,* 1 Th 2:9; 2 Th 3:8; *to bear hard upon, overcharge,* 2 Co 2:5* [1912]

[2097] ἐπιβιβάζω *epibibazō* 3x *to cause to ascend* or *mount, to set upon,* Lk 10:34; 19:35; Ac 23:24* [1913]

[2098] ἐπιβλέπω *epiblepō* 3x *to look upon; to regard* with partiality, Jas 2:3; *to regard* with kindness and favor, Lk 1:48; 9:38* [1914]

[2099] ἐπίβλημα *epiblēma* 4x *that which is put over* or *upon;* in N.T. *a patch,* Mt 9:16; Mk 2:21; Lk 5:36 (2t)* [1915]

[2101] ἐπιβουλή *epiboulē* 4x *a purpose* or *design against* any one; *conspiracy, plot,* Ac 9:24; 20:3, 19; 23:30* [1917]

[2102] ἐπιγαμβρεύω *epigambreuō* 1x *to marry* a wife *by the law of affinity,* Mt 22:24* [1918]

[2103] ἐπίγειος *epigeios* 7x pr. *on the earth,* Phil 2:10; *earthly, terrestrial,* Jn 3:12; 1 Co 15:40; 2 Co 5:1; Phil 3:19; *earthly, low, grovelling,* Jas 3:15* [1919]

[2104] ἐπιγίνομαι *epiginomai* 1x *to come on, spring up,* as the wind, Ac 28:13* [1920]

[2105] ἐπιγινώσκω *epiginōskō* 44x pr. *to make* a thing *a subject of observation;* hence, *to arrive at knowledge from preliminaries; to attain to a knowledge of,* Mt 11:27; *to ascertain,* Lk 7:37; 23:7; *to perceive,* Mk 2:8; 5:30; *to discern, detect,* Mt 7:16, 20; *to recognize,* Mk 6:33; Lk

24:16, 31; Ac 3:10; *to acknowledge, admit,*
1 Co 14:37; 1 Ti 4:3; pass. *to have one's*
character discerned and acknowledged, 2 Co
6:9; from the Hebrew, *to regard* with favor
and kindness, 1 Co 16:18 [1921]

[2106] ἐπίγνωσις *epignōsis* 20x *the*
coming at the knowledge of a thing, *ascer-*
tainment, Ro 3:20; *a distance perception* or
impression, acknowledgment, insight, Col
2:2 [1922]

[2107] ἐπιγραφή *epigraphē* 5x *an in-*
scription; a legend of a coin, Mt 22:20; Mk
12:16; Lk 20:24; *a label* of a criminal's
name and offence, Mk 15:26; Lk 23:38*
[1923]

[2108] ἐπιγράφω *epigraphō* 5x pluperfect pass., ἐπεγεγράμμην, *to imprint a mark*
on; to inscribe, engrave, write on, Mk 15:26;
Ac 17:23; Rev 21:12; met. *to imprint, im-*
press deeply on, Heb 8:10; 10:16* [1924]

[2109] ἐπιδείκνυμι *epideiknymi* 7x *to*
exhibit, Mt 16:1; Ac 9:39; *to show,* Mt
22:19; Lk 17:14; *to point out,* Mt 24:1; *to*
demonstrate, prove, Ac 18:28; Heb 6:17*
[1925]

[2110] ἐπιδέχομαι *epidechomai* 2x *to*
admit; to receive kindly, welcome, entertain,
3 Jn 10; met. *to admit, approve, assent to,*
3 Jn 9* [1926]

[2111] ἐπιδημέω *epidēmeō* 2x *to dwell*
among a people; to be at home among one's
own people; and in N.T. *to sojourn as a*
stranger among another people, Ac 2:10;
17:21* [1927]

[2112] ἐπιδιατάσσομαι *epidiatassomai*
1x *to enjoin* anything *additional, superadd*
an injunction, Gal 3:15* [1928]

[2113] ἐπιδίδωμι *epididōmi* 9x *to give in*
addition; also, *to give to, deliver to, give into*
one's hands, Mt 7:9, 10; Lk 4:17; 11:11f.;
24:30, 42; Ac 15:30; intrans. probably a
nautical term, *to commit a ship to the wind,*
let her drive, Ac 27:15* [1929]

[2114] ἐπιδιορθόω *epidiorthoō* 1x *to set*
further to rights, to carry on an amendment,
correct, Tit 1:5* [1930]

[2115] ἐπιδύω *epidyō* 1x *to set upon, to*
set during, Eph 4:26* [1931]

[2116] ἐπιείκεια *epieikeia* 2x also
spelled ἐπιεικία, *reasonableness, equity;* in
N.T. *gentleness, mildness,* 2 Co 10:1; *clem-*
ency, Ac 24:4* [1932]

[2117] ἐπιεικής *epieikēs* 5x pr. *suit-*
able; fair, reasonable; gentle, mild, patient,
1 Ti 3:3; Tit 3:2; Jas 3:17; 1 Pe 2:18;
τὸ ἐπιεικές, *mildness, gentleness,* Phil 4:5*
[1933]

[2118] ἐπιζητέω *epizēteō* 13x *to seek for,*
make search for, Ac 12:19; *to require, de-*
mand, Mt 12:39; 16:4; Ac 19:39; *to desire,*
endeavor to obtain, Ro 11:7; Heb 11:14; *to*
seek with care and anxiety, Mt 6:32 [1934]

[2119] ἐπιθανάτιος *epithanatios* 1x
condemned to death, under sentence of death,
1 Co 4:9* [1935]

[2120] ἐπίθεσις *epithesis* 4x *the act of*
placing upon, imposition of hands, Ac 8:18;
1 Ti 4:14; 2 Ti 1:6; Heb 6:2* [1936]

[2121] ἐπιθυμέω *epithumeō* 16x with
the gen. or acc., *to set the heart upon; to de-*
sire, long for, have earnest desire, Mt 13:17;
Lk 15:16; *to lust after,* Mt 5:28; spc. *to*
covet, Ro 13:9 [1937]

[2122] ἐπιθυμητής *epithumētēs* 1x *one*
who has an ardent desire for anything, 1 Co
10:6* [1938]

[2123] ἐπιθυμία *epithumia* 38x *earnest*
desire, Lk 22:15; *irregular* or *violent desire,*
Mk 4:19; spc. impure *desire, lust,* Ro 1:24;
met. *the object of desire, what enkindles*
desire, 1 Jn 2:16, 17 [1939]

[2125] ἐπικαθίζω *epikathizō* 1x *to cause*
to sit upon, seat upon, Mt 21:7 (where
some mss read ἐπεκάθισεν, intrans. *to sit*
*upon)** [1940]

[2126] ἐπικαλέω *epikaleō* 30x pluperfect, ἐπεκέκλητο (3 sg), *to call on; to attach*
or *connect a name,* Ac 15:17; Jas 2:7; *to*
attach an additional name, to surname,
Mt 10:3; pass. *to receive an appellation* or
surname, Heb 11:16; mid. *to call upon,*
invoke, 2 Co 1:23; *to appeal to,* Ac 25:11,
12, 21 [1941]

[2127] ἐπικάλυμμα *epikalymma* 1x *a*
covering, veil; met. *a cloak,* 1 Pe 2:16*
[1942]

[2128] ἐπικαλύπτω *epikalyptō* 1x *to cov-*
er over; met. *to cover* or *veil* by a pardon,
Ro 4:7* [1943]

[2129] ἐπικατάρατος *epikataratos* 2x
cursed, accursed; subject to the curse of
condemnation, Gal 3:10; *infamous,* Gal
3:13* [1944]

[2130] ἐπίκειμαι *epikeimai* 7x *to lie*
upon, be placed upon, Jn 11:38; 21:9; *to*
press, urge upon, Lk 5:1; Ac 27:20; *be*
urgent, importunate upon, Lk 23:23; *to*
be imposed upon, be imposed by law, Heb
9:10; *by necessity,* 1 Co 9:16 [1945]

[2131] ἐπικέλλω *epikellō* 1x *to push* a
ship *to shore,* Ac 27:41* [2027]

[2134] Ἐπικούρειος *Epikoureios* 1x
an Epicurean, follower of the philosophy of
Epicurus, Ac 17:18* [1946]

[2135] ἐπικουρία *epikouria* 1x *help, as-*
sistance, Ac 26:22* [1947]

[2137] ἐπικρίνω *epikrinō* 1x *to decide; to*
decree, Lk 23:24* [1948]

[2138] ἐπιλαμβάνομαι *epilambanomai*
19x *to take hold of,* Mt 14:31; Mk 8:23;
to lay hold of, seize, Lk 23:26; Ac 16:19;
met. *to seize on* as a ground of accusation, Lk 20:20, 26; *to grasp, obtain* as if by
seizure, 1 Ti 6:12, 19; *to assume a portion*
of, to assume the nature of, or, *to attach* or
ally one's self to, Heb 2:16 [1949]

[2140] ἐπιλανθάνομαι *epilanthano-*
mai 8x *to forget,* Mt 16:5; *to be forgetful,*
neglectful of, to disregard, Phil 3:13; Heb
6:10; in N.T. in a passive sense, *forgotten,*
Lk 12:6 [1950]

[2141] ἐπιλέγω *epilegō* 2x *to call,* Jn
5:2; mid. *to select for one's self, choose,* Ac
15:40* [1951]

[2142] ἐπιλείπω *epileipō* 1x *to be insuf-*
ficient, to run short, to fail, Heb 11:32*
[1952]

[2143] ἐπιλείχω *epileichō* 1x *to lick,* Lk
16:21* [621]

[2144] ἐπιλησμονή *epilēsmonē* 1x *forget-*
fulness, oblivion, Jas 1:25* [1953]

[2145] ἐπίλοιπος *epiloipos* 1x *remain-*
ing, still left, 1 Pe 4:2* [1954]

[2146] ἐπίλυσις *epilysis* 1x *a loos-*
ing, liberation; met. *interpretation of* what
is enigmatical and obscure, 2 Pe 1:20*
[1955]

[2147] ἐπιλύω *epilyō* 2x *to loose* what
has previously been fastened or entangled, as a knot; met. *to solve, to explain,*
what is enigmatical, as a parable, Mk
4:34; *to settle, put an end to* a matter of
debate, Ac 19:39* [1956]

[2148] ἐπιμαρτυρέω *epimartyreō* 1x *to*
bear testimony to; to testify solemnly, 1 Pe
5:12* [1957]

[2149] ἐπιμέλεια *epimeleia* 1x *care, at-*
tention, Ac 27:3* [1958]

[2150] ἐπιμελέομαι *epimeleomai* 3x
gen., *to take care of,* Lk 10:34f.; 1 Ti 3:5*
[1959]

[2151] ἐπιμελῶς *epimelōs* 1x *carefully,*
diligently, Lk 15:8* [1960]

[2152] ἐπιμένω *epimenō* 16x *to stay*
longer, prolong a stay, remain on, Ac 10:48;
15:34; *to continue, persevere,* Jn 8:7; Ac
12:16; *to adhere to, continue to embrace,*
Ac 13:43; Ro 11:22; *to persist in,* Ro 6:1;
1 Co 16:8 [1961]

[2153] ἐπινεύω *epineuō* 1x *to nod to;* met. *to assent to, consent,* Ac 18:20★ [1962]

[2154] ἐπίνοια *epinoia* 1x *thought, purpose, device, intent,* Ac 8:22★ [1963]

[2155] ἐπιορκέω *epiorkeō* 1x *to forswear one's self, to fail of observing one's oath,* Mt 5:33★ [1964]

[2156] ἐπίορκος *epiorkos* 1x *one who violates his oath, perjured,* 1 Ti 1:10★ [1965]

[2157] ἐπιούσιος *epiousios* 2x This word occurs nowhere else in Greek literature except in the context of the Lord's prayer. Guesses include, *necessary for today, necessary for tomorrow, daily, sufficient,* Mt 6:11; Lk 11:3★ [1967]

[2158] ἐπιπίπτω *epipiptō* 11x *to fall upon; to throw one's self upon,* Lk 15:20; Jn 13:25; Ac 20:10, 37; *to press, urge upon,* Mk 3:10; *to light upon,* Ro 15:3; *to come over,* Ac 13:11; *to come upon, fall upon* mentally or spiritually, Lk 1:12; Ac 8:16; 10:10, 44; 11:15; 19:17 [1968]

[2159] ἐπιπλήσσω *epiplēssō* 1x pr. *to inflict blows upon;* met. *to chide, reprove,* 1 Ti 5:1★ [1969]

[2160] ἐπιποθέω *epipotheō* 9x *to desire besides;* also, *to desire earnestly, long for,* 2 Co 5:2; *to have a strong bent,* Jas 4:5; by impl. *to love, have affection for,* 2 Co 9:14 [1971]

[2161] ἐπιπόθησις *epipothēsis* 2x *earnest desire, strong affection,* 2 Co 7:7, 11★ [1972]

[2162] ἐπιπόθητος *epipothētos* 1x *earnestly desired, longed for,* Phil 4:1★ [1973]

[2163] ἐπιποθία *epipothia* 1x *earnest desire,* Ro 15:23★ [1974]

[2164] ἐπιπορεύομαι *epiporeuomai* 1x *to travel to; to come to,* Lk 8:4★ [1975]

[2165] ἐπιράπτω *epiraptō* 1x also ἐπιρράπτω, *to sew on,* Mk 2:21★ [1976]

[2166] ἐπιρίπτω *epiriptō* 2x *to throw upon, cast upon,* Lk 19:35; 1 Pe 5:7★ [1977]

[2168] ἐπίσημος *episēmos* 2x pr. *bearing a distinctive mark* or *device; noted, eminent,* Ro 16:7; *notorious,* Mt 27:16★ [1978]

[2169] ἐπισιτισμός *episitismos* 1x *supply of food, provisions,* Lk 9:12★ [1979]

[2170] ἐπισκέπτομαι *episkeptomai* 11x *to look at observantly, to inspect; to look out, select,* Ac 6:3; *to go see, visit,* Ac 7:23; 15:36; *to visit* for the purpose of comfort and relief, Mt 25:36, 43; Jas 1:27; from the Hebrew, of God, *to visit,* Lk 1:68, 78 [1980]

[2171] ἐπισκευάζομαι *episkeuazomai* 1x *to prepare for a journey,* Ac 21:15★ [643]

[2172] ἐπισκηνόω *episkēnoō* 1x *to quarter in* or *at;* met. *to abide upon,* 2 Co 12:9★ [1981]

[2173] ἐπισκιάζω *episkiazō* 5x *to overshadow,* Mt 17:5; met. *to shed influence upon,* Lk 1:35 [1982]

[2174] ἐπισκοπέω *episkopeō* 2x *to look at, inspect;* met. *to be circumspect, heedful,* Heb 12:15; *to oversee, to exercise the office of* ἐπίσκοπος, 1 Pe 5:2★ [1983]

[2175] ἐπισκοπή *episkopē* 4x *inspection, oversight, visitation;* of God, *visitation, interposition,* whether in mercy or judgment, Lk 19:44; 1 Pe 2:12; *the office of an ecclesiastical overseer,* 1 Ti 3:1; from the Hebrew, *charge, function,* Ac 1:20★ [1984]

[2176] ἐπίσκοπος *episkopos* 5x pr. *an inspector, overseer; a watcher, guardian,* 1 Pe 2:25; in N.T. *an ecclesiastical overseer,* Ac 20:28; Phil 1:1; 1 Ti 3:2; Tit 1:7★ [1985]

[2177] ἐπισπάομαι *epispaomai* 1x *to draw upon* or *after;* in N.T. mid. *to obliterate circumcision* by artificial extension of the foreskin, 1 Co 7:18★ [1986]

[2178] ἐπισπείρω *epispeirō* 1x *to sow in* or *among,* Mt 13:25★ [4687]

[2179] ἐπίσταμαι *epistamai* 14x *to be versed in, to be master of,* 1 Ti 6:4; *to be acquainted with,* Ac 18:25; 19:15; Jude 10: *to know,* Ac 10:28; *to remember, comprehend, understand,* Mk 14:68 [1987]

[2180] ἐπίστασις *epistasis* 2x pr. *care of, attention to,* 2 Co 11:28 [1999]

[2181] ἐπιστάτης *epistatēs* 7x pr. *one who stands by; one who is set over;* in N.T. in voc., equivalent to διδάσκαλε, or ῥαββί, *master, doctor,* Lk 5:5; 8:24, 45; 9:33, 49; 17:13★ [1988]

[2182] ἐπιστέλλω *epistellō* 3x *to send word to, to send injunctions,* Ac 15:20; 21:25; *to write to, write* a letter, Heb 13:22★ [1989]

[2184] ἐπιστήμων *epistēmōn* 1x *knowing, discreet, understanding,* Jas 3:13★ [1990]

[2185] ἐπιστηρίζω *epistērizō* 4x pr. *to cause to rest* or *lean on, to settle upon;* met. *to conform, strengthen, establish,* 14:22; 15:32, 41; 18:23★ [1991]

[2186] ἐπιστολή *epistolē* 24x *word sent; an order, command; an epistle, letter,* Ac 9:2; 15:30 [1992]

[2187] ἐπιστομίζω *epistomizō* 1x *to apply a curb* or *muzzle;* met. *to put to silence,* Tit 1:11★ [1993]

[2188] ἐπιστρέφω *epistrephō* 36x trans. *to turn towards; to turn round; to bring back, convert,* Lk 1:16, 17; Jas 5:19, 20; intrans. and mid. *to turn one's self upon* or *towards,* Ac 9:40; Rev 1:12; *to turn about,* Mt 9:22; *to turn back, return,* Mt 12:44; met. *to be converted,* Ac 28:27 [1994]

[2189] ἐπιστροφή *epistrophē* 1x *a turning towards, a turning about;* in N.T. met. *conversion,* Ac 15:3★ [1995]

[2190] ἐπισυνάγω *episynagō* 8x *to gather to* a place; *to gather together, assemble, convene,* Mt 23:37; 24:31; Lk 17:37 [1996]

[2191] ἐπισυναγωγή *episynagōgē* 2x *the act of being gathered together* or *assembled,* 2 Th 2:1; *an assembling together,* Heb 10:25ᴧ [1997]

[2192] ἐπισυντρέχω *episyntrechō* 1x *to run together* to a place, Mk 9:25★ [1998]

[2195] ἐπισφαλής *episphalēs* 1x *on the verge of falling, unsteady;* met. *insecure, hazardous, dangerous,* Ac 27:9★ [2000]

[2196] ἐπισχύω *epischuō* 1x *to strengthen;* intrans. *to gather strength;* met. *to be urgent, to press on* a point, *insist,* Lk 23:5★ [2001]

[2197] ἐπισωρεύω *episōreuō* 1x *to heap up, accumulate largely;* met. *to procure in abundance,* 2 Ti 4:3★ [2002]

[2198] ἐπιταγή *epitagē* 7x *injunction,* 1 Co 7:6, 25; 2 Co 8:8; *a decree,* Ro 16:26; 1 Ti 1:1; Tit 1:3; *authoritativeness, strictness,* Tit 2:15★ [2003]

[2199] ἐπιτάσσω *epitassō* 10x with dat., *to set over* or *upon; to enjoin, charge,* Mk 1:27; 6:39; Lk 4:36 [2004]

[2200] ἐπιτελέω *epiteleō* 10x *to bring to an end; to finish, complete, perfect,* Ro 15:28; 2 Co 8:6, 11; *to perform,* Lk 13:32; *to carry into practice, to realize,* 2 Co 7:1; *to discharge,* Heb 9:6; *to execute,* Heb 8:5; *to carry out to completion,* Phil 1:6; mid. *to end, make an end,* Gal 3:3; pass. *to be fully undergone, endured,* 1 Pe 5:9 [2005]

[2201] ἐπιτήδειος *epitēdeios* 1x *fit, suitable, necessary,* Jas 2:16★ [2006]

[2202] ἐπιτίθημι *epitithēmi* 39x *to put, place,* or *lay upon,* Mt 9:18; Lk 4:40; *to impose* a name, Mk 3:16, 17; *to inflict,* Ac 16:23; Lk 10:30; Rev 22:18; mid. *to* *impose* with authority, Ac 15:28; 28:10; *to set* or *fall upon, assail, assault, attack,* Ac 18:10 [2007]

[2203] ἐπιτιμάω *epitimaō* 29x pr. *to set a value upon; to assess a penalty; to allege as a crimination;* hence, *to reprove, chide, censure, rebuke, reprimand,* Mt 19:13; Lk 23:40; in N.T. *to admonish strongly, enjoin strictly,* Mt 12:16; Lk 17:3 [2008]

[2204] ἐπιτιμία *epitimia* 1x *a punishment, penalty,* 2 Co 2:6* [2009]

[2205] ἐπιτρέπω *epitrepō* 18x *to give over, to leave to the entire trust* or *management of* any one; hence, *to permit, allow, suffer,* Mt 8:21; Mk 5:13 [2010]

[2207] ἐπιτροπή *epitropē* 1x *a trust; a commission, permission,* Ac 26:12* [2011]

[2208] ἐπίτροπος *epitropos* 3x *one to whose charge* or *control a thing is left; a steward, bailiff, agent, manager,* Mt 20:8; *steward* or *overseer of the revenue, treasurer,* Lk 8:3; *a guardian* of children, Gal 4:2* [2012]

[2209] ἐπιτυγχάνω *epitynchanō* 5x *to light upon, find; to hit, reach; to acquire, obtain, attain,* Ro 11:7 (2t); Heb 6:15; 11:33; Jas 4:2* [2013]

[2210] ἐπιφαίνω *epiphainō* 4x *to make to appear, to display;* pass. *to be manifested, revealed,* Tit 2:11; 3:4; intrans. *to give light, shine,* Lk 1:79; Ac 27:20* [2014]

[2211] ἐπιφάνεια *epiphaneia* 6x *appearance, manifestation,* 1 Ti 6:14; 2 Ti 1:10; *glorious display,* 2 Th 2:8; 2 Ti 4:1, 8; Tit 2:13* [2015]

[2213] ἐπιφαύσκω *epiphauskō* 1x *to shine upon, give light to, enlighten,* Eph 5:14* [2017]

[2214] ἐπιφέρω *epipherō* 2x *to bring upon* or *against,* Jude 9; *to inflict,* Ro 3:5* [2018]

[2215] ἐπιφωνέω *epiphōneō* 4x *to cry aloud, raise a shout* at a speaker, whether applaudingly, Ac 12:22; or the contrary, *to clamor at,* Lk 23:21; Ac 21:34; 22:24* [2019]

[2216] ἐπιφώσκω *epiphōskō* 2x *to dawn,* Mt 28:1; hence, used of the reckoned commencement of the day, *to be near commencing, to dawn on,* Lk 23:54* [2020]

[2217] ἐπιχειρέω *epicheireō* 3x *to put hand to* a thing; *to undertake, attempt,* Lk 1:1; Ac 9:29; 19:13* [2021]

[2219] ἐπιχέω *epicheō* 1x *to pour upon,* Lk 10:34* [2022]

[2220] ἐπιχορηγέω *epichorēgeō* 5x *to supply further; to superadd,* 2 Pe 1:5; *to supply, furnish, give,* 2 Co 9:10; Gal 3:5; 2 Pe 1:11; pass. *to gather vigor,* Col 2:19* [2023]

[2221] ἐπιχορηγία *epichorēgia* 2x *supply, aid, support,* Eph 4:16; Phil 1:19* [2024]

[2222] ἐπιχρίω *epichriō* 2x *to smear upon, to anoint,* Jn 9:6, 11* [2025]

[2224] ἐποικοδομέω *epoikodomeō* 7x *to build upon,* 1 Co 3:10, 12, 14; pass. met. *to be built upon* as parts of a spiritual structure, Eph 2:20; *to build up, carry up a building;* met. *to build up in spiritual advancement,* Col 2:7; Jude 20* [2026]

[2226] ἐπονομάζω *eponomazō* 1x *to attach a name to;* pass. *to be named,* Ro 2:17* [2028]

[2227] ἐποπτεύω *epopteuō* 2x *to look upon, observe, watch; to witness, be an eye-witness of,* 1 Pe 2:12; 3:2* [2029]

[2228] ἐπόπτης *epoptēs* 1x *a looker-on, eye-witness,* 2 Pe 1:16* [2030]

[2229] ἔπος *epos* 1x *a word, that which is expressed by words;* ὡς ἔπος εἰπεῖν, *so to say, if the expression may be allowed,* Heb 7:9* [2031]

[2230] ἐπουράνιος *epouranios* 19x *heavenly,* in respect of locality, Eph 1:20; Phil 2:10; τὰ ἐπουράνια, *the upper regions* of the air, Eph 6:12; *heavenly,* in respect of essence and character, *unearthly,* 1 Co 15:48, 49; met. *divine, spiritual,* Jn 3:12 [2032]

[2231] ἑπτά *hepta* 88x *seven,* indecl. numeral, Mt 15:34, 37; by Jewish usage for a round number, Mt 12:45; Lk 11:26 [2033]

[2232] ἑπτάκις *heptakis* 4x *seven times,* Mt 18:21, 22; Lk 17:4 (2t)* [2034]

[2233] ἑπτακισχίλιοι *heptakischilioi* 1x *seven thousand,* Ro 11:4* [2035]

[2235] Ἔραστος *Erastos* 3x *Erastus,* pr. name, Ac 19:22; Ro 16:23; 2 Ti 4:20* [2037]

[2236] ἐραυνάω *eraunaō* 6x *to search, examine, investigate,* Jn 5:39; 7:52; Ro 8:27; 1 Co 2:10; 1 Pe 1:11; Rev 2:23* [2045]

[2237] ἐργάζομαι *ergazomai* 41x intrans. *to work, labor,* Mt 21:28; Lk 13:14; *to trade, traffic, do business,* Mt 25:16; Rev 18:17; *to act, exert one's power, be active,* Jn 5:17; trans. *to do, perform, commit,* Mt 26:10; Jn 6:28; *to be engaged in, occupied*

upon, 1 Co 9:13; Rev 18:17; *to acquire, gain by one's labor,* Jn 6:27 [2038]

[2238] ἐργασία *ergasia* 6x *work, labor;* in N.T. ἐργασίαν διδόναι, *to endeavor, strive,* Lk 12:58; *performance, practice,* Eph 4:19; *a trade, business, craft,* Ac 19:25, *gain* acquired by labor or trade, *profit,* Ac 16:16, 19; 19:24* [2039]

[2239] ἐργάτης *ergatēs* 16x *a workman, laborer,* Mt 9:37, 38; 20:1, 2, 8; met. *a spiritual workman* or *laborer,* 2 Co 11:13; *an artisan, artificer,* Ac 19:25; *a worker, practicer,* Lk 13:27 [2040]

[2240] ἔργον *ergon* 169x *anything done* or *to be done; a deed, work, action,* Jn 3:21; Eph 2:10; 2 Co 9:8, et al. freq.; *duty enjoined, office, charge, business,* Mk 13:34; Jn 4:34, et al. freq.; *a process, course of action,* Jas 1:4; *a work, product of an action* or *process,* Ac 7:41; Heb 1:10; *substance in effect,* Ro 2:15 [2041]

[2241] ἐρεθίζω *erethizō* 2x *to provoke, to irritate, exasperate,* Col 3:21; *to incite, stimulate,* 2 Co 9:2* [2042]

[2242] ἐρείδω *ereidō* 1x *to make to lean upon; to fix firmly;* intrans. *to become firmly fixed, stick fast,* Ac 27:41* [2043]

[2243] ἐρεύγομαι *ereugomai* 1x *to vomit;* met. *to utter, declare openly,* Mt 13:35* [2044]

[2244] ἐρημία *erēmia* 4x *a solitude, uninhabited region, waste, desert,* Mt 15:33; Mk 8:4; 2 Co 11:26; Heb 11:38* [2047]

[2245] ἔρημος *erēmos* 48x *lone, desert, waste, uninhabited,* Mt 14:13, 15; Mk 6:31, 32, 35; *lone, abandoned* to ruin, Mt 23:38; Lk 13:35; met. *lone, unmarried,* Gal 4:27; as a subst. *a desert, uninhabited region, waste,* Mt 3:1; 24:26; Ac 7:36 [2048]

[2246] ἐρημόω *erēmoō* 5x *to lay waste, make desolate, bring to ruin,* Mt 12:25; Lk 11:17; Rev 17:16; 18:17, 19* [2049]

[2247] ἐρήμωσις *erēmōsis* 3x *desolation, devastation,* Mt 24:15; Mk 13:14; Lk 21:20* [2050]

[2248] ἐρίζω *erizō* 1x *to quarrel; to wrangle; to use the harsh tone of a wrangler* or *brawler, to grate,* Mt 12:19* [2051]

[2249] ἐριθεία *eritheia* 7x *the service of a party, party spirit; feud, faction,* 2 Co 12:20; *contentious disposition, selfish ambition,* Gal 5:20; Phil 1:17; 2:3; Jas 3:14; by impl. *untowardness, disobedience,* Ro 2:8; Jas 3:16* [2052]

[2250] ἔριον *erion* 2x *wool,* Heb 9:19; Rev 1:14* [2053]

[2251] ἔρις *eris* 9x *altercation, strife,* Ro 13:13; *contentious disposition,* Ro 1:29; Phil 1:15 [2054]

[2252] ἐρίφιον *eriphion* 1x *a goat, kid,* Mt 25:33* [2055]

[2253] ἔριφος *eriphos* 2x *a goat, kid,* Mt 25:32; Lk 15:29* [2056]

[2254] Ἑρμᾶς *Hermas* 1x *Hermas,* pr. name, Ro 16:14* [2057]

[2255] ἑρμηνεία *hermēneia* 2x *interpretation, explanation,* 1 Co 14:26; meton. *the power* or *faculty of interpreting,* 1 Co 12:10* [2058]

[2257] ἑρμηνεύω *hermēneuō* 3x *to explain, interpret, translate,* Jn 1:42; 9:7; Heb 7:2* [2059]

[2258] Ἑρμῆς *Hermēs* 2x *Hermes* or *Mercury,* son of Jupiter and Maia, the messenger and interpreter of the gods, and the patron of eloquence, learning, etc., Ac 14:12; Ro 16:14* [2060]

[2259] Ἑρμογένης *Hermogenēs* 1x *Hermogenes,* pr. name, 2 Ti 1:15* [2061]

[2260] ἑρπετόν *herpeton* 4x *a creeping animal, a reptile,* Ac 10:12; 11:6; Ro 1:23; Jas 3:7* [2062]

[2261] ἐρυθρός *erythros* 2x *red,* Ac 7:36; Heb 11:29* [2063]

[2262] ἔρχομαι *erchomai* 632x *to come, to go, to pass.* By the combination of this verb with other terms, a variety of meaning results, which, however, is due, not to a change of meaning in the verb, but to the adjuncts. Ὁ ἐρχόμενος, *He who is coming, the expected Messiah,* Mt 11:3 [2064]

[2263] ἐρωτάω *erōtaō* 63x *to ask, interrogate, inquire of,* Mt 21:24; Lk 20:3; in N.T. *to ask, request, beg, beseech,* Mt 15:23; Lk 4:38; Jn 14:16 [2065]

[2264] ἐσθής *esthēs* 8x also spelled ἔσθησις, *a robe, vestment, raiment, garment,* Lk 23:11; 24:4; Ac 1:10; 10:30; 12:21; Jas 2:2, 3* [2066]

[2266] ἐσθίω *esthiō* 158x *to eat,* Mt 12:1; 15:27; ἐσθίειν καὶ πίνειν, *to eat and drink, to eat and drink* in the usual manner, *follow the common mode of living,* Mt 11:18; also with the associated notion of supposed security, Lk 17:27; *to feast, banquet,* Mt 24:49; met. *to devour, consume,* Heb 10:27; Jas 5:3; from the Hebrew, ἄρτον ἐσθίειν, *to eat bread, to take food, take the usual meals,* Mt 15:2 [2068, 5315]

[2268] Ἐσλί *Hesli* 1x *Esli,* pr. name, indecl., Lk 3:25* [2069]

[2269] ἔσοπτρον *esoptron* 2x *mirror,* Jas 1:23; 1 Co 13:12* [2072]

[2270] ἑσπέρα *hespera* 3x *evening,* Lk 24:29; Ac 4:3; 28:23* [2073]

[2272] Ἑσρώμ *Hesrōm* 3x *Hezron,* pr. name, indecl., Mt 1:3; Lk 3:33* [2074]

[2274] ἔσχατος *eschatos* 52x *farthest; last, latest,* Mt 12:45; Mk 12:6; *lowest,* Mt 19:30; 20:16; *in the lowest plight,* 1 Co 4:9 [2078]

[2275] ἐσχάτως *eschatōs* 1x *to be in the last extremity,* Mk 5:23* [2079]

[2276] ἔσω *esō* 9x can function as an improper prep., *in, within, in the interior of,* Mt 26:58; Jn 20:26; ὁ, ἡ, τὸ ἔσω, *inner, interior, internal;* met. *within* the pale of community, 1 Co 5:12; ὁ ἔσω ἄνθρωπος, *the inner man, the mind, soul,* Ro 7:22 [2080]

[2277] ἔσωθεν *esōthen* 12x *from within, from the interior,* Mk 7:21, 23; *within, in the internal parts,* Mt 7:15; ὁ, ἡ, τὸ ἔσωθεν, *interior, internal,* Lk 11:39, 40; ὁ ἔσωθεν ἄνθρωπος, *the mind, soul,* 2 Co 4:16 [2081]

[2278] ἐσώτερος *esōteros* 2x *inner, interior,* Ac 16:24; Heb 6:19* [2082]

[2279] ἑταῖρος *hetairos* 3x *a companion, associate, fellow-comrade, friend,* Mt 20:13; 22:12; 26:50* [2083]

[2280] ἑτερόγλωσσος *heteroglōssos* 1x *one who speaks another* or *foreign language,* 1 Co 14:21* [2084]

[2281] ἑτεροδιδασκαλέω *heterodidaskaleō* 2x *to teach other* or *different doctrine,* and spc. *what is foreign to the Christian religion,* 1 Ti 1:3; 6:3* [2085]

[2282] ἑτεροζυγέω *heterozygeō* 1x *to be unequally yoked* or *matched,* 2 Co 6:14* [2086]

[2283] ἕτερος *heteros* 98x *other,* Mt 12:45; *another, some other,* Mt 8:21; *besides,* Lk 23:32; ὁ ἕτερος, *the other* of two, Mt 6:24; τῇ ἑτέρᾳ, *on the next* day, Ac 20:15; 27:3; ὁ ἕτερος, *one's neighbor,* Ro 13:8; *different,* Lk 9:29; *foreign, strange,* Ac 2:4; 1 Co 14:21; *illicit,* Jude 7 [2087]

[2284] ἑτέρως *heterōs* 1x *otherwise, differently,* Phil 3:15* [2088]

[2285] ἔτι *eti* 93x *yet, still,* Mt 12:46; *still, further, longer,* Lk 16:2; *further, besides, in addition,* Mt 18:16; with a compar. *yet, still,* Phil 1:9 [2089]

[2286] ἑτοιμάζω *hetoimazō* 40x *to make ready, prepare,* Mt 22:4; 26:17 [2090]

[2288] ἑτοιμασία *hetoimasia* 1x *preparation; preparedness, readiness,* Eph 6:15* [2091]

[2289] ἕτοιμος *hetoimos* 17x *ready, prepared,* Mt 22:4, 8; Mk 14:15 [2092]

[2290] ἑτοίμως *hetoimōs* 3x *in readiness, preparedly,* Ac 21:13; 2 Co 2:14; 1 Pet 4:5* [2093]

[2291] ἔτος *etos* 49x *a year,* Lk 2:41; 3:23 [2094]

[2293] Εὔα *heua* 2x *Eve,* pr. name, 2 Co 11:3; 1 Ti 2:13* [2096]

[2294] εὐαγγελίζω *euangelizō* 54x *to address with good tidings,* Rev 10:7; 14:6; but elsewhere *to proclaim as good tidings, to announce good tidings of,* Lk 1:19; *to address with good tidings,* Ac 13:32; 14:15; *to address with the Gospel teaching, evangelize,* Ac 16:10; Gal 1:9; absol. *to announce the good tidings* of the Gospel, Lk 4:18; 9:6; pass. *to be announced as good tidings,* Lk 16:16; *to be addressed with good tidings,* Mt 11:5; Lk 7:22; Heb 4:2 [2097]

[2295] εὐαγγέλιον *euangelion* 76x *glad tidings, good* or *joyful news,* Mt 4:23; 9:35; *the Gospel; doctrines of the Gospel,* Mt 26:13; Mk 8:35; meton. *the preaching of,* or *instruction in, the Gospel,* 1 Co 4:15; 9:14 [2098]

[2296] εὐαγγελιστής *euangelistēs* 3x pr. *one who announces glad tidings; an evangelist, preacher of the Gospel, teacher of the Christian religion,* Ac 21:8; Eph 4:11; 2 Ti 4:5* [2099]

[2297] εὐαρεστέω *euaresteō* 3x *to please,* Heb 11:5, 6; pass. *to take pleasure in, be well pleased with,* Heb 13:16* [2100]

[2298] εὐάρεστος *euarestos* 9x *well-pleasing, acceptable, grateful,* Ro 12:1, 2 [2101]

[2299] εὐαρέστως *euarestōs* 1x *acceptably,* Heb 12:28 [2102]

[2300] Εὔβουλος *euboulos* 1x *Eubulus,* pr. name, 2 Ti 4:21* [2103]

[2301] εὖγε *euge* 1x *Well done!* Lk 19:17* [2095]

[2302] εὐγενής *eugenēs* 3x *well-born, of high rank, honorable,* Lk 19:12; 1 Co 1:26; *generous, candid,* Ac 17:11* [2104]

[2304] εὐδία *eudia* 1x *serenity of the heavens, a cloudless sky, fair* or *fine weather,* Mt 16:2* [2105]

[2305] εὐδοκέω *eudokeō* 21x *to think well, approve, consent, take delight* or *pleasure,* Mt 3:17; 17:5; Mk 1:11; Lk 3:22; 12:32 [2106]

[2306] εὐδοκία *eudokia* 9x *good will, favor,* Lk 2:14; *good pleasure, purpose, intention,* Mt 11:26; Lk 10:21; Eph 1:5, 9; Phil 2:13; by impl. *desire,* Ro 10:1; Phil 1:15; 2 Th 1:11* [2107]

[2307] εὐεργεσία *euergesia* 2x *well-doing, a good deed, benefit conferred,* Ac 4:9; *duty, good offices,* 1 Ti 6:2* [2108]

[2308] εὐεργετέω *euergeteō* 1x *to do good, exercise beneficence,* Ac 10:38* [2109]

[2309] εὐεργέτης *euergetēs* 1x *a well-doer; a benefactor,* Lk 22:25* [2110]

[2310] εὔθετος *euthetos* 3x pr. *well arranged, rightly disposed; fit, proper, adapted,* Lk 9:62; 14:35; *useful,* Heb 6:7* [2111]

[2311] εὐθέως *eutheōs* 36x *immediately, instantly, at once,* Mt 8:3; 13:5 [2112]

[2312] εὐθυδρομέω *euthudromeō* 2x *to run on a straight course; to sail on a direct course,* Ac 16:11; 21:1* [2113]

[2313] εὐθυμέω *euthumeō* 3x *to be cheerful, be in good spirits, take courage,* Ac 27:22, 25; Jas 5:13* [2114]

[2314] εὔθυμος *euthumos* 1x *good cheer* or *courage, cheerful,* Ac 27:36* [2115]

[2315] εὐθύμως *euthumōs* 1x *cheerfully,* Ac 24:10* [2115]

[2316] εὐθύνω *euthunō* 2x *to guide straight; to direct, guide, steer* a ship, Jas 3:4; *to make straight,* Jn 1:23* [2116]

[2317] εὐθύς *euthus* 59x *straight forwards; directly, immediately, instantly,* Mt 3:16; 13:20, 21 [2117]

[2319] εὐθύτης *euthutēs* 1x *righteousness, uprightness, equity,* Heb 1:8* [2118]

[2320] εὐκαιρέω *eukaireō* 3x *to have convenient time* or *opportunity, have leisure,* Mk 6:31; 1 Co 16:12; *to be at leisure* for a thing, *to be disposed to attend, to give time,* Ac 17:21* [2119]

[2321] εὐκαιρία *eukairia* 2x *convenient opportunity, favorable occasion,* Mt 26:16; Lk 22:6* [2120]

[2322] εὔκαιρος *eukairos* 2x *timely, opportune, seasonable, convenient,* Mk 6:21; Heb 4:16* [2121]

[2323] εὐκαίρως *eukairōs* 2x *opportunely, seasonable, conveniently,* Mk 14:11; 2 Ti 4:2* [2122]

[2324] εὔκοπος *eukopos* 7x *easy,* Mt 9:5; 19:24; Mk 2:9; 10:25; Lk 5:3; 16:17; 18:25 [2123]

[2325] εὐλάβεια *eulabeia* 2x *the disposition of one who is* εὐλαβής, *caution, circum-*

spection; in N.T. *reverence* to God, *piety,* Heb 5:7; 12:28* [2124]

[2326] εὐλαβέομαι *eulabeomai* 1x *to fear, be afraid* or *apprehensive;* in N.T. absol. *to reverence* God, *to be influenced by pious awe,* Heb 11:7* [2125]

[2327] εὐλαβής *eulabēs* 4x pr. *taking hold of well,* i.e., *warily;* hence, *cautious, circumspect; full of reverence* towards God, *devout, pious, religious,* Lk 2:25; Ac 2:5; 8:2; 22:12* [2126]

[2328] εὐλογέω *eulogeō* 41x pr. *to speak well of,* in N.T. *to bless, ascribe praise and glorification,* Lk 1:64; *to bless, invoke a blessing upon,* Mt 5:44; *to bless, confer a favor* or *blessing upon,* Eph 1:3; Heb 6:14; pass. *to be blessed, to be an object of favor* or *blessing,* Lk 1:28 [2127]

[2329] εὐλογητός *eulogētos* 8x *worthy of praise* or *blessing, blessed,* Mk 14:61; Lk 1:68 [2128]

[2330] εὐλογία *eulogia* 16x pr. *good speaking; fair speech, flattery,* Ro 16:18; in N.T. *blessing, praise, celebration,* 1 Co 10:16; Rev 5:12, 13; *invocation of good, benediction,* Jas 3:10; *a divine blessing,* Ro 15:29; *a gift, benevolence,* 2 Co 9:5; *a frank gift,* as opposed to πλεονεξία, 2 Co 9:5; ἐπ' εὐλογίαις, *liberally,* 2 Co 9:6 [2129]

[2331] εὐμετάδοτος *eumetadotos* 1x *liberal, bountiful, generous,* 1 Ti 6:18* [2130]

[2332] Εὐνίκη *eunikē* 1x *Eunice,* pr. name, 2 Ti 1:5* [2131]

[2333] εὐνοέω *eunoeō* 1x *to have kind thoughts, be well affected* or *kindly disposed* towards, *make friends,* Mt 5:25* [2132]

[2334] εὔνοια *eunoia* 1x *good will, kindliness; heartiness, enthusiasm,* Eph 6:7* [2133]

[2336] εὐνοῦχος *eunouchos* 8x pr. *one who has charge of the bedchamber;* hence, *a eunuch, one emasculated,* Mt 19:12; as eunuchs in the East often rose to places of power and trust, hence, *a minister of a court,* Ac 8:27, 34, 36, 38f.* [2135]

[2337] Εὐοδία *euodia* 1x *Euodia,* pr. name, Phil 4:2* [2136]

[2338] εὐοδόω *euodoō* 4x *to give a prosperous journey; cause to prosper* or *be successful;* pass. *to have a prosperous journey, to succeed in a journey,* Ro 1:10; met. *to be furthered, to prosper,* temporally or spiritually, 1 Co 16:2; 3 Jn 2 (2t)* [2137]

[2339] εὐπάρεδρος *euparedros* 1x *constantly attending; devoted to;*

τὸ εὐπάρεδρον, *devotedness,* 1 Co 7:35* [2145]

[2340] εὐπειθής *eupeithēs* 1x *easily persuaded, compliant,* Jas 3:17* [2138]

[2342] εὐπερίστατος *euperistatos* 1x *easily* or *constantly distracted,* Heb 12:1* [2139]

[2343] εὐποιΐα *eupoiia* 1x *doing good, beneficence,* Heb 13:16* [2140]

[2344] εὐπορέω *euporeō* 1x *to be in prosperous circumstances, enjoy plenty,* Ac 11:29* [2141]

[2345] εὐπορία *euporia* 1x *wealth, abundance,* Ac 19:25* [2142]

[2346] εὐπρέπεια *euprepeia* 1x *grace, beauty,* Jas 1:11* [2143]

[2347] εὐπρόσδεκτος *euprosdektos* 5x *acceptable, grateful, pleasing,* Ro 15:16, 31; 2 Co 6:2; 8:12; 1 Pe 2:5; in N.T. *gracious** [2144]

[2349] εὐπροσωπέω *euprosōpeō* 1x *to carry* or *make a fair appearance,* Gal 6:12* [2146]

[2350] εὐρακύλων *eurakylōn* 1x *the northeaster,* Ac 27:14* [2148]

[2351] εὑρίσκω *heuriskō* 176x *to find, to meet with;* Mt 18:28; 20:6; *to find out, to detect, discover,* Lk 23:2, 4, 14; *to acquire, obtain, win, gain,* Lk 1:30; 9:12; *to find mentally, to comprehend, recognize,* Ac 17:27; Ro 7:21; *to find* by experience, *observe, gather,* Ro 7:18; *to devise* as feasible, Lk 5:19; 19:48 [2147]

[2352] εὐρακύλων *eurakylōn* 1x also spelled εὐρυκλύδων and εὐροκλύδων, which *BAGD* says was probably due to scribal error, *euracylon,* the name of a tempestuous southeast wind, Ac 27:14* [2148]

[2353] εὐρύχωρος *eurychōros* 1x *spacious; broad, wide,* Mt 7:13* [2149]

[2354] εὐσέβεια *eusebeia* 15x *reverential feeling; piety, devotion, godliness,* Ac 3:12; 1 Ti 2:2; 4:7, 8; *religion, the* Christian *religion,* 1 Ti 3:16 [2150]

[2355] εὐσεβέω *eusebeō* 2x *to exercise piety;* towards a deity, *to worship,* Ac 17:23; towards relatives, *to be dutiful towards,* 1 Ti 5:4* [2151]

[2356] εὐσεβής *eusebēs* 3x *reverent; pious, devout, religious,* Ac 10:2, 7; 2 Pe 2:9* [2152]

[2357] εὐσεβῶς *eusebōs* 2x *piously, religiously,* 2 Ti 3:12; Tit 2:12* [2153]

[2358] εὔσημος *eusēmos* 1x pr. *well marked, strongly marked;* met. *significant, intelligible,* 1 Co 14:9★ [2154]

[2359] εὔσπλαγχνος *eusplanchnos* 2x *tender-hearted, compassionate,* Eph 4:32; 1 Pe 3:8★ [2155]

[2361] εὐσχημόνως *euschēmonōs* 3x *in a becoming manner, with propriety, decently, gracefully,* Ro 13:13; 1 Co 14:40; 1 Th 4:12★ [2156]

[2362] εὐσχημοσύνη *euschēmosynē* 1x *comeliness, gracefulness;* artificial *comeliness, ornamental array, embellishment,* 1 Co 12:23★ [2157]

[2363] εὐσχήμων *euschēmōn* 5x *of good appearance, pleasing to look upon, comely,* 1 Co 12:24; met. *becoming, decent,* τὸ εὔσχημον, *decorum, propriety,* 1 Co 7:35; *honorable, reputable, of high standing and influence,* Mk 15:43; Ac 13:50; 17:12★ [2158]

[2364] εὐτόνως *eutonōs* 2x *intensely, vehemently, strenuously,* Lk 23:10; Ac 18:28★ [2159]

[2365] εὐτραπελία *eutrapelia* 1x *facetiousness, pleasantry;* hence, *buffoonery, coarse laughter,* Eph 5:4★ [2160]

[2366] Εὔτυχος *eutychos* 1x *Eutychus,* pr. name, Ac 20:9★ [2161]

[2367] εὐφημία *euphēmia* 1x pr. *use of words of good omen;* hence, *favorable expression, praise, commendation,* 2 Co 6:8★ [2162]

[2368] εὔφημος *euphēmos* 1x pr. *of good omen, auspicious;* hence, *of good report, commendable, laudable, reputable,* Phil 4:8★ [2163]

[2369] εὐφορέω *euphoreō* 1x *to bear* or *bring forth well* or *plentifully, yield abundantly,* Lk 12:16★ [2164]

[2370] εὐφραίνω *euphrainō* 14x *to gladden,* 2 Co 2:2; pass. *to be glad, exult, rejoice,* Lk 12:19; Ac 2:26; mid. *to feast in token of joy, keep a day of rejoicing,* Lk 15:23, 24, 29, 32 [2165]

[2371] Εὐφράτης *euphratēs* 2x the river *Euphrates,* Rev 9:14; 16:12★ [2166]

[2372] εὐφροσύνη *euphrosynē* 2x *joy, gladness, rejoicing,* Ac 2:28; 14:17★ [2167]

[2373] εὐχαριστέω *eucharisteō* 38x *to thank,* Lk 17:16; absol. *to give thanks,* Mt 15:36; 26:27; pass. *to be made a matter of thankfulness,* 2 Co 1:11 [2168]

[2374] εὐχαριστία *eucharistia* 15x *gratitude, thankfulness,* Ac 24:3; *thanks, the act of giving thanks, thanksgiving,*

1 Co 14:16; *conversation marked by the gentle cheerfulness of a grateful heart,* as contrasted with the unseemly mirth of εὐτραπελία, Eph 5:4 [2169]

[2375] εὐχάριστος *eucharistos* 1x *grateful, pleasing; mindful of benefits, thankful,* Col 3:15★ [2170]

[2376] εὐχή *euchē* 3x *a wish, prayer,* Jas 5:15; *a vow,* Ac 21:23; Ac 18:18★ [2171]

[2377] εὔχομαι *euchomai* 7x *to pray, offer prayer,* Ac 26:29; 2 Co 13:7, 9; Jas 5:16; *to wish, desire,* Ac 27:29; Ro 9:3; 3 Jn 2★ [2172]

[2378] εὔχρηστος *euchrēstos* 3x *highly useful, very profitable,* 2 Ti 2:21; 4:11; Phlm 11★ [2173]

[2379] εὐψυχέω *eupsycheō* 1x *to be animated, encouraged, in good spirits,* Phil 2:19★ [2174]

[2380] εὐωδία *euōdia* 3x *a sweet smell, grateful odor, fragrance,* 2 Co 2:15; Eph 5:2; Phil 4:18★ [2175]

[2381] εὐώνυμος *euōnymos* 9x *of good name* or *omen;* used also as an euphemism by the Greeks instead of ἀριστερός, which was a word of bad import, as all omens on the left denoted misfortune; *the left,* Mt 20:21, 23; 25:33, 41 [2176]

[2383] ἐφάλλομαι *ephallomai* 1x *to leap* or *spring upon, assault,* Ac 19:16★ [2177]

[2384] ἐφάπαξ *ephapax* 5x *once for all,* Ro 6:10; Heb 7:27; 9:12; 10:10; *at once,* 1 Co 15:6★ [2178]

[2386] Ἐφέσιος *Ephesios* 5x *Ephesian,* belonging to Ephesus, Ac 19:28, 34, 35; 21:29★ [2180]

[2387] Ἔφεσος *Ephesos* 16x *Ephesus,* a celebrated city of Asia Minor, Ac 18:19, 21, 24; 1 Co 15:32★ [2181]

[2388] ἐφευρετής *epheuretēs* 1x *an inventor, deviser,* Ro 1:30★ [2182]

[2389] ἐφημερία *ephēmeria* 2x pr. *daily course; the daily service* of the temple; *a class* of priests to which the daily service for a week was allotted in rotation, Lk 1:5, 8★ [2183]

[2390] ἐφήμερος *ephēmeros* 1x *lasting for a day; daily sufficient for a day, necessary for every day,* Jas 2:15★ [2184]

[2391] ἐφικνέομαι *ephikneomai* 2x *to come* or *reach to, to reach* a certain point or end; *to reach, arrive at,* 2 Co 10:13, 14★ [2185]

[2392] ἐφίστημι *ephistēmi* 21x trans. *to place upon, over, close by;* intrans. *to stand by* or *near,* Lk 2:38; 4:39; *to come suddenly*

upon, Lk 2:9; 24:4; *to come upon, assault,* Ac 6:12; 17:5; *to come near, approach,* Lk 10:40; *to impend, be instant, to be at hand,* 1 Th 5:3; *to be present,* Ac 28:2; *to be pressing, urgent, earnest,* 2 Ti 4:2 [2186]

[2393] ἐφοράω *ephoraō* 2x a proposed lexical form for the second aorist ἐπεῖδον [1896]

[2394] Ἐφραΐμ *Ephraim* 1x *Ephraim,* pr. name, indecl. Jn 11:54★ [2187]

[2395] ἐφφαθά *ephphatha* 1x Aramaic, *be thou opened,* Mk 7:34★ [2188]

[2396] ἐχθές *echthes* 3x *yesterday,* Jn 4:52; Ac 7:28; Heb 13:8★ [5504]

[2397] ἔχθρα *echthra* 6x *enmity, discord, feud,* Lk 23:12; Gal 5:20; *alienation,* Eph 2:14, 16; *a principle* or *state of enmity,* Ro 8:7; Jas 4:4★ [2189]

[2398] ἐχθρός *echthros* 32x *hated, under disfavor,* Ro 11:28; *inimical, hostile,* Mt 13:28; Col 1:21; as a subst., *an enemy, adversary,* Mt 5:43, 44; 10:36; Lk 27:35 [2190]

[2399] ἔχιδνα *echidna* 5x *a viper, poisonous serpent,* Ac 28:3; used also fig. of persons, Mt 3:7; 12:34; 23:33; Lk 3:7★ [2191]

[2400] ἔχω *echō* 708x pluperfect., ἐσχήκειν, *to hold,* Rev 1:16; *to seize, possess* a person, Mk 16:8; *to have, possess,* Mt 7:29, et al. freq.; *to have, have ready, be furnished with,* Mt 5:23; Jn 5:36; 6:68; *to have* as a matter of crimination, Mt 5:23; Mk 11:25; *to have* at command, Mt 27:65; *to have* the power, *be able,* Mt 18:25; Lk 14:14; Ac 4:14; *to have in marriage,* Mt 14:4; *to have, be affected by, subjected to,* Mt 3:14; 12:10; Mk 3:10; Jn 12:48; 15:22, 24; 16:21, 22; Ac 23:29; 1 Ti 5:12; Heb 7:28; 1 Jn 1:8; 4:18; χάραν ἔχειν, *to feel gratitude, be thankful,* 1 Ti 1:12; 2 Ti 1:3; Phlm 7; *to hold, esteem, regard,* Mt 14:5; Lk 14:18, 19; *to have* or *hold* as an object of knowledge, faith, or practice, Jn 5:38, 42; 14:21; 1 Jn 5:12; 2 Jn 9; *to hold on* in entire possession, *to retain,* Ro 15:4; 2 Ti 1:13; Heb 12:28; intrans. with adverbs or adverbial expression, *to be, to fare,* Mt 9:12; Mk 2:17; 5:23; Lk 5:31; Jn 4:52; Ac 7:1; 12:15; 15:36; 21:13; 2 Co 10:6; 12:14; 1 Ti 5:25; 1 Pe 4:5; τὸ νῦν ἔχον, *for the present;* in N.T. ἔχειν ἐν γαστρί, *to be pregnant,* Mt 1:18; as also ἔχειν κοίτην, Ro 9:10; ἔχειν δαιμόνιον, *to be possessed,* Mt 11:18; of time, *to have continued, to have lived,* Jn 5:5, 6; 8:57; of space, *to embrace, be distant,* Ac 1:12; mid. pr. *to hold by, cling to;* hence, *to border upon, be next,* Mk 1:38;

Lk 13:33; Ac 20:15; 21:26; *to tend immediately to*, Heb 6:9 [2192]

[2401] ἕως *heōs* 146x can function as an improper prep., *while, as long as,* Jn 9:4; *until,* Mt 2:9; Lk 15:4; as also in N.T. ἕως οὗ, ἕως ὅτου, Mt 5:18, 26; ἕως ἄρτι, *until now,* Mt 11:12; ἕως πότε, *until when, how long,* Mt 17:17; ἕως σήμερον, *until this day, to this time,* 2 Co 3:15; as a prep. of time, *until,* Mt 24:21; of place, *unto, even to,* Mt 11:23; Lk 2:15; ἕως ἄνω, *to the brim,* Jn 2:7; ἕως εἰς, *even to, as far as,* Lk 24:50; ἕως κάτω, *to the bottom;* ἕως ὧδε, *to this place,* Lk 23:5; of state, *unto, even to,* Mt 26:38; of number, *even, so much as,* Ro 3:12, et al. freq. [2193]

[2404] Ζαβουλών *Zaboulōn* 3x *Zebulun,* pr. name, indecl., an Israelite tribe, Mt 4:13, 15; Rev 7:8* [2194]

[2405] Ζακχαῖος *Zakchaios* 3x *Zaccheus,* pr. name, Lk 19:2, 5, 8* [2195]

[2406] Ζάρα *Zara* 1x *Zerah,* pr. name, indecl., Mt 1:3* [2196]

[2408] Ζαχαρίας *Zacharias* 11x *Zacharias,* pr. name. (1) *Son of Barachias,* Mt 23:35; Lk 11:51. (2) *Father of Jn the Baptist,* Lk 1:5 [2197]

[2409] ζάω *zaō* 140x *to live, to be possessed of vitality, to exercise the functions of life,* Mt 27:63; Ac 17:28; τὸ ζῆν, *life,* Heb 2:15; *to have means of subsistence,* 1 Co 9:14; *to live, to pass existence* in a specific manner, Lk 2:36; 15:13; *to be instinct with life and vigor;* hence, ζῶν, *living,* an epithet of God, in a sense peculiar to Himself; ἐλπὶς ζῶσα, *a living hope* in respect of vigor and constancy, 1 Pe 1:3; ὕδωρ ζῶν, *living water* in respect of a full and unfailing flow, Jn 4:10, 11; *to be alive with cheered and hopeful feelings,* 1 Th 3:8; *to be alive* in a state of salvation from spiritual death, 1 Jn 4:9 [2198]

[2411] Ζεβεδαῖος *Zebedaios* 12x *Zebedee,* pr. name, the father of Jas and John, Mt 4:21; Mk 10:35; Lk 5:10; Jn 21:1* [2199]

[2412] ζεστός *zestos* 3x pr. *boiled; boiling, boiling hot;* met. *glowing with zeal, fervent,* Rev 3:15, 16* [2200]

[2414] ζεῦγος *zeugos* 2x *a yoke* of animals; *a pair, couple,* Lk 2:24; 14:19* [2201]

[2415] ζευκτηρία *zeuktēria* 1x *a fastening, band,* Ac 27:40* [2202]

[2416] Ζεύς *Zeus* 2x the supreme god of the Greeks answering to the *Jupiter* of the Romans, Ac 14:12, 13* [2203]

[2417] ζέω *zeō* 2x *to boil, to be hot,* in N.T. met. *to be fervent, ardent, zealous,* Ac 18:25; Ro 12:11* [2204]

[2418] ζηλεύω *zēleuō* 1x *to be zealous, earnest, eager,* Rev 3:19* [2206]

[2419] ζῆλος *zēlos* 16x *generous rivalry; noble aspiration;* in N.T. *zeal, ardor* in behalf of, *ardent affection,* Jn 2:17; Ro 10:2; in a bad sense, *jealousy, envy, malice,* Ac 13:45; Ro 13:13; *indignation, wrath,* Ac 5:17 [2205]

[2420] ζηλόω *zēloō* 11x *to have strong affection towards, be ardently devoted to,* 2 Co 11:2; *to make a show of affection and devotion towards,* Gal 4:17; *to desire earnestly, aspire eagerly after,* 1 Co 12:31; 14:1, 39; absol. *to be fervent, to be zealous,* Rev 3:19; *to be jealous, envious, spiteful,* Ac 7:9; 17:5; 1 Co 13:4; Jas 4:2; pass. *to be an object of warm regard and devotion,* Gal 4:18 [2206]

[2421] ζηλωτής *zēlōtēs* 8x pr. *a generous rival, an imitator;* in N.T. *an aspirant,* 1 Co 14:12; Tit 2:14; *a devoted adherent, a zealot,* Ac 21:20; 22:3; Gal 1:14 [2207, 2208]

[2422] ζημία *zēmia* 4x *damage, loss, detriment,* Ac 27:10, 21; Phil 3:7, 8* [2209]

[2424] Ζηνᾶς *Zēnas* 1x *Zenas,* pr. name, Tit 3:13* [2211]

[2426] ζητέω *zēteō* 117x *to seek, look for,* Mt 18:12; Lk 2:48, 49; *to search after,* Mt 13:45; *to be on the watch for,* Mt 26:16; *to pursue, endeavor to obtain,* Ro 2:7; 1 Pe 3:11; *to desire, wish, want,* Mt 12:47; *to seek, strive for,* Mt 6:33; *to endeavor,* Mt 21:46; *to require, demand, ask for,* Mk 8:11; Lk 11:16; 12:48; *to inquire* or *ask questions, question,* Jn 16:19; *to deliberate,* Mk 11:18; Lk 12:29; in N.T. from Hebrew, ζητεῖν τὴν ψυχήν, *to seek the life* of any one, *to seek to kill,* Mt 2:20 [2212]

[2427] ζήτημα *zētēma* 5x *a question; a subject of debate* or *controversy,* Ac 15:2; 18:15; 23:29; 25:19; 26:3* [2213]

[2428] ζήτησις *zētēsis* 7x *a seeking; an inquiry, a question; a dispute, debate, discussion,* Jn 3:25; 1 Ti 6:4; *a subject of dispute* or *controversy,* Ac 15:2, 7; 25:20; 2 Ti 2:23; Tit 3:9 [2214]

[2429] ζιζάνιον *zizanion* 8x *zizanium, darnel, spurious wheat,* a plant found in Palestine, which resembles wheat both in its stalk and grain, but is worthless, Mt 13:25, 26, 27, 29, 30, 36, 38, 40* [2215]

[2431] Ζοροβαβέλ *Zorobabel* 3x *Zorobabel,* pr. name, indecl. (Ezra 2:2; 3:8), Mt 1:12, 13; Lk 3:27* [2216]

[2432] ζόφος *zophos* 5x *gloom, thick darkness,* Heb 12:18; 2 Pe 2:4, 17; Jude 6, 13* [2217]

[2433] ζυγός *zygos* 6x also spelled zugovn, ou, tov (n-2c), pr. *a cross bar* or *band; a yoke;* met. *a yoke* of servile condition, 1 Ti 6:1; *a yoke* of service or obligation, Mt 11:29, 30; Ac 15:10; Gal 5:1; *the beam* of a balance; *a balance,* Rev 6:5* [2218]

[2434] ζύμη *zymē* 13x *leaven, yeast,* Mt 16:12; 13:33; met. *leaven* of the mind and conduct, by a system of doctrine or morals, used in a bad sense, Mt 16:6, 11; 1 Co 5:6 [2219]

[2435] ζυμόω *zymoō* 4x *to leaven, cause to ferment,* Mt 13:33; Lk 13:21; 1 Co 5:6; Gal 5:9* [2220]

[2436] ζωγρέω *zōgreō* 2x pr. *to take alive, take prisoner in war* instead of killing; *to take captive, enthral,* 2 Ti 2:26; also, *to catch* animals, as fish; in which sense it is used figuratively, Lk 5:10* [2221]

[2437] ζωή *zōē* 135x *life, living existence,* Lk 16:25; Ac 17:25; in N.T. spiritual *life* of deliverance from the proper penalty of sin, which is expressed by θάνατος, Jn 6:51; Ro 5:18; 6:4; the final *life* of the redeemed, Mt 25:46; *life, source of* spiritual *life,* Jn 5:39; 11:25; Col 3:4 [2222]

[2438] ζώνη *zōnē* 8x *a zone, belt, girdle,* Mt 3:4; 10:9; Mk 1:6; 6:8; Ac 21:11; Rev 1:13; 15:6* [2223]

[2439] ζώννυμι *zōnnymi* 3x also spelled ζωννύω, *to gird, gird on, put on one's girdle,* Jn 21:18 (2t), Ac 12:8* [2224]

[2441] ζωογονέω *zōiogoneō* 3x pr. *to bring forth living creatures;* in N.T. *to preserve alive, save,* Lk 17:33; Ac 7:19; 1 Ti 6:13* [2225]

[2442] ζῷον *zōon* 23x *a living creature, animal,* Heb 13:11; 2 Pe 2:12 [2226]

[2443] ζωοποιέω *zōiopoieō* 11x pr. *to engender living creatures; to quicken, make alive,* Ro 4:17; 8:11; 1 Co 15:36; in N.T. met. *to quicken* with the life of salvation, Jn 6:63; 2 Co 3:6 [2227]

[2445] ἤ *ē* 343x can function as a conj (298t), *either, or,* Mt 6:24; after comparatives, and ἄλλος, ἕτερος, expressed or implied, *than,* Mt 10:15; 18:8; Ac 17:21; 24:21; intensive after ἀλλά and πρίν, Lk 12:51; Mt 1:18; it also serves to point an interrogation, Ro 3:29 [2228]

[2448] ἡγεμονεύω *hēgemoneuō* 2x *to be a guide, leader, chief;* in N.T. *to hold the of-*

fice of a Roman provincial governor, Lk 2:2; 3:1* [2230]

[2449] ἡγεμονία *hēgemonia* 1x *leadership, sovereignty;* in N.T. *a reign,* Lk 3:1* [2231]

[2450] ἡγεμών *hēgemōn* 20x *a guide; a leader; a chieftain, prince,* Mt 2:6; *a Roman provincial governor,* under whatever title, Mt 10:18; 27:2; Lk 20:20; Ac 23:24 [2232]

[2451] ἡγέομαι *hēgeomai* 28x *to lead the way; to take the lead,* Ac 14:12; *to be chief, to preside, govern, rule,* Mt 2:6; Ac 7:10; ἡγούμενος, *a chief officer* in the church, Heb 13:7, 17, 24; also, *to think, consider, count, esteem, regard,* Ac 26:2; 2 Co 9:5 [2233]

[2452] ἡδέως *hēdeōs* 5x *with pleasure, gladly, willingly,* Mk 6:20; 12:37; 2 Co 11:19 [2234, 2236]

[2453] ἤδη *ēdē* 62x *before now, now, already,* Mt 3:10; 5:28; ἤδη ποτέ, *at length,* Ro 1:10; Phil 4:10 [2235]

[2454] ἡδονή *hēdonē* 5x *pleasure, gratification;* esp. *sensual pleasure,* Lk 8:14; Tit 3:3; Jas 4:3; 2 Pe 2:13; *a passion,* Jas 4:1* [2237]

[2455] ἡδύοσμον *hēdyosmon* 2x *garden mint,* Mt 23:23; Lk 11:42* [2238]

[2456] ἦθος *ēthos* 1x pr. *a place of customary resort;* hence, *a settled habit of mind and manners,* 1 Co 15:33* [2239]

[2457] ἥκω *hēkō* 26x *to become, have arrived,* Mt 8:11; Mk 8:3; Lk 15:27; Rev 15:4* [2240]

[2458] ἠλί *ēli* 2x *My God!,* Mt 27:46 (2x)* [2241]

[2459] Ἠλί *ēli* 1x *Heli,* the father of Joseph, Lk 3:23* [2242]

[2460] Ἠλίας *ēlias* 29x *Elijah,* pr name, (1 Kgs 17-20), Mt 11:14; 17:3f.; Mk 15:35f.; Lk 1:7; Jn 1:21; Jas 5:17 [2243]

[2461] ἡλικία *hēlikia* 8x *a particular period of life; the period fitted for a particular function, prime,* Heb 11:11; *full age, years of discretion,* Jn 9:21, 23; perhaps, *the whole duration of life,* Mt 6:27; Lk 12:25; otherwise, *stature,* Lk 2:52; 19:3; Eph 4:13* [2244]

[2462] ἡλίκος *hēlikos* 3x *as great as; how great,* Col 2:1; Jas 3:5 (2t)* [2245]

[2463] ἥλιος *hēlios* 32x *the sun,* Mt 13:43; 17:2; Mk 1:32; meton. *light of the sun, light,* Ac 13:11 [2246]

[2464] ἧλος *hēlos* 2x *a nail,* Jn 20:25 (2t)* [2247]

[7005] ἡμεῖς *hēmeis* 864x see ἐγώ

[2465] ἡμέρα *hēmera* 389x *day, a day, the interval from sunrise to sunset,* opp. to νύξ, Mt 4:2; 12:40; Lk 2:44; *the interval of twenty-four hours,* comprehending day and night, Mt 6:34; 15:32; from the Hebrew, ἡμέρα καὶ ἡμέρα, *day by day, every day,* 2 Co 4:16; ἡμέραν ἐξ ἡμέρας, *from day to day, continually,* 2 Pe 2:8; καθ' ἡμέραν, *every day, daily,* Ac 17:17; Heb 3:13; *a point* or *period of time,* Lk 19:42; Ac 15:7; Eph 6:13; *a judgement, trial,* 1 Co 4:3 [2250]

[2466] ἡμέτερος *hēmeteros* 7x *our,* Lk 16:12; Ac 2:11; 24:6; 26:5; Ro 15:4; 2 Ti 4:15; Tit 3:14; 1 Jn 1:3; 2:2* [2251]

[2467] ἡμιθανής *hēmithanēs* 1x *half dead,* Lk 10:30* [2253]

[2468] ἥμισυς *hēmisys* 5x *half,* Mk 6:23; Lk 19:8; Rev 11:9, 11; 12:14* [2255]

[2469] ἡμιώριον *hēmiōrion* 1x also spelled ἡμίωρον, *half an hour,* Rev 8:1* [2256]

[2471] ἡνίκα *hēnika* 2x *when,* 2 Co 3:15, 16* [2259]

[2472] ἤπερ *ēper* 1x strengthened form of ἤ, *than,* Jn 12:43* [2260]

[2473] ἤπιος *ēpios* 2x *mild, gentle, kind,* 2 Ti 2:24; 1 Th 2:7* [2261]

[2474] Ἤρ *ēr* 1x *Er,* pr. name, indecl., Lk 3:28* [2262]

[2475] ἤρεμος *ēremos* 1x *tranquil, quiet,* 1 Ti 2:2* [2263]

[2476] Ἡρῴδης *hērōdēs* 43x *Herod,* pr. name. (1) *Herod the Great,* Mt 2:1. (2) *Herod Antipas,* tetrarch of Galilee and Peraea, Mt 14:1. (3) *Herod Agrippa,* Ac 12:1 [2264]

[2477] Ἡρῳδιανοί *hērōidianoi* 3x *Herodians,* partisans of Ἡρῴδης, *Herod Antipas,* Mt 22:16; Mk 3:6; 12:13* [2265]

[2478] Ἡρῳδιάς *hērōidias* 6x *Herodias,* pr. name, the wife of Herod Antipas, Mt 14:3, 6; Mk 6:17, 19, 22; Lk 3:19* [2266]

[2479] Ἡρῳδίων *hērōidiōn* 1x *Herodian,* pr. name, Ro 16:11* [2267]

[2480] Ἡσαΐας *ēsaias* 22x *Isaiah,* pr. name, Mt 3:3; 13:14; Mk 1:2; Lk 4:17; Jn 1:23; 12:38, 39, 41; Ac 8:28; Ro 9:27, 29 [2268]

[2481] Ἠσαῦ *ēsau* 3x *Esau,* pr. name, indecl. (Gen 27-28), Ro 9:13; Heb 11:20; 12:16* [2269]

[2482] ἥσσων *hēssōn* 2x *lesser, inferior, weaker,* 1 Co 11:17; 2 Co 12:15* [2276]

[2483] ἡσυχάζω *hēsychazō* 5x *to be still, at rest; to live peaceably, be quiet,* 1 Th 4:11; *to rest* from labor, Lk 23:56; *to be silent* or *quiet, acquiesce, to desist* from discussion, Lk 14:4; Ac 11:18; 21:14* [2270]

[2484] ἡσυχία *hēsychia* 4x *rest, quiet, tranquillity; a quiet, tranquil life,* 2 Th 3:12; *silence, silent attention,* Ac 22:2; 1 Ti 2:11, 12* [2271]

[2485] ἡσύχιος *hēsychios* 2x *quiet, tranquil, peaceful,* 1 Ti 2:2; 1 Pe 3:4* [2272]

[2486] ἤτοι *ētoi* 1x *whether,* with an elevated tone, Ro 6:16* [2273]

[2487] ἡττάομαι *hēttaomai* 2x *to be less, inferior to; to fare worse;* by impl. *to be overcome, vanquished,* 2 Pe 2:19, 20* [2274]

[2488] ἥττημα *hēttēma* 2x *an inferiority, to a particular standard; default, defeat, failure, shortcoming,* Ro 11:12; 1 Co 6:7* [2275]

[2490] ἠχέω *ēcheō* 1x *to sound, ring,* 1 Co 13:1* [2278]

[2491] ἦχος *ēchos* 3x *roar, sound, noise,,* Heb 12:19; *report,* Lk 4:37; Ac 2:2* [2279]

[2492] ἦχος *ēchos* 1x *sound, noise,* Lk 21:25* [2279]

[2497] Θαδδαῖος *thaddaios* 2x *Thaddaeus,* pr. name, Mt 10:3; Mk 3:18* [2280]

[2498] θάλασσα *thalassa* 91x *the sea,* Mt 23:15, Mk 9:42; *a sea,* Ac 7:36; *an inland sea, lake,* Mt 8:24 [2281]

[2499] θάλπω *thalpō* 2x *to impart warmth;* met. *to cherish, nurse, foster, comfort,* Eph 5:29; 1 Th 2:7* [2282]

[2500] Θαμάρ *thamar* 1x *Tamar,* (Gen 38), pr. name, indecl., Mt 1:3* [2283]

[2501] θαμβέω *thambeō* 3x *to be astonished, amazed, awestruck* Mt 1:27; 10:24, 32* [2284]

[2502] θάμβος *thambos* 3x *astonishment, amazement, awe,* Lk 4:36; 5:9; Ac 3:10* [2285]

[2503] θανάσιμος *thanasimos* 1x *deadly, mortal, fatal,* Mk 16:18* [2286]

[2504] θανατηφόρος *thanatēphoros* 1x *bringing* or *causing death, deadly, fatal,* Jas 3:8* [2287]

[2505] θάνατος *thanatos* 120x *death, the extinction of life,* whether naturally, Lk 2:26; Mk 9:1; *or violently,* Mt 10:21; 15:4; *imminent danger of death,* 2 Co 4:11, 12; 11:23; *in N.T. spiritual death,* as opposed to ζωή *in its spiritual sense, in respect of a forfeiture of salvation,* Jn 8:51; Ro 6:16 [2288]

[2506] θανατόω *thanatoō* 11x *to put to death, deliver to death,* Mt 10:21; 26:59; Mk 13:12; *pass. to be exposed to imminent danger of death,* Ro 8:36; *in N.T. met. to subdue,* Ro 8:13; *pass. to be dead to, to be rid, parted from,* as if by the intervention of death, Ro 7:4 [2289]

[2507] θάπτω *thaptō* 11x *to bury,* Mt 8:21, 22; 14:12 [2290]

[2508] Θάρα *Thara* 1x *Terah,* Abraham's father, pr. name, indecl., Lk 3:34* [2291]

[2509] θαρρέω *tharreō* 6x *to be confident, courageous,* 2 Co 5:6, 8; 7:16; 10:1, 2; Heb 13:6* [2292]

[2510] θαρσέω *tharseō* 7x *to be of good courage, be of good cheer,* Mt 9:2; *to be confident, hopeful; to be bold, maintain a bold bearing,* Mt 9:22; 14:27; Mk 6:50; 10:49; Jn 16:33; Ac 23:11* [2293]

[2511] θάρσος *tharsos* 1x *courage, confidence,* Ac 28:15* [2294]

[2512] θαῦμα *thauma* 2x *a wonder; wonder, admiration, astonishment,* 2 Co 11:14; Rev 17:6* [2295]

[2513] θαυμάζω *thaumazō* 43x *to admire, regard with admiration, wonder at,* Lk 7:9; Ac 7:31; *to reverence, adore,* 2 Th 1:10; *absol. to wonder, be filled with wonder, admiration,* or *astonishment,* Mt 8:10; Lk 4:22 [2296]

[2514] θαυμάσιος *thaumasios* 1x *wonderful, admirable, marvellous;* τὸ θαυμάσιον, *a wonder, wonderful work,* Mt 21:15* [2297]

[2515] θαυμαστός *thaumastos* 6x *wondrous, glorious,* 1 Pe 2:9; Rev 15:1; *marvellous, strange, uncommon,* Mt 21:42; Mk 12:11; Jn 9:30; Rev 15:3* [2298]

[2516] θεά *thea* 1x *a goddess,* Ac 19:27* [2299]

[2517] θεάομαι *theaomai* 22x *to gaze upon,* Mt 6:1; 23:5; Lk 7:24; *to see, discern with the eyes,* Mk 16:11, 14; Lk 5:27; Jn 1:14, 32, 38; *to see, visit,* Ro 15:24 [2300]

[2518] θεατρίζω *theatrizō* 1x *to be exposed as in a theater, to be made a gazing-stock, object of scorn,* Heb 10:33* [2301]

[2519] θέατρον *theatron* 3x *a theater, a place where public games and spectacles are exhibited,* Ac 19:29, 31; *meton. a show, gazing-stock,* 1 Co 4:9* [2302]

[2520] θεῖον *theion* 7x *brimstone, sulphur,* Lk 17:29; Rev 9:17; 14:10; 19:20; 20:10; 21:8* [2303]

[2521] θεῖος *theios* 3x *divine, pertaining to God,* 2 Pe 1:3, 4; τὸ θεῖον, *the divine nature, divinity,* Ac 17:29* [2304]

[2522] θειότης *theiotēs* 1x *divinity, deity, godhead, divine majesty,* Ro 1:20* [2305]

[2523] θειώδης *theiōdēs* 1x *of brimstone, sulphurous,* Rev 9:17* [2306]

[2525] θέλημα *thelēma* 62x *will, bent, inclination,* 1 Co 16:12; Eph 2:3; 1 Pe 4:3; *resolve,* 1 Co 7:37; *will, purpose, design,* 2 Ti 2:26; 2 Pe 1:21; *will, sovereign pleasure, behest,* Mt 18:14; Lk 12:47; Ac 13:22, et al. freq.; ἐν τῷ θελήματι θεοῦ, *Deo permittente, if God please* or *permit,* Ro 1:10 [2307]

[2526] θέλησις *thelēsis* 1x *will, pleasure,* Heb 2:4* [2308]

[2527] θέλω *thelō* 208x *to exercise the will,* properly by an unimpassioned operation; *to be willing,* Mt 17:4; *to be inclined, disposed,* Ro 13:3; *to choose,* Lk 1:62; *to intend, design,* Lk 14:28; *to will,* Jn 5:21; 21:22; ἤθελον, *I could wish,* Gal 4:20 [2309]

[2528] θεμέλιον *themelion* 1x can also be θεμέλιος, ου, ὁ, *a foundation,* Lk 6:48, 49; Heb 11:10; *met. a foundation* laid in elementary instruction, Heb 6:1; *a foundation* of a superstructure of faith, doctrine, or hope, 1 Co 3:10, 11, 12; Eph 2:20; 1 Ti 6:19; *a foundation* laid in a commencement of preaching the Gospel, Ac 16:26; Ro 15:20* [2310]

[2529] θεμέλιος *themelios* 15x see θεμέλιον [2310]

[2530] θεμελιόω *themelioō* 5x *to found, lay the foundation of,* Mt 7:25; Heb 1:10; *met. to ground, establish, render firm and unwavering,* Eph 3:17; Col 1:23; 1 Pe 5:10* [2311]

[2531] θεοδίδακτος *theodidaktos* 1x *taught of God, divinely instructed,* 1 Th 4:9* [2312]

[2534] θεομάχος *theomachos* 1x *fighting against God, in conflict with God,* Ac 5:39* [2314]

[2535] θεόπνευστος *theopneustos* 1x *divinely inspired,* 2 Ti 3:16* [2315]

[2536] θεός *theos* 1,317x *a deity,* Ac 7:43; 1 Co 8:5; *an idol,* Ac 7:40; *God,*

the true God, Mt 3:9, et al. freq.; *God, possessed of true godhead,* Jn 1:1; Ro 9:5; from the Hebrew, *applied to potentates,* Jn 10:34, 35; τῷ θεῷ, *an intensive term,* from the Hebrew, *exceedingly,* Ac 7:20, and, perhaps, 2 Co 10:4 [2316]

[2537] θεοσέβεια *theosebeia* 1x *worshipping of God, reverence towards God, piety,* 1 Ti 2:10* [2317]

[2538] θεοσεβής *theosebēs* 1x *reverencing God, pious, godly, devout, a sincere worshipper of God,* Jn 9:31* [2318]

[2539] θεοστυγής *theostygēs* 1x *God-hated; in N.T. a hater and despiser of God,* Ro 1:30* [2319]

[2540] θεότης *theotēs* 1x *divinity, deity, godhead,* Col 2:9* [2320]

[2541] Θεόφιλος *Theophilos* 2x *Theophilus,* pr. name, Lk 1:3; Ac 1:1* [2321]

[2542] θεραπεία *therapeia* 3x *service, attendance; healing, cure,* Lk 9:11; Rev 22:2; *meton. those who render service, servants, domestics, family household,* Lk 12:42* [2322]

[2543] θεραπεύω *therapeuō* 43x *to heal, cure,* Mt 4:23, 24; 8:16; *pass. to receive service,* Ac 17:25; *to serve, minister to, render service and attendance; to render divine service, worship,* Ac 17:25 [2323]

[2544] θεράπων *therapōn* 1x *an attendant, a servant; a minister,* Heb 3:5* [2324]

[2545] θερίζω *therizō* 21x *to gather in harvest, reap,* Mt 6:26; 25:24, 26; *met. to reap* the reward of labor, 1 Co 9:11; 2 Co 9:6; *to reap* the harvest of vengeance, Rev 14:15, 16 [2325]

[2546] θερισμός *therismos* 13x *a harvest, the act of gathering in the harvest, reaping,* Jn 4:35; *met. the harvest* of the Gospel, Mt 9:37, 38; Lk 10:2; *a crop; met. the crop* of vengeance, Rev 14:15 [2326]

[2547] θεριστής *theristēs* 2x *one who gathers in the harvest, a reaper,* Mt 13:30, 39* [2327]

[2548] θερμαίνω *thermainō* 6x *to warm; mid. to warm one's self,* Mt 14:54, 67; Jn 18:18, 25; Jas 2:16* [2328]

[2549] θέρμη *thermē* 1x also formed as θέρμα, *heat, warmth,* Ac 28:3* [2327]

[2550] θέρος *theros* 3x *the warm season of the year, summer,* Mt 24:32; Mk 13:28; Lk 21:30* [2330]

[2552] Θεσσαλονικεύς *Thessalonikeus* 4x *Thessalonian, of Thessalonica,* Ac

20:4; 27:2; inscription to 1 and 2 Thess★ [2331]

[2553] Θεσσαλονίκη *Thessalonikē* 5x *Thessalonica*, a city of Macedonia, Ac 17:1, 11, 13; Phil 4:16; 2 Ti 4:10★ [2332]

[2554] Θευδᾶς *Theudas* 1x *Theudas*, pr. name, Ac 5:36★ [2333]

[2555] θεωρέω *theōreō* 58x *to be a spectator, to gaze on, contemplate; to behold, view with interest and attention*, Mt 27:55; 28:1; *to contemplate* mentally, *consider*, Heb 7:4; in N.T. *to see, perceive*, Mk 3:11; *to come to a knowledge of*, Jn 6:40; from the Hebrew, *to experience, undergo*, Jn 8:51 [2334]

[2556] θεωρία *theōria* 1x *a beholding; a sight, spectacle*, Lk 23:48★ [2335]

[2557] θήκη *thēkē* 1x *a repository, receptacle; a case, sheath, scabbard*, Jn 18:11★ [2336]

[2558] θηλάζω *thēlazō* 5x *to suckle, give suck*, Mt 24:19; Mk 13:17; Lk 21:23; *to suck*, Mt 21:16; Lk 11:27★ [2337]

[2559] θῆλυς *thēlys* 5x *female;* τὸ θῆλυ, σχ. γένος, *a female*, Mt 19:4; Mk 10:6; Gal 3:28; ἡ θήλεια, *woman*, Ro 1:26, 27★ [2338]

[2560] θήρα *thēra* 1x *hunting, the chase;* met. *means of capture, a cause of destruction*, Ro 11:9★ [2339]

[2561] θηρεύω *thēreuō* 1x *to hunt, catch;* met. *to seize on, lay hold of*, Lk 11:54★ [2340]

[2562] θηριομαχέω *thēriomacheō* 1x *to fight with wild beasts;* met. *to be exposed to furious hostility*, 1 Co 15:32★ [2341]

[2563] θηρίον *thērion* 46x *a beast, wild animal*, Mk 1:13; Ac 10:12; met. *a brute, brutish man*, Tit 1:12 [2342]

[2564] θησαυρίζω *thēsaurizō* 8x *to collect and lay up stores* or *wealth, treasure*, Mt 6:19, 20; Lk 12:21; 2 Co 12:14; Jas 5:3; *to heap up, accumulate*, Ro 2:5; 1 Co 16:2; *to reserve, keep in store*, 2 Pe 3:7 [2343]

[2565] θησαυρός *thēsauros* 17x *a treasury, a store, treasure, precious deposit*, Mt 6:19, 20, 21; *a receptacle in which precious articles are kept, a casket*, Mt 2:11; *a storehouse*, Mt 12:35 [2344]

[2566] θιγγάνω *thinganō* 3x *to touch*, Col 2:21; Heb 12:20; *to harm*, Heb 11:28★ [2345]

[2567] θλίβω *thlibō* 10x *to squeeze, press; to press upon, encumber, throng, crowd*, Mk 3:9; met. *to distress, afflict*, 2 Co 1:6; 4:8;

pass. *to be compressed, narrow*, Mt 7:14 [2346]

[2568] θλῖψις *thlipsis* 45x pr. *pressure, compression;* met. *affliction, distress* of mind, 2 Co 2:4; *distressing circumstances, trial, affliction*, Mt 25:9 [2347]

[2569] θνήσκω *thnēskō* 9x *to die;* in N.T. *to be dead*, Mt 2:20; Mk 15:44 [2348]

[2570] θνητός *thnētos* 6x *mortal, subject to death*, Ro 6:12; 8:11; 2 Co 4:11; τὸ θνητόν, *mortality*, 1 Co 15:53, 54; 2 Co 5:4★ [2349]

[2571] θορυβάζω *thorybazō* 1x *to be troubled, disturbed*, Lk 10:41★ [5182]

[2572] θορυβέω *thorybeō* 4x *to make a din, uproar;* trans. *to disturb, throw into commotion*, Ac 17:5; in N.T. mid. *to manifest agitation of mind, to raise a lament*, Mt 9:23; Mk 5:39; Ac 20:10★ [2350]

[2573] θόρυβος *thorybos* 7x *an uproar, din; an outward expression of mental agitation, outcry*, Mk 5:38; *a tumult, commotion*, Mt 26:5 [2351]

[2575] θραύω *thrauō* 1x *to break, shiver;* met., *shattered, crushed* by cruel oppression, Lk 4:18★ [2352]

[2576] θρέμμα *thremma* 1x *that which is reared* (especially sheep and goats); pl. *cattle*, Jn 4:12★ [2353]

[2577] θρηνέω *thrēneō* 4x *to lament, bewail*, Mt 11:17; Lk 7:32; 23:27; Jn 16:20★ [2354]

[2579] θρησκεία *thrēskeia* 4x *religious worship*, Col 2:18; *religion, a religious system*, Ac 26:5; *religion, piety*, Jas 1:26, 27★ [2356]

[2581] θριαμβεύω *thriambeuō* 2x pr. *to celebrate a triumph;* trans. *to lead in triumph, celebrate a triumph over*, Col 2:15; in N.T. *to cause to triumph*, or, *to render conspicuous*, 2 Co 2:14★ [2358]

[2582] θρίξ *thrix* 15x *a hair; the hair* of the head, Mt 5:36; 10:30; of an animal, Mt 3:4; Mk 1:6 [2359]

[2583] θροέω *throeō* 3x *to cry aloud;* in N.T. pass., *to be disturbed, disquieted, alarmed, terrified*, Mt 24:6; Mk 13:7; 2 Th 2:2★ [2360]

[2584] θρόμβος *thrombos* 1x *a lump;* espec. *a clot* of blood, *drop*, Lk 22:44★ [2361]

[2585] θρόνος *thronos* 62x *a seat, a throne*, Mt 5:34; 19:28; Lk 1:52; meton. *power, dominion*, Lk 1:32; Heb 1:8; *a potentate*, Col 1:16 [2362]

[2587] Θυάτειρα *Thuateira* 4x *Thyatira*, a city of Lydia, Ac 16:14; Rev 1:11; 2:18, 24★ [2363]

[2588] θυγάτηρ *thugatēr* 28x *a daughter*, Mt 9:18; 10:35, 37; in the vocative, an expression of affection and kindness, Mt 9:22; from the Hebrew, *one of the female posterity* of any one, Lk 1:5; met. *a city*, Mt 21:5; Jn 12:15; pl. *female inhabitants*, Lk 23:28 [2364]

[2589] θυγάτριον *thugatrion* 2x *a little daughter, female child*, Mk 5:23; 7:25★ [2365]

[2590] θύελλα *thuella* 1x *a tempest, whirlwind, hurricane*, Heb 12:18★ [2366]

[2591] θύϊνος *thuinos* 1x *thyme*, of θυΐα, *thya*, an aromatic evergreen tree, arbor vitae, resembling the cedar, and found in Libya, Rev 18:12★ [2367]

[2592] θυμίαμα *thumiama* 6x *incense, any odoriferous substance burnt in religious worship*, Rev 5:8; 8:3, 4; 18:13; or, *the act of burning incense*, Lk 1:10, 11★ [2368]

[2593] θυμιατήριον *thumiatērion* 1x *an altar* of burning incense, Heb 9:4★ [2369]

[2594] θυμιάω *thumiaō* 1x *to burn incense*, Lk 1:9★ [2370]

[2595] θυμομαχέω *thumomacheō* 1x *to wage war fiercely; to be warmly hostile to, be enraged against*, Ac 12:20★ [2371]

[2596] θυμός *thumos* 18x pr. *the soul, mind;* hence, *a strong passion* or *emotion of the mind; anger, wrath*, Lk 4:28; Ac 19:28; pl. *swellings of anger*, 2 Co 12:20; Gal 5:20 [2372]

[2597] θυμόω *thumoō* 1x *to provoke to anger;* pass. *to be angered, enraged*, Mt 2:16★ [2373]

[2598] θύρα *thura* 39x *a door, gate*, Mt 6:6; Mk 1:33; *an entrance*, Mt 27:60; in N.T. met. *an opening, occasion, opportunity*, Ac 14:27; 1 Co 16:9; meton. *a medium* or *means of entrance*, Jn 10:7, 9 [2374]

[2599] θυρεός *thureos* 1x *a stone* or *other material employed to close a doorway;* later, *a large oblong shield*, Eph 6:16★ [2375]

[2600] θυρίς *thuris* 2x *a small opening; a window*, Ac 20:9; 2 Co 11:33★ [2376]

[2601] θυρωρός *thurōros* 4x *a doorkeeper, porter*, Mk 13:34; Jn 10:3; 18:16, 17★ [2377]

[2602] θυσία *thusia* 28x *sacrifice, the act of sacrificing*, Heb 9:26; *the thing sacrificed, a victim*, Mt 9:13; 12:7; *the flesh of victims eaten by the sacrificers*, 1 Co 10:18; in

N.T. *an offering* or *service* to God, Phil
4:18 [2378]

[2603] θυσιαστήριον *thusiastērion* 23x
an altar, Mt 5:23, 24; Lk 1:11; spc. *the
altar of burnt-offering*, Mt 23:35; Lk
11:51; meton. *a class of sacrifices*, Heb
13:10 [2379]

[2604] θύω *thuō* 14x *to offer; to kill in
sacrifice, sacrifice, immolate*, Ac 14:13, 18;
in N.T. *to slaughter* for food, Mt 22:4
[2380]

[2605] Θωμᾶς *Thōmas* 11x *Thomas*,
pr. name, Mt 10:3; Mk 3:18; Lk 6:15; Jn
11:16; 14:5; 20:24, 26, 27, 28; 21:2; Ac
1:13* [2381]

[2606] θώραξ *thōrax* 5x *a breast-plate,
armor for the body*, consisting of two parts,
one covering the breast and the other the
back, Rev 9:9, 17; Eph 6:14; 1 Th 5:8*
[2382]

[2608] Ἰάϊρος *Iairos* 2x also spelled
Ἰάειρος, *Jairus*, pr. name, Mk 5:22; Lk
8:41* [2383]

[2609] Ἰακώβ *Iakōb* 27x *Jacob*, pr.
name, indecl. (1) Son of Issac, Matt 1:2.
(2) Father of Joseph, Mary,Äôs husband,
Matt 1:15, 16 [2384]

[2610] Ἰάκωβος *Iakōbos* 42x *James*,
pr. name (1) *Son of Zebedee*, Mt 4:21. (2)
Son of Alphaeus and Mary, brother of Jude,
Mt 10:3. (3) *James the less, brother of Jesus*,
Gal 1:19 [2385]

[2611] ἴαμα *iama* 3x *healing, cure*, 1 Co
12:9, 28, 30* [2386]

[2612] Ἰαμβρῆς *Iambrēs* 1x *Jambres*, pr.
name, 2 Ti 3:8* [2387]

[2613] Ἰανναί *Iannai* 1x *Jannai*, pr.
name, indecl., Lk 3:24* [2388]

[2614] Ἰάννης *Iannēs* 1x *Jannes*, pr.
name, 2 Ti 3:8* [2389]

[2615] ἰάομαι *iaomai* 26x *to heal, cure*,
Mt 8:8; Lk 9:2; met. *to heal*, spiritually,
restore from a state of sin and condemnation,
Mt 13:15; Heb 12:13 [2390]

[2616] Ἰάρετ *Iaret* 1x *Jared*, pr. name,
indecl., Lk 3:37* [2391]

[2617] ἴασις *iasis* 3x *healing, cure*, Lk
13:32; Ac 4:22, 30* [2392]

[2618] ἴασπις *iaspis* 4x *jasper*, a precious stone of various colors, as purple,
cerulian green, etc. Rev 4:3; 21:11, 18,
19* [2393]

[2619] Ἰάσων *Iasōn* 5x *Jason*, Ac 17:5-
7 (3t), 9; Ro 16:21* [2394]

[2620] ἰατρός *iatros* 7x *physician*, Mt
9:12; Mk 2:17; 5:26; Lk 4:23; 5:31; 8:43;
Col 4:14* [2395]

[2623] ἴδε *ide* 29x the imperative of
εἶδον used as a particle, *Lo! Behold!* Jn
16:29; 19:4, 5 [2396]

[2625] ἴδιος *idios* 114x *one's own*, Mk
15:20; Jn 7:18; *due, proper, specially assigned*, Gal 6:9; 1 Ti 2:6; 6:15; Tit 1:3;
also used in N.T. as a simple possessive,
Eph 5:22; τὰ ἴδια, *one's home, household,
people*, Jn 1:11; 16:32; 19:17; οἱ ἴδιοι,
members of one's own household, friends,
Jn 1:11; Ac 24:23; ἰδίᾳ, *adverbially,
respectively*, 1 Co 12:11; κατ᾽ ἰδίαν, *adv.,
privately, aside, by one's self, alone*, Mt
14:13, 23 [2398]

[2626] ἰδιώτης *idiōtēs* 5x pr. *one in
private life, one devoid of special learning* or
gifts, a plain person, Ac 4:13; 2 Co 11:6;
ungifted, 1 Co 14:16, 23, 24* [2399]

[2627] ἰδού *idou* 200x aorist middle
imperative of εἶδον used as an interjec-
tion, *Look! See! Lo!* Mt 1:23; Lk 1:38; Ac
8:36 [2400]

[2628] Ἰδουμαία *Idoumaia* 1x *Idu-
maea*, a country south of Judea, Mk 3:8*
[2401]

[2629] ἱδρώς *hidrōs* 1x *sweat*, Lk
22:44* [2402]

[2630] Ἰεζάβελ *Iezabel* 1x *Jezebel*, (1
Kgs 16:31), pr. name, indecl., Rev 2:20*
[2403]

[2631] Ἱεράπολις *Hierapolis* 1x *Hierapolis*, a city of Phrygia, Col 4:13* [2404]

[2632] ἱερατεία *hierateia* 2x *priesthood, sacerdotal office*, Lk 1:9; Heb 7:5*
[2405]

[2633] ἱεράτευμα *hierateuma* 2x *a
priesthood;* meton. *a body of priests*, 1 Pe
2:5, 9* [2406]

[2634] ἱερατεύω *hierateuō* 1x *to officiate as a priest, perform sacred rites*, Lk 1:8*
[2407]

[2635] Ἱερεμίας *Ieremias* 3x *Jeremiah*,
pr. name, Mt 2:17; 16:14; 27:9* [2408]

[2636] ἱερεύς *hiereus* 31x *a priest, one
who performs sacrificial rites*, Mt 8:4; Lk
1:5; Jn 1:19 [2409]

[2637] Ἱεριχώ *Ierichō* 7x *Jericho*, a city
of Palestine, Mt 20:29; Mk 10:46; Lk
10:30; 18:35; 19:1; Heb 11:30* [2410]

[2638] ἱερόθυτος *hierothutos* 1x *offered
in sacrifice*, 1 Co 10:28* [1494]

[2639] ἱερόν *hieron* 72x *temple, sanctuary*, Mt 4:5; Lk 4:9; Ac 19:27 [2411]

[2640] ἱεροπρεπής *hieroprepēs* 1x *reverent*, Tit 2:13* [2412]

[2641] ἱερός *hieros* 2x *holy, divine, set
apart*, 2 Ti 3:15; τὰ ἱερά, *sacred rites*,
1 Co 9:13* [2413]

[2642] Ἱεροσόλυμα *Hierosolyma* 62x
see Ἱερουσαλήμ [2414]

[2643] Ἱεροσολυμίτης *Hierosolymitēs*
2x *a native of Jerusalem*, Mk 1:5; Jn
7:25* [2415]

[2644] ἱεροσυλέω *hierosyleō* 1x *to
despoil temples, commit sacrilege*, Ro 2:22*
[2416]

[2645] ἱερόσυλος *hierosylos* 1x *one
who despoils temples, commits sacrilege*, Ac
19:37* [2417]

[2646] ἱερουργέω *hierourgeō* 1x *to officiate as priest, perform sacred rites;* in N.T.
to minister in a divine commission, Ro
15:16* [2418]

[2647] Ἱερουσαλήμ *Ierousalēm* 77x
Jerusalem, pr. name, indecl., spelled
Ἱερουσαλήμ 77x and Ἱεροσόλυμα 62x in
our text [2419]

[2648] ἱερωσύνη *hierōsynē* 3x *a priesthood, sacerdotal office*, Heb 7:11, 12, 24*
[2420]

[2649] Ἱεσσαί *Iessai* 5x *Jesse*, father
of David (1 Sam 16), pr. name, indecl.,
Mt 1:5f.; Lk 3:32; Ac 13:22; Ro 15:12*
[2421]

[2650] Ἰεφθάε *Iephthae* 1x *Jephthah*,
(Judges 11f.), pr. name, indecl., Heb
11:32* [2422]

[2651] Ἰεχονίας *Iechonias* 2x *Jecho-
niah*, pr. name, Mt 1:11, 12; Lk 3:23ff.*
[2423]

[2652] Ἰησοῦς *Iēsous* 917x *a Sav-
ior, Jesus*, Mt 1:21, 25; 2:1, et al. freq.;
Joshua, Ac 7:45; Heb 4:8; *Jesus*, a Jewish
Christian, Col 4:11 [2424]

[2653] ἱκανός *hikanos* 39x *befit-
ting; sufficient, enough*, Lk 22:38;
ἱκανὸν ποιεῖν τινι, *to satisfy, gratify*,
Mk 15:15; τὸ ἱκανὸν λαμβάνειν, *to take
security* or *bail of any one*, Ac 17:9; *or
persons, adequate, competent, qualified*,
2 Co 2:16; *fit, worthy*, Mt 3:11; 8:8; of
number or quantity, *considerable, large,
great, much*, and pl. *many*, Mt 28:12; Mk
10:46 [2425]

[2654] ἱκανότης *hikanotēs* 1x *sufficiency,
ability, fitness, qualification*, 2 Co 3:5*
[2426]

[2655] ἱκανόω *hikanoō* 2x *to make sufficient* or *competent, qualify,* 2 Co 3:6; Col 1:12* [2427]

[2656] ἱκετηρία *hiketēria* 1x pr. *an olive branch* borne by suppliants in their hands; *prayer, supplication,* Heb 5:7* [2428]

[2657] ἰκμάς *ikmas* 1x *moisture,* Lk 8:6* [2429]

[2658] Ἰκόνιον *Ikonion* 6x *Iconium,* a city of Lycaonia, in Asia Minor, Ac 13:51; 14:1, 19, 21; 16:2; 2 Ti 3:11* [2430]

[2659] ἱλαρός *hilaros* 1x *cheerful, not grudging,* 2 Co 9:7* [2431]

[2660] ἱλαρότης *hilarotēs* 1x *cheerfulness, graciousness,* Ro 12:8* [2432]

[2661] ἱλάσκομαι *hilaskomai* 2x *to appease, render propitious;* in N.T. *to expiate, make an atonement* or *expiation for,* Heb 2:17; ἱλάσθητι, *be gracious, show mercy, pardon,* Lk 18:13* [2433]

[2662] ἱλασμός *hilasmos* 2x *atoning sacrifice, sin offering, propitiation, expiation; one who makes propitiation/expiation,* 1 Jn 2:2; 4:10* [2434]

[2663] ἱλαστήριον *hilastērion* 2x *the cover of the ark of the covenant, the mercy-seat, the place of propitiation,* Ro 3:25; Heb 9:5* [2435]

[2664] ἵλεως *hileōs* 2x *propitious, favorable, merciful, gracious,* Heb 8:12; from the Hebrew, ἵλεως σοι (ὁ θεός) *God have mercy on thee, God forbid, far be it from thee,* Mt 16:22* [2436]

[2665] Ἰλλυρικόν *Illyrikon* 1x *Illyricum,* a country between the Adriatic and the Danube, Ro 15:19* [2437]

[2666] ἱμάς *himas* 4x *a strap* or *thong of leather,* Ac 22:25; *a shoe-latchet,* Mk 1:7; Lk 3:16; Jn 1:27* [2438]

[2667] ἱματίζω *himatizō* 2x *to clothe;* pass. *to be clothed,* Mk 5:15; Lk 8:35* [2439]

[2668] ἱμάτιον *himation* 60x *a garment; the upper garment, mantle,* Mt 5:40; 9:16, 20, 21; pl. *the mantle and tunic together,* Mt 26:65; pl. genr. *garments, raiment,* Mt 11:8; 24:18 [2440]

[2669] ἱματισμός *himatismos* 5x *garment; raiment, apparel, clothing,* Lk 7:25; 9:29; Jn 19:24; Ac 20:33; 1 Ti 2:9* [2441]

[2671] ἵνα *hina* 663x *that, in order that,* Mt 19:13; Mk 1:38; Jn 1:22; 3:15; 17:1; ἵνα μή, *that not, lest,* Mt 7:1; in N.T. equivalent to ὥστε, *so that, so as that,* Jn

9:2; also, marking a simple circumstance, *the circumstance that,* Mt 10:25; Jn 4:34; 6:29; 1 Jn 4:17; 5:3 [2443]

[2672] ἱνατί *hinati* 6x *Why is it that? For what reason? Why?* Mt 9:4; 27:46; Lk 13:7; Ac 4:25; 7:26; 1 Co 10:29* [2444]

[2673] Ἰόππη *Ioppē* 10x *Joppa,* a city of Palestine, Ac 9:36, 38, 42f.; 10:5, 8, 23, 32; 11:5, 13* [2445]

[2674] Ἰορδάνης *Iordanēs* 15x *the river Jordan,* Mt 3:5; Mk 10:1; Lk 4:1; Jn 3:26 [2446]

[2675] ἰός *ios* 3x *a missile weapon, arrow, dart; venom, poison,* Ro 3:13; Jas 3:8; *rust,* Jas 5:3* [2447]

[2677] Ἰουδαία *Ioudaia* 44x *Judea,* the southern party of the country, below Samaria, Mt 2:1, 5, 22; 3:1; meton. *the inhabitants of Judea* [2449]

[2679] Ἰουδαϊκός *Ioudaikos* 1x *Jewish, current among the Jews,* Tit 1:14* [2451]

[2680] Ἰουδαϊκῶς *Ioudaikōs* 1x *in the manner of Jews, according to Jewish custom,* Gal 2:14* [2452]

[2681] Ἰουδαῖος *Ioudaios* 194x *Jewish,* Mk 1:5; Jn 3:22; Ac 16:1; 24:24; pr. *one sprung from the tribe of Judah,* or *a subject of the kingdom of Judah;* in N.T. *a descendant of Jacob, a Jew,* Mt 28:15; Mk 7:3; Ac 19:34; Ro 2:28, 29 [2453]

[2682] Ἰουδαϊσμός *Ioudaismos* 2x *Judaism, the character and condition of a Jew; practice of the Jewish religion,* Gal 1:13, 14* [2454]

[2683] Ἰούδας *Ioudas* 44x *Judas, Jude,* pr. name. (1) *Judah, son of Jacob; the tribe of Judah,* Mt 1:2; Lk 1:39. (2) *Juda, son of Joseph, of the ancestry of Jesus,* Lk 3:30. (3) *Juda, son of Joanna, of the ancestry of Jesus,* Lk 3:26. (4) *Judas, brother of James, Jude,* Lk 6:16; Jude 1. (5) *Judas Iscariot, son of Simon,* Mt 10:4; Jn 6:71. (6) *Judas, brother of Jesus,* Mt 13:55; Mk 6:3. (7) *Judas of Galilee,* Ac 5:37 . (8) *Judas, surnamed Barsabas,* Ac 15:22. (9) *Judas of Damascus,* Ac 9:11 [2455]

[2684] Ἰουλία *Ioulia* 1x *Julia,* pr. name, Ro 16:15* [2456]

[2685] Ἰούλιος *Ioulios* 2x *Julius,* pr. name, Ac 27:1, 3* [2457]

[2687] Ἰουνιᾶς *Iounias* 1x *Junia,* pr. name, Ro 16:7* [2458]

[2688] Ἰοῦστος *Ioustos* 3x *Justus,* pr. name (1) *Joseph Barsabas,* Ac 1:23 (2) *Justus of Corinth,* Ac 18:7 (3) *Jesus, called Justus,* Col 4:11* [2459]

[2689] ἱππεύς *hippeus* 2x *a horseman;* pl. ἱππεῖς, *horsemen, cavalry,* Ac 23:23, 32* [2460]

[2690] ἱππικός *hippikos* 1x *equestrian;* τὸ ἱππικόν, *cavalry, horse,* Rev 9:16* [2461]

[2691] ἵππος *hippos* 17x *a horse,* Jas 3:3; Rev 6:2, 4, 5, 8; 9:7, 17; 18:13; 19:11, 14 [2462]

[2692] ἶρις *iris* 2x *a rainbow, iris,* Rev 4:3; 10:1* [2463]

[2693] Ἰσαάκ *Isaak* 20x *Isaac,* pr. name, indecl., Mt 1:2; 8:11; 23:32; Ac 3:13;. Ro 9:7f.; Gal 4:28; Heb 11:9ff.; Jas 2:21 [2464]

[2694] ἰσάγγελος *isangelos* 1x *equal* or *similar to angels,* Lk 20:36* [2465]

[2696] Ἰσκαριώθ *Iskariōth* 3x see Ἰσκαριώτης [2469]

[2697] Ἰσκαριώτης *Iskariōtēs* 8x *Iscariot,* surname of Judas. Also spelled Ἰσκαριώθ in our text 3x (Mk 3:19; 14:10; Lk 6:16), which is indeclinable. This declinable form is found 8x in our text, Mt 10:4; 26:14; Lk 22:3; Jn 6:71; Jn 12:4; 13:2, 26; 14:22* [2469]

[2698] ἴσος *isos* 8x *equal, like,* Mt 20:12; Lk 6:34; *on an equality,* Phil 2:6; met. *correspondent, consistent,* Mk 14:56, 59 [2470]

[2699] ἰσότης *isotēs* 3x *equality, equal proportion,* 2 Co 8:13, 14; *fairness, equity, what is equitable,* Col 4:1* [2471]

[2700] ἰσότιμος *isotimos* 1x *of equal price, equally precious* or *valuable,* 2 Pe 1:1* [2472]

[2701] ἰσόψυχος *isopsychos* 1x *likeminded, of the same mind and spirit,* Phil 2:20* [2473]

[2702] Ἰσραήλ *Israēl* 68x *Israel,* pr. name, indecl. [2474]

[2703] Ἰσραηλίτης *Israēlitēs* 9x *an Israelite, a descendant of* Ἰσραήλ, *Israel* or *Jacob,* Jn 1:47; Ac 2:22 [2475]

[2704] Ἰσσαχάρ *Issachar* 1x *Issachar,* pr. name, indecl., Rev 7:7* [2466]

[2705] ἵστημι *histēmi* 154x pluperfect, ἑστάμην, also formed as στήκω 10x, trans. *to make to stand, set, place,* Mt 4:5; *to set forth, appoint,* Ac 1:23; *to fix, appoint,* Ac 17:31; *to establish, confirm,* Ro 10:3; Heb 10:9; *to set down, impute,* Ac 7:60; *to weigh out, pay,* Mt 26:15; intrans. *to stand,* Mt 12:46; *to stand fast, be firm, be permanent, endure,* Mt 12:25; Eph 6:13; *to be* *confirmed, proved,* Mt 18:16; 2 Co 13:1; *to stop,* Lk 7:14; 8:44; Ac 8:38 [2476]

[2707] ἱστορέω *historeō* 1x *to ascertain by inquiry and examination; to inquire of;* in N.T. *to visit* in order to become acquainted with, Gal 1:18* [2477]

[2708] ἰσχυρός *ischuros* 29x *strong, mighty, robust,* Mt 12:29; Lk 11:21; *powerful, mighty,* 1 Co 1:27; 4:10; 1 Jn 2:14; *strong, fortified,* Rev 18:10; *vehement,* Mt 14:20; *energetic,* 2 Co 10:10; *sure, firm,* Heb 6:18 [2478]

[2709] ἰσχύς *ischus* 10x *strength, might, power,* Rev 18:2; Eph 1:19; *faculty, ability,* 1 Pe 4:11; Mk 12:30, 33; Lk 10:27 [2479]

[2710] ἰσχύω *ischuō* 28x *to be strong, be well, be in good health,* Mt 9:12; *to have power, be able,* Mt 8:28; 26:40; *to have power* or *efficiency, avail, be valid,* Gal 5:6; Heb 9:17; *to be of service, be serviceable,* Mt 5:13; meton. *to prevail,* Ac 19:16; Rev 12:8 [2480]

[2711] ἴσως *isōs* 1x *equally; perhaps, it may be that,* Lk 20:13* [2481]

[2712] Ἰταλία *Italia* 4x *Italy,* Ac 18:2; 27:1, 6; Heb 13:24* [2482]

[2713] Ἰταλικός *Italikos* 1x *Italian,* Ac 10:1* [2483]

[2714] Ἰτουραῖος *Itouraios* 1x *Ituraea,* a district of Palestine beyond Jordan, Lk 3:1* [2484]

[2715] ἰχθύδιον *ichthudion* 2x *a small fish,* Mt 15:34; Mk 8:7* [2485]

[2716] ἰχθύς *ichthus* 20x *a fish,* Mt 15:36; 17:27; Lk 5:6 [2486]

[2717] ἴχνος *ichnos* 3x *a footstep, track;* in N.T. pl. *footsteps, line of conduct,* Ro 4:12; 2 Co 12:18; 1 Pe 2:21* [2487]

[2718] Ἰωαθάμ *Iōatham* 2x *Joatham,* pr. name, indecl., Mt 1:9* [2488]

[2720] Ἰωανάν *Iōanan* 1x *Joanan,* pr. name, indecl., Lk 3:27* [2489]

[2721] Ἰωάννα *Iōanna* 2x also spelled Ἰωάνα, *Joanna,* pr. name, Lk 8:3; 24:10* [2489, 2490]

[2722] Ἰωάννης *Iōannēs* 135x also spelled Ἰωάνης, *Joannes, John,* pr. name (1) *Jn the Baptist,* Mt 3:1, et al. (2) *John, son of Zebedee, the apostle,* Mt 4:21, et al. (3) *John, surnamed Mark,* Ac 12:12, et al. (4) *John, the high-priest,* Ac 4:6 [2491]

[2724] Ἰώβ *Iōb* 1x *Job,* pr. name, indecl., Jas 5:11* [2492]

[2725] Ἰωβήδ *Iōbēd* 3x *Obed,* David's grandfather, pr. name, indecl., Mt 1:5; Lk 3:32* [5601]

[2726] Ἰωδά *Iōda* 1x *Joda,* pr. name, indecl., Lk 3:26* [2455]

[2727] Ἰωήλ *Iōēl* 1x *Joel,* an Old Testament prophet, pr. name, indecl., Ac 2:16* [2493]

[2729] Ἰωνάμ *Iōnam* 1x *Jonam,* pr. name, indecl., Lk 3:30* [2494]

[2731] Ἰωνᾶς *Iōnas* 9x *Jonas,* pr. name *Jonah, the prophet,* Mt 12:39; Lk 11:29 [2495]

[2732] Ἰωράμ *Iōram* 2x *Joram,* king of Judah (2 Kgs 8:16ff.), pr. name, indecl., Mt 1:8* [2496]

[2733] Ἰωρίμ *Iōrim* 1x *Jorim,* pr. name, indecl., Lk 3:29* [2497]

[2734] Ἰωσαφάτ *Iōsaphat* 2x *Josaphat,* king of Judah (1 Kgs 22:41), pr. name, indecl., Mt 1:8* [2498]

[2736] Ἰωσῆς *Iōsēs* 4x *Joses, Joseph* pr. name Mt 27:56; Mk 6:3; 15:40, 47* [2500]

[2737] Ἰωσήφ *Iōsēph* 35x *Joseph,* pr. name, indecl. (1) *Joseph, son of Jacob,* Jn 4:5. (2) *Joseph, son of Jonan,* Lk 3:30. (3) *Joseph, son of Judas,* Lk 3:26. (4) *Joseph, son of Mattathias,* Lk 3:24. (5) *Joseph, the husband of Mary,* Mt 1:16. (6) *Joseph of Arimathea,* Mt 27:57. (7) *Joseph Barsabas,* Ac 1:23. (8) *Joseph Barnabas,* Ac 4:36 [2501]

[2738] Ἰωσήχ *Iōsēch* 1x *Josech,* pr. name, indecl., Lk 3:26* [2501]

[2739] Ἰωσίας *Iōsias* 2x *Josiah,* king of Judah (2 Kgs 22), Mt 1:10, 11* [2502]

[2740] ἰῶτα *iōta* 1x *iota;* in N.T. used like the Hebrew/Aramaic *yod,* the smallest letter in the Hebrew/Aramaic alphabet, as an expression for *the least* or *minutest part; a jot,* Mt 5:18* [2503]

[2743] κἀγώ *kagō* 84x *and I, I also, but I,* a crasis of καί and ἐγώ, dat., κἀμοί, acc., κἀμέ [2504]

[2745] καθά *katha* 1x can function as an adverb, *just as,* Mt 27:10* [2505]

[2746] καθαίρεσις *kathairesis* 3x *tearing down, destruction,* 2 Co 10:4, 8; 13:10* [2506]

[2747] καθαιρέω *kathaireō* 9x *take* or *bring down,* Mk 15:36, 46; Lk 1:52; 23:53; Ac 13:29; *tear down, destroy,* Lk 12:18; Ac 13:19; 19:27; 2 Co 10:4* [2507]

[2748] καθαίρω *kathairō* 1x *to cleanse* from filth; *to clear* by pruning, *prune,* Jn 15:2; met. *to cleanse* from sin, *make expiation* [2508]

[2749] καθάπερ *kathaper* 13x can function as an adverb, *even as, just as,* Ro 3:4; 4:6; 9:13; 10:15; 11:8; 12:4; 1 Co 10:10; 12:12; 2 Co 1:14; 3:13, 18; 8:11; 1 Th 2:11; 3:6, 12; 4:5; Heb 4:2* [2509]

[2750] καθάπτω *kathaptō* 1x trans. *to fasten* or *fit to;* in N.T. equivalent to καθαπτομαι, *to fix one's self upon, fasten upon, take hold of, seize,* Ac 28:3* [2510]

[2751] καθαρίζω *katharizō* 31x *to cleanse, render pure, purify,* Mt 23:25; Lk 11:39; *to cleanse* from leprosy, Mt 8:2, 3; 10:8; met. *to cleanse* from sin, *purify by an expiatory offering, make expiation for,* Heb 9:22, 23; 1 Jn 1:7; *to cleanse* from sin, *free from the influence of error and sin,* Ac 15:9; 2 Co 7:1; *to pronounce* ceremonially *clean,* Ac 10:15; 11:9 [2511]

[2752] καθαρισμός *katharismos* 7x ceremonial *cleansing, purification,* Lk 2:22; 5:14; *mode of purification,* Jn 2:6; 3:25; *cleansing* of lepers, Mk 1:44; met. *expiation,* Heb 1:3; 2 Pe 1:9* [2512]

[2754] καθαρός *katharos* 27x *clean, pure, unsoiled,* Mt 23:26; 27:59; met. *clean* from guilt, *guiltless, innocent,* Ac 18:6; 20:26; *sincere, upright, virtuous, void of evil,* Mt 5:8; Jn 15:3; *clean* ceremonially and morally, Lk 11:41 [2513]

[2755] καθαρότης *katharotēs* 1x *cleanness;* ceremonial *purity,* Heb 9:13* [2514]

[2756] καθέδρα *kathedra* 3x *chair, seat,* Mt 21:12; 23:2; Mk 11:15* [2515]

[2757] καθέζομαι *kathezomai* 7x *to seat one's self, sit down,* Mt 26:55; Lk 2:46; Jn 4:6; 1:20; 20:12; Ac 6:15; 20:9* [2516]

[2759] καθεξῆς *kathexēs* 5x *in a continual order* or *series, successively, consecutively,* Lk 1:3; Ac 11:4; 18:23; ὁ, ἡ, καθεξῆς, *succeeding, subsequent,* Lk 8:1; Ac 3:24* [2517]

[2761] καθεύδω *katheudō* 22x *to sleep, be fast asleep,* Mt 8:24; 9:24; met. *to sleep* in spiritual sloth, Eph 5:14; 1 Th 5:6; *to sleep* the sleep of death, *to die,* 1 Th 5:10 [2518]

[2762] καθηγητής *kathēgētēs* 2x pr. *a guide, leader;* in N.T. *a teacher, instructor,* Mt 23:10* [2519]

[2763] καθήκω *kathēkō* 2x *to reach, extend to;* καθήκει, impers. *it is fitting, meet,* Ac 22:22; τὸ καθῆκον, *what is fit, right, duty;* τὰ μὴ καθήκοντα, by litotes for *what is abominable* or *detestable*, Ro 1:28* [2520]

[2764] καθημαι *kathēmai* 91x *to sit, be sitting*, Mt 9:9; Lk 10:13; *to be seated*, 1 Co 14:30; *to be enthroned*, Rev 18:7; *to dwell, reside*, Mt 4:16; Lk 1:79; 21:35 [2521]

[2766] καθημερινός *kathēmerinos* 1x *daily, day by day*, Ac 6:1* [2522]

[2767] καθίζω *kathizō* 46x (1) trans. *to cause to sit, place;* καθίζομαι, *to be seated, sit*, Mt 19:28; Lk 22:30; *to cause to sit as judges, place, appoint*, 1 Co 6:4; (2) intrans. *to sit, sit down*, Mt 13:48; 26:36; *to remain, settle, stay, continue, live*, Lk 24:49 [2523]

[2768] καθίημι *kathiēmi* 4x *to let down, lower*, Lk 5:19; Ac 9:25; 10:11; 11:5* [2524]

[2770] καθίστημι *kathistēmi* 21x also formed as καθιστάνω, *to place, set*, Jas 3:6; *to set, constitute, appoint*, Mt 24:45, 47; Lk 12:14; *to set down* in a place, *conduct*, Ac 17:15; *to make, render*, or *cause to be*, 2 Pe 1:8; pass. *to be rendered*, Ro 5:19 [2525]

[2771] καθό *katho* 4x *as*, Ro 8:26; *according as, in proportion as, to the degree that*, 2 Co 8:12; 1 Pe 4:13* [2526]

[2773] καθόλου *katholou* 1x *on the whole, entirely, in general, altogether, completely;* with a negative, *not at all*, Ac 4:18* [2527]

[2774] καθοπλίζω *kathoplizō* 1x middle, *to arm oneself (completely)*, Lk 11:21* [2528]

[2775] καθοράω *kathoraō* 1x pr. *to look down upon*, in the N.T. *to mark, perceive, discern*, Ro 1:20* [2529]

[2776] καθότι *kathoti* 6x *as, just as, according as, in proportion as*, Ac 2:45; 4:35; *inasmuch as*, Lk 1:7; 19:9; Ac 2:24; 17:31* [2530]

[2777] καθώς *kathōs* 182x *as, just as, in the manner that*, Mt 21:6; 26:24; *how, in what manner*, Ac 15:14; *according as*, Mk 4:33; *inasmuch as*, Jn 17:2; *of time, when*, Ac 7:17 [2531]

[2778] καθώσπερ *kathōsper* 1x *just as, exactly as*, Heb 5:4* [2509]

[2779] καί *kai* 9,160x (1) *and*, Mt 2:2, 3, 11; 4:22; (2) καί ... καί, *both ... and;* (3) as a cumulative particle, *also, too*, Mt 5:39; Jn 8:19; 1 Co 11:6; (4) emphatic, *even, also*, Mt 10:30; 1 Co 2:10; in N.T. adversative, *but*, Mt 11:19; also introductory of the apodosis of a sentence, Jas 2:4; Gal, 3:28 [2532]

[2780] Καϊάφας *Kaiaphas* 9x *Caiaphas*, pr. name, the high priest from A.D. 18-36, Mt 26:3, 57; Lk 3:2; Jn 11:49; 18:13f., 24, 28; Ac 4:6* [2533]

[2782] Κάϊν *Kain* 3x *Cain*, pr. name, indecl., Heb 11:4; 1 Jn 3:12; Jude 11* [2535]

[2783] Καϊνάμ *Kainam* 2x *Cainan*, pr. name, indecl., Lk 3:36, 37* [2536]

[2785] καινός *kainos* 41x *new, recently made*, Mt 9:17; Mk 2:22; *new* in species, character, or mode, Mt 26:28, 29; Mk 14:24, 25; Lk 22:20; Jn 13:34; 2 Co 5:17; Gal 6:15; Eph 2:15; 4:24; 1 Jn 2:7; Rev 3:12; *novel, strange*, Mk 1:27; Ac 17:19; *new to the possessor*, Mk 16:17; *unheard of, unusual*, Mk 1:27; Ac 17:19; met. *renovated, better, of higher excellence*, 2 Co 5:17; Rev 5:9 [2537]

[2786] καινότης *kainotēs* 2x *newness*, Ro 6:4; 7:6* [2538]

[2788] καίπερ *kaiper* 5x *though, although;* Phil 3:4; Heb 5:8; 7:5; 12:17; 2 Pe 1:12* [2539]

[2789] καιρός *kairos* 85x pr. *fitness, proportion, suitableness; a fitting situation, suitable place*, 1 Pe 4:17; *a limited period of time marked by a suitableness of circumstances, a fitting season*, 1 Co 4:5; 1 Ti 2:6; 6:15; Tit 1:3; *opportunity*, Ac 24:25; Gal 6:10; Heb 11:15; *a limited period of time marked by characteristic circumstances, a signal juncture, a marked season*, Mt 16:3; Lk 12:56; 21:8; 1 Pe 1:11; *a destined time*, Mt 8:29; 26:18; Mk 1:15; Lk 21:24; 1 Th 5:1; *a season* in ordinary succession, equivalent to ὥρα, Mt 13:30; Ac 14:17; in N.T. *a limited time, a short season*, Lk 4:13; simply, *a point of time*, Mt 11:25; Lk 13:1 [2540]

[2790] Καῖσαρ *Kaisar* 29x *Caesar*, pr. name [2541]

[2791] Καισάρεια *Kaisareia* 17x *Caesarea* (1) *Caesarea Philippi*, Mt 16:13; Mk 8:27; (2) *Caesarea Augusta*, Ac 8:40 [2542]

[2792] καίτοι *kaitoi* 2x *and yet, though, although*, Ac 14:17; Heb 4:3* [2543]

[2793] καίτοιγε *kaitoige* 1x *although indeed, and yet*, Jn 4:2* [2544]

[2794] καίω *kaiō* 11x *to cause to burn, kindle, light*, Mt 5:15; pass. *to be kindled, burn, flame*, Lk 12:35; met. *to be kindled into emotion*, Lk 24:32; *to consume with fire*, Jn 15:6; 1 Co 13:3 [2545]

[2795] κἀκεῖ *kakei* 10x crasis, *and there*, Mt 5:23; 10:11; *there also*, Ac 17:13 [2546]

[2796] κἀκεῖθεν *kakeithen* 10x crasis, *and there*, Mk 10:1; Ac 7:4; 14:26; 20:15; 21:1; 27:4, 12; 28:15; *and then, afterwards*, Ac 13:21 [2547]

[2797] κἀκεῖνος *kakeinos* 22x crasis, *and he, she, it; and this, and that*, Mt 15:18; 23:23; *he, she, it also; this also, that also*, Mt 20:4 [2548]

[2798] κακία *kakia* 11x *malice, malignity*, Ro 1:29; Eph 4:31; *wickedness, depravity*, Ac 8:22; 1 Co 5:8; in N.T. *evil, trouble, calamity, misfortune*, Mt 6:34 [2549]

[2799] κακοήθεια *kakoētheia* 1x *disposition for mischief, misfortune, malignity*, Ro 1:29* [2550]

[2800] κακολογέω *kakologeō* 4x *to speak evil of, revile, abuse, insult*, Mk 9:39; Ac 19:9; *to address with offensive language, to treat with disrespect*, Matt, 15:4; Mk 7:10* [2551]

[2801] κακοπάθεια *kakopatheia* 1x *a state of suffering, affliction, trouble*, in N.T. *endurance in affliction, perseverance*, Jas 5:10* [2552]

[2802] κακοπαθέω *kakopatheō* 3x *to suffer evil* or *afflictions*, 2 Ti 2:9; *to be afflicted, troubled, dejected*, Jas 5:13; in N.T. *to show endurance in trials and afflictions*, 2 Ti 4:5* [2553]

[2803] κακοποιέω *kakopoieō* 4x *to cause evil, injure, do harm*, Mk 3:4; Lk 6:9; *to do evil, commit sin*, 1 Pe 3:17; 3 Jn 11* [2554]

[2804] κακοποιός *kakopoios* 3x *an evildoer*, 1 Pe 2:12, 14; 4:15* [2555]

[2805] κακός *kakos* 50x *bad, of a bad quality* or *disposition, worthless, corrupt, depraved*, Mt 21:41; 24:48; Mk 7:21; *wicked, criminal, morally bad;* τὸ κακόν, *evil, wickedness, crime*, Mt 27:23; Ac 23:9; *deceitful*, 1 Pe 3:10; *mischievous, harmful, destructive;* τὸ κακόν, *evil mischief, harm, injury*, Tit 1:12; *afflictive;* τὸ κακόν, *evil, misery, affliction, suffering*, Lk 16;25 [2556]

[2806] κακοῦργος *kakourgos* 4x *an evildoer, malefactor, criminal*, Lk 23:32, 33, 39; 2 Ti 2:9* [2557]

[2807] κακουχέω *kakoucheō* 2x *to torment, afflict, harass;* pass. *to be afflicted, be oppressed with evils*, Heb 11:37 13:3* [2558]

[2808] κακόω *kakoō* 6x *to harm, mistreat, cause evil to, oppress*, Ac 7:6, 19; 12:1; 18:10; 1 Pe 3:13; in N.T. *to make angry, embitter*, Ac 14:2* [2559]

[2809] κακῶς *kakōs* 16x *ill, badly;* physically *ill, sick,* Mt 4:24; 8:16; *grievously, vehemently,* Mt 15:22; *wretchedly, miserably,* Mt 21:41; *wickedly, reproachfully,* Ac 23:5; *wrongly, criminally,* Jn 18:23; *amiss,* Jas 4:3 [2560]

[2810] κάκωσις *kakōsis* 1x *ill-treatment, affliction, oppression, misery,* Ac 7:34* [2561]

[2811] καλάμη *kalamē* 1x *the stalk* of grain, *straw, stubble,* 1 Co 3:12* [2562]

[2812] κάλαμος *kalamos* 12x *a reed, cane,* Mt 11:7; 12:20; Lk 7:24; *a reed* in its various appliances, as, a wand, a staff, Mt 27:29, 30, 48; Mk 15:19, 36; *a measuring-rod,* Rev 11:1; 21:15f.; *a writer's reed,* 3 Jn 13* [2563]

[2813] καλέω *kaleō* 148x *to call, call to,* Jn 10:3; *to call* into one's presence, *send for* a person, Mt 2:7; *to summon,* Mt 2:15; 25:14; *to invite,* Mt 22:9; *to call* to the performance of a certain thing, Mt 9:13; Heb 11:8; *to call* to a participation in the privileges of the Gospel, Ro 8:30; 9:24; 1 Co 1:9; 7:18; *to call* to an office or dignity, Heb 5:4; *to name, style,* Mt 1:21; pass. *to be styled, regarded,* Mt 5:9, 19 [2564]

[2814] καλλιέλαιος *kallielaios* 1x pr. adj. *productive of good oil;* as subst. *a cultivated olive tree,* Ro 11:24* [2565]

[2815] καλοδιδάσκαλος *kalodidaskalos* 1x *teaching what is good; a teacher of good,* Tit 2:3* [2567]

[2818] καλοποιέω *kalopoieō* 1x *to do well, do good, do what is right,* 2 Th 3:13* [2569]

[2819] καλός *kalos* 101x pr. *beautiful; good, of good quality* or *disposition; fertile, rich,* Mt 13:8, 23; *useful, profitable,* Lk 14:34; καλόν ἐστι[ν], *it is profitable, it is well,* Mt 18:8, 9; *excellent, choice, select, goodly,* Mt 7:17, 19; καλόν ἐστι[ν], *it is pleasant, delightful,* Mt 17:4; *just, full* measure, Lk 6:38; *honorable, distinguished,* Jas 2:7; *good, possessing moral excellence, worthy, upright, virtuous,* Jn 10:11, 14; 1 Ti 4:6; τὸ καλόν, and τὸ καλὸν ἔργον, *what is good and right, a good deed, rectitude, virtue,* Mt 5:16; Ro 7:18, 21; *right, duty, propriety,* Mt 15:26; *benefit, favor,* Jn 10:32, 33 [2566, 2570]

[2820] κάλυμμα *kalymma* 4x *a covering; a veil,* 2 Co 3:13; met. *a veil, a blind* to spiritual vision, 2 Co 3:14, 15, 16* [2571]

[2821] καλύπτω *kalyptō* 8x *to cover,* Mt 8:24; Lk 8:16; 23:30; *to hide, conceal,* Mt 10:26; 2 Co 4:3; met. *to cover, throw a veil* of oblivion *over,* Jas 5:20; 1 Pe 4:8 [2572]

[2822] καλῶς *kalōs* 37x *well, rightly, suitable, with propriety, becomingly,* 1 Co 7:37; 14:17; Gal 4:17; 5:7; *truly, justly, correctly,* Mk 12:32; Lk 20:39; Jn 4:17; *appositely,* Mt 15:7; Mk 7:6; *becomingly, honorably,* Jas 2:3; *well, effectually,* Mk 7:9, 37; καλῶς εἰπεῖν, *to speak well, praise, applaud,* Lk 6:26; καλῶς ἔχειν, *to be convalescent,* Mk 16:18; καλῶς ποιεῖν, *to do good, confer benefits,* Mt 5:44; 12:12; *to do well, act virtuously,* Phil 4:14 [2573]

[2823] κάμηλος *kamēlos* 6x *a camel,* Mt 3:4; 23:24 [2574]

[2825] κάμινος *kaminos* 4x *a furnace, oven, kiln,* Mt 13:42, 50; Rev 1:15; 9:2* [2575]

[2826] καμμύω *kammyō* 2x *to shut, close* the eyes, Mt 13:15; Ac 28:27* [2576]

[2827] κάμνω *kamnō* 2x *to tire with exertion, labor to weariness; to be wearied, tired out, exhausted, be discouraged,* Heb 12:3; *to labor* under disease, *be sick,* Jas 5:15* [2577]

[2828] κάμπτω *kamptō* 4x trans. *to bend, inflect* the knee, Ro 11:4; Eph 3:14 intrans. *to bend, bow,* Ro 14:11; Phil 2:10* [2578]

[2829] κἄν *kan* 17x crasis, *and if,* Mk 16:18; *also if,* Mt 21:21; *even if, if even, although,* Jn 10:38; *if so much as,* Heb 12:20; also in N.T. simply equivalent to καί, as a particle of emphasis, by a pleonasm of ἄν, *at least, at all events,* Mk 6:56; Ac 5:15; 2 Co 11:16 [2579]

[2830] Κανά *Kana* 4x indecl. *Cana,* a town in Galilee, Jn 2:1, 11; 4:46; 21:2* [2580]

[2831] Καναναῖος *Kananaios* 2x *a Canaanite,* Mt 10:4; Mk 3:18* [2581]

[2833] Κανδάκη *Kandakē* 1x *Candace,* pr. name, Ac 8:27* [2582]

[2834] κανών *kanōn* 4x *a measure, rule;* in N.T. *prescribed range* of action or duty, 2 Co 10:13, 15, 16; met. *rule* of conduct or doctrine, Gal 6:16* [2583]

[2836] καπηλεύω *kapēleuō* 1x pr. *to be* κάπηλος, *a retailer; to peddle with; to corrupt, adulterate,* 2 Co 2:17* [2585]

[2837] καπνός *kapnos* 13x *smoke,* Ac 2:19; Rev 8:4 [2586]

[2838] Καππαδοκία *Kappadokia* 2x *Cappadocia,* a district of Asia Minor, Ac 2:9; 1 Pe 1:1* [2587]

[2840] καρδία *kardia* 156x *the heart,* regarded as the seat of feeling, impulse, affection, desire, Mt 6:21; 22:37; Phil 1:7; *the heart,* as the seat of intellect, Mt 13:15; Ro 1:21; *the heart,* as the inner and mental frame, Mt 5:8; Lk 16:15; 1 Pe 3:4; *the conscience,* 1 Jn 3:20, 21; *the heart, the inner part, middle, center,* Mt 12:40 [2588]

[2841] καρδιογνώστης *kardiognōstēs* 2x *heart-knower, searcher of hearts,* Ac 1:24; 15:8* [2589]

[2842] Κάρπος *Karpos* 1x *Carpus,* pr. name, 2 Ti 4:13* [2591]

[2843] καρπός *karpos* 66x *fruit,* Mt 3:10; 21:19, 34; from the Hebrew, καρπὸς κοιλίας, *fruit of the womb, offspring,* Lk 1:42; καρπὸς ὀσφύος, *fruit of the loins, offspring, posterity,* Ac 2:30; καρπὸς χειλέων, *fruit of the lips, praise,* Heb 13:15; met. *conduct, actions,* Mt 3:8; 7:16; Ro 6:22; *benefit, profit,* Ro 1:13; 6:21; *reward,* Phil 4:17 [2590]

[2844] καρποφορέω *karpophoreō* 8x *to bear fruit, yield,* Mk 4:28; met. *to bring forth the fruit* of action or conduct, Mt 13:23; Ro 7:5; mid. *to expand by fruitfulness, to develop itself by success,* Col 1:6, 10 [2592]

[2845] καρποφόρος *karpophoros* 1x *fruitful, adapted to bring forth fruit,* Ac 14:17* [2593]

[2846] καρτερέω *kartereō* 1x *to be stout; to endure patiently, persevere, bear up with fortitude,* Heb 11:27* [2594]

[2847] κάρφος *karphos* 6x *any small dry thing,* as *chaff, stubble, splinter,* Mt 7:3, 4, 5; Lk 6:41, 42* [2595]

[2848] κατά *kata* 473x *down from,* Mt 8:32; *down upon, upon,* Mk 14:3; Ac 27:14; *down into;* κατὰ βάθους, *profound, deepest,* 2 Co 8:2; *down over, throughout* a space, Lk 4:14; 23:5; *concerning,* in cases of pointed allegation, 1 Co 15:15; *against,* Mt 12:30; *by,* in oaths, Mt 26:63; with an acc. of place, *in the quarter of, about, near, at,* Lk 10:32; Ac 2:10; *throughout,* Lk 8:39; *in,* Ro 16:5; *among,* Ac 21:21; *in the presence of,* Lk 2:31; *in the direction of, towards,* Ac 8:26; Phil 3:14; *of time, within the range of; during, in the course of, at, about,* Ac 12:1; 27:27; distributively, κατ᾽ οἶκον, *by houses, from house to house,* Ac 2:46; kata; duvo, *two and two,* 1 Co 14:27; καθ᾽ ἡμέραν, *daily,* Mt 26:55; trop., *according to, conformable to, in proportion to,* Mt 9:29; 25:15; *after the fashion* or *likeness of,* Heb 5:6; *in virtue of,* Mt

19:3; *as respects,* Ro 11:3; Ac 25;14; Heb 9:9 [2596]

[2849] καταβαίνω *katabainō* 81x *to come* or *go down, descend,* Mt 8:1; 17:9; *to lead down,* Ac 8:26; *to come down, fall,* Mt 7:25, 27; *to be let down,* Ac 10:11; 11:5 [2597]

[2850] καταβάλλω *kataballō* 2x *to cast down,* 2 Co 4:9; mid. *to lay down, lay* a foundation, Heb 6:1* [2598]

[2851] καταβαρέω *katabareō* 1x pr. *to weigh down,* met. *to burden, be burdensome to,* 2 Co 12:16* [2599]

[2852] καταβαρύνω *katabarynō* 1x *to weigh down, depress,* pass., *be heavy,* Mk 14:40* [925]

[2853] κατάβασις *katabasis* 1x *the act of descending; a way down, descent,* Lk 19:37* [2600]

[2856] καταβολή *katabolē* 11x pr. *a casting down; laying the foundation, foundation; beginning, commencement,* Mt 13:35; 25:34; *conception* in the womb, Heb 11:11 [2602]

[2857] καταβραβεύω *katabrabeuō* 1x pr. *to give an unfavorable decision as respects a prize;* hence, *to decide against,* Col 2:18* [2603]

[2858] καταγγελεύς *katangeleus* 1x *one who announces* anything, *a proclaimer, publisher,* Ac 17:18* [2604]

[2859] καταγγέλλω *katangellō* 18x *to announce, proclaim,* Ac 13:38; in N.T. *to laud, celebrate,* Ro 1:8 [2605]

[2860] καταγελάω *katagelaō* 3x *to deride, laugh at, jeer,* Mt 9:24; Mk 5:40; Lk 8:53* [2606]

[2861] καταγινώσκω *kataginōskō* 3x *to determine against, condemn, blame, reprehend,* Gal 2:11; 1 Jn 3:20, 21 [2607]

[2862] κατάγνυμι *katagnymi* 4x *to break in pieces, crush, break in two,* Mt 12:20; Jn 19:31, 32, 33* [2608]

[2863] καταγράφω *katagraphō* 1x *to trace, draw in outline, write,* Jn 8:6* [1125]

[2864] κατάγω *katagō* 9x *to lead, bring,* or *conduct down,* Ac 9:30; 22:30; 23:15, 20, 28; *to bring* a ship *to land;* pass. κατάγομαι, aor. κατήχθην, *to come to land, land, touch,* Lk 5:11 [2609]

[2865] καταγωνίζομαι *katagōnizomai* 1x *to subdue, vanquish, overcome, conquer,* Heb 11:33* [2610]

[2866] καταδέω *katadeō* 1x *to bind up; to bandage* a wound, Lk 10:34* [2611]

[2867] κατάδηλος *katadēlos* 1x *quite clear* or *evident,* Heb 7:15* [2612]

[2868] καταδικάζω *katadikazō* 5x *to give judgment against, condemn,* Mt 12:7, 37; Lk 6:37; Jas 5:6* [2613]

[2869] καταδίκη *katadikē* 1x *condemnation, sentence of condemnation,* Ac 25:15* [1349]

[2870] καταδιώκω *katadiōkō* 1x *to follow hard upon; to track, search for, follow perseveringly,* Mk 1:36* [2614]

[2871] καταδουλόω *katadouloō* 2x *to reduce to absolute servitude, make a slave of,* 2 Co 11:20; Gal 2:4* [2615]

[2872] καταδυναστεύω *katadynasteuō* 2x *to tyrannize over, oppress, exploit,* Ac 10:38; Jas 2:6* [2616]

[2873] κατάθεμα *katathema* 1x *an execration, curse;* by meton. *what is worthy of cursing* or *condemnation,* Rev 22:3* [2652]

[2874] καταθεματίζω *katathematizō* 1x *to curse,* Mt 26:74* [2653]

[2875] καταισχύνω *kataischunō* 13x *to humiliate, shame, put to shame,* 1 Co 1:27; pass. *to be ashamed, be put to shame,* Lk 13:17; *to dishonor, disgrace,* 1 Co 11:4, 5; from the Hebrew, *to frustrate, disappoint,* Ro 5:5; 9:33; 1 Pe 2:6 [2617]

[2876] κατακαίω *katakaiō* 12x *to burn up, consume with fire,* Mt 3:12; 13:30, 40 [2618]

[2877] κατακαλύπτω *katakalyptō* 3x *to veil;* mid. *to veil one's self, be veiled* or *covered,* 1 Co 11:6, 7. In the pres act ind., 2nd sg, the personal ending sai does not simplify as normal, κατακαυχᾶσαι* [2619]

[2878] κατακαυχάομαι *katakauchaomai* 4x *to boast, glory over, assume superiority over,* Ro 11:18 (2t); Jas 2:13; 3:14* [2620]

[2879] κατάκειμαι *katakeimai* 12x *to lie, be in a recumbent position, be laid down,* Mk 1:30; 2:4; Lk 5:25; Jn 5:3, 6; Ac 9:33; 28:8; *to recline* at table, Mk 2:15; 14:3; Lk 5:29; 7:37; 1 Co 8:10* [2621]

[2880] κατακλάω *kataklaō* 2x *to break, break in pieces,* Mk 6:41; Lk 9:16* [2622]

[2881] κατακλείω *katakleiō* 2x *to close, shut fast; to shut up, confine,* Lk 3:20; Ac 26:10* [2623]

[2883] κατακληρονομέω *kataklēronomeō* 1x *to give as inheritance,* Ac 13:19* [2624]

[2884] κατακλίνω *kataklinō* 5x *to cause to lie down, cause to recline* at table, Lk

9:14, 15; mid. *to lie down, recline,* Lk 7:36; 14:8; 24:30* [2625]

[2885] κατακλύζω *kataklyzō* 1x *to inundate, flood, deluge,* 2 Pe 3:6* [2626]

[2886] κατακλυσμός *kataklysmos* 4x *flood, deluge,* Mt 24:38, 39; Lk 17:27; 2 Pe 2:5* [2627]

[2887] κατακολουθέω *katakoloutheō* 2x *to follow closely* or *earnestly,* Lk 23:55; Ac 16:17* [2628]

[2888] κατακόπτω *katakoptō* 1x *to cut* or *dash in pieces; to mangle, wound,* Mk 5:5* [2629]

[2889] κατακρημνίζω *katakrēmnizō* 1x *to cast down headlong,* Lk 4:29* [2630]

[2890] κατάκριμα *katakrima* 3x *punishment, condemnation, condemning sentence,* Ro 5:16, 18; 8:1* [2631]

[2891] κατακρίνω *katakrinō* 18x *to give judgment against, condemn,* Mt 27:3; Jn 8:10, 11; *to condemn, to place in a guilty light* by contrast, Mt 12:41, 42; Lk 11:31, 32; Heb 11:7 [2632]

[2892] κατάκρισις *katakrisis* 2x *condemnation,* 2 Co 3:9; *censure,* 2 Co 7:3* [2633]

[2893] κατακύπτω *katakyptō* 1x *to bend down,* Jn 8:8* [2596 + 2955]

[2894] κατακυριεύω *katakyrieuō* 4x *to get into one's power;* in N.T. *to bring under, master, overcome,* Ac 19:16; *to domineer over,* Mt 20:25; Mk 10:42; 1 Pe 5:3* [2634]

[2895] καταλαλέω *katalaleō* 5x *to blab out; to speak against, slander,* Jas 4:11; 1 Pe 2:12; 3:16* [2635]

[2896] καταλαλιά *katalalia* 2x *evil-speaking, detraction, backbiting, slandering,* 2 Co 12:20; 1 Pe 2:1* [2636]

[2897] κατάλαλος *katalalos* 1x *slanderous; a detractor, slanderer,* Ro 1:30* [2637]

[2898] καταλαμβάνω *katalambanō* 15x *to lay hold of, grasp; to obtain, attain,* Ro 9:30; 1 Co 9:24; Phil 3:12, 13; *to seize, to take possession of,* Mk 9:18; *to come suddenly upon; overtake, surprise,* Jn 12:35; 1 Th 5:4; *to detect in the act, seize,* Jn 8:3, 4; met. *to comprehend, apprehend,* Jn 1:5; mid. *to understand, perceive,* Ac 4:13; 10:34; 25:25; Eph 3:18* [2638]

[2899] καταλέγω *katalegō* 1x *to select, enter in a list* or *catalog, enroll,* 1 Ti 5:9* [2639]

[2901] καταλείπω *kataleipō* 24x *to leave behind; to leave behind* at death, Mk 12:19; *to relinquish, let remain,* Mk 14:52; *to quit,* depart from, forsake, Mt 4:13; 16:4; *to neglect*, Ac 6:2; *to leave alone*, or *without assistance*, Lk 10:40; *to reserve*, Ro 11:4 [2641]

[2902] καταλιθάζω *katalithazō* 1x *to stone, kill by stoning*, Lk 20:6* [2642]

[2903] καταλλαγή *katallagē* 4x pr. *an exchange; reconciliation, restoration to favor*, Ro 5:11; 11:15; 2 Co 5:18, 19* [2643]

[2904] καταλλάσσω *katallassō* 6x *to change, exchange; to reconcile*; pass. *to be reconciled*, Ro 5:10 (2t); 1 Co 7:11; 2 Co 5:18, 19, 20* [2644]

[2905] κατάλοιπος *kataloipos* 1x *remaining*; οἱ κατάλοιποι, *the rest*, Ac 15:17* [2645]

[2906] κατάλυμα *katalyma* 3x *lodging, inn*, Lk 2:7; *a guest-chamber*, Mk 14:14; Lk 22:11* [2646]

[2907] καταλύω *katalyō* 17x *to dissolve; to destroy, demolish, overthrow, throw down*, Mt 24:2; 26:61; met. *to nullify, abrogate*, Mt 5:17; Ac 5:38, 39; absol. *to unloose* harness, etc., *to halt, to stop for the night, lodge*, Lk 9:12 [2647]

[2908] καταμανθάνω *katamanthanō* 1x *to learn* or *observe thoroughly; to consider accurately and diligently, contemplate*, Mt 6:28* [2648]

[2909] καταμαρτυρέω *katamartyreō* 3x *to witness* or *testify against*, Mt 26:62; 27:13; Mk 14:60* [2649]

[2910] καταμένω *katamenō* 1x *to remain; to abide, dwell*, Ac 1:13* [2650]

[2914] καταναλίσκω *katanaliskō* 1x *to consume*, as fire, Heb 12:29* [2654]

[2915] καταναρκάω *katanarkaō* 3x in N.T. *to be burdensome to the disadvantage of* any one, *to be a dead weight upon*; by impl. *to be troublesome, burdensome to*, in respect of maintenance, 2 Co 11:9; 12:13, 14* [2655]

[2916] κατανεύω *kataneuō* 1x pr. *to nod, signify assent by a nod*; genr. *to make signs, beckon*, Lk 5:7* [2656]

[2917] κατανοέω *katanoeō* 14x *to perceive, understand, apprehend*, Lk 20:23; *to observe, consider, contemplate*, Lk 12:24, 27; *to discern, detect*, Mt 7:3; *to have regard to, make account of*, Ro 4:19 [2657]

[2918] καταντάω *katantaō* 13x *to come to, arrive at*, Ac 16:1; 20:15; of an epoch, *to come upon*, 1 Co 10:11; met. *to reach, attain to*, Ac 26:7 [2658]

[2919] κατάνυξις *katanyxis* 1x in N.T. *deep sleep, stupor, dullness*, Ro 11:8* [2659]

[2920] κατανύσσομαι *katanyssomai* 1x *to pierce through; to pierce* with compunction and pain of heart, Ac 2:37* [2660]

[2921] καταξιόω *kataxioō* 3x *to consider worthy of*, Lk 20:35; Ac 5:41; 2 Th 1:5* [2661]

[2922] καταπατέω *katapateō* 5x *to trample upon, tread down* or *under feet*, Mt 5:13; 7:6; Lk 8:5; 12:1; met. *to trample on* by indignity, *spurn*, Heb 10:29* [2662]

[2923] κατάπαυσις *katapausis* 9x pr. *the act of giving rest; a state of settled* or *final rest*, Heb 3:11, 18; 4:1, 3, 4, 5, 11; *a place of rest, place of abode, dwelling, habitation*, Ac 7:49* [2663]

[2924] καταπαύω *katapauō* 4x *to cause to cease, restrain*, Ac 14:18; *to cause to rest, give final rest to, settle finally*, Heb 4:8; intrans. *to rest, desist from*, Heb 4:4, 10* [2664]

[2925] καταπέτασμα *katapetasma* 6x *a veil, curtain*, Mt 27:51; Mk 15:38; Lk 23:45; Heb 6:19; 9:3; 10:20* [2665]

[2927] καταπίνω *katapinō* 7x *to drink, swallow, gulp down*, Mt 23:24; *to swallow up, absorb*, Rev 12:16; 2 Co 5:4; *to engulf, submerge, overwhelm*, Heb 11:29; *to swallow greedily, devour*, 1 Pe 5:8; *to destroy, annihilate*, 1 Co 15:54; 2 Co 2:7* [2666]

[2928] καταπίπτω *katapiptō* 3x *to fall down, fall prostrate*, Lk 8:6; Ac 26:14; 28:6* [2667]

[2929] καταπλέω *katapleō* 1x *to sail towards land, to come to land*, Lk 8:26* [2668]

[2930] καταπονέω *kataponeō* 2x *to exhaust by labor* or *suffering; to wear out*, 2 Pe 2:7; *to overpower, oppress*, Ac 7:24* [2669]

[2931] καταποντίζω *katapontizō* 2x *to sink in the sea*; pass. *to sink*, Mt 14:30; *to be plunged, submerged, drowned*, Mt 18:6* [2670]

[2932] κατάρα *katara* 6x *a cursing, execration, imprecation*, Jas 3:10; from the Hebrew, *condemnation, doom*, Gal 3:10; Heb 6:8; 2 Pe 2:14; meton., *a doomed one, one on whom condemnation falls*, Gal 3:13* [2671]

[2933] καταράομαι *kataraomai* 5x *to curse, to wish evil to, imprecate evil upon*, Mk 11:21; Lk 6:28; Ro 12:14; Jas 3:9; in N.T. pass. *to be cursed*, Mt 25:41* [2672]

[2934] καταργέω *katargeō* 27x *to render useless* or *unproductive, occupy unprofitable*, Lk 13:7; *to render powerless*, Ro 6:6; *to make empty and unmeaning*, Ro 4:14; *to render null, to abrogate, cancel*, Ro 3:3,

31; Eph 2:15; *to bring to an end*, 1 Co 2:6; 13:8; 15:24, 26; 2 Co 3:7; *to destroy, annihilate*, 2 Th 2:8; Heb 2:14; *to free from, dissever from*, Ro 7:2, 6; Gal 5:4 [2673]

[2935] καταριθμέω *katarithmeō* 1x *to enumerate, number with, count with*, Ac 1:17* [2674]

[2936] καταρτίζω *katartizō* 13x *to adjust thoroughly; to knit together, unite completely*, 1 Co 1:10; *to frame*, Heb 11:3; *to prepare, provide*, Mt 21:16; Heb 10:5; *to qualify fully, to complete* in character, Lk 6:40; Heb 13:21; 1 Pe 5:10; perf. pass. κατηρτισμένα, *fit, ripe*, Ro 9:22; *to repair, refit*, Mt 4:21; Mk 1:19; *to supply, make good*, 1 Th 3:10; *to restore* to a forfeited condition, *to reinstate*, Gal 6:1; 2 Co 13:11* [2675]

[2937] κατάρτισις *katartisis* 1x pr. *a complete adjustment; completeness* of character, *perfection*, 2 Co 13:9* [2676]

[2938] καταρτισμός *katartismos* 1x *a perfectly adjusted adaptation; complete qualification* for a specific purpose, Eph 4:12* [2677]

[2939] κατασείω *kataseiō* 4x *to shake down* or *violently*, Ac 19:33; τὴν χεῖρα, or τῇ χειρί, *to wave the hand, beckon; to signal silence by waving the hand*, Ac 12:17; 13:16; 21:40* [2678]

[2940] κατασκάπτω *kataskaptō* 2x pr. *to dig down under, undermine;* by impl. *to overthrow; demolish, raze*, Ro 11:3; τὰ κατεσκαμμένα, *ruins*, Ac 15:16* [2679]

[2941] κατασκευάζω *kataskeuazō* 11x *to prepare, put in readiness*, Mt 11:10; Mk 1:2; Lk 1:17; 7:27; *to construct, form, build*, Heb 3:3, 4; 9:2, 6; 11:7; 1 Pe 3:20* [2680]

[2942] κατασκηνόω *kataskēnoō* 4x *to pitch one's tent;* in N.T. *to rest in* a place, *settle, abide*, Ac 2:26; *to haunt, roost*, Mt 13:32; Mk 4:32; Lk 13:19* [2681]

[2943] κατασκήνωσις *kataskēnōsis* 2x pr. *the pitching a tent; a tent;* in N.T. *a dwelling-place*, Mt 8:20; Lk 9:58* [2682]

[2944] κατασκιάζω *kataskiazō* 1x *to overshadow*, Heb 9:5* [2683]

[2945] κατασκοπέω *kataskopeō* 1x *to view closely and accurately; to spy out*, Gal 2:4* [2684]

[2946] κατάσκοπος *kataskopos* 1x *a scout, spy*, Heb 11:31* [2685]

[2947] κατασοφίζομαι *katasophizomai* 1x *to exercise cleverness to the detriment of* any one, *to outwit; to make a victim of*

subtlety, to practice on the insidious dealing, Ac 7:19★ [2686]

[2948] καταστέλλω *katastellō* 2x *to arrange, dispose in regular order; to appease, quiet, pacify,* Ac 19:35, 36★ [2687]

[2949] κατάστημα *katastēma* 1x *determinate state, behavior, condition; personal appearance,* Tit 2:3★ [2688]

[2950] καταστολή *katastolē* 1x pr. *an arranging in order; adjustment of dress;* in N.T. *apparel, dress,* 1 Ti 2:9★ [2689]

[2951] καταστρέφω *katastrephō* 2x *to invert; to overturn, upset, overthrow, throw down,* Mt 21:12; Mk 11:15★ [2690]

[2952] καταστρηνιάω *katastrēniaō* 1x *to be headstrong* or *wanton towards,* 1 Ti 5:11★ [2691]

[2953] καταστροφή *katastrophē* 2x *an overthrow, destruction,* 2 Pe 2:6; met. *overthrow* of right principle or faith, *utter detriment, perversion,* 2 Ti 2:14★ [2692]

[2954] καταστρώννυμι *katastrōnnymi* 1x *to lay flat;* pass. *to be laid prostrate* in death, 1 Co 10:5★ [2693]

[2955] κατασύρω *katasyrō* 1x *to drag down, to drag away* by force, Lk 12:58★ [2694]

[2956] κατασφάζω *katasphazō* 1x also spelled κατασφάττω, *to slaughter, slay,* Lk 19:27★ [2695]

[2958] κατασφραγίζω *katasphragizō* 1x *to seal up,* Rev 5:1★ [2696]

[2959] κατάσχεσις *kataschesis* 2x *a possession, thing possessed,* Ac 7:5, 45★ [2697]

[2960] κατατίθημι *katatithēmi* 2x mid. *to lay up for one's self;* χάριν, or χάριτας, *to lay up a store of favor for one's self, earn a title to favor* at the hands of a person, *to curry favor with,* Ac 24:27; 25:9★ [2698]

[2961] κατατομή *katatomē* 1x *mutilation,* Phil 3:2★ [2699]

[2963] κατατρέχω *katatrechō* 1x *to run down,* Ac 21:32★ [2701]

[2965] καταφέρω *katapherō* 4x *to bear down; to overpower,* as sleep, Ac 20:9; καταφέρειν ψῆφον, *to give a vote* or *verdict,* Ac 26:10; *to bring charges,* Ac 25:7★ [2702]

[2966] καταφεύγω *katapheugō* 2x *to flee to* for refuge, Ac 14:6; Heb 6:18★ [2703]

[2967] καταφθείρω *kataphtheirō* 1x *to destroy, corrupt, deprave,* 2 Ti 3:8★ [2704]

[2968] καταφιλέω *kataphileō* 6x *to kiss affectionately* or *with a semblance of affection, to kiss with earnest gesture,* Mt 26:49;

Mk 14:45; Lk 7:38, 45; 15:20; Ac 20:37★ [2705]

[2969] καταφρονέω *kataphroneō* 9x pr. *to look down on; to scorn, despise,* Mt 18:10; Ro 2:4; *to slight,* Mt 6:24; Lk 16:13; 1 Co 11:22; 1 Ti 4:12; 6:2; 2 Pe 2:10; *to disregard,* Heb 12:2★ [2706]

[2970] καταφρονητής *kataphronētēs* 1x *despiser, scorner,* Ac 13:41★ [2707]

[2972] καταχέω *katacheō* 2x *to pour out* or *down upon,* Mt 26:7; Mk 14:3★ [2708]

[2973] καταχθόνιος *katachthonios* 1x *under the earth, subterranean, infernal,* Phil 2:10★ [2709]

[2974] καταχράομαι *katachraomai* 2x *to use downright; to use up, consume; to make an unrestrained use of, use eagerly,* 1 Co 7:31; *to use to the full, stretch to the utmost, exploit,* 1 Co 9:18★ [2710]

[2976] καταψύχω *katapsychō* 1x *to cool, refresh,* Lk 16:24★ [2711]

[2977] κατείδωλος *kateidōlos* 1x *rife with idols, sunk in idolatry, grossly idolatrous,* Ac 17:16★ [2712]

[2978] κατέναντι *katenanti* 8x can function as an improper prep., *over against, opposite to,* Mk 11:2; 12:41; 13:3; ὁ, ἡ, τό, κατέναντι, *opposite,* Lk 19:30; *before, in the presence of, in the sight of,* Ro 4:17 [2713]

[2979] κατενώπιον *katenōpion* 3x can function as an improper prep., *in the presence of, in the sight of, before;* Eph 1:4; Col 1:22; Jude 24★ [2714]

[2980] κατεξουσιάζω *katexousiazō* 2x *to exercise lordship* or *authority over, domineer over,* Mt 20:25; Mk 10:42★ [2715]

[2981] κατεργάζομαι *katergazomai* 22x *to work out; to effect, produce, bring out as a result,* Ro 4:15; 5:3; 7:13; 2 Co 4:17; 7:10; Phil 2:12; 1 Pe 4:3; Jas 1:3; *to work, practice, realize in practice,* Ro 1:27; 2:9; *to work* or *mould into fitness,* 2 Co 5:5, *despatch,* Eph 6:13 [2716]

[2982] κατέρχομαι *katerchomai* 16x *to come* or *go down,* Lk 4:31; 9:37; Ac 8:5; 9:32; *to land at, touch at,* Ac 18:22; 27:5 [2718]

[2983] κατεσθίω *katesthiō* 14x also spelled κατέσθω, *to eat up, devour,* Mt 13:4; *to consume,* Rev 11:5, *to expend, squander,* Lk 15:30; met. *to make a prey of, plunder,* Mt 23:13; Mk 12:40; Lk 20:47; 2 Co 11:20; *to annoy, injure,* Gal 5:15 [2719]

[2985] κατευθύνω *kateuthunō* 3x optative, κατευθύναι (3rd sg), *to make straight;*

to direct, guide aright, Lk 1:79; 1 Th 3:11; 2 Th 3:5★ [2720]

[2986] κατευλογέω *kateulogeō* 1x *to bless,* Mk 10:16★ [2127]

[2987] κατεφίσταμαι *katephistamai* 1x *to come upon suddenly, rush upon, assault,* Ac 18:12★ [2721]

[2988] κατέχω *katechō* 17x (1) transitive, *to hold down; to detain, retain,* Lk 4:42; Ro 1:18; Phlm 13; *to hinder, restrain,* 2 Th 2:6, 7; *to hold downright, hold in a firm grasp, to have in full and secure possession,* 1 Co 7:30; 2 Co 6:10; *to come into full possession of, seize upon; to keep, retain,* 1 Th 5:21; *to occupy,* Lk 14:9; met. *to hold fast* mentally, *retain,* Lk 8:15; 1 Co 11:2; 15:2; *to maintain,* Heb 3:6, 14; 10:23; (2) intransitive, a nautical term, *to land, touch,* Ac 27:40; pass. *to be in the grasp of, to be bound by,* Ro 7:6★ [2722]

[2989] κατηγορέω *katēgoreō* 23x *to speak against, accuse,* Mt 12:10; 27:12; Jn 5:45 [2723]

[2990] κατηγορία *katēgoria* 3x *an accusation, crimination,* Jn 18:29; 1 Ti 5:19; Tit 1:6★ [2724]

[2991] κατήγορος *katēgoros* 4x *an accuser,* Ac 23:30, 35; Ac 25:16, 18★ [2725]

[2992] κατήγωρ *katēgōr* 1x *an accuser,* Rev 12:10, a barbarous form for κατήγορος★ [2725]

[2993] κατήφεια *katēpheia* 1x *dejection, sorrow,* Jas 4:9★ [2726]

[2994] κατηχέω *katēcheō* 8x pr. *to sound in the ears, make the ears ring; to instruct orally, to instruct, inform,* 1 Co 14:19; pass. *to be taught, be instructed,* Lk 1:4; Ro 2:18; Gal 6:6; *to be made acquainted,* Ac 18:25; *to receive information, hear report,* Ac 21:21, 24★ [2727]

[2995] κατιόω *katioō* 1x *to cover with rust;* pass. *to rust, become rusty* or *tarnished,* Jas 5:3★ [2728]

[2996] κατισχύω *katischuō* 3x *to overpower,* Mt 16:18; absol. *to predominate, get the upper hand,* Lk 21:36; 23:23★ [2729]

[2997] κατοικέω *katoikeō* 44x trans. *to inhabit,* Ac 1:19; absol. *to have an abode, dwell,* Lk 13:4; Ac 11:29; *to take up* or *find an abode,* Ac 7:2; *to indwell,* Eph 3:17; Jas 4:5 [2730]

[2998] κατοίκησις *katoikēsis* 1x *an abode, dwelling, habitation,* Mk 5:3★ [2731]

[2999] κατοικητήριον *katoikētērion* 2x *an abode, dwelling, habitation,* the same as κατοίκησις, Eph 2:22; Rev 18:2★ [2732]

[3000] κατοικία *katoikia* 1x *habitation,* i.q. κατοίκησις, Ac 17:26* [2733]

[3001] κατοικίζω *katoikizo* 1x *to cause to dwell,* Jas 4:5* [2730]

[3002] κατοπτρίζω *katoptrizo* 1x *to show in a mirror; to present a clear and correct image of* a thing, mid. *to have presented in a mirror, to have a clear image presented,* or, *to reflect,* 2 Co 3:18* [2734]

[3004] κάτω *kato* 9x (1) *down, downwards,* Mt 4:6; Lk 4:9; Jn 8:6; Ac 20:9; (2) *beneath, below, under,* Mt 27:51; Mk 14:66; 15:38; Ac 2:19; ὁ, ἡ, τό, κάτω, *what is below, earthly,* Jn 8:23* [2736]

[3005] κατώτερος *katoteros* 1x *lower,* Eph 4:9* [2737]

[3006] κατωτέρω *katotero* 1x *lower, farther down;* of time, *under,* Mt 2:16* [2736]

[3007] Καῦδα *Kauda* 1x also spelled Κλαῦδα (3084) and Κλαύδη (3085), *Cauda,* indecl. prop. name of an island, Ac 27:16* [2802]

[3008] καῦμα *kauma* 2x *heat, scorching* or *burning heat,* Rev 7:16; 16:9* [2738]

[3009] καυματίζω *kaumatizo* 4x *to scorch, burn,* Mt 13:6; Mk 4:6; Rev 16:8, 9* [2739]

[3011] καῦσις *kausis* 1x *burning, being burned,* Heb 6:8* [2740]

[3012] καυσόω *kausoo* 2x *to be on fire, burn intensely,* 2 Pe 3:10, 12* [2741]

[3013] καυστηριάζω *kausteriazo* 1x also spelled καυτηριάζω, *to cauterize, brand;* pass. met. *to be branded* with marks of guilt, or, *to be seared* into insensibility, 1 Ti 4:2* [2743]

[3014] καύσων *kauson* 3x *fervent scorching heat; the scorching* of the sun, Mt 20:12; *hot weather, a hot time,* Lk 12:55; *the scorching wind of the East, Eurus,* Jas 1:11* [2742]

[3016] καυχάομαι *kauchaomai* 37x *to glory, boast,* Ro 2:17, 23; ὑπέρ τινος, *to boast of* a person or thing, *to undertake a complimentary testimony to,* 2 Co 12:5; *to rejoice, exult,* Ro 5:2, 3, 11 [2744]

[3017] καύχημα *kauchema* 11x *a glorying, boasting,* 1 Co 5:6; *a ground* or *matter of glorying* or *boasting,* Ro 4:2; *joy, exultation,* Phil 1:26; *complimentary testimony,* 1 Co 9:15, 16; 2 Co 9:3 [2745]

[3018] καύχησις *kauchesis* 11x *boasting, pride,* a later equivalent to καύχημαι, Ro 3:27; 2 Co 7:4, 14; 11:10 [2746]

[3019] Καφαρναούμ *Kapharnaoum* 16x indecl. pr. name, *Capernaum* [2584]

[3020] Κεγχρεαί *Kenchreai* 2x *Cenchreae,* the port of Corinth on the Saronic Gulf; Ac 18:18; Ro 16:1* [2747]

[3022] Κεδρών *Kedron* 1x indecl. pr. name, *Kidron,* a valley near Jerusalem, Jn 18:1* [2748]

[3023] κεῖμαι *keimai* 24x *to lie, to be laid; to recline, to be lying, to have been laid down,* Mt 28:6; Lk 2:12; *to have been laid, placed, set,* Mt 3:10; Lk 3:9; Jn 2:6; *to be situated,* as a city, Mt 5:14; Rev 21:16; *to be in store,* Lk 12:19; met. *to be constituted, established* as a law, 1 Ti 1:9; in N.T. of persons, *to be specially set, solemnly appointed, destined,* Lk 2:34; Phil 1:16; 1 Th 3:3; *to lie* under an influence, *to be involved in,* 1 Jn 5:19 [2749]

[3024] κειρία *keiria* 1x *a bandage, swath,* in N.T. pl. *graveclothes,* Jn 11:44* [2750]

[3025] κείρω *keiro* 4x *to cut off* the hair, *shear, shave,* Ac 8:32; 18:18; 1 Co 11:6 (2t)* [2751]

[3026] κέλευσμα *keleusma* 1x *a word of command; a mutual cheer;* hence, in N.T. *a loud shout, an arousing outcry,* 1 Th 4:16* [2752]

[3027] κελεύω *keleuo* 25x *to order, command, direct, bid,* Mt 8:18; 14:19, 28 [2753]

[3029] κενοδοξία *kenodoxia* 1x *empty conceit,* Phil 2:3* [2754]

[3030] κενόδοξος *kenodoxos* 1x *boastful,* Gal 5:26* [2755]

[3031] κενός *kenos* 18x *empty; having nothing, empty-handed,* Mk 12:3; met. *vain, fruitless, void of effect,* Ac 4:25; 1 Co 15:10; εἰς κενόν, *in vain, to no purpose,* 2 Co 6:1; *hollow, fallacious, false,* Eph 5:6; Col 2:8; *inconsiderate, foolish,* 1 Th 3:5; Jas 2:20 [2756]

[3032] κενοφωνία *kenophonia* 2x *vain, empty babbling, vain disputation, fruitless discussion,* 1 Ti 6:20; 2 Ti 2:16* [2757]

[3033] κενόω *kenoo* 5x *to empty, evacuate;* ἑαυτόν, *to divest one's self of one's prerogatives, abase one's self,* Phil 2:7; *to deprive a thing* of its proper functions, Ro 4:14; 1 Co 1:17; *to show to be without foundation, falsify,* 1 Co 9:15; 2 Co 9:3* [2758]

[3034] κέντρον *kentron* 4x *a sharp point; a sting* of an animal, Rev 9:10; *a prick, stimulus, goad,* Ac 26:14; met. of death, *destructive power, deadly venom,* 1 Co 15:55, 56* [2759]

[3035] κεντυρίων *kentyrion* 3x in its original signification, *a commander of a hundred foot-soldiers, a centurion,* Mk 15:39, 44, 45* [2760]

[3036] κενῶς *kenos* 1x *in vain, to no purpose, unmeaning,* Jas 4:5* [2761]

[3037] κεραία *keraia* 2x pr. *a horn-like projection, a point, extremity;* in N.T. *an apex,* or *fine point;* as of letters, used for *the minutest part, a tittle,* Mt 5:18; Lk 16:17* [2762]

[3038] κεραμεύς *kerameus* 3x *a potter,* Mt 27:7, 10; Ro 9:21* [2763]

[3039] κεραμικός *keramikos* 1x *made by a potter, earthen,* Rev 2:27* [2764]

[3040] κεράμιον *keramion* 2x *an earthenware vessel, a pitcher, jar,* Mk 14:13; Lk 22;10* [2765]

[3041] κέραμος *keramos* 1x *potter's clay; earthenware; a roof, tile, tiling,* Lk 5:19* [2766]

[3042] κεράννυμι *kerannymi* 3x *to mix, mingle,* drink; *to prepare* for drinking, Rev 14:10; 18:6 (2t)* [2767]

[3043] κέρας *keras* 11x *a horn,* Rev 5:6; 12:3; *a horn-like projection* at the corners of an altar, Rev 9:13; from the Hebrew, *a horn* as a symbol of power, Lk 1:69 [2768]

[3044] κεράτιον *keration* 1x pr. *a little horn;* in N.T. *a pod, the pod of the carob tree,* or *Ceratonia siliqua* of Linnaeus, a common tree in the East and the south of Europe, growing to a considerable size, and producing long slender pods, with a pulp of a sweetish taste, and several brown shining seeds like beans, sometimes eaten by the poorer people in Syria and Palestine, and commonly used for fattening swine, Lk 15:16* [2769]

[3045] κερδαίνω *kerdaino* 17x *to gain* as a matter of profit, Mt 25:17; *to win, acquire possession of,* Mt 16:26; *to profit in the avoidance of, to avoid,* Ac 27:21; in N.T. Χριστόν, *to win* Christ, *to become possessed of* the privileges of the Gospel, Phil 3:8; *to win over* from estrangement, Mt 18:15; *to win over* to embrace the Gospel, 1 Co 9:19, 20, 21, 22; 1 Pe 3:1; absol. *to make gain,* Jas 4:13 [2770]

[3046] κέρδος *kerdos* 3x *gain, profit,* Phil 1:21; 3:7; Tit 1:11* [2771]

[3047] κέρμα *kerma* 1x *something clipped small; small change, small pieces of money, coin,* Jn 2:15* [2772]

[3048] κερματιστής *kermatistēs* 1x *a money changer*, Jn 2:14* [2773]

[3049] κεφάλαιον *kephalaion* 2x *a sum total; a sum of money, capital*, Ac 22:28; *the crowning* or *ultimate point* to preliminary matters, Heb 8:1* [2774]

[3051] κεφαλή *kephalē* 75x *the head*, Mt 5:36; 6:17; *the head, top;* κεφαλὴ γωνίας, *the head of the corner, the chief corner-stone*, Mt 21:42; Lk 20:17; met. *the head, superior, chief, principal, one to whom others are subordinate*, 1 Co 11:3; Eph 1:22 [2776]

[3052] κεφαλιόω *kephalioō* 1x *to hit the head*, Mk 12:4* [2775]

[3053] κεφαλίς *kephalis* 1x in N.T. *a roll, volume, division* of a book, Heb 10:7* [2777]

[3055] κημόω *kēmoō* 1x *to muzzle*, 1 Co 9:9* [5392]

[3056] κῆνσος *kēnsos* 4x *a census, assessment, enumeration of the people and a valuation of their property;* in N.T. *tribute, tax*, Mt 17:25; *poll-tax*, Mt 22.17, 19; Mk 12:14* [2778]

[3057] κῆπος *kēpos* 5x *a garden, any place planted with trees and herbs*, Lk 13:19; Jn 18:1, 26; 19:41* [2779]

[3058] κηπουρός *kēpouros* 1x *a garden-keeper, gardener*, Jn 20:15* [2780]

[3060] κήρυγμα *kērygma* 9x *proclamation, proclaiming, public annunciation*, Mt 12:41; *public inculcation, preaching*, 1 Co 2:4; 15:14; meton. *what is publicly inculcated, doctrine*, Ro 16:25; Tit 1:3* [2782]

[3061] κῆρυξ *kēryx* 3x *a herald, public messenger;* in N.T. *a proclaimer, publisher, preacher*, 1 Ti 2:7; 2 Ti 1:11; 2 Pe 2:5* [2783]

[3062] κηρύσσω *kēryssō* 61x *to publish, proclaim, as a herald*, 1 Co 9:27; *to announce openly and publicly*, Mk 1:4; Lk 4:18; *to noise abroad*, Mk 1:45; 7:36; *to announce as a matter of doctrine, inculcate, preach*, Mt 24:14; Mk 1:38; 13:10; Ac 15:21; Ro 2:21 [2784]

[3063] κῆτος *kētos* 1x *a large fish, sea monster, whale*, Mt 12:40* [2785]

[3064] Κηφᾶς *Kēphas* 9x *Cephas, Rock*, rendered into Greek by Πέτρος, Jn 1:42; 1 Co 1:12; 3:22; 9:5; 15:5; Gal 1:18; 2:9, 11, 14* [2786]

[3066] κιβωτός *kibōtos* 6x *a chest, coffer; the ark* of the covenant, Heb 9:4; Rev 11:19; *the ark* of Noah, Mt 24:38; Lk 17:27; Heb 11:7; 1 Pe 3:20* [2787]

[3067] κιθάρα *kithara* 4x *a lyre, harp*, 1 Co 14:7; Rev 5:8; 14:2; 15:2* [2788]

[3068] κιθαρίζω *kitharizō* 2x *to play on a lyre* or *harp*, 1 Co 14:7; Rev 14:2* [2789]

[3069] κιθαρῳδός *kitharōidos* 2x *one who plays on the lyre and accompanies it with his voice*, Rev 14:2; 18:22* [2790]

[3070] Κιλικία *Kilikia* 8x *Cilicia*, a province of Asia Minor, Gal 1:21 [2791]

[3073] κινδυνεύω *kindyneuō* 4x *to be in danger* or *peril*, Lk 8:23; Ac 19:27, 40; 1 Co 15:30* [2793]

[3074] κίνδυνος *kindynos* 9x *danger, peril*, Ro 8:35; 2 Co 11:26* [2794]

[3075] κινέω *kineō* 8x *to set a-going; to move*, Mt 23:4; *to excite, agitate*, Ac 21:30; 24:5; *to remove*, Rev 2:5; 6:14; in N.T. κεφαλήν, *to shake the head* in derision, Mt 27:39; Mk 15:29; mid., *to move, possess the faculty of motion, exercise the functions of life*, Ac 17:28* [2795]

[3077] κιννάμωμον *kinnamōmon* 1x *cinnamon*, Rev 18:13* [2792]

[3078] Κίς *Kis* 1x *Kish*, the father of Saul, pr. name, indecl., Ac 13:21* [2797]

[3079] κίχρημι *kichrēmi* 1x *to lend*, Lk 11:5* [5531]

[3080] κλάδος *klados* 11x *a bough, branch, shoot*, Mt 13:32; 21:8; met. *a branch* of a family stock, Ro 11:16, 21 [2798]

[3081] κλαίω *klaiō* 40x intrans. *to weep, shed tears*, Mt 26:75; Mk 5:38, 39; Lk 19:41; 23:28; trans. *to weep for, bewail*, Mt 2:18 [2799]

[3082] κλάσις *klasis* 2x *a breaking, the act of breaking*, Lk 24:35; Ac 2:42 [2800]

[3083] κλάσμα *klasma* 9x *a piece broken off, fragment*, Mt 14:20; 15:37; Mk 6:43; 8:8, 19, 20; Lk 9:17; Jn 6:12f.* [2801]

[3086] Κλαυδία *Klaudia* 1x *Claudia*, pr. name, 2 Ti 4:21* [2803]

[3087] Κλαύδιος *Klaudios* 3x *Claudius*, pr. name (1) *The fourth Roman Emperor*, Ac 11:28; 18:2. (2) *Claudius Lysias, a Roman captain*, Ac 23:26* [2804]

[3088] κλαυθμός *klauthmos* 9x *weeping, crying*, Mt 2:18; 8:12 [2805]

[3089] κλάω *klaō* 14x *to break off;* in N.T. *to break* bread, Mt 14:19; with figurative reference to the violent death of Christ, 1 Co 11:24 [2806]

[3090] κλείς *kleis* 6x *a key*, used in N.T. as the symbol of power, authority, etc. Mt 16:19; Rev 1:18; 3:7; 9:1; 20:1; met. *the key* of entrance into knowledge, Lk 11:52* [2807]

[3091] κλείω *kleiō* 16x *to close, shut*, Mt 6:6; 25:10; *to shut up* a person, Rev 20:3; met. of the heavens, Lk 4:25; Rev 11:6; κλεῖσαι τὰ σπλάγχνα, *to shut one's bowels, to be hard-hearted, void of compassion*, 1 Jn 3:17; κλείειν τὴν βασιλεία τῶν οὐρανῶν, *to endeavor to prevent entrance into the kingdom of heaven*, Mt 23:13 [2808]

[3092] κλέμμα *klemma* 1x *theft*, Rev 9:21* [2809]

[3093] Κλεοπᾶς *Kleopas* 1x *Cleopas*, pr. name, Lk 24:18* [2810]

[3094] κλέος *kleos* 1x pr. *rumor, report; good report, praise, credit*, 1 Pe 2:20* [2811]

[3095] κλέπτης *kleptēs* 16x *a thief*, Mt 6:19, 20; 24:43; trop. *a thief* by imposture, Jn 10:8 [2812]

[3096] κλέπτω *kleptō* 13x *to steal*, Mt 6:19, 20; 19:18; *to take away stealthily, remove secretly*, Mt 27:64; 28:13 [2813]

[3097] κλῆμα *klēma* 4x *a branch, shoot, twig*, esp. of the vine, Jn 15:2, 4-6* [2814]

[3098] Κλήμης *Klēmēs* 1x *Clemens, Clement*, pr. name, Latin, Phil 4:3* [2815]

[3099] κληρονομέω *klēronomeō* 18x pr. *to acquire by lot; to inherit, obtain by inheritance;* in N.T. *to obtain, acquire, receive possession of*, Mt 5:5; 19:29; absol. *to be heir*, Gal 4:30 [2816]

[3100] κληρονομία *klēronomia* 14x *an inheritance, patrimony*, Mt 21:38; Mk 12:7; *a possession, portion, property*, Ac 7:5; 20:32; in N.T. *a share, participation* in privileges, Ac 20:32; Eph 1:14; 5:5 [2817]

[3101] κληρονόμος *klēronomos* 15x *an heir*, Mt 21:38; Gal 4:1; *a possessor*, Ro 4:13; Heb 11:7; Jas 2:5 [2818]

[3102] κλῆρος *klēros* 11x *a lot, die, a thing used in determining chances*, Mt 27:35; Mk 15:24; Lk 23:34; Jn 19:24; Ac 1:26; *assignment, investiture*, Ac 1:17; *allotment, destination*, Col 1:12; *a part, portion, share*, Ac 8:21; 26:18; *a constituent portion* of the Church, 1 Pe 5:3* [2819]

[3103] κληρόω *klēroō* 1x *to obtain by lot* or *assignment; to obtain a portion, receive a share*, Eph 1:11* [2820]

[3104] κλῆσις *klēsis* 11x *a call, calling, invitation;* in N.T. *the call* or *invitation* to the privileges of the Gospel, Ro 11:29;

Eph 1:18; *the favor and privilege of the invitation,* 2 Th 1:11; 2 Pe 1:10; *the temporal condition in which the call found a person,* 1 Co 1:26; 7:20 [2821]

[3105] κλητός *klētos* 10x *called, invited,* in N.T. *called* to privileges or function, Mt 20:16; 22:14; Ro 1:1, 6, 7; 8:28; 1 Co 1:1, 2, 24; Jude 1; Rev 17:14 [2822]

[3106] κλίβανος *klibanos* 2x *an oven,* Mt 6:30; Lk 12:28* [2823]

[3107] κλίμα *klima* 3x pr. *a slope; a portion of the* ideal *slope* of the earth's surface; *a tract* or *region* of country, Ro 15:23; 2 Co 11:10; Gal 1:21* [2824]

[3108] κλινάριον *klinarion* 1x *a small bed* or *couch,* Ac 5:15* [2825]

[3109] κλίνη *klinē* 9x *a couch, bed,* Mt 9:2, 6; Mk 4:21; Rev 2:22 [2825]

[3110] κλινίδιον *klinidion* 2x *a small couch* or *bed,* Lk 5:19, 24* [2826]

[3111] κλίνω *klinō* 7x pr. trans. *to cause to slope* or *bend; to bow down,* Lk 24:5; Jn 19:30; *to lay down* to rest, Mt 8:20; Lk 9:58; *to put to flight* troops, Heb 11:34; intrans. of the day, *to decline,* Lk 9:12; 24:29* [2827]

[3112] κλισία *klisia* 1x pr. *a place for reclining; a tent, seat, couch;* in N.T. *a group of persons reclining* at a meal. Lk 9:14* [2828]

[3113] κλοπή *klopē* 2x *theft,* Mt 15:19; Mk 7:21* [2829]

[3114] κλύδων *klydōn* 2x *a wave, billow, surge,* Lk 8:24; Jas 1:6* [2830]

[3115] κλυδωνίζομαι *klydōnizomai* 1x *to be tossed by waves;* met. *to fluctuate* in opinion, *be agitated, tossed to and fro,* Eph 4:14* [2831]

[3116] Κλωπᾶς *Klōpas* 1x *Cleopas,* pr. name, Jn 19:25* [2832]

[3117] κνήθω *knēthō* 1x *to scratch; to tickle, cause titillation;* in N.T. mid. met. *to procure pleasurable excitement for, to indulge an itching,* 2 Ti 4:3* [2833]

[3118] Κνίδος *Knidos* 1x *Cnidus,* a city of Caria, in Asia Minor, Ac 27:7* [2834]

[3119] κοδράντης *kodrantēs* 2x *a Roman brass coin,* equivalent to the *fourth part* of an *as,* or ἀσσάριον, or to δύο λεπτά, Mt 5:26; Mk 12:42* [2835]

[3120] κοιλία *koilia* 22x *a cavity; the belly,* Mt 15:17; Mk 7:19; *the stomach,* Mt 12:40; Lk 15:16; *the womb,* Mt 19:12; Lk 1:15; from the Hebrew, *the inner self,* Jn 7:38 [2836]

[3121] κοιμάω *koimaō* 18x *to lull to sleep;* pass. *to fall asleep, be asleep,* Mt 28:13; Lk 22:45; met. *to sleep* in death, Ac 7:60; 13:36; 2 Pe 3:4 [2837]

[3122] κοίμησις *koimēsis* 1x *sleep;* meton. *rest, repose,* Jn 11:13* [2838]

[3123] κοινός *koinos* 14x *common, belonging equally to several,* Ac 2:44; 4:32; in N.T. *common, profane,* Heb 10:29; Rev 21:27; *ceremonially unclean,* Mk 7:2; Ac 10:14 [2839]

[3124] κοινόω *koinoō* 14x *to make common,* in N.T. *to profane, desecrate,* Ac 21:28; *to render* ceremonially *unclean, defile, pollute,* Mt 15:11, 18, 20; 7:15, 18, 20, 23; Heb 9:13; *to pronounce unclean* ceremonially, Ac 10:15; 11:9* [2840]

[3125] κοινωνέω *koinōneō* 8x *to have in common, share,* Heb 2:14; *to be associated in, to become a sharer in,* Ro 15:27; 1 Pe 4:13; *to become implicated in, be a party to,* 1 Ti 5:22; 2 Jn 11; *to associate one's self with* by sympathy and assistance, *to communicate with* in the way of aid and relief, Ro 12:13; Gal 6:6; Phil 4:15* [2841]

[3126] κοινωνία *koinōnia* 19x *fellowship, partnership,* Ac 2:42; 2 Co 6:14; 13:13; Gal 2:9; Phil 3:10; 1 Jn 1:3; *participation, communion,* 1 Co 10:16; *aid, relief,* Heb 13:16; *contribution in aid,* Ro 15:26 [2842]

[3127] κοινωνικός *koinōnikos* 1x *social;* in N.T. *generous, liberal, beneficent,* 1 Ti 6:18* [2843]

[3128] κοινωνός *koinōnos* 10x *a fellow, partner, companion,* Mt 23:30; Lk 5:10; 1 Co 10:18, 20; 2 Co 8:23; Phlm 17; Heb 10:33; *a sharer, partaker,* 2 Co 1:7; 1 Pe 5:1; 2 Pe 1:4* [2844]

[3130] κοίτη *koitē* 4x *a bed,* Lk 11:7; *the* conjugal *bed,* Heb 13:4; meton. *sexual intercourse, concubitus;* hence, *lewdness, whoredom, chambering,* Ro 13:13; in N.T. *conception,* Ro 9:10* [2845]

[3131] κοιτών *koitōn* 1x *a bed-chamber,* Ac 12:20* [2846]

[3132] κόκκινος *kokkinos* 6x *dyed with coccus, crimson, scarlet,* Mt 27:28; Heb 9:19; Rev 17:3, 4; 18:12, 16* [2847]

[3133] κόκκος *kokkos* 7x *a kernel, grain, seed,* Mt 13:31; 17:20; Mk 4:31; Lk 13:19; 17:6; Jn 12:24; 1 Co 15:37* [2848]

[3134] κολάζω *kolazō* 2x pr. *to curtail, to coerce; to chastise, punish,* Ac 4:21; 2 Pe 2:9* [2849]

[3135] κολακεία *kolakeia* 1x *flattery, adulation, obsequiousness,* 1 Th 2:5* [2850]

[3136] κόλασις *kolasis* 2x *chastisement, punishment,* Mt 25:46; *painful disquietude, torment,* 1 Jn 4:18* [2851]

[3139] κολαφίζω *kolaphizō* 5x *to beat with the fist, buffet,* Mt 26:67; Mk 14:65; met. *to maltreat, treat with excessive force,* 1 Co 4:11; *to punish,* 1 Pe 2:20; *to buffet, fret, afflict,* 2 Co 12:7* [2852]

[3140] κολλάω *kollaō* 12x *to glue* or *weld together;* mid. *to adhere to,* Lk 10:11; met. *to attach one's self to, unite with, associate with,* Lk 15:15; Ac 5:13; Rev 18:5 [2853]

[3141] κολλούριον *kollourion* 1x also spelled κολλύριον, *collyrium, eye-salve,* Rev 3:18* [2854]

[3142] κολλυβιστής *kollybistēs* 3x *a money-changer,* Mt 21:12; Mk 11:15; Jn 2:15* [2855]

[3143] κολοβόω *koloboō* 4x in N.T. of time, *to cut short, shorten,* Mt 24:22; Mk 13:20* [2856]

[3145] Κολοσσαί *Kolossai* 1x also spelled Κολασσαεύς, *Colossae,* a city of Phrygia, Col 1:2* [2857]

[3146] κόλπος *kolpos* 6x *the bosom,* Lk 16:22, 23; Jn 1:18; 13:23; *the bosom of a garment,* Lk 6:38; *a bay, creek, inlet,* Ac 27:39* [2859]

[3147] κολυμβάω *kolymbaō* 1x *to dive;* in N.T. *to swim,* Ac 27:43* [2860]

[3148] κολυμβήθρα *kolymbēthra* 3x *a place where any one may swim; a pond, pool,* Jn 5:2, 4, 7; 9:7* [2861]

[3149] κολωνία *kolōnia* 1x *a Roman colony,* Ac 16:12* [2862]

[3150] κομάω *komaō* 2x *to have long hair, wear the hair long,* 1 Co 11:14, 15* [2863]

[3151] κόμη *komē* 1x *the hair; a head of long hair,* 1 Co 11:15* [2864]

[3152] κομίζω *komizō* 10x pr. *to take into kindly keeping, to provide for; to convey, bring,* Lk 7:37; mid. *to bring for one's self; to receive, obtain,* 2 Co 5:10; Eph 6:8; *to receive again, recover,* Mt 25:27; Heb 11:19 [2865]

[3153] κομψότερον *kompsoteron* 1x in N.T. *in better health,* Jn 4:52* [2866]

[3154] κονιάω *koniaō* 2x *to whitewash,* or, *plaster,* Mt 23:27; Ac 23:3* [2867]

[3155] κονιορτός *koniortos* 5x *dust*, Mt 10:14; Lk 9:5; 10:11; Ac 13:51; 22:23* [2868]

[3156] κοπάζω *kopazō* 3x pr. *to grow weary, suffer exhaustion; to abate, be stilled*, Mt 14:32; Mk 4:39; 6:51* [2869]

[3157] κοπετός *kopetos* 1x pr. *a beating of the breast, etc., in token of grief; a wailing, lamentation*, Ac 8:2* [2870]

[3158] κοπή *kopē* 1x *a stroke, smiting;* in N.T. *slaughter*, Heb 7:1* [2871]

[3159] κοπιάω *kopiaō* 23x *to be wearied* or *spent with labor, faint from weariness*, Mt 11:28; Jn 4:6; in N.T. *to labor hard, to toil*, Lk 5:5; Jn 4:38 [2872]

[3160] κόπος *kopos* 18x *trouble, difficulty, uneasiness*, Mt 26:10; Mk 14:6; *labor, wearisome labor, travail, toil*, 1 Co 3:8; 15:58; meton. *the fruit* or *consequence of labor*, Jn 4:38; 2 Co 10:15 [2873]

[3161] κοπρία *kopria* 1x *dung, manure*, Lk 14:35* [2874]

[3162] κόπριον *koprion* 1x *dung, manure*, Lk 13:8* [2874]

[3164] κόπτω *koptō* 8x *to smite, cut; to cut off* or *down*, Mt 21:8; Mk 11:8; mid. *to beat one's self* in mourning, *lament, bewail*, Mt 11:17; 24:30; Lk 8:52; 23:27; Rev 1:7; 18:9* [2875]

[3165] κόραξ *korax* 1x *a raven, crow*, Lk 12:24* [2876]

[3166] κοράσιον *korasion* 8x *a girl, damsel, maiden*, Mt 9:24, 25; 14:11; Mk 5:41, 42; 6:22, 28* [2877]

[3167] κορβᾶν *korban* 1x *corban, a gift, offering, oblation, anything consecrated to God*, Mk 7:11* [2878]

[3168] κορβανᾶς *korbanas* 1x *temple treasury, the sacred treasury*, Mt 27:6* [2878]

[3169] Κόρε *Kore* 1x *Korah*, Jude 11* [2879]

[3170] κορέννυμι *korennymi* 2x *to satiate, satisfy*, Ac 27:38; 1 Co 4:8* [2880]

[3171] Κορίνθιος *Korinthios* 2x *Corinthian; an inhabitant of* Κόρινθος, *Corinth*, Ac 18:8; 2 Co 6:11* [2881]

[3172] Κόρινθος *Korinthos* 6x *Corinth*, a celebrated city of Greece, Ac 18:1; 19:1: 1 Co 1:2; 2 Co 1:1, 23; 2 Ti 4:20* [2882]

[3173] Κορνήλιος *Kornēlios* 8x *Cornelius*, a Latin pr. name, Ac 10:1, 3, 17, 22, 24f., 30f.* [2883]

[3174] κόρος *koros* 1x *a cor*, the largest Jewish measure for things dry, equal to the homer, and about fifteen bushels English, according to Josephus, Lk 16:7* [2884]

[3175] κοσμέω *kosmeō* 10x pluperfect, ἐκεκόσμητο (3 sg), *to arrange, set in order; to adorn, decorate, embellish*, Mt 12:44; 23:29; *to prepare, put in readiness, trim*, Mt 25:7; met. *to honor, dignify*, Tit 2:10 [2885]

[3176] κοσμικός *kosmikos* 2x pr. *belonging to the universe*, in N.T. *accommodated to the present state of things, adapted to this world, worldly*, Tit 2:12; τὸ κοσμικόν, as a subst. *the apparatus* for the service of the tabernacle, Heb 9:1* [2886]

[3177] κόσμιος *kosmios* 2x *decorous, respectable, well-ordered*, 1 Ti 2:9; 3:2* [2887]

[3179] κοσμοκράτωρ *kosmokratōr* 1x pr. *monarch of the world;* in N.T. *a worldly prince, a power paramount in the world* of the unbelieving and ungodly, Eph 6:12* [2888]

[3180] κόσμος *kosmos* 186x (1) pr. *order, regular disposition; ornament, decoration, embellishment*, 1 Pe 3:3; (2) *the world, the material universe*, Mt 13:35; *the world, the aggregate of sensitive existence*, 1 Co 4:9; *the lower world, the earth*, Mk 16:15; *the world, the aggregate of mankind*, Mt 5:14; *the world, the public*, Jn 7:4; in N.T. *the present order of things, the secular world*, Jn 18:36; *the human race* external to the Jewish nation, *the heathen world*, Ro 11:12, 15; *the world* external to the Christian body, 1 Jn 3:1, 13; *the world* or *material system* of the Mosaic covenant, Gal 4:3; Col 2:8, 20 [2889]

[3181] Κούαρτος *Kouartos* 1x *Quartus*, a Latin pr. name, Ro 16:23* [2890]

[3182] κούμ *koum* 1x an Aramaic imperative, also spelled κοῦμι, *stand up*, Mk 5:41* [2891]

[3184] κουστωδία *koustōdia* 3x *a watch, guard*, Mt 27:65, 66; 28:11* [2892]

[3185] κουφίζω *kouphizō* 1x *to lighten, make light* or *less heavy*, Ac 27:38* [2893]

[3186] κόφινος *kophinos* 6x *a large basket*, Mt 14:20; 16:9; Mk 6:43; 8:19; Lk 9:17; Jn 6:13* [2894]

[3187] κράβαττος *krabattos* 11x also spelled κράββατος, *mattress, pallet, bed*, Mk 2:4, 9, 11f.; 6:55; Jn 5:8-11; Ac 5:15; 9:33* [2895]

[3189] κράζω *krazō* 55x *to utter a cry*, Mt 14:26; *to exclaim, cry out*, Mt 9:27; Jn 1:15; *to cry* for vengeance, Jas 5:4; *to cry* in supplication, Ro 8:15; Gal 4:6 [2896]

[3190] κραιπάλη *kraipalē* 1x also spelled κρεπάλη, *drunken dissipation*, Lk 21:34* [2897]

[3191] κρανίον *kranion* 4x *a skull*, Mt 27:33; Mk 15:22; Lk 23:33; Jn 19:17* [2898]

[3192] κράσπεδον *kraspedon* 5x *a margin, border, edge*, in N.T. *a fringe, tuft, tassel*, Mt 9:20; 14:36; 23:5; Mk 6:56; Lk 8:44* [2899]

[3193] κραταιός *krataios* 1x *strong, mighty, powerful*, 1 Pe 5:6* [2900]

[3194] κραταιόω *krataioō* 4x *to strengthen, render strong, corroborate, confirm;* pass. *to grow strong, acquire strength*, Lk 1:80; 2:40; Eph 3:16; *to be firm, resolute*, 1 Co 16:13* [2901]

[3195] κρατέω *krateō* 47x pr. *to be strong; to be superior* to any one, *subdue, vanquish*, Ac 2:24; *to get into one's power, lay hold of, seize, apprehend*, Mt 14:3; 18:28; 21:46; *to gain, compass, attain*, Ac 27:13; in N.T. *to lay hold of, grasp, clasp*, Mt 9:25; Mk 1:31; 5:41; *to retain, keep under reserve*, Mk 9:10; met, *to hold fast, observe*, Mk 7:3, 8; 2 Th 2:15; *to hold to, adhere to*, Ac 3:11; Col 2:19; *to restrain, hinder, repress*, Lk 24:16; Rev 7:1; *to retain, not to remit*, sins, Jn 20:23 [2902]

[3196] κράτιστος *kratistos* 4x *strongest;* in N.T. κράτιστε, a term of respect, *most excellent, noble*, or *illustrious*, Lk 1:3; Ac 23:26; 24:3; 26:25* [2903]

[3197] κράτος *kratos* 12x *strength, power, might, force*, Ac 19:20; Eph 1:19; meton. *a display of might*, Lk 1:51; *power, sway, dominion*, Heb 2:14; 1 Pe 4:11; 5:11 [2904]

[3198] κραυγάζω *kraugazō* 9x *to cry out, exclaim, shout*, Mt 12:19; Ac 22:23 [2905]

[3199] κραυγή *kraugē* 6x *a cry, outcry, clamor, shouting*, Mt 25:6; Lk 1:42; Ac 23:9; Eph 4:31; *a cry* of sorrow, *wailing, lamentation*, Rev 21:4; *a cry* for help, *earnest supplication*, Heb 5:7* [2906]

[3200] κρέας *kreas* 2x *flesh, meat*, a later form of κρέατος, Ro 14:21; 1 Co 8:13* [2907]

[3202] κρείττων *kreittōn* 19x can also be spelled κρείσσων, *better, more useful* or *profitable, more conducive to good*, 1 Co 7:8, 38; *superior, more excellent, of a higher* *nature, more valuable,* Heb 1:4; 6:9; 7:7, 19, 22 [2908, 2909]

[3203] κρεμάννυμι *kremannymi* 7x also spelled κρέμαμαι and κρεμάζω, *to hang, suspend,* Ac 5:30; 10:39; pass. *to be hung, suspended,* Mt 18:6; Lk 23:39; mid. κρέμαμαι, *to hang, be suspended,* Ac 28:4; Gal 3:13; met. κρέμαμαι ἐν, *to hang upon, to be referable to* as an ultimate principle, Mt 22:40 [2910]

[3204] κρημνός *krēmnos* 3x *a hanging steep, precipice, a steep bank,* Mt 8:32; Mk 5:13; Lk 8:33★ [2911]

[3205] Κρής *Krēs* 2x *a Cretan, an inhabitant of* Κρήτη, Ac 2:11; Tit 1:12★ [2912]

[3206] Κρήσκης *Krēskēs* 1x *Crescens,* a Latin pr. name, 2 Ti 4:10★ [2913]

[3207] Κρήτη *Krētē* 5x *Crete,* a large island in the eastern part of the Mediterranean, Ac 27:7, 12f., 21, Tit 1:5★ [2914]

[3208] κριθή *krithē* 1x *barley,* Rev 6:6★ [2915]

[3209] κρίθινος *krithinos* 2x *made of barley,* Jn 6:9, 13★ [2916]

[3210] κρίμα *krima* 27x *judgment; a sentence, award,* Mt 7:2; *a judicial sentence,* Lk 23:40; 24:20; Ro 2:2; 5:16; *an adverse sentence,* Mt 23:14; Ro 13:2; 1 Ti 5:12; Jas 3:1; *judgment, administration of justice,* Jn 9:39; Ac 24:25; *execution of justice,* 1 Pe 4:17; *a lawsuit;* 1 Co 6:7; in N.T. *judicial visitation,* 1 Co 11:29; 2 Pe 2:3; *an administrative decree,* Ro 11:33 [2917]

[3211] κρίνον *krinon* 2x *a lily,* Mt 6:28; Lk 12:27★ [2918]

[3212] κρίνω *krinō* 114x pluperfect, kekrivkei (3 sg), pr. *to separate; to make a distinction between; to exercise judgment upon; to estimate,* Ro 14:5; *to judge, to assume censorial power over, to call to account,* Mt 7:1; Lk 6:37; Ro 2:1, 3; 14:3, 4, 10, 13; Col 2:16; Jas 4:11, 12; *to bring under question,* Ro 14:22; *to judge judicially, to try* as a judge, Jn 18:31; *to bring to trial,* Ac 13:27; *to sentence,* Lk 19:22; Jn 7:51; *to resolve on, decree,* Ac 16:4; Rev 16:5; absol. *to decide, determine, resolve,* Ac 3:13; 15:19; 27:1; *to deem,* Ac 13:46; *to form a judgment, pass judgment,* Jn 8:15; pass. *to be brought to trial,* Ac 25:10, 20; Ro 3:4; *to be brought to account, to incur arraignment, be arraigned,* 1 Co 10:29; mid. *to go to law, litigate,* Mt 5:40; in N.T. *to judge, to visit judicially,* Ac 7:7; 1 Co 11:31, 32; 1 Pe 4:6; *to judge, to right, to vindicate,* Heb 10:30; *to administer government over, to govern,* Mt 19:28; Lk 22:30 [2919]

[3213] κρίσις *krisis* 47x pr. *distinction; discrimination; judgment, decision, award,* Jn 5:30; 7:24; 8:16; *a judicial sentence,* Jn 3:19; Jas 2:13; *an adverse sentence,* Mt 23:33; Mk 3:29; *judgment, judicial process, trial,* Mt 10:15; Jn 5:24; 12:31; 16:8; *judgment, administration of justice,* Jn 5:22, 27; in N.T. *a court of justice, tribunal,* Mt 5:21, 22; *an impeachment,* 2 Pe 2:11; Jude 9; from the Hebrew, *justice, equity,* Mt 12:18, 20; 23:23; Lk 11:42 [2920]

[3214] Κρίσπος *Krispos* 2x *Crispus,* a Latin pr. name, Ac 18:8; 1 Co 1:14★ [2921]

[3215] κριτήριον *kritērion* 3x pr. *a standard* or *means by which to judge, criterion; a court of justice, tribunal,* Jas 2:6; *a cause, controversy,* 1 Co 6:2, 4★ [2922]

[3216] κριτής *kritēs* 19x *a judge,* Mt 5:25; from the Hebrew, *a magistrate, ruler,* Ac 13:20; 24:10 [2923]

[3217] κριτικός *kritikos* 1x *able* or *quick to discern* or *judge,* Heb 4:12★ [2924]

[3218] κρούω *krouō* 9x *to knock* at a door, Mt 7:7, 8; Lk 11:9, 10; 12:36; 13:25; Ac 12:13, 16; Rev 3:20★ [2925]

[3219] κρύπτη *kryptē* 1x *a vault* or *closet, a cell* for storage, *dark secret place,* Lk 11:33★ [2926]

[3220] κρυπτός *kryptos* 17x *hidden, concealed, secret, clandestine,* Mt 6:4, 6; τὰ κρυπτά, *secrets,* Ro 2:16; 1 Co 14:25 [2927]

[3221] κρύπτω *kryptō* 18x *to hide, conceal,* Mt 5:14; in N.T. *to lay up in store,* Col 3:3; Rev 2:17; κεκρυμμένος, *concealed, secret,* Jn 19:38 [2928]

[3222] κρυσταλλίζω *krystallizō* 1x *to be clear, brilliant like crystal,* Rev 21:11★ [2929]

[3223] κρύσταλλος *krystallos* 2x pr. *clear ice; crystal,* Rev 4:6; 22:1★ [2930]

[3224] κρυφαῖος *kryphaios* 2x *secret, hidden,* Mt 6:18★ [2927]

[3225] κρυφῇ *kryphē* 1x *in secret, secretly, not openly,* Eph 5:12★ [2931]

[3227] κτάομαι *ktaomai* 7x *to get, procure, provide,* Mt 10:9; *to make gain, gain,* Lk 18:12; *to purchase,* Ac 8:20; 22:28; *to be the cause* or *occasion of purchasing,* Ac 1:18; *to preserve, save,* Lk 21:19; *to get under control, to be winning the mastery over,* 1 Th 4:4; perf.κέκτημαι, *to possess*★ [2932]

[3228] κτῆμα *ktēma* 4x *a possession, property, field,* Mt 19:22; Mk 10:22; Ac 2:45; 5:1★ [2933]

[3229] κτῆνος *ktēnos* 4x pr. *property,* generally used in the plural, τὰ κτήνη; *property* in animals; *a beast of burden, domesticated animal,* Lk 10:34; Ac 23:24; *beasts, cattle,* 1 Co 15:39; Rev 18:13★ [2934]

[3230] κτήτωρ *ktētōr* 1x *a possessor, owner,* Ac 4:34★ [2935]

[3231] κτίζω *ktizō* 15x pr. *to reduce from a state of disorder and wildness;* in N.T. *to call into being, to create,* Mk 13:19; *to call into individual existence, to frame,* Eph 2:15; *to create spiritually, to invest with a* spiritual *frame,* Eph 2:10; 4:24 [2936]

[3232] κτίσις *ktisis* 19x (1) pr. *a framing, founding;* (2) in N.T. *creation, the act of creating,* Ro 1:20; *creation, the material universe,* Mk 10:6; 13:19; Heb 9:11; 2 Pe 3:4; *a created thing, a creature,* Ro 1:25; 8:39; Col 1:15; Heb 4:13; *the* human *creation,* Mk 16:15; Ro 8:19, 20, 21, 22; Col 1:23; *a spiritual creation,* 2 Co 5:17; Gal 6:15; (3) *an institution, ordinance,* 1 Pe 2:13 [2937]

[3233] κτίσμα *ktisma* 4x pr. *a thing founded;* in N.T. *a created being, creature,* 1 Ti 4:4; Jas 1:18; Rev 5:13; 8:9★ [2938]

[3234] κτίστης *ktistēs* 1x *a founder;* in N.T. *a creator,* 1 Pe 4:19★ [2939]

[3235] κυβεία *kybeia* 1x also spelled κυβία, pr. *dice playing;* met. *craftiness, trickery,* Eph 4:14★ [2940]

[3236] κυβέρνησις *kybernēsis* 1x *government, office of a governor* or *director;* meton. *a director,* 1 Co 12:28★ [2941]

[3237] κυβερνήτης *kybernētēs* 2x *a pilot, helmsman,* Ac 27:11; Rev 18:17★ [2942]

[3238] κυκλεύω *kykleuō* 1x *to encircle, surround, encompass,* Rev 20:9★ [2944]

[3239] κυκλόθεν *kyklothen* 3x *all around, round about,* Rev 4:3, 4, 8★ [2943]

[3240] κυκλόω *kykloō* 4x *to encircle, surround, encompass, come around.* Jn 10:24; Ac 14:20; spc. *to lay siege to,* Lk 21:20; *to march round,* Heb 11:30★ [2944]

[3241] κύκλῳ *kyklōi* 8x from κύκλος, functions in the N.T. only as an improper prep., *a circle;* in N.T. κύκλῳ functions adverbially, *round, round about, around,* Mk 3:34; 6:6, 36 [2945]

[3243] κυλισμός *kylismos* 1x also spelled κύλισμα, *a rolling, wallowing,* 2 Pe 2:22★ [2946]

[3244] κυλίω *kyliō* 1x *to roll;* mid. *to roll one's self, to wallow,* Mk 9:20 [2947]

[3245] κυλλός *kyllos* 4x pr. *crooked, bent, maimed, lame, crippled,* Mt 18:8; Mk 9:43, used as a noun meaning *cripple,* Mt 15:30ff.* [2948]

[3246] κῦμα *kyma* 5x *a wave, surge, billow,* Mt 8:24; 14:24; Mk 4:37; Ac 27:41; Jude 13* [2949]

[3247] κύμβαλον *kymbalon* 1x *a cymbal,* 1 Co 13:1* [2950]

[3248] κύμινον *kyminon* 1x *cumin, cuminum salivum* of Linnaeus, a plant, a native of Egypt and Syria, whose seeds are of an aromatic, warm, bitterish taste, with a strong but not disagreeable smell, and used by the ancients as a condiment, Mt 23:23* [2951]

[3249] κυνάριον *kynarion* 4x *a little* or *worthless dog,* Mt 15:26, 27; Mk 7:27, 28* [2952]

[3250] Κύπριος *Kyprios* 3x *a Cypriot, an inhabitant of Cyprus,* Ac 4:36; 11:20; 21:16* [2953]

[3251] Κύπρος *Kypros* 5x *Cyprus,* an island in the eastern part of the Mediterranean, Ac 11:19; 13:4; 15:39; 21:3; 27:4* [2954]

[3252] κύπτω *kyptō* 2x *to bend forwards, stoop down,* Mk 1:7; Jn 8:6* [2955]

[3254] Κυρηναῖος *Kyrēnaios* 6x *a Cyrenian, an inhabitant of Cyrene,* Mt 27:32; Mk 15:21; Lk 23:26; Ac 6:9; 11:20; 13:1* [2956]

[3255] Κυρήνη *Kyrēnē* 1x *Cyrene,* a city founded by a colony of Greeks, in Northern Africa, Ac 2:10* [2957]

[3256] Κυρήνιος *Kyrēnios* 1x *Cyrenius* (perhaps *Quirinus*) pr. name, the governor of Syria, Lk 2:2* [2958]

[3257] κυρία *kyria* 2x *a lady,* 2 Jn 1:1, 5* [2959]

[3258] κυριακός *kyriakos* 2x *pertaining to the Lord Jesus Christ, the Lord's,* 1 Co 11:20; Rev 1:10* [2960]

[3259] κυριεύω *kyrieuō* 7x *to be lord over, to be possessed of, mastery over,* Ro 6:9, 14; 7:1; 14:9; 2 Co 1:24; 1 Ti 6:15; *to exercise control over,* Lk 22:25* [2961]

[3261] κύριος *kyrios* 717x *a lord, master,* Mt 12:8; *an owner, possessor,* Mt 20:8; *a potentate, sovereign,* Ac 25:26; *a power, deity,* 1 Co 8:5; *the Lord, Jehovah,* Mt 1:22; *the Lord* Jesus Christ, Mt 24:42; Mk 16:19; Lk 10:1; Jn 4:1; 1 Co 4:5; freq.; κύριε, a term of respect of various force, *Sir, Lord,* Mt 13:27; Ac 9:6, et al. freq. [2962]

[3262] κυριότης *kyriotēs* 4x *lordship; constituted authority,* Eph 1:21; 2 Pe 2:10; Jude 8; pl. *authorities, potentates,* Col 1:16. The Ephesian and Colossian passage could also be speaking about angelic powers.* [2963]

[3263] κυρόω *kyroō* 2x *to confirm, ratify,* Gal 3:15; *to reaffirm, assure,* 2 Co 2:8* [2964]

[3264] κύων *kyōn* 5x *a dog,* Mt 7:6; Lk 16:21; 2 Pe 2:22; met. *a dog, a religious corrupter,* Phil 3:2; *miscreant,* Rev 22:15* [2965]

[3265] κῶλον *kōlon* 1x lit., *a member* or *limb of the body,* fig., *dead body, corpse,* Heb 3:17* [2966]

[3266] κωλύω *kōlyō* 23x *to hinder, restrain, prevent,* Mt 19:14; Ac 8:36; Ro 1:13 [2967]

[3267] κώμη *kōmē* 27x *a village, a country town,* Mt 9:35; 10:11; Lk 8:1 [2968]

[3268] κωμόπολις *kōmopolis* 1x *a large village, market town,* Mk 1:38* [2969]

[3269] κῶμος *kōmos* 3x pr. *a festive procession, a merry-making;* in N.T. *a revel, lewd, immoral feasting,* Ro 13:13; Gal 5:21; 1 Pe 4:3* [2970]

[3270] κώνωψ *kōnōps* 1x *a gnat, mosquito,* which is found in wine when becoming sour, Mt 23:24* [2971]

[3272] Κωσάμ *Kōsam* 1x *Cosam,* pr. name, indecl., Lk 3:28* [2973]

[3273] κωφός *kōphos* 14x pr. *blunt, dull,* as a weapon; *dull* of hearing, *deaf,* Mt 11:5; Mk 7:32, 37; 9:25; Lk 7:22; *dumb, mute,* Mt 9:32, 33; 12:22; 15:30, 31; Lk 1:22; meton. *making dumb, causing dumbness,* Lk 11:14* [2974]

[3275] λαγχάνω *lanchanō* 4x *to have assigned to one, to obtain, receive,* Ac 1:17; 2 Pe 1:1; *to have fall to one by lot,* Lk 1:9; absol. *to cast lots,* Jn 19:24* [2975]

[3276] Λάζαρος *Lazaros* 15x *Lazarus,* pr. name [2976]

[3277] λάθρα *lathrai* 4x *secretly, privately,* Mt 1:19; 2:7; Jn 11:28; Ac 16:37* [2977]

[3278] λαῖλαψ *lailaps* 3x *a squall of wind, a hurricane,* Mk 4:37; Lk 8:23; 2 Pe 2:17* [2978]

[3279] λακάω *lakaō* 1x *burst open,* Ac 1:18* [2997]

[3280] λακτίζω *laktizō* 1x *to kick,* Ac 26:14* [2979]

[3281] λαλέω *laleō* 296x *to make vocal utterance; to babble, to talk;* in N.T. absol. *to exercise the faculty of speech,* Mt 9:33; *to speak,* Mt 10:20; *to hold converse with, to talk with,* Mt 12:46; Mk 6:50; Rev 1:12; *to discourse, to make an address,* Lk 11:37; Ac 11:20; 21:39; *to make announcement, to make a declaration,* Lk 1:55; *to make mention,* Jn 12:41; Ac 2:31; Heb 4:8; 2 Pe 3:16; trans. *to speak, address, preach,* Mt 9:18; Jn 3:11; Tit 2:1; *to give utterance to, utter,* Mk 2:7; Jn 3:34; *to declare, announce, reveal,* Lk 24:25 et al.; *to disclose,* 2 Co 12:4 [2980]

[3282] λαλιά *lalia* 3x *talk, speech;* in N.T. *matter of discourse,* Jn 4:42; 8:43; *language, dialect,* Mt 26:73* [2981]

[3284] λαμβάνω *lambanō* 258x *to take, take up, take in the hand,* Mt 10:38; 13:31, 33; *to take on one's self, sustain,* Mt 8:17; *to take, seize, seize upon,* Mt 5:40; 21:34; Lk 5:26; 1 Co 10:13; *to catch,* Lk 5:5; 2 Co 12:16; *to assume, put on,* Phil 2:7; *to make a rightful* or *successful assumption of,* Jn 3:27; *to conceive,* Ac 28:15; *to take* by way of provision, Mt 16:5; *to get, get together,* Mt 16:9; *to receive* as payment, Mt 17:24; Heb 7:8; *to take* to wife, Mk 12:19; *to admit, give reception to,* Jn 6:21; 2 Jn 10; met. *to give* mental *reception to,* Jn 3:11; *to be simply recipient of, to receive,* Mt 7:8; Jn 7:23, 39; 19:30; Ac 10:43; in N.T. λαμβάνειν πεῖραν, *to make encounter of* a matter of difficulty or trial, Heb 11:29, 36; λαμβάνειν ἀρχήν, *to begin,* Heb 2:3; λαμβάνειν συμβούλιον, *to take counsel, consult,* Mt 12:14; λαμβάνειν λήθην, *to forget,* 2 Pe 1:9; λαμβάνειν ὑπόμνησιν, *to recollect, call to mind,* 2 Ti 1:5; λαμβάειν περιτομήν, *to receive circumcision, be circumcised,* Jn 7:23; λαμβάνειν καταλλαγήν, *to be reconciled,* Ro 5:11; λαμβάνειν κρίμα, *to receive condemnation* or *punishment, be punished,* Mk 12:40; from the Hebrew, πρόσωπον λαμβάνειν, *to accept the person of any one, show partiality towards,* Lk 20:21 [2983]

[3285] Λάμεχ *Lamech* 1x *Lamech,* pr. name, indecl., Lk 3:36* [2984]

[3286] λαμπάς *lampas* 9x *a light,* Ac 20:8; *a lamp,* Rev 4:5; 8:10, a portable *lamp, lantern, torch,* Mt 25:1, 3, 4, 7, 8; Jn 18:3* [2985]

[3287] λαμπρός *lampros* 9x *bright, resplendent, shining,* Rev 22:16; *clear, transparent,* Rev 22:1; *white, glistening,* Ac 10:30; Rev 15:6; Rev 19:8; *of a bright color, gaudy,* Lk 23:11; by impl. *splendid, magnificent, sumptuous,* Jas 2:2, 3; Rev 18:14* [2986]

[3288] λαμπρότης *lamprotēs* 1x *brightness, splendor*, Ac 26:13* [2987]

[3289] λαμπρῶς *lamprōs* 1x *splendidly; magnificently, sumptuously*, Lk 16:19* [2988]

[3290] λάμπω *lampō* 7x *to shine, give light*, Mt 5:15, 16; 17:2; *to flash, shine*, Lk 17:24; Ac 12:7; 2 Co 4:6* [2989]

[3291] λανθάνω *lanthanō* 6x *to be unnoticed; to escape the knowledge* or *observation of* a person, Ac 26:26; 2 Pe 3:5, 8; absol. *to be concealed* or *hidden, escape detection*, Mk 7:24; Lk 8:47; with a participle of another verb, *to be unconscious* of an action while the subject or object of if, Heb 13:2* [2990]

[3292] λαξευτός *laxeutos* 1x *cut in stone, hewn out of stone* or *rock*, Lk 23:53* [2991]

[3293] Λαοδίκεια *Laodikeia* 6x *Laodicea*, a city of Phrygia in Asia Minor, Rev 3:14* [2993]

[3294] Λαοδικεύς *Laodikeus* 1x *a Laodicean, an inhabitant of Laodicea*, Col 4:16* [2994]

[3295] λαός *laos* 142x *a body of people; a concourse of people, a multitude*, Mt 27:25; Lk 8:47; *the common people*, Mt 26:5; *a people, nation*, Mt 2:4; Lk 2:32; Tit 2:14; ὁ λαός, *the people* of Israel, Lk 2:10 [2992]

[3296] λάρυγξ *larynx* 1x *the throat, gullet*, Ro 3:13* [2995]

[3297] Λασαία *Lasaia* 1x *Lasaea*, also spelled Λασέα, a maritime town in Crete, Ac 27:8 [2996]

[3300] λατομέω *latomeō* 2x *to hew stones; to cut out of stone, hew from stone*, Mt 27:60; Mk 15:46; Lk 23:53* [2998]

[3301] λατρεία *latreia* 5x *service, servitude; religious service, worship*, Jn 16:2; Ro 9:4; 12:1; Heb 9:1, 6* [2999]

[3302] λατρεύω *latreuō* 21x *to be a servant, to serve*, Ac 27:23; *to render religious service and homage, worship*, Mt 4:10; Lk 1:74; spc. *to offer sacrifices, present offerings*, Heb 8:5; 9:9 [3000]

[3303] λάχανον *lachanon* 4x *a garden herb, vegetable*, Mt 13:32; Mk 4:32; Lk 11:42; Ro 14:2* [3001]

[3305] λεγιών *legiōn* 4x also spelled λεγεών, *a* Roman *legion;* in N.T. used indefinitely for a great number, Mt 26:53; Mk 5:9, 15, Lk 8:30* [3003]

[3306] λέγω *legō* 2,353x *to lay, to arrange, to gather; to say*, Mt 1:20; *to speak,* *make an address* or *speech*, Ac 26:1; *to say* mentally, in thought, Mt 3:9; Lk 3:8; *to say* in written language, Mk 15:28; Lk 1:63; Jn 19:37; *to say*, as distinguished from acting, Mt 23:3; *to mention, speak of*, Mk 14:71; Lk 9:31; Jn 8:27; *to tell, declare, narrate*, Mt 21:27; Mk 10:32; *to express*, Heb 5:11; *to put forth, propound*, Lk 5:36; 13:6; Jn 16:29; *to mean, to intend to signify*, 1 Co 1:12; 10:29; *to say, declare, affirm, maintain*, Mt 3:9; 5:18; Mk 12:18; Ac 17:7; 26:22; 1 Co 1:10; *to enjoin*, Ac 15:24; 21:21; Ro 2:22; *to term, designate, cull*, Mt 19:17; Mk 12:37; Lk 20:37; 23:2; 1 Co 8:5; *to call* by a name, Mt 2:23; pass. *to be further named, to be surnamed*, Mt 1:16; *to be explained, interpreted*, Jn 4:25; 20:16, 24; in N.T. σὺ λέγεις, *you say*, a form of affirmative answer to a question Mt 27:11; Mk 15:2; Jn 18:37 [2036, 2046, 3004, 4483]

[3307] λεῖμμα *leimma* 1x pr. *a remnant;* in N.T. *a small residue*, Ro 11:5* [3005]

[3308] λεῖος *leios* 1x *smooth, level, plain*, Lk 3:5* [3006]

[3309] λείπω *leipō* 6x trans. *to leave, forsake;* pass. *to be left, deserted;* by impl. *to be destitute of, deficient in*, Jas 1:4, 5; 2:15; intrans. *to fail, be wanting, be deficient*, Lk 18:22; Tit 1:5; 3:13* [3007]

[3310] λειτουργέω *leitourgeō* 3x pr. *to perform some public service at one's own expense;* in N.T. *to officiate* as a priest, Heb 10:11; *to minister* in the Christian Church, Ac 13:2; *to minister to, assist, succor*, Ro 15:27* [3008]

[3311] λειτουργία *leitourgia* 6x pr. *a public service discharged by a citizen at his own expense;* in N.T. *a* sacred *ministration*, Lk 1:23; Phil 2:17; Heb 8:6; 9:21; *a kind office, aid, relief*, 2 Co 9:12; Phil 2:30* [3009]

[3312] λειτουργικός *leitourgikos* 1x *ministering; engaged in holy service*, Heb 1:14* [3010]

[3313] λειτουργός *leitourgos* 5x pr. *a person of property who performed a public duty* or *service to the state at his own expense;* in N.T. *a minister* or *servant*, Ro 13:6; 15:16; Heb 1:7; 8:2; *one who ministers relief*, Phil 2:25* [3011]

[3316] λεμά *lema* 2x *For what? Why? Wherefore?* Mt 27:46; Mk 15:34* [2982]

[3317] λέντιον *lention* 2x *a coarse cloth, with which servants were girded, a towel, napkin, apron*, Jn 13:4, 5* [3012]

[3318] λεπίς *lepis* 1x *a scale, shell, rind, crust, incrustation*, Ac 9:18* [3013]

[3319] λέπρα *lepra* 4x *the leprosy*, Mt 8:3; Mk 1:42; Lk 5:12, 13* [3014]

[3320] λεπρός *lepros* 9x *leprous; a leper*, Mt 8:2; 10:8 [3015]

[3322] Λευί *Leuu* 8x *Levi*, also spelled Λευίς (3323), pr. name. When the N.T. refers to the Λευί of the O.T., the word is indecl. (n-3g[2]); when it refers to a N.T. person, it is partially declined (n-3g[1]): Λευίς (nom); Λευίν (acc). (1) *Levi, son of Jacob*, Heb 7:5, 9; Rev 7:7. (2) *Levi, son of Symeon*, Lk 3:29 (3) *Levi, son of Melchi*, Lk 3:24 [3017]

[3324] Λευίτης *Leuutēs* 3x *a Levite, one of the posterity of Levi*, Jn 1:19; Lk 10:32; Ac 4:36* [3019]

[3325] Λευιτικός *Leuutikos* 1x *Levitical, pertaining to the Levites*, Heb 7:11* [3020]

[3326] λευκαίνω *leukainō* 2x *to brighten, to make white*, Mk 9:3; Rev 7:14* [3021]

[3328] λευκός *leukos* 25x pr. *light, bright; white*, Mt 5:36; 17:2; *whitening, growing white*, Jn 4:35 [3022]

[3329] λέων *leōn* 9x *a lion*, Heb 11:33; 1 Pe 5:8; Rev 4:7; 9:8, 17; 10:3; 13:2; met. *a lion, cruel adversary, tyrant*, 2 Ti 4:17; *a lion, a hero, deliverer*, Rev 5:5* [3023]

[3330] λήθη *lēthē* 1x *forgetfulness, oblivion*, 2 Pe 1:9* [3024]

[3331] λῆμψις *lēmpsis* 1x also spelled λῆψις, *taking, receiving*, Phil 4:15* [3028]

[3332] ληνός *lēnos* 5x pr. *a tub. trough; a wine-press*, into which grapes were cast and trodden, Rev 14:19, 20; 19:15; *a wine-vat*, i.q. ὑπολήνιον, the lower vat into which the juice of the trodden grapes flowed, Mt 21:33* [3025]

[3333] λῆρος *lēros* 1x *idle talk; an empty tale, nonsense*, Lk 24:11* [3026]

[3334] ληστής *lēstēs* 15x *a plunderer, robber, highwayman*, Mt 21:13; 26:55; Mk 11:17; Lk 10:30; 2 Co 11:26; *a bandit, brigand*, Mt 27:38, 44; Mk 15:27; Jn 18:40; trop. *a robber, rapacious imposter*, Jn 10:1, 8 [3027]

[3336] λίαν *lian* 12x *much, greatly, exceedingly*, Mt 2:16; 4:8; 8:28 [3029]

[3337] λίβανος *libanos* 2x *arbor thurifera*, the tree producing frankincense, growing in Arabia and Mount Lebanon; in N.T. *frankincense*, the transparent gum that distils from incisions in the tree, Mt 2:11; Rev 18:13* [3030]

[3338] λιβανωτός *libanōtos* 2x *frankincense;* in N.T. *a censer,* Rev 8:3, 5* [3031]

[3339] Λιβερτῖνος *Libertinos* 1x *a freedman, one who having been a slave has obtained his freedom,* or *whose father was a freed-man;* in N.T. the λιβερτῖνοι probably denote Jews who had been carried captive to Rome, and subsequently manumitted, Ac 6:9* [3032]

[3340] Λιβύη *Libyē* 1x *Libya,* a part of Africa, bordering on the west of Egypt, Ac 2:10* [3033]

[3342] λιθάζω *lithazō* 9x *to stone, pelt* or *kill with stones,* Jn 8:5; 10:31, 32, 33; 11:8; Ac 5:26; 14:19; 2 Co 11:25; Heb 11:37* [3034]

[3343] λίθινος *lithinos* 3x *made of stone,* Jn 2:6; 2 Co 3:3; Rev 9:20* [3035]

[3344] λιθοβολέω *lithoboleō* 7x *to stone, pelt with stones,* in order to kill, Mt 21:35; 23:37 [3036]

[3345] λίθος *lithos* 59x *a stone,* Mt 3:9; 4:3, 6; used figuratively, of Christ, Eph 2:20; 1 Pe 2:6, of believers, 1 Pe 2:5; meton. *a tablet of stone,* 2 Co 3:7; *a precious stone,* Rev 4:3 [3037]

[3346] λιθόστρωτος *lithostrōtos* 1x *a pavement made of blocks of stone,* Jn 19:13* [3038]

[3347] λικμάω *likmaō* 2x pr. *to winnow grain;* in N.T. *to scatter like chaff, crush,* Mt 21:44; Lk 20:18* [3039]

[3348] λιμήν *limēn* 3x *a port, haven, harbor,* Καλὰ Λιμένες, Ac 27:8, 12* [3040]

[3349] λίμνη *limnē* 11x *a tract of standing water; a lake,* Lk 5:1; Rev 20:14 [3041]

[3350] λιμός *limos* 12x *famine, scarcity of food, want of grain,* Mt 24:7; *famine, hunger, famishment,* Lk 15:17; Ro 8:35 [3042]

[3351] λίνον *linon* 2x *flax;* by meton. *a flaxen wick,* Mt 12:20; *linen,* Rev 15:6* [3043]

[3352] Λίνος *Linos* 1x some accent as Λῖνος, *Linus,* pr. name, 2 Ti 4:21* [3044]

[3353] λιπαρός *liparos* 1x lit., *fat;* fig., *rich, sumptuous,* Rev 18:14* [3045]

[3354] λίτρα *litra* 2x *a pound, libra,* equivalent to about twelve ounces (American), Jn 12:3; 19:39* [3046]

[3355] λίψ *lips* 1x pr. *the south-west wind;* meton. *the south-west quarter of the heavens,* Ac 27:12* [3047]

[3356] λογεία *logeia* 2x *collection* of money, 1 Co 16:1f.* [3048]

[3357] λογίζομαι *logizomai* 40x (1) pr. *to count, calculate; to count, enumerate,* Mk 15:28; Lk 22:37; *to set down* as a matter of account, 1 Co 13:5; 2 Co 3:5; 12:6; *to impute,* Ro 4:3; 2 Co 5:19; 2 Ti 4:16; *to account,* Ro 2:26; 8:36; εἰς οὐδὲν λογισθῆναι, *to be set at nought, despised,* Ac 19:27; *to regard, deem, consider,* Ro 6:11; 14:14; 1 Co 4:1; 2 Co 10:2; Phil 3:13; (2) *to infer, conclude, presume,* Ro 2:3; 3:28; 8:18; 2 Co 10:2, 7, 11; Heb 11:19; 1 Pe 5:12; (3) *to think upon, ponder,* Phil 4:8; absol. *to reason,* Mk 11:31; 1 Co 13:11 [3049]

[3358] λογικός *logikos* 2x *pertaining to speech; pertaining to reason;* in N.T. *rational, spiritual, pertaining to the mind and soul,* Ro 12:1; 1 Pe 2:2* [3050]

[3359] λόγιον *logion* 4x *an oracle, a divine communication* or *revelation,* Ac 7:38; Ro 3:2; Heb 5:12; 1 Pe 4:11* [3051]

[3360] λόγιος *logios* 1x *gifted with learning* or *eloquence,* Ac 18:24* [3052]

[3361] λογισμός *logismos* 2x pr. *a computation, act of computing; a thought, cogitation,* Ro 2:15; *a conception, device,* 2 Co 10:4* [3053]

[3362] λογομαχέω *logomacheō* 1x *to contend about words;* by impl. *to dispute about trivial things,* 2 Ti 2:14* [3054]

[3363] λογομαχία *logomachia* 1x *contention* or *strife about words;* by impl. *a dispute about trivial things, unprofitable controversy,* 1 Ti 6:4* [3055]

[3364] λόγος *logos* 330x *a word, a thing uttered,* Mt 12:32, 37; 1 Co 14:19; *speech, language, talk,* Mt 22:15; Lk 20:20; 2 Co 10:10; Jas 3:2; *converse,* Lk 24:17; *mere talk, wordy show,* 1 Co 4:19, 20; Col 2:23; 1 Jn 3:18; *language, mode of discourse, style of speaking,* Mt 5:37; 1 Co 1:17; 1 Th 2:5; *a saying, a speech,* Mk 7:29; Eph 4:29; *an expression, form of words, formula,* Mt 26:44; Ro 13:9; Gal 5:14; *a saying, a thing propounded in discourse,* Mt 7:24; 19:11; Jn 4:37; 6:60; 1 Ti 1:15; *a message, announcement,* 2 Co 5:19; *a prophetic announcement,* Jn 12:38; *an account, statement,* 1 Pe 3:15; *a story, report,* Mt 28:15; Jn 4:39; 21:23; 2 Th 2:2; *a written narrative, a treatise,* Ac 1:1; *a set discourse,* Ac 20:7; *doctrine,* Jn 8:31, 37; 2 Ti 2:17; *subject-matter,* Ac 15:6; *reckoning, account,* Mt 12:36; 18:23; 25:19; Lk 16:2; Ac 19:40; 20:24; Ro 9:28; Phil 4:15, 17; Heb 4:13; *a plea,* Mt 5:32; Ac 19:38; *a motive,* Ac 10:29; *reason,* Ac 18:14; ὁ λόγος, *the*

word of God, especially in the Gospel, Mt 13:21, 22; Mk 16:20; Lk 1:2; Ac 6:4; ὁ λόγος, *the* divine *WORD,* or *Logos,* Jn 1:1 [3056]

[3365] λόγχη *lonchē* 1x pr. *the head of a javelin; a spear, lance,* Jn 19:34* [3057]

[3366] λοιδορέω *loidoreō* 4x *to revile, rail at, abuse,* Jn 9:28; Ac 23:4; 1 Co 4:12; 1 Pe 2:23* [3058]

[3367] λοιδορία *loidoria* 3x *reviling, railing, verbal abuse,* 1 Ti 5:14; 1 Pe 3:9* [3059]

[3368] λοίδορος *loidoros* 2x *reviling, railing;* as a subst. *a reviler, railer,* 1 Co 5:11; 6:10* [3060]

[3369] λοιμός *loimos* 2x *a pestilence, plague,* Lk 21:11; met. *a pest, pestilent fellow,* Ac 24:5* [3061]

[3370] λοιπός *loipos* 55x *remaining; the rest, remainder,* Mt 22:6; as an adv., οὗ λοιποῦ, *henceforth,* Gal 6:17; τὸ λοιπόν, or λοιπόν, *henceforward,* Mt 26:45; 2 Ti 4:8; Ac 27:20; *as to the rest, besides,* 1 Co 1:16; *finally,* Eph 6:10; ὁ δὲ λοιπόν, *but, now, furthermore,* 1 Co 4:2 [3062, 3063, 3064]

[3371] Λουκᾶς *Loukas* 3x *Luke,* pr. name [3065]

[3372] Λούκιος *Loukios* 2x *Lucius,* pr. name, (1) a person from Cyrene of Antioch, Ac 13:1. (2) a person who sends his greeting with Paul, Ro 16:21* [3066]

[3373] λουτρόν *loutron* 2x *a bath, water for bathing; a bathing, washing, ablution,* Eph 5:26; Tit 3:5* [3067]

[3374] λούω *louō* 5x pr. *to bathe the body,* as distinguished from washing only the extremities, Jn 13:10; *to bathe, wash,* Ac 9:37; 16:33; Heb 10:22; 2 Pe 2:22* [3068]

[3375] Λύδδα *Lydda* 3x *Lydda,* a town in Palestine, Ac 9:32, 35, 38* [3069]

[3376] Λυδία *Lydia* 2x *Lydia,* pr. name of a woman, Ac 16:14, 40* [3070]

[3377] Λυκαονία *Lykaonia* 1x *Lycaonia,* a province of Asia Minor, Ac 14:6* [3071]

[3378] Λυκαονιστί *Lykaonisti* 1x *in the dialect of Lycaonia,* Ac 14:11* [3072]

[3379] Λυκία *Lykia* 1x *Lycia,* a province of Asia Minor, Ac 27:5* [3073]

[3380] λύκος *lykos* 6x *a wolf,* Mt 10:16; Lk 10:3; Jn 10:12; met. *a person of wolf-like character,* Mt 7:15; Ac 20:29* [3074]

[3381] λυμαίνω *lymainō* 1x some list as a deponent, λυμαίνομαι, *to outrage, harm, violently maltreat;* in N.T. *to make havoc of, ruin,* Ac 8:3* [3075]

[3382] λυπέω *lypeō* 26x *to occasion grief* or *sorrow to, to distress,* 2 Co 2:2, 5; 7:8; pass. *to be grieved, pained, distressed, sorrowful,* Mt 17:23; 19:22; *to aggrieve, cross, vex,* Eph 4:30; pass. *to feel pained,* Ro 14:15 [3076]

[3383] λύπη *lypē* 16x *pain, distress,* Jn 16:21; *grief, sorrow,* Jn 16:6, 20, 22; meton. *cause of grief, trouble, affliction,* 1 Pe 2:19 [3077]

[3384] Λυσανίας *Lysanias* 1x *Lyssanias,* pr. name, Lk 3:1* [3078]

[3385] Λυσίας *Lysias* 2x *Lysias,* pr. name, Ac 23:26; 24:7, 22* [3079]

[3386] λύσις *lysis* 1x *a loosing;* in N.T. *a release* from the marriage bond, *a divorce,* 1 Co 7:27* [3080]

[3387] λυσιτελέω *lysiteleō* 1x pr. *to compensate for incurred expense;* by impl. *to be advantageous to, to profit, advantage;* impers. Lk 17:2* [3081]

[3388] Λύστρα *Lystra* 6x *Lystra,* a city of Lycaonia, in Asia Minor, Ac 14:6, 8, 21; 16:1f.; 2 Ti 3:11* [3082]

[3389] λύτρον *lytron* 2x pr. *price paid; a ransom,* Mt 20:28; Mk 10:45* [3083]

[3390] λυτρόω *lytroō* 3x *to release for a ransom;* mid, *to ransom, redeem, deliver, liberate,* Lk 24:21; Tit 2:14; 1 Pe 1:18* [3084]

[3391] λύτρωσις *lytrōsis* 3x *redemption,* Heb 9:12; *liberation, deliverance,* Lk 1:68; 2:38* [3085]

[3392] λυτρωτής *lytrōtēs* 1x *a redeemer; a deliverer,* Ac 7:35* [3086]

[3393] λυχνία *lychnia* 12x *a candlestick, lampstand,* Mt 5:15; met. *a candlestick,* as a figure of a Christian church, Rev 1:12, 13, 20; of a teacher or prophet, Rev 11:4 [3087]

[3394] λύχνος *lychnos* 14x *a light, lamp, candle,* etc., Mt 5:15; Mk 4:21; met. *a lamp,* as a figure of a distinguished teacher, Jn 5:35 [3088]

[3395] λύω *lyō* 42x *to loosen, unbind, unfasten,* Mk 1:7; *to loose, untie,* Mt 21:2; Jn 11:44; *to disengage,* 1 Co 7:27; *to set free, set at liberty, deliver,* Lk 13:16; *to break,* Ac 27:41; Rev 5:2, 5; *to break up, dismiss,* Ac 13:43; *to destroy, demolish,* Jn 2:19; Eph 2:14; met *to infringe,* Mt 5:19; Jn 5:18; 7:23; *to make void, nullify,* Jn

10:35; in N.T. *to declare free,* of privileges, or, in respect of lawfulness, Mt 16:19 [3089]

[3396] Λωΐς *Lōis* 1x *Lois,* pr. name of a woman, 2 Ti 1:5* [3090]

[3397] Λώτ *Lōt* 4x *Lot,* pr. name, indecl., Lk 17:28, 29, 32; 2 Pe 2:7* [3091]

[3399] Μάαθ *Maath* 1x *Maath,* pr. name, indecl., Lk 3:26* [3092]

[3400] Μαγαδάν *Magadan* 1x *Magadan,* pr. name, indecl., Mt 15:39* [3093]

[3402] Μαγδαληνή *Magdalēnē* 12x *Magdalene,* pr. name (*of Magdala*), Jn 20:18 [3094]

[3404] μαγεία *mageia* 1x pr. *the system of the magians; magic,* Ac 8:11* [3095]

[3405] μαγεύω *mageuō* 1x *to be a magician; to use magical arts, practise magic, sorcery,* Ac 8:9* [3096]

[3407] μάγος *magos* 6x (1) *a magus, sage of the magician religion, magician, astrologer, wise man,* Mt 2:1, 7, 16; (2) *a magician, sorcerer,* Ac 13:6, 8* [3097]

[3408] Μαγώγ *Magōg* 1x *Magog,* pr. name, indecl., Rev 20:8* [3098]

[3409] Μαδιάμ *Madiam* 1x *Madian,* a district of Arabia Petra, Ac 7:29* [3099]

[3411] μαθητεύω *mathēteuō* 4x intrans. *to be a disciple, follow as a disciple,* Mt 27:57; in N.T. trans. *to make a disciple of, to train in discipleship,* Mt 28:19; Ac 14:21; pass. *to be trained, disciplined, instructed,* Mt 13:52* [3100]

[3412] μαθητής *mathētēs* 261x *a disciple,* Mt 10:24, 42, et al. [3101]

[3413] μαθήτρια *mathētria* 1x *a female disciple; a female Christian,* Ac 9:36* [3102]

[3415] Μαθθάτ *Maththat* 2x also spelled Ματθάτ, *Mathat,* pr. name, indecl., Lk 3:24, 29* [3158]

[3416] Μαθθίας *Maththias* 2x also spelled Ματθίας, *BAGD* suggest it is a shortened form of Ματταθίας, *Matthias,* pr. name, Ac 1:23, 26* [3159]

[3419] μαίνομαι *mainomai* 5x *to be disordered in mind, mad,* Jn 10:20; Ac 12:15; 26:24, 25; 1 Co 14:23* [3105]

[3420] μακαρίζω *makarizō* 2x *to pronounce happy, fortunate,* Lk 1:48; Jas 5:11* [3106]

[3421] μακάριος *makarios* 50x *happy, blessed,* as a noun it can depict someone

who receives divine favor, Mt 5:3, 4, 5, 7; Lk 1: 45 [3107]

[3422] μακαρισμός *makarismos* 3x *a happy calling, the act of pronouncing happy,* Ro 4:6, 9; *self-congratulation,* Gal 4:15* [3108]

[3423] Μακεδονία *Makedonia* 22x *Macedonia,* Ac 16:9; Ro 15:26; 1 Co 16:5; 1 Th 1:7; 1 Ti 1:3 [3109]

[3424] Μακεδών *Makedōn* 5x *a native of Macedonia,* Ac 16:9; 19:29; 27:2; 2 Co 9:2, 4* [3110]

[3425] μάκελλον *makellon* 1x *meat market, marketplace, slaughter house,* 1 Co 10:25* [3111]

[3426] μακράν *makran* 10x *far, far off, at a distance, far distant,* Mt 8:30; Mk 12:34; met. οἱ μακράν, *remote, alien,* Eph 2:13, 17; so οἱ εἰς μακράν, Ac 2:39 [3112]

[3427] μακρόθεν *makrothen* 14x *far off, at a distance, from afar, from a distance,* Mk 8:3; 11:13; preceded by ἀπό, in the same sense, Mt 26:58 [3113]

[3428] μακροθυμέω *makrothumeō* 10x *to be slow towards, be long-enduring; to exercise patience, be long-suffering, clement,* or *indulgent, to forbear,* Mt 18:26, 29; 1 Co 13:4; 1 Th 5:14; 2 Pe 3:9; *to have patience, endure patiently, wait with patient expectation,* Heb 6:15; Jas 5:7, 8; *to bear long* with entreaties for deliverance and avengement, Lk 18:7* [3114]

[3429] μακροθυμία *makrothumia* 14x *patience; patient enduring of evil, fortitude,* Col 1:11; Col 3:12; 1 Ti 1:16; 1 Pe 3:20; *slowness of avenging injuries, long-suffering, forbearance, clemency,* Ro 2:4; 9:22; 2 Co 6:6; Gal 5:22; Eph 4:2; 2 Ti 4:2; Jas 5:10; *patient expectation,* 2 Ti 3:10; Heb 6:12; 2 Pe 3:15* [3115]

[3430] μακροθύμως *makrothumōs* 1x *patiently,* Ac 26:3* [3116]

[3431] μακρός *makros* 4x *long;* of space, *far, distant, remote,* Lk 15:13; 19:12; of time, *of long duration,* Mk 12:40; Lk 20:47* [3117]

[3432] μακροχρόνιος *makrochronios* 1x *of long duration; long-lived,* Eph 6:3* [3118]

[3433] μαλακία *malakia* 3x *softness; listlessness, indisposition, weakness, infirmity of body,* Mt 4:23; 9:35; 10:1* [3119]

[3434] μαλακός *malakos* 4x *soft; soft to the touch, delicate,* Mt 11:8; Lk 7:25; met. *an instrument of unnatural lust, effeminate,* 1 Co 6:9* [3120]

[3435] Μαλελεήλ *Maleleēl* 1x *Maleleel,* pr. name, indecl., Lk 3:37★ [3121]

[3436] μάλιστα *malista* 12x *most, most of all, chiefly, especially,* Ac 20:38; 25:26 [3122]

[3437] μάλλον *mallon* 81x *more, to a greater extent, in a higher degree,* Mt 18:13; 27:24; Jn 5:18; 1 Co 14:18; *rather, in preference,* Mt 10:6; Eph 4:28; used in a periphrasis for the comparative, Ac 20:35; as an intensive with a comparative term, Mt 6:26; Mk 7:36; 2 Co 7:13; Phil 1:23; μάλλον δέ, *yea rather, or, more properly speaking,* Ro 8:34; Gal 4:9; Eph 5:11 [3123]

[3438] Μάλχος *Malchos* 1x *Malchus,* pr. name, Jn 18:10★ [3124]

[3439] μάμμη *mammē* 1x *a mother;* later, *a grandmother,* 2 Ti 1:5★ [3125]

[3440] μαμωνᾶς *mamōnas* 4x *wealth, riches,* Lk 16:9, 11; personified, like the Greek Πλοῦτος, *Mammon,* Mt 6:24; Lk 16:13★ [3126]

[3441] Μαναήν *Manaēn* 1x *Manaen,* pr. name, indecl., Ac 13:1★ [3127]

[3442] Μανασσῆς *Manassēs* 3x *Manasses,* pr. name (1) *the tribe of Manasseh,* Rev 7:6 (2) *Manasseh, king of Judah,* Mt 1:10★ [3128]

[3443] μανθάνω *manthanō* 25x *to learn, be taught,* Mt 9:13; 11:29; 24:32; *to learn by practice or experience, acquire a custom or habit,* Phil 4:11; 1 Ti 5:4, 13; *to ascertain, be informed,* Ac 23:27; *to understand, comprehend,* Rev 14:3 [3129]

[3444] μανία *mania* 1x *madness, insanity,* Ac 26:24★ [3130]

[3445] μάννα *manna* 4x *manna,* the miraculous food of the Israelites while in the desert, Jn 6:31, 49; Heb 9:4; Rev 2:17★ [3131]

[3446] μαντεύομαι *manteuomai* 1x *to speak oracles, to divine,* Ac 16:16★ [3132]

[3447] μαραίνω *marainō* 1x *to quench, cause to decay, fade, or wither;* pass. *to wither, waste away,* met. *to fade away, disappear, perish,* Jas 1:11★ [3133]

[3449] μαργαρίτης *margaritēs* 9x *a pearl,* Mt 7:6; 13:45, 46; 1 Ti 2:9; Rev 17:4; 18:12, 16; 21:21★ [3135]

[3450] Μάρθα *Martha* 13x *Martha,* pr. name, Jn 12:2 [3136]

[3451] Μαρία *Maria* 27x *Mary,* pr. name (1) The mother of Jesus, Mt 1:16; Ac 1:14. (2) *Mary,* wife of Clopas, mother of James, Mk 15:40; Lk 24:10; Jn 19:25. (3) *Mary Magdalene,* Mt 27:56; Lk 20:18. (4) Sister of Martha and Lazarus, Lk 10:39; Jn 11:1; 12:3. (5) Mother of Jn surnamed Mark, Ac 12:12 (6) A Christian at Rome, Ro 16:6 [3137]

[3452] Μαριάμ *Mariam* 27x the indeclinable form of Μαρία [3137]

[3453] Μάρκος *Markos* 8x *Mark,* pr. name [3138]

[3454] μάρμαρος *marmaros* 1x *a white glistening stone; marble,* Rev 18:12★ [3139]

[3455] μαρτυρέω *martyreō* 76x trans. *to testify, depose,* Jn 3:11, 32; 1 Jn 1:2; Rev 1:2; 22:20; absol. *to give evidence,* Jn 18:23; *to bear testimony, testify,* Lk 4:22; Jn 1:7, 8; *to bear testimony* in confirmation, Ac 14:3; *to declare* distinctly and formally, Jn 4:44; pass. *to be the subject of testimony, to obtain attestation* to character, Ac 6:3; 10:22; 1 Ti 5:10; Heb 11:2, 4; mid. equivalent to μαρτύρομαι, *to make a solemn appeal,* Ac 26:22; 1 Th 2:12 [3140]

[3456] μαρτυρία *martyria* 37x *judicial evidence,* Mk 14.55, 56, 59, Lk 22:71; *testimony* in general, Tit 1:13; 1 Jn 5:9 *testimony, declaration* in a matter of fact or doctrine, Jn 1:19; 3:11; Ac 22:18; *attestation* to character, Jn 5:34, 36; *reputation,* 1 Ti 3:7 [3141]

[3457] μαρτύριον *martyrion* 19x *testimony, evidence,* 2 Co 1:12; Jas 5:3; Ac 4:33; in N.T. *testimony, mode of solemn declaration,* Mt 8:4; Lk 9:5; *testimony, matter of solemn declaration,* 1 Co 1:6; 2:1; 1 Ti 2:6; σκηνὴ τοῦ μαρτυρίου, a title of the Mosaic tabernacle, Ac 7:44; Rev 15:5 [3142]

[3458] μαρτύρομαι *martyromai* 5x *to call to witness;* intrans. *to make a solemn affirmation* or *declaration,* Ac 20:26; 26:22; Gal 5:3; *to make a solemn appeal,* Eph 4:17; 1 Th 2:12★ [3143]

[3459] μάρτυς *martys* 35x (1) *a judicial witness, deponent,* Mt 18:16; Heb 10:28; (2) generally, *a witness* to a circumstance, Lk 24:48; Ac 10:41; in N.T. *a witness, a testifier,* of a doctrine, Rev 1:5; 3:14; 11:3; (3) *a martyr,* Ac 22:20; Rev 2:13 [3144]

[3460] μασάομαι *masaomai* 1x *to chew, masticate,* in N.T. *to gnaw,* Rev 16:10★ [3145]

[3463] μαστιγόω *mastigoō* 7x *to scourge, whip,* Mt 10:17; 20:19; 23:34; Mk 10:34; Lk 18:33; Jn 19:1; met. *to chastise,* Heb 12:6★ [3146]

[3464] μαστίζω *mastizō* 1x *to scourge,* Ac 22:25★ [3147]

[3465] μάστιξ *mastix* 6x *a scourge, whip,* Ac 22:24; Heb 11:36; met. *a scourge* of disease, Mk 3:10; 5:29, 34; Lk 7:21★ [3148]

[3466] μαστός *mastos* 3x *the breast, pap,* Lk 11:27; 23:29; Rev 1:13★ [3149]

[3467] ματαιολογία *mataiologia* 1x *vain talking, idle disputation,* 1 Ti 1:6★ [3150]

[3468] ματαιολόγος *mataiologos* 1x *a vain talker, given to vain talking* or *trivial disputation,* Tit 1:10★ [3151]

[3469] μάταιος *mataios* 6x *idle, ineffective, worthless,* 1 Co 3:20; *groundless, deceptive, fallacious,* 1 Co 15:17; *useless, fruitless, unprofitable,* Tit 3:9; Jas 1:26; from the Hebrew, *erroneous* in principle, *corrupt, perverted,* 1 Pe 1:18; τὰ μάταια, *superstition, idolatry,* Ac 14:15★ [3152]

[3470] ματαιότης *mataiotēs* 3x *vanity, folly, futility,* from the Hebrew, *religious error,* Eph 4:17; 2 Pe 2:18; *false religion,* Ro 8:20★ [3153]

[3471] ματαιόω *mataioō* 1x *to make vain;* from the Hebrew, pass. *to fall into religious error, to be perverted,* Ro 1:21★ [3154]

[3472] μάτην *matēn* 2x *in vain, fruitlessly, without profit,* Mt 15:9; Mk 7:7★ [3155]

[3474] Ματθάν *Matthan* 2x *Matthan,* pr. name, indecl., Mt 1:15 (2t)★ [3157]

[3477] Ματταθά *Mattatha* 1x *Mattatha,* pr. name, indecl.; Lk 3:31★ [3160]

[3478] Ματταθίας *Mattathias* 2x see also Μαθθίας, *Mattathias,* pr. name, Lk 3:25, 26★ [3161]

[3479] μάχαιρα *machaira* 29x *a large knife, dagger; a sword,* Mt 26:47, 51; *the sword* of the executioner, Ac 12:2; Ro 8:35; Heb 11:37; hence, φορεῖν μάχαιραν, *to bear the sword, to have the power of life and death,* Ro 13:4; meton. *war,* Mt 10:34 [3162]

[3480] μάχη *machē* 4x *a fight, battle, conflict;* in N.T. *contention, dispute, strife, controversy,* 2 Co 7:5; 2 Ti 2:23; Tit 3:9; Jas 4:1★ [3163]

[3481] μάχομαι *machomai* 4x *to fight; to quarrel,* Ac 7:26; 2 Ti 2:24; *to contend, dispute,* Jn 6:52; Jas 4:2★ [3164]

[3483] μεγαλεῖος *megaleios* 1x *magnificent, splendid;* τὰ μεγαλεῖα, *great things, wonderful works,* Ac 2:11★ [3167]

[3484] μεγαλειότης *megaleiotēs* 3x *majesty, magnificence, glory,* Lk 9:43; Ac 19:27; 2 Pe 1:16* [3168]

[3485] μεγαλοπρεπής *megaloprepēs* 1x pr. *becoming a great man; magnificent, glorious, most splendid,* 2 Pe 1:17* [3169]

[3486] μεγαλύνω *megalynō* 8x lit., *to enlarge, amplify,* Mt 23:5; 2 Co 10:15; *to manifest in an extraordinary degree,* Lk 1:58; fig., *to magnify, exalt, extol,* Lk 1:46; Ac 5:13; Ac 10:46; 19:17; Phil 1:20* [3170]

[3487] μεγάλως *megalōs* 1x *greatly, very much, vehemently,* Phil 4:10* [3171]

[3488] μεγαλωσύνη *megalōsynē* 3x *greatness, majesty,* Heb 1:3; 8:1; ascribed *majesty,* Jude 25* [3172]

[3489] μέγας *megas* 243x *great, large in size,* Mt 27:60; Mk 4:32; *great, much, numerous,* Mk 5:11; Heb 11:26; *great, grown up, adult,* Heb 11:24; *great, vehement, intense,* Mt 2:10; 28:8; *great, sumptuous,* Lk 5:29; *great, important, weighty, of high importance,* 1 Co 9:11; 13:13; *great, splendid, magnificent,* Rev 15:3; *extraordinary, wonderful,* 2 Co 11:15; *great, solemn,* Jn 7:37; 19:31; *great in rank, noble,* Rev 11:18; 13:16; *great in dignity, distinguished, eminent, illustrious, powerful,* Mt 5:19; 18:1, 4; *great, arrogant, boastful,* Rev 13:5 [3173]

[3490] μέγεθος *megethos* 1x *greatness, vastness,* Eph 1:19* [3174]

[3491] μεγιστάν *megistan* 3x *great men, lords, chiefs, nobles, princes,* Mk 6:21; Rev 6:15; 18:23* [3175]

[3493] μεθερμηνεύω *methermēneuō* 8x *to translate, interpret,* Mt 1:23; Mk 5:41; 15:22, 34; Jn 1:38, 41; Ac 4:36; 13:8* [3177]

[3494] μέθη *methē* 3x *strong drink; drunkenness,* Lk 21:34; *an indulgence in drinking,* Ro 13:13; Gal 5:21* [3178]

[3496] μεθίστημι *methistēmi* 5x *to cause a change of position; to remove, transport,* 1 Co 13:2; *to transfer,* Col 1:13; met. *to cause to change sides;* by impl. *to pervert, mislead,* Ac 19:26; *to remove from office, dismiss, discard,* Lk 16:4; Ac 13:22* [3179]

[3497] μεθοδεία *methodeia* 2x *wile, scheme, scheming, craftiness,* Eph 4:14; 6:11* [3180]

[3499] μεθύσκω *methuskō* 5x *to inebriate, make drunk;* pass. *to be intoxicated, to be drunk,* Lk 12:45; Eph 5:18; 1 Th 5:7; Rev 17:2; *to drink freely,* Jn 2:10* [3182]

[3500] μέθυσος *methusos* 2x *drunken; a drunkard,* 1 Co 5:11; 6:10* [3183]

[3501] μεθύω *methuō* 5x *to be intoxicated, be drunk,* Mt 24:49; Ac 2:15; 1 Co 11:21; 1 Th 5:7; Rev 17:6* [3184]

[3505] μείζων *meizōn* 48x *greater,* comparative of μέγας [3185, 3187]

[3506] μέλας *melas* 6x *black,* Mt 5:36; Rev 6:5, 12, the form μέλαν means *ink,* 2 Co 3:3; 2 Jn 12; 3 Jn 13 [3188, 3189]

[3507] Μελεά *Melea* 1x *Melea,* indecl. pr. name, Lk 3:31* [3190]

[3508] μέλει *melei* 10x *there is a care, it concerns,* Mt 22:16; Ac 18:17; 1 Co 7:21; 9:9 [3199]

[3509] μελετάω *meletaō* 2x *to care for; to bestow careful thought upon, to give painful attention to, be earnest in,* 1 Ti 4:15; *to devise,* Ac 4:25* [3191]

[3510] μέλι *meli* 4x *honey,* Mt 3:4; Mk 1:6; Rev 10:9, 10* [3192]

[3514] Μελίτη *Melitē* 1x *also spelled* Μελιτήνη, *Malta,* an island in the Mediterranean, Ac 28:1* [3194]

[3516] μέλλω *mellō* 109x *to be about to, be on the point of,* Mt 2:13; Jn 4:47; it serves to express in general a settled futurity, Mt 11:14; Lk 9:31; Jn 11:51; *to intend,* Lk 10:1; participle μέλλων, μέλλουσα, μέλλον, *future* as distinguished from past and present, Mt 12:32; Lk 13:9; *to be always, as it were, about to do, to delay, linger,* Ac 22:16 [3195]

[3517] μέλος *melos* 34x *a member, limb, any part of the body,* Mt 5:29, 30; Ro 12:4; 1 Co 6:15; 12:12 [3196]

[3518] Μελχί *Melchi* 2x *Melchi,* pr. name, indecl., Lk 3:24, 28* [3197]

[3519] Μελχισέδεκ *Melchisedek* 8x *Melchisedek,* pr. name, indecl., Heb 5:6, 10; 6:20; 7:1, 10f., 15, 17* [3198]

[3521] μεμβράνα *membrana* 1x *parchment, vellum,* 2 Ti 4:13* [3200]

[3522] μέμφομαι *memphomai* 2x *to find fault with, blame, censure; to intimate dissatisfaction with,* Heb 8:8; absol. *to find fault,* Ro 9:19* [3201]

[3523] μεμψίμοιρος *mempsimoiros* 1x *finding fault* or *being discontented with one's lot, querulous; a discontented, querulous person, a complainer,* Jude 16* [3202]

[3525] μέν *men* 179x *a particle serving to indicate that the term or clause with which it is used stands distinguished from another,* usually in the sequel, and then mostly with δέ correspondent, Matt 3:11; 9:39; Acts 1:1; ὁ μέν ... ὁ δέ, *this ... that, the one ... the other,* Phil 1:16, 17; *one ... another,* οἱ μέν ... οἱ δέ, *some ... others,* Matt 22:5; ἄλλος μέν ... ἄλλος δέ, *one ... another,* pl. *some ... others,* Matt 13:8; 21:35; ἄλλος μέν ... ἄλλος δέ, *one ... another,* 1 Cor 15:39; ὧδε μέν ... ἐκεῖ δέ, *here ... there,* Heb 7:8; τοῦτο μέν ... τοῦτο δέ, *partly ... partly,* Heb 10:33 [3303]

[3527] Μεννά *Menna* 1x *Menna,* pr. name, indecl., Lk 3:31* [**]

[3528] μενοῦν *menoun* 1x *see* μενοῦνγε [3304]

[3529] μενοῦνγε *menounge* 3x *also spelled as two words,* μενοῦν γε (Lk 11:28), a combination of particles serving to take up what has just preceded, with either emphasize or to correct; *indeed, really, truly, rather,* Ro 9:20; 10:18; Phil 3:8* [3304]

[3530] μέντοι *mentoi* 8x *truly, certainly, sure,* John 4:27; Jude 8 [3305]

[3531] μένω *menō* 118x *pluperfect,* μεμενηκειν, *to stay,* Mt 26:38; Ac 27:31; *to continue;* 1 Co 7:11; 2 Ti 2:13; *to dwell, lodge, sojourn,* Jn 1:39; Ac 9:43; *to remain,* Jn 9:41; *to rest, settle,* Jn 1:32, 33; 3:36; *to last, endure,* Mt 11:23; Jn 6:27; 1 Co 3:14; *to survive,* 1 Co 15:6; *to be existent,* 1 Co 13:13; *to continue unchanged,* Ro 9:11; *to be permanent,* Jn 15:16; 2 Co 3:11; Heb 10:34; 13:14; 1 Pe 1:23; *to persevere, be constant, be steadfast,* 1 Ti 2:15; 2 Ti 3:14; *to abide, to be in close and settled union,* Jn 6:56; 14:10; 15:4; *to indwell,* Jn 5:38; 1 Jn 2:14; trans. *to wait for,* Ac 20:5, 23 [3306]

[3532] μερίζω *merizō* 14x *to divide; to divide out, distribute,* Mk 6:41; *to assign, bestow,* Ro 12:3; 1 Co 7:17; 2 Co 10:13; Heb 7:2; mid. *to share,* Lk 12:13; pass. *to be subdivided, to admit distinctions,* Mk 3:24-26; 1 Co 1:13; *to be severed* by discord, *be at variance,* Mt 12:25, 26; *to differ,* 1 Co 7:34* [3307]

[3533] μέριμνα *merimna* 6x *care,* Mt 13:22; Mk 4:19; Lk 8:14; 21:34; *anxiety, anxious interest,* 2 Co 11:28; 1 Pe 5:7* [3308]

[3534] μεριμνάω *merimnaō* 19x *to be anxious,* or *solicitous,* Phil 4:6; *to expend careful thought,* Mt 6:27, 28, 31, 34a; 10:19; Lk 10:41; 12:11, 22, 25, 26; *to concern one's self,* Mt 6:25; 1 Co 12:25; *to have the thoughts occupied with,* 1 Co 7:32, 33, 34; *to feel an interest in,* Phil 2:20* [3309]

[3535] μερίς *meris* 5x *a part; a division* of a country, *district, region, tract,* Ac 16:12; *a portion,* Lk 10:42; *an allotted portion,* Col 1:12; *a portion* in common, *share,* Ac 8:21; 2 Co 6:15★ [3310]

[3536] μερισμός *merismos* 2x *a dividing, act of dividing,* Heb 4:12; *distribution, gifts distributed,* Heb 2:4★ [3311]

[3537] μεριστής *meristēs* 1x *a divider, arbitrator,* Lk 12:14★ [3312]

[3538] μέρος *meros* 42x *a part, portion, division,* of a whole, Lk 11:36; 15:12; Ac 5:2; Eph 4:16; *a piece, fragment,* Lk 24:42; Jn 19:23; *a party, faction,* Ac 23:9; *allotted portion, lot, destiny,* Mt 24:51; Lk 12:46; *a calling, craft,* Ac 19:27; *a partner's portion, partnership, fellowship,* Jn 13:8; pl. mevrh, a local *quarter, district, region,* Mt 2:22; 16:13; Ac 19:1; Eph 4:9; *side of a ship,* Jn 21:6; ἐν μέρει, *in respect,* 2 Co 3:10; 9:3; Col 2:16; 1 Pe 4:16; μέρος τι, *partly, in some part,* 1 Co 11:18; ἀνὰ μέρος, *alternately, one after another,* 1 Co 14:27; ἀπὸ μέρους, *partly, in some part* or *measure,* 2 Co 1:14; ἐκ μέρους, *individually,* 1 Co 12:27; *partly, imperfectly,* 1 Co 13:9; κατὰ μέρος, *particularly, in detail,* Heb 9:5 [3313]

[3540] μεσημβρία *mesēmbria* 2x *midday, noon,* Ac 22:6; meton. *the south,* Ac 8:26★ [3314]

[3541] μεσιτεύω *mesiteuō* 1x *to perform offices between two parties; to intervene, interpose,* Heb 6:17★ [3315]

[3542] μεσίτης *mesitēs* 6x *one that acts between two parties; a mediator, one who interposes to reconcile two adverse parties,* 1 Ti 2:5; *an arbitrator, one who is the medium of communication between two parties, a mid-party,* Gal 3:19, 20; Heb 8:6; 9:15; 12:24★ [3316]

[3543] μεσονύκτιον *mesonyktion* 4x *midnight,* Lk 11:5, Mk 13:35; Lk 11:5; Ac 16:25; 20:7★ [3317]

[3544] Μεσοποταμία *Mesopotamia* 2x *Mesopotamia,* the country lying between the rivers Tigris and Euphrates, Ac 2:9; 7:2★ [3318]

[3545] μέσος *mesos* 58x *mid, middle,* Mt 25:6; Ac 26:13; ἀνὰ μέσον, *in the midst;* from the Hebrew, *in, among,* Mt 13:25; *between,* 1 Co 6:5; διὰ μέσου, *through the midst of,* Lk 4:30; εἰς τὸ μέσον, *into,* or *in the midst,* Mk 3:3; Lk 6:8; ἐκ μέσου, *from the midst, out of the way,* Col 2:14; 2 Th 2:7; from the Hebrew, *from, from among,* Mt 13:49; ἐν τῷ μέσῳ, *in the midst,* Mt 10:16; *in the midst, in public, publicly,* Mt 14:6 ἐν μέσῳ, *in the midst of; among,*

Mt 18:20; κατὰ μέσον τῆς νυκτός, *about midnight,* Ac 27:27 [3319]

[3546] μεσότοιχον *mesotoichon* 1x *a middle wall; a partition wall, a barrier,* Eph 2:14★ [3320]

[3547] μεσουράνημα *mesouranēma* 3x *the mid-heaven, mid-air,* Rev 8:13; 14:6; 19:17★ [3321]

[3548] μεσόω *mesoō* 1x *to be in the middle* or *midst; to be advanced midway,* Jn 7:14★ [3322]

[3549] Μεσσίας *Messias* 2x *the Messiah, the Anointed One,* i.q. ὁ Χριστός, Jn 1:42, 4:25★ [3323]

[3550] μεστός *mestos* 9x *full, full of, filled with,* Jn 19:29; 21:11; *replete,* Mt 23:28; Ro 1:29; 15:14; Jas 3:8, 17; 2 Pe 2:14★ [3324]

[3551] μεστόω *mestoō* 1x *to fill;* pass. *to be filled, be full,* Ac 2:13★ [3325]

[3552] μετά *meta* 469x (1) gen., *with, together with,* Mt 16:27; 12:41; 26:55; *with, on the same side* or *party with, in aid of,* Mt 12:30; 20:20; *with, by means of,* Ac 13:17; *with,* of conflict, Rev 11:7; *with, among,* Lk 24:5; *with, to, towards,* Lk 1:58, 72; (2) acc., *after,* of place, *behind,* Heb 9:3; of time, *after,* Mt 17:1; 24:29; followed by an infin. with the neut. article, *after, after that,* Mt 26:32; Lk 22:20 [3326]

[3553] μεταβαίνω *metabainō* 12x *to go* or *pass from one place to another,* Jn 5:24; *to pass away, be removed,* Mt 17:20; *to go away, depart,* Mt 8:34 [3327]

[3554] μεταβάλλω *metaballō* 1x *to change;* mid. *to change one's mind,* Ac 28:6★ [3328]

[3555] μετάγω *metagō* 2x *to lead* or *move from one place to another; to change direction, turn about,* Jas 3:3, 4★ [3329]

[3556] μεταδίδωμι *metadidōmi* 5x *to give a part, to share,* Lk 3:11; *to impart, bestow,* Ro 1:11; 12:8; Eph 4:28; 1 Th 2:8★ [3330]

[3557] μετάθεσις *metathesis* 3x *a removal, translation,* Heb 11:5; 12:27; *a transmutation, change by the abolition of one thing, and the substitution of another,* Heb 7:12★ [3331]

[3558] μεταίρω *metairō* 2x *to remove, transfer;* in N.T. intrans. *to go away, depart,* Mt 13:53; 19:1★ [3332]

[3559] μετακαλέω *metakaleō* 4x *to call from one place into another;* mid. *to call* or *send for, invite to come to oneself,* Ac 7:14; 10:32; 20:17; 24:25★ [3333]

[3560] μετακινέω *metakineō* 1x *to move away, remove;* pass. met. *to stir away from, to swerve,* Col 1:23★ [3334]

[3561] μεταλαμβάνω *metalambanō* 7x *to partake of, share in,* Ac 2:46; 27:33f.; 2 Ti 2:6; Heb 6:7; 12:10; *to get, obtain, find,* Ac 24:25★ [3335]

[3562] μετάλημψις *metalēmpsis* 1x *a partaking of, a being partaken of,* 1 Ti 4:3★ [3336]

[3563] μεταλλάσσω *metallassō* 2x *to exchange, change for* or *into, transmute,* Ro 1:25, 26★ [3337]

[3564] μεταμέλομαι *metamelomai* 6x *to change one's judgment on past points of conduct; to change one's mind and purpose,* Heb 7:21; *to repent, regret,* Mt 21:29, 32; 27:3; 2 Co 7:8★ [3338]

[3565] μεταμορφόω *metamorphoō* 4x *to change the external form, transfigure;* mid. *to change one's form, be transfigured,* Mt 17:2; Mk 9:2; *to undergo* a spiritual *transformation* Ro 12:2; 2 Co 3:18★ [3339]

[3566] μετανοέω *metanoeō* 34x *to undergo a change in frame of mind and feeling, to repent,* Lk 17:3, 4; *to make a change of principle and practice, to reform,* Mt 3:2 [3340]

[3567] μετάνοια *metanoia* 22x *a change of mode of thought and feeling, repentance,* Mt 3:8; Ac 20:21; 2 Ti 2:25; *practical reformation,* Lk 15:7; *reversal* of the past, Heb 12:17 [3341]

[3568] μεταξύ *metaxy* 9x can function as an improper prep., *between,* Mt 23:35; Lk 11:51; 16:26; Ac 15:9; ἐν τῷ μεταξύ, sc. χρόνῳ, *in the meantime, meanwhile,* Jn 4:31; in N.T. ὁ μεταξύ, *following, succeeding,* Ac 13:42 [3342]

[3569] μεταπέμπω *metapempō* 9x *to send after;* mid. *to send after* or *for* any one, *invite to come to one's self,* Ac 10:5, 22, 29; 11:13; 20:1; 24:24, 26; 25:3★ [3343]

[3570] μεταστρέφω *metastrephō* 2x *to turn about; convert* into something else, *change,* Ac 2:20; by impl. *to pervert,* Gal 1:7★ [3344]

[3571] μετασχηματίζω *metaschēmatizō* 5x *to remodel, transfigure,* Phil 3:21; mid. *to transform one's self,* 2 Co 11:13, 14, 15; *to transfer* an imagination, 1 Co 4:6★ [3345]

[3572] μετατίθημι *metatithēmi* 6x *to transport,* Ac 7:16; *to transfer,* Heb 7:12; *to translate* out of the world, Heb 11:5; met. *to transfer* to other purposes, *to pervert,* Jude 4; mid. *to transfer one's self, to change over,* Gal 1:6★ [3346]

[3573] μετατρέπω *metatrepō* 1x *to turn around, change, alter,* Jas 4:9★ [3344]

[3575] μετέπειτα *metepeita* 1x *afterwards,* Heb 12:17★ [3347]

[3576] μετέχω *metechō* 8x *to share in, partake,* 1 Co 9:10, 12; 10:17, 21; 1 Co 10:30; Heb 2:14; 5:13; *to be a member of,* Heb 7:13★ [3348]

[3577] μετεωρίζομαι *meteōrizomai* 1x *to raise aloft;* met. *to unsettle in mind;* pass. *to be excited with anxiety, be in anxious suspense,* Lk 12:29★ [3349]

[3578] μετοικεσία *metoikesia* 4x *change of abode* or *country, migration,* Mt 1:11, 12, 17★ [3350]

[3579] μετοικίζω *metoikizō* 2x *to cause to change abode, cause to emigrate,* Ac 7:4, 43★ [3351]

[3580] μετοχή *metochē* 1x *a sharing, partaking; communion, fellowship,* 2 Co 6:14★ [3352]

[3581] μέτοχος *metochos* 6x *a partaker,* Heb 3:1, 14; 6:4; 12:8; *an associate, partner, fellow,* Lk 5:7; Heb 1:9★ [3353]

[3582] μετρέω *metreō* 11x *to allot, measure,* Mt 7:2; Mk 4:24; Lk 6:38; Rev 11:1, 2; 21:15-17; met. *to estimate,* 2 Co 10:12★ [3354]

[3583] μετρητής *metrētēs* 1x pr. *a measurer;* also, *metretes,* Latin *metreta,* equivalent to the Attic ἀμφορεύς, i.e., three-fourths of the Attic μέδιμνος, and therefore equal to about nine gallons, Jn 2:6★ [3355]

[3584] μετριοπαθέω *metriopatheō* 1x *to moderate one's passions; to be gentle, compassionate,* Heb 5:2★ [3356]

[3585] μετρίως *metriōs* 1x *moderately; slightly;* ouj metrivw" *no little, not a little, much, greatly,* Ac 20:12★ [3357]

[3586] μέτρον *metron* 14x *measure,* Mt 7:2; Mk 4:24; Lk 6:38; Rev 21:17; *measure, standard,* Eph 4:13; *extent, compass,* 2 Co 10:13; allotted *measure, specific portion,* Ro 12:3; Eph 4:7, 16; ἐκ μέτρον, *by measure, with definite limitation,* Jn 3:34 [3358]

[3587] μέτωπον *metōpon* 8x *forehead, front,* Rev 7:3; 9:4; 13:16; 14:1, 9; 17:5; 20:4; 22:4★ [3359]

[3588] μέχρι *mechri* 17x improper prep. and a conj (*until*), can also spelled μέχρις, *unto, even to,* Ro 15:19; of time, *until, till,* Mt 11:23; Mk 13:30 [3360]

[3590] μή *mē* 1,042x *a negative particle,* can function as a conj, *not, for*

the particulars of its usage, especially as distinguished from that of οὐ, consult a grammar; as a conj., *lest, that not,* Mt 5:29, 30; 18:10; 24:6; Mk 13:36; μή, or μήτι, or μήποτε, prefixed to an interrogative clause, is a mark of tone, since it expresses an intimation either of the reality of the matters respecting which the question is asked, Mt 12:23; or the contrary, Jn 4:12 [3361]

[3592] μηδαμῶς *mēdamōs* 2x *by no means,* Ac 10:14; 11:8★ [3365]

[3593] μηδέ *mēde* 56x *negative disjunctive particle,* can function as an adverb and a conj, *neither,* and repeated, *neither-nor,* Mt 6:25; 7:6; 10:9, 10; *not even, not so much as,* Mk 2:2 [3366]

[3594] μηδείς *mēdeis* 90x *not one, none, no one,* Mt 8:4 [3367]

[3595] μηδέποτε *mēdepote* 1x *not at any time, never,* 2 Ti 3:7★ [3368]

[3596] μηδέπω *mēdepō* 1x *not yet, not as yet,* Heb 11:7★ [3369]

[3597] Μῆδος *Mēdos* 1x *a Mede, a native of Media* in Asia, Ac 2:9★ [3370]

[3600] μηκέτι *mēketi* 22x *no more, no longer,* Mk 1:45; 2:2 [3371]

[3601] μῆκος *mēkos* 3x *length,* Eph 3:18; Rev 21:16★ [3372]

[3602] μηκύνω *mēkynō* 1x *to lengthen, prolong;* mid. *to grow up,* as plants, Mk 4:27★ [3373]

[3603] μηλωτή *mēlōtē* 1x *a sheepskin,* Heb 11:37★ [3374]

[3604] μήν *mēn* 19x *a month,* Lk 1:24, 26, 36, 56; in N.T. *the new moon, the day of the new moon,* Gal 4:10 [3375]

[3606] μηνύω *mēnyō* 4x *to disclose* what is secret, Jn 11:57; Ac 23:30; 1 Co 10:28; *to declare, indicate,* Lk 20:37★ [3377]

[3607] μήποτε *mēpote* 25x can function as an adverb, *BAGD* list it as a negative part., conj., and interrogative part., same signif. and usage as μή, Heb 9:17; Mt 4:6; 13:15; also, *whether,* Lk 3:15 [3379]

[3609] μήπω *mēpō* 2x *not yet, not as yet,* Ro 9:11; Heb 9:8★ [3380]

[3611] μηρός *mēros* 1x *the thigh,* Rev 19:16★ [3382]

[3612] μήτε *mēte* 34x *neither;* μήτε ... μήτε, or μή ... μήτε, or μηδὲ ... μητέ, *neither ... nor,* Mt 5:34, 35, 36; Ac 23:8; 2 Th 2:2; in N.T. also equivalent to μηδέ, *not even, not so much as,* Mk 3:20 [3383]

[3613] μήτηρ *mētēr* 83x *a mother,* Mt 1:18; 12:49, 50, et al. freq.; *a parent* city, Gal 4:26; Rev 17:5 [3384]

[3614] μήτι *mēti* 18x interrogative particle, used in questions expecting a negative answer; has the same use as mhv in the form εἰ μήτε, Lk 9:3; also when prefixed to an interrogative clause, Mt 7:16; Jn 4:29 [3385, 3387]

[3616] μήτρα *mētra* 2x *the womb,* Lk 2:23; Ro 4:19★ [3388]

[3618] μητρολῴας *mētrolōas* 1x *one who murders* or *strikes his mother, matricide,* 1 Ti 1:9★ [3389]

[3620] μιαίνω *miainō* 5x pr. *to tinge, dye, stain; to pollute, defile,* ceremonially, Jn 18:28; *to corrupt, deprave,* Tit 1:15 (2t); Heb 12:15; Jude 8★ [3392]

[3621] μίασμα *miasma* 1x *pollution,* moral *defilement, corruption,* 2 Pe 2:20★ [3393]

[3622] μιασμός *miasmos* 1x *pollution, corruption, defiling,* 2 Pe 2:10★ [3394]

[3623] μίγμα *migma* 1x *a mixture,* Jn 19:39★ [3395]

[3624] μίγνυμι *mignymi* 4x also spelled μείγνυμι, *to mix, mingle,* Mt 27:34; Lk 13:1; Rev 8:7 [3396]

[3625] μικρός *mikros* 46x *little, small* in size quantity, etc. Mt 13:32; Lk 12:32; Rev 3:8; *small, little* in age, *young, not adult,* Mk 15:40; *little, short* in time, Jn 7:33; μικρόν, sc. χρόνον, *a little while, a short time,* Jn 13:33; μετὰ μικρόν, *after a little while, a little while afterwards,* Mt 26:73; *little* in number, Lk 12:32; *small, little* in dignity, *low, humble,* Mt 10:42; 11:11; μικρόν, as an adv., *little, a little,* Mt 26:39 [3397, 3398]

[3626] Μίλητος *Milētos* 3x *Miletus,* a seaport city of Caria, on the west coast of Asia Minor, Ac 20:15, 17; 2 Ti 4:20★ [3399]

[3627] μίλιον *milion* 1x *a Roman mile,* which contained *mille passuum,* 1000 paces, or 8 stadia, 4, 854 feet, Mt 5:41★ [3400]

[3628] μιμέομαι *mimeomai* 4x *to imitate, follow* as an example, *strive to resemble,* 2 Th 3:7, 9; Heb 13:7; 3 Jn 11★ [3401]

[3629] μιμητής *mimētēs* 6x *an imitator, follower,* 1 Co 4:16; 11:1; Eph 5:1; 1 Th 1:6; 2:14; Heb 6:12★ [3402]

[3630] μιμνῄσκομαι *mimnēskomai* 23x *to remember, recollect, call to mind,* Mt 26:75; Lk 1:54, 72; 16:25; in N.T., in a passive sense, *to be called to mind, be borne in mind*, Ac 10:31; Rev 16:19   [3403]

[3631] μισέω *miseō* 40x *to hate, regard with ill-will*, Mt 5:43, 44; 10:22; *to detest, abhor*, Jn 3:20; Ro 7:15; in N.T. *to regard with less affection, love less, esteem less*, Mt 6:24; Lk 14:26   [3404]

[3632] μισθαποδοσία *misthapodosia* 3x pr. *the discharge of wages; requital; reward*, Heb 10:35; 11:26; *punishment*, Heb 2:2*   [3405]

[3633] μισθαποδότης *misthapodotēs* 1x *a bestower of remuneration; recompenser, rewarder*, Heb 11:6*   [3406]

[3634] μίσθιος *misthios* 2x *hired;* as a subst., *a hired servant, hireling*, Lk 15:17, 19*   [3407]

[3635] μισθός *misthos* 29x *hire, wages*, Mt 20:8; Jas 5:4; *reward*, Mt 5:12, 46; 6:1, 2, 5, 16; *punishment*, 2 Pe 2:13   [3408]

[3636] μισθόω *misthoō* 2x *to hire out, let out to hire;* mid. *to hire*, Mt 20:1, 7*   [3409]

[3637] μίσθωμα *misthōma* 1x *hire, rent;* in N.T. *a hired dwelling*, Ac 28:30*   [3410]

[3638] μισθωτός *misthōtos* 3x *a hireling*, Mk 1:20; Jn 10:12, 13*   [3411]

[3639] Μιτυλήνη *Mitylēnē* 1x *Mitylene*, the capital city of Lesbos, in the Aegean sea, Ac 20:14*   [3412]

[3640] Μιχαήλ *Michaēl* 2x *Michael, the archangel*, indecl., Jude 9; Rev 12:7*   [3413]

[3641] μνᾶ *mna* 9x Latin *mina; a weight*, equivalent to 100 drachmae; also *a sum*, equivalent to 100 drachmas and the sixtieth part of a talent, Lk 19:13, 16, 18, 20, 24f.*   [3414]

[3643] Μνάσων *Mnasōn* 1x *Mnason*, pr. name, Ac 21:16*   [3416]

[3644] μνεία *mneia* 7x *remembrance, recollection*, Phil 1:3; 1 Th 3:6; 2 Ti 1:3; *mention;* μνείαν ποιεῖσθαι, *to make mention*, Ro 1:9; Eph 1:16; 1 Th 1:2; Phlm 4*   [3417]

[3645] μνῆμα *mnēma* 8x pr. *a memorial, monument; a tomb, sepulchre*, Mk 5:3, 5; Lk 8:27; 23:53; 24:1; Ac 2:29; 7:16; Rev 11:9*   [3418]

[3646] μνημεῖον *mnēmeion* 39x *monument, memorial*, Lk 11:47; *grave, tomb*, Mt 23:39; Mk 5:2; Lk 11:44; Jn 11:17, 31, 38; Ac 13:29   [3419]

[3647] μνήμη *mnēmē* 1x *remembrance, recollection, memory;* μνήμην ποιεῖσθαι, *to make mention*, 2 Pe 1:15*   [3420]

[3648] μνημονεύω *mnēmoneuō* 21x *to remember, recollect, call to mind*, Mt 16:9; Lk 17:32; Ac 20:31; *to be mindful of, to fix the thoughts upon*, Heb 11:15; *to make mention, mention, speak of*, Heb 11:22   [3421]

[3649] μνημόσυνον *mnēmosynon* 3x *a record, memorial*, Ac 10:4; *honorable remembrance*, Mt 26:13; Mk 14:9*   [3422]

[3650] μνηστεύω *mnēsteuō* 3x *to ask in marriage; to betroth;* pass. *to be betrothed, engaged*, Mt 1:18; Lk 1:27; 2:5*   [3423]

[3652] μογιλάλος *mogilalos* 1x *having an impediment in one's speech, speaking with difficulty, a stammerer*, Mk 7:32*   [3424]

[3653] μόγις *mogis* 1x *with difficulty, scarcely, hardly*, Lk 9:39*   [3425]

[3654] μόδιος *modios* 3x *a modius*, a Roman measure for things dry, containing 16 sextarii, and equivalent to about *a peck* (8.75 liters); in N.T. *a corn measure*, Mt 5:15; Mk 4:21; Lk 11:33*   [3426]

[3655] μοιχαλίς *moichalis* 7x *an adulteress*, Ro 7:3; Jas 4:4; by meton., *an adulterous appearance, lustful significance*, 2 Pe 2:14; from the Hebrew, spiritually *adulterous, faithless, ungodly*, Mt 12:39; 16:4; Mk 8:38*   [3428]

[3656] μοιχάω *moichaō* 4x act., *to cause to commit adultery*, pass., *to commit* or *be guilty of adultery*, Mt 5:32; 19:9; Mk 10:11f.*   [3429]

[3657] μοιχεία *moicheia* 3x *adultery*, Mt 15:19; Mk 7:22; Jn 8:3*   [3430]

[3658] μοιχεύω *moicheuō* 15x trans. *to commit adultery with, debauch*, Mt 5:28; absol. and mid. *to commit adultery*, Mt 5:27; Jn 8:4; *to commit* spiritual *adultery, be guilty of idolatry*, Rev 2:22   [3431]

[3659] μοιχός *moichos* 3x *an adulterer*, Lk 18:11; 1 Co 6:9; Heb 13:4*   [3432]

[3660] μόλις *molis* 6x *with difficulty, scarcely, hardly*, Ac 14:18; 27:7, 8, 16; Ro 5:7; 1 Pe 4:18*   [3433]

[3661] Μολόχ *Moloch* 1x *Moloch*, pr. name, indecl., Ac 7:43*   [3434]

[3662] μολύνω *molynō* 3x pr. *to stain, sully; to defile, contaminate* morally, 1 Co 8:7; Rev 14:4; *to soil*, Rev 3:4*   [3435]

[3663] μολυσμός *molysmos* 1x *pollution, defilement*, 2 Co 7:1*   [3436]

[3664] μομφή *momphē* 1x *a complaint, cause* or *ground of complaint*, Col 3:13*   [3437]

[3665] μονή *monē* 2x *a stay in any place; an abode, dwelling, mansion*, Jn 14:2, 23*   [3438]

[3666] μονογενής *monogenēs* 9x *only-begotten, only-born*, Lk 7:12; 8:42; 9:38; Heb 11:17; *only-begotten* in respect of peculiar generation, *unique*, Jn 1:14, 18; 3:16, 18; 1 Jn 4:9*   [3439]

[3668] μόνος *monos* 114x *without accompaniment, alone*, Mat. 14:23; 18:15; Lk 10:40; *singly existent, sole, only*, Jn 17:3; *lone solitary*, Jn 8:29; 16:32; *alone* in respect of restriction, *only*, Mt 4:4; 12:4; *alone* in respect of circumstances, *only*, Lk 24:18; *not multiplied by reproduction, lone, barren*, Jn 12:24   [3441]

[3669] μονόφθαλμος *monophthalmos* 2x *one-eyed; deprived of an eye*, Mt 18:9; Mk 9:47*   [3442]

[3670] μονόω *monoō* 1x *to leave alone;* pass. *to be left alone, be lone*, 1 Ti 5:5*   [3443]

[3671] μορφή *morphē* 3x *form, outward appearance*, Mk 16:12; Phil 2:6, 7*   [3444]

[3672] μορφόω *morphoō* 1x *to give shape to, mold, fashion*, Gal 4:19*   [3445]

[3673] μόρφωσις *morphōsis* 2x pr. *a shaping, moulding;* in N.T. *external form, appearance*, 2 Ti 3:5; *a settled form.* prescribed *system*, Ro 2:20*   [3446]

[3674] μοσχοποιέω *moschopoieō* 1x *to form an image of a calf*, Ac 7:41*   [3447]

[3675] μόσχος *moschos* 6x pr. *a tender branch, shoot; a young animal; a calf, young bull*, Lk 15:23, 27, 30; Heb 12:19; Rev 4:7*   [3448]

[3676] μουσικός *mousikos* 1x pr. *devoted to the arts of the Muses; a musician;* in N.T., perhaps, *a singer*, Rev 18:22*   [3451]

[3677] μόχθος *mochthos* 3x *wearisome labor, toil, travail*, 2 Co 11:27; 1 Th 2:9; 2 Th 3:8*   [3449]

[3678] μυελός *myelos* 1x *marrow*, Heb 4:12*   [3452]

[3679] μυέω *myeō* 1x *to initiate, instruct* in the sacred mysteries; in N.T. pass. *to be disciplined* in a practical lesson, *to learn* a lesson, Phil 4:12*   [3453]

[3680] μῦθος *mythos* 5x *a word, speech, a tale; a fable, figment*, 1 Ti 1:4; 4:7; 2 Ti 4:4; Tit 1:14; 2 Pe 1:16*   [3454]

[3681] μυκάομαι *mykaomai* 1x *to low, bellow,* as a bull; also, *to roar,* as a lion, Rev 10:3★ [3455]

[3682] μυκτηρίζω *myktērizō* 1x *to contract the nose in contempt and derision, toss up the nose; to mock, deride,* Gal 6:7★ [3456]

[3683] μυλικός *mylikos* 1x *of a mill, belonging to a mill,* Lk 17:2★ [3457]

[3684] μύλινος *mylinos* 1x *belonging to a mill,* Rev 18:21★ [3458]

[3685] μύλος *mylos* 4x *a millstone,* Mt 18:6; 24:41; Mk 9:42; Rev 18:22★ [3458]

[3688] Μύρα *Myra* 1x neuter plural, *Myra,* a city of Lycia, Ac 27:5★ [3460]

[3689] μυριάς *myrias* 8x *a myriad, ten thousand,* Ac 19:19; indefinitely, *a vast multitude,* Lk 12:1; Ac 21:20; Heb 12:22; Jude 14; Rev 5:11; 9:16★ [3461]

[3690] μυρίζω *myrizō* 1x *to anoint,* Mk 14:8★ [3462]

[3691] μύριοι *myrioi* 1x indefinitely, *a great number;* specifically, μύριοι, *a myriad, ten thousand,* Mt 18:24★ [3463]

[3692] μυρίος *myrios* 2x *innumerable,* 1 Co 4:15; 14:19★ [3463]

[3693] μύρον *myron* 14x pr. *aromatic juice which distills from trees; ointment, unguent,* usually perfumed, Mt 26:7, 12; Mk 14:3, 4 [3464]

[3695] Μυσία *Mysia* 2x *Mysia,* a province of Asia Minor, Ac 16:7f.★ [3465]

[3696] μυστήριον *mystērion* 28x *a matter to the knowledge of which initiation is necessary; a secret* which would remain such but for revelation, Mt 3:11; Ro 11:25; Col 1:26; *a concealed power* or *principle,* 2 Th 2:7; *a hidden meaning* of a symbol, Rev 1:20: 17:7 [3466]

[3697] μυωπάζω *myōpazō* 1x pr. *to close the eyes, contract the eyelids, wink; to be nearsighted, partially blinded, slow to understand,* 2 Pe 1:9★ [3467]

[3698] μώλωψ *mōlōps* 1x *the mark of a blow; a stripe, a wound,* 1 Pe 2:24★ [3468]

[3699] μωμάομαι *mōmaomai* 2x *to find fault with, censure, blame,* 2 Co 8:20; passively, 2 Co 6:3★ [3469]

[3700] μῶμος *mōmos* 1x *blame, ridicule; a disgrace* to society, *a stain,* 2 Pe 2:13★ [3470]

[3701] μωραίνω *mōrainō* 4x *to be foolish, to play the fool;* in N.T. trans. *to make foolish, convict of folly,* 1 Co 1:20; pass. *to be convicted of folly, to incur the character*

of folly, Ro 1:22; *to be rendered insipid,* Mt 5:13; Lk 14:34★ [3471]

[3702] μωρία *mōria* 5x *foolishness,* 1 Co 1:18, 21, 23; 2:14; 3:19★ [3472]

[3703] μωρολογία *mōrologia* 1x *foolish talk,* Eph 5:4★ [3473]

[3704] μωρός *mōros* 12x pr. *dull; foolish,* Mt 7:26; 23:17; 25:2f., 8; 1 Co 1:25, 27; 3:18; 4:10; 2 Ti 2:23; Tit 3:9; from the Hebrew, *a fool* in senseless wickedness, Mt 5:22★ [3474]

[3707] Μωϋσῆς *Mōysēs* 80x also spelled Μωσῆς and Μεσευς (3705), *Moses,* pr. name, Mt 8:4; Jn 1:17; Ro 5:14 [3475]

[3709] Ναασσών *Naassōn* 3x *Naasson,* pr. name, indecl., Mt 1:4; Lk 3:32★ [3476]

[3710] Ναγγαί *Nangai* 1x *Naggai, Nagge,* pr. name, indecl., Lk 3:25★ [3477]

[3711] Ναζαρά *Nazara* 2x see Ναζαρέθ, Mt 4:13; Lk 4:16★ [3478]

[3714] Ναζαρέθ *Nazareth* 6x an indeclinable form, *Nazareth,* is spelled Ναζαρέτ (4x) and Ναζαρά (2x) [3478]

[3715] Ναζαρέτ *Nazaret* 4x see Ναζαρέθ, Mt 2:23; Mk 1:9; Jn 1:45, 46★ [3478]

[3716] Ναζαρηνός *Nazarēnos* 6x *an inhabitant of Nazareth,* Mk 1:24; 10:47; 4:67; 16:6; Lk 4:34; 24:19★ [3479]

[3717] Ναζωραῖος *Nazōraios* 13x also spelled Ναζαρηνός, *a Nazarite; an inhabitant of Nazareth,* Mt 2:23; 26:71; Lk 18:37; Jn 18:5, 7; 19:19; Ac 2:22; 3:6; 4:10; 6:14; 22:8; 24:5; 26:9★ [3480]

[3718] Ναθάμ *Natham* 1x also spelled Ναθάν, *Nathan,* pr. name, indecl., Lk 3:31★ [3481]

[3720] Ναθαναήλ *Nathanaēl* 6x *Nathanael,* pr. name, indecl., Jn 1:45-49; 21:2 [3482]

[3721] ναί *nai* 33x a particle, used to strengthen an affirmation, *certainly,* Rev 22:20; to make an affirmation, or express an assent, *yea, yes,* Mt 5:37; Ac 5:8 [3483]

[3722] Ναιμάν *Naiman* 1x also spelled Νεεμάν, *Naaman,* pr. name, indecl., Lk 4:27★ [3497]

[3723] Ναΐν *Nain* 1x *Nain,* a town of Palestine, indecl., Lk 7:11★ [3484]

[3724] ναός *naos* 45x pr. *a dwelling; the dwelling* of a deity, *a temple,* Mt 26:61; Ac 7:48; used figuratively of individuals, Jn

2:19; 1 Co 3:16; spc. *the cell of a temple;* hence, *the Holy Place* of the Temple of Jerusalem, Mt 23:35; Lk 1:9; *a model of a temple, a shrine,* Ac 19:24 [3485]

[3725] Ναούμ *Naoum* 1x *Naum,* pr. name, indecl., Lk 3:25★ [3486]

[3726] νάρδος *nardos* 2x *spikenard, andropogon nardus* of Linn., a species of aromatic plant with grassy leaves and a fibrous root, of which the best and strongest grows in India; in N.T. *oil of spikenard,* an oil extracted from the plant, which was highly prized and used as an ointment either pure or mixed with other substances, Mk 14:3; Jn 12:3★ [3487]

[3727] Νάρκισσος *Narkissos* 1x *Narcissus,* pr. name, Ro 16:11★ [3488]

[3728] ναυαγέω *nauageō* 2x *to make shipwreck, be shipwrecked,* 2 Co 11:25; 1 Ti 1:19★ [3489]

[3729] ναύκληρος *nauklēros* 1x *the master* or *owner of a ship,* Ac 27:11★ [3490]

[3730] ναῦς *naus* 1x *a ship, vessel,* Ac 27:41★ [3491]

[3731] ναύτης *nautēs* 3x *sailor, seaman,* Ac 27:27, 30; Rev 18:17★ [3492]

[3732] Ναχώρ *Nachōr* 1x *Nachor,* pr. name, indecl., Lk 3:34★ [3493]

[3733] νεανίας *neanias* 3x *a young man, youth,* Ac 20:9; 23:17; used of *one who is in the prime of life,* Ac 7:58★ [3494]

[3734] νεανίσκος *neaniskos* 11x *a young man, youth,* Mk 14:51; 16:5; used of *one in the prime of life,* Mat. 19:20, 22; νεανίσκοι, *soldiers,* Mk 14:51 [3495]

[3735] Νέα πολις *Neapolis* 1x *Neapolis,* a city of Thrace on the Strymonic gulf, Ac 16:11★ [3496]

[3738] νεκρός *nekros* 129x *dead, without life,* Mt 11:5; 22:31; met. νεκρός τινι, *dead to a thing, no longer devoted to,* or *under the influence of a thing,* Ro 6:11; *dead in respect of fruitlessness,* Jas 2:17, 20, 26; *morally* or *spiritually dead,* Ro 6:13; Eph 5:14; *dead in alienation from God,* Eph 2:1, 5; Col 2:13; *subject to death, mortal,* Ro 8:10; *causing death and misery, fatal, having a destructive power,* Heb 6:1; 9:14 [3498]

[3739] νεκρόω *nekroō* 3x pr. *to put to death, kill;* in N.T. met. *to deaden, mortify,* Col 3:5; pass. *to be rendered impotent,* Ro 4:19; Heb 11:12★ [3499]

[3740] νέκρωσις *nekrōsis* 2x pr. *a putting to death; dying, abandonment to death,*

2 Co 4:10; *deadness, impotency*, Ro 4:19* [3500]

[3741] νεομηνία *neomēnia* 1x *new moon, first of the month*, Col 2:16* [3561]

[3742] νέος *neos* 24x *recent, new, fresh*, Mt 9:17; 1 Co 5:7; Col 3:10; Heb 12:24; *young, youthful*, Tit 2:4. In Ac 16:11 is used in the name Νέαν πολις, which some lexicons list as its own lexical form. This occurrence is not included in the word's frequency count. [3501]

[3744] νεότης *neotēs* 4x *youth*, Mt 19:20 [3503]

[3745] νεόφυτος *neophytos* 1x *newly* or *recently planted* met. *a neophyte, one newly implanted* into the Christian Church, *a new convert*, 1 Ti 3:6* [3504]

[3748] νεύω *neuō* 2x *to nod; to intimate by a nod* or *significant gesture*, Jn 13:24; Ac 24:10* [3506]

[3749] νεφέλη *nephelē* 25x *a cloud*, Mt 17:5; 24:30; 26:64 [3507]

[3750] Νεφθαλίμ *Nephthalim* 3x *Nephthalim*, pr. name, indecl., Mt 4:13, 15; Rev 5:6* [3508]

[3751] νέφος *nephos* 1x *a cloud; trop. a cloud, a throng* of persons, Heb 12:1* [3509]

[3752] νεφρός *nephros* 1x *a kidney; pl.* νεφροί, *the kidneys, reins;* from the Hebrew *the reins* regarded as a seat of desire and affection, Rev 2:23* [3510]

[3753] νεωκόρος *neōkoros* 1x pr. *one who sweeps* or *cleanses a temple;* generally, *one who has the charge of a temple;* in N.T. *a devotee* city, as having specially dedicated a temple to some deity, Ac 19:35* [3511]

[3754] νεωτερικός *neōterikos* 1x *juvenile, natural to youth, youthful*, 2 Ti 2:22* [3512]

[3755] νή *nē* 1x *by*, BAGD calls it a "particle of strong affirmation," and is followed by the person or thing (in the acc) by which the person swears, 1 Co 15:31* [3513]

[3756] νήθω *nēthō* 2x *to spin*, Mt 6:28; Lk 12:27* [3514]

[3757] νηπιάζω *nēpiazō* 1x *to be childlike*, 1 Co 14:20* [3515]

[3758] νήπιος *nēpios* 15x pr. *not speaking*, Latin *infans; an infant, babe, child*, Mt 21:16; 1 Co 13:11; *one below the age of manhood, a minor*, Gal 4:1; met. *a babe* in knowledge, *unlearned, simple*, Mt 11:25; Ro 2:20 [3516]

[3759] Νηρεύς *Nēreus* 1x *Nereus*, pr. name, Ro 16:15* [3517]

[3760] Νηρί *Nēri* 1x *Neri*, pr. name, indecl., Lk 3:27* [3518]

[3761] νησίον *nēsion* 1x *a small island*, Ac 27:16* [3519]

[3762] νῆσος *nēsos* 9x *an island*, Ac 13:6; 27:26 [3520]

[3763] νηστεία *nēsteia* 5x *fasting, want of food*, 2 Co 6:5; 11:27; *a fast*, religious *abstinence from food*, Mt 17:21; Lk 2:37; spc. *the annual public fast of the Jews, the great day of atonement*, occurring in the month Tisri, corresponding to the new moon of October, Ac 27:9* [3521]

[3764] νηστεύω *nēsteuō* 20x *to fast*, Mt 4:2; 6:16, 17, 18; 9:15 [3522]

[3765] νῆστις *nēstis* 2x can also be masc. with a gen. in ιδος (n-3c[2]), *fasting, hungry*, Mt 15:32; Mk 8:3* [3523]

[3767] νηφάλιος *nēphalios* 3x *somber, temperate, abstinent in respect to wine*, etc.; in N.T. met., *vigilant, circumspect, self-controlled*, 1 Ti 3:2, 11; Tit 2:2* [3524]

[3768] νήφω *nēphō* 6x *to be sober, not intoxicated;* in N.T. met., *to be vigilant, circumspect*, 1 Th 5:6, 8 [3525]

[3769] Νίγερ *Niger* 1x *Niger*, pr. name, probably not declined, Ac 13:1* [3526]

[3770] Νικάνωρ *Nikanōr* 1x *Nicanor*, pr. name, Ac 6:5* [3527]

[3771] νικάω *nikaō* 28x *to conquer, overcome, vanquish, subdue*, Lk 1:22; Jn 16:33; absol. *to overcome, prevail*, Rev 5:5; *to come off superior* in a judicial cause, Ro 3:4 [3528]

[3772] νίκη *nikē* 1x *victory;* meton. *a victorious principle*, 1 Jn 5:4* [3529]

[3773] Νικόδημος *Nikodēmos* 5x *Nicodemus*, pr. name, Jn 3:1, 4, 9; 7:50; 19:39* [3530]

[3774] Νικολαΐτης *Nikolaitēs* 2x *a Nicolaitan*, or follower of Nicolaus, a heresy of the Apostolic age, Rev 2:6, 15* [3531]

[3775] Νικόλαος *Nikolaos* 1x *Nicolaus*, pr. name, Ac 6:5* [3532]

[3776] Νικόπολις *Nikopolis* 1x *Nicopolis*, a city of Macedonia, Tit 3:12* [3533]

[3777] νῖκος *nikos* 4x *victory*, Mt 12:20; 1 Co 15:54, 55, 57* [3534]

[3780] Νινευίτης *Nineuitēs* 3x *a Ninevite, an inhabitant of Nineveh*, Mt 12:41; Lk 11:30, 32* [3536]

[3781] νιπτήρ *niptēr* 1x *a basin* for washing some part of the person, Jn 13:5* [3537]

[3782] νίπτω *niptō* 17x *to wash;* spc. *to wash* some part of the person, as distinguished from λούω, Mt 6:17; Jn 13:8 [3538]

[3783] νοέω *noeō* 14x *to perceive, observe; to mark* attentively, Mt 24:15; Mk 13:14; 2 Ti 2:7; *to understand, comprehend*, Mt 15:17; *to conceive*, Eph 3:20 [3539]

[3784] νόημα *noēma* 6x *the mind, the understanding, intellect*, 2 Co 3:14; 4:4; Phil 4:7; *the heart, soul, affections, feelings, disposition*, 2 Co 11:3; *a conception of the mind, thought, purpose, device*, 2 Co 2:11; 10:5* [3540]

[3785] νόθος *nothos* 1x *spurious, bastard*, Heb 12:8* [3541]

[3786] νομή *nomē* 2x *pasture, pasturage*, Jn 10:9; ἔχειν νομήν, *to eat its way, spread corrosion*, 2 Ti 2:17* [3542]

[3787] νομίζω *nomizō* 15x *to own as settled and established; to deem*, 1 Co 7:26; 1 Ti 6:5; *to suppose, presume*, Mt 5:17; 20:10; Lk 2:44; *to be usual, customary*, Ac 16:13 [3543]

[3788] νομικός *nomikos* 9x *pertaining to law; relating to the* Mosaic *law*, Tit 3:9; as a subst., *one skilled in law, a jurist, lawyer*, Tit 3:13; spc. *an interpreter and teacher of the* Mosaic *law*, Mt 22:35 [3544]

[3789] νομίμως *nomimōs* 2x *lawfully, agreeably to law* or *custom, rightfully*, 1 Ti 1:8; 2 Ti 2:5* [3545]

[3790] νόμισμα *nomisma* 1x pr. *a thing sanctioned by law* or *custom; lawful money, coin*, Mt 22:19* [3546]

[3791] νομοδιδάσκαλος *nomodidaskalos* 3x *a teacher and interpreter of the* Mosaic *law*, Lk 5:17; Ac 5:34; 1 Ti 1:7 [3547]

[3792] νομοθεσία *nomothesia* 1x *legislation;* ἡ νομοθεσία, *the gift of the* Divine *law*, or *the* Mosaic *law* itself, Ro 9:4* [3548]

[3793] νομοθετέω *nomotheteō* 2x *to impose a law, give laws;* in N.T. pass., *to have a law imposed on one's self, receive a law*, Heb 7:11; *to be enacted, constituted*, Heb 8:6* [3549]

[3794] νομοθέτης *nomothetēs* 1x *a legislator, lawgiver*, Jas 4:12* [3550]

[3795] νόμος *nomos* 194x *a law*, Ro 4:15; 1 Ti 1:9; *the* Mosaic *law*, Mt 5:17, et al. freq.; *the Old Testament Scripture*, Jn 10:34; *a legal tie*, Ro 7:2, 3; *a law, a* *rule, standard*, Ro 3:27; *a rule* of life and conduct, Gal 6:2, Jas 1:25 [3551]

[3796] νοσέω *noseō* 1x *to be sick;* met. *to have a diseased appetite* or *craving for* a thing, *have an excessive and vicious fondness for* a thing, 1 Ti 6:4* [3552]

[3798] νόσος *nosos* 11x *a disease, sickness, distemper*, Mt 4:23, 24; 8:17; 9:35 [3554]

[3799] νοσσιά *nossia* 1x *a brood* of young birds, Lk 13:34* [3555]

[3800] νοσσίον *nossion* 1x *the young of birds, a chick;* pl. *a brood* of young birds, Mt 23:37* [3556]

[3801] νοσσός *nossos* 1x also spelled νεοσσός, *the young of birds, a young bird, chick*, Lk 2:24* [3502]

[3802] νοσφίζω *nosphizō* 3x *to deprive, rob;* mid. *to misappropriate; to make secret reservation*, Ac 5:2, 3; *to purloin*, Tit 2:10* [3557]

[3803] νότος *notos* 7x *the south wind*, Lk 12:55; Ac 27:13; 28:13; meton. *the south, the southern quarter of the heavens*, Mt 12:42; Lk 11:31; 13:29; Rev 21:13* [3558]

[3804] νουθεσία *nouthesia* 3x *warning, admonition*, 1 Co 10:11; Eph 6:4; Tit 3:10* [3559]

[3805] νουθετέω *noutheteō* 8x pr. *to put in mind; to admonish, warn*, Ac 20:31; Ro 15:14 [3560]

[3807] νουνεχῶς *nounechōs* 1x *understandingly, sensibly, discreetly*, Mk 12:34* [3562]

[3808] νοῦς *nous* 24x *the mind, intellect*, 1 Co 14:15, 19; *understanding, intelligent faculty*, Lk 24:45; *intellect, judgment*, Ro 7:23, 25; *opinion, sentiment*, Ro 14:5; 1 Co 1:10; *mind, thought, conception*, Ro 11:34; 1 Co 2:16; Phil 4:7; *settled state of mind*, 2 Th 2:2; *frame of mind*, Ro 1:28; 12:2; Col 2:18; Eph 4:23; 1 Ti 6:5; 2 Ti 3:8; Tit 1:15 [3563]

[3811] νύμφη *nymphē* 8x *a bride*, Jn 3:29; Rev 18:23; 21:2, 9; 22:17; opposed to πενθερά, *a daughter-in-law*, Mt 10:35; Lk 12:53* [3565]

[3812] νυμφίος *nymphios* 16x *a bridegroom*, Mt 9:15; 25:1, 5, 6, 10 [3566]

[3813] νυμφών *nymphōn* 3x *a bridal-chamber;* in N.T. υἱοὶ τοῦ νυμφῶνος, *sons of the bridal-chamber, the bridegroom's attendant friends, groomsmen*, Mt 9:15; Mk 2:19; Lk 5:34* [3567]

[3814] νῦν *nyn* 147x *now, at the present time*, Mk 10:30; Lk 6:21, et al. freq.; *just now*, Jn 11:8; *forthwith*, Jn 12:31; καὶ νῦν, *even now, as matters stand*, Jn 11:22; *now*, expressive of a marked tone of address, Ac 7:34; 13:11; Jas 4:13; 5:1; τὸ νῦν, *the present time*, Lk 1:48; τανῦν, or τὰ νῦν, *now*, Ac 4:29 [3568]

[3815] νυνί *nyni* 20x of time, *now, at this very moment*, an emphatic form of νῦν although it now carries the same meaning [3570]

[3816] νύξ *nyx* 61x *night*, Mt 2:14; 28:13; Jn 3:2; met. spiritual *night*, moral *darkness*, Ro 13:12; 1 Th 5:5 [3571]

[3817] νύσσω *nyssō* 1x *to prick* or *pierce*, Jn 19:34* [3572]

[3818] νυστάζω *nystazō* 2x *to nod; to nod in sleep; to sink into a sleep*, Mt 25:5; *to slumber* in inactivity, 2 Pe 2:3* [3573]

[3819] νυχθήμερον *nychthēmeron* 1x *a day and night, twenty-four hours*, 2 Co 11:25* [3574]

[3820] Νῶε *Nōe* 8x *Noah*, pr. name, indecl., Mt 24:37ff; Lk 3:36; 17:26f.; Heb 11:7; 1 Pe 3:20; 2 Pe 2:25* [3575]

[3821] νωθρός *nōthros* 2x *slow, sluggish, lazy*, Heb 5:11; 6:12* [3576]

[3822] νῶτος *nōtos* 1x *the back* of men or animals, Ro 11:10* [3577]

[3825] ξενία *xenia* 2x pr. *state of being a guest;* then, *the reception of a guest* or *stranger, hospitality*, in N.T. *a lodging*, Ac 28:23; Phlm 22* [3578]

[3826] ξενίζω *xenizō* 10x *to receive as a guest, entertain*, Ac 10:23; 28:7; Heb 13:2; pass. *to be entertained as a guest, to lodge* or *reside with*, Ac 10:6, 18, 32; 21:16; *to strike with a feeling of strangeness, to surprise;* pass. or mid. *to be struck with surprise, be staggered, be amazed*, 1 Pe 4:4, 12; intrans. *to be strange;* ξενίζοντα, *strange matters, novelties*, Ac 17:20* [3579]

[3827] ξενοδοχέω *xenodocheō* 1x *to receive and entertain strangers, exercise hospitality*, 1 Ti 5:10* [3580]

[3828] ξένος *xenos* 14x *strange, foreign, alien*, Eph 2:12, 19; *strange, unexpected, surprising*, 1 Pe 4:12; *novel*, Heb 13:9; subst. *a stranger*, Mt 25:35, et al.; *a host*, Ro 16:23 [3581]

[3829] ξέστης *xestēs* 1x *a sextarius*, a Roman measure, containing about one pint English; in N.T. used for *a small vessel, cup, pot*, Mk 7:4* [3582]

[3830] ξηραίνω *xērainō* 15x *to dry up, parch*, Jas 1:11; pass. *to be parched,*

Mt 13:6, et al.; *to be ripened* as corn, Rev 14:15; *to be withered, to wither*, Mk 11:20; of parts of the body, *to be withered*, Mk 3:1, 3; *to pine*, Mk 9:18 [3583]

[3831] ξηρός *xēros* 8x *dry, withered*, Lk 23:31; ἡ ξηρά, sc. γῆ, *the dry land, land*, Mt 23:15; Heb 11:29; of parts of the body, *withered*, Mt 12:10 [3584]

[3832] ξύλινος *xylinos* 2x *wooden, of wood, made of wood*, 2 Ti 2:20; Rev 9:20* [3585]

[3833] ξύλον *xylon* 20x *wood, timber*, 1 Co 3:12; Rev 18:12; *stocks*, Ac 16:24; *a club*, Mt 26:47, 55; *a post, cross, gibbet*, Ac 5:30; 10:29; 13:29; *a tree*, Lk 23:31; Rev 2:7 [3586]

[3834] ξυράω *xyraō* 3x *to cut off the hair, shear, shave*, Ac 21:24; 1 Co 11:5, 6* [3587]

[3836] ὁ *ho* 19,867x *the* prepositive article, answering, to a considerable extent, to the English definite article; but, for the principle and facts of its usage, consult a grammar; ὁ μὲν ... ὁ δέ, *the one ... the other*, Phil 1:16, 17; Heb 7:5, 6, 20, 21, 23, 24; pl. *some ... others*, Mt 13:23; 22:5, 6; ὁ δέ, *but he*, Mt 4:4; 12:48; οἱ δέ, *but others*, Mt 28:17; used, in a poetic quotation, for a personal pronoun, Ac 17:28 [3588, 5120]

[3837] ὀγδοήκοντα *ogdoēkonta* 2x indecl. numeral, *eighty*, Lk 2:37; 16:7* [3589]

[3838] ὄγδοος *ogdoos* 5x *the eighth*, Lk 1:59; Ac 7:8; 2 Pet 2:5; Rev 17:11; 21:20* [3590]

[3839] ὄγκος *onkos* 1x pr. *bulk, weight; a burden, impediment*, Heb 12:1* [3591]

[3840] ὅδε *hode* 10x *this, that, he, she, it*, Lk 10:39; 16:25; Ac 15:23 [3592]

[3841] ὁδεύω *hodeuō* 1x *to journey, travel*, Lk 10:33* [3593]

[3842] ὁδηγέω *hodēgeō* 5x *to lead, guide*, Mt 15:14; Lk 6:39; Rev 7:17; met. *to instruct, teach*, Jn 16:13; Ac 8:31* [3594]

[3843] ὁδηγός *hodēgos* 5x *a guide, leader*, Ac 1:16; met. *an instructor, teacher*, Mt 15:14; 23:16, 24; Ro 2:19* [3595]

[3844] ὁδοιπορέω *hodoiporeō* 1x *to journey, travel*, Ac 10:9* [3596]

[3845] ὁδοιπορία *hodoiporia* 2x *to journey, journeying, travel*, Jn 4:6; 2 Co 11:26* [3597]

[3847] ὁδός *hodos* 101x *a way, road*, Mt 2:12; 7:13, 14; 8:28; 22:9, 10; *means* *of access, approach, entrance,* Jn 14:6; Heb 9:8; *direction, quarter, region,* Mt 4:15; 10:5 *the act of journeying, a journey, way, course,* Mt 10:10; Mk 2:23; 1 Th 3:11; *a journey,* as regards extent, Ac 1:12; met. *a way,* systematic *course* of pursuit, Lk 1:79; Ac 2:28; 16:17; *a way,* systematic *course* of action or conduct, Mt 21:32; Ro 11:33; 1 Co 4:17; *a way, system of doctrine,* Ac 18:26; ἡ ὁδός, *the way of the Christian faith,* Ac 19:9, 23, 24:22 [3598]

[3848] ὁδούς *odous* 12x *a tooth,* Mt 5:38; 8:12 [3599]

[3849] ὀδυνάω *odynaō* 4x *to pain* either bodily or mentally; pass. *to be in an agony, be tormented,* Lk 2:48; 16:24, 25; *to be distressed, grieved,* Ac 20:38★ [3600]

[3850] ὀδύνη *odynē* 2x *pain* of body of mind; *sorrow, grief,* Ro 9:2; 1 Ti 6:10★ [3601]

[3851] ὀδυρμός *odyrmos* 2x *bitter lamentation, wailing,* Mt 2:18; meton. *sorrow, mourning,* 2 Co 7:7★ [3602]

[3852] Ὀζίας *Ozias* 2x *Uzziah,* pr. name, indeclinable, Lk 3:23ff.★ [3604]

[3853] ὄζω *ozō* 1x *to smell, emit an odor; to have an offensive smell, stink,* Jn 11:39★ [3605]

[3854] ὅθεν *hothen* 15x *whence,* Mt 12:44; Ac 14:26; *from the place where,* Mt 25:24, 26; *whence, from which circumstance,* 1 Jn 2:18; *wherefore, whereupon,* Mt 14:7 [3606]

[3855] ὀθόνη *othonē* 2x pr. *fine linen; a linen cloth; a sheet,* Ac 10:11; 11:5★ [3607]

[3856] ὀθόνιον *othonion* 5x *a linen cloth;* in N.T. *a swath, bandage* for a corpse, Lk 24:12 [3608]

[3857] οἶδα *oida* 318x *to know,* Mt 6:8; *to know how,* Mt 7:11; from the Hebrew, *to regard with favor,* 1 Th 5:12. οἶδα is actually a perfect form functioning as a present, and ᾔδειν is actually a pluperfect form functioning as an aorist. [1492]

[3858] οἰκεῖος *oikeios* 3x *belonging to a house, domestic;* pl. *members of a family, immediate kin,* 1 Ti 5:8; *members of a* spiritual *family,* Eph 2:19; *members of a* spiritual *brotherhood,* Gal 6:10★ [3609]

[3859] οἰκετεία *oiketeia* 1x *the members, of a household,* Mt 24:45★ [2322]

[3860] οἰκέτης *oiketēs* 4x pr. *an inmate of a house; a domestic servant, household slave,* Lk 16:13; Ac 10:7; Ro 14:4; 1 Pe 2:18★ [3610]

[3861] οἰκέω *oikeō* 9x *to dwell in, inhabit,* 1 Ti 6:16; intrans. *to dwell, live;*

to cohabit, 1 Co 7:12, 13; *to be indwelling, indwell,* Ro 7:17, 18, 20; 8:9, 11; 1 Co 3:16★ [3611]

[3862] οἴκημα *oikēma* 1x *a dwelling;* used in various conventional senses, and among them, *a prison, cell,* Ac 12:7★ [3612]

[3863] οἰκητήριον *oikētērion* 2x *a habitation, dwelling, an abode,* Jude 6; trop. *the* personal *abode* of the soul, 2 Co 5:2★ [3613]

[3864] οἰκία *oikia* 93x *a house, dwelling, an abode,* Mt 2:11; 7:24, 27; trop. *the* bodily *abode* of the soul, 2 Co 5:1; meton. *a household, family,* Mt 10:13; 12:25; meton. *goods, property, means,* Mt 23:13 [3614]

[3865] οἰκιακός *oikiakos* 2x *belonging to a house;* pl. *the members of a household* or *family, kindred,* Mt 10:25, 36★ [3615]

[3866] οἰκοδεσποτέω *oikodespoteō* 1x pr. *to be master of a household; to occupy one's self in the management of a household,* 1 Ti 5:14★ [3616]

[3867] οἰκοδεσπότης *oikodespotēs* 12x *the master* or *head of a house* or *family,* Mt 10:25; 13:27, 52 [3617]

[3868] οἰκοδομέω *oikodomeō* 40x pluperfect, ᾠκοδόμητο (3 sg), *to build a house; to build,* Mt 7:24; *to repair, embellish, and amplify* a building, Mt 23:29; *to construct, establish,* Mt 16:18; met. *to contribute to advancement* in religious knowledge, *to edify,* 1 Co 14:4, 17; *to advance* a person's spiritual condition, *to edify,* 1 Co 8:1; pass. *to make spiritual* advancement, *be edified,* Ac 9:31; *to advance* in presumption, 1 Co 8:10 [3618]

[3869] οἰκοδομή *oikodomē* 18x pr. *the act of building; a building, structure,* Mt 24:1; in N.T. *a spiritual structure,* as instanced in the Christian body, 1 Co 3:9; Eph 2:21; religious *advancement, edification,* Ro 14:19; 1 Co 14:3 [3619]

[3871] οἰκοδόμος *oikodomos* 1x *a builder, architect,* Ac 4:11★ [3618]

[3872] οἰκονομέω *oikonomeō* 1x *to manage a household; to manage the affairs* of any one, *be steward,* Lk 16:2★ [3621]

[3873] οἰκονομία *oikonomia* 9x pr. *the management of a household; a stewardship,* Lk 16:2, 3, 4; in N.T. *an* apostolic *stewardship,* a ministerial *commission* in the publication and furtherance of the Gospel, 1 Co 9:17; 3:2; Col 1:25; or, *an arranged plan, a scheme,* Eph 1:10; *a due discharge of a commission,* 1 Ti 1:4, Eph 3:9★ [3622]

[3874] οἰκονόμος *oikonomos* 10x *the manager of a household; a steward,* Lk 12:42; 16:1, 3, 8; 1 Co 4:2; *a manager, trustee,* Gal 4:2; *a* public *steward, treasurer,* Ro 16:23; *a* spiritual *steward, the holder of a commission* in the service of the Gospel, 1 Co 4:1; Tit 1:7; 1 Pe 4:10★ [3623]

[3875] οἶκος *oikos* 114x *a house, dwelling,* Mt 9:6, 7; Mk 2:1, 11; 3:20; *place of abode, seat, site,* Mt 23:38; Lk 13:35; met. *a* spiritual *house* or *structure,* 1 Pe 2:5; meton. *a household, family,* Lk 10:5; 11:17; *a* spiritual *household,* 1 Ti 3:15; Heb 3:6; *family, lineage,* Lk 1:27, 69; 2:4; from the Hebrew, *a people, nation,* Mt 10:6; 15:24 [3624]

[3876] οἰκουμένη *oikoumenē* 15x some list as a participle, *the habitable earth, world,* Matt 24:14; Ro 10:18; Heb 1:6; used, however, with various restrictions of meaning, according to the context, Lk 2:1; Ac 17:6; meton. *the inhabitants of the earth, the whole human race, mankind,* Ac 17:31; 19:27; Rev 3:10. Some view this word as a participial form of οἰκέω. [3625]

[3877] οἰκουργός *oikourgos* 1x *one who is occupied in domestic affairs,* Tit 2:5★ [3626]

[3880] οἰκτιρμός *oiktirmos* 5x *compassion; kindness,* in relieving sorrow and want, Phil 2:1; Col 3:12; Heb 10:28; *favor, grace, mercy,* Ro 12:1; 2 Co 1:3★ [3628]

[3881] οἰκτίρμων *oiktirmōn* 3x *compassionate, merciful,* Lk 6:36; Jas 5:11★ [3629]

[3882] οἰκτίρω *oiktirō* 2x also spelled οἰκτείρω, *to have compassion on, exercise grace* or *favor towards,* Ro 9:15★ [3627]

[3884] οἰνοπότης *oinopotēs* 2x *wine-drinking;* in a bad sense, *a wine-bibber, tippler,* Mt 11:19; Lk 7:34★ [3630]

[3885] οἶνος *oinos* 34x *wine,* Mt 9:17; Mk 2:22; meton. *the vine and its clusters,* Rev 6:6 met. οἶνος, *a potion,* οἶνος τοῦ θυμοῦ, *a furious potion,* Rev 14:8, 10; 16:19; 17:2, 18:3 [3631]

[3886] οἰνοφλυγία *oinophlygia* 1x *a debauch with wine, drunkenness,* 1 Pe 4:3★ [3632]

[3887] οἴομαι *oiomai* 3x *to think, suppose, imagine, presume,* Jn 21:25; Phil 1:17. οἴεσθω in Jas 1:7 formed from the contracted form οἶμαι★ [3633]

[3888] οἷος *hoios* 14x *what, of what kind* or *sort, as,* Mt 24:21; Mk 9:3; οὐχ, οἷον, *not so as, not as implying,* Ro 9:6 [3634]

[3890] ὀκνέω *okneō* 1x *to be slow; to delay, hesitate,* Ac 9:38★ [3635]

[3891] ὀκνηρός *oknēros* 3x *slow; slothful, indolent, idle,* Mt 25:26; Ro 12:11; *tedious, troublesome,* Phil 3:1★ [3636]

[3892] ὀκταήμερος *oktaēmeros* 1x *on the eighth day,* Phil 3:5★ [3637]

[3893] ὀκτώ *oktō* 8x *eight,* Lk 2:21; 9:28 [3638]

[3897] ὄλεθρος *olethros* 4x *perdition, destruction,* 1 Co 5:5, 1 Th 5:3; 2 Th 1:9; 1 Ti 6:9★ [3639]

[3898] ὀλιγοπιστία *oligopistia* 1x *littleness* or *imperfectness of faith,* Mt 17:20★ [570]

[3899] ὀλιγόπιστος *oligopistos* 5x *scant of faith, of little faith, one whose faith is small and weak,* Mt 6:30; 8:26; 14:31; 16:18; Lk 12:28★ [3640]

[3900] ὀλίγος *oligos* 40x *little, small,* in number, etc.; pl. *few,* Mt 7:14; 9:37; 20:16; Lk 13:23; δι ὀλίγων, sc. λόγων, *in a few words, briefly,* 1 Pe 5:12; *little* in time, *short, brief,* Ac 14:28; Rev 12:12; πρὸς ὀλίγον, sc. χρόνον, *for a short time, for a little while,* Jas 4:14; *little, small, light,* etc., in magnitude, amount, etc., Lk 7:47; Ac 12:18; 15:2; ἐν ὀλίγῳ, *concisely, briefly,* Eph 3:3; *almost,* Ac 26:28, 29 [3641]

[3901] ὀλιγόψυχος *oligopsychos* 1x *fainthearted, desponding,* 1 Ti 5:14★ [3642]

[3902] ὀλιγωρέω *oligōreō* 1x *to neglect, regard slightly, make light of, despise,* Heb 12:5★ [3643]

[3903] ὀλίγως *oligōs* 1x *little, scarcely,* 2 Pe 2:18★ [3689]

[3904] ὀλοθρευτής *olothreutēs* 1x *a destroyer,* 1 Co 10:10★ [3644]

[3905] ὀλοθρεύω *olothreuō* 1x also spelled ὀλεθρεύω, *to destroy, cause to perish,* Heb 11:28★ [3645]

[3906] ὁλοκαύτωμα *holokautōma* 3x *a holocaust, whole burnt-offering,* Mk 12:33; Heb 10:6, 8★ [3646]

[3907] ὁλοκληρία *holoklēria* 1x *perfect soundness,* Ac 3:16★ [3647]

[3908] ὁλόκληρος *holoklēros* 2x *whole, having all its parts, sound, perfect, complete in every part;* in N.T. *the whole,* 1 Th 5:23; morally, *perfect, faultless, blameless,* Jas 1:4★ [3648]

[3909] ὀλολύζω *ololyzō* 1x pr. *to cry aloud in invocation; to howl, utter cries of distress, lament, bewail,* Jas 5:1★ [3649]

[3910] ὅλος *holos* 109x *all, whole, entire,* Mt 1:22; 4:23, 24 [3650]

[3911] ὁλοτελής *holotelēs* 1x *complete; all, the whole,* 1 Th 5:23★ [3651]

[3912] Ὀλυμπᾶς *Olympas* 1x *Olympas,* pr. name, Ro 16:15★ [3652]

[3913] ὄλυνθος *olynthos* 1x *an unripe* or *unseasonable fig, such as, shaded by the foliage, does not ripen at the usual season, but hangs on the trees during winter,* Rev 6:13★ [3653]

[3914] ὅλως *holōs* 4x *wholly, altogether; actually, really,* 1 Co 5:1; 6:7; 15:29; with a negative, *at all,* Mt 5:34★ [3654]

[3915] ὄμβρος *ombros* 1x *rain, a storm of rain,* Lk 12:54★ [3655]

[3916] ὁμείρομαι *homeiromai* 1x also spelled ἱμείρομαι, *to desire earnestly, have a strong affection for,* 1 Th 2:8★ [2442]

[3917] ὁμιλέω *homileō* 4x *to be in company with, associate with; to converse with, talk with,* Lk 24:14, 15; Ac 20:11; 24:26★ [3656]

[3918] ὁμιλία *homilia* 1x *intercourse, communication, converse,* 1 Co 15:33★ [3657]

[3920] ὁμίχλη *homichlē* 1x *a mist, fog, a cloud,* 2 Pet 2:17★ [★★]

[3921] ὄμμα *omma* 2x *the eye,* Mt 20:34; Mk 8:23★ [3659]

[3923] ὀμνύω *omnyō* 26x *to swear,* Mt 5:34; *to promise with an oath,* Mk 6:23; Ac 2:30; 7:17 [3660]

[3924] ὁμοθυμαδόν *homothumadon* 11x *with one mind, with one accord, unanimously,* Ac 1:14; Ro 15:6; *together, at once, at the same time,* Ac 2:1, 46; 4:24 [3661]

[3926] ὁμοιοπαθής *homoiopathēs* 2x *being affected in the same way* as another, *subject to the same incidents, of like infirmities, subject to the same frailties and evils,* Ac 14:15; Jas 5:17★ [3663]

[3927] ὅμοιος *homoios* 45x *like, similar, resembling,* Mt 11:16; 13:31, 33, 44, 45, 47, 52; Jn 8:55, et al. freq.; *like, of similar drift and force,* Mt 22:39 [3664]

[3928] ὁμοιότης *homoiotēs* 2x *likeness, similitude,* Heb 4:15; 7:15★ [3665]

[3929] ὁμοιόω *homoioō* 15x *to make like, cause to be like* or *resemble, assimilate;* pass. *to be made like, become like, resemble,* Mt 6:8; 13:24; 18:23; *to liken, compare,* Mt 7:24, 26; 11:16 [3666]

[3930] ὁμοίωμα *homoiōma* 6x pr. *that which is conformed* or *assimilated; form,* shape, figure, Rev 9:7; *likeness, resemblance, similitude,* Ro 1:23; 5:14; 6:5; 8:3; Phil 2:7★ [3667]

[3931] ὁμοίως *homoiōs* 30x *likewise, in a similar manner,* Mt 22:26; 27:41 [3668]

[3932] ὁμοίωσις *homoiōsis* 1x pr. *assimilation; likeness, resemblance,* Jas 3:9★ [3669]

[3933] ὁμολογέω *homologeō* 26x *to speak in accordance, adopt the same terms of language; to engage, promise,* Mt 14:7; *to admit, avow frankly,* Jn 1:20; Ac 24:14; *to confess,* 1 Jn 1:9; *to profess, confess,* Jn 9:22; 12:42; Ac 23:8; *to avouch, declare openly and solemnly,* Mt 7:23; in N.T. ὁμολογεῖν ἐν, *to accord belief,* Mt 10:32; Lk 12:8; *to accord approbation,* Lk 12:8; from the Hebrew, *to accord praise,* Heb 13:15 [3670]

[3934] ὁμολογία *homologia* 6x *assent, consent; profession,* 2 Co 9:13; 1 Ti 6:12, 13; Heb 3:1; 4:14; 10:23★ [3671]

[3935] ὁμολογουμένως *homologoumenōs* 1x *confessedly, avowedly, without controversy,* 1 Ti 3:16★ [3672]

[3937] ὁμότεχνος *homotechnos* 1x *to the same trade* or *occupation,* Ac 18:3★ [3673]

[3938] ὁμοῦ *homou* 4x *together; in the same place,* Jn 21:2; *together at the same time,* Jn 4:36; 20:4; Ac 2:1★ [3674]

[3939] ὁμόφρων *homophrōn* 1x *of like mind, of the same mind, like-minded,* 1 Pe 3:8★ [3675]

[3940] ὅμως *homōs* 3x *yet, nevertheless;* with μέντοι, *but nevertheless, but for all that,* Jn 12:42; *even, though it be but,* 1 Co 14:7; Gal 3:15★ [3676]

[3941] ὄναρ *onar* 6x *a dream,* Mt 1:20; 2:12, 13, 19, 22; 27:19★ [3677]

[3942] ὀνάριον *onarion* 1x *a young ass, an ass's colt,* Jn 12:14★ [3678]

[3943] ὀνειδίζω *oneidizō* 9x *to censure, inveigh against,* Mt 11:20; Mk 16:14; *to reproach* or *revile,* Jas 1:5; *to revile, insult with insulting language,* Mt 5:11 [3679]

[3944] ὀνειδισμός *oneidismos* 5x *censure,* 1 Ti 3:7; *reproach, reviling,* Ro 15:3 [3680]

[3945] ὄνειδος *oneidos* 1x pr. *fame, report, character;* usually, *reproach, disgrace,* Lk 1:25★ [3681]

[3946] Ὀνήσιμος *Onēsimos* 2x *Onesimus,* pr. name, Col 4:9; Phlm 10★ [3682]

[3947] Ὀνήσιφορος *Onēsiphoros* 2x *Onesiphorus,* pr. name, 2 Ti 1:16; 4:19★ [3683]

[3948] ὀνικός *onikos* 2x *pertaining to an ass;* μύλος ὀνικός, *a millstone turned by an ass, a large* or *an upper millstone,* Mt 18:6; Mk 9:42* [3684]

[3949] ὀνίνημι *oninēmi* 1x optative, ὀναίμην, *to receive profit, pleasure,* etc.; with a gen., *to have joy of,* Phlm 20* [3685]

[3950] ὄνομα *onoma* 231x *a name; the proper name* of a person, etc., Mt 1:23, 25; 10:2; 27:32; *a mere name* or *reputation,* Rev 3:1; in N.T. *a name* as the representative of a person, Mt 6:9; Lk 6:22; 11:2; *the name* of the author of a commission, delegated authority, or religious profession, Mt 7:22; 10:22; 12:21; 18:5, 20; 19:29; 21:9; 28:19; Ac 3:16; 4:7, 12; εἰς ὄνομα, ἐν ὀνόματι, *on the score of being* possessor of a certain character, Mt 10:41, 42; Mk 9:41 [3686]

[3951] ὀνομάζω *onomazō* 10x *to name,* Lk 6:14; *to style, entitle,* Lk 6:13; 1 Co 5:11; *to make mention of,* Eph 5:3; *to make known,* Ro 15:20; *to pronounce* in exorcism, Ac 19:13; in N.T. *to profess,* 2 Ti 2:19 [3687]

[3952] ὄνος *onos* 5x *donkey, ass,* male or female, Mt 21:2, 5, 7 [3688]

[3953] ὄντως *ontōs* 10x *really, in truth, truly,* Mk 11:32; Lk 23:47. [3689]

[3954] ὄξος *oxos* 6x *vinegar; a wine of sharp flavor, posca,* which was an ordinary beverage, and was often mixed with bitter herbs, etc., and this given to the condemned criminals in order to stupefy them, and lessen their sufferings, Mt 27:48; Mk 15:36; Lk 23:36; Jn 19:29, 30 [3690]

[3955] ὀξύς *oxys* 8x *sharp, keen,* Rev 1:16; 2:12; 14:14, 17, 18; 19:15; *swift, nimble,* Ro 3:15* [3691]

[3956] ὀπή *opē* 2x *a hole; a hole, vent, opening,* Jas 3:11; *a hole, cavern,* Heb 11:38* [3692]

[3957] ὄπισθεν *opisthen* 7x can function as an improper prep., *from behind, behind, after, at the back of,* Mt 9:20; 15:23 [3693]

[3958] ὀπίσω *opisō* 35x can function as an improper prep., *behind, after, at one's back,* Mt 4:10; Lk 7:38; Rev 1:10; τὰ ὀπίσω, *the things which are behind,* Phil 3:13; ὀπίσω and εἰς τὰ ὀπίσω, *back, backwards,* Mt 24:18; Mk 13:16; Lk 9:62, when an improper prep., takes the gen. [3694]

[3959] ὁπλίζω *hoplizō* 1x *to arm, equip;* mid. *to arm one's self, equip one's self,* 1 Pe 4:1* [3695]

[3960] ὅπλον *hoplon* 6x *an implement,* Ro 6:13; pl. τὰ ὅπλα, *arms, armor, weapons,* whether offensive or defensive, Jn 18:3; Ro 13:12; 2 Co 6:7; 10:4* [3696]

[3961] ὁποῖος *hopoios* 5x *what, of what sort* or *manner,* 1 Co 3:13; Gal 2:6; 1 Th 1:9; Jas 1:24; after τοιοῦτος, *as,* Ac 26:29* [3697]

[3963] ὅπου *hopou* 82x *where, in which place, in what place,* Mt 6:19, 20, 21; Rev 2:13; *whither, to what place,* Jn 8:21; 14:4; ὅπου ἄν, or ἐάν, *wherever, in whatever place,* Mt 24:28; *whithersoever,* Mt 8:19; Jas 3:4; met. *where, in which thing, state,* etc., Col 3:11; *whereas,* 1 Co 3:3; 2 Pe 2:11 [3699]

[3964] ὀπτάνομαι *optanomai* 1x *to be seen, appear,* Ac 1:3* [3700]

[3965] ὀπτασία *optasia* 4x *a vision, apparition,* Lk 1:22; 24:23; Ac 26:19; 2 Co 12:1* [3701]

[3966] ὀπτός *optos* 1x *dressed by fire, roasted, broiled,* etc., Lk 24:42* [3702]

[3967] ὀπώρα *opōra* 1x *autumn; the fruit season;* meton. *fruits,* Rev 18:14* [3703]

[3968] ὅπως *hopōs* 53x can function as a conj., *how, in what way* or *manner, by what means,* Mt 22:5; Lk 24:20; conj. *that, in order that,* and ὅπως μή, *that not, lest,* Mt 6:2, 4, 5, 16, 18; Ac 9:2, et al. freq. [3704]

[3969] ὅραμα *horama* 12x *a thing seen, sight, appearance,* Ac 7:31; *a vision,* Mt 17:9; Ac 9:10, 12 [3705]

[3970] ὅρασις *horasis* 4x *seeing, sight; appearance, aspect, a vision,* Ac 2:17; Rev 9:17; 4:3* [3706]

[3971] ὁρατός *horatos* 1x *visible,* Col 1:16* [3707]

[3972] ὁράω *horaō* 454x pluperfect, ἑωράκειν, some list εἶδον as the second aorist of ὁράω, *to see, behold,* Mt 2:2, et al. freq.; *to look,* Jn 19:37; *to visit,* Jn 16:22; Heb 13:23; *to mark, observe,* Ac 8:23; Jas 2:24; *to be admitted to witness,* Lk 17:22; Jn 3:36; Col 2:18; with Θεόν, *to be admitted into the more immediate presence of God,* Mt 5:8; Heb 12:14; *to attain to a true knowledge of God,* 3 Jn 11; *to see to* a thing, Mt 27:4; Ac 18:15; ὅρα, *see, take care,* Mt 8:4; Heb 8:5; pass. *to appear,* Lk 1:11; Ac 2:3; *to reveal one's self,* Ac 26:16; *to present one's self,* Ac 7:26 [3708]

[3973] ὀργή *orgē* 36x pr. *mental bent, impulse; anger, indignation, wrath,* Eph 4:31; Col 3:8; μετ᾽ ὀργῆς, *indignantly,* Mk 3:5; *vengeance, punishment,* Mt 3:7; Lk 3:7; 21:23; Ro 13:4, 5 [3709]

[3974] ὀργίζω *orgizō* 8x some list as deponent, ὀργίζομαι, *to provoke to anger, irritate;* pass. *to be angry, indignant, enraged,* Mt 5:22; 18:34 [3710]

[3975] ὀργίλος *orgilos* 1x *prone to anger, irascible, passionate,* Tit 1:7* [3711]

[3976] ὀργυιά *orgyua* 2x *the space measured by the arms outstretched; a fathom,* Ac 27:28 (2t)* [3712]

[3977] ὀρέγω *oregō* 3x *to extend, stretch out;* mid. *to stretch one's self out, to reach forward to,* met. *to desire earnestly, long after,* 1 Ti 3:1; Heb 11:16; by impl. *to indulge in, be devoted to,* 1 Ti 6:10* [3713]

[3978] ὀρεινός *oreinos* 2x *mountainous, hilly,* Lk 1:39, 65* [3714]

[3979] ὄρεξις *orexis* 1x *desire, longing; lust, concupiscence,* Ro 1:27* [3715]

[3980] ὀρθοποδέω *orthopodeō* 1x *to walk in a straight course; to be straightforward* in moral conduct, Gal 2:14* [3716]

[3981] ὀρθός *orthos* 2x *erect, upright,* Ac 14:10; *plain, level, straight,* Heb 12:13* [3717]

[3982] ὀρθοτομέω *orthotomeō* 1x *to cut straight; to set forth truthfully, without perversion* or *distortion,* 2 Ti 2:15* [3718]

[3983] ὀρθρίζω *orthrizō* 1x *to rise early in the morning; to come with the dawn,* Lk 21:38* [3719]

[3984] ὀρθρινός *orthrinos* 1x *a later form of* ὄρθριος, *of* or *belonging to the morning, morning,* Lk 24:22* [3720]

[3986] ὄρθρος *orthros* 3x *the dawn; the morning,* Jn 8:2; Ac 5:21; ὄρθος βαθύς, *the first streak of dawn, the early dawn,* Lk 24:1* [3722]

[3987] ὀρθῶς *orthōs* 4x *straightly; rightly, correctly,* Mk 7:35; Lk 7:43; 10:28; 20:21* [3723]

[3988] ὁρίζω *horizō* 8x *to set bounds to, to bound; to restrict,* Heb 4:7; *to settle, appoint definitively,* Ac 17:26; *to fix determinately,* Ac 2:23; *to decree, destine,* Lk 22:22; *to constitute, appoint,* Ac 10:42; 17:31; *to characterize with precision, to set forth distinctively,* Ro 1:4; absol. *to resolve,* Ac 11:29* [3724]

[3990] ὅριον *horion* 12x *a limit, bound, border of a territory* or *country;* pl. τὰ ὅρια, region, territory, district, Mt 2:16; 4:13; 8:34 [3725]

[3991] ὁρκίζω *horkizō* 2x *to put to an oath; to obtest, adjure, conjure,* Mk 5:7; Ac 19:13* [3726]

[3992] ὅρκος *horkos* 10x *an oath,* Mt 14:7, 9; 26:72; meton. *that which is solemnly promised, a vow,* Mt 5:33 [3727]

[3993] ὁρκωμοσία *horkōmosia* 4x *the act of taking an oath; an oath,* Heb 7:20, 21, 28* [3728]

[3994] ὁρμάω *hormaō* 5x pr. trans. *to put in motion, incite;* intrans. *to rush,* Mt 8:32; Mk 5:13; Lk 8:33 [3729]

[3995] ὁρμή *hormē* 2x *impetus, impulse; assault, violent attempt,* Ac 14:5; met. *impulse of mind, purpose, will,* Jas 3:4 [3730]

[3996] ὅρμημα *hormēma* 1x *violent* or *impetuous motion; violence,* Rev 18:21* [3731]

[3997] ὄρνεον *orneon* 3x *a bird, fowl,* Rev 18:2; 19:17, 21* [3732]

[3998] ὄρνις *ornis* 2x *bird, fowl;* domestic *hen,* Mt 23:37; Lk 13:34* [3733]

[3999] ὁροθεσία *horothesia* 1x pr. *the act of fixing boundaries; a bound set, certain bound, fixed limit,* Ac 17:26* [3734]

[4001] ὄρος *oros* 63x *a mountain, hill,* Mt 5:1, 14; 8:1; 17:20 [3735]

[4002] ὀρύσσω *oryssō* 3x *to dig, excavate,* Mt 21:33; 25:18; Mk 12:1* [3736]

[4003] ὀρφανός *orphanos* 2x *bereaved of parents, orphan,* Jas 1:27; *bereaved, desolate,* Jn 14:18 [3737]

[4004] ὀρχέομαι *orcheomai* 4x *to dance,* Mt 11:6, 17; Mk 6:22; Lk 7:32* [3738]

[4005] ὅς *hos* 1,407x *who, which, what, that,* Mt 1:16, 23, 25; in N.T. interrog. ἐφ᾽ ὅ, *wherefore, why,* Mt 26:50; in N.T. ὅς μὲν ... ὅς δέ, for ὁ μὲν ... ὁ δέ, Mt 21:35; 2 Co 2:16 [3739]

[4006] ὁσάκις *hosakis* 3x *as often as,* 1 Co 11:25, 26; Rev 11:6* [3740]

[4008] ὅσιος *hosios* 8x pr. *sanctioned by the supreme law of God, and nature; pious, devout,* Tit 1:8; *pure,* 1 Ti 2:8; *supremely holy,* Ac 2:27; 13:35; Heb 7:26; Rev 15:4; 16:5; τὰ ὅσια, *pledged bounties, mercies,* Ac 13:34* [3741]

[4009] ὁσιότης *hosiotēs* 2x *piety, sacred observance of all duties towards God, holiness,* Lk 1:75; Eph 4:24* [3742]

[4010] ὁσίως *hosiōs* 1x *piously,* 1 Th 2:10* [3743]

[4011] ὀσμή *osmē* 6x *smell, odor; fragrant odor,* Jn 12:3; Eph 5:2; Phil 4:18; met. 2 Co 2:14, 16* [3744]

[4012] ὅσος *hosos* 110x *as great, as much,* Mk 7:36; Jn 6:11; Heb 1:4; 8:6; 10:25; ἐφ᾽ ὅσον χρόνον, *for how long a time, while, as long as,* Ro 7:1; so, ἐφ᾽ ὅσον, sc. χρόνον, Mt 9:15; ὅσον χρόνον, *how long,* Mk 2:19; neut. ὅσον repeated, ὅσον ὅσον, used to give intensity to other qualifying words, e.g., μικρόν, *the very least, a very little while,* Heb 10:37; ἐφ᾽ ὅσον, *in as much as,* Mt 25:40, 45; καθ᾽ ὅσον, *by how much, so far as,* Heb 3:3; or, *in as much as, as, so,* Heb 7:20; 9:27; pl. ὅσα, *so far as, as much as,* Rev 1:2; 18:7; *how great, how much, how many, what,* Mk 3:8; 5:19, 20; *how many, as many as, all who,* 2 Co 1:20; Phil 3:15; 1 Ti 6:1; ὅσος ἄν, or ἐάν, *whoever, whatsoever,* Mt 7:12; 18:18 [3745]

[4014] ὀστέον *osteon* 4x contracted form, ὀστοῦν, οῦ, τό, *a bone,* Mt 23:27; Lk 24:39; Jn 19:36; Heb 11:22* [3747]

[4015] ὅστις *hostis* 144x *whoever, whatever; whosoever, whatsoever,* Mt 5:39, 41; 13:12; 18:4; its use in place of the simple relative is also required in various cases, which may be learned from the grammars; ἕως ὅτου, sc. χρόνου, *until,* Lk 13:8; *while,* Mt 5:25 [3748, 3755]

[4017] ὀστράκινος *ostrakinos* 2x *earthen, of earthenware,* 2 Co 4:7; 2 Ti 2:20* [3749]

[4018] ὄσφρησις *osphrēsis* 1x *smell, the sense of smelling,* 1 Co 12:17* [3750]

[4019] ὀσφῦς *osphys* 8x *the loins,* Mt 3:4; Mk 1:6. On the accent see BDF, 13. [3751]

[4020] ὅταν *hotan* 123x *when, whenever,* Mt 5:11; 6:2; Mk 3:11; Rev 4:9, et al. freq.; in N.T. *in case of, on occasion of,* Jn 9:5; 1 Co 15:27; Heb 1:6 [3752]

[4021] ὅτε *hote* 103x *when, at the time that, at what time,* Mt 7:28; 9:25; Lk 13:35, et al. freq. [3753]

[4022] ὅτι *hoti* 1,296x originally was the neuter of ὅστις, *that,* Mt 2:16, 22, 23; 6:5, 16; often used pleonastically in reciting another's words, Mt 9:18; Lk 19:42; Ac 5:23; as a causal particle, *for that, for, because,* Mt 2:18; 5:3, 4, 5; 13:13; *because, seeing that, since,* Lk 23:40; Ac 1:17 [3754]

[4023] οὗ *hou* 24x *where, in what place,* Mt 2:9; 18:20; *whither, to what place,* Lk 10:1; 22:10; 24:28; οὗ ἐάν, *whithersoever,* 1 Co 16:6 [3757]

[4024] οὐ *ou* 1,623x *negative adverb,* originally the gen. of ὅς, spelled οὐκ if followed by a word beginning with a vowel and a smooth breathing, οὐχ if followed by a vowel and rought breathing, *not, no,* Mt 5:37; 12:43; 23:37; for the peculiarities of its usage (especially as distinct from μή) consult a grammar [3756]

[4025] οὐά *oua* 1x *expressive of insult and derision, Ah! Ah!,* Mk 15:29* [3758]

[4026] οὐαί *ouai* 46x *Wo! Alas!* Mt 11:21; 18:7; 23:13, 14, 15, 16; ἡ οὐαί, subst., *a woe, calamity,* Rev 9:12; 11:14 [3759]

[4027] οὐδαμῶς *oudamōs* 1x *by no means,* Mt 2:6* [3760]

[4028] οὐδέ *oude* 143x *negative conj., neither, nor, and not, also not,* Mt 5:15; 6:15, 20, 26, 28; when single, *not even* Mt 6:29; 8:10 [3761]

[4029] οὐδείς *oudeis* 227x latter form, οὐθείς (4032), *not one, no one, none, nothing,* Mt 5:13; 6:24; 19:17; met. οὐδέν, *nothing, of no account, naught,* Jn 8:54; Ac 21:24 [3762]

[4030] οὐδέποτε *oudepote* 16x *never,* Mt 7:23; 21:16, 42, et al. freq. [3763]

[4031] οὐδέπω *oudepō* 4x *not yet, never yet, never,* Jn 7:39; 19:41; 20:9; Ac 8:16* [3764]

[4032] οὐθείς *outheis* 7x *see* οὐδείς [3762]

[4033] οὐκέτι *ouketi* 47x *no longer, no more,* Mt 22:46 [3765]

[4034] οὐκοῦν *oukoun* 1x *then, therefore;* used interrogatively, Jn 18:37* [3766]

[4036] οὖν *oun* 499x *then, now then,* Mt 13:18; Jn 19:29; *then, thereupon,* Lk 15:28; Jn 6:14; *therefore, consequently,* Mt 5:48; Mk 10:9; it also serves to mark the resumption of discourse after an interruption by a parenthesis, 1 Co 8:4. Sometimes it is not translated. [3767]

[4037] οὔπω *oupō* 26x *not yet,* Mt 15:17; 16:9; 24:6 Jn 2:4 [3768]

[4038] οὐρά *oura* 5x *a tail,* Rev 9:10, 19; 12:4* [3769]

[4039] οὐράνιος *ouranios* 9x *heavenly, celestial,* Mt 6:14, 26, 32; 15:13 [3770]

[4040] οὐρανόθεν *ouranothen* 2x *from heaven,* Ac 14:17; 26:13* [3771]

[4041] οὐρανός *ouranos* 273x *heaven, the heavens, the visible heavens and all their phenomena,* Mt 5:18; 16:1; 24:29, et al. freq.; *the air, atmosphere,* in which the clouds and tempests gather, the birds fly, etc., Mt 6:26; 16:2, 3; *heaven* as the peculiar seat and abode of God, of angels, of glorified spirits, etc., Mt 5:34, 45, 48; 6:1, 9, 10; 12:50; Jn 3:13, 31; 6:32, 38, 41, 42, 50, 51, 58; in N.T. *heaven* as a term expressive of the Divine Being, His administration, etc., Mt 19:14; 21:25; Lk 20:4, 5; Jn 3:27 [3772]

[4042] Οὐρβανός *ourbanos* 1x *Urbanus, Urban*, pr. name, Ro 16:9★ [3773]

[4043] Οὐρίας *ourias* 1x *Urias, Uriah*, pr. name (2 Sam 11; 12:24), Mt 1:6★ [3774]

[4044] οὖς *ous* 36x *the ear*, Mt 10:27; Mk 7:33; Lk 22:50; Ac 7:57 [3775]

[4045] οὐσία *ousia* 2x *substance, property, goods, fortune*, Lk 15:12, 13★ [3776]

[4046] οὔτε *oute* 87x *neither, nor*, Lk 20:36; οὔτε ... οὔτε, ορ οὔτε ... οὔτε, *neither ... nor*, Lk 20:35; Gal 1:12; in N.T. also used singly in the sense of οὐδέ, *not even*, Mk 5:3; Lk 12:26; 1 Co 3:2 [3777]

[4047] οὗτος *houtos* 1,387x *this, this* person or thing, Mt 3:3, 9, 17; 8:9; 10:2; 24:34, et al. freq.; used by way of contempt, *this fellow*, Mt 13:55; 27:47; αὐτὸ τοῦτο, *this very thing, this same thing*, 2 Co 2:3; 7:11; εἰς αὐτὸ τοῦτο, and elliptically, αὐτὸ τοῦτο, *for this same purpose, on this account*, Eph 6:18, 22; 2 Pe 1:5; καὶ οὗτος, *and moreover*, Lk 7:12; 16:1; 20:30; καὶ τοῦτο, *and that too*, 1 Co 6:6, 8; τοῦτο μὲν ... τοῦτο δέ, *partly ... partly*, Heb 10:33 [3778, 5023, 5025, 5026, 5123, 5124, 5125, 5126, 5127, 5128, 5129, 5130]

[4048] οὕτως *houtōs* 208x *thus, in this way*, Mt 1:18; 2:5; 5:16; et al. freq.; ὃς μὲν οὕτως, ὃς δὲ οὕτως, *one so, and another so, one in one way, and another in another*, 1 Co 7:7; *so*, Mt 7:12; 12:40; 24:27, 37, et al. freq.; *thus, under such circumstances*, Ac 20:11; *in such a condition*, viz., one previously mentioned, Ac 27:17; 1 Co 7:26, 40; and, perhaps, Jn 4:6; *in an ordinary way, at ease*, like Latin *sic*, perhaps, Jn 4:6 [3779]

[4049] οὐχί *ouchi* 54x *a strengthened form of* οὐ, *not*, Jn 13:10, 11; when followed by ἀλλά, *nay, not so, by no means*, Lk 1:60; 12:51; used also in negative interrogations, Mt 5:46, 47; 6:25 [3780]

[4050] ὀφειλέτης *opheiletēs* 7x *a debtor, one who owes*, Mt 18:24; met. *one who is in any way bound*, or *under obligation* to perform any duty, Ro 1:14; 8:12; 15:27; Gal 5:3; in N.T. *one who fails in duty, a delinquent, offender*, Mt 6:12; *a sinner*, Lk 13:4, cf. v. 2★ [3781]

[4051] ὀφειλή *opheilē* 3x *a debt*, Mt 18:32; met. *a duty, due*, Ro 13:7; 1 Co 7:3★ [3782]

[4052] ὀφείλημα *opheilēma* 2x *a debt; a due*, Ro 4:4, in N.T. *a delinquency, offence, fault, sin*, Mt 6:12, cf. v. 14★ [3783]

[4053] ὀφείλω *opheilō* 35x *to owe, be indebted*, Mt 18:28, 30, 34; *to incur a bond, to be bound to make discharge*, Mt 23:16, 18; *to be bound* or *obliged* by what is due or fitting or consequently necessary, Lk 17:10; Jn 13:14; *to incur desert, to deserve*, Jn 19:7; *to be due* or *fitting*, 1 Co 7:3, 36; from the Aramaic, *to be delinquent*, Lk 11:4 [3784]

[4054] ὄφελον *ophelon* 4x originally a ptcp (aor act ptcp nom sg neut) from ὀφείλω, used in N.T. as an interj. to introduce a wish that cannot be attained, *O that! Would that!* 1 Co 4:8; 2 Co 11:1; Gal 5:12; Rev 3:15★ [3785]

[4055] ὄφελος *ophelos* 3x *profit, benefit, advantage*, 1 Co 15:32; Jas 2:14, 16★ [3786]

[4056] ὀφθαλμοδουλία *ophthalmodoulia* 2x also written ὀφθαλμοδουλεία, *eye-service, service rendered only while under inspection*, Eph 6:6; Col 3:22★ [3787]

[4057] ὀφθαλμός *ophthalmos* 100x *an eye*, Mt 5:29, 38; 6:23; 7:3, 4, 5; ὀφθαλμὸς πονηρός, *an evil eye, an envious eye, envy*, Mt 20:15; Mk 7:22; met. *the intellectual eye*, Mt 13:15; Mk 8:18; Jn 12:40; Ac 26:18 [3788]

[4058] ὄφις *ophis* 14x *a serpent*, Mt 7:10; 10:16; *an artificial serpent*, Jn 3:14; used of *the devil* or *Satan*, Rev 12:9, 14, 15; 20:2; met. *a man of serpentine character*, Mt 23:33 [3789]

[4059] ὀφρῦς *ophrys* 1x *a brow, eyebrow; the brow* of a mountain, *edge* of a precipice, Lk 4:29★ [3790]

[4061] ὀχλέω *ochleō* 1x pr. *to mob; to disturb, trouble*, Ac 5:16★ [3791]

[4062] ὀχλοποιέω *ochlopoieō* 1x *to collect a mob, create a tumult*, Ac 17:5★ [3792]

[4063] ὄχλος *ochlos* 175x *a crowd, a confused multitude of people*, Mt 4:25; 5:1; 7:28; spc. *the common people*, Jn 7:49; *a multitude, great number*, Lk 5:29; 6:17; Ac 1:15; by impl. *tumult, uproar*, Lk 22:6; Ac 24:18 [3793]

[4065] ὀχύρωμα *ochurōma* 1x *a stronghold*; met. *an* opposing *bulwark* of error or vice, 2 Co 10:4★ [3794]

[4066] ὀψάριον *opsarion* 5x *a little fish*, Jn 6:9, 11; 21:9, 10, 13★ [3795]

[4067] ὀψέ *opse* 3x can function as an improper prep., *late;* put for *the first watch, at evening*, Mk 11:19; 13:35; ὀψὲ σαββάτων, *after the close of the Sabbath*, Mt 28:1 [3796]

[4068] ὀψία *opsia* 15x see ὄψιος [3798]

[4069] ὄψιμος *opsimos* 1x *late; latter*, Jas 5:7; poetic and later prose for ὄψιος★ [3797]

[4071] ὄψις *opsis* 3x *a sight; the face, countenance*, Jn 11:44; Rev 1:16; *external appearance*, Jn 7:24★ [3799]

[4072] ὀψώνιον *opsōnion* 4x *provisions; a stipend* or *pay* of soldiers, Lk 3:14; 1 Co 9:7; *wages* of any kind, 2 Co 11:8; *due wages*, a stated *recompense*, Ro 6:23★ [3800]

[4074] παγιδεύω *pagideuō* 1x *to ensnare, entrap, entangle*, Mt 22:15★ [3802]

[4075] παγίς *pagis* 5x *a snare, trap*, Lk 21:35; met. *stratagem, device, wile*, 1 Ti 3:7; 6:9; 2 Ti 2:26; met. *a trap* of ruin, Ro 11:9★ [3803]

[4076] πάγος *pagos* 2x *a hill*, Ἄρειος πάγος, *Areopagus, the hill of Mars*, at Athens, Ac 17:19, 22 [697]

[4077] πάθημα *pathēma* 16x *what is suffered; suffering, affliction*, Ro 8:18; 2 Co 1:5, 6, 7; Phil 3:10; *emotion, passion*, Ro 7:5; Gal 5:24 [3804]

[4078] παθητός *pathētos* 1x *passible, capable of suffering, liable to suffer;* in N.T. *destined to suffer*, Ac 26:23★ [3805]

[4079] πάθος *pathos* 3x *suffering; an affection, passion*, especially sexual, Ro 1:26 [3806]

[4080] παιδαγωγός *paidagōgos* 3x *a pedagogue, childtender*, a person, usually a slave or freedman, to whom the care of the boys of a family was committed, whose duty it was to attend them at their play, lead them to and from the public school, and exercise a constant superintendence over their conduct and safety; in N.T. an ordinary *director* or *minister* contrasted with an Apostle, as a pedagogue occupies an inferior position to a parent, 1 Co 4:15; a term applied to the Mosaic law, as dealing with men as in a state of mere childhood and tutelage, Gal 3:24, 25★ [3807]

[4081] παιδάριον *paidarion* 1x *a little boy, child; a boy, lad*, Jn 6:9★ [3808]

[4082] παιδεία *paideia* 6x *education, training up, nurture* of children, Eph 6:4; *instruction, discipline,* 2 Ti 3:16; in N.T. *correction, chastisement,* Heb 12:5, 7, 8, 11* [3809]

[4083] παιδευτής *paideutēs* 2x *a preceptor, instructor, teacher,* pr. of boys; gener. Ro 2:20; in N.T. *a chastiser,* Heb 12:9* [3810]

[4084] παιδεύω *paideuō* 13x *to educate, instruct* children, Ac 7:22; 22:3; genr. παιδεύομαι, *to be taught, learn,* 1 Ti 1:20; *to admonish, instruct by admonition,* 2 Ti 2:25; Tit 2:12; in N.T. *to chastise, chasten,* 1 Co 11:32; 2 Co 6:9; Heb 12:6, 7, 10; Rev 3:19; of criminals, *to scourge,* Lk 23:16, 22* [3811]

[4085] παιδιόθεν *paidiothen* 1x *from childhood, from a child,* Mk 9:21* [3812]

[4086] παιδίον *paidion* 52x *an infant, babe,* Mt 2:8; but usually in N.T. as equiv. to παῖς, Mt 14:21; Mk 7:28, et al. freq.; pl. voc. used by way of endearment, *my dear children,* 1 Jn 2:18; also as a term of familiar address, *children, my lads,* Jn 21:5 [3813]

[4087] παιδίσκη *paidiskē* 13x *a girl, damsel, maiden; a female slave* or *servant,* Mt 26:69; Mk 14:66, 69 [3814]

[4089] παίζω *paizō* 1x *to play in the manner of children; to sport, to practise the festive gestures* of idolatrous worship, 1 Co 10:7* [3815]

[4090] παῖς *pais* 24x *a child* in relation to parents, of either sex, Jn 4:51; *a child* in respect of age, either male or female, and of all ages from infancy up to manhood, *a boy, youth, girl, maiden,* Mt 2:16; 17:18; Lk 2:43; 8:54; *a servant, slave,* Mt 8:6, 8, 13, cf. v. 9; Lk 7:7, cf. v. 3, 10; *an attendant, minister,* Mt 14:2; Lk 1:69; Ac 4:25; also, Lk 1:54; or, perhaps, *a child* in respect of fatherly regard [3816]

[4091] παίω *paiō* 5x *to strike, smite,* with the fist, Mt 26:68; Lk 22:64; with a sword, Mk 14:47; Jn 18:10; *to strike* as a scorpion, *to sting,* Rev 9:5* [3817]

[4093] πάλαι *palai* 6x *of old, long ago,* Mt 11:21; Lk 10:13; Heb 1:1; Jude 4; οἱ πάλαι, *old, former,* 2 Pe 1:9; *some time since, already,* Mk 15:44 [3819]

[4094] παλαιός *palaios* 19x *old, not new* or *recent,* Mt 9:16, 17; 13:52; Lk 5:36 [3820]

[4095] παλαιότης *palaiotēs* 1x *oldness, obsoleteness,* Ro 7:6* [3821]

[4096] παλαιόω *palaioō* 4x *to make old;* pass. *to grow old, to become worn,* Lk 12:33; Heb 1:11; met. *to treat as antiquated, to abrogate, supersede,* Heb 8:13* [3822]

[4097] πάλη *palē* 1x *wrestling; struggle, contest,* Eph 6:12* [3823]

[4098] παλιγγενεσία *palingenesia* 2x *a new birth; regeneration, renovation,* Mt 19:28; Tit 3:5. See unpublished Ph.D. dissertation, William D. Mounce, *The Origin of the New Testament Metaphor of Rebirth,* University of Aberdeen, Scotland* [3824]

[4099] πάλιν *palin* 141x pr. *back; again, back again,* Jn 10:17; Ac 10:16; 11:10; *again* by repetition, Mt 26:43; *again* in continuation, *further,* Mt 5:33; 13:44, 45, 47, 18:19; *again, on the other hand,* 1 Jn 2:8 [3825]

[4101] παμπληθεί *pamplēthei* 1x *the whole multitude together, all at once,* Lk 23:18* [3826]

[4103] Παμφυλία *Pamphylia* 5x *Pamphylia,* a country of Asia Minor, Ac 2:10; 13:13; 14:24; 15:38; 27:5* [3828]

[4106] πανδοχεῖον *pandocheion* 1x *a public inn, place where travelers may lodge,* called in the East by the name of *menzil, khan, caravanserai,* Lk 10:34* [3829]

[4107] πανδοχεύς *pandocheus* 1x *the keeper of a public inn* or *caravanserai, a host,* Lk 10:35* [3830]

[4108] πανήγυρις *panēgyris* 1x pr. *an assembly of an entire people; a solemn gathering at a festival; a festive convocation,* Heb 12:22* [3831]

[4109] πανοικεί *panoikei* 1x also spelled πανοικί, *with one's whole household* or *family,* Ac 16:34* [3832]

[4110] πανοπλία *panoplia* 3x *panoply, complete armor, a complete suit of armor,* both offensive and defensive, as the shield, sword, spear, helmet, breastplate, etc., Lk 11:22; Eph 6:11, 13* [3833]

[4111] πανουργία *panourgia* 5x *knavery, craft, cunning,* Lk 20:23; 1 Co 3:19 [3834]

[4112] πανοῦργος *panourgos* 1x pr. *ready to do anything;* hence, *crafty, cunning, artful, wily,* 2 Co 12:16* [3835]

[4114] πανταχῆ *pantachē* 1x *everywhere,* Ac 21:28* [3837]

[4116] πανταχοῦ *pantachou* 7x *in all places, everywhere,* Mk 16:20; Lk 9:6 [3837]

[4117] παντελής *pantelēs* 2x *perfect, complete;* εἰς τὸ παντελές, adverbially, *throughout, through all time, ever,* Heb 7:25; with a negative, *at all,* Lk 13:11* [3838]

[4118] πάντη *pantē* 1x *everywhere; in every way, in every instance,* Ac 24:3* [3839]

[4119] πάντοθεν *pantothen* 3x *from every place, from all parts, on all sides, on every side, round about,* Mk 1:45; Lk 19:43; Heb 9:4* [3840]

[4120] παντοκράτωρ *pantokratōr* 10x *almighty, omnipotent,* 2 Co 6:18; Rev 1:8; 4:8 [3841]

[4121] πάντοτε *pantote* 41x *always, at all times, ever,* Mt 26:11; Mk 14:7; Lk 15:31; 18:1 [3842]

[4122] πάντως *pantōs* 8x *wholly, altogether; at any rate, by all means,* 1 Co 9:22; by impl. *surely, assuredly, certainly,* Lk 4:23; Ac 21:22; 28:4; 1 Co 9:10; οὐ πάντως, *in nowise, not in the least,* Ro 3:9; 1 Co 5:10; 16:12* [3843]

[4123] παρά *para* 194x (1) gen., *from,* indicating source or origin, Mt 2:4, 7; Mk 8:11; Lk 2:1; οἱ παρ' αὐτοῦ, *his relatives* or *kinsmen,* Mk 3:21; τὰ παρ' αὐτῆς πάντα, *all her substance, property,* etc., Mk 5:26. (2) dat., *with, in, among,* etc., Mt 6:1; 19:26; 21:25; 22:25; παρ' ἑαυτῷ, *at home,* 1 Co 16:2; *in the sight of, in the judgment* or *estimation of,* 1 Co 3:19; 2 Pe 2:11; 3:8. (3) acc., motion, *by, near to, along,* Mt 4:18; motion, *towards, to, at,* Mt 15:30; Mk 2:13; motion terminating in rest, *at, by, near, by the side of,* Mk 4:1, 4; Lk 5:1; 8:5; *in deviation from, in violation of, inconsistently with,* Ac 18:13; Ro 1:26; 11:24; *above, more than,* Lk 13:2, 4; Ro 1:25. (4) Misc., after comparatives, Lk 3:13; 1 Co 3:11; *except, save,* 2 Co 11:24; *beyond, past,* Heb 11:11; *in respect of, on the score of,* 1 Co 12:15, 16 [3844]

[4124] παραβαίνω *parabainō* 3x pr. *to step by the side of; to deviate;* met. *to transgress, violate,* Mt 15:2, 3; *to incur forfeiture,* Ac 1:25* [3845]

[4125] παραβάλλω *paraballō* 1x *to cast* or *throw by the side of;* absol., a nautical term, *to bring-to, land,* Ac 20:15* [3846]

[4126] παράβασις *parabasis* 7x *a stepping by the side, deviation; a transgression, violation of law,* Ro 2:23; 4:15 [3847]

[4127] παραβάτης *parabatēs* 5x *transgressor, violator of law,* Ro 2:25, 27; Gal 2:18; Jas 2:9, 11* [3848]

[4128] παραβιάζομαι *parabiazomai* 2x *to force; to constrain press* with urgent entreaties, Lk 24:29; Ac 16:15★ [3849]

[4129] παραβολεύομαι *paraboleuomai* 1x also spelled παραβουλεύομαι, *to stake* or *risk one's self*, Phil 2:30★ [3851]

[4130] παραβολή *parabole* 50x *a placing one thing by the side of another; a comparing; a parallel case cited in illustration; a comparison, simile, similitude,* Mk 4:30; Heb 11:19; *a parable,* a short relation under which something else is figured, or in which that which is fictitious is employed to represent that which is real, Mt 13:3, 10, 13, 18, 24, 31, 33, 34, 36, 53; 21:33, 45; 22:1; 24:32; in N.T. *a type, pattern, emblem,* Heb 9:9; *a sentiment, grave and significant precept, maxim,* Lk 14:7; *an obscure and enigmatical saying,* anything expressed in remote and ambiguous terms, Mt 13:35; Mk 7:17; *a proverb, adage,* Lk 4:23 [3850]

[4132] παραγγελία *parangelia* 5x *a command, order, charge,* Ac 5:28; 16:24; *direction, precept,* 1 Th 4:2; 1 Ti 1:5, 18★ [3852]

[4133] παραγγέλλω *parangello* 32x *to announce, notify; to command, direct, charge,* Mt 10:5; Mk 6:8, 8:6; Lk 9:21; *to charge, entreat solemnly,* 1 Ti 6:13 [3853]

[4134] παραγίνομαι *paraginomai* 37x pluperfect, παραγεγόνει (3 sg), *to be by the side of; to come, approach, arrive,* Mt 2:1; 3:13; Mk 14:43; Lk 7:4; seq. ἐπί, *to come upon* in order to seize, Lk 22:52; *to come forth in public, make appearance,* Mt 3:1; Heb 9:11 [3854]

[4135] παράγω *parago* 10x *to lead beside;* intrans. *to pass along* or *by,* Mt 20:30; Jn 9:1; *to pass on,* Mt 9:9, 27; intrans. and mid. *to pass away, be in a state of transition,* 1 Co 7:31; 1 Jn 2:8, 17 [3855]

[4136] παραδειγματίζω *paradeigmatizo* 1x *to make an example of; to expose to ignominy and shame,* Heb 6:6★ [3856]

[4137] παράδεισος *paradeisos* 3x *a park, a forest where wild beasts were kept for hunting; a pleasure-park, a garden of trees of various kinds;* used in the LXX for *the Garden of Eden;* in N.T. the celestial *paradise,* Lk 23:43; 2 Co 12:4; Rev 2:7★ [3857]

[4138] παραδέχομαι *paradechomai* 6x *to accept, receive,* met. *to receive, admit, yield assent to,* Mk 4:20; Ac 15:4; 16:21; 22:18; 1 Ti 5:19; in N.T. *to receive* or *embrace with favor, approve, love,* Heb 12:6★ [3858]

[4140] παραδίδωμι *paradidomi* 119x pluperfect, παραδεδώκεισαν (3 pl), *to give over, hand over, deliver up,* Mt 4:12; 5:25; 10:4, 17; *to commit, intrust,* Mt 11:27; 25:14; *to commit, commend,* Ac 14:26; 15:40; *to yield up,* Jn 19:30; 1 Co 15:24; *to abandon,* Ac 7:42; Eph 4:19; *to stake, hazard,* Ac 15:26; *to deliver* as a matter of injunction, instruction, etc., Mk 7:13; Lk 1:2; Ac 6:14; absol. *to render a yield, to be matured, Mk 4:29* [3860]

[4141] παράδοξος *paradoxos* 1x *unexpected; strange, wonderful, astonishing,* Lk 5:26★ [3861]

[4142] παράδοσις *paradosis* 13x *delivery, handing over, transmission;* in N.T. *what is transmitted* in the way of teaching, precept, doctrine, 1 Co 11:2; 2 Th 2:15; 3:6; *tradition, traditionary law,* handed down from age to age, Mt 15:2, 3, 6 [3862]

[4143] παραζηλόω *parazeloo* 4x *to provoke to jealousy,* Ro 10:19; *to excite to emulation,* Ro 11:11, 14; *to provoke to indignation,* 1 Co 10:22★ [3863]

[4144] παραθαλάσσιος *parathalassios* 1x *by the sea-side, situated on the sea-coast, maritime,* Mt 4:13★ [3864]

[4145] παραθεωρέω *paratheoreo* 1x *to look at things placed side by side,* as in comparison, *to compare in thus looking, to regard less in comparison, overlook, neglect,* Ac 6:1★ [3865]

[4146] παραθήκη *paratheke* 3x *a deposit, a thing committed to one's charge, a trust,* 2 Ti 1:12; 1 Ti 6:20; 2 Ti 1:14★ [3866]

[4147] παραινέω *paraineo* 2x *to advise, exhort,* Ac 27:9, 22★ [3867]

[4148] παραιτέομαι *paraiteomai* 12x *to entreat; to beg off, excuse one's self,* Lk 14:18, 19; *to deprecate, entreat against,* Ac 25:11; Heb 12:19; *to decline receiving, refuse, reject,* 1 Ti 4:7; 5:11; Tit 3:10; Heb 12:25; *to decline, avoid, shun,* 2 Ti 2:23 [3868]

[4149] παρακαθέζομαι *parakathezomai* 1x *to sit down by,* Lk 10:39★ [3869]

[4151] παρακαλέω *parakaleo* 109x *to call for, invite to come, send for,* Ac 28:20; *to call upon, exhort, admonish, persuade,* Lk 3:18; Ac 2:40; 11:23; *to beg, beseech, entreat, implore,* Mt 8:5, 31; 18:29; Mk 1:40; *to animate, encourage, comfort, console,* Mt 2:18; 5:4; 2 Co 1:4, 6; pass. *to be cheered, comforted,* Lk 16:25; Ac 20:12; 2 Co 7:13 [3870]

[4152] παρακαλύπτω *parakalypto* 1x *to cover over, veil;* met. pass. *to be veiled* from comprehension, Lk 9:45★ [3871]

[4154] παράκειμαι *parakeimai* 2x *to lie near, be adjacent;* met. *to be at hand, be present,* Ro 7:18, 21★ [3873]

[4155] παράκλησις *paraklesis* 29x *a calling upon, exhortation, incitement, persuasion,* Ro 12:8; 1 Co 14:3; *hortatory instruction,* Ac 13:15; 15:31; *entreaty, importunity, earnest supplication,* 2 Co 8:4; *solace, consolation,* Lk 2:25; Ro 15:4, 5; 2 Co 1:3, 4, 5, 6, 7; *cheering and supporting influence,* Ac 9:31; *joy, gladness, rejoicing,* 2 Co 7:13; *cheer, joy, enjoyment,* Lk 6:24 [3874]

[4156] παράκλητος *parakletos* 5x *one called* or *sent for to assist another; an advocate, one who pleads the cause of another,* 1 Jn 2:1; genr. *one present to render various beneficial service,* and thus *the Paraclete,* whose influence and operation were to compensate for the departure of Christ himself, Jn 14:16, 26; 15:26; 16:7★ [3875]

[4157] παρακοή *parakoe* 3x *an erroneous* or *imperfect hearing; disobedience,* Ro 5:19; *a deviation from obedience,* 2 Co 10:6; Heb 2:2★ [3876]

[4158] παρακολουθέω *parakoloutheo* 3x *to follow* or *accompany closely; to accompany, attend, characterize,* Mk 16:17; *to follow* with the thoughts, *trace,* Lk 1:3; *to conform to,* 1 Ti 4:6; 2 Ti 3:10★ [3877]

[4159] παρακούω *parakouo* 3x *to overhear,* Mk 5:36; *to hear amiss, to fail to listen, neglect to obey, disregard,* Mt 18:17 (2t)★ [3878]

[4160] παρακύπτω *parakypto* 5x *to stoop beside; to stoop down* in order to take a view, Lk 24:12; Jn 20:5, 11; *to bestow a close and attentive look, to look intently, to penetrate,* Jas 1:25; 1 Pe 1:12★ [3879]

[4161] παραλαμβάνω *paralambano* 49x pr. *to take to one's side; to take, receive to one's self,* Mt 1:20; Jn 14:3; *to take* with one's self, Mt 2:13, 14, 20, 21; 4:5, 8; *to receive* in charge or possession, Col 4:17; Heb 12:28; *to receive* as a matter of instruction, Mk 7:4; 1 Co 11:23; 15:3; *to receive, admit, acknowledge,* Jn 1:11; 1 Co 15:1; Col 2:6; pass. *to be carried off,* Mt 24:40, 41; Lk 17:34, 35, 36 [3880]

[4162] παραλέγομαι *paralegomai* 2x *to gather* a course *along; to sail by, coast along,* Ac 27:8, 13★ [3881]

[4163] παράλιος *paralios* 1x *adjacent to the sea, maritime;* ἡ παράλιος, sc. χώρα, *the sea-coast,* Lk 6:17★ [3882]

[4164] παραλλαγή *parallagē* 1x *a shifting, mutation, change,* Jas 1:17★ [3883]

[4165] παραλογίζομαι *paralogizomai* 2x *to misreckon, make a false reckoning; to impose upon, deceive, delude, circumvent,* Col 2:4; Jas 1:22★ [3884]

[4166] παραλυτικός *paralytikos* 10x *lame, palsied,* used only as a noun in N.T., *paralytic,* Mt 4:24; 8:6; 9:2, 6 [3885]

[4168] παραλύω *paralyō* 5x *to unloose from proper fixity* or *consistency of substance; to enervate* or *paralyze* the body or limbs; pass. *to be enervated* or *enfeebled,* Heb 12:12; pass. perf. part. παραλελυμένος, *paralytic,* Lk 5:18, 24 [3886]

[4169] παραμένω *paramenō* 4x *to stay beside; to continue, stay, abide,* 1 Co 16:6; Heb 7:23; met. *to remain constant in, persevere in,* Phil 1:25; Jas 1:25★ [3887]

[4170] παραμυθέομαι *paramytheomai* 4x *to exercise a gentle influence by words; to soothe, comfort, console,* Jn 11:19, 31; 1 Th 5:14; *to cheer, exhort,* 1 Th 2:12★ [3888]

[4171] παραμυθία *paramythia* 1x *comfort, encouragement,* 1 Co 14:3★ [3889]

[4172] παραμύθιον *paramythion* 1x *gentle cheering, encouragement,* Phil 2:1★ [3890]

[4174] παρανομέω *paranomeō* 1x *to violate* or *transgress the law,* Ac 23:3★ [3891]

[4175] παρανομία *paranomia* 1x *violation of the law, transgression,* 2 Pe 2:16★ [3892]

[4176] παραπικραίνω *parapikrainō* 1x pr. *to incite to bitter feelings; to provoke;* absol. *to act provokingly, be rebellious,* Heb 3:16★ [3893]

[4177] παραπικρασμός *parapikrasmos* 2x *exasperation, provocation; rebellion,* Heb 3:8, 15★ [3894]

[4178] παραπίπτω *parapiptō* 1x pr. *to fall by the side of;* met. *to fall off* or *away from, make defection from,* Heb 6:6★ [3895]

[4179] παραπλέω *parapleō* 1x *to sail by* or *past* a place, Ac 20:16★ [3896]

[4180] παραπλήσιος *paraplēsios* 1x pr. *near alongside;* met. *like, similar;* neut. παραπλήσιον, adverbially, *near to, nearly, with a near approach to,* Phil 2:27★ [3897]

[4181] παραπλησίως *paraplēsiōs* 1x *like, in the same* or *like manner,* Heb 2:14★ [3898]

[4182] παραπορεύομαι *paraporeuomai* 5x *to pass by the side of; to pass along,* Mt 27:39; Mk 2:23; 9:30; 11:20; 15:29★ [3899]

[4183] παράπτωμα *paraptōma* 19x pr. *a stumbling aside, a false step;* in N.T. *a trespass, fault, offence, transgression,* Mt 6:14, 15; Mk 11:25, 26; Ro 4:25; *a fall* in faith, Ro 11:11, 12 [3900]

[4184] παραρρέω *pararreō* 1x *to flow beside; to glide aside from; to fall off* from profession, *decline* from steadfastness, *make forfeit* of faith, Heb 2:1★ [3901]

[4185] παράσημος *parasēmos* 1x *a distinguishing mark; an ensign* of a ship, Ac 28:11★ [3902]

[4186] παρασκευάζω *paraskeuazō* 4x *to prepare, make ready,* 2 Co 9:2, 3; mid. *to prepare one's self, put one's self in readiness,* Ac 10:10; 1 Co 14:8★ [3903]

[4187] παρασκευή *paraskeuē* 6x *a getting ready, preparation,* in N.T. *preparation* for a feast, *day of preparation,* Mt 27:62; Mk 15:42 [3904]

[4189] παρατείνω *parateinō* 1x *to extend, stretch out; to prolong, continue,* Ac 20:7★ [3905]

[4190] παρατηρέω *paratēreō* 6x *to watch narrowly,* Ac 9:24; *to observe* or *watch insidiously,* Mk 3:2; Lk 6:7; 14:1; 20:20; *to observe scrupulously,* Gal 4:10★ [3906]

[4191] παρατήρησις *paratērēsis* 1x *careful watching, intent observation,* Lk 17:20★ [3907]

[4192] παρατίθημι *paratithēmi* 19x *to place by the side of,* or *near; to set before,* Mk 6:41; 8:6, 7; Lk 9:16; met. *to set* or *lay before, propound,* Mt 13:24, 31; *to inculcate,* Ac 17:3; *to deposit, commit to the charge of, entrust,* Lk 12:48; 23:46; *to commend,* Ac 14:23 [3908]

[4193] παρατυγχάνω *paratynchanō* 1x *to happen, to chance upon, chance to meet,* Ac 17:17★ [3909]

[4194] παραυτίκα *parautika* 1x *instantly, immediately;* ὁ, ἡ, τό, παραυτίκα, *momentary, transient,* 2 Co 4:17★ [3910]

[4195] παραφέρω *parapherō* 4x *to carry past; to cause to pass away,* Mk 14:36; Lk 22:42; pass. *to be swept along,* Jude 12; *to be led away, misled, seduced,* Heb 13:9★ [3911]

[4196] παραφρονέω *paraphroneō* 1x *to be beside one's wits;* παραφρονῶν, *in foolish style,* 2 Co 11:23★ [3912]

[4197] παραφρονία *paraphronia* 1x *madness, folly,* 2 Pe 2:16★ [3913]

[4199] παραχειμάζω *paracheimazō* 4x *to winter, spend the winter,* Ac 27:12; 28:11; 1 Co 16:6; Tit 3:12★ [3914]

[4200] παραχειμασία *paracheimasia* 1x *a wintering* in a place, Ac 27:12★ [3915]

[4202] παραχρῆμα *parachrēma* 18x *at once, immediately,* Mt 21:19, 20; Lk 1:64 [3916]

[4203] πάρδαλις *pardalis* 1x *a leopard* or *panther,* Rev 13:2★ [3917]

[4204] παρεδρεύω *paredreuō* 1x *to sit near; to attend, serve,* 1 Co 9:13★ [4332]

[4205] πάρειμι *pareimi* 24x *to be beside; to be present,* Lk 13:1; *to have come,* Mt 26:50; Jn 7:6; 11:28; Col 1:6; *to be in possession,* Heb 13:5; 2 Pe 1:9, 12; part. παρών, οὖσα, όν, *present,* 1 Co 5:3; τὸ παρόν, *the present time, the present,* Heb 12:11 [3918]

[4206] παρεισάγω *pareisagō* 1x *to introduce stealthily,* 2 Pe 2:1★ [3919]

[4207] παρείσακτος *pareisaktos* 1x *secretly introduced, brought in stealthily,* Gal 2:4★ [3920]

[4209] παρεισέρχομαι *pareiserchomai* 2x *to supervene,* Ro 5:20; *to steal in,* Gal 2:4★ [3922]

[4210] παρεισφέρω *pareispherō* 1x *to bring in beside; to bring into play, exhibit in addition,* 2 Pe 1:5★ [3923]

[4211] παρεκτός *parektos* 3x can function as an improper prep., *without, on the outside; except,* Mt 5:32; Ac 26:29; τὰ παρεκτός, *other matters,* 2 Co 11:28 [3924]

[4212] παρεμβάλλω *paremballō* 1x *to cast up, set up, throw up* a palisade, Lk 19:43★ [4016]

[4213] παρεμβολή *parembolē* 10x *an insertion besides;* later, *a marshalling* of an army; *an array* of battle, *army,* Heb 11:34; *a camp,* Heb 13:11, 13; Rev 20:9; *a standing camp, fortress, citadel, castle,* Ac 21:34, 37; 22:24; 23:10, 16, 32★ [3925]

[4214] παρενοχλέω *parenochleō* 1x *to trouble, harass,* Ac 15:19★ [3926]

[4215] παρεπίδημος *parepidēmos* 3x *residing in a country not one's own, a sojourner, stranger,* Heb 11:13; 1 Pe 1:1; 2:11★ [3927]

[4216] παρέρχομαι *parerchomai* 29x *to pass beside, pass along, pass by,* Mt 8:28; Mk 6:48; *to pass, elapse,* as time, Mt 14:15; Ac 27:19; *to pass away, be removed,*

Mt 26:39, 42; Mk 14:35; met. *to pass away, disappear, vanish, perish,* Mt 5:18; 24:34, 35; *to become vain, be rendered void,* Mt 5:18; Mk 13:31; trans. *to pass by, disregard, neglect,* Lk 11:42; 15:29; *to come to the side of, come to,* Lk 12:37; 17:7 [3928]

[4217] παρεσις *paresis* 1x *a letting pass; a passing over,* Ro 3:25* [3929]

[4218] παρέχω *parechō* 16x *to hold beside; to hold out to, offer, present,* Lk 6:29; *to confer, render,* Lk 7:4; Ac 22:2; 28:2; Col 4:1; *to afford, furnish,* Ac 16:16; 17:31; 19:24; 1 Ti 6:17; *to exhibit,* Tit 2:7; *to be the cause of, occasion,* Mt 26:10; Mk 14:6; Lk 11:7 [3930]

[4219] παρηγορία *parēgoria* 1x *exhortation; comfort, solace, consolation,* Col 4:11* [3931]

[4220] παρθενία *parthenia* 1x *virginity,* Lk 2:36* [3932]

[4221] παρθένος *parthenos* 15x *a virgin, maid,* Mt 1:23; 25:1, 7, 11; Ac 21:9; in N.T. also masc., *chaste,* Rev 14:4 [3933]

[4222] Πάρθοι *Parthoi* 1x *a Parthian, a native of Parthia, in central Asia,* Ac 2:9 [3934]

[4223] παρίημι *pariēmi* 2x *to let pass beside, let fall beside; to relax,* Lk 11:42; perf. pass. part. παρειμένος, *hanging down helplessly, unstrung, feeble,* Heb 12:12* [3935]

[4225] παρίστημι *paristēmi* 41x pluperfect, παρειστήκειν, also formed as παριστάνω, trans. *to place beside; to have in readiness, provide,* Ac 23:24; *to range beside, to place at the disposal of,* Mt 26:53; Ac 9:41; *to present to God, dedicate, consecrate, devote,* Lk 2:22; Ro 6:13, 19; *to prove, demonstrate, show,* Ac 1:3; 24:13; *to commend, recommend,* 1 Co 8:8; intrans. perf. παρέστηκα, part. παρεστώς, pluperf. παρειστήκειν, 2 aor. παρέστην, and mid., *to stand by* or *before,* Ac 27:24; Ro 14:10; *to stand by, to be present,* Mk 14:47, 69, 70; *to stand in attendance, attend,* Lk 1:19; 1:24; of time, *to be present, have come,* Mk 4:29; *to stand by* in aid, *assist, support,* Ro 16:2 [3936]

[4226] Παρμενᾶς *Parmenas* 1x *Parmenas,* pr. name, Ac 6:5* [3937]

[4227] πάροδος *parodos* 1x *a way by; a passing by;* ἐν παρόδῳ, *in passing, by the way,* 1 Co 16:7* [3938]

[4228] παροικέω *paroikeō* 2x *to dwell beside;* later, *to reside in a place as a stranger, sojourn, be a stranger* or *sojourner,* Lk 24:18; Heb 11:9* [3939]

[4229] παροικία *paroikia* 2x *a sojourning, temporary residence in a foreign land,* Ac 13:17; 1 Pe 1:17* [3940]

[4230] πάροικος *paroikos* 4x *a neighbor;* later, *a sojourner, temporary resident, stranger,* Ac 7:6, 29; Eph 2:19; 1 Pe 2:11* [3941]

[4231] παροιμία *paroimia* 5x *a byword, proverb, adage,* 2 Pe 2:22; in N.T. *an obscure saying, enigma,* Jn 16:25, 29; *a parable, similitude, figurative discourse,* Jn 10:6* [3942]

[4232] πάροινος *paroinos* 2x pr. *pertaining to wine, drunken;* hence, *quarrelsome, insolent, overbearing,* 1 Ti 3:3; Tit 1:7* [3943]

[4233] παροίχομαι *paroichomai* 1x *to have gone by;* perf. part. παρῳχημένος, *bygone,* Ac 14:16* [3944]

[4234] παρομοιάζω *paromoiazō* 1x *to be like, to resemble,* Mt 23:27* [3945]

[4235] παρόμοιος *paromoios* 1x *nearly resembling, similar, like,* Mk 7:13* [3946]

[4236] παροξύνω *paroxynō* 2x *to sharpen;* met. *to incite, stir up,* Ac 17:16; *to irritate, provoke,* 1 Co 13:5* [3947]

[4237] παροξυσμός *paroxysmos* 2x *an inciting, incitement,* Heb 10:24; *a sharp fit of anger, sharp contention, angry dispute,* Ac 15:39* [3948]

[4239] παροργίζω *parorgizō* 2x *to provoke to anger, irritate, exasperate,* Ro 10:19; Eph 6:4* [3949]

[4240] παροργισμός *parorgismos* 1x *provocation to anger; anger excited, indignation, wrath,* Eph 4:26* [3950]

[4241] παροτρύνω *parotrynō* 1x *to stir up, incite, instigate,* Ac 13:50* [3951]

[4242] παρουσία *parousia* 24x *presence,* 2 Co 10:10; Phil 2:12; *a coming, arrival, advent,* Phil 1:26; Mt 24:3, 27, 37, 39; 1 Co 15:23 [3952]

[4243] παροψίς *paropsis* 1x pr. *a dainty side-dish;* meton. *a plate, platter,* Mt 23:25* [3953]

[4244] παρρησία *parrēsia* 31x *freedom in speaking, boldness of speech,* Ac 4:13; παρρησίᾳ, as an adv., *freely, boldly,* Jn 7:13, 26; so μετὰ παρρησίας, Ac 2:29; 4:29, 31; *license, authority,* Phlm 8; *confidence, assurance,* 2 Co 7:4; Eph 3:12; Heb 3:6; 10:19; *openness, frankness,* 2 Co 3:12; παρρησίᾳ, and ἐν παρρησίᾳ, adverbially, *openly, plainly, perspicuously, unambiguously,* Mk 8:32; Jn 10:24; *publicly, before all,* Jn 7:4 [3954]

[4245] παρρησιάζομαι *parrēsiazomai* 9x *to speak plainly, freely, boldly, and confidently,* Ac 13:46; 14:3 [3955]

[4246] πᾶς *pas* 1,243x *all;* in the sg. *the whole, entire,* usually when the substantive has the article, Mt 6:29; 8:32; Ac 19:26; *every,* only with an anarthrous subst., Mt 3:10; 4:4; pl. *all,* Mt 1:17, et al. freq.; πάντα, *in all respects,* Ac 20:35; 1 Co 9:25; 10:33; 11:2; by a Hebraism, a negative with πᾶς is sometimes equivalent to οὐδείς or μηδείς, Mt 24:22; Lk 1:37; Ac 10:14; Ro 3:20; 1 Co 1:29; Eph 4:29 [3956]

[4247] πάσχα *pascha* 29x *the passover, the paschal lamb,* Mt 26:17; Mk 14:12; met. used of Christ, the true *paschal lamb,* 1 Co 5:7; *the feast of the passover, the day on which the paschal lamb was slain and eaten,* the 14th of Nisan, Mt 26:18; Mk 14:1; Heb 11:28; more genr. *the whole paschal festival,* including the seven days of *the feast of unleavened bread,* Mt 26:2; Lk 2:41; Jn 2:13 [3957]

[4248] πάσχω *paschō* 42x *to be affected by* a thing, whether good or bad, *to suffer, endure* evil, Mt 16:21; 17:12, 15; 27:19; absol. *to suffer* death, Lk 22:15; 24:26 [3958]

[4249] Πάταρα *Patara* 1x *Patara,* a city on the sea-coast of Lycia, in Asia Minor, Ac 21:1* [3959]

[4250] πατάσσω *patassō* 10x *to strike, beat upon; to smite, wound,* Mt 26:51; Lk 22:49, 50; by impl. *to kill, slay,* Mt 26:31; Mk 14:27; Ac 7:24; *to strike gently,* Ac 12:7; from the Hebrew, *to smite with* disease, plagues, etc., Ac 12:23; Rev 11:6; 19:15* [3960]

[4251] πατέω *pateō* 5x intrans. *to tread,* Lk 10:19; trans. *to tread* the winepress, Rev 14:20; 19:15; *to trample,* Lk 21:24; Rev 11:2* [3961]

[4252] πατήρ *patēr* 413x *a father,* Mt 2:22; 4:21, 22; spc. used of God, as the *Father* of man by creation, preservation, etc., Mt 5:16, 45, 48; and peculiarly as the *Father* of our Lord Jesus Christ, Mt 7:21; 2 Co 1:3; *the founder of a race, remote progenitor, forefather, ancestor,* Mt 3:9; 23:30, 32; *an elder, senior, father* in age, 1 Jn 2:13, 14; *a spiritual father,* 1 Co 4:15; *father* by origination, Jn 8:44; Heb 12:9; used as an appellation of honor, Mt 23:9; Ac 7:2 [3962]

[4253] Πάτμος *Patmos* 1x *Patmos,* an island in the Aegean sea, Rev 1:9* [3963]

[4255] πατριά *patria* 3x *descent, lineage; a family, tribe, race,* Lk 2:4; Ac 3:25; Eph 3:15* [3965]

[4256] πατριάρχης *patriarchēs* 4x *a patriarch, head* or *founder of a family,* Ac 2:29; 7:8, 9; Heb 7:4* [3966]

[4257] πατρικός *patrikos* 1x *from fathers* or *ancestors, ancestral, paternal,* Gal 1:14* [3967]

[4258] πατρίς *patris* 8x *one's native place, country,* or *city,* Mt 13:54, 57; Mk 6:1, 4; Lk 4:23, 24; Jn 4:44; *a heavenly country,* Heb 11:14* [3968]

[4259] Πατροβᾶς *Patrobas* 1x *Patrobas,* pr. name, Ro 16:14* [3969]

[4260] πατρολῴας *patrolōas* 1x also spelled πατραλῴας, *one who kills one's father, a patricide,* 1 Ti 1:9* [3964]

[4261] πατροπαράδοτος *patroparadotos* 1x *handed down* or *received by tradition from one's fathers* or *ancestors,* 1 Pe 1:18* [3970]

[4262] πατρῷος *patrōos* 3x *received from one's ancestors, paternal, ancestral,* Ac 22:3; 24:14; 28:17* [3971]

[4263] Παῦλος *Paulos* 158x *Paulus, Paul,* pr. name. (1) *Paul, the Apostle,* Ac 13:9, et al. freq. (2) *Sergius Paulus, the deputy* or *proconsul of Cyprus,* Ac 13:7 [3972]

[4264] παύω *pauō* 15x *to cause to pause* or *cease, restrain, prohibit,* 1 Pe 3:10; mid. perf. πέπαυται, *to cease, stop, leave off, desist, refrain,* 1 Pe 4:1 [3973]

[4265] Πάφος *Paphos* 2x *Paphos,* the chief city in the island of Cyprus [3974]

[4266] παχύνω *pachunō* 2x *to fatten, make gross;* met. pass. *to be rendered gross, dull, unfeeling,* Mt 13:15; Ac 28:27* [3975]

[4267] πέδη *pedē* 3x *a fetter, shackle,* Mk 5:4; Lk 8:29* [3976]

[4268] πεδινός *pedinos* 1x *level, flat,* Lk 6:17* [3977]

[4269] πεζεύω *pezeuō* 1x pr. *to travel on foot; to travel by land,* Ac 20:13* [3978]

[4270] πεζῇ *pezē* 2x *on foot,* or, *by land,* Mt 14:13; Mk 6:33 [3979]

[4272] πειθαρχέω *peitharcheō* 4x *to obey* one *in authority,* Ac 5:29, 32; Tit 3:1; genr. *to obey, follow,* or *conform to advice,* Ac 27:21* [3980]

[4273] πειθός *peithos* 1x also spelled πιθός, *persuasive, skillful,* 1 Co 2:4* [3981]

[4275] πείθω *peithō* 52x pluperfect, ἐπεποίθειν, *to persuade, seek to persuade, endeavor to convince,* Ac 18:4; 19:8, 26; 28:23; *to persuade, influence by persuasion,* Mt 27:20; Ac 13:43; 26:28; *to incite, instigate,* Ac 14:19; *to appease, render tranquil, to quiet,* 1 Jn 3:19; *to strive to conciliate, aspire to the favor of,* Gal 1:10; *to pacify, conciliate, win over,* Mt 28:14; Ac 12:20; pass. and mid. *to be persuaded of, be confident of,* Lk 20:6; Ro 8:38; Heb 6:9; *to suffer one's self to be persuaded, yield to persuasion, to be induced,* Ac 21:14; *to be convinced, to believe, yield belief,* Lk 16:31; Ac 17:4; *to assent, listen to, obey, follow,* Ac 5:36, 37, 40; 2 perf. πέποιθα, *to be assured, be confident,* 2 Co 2:3; Phil 1:6; Heb 13:18; *to confide in, trust, rely on, place hope and confidence in,* Mt 27:43; Mk 10:24; Ro 2:19 [3982]

[4277] πεινάω *peinaō* 23x *to hunger, be hungry,* Mt 4:2; Mk 11:12; *to be exposed to hunger, be famished,* 1 Co 4:11; Phil 4:12; met. *to hunger after, desire earnestly, long for,* Mt 5:6 [3983]

[4278] πεῖρα *peira* 2x *a trial, attempt, endeavor;* λαμβάνειν πεῖραν, *to attempt,* Heb 11:29; also, *to experience,* Heb 11:36* [3984]

[4279] πειράζω *peirazō* 38x *to make proof* or *trial of, put to the proof,* whether with good or mischievous intent, Mt 16:1; 22:35; absol. *to attempt,* Ac 16:7; 24:6; in N.T. *to tempt,* Mt 4:1; *to try, subject to trial,* 1 Co 10:13 [3985]

[4280] πειρασμός *peirasmos* 21x *a putting to the proof, proof, trial,* 1 Pe 4:12; Heb 3:8; direct *temptation to sin,* Lk 4:13; *trial, temptation,* Mt 6:13; 26:41; 1 Co 10:13; *trial, calamity, affliction,* Lk 22:28 [3986]

[4281] πειράω *peiraō* 1x *to try, attempt, essay, endeavor,* Ac 26:21* [3987]

[4282] πεισμονή *peismonē* 1x *a yielding to persuasion, assent,* Gal 5:8* [3988]

[4283] πέλαγος *pelagos* 2x *the deep, the open sea,* Mt 18:6; *a sea,* distinguished from the sea in general, and named from an adjacent country, Ac 27:5* [3989]

[4284] πελεκίζω *pelekizō* 1x *to strike* or *cut with an axe; to behead,* Rev 20:4* [3990]

[4286] πέμπτος *pemptos* 4x *fifth,* Rev 6:9; 9:1; 16:10; 21:20* [3991]

[4287] πέμπω *pempō* 79x *to send, to despatch on any message, embassy, business,* etc., Mt 2:8; 11:2; 14:10; *to transmit,* Ac 11:29; Rev 1:11; *to dismiss, permit to go,* Mk 5:12; *to send in* or *among,* 2 Th 2:11; *to thrust in,* or *put forth,* Rev 14:15, 18 [3992]

[4288] πένης *penēs* 1x pr. *one who labors for his bread; poor, needy,* 2 Co 9:9* [3993]

[4289] πενθερά *penthera* 6x *a mother-in-law,* Mt 8:14; 10:35; Mk 1:30; Lk 4:38; 12:53* [3994]

[4290] πενθερός *pentheros* 1x *a father-in-law,* Jn 18:13* [3995]

[4291] πενθέω *pentheō* 10x trans. *to lament over,* 2 Co 12:21; absol. *to lament, be sad, mourn,* Mt 5:4; 9:15; Mk 16:10; mid. *to bewail one's self, to feel guilt,* 1 Co 5:2 [3996]

[4292] πένθος *penthos* 5x *mourning, sorrow, sadness, grief,* Jas 4:9 [3997]

[4293] πενιχρός *penichros* 1x *poor, needy,* Lk 21:2* [3998]

[4294] πεντάκις *pentakis* 1x *five times,* 2 Co 11:24* [3999]

[4295] πεντακισχίλιοι *pentakischilioi* 6x *five times one thousand, five thousand,* Mt 14:21; 16:9 [4000]

[4296] πεντακόσιοι *pentakosioi* 2x *five hundred,* Lk 7:41; 1 Co 15:6* [4001]

[4297] πέντε *pente* 38x *five,* Mt 14:17, 19; 16:9 [4002]

[4298] πεντεκαιδέκατος *pentekaidekatos* 1x *fifteenth,* Lk 3:1* [4003]

[4299] πεντήκοντα *pentēkonta* 7x *fifty,* Mk 6:40; Lk 7:41 [4004]

[4300] πεντηκοστή *pentēkostē* 3x *Pentecost,* or *the Feast of Weeks;* one of the three great Jewish festivals, so called because it was celebrated on the *fiftieth* day, reckoning from the second day of the feast of unleavened bread, i.e., from the 16th day of Nisan, Ac 2:1; 20:16; 1 Co 16:8* [4005]

[4301] πεποίθησις *pepoithēsis* 6x *trust, confidence, reliance,* 2 Co 1:15 [4006]

[4304] περαιτέρω *peraiterō* 1x compar. adv. of πέραν, Ac 19:39* [4012 + 2087]

[4305] πέραν *peran* 23x can function as an improper prep., *across, beyond, over, on the other side,* Mt 4:15, 25; 19:1; Jn 6:1, 17; ὁ, ἡ, τό, πέραν, *farther, on the farther side,* and τὸ πέραν, *the farther side, the other side,* Mt 8:18, 28; 14:22 [4008]

[4306] πέρας *peras* 4x *an extremity, end,* Mt 12:42; Lk 11:31; Ro 10:18; *an end, conclusion, termination,* Heb 6:16* [4009]

[4307] Πέργαμος *Pergamos* 2x *Pergamus*, a city of Mysia, in Asia Minor, Rev 1:11; 2:12* [4010]

[4308] Πέργη *Pergē* 3x *Perga*, the chief city of Pamphylia, in Asia Minor, Ac 13:13f.; 14:25 [4011]

[4309] περί *peri* 333x pr. of place, (1) gen., *about, around; about, concerning, respecting*, Mt 2:8; 11:10; 22:31; Jn 8:18; Ro 8:3, et al. freq.; (2) acc., of place, *about, around, round about*, Mt 3:4; Mk 3:34; Lk 13:8; οἱ περί τινα, *the companions* of a person, Lk 22:49; *a person and his companions*, Ac 13:13; simply *a person*, Jn 11:19; τὰ περί τινα, *the condition, circumstances of* any one, Phil 2:23; of time, *about*, Mt 20:3, 5, 6, 9; *about, concerning, respecting, touching*, Lk 10:40; 1 Ti 1:19; 6:21; Tit 2:7 [4012]

[4310] περιάγω *periagō* 6x *to lead around, carry about* Ac 13:11 in one's company, 1 Co 9:5; *to traverse*, Mt 4:23; 9:35; 23:15; Mk 6:6 [4013]

[4311] περιαιρέω *periaireō* 5x *to take off, lift off, remove*, 2 Co 3:16; *to cast off*, Ac 27:40; met. *to cut off* hope, Ac 27:20; met. *to take away* sin, *remove the guilt* of sin, *make expiation for* sin, Heb 10:11 [4014]

[4312] περιάπτω *periaptō* 1x *to light a fire, kindle*, Lk 22:55* [681]

[4313] περιαστράπτω *periastraptō* 2x *to lighten around, shine like lightning around*, Ac 9:3; 22:6* [4015]

[4314] περιβάλλω *periballō* 23x *to cast around; to clothe*, Mt 25:36, 38, 43; mid. *to clothe one's self, to be clothed*, Mt 6:29, 31; Lk 23:11; Jn 19:2; Ac 12:8; Rev 4:4 [4016]

[4315] περιβλέπω *periblepō* 7x trans. *to look around upon*, Mk 3:5, 34; 11:11; Lk 6:10; absol. *to look around*, Mk 5:32; 9:8; 10:23* [4017]

[4316] περιβόλαιον *peribolaion* 2x *that which is thrown around* any one, *clothing, covering; a cloak*, Heb 1:12; *a covering*, 1 Co 11:15* [4018]

[4317] περιδέω *perideō* 1x pluperfect, περιεδέδετο (pass., 3 sg), *to bind round about*; pass. *to be bound around, be bound up*, Jn 11:44* [4019]

[4318] περιεργάζομαι *periergazomai* 1x *to do a thing with excessive* or *superfluous care; to be a busy-body*, 2 Th 3:11* [4020]

[4319] περίεργος *periergos* 2x *over careful; officious, a busy-body*, 1 Ti 5:13;

in N.T. περίεργα, *magic arts, sorcery*, Ac 19:19* [4021]

[4320] περιέρχομαι *perierchomai* 3x *to go about, wander about, rove*, Ac 19:13; Heb 11:37; *to go about, visit* from house to house, 1 Ti 5:13* [4022]

[4321] περιέχω *periechō* 2x *to encompass, enclose*; met. *to encompass, seize on the mind*, Lk 5:9; περιέχει, impers. *it is contained, it is among the contents* of a writing, 1 Pe 2:6* [4023]

[4322] περιζώννυμι *perizōnnymi* 6x also spelled περιζωννύω, *to bind around with a girdle, gird*; in N.T. mid. *to gird one's self* in preparation for bodily motion and exertion, Lk 12:37; 17:8; *to wear a girdle*, Rev 1:13; 15:6 [4024]

[4324] περίθεσις *perithesis* 1x *a putting on, wearing* of dress, etc., 1 Pe 3:3* [4025]

[4325] περιΐστημι *periistēmi* 4x *to place around*; intrans. 2 aor. περιέστην, perf. part. περιεστώς, *to stand around*, Jn 11:42; Ac 25:7; mid. *to keep aloof from, avoid, shun*, 2 Ti 2:16; Tit 3:9* [4026]

[4326] περικάθαρμα *perikatharma* 1x pr. *filth*; met. *refuse, outcast*, 1 Co 4:13* [4027]

[4328] περικαλύπτω *perikalyptō* 3x *to cover round about, cover over; to cover* the face, Mk 14:65; *to blindfold*, Lk 22:64; pass. *to be overlaid*, Heb 9:4* [4028]

[4329] περίκειμαι *perikeimai* 5x *to lie around, be surround*, Heb 12:1; *to be hung around*, Mk 9:42; Lk 17:2; *to have around one's self, to wear*, Ac 28:20; *to be in submission to*, Heb 5:2* [4029]

[4330] περικεφαλαία *perikephalaia* 2x *a helmet*, Eph 6:17; 1 Th 5:8* [4030]

[4331] περικρατής *perikratēs* 1x *overpowering*; περικρατὴς γενέσθαι, *to become master of, to secure*, Ac 27:16* [4031]

[4332] περικρύβω *perikrybō* 1x also spelled περικρύπτω, *to hide* or *keep from sight, to conceal by envelopment; to conceal*, Lk 1:24* [4032]

[4333] περικυκλόω *perikykloō* 1x *to encircle, surround*, Lk 19:43* [4033]

[4334] περιλάμπω *perilampō* 2x *to shine around*, Lk 2:9; Ac 26:13* [4034]

[4335] περιλείπομαι *perileipomai* 2x *to leave remaining*; pass. *to remain, survive*, 1 Th 4:15, 17* [4035]

[4337] περίλυπος *perilypos* 5x *greatly grieved, exceedingly sorrowful*, Mt 26:38; Mk 14:34 [4036]

[4338] περιμένω *perimenō* 1x *to await, wait for*, Ac 1:4* [4037]

[4339] πέριξ *perix* 1x *neighboring*, Ac 5:16* [4038]

[4340] περιοικέω *perioikeō* 1x *to dwell around*, or *in the vicinity; to be a neighbor*, Lk 1:65* [4039]

[4341] περίοικος *perioikos* 1x *one who dwells in the vicinity, a neighbor*, Lk 1:58* [4040]

[4342] περιούσιος *periousios* 1x *chosen; peculiar, special*, Tit 2:14* [4041]

[4343] περιοχή *periochē* 1x lit., *a compass, circumference, contents*; fig., *a section, a portion* of Scripture, Ac 8:32* [4042]

[4344] περιπατέω *peripateō* 95x pluperfect, περι[ε]πεπατήκει (3 sg), *to walk, walk about*, Mt 9:5; 11:5; 14:25, 26, 29; *to rove, roam*, 1 Pe 5:8; with μετά, *to accompany, follow*, Jn 6:66; Rev 3:4; *to walk, frequent* a locality, Jn 7:1; 11:54; from the Hebrew, *to maintain* a certain *walk* of life and conduct, Gal 5:16; Eph 2:10 [4043]

[4345] περιπείρω *peripeirō* 1x *to put on a spit, transfix*; met. *to pierce, wound deeply*, 1 Ti 6:10* [4044]

[4346] περιπίπτω *peripiptō* 3x *to fall around* or *upon, to fall in with*, Lk 10:30; *to fall into, light upon*, Ac 27:41; *to be involved in*, Jas 1:2* [4045]

[4347] περιποιέω *peripoieō* 3x *to cause to remain over and above, to reserve, save*, Lk 17:33; mid. *to acquire, gain, earn*, 1 Ti 3:13; *to purchase*, Ac 20:28* [4046]

[4348] περιποίησις *peripoiēsis* 5x *a laying up, keeping; an acquiring* or *obtaining, acquisition*, 1 Th 5:9; 2 Th 2:14; *a saving, preservation*, Heb 10:39; *a peculiar possession, specialty*, Eph 1:14; 1 Pet 2:9* [4047]

[4351] περιρήγνυμι *perirēgnymi* 1x also spelled περιρρήγνυμι, *to break* or *tear all around; to strip off*, Ac 16:22* [4048]

[4352] περισπάω *perispaō* 1x *to draw off from around; to wheel about; to distract*; pass. *to be distracted, over-busied*, Lk 10:40* [4049]

[4353] περισσεία *perisseia* 4x *superabundance*, Ro 5:17; 2 Co 8:2; 10:15; Jas 1:21* [4050]

[4354] περίσσευμα *perisseuma* 5x *more than enough, residue over and above*, Mk 8:8; *abundance, exuberance*, Mt 12:34; Lk 6:45; *superabundance, affluence*, 2 Co 8:14* [4051]

[4355] περισσεύω *perisseuō* 39x *to be over and above, to be superfluous,* Mt 14:20; Mk 12:44; Lk 21:4; *to exist in full quantity, to abound, be abundant,* Ro 5:15; 2 Co 1:5; *to increase, be augmented,* Ac 16:5; *to be advanced, be rendered more prominent,* Ro 3:7; *of persons, to be abundantly gifted, richly furnished, abound,* Lk 15:17; Ro 15:13; 1 Co 14:12; 2 Co 8:7; *to be possessed of a full sufficiency,* Phil 4:12, 18; *to abound* in performance, 1 Co 15:58; *to be a gainer,* 1 Co 8:8; in N.T. trans., *to cause to be abundant,* 2 Co 4:15; 9:8; Eph 1:8; *to cause to be abundantly furnished, cause to abound,* 1 Th 3:12; pass. *to be gifted with abundance,* Mt 13:12; 25:29 [4052]

[4356] περισσός *perissos* 6x *over and above,* Mt 5:37; *superfluous,* 2 Co 9:1; *extraordinary,* Mt 5:47; compar. *more, greater,* Mt 11:9; 23:14; *excessive,* 2 Co 2:7; adverbially, περισσόν, *in full abundance,* Jn 10:10; περισσότερον, and ἐκ περισσοῦ, *exceedingly, vehemently,* Mk 6:51; 7:36; 1 Co 15:10; Eph 3:20; τὸ περισσόν, *pre-eminence, advantage,* Ro 3:1 [4053]

[4358] περισσότερος *perissoteros* 16x comparative adj. from περισσός, *greater, more,* Mk 12:40; Lk 20:47; *even more,* Lk 12:48; 1 Co 15:10; *even more, so much more,* Mk 7:36 [4055]

[4359] περισσοτέρως *perissoterōs* 12x *more, more abundantly, more earnestly, more vehemently,* 2 Co 7:13; *exceedingly,* Gal 1:14 [4056]

[4360] περισσῶς *perissōs* 4x *much, abundantly, vehemently,* Ac 26:11; *more, more abundantly,* Mt 27:23; Mk 10:26; 15:14* [4057]

[4361] περιστερά *peristera* 10x *a dove, pigeon,* Mt 3:16; 10:16 [4058]

[4362] περιτέμνω *peritemnō* 17x *to cut around; to circumcise, remove the prepuce,* Lk 1:59; 2:21; met. Col 2:11; mid. *to submit to circumcision,* Ac 15:1 [4059]

[4363] περιτίθημι *peritithēmi* 8x *to place around, put about* or *around,* Mt 21:33; 27:28; met. *to attach, bestow,* 1 Co 12:23 [4060]

[4364] περιτομή *peritomē* 36x *circumcision, the act* or *custom of circumcision,* Jn 7:22, 23; Ac 7:8; *the state of being circumcised, the being circumcised,* Ro 2:25, 26, 27; 4:10; meton. *the circumcision, those who are circumcised,* Ro 3:30; 4:9 met. spiritual *circumcision* of the heart and affection, Ro 2:29; Col 2:11; meton. *persons* spiritually *circumcised,* Phil 3:3 [4061]

[4365] περιτρέπω *peritrepō* 1x *to turn about; to bring round* into any state, Ac 26:24* [4062]

[4366] περιτρέχω *peritrechō* 1x *to run about, run up and down,* Mk 6:55* [4063]

[4367] περιφέρω *peripherō* 3x *to bear* or *carry about,* Mk 6:55; 2 Co 4:10; pass. *to be borne about hither and thither, driven to and fro,* Eph 4:14* [4064]

[4368] περιφρονέω *periphroneō* 1x *to contemplate, reflect on; to despise, disregard,* Tit 2:15* [4065]

[4369] περίχωρος *perichōros* 9x *neighboring;* ἡ περίχωρος, sc. γῆ, *an adjacent region, country round about,* Mt 14:35; Mk 1:28; meton. *inhabitants of the region round about,* Mt 3:5 [4066]

[4370] περίψημα *peripsēma* 1x *filth which is wiped off;* met. 1 Co 4:13* [4067]

[4371] περπερεύομαι *perpereuomai* 1x *to vaunt one's self,* 1 Co 13:4* [4068]

[4372] Περσίς *Persis* 1x *Persis,* pr. name, Ro 16:12* [4069]

[4373] πέρυσι *perysi* 2x *last year, a year ago,* 2 Co 8:10; 9:2* [4070]

[4374] πετεινόν *peteinon* 14x *a bird, fowl,* Mt 6:26; 8:20 [4071]

[4375] πέτομαι *petomai* 5x also spelled πετάομαι, *to fly,* Rev 4:7; 8:13; 12:14; 14:6; 19:17* [4072]

[4376] πέτρα *petra* 15x *a rock,* Mt 7:24, 25; met. Ro 9:33; 1 Pe 2:8; *crags, clefts,* Rev 6:15, 16; *stony ground,* Lk 8:6, 13 [4073]

[4377] Πέτρος *Petros* 156x *a stone;* in N.T. the Greek rendering of the surname Cephas, given to the Apostle Simon, and having, therefore, the same sense as πέτρα, *Peter,* Mt 4:18; 8:14 [4074]

[4378] πετρώδης *petrōdēs* 4x *like rock; stony, rocky,* Mt 13:5, 20; Mk 4:5, 16* [4075]

[4379] πήγανον *pēganon* 1x *rue,* a plant, *ruta graveolens* of Linnaeus, Lk 11:42* [4076]

[4380] πηγή *pēgē* 11x *a source, spring, fountain,* Jas 3:11, 12; *a well,* Jn 4:6; *an issue, flux, flow,* Mk 5:29; met. Jn 4:14 [4077]

[4381] πήγνυμι *pēgnymi* 1x *to fasten; to pitch* a tent, Heb 8:2* [4078]

[4382] πηδάλιον *pēdalion* 2x *a rudder,* Ac 27:40; Jas 3:4* [4079]

[4383] πηλίκος *pēlikos* 2x *how large,* Gal 6:11; *how great* in dignity, Heb 7:4* [4080]

[4384] πηλός *pēlos* 6x *moist earth, mud, slime,* Jn 9:6, 11, 14, 15; *clay,* potter's *clay,* Ro 9:21* [4081]

[4385] πήρα *pēra* 6x *a leather bag* or *sack* for provisions, *wallet,* Mt 10:10; Mk 6:8 [4082]

[4388] πῆχυς *pēchus* 4x pr. *cubitus, the forearm;* hence, *a cubit,* a measure of length, equal to the distance from the elbow to the extremity of the little finger, usually considered as equivalent to a foot and one half, or 17 inches and one half, Jn 21:8; Rev 21:17; met. of time, *a span,* Mt 6:27; Lk 12:25* [4083]

[4389] πιάζω *piazō* 12x *to press;* in N.T. *to take* or *lay hold of,* Ac 3:7; *to take, catch* fish, etc., Jn 21:3, 10; Rev 19:20; *to take, seize, apprehend, arrest,* Jn 7:30, 32, 44 [4084]

[4390] πιέζω *piezō* 1x *to press, to press* or *squeeze down, make compact by pressure,* Lk 6:38* [4085]

[4391] πιθανολογία *pithanologia* 1x *persuasive speech, plausible discourse,* Col 2:4* [4086]

[4393] πικραίνω *pikrainō* 4x *to embitter, render bitter,* Rev 10:9; pass. *to be embittered, be made bitter,* Rev 8:11; 10:10; met. pass. *to be embittered, to grow angry, harsh,* Col 3:19* [4087]

[4394] πικρία *pikria* 4x *bitterness,* Ac 8:23; Heb 12:15; met. *bitterness* of spirit and language, *harshness,* Ro 3:14; Eph 4:31* [4088]

[4395] πικρός *pikros* 2x *bitter,* Jas 3:11; met. *bitter, harsh,* Jas 3:14* [4089]

[4396] πικρῶς *pikrōs* 2x *bitterly,* Mt 26:75; Lk 22:62* [4090]

[4397] Πιλᾶτος *Pilatos* 55x *Pilate,* pr. name [4091]

[4398] πίμπλημι *pimplēmi* 24x *to fill,* Mt 27:48; pass. *to be filled* mentally, *be under full influence,* Lk 1:15; 4:28; *to be fulfilled,* Lk 21:22; of stated time, *to be brought to a close, arrive at its close,* Lk 1:23, 57; 2:6, 21, 22 [4130]

[4399] πίμπρημι *pimprēmi* 1x *to set on fire, burn, inflame;* in N.T. pass., *to swell from inflamation,* Ac 28:6* [4092]

[4400] πινακίδιον *pinakidion* 1x *a small tablet* for writing, Lk 1:63* [4093]

[4402] πίναξ *pinax* 5x pr. *a board* or *plank;* in N.T. *a plate, platter, dish* on which food was served, Mk 14:8, 11 [4094]

[4403] πίνω *pinō* 73x *to drink*, Mt 6:25, 31; 26:27, 29, et al. freq.; *trop.* of the earth, *to drink in, imbibe*, Heb 6:7 [4095]

[4404] πιότης *piotēs* 1x *fatness, richness*, Ro 11:17* [4096]

[4405] πιπράσκω *pipraskō* 9x *to sell*, Mt 13:46; 18:25; met. with ὑπό, pass. *to be sold under, to be a slave to, be devoted to*, Ro 7:14 [4097]

[4406] πίπτω *piptō* 90x *to fall*, Mt 15:27; Lk 10:18; *to fall, fall prostrate, fall down*, Mt 17:6; 18:29; Lk 17:16; *to fall down dead*, Lk 21:24; *to fall, fall in ruins*, Mt 7:25, 27; Lk 11:17; met. *to fall, come by chance*, as a lot, Ac 1:26; *to fall, to fail, become null and void, fall to the ground*, Lk 16:17; *to fall into a worse state*, Rev 2:5; *to come to ruin*, Ro 11:11; Heb 4:11; *to fall into sin*, Ro 11:22; 1 Co 10:2; *to fall in judgment, by condemnation*, Rev 14:8; *to fall upon, seize*, Rev 11:11; *to light upon*, Rev 7:16; *to fall under, incur*, Jas 5:12 [4098]

[4407] Πισιδία *Pisidia* 1x *Pisidia*, a country of Asia Minor, Ac 14:24* [4099]

[4409] πιστεύω *pisteuō* 241x pluperfect, πεπιστεύκειν, *to believe, give credit to*, Mk 1:15; 16:13; Lk 24:25; intrans. *to believe, have a mental persuasion*, Mt 8:13; 9:28; Jas 2:19; *to believe, be of opinion*, Ro 14:2; in N.T. πιστεύειν ἐν, εἰς, ἐπί, *to believe in or on*, Mt 18:6; 27:42; Jn 3:15, 16, 18; absol. *to believe, be a believer* in the religion of Christ, Ac 2:44; 4:4, 32; 13:48; trans. *to intrust, commit to the charge or power of*, Lk 16:11; Jn 2:24; pass. *to be intrusted with*, Ro 3:2; 1 Co 9:17 [4100]

[4410] πιστικός *pistikos* 2x *genuine, unadulterated*, or (πίνω) *liquid*, Mk 14:3; Jn 12:3* [4101]

[4411] πίστις *pistis* 243x *faith, belief, firm persuasion*, 2 Co 5:7; Heb 11:1; *assurance, firm conviction*, Ro 14:23; *ground of belief, guarantee, assurance*, Ac 17:31; *good faith, honesty, integrity*, Mt 23:23; Gal 5:22; Tit 2:10; *faithfulness, truthfulness*, Ro 3:3; in N.T. *faith* in God and Christ, Mt 8:10; Ac 3:16, et al. freq.; ἡ πίστις, *the* matter of Gospel *faith*, Ac 6:7; Jude 3 [4102]

[4412] πιστός *pistos* 67x *faithful, true, trusty*, Mt 24:45; 25:21, 23; Lk 12:42; 2 Ti 2:2; *put in trust*, 1 Co 7:25; *true, veracious*, Rev 1:5; 2:13; *credible, sure, certain, indubitable*, Ac 13:34; 1 Ti 1:15; *believing, yielding belief and confidence*, Jn 20:27; Gal 3:9; spc. *a* Christian *believer*,

Ac 10:45; 16:1, 15; 2 Co 6:15; πιστόν, *in a true-hearted manner, right-mindedly*, 3 Jn 5 [4103]

[4413] πιστόω *pistoō* 1x *to make trustworthy*; pass. *to be assured, feel sure belief*, 2 Ti 3:14* [4104]

[4414] πλανάω *planaō* 39x *to lead astray, cause to wander*; pass. *to go astray, wander about, stray*, Mt 18:12, 13; 1 Pe 2:25; met. *to mislead, deceive*, Mt 24:4, 5, 11, 24; pass. *to be deceived, err, mistake*, Mt 22:29; *to seduce, delude*, Jn 7:12; pass. *to be seduced* or *wander* from the path of virtue, *to sin, transgress*, Tit 3:3; Heb 5:2; Jas 5:19 [4105]

[4415] πλάνη *planē* 10x *a wandering; deceit, deception, delusion, imposture, fraud*, Mt 27:64; 1 Th 2:3; *seduction, deceiving*, Eph 4:14; 2 Th 2:11; 1 Jn 4:6; *error, false opinion*, 2 Pe 3:17; *wandering* from the path of truth and virtue, *perverseness, wickedness, sin*, Ro 1:27; Jas 5:20; 2 Pe 2:18; Jude 11* [4106]

[4417] πλανήτης *planētēs* 1x *a rover, roving, a wanderer, wandering*; ἀστὴρ πλανήτης, *a wandering star*, Jude 13* [4107]

[4418] πλάνος *planos* 5x *a wanderer, vagabond*; also act. *deceiving, seducing; a deceiver, impostor*, Mt 27:63; 2 Co 6:8; 1 Ti 4:1; 2 Jn 7* [4108]

[4419] πλάξ *plax* 3x *a flat broad surface; a table, tablet*, 2 Co 3:3; Heb 9:4* [4109]

[4420] πλάσμα *plasma* 1x *a thing formed* or *fashioned*; spc. *a potter's vessel*, Ro 9:20* [4110]

[4421] πλάσσω *plassō* 2x *to form, fashion, mould*, Ro 9:20; 1 Ti 2:13* [4111]

[4422] πλαστός *plastos* 1x *formed, fashioned, moulded*; met. *fabricated, counterfeit, delusive*, 2 Pe 2:3* [4112]

[4423] πλατεῖα *plateia* 10x *a street, broad way*, Mt 6:5; 12:19; Lk 10:10 [4113]

[4424] πλάτος *platos* 4x *breadth*, Eph 3:18; Rev 20:9; 21:16* [4114]

[4425] πλατύνω *platynō* 3x *to make broad, widen, enlarge*, Mt 23:5; pass. met. of the heart, from the Hebrew, *to be expanded* with kindly and genial feelings, 2 Co 6:11, 13* [4115]

[4426] πλατύς *platys* 1x *broad, wide*, Mt 7:13* [4116]

[4427] πλέγμα *plegma* 1x *anything plaited* or *intertwined; a braid* of hair, 1 Ti 2:9* [4117]

[4428] πλέκω *plekō* 3x *to interweave, weave, braid, plait*, Mt 27:29; Mk 15:17; Jn 19:2* [4120]

[4429] πλεονάζω *pleonazō* 9x *to be more than enough; to have more than enough, to have in abundance*, 2 Co 8:15; *to abound, be abundant*, 2 Th 1:3; 2 Pe 1:8; *to increase, be augmented*, Ro 5:20; *to come into wider action, be more widely spread*, Ro 6:1; 2 Co 4:15; in N.T. trans. *to cause to abound* or *increase, to augment*, 1 Th 3:12 [4121]

[4430] πλεονεκτέω *pleonekteō* 5x *to have more* than another; *to take advantage of; to overreach, make gain of*, 2 Co 7:2; 12:17, 18; *to wrong*, 1 Th 4:6; *to get the better*, or *an advantage of*, 2 Co 2:11* [4122]

[4431] πλεονέκτης *pleonektēs* 4x *one who has* or *claims to have more than his share; a covetous, avaricious person, one who defrauds for the sake of gain*, 1 Co 5:10, 11; 6:10; Eph 5:5* [4123]

[4432] πλεονεξία *pleonexia* 10x *some advantage which one possesses over another; an inordinate desire of riches, covetousness*, Lk 12:15; *grasping, overreaching, extortion*, Ro 1:29; 1 Th 2:5; *a gift exacted by importunity and conferred with grudging, a hard-wrung gift*, 2 Co 9:5; *a scheme of extortion*, Mk 7:22 [4124]

[4433] πλευρά *pleura* 5x pr. *a rib; the side* of the body, Jn 19:34; 20:20, 25, 27; Ac 12:7* [4125]

[4434] πλέω *pleō* 6x *to sail*, Lk 8:23; Ac 21:3; 27:2, 6, 24; Rev 18:17* [4126]

[4435] πληγή *plēgē* 22x *a blow, stroke, stripe*, Lk 10:30; 12:48; meton. *a wound*, Ac 16:33; Rev 13:3, 12, 14; from the Hebrew, *a plague, affliction, calamity*, Rev 9:20; 11:6 [4127]

[4436] πλῆθος *plēthos* 31x *fullness, amplitude, magnitude; a multitude, a great number*, Lk 1:10; 2:13; 5:6; *a multitude, a crowd, throng*, Mk 3:7, 8; Lk 6:17 [4128]

[4437] πληθύνω *plēthunō* 12x optative, πληθύναι (3 sg), trans. *to multiply, cause to increase, augment*, 2 Co 9:10; Heb 6:14; pass. *to be multiplied, increase, be accumulated*, Mt 24:12; Ac 6:7; 7:17; intrans. *to multiply, increase, be augmented*, Ac 6:1 [4129]

[4438] πλήκτης *plēktēs* 2x *a striker, one apt to strike; a quarrelsome, violent person*, 1 Ti 3:3; Tit 1:7* [4131]

[4439] πλήμμυρα *plēmmyra* 1x *the flood-tide; a flood*, Lk 6:48* [4132]

[4440] πλήν *plēn* 31x can function as an improper prep., *besides, except,* Mk 12:32; Ac 8:1; 20:23; as a conj. *but, however, nevertheless,* Mt 18:7; Lk 19:27; Eph 5:33; equivalent to ἀλλά, Lk 6:35; 12:31; Ac 27:22 [4133]

[4441] πλήρης *plērēs* 16x *full, filled,* Mt 14:20; 15:37; *full* of disease, Lk 5:12; met. *full of, abounding in, wholly occupied with, completely under the influence of,* or *affected by,* Lk 4:1; Jn 1:14; Ac 9:36; *full, complete, perfect,* Mk 4:28 [4134]

[4442] πληροφορέω *plērophoreō* 6x *to bring full measure, to give in full; to carry out fully, to discharge completely,* 2 Ti 4:5, 17; pass. of things, *to be fully established* as a matter of certainty, Lk 1:1; of persons, *to be fully convinced, assured,* Ro 4:21; 14:15; Col 4:12★ [4135]

[4443] πληροφορία *plērophoria* 4x *full conviction, firm persuasion, assurance,* 1 Th 1:5; Col 2:2 [4136]

[4444] πληρόω *plēroō* 86x pluperf., πεπληρώκει (3 sg), *to fill, make full, fill up,* Mt 13:48; 23:32; Lk 3:5; *to fill up* a deficiency, Phil 4:18, 19; *to pervade,* Jn 12:3; Ac 2:2; *to pervade* with an influence, *to influence fully, possess fully,* Jn 16:6; Ac 2:28; 5:3; Ro 1:29; Eph 5:18; *to complete, perfect,* Jn 3:29; Eph 3:19; *to bring to an end,* Lk 7:1; *to perform fully, discharge,* Mt 3:15; Ac 12:25; 13:25; 14:26; Ro 13:8; Col 4:17; *to consummate,* Mt 5:17; *to realize, accomplish, fulfil,* Lk 1:20; 9:31; Ac 3:18; 13:27; from the Hebrew; *to set forth fully,* Ro 15:19; Col 1:25; pass. of time, *to be fulfilled, come to an end, be fully arrived,* Mk 1:15; Lk 21:24; Jn 7:8; of prophecy, *to receive fulfillment,* Mt 1:22, et al. freq. [4137]

[4445] πλήρωμα *plērōma* 17x *that which fills up; full measure, entire content,* Mk 8:20; 1 Co 10:26, 28; *complement, full extent, full number,* Gal 4:4; Eph 1:10; *that which fills up a deficiency, a supplement, a patch,* Mt 9:16; *fulness, abundance,* Jn 1:16; *full measure,* Ro 15:29; *a fulfilling, perfect performance,* Ro 13:10; *complete attainment* of entire belief, *full acceptance,* Ro 11:12; *full development, plenitude,* Eph 4:13; Col 1:19; 2:9 [4138]

[4446] πλησίον *plēsion* 17x can function as an improper prep., *near, near by,* Jn 4:5; ὁ πλησίον, *a neighbor,* Mt 19:19; Ro 15:2; a friendly *neighbor,* Mt 5:43 [4139]

[4447] πλησμονή *plēsmonē* 1x *a filling up;* met. *gratification, satisfaction,* Col 2:23★ [4140]

[4448] πλήσσω *plēssō* 1x also spelled πλήττω, *to strike, smite;* from the Hebrew, *to smite, to plague, blast,* Rev 8:12 [4141]

[4449] πλοιάριον *ploiarion* 5x *a small vessel, boat,* Mk 3:9; Jn 6:22, 23, 24 [4142]

[4450] πλοῖον *ploion* 67x *a vessel, ship, bark,* whether large or small, Mt 4:21, 22; Ac 21:2, 3 [4143]

[4454] πλούσιος *plousios* 28x *rich, opulent, wealthy;* and pl. οἱ πλούσιοι, *the rich,* Mt 19:23, 24; 27:57; met. *rich, abounding in, distinguished for,* Eph 2:4; Jas 2:5; Rev 2:9; 3:17; *rich in glory, dignity, bliss,* etc., 2 Co 8:9 [4145]

[4455] πλουσίως *plousiōs* 4x *rich, largely, abundantly,* Col 3:16 [4146]

[4456] πλουτέω *plouteō* 12x *to be* or *become rich,* Lk 1:25; 1 Ti 6:9; trop. Lk 12:21; met. *to abound in, be abundantly furnished with,* 1 Ti 6:18; *to be* spiritually *enriched,* 2 Co 8:9 [4147]

[4457] πλουτίζω *ploutizō* 3x *to make rich, enrich;* met. *to enrich* spiritually, 1 Co 1:5; 2 Co 6:10; 9:11★ [4148]

[4458] πλοῦτος *ploutos* 22x *riches, wealth, opulence,* Mt 13:22; Lk 8:14; in N.T., πλοῦτος τοῦ Θεοῦ, or Χριστοῦ, *those rich benefits, those abundant blessings which flow from God* or *Christ,* Eph 3:8; Phil 4:19; meton. *richness, abundance,* Ro 2:4; 11:33; 2 Co 8:2; meton. *a spiritual enriching,* Ro 11:12 [4149]

[4459] πλύνω *plynō* 3x *to wash* garments, Lk 5:1; Rev 7:14; 22:14★ [4150]

[4460] πνεῦμα *pneuma* 379x *wind, air in motion,* Jn 3:8; *breath,* 2 Th 2:8; the substance *spirit,* Jn 3:6; *a spirit, spiritual being,* Jn 4:24; Ac 23:8, 9; Heb 1:14; *a bodiless spirit, specter,* Lk 24:37; *a foul spirit,* δαιμόνιον, Mt 8:16; Lk 10:20; *spirit,* as a vital principle, Jn 6:63; 1 Co 15:45; *the* human *spirit, the soul,* Mt 26:41; 27:50; Ac 7:59; 1 Co 7:34; Jas 2:26; *the spirit* as the seat of thought and feeling, *the mind,* Mk 8:12; Ac 19:21; *spirit, mental frame,* 1 Co 4:21; 1 Pe 3:4; *a characteristic spirit, an influential principle,* Lk 9:55; 1 Co 2:12; 2 Ti 1:7; *a pervading influence,* Ro 11:8; *spirit, frame of mind,* as distinguished from outward circumstances and action, Mt 5:3; *spirit* as distinguished from outward show and form, Jn 4:23; *spirit, a divinely bestowed spiritual frame,* characteristic of true believers, Ro 8:4; Jude 19; *spirit,* latent *spiritual import, spiritual significance,* as distinguished from the mere letter, Ro 2:29; 7:6; 2 Co 3:6, 17; *spirit,* as a term for a process superior to a merely natural or

carnal course of things, by the operation of the Divine Spirit, Ro 8:4; Gal 4:29; *a spiritual dispensation,* or *a sealing energy of the Holy Spirit,* Heb 9:14; the Holy Spirit, Mt 3:16; 12:31; Jn 1:32, 33; *a gift of the Holy Spirit,* Jn 7:39; Ac 19:2; 1 Co 14:12; *an operation* or *influence of the Holy Spirit,* 1 Co 12:3; *a spiritual influence, an inspiration,* Mt 22:43; Lk 2:27; Eph 1:17; *a professedly divine communication,* or, *a professed possessor of a spiritual communication,* 1 Co 12:10; 2 Th 2:2; 1 Jn 4:1, 2, 3 [4151]

[4461] πνευματικός *pneumatikos* 26x *spiritual, pertaining to the soul,* as distinguished from what concerns the body, Ro 15:27; 1 Co 9:11; *spiritual, pertaining to the nature of spirits,* 1 Co 15:44; τὰ πνευματικα; τῆς πονηρίας, i.q. τὰ πνεύματα τὰ πονηρά, *evil spirits,* Eph 6:12; *spiritual, pertaining* or *relating to the influences of the Holy Spirit,* of things, Ro 1:11; 7:14; τὰ πνευματικά, *spiritual gifts,* 1 Co 12:1; 14:1; *superior in process to the natural course of things, miraculous,* 1 Co 10:3; of persons, *gifted with a spiritual frame of mind, spiritually affected,* 1 Co 2:13, 15; *endowed with spiritual gifts, inspired,* 1 Co 14:37 [4152]

[4462] πνευματικῶς *pneumatikōs* 2x *spiritually, through spiritual views and affections,* 1 Co 2:14; *spiritually, in a spiritual sense, allegorically,* Rev 11:8★ [4153]

[4463] πνέω *pneō* 7x *to breathe; to blow,* as the wind, Mt 7:25, 27 [4154]

[4464] πνίγω *pnigō* 3x *to stifle, suffocate, choke,* Mk 5:13; *to seize by the throat,* Mk 13:17; 18:28★ [4155]

[4465] πνικτός *pniktos* 3x *strangled, suffocated;* in N.T. τὸ πνικτόν, *the flesh of animals killed by strangulation* or *suffocation,* Ac 15:20, 29; 21:25★ [4156]

[4466] πνοή *pnoē* 2x *breath, respiration,* Ac 17:25; *a wind, a blast of wind, breeze,* Ac 2:2★ [4157]

[4468] ποδήρης *podērēs* 1x *reaching to the feet;* as subst. sc. ἐσθής, *a long, flowing robe reaching down to the feet,* Rev 1:13★ [4158]

[4470] πόθεν *pothen* 29x *whence? from where,* used of place, etc., Mt 15:33; met. of a state of dignity, Rev 2:5; used of origin, Mt 21:25; of cause, source, author, etc., Mt 13:27, 54, 56; Lk 1:43; *how? in what way?* Mk 8:4; 12:37 [4159]

[4472] ποιέω *poieō* 568x pluperf., πεποιήκειν, *to make, form, construct,* Mt 17:4; Mk 9:5; Jn 2:15; of God, *to create,* Mt 19:4; Ac 4:24; *to make, prepare* a feast, etc., Mt 22:2; Mk 6:21; met. *to make, establish, ratify,* a covenant, Heb 8:9; *to make, assume, consider, regard,* Mt 12:33; *to make, effect, bring to pass, cause to take place, do, accomplish,* Mt 7:22; 21:21; Mk 3:8; 6:5; 7:37; met. *to perfect, accomplish, fulfil, put in execution* a purpose, promise, etc., Lk 16:4; 19:48; *to cause, make,* Mt 5:32; Jn 11:37; Ac 24:12; *to make* gain, *gain, acquire,* Mt 25:16; Lk 19:18; *to get, procure,* Lk 12:33; *to make, to cause to be* or *become* a thing, Mt 21:13; 23:15; *to use, treat,* Lk 15:19; *to make, constitute, appoint* to some office, Mt 4:19; Mk 3:14; *to make, declare to be,* 1 Jn 1:10; 5:10; *to do, to perform, execute, practise, act,* Mt 5:46, 47, 6:2, 3; *to commit* evil, Mt 13:41; 27:23; *to be devoted to, follow, practise,* Jn 3:21; 5:29; Ro 3:12; *to do, execute, fulfil, keep, observe, obey,* precepts, etc., Mt 1:24; 5:19; 7:21, 24, 26; *to bring evil upon, inflict,* Ac 9:13; *to keep, celebrate* a festival, Mt 26:18; *to institute the celebration of* a festival, Heb 11:28; ποιεῖν τινα ἔξω, *to cause to leave* a place, i.q. ἔξω ἄγειν, *to lead* or *conduct out,* Ac 5:34; *to pass, spend* time, *continue for* a time, Mt 20:12; Ac 15:33; 18:23; Jas 4:13; *to bear,* as trees, *yield, produce,* Mt 3:8, 10; 7:17, 18, 19; with a substantive or adjective it forms a periphrasis for the verb corresponding to the noun or adjective, e.g. δῆλον ποιεῖν, i.q. δηλοῦν, *to make manifest, betray,* Mt 26:73; ἐκδίκησιν ποιεῖν, i.q. ἐκδικεῖν, *to vindicate, avenge,* Lk 18:7, 8; ἔκθετον ποιεῖν, i.q. ἐκτιθέναι, *to expose* infants, Acts 7:19; ἐνέδραν ποιεῖν, i.q. ἐνεδρεύειν, *to lie in wait,* Acts 25:3; ἐξουσίαν ποιεῖν, i.q. ἐξουσιάζειν, *to exercise power* or *authority,* Rev 13:12; κρίσιν ποιεῖν, i.q. κρίνειν, *to judge, act as judge,* John 5:27; λύτρωσιν ποιεῖν, i.q. λυτροῦν, *to deliver, set free,* Luke 1:68; μονὴν ποιεῖν, i.q. μένειν, *to remain, dwell,* John 14:23; πόλεμον ποιεῖν, i.q. πολεμεῖν, *to make* or *wage war, fight,* Rev 11:7; συμβούλιον ποιεῖν, i.q. συμβουλεύεσθαι, *to consult together, deliberate,* Mark 3:6; συνωμοσίαν ποιεῖν, i.q. συνομνύναι, and συστροφὴν ποιεῖν, i.q. συστρέφεσθαι, *to conspire together, form a conspiracy,* Acts 23:12, 13; φανερὸν ποιεῖν, i.q. φανεροῦν, *to make known, betray,* Matt 12:16; ἀναβολὴν ποιεσθαι, i.q. ἀναβάλλεσθαι, *to delay, procrastinate,* Acts 25:17; βέβαιον ποιεῖσθαι, i.q. βεβαιοῦν, *to confirm, render firm and sure,* 2 Peter 1:10; δεήσεις ποιεῖσθαι, i.q. δεῖσθαι, *to pray, offer prayer,* Luke 5:33; ἐκβολὴν ποιεῖσθαι, i.q. ἐκβάλλειν, *to cast out, throw overboard,* Acts 27:18; καθαρισμὸν ποιεῖσθαι, i.q. καθαρίζειν, *to cleanse* from sin, Heb 1:3; κοινωνίαν ποιεῖσθαι, i.q. κοινωνεῖν, *to communicate in liberality, bestow alms,* Rom 15:26; κοπετὸν ποιεῖν, i.q. κόπτεσθαι, *to lament, bewail,* Acts 8:2; λόγον ποιεῖσθαι, *to regard, make account of,* Acts 20:24; μνείαν ποιεῖσθαι, i.q. μνησθῆναι, *to call to mind,* Rom 1:9; μνήμην ποιεῖσθαι, *to remember, retain in memory,* 2 Peter 1:15; πορείαν ποιεῖσθαι, i.q. πορεύεσθαι, *to go, journey, travel,* Luke 13:22; πρόνοιαν ποιεῖσθαι, i.q. προνοεῖσθαι, *to take care of, provide for,* Rom 13:14; σπουδὴν ποιεῖσθαι, *to act with diligence and earnestness,* Jude 3 [4160]

[4473] ποίημα *poiēma* 2x *that which is made* or *done; a work, workmanship, creation,* Ro 1:20; met. Eph 2:10* [4161]

[4474] ποίησις *poiēsis* 1x *a making; an acting, doing, performance; observance* of a law, Jas 1:25* [4162]

[4475] ποιητής *poiētēs* 6x *a maker; the maker* or *author* of a song or poem, *a poet,* Ac 17:28; *a doer; a performer* of the enactments of a law, Ro 2:13 [4163]

[4476] ποικίλος *poikilos* 10x *of various colors, variegated, checkered; various, diverse, manifold,* Mt 4:24 [4164]

[4477] ποιμαίνω *poimainō* 11x *to feed, pasture, tend a flock,* Lk 17:7; 1 Co 9:7; trop. *to feed* with selfish indulgence, *to pamper,* Judc 12; met. *to tend, direct, superintend,* Mt 2:6; Jn 21:16; *to rule,* Rev 2:27 [4165]

[4478] ποιμήν *poimēn* 18x *one who tends flocks* or *herds, a shepherd, herdsman,* Mt 9:36; 25:32; met. *a pastor, superintendent, guardian,* Jn 10:11, 14, 16 [4166]

[4479] ποίμνη *poimnē* 5x *a flock* of sheep, Lk 2:8; 1 Co 9:7; meton. *a flock* of disciples, Mt 26:31; Jn 10:16* [4167]

[4480] ποίμνιον *poimnion* 5x *a flock;* met. *a flock* of Christian disciples, Lk 12:32; Ac 20:28, 29; 1 Pe 5:2, 3* [4168]

[4481] ποῖος *poios* 33x *of what kind, sort* or *species,* Jn 12:33; 21:19; *what? which?* Mt 19:18; 21:23, 24, 27 [4169]

[4482] πολεμέω *polemeō* 7x *to make* or *wage war, fight,* Rev 2:16; 12:7; *to battle, quarrel,* Jas 4:2 [4170]

[4483] πόλεμος *polemos* 18x *war,* Mt 24:6; Mk 13:7; *battle, engagement, combat,* 1 Co 14:8; Heb 11:34; *battling, strife,* Jas 4:1 [4171]

[4484] πόλις *polis* 162x *a city, an enclosed and walled town,* Mt 10:5, 11; 11:1; meton. *the inhabitants of a city,* Mt 8:34; 10:15; with a gen. of person, or a personal pronoun, *the city* of any one, *the city* of one's birth or residence, Mt 9:1; Lk 2:4, 11; ἡ πόλις, *the city,* κατ᾽ ἐξοχήν, *Jerusalem,* Mt 21:18; 28:11; met. *a place of permanent residence, abode, home,* Heb 11:10, 16; 13:14. The frequency count does not include its occurrence in the name Νέαν πόλιν in Ac 16:11 [4172]

[4485] πολιτάρχης *politarchēs* 2x *a ruler* or *prefect of a city, city magistrate,* Ac 17:6, 8* [4173]

[4486] πολιτεία *politeia* 2x *the state of being a citizen; citizenship, the right* or *privilege of being a citizen, freedom of a city* or *state,* Ac 22:28; *a commonwealth, community,* Eph 2:12* [4174]

[4487] πολίτευμα *politeuma* 1x *the administration of a commonwealth;* in N.T. equivalent to πολιτεία, *a community, commonwealth,* Phil 3:20* [4175]

[4488] πολιτεύομαι *politeuomai* 2x intrans. *to be a citizen;* trans. *to govern a city* or *state, administer the affairs of a state;* pass. *to be governed;* in N.T. *to order one's life and conduct, converse, live,* in a certain manner as to habits and principles, Ac 23:1; Phil 1:27* [4176]

[4489] πολίτης *politēs* 4x *a citizen,* Lk 15:15; 19:14; Ac 21:39; Heb 8:11* [4177]

[4490] πολλάκις *pollakis* 18x *many times, often, frequently,* Mt 17:15; Mk 5:4; 9:22 [4178]

[4491] πολλαπλασίων *pollaplasiōn* 1x *manifold, many times more,* Lk 18:30* [4179]

[4494] πολυλογία *polylogia* 1x *wordiness, loquacity,* Mt 6:7* [4180]

[4495] πολυμερῶς *polymerōs* 1x *in many parts* or *ways,* Heb 1:1* [4181]

[4497] πολυποίκιλος *polypoikilos* 1x *exceedingly various, multiform, manifold;* by impl. *immense, infinite,* Eph 3:10* [4182]

[4498] πολύς *polys* 416x *great in* magnitude or quantity, *much, large,* Mt 13:5; Jn 3:23; 15:8; pl. *many,* Mt 3:7; in time, *long,* Mt 25:19; Mk 6:35; Jn 5:6; οἱ πολλοί, *the many, the mass,* Ro 5:15; 12:5; 1 Co 10:33; τὸ πολύ, *much,* 2 Co 8:15; πολύ, as an adv., *much, greatly,* Mk 12:27; Lk 7:47; of time, ἐπὶ πολύ, *a long time,* Ac 28:6; μετ᾽ οὐ πολύ, *not long after,* Ac 27:14; followed by a compar., *much,* 2 Co 8:22; πολλῷ, *much, by much,* Mt 6:30; Mk 10:48; τὰ πολλά, as an adv., *most frequently, generally,* Ro 15:22; πολλά, as an adv., *much, greatly, vehemently,* Mk 1:45; 3:12; of time, *many times, frequently, often,* Mt 9:14 [4118, 4119, 4183]

[4499] πολύσπλαγχνος *polysplanchnos* 1x *very merciful, very compassionate,* Jas 5:11* [4184]

[4500] πολυτελής *polytelēs* 3x *expensive, costly,* Mk 14:3; 1 Ti 2:9; *of great value, very precious,* 1 Pe 3:4* [4185]

[4501] πολύτιμος *polytimos* 3x *of great price, costly, precious,* Mt 13:46; Jn 12:3; 1 Pet 1:7* [4186]

[4502] πολυτρόπως *polytropōs* 1x *in many ways, in various modes,* Heb 1:1* [4187]

[4503] πόμα *poma* 2x *drink,* 1 Co 10:4; Heb 9:10* [4188]

[4504] πονηρία *ponēria* 7x pr. *badness, bad condition;* in N.T. *evil disposition* of mind, *wickedness, mischief, malignity,* Mt 22:18; pl. πονηρίαι, *wicked deeds, villanies,* Mk 7:23; Ac 3:26 [4189]

[4505] πονηρός *ponēros* 78x *bad, unsound,* Mt 6:23; 7:17, 18; *evil, afflictive,* Eph 5:16; 6:13; Rev 16:2; *evil, wrongful, malignant, malevolent,* Mt 5:11, 39; Ac 28:21; *evil, wicked, impious,* and τὸ πονηρόν, *evil, wrong, wickedness,* Mt 5:37, 45; 9:4; *slothful, inactive,* Mt 25:26; Lk 19:22; ὁ πονηρός, *the evil one, the devil,* Mt 13:19, 38; Jn 17:15; *evil* eye, i.q. φθονερός *envious,* Mt 20:15; Mk 7:22; impl. *covetous,* Mt 7:11 [4190, 4191]

[4506] πόνος *ponos* 4x *labor, travail; pain, misery, anguish,* Col 4:13; Rev 16:10, 11; 21:4* [4192]

[4507] Ποντικός *Pontikos* 1x *belonging to* or *an inhabitant of Pontus,* Ac 18:2* [4193]

[4508] Πόντιος *Pontios* 3x *Pontius,* pr. name, Ac 4:27 [4194]

[4509] Πόντος *Pontos* 1x *Pontus,* country of Asia Minor, Ac 2:9; 1 Pe 1:1* [5117]

[4511] Πόπλιος *Poplios* 2x *Publius,* pr. name, Ac 28:7, 8* [4196]

[4512] πορεία *poreia* 2x *a going, progress; a journey, travel,* Lk 13:22; from the Hebrew, *way of life, business, occupation,* Jas 1:11* [4197]

[4513] πορεύω *poreuō* 153x also listed as a deponent, πορεύομαι, *to go, pass from one place to another,* Mt 17:27; 18:12; *to go away, depart,* Mt 24:1; 25:41; Jn 14:2, 3; trop. *to go away, depart,* from life, *to die,* Lk 22:22; *to go, pass on one's way, journey, travel,* Mt 2:8, 9; Lk 1:39; 2:41; πορεύομαι ὀπίσω, *to go after, to become a follower* or *partisan,* Lk 21:8; or, *to pursue after, be devoted to,* 2 Pe 2:10; from the

Hebrew, *to go* or *proceed* in any way or course of life, *live* in any manner, Lk 1:6; 8:14; Ac 9:31 [4198]

[4514] πορθέω *portheō* 3x *to lay waste, destroy;* impl. *to harass, ravage,* Ac 9:21; Gal 1:13, 23* [4199]

[4516] πορισμός *porismos* 2x *a providing, procuring;* meton. *source of gain,* 1 Ti 6:5, 6* [4200]

[4517] Πόρκιος *Porkios* 1x *Porcius,* pr. name, Ac 24:27* [4201]

[4518] πορνεία *porneia* 25x *fornication, whoredom,* Mt 15:19; Mk 7:21; Ac 15:20, 29; *concubinage,* Jn 8:41; *adultery,* Mt 5:32; 19:9; *incest,* 1 Co 5:1; *lewdness, uncleanness,* genr., Ro 1:29; from the Hebrew, put symbolically for *idolatry,* Rev 2:21; 14:8 [4202]

[4519] πορνεύω *porneuō* 8x *to commit fornication,* 1 Co 6:18; 10:8; Rev 2:14, 20; from the Hebrew, *to commit* spiritual *fornication, practise idolatry,* Rev 17:2; 18:3, 9* [4203]

[4520] πόρνη *pornē* 12x *a prostitute, a whore, harlot, an unchaste female,* Mt 21:31, 32; from the Hebrew, an *idolatress,* Rev 17:1, 5, 15 [4204]

[4521] πόρνος *pornos* 10x *a catamite;* in N.T. *a fornicator, impure person,* 1 Co 5:9, 10, 11; 6:9 [4205]

[4522] πόρρω *porrō* 4x *in advance, far advanced; far, far off, at a distance,* Mt 15:8; Mk 7:6; Lk 14:32, can be an improper prep. with the gen. The comparative form of the adverb appears as πορρώτερον at Lk 24:28.* [4206]

[4523] πόρρωθεν *porrōthen* 2x *from a distance, from afar,* Heb 11:13; *at a distance, far, far off,* Lk 17:12* [4207]

[4525] πορφύρα *porphyra* 4x *purpura, murex,* a species of shell-fish that yielded the purple dye, highly esteemed by the ancients, its tint being a bright crimson; in N.T. *a purple garment, robe of purple,* Lk 16:19; Rev 18:12 [4209]

[4527] πορφυρόπωλις *porphyropōlis* 1x *a female seller of purple cloths,* Ac 16:4* [4211]

[4528] πορφυροῦς *porphyrous* 4x contracted form is πορφύρεος, *purple,* Jn 19:2, 5; *purple clothing,* Rev 17:4; 18:16* [4210]

[4529] ποσάκις *posakis* 3x *How many times? How often?* Mt 18:21; 23:37; Lk 13:34* [4212]

[4530] πόσις *posis* 3x *drinking; drink, beverage,* Jn 6:55; Ro 14:17; Col 2:16* [4213]

[4531] πόσος *posos* 27x *How great? How much?* Mt 6:23; Lk 16:5, 7; 2 Co 7:11; πόσῳ, adverbially before a comparative, *How much? By how much?* Mt 7:11; 10:25; Heb 10:29; of time, *How long?* Mk 9:21; of number, pl. *How many?* Mt 15:34; 16:9, 10 [4214]

[4532] ποταμός *potamos* 17x *a river, stream,* Mk 1:5; Ac 16:13; met. and allegor. Jn 7:38; Rev 22:1, 2; *a flood, winter torrent,* for χείμαρρος ποταμός, Mt 7:25, 27 [4215]

[4533] ποταμοφόρητος *potamophorētos* 1x *borne along* or *carried away by a flood* or *torrent,* Rev 12:15* [4216]

[4534] ποταπός *potapos* 7x *Of what country?* in N.T. equivalent to ποῖος, *What? Of what manner? Of what kind* or *sort?* Lk 1:29; 7:37; denoting admiration, *What? What kind of? How great?* Mt 8:27; Mk 13:1 [4217]

[4536] πότε *pote* 19x interrogative adverb, *When? At what time?* Mt 24:3; 25:37, 38, 39, 44; ἕως πότε, *until when? how long?* Mt 17:17 [4219]

[4537] ποτέ *pote* 29x enclitic particle, *once, some time* or *other,* either past or future; *formerly,* Jn 9:13; *at length,* Lk 22:32; *at any time, ever,* Eph 5:29; Heb 2:1; intensive after interrogatives, *ever,* 1 Co 9:7; Heb 1:5 [4218]

[4538] πότερον *poteron* 1x interrogative of πότερος, α, ον, which never occurs in N.T. other than in this form, *whether?,* Jn 7:17* [4220]

[4539] ποτήριον *potērion* 31x *a vessel for drinking, cup,* Mt 10:42; 23:25, 26; meton. *the contents of a cup, liquor contained in a cup,* Lk 22:20; 1 Co 10:16; from the Hebrew, *the cup* or *potion* of what God's administration deals out, Mt 20:22, 23; Rev 14:10 [4221]

[4540] ποτίζω *potizō* 15x *to cause to drink, give drink to,* Mt 10:42; met. 1 Co 3:2; Rev 14:8; *to water, irrigate,* met. 1 Co 3:6, 7, 8 [4222]

[4541] Ποτίολοι *Potioloi* 1x *Puteoli,* a town of Italy, Ac 28:13* [4223]

[4542] πότος *potos* 1x *a drinking; a drinking together, drinking-bout,* 1 Pe 4:3* [4224]

[4543] που *pou* 4x enclitic, *somewhere, in a certain place,* Heb 2:6; 4:4; with numerals, *thereabout,* Ro 4:19* [4225]

[4544] ποῦ *pou* 48x interrogative, *where? In what place?* direct, Mt 2:2; Lk 8:25; Jn 1:39; indirect, Mt 2:4; Jn 1:40; *whither*, Jn 3:8; 7:35; 13:36 [4226]

[4545] Πούδης *Poudēs* 1x *Pudens*, pr. name, Latin, 2 Ti 4:21★ [4227]

[4546] πούς *pous* 93x *the foot*, Mt 4:6; 5:35; 7:6; 22:44; 28:9; Lk 1:79; Ac 5:9; Ro 3:15 [4228]

[4547] πρᾶγμα *pragma* 11x *a thing done, fact, deed, work, transaction*, Lk 1:1; Jas 3:16; *a matter, affair*, Mt 18:19; Ro 16:2; *a matter* of dispute, 1 Co 6:1; *a thing*, genr., Heb 10:1; 11:1; τὸ πρᾶγμα, a euphemism for *unlawful sexual conduct*, perhaps, 1 Th 4:6 [4229]

[4548] πραγματεία *pragmateia* 1x *an application to a matter of business;* in N.T. *business, affair, transaction*, 2 Ti 2:4★ [4230]

[4549] πραγματεύομαι *pragmateuomai* 1x *to be occupied with* or *employed in any business, do business; to trade traffic*, Lk 19:13★ [4231]

[4550] πραιτώριον *praitōrion* 8x when used in reference to a camp, *the tent of the general* or *commander-in-chief;* hence, in reference to a province, *the palace in which the governor of the province resided*, Mt 27:27; Mk 15:16; Ac 23:35; *the camp occupied by the praetorian cohorts at Rome, the praetorian camp*, or, *the Roman emperor's palace*, Phil 1:13 [4232]

[4551] πράκτωρ *praktōr* 2x *an exactor of dues* or *penalties; an officer* who enforced payment of debts by imprisonment, Lk 12:58★ [4233]

[4552] πρᾶξις *praxis* 6x *operation, business, office*, Ro 12:4; πρᾶξις, and πράξεις, *actions, mode of acting, ways, deeds, practice, behavior*, Mt 16:27; Lk 23:51 [4234]

[4555] πρασιά *prasia* 2x *a small area* or *bed in a garden;* trop. *a company of persons disposed in squares;* from the Hebrew, πρασιαὶ πρασιαί, *by areas, by squares*, like beds in a garden, Mk 6:40★ [4237]

[4556] πράσσω *prassō* 39x *to do, execute, perform, practise, act, transact*, and of evil, *to commit*, Lk 22:23; 23:15; Jn 3:20; Ac 26:9, 20, 26, 31; *to fulfil, obey, observe* a law, Ro 2:25; *to do to* any one, Ac 16:28; 5:35; *to occupy one's self with, be engaged in, busy one's self about*, Ac 19:19; 1 Th 4:11; absol. *to fare*, Ac 15:29; Eph 6:21; *to exact, require, collect* tribute, money lent, etc., Lk 3:13; 19:23 [4238]

[4557] πραϋπάθεια *praupatheia* 1x *meekness, gentleness of mind, kindness*, 1 Ti 6:11★ [4236]

[4558] πραΰς *praus* 4x also spelled πρᾶος, *meek, gentle, kind, forgiving*, Mt 5:5; *mild, benevolent, humane*, Mt 11:29; 21:5; 1 Pe 3:4★ [4239]

[4559] πραΰτης *prautēs* 11x also spelled πραότης, ητος, ἡ, *meekness, mildness, forbearance*, 1 Pe 3:15; *gentleness, kindness*, Jas 1:21; 3:13; Gal 5:23 [4240]

[4560] πρέπω *prepō* 7x *it becomes, it is fitting, it is proper, it is right*, etc., and part. πρέπον, *becoming, suitable, decorous*, etc., Mt 3:15; 1 Co 11:13; Eph 5:3; 1 Ti 2:10 [4241]

[4561] πρεσβεία *presbeia* 2x *eldership, seniority; an embassy, legation; a body of ambassadors, legates*, Lk 14:32; 19:14★ [4242]

[4563] πρεσβεύω *presbeuō* 2x *to be elder; to be an ambassador, perform the duties of an ambassador*, 2 Co 5:20; Eph 6:20★ [4243]

[4564] πρεσβυτέριον *presbyterion* 3x *a body of old men, an assembly of elders; the Jewish Sanhedrin*, Lk 22:66; Ac 22:5; *a body of elders* in the Christian church, *a presbytery*, 1 Ti 4:14★ [4244]

[4565] πρεσβύτερος *presbyteros* 66x *elder, senior; older, more advanced in years*, Lk 15:25; Jn 8:9; Ac 2:17; *an elder* in respect of age, *person advanced in years*, 1 Ti 5:1, 2; pl. spc. *ancients, ancestors, fathers*, Mt 15:2; Heb 11:2; as an appellation of dignity, *an elder, local dignitary*, Lk 7:3; *an elder, member of the Jewish Sanhedrin*, Mt 16:21; 21:23; 26:3, 47, 57, 59; *an elder* or *presbyter* of the Christian church, Ac 11:30; 14:23, et al. freq. [4245]

[4566] πρεσβύτης *presbytēs* 3x *an old man, aged person*, Lk 1:18; Tit 2:2; Phlm 9★ [4246]

[4567] πρεσβῦτις *presbytis* 1x *an aged woman*, Tit 2:3★ [4247]

[4568] πρηνής *prēnēs* 1x *prone, head-foremost;* πρηνὴς γενόμενος, *falling head-long*, Ac 1:18★ [4248]

[4569] πρίζω *prizō* 1x also spelled πρίω, *to saw, saw in two*, Heb 11:37★ [4249]

[4570] πρίν *prin* 13x can function as a temporal conj. and an improper prep., *before*, of time, Mt 26:34, 75; Mk 14:72; πρὶν ἤ, *sooner than, before*, Mt 1:18; Lk 2:26 [4250]

[4571] Πρίσκα *Priska* 3x see also Πρόσκιλλα, *Prisca*, pr. name, Ro 16:3; 1 Co 16:19; 2 Ti 4:19★ [4251]

[4572] Πρίσκιλλα *Priskilla* 3x *Priscilla*, pr. name, the diminutive form of Πρίσκα, both words forms referring to the same person, the wife of Apollo, Ac 18:2, 18, 26★ [4252]

[4574] πρό *pro* 47x *before*, of place, *in front of, in advance of*, Mt 11:10; Lk 1:76; Ac 5:23; *before*, of time, Mt 5:12; Lk 11:38; before an infin. with the gen. of the article, *before, before that*, Mt 6:8; Lk 2:21; *before, above, in preference*, Jas 5:12; 1 Pe 4:8 [4253]

[4575] προάγω *proagō* 20x *to lead, bring*, or *conduct forth, produce*, Ac 12:6; 16:30; 25:26; intrans. *to go before, to go first*, Mt 2:9; 21:9; Mk 6:45; 1 Ti 5:24; part. προάγων, ουσα, ον, *preceding, previous, antecedent*, 1 Ti 1:18; Heb 7:18; hence, in N.T., trans. *to precede*, Mt 14:22; *to be in advance of*, Mt 21:31 [4254]

[4576] προαιρέω *proaireō* 1x *to prefer, choose;* met. *to purpose, intend considerately*, 2 Co 9:7★ [4255]

[4577] προαιτιάομαι *proaitiaomai* 1x pr. *to charge beforehand; to convince beforehand*, Ro 3:9, since the charges in the case in question were drawn from Scripture.★ [4256]

[4578] προακούω *proakouō* 1x *to hear beforehand* or *already*, Col 1:5★ [4257]

[4579] προαμαρτάνω *proamartanō* 2x *to sin before;* perf., *to have already sinned, have sinned heretofore*, 2 Co 12:21; 13:2★ [4258]

[4580] προαύλιον *proaulion* 1x *the exterior court* before an edifice, Mk 14:68★ [4259]

[4581] προβαίνω *probainō* 5x *to go forward, advance*, Mt 4:21; Mk 1:19; *to advance* in life, Lk 1:7, 18; 2:36★ [4260]

[4582] προβάλλω *proballō* 2x *to cast before, project; to put* or *urge forward*, Ac 19:33; *to put forth*, as a tree its blossoms, etc., Lk 21:30★ [4261]

[4583] προβατικός *probatikos* 1x *belonging* or *pertaining to sheep;* ἡ προβατικὴ, (πύλη) *the sheep-gate*, Jn 5:2★ [4262]

[4585] πρόβατον *probaton* 39x *a sheep*, Mt 7:15; 9:36; 10:16; met. Mt 10:6; 15:24 [4263]

[4586] προβιβάζω *probibazō* 1x *to cause* any one *to advance, to lead forward;* met. *to incite, instigate*, Mt 14:8★ [4264]

[4587] προβλέπω *problepō* 1x *to foresee;* mid. *to provide beforehand,* Heb 11:40* [4265]

[4588] προγίνομαι *proginomai* 1x *to be* or *happen before, be previously done* or *committed;* προγεγονώς, *bygone, previous,* Ro 3:25 [4266]

[4589] προγινώσκω *proginōskō* 5x *to know beforehand, to be previously acquainted with,* Ac 26:5; 2 Pe 3:17; *to determine on beforehand, to fore-ordain,* 1 Pe 1:20; in N.T., from the Hebrew, *to foreknow, to appoint as the subject of future privileges,* Ro 8:29; 11:2* [4267]

[4590] πρόγνωσις *prognōsis* 2x *foreknowledge;* in N.T. *previous determination, purpose,* Ac 2:23; 1 Pe 1:2* [4268]

[4591] πρόγονος *progonos* 2x *born earlier, elder; a progenitor,* pl. *progenitors; parents,* 1 Ti 5:4; *forefathers, ancestors,* 2 Ti 1:3* [4269]

[4592] προγράφω *prographō* 4x *to write before,* Ro 15:4; Eph 3:3; *to make a subject of public notice; to set forth unreservedly and distinctly,* Gal 3:1; *to designate clearly,* Jude 4* [4270]

[4593] πρόδηλος *prodēlos* 3x *previously manifest, before known; plainly manifest, very clear, prominently conspicuous,* 1 Ti 5:24, 25; Heb 7:14* [4271]

[4594] προδίδωμι *prodidōmi* 1x *to give before, precede in giving;* Ro 11:35* [4272]

[4595] προδότης *prodotēs* 3x *a betrayer, traitor,* Lk 6:16; Ac 7:52; 2 Ti 3:4* [4273]

[4596] πρόδρομος *prodromos* 1x *a precursor, forerunner, one who advances to explore and prepare the way,* Heb 6:20* [4274]

[4598] προελπίζω *proelpizō* 1x *to have hope and confidence* in a person or thing *beforehand,* Eph 1:12* [4276]

[4599] προενάρχομαι *proenarchomai* 2x *to begin before* a particular time, 2 Co 8:6, 10* [4278]

[4601] προέρχομαι *proerchomai* 9x *to go forwards, advance, proceed,* Mt 26:39; Mk 14:35; Ac 12:10; *to precede, go before* any one, Lk 22:47; *to precede* in time, *be a forerunner* or *precursor,* Lk 1:17; *to outgo, outstrip in going,* Mk 6:33; *to travel in advance of* any one, *precede,* 20:5, 13; 2 Co 9:5* [4281]

[4602] προετοιμάζω *proetoimazō* 2x *to prepare beforehand;* in N.T. *to appoint beforehand,* Ro 9:23; Eph 2:10* [4282]

[4603] προευαγγελίζομαι *proeuangelizomai* 1x *to announce joyful tidings beforehand,* Gal 3:8* [4283]

[4604] προέχω *proechō* 1x *to have* or *hold before;* intrans. and mid. *to excel, surpass, have advantage* or *pre-eminence,* Ro 3:9* [4284]

[4605] προηγέομαι *proēgeomai* 1x *to go before, precede, lead onward;* met. *to endeavor to take the lead of, vie with,* or, *to give precedence to, to prefer,* Ro 12:10* [4285]

[4606] πρόθεσις *prothesis* 12x *a setting forth* or *before;* οἱ ἄρτοι τῆς προθέσεως, and ἡ πρόθεσις τῶν ἄρτων, *the shewbread,* the twelve loaves of bread, corresponding to the twelve tribes, which were *set out* in two rows upon the golden table in the sanctuary, Mt 12:4; Mk 2:26; Lk 6:4; Heb 9:2; *predetermination, purpose,* Ac 11:23; 27:13; Ro 8:28; 2 Ti 3:10 [4286]

[4607] προθεσμία *prothesmia* 1x *a time before appointed, set* or *appointed time,* Gal 4:2* [4287]

[4608] προθυμία *prothumia* 5x *promptness, readiness, eagerness of mind, willingness,* Ac 17:11; 2 Co 8:11, 12, 19; 9:2* [4288]

[4609] πρόθυμος *prothumos* 3x *ready in mind, prepared, prompt, willing,* Mt 26:41; Mk 14:38; τὸ πρόθυμον, i.q. ἡ προθυμία, *readiness, eagerness of mind,* Ro 1:15* [4289]

[4610] προθύμως *prothumōs* 1x *promptly, readily, willingly, heartily, cheerfully,* 1 Pe 5:2* [4290]

[4611] πρόϊμος *proimos* 1x also spelled πρώϊμος, *early,* Jas 5:7* [4406]

[4613] προΐστημι *proistēmi* 8x *to set before;* met. *to set over, appoint with authority;* intrans. 2 aor. προύστην, perf. προέστηκα, part. proestwv", and mid. προΐσταμαι, *to preside, govern, superintend,* Ro 12:8; 1 Th 5:12; 1 Ti 3:4, 5, 12; 5:17; mid. *to undertake resolutely, to practise diligently, to maintain the practice of,* Tit 3:8, 14* [4291]

[4614] προκαλέω *prokaleō* 1x *to call out, challenge to fight; to provoke, irritate, with feelings of ungenerous rivalry,* Gal 5:26* [4292]

[4615] προκαταγγέλλω *prokatangellō* 2x *to declare* or *announce beforehand, foretell, predict,* Ac 3:18; 7:52* [4293]

[4616] προκαταρτίζω *prokatartizō* 1x *to make ready, prepare,* or *complete beforehand,* 2 Co 9:5* [4294]

[4618] πρόκειμαι *prokeimai* 5x *to lie* or *be placed before;* met. *to be proposed* or *set before,* as a duty, example, reward, etc., Heb 6:18; 12:1, 2; Jude 7; *to be at hand, be present,* 2 Co 8:12* [4295]

[4619] προκηρύσσω *prokēryssō* 1x *to announce publicly;* in N.T. *to announce before,* Ac 13:24* [4296]

[4620] προκοπή *prokopē* 3x *advance upon a way;* met. *progress, advancement, furtherance,* Phil 1:12, 25; 1 Ti 4:15* [4297]

[4621] προκόπτω *prokoptō* 6x pr. *to cut* a passage *forward; to advance, make progress; to advance,* as time, *to be far spent,* Ro 13:12; met. *to advance* in wisdom, age, or stature, Lk 2:52; seq. ejn, *to make progress* or *proficiency in,* Gal 1:14; προκόπτω ἐπὶ πλεῖον, *to proceed* or *advance further,* 2 Ti 2:16; 3:9; προκόπτω ἐπὶ τὸ χεῖρον, *to grow* worse and worse, 2 Ti 3:13* [4298]

[4622] πρόκριμα *prokrima* 1x *previous judgment, prejudice,* or, *preference, partiality,* 1 Ti 5:21* [4299]

[4623] προκυρόω *prokyroō* 1x *to sanction and establish previously, ratify and confirm before,* Gal 3:17* [4300]

[4624] προλαμβάνω *prolambanō* 3x *to take before* another, 1 Co 11:21; trop. *to anticipate, do beforehand,* Mk 14:8; *to take by surprise;* pass. *be taken unexpectedly, be overtaken, be taken by surprise,* Gal 6:1* [4301]

[4625] προλέγω *prolegō* 15x *to tell beforehand, to foretell,* Mt 24:25; Ac 1:16; Ro 9:29; 2 Co 13:2; Gal 5:21; 1 Th 3:4 [4302, 4277, 4280]

[4626] προμαρτύρομαι *promartyromai* 1x pr. *to witness* or *testify beforehand; to declare beforehand, predict,* 1 Pe 1:11* [4303]

[4627] προμελετάω *promeletaō* 1x *to practise beforehand; to premeditate,* Lk 21:14* [4304]

[4628] προμεριμνάω *promerimnaō* 1x *to be anxious* or *solicitous beforehand, to ponder beforehand,* Mk 13:11* [4305]

[4629] προνοέω *pronoeō* 3x *to perceive beforehand, foresee; to provide for,* 1 Ti 5:8; mid. *to provide for one's self;* by impl. *to apply one's self to* a thing, *practice, strive to exhibit,* Ro 12:17; 2 Co 8:21* [4306]

[4630] πρόνοια *pronoia* 2x *forethought; providence, provident care,* Ac 24:2; *provision,* Ro 13:14* [4307]

[4632] προοράω *prooraō* 4x *to foresee,* Ac 2:31; Gal 3:8; *to see before,* Ac 21:29;

in N.T. *to have vividly present to the mind, to be mindful of,* Ac 2:25* [4275, 4308]

[4633] προορίζω *proorizō* 6x *to limit or mark out beforehand; to design definitely beforehand, ordain beforehand, predestine,* Ac 4:28; Ro 8:29, 30 [4309]

[4634] προπάσχω *propaschō* 1x *to experience previously,* of ill treatment, 1 Th 2:2* [4310]

[4635] προπάτωρ *propatōr* 1x *a grandfather; a progenitor,* or *ancestor,* Ro 4:1* [3962]

[4636] προπέμπω *propempō* 9x *to send on before; to accompany* or *attend out of respect, escort, accompany for a certain distance on setting out on a journey,* Ac 15:3; 20:38; 21:5; *to furnish with things necessary for a journey,* Tit 3:13; 3 Jn 6 [4311]

[4637] προπετής *propetēs* 2x *falling forwards;* meton. *precipitate, rash,* Ac 19:36; 2 Ti 3:4* [4312]

[4638] προπορεύομαι *proporeuomai* 2x *to precede, go before,* Ac 7:40; Lk 1:76* [4313]

[4639] πρός *pros* 700x *from;* met. *for the benefit of,* Ac 27:34; with a dative, *near, by, at, by the side of, in the vicinity of,* Mk 5:11; Lk 19:37; with an accusative, used of the place to which anything tends, *to, unto, towards,* Mt 2:12; 3:5, 13; *at, close upon,* Mt 3:10; Mk 5:22; *near to, in the vicinity of,* Mk 6:45; after verbs of speaking, praying, answering to a charge, etc., *to,* Mt 3:15; 27:14; of place where, *with, in, among, by, at,* etc., Mt 26:55; Mk 11:4; Lk 1:80; of time, *for, during,* Lk 8:13; 1 Co 7:5; *near, towards,* Lk 24:29; of the end, object, purpose for which an action is exerted, or to which any quality, etc., has reference, *to,* Jn 4:35; Ac 3:10; 27:12; before an infin. with τό, *in order to, that, in order that,* Mt 6:1; 13:30; 26:12; *so as to, so that,* Mt 5:28; of the relation which any action, state, quality, etc., bears to any person or thing, *in relation to, of, concerning, in respect to, with reference to,* Mt 19:8; Lk 12:41; 18:1; 20:19; *as it respects, as it concerns, with relation to,* Mt 27:4; Jn 21:22, 23; *according to, in conformity with,* Lk 12:47; 2 Co 5:10; *in comparison with,* Ro 8:18; *in attention to,* Eph 3:4; of the actions, dispositions, etc., exhibited with respect to any one, whether friendly, *towards,* Gal 6:10; Eph 6:9; or unfriendly, *with, against,* Lk 23:12; Ac 23:30; after verbs signifying to converse, dispute, make a covenant, etc., *with,* Lk 24:14; Ac 2:7; 3:25 [4314]

[4640] προσάββατον *prosabbaton* 1x *the day before the sabbath, sabbath-eve,* Mk 15:42* [4315]

[4641] προσαγορεύω *prosagoreuō* 1x *to speak to, accost, to name, declare,* Heb 5:10* [4316]

[4642] προσάγω *prosagō* 4x *to lead* or *conduct to, bring,* Lk 9:41; Ac 16:20; *to conduct to the presence of, to procure access for,* 1 Pe 3:18; *to bring near; to near,* in a nautical sense, Ac 27:27* [4317]

[4643] προσαγωγή *prosagōgē* 3x *approach; access, admission,* to the presence of any one, Ro 5:2; Eph 2:18; 3:12* [4318]

[4644] προσαιτέω *prosaiteō* 1x *to ask for in addition; to ask earnestly, beg; to beg alms,* Jn 9:8* [4319]

[4645] προσαίτης *prosaitēs* 2x *a beggar, mendicant,* Mk 10:46; Jn 9:8* [4319]

[4646] προσαναβαίνω *prosanabainō* 1x *to go up further,* Lk 14:10* [4320]

[4649] προσαναλόω *prosanaloō* 1x *to spend,* Lk 8:43* [4321]

[4650] προσαναπληρόω *prosanaplēroō* 2x *to fill up by addition; to supply* deficiencies, 2 Co 9:12; 11:9* [4322]

[4651] προσανατίθημι *prosanatithēmi* 2x occurs in the N.T. only as a middle, *to lay upon over and above;* mid. *to put one's self in free communication with, to confer with,* Gal 1:16; *to confer upon, to propound as a matter of consideration,* Gal 2:6* [4323]

[4653] προσαπειλέω *prosapeileō* 1x *to threaten in addition, utter additional threats,* Ac 4:21* [4324]

[4655] προσδαπανάω *prosdapanaō* 1x *to spend besides, expend over and above,* Lk 10:35* [4325]

[4656] προσδέομαι *prosdeomai* 1x *to want besides* or *in addition, need,* Ac 17:25* [4326]

[4657] προσδέχομαι *prosdechomai* 14x *to receive, accept; to receive, admit, grant access to,* Lk 15:2; *to receive, admit, accept,* and with οὐ, *to reject,* Heb 11:35; *to submit to,* Heb 10:34; *to receive kindly,* as a guest, *entertain,* Ro 16:2; *to receive, admit,* as a hope, Ac 24:15; *to look* or *wait for, expect, await,* Mk 15:43; Lk 2:25 [4327]

[4659] προσδοκάω *prosdokaō* 16x *to look for, be expectant of,* Mt 11:3; Lk 7:19, 20; Ac 3:5; 2 Pe 3:12, 13, 14; *to expect,* Ac 28:6; *to wait for,* Lk 1:21; 8:40; Ac 10:24; 27:33; absol. *to think, anticipate,* Mt 24:50; Lk 12:46 [4328]

[4660] προσδοκία *prosdokia* 2x *a looking for, expectation, anticipation,* Lk 21:26; meton. *expectation, what is expected* or *anticipated,* Ac 12:11* [4329]

[4661] προσεάω *proseaō* 1x *to permit an approach,* Ac 27:7* [4330]

[4664] προσεργάζομαι *prosergazomai* 1x pr. *to work in addition; to gain in addition in trade,* Lk 19:16* [4333]

[4665] προσέρχομαι *proserchomai* 86x *to come* or *go to any one, approach,* Mt 4:3, 11; 5:1; 8:19, 25, et al. freq.; trop. *to come* or *go to, approach, draw near,* spiritually, Heb 7:25; 11:6; 4:16; 1 Pe 2:4; met. *to assent to, accede to, concur in,* 1 Ti 6:3 [4334]

[4666] προσευχή *proseuchē* 36x *prayer,* Mt 17:21; 21:13, 22; Lk 6:12; Ac 1:14; meton. *a place where prayer is offered, an oratory,* perhaps, Ac 16:13, 16 [4335]

[4667] προσεύχομαι *proseuchomai* 85x *to pray, offer prayer,* Mt 5:44; 6:5, 6 [4336]

[4668] προσέχω *prosechō* 24x *to have in addition; to hold to, bring near;* absol. *to apply* the mind to a thing, *to give heed to, attend to, observe, consider,* Ac 5:35; Heb 2:1; 2 Pe 1:19; *to take care of, provide for,* Ac 20:28; when followed by ἀπό, μή, or μήποτε, *to beware of, take heed of, guard against,* Mt 6:1; 7:15; *to assent to, yield credence to, follow, adhere* or *be attached to,* Ac 8:6, 10, 11; 16:14; *to give one's self up to, be addicted to, engage in, be occupied with,* 1 Ti 1:4, 3:8 [4337]

[4669] προσηλόω *proseloō* 1x *to nail to, affix with nails,* Col 2:14* [4338]

[4670] προσήλυτος *proselytos* 4x pr. *a newcomer, a stranger;* in N.T. *a proselyte, convert from paganism to Judaism,* Mt 23:15; Ac 2:11; 6:5; 13:43* [4339]

[4672] πρόσκαιρος *proskairos* 4x *opportune,* in N.T. *continuing for a limited time, temporary, transient,* Mt 13:21; Mk 4:17; 2 Co 4:18; Heb 11:25* [4340]

[4673] προσκαλέω *proskaleō* 29x *to call to one's self, summon,* Mt 10:1; 15:10, 32; 18:2; *to invite,* Ac 2:39; *to call* to the performance of a thing, *appoint,* Ac 13:2; 16:10 [4341]

[4674] προσκαρτερέω *proskartereō* 10x *to persist in adherence to* a thing; *to be intently engaged in, attend constantly to,* Ac 1:14; 2:42; Ro 13:6; *to remain constantly in a place,* Ac 2:46; *to constantly attend upon, continue near to, be at hand,* Mk 3:9; Ac 8:13; 10:7 [4342]

[4675] προσκαρτέρησις *proskarterēsis* 1x *perseverance, unremitting continuance in* a thing, Eph 6:18★ [4343]

[4676] προσκεφάλαιον *proskephalaion* 1x pr. *a cushion for the head, pillow;* also, *a boat-cushion,* Mk 4:38★ [4344]

[4677] προσκληρόω *prosklēroō* 1x pr. *to assign by lot;* in N.T., *to adjoin one's self to, associate with, follow as a disciple,* Ac 17:4★ [4345]

[4679] προσκλίνω *prosklinō* 1x pr. *to make to lean upon* or *against* a thing; met., *to join one's self to, follow as an adherent,* Ac 5:36★ [4347]

[4680] πρόσκλισις *prosklisis* 1x pr. *a leaning upon* or *towards* a thing; met. *a leaning towards* any one, *inclination* of mind *towards, partiality,* 1 Ti 5:21★ [4346]

[4681] προσκολλάω *proskollaō* 2x pr. *to glue to; to cleave closely to,* Mk 10:7; Eph 5:31★ [4347]

[4682] πρόσκομμα *proskomma* 6x *a stumbling,* Ro 9:32, 33; 1 Pe 2:8; met. *a stumbling-block, an occasion of sinning, means of inducing to sin,* Ro 14:13; 1 Co 8:9; met. *a* moral *stumbling, a shock* to the moral or religious sense, *a* moral *embarrassment,* Ro 14:20★ [4348]

[4683] προσκοπή *proskopē* 1x pr. *a stumbling; offence;* in N.T. *an offence, shock, ground of exception,* 2 Co 6:3★ [4349]

[4684] προσκόπτω *proskoptō* 8x *to dash against, to beat upon,* Mt 7:27; *to strike* the foot *against,* Mt 4:6; Lk 4:11; *to stumble,* Jn 11:9, 10; met. *to stumble at, to take offence at,* Ro 9:32; 14:21; 1 Pe 2:8★ [4350]

[4685] προσκυλίω *proskyliō* 2x *to roll to* or *against,* Mt 27:60; Mk 15:46★ [4351]

[4686] προσκυνέω *proskyneō* 60x *to do reverence* or *homage by kissing the hand;* in N.T. *to do reverence* or *homage by prostration,* Mt 2:2, 8, 11; 20:20; Lk 4:7; 24:52; *to pay* divine *homage, worship, adore,* Mt 4:10; Jn 4:20, 21; Heb 1:6; *to bow one's self in adoration,* Heb 11:21 [4352]

[4687] προσκυνητής *proskynētēs* 1x *a worshipper,* Jn 4:23★ [4353]

[4688] προσλαλέω *proslaleō* 2x *to speak to, converse with,* Ac 13:43; 28:20★ [4354]

[4689] προσλαμβάνω *proslambanō* 12x *to take to one's self, assume, take as a companion* or *associate,* Ac 17:5; 18:26; *to take,* as food, Ac 27:33, 36; *to receive kindly* or *hospitably, admit to one's society and friendship, treat with kindness,* Ac 28:2; Ro 14:1, 3; 15:7; Phlm 17; *to take* or *draw*

to one's self as a preliminary to an address of admonition, Mt 16:22; Mk 8:32★ [4355]

[4691] πρόσλημψις *proslēmpsis* 1x also spelled πρόσληψις, *acceptance,* Ro 11:15★ [4356]

[4693] προσμένω *prosmenō* 7x *to continue, remain, stay* in a place, 1 Ti 1:3; *to remain* or *continue with* any one, Mt 15:32; Mk 8:2; Ac 18:18; *to adhere to,* Ac 11:23; met. *to remain constant in, persevere in,* Ac 13:43; 1 Ti 5:5★ [4357]

[4694] προσορμίζω *prosormizō* 1x *to bring a ship to its station* or *to land;* mid. *to come to the land,* Mk 6:53★ [4358]

[4695] προσοφείλω *prosopheilō* 1x *to owe besides* or *in addition,* Phlm 19★ [4359]

[4696] προσοχθίζω *prosochthizō* 2x *to be vexed* or *angry at,* Heb 3:10, 17★ [4360]

[4698] πρόσπεινος *prospeinos* 1x *very hungry,* Ac 10:10★ [4361]

[4699] προσπήγνυμι *prospēgnymi* 1x *to fix to, affix to,* Ac 2:23★ [4362]

[4700] προσπίπτω *prospiptō* 8x *to fall* or *impinge upon* or *against* a thing; *to fall down to* any one, Mk 3:11; 7:25; *to rush violently upon, beat against,* Mt 7:25 [4363]

[4701] προσποιέω *prospoieō* 1x *to add* or *attach;* mid. *to attach to one's self; to claim* or *arrogate to one's self; to assume the appearance of, make a show of, pretend,* Lk 24:28★ [4364]

[4702] προσπορεύομαι *prosporeuomai* 1x *to go* or *come to* any one, Mk 10:35★ [4365]

[4704] προσρήσσω *prosrēssō* 2x also spelled προσρήγνυμι, *to break* or *burst upon, dash against,* Lk 6:48, 49★ [4366]

[4705] προστάσσω *prostassō* 7x pr. *to place* or *station at* or *against; to enjoin, command, direct,* Mt 1:24; 8:4; Mk 1:44; *to assign, constitute, appoint,* Ac 17:26★ [4367]

[4706] προστάτις *prostatis* 1x *a patroness, protectress,* Ro 16:2★ [4368]

[4707] προστίθημι *prostithēmi* 18x *to put to* or *near; to lay with* or *by the side of,* Ac 13:36; *to add, super-add, adjoin,* Mt 6:27, 33; Lk 3:20; Ac 2:41; from the Hebrew, denote *continuation,* or *repetition,* Lk 19:11; 20:11, 12; Ac 12:3 [4369]

[4708] προστρέχω *prostrechō* 3x *to run to,* or *up,* Mk 9:15; 10:17; Ac 8:30★ [4370]

[4709] προσφάγιον *prosphagion* 1x *what is eaten besides;* hence, genr. *victuals, food,* Jn 21:5★ [4371]

[4710] πρόσφατος *prosphatos* 1x pr. *recently killed;* hence, genr. *recent, new, newly* or *lately made,* Heb 10:20★ [4372]

[4711] προσφάτως *prosphatōs* 1x *newly, recently, lately,* Ac 18:2★ [4373]

[4712] προσφέρω *prospherō* 47x *to bear* or *bring to,* Mt 4:24; 25:20; *to bring to* or *before* magistrates, Lk 12:11; 23:14; *to bring near to, apply to,* Jn 19:29; *to offer, tender, proffer,* as money, Ac 8:18; *to offer, present,* as gifts, oblations, etc., Mt 2:11; 5:23; Heb 5:7; *to offer* in sacrifice, Mk 1:44; Lk 5:14; *to offer up* any one as a sacrifice to God, Heb 9:25, 28; 11:17; mid. *to bear one's self towards, behave* or *conduct one's self towards, to deal with, treat* any one, Heb 12:7 [4374]

[4713] προσφιλής *prosphilēs* 1x *friendly, grateful, acceptable,* Phil 4:8★ [4375]

[4714] προσφορά *prosphora* 9x pr. *a bringing to;* in N.T. *an offering, an act of offering up* or *sacrificing,* Heb 10:10, 14, 18; trop. Ro 15:16; *an offering, oblation, a thing offered,* Eph 5:2; Heb 10:5, 8; *a sacrifice, victim offered,* Ac 21:26; 24:17★ [4376]

[4715] προσφωνέω *prosphōneō* 7x *to speak to, address,* Mt 11:16; Lk 7:32; 13:12; *to address, harangue,* Ac 22:2; *to call to one's self,* Lk 6:13 [4377]

[4717] πρόσχυσις *proschusis* 1x *an effusion, sprinkling,* Heb 11:28★ [4378]

[4718] προσψαύω *prospsauō* 1x *to touch upon, touch lightly,* with the dative, Lk 11:46★ [4379]

[4719] προσωπολημπτέω *prosōpolēmpteō* 1x *show partiality,* Jas 2:9★ [4380]

[4720] προσωπολήμπτης *prosōpolēmptēs* 1x *one who shows partiality,* Ac 10:34★ [4381]

[4721] προσωπολημψία *prosōpolēmpsia* 4x *respect of persons, partiality,* Ro 2:11; Eph 6:9; Col 3:25; Jas 2:1★ [4382]

[4725] πρόσωπον *prosōpon* 76x *the face, countenance, visage,* Mt 6:16, 17; 17:2, 6; according to late usage, *a person, individual,* 2 Co 1:11; hence, *a personal presence,* 1 Th 2:17; from the Hebrew, πρόσωπον πρὸς πρόσωπον, *face to face, clearly, perfectly,* 1 Co 13:12; *face, surface, external form, figure, appearance,* Mt 16:3; Lk 12:56; *external circumstances,* or *condition* of any one, Mt 22:16; Mk 12:14; πρόσωπον λαμβάνειν, *to have* respect to the external circumstances of any one, Lk 20:21; Gal 2:6; ἐν προσώπῳ, *in presence of*, 2 Co 2:10; ἀπὸ προσώπου, *from the presence of, from*, Ac 3:19; also, *from before*, Ac 7:45; εἰς πρόσωπον, and κατὰ πρόσωπον, *in the presence of, before*, Ac 3:13; 2 Co 8:24; also, *openly*, Gal 2:11; κατὰ πρόσωπον, ἔχειν, *to have before one's face, to have* any one *present*, Ac 25:16; ἀπὸ προσώπου, *from*, Rev 12:14; πρὸ προσώπου, *before*, Ac 13:24 [4383]

[4727] προτείνω *proteinō* 1x *to extend before; to stretch out*, Ac 22:25★ [4385]

[4728] πρότερος *proteros* 11x *former, prior*, Eph 4:22; *before, formerly*, Jn 6:62 [4386, 4387]

[4729] προτίθημι *protithēmi* 3x *to place before; to set forth, propose publicly*, Ro 3:25; mid. προτίθεμαι, *to purpose, determine, design beforehand*, Ro 1:13; Eph 1:9★ [4388]

[4730] προτρέπω *protrepō* 1x *to turn forwards; to impel; to excite, urge, exhort*, Ac 18:27★ [4389]

[4731] προτρέχω *protrechō* 2x *to run before*, or *in advance*, Lk 19:4; Jn 20:4★ [4390]

[4732] προϋπάρχω *prouparchō* 2x *to be before*, or *formerly*, Lk 23:12; Ac 8:9★ [4391]

[4733] πρόφασις *prophasis* 6x pr. *that which appears in front, that which is put forward to hide the true state of things; a fair show* or *pretext*, Ac 27:30; *a specious cloak*, Mt 23:13; 1 Th 2:5; *an excuse*, Jn 15:22 [4392]

[4734] προφέρω *propherō* 2x *to bring before, present; to bring forth* or *out, produce*, Lk 6:45 (2t)★ [4393]

[4735] προφητεία *prophēteia* 19x *prophecy, a prediction of future events*, Mt 13:14; 2 Pe 1:20, 21; *prophecy, a gifted faculty of setting forth and enforcing revealed truth*, 1 Co 12:10; 13:2; *prophecy, matter of divine teaching set forth by special gift*, 1 Ti 1:18 [4394]

[4736] προφητεύω *prophēteuō* 28x *to exercise the function of a* προφήτης; *to prophesy, to foretell the future*, Mt 11:13; *to divine*, Mt 26:68; Mk 14:65; Lk 22:64; *to prophesy, to set forth matter of divine teaching by special faculty*, 1 Co 13:9; 14:1 [4395]

[4737] προφήτης *prophētēs* 144x pr. *a spokesman for* another; spc. *a spokesman* or *interpreter* for a deity; *a prophet, seer*, Tit 1:12; in N.T. *a prophet, a divinely commissioned and inspired person*, Mt 14:5; Lk 7:16, 39; Jn 9:17; *a prophet* in the Christian church, *a person gifted for the exposition of divine truth*, 1 Co 12:28, 29; *a prophet, a foreteller of the future*, Mt 1:22, et al. freq.; οἱ προφῆται, *the prophetic scriptures of the Old Testament*, Lk 16:29 [4396]

[4738] προφητικός *prophētikos* 2x *prophetic, uttered by prophets*, Ro 16:26; 2 Pe 1:19★ [4397]

[4739] προφῆτις *prophētis* 2x *a prophetess, a divinely gifted female teacher*, Lk 2:36; Rev 2:20★ [4398]

[4740] προφθάνω *prophthanō* 1x *to outstrip, anticipate; to anticipate* any one *in doing* or *saying a thing, be beforehand with*, Mt 17:25★ [4399]

[4741] προχειρίζω *procheirizō* 3x also listed as a deponent, proceirivzomai, *to take into the hand, to make ready for use* or *action; to constitute, destine*, Ac 3:20; 22:14; 26:16★ [4400]

[4742] προχειροτονέω *procheirotoneō* 1x pr. *to elect before* Ac 10:41★ [4401]

[4743] Πρόχορος *Prochoros* 1x *Prochorus*, pr. name, Ac 6:5★ [4402]

[4744] πρύμνα *prymna* 3x *the hinder part of a vessel, stern*, Mk 4:38; Ac 27:29, 41★ [4403]

[4745] πρωΐ *prōi* 12x *in the morning, early*, Mt 16:3; 20:1; Mk 15:1; Ac 28:23; *the morning watch*, which ushers in the dawn, Mk 13:35 [4404]

[4746] πρωΐα *prōia* 2x *morning, the morning hour*, Mt 27:1; Jn 21:4★ [4405]

[4748] πρωϊνός *prōinos* 2x *belonging to the morning, morning*, Rev 2:28; 22:16★ [4407]

[4749] πρῷρα *prōra* 2x *the forepart of a vessel, prow*, Ac 27:30, 41★ [4408]

[4750] πρωτεύω *prōteuō* 1x *to be first, to hold the first rank* or *highest dignity, have the pre-eminence, be chief*, Col 1:18★ [4409]

[4751] πρωτοκαθεδρία *prōtokathedria* 4x *the first* or *uppermost seat, the most honorable seat*, Mt 23:6; Mk 12:39; Lk 11:43; 20:46★ [4410]

[4752] πρωτοκλισία *prōtoklisia* 5x *the first place of reclining* at table, *the most honorable place at table*, Mt 23:6; Mk 12:39; Lk 14:7, 8; 20:46 [4411]

[4755] πρῶτος *prōtos* 155x *first* in time, order, etc., Mt 10:2; 26:17; *first* in dignity, importance, etc., *chief, principal, most important*, Mk 6:21; Lk 19:47; Ac 13:50; 16:12; as an equivalent to the compar. πρότερος, *prior*, Jn 1:5, 30; 15:18; Mt 27:64; adverbially, *first*, Jn 1:42; 5:4; 8:7 [4413]

[4756] πρωτοστάτης *prōtostatēs* 1x pr. *one stationed in the first rank* of an army; *a leader; a chief, ringleader*, Ac 24:5★ [4414]

[4757] πρωτοτόκια *prōtotokia* 1x *the rights of primogeniture, birthright*, Heb 12:16 [4415]

[4758] πρωτότοκος *prōtotokos* 8x *first-born*, Lk 2:7; Heb 11:28; in N.T. *prior in generation*, Col 1:15; *a first-born* head of a spiritual family, Ro 8:29; Heb 1:6; *first-born*, as possessed of the peculiar privilege of spiritual generation, Heb 12:23 [4416]

[4759] πρώτως *prōtos* 1x *for the first time*, Ac 11:26★ [4412]

[4760] πταίω *ptaiō* 5x *to cause to stumble*; intrans. *to stumble, stagger, fall; to make a false step*; met. *to err, transgress*, Ro 11:11; Jas 2:10; 3:2 (2t); met. *to fail* of an object, 2 Pe 1:10★ [4417]

[4761] πτέρνα *pterna* 1x *the heel*, Jn 13:18★ [4418]

[4762] πτερύγιον *pterygion* 2x *a little wing; the extremity, the extreme point* of a thing; *a pinnacle*, or *apex* of a building, Mt 4:5; Lk 4:9★ [4419]

[4763] πτέρυξ *pteryx* 5x *a wing, pinion*, Mt 23:37; Lk 13:34 [4420]

[4764] πτηνός *ptenos* 1x as adj., *winged, with feathers;* as noun, *a bird, fowl*, 1 Co 15:39★ [4421]

[4765] πτοέω *ptoeō* 2x *to terrify, affright;* pass. *to be terrified*, Lk 21:9; 24:37★ [4422]

[4766] πτόησις *ptoēsis* 1x *consternation, dismay*, 1 Pe 3:6★ [4423]

[4767] Πτολεμαΐς *Ptolemais* 1x *Ptolemais*, a city on the sea-coast of Galilee: the modern *Acre*, Ac 21:7★ [4424]

[4768] πτύον *ptyon* 2x *a fan, winnowing-shovel*, Mt 3:12; Lk 3:17★ [4425]

[4769] πτύρω *ptyrō* 1x *to scare, terrify;* pass. *to be terrified, be in consternation*, Phil 1:28★ [4426]

[4770] πτύσμα *ptysma* 1x *spittle, saliva*, Jn 9:6★ [4427]

[4771] πτύσσω *ptyssō* 1x *to fold; to roll up* a scroll, Lk 4:20★ [4428]

[4772] πτύω *ptyō* 3x *to spit, spit out*, Mk 7:33; 8:23; Jn 9:6 [4429]

[4773] πτῶμα *ptōma* 7x *a fall; a dead body, carcass, corpse,* Mt 24:28; Mk 6:29 [4430]

[4774] πτῶσις *ptōsis* 2x *a fall, crash, ruin,* Mt 7:27; met. *downfall, ruin,* Lk 2:34* [4431]

[4775] πτωχεία *ptōcheia* 3x *begging; beggary; poverty,* 2 Co 8:2, 9; Rev 2:9* [4432]

[4776] πτωχεύω *ptōcheuō* 1x *to be a beggar; to be* or *become poor, be in poverty,* 2 Co 8:9* [4433]

[4777] πτωχός *ptōchos* 34x *reduced to beggary, mendicant; poor, indigent,* Mt 19:21; 26:9, 11; met. spiritually *poor,* Rev 3:17; by impl. *a person of low condition,* Mt 11:4; Lk 4:18; 7:22; met. *beggarly, sorry,* Gal 4:9; met. *lowly,* Mt 5:3; Lk 6:20 [4434]

[4778] πυγμή *pygmē* 1x *together with the fore-arm,* or, *with care, carefully,* Mk 7:3* [4435]

[4781] πυκνός *pyknos* 3x *dense, thick; frequent,* 1 Ti 5:23; πυκνά, as an adverb, *frequently, often,* Lk 5:33; so the compar. πυκνότερον, *very frequently,* Ac 24:26* [4437]

[4782] πυκτεύω *pykteuō* 1x *to box, fight as a boxer,* 1 Co 9:26* [4438]

[4783] πύλη *pylē* 10x *a gate,* Mt 7:13, 14; Lk 7:12; Ac 12:10; πύλαι ᾅδου, *the gates of hades, the nether world and its powers, the powers of destruction, dissolution,* Mt 16:18 [4439]

[4784] πυλών *pylōn* 18x *a gateway, vestibule,* Mt 26:71; Lk 16:20; *a gate,* Ac 14:13; Rev 21:12, 13, 15, 21, 25 [4440]

[4785] πυνθάνομαι *pynthanomai* 12x *to ask, inquire,* Mt 2:4; Lk 15:26; *to investigate, examine* judicially, Ac 23:20; *to ascertain by inquiry, understand,* Ac 23:34 [4441]

[4786] πῦρ *pyr* 71x *fire,* Mt 3:10; 7:19; 13:40, et al. freq.; πυρός, used by Hebraism with the force of an adjective, *fiery, fierce,* Heb 10:27; *fire* used figuratively to express various circumstances of severe trial, Lk 12:49; 1 Co 3:13; Jude 23 [4442]

[4787] πυρά *pyra* 2x *a fire, heap of combustibles,* Ac 28:2, 3* [4443]

[4788] πύργος *pyrgos* 4x *a tower,* Mt 21:33; Mk 12:1; Lk 13:4; genr. *a castle, palace,* Lk 14:28* [4444]

[4789] πυρέσσω *pyressō* 2x *to be feverish, be sick of a fever,* Mt 8:14; Mk 1:30* [4445]

[4790] πυρετός *pyretos* 6x *scorching and noxious heat; a fever,* Mt 8:15; Mk 1:31 [4446]

[4791] πύρινος *pyrinos* 1x pr. *of fire, fiery, burning; shining, glittering,* Rev 9:17* [4447]

[4792] πυρόω *pyroō* 6x *to set on fire, burn;* pass. *to be kindled, be on fire, burn, flame,* Eph 6:16; 2 Pe 3:12; Rev 1:15; met. *to fire with distressful feelings,* 2 Co 11:29; of lust, *to be inflamed, burn,* 1 Co 7:9; *to be tried with fire,* as metals, Rev 3:18* [4448]

[4793] πυρράζω *pyrrazō* 2x *to be fiery-red,* Mt 16:2, 3* [4449]

[4794] πυρρός *pyrros* 2x *of the color of fire, fiery-red,* Rev 6:4; 12:3* [4450]

[4795] Πύρρος *Pyrros* 1x *Pyrrhus,* pr. name, Ac 20:4* [**]

[4796] πύρωσις *pyrōsis* 3x *a burning, conflagration,* Rev 18:9, 18; met. *a fiery test* of trying circumstances, 1 Pe 4:12* [4451]

[4797] πωλέω *pōleō* 22x *to sell,* Mt 10:29; 13:44 [4453]

[4798] πῶλος *pōlos* 12x *a youngling; a foal* or *colt,* Mt 21:2, 5, 7; Mk 11:2 [4454]

[4799] πώποτε *pōpote* 6x *ever yet, ever, at any time,* Lk 19:30; Jn 1:18 [4455]

[4800] πωρόω *pōroō* 5x *to petrify; to harden;* in N.T. *to harden* the feelings, Jn 12:40; pass. *to become callous, unimpressible,* Mk 6:52; 8:17; Ro 11:7; 2 Co 3:14* [4456]

[4801] πώρωσις *pōrōsis* 3x *a hardening;* met. *hardness* of heart, *callousness, insensibility,* Mk 3:5; Ro 11:25; Eph 4:18* [4457]

[4802] πῶς *pōs* 103x interrogative particle, *How? In what manner? By what means?* Mt 7:4; 22:12; Jn 6:52; used in interrogations which imply a negative, Mt 12:26, 29, 34; 22:45; 23:33; Ac 8:31; put concisely for *How is it that? How does it come to pass that?* Mt 16:11; 22:43; Mk 4:40; Jn 7:15; with an indirect interrogation, *how, in what manner,* Mt 6:28; 10:19; Mk 11:18; put for τί, *What?* Lk 10:26; put for ὡς, as a particle of exclamation, *how, how much, how greatly,* Mk 10:23, 24 [4459]

[4803] πως *pōs* 15x enclitic particle, *in any way, by any means,* Ac 27:12; Ro 1:10 [4452, 4458]

[4805] Ῥαάβ *Rhaab* 2x *Rahab,* pr. name, indecl (Josh 2; 6:17, 25) Heb 11:31; Jas 2:25* [4460]

[4806] ῥαββί *rhabbi* 15x also spelled ῥαββεί, *rabbi, my master, teacher,* Mt 23:7, 8; 26:25, 49 [4461]

[4808] ῥαββουνί *rhabbouni* 2x see ῥαββονί [4462]

[4810] ῥαβδίζω *rhabdizō* 2x *to beat with rods,* Ac 16:22; 2 Co 11:25* [4463]

[4811] ῥάβδος *rhabdos* 12x *a rod, wand,* Heb 9:4; Rev 11:1; *a rod* of correction, 1 Co 4:21; *a staff,* Mt 10:10; Heb 11:21; *a scepter,* Heb 1:8; Rev 2:27 [4464]

[4812] ῥαβδοῦχος *rhabdouchos* 2x *the bearer of a wand* of office; *a lictor, sergeant,* a public servant who bore a bundle or rods before the magistrates as insignia of their office, and carried into execution the sentences they pronounced, Ac 16:35, 38* [4465]

[4814] Ῥαγαύ *Rhagau* 1x *Ragau,* pr. name, indecl. Lk 3:35* [4466]

[4815] ῥαδιούργημα *rhadiourgēma* 1x pr. *anything done lightly, levity; reckless conduct, crime,* Ac 18:14* [4467]

[4816] ῥαδιουργία *rhadiourgia* 1x *facility of doing anything; levity in doing; recklessness, wickedness,* Ac 13:10* [4468]

[4818] Ῥαιφάν *Rhaiphan* 1x pr. name., *Rephan,* Ac 7:43* [4481]

[4819] ῥακά *rhaka* 1x *raca,* an Aramaic term of bitter contempt, *worthless fellow, fool,* Mt 5:22* [4469]

[4820] ῥάκος *rhakos* 2x *a piece torn off; a bit of cloth, cloth,* Mt 9:16; Mk 2:21* [4470]

[4821] Ῥαμά *Rhama* 1x *Rama,* a city of Judea [4471]

[4822] ῥαντίζω *rhantizō* 4x *to sprinkle,* Heb 9:13, 19, 21; met. and by impl. *to cleanse by sprinkling, purify, free from pollution,* Heb 10:22* [4472]

[4823] ῥαντισμός *rhantismos* 2x pr. *a sprinkling;* met. *a cleansing, purification,* Heb 12:24; 1 Pe 1:2* [4473]

[4824] ῥαπίζω *rhapizō* 2x *to beat with rods; to strike with the palm of the hand, cuff, clap,* Mt 5:39; 26:67* [4474]

[4825] ῥάπισμα *rhapisma* 3x *a blow with the palm of the hand, cuff, slap,* Mk 14:65; Jn 18:22; 19:3* [4475]

[4827] ῥαφίς *rhaphis* 2x *a needle,* Mt 19:24; Mk 10:25* [4476]

[4829] Ῥαχάβ *Rhachab* 1x *Rachab*, pr. name, indecl., Mt 1:5* [4477]

[4830] Ῥαχήλ *Rhachēl* 1x *Rachel*, pr. name, indecl., Mt 2:18* [4478]

[4831] Ῥεβέκκα *Rhebekka* 1x *Rebecca*, pr. name, Ro 9:10* [4479]

[4832] ῥέδη *rhedē* 1x *a carriage with four wheels* for travelling, *a chariot*, Rev 18:13* [4480]

[4835] ῥέω *rheō* 1x *flow, overflow with*, Jn 7:38* [4482]

[4836] Ῥήγιον *Rhēgion* 1x *Rhegium*, a city at the southwestern extremity of Italy, Ac 28:13* [4484]

[4837] ῥῆγμα *rhēgma* 1x *a rent; a crash, ruin*, Lk 6:49* [4485]

[4838] ῥήγνυμι *rhēgnymi* 1x see ῥήσσω [4486]

[4839] ῥῆμα *rhēma* 68x *that which is spoken; declaration, saying, speech, word*, Mt 12:36; 26:75; Mk 9:32; 14:72; *a command, mandate, direction*, Lk 3:2; 5:5; *a promise*, Lk 1:38; 2:29; *a prediction, prophecy*, 2 Pe 3:2; *a doctrine* of God or Christ, Jn 3:34; 5:47; 6:63, 68; Ac 5:20; *an accusation, charge, crimination*, Mt 5:11; 27:14; from the Hebrew, *a thing*, Mt 4:4; Lk 4:4; *a matter, affair, transaction, business*, Mt 18:16; Lk 1:65; 2 Co 13:1 [4487]

[4840] Ῥησά *Rhēsa* 1x *Rhesa*, pr. name, indecl., Lk 3:27* [4488]

[4841] ῥήσσω *rhēssō* 6x also spelled ῥήγνυμι 1x in our text (Mt 9:17). *to rend, shatter; to break* or *burst in pieces* Mt 9:17; Mk 2:22; Lk 5:37; *to rend, lacerate*, Mt 7:6; *to cast* or *dash* upon the ground, *convulse*, Mk 9:18; Lk 9:42; absol. *to break forth* into exclamation, Gal 4:27 [4486]

[4842] ῥήτωρ *rhētōr* 1x *an orator, advocate*, Ac 24:1* [4489]

[4843] ῥητῶς *rhētōs* 1x *in express words, expressly*, 1 Ti 4:1* [4490]

[4844] ῥίζα *rhiza* 17x *a root* of a tree, Mt 3:10; 13:6; met. ἔχειν ῥίζαν, or ἔχειν ῥίζαν ἐν ἑαυτῷ, *to be rooted* in faith, Mt 13:21; Mk 4:17; Lk 8:13; met. *cause, source, origin*, 1 Ti 6:10; Heb 12:15; by synec. *the trunk, stock* of a tree, met. Ro 11:16, 17, 18; met. *offspring, progeny, a descendant*, Ro 15:12; Rev 5:5; 22:16 [4491]

[4845] ῥιζόω *rhizoō* 2x *to root, cause to take root; firmly rooted, strengthened with roots;* met. *firm, constant, firmly fixed*, Eph 3:17; Col 2:7* [4492]

[4846] ῥιπή *rhipē* 1x pr. *a rapid sweep, jerk; a wink, twinkling* of the eye, 1 Co 15:52* [4493]

[4847] ῥιπίζω *rhipizō* 1x *to fan, blow, ventilate; to toss, agitate*, e.g. the ocean by the wind, Jas 1:6* [4494]

[4848] ῥιπτέω *rhipteō* 1x also spelled ῥίπτω, frequent and repeated action, *to toss repeatedly, toss up* with violent gesture, Ac 22:23 (ῥιπτούντων)* [4495]

[4849] ῥίπτω *rhiptō* 7x also spelled ῥιπτέω, *to hurl, throw, cast; to throw* or *cast down*, Mt 27:5; Lk 4:35; 17:2; *to throw* or *cast out*, Ac 27:19, 29; *to lay down, set down*, Mt 15:30; pass. *to be dispersed, scattered*, Mt 9:36* [4496]

[4850] Ῥοβοάμ *Rhoboam* 2x *Roboam*, pr. name, indecl., Mt 1:7* [4497]

[4851] Ῥόδη *Rhodē* 1x *Rhoda*, pr. name, Ac 12:13* [4498]

[4852] Ῥόδος *Rhodos* 1x *Rhodes*, an island in the Mediterranean, south of Caria, Ac 21:1* [4499]

[4853] ῥοιζηδόν *rhoizēdon* 1x *with a noise, with a crash*, etc., 2 Pe 3:10* [4500]

[4855] ῥομφαία *rhomphaia* 7x pr. *a Thracian broad-sword; a sword*, Rev 1:16; 2:12; by meton. *war*, Rev 6:8; met. *a thrill of anguish*, Lk 2:35 [4501]

[4857] Ῥουβήν *Rhoubēn* 1x *Reuben*, pr. name, indecl., Rev 7:5* [4502]

[4858] Ῥούθ *Rhouth* 1x *Ruth*, pr. name, indecl., Mt 1:5* [4503]

[4859] Ῥοῦφος *Rhouphos* 2x *Rufus*, pr. name, Mk 15:21; Ro 16:13* [4504]

[4860] ῥύμη *rhymē* 4x pr. *a rush* or *sweep* of a body in motion; *a street*, Ac 9:11; 12:10; *a narrow street, lane, alley*, as distinguished from πλατεῖα, Mt 6:2; Lk 14:21* [4505]

[4861] ῥύομαι *rhyomai* 17x *to drag* out of danger, *to rescue, save*, Mt 6:13; 27:43; *to be rescued, delivered*, Lk 1:74; Ro 15:31; 2 Th 3:2; 2 Ti 4:17 [4506]

[4862] ῥυπαίνω *rhypainō* 1x *to make filthy, defile*, Rev 22:11* [4510]

[4864] ῥυπαρία *rhyparia* 1x *filth;* met. moral *filthiness, uncleanness, pollution*, Jas 1:21* [4507]

[4865] ῥυπαρός *rhyparos* 2x *filthy, squalid, sordid, dirty*, Jas 2:2; met. *defiled, polluted*, Rev 22:11* [4508]

[4866] ῥύπος *rhypos* 1x *filth, squalor*, 1 Pe 3:21* [4509]

[4868] ῥύσις *rhysis* 3x *a flowing; a morbid flux*, Mk 5:25; Lk 8:43, 44* [4511]

[4869] ῥυτίς *rhytis* 1x *a wrinkle;* met. *a disfiguring wrinkle, flaw, blemish*, Eph 5:27* [4512]

[4871] Ῥωμαῖος *Rhōmaios* 12x *Roman; a Roman citizen*, Jn 11:48; Ac 2:10; 16:21 [4514]

[4872] Ῥωμαϊστί *Rhōmaisti* 1x *in the Roman language, in Latin*, Jn 19:20* [4515]

[4873] Ῥώμη *Rhōmē* 8x *Rome*, Ac 18:2; 19:21; 23:11; 28:14, 16; Ro 1:7, 15; 2 Ti 1:17* [4516]

[4874] ῥώννυμι *rhōnnymi* 1x *to strengthen, render firm; to be well, enjoy firm health;* at the end of letters, like the Latin *vale, farewell*, Ac 15:29* [4517]

[4876] σαβαχθάνι *sabachthani* 2x (Aramaic) *sabacthani, you have forsaken me;* interrogatively, *have you forsaken me?* preceded with λαμᾶ, *Why?* Mt 27:46; Mk 15:34* [4518]

[4877] Σαβαώθ *Sabaōth* 2x (Hebrew) *hosts, armies*, indecl., Ro 9:29; Jas 5:4* [4519]

[4878] σαββατισμός *sabbatismos* 1x pr. *a keeping of a sabbath; a state of rest, a sabbath-state*, Heb 4:9* [4520]

[4879] σάββατον *sabbaton* 68x pr. *cessation from labor, rest; the* Jewish *sabbath*, both in the sg. and pl., Mt 12:2, 5, 8; 28:1; Lk 4:16; *a week*, sg. and pl., Mt 28:1; Mk 16:9; pl. *sabbaths*, or *times of sacred rest*, Col 2:16 [4521]

[4880] σαγήνη *sagēnē* 1x *a large net*, Mt 13:47* [4522]

[4881] Σαδδουκαῖος *Saddoukaios* 14x *a Sadducee*, one belonging to the sect of the Sadducees, which, according to the Talmudists, was founded by one, *Sadoc*, about three centuries before the Christian era: they were directly opposed in sentiments to the Pharisees, Mt 3:7; 16:1, 6, 11, 12; 22:23, 34; Mk 12:18; Lk 20:27; Ac 4:1; 5:17; 23:6-8* [4523]

[4882] Σαδώκ *Sadōk* 2x *Zadok*, pr. name, indecl., Mt 1:14* [4524]

[4883] σαίνω *sainō* 1x pr. *to wag* the tail; *to fawn, flatter, cajole;* pass. *to be cajoled; to be wrought upon, to be perturbed*, 1 Th 3:3* [4525]

[4884] σάκκος *sakkos* 4x *sackcloth*, a coarse black cloth made of hair (goat or camel), Rev 6:12; *a mourning garment of sackcloth*, Mt 11:21; Lk 10:13; Rev 11:3* [4526]

[4885] Σαλά *Sala* 2x *Sala*, pr. name, indecl., Lk 3:32, 35★ [4527]

[4886] Σαλαθιήλ *Salathiēl* 3x *Shealtiel*, pr. name, indecl., Mt 1:12; Lk 3:27★ [4528]

[4887] Σαλαμίς *Salamis* 1x *Salamis*, a city in the island of Cyprus, Ac 13:5★ [4529]

[4887.5] Σαλείμ *Saleim* 1x *Saleim*, also formed as Σαλίμ (*#4890*). John was baptizing at Aenon near Saleim, Jn 3:26★ [4529]

[4888] σαλεύω *saleuō* 15x *to make to rock, to shake,* Mt 11:7; 24:29; Mk 13:25; Lk 6:38, 48; 7:24; 21:26; Ac 4:31; 16:26; Heb 12:26; met. *to stir up, excite* the people, Ac 17:13; *to agitate, disturb* mentally, Ac 2:25; 2 Th 2:2; pass. impl. *to totter, be ready to fall, be near to ruin,* met. Heb 12:36, 27★ [4531]

[4889] Σαλήμ *Salēm* 2x (Hebrew, meaning *peace*), *Salem,* pr. name, indecl., Heb 7:1f.★ [4532]

[4891] Σαλμών *Salmōn* 2x *Salmon,* pr. name, indecl., Mt 1:4f.★ [4533]

[4892] Σαλμώνη *Salmōnē* 1x *Salmone,* a promontory, the eastern extremity of Crete, Ac 27:7★ [4534]

[4893] σάλος *salos* 1x *agitation, tossing, rolling,* spc. of the sea, Lk 21:25★ [4535]

[4894] σάλπιγξ *salpinx* 11x *trumpet,* 1 Co 14:8; Heb 12:19; Rev 1:10; 4:1; 8:2, 6; 13:9; 1 Th 4:16; *sound of the trumpet,* Mt 24:31; 1 Co 15:52; 1 Th 4:16★ [4536]

[4895] σαλπίζω *salpizō* 12x *to sound a trumpet,* Mt 6:2; 1 Co 5:52; Rev 8:6, 7, 8, 10, 12, 13; 9:1, 13; 10:7; 11:15★ [4537]

[4896] σαλπιστής *salpistēs* 1x *a trumpeter,* Rev 18:22★ [4538]

[4897] Σαλώμη *Salōmē* 2x *Salome,* pr. name, a Galilean woman who followed Jesus, Mt 27:56; Mk 15:40; 16:1★ [4539]

[4899] Σαμάρεια *Samareia* 11x *Samaria,* the city and region so called, Ac 8:14 [4540]

[4901] Σαμαρίτης *Samaritēs* 9x *a Samaritan, an inhabitant of the city* or *region of Samaria,* applied by the Jews as a term of reproach and contempt, Mt 10:5; Jn 4:9, 39f.; 8:48; Lk 9:52; 10:33; 17:16; Ac 8:25★ [4541]

[4902] Σαμαρῖτις *Samaritis* 2x *a Samaritan woman,* Jn 4:9★ [4542]

[4903] Σαμοθράκη *Samothrakē* 1x *Samothrace,* an island in the northern part of the Aegean sea, Ac 16:11★ [4543]

[4904] Σάμος *Samos* 1x *Samos,* a celebrated island, in the Aegean sea, Ac 20:15★ [4544]

[4905] Σαμουήλ *Samouēl* 3x (1 Sam 1:1-25:1), *Samuel,* pr. name, indecl., Ac 3:24; 13:20; Heb 11:32★ [4545]

[4907] Σαμψών *Sampsōn* 1x (Judges 13-16), *Samson,* pr. name, indecl., Heb 11:32★ [4546]

[4908] σανδάλιον *sandalion* 2x *a sandal,* a sole of wood or hide, covering the bottom of the foot, and bound on with leathern thongs, Mk 6:9, Ac 12:8★ [4547]

[4909] σανίς *sanis* 1x *a board, plank,* Ac 27:44★ [4548]

[4910] Σαούλ *Saoul* 9x *Saul,* pr. name, indecl. I. *Saul, king of Israel,* Ac 13:21; II. *The Apostle Paul,* Ac 9:4, 17; 22:7, 13; 26:14★ [4549]

[4911] σαπρός *sapros* 8x pr. *rotten, putrid;* hence, *bad, of a bad quality,* Mt 7:17, 18; 12:33; Lk 6:43; *refuse,* Mt 13:48; met. *corrupt, depraved, vicious, foul, impure,* Eph 4:29★ [4550]

[4912] Σάπφιρα *Sapphira* 1x *Sapphira,* wife of Ananias and a member of the Jerusalem church, Ac 5:1★ [4551]

[4913] σάπφιρος *sapphiros* 1x *a sapphire,* a precious stone of a blue color in various shades, next in hardness and value to the diamond, Rev 21:19 [4552]

[4914] σαργάνη *sarganē* 1x *twisted* or *plaited work; a netword of cords like a basket, basket of ropes,* etc. 2 Co 11:33★ [4553]

[4915] Σάρδεις *Sardeis* 3x *Sardis,* the capital city of Lydia, in Asia Minor Rev 1:11; 3:1, 4★ [4554]

[4917] σάρδιον *sardion* 2x *carnelian,* a reddish precious stone, Rev 4:3; 21:20★ [4556]

[4918] σαρδόνυξ *sardonyx* 1x *sardonyx,* a gem exhibiting the color of the carnelian and the white of the calcedony, intermingled in alternate layers, Rev 21:20★ [4557]

[4919] Σάρεπτα *Sarepta* 1x *Sarepta,* a city of Phoenicia, between Tyre and Sidon, Lk 4:26★ [4558]

[4920] σαρκικός *sarkikos* 7x *fleshly; pertaining to the body, corporeal, physical,* Ro 15:27; 1 Co 9:11; *carnal, pertaining to the flesh,* 1 Pe 2:11; *carnal, low in spiritual knowledge and frame,* 1 Co 3:3 (2t); *carnal, human* as opposed to divine, 2 Co 1:12; 10:4★ [4559]

[4921] σάρκινος *sarkinos* 4x *of flesh, fleshly,* 2 Co 3:3; Ro 7:14; 1 Co 3:1; Heb 7:16★ [4560]

[4922] σάρξ *sarx* 147x *flesh,* Lk 24:39; Jn 3:6; *the* human *body,* 2 Co 7:5; *flesh, human nature, human frame,* Jn 1:13, 14; 1 Pe 4:1; 1 Jn 4:2; *kindred,* Ro 11:14; *lineage,* Ro 1:3; 9:3; *flesh, humanity, human beings,* Mt 24:22; Lk 3:6; Jn 17:2; *the circumstances of the body, material condition,* 1 Co 5:5; 7:28; Phlm 16; *flesh, mere humanity, human fashion,* 1 Co 1:26; 2 Co 1:17; *flesh as the seat of passion and frailty,* Ro 8:1, 3, 5; *carnality,* Gal 5:24; *materiality, material circumstance,* as opposed to the spiritual, Phil 3:3, 4; Col 2:18; *a material system* or *mode,* Gal 3:3; Heb 9:10 [4561]

[4924] σαρόω *saroō* 3x *to sweep, to clean with a broom,* Mt 12:44; Lk 11:25; 15:8★ [4563]

[4925] Σάρρα *Sarra* 4x *Sara, Sarah,* pr. name, the wife of Abraham, Ro 4:19; 9:9; Heb 11:11; 1 Pe 3:6★ [4564]

[4926] Σαρών *Sarōn* 1x *Saron,* a level tract of Palestine, between Caesarea and Joppa, Ac 9:35★ [4565]

[4928] Σατανᾶς *Satanas* 36x *an adversary, opponent, enemy,* perhaps, Mt 16:23; Mk 8:33; Lk 4:8; elsewhere, *Satan, the devil,* Mt 4:10; Mk 1:13 [4567]

[4929] σάτον *saton* 2x *a satum* or *seah,* a Hebrew measure for things dry, containing, as Josephus testifies, (*Ant.* 9.85) an Italian modius and one half, or 24 sextarii, and therefore equivalent to somewhat less than three gallons English, Mt 13:33; Lk 13:21★ [4568]

[4930] Σαῦλος *Saulos* 15x *Saul,* the Hebrew name of the Apostle Paul, Σαούλ with a Greek termination, Ac 7:58; 8:1, 3; 9:1 [4569]

[4931] σβέννυμι *sbennymi* 6x *to extinguish, quench,* Mt 12:20; 25:8; Mk 9:44, 46, 48; Eph 6:16; Heb 11:34; met. *to quench, damp, hinder, thwart,* 1 Th 5:19★ [4570]

[4932] σεαυτοῦ *seautou* 43x *of yourself, to yourself,* etc. Mt 4:6; 8:4; 19:19 [4572]

[4933] σεβάζομαι *sebazomai* 1x *to feel dread of* a thing; *to venerate, adore, worship,* Ro 1:25★ [4573]

[4934] σέβασμα *sebasma* 2x *an object of religious veneration and worship,* Ac 17:23; 2 Th 2:4★ [4574]

[4935] σεβαστός *sebastos* 3x pr. *venerable, august;* ὁ Σεβαστός, i.q. Latin *Augus-*

tus, Ac 25:21, 25; *Augustan*, or, *Sebastan*, named from the city Sebaste, Ac 27:1* [4575]

[4936] σέβω *sebō* 10x mid., *to stand in awe; to venerate, reverence, worship, adore*, Mt 15:9; Mk 7:7; Ac 18:13; 19:27; part. σεβόμενος, η, ον, *worshiping, devout, pious*, a term applied to proselytes to Judaism, Ac 13:43; 16:14; 18:7; 13:50; 17:4, 17* [4576]

[4937] σειρά *seira* 1x *a cord, rope, band*; in N.T. *a chain*, 2 Pe 2:4* [4577]

[4939] σεισμός *seismos* 14x pr. *a shaking, agitation, concussion; an earthquake*, Mt 24:7; 27:54; *a tempest*, Mt 8:24 [4578]

[4940] σείω *seiō* 5x *to shake, agitate*, Heb 12:26; pass. *to quake*, Mt 27:51; 28:4; Rev 6:13; met. *to put in commotion, agitate*, Mt 21:10 [4579]

[4941] Σεκοῦνδος *Sekoundos* 1x *Secundus*, pr. name, Ac 20:4* [4580]

[4942] Σελεύκεια *Seleukeia* 1x *Seleucia*, a city of Syria, west of Antioch, on the Orontes, Ac 13:4* [4581]

[4943] σελήνη *selēnē* 9x *the moon*, Mt 24:29; Mk 13:24 [4582]

[4944] σεληνιάζομαι *selēniazomai* 2x *to be a lunatic*, Mt 4:24; 17:15* [4583]

[4946] Σεμεΐν *Semein* 1x *Semei*, pr. name, indecl., Lk 3:26* [4584]

[4947] σεμίδαλις *semidalis* 1x *the finest flour*, Rev 18:13* [4585]

[4948] σεμνός *semnos* 4x *august, venerable; honorable, reputable*, Phil 4:8; *grave, serious, dignified*, 1 Ti 3:8, 11; Tit 2:2* [4586]

[4949] σεμνότης *semnotēs* 3x pr. *majesty; gravity, dignity, dignified seriousness*, 1 Ti 2:2; 3:4; Tit 2:7* [4587]

[4950] Σέργιος *Sergios* 1x *Sergius*, pr. name, Ac 13:7* [4588]

[4952] Σερούχ *Serouch* 1x *Serug*, proper name, Lk 3:35* [4562]

[4953] Σήθ *Sēth* 1x *Seth*, (Gen. 4:25f.) pr. name, indecl., Lk 3:38* [4589]

[4954] Σήμ *Sēm* 1x *Shem*, (Gen. 5:32) pr. name, indecl., Lk 3:36* [4590]

[4955] σημαίνω *sēmainō* 6x *to indicate by a sign, to signal; to indicate, intimate*, Jn 12:33; 18:32; 21:19; *to make known, communicate*, Ac 11:28; Rev 1:1; *to specify*, Ac 25:27* [4591]

[4956] σημεῖον *sēmeion* 77x *a sign, a mark, token*, by which anything is known

or distinguished, Mt 16:3; 24:3; 2 Th 3:17; *a token, pledge, assurance*, Lk 2:12; *a proof, evidence, convincing token*, Mt 12:38; 16:1; Jn 2:18; in N.T. *a sign, wonder, remarkable event, wonderful appearance, extraordinary phenomenon*, 1 Co 14:22; Rev 12:1, 3; 15:1; *a portent, prodigy*, Mt 24:30; Ac 2:19; *a wonderful work, miraculous operation, miracle*, Mt 24:24; Mk 16:17, 20; meton. *a sign, a signal character*, Lk 2:34 [4592]

[4957] σημειόω *sēmeioō* 1x mid., *to mark, inscribe marks upon*; mid. *to mark for one's self, note*, 2 Th 3:14* [4593]

[4958] σήμερον *sēmeron* 41x *to-day, this day*, Mt 6:11, 30; 16:3; 21:28; *now, at present*, Heb 13:8; 2 Co 3:15; ἡ σήμερον, sc. ἡμέρα, sometimes expressed, *this day, the present day*, Ac 20:26; ἕως or ἄχρι τῆς σήμερον, *until this day, until our times*, Mt 11:23; 27:8 [4594]

[4960] σήπω *sēpō* 1x *to cause to putrify, rot, be corrupted* or *rotten*, Jas 5:2* [4595]

[4962] σής *sēs* 3x *a moth*, Lk 12:33; Mt 6:19f.* [4597]

[4963] σητόβρωτος *sētobrōtos* 1x *motheaten*, Jas 5:2* [4598]

[4964] σθενόω *sthenoō* 1x *to strengthen, impart strength*, 1 Pe 5:10* [4599]

[4965] σιαγών *siagōn* 2x *the jaw-bone*; in N.T. *the cheek*, Mt 5:39; Lk 6:29* [4600]

[4967] σιγάω *sigaō* 10x *to be silent, keep silence*, Lk 9:36; 20:26; Ac 15:12f.; 1 Co 14:28, 30, 34; Lk 18:39; trans. *to keep in silence, not to reveal, to conceal*; pass. *to be concealed, not to be revealed*, Ro 16:25* [4601]

[4968] σιγή *sigē* 2x *silence*, Ac 21:40; Rev 8:1* [4602]

[4970] σίδηρος *sidēros* 1x *iron*, Rev 18:12* [4604]

[4971] σιδηροῦς *sidērous* 5x *made of iron*, Ac 12:10; Rev 2:27; 9:9; 12:5; 19:15* [4603]

[4972] Σιδών *Sidōn* 9x *Sidon*, a celebrated city of Phoenicia, Mt 11:21f.; Mk 3:8; 7:31; Lk 6:17; Ac 27:3 [4605]

[4973] Σιδώνιος *Sidōnios* 2x *Sidonian; an inhabitant of* Σιδών, *Sidon*, Ac 12:20; Lk 4:26* [4606]

[4974] σικάριος *sikarios* 1x *an assassin, bandit, robber*, Ac 21:38* [4607]

[4975] σίκερα *sikera* 1x *strong* or *inebriating drink*, Lk 1:15* [4608]

[4976] Σίλας *Silas* 12x *Silas*, pr. name, in Luke, Ac 15:22; see Σιλουανός [4609]

[4977] Σιλουανός *Silouanos* 4x *Silvanus*, pr. name, 2 Co 1:19; 1 Th 1:1; 2 Th 1:1; 1 Pe 5:12, see Σίλας* [4610]

[4978] Σιλωάμ *Silōam* 3x *Siloam*, a pool or fountain near Jerusalem, Lk 13:4; Jn 9:7, 11* [4611]

[4980] σιμικίνθιον *simikinthion* 1x *an apron*, Ac 19:12* [4612]

[4981] Σίμων *Simōn* 75x *Simon*, pr. name. (1) *Simon Peter*, Mt 4:18. (2) *Simon (the Canaanite) the Zealot*, Mt 10:4; Ac 1:13 . (3) *Simon, brother of Jesus*, Mt 13:55; Mk 6:3. (4) *Simon, the leper*, Mt 26:6; Mk 14:3. (5) *Simon, the Pharisee*, Lk 7:40. (6) *Simon of Cyrene*, Mt 27:32. (7) *Simon, father of Judas Iscariot*, Jn 6:71. (8) *Simon, the sorcerer*, Ac 8:9. (9) *Simon, the tanner, of Joppa*, Ac 9:43; 10:6 [4613]

[4982] Σινᾶ *Sina* 4x *Mount Sinai*, in Arabia, Ac 7:30, 38; Gal 4:24, 25* [4614]

[4983] σίναπι *sinapi* 5x *mustard;* in N.T. probably the shrub, not the herb, *Khardal, Salvadora Persica L.*, the fruit of which possesses the pungency of mustard, Mt 13:31; 17:20; Mk 4:31; Lk 13:19; 17:6* [4615]

[4984] σινδών *sindōn* 6x *sindon;* pr. *fine Indian cloth; fine linen;* in N.T. *a linen garment, an upper garment* or *wrapper of fine linen*, worn in summer by night, and used to envelope dead bodies, Mt 27:59; Mk 14:51, 52; 15:46; Lk 23:53* [4616]

[4985] σινιάζω *siniazō* 1x *to sift;* met. *to sift* by trials and temptations, Lk 22:31* [4617]

[4986] σιρικός *sirikos* 1x see also σηρικός, *silk, of silk, silken;* τὸ σηρικόν, *silken stuff*, Rev 18:12* [4596]

[4988] σιτευτός *siteutos* 3x *fed, fatted*, Lk 15:23, 27, 30* [4618]

[4989] σιτίον *sition* 1x *provision of corn, food*, Ac 7:12* [4621]

[4990] σιτιστός *sitistos* 1x *fatted, a fatling, cattle*, Mt 22:4* [4619]

[4991] σιτομέτριον *sitometrion* 1x *a certain measure of grain* distributed for food at set times to the slaves of a family, *a ration*, Lk 12:42* [4620]

[4992] σῖτος *sitos* 14x *corn, grain, wheat*, Mt 3:12; 13:25, 29, 30; Mk 4:28 [4621]

[4994] Σιών *Siōn* 7x *Zion, Mt. Zion*, a hill within the city of Jerusalem, indecl., Heb 12:22; Rev 14:1; *poetic use*, Mt 21:5;

Jn 12:15; *people of Israel*, Ro 9:33; 11:26; *new Jerusalem of Christianity*, 1 Pe 2:6* [4622]

[4995] σιωπάω *siōpaō* 10x *to be silent, keep silence, hold one's peace*, Mt 20:31; 26:63; Mk 3:4; 9:34; 10:48; 14:61; Lk 19:40; Ac 18:9; σιωπῶν, *silent, dumb*, Lk 1:20; met. *to be silent, still, hushed, calm*, as the sea, Mk 4:39* [4623]

[4997] σκανδαλίζω *skandalizō* 29x pr. *to cause to stumble*; met. *offend*, Mt 17:27; *to offend, shock, excite feeling of repugnance*, Jn 6:61; 1 Co 8:13; pass. *to be offended, shocked, pained*, Mt 15:12; Ro 14:21; 2 Co 11:29; σκανδαλίζεσθαι ἔν τινι, *to be affected with scruples of repugnance towards any one* as respects his claims or pretensions, Mt 11:6; 13:57; met. *to cause to stumble* morally, *to cause to falter* or *err*, Mt 5:29; 18:6; pass. *to falter, fall away*, Mt 13:21 [4624]

[4998] σκάνδαλον *skandalon* 15x pr. *a trap-spring*; also genr. *a stumbling-block, anything against which one stumbles, an impediment*; met. *a cause of ruin, destruction, misery*, etc., Ro 9:33; 11:9; 1 Pe 2:8; *a cause* or *occasion of sinning*, Mt 16:23; 18:7 (3t); Lk 17:1; Ro 14:13; 16:17; Rev 2:14; *scandal, offence, cause of indignation*, Mt 13:41; 1 Co 1:23; Gal 5:11; 1 Jn 2:10* [4625]

[4999] σκάπτω *skaptō* 3x *to dig, excavate*, Lk 6:48; 13:8; 16:3* [4626]

[5002] σκάφη *skaphē* 3x pr. *anything excavated* or *hollowed; a boat, skiff*, Ac 27:16, 30, 32* [4627]

[5003] σκέλος *skelos* 3x *the leg*, Jn 19:31, 32, 33* [4628]

[5004] σκέπασμα *skepasma* 1x *covering; clothing, raiment*, 1 Ti 6:8* [4629]

[5005] Σκευᾶς *Skeuas* 1x *Sceva*, pr. name, Ac 19:14* [4630]

[5006] σκευή *skeuē* 1x *apparatus; tackle*, Ac 27:19* [4631]

[5007] σκεῦος *skeuos* 23x *a vessel, utensil* for containing anything, Mk 11:16; Lk 8:16; Ro 9:21; *any utensil, instrument*; σκεύη, *household stuff, furniture, goods*, etc., Mt 12:29; Mk 3:27; *the mast of a ship*, or, *the sail*, Ac 27:17; met. *an instrument, means, organ, minister*, Ac 9:15; σκεύη ὀργῆς and σκεύη ἐλέους, *vessels of wrath*, or, *of mercy, persons visited by punishment*, or, *the divine favor*, Ro 9:22, 23; *the vessel* or *frame* of the human individual, 1 Th 4:4; 1 Pe 3:7 [4632]

[5008] σκηνή *skēnē* 20x *a tent, tabernacle*; genr. *any temporary dwelling; a tent, booth*, Mt 17:4; Heb 11:9; *the tabernacle* of the covenant, Heb 8:5; 9:1, 21; 13:10; allegor. *the* celestial or true *tabernacle*, Heb 8:2; 9:11; *a division* or *compartment of the tabernacle*, Heb 9:2, 3, 6; *a small portable tent* or *shrine*, Ac 7:43; *an abode* or *seat* of a lineage, Ac 15:16; *a mansion, habitation, abode, dwelling*, Lk 16:9; Rev 13:6 [4633]

[5009] σκηνοπηγία *skēnopēgia* 1x pr. *a pitching of tents* or *booths*; hence, *the feast of tabernacles* or *booths*, instituted in memory of the forty years' wandering of the Israelites in the desert, and as a season of gratitude for the ingathering of harvest, celebrated for eight days, commencing on the 15th of Tisri, Jn 7:2* [4634]

[5010] σκηνοποιός *skēnopoios* 1x *a tent-maker*, Ac 18:3* [4635]

[5011] σκῆνος *skēnos* 2x *a tent, tabernacle, lodging*; met. *the corporeal tabernacle*, 2 Co 5:1, 4* [4636]

[5012] σκηνόω *skēnoō* 5x *to pitch tent, encamp; to tabernacle, dwell in a tent; to dwell, have one's abode*, Jn 1:14; Rev 7:15; 12:12; 13:6; 21:3* [4637]

[5013] σκήνωμα *skēnōma* 3x *a habitation, abode, dwelling*, Ac 7:46; *the corporeal tabernacle* of the soul, 2 Pe 1:13, 14* [4638]

[5014] σκιά *skia* 7x *a shade, shadow*, Mk 4:32; Ac 5:15; met. *a shadow, a foreshadowing, a vague outline*, in distinction from ἡ εἰκών, the perfect image or delineation, and τὸ σῶμα, the reality, Col 2:17; Heb 8:5; 10:1; *gloom*; σκιὰ θανάτου, *death-shade, the thickest darkness*, Mt 4:16; Lk 1:79* [4639]

[5015] σκιρτάω *skirtaō* 3x *to leap*, Lk 1:41, 44; *to leap, skip, bound* for joy, Lk 6:23* [4640]

[5016] σκληροκαρδία *sklērokardia* 3x *hardness of heart, obstinacy, perverseness*, Mt 19:8; Mk 10:5; 16:14* [4641]

[5017] σκληρός *sklēros* 5x *dry, hard* to the touch; met. *harsh, severe, stern*, Mt 25:24; *vehement, violent, fierce*, Jas 3:4; *grievous, painful*, Ac 26:14; *grating* to the mind, *repulsive, offensive*, Jn 6:60; *stubborn, resistance to authority*, Jude 15* [4642]

[5018] σκληρότης *sklērotēs* 1x *hardness*; met. σκληρότης τῆς καρδίας, *hardness of heart, obstinacy, perverseness*, Ro 2:5* [4643]

[5019] σκληροτράχηλος *sklērotrachēlos* 1x *stiff-necked, obstinate*, Ac 7:51* [4644]

[5020] σκληρύνω *sklērynō* 6x *to harden*; met. *to harden* morally, *to make stubborn*, Heb 3:8, 15; 4:7; as a negation of ἐλεεῖν, *to leave to stubbornness and contumacy*, Ro 9:18; mid. and pass. *to put on a stubborn frame*, Ac 19:9; Heb 3:13* [4645]

[5021] σκολιός *skolios* 4x *crooked, tortuous*, Lk 3:5; met. *perverse, wicked*, Ac 2:40; Phil 2:15; *crooked, peevish, morose*, 1 Pe 2:18* [4646]

[5022] σκόλοψ *skolops* 1x *anything pointed*; met. *a thorn, a plague*, 2 Co 12:7* [4647]

[5023] σκοπέω *skopeō* 6x *to view attentively, watch; to see, observe, take care, beware*, Lk 11:35; Gal 6:1; *to regard, have respect to*, 2 Co 4:18; Phil 2:4; *to mark, note*, Ro 16:17; Phil 3:17* [4648]

[5024] σκοπός *skopos* 1x *a watcher*; also, *a distant object on which the eye is kept fixed; a mark, goal*, Phil 3:14* [4649]

[5026] σκορπίος *skorpios* 5x *a scorpion*, a large insect, sometimes several inches in length, shaped somewhat like a crab and furnished with a tail terminating in a stinger from which it emits a dangerous poison, Lk 10:19; 11:12; Rev 9:3, 5, 10* [4651]

[5027] σκοτεινός *skoteinos* 3x *dark*, Mt 6:23; Lk 11:34, 36* [4652]

[5028] σκοτία *skotia* 16x *darkness*, Jn 6:17; 20:1; *privacy*, Mt 10:27; Lk 12:3; met. moral or spiritual *darkness*, Jn 1:5 (2t); 8:12; 12:35, 46; 1 Jn 1:5; 2:8, 9, 11* [4653]

[5030] σκότος *skotos* 31x *darkness*, Mt 27:45; Ac 2:20; *gloom* of punishment and misery, Mt 8:12; 2 Pe 2:17; met. moral or spiritual *darkness*, Mt 4:16; Jn 3:19; Eph 5:11; *a realm of* moral *darkness*, Eph 5:8; 6:12 [4655]

[5031] σκοτόω *skotoō* 3x *to darken, shroud in darkness*, Eph 4:18; Rev 9:2; 16:10 [4656]

[5032] σκύβαλον *skybalon* 1x *dung, sweepings, refuse, rubbish*, Phil 3:8* [4657]

[5033] Σκύθης *Skythēs* 1x *A Scythian, a native of Scythia*, the modern Mongolia and Tartary, Col 3:11* [4658]

[5034] σκυθρωπός *skythrōpos* 2x *of a stern, morose, sour, gloomy*, or *dejected countenance*, Mt 6:16; Lk 24:17* [4659]

[5035] σκύλλω *skyllō* 4x *to flay, lacerate*; met. *to vex, trouble, annoy*, Mk 5:35; Lk 7:6; 8:49; pass. met. ἐσκυλμένοι, *in sorry plight*, Mt 9:36* [4660]

[5036] σκῦλον *skylon* 1x *spoils stripped off an enemy*; σκῦλα, *spoil, plunder, booty*, Lk 11:22* [4661]

[5037] σκωληκόβρωτος *skōlēkobrōtos* 1x *eaten of worms, consumed by worms,* Ac 12:23* [4662]

[5038] σκώληξ *skōlēx* 1x *a worm;* met. *gnawing anguish,* Mk 9:48* [4663]

[5039] σμαράγδινος *smaragdinos* 1x *of smaragdus* or *emerald,* Rev 4:3* [4664]

[5040] σμάραγδος *smaragdos* 1x *smaragdus, the emerald,* a gem of a pure green color; but under this name the ancients probably comprised all stones of a fine green color, Rev 21:19* [4665]

[5043] σμύρνα *smyrna* 2x *myrrh,* an aromatic bitter resin, or gum, issuing by incision, and sometimes spontaneously, from the trunk and larger branches of a small thorny tree growing in Egypt, Arabia, and Abyssinia, much used by the ancients in unguents, Mt 2:11; Jn 19:39* [4666]

[5044] Σμύρνα *Smyrna* 2x *Smyrna,* a maritime city of Ionia, in Asia Minor, Rev 1:11; 2:8* [4667]

[5046] σμυρνίζω *smyrnizō* 1x *to mingle* or *flavor with myrrh,* Mk 15:23* [4669]

[5047] Σόδομα *Sodoma* 9x *Sodom,* (Gen. 19:24) one of the four cities of the vale of Siddim, now covered by the Dead sea, Mt 11:23f.; Lk 17:29; Ro 9:29; 2 Pe 2:6; Rev 11:8 [4670]

[5048] Σολομών *Solomōn* 12x *Solomon,* also spelled Σολομῶν, ῶντος, ὁ (n-3f[1a]), pr. name, son and successor of David, Mt 1:6f.; 6:29; Lk 11:31; Jn 10:23; Ac 3:11; 7:47 [4672]

[5049] σορός *soros* 1x *a coffer; an urn for receiving the ashes of the dead; a coffin;* in N.T. *a bier,* Lk 7:14* [4673]

[5050] σός *sos* 26x *yours,* Mt 7:3, 22; οἱ σοί, *your kindred, friends,* etc., Mk 5:19; τὸ σόν and τὰ σά, *what is yours, your property, goods,* etc., Mt 20:14; 25:25; Lk 6:30 [4674]

[5051] σουδάριον *soudarion* 4x *a handkerchief, napkin,* etc., Lk 19:20; Jn 11:44; 20:7; Ac 19:12* [4676]

[5052] Σουσάννα *Sousanna* 1x *Susanna,* pr. name, Lk 8:3* [4677]

[5053] σοφία *sophia* 51x *wisdom* in general, *knowledge,* Mt 12:42; Lk 2:40, 52; 11:31; Ac 7:10; *ability,* Lk 21:15; Ac 6:3, 10; practical *wisdom, prudence,* Col 4:5; *learning, science,* Mt 13:54; Mk 6:2; Ac 7:22; scientific *skill,* 1 Co 1:17; 2:1; professed *wisdom,* human *philosophy,* 1 Co 1:19, 20, 22; 2:4, 5, 6; superior *knowledge and enlightenment,* Col 2:23; in

N.T. divine *wisdom,* Ro 11:33; Eph 3:10; Col 2:3; revealed *wisdom,* Mt 11:19; Lk 11:49; 1 Co 1:24, 30; 2:7; Christian *enlightenment,* 1 Co 12:8; Eph 1:8, 17; Col 1:9, 28, 3:16; Jas 1:5; 3:13 [4678]

[5054] σοφίζω *sophizō* 2x *to make wise, enlighten,* 2 Ti 3:15; mid. *to invent skilfully, devise artfully,* pass. 2 Pe 1:16* [4679]

[5055] σοφός *sophos* 20x *wise* generally, 1 Co 1:25; *shrewd, clever,* Ro 16:19; 1 Co 3:10; 6:5; *learned, intelligent,* Mt 11:25; Ro 1:14, 22; 1 Co 1:19, 20, 26, 27; 3:18; in N.T. divinely *instructed,* Mt 23:34; *furnished with* Christian *wisdom,* spiritually *enlightened,* Jas 3:13; *all-wise,* Ro 16:27; 1 Ti 1:17; Jude 25 [4680]

[5056] Σπανία *Spania* 2x *Spain,* Ro 15:24, 28* [4681]

[5057] σπαράσσω *sparassō* 3x pr. *to tear, lacerate;* by impl. *to agitate greatly, convulse, distort by convulsion,* Mk 1:26; 9:26; Lk 9:39* [4682]

[5058] σπαργανόω *sparganoō* 2x *to swathe, wrap in swaddling-cloths,* Lk 2:7, 12* [4683]

[5059] σπαταλάω *spatalaō* 2x *to live luxuriously, voluptuously, wantonly,* 1 Ti 5:6; Jas 5:5* [4684]

[5060] σπάω *spaō* 2x *to draw, pull; to draw* a sword, Mk 14:47; Ac 16:27* [4685]

[5061] σπεῖρα *speira* 7x *anything twisted* or *wreathed, a cord, coil, band,* etc.; *a band of soldiers, company, troop;* used for a Roman *cohort,* about 600 soldiers, Mt 27:27; Ac 10:1; *the* temple *guard,* Jn 18:3, 12; Mk 15:16; Ac 21:31; 27:1* [4686]

[5062] σπείρω *speirō* 52x *to sow* seed, Mt 6:26; 13:3, 4, 18, 24, 25, 27, 37, 3 [4687]

[5063] σπεκουλάτωρ *spekoulatōr* 1x *a sentinel, life-guardsman,* a kind of soldiers who formed the body-guard of princes, etc., one of whose duties was to put criminals to death, Mk 6:27* [4688]

[5064] σπένδω *spendō* 2x *to pour out a libation* or *drink-offering;* in N.T. mid. *to make a libation of one's self* by expending energy and life in the service of the Gospel, Phil 2:17; pass. *to be in the act of being sacrificed* in the cause of the Gospel, 2 Ti 4:6* [4689]

[5065] σπέρμα *sperma* 43x *seed,* Mt 13:24, 27, 37, 38; *semen virile,* Heb 11:11; *offspring, posterity,* Mt 22:24, 25; Jn 7:42; *a seed* of future generations, Ro 9:29; in N.T. met. *a seed* or *principle* of spiritual life, 1 Jn 3:9 [4690]

[5066] σπερμολόγος *spermologos* 1x pr. *seed-picking; one who picks up and retails scraps of information; a gossip; a babbler,* Ac 17:18* [4691]

[5067] σπεύδω *speudō* 6x trans. *to urge on, impel, quicken; to quicken* in idea, *to be eager for the arrival of,* 2 Pe 3:12; intrans. *to hasten, make haste,* Ac 20:16; 22:18; the part. has the force of an adverb, *quickly, hastily,* Lk 2:16; 19:5, 6* [4692]

[5068] σπήλαιον *spēlaion* 6x *a cave, cavern, den, hideout,* Mt 21:13; Mk 11:17; Lk 19:46; Jn 11:38; Heb 11:38; Rev 6:5* [4693]

[5069] σπιλάς *spilas* 1x *a sharply-cleft portion of rock;* in N.T. *a flaw, stigma,* Jude 12* [4694]

[5070] σπίλος *spilos* 2x *a spot, stain, blot;* a moral *blemish,* Eph 5:27; 2 Pe 2:13* [4696]

[5071] σπιλόω *spiloō* 2x *to spot, soil; to contaminate, defile,* Jas 3:6; Jude 23* [4695]

[5072] σπλαγχνίζομαι *splanchnizomai* 12x *to be moved with pity* or *compassion,* Mt 9:36; 14:14; 20:34; Lk 7:13; *to be compassionate,* Mt 18:27 [4697]

[5073] σπλάγχνον *splanchnon* 11x *the chief intestines, viscera; the entrails, bowels,* Ac 1:18; met. *the heart, the affections of the heart, the tender affections,* Lk 1:78; 2 Co 6:12; 7:15; Phil 1:8, 2:1; Col 3:12; Phlm 7, 20; 1 Jn 3:17; meton. *a cherished one, dear as one's self,* Phlm 12* [4698]

[5074] σπόγγος *spongos* 3x *a sponge,* Mt 27:48; Mk 15:36; Jn 19:29* [4699]

[5075] σποδός *spodos* 3x *ashes,* Mt 11:21; Lk 10:13; Heb 9:13* [4700]

[5076] σπορά *spora* 1x *a sowing; seed sown;* met. generative *seed, generation,* 1 Pe 1:23* [4701]

[5077] σπόριμος *sporimos* 3x *sown, fit to be sown;* in N.T. τὰ σπόριμα, *fields which are sown, fields of grain, cornfields,* Mt 12:1; Mk 2:23; Lk 6:1* [4702]

[5078] σπόρος *sporos* 6x *a sowing;* in N.T. *seed, that which is sown,* Mk 4:26, 27; Lk 8:5, 11; met. *the seed sown* in almsgiving, 2 Co 9:10* [4703]

[5079] σπουδάζω *spoudazō* 11x *to hurry; be bent upon,* Gal 2:10; *to endeavor earnestly, strive,* Eph 4:3 [4704]

[5080] σπουδαῖος *spoudaios* 3x *earnest, eager, forward, zealous,* 2 Co 8:17, 22 (2t)* [4705, 4706, 4707]

[5081] σπουδαίως *spoudaiōs* 4x *earnestly, eagerly, diligently,* Lk 7:4; 2 Ti 1:17; Tit 3:13; compar. σπουδαιοτέρως, *more earnestly, with special urgency,* Phil 2:28 [4708, 4709]

[5082] σπουδή *spoudē* 12x *haste;* μετὰ σπουδῆς, *with haste, hastily, quickly,* Mk 6:25; Lk 1:39; *earnestness, earnest application, diligence, enthusiasm,* Ro 12:8, 11; 2 Co 7:11, 12; 8:16; 8:7f. [4710]

[5083] σπυρίς *spyris* 5x *also spelled* σφυρίς, *a basket, hand-basket* for provision, Mt 15:37; 16:10; Mk 8:8, 20; Ac 9:25* [4711]

[5084] στάδιον *stadion* 7x pr. *a fixed standard of measure; a stadium,* the eighth part of a Roman mile, and nearly equal to a furlong, containing 201.45 yards, *about 192 meters,* Lk 24:13; Mt 14:24; Jn 6:19; 11:18; Rev 14:20; 21:16; *a race-course, a race,* 1 Co 9:24* [4712]

[5085] στάμνος *stamnos* 1x can be masculine, but not in the N.T., *a wine-jar; a pot, jar, urn, vase,* Heb 9:4* [4713]

[5086] στασιαστής *stasiastēs* 1x *a partisan, rebel, revolutionary,* Mt 15:7* [4955]

[5087] στάσις *stasis* 9x *a setting; a standing; an effective position,* an unimpaired *standing* or *dignity,* Heb 9:8; *a gathered party, a group;* hence, *a tumultuous assemblage, popular outbreak,* Mk 15:7; Ac 19:40; Lk 23:19, 25; *seditious movement,* Ac 24:5; *discord, dispute, dissension,* Ac 15:2; 23:7, 10* [4714]

[5088] στατήρ *statēr* 1x pr. *a weight; a stater,* an Attic silver coin, equal in value to the Jewish shekel, or to four Attic or two Alexandrian drachmas, Mt 17:27* [4715]

[5089] σταυρός *stauros* 27x *a stake; a cross,* Mt 27:32, 40, 42; Phil 2:8; by impl. *the punishment of the cross, crucifixion,* Eph 2:16; Heb 12:2; meton. *the crucifixion* of Christ in respect of its import, *the doctrine of the cross,* 1 Co 17:18; Gal 5:11; 6:12, 14; met. *to take up,* or bear one's cross, *to be ready to encounter any extremity,* Mt 10:38; 16:24 [4716]

[5090] σταυρόω *stauroō* 46x *to fix stakes;* later, *to crucify, affix to the cross,* Mt 20:19; 23:34; met. *to crucify, to mortify, to deaden, to make a sacrifice of,* Gal 5:24; pass. *to be cut off* from a thing, as by a violent death, *to be come dead to,* Gal 6:14 [4717]

[5091] σταφυλή *staphylē* 3x *a cluster* or *bunch of grapes,* Mt 7:16; Lk 6:44, Rev 14:18* [4718]

[5092] στάχυς *stachus* 5x *an ear of corn, head of grain,* Mt 12:1; Mk 2:23; 4:28; Lk 6:1* [4719]

[5093] Στάχυς *Stachus* 1x *Stachys,* pr. name, Ro 16:9* [4720]

[5094] στέγη *stegē* 3x *a roof, flat roof* of a house, Mt 8:8; Mk 2:4; Lk 7:6* [4721]

[5095] στέγω *stegō* 4x *to cover; to hold off, to hold in;* hence, *to hold out against, to endure patiently,* 1 Co 9:12; 13:7; absol. *to contain one's self,* 1 Th 3:1, 5* [4722]

[5096] στεῖρα *steira* 5x *barren, incapable of bearing children,* Lk 1:7, 36; 23:29; Gal 4:27; Heb 11:11* [4723]

[5097] στέλλω *stellō* 2x pr. *to place in set order, to arrange; to equip; to despatch; to stow;* mid. *to contract one's self, to shrink; to withdraw from, avoid, shun,* 2 Co 8:20; 2 Th 3:6* [4724]

[5098] στέμμα *stemma* 1x *a crown, wreath,* Ac 14:13* [4725]

[5099] στεναγμός *stenagmos* 2x *a sighing, groaning, groan,* Ac 7:34; *an inward sighing,* Ro 8:26* [4726]

[5100] στενάζω *stenazo* 6x *to groan, sigh,* Ro 8:23; 2 Co 5:2, 4; Heb 13:17; *to sigh* inwardly, Mk 7:34; *to give vent to querulous* or *censorious feelings,* Jas 5:9* [4727]

[5101] στενός *stenos* 3x *narrow, strait,* Mt 7:13, 14; Lk 13:24* [4728]

[5102] στενοχωρέω *stenochōreo* 3x *to crowd together into a narrow place, straiten;* pass. met. *to be in straits, to be cooped up, to be cramped* from action, 2 Co 4:8; *to be cramped* in feeling, 2 Co 6:12* [4729]

[5103] στενοχωρία *stenochōria* 4x pr. *narrowness of place, a narrow place;* met. *straits, distress, anguish,* Ro 2:9; 8:35; 2 Co 6:4; 12:10* [4730]

[5104] στερεός *stereos* 4x *stiff, hard;* of food, *solid,* as opposed to what is liquid and light, Heb 5:12, 14; *firm, steadfast,* 2 Ti 2:19; 1 Pe 5:9* [4731]

[5105] στερεόω *stereoō* 3x *to make firm; to strengthen,* Ac 3:7, 16; *to settle,* Ac 16:5* [4732]

[5106] στερέωμα *stereōma* 1x pr. *what is solid and firm;* met. *firmness, steadfastness, constancy,* Col 2:5* [4733]

[5107] Στεφανᾶς *Stephanas* 3x *Stephanas,* pr. name, 1 Co 1:16; 16:15, 17* [4734]

[5108] Στέφανος *Stephanos* 7x *Stephen,* pr. name, Ac 6:5, 8f.; 7:59; 8:2; 11:19; 22:20* [4736]

[5109] στέφανος *stephanos* 18x *that which forms an encirclement; a crown,* Mt 27:29; Rev 4:4, 10; *wreath,* conferred on a victor in the public games, 1 Co 9:25; met. *a crown, reward, prize,* 2 Ti 4:8; Jas 1:12; *a crown, ornament, honor, glory* [4735]

[5110] στεφανόω *stephanoō* 3x *to crown; to crown* as victor in the games, [4737]

[5111] στῆθος *stēthos* 5x *the breast, chest,* Lk 18:13; 23:48; Jn 13:25; 21:20; Rev 15:6* [4738]

[5112] στήκω *stēkō* 9x *to stand,* Mk 3:31; 11:25; met. *to stand* when under judgment, *to be approved,* Ro 14:4; *to stand firm, be constant, persevere,* 1 Co 16:13; Gal 5:1; Phil 1:27; 4:1; 1 Th 3:8; 2 Th 2:15* [4739]

[5113] στηριγμός *stērigmos* 1x pr. *a fixing, settling; a state of firmness, fixedness;* met. *firmness* of belief, *settle frame* of mind, 2 Pe 3:17* [4740]

[5114] στηρίζω *stērizō* 13x *to set fast; to set* in a certain position or direction, Lk 9:51; met. *to render* mentally *steadfast, to settle, confirm,* Lk 22:32; Ro 1:11; *to stand immovable,* Lk 16:26; met. *to be* mentally *settled,* 2 Pe 1:12 [4741]

[5115] στιβάς *stibas* 1x *a stuffing* of leaves, boughs, etc., meton. *a bough, branch,* Mk 11:8* [4746]

[5116] στίγμα *stigma* 1x *a brand-mark,* Gal 6:17* [4742]

[5117] στιγμή *stigmē* 1x pr. *a point;* met. *a point* of time, *moment, instant,* Lk 4:5* [4743]

[5118] στίλβω *stilbō* 1x *to shine, glisten, be radiant,* Mk 9:3* [4744]

[5119] στοά *stoa* 4x *a colonnade, cloister, covered walk supported by columns,* Jn 5:2; 10:23; Ac 3:11; 5:12* [4745]

[5121] Στοϊκός *Stoikos* 1x *Stoic,* Ac 17:18* [4770]

[5122] στοιχεῖον *stoicheion* 7x *an element; an element* of the natural universe, 2 Pe 3:10, 12; *an element* or *rudiment* of any intellectual or religious system, Gal 4:3, 9; Col 2:8, 20; Heb 5:12* [4747]

[5123] στοιχέω *stoicheō* 5x pr. *to advance in a line;* met. *to frame one's conduct* by a certain rule, Ac 21:24; Ro 4:12; Gal 5:25; 6:16; Phil 3:16* [4748]

[5124] στολή *stolē* 9x *equipment; dress; a long garment, flowing robe,* worn by priests, kings, and persons of distinction, Mt 12:38; 16:5; Lk 15:22; Rev 6:11 [4749]

[5125] στόμα *stoma* 78x *the mouth,* Mt 12:34; 15:11, 17, 18; 21:16; *speech, words,* Mt 18:16; 2 Co 13:1; *command of speech, facility of language,* Lk 21:15; from the Hebrew, ἀνοίγειν τὸ στόμα, *to utter, to speak,* Mt 5:2, 13:35; also, used of the earth, *to rend, yawn,* Rev 12:16; στόμα πρὸς στόμα λαλεῖν, *to speak mouth to mouth, face to face,* 2 Jn 12; 3 Jn 14; *the edge* or *point* of a weapon, Lk 21:24; Heb 11:34 [4750]

[5126] στόμαχος *stomachos* 1x pr. *the gullet* leading to the stomach; hence, later, *the stomach* itself, 1 Ti 5:23* [4751]

[5127] στρατεία *strateia* 2x *a military expedition, campaign;* and genr. *military service, warfare;* met. *the* Christian *warfare,* 2 Co 10:4; *fight,* 1 Ti 1:18* [4752]

[5128] στράτευμα *strateuma* 8x *an army,* Mt 22:7; Rev 19:14, 19; *an armed force, corps,* Ac 23:10, 27; *troops, guards,* Lk 23:11; Rev 9:16* [4753]

[5130] στρατηγός *stratēgos* 10x *a leader* or *commander of an army, general; a* Roman *praetor, provincial magistrate,* Ac 16:20, 22, 35, 36, 38; στρατηγός τοῦ ἱεροῦ, *the captain* or *prefect of the temple,* the chief of the Levites who kept guard in and around the temple, Lk 22:4, 52; Ac 4:1; 5:24, 26* [4755]

[5131] στρατιά *stratia* 2x *an army, host;* from the Hebrew, στρατιὰ οὐράνιος, or τοῦ οὐρανοῦ, *the heavenly host, the host of heaven, the hosts of angels,* Lk 2:13; *the stars,* Ac 7:42* [4756]

[5132] στρατιώτης *stratiōtēs* 26x *a soldier,* Mt 8:9; 27:27; met. *a soldier of* Christ, 2 Ti 2:3 [4757]

[5133] στρατολογέω *stratologeō* 1x *to collect* or *gather an army, enlist troops,* 2 Ti 2:4* [4758]

[5136] στρατόπεδον *stratopedon* 1x pr. *the site of an encampment; an encampment;* meton. *an army,* Lk 21:20* [4760]

[5137] στρεβλόω *strebloō* 1x pr. *to distort* the limbs *on a rack;* met. *to wrench, distort, pervert,* 2 Pe 3:16* [4761]

[5138] στρέφω *strephō* 21x *to twist; to turn,* Mt 5:39; *to make a change* of substance, *to change,* Rev 11:6; absol. *to change* or *turn* one's course of dealing, Ac 7:42; mid. *to turn one's self about,* Mt 16:23; Lk 7:9; *to turn back,* Ac 7:39; *to change one's direction, to turn* elsewhere, Ac 13:46; *to change one's course of principle and conduct, to be converted,* Mt 18:3 [4762]

[5139] στρηνιάω *strēniaō* 2x *to be wanton, to revel, riot,* Rev 18:7, 9* [4763]

[5140] στρῆνος *strēnos* 1x *luxury, sensuality,* Rev 18:3* [4764]

[5141] στρουθίον *strouthion* 4x *any small bird,* spc. *a sparrow,* Mt 10:29, 31; Lk 12:6, 7* [4765]

[5143] στρωννύω *strōnnyō* 6x the thematic form of στρώννυμι, the μι form never being visible in the N.T., *to spread, to strew,* Mt 21:8; Mk 11:8; *to spread* a couch, *make your own bed,* Ac 9:34; used of a supper-chamber, pass. *to have the couches spread, to be prepared, furnished,* Mk 14:15; Lk 22:12* [4766]

[5144] στυγητός *stygētos* 1x *hateful, disgusting, detested,* Tit 3:3* [4767]

[5145] στυγνάζω *stygnazō* 2x *to put on a gloomy and downcast look, to be shocked, appalled,* Mk 10:22; of the sky, *to lower,* Mt 16:3* [4768]

[5146] στῦλος *stylos* 4x *a pillar, column,* Rev 10:1; used of persons of authority, influence, etc., *a support* or *pillar* of the Church, Gal 2:9; Rev 3:12; *a support* of true doctrine, 1 Ti 3:15* [4769]

[5148] σύ *sy* 2,906x *you,* gen., sou', dat., soiv, acc., se, Mt 1:20; 2:6 [4571, 4671, 4675, 4771, 5209, 5210, 5213, 5216]

[5149] συγγένεια *syngeneia* 3x *kindred; kinsfolk, kinsmen, relatives,* Lk 1:61; Ac 7:3, 14* [4772]

[5150] συγγενής *syngenēs* 11x *kindred, akin;* as a subst. *a kinsman* or *kinswoman, relative;* Mk 6:4; Lk 1:58; 2:44; 14:12; 21:16; Jn 18:26; Ac 10:24; *one* nationally *akin, a fellow-countryman,* Ro 9:3; 16:7, 11, 21* [4773]

[5151] συγγενίς *syngenis* 1x *a kinswoman, female relative,* Lk 1:36* [4773]

[5152] συγγνώμη *syngnōmē* 1x *pardon; concession, leave, permission,* 1 Co 7:6* [4774]

[5153] συγκάθημαι *synkathēmai* 2x *to sit in company with,* Mk 14:54; Ac 26:30* [4775]

[5154] συγκαθίζω *synkathizō* 2x trans. *to cause to sit down with, seat in company with,* Eph 2:6; intrans. *to sit in company with; to sit down together,* Lk 22:55* [4776]

[5155] συγκακοπαθέω *synkakopatheō* 2x *to suffer evils along with* someone; *to be enduringly adherent,* 2 Ti 1:8; 2:3* [4777]

[5156] συγκακουχέομαι *synkakoucheomai* 1x *to encounter adversity along with* any one, Heb 11:25* [4778]

[5157] συγκαλέω *synkaleō* 8x *to call together,* Mk 15:16; Lk 15:6, 9; Ac 5:21; mid. *to call around one's self,* Lk 9:1; 23:13; Ac 10:24; 28:17* [4779]

[5158] συγκαλύπτω *synkalyptō* 1x *to cover completely, to cover up;* met. *to conceal,* Lk 12:2* [4780]

[5159] συγκάμπτω *synkamptō* 1x *to bend* or *bow together; to bow down* the back of any one afflictively, Ro 11:10* [4781]

[5160] συγκαταβαίνω *synkatabainō* 1x *to go down with* anyone, Ac 25:5* [4782]

[5161] συγκατάθεσις *synkatathesis* 1x *assent;* in N.T. *accord, alliance, agreement,* 2 Co 6:16* [4783]

[5163] συγκατατίθημι *synkatatithēmi* 1x *to set down together with;* mid. *to agree, accord,* Lk 23:51* [4784]

[5164] συγκαταψηφίζομαι *synkatapsēphizomai* 1x *to count, number with, be chosen together with,* Ac 1:26* [4785]

[5166] συγκεράννυμι *synkerannymi* 2x pluperf., συνεκέκρατο (3 sg), *to mix with, mingle together; to blend,* 1 Co 12:24; pass. *to be combined, united,* Heb 4:2* [4786]

[5167] συγκινέω *synkineō* 1x *to agitate, put in turmoil; to excite,* Ac 6:12* [4787]

[5168] συγκλείω *synkleiō* 4x *to shut up together, to hem in; to enclose,* Lk 5:6; met. *to band* under a sweeping sentence, Ro 11:32; Gal 3:22; pass. *to be banded* under a bar of disability, Gal 3:23* [4788]

[5169] συγκληρονόμος *synklēronomos* 4x pr. *a coheir,* Ro 8:17; *a fellow-participant,* Eph 3:6; Heb 11:9; 1 Pe 3:7* [4789]

[5170] συγκοινωνέω *synkoinōneō* 3x *to be a joint partaker, participate with* a person; in N.T. *to mix one's self up* in a thing, *to involve one's self, be an accomplice in,* Eph 5:11; Rev 18:4; *to sympathize actively in, to relieve,* Phil 4:14* [4790]

[5171] συγκοινωνός *synkoinōnos* 4x *one who partakes jointly; a coparticipant,* Ro 11:17; *a copartner* in service, *fellow,* 1 Co 9:23; Phil 1:7; *a sharer,* 1 Co 9:23; Rev 1:9* [4791]

[5172] συγκομίζω *synkomizō* 1x *to prepare for burial, take charge of the funeral* of any one, *bury,* Ac 8:2* [4792]

[5173] συγκρίνω *synkrinō* 3x *to combine, compound; to compare, to estimate by comparing with* something else, or, *to* *match*, 2 Co 10:12 (2t); *to explain, to illustrate, or, to suit*, 1 Co 2:13* [4793]

[5174] συγκύπτω *synkyptō* 1x *to bend* or *bow together; to be bowed together, bent over*, Lk 13:11* [4794]

[5175] συγκυρία *synkyria* 1x *concurrence, coincidence, chance, accident;* κατὰ συγκυρίαν, *by chance, accidentally*, Lk 10:31* [4795]

[5176] συγχαίρω *synchairō* 7x *to rejoice with* any one, *sympathize in joy*, Lk 1:58; 15:6, 9; Phil 2:17, 18; met. 1 Co 12:26; *to sympathize in the advancement of, congratulate*, 1 Co 13:6* [4796]

[5177] συγχέω *syncheō* 5x *to pour together, mingle by pouring together;* hence, *to confound, perplex, amaze*, Ac 2:6; *to confound* in dispute, Ac 9:22; *to throw into confusion, fill with uproar*, Ac 19:32; 21:27, 31* [4797]

[5178] συγχράομαι *synchraomai* 1x *use in common; associate with, have dealings with*, Jn 4:9* [4798]

[5180] σύγχυσις *synchusis* 1x pr. *a pouring together;* hence, *confusion, commotion, tumult, uproar*, Ac 19:29* [4799]

[5182] συζάω *syzaō* 3x *to live with; to continue in life with* someone, 2 Co 7:3; *to coexist in life with* another, Ro 6:8; 2 Ti 2:11* [4800]

[5183] συζεύγνυμι *syzeugnymi* 2x *to join together;* trop. *join together, unite*, Mt 19:6; Mk 10:9* [4801]

[5184] συζητέω *syzēteō* 10x *to seek, ask,* or *inquire with* another; *to deliberate, debate*, Mk 1:27; 9:10; Lk 24:15; *to hold discourse with, argue, reason*, Mk 8:11; 12:28; Lk 22:23; Ac 6:9; 9:29; *to question, dispute, quibble*, Mk 9:14, 16* [4802]

[5186] συζητητής *syzētētēs* 1x *a disputant, controversial reasoner, sophist*, 1 Co 1:20* [4804]

[5187] σύζυγος *syzygos* 1x *an associate, comrade, fellow-laborer*, or it could be the person's name, Phil 4:3* [4805]

[5188] συζωοποιέω *syzōopoieō* 2x *to make alive together with another; to make a sharer in the quickening of another*, Eph 2:5; Col 2:13* [4806]

[5189] συκάμινος *sykaminos* 1x *a sycamore-tree, mulberry tree,* i.q. συκομοραία, q.v., Lk 17:6* [4807]

[5190] συκῆ *sykē* 16x *a fig tree*, Mt 21:19 [4808]

[5191] συκομορέα *sykomorea* 1x *the fig-mulberry tree, sycamore fig*, Lk 19:4* [4809]

[5192] σῦκον *sykon* 4x *a fig, a ripe fig*, Mt 7:16; Mk 11:13; Lk 6:44; Jas 3:12* [4810]

[5193] συκοφαντέω *sykophanteō* 2x *to inform against; to accuse falsely;* by impl. *to wrong by false accusations; to extort* money *by false informations*, Lk 3:14; 19:8* [4811]

[5194] συλαγωγέω *sylagōgeō* 1x *to carry off as a prey* or *booty;* met. *to make victims of fraud*, Col 2:8* [4812]

[5195] συλάω *sylaō* 1x *to strip; to rob*, 2 Co 11:8* [4813]

[5196] συλλαλέω *syllaleō* 6x *to talk, converse,* or *discuss with*, Mt 17:3; Mk 9:4; Lk 4:36; 9:30; 22:4; Ac 25:12* [4814]

[5197] συλλαμβάνω *syllambanō* 16x *to catch; to seize, apprehend*, Mt 26:55; Ac 1:16; *to catch,* as prey, Lk 5:9; *to conceive, become pregnant*, Lk 1:24, 31, 36; 2:21; met. Jas 1:15; mid. *to help, aid, assist*, Lk 5:7; Phil 4:3 [4815]

[5198] συλλέγω *syllegō* 8x *to collect, gather*, Mt 7:16, 13:28-30, 40f., 48; Lk 6:44* [4816]

[5199] συλλογίζομαι *syllogizomai* 1x *to reason together; to consider, deliberate, reason*, Lk 20:5* [4817]

[5200] συλλυπέω *syllypeō* 1x *to be grieved together with; to be grieved*, Mk 3:5* [4818]

[5201] συμβαίνω *symbainō* 8x *to step* or *come together; to happen, meet, fall out*, Mk 10:32; Ac 20:19; 21:35; 1 Co 10:11; 1 Pe 4:12; 2 Pe 2:22; Ac 3:10; Lk 24:14* [4819]

[5202] συμβάλλω *symballō* 6x pr. *to throw together;* absol. *to meet and join*, Ac 20:14; *to meet in war, to encounter, engage with*, Lk 14:31; *to encounter in discourse or dispute*, Ac 17:18; *to consult together*, Ac 4:15; mid. *to contribute, be of service to, to aid*, Ac 18:27; συμβάλλειν ἐν τῇ καρδίᾳ, *to revolve in mind, ponder upon*, Lk 2:19* [4820]

[5203] συμβασιλεύω *symbasileuō* 2x *to reign with;* met. *to enjoy honor with*, 1 Co 4:8; 2 Ti 2:12* [4821]

[5204] συμβιβάζω *symbibazō* 7x pr. *to cause to come together; to unite, knit together*, Eph 4:16; Col 2:2, 19; *to infer, conclude*, Ac 16:10; by impl. *to prove, demonstrate*, Ac 9:22; in N.T. *to teach, instruct*, 1 Co 2:16; Ac 19:33* [4822]

[5205] συμβουλεύω *symbouleuō* 4x *to counsel, advise, exhort*, Jn 18:14; Rev 3:18; mid. *to consult together, plot*, Mt 26:4; Ac 9:23* [4823]

[5206] συμβούλιον *symboulion* 8x *counsel, consultation, mutual consultation*, Mt 12:14; 22:15; 27:1, 7; 28:12; Mk 3:6; Ac 27:1, 7; 28:12; *a council of counsellors*, Ac 25:12* [4824]

[5207] σύμβουλος *symboulos* 1x *a counsellor; advisor, one who shares one's counsel*, Ro 11:34* [4825]

[5208] Συμεών *Symeōn* 7x *Symeon, Simeon*, pr. name. indecl. (1) *Simeon,* son of Juda, Lk 3:30. (2) *Simeon,* son of Jacob, Rev 7:7. (3) *Simeon,* a prophet of Jerusalem, Lk 2:25, 34. (4) *Simeon,* or *Simon Peter*, Ac 15:14; 2 Pe 1:1. (5) *Simeon,* called Niger, Ac 13:1* [4826]

[5209] συμμαθητής *symmathētēs* 1x *a fellow-disciple*, Jn 11:16* [4827]

[5210] συμμαρτυρέω *symmartyreō* 3x *to testify* or *bear witness together with* another, *confirm, add testimony*, Ro 2:15; 8:16; 9:1* [4828]

[5211] συμμερίζω *symmerizō* 1x *to divide with* another so as to receive a part to one's self, *share with, partake with*, 1 Co 9:13* [4829]

[5212] συμμέτοχος *symmetochos* 2x *a partaker with* any one, *a joint partaker*, Eph 3:6; 5:7* [4830]

[5213] συμμιμητής *symmimētēs* 1x *an imitator together with* any one, *a joint-imitator*, Phil 3:17* [4831]

[5214] συμμορφίζω *symmorphizō* 1x *to conform to, take on the same form as*, Phil 3:10* [4833]

[5215] σύμμορφος *symmorphos* 2x *of like form, assimilated, conformed, similar in form*, Ro 8:29; Phil 3:21* [4832]

[5217] συμπαθέω *sympatheō* 2x *to sympathize with*, Heb 4:15; *to be compassionate*, Heb 10:34* [4834]

[5218] συμπαθής *sympathēs* 1x *sympathizing, compassionate*, 1 Pe 3:8* [4835]

[5219] συμπαραγίνομαι *symparaginomai* 1x *to be present together with; to come together, convene*, Lk 23:48* [4836]

[5220] συμπαρακαλέω *symparakaleō* 1x *to invite, exhort along with others;* pass. *to share in mutual encouragement*, Ro 1:12* [4837]

[5221] συμπαραλαμβάνω *symparalambanō* 4x *to take along with, take as a* companion, Ac 12:25; 15:37, 38; Gal 2:1* [4838]

[5223] συμπάρειμι *sympareimi* 1x *to be present with* any one, Ac 25:24* [4840]

[5224] συμπάσχω *sympaschō* 2x *to suffer with, sympathize,* 1 Co 12:26; *to suffer as* another, *endure corresponding sufferings,* Ro 8:17* [4841]

[5225] συμπέμπω *sympempō* 2x *to send with* any one, 2 Co 8:18, 22* [4842]

[5227] συμπεριλαμβάνω *symperilambanō* 1x *to embrace together; to embrace,* Ac 20:10* [4843]

[5228] συμπίνω *sympinō* 1x *to drink with* any one, Ac 10:41* [4844]

[5229] συμπίπτω *sympiptō* 1x *fall together, collapse,* Lk 6: 49* [4098]

[5230] συμπληρόω *symplēroō* 3x *to fill, fill up,* Lk 8:23; pass., of time, *to be completed, have fully come,* Lk 9:51; Ac 2:1* [4845]

[5231] συμπνίγω *sympnigō* 5x *to throttle, choke;* trop. *to choke* the growth or increase of seed or plants, Mt 13:22; Mk 4:7, 19; Lk 8:14; *to press upon, crowd,* Lk 8:42* [4846]

[5232] συμπολίτης *sympolitēs* 1x *a fellow-citizen,* met. Eph 2:19* [4847]

[5233] συμπορεύομαι *symporeuomai* 4x *to go with, accompany,* Lk 7:11; 14:25; 24:15; *to come together, assemble,* Mk 10:1* [4848]

[5235] συμπόσιον *symposion* 2x *a drinking together; a feast, banquet; a festive company;* in N.T., pl. συμπόσια, *eating party,* Mk 6:39* [4849]

[5236] συμπρεσβύτερος *sympresbyteros* 1x *a fellow-elder, fellow-presbyter,* 1 Pe 5:1* [4850]

[5237] συμφέρω *sympherō* 15x *to bring together, collect,* Ac 19:19; absol. *be for the benefit* of any one, *be profitable, advantageous, expedient,* 1 Co 6:12; *to suit best, be appropriate,* 2 Co 8:10; *good, benefit, profit, advantage,* Ac 20:20; 1 Co 7:35; *it is profitable, advantageous, expedient,* Mt 5:29, 30; 19:10 [4851]

[5238] σύμφημι *symphēmi* 1x pr. *to agree with,* Ro 7:16* [4852]

[5239] σύμφορος *symphoros* 2x *profitable, expedient,* 1 Co 7:35; 10:33* [4851]

[5241] συμφυλέτης *symphyletēs* 1x pr. *one of the same tribe; a fellow-citizen, fellow-countryman,* 1 Th 2:14* [4853]

[5242] σύμφυτος *symphytos* 1x pr. *planted together, grown together;* in N.T. met. *grown together, closely entwined* or *united with,* Ro 6:5* [4854]

[5243] συμφύω *symphyō* 1x *to make to grow together;* pass. *to grow* or *spring up with,* Lk 8:7* [4855]

[5244] συμφωνέω *symphōneō* 6x *to sound together, to be in unison, be in accord;* trop. *to agree with, accord with* in purport, Ac 15:15; *to harmonize with, suit with,* Lk 5:36; *to agree with, make an agreement,* Mt 18:19; 20:2, 13; Ac 5:9* [4856]

[5245] συμφώνησις *symphōnēsis* 1x *unison, accord; agreement,* 2 Co 6:15* [4857]

[5246] συμφωνία *symphōnia* 1x *symphony, harmony of sounds, concert of instruments, music,* Lk 15:25* [4858]

[5247] σύμφωνος *symphōnos* 1x *agreeing in sound;* met. *harmonious, agreeing, accord, agreement,* 1 Co 7:5* [4859]

[5248] συμψηφίζω *sympsēphizō* 1x *to calculate together, compute, reckon up,* Ac 19:19* [4860]

[5249] σύμψυχος *sympsychos* 1x *united in mind, at unity,* Phil 2:2 [4861]

[5250] σύν *syn* 128x *with, together with,* Mt 25:27; 26:35; 27:38; *attendant on,* 1 Co 15:10; *besides,* Lk 24:21; *with, with the assistance of,* 1 Co 5:4; *with, in the same manner as,* Gal 3:9; εἶναι σύν τινι, *to be with any one, to be in company with, accompany,* Lk 2:13; 8:38; *to be on the side of, be a partisan of any one,* Ac 4:13; 14:4; οἱ σύν τινι, *those with any one, the companions of any one,* Mk 2:26; Ac 22:9; *the colleagues, associates of any one,* Ac 5:17, 21 [4862]

[5251] συνάγω *synagō* 59x *to bring together, collect, gather,* as grain, fruits, etc., Mt 3:12 6:26; 13:30, 47; *to collect* an assembly; pass. *to convene, come together, meet,* Mt 2:4; 13:2; 18:20; 22:10; in N.T. *to receive with kindness and hospitality, to entertain,* Mt 25:35, 38, 43 [4863]

[5252] συναγωγή *synagōgē* 56x *a collecting, gathering; a* Christian *assembly* or *congregation,* Jas 2:2; *the congregation* of a synagogue, Ac 9:2; hence, *the place itself, a synagogue,* Lk 7:5 [4864]

[5253] συναγωνίζομαι *synagōnizomai* 1x *to combat in company with* any one; *to exert one's strength with, to be earnest in aiding, help,* Ro 15:30* [4865]

[5254] συναθλέω *synathleō* 2x pr. *to fight* or *work on the side of* any one; in N.T. *to cooperate vigorously with* a person, Phil 4:3; *to make effort in the cause of, in support of* a thing, Phil 1:27* [4866]

[5255] συναθροίζω *synathroizō* 2x *to gather; to bring together,* Ac 19:25; pass. *to come together, convene,* Ac 12:12* [4867]

[5256] συναίρω *synairō* 3x *to take up* a thing *with* any one; in N.T. συναίρειν λόγον, *to settle accounts, reckon* in order to payment, Mt 18:23, 24; 25:19* [4868]

[5257] συναιχμάλωτος *synaichmalōtos* 3x *a fellow-captive,* Ro 16:7; Col 4:10; Phlm 23* [4869]

[5258] συνακολουθέω *synakoloutheō* 3x *to follow in company with, accompany,* Mk 5:37; 14:51; Lk 23:49* [4870]

[5259] συναλίζω *synalizō* 1x *to cause to come together, collect, assemble, congregate;* mid. *to convene to one's self,* Ac 1:4* [4871]

[5261] συναλλάσσω *synallassō* 1x *to negotiate* or *bargain with* someone; *to reconcile,* Ac 7:26* [4900]

[5262] συναναβαίνω *synanabainō* 2x *to go up, ascend with* someone, Mk 15:41; Ac 13:31* [4872]

[5263] συνανάκειμαι *synanakeimai* 7x *to recline with* someone at table, Mt 9:10; 14:9; Mk 2:15; 6:22; Lk 7:49; 14:10, 15* [4873]

[5265] συναναπαύομαι *synanapauomai* 1x *to experience refreshment* or *rest in company with* someone, Ro 15:32* [4875]

[5267] συναντάω *synantaō* 6x *to meet with, fall in with, encounter,* Lk 9:37; 22:10; Ac 10:25; Heb 7:1, 10; *to occur, happen to, befall,* Ac 20:22* [4876]

[5269] συναντιλαμβάνομαι *synantilambanomai* 2x pr. *to take hold of with* someone; *to support, help, aid,* Lk 10:40; Ro 8:26* [4878]

[5270] συναπάγω *synapagō* 3x *to lead* or *carry away with; to seduce;* pass. *to be led away* [4879]

[5271] συναποθνήσκω *synapothnēskō* 3x *to die together with* any one, Mk 14:31; 2 Co 7:3; met. *to die with,* in respect of a spiritual likeness, 2 Ti 2:11* [4880]

[5272] συναπόλλυμι *synapollymi* 1x *to destroy together with* others; mid. *to perish* or *be destroyed with* others, Heb 11:31* [4881]

[5273] συναποστέλλω *synapostellō* 1x *to send forth together with* someone, 2 Co 12:18* [4882]

[5274] συναρμολογέω *synarmologeō* 2x *to join together fitly, fit* or *frame together, compact,* Eph 2:21; 4:16* [4883]

[5275] συναρπάζω *synarpazō* 4x pluperf., συνηρπάκειν, *to snatch up, clutch; to seize and carry off suddenly,* Ac 6:12; *to seize with force and violence,* Lk 8:29; Ac 19:29; pass. of a ship, *to be caught and swept on* by the wind, Ac 27:15* [4884]

[5277] συναυξάνω *synauxanō* 1x pas., *to grow together* in company, Mt 13:30* [4885]

[5278] σύνδεσμος *syndesmos* 4x *that which binds together,* Col 2:19; *a band* of union, Eph 4:3; Col 3:14; *a bundle,* or, *bond,* Ac 8:23* [4886]

[5279] συνδέω *syndeō* 1x *to bind together;* in N.T. pass. *to be in bonds together,* Heb 13:3* [4887]

[5280] συνδοξάζω *syndoxazō* 1x in N.T. *to glorify together with, to exalt to a state of dignity and happiness in company with, to make to partake in the glorification* of another, Ro 8:17* [4888]

[5281] σύνδουλος *syndoulos* 10x *a fellow-slave, fellow-servant,* Mt 24:49; 18:28f., 31, 33; Col 4:7; Rev 6:11; 19:10; 22:9; *a fellow-minister* of Christ, Col 1:7* [4889]

[5282] συνδρομή *syndromē* 1x *a running together, forming a mob,* Ac 21:30* [4890]

[5283] συνεγείρω *synegeirō* 3x *to raise up with* any one; *to raise up with* Christ by spiritual resemblance of His resurrection, Eph 2:6; Col 2:12; 3:1* [4891]

[5284] συνέδριον *synedrion* 22x pr. *a sitting together, assembly,* etc., in N.T. *the Sanhedrin,* the supreme council of the Jewish nation, Mt 5:22; 26:59; meton. *the Sanhedrin,* as including the members and place of meeting, Lk 22:66; Ac 4:15; genr. *a* judicial *council, tribunal,* Mt 10:17; Mk 13:9 [4892]

[5287] συνείδησις *syneidēsis* 30x *consciousness,* Heb 10:2; *a present idea, persisting notion, impression of reality,* 1 Pe 2:19; *conscience,* as an inward moral impression of one's actions and principles, Ac 23:1; 24:16; Ro 9:1; 2 Co 1:12; *conscience,* as the inward faculty of moral judgment, Ro 2:15; 13:5; 1 Co 8:7b, 10, 12; 10:25, 27, 28, 29; 2 Co 4:2; 5:11; 1 Ti 1:5, 19; 3:9; 4:2; 2 Ti 1:3; *conscience,* as the inward moral and spiritual frame, Tit 1:15; Heb 9:9, 14; 10:22; 13:18; 1 Pe 3:16, 21* [4893]

[5289] σύνειμι *syneimi* 2x (1) from εἰμί, *to be with, be in company with,* Lk 9:18; Ac 22:11* [4895]

[5290] σύνειμι *syneimi* 1x (1) from εἶμι, *to come together,* Lk 8:4* [4896]

[5291] συνεισέρχομαι *syneiserchomai* 2x *to enter with* someone, Jn 18:15; *to embark with,* Jn 6:22* [4897]

[5292] συνέκδημος *synekdēmos* 2x *one who accompanies* another *to foreign countries, fellow-traveller,* Ac 19:29; 2 Co 8:19* [4898]

[5293] συνεκλεκτός *syneklektos* 1x *chosen along with* others; *elected* to Gospel privileges *along with,* 1 Pe 5:13* [4899]

[5296] συνεπιμαρτυρέω *synepimartyreō* 1x *to join in according testimony; to support by testimony, to confirm, sanction,* Heb 2:4* [4901]

[5298] συνεπιτίθημι *synepitithēmi* 1x can also be spelled συνεπιτίθεμαι, mid., *to set upon along with, join with others* in an attack; *to unite in impeaching,* Ac 24:9* [4934]

[5299] συνέπομαι *synepomai* 1x *to follow with, attend, accompany,* Ac 20:4* [4902]

[5300] συνεργέω *synergeō* 5x *to work together with, to cooperate,* etc., 1 Co 16:16; 2 Co 6:1; *to assist, afford aid to,* Mk 16:20; Jas 2:22; absol. *to conspire actively* to a result, Ro 8:28* [4903]

[5301] συνεργός *synergos* 13x *a fellow-laborer, associate, helper,* Ro 16:3, 9, 21; 2 Co 1:24 [4904]

[5302] συνέρχομαι *synerchomai* 30x pluperf., συνεληλύθεισαν (3 pl), *to come together; to assemble,* Mk 3:20; 6:33; 14:53; *to cohabit* matrimonially, Mt 1:18; 1 Co 7:5; *to go* or *come with* any one, *to accompany,* Lk 23:55; Ac 9:39; *to company with, associate with,* Ac 1:21 [4905]

[5303] συνεσθίω *synesthiō* 5x *to eat with,* Ac 10:41; 11:3; 1 Co 5:11; by impl. *to associate with, live on familiar terms with,* Lk 15:2; Gal 2:12* [4906]

[5304] σύνεσις *synesis* 7x pr. *a sending together, a junction,* as of streams; met. *understanding, intelligence, discernment,* Lk 2:47; 1 Co 1:19; meton. *the understanding, intellect, mind,* Mk 12:33; Eph 3:4; Col 1:9; 2:2; 2 Ti 2:7* [4907]

[5305] συνετός *synetos* 4x *intelligent, discerning, wise, prudent,* Mt 11:25; Lk 10:21; Ac 13:7; 1 Co 1:19* [4908]

[5306] συνευδοκέω *syneudokeō* 6x *to approve with* another; *to agree with in principle,* Ro 1:32; *to stamp approval,* Lk 11:48; Ac 8:1; 22:20; *to be willing, agreeable,* 1 Co 7:12, 13* [4909]

[5307] συνευωχέομαι *syneuōcheomai* 2x *to feast together with,* 2 Pe 2:13; Jude 12* [4910]

[5308] συνεφίστημι *synephistēmi* 1x *to set together upon, join in an attack,* Ac 16:22* [4911]

[5309] συνέχω *synechō* 12x pr. *to hold together; to confine, shut up, close;* τὰ ωτα, *to stop the ears,* Ac 7:57; *to confine,* as a besieged city, Lk 19:43; *to hold, hold fast, have the custody of* any one, Lk 22:63; *to hem in, urge, press upon,* Lk 8:45; *to exercise a constraining influence on,* 2 Co 5:14; pass. *to be seized with, be affected with,* as fear, disease, etc., Mt 4:24; Lk 4:38; 8:37; Ac 28:8; *to be in a state of* mental *constriction, to be hard pressed* by urgency of circumstances, Lk 12:50; Ac 18:5; Phil 1:23* [4912]

[5310] συνήδομαι *synēdomai* 1x *to be pleased along with* others; *to congratulate; to delight in, approve cordially,* Ro 7:22* [4913]

[5311] συνήθεια *synētheia* 3x *use, custom; an established custom, practice,* Jn 18:39; 1 Co 8:7; 11:16* [4914]

[5312] συνηλικιώτης *synēlikiōtēs* 1x *one of the same age, an equal in age,* Gal 1:14* [4915]

[5313] συνθάπτω *synthaptō* 2x *to bury with;* pass. in N.T. *to be buried with* Christ symbolically, Ro 6:4; Col 2:12* [4916]

[5314] συνθλάω *synthlaō* 2x *to crush together; to break in pieces, shatter,* Mt 21:44; Lk 20:18* [4917]

[5315] συνθλίβω *synthlibō* 2x *to press together; to press upon, crowd,* Mk 5:24, 31* [4918]

[5316] συνθρύπτω *synthryptō* 1x *to crush to pieces;* met. *to break* the heart of any one, *to make to recoil in fear,* Ac 21:13* [4919]

[5317] συνίημι *syniēmi* 26x also συνίω, see *BAGD* for a discussion, pr. *to send together;* met. *to understand, comprehend thoroughly,* Mt 13:51; Lk 2:50; 18:34; 24:45; *to perceive clearly,* Mt 16:12; 17:13; Ac 7:25; Ro 15:21; Eph 5:17; absol. *to be well-judging, sensible,* 2 Co 10:12; *to be* spiritually *intelligent,* Mt 13:13, 14, 15; Ac 28:26, 27; *to be* religiously *wise,* Ro 3:11 [4920]

[5319] συνίστημι *synistēmi* 16x also spelled συνιστάνω and συνιστάω, *to place together; to recommend to favorable attention*, Ro 16:1; 2 Co 3:1; 10:18; *to place in a striking point of view*, Ro 3:5; 5:8; Gal 2:18; *to stand beside*, Lk 9:32; *to have been permanently framed*, Col 1:17; *to possess consistence*, 2 Pe 3:5 [4921]

[5321] συνοδεύω *synodeuō* 1x *to journey or travel with, accompany on a journey*, Ac 9:7* [4922]

[5322] συνοδία *synodia* 1x pr. *a journeying together;* meton. *a company of fellow-travellers, caravan*, Lk 2:44* [4923]

[5323] σύνοιδα *synoida* 2x a defective verb that is actually perfect in form but present in meaning, *to share in the knowledge* of a thing; *to be privy to*, Ac 5:2; *to be conscious;* οὐδὲν σύνοιδα, *to have a clear conscience*, 1 Co 4:4* [4894]

[5324] συνοικέω *synoikeō* 1x *to dwell with; to live or cohabit with*, 1 Pe 3:7* [4924]

[5325] συνοικοδομέω *synoikodomeō* 1x *to build in company with* someone; pass. *to be built up, form a constituent part of a structure*, Eph 2:22* [4925]

[5326] συνομιλέω *synomileō* 1x pr. *to be in company with; to talk or converse with*, Ac 10:27* [4926]

[5327] συνομορέω *synomoreō* 1x *to be next to, be next door*, Ac 18:7* [4927]

[5328] συνοράω *synoraō* 2x *perceive, become aware of, realize*, Ac 12:12; 14:6* [4894]

[5330] συνοχή *synochē* 2x pr. *a being held together; compression;* in N.T. met. *distress of mind, anxiety*, Lk 21:25; 2 Co 2:4 [4928]

[5332] συντάσσω *syntassō* 3x pr. *to arrange or place in order together;* in N.T. *to order, charge, direct*, Mt 21:6, 26:19; 27:10* [4929]

[5333] συντέλεια *synteleia* 6x *a complete combination, a completion, consummation, end*, Mt 13:39, 40, 49; 24:3; 28:20; Heb 9:26* [4930]

[5334] συντελέω *synteleō* 6x pr. *to bring to an end altogether; to finish, end*, Lk 4:13; *to consummate*, Ro 9:28; *to ratify* a covenant, Heb 8:8; pass. *to be terminated*, Lk 4:2; Ac 21:27; *to be fully realized*, Mk 13:4* [4931]

[5335] συντέμνω *syntemnō* 1x pr. *to cut short, contract by cutting off;* met. *to execute speedily*, or from the Hebrew, *to determine, decide, decree*, Ro 9:28 (2t)* [4932]

[5337] συντηρέω *syntēreō* 3x *to keep safe and sound*, Mt 9:17; *to observe strictly*, or, *to secure from harm, protect*, Mk 6:20; *to preserve in memory, keep carefully in mind*, Lk 2:19* [4933]

[5338] συντίθημι *syntithēmi* 3x *to agree together, come to a mutual understanding*, Jn 9:22; Ac 23:20; *to bargain, to pledge one's self*, Lk 22:5* [4934]

[5339] συντόμως *syntomōs* 1x *concisely, briefly*, Ac 24:4* [4935]

[5340] συντρέχω *syntrechō* 3x *to run together, flock together*, Mk 6:33; Ac 3:11; *to run in company with* others, met. 1 Pe 4:4* [4936]

[5341] συντρίβω *syntribō* 7x *to rub together; to shiver*, Mk 14:3; Rev 2:27; *to break, break in pieces*, Mk 5:4; Jn 19:36; *to break down, crush, bruise*, Mt 12:20; met. *to break the power of* any one, *deprive of strength, debilitate*, Lk 9:39; Ro 16:20* [4937]

[5342] σύντριμμα *syntrimma* 1x *a breaking, bruising;* in N.T. *destruction, ruin*, Ro 3:16* [4938]

[5343] σύντροφος *syntrophos* 1x *nursed with* another; *one brought up* (*NIV*) or *educated with* another, *intimate friend, friend of the court* (*RSV*) Ac 13:1* [4939]

[5344] συντυγχάνω *syntynchanō* 1x *to meet or fall in with; join*, in N.T. *to get to, approach*, Lk 8:19* [4940]

[5345] Συντύχη *Syntychē* 1x *Syntyche*, pr. name, Phil 4:2* [4941]

[5347] συνυποκρίνομαι *synypokrinomai* 1x *to dissemble, feign with*, or *in the same manner as* another, *join in the playing of the hypocrite*, Gal 2:13* [4942]

[5348] συνυπουργέω *synypourgeō* 1x *to aid along with* another, *help together*, 2 Co 1:11* [4943]

[5349] συνωδίνω *synōdinō* 1x pr. *to travail at the same time with;* trop. *suffer together*, Ro 8:22* [4944]

[5350] συνωμοσία *synōmosia* 1x *a banding by oath; a combination, conspiracy*, Ac 23:13* [4945]

[5352] Συράκουσαι *Syrakousai* 1x *Syracuse*, a celebrated city of Sicily, Ac 28:12* [4946]

[5353] Συρία *Syria* 8x *Syria*, an extensive country of Asia, Mt 4:24; Lk 2:2; Ac 15:23 [4947]

[5354] Σύρος *Syros* 1x *a Syrian*, Lk 4:27* [4948]

[5355] Συροφοινίκισσα *Syrophoinikissa* 1x *a Syrophoenician woman*, Phoenicia being included in Syria, Mk 7:26* [4949]

[5358] Σύρτις *Syrtis* 1x *a shoal, sandbank, a place dangerous on account of shoals*, two of which were particularly famous on the northern coast of Africa, one lying near Carthage, and the other, *the syrtis major*, lying between Cyrene and Leptis, which is probably referred to in Ac 27:17* [4950]

[5359] σύρω *syrō* 5x *to draw, drag*, Jn 21:8; Rev 12:4; *to force away, hale* before magistrates, etc., Ac 8:3; 14:19; 17:6* [4951]

[5360] συσπαράσσω *sysparassō* 2x *to tear to pieces; to convulse altogether*, Mk 9:20; Lk 9:42* [4952]

[5361] σύσσημον *syssēmon* 1x *a signal*, Mk 14:44* [4953]

[5362] σύσσωμος *syssōmos* 1x *united in the same body;* met. pl. *joint members* in a spiritual body, Eph 3:6* [4954]

[5364] συστατικός *systatikos* 1x *commendatory, recommendatory*, 2 Co 3:1 (2t)* [4956]

[5365] συσταυρόω *systauroō* 5x *to crucify with* another, Mt 27:44; Mk 15:32; Jn 19:32; pass. met. *to be crucified with* another in a spiritual resemblance, Ro 6:6; Gal 2:20* [4957]

[5366] συστέλλω *systellō* 2x *to draw together, contract, straiten; to enwrap;* hence, i.q. περιστέλλω, *to lay out, prepare for burial*, Ac 5:6; pass. *to be shortened*, 1 Co 7:29* [4958]

[5367] συστενάζω *systenazō* 1x *to groan or lament together*, Ro 8:22* [4959]

[5368] συστοιχέω *systoicheō* 1x pr. *to be in the same row with;* met. *to correspond to*, Gal 4:25* [4960]

[5369] συστρατιώτης *systratiōtēs* 2x *a fellow-soldier, co-militant*, in the service of Christ, Phil 2:25; Phlm 2* [4961]

[5370] συστρέφω *systrephō* 2x *to turn or roll together; to collect, gather*, Ac 28:3; Mt 17:22* [4962]

[5371] συστροφή *systrophē* 2x *a gathering, tumultuous assembly*, Ac 19:40; *a combination, conspiracy*, Ac 23:12* [4963]

[5372] συσχηματίζω *syschēmatizō* 2x *to fashion in accordance with;* mid/pass. *to conform or assimilate one's self to*, met. Ro 12:2; 1 Pe 1:14* [4964]

[5373] Συχάρ *Sychar* 1x *Sychar*, indecl., a city of Samaria, Jn 4:5* [4965]

[5374] Συχέμ *Sychem* 2x *Shechem,* indecl., fem., a city of Samaria, Ac 7:16★ [4966]

[5375] σφαγή *sphagē* 3x *slaughter,* Ac 8:32; Ro 8:36; Jas 5:5★ [4967]

[5376] σφάγιον *sphagion* 1x *a victim* slaughtered in sacrifice, *offering,* Ac 7:42★ [4968]

[5377] σφάζω *sphazō* 10x also spelled σφάττω, *to slaughter, kill, slay;* pr. used of animals killed in sacrifice, etc., Rev 5:6, 9, 12; 13:8; of persons, etc., 1 Jn 3:12; Rev 6:4, 9; 18:24; *to wound mortally,* Rev 13:3★ [4969]

[5379] σφόδρα *sphodra* 11x *much, greatly, exceedingly,* Mt 2:10; 17:6; Mk 16:4; Lk 18:23; Ac 6:7 [4970]

[5380] σφοδρῶς *sphodrōs* 1x *exceedingly, vehemently,* Ac 27:18★ [4971]

[5381] σφραγίζω *sphragizō* 15x *to seal, stamp with a seal,* Mt 27:66; Rev 20:3; *to seal up, to close up, conceal,* Rev 10:4; 22:10; *to set a mark upon, distinguish by a mark,* Eph 1:13; 4:30; Rev 7:3, 4, 5, 8; *to seal, to mark distinctively* as invested with a certain character, Jn 6:27; mid. *to set one's own mark upon, seal as one's own, to impress with a mark of acceptance,* 2 Co 1:22; *to deliver over safely to* someone, Ro 15:28; absol. *to set to one's seal, to make a solemn declaration,* Jn 3:33★ [4972]

[5382] σφραγίς *sphragis* 16x *a seal, a signet ring,* Rev 7:2; *an inscription on a seal, motto,* 2 Ti 2:19; *a seal, the impression of a seal,* Rev 5:1, 2, 5, 9; 6:1, 3, 5, 7, 9, 12; 8:1; *a seal, a distinctive mark,* Rev 9:4; *a seal, a token, proof,* 1 Co 9:2; *a token* of guarantee, Ro 4:11★ [4973]

[5383] σφυδρόν *sphydron* 1x *ankle,* Ac 3:7★ [4974]

[5385] σχεδόν *schedon* 3x pr. *near,* of place; hence, *nearly, almost,* Ac 13:44; 19:26; Heb 9:22★ [4975]

[5386] σχῆμα *schēma* 2x *fashion, form; fashion, external show,* 1 Co 7:31; Phil 2:7★ [4976]

[5387] σχίζω *schizō* 11x *to split,* Mt 27:51; Mk 15:38; *to rend, tear asunder,* Mt 27:51; Lk 5:36; 23:45; Jn 19:24; 21:11); mid. *to open* or *unfold* with a chasm, Mk 1:10; pass. met. *to be divided* into parties or factions, Ac 14:4; 23:7★ [4977]

[5388] σχίσμα *schisma* 8x *a split,* Mt 9:16; Mk 2:21; met. *a division* into parties, *schism,* Jn 7:43; 9:16; 10:19; 1 Co 1:10; 11:18; 12:25★ [4978]

[5389] σχοινίον *schoinion* 2x pr. *a cord made of rushes;* genr. *a rope, cord,* Jn 2:15; Ac 27:32★ [4979]

[5390] σχολάζω *scholazō* 2x *to be unemployed, to be at leisure; to be at leisure* for a thing, *to devote one's self entirely* to a thing, 1 Co 7:5; *to be unoccupied, empty,* Mt 12:44★ [4980]

[5391] σχολή *scholē* 1x *freedom from occupation;* later, *ease, leisure; a school,* Ac 19:9★ [4981]

[5392] σῴζω *sōzō* 106x *to save, rescue; to preserve safe and unharmed,* Mark. 8:25; 10:22; 24:22; 27:40, 42, 49; 1 Ti 2:15; σῴζειν εἰς, *to bring safely to,* 2 Ti 4:18; *to cure, heal, restore to health,* Mt 9:21, 22; Mk 5:23, 28, 34; 6:56; *to save, preserve* from being lost, Mt 16:25; Mk 3:4; 8:35; σῴζειν ἀπό, *to deliver from, set free from,* Mt 1:21; Jn 12:27; Ac 2:40; in N.T. *to rescue* from unbelief, *convert,* Ro 11:14; 1 Co 1:21; 7:16; *to bring within the pale of saving privilege,* Tit 3:5; 1 Pe 3:21; *to save* from final ruin, 1 Ti 1:15; pass. *to be brought within the pale of saving privilege,* Ac 2:47; Eph 2:5, 8; *to be in the way of salvation,* 1 Co 15:2; 2 Co 2:15 [4982]

[5393] σῶμα *sōma* 142x *the body* of an animal; *a living body,* Mt 5:29, 30; 6:22, 23, 25; Jas 3:3; *a person, individual,* 1 Co 6:16; *a dead body; corpse, carcass,* Mt 14:12; 27:52, 58; Heb 13:11; *the human body* considered as the seat and occasion of moral imperfection, as inducing to sin through its appetites and passions, Ro 7:24; 8:13; genr. *a body, a material substance,* 1 Co 15:37, 38, 40; *the substance, reality,* as opposed to ἡ σκιά, Col 2:17; in N.T. met., *the aggregate body* of believers, *the body* of the Church, Ro 12:5; Col 1:18 [4983]

[5394] σωματικός *sōmatikos* 2x *bodily, of* or *belonging to the body,* 1 Ti 4:8; *corporeal, material,* Lk 3:22★ [4984]

[5395] σωματικῶς *sōmatikōs* 1x *bodily, in a bodily frame,* Col 2:9★ [4985]

[5396] Σώπατρος *Sōpatros* 1x *Sopater,* pr. name, Ac 20:4★ [4986]

[5397] σωρεύω *sōreuō* 2x *to heap* or *pile up,* Ro 12:20; met. pass. *to be filled* with sins, 2 Ti 3:6★ [4987]

[5398] Σωσθένης *Sōsthenēs* 2x *Sosthenes,* pr. name, Ac 18:17; 1 Co 1:1★ [4988]

[5399] Σωσίπατρος *Sōsipatros* 1x *Sosipater,* pr. name, Ro 16:21★ [4989]

[5400] σωτήρ *sōtēr* 24x *a savior, preserver, deliverer,* Lk 1:47; 2:11; Ac 5:31 [4990]

[5401] σωτηρία *sōtēria* 46x *a saving, preservation,* Ac 27:34; Heb 11:7; *deliverance,* Lk 1:69, 71; Ac 7:25; *salvation,* spiritual and eternal, Lk 1:77; 19:9; Ac 4:12; Rev 7:10; *a being placed in a condition of salvation* by an embracing of the Gospel, Ro 10:1, 10; 2 Ti 3:15; *means* or *opportunity of salvation,* Ac 13:26; Ro 11:11; Heb 2:3; ἡ σωτηρία, *the* promised *deliverance* by the Messiah, Jn 4:22 [4991]

[5403] σωτήριος *sōtērios* 1x *imparting salvation, saving,* Tit 2:11; Lk 2:30; 3:6; Ac 28:28; Eph 6:17★ [4992]

[5404] σωφρονέω *sōphroneō* 6x *to be of a sound mind, be in one's right mind, be sane,* Mk 5:15; Lk 8:35; *to be calm,* 2 Co 5:13; *to be sober-minded, sedate,* Tit 2:6; 1 Pe 4:7; *to be of a modest, humble mind,* Ro 12:3★ [4993]

[5405] σωφρονίζω *sōphronizō* 1x *encourage, to restore to a right mind; to make sober-minded, to steady* by exhortation and guidance, Tit 2:4★ [4994]

[5406] σωφρονισμός *sōphronismos* 1x *self discipline, prudence,* 2 Ti 1:7★ [4995]

[5407] σωφρόνως *sōphronōs* 1x *in the manner of a person in his right mind; soberly, temperately,* Tit 2:12★ [4996]

[5408] σωφροσύνη *sōphrosynē* 3x *sanity, soundness of mind, a sane mind,* Ac 26:25; *female modesty,* 1 Ti 2:9, 15★ [4997]

[5409] σώφρων *sōphrōn* 4x *of a sound mind, sane; temperate, discreet,* 1 Ti 3:2; Tit 1:8; 2:2; *modest, chaste,* Tit 2:5★ [4998]

[5411] ταβέρναι *tabernai* 1x *taverns,* used in the NT only in the transliterated Latin name of "Three Taverns" (Τριῶν ταβερνῶν), see #5553, Ac 28:15★ [4999]

[5412] Ταβιθά *Tabitha* 2x *antelope, Tabitha,* pr. name, Ac 9:36, 40★ [5000]

[5413] τάγμα *tagma* 1x pr. *anything placed in order;* in N.T. *order of* succession, *class, group,* 1 Co 15:23★ [5001]

[5414] τακτός *taktos* 1x pr. *arranged; fixed, appointed, set,* Ac 12:21★ [5002]

[5415] ταλαιπωρέω *talaipōreō* 1x *to endure severe labor and hardship; to be harassed; complain,* Jas 4:9★ [5003]

[5416] ταλαιπωρία *talaipōria* 2x *toil, difficulty, hardship; calamity, misery, distress,* Ro 3:16; Jas 5:1★ [5004]

[5417] ταλαίπωρος *talaipōros* 2x pr. *enduring severe effort and hardship;* hence, *wretched, miserable, afflicted,* Ro 7:24; Rev 3:17★ [5005]

[5418] ταλαντιαῖος *talantiaios* 1x *of a talent weight, weighing a talent,* Rev 16:21★ [5006]

[5419] τάλαντον *talanton* 14x *the scale of a balance; a talent,* which as a weight was among the Jews equivalent to 3000 shekels, i.e., as usually estimated, 114 lbs. 15 dwts. Troy; while the Attic talent, on the usual estimate, was only equal to 56 lbs. 11 oz. Troy, Mt 18:24; 25:15, 16, 20, 22, 24, 25, 28★ [5007]

[5420] ταλιθά *talitha* 1x Aramaic, *(little) girl,* Mk 5:41★ [5008]

[5421] ταμεῖον *tameion* 4x *a storehouse, granary, barn,* Lk 12:24; *a chamber, closet, place of retirement and privacy,* Mt 6:6; 24:26; Lk 12:3★ [5009]

[5423] τάξις *taxis* 9x *order, regular disposition, arrangement; order, series, succession,* Lk 1:8; *an order, distinctive class,* as of priests, Heb 5:6, 10; 6:20; 7:11(2t), 17; *order, good order,* 1 Co 14:40; *orderliness, well-regulated conduct,* Col 2:5★ [5010]

[5424] ταπεινός *tapeinos* 8x *low* in situation; of condition, *humble, poor, mean, depressed,* Lk 1:52; 2 Co 7:6; Jas 1:9; met. of the mind, *humble, lowly, modest,* Mt 11:29; Ro 12:16; 2 Co 10:1; Jas 4:6; 1 Pe 5:5★ [5011]

[5425] ταπεινοφροσύνη *tapeinophrosynē* 7x *lowliness* or *humility of mind, modesty,* Ac 20:19; Eph 4:2; Phil 2:3; Col 2:18, 23; 3:12; 1 Pe 5:5★ [5012]

[5426] ταπεινόφρων *tapeinophrōn* 1x *humble-minded,* 1 Pe 3:8★ [5391]

[5427] ταπεινόω *tapeinoō* 14x *to bring low, depress, level,* Lk 3:5; met. *to humble, abase,* Phil 2:8; mid. *to descend to,* or *live in, a humble condition,* 2 Co 11:7; Phil 4:12; *to humble, depress the pride of,* any one, Mt 18:4; mid. *to humble one's self, exhibit humility and contrition,* Jas 4:10; 1 Pe 5:6; *to humble* with respect to hopes and expectations, *to depress* with disappointment, Mt 23:12; Lk 14:11; 18:14; 2 Co 12:21★ [5013]

[5428] ταπείνωσις *tapeinōsis* 4x *depression; low estate, abject condition,* Lk 1:48; Ac 8:33; Phil 3:21; Jas 1:10★ [5014]

[5429] ταράσσω *tarassō* 17x *to agitate, trouble,* as water, Jn 5:7; met. *to agitate, trouble* the mind; with fear, *to terrify, put in consternation,* Mt 2:3; 14:26; with grief, etc., *affect with grief, anxiety,* etc., Jn 12:27; 13:21; with doubt, etc., *to unsettle, perplex,* Ac 15:24; Gal 1:7 [5015]

[5431] τάραχος *tarachos* 2x *agitation, commotion; consternation, terror,* Ac 12:18; *excitement, tumult, public contention,* Ac 19:23★ [5017]

[5432] Ταρσεύς *Tarseus* 2x *of,* or *a native of* Ταρσός, *Tarsus,* the metropolis of Cilicia, Ac 9:11; 21:39★ [5018]

[5433] Ταρσός *Tarsos* 3x *Tarsus,* the chief city of Cilicia, and birth-place of the Apostle Paul, Ac 9:30; 11:25; 22:3★ [5019]

[5434] ταρταρόω *tartaroō* 1x *to cast* or *thrust down to Tartarus* or *Gehenna,* 2 Pe 2:4★ [5020]

[5435] τάσσω *tassō* 8x *to arrange; to set, appoint,* in a certain station, Lk 7:8; Ro 13:1; *to set, devote,* to a pursuit, 1 Co 16:15; *to dispose, frame,* for an object, Ac 13:48; *to arrange, appoint,* place or time, Mt 28:16; Ac 28:23; *to allot, assign,* Ac 22:10; *to settle, decide,* Ac 15:2★ [5021]

[5436] ταῦρος *tauros* 4x *a bull, ox,* Mt 22:4; Ac 14:13; Heb 9:13; 10:4★ [5022]

[5438] ταφή *taphē* 1x *burial, the act of burying, burial place,* Mt 27:7★ [5027]

[5439] τάφος *taphos* 7x *a sepulchre, grave, tomb,* Mt 23:27, 29; 27:61, 64, 66; 28:1; met. Ro 3:13★ [5028]

[5440] τάχα *tacha* 2x pr. *quickly, soon; perhaps, possibly,* Ro 5:7; Phlm 15★ [5029]

[5441] ταχέως *tacheōs* 15x adverb of ταχύς, *quickly, speedily; soon, shortly,* 1 Co 4:19; Gal 1:6; *hastily,* Lk 14:21; 16:6; *with inconsiderate haste,* 1 Ti 5:22 [5030, 5032, 5033]

[5442] ταχινός *tachinos* 2x *swift, speedy,* 2 Pe 2:1; *near at hand, impending,* 2 Pe 1:14★ [5031]

[5443] τάχος *tachos* 8x *swiftness, speed, quickness;* ἐν τάχει, *with speed, quickly, speedily; soon, shortly,* Lk 18:8; Ac 25:4; *hastily, immediately,* Ac 12:7; 22:18; Ro 16:20; 1 Ti 3:14; Rev 1:1; 22:6★ [5034]

[5444] ταχύς *tachus* 13x *swift, fleet, quick;* met. *ready, prompt,* Jas 1:19; Mt 28:7f.; Mk 9:39; Lk 15:22; Jn 11:29 [5035, 5036]

[5445] τε *te* 215x enclitic, can function as a conj., serving either as a lightly-appending link, Ac 1:15; *and,* Ac 2:3; or as an inclusive prefix, Lk 12:45; *both,* Lk 24:20; Ac 26:16 [5037]

[5446] τεῖχος *teichos* 9x *a wall* of a city, Ac 9:25; 2 Co 11:33; Heb 11:30; Rev 21:12, 14f., 17-19★ [5038]

[5447] τεκμήριον *tekmērion* 1x *a sign, indubitable token, clear proof,* Ac 1:3★ [5039]

[5448] τεκνίον *teknion* 8x *a little child;* τεκνία, an endearing appellation, *my dear children,* Jn 13:33; 1 Jn 2:1, 12, 28; 3:7, 18; 4:4; 5:21★ [5040]

[5449] τεκνογονέω *teknogoneō* 1x *to bear children, to rear a family,* 1 Ti 5:14★ [5041]

[5450] τεκνογονία *teknogonia* 1x *the bearing of children, the rearing of a family,* 1 Ti 2:15★ [5042]

[5451] τέκνον *teknon* 99x *a child, a son* or *daughter,* Mt 2:18; Lk 1:7; pl. *descendants, posterity,* Mt 3:9; Ac 2:39; *child, son,* as a term of endearment, Mt 9:2; Mk 2:5; 10:24; pl. *children, inhabitants, people,* of a city, Mt 23:37; Lk 19:44; from the Hebrew, met. *a child* or *son* in virtue of discipleship, 1 Co 4:17; 1 Ti 1:2; 2 Ti 1:2; Tit 1:4; Phlm 10; 3 Jn 4; *a child* in virtue of gracious acceptance, Jn 1:12; 11:52; Ro 8:16, 21; 1 Jn 3:1; *a child* in virtue of spiritual conformity, Jn 8:39; Phil 2:15; 1 Jn 3:10; *a child of,* one characterized by some condition or quality, Mt 11:19; Eph 2:3; 5:8; 1 Pe 1:14; 2 Pe 2:14 [5043]

[5452] τεκνοτροφέω *teknotropheō* 1x *to rear a family,* 1 Ti 5:10★ [5044]

[5454] τέκτων *tektōn* 2x *an artisan;* and spc. *one who works with wood, a carpenter,* Mt 13:55; Mk 6:3★ [5045]

[5455] τέλειος *teleios* 19x *brought to completion; fully accomplished, fully developed,* Jas 1:4a; *fully realized, thorough,* 1 Jn 4:18; *complete, entire,* as opposed to what is partial and limited, 1 Co 13:10; *full grown of ripe age,* 1 Co 14:20; Eph 4:13; Heb 5:14; *fully accomplished* in Christian enlightenment, 1 Co 2:6; Phil 3:15; Col 1:28; *perfect* in some point of character, *without shortcoming* in respect of a certain standard, Mt 5:48; 19:21; Col 4:12; Jas 1:4b; 3:2; *perfect, consummate,* Ro 12:2; Jas 1:17, 25; compar. *of higher excellence and efficiency,* Heb 9:11★ [5046]

[5456] τελειότης *teleiotēs* 2x *completeness, perfectness,* Col 3:14; *ripeness* of knowledge or practice, *maturity,* Heb 6:1★ [5047]

[5457] τελειόω *teleioō* 23x *to execute fully, discharge,* Jn 4:34; 5:36; 17:4; *to reach the end of, run through, finish,* Lk 2:43; Ac 20:24; *to consummate, place in a* condition of finality, Heb 7:19; *to perfect* a person, *advance* a person *to final completeness* of character, Heb 2:10; 5:9; 7:28; *to perfect* a person, *advance* a person *to a completeness* of its kind, which needs no further provision, Heb 9:9; 10:1, 14; pass. *to receive fulfillment*, Jn 19:28; *to be brought to the goal, to reach the end of one's course*, Lk 13:32; Phil 3:12; Heb 11:40; 12:23; *to be fully developed*, 2 Co 12:9; Jas 2:22; 1 Jn 2:5; 4:12, 17; *to be completely organized, to be closely embodied*, Jn 17:23 [5048]

[5458] τελείως *teleiōs* 1x *perfectly, completely*, 1 Pe 1:13★ [5049]

[5459] τελείωσις *teleiōsis* 2x *a completing; a fulfillment, an accomplishment* of predictions, promised, etc., Lk 1:45; *finality* of function, *completeness* of operation and effect, Heb 7:11★ [5050]

[5460] τελειωτής *teleiōtēs* 1x *a finisher, one who completes and perfects* a thing; *one who brings through to final attainment, perfecter*, Heb 12:2★ [5051]

[5461] τελεσφορέω *telesphoreō* 1x *to bring to maturity*, as fruits, etc.; met. Lk 8:14★ [5052]

[5462] τελευτάω *teleutaō* 11x *to end, finish, complete*; absol. *to end* [5053]

[5463] τελευτή *teleutē* 1x *a finishing, end*; hence, *end* of life, *death, decease*, Mt 2:15★ [5054]

[5464] τελέω *teleō* 28x *to finish, complete, conclude*, an operation, Mt 11:1; 13:53; 19:1; *to finish* a circuit, Mt 10:23; *to fulfil, to carry out into full operation*, Ro 2:27; Gal 5:16; Jas 2:8; *to pay* dues, Mt 17:24; pass. *to be fulfilled, realized*, Lk 12:50; 18:31; of time, *to be ended, elapse*, Ro 15:8; 20:3, 5, 7 [5055]

[5465] τέλος *telos* 40x *an end attained, consummation; an end, closing act*, Mt 24:6, 14; 1 Co 15:24; *full performance, perfect discharge*, Ro 10:4; *fulfillment, realization*, Lk 22:37; *final dealing*, developed *issue*, Jas 5:11; *issue, final stage*, 1 Co 10:11; *issue, result*, Mt 26:58; Ro 6:21, 22; 1 Pe 1:9; antitypical *issue*, 2 Co 3:13; practical *issue*, 1 Ti 1:5; *ultimate destiny*, Phil 3:19; Heb 6:8; 1 Pe 4:17; *a tax* or *dues*, Mt 17:25; Ro 13:7; εἰς τέλος, *to the full*, 1 Th 2:16; εἰς τέλος, *continually*, Lk 18:5; εἰς τέλος, μέχρι, ἄχρι τέλους, *throughout*, Mt 10:22; Mk 13:13; Jn 13:1; Heb 3:6, 14; 6:11; Rev 2:26 [5056]

[5467] τελώνης *telōnēs* 21x *one who farms the public revenues;* in N.T. *a publican, collector of imposts, revenue officer,* tax gatherer, Mt 5:46; 9:10, 11; 10:3; Mk 2:15f.; Lk 3:12 [5057]

[5468] τελώνιον *telōnion* 3x *a custom-house, toll-house; collector's office*, Mt 9:9; Mk 2:14; Lk 5:27★ [5058]

[5469] τέρας *teras* 16x *a prodigy, portent*, Ac 2:19; *a signal act, wonder, miracle*, Mt 13:22; Jn 4:48; Ac 2:43 [5059]

[5470] Τέρτιος *Tertios* 1x *Tertius*, pr. name, a helper of Paul, Ro 16:22★ [5060]

[5472] Τέρτυλλος *Tertyllos* 2x *Tertullus*, pr. name, an attorney, Ac 24:1f.★ [5061]

[5475] τέσσαρες *tessares* 41x *four*, Mt 24:31; Mk 2:3 [5064]

[5476] τεσσαρεσκαιδέκατος *tessareskaidekatos* 2x *the fourteenth*, Ac 27:27, 33★ [5065]

[5477] τεσσεράκοντα *tesserakonta* 22x *forty*, indecl., Mt 4:2; Jn 2:20; Ac 1:3; 23:13, 21; Heb 3:9; Rev 11:2; 21:17 [5062]

[5478] τεσσερακονταετής *tesserakontaetēs* 2x *forty years*, Ac 7:23; 13:18★ [5063]

[5479] τεταρταῖος *tetartaios* 1x *on the fourth day*, Jn 11:39★ [5066]

[5480] τέταρτος *tetartos* 10x *fourth*, Mt 14:25; *the fourth part, quarter*, Rev 6:8 [5067]

[5481] τετράγωνος *tetragōnos* 1x *four-angled, quadrangular, square*, Rev 21:16★ [5068]

[5482] τετράδιον *tetradion* 1x *a set of four; a detachment of four men*, Ac 12:4★ [5069]

[5483] τετρακισχίλιοι *tetrakischilioi* 5x *four thousand*, Mt 15:38; 16:10; Mk 8:9, 20; Ac 21:38★ [5070]

[5484] τετρακόσιοι *tetrakosioi* 4x *four hundred*, Ac 5:36; 7:6; 13:20; Gal 3:17★ [5071]

[5485] τετράμηνος *tetramēnos* 1x *of four months, four months in duration*, Jn 4:35★ [5072]

[5487] τετραπλοῦς *tetraplous* 1x contracted form of τετραπλόος, *four times (as much), fourfold, quadruple*, Lk 19:8★ [5073]

[5488] τετράπους *tetrapous* 3x *four-footed; quadrupeds*, Ac 10:12; 11:6; Ro 1:23★ [5074]

[5489] τετρααρχέω *tetraarcheō* 3x also spelled τετραρχέω, *be tetrarch*, Lk 3:1 (3t)★ [5075]

[5490] τετραάρχης *tetraarchēs* 4x also spelled τετράρχης, *a tetrarch*, title of a prince, whose rank was lower than a king, Mt 14:1; Lk 3:19; 9:7; Ac 13:1★ [5076]

[5491] τεφρόω *tephroō* 1x *to reduce to ashes, to consume, destroy*, 2 Pe 2:6★ [5077]

[5492] τέχνη *technē* 3x *art, skill*, Ac 17:29; *an art, trade, craft*, Ac 18:3; Rev 18:22★ [5078]

[5493] τεχνίτης *technitēs* 4x *an artisan; workman, mechanic*, Ac 19:24, 38; Rev 18:22; *an architect, builder*, Heb 11:10★ [5079]

[5494] τήκω *tēkō* 1x *to dissolve*; pass. *to melt*, 2 Pe 3:12★ [5080]

[5495] τηλαυγῶς *tēlaugōs* 1x *clearly, plainly, distinctly*, Mk 8:25★ [5081]

[5496] τηλικοῦτος *tēlikoutos* 4x *so great, large, important*, 2 Co 1:10; Heb 2:3; Jas 3:4; Rev 16:18★ [5082]

[5498] τηρέω *tēreō* 70x *to keep watch upon, guard*, Mt 27:36, 54; 28:4; Ac 12:6; *to watch over* protectively, *guard*, 1 Jn 5:18; Rev 16:15; *to mark attentively, to heed*, Rev 1:3; *to observe* practically, *keep strictly*, Mt 19:17; 23:3; 28:20; Mk 7:9; Jn 8:51; *to preserve, shield*, Jn 17:15; *to store up, reserve*, Jn 2:10; 12:7; 1 Pe 1:4; 2 Pe 2:4, 9, 17; *to keep in custody*, Ac 12:5; 16:23; *to maintain*, Eph 4:3; 2 Ti 4:7; *to keep* in a condition, Jn 17:11, 12; 1 Co 7:37; 2 Co 11:9; 1 Ti 5:22; Jas 1:27 [5083]

[5499] τήρησις *tērēsis* 3x *a keeping, custody*; meton. *a place of custody, prison, ward*, Ac 4:3; 5:18; met. practical *observance, strict performance*, 1 Co 7:19★ [5084]

[5500] Τιβεριάς *Tiberias* 3x *Tiberias*, a city of Galilee, built by Herod Antipas, and named in honor of Tiberius, Jn 6:1, 23; 21:1★ [5085]

[5501] Τιβέριος *Tiberios* 1x *Tiberius*, the third Roman emperor, *14-37 A.D.*, Lk 3:1★ [5086]

[5502] τίθημι *tithēmi* 100x by-form of τιθέω, *to place, set, lay*, Mt 5:15; Mk 6:56; Lk 6:48; *to produce* at table, Jn 2:10; *to deposit, lay*, Mt 27:60; Lk 23:53; Ac 3:2; *to lay down*, Lk 19:21, 22; Jn 10:11, 15, 17, 18; 1 Jn 3:16; *to lay aside, put off*, Jn 13:4; *to allocate, assign*, Mt 24:51; Lk 12:46; *to set, appoint*, Jn 15:16; Ac 13:47; Heb 1:2; *to render, make*, Mt 22:44; Ro 4:17; 1 Co 9:18; mid. *to put* in custody, Mt 14:3; Ac 4:3; *to reserve*, Ac 1:7; *to commit* as a matter of charge, 2 Co 5:19; *to set*, with design, in a certain arrangement or position, Ac 20:28; 1 Co 12:18, 28; 1 Th 5:9; 1 Ti 1:12; pass. 1 Ti 2:7; 2 Ti 1:11; 1 Pe 2:8; τιθέναι τὰ γόνατα, *to kneel down*, Mk 15:19; Lk 22:41; Ac 7:60; 9:40; 20:36; 21:5; τίθεσθαι ἐν τῇ καρδίᾳ, *to lay to heart, ponder*, Lk 1:66; also, εἰς τὰς καρδίας, Lk 21:14; *to design, resolve*, Ac 5:4; also, ἐν πνεύματι, Ac 19:21; also, βουλήν, Ac 17:12; τίθεσθαι εἰς τὰ ὦτα, *to give attentive audience to, to listen to retentively*, Lk 9:44 [5087]

[5503] τίκτω *tiktō* 18x *to bear, bring forth* children, Mt 1:21, 23; trop. *to bear, produce*, as the earth, *yield*, Heb 6:7; met. *to give birth to*, Jas 1:15 [5088]

[5504] τίλλω *tillō* 3x *to pull, pluck off*, Mt 12:1; Mk 2:23; Lk 6:1* [5089]

[5505] Τιμαῖος *Timaios* 1x *Timaeus*, pr. name, Mk 10:46* [5090]

[5506] τιμάω *timaō* 21x *to estimate in respect of worth; to hold in estimation, respect, honor, reverence*, Mt 15:4, 5, 8; 19:19; Mk 7:10; *to honor* with reverent service, Jn 5:23 (4t); 8:49; *to treat with honor, manifest consideration towards*, Ac 28:10; *to treat graciously, visit with marks of favor*, Jn 12:26; mid. *to price*, Mt 27:9 [5091]

[5507] τιμή *timē* 41x *a pricing, estimate of worth; price, value*, Mt 27:9; *price* paid, Mt 27:6; meton. *a thing of price*, and collectively, *precious things*, Rev 21:24, 26; *preciousness*, 1 Pe 2:7; substantial *value, real worth*, Col 2:23; *careful regard, honor, state of honor, dignity*, Ro 9:21; Heb 5:4; *honor* conferred, *observance, veneration*, Ro 2:7, 10; 12:10; *mark of favor and consideration*, Ac 28:10, *honorarium, compensation*, 1 Ti 5:7 [5092]

[5508] τίμιος *timios* 13x *precious, costly, of great price*, 1 Co 3:12; Rev 18:12; *precious, dear, valuable*, Ac 20:24; 1 Pe 1:7, 19; *honored, esteemed, respected*, Ac 5:34; Heb 13:4 [5093]

[5509] τιμιότης *timiotēs* 1x *preciousness, costliness;* meton. *precious things, valuable merchandise*, Rev 18:19* [5094]

[5510] Τιμόθεος *Timotheos* 24x *Timotheus, Timothy*, pr. name, *son of Eunice, traveling companion of Paul*, Ac 16:1; Ro 16:21; 1 Co 4:17; 2 Co 1:1; Phil 1:1; Col 1:1; 1 Th 1:1; 1 Ti 1:2, 18; 6:20; 2 Ti 1:2 [5095]

[5511] Τίμων *Timōn* 1x *Timon*, pr. name, Ac 6:5* [5096]

[5512] τιμωρέω *timōreō* 2x *to avenge, someone;* in N.T. *to punish*, Ac 22:5; 26:11* [5097]

[5513] τιμωρία *timōria* 1x *punishment*, Heb 10:29* [5098]

[5514] τίνω *tinō* 1x *to pay; to pay* a penalty, *incur* punishment, 2 Th 1:9* [5099]

[5515] τίς *tis* 555x *Who? What?* Mt 3:7; 5:13; 19:27; equivalent to πότερος, *Whether? which* of two things? Mt 9:5; Mk 2:9; Phil 1:22; *Why?* Mt 8:26; 9:11, 14; τί ὅτι, *Why is it that?* Mk 2:16; Jn 14:22; *What?* as an emphatic interrogative, Ac 26:8; τί, *How very!* Mt 7:14; in indirect question, Mt 10:11 [5101]

[5516] τις *tis* 534x enclitic, indefinite pronoun, *a certain one, someone*, Mt 12:47; pl. *some, certain, several*, Lk 8:2; Ac 9:19; 2 Pe 3:16; *one, a person*, Mt 12:29; Lk 14:8; Jn 6:50; combined with the name of an individual, *one*, Mk 15:21; *as it were in a manner, a kind of*, Heb 10:27; Jas 1:18; *any* whatever, Mt 8:28; Lk 11:36; Ro 8:39; τις, *somebody* of consequence, Ac 5:36; τι, *something* of consequence, Gal 2:6; 6:3; τι, *anything* at all, *anything* worth account, 1 Co 3:7; 10:19; τι *at all*, Phil 3:15; Phlm 18 [5100]

[5517] Τίτιος *Titios* 1x *Titius*, pr. name, Ac 18:7* [2459]

[5518] τίτλος *titlos* 2x *an inscribed roll, superscription*, Jn 19:19, 20* [5102]

[5519] Τίτος *Titos* 13x *Titus*, pr. name, friend and helper of Paul, 2 Co 2:13; 7:6; Gal 2:1; 2 Ti 4:10; Tit 1:4 [5103]

[5521] τοιγαροῦν *toigaroun* 2x *well then, so then, wherefore, for that reason*, 1 Th 4:8; Heb 12:1* [5105]

[5524] τοιόσδε *toiosde* 1x *such as this; such as follows*, 2 Pe 1:17* [5107]

[5525] τοιοῦτος *toioutos* 57x *such, such like, of this kind* or sort, Mt 18:5; 19:14; *such, so great*, Mt 9:8; Mk 6:2; ὁ τοιοῦτος, *such a fellow*, Ac 22:22; also, *the one alluded to*, 1 Co 1:5; 2 Co 2:6, 7; 12:2, 3, 5 [5108]

[5526] τοῖχος *toichos* 1x *a wall* of a building, as distinct from a city wall or fortification (τεῖχος) Ac 23:3* [5109]

[5527] τόκος *tokos* 2x *a bringing forth; offspring;* met. *produce* of money lent, *interest, usury*, Mt 25:27; Lk 19:23* [5110]

[5528] τολμάω *tolmaō* 16x *to assume resolution* to do a thing, Mk 15:43; Ro 5:7; Phil 1:14; *to make up the mind*, 2 Co 10:12; *to dare*, Ac 5:13; 7:32; *to presume*, Mt 22:46; Mk 12:34; Lk 20:40; Jn 21:12; Ro 15:18; Jude 9; *to have the face*, 1 Co 6:1; absol. *to assume a bold bearing, courageous*, 2 Co 10:2; 11:21* [5111]

[5529] τολμηρός *tolmēros* 1x *bold, daring*, Ro 15:15* [5112]

[5532] τολμητής *tolmētēs* 1x *one who is bold;* in a bad sense, *a presumptuous, audacious person*, 2 Pe 2:10* [5113]

[5533] τομός *tomos* 1x *cutting, sharp, sharper*, Heb 4:12* [5114]

[5534] τόξον *toxon* 1x *a bow*, Rev 6:2* [5115]

[5535] τοπάζιον *topazion* 1x *a topaz*, a gem of a yellowish color, different from the modern topaz, Rev 21:20* [5116]

[5536] τόπος *topos* 94x *a place, locality*, Mt 12:43; Lk 6:17; *a limited spot* or *ground*, Mt 24:15; 27:33; Jn 4:20; Ac 6:13; *a precise spot* or *situation*, Mt 28:6; Mk 16:6; Lk 14:9; *a dwelling place, abode, mansion, dwelling, seat*, Jn 14:2, 3; Ac 4:31; *a place* of ordinary deposit, Mt 26:52; *a place, passage* in a book, Lk 4:17; *place* occupied, *room, space*, Lk 2:7; 14:9, 22; *place, opportunity*, Ac 25:16; Heb 12:17; *place, condition, position*, 1 Co 14:16 [5117]

[5537] τοσοῦτος *tosoutos* 20x *so great, so much*, Mt 8:10; 15:33; *so long*, of time, Jn 14:9; pl. *so many*, Mt 15:33 [5118]

[5538] τότε *tote* 160x *then, at that time*, Mt 2:17; 3:5; 11:20; *then*, Mt 12:29; 13:26; 25:31; ἀπὸ τότε, *from that time*, Mt 4:17; 16:21; ὁ τότε, *which then was*, 2 Pe 3:6 [5119]

[5543] τράγος *tragos* 4x *a he-goat*, Heb 9:12, 13, 19; 10:4* [5131]

[5544] τράπεζα *trapeza* 15x *a table, an eating-table*, Mt 15:27; Mk 7:28; Heb 9:2; by impl. *a meal, feast*, Ro 11:9; 1 Co 10:21; *a table* or *counter* of a money-changer, Mt 21:12; *a bank*, Lk 19:23; by impl. pl. *money matters*, Ac 6:2 [5132]

[5545] τραπεζίτης *trapezitēs* 1x *a money-changer, broker, banker*, who exchanges or loans money for a premium, Mt 25:27* [5133]

[5546] τραῦμα *trauma* 1x *a wound*, Lk 10:34* [5134]

[5547] τραυματίζω *traumatizō* 2x *to wound*, Lk 20:12; Ac 19:16* [5135]

[5548] τραχηλίζω *trachēlizō* 1x pr. *to grip the neck; to bend the neck back*, so as to make bare or expose the throat, as in slaughtering animals, etc.; met. *to lay bare in view*, Heb 4:13* [5136]

[5549] τράχηλος *trachēlos* 7x *the neck*, Mt 18:6; Mk 9:42; Lk 15:20; 17:2; ἐπιθεῖναι ζυγὸν ἐπὶ τὸν τράχηλον, *to put* *a yoke upon the neck* of someone, met. *to bind to a burdensome observance,* Ac 15:10; 20:37; ὑποτιθέναι τὸν τράχηλον, *to lay down one's neck* under the axe of the executioner, *to imperil one's life,* Ro 16:4★ [5137]

[5550] τραχύς *trachus* 2x *rough, rugged, uneven,* Lk 3:5; εἰς τραχεῖς τόπους, *on a rocky shore,* Ac 27:29★ [5138]

[5551] Τραχωνῖτις *Trachōnitis* 1x *Trachonitis,* part of the tetrarchy of Herod Antipas, the north-easternmost habitable district east of the Jordan, Lk 3:1★ [5139]

[5552] τρεῖς *treis* 68x *three,* Mt 12:40. The frequency count does not include its occurrence in the name Τριῶν ταβερνῶν in Ac 28:15 (#5553) [5140]

[5553] Τρεῖς ταβέρναι *treis tabernai* 1x *Three Taverns,* the name of a station on the Appian Way in Ac 28:15 (Τριῶν ταβερνῶν). The Latin *taberna* is an inn or shop [5992]

[5554] τρέμω *tremō* 3x *to tremble, be agitated from fear,* Mk 5:33; Lk 8:47; by impl. *to fear, be afraid,* 2 Pe 2:10★ [5141]

[5555] τρέφω *trephō* 9x *to nourish; to feed, support, cherish, provide for,* [5142]

[5556] τρέχω *trechō* 20x *to run,* Mt 27:48; 28:8; *to run a race,* 1 Co 9:24; met. 1 Co 9:24, 26; Heb 12:1; in N.T. *to run* a certain course of conduct, Gal 5:7; *to run* a course of exertion, Ro 9:16; Gal 2:2; Phil 2:16; *to run, to progress freely, to advance rapidly,* 2 Th 3:1 [5143]

[5557] τρῆμα *trēma* 1x *an aperture, hole, eye of a needle,* Lk 18:25★ [5169]

[5558] τριάκοντα *triakonta* 11x *thirty,* indecl., Mt 13:8, 23; Mk 4:8; Lk 3:23 [5144]

[5559] τριακόσιοι *triakosioi* 2x *three hundred,* Mk 14:5; Jn 12:5★ [5145]

[5560] τρίβολος *tribolos* 2x pr. *three-pronged; a thistle, thorn,* Mt 7:16; Heb 6:8★ [5146]

[5561] τρίβος *tribos* 3x *a beaten track; a road, highway,* Mt 3:3; Mk 1:3; Lk 3:4★ [5147]

[5562] τριετία *trietia* 1x *the space of three years,* Ac 20:31★ [5148]

[5563] τρίζω *trizō* 1x *to creak, grating sound; to gnash, grind* the teeth, Mk 9:18★ [5149]

[5564] τρίμηνος *trimēnos* 1x *the space of three months,* Heb 11:23★ [5150]

[5565] τρίς *tris* 12x *three times, thrice,* Mt 26:34, 75; ἐπὶ τρίς, *to the extent of thrice, as many as three times,* Ac 10:16; 11:10 [5151]

[5566] τρίστεγον *tristegon* 1x *the third floor, third story,* Ac 20:9★ [5152]

[5567] τρισχίλιοι *trischilioi* 1x *three thousand,* Ac 2:41★ [5153]

[5569] τρίτος *tritos* 56x *third,* Mt 20:3; 27:64; ἐκ τρίτου, *the third time, for the third time,* Mt 26:44; τὸ τρίτον, sc. μέρος, *the third part,* Rev 8:7, 12; τρίτον + τὸ τρίτον, as an adv., *the third time, for the third time,* Mk 14:21; Lk 23:22 [5154]

[5570] τρίχινος *trichinos* 1x *of hair, made of hair,* Rev 6:12★ [5155]

[5571] τρόμος *tromos* 5x pr. *a trembling, quaking; trembling* from fear, *fear, terror, agitation of mind,* Mk 16:8; *anxious,* under solemn responsibility, 1 Co 2:3; *reverence, veneration, awe,* 2 Co 7:15; Eph 6:5; Phil 2:12★ [5156]

[5572] τροπή *tropē* 1x *a turning round; a turning back, change, mutation,* Jas 1:17★ [5157]

[5573] τρόπος *tropos* 13x *a turn; mode, manner, way,* Jude 7; ὃν τρόπον, + καθ᾽ ὃν τρόπον, *in which manner, as, even as,* Mt 23:37; Ac 15:11; κατὰ μηδένα τρόπον, *in no way, by no means,* 2 Th 2:3; ἐν παντὶ τρόπῳ, and παντὶ τρόπῳ *in every way, by every means,* Phil 1:18; 2 Th 3:16; *turn* of mind or action, *habit, disposition,* Heb 13:5 [5158]

[5574] τροποφορέω *tropophoreō* 1x *to bear with the disposition, manners, and conduct* of any one, *to put up with,* Ac 13:18★ [5159]

[5575] τροφή *trophē* 16x *nourishment, food,* Mt 3:4; Lk 12:23; Jn 4:8; Ac 9:19; Jas 2:15; *provision,* Mt 24:45; *sustenance, maintenance,* Mt 10:10; met. *nourishment* of the mind, *of spiritual nourishment,* Heb 5:12, 14 [5160]

[5576] Τρόφιμος *Trophimos* 3x *Trophimus,* pr. name, of Ephesus, a friend of Paul, Ac 20:4; 21:29; 2 Ti 4:20★ [5161]

[5577] τροφός *trophos* 1x *a nurse,* 1 Th 2:7★ [5162]

[5579] τροχιά *trochia* 1x *a wheel-track; a track, way, path,* met. Heb 12:13★ [5163]

[5580] τροχός *trochos* 1x pr. *a runner; anything spherical, a wheel; drift, course,* with which signification the word is usually written τρόχος, Jas 3:6★ [5164]

[5581] τρύβλιον *tryblion* 2x *a bowl, dish,* Mt 26:23; Mk 14:20★ [5165]

[5582] τρυγάω *trygaō* 3x *to harvest, gather,* fruits, and spc. grapes, Lk 6:44; Rev 14:18, 19★ [5166]

[5583] τρυγών *trygōn* 1x *a turtle-dove,* Lk 2:24★ [5167]

[5584] τρυμαλιά *trymalia* 1x *a hole, perforation; eye* of a needle, Mk 10:25★ [5168]

[5585] τρύπημα *trypēma* 1x *a hole; eye* of a needle, Mt 19:24★ [5169]

[5586] Τρύφαινα *Tryphaina* 1x *Tryphaena,* pr. name, Ro 16:12★ [5170]

[5587] τρυφάω *tryphaō* 1x *to live self-indulgently, luxuriously,* Jas 5:5★ [5171]

[5588] τρυφή *tryphē* 2x *indulgent living, luxury,* Lk 7:25; 2 Pet 2:13★ [5172]

[5589] Τρυφῶσα *Tryphōsa* 1x *Tryphosa,* pr. name, Ro 16:12★ [5173]

[5590] Τρωάς *Trōias* 6x *Troas,* a city on the coast of Phrygia, near the site of ancient Troy, Ac 16:8, 11; 20:5f.; 2 Co 2:12; 2 Ti 4:13★ [5174]

[5592] τρώγω *trōgō* 6x pr. *to crunch; to eat,* Mt 24:38; from the Hebrew, ἄρτον τρώγειν, *to take food, partake of a meal,* Jn 6:54, 56-58; 13:18★ [5176]

[5593] τυγχάνω *tynchanō* 12x *to hit* an object; *to attain to, to obtain, acquire, enjoy,* Lk 20:35; Ac 24:2; 26:22; 27:3; 2 Ti 2:10; Heb 8:6; 11:35; intrans. *to happen, fall out, chance; common, ordinary,* Ac 19:11; 28:2; as an adv., *it may be, perchance, perhaps,* 1 Co 16:6; εἰ τύχοι, *as it so happens, as the case may be,* 1 Co 14:10; 15:37★ [5177]

[5594] τυμπανίζω *tympanizō* 1x pr. *to beat a drum; to drum upon;* in N.T. *to torture, beat to death with rods and clubs,* Heb 11:35★ [5178]

[5595] τυπικῶς *typikōs* 1x *figuratively, typically,* 1 Co 10:11★ [5179]

[5596] τύπος *typos* 15x pr. *an impress; a print, mark,* of a wound inflicted, Jn 20:25; *a delineation; an image, statue,* Ac 7:43; *a formula, scheme,* Ro 6:17; *form,* Ac 23:25; *a figure, counterpart,* 1 Co 10:6; *an anticipative figure, type,* Ro 5:14; *a model pattern,* Ac 7:44; Heb 8:5; *a moral pattern,* Phil 3:17; 1 Th 1:7; 2 Th 3:9; 1 Ti 4:12; Tit 2:7; 1 Pe 5:3★ [5179]

[5597] τύπτω *typtō* 13x *to beat, strike, smite,* Mt 24:49; 27:30; *to beat* the breast, as expressive of grief or strong emotion, Lk 18:13; 23:48; in N.T. met. *to wound* or *shock* the conscience of any one, 1 Co 8:12; from the Hebrew, *to smite* with evil, *punish,* Ac 23:3 [5180]

[5598] Τύραννος *Tyrannos* 1x *Tyrannus, an Ephesian,* Ac 19:9* [5181]

[5601] Τύριος *Tyrios* 1x *a Tyrian, an inhabitant of Tyre,* Ac 12:20* [5183]

[5602] Τύρος *Tyros* 11x *Tyre,* a celebrated and wealthy commercial city of Phoenicia, Mt 11:21; 15:21; Mk 7:24; Ac 21:3, 7 [5184]

[5603] τυφλός *typhlos* 50x *blind,* Mt 9:27, 28; 11:5; 12:22; met. *mentally blind,* Mt 15:14; 23:16 [5185]

[5604] τυφλόω *typhloō* 3x *to blind, render blind;* met. Jn 12:40; 2 Co 4:4; 1 Jn 2:11* [5186]

[5605] τυφόω *typhoō* 3x *to besmoke;* met. *to possess with the fumes* of conceit; pass. *to be demented with conceit, puffed up,* 1 Ti 3:6; 6:4; 2 Ti 3:4; 1 Ti 6:4* [5187]

[5606] τύφω *typhō* 1x *to raise a smoke;* pass. *to emit smoke, smoke, smoulder,* Mt 12:20* [5188]

[5607] τυφωνικός *typhōnikos* 1x *stormy, tempestuous;* with ἄνεμος it means *hurricane, typhoon, whirlwind,* Ac 27:14* [5189]

[5608] Τυχικός *Tychikos* 5x *Tychicus,* pr. name, a friend or companion of Paul, Ac 20:4; Eph 6:21; Col 4:7; 2 Ti 4:12; Tit 3:12; Eph subscr.; Col subscr.* [5190]

[5610] ὑακίνθινος *hyakinthinos* 1x *hyacinthine, resembling the hyacinth in color, dark blue,* Rev 9:17* [5191]

[5611] ὑάκινθος *hyakinthos* 1x *a hyacinth,* a gem resembling the color of the *hyacinth flower, dark blue,* Rev 21:20* [5192]

[5612] ὑάλινος *hyalinos* 3x *made of glass; glassy, translucent,* Rev 4:6; 15:2* [5193]

[5613] ὕαλος *hyalos* 2x *a transparent stone, crystal;* also, *glass,* Rev 21:18, 21* [5194]

[5614] ὑβρίζω *hybrizō* 5x *to run riot;* trans. *to outrage, to treat in an arrogant* or *spiteful manner,* Mt 22:6; Lk 11:45; 18:32; Ac 14:5; 1 Th 2:2* [5195]

[5615] ὕβρις *hybris* 3x *insolence; shame, insult, outrage,* 2 Co 12:10; *damage* by sea, Ac 27:10, 21* [5196]

[5616] ὑβριστής *hybristēs* 2x *an overbearing, violent person,* Ro 1:30; 1 Ti 1:13* [5197]

[5617] ὑγιαίνω *hygiainō* 12x *to be sound, in health,* Lk 5:31; 7:10; *to be safe and sound,* Lk 15:27; 3 Jn 2; met. *to be healthful* or *sound* in faith, doctrine, etc.,

Tit 1:9, 13; 2:1, 2; *sound, pure, uncorrupted,* 1 Ti 1:10; 6:3; 2 Ti 1:13; 4:3* [5198]

[5618] ὑγιής *hygiēs* 11x *sound, in health,* Mt 12:13; 15:31; met. of doctrine, *sound, pure, wholesome,* Tit 2:8 [5199]

[5619] ὑγρός *hygros* 1x pr. *wet, moist, humid;* used of a tree, *full of sap, fresh, green,* Lk 23:31* [5200]

[5620] ὑδρία *hydria* 3x *a water-pot, pitcher,* Jn 2:6, 7; *a bucket, pail,* Jn 4:28* [5201]

[5621] ὑδροποτέω *hydropoteō* 1x *to be only a water-drinker,* 1 Ti 5:23* [5202]

[5622] ὑδρωπικός *hydrōpikos* 1x *dropsical, suffering from dropsy,* Lk 14:2* [5203]

[5623] ὕδωρ *hydōr* 76x *water,* Mt 3:11, 16; 14:28, 29; 17:15; Jn 5:3, 4, 7; *watery fluid,* Jn 19:34; ὕδωρ ζῶν, *living water, fresh flowing water,* Jn 4:11; met. of spiritual refreshment, Jn 4:10; 7:38 [5204]

[5624] ὑετός *hyetos* 5x *rain,* Ac 14:17; 28:2; Heb 6:7; Jas 5:18; Rev 11:6* [5205]

[5625] υἱοθεσία *hyuothesia* 5x *adoption, a placing in the condition of a son,* Ro 8:15, 23; 9:4; Gal 4:5; Eph 1:5* [5206]

[5626] υἱός *hyuos* 377x *a son,* Mt 1:21, 25; 7:9; 13:55 freq.; *a legitimate son,* Heb 12:8; *a son* artificially constituted, Ac 7:21; Heb 11:24; *a descendant,* Mt 1:1, 20; Mk 12:35; in N.T. *the young* of an animal, Mt 21:5; *a spiritual son* in respect of conversion or discipleship, 1 Pe 5:13; from the Hebrew, *a disciple,* perhaps, Mt 12:27; *a son* as implying connection in respect of membership, service, resemblance, manifestation, destiny, etc., Mt 8:12; 9:15; 13:38; 23:15; Mk 2:29; 3:17; Lk 5:34; 10:6; 16:8; 20:34, 36; Jn 17:12; Ac 2:25; 4:36; 13:10; Eph 2:2; 5:6; Col 3:6; 1 Th 5:5; 2 Th 2:3; υἱὸς θεοῦ, κ.τ.λ., *son of God* in respect of divinity, Mt 4:3, 6; 14:33; Ro 1:4; also, in respect of privilege and character, Mt 5:9, 45; Lk 6:35; Ro 8:14, 19; 9:26; Gal 3:26; ὁ υἱὸς τοῦ θεοῦ, κ.τ.λ., a title of the Messiah, Mt 26:63; Mk 3:11; 14:61; Jn 1:34, 50; 20:31; υἱὸς ἀνθρώπου, *a son of man, a man,* Mk 3:28; Eph 3:5; Heb 2:6; ὁ υἱὸς τοῦ ἀνθρώπου, a title of the Messiah, Mt 8:20 freq.; as also, ὁ υἱὸς Δαβίδ, (Δαυίδ) Mt 12:23 [5207]

[5627] ὕλη *hylē* 1x *wood, a forest;* in N.T. *firewood, a mass of fuel,* Jas 3:5* [5208]

[7007] ὑμεῖς *hymeis* 1,840x see σύ

[5628] Ὑμέναιος *Hymenaios* 2x *Hymenaeus,* pr. name, 1 Ti 1:20; 2 Ti 2:17* [5211]

[5629] ὑμέτερος *hymeteros* 11x *your, yours,* Lk 6:20; Jn 7:6; 15:20 [5212]

[5630] ὑμνέω *hymneō* 4x *to hymn, praise, celebrate* or *worship with hymns,* Ac 16:25; Heb 2:12; absol. *to sing a hymn,* Mt 26:30; Mk 14:26* [5214]

[5631] ὕμνος *hymnos* 2x *a song; a hymn, song of praise* to God, Eph 5:19; Col 3:16* [5215]

[5632] ὑπάγω *hypagō* 79x *to lead* or *bring under; to lead* or *bring from under; draw on* or *away;* in N.T. intrans. *to go away, depart,* Mt 8:4, 13; 9:6; ὕπαγε ὀπίσω μου, *Get behind me! Away! Begone!* Mt 4:10; 16:23; *to go,* Mt 5:41; Lk 12:58; *to depart* life, Mt 26:24 [5217]

[5633] ὑπακοή *hypakoē* 15x *a hearkening to; obedience,* Ro 5:19; 6:16; 1 Pe 1:14; *submissiveness,* Ro 16:19; 2 Co 7:15; *submission,* Ro 1:5; 15:18; 16:26; 2 Co 10:5; Heb 5:8; 1 Pe 1:2, 22; *compliance,* Phlm 21 [5218]

[5634] ὑπακούω *hypakouō* 21x *to give ear; to listen,* Ac 12:13; *to obey,* Mt 8:27; Mk 1:27; in N.T. *to render submissive acceptance,* Ac 6:7; Ro 6:17; 2 Th 1:8; Heb 5:9; absol. *to be submissive,* Phil 2:12 [5219]

[5635] ὕπανδρος *hypandros* 1x *bound to a man, married,* Ro 7:2* [5220]

[5636] ὑπαντάω *hypantaō* 10x *to meet,* Mt 8:28; Lk 8:27; Jn 11:20, 30; 12:18 [5221]

[5637] ὑπάντησις *hypantēsis* 3x *a meeting, act of meeting,* Mt 8:34; 25:1; Jn 12:13^ [5222]

[5638] ὕπαρξις *hyparxis* 2x *goods possessed, substance, property,* Ac 2:45; Heb 10:34* [5223]

[5639] ὑπάρχω *hyparchō* 60x *to begin; to come into existence; to exist; to be, subsist,* Ac 19:40; 28:18; *to be in possession, to belong,* Ac 3:6; 4:37; *goods, possessions, property,* Mt 19:21; Lk 8:3; *to be,* Lk 7:25; 8:41 [5224, 5225]

[5640] ὑπείκω *hypeikō* 1x *to yield, give way;* absol. *to be submissive,* Heb 13:17* [5226]

[5641] ὑπεναντίος *hypenantios* 2x *over against; contrast, adverse,* Col 2:14; ὁ ὑπεναντίος, *an opponent, adversary,* Heb 10:27* [5227]

[5642] ὑπέρ *hyper* 150x (1) gen., *above, over;* met. *in behalf of,* Mt 5:44; Mk 9:40; Jn 17:19; *instead of* beneficially, Phlm 13; *in maintenance of,* Ro 15:8; *for the furtherance of,* Jn 11:4; 2 Co 1:6, 8; *for*

the realization of, Phil 2:13; equivalent to περί, *about, concerning,* with the further signification of interest or concern in the subject, Ac 5:41; Ro 9:27; 2 Co 5:12; 8:23; 2 Th 2:1. (2) acc., *over, beyond;* met. *beyond, more than,* Mt 10:37; 2 Co 1:8; used after comparative terms, Lk 16:8; 2 Co 12:13; Heb 4:12. (3) in N.T. as an adv., *in a higher degree, in fuller measure,* 2 Co 11:23 [5228]

[5643] ὑπεραίρω *hyperairō* 3x *to raise* or *lift up above* or *over;* mid. *to lift up one's self;* met. *to be over-elated,* 2 Co 12:7 (2x); *to bear one's self arrogantly, to rear a haughty front,* 2 Th 2:4* [5229]

[5644] ὑπέρακμος *hyperakmos* 1x *past the bloom of life, past one's prime,* 1 Co 7:36* [5230]

[5645] ὑπεράνω *hyperanō* 3x can function as an improper prep., *above, over, far above;* of place, Eph 4:10; Heb 9:5; of rank, dignity, Eph 1:21* [5231]

[5647] ὑπεραυξάνω *hyperauxanō* 1x *to increase exceedingly,* 2 Th 1:3* [5232]

[5648] ὑπερβαίνω *hyperbainō* 1x *to overstep; to wrong, transgress,* 1 Th 4:6* [5233]

[5649] ὑπερβαλλόντως *hyperballontōs* 1x *exceedingly, above measure,* 2 Co 11:23* [5234]

[5650] ὑπερβάλλω *hyperballō* 5x pr. *to cast* or *throw over* or *beyond, to overshoot;* met. *to surpass, excel; surpassing,* 2 Co 3:10; 9:14; Eph 1:19; 2:7; 3:19* [5235]

[5651] ὑπερβολή *hyperbolē* 8x pr. *a throwing beyond, an overshooting; extraordinary amount* or *character, transcendency,* 2 Co 12:7; 4:7; καθ᾽ ὑπερβολήν, adverbially, *exceedingly, extremely,* Ro 7:13; 2 Co 1:8; Gal 1:13; *a far better way,* 1 Co 12:31; *beyond all measure,* 2 Co 4:17* [5236]

[5654] ὑπερέκεινα *hyperekeina* 1x *BAGD* list as an adverb used with the gen., others list as an improper prep., *beyond,* 2 Co 10:16* [5238]

[5655] ὑπερεκπερισσοῦ *hyperekperissou* 3x *in over abundance; beyond all measure, superabundantly,* Eph 3:20; 1 Th 3:10; 5:13* [5240]

[5657] ὑπερεκτείνω *hyperekteinō* 1x *to over-extend, over-stretch,* 2 Co 10:14* [5239]

[5658] ὑπερεκχύννω *hyperekchunnō* 1x *to pour out above measure* or *in excess;* pass. *to run over, overflow,* Lk 6:38* [5240]

[5659] ὑπερεντυγχάνω *hyperentynchanō* 1x *to intercede for,* Ro 8:26* [5241]

[5660] ὑπερέχω *hyperechō* 5x *to hold above;* intrans. *to stand out above, to over-top;* met. *to surpass, excel,* Phil 2:3; 4:7; τὸ ὑπερέχον, *excellence, pre-eminence,* Phil 3:8; *to be higher, superior,* Ro 13:1; 1 Pe 2:13* [5242]

[5661] ὑπερηφανία *hyperēphania* 1x *haughtiness, arrogance,* Mk 7:22* [5243]

[5662] ὑπερήφανος *hyperēphanos* 5x *assuming, haughty, arrogant,* Lk 1:51; Ro 1:30; 2 Ti 3:2; Jas 4:6; 1 Pe 5:5* [5244]

[5663] ὑπερλίαν *hyperlian* 2x *in the highest degree, pre-eminently, especially, superlatively,* 2 Co 11:5; 12:11* [5244]

[5664] ὑπερνικάω *hypernikaō* 1x *to overpower in victory; to be abundantly victorious, prevail mightily,* Ro 8:37* [5245]

[5665] ὑπέρογκος *hyperonkos* 2x pr. *swollen, overgrown;* of language, *swelling, pompous, boastful,* 2 Pe 2:18; Jude 16* [5246]

[5666] ὑπεροράω *hyperoraō* 1x *overlook, disregard,* Ac 17:30* [5237]

[5667] ὑπεροχή *hyperochē* 2x *prominence;* met., *excellence, rare quality,* 1 Co 2:1; *eminent station, authority,* 1 Ti 2:2* [5247]

[5668] ὑπερπερισσεύω *hyperperisseuō* 2x *to superabound; to abound still more,* Ro 5:20; mid. *to be abundantly filled, overflow,* 2 Co 7:4* [5248]

[5669] ὑπερπερισσῶς *hyperperissōs* 1x *superabundantly, most vehemently, above all measure,* Mk 7:37* [5249]

[5670] ὑπερπλεονάζω *hyperpleonazō* 1x *to superabound, be in exceeding abundance, over-exceed,* 1 Ti 1:14* [5250]

[5671] ὑπερυψόω *hyperypsoō* 1x *to exalt supremely,* Phil 2:9* [5251]

[5672] ὑπερφρονέω *hyperphroneō* 1x *to have lofty thoughts, be elated, haughty,* Ro 12:3* [5252]

[5673] ὑπερῷον *hyperōon* 4x *the upper part of a house, upper room,* or *chamber,* Ac 1:13; 9:37, 39; 20:8* [5253]

[5674] ὑπέχω *hypechō* 1x pr. *to hold under; to render, undergo, suffer,* Jude 7* [5254]

[5675] ὑπήκοος *hypēkoos* 3x *giving ear; obedient, submissive,* Ac 7:39; 2 Co 2:9; Phil 2:8* [5255]

[5676] ὑπηρετέω *hypēreteō* 3x *to subserve,* Ac 13:36; *to relieve, supply,* Ac 20:34; *to render kind offices,* Ac 24:23* [5256]

[5677] ὑπηρέτης *hypēretēs* 20x pr. *an under-rower, a rower, one of a ship's crew; a minister, attendant, servant; an attendant* on a magistrate, *officer,* Mt 5:25; *an attendant* or *officer* of the Sanhedrin, Mt 26:58; *an attendant,* or *servant* of a synagogue, Lk 4:20; *a minister, attendant, assistant* in any work, Lk 1:2; Jn 18:36 [5257]

[5678] ὕπνος *hypnos* 6x *sleep,* Mt 1:24; Lk 9:32; Jn 11:13; Ac 20:9; met. spiritual *sleep,* religious *slumber,* Ro 13:11* [5258]

[5679] ὑπό *hypo* 220x (1) gen., *under;* hence, used to express influence, causation, agency; *by,* Mt 1:22 freq.; *by the agency of, at the hands of,* 2 Co 11:24; Heb 12:3. (2) acc., *under,* with the idea of motion associated, Mt 5:15; *under,* Jn 1:49; 1 Co 10:1; *under subjection to,* Ro 6:14; 1 Ti 6:1; of time, *at, about,* Ac 5:21 [5259]

[5680] ὑποβάλλω *hypoballō* 1x *to cast under;* met. *to suggest, instigate,* Ac 6:11* [5260]

[5681] ὑπογραμμός *hypogrammos* 1x pr. *a copy to write after;* met. *an example for imitation, pattern,* 1 Pe 2:21* [5261]

[5682] ὑπόδειγμα *hypodeigma* 6x *a token, intimation; an example, model,* proposed for imitation or admonition, Jn 13:15; Heb 4:11; Jas 5:10; 2 Pe 2:6; *a copy,* Heb 8:5; 9:23* [5262]

[5683] ὑποδείκνυμι *hypodeiknymi* 6x also spelled ὑποδεικνύω, *to indicate,* Ac 20:35; *to intimate, suggest, show, prove,* Mt 3:7; Lk 3:7; 6:47; 12:5; Ac 9:16* [5263]

[5685] ὑποδέχομαι *hypodechomai* 4x *to give reception to; to receive as a guest, welcome, entertain,* Lk 10:38; 19:6; Ac 17:7; Jas 2:25* [5264]

[5686] ὑποδέω *hypodeō* 3x *to bind under,* mid. *to bind under one's self, put on one's own feet,* Ac 12:8; *to shoe,* Eph 6:15; pass. *to be shod,* Mk 6:9* [5265]

[5687] ὑπόδημα *hypodēma* 10x *anything bound under; a sandal,* Mt 3:11; 10:10 [5266]

[5688] ὑπόδικος *hypodikos* 1x *under a legal process;* also, *under a judicial sentence; under verdict* to an opposed party in a suit, *liable to penalty,* Ro 3:19* [5267]

[5689] ὑποζύγιον *hypozygion* 2x *an animal subject to the yoke, a beast of burden;* in N.T. spc. *an ass, donkey,* Mt 21:5; 2 Pe 2:16* [5268]

[5690] ὑποζώννυμι *hypozōnnymi* 1x *to gird under*, of persons; *to undergird* a ship with cables, chains, etc., Ac 27:17★ [5269]

[5691] ὑποκάτω *hypokatō* 11x can function as an improper prep., *under*, *beneath, underneath*, Mk 6:11; 7:28; met. Heb 2:8 [5270]

[5693] ὑποκρίνομαι *hypokrinomai* 1x *to answer, respond; to act a part* upon the stage; hence, *to assume a counterfeit character; to pretend, feign*, Lk 20:20★ [5271]

[5694] ὑπόκρισις *hypokrisis* 6x *a response, answer; an over-acting personification, acting; hypocrisy, simulation*, Mt 23:28; Mk 12:15; Lk 12:1; Gal 2:13; 1 Ti 4:2; 1 Pe 2:1★ [5272]

[5695] ὑποκριτής *hypokritēs* 17x *the giver of an answer* or *response; a stageplayer, actor;* in N.T. a moral or religious *counterfeit, a hypocrite*, Mt 6:2, 5, 16; 7:5 [5273]

[5696] ὑπολαμβάνω *hypolambanō* 5x *to take up*, by placing one's self underneath what is taken up; *to catch away, withdraw*, Ac 1:9; *to take up* discourse by continuation; hence, *to answer*, Lk 10:30; *to take up* a notion, *to think, suppose*, Lk 7:43; Ac 2:15; *receive as a guest*, 3 Jn 8★ [5274]

[5698] ὑπόλειμμα *hypoleimma* 1x *a remnant*, Ro 9:27★ [2640]

[5699] ὑπολείπω *hypoleipō* 1x *to leave remaining, leave behind;* pass. *to be left surviving*, Ro 11:3★ [5275]

[5700] ὑπολήνιον *hypolēnion* 1x *a vat*, placed under the press, ληνός, to receive the juice, Mk 12:1★ [5276]

[5701] ὑπολιμπάνω *hypolimpanō* 1x *to leave behind*, 1 Pe 2:21★ [5277]

[5702] ὑπομένω *hypomenō* 17x intrans. *to remain* or *stay behind*, when others have departed, Lk 2:43; trans. *to bear up under, endure, suffer patiently*, 1 Co 13:7; Heb 10:32; absol. *to continue firmly, hold out, remain constant, persevere*, Mt 10:22; 24:13 [5278]

[5703] ὑπομιμνήσκω *hypomimnēskō* 7x *remember, remind*, Jn 14:26; Tit 3:1; 2 Pe 1:12; Jude 5; *to suggest recollection of, remind* others of, 2 Ti 2:14; 3 Jn 10; *to call to mind, recollect, remember*, Lk 22:61★ [5279]

[5704] ὑπόμνησις *hypomnēsis* 3x *a putting in mind, act of reminding*, 2 Pe 1:13; 3:1; *remembrance, recollection*, 2 Ti 1:5★ [5280]

[5705] ὑπομονή *hypomonē* 32x *patient endurance*, 2 Co 12:12; Col 1:11; *patient awaiting*, Lk 21:19; *a patient frame of mind, patience*, Ro 5:3, 4; 15:4, 5; Jas 1:3; *perseverance*, Ro 2:7; *endurance* in adherence to an object, 1 Th 1:3; 2 Th 3:5; Rev 1:9; ἐν ὑπομονῇ and δι᾽ ὑπομονῆς, *constantly, perseveringly*, Lk 8:15; Ro 8:25; Heb 12:1; *an enduring* of affliction, etc., *the act of suffering, undergoing*, etc., 2 Co 1:6; 6:4 [5281]

[5706] ὑπονοέω *hyponoeō* 3x *to suspect; to suppose, deem*, Ac 13:25; 25:18; 27:27★ [5282]

[5707] ὑπόνοια *hyponoia* 1x *suspicion, surmise*, 1 Ti 6:4★ [5283]

[5709] ὑποπλέω *hypopleō* 2x *to sail under; to sail under* the lee, or, *to the south of*, an island, etc., Ac 27:4, 7★ [5284]

[5710] ὑποπνέω *hypopneō* 1x *to blow gently*, as the wind, Ac 27:13★ [5285]

[5711] ὑποπόδιον *hypopodion* 7x *a footstool*, Jas 2:3 [5286]

[5712] ὑπόστασις *hypostasis* 5x pr. *a standing under; a taking* of a thing *upon one's self; an assumed position, an assumption* of a specific character, 2 Co 11:17; *an engagement undertaken* with regard to the conduct of others, *a vouching*, 2 Co 9:4; or of one's self, *a pledged profession*, Heb 3:14; *an assured impression, a mental realizing*, Heb 11:1; *a substructure, basis; subsistence, essence*, Heb 1:3★ [5287]

[5713] ὑποστέλλω *hypostellō* 4x pr. *to let down, to stow away; to draw back, withdraw*, Gal 2:12; mid. *to shrink back, recoil*, Heb 10:38; *to keep back, suppress, conceal*, Ac 20:20, 27★ [5288]

[5714] ὑποστολή *hypostolē* 1x *a shrinking back*, Heb 10:39★ [5289]

[5715] ὑποστρέφω *hypostrephō* 35x *to turn back, return*, Mk 14:40; Lk 1:56; 2:39, 43, 45 [5290]

[5716] ὑποστρωννύω *hypostrōnnyō* 1x *to stow under, spread underneath*, Lk 19:36★ [5291]

[5717] ὑποταγή *hypotagē* 4x *subordination*, 1 Ti 3:4; *submissiveness, obedience*, 2 Co 9:13; Gal 2:5; 1 Ti 2:11★ [5292]

[5718] ὑποτάσσω *hypotassō* 38x *to place* or *arrange under; to subordinate*, 1 Co 15:27; *to bring under influence*, Ro 8:20; pass. *to be subordinated*, 1 Co 14:32; *to be brought under a state* or *influence*, Ro 8:20; mid. *to submit one's self, render obedience, be submissive*, Lk 2:51; 10:17 [5293]

[5719] ὑποτίθημι *hypotithēmi* 2x *to place under; to lay down* the neck beneath the sword of the executioner, *to set on* imminent risk, Ro 16:4; mid. *to suggest, recommend to attention*, 1 Ti 4:6★ [5294]

[5720] ὑποτρέχω *hypotrechō* 1x *to run under;* as a nautical term, *to sail under* the lee of, Ac 27:16★ [5295]

[5721] ὑποτύπωσις *hypotypōsis* 2x *a sketch, delineation; a form, formula, presentment, sample*, 2 Ti 1:13; *a pattern, a model representation*, 1 Ti 1:16★ [5296]

[5722] ὑποφέρω *hypopherō* 3x *to bear under; to bear up under, support, sustain*, 1 Co 10:13; *to endure patiently*, 1 Pe 2:19; *to undergo*, 2 Ti 3:11★ [5297]

[5723] ὑποχωρέω *hypochōreō* 2x *to withdraw, retire, retreat*, Lk 5:16; 9:10★ [5298]

[5724] ὑπωπιάζω *hypōpiazō* 2x pr. *to strike one upon the parts beneath the eye; to beat black and blue;* hence, *to discipline by hardship, coerce*, 1 Co 9:27; met. *to weary by continual importunities, pester*, Lk 18:5★ [5299]

[5725] ὗς *hys* 1x *a hog, swine, boar, sow*, 2 Pe 2:22★ [5300]

[5727] ὕσσωπος *hyssōpos* 2x *hyssop*, in N.T., however, not the plant usually so named, but probably the caper plant; *a bunch of hyssop*, Heb 9:19; *a hyssop stalk*, Jn 19:29★ [5301]

[5728] ὑστερέω *hystereō* 16x *to be behind* in place or time, *to be in the rear; to fall short of, be inferior to*, 2 Co 11:5; 12:11; *to fail of, fail to attain*, Heb 4:1; *to be in want of, lack*, Lk 22:35; *to be wanting*, Mk 10:21; absol. *to be defective, in default*, Mt 19:20; 1 Co 12:24; *to run short*, Jn 2:3; mid. *to come short of* a privilege or standard, *to miss*, Ro 3:23; absol. *to come short, be below standard*, 1 Co 1:7; *to come short* of sufficiency, *to be in need, want*, Lk 15:14; 2 Co 11:9; Phil 4:12; Heb 11:37; *to be a loser, suffer detriment*, 1 Co 8:8; in N.T. ὑστερεῖν ἀπό, *to be backwards with respect to, to slight*, Heb 12:15★ [5302]

[5729] ὑστέρημα *hysterēma* 9x *a shortcoming, defect;* personal *shortcoming*, 1 Co 16:17; Phil 2:30; Col 1:24; 1 Th 3:10; *want, need, poverty, penury*, Lk 21:4; 2 Co 8:14; 9:12; 11:9★ [5303]

[5730] ὑστέρησις *hysterēsis* 2x *want, need*, Mk 12:44; Phil 4:11★ [5304]

[5731] ὕστερος *hysteros* 12x *posterior* in place or time; *subsequent, later, last, finally*, 1 Ti 4:1; Mt 21:31 [5305, 5306]

[5733] ὑφαντός *hyphantos* 1x *woven*, Jn 19:23★ [5307]

[5734] ὑψηλός *hypsēlos* 11x *high, lofty, elevated,* Mt 4:8; 17:1; τὰ ὑψηλά, *the highest* heaven, Heb 1:3; *upraised,* Ac 13:17; met. *highly esteemed,* Lk 16:15; φρονεῖν τὰ ὑψηλά, *to have lofty thoughts, be proud, arrogant,* Ro 12:16 [5308]

[5735] ὑψηλοφρονέω *hypsēlophroneō* 1x *to have lofty thoughts, be proud, haughty,* 1 Ti 6:17* [5309]

[5736] ὕψιστος *hypsistos* 13x *highest, loftiest, most elevated;* τὰ ὕψιστα, from the Hebrew, *the highest* heaven, Mt 21:9; Mk 11:10; met. ὁ ὕψιστος, *the Most High,* Mk 5:7 [5310]

[5737] ὕψος *hypsos* 6x *height,* Eph 3:18; Rev 21:16; met. *exaltation, dignity, eminence,* Jas 1:9; from the Hebrew, *the height* of heaven, Lk 1:78; 24:49; Eph 4:8* [5311]

[5738] ὑψόω *hypsoō* 20x *to raise aloft, lift up,* Jn 3:14; 8:28; met. *to elevate* in condition, *uplift, exalt,* Mt 11:23; 23:12; Lk 1:52 [5312]

[5739] ὕψωμα *hypsōma* 2x *height,* Ro 8:39; *a towering* of self-conceit, *presumption,* 2 Co 10:5* [5313]

[5741] φάγος *phagos* 2x *a glutton,* Mt 11:19; Lk 7:34* [5314]

[5742] φαιλόνης *phailonēs* 1x *a thick cloak* for travelling, with a hood, 2 Ti 4:13* [5341]

[5743] φαίνω *phainō* 31x *to cause to appear, bring to light;* absol. *to shine,* Jn 1:5; 5:35; 2 Pe 1:19; 1 Jn 2:8; Rev 1:16; 8:12; 21:23; mid./pass. *to be seen, appear, be visible,* Mt 1:20; 2:7, 13, 19; τὰ φαινόμενα, *things visible, things obvious to the senses,* Heb 11:3; φαίνομαι, *to appear, seen, be in appearance,* Mt 23:27; Lk 24:11; *to appear* in thought, *seen* in idea, *be a notion,* Mk 14:64 [5316]

[5744] Φάλεκ *Phalek* 1x *Peleg,* also spelled Φάλεγ, pr. name, indecl., Lk 3:35* [5317]

[5745] φανερός *phaneros* 18x *apparent, manifest, clear, known, well-known,* Mk 4:22; 6:14; Gal 5:19; *in outward guise, externally,* Ro 2:28 [5318]

[5746] φανερόω *phaneroō* 49x *to bring to light, to set in a clear light; to manifest, display,* Jn 2:11; 7:4; 9:3; *to show,* Ro 1:19; 2 Co 7:12; *to declare, make known,* Jn 17:6; *to disclose,* Mk 4:22; 1 Co 4:5; Col 4:4; *to reveal,* Ro 3:21; 16:26; Col 1:26; *to present to view,* Jn 21:1, 14; pass. *to make an appearance,* Mk 16:12, 14; spc. of Christ, *to be* personally *manifested,* Jn 1:31; Col 3:4; 1 Pe 1:20; 5:4; 1 Jn 3:5; *to*

be laid bare, appear in true character, 2 Co 5:10, 11 [5319]

[5747] φανερῶς *phanerōs* 3x *manifestly; clearly, plainly, distinctly,* Ac 10:3; *openly, publicly,* Mk 1:45; Jn 7:10* [5320]

[5748] φανέρωσις *phanerōsis* 2x *a disclosure, clear display,* 2 Co 4:2; *an* outward *evidencing* of a latent principle, *active exhibition,* 1 Co 12:7* [5321]

[5749] φανός *phanos* 1x *a torch, lantern, light,* Jn 18:3* [5322]

[5750] Φανουήλ *Phanouēl* 1x *Phanuel,* pr. name, indecl., Lk 2:36* [5323]

[5751] φαντάζω *phantazō* 1x *to render visible, cause to appear;* pass. *to appear, be seen;* τὸ φανταζόμενον, *the sight, spectacle,* Heb 12:21* [5324]

[5752] φαντασία *phantasia* 1x pr. *a rendering visible; a display; pomp, parade,* Ac 25:23* [5325]

[5753] φάντασμα *phantasma* 2x *a phantom, specter,* Mt 14:26; Mk 6:49* [5326]

[5754] φάραγξ *pharanx* 1x *a cleft, ravine, valley,* Lk 3:5* [5327]

[5755] Φαραώ *Pharaō* 5x *Pharaoh,* pr. name, indecl., Ac 7:10, 13, 21; Ro 9:17; Heb 11:24* [5328]

[5756] Φαρές *Phares* 3x *Perezs,* pr. name, indecl., Mt 1:3; Lk 3:33* [5329]

[5757] Φαρισαῖος *Pharisaios* 98x *a Pharisee, a follower of the sect of the Pharisees,* a numerous and powerful sect of the Jews, distinguished for their ceremonial observances, and apparent sanctity of life, and for being rigid interpreters of the Mosaic law; but who frequently violated its spirit by their traditional interpretations and precepts, to which they ascribed nearly an equal authority with the Old Testament Scriptures, Mt 5:20; 12:2; 23:14 [5330]

[5758] φαρμακεία *pharmakeia* 2x *employment of drugs* for any purpose; *sorcery, magic, enchantment,* Rev 18:23; Gal 5:20* [5331]

[5760] φάρμακον *pharmakon* 1x *a drug; an enchantment; magic potion, charm,* Rev 9:21* [5331]

[5761] φάρμακος *pharmakos* 2x *a sorcerer, magician,* Rev 21:8; 22:15* [5333]

[5762] φάσις *phasis* 1x *report, information,* Ac 21:31* [5334]

[5763] φάσκω *phaskō* 3x *to assert, affirm,* Ac 24:9; 25:19; Ro 1:22* [5335]

[5764] φάτνη *phatnē* 4x *a manger, stall,* Lk 2:7, 12, 16; 13:15* [5336]

[5765] φαῦλος *phaulos* 6x *vile, refuse; evil, wicked;* Jn 3:20; 5:29; Ro 9:11; 2 Co 5:10; Tit 2:8; Jas 3:16* [5337]

[5766] φέγγος *phengos* 2x *light, splendor, radiance,* Mt 24:29; Mk 13:24* [5338]

[5767] φείδομαι *pheidomai* 10x *to spare; to be tender of,* Ro 8:32; *to spare,* in respect of hard dealing, Ac 20:29; Ro 11:21; 1 Co 7:28; 2 Co 1:23; 13:2; 2 Pe 2:4, 5; absol. *to forbear, abstain,* 2 Co 12:6* [5339]

[5768] φειδομένως *pheidomenōs* 2x *sparingly,* 2 Co 9:6 (2t)* [5340]

[5770] φέρω *pherō* 66x *to bear, carry,* Mk 2:3; *to bring,* Mt 14:11, 18; *to conduct,* Mt 17:17; Jn 21:18; *to bear, endure,* Ro 9:22; Heb 12:20; 13:13; *to uphold, maintain, conserve,* Heb 1:3; *to bear, bring forth, produce,* Mk 4:8; Jn 12:24; 15:2; *to bring forward, advance, allege,* Jn 18:29; Ac 25:7; 2 Pe 2:11; *to offer, ascribe,* Rev 21:24, 26; absol. used of a gate, *to lead,* Ac 12:10; pass. *to be brought* within reach, *offered,* 1 Pe 1:13; *to be brought in, to enter,* Heb 9:16; *to be under a moving influence, to be moved,* 2 Pe 1:21; mid. *to rush, sweep,* Ac 2:2; *to proceed, come forth, have utterance,* 2 Pe 1:17, 18, 21; *to proceed, make progress,* Heb 6:1; used of a ship, *to drive before the wind,* Ac 27:15, 17 [5342]

[5771] φεύγω *pheugō* 29x absol. *to flee, take to flight,* Mt 2:13; 8:33; *to shrink, stand fearfully aloof,* 1 Co 10:14; *to make escape,* Mt 23:33; trans. *to shun,* 1 Co 6:18; 1 Ti 6:11; 2 Ti 2:22; *to escape,* Heb 11:34 [5343]

[5772] Φῆλιξ *Phēlix* 9x *Felix,* pr. name, Ac 23:24, 26; 24:3, 22, 24f., 27; 25:14* [5344]

[5773] φήμη *phēmē* 2x pr. *a celestial* or *oracular utterance; an utterance; fame, rumor, report,* Mt 9:26; Lk 4:14* [5345]

[5774] φημί *phēmi* 66x *to utter; to say, speak,* Mt 8:8; 14:8; 26:34, 61; *to say, allege, affirm,* Ro 3:8 [5346]

[5776] Φῆστος *Phēstos* 13x *Festus,* pr. name, Ac 24:27; 25:1, 4, 12ff., 22ff.; 26:24f., 32* [5347]

[5777] φθάνω *phthanō* 7x *come before, precede,* 1 Th 4:15; absol. *to advance, make progress,* 2 Co 10:14; Phil 3:16; *to come up* with, *come upon, be close at hand,* Mt 12:28; Lk 11:20; 1 Th 2:16; *to attain* an object of pursuit, Ro 9:31* [5348]

[5778] φθαρτός *phthartos* 6x *corruptible, perishable,* Ro 1:23; 1 Co 9:25; 15:53f.; 1 Pe 1:18, 23* [5349]

[5779] φθέγγομαι *phthengomai* 3x *to emit a sound; to speak,* Ac 4:18; 2 Pe 2:16, 18* [5350]

[5780] φθείρω *phtheirō* 9x *to spoil, ruin,* 1 Co 3:17; 2 Co 7:2; *to corrupt,* morally *deprave,* 1 Co 15:33; 2 Co 11:3 [5351]

[5781] φθινοπωρινός *phthinopōrinos* 1x *autumnal, bare,* Jude 12* [5352]

[5782] φθόγγος *phthongos* 2x *a vocal sound,* Ro 10:18; 1 Co 14:7* [5353]

[5783] φθονέω *phthoneō* 1x *to envy,* Gal 5:26* [5354]

[5784] φθόνος *phthonos* 9x *envy, jealously, spite,* Mt 27:18; Mk 15:10; Ro 1:29; Gal 5:21; Phil 1:15; 1 Ti 6:4; Tit 3:3; Jas 4:5; 1 Pe 2:1* [5355]

[5785] φθορά *phthora* 9x *corruption, decay, ruin, corruptibility, mortality,* Ro 8:21; 1 Co 15:42; meton. *corruptible, perishable substance,* 1 Co 15:50; *killing, slaughter,* 2 Pe 2:12; spiritual *ruin,* Gal 6:8; Col 2:22; met. moral *corruption, depravity,* 2 Pe 1:4; 2:19^ [5356]

[5786] φιάλη *phialē* 12x *a bowl, shallow cup,* Rev 5:8; 15:7; 16:1, 2, 3, 4 [5357]

[5787] φιλάγαθος *philagathos* 1x *a lover of goodness,* or, *of the good, a fosterer of virtue,* Tit 1:8* [5358]

[5788] Φιλαδέλφεια *Philadelpheia* 2x *Philadelphia,* a city of Lydia, near Mount Tmolus, Rev 1:11; 3:7* [5359]

[5789] φιλαδελφία *philadelphia* 6x *brotherly love;* in N.T. *love of the* Christian *brotherhood,* Ro 12:10; 1 Th 4:9; Heb 13:1; 1 Pe 1:22; 2 Pe 1:7* [5360]

[5790] φιλάδελφος *philadelphos* 1x *brother-loving;* in N.T. *loving the members of the* Christian *brotherhood,* 1 Pe 3:8* [5361]

[5791] φίλανδρος *philandros* 1x *husband-loving; conjugal,* Tit 2:4* [5362]

[5792] φιλανθρωπία *philanthrōpia* 2x *philanthropy, love of mankind,* Tit 3:4; *benevolence, humanity,* Ac 28:2* [5363]

[5793] φιλανθρώπως *philanthrōpōs* 1x *humanely, benevolently, kindly,* Ac 27:3* [5364]

[5794] φιλαργυρία *philargyria* 1x *love of money, covetousness,* 1 Ti 6:10* [5365]

[5795] φιλάργυρος *philargyros* 2x *money-loving, covetous,* Lk 16:14; 2 Ti 3:2* [5366]

[5796] φίλαυτος *philautos* 1x *self-loving; selfish,* 2 Ti 3:2* [5367]

[5797] φιλέω *phileō* 25x pr. *to manifest some act* or *token of kindness* or *affection; to kiss,* Mt 26:48; Mk 14:44; Lk 22:47; *to love, regard with affection, have affection for,* Mt 10:37; Jn 5:20; *to like, be fond of, delight in* a thing, Mt 23:6; Rev 22:15; *to cherish inordinately, set store by,* Jn 12:25; followed by an infin. *to be wont,* Mt 6:5 [5368]

[5798] φιλήδονος *philēdonos* 1x *pleasure-loving; a lover of pleasure,* 2 Ti 3:4* [5369]

[5799] φίλημα *philēma* 7x *a kiss,* Lk 7:45; 22:48; Ro 16:16; 1 Co 16:20; 2 Co 13:12; 1 Th 5:26; 1 Pe 5:14* [5370]

[5800] Φιλήμων *Philēmōn* 1x *Philemon,* pr. name, Phlm 1; subscr. and title* [5371]

[5801] Φίλητος *Philētos* 1x *Philetus,* pr. name, 2 Ti 2:17* [5372]

[5802] φιλία *philia* 1x *affection, fondness, love,* Jas 4:4* [5373]

[5803] Φιλιππήσιος *Philippēsios* 1x *a Philippian,* a citizen of Φίλιπποι, *Philippi,* Phil 4:15; title* [5374]

[5804] Φίλιπποι *Philippoi* 4x *Philippi,* a considerable city of Macedonia, east of Amphipolis, Ac 16:12; 20:6; Phil 1:1; 1 Th 2:2; 1 & 2 Co subscr.* [5375]

[5805] Φίλιππος *Philippos* 36x *Philip,* pr. name . (1) *Philip, the Apostle,* Mt 10:3. (2) *Philip, the Evangelist,* Ac 6:5. (3) *Philip, son of Herod the Great and Mariamne,* Mt 14:3 . (4) *Philip, son of Herod the Great and Cleopatra,* Mt 16:13; Lk 3:1 [5376]

[5806] φιλόθεος *philotheos* 1x *God-loving, pious; a lover of God,* 2 Ti 3:4* [5377]

[5807] Φιλόλογος *Philologos* 1x *Philologus,* pr. name, Ro 16:15* [5378]

[5808] φιλονεικία *philoneikia* 1x *a love of contention; rivalry, contention,* Lk 22:24* [5379]

[5809] φιλόνεικος *philoneikos* 1x *fond of contention; contentious, disputatious,* 1 Co 11:16* [5380]

[5810] φιλοξενία *philoxenia* 2x *kindness to strangers, hospitality,* Ro 12:13; Heb 13:2* [5381]

[5811] φιλόξενος *philoxenos* 3x *kind to strangers, hospitable,* 1 Ti 3:2; Tit 1:8; 1 Pe 4:9* [5382]

[5812] φιλοπρωτεύω *philoprōteuō* 1x *to love* or *desire to be first* or *chief, affect pre-eminence,* 3 Jn 9* [5383]

[5813] φίλος *philos* 29x *loved, dear; devoted;* Ac 19:31; as a subst., *a friend,* Lk 7:6; 11:5, 6, 8; *a congenial associate,* Mt 11:19; Lk 7:34; Jas 4:4; used as a word of courteous appellation, Lk 14:10 [5384]

[5814] φιλοσοφία *philosophia* 1x *a love of science;* systematic *philosophy;* in N.T. *the philosophy* of the Jewish gnosis, Col 2:8* [5385]

[5815] φιλόσοφος *philosophos* 1x pr. *a lover of science,* a systematic *philosopher,* Ac 17:18* [5386]

[5816] φιλόστοργος *philostorgos* 1x *tenderly affectionate,* Ro 12:10* [5387]

[5817] φιλότεκνος *philoteknos* 1x *loving one's children, duly parental,* Tit 2:4* [5388]

[5818] φιλοτιμέομαι *philotimeomai* 3x pr. *to be ambitious of honor;* by impl. *to exert one's self* to accomplish a thing, *use one's utmost efforts, endeavor earnestly,* Ro 15:20; 2 Co 5:9; 1 Th 4:11* [5389]

[5819] φιλοφρόνως *philophronōs* 1x *with kindly feeling* or *manner, courteously,* Ac 28:7* [5390]

[5821] φιμόω *phimoō* 7x *to muzzle,* 1 Ti 5:18; met. and by impl. *to silence, put to silence;* pass. *to be silent, speechless,* Mt 22:12, 34; 1 Pe 2:15; Mk 1:25; trop. pass. *to be hushed,* as winds and waves, Mk 4:39; Lk 4:35* [5392]

[5823] Φλέγων *Phlegōn* 1x *Phlegon,* pr. name, Ro 16:14* [5393]

[5824] φλογίζω *phlogizō* 2x *to set in a flame, kindle, inflame,* Jas 3:6 (2t)* [5394]

[5825] φλόξ *phlox* 7x *a flame,* Lk 16:24; Ac 7:30 [5395]

[5826] φλυαρέω *phlyareō* 1x *to talk folly* or *nonsense;* in N.T. trans., *bring unjustified charges against,* 3 Jn 10* [5396]

[5827] φλύαρος *phlyaros* 1x *a gossip, tattler,* 1 Ti 5:13* [5397]

[5828] φοβέομαι *phobeomai* 95x has an active form, φοβέω (5828), but only occurs as a passive (deponent) in our literature, *to fear, dread,* Mt 10:26; 14:5; *to fear reverentially, to reverence,* Mk 6:20; Lk 1:50; Ac 10:2; Eph 5:33; Rev 11:18; *to be afraid* to do a thing, Mt 2:22; Mk 9:32; *to be reluctant, to scruple,* Mt 1:20; *to fear, be apprehensive,* Ac 27:17; 2 Co 11:3; 12:20; *to be fearfully anxious,* Heb 4:1; absol. *to be fearful, afraid, alarmed,* Mt 14:27; 17:6,

7; Mk 16:8; *to be fearfully impressed*, Ro 11:20 [5399]

[5829] φοβερός *phoberos* 3x *fearful; terrible*, Heb 10:27, 31; 12:21* [5398]

[5831] φόβητρον *phobētron* 1x *something which inspires terror; terrible sight* or *event*, Lk 21:11* [5400]

[5832] φόβος *phobos* 47x *fear, terror, affright*, Mt 14:26; Lk 1:12; *astonishment, amazement*, Mt 28:8; Mk 4:41; *trembling concern*, 1 Co 2:3; 2 Co 7:15; meton. *a terror, an object* or *cause of terror*, Ro 13:5; *reverential fear, awe*, Ac 9:31; Ro 3:18; *respect, deference*, Ro 13:7; 1 Pe 2:18 [5401]

[5833] Φοίβη *Phoibē* 1x *Phoebe*, pr. name, Ro 16:1* [5402]

[5834] Φοινίκη *Phoinikē* 3x *Phoenice, Phoenicia*, a country on the east of the Mediterranean, between Palestine and Syria, anciently celebrated for commerce, Ac 11:19; 15:3; 21:2* [5403]

[5836] φοῖνιξ *phoinix* 2x *the palm-tree, the date-palm*, Jn 12:13; Rev 7:9. Identical in form to the word meaning *phoenix*, the Egyptian bird.* [5404]

[5837] Φοῖνιξ *Phoinix* 1x *Phoenix, Phoenice*, a city, with a harbor, on the southeast coast of Crete, Ac 27:12* [5405]

[5838] φονεύς *phoneus* 7x *a homicide, murderer*, Mt 22:7; Ac 3:14; 7:52; 28:4; 1 Pe 4:15; Rev 21: 8; 22:15* [5406]

[5839] φονεύω *phoneuō* 12x *to put to death, kill, stay*, Mt 23:31, 35; absol. *to commit murder*, Mt 5:21 [5407]

[5840] φόνος *phonos* 9x *a killing, slaughter, murder*, Mt 15:19; Mk 7:21; 15:7 [5408]

[5841] φορέω *phoreō* 6x *to bear; to wear*, Mt 11:8; Jn 19:5; Ro 13:4; 1 Co 15:49; Jas 2:3 [5409]

[5842] φόρον *phoron* 1x *a forum, marketplace*; Φόρον Ἀππίου, *Forum Appii*, the name of a small town on the Appian way, according to Antoninus, forty-three Roman miles from Rome, or about forty English miles, Ac 28:15* [5410]

[5843] φόρος *phoros* 5x *tribute, tax*, strictly such as is laid on dependent and subject people, Lk 20:22; 23:2; Ro 13:6, 7* [5411]

[5844] φορτίζω *phortizō* 2x *to load, burden;* met. Mt 11:28; Lk 11:46* [5412]

[5845] φορτίον *phortion* 6x *a load, burden;* of a ship, *freight, cargo*, Ac 27:10; met. *a burden* of imposed precepts, etc.,

Mt 11:30; 23:4; Lk 11:46 (2t); of faults, sins, etc., Gal 6:5* [5413]

[5847] Φορτουνᾶτος *Phortounatos* 1x *Fortunatus*, pr. name, 1 Co 16:17* [5415]

[5848] φραγέλλιον *phragellion* 1x *a whip, scourge*, Jn 2:15* [5416]

[5849] φραγελλόω *phragelloō* 2x *to scourge*, Mt 27:26; Mk 15:15* [5417]

[5850] φραγμός *phragmos* 4x *a fence, hedge; a hedgeside path*, Mt 21:33; Mk 12:1; Lk 14:23; met. *a parting fence*, Eph 2:14* [5418]

[5851] φράζω *phrazō* 1x pr. *to propound in distinct terms, to tell;* in N.T. *to explain, interpret, expound*, Mt 15:15* [5419]

[5852] φράσσω *phrassō* 3x *to fence in;* by impl. *to obstruct, stop, close up*, Heb 11:33; met. *to silence, put to silence*, Ro 3:19; 2 Co 11:10* [5420]

[5853] φρέαρ *phrear* 7x *a well, cistern*, Lk 14:5; Jn 4:11, 12; *a pit*, Rev 9:1, 2* [5421]

[5854] φρεναπατάω *phrenapataō* 1x *to deceive the mind; to deceive, impose on*, Gal 6:3* [5422]

[5855] φρεναπάτης *phrenapatēs* 1x *a deceiver, seducer*, Tit 1:10* [5423]

[5856] φρήν *phrēn* 2x pr. *the diaphragm, midriff; the mind, intellect, understanding*, 1 Co 14:20 (2t)* [5424]

[5857] φρίσσω *phrissō* 1x *to be ruffled, to bristle; to shiver, shudder* from fear, Jas 2:19* [5425]

[5858] φρονέω *phroneō* 26x *to think, to mind; to be of opinion*, Ac 28:22; Phil 1:7; *to take thought, be considerate*, Phil 4:10; *to entertain sentiments* or *inclinations* of a specific kind, *to be minded*, Ro 12:16; 15:5; 1 Co 13:11; 2 Co 13:11; Gal 5:10; Phil 2:2; 3:16; 4:2; *to be in a* certain *frame of mind*, Ro 12:3; Phil 2:5; *to imagine, entertain conceit*, 1 Co 4:6; *to heed, pay regard to*, Ro 14:6; *to incline to, be set upon, mind*, Mt 16:23; Mk 8:33; Ro 8:5; Phil 3:15, 19; Col 3:2 [5426]

[5859] φρόνημα *phronēma* 4x *frame of thought, will, aspirations*, Ro 8:6, 7, 27* [5427]

[5860] φρόνησις *phronēsis* 2x *a thoughtful frame, sense, rightmindedness*, Lk 1:17; *intelligence*, Eph 1:8* [5428]

[5861] φρόνιμος *phronimos* 14x *considerate, thoughtful, prudent, discreet*, Mt 7:24; 10:16; 24:45; 25:2, 4, 8, 9; Lk 12:42; *sensible, wise*, Ro 11:25; 12:16; 1 Co 4:10; 10:15; 2 Co 11:19* [5429]

[5862] φρονίμως *phronimōs* 1x *considerately, providently*, Lk 16:8* [5430]

[5863] φροντίζω *phrontizō* 1x *to be considerate, be careful*, Tit 3:8* [5431]

[5864] φρουρέω *phroureō* 4x *to keep watch;* trans. *to guard, watch*, with a military guard, 2 Co 11:32; *to keep* in a condition of restraint, Gal 3:23; *to keep* in a state of settlement or security, Phil 4:7; 1 Pe 1:5* [5432]

[5865] φρυάσσω *phryassō* 1x pr. *to snort, neigh, stamp*, etc.; as a high-spirited horse; hence, *to be noisy, fierce, insolent, and tumultuous, to rage, tumultuate*, Ac 4:25* [5433]

[5866] φρύγανον *phryganon* 1x *a dry twig, branch*, etc., Ac 28:3* [5434]

[5867] Φρυγία *Phrygia* 3x *Phrygia*, an inland province of Asia Minor, Ac 2:10; 16:6; 18:23; 1 Ti subscr.* [5435]

[5869] Φύγελος *Phygelos* 1x *Phygellus*, pr. name, 2 Ti 1:15* [5436]

[5870] φυγή *phygē* 1x *a fleeing, flight*, Mt 24:20* [5437]

[5871] φυλακή *phylakē* 47x *a keeping watch, ward, guard*, Lk 2:8; *a place of watch*, Rev 18:2; *a watch, guard, body of guards*, Ac 12:10; *ward, custody, imprisonment*, 2 Co 6:5; 11:23; Heb 11:36; *prison*, 1 Pe 3:19; *a place of custody, prison*, Mt 14:10; 25:39, 44; *a watch* or *division*, of the night, which in the time of our Savior was divided into watches of three hours each, called ὀψέ, μεσονύκτιον, ἀλεκτοροφωνία and πρωία, or πρωΐ, Mt 14:25; 24:43; Mk 6:48; Lk 12:38 (2t) [5438]

[5872] φυλακίζω *phylakizō* 1x *to deliver into custody, put in prison, imprison*, Ac 22:19* [5439]

[5873] φυλακτήριον *phylaktērion* 1x *the station of a guard* or *watch; a preservative, safeguard;* hence, *a phylactery* or *amulet*, worn about the person; from which circumstance the word is used in the N.T. as a term for the Jewish *Tephillin* or *prayer-fillets*, which took their rise from the injunction in Deut 6:8; 11:18; Mt 23:5* [5440]

[5874] φύλαξ *phylax* 3x *a watchman, guard, sentinel*, Ac 5:23; 12:6, 19* [5441]

[5875] φυλάσσω *phylassō* 31x *to be on watch, keep* watch, Lk 2:8; *to have in keeping*, Ac 20:20; *to have in custody*, Ac 28:16; *to keep* under restraint, *confine*, Lk 8:29; Ac 12:4; 23:35; *to guard, defend*, Lk 11:21; *to keep safe, preserve*, Jn 12:25;

17:12; 2 Th 3:3; 2 Pe 2:5; Jude 24; *to keep* in abstinence, Ac 21:25; 1 Jn 5:21; *to observe* a matter of injunction or duty, Mk 10:20; Lk 11:28; Ac 7:53; 16:4; 21:24; mid. *to be on one's guard, beware,* Lk 12:15; 2 Ti 4:15; 2 Pe 3:17 [5442]

[5876] φυλή *phylē* 31x *a tribe,* Mt 19:28; 24:30; Lk 2:36; *a people, nation,* Rev 1:7; 5:9 [5443]

[5877] φύλλον *phyllon* 6x *a leaf,* Mt 21:19 [5444]

[5878] φύραμα *phyrama* 5x *that which is mingled and reduced to a uniform consistence, by kneading, beating, treading,* etc.; *a mass* of potter's clay, Ro 9:21; of dough, 1 Co 5:6, 7; Gal 5:9; met. Ro 11:16* [5445]

[5879] φυσικός *physikos* 3x *natural, agreeable to nature,* Ro 1:26, 27; *following the instinct of nature,* as animals, 2 Pe 2:12* [5446]

[5880] φυσικῶς *physikōs* 1x *naturally, by natural instinct,* Jude 10* [5447]

[5881] φυσιόω *physioō* 7x *to inflate puff up;* met. *to inflate* with pride and vanity, 1 Co 8:1; pass. *to be inflated* with pride, *to be proud, vain, arrogant,* 1 Co 4:6, 18, 19; 5:2; 13:4; Col 2:18* [5448]

[5882] φύσις *physis* 14x *essence,* Gal 4:8; *native condition, birth,* Ro 2:27; 11:21, 24; Gal 2:15; Eph 2:3; *native species, kind,* Jas 3:7; *nature, natural frame,* 2 Pe 1:4; *nature, native instinct,* Ro 2:14; 1 Co 11:14; *nature, prescribed course of nature,* Ro 1:26* [5449]

[5883] φυσίωσις *physiōsis* 1x pr. *inflation;* met. *inflation* of mind, *pride,* 2 Co 12:20* [5450]

[5884] φυτεία *phyteia* 1x *plantation, the act of planting; a plant,* met. Mt 15:13* [5451]

[5885] φυτεύω *phyteuō* 11x *to plant, set,* Mt 21:33; Lk 13:6; 17:6, 28; 20:9; met. Mt 15:13; Mk 12:1; *to plant* the Gospel, 1 Co 3:6, 7, 8; 9:7* [5452]

[5886] φύω *phyō* 3x *to generate, produce;* pass. *to be generated, produced;* of plants, *to germinate, sprout,* Lk 8:6, 8; intrans. *to germinate, spring* or *grow up,* Heb 12:15* [5453]

[5887] φωλεός *phōleos* 2x *a den, lair, burrow,* Mt 8:20; Lk 9:58* [5454]

[5888] φωνέω *phōneō* 43x *to sound, utter a sound;* of the cock, *to crow,* Mt 26:34, 74, 75; *to call,* or *cry out, exclaim,* Lk 8:8, 54; 16:24; 23:46; *to call to,* Mt 27:47; Mk 3:31; *to call,* Jn 13:13; *to call, summon,*

Mt 20:32; *to invite* to a feast, Lk 14:12 [5455]

[5889] φωνή *phōnē* 139x *a sound,* Mt 24:31; Jn 3:8; Rev 4:5; 8:5; *a cry,* Mt 2:18; *an* articulate *sound, voice,* Mt 3:3, 17; 17:5; 27:46, 50; *voice, speech, discourse,* Jn 10:16, 27; Ac 7:31; 12:22; 13:27; Heb 3:7, 15; *tone* of address, Gal 4:20; *language, tongue, dialect,* 1 Co 14:10 [5456]

[5890] φῶς *phōs* 73x *light,* Mt 17:2; 2 Co 4:6; *daylight, broad day,* Mt 10:27; Lk 12:3; *radiance, blaze of light,* Mt 4:16; Ac 9:3; 12:7; *an instrument* or *means of light, a light,* Mt 6:23; Ac 16:29; *a fire,* Mk 14:54; Lk 22:56; from the Hebrew, *the light* of God's presence, 2 Co 11:14; 1 Ti 6:16; met. *the light* of Divine truth, spiritual *illumination,* Lk 16:8; Jn 3:19; Ro 13:12; Eph 5:8; 1 Pe 2:9; 1 Jn 1:7; 2:8, 9, 10; *a source* or *dispenser of* spiritual *light,* Mt 5:14; Jn 1:4, 5, 7, 8, 9; 8:12; 9:5; pure *radiance,* perfect *brightness,* 1 Jn 1:5 [5457]

[5891] φωστήρ *phōstēr* 2x *a cause of light, illuminator; a light, luminary, star,* Phil 2:15; *radiance,* or, *luminary,* Rev 21:11* [5458]

[5892] φωσφόρος *phōsphoros* 1x *light-bringing;* sc. ἀστήρ, *Lucifer, the morning star,* met. 2 Pe 1:19* [5459]

[5893] φωτεινός *phōteinos* 5x *radiant, lustrous,* Mt 17:5; *enlightened, illuminated,* Mt 6:22; Lk 11:34, 36 (2t)* [5460]

[5894] φωτίζω *phōtizō* 11x *to light, give light to, illuminate, shine upon,* Lk 11:36; Rev 18:1; 21:23; met. *to enlighten* spiritually, Jn 1:9; Eph 1:18; 3:9; Heb 6:4; 10:32; *to reveal, to bring to light, make known,* 1 Co 4:5; 2 Ti 1:10; intrans. *shine,* Rev 22:5* [5461]

[5895] φωτισμός *phōtismos* 2x *illumination; a shining forth, bringing to light, enlightenment,* 2 Co 4:4, 6* [5462]

[5897] χαίρω *chairō* 74x *to rejoice, be glad, be joyful, be full of joy,* Mt 2:10; 5:12; 18:13; Mk 14:11; Ro 12:12; 2 Co 2:3; a term of salutation, *Hail!* Mt 26:49; λέγω χαίρειν, *to greet,* 2 Jn 10:11; an epistolary forth, *Health!* Ac 15:23 [5463]

[5898] χάλαζα *chalaza* 4x *hail,* Rev 8:7; 11:19; 16:21 (2t)* [5464]

[5899] χαλάω *chalaō* 7x *to slacken; to let down, lower,* Mk 2:4; Lk 5:4, 5; Ac 9:25; 27:17, 30; 1 Co 11:33* [5465]

[5900] Χαλδαῖος *Chaldaios* 1x *a Chaldean, a native of Chaldea,* a country of central Asia, which seems to have included Mesopotamia, Ac 7:4* [5466]

[5901] χαλεπός *chalepos* 2x *hard, rugged; furious, ferocious,* Mt 8:28; *difficult, trying,* 2 Ti 3:1* [5467]

[5902] χαλιναγωγέω *chalinagōgeō* 2x pr. *to guide with a bridle;* met. *to bridle, control, sway,* Jas 1:26; 3:2* [5468]

[5903] χαλινός *chalinos* 2x *a bridle, bit,* Jas 3:3; Rev 14:20* [5469]

[5906] χαλκεύς *chalkeus* 1x pr. *a coppersmith;* hence, genr. *a worker in metals, smith,* 2 Ti 4:14* [5471]

[5907] χαλκηδών *chalkēdōn* 1x *chalcedony,* the name of a gem, generally of a whitish, bluish, or gray color, susceptible of a high and beautiful polish, and of which there are several varieties, as the onyx, modern carnelian, etc., Rev 21:19* [5472]

[5908] χαλκίον *chalkion* 1x *a vessel, copper, brazen utensil,* Mk 7:4* [5473]

[5909] χαλκολίβανον *chalkolibanon* 2x *orichalcum, fine bronze,* a factitious metal of which there were several varieties, the white being of the highest repute, or, *deep-tinted frankincense,* Rev 1:15; 2:18* [5474]

[5910] χαλκός *chalkos* 5x *copper,* also, *bronze,* Rev 18:12; *a brazen musical instrument,* 1 Co 13:1; *copper money,* Mt 10:9; *money* in general, Mk 6:8; 12:41* [5475]

[5911] χαλκοῦς *chalkous* 1x contracted form of χάλκεος, *made of copper, brass,* or *bronze,* Rev 9:20* [5470]

[5912] χαμαί *chamai* 2x *on the ground, to the earth,* Jn 9:6; 18:6* [5476]

[5913] Χανάαν *Chanaan* 2x *Canaan,* the ancient name of Palestine, Ac 7:11; 13:19 [5477]

[5914] Χαναναῖος *Chananaios* 1x *Canaanitish, of Canaan,* Mt 15:22* [5478]

[5915] χαρά *chara* 59x *joy, gladness, rejoicing,* Mt 2:10; 13:20, 44; 28:8; meton, *joy, cause of joy, occasion of rejoicing,* Lk 2:10; Phil 4:1; 1 Th 2:19, 20; *bliss,* Mt 25:21, 23 [5479]

[5916] χάραγμα *charagma* 8x *an imprinted mark,* Rev 13:16, 17; 14:9, 11; 16:2; 19:20; 20:4; *sculpture,* Ac 17:29* [5480]

[5917] χαρακτήρ *charaktēr* 1x *a graver, graving-tool; an engraven* or *impressed device; an impress, exact expression,* Heb 1:3* [5481]

[5918] χάραξ *charax* 1x *a stake; a* military *palisade, rampart,* formed from the earth thrown out of the ditch, and stuck with sharp stakes or palisades, Lk 19:43★ [5482]

[5919] χαρίζομαι *charizomai* 23x *to gratify; to bestow* in kindness, *grant* as a free favor, Lk 7:21; Ro 8:32; *to grant the deliverance* of a person in favor to the desire of others, Ac 3:14; 27:24; Phlm 22; *to sacrifice* a person to the demand of enemies, Ac 25:11; *to remit, forgive*, Lk 7:42; 2 Co 2:7, 10 [5483]

[5920] χάριν *charin* 9x the acc. sg form of the noun χάριν which can be used as an improper prep., *on account of*, Lk 7:47; Eph 3:1, 14; 1 Jn 3:12; *for the sake of, in order to*, Gal 3:19; Tit 1:5, 11; Jude 16; *on the score of*, 1 Ti 5:14★ [5484]

[5921] χάρις *charis* 155x *pleasing show, charm; beauty, gracefulness; a pleasing circumstance, matter of approval*, 1 Pe 2:19, 20; *kindly bearing, graciousness*, Lk 4:22; *a beneficial opportunity, benefit*, 2 Co 1:15; Eph 4:29; *a charitable act, generous gift*, 1 Co 16:3; 2 Co 8:4, 6; *an act of favor*, Ac 25:3; *favor, acceptance*, Lk 1:30, 52; Ac 2:47; 7:10, 46; *free favor, free gift, grace*, Jn 1:14, 16, 17; Ro 4:4, 16; 11:5, 6; Eph 2:5, 8; 1 Pe 3:7; *free favor* specially manifested by God towards man in the Gospel scheme, *grace*, Ac 15:11; Ro 3:24; 5:15, 17, 20, 21; 6:1; 2 Co 4:15; *a gracious provision, gracious scheme, grace*, Ro 6:14, 15; Heb 2:9; 12:28; 13:9; *gracious dealing* from God, *grace*, Ac 14:26; 15:40; Ro 1:7; 1 Co 1:4; 15:10; Gal 1:15; *a commission graciously devolved* by God upon a human agent, Ro 1:5; 12:3; 15:15; 1 Co 3:10; 2 Co 1:12; Gal 2:9; Eph 3:8; *grace, graciously bestowed* divine *endowment* or *influence*, Lk 2:40; Ac 4:33; 11:23; Ro 12:6; 2 Co 12:9; *grace*, Ac 11:43; Ro 5:2; Gal 5:4; 2 Pe 3:18; *an emotion correspondent to what is pleasing* or *kindly; sense of obligation*, Lk 17:9; *a grateful frame of mind*, 1 Co 10:30; *thanks*, Lk 6:32, 33, 34; Ro 6:17; 1 Co 15:57; χάριν or χάριτας καταθέσθαι, *to oblige, gratify*, Ac 24:27; 25:9 [5485]

[5922] χάρισμα *charisma* 17x *a free favor, free gift*, Ro 5:15, 16; 6:23; 2 Co 1:11; *benefit*, Ro 1:11; *a divinely conferred endowment*, 1 Co 12:4, 9, 28, 30, 31 [5486]

[5923] χαριτόω *charitoō* 2x *to favor, visit with favor, to make an object of favor, to gift*, Eph 1:6; pass. *to be visited with free favor, be an object of gracious visitation*, Lk 1:28★ [5487]

[5924] Χαρράν *Charran* 2x *Charran*, a city in the northern part of Mesopotamia, 7:2, 4★ [5488]

[5925] χάρτης *chartēs* 1x *paper*, 2 Jn 12★ [5489]

[5926] χάσμα *chasma* 1x *a chasm, gulf*, Lk 16:26★ [5490]

[5927] χεῖλος *cheilos* 7x *a lip*, and pl. τὰ χείλη, *the lips*, Mt 15:8; Mk 7:6; Ro 3:13; Heb 13:15; 1 Pe 3:10; trop. χεῖλος τῆς θαλάσσης, *the seashore*, Heb 11:12; meton. *language, dialect*, 1 Co 14:21★ [5491]

[5928] χειμάζω *cheimazō* 1x *to excite a tempest, toss with a tempest;* pass. *to be storm-tossed*, Ac 27:18★ [5492]

[5930] χειμών *cheimōn* 6x *stormy weather*, Mt 16:3; *a storm, tempest*, Ac 27:20; *winter*, Mt 24:20; Mk 13:18; Jn 10:22; 2 Ti 4:21★ [5494]

[5931] χείρ *cheir* 177x *a hand*, Mt 3:12; 4:6; 8:15 freq.; from the Hebrew, χεὶρ Κυρίου, a special *operation of God*, Ac 11:21; 13:3; ἐν χειρί, *by agency*, Ac 7:35; Gal 3:19 [5495]

[5932] χειραγωγέω *cheiragōgeō* 2x *to lead by the hand*, Ac 9:8; 22:11★ [5496]

[5933] χειραγωγός *cheiragōgos* 1x *one who leads another by the hand*, Ac 13:11★ [5497]

[5934] χειρόγραφον *cheirographon* 1x *handwriting; a written form, literal instrument*, as distinguished from a spiritual dispensation, Col 2:14★ [5498]

[5935] χειροποίητος *cheiropoiētos* 6x *made by hand, artificial, material*, Mk 14:58; Ac 7:48; 17:24; Eph 2:11; Heb 9:11, 24★ [5499]

[5936] χειροτονέω *cheirotoneō* 2x *to stretch out the hand; to constitute by voting; to appoint, constitute*, Ac 14:23; 2 Co 8:19★ [5500]

[5937] χείρων *cheirōn* 11x *worse*, Mt 9:16; *more severe*, Jn 5:14; Heb 10:29 [5501]

[5938] Χερούβ *Cheroub* 1x also spelled Χερουβείν and Χερουβίμ, indecl. *cherub*, a two-winged figure over the ark of the covenant, Heb 9:5★ [5502]

[5939] χήρα *chēra* 26x *a widow*, Mt 23:14; Lk 4:26 [5503]

[5941] χιλίαρχος *chiliarchos* 21x *commander of a thousand men;* hence, genr. *a commander, military chief*, Mk 6:21; Rev 6:15; 19:18; spc. *a legionary tribune*, Ac 21:31, 32, 33, 37; *the prefect* of the temple, Jn 18:12 [5506]

[5942] χιλιάς *chilias* 23x the number *one thousand, a thousand*, Lk 14:31; Ac 4:4 [5505]

[5943] χίλιοι *chilioi* 11x *a thousand*, 2 Pe 3:8; Rev 11:3; 12:6; 14:20; 20:2-7★ [5507]

[5945] χιτών *chitōn* 11x *a tunic, vest*, the inner garment which fitted close to the body, having armholes, and sometimes sleeves, and reaching below the knees, worn by both sexes, Mt 5:40; 10:10; pl. χιτῶνες, *clothes, garments* in general, Mk 14:63 [5509]

[5946] χιών *chiōn* 2x *snow*, Mt 28:3; Rev 1:14★ [5510]

[5948] χλαμύς *chlamys* 2x *chlamys*, a type of *cloak;* a Roman military commander's *cloak*, Mt 27:28, 31★ [5511]

[5949] χλευάζω *chleuazō* 1x *to jeer, scoff*, Ac 17:32★ [5512]

[5950] χλιαρός *chliaros* 1x *warm, tepid; lukewarm*, Rev 3:16★ [5513]

[5952] χλωρός *chlōros* 4x *pale green; green, verdent*, Mk 6:39; Rev 8:7; 9:4; *pale, sallow*, Rev 6:8★ [5515]

[5954] χοϊκός *choikos* 4x *of earth, earthy*, 1 Co 15:47, 48, 49★ [5517]

[5955] χοῖνιξ *choinix* 2x *a choenix*, an Attic measure for things dry, being the 48th part of a medimnus, consequently equal to the 8th part of the Roman modius, and nearly equivalent to about one quart, being considered a sufficient daily allowance for the sustenance of one man, Rev 6:6 (2t)★ [5518]

[5956] χοῖρος *choiros* 12x pr. *a young swine; a swine, hog*, or *sow*, Mt 8:30, 31, 32 [5519]

[5957] χολάω *cholaō* 1x pr. *to be melancholy;* used later as an equivalent to χολοῦμαι, *to be angry, incensed*, Jn 7:23★ [5520]

[5958] χολή *cholē* 2x *the bile, gall;* in N.T. *a bitter ingredient*, as *wormwood*, Mt 27:34; χολὴ πικρίας, *intense bitterness*, met. *thorough disaffection* to divine truth, *utter estrangement*, Ac 8:23★ [5521]

[5960] Χοραζίν *Chorazin* 2x also spelled Χωραζίν and Χοραζείν, *Chorazin*, a town of Galilee, probably near Bethsaida and Capernaum, indecl., Mt 11:21; Lk 10:13★ [5523]

[5961] χορηγέω *chorēgeō* 2x *to lead a chorus;* at Athens, *to defray the cost of a chorus;* hence, *to supply funds; to supply, furnish*, 2 Co 9:10; 1 Pe 4:11★ [5524]

[5962] χορός *choros* 1x *dancing* with music, Lk 15:25* [5525]

[5963] χορτάζω *chortazō* 16x pr. *to feed* or *fill with grass, herbage*, etc., *to fatten*; used of animals of prey, *to satiate, gorge*, Rev 19:21; of persons, *to satisfy with food*, Mt 14:20; 15:33, 37; met. *to satisfy* the desire of any one, Mt 5:6 [5526]

[5964] χόρτασμα *chortasma* 1x *pasture, provender* for cattle; *food, provision, sustenance*, for men, Ac 7:11* [5527]

[5965] χόρτος *chortos* 15x *an enclosure; pasture-ground; fodder* for beasts; in N.T. *herbage, grass*, Mt 6:30; 14:19; *a plant* of corn, Mt 13:26; Mk 4:28 [5528]

[5967] χοῦς *chous* 2x uncontracted form χόος, *dust*, acc., χοῦν, Mk 6:11; Rev 18:19* [5522]

[5968] χράομαι *chraomai* 11x *to use, make use of, employ*, Ac 27:17; 1 Co 7:31; *to take advantage of*, 1 Co 7:21; 9:12, 15; *to use, to treat, behave towards*, Ac 27:3; 2 Co 13:10 [5530]

[5970] χρεία *chreia* 49x *use; need, necessity, requisiteness*, Eph 4:29; Heb 7:11; personal *need*, an individual *want*, Ac 20:34; Ro 12:13; Phil 2:25; 4:16, 19; χρείαν ἔχω, *to need, require, want*, Mt 6:8; 14:16; Mk 2:25; Jn 2:25; ἐστὶ χρεία, *there is need*, Lk 10:42; τὰ πρὸς τὴν χρείαν, *necessary things*, Ac 28:10; *a necessary business, affair*, Ac 6:3 [5532]

[5971] χρεοφειλέτης *chreopheiletēs* 2x *debtor*, Lk 7:41; 16:5* [5533]

[5973] χρή *chrē* 1x impersonal verb, *there is need* or *occasion, it is necessary, it is requisite; it becomes, it is proper*, Jas 3:10* [5534]

[5974] χρῄζω *chrēzō* 5x *to need, want, desire*, Mt 6:32; Lk 11:8; 12:30; Ro 16:2; 2 Co 3:1* [5535]

[5975] χρῆμα *chrēma* 6x *anything useful*, or *needful*; pl. *wealth, riches*, Mk 10:23; Lk 18:24; *money*, Ac 8:18, 20; 24:26; sg. *price*, Ac 4:37* [5536]

[5976] χρηματίζω *chrēmatizō* 9x *to have dealings, transact business; to negotiate; to give answer on deliberation*; in N.T. *to utter a divine communication*, Heb 12:25; pass. *to be divinely instructed, receive a revelation* or *warning from God*, Mt 2:12, 22; Lk 2:26; Ac 10:22; Heb 8:5; 11:7; intrans. *to receive an appellation*, Ac 11:26; Ro 7:3* [5537]

[5977] χρηματισμός *chrēmatismos* 1x in N.T. *a response from God, a divine communication, oracle*, Ro 11:4* [5538]

[5978] χρήσιμος *chrēsimos* 1x *useful, profitable*, 2 Ti 2:14* [5539]

[5979] χρῆσις *chrēsis* 2x *use, employment; manner of using*, Ro 1:26, 27* [5540]

[5980] χρηστεύομαι *chrēsteuomai* 1x *to be gentle, benign, kind*, 1 Co 13:4* [5541]

[5981] χρηστολογία *chrēstologia* 1x *bland address, fair speaking*, Ro 16:18* [5542]

[5982] χρηστός *chrēstos* 7x *useful, profitable; good, agreeable*, Lk 5:39; *easy*, as a yoke, Mt 11:30; *gentle, benign, kind, obliging, gracious*, Lk 6:35; Eph 4:32; Ro 2:4; 1 Pe 2:3; *good* in character, disposition, etc., *virtuous*, 1 Co 15:33* [5543]

[5983] χρηστότης *chrēstotēs* 10x pr. *goodness, kindness, gentleness*, Ro 2:4; 11:22(3t); 2 Co 6:6; Gal 5:22; Col 3:12; Tit 3:4; *kindness* shown, *beneficence*, Eph 2:7; *goodness, virtue*, Ro 3:12* [5544]

[5984] χρῖσμα *chrisma* 3x pr. *anything which is applied by smearing; ointment*; in N.T. *an anointing*, in the reception of spiritual privileges, 1 Jn 2:20, 27* [5545]

[5985] Χριστιανός *Christianos* 3x *a Christian, follower of Christ*, Ac 11:26; 26:28; 1 Pe 4:16* [5546]

[5986] Χριστός *Christos* 529x pr. *anointed*; ὁ Χριστός, *the Christ, the Anointed One*, i.q. Μεσσίας, *the Messiah*, Mt 1:16, 17; Jn 1:20, 25, 42; meton. *Christ, the word* or *doctrine of Christ*, 2 Co 1:19; 21; Eph 4:20; *Christ, a truly Christian frame* of doctrine and affection, Ro 8:10; Gal 4:19; *Christ, the Church of Christ*, 1 Co 12:12; *Christ the distinctive privileges of the Gospel of Christ*, Gal 3:27; Phil 3:8; Heb 3:14 [5547]

[5987] χρίω *chriō* 5x *to anoint*; in N.T. *to anoint*, by way of instituting to a dignity, function, or privilege, Lk 4:18; Ac 4:27; 10:38; 2 Co 1:21; Heb 1:9* [5548]

[5988] χρονίζω *chronizō* 5x *to spend time; to linger, delay, be long*, Mt 24:48; 25:5; Lk 1:21; 12:45; Heb 10:37* [5549]

[5989] χρόνος *chronos* 54x *time*, whether in respect of duration or a definite point of its lapse, Mt 2:7; 25:19 freq.; *an epoch, era*, marked *duration*, Ac 1:7; 1 Th 5:1 [5550]

[5990] χρονοτριβέω *chronotribeō* 1x *to spend time, waste time, linger, delay*, Ac 20:16* [5551]

[5992] χρυσίον *chrysion* 12x *gold*, Heb 9:4; 1 Pe 1:7; Rev 3:18; 21:18, 21; spc. *gold when coined* or *manufactured; golden ornaments*, 1 Ti 2:9; 1 Pe 3:3; Rev 17:4; 18:16; *gold coin, money*, Ac 3:6; 20:33; 1 Pe 1:18* [5553]

[5993] χρυσοδακτύλιος *chrysodaktylios* 1x *having rings of gold on the fingers*, Jas 2:2* [5554]

[5994] χρυσόλιθος *chrysolithos* 1x *chrysolite*, a name applied by the ancients to all gems of a gold color; spc. the modern *topaz*, Rev 21:10* [5555]

[5995] χρυσόπρασος *chrysoprasos* 1x *a chrysoprase*, a species of gem of a golden green color like that of a leek, Rev 21:20* [5556]

[5996] χρυσός *chrysos* 10x *gold*, Mt 2:11; 23:16, 17; meton. *gold ornaments*, 1 Ti 2:9; *gold coin, money*, Mt 10:9 [5557]

[5997] χρυσοῦς *chrysous* 18x *golden, made of* or *adorned with gold*, 2 Ti 2:20; Heb 9:4; Rev 1:12, 13, 20; 9:13, 20; 21:15 [5552]

[5998] χρυσόω *chrysoō* 2x *to gild, overlay with gold, adorn* or *deck with gold*, Rev 17:4; 18:16* [5558]

[5999] χρώς *chrōs* 1x *the skin; the body surface;* Ac 19:12* [5559]

[6000] χωλός *chōlos* 14x *crippled in the feet, limping, halting, lame*, Mt 11:5; 15:30, 31; met. *limping, weak*, spiritually, Heb 12:13; *maimed, deprived of a foot*, for ἀναπηρός, Mk 9:45 [5560]

[6001] χώρα *chōra* 28x *space, room; a country, region, tract, province*, Mk 5:10; Lk 2:8; *a district, territory, suburbs*, Mt 8:28; meton. *the inhabitants of a country, region*, etc., Mk 1:5; Ac 12:20; *the country*, as opposed to the city or town, Lk 21:21; *a field, farm*, Lk 12:16; Jn 4:35 [5561]

[6003] χωρέω *chōreō* 10x *to make room*, either by motion or capacity; *to move, pass*, Mt 15:17; *to proceed, go on*, 2 Pet 3:9; *to progress, make way*, Jn 8:37; trans. *to hold* as contents, *contain, afford room for*, Mk 2:2; Jn 2:6; 21:25; met. *to give mental admittance to, to yield accordance*, Mt 19:11, 12; *to admit* to approbation and esteem, *to regard cordially*, 2 Co 7:2* [5562]

[6004] χωρίζω *chōrizō* 13x *to divide, separate*, Mt 19:6; Mk 10:9; Ro 8:35, 39; *to dissociate one's self, to part*, 1 Co 7:10, 11, 15; *to withdraw, depart*, Ac 1:4; 18:1, 2; Phlm 15; *to be aloof*, Heb 7:26* [5563]

[6005] χωρίον *chōrion* 10x *a place, spot;* Mt 26:36; Mk 14:32; *a field, farm, estate, domain,* Jn 4:5; Ac 1:18, 19(2t); 4:34; 5:3, 8; 28:7* [5564]

[6006] χωρίς *chōris* 41x can function as an improper prep., *apart,* Jn 20:7; *apart from, parted from,* Jn 15:5; Jas 2:18, 20, 26; *alien from,* Eph 2:12; *apart from, on a distinct footing from,* 1 Co 11:11; *apart from, distinct from, without the intervention of,* Ro 3:21, 28; 4:6; *apart from the company of, independently of,* 1 Co 4:8; Heb 11:40 *without* the presence of, Heb 9:28; *without* the agency of, Jn 1:3; Ro 10:14; *without* the employment of, Mt 13:34; Mk 4:34; Heb 7:20, 21; 9:7, 18, 22; *without,* Lk 6:49; Phil 2:14; 1 Ti 2:8; 5:21; Phlm 14; Heb 10:28; 11:6; 12:8, 14; *clear from,* Heb 7:7; *irrespectively of,* Ro 7:8, 9; *without reckoning, besides,* Mt 14:21; 15:38; 2 Co 11:28; *with the exception of,* Heb 4:15 [5565]

[6008] χῶρος *chōros* 1x *Corus,* or *Caurus, the northwest wind;* meton, *the northwest* quarter of the heavens, Ac 27:12* [5566]

[6010] ψάλλω *psallō* 5x *to move by a touch, to twitch; to touch, strike* the strings or chords of an instrument; absol. *to play on a stringed instrument; to sing to music;* in N.T. *to sing praises,* Ro 15:9; 1 Co 14:15; Eph 5:19; Jas 5:13* [5567]

[6011] ψαλμός *psalmos* 7x *impulse, touch* of the chords of a stringed instrument; in N.T. *a sacred song, psalm,* Lk 20:42; 24:44; Ac 1:20; 13:33; 1 Co 14:26; Eph 5:19; Col 3:16* [5568]

[6012] ψευδάδελφος *pseudadelphos* 2x *a false brother, a pretended Christian,* 2 Co 11:26; Gal 2:4* [5569]

[6013] ψευδαπόστολος *pseudapostolos* 1x *a false apostle, pretended minister of Christ,* 2 Co 11:13* [5570]

[6014] ψευδής *pseudēs* 3x *false, lying,* Ac 6:13; Rev 2:2; in N.T. pl. *maintainers of* religious *falsehood, corrupters of the truth* of God, Rev 21:8* [5571]

[6015] ψευδοδιδάσκαλος *pseudodidaskalos* 1x *a false teacher, one who teaches false doctrines,* 2 Pe 2:1* [5572]

[6016] ψευδολόγος *pseudologos* 1x *false-speaking,* 1 Ti 4:2* [5573]

[6017] ψεύδομαι *pseudomai* 12x *lie,* Mt 5:11; Ac 5:4; Ro 9:1; 2 Co 11:31 [5574]

[6018] ψευδομαρτυρέω *pseudomartyreō* 5x *to bear false witness, give false testimony,* Mt 19:18; Mk 10:19; 14:56, 57; Lk 18:20* [5576]

[6019] ψευδομαρτυρία *pseudomartyria* 2x *false witness, false testimony,* Mt 15:19; 26:59* [5577]

[6020] ψευδόμαρτυς *pseudomartys* 2x *a false witness,* Mt 26:60 (2t); 1 Co 15:15* [5575]

[6021] ψευδοπροφήτης *pseudoprophētēs* 11x *a false prophet, one who falsely claims to speak by divine inspiration,* whether as a foreteller of future events, or as a teacher of doctrines, Mt 7:15; 24:24; Mk 13:22; Ac 13:6; 1 Jn 4:1; Rev 16:13 [5578]

[6022] ψεῦδος *pseudos* 10x *falsehood,* Jn 8:44; Eph 4:25; 2 Th 2:9, 11; 1 Jn 2:21, 27; in N.T. religious *falsehood, perversion* of religious truth, *false religion,* Ro 1:25; *the practices of false religion,* Rev 14:15; 21:27; 22:15* [5579]

[6023] ψευδόχριστος *pseudochristos* 2x *a false Christ, pretended Messiah,* Mt 24:24; Mk 13:22* [5580]

[6024] ψευδώνυμος *pseudōnymos* 1x *falsely named, falsely called,* 1 Ti 6:20* [5581]

[6025] ψεῦσμα *pseusma* 1x *a falsehood, lie;* in N.T. *untruthfulness,* Ro 3:7* [5582]

[6026] ψεύστης *pseustēs* 10x *one who utters a falsehood, a liar,* Jn 8:44, 55; Ro 3:4; 1 Ti 1:10; Tit 1:12; 1 Jn 1:10; 2:4, 22; 4:20; 5:10* [5583]

[6027] ψηλαφάω *psēlaphaō* 4x *to feel, handle,* Lk 24:39; *to feel* or *grope for* or *after,* as persons in the dark, Ac 17:27; Heb 12:18; 1 Jn 1:1* [5584]

[6028] ψηφίζω *psēphizō* 2x *to reckon by means of pebbles, compute by counters;* hence genr. *to compute, reckon, calculate,* Lk 14:28; Rev 13:18* [5585]

[6029] ψῆφος *psēphos* 3x *a small stone, pebble; a pebble* variously employed, especially in a ballot; hence, *a vote, suffrage,* Ac 26:10; *a pebble* or *stone;* probably given as a token, Rev 2:17 (2t)* [5586]

[6030] ψιθυρισμός *psithurismos* 1x *a whispering; a* calumnious *whispering, gossip,* 2 Co 12:20* [5587]

[6031] ψιθυριστής *psithuristēs* 1x *a whisperer; a whisperer, gossip,* Ro 1:29* [5588]

[6033] ψιχίον *psichion* 2x *a morsel, crumb, bit,* Mt 15:27; Mk 7:28* [5589]

[6034] ψυχή *psyche* 103x *breath; the principle of animal life; the life,* Mt 2:20; 6:25; Mk 3:4; Lk 21:19; Jn 10:11; *an inanimate being,* 1 Co 15:45; *a human individual, soul,* Ac 2:41; 3:23; 7:14; 27:37; Ro 13:1; 1 Pe 3:20; *the* immaterial *soul,* Mt 10:28; 1 Pe 1:9; 2:11, 25; 4:19; *the soul* as the seat of religious and moral sentiment, Mt 11:29; Ac 14:2, 22; 15:24; Eph 6:6; *the soul,* as a seat of feeling, Mt 12:18; 26:38; *the soul, the* inner *self,* Lk 12:19 [5590]

[6035] ψυχικός *psychikos* 6x *pertaining to the life* or *soul;* in N.T. *animal,* as distinguished from spiritual subsistence, 1 Co 15:44, 46; *occupied with mere animal things, animal, sensual,* 1 Co 2:14; Jas 3:15; Jude 19* [5591]

[6036] ψῦχος *psychos* 3x *cold,* Jn 18:18; Ac 28:2; 2 Co 11:27* [5592]

[6037] ψυχρός *psychros* 4x *cool, cold,* Mt 10:42; met. Rev 3:15, 16* [5593]

[6038] ψύχω *psychō* 1x *to breathe; to cool;* pass. *to be cooled;* met. of affection, Mt 24:12* [5594]

[6039] ψωμίζω *psōmizō* 2x pr. *to feed by morsels;* hence, genr. *to feed, supply with food,* Ro 12:20; *to bestow in supplying food,* 1 Co 13:3* [5595]

[6040] ψωμίον *psōmion* 4x *a bit, morsel, mouthful,* Jn 13:26, 27, 30* [5596]

[6041] ψώχω *psōchō* 1x *to rub in pieces,* as the ears of grain, Lk 6:1* [5597]

[6042] Ὦ *ō* 3x *Omega,* the last letter of the Greek alphabet, hence, met. τὸ Ω, *the last,* Rev 1:8; 21:6; 22:13* [5598]

[6043] ὦ *ō* 17x *O!,* Mt 15:28; Mk 9:19; Ac 1:1; Ro 2:1, 3; 11:33 [5599]

[6045] ὧδε *hōde* 61x *here, in this place,* Mt 12:6, 41; ὧδε ἤ ὧδε, *here* or *there,* Mt 24:23; τὰ ὧδε, *the state of things here,* Col 4:9; met. *herein, in this thing,* Rev 13:10, 18; *to this place,* Mt 8:29; 14:18 [5602]

[6046] ὠδή *ōdē* 7x *an ode, song, hymn,* Eph 5:19; Col 3:16; Rev 5:9; 14:3; 15:3* [5603]

[6047] ὠδίν *ōdin* 4x *the spasms* or *pains,* of a woman in travail, *a birth-pang,* 1 Th 5:3; pl. met. *birth-throes, preliminary troubles* to the development of a catastrophe, Mt 24:8; Mk 13:8; from the Hebrew, *a stringent band, a snare, noose,* Ac 2:24* [5604]

[6048] ὠδίνω *ōdinō* 3x *to be in travail,* Gal 4:27; Rev 12:2; met. *to travail with, suffer birth pangs, to make effort to bring to* spiritual birth, Gal 4:19* [5605]

[6049] ὦμος *ōmos* 2x *the shoulder,* Mt 23:4; Lk 15:5* [5606]

[6050] ὠνέομαι *ōneomai* 1x *to buy, purchase*, Ac 7:16* [5608]

[6051] ᾠόν *ōon* 1x *an egg*, Lk 11:12* [5609]

[6052] ὥρα *hōra* 106x *a limited portion of time*, marked out by part of a settled routine or train of circumstances; *a season of the year; time of day*, Mt 14:15; Mk 6:35; 11:11; *an hour*, Mt 20:3; Jn 11:9; in N.T. *an eventful season*, 1 Jn 2:18 (2t); Rev 3:10; 14:7; *due time*, Jn 16:21; Ro 13:11; *a destined period, hour*, Mt 26:45; Mk 14:35; Jn 2:4; 7:30; *a short period*, Mt 26:40; Jn 5:35; 2 Co 7:8; Gal 2:5; 1 Th 2:17; Phlm 15; *a point of time, time*, Mt 8:13; 24:42; Lk 2:38 [5610]

[6053] ὡραῖος *hōraios* 4x *timely, seasonable; in prime, blooming;* in N.T. *beautiful*, Mt 23:27; Ac 3:2, 10; Ro 10:15* [5611]

[6054] ὠρύομαι *ōryomai* 1x *to howl; to roar*, as a lion, 1 Pe 5:8* [5612]

[6055] ὡς *hōs* 504x conjunction formed from the relative pronoun ὅς, used as a comparative part. and conj., *as*, correlatively, Mk 4:26; Jn 7:46; Ro 5:15; *as, like as*, Mt 10:16; Eph 5:8; *according as*, Gal 6:10; *as, as it were*, Rev 8:8; *as*, Lk 16:1; Ac 3:12; before numerals, *about*, Mk 5:13; conj. *that*, Ac 10:28; *how*, Ro 11:2; *when*, Mt 28:9; Phil 2:23; as an exclamatory particle, *how*, Ro 10:15; equivalent to ὥστε, *accordingly*, Heb 3:11; also, *on condition that, provided that*, Ac 20:24; ὡς εἰπεῖν, *so to speak*, Heb 7:9 [5613]

[6057] ὡσαννά *hōsanna* 6x *Hosanna! save now, help now*, Mt 21:9, 15; Mk 11:9, 10; Jn 12:13* [5614]

[6058] ὡσαύτως *hōsautōs* 17x *just so, in just the same way* or *manner, likewise*, Mt 20:5; 21:30 [5615]

[6059] ὡσεί *hōsei* 21x *as if; as it were, as, like*, Mt 3:16; 9:36; with terms of number or quantity, *about*, Mt 14:21; Lk 1:56; 22:41, 59 [5616]

[6060] Ὡσηέ *hōsēe* 1x *Hosea*, pr. name, indecl., Ro 9:25* [5617]

[6061] ὥσπερ *hōsper* 36x *just as, as*, Mt 6:2; 24:37; 1 Th 5:3 [5618]

[6062] ὡσπερεί *hōsperei* 1x *just as if; as it were*, 1 Co 15:8* [5619]

[6063] ὥστε *hōste* 83x *so that, so as that, so as to*, Mt 8:24; Mk 2:12; Ac 14:1; Gal 2:13; as an illative particle, *therefore, consequently*, Mt 12:12; 23:31 [5620]

[6064] ὠτάριον *ōtarion* 2x *an ear*, Mt 14:47; Jn 18:10* [5621]

[6065] ὠτίον *ōtion* 3x in N.T. simply equivalent to οὖς, *an ear*, Mt 26:51; Lk 22:51; Jn 18:26* [5621]

[6066] ὠφέλεια *ōpheleia* 2x *help; profit, gain, advantage, benefit*, Ro 3:1; Jude 16* [5622]

[6067] ὠφελέω *ōpheleō* 15x *to help, profit, benefit, accomplish*, Mt 27:24; Mk 7:11; Ro 2:25; *be of value*, Jn 6:63 [5623]

[6068] ὠφέλιμος *ōphelimos* 4x *profitable, useful, beneficial; serviceable*, 1 Ti 4:8 (2t); 2 Ti 3:16; Tit 3:8* [5624]